The INTERNATIONAL STANDARD BIBLE ENCYCLOPEDIA

The INTERNATIONAL STANDARD BIBLE ENCYCLOPEDIA

VOLUME TWO • E-J

GENERAL EDITOR

GEOFFREY W. BROMILEY
Church History and Doctrine

ASSOCIATE EDITORS

EVERETT F. HARRISON
New Testament

ROLAND K. HARRISON
Old Testament

WILLIAM SANFORD LASOR
Biblical Geography and Archeology

CONSULTING EDITOR

LAWRENCE T. GERATY
Archeology

PROJECT EDITOR

EDGAR W. SMITH, JR.

FULLY REVISED • ILLUSTRATED • IN FOUR VOLUMES

THE PATERNOSTER PRESS
EXETER

This British edition published through special arrangement with Eerdmans by The Paternoster Press, Exeter, England.

Publication History:

First published 1915; copyright 1915 by the Howard-Severance Company, Chicago. New and revised edition, edited by Melvin Grove Kyle, copyright 1929 by the Howard-Severance Company. Copyright renewed, 1956, by William B. Eerdmans Publishing Company. Completely revised and reset.
Volume II: first printing, 1982.

AUSTRALIA:
Bookhouse Australia Ltd.,
P.O. Box 115, Flemington Markets,
N.S.W. 2129

SOUTH AFRICA:
Oxford University Press,
P.O. Box 1141,
Cape Town

British Library Cataloguing in Publication Data

The International standard Bible encyclopaedia.
Vol. 2 (E-J)
1. Bible — Dictionaries
I. Bromiley, Geoffrey W.
220.3'21 BS440

ISBN 0-85364-304-0

Printed and Bound at Eerdmans Printing Company, Grand Rapids.

CONTRIBUTORS†

ARMERDING, CARL EDWIN
A.B., B.D., M.A., Ph.D., Professor of Old Testament, Regent College, Vancouver, British Columbia, Canada.

AUNE, DAVID E.
B.A., M.A., M.A., Ph.D., Professor of Religion, Saint Xavier College, Chicago, Illinois.

BAKER, DAVID W.
A.B., M.C.S., M.Phil., Pastoral Staff, Westminster Gospel Chapel, Burnaby, British Columbia, Canada.

BALCHIN, JOHN A.
M.A., B.D., Pastor, First Presbyterian Church, Papakura, New Zealand.

BALL, EDWARD
M.A., Lecturer in Old Testament, St. John's College, Nottingham, England.

BALY, A. DENIS
B.A., Professor of Religion, Kenyon College, Gambier, Ohio.

BANDSTRA, ANDREW J.
A.B., B.D., Th.D., Professor of New Testament, Calvin Theological Seminary, Grand Rapids, Michigan.

BANKS, EDGAR J.*
Ph.D., Professor of Ancient History, Robert College, Constantinople, Turkey, and Field Director of the Babylonian Expedition of the University of Chicago.

BAUR, WILLIAM*
D.D., Professor of Church History, Eden Seminary, St. Louis, Missouri.

BEECHER, WILLIS JUDSON*
M.A., D.D., Professor of Hebrew Language and Literature, Auburn Theological Seminary, Auburn, New York.

BEITZEL, BARRY
B.A., M.A., Ph.D., Associate Professor of Old Testament and Semitic Languages, Trinity Evangelical Divinity School, Deerfield, Illinois.

BIRKEY, ARLAN J.
A.B., Th.B., M.Div., Associate Professor of Greek and Bible, Fort Wayne Bible College, Fort Wayne, Indiana.

BORCHERT, GERALD L.
B.A., LL.B., M.Div., Th.M., Ph.D., Professor of New Testament, Southern Baptist Theological Seminary, Louisville, Kentucky.

BREMER, PAUL L.
A.B., B.D., Ph.D., Associate Professor of Bible and Greek Language, Reformed Bible College, Grand Rapids, Michigan.

BRESLICH, ARTHUR LOUIS*
B.D., Ph.D., President of Baldwin-Wallace College and Nast Theological Seminary, Berea, Ohio.

BRISCO, THOMAS V.
B.A., Ph.D., Instructor of Biblical Backgrounds and Archaeology, Southwestern Baptist Theological Seminary, Fort Worth, Texas.

BROMILEY, GEOFFREY W.
M.A., Ph.D., Emeritus Professor of Church History and Historical Theology, Fuller Theological Seminary, Pasadena, California.

BROWNLEE, WILLIAM H.
Th.M., Ph.D., Professor of Religion, Claremont Graduate School, Claremont, California.

BRUCE, FREDERICK FYVIE
M.A., D.D., F.B.A., Emeritus Professor of Biblical Criticism and Exegesis, University of Manchester, England.

BUCHANAN, GEORGE WESLEY
B.A., M.Div., M.A., Ph.D., Professor of New Testament, Wesley Theological Seminary, Washington, D.C.

BUEHLER, WILLIAM W.
B.S., B.D., D.Th., Professor of Biblical Studies and Chairman of the Department of Religious Studies, Barrington College, Barrington, Rhode Island.

BURDICK, DONALD W.
A.B., B.D., Th.M., Th.D., Professor of New Testament, Conservative Baptist Theological Seminary, Denver, Colorado.

BURKE, DAVID G.
A.B., B.D., Th.M., Ph.D., Lutheran Campus Pastor, Rutgers, The State University, New Brunswick, New Jersey.

BUSH, FREDERICK W.
B.A., M.Div., Th.M., M.A., Ph.D., Assistant Professor of Old Testament, Fuller Theological Seminary, Pasadena, California.

CALDECOTT, W. SHAW*
M.R.A.S., Minister of the Wesleyan Conferences of Great Britain and South Africa.

†An asterisk (*) indicates a contributor to the 1915/1929 *ISBE* whose work has been retained with editorial changes.

CAMPBELL, ANTONY F., S.J.
B.A., M.A., S.T.L., L.S.S., Ph.D., Professor of Old Testament, Jesuit Theological College, United Faculty of Theology, Parkville, Victoria, Australia.

CARVER, WILLIAM OWEN*
M.A., Th.D., LL.D., Professor of Comparative Religion and Missions, Southern Baptist Theological Seminary, Louisville, Kentucky.

CHRISTIANS, CLIFFORD G.
A.B., B.D., Th.M., M.A., Ph.D., Associate Professor of Communications, University of Illinois at Urbana, Illinois.

CLEMONS, JAMES T.
A.B., B.D., Ph.D., Professor of New Testament, Wesley Theological Seminary, Washington, D.C.

CLIPPINGER, WALTER GILLAN*
B.A., D.D., LL.D., President of Otterbein College, Westerville, Ohio.

COLLINS, ADELA YARBRO
B.A., M.A., Ph.D., Associate Professor of New Testament, McCormick Theological Seminary, Chicago, Illinois.

CONRAD, EDGAR W.
A.B., M.Div., Th.M., Ph.D., Teacher in the Department of Religious Studies, University of Queensland, St. Lucia, Queensland, Australia.

CONDOR, CLAUDE REIGNIER*
LL.D., M.R.A.S., Archeologist and Topographer.

COTTLE, RONALD E.
A.B., B.D., Ph.D., M.S.Ed., Ed.D., Executive Vice President, Assemblies of God Graduate School, Springfield, Missouri.

COTTON, JESSE L.*
D.D., LL.D., Professor of Old Testament Exegesis, Louisville Presbyterian Theological Seminary, Louisville, Kentucky.

COUGHENOUR, ROBERT A.
B.S., B.D., M.A., Ph.D., Professor of Old Testament, Western Theological Seminary, Holland, Michigan.

COX, JAMES J. C.
B.A., M.A., Ph.D., Professor and Chairman of the Department of New Testament, Andrews University, Berrien Springs, Michigan.

CRANNELL, PHILIP WENDELL*
D.D., President, Kansas City Baptist Theological Seminary, Kansas City, Kansas.

CRICHTON, JAMES*
B.D., M.A., Senior Minister of the United Free Church, Airdrie, Scotland.

CULPEPPER, R. ALAN
B.A., M.Div., Ph.D., Associate Professor of New Testament Interpretation, Southern Baptist Theological Seminary, Louisville, Kentucky.

DAANE, JAMES
A.B., Th.B., Th.D., Senior Professor of Theology and Ministry, Fuller Theological Seminary, Pasadena, California.

DANKER, FREDERICK W.
B.D., M.Div., Ph.D., Professor, Department of Exegetical Theology, Christ Seminary–Seminex, St. Louis, Missouri.

DAVIES, T. WITTON*
B.A., D.D., Ph.D., Professor of Semitic Languages, University College, Bangor, North Wales.

DAY, ALFRED ELY*
M.A., M.Sc., Professor of Natural Sciences, American University of Beirut.

DEERE, DERWARD W.
Th.D., Late Professor of Old Testament, Golden Gate Theological Seminary, Mill Valley, California.

DEHOOG, JOHN W.
A.B., Former Project Editor, *ISBE* Revision.

DEMENT, BYRON H.*
Th.D., Professor of Sunday School Pedagogy, Southern Baptist Theological Seminary, Louisville, Kentucky.

DENNISON, JAMES T., JR.
B.S., B.D., M.Div., Th.M., Librarian, Westminster Theological Seminary in California, Escondido, California.

DEVRIES, CARL E.
B.S., M.A., B.D., Ph.D., Former Research Associate (Associate Professor), Oriental Institute, Chicago, Illinois.

DICKIE, ARCHIBALD CAMPBELL*
M.A., F.S.A., A.R.I.B.A., Professor of Architecture, University of Manchester, England.

DOOLAN, LEONARD W.*
B.A., Th.D., Pastor, First Baptist Church, Danville, Kentucky.

DOWNER, BENJAMIN RENO*
B.A., Th.D., Professor of Hebrew and Old Testament, Kansas City Theological Seminary, Kansas City, Kansas.

DUGAN, ROBERT P., JR.
B.A., M.Div., Director, Office of Public Affairs of the National Association of Evangelicals, Washington, D.C.

DUNGAN, DAVID ROBERTS*
M.A., LL.D., Author, Des Moines, Iowa.

EARLE, RALPH
A.B., B.D., M.A., Th.D., Emeritus Professor of New Testament, Nazarene Theological Seminary, Kansas City, Missouri.

EASTON, BURTON SCOTT*
D.D., Ph.D., Professor of the Interpretation and Literature of the New Testament, General Theological Seminary, New York, New York.

EDWARDS, DAVID MIALL*
M.A., Ph.D., D.D., Professor of Doctrinal Theology and Philosophy of Religion, Memorial College (Congregational), Brecon, South Wales.

ELLISON, HENRY LEOPOLD
B.A., B.D., Senior Tutor, Moorlands Bible College, Dawlish, Devon, England.

EMMERSON, GRACE I.
M.A., Dip. Or. Lang., Lecturer, Department of Theology, University of Birmingham, England.

ESTES, DAVID FOSTER*
M.A., D.D., Professor of New Testament Interpretation, Colgate University, Hamilton, New York.

EVANS, MORRIS O.*
D.D., Ph.D., Lecturer on English Bible and Literature, Congregational College, Bangor, North Wales.

EVANS, WILLIAM*
D.D., Ph.D., Bible Teacher, Author, and Lecturer, Pomona, California.

EWING, WILLIAM*
M.C., M.A., D.D., Minister, Grange United Free Church, Edinburgh, Scotland.

FARR, F. K.*
A.M., D.D., Professor of Hebrew and Old Testament Exegesis, Lane Seminary, Cincinnati, Ohio.

FAULKNER, JOHN ALFRED*
M.A., B.D., LL.D., Professor of Church History, Theological College of Drew University, Madison, New Jersey.

FEINBERG, CHARLES L.
A.B., A.M., Th.B., Th.M., Th.D., Ph.D., Dean Emeritus and Professor of Semitics and Old Testament, Talbot Theological Seminary, La Mirada, California.

FENSHAM, F. CHARLES
B.A., B.D., M.A., D.D., Ph.D., Professor of Semitic Languages and Head of the Department, University of Stellenbosch, Republic of South Africa.

FILSON, FLOYD V.
B.A., B.D., Th.D., Late Dean and Professor of New Testament Literature and History, McCormick Theological Seminary, Chicago, Illinois.

FISHER, MILTON C.
B.A., M.A., B.D., Th.M., Ph.D., Professor of Old Testament and President, The Theological Seminary of the Reformed Episcopal Church, Philadelphia, Pennsylvania.

FORTUNE, A. W.*
B.D., M.A., Professor of New Testament, College of the Bible, Lexington, Kentucky.

FULLER, DANIEL P.
B.A., B.D., Th.M., Th.D., D.Th., Professor of Hermeneutics, Fuller Theological Seminary, Pasadena, California.

GARBER, PAUL LESLIE
Th.M., Ph.D., Professor Emeritus of Bible and Religion, Agnes Scott College, Decatur, Georgia.

GASQUE, W. WARD
B.A., B.D., M.Th., Ph.D., President and Professor of New Testament, New College, Berkeley, California.

GERATY, LAWRENCE T.
B.A., M.A., M.Div., Ph.D., Associate Professor of Archeology and History of Antiquity, Andrews University Theological Seminary, Berrien Springs, Michigan.

GIBBS, JOHN G.
A.B., M.Div., Th.M., Ph.D., Professor of Humanities, Moorhead State University, Moorhead, Minnesota.

GILCHRIST, PAUL R.
B.A., B.D., Ph.D., Associate Professor of Biblical Studies, Covenant College, Lookout Mountain, Tennessee.

GILLESPIE, V. BAILEY
B.A., M.A., M.Div., Ph.D., Associate Professor of Theology and Christian Personality, Loma Linda University, Riverside, California.

GOLDSTEIN, SIDNEY M.
B.A., M.A., Ph.D., Chief Curator, Corning Museum of Glass, Corning, New York.

GORDON, ROBERT P.
M.A., Ph.D., Lecturer in Divinity, Cambridge University, Cambridge, England.

GRANT, ALEXANDER C.*
M.A., Missionary of the United Free Church of Scotland, Rajputana, India.

GRAY, JAMES M.*
D.D., President, Moody Bible Institute, Chicago, Illinois.

GRAYBILL, JOHN B.
B.A., B.D., Ph.D., Emeritus Professor, Department of Bible and Theology, Barrington College, Barrington, Rhode Island.

GUNDRY, ROBERT H.
B.A., B.D., Ph.D., Professor of New Testament and Greek, Westmont College, Santa Barbara, California.

GUTHRIE, DONALD
B.D., M.Th., Ph.D., Vice Principal and Senior New Testament Lecturer, London Bible College, London, England.

GWINN, RALPH A.
A.B., B.D., Ph.D., Professor of Philosophy and Religion, Tarkio College, Tarkio, Missouri.

HAGNER, DONALD A.
B.A., B.D., Th.M., Ph.D., Associate Professor of New Testament, Fuller Theological Seminary, Pasadena, California.

HALPERIN, DAVID J.
B.A., M.A., Ph.D., Assistant Professor of Religion, University of North Carolina, Chapel Hill, North Carolina.

HARRINGTON, CLYDE E.
Ph.D., Former Editor, American Sunday School Union, Philadelphia, Pennsylvania.

HARRIS, MURRAY J.
M.A., Dip.Ed., B.D., Ph.D., Lecturer in New Testament, Bible College of New Zealand, Auckland, New Zealand.

HARRIS, R. LAIRD
Th.B., Th.M., Ph.D., Professor of Old Testament, Covenant Theological Seminary, St. Louis, Missouri.

HARRISON, EVERETT F.
B.A., Th.B., M.A., Ph.D., Th.D., Professor Emeritus of New Testament, Fuller Theological Seminary, Pasadena, California.

HARRISON, ROLAND K.
B.D., M.Th., Ph.D., Professor of Old Testament, Wycliffe College, Toronto, Ontario, Canada.

HARTLEY, JOHN E.
B.A., B.D., M.A., Ph.D., Chairman of the Division of Philosophy and Religion, Azusa Pacific College; Visiting Professor of Biblical Literature, Fuller Theological Seminary, Pasadena, California.

HASEL, GERHARD F.
M.A., B.D., Ph.D., Professor of Old Testament and Biblical Theology and Assistant Academic Dean, Andrews University, Berrien Springs, Michigan.

HAWTHORNE, GERALD F.
B.A., M.A., Ph.D., Professor of Greek, Wheaton College, Wheaton, Illinois.

HAYDEN, ROY E.
B.A., B.D., Th.M., M.A., Ph.D., Professor of Biblical Literature, Oral Roberts University, Tulsa, Oklahoma.

HEIDEL, WILLIAM ARTHUR*
M.A., Ph.D., Research Professor of Greek Language and Literature, Wesleyan University, Middletown, Connecticut.

HEMER, COLIN J.
M.A., Ph.D., Research Scholar in New Testament History, Tyndale House, Cambridge, England.

HEWETT, JAMES ALLEN
B.A., B.D., M.A., Ph.D., Associate Professor of Theology, Oral Roberts University, Tulsa, Oklahoma.

HIRSCH, FRANK E.*
M.A., D.D., LL.D., President of Charles City College, Charles City, Iowa.

HODGE, CASPAR WISTAR*
Ph.D., Charles Hodge Professor of Systematic Theology, Princeton Theological Seminary, Princeton, New Jersey.

HOEHNER, HAROLD W.
B.A., Th.M., Th.D., Ph.D., Director of Doctoral Studies and Professor of New Testament Literature and Exegesis, Dallas Theological Seminary, Dallas, Texas.

HOFFINE, JAMES E.
B.A., M.A.B.S., M.A., Editorial Associate, *ISBE* Revision Project.

HOLWERDA, DAVID E.
A.B., B.D., D.Th., Professor of Religion and Theology, Calvin College, Grand Rapids, Michigan.

HOVEE, GENE H.
B.A., M.Div., M.A., Ph.D., Associate Professor of Bible and Vice President, Fort Wayne Bible College, Fort Wayne, Indiana.

HOVEY, BARRY E.
B.A., B.D., Th.M., Software Support Representative, Sperry Univac, Blue Bell, Pennsylvania.

HOVEY, GEORGE RICE*
M.A., D.D., Secretary of Education, American Baptist Home Mission Society, New York, New York.

HUBBARD, DAVID A.
B.A., B.D., Th.M., Ph.D., President and Professor of Old Testament, Fuller Theological Seminary, Pasadena, California.

HUBBARD, ROBERT L., JR.
A.B., B.D., M.A., Ph.D., Assistant Professor of Old Testament, Conservative Baptist Theological Seminary, Denver, Colorado.

HUGHES, PHILIP C.
B.S., S.D.M., S.T.B., M.S., Ph.D., Vice President, Duro-Test Corporation, North Bergen, New Jersey.

HUGHES, ROBERT J., III
D.V.M., M.Div., Th.M., Professor of Science and Chairman of the Division of General Studies, Fort Wayne Bible College, Fort Wayne, Indiana.

HUNT, LESLIE
B.A., B.D., M.Th., D.D., Principal Emeritus and Professor of New Testament, Wycliffe College, Toronto, Ontario, Canada.

HUNTER, S. F.*
M.A., B.D., Professor of Knox College, Dunedin, New Zealand.

HUTCHISON, JOHN*
M.A., LL.D., Rector of the High School, Glasgow, Scotland.

ISAACS, ELLA DAVIS*
M.A., Cambridge, Massachusetts.

JACOBS, HENRY E.*
D.D., LL.D., Norton Professor of Systematic Theology, Lutheran Theological Seminary, Philadelphia, Pennsylvania.

JOHNSON, MARSHALL D.
B.A., Th.B., Th.D., Professor of Religion, Wartburg College, Waverly, Iowa.

JOHNSTON, ELEANOR B.
B.A., M.A., Assistant to the President, Swarthmore College, Swarthmore, Pennsylvania.

JOY, ALFRED H.*
Ph.B., M.A., F.R.A.S., Astronomer and Secretary of the Mount Wilson Observatory, Pasadena, California.

JUNG, KURT GERHARD
Th.D., U.S. Army Chaplain, Berlin, Germany.

KELLY, DAVID J.
B.A., M.Div., Th.M., Ph.D., Minister, Exeter and Milligan United Methodist Churches, Nebraska.

KENYON, KATHLEEN M.
M.A., D.Litt., L.H.D., Late Principal of St. Hugh's College, Oxford, England.

KERR, COLIN M.*
B.Sc., B.D., M.A., Ph.D., Professor of Political Philosophy in Scottish Churches College, Calcutta, India.

KITCHEN, KENNETH A.
B.A., Ph.D., Reader in Egyptian and Coptic Studies, School of Archaeology and Oriental Studies, University of Liverpool, England.

KLOOSTER, FRED H.
A.B., B.D., Th.M., Th.D., Professor of Systematic Theology, Calvin Theological Seminary, Grand Rapids, Michigan.

KNUTSON, F. BRENT
B.S., M.A., Ph.D., Associate Professor of Philosophy and Religion, University of Arkansas at Little Rock, Arkansas.

LADD, GEORGE ELDON
Th.B., B.D., Ph.D., Emeritus Professor of New Testament Theology and Exegesis, Fuller Theological Seminary, Pasadena, California.

LASOR, WILLIAM SANFORD
A.B., A.M., Th.B., Th.M., Ph.D., Th.D., Emeritus Professor of Old Testament, Fuller Theological Seminary, Pasadena, California.

LAY, HAROLD W.
B.A., M.Div., Pastor, English Neighborhood Reformed Church, Ridgefield, New Jersey.

CONTRIBUTORS

LEE, GARY A.
B.A., M.T.S, Chief Editorial Associate, *ISBE* Revision Project.

LEVENSON, DAVID B.
M.A., Ph.D., Assistant Professor of Religion, Florida State University, Tallahassee, Florida.

LEVERTOFF, PAUL*
B.D., Professor of Old Testament and Talmudic Literature, Institutum Delitzschianum, Leipzig, Germany.

LEWIS, ARTHUR H.
B.A., M.A., B.D., Ph.D., Professor of Old Testament, Bethel College, St. Paul, Minnesota.

LEWIS, THOMAS*
B.D., M.A., Principal of Memorial College (Congregational), Brecon, South Wales.

LINTON, CALVIN D.
A.B., M.A., Ph.D., Professor of English and Dean, Columbian College of Arts and Sciences, George Washington University, Washington, D.C.

LITTMANN, ENNO*
Ph.D., Professor of Semitic Philology, University of Göttingen, Germany.

LOWN, JOHN S.
B.A., M.A., B.D., Ph.D., Professor of Biblical Languages and Literature and Director of Graduate Studies and Continuing Education in Religion, Point Loma College, San Diego, California.

LUERING, HEINRICH LUDWIG EMIL*
Ph.D., Professor of Dogmatic Theology and New Testament Greek, Martin Theological Seminary of the Methodist Episcopal Church, Frankfurt-am-Main, Germany.

MAAHS, KENNETH H.
B.A., M.Div., Th.M., Ph.D., Associate Professor of Religion, Eastern College, St. Davids, Pennsylvania.

MACALISTER, ALEXANDER*
M.D., M.A., D.Sc., LL.D., F.R.S., F.S.A., Professor of Anatomy, Cambridge University, Cambridge, England.

MACDONALD, BURTON
B.A., M.Th., M.A., Ph.D., Associate Professor of Theology, St. Francis Xavier University, Antigonish, Nova Scotia, Canada.

MACK, EDWARD*
Ph.D., D.D., LL.D., McCormick Professor of Old Testament Interpretation, Union Theological Seminary, Richmond, Virginia.

MACLEOD, MURDO A.
M.A., Director and General Secretary, Christian Witness to Israel, Chislehurst, Kent, England.

MADVIG, DONALD H.
A.B., B.D., Th.M., M.A., Ph.D., Pastor, Ravenswood Evangelical Covenant Church, Chicago, Illinois.

MARSHALL, I. HOWARD
B.A., M.A., B.D., Ph.D., Professor of New Testament Exegesis, University of Aberdeen, Scotland.

MARTIN, RALPH P.
B.A., M.A., Ph.D., Professor of New Testament and Director of the Graduate Studies Program, Fuller Theological Seminary, Pasadena, California.

MAST, EDWIN S.
A.B., M.Div., Principal, Fountain Hills Christian Academy, and Pastor, Fountain Hills Community Church, Fountain Hills, Arizona.

MASTERMAN, ERNEST W. G.*
M.D., F.R.C.S., F.R.G.S., Honorary Secretary of the Palestine Exploration Fund, London, England.

MCALLISTER, J. GRAY*
B.A., D.D., Professor of Biblical Introduction, English Bible, and Biblical Theology, Louisville Presbyterian Theological Seminary, Louisville, Kentucky.

MCCARTER, P. KYLE
B.A., M.Div., Ph.D., Associate Professor of Religious Studies, University of Virginia, Charlottesville, Virginia.

MCCOMISKEY, THOMAS EDWARD
B.A., M.Div., Th.M., M.A., Ph.D., Professor of Old Testament and Semitic Languages, Trinity Evangelical Divinity School, Deerfield, Illinois.

MCFALL, LESLIE
B.A., Ph.D., Lecturer in Old Testament and Hebrew Language, Belfast Bible College, Belfast, Northern Ireland.

MCKIM, DONALD K.
B.A., M.Div., Ph.D., Pastor of Friendship United Presbyterian Parish, Slippery Rock, Pennsylvania.

MICKELSEN, A. BERKELEY
B.A., M.A., B.D., Ph.D., Professor of New Testament, Bethel Theological Seminary, St. Paul, Minnesota.

MILLARD, ALAN R.
M.A., M.Phil., Rankin Senior Lecturer in Hebrew and Ancient Semitic Languages, University of Liverpool, England.

MILLER, RUSSELL BENJAMIN*
M.A., B.D., Ph.D., Professor of Biblical Literature, Ohio Wesleyan University, Delaware, Ohio.

MORGAN, DONN F.
B.A., B.D., M.A., Ph.D., Associate Professor of Old Testament, Church Divinity School of the Pacific, Berkeley, California.

MORRIS, LEON
B.Sc., M.Sc., M.Th., Ph.D., Former Principal of Ridley College, Melbourne, Australia.

MORRO, WILLIAM CHARLES*
B.D., M.A., Ph.D., Chair of New Testament, Brite College of the Bible, Texas Christian University, Fort Worth, Texas.

MOSIMAN, SAMUEL K.*
Ph.D., Litt.D., President of Bluffton College, Bluffton, Ohio.

MOYER, JAMES C.
A.B., M.Div., M.A., Ph.D., Associate Professor of History, Southwest Missouri State University, Springfield, Missouri.

MURRAY, JOHN
M.A., Th.B., Th.M., Late Professor of Systematic Theology, Westminster Theological Seminary, Philadelphia, Pennsylvania.

MYERS, ALLEN C.
B.A., M.Div., Editor, Reference Books, Eerdmans Publishing Company.

NICOL, THOMAS*
D.D., Professor of Divinity and Biblical Criticism, University of Aberdeen, Scotland.

NORMAN, JAMES GARTH GIFFORD
B.D., M.Th., Late Pastor of Rosyth Baptist Church, Fife, Scotland.

OPPERWALL, NOLA J.
A.B., M.Div., Former Editorial Associate, *ISBE* Revision Project.

ORR, JAMES*
M.A., D.D., Professor of Apologetics and Theology, Theological College of United Free Church, Glasgow, Scotland.

PALMER, EDWIN H.
B.A., Th.B., Th.D., Late Executive Secretary for the Committee on Bible Translation for the New International Version Bible, Zondervan Corporation, Grand Rapids, Michigan.

PATCH, JAMES A.*
B.S., Professor of Chemistry, American University of Beirut.

PAYNE, DAVID F.
B.A., M.A., Senior Lecturer and Head of the Department of Semitic Studies, The Queen's University, Belfast, Northern Ireland.

PAYNE, J. BARTON
B.A., B.D., M.A., Th.M., Ph.D., Late Professor and Chairman of the Department of Old Testament, Covenant Theological Seminary, St. Louis, Missouri.

PECOTA, DANIEL B.
B.A., M.Div., Th.M., D.Min., Professor of Greek and Theology, Northwest College, Kirkland, Washington.

PERKIN, HAZEL W.
B.A., M.A., Principal, St. Clement's School, Toronto, Ontario, Canada.

PERLMAN, ALICE L.
B.A., Ph.D., Former Assistant Editor, Scholars Press, Chico, California.

PFEIFFER, CHARLES F.
B.A., B.D., S.T.M., Ph.D., Late Professor of Ancient Literature, Central Michigan University, Mt. Pleasant, Michigan.

PINCHES, THEOPHILUS GOLDRIDGE*
LL.D., M.R.A.S., Lecturer in Assyrian, University College, London, England; Department of Egyptian and Assyrian Antiquities, British Museum, London.

POLLARD, EDWARD BAGBY*
M.A., D.D., Ph.D., Professor of Homiletics, Crozer Theological Seminary, Chester, Pennsylvania.

PORTER, H.*
Ph.D., Professor of History and Psychology, American University of Beirut, Lebanon.

PREWITT, J. FRANKLIN
B.A., B.Th., D.D., Professor of Bible and History, Western Baptist Bible College, Salem, Oregon.

PRICE, JAMES R.
A.B., M.Div., A.M., Pastor, Faith United Methodist Church, Joliet, Illinois.

RAINEY, ANSON F.
B.A., M.A., B.D., M.Th., Ph.D., Associate Professor of Ancient Near Eastern Cultures, Tel Aviv University, Tel Aviv, Israel.

RAMSAY, WILLIAM M.*
D.D., Litt.D., D.C.L., LL.D., New Testament Scholar and Archeologist.

REEVE, JAMES JOSIAH*
B.A., B.D., Th.D., Professor of Hebrew and Cognate Languages and Old Testament Theology, Southwestern Baptist Theological Seminary, Fort Worth, Texas.

REID, W. STANFORD
B.A., M.A., Th.B., Th.M., Ph.D., L.H.D., Retired Professor of History, University of Guelph, Ontario, Canada.

RENWICK, A. M.
M.A., B.D., D.Litt., D.D., Late Professor of Church History, Free Church of Scotland College, Edinburgh, Scotland.

RIDDERBOS, HERMAN N.
D.D., Professor Emeritus of New Testament Theology, Theological Seminary of the Reformed Churches, Kampen, the Netherlands.

RIENSTRA, MARCHIENNE V.
B.A., M.A., Pastor, Port Sheldon Presbyterian Church, Port Sheldon, Michigan.

RIFE, J. MERLE
A.B., M.A., Ph.D., Former Professor of Classical Languages and Bible, Muskingum College, New Concord, Ohio.

ROBERTS, DAVID FRANCIS*
B.A., B.D., Minister, Fitzclarence Street Welsh Presbyterian Church, Liverpool, England.

ROBINSON, GEORGE L.*
M.A., Ph.D., D.D., LL.D., Professor of Biblical Literature and English Bible, Presbyterian Theological Seminary, Chicago, Illinois.

ROBINSON, WILLIAM CHILDS
A.B., M.A., B.D., Th.M., Th.D., Professor Emeritus, Columbia Theological Seminary, Decatur, Georgia.

RUNNING, LEONA GLIDDEN
M.A., Ph.D., Professor of Biblical Languages, Andrews University Theological Seminary, Berrien Springs, Michigan.

RUTHERFURD, JOHN*
B.D., M.A., Minister, Moorpark United Free Church, Renfrew, Scotland.

SAARISALO, AAPELI A.
Th.D., Professor Emeritus of Oriental Literature, Helsinki University, Helsinki, Finland.

SAMPEY, JOHN RICHARD*
B.A., D.D., LL.D., Professor of Old Testament Interpretation, Southern Baptist Theological Seminary, Louisville, Kentucky.

SCHENK, CHARLES E.*
D.D., President, Cincinnati Missionary Training School, Cincinnati, Ohio.

CONTRIBUTORS

SCHOONHOVEN, CALVIN R.
B.A., B.D., D.Th., Director of McAlister Library and Associate Professor of Biblical Interpretation, Fuller Theological Seminary, Pasadena, California.

SCHOVILLE, KEITH N.
B.A., M.A., Ph.D., Associate Professor and Chairman of the Department of Hebrew and Semitic Studies, University of Wisconsin, Madison, Wisconsin.

SCHRECKENBERG, HEINZ
Ph.D., Lecturer, University of Münster, West Germany.

SCHULTZ, SAMUEL J.
Th.D., Emeritus Professor of Biblical Studies and Theology, Wheaton College and Graduate School, Wheaton, Illinois.

SEALE, MORRIS S.
B.A., Ph.D., D.D., Former Professor, Near East School of Theology, Beirut, Lebanon.

SHEA, WILLIAM
Ph.D., Associate Professor of Old Testament, Andrews University Theological Seminary, Berrien Springs, Michigan.

SHELL, WILLIAM A.
B.A., M.Div., M.A., Assistant Professor of Biblical Studies, Reformed Bible College, Grand Rapids, Michigan.

SMALLEY, STEPHEN S.
M.A., B.D., Ph.D., Canon Residentiary and Precentor, Coventry Cathedral, Coventry, England.

SMEDES, LEWIS B.
A.B., B.D., Th.D., Professor of Theology and Ethics, Fuller Theological Seminary, Pasadena, California.

SMITH, EDGAR W., JR.
B.A., B.D., Ph.D., Project Editor, *ISBE* Revision.

SMITH, WILBUR M.
D.D., D.Litt., Late Professor of English Bible, Fuller Theological Seminary, Pasadena, California.

SODERLUND, SVEN K.
B.A., M.C.S., Ph.D., Assistant Professor of Biblical Languages, Regent College, Vancouver, British Columbia, Canada.

STEARNS, WALLACE NELSON*
B.D., Ph.D., Professor of Biblical History and Literature, Fargo College, Fargo, North Dakota.

STEIN, ROBERT H.
B.A., B.D., S.T.M., Ph.D., Professor of New Testament, Bethel Theological Seminary, St. Paul, Minnesota.

STEK, JOHN H.
A.B., B.D., Th.M., Associate Professor of Old Testament, Calvin Theological Seminary, Grand Rapids, Michigan.

STEWART, ROY A.
M.A., B.D., M.Litt., Retired Minister and Biblical Scholar, Church of Scotland, Edinburgh, Scotland.

STRANGE, JAMES F.
B.A., M.Div., Ph.D., Associate Professor of Religious Studies, University of South Florida, Tampa, Florida.

STRATTON-PORTER, GENE*
Author and Illustrator; Special Writer on Birds and Nature.

SWEET, LOUIS MATTHEWS*
M.A., S.T.D., Ph.D., Professor of Christian Theology and Apologetics, The Biblical Seminary, New York, New York.

TAPPEINER, DANIEL A.
B.S., B.D., Ph.D., President and Associate Professor of Theology, Center for Theological Studies, Newport Beach, California.

TERIAN, ABRAHAM
B.A., M.A., Associate Professor of Intertestamental and Early Christian Literatures, Andrews University, Berrien Springs, Michigan.

THOMPSON, JAMES W.
B.A., M.A., B.D., Ph.D., Instructor of Biblical Studies, University of Texas, Austin, Texas.

TIFFANY, FREDERICK C.
B.A., M.Div., Ph.D., Assistant Professor of Old Testament, Earlham School of Religion, Richmond, Indiana.

TOGTMAN, RAYMOND C.
A.B., Former Editorial Assistant, *ISBE* Revision Project.

TURNER, GEORGE A.
A.B., B.D., S.T.B., S.T.M., Ph.D., Professor Emeritus of Biblical Literature, Asbury Theological Seminary, Wilmore, Kentucky.

URQUHART, JOHN*
Minister, Author, Editor, Member of the Victoria Institute, Melbourne, Australia.

VAN ALSTINE, GEORGE A.
B.A., B.D., Th.M., Pastor, Altadena Baptist Church, Altadena, California.

VAN BROEKHOVEN, HAROLD, JR.
B.A., M.A., M.Div., Th.M., Pastor, Tabernacle Baptist Church, Hope, Rhode Island.

VANELDEREN, BASTIAAN
A.B., B.D., M.A., Th.D., Professor of New Testament, Calvin Theological Seminary, Grand Rapids, Michigan.

VAN SELMS, ADRIANUS
D.Th., Emeritus Professor of Semitic Languages, University of Pretoria, Republic of South Africa.

VERHEY, ALLEN D.
B.A., B.D., Ph.D., Associate Professor of Religion, Hope College, Holland, Michigan.

VOGEL, ELEANOR K.
B.A., M.Ed., Former Archeological Assistant to Nelson Glueck, Cincinnati, Ohio.

VOS, HOWARD F.
B.A., Th.M., Th.D., M.A., Ph.D., Professor of History and Archaeology, The King's College, Briarcliff Manor, New York.

VUNDERINK, RALPH W.
A.B., B.D., M.A., Ph.D., Former Editorial Associate, *ISBE* Revision Project.

WALKER, W. L.*
D.D., Congregational Minister, Glasgow, Scotland.

WALLACE, HENRY*
Pastor, Parkhead Congregational Church, Glasgow, Scotland.

WALLACE, RONALD STEWART
B.S., M.A., Ph.D., Professor Emeritus of Biblical Theology, Columbia Theological Seminary, Decatur, Georgia.

WALTERS, STANLEY D.
B.A., B.D., Th.M., Ph.D., Professor of Old Testament Languages and Literature, Knox College, Toronto, Ontario, Canada.

WALTKE, BRUCE K.
A.B., Th.M., Th.D., Ph.D., Professor of Old Testament, Regent College, Vancouver, British Columbia, Canada.

WARFIELD, BENJAMIN BRECKINRIDGE*
D.D., LL.D., Litt.D., Professor of Didactic and Polemic Theology, Theological Seminary of the Presbyterian Church in the U.S.A., Princeton, New Jersey.

WATSON, D. M.
B.A., M. Div., Pastor, Aalen, West Germany.

WATTS, JOHN D. W.
B.A., Th.M., Ph.D., Professor of Old Testament, Fuller Theological Seminary, Pasadena, California.

WEAD, DAVID W.
A.B., B.Th., B.D., D.Th., Minister of Boones Creek Church of Christ, Johnson City, Tennessee.

WEDDLE, FOREST
A.B., M.S., Ph.D., Professor of Biblical Archaeology and Geography, Fort Wayne Bible College, Fort Wayne, Indiana.

WEIR, THOMAS HUNTER*
B.D., M.A., M.R.A.S., Lecturer in Arabic, University of Glasgow, Scotland.

WELCH, E. DOUGLAS
B.S., M.Div., M.A., Ph.D., Scholar in Biblical and Ancient Near Eastern Studies.

WESSEL, WALTER W.
B.A., M.A., Ph.D., Professor of New Testament and Chairman of the Department of Biblical and Theological Studies, Bethel College, St. Paul, Minnesota.

WHITELAW, THOMAS*
M.A., D.D., Minister of King Street United Free Church, Kilmarnock, Scotland.

WIEAND, DAVID JOHN
A.B., M.A., B.D., Ph.D., Professor of Biblical Literature, Bethany Theological Seminary, Oak Brook, Illinois.

WILLIAMS, CHARLES B.*
M.A., B.D., Ph.D., Professor of Greek and Ethics, Union University, Jackson, Tennessee.

WILLIAMS, WILLIAM C.
B.A., M.A., M.A.Rel., Ph.D., Professor of Old Testament, Southern California College, Costa Mesa, California.

WILLIAMSON, H. G. M.
B.A., M.A., Ph.D., Lecturer in Hebrew and Aramaic, Cambridge University, Cambridge, England.

WILLIS, LLOYD
B.A., M.A., Assistant Professor of Religion, Spicer Memorial College, Pune, India.

WOLF, HERBERT M.
B.A., Th.M., Ph.D., Associate Professor of Old Testament, Wheaton Graduate School, Wheaton, Illinois.

WOLF, HORACE J.*
B.H.L., M.A., Associate Rabbi of Berith Kodish Congregation, Rochester, New York.

WOUDSTRA, SIERD
A.B., B.D., Th.M., Th.D., Associate Professor of Religion and Theology, Calvin College, Grand Rapids, Michigan.

WRIGHT, CHRISTOPHER J. H.
M.A., Ph.D., Lecturer in Old Testament, Union Biblical Seminary, Pune, India.

WYATT, ROBERT J.
B.A., M.A., Editorial Associate, *ISBE* Revision Project.

WYPER, GLENN
B.A., B.D., Th.M., Registrar and Chairman of the Department of Biblical Studies, Ontario Bible College, Willowdale, Ontario, Canada.

YOUNG, FREDERICK E.
A.B., B.D., Ph.D., Dean of the Seminary and Professor of Old Testament, Central Baptist Theological Seminary, Kansas City, Kansas.

YOUNGBLOOD, RONALD F.
B.A., B.D., Ph.D., Professor of Old Testament, Trinity Evangelical Divinity School, Deerfield, Illinois.

PUBLISHERS' NOTES TO VOLUME TWO

As a convenience to the readers, the Abbreviations (with a few additions), the Transliteration Scheme, and the Pronunciation Key are included in this volume as well as in Volume I. Volume II also has its own list of Contributors. It does not appear necessary, however, to repeat in this volume the Introduction that appears in Volume I or to reprint the full-color map section with its index. Omission of the maps has allowed the section of full-color photographs to be doubled in size.

Completion of Volume II, as well as the work on the forthcoming Volumes III and IV, has been aided considerably by the addition of Consulting Editor Lawrence T. Geraty to the editorial team. The publishers' staff, too, has seen some changes: in addition to the persons mentioned in the Preface of Volume I, we are grateful to Gary A. Lee, Robert J. Wyatt, and James E. Hoffine for their work as Editorial Associates; to Kimberly Adams for work with the photographs and editing of English style; to Norma Garthe for typesetting; and to Louise Bauer for mapmaking and other technical help in the final stages of production.

THE PUBLISHERS

Abbreviations

GENERAL

A	Codex Alexandrinus (*See* Text and MSS of the NT I.B)
abbr.	abbreviated, abbreviation
act.	active
Akk.	Akkadian
Amer. Tr.	J. M. P. Smith and E. J. Goodspeed, *The Complete Bible: An American Translation*
Am.Tab.	el-Amarna Letters (*See* Amarna Tablets)
Apoc.	Apocrypha
Apost. Const.	Apostolic Constitutions
Aq.	Aquila's Greek version of the OT (*See* Septuagint)
Arab.	Arabic
Aram.	Aramaic
art.	article
Assyr.	Assyrian
ASV	American Standard Version
AT	Altes (or Ancien) Testament
AV	Authorized (King James) Version
b.	born
B	Codex Vaticanus (*See* Text and MSS of the NT I.B)
Bab.	Babylonian
bk.	book
Boh.	Bohairic (dialect of Coptic)
ca.	*circa,* about
Can.	Canaanite
cent., cents.	century, centuries
CG	Coptic Gnostic (*See* Nag Hammadi Literature)
ch., chs.	chapter(s)
Chald.	Chaldean, Chaldaic
col., cols.	column(s)
comm., comms.	commentary, commentaries
Copt.	Coptic
d.	died
D	Deuteronomist (*See* Criticism II.D.4); also Codex Bezae (*See* Text and MSS of the NT I.B)
diss.	dissertation
DSS	Dead Sea Scrolls
E	Elohist (*See* Criticism II.D.4); east
E.B.	Early Bronze (Age)
ed., eds.	editor, edition, edited (by), editors, editions
Egyp.	Egyptian
E.I.	Early Iron (Age)
Einl.	*Einleitung* (Introduction)
Eng. tr.	English translation
ERV	English Revised Version (1881-1885)
esp.	especially
et al.	and others
Eth.	Ethiopic, Ethiopian
f., ff.	following
fem.	feminine
fig.	figuratively
ft.	foot, feet
gal., gals.	gallon(s)
gen.	genitive
Ger.	German
Gk.	Greek
gm.	gram(s)
H	Law of Holiness (Lev. 17–26; *See* Criticism II.D.5)
ha.	hectare(s)
Heb.	Hebrew
Hist.	History
Hitt.	Hittite
Hom.	Homily
impf.	imperfect (tense)
in.	inch(es)
in loc.	at/on this passage
inscr.	inscription
intrans.	intransitive
intro., intros.	introduction(s)
J	Yahwist (*See* Criticism II.D.4)
JB	Jerusalem Bible
K	*kethibh* (*See* Text and MSS of the OT)
km.	kilometer(s)
l.	liter(s)
L	Lukan source (*See* Gospels, Synoptic V)
Lat.	Latin
L.B.	Late Bronze (Age)
lit.	literally
loc. cit.	in the place cited
LXX	Septuagint
m.	meter(s)
M	Matthaean source (*See* Gospels, Synoptic V)
masc.	masculine
M.B.	Middle Bronze (Age)
mg.	margin
mi.	mile(s)
mid.	middle voice

Midr. — Midrash
Mish. — Mishna (*See* TALMUD I)
Moff. — J. Moffatt, *A New Translation of the Bible* (1926)
MS, MSS — manuscript(s)
MT — Mas(s)oretic Text (*See* TEXT AND MSS OF THE OT)
N — north
n., nn. — note(s)
NAB — New American Bible
NASB — New American Standard Bible
n.d. — no date
NEB — New English Bible
neut. — neuter
N.F. — *Neue Folge* (New Series)
NIV — New International Version
NJV — New Jewish Version
no., nos. — number(s)
N.S. — New Series
NT — New (Neues, Nouveau) Testament
Onk. — Onkelos (Targum)
op. cit. — in the work quoted
OT — Old Testament
Oxy. P. — Oxyrhynchus papyrus
p — papyrus (used only with superscript number of the papyrus)
P — Priestly Code (*See* CRITICISM II.D.5)
par. — (and) parallel passage(s)
para. — paragraph
part. — participle
pass. — passive
Pent. — Pentateuch
Pers. — Persian
Pesh. — Peshito, Peshitta (*See* VERSIONS)
pf. — perfect (tense)
Phoen. — Phoenician
pl. — plural
prob. — probably
pt., pts. — part(s)
Q — *Quelle* (*See* GOSPELS, SYNOPTIC V)
Q — *qere* (*See* TEXT AND MSS OF THE OT)
repr. — reprinted
rev. — revised (by)
RSV — Revised Standard Version
RV — Revised Version (ERV or ASV)
S — south
Sah. — Sahidic (dialect of Coptic)
Sam. — Samaritan
Sem. — Semitic
sing. — singular
sq. — square
subst. — substantive
Sum. — Sumerian
supp. — supplement(ary)
s.v. — *sub voce* (*vocibus*), under the word(s)
Symm. — Symmachus' Greek version of the OT (*See* SEPTUAGINT)
Syr. — Syriac
Talm. — Talmud
T.B. — Babylonian Talmud
Tg., Tgs. — Targum(s)
Th. — Theodotion's revision of the LXX (*See* SEPTUAGINT)
T.P. — Palestinian (Jerusalem) Talmud
TR — Textus Receptus (*See* TEXT AND MSS OF THE NT IV)
tr. — translation, translated (by)
trans. — transitive
Ugar. — Ugaritic
v., vv. — verse(s)
v. — *versus*
var. — variant
vb., vbs. — verb(s)
viz. — namely
vol., vols. — volume(s)
Vulg. — Vulgate (*See* VERSIONS)
W — west
yd., yds. — yard(s)

SYMBOLS

א — Codex Sinaiticus (*See* TEXT AND MSS OF THE NT I.B)
< — derived from (etymological)
= — is equivalent to
* — theoretical or unidentified form
§ — section

PUBLICATIONS

AASOR — *Annual of the American Schools of Oriental Research*
AB — *Anchor Bible*
ADAJ — *Annual of the Department of Antiquities of Jordan*
AfO — *Archiv für Orientforschung*
AJSL — *American Journal of Semitic Languages and Literatures*
Alf. — Henry Alford, *Greek Testament* (4 vols., 1857-1861)
ANEP — J. B. Pritchard, ed., *The Ancient Near East in Pictures* (1954; 2nd ed. 1969)
ANET — J. B. Pritchard, ed., *Ancient Near Eastern Texts Relating to the Old Testament* (1950; 3rd ed. 1969)
ANT — M. R. James, *The Apocryphal New Testament* (1924; repr. 1953)
AOTS — D. W. Thomas, ed., *Archaeology and Old Testament Study* (1967)
AP — W. F. Albright, *The Archaeology of Palestine* (1949; rev. 1960)
APC — L. Morris, *Apostolic Preaching of the Cross* (3rd ed. 1965)
APOT — R. H. Charles, ed., *The Apocrypha and Pseudepigrapha of the Old Testament* (2 vols., 1913; repr. 1963)
ARAB — D. D. Luckenbill, ed., *Ancient Records of Assyria and Babylonia* (2 vols., 1926-1927)
ARI — W. F. Albright, *Archaeology and the Religion of Israel* (4th ed. 1956)
ARM — *Archives Royales de Mari* (1941–)
ATD — *Das Alte Testament Deutsch*
ATR — *Anglican Theological Review*
BA — *The Biblical Archaeologist*
BANE — G. E. Wright, ed., *The Bible and the Ancient Near East: Essays in Honor of William Foxwell Albright* (1961; repr. 1965, 1979)
BASOR — *Bulletin of the American Schools of Oriental Research*
Bauer — W. Bauer, *A Greek-English Lexicon of the New Testament,* tr. W. F. Arndt and F. W. Gingrich (1957; rev. ed.

ABBREVIATIONS

[tr. F. W. Gingrich and F. W. Danker from 5th Ger. ed.] 1979)

BC — F. J. Foakes Jackson and K. Lake, eds., *The Beginnings of Christianity* (5 vols., 1920-1933)

BDB — F. Brown, S. R. Driver, and C. A. Briggs, *Hebrew and English Lexicon of the Old Testament* (1907)

BDF — F. Blass and A. Debrunner, *A Greek Grammar of the New Testament*, tr. and rev. R. W. Funk (1961)

BDTh — *Baker's Dictionary of Theology* (1960)

BH — R. Kittel, ed., *Biblia Hebraica* (3rd ed. 1937)

BHS — K. Elliger and W. Rudolph, eds., *Biblia Hebraica Stuttgartensia* (1967-1977)

BhHW — *Biblisch-historisches Handwörterbuch* (1962–)

BHI — J. Bright, *A History of Israel* (1959; 2nd ed. 1972)

Bibl. — *Biblica*

BJRL — *Bulletin of the John Rylands Library*

BKAT — *Biblischer Kommentar, Altes Testament*

Bousset-Gressmann — W. Bousset, *Die Religion des Judentums im späthellenistischen Zeitalter*, rev. H. Gressmann (*HNT*, 21, 1926)

BZ — *Biblische Zeitschrift*

BZAW — *Beihefte zur Zeitschrift für die alttestamentliche Wissenschaft*

BZNW — *Beihefte zur Zeitschrift für die neutestamentliche Wissenschaft*

CAD — I. J. Gelb, *et al.*, eds., *Assyrian Dictionary of the Oriental Institute of the University of Chicago* (1956–)

CAH — *Cambridge Ancient History* (12 vols., rev. ed. 1962; 1970)

CBC — *Cambridge Bible Commentary on the New English Bible*

CBP — W. M. Ramsay, *Cities and Bishoprics of Phrygia* (1895-1897)

CBQ — *Catholic Biblical Quarterly*

CBSC — *Cambridge Bible for Schools and Colleges*

CCK — D. J. Wiseman, *Chronicles of Chaldaean Kings* (1956)

CD — K. Barth, *Church Dogmatics* (Eng. tr., 4 vols., 1936-1962)

CD — See Biblical and Extrabiblical Literature: Dead Sea Scrolls

CERP — A. H. M. Jones, *Cities of the Eastern Roman Provinces* (1937)

CG — P. Kahle, *The Cairo Geniza* (2nd ed. 1959)

CGT — *Cambridge Greek Testament* (20 vols., 1881-1933)

CHAL — W. L. Holladay, *A Concise Hebrew and Aramaic Lexicon of the Old Testament* (1971)

CIG — *Corpus Inscriptionum Graecarum* (1825-1859; index 1877)

CIL — *Corpus Inscriptionum Latinarum* (1862–)

ConNT — *Coniectanea Neotestamentica*

CRE — W. M. Ramsay, *The Church in the Roman Empire Before A.D. 170* (1903)

DBSup. — L. Pirot, *et al.*, eds., *Dictionnaire de la Bible: Supplement* (1928–)

DCG — J. Hastings, *Dictionary of Christ and the Gospels* (2 vols., 1906, 1908)

Deiss.LAE — G. A. Deissmann, *Light from the Ancient East* (Eng. tr., 2nd ed. 1927 [from German 4th ed.]; repr. 1978)

Dessau — H. Dessau, ed., *Inscriptiones Latinae Selectae* (3 vols., 2nd ed. 1954-1955)

DJD — *Discoveries in the Judean Desert*

DNTT — C. Brown, ed., *Dictionary of New Testament Theology* (3 vols., Eng. tr. 1975-1978)

DOTT — D. W. Thomas, ed., *Documents from Old Testament Times* (1958)

DTC — *Dictionnaire de Théologie Catholique* (15 vols., 1903-1950)

EAEHL — M. Avi-Yonah and E. Stern, eds., *Encyclopedia of Archaeological Excavations in the Holy Land* (4 vols., Eng. tr. 1975-1978)

EB — T. K. Cheyne and J. S. Black, eds., *Encyclopaedia Biblica* (4 vols., 1899)

Enc.Brit. — *Encyclopaedia Britannica*

EQ — *Evangelical Quarterly*

ERE — J. Hastings, *Encyclopaedia of Religion and Ethics* (12 vols., 1908-1926)

EtB — *Études Bibliques*

EvTh — *Evangelische Theologie*

Expos. — *The Expositor*

Expos.B. — *The Expositor's Bible* (3rd ed. 1903; rev. 1956)

Expos.G.T. — *The Expositor's Greek Testament*

Expos.T. — *Expository Times*

FRLANT — *Forschungen zur Religion und Literatur des Alten und Neuen Testaments*

FSAC — W. F. Albright, *From the Stone Age to Christianity* (2nd ed. 1957)

GAB — L. H. Grollenberg, *Atlas of the Bible* (1956)

GB — D. Baly, *Geography of the Bible* (1957; 2nd ed. 1974)

GJV — E. Schürer, *Geschichte des jüdischen Volkes im Zeitalter Jesu Christi* (3 vols., 4th ed. 1901-1909) (Converted to *HJP* when possible; but Eng. tr. not complete)

GKC — W. Gesenius, E. Kautzsch, and A. E. Cowley, *Gesenius' Hebrew Grammar* (2nd ed. 1910)

GP — F.-M. Abel, *Géographie de la Palestine* (2 vols., 2nd ed. 1933-1938)

GTTOT — J. Simons, *Geographical and Topographical Texts of the Old Testament* (1959)

HAT — *Handbuch zum Alten Testament*

HBD — M. S. Miller and J. L. Miller, eds., *Harper's Bible Dictionary* (1952; 2nd ed. 1961; 8th ed. [rev.] 1973)

HDB — J. Hastings, ed., *Dictionary of the Bible* (4 vols., 1898-1902, extra vol., 1904; rev. one-vol. ed. 1963)

HGHL — G. A. Smith, *Historical Geography of the Holy Land* (rev. ed. 1932)

HibJ — *The Hibbert Journal*

HJP — E. Schürer, *A History of the Jewish People in the Time of Jesus Christ* (tr. [of German *3rd* ed.] 1892-1901)

HJP[2] — E. Schürer, *The History of the Jewish People in the Age of Jesus Christ*, ed. G. Vermes and F. Millar (Eng. tr. and rev. 1973–)

HNT — *Handbuch zum Neuen Testament*

HNTC — *Harper's New Testament Commentaries = Black's New Testament Commentaries*

HNTT R. H. Pfeiffer, *A History of New Testament Times with an Introduction to the Apocrypha* (1949)
HR E. Hatch and H. A. Redpath, *Concordance to the Septuagint* (1897)
H-S E. Hennecke and W. Schneemelcher, eds., *New Testament Apocrypha* (2 vols., Eng. tr. 1963, 1965)
HST R. Bultmann, *History of the Synoptic Tradition* (Eng. tr., 2nd ed. 1968)
HTK *Herders Theologischer Kommentar zum Neuen Testament*
HTR *Harvard Theological Review*
HUCA *Hebrew Union College Annual*
IB *Interpreter's Bible* (12 vols., 1952-1957)
ICC *International Critical Commentary*
IDB *Interpreter's Dictionary of the Bible* (4 vols., 1962; Supplementary Volume, 1976)
IEJ *Israel Exploration Journal*
ILC J. Pedersen, *Israel: Its Life and Culture* (vols. I-II, Eng. tr. 1926; III-IV, Eng. tr. 1940)
Interp. *Interpretation: A Journal of Bible and Theology*
IOTG H. B. Swete, *Introduction to the Old Testament in Greek* (1902)
IP M. Noth, *Die israelitischen Personennamen in Rahmen der gemeinsemitischen Namengebung* (1928)
ISBE J. Orr, *et al.*, eds., *International Standard Bible Encyclopaedia* (2nd ed. 1929)
JAOS *Journal of the American Oriental Society*
Jastrow M. Jastrow, *Dictionary of the Targumim, the Talmud Babli, and the Midrashic Literature* (2 vols., 1950)
JBL *Journal of Biblical Literature*
JBR *Journal of Bible and Religion*
JCS *Journal of Cuneiform Studies*
JEA *Journal of Egyptian Archaeology*
JETS *Journal of the Evangelical Theological Society*
Jew.Enc. *Jewish Encyclopedia* (12 vols., 1901-1906)
JJS *Journal of Jewish Studies*
JNES *Journal of Near Eastern Studies*
JPOS *Journal of the Palestinian Oriental Society*
JQR *Jewish Quarterly Review*
JR *Journal of Religion*
JSS *Journal of Semitic Studies*
JTS *Journal of Theological Studies*
KAI H. Donner and W. Röllig, *Kanaanäische und Aramäische Inschriften* (3 vols., 2nd ed. 1966-1968)
KAT E. Schrader, ed., *Die Keilinschriften und das Alte Testament* (3rd ed. 1903)
KD K. F. Keil and F. Delitzsch, *Commentary on the Old Testament* (Eng. tr. 1864-1901; repr. 1973)
KEK *Kritisch-exegetischer Kommentar über das Neue Testament*
KoB L. Koehler and W. Baumgartner, *Lexicon in Veteris Testamenti Libros* (1953)
KS A. Alt, *Kleine Schriften zur Geschichte des Volkes Israel* (3 vols., 1953-1959)
KZAT *Kommentar zum Alten Testament*
KZNT *Kommentar zum Neuen Testament*
Lange Lange Commentaries
LAP J. Finegan, *Light from the Ancient Past* (1946; rev. 1959)
LBHG Y. Aharoni, *Land of the Bible: A Historical Geography* (Eng. tr. 1967)
LCC *Library of Christian Classics*
LCL *Loeb Classical Library*
LSC W. M. Ramsay, *Letters to the Seven Churches of Asia* (1905)
LSJ H. G. Liddell, R. Scott, H. S. Jones, *Greek-English Lexicon* (9th ed. 1940)
LTJM A. Edersheim, *Life and Times of Jesus the Messiah* (8th ed., rev., 1904; repr. 1977)
LTK Herder, *Lexicon für Theologie und Kirche* (2nd ed. 1957–)
MM J. M. Moulton and G. Milligan, *The Vocabulary of the Greek New Testament* (1930)
MNHK E. R. Thiele, *The Mysterious Numbers of the Hebrew Kings* (1965 ed.)
MNTC *Moffatt New Testament Commentary*
MPB H. N. and A. L. Moldenke, *Plants of the Bible* (1952)
MSt J. McClintock and J. Strong, *Cyclopaedia of Biblical, Theological and Ecclesiastical Literature* (1891)
NBC F. Davidson, ed., *New Bible Commentary* (1953)
NBD J. D. Douglas, ed., *New Bible Dictionary* (1962)
NHI M. Noth, *History of Israel* (Eng. tr. 1958; 2nd ed. 1960)
NICNT *New International Commentary on the New Testament*
NICOT *New International Commentary on the Old Testament*
Nov.Test. *Novum Testamentum: An International Quarterly*
NTD *Das Neue Testament Deutsch*
NTS *New Testament Studies*
ODCC *Oxford Dictionary of the Christian Church* (1957; 2nd ed. 1974)
ORHI W. O. E. Oesterley and T. H. Robinson, *History of Israel* (2 vols., 1932)
OTG H. B. Swete, *The Old Testament in Greek According to the Septuagint* (4th ed. 1912)
OTL *Old Testament Library*
OTMS H. H. Rowley, ed., *The Old Testament and Modern Study* (1951)
Pauly-Wissowa A. Pauly and G. Wissowa, eds., *Real-Encyclopädie der classischen Altertumswissenschaft*
PEF *Palestine Exploration Fund Memoirs*
PEQ *Palestine Exploration Quarterly*
PG J. P. Migne, ed., *Patrologia Graeca* (162 vols., 1857-1866)
PIOT R. H. Pfeiffer, *Introduction to the Old Testament* (1952 [1957] ed.)
PJ *Palästinajahrbuch*
PL J. P. Migne, ed., *Patrologia Latina* (221 vols., 1844-1864)
PSBA *Proceedings of the Society of Biblical Archaeology*
QHJ A. Schweitzer, *The Quest of the Historical Jesus* (1906; Eng. tr., 2nd ed. 1936)
RAC *Reallexikon für Antike und Christentum*

ABBREVIATIONS

RB	*Revue Biblique*
RGG	*Religion in Geschichte und Gegenwart* (5 vols., 3rd ed. 1957-1965)
RGJ	K. L. Schmidt, *Der Rahmen der Geschichte Jesu* (1919)
RHR	*Revue de l'histoire des religions*
RQ	*Revue de Qumran*
RRAM	D. Magie, *Roman Rule in Asia Minor* (2 vols., 1950)
RTWB	A. Richardson, ed., *A Theological Word Book of the Bible* (1950)
SB	H. L. Strack and P. Billerbeck, *Kommentar zum Neuen Testament aus Talmud und Midrasch* (5 vols., 1922-1961)
SBT	*Studies in Biblical Theology*
Sch.-Herz.	*The New Schaff-Herzog Encyclopedia of Religious Knowledge* (2nd ed. 1949-1952)
SE	*Studia Evangelica*
SJT	*Scottish Journal of Theology*
SPT	W. Ramsay, *St. Paul the Traveller and Roman Citizen* (1920)
SQE	K. Aland, ed., *Synopsis Quattor Evangeliorum* (2nd ed. 1964)
SSW	G. Dalman, *Sacred Sites and Ways* (1935)
ST	*Studia Theologica*
SVT	*Supplements to Vetus Testamentum*
SWP	C. R. Conder, *et al.*, eds., *Survey of Western Palestine* (9 vols., 1881-1888)
TDNT	G. Kittel and G. Friedrich, eds., *Theological Dictionary of the New Testament* (10 vols., Eng. tr. 1964-1976)
TDOT	G. J. Botterweck and H. Ringgren, eds., *Theological Dictionary of the Old Testament* (1974–)
THAT	E. Jenni and C. Westermann, eds., *Theologisches Handwörterbuch zum Alten Testament* (2 vols., 1971)
Thayer	Thayer's *Greek-English Lexicon of the New Testament*
ThHK	*Theologischer Handkommentar zum Neuen Testament mit Text und Paraphrase* (7 vols., 1928-1939; rev. 1957–)
TLZ	*Theologische Literaturzeitung*
Torch	*Torch Bible Commentaries*
TR	*Theologische Rundschau*
TU	*Texte und Untersuchungen zur Geschichte der altchristlichen Literatur*
UT	C. Gordon, *Ugaritic Textbook* (*Analecta Orientalia*, 38, 1965)
VC	*Vigiliae Christianae*
VE	*Vox Evangelica*
VT	*Vetus Testamentum*
WA	Luther's *Werke*, Weimar Ausgabe (1883–)
Wace	H. Wace, ed., *Apocrypha* (*Speaker's Commentary*, 1888)
WBA	G. E. Wright, *Biblical Archaeology* (1962)
WC	*Westminster Commentaries*
WHAB	G. E. Wright and F. V. Filson, eds., *Westminster Historical Atlas to the Bible* (1956)
WMANT	*Wissenschaftliche Monographien zum Alten und Neuen Testament*
WTJ	*Westminster Theological Journal*
ZAW	*Zeitschrift für die alttestamentliche Wissenschaft*
ZDPV	*Zeitschrift des deutschen Palästina-Vereins*
ZNW	*Zeitschrift für die neutestamentliche Wissenschaft*
ZTK	*Zeitschrift für Theologie und Kirche*

ANCIENT AUTHORS AND DOCUMENTS

Appian *Syr.*	*Syrian Wars*
Aquinas *Summa Theol.*	*Summa Theologica*
Aristotle *De an.*	*De anima* (*On the Soul*)
Eth. Nic.	*Nicomachaean Ethics*
Eth. Eud.	*Eudemaean Ethics*
Meta.	*Metaphysics*
Phys.	*Physics*
Pol.	*Politics*
Anal. post.	*Posterior Analytics*
Anal. pr.	*Prior Analytics*
Rhet.	*Rhetoric*
Poet.	*Poetics*
Augustine *Civ. Dei*	*De civitate Dei* (*The City of God*)
Conf.	*Confessiones*
De trin.	*De trinitate*
Ench.	*Enchiridion*
Ep.	*Epistulae*
Retr.	*Retractiones*
Calvin *Inst.*	*Institutes of the Christian Religion*
Chrysostom	
Hom. in Gen.	Homily on Genesis
Hom. in Heb.	Homily on Hebrews
Hom. in Jn.	Homily on John
Hom. in Mt.	Homily on Matthew
Clement of Alexandria	
Misc.	*Miscellanies* (*Stromateis*)
Paed.	*Paedagogus*
Curtius Rufus	Quintus Curtius Rufus
Digest	*See* ROMAN LAW II.G
Dio Cassius *Hist.*	*Roman History*
Hist. Epit.	Epitome of the *History*
Diodorus	Diodorus Siculus, *Library of History*
Diogenes	Diogenes Laertius, *Vitae philosophorum*
Epiphanius *Haer.*	*Adversus lxxx haereses* (*Panarion*)
Eusebius *HE*	*Historia ecclesiastica*
Onom.	*Onomasticon*
Praep. ev.	*Praeparatio evangelica*
HE	*Historia ecclesiastica* (*Church History*)
Herodotus	Herodotus *History*

Hippolytus *Ref.*	*Refutatio omnium haeresium (Philosophoumena)*
Homer *Il.*	*Iliad*
Od.	*Odyssey*
Irenaeus *Adv. haer.*	*Adversus omnes haereses*
Jerome *Ep.*	*Epistula(e)*
De vir. ill.	*De viris illustribus*
Adv. Pelag.	*Dialogi adversus Pelagianos*
Josephus *Ant.*	*Antiquities of the Jews*
BJ	*Bellum Judaicum (The Jewish War)*
CAp	*Contra Apionem*
Vita	*Life*
Justin Martyr *Apol.*	*Apologia*
Dial.	*Dialogus contra Tryphonem*
Livy *Epit.*	Epitomes of *Annals of the Roman People*
Origen *De prin.*	*De principiis*
Orosius	Orosius *Historiae*
Pliny (the Elder)	
Nat. hist.	*Naturalis historia*
Pliny (the Younger) *Ep.*	*Epistulae*
Ptolemy *Geog.*	*Geography*
Sallust	*Bellum Catilinae*
Strabo *Geog.*	*Geography*
Sulpicius Severus	
Chronicorum	*Historia sacra*
Tacitus *Ann.*	*Annals (Annales ab excessu divi Augusti)*
Hist.	*Histories*
Tertullian *Adv. Judaeos*	*Adversus Judaeos*
Adv. Marc.	*Adversus Marcionem*
Adv. Prax.	*Adversus Praxeam*
Apol.	*Apologeticum*
De orat.	*De oratione*
De praescr. haer.	*De praescriptione haereticorum*
De res.	*De resurrectione carnis*
Vergil *Aen.*	*Aeneid*

BIBLICAL AND EXTRABIBLICAL LITERATURE

OLD TESTAMENT

Gen.	Genesis
Ex.	Exodus
Lev.	Leviticus
Nu.	Numbers
Dt.	Deuteronomy
Josh.	Joshua
Jgs.	Judges
	Ruth
1, 2 S.	1, 2 Samuel
1, 2 K.	1, 2 Kings
1, 2 Ch.	1, 2 Chronicles
Ezr.	Ezra
Neh.	Nehemiah
Est.	Esther
Job	Job
Ps.	Psalm(s)
Prov.	Proverbs
Eccl.	Ecclesiastes
Cant.	Canticles (Song of Songs)
Isa.	Isaiah
Jer.	Jeremiah
Lam.	Lamentations
Ezk.	Ezekiel
Dnl.	Daniel
Hos.	Hosea
	Joel
Am.	Amos
Ob.	Obadiah
	Jonah
Mic.	Micah
Nah.	Nahum
Hab.	Habakkuk
Zeph.	Zephaniah
Hag.	Haggai
Zec.	Zechariah
Mal.	Malachi

NEW TESTAMENT

Mt.	Matthew
Mk.	Mark
Lk.	Luke
Jn.	John
	Acts
Rom.	Romans
1, 2 Cor.	1, 2 Corinthians
Gal.	Galatians
Eph.	Ephesians
Phil.	Philippians
Col.	Colossians
1, 2 Thess.	1, 2 Thessalonians
1, 2 Tim.	1, 2 Timothy
Tit.	Titus
Philem.	Philemon
He.	Hebrews
Jas.	James
1, 2 Pet.	1, 2 Peter
1, 2, 3 Jn.	1, 2, 3 John
	Jude
Rev.	Revelation

APOCRYPHA

1, 2 Esd.	1, 2 Esdras
Tob.	Tobit
Jth.	Judith
Ad. Est.	Additions to Esther
Wisd.	Wisdom of Solomon
Sir.	Sirach (Ecclesiasticus)
Bar.	Baruch
Ep. Jer.	Epistle (Letter) of Jeremiah
Song Three	Song of the Three Young Men
Sus.	Susanna
Bel	Bel and the Dragon
Pr. Man.	Prayer of Manasseh
1, 2 Macc.	1, 2 Maccabees

PSEUDEPIGRAPHA

Asc. Isa.	Ascension of Isaiah
Asm. M.	Assumption of Moses
2 Bar.	2 (Syriac Apocalypse of) Baruch
3 Bar.	3 (Greek Apocalypse of) Baruch
1, 2 En.	1, 2 Enoch
Jub.	Jubilees
Ps. Sol.	Psalms of Solomon
Sib. Or.	Sibylline Oracles
XII P.	Testaments of the Twelve Patriarchs
T. Reub.	Testament of Reuben
T. Sim.	Testament of Simeon
T. Levi	Testament of Levi
T. Jud.	Testament of Judah
T. Iss.	Testament of Issachar
T. Zeb.	Testament of Zebulun
T. Dan	Testament of Dan
T. Naph.	Testament of Naphtali
T. Gad	Testament of Gad
T. Ash.	Testament of Asher
T. Jos.	Testament of Joseph
T. Benj.	Testament of Benjamin

APOSTOLIC FATHERS

Barn.	Epistle of Barnabas
1 Clem.	1 Clement
2 Clem.	2 Clement
Did.	Didache
Ign.	Ignatius of Antioch
Eph.	Epistle to the Ephesians
Magn.	Epistle to the Magnesians
Trall.	Epistle to the Trallians
Rom.	Epistle to the Romans
Philad.	Epistle to the Philadelphians
Smyrn.	Epistle to the Smyrnaeans
Polyc.	Epistle to Polycarp
Polyc. Phil.	Polycarp of Smyrna, Epistle to the Philippians
M. Polyc.	Martyrdom of Polycarp
Shep. Herm.	Shepherd of Hermas
Vis.	Visions
Mand.	Mandates
Sim.	Similitudes
Diogn.	Epistle to Diognetus

DEAD SEA SCROLLS

Initial arabic numeral indicates cave number; Q = Qumrân; p = pesher (commentary).

CD	Damascus Document (Zadokite Fragment)
1QapGen	Genesis Apocryphon
1QH	Thanksgiving Hymns
1QIsa[a]	First copy of Isaiah from Qumrân Cave 1
1QIsa[b]	Second copy of Isaiah
1QM	War Scroll
1QpHab	Pesher (Commentary) on Habakkuk
1QpMic	Pesher on Micah
1QpPs	Pesher on Psalms
1QS	Manual of Discipline
1Q*34*[bis]	Prayer for the Feast of Weeks (Fragment of Liturgical Prayer Scroll = 1Q Prayers)
1QDM (or 1Q*22*)	Sayings of Moses
3QInv (or 3Q*15*)	Copper (Treasure) Scroll
4QFlor	Florilegium (eschatological midrashim) from Cave 4
4QPBless	Patriarchal Blessings
4QpIsa[a, b, c, d]	Copies of Isaiah pesher from Cave 4
4QpNah	Pesher on Nahum
4QpPs37	Pesher on Ps. 37
4QSam[a, b, c]	Copies of Samuel
4QTestim	Testimonia text from Cave 4
6QD (or 6Q*15*)	Fragments of the Damascus Document

The eagle was the patron of the armies of Hatra (a city 50 km. [30 mi.] NW of Asshur). Relief, 1st cent. A.D. (State Antiquities Organization, Republic of Iraq)

E (ELOHIST). *See* CRITICISM II.

EAGLE [Heb. *nešer*; Aram. *nᵉšar* (Dnl. 4:30; 7:4); Gk. *aetós* (Mt. 24:28; Lk. 17:37; Rev. 4:7; 8:13; 12:14)]; NEB also VULTURE, GRIFFON VULTURE (15 times). Two root meanings have been suggested for *nešer*: "gleaming flash" or "rushing sound" (G. R. Driver) and "tear with the beak" (H. B. Tristram). Both apply equally well to the Old World vulture and to the eagle.

The ambiguity of the term *nešer,* which poses a problem for translators, has been explained as a result of the distance from which these great birds are seen in flight (e.g., Cansdale, p. 124). The Bible, however, gives evidence of close and accurate observation of these diurnal birds of prey, great numbers of which lived in ancient Palestine. Thus the ambiguity in *nešer* derives not so much from confusion of eagles with vultures as from interest in their similarities rather than their differences. Both birds were notably similar in: size, strength, and longevity; magnificent flight; regal appearance (often symbolizing monarchal power and authority); nesting patterns; and feeding habits — both ate carrion and prey, although the eagle was better equipped for hunting. Their differences, therefore, are rarely important in the Bible.

In fact, the Hebrews were not wholly incorrect in grouping the vulture and the eagle together. Although superficially like the New World vultures (e.g., the Andean or California Condor) of the family *Cathartidae,* the Old World vultures of the Middle East are classed with eagles in family *Accipitridae* because of their similar structure.

While *nešer* may refer to large diurnal birds of prey in general, especially in flight, it is possible to be more specific by elimination. Eight species of eagles and four of vultures appear in Palestine. Most of the eagles are passing migrants and are too small to be called *nešer* (which appears to designate the largest group of birds; cf. Driver). Of the eagles, then, the Golden (*Aquila chrysaetos*) and perhaps the Imperial (*Aquila heliaca heliaca*) are most probably in mind. Two vultures (the Lammergeier, or Great Bearded, and the Black Vulture) fit most of the qualifications but are less frequently observed in Palestine and may be more specifically designated *peres* and *ʿoznîyâ,* respectively. A third, the Egyptian, is rather too small. Therefore, the fourth vulture, the Griffon, best fits all the requirements. It is a huge, handsome bird that must have been very numerous and thus a constant feature of ancient Palestine, especially in temple areas and battlefields. Its likeness appears in ancient Egyptian and Assyrian pictures. Although certainty is not important, the Griffon Vulture is probably in mind more often than the eagle in the biblical references.

Except for Lev. 11:13 and Dt. 14:12, in which *nešer* heads the list of unclean birds, all other references are metaphorical or illustrative, which may be grouped as follows:

(1) Flight (Ex. 19:4; Dt. 28:49; 2 S. 1:23; Job 9:26; Prov. 23:5; 30:19; Isa. 40:31; Jer. 4:13; 48:40; 49:22; Lam. 4:19; Ob. 4; Hab. 1:8; Rev. 4:7; 8:13; 12:14). The ancient Hebrew's fascination with the "eagle's" flight is expressed in Prov. 30:18f.: "Three things are too wonderful for me . . . the way of an eagle in the sky." Except for descriptions of the bird's carrying away its prey in flight (for which vultures' talons are too weak), the references may be to either the vulture or the eagle.

(2) Portents of death and destruction (Jer. 48:40; 49:22; Hos. 8:1; Mt. 24:28; Lk. 17:37; perhaps Lam. 4:19; Hab. 1:8). The prophetic references seem to picture carrion birds wheeling over a dying victim, Jerusalem or Israel. Jesus' reference is to vultures, for eagles do not gather. Besides these uses of *nešer* or *aetós* there are many allusions in the OT to scavenger birds (vultures) over battlefields (cf. Parmelee, pp. 125ff.).

(3) Nesting patterns (Dt. 32:11; Job 39:27-30; Jer. 49:16; Ob. 4). One of the best biblical descriptions of animal life (from a naturalist's viewpoint) is Job 39:27-30, which applies to both birds, although more completely to the vulture. The image is, on the one hand, of the bird's solicitude for its young, an illustration of God's care for Israel (Dt. 32:11). On the other hand, it is of the bird's security in its inaccessible cliff nest, although the point is made with regard to Edom's false security in Petra (Jer. 49:16; Ob. 4). *See also* NEST.

(4) Appearance (Ezk. 1:10; 10:14; Dnl. 4:33 [MT 30]; 7:4; Mic. 1:16). Mic. 1:16 is the most obvious OT allusion to the Griffon Vulture and its bald head (the RSV translation is poor). While the bird's regal bearing is usually intended, the reference in Dnl. 4:33 is hardly complimentary to the king!

(5) Youthful vigor (Ps. 103:5; Isa. 40:31). Ps. 103:5 may refer to the eagle's molting (cf. JB mg.) or to its incredible longevity (100 years); or the "youth" may be synonymous with "strength," as in Isa. 40:31 (so J. Duns, *Biblical Natural Science*, II [1863], 419f.).

Perhaps the most complete and best use of the eagle image is in the parable or riddle of Ezk. 17:1-21, where the eagle is a symbol of royal splendor and power over his prey (as explained in vv. 11-21).

Bibliography.–F. S. Bodenheimer, *Animal and Man in Bible Lands* (1960), pp. 53f.; G. S. Cansdale, *Animals of the Bible* (1970); G. R. Driver, *PEQ*, 87 (1955), 5-20, 129-140; A. Parmelee, *All the Birds of the Bible* (1959); R. Pinney, *Animals of the Bible* (1964); H. B. Tristram, *Natural History of the Bible* (1867); United Bible Society, *Fauna and Flora of the Bible* (1972).

H. VAN BROEKHOVEN, JR.

EANES ē'ə-nēz (AV, 1 Esd. 9:21). *See* MAASEIAH.

EAR [Heb. *'āḇîḇ* (Ex. 9:31), *'āzan, 'ōzen, karmel* (Lev. 2:14), *m^e lîlâ* (Dt. 23:25 [MT 26]), *šāma'* (1 K. 8:52; Ps. 55:19 [MT 20]), *šibbōleṯ*; Gk. *akoḗ, akoúō* (Mt. 28:14), *enōtízomai* (Acts 2:14), *oús, stáchys, ōtíon*]; AV also AUDIENCE, HEAR, HEARING, HEARKEN; NEB also ATTEND, "by report," HEAR, HEARD, HEARING, LISTEN, "pay attention," "pay heed," TURN (Ps. 86:1), etc. The physical organ for the reception of sound in both man (Ps. 49:4 [MT 5]) and beast (Prov. 26:17). The most important function of ears was the receiving of information and thereby correctly aligning life to the realities in control of existence.

As external parts of the body, the ears were subject to beautification (Gen. 35:4; Ezk. 16:12) and, in time of war, sadistic torture (Ezk. 23:25). The ear of the slave who voluntarily commited himself to perpetual service was to be pierced with an awl by the master (Ex. 21:6; Dt. 15:17). This was a public (at "the door"), legal ceremony binding the servant to his master forever. Similarly, the marking of the priests with blood on the right toe, thumb, and ear (Lev. 8:23f.) ordained them for perpetual servitude to their master by giving their ears over to His exclusive control.

Anthropomorphically, God too has ears and can hear the petitions of those who call upon Him (1 S. 8:21; Isa. 59:1; Jas. 5:4). This is in stark contrast to the gods of other nations (Ps. 135:17) and highlights through anthropomorphic language the accessibility and personal relationship of Yahweh to man. But He also hears the arrogance of man, responds appropriately (2 K. 19:28), and may even close His ears (Ezk. 8:18).

In typical Semitic fashion, the ear also stands for the totality of its function, i.e., the whole faculty of hearing in the fullest range of its possibilities. The ear is considered the organ that both receives and understands communications of every sort (Dt. 31:30; Job 12:11; 13:1; Prov. 18:15; Isa. 33:15). The function of the ear makes it often synonymous with the "heart" or "mind" as the organ of cognition (Prov. 2:2; 18:15). This relationship between "hearing" and "understanding" leads to many idiomatic uses: "to incline" or "give" ear means to hear and be favorably disposed toward what is heard (Ps. 31:2 [MT 3]; Isa. 1:10); the opposite of a willingness to receive or accept is having "uncircumcised," "heavy," or "deaf" ears (AV, NEB, Jer. 6:10; RSV "closed"; Acts 7:51; Isa. 6:10; 43:8); "itching" ears are ears disposed to hear only what is agreeable to their understanding (2 Tim. 4:3).

God has created the ear (Prov. 20:12). Therefore, man has a great responsibility to use his ears wisely, allowing God to open them so life can be aligned with reality. There is, then, the ear that hears without comprehension or appreciation (Dt. 29:4 [MT 3]; Ps. 115:6; Isa. 48:8; Ezk. 12:2); on the other hand, if one is willing, God can open the ear to life (Job 36:10, 15; Ps. 40:6 [MT 7]). The greatest achievement of the ear is to hear as a prophet (Isa. 22:14; 50:4f.), for the ear is almost always given priority over the eye for the reception of revelation. "Hear, O Israel" is the most important challenge of Israel's faith (Dt. 5:1; 6:3f.; Jer. 2:4). The theologically troublesome charge to Isaiah (6:9), "Go, and say to this people: 'Hear and hear, but do not understand,'" which is echoed in the NT (Mt. 13:14f.; Mk. 8:18), has often been explained in terms of divine sovereignty (so *TDNT*, V, 548). If this command is an exercise of biblical irony, however, then there is no question of divine morality involved; "the command is the counterpart of the ironic quotation in ch. 5:19, where the people sarcastically express their eagerness to see and hear. And the command ironically says, 'Try to make them worse than they are! Give them more ignorance, extend their incomprehension!'" (Good, p. 137). This is not what Isaiah consciously does, of course, but it is what results from further preaching to a people who refuse to hear aright.

The NT also recognizes the importance of the ear in receiving revelation, noting that such hearing must be accompanied by a willingness to appropriate what is heard; hence the frequent challenge, "He who has ears to hear, let him hear" (Mt. 11:15; Mk. 4:9; Lk. 14:35).

The importance of this challenge is heightened by the clarification given by John: "He who has an ear, let him hear *what the Spirit says*" (Rev. 2:7, 11, 17, 29; 3:6, 13, 22). Therefore, Jesus heals the deaf (Mk. 7:31-37) in response to OT prophecy (Isa. 35:5), for the Kingdom cannot come if men cannot hear the word of God.

The OT and NT mention "ears of grain," not of corn, which was unknown, but of barley (Ex. 9:31), wheat (Dt. 23:25), and no doubt other cereals (Lev. 2:14). The first month of the Hebrew calendar took its name *ʾāḇîḇ* from the barley ear, which ripened at this time of year (BDB, p. 1).

Bibliography.–E. M. Good, *Irony in the OT* (1965); *TDNT,* V, *s.v.* οὖς (Horst); *THAT,* I, *s.v.* אֹזֶן (Liedke). K. H. MAAHS

EAR; EARED; EARING. The Hebrew verbs *ḥāraš* (1 S. 8:12) and *ʿāḇaḏ* (Dt. 21:4; Isa. 30:24) are rendered by the AV "ear," "eared," an obsolete term meaning "to plow" (cf. RSV). The participle *ḥārîš* is rendered "earing" by the AV in Gen. 45:6 and Ex. 34:21 (RSV "plowing"). *See* PLOW.

EARLY. In the OT "early" occurs most frequently to translate the Hebrew verb *šāḵam* (e.g., "rise early" in Gen. 20:8; 21:14; 22:3; 26:31; 28:18; Ex. 24:4; etc.; "rise up early" in Gen. 19:2; Ex. 8:20; 9:13; 32:6; etc.). The RSV uses "early morning" twice to translate *ʾôr* (Ruth 2:7; Neh. 8:3), and renders "early rain" for *yôreh* (Dt. 11:14) and *môreh* (Ps. 84:6 [MT 7]; Joel 2:23). In Palestine the early rain is that which falls between late October and early December (cf. Jas. 5:7; *see* RAIN). In Ezk. 27:17 the RSV employs "early figs" to translate Heb. *pannag* (AV "pannag"; NEB "meal"). This is the only occurrence of the Hebrew term, so its meaning is uncertain; it represents one of the articles of commerce of Judah and Israel, probably some kind of food. The LXX reads *kasía,* which is an Arabian spice. In Ps. 46:5 (MT 6) "early" has the sense of "speedily," rendering Heb. *bōqer.*

In the NT "early" renders Gk. *órthros* and related words (Lk. 21:38; 24:1, 22; Jn. 8:2), *prōí* with related *prōía* (Mt. 20:1; Mk. 16:2; Jn. 18:28; 20:1) and *próïmos* (Jas. 5:7), and *archaíos* (Acts 15:7, 21; 21:16). *Órthros* and *prōí,* along with their cognates, refer exclusively to the morning. *Próïmos* is derived from *pró* rather than *prōí* (cf. Bauer, p. 713; see above on Dt. 11:4; Ps. 84:6; Joel 2:23). In Acts 15:7, 21 *archaíos* denotes the ancient times, while in 21:16 it is used of a disciple "of long standing" (Bauer, p. 110).

EARNEST. *See* GUARANTEE.

EARRING [Heb. *nezem*] (Ex. 35:22; Jgs. 8:24-26); [*ʿāgîl*] (Nu. 31:50; Ezk. 16:12); NEB PENDANT. An ornament of some kind hanging from the ears, apparently worn by both sexes in oriental lands including Palestine from the earliest times. The Ishmaelite men were known for their golden earrings (Jgs. 8:24-26). Among the Greeks and Romans, as with Western peoples in general, its use was confined to females.

The first people known to have used earrings are the Sumerians, for whom they were magical amulets designed to protect the ear openings from infiltration by evil spirits that were thought to be the cause of disease.

Ancient earrings were usually fashioned from gold, finely wrought, and often set with precious stones, as supported by archeological discoveries. The jewels were worn for protection as well as for decoration. Various kinds of earrings have been unearthed from different levels at numerous Palestinian sites, including Gezer, Megiddo, Tell Jemmeh, Taanach, and Tell el-ʿAjjûl.

See also AMULET; ORNAMENT. R. K. H.

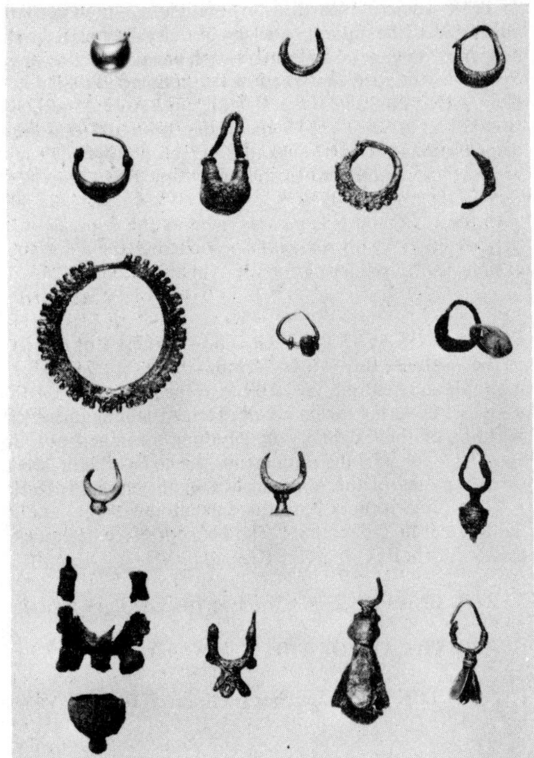

Copper, gold, and silver earrings from graves at Asshur (predominantly 9th-7th cents. B.C.) (Staatliche Museen, Berlin)

EARTH [Heb. *ʾereṣ, ʾ^{a}ḏāmâ,* also *ʿāp̄ār*–'dust' (Gen. 26:15; Job 7:21; etc.), *ʾaḏmaṯ-ʿāp̄ār* ("dust of the earth," Dnl. 12:2); Aram. *ʾ^{a}raʿ* (Ezr. 5:11; Jer. 10:11; Dnl. 2–7), *ʾ^{a}raq* (Jer. 10:11), *yabbeštāʾ* (Dnl. 2:10); Gk. *gḗ,* also *katachthónios*–'under the earth,' 'subterranean' (Phil. 2:10)].

While used in most of the senses of *ʾaḏāmâ, ʾereṣ* often indicated the earth as a planet rather than as soil or ground. Although the Hebrews occasionally thought of the earth as spherical (Isa. 40:22), they generally imagined it to be flat (cf. Isa. 42:5; 44:24), poised in space (Job 26:7) or situated on a vast ocean (Ps. 24:2; 136:6), and established on firm foundations (Ps. 104:5) that were sometimes described in terms of pillars (1 S. 2:8; Job 9:6; Ps. 75:3 [MT 4]) or props (Prov. 8:29; cf. 2 S. 22:16). The WORLD was thought to have four edges or corners (Isa. 11:12; cf. Ezk. 7:2; Job 38:13), but apart from this there was no speculation about the physical shape of the earth. It should be remembered that many of the foregoing descriptions occur in poetic passages and must be evaluated accordingly. The Sumerian pictograph for earth (ki), comprising a sphere with shading in the middle to afford perspective, indicated an early acceptance of a round rather than a flat earth. The outlook of the ancient Near Eastern peoples was regional, and areas that extended beyond known boundaries were usually described by such vague terms as "the islands" (cf. Isa. 40:15).

The earth and its fulness were the Lord's (Ps. 24:1; 1 Cor. 10:26), and its productivity depended largely upon man's obedience to God's will. The Israelites were promised repeatedly that an increase of crops would result from following the divine precepts (cf. Dt. 28:4f.; etc.), while disobedience would be punished by failure and famine (cf. Dt. 28:16-18; etc.). This type of theological monism stood in sharp contrast to the fertility notions of other ancient Near Eastern religions, in which the earth had to be impregnated by a deity before it could bear fruit. In general agreement with pagan thought, however, was the idea that shed blood polluted the land (cf. Gen. 4:11f.; Nu. 35:33f.; 2 S. 1:21; cf. 3 Aqht 35 [AQHT B iv 35 in *ANET,* p. 153]). Under both old and new dispensations the earth was to be given renewed life and productivity at the end of the age (Am. 9:13; Zec. 14:8; Rev. 21:1).

In the LXX and NT, *gḗ* was used as the equivalent of the MT *ʾereṣ,* with *oikouménē* occurring on a few occasions as the rendering for the "inhabited earth."

R. K. H.

EARTH, CORNERS OF THE. The "corners" or "ends" of the earth are its "wings" (Heb. *kanᵉpôṯ hāʾāreṣ*), i.e., its borders or extremities. Because the wing of a bird is used as a covering for its young, Heb. *kānāp* acquires the meaning of the extremity of anything stretched out. In Isa. 11:12; Job 37:3 the term means the coasts, boundaries, or extremities of the land surface of the earth. In Ezk. 7:2 the "four-corners" are the extremities of the land in the four cardinal directions. The concept of "extremities" also occurs in Rev. 7:1; 20:8 (Gk. *gonía*). R. K. H.

EARTH, ENDS OF THE. *See* EARTH, CORNERS OF THE.

EARTH, PILLARS OF THE. *See* WORLD.

EARTH, THE NEW. *See* ESCHATOLOGY III; HEAVENS, NEW.

EARTH, VAULT OF THE. In one passage it is said that God "founds his vault [Heb. *ʾᵃguddâ*] upon the earth" (Am. 9:6). It is not quite certain whether this dome or vault refers to the earth itself, or to the heavens arched above it. The latter is the usual interpretation, but in either case the reference is rather to the strength of the structure than to its form. The word implies something that is firmly bound together, hence an arch or dome because of its stability. *See also* WORLD.

EARTHEN VESSELS; EARTHEN FLASK; EARTHEN POT; EARTHENWARE [Heb. *ḥereś* (Prov. 26:23; Isa. 45:9), *kᵉlî-ḥereś* (Lev. 6:28 [MT 21]; 11:33; 14:5, 50; 15:12; Nu. 5:17; Jer. 32:14), *baqbuq ḥereś* (Jer. 19:1), *niḇlê-ḥereś* (Lam. 4:2), *kᵉlî-yôṣēr* (2 S. 17:28); Gk. *ostrákinos* (2 Cor. 4:7; 2 Tim. 2:20), *keramikós* (Rev. 2:27)]; AV also POTSHERD, EARTHEN BOTTLE, EARTHEN PITCHER, etc.; NEB also EARTHENWARE VESSEL, JUG, etc. These fired pottery vessels were heat-resisting and so could be used for cooking and for boiling clothes (Lev. 6:28; 11:33; 14:5, 50). Demonstrating typical Near Eastern hospitality, the generous natives brought David not only gifts of food but also the necessary vessels in which to cook it (2 S. 17:28). An earthen vessel was also used to preserve a deed for land (Jer. 32:14).

In 2 Tim. 2:20 a comparison of earthenware vessels with vessels of gold and silver is used metaphorically. Breaking of an earthen vessel is symbolic of the destruction of Jerusalem (Jer. 19:1, 10), or of the "nations" (Rev. 2:27). Earthen vessels were also used to illustrate the commonness (Lam. 4:2) and frailty (2 Cor. 4:7) of our bodies.

See also POTTERY; CLAY. J. A. PATCH

EARTHLY [Gk. *epígeios*] (Jn. 3:12; 2 Cor. 5:1; Phil. 3:19; Jas. 3:15); NEB also "things on earth," EARTH-BOUND; [*epí tḗs gḗs*] (Col. 3:5); AV "upon the earth"; NEB "which belong to the earth"; [*katá sárka, tḗs sarkós*] (Eph. 6:5; Col. 3:22; He. 12:9); AV "according to the flesh," "of flesh"; [*sarkikós*] (2 Cor. 1:12); AV FLESHLY; NEB WORLDLY; [*kosmikós*] (He. 9:1); AV WORLDLY; NEB MATERIAL.

As used by the RSV, "earthly" does not have a negative moral connotation, with the exceptions of Phil. 3:19 and Jas. 3:15. The term *epígeios* is from *epí,* "upon," and *gḗ,* "earth." It simply means "of or pertaining to the earth, or to the present state of existence." In Phil. 3:19 and Jas. 3:15, where earth is spoken of as the place of sin, "earthly" takes on the connotation of moral inferiority, suggesting that which is opposed to the spiritual in character. *Sárx* and adj. *sarkikós* as used in 2 Cor. 1:12; Eph. 6:5; Col. 3:22; He. 12:9 are ethically neutral terms. *Sárx* here denotes the sphere of human existence, which is limited and temporary, in contrast with the heavenly and spiritual sphere. *Kosmikós,* likewise, is used of the tabernacle in He. 9:1 not in its usual sense of "worldly" but in the sense of "belonging to this world," i.e., a transitory, now obsolete, institution. N. J. O.

EARTHQUAKE [Heb. *raʿaš*; Gk. *seismós*]; AV, NEB, also RUSHING. A shaking of the earth's crust, usually a tectonic activity of variable intensity. Egypt is relatively free from this hazard, but the area from Greece to Iran is especially vulnerable, as many catastrophes in the area indicate: a quake in Iran in the spring of 1972 took four thousand lives, and two decades earlier Greece suffered severely. Palestine is at the edge of this quake-prone area, the center of which lies in Turkey.

In the past two millennia Palestine has had seventeen recorded quakes of major proportions, an average of slightly less than one in each century. Amos alluded to one in his day (*ca.* 760 B.C.): "two years before the earthquake" (Am. 1:1). Josephus (*Ant.* xv.5.2) reported the loss of ten thousand lives in a quake in 31 B.C., the effects of which may still be seen in the steps of a cistern constructed by the Qumrân community near the Dead Sea. On Jan. 1, 1837, an earthquake centered in Safat took nearly five thousand lives. Another, centered in Nâblus, resulted in the loss of 350 lives in 1927. The Ludd-Ramla area is also subject to earthquakes.

It is believed that the source of the major quakes is the Jordan or rift-valley. Antioch in Syria has often been an epicenter. Jerusalem is relatively free from severe

Earthquake damage to steps leading to a cistern at Qumrân (D. Baly)

quakes (though it seems to have been hit more frequently by small ones). A quake in 64 B.C. damaged the temple in Jerusalem, as did another in A.D. 33. This may have coincided with the disturbance mentioned at the time of Jesus' crucifixion (Mt. 27:54; 28:2).

In addition to the major quakes reported above, seismic activity has been recorded in many places since NT times. A severe quake hit central Palestine in A.D. 130, and in 365 the fortress at Kerak in Transjordan was severely damaged. Severe shocks were experienced at Imwas in 498, at Acco in 502, in Galilee in 551, and at Jerusalem in 746. In 1016 the cupola of the Dome of the Rock in Jerusalem collapsed. The quake in 1033 was very severe and widespread. In 1546 and again in 1834 severe damage was done to the domes of both the Holy Sepulchre and the Dome of the Rock. Earthquakes dammed the Jordan River (as perhaps in the time of Joshua) at Damiya in 1546 and again in 1927; the latter shock left 860 dead.

The number of casualties normally depends not so much on the severity of the quake as on its location; when populated areas are hit, as at Safat in 1837, the loss of life is far more extensive than if the quake occurs in open country. Obviously buildings constructed of earth or stone are much more liable to damage than structures of wood, steel, or reinforced concrete.

The Bible sometimes refers to earthquakes as accompanying divine revelation (Ex. 19:18; 1 K. 19:11f.; Isa. 6:4) or demonstrating God's power (Job 9:6) and presence (Ps. 68:8 [MT 9]) or divine judgments (Ps. 18:7 [MT 8]; Nah. 1:5; Isa. 13:13; 29:6; Am. 9:1; Ezk. 38:19f.; cf. Zec. 14:5). An earth tremor sufficed to free Paul and Silas at a very opportune time (Acts 16:26). Earthquakes are predicted to precede the end of the age (Mt. 24:7; Mk. 13:8; Lk. 21:11; Rev. 6:12; 8:5; 11:13, 19; 16:18).

Bibliography.–D. H. K. Amiran, *IEJ,* 1 (1950/51), 223-246; C. F. Richter, *Elementary Seismology* (1958); E. J. Arieh, *Geological Survey of Israel,* 43 (1967), 1-14; *Encyclopedia Judaica,* VI, *s.v.*; D. P. McKenzie, *Nature* (London), 226 (1970), 237-243.

G. A. TURNER

EARTHY (1 Cor. 15:47-49, AV). *See* DUST.

EASE; AT EASE; etc. [Heb. *šā'an, ša'ᵃnān*]; AV also REST, QUIET; NEB also PEACE, UNDISTURBED, PROSPEROUS, PROUD; [*šal'ᵃnan*] (Job 21:23); NEB COMFORT; [hiphil of *rāga'*] (Dt. 28:65); NEB PEACE; [*šālēw, šᵉlêw*] (Job 16:12; Ps. 73:12; Jer. 49:31); AV also PROSPER, WEALTHY; NEB also PROSPER, AT PEACE; [*šāqaṭ*] (Job 3:26; Ezk. 16:49); AV REST, IDLENESS; NEB also "peace of mind"; [*nāśā'*] (Job 7:13); NEB RELIEVE; [hiphil part. of *rûm*] (Hos. 11:4); AV "take off"; NEB LIFT; [Aram. *šᵉlēh*] (Dnl. 4:4 [MT 1]); AV REST; NEB PEACEFULLY; [Gk. *anapaúō*] ("take your ease," Lk. 12:19); NEB EASY; [*aphóbōs*] (1 Cor. 16:10); AV "without fear"; [*ánesis*] (2 Cor. 8:13); NEB RELIEVE.

House at Hazor apparently destroyed by earthquake in Amos's time (Am. 1:1) (Institute of Archaeology, Hebrew University of Jerusalem)

The OT terms most commonly rendered "ease" are the verb *šā'an* and the noun *ša'ᵃnān,* which generally express tranquility, security, or comfort of mind; in the ethical sense, however, they indicate indifference to moral or religious concerns (cf. Job 12:5; Ps. 123:4; Isa. 32:9, 11; Jer. 48:11; Am. 6:1; Zec. 1:15). This ethical sense applies also to *šāqaṭ* in Ezk. 16:49, referring to Sodom, and to *šālēw* in Ps. 73:12 and *šᵉlēw* in Jer. 49:31.

The only occurrence of "ease" in the Gospels is in the story of the rich fool, where the use of *anapaúō* reflects the common OT ethical sense. In 1 Cor. 16:10 the RSV and NEB render *aphóbōs génētai* (AV lit. "that he may be . . . without fear") by "put him at ease."

"Ease" occurs as a verb twice in the OT and once in the NT. The verbs *nāśā'* and (hiphil) *rûm* both mean "lift" or "raise." The Gk. *ánesis* denotes a "relaxing" or "relief."

N. J. O.

EAST, PEOPLE OF THE [Heb. *mizrāḥ, qeḏem, qēḏem,* and other derivatives of the same root; Gk. *anatolḗ*]. *Mizrāḥ* is the equivalent of the Arab. *meshriq,* "the orient" or "place of sunrise." *Qāḏam,* "precede" (whence *qeḏem,* "east"), and its derivatives correspond closely to the Arab. *qadam,* except that the Arabic derivatives do not include the signification "east." In the majority of cases "east" and other words of direction require no explanation, but the expressions "the people of the east" (*bᵉnê qeḏem*), "land of the people of the east" (*'ereṣ bᵉnê qeḏem*), and "the east country" (*'ereṣ qeḏem*) belong to a different category. In the story of Gideon we find several times the expression "the Midianites and the Amalekites and [all] the people of the East" (Jgs. 6:3, 33; 7:12; cf. 8:10). In Jgs. 8:24 it is said of the same host: "For they had golden earrings, because they were Ishmaelites"; in Jer. 49:28f.: "Rise up, advance against Kedar! Destroy the people of the East! Their tents and their flocks shall be taken"; in Gen. 25:6: "But to the sons of his concubines Abraham gave gifts, and while he was still living he sent them away from his son Isaac, eastward to the east country." Now Ishmael is the son of Abraham and Hagar, Midian of Abraham and Keturah, Kedar the son of Ishmael, and Amalek the grandson of Esau, dwelling in Edom. It is evident that the references are to the Syrian desert and in a general way to Arabia, especially its northern part, and to peoples like the Bedouin who kept camels and dwelt in tents, "houses of hair" (*buyût sha'r*) as they are called by modern Arabs.

A striking passage is Gen. 29:1: "Then Jacob went on his journey, and came to the land of the people of the east" in Paddan-aram. Journeying eastward from Jordan one traverses first a region of towns and villages with fields of grain, and then the wide desert where the Bedouin wander with their herds. The line is a sharp one. Within a very short time one passes from the settled part, where the rain, though scanty, is sufficient to bring the grain to maturity, to the bare desert.

Job was "the greatest of all the people of the east" (Job 1:3). These desert people were renowned for their wisdom, as attested by 1 K. 4:30: "Solomon's wisdom surpassed the wisdom of all the people of the east, and all the wisdom of Egypt"; and Mt. 2:1: "Now when Jesus was born . . . wise men from the East came."

The biblical references make it clear that any nation living to the east of the Israelites could be included in this designation. A. E. DAY

EAST COUNTRY [Heb. *'ereṣ mizrāḥ*]. Literally "country of the sunrise" over against the "country of the sunset" (Zec. 8:7). The two together form a poetical expression (merism) indicating the whole earth. Abraham sent the sons of his concubines to the east country (*'ereṣ qeḏem,* Gen. 25:6), the area SE of Palestine.

EAST GATE. *See* GATE, EAST; POTSHERD GATE.

EAST WIND. *See* WIND.

EASTER (AV Acts 12:4). An anachronistic mistranslation of the Gk. *páscha* (RSV, NEB, "Passover"), in which the AV followed such earlier versions as Tyndale and Coverdale. The Acts passage refers to the seven-day Passover festival (including the Feast of Unleavened Bread). It is reasonably certain that the NT contains no reference to a yearly celebration of the resurrection of Christ.

I. Origin of the Term.–The term Easter was derived from the Anglo-Saxon "Eostre," the name of the goddess of spring. In her honor sacrifices were offered at the time of the vernal equinox. By the 8th cent. the term came to be applied to the anniversary of Christ's resurrection.

II. Controversy about the Time of Celebration.–The date for the celebration of the Resurrection was the subject of extensive disagreement for centuries. Among early Jewish Christians the time of the observance was determined by the date of the Hebrew Passover festival (Heb. *pesaḥ*), which began on the 14th day of Nisan. Gentile Christians, however, tended to celebrate the Resurrection on a Sunday. The result was that Christians in the East generally observed the same day of the month, regardless of the day of the week on which it fell, whereas Christians in Rome and the West observed the same day of the week (the first), regardless of the day of the month on which it came. The issue was bitterly debated, but as time passed an increasing number of people celebrated the anniversary of the Resurrection on the first day of the week.

Steps toward settlement of the disagreement were taken at the Council of Nicea (A.D. 325). Although Syrian leaders argued for dating Easter according to the Jewish Passover, the Council unanimously decided that the Resurrection was to be celebrated in all churches on the same Sunday. No fixed rule was established for deciding which Sunday was to be observed. Instead, it was left for church leaders of Alexandria to determine the date each year. Disagreement continued to surround the matter. Some, who were called "Quarto-decimans," persisted in relating Easter to the 14th of Nisan.

By the 7th cent. the practice of the Church had become reasonably uniform. The time agreed upon was the first Sunday following the full moon that comes on or after the vernal equinox. The date of the equinox was set at Mar. 21. This allowed for a variation in Easter dates from Mar. 22 to Apr. 25. The uniformity of practice which prevailed for a number of centuries was again disturbed for a time with the adoption of the Gregorian calendar in 1582.

III. Current Practice.–In the 20th cent. there is agreement on the determination of the Easter date except in the Eastern Orthodox Church, which employs a somewhat different method of calculation. The advisability of fixing the date of Easter on a set Sunday, such as the first Sunday of April, has been discussed by some church leaders in recent years.

Bibliography.–N. M. Denis-Boulet, *Christian Calendar* (1960), pp. 40-49; *EB,* VII, *s.v.* (E. O. James); *ODCC, s.v.*

D. W. BURDICK

EASTERN SEA (Ezk. 47:18; Joel 2:20; Zec. 14:8). *See* DEAD SEA.

EAT. ***I. Word Usage.*** The Hebrew verb for "eat" is *'āḵal* and the corresponding Greek word is *esthíō/éphagon*. Both terms stand for a basic act necessary for the sustaining of life and as such are widely used in both OT and NT, often in combination with drinking (e.g., Gen. 25:34; 26:30; Jgs. 9:27; 19:4, 21; Ruth 3:3; 1 K. 13:18). In the NT Paul directed that if anyone refused to work he should not be permitted to eat, either (2 Thess. 3:10). Closely associated, directly or indirectly, with eating and drinking is the enjoyment of life (e.g., 2 S. 11:11; 1 K. 1:25; 4:20; Job 1:4; Eccl. 3:13; 5:18 [MT 17]; Lk. 15:23).

In the OT the verb is also used figuratively, e.g., Israel "devours" its enemies, meaning that it suppresses or destroys them (Dt. 7:16; Ezk. 19:3, 6; 36:13; Zec. 12:6). Similarly other nations can "devour" or "consume" Israel and its land (Ps. 79:7; Isa. 1:7; Jer. 8:16; 10:25; 50:7; cf. Nu. 13:32). "To devour the poor" is to treat them unjustly (Prov. 30:14; Hab. 3:14). Grave social disorder and injustice is an eating of the flesh of the people (Mic. 3:3). According to Isaiah (49:26) Yahweh will make Israel's oppressors "eat their own flesh," i.e., they will be reduced to utter helplessness (cf. *TDOT,* I, 238). The prophetic announcement that covenant breaking would result in severe famine, driving people to eat the flesh of their sons and daughters (Lev. 26:29; Dt. 28:53-57), became historical reality (2 K. 6:28f.; cf. Lam. 2:20).

In other figurative uses Heb. *'āḵal* is conjoined with Yahweh. In battle His sword devours enemies (Dt. 32:42; Jer. 46:10), and in judgment it devours Israel (Isa. 1:20; Jer. 12:12; etc.; cf. Hos. 13:8). God is a devouring fire (Ex. 24:17; Dt. 4:24; He. 12:29). Heb. *'āḵal* also is used in reference to humans. In Ps. 14:4 evildoers eat up God's people the way they eat bread (cf. Ps. 50:3; etc.); heat consumes Jacob (Gen. 31:40), and zeal for the house of God consumes the psalmist (Ps. 69:9 [MT 10]; cf. Jn. 2:17 for a later application of this verse to Jesus). To the wide range of meaning belongs also that of "using" or "enjoying" something, e.g., Eccl. 5:11 (MT 10), which speaks of the consumption of one's goods by others.

II. Regulations and Customs.–The OT and the Jewish world in general observed certain rituals with respect to food and its consumption. The Mosaic law prescribed which portion of the sacrifices was to be for the priests (Lev. 2:3; 5:13; 6:14-30; 7:9, 29-36; 10:12-15. The law also specified which foods were clean and which unclean (Lev. 11; Dt. 14:3-21; cf. Gen. 9:3). Specifically, swine's flesh was an abomination (Isa. 65:4; 66:3, 17). Daniel and his friends refused to eat from the king's table because they did not wish to violate Jewish dietary laws (Dnl. 1:8, 12; cf. 2 Macc. 5:27). Special regulations pertained to food for Nazirites and soldiers (Nu. 6:1-4). According to an editorial note in Mk. 7:19 Jesus did away with the distinction between foods (cf. He. 9:10; 13:9). The early Church was troubled by the propriety of eating flesh sacrificed to idols (Acts 15:29; Rom. 14; 1 Cor. 8; 10:19-33). The Pharisees carefully observed the prior washing of hands (Mk. 7:3f.), but Jesus regarded Himself free from such obligations (Mt. 15:16-20).

Fasting, the refraining from eating and drinking, was

prominent in biblical Israel. During the forty days that he was on the mountain with God, Moses neither ate bread nor drank water (Ex. 34:28; cf. Dt. 9:9). Jesus fasted forty days and forty nights in the wilderness (Mt. 4:2). Part of Jonah's call of repentance to Nineveh was the call to fast (Jonah 3:7). In the Babylonian Exile, and also afterwards upon their return to Palestine, the Jews observed stated fasts (Zec. 7:5; cf. also Acts 9:9). Fasting was often observed in connection with vows (Acts 23:12, 14).

Feasting was also common in the ancient Near East. The Ugaritic myths have frequent references to it (e.g., *UT,* 51:iv:35; 52:6; 67:i:24; ii:23), some of which have close parallels in the OT. In view of the cultic nature of these Ugaritic texts, the OT parallels may be further instances of "archaic demythologizing" (W. F. Albright's term in *Yahweh and the Gods of Canaan* [1968], pp. 183-193), which was an attempt by OT authors to transform pagan ideas or associations. Thus in Prov. 9:1-6 the personified Wisdom calls for people to join in a feast, which apparently will enlighten them (v. 6; cf. Isa. 55:1; on Cant. 5:1 see M. Pope, *Song of Songs* [*AB,* 1977], pp. 507-510).

Attendants bring food, whisk away flies, and make music for King Ashurbanipal (reclining) and his queen, who drink wine from bowls in their garden. Palace relief from Kuyunjik (Nineveh), 668-633 B.C. (Trustees of the British Museum)

III. Theological Use.–In the story of mankind's FALL into sin (Gen. 3), the actual fall from grace occurs in connection with Adam and Eve's eating from the tree of the knowledge of good and evil. This tree seems to represent omniscience, which is solely God's domain. The eating of the forbidden fruit represents humanity's sinful determination to set for itself the standard of right and wrong. By this act of usurping what belongs to God alone, the human race incurs God's punishment. Hard labor is now man's lot; he is subject to death and barred from the strength-renewing and healing powers of the tree of life (cf. Rev. 22:2), and must work hard for his food (cf. Gen. 3:17-19).

The Mosaic law contains detailed regulations pertaining to the preparation and eating of the PASSOVER lamb (Ex. 12:1-13). These details served as reminders of aspects of the bondage the Israelites had endured in Egypt and of Yahweh's gracious deliverance.

An agreement or reconciliation reached between parties was frequently sealed and celebrated with eating and drinking together, e.g., when Laban and Jacob covenanted not to treat each other ill (Gen. 31:54). Sharing a meal was in antiquity often an expression of mutual fellowship and trust. In contrast, turning against someone with whom one had shared table fellowship was a vile act of the lowest sort; Jesus was not betrayed by an outsider but by "one who is eating with me" (Mk. 14:18; cf. also v. 20; Lk. 22:21; Ps. 41:9 [MT 10]). After Jesus' resurrection the disciples whom He had chosen to be His witnesses ate and drank with Him (Acts 10:41). Refusal to eat with someone expressed repudiation of fellowship with that person (1 Cor. 5:11).

The covenantal meal described in Ex. 24:9-11 is particularly apt. Following the formal ratification of the covenant between Yahweh and Israel (vv. 1-8), Moses, Aaron, Nadab, Abihu, and seventy of the elders went up the mountain, where they saw the God of Israel, ate and drank in His presence, and yet were not consumed by Him. This meal symbolized the covenantal unity and trust that now existed between Yahweh and Israel. (*See also* COVENANT [OT] II; IV.A, C.)

Not surprisingly the symbolism of a meal can also be used metaphorically to describe Israel's messianic future. Thus Isa. 25:6-9 speaks of a great feast which the Lord will prepare on Mt. Zion, with the best of foods and wines, and with all the nations of the world sharing in it. Symbolically this feast expresses the prophetic hope of the golden age to come, when suffering and mourning, sin and death, will be banished forever (cf. 1 Cor. 15:54; Rev. 21:4).

In the NT much of the OT imagery of eating and drinking recurs, though updated in the light of the redemptive events of Jesus Christ and the coming of the Holy Spirit. Jesus habitually ate with tax collectors and sinners (Mt. 9:11; cf. Lk. 14:12-14), thereby signifying His solidarity with them. Banquets were a familiar theme in His parables describing aspects of His coming kingdom (Mt. 8:11; 22:1-10; Lk. 14:16-24; etc.). He also spoke of the necessity of eating His flesh and drinking His blood, thereby describing the intimate acceptance of Him that is needed for eternal life (Jn. 6:48-53; note that He also called Himself the bread of life [vv. 35, 51, 58]).

The LORD'S SUPPER combines the imagery of the OT Passover and of the great feast to be prepared by God. Jesus Himself is now the Passover lamb (cf. 1 Cor. 5:7) and the believers' eating and drinking together symbolize their sharing in Christ, their fellowship and oneness with each other, and their common expectation of the blessed future to come. The Lord's Supper, particularly its fulfillment in the consummation of the Kingdom, may also be viewed as a NT counterpart of the meal that Moses and the elders of Israel ate in the presence of the Lord; both sacramentally represent the future inherent in the present reality. The traditionally heavy theological emphasis on the Lord's Supper as a commemoration of Christ's sacrificial and atoning death should not be allowed to obscure the meal character of the Supper. As celebrated by the NT Church, the Lord's Supper foreshadowed the believers' participation in the coming marriage supper of the Lamb (Rev. 19:9; cf. Mt. 26:29 par.). In turn this image of the marriage supper of the Lamb may also be regarded as the climactic fulfillment of the meal of Israel's elders in the presence of the Lord and of the prophecy of Isaiah 25.

The tree of life in Rev. 22:1f., with its twelve kinds of fruit and its leaves for the healing of the nations, stood on either side of the river flowing through the city of God. This scene combines the imagery of the tree of life in the garden of Eden (Gen. 3) and of Ezekiel's vision of the new temple (Ezk. 47:12). In the consummation mankind will have unlimited access to the tree of life and will fully enjoy the blessings of the unbroken fellowship with God in the new Jerusalem.

Eating and drinking frequently meant participation in what the food and drink represented. Paul was convinced that an idol was nothing and thus food offered to an idol remained ordinary food. Yet in order to spare those who might be offended at the eating of such food, he counseled against eating it on the ground that one cannot partake of the table of the Lord and of the table of demons (1 Cor.

8:10). He also exhorted his readers not to cause (by their eating) the ruin of one for whom Christ died, for the kingdom of God is not a matter of food and drink but of righteousness, peace, and joy in the Holy Spirit (Rom. 14:15, 17; see the whole chapter). In the case of the Lord's Supper, the disrespectful eating of the bread and drinking of the cup is tantamount to profaning the body and blood of the Lord (1 Cor. 11:27). The writer of Hebrews speaks of an altar from which those who serve the tabernacle have no right to eat (13:10); unlike Jewish priests who were not permitted to eat of the sacrifice on the altar, Christians may eat Christ's own sacrifice on the cross, i.e., to the fullest extent share in Christ's atoning sacrifice, which is something adherents of Judaism, those who hold on to the old dispensation, cannot do.

The final thing that can be said of eating and drinking is that, like everything else, they must be done to the glory of God (1 Cor. 10:31).

See *TDOT*, I, *s.v.* "ākhal" (Ottoson).

See also BREAD V; DRINK; FEASTS; FOOD; MEALS.

S. WOUDSTRA

EBAL ē'bäl [Heb. *'êḇāl*–'bare'].

1. A variant reading (1 Ch. 1:22) for Obal, a son of Joktan and ancestor of an Arab tribe (Gen. 10:28). The locality where they settled, which the name designates in 1 Ch. 1:22, is of uncertain identification.

2. A son of Shobal son of Seir the Horite (Gen. 36:23; 1 Ch. 1:40).

EBAL, MOUNT ē'bəl [Heb. *har 'êḇāl*; LXX Gk. *Gaibal*] (Dt. 11:29; 27:4, 13; Josh. 8:30, 33 [LXX 9:2]). The modern Jebel Eslāmîyeh, located N of SHECHEM and opposite Mt. Gerizim (*see* GERIZIM, MOUNT). These two mountains overlook the pass through which runs the main E-W route, and an important N-S crossroad lies just to the east; thus Ebal was strategically important. It stands 427 m. (1402 ft.) above its base (940 m. [3080 ft.] above sea level), and thus is visible from afar (Dt. 11:29f.).

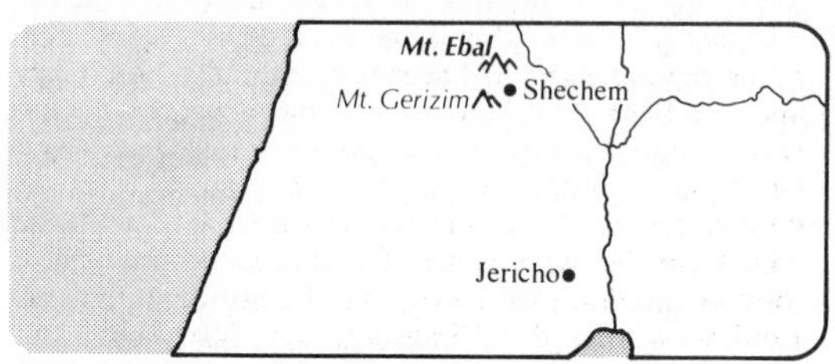

Joshua led the people to Ebal to renew the covenant after the conquest of AI. As Moses had directed, Joshua erected "an altar of unhewn stones" (Josh. 8:30f.; cf. Dt. 27:4-6), which he presumably plastered (in accordance with Dt. 27:4) in order to write upon it the copy of the law (Josh. 8:32; cf. P. C. Craigie, *Book of Deuteronomy* [*NICOT*, 1976], pp. 328f.). Placing half the tribes on the slope of Gerizim, half on the slope of Ebal, and the ark with the priests and Levites between, Joshua proceeded to read the blessings and the curses of the law, probably with the two divisions of the people responding appropriately (cf. Dt. 27:13-26). It has sometimes been questioned if the reading of the law could have been heard by the people in the way here described. But the formation of the sides of the valley at the narrowest part and the acoustics, which have been tested more than once, leave no reasonable doubt about the possibility.

The religious associations of Ebal continued even in postbiblical times. The head of John the Baptist is said to be buried there, and in the Middle Ages the Moslems erected a monument over this traditional site. The ruins of a church have also been found there.

G. A. L.

EBED ē'bed [Heb. *'eḇeḏ*–'servant'].

1. Father of Gaal, who rebelled against Abimelech (Jgs. 9:26, 35).

2. A companion of Ezra in his return (Ezr. 8:6). In 1 Esd. 8:32 he is called Obed (AV, NEB, "Obeth").

EBED-MELECH ē-bed-mē'lek, eb-ed-me'lek [Heb. *'eḇeḏ-meleḵ*–'servant of the king']. An Ethiopian eunuch in the service of King Zedekiah, who interceded with the king for the prophet Jeremiah and rescued him from the cistern into which he had been cast to die (Jer. 38:7-13). For this, the word of Yahweh through Jeremiah promised Ebed-melech that his life should be spared in the fall of Jerusalem (Jer. 39:15-18).

From the early monarchy the description of a court official as "slave" helped to differentiate him from those who were functioning in their capacity as tribal elders. Sometimes it was indicated that the "slave" was a paid official. The practice originated in Babylonia, and among the Assyrians "Ebed-melech" became a proper name.

EBENEZER eb-ə-nē'zər [Heb. *'eḇen hā'ezer*–'stone of the help'; Gk. *Abenezer*].

1. Here Israel was defeated by the Philistines, four thousand men falling in the battle (1 S. 4:1ff.). It appears also to have been the scene of the disaster when the ark of God was captured (vv. 3ff.). The place is not identified. It was across from Aphek; but this site also is unknown (cf. Josh. 12:18). In *Onom.* Eusebius places it between Jerusalem and Ascalon, in the neighborhood of Beth-shemesh.

2. A stone set up by Samuel to perpetuate the memory of the signal victory granted to Israel over the Philistines in answer to his prayer (1 S. 7:12). It stood between Mizpeh and "Jeshanah," an emended reading followed by the RSV and NEB (cf. 2 Ch. 13:19). The AV, following the MT, reads "Shen" (tooth). A location on the border between Israel and Judah appears likely, but proper identification has not yet been made.

W. EWING

EBER ē'bər [Heb. *'ēḇer*; LXX Gk. *Eber* in Genesis, *Ōbēd* in Chronicles].

1. Occurs in the genealogies (Gen. 10:21, 25; 11:14-17) as the great-grandson of Shem and father of Peleg and Joktan. The word means "beyond," "across." Some scholars contend the related form "Hebrew" (Heb. *'iḇrî*) denotes the people or tribe who came "from the other side of the river" (i.e., the Euphrates), from Haran (Gen. 11:31), whence Abraham and his dependents migrated to Canaan. In Nu. 24:24 Eber should most probably not be read as a proper name, but rendered "region beyond," i.e., beyond the Euphrates. *See also* TELL MARDIKH.

2. A Gadite (1 Ch. 5:13).

3, 4. Two Benjaminites (1 Ch. 8:12, 22).

5. The head of a priestly family (Neh. 12:20).

A. C. GRANT

EBEZ ē'bez [Heb. *'eḇeṣ*; LXX Gk. *Rhebes*]; AV ABEZ. One of the sixteen cities in Issachar (Josh. 19:20). The name seems to be cognate to that of the judge Ibzan (Jgs. 12:8-10). The site is unknown, though *Westminster Dictionary of the Bible* (1944) conjectures 'Ain el-Ḥbuṣ, or el-'Abuṣ, between 'Aulam and Sitīn.

EBIASAPH ə-bī'ə-saf [Heb. *'eḇyāsāp̄*; LXX Gk. *Abiasaph*].

A descendant of Kohath the son of Levi (1 Ch. 6:37 [MT 22]). *See* ABIASAPH.

EBIONITES; EBIONISM. A Jewish-Christian heretical sect flourishing in the 2nd, 3rd, and 4th cents. A.D.

I. Origin
II. Sources
  A. Gospel of the Ebionites
  B. Pseudo-Clementine Literature
III. Theology
IV. Ebionites and Qumrân

I. Origin.–The name Ebionite seems to be derived from Heb. *'eḇyôn,* "poor." It first appears in the writings of Irenaeus (*Adv. haer.* i.26.2), who gave no explanation of the term. Other writers in antiquity, however, variously explained why the Ebionites were so called. Origen in his commentary on Mt. 12:2 said that their name came from the poverty of their faith in Jesus. In *Contra Celsum* ii.1 he stated that they were named for the poverty of their interpretation of the law. Eusebius reiterated the sentiment of Origen by saying that "from these practices [observing the law, rejecting Paul, and using exclusively the Gospel according to the Hebrews] they have obtained their name, for their name means 'poor' in Hebrew" (*HE* iii.27.2). He also said they got their name from the first Christians because they held such poor and lowly opinions of Jesus Christ. None of these polemical explanations of the origin of the name is taken seriously by scholars today.

About two hundred years after Irenaeus's first mention of the Ebionites by name, Epiphanius wrote extensively of them in his *Panarion* (*Haer.*). He derived their name from Ebion, the alleged founder of the sect, and traced their history back to the period immediately following the destruction of Jerusalem in A.D. 70. This explanation, too, is highly unlikely, although there is some evidence that there was a historical person named Ebion. Some scholars think that certain fragments of *Doctrina patrum de incarnatione Verbi* are by him.

J. A. Fitzmyer suggested that the name *Ebionaioi* grew out of the practice of referring to the first Christians in Jerusalem as "the poor," especially after the destruction of the city in A.D. 70. "At some time during the first two centuries . . . this designation was restricted to those who lived in Palestine and Syria, and who continued to observe the Mosaic Law. It seems likely that the original use of the word was in no way connected with a heretical sect" (Fitzmyer, p. 210). This group of Jewish Christians is usually associated with James the brother of Jesus, the head of the Jerusalem church. "It is not unlikely that remnants of this group, after the destruction of Jerusalem, developed into the Ebionite sect, acquiring heterodox notions in time from other sources, such as Cerinthus and the Elchesaites" (p. 210). How long the Ebionites existed before Irenaeus' explicit mention of them is not known, but that there was such a group by his time is clear. He calls them heretical (*Adv. haer.* i.26.2) and classifies them among the Gnostics.

L. E. Keck proposed a similar explanation of their origin: "After the refugees [either from the Jewish War of A.D. 66-70 or the Hadrianic War in A.D. 135] from Jerusalem found themselves destitute, they cherished more than ever the words of Jesus about the poor and the threat of possessions, and so made of their poverty a virtue and probably named themselves 'the Poor.' In the region where they now lived, they came into contact with dualistic and syncretistic movements which provided a cosmological rationale of their poverty and intensified certain elements of their theology in general. The link with the practice of the primitive church in sharing wealth came much later as an apologetic device and cannot be taken at face value" (*ZNW,* 57 [1966], 65f.).

II. Sources.–*A. Gospel of the Ebionites.* This is an abridged and falsified Gospel of Matthew known only through the accounts and quotations of Epiphanius. Since it presupposes the Synoptics, the earliest it could have been written is the 2nd century. The Gospel begins not with the Nativity narrative but with the appearance of John the Baptist. This is followed by the Call of the Disciples and the Baptism of Jesus. It also contains parallels to Mt. 5:17; 12:46-50; 26:17ff.; and Lk. 22:15 (*SQE*). Epiphanius said that it included the story of the Last Supper, the Passion of Christ, and the Resurrection, but we have no details.

B. Pseudo-Clementine Literature. Apart from the Ebionite Gospel, there is little agreement among scholars about authentic Ebionite sources. The nineteenth-century Tübingen scholars isolated a source — *Kerygmata Petrou* (Sermons of Peter)—in the Pseudo-Clementine literature and identified it as Ebionite. This reconstruction has been followed by more recent scholars. H. J. Schoeps bases his reconstruction of the history and theology of early Jewish Christianity on the *Kerygmata Petrou,* and both O. Cullmann and J. A. Fitzmyer use the *Kerygmata* as a primary source to compare the beliefs of the Qumrân community with those of the Ebionites. Considerable doubt exists, however, about the genuineness of the *Kerygmata Petrou* as an Ebionite source. Keck points out that even though the Pseudo-Clementine literature has been subjected for more than a hundred years to discussion and analysis, "there is still little agreement on the elemental point of whether or not there is any relation whatsoever between this pot-pourri of tradition and the Ebionites" (p. 60).

III. Theology.–Origen was the first to distinguish between two types of Ebionites theologically: those who believed in the Virgin Birth and those who rejected it (*Contra Celsum* v.61). Eusebius also distinguished between two groups, describing them as follows (*HE* iii.27):

> They held him [Christ] to be a plain and ordinary man who had achieved righteousness merely by the progress of his character and had been born naturally from Mary and her husband. They insisted on the complete observation of the Law, and did not think that they would be saved by faith in Christ alone and by a life in accordance with it. But there were others besides these who have the same name. These escaped the absurd folly of the first mentioned, and did not deny that the Lord was born of a Virgin and the Holy Spirit, but nevertheless agreed with them in not confessing his pre-existence as God, being the Logos and Wisdom. Thus they shared in the impiety of the former class, especially in that they were equally zealous to insist on the literal observance of the Law. They thought that the letters of the Apostle ought to be wholly rejected and called him an apostate from the Law. They used only the Gospel called according to the Hebrews and made little account of the rest. Like the former they used to observe the sabbath and the rest of the Jewish ceremonial, but on Sundays celebrated rites like ours in commemoration of the Saviour's resurrection.

Epiphanius likewise differentiated between a more orthodox group (those who believed in the Virgin Birth) and a more heterodox group. The former he called Nazoreans and the latter Ebionites (*Haer.* 29f.). The Ebionites, he said, were influenced by the Elchasaites, an early heretical group with certain Gnostic ideas. It is also possible that the Ebionites came under the influence of the Essenes.

Although strict observance of the law was enjoined, not

all of the law of Moses was accepted as valid. They held that the true law had been adulterated by the addition of certain falsehoods, post-Mosaic in origin. These had to be purged, because they contained doctrines that were actually inimical to Moses' teaching. By means of this approach to the Pentateuch the Ebionites were able to eliminate concepts of God contrary to their own. In the *Pseudo-Clementines* (Homily 2.52) the apostle says, "Neither was Adam a transgressor, who was fashioned by the hands of God; nor was Noah drunken, who was found righteous above all the world; nor did Abraham live with three wives at once, who, on account of his sobriety, was thought worthy of a numerous posterity; nor did Jacob associate with four — of whom two were sisters — who was the father of the ten tribes, and who intimated the coming of the presence of our Master; nor was Moses a murderer, nor did he learn to judge from an idolatrous priest. . . ." Jesus was for them the great reformer of the law, whereas Paul was its distorter.

The Ebionites also believed that the grace of baptism put an end to all sacrifices. The destruction of the temple was brought about by God because of the Jews' refusal to discontinue the temple sacrificial system. The priesthood, too, was considered no longer valid, since sacrifices were at an end.

Christianity was for them not a religion of salvation. Jesus came not to save but to teach. He stood in a direct line with the great prophets — prophetism climaxed in Him. He came after Adam and Moses to reform and purify Judaism.

Ebionism's most important deviations from orthodox Christianity were in the realm of Christology. Although, as seen from the above quotations from Origen and statements in Epiphanius, there was no unanimity among them in their christological beliefs, they generally rejected the orthodox doctrine of the Virgin Birth. They also denied the Incarnation. Although they believed in Jesus (this distinguished them from the orthodox Jews), they regarded Him simply as a man chosen by God, who at His baptism received a power from God. It is generally believed that the christological tenets of the Ebionites showed Cerinthian influence.

IV. Ebionites and Qumrân.–Since the discovery of the Dead Sea Scrolls, vigorous discussions have been carried on about the relationship of the Ebionites to the people of the Scrolls. J. L. Teicher maintained that the Qumrân sect was Ebionite, that Christ was the "Teacher of Righteousness," and the apostle Paul was the "Man of Lies." Teicher's theory faces several difficulties, the most telling of which are: (1) the Ebionites appear too late to be identified with the Qumrân sect (the earliest mention of the Ebionites is *ca.* A.D. 175); and (2) the religious background of the Ebionites, though heretical, is definitely Christian, whereas that of the people of Qumrân is pre-Christian and oriented to the OT, not the NT.

Although Cullmann did not identify the Qumrân sect with the Ebionites, he argued for a connection between the two: what was left of the Qumrân sect (which he identified with the Essenes) went over to the Ebionites. This theory, of course, would necessitate the conversion of the Essenes to Christianity. While this is not impossible, there seems to be little evidence to support it.

Fitzmyer, after a careful comparison of the theological beliefs and practices of the two groups, found too great a divergence between them to accept either Teicher's or Cullmann's theories. He concluded: "It seems that the most we can say is that the sect of Qumran influenced the Ebionites in many ways; Essene tenets and practices were undoubtedly adopted or adapted into the Ebionite way of life. To try to state more than this is to overstep the limits set by the evidence we have at our disposal" (p. 231). This appears to be a more tenable view of the relationship between Qumrân and the Ebionites.

Bibliography.–O. Cullmann, "Die neuentdeckten Qumrantexte und das Judenchristentum der Pseudo-klementinen," in *NT Studien für Rudolf Bultmann* (*BZNW*, 21, 1954), 35-51; "Significance of the Qumran Texts for Research into the Beginnings of Christianity," in K. Stendahl, ed., *The Scrolls and the NT* (1957), pp. 18-32; J. A. Fitzmyer, "The Qumran Scrolls, the Ebionites and their Literature," in Stendahl, pp. 208-210 (= *Theological Studies*, 16 [1955], 335-372); H-S, I, 153-58; F. J. A. Hort, *Judaistic Christianity* (1898); L. E. Keck, *ZNW*, 57 (1966), 54-78; H. J. Schoeps, *Theologie and Geschichte des Judenchristentums* (1949); *JTS*, 4 (1953), 223ff.; J. L. Teicher, *JJS*, 2 (1951), 67-99.

W. W. WESSEL

EBIONITES, GOSPEL OF THE. *See* APOCRYPHAL GOSPELS IV.B: EBIONITES II.A

EBLA eb'lə. The capital of a great Canaanite empire that flourished during the 3rd and 2nd millennia B.C. The significance of this major urban center of ancient Syria was not known until the early 1970's, when excavations at TELL MARDIKH in northwest Syria (67 km. [41 mi.] SW of Aleppo, just E of the highway from Aleppo to Hama and Damascus) led to its identification with Ebla. Under the great king Ibrum the kingdom of Ebla controlled all the territory between Egypt and the Persian Gulf, including Palestine and Syria, Sumer and Akkad.

EBONY [Heb. *K hôḇānîm, Q hoḇnîm*] (Ezk. 27:15). Of uncertain vocalization, this term, omitted by the LXX, doubtless refers to two species of ebony, *Diospyros ebenaster* Retz. and *D. melanoxylon* Roxb., native to India and shipped to Tyre by Phoenician merchants. The exterior sapwood is stripped off, leaving an interior portion of about 2 ft. (.6 m.) in diameter in mature trees. When old, ebony becomes black, heavy, and durable, and from antiquity has been widely used for cabinet-making and ornamental work. *See* picture of hounds-and-jackals game in GAMES. R. K. H.

EBRON ē'brən [Heb. *ʿeḇrōn*]; AV HEBRON; NEB ABDON. A town in the territory of Asher (Josh. 19:28), probably the same as ABDON (Josh. 21:30; 1 Ch. 6:74), conjecturing a copyist's error of *resh* (ר) for *daleth* (ד).

EBRONAH ə-brō'nə (AV, NEB, Nu. 33:34f.). *See* ABRONAH.

ECANUS e-kā'nəs (AV 2 Esd. 14:24). *See* ETHANUS.

ECBATANA ek-ba'tə-nə [Aram. *'aḥmᵉṯā'* (Ezr. 6:2); Gk. *Amatha*; Pesh. Syr. *'aḥmāṯān*; Tiglath-pileser's inscr. (*ca.* 1100 B.C.) *Amadāna*; Darius' Behistun inscr. ii.76-78 *Hañgmatāna*–'place of assembly'; Herodotus *Agbatana*; Xenophon *Ekbatana*; so 1 Esd. 6:23; Tob. 3:7; 6:5; 7:1; 14:12, 14; Jth. 1:1f., 14; 2 Macc. 9:3; Talm. Heb. *hamdān*; now Arab. *hamadān*]; AV ACHMETHA; AV Apoc. ECBATANE. The ancient capital of Media, now buried under modern Hamadân, 290 km. (180 mi.) WSW of Tehran at about the 1830-m. (6000-ft.) level near the foot of Mt. Orontes (Aurvant). It was situated on a strategic trade route along the Elburz (now the modern Kazvin-Kermanshah highway), which ran from Central Asia to Rhages (near Tehran), then by way of Ecbatana and Kermanshah to northwestern Mesopotamia. During the Parthian period this site was on one of the three stretches of the great "Silk Road," which passed through Merv, Hecatompylos, and Ecbatana, crossed the Euphrates, and

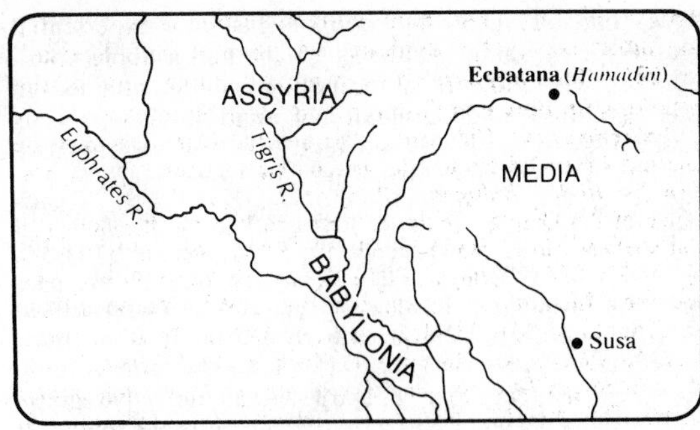

Achaemenian gold dagger with two lion heads at pommel (5th cent. B.C.), reputedly from Ecbatana (Hamadân) (Metropolitan Museum of Art, Harris Brisbane Dick Fund, 1954)

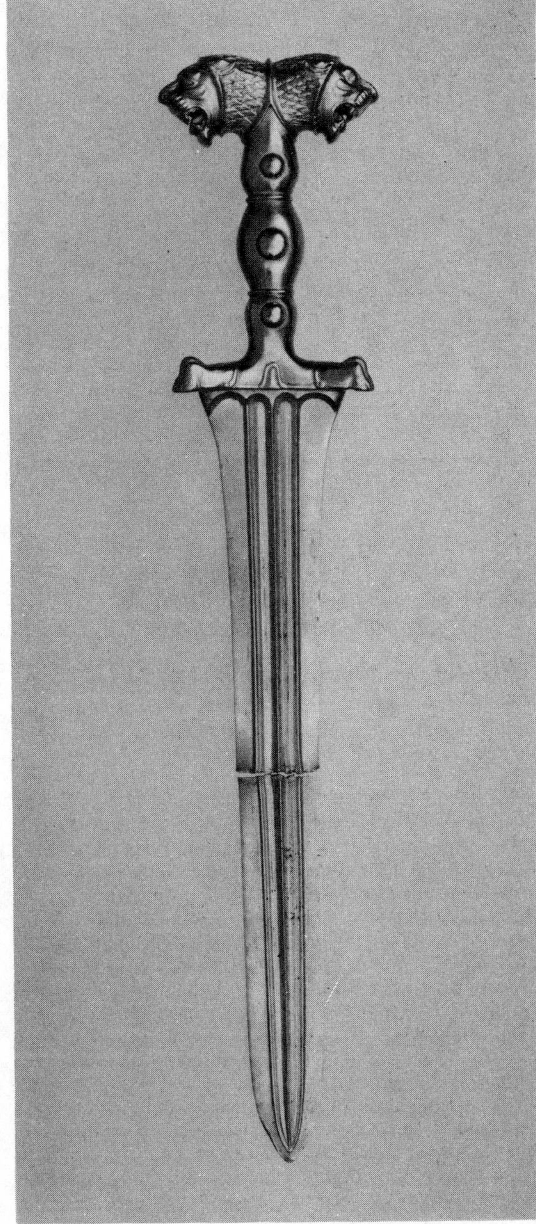

passed on to the Mediterranean. It is still one of the chief trade and distribution centers of Iran.

The city is mentioned in cuneiform inscriptions from Tiglath-pileser I (*ca.* 1100 B.C.) as *kar-kassi,* "Kassite town." Ctesias attributed the founding of the city to Semiramis (*ca.* 800 B.C.), who built a palace there for herself; but Herodotus (i.96ff.) claimed the city was founded or rebuilt by Deioces (Daiaukku) the Mede (*ca.* 700 B.C.) on the site of Elippi, an ancient city of the Mandā. Cyrus captured the city from Astyages (548 B.C.), and later brought Croesus there as captive. Cyrus and other Persian kings used to spend the two summer months there yearly, owing to the comparative coolness of the climate. The winters, however, are long and severe, with much snow.

Herodotus (i.98) described it as a magnificent city fortified with seven concentric walls. Its citadel (Aram. *bîr^{e}ṯā'*, Ezr. 6:2) is mentioned by Arrian, who says that when Alexander took the city in 324 B.C. he stored his enormous amount of booty there. In it the royal archives were kept. It stood on a hill, where later was built a temple of Mithra. Polybius (x.27) spoke of the great strength of the citadel. Diodorus indicated that the city was 250 stadia in circumference. On Mt. Aurvant (3268 m.; 10,728 ft.) have been found inscriptions of Xerxes. Doubtless Ecbatana was one of the "cities of the Medes" to which Israel was carried captive (2 K. 17:6). It should be noted that Greek writers mention several Ecbatanas. One of these, afterward called Gazaca (Takhti Sulaimān, just S of Lake Urmia), was capital of Atropatene. H. Rawlinson identified the Ecbatana of Tobit and Herodotus with this northern city. The southern and far more important Ecbatana is certainly that of 2 Macc. 9:3. It was Cyrus' Median capital, and is doubtless that of Ezr. 6:2. In 1971 Hamadân had a population of about 125,000, including some five thousand Jews and a few Armenians. Jews from other countries make pilgrimages to the alleged tombs of Esther and Mordecai in the middle of the city.

Ecbatana still awaits the spade of the archeologist. The only artifacts have come from chance findings. Among these was a gold tablet written in cuneiform, the oldest Achaemenian object known and containing the earliest Old Persian text. R. E. HAYDEN

ECCLESIASTES e-klē-zi-as'tēz [Heb. *qōheleṯ*; Gk. *Ekklēsiastēs*]. A book of the OT, part of the wisdom literature.

I. Name
II. Structure
III. Contents
IV. Date and Authorship
V. Canonicity

I. Name.–The speaker in Ecclesiastes calls himself Heb. *qōheleṯ* (1:1f., 12; 7:27; 12:8-10; twice with the article), rendered "the Preacher" in most English versions. The term occurs nowhere else in Hebrew writings, although it is from a stem that is in common use. In form it is a feminine participle of a verb *qhl,* meaning "assemble," though this form is always (with the possible exception of 7:27) rendered with a masculine verb. Various theories have attempted to explain the enigma, but it is probably best to conclude that *qōheleṯ* originally signified some kind of office, e.g., "one who collects" or "one who calls an assembly together" or "one who speaks to an assembly." The Hebrew word for assembly (*qāhāl*) is often rendered in the LXX by Gk. *ekklēsía* and its cognates (e.g., Dt. 4:10; 9:10; Jgs. 20:2; 21:5, 8), a fact that probably influenced the LXX translation of *qōheleṯ* by Gk. *ekklēsiastēs,* from which are derived the present Latin and English forms of the name.

II. Structure.–Attempts to determine a rigid structural development within Ecclesiastes have foundered for lack of convincing evidence, but that is not to say that the book lacks unity or structure. Beginning with a title (1:1) and a prefatory section that establishes the general theme (1:2-11), the book continues with a series of autobiographical wisdom reflections followed by various admonitions and observations in the style of standard didactic wisdom, and concludes with a brief prose appendix (12:9-14) in which a definite conclusion is drawn. Although certain sections seem to conclude an argument (e.g., 2:24-26; 3:12-22; 5:18-20) in a manner that contrasts with the sections immediately preceding, it is not clear that the book is intended to be a simple presentation of the opposing sides of any issue. In the less autobiographical and more gnomic sections toward the latter part of Ecclesiastes the conclusions are an integral part of the argument (e.g., 8:17). The idea of the vanity of all things and the concomitant hope resulting from a basic belief in the goodness of God and creation characterize both the personal ("I") and the gnomic ("thou") sections.

III. Contents.–Qoheleth's thesis is set forth at the beginning, and the remainder of the treatise stands in relation to it. "Vanity of vanities! All is vanity and a striving after wind"; that is the premise. All things are empty and the results of human effort are illusive (1:2f.). Human generations, day and night, the wind, the streams, are alike the repetition of an unending cycle (1:4-7). The same holds true for human study and thought (1:8-11). Nothing is new. Every effort of nature or of man is the doing again of something that has already been done.

But the idea that all things consist of vapor, that all is momentary, profitless, and empty, is clearly set in a context of Jewish wisdom and piety. Qoheleth is a believer, and this is what creates the dynamic of his book. It is not a question of nihilism, hedonism, or determinism. These he has considered, and in some ways each system has its appeal; but in his thought are also elements of purpose, eternity, value, and individual worth. Although there are and must continue to be great unanswered questions, and their presence must function as a counter to smug assurance and unreflective belief, there is also value and meaning. Human beings must accept their own lot and not confuse that lot with what is reserved for God alone (3:11; 5:2). Despite the enigma of existence, they can enjoy life and work, sleeping the sweet sleep of those who have put their shoulders to the wheel (3:12-14; 5:12; 9:10), knowing that both the good days and the bad are made by the one God (7:14). And although there is little developed sense of the hereafter, Qoheleth has no doubt that God, who rules over all, will some day or in some manner bring every act to judgment, whether good or evil (12:14). Such judgments do not resolve the problem of existence, but they do reduce to an acceptable level the absurdity of life as it appears to a thoughtful observer.

Qoheleth's conclusions, often set over against his own sharply contrasting and pessimistic speculation, convince him that life is still worth living, even in the worst of times. It is the ultimate faith in the historical process, a faith derived from his faith in a God who is often hidden but never really doubted, that separates Ecclesiastes from all forms of agnostic speculative philosophy. Qoheleth's life may contain a host of unanswered and unanswerable questions, but his God is consistent. God's way and will may not be known; but His is not the way and will of the Babylonian deities, to whom appeal may be made but to whom no final and consistent will may ever be attributed (cf. *ANET,* pp. 438-440).

In developing these ideas, Qoheleth begins with his general observations on the order of things natural and intellectual (1:2-11). After the preface the speaker introduces himself again and recounts his own experiential search for meaning. At the outset he had a noble ambition for wisdom and discipline, but all he attained to was emptiness and perplexity of mind (1:12-18; this is equally the meaning of the text, whether we translate "vanity and vexation of spirit" [AV] or "vanity and a striving after wind" [RSV and most modern translations]).

Finding no adequate satisfaction in the pursuits of the scholar and wisdom teacher, he seeks to combine with these the pursuit of pleasure, both that which comes from external stimuli and that which arises from his own enterprise and achievement (2:1-11). Again he attains only emptiness and perplexity of spirit. A concluding paragraph puts wisdom ahead of pleasure (the pursuit of the fool), but realizes that inevitable and ubiquitous death finally reduces wise man and fool to the same end (2:12-23). There is no solution but to view the problem in the light of God's purpose for mankind (2:24-26): "There is no (greater) good for a man than to eat and drink and cause his soul to see good in his labor" (v. 24, as most naturally translated, although "greater" must be seen as an interpolation), because this is what God has given him to do.

Chapter 3 begins with a simple but majestic ode to time. Every human activity has its own appointed time (3:1-8), but time also creates a problem. If human beings were merely creatures of time, they would not concern themselves with the further dimension of eternity (3:9-11). But it is God who has "set eternity in their heart," though keeping from them the real secret of what will be in the future. To be made for eternity, but limited to time, is a tragedy of manifest proportions; the conclusion (3:12-22) is again simply to live with the enigma. What God does will remain forever; in that light the cyclical motions of mankind and beast, endlessly moving from the cradle to the grave, must be accepted. "Nothing is better than that a man should enjoy his work, for that is his lot." Human beings cannot move beyond the pale to see what will be after them.

And so the record of experiences continues, hopeful passages alternating with pessimistic passages. Later in the book the agnosticism and pessimism recede somewhat, and the hopeful passages become more positive. Experience gives way to gnomic wisdom, with collections of maxims on prudent behavior. The words of the wise, though sometimes despised (9:15), are to be preferred to the shouting of a ruler among fools (v. 17). Also toward the end of the book is an increase in the passages that encourage piety. "I know that it will be well with those who fear God" (8:12), says Qoheleth, and he closes his book with a strong admonition to that effect: "Fear God, and keep His commandments; for this is the whole duty of man" (12:13).

We should be wary of any attempt to separate the writer of Ecclesiastes from his arguments, whether positive or negative. It is because Qoheleth feels deeply the illusive nature of all human striving, whether to know or to do, that his hopeful passages ring with reality. Disregard the agnostic passages, and we are left with a series of somewhat hesitant affirmations that hardly fit together. But disregard the affirmative passages, and we are left with a world view considerably less than acceptable to Jewish or Christian piety. When put together in their canonical sequence, we have the experience of the finest of Jewish faith — faith that can live with the enigma and still affirm the goodness of God, and hence the meaning of life and toil. We learn that it is possible to live and even flourish apart from some of the answers we are born to crave. In all of this the solution is that of the wisdom teacher. Fear God, live in your own sphere, accept the fact that there is meaning even when you do not know what it is, avoid extremes, and enter fully into those limited joys that life can supply. Although all is vanity and all will pass away, there are still degrees of value. Wisdom is better than folly, good stands out from evil. Above all, Qoheleth warns the youth, remember your Creator while it is still possible (12:1), even as you devote yourself to the sayings of the wise (v. 11).

IV. Date and Authorship.–In addition to his title "Qoheleth," the speaker is represented as "the son of David, king in Jerusalem" (1:1). So far as this clause is concerned, the king in question might be either Solomon or any other king of the dynasty, or he might be a composite or an ideal king. Two obvious anachronisms are alleged to militate against Solomonic authorship, although most arguments for a later date center on other data. In 1:12 the speaker writes, "I . . . have been [Heb. *hāyîṯî*] king . . . in Jerusalem," and v. 16 favorably compares the speaker's wisdom with "all who were over Jerusalem before me." However, v. 12 can also be translated "I became king . . . ," and v. 16 may refer to wisdom teachers rather than a long line of previous monarchs. But either way, Solomonic authorship is not conclusively ruled out by such fragmentary evidence. Evidence from other sources does point to a later date; but it is probably safe to say that if the speaker is not Solomon, he is some other actual or composite or ideal king of the dynasty of David. In any case the book is not pseudepigraphical, since its reference to the role and background of the speaker does not specifically mention Solomon, but uses instead the self-designation "Qoheleth."

Evidence for dating the book comes from both its ideas and its linguistic peculiarities. A widely held opinion is that the skepticism of the book could represent only a late period in Hebrew thought, when Judaism had spent its early vigor (see O. Eissfeldt, *The OT: An Intro.* [Eng. tr. 1965], p. 496). It is true that the work reflects a time of misery and decline (Eccl. 1:2-11; 3:1-15; etc.), but given the vicissitudes of national fortune observable in any society, this is hardly as conclusive an argument as has been suggested. Among those still committed to Solomonic authorship, the tradition of a time late in that monarch's reign, as reflected in one Midrashic source (*Cant. Rabbah* i.1.10), seems equally appropriate.

Traces of both Greek and Egyptian thought have been discovered in Qoheleth, but neither has been conclusively demonstrated. If indeed the book is to be dated in the postexilic period, it would not be surprising if some affinities to Greek thought were demonstrable; but most of the attempts to link Ecclesiastes with Stoics or Epicureans, with the Cynics or Heraclitus, have met with stern rebuttal in the scholarly discussions (cf. Gordis, *Koheleth*, pp. 51-57). Egyptian sources present similarities both in form and content, including not only the general tone (cf. *ANET*, p. 467) but specific references to belief and custom (e.g., the sacred oath of 8:2 and the funeral customs of 8:10; cf. Eissfeldt, p. 499). Egyptian influence would not of itself establish any date for the book, as it is known to have been felt in Israel as early as Solomon and as late as the postexilic period.

Linguistic arguments have traditionally focused on the presence of Aramaisms and Grecisms. Gordis, who contends that "the *abundance* of evidence points overwhelmingly to a period when Aramaic was becoming the dominant language of Western Asia" (*Koheleth*, p. 59), further states: "Koheleth does not really include Aramaic words, but rather their Hebrew or Hebraized parallels" (p. 61). Rejecting arguments for an Aramaic original, Gordis finds evidence rather for a language standing "midway between classical Biblical Hebrew and the Mishnaic idiom, though . . . closer to the latter" (p. 60). Gordis is representative of the majority of scholars, although there have always been a variety of opposing positions.

Along with arguments for a dependence upon Greek philosophy, many have alleged the presence of Grecisms. Although this is by no means a dead issue, there is now more agreement that evidence of Greek forms is limited to a few possible, but by no means certain, expressions. Gordis even goes so far as to claim, ". . . there are no indubitable Greek constructions or idioms in the text and not a single instance of a Greek word" (*Koheleth*, p. 62).

Much more influential has been the work of M. Dahood, whose article "Canaanite-Phoenician Influence in Qoheleth" (*Bibl.*, 33 [1952], pp. 30-52, 191-221) tries to prove considerable dependence by the author of Ecclesiastes on Phoenician orthography, grammar, and syntax. The evidence marshaled is impressive and not unlike some of the evidence set forth by the same author for Canaanite-Phoenician affinities in other biblical literature. But Dahood retains a postexilic date for the composition, in contrast to some who have used his arguments to support the more immediately appealing idea that Solomon, with his Phoenician contacts, may have employed northern scribes in compiling the work.

In truth, the language of Ecclesiastes is unique. Frag-

Fragment of Ecclesiastes Scroll from Qumrân, probably dating from the middle of the 2nd cent. B.C. (Israel Department of Antiquities and Museums)

ments of the work have been found in the corpus of texts from Qumrân Cave 4 (J. Muilenburg, *BASOR*, 135 [Oct. 1954], 20-28), dated generally to the 2nd cent. B.C.; so the book is known to predate that era. The Wisdom of Ben Sira (Sirach or Ecclesiasticus) was influenced by Ecclesiastes (although some have alleged that the influence was the other way), making it highly probable that the latter work was circulating by *ca.* 300 B.C. Any attempt to compare the language of the book to other postexilic or intertestamental works has foundered, probably because of the unique genre of Ecclesiastes. Comparisons with Aramaic forms, however, together with the evidence for a stage of Hebrew approaching Mishnaic, lead to the conclusion that Ecclesiastes as presently composed embodies a late form of the language, and the work may safely be dated in the late 5th or early 4th century. The suggestion that such a date would make the work spurious or fictional ignores the obvious fact that the book itself does not identify its author in other than general terms.

V. Canonicity.–Ecclesiastes appears in the third section of the Hebrew Bible (Kethubhim, or Writings), where it is grouped among the five Megilloth or Scrolls. Although it has been widely assumed that such a grouping itself insures the lateness of a book, and with lateness a relatively slow process of canonization, such a conclusion is by no means certain. Both the date of the rise of a threefold division of the canon and the reasons for placing a book within the third division have been hotly debated by conservative scholars within this century. Most of the books in the third division do represent the later collections of the Hebrew Bible, but this does not mean that these books could not have been received as canonical before the 1st cent. of the Christian era. When extensive discussion arose over the place of Ecclesiastes among the books that "[ritually] defiled the hands," it came not as a question of admitting a new book to the canon but as an attack on the book's traditional place among the canonical writings. The book's relative skepticism made it an offense to some of the conservative school (Shammai) within Judaism. Its eventual confirmation was probably assured because of the tradition of Solomonic authorship, reflected in its placement with Proverbs and Canticles in the LXX and certain rabbinic sources, and because of the tradition of usage dating back to Ben Sira. The book was generally accepted by the Christian Church, which took over its OT canon from the Jews. *See also* CANON OF THE OT.

Bibliography.–Standard intros. and comms., including those by F. Delitzsch (KD, 1878); G. A. Barton (*ICC*, 1908); A. L. Williams (*CBSC*, 1922); O. S. Rankin and G. G. Atkins (*IB*, 1956); R. B. Y. Scott (*AB*, 1965). Other works of value include: H. L. Ginsberg, *Studies in Koheleth* (1950); "Structure and Contents of the Book of Koheleth," in M. Noth and D. W. Thomas, eds., *Wisdom in Israel and in the Ancient Near East* (*SVT*, 3, 1955), pp. 138-149; R. Gordis, *Wisdom of Ecclesiastes* (1945); *Koheleth, The Man and His World* (3rd ed. 1968); *JBL*, 74 (1955), 103-114; *Biblica*, 41 (1960), 395-410; M. Jastrow, *A Gentle Cynic* (1916); R. Murphy, *CBQ*, 17 (1955), 304-314; *Wisdom Literature* (*Forms of the OT Literature*, 1981), pp. 125-149.

W. J. BEECHER C. E. ARMERDING

ECCLESIASTICUS e-klē-zi-as'tə-kəs. *See* SIRACH.

ECLIPSE. *See* ASTRONOMY II.B.

ECSTASY. Defined in a distinctively religious sense, an abnormal state of consciousness in which revelatory communications (both visionary and auditory) are believed to be received from supernatural beings.

- I. General
  - A. Definition
  - B. Biblical Occurrences
  - C. Psycho-Social Approaches
  - D. Controlled and Uncontrolled Possession
- II. In the OT
  - A. Nature of Revelatory Experience
  - B. Descriptive Phrases
  - C. Types of Revelatory Experience
- III. In the NT
  - A. Uses of the Term
  - B. Behavioral Features
  - C. Descriptive Phrases

I. General.–*A. Definition.* "Ecstasy" is a transliteration of the Greek noun *ékstasis,* derived from the verb *exístēmi* (or *existánō*), the root meaning of which is "displace," "stand apart from," or "put out of place." While the Greek words literally mean displacement or change, metaphorically they refer to at least three states of mind, each having characteristic behavioral features: (1) mental or psychological distractions such as excitement and astonishment, fear and terror; (2) the pathological mental state of madness or insanity (whether temporary or permanent); and (3) the trancelike state in which people are considered particularly susceptible to communications from supernatural beings. These types of *ékstasis* were distinguished by Philo (*Quis rerum divinarum heres* 249), who was dependent on Plato (*Phaedrus* 244a-245a), though Plato used different terms. This article will focus on the third type of *ékstasis*; but since this category exhibits such a wide variety of behavioral characteristics, and since such designations as "trancelike state" or "ecstatic state" are vague and subject to misunderstanding, we shall refer to this phenomenon as the *revelatory state* of consciousness.

B. Biblical Occurrences. The term "ecstasy" is not used in the AV, RSV, or NEB. In three NT passages (Acts 10:10; 11:5; 22:17), however, *ékstasis* is appropriately translated "trance" in all three versions. The AV also uses "trance" in Nu. 24:4, 16 in a periphrastic, though not inappropriate, interpretation of the Hebrew text, which describes Balaam's experience of a revelatory state of consciousness. In the OT there is no single Hebrew word which, like the Gk. *ékstasis,* describes the revelatory state. The LXX uses *ékstasis* thirty times to translate eleven different Hebrew words, the majority of which are synonyms for "fear" or "terror." In two passages (Gen. 2:21; 15:12) *ékstasis* represents the Hebrew noun *tardēmâ* ("deep sleep"); in 15:12 God is said to have caused a deep sleep to fall upon Abraham, during which the patriarch received a revelation in a vision. In the NT the Gk. *exístēmi* (or *existánō*) can refer to irrationality or madness (Mk. 3:21), but in most instances it refers to "amazement" or "astonishment" (Mt. 10:23; Mk. 2:12; 5:42; 6:51; Lk. 2:47; 8:56; Acts 2:7, 12; 8:13; 9:21; 10:45; 12:16). In one instance (2 Cor. 5:13, discussed below) *exístēmi* refers to the revelatory state. The LXX uses *exístēmi* and *existánō* about seventy-five times as translations for twenty-nine Hebrew words, all of which are synonyms for "fear" or "amazement."

C. Psycho-Social Approaches. From the psychological point of view the revelatory state is an abnormal state of consciousness in which intense absorption in one restricted set of feelings or ideas dominates the consciousness to the exclusion of normal external sensory impressions. The subject experiences the control and domination of his consciousness by a supernatural force or power outside of himself. From the psychological perspective the resulting visions and auditions are subjective rather than objective experiences. From the sociological perspective, the revelatory state is an experience characterized by abnormal behavioral features that are accepted as proving that the subject has received visionary and/or suggesting communication with supernatural beings by means of contact or possession. The revelatory state, often referred to as "ecstatic experience," is a universal religious phenomenon (Lewis, *passim*). If the supernatural beings that communicate with man are regarded as affecting him in primarily an *external* manner, the experience can be referred to as "divine inspiration." If the supernatural beings are thought to enter into a man's body or personality, the experience may be referred to as "divine possession." In general the ancient Greek view up to the 1st cent. A.D. was that of "divine inspiration," while the Judeo-Christian view was that of "divine possession."

D. Controlled and Uncontrolled Possession. Two other distinctions must be made. The experience of the revelatory state in terms of inspiration or possession can occur in an *uncontrolled* or a *controlled* manner (Lewis, p. 64). Uncontrolled inspiration or possession cannot be limited by the subject to particular places and times, while controlled inspiration or possession is subject to the will of the practitioner and occurs only within scheduled situations. Frequently the initial experience of uncontrolled possession or inspiration is gradually transformed into the kind of controlled possession practiced, for example, by Siberian shamans (Lewis, p. 55). For biblical examples of uncontrolled possession we may point to the revelatory trances experienced by Peter (Acts 10:10; 11:5), Paul (Acts 22:17), and John (Rev. 1:10; 4:1), while examples of controlled possession are exhibited by Balaam (Nu. 24:4, 16) and the Corinthian prophets (1 Cor. 14:27-33). In general it may be said that controlled inspiration characterized the Greek conception of divine revelation, since oracular utterances were normally given in response to inquiries at defined times and places, and that ancients regularly consulted such oracles to minimize the risks inherent in human decisions. Prophets of the ancient Near East (Canaan, Egypt, Mari, Israel), on the other hand, knew both controlled and uncontrolled possession. Classical Israelite prophecy was frequently of the uncontrolled type, since divine revelations were spontaneously delivered in situations of extraordinary social and political crisis.

II. In the OT.–*A. Nature of Revelatory Experience.* In ancient Palestine, during the period of Israelite occupation until the beginning of classical Israelite prophecy with Amos and Hosea in the 8th cent. B.C., the revelatory state of consciousness was primarily achieved and practiced in controlled situations. Though it has often been claimed that Canaanite and early Israelite prophets induced the revelatory state by artificial means, it is more probable that references to the use of music (1 S. 10:5; 2 K. 3:15; 1 Ch. 25:1) and the dance (1 K. 18:26) were part of the normal ritual setting within which versified oracles were chanted. Although the band of prophets depicted in 1 S. 10:5-13; 19:8-24 appears to have experienced a controlled revelatory state, Saul and his messengers are described as falling into the revelatory state involuntarily. The revelatory state into which the band of prophets had fallen was infectious and produced a catatonic state in Saul, for whom the experience was both new and alien (19:24). The controlled nature of the revelatory state for some OT prophets is indicated by the fact that it was preceded by prayer (Jer. 33:3; 37:3, 6-10; 42:2-4; Dnl. 9:20-23), and sometimes by fasting (Dnl. 10:2-9), features that often provide a context for the onset of the revelatory state in the NT. Presumably the cult prophets, who had to respond to specific questions posed by those who came "to inquire of the Lord" (1 S. 9:9; 1 K. 22:5, 7; 2 K. 3:11; Jer. 21:2), were able to achieve the revelatory state at will.

B. Descriptive Phrases. The onset of the revelatory state is frequently described with such stereotyped phrases as "the Spirit of God came upon" a certain one (Nu. 24:2; 1 S. 10:10; 11:6; 19:20, 23; 2 Ch. 15:1; Isa. 61:1), or "the hand of the Lord came/was upon" someone (Ezk. 3:14, 22; 8:1; 33:22; 37:1), or "the word of the Lord came to" a certain prophet (1 K. 19:9; 1 S. 15:10; 2 S. 24:11; Jonah 1:1; Hag. 1:1; 2:1, 20; Zec. 7:1, 8; 8:1). These formal descriptions tell us very little about the nature of the revelatory state except that those who so described the experience (in some cases the prophets themselves) carefully distinguished the onset of the revelatory state from the normal state of consciousness.

C. Types of Revelatory Experience. The kinds of experience that characterized the revelatory state are rarely described in the OT, with the exception of the prophet Ezekiel (cf. 1:1–3:15) and some of the visions described by other prophets (Amos 7:1–8:14; Zec. 4–6). In opposing false prophets, Jeremiah affirmed that only those who had stood in the council of the Lord were true prophets (Jer. 23:18, 22). This kind of visionary experience is presented in more detail in 1 K. 22:19-23, where Micaiah ben Imlah describes an experience he had while in a revelatory state: he heard and saw the conversations and activities of the council of God in heaven regarding the imminent events on earth. Another type of revelatory experience, which is an example of uncontrolled inspiration, is the call reported by many prophets (Ex. 3:1–4:17; 1 S. 3:2-14; 2 K. 2:9-14; Jer. 1:4-10; Isa. 6:1-13). In considering the full spectrum of revelatory experiences narrated in the OT, neither the type of revelatory state nor the conditions within which it is experienced is the subject of criticism or disapproval. The distinction which some modern scholars have made between the "ecstasy of absorption" and the "ecstasy of concentration" is not found in the OT, but rather imposed on it.

III. In the NT.–*A. Uses of the Term.* In the NT, the Gk. *ékstasis* ("trance," AV, RSV, NEB) refers to the revelatory state in Acts 10:10; 11:15; 22:17. In the first two references Peter is said to have fallen into a revelatory state after prayer and then to have received a revelatory vision; in the third reference Paul similarly receives a vision while praying in the temple in Jerusalem. In another important passage, Paul uses the verb *exístēmi* to describe a state of revelatory ecstasy in a way not clearly communicated by the RSV or other major versions. In 2 Cor. 5:13 Paul observes: "For if we are beside ourselves [*exéstēmen*] it is for God; if we are in our right mind [*sōphronoúmen*], it is for you." Paul here contrasts two states of consciousness, not irrationality and rationality, but rather the revelatory state, i.e., the extraordinary experience of full possession of the Spirit, in contrast to the normal, rational state of consciousness (F. Pfister, p. 187). Paul makes a similar distinction in 1 Cor. 14:2, where glossolalia is specifically defined as speech directed to God, whereas comprehensible speech is addressed to man.

B. Behavioral Features. In the NT the revelatory state of consciousness has external behavioral features that allow it to be confused with drunkenness (Acts 2:13, 15; Eph. 5:18) or insanity (Mk. 3:21; 1 Cor. 14:23). A revelatory state is often exhibited by an abnormally loud voice (Mk. 1:24; 3:11; 5:7; Lk. 1:42; Acts 2:14; 16:17; cf. F. J. Dölger), or even by incomprehensible speech (1 Cor. 14:2, 9, 18). At times it is accompanied by bizarre behavior (Mk. 5:2-5; 9:22; Acts 16:17f.; 21:11). In most NT instances the onset of the revelatory state is unexpected and uncontrolled, though it is occasionally said to be preceded by prayer (Lk. 3:21; 9:28f.; Acts 10:10; 11:5; 22:17; 2 Cor. 12:8f.), and on one occasion by fasting (Acts 13:2). The revelatory experience itself is described in a number of ways. A vision may be received by one in the revelatory state (Acts 10:10; 11:5; 22:17-21) in the form of a journey to heaven (2 Cor. 12:1-4; Rev. 4:1) or of an appearance of a supernatural being (God, Christ, or an angel) from heaven (Acts 9:3-6; 22:6-8; 26:13-18). The experience may be regarded as subjective in the sense that not all those present see or hear the same thing (compare Acts 9:7 with 22:9, and compare the various accounts of Jesus' revelatory experience at His baptism in Mt. 3:16f.; Mk. 1:10f.; Lk. 3:21f.).

C. Descriptive Phrases. The phrase "(be) in the Spirit" (Rev. 1:10; 4:1) is another way of describing the revelatory state, the opposite of which is to "be oneself" (Acts 12:11). The concept of the central role played by the Spirit of God in producing the revelatory state is derived from the OT (Nu. 24:2; 1 S. 10:10; 11:6; 19:20; Ezk. 8:3; Isa. 61:1), and early Christians emphasized the Spirit's role as the cause of the revelatory state within which OT prophets uttered their inspired oracles (Acts 1:16; 1 Pet. 1:11; 2 Pet. 1:21). Though all Christians can be described as being "in the Spirit" (Rom. 8:9-11; Gal. 3:3; 5:16), that status does not refer to the extraordinary and abnormal revelatory state, which is a temporary rather than a permanent experience. In the NT, as in the OT, the revelatory state is not always attained in an uncontrolled manner, for the very fact that prophecy and other manifestations of the Spirit occur within the framework of Christian worship (Acts 11:27f.; 13:1; 1 Cor. 14:26-33) indicates that both the time and place of the onset of the revelatory state is subject to control. Paul urges even greater control in 1 Cor. 14:27-32. It is probable that Paul himself, who claims to have had many experiences while in a revelatory state (1 Cor. 14:6, 26; 2 Cor. 12:1, 7; Gal. 1:12; 2:2), learned to control the experience and on that basis could exhort the Corinthian community to exercise control over their experiences.

See also INSPIRATION; PROPHECY.

Bibliography.–E. Benz, *Paulus als Visionär* (1952); F. J. Dölger, *Antike und Christentum,* 5 (1936), 218-223; I. M. Lewis, *Ecstatic Religion: An Anthropological Study of Spirit Possession and Shamanism* (1971); F. Pfister, "Ekstasis," in T. Klauser and A. Rücker, eds., *Pisculi: Studien zur Religion und Kultur des Altertums* (1939), pp. 320-333; W. D. Smith, *Proceedings of the American Philological Association,* 96 (1965), 403-436; *TDNT,* II, *s.v.* ἔκστασις, ἐξίστημι (Oepke).

D. E. AUNE

ED ed [Heb. *ʿēḏ*–'witness'] (AV Josh. 22:34). *See* WITNESS. The name of the altar erected by the trans-Jordanic tribes upon finally taking possession of Gilead (Josh. 22:10f., 34).

EDAR ē'där. *See* EDER, TOWER OF.

EDDIAS ed-ī'əs (AV 1 Esd. 9:26). *See* IZZIAH.

EDDINUS ed'i-nəs [Gk. B *Eddeinous,* A *Eddinous*); AV JEDUTHUN; NEB EDDINOUS. One of the temple singers at Josiah's Passover (1 Esd. 1:15). AV reads here "Jeduthun," the corresponding name in the parallel passage (2 Ch. 35:15). *See also* JEDUTHUN.

EDEN ē'dən [Heb. *ʿēḏen*] (2 Ch. 29:12; 31:15). A Levite who participated in Hezekiah's reform. It is not certain whether both passages refer to the same man or if there were two Levites by this name.

EDEN [Heb. *ʿēḏen*; Gk. *Edem*].

1. The area where God planted a garden of trees to form the first dwelling place of Adam and Eve. The etymology of the word is uncertain, although some scholars have attempted to explain it in terms of the Sum. edinu, "plain," "wilderness." The meaning "delight" conveyed by the LXX resulted from the assumed derivation of Eden from *ʿēḏen,* "loveliness," "delight," while the rendering *parádeisos tḗs tryphḗs* ("garden of delight") as the equivalent of "garden of Eden" not unnaturally led to the association of the latter with Paradise.

Aside from those in Gen. 2 and 3, other references to Eden in the OT are: Gen. 4:16; 2 K. 19:12; Isa. 37:12; 51:3; Ezk. 28:13; 31:9, 16, 18; 36:35; Joel 2:3. The name occurs thirteen times in the singular to designate a location. In Gen. 2:8 the garden was said to be "in Eden, in the east" (NEB "in Eden, away to the east"; cf. 4:16), where the vegetation was luxurious (2:9), where the fig tree, among others, was indigenous (3:7), and where irrigation canals supplied water. As distinct from a geographical locale in which a garden was situated, Gen. 2:15; 3:23f. refer to "the garden of Eden" as a separate topographical entity. In a metaphorical sense Eden paralleled "the garden of the Lord" (Isa. 51:3), an image which also appears in Ezk. 28:13; 31:9. The splendor of the trees in Eden is alluded to in Ezk. 31:16, 18; cf. 36:35; Joel 2:3. *See also* BETH-EDEN.

The location of Eden can be partially determined from the description already given. It must obviously be situated where the climate was suitable for the growth of fruit trees and where animals capable of domestication could live alongside the earliest members of the species *homo sapiens.* In particular the location of Eden must be considered by reference to the river from which the garden was watered. Before this is attempted, however, it is necessary to examine the nature of the source material containing the description of the area. Most modern scholars dismiss the passage in question as either legend or myth, having no significant basis in historical reality. However, the present writer views the bulk of Genesis as having been transmitted in a readily recognizable tablet form from a very early period of Mesopotamian history (see R. K. Harrison, *Intro. to the OT* [1969], pp. 543-553); thus this kind of material represents early attempts at the writing of history. The source in question is therefore taken as being fundamentally historical in nature, so that it is the responsibility of the exegete to interpret what the ancient author was endeavoring to describe.

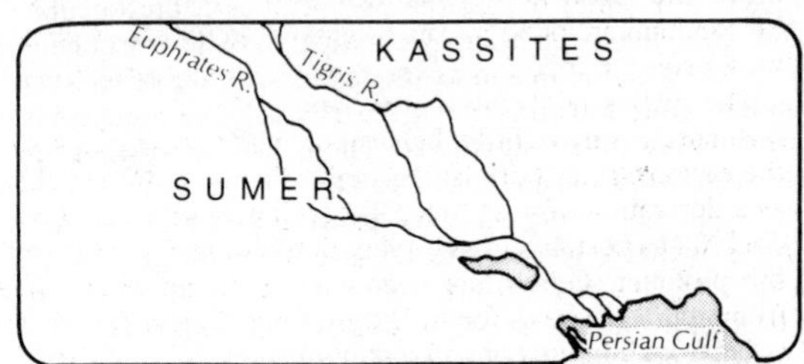

While there must always be a certain amount of conjecture in any reconstruction, it seems at least possible to make the following observations. The principal river (*nāhār*) of Gen. 2:10 parted and became four "heads" (MT *rā'šîm*; RSV "rivers"; NEB "streams"), a word that in Jgs. 7:16; Job 1:17 denotes the main detachments into which an army was divided, and therefore would more properly signify "branches" than "heads" of a river. Such branches were named respectively Pishon, which flowed round the whole land of Havilah; Gihon, which encompassed the land of Cush; Hiddekel, the river Tigris flowing E of Assyria; and the Euphrates.

The fact that two of the four branches are historic and familiar rivers suggests that, at the time of the original writer, the other two were also. Attempts to identify the latter have depended to some extent upon the location of Havilah and Cush. Havilah is mentioned in Gen. 10:29 as the name of one of the sons of Joktan, while in Gen. 25:18 it occurs as a place, perhaps located in the area of Sinai and northwestern Arabia. In Gen. 10:7 the name Havilah is found again to describe a descendant of Ham through Cush. These could represent quite distinct persons and places or could perhaps indicate that some area of settlement in South Arabia was associated with the two persons named Havilah, along with their descendants. This, however, throws no light upon a Mesopotamian location for Havilah, unless those scholars are right who relate the name to the Heb. *ḥôl,* "sand," to designate a desert area. The mention of the presence of "gold" in the land (Gen. 2:10) is certainly a questionable translation, and the NEB margin quite properly draws attention to the alternative rendering "frankincense." Similarly the meaning of the word "bdellium" is open to some doubt, and the most satisfactory translation is "gum resin," as also in the NEB margin. Aromatic resins and gums are a typical product of Arabia, which would again suggest that Havilah was located somewhere in that area. However, the *šōham* stone (RSV "onyx stone"; NEB "cornelians") is most probably a form of onyx, which occurs primarily in South America and India, suggesting a location E rather than W of Mesopotamia. If Havilah can be placed in some part of Arabia, this need only mean that it was a western colony of an original Havilah in Mesopotamia, though certainty in this matter is lacking.

Cush, the land encircled by the river branch known as Gihon, usually signifies Ethiopia in the OT, although not uniformly so (cf. Gen. 10:8). Those who postulate an Egyptian location for Cush think of the Ethiopia mentioned by classical authors, i.e., some region S of Egypt proper, such as the northern Sudan or Nubia. In the late 3rd millennium B.C. "Kush" was a district located somewhere between the second and third cataracts of the Nile. The area encompassed by the Gihon, however, was most probably in western Asia, and as such entirely unrelated to the region in Egypt. In the 2nd millennium B.C. a district E of the Tigris bore the name "Kush," and it was from this area that the Kassites came. Since the Garden of Eden narrative clearly implies a Mesopotamian location, the original home of the Kassites would suit the topography better than some area of Egypt.

The names of the two branches mentioned above unfortunately throw little light upon their location, since the etymology of both is uncertain. Pishon has been seen as a derivation of *pûš,* "leap," "spring forth," but this is doubtful as best and in any event does not help to elucidate the problem. Gihon has been viewed as an appellative from *gû(a)ḥ,* "break forth," "burst out," though this too is far from convincing and again does not resolve the difficulty. Probably the most suitable answer concerning the actual location of the Garden of Eden is to think of the river that watered the garden and thereafter became four "branches" as actually comprising the beginning or junction of tributaries going upstream from a point in southern Mesopotamia. Less probably the word *rô'š* ("head," "beginning," "top") means the root of a branch going downstream, as in a delta formation. If the original author was in an area close to the Persian Gulf that was being watered by the confluence of the Tigris and Euphrates, the branching of the river might well have referred to the upstream bifurcation of the rivers. Since from Gen. 2:6 it appears that a river (AV, RSV, "mist"; NEB "flood") overflowed in the garden to provide irrigation, it is probable that the inhabitants of Eden were living in an irrigation culture. Thus it is very likely that Pishon and Gihon were the names, not of rivers as commonly understood, but of major irrigation canals, which because of their nature have disappeared over the millennia. The narrative makes it clear that the author regarded these two waterways as equally renowned in his day with the Tigris and Euphrates, and that he was also describing an actual geographical location in rather primitive terminology. The location of the Garden could thus be placed with considerable assurance in ancient Sumer. The phrase "in Eden, in the east" (Gen. 2:8; NEB "away to the east") is literally "in Eden from in front," and indicates that perhaps the garden was located to the east of the author or that it was in the eastern part of the general area known as Eden. Nevertheless, it is impossible in the light of current information to be absolutely specific about the area's location.

By assuming the author's ignorance of geography, numerous fanciful identifications for Eden have been proposed. When Columbus passed the mouth of the Orinoco river, he supposed that its waters came down from the Garden of Eden. At that time, however, he imagined himself to be on the east coast of Asia. Those anthropologists who support a Near Eastern, rather than an African, home for earliest man, have located Eden somewhere in central Asia. Some in particular have placed it in that area stretching E from the Pamir, from which flow four rivers — the Indus, the Tarim, the Jaxartes, and the Oxus. One nineteenth-century author, W. F. Warren, went so far as to locate the original Eden at the North Pole, adducing as evidence the contention that in northern Greenland and in Spitzbergen abundant remains of fossil plants show that during the middle of the Tertiary period the whole circumpolar region manifested a climate similar to that occurring at present in southern Europe. Unfortunately, there is absolutely no evidence whatever that Adamic man (*homo sapiens*) goes back to the middle Tertiary period. A more realistic identification of Eden is with Armenia, where the Tigris and Euphrates have their origin. The Pishon and Gihon branches have been supposed to be the Choruk (thought by some to be the Phasis) and the Aras (Araxes), which empty into the Black Sea and the Caspian Sea respectively. On this identification Havilah would represent the area around Colchis; it is impossible, however, to place Cush in that region. Furthermore, these four rivers could not possibly be regarded as branches of one parent stream.

Quite clearly no theory, ancient or modern, of the location of Eden and its celebrated garden is entirely free from difficulties. On the basis of currently available information it would appear that the one that locates Eden near the head of the Persian Gulf combines the greatest number of probabilities of every kind.

Bibliography.–F. Delitzsch, *Wo lag das Paradies?* (1881); W. F. Albright, *AJSL,* 39 (1922/23), 15-31; T. C. Vriezen, *Onderzoek naar de Paradijsvoortstelling bij de oude semietische Volken* (1937); E. A. Speiser, *Festschrift Johannes Friedrich* (1959), pp. 473-485; M. G. Kline, *WTJ,* 20 (1957/58), 146-49.

R. K. HARRISON

2. (Ezk. 27:23). *See* BETH-EDEN.

EDEN, CHILDREN OF. *See* PEOPLE OF EDEN.

EDEN, HOUSE OF (AV Am. 1:5). *See* BETH-EDEN; PEOPLE OF EDEN.

EDEN, PEOPLE OF. *See* PEOPLE OF EDEN.

EDER ē'dər [Heb. *'ēḏer*–'flock'].

1. A Merarite Levite in the days of David (1 Ch. 23:23; 24:30); he was the son of Mushi.

2. A Benjaminite (1 Ch. 8:15; AV, NEB, Ader).

EDER ē'dər [Heb. *ʿēḏer*–'flock']. One of the outlying cities of Judah in the Negeb near the border of Edom (Josh. 15:21). Identification with Khirbet el-ʿAdar 8 km. (5 mi.) S of Gaza has been suggested, but this is too far west. The biblical text would seem to indicate that the site is to be found E of Beer-sheba, probably in the Arabah.

J. F. PREWITT

EDER, TOWER OF [Heb. *migdal-ʿēḏer*–'tower of the flock']; AV TOWER OF EDAR; NEB MIGDAL-EDER. After Rachel died and was buried near Bethlehem, Jacob continued his journey toward Hebron "and pitched his tent beyond the tower of Eder" (Gen. 35:21). This "tower of the flock" must, therefore, be looked for between Bethlehem and Hebron. Jerome says it was 1 Roman mi. (1.5 km., 0.9 mi.) from Bethlehem. It was probably not a town but simply a tower for guarding flocks against robbers (cf. "watchtower," 2 K. 18:8).

The phrase *migdal-ʿēḏer* occurs in Mic. 4:8, where Jerusalem is compared to such a tower. There the AV and RSV translate "tower of the flock," while the NEB renders "rocky bastion."

E. W. G. MASTERMAN
J. F. PREWITT

EDES ē'dēz (AV 1 Esd. 9:35). *See* IDDO **3.**

EDGE [Heb. *qāṣeh* (Ex. 28:7; Nu. 20:16; 33:37; etc.), *qāṣâ* (Ex. 28:23f.; 39:16f.), *peh* (Ex. 17:13; Dt. 13:15 [MT 16]; Jgs. 3:16; etc.), *qᵉṣāṯ* (Ex. 39:4), *pēʾâ* (Lev. 19:27; 21:5), *śāpâ* (Ex. 26:4, 10; 36:11, 17; Ezk. 43:13; etc.), *ʿēḇer* (Ex. 28:26; 39:19), *pānîm* (Eccl. 10:10; Ezk. 21:16 [MT 21]), *qāhâ* (Jer. 31:29f.; Ezk. 18:2), *ṣûr* (Ps. 89:43), *ʿal* (Dt. 3:12); Gk. *stóma* (Lk. 21:24; He. 11:34)]; AV also SIDE, BRINK, BANK, FACE, END, CORNER, etc.; NEB also CORNER, SIDE, FRONTIER, OUTSKIRTS, etc. Used frequently in the OT for Heb. *peh,* "mouth," in the phrase "smote with the edge of the sword" (e.g., Josh. 8:24; 10:28ff.; 11:12, 14; Jgs. 1:18, 25; cf. Josh. 6:21; Jgs. 4:15f.; etc.; NEB "put to the sword"), and similarly in the NT for Gk. *stóma,* "mouth" (Lk. 21:24; He. 11:34). Also occurring frequently in the OT is the phrase "edge of the valley" (Dt. 2:36; 4:48; Josh. 12:2; 13:9, 16; etc.) from the Heb. *śāpâ,* "lip." *Qāṣeh* and *qāṣâ* ("end," "border," "extremity") are used in reference to the wilderness (Ex. 13:20; Nu. 33:6), a curtain in the tabernacle (Ex. 26:5; 36:12), the camp (2 K. 7:5, 8), etc.

Jeremiah (31:29) and Ezekiel (18:2) quote an ancient proverb: "The fathers have eaten sour grapes, and the children's teeth are set on edge." The Hebrew term here is *qāhâ,* which means "become blunt." The proverb expresses the old covenant teaching that children are punished for the sins of their fathers (cf. Ex. 20:5). Both prophets affirm that a day is coming when each man will be responsible for his own sins (Jer. 31:30-32; Ezk. 18:3-32).

N. J. O.

EDICT. *See* DECREE.

EDIFICATION; EDIFY. The Gk. *oikodoméō,* "build," and *oikodomḗ,* "the act of building," are used both literally and figuratively in the NT (cf. literal use in Mt. 7:24, 26 par. Lk. 6:47, 49; Mt.; 16:18; 21:33; 26:61 par. Mk. 14:58; Lk. 4:29; etc.). "Edify," "edifying," "edification," are the translation of the AV in some twenty passages, all in the figurative sense of the promotion of growth in Christian character. The RSV renders these terms in this sense only seven times (Rom. 15:2; 1 Cor. 14:4f., 17, 26; Eph. 4:29); in the other instances it renders "building up" or "upbuilding" (Acts 9:31; Rom. 14:19; 1 Cor. 8:1; 10:23; 14:3, 12; 2 Cor. 10:8; 12:19; 13:10; Eph. 4:12, 16; 1 Thess. 5:11). In 1 Tim. 1:4 the Greek text followed by the RSV has *oikonomía,* "training," instead of *oikodomía,* "edifying" (AV). *See also* BUILD.

F. K. FARR

EDNA ed'nə [Gk. *Edna*]. Wife of Raguel and mother of Sarah, who married Tobias (Tob. 7:2, etc., 10:12; 11:1). "Edna" in Hebrew means "pleasure" and corresponds to Lat. *Anna.*

EDOM ē'dəm; **EDOMITES** ē'dəm-īts [Heb. *ʾᵉḏôm, ʾᵃḏōmîm*; Gk. *Edōm*; Ugar. *ʾudm*; Akk. *Udumu*; Egyp. *ʾdm, Aduma*]. The country S of Moab and E and W of the Arabah, and its people. The name Edom is derived from the Semitic root meaning "red," "ruddy"; it may have been given to the land because of the reddish color of the sandstone in that district.

I. Origins
II. Territory
III. History
IV. Economy
V. Religion
VI. Language
VII. Israel and Edom

I. Origins.–The Edomites are said to be the descendants of Jacob's brother ESAU (Gen. 36:9), who is sometimes called Edom (25:30; 36:1, 8, 43). Esau/Seir (36:8) is the ancestor of the Edomites in the same way that Jacob/Israel is the eponym of the Israelites. The children of Esau apparently had to drive the Horites out of the land of Seir (Dt. 2:22). Like the Israelites, the Edomites probably came originally from Aram; but they appear to have been a composite group (Gen. 36).

II. Territory.–Edom was situated S of the Dead Sea, extending from the Wâdī el-Ḥesā to the Gulf of Aqabah. Its eastern and western boundaries are indeterminate, although Nu. 20:16 places Kadesh on the edge of Edomite territory (cf. Nu. 20:23; Josh. 15:1, 21). In the OT Edom is often identified with the country or mountain of Seir (e.g., Gen. 32:3; 36:8; Jgs. 5:4).

The western and eastern sections of Edom are separated by the Wâdī el-ʿArabah, the continuation of the Jordan rift between the Dead Sea and the Gulf of Aqabah, a distance of about 175 km. (110 mi.). About 95 km. (60 mi.) S of the Dead Sea it reaches a height of about 600 m. (2000 ft.) above the Dead Sea. From this point it descends

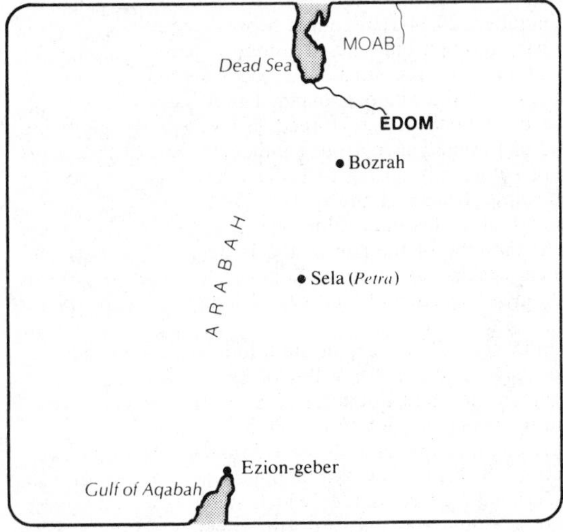

about 215 m. (700 ft.) until it reaches the shores of the Gulf of Aqabah. On both sides the mountains rise steeply from the Arabah. On the east the mountains are mainly red Nubian sandstone, reaching an altitude that exceeds 1520 m. (5000 ft.) in many instances and occasionally 1700 m. (5600 ft.) and more to the south. Because of their height the mountains enjoy an adequate rainfall in winter, but only on the western ascents and the western edge of the plateau. The eastern and southern sections are, for the most part, desert regions. On the western side of the Arabah in the north, the mountains are from 450 m. (1500 ft.) to a little over 600 m. (2000 ft.) high, and they rise gradually until they reach as high as 800 m. (2600 ft.) in the south. This is mostly desert region. The mountains on both sides of the Arabah are cut by deep gorges, which add to the forbidding character of the land. *See* Plates 1, 2.

III. History.–According to Glueck, a "Pre-Pottery Neolithic village of the first part of the seventh millennium B.C. has been excavated," and there is "clear evidence of late fourth millennium B.C. Chalcolithic settlements in Edom" (*AOTS*, pp. 444f.). Much more evidence has been found of a highly advanced Early Bronze Age agricultural civilization, which flourished from the 23rd to 20th cents. B.C. (Glueck, *AASOR*, 15 [1934/35], 138; 18-19 [1938/39], 268). But *ca.* 1900 this civilization was destroyed, perhaps by the Hyksos or some other rising power; it may even be that Gen. 14:6 refers to this destruction. For the next six centuries only bedouin inhabited the land of Edom (*AOTS*, pp. 443f.).

The earliest discovered references to the land and people of Edom/Seir come from Egyptian texts. One of the Amarna Letters (early 14th cent. B.C.) mentions the "lands of Seir" (Am.Tab. 288; *ANET*, p. 488; cf. "Udumu," Am.Tab. 256; *ANET*, p. 486). The Shasu tribes (bedouin) of Edom are mentioned as crossing the border into Egypt in the reign of Seti II (1214-1208 B.C.; *ANET*, p. 259); and Ramses III (1198-1166 B.C.) claimed to have destroyed the nomadic Shasu of Seir (*ANET*, p. 262). During this period we hear only of Shasu peoples or bedouin of Seir/Edom. No Edomite/Seirite towns or leaders are named, and nothing suggests that Edom and Seir had any real political or national significance at this time.

Although Gen. 36:31-39 suggests that an Edomite kingdom existed before there was an Israelite kingdom (cf. 1 Ch. 1:43-53), this text may refer to tribal chieftains or nondynastic leaders like the Israelite judges. Thus in Gen. 36:15-19, 40-43; Ex. 15:15, Edomite leaders are called "chiefs" (Heb. *'allupîm*).

Numbers 20:14-21 recounts Moses' request at Kadesh to pass through the land of Edom in order to reach the territory E of the Jordan as the starting-point of the conquest of the land of Canaan. The request was refused, and the Israelites were forced to make a detour to the east of Edom. This narrative indicates that the Edomites were sufficiently strong to prevent the Israelite passage along the King's Highway (vv. 17-19), but it does not mean that at this time Edom was a well-unified country.

At the time of the rise of the Israelite monarchy Saul fought successfully against Edom (1 S. 14:47). Doeg, an Edomite, was chief of Saul's herdsmen (1 S. 21:7 [MT 8]; 22:9, 18, 22).

In David's wars of expansion Edom was conquered after a decisive defeat in the Valley of Salt, where David slew eighteen thousand Edomites (2 S. 8:13f.; cf. 1 Ch. 18:12 and the superscription to Ps. 60 [MT v. 2]). David placed garrisons in Edom and all the Edomites became his subjects (2 S. 8:14). The thoroughness of the operation is underlined by 1 K. 11:15f., which states twice that every male in Edom was put to death. David's motive for the conquest of the Edomites may lie not so much in that they were a threat to him as in the prospect of wealth from the abundant copper in their territory and from control of the trade routes that passed through it.

David's victory resulted in the flight to Egypt of a young man called Hadad (1 K. 11:17f.) who "was of the royal house in Edom" (v. 14). There he married a member of the Egyptian royal family (v. 19). After David's death he returned to Edom as king and became an adversary of Solomon (vv. 14, 21, 25; in v. 25 read "Edom" with the LXX, NEB, *contra* the MT, RSV, AV). It would appear from this narrative that a monarchical form of government became a reality in Edom about the same time as the emergence of the monarchy in Israel. How widespread, successful, or lasting Hadad's rule over Edom was is uncertain. Solomon, nevertheless, seems to have had sufficient supplies of copper (7:14, 45-47) and access to his port at EZION-GEBER (9:26). It is possible that Ezion-geber was destroyed during the invasion by Sheshonq (Shishak) of Egypt in the fifth year of Rehoboam's reign (14:25f.; 2 Ch. 12:2-9). Sheshonq's invasion of Palestine and Transjordan gave Edom a chance to regain its independence.

We have no information about Edom from the end of Solomon's reign until Jehoshaphat's (873-849 B.C.). In the time of Jehoshaphat Judah expanded southward, ruled Edom (1 K. 22:47), and used the port of Ezion-geber (vv. 48f.; 2 Ch. 20:35f.). The ships of Jehoshaphat were wrecked at Ezion-geber, perhaps by Edomites (1 K. 22:48; 2 Ch. 20:36f.).

The narrative of 2 K. 3:4-27 describes an unsuccessful campaign of Jehoram king of Israel, Jehoshaphat king of Judah, and the king of Edom against Mesha king of Moab. The Lucianic version of this passage does not name Jehoshaphat as this king of Judah, however, and the Moabite campaign is best placed under the two kings Jehoram (or the coregency of Jehoshaphat and his son Jehoram).

Edom successfully revolted under Jehoram of Judah (849-842 B.C.) and set up a king of its own (2 K. 8:20-22); it probably regained control of the Wâdī el-ʿArabah and seized Ezion-geber. Edom maintained its independence for about fifty or sixty years until the middle of Amaziah's reign (800-783). Amaziah achieved a partial conquest as far S as Sela, and defeated an army of ten thousand Edomites in the Valley of Salt (2 K. 14:7; cf. 2 Ch. 25:11f.). This victory assured Judah of control over northern Edom and the copper mines of the Punon area. It is unlikely, however, that Amaziah made any lasting conquest of Edom. Uzziah (= Azariah, 783-742), Amaziah's son, restored ELATH (Ezion-geber) to Judah (2 K. 14:22; 2 Ch. 26:1f.). But in the time of Ahaz (735-715), Edom defeated Judah (2 Ch. 28:17) and recovered Elath (2 K. 16:6; note that "Edom" is to be read for MT "Aram," requiring only the smallest consonantal change; also in 2 S. 8:13; 2 Ch. 20:2). Judah was never again able to exercise control over Edom. During the whole period from *ca.* 842 Judah's control over Edom could not have been very strong; for during the 8th and at least the first half of the 7th cents., Edom was usually a vassal of Assyria.

The first Assyrian contact with Edom on record occurred *ca.* 800 B.C., when Adadnirari III (810-782) conquered "the country of the Hittites, Amurru-country in its full extent, Tyre, Sidon, Israel, Edom, Palestine" and imposed "upon them tribute" (*ANET*, p. 281). When Tiglath-pileser III (745-727) appeared in the west, Qauš-Malaku of Edom paid him tribute (*ca.* 734; *ANET*, p. 282). Sargon II (722-705) listed an unnamed ruler of Edom among those involved in the rebellion of Ashdod in 713 (*ANET*, p. 287). Sennacherib (705-681) reported that

Aiarammu from Edom brought gifts (*ANET,* p. 287). Esarhaddon (680-669) mentioned Qauš-gabri king of Edom with twenty-two vassal kings whom he swore to loyalty at Nineveh (*ANET,* p. 291). Finally, Qauš-gabri king of Edom paid tribute and submitted also to Ashurbanipal (669-627; *ANET,* p. 294), who in his ninth campaign (against Uate' king of Arabia) pursued his quarry into Edom (*ANET,* p. 298). From the Assyrian records it appears that Edom was known and recognized by Assyria as a clearly identifiable and even important kingdom from the beginning of the 8th cent. B.C. onward.

This is substantiated by the archeological evidence from three sites in central Edom (Umm el-Bayyârah, Tawīlân, and Buṣeirah) excavated by C.-M. Bennett. None of these sites produced any clear evidence of sedentary occupation before the beginning of the 8th cent. B.C. The excavations at Buṣeirah — probably the site of Bozrah, the chief royal city of the Edomites (Gen. 36:33; Isa. 34:6; 63:1; Jer. 49:13, 22; Am. 1:12), which flourished mainly from the end of the 8th cent. to the end of the 7th cent. B.C. — have been especially crucial for establishing the importance of Edom during this period.

These excavations by C.-M. Bennett complement earlier excavations by N. Glueck at Tell el-Kheleifeh (probably Ezion-geber = Elath; but *see* TELL EL-KHELEIFEH) on the north shore of the Gulf of Aqabah. The pottery of Period IV (from about the end of the 8th to the end of the 6th cent. B.C.) from this site is comparable to that found in the Edomite sites excavated by Bennett. Period IV at Tell el-Kheleifeh is completely Edomite and testifies to a vigorous Edomite civilization "in the seventh–sixth centuries B.C. beginning with the end of the eighth century B.C." (N. Glueck, *BASOR,* 188 [1967], 23).

Two Hebrew ostraca discovered by Y. Aharoni at Tell Arad in southeastern Judah also testify to Edom's power *ca.* 700-600 B.C. One ostracon, which may be associated with the campaign of Sennacherib in 701, refers to some sort of negotiations between Judahite and Edomite authorities. The other deals with the urgency of gathering men in anticipation of an Edomite attack, possibly associated with one of Nebuchadrezzar's campaigns (Y. Aharoni, *BASOR,* 197 [Feb. 1970], 16-42).

While the 7th cent. B.C. saw the height of Edom's prosperity, it also saw the beginning of its end. Edom, like Judah, was subject to destruction by the Babylonians in the 6th cent. B.C. (Jer. 27:2f., 6; 49:7-22; Ezk. 32:29). The oracle of Mal. 1:2-4 indicates that by the time of its writing Edom was in ruin. The archeological evidence also indicates the downfall of Edom by the end of the 6th century. Nomadic tribes infiltrated Edom and it lost the power to control and profit from the trade between Arabia and the Mediterranean coast and Egypt. In the 5th cent. an Arabian tribe, the Nabateans, forced their way into Edom and replaced the Edomites, many of whom went westward to southern Judea (later to become Idumea; cf. 1 Macc. 5:3, 65), while others were absorbed into the newcomers. By 312 B.C. the area around Petra also was inhabited by the Nabateans.

IV. Economy.–The economy of Edom was based on agriculture and commerce rather than on the control of the copper mines of the Wâdī el-ʿArabah. Agriculture was possible especially in the northeastern region of the country. But Edom's prosperity depended on the caravan routes from India and south Arabia to the Mediterranean coast and Egypt. Whenever Edom lost control of these routes its civilization declined.

V. Religion.–The Edomites were devoted to the gods and goddesses of fertility. Townspeople and peasants had in their houses crude pottery figurines, representing the deities whose good will they sought. Near Buṣeirah was found a pottery figurine (9th-8th cents. B.C.) of a fertility goddess, wearing a lamp as a crown and holding in her hand some sacred object. From Tell el-Kheleifeh has come a crude pottery plaque representing the pregnant mother-goddess, a figure of the same type of fertility goddess with what may be an incense cup, and evidence of foundation offerings.

The deity peculiar to Edom was Qauš (Koze in Josephus *Ant.* xv.7.9), as is evident from personal names found in inscriptions (cf. N. Glueck, *BASOR,* 72 [Dec. 1938], pp. 2ff., 11ff.; 82 [Apr. 1941], 3-11; *RB,* 73 [1966], 372ff., 399ff.). Another divine name perhaps known in Edom was Eloah, who, according to the prophet Habakkuk, came from Teman (Hab. 3:31); this name appears most frequently in Job, which some suppose to be Edomite (cf. Pfeiffer). In the Hebrew tradition Eloah (the singular form of the more familiar Elohim) was identified with Yahweh, who was said to have marched from Edom, among other places of the south (Dt. 33:2; Jgs. 5:4).

VI. Language.–Written materials recovered from Edom are scant, being limited primarily to ostraca, seals, and stamped jar handles of the 9th to 5th cents. from the sites mentioned above. Among the most interesting discoveries are a seal bearing the name Qauš-gabri, found at Umm el-Bayyârah, the "Jotham" signet ring from Tell el-Kheleifeh, and twelve seventh- or sixth-century stamped jar handles reading "belonging to Qausʿanal, servant of the king," also from Tell el-Kheleifeh (J. R. Bartlett, "Moabites and Edomites," pp. 247f.; *see also* TELL EL-KHELEIFEH). Study of these written materials suggests that the Edomite language was not very different from Moabite and Hebrew.

VII. Israel and Edom.–According to the biblical account, the brotherly relationship between Edom and Israel stemmed from the identification of Edom with Esau, Jacob's brother (cf. Dt. 23:7 [MT 8]; see I above). A contributing factor in this identification may have been that the Israelites were conscious that they had many things in common with the Edomites. Their brotherly relationship may have been based both on racial ties and on a brotherly covenant treaty (cf. Am. 1:11).

Edom was renowned in Israel for its wisdom (Jer. 49:7; Ob. 8; Bar. 3:22f.). The book of JOB seems to reflect an

Enlarged impression of seal of *Qwsʿnl* in Edomite(?) lapidary script from Tell el-Kheleifeh. The actual impression is about 1.2 cm. (0.5 in.) long (E. K. Vogel; picture American Schools of Oriental Research)

Edomite setting. Probably Job's friend Eliphaz the Temanite and possibly Bildad and Zophar came from Edom (Job 2:11; cf. Gen. 36:4, 10-12). The LXX identifies Job with Jobab king of the Edomites (Gen. 36:33). Also, the land of Uz (Job 1:1) may have been in Edom (cf. Lam. 4:21).

From the time of the Israelite kings, the relationship between Edom and Israel was one of continual hostility. As foreshadowed in the blessings of Isaac (Gen. 27:27-29, 39f.), Edom was subjugated by Israel in the time of David but regained its independence in the 8th cent. B.C. The prophets of Judah were extremely bitter toward Edom for its stance in the destruction of Jerusalem by Babylon in 587/586 B.C., and they predicted Edom's desolation (e.g., Obadiah). It is not certain whether Edom simply stood aloof and rejoiced in Judah's calamity or actually assisted in Jerusalem's destruction, as seems to be implied by Ps. 137:7; Isa. 34:5-15; Jer. 49:7-22; Lam. 4:21f.; Ezk. 35:3-15 (cf. Jth. 7:8, 18; 1 Esd. 4:45). According to Jer. 40:11 Edom offered a home to some of the Judean refugees.

See also IDUMEA; SEIR.

Bibliography.–J. R. Bartlett, *JTS*, N.S. 16 (1965), 301-314; 20 (1969), 1-20; *PEQ*, 104 (1972), 26-37; "Moabites and Edomites," in D. J. Wiseman, ed., *Peoples of OT Times* (1973), pp. 229-258; *Journal for the Study of the OT*, 4 (1977), 2-27; C.-M. Bennett, *Perspective*, 12 (1971), 35-44; F. Buhl, *Geschichte der Edomiter* (1893); *GB*; N. Glueck, *AASOR*, 15 (1934/35); 18-19 (1938/39); 25-28 (1945-1949); "Civilization of the Edomites," in D. N. Freedman and E. F. Campbell, eds., *Biblical Archaeologist Reader*, 2 (1964), 51-58; *HUCA*, 11 (1936), 141-157; "Transjordan," in *AOTS*, pp. 429-453; *Other Side of the Jordan* (rev. ed. 1970); *GTTOT*; *LBHG*; G. Moritz, *Muséon*, 1 (1937), 101-122; R. H. Pfeiffer, *ZAW*, 44 (1926), 13-25; J. Starcky, *BA*, 28 (1955), 84-106; R. de Vaux, *RB*, 50 (1941), 16-47; T. C. Vriezen, "The Edomite Deity Qaus," *Oudtestamentische Studiën*, 14 (1965), 330-353; *WHAB*.

B. MACDONALD

EDREI ed'rə-ī [Heb. *'edrᵉ'î*; Gk. *Edraein*].

1. A chief metropolitan city of the Amorite kingdom of Og king of Bashan. Situated on one of the eastern tributaries of the Yarmuk and overlooking the uplands between Gilead and Hermon, it is 16 km. (10 mi.) N of Ramoth-gilead and 48 km. (30 mi.) E and slightly S of Galilee. Here the invading Israelites killed Og and defeated his armies, whereupon Edrei was assigned to Machir son of Manasseh (Josh. 13:31). Dt. 3:10 suggests that it was the western limit of Bashan as Salecah was on the east, and probably marked the northern limit of Israel's penetration to that time. Edrei appears in a list of cities ruled by Thutmose III (*ca.* 1501-1447 B.C.), which list was found in the temple of Ammon in Karnak, Egypt (*ANET*, p. 242).

It is probably modern Der'ā, a town of about five thousand people in a very fertile district. The accumulated ruins in the town cover many remains of antiquity. Most remarkable, however, is the series of subterranean dwellings cut in the rock under the town to serve as a refuge in times of siege. The average depth was 21 m. (70 ft.); the system was supported by air holes.

2. An unidentified city in Naphtali between Kedesh and En-hazor (Josh. 19:37).

D. B. PECOTA

EDUCATED [Heb. piel of *gāḏal*] (Dnl. 1:5); AV NOURISHING; NEB TRAINING; [Gk. *paideúō*] (Acts 22:3); AV TAUGHT; NEB THOROUGHLY TRAINED; **UNEDUCATED** [Gk. *agrámmatos*] (Acts 4:13); AV UNLEARNED; NEB UNTRAINED. Heb. *gāḏal* (in qal "grow up," "become great") is used in the piel also in 2 K. 10:6; Isa. 1:2; 23:4; 51:18 with the meaning "bring up." Several other Hebrew terms also refer to the process or result of education; e.g., the RSV gives "learned" for Heb. *sōpēr* in Ezr. 7:11 (AV "scribe"; NEB "scribe versed in"); the AV gives "learned" in Isa. 29:11f. for Heb. *yāḏa' hassēper* (lit. "know the book"; RSV, NEB, "one who can read") and in Isa. 50:4 for *limmûḏ* (RSV "those who are taught"; NEB "teacher"). With the piel of *gāḏal* the emphasis is on the discipline, training, and general education involved in bringing up a child. The other Hebrew terms cited refer to the knowledge of books, especially the Law.

Greek *paideúō* emphasizes the grueling discipline that would be involved in learning at the feet of one like Gamaliel "according to the strict manner of the law" (Acts 22:3); cf. 7:22, where the RSV renders *paideúō* with "instructed" (AV "learned"; NEB "trained"). *Agrámmatos* is one of several Greek terms denoting illiteracy or ignorance, rendered "unlearned" by the AV, including also *apaídeutos* (2 Tim. 2:23), *amathḗs* (2 Pet. 3:16), *idiṓtēs* (1 Cor. 14:16, 23f.).

G. A. VAN ALSTINE

EDUCATION. The chief source of information regarding education in ancient Israel is the OT. While the OT writers were not interested in education per se, they were concerned about the transmission of religious traditions, and they provided incidental information concerning other educational processes. This evidence may be supplemented and set in context by other literary sources and archeological discoveries. Although the term "school" does not occur in the OT, both Sumer and Egypt had developed schools prior to Israel's conquest of Canaan (13th cent. B.C.). These cultures may have exerted some influence on education and the development of schools in Israel. Education in ancient Israel, however, was largely informal and related to the family unit.

I. In the Ancient Near East.–Following the invention of cuneiform writing, scribal schools emerged in Sumer. The principal aim of these schools was to teach this difficult form of writing to scribes for work in the palace, temples, and administrative offices. The school system flourished between 2500 and 2000 B.C., and the variety of positions held by the scribes suggests that the schools were numerous and sizeable. Almost without exception, the students at these schools were the sons of the wealthier families; records indicate that the fathers of the students generally held responsible positions. The head of the school was the ummia ("expert," "professor," or "school father"). His assistants were "big brothers," and the students were called "school sons" or "sons of the tablet house." The curriculum included both oral and written exercises. Discipline (which appears to have been a problem) was enforced by whipping or "caning." School texts have been recovered bearing the writing of students at various stages along the way toward mastery of the script. In addition to learning to write, young scribes-to-be were taught lists of words and terms which would be needed for writing various documents; and they practiced copying sample documents. Identification of the ruins of these schools is difficult; but rooms possibly used for classes have been found in Nippur, Sippar, Ur, and Mari (destroyed shortly after 1697 B.C.). The teachers evidently were paid out of tuition fees. A "school days" essay written about 2000 B.C. by an anonymous teacher vividly describes the daily routine at the schools and a successful attempt at "apple polishing." Sumerian texts were later collected by the Assyrian king Ashurbanipal, whose library also contained interlinear texts of Sumerian and Assyrian.

In Egypt "formal" education was established sometime during the third millennium B.C. Such education was primarily vocational in aim, teaching the skills necessary to become a priest, engineer, noble, or soldier. The priests were probably the first to use writing, which may have been taught originally in temple schools, since lives of the dead were written and buried with them. The temple schools also taught dancing and music because of their religious significance. School texts recovered from trash heaps near the temples suggest that great attention was paid to calligraphy. In addition to various letters and documents used as exercises to be copied by the students, there are writings which praise the scribe's occupation and exhort the student to diligence. Learning the staggering number of necessary characters took a great deal of time; the student's memory was taxed, and discipline was harsh. These schools also used wisdom sayings in their curriculum, since they were brief (i.e., easily copied) and generally edifying. Students in the temple schools, court schools, and military schools were males from the higher strata of Egyptian society. Writing was taught because of its necessity in various vocations; and, as in Sumerian culture, the specialties, functions, and resulting social positions among the scribes were quite diverse.

Although there were schools in Sumer and Egypt prior to the settlement of the tribes of Israel in Canaan, it would be a mistake to assume that the nomadic Israelites were influenced by these schools directly or immediately. One can only speculate about Moses' education among the Egyptians and his role as a mediator of Egyptian pedagogy to the Israelites (Acts 7:22; cf. Ex. 2:10-15). After the Conquest the Israelites probably adopted Canaanite educational practices. The relative simplicity of alphabetic writing meant that more youths could be taught to write. Hence, its impact upon Israelite education must be noted. Alphabetic writing appears to have been developed during the Hyksos period (1730-1580 B.C.), and the earliest known alphabet is the North Semitic. The early Phoenician alphabet influenced the development of early Hebrew writing.

Painted statue from Saqqârah (5th Dynasty) of an Egyptian scribe holding a papyrus roll (Egyptian Museum, Cairo; picture W. S. LaSor)

A well-written cuneiform letter dated *ca.* 1400 B.C. is vivid evidence for the kind of education enjoyed by well-to-do Canaanites in the period preceding the Israelite conquest. Found in the house of a wealthy Shechemite, the letter was written by the teacher of one of his children as a request for payment. The teacher claims that for three years no payment had been made even though he had been father and mother to the children and the children continued to learn. There is no reference to what the children were being taught, nor is there any indication of whether the teacher was male or female. A further clue to the existence of schools among the Canaanites may be seen in the name of a Canaanite city Kiriath-sepher ("City of the Book" [or "Scribe"]; Josh. 15:15f.; Jgs. 1:11f.). Moreover, the Oak of Moreh ("teaching" or "teacher," Gen. 12:6; Dt. 11:30; cf. Isa. 30:20) was probably originally a Canaanite cultic center.

II. In Preexilic Israel.–For ancient Israelites, the education of one's children was a religious duty, and much of the content of what was taught in the homes was the religious tradition of Israel: ". . . for I have chosen him [Abraham], *that he may charge his children and his household after him to keep the way of the Lord* by doing righteousness and justice; so that the Lord may bring to Abraham what he has promised him" (Gen. 18:19). This verse underscores the importance of instruction within the family, the religious content of this instruction, its purpose (that the children might live righteously and justly), and the integral relationship of this kind of instruction to the hope of the nation ("that the Lord may bring to Abraham what he has promised him").

At least from the time of Josiah, the Shema (Dt. 6:4-9) was the core of religious instruction given in the home. Within the Shema is the injunction to teach it to one's children: "Hear, O Israel: The Lord our God is one Lord . . . and you shall teach them [i.e., these words] diligently to your children, and shall talk of them when you sit in your house . . ." (Dt. 6:4, 7). Along with the Shema the children were taught the commandments for righteous living (Dt. 4:9f.), and it was the father's duty to explain the meaning of the commandments by telling the story of the nation's history (Dt. 6:20-25). Since the religious teaching given in the home was the heart of the education of Hebrew children, it was the solemn duty of every parent (Dt. 11:19).

This instruction was reinforced by the celebration of the major festivals in the home and in the community. The children's participation in the preparations, excitement, and observance of the festivals created a natural context in which indelible lessons could be learned. The educational importance of these events was not overlooked: "And when your children say to you, 'What do you mean by this service?' you shall say, 'It is the sacrifice of the Lord's passover . . .'" (Ex. 12:26f.). In fact, it came to be the practice for the youngest child in the family to ask the father this question at the appropriate point in the family's observance of the Passover so that the father could then recite the story of the Lord's deliverance of His people from bondage (cf. Ex. 13:8, 14). The other festivals were also regarded as teaching opportunities (Lev. 23:42f.). Through the father's instruction in the home and his explanations of the significance of the festivals, the Hebrew children were taught how God had manifested Himself to them in the past, how they were to live in the present, and what God's promises were regarding the future of His people.

Hebrew children were also taught the skills they would need to be successful members of their community. Girls were taught baking (2 S. 13:8), spinning (Ex. 35:25), and all the skills required to run a household. Boys were taught the agricultural cycle of the year and how to work in the fields or tend sheep (1 S. 16:11). It was common for a son to enter his father's profession (cf. the proverb in Jn. 5:19), and the father's instruction involved the secrets of the trade or craft.

Craftsmen were also educators. Members of the same craft or trade often lived together in a particular district (Neh. 3:2, 15) and had a leader or chief officer (1 Ch. 4:14). Craftsmen's and merchants' guilds may have existed in Palestine as early as the Hyksos period. A man would often be designated by his profession, as "A. son of B. of the goldsmiths" or simply "A. one of the goldsmiths" (Neh. 3:8, 31; AV "the goldsmith's son"). The guilds were even referred to as families (1 Ch. 2:55). During the postexilic period they became powerful legal entities having some measure of authority over their districts (Tosefta *Baba Metzia* [ed. Zuckermandel], xi.16, 24-26). They also provided a sort of occupational insurance for their members whereby his tools, ass, boat, or other means of livelihood would be replaced if lost for reasons other than negligence. In Jerusalem, and doubtless in other cities as well, members of each trade or guild lived in separate parts of the city. It has been argued that Mic. 1:14b is clarified by 1 Ch. 4:21-23 as a reference to guild workshops or factories and should be translated "the factories of Achzib are a loss to the kings of Israel" (cf. Jer. 18:2; Cant. 2:4; Am. 3:15; Mish. *Shabbath* i.9). Wherever such guilds were organized, one might expect that they served an educational function by teaching young apprentices their craft.

An important vocation during the preexilic period was that of the scribe. As with the other vocations, one may assume that a scribe would teach his sons how to read and write, but it is unknown how widespread this ability was among the Israelites. A very early inscription, the GEZER CALENDAR, provides evidence of the teaching of writing among the Israelites. The calendar is inscribed on a writing tablet, a smooth piece of limestone with rounded edges which would fit easily into the hand of a twelve-year-old boy. W. F. Albright dated it to a brief Israelite occupation of Gezer between *ca.* 950 and 918 B.C., and identified it as a school exercise. The surface has been scraped clean several times for repeated use, and the Yahwist name of the scribe, "Abijah" (lit. "Yahweh is my father"), appears on the lower left hand corner of the stone. The text is a mnemonic ditty designed to teach the succession of agricultural activities.

Other references to writing can be found in some of the earlier books of the OT. Josh. 18:9, for example, relates how each tribe provided three men who traveled through the land writing a description of it. Jgs. 8:14 narrates the following incident during Gideon's career: "And he caught a young man of Succoth, and questioned him; and he wrote down for him the officials and elders of Succoth, seventy-seven men." This verse has been cited in the past as evidence that the ability to write was common, but no youth who knew the names (and possibly the positions) of seventy-seven men can be considered average or typical. Rather, he was probably a young scribe who had been taught the names of the officials as part of his training. Another early reference to a scribe is found in 2 S. 8:17 (RSV "secretary"). Other references to writing can be found in Dt. 24:1, 3; Job 31:35; Jer. 32:12; Isa. 10:19; but there is no compelling evidence that most Israelites could read and write prior to the Exile. On the contrary, references to signet rings (e.g. Gen. 38:18) suggest that the rings were often used instead of a signature. In preexilic Israel, at least, the ability to write was probably limited largely to officials, priests, scribes, and the upper class. The number of scribes and the variety of positions they filled increased greatly during the reign of Solomon (1 K. 4:3; 2 K. 25:19). Hence, the need to train these men probably surpassed the ability of individual families, and the court may have looked for other ways to fill this need.

As described above, the Sumerians and Egyptians had developed schools for scribes long before the time of Solomon. To the extent that the monarchy under Solomon was influenced (directly or indirectly) by Egyptian institutions and administrative structures, it is reasonable to assume that it adopted the model of Egyptian schools. The Canaanite culture may have been the mediator of this influence, and since the Amarna texts reveal that Akkadian was the language of diplomatic correspondence in Syria and Palestine during the latter part of the 2nd millennium B.C., the model of the Sumerian schools may have had some influence also. Men would have been needed who had been trained in schools that taught the Akkadian scribal art. Although there are no direct references to such schools and it is conjectural to suggest how they might have arisen, that such schools developed during Solomon's reign or shortly thereafter is likely. Moreover, such schools were probably the spawning ground for the earliest written traditions now contained in the OT. Oral traditions were written down for transmission and use in the court, temple, and local worship centers. As these writings became more numerous, the ability to read and write probably also began to spread in Israel. An echo of an ancient elementary lesson in the alphabet may be preserved in Isa. 28:9-13. Verse 10 can be understood as the quotation of a lesson teaching the Hebrew letters *ṣāḏê* and *qôp̄*. Isaiah's opponents mock his teaching: "For it is *ṣaw lāṣāw, ṣaw lāṣāw, qaw lāqāw, qaw lāqāw*" (here a little, there a little).

Alongside the schools in the temple and palace in which scribes were trained for various positions, priests for temple service (Jer. 36:10, 12-21) and princes for positions of authority, wisdom schools emerged. The relation of the latter to other schools in the preexilic period is unclear. When many activities became focused upon the second temple, some wisdom schools probably merged with the temple school. Earlier, however, they may have been independent institutions and separate bearers of written tradition. Little is known about these schools apart from what can be deduced from the writings that they produced. Proverbs, for example, was probably used both for practice in writing and grammar through the dictation of its short sayings and also for instruction in its content. Proverbs is similar to the materials found in the Egyptian schools and would have been suitable for teaching the young how to associate with peers, elders, men in authority, and children. In short, the wisdom schools taught one how to live a pleasant and successful life and avoid trouble. Although this may not have been the original or exclusive purpose of the wisdom literature, and although this literature may not have been the sole content of the curriculum in the wisdom schools, it does convey a vivid impression of what was taught at these schools.

According to Prov. 1:7 true wisdom is anchored in the fear of the Lord: "The fear of the Lord is the beginning of knowledge; fools despise wisdom and instruction." The educational intent of the book is confirmed by its proem:

That men may know wisdom and instruction,
 understand words of insight,

receive instruction in wise dealing,
righteousness, justice, and equity;
that prudence may be given to the simple,
knowledge and discretion to the youth (Prov. 1:2-4).

Although these verses were probably written at the time that the book was compiled (3rd or 4th cent. B.C.), much of the material in Proverbs is older and may have been used for instruction during the preexilic period. The student was addressed as "my son" (Prov. 1:8, 10; 2:1; 3:1; *passim*), as in the Sumerian schools, and discipline was harsh (Prov. 13:24; 22:15). The schools were organized on the premise contained in Prov. 22:6: "Train up a child in the way he should go, and when he is old he will not depart from it." Those who were able sent their sons to receive instruction in the proper conduct of life at the wisdom schools.

One passage is particularly revealing of the way students were taught:

Incline your ear, and hear the words of the wise,
and apply your mind to my knowledge;
for it will be pleasant if you keep them with you,
if all of them are ready on your lips.
That your trust may be in the Lord,
I have made them known to you today, even to you.
Have I not written for you thirty sayings
of admonition and knowledge,
to show you what is right and true,
that you may give a true answer
to those who sent you?

(Prov. 22:17-21; cf. "Instruction of Amen-em-opet," *ANET,* pp. 421-24). The italicized words imply that the teachers (cf. Prov. 5:13) taught by reciting maxims orally and writing them for the students. These sayings were to be kept in the student's heart, or memorized (Prov. 3:3; 7:3; 13:14) and understood, so that his trust would be in the Lord and he would be able to give an acceptable answer to his parents.

Another passage (Prov. 31:10-31) may have been used as a memorandum in a school for young women. These verses form an acrostic in which the first letters of each line are the letters of the Hebrew alphabet; the form is a device to aid the memory. It has been argued that the verses provide not a picture of typical domestic life, but the resume of a course of training for young women who would shortly assume positions of responsibility as wives in well-to-do households. After completing her training in household management, horticulture, the arts of weaving and design, and the instruction of children (Prov. 31:26), the girl may have taken this passage home to keep for future guidance. Such schools, however, are not likely to have been very common, and would have been reserved for the daughters of wealthy families.

Even further removed from official control than the wisdom schools were the bands of prophets. Regardless of whether prophetic bands should be called schools, associations, or brotherhoods, the followers of the prophets were called their disciples (*limmûḏîm*) and children (*yᵉlāḏîm*): "Bind up the testimony, seal the teaching among my disciples . . . Behold, I and the children whom the Lord has given me are signs and portents in Israel . . ." (Isa. 8:16, 18). What the prophet Isaiah could not say publicly he sealed or entrusted to his disciples. The reference to "children" may be a figurative reference to his disciples, but can also be understood literally. The disciples were also called "sons (*bᵉnê*) of the prophets" (2 K. 2:3, 5; 4:38). Teaching was integral to the prophetic role. Isa. 50:4 suggests that the principal function of the disciple was to listen and remember the words of his teacher. The schools or brotherhoods which formed around the prophets regarded the prophets as teachers, memorized their sayings, and transmitted orally the tradition of the life and sayings of their prophet for some time before these traditions were collected and written down (2 K. 8:4; cf. Jer. 26:17f.). Moreover, the prophetic ideal for the future involved the religious instruction of the people: ". . . for the earth shall be full of the knowledge of the Lord as the waters cover the sea" (Isa. 11:9). Even the vision of universal education may have been seen first by the prophets: "*All* your sons shall be taught by the Lord, and great shall be the prosperity of your sons" (Isa. 54:13; cf. Jn. 6:45). As in the wisdom schools, so among the prophets, wisdom and knowledge came from the Lord (cf. Isa. 19:11; Jer. 8:8f.), and prosperity came to him who had gained a full measure of this knowledge.

In addition to their other priestly duties, the Levites also taught the people. Moses' blessing to Levi describes their position:

They shall teach Jacob thy ordinances,
and Israel thy law;
they shall put incense before thee,
and whole burnt offering upon thy altar

(Dt. 33:10; cf. Lev. 10:11). At times they seem to have been itinerant teachers (2 Ch. 17:7-9), and some were scribes as well (1 Ch. 24:6). During Josiah's reign they were regarded as teachers (2 Ch. 35:3), and they maintained this role until the time of Ezra (Neh. 8:7-9). Even the prophets recognized their role as teachers of the people and interpreters of the Law (Mal. 2:6-9) and rebuked the Levites only for accepting payment for their teaching (Mic. 3:11).

Reference should be made to the impact of the Exile on education in Israel. Dnl. 1:3-5 may preserve a historical recollection about how some Hebrew youths were provided with tutors and educated in Babylonian ways during the Exile. According to this reference, Daniel and his companions were given an instructor who was ". . . to teach them the letters and language of the Chaldeans. . . . They were to be educated for three years, and at the end of that time they were to stand before the king." Other evidence suggests that the sons of Joiachin were given a Jewish attendant. In addition to the influence of Babylonian culture, and indeed in reaction to it, the Exile was a period of prolific literary activity among the priests and prophets in exile. Much of this activity centered on the Law (Torah) which Ezra brought to the people after the return. (The term "Torah" originally meant "instruction" rather than "Law" [cf. Isa. 8:16; Prov. 4:2].)

III. In Postexilic Israel.–Ezra, who was both priest and scribe (Neh. 8:9), undertook the task of calling the people back to their religious heritage by teaching and explaining to them the Law: "This Ezra went up from Babylonia. He was a scribe skilled in the law of Moses which the Lord the God of Israel had given. . . . For Ezra had set his heart to study the law of the Lord, and to do it, and to teach his statutes and ordinances in Israel" (Ezr. 7:6, 10). In this task of teaching the Law section by section (Neh. 8:8) he was aided by the Levites, who "helped the people to understand" (Neh. 8:7, 9; Ezr. 8:16). Ezra interpreted the Law in the language of the people — Aramaic. Biblical commentaries (Midrashim) and loose translations (Targums) later developed from this form of teaching. Under the influence of Ezra's reform, teaching came to have a new prominence among the Jews, and the scribes became the leading educators of the people. The priests and Levites increasingly confined their activities to the temple, and the role of the prophets declined rapidly. Simultaneously, the scribes emerged as a professional class of men trained in the Law and its interpretation. (2 Macc. 2:13 refers to a library established by Nehemiah, but the report is very likely fictitious.)

Information about Jewish education during the Persian period is sparse. Official documents were written in the style used by Persian officials (Ezr. 5:6-17). Wisdom schools continued to hand on their tradition (e.g., Proverbs, Ecclesiastes), but probably came to be linked with the temple. During this period the synagogue may have emerged as a place for worship and study of the Scriptures (see below).

IV. In Hellenistic Judaism.–After the illustrious career of Alexander the Great, Palestine fell under the pervasive influence of Hellenistic culture. During the centuries that followed, most Jews resisted every attempt to impose Hellenism upon them, but simultaneously absorbed many Hellenistic viewpoints and practices. The general importance of this period for the development of education in postbiblical Judaism and early Christianity can hardly be overestimated, but the particular effects of Hellenism upon Jewish education are difficult to assess. Because education had been practiced as a religious duty prior to the advent of Hellenistic culture in Palestine, to say that education or schools arose among the Jews as a result of the influence of Hellenism is a gross exaggeration. It is no exaggeration, however, to say that Hellenism had a profound effect upon the development of education among the Jews. Learning was one of the hallmarks of the Greek spirit, and education one of the primary vehicles in the spread of Hellenism. A non-Greek's "hellenization" meant primarily his learning to speak Greek and secondarily his learning to live as a Greek. It is not surprising, therefore, that the hellenizing party in Jerusalem secured permission to build a Greek gymnasium in that city in order to educate "the noblest of the young men" in Greek culture (2 Macc. 4:9, 12; 1 Macc. 1:14; cf. Dnl. 1:3-5). Knowledge of the Greek language spread quickly in Palestine, and the use of double names (Aramaic and Greek; e.g., Saul/Paul) became commonplace. Instruction in the gymnasium included not only athletic activity, but instruction in music and literary subjects (especially Homer). The continued presence of these schools in Palestine after the Maccabean period can be seen in Josephus' reference to a conversation between Herod and an Essene when Herod was a child going to school (*Ant.* xv.10.5).

In reaction against the spread of Hellenism through the education of young men in Greek culture, Hasidic Jews (who were separatistic or inclined to be zealous for national traditions) moved to make education in the Law available to a broader spectrum of Jewish young men (cf. Jub. 11:16; 19:14). This reaction to Hellenism stimulated the spread of elementary schools and synagogues in Jewish communities and lent added motivation to the regulation of Jewish life according to the Law through its study, interpretation, and application to the affairs of daily life. The earliest reference to a *bēṯ hammiḏrāš* is Sir. 51:23. Sirach was written *ca.* 180 B.C. by a wisdom teacher whose school was probably located in Jerusalem and portrays a wisdom teacher in the process of becoming a scribe (i.e., an interpreter of the Law). Another probable effect of the encounter with Hellenism was the practice of affirming the authority of one's tradition by tracing it back through a succession of teachers. Previously, one might have quoted his teacher or collected his sayings (e.g., the sayings of a prophet) or affirmed the authority of a teaching by claiming that it came from a venerable figure in antiquity such as Moses, David, or Solomon; but the practice of tracing the succession of teachers in the pattern of the Greek philosophical schools did not emerge in Judaism until after its encounter with Hellenism. It probably should not be said, however, that the movement toward universal education among the Jews reflects the influence of the Platonic concept that virtue is teachable. From the earliest days Jewish education had been primarily religious, directed at teaching the children how to live by the commandments of their God.

The origins of both the synagogue and the Jewish elementary school are obscure. Whether the origin of the synagogue is to be traced to the Exile or to Ezra is uncertain. The first inscriptional evidence for the existence of a synagogue comes from Schedia in Egypt and is dated in the 3rd cent. B.C. (R. P. Jean-Baptiste Frey, ed., *Corpus Inscriptionum Judaicarum,* II [1952], 1440). Other synagogues are attested from the 2nd cent. B.C. (V.A. Tcherikover and A. Fuks, eds., *Corpus Papyrorum Judaicarum* [1957-1964], no. 134; Josephus *BJ* vii.44; cf. *TDNT,* VII, 811f. [Schrage]). The synagogue's primary purpose was to provide a place where the Jews in every city in Palestine and the diaspora could gather to study the law. Although the synagogue had achieved a central position in most Jewish communities by A.D. 70, its importance (and the importance of the study of the Torah) was further enhanced during the reorganization of Judaism following the destruction of the temple.

Emphasis in the synagogues on the study of the Torah gave them much of the character of a school. Philo relates that Jews everywhere met every seventh day (presumably in the synagogues) for study of the Law (*De vita Mosis* ii.215f.; *De specialibus legibus* II,62). Josephus also refers to the pride the Jews took in the education of their children (*CAp* i.60; ii.204; *Ant.* iv.211; cf. also Philo *De legatione ad Gaium* 115).

One of the scrolls discovered near Qumrân contains a reference to the education of children associated with that community:

> And this is the rule for all the hosts of the Congregation, concerning every native in Israel. From [his] you[th] [he shall be in]structed in the Book of Meditation and shall be taught the precepts of the Covenant in accordance with his age, and [shall receive] his [edu]cation in their ordinances for ten years [from] the time of entry into the children's [class]. Then at the age of twenty [he shall be subject] [to] the census . . . (1QSa 1:6-9; tr. A. Dupont-Sommer and G. Vermes).

This reference predates all of the talmudic references to Jewish schools, but it cannot be used as a basis from which to generalize about the education of Jewish children apart from the community at Qumrân.

The origins of the Jewish elementary school (*bēṯ sēper*) are obscure. The Palestinian Talmud (*Ketuboth* viii.8) attributes its origin to Simeon ben Shetah (*ca.* 100 B.C.) and the Babylonian Talmud (*Baba Bathra* 21a) records a tradition from R. Judah-Rav that Joshua ben Gamla (*ca.* A.D. 64) introduced a decree that teachers should be appointed in every district and town. Neither of these traditions can be authenticated, but even if the latter is correct, it implies that at least some children received instruction in schools prior to the decree. Whether the decree was issued by Joshua ben Gamla or merely attributed to him at a later time remains highly problematic. It does appear that the elementary schools originated independently of the synagogue and were private enterprises at first (T.B. *Baba Bathra* 21b). While some schools may have met in synagogues, it was not until after A.D. 200 that the elementary school came to be firmly related to the synagogue (cf. Morris, p. 52).

When a boy entered the *bēṯ sēper* at the age of five to seven years he began to learn to read the Torah. The teaching methods were very mechanical, and the students

Illustration from the *Leipzig Maḥzor* (*ca.* A.D. 1320) showing pupils being introduced to the study of Torah. From left, a gift of honey signifies Torah's sweetness; a father carries his son, wrapped in a Torah binder, to the synagogue; children learn that people without Torah are like fish without water (facsimile Yale University Library)

read or recited passages aloud until they were able to read the Scriptures accurately. Rote memorization and repetition played major roles in the learning process. According to rabbinic tradition (*Aboth* v.21), at the age of ten a youth was ready for the study of Mishnah or oral law. The traditional interpretations of the written Torah were the primary curriculum of the *bēṯ hammiḏrāš*. Again, repetition and memorization were stressed, and various devices were employed to aid the memory. According to the same tradition, at the age of fifteen a youth was ready for the study of Talmud (the Mishnah or oral law plus the commentary on it). Our sources do not allow us to reconstruct the development of this graduated system of schools, its spread, precisely what forms the *bēṯ hammiḏrāš* took, or how it was related to the *bēṯ sēp̄er*. Clearly, however, study of the Law preceded the study of its interpretation; in all Jewish schools the Torah was the heart of the curriculum, and memorization was emphasized.

V. In the Early Church.–The role of education in early Christianity cannot be properly assessed apart from the recognition that Jesus was a teacher and looked upon teaching as integral to His ministry. His disciples, i.e., students, later handed on and interpreted His teachings for the early Church, which itself emphasized the importance of teaching.

In view of the Christology of the NT writings, it is significant that one of the most common titles for addressing Jesus was "teacher" or "rabbi." The latter, however, meant simply "teacher" and had not yet acquired the technical meaning which it has in later Jewish writings. In addition, Jesus taught in synagogues and public places and disputed with the scribes and Pharisees (Mt. 26:55; Lk. 21:37; Jn. 18:20). The crowds showed Him the respect normally accorded to teachers, and Jesus was held accountable for the practices of His "students" (Mk. 2:18, 23f.). Like other Jewish teachers, Jesus sat while He taught (Mt. 5:1; Lk. 4:20f.). Unlike others, however, Jesus called His disciples; they did not seek Him out. He was an itinerant teacher and taught the crowds as well as His disciples. Jesus also distinguished Himself from other Jewish teachers by placing His personal authority above that of the Law. Although He did not dismiss the Law (Mt. 5:17-20), He used it to defend His actions and buttress His teachings in a way unheard of among the rabbis, and brought to it an interpretation which differed radically from theirs. In addition to His unique stance toward the Law, Jesus stood apart from other Hellenistic and Jewish teachers by claiming no teachers as His authority (Lk. 20:8). He was untrained (Jn. 7:15; cf. Mt. 13:54-56) and yet taught as one with authority which surpassed that of the scribes (Mt. 7:29). Moreover, He offered a new teaching in a milieu in which all knowledge came from the past or was revealed by God. His claim "but I say to you . . ." in Mt. 5:22-44 surpassed the form of address used by the prophets: "thus says the Lord . . . ," and identified Him with the fulfillment of the Law (Mt. 5:17; Lk. 24:27). This claim to authority should be interpreted in connection with His emphasis on the urgency of His message and the imminent eschatological crisis. Against this background, it is not surprising that the three themes which dominated the teachings of Jesus were the kingdom of God, the Son of Man, and the nature of discipleship.

Recent discussion about Jesus as teacher has polarized over the issue of whether Jesus made His disciples memorize His teaching. This polarization is unfortunate. It is wise to distinguish between "memorizing" and "remembering." The claim that the disciples memorized sayings is supported by the generally shared view that many of the sayings and parables are authentic and must have been remembered by the disciples. This does not necessarily mean that they made a systematic effort to memorize His sayings from the beginning or that He instructed them to do so. However, assuming that the role of Jesus' disciples was to participate in the proclamation of the Kingdom, it is probable that they received some instruction in the demands of the life of discipleship and the nature of the kingdom of God.

From Paul's letters and from Acts one sees that teaching was important in the life of the early Church. Acts describes the apostles as teaching both in public (4:18; 5:21, 25) and in private (2:42). Moreover, using the Greek equivalents of Hebrew verbs that had the technical meaning of "receive" and "hand on" tradition, Paul alluded to his use of traditional teachings (1 Cor. 11:2, 23; 15:3; 2 Thess. 2:15; 3:6). 1 Cor. 11:23 suggests that Paul regarded Jesus as the ultimate source of the traditions and that they had the same authority as the Lord Himself. It is therefore not surprising that teaching was an essential part of Paul's work also (see 1 Cor. 4:17; Col. 2:7; Rom. 6:17; 16:17; 2 Thess. 2:15; cf. 1 Thess. 4:6). The importance of teaching in the early Church is underscored by references to "remembering" the teachings of Paul (1 Cor. 4:17; 2 Thess. 2:5) and of the apostles (2 Pet. 3:2; Jude 17), and the words of Jesus (Lk. 24:6, 8; Acts 11:16; 20:35).

Another dimension of teaching in the early Church may be seen in its instruction of recent converts in the rudimentary Christian doctrines. Such instruction is commonly called catechesis. While its content cannot be systematically outlined, early Christian catechesis appears to have involved material from the OT and Jesus' teachings; material about Jesus, the Church, and the Christian life; and also traditional Hellenistic ethical teachings drawn from Judaism and the Greek philosophies (e.g., Jas. 1:27; 3:3-6; Phil. 4:8; Gal. 5:22f.). These hortatory and ethical materials were used by Christian teachers in much the same way they had been used in the instruction of converts to a philosophy or to Judaism: to guide the convert along the path of prudence, wisdom, and righteousness. Paul refers to the duty of the catechumens to support their teacher (Gal. 6:6). The reference in 1 Thess. 4:1f. to the teaching his readers had received may again allude to catechetical instruction, since Paul wrote 1 Thessalonians shortly after establishing the church there. The office of teacher, moreover, probably developed in the early churches largely in response to the need to instruct recent converts. Paul seems to place teachers nearest in rank and function to the apostles (1 Cor. 4:17; 2 Thess. 2:15; cf. Col. 2:7; Eph. 4:21), and the later NT writings show that "teacher" increasingly came to denote an office rather than a function (cf. 1 Cor. 12:28f.; Acts 13:1; He. 5:12; Eph. 4:11; 1 Tim. 2:7; 2 Tim. 1:11; 4:3; Jas. 3:1).

Finally, while the NT gives surprisingly little attention to the instruction of children, this instruction appears to have remained primarily the responsibility of the family, just as it was among the Jews (Eph. 6:4; 2 Tim. 3:15). If the Christian child received a formal education he did so only in pagan schools (Tertullian *De idololatria* 10), yet Tertullian prohibited Christians from teaching in these schools. Education in first-century A.D. Roman schools reflected the system of education developed in the Greek schools of the Hellenistic age, and most schools continued to be supported by private benefactors. Children between the ages of seven and eleven were taught reading, writing, and arithmetic. In this part of their education pupils learned sections of Homer selected for their moral content. By the 1st cent. Virgil and other poets were also studied; but Homer remained, as he had been for centuries, the center of the curriculum. Secondary education (for students between twelve and fifteen) consisted of further study of Homer, grammar, composition, mathematics, and science. These subjects formed the core of the ancient ideal of *enkýklios paideía* ("general education"). Higher education generally meant the study of rhetoric, since the ability to speak persuasively was essential in most public careers. Gifted students, however, might also seek further education at schools of philosophy, medicine, or law. By late in the 2nd cent. Christian schools began to emerge. Prior to this development churches probably supplemented the education of their children with instruction in the Scriptures, the teachings of Jesus, and ethical materials. That churches did not provide separate schools for the education of their children during the 1st cent. has been attributed to the following factors: they expected the Second Coming imminently, they were poor, and Christianity had no official recognition within the Roman empire. Nevertheless, both the Jewish heritage and the example of Jesus insured that Christianity was fundamentally and essentially a teaching religion, which transmitted the revelation of God it had received and the wisdom of human experience it had acquired (Col. 2:6f.).

***Bibliography.**–General:* R. F. Butts, *Education of the West* (1973); M. L. Clarke, *Higher Education in the Ancient World* (1971); B. Gerhardsson, *Memory and Manuscript* (*Acta Seminarii Neotestamentici Upsaliensis*, 22; Eng. tr. 1961); W. Jaeger, *Paideia: The Ideals of Greek Culture* (3 vols.; Eng. tr. 1939-1944); H. I. Marrou, *History of Education in Antiquity* (Eng. tr. 1956).

Ancient Near East: W. F. Albright, *BASOR*, 86 (Apr. 1942), 28-31; D. Diringer, *Writing* (1962); G. R. Driver, *Semitic Writing—From Pictograph to Alphabet* (1948); A. Erman, *Literature of the Ancient Egyptians* (Eng. tr. 1927); C. H. Kraeling and R. M. Adams, eds., *City Invincible: A Symposium on Urbanization and Cultural Development in the Ancient Near East* (1960); S. N. Kramer, *From the Tablets of Sumer* (1956); *JAOS*, 59 (1949), 199-215; *The Sumerians: Their History, Culture, and Character* (1963); G. E. Mendenhall, *BA*, 11 (1949), 1-19.

Israel and Postbiblical Judaism: W. F. Albright, *BASOR*, 92 (Dec. 1943), 16-26; *BA*, 5 (1942), 49-55; M. B. Crook, *JNES*, 13 (1954), 137-140; A. Demsky, *Encyclopedia Judaica*, VI, 382-398; *IEJ*, 16 (1966), 211-15; N. Drazin, *History of Jewish Education from 515 B.C.E. to 220 C.E.* (1940); E. Ebner and S. Eliezer, *Elementary Education in Ancient Israel During the Tannaitic Period (10-220 C. E.)* (1956); M. Hengel, *Judaism and Hellenism* (Eng. tr. 1974), I, 65-83; H.-J. Hermisson, *Studien zur Israelitischen Spruchweisheit* (1968); W. McKane, *Prophets and Wise Men* (*SBT*, 44, 1965); I. Mendelsohn, *BASOR*, 80 (Dec. 1940), 17-21; N. Morris, *The Jewish School: An Introduction to the History of Jewish Education* (1937); S. Safrai, "Education and the Study of Torah," in S. Safrai and M. Stern, eds., *Jewish People of the First Century*, II (1976), 945-970; F. H. Swift, *Education in Ancient Israel: From Earliest Times to 70 A.D.* (1919); E. Weidner, *Melanges Syriens*, II (1939), 923-935; R. N. Whybray, *Intellectual Tradition in the OT* (*BZAW*, 135, 1974).

Early Church: W. Barclay, *Educational Ideals in the Ancient World* (1959); R. A. Culpepper, *The Johannine School* (1975); D. Daube, *NTS*, 19 (1972), 1-15; W. D. Davies, *Setting of the Sermon on the Mount* (1966), pp. 415-435; C. H. Dodd, "Jesus as Teacher and Prophet," in G. K. A. Bell and A. Deissmann, eds., *Mysterium Christi* (1930); "The 'Primitive Catechism' and the Sayings of Jesus," in A. J. B. Higgins, ed., *NT Essays: Studies in Memory of Thomas Walter Manson* (1959), pp. 106-118 (= *More NT Studies* [1968], pp. 11-29); E. Fascher, *TLZ*, 79 (1954), 325-342; J. A. Grassi, *The Teacher in the Primitive Church and the Teacher Today* (1973); W. Jaeger, *Early Christianity and Greek Paideia* (1965); I. A. Muirhead, *Education in the NT* (*Monographs in Christian Education*, 2, 1965); L. J. Sherill, *Rise of Christian Education* (1944).

R. A. CULPEPPER

EDUTH ē'duth [Heb. *ʿēḏûṯ*–'testimony,' a technical term for the Ten Commandments or for the Law]. The term "Eduth" occurs in the title to Ps. 60 (MT v. 1), "according to Shushan Eduth" (lit. "lily of the testimony" [?]). The title of Ps. 80 (MT v. 1), Heb. *ʾel-šōšannîm ʿēḏûṯ lᵉʾāsāp̱*, is rendered by the RSV "according to Lilies. A Testimony of Asaph." These words may be intended to designate the melody to which these Psalms were usually sung. *See* PSALMS II.C.

EGG [Heb. *bêṣâ*; OT only pl.; Gk. *ōón*]. It is not likely that the egg was used by the Israelites as food until about the Persian period, when the domestic fowl was first introduced to Palestine, though by the 1st cent. A.D. it was well established (Lk. 11:12; Mt. 23:27; Lk. 13:34). The Mishnah has frequent references to eggs and how they may be cooked. In Dt. 22:6 they are mentioned in a law that allows for taking the young birds but not the mother; it is significant that the taking of the eggs is not mentioned.

In Job 6:6, the AV "white of an egg" is no doubt a mistranslation for "slime of the purslane" (RSV, BDB; NEB "juice of mallows"); purslane is a plant whose flower resolves into an insipid mucilaginous jelly.

Job 39:14 speaks of the habit of the ostrich, who stupidly wanders away from her eggs and forgets where she has left them. The verse has given rise to the popular but false belief that she leaves them to hatch in the sun. (Cf. Isa. 10:14.)

The reference in Isa. 59:5 is to the egg of a serpent and is figurative of the schemes of evil men. J. A. BALCHIN

EGLAH eg'lə [Heb. *'eglâ*–'heifer']. Wife of David and mother of Ithream (2 S. 3:5 par. 1 Ch. 3:3).

EGLAIM eg'lə-im [Heb. *'eglayim*] (Isa. 15:8). A town which, to judge from the poetic statement in Isaiah, was at one of the extremes of Moab. Eusebius mentions an Agallim 8 Rom. mi. S of Areopolis (Rabbah, now Amman). About 12 km. (7½ mi.) S of Rabbah, near Kerak, a pile of stones known as Rujm el-Jilîmeh preserves the Byzantine name Aegallim. About 6½ km. (4 mi.) further S Khirbet Jaljul is sometimes identified as Eglaim. Aharoni suggests that Eglaim was located at Mazra', NE of the Lisan — which would more accurately be an extremity of Moab, but the identification is uncertain.

Bibliography.–Y. Aharoni, *LBHG*, p. 32; Y. Aharoni and M. Avi-Yonah, *Macmillan Bible Atlas* (1968), maps 155, 213; *EAEHL*, I, *s.v.* "El-'Ajjul, Tell" (O. Tufnell); *GP*, II, 310f. W. S. L. S.

EGLATH-SHELISHIYAH eg'lath-shə-lə-shī'yə [Heb. *'eglaṯ šelišîyâ*]. Found in Isa. 15:5; Jer. 48:34 in the oracles against Moab. The AV translates "an heifer of three years old"; the RSV takes it as the name of a place. In the former case strong and unconquered cities, Zoar and Horoniam, are compared to the heifer not yet broken to the yoke. Such use of "heifer" is not infrequent (cf. Jer. 46:20; Hos. 10:11; etc.). The majority of scholars, however, take it as a place name. Some would read "the third Eglath," as if there were three towns of that name. The NEB omits it in Isa. 15:5 and takes it as a place name in Jer. 48:34. No probable identification has been suggested. W. EWING

EGLON eg'lon [Heb. *'eglôn*–'circle']. A king of Moab in the period of the judges who, in alliance with Ammon and Amalek, overcame Israel and made Jericho his capital. He was presumably driven across the Jordan by the turmoil in his own kingdom, which at that time was probably being used as a battle ground by Edom and the desert tribes (cf. Gen. 36:35). After eighteen years of servitude the Israelites were delivered by Ehud the Benjaminite, who like many other Benjaminites (cf. Jgs. 20:16) was left-handed. Under the pretext of carrying a present to the tyrant, he secured a private interview and assassinated him with the two-edged sword which he had carried concealed on his right side (Jgs. 3:19-22). Ehud made his escape, rallied the Israelites about him, and returned to conquer the Moabites (Jgs. 3:30). *See also* EHUD 1. E. D. ISAACS

EGLON eg'lon [Heb. *'eglôn*; the LXX usually confused this town with ADULLAM, thus in Josh. 10 *passim*, Gk. *Odol(l)am*; other variants, Gk. *Aglōn, Aiglōn, Ailam, Eglōm, Eglōn, Ideadalea, Odolloch*]. An Amorite city at the eastern margin of the Shephelah (Josh. 10:33ff.; 12:12; 15:39).

I. Identification.–Robinson, and later Conder and Kitchener, found the name Eglon preserved in the Arabic form Khirbet 'Ajlân. This is undoubtedly the Gk. *Agla* of Eusebius (Onom. 48.18), although, led astray by the LXX substitution of Adullam for Eglon (cf. *Onom.* 24.21f.; 84.22-24; 172.7), the church father had wrongly identified *Agla* with Beth-hoglah (Josh. 15:6). Because the nearby Khirbet Umm Lâqis, which the British surveyors took for a reflex of the biblical Lachish, was so small and insignificant, they sought the latter city at Tell el-Ḥesī, the largest ancient site in the vicinity. Petrie accepted this view and proposed to identify ancient Eglon with Tell en-Nejîleh, as did his successor Bliss. Bliss's discovery of a cuneiform tablet at Tell el-Ḥesī that mentioned Zimreddu, ruler of Lachish in the Amarna Letters, gave superficial support to this view.

Albright, however, rejected that equation and identified Tell el-Ḥesī with Eglon; Garstang concurred. Excavations at Tell ed-Duweir have established almost beyond doubt that it is the site of Lachish. Therefore the case for Eglon = Tell el-Ḥesī is strengthened. However, although the nearness of Khirbet 'Ajlân supports Albright's view, it is hard to believe that the Judean Shephelah extended that far west. The biblical references (see below) would favor a site E of Lachish. Other proposals for Eglon are Tell Beit Mirsim by Elliger, and Khirbet 'Aiṭûn by Noth. The latter, occupied in the Middle and Late Bronze Ages as well as the Iron Age, would more logically fit the line of march from Lachish to Hebron (Josh. 10:34-37).

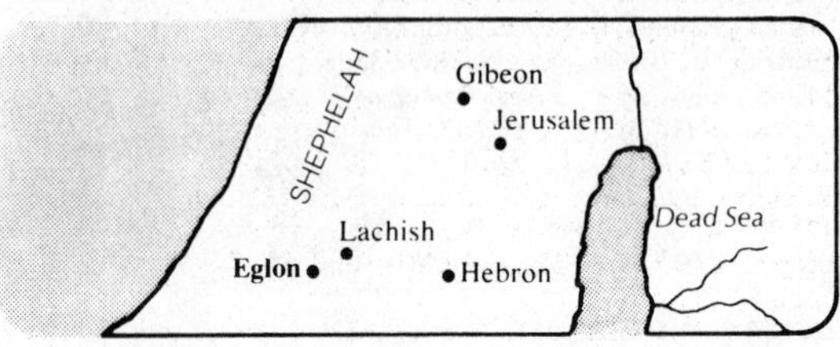

II. Excavation.–Because Tell el-Ḥesī is still viewed by many as the site of Eglon, a review of the archeological finds there is in order. The work started by Petrie in 1890 and continued by Bliss from 1891 to 1893 uncovered eight "towns" built one upon the other and marked the real beginning of modern archeological excavation in Palestine. Although the methods have been refined and corrected by other scholars, the general picture of the site's history remains fairly well established.

The deepest observed stratum evidently belongs to E.B. III. During the Middle Bronze Age the city was fortified with a wall supported by a sloping stone revetment coated with hard clay or lime plaster, typical of that period in Palestine. The L.B. city produced a cuneiform tablet of the Amarna type, and, from a somewhat later stratum, an ostracon bearing an early West Semitic inscription. As were most towns of the region, the L.B. city was destroyed *ca.* 1200 B.C.

During the Iron Age the town was only a relatively minor urban center, confined to the small upper citadel, and thus characterized by a fortress from which the surrounding villages were governed. Recent excavations and surveys have shown small Iron Age farming communities in the region around Tell el-Ḥesī, including Tell Idbîs and an unnamed site above Wâdi Jemmâmeh, both on natural hills. The Iron Age settlement at Tell Idbîs had been severely eroded, but it provides a useful comparison with Tell en-Negîleh, where abundant Iron II pottery suggested a prominent Israelite or Philistine town. Because excavations showed immediately no building remains were left that could be associated with the Iron Age settlement, it was evidently only a small farming community, founded on top of a mighty Bronze Age tell in the same way as that at Tell Idbîs had been set up on a natural hill. The mother city was apparently at Tell el-Ḥesî, with daughter villages dispersed round about (cf. Josh. 15:39b, 41b).

III. History.–The earliest mention of Eglon in a historical source is evidently in the Egyptian Execration Texts (G. Posener, *Princes et pays d'Asie et de Nubie* [1940], p. 92, no. E 58). A L.B. cuneiform tablet discovered at Tell el-Ḥesī, shown by its language and general appearance to be contemporary with the Amarna texts (included in modern editions as Am.Tab. 333), is a letter from a certain Pa'pu to the "Great One," undoubtedly the ruler of Tell el-Ḥesī; the writer describes the high treason brewing among Zimreddu, Shipti-baʿlu (i.e., the ruler of Lachish and his successor; cf. Am.Tab. 329:5f and probably 332.3), and the ruler of Yaramu against the pharaoh.

During the Israelite invasion of Canaan, Adonizedek king of Jerusalem was galvanized into action against his subjects at Gibeon, who had made a pact with Joshua. The king sought aid from Jerusalem's Amorite allies, the kings of Jarmuth, Hebron, and Lachish, as well as Debir king of Eglon (Josh. 10:3-6). The Israelites came to the defense of Gibeon, winning a decisive victory over the coalition. The five Amorite kings were captured (Josh. 10:23), and Eglon was seized in the conquest of southern Palestine (Josh. 10:34-37; 12:12). The city was included in the second district, the lowland Shephelah region, of the inheritance of Judah (Josh. 15:39).

***Bibliography*.**–W. F. Albright, *ZAW,* 47 (1929), 3; *BASOR,* 15 (Oct. 1924), 7f.; 87 (Oct. 1942), 32-38; R. Amiran, *IEJ,* 13 (1963), 143-45, 333f.; F. J. Bliss, *Mound of Many Cities, or Tell Hesy Excavated* (1898); C. R. Conder, *Tent Work in Palestine* (1878), II, 168f.; *EAEHL,* II, *s.v.* "Ḥesi, Tel" (R. Amiran and J. E. Worrell); R. Gofna, *Bulletin of the Israel Exploration Society,* N.S. 3 (1963), 173-77; W. M. F. Petrie, *Tell el Hesy (Lachish)* (1891); L. E. Stager, *HTR,* 64 (1971), 448-450 = *BA,* 34 (1971), 86-88; L. E. Toombs, *IEJ,* 21 (1971), 177f.; J. E. Worrell and L. E. Toombs, *IEJ,* 21 (1971), 232f.; J. E. Worrell, *IEJ,* 24 (1974), 139-141; G. E. Wright, *HTR,* 64 (1971), 437-448 = *BA,* 34 (1971), 76-86.

A. F. RAINEY

EGREBEL eg'rə-bel. *See* ACRABA.

EGYPT ē'jipt [Heb. *miṣrayim*; Gk. *Aigyptos*]. The land along the Nile from the Fourth, Third, Second, or First Cataract northward to the Mediterranean Sea.

- I. Name
- II. Location and Size
- III. Geography
  - A. White Nile
  - B. Blue Nile
  - C. Nile Proper
  - D. Annual Flooding of the Nile
  - E. Faiyûm
  - F. Western Desert
  - G. Eastern Desert
- IV. Climate
- V. People and Language
  - A. People
  - B. Language
  - C. Form of Writing
  - D. Direction of Writing
  - E. Decipherment of the Language
  - F. Writing Materials
- VI. Calendar and Chronology
  - A. Calendar
  - B. Chronology
- VII. Science and Metrology
- VIII. History
  - A. Predynastic Period
  - B. Archaic Period
  - C. Old Kingdom
  - D. First Intermediate Period
  - E. Middle Kingdom
  - F. Second Intermediate Period
  - G. New Kingdom (Empire)
  - H. The Hebrews in Egypt
  - I. Late Dynastic Period
- IX. Egypt and the Bible

I. Name.–The Heb. *miṣrayim* is apparently related to Ugar. *mṣrm,* "Egypt," *mṣrym,* "Egyptian"; Amarna *miṣri,* "Egyptian"; Akk. *muṣur, muṣri,* "Egypt/Egyptian," and also *"Musri"* in northern Syria (which may be intended in 1 K. 10:28). The Hebrew word was formerly taken as a dual, referring to the "two lands" of Egypt, but this view has been strongly challenged on the basis of the forms in cognate languages. The word first occurs in nonbiblical texts in the 14th cent. B.C., and seems to have been used only by outsiders, since the name has not been found in Egyptian sources.

The Gk. *Aigyptos* first occurs in Homer (*Odyssey*), with the masculine article for the Nile and with the feminine article for Egypt. The suggestion by Brugsch, adopted by Gardiner, that the Greek comes from Egyptian *ḥwt-kȝ-ptḥ* (cf. Amarna *ḫikuptaḫ,* "mansion of the Ka of Ptah") has been generally accepted (cf. Am.Tab. 84:37), even though Hikuptah is Memphis, capital of Lower Egypt, and not the entire land. The use of the name "Memphis" to refer to all of Egypt has support in the Hebrew Bible, where both *môp* and *nôp,* derived from Egyp. *mn-nfr* (vocalized something like *mennufe(r)*; cf. Copt. *menpi, mempi*), "established and goodly," stand for "Egypt" (cf. Hos. 9:6; Isa. 19:13). The name *mn-nfr* was given to the pyramid of Pepi I of the 6th Dynasty, and then transferred to the capital at Memphis (Gardiner, *Egypt of the Pharaohs,* p. 91).

The Egyptians called their land *kmt,* vocalized in Coptic as *kēme,* "black land," referring to the rich alluvial soil along the banks of the Nile, in contrast to *dašre(t),* "red land," the desert region on either side of the fertile Nile Valley. They also called their land *tȝwy,* "two lands," referring to the ancient division into Upper and Lower Egypt, and *tȝ-mrȝi,* "beloved land," usually translated "Egypt."

II. Location and Size.–Egypt is located in the northeastern part of Africa. Because its borders were not the same throughout its history, a precise definition of its boundaries cannot be stated generally. The Delta extends from about 30° to 32° East Longitude, and the Nile from the First Cataract (Aswân) to the Mediterranean lies between 24° and 31°30′ North Latitude. The Second Cataract is about 22° North Latitude, and the Fourth Cataract about 19° North Latitude. Each of these locations was at some time the southern boundary of Egypt. Modern Egypt extends from the Second Cataract to the Mediterranean, and from the border with Libya (25° East Longitude) to the Red Sea. The SINAI Peninsula, part of Asia, is included in modern Egypt, but will not be considered in this article. The total area of Egypt is about 1,000,000 sq. km. (390,000 sq. mi.), of which less than 4 percent is habitable. Perhaps more accurate than measurements based on geographical boundaries is the simple statement, "Egypt is the Nile."

III. Geography.–Since Egypt is "the gift of the Nile" (attributed to Herodotus [cf. ii.5] by Strabo *Geog.* xii.2.4) it seems relevant to begin the study of the geography of Egypt with the Nile River system, possibly the world's greatest river complex. The Nile proper is formed by tributaries, the major ones being the White Nile, the Blue Nile, and the Atbara. At a point near modern Cairo the Nile divides, having formed an alluvial fan known from ancient times as the Delta of the Nile. Although the tributaries lie outside the boundaries of Egypt, we must consider them because of their importance in the phenomenon of the annual flooding of the Nile and the part it has played throughout history in the life of Egypt.

A. White Nile. The sources of this river system are found in equatorial Africa, a few degrees S of the equator, in the region where the modern nations of Zaïre, Burundi,

Ruwanda, Uganda, Sudan, Kenya, and Tanzania are close to each other. The Lake Albert system and the Lake Victoria system join to form the Albert Nile (Baḥr ej-Jebel). This divides in a flat region, where the river is frequently blocked by vegetation (the Sudd), to form the Baḥr ej-Jebel and the Baḥr ez-Zeraf. These rejoin, along with the Baḥr el-Ghazal, to form the White Nile near Malakal in Sudan. There are also other tributaries from the east. *See* Plate 27.

B. Blue Nile. A spring in Ethiopia that flows through the Little Abbai into Lake Tana, located near Bahar Dar in Ethiopia, is considered the source of the Blue Nile. Lake Tana, about 12° North Latitude, lies at an altitude of 1785 m. (5856 ft.). (By way of comparison, Lake Victoria lies at an altitude of 1139 m. [3720 ft.], and Lake Albert at 679 m. [2030 ft.].) From Lake Tana the Abbai, called in Sudan Baḥr el-Azrâq, "the Blue River," drops rapidly in a gorge, flowing first southward, then westward, and finally northwestward, to join the White Nile at Khartoum (about 16° North Latitude). Lake Tana furnishes only a small part of the water of the Blue Nile, the balance coming from numerous tributaries that drain the mountains of Ethiopia, which rise to the height of 4500 m. (15,000 ft.). The seasonal torrential rains in the Ethiopian highlands cause the annual flooding of the Nile. *See* picture in ETHIOPIA.

C. Nile Proper. From Khartoum the Nile flows generally northward, bordered by a narrow strip of vegetation and the wide expanse of the deserts on each side. The northern direction is broken by a huge S-bend between Atbara and Dongola, a distance of about 700 km. (435 mi.). The Atbara River, the last main tributary of the Nile, joins the Nile at Atbara (around 17° North Latitude). Like the Blue Nile, it drains the highlands of Ethiopia and contributes to the flooding of the Nile.

Between Khartoum and Aswân the Nile has cut its way through six granite barriers, with resultant rapids or cataracts. Since they were numbered by explorers, their sequence is in reverse order to the river's current. The Sixth Cataract is at Wâdī Hamid, about 100 km. (60 mi.) N of Khartoum. The Fifth, Fourth, and Third Cataracts seem to have been caused by the same granite formation, as the river crosses it three times in the course of the S-bend, the Fifth Cataract N of Atbara, the Fourth Cataract N of (but upstream from) Meroë, and the Third Cataract near Kerma. The Second Cataract was near Wâdī Halfa, almost on the border between Sudan and Egypt (now covered by Lake Nasser), and the First Cataract is just N of (below) the Aswan Dam. The cataracts make navigation on the Nile above Wâdī Halfa impossible, and in recent times a railroad joined Wâdī Halfa and Khartoum, bypassing the lower portion of the great S-bend of the river. The region between the First and Sixth Cataracts was known in antiquity as Nubia — Lower Nubia from the First to the Second Cataract, and Upper Nubia from the Second to the Sixth. The Egyptians controlled part or all of Nubia only at certain periods. The High Dam at Aswân was constructed (1960-1970) to form a lake (Lake Nasser) extending to the Second Cataract.

From Aswân to Cairo (more properly, to just S of ancient Memphis) is "Upper Egypt." Except for a large bend between Luxor and Nag Hammadi, the course is almost directly northward for a distance of about 1200 km. (750 mi.). The arable land is a narrow strip of alluvial soil on each bank of the Nile, sometimes less than a kilometer (0.6 mi.) in width, and never more than about 10 km. (6 mi.) wide on each side. In predynastic times this was divided into twenty-two "nomes" or districts, numbered from south to north, each of which was ruled by a "nomarch." The principal cities of these nomes continued in

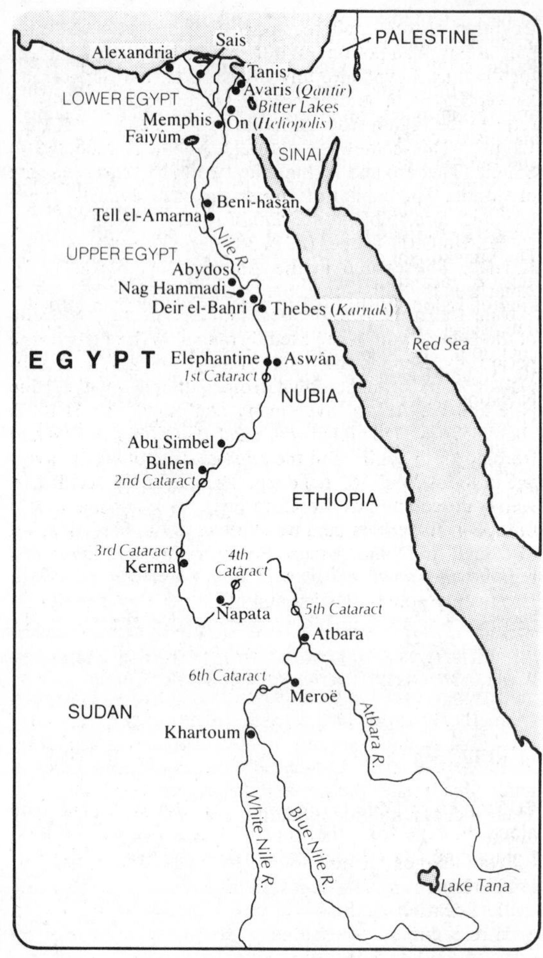

Second Cataract of the Nile (W. S. LaSor)

Egyptian history, and the local divisions also played a part in Egyptian politics. While there is no historical basis for dividing Egypt into any other parts than Upper and Lower Egypt, it is common in some modern works to refer to the region from Akhmim to Memphis as "Middle Egypt." This somewhat natural division is reflected in Saʿidic (Theban) and Akhmimic, two of the early dialects of Coptic. The capital of Upper Egypt in dynastic times was *nw.t ỉmn,* biblical *nō' 'āmûn* (Nah. 3:8) or *nō'* (Jer. 46:25), Homeric Thebes (*Il.* ix.383-85), modern Luxor and Karnak. The capital in the Amarna period was at el-Amarna in the 15th Nome, hence in Middle Egypt.

Near Cairo the Nile divides, fanning out into the Delta of the Nile. A gulf of the Mediterranean in the Pleistocene period, the Delta is the result of an accumulation of alluvial deposits brought down from Ethiopia by the Blue Nile and the Atbara over many centuries. The Delta is about 250 km. (150 mi.) in width and about 160 km. (100 mi.) from north to south, and the alluvial deposit on the average is about 20 m. (65 ft.) deep. The extremely fertile and well-watered soil has therefore been an important source of food in all periods, and was known as "the breadbasket of Rome" in Roman times. From predynastic times this region was known as "Lower Egypt," and was divided into twenty nomes. The capital of Lower Egypt in dynastic times was at Memphis. In the 19th and 20th Dynasties (the Ramesside period), there was also a capital at Avaris in the eastern Delta. The two branches of the Nile in modern times are the Rosetta (Rashid, at the west) and the Damietta (Dumyat, at the east). In antiquity there were, according to one tradition, twelve branches of the Nile. Strabo names seven: Canobic, Bolbitine, Sebennytic, Phatnitic, Mendesian, Tanitic, and Pelusiac (*Geog.* xvii.1.18). Their location and identification are not generally agreed upon.

From its most distant source to the Mediterranean the Nile measures 6670 km. (4145 mi.), making it probably the longest river in the world (the Amazon, which has not been as accurately measured, is sometimes awarded this distinction), and the Nile basin extends over about 2,850,000 sq. km. (1,100,000 sq. mi.), roughly 10 percent of the area of the continent of Africa. Approximately 58 percent of the water is supplied by the Blue Nile, 29 percent by the White Nile, and 13 percent by the Atbara.

D. Annual Flooding of the Nile. From the earliest periods of civilization the cultivation of land along the Nile depended on a unique phenomenon, the annual flooding of the Nile. The constant source of water in the Nile is largely the result of the drainage of the plateaus of equatorial Africa accomplished by the White Nile and its tributaries. This water is greatly augmented by the Blue Nile and the Atbara, which drain the seasonal rains of the Ethiopian highlands. The rains in Ethiopia begin in May, and the season of heavy rains (the *kremt*) occurs in the months of July-September. At Wâdī Halfa, on the northern border of modern Egypt, the Nile begins to rise in June and reaches its maximum height in September. At that time the flow is nearly 800,000,000 cubic m. (28,290,000,000 cubic ft.) per day. The river begins to drop until it reaches its low point in late January. At that time the flow is less than 100,000,000 cubic m. (3,530,000,000 cubic ft.) per day. While the Blue Nile is in flood, it serves to hold back some of the water of the White Nile, forming a sort of natural reservoir, and this prolongs the seasonal flood.

The flood served two major purposes for the Egyptians. First, it provided fresh alluvial deposits each year, making the use of any other fertilizer unnecessary. The silt content of the Nile at the height of flood averaged 2500 parts per million by weight, and during the flood season averaged 1600 parts per million. The building of dams, particularly the High Dam at Aswân, has seriously disturbed this deposit of alluvium and made extensive use of fertilizers necessary. At the same time, the dam has served to control excessive flooding while providing hydroelectric power. The second service the Nile flood rendered was the irrigation of the fields for the major part of the growing season. However, the flood stage of the Nile was not uniform. The difference between the maximum and minimum flood stages has been measured at 34 cm. (13.4 in.); thus in some years the level would be insufficient for satisfactory irrigation. Nilometers were used, both in antiquity and in more recent times, to record the height of the flood. One of these, described by Strabo (*Geog.* xvii.1.3, 48), can be seen today at Elephantine island near Aswân. According to J. H. Breasted (*History of Egypt* [1905], p. 191), the Nilometer shows that the Nile in antiquity rose "twenty five to thirty feet higher than the Nile rises at the present day." Strabo records (xvii.1.3) that the Nile rose to fourteen cubits *(pḗcheis)* at its greatest and to eight cubits at its lowest flood stage. Taking the *pēchys* to be about 46 cm. (18 in.; the length from the point of the elbow to the tip of the middle finger; cf. LSJ, *s.v.*), this would be the equivalent of 640 cm. (252 in.) and 365 cm. (144 in.), respectively. The Egyptian calendar of 365 days was not precisely correlated with the solar year, so the rising of the Nile could not be predetermined by reference to the calendar. The Egyptians discovered, at an early date, that the rising of the Nile coincides with the heliacal rising of the Dog Star, Sothis, called "the going up of Sothis." *See* ASTRONOMY I.A.

E. Faiyûm. The only exception to the description of the Nile as a narrow valley is found in the region about 100 km. (60 mi.) S of Cairo and W of the Nile, known as the Faiyûm. Near Abydos is a small branch of the Nile called Baḥr Yûsûf ("river of Joseph"). This feeds the Faiyûm depression and empties into Lake Karûn (Qarûn), which lies 45 m. (148 ft.) below sea level. Amenemhet III either built or rebuilt a canal by which the water of the Nile in flood could be stored in this lake and used for irrigation while the Nile was at low-water stage. Strabo refers to this as "the lake of Moeris" and gives a rather full description of the locks and other buildings (*Geog.* xvii.1.37; cf. Herodotus ii.149). Because of the name "river of Joseph," local guides sometimes tell visitors that this was the location of the Hebrews in the days of Joseph and Moses. This identification is worthless. Of great significance, however, is the fact that Crocodilopolis, where the crocodile god Sebek was honored, yielded numerous mummified crocodiles wrapped or stuffed with papyri. These were the famous papyri recovered by Grenfell, Hunt, and Hogarth in 1895ff.

F. Western Desert. The region west of the Nile (the Western Desert, eṣ-Ṣaḥra el-Gharbîya, or the Libyan Desert, eṣ-Ṣaḥra el-Libîya) is almost entirely a vast desert, extending from the Mediterranean to Khartoum, described as perhaps the most arid region in the world. It is part of the great Sahara. In modern Egypt, it covers about 675,000 sq. km. (260,000 sq. mi.), roughly three-quarters of the modern country. A limestone plateau, reaching its greatest height (1934 m., 6345 ft.) at Jebel el-ʿUwaynât in the extreme southwest, it is covered largely by rocks and sand. The plateau slopes gently toward the north, and is broken only by a few depressions or oases, namely, el-Wâḥât el-Dakhla, el-Wâḥât el-Farâfra, and el-Wâḥât el-Baḥarîya in the central part of the Western Desert, and the greater depressions, el-Wâḥât es-Siwa (ancient Ammonium, or Siwah, where Alexander the Great consulted the oracle of Amon), and Munkhafad el-Qaṭṭara, the Qattara Depression, which lies 132 m. (435 ft.) below sea level. The plateau ends in a shelf or escarpment about 180 m. (600 ft.) high near the Mediterranean coast. The narrow strip along the shore is watered by rains and is habitable. The oases, except the Qattara Depression, are also habitable due to ground water supplies. A notable feature of the desert is the formation of parallel sand dunes 60 m. (200 ft.) or more in height in the region between Siwah in the northwest and Jifr el-Kebîr, the mountains in the southwest.

G. Eastern Desert. East of the Nile and extending to the Red Sea is the Eastern Desert (eṣ-Ṣaḥra eš-Šarqîya), also called the Arabian Desert, an area of 222,750 sq. km. (86,000 sq. mi.). This region is a striking contrast to the Western Desert, for while it is also arid, it consists partly of a mountain chain with peaks of 1977 m. (6486 ft., Jebel Ḥamâtâ), 2187 m. (7175 ft., Jebel Šâyib el-Banât), and 1751 m. (5745 ft., Jebel Ghârib), plus several lower peaks. The region is cut by numerous wadis and several larger valleys that extend from the Nile to the Red Sea. The most important is Wâdī Ḥammâmât, extending from Qift (Koptos, N of Karnak) to Quseir, a distance of 193 km. (120 mi.) on the modern map. Stone quarries were worked in Wâdī Ḥammâmât from early times. Erman records that, with the exception of granite, all the hard, dark-colored stone used by Egyptian sculptors came from the quarries in Wâdī Ḥammâmât (A. Erman and H. Ranke, *La Civilisation égyptienne* [1952], p. 38). The route through Wâdī Ḥammâmât was the shortest to Punt, and was used by pharaohs in their military and commercial ventures. More than fifty inscriptions tell of the exploitation of these quarries or expeditions through the wadi.

A more important modern route lies slightly to the north, from Qena (opposite Dendera) to Port Safaga. Other routes are located from a point opposite Edfu to Marsa Alam and from Aswân to Bit Shalatein. Although the Eastern Desert generally tapers out at the edge of the Delta, a more significant boundary is Wâdī Ṭumilât, which runs from Bubastis (near modern Zagazig) to Lake Timsâḥ (near modern Ismailia). At an early date, a canal was cut through this wadi, connecting the Nile with the Red Sea. The canal fell into ruin, and was restored by Pharaoh Neco and later by Darius. Amenemhet I built a fortress at the eastern end of Wâdī Ṭumilât, called "the Walls of the Ruler," to protect the northern border against Asiatic invaders.

IV. Climate.–Lower Egypt has Mediterranean weather, which means that the winds are prevailingly from the west, either southwest (in summer) or northwest (in winter). Rainfall in winter in the Delta ranges from 20 cm. (8 in.) per annum at Alexandria to 3.3 cm. (1.3 in.) at Cairo. From April to June there will be days when the Saharan weather dominates, resulting in much heat and excessive aridity (the *khamsîn*). The rest of Egypt rarely has any rainfall whatever. The temperature ranges between 11° and 27° C (53° and 81° F) during the day at Cairo in summer and averages between 12° and 15° C (55° and 60° F) in January. In Upper Egypt, temperatures are considerably higher, often going above 38° C (100° F). Nights are sometimes 17° C (30° F) cooler than the days. The winds generally blow up the Nile Valley, making it possible to sail upstream (i.e., from north to south).

V. People and Language.–*A. People.* Some would trace the origin of the Egyptians to Asia, others to Africa. D. Garrod speculates that survivors of a Neanderthal race, producing artifacts with Levalloisian affinities, may have been displaced by men of the modern type in Mesolithic times (*CAH* [3rd ed.], I/1 [1970], 70). This subject lies beyond the limits of our present study. On the basis of linguistic evidence, however, it seems reasonable to assume that the Egyptians of historic times were partly of Semitic stock and partly of Hamitic (or Berber) stock. The direction of the movements of these peoples and the approximate dates cannot be determined at present. On the basis of my studies of Semitic phonemes, I formulated a hypothesis that the Semites penetrated from the northeast, moved up the Nile and into what is now known as Ethiopia, thence across Bab el-Mandeb into South Arabia, and from there bifurcated, one branch migrating into North Arabia and the other into the Mesopotamian valley ("Semitic Phonemes," dissertation, Dropsie College, 1949). This movement, if it did take place in such fashion, was well before the historic period, for the languages of the specified areas had already developed in distinctly different ways by the end of the Chalcolithic Age. The Hamitic group most likely penetrated Egypt from Libya. This also must have been before the historic age, for Hamitic elements are found in Egyptian at the earliest known level of the language. On the other hand, the Hamitic penetration must have been later than the Semitic movement into Ethiopia and South Arabia, for no Hamitic elements are found in the early Semitic languages of those regions.

There are other mixtures in the Egyptian people. The peoples of sub-Saharan Africa made their way down the Nile, reaching Khartoum probably by 3200 B.C. To what extent the Nubians are Negroid is a matter of debate, for while they have dark skin pigmentation, the facial characteristics and the hair are not those generally described as Negroid. One of the chests from the tomb of Tutankhamen shows the king engaging in battle with Negroes, clearly indicated by hair and facial characteristics as well as by color. By the end of the 18th Dynasty dark-skinned people had taken over large portions of Nubia and established a capital at Napata. For the 25th Dynasty Manetho lists three "Ethiopian" kings, Sabacon, Sebichos, and Tarcos. The founder of the dynasty was Kashta, who was succeeded by Piankhy. But the first to rule all of Egypt was Shabaka (Manetho's Sabacon), who was succeeded by Shebiktu (Shabataka) and Taharqa (Tirhakah; cf. 2 K. 19:9 par. Isa. 37:9). Whether these "Ethiopians" were Negroid or not depends in part on definitions. Figures with clearly Negroid characteristics can be found in Egyptian art. Unfortunately, the Egyptian word for "Negro" [*neḥes*] does not help us, for the word seems to have been used indiscriminately for other foreigners besides the Nubians or Negroes. Further complicating the problem is the fact that the terms "Hamitic," "Berber," and "Nilotic" are sometimes used by scholars for subclasses of the Negro race, whereas the Hamitic peoples in the OT are Caucasoid, the Berbers are generally considered to be a Caucasoid Mediterranean people, and "Nilotic" is sometimes used to describe the Nubians in contradistinction to the Negroes. Perhaps the most that can be said is that some Negro peoples were in Egypt from the 18th Dynasty on, if not earlier. Cf. Gardiner, *Egypt of the Pharaohs,* p. 133; T. Säve-Söderbergh, *Ägypten und Nubien* (1941), pp. 39ff.

The last great invasion of peoples in Egypt was the Moslem advance in A.D. 640. This lies beyond the limits of the present article, yet it has left influences (such as the modern place names) that need to be recognized to clarify our present understanding. The Moslem conquest brought in a new wave of Semitic peoples and a late level of the Semitic language, namely, Arabic, which today has developed into an Egyptian dialect. The Copts claim that they are the descendants of the earlier Egyptians, and certainly their liturgical language as well as the name "Copt" does preserve a late stage of the Egyptian language. The modern language of Egypt is *not* Egyptian, even though it is called such, and has little relationship to ancient Egyptian. Coptic, on the other hand, is a direct descendant of ancient Egyptian.

B. Language. The Egyptian language, like the people, is a mixture of two or more elements, generally described as Semitic and Hamitic. The Semitic elements include characteristic triconsonantal roots, phonemic-phonetic elements (such as the diversity of guttural sounds), feminine nouns and second-person verbal forms ending in *-t*, gemination (doubling) of the middle radical (though this feature is denied by W. Till and is generally observable only in Coptic), similarities of the pronominal suffixes and the independent personal pronouns, preformative elements (such as the Ś-causative and the N-reflexive), and many similarities in etymology. Not all of these elements are clearly observable, and there is some difference of opinion among scholars. For example, W. F. Albright has maintained that all of the numerals from 1 to 9 in Egyptian are cognate with the Semitic numerals, but I have demonstrated that several of the identifications are phonemically impossible or highly improbable. Less certain, but worthy of further research, is the possible relationship between the Egyptian *wn* and the Hebrew *waw*-conversive. On the other hand there are several elements that are more closely related to Hamitic (or Libyco-Berber), including numerous etymologies, reduplication of the entire root or of part of the root (e.g., the *qalqal,* the *qatlal,* and the *qᵉtaltal* — these are also found in several Semitic languages and may therefore be either Proto-Semitic or very early Semitic borrowings from Hamitic when the first Semites moved through Egypt and Abyssinia into the Arabian peninsula, if my hypothesis is sound), and other features noted by Hamitic scholars. The Egyptian verbal system seems to be somewhat different from either of these parent groups, lacking for one thing the formation of verbal forms with preformative pronominal elements (e.g., Heb. *yiqtōl,* Arab. *yaqtulu,* and Akk. *iprus* and *iparras*). There are also later additions to Egyptian, some of which may be identified as Cushitic (Abyssinian or Nilotic from the upper Nile regions), and of course Greek elements that entered Coptic.

The history of the Egyptian language may be divided into several periods. We may assume (1) a Proto-Egyptian or formative period when the earliest known elements were in the process of becoming the language. This is necessary to account for the well-developed language at its earliest historical stage, commonly called (2) Old Egyptian (1st-8th Dynasties). Perhaps the most important survivals of Old Egyptian are the Pyramid Texts, largely of religious and funerary character. (3) Middle Egyptian (9th-18th Dynasties) is the classical period of the language. Many literary compositions as well as official documents have been preserved in Middle Egyptian. It is also the most familiar stage of the language, since most students begin (and usually end) their studies in Middle Egyptian. (4) Neo-Egyptian (from the Amarna age to the 24th Dynasty) is the popular language of the New Empire, preserved in correspondence, official records, stories, and other examples, as well as the official language of numerous inscriptions and literary compositions. (5) Late (or Low) Egyptian is the language of the period from the 25th Dynasty to Roman times. It is preserved in numerous documents, both private and administrative, written in demotic (see below), and in inscriptions, mostly Saite and Ptolemaic, where the scribes were attempting some sort of classical revival. (This same feature is true of the art of this period.) Finally, there is (6) Coptic, often described as the language of the Christians of Egypt. However, early evidences of Coptic are found two or three centuries before the Christian era. Coptic occurs in several dialects, including (a) Bohairic, from Alexandria and Lower Egypt, (b) Akhmimic, from "Middle Egypt" (see III.C above), (c) Saʿidic (often and less correctly spelled Sahidic; cf. Arab. *eṣ-Ṣaʿid,* "Upper Egypt") from Thebes, gradually spreading through all of Upper and Middle Egypt, and (d) Faiyumic, used in the Faiyûm. The Bohairic and Saʿidic versions of the NT are significant for textual studies. The Gnostic documents from Chenoboskion (Nag Hammadi) are written in Coptic.

C. Form of Writing. Egyptian is written in hieroglyphic, hieratic, demotic, and Coptic forms or styles of writing. These terms are sometimes understood either as chronological developments or as linguistic subdivisions (and of course both elements are present), but strictly speaking the first three are forms of writing.

(1) Hieroglyphic ("priestly carving") is the most familiar, since it is the form used on wall inscriptions. The name was given to the writing before the decipherment was accomplished, when it was thought that the inscriptions were sacred and esoteric writings of the priests. It was initially pictographic (expressing the idea in pictures), hence the large number of recognizable characters such as birds, reptiles, animals, parts of the body, and flowers and plants. But by the time of the first known inscriptions, ideograms (the character suggests an idea), logograms (the character represents a word), phonograms (the character suggests a sound, an alphabetic character), and phonetic complements (suggesting the pronunciation of the word) are found. All methods may be used simultaneously. Vowels were not written (although the signs for *-w, 3,* and *ỉ* often indicate the vowel sound to be used). It has been customary to vocalize Egyptian words with *e*-vowels (e.g., Amenemhet and Wenes), even though the evidence of Coptic or foreign transcriptions may indicate otherwise.

(2) Hieratic is a cursive form of writing, in which the

The hieroglyphic biography (*ca.* 2400 B.C.) of Metjetjy, a nobleman. Painted relief from his tomb at Saqqârah (Royal Ontario Museum, Toronto)

Part of the Theban Book of the Dead in cursive hieroglyphs with some hieratic signs (University Museum, University of Pennsylvania)

beautiful characters of hieroglyphic may still be recognized. Champollion described hieratic as "a hasty writing of hieroglyphs" (*tachygraphie des hiéroglyphes*). It is not a different language or a different stage of development of the language, but simply a different style used for a different medium, much as our hand printing is used for signs and our writing is used for documents or letters. Hieratic is written with a sharpened reed and ink on papyrus, wood, and fragments of pottery. (Hieroglyphic writing is also found on papyrus.) Hieroglyphic writing is found from the 1st Dynasty until about the 3rd cent. A.D., and hieratic writing from about the 3rd Dynasty to the same *terminus ad quem*.

(3) Demotic is a further simplification of hieratic, much more cursive and much more difficult to read. It first occurred around the 25th Dynasty, and is therefore related to Late Egyptian, which is sometimes called "Demotic," thus confusing the style of writing with the linguistic development. The latest document in demotic comes from Philae and is dated A.D. 473. It was more the "popular" writing (hence the name given by the Greeks, *dēmotikós*, "of the people"), and was used for everyday documents and profane literature.

(4) Coptic is in a completely different style of writing, borrowed almost entirely from Greek uncial letters. In order to provide for certain phonemes not found in Greek, Coptic scribes adapted certain demotic characters, namely, *šai* [š], *fai* [f], *ḫai* [ḫ], *ḥori* [ḥ], *ǧanǧia* [ǧ or ž], *čima* [č], and *ti* [ti]. The phonetic nature of the *ti*, and why it was added when there was already the *tau*, is not clear, but there appears to have been a glottal element in the *ti* (Egyp. *ti3*). Since the Gk. *theta*, *phi*, and *chi* were at that period pronounced as aspirates (*th* as in hothouse, *ph* as in upholstery, and *kh* as in backhand), they were used in Coptic only for *t+h*, *p+h*, and *k+h*, and it was necessary to borrow signs for *f* and *ḫ*/*ḥ*. Certain phonetic shifts had taken place in Egyptian, and as a result the dentals *d* and *t* fell together as *t*, the prepalatals *ḏ* [ǧ] and *ṯ* [č] developed either to *t* or to *ǧ*, suggesting a conditioned sound-shift, and ḫ developed either to *š* or to *ḥ*, suggesting that it may have been an *Ichlaut* conditioned by a neighboring sound. Some final consonants have fallen away and are not written in Coptic (note especially the final *-t* in Egyptian, lacking in Coptic). Of particular importance is the presence of *l* in Coptic, which sometimes represents an Egyp. *r*, and at other times (rarely) an Egyp. *n* or *m*. The fact that *r*, *n*, and *m* usually are the same in Coptic as in Egyptian clearly indicates that there was an *l*-sound in Egyptian, preserved in the Copt. *l*. Coptic writing continues to be used in the liturgical and scriptural writings of the Coptic Church.

D. Direction of Writing. Egyptian was written either vertically or horizontally. When written vertically it is from top to bottom, but when written horizontally, it may be from left to right (dextrograde), but is more often from right to left (sinistrograde). Bustrophedon writing (each succeeding line reading in the opposite direction) is rarely if ever found. The direction is always apparent, for the characters are reversed, and we always read in the opposite direction from the way the birds are facing. (Since there are about fifty-three different bird-characters, some are always present. The same phenomenon is found for other beings, human or animal.) This description, however, is an oversimplification. From the Middle Kingdom on, hieratic is always written from right to left, as is demotic. Coptic is written from left to right. Hieroglyphic on monuments is composed to fit the monument, and may consist of two or three different directions of writing. Furthermore, certain characters fit together, either vertically or side by side, and the characters of a word may be arranged in a square-formation, with a long-and-narrow character placed alongside two or three short-and-wide characters, regardless of their order in the word. This accounts for different readings of the same name; e.g., *wśrt-s-n* is sometimes read "Usertsen" rather than "Senwosre(t)," i.e., Sesostris. The characters are faced toward the important part of the monument, so that on the left the writing may be dextrograde whereas on the right side the writing may be sinistrograde. Further complicating the description is the fact that certain words or elements, e.g., names of deities and the words *nsw* ("king") and *nṯr* ("god"), are placed first, regardless of their proper place. The names of kings (specifically the Prenomen and Nomen) are customarily written within an oval or oblong figure called a cartouche.

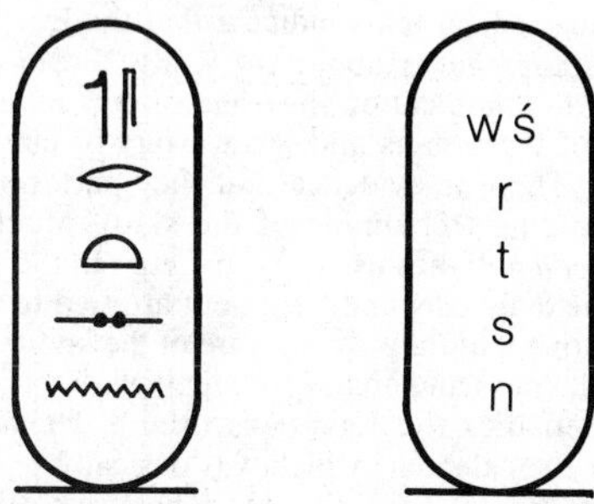

Cartouche of Sesostris (Sen-Wosret): "Man of [goddess] Wosret." Here the two lower signs are read first, then the other four signs, starting at the top left (the second and third signs repeat part of the first to clarify the reading).

E. Decipherment of the Language. Until the efforts by the German Jesuit A. Kircher in the mid-seventeenth cent., the hieroglyphs were considered as such: sacred and secret writings. Kircher, a Coptic scholar, failed in his efforts to decipher them, thinking they were written in alphabetic characters. But when Napoleon's expedition to Egypt discovered the Rosetta Stone in 1799, the desideratum of all who would decipher an unknown language was provided, namely, an inscription in two languages (not three, as sometimes stated; the Egyptian is written in both hieroglyphic and hieratic). *See* picture in ARCHEOLOGY OF EGYPT. The names of S. de Sacy, J. D. Åkerblad, and T. Young are connected with the first attempts to decipher the language, but credit for fully translating the stone is usually given to Jean-François Champollion (d. 1832). He subsequently prepared an Egyptian grammar and a dictionary (published posthumously). The date given for the decipherment, based on his letter to M. Dacier, is 1822, when Champollion was thirty-two years of age.

The following phonemes (indicated in Egyptian by alphabetic characters) are found: *b, p, f* (both *p* and *f* are phonemic; they are not allophones as in Hebrew and Aramaic), *m, n, r, s, ś, š, d, t, ṯ (č), g, k, ḏ (ǧ), q (ḳ), ẖ* (perhaps an *Ichlaut*), *ḫ* (perhaps an *Achlaut*), *ḥ, h, 3* (like Heb. *ʾaleph*), *ỉ* (also like *ʾaleph,* often transcribed as *i* or *y*), *ʿ* (like Heb. *ʿayin*), *w, y.* No symbol for *l* occurs, either *n* or *r* being used to represent the phoneme. That there must have been an *l* is indicated by its presence in Coptic words of Egyptian origin (cf. Egyp. *ỉ3rrt,* Copt. *eloole,* "vine"; Egyp. *ns,* Copt. *las,* "tongue"). That numerous phonetic shifts must have taken place in the course of 3000 years is a linguistic certainty. Evidence of some of the shifts can be seen in Coptic words. Particularly noteworthy is the loss of final *-t* (cf. Egyp. *nw.t ỉmn,* Heb. *nōʾ ʾāmûn,* "Thebes").

F. Writing Materials. The Egyptian scribe used a sharpened reed and usually wrote with ink on papyrus. His equipment included a palette, an ink box, and a pen or two. Examples of writing in both black and red inks have been preserved. Papyrus was made from the stalk of the papyrus plant (which is no longer found in Egypt except in front of the archeological museum). The rind was removed and the pithy stalk was split and laid out in vertical strips. Over these were placed horizontal strips of the same material. They either adhered because of the fluids in the stalk or because of an unknown adhesive. (Pliny [*Nat. hist.* xiii.11-13] says that Nile water was used as the adhesive.) The sheets were then held together under pressure until dry and afterward rubbed until smooth. Writing was done on both sides, because of the cost of papyrus, but the side laid horizontally was considered the *recto.* The use of potsherds (ostraca) by student scribes was common. Hieroglyphics were carved or painted on wall surfaces.

VI. Calendar and Chronology.–*A. Calendar.* The date when the Egyptian calendar was first used is unknown, but from the Archaic Period until the Julian calendar was forced on Egypt (30 B.C.) the year was composed of twelve months of thirty days each, with five epagomenal days at the end of the year. Thus a year of 365 days was established. The year was divided into three seasons: *3ḫt* (Copt. *ḥate*), "Inundation"; *prt* (Copt. *prou*), "Emerging (soil), winter," the season of planting; and *šmw* (Copt. *šōm*), "deficiency(?) of water, summer," the season of harvesting. A date would be given as *tpy 3ḫt śśw* ("first [month] of Inundation, day 1). Obviously, a calendar of 365 days would get out of phase with the actual seasons within a short time, for the solar year is approximately 365¼ days. Accordingly we find such statements as "winter is come in summer," and the actual flooding of the Nile would not occur in the calendar season of Inundation. The Egyptians made no attempt to correct this until the time of Ptolemy III Euergetes (237 B.C.), and even then his suggestion to add an extra day was rejected.

At an early date it was observed that the flooding of the Nile occurred at the same time as the heliacal rising of the Dog Star (Sirius or Sothis). At the latitude of Memphis this was 19 July by our calendar (*see* ASTRONOMY I.A). Instead of correcting their calendar to bring it into coincidence with the inundation, the Egyptians marked "the going up of Sothis" *(prt spdt)* and recorded when it occurred by their calendar. This idiosyncrasy has made it possible to establish a number of fixed points in Egyptian chronology. (O. Neugebauer says, "This calendar is, indeed, the only intelligent calendar which ever existed in human history" [*Exact Sciences in Antiquity* (1957), p. 81], since a fixed time scale without any intercalation is exactly what is needed for astronomical calculations.) The Latin scholar Censorinus records (21.10) that the beginning of a Sothic cycle coincided with the New Year of the Egyptian calendar (*wpt-rnpt,* "opening of the year") in the second year of Antoninus Pius, i.e., A.D. 139. The difference between the 365-day year and a solar year is approximately ¼ day per year or one day in four years, or one year in 1460 years (1461 calendar years = 1460 solar years), which is called a Sothic cycle. The Egyptians did not use the term Sothic cycle, but they did refer to the "perfect year" when the calendar New Year (*wpt-rnpt*) coincided with the "going up of Sothis" (*prt-spdt*). If a Sothic cycle began in the year A.D. 139 of the Julian calendar, other cycles would have coincided with the New Year in approximately 1321 B.C., 2781 B.C., and 4241 B.C. (Other scholars calculate these dates slightly differently, but on a basis unclear to me.) It was the hypothesis of Sir Flinders Petrie, followed by other Egyptologists, that the invention of the Egyptian calendar must have coincided with the beginning of a Sothic cycle; in other words, the going up of Sothis would have been marked as the first day of the newly instituted calendar. Since 2781 B.C. was patently too late for the beginning of the dynastic era, the date 4241 B.C. was assumed. This hypothesis was rejected (cf. O. Neugebauer, *Acta Orientalia,* 17 [1938], 169-195; *JNES,* 1 [1942], 396-403), and Egyptologists were free to establish the date of the 1st Dynasty on the basis of other evidence. There is general agreement at the time of this article that the 1st Dynasty began *ca.* 3100 B.C. ± 150 years.

From the Persian period on, the Egyptians named their months. They also made a table of the stars according to which they could determine the hours of the night; they divided the day, as well as the night, into twelve hours, but the less accurate basis for the hours of the day was a water clock, or a sundial. Their *3t,* "minute," was an indefinite short period, like our "moment."

B. Chronology. In the days of Ptolemy II Philadelphus (283-247 B.C.), the Egyptian priest Manetho attempted to write a history of Egypt in which he listed the kings and the lengths of each reign, dividing them into thirty dynasties. The work is extant only in the versions of Africanus and Eusebius, the latter of which adds a 31st Dynasty. The two versions are not always in agreement. Manetho's figures for the length of each king's reign, and his names as he transcribed them in Greek, are not always reliable, but in general his outline is satisfactory and has become the basis for all modern histories of Egypt. See Gardiner, *Egypt of the Pharaohs,* pp. 429-453, for the complete list of kings and dynasties with Gardiner's notes.

Other works also furnish information. The Turin Canon of Kings is a papyrus list written in hieratic about the time of Ramses II, reportedly in good condition in the 17th cent. (A.D.) but now in fragments. The number of names is approximately the same as in Manetho's list. The Table of Abydos, inscribed on the walls of the temple, shows Seti I and his son making offerings to seventy-six of his ancestors whose names are written in hieroglyphic. The Table of Saqqârah, discovered in 1861, at one time had the names of fifty-seven kings honored by Ramses II, but because of damage to the inscription only fifty can be read. The Table of Karnak likewise is a wall inscription, this one dating from the reign of Thutmose III. It lists sixty-one names, of which forty-eight could be read when it was discovered (1825), but the names are not in chronological order. The Palermo Stone, fragments of which are in the museums at Palermo and Cairo, gives a year-by-year record of the kings and the principal events for the first six dynasties, but its condition makes it only of occasional use.

From these lists, together with synchronisms from other ancient Near Eastern documents and the correlations with the Sothic cycle in the reigns of Sesostris III and Amenhotep I, Egyptologists have been able to put together a reasonably complete and accurate chronology of the kings of Egypt. For portions of the history other data are available, such as the years of the "(cattle) count" (a kind of taxation), the *hb-śd* or Sed-Festivals, and the records of the precise dates of the birth and death of Apis bulls correlated with the dates of reigning kings. Because P. van der Meer (*Chronology of Ancient Western Asia and Egypt* [1955], pp. 83-85) has put so much value on the Sed-Festivals, claiming that they occurred regularly at thirty-year intervals, a word of caution is necessary. From records available it appears that some kings celebrated Sed-Festivals every *third* year, beginning with their thirtieth anniversary. Thus Ramses II celebrated six from his thirtieth to his forty-second year, and altogether celebrated twelve or thirteen such festivals. (Cf. R. A. Parker, *Calendars of Ancient Egypt* [1950]; A. H. Gardiner, *Royal Canon of Turin* [1959]; G. Steindorff, *Urkunden des ägyptischen Altertums* [1903-1917].)

VII. Science and Metrology.–The Egyptians were unusually clever in their powers of observation but lacking in their ability to abstract principles; hence, we give the Greeks credit for many discoveries in mathematics, geometry, and astronomy, whereas the foundations seem to have been laid by the Egyptians, and the principles abstracted by the Greeks.

We have already discussed some of the astronomical observations. To these we must add the ability to work from sightings of the stars to the orientation of the pyramids. The Great Pyramid deviates from true north by only 0°2′30″.

Egyptian medical texts indicate that the Egyptians had observed many facts about the body. From preparing bodies for mummification they had of course learned the positions of the organs and were aware of circulation of the blood. There is evidence that they performed operations, including trepanning of the skull. Much of their *materia medica* makes use of herbs, etc., but it is interesting that the diagnosis and treatment are tied to the calendar, indicating that they were aware of the interrelationship between sickness and climate or weather.

In mathematics the Egyptians used a decimal system except for the calendar, which was basically sexagesimal. There were figures for units, tens, hundreds, thousands, tens of thousands, hundreds of thousands, and even millions. There were also figures for fractions, but here the Egyptian inability to abstract a principle shows itself, for the numerator is always 1 and the denominator is 2 or a multiple, i.e., ½, ¼, ⅛, 1/16, 1/32, and 1/64. These added, the Egyptian knew, to only 63/64, and Thoth was supposed to supply the remainder. Other values could be expressed by hieroglyphs. Multiplication and division were accomplished by factoring, i.e., multiplying or dividing by 2, obviously a long and complicated process.

Geometry is illustrated on Papyrus Rhind, and is rather elementary, but it sufficed to lay out plots of ground as well as to build great pyramids and other structures.

The units of length were the *mḥ,* "cubit" (523 mm. or 20.6 in.), the *šsp* or palm (1/7 cubit), the *ḏbʿ* or finger (¼ palm), and for larger measures the *ḫt* or rod (100 cubits) and the *3trw* or river-measure (20,000 cubits, 10.46 km., or 6.50 mi.). This was satisfactory even for great distances, and the Egyptians had measured Upper Egypt at 86 atours (900 km. or 559 mi.) and Lower Egypt at 20 atours (209 km. or 130 mi.), figures which are remarkably accurate.

Units of area were the *sṯ3t* (one square *ḫt* or 2735 sq. m. — about ½ acre), the land mile (1000 square cubits), and the *atour* (one square atour).

The measure of capacity was the *ḥq3t* (about 4.8 liters), which was divided into ½, ¼, etc., with the missing 1/64 from Thoth.

The unit of weight was the *dbn* (91 gm., 3.2 oz.). A smaller unit was the *qdt* (1/10 of the *dbn*; cf. A. H. Gardiner, *Egyptian Grammar* [3rd ed. 1957], pp. 191-200).

VIII. History.–We shall concern ourselves here with the history of Egypt from late predynastic times to the Roman period, with emphasis on the periods that seem to have more relevance to biblical studies. (For the modern discovery of Egypt *see* ARCHEOLOGY OF EGYPT.)

A. Predynastic Period (*ca.* 5000-3200 B.C.). When the gulf that was formed in the Pliocene began to dry, the waters descended irregularly, leaving gravel terraces at heights of 90 m. (296 ft.) to 45 m. (148 ft.). These contain no trace of human habitation. The first artifacts indicating the presence of human beings are found in the 30-m. (98-ft.) level. After the 9-m. (30-ft.) stage, the river dropped below its present level, and the remains of human occupation there have been obliterated. We may assume that there was continuous occupation, perhaps with some penetration of peoples from other areas. Cf. *CAH* (3rd ed.), I/1 (1970), 62-69.

The Neolithic "revolution," which appears to have left its earliest traces in the Zagros Mountains between modern Iraq and Iran, reached Egypt *ca.* 5000 B.C. Neolithic communities have been discovered at Merimda (Beni Salameh), about 48 km. (30 mi.) NW of Cairo, and at Der Tasa and Badari, between Akhmîm and Asyût in Upper Egypt. Typical finds are classified as "Tasian" and "Badarian." At Nagada (Naqada) on the west bank N of Luxor, the "Amratian" and "Gerzean" types were found. The presence of copper artifacts leads to the conclusion that the inhabitants had passed into the Chalcolithic Age. According to a modification of Petrie's system of Sequence Dating (abbr. S.D.), Amratian was assigned S.D. 30-37 and Badarian S.D. 38-63. More recent scholars have tended to use the terms "Naqada I" for the earlier (*ca.* 4500 B.C.), and "Naqada II" for the later (*ca.* 3500 B.C.). (Cf. *CAH* [3rd ed.], I/1 [1970], 463-497.) Newcomers, possibly Semitic, seem to have been responsible for the new vitality found in Naqada II. Cylinder seals and two original seals of the Jemdet Nasr period found in Naqada II tombs provide a synchronism with Mesopotamian prehistory and lend support to the theory of a Semitic invasion.

The geography of Egypt encouraged the development of individual kingdoms rather than a central government. Accordingly we find these petty states, to which Herodotus gave the name "nomes," each of which was ruled by a "nomarch," at the beginning of the dynastic era (cf. Herodotus ii.177). At an indeterminate date before the dynastic period the twenty-two nomes of southern Egypt federated to form Upper Egypt and the twenty nomes of northern Egypt formed Lower Egypt.

B. Archaic Period (*ca.* 3200-2700 B.C.). The union of Upper and Lower Egypt was accomplished by Narmer, who is often identified as Menes, though not without scholarly objection. The Narmer palette shows Narmer wearing the crown of Upper Egypt, and hieroglyphic signs have been interpreted to mean "Horus brings the captives of Lower Egypt," leading to the conclusion that Narmer unified the land by conquering Lower Egypt. The Turin Canon and the Abydos king list name the first king as Meni, the Min of Herodotus and the Menes who founded Manetho's 1st Dynasty. But W. B. Emery (*Archaic Egypt* [1961], pp. 32-37) gives arguments for and against this identification, concluding that Ḥor-aha and not Menes was Narmer. According to Herodotus, Menes founded a new capital at Memphis, named "White Wall(s)" or simply "Wall(s)." Since white was the color of Upper Egypt, to locate the new capital on the edge of Lower Egypt and to name it "White Wall(s)" may have been intended to emphasize the victory of the southern kingdom. On the other hand, it may simply have been descriptive of the color of the walls (cf. Thucydides i.104).

Since the division of the kings of Egypt into "dynasties" by the priest Manetho, historians have followed this general outline. The Archaic Period includes the 1st Dynasty, for which Manetho lists eight kings with a total of 253 years, and the 2nd Dynasty, nine kings with a total of about 300 years (297 or 302, according to the versions of Africanus and Eusebius). The average length of a king's reign in a dynastic sequence is usually around twenty or twenty-five years, so these totals seem to be somewhat high. Evidence from a later period that Egyptians practiced the custom of co-regencies suggests that these figures incorporate some overlapping of reigns.

It was formerly held that the historic period must have begun with the beginning of a Sothic cycle, and 4241 B.C. was taken as the date for the beginning of the 1st Dynasty, but, as we have seen, this view has been rejected. The 1st Dynasty must be dated within a century or two of 3200 B.C.

In the Archaic Period there was a strong central government, and significant progress was made. Irrigation canals were maintained, writing was introduced or at least first used extensively, and architecture was revolutionized by the introduction of stone as a building material. Stone was used for vessels and sculptors were showing mastery in carved reliefs and in representing the human figure (cf. W. S. Smith, *Art and Architecture of Ancient Egypt* [1958], pp. 11-29; I. Woldering, *Art of Egypt* [1963], chs. 2–4).

C. Old Kingdom (*ca.* 2700-2400 B.C.). The Old Kingdom includes the 3rd-6th Dynasties. Manetho lists nine kings of Memphis totalling 214 years for the 3rd Dynasty, eight kings of Memphis of a different line totalling 277 years for the 4th Dynasty, eight kings of Elephantine totalling 248 years for the 5th Dynasty, and six kings of Memphis totalling 203 years for the 6th Dynasty. The total for the four dynasties is therefore 942 years. By way of comparison, A. H. Gardiner (*Egypt of the Pharaohs*, pp. 433-36) gives the following dates for the beginning of each

The Tjeḥnu Palette. Left: the seven squares probably represent towns (signified by the hieroglyphs), and the seven animals, each breaking its way through the wall with a pick, probably represent provinces or nomes. Right: the booty captured from the towns(?) (Service des musées, Cairo)

dynasty: 3rd, 2700 B.C.; 4th, 2620 B.C.; 5th, 2480 B.C.; and 6th, 2340 B.C. Other scholars give somewhat different dates, but all in approximately the same time framework. The dates are self-consistent, and can be synchronized at points with other datable persons or events of the ancient Near East. Thus, e.g., the discovery of vase inscriptions of Chephren of the 4th Dynasty and of Pepi I of the 6th Dynasty at Tell Mardikh (Ebla) give approximate synchronisms with Iblul-Il of Mari and with Mesalim of Kish, according to G. Pettinato (*Catalogo dei testi cuneiformi di Tell Mardikh–Ebla* [1979], p. xxxviii); thus these Egyptian kings must be dated to the middle of the 3rd millennium B.C.

Of the kings in Manetho's 3rd Dynasty, only two are known from the monuments, Djoser (Zoser, Manetho's Tosorthros) and Ḥuny. Five are known from the king lists (adding Djoser-teti, Sedjes or Nebkare, and Neferkare, possibly Manetho's Kerpheres), and the total reigns of the four listed in the Turin Canon add up to fifty-five years. We can see that Manetho's lists and totals must be handled critically. Best known of these kings is Djoser, whose step-pyramid at Saqqârah (Sakkara) is considered to be the first sizable stone structure built by man. Djoser's architect and scribe was Imhotep, also considered a physician and a magician. Imhotep must have been a genius by any standards, and the nineteen years allotted to Djoser's reign by the Turin Canon, or the twenty-nine years of Manetho, do not seem to be sufficient for his accomplishments.

The 4th Dynasty consists of eight kings of a different Memphite line (Manetho), of whom three are well known: Cheops (Khufu), Chephren (Khafre), and Mycerinus (Menkaure), builders of the largest pyramids. Gardiner suggests 2620 B.C., W. S. Smith 2680 B.C., for the beginning of the 4th Dynasty. Snefru, founder of the dynasty, conducted raids on both Nubians and Libyans, and is credited with three pyramids, two at Dahshur and one at Meidum. Forty ships are reported to have brought cedar wood from Lebanon. From this time on, the nomen of the king seems to have been preferred to the Horus name, and was enclosed in a cartouche on monuments.

Since the names of the kings have been, and to some extent continue to be, one of the problems in reconstructing the history of Egypt, a brief description is needed. The "titulary" (*nḫbt*) of the king consisted of five "great names" (*rn wr*): (1) the Horus name, representing the king as an embodiment of Horus; (2) the "Two Ladies" (*nbty*) name, identifying the king with the ancient goddesses of the Upper Egyptian city of El Kâb and the Lower Egyptian city of *Dp*; (3) the Golden Horus name, the significance of which is not entirely clear; (4) the prenomen, which is always preceded by the title *n-sw-bỉt,* written as *insibya* in Babylonian cuneiform documents, and almost always compounded with Reᶜ; and (5) the nomen, introduced by *s3 rᶜ*, "son of Reᶜ." The prenomen and the nomen were usually written in cartouches, and the nomen was usually the name by which the king was known — something like a family name — before his accession to the throne. The principal name is the prenomen, which often stands alone or accompanied only by the nomen. The Horus name, prominent in the early dynasties, was of less importance than the nomen from the 4th Dynasty on. The prenomen is the more personal, and the nomen the more familial name, but we generally use the nomen and attach a Roman number to designate which of the Thutmoses or Amenhoteps is meant. On the other hand, the prenomen often occurs on cuneiform documents. The Table of Abydos, by way of contrast, lists only the prenomen. Cf. A. H. Gardiner, *Egyptian Grammar* (3rd ed. 1957), pp. 71-76.

Cheops (Khufu) is best remembered for his Great Pyramid, one of the seven wonders of the ancient world. Much has been written about this pyramid, some of it nonsense. It was designed as a tomb, not as a calendar for predicting the future. But when we have made that distinction, it remains a marvel of engineering skill because of its size, proportions, and almost exact orientation north-south and east-west. (For a discussion, see I. E. S. Edwards, *Pyramids of Egypt* [2nd ed. 1961]; A. Fakhry, *The Pyramids* [1961].) His son Chephren (Khafre) built a pyramid almost as large (originally only 3 m. [10 ft.] less in height and 15 m. [48 ft.] less on each side) and as splendid as Khufu's. The approach to the pyramid was guarded by a huge figure that has come to be known as the Sphinx, a covered causeway, and a funerary temple. The Sphinx was carved from a rock outcropping, but the monolithic pillars of the Valley Temple are of rose granite from the quarries near Aswân. The pyramids were built of limestone blocks averaging 2500 kg. (2½ tons) each, brought from the quarries on the Muqattem hills, on the opposite side of the Nile. Originally the pyramids were covered with a layer of polished white granite also from the Aswân quarries, but only at the top and the base (which had been covered with sand) of Chephren's pyramid can the original covering be seen; the rest was robbed in antiquity for other building projects. The pyramid of Mycerinus (Menkaure) is only a little over half the size of the pyramids of Cheops and Chephren, but the covering with rose granite, originally planned, would have made it somewhat larger. It still ranks as the third greatest of the pyramids of Egypt.

There are numerous works of art from this period, including a splendid statue of Menkaure and his wife, now in the Boston Museum of Fine Arts. Little else is known of Egypt in the 4th Dynasty. We may assume that much of the strength of the country was spent in building the pyramids and their surrounding structures. According to Manetho, Khufu (Suphis) reigned sixty-three years, and his son Khafre (also called Suphis) reigned sixty-six years. Between them, another son Raᶜdjedef is named in the king lists. Menkaure is also credited by Manetho with a reign of sixty-three years. We may assume that these figures either are exaggerated or include co-regencies.

After Menkaure the dynasty declined rapidly. Manetho lists four more kings but the Abydos king list gives only one. The 5th Dynasty was founded by Userkaf, a priest of Re from On (Heliopolis, near Cairo). He and his successors worshiped Re, the sun-god, rather than Horus, and adopted the custom of using a Re name. There are long religious and magical texts from this period, and detailed

Step pyramid of Djoser at Saqqârah (W. S. LaSor)

EGYPT

The Sphinx at Gîzeh (A. C. Myers)

The Great Pyramids at Gîzeh. The large one on the left is Khufu's (Cheops) and that on the right Khafre's (Chefren) (W. S. LaSor)

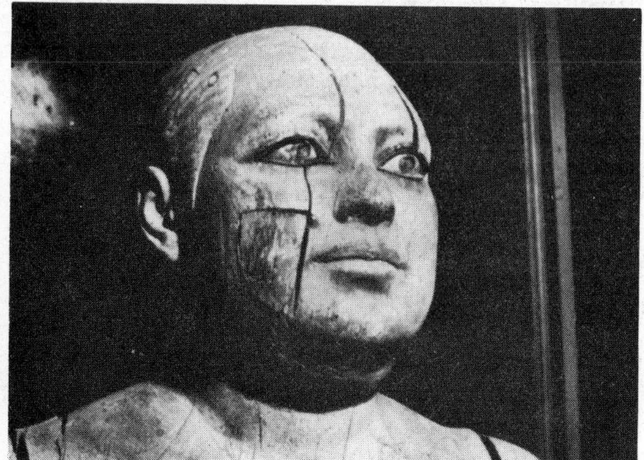

Head of the so-called Sheik el-Beled, an innovative wooden statue (4th-5th Dynasties, *ca.* 2500 B.C.) with realistic as well as stylized features (Egyptian Museum, Cairo; picture W. S. LaSor)

scenes of many aspects of everyday life portrayed in wall carvings. The Palermo Stone was engraved at this time.

The 6th Dynasty consisted of six Memphite kings and was founded *ca.* 2340 B.C. by Teti (Othoes in Manetho). The repression in art and literature that seems apparent until the 5th Dynasty now gave way to inscribed tombs throughout the country. During the reign of Pepi I, Weni, a commoner who rose to "friend" of the king and later to governor, organized expeditions to Sinai, south Palestine, and Elephantine; and Har-khuf, overseer of the interpreters, led caravans to southern Nubia and to oases in southern Libya. Among other items he brought back a pygmy dancer from the Sudan. After the long reign of Pepi II (99 years according to Manetho — a figure supported in the Turin Canon, where 90 plus a broken-away figure appears), the dynasty and the entire country fell into disarray. Civil war broke out, and the unity of the nation was gone.

D. First Intermediate Period (*ca.* 2258-2134 B.C.). Some idea of the turbulence of this period is conveyed by Manetho's treatment. For the 7th Dynasty he reports that "seventy kings from Memphis reigned for seventy days." There is no record of any king of this line. For the 8th Dynasty he reports that twenty-seven kings reigned for 146 years, an average of only 5.4 years per reign. He does not give their names. The Abydos list names eighteen successors to Pepi II. The 9th Dynasty, according to Manetho, consisted of nineteen kings who reigned 409 years, a reasonable if somewhat high average of 27.5 years. The dynastic capital was at Heracleopolis Magna, 90 km. (55 mi.) S of Memphis. The 10th Dynasty, according to the same source, consisted of nineteen kings who reigned 185 years (average 9.7 years). The total of these four dynasties, according to Manetho, was 740 years, which we must compress into not much more than 125 years. The impression left is that of rival kings in various parts of Egypt, each possibly controlling only a few nomes. The Turin Canon, like the Abydos list, apparently named eighteen kings, but there is little agreement between the names in the two lists. If we assume that there were indeed eighteen kings in 125 years, this averages less than 7 years per king, again indicating the very unstable conditions. From this period come some of the finest pessimistic writings, which began a literary genre used ever after, and indicated a complete upheaval of the social order. At the same time there is a paucity of monuments. Expeditions to the turquoise mines in Sinai ceased, and there were years of famine. Above all, Thebes, which had been very insignificant, began to increase in importance.

E. Middle Kingdom (*ca.* 2134-1786 B.C.). The priests at Thebes, probably led by Antef (Inyotef), asserted their independence of Lower Egypt, then pushed their borders northward, becoming rulers of all Egypt. The 11th Dynasty consisted of sixteen kings of Diospolis (Thebes), according to Manetho, but we can account for only six — three Antef's and three Mentuhotep's — from the monuments and king lists. Mentuhotep (perhaps II, but Gardiner credits the first of that name) established rule over Upper and Lower Egypt *ca.* 2040 B.C. He designed and began to build a magnificent funerary monument at Deir el-Baḥri, which became the model for the one built by Hatshepsut several centuries later. He also attempted to conquer Nubia. In his days, and those of his successor, a large expedition was sent to Wâdī Ḥammâmât to work the quarries and to open a more direct trade route to Punt. Tombs of the period contain many models depicting scenes from everyday life.

The 12th Dynasty is in many respects the zenith of Egyptian culture. Founded by Amenemhet I (Ammenemes), it consisted of eight kings, four named Amenemhet, three named Sesostris (Senwosre), and the female "king" Sebeknofru. Amenemhet I moved from Thebes to It-Tawi (El-Lisht), 32 km. (20 mi.) S of Memphis. It is in this dynasty that we get our first firm date, for a papyrus from El-Lahûn in the Faiyûm records a heliacal rising of Sothis in month 4 of *prt* (i.e., the eighth month of the year), day 16, of the seventh year of the reign of Sesostris III. On that date the year was 226 days out of phase, or 904 years from the "perfect year." The only reasonable

Sothic cycle for this king would be the one that began in 2781 B.C., hence the seventh year of his reign was 1877 B.C., and his reign began in 1883 B.C. (Because the observation of the heliacal rising cannot be precisely established, and because the difference of a day makes a difference in the calendar of four years, this date must be bracketed with a plus-or-minus of approximately six years. Cf. W. F. Edgerton, *AJSL,* 53 [1937], 188-197; *JNES,* 1 [1942], 307-314.) Gardiner (*Egypt of the Pharaohs,* p. 66) accepts 1872 B.C. for the seventh year of Sesostris III.

During the 12th Dynasty, the country was completely reorganized and foreign expansion was undertaken. Sesostris I and Sesostris III subdued Nubia to the Second Cataract, and Sesostris III invaded Palestine as far as Sekmem (believed to be Shechem). Evidences of Egyptian penetration have been found at Byblos, Qatna, Ugarit, and Atchana, and the court at Byblos seems to have been highly Egyptianized (but probably not under Egyptian control). Gold was brought from Nubia; ivory, ebony, leopard skins, and ostrich feathers from Sudan; and a trading post was established at Kerma near the Third Cataract. Expeditions were sent to Punt (referring, it seems, to both sides of the Red Sea at Bab el-Mandeb) and the Somali coast. Basalt was obtained from Wâdī Ḥammâmât, alabaster from Hatnub, diorite from the region NW of Abu Simbel, turquoise from the mines at Serābîṭ el-Khâdim in Sinai, and amethyst from Wâdī el-Hudi.

The region of the Faiyûm was developed, probably beginning with Sesostris I. Lake Moeris was made a reservoir for the waters of the Nile inundation. A mortuary temple was built at Hawwara, which came to be known as the Labyrinth, the wonder of visitors of classical times. (The name is probably not to be related to the Lydian *labrys* or the Cretan Labyrinth, but rather to the Egyptian king Nemaʿre [Amenemhet III], rendered by Manetho as Lacharēs, which suggests that the character *n* may have represented the *l*-sound, resulting in something like "Lamaʿre.")

Tombs and pyramids were built at numerous sites, including Lisht, Beni-hasan, Al-Bersha, Asyut, and Deir Rifah. The paintings in the tombs at Beni-hasan include scenes with Libyan and Asiatic merchants. Amon of Thebes began to be fused with Re, and the compound name Amon-Reʿ became prominent. Art and literature were developed. Among the literary compositions are "The Tale of the Eloquent Peasant" (T. E. Peet, *Comparative Study of the Literatures of Egypt, Palestine, and Mesopotamia* [1931], pp. 39-42; *ANET,* pp. 407-410), "Hymns to Senusret III from El-Lahûn" (Peet, pp. 67f.), "Instructions of King Amenemhet" (Peet, pp. 107-111; *ANET,* pp. 418f.), "The Shipwrecked Sailor" (Peet, pp. 28f.), and "The Tale of Sinuhe" (*ANET,* pp. 18-22). The last tells of the wanderings of a voluntary exile in Syria in the days of Sesostris I. (Cf. A. Erman, *Literature of the Ancient Egyptians* [1923], pp. 14-29.)

The most probable time for the visit of Abraham to Egypt, in the opinion of many scholars, is in the Middle Kingdom, although discoveries at Tell Mardikh (Ebla) have led a few scholars to place the time of the existence of the Cities of the Plain (Sodom, Gomorrah, etc.), and therefore the time of Abraham, two or three centuries earlier. Other scholars have attempted to date Abraham much later. *See* CHRONOLOGY OF THE OT III.A.

F. Second Intermediate Period (*ca.* 1786-1575 B.C.). The period between the end of the 12th Dynasty and the beginning of the 18th is difficult for scholars to study. Manetho lists sixty kings for the 13th (Theban) Dynasty, totaling 453 years, and seventy-six kings of the 14th (Xoite) Dynasty, totaling 184 (or 484) years. The 15th Dynasty consisted of six Hyksos or "Shepherd Kings" who ruled 284 years; the 16th Dynasty of thirty-two shepherd kings for 518 years; and the 17th Dynasty, forty-three shepherd kings and forty-three Theban kings ruling at the same time during a period of 151 years. This adds up to no less than 1590 (or 1890) years. To solve the problem Petrie would have added another Sothic cycle to the date for Sesostris III — but that makes nonsense out of Egyptian history, with respect to both foreign synchronisms and Egyptian monuments. Some of Manetho's figures are clearly absurd (e.g., six kings ruling 284 years). The king lists here are of little or no help, except for the Turin Canon, which supports Manetho to the extent of listing a large number of kings (more than a hundred) in a short period of time. We must conclude that many of them reigned over small parts of Egypt in concurrent or overlapping periods.

According to Manetho the 15th-17th Dynasties included the Hyksos. The word Hyksos may be derived from Egyptian *ḥiq-khase* (Gardiner) or *ḥq3w ḫswt,* pronounced something like *heku shoswet* (cf. G. Steindorff and K. C. Seele, *When Egypt Ruled the East* [1942], p. 24), "rulers of foreign lands." The term had been used as early as the Old Kingdom for Nubian chiefs (cf. K. Sethe, in G. Steindorff, ed., *Urkunden,* I [1903], 109, 134). As reconstructed by W. C. Hayes (*CAH* [3rd ed.], II/1 [1973], 44-64), the 13th Dynasty consisted of a large number of puppets or appointed officials who reigned for brief periods during a century and a half (*ca.* 1786-1633 B.C.), probably from the location at It-Tawi near Memphis. They were Thebans, and when Memphis fell in 1674 B.C., this line continued at Thebes where a new dynasty (the 17th) arose in 1650 B.C. Meanwhile, foreign peoples had invaded the eastern Delta, probably around 1720 B.C. They were not a single ethnic group, but were a mixture, with Semitic, Hurrian, and Indo-European chieftains, and they seem to have come in two waves, the second around 1674 B.C.

When the 12th Dynasty began to collapse, Hayes suggests that the western Delta became independent, with its capital at Xois (Khois). The line of kings ruling here formed Manetho's 14th Dynasty. The strong Hyksos rulers of the second wave include the six kings of the 15th Dynasty. The Hyksos of the 16th and 17th Dynasties, according to Hayes, were chiefs of the many Asiatic tribes. The Theban kings of the 17th Dynasty were the successors to the 13th Dynasty who organized the opposition, probably with the help of the "Pan Grave" people from Lower Nubia, and ultimately drove out the Hyksos under Kamose in 1567 B.C.

This reconstruction, it is granted, lacks support of a continuous record, although many of the individual names are found on the monuments which Hayes has cited. On the other hand, it does seem to fit the available time between the end of the 12th and the beginning of the 18th Dynasties, and it does commend itself as self-consistent. It is offered here as one plausible solution to the problem.

The expulsion of the Hyksos occurred *ca.* 1567 at the hands of Ahmose I — but the records of the period are scanty and the evidence is somewhat confusing. A stele discovered at Karnak in 1954 tells of the efforts of Kamose. The Hyksos were under Auserre Apophis I and apparently ruled Egypt from the Delta to Cusae a few miles N of Asyut. At the same time, the Nubians ruled the territory from the First Cataract to the Second, and possibly to Kerma near the Third Cataract. Kamose recorded, "My desire is to deliver Egypt and to smite the Asiatics" (cf. Gardiner, *Egypt of the Pharaohs,* p. 166). Kamose did succeed in driving the Hyksos out of Middle Egypt, but the final deliverance apparently was accomplished by his successor Ahmose I (Amosis). According to an inscription on the wall of a tomb at El Kâb, Avaris fell after a siege. This was followed by a siege of the Hyksos stronghold at Sharuhen in southwest Palestine (cf. Josh. 19:6). Ahmose may have penetrated deeper into *Ḍhy* (Palestine-Syria), but this seems unlikely, for he had to turn his attention to the Nubians. He seems to have driven them back to the Second Cataract at least, for there are remains of a temple connected with his name at Buhen (Wâdī Halfa), just below the Second Cataract. Ahmose reigned at least twenty-two years (the highest recorded regnal year — but he may have reigned longer, as indicated by Manetho), and was succeeded by his son Amenhotep I. (Cf. P. Labib; H. Stock; also J. Van Seters; D. B. Redford.)

G. New Kingdom (Empire) (*ca.* 1570-1085 B.C.). With the expulsion of the Hyksos, Egypt entered into a brilliant period of expansion. For convenience, this can be divided into three parts: (1) the 18th Dynasty from Ahmose to Amenhotep III; (2) the Amarna period, Amenhotep IV (Akhenaten) to Haremhab; and (3) the 19th and 20th Dynasties. This covers a period of nearly four hundred years and includes military campaigns that extended Egypt's borders at times to the Euphrates River or Qadesh on the Orontes and also deep into Nubia. It was also the time of colossal works in architecture and sculpture.

Amenhotep I (Amenophis, 1546-1527 B.C.) succeeded Ahmose, and thus the 18th Dynasty was established. Records are not plentiful, but we may assume that Ahmose had succeeded in stabilizing Egypt, and Amenhotep was able to express a desire to "extend the boundaries." From the claims of his successor Thutmose in his second year that his boundaries extended from the Third Cataract to the Euphrates, even allowing for considerable exaggeration, we may further assume that Amenhotep had succeeded in realizing that desire.

The extent to which we may credit the Hyksos period with this new attitude on the part of Egypt is not clear. There were contacts with the outer world long before the Hyksos period, but the new militarism of the 18th Dynasty has often been looked upon as a result of the period under foreign rulers. The Hyksos have also been credited with introducing the horse and chariot into Egypt, as well as the compound bow and other implements of war. Some of these claims have been seriously disputed by more recent scholarship. But whatever the cause, there can be no doubt that Egypt now embarked on an empire-building period.

We have an astronomical date for the reign of Amenhotep I. In Papyrus Ebers it is recorded that the going up of Sothis occurred in the ninth year of the king's reign on month 3 of *šmw* (i.e., the eleventh month of the year), day 9. From this we can calculate that the civil year was 308 days out of phase with the "perfect year," which occurred, as we have seen above, in 2781 B.C. (± 6 years). We can therefore date the beginning of the reign of Amenhotep I *ca.* 1557 B.C. (By another reckoning, the ninth year of Amenhotep I was 1537 B.C., hence his reign began in 1545 B.C.)

Thutmose I (*ca.* 1526-1512 B.C.) subdued Cush to Napata at the Fourth Cataract, and advanced in Asia to the Euphrates; hence he must be recognized as a ruler with military prowess. He made the first of the many additions to the temple of Amon at Karnak, and was the first king to be buried in the Valley of the Kings. He was succeeded by his son Thutmose II, who was married to his half-sister Hatshepsut. Thutmose II reigned only a few years, and when he died his son Thutmose III was merely a child. Hatshepsut seized the opportunity and had herself crowned king (1503-1482 B.C.) with all the royal honors. In representations of herself she appears in man's garb. A strong woman, Hatshepsut cultivated the art of peace, completed and decorated her funerary monument at Deir el-Baḥri, sent an expedition to Punt, and transported two granite obelisks by water from the quarries near Aswân to Karnak. The portrayal of this feat in relief on the wall of her temple at Deir el-Baḥri gives us some idea of how such tremendous achievements were accomplished. Meanwhile, Thutmose III was attempting to wrest the throne from her, and succeeded in doing so in his twenty-second regnal year. He reigned thirty-two years after that, and is considered by some to be the greatest king in Egypt's long history.

During his reign Thutmose III (1482-1450 B.C.) retook Syria, which had revolted under Hatshepsut's reign, conducting six campaigns against Qadesh on the Orontes and a total of seventeen campaigns into Syria and Palestine. (For a graphic account, see *ANET,* pp. 234ff.) In his thirty-third year he crossed the Euphrates at Carchemish and penetrated the territory of the Hurrian king of the Mitanni. Between military campaigns he carried out extensive building programs, led an expedition to Nubia, and put the empire on a sound administrative basis.

Amenhotep II (1450-1425 B.C.) was renowned as an athlete; his feats rival those of Hercules, if we can believe his modest accounts. One example: as an oarsman with an oar 20 cubits long (10 m. or 33 ft.!) he was the equal of 200 men, rowing six times as far as they could without stopping (cf. Gardiner, *Egypt of the Pharaohs,* p. 198). In the seventh year of his twenty-six-year reign he led an army to the Orontes in Syria. His successor Thutmose IV (1425-1416 B.C.) waged wars in Syria and, probably as protection against the growing Hittite power, married a Mitannian princess.

Amenhotep III (1416-1379 B.C.) was a mighty builder, especially at Thebes, which has been called the zenith of the magnificence of the 18th Dynasty. He built the temple at Luxor as well as the avenue of rams and the pylons at Karnak, and he constructed temples in Sedeinga and Soleb in Nubia. The so-called Colossi of Memnon, figures of himself 21 m. (70 ft.) high, were part of the approach to his funerary temple. The remains of the temple now lie beneath the cultivated fields behind the statues. He also built a lake for Queen Tiy, 3700 by 700 cubits (1880 by 178 m. or 6167 by 583 ft.), believed to be Birket Habu S of the temple at Medinet Habu. He carried on extensive international relations, and correspondence with the Hittites and the Mitanni, as well as with Alashia (Cyprus), has been recovered from Tell el-Amarna. He married Gilukhepa the daughter of the Mitannian king Shuttarna. But though he took the Golden Horus name of "Great of Strength who Smites the Asiatics," he let the influence of Egypt over its Asian holdings deteriorate. In his building projects he dismantled the works of predecessors in order to use their materials for his own.

The Amarna age spans three-quarters of a century, *ca.* 1379-1300 B.C. The son of Amenhotep III and Queen Tiy ascended the throne as Amenhotep IV. At that time the Amon priesthood was strong in Thebes, and the fact that three kings had been given names compounded with "Amen" indicates that the dynasty supported the Amon religion. The worship of the solar deity Reʿ had existed for a considerable time, and other divine names had been connected with the name Reʿ, much as the name Amon had become Amon-reʿ. So a monotheism of the solar god was already developing, according to some scholars. Amenhotep is still named *ỉmn-ḥtpw* and portrayed as worshiping Amon in his fifth regnal year, but in the sixth

Colossi of Memnon built by Amenhotep III *ca.* 1400 B.C. that guard the entrance to his funerary temple at Thebes. Their size is indicated by the six-foot man beside the left colossus (W. S. LaSor)

Some of the sphinxes that once lined the avenue from Luxor to Karnak (W. S. LaSor)

year he broke with the Amon religion and took the name Akhenaten, "serviceable to Aten." He removed his capital from Thebes, the center of Amon worship, to el-Amarna, about halfway between Memphis and Thebes. This location, a plain on the east bank of the Nile about 13 by 5 km. (8 by 3 mi.), was hastily developed into the seat of government. The excavations, begun by Petrie in 1891 and continuing with some interruptions until 1937, show haste in the shoddy workmanship. The new capital was called Akhetaten, "horizon of Aten." Akhenaten introduced the Amarna age in art, of which the principal characteristic is the rejection of the stylized form that had dominated Egyptian art from early dynastic times in favor of an informal realism. One of the best-known products of his time is the beautiful head of his queen, Nefernefruaten-Nefertiti, now in West Berlin. His "Hymn to Aten" (*ANET,* pp. 369-371) has often been compared to Ps. 104.

The AMARNA TABLETS, discovered in 1887, are addressed to two (or three) Egyptian kings (among other addressees): to Nibmuaria or Nimmuria, which probably approximates the pronunciation of the prenomen of Nebmaʿreʿ Amenhotep III; and to Napḫururia or Napḫururia or Napḫuriria, i.e., Neferheprureʿ Amenhotep IV (Akhenaten). In Am.Tab. 28 and 29, Tushratta king of Mitanni makes reference to "Taduḫepa my daughter your wife," which has led some scholars to conclude that Amenhotep IV had taken over the marriage-alliance wife of his father.

The daughter of Akhenaten married Smenkhkareʿ, and he succeeded Akhenaten on the throne. He appears to have been the first to reject the Aten heresy. After three years he was succeeded by Tutankhaten, who must have been about ten years of age at the time. Whether one so young could have managed the restoration of Amon worship and of Amon monuments at Thebes unless he was being manipulated by the Amon priesthood is debatable. He did not abandon Tell el-Amarna, but he did change his name to Tutankhamen, and was buried, as had been all the kings of the dynasty before Akhenaten, at the Valley of the Kings. His tomb, discovered by H. Carter in 1922, yielded fabulous wealth, although he reigned only eight years and was about eighteen when he was embalmed for mummification.

Prior to the 19th and 20th Dynasties (*ca.* 1320-1085 B.C.), Ay reigned for five years, and then Haremhab took control. The connection of Ay with the preceding dynasty is not clear. Haremhab was a soldier with no recorded genealogy, hence in all likelihood a commoner. The Amarna Letters show that there was considerable turmoil in the Syro-Palestine areas once controlled by Egypt, and

Head of Nefertiti, queen of Amenhotep IV (Staatliche Museen Preussischer Kulturbesitz, Egyptian Museum, Berlin [West]; picture W. S. LaSor)

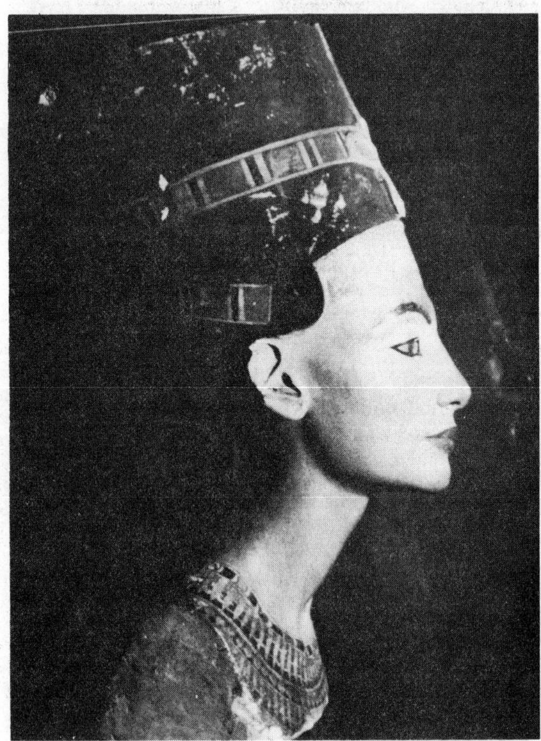

the Amarna revolution had not added to Egyptian stability, much less taken care of the Palestine situation. The time called for a strong man, and Haremhab seems to have filled the need. In addition to his military deeds, he also found time for building. The magnificent Hypostyle Hall at Karnak was planned and begun by him, and some attribute to him also the avenue of the ram-headed sphinxes. Perhaps his most valuable contribution to Egyptian history, however, was the appointing of a certain Peraʿmesse to the office of vizier. Peraʿmesse dropped the definite article (*p-*) and called himself Ramses (Raʿmesse) when he ascended the throne after Haremhab had reigned for about thirty years. Ramses I was then an old man, and he instituted the 19th Dynasty with a reign of but a little more than a year.

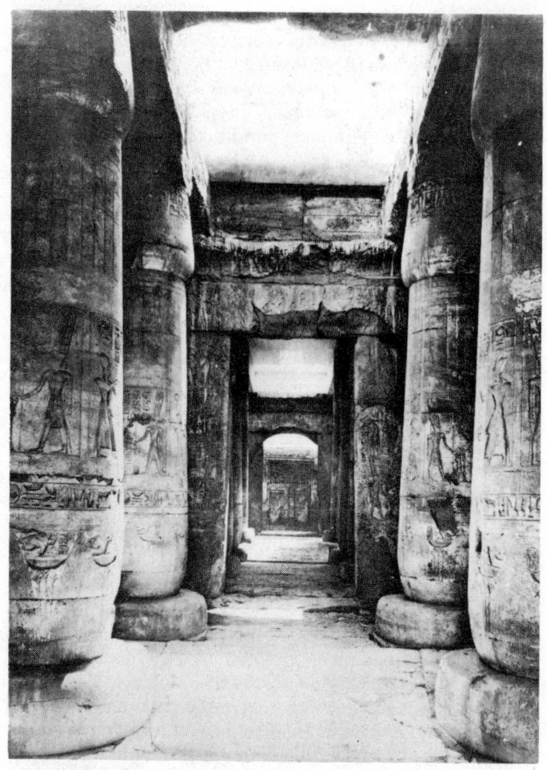

Hypostyle Hall at Abydos, completed by Ramses II (Oriental Institute, University of Chicago)

Seti I (*ca.* 1317-1304 B.C.) was a strong king who was fated to stand in the shadow of his son. In his first year he invaded Palestine and Syria, and restored a measure of Egyptian control. Two inscriptions of his have been found at Beisan (Beth-shean) in the Jordan Valley S of the Sea of Galilee. He built a magnificent temple at Abydos and continued the building of the Hypostyle Hall at Karnak. During the closing years of his reign his son Ramses II was co-regent.

Ramses II (*ca.* 1304-1227 B.C.) had a long and splendid reign. He waged wars with the Nubians, the Libyans, the Syrians, and the Hittites. In his fourth year he erected a stele at Nahr el-Kelb (Dog River) N of Beirut. In the fifth year he engaged the Hittites at Qadesh, which had been taken by Seti I and retaken by the Hittites. From a comparison of Hittite and Egyptian accounts, it would appear that Ramses barely escaped losing his entire army and his life (cf. J. H. Breasted, *Battle of Kadesh* [1903]). In his twenty-first year he made a treaty with Ḫattusilis of the Hittites and concluded it with a marriage alliance. The treaty is inscribed in hieroglyphs on the walls of the temple of Amon at Karnak and was found at Boghazköy written on clay tablets in Hittite cuneiform (cf. *ANET*, pp. 199-203). One of the greatest builders in history, Ramses II completed the Hypostyle Hall at Karnak, built the Ramesseum, and left colossal statues of himself in many places from Abu Simbel (near the Second Cataract) to Tanis in the eastern Delta. In order to strengthen the Delta frontier he built a capital at Pi-Raʿmesse, probably the biblical Raamses (Ex. 1:11; *see* RAMESES), most likely on the site of the Hyksos Avaris. According to some scholars Avaris was Egyptian Djaʿne, Greek Tanis, Hebrew Zoan, but others on the basis of later excavations would locate Pi-Raʿmesse at Qanṭîr, 17 km. (11 mi.) further south.

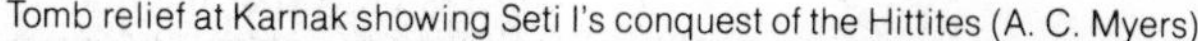

Tomb relief at Karnak showing Seti I's conquest of the Hittites (A. C. Myers)

Statue of Ramses II at Karnak (W. S. LaSor)

Ramses II also produced a great progeny. Starting early with the gift of a harem from his father when he was only twelve, he managed to record the names of over one hundred sons and daughters of royal line — which probably does not include those who were commoners.

Ramses II was succeeded by his thirteenth son MERNEPTAH (*ca.* 1227-1217 B.C.), who was probably well advanced in years. The most noteworthy datum from his reign is his stele on which the name Israel occurs for the first time in history. In Merneptah's day the great movement of peoples was taking place which, among other effects, would push the Hittites out of Anatolia and would bring the sea-peoples to Egypt and the coast of Palestine. Merneptah's reign was probably weak, and it was followed by a succession of weak kings. *See* Plate 26.

The 20th Dynasty (*ca.* 1200-1085 B.C.) was inaugurated by Sethnakht, of whom we know little. He appears to have had a short reign (possibly 1200-1198 B.C.) during which he brought some stability to the Delta. His son, who was obviously impressed with Ramses II (but in no way related to him), took parts of the prenomen and nomen of Ramses II for his own names. He is known to history as Ramses III. His successors were all named Ramses (IV to XI), and this is known as the Ramesside era. Ramses III was the only great king of the dynasty. He repulsed an attempt of the sea-peoples to land in the Delta, with the result that many of them landed along the coast of Palestine, including the Pelest (Philistines) and the Tjekker who located at Dor. From the 20th Dynasty we have a great quantity of written material, including the most magnificent of state archives, Papyrus Harris No. 1, which is 41 m. (133 ft.) long by 42 cm. (16½ in.) high and contains 117 columns of hieratic writing. Also from this period comes the delightful story of the journey of Wen-Amon to Phoenicia (*ANET,* pp. 25-29).

H. The Hebrews in Egypt. By any system of reckoning we must place the Israelites in Egypt for some portion of the New Kingdom (Empire) period. The two most widely held theories of the date of the Exodus would place the Exodus either in the time of Thutmose III (specifically 1446 B.C.) or in the time of Ramses II (approximately 1290 B.C.). This is discussed at length elsewhere (*see* EXODUS, DATE OF THE). From our survey of Egyptian geography and history in this article at least two points stand out. (1) The Israelites were almost certainly in the eastern Delta, within a short journey from Yam Suph (translated "Red Sea" but more likely the Bitter Lakes). There is no other part of Egypt that allows, geographically, for the Exodus as it is described, in no little detail, in the book of Exodus. (2) The Egyptian ruler almost certainly was located somewhere near the Hebrews, for only in such a location could the baby Moses have been placed in the reed vessel where Pharaoh's daughter came to bathe, and only in such a location could the man Moses have made frequent journeys to plead his case with the ruler. A Theban dynasty is out of the question, unless it can be demonstrated that the king had a palace in the Delta. The mention of the store-cities of Pithom (Pi-Atom or Pr-Atom) and Raamses (Pr-Raʿmesse) in Exodus seems further to limit the time to a period of such building operations.

I. Late Dynastic Period (*ca.* 1085-332 B.C.). The great days of ancient Egypt were now in the past, and a period of decline, not unbroken, had set in. Yet for biblical study this period is of considerable importance, for in it we have the first definite interconnections with the OT.

The 21st Dynasty (*ca.* 1085-945 B.C.) was located at Tanis, while at the same time descendants of Herihor were a priestly ruling caste at Thebes. Records are scanty, but it is clear that internal instability made it impossible for Egypt to control Palestine. About this time, the monarchy in Israel was established by Saul. The 22nd Dynasty (*ca.* 945-730 B.C.) was located at Bubastis, near the entrance to Wâdī Ṭumilât, also in the eastern Delta. Sheshonq (Shoshenq, Shishak of 1 K. 11:40) married into the pharaonic house at Tanis, thus establishing peaceably a Libyan dynasty. He managed to install his son as high priest at Thebes and brought Upper Egypt under control, and then he set about regaining control of Palestine (cf. 1 K. 14:25), erecting a stele at Megiddo (*ANEP,* p. 118 figure 349). Osorkon I sent Zerah, described in 2 Ch. 14:9 as "the Ethiopian," to Israel with a large army. Asa of Judah (910-870 B.C.) defeated him at Mareshah. The following kings of the dynasty were apparently weak, for a rival dynasty, the 23rd (*ca.* 817-730 B.C.), was established at Tanis according to Manetho, but more likely at Thebes in Upper Egypt.

Temple of Ramses III at Medinet Habu (Oriental Institute, University of Chicago)

When David had invaded Edom, Joab "slew every male in Edom," but the royal child Hadad was taken to Egypt for safety (1 K. 11:14-21). Hadad married the sister of Pharaoh, and later became an adversary against Solomon. In an attempt to develop peaceful relations with Egypt, Solomon entered into a marriage alliance with Pharaoh's daughter (1 K. 3:1), and had received "Gezer" (probably to be read Gerar) as a dowry (1 K. 9:16). But it is obvious that Egypt was not a trusted friend of Israel, for when Jeroboam appeared as a potential threat to Solomon's kingdom, he was given asylum in Egypt (1 K. 11:40; 12:2). Osorkon II appears to have had an alliance with the northern kingdom in the days of Omri or Ahab. When Rezin of Syria and Pekah of Israel besieged Ahaz in Jerusalem, the Edomites used the occasion to "recover" Elath for Edom (2 K. 16:5f.). And in the closing days of Israel, Hoshea turned to the Egyptian king So for help (2 K. 17:4), suggesting that an Edomite-Israelite-Egyptian alliance against Judah had continued throughout the period of the divided kingdom.

About 730 B.C., just before the fall of Samaria, two new dynasties appeared in Egypt. The 24th Dynasty, located at Sais in the western Delta, was short-lived (*ca.* 730-715 B.C.). The 25th Dynasty (*ca.* 730-656 B.C.) was foreign (Cushite or Ethiopian), with its capital at Napata near the Fourth Cataract. The Nubians had been a growing threat to Egypt since at least the days of Ramses II, and now the warrior Piankhy, son of the king Kashta, subdued Tafnekht the Saite pharaoh to "protect" Thebes, and returned to Napata. Piankhy was succeeded by his brother Shabaka (Sabacon), who proceeded to bring all Egypt under his rule (*ca.* 715 or 711 B.C.). A new power had arisen in the east, namely, Assyria under Tiglath-pileser III (745-727 B.C.). The Assyrian king had, according to his own claim (*ANET,* p. 284; *ARAB,* I, § 816), set Hoshea over Israel, and the biblical record confirms that Hoshea had been a tributary of Assyria (2 K. 17:3). It is probable that Hoshea's revolt against Assyria occurred soon after Tiglath-pileser died (cf. 2 K. 17:4), hence *ca.* 726 or 725. The identity of "So" has not been established, but obviously he cannot have been Shabaka; one suggestion is Osorkon IV, last king of the 23rd Dynasty, and another (by S. Yeivin) is that the Hebrew *sô'* is a transcription of Egyptian *ṯ3*, "vizier," hence 2 K. 17:4 would read, "to the vizier of the king of Egypt" (*VT,* 2 [1952], 164-68).

Shabaka was succeeded by Shabataka (Shebiktu), a son of Piankhy, perhaps about the time that Sennacherib was marching against the coastal cities of Judah (701 B.C.). According to 2 K. 19:9, Tirhakah "king of Ethiopia" set out to engage the Assyrian army, but Tirhakah (Taharqa) did not become king until 689 B.C., according to Apis inscriptions. Several attempts have been made to resolve this problem, including the theory that Sennacherib actually made two attempts on Jerusalem. Scholarly opinion at this writing seems to favor the suggestion that Tirhakah was commander of the forces of his brother Shabataka. Sennacherib reported that Hezekiah king of Judah had appealed to the king of Egypt for help (*ANET,* p. 287; *ARAB,* II, § 240). (On the problem of Sennacherib's campaigns in Palestine, see *BHI* [2nd ed. 1972], 296-308, and references therein.) Tirhakah as king was defeated twice more in battles with Assyria, the first time (671 B.C.) by Esarhaddon, who made a punitive raid into Egypt and besieged Memphis, and the second (666 B.C.) by Ashurbanipal, who succeeded Esarhaddon in 669 B.C. Tiring of Egypt's attitude, Ashurbanipal launched a bitter attack against Ta-net-Amon (Urdamane), who had succeeded Tirhakah, and sacked Thebes in 664 B.C. (cf. Nah. 3:8-10). Neco was installed as governor in Sais. Ta-net-Amon continued to claim the kingship, but ultimately retired to Napata, the last of the Ethiopian dynasty.

Psamtik I (Psammetichus) appears to be the real founder of the 26th Dynasty, located at Sais in the western Delta. As Gardiner observes, "the history of Egypt now becomes increasingly merged into that of the Middle East and of Greece, and our main authorities besides Herodotus are the cuneiform chronicles, the Jewish historian Josephus and the Old Testament" (*Egypt of the Pharaohs,* p. 355). Psamtik reigned fifty-four years, according to an Apis stele, and was succeeded by his son Neco II in 610 B.C. Nineveh had fallen in 612 B.C. and a government-in-exile had been formed by Aššur-uballiṭ at Ḫarran. Neco, for reasons unclear, but possibly because there was a link between his dynasty and the Assyrians, went to the aid of the Assyrians (this seems to be the best translation of the preposition *'al* in 2 K. 23:29). Josiah of Judah attempted to stop the Egyptians and was killed in the battle at Megiddo (609 B.C.). The Egyptians defeated the Babylonians at Quramati, near Carchemish, but in 605 B.C. Nabopolassar mounted a great battle at Carchemish led by his son Nebuchadrezzar. On the death of Nabopolassar that same year, Nebuchadrezzar became king of the young Babylonian empire, and proceeded to conquer all of "Khatti," the name for Syria and Palestine (cf. *ANET,* p. 307; *CCK,* pp. 25,69).

In 601 B.C. Nebuchadrezzar marched against Egypt and was met by Neco, who drove him back. Both armies suffered heavy losses, and Nebuchadrezzar did not again attempt a campaign against Egypt (cf. *CCK,* pp. 29, 71). It was possibly this Babylonian setback that caused Jehoiakim to revolt against Babylon and turn to Egypt (2 K. 24:1), in spite of Jeremiah's warning (Jer. 46:14-24).

Psamtik II (595-589 B.C.) succeeded Neco, and was in turn succeeded by Apries (Uaphris, Hophra of Jer. 44:30). When Jerusalem had revolted against Babylonia in 597 B.C., the Egyptian king did not become involved, but Apries followed a different course. Zedekiah of Jerusalem had revolted in 589 B.C., and had turned to Egypt for support (Ezk. 17:15), which Hophra apparently was willing to give (cf. Jer. 37:5). The relief for Jerusalem was only the calm before the storm, for Nebuchadrezzar sacked the city in 586 B.C. Meanwhile Apries turned his attention to Cyrene on the Libyan coast and was soundly defeated. Amasis (Ahmose II, 570-526 B.C.) succeeded him, and was a man of peace (Herodotus called him "Philhellene," ii.178).

Cyrus the Mede defeated the Babylonian empire in 539 B.C., and recognized that Egypt must be brought under control. It was Cambyses, however, who defeated Psamtik III in the Battle of Pelusium (525 B.C.), and who is listed by Manetho as the first of the 27th Dynasty consisting of "eight Persian kings" (525-404 B.C.). After the Greek defeat of the Persians at Marathon, Egypt attempted to revolt, and Xerxes, who had succeeded Darius, put down the revolt and "reduced all Egypt to slavery" (Herodotus vii.7). According to the Persian system of ruling conquered peoples, Egypt was a satrapy, ruled by a local governor. From the Jewish colony at Elephantine we have numerous Aramaic papyri which provide details of local administration. We also know that the temple at Elephantine was destroyed and that the Jews appealed to Bagoas, governor of Judah, for aid in rebuilding it. Herodotus the "father of history" toured Egypt *ca.* 450 B.C.

In 404 B.C. Amyrtaeus of Sais became the sole king of Manetho's 28th Dynasty. The 29th and 30th Dynasties consist of four and three kings, respectively. To Manetho's original thirty dynasties, a thirty-first has been added by a later record preserved in Eusebius's text; it consisted of three Persian kings, Artaxerxes III Ochus, Arses, and Darius III. Alexander the Great entered Egypt in 332 B.C. and proceeded to Memphis, where he made a sacrifice to Apis and was proclaimed pharaoh. Then he laid out the site of the future city of Alexandria, and went to the oasis at Siwah where he consulted the oracle of Amon. According to some writers, Alexander conceived the idea of his own divinity at this time.

There is little else to add to the history of ancient Egypt. Upon the death of Alexander, Egypt passed to Ptolemy I Soter, son of Lagos and one of the Diadochoi in Alexander's campaigns. He organized Egypt and established the line of rulers each named Ptolemy (I-XVI). Palestine was under the Ptolemies until *ca.* 198 B.C., when it was taken by the Seleucid Antiochus III. The famous (or infamous) Cleopatra had ruled as queen with Ptolemy XIV, and her son from the union with Caesar ruled as Ptolemy XVI Caesarion (45-44 B.C.). When Cleopatra committed suicide in 30 B.C., Egypt came under Roman rule.

IX. Egypt and the Bible.–From this survey it may appear at first glance that Egyptian history, literature, or religion has little of value for the biblical student. If we are looking for close relationships, such as may be found between Ugaritic and the Bible or Assyrian and Babylonian and the Bible, we shall be disappointed. After all, the origins of the patriarchal line were in Mesopotamia, the closest contacts of the Israelites were with the Canaanites, and the exile was in Babylonia. Joseph and his brothers moved to Egypt and the Israelites lived there for a long period of time, but they were isolated from the Egyptians both by geography and by the Egyptian antipathy to foreigners. Nevertheless, a survey of Egypt is valuable to the student of the Bible for several reasons.

For one, Egypt was the custodian of young Israel when it was only a band of seminomadic tribes. If the Israelite people did not learn how to organize as a nation while living in Egypt, it certainly appears that Moses had learned something of the necessary elements of national leadership. Israelite law and historiography seem to be influenced more by Mesopotamia, for these genres are found in the literary remains of Mesopotamia to a greater extent than in Egypt. But the Egyptian contributions of story telling, of wisdom, and perhaps even of medicine, seem to have had some influence on Israel. The skilled workmanship required for building the tabernacle in the wilderness probably had Egyptian roots. It has been pointed out many times that the Joseph cycle (Gen. 37–50) and the book of Exodus show marked familiarity with Egypt and Egyptian customs. Much more can be learned by carefully controlled study of this Egyptian background.

During the days when Israel was just getting settled in the land of the Canaanites, Palestine was to a greater or lesser extent under Egyptian influence. It is true that Palestine was often the scene of battles between nations that came from beyond the northern and southern boundaries, but it is also true that Palestine enjoyed periods of peace and opportunities for development when Egyptian power was strong enough to maintain peace, or when there was a power vacuum in that part of the world. Once again, carefully controlled study of the historical situation, including the part Egypt played, can be of value to the student of the Bible.

Egypt was a place of refuge. Jews fled to Egypt when Assyria and Babylonia were waging war on Judah and Jerusalem. Jewish colonies were founded in Egypt, one at Elephantine, as we know from the Elephantine Aramaic papyri of the 5th cent., and another at Alexandria, as we know from the production of the OT in Greek (the Septuagint). The prophet Jeremiah was taken to Egypt toward the close of his life, and some of his prophecy has close relationship with Egypt. The baby Jesus was taken to Egypt to escape the bloody action of Herod. Perhaps we should look for further implications of these facts.

The study of the religion of Egypt is reserved for the article RELIGIONS OF THE BIBLICAL WORLD: EGYPT. Here only one fact may be mentioned: something approaching a monotheism was in the process of development in Egypt at about the same time that the Israelites were in Egypt. This is not to suggest that Israelite monotheism was fashioned in Egypt, or that Moses got his ideas from Akhenaten. But it is a fact of human nature, as well as of history, that the times influence all of us. In a philosophical age people are more likely to talk and think about philosophical subjects, whereas in a materialistic age, such as the present day, we have time only for materialistic subjects. In the providence of God, the Hebrew people were placed in Egypt for "four hundred years" prior to the revelations of Sinai and the conflicts of the prophets of Yahweh with the Canaanite religious concepts. Was there a divine plan in this? To deny it would seem to be a denial of God's wisdom. To admit it lays a burden on the biblical student to devote more study to the religious ideas as well as the other contributions of Egypt.

Bibliography.–*People and Culture:* C. Aldred, *Development of Egyptian Art* (3 vols., 1952); *Egyptians* (1961); E. J. Baumgartel, *Cultures of Prehistoric Egypt* (rev. ed. 1955); J. Černý, *Ancient Egyptian Religion* (1952); C. Desroches-Noblecourt, *Le Style égyptien* (1946); E. Drioton, *La Religion égyptienne* (1955); E. Drioton and J. Vandier, *Les Peuples de l'orient meditérranéen, II: L'Égypte* (3rd ed. 1952); I. E. S. Edwards, *Pyramids of Egypt* (2nd ed. 1961); *Enc.Brit.* (1970), VIII, *s.v.* "Egypt," "Egyptian Architecture," "Egyptian Language," and bibliographies; A. Erman, *Handbook of Egyptian Religion* (1907); A. Fakhry, *Pyramids* (1961); H. Frankfort, *et al.*, *Intellectual Adventure of Ancient Man* (1946); J.-P. Lauer, *Sakkarah: The Monuments of Zoser* (2nd ed. 1951); A. Lucas, *Ancient Egyptian Materials and Industries* (3rd ed. 1948); P. Montet, *Everyday Life in Egypt in the Days of Ramses the Great* (Eng. tr. 1958); *Les Scènes de la vie privée dans les tombeaus égyptiens de l'ancien empire* (1925); J. D. S. Pendlebury, *Tell el-Amarna* (1935); B. Porter and R. L. B. Moss, *Topographical Bibliography of Ancient Hieroglyphic Texts, Reliefs, and Paintings* (7 vols., 1927-1951); G. Posener, *Littérature et politique dans l'Égypte de la XII dynastie* (1956); G. Posener, *et al.*, *Dictionary of Egyptian Civilization* (1961); H. Schäfer, *Die Kunst Ägyptens* (3rd ed. 1925); W. S. Smith, *Art and Architecture of Ancient Egypt* (1958); N. F. Wheeler, *Antiquity*, 9 (1935), 5-21, 161-189, 292-304; H. E. Winlock, *Models of Daily Life in Ancient Egypt* (1955); I. Woldering, *Art of Egypt* (1963).

Language and Literature: ANET; W. F. Edgerton and J. A. Wilson, *Historical Records of Ramses III* (1936); A. Erman, *Literature of the Ancient Egyptians* (Eng. tr. 1927); A. Erman and H. Grapow, *Wörterbuch der ägyptischen Sprache* (6 vols., 1926-1950); A. H. Gardiner, *Egyptian Grammar* (3rd ed. 1957); *Kadesh Inscriptions of Ramesses II* (1960); C. D. Leake, *Old Egyptian Medical Papyri* (1952); G. Lefebvre, *Grammaire de l'égyptien classique* (2nd ed. 1955); *Romans et contes égyptiens de l'époque pharaonique* (1949); S. A. B. Mercer, *Pyramid Texts in Translation and Commentary* (4 vols., 1952); T. E. Peet, *Comparative Study of the Literatures of Egypt, Palestine, and Mesopotamia* (1931); H. D. Schaedel, *Die Listen des grossen Papyrus Harris* (1936); T. W. Thacker, *Relationship of the Semitic and Egyptian Verbal Systems* (1954).

Calendar and Chronology: R. W. Ehrich, ed., *Chronologies in Old World Archaeology* (1965); O Neugebauer, *Acta Orientalia*, 17 (1938); *JNES*, 1 (1942), 396-403; R. A. Parker, *Calendars of Ancient Egypt* (1950); *JNES*, 16 (1957), 39-43; H. S. Smith, *Antiquity*, 38 (1964), 32-37; P. van der Meer, *Chronology of Ancient Western Asia and Egypt* (1955); W. Wolf, *Die Welt der Ägypter* (1955).

History: J. H. Breasted, *Ancient Records of Egypt* (5 vols., 1906-1907); *Battle of Kadesh* (1903); *History of Egypt* (2nd ed. 1919); *CAH* (3rd ed.), I/1 (1970), 5-9, 62-74. 106-114, 132-38, 173-193, 463-498; I/2 (1971), 1-70, 145-207, 464-531; II/1 (1973), 42-76, 289-416, 526-555, bibliography; W. R. Dawson, *Who Was Who in*

Egyptology (1951); W. B. Emery, *Archaic Egypt* (1961); R. M. Engberg, *The Hyksos Reconsidered* (1939); A. Erman and H. Ranke, *La Civilisation égyptienne* (Fr. tr. 1952); H. Frankfort, *Kingship and the Gods* (1948), pp. 19ff.; A. H. Gardiner, *Egypt of the Pharaohs* (1961); *Royal Canon of Turin* (1959); H. R. Hall, *Ancient History of the Near East* (11th ed. 1950); W. C. Hayes, *Most Ancient Egypt* (1965); *Scepter of Egypt* (2 vols., 1953, 1959); Herodotus ii; W. Hölscher, *Libyer und Ägypter* (1937); P. Labib, *Die Herrschaft der Hyksos in Ägypten und ihr Sturz* (1937); E. Meyer, *Geschichte des Altertums* I-III (1925-1937); P. Montet, *Eternal Egypt* (Eng. tr. 1965); D. B. Redford, *Orientalia*, 39 (1970), 1-51; T. Säve-Söderbergh, *Ägypten und Nubien* (1941); *JEA*, 37 (1951), 53-71; A. Scharff and A. Moortgat, *Ägypten und Vorderasien im Altertum* (1950); G. Steindorff, ed., *Urkunden des ägyptischen Altertums* (1903-); G. Steindorff and K. C. Seele, *When Egypt Ruled the East* (2nd ed. 1957); H. Stock, *Studien zur Geschichte und Archäologie der 13. bis 17. Dynastie Ägyptens* (1942); J. Van Seters, *The Hyksos: A New Investigation* (1966); J. Vandier, *La Famine dans l'Égypte ancienne* (1936); W. G. Waddell, *Manetho* (Eng. tr. 1940); J. Wilson, *Burden of Egypt* (1951); H. E. Winlock, *Rise and Fall of the Middle Kingdom in Thebes* (1947); Y. Yadin, *IEJ*, 5 (1955), 1ff.; *see also* ARCHEOLOGY OF EGYPT, Bibliography.

Egypt and the Bible: K. A. Kitchen, *Joseph Narrative and Its Egyptian Background* (1962); P. Montet, *Egypt and the Bible* (Eng. tr. 1968); T. E. Peet, *Egypt and the Old Testament* (1922); J. Vergote, *Joseph en Égypte* (1959).

W. S. LASOR

EGYPT, ARCHEOLOGY OF. *See* ARCHEOLOGY OF EGYPT.

EGYPT, BROOK (RIVER, STREAM) OF. *See* BROOK OF EGYPT.

EGYPTIAN, THE [Gk. *ho Aigýptios*]. Mentioned in Acts 21:38 by Claudius Lysias as having "recently stirred up a revolt and led the four thousand men of the Assassins out into the wilderness." Reference to this Egyptian and to the suppression of his rebellion by the procurator Felix is likewise found in Josephus (*Ant.* xx.8.6; *BJ* ii.13.5).

See ASSASSINS.

EGYPTIAN VERSIONS. *See* VERSIONS.

EGYPTIANS, GOSPEL ACCORDING TO THE. *See* APOCRYPHAL GOSPELS V.E.

EHI ē'hī [Heb. *'ēḥî*] (Gen. 46:21). Apparently a contracted form of AHIRAM.

EHUD ē'hud [Heb. *'ēhûḏ*–'united,' 'strong'].

1. A left-handed Benjaminite, son of Gera, deliverer of Israel from oppression by Moab (Jgs. 3:15-30; 1 Ch. 8:6). Having gained a private interview with King EGLON under pretense of a secret errand connected with the payment of Israel's tribute, Ehud drew the sword he had concealed on his right side and thrust it through the king. After making his escape he gathered the Israelite forces and overcame Moab at the fords of the Jordan, slaying some ten thousand.

2. The son of Bilhan and great-grandson of Benjamin in 1 Ch. 7:10. Some scholars have supposed that the inclusion of a Benjaminite name in a chapter dealing partly with Zebulunite genealogy rests on the erroneous substitution of Benjamin for Zebulun in 1 Ch. 7:6. While some of the descendants of Benjamin appear under different names in genealogical records, there is no evidence that the name "Ehud" was ever restricted to that one tribe.

F. K. FARR
R. K. H.

EITHER. Sometimes used in the AV in the now uncommon sense of "or" (Lk. 6:42; 15:8; Phil. 3:12; Jas. 3:12).

EKER ē'kər [Heb. *'ēqer*–'root']. A Jerahmeelite (1 Ch. 2:27).

EKREBEL ek'rə-bel. *See* ACRABA.

EKRON ek'ron; **EKRONITE** ek'rən-īt [Heb. *'eqrôn*–perhaps 'deep-rooted' (cf. Zeph. 2:4); Akk. *Amqarruna*; Gk. *Akkarōn*]. One of the five cities ruled by a Philistine "tyrant" (Josh. 13:3; 1 S. 6:17). The ancient Hebrew name may be preserved by the modern Arabic village name *'Âqir*, which means "barren, childless, sterile."

Its territorial boundary marked the northern extension of the coastal area not taken on the Israelites' initial invasion of the land (Josh. 13:3); cf. LXX Jgs. 1:18, "Judah took not . . . Ekron with its territory," a rendering proved by the further statement in v.19b that Judah "could not drive out the inhabitants of the plain, because they had chariots of iron." In the tribal allotments Ekron was assigned to the Danites (Josh. 19:43), but they failed to break out of the hill country (Jgs. 1:34), leaving their coastal territory to be absorbed by Judah (Josh. 15:45f.). Thus, the border of Judah passed along the ridge to the north of Ekron (Josh. 15:11).

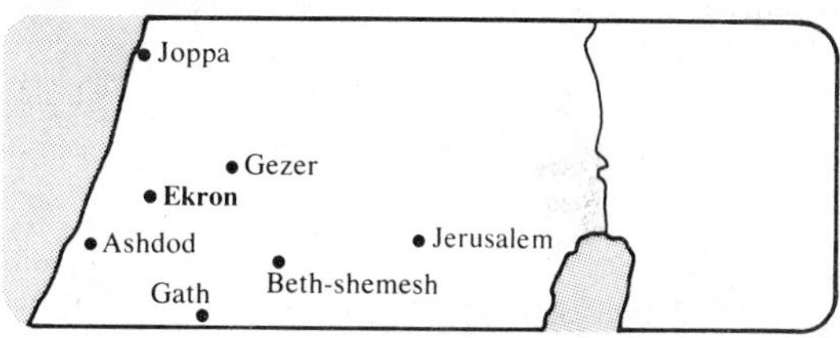

As one of the two Philistine cities facing the Judean Shephelah (see below), Ekron played an important role in the conflicts between the two peoples. Ekron was the last place to which the captured ark of the covenant was brought before its return to Israel (1 S. 5:10–6:16); the narrative indicates a certain topographical connection with Beth-shemesh (6:16). Later, led by the prophet Samuel, the Israelites regained control of the towns formerly lost to Ekron (7:14). Finally, the Philistines who retreated from the Vale of Elah ran toward Gath and toward Ekron (17:52).

During the prophet Elijah's ministry the deity of Ekron was known as Baal-zebub, of whom the stricken Ahaziah of Israel sought to inquire concerning his chances of recovery (2 K. 1:2-16). Toward the end of the 8th cent. B.C. the prophet Amos included Ekron in his imprecation against the land of the Philistines (Am. 1:8).

In 712 B.C. Sargon II of Assyria conquered Ekron; previously Ekron may have come under Assyrian domination when Tiglath-pileser III passed through Philistia in his campaign of 734. Furthermore, Sargon II had made invasions in 720 and 716; but Ekron is not specifically mentioned until 712 when it fell to Sargon's troops along with Gath, Gibbethon, and Ashdod.

A few years later Padi king of Ekron remained loyal to the Assyrians even though Sargon had died and his successor Sennacherib faced rebellion throughout the empire. The aristocrats of Ekron, however, had succumbed to the blandishments of Hezekiah king of Judah and chose to revolt againt their Assyrian overlords. To succeed they had to depose Padi, handing him over to Hezekiah to be held as a political prisoner in Jerusalem. All of this was part of the combined effort of several Palestinian states to free themselves from Assyrian oppression; but in 701 Sennacherib led his army into Palestine for a showdown. After securing Joppa and the surrounding hinterland, he met the Egyptian forces rushing to aid the conspirators at Ekron. The Assyrians severely defeated the Egyptians in the plain near Eltekeh, thus opening the way to subdue Ekron. After Eltekeh itself was taken, Sennacherib severed Ekron from its Judean allies by the conquest of Timnah. Ekron was now isolated from both the east and the west, and the expected Egyptian help from the south was crushed. Sennacherib ordered a full-scale assault on the hapless Ekron, and it quickly succumbed. The leading officials and nobility who had fomented the revolt were impaled on stakes outside the city. Common citizens who had supported the rebellion were taken into captivity, but the rest of the population was set free. During the ensuing conflict with Judah, Hezekiah agreed to release Padi, who was restored to his throne in Ekron by Sennacherib. Some of the territories taken from Judah were given to Padi as a reward for his loyalty.

The king of Ekron during the 7th cent. B.C. was a certain Ikausu (or Ikašamsu), whom Esarhaddon called to Nineveh for corvée service with other Levantine rulers (*ANET,* p. 291). When Ashurbanipal (669-633 B.C.) passed through Palestine on his way to Egypt (663 B.C.) the same king paid tribute to the Assyrian monarch (*ANET,* p. 294). During the reign of Josiah, Zephaniah prophesied that Ekron and other peoples of Philistia would be removed from their lands (Zeph. 2:4; cf. Jer. 25:20; Am. 1:8; Zec. 9:5,7). Ekron's actual fate during the Babylonian conquest of Palestine and the subsequent transfer to Persian hands is not known. Not until the Hellenistic age is Ekron again mentioned by historical sources. After Jonathan Maccabeus had demonstrated his military prowess by the defeat of Demetrius (147 B.C.) and the subsequent conquest of Ashdod (Ashkelon came to terms with him), Alexander Balas rewarded him with "Ekron and all its environs [toparchy]" (1 Macc. 10:89; Josephus *Ant.* xiii.4.4).

J. Naveh's 1957 researches confirm that Ekron was located at Khirbet el-Muqennaʿ, a relatively low-standing tell just S of the Wâdī el-Majanne in a sort of depression surrounded by the rolling swells of the Philistine plain. In surface area, however, the fortified city covered about 16 ha. (40 acres), more than any other known Iron Age site. Numerous impressive architectural remains visible on the surface include an apparent gate area defended by a heavy stone glacis (on the southern side). The ceramic evidence ranged from some E.B. sherds through nearly all the Iron Age periods (including Persian material). Philistine ware was much in evidence; the lack of any from the M.B., the L.B., or the E.I. I periods suggests that the great city was founded by the Philistines on the ruins of an abandoned E.B. village. The ample water sources, namely, the springs just N of the tell in the wadi bed, were apparently a strong attraction for the Philistines, who were spreading their influence to the north and west.

A principal evidence for identifying Tell el-Muqennaʿ with Ekron is the boundary description of Judah (Josh. 15:10f.), which traces the line from Beth-shemesh (Tell er-Rumeileh) to Timnah (Tell Baṭâshī) and then to "the shoulder [ridge] of the hill north of Ekron." The next station on the line was Shikkeron (probably Tell el-Fûl), followed by Mt. Baalah (the el-Mughar hills) and Jabneel. If all these identifications be accepted, especially that of Ekron, then the stations along the border were spaced about 5-6½ km. (3-4 mi.) apart. Furthermore, a very prominent ridge of high ground separating the "basin" of Khirbet el-Muqennaʿ from the Sorek Valley and Tell el-Baṭâshī appears from the north as the most likely feature that could be described as "the shoulder north of Ekron."

The Philistines' flight toward Gath and Ekron from their defeat in the Vale of Elah favors the Tell el-Muqennaʿ identification. When the retreating Philistines debouched from the narrow defile created by the Wâdī ʿAjjûr as it

Assyrian guard with Israelite captives being deported from Ekron. Relief from Nineveh, 7th cent. B.C. (Louvre; picture W. S. LaSor)

passes between Khirbet ʿAṭrabā and Khirbet esh-Shāh, they had only to cross over the high ground by Mughallis and follow a branch of the Wâdī Majanne directly to Khirbet el-Muqennaʿ. In addition, Sennacherib's campaign (see above) is better explained by locating Ekron between Tell el-Baṭâshī on the east and Eltekeh further to the west.

Though remains of Jonathan's Hellenistic estate have not yet been found in the vicinity of Khirbet el-Muqennaʿ, the district of Ekron (called a toparchy by Josephus) was evidently taken from Ashdod (the regional capital since Persian, even Assyrian times), and the territory of Ashdod had been adjacent to that of Gezer (1 Macc. 14:34). Beyer therefore argued that the toparchy of Ekron must have been located between those of Ashdod and Gezer. Khirbet el-Muqennaʿ meets this requirement admirably.

Citizens of Ekron, called Ekronite(s) (Heb. *ʿeqrônî[m]*; Gk. *ʾAkkarōneítēs*), are mentioned in Josh. 13:3 and 1 S. 5:10.

Bibliography.–LBHG, pp. 248-250, 337-39; W. F. Albright, *AASOR,* 2f. (1923), 1-17; Z. Kallai (-Kleinmann), *VT,* 8 (1958), 134-160; J. Naveh, *IEJ,* 8 (1958), 87-100, 165-170; H. Tadmor, *BA,* 29 (1966), 86-102; G. E. Wright, *BA,* 29 (1966), 70-86.

A. F. RAINEY

EL. *See* GOD II.B; GOD, NAMES OF II.A.1.

EL ELYON el el-yōn′, ē-lī′ən. *See* GOD, NAMES OF II.B.2.

EL ROI el rō′ī (Gen. 16:13, NEB mg.). *See* GOD, NAMES OF II.B.4.

EL SHADDAI el shad′ī. *See* GOD, NAMES OF II.B.1.

ELA ē′lə [Heb. *ʾēlāʾ*; Gk. *Ēla*].

1. Father of Shimei (1 K. 4:18; AV, NEB, "Elah").

2. (AV, NEB, 1 Esd. 9:27). The same as Elam in Ezr. 10:26.

ELADAH el′ə-də. *See* ELEADAH.

ELAH ē′lə [Heb. *ʾēlâ*–'oak' or 'terebinth'].

1. A chief (head of a clan) of Edom (Gen. 36:41; 1 Ch. 1:52).

2. (AV, NEB, 1 K. 4:18). *See* ELA **1.**

3. A son of Caleb the son of Jephunneh (1 Ch. 4:15).

4. Father of Hoshea, the last king of Israel (2 K. 15:30; 17:1; 18:1, 9).

5. A Benjaminite, son of Uzzi, one of the chiefs of the tribes when the country was settled (1 Ch. 9:8).

6. Son of BAASHA, fourth king of Israel (1 K. 16:6-14). He reigned two years, 886-885 B.C. The statement that he came to the throne in the twenty-sixth year of Asa, reigned two years, and died in the twenty-seventh year of Asa, illustrates the Hebrew method of synchronizing the reigns of the kings of Israel and Judah (cf. 1 K. 15:33; 16:8). Elah appears to have been a debauchee. While he was drinking himself drunk in the house of Azra, his servant Zimri, one of his military leaders, conspired against him and murdered him. According to Josephus (*Ant.* viii.12.4) Zimri took advantage of the absence of the army, which was at Gibbethon, to kill Elah. The extirpation of the royal family followed the murder of the king. Baasha's dynasty had its origin in a murder and it ended in a murder.

S. K. MOSIMAN

ELAH, VALE OF [Heb. *ʿēmeq hāʾēlâ*–'valley of the terebinth'; Gk. B *hē koilás Ēla,* A *tḗs dryós*]. The scene of the events of 1 S. 17:2ff., referred to also in 1 S. 21:9. The location of this valley is established by reference to the towns in the former passage. Socoh is to be identified with the large Khirbet ʿAbâd, an Iron Age site beside the Byzantine Khirbet esh-Shuweikeh. This ancient ruin stands on the southern edge of Wâdī es-Sanṭ, a valley whose Arabic name apparently means "valley of the acacia." Azekah was the lofty Tell ez-Zakarîyeh, perched atop a prominent ridge of the Shephelah around the foot of which the Wâdī es-Sanṭ is forced to twist northward before continuing its flow westward to the sea.

During the military confrontation described in 1 S. 12 the Philistines encamped upon the southern side of the valley, between Socoh and Azekeh. The significance and possible location of Saul's forces are difficult to ascertain; they must have been ranged along the northern ridge somewhere between the village of Beit Nettif and the slope opposite Azekeh. The contest between David and Goliath evidently took place in the broad valley on the southern side of the creek bed (which clings to the foot of the northern ridge). The Philistine retreat probably took them around the bend below Azekeh and westward along the course of the valley (1 S. 17:52; cf. esp. LXX). This would take them in the direction of Ekron (Khirbet el-Muqennaʿ) and Gath (which strengthens its identification with Tell eṣ-Ṣâfī).

Bibliography.–G. Dalman, *PJ,* 5 (1909), 60; J. Naveh, *IEJ,* 8 (1958), 169.

A. F. RAINEY

The (dry) brook in the vale of Elah (W. S. LaSor)

ELAM ē'ləm [Heb. *ʿêlām*].

1. A son of Shem (Gen. 10:22; 1 Ch. 1:17); *see* ELAMITES.

2. A Benjaminite (1 Ch. 8:24).

3. A Korahite (1 Ch. 26:3).

4. Heads of families in the return from exile (Ezr. 2:7 par. Neh. 7:12; Ezr. 2:31 par. Neh. 7:34; Ezr. 8:7; 10:2, 26).

5. A chief of the people (Neh. 10:14).

6. A priest (Neh. 12:42).

ELAM; ELAMITES ē'lə-mīts [Heb. *ʿêlām*; Gk. *Ailam*]. A land and people E of the lower Tigris.

I. Name
II. The Land
III. History
IV. Writing and Language
V. Art
VI. Religion

I. Name.–The native name *ḫal-tamti* may mean "land of god." It is represented in Akkadian cuneiform texts by the Sumerogram NIM, "high land," and by *elamtu,* a normalized form of the Elamite word. The Hebrew with initial *ayin* may have come by way of Akkadian, where there is slight evidence for pronunciation of an initial guttural, or equally well directed from Elamite.

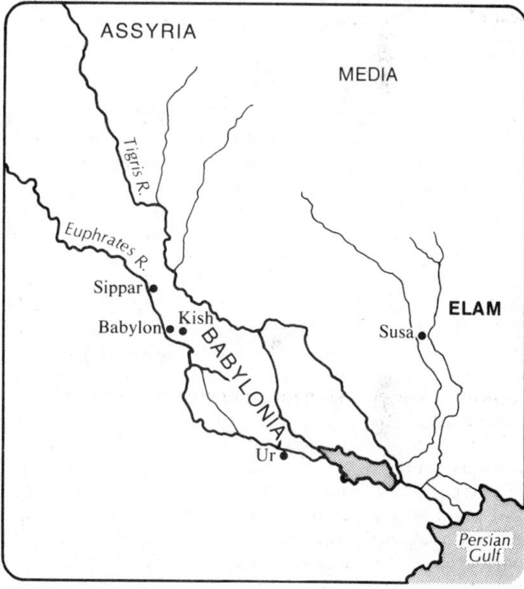

II. The Land.–Topographical reasons underlie the Sumerian designation "high land," for the country is partly hidden in the southern Zagros Mountains E of the Tigris. The center of Elam is the area known today as the plain of Khuzistan in southwestern Iran. To the north it is bounded by the mountains of Luristan, to the east by the Bakhtiari range; to the south the Ahwaz hills form a slight barrier, and the Pusht-i-Kuh lie to the northwest. Three major rivers, the Karkho, Diz, and Karun water this plain, the last two combining to continue to the Shatt al-Arab. Tracts of land beside the rivers are cultivated, and after the winter rain there is abundant pasture over the whole plain. The ancient capital city SUSA lay beside a branch of the Karkho, the Shaur, in the center of the most fertile area.

Elam extended N and E of the riverine territory into the hills and mountain valleys, making a broken land, hard to unify. The mainstay of Elamite prosperity lay in this mountainous country, for here were the sources of timber and metals which the cities of Babylonia lacked.

Thus Elam was naturally provided with valuable trading materials. Routes ran to each of the cardinal points: westward past the foot of the Pusht-i-Kuh to Babylon, either following the marshy Tigris or the frontier as far as Der (modern Badrah) then across to Babylon; northward up the Karkho toward the modern towns of Horramabad or Kermanshah on the Iranian plateau; eastward along the course of the Karun ascending the Bakhtiari Mountains into the plateau near Isfahan; southward to the Persian Gulf for sea voyages.

III. History.–It is apparent from the geography that Elam is really a part of lower Mesopotamia (whence, perhaps, its representation as a son of Shem in Gen. 10:22). The two districts have been very closely related since prehistoric times, and the story of Elam is one of incessant struggle between the two areas. Two major excavations supply most of our information, those at Susa (ancient Shushan) and at Choga Zambil (Dur-Untash). At an early period ideas flowed from Elam into Iraq (Susa A: Ubaid, *ca.* 4000 B.C.), whereas subsequently strong Mesopotamian influences are traceable in Elam, the most important being the concept of writing (see IV below). During the earliest historic periods Elamite culture shows indigenous development, but to this time (Susa D: Early Dynastic I) refer the earliest international incidents mentioned in later epics such as the story of "Enmerkar and the Lord of Aratta." A Sumerian notice records a raid by a king of Kish into Elam *ca.* 2700 B.C., and a similar achievement is accredited to Gilgamesh slightly later.

After this time a dynasty arose in the city of Awan, a site as yet unidentified, situated E of Susa and near Shushtar. A raid into Iraq destroyed the current Sumerian dynasty at Ur and established Elamite independence until Sargon of Agade marched through the land *ca.* 2325 B.C. Sargon's descendant Naram-Sin made a suzerainty treaty with his Elamite vassal, which survives as one of the oldest examples of the covenant formulations found throughout the ancient Near East (*see* COVENANT II). It is written in Elamite and invokes Elamite deities, which may indicate that there were separate versions: in his native Akkadian for the overlord Naram-Sin, and in Elamite for the vassal.

The last monarch of the Awan dynasty, Kutik-In-šušinak, had been viceroy of Susa at first and left some inscriptions there. Incursions by mountain tribes cut short the might of this dynasty. For a century Elam was subject to the Sumerian city of Lagash to some degree, and thereafter to the 3rd Dynasty of Ur (*ca.* 2110-2005 B.C.). However, a local dynasty continued in Simash, possibly modern Horram-abad, eventually leading a coalition that conquered Ur and inaugurated a period of intercity rivalry in Babylonia. One family that gained power in the city of Larsa certainly owed something to Elamite favor, but of events within Elam little is known beyond names of kings. The attack on the cities in the Dead Sea plain recorded in Gen. 14 is probably to be dated in this era. The name of the Elamite king, CHEDORLAOMER, has a plausible form (Elamite Kutir-Lagamar), but no trace of him has been discovered.

Elam shared in the general round of intrigues and alliances of the Babylonian states, and was presently contained by the power of Hammurabi of Babylon. Although Kutir-Naḫḫunte I raided Babylon, *ca.* 1725 B.C., Hammurabi's successors seem to have held some dominion over Elam until their dynasty was ended *ca.* 1595 B.C. The darkness that hangs over the following centuries of Babylonian history is shared by Elam. Kassites and Hurrians from the North are attested among the citizens of Susa, and may have predominated in some areas. The country was no longer a single state, but a number of independent counties. One major event is recorded near the end of the dark age, an invasion by the Kassite king of Babylon, Kurigalzu II, *ca.* 1330 B.C.

At about that time a new native dynasty was gaining strength E of Susa and expanded to control most of Elam early in the 13th cent. B.C. Under Ḫumban-numena (*ca.* 1285-1266 B.C.) there was again a single realm of Elam. His son Untaš-^{d}GAL (the second element is a Sumerian writing "great god," variously rendered by the god's name Ḫumban or the epithet *napiriša*) built many temples and founded a new shrine and city called Dur-Untaš, "fortress of Untaš," after himself. In addition, Untaš-^{d}GAL took advantage of the waning Kassite power to raid the Babylonian territory E of the Tigris. However, this and Elamite land were soon lost to the newly powerful Assyria, which under Tukulti-Ninurta I (*ca.* 1244-1208 B.C.) installed a subject king in Babylon. The weakness of Babylon provided opportunity for the Elamite Kidin-Ḫutran (*ca.* 1244-1222 B.C.) to make two raids across the country, dethroning the Assyrian puppet on the first. Tukulti-Ninurta's strength was the greater, however; the Elamite disappeared, perhaps in a revolt, and with him his dynasty.

A further half-century of darkness gives way to the rise of another dynasty, probably centered at Susa, which raised Elam to its zenith for a few decades. Assyria had declined, and Babylonia too, after a brief resurgence. Thus Šutruk-Naḫḫunte, first of the new line, was able to establish an enlarged Elam, reaching S to Bushire, and then to invade Babylonia. He took a heavy tribute, including such famous monuments as the Law Code stele of Hammurabi, and set his son Kutir-Naḫḫunte on the throne of Babylon (*ca.* 1160 B.C.). The son faced the Babylonians after his father's death and defeated them in a three-year struggle, bringing the Kassite dynasty to an end and deporting many people and their gods. Another son of Šutruk-Naḫḫunte succeeded *ca.* 1150 B.C., Šilhak-In-šušinak. His various expeditions in eastern Iraq are recorded in detail, with long lists of the places conquered, stretching as far N as the regions of Kirkuk and Kirmanshah, although Babylon proper was gradually lost to Elamite sway. Unruly hill people in the mountains were also quelled. Šilhak-In-šušinak died *ca.* 1120 B.C., leaving a large empire to his successor (whether son or nephew is uncertain, for the second son of Šutruk-Naḫḫunte had married his brother's widow, who was probably their sister, according to Elamite royal custom). The new king was unable to keep up the might of his fathers. Babylonia and Assyria were rising again, and the king of Babylon was determined to recapture the cult-statue of his patron god from Susa. His first attack was unsuccessful; in the second his army was aided by various troops from Elam's borders and sacked Susa. With this disaster Elam entered a long period of obscurity (*ca.* 1110 B.C.).

An Assyrian inscription referring to events in 821 B.C. tells of the submission of an Elamite ruler, the first historical notice of that state since the sack of Susa. In the intervening years Elam had suffered pressure from Indo-Aryan invaders in the east and north. The MEDES gradually settled N of Elam, the Persians to the southeast, around Pasargadae and Persepolis. In the mountains enclosing the Elamite plain were the nameless tribes whose metalwork survives as the Luristan bronzes.

Elam enjoyed one more period of importance in world history within the decades following the battle of Der in 720 B.C., when Elamite troops, allied with the Babylonian king Merodach-baladan II, prevented the forces of Sargon II of Assyria from marching southward. Aid to Babylonia against Assyrian attempts at subjugation absorbed much of Elam's strength and eventually ruined the country.

Ḫumban-nikaš I (*ca.* 742-717 B.C.), whose army fought

at Der, was succeeded by his nephew Šutruk-Naḫḫunte II. In 710 B.C. Sargon made a show of force in western Elam causing the king to flee to the mountains, then marched into Babylonia. The Assyrian threat was effective; Merodach-baladan attempted to gain Elamite assistance with costly presents; they were accepted, but he was not granted asylum on Elamite soil. When he again seized the throne of Babylon (703 B.C.) his gifts persuaded Šutruk-Naḫḫunte to send a large force to his aid, including eighty thousand archers (cf. Isa. 22:6; Jer. 49:35). This was insufficient to contain the Assyrian might, despite a fierce battle, so the Elamites withdrew. Assyria reannexed two territories on the northwest border of Elam. In 700 B.C. Merodach-baladan received further support from Elam as the Assyrians advanced into southern Babylonia; but he could not withstand them, and fled to the Elamite coast where he died.

At this time (*ca.* 699 B.C.) Šutruk-Naḫḫunte was removed from the throne by his brother Ḫallutuš-In-šušinak, who ruled until 693 B.C. The policy of aiding Babylonian nationalists was continued, and refuge and help were given to the members of the royal family in the marshes about the head of the Persian Gulf. Sennacherib took his forces to crush this center of disaffection in 694 B.C.; and as soon as the Assyrians had passed to the south the Elamite king struck out, raiding Sippar and capturing Sennacherib's son, the Assyrian king of Babylon. A Babylonian noble was set on the throne in his place, but the Elamites were defeated by the returning Assyrian army and their protégé removed. Ḫallutuš-In-šušinak was deposed in 693 B.C.

Kudur-Naḫḫunte, who next took the throne, ruled for ten months only, bearing the defeat of the Assyrian return attack and losing more territory. A rebellion made Ḫumban-numena king, without changing the political orientation. Anti-Assyrian movements in Babylonia found more Elamite support, culminating in the indecisive battle at Ḫalule E of the Tigris. According to the Babylonian Chronicle the Elamite king was in command. However, he could not take up any advantage, for he suffered a stroke and died after a ten-month illness (688 B.C.).

The reign of Ḫumba-Ḫaldaš I (688-681 B.C.) was uneventful; a second Ḫumban-Ḫaldaš ruled until 674 B.C. He favored Assyria at first, executing Babylonian rebels who had fled to Elam; but while the Assyrians were campaigning in Egypt he made a raid across the Tigris and massacred men of Sippar (*ca.* 675 B.C.). His brother and successor is known solely from Assyrian texts which name him Urtaki. Early in his reign fear of reprisal, or an actual Assyrian threat, caused the return from Elam of certain divine images taken there as booty. On the other side, Assyria contributed to famine–relief measures in the borderlands. The Elamite broke the entente by raiding Babylonia in 665 B.C. while the main Assyrian army was again in Egypt. Local forces repulsed the Elamites; Urtaki was assassinated, and his son took refuge in Assyria (664 B.C.).

The next king, Tept-Ḫumban-In-šušinak (Assyr. Te-Umman), figures prominently in the sculptures and annals of Ashurbanipal. His early years were spent in enlarging Elam's domains to the north and southeast, perhaps exacting tribute even from the Persian tribes. Attempts to extradite Elamites who found asylum in Assyria provoked war. The Elamites were defeated by the Assyrians at the Ulai River, where they were defending Susa. The main cities were occupied by Assyrian armies; Te-Umman was decapitated, to Ashurbanipal's great satisfaction; and his domain was given to that son of Urtaki who had found refuge in Assyria, Ḫumban-nikaš (653 B.C.). A brother, Tammaritu, was made king in the southern province of Ḫidalu. Ḫumban-nikaš shifted his loyalties, aiding Šamaš-šum-ukīn of Babylon in his revolt. But his cousin, another Tammaritu, supplanted him (651 B.C.); this Tammaritu continued his policy, only to be deposed by a general, Indabigaš, after which he fled to Assyria (649 B.C.). Indabigaš adopted a more conciliatory attitude to Assyria.

In Susa ruled Atta-Ḫamiti-In-šušinak (Assyr. Attametu), who left an inscription recording his rule over the south-

Elamite archers of the Persian army. Relief from Susa (5th cent. B.C.) (Louvre)

eastern region. When he died in 648 B.C. his son Ḫumban-Ḫaldaš III (Assyr. Ummanaldasi) became the last Elamite king and dethroned Indabigaš. This monarch realized that a major cause of Assyrian hostility was the shelter Elam afforded to Nabû-bēl-šumāti, a rebel Babylonian descended from Merodach-baladan II. His attempt to deliver the Babylonian to Assyria was thwarted by his officers, precipitating an Assyrian campaign which drove Ḫumban-Ḫaldaš from Susa and reinstated Tammaritu, *ca.* 647 B.C. The latter rebelled but was forced to take refuge in Assyria once more.

A final campaign in the next year accomplished Ashurbanipal's desire: Elam was devastated and Susa despoiled, and the situation became so inimical that Nabû-bēl-šumati killed himself. Ḫumban-Ḫaldaš ruled his ravaged realm for a little longer until he lost his throne during a revolt and also fled to Assyria, *ca.* 644 B.C.

Thereafter little is known of Elam's history; it passed into the Persian empire as the third satrapy and attempted unsuccessfully to break away under another Atta-Ḫamiti-In-šušinak at the accession of Darius I. In the Hellenistic period Elymais existed as a small state under the Parthians and retained some national characteristics long after. It is profitable to compare the vicissitudes of Elamite history with those of two other minor states, Israel and Judah, in their similar contexts.

IV. Writing and Language.–Clay tablets from Susa and from Sialk (by Kashan) show that a local pictographic script ("proto-Elamite") was widely used *ca.* 2900 B.C., stimulated by the invention of writing in Sumer shortly before. Judging by the recognizable signs, these texts are accounts of livestock. The signs developed into a linear script with a very much reduced syllabary of about seventy characters, attested in a few inscriptions of Kutik-In-šušinak *ca.* 2250 B.C. The ensuing Akkadian domination brought the Akkadian script into official use, and a local form of this remained the vehicle for Elamite texts until the end of Elam, even though it was basically unsuited to the Elamite phonetics.

The Elamite language has no known relation, is agglutinative, and is only partially understood. The treaty imposed by Naram-Sin is the oldest text in Elamite. The resurgence in the 13th cent. B.C. included a revival of its use for royal inscriptions and private contracts, which was maintained into the Achaemenid era. In the mid-2nd millennium B.C. Babylonian was employed for legal contracts and economic documents. The exercise tablets of a scribal school have been found in Susa, based on Babylonian exemplars, including the myth of the bird Zu (cf. *ANET,* pp. 111ff., 515ff.). No native literature has been recovered.

V. Art.–Prehistoric Elam has become famous for its flowing abstract designs and more formal patterns painted on pottery and engraved on cylinder seals. Sumerian influence is very apparent in the early 3rd millennium B.C., yet, as is the case throughout Elamite culture, local characteristics are obvious. Lions loom large, symbolizing, perhaps, the awesome mountain spirits. The impressions of seals on clay tablets, which represent many aspects of daily life, are the chief source of knowledge. Naram-Sin's conquest introduced Akkadian styles, noticeable in rock-reliefs and seals. Hurrian influence appears in the seals of *ca.* 1500 B.C., bringing a rather barbaric touch. From slightly earlier there survive a few remarkable vessels of bitumen carved with naturalistic animals in high relief.

While the few stone sculptures of Šilhak-In-šušinak's period are generally unexciting, several bronze figures are outstanding. Most interest attaches to a model depicting a temple ritual with two squatting priests, offering tables, and sacred trees. Polychrome glazed tiles were introduced as wall plates, the designs depicting mythical creatures.

Elamite copper head of man with curled beard and banded hair from the late 2nd millennium B.C. (Metropolitan Museum of Art, Rogers Fund, Purchase, 1947)

This was the period of the Luristan bronzes, which, although not actually Elamite, have affinities with Elamite art and may owe their technical excellence to Elamite smithery. Detailed comparison of numerous bronzes has led to the distinction of a few as Elamite, mainly plaques and vessels with repoussé decoration.

VI. Religion.–Indirect evidence supplies a good deal of disjointed information about religious beliefs in Elam. A mother-goddess (called Pinikir in Susa, Kiririsha in the southwest) headed the pantheon and was considered wife of the chief god Ḫumban. Naḫḫunte was the son-god. There were many patron city deities, In-šušinak ("lord of Susa," a Sumerian phrase) being well known, and a host of others. A pair of serpents frequently occur in sculptures, probably as fertility emblems; and flowing water had an important place. Temple towers, like the ziggurats of Babylonia, dominated major cities. A feature peculiar to Elam was the tradition of horns in their decoration. Sacred groves were planted on or near the towers.

Lack of source material prevents analysis of any but the official or royal cult; mother-goddess figurines are about the only representatives of "popular" religion.

Bibliography.–G. G. Cameron, *History of Early Iran* (1936); R. Ghirshman, *Iran* (1954), pp. 32-72; W. Hinz, *Lost World of Elam* (Eng. tr. 1972); *CAH,* I, ch. 23; II, ch. 7; *Iranica Antiqua,* 2 (1962), 1-17; R. Labat, *CAH,* II, chs. 29, 32; L. Le Breton, *Iraq,* 19 (1957), 79-124; E. Porada, *Ancient Iran* (1965); E. Reiner, *Handbuch der Orientalistik,* 1.II.1-2.2 (1969).

A. R. MILLARD

ELASA el'ə-sə [Gk. *Alasa*]; AV ELEASA; NEB ALASA. The place where Judas Maccabeus pitched his camp before the battle in which he was overwhelmed by the Syrians and slain in 161 B.C. (1 Macc. 9:5). It probably corresponds to the modern Khirbet el- ʿAshshī between Lower and Upper Beth-horon.

ELASAH el-ə-sə [Heb. *ʾelʿāśâ*–'God has made'].

1. An Israelite, son of Pashhur the priest, who had a foreign wife (Ezr. 10:22).

2. A son of Shaphan, by whom, with Gemariah, King Zedekiah sent a message to Babylon (Jer. 29:3). The same as ELEASAH **2.**

ELATH ē'lath, ā-lät'; **ELOTH** ē'loth [Heb. *ʾêlaṯ, ʾêlôṯ, ʾēlôṯ*]. A settlement in EDOM, near the present port city of Aqabah, Jordan, on the north shore of the Gulf of Aqabah. It is mentioned with EZION-GEBER in three OT passages (Dt. 2:8; 1 K. 9:26; 2 Ch. 8:17). Most modern scholars believe that the two names are applied to the same town, Elath being a later name of Edomite origin.

Elath lay along the route traveled by the Israelites on their journey from Egypt to Canaan (Dt. 2:8). It presumably came under Israelite rule when David conquered the Edomites (2 S. 8:13f.). During the reign of Jehoram (Joram) of Judah (848-841 B.C.) Edom revolted and regained independence (2 K. 8:20-22; 2 Ch. 21:8-10). Uzziah (Azariah) of Judah (767-740) recaptured Elath and rebuilt it (2 K. 14:22; 2 Ch. 26:1f.). During the reign of Ahaz (*ca.* 735) the king of Edom recovered Elath (2 K. 16:6).

In Roman times Elath was called Aila (Aelath, Aelana), also Berenike. Trajan's highway extended along the old King's Highway (cf. Nu. 20:17, etc.) from Damascus to Aila, where the Tenth Roman Legion was stationed. The names of four bishops from the Aila Bishopric appear in records of several church councils of the 4th to 6th centuries.

After the Moslem victory *ca.* A.D. 630, John, the Christian ruler of Aila, paid an annual tribute of three hundred gold pieces. The site became known as Aqabah and was an important station on the pilgrimage route to Mecca.

For archeology of the area *see* TELL EL-KHELEIFEH.

E. K. VOGEL

EL-BERITH el-ber'ith [Heb. *ʾēl beʳrîṯ*; Gk. *Baal diathḗkēs*] (Jgs. 9:46). A Canaanite deity, known also as BAAL-BERITH, whose temple was at Shechem.

Cross regards the name as a specific epithet of the patriarchal god 'El (*TDOT,* I, 250). He refers to the Hurrian hymn to 'El (*Ugaritica,* V, 510ff.), which speaks of *il brt* and *il dn*. In any event Jgs. 9:46 clearly refers to a pagan deity.

EL-BETHEL el-beth'əl [Heb. *ʾēl bêṯ-ʾēl*] (Gen. 35:7). Probably "God of Bethel" (RSV mg.). Another possibility is that El-bethel is a divine title ("God Bethel") like El Elyon, El Shaddai, El Olam, and El Roi (*see* GOD, NAMES OF II.B.5). This possibility is supported by the use of the term as a title in the Elephantine papyri of the 5th cent. B.C. The MT of Gen. 31:13 reads *hāʾēl bêṯ-ʾēl* ("the God [of] Bethel"; cf. AV, RSV); but this text is probably defective and should read "the God who appeared to you at Bethel" with the LXX and some Targums (cf. NEB). In any case it is clear that Jacob named the altar not after a pagan Canaanite deity but after Yahweh, the God who had appeared to him at BETHEL (1) (28:12-22).

N. J. O.

ELCIA el-sī'-ə (AV Jth. 8:1). *See* ELKIAH.

ELDAAH el-dā'ə [Heb. *ʾeldāʿâ*]. A son of Midian (Gen. 25:4; 1 Ch. 1:33).

ELDAD el'dad [Heb. *ʾeldāḏ*–'God has loved'(?)]. One of the seventy elders chosen by Moses at the command of Yahweh to share "the burden of the people" (Nu. 11:16-25). Eldad and his companion Medad were not present with the rest at the tent meeting, yet the Spirit rested also upon them and they prophesied in the camp (vv. 26-29).

ELDAD AND MODAD mō'dad, **BOOK OF.** An apocryphal book that was supposed to contain the prophecy of ELDAD and MEDAD (cf. Nu. 11:26-29; RSV "Medad"; LXX "Modad"). The nature of their prophecy is not recorded in the OT account, and thus it naturally became a good subject for the play of the imagination. It furnished the basis for a lost work, which was quoted by Hermas (Vis. 2:3): "The Lord is near to them who return unto Him, as it is written in Eldad and Modad, who prophesied to the people in the wilderness." The Palestine Targums also filled in the subject of the prophecy of Eldad and Modad; as they have it, it related to the coming of Gog and Magog against Israel at the end of the days. One of the Targums has the expression, "The Lord is near to them that are in the hour of tribulation." The authors of the Targums were either dependent upon that work or upon a similar tradition, the former view being the more probable.

Some scholars (e.g., J. B. Lightfoot, *Apostolic Fathers* [1890; repr. 1973], I/2, 80f.) think the lengthy quotation in 1 Clem. 23 and 2 Clem. 11 is from the Book of Eldad and Modad. The work is listed as part of the OT Apocrypha in the Stichometry of Nicephorus (*ca.* A.D. 850?) and consists of four hundred lines, which would make it about twice the length of the Canticles.

A. W. FORTUNE

ELDER IN THE OT [Heb. *zāqēn*–'beard'; cf. Akk. *ziqnu*; Ugar. *dqn*; etc.]; AV also ANCIENT. An elderly person; also, an authority, or a person with judicial office. It is commonly accepted that the origin of this latter meaning is to be sought in the ancient patriarchal family institution of the Hebrews. The elder was similar to a sheikh among the Arabian bedouin.

Moses got the command from God to gather the elders of Israel to give to them the message of Yahweh (Ex. 3:16). These elders were probably the heads of certain family groups. Throughout the wanderings in the desert Moses continued his contact with the elders and even gave them delegated authority to judge in certain minor cases (cf. Ex. 18:13-27; Nu. 11:16, 24). The number of these elders is given as seventy; this number was probably not uniform.

Elder as a title continues in use throughout the times of the judges (e.g., Jgs. 8:16) into the kingdom. Saul asked to be honored before the elders (1 S. 15:30); the elders appeared before David in Hebron (2 S. 17:15); elders took part in the temple procession of Solomon (1 K. 8:3). It is obvious from these passages that the elders played a very important role in the election of the king and in advising the king. If the king did not accept their advice, he could anticipate evil consequences, as in the case of Rehoboam (1 K. 12:1ff.).

The elders served as local magistrates in bringing murderers to trial (Dt. 19:12; 21:1ff.; Josh. 20:4), punishing a disobedient son (Dt. 21:19), inflicting penalty for slander (22:15) and for noncompliance with the Levirate marriage law (25:7ff.), enforcing the law (27:1), and conducting the service of expiating an unwitting violation of the law (Lev. 4:13ff.).

From earliest times a judicial body of elders was formed to give judgment on certain cases. They gathered in the gates of the city where their jurisprudence was pronounced. Even parts of Job might be understood in the light of this legal activity, according to L. Koehler.

The term elder thus has various meanings which must be carefully distinguished from each other. The most important are elders with certain governing rights and those with judicial rights.

See also CHIEF.

Bibliography.–*TDNT*, VI, *s.v.* πρεσβύτερος (G. Bornkamm); L. Koehler, *Hebrew Man* (1956); R. de Vaux, *Ancient Israel*, I (1961).

F. C. FENSHAM

ELDER IN THE NT [Gk. *presbýteros*].

1. The word is used adjectivally to denote seniority (Lk. 15:25; 1 Tim. 5:2).

2. It is used in reference to the Jewish elders of the synagogue, usually associated with the scribes and Pharisees, and occurs in the NT passages cited in the preceding article.

3. It denotes certain persons appointed to hold office in the Christian church, and to exercise spiritual oversight of the flock entrusted to them. From the references in Acts (14:23; 20:17) it may be inferred that the churches generally had elders appointed over them. That "elders" and "bishops" were in apostolic and subapostolic times the same is now almost universally admitted; in all NT references their functions are identical. The most probable explanation of the difference of names is that "elder" refers mainly to the person and "bishop" to the office; the name "elder" emphasizes what he is, while "bishop," i.e., "overseer," emphasizes what the elder or presbyter does. *See* BISHOP; CHURCH GOVERNMENT; MINISTRY III.B, C; PRESBYTER.

A. C. GRANT

ELDEST [Heb. *gāḏôl*–'great'] (Gen. 44:12; 1 S. 17:13f., 28); [*b^e^ḵôr*–'firstborn'] (2 K. 3:27; Job 1:13, 18); [Gk. *presbýteros*] (Jn. 8:9). The eldest son in a family took precedence over his brothers while the father lived. When the father died the eldest became the head of the family, inheriting a double portion of the estate. Because the eldest sons were the FIRSTBORN they belonged to God — as did all "first fruits" — and had to be redeemed. The Levites were chosen to serve God as their substitutes.

ELEAD el'ē-ad [Heb. *'el'āḏ*–'God has testified']. An Ephraimite, slain by the men of Gath while he was making a raid (1 Ch. 7:21).

ELEADAH el-e-ā'də [Heb. *'el'āḏâ*–'God has adorned']; AV, NEB, ELADAH. An Ephraimite (1 Ch. 7:20).

ELEALEH e-lə-ā'lə [Heb. *'el'ālēh*–'God has ascended']. A city in Moab, part of the tribal allotment of Reuben, and, along with several other cities, rebuilt by Reuben (Nu. 32:3, 37). The cities that were rebuilt were renamed, but the new names are not given. Later Elealeh is mentioned in the oracles against Moab (Isa. 15:4; 16:9; Jer. 48:34). According to Eusebius (*Onom.* 84.10) it was still a large village in the 4th cent. A.D., located a little more than 1 Rom. mi. (1.5 km.; 0.9 mi.) from Heshbon. It is identified today with the ruins of el-'Al, 3 km. (2 mi.) NNE of Heshbon.

W. S. L. S.

ELEASA el-ə-ā'sə (AV 1 Macc. 9:5). *See* ELASA.

ELEASAH el-ə-ā'sə [Heb. *'el'āśâ*–'God has made']; NEB ELASAH.

1. A descendant of Judah (1 Ch. 2:39f.).

2. A Benjaminite, a descendant of Saul (1 Ch. 8:37; 9:43). The same as ELASAH **2.**

ELEAZAR el-ē-ā'zər [Heb. *'el'āzār*–'God has helped'; Gk. *Eleazar*].

1. The third son of Aaron by Elisheba (Ex. 6:23; Nu. 3:2). He married one of the daughters of Putiel, who bore him Phinehas (Ex. 6:25). With his father and three brothers he was consecrated to the priest's office (Ex. 28:1). After the destruction of Nadab and Abihu, he occupied a more important position, and he and Ithmar "served as priests in the lifetime of Aaron their father" (Lev. 10:6f.; Nu. 3:4; 1 Ch. 24:2ff.). He was given the oversight of the Levites and had charge of the tabernacle and all within it (Nu. 3:32; 4:16). To Eleazar fell the duty of hammering out for an altar covering the censers of Korah and his fellow conspirators who had attempted to seize the priesthood (Nu. 16:37, 39).

On the death of Aaron, Eleazar succeeded him (20:25ff.). He assisted Moses with the census after the plague in the plains of Moab (26:1ff.) and with Moses and the elders heard the petition of the daughters of Zelophehad who wished to receive the inheritance of their father (27:1ff.). After the entrance into Canaan, Eleazar and Joshua gave effect to the decision arrived at by giving the daughters of Zelophehad a share in the land of Manasseh (Josh. 17:4). He was priest and adviser to Joshua, the successor of Moses (Nu. 27:19; 31:12ff.), whom he also assisted in partitioning Canaan among the tribes (Nu. 34:17; Josh. 14:1; 19:51; 21:1). He was buried at Gibeah, the town of Phinehas his son in the hill country of Ephraim (Josh. 24:33).

For some unknown reason the descendants of Ithamar seem to have held the chief position among the priests from Eli until the accession of Solomon, when Abiathar was sent into retirement and Zadok, the descendant of Eleazar, was appointed in his place (1 K. 2:26ff.). Ezra was a descendant of Zadok (Ezr. 7:1ff.); and the high priest's office was in the family of Zadok until the time of the Maccabees.

2. The son of Abinadab, sanctified to keep the ark of Yahweh when it was brought from Beth-shemesh to Kiriath-jearim after being sent back by the Philistines (1 S. 7:1).

3. The son of Dodo, one of David's three mighty men. A famous feat of arms with David at Pas-dammin is recorded (2 S. 23:9f.; 1 Ch. 11:12f.).

4. A Levite, a son of Mahli, a Merarite. It is recorded that he had no sons, but daughters only, who were married to their cousins (1 Ch. 23:21f; 24:28).

5. A priest who accompanied Ezra from Babylon (Ezr. 8:33); the son of Phinehas. **5** may be identical with **7.**

6. A son of Parosh, among those who put away their foreign wives and children in accordance with Ezra's ban (Ezr. 10:25).

7. A priest who took part in the dedication of the wall of Jerusalem (Neh. 12:42).

8. A son of Mattathias and brother of Judas Maccabeus (1 Macc. 2:5; 6:43f.; 2 Macc. 8:23). *See* HASMONEANS; MACCABEES.

9, 10. Two others are mentioned in 1 Macc. 8:17; 2 Macc. 6:18ff.

11. An ancestor of Jesus, three generations before Joseph (Mt. 1:15).

S. F. HUNTER

ELEAZURUS el'ē-ə-zoo'rəs (AV 1 Esd. 9:24). *See* ELIASHIB **4.**

ELECT [Heb. *bāḥîr*; Gk. *eklektós*]; AV also ELECTION (Rom. 11:7); NEB CHOSEN, CHOSEN ONES, CHOSEN PEOPLE. The basic meaning is that of a people or persons "selected" or "chosen" by divine action. A secondary, though infrequent, meaning is "choice" or "precious." The biblical references to "the elect" are of four main types: (1) in the OT, Israel, (2) in the NT, heirs of salvation, (3) Jesus Christ as the Messiah, and (4) the good angels (only 1 Tim. 5:21).

(1) The OT covenant people, Israel, descendants of Abraham and Jacob, are God's "elect" (RSV "chosen," Isa. 45:4; 65:9, 15, 22). This choice of Israel from among all the nations is also expressed in other ways (Dt. 4:37; 7:6f.; 1 K. 3:8; Isa. 44:1f.; Am. 3:2). The election of Israel stems from God's sovereign choice, expresses His love, and has for its purpose the redemptive history culminating in Jesus Christ. The elect nation Israel is made to be God's people and is given covenantal privilege and blessing. While God's electing purpose for Israel is salvation, not all members of the nation are so elect. Within the election of the nation God exercises an individual election by which He distinguishes Isaac and Ishmael, Jacob and Esau (cf. Rom. 9:1-13). The LXX displays a fondness for *eklektós* so that the term becomes "a single catchword for a whole series of terms in the OT" (*TDNT,* IV, 179).

(2) In the NT the term likewise has a pregnant meaning. The most frequent reference to "the elect" relates to the "spiritual Israel" who are the heirs of salvation. The elect are those whom God has chosen (Mk. 13:20); they are now both Jews and Gentiles who come to believe in Jesus Christ and are gathered worldwide (Mk. 13:27; Mt. 24:31). As God had promised Abraham, the gospel is now preached to all nations. Yet, while many are called, "few are chosen" (Mt. 22:14). In Rom. 8:33 Paul uses the term "God's elect" as an emphatic summary of 8:14ff. The elect are those whom God "foreknew . . . predestined . . . called . . . justified . . . also glorified" (Rom. 8:29f.). The salvation of the elect has an origin before time, is realized in history, and culminates in eternal glorification. Hence there is no accusation nor condemnation of the elect (8:1, 33) and nothing can separate them from the love of God (vv. 35-39). The elect are to be "conformed to the image" of the Son (v. 29); they were chosen in Christ to be "holy and blameless before him" (Eph. 1:4). Thus the elect are exhorted to responsible Christian living (Col. 3:12ff.; Tit. 1:1-3), and they have an evangelistic task in the world (1 Pet. 2:9). Yet their preservation, also in the difficult last days, and their final glorification is God's gracious work in them (Mk. 13:19-17; Mt. 24:21-31; Lk. 18:7).

Although most NT references are to "the elect" in a general or comprehensive way, individuals are meant and some are even mentioned by name (cf. Rom. 9:6-13; cf. 1 Pet. 5:13; 2 Jn. 1, 13; *see* ELECT LADY). This does not mean individualism. The chosen "exiles of the Dispersion" addressed by Peter are designated "a chosen race, a royal priesthood, a holy nation, God's own people" (1 Pet. 1:1; 2:9). The elect in Christ comprise an organic unity that comes to partial manifestation in the Church and will be perfectly realized upon the Son's return when His angels will gather together all the elect (Mk. 13:27; Mt. 24:31).

(3) Jesus as the Messiah is also referred to as "the elect" or "chosen one." At the transfiguration the voice of the Father from heaven speaks of "my Son, my Chosen" (*eklelegménos,* Lk. 9:35); however, Mark and Matthew refer only to "my beloved Son" (Mk. 9:7; Mt. 17:5). And again in Luke at Jesus' crucifixion the rulers sneer at "his Chosen One" (Lk. 23:35), while Mark and Matthew refer the scoff to "the King of Israel" (Mk. 15:32; Mt. 27:42). (An alternate reading for Jn. 1:34 refers to Jesus as *eklektós.*) These references to the Messiah as the "Chosen One" reflect Isa. 42:1 in the LXX. Similar references are found in the Book of Enoch (40:5; 45:3ff.), which might indicate that this was a more common messianic designation in Jesus' day. Peter, quoting Isa. 28:16, refers to Jesus Christ as the living stone and as the cornerstone "chosen and precious" (1 Pet. 2:4, 6; cf. Mt. 12:18). Reference to Jesus as "the elect" thus refers to His unique and distinctive messianic office. In this term is an expression of the Father's peculiar delight in His beloved Son. Furthermore, everything that "the elect" heirs of salvation receive, they receive in and from Jesus Christ, "the Chosen One."

(4) Only once does the term "the elect" refer to the angels (1 Tim. 5:21). (Cf. other references to the angels such as 1 Cor. 6:3; 2 Pet. 2:4; Jude 6.)

Bibliography.–*TDNT,* IV, 181-192 (Schrenk); *TDOT,* II, *s.v.* "bāchar."

F. H. KLOOSTER

ELECT LADY [Gk. *eklektḗ kyría*]; NEB LADY CHOSEN BY GOD. This phrase in 2 Jn. 1 designates the addressee of the brief epistle. Much discussion has been devoted to the attempt to determine its precise meaning. Four translations are possible grammatically: (1) to the elect lady; (2) to an elect lady; (3) to the elect Kyria; (4) to the lady Electa. All interpretations come down to two main types: (1) the phrase is to be taken literally and refers to a particular person; or (2) the phrase is to be taken figuratively and refers to a particular church or congregation. The first two translations are open to either of these interpretations; the last two allow only for the interpretation of a particular individual. Good arguments are adduced in favor of each of the two main interpretations and responsible exegetes have taken opposite sides throughout Christian history. No particular theological bias is evident in the choices made. At present no convincing evidence exists to decide the issue clearly, and interpreters express their preference in the light of the arguments judged most convincing.

(1) The literal interpretation referring to a particular person. Many who favor this interpretation regard the identity of the lady addressed as unknown. Others have made conjectures about her name or identity. Clement of Alexandria took the first of the two words as her name and held that the epistle was addressed to "the lady Electa." This position hardly seems tenable since her sister mentioned in v. 13 would then have the same name. J. R. Harris also favored this view, and, on the basis of papyrus evidence that *kýrios* and *kyría* were used in ancient letters to express intimacy, rendered the phrase "my dear Electa." He thought she was a gentile proselyte of the tribe of Ruth and also a widow. This ingenious suggestion has gained little support.

Athanasius as well as later interpreters favored the translation "to the elect Kyria," thinking her name was *Kyria,* the Greek word for "lady." The name of Mary, the mother of Jesus, has been suggested with an appeal to Jn.19:27, but this conjecture is untenable. Martha of Bethany has also been suggested, since Gk. *kyría* means "mistress" and corresponds to Aram. *mārᵉṯā'* (Martha) and Lat. *Dom(i)na.*

All these suggestions concerning the name of the addressee are conjectural; if the phrase refers to a distinct individual, her name and identity remain unknown. Yet the literal interpretation is the simplest and most natural, and taken as a personal letter 2 John parallels 3 John.

(2) The figurative interpretation referring to a particular church or congregation. Clement and Jerome favored this interpretation and it is widely held by recent interpreters. Arguments are drawn from the general character of the Epistle: the subject with which it deals concerns a community rather than an individual or a family; the language of the first three verses fits a community more readily than an individual; the interchange of the singular and plural throughout the Epistle is easier to account for if the addressee is a church; the reference to a new commandment in v. 5 suggests a church rather than an individual; the message of vv. 6, 8, 10, 12 relates better to church members than to children in a family; the saluta-

tion of v. 13 is more understandable if it comes from a church rather than the lady's sister. Appeal is also made to the possible parallel in 1 Pet. 5:13, which personifies a church in feminine terms as Scripture does elsewhere (cf. also Bar. 4f.). If the figurative interpretation of "the elect lady" is favored, the specific identity of the church addressed is not known and depends, in part, on the identity of "the elder" in v. 1.

See J. R. Harris, *Expos.* 3 (6th ser., 1901), 194-203.

F. H. KLOOSTER

ELECTION [Heb. *bāḥar*–'choose'; Gk. *eklogḗ*–'chosen']. In both the OT and NT, a divine choosing of man, individually or corporately, either to salvation and eternal life, or to a special office or work. The term "the elect" in both Testaments applies mainly to God's elect people, chosen unto eternal life (2 S. 21:6; 1 Ch. 16:13; Ps. 105:6, 43; 106:5, 23; Isa. 42:1; 43:20; Mt. 24:22, 24, 31; Rom. 8:33; Col. 3:12; 1 Pet. 1:2, etc.). *See* ELECT.

When man first sinned his fellowship with God suffered a disastrous breach, for man declared his independence of his Creator (Gen. 3; Rom. 1:21ff.). Yet at the same time God in His grace introduced immediately into history (Gen. 3:15f.) the revelation of redemption, so that from the beginning one finds redeemed men who walked in faith and obedience to God (He. 11:4-7). Thus from Gen. 4 on there is a people of God who live in righteousness and truth. Yet, while such is the case, no direct reference appears in the early chapters of Genesis to the idea of election.

The first clear statement of election is in connection with Abraham, although the account of God's call to him to go into Canaan (Gen. 12:1) does not specifically state this. One finds such an explanation given later in Israel's history (Neh. 9:7; cf. Dt. 7:6ff.). Within two generations of Abraham, however, the idea of election had become clear, for it is stated that God chose Jacob rather than Esau (Gen. 25:24ff.; cf. Mal. 1:2ff.; Rom. 9:13f.). In all the cases of specific divine election and calling during the patriarchal age, one finds that God took action in order to bring His elect into a covenant relation with Himself. Thus neither at this point nor later may one separate election from God's covenant grace. On His own initiative He made His covenant, which applied not merely to elect individuals but also to their descendants, circumcision being the covenant sign and seal (Gen. 17:9ff.; Ex. 12:44ff.; Josh. 5:2ff.).

By virtue of God's election of the fathers, Israel became God's elect nation (Dt. 4:37; 7:6f., 10:15; 14:2), and for this reason God, after He had delivered them from Egypt (Ex. 19:3ff.), entered into a covenant relation with the people as a whole at Mt. Sinai. By this covenant Israel became a nation separated from all others that it might act as the repository of God's revelation for the rest of mankind (Rom. 9:5). Thus, although Israel experienced God's special favor, at the same time it had a special worldwide obligation.

Yet the election of Israel did not mean that every Israelite trusted in God's promises and faithfully served Him. Throughout the history of Israel one sees that the nation varied greatly in its obedience to its covenant Lord. Only too frequently Israelites believed that because they had descended physically from Abraham, Isaac, and Jacob, God's covenant remained inalienable despite their unbelief and their disobedience. As long as they fulfilled the ritual requirements of the law most Israelites felt they would remain secure in God's favor. Against this assumption Moses warned them, as did the prophets, both early and late, in no uncertain terms (Dt. 28:15ff.; 1 K. 21:21; Isa. 1:10ff.; Hos. 1:1ff.; Rom. 10:19ff.). Yet the nation as a whole refused to hear, and eventually God carried them off into captivity. In this way He showed that the external election of a group or of a nation to political and ecclesiastical favor did not necessarily constitute a vital covenant relationship between the creature and the Creator. This could come only by God's entering into this relationship with elect *individuals*.

The existence at all times within Israel of a faithful, believing remnant made this quite clear. One might liken Israel to two concentric circles, the inner circle consisting of those individuals whom God had chosen and effectually called to faith and obedience, and who consequently sought to serve Him. The outer circle was made up of Israelites who, while outwardly professing the covenant and so claiming to be of the elect, in truth were not of the covenant people. The kingdom consisted of these two groups, the remnant real but invisible (except to the eye of God) in the visible outward kingdom. One finds them referred to in a number of places throughout the OT (1 K. 19:18; Isa. 1:9; 6:13; Zeph. 2:9; Joel 2:32; cf. Rom. 9:6ff.). From this remnant God chose the judges, David, the prophets, Zerubbabel, and others to serve Him as leaders of the people (1 S. 10:24; 16:8ff.; Ps. 105:26; Isa. 41:9). Thus the election to favor and salvation lay at the basis of election to service.

At the same time as God made clear by the prophets that only the elect remnant within Israel truly were His people, He also indicated that eventually the Gentiles too would enter the kingdom. This would take place according to His plan and purpose and would be effected by His election and calling (Isa. 2:2ff.; Hos. 2:23; Acts 15:15ff.; Rom. 9:22ff.; 11:13ff.). In this way individual election took precedence over national election, which meant in turn that the covenant with Israel rested upon that with Abraham, for only as God sovereignly chose and called individuals could they truly come to Him in reconciliation (cf. Gal. 3:15ff.), and so truly become Abraham's seed (Rom. 9:7; Gal. 3:26ff.).

Yet while considering the OT doctrine of election one also finds a number of references, particularly in Isaiah, to the Lord's "elect servant" (Isa. 42:1; 65:9). The references appear to point to one individual specially called to a particular office and in whom the covenant God had a particular delight. This would seem to be the Messiah, who would save Israel from its sins, its election thus culminating with a redeemer.

As in all other aspects of God's revelation the NT both continues and fulfils that which was revealed in the OT. Christ's teachings contain many references to the elect and to God's action in choosing and calling men to Himself in and through Christ (Mt. 24:22ff.; Mk. 13:20ff.; Lk. 18:7; Jn. 6:37, 65; 10:15f.). After His ascension He led the Church to see that God had chosen Gentiles to become members of the covenant people (Acts 15:5ff.; Gal. 2:11f.), and through the instrumentality of the apostle Paul in particular, revealed the doctrine in all its fulness (Rom. 9–11; Eph. 1).

As one attempts to understand the whole NT doctrine of election, one finds that, as in the OT, it centers upon the covenant of which Christ is the head. He is *the elect* of God (Lk. 23:35; 1 Pet. 2:4, 6). In the eternal covenant He is the one chosen to redeem sinners as their Representative. There is no teaching that Christ saves all men. Rather it is perfectly clear that God has elected certain individuals in Christ (Jn. 6:37; Eph. 1:4f.; cf. Rom. 8:28ff.). God the Father bestows His love upon the elect sinners because He sees them at all times in Christ, the Son, the elect Redeemer.

The apostle Paul points out quite clearly that God has chosen individuals that they might be His people in Christ. He has not chosen them because of any foreseen faith or good works, but simply according to His own holy and sovereign will (Rom. 9–11; Eph. 1:3-12). This choice by God is a selection for salvation. Some would hold that He had chosen them to receive the offer of salvation, but Paul repeatedly points out that, like the Jews of the OT, all men are in rebellion against God. Therefore, when He chooses men to redemption He actually predestines them to adoption as His children in Jesus Christ (Eph. 1:5). Christ has paid the penalty of sin for them as the head of the covenant people, and by His atonement He has merited for His elect the gift of the Holy Spirit who regenerates and converts the elect sinner, so that he places his faith in Christ (Jn. 6:39; 63ff.; 10:11ff.; 17:6ff.; Rom. 8:7ff., 29ff.; Eph. 2:4ff.; 1 Pet. 1:2).

The elect of God are chosen not only for salvation, but also for service. They should have the assurance of their calling and election which gives them confidence, strength, and a sense of responsibility (2 Pet. 1:10f.). This leads the Christian to a knowledge of his responsibility to serve Christ as his Lord in this world (Rom. 12; Eph. 1:4). In this way the elect glorify Christ as their covenant Lord to whom they owe all that they are and have (1 Cor. 6:20; 7:23).

But what of the nonelect? Even though they hear the gospel offering to them eternal life in Christ, they refuse to accept it. Consequently they come under the judgment and condemnation of God, not because they are nonelect, but because despite God's revelation of His power and Godhead to all men, they have refused to glorify Him as God (Rom. 1:19-23). Therefore, God has given them up to sin so that their hearts are hardened against Him (Rom. 1:26ff.; 9:13ff.). Upon these rebels against His law will come God's wrath in the final day of judgment (Mt. 12:24, 50; 25:14-46; Rev. 20:12-15).

Up to this point we have dealt with what the Scriptures teach. Yet many problems for which one can find no rational solution remain unresolved, nor do the Scriptures even hint at any kind of answer. As Paul points out in Rom. 9:19ff., one cannot call God to account for an answer but must simply submit to the revelation that God in His wisdom has seen fit to give men.

Probably the most pressing question that arises is: Why has God chosen some and not others? Men have endeavored through the ages to offer explanations by referring to foresight of faith, universal grace that must be improved, or some other rationalization. Barth finds the answer in the fact that everyone is chosen in Christ, who Himself is rejected on man's behalf (*CD,* II/2, pp. 176ff.). But the only answer seems to be that man by virtue of his sinful corruption can and will do nothing for himself. Therefore God, under no obligation to save any of His rebellious creatures, of His own free, sovereign, and holy will determines to save some. Beyond this lies the mystery of the very nature and being of God Himself. Man may not and cannot go further.

See also PREDESTINATION; CHOOSE.

Bibliography.–Calvin *Inst.* iii.21ff.; L. Boettner, *Reformed Doctrine of Predestination* (1932), ch. 21; C. Hodge, *Systematic Theology* (1871-73), pt. III, ch. 1; B. B. Warfield, *Biblical Doctrines* (1929), pp. 3-67; G. C. Berkouwer, *Divine Election* (Eng. tr. 1960).

W. S. REID

ELECTRUM. The RV mg. rendering of Heb. *ḥašmal* in Ezk. 1:4, 27; 8:2 (LXX *ēlektron* [which LSJ, p. 768, connects with *ēléktōr,* "the beaming sun"]; Vulg. *electrum*). Ancient writers used the term "electrum" to describe a native argentiferous gold, pale yellow in color, containing from 20 to 50 percent silver. (Modern electrum is an alloy of copper, zinc, tin, and sometimes nickel.) Both the AV and the ERV have "amber," while the RSV has "gleaming bronze" and the NEB reads "brass." Although various scholars (e.g., Cameron, Irwin, KoB, Staples) cite Akk. *ešmarû* ("inlay," from Elamite *ilmasu,* or "brass") as a cognate, *CAD* rejects that connection and suggests rather *elmešu,* a "quasi-mythical precious stone of great brilliancy" (note also the contexts given here; cf. G. R. Driver, *VT,* 1 [1951], 60-62, who connects Heb. *ḥašmal,* Akk. *elmešu,* and Egypt. *ḥsmn,* "bronze"; cf. also *IB,* VI, 70. The suggestion (KoB, Staples) that Ugar. *ṯrml* ("alabaster" or "limestone," *UT,* pp. 506f.) is a cognate is likewise to be rejected, since the interchange of Hebrew *ḥ* and Ugaritic *r* (in linguistic terms a fricative pharyngeal for a rolled dental) is unattested and extremely unlikely.

Bibliography.–*CAD,* IV, 107f., 366f.; G. G. Cameron, *Persepolis Treasury Tablets* (1948), pp. 129f.; *IDB,* I, *s.v.* "amber" (W. E. Staples); W. A. Irwin, *VT,* 2 (1952), 169f.; KoB, p. 342.

G. A. L.

EL-ELOHE-ISRAEL el-e-lō'he-iz'rē-əl; el-el'ō-he-iz'rē-əl [Heb. *'ēl 'ᵉlōhê yiśrā'ēl*] (Gen. 33:20); NEB EL-ELOHEY-ISRAEL; AV mg., NEB mg., "God, the God of Israel." Found only in Gen. 33:20 as the name given to the altar erected at Shechem by Jacob, henceforth known as Israel, on the parcel of ground purchased by him from the inhabitants of Shechem during his first encampment of length since the return to Palestine from Paddan-aram and the eventful night at Peniel (32:30). Most probably the compound name was actually engraved on the structure.

This unusual combination of names has given occasion for much speculation and for various text emendations. Already the LXX sought to meet the difficulty by reading *wayyiqrā' 'el 'ᵉlōhê yiśrā'ēl,* "and he called *upon* the God of Israel," instead of the *wayyiqrā' -lô 'ēl 'ᵉlōhê yiśrā'ēl* of the MT, "and he called it El, the God of Israel." The phrase is best understood in its close connection with the struggle at Peniel, recorded in Gen. 32. Being victorious in that struggle, Jacob received the new name "Israel," and to his first altar in Palestine he gave the name of God that appeared in his own new name, further explaining it by the appositive phrase "Elohe-Israel." Thus his altar was called, or dedicated to, "El, the God of Israel."

E. MACK

ELEMENT; ELEMENTAL [Gk. *stoicheíon,* pl. *tá stoicheía*]. The Greek word occurs seven times in the NT: Gal. 4:3, 9; Col. 2:8, 20; He. 5:12; 2 Pet. 3:10, 12. The various translations given to the word by the AV, the RSV, and the NEB show the need for careful study to determine the precise meaning intended.

In Gal. 4:3 the AV has "the elements of the world" (mg. "rudiments"); RSV and NEB "the elemental spirits of the universe" (NEB mg. "elements of the natural world, *or* elementary ideas belonging to this world"). In Gal. 4:9 the AV has "the weak and beggarly elements"; RSV "the weak and beggarly elemental spirits"; NEB "the mean and beggarly spirits of the elements."

In Col. 2:8 the AV reads "the rudiments of the world" (mg. "elements"); RSV "the elemental spirits of the universe"; NEB "the elemental spirits of the world" (mg. "rudimentary notions").

In He. 5:12 the AV has "the first principles of the oracles of God"; RSV "the first principles of God's word"; NEB "the ABC of God's oracles."

In 2 Pet. 3:10, 12, the AV, RSV, and NEB all render the word *stoicheía* as "the elements."

I. Greek Literature Outside the NT.–The following six meanings show how diversified is the use of this word: (1) It designates the lengths of shadows. (2) As an ancient linguistic term it refers to a syllable or constituent part of a word. (3) It refers to cosmic or elemental substances. (4) It is a descriptive term for the elementary details of music instruction or the basic matters of mathematics. (5) It designates the stars or heavenly bodies. (6) It refers to spirit beings or elemental spirits of the stars. (For all of these meanings and related aspects see *TDNT*.)

II. Meanings and Theological Importance in the NT.–In 2 Pet. 3:10-13 the word *stoicheía* occurs twice (vv. 10, 12). Here it means "the elemental substances of the universe." In the day of the Lord the heavens will pass away with a roar, and these elemental substances, being on fire, will break up into their component parts (v. 10), or melt (v. 12). Thus, says Peter, there is no permanence or stability in material things. Because Christians are expecting these catastrophic changes, they are to make every effort to be spotless and without blemish. They want to be found by Christ in peace (2 Pet. 3:14). Since all things will be in the process of being dissolved, Christians are to be persons of quality in a holy manner of life doing godly acts (3:11).

The use in Hebrews is in the context of the writer's concern about his readers. They had become sluggish in their hearing. They had not matured. They were not able to be teachers but needed someone to teach them the initial elements of God's oracles (He. 5:11). The NEB renders the term *tá stoicheía* as "the ABC of God's oracles." These initial elements are listed in He. 6:1f. The basic principles referred to here certainly parallel the basic principles of mathematics or the elemental principles of music. (*See also* ELEMENTARY DOCTRINES OF CHRIST.)

Any agreement about how to translate *tá stoicheía* disappears when we consider the use of the term in Gal. 4:3, 9. The context in 4:1-11 must determine what meaning is given the word. At the close of ch. 3 those who are Christ's are Abraham's offspring and heirs according to God's promise. In the legal system of Judaism an heir was controlled closely by his father. He did not enter into the rights of manhood until the date set by his father (4:2). When the fulness of time came, God sent forth His Son to redeem those who were under the law (4:4) and thus made it possible for all men to receive sonship (5:5).

In this context the idea that Paul is referring to "the elemental spirits of the universe" does not make good sense. The context surrounding Gal. 4:3 favors the idea that when the readers were children and when Paul was younger, they were all part of a Jewish or gentile religion. In their former states they were in bondage to a way of life that did not give them freedom. Judaism, the religious expression of Paul and his contemporaries, was not a pure interpretation of the OT. Legalism had replaced law. The Gentiles knew neither God nor the law of the OT in its right meaning. They were tied up with idolatries (4:8). To return to any type of legalism would be to return to the weak and miserable religious expressions that preceded Christ and His freedom (v. 9). The "elements of this world" here are the constitutive elements of man's existence prior to God's sending His Son in the fulness of time. Christ's life and deeds made a radical change in how man's existence is to be constituted. Hence, as Delling has pointed out, "the elements of the world" is a Pauline term — not that of the Galatian readers (*TDNT*, VII, 684f.). For Paul, it summarized life before the fulness of time, before Christ's coming.

The phrase *tá stoicheía* occurs twice in Col. 2 (vv. 8, 20). In v. 8 it is parallel to the phrase "the traditions of men." It is contrasted with "being according to Christ." Paul is concerned about the Colossians. Living in the world, they have become subject to rules and regulations (v. 19). In this context, the "elemental spirits of the universe" is too specific a translation. Rather, if we translate *tá stoicheía* as "the elements of the world" (vv. 8, 20), the passage would seem to teach that religious activities not centered in Christ are judged by God to be invalid. To die with Christ is to be set free from these elements of the world (v. 20). They come under Christ's judgment because they are only commandments and teachings of men (v. 22). Those Colossians who may have been involved with worship of angels (v. 18) needed to break with this as well as with any of the other elements in their existence. But there is never any explicit connection between the elements of the world and the worship of angels. In Colossians, "the elements of the world" is again a broad term for human existence apart from Christ.

III. Creativity of Paul.–The expression "the elements of the world" in Galatians and Colossians is a vivid description by Paul of elements that characterize man in revolt. These elements show man's busy activities in which allegiance to God and Christ is absent. They denote a way of life that is not according to Christ. They designate the busy round of activities that discloses man's estrangement from God and from which man is set free when he genuinely identifies himself with Christ's death. Functioning in this way, the phrase "elements of the world" stands for all that is involved in bondage as contrasted with the freedom that comes in Christ.

Bibliography.–A. J. Bandstra, *Law and the Elements of the World* (1964); *TDNT*, VII, *s.v.* στοιχεῖον (Delling).

A. B. MICKELSEN

ELEMENTARY DOCTRINES OF CHRIST [Gk. *ho tḗs archḗs toú Christoú lógos*] (He. 6:1); AV PRINCIPLES OF THE DOCTRINE OF CHRIST; NEB RUDIMENTS OF CHRISTIANITY. Here *lógos* is to be understood as "doctrine(s)," *archḗ* ("beginning") in the genitive as adjectival, and *toú Christoú* as modifying *lógos* (not *archḗ*). Thus, the whole expression refers to the teachings about Christ that come first, not to teachings about the beginning (origin) of Christ. *See also* ELEMENT II.

ELEPH ēl'ef (Josh. 18:28). *See* HA-ELEPH.

ELEPHANT [Gk. *eléphas*] (1 Macc. 3:34; 6:30ff.; 8:6). During the Hellenistic age elephants were used militarily. These were mainly imported from India, although some evidence points to the breeding of the animals by the Seleucids in Syria. Lysias included thirty-two of them in his army mustered against the Jews in 163 B.C.

ELEPHANTINE PAPYRI el-ə-fan-tē'nē pə-pī'rī. A collection of fifth-century B.C. papyri recovered from a settlement on an island in the Nile in Upper Egypt opposite Aswân (about 885 km., 550 mi. S of Cairo). The colony is known by the Greek name *Elephantinē* ("elephant location"), but the Egyptians called it *Iebew*. Situated at the First Cataract of the Nile, the island was often considered to mark the southern extremity of ancient Egypt, along with the city Syene, which was located across the Nile on the east bank.

The papyri, written in Aramaic, were acquired in two principal sections. In 1893 C. E. Wilbour obtained some Aramaic legal texts from a dealer in Aswân, but the documents were placed in the Brooklyn Museum and lay unread

Bearded and barefoot men from Musri (Egypt?) bring elephants and monkeys as tribute. Panel of the Black Obelisk of Shalmaneser III (858-824 B.C.) (Trustees of the British Museum)

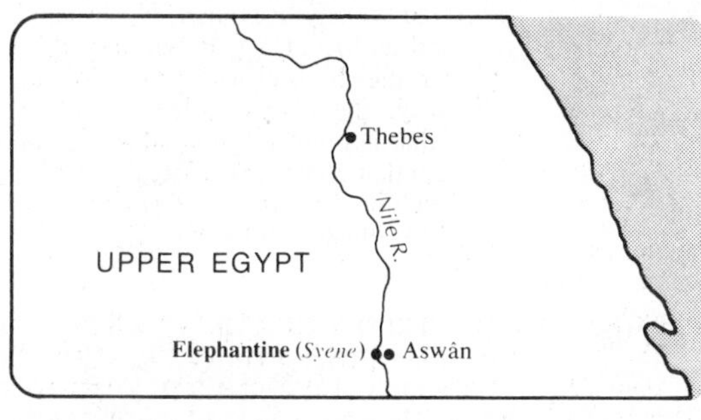

The island of Elephantine in the Nile near Aswân (W. S. LaSor)

until they were published in 1953 by E. G. Kraeling. The second batch, which also comprised legal and some literary texts, was also purchased from Aswân dealers in antiquities, and appeared in separate publications by A. H. Sayce, A. E. Cowley, and E. Sachau between 1906 and 1911.

The colony from which these texts originated was a Jewish military settlement. In the documents the outpost is called "Yeb the fortress," preserving in modified form the older Egyptian name of the area (*Yeb* is Egyptian for "elephant"). Because of limited space on the island, the inhabitants bought residences in nearby Syene and in effect established a similar defensive post there. While Elephantine is not mentioned by name in the OT, its destiny was doubtless subsumed under that of Syene in the prophecies of Ezekiel (29:10; 30:6).

Origins of the establishment at Elephantine are obscure. The papyri imply that it had been in existence long before Cambyses, son of Cyrus, conquered Egypt in 525 B.C. Perhaps it had originated as a Jewish settlement far to the south of troubled Palestine when the Babylonians were threatening the future of that land in the time of Jeremiah. If so, it would have formed a natural basis for a military garrison organized by Cambyses to maintain Persian control over Egypt, and it was perhaps this latter circumstance that precipitated the trouble of which some of the papyri complain. At all events, the settlement began when Egypt and the Judeans were on friendly terms, perhaps during the reign of Pharaoh Hophra (Apries, 588-566 B.C.), mentioned in Jer. 44:30. The papyri indicate that the settlement survived well into the postexilic period. There are some grounds for thinking that the Jewish garrison was removed after the accession of Nepherites in 399 B.C., but that Jews continued to live in the general area up to the beginning of the Christian era.

One of the principal concerns of the papyri was with a temple at Yeb dedicated to *Yhw* (a modified form of the sacred Hebrew name for God). This temple had apparently been constructed before the invasion of Egypt by Cambyses II, but had been destroyed by Egyptian insurgents in 410 B.C. That worship in this shrine was syncretistic may be inferred from the long list of contributors (many of them women) to the upkeep of the

Two of the Elephantine Papyri — a sealed marriage contract (bottom) and a deed for a house (top) — from the time of Darius II (*ca.* 420 B.C.) (Brooklyn Museum)

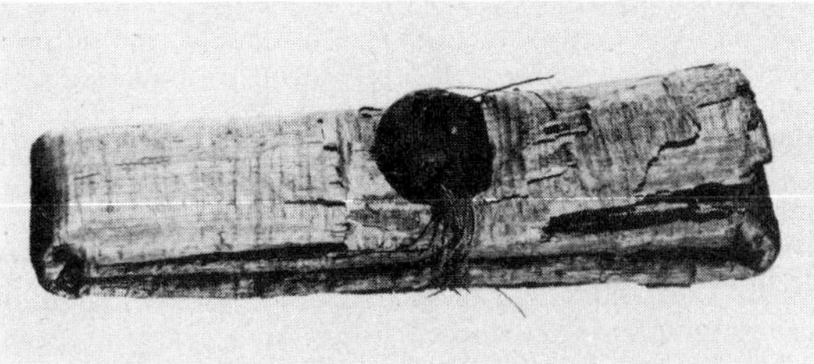

temple, for besides *Yhw* the donors honor also *Ishum-bethel, Anath-bethel,* and *Herem-bethel.* The *bethel* ("house of God") part of the name has been regarded by scholars as a mere designation of deity, and not as the proper name of a deity or a place. The deity designated by the compound name *Anath-Yhw,* a variant in the texts for *Anath-bethel,* may have been regarded as a consort of *Yhw* and was possibly the "queen of heaven" whose worship by the seventh-century B.C. Judeans was castigated in Jer. 7:18; 44:17. Certain of the letters request the blessing of "the gods" on the recipients, which indicates an accommodation to Egyptian polytheism at least in the use of the epistolary formula, but in other respects traditional Hebrew phrases such as "God of heaven" and "Lord of hosts" are also found, the latter on a potsherd.

Older liberal scholars professed "surprise" that a Jewish temple should have been standing in Elephantine in the 5th cent. B.C. (so H. H. Rowley in *DOTT,* p. 257). This perplexity was based on the theory that King Josiah had promulgated the "law of Deuteronomy" in 621 B.C., which, according to the interpretations of nineteenth-century exponents of literary criticism, had centralized worship in Jerusalem and prohibited the use of any other sacrificial altar. There is no evidence, however, that the scroll recovered in the time of Josiah consisted of the book of Deuteronomy, either in part or in whole; nor is there any objective support for the assumption that either the law scroll found by Hilkiah or the extant book of Deuteronomy prescribed Jerusalem as the place where a single sanctuary was to be established. (*See* DEUTERONOMY IV.) Deuteronomy simply does not consider the matter of erecting shrines in other countries, because in the time of Moses the expectation was that the Israelites would live as a spiritual community in the land that God had provided for them. But these conditions changed as the result of continued Israelite apostasy and the prospect of consequent destruction by enemies of the nation. Those who left Judah in the 7th cent. B.C. for less troubled areas were certainly not prohibited by Deuteronomy or any other part of the Mosaic legislation from building a shrine outside of Palestine, and thus the construction of a Jewish temple at Yeb for the worship of *Yhw* would have been both legitimate and normal.

One of the documents, the so-called Passover papyrus, throws light on the patterns of worship in the Yeb shrine. The text has been poorly preserved, but with some restoration it has been shown to deal with a festival celebrated in the month of Nisan. The document was sent in 419 B.C., by authority of Darius II, instructing the colony to observe the feast of Unleavened Bread. It mentions a count of fourteen days in Nisan, after which a gap in the text is followed by an injunction regarding a period from the fifteenth to the twenty-first day of the same month. There is no specific reference to the Passover, but this may have occurred originally in the portion that is now missing. Some scholars have maintained that there was never any reference to the Passover in the text, suggesting that the killing of an animal would have antagonized the local Egyptians, who venerated almost every animal in some manner as a god. Whatever the nature of the original document, it was issued by authority of the Persian king, like similar edicts in the time of Ezra and Nehemiah.

One of the most interesting of the letters is that addressed by the colonists of Yeb to Bagoas, the Persian governor of Judea. It seems to have been the successor to an earlier complaint sent to a Persian official in Egypt about the wanton destruction of the temple by rebellious Egyptians in 410 B.C. That letter had apparently gone unanswered, hence the petition in 407 B.C. to Bagoas, a copy of which was kept at Yeb. The document was sent by "your servants Yedoniah and his colleagues," and reports the shameless pillaging of the shrine. A concluding section requests official approval for the reconstruction of the building, and also states that the sons of Sanballat, governor of Samaria in the time of Nehemiah, have been requested to help.

If an official reply was received by the priests of Yeb, it has not survived. A memorandum has been recovered, however, which indicates that a verbal response sent to Arsames, the Persian governor in Egypt, supported the request for permission to rebuild. This is evidence that the Persian rulers took a genuine interest in the lives of their subjects, taking care to accommodate religious traditions. Meal offerings and incense are specified as the only ritual procedures to be followed, "as was done formerly." Another smaller Aramaic text dealing with the proposed reconstruction of the temple states specifically that sheep, oxen, and goats were not offered there. Thus it is far from certain that the Passover was ever observed at Yeb, at least in its traditional form.

Other papyri from Elephantine include marriage contracts, documents relating to adoption, and texts containing a number of business procedures connected especially with two families in the colony. All the transactions had been drawn up in an approved legal fashion, attested by witnesses, and then sealed. A notation or "docket" on the exterior of the papyrus gave an indication of its contents. All of this was thoroughly in accord with the Babylonian tradition adopted by the Persians. Estate transactions are well represented among the texts, and they show that both men and women could engage in business. Among the other facets of civil life at Yeb and Syene revealed by the papyri is the extremely high rate of interest charged on loans, a circumstance that frequently resulted in civil litigation.

The Elephantine papyri are the principal witnesses to the existence of Aramaic in Egypt. The extent to which Aramaic had by this time become the language of commerce and diplomacy is also made abundantly clear. That members of the community at Yeb spoke and wrote in Aramaic is evidence that this language was popular in Palestine before the Exile. The language of the papyri is a rather early form of the official Aramaic appearing in Daniel and Ezra, and is of great importance for the period of Ezra and Nehemiah. The letters in Ezr. 4 particularly exhibit a great many of the characteristics of fifth-century B.C. Aramaic. The documents are all the more significant as external evidence because of the scarcity of such material as background for the fifth-century B.C. OT writings.

Bibliography.–A. H. Sayce and A. E. Cowley, *Aramaic Papyri Discovered at Assuan* (1906); E. Sachau, *Aramäische Papyrus und Ostraka* (1911); A. Ungnad, *Aramäische Papyrus aus Elephantine* (1911); W. Staerk, *Jüdisch-Aramäische Papyrus aus Elephantine* (2nd ed. 1912); A. E. Cowley, *Aramaic Papyri of the Fifth Century B.C.* (1932); E. G. Kraeling, *Brooklyn Museum Aramaic Papyri* (1953); *ANET,* pp. 222f., 548f.; *DOTT,* pp. 256-269.

R. K. HARRISON

ELEUTHERUS e-loo'thər-əs [Gk. *Eleútheros*] (1 Macc. 11:7; 12:30). A river in Syria flowing from the base of the Lebanon to the sea. It formed an important boundary and is mentioned in the account of Jonathan Maccabeus in 1 Maccabees. It is probably to be identified with Nahr el-Kebir, 30 km. (19 mi.) N of Tripoli in Lebanon.

Bibliography.–Y. Aharoni and M. Avi-Yonah, *Macmillan Bible Atlas* (1968), map 203; Strabo *Geog.* xvi.2.12. W. S. L. S.

ELEVEN, THE [Gk. *hoi héndeka*] (Lk. 24:9, 33; Acts 2:14). The eleven apostles remaining after the death of Judas. The definite article serves to designate them as a distinct group whose integrity was not destroyed by the loss of one of the twelve. The company of "the twelve" had come to be so well recognized that all the Gospel writers used on occasions the word with the definite article to represent the twelve apostles chosen by Jesus. This custom remained and the numeral merely changed, as, "Afterward he appeared to the eleven" (Mk. 16:14). On the other hand, the substantive is also sometimes used, as, "Now the eleven disciples went to Galilee" (Mt. 28:16; cf. also Acts 1:26). As an illustration of the fixedness of usage, Paul refers to the eleven as "the twelve" when he recounts the appearances of Jesus after His resurrection: "and that he appeared to Cephas, then to the twelve" (1 Cor. 15:5). W. G. CLIPPINGER

ELHANAN el-hā'nən [Heb. *'elḥānān*–'God is gracious'].

1. A great warrior in the army of David who slew a Philistine giant. There is a discrepancy between 2 S. 21:19 and 1 Ch. 20:5. In the former passage we read, "And there was again war with the Philistines at Gob; and Elhanan the son of Jaareoregim, the Bethlehemite, slew Goliath the Gittite, the shaft of whose spear was like a weaver's beam"; while in the latter we are told, "And there was again war with the Philistines; and Elhanan the son of Jair slew Lahmi the brother of Goliath the Gittite, the shaft of whose spear was like a weaver's beam."

On careful comparison it is possible to discern a distinct relationship between the two passages, with the former containing certain transcriptional errors. The name of Elhanan's father should not contain the Hebrew word *'ōr^e^gîm,* which is an obvious copyist's mistake resulting from the occurrence of the term (Eng. "beam," "shuttle") at the end of that same verse. The name "Jaare" should be revised to agree with the textual variant in the Chronicles reference, i.e., Jairi. J. R. SAMPEY

In addition, the accusative particle *'ēṯ* in 2 S. 21:19 should read *'^a^ḥî* ("the brother of"), as in 1 Ch. 20:5. Finally, the term in Chronicles from which the name Lahmi is derived should be corrected to read "Bethlehemite," following the text of 2 Samuel. As corrected, the verse would then read: "And Elhanan, the son of Jairi the Bethlehemite, slew the brother of Goliath . . . ," thus removing the apparent discrepancy. R. K. H.

The resemblance to the story of David has been explained in two other ways. (1) With Jerome, it has been proposed that Elhanan is a name for David (some more recent scholars even supposing that "David" is the throne-name). (2) Following Ewald, it has been asserted that the name "Goliath" from the Elhanan story was inserted in 1 S. 17 and 21. Most conservative scholars consider these conjectures unnecessary.

2. The son of Dodo of Bethlehem, one of David's mighty men (2 S. 23:24; 1 Ch. 11:26). Some scholars think that there was only one Elhanan, and that he was the son of Dodo of the clan of Jair.

ELI ē'lī [Heb. *'ēlî*]; AV also HELI (2 Esd. 1:2). A descendant of Ithamar, the fourth son of Aaron, who exercised the office of high priest in Shiloh at the time of Samuel's birth. For the first time in Israel, Eli combined in his own person the functions of high priest and judge, judging Israel for forty years (1 S. 4:18).

The recorded events in Eli's life are few; indeed, the main interest of the narrative is in the other characters who are associated with him, particularly Samuel. In Eli's first interview with Hannah (1 S. 1:12ff.) she is the central figure; in the second interview (vv. 24ff.) it is the child Samuel. Eli next appears as the father of Hophni and Phinehas, whose licentious lives had profaned their priestly office and earned for them the title "men of Belial" (or "worthlessness"). Eli administered no stern rebuke to his sons, but only a gentle chiding of their greed and immorality. Thereafter he was warned by an unnamed prophet of the downfall of his house and of the death of both of his sons in one day (2:27-36); this was later confirmed by Samuel, who had received this word directly from Yahweh Himself (3:11ff.). The prophecy was not long in fulfillment. During the next invasion by the Philistines the Israelites were utterly routed, the ark of God was captured, and Hophni and Phinehas were both slain. When the news reached Eli he was so overcome that he "fell over backward from his seat by the side of the gate; and his neck was broken and he died" (4:18).

Eli, while sincere and devout, seems to have been lacking in firmness. He appears from the history to have been a good man, full of humility and gentleness, but weak and indulgent. He is always overshadowed by some more commanding or interesting figure. A. C. GRANT

ELI, ELI, LAMA SABACHTHANI ā'lē, ā'lē, lä'mə sə-bäk-thä'nē [Gk. *ēlí ēlí lemá sabachtháni*] (Mt. 27:46); NEB *"Eli, Eli, lema sabachthani";* **ELOI** ē'loi or e-lō'ī, **ELOI, LAMA SABACHTHANI** [Gk. *elōí elōí lamá sabachtháni*] (Mk. 15:34); NEB *"Eli, Eli, lema sabachthani."* A statement uttered by Jesus on the cross just before His death, translated, "My God, my God, why hast thou forsaken me?" With some changes of form, it is probably from Ps. 22:1 [MT 2]: Heb. *'ēlî 'ēlî lāmâ ʿᵃzaḇtānî*.

Variations exist on the readings of both Matthew and Mark. In some Matthaean MSS *elōí* occurs for *ēlí* and in some Markan MSS *ēlí* for *elōí*. The passage seems to be a mixture of Hebrew and Aramaic. The *elōí* of Mark and *lemá* of Matthew are closer to the Aramaic. Scholars do not agree about whether Jesus uttered this cry in Hebrew or Aramaic. In either language the first two words bear sufficient similarity to the name Elias to explain the jeer that Jesus was calling upon Elias (Elijah).

The Gospel writers note several instances of correspondence between the suffering of Jesus and the experience of the psalmist described in Ps. 22 (cf. Mk. 15:29 with Ps. 22:7, Mt. 27:43 with Ps. 22:8, and Mt. 27:35; Mk. 15:24; Lk. 23:34; Jn. 19:23f. with Ps. 22:18). Jesus may have been meditating upon this Psalm, as the Jews sometimes did in times of suffering. In any case, He used the opening lines to express His sense of being abandoned by God. It should be noted that Ps. 22 ends in a hymn of triumph and thanksgiving to God for His deliverance; thus, this lament does not indicate a loss of faith in God. N. J. O.

ELIAB ē-lī'əb [Heb. *'ᵉlî'āḇ*–'God is father'].

1. Prince of the tribe of Zebulun in the Exodus (Nu. 1:9; 2:7; 7:24, 29; 10:16).

2. A Reubenite, father of Dathan and Abiram (Nu. 16:1, 12; 26:8f.; Dt. 11:6).

3. Eldest son of Jesse and brother of David (1 Ch. 2:13; 1 S. 16:6), once called Elihu (1 Ch. 27:18). He was of commanding appearance (1 S. 16:6) and, serving with Saul's army when it was confronting the Philistines and Goliath, was inclined to lord it over his brother David (17:28f.). His daughter Abihail became a wife of Rehoboam (2 Ch. 11:18).

4. An Ephraimite, an ancestor of Samuel (1 Ch. 6:27); called Eliel in v. 34 and Elihu in 1 S. 1:1.

5. A Gadite warrior with David (1 Ch. 12:9), one of eleven mighty men (vv. 8, 14).

6. A Levite musician (1 Ch. 15:18, 20; 16:5).

7. An ancestor of Judith (Jth. 8:1; cf. 9:2).

F. K. FARR

ELIADA ē-lī'ə-də [Heb. *'elyāḏāʿ*–'God knows'].

1. One of the sons of David (2 S. 5:16; 1 Ch. 3:8; called BEELIADA in 1 Ch. 14:7).

2. A descendant of Benjamin and a captain in the army of Jehoshaphat, commander of 200,000 men (2 Ch. 17:17).

3. Father of Rezon, an "adversary" of Solomon (1 K. 11:23, AV "Eliadah").

ELIADAS ē-lī'ə-dəs (AV, RSV mg., NEB, 1 Esd. 9:28). *See* ELIOENAI **5.**

ELIADUN ē-lī'ə-dən (AV 1 Esd. 5:58). *See* ILIADUN.

ELIAH ē-lī'ə (AV 1 Ch. 8:27; Ezr. 10:26; NEB 1 Ch. 8:27). *See* ELIJAH **2, 4.**

ELIAHBA ē-lī'ə-bə [Heb. *'elyaḥbā'*–'God hides']. One of David's thirty mighty men (2 S. 23:32; 1 Ch. 11:33).

ELIAKIM ē-lī'ə-kim [Heb. *'elyāqîm*; Gk. *Eliakeim*–'God raises up'].

1. The son of Hilkiah who succeeded Shebna as governor of the palace and "grand vizier" under Hezekiah (Isa. 22:20). The functions of his office are seen from the oracle of Isaiah in which Shebna is deposed and Eliakim set in his place (22:15ff.). He is the "steward" and is "over the household" (v. 15). At his installation he is clothed with a robe and girdle, the insignia of his office, and, having the government committed into his hand, is the "father to the inhabitants of Jerusalem and to the house of Judah" (v. 21). The key of the house of David is laid on his shoulder, and he alone has power to open and shut, this being symbolic of his absolute authority as the king's representative (v. 22).

One of Solomon's officials is the first mentioned as occupying this position (1 K. 4:6); the office was continued in both the northern and southern kingdoms (1 K. 16:9; 18:3; 2 K. 10:5; 15:5). Its importance is seen from the fact that after Azariah was smitten with leprosy, Jotham his heir "was over the household, governing the people of the land" (2 K. 15:5).

When Sennacherib sent an army against Jerusalem in 701, Eliakim was one of those Jewish princes who held, on behalf of Hezekiah, a parley with the Assyrian officers (2 K. 18:18, 26, 37; Isa. 36:3, 11, 22). As a result of the invader's threats, he was sent by Hezekiah in sackcloth to Isaiah, entreating his prayers to Yahweh on behalf of Jerusalem (2 K. 19:2; Isa. 37:2).

2. The original name of JEHOIAKIM, the son of Josiah, whom Pharoah Neco made king of Judah (2 K. 23:34; 2 Ch. 36:4).

3. A priest who assisted at the dedication of the wall of Jerusalem, rebuilt after his return from Babylon (Neh. 12:41).

4. A grandson of Zerubbabel and ancestor of Jesus (Mt. 1:13).

5. An ancestor of Jesus (Lk. 3:30). S. F. HUNTER

ELIALI ē-lī'ə-lī. *See* ELIALIS.

ELIALIS ē-lī'ə-lis [Gk. *Elialis*] (1 Esd. 9:34); AV, NEB, ELIALI. One of the sons of Bani who put away foreign wives and children.

ELIAM ē-lī'əm [Heb. *'ᵉlîʿām*–'people's God'(?)].

1. Father of Bathsheba (2 S. 11:3); in 1 Ch. 3:5 called Ammiel.

2. One of David's "thirty," son of Ahithophel the Gilonite (2 S. 23:34).

ELIAONIAS ē-lī-ə-ō-nī'əs (AV, NEB, 1 Esd. 8:31). *See* ELIEHOENAI.

ELIAS ē-lī'əs. *See* ELIJAH.

ELIASAPH ē'lī'ə-saf [Heb. *'elyāsāp*–'God has added'].

1. Son of Deuel; prince of the tribe of Gad in the Exodus (Nu. 1:14; 2:14; 7:42, 47; 10:20).

2. Son of Lael; prince of the Gershonites (Nu. 3:24).

ELIASHIB ē-lī'ə-shib [Heb. *'elyāšîḇ*–'God restores'; Gk. *Eliasibos* (1 Esd. 9:1, 24), *Eliasimos* (1 Esd. 9:28), *Enasibos* (1 Esd. 9:34)]; AV also ELEAZURUS, ELISIMUS, ELIASIB, ENASIBUS; NEB also ELIASIBUS, ELIASIMUS, ENASIBUS.

1. A descendant of David (1 Ch. 3:24).

2. Head of the eleventh course of priests (1 Ch. 24:12).

3. The high priest in the time of Nehemiah (Neh. 3:1, 20f.; 12:10, 22f.; 13:4, 7, 28). He, with his brethren the priests, helped in the rebuilding of the wall (3:1). But later he was "connected with Tobiah" the Ammonite (13:4) and allowed that enemy of Nehemiah the use of a large chamber in the temple (v. 5); one of his grandsons, a son of Jehoiada, married a daughter of SANBALLAT the Horonite and was for this reason expelled from the community by Nehemiah (v. 28).

4, 5, 6. Three Israelites, one a "singer," who had married foreign wives (Ezr. 10:24, 27, 36; 1 Esd. 9:24, 28, 34).

7. Father of Jehohanan (Ezr. 10:6; 1 Esd. 9:1); probably identical with **3** above. F. K. FARR

ELIASIB ē-lī'ə-sib. *See* ELIASHIB **7.**

ELIASIBUS ē-li-as'i-bəs. *See* ELIASHIB **4, 7.**

ELIASIMUS ē-li-as'i-məs. *See* ELIASHIB **5.**

ELIASIS ē-lī'ə-sis [Gk. *Eliasis*]. One who had married a foreign wife (1 Esd. 9:34). Attempts to identify him with Jaasu (Ezr. 10:37) or Binnui (Ezr. 10:38) are unconvincing.

ELIATHAH ē-lī'ə-thə [Heb. *'ĕlî'āṯâ*–'God has come']. A Hemanite, head of the twentieth division of the temple musicians (1 Ch. 25:4, 27). *See also* JOSHBEKASHAH.

ELIDAD ē-lī'dad [Heb. *'ĕlîḏāḏ*–'God has loved']. A leader of the tribe of Benjamin appointed by Moses to help in the division of the land of Canaan (Nu. 34:21); perhaps the same as ELDAD.

ELIEHOENAI ē-lī'ə-hō-ē'-nī [Heb. *'elyᵉhô'ênay*–'to Yahweh are my eyes'].

1. (AV, NEB, "Elioenai"). A gatekeeper of the family of Korah (1 Ch. 26:3).

2. (AV, NEB, "Elihoenai"). Head of a family that returned from the Exile (Ezr. 8:4). The RSV also renders Eliehoenai in 1 Esd. 8:31 for Gk. *Elialōnias* (AV, NEB, "Eliaonias").

ELIEL ē-lī'əl [Heb. *'ĕlî'ēl*–'El is God,' or 'my God is God'].

1, 2, 3. Mighty men of David (1 Ch. 11:46f.; 12:11).

4. A chief of Manasseh, E of the Jordan (1 Ch. 5:24).

5, 6. Two chiefs of Benjamin (1 Ch. 8:20, 22).

7. A chief Levite from Hebron (1 Ch. 15:9, 11).

8. A Kohathite in the line of Elkanah, Samuel, and Heman (1 Ch. 6:34). *See* ELIAB **4.**

9. A Levite of the time of Hezekiah (2 Ch. 31:13).

ELIENAI el-i-ē'nī [Heb. *'ĕlî'ênay*]. A Benjaminite chief (1 Ch. 8:20).

ELIEZER el-i-ē'zər [Heb. *'ĕlî'ezer*; Gk. *Eliezer*–'my God is help'].

1. The chief servant of Abraham (Gen. 15:2; AV, RSV, NEB, "Eliezer of Damascus"). The Hebrew is peculiar: lit. "and the son of the possession (*mešeq*) of my house is *dammeśeq* (of) Eliezer." A possible but unlikely meaning is that his property would become the possession of Damascus, the city of Eliezer. The Syriac Targum reads "Eliezer the Damascene"; this supposes a reading, "Eliezer *haddammaśqî*" or "*middammeśeq*". The text may be corrupt: the assonance between *mešeq* and *dammeśeq* is suspicious. Abraham calls Eliezer "a slave born in my house" (v. 3), i.e., a dependent, a member of his household, and so regards him as his heir in place of Lot, who had left his house (ch. 13). Eliezer is probably the servant described as "the oldest of his house, who had charge of all that he had" (24:2), whom Abraham sent to find a wife for Isaac.

2. The second son of Moses and Zipporah, called thus because "the God of my father was my help, and delivered me from the sword of Pharaoh" (Ex. 18:4; 1 Ch. 23:15, 17; 26:25).

3. A son of Becher, one of the sons of Benjamin (1 Ch. 7:8).

4. A priest who assisted in bringing up the ark from the house of Obed-edom to Jerusalem (1 Ch. 15:24).

5. The son of Zichri, ruler over the Reubenites in the time of David (1 Ch. 27:16).

6. The son of Dodavahu of Mareshah who prophesied the destruction of the ships which Jehoshaphat king of Judah built, because he had done so in cooperation with Ahaziah king of Israel (2 Ch. 20:35ff.).

7. One of the messengers whom Ezra sent to Iddo, the chief of Casiphia, with the request for ministers for the temple (Ezr. 8:16ff.).

8, 9, 10. A priest (Ezr. 10:18), a Levite (v. 23), and one of the sons of Harim (v. 31), all of whom were required to divorce their foreign wives.

11. An ancestor of Jesus in the genealogy given by Luke (3:29). S. F. HUNTER

ELIHOENAI (AV Ezr. 8:4). *See* ELIEHOENAI **2.**

ELIHOREPH el-ə-hō'ref [Heb. *'ĕlîḥōrep*–'God of autumn'?]; NEB "in charge of the calendar." A son of Shisha who with his brother Ahijah held the office of secretary to king Solomon (1 K. 4:3). For the NEB reading, see J. A. Montgomery, *Books of the Kings* (*ICC*, 1955).

ELIHU ē-lī'hū, ē-lī'hōō [Heb. *'ĕlîhû'*, *'ĕlîhû*–'He is (my) God'; Gk. *Ēliou*].

1. Samuel's great-grandfather (1 S. 1:1), called ELIAB (**4**) in 1 Ch. 6:27 and Eliel in 1 Ch. 6:34.

2. David's eldest brother ELIAB (**3**) is so called in 1 Ch. 27:18; since the LXX has Eliab here, the MT reading is probably a scribal error, though his eldest brother may well be intended.

3. A Manassite who joined David at Ziklag (1 Ch. 12:20).

4. A gatekeeper of the family of Korah, a descendant of Obed-edom (1 Ch. 26:7).

5. A character in the book of Job. He is of the tribe of Buz (cf. Gen. 22:21), a brother tribe of Uz (Job 1:1); thus (with the other characters in the book) from Transjordan. Elihu is the only character whose genealogy is given (32:2); thus, while the earlier speakers have been speaking from the standpoint of the wise, Elihu gives the well-bred aristocrat's point of view. After his introduction (32:6-22) he has three answers to Job (chs. 33, 34, 35–37). In spite of his indignation against Job's friends for their failure to prove Job wrong, he does little better. Elihu makes some new points in ch. 33, but in ch. 34 he fails to equal Bildad's argument, and in chs. 35–37 shows himself unable to cope with the greatness of God.

Most modern commentators see Elihu as a later interpolation, though some consider him an afterthought by the original author. No adequate reason is suggested why he should have been interpolated; nor is there much force in the suggestion that he had not been mentioned before, for had he been, the tension of the work would have been seriously affected, as the reader waited for his contribution. As it is, he enables Job to relax sufficiently to receive the divine revelation. The argument that God ignores Elihu's intervention (38:2 refers to Job), thereby showing that he was not in the original version, is valueless, for Job's friends are equally ignored.

A more cogent argument for regarding Elihu as a later interpolation is that the Epilogue (42:7-9) mentions the others but not Elihu. Critics point also to the peculiar language and style of the Elihu section, claiming that it interrupts the natural progression from ch. 31 (Job's challenge) to ch. 38 (God's reply).

But none of these arguments is decisive, and Elihu does serve to show that the mystery of God's working surpasses all wisdom of man, not merely that of one class or age. In addition, his speeches can be seen as providing a further dramatic basis for the Lord's discourses in the following chapters.

See also JOB. H. L. ELLISON

ELIJAH [Heb. *'ēlîyāhû* or *'ēlîyâ* (Mal. 4:5 [MT 3:23])–'my God is Yah(weh)'; Gk. *Ēleias*]; AV ELIAS (NT).

1. The Prophet.

- I. Introduction
  - A. Elijah the Man
  - B. Circumstances of His Ministry
  - C. Primary Sources
- II. Elijah's Ministry
  - A. Baal Challenged
  - B. Judgment on Ahab and Jezebel Announced
  - C. Elijah and Ahaziah
  - D. Elijah's Translation
  - E. A Letter to Jehoram
- III. In the Latter Prophets
- IV. In the Intertestamental Literature
- V. In the NT
  - A. Elijah and John the Baptist
  - B. Elijah and Jesus
  - C. In the Epistles and Revelation
- VI. In Early A.D. Extrabiblical Literature
  - A. Judaic
  - B. Christian

***I. Introduction.**–A. Elijah the Man.* His name and memory have defied the passage of time, but about Elijah the man very little is known. Biblical traditions concerning him lack even a genealogy. He was a Tishbite, but it is unclear whether he came from Tishbe near Kedesh Naphtali (mentioned in Tobit 1:2 as "Thisbe") or from some otherwise unknown Tishbe in Gilead (based on the LXX rendering of *mittōšāḇê* ["from the inhabitants of," 1 K. 17:1]; cf. Josephus *Ant.* viii.13.2). His haunts were far from the cities, and his distinctive garb was a mantle (1 K. 19:13, 19; 2 K. 2:8, 13f.), perhaps woven of hair, with a rawhide rope tied around his waist (2 K. 1:8)—later recognized as the traditional garb of a prophet (Zech. 13:4; Mt. 3:4). Of his physical characteristics we know nothing; even his age is a matter of some conjecture, although he must have been well on in years when first we meet him in the Kings narrative.

B. Circumstances of His Ministry. In Elijah's day the religious life of the northern kingdom was in crisis. The political policies of Omri had tended toward an amalgamation of Israel with the Canaanite enclaves remaining in the land. Ahab carried his father's policies even farther. Spurred on by the haughty and strong-willed Jezebel, a devotee of the Tyrian Baal Melqart and his consort Asherah/Astarte (Jezebel's father was Ethbaal king of Sidon, who was, or had been, a priest of Astarte; cf. Josephus *CAp* i.18), Ahab established the cult of Baal and Asherah in his capital city of Samaria (1 K. 16:32f.). The large number of Baal and Asherah prophets maintained under Jezebel's sponsorship at court (18:19), and her brazen attempt to purge the realm of the prophets of Yahweh (v. 13), give striking evidence of her powerful influence. Ahab, though he gave his children Yahwist names (Azariah, Jehoram, Athaliah), apparently acquiesced in her designs. Elijah's prophetic ministry is presented as Yahweh's response to this crisis.

C. Primary Sources. All that we know of Elijah is based on the account of his ministry found in Kings, together with a brief notice in 2 Ch. 21. Other sources add nothing of substance.

The author of KINGS evidently had available to him an account of Elijah's ministry. From this source he selected what was useful and wove it into his narrative. This no doubt explains the abruptness with which Elijah is introduced. It appears that this earlier source already linked the ministries of Elijah and Elisha as one continuous story, and that it depicted their ministries as embodying singular analogies to the sequential ministries of Moses and Joshua. Even the names Elijah ("my God is Yahweh") and Elisha ("my God saves") evoked memory of Moses (under whose ministry Israel came to know God as Yahweh) and Joshua ("Yahweh saves"). (For the analogies to Moses, see II and V below.)

In Kings the Elijah material has been broken up into four sections of unequal length: 1 K. 17–19; 21:17-29; 2 K. 1:2-16; 2:1-12. The first of these presents a cycle of episodes that centers on the dramatic trial on Mt. Carmel; the second narrates Elijah's involvement in the episode concerning Naboth's vineyard; the third tells of the confrontation between Elijah and King Ahaziah; the fourth relates the manner in which Elijah's ministry was terminated and his prophet's mantle passed on to ELISHA.

***II. Elijah's Ministry.**–A. Baal Challenged: 1 K. 17–19. 1. Initial Confrontation of Ahab (1 K. 17:1).* As if from nowhere, Elijah abruptly appears in the narrative to announce to Ahab: "As Yahweh the God of Israel lives, before whom I stand, there shall be neither dew nor rain these years, except by my word" (17:1). In that brief but dramatic moment the great issues at stake in Elijah's ministry are sharply focused; the humble servant of Yahweh stands athwart the royal devotee of Baal and announces that only at the word of Yahweh's servant will the fertilizing rains return to the Promised Land. They are Yahweh's gift, not Baal's, though Baal be hailed as "Rider of the Clouds" (see, e.g., *ANET,* p. 132) and Lightning and Dew as his wives or daughters (*ANET,* p. 131). Yahweh will now make the land of milk and honey become like the desert through which Israel passed long ago on its way to the Promised Land.

2. By the Wadi Cherith (1 K. 17:2-7). The word of Yahweh then directs Elijah to get away to a remote place, E of the Jordan. There, outside the Promised Land, Yahweh provides bread and meat (1 K. 17:4f.; cf. Ex. 16; Nu. 11; Ps. 78:23-29), carried to him by ravens, and water (cf. Ex. 15:25; 17:6; Nu. 20:2-13; Dt. 8:15; Ps. 78:16, 20) from the Wâdī CHERITH. Thus, while the land that looks to the god of dew and rain suffers drought, Yahweh nourishes His servant with food and water.

3. At Zarephath (1 K. 17:8-24). a. Elijah and the Widow Sustained (vv. 8-16). When the source of water dries up, the word of Yahweh directs Elijah to go to the home of a widow in ZAREPHATH, a small town under the jurisdiction of Sidon. Both the location and circumstances are significant. In Phoenicia too — the homeland of Jezebel and her god Baal Melqart — the drought has struck (as Menander reports; cf. Josephus *Ant.* viii.13.2); Yahweh has shut up Baal's heavens. (According to an early Phoenician [Ugaritic] myth, when drought is upon the land Baal is dead, but when he lives "the heavens rain oil, the wadis run with honey" [see Coogan, p. 112].) But the life-sustaining blessings that are being withheld from Israel, because Yahweh's word is no longer heeded there while Baal is worshiped, are now bestowed on Elijah in Baal's own land and shared with a Phoenician widow who took Yahweh's word seriously enough to share her last morsel with His prophet (cf. Dt. 32:15-21).

b. The Widow's Son Revived (vv. 17-24). Through Elijah's ministry an even greater blessing is in store for this Phoenician widow: the supreme blessing of the covenant, the gift of life (Dt. 30:19f.; 32:47). In ancient Near Eastern societies the situation of a WIDOW was desperate — especially if she had no son. Such is the prospect of this Phoenician widow when her son dies. But Elijah intercedes for her and the life of her son is restored. In this episode, too, reliance on Baal and his associate gods for the restoration of life seems to be directly challenged (cf. Coogan, p. 31).

4. Trial on Mt. Carmel (1 K. 18:1-46). "In the third year" (according to later tradition the drought lasted three years and six months; cf. Lk. 4:25; Jas. 5:17) Yahweh directs Elijah to announce to Ahab that He is about to send rain. Elijah's approach is indirect. He shows himself first to Obadiah, one of Ahab's high officials, and asks him to announce his coming. From Obadiah's lips we learn how far Ahab had searched for Elijah (among all nations) and of the popular opinion that the Spirit of God had carried the prophet away to unknown hiding places.

When the king and Elijah meet again, the issues at stake are once more clearly exhibited: Ahab hails the prophet as "you troubler of Israel" (v. 17), and Elijah replies, It is you and your dynasty that have troubled Israel, "because you have forsaken the commandments of Yahweh and followed the Baals" (v. 18).

Elijah then issues a challenge to the gods of Ahab and Jezebel, a test of their power in the presence of "all Israel" (v. 19). The lone prophet of Yahweh will face the 450 prophets of Baal and the 400 prophets of Asherah on Mt. Carmel. The site was chosen no doubt because it was normally crowned with luxuriant growth (*see* CARMEL **1**) and was thought to be a place where the power of Baal was especially potent.

Elijah first rebukes his watching countrymen ("How long will you go limping with two different opinions?") and calls them to decision ("If Yahweh is God, follow him; but if Baal, then follow him," v. 21). He then lays down the conditions of the test. Two bulls are to be presented for sacrifice, from which the devotees of Baal will have first choice. Elijah and the prophets of Baal will each prepare their sacrifice and lay it on the wood. Then they will pray; "and the God who answers by fire, he is God" (v. 24). To this the people assent, and the prophets of Baal can hardly demur, since Baal is the storm-god, "flashing his lightnings to the earth" (see *ANET,* p. 133).

Throughout the clear, hot day, the prophets of Baal implore their god to hear, hopping about the altar, raising their cultic cries, finally in desperation gashing their bodies with knives and lances. But Baal remains silent. At noon Elijah mocks with merciless sarcasm; "Cry louder, for he is a god. He may be off somewhere meditating; maybe he has been side-tracked; maybe he is on a journey; perhaps he is sleeping and has to be awakened" (author's *ad sensum* tr. of v. 27). Yet Baal does not act.

As evening approaches Elijah calls the Israelites to gather around him. He rebuilds a crumbled altar of Yahweh (using twelve stones to represent the twelve tribes of Israel, v. 31), digs a trench around the altar, prepares the sacrifice, and has the whole thing drenched with water until the trench itself is filled. Then, when the hour of sacrifice has come, he prays that Yahweh will let it be known that He is God in Israel, that Elijah is truly His prophet and has been acting on His instructions, and that He is reclaiming Israel for Himself (vv. 36f.). Then Yahweh answers by fire, which consumes the sacrifice, the wood, the altar, and the water. At this the people acknowledge, "Yahweh, He is God; Yahweh, He is God" (v. 39).

But the confrontation is not finished until the land is purged of those who devoted themselves to Baal (cf. Dt. 13). Imperiously ignoring the king, Elijah orders the execution of the prophets of Baal, and the people obey him (v. 40). By day's end King Ahab stands alone over against the prophet and the people.

The time has now come for Yahweh to give rain once more. Elijah announces it and urges Ahab to feast in anticipation (v. 41). Returning to the top of Carmel, Elijah bows down and prays. At last a small cloud "like a man's hand" rises from the sea, and Elijah warns Ahab of the approaching storm. While the darkened heavens pour down a "great rain," Elijah, strengthened by Yahweh, runs before Ahab the 27 km. (17 mi.) to the king's residence in Jezreel.

5. At Mt. Horeb (1 K. 19:1-21). Ahab's report to Jezebel does not subdue her. Boldly she informs Elijah that she will kill him within a day's time. Triumphant one day, a fugitive the next, Elijah flees southward. Deep within the Negeb and alone, he prays that he might die and be released from his burdensome and apparently hopeless mission (v. 4; cf. Nu. 11:11-15). But Yahweh's work for Elijah is not finished; so He sends food and water rather than the sleep of death.

Thus sustained, Elijah travels forty days and nights to Mt. Horeb/Sinai (vv. 5-8) — the mountain where Moses had received the tables of the covenant during a stay of forty days and nights, had interceded for the Israelites after they had sacrificed to a golden calf (Ex. 24:12-18; 32:30-35), and had been hidden in a "cleft of the rock" while Yahweh passed by and His mercy and justice were proclaimed (33:12–34:7). Now Elijah sits in a cave on Mt. Horeb and pleads his own case *against* Israel, calling for judgment upon Israel for its apostasy. But when Yahweh passes by He is not in the wind, the earthquake, or the fire; He is present in the quiet stillness (1 K. 19:11f.). When questioned a second time about his purpose at the mount of God, Elijah renews his accusations against Israel (v. 14) — a complete reversal of Moses' intercession.

This time it is Yahweh who refuses to give up on Israel. Elijah must return and continue his mission. Two kings (Hazael of Syria and Jehu of Israel) and a prophet (Elisha) are to be anointed as Yahweh's agents to bring judgment on Israel — judgment for Israel's purging, not its destruction; Yahweh will leave a REMNANT in Israel who have not "bowed to Baal" nor "kissed him" (v. 18). The narrator evidently recognizes that in the anointing of Elisha, Elijah is to receive his "Joshua" who will finish his work. Is Elijah, like Moses, kept from completing his mission because he faltered under the severe aggravation of Israel's stubbornness? That analogy, too, is hinted at.

Having returned from Horeb, Elijah immediately seeks out Elisha; he finds him plowing the fields (the drought has been broken). Elijah casts his mantle on the young man and departs. This symbolic act is understood by Elisha, who holds a feast with his family and then leaves all to "minister" to Elijah (cf. Josh. 1:1).

B. Judgment on Ahab and Jezebel Announced (1 K. 21:17-29). Jezebel's continuing influence over Ahab is illustrated in the story of Naboth's vineyard. With blatant disregard for justice, she secures Naboth's execution on false charges and delivers to her husband the property he coveted. Although he may have been innocent of his queen's procedures, Ahab asks no questions when Jezebel triumphantly announces to him that Naboth is dead and his vineyard can be had for the taking.

Yahweh then sends Elijah yet again to confront Ahab, while he is still in the vineyard asserting his royal claim (vv. 17-24). Elijah's accusation lays responsibility directly on the king, and the judgment falls on him and his dynasty. They will share the fate of Naboth and that of the dynasties of Jeroboam I and of Baasha. Jezebel, too, will not be spared (v. 23).

This would have been the end of the matter had Ahab not humbled himself before so radical a judgment. Elijah is told that because of Ahab's response Yahweh's judgment will be postponed until the days of Ahab's sons (vv. 27-29).

C. Elijah and Ahaziah (2 K. 1:2-16). Ahaziah is perhaps even more exclusively devoted to Baal than his father Ahab. Seriously injured by a fall, he sends to inquire of BAAL-ZEBUB, a god worshiped in the Philistine city of Ekron. This blatantly disloyal act moves Yahweh once more to send His servant Elijah to challenge the house of Omri. Through His angel He commissions the prophet to announce the king's death — for it is Yahweh the God of Israel who heals or takes away life. The prophet accosts the king's emissaries and delivers his message, and they return to Ahaziah with a word from Yahweh, not from Baal-zebub.

Recognizing Elijah by the description of his garb, the king sends a company of soldiers to arrest him. They find him sitting high on a promontory and demand that he come down to them: "O man of God, the king says, 'Come down'" (v. 9). But the servant of Yahweh replies with fitting irony: "If I be a man (*'îš*) of God, let fire (*'ēš*) come down from heaven and consume you and your fifty" (v. 10). Then — as with Moses in the wilderness (Nu. 16:35) — Yahweh sends fire from heaven to vindicate His servant. The whole procedure is repeated (vv. 11f.); but when the king's third emissary shows Yahweh's servant due respect, Yahweh's angel instructs Elijah to accompany the king's officer and deliver His message to the king's face (vv. 13–15a). The episode concludes with Elijah's prophecy being fulfilled (v. 17).

D. Elijah's Translation (2 K. 2:1-12). The final episode tells of the events surrounding the termination of Elijah's ministry and the transfer of his prophetic mission to Elisha. Concerning the significance of Elijah's final movements in the land we can only conjecture. The places visited (Gilgal, Bethel, Jericho) are all memorable sites in Israel's traditions; but they appear also to have been towns to which the communities of the prophets were attached. In any case, a central concern of the whole narrative unit appears to be Elisha's special qualifications and his designation to continue Elijah's mission as mediator of Yahweh's royal presence in Israel, at this time when its kings had become apostate.

Recognizing that the day has come when Yahweh will take him away, Elijah seeks to release Elisha from further service to him. But Elisha refuses to accept release — not once, but three times (vv. 2, 4, 6). His tenacious refusal to leave his master's side suggests that he recognizes that his work as "minister" to Elijah is not finished and indicates his determination to carry on Elijah's work.

At the Jordan Elijah's mantle (like Moses' rod at the Red Sea) opens a path through the waters, and Elijah and Elisha cross the river to a region outside the Promised Land (v. 8). There Elijah asks his faithful "minister" what final bequest he desires of him. Elisha's answer (v. 9) further bespeaks his dedication to carry on Elijah's ministry; he requests the firstborn's portion of Elijah's only legacy.

In Elijah's response the text contains a troublesome ambiguity. The whole context, however, points to a reading that reflects Elijah's sense of relief at his imminent release from his mission, and his reluctance to pass on so onerous a task to his young friend. On this reading, Elijah's words should be rendered: "You have asked for a grievous burden." His further word makes clear his recognition that what Elisha requests is not his to grant — it lies with Him who commissions the prophets (v. 10).

The moment of Elijah's final departure, like so much of his ministry, is charged with significance. (1) It evokes memory of Moses' death and mysterious burial: both men are taken by Yahweh — outside the promised land, as a testimony against wayward Israel — with no tomb for Israel to convert into a shrine to rival the sanctuary of Yahweh. (2) The fiery host sent to escort Elijah discloses that Yahweh's host has accompanied Elijah's ministry and thus constitutes a divine vindication of Elijah as a true man of God (cf. 2 K. 6:17). (3) Yahweh's translation of Elijah demonstrates that it is to Yahweh, not to Baal, that the fiery chariots of heaven belong; and to Him, not to the gods of Baal's pantheon, belongs the power to bestow immortality on man. (4) That Elisha sees Elijah as he is taken up to heaven, and that Elijah's mantle is left for Elisha, disclose that Elisha has received his request and that the prophet's commission has been placed upon him — the second Moses has truly been given his Joshua (*see* ELISHA). (5) Elisha's epithet concerning Elijah ("My father, my father! the chariots of Israel and its horsemen!" v. 12) not only betokens Elisha's devotion to Elijah but also hails the departing prophet as the true source of Israel's power, in distinction from the apostate royal house.

E. A Letter to Jehoram (2 Ch. 21:12-15). The author of Chronicles adds one more episode to Elijah's ministry. He relates the substance of a letter sent by Elijah to King Jehoram of Judah. With his wife Athaliah, that apostate king had introduced the policies of Ahab into the southern kingdom and executed his royal brothers to cut off any political opposition. Elijah sets himself against this king also. He boldly lays out the charges against him in Yahweh's name (v. 12) and pronounces Yahweh's fearful judgment on him (vv. 14f.).

This account has occasioned lengthy discussions because of the chronological problems involved. According to 2 K. 3 it is Elisha who earlier accompanies the combined forces of Jehoshaphat (Jehoram's father) of Judah and Jehoram of Israel in a campaign against Moab. The best solution is that Elisha accompanied these armies on behalf of an aged Elijah; Elijah, then, outlived Jehoshaphat and, when he heard of Jehoram's apostasy and executions, sent him a sharp letter of condemnation, lacking the physical strength to face the king in person. If, as is likely, Jehoram committed these atrocities shortly after his father's death in 848 B.C., this letter may be dated as early as 847, and Elijah's translation may have taken place the same year.

III. In the Latter Prophets (Mal. 4:5).–Although Elijah's ministry marked a point of transition in the ministry of the prophets (*see* PROPHECY), and he completed his work some fifty years before Amos, he is mentioned but once in the literature of the writing prophets. At the very end of his prophecy, Malachi makes the momentous announcement: "Behold, I will send you Elijah the prophet before the great and terrible day of Yahweh comes. . . ." Just as other prophets announced the coming of another "David" (Ezk. 34:23f.; 37:24f.; etc.), so Malachi announces the coming of another "Elijah." Through his mission the generations in Israel will be united in a purified service of Yahweh, lest the Day of Yahweh (*see* DAY OF THE LORD) bring only a curse on the land. The announcement in 3:1 probably has reference to the same prophetic ministry: "Behold, I send my messenger to prepare the way before me. . . ." Against the background of the Elijah-Elisha narrative as preserved in Kings, this announcement of the coming of another Elijah, to be followed by a climactic redemptive event, strongly suggests that the Elijah to come will also have his Elisha.

IV. In Intertestamental Literature.–In his "praise of famous men," Ben Sira summarizes what is known of

Elijah from Kings and Chronicles and echoes Malachi's prophecy concerning the coming Elijah (Sir. 48:1-14). 1 Maccabees reports Mattathias' statement that "Elijah because of a great zeal for the law was taken up into heaven" (2:58). Two subsequent references to a prophet who will come and give decisions regarding uncertain matters are probably allusions to the expected Elijah (4:46; 14:41). In an apocalyptic dream-vision 1 Enoch foretells the return of Elijah before the judgment and before the appearance of the great apocalyptic lamb (89:12). A later reference to a man who "shall ascend" during the apostate sixth world-week is probably a reference to Elijah (93:8). In the Assumption of Moses is found a brief recounting of Elijah's reproof of Ahaziah (Asm. M. 2:14).

V. In the NT.–As is evident from Ben Sira and 1 Enoch (cf. also 1 Macc. 4:46; 14:41), Jewish eschatology in the intertestamental period picked up the reference to Elijah in the prophecy of Malachi and — in part, no doubt, due to the dramatic translation of Elijah — included the return of Elijah as a distinct element in its expectations for the end time. From the NT also it is evident that the expectation of Elijah was widespread in Palestine in the 1st cent. A.D. (No explicit reference to Elijah is found in the sectarian literature from Qumrân, though some have thought that the "prophet" of 1QS 9:11 may be Elijah

Statue from Mt. Carmel showing Elijah victorious over a Baal prophet. The Latin text on the front panel is Sir. 48:1 (D. Baly)

in the role of messianic herald; cf. P. Wernberg-Møller, *Manual of Discipline* [1957], pp. 135f.)

A. Elijah and John the Baptist. According to Mt. 17:9-13 par. the disciples at one point asked Jesus about the scribal teaching that "first Elijah must come." Jesus replied that Elijah had already come, and then alluded to John the Baptist. Jesus' identification of John the Baptist as the promised Elijah is even more explicit in Mt. 11:14. This accords with Luke's account of the angelic announcement to Zechariah, which points to John as the fulfillment of Malachi's prophecy (1:17; cf. also Mk. 1:2). (By this identification Jesus was offering a subtle self-disclosure as the Elisha/Joshua — His Semitic name — who would complete John's ministry.) According to Jn. 1:21, 23 John the Baptist, when questioned by the Jews, refused identification of himself with Elijah, as well as with Messiah or "the prophet." But his garb (Mk. 1:6 par.), his asceticism (Mk. 1:6 par.; Mt. 11:18 par.), his ministry in the wilderness (Mk. 1:4 par.; Mt. 11:7 par.), and his bold rebuke of the powerful (Lk. 3:7-14; Mk. 6:18 par.) all evoked the memory of Elijah and suggested that he was indeed the Elijah to come, the one in whom prophecy was once more renewed as a sign of the dawn of the messianic age.

B. Elijah and Jesus. When John the Baptist described Jesus as the one who would "baptize with the Holy Spirit and with fire" (Mt. 3:11 par.), he may have hinted at an analogy between Jesus' ministry and Elijah's. James and John clearly made the association when they asked Jesus if He wished them to "bid fire to come down from heaven and consume" the Samaritans (Lk. 9:54). The nature of Jesus' ministry itself suggested to many that He was the Elijah to come (Mk. 6:15 par.; cf. 8:28 par.). Jesus Himself alluded to Elijah's journey to Zarephath and suggested a parallel between His own ministry and Elijah's (Lk. 5:25f.) He may also have alluded to Elijah's ministry when He said of Himself, "I came to cast fire upon the earth" (Lk. 12:49).

On the mount of transfiguration Elijah appeared with Moses and together they conversed with Jesus (Mk. 9:4 par.) about the "passage" (*éxodos*) He was to accomplish through His suffering at Jerusalem (Lk. 9:31f.). As fellow servants in God's mission, they were speaking with the last Joshua/Elisha, who would finish their work and lead Israel into God's promised "rest."

C. In the Epistles and Revelation. Elijah is mentioned twice in the Epistles. Paul recalls how Elijah pleaded with God against Israel, and how God replied by referring to a faithful remnant, the seven thousand "who had not bowed the knee to Baal" (Rom. 11:2-4). James points to Elijah, "a man of like nature with ourselves," to illustrate that "the prayer of a righteous man has great power in its effects" (Jas. 5:17f.).

The "two witnesses" in Rev. 11, from whose mouths fire proceeds to destroy their enemies (v. 5), who have "power to shut the sky, that no rain may fall . . . and . . . power over the waters to turn them to blood, and to smite the earth with every plague" (v. 6), and who go "up to heaven in a cloud" (v. 12), are usually understood to refer to Moses and Elijah. Some also suppose that the three and a half years of Rev. 12:14 has its prototype in the years of drought called down upon the land by Elijah (cf. Lk. 4:25; Jas. 5:17).

VI. In Early A.D. Extrabiblical Literature.–*A. Judaic.* Philo recalls "that [Elijah] did not die but was carried up with a whirlwind as it were into heaven and went up there to be among the angels" (*Quaestiones et solutiones in Genesin* i.86). Elsewhere he speaks of a coming redeemer, who seems to correspond to the Elijah figure of Malachi (*De praemiis et poenis* 28.163; 29.16). 2 Baruch (*ca.* A.D.

70) refers to Elijah's being fed by ravens (77:24f.). 4 Ezra mentions the answers to Elijah's prayers for rain and for the resuscitation of the widow's son (7:109). It also refers to "the men who have been taken up" and who will appear before the Messiah, presumably alluding to Enoch and Elijah (6:26). In the Mishnah Elijah appears as the one who will: (1) return to prepare the tribes of Israel for the messianic age, (2) resolve all the religious and judicial controversies with which the rabbis have wrestled, (3) restore the flask of manna, the flask of water for purification, the flask of oil for anointing, and Aaron's rod, (4) anoint the Messiah, and (5) have a part in the resurrection of the dead (see Friedmann; Klausner). According to Justin Martyr, the Jew Trypho insisted that even if Messiah had come he could not be known "until Elijah comes, and anoints him and makes him manifest to all" (*Dial.*8.14; cf. 49.1). (For the many references to Elijah in the Talmud, and for his continuing role in the Jewish sabbath liturgy and Passover ritual, see Friedmann and Wiener.)

B. Christian. In NT Apocrypha and Pseudepigrapha, Elijah is frequently mentioned as a model both of ascetic piety and of bold rebuke of apostasy. His translation is recalled as analogous to Jesus' ascension; and, as one who was taken up to heaven in the body, he is frequently paired with Enoch, appearing with him in heaven or playing a role in the final eschatological events. (For the references, see H-S.)

For the church fathers Elijah was the greatest of the prophets, a model of piety and righteous zeal. His miracles were regularly interpreted as allegorical references to NT realities, and his relation to John the Baptist was thoroughly explored. As John heralded Jesus' first appearance, so, it was thought, Elijah would appear to announce His return in the day of judgment. (For a succinct overview of patristic references, see Wiener, pp. 145-47.)

Bibliography.–L. Bronner, *The Stories of Elijah and Elisha* (1968); M. D. Coogan, *Stories from Ancient Canaan* (1978); O. Eissfeldt, *Der Gott Karmel* (1953); G. Fohrer, *Elia* (1957); M. Friedmann, *Seder Eliyahu* (1902), pp. 2-44; K. Galling, "Der Gott Karmel und die Ächtung der Fremden Götter," in W. F. Albright, *et al.*, eds., *Alt-Festschrift* (1953), pp. 105-125; H-S; J. Klausner, *Messianic Idea in Israel* (1956), pp. 451-57; *KS,* II (1953), 135-149; A. S. Peake, *BJRL,* 11 (1927), 296-321; H. H. Rowley, *Men of God* (1963), pp. 37-65; O. H. Steck, *Überlieferung und Zeitgeschichte in den Elia-Erzählungen* (1968); R. S. Wallace, *Elijah and Elisha* (1957); A. Wiener, *The Prophet Elijah in the Development of Judaism* (1978).

2. [Heb. *'ēlîyâ*] (1 Ch. 8:27); AV ELIAH. A "head of a father's house" of the tribe of Benjamin.

3. [Heb. *'ēlîyâ*]. (Ezr. 10:21). A priest in the time of Ezra, one of the "sons of Harim," who is listed among those who had married foreign women.

4. [Heb. *'ēlîyâ*] (Ezra 10:26); AV ELIAH. An Israelite in the time of Ezra, one of "the sons of Elam," who is listed among those who had married foreign women.

5. [Gk. *Ēlion*] (Jth. 8:1); AV ELIHU; NEB ELIAS. An ancestor of Judith.

J. H. STEK

ELIJAH, APOCALYPSE OF (COPTIC). An anonymous series of oracles attributed to Elijah only in the title. The work as a whole is known today only in Coptic. The existence of a brief Greek fragment suggests that the Coptic is a translation from the Greek.

The Apocalypse of Elijah is clearly Christian in its present form. Scholars disagree whether it is a Christian composition based on Jewish traditions or a Christian edition of one or more originally Jewish documents. The current form of the work can be dated to the second half of the 3rd cent. A.D., on the basis of 2:23-45, a passage that reflects Palmyrene domination of Egypt and antagonism between Palmyrenes and Sassanians. J. M. Rosenstiehl (pp. 75f.) argues that 2:23-45 is a late addition, and that most of the work is an Egyptian Jewish document with Essene traits dating to the 1st cent. A.D.

The document contains a review of history in the form of prediction. Eschatological motifs include a physical description of the eschatological adversary, the return of Enoch and Elijah, the destruction of the world, cosmic transformation, and personal afterlife.

Bibliography.–Coptic text, German translation: G. Steindorff, *Die Apokalypse des Elias* (*TU,* N.F. 2/3a, 1899); English translation: H. P. Houghton, *Aegyptus,* 39 (1959), 43-91, 179-210; Study and French translation: J. M. Rosenstiehl, *L'Apocalypse d'Elie* (1972). Introduction and bibliography: J. H. Charlesworth, *Pseudepigrapha and Modern Research* (1976), pp. 95-98.

A. Y. COLLINS

ELIJAH, APOCALYPSE OF (HEBREW) [*sēper 'ēlîyāhû*–'The Book of Elijah']. An Aramaic and Hebrew account of the eschatological secrets that Michael revealed to Elijah on Mt. Carmel. In midrashic style the events are related to verses in Isaiah, Ezekiel, Zechariah, Daniel, and Deuteronomy.

A detailed eschatological timetable follows a report of Elijah's divinely conducted journey to the ends of the earth. It includes: (1) wars between Rome and Persia; (2) appearance of the eschatological adversary whose name (or mother's name) Gigit and physical description are provided; (3) return of the three exiles; (4) advent of the Messiah ("Yinnon," cf. T. B. *Sanhedrin* 98b) accompanied by Gabriel, angels of destruction, and thirty thousand righteous; (5) defeat of Gog and Magog; (6) defense of Jerusalem by God and Messiah; (7) destruction of non-Jewish cities; (8) resurrection of the dead, punishment of the wicked in Abaddon, and reward of the righteous who enjoy the marvelous material blessings of the new age in which Torah and Peace reign; (9) descent of heavenly Jerusalem.

Various scholars have attempted to date the work by identifying the personalities and events involved in the Roman-Persian wars. Buttenwieser placed the work in A.D. 261 and identified the "last king of Persia" as Shapur I and the eschatological adversary as Odenathus of Palmyra. According to S. Krauss (*Monumenta Talmudica,* 5/1 [1914], 53f.) the work was written a decade earlier (Persian king = Adashir; adversary = Alexander Severus). Y. Even-Shemuel (pp. 31-54) is more likely correct in assigning the work to the early 7th cent. A.D. (Persian king = Chosroes II; adversary = Phocas).

The work entitled *Pereq 'Ēlîyāhû* (a later recension of *Sēper 'Ēlîyāhû*) was produced after the rise of Islam.

Bibliography.–M. Buttenwieser, *Die hebräische Elias-Apokalypse* (1897) (includes Ger. tr.); Y. Even-Shemuel, *Midreshi Ge'ulah* (1953-54) (includes *Pereq 'Ēlîyāhû*). Eng. tr. in G. W. Buchanan, *Revelation and Redemption* (1978), pp. 426-441.

D. B. LEVENSON

ELIKA ē-lī'kə [Heb. *'ĕlîqā'*]. A Harodite (Uradite), one of David's "thirty" guards (2 S. 23:25); omitted from the list in 1 Ch. 11:27.

ELIM ē'lim [Heb. *'êlim*–derivation uncertain, perhaps pl. of *'ayil,* 'robust tree' or of *'ēl,* 'god']. One of the places where the Israelites under Moses stopped in their journey from the Red Sea (or Sea of Reeds) to Mt. Sinai. From the text of Ex. 15:22–16:1 it appears that Elim lay between MARAH and the Wilderness of Sin (but cf. Nu. 33:8-12, where an encampment by the Red Sea comes between Elim and the wilderness of Sin). Many scholars, however, feel that the text is composite here and that the section mentioning Marah was not originally part of the itinerary that listed Elim as a place of encampment.

The traditional site of the oasis at Elim where the Israelites camped en route from Egypt to Sinai (D. Baly)

In this view, Elim was an oasis in the general area known as the Wilderness of SHUR.

The location of Elim remains uncertain despite wide acceptance of the proposal to locate it in the Wâdī Gharandel. The question is closely tied to the whole problem of the route of the Exodus. (*See* EXODUS, ROUTE OF; WANDERINGS OF ISRAEL.) E. D. WELCH

ELIMELECH ē-lim'ə-lek [Heb. *'ĕlîmeleḵ*–'God is king'; Gk. *Abeimelech, Alimelek*]. A member of the tribe of Judah, a native of Bethlehem, a man of wealth, and probably head of a family or clan (Ruth 1:2f.; 2:1, 3; 4:3, 9). He lived during the period of the judges, had a hereditary possession near Bethlehem, and is chiefly known as the husband of Naomi the mother-in-law of Ruth. Because of a severe famine in Judea he emigrated to Moab with his wife and sons, Mahlon and Chilion. Not long afterward he died, and his two sons married Moabite women, Ruth and Orpah. During the ten years spent in Moab the two sons died and the three widows were left. The sequel is told in the book of Ruth. *See also* NAOMI; RUTH.

J. J. REEVE

ELIOENAI el-i-ō-ē'nī [Heb. *'elyô'ênay*; Gk. *Eliōnas, Eliadas*]; AV, NEB, also ELIONAS (1 Esd. 9:22), ELIADAS (1 Esd. 9:28).

1. A descendant of the house of David (1 Ch. 3:22-24).

2. A Simeonite tribal chieftain (1 Ch. 4:36).

3. A member of a Benjaminite family (1 Ch. 7:8).

4. A member of the priestly house of Pashhur who divorced his foreign wife (Ezr. 10:22; 1 Esd. 9:22). The latter reference is apparently to the Eliezer of Ezr. 10:31.

5. A descendant of Zattu who divorced his foreign wife (Ezr. 10:27; 1 Esd. 9:28).

6. A priest in the time of Nehemiah (Neh. 12:41).

ELIONAS el-i-ō'nəs (AV 1 Esd. 9:22). *See* ELIOENAI **4.**

ELIPHAL ē-lī'fəl, el'i-fəl [Heb. *'ĕlîpāl*–'God has judged']. Son of Ur, one of the mighty men of David's armies (1 Ch. 11:35). He should probably be identified with ELIPHELET **(2)**, son of AHASBAI of Maacah (2 S. 23:34).

ELIPHALAT ē-lif'ə-lat (1 Esd. 9:33, AV); **ELIPHALET** ē-lif'ə-let (1 Esd. 8:39, AV). *See* ELIPHELET.

ELIPHAZ el'i-faz, ē-lī'faz [Heb. *'ĕlîpaz*–'God is victorious'(?)].

1. Son of Esau by Adah, and father of Teman, Omar, Zepho (or Zephi), Gatam, Kenaz, and Amalek (Gen. 36:4, 10-12, 15; 1 Ch. 1:35f., which includes a sister Timna).

2. One of Job's three friends, who came to "condole" and "comfort" him (Job 2:11). He is always given the precedence (cf. esp. Job 42:7), probably because of both his character and his age. He came from Teman, doubtless in Edom. Though he is evidently a rich chief, he is presented, like his friends, primarily as one of the wise; hence no details of his family are given, in contrast to Elihu.

He was a kindly man, whose outlook on life was dominated by a dream he once had (4:12-21; cf. 15:14-16; 22:2-4). Like his two companions, he was limited by the contemporary view that suffering must be the outcome and punishment of sin, so he had assumed that Job must have sinned grievously. But this assumption did not become clear until Job had challenged the justice of God, thereby shaking the rock on which Eliphaz stood (ch. 21); he then (22:5-11) charged Job with sins for which there was no evidence.

He has three speeches: chs. 4f., 15, and 22. In the first he is kindly, treating Job's sufferings as merely an example of the universal experience of sinful men and promising forgiveness and restoration if Job repents. In his second he shows his shock at Job's self-justification and challenges his whole concept of life; hence there is a sharper edge to his words: the picture of man's sin is darker and ends in an exaggerated description of the fate of the wicked. The third reveals his inward thoughts about Job and directly charges him with being one of the wicked; even here, however, he ends with a moving account of God's mercy to the penitent.

Eliphaz was a man of sterling character and sympathy, but his dogmatic insistence on explaining everything by the pattern of his own experience and understanding of God prevented his understanding Job. Job's failure to appreciate his remonstrances drew out the expression of wounded pride.

See also JOB. H. L. ELLISON

ELIPHELEHU ē-lif'ə-lē'hū [Heb. *'ĕlîpᵉlēhû*–'may God distinguish him']; AV ELIPHELEH. A Levite of the second order appointed with five others to "lead with lyres" when the ark was brought up to Jerusalem by David (1 Ch. 15:18, 21).

ELIPHELET ē-lif'ə-let [Heb. *'ĕlîpeleṭ*; Gk. *Eliphalatos* (1 Esd. 8:39), *Eliphalat* (1 Esd. 9:33)]; AV also ELIPHALET, ELIPHALAT; NEB also ELIPHALATUS, ELIPHALAT.

1. A descendant of David (2 S. 5:16; 1 Ch. 3:6, 8; 14:7).

2. Son of AHASBAI; one of David's heroes (2 S. 23:34), probably the Eliphal of 1 Ch. 11:35.

3. A Benjaminite descendant of Saul and Jonathan (1 Ch. 8:39).

4. A person who returned to Palestine in the time of Ezra (Ezr. 8:13; 1 Esd. 8:29).

5. A man who divorced his foreign wife during Ezra's reforms (Ezr. 10:33; 1 Esd. 9:33).

ELISABETH. *See* ELIZABETH.

ELISEUS el-i-sē'əs. *See* ELISHA.

ELISHA ē-lī'shə [Heb. *'ĕlîšā'*–'(my) God saves'; Gk. *Elisaios*]; AV also ELISEUS (Sir. 48:12; Lk. 4:27).

I. Introduction

A. Elisha the Man

B. Circumstances of His Ministry
C. Primary Sources
II. Elisha's Ministry
A. Call
B. Investiture
C. Deeds
D. Involvement in the Israel-Syria Conflicts
E. Restitution of the Shanammite's Estates
F. Anointing Kings
G. Death and Burial
III. Later Tradition

***I. Introduction.**–A. Elisha the Man.* In youth a son of the soil, Elisha hailed from Abel-meholah E of the Jordan (N. Glueck, *River Jordan* [1946], pp. 168-172; traditionally in the Jordan Valley S of Beth-shean [Eusebius, *Onom.*]), where his father Shaphat must have been a man of some means, for he was able to field twelve yoke of oxen. When Elisha was still a young man Elijah summoned him to take up the prophetic vocation (1 K. 19:19-21); he then spent some years as Elijah's assistant (until *ca.* 847 B.C.; *see* ELIJAH II.E). For the next fifty years (during the reigns of Jehoram, Jehu, Jehoahaz, and Jehoash) he continued with his own ministry in the northern kingdom. Like his predecessor, he remained unmarried, accompanied only by his servant Gehazi. Unlike Elijah, he lived among the people. His connections with the several prophetic communities (2 K. 2:1, 3, 5; 4:38; 6:1; 9:1) were close, and he was held in high regard by them, but his precise relationship with them remains uncertain. Although he made Samaria his home (2:25; 5:3, 9; 6:32), apparently he traveled often, at times ranging as far as Edom and Moab to the south (ch. 3) and Damascus to the northeast (8:7). Persons of all stations in life had ready access to him, and he had access to the highest in the land (4:13). He was bald (2:23 — apparently rare among the ancient Semites) and walked with a staff (4:29). Whether he wore Elijah's mantle as a sign of office is not known. At the time of Elijah's departure he apparently was garbed in conventional clothes (2 K. 2:12). From the day of his call his dedication to Elijah and Elijah's God was complete and did not wane (13:14-19). Confident in his commission from the God of Elijah, he feared no one (2 K. 3:13f.; 5:10-12; 6:32). When he died (shortly after 798 B.C.), he was buried in his homeland E of the Jordan (13:20).

B. Circumstances of His Ministry. His association with Elijah began shortly after the confrontation between Elijah and Ahab on Mt. Carmel, and he began his own ministry early in the reign of Jehoram (852-841 B.C.). Although the new king broke partially with the religious practices of his parents (2 K. 3:2), he continued in the ways of Jeroboam I and made no effort to uproot baalism among the people. Jehu's revolt brought a bloody end to the Omride dynasty and the Baal worship it had encouraged (chs. 9–10). Friendly relations continued between Judah and Israel, but Syria under Ben-hadad and Hazael was a constant threat. At times Syria raided Israel at will (6:8-10), and once even subjected Samaria to a long and devastating siege (6:24-31). Hazael took all Transjordan from Jehu (10:32f.), and Hazael and his son reduced Jehoahaz to vassalage, allowing him only a small police force (13:1-7). Politically, Israel's very existence was threatened, a condition from which Elisha foresaw relief only on his deathbed (13:14-19). Faithfulness to Yahweh was relatively rare and yet was manifested by various groups and individuals: the communities of the prophets, the Shunammite (ch. 4), the farmer from Baal-shalisha (4:42), the captive girl in Damascus (5:2f.), some of the elders in Samaria (6:32), Jehu (10:16-30), and Jehonadab son of Rechab (10:15f.). Elijah's bold ministry had failed to reform the house of Ahab or the nation generally. It was Elisha's role to carry forward that ministry and mediate Yahweh's redemptive presence among His people during these very troubled times.

C. Primary Sources. All that we know of Elisha comes from the narrative of his ministry found in Kings. The compiler apparently had an account that viewed the interlocking ministries of Elijah and Elisha against the background of Yahweh's ways with Israel in the days of Moses and Joshua (*see* ELIJAH I.C).

In Kings the story of Elisha's ministry is found for the most part in a single block of narrative (2 K. 2:1–8:6 — interrupted only at 3:1-3 to introduce the reign of Jehoram), to which 8:1-6 constitutes a conclusion. This is followed by accounts of Elisha's involvement in the anointings of Hazael (8:7-15) and Jehu (9:1-3) and of events surrounding Elisha's death (13:14-21). The order of materials in the major segment is not chronological (see the comms.), but neither is it haphazard. Following the account of Elisha's investiture (2:1-18), three large narrative units (3:4-27; 4:8-37; 5:1-27) are interspersed between four smaller segments offering brief accounts of additional acts of Elisha (2:19-25; 4:1-7; 4:38-44; 6:1-7), each of which refers to acts performed on behalf of the prophetic communities. Central to this structure is the account of Elisha's dealings with the Shunammite.

Later, after two extended narrative panels (6:8-23; 6:24–7:20) concerning Elisha's involvement in the Israel-Syria conflicts (each resulting in deliverance for Israel), we are told how the recital of "all the great things Elisha has done" moved the king to restore the Shunammite's family inheritance (8:1-6). The subsequent accounts of Elisha's fulfillment of Elijah's commission to anoint Hazael and Jehu (1 K. 19:15f.) are integrated by the author into his story of the kings of Israel and Judah, as is also his account of Elisha's death and accompanying events. Thus the author shows that Elisha ("my God saves") completed Elijah's mission; he depicts Elisha's ministry as one through which Yahweh was savingly present among His people.

***II. Elisha's Ministry.**–A. Call* (1 K. 19:15-21). At Horeb Elijah's mission to Israel was renewed, with specific commission to anoint Hazael king of Syria, Jehu king of Israel, and Elisha to be prophet in his place. Each of these three was to be used by Yahweh to chastise and purge Israel. Elijah sought out Elisha first, finding him plowing in his father's fields. He cast his mantle on the young man's shoulders and passed on without a word. Elisha understood and committed himself immediately, the firmness of his decision evident in the formal leave he took of his family, which included symbolically divesting himself of the implements of the soil — his slaughtering of the oxen and boiling them with their yokes (and plow?). Henceforth he would be the devoted servant of Elijah and Elijah's God.

B. Investiture (2 K. 2:1-18). Elisha knew when it was time for Yahweh to take Elijah (vv. 3, 5), but when Elijah offered to release him from his vocation (three times: at Gilgal, v. 2, at Bethel, v. 4, and at Jericho, v. 6), he steadfastly refused. Accordingly, his final request of his master was that he might inherit a "double share" of his spirit (v. 9), i.e., the inheritance of the firstborn. Elijah's response (*see also* ELIJAH II.D), "If you see me as I am being taken from you, it shall be so for you," was charged with double meaning: (1) if God allows it — only He can grant your request — and (2) if your resolve remains firm and you stay with me to the end. When Elijah was taken, Elisha was there, and he saw. And Elijah's mantle remained! Elisha's investiture was of Yahweh. Hailing the departing Elijah as "father" and as the "chariots and horsemen of Israel" — Israel's true source of strength — he took up Elijah's mantle and returned in the spirit and power of Elijah back across the Jordan to the scene of Elijah's labors. There he was greeted by the sons of the prophets as Elijah's successor (v. 15).

C. Deeds (2 K. 2:19–8:6). 1. *Initial Signs Characterizing His Ministry* (2 K. 2:19-25). *a. Healing the Spring by Jericho* (2 K. 2:19-22). Elisha cast salt into the spring and pronounced the healing word of Yahweh. As a result its water no longer caused death or miscarriage (cf. Ex. 15:25).

b. Cursing the Youths of Bethel (2 K. 2:23-25). Proceeding past Bethel to Mt. Carmel, Elisha was ridiculed by the sons of the Bethelites, who had learned from their fathers to despise the representatives of Yahweh. When he cursed them in the name of Yahweh, two she-bears attacked them and killed forty-two of them.

Elisha's ministry would mean life for those who honored Yahweh but death for those who despised him.

2. Prophecy Against Moab (2 K. 3:4-27). Elisha accompanied the army of Israel (no doubt as Elijah's proxy; *see* ELIJAH II.E) when Jehoram went to suppress Moab's rebellion early in his reign. Refusing to serve Jehoram (v. 13), he responded to Jehoshaphat's inquiry. This one time he sought musical inducement to obtain an answer from Yahweh (*see* PROPHECY). Though victorious, the Israelites left the land without accomplishing their purpose (v. 27).

3. Multiplying the Widow's Oil (2 K. 4:1-7). A poor widow whose two sons were to be taken as bondmen for a debt she could not pay appealed to Elisha, at whose word her one jar of oil in the house filled many others borrowed from her neighbors. The market value of the oil thus supplied enough to pay her debt and provide for her and her sons (cf. 1 K. 17:8-16).

4. A Son for the Shunammite (2 K. 4:8-37). *a. The Son Given* (4:8-17). Having enjoyed the gracious hospitality of a wealthy woman of Shunem (4.8 km. [3 mi.] N of Jezreel) on his frequent passage through the town, Elisha sought to recompense her. When she declined and he learned that she was childless and her husband already old (she faced the prospect of early and desolate widowhood), Elisha promised her a son. Within a year the child was born.

b. The Son Revived (4:18-37). A few years later, when the Shunammite's son suddenly sickened and died, she turned to Elisha again and Elisha revived her son (cf. 1 K. 17:17-24; Lk. 7:11-17).

By centering this two-part narrative in his account of Elisha's deeds, the author demonstrated the significance of Elisha's ministry, namely, that God was present with His people to save.

5. Food for a Community of the Prophets (2 K. 4:38-44). *a. Cleansing the Poison Pottage* (4:38-41). When he visited the community of the prophets at Gilgal during a famine, Elisha played the host and instructed his servant to prepare a pot of gruel for the brothers. When some poisonous wild gourds (probably *citrullus colocynthis,* a strong purgative) were innocently added to the ingredients, Elisha threw some meal into the pottage and the brothers ate it without harm.

b. Multiplying the Loaves (2 K. 4:42-44). Circumstantial connections with the preceding episode can be deduced from the juxtaposition of the two accounts and the parallels that link them. A man from Baal-shalisha brought Elisha the first fruits of his barley harvest. These were to be consecrated to Yahweh (Lev. 23:15-17; Dt. 16:9-11) and were normally for the priests (Lev. 23:20). In bringing them to Elisha the man acknowledged that Elisha was the true representative of Yahweh. Elisha commanded that the loaves be distributed among the hundred men present (presumably the members of the prophetic brotherhood). Although his servant protested that the amount was insufficient, all ate their fill, and there was surplus, according to Yahweh's word (cf. Mt. 14:13-21, par.; Mt. 15:32-39).

6. Healing Naaman (2 K. 5:1-27). Naaman, a Syrian general afflicted with leprosy, heard about Elisha and went to Samaria bearing large gifts and requesting healing from the king of Israel (Jehoram?). Elisha requested that Naaman be sent to him (v. 8), and then instructed him to wash seven times in the Jordan. Reluctant at first, Naaman ultimately obeyed and was healed. He committed himself to worship only Yahweh and sought assurance from Elisha that he would be pardoned when his official duties required him to participate in the cult in the temple of Rimmon (Hadad). Elisha assured him with his parting word, "Go in peace" (v. 19). The greed of Elisha's servant Gehazi brought Naaman's leprosy on his own head. This episode shows that the true power of healing the world's sickness was present only in Israel, with the God of Elisha.

7. Recovering the Axe Head (2 K. 6:1-7). Apparently, in this time of widespread apostasy, membership in the prophetic brotherhoods was expanding. The community (at Jericho? Gilgal?) undertook to enlarge their domicile. In the process one of them lost the iron head of his borrowed axe in the Jordan. The distress with which he turned to Elisha for help suggests that, unable in his poverty to pay for the expensive tool, he was threatened with a debtor's bondage. Elisha threw a stick into the Jordan where the axe head had sunk; the axe head rose to the surface and the distraught man recovered it.

D. Involvement in the Israel-Syria Conflicts (2 K. 6:8–7:20). To the above account of the acts of Elisha the author of Kings appends two stories of Elisha's involvement in the Israel-Syria wars. The king of Israel is not named (Jehoram, M. Noth, *History of Israel* [2nd ed. 1960], p. 243 n. 1; Jehoahaz or Jehu, *BHI,* p. 244 n. 59; Jehu or Joash, Gray, pp. 513, 518), so the dates of the events are not known.

1. Syrian Raids Frustrated (2 K. 6:8-23). During a period of frequent Syrian incursions into Israel, Elisha provided his king with crucial intelligence that saved him repeatedly from Syrian ambushment. The Syrians retaliated by trying to capture Elisha at Dothan, but were struck with blindness (*sanwērîm,* cf. Gen. 19:11) and led into Samaria. In this episode Elisha is depicted as the eyes of Israel's army and the captain of the hosts of Yahweh; he, not the king, is Israel's defense.

2. Siege of Samaria Lifted (2 K. 6:24–7:20). During a long and bitter siege of Samaria by Ben-hadad, when the poorest of the city, the widows, were reduced to eating their children, the king vowed to kill Elisha. But Elisha told him that before another day passed, food would be so abundant in the city that the market would be glutted. Four desperate lepers found the Syrian camp deserted, and before sunset the next day, food was cheap in the market of Samaria.

E. Restitution of the Shunammite's Estates (2 K. 8:16). This episode constitutes the conclusion to the main body of the acts of Elisha, although it is itself not one of Elisha's acts but only a recounting of some of his deeds. Having been advised by Elisha to take up temporary residence outside the land to escape the seven-year famine Yahweh was about to bring on Israel (perhaps the famine of 4:38-41), the Shunammite, evidently now a widow, returned at the end of the seven years and appealed to the king for her expropriated property. She interrupted Gehazi's story of Elisha's great deeds (which the king [unnamed] had asked him to recount) just as Gehazi was telling of Elisha's restoration of her son to life. When the Shunammite confirmed Gehazi's account, the king commanded that her property be restored, together with all the produce that had been harvested from her fields.

F. Anointing Kings (2 K. 8:7–9:13). Following the account of the acts of Elisha, the author of Kings returns to his narrative of royal affairs. Interwoven with this narrative are his accounts of how Elisha completed Elijah's commission to anoint Hazael king of Syria and Jehu king of Israel (cf. 1 K. 19:15f.).

1. Hazael (2 K. 8:7-15). While on a journey to Damascus, Elisha was approached by Hazael, who had been sent by Ben-hadad (I? II?) to inquire about the outcome of his sickness (cf. 1:2). In reply, Elisha foretold the evil that Hazael would do to Israel. In spite of his innocent protestations, Hazael returned with Elisha's word to the king and the next day smothered him in his bed and took the throne. The year was *ca.* 842 B.C. (*BHI*, p. 250).

2. Jehu (2 K. 9:1-13). Shortly after Hazael's accession to the throne in Damascus, Jehoram, with the help of the recently crowned Ahaziah of Judah, attempted to recover Ramoth-gilead from the Syrians. He was wounded in the fighting and withdrew to recover in Jezreel. Elisha then sent one of the sons of the prophets to anoint Jehu, an officer in Jehoram's chariot corps. In the bloodbath that followed Jehu swept away the descendants of Ahab in both Israel and Judah. The sword of Elisha (1 K. 19:17) proved to be the sword of Yahweh's judgment in the hands of Hazael and Jehu.

G. Death and Burial (2 K. 13:11-21). *1. Prophecy to Jehoash* (13:11-19). Shortly after Jehoash came to the throne (798), Elisha fell ill. Jehoash went to visit the prophet and wept to see that the aged Elisha was dying. The words with which he hailed him, "My father, my father! The chariots of Israel and its horsemen!" are a duplicate of those with which Elisha summed up the significance of Elijah (2 K. 2:12).

Elisha's final deed was to lay his hands on the hands of Jehoash and shoot "Yahweh's arrow of victory, the arrow of victory over Syria!" (v. 17). Commanding the king to take arrows and strike the ground with them, Elisha was angered when the king did so only three times, for that meant that the king's triumphs would be limited to three victories.

2. Elisha's Grave Yields Life (2 K. 13:20f.). Shortly thereafter, Elisha died and was buried in his homeland E of the Jordan. When a dead body was hastily thrown into Elisha's tomb, it touched his bones and the man revived. Even in death, Elisha was the mediator of Yahweh's gift of life.

III. Later Tradition.–Elisha is mentioned but once in the intertestamental literature that has survived. In his praise of famous men, Ben Sira devotes a few lines to Elisha (Sir. 48:12-14) at the conclusion of his eulogy of Elijah. He recalls that Elisha was filled with Elijah's spirit and did not tremble before anyone.

In the NT Elisha is mentioned only once (Lk. 4:27), where his healing of Naaman is recalled as one of two instances in which prophets mediated God's mercies to Gentiles rather than to Israelites.

Although the authors of the Gospels seem clearly to have discerned in Jesus' ministry a fulfillment of that of Elijah (*see* ELIJAH V.B), there is some evidence that they also saw Jesus as being John the Baptist's Elisha. Note especially: (1) Jesus' baptism by John in the Jordan, at which time He received the Spirit that qualified Him for His ministry (Mk. 1:9-11 par.); (2) His continuing in a ministry like John's until John was removed from the scene, at which time He undertook His own distinctive ministry (Mk. 1:14; Mt. 4:12); (3) His movement among the people, together with His special association with the poor and outcasts; (4) His peripatetic ministry in Galilee and Samaria; (5) His miracles, which played a considerable role in His ministry and which were similar to those of Elisha: cf. (a) Jesus' healing of the ten lepers (Lk. 17:11-19) and Elisha's healing of Naaman (2 K. 5); (b) His multiplication of the loaves (Mt. 14:13-21 par.; 15:29-39; esp. Jn. 6:1-15) and Elisha's similar deed (2 K. 4:42-44); (c) His raising of the son of the widow of Nain (Lk. 7:11-17) and Elisha's raising of the son of the Shunammite (2 K. 4:17-37). For other possible parallels between the Gospel accounts of Jesus' ministry and that of Elisha, see Brown.

Bibliography.–M. A. Beek, *Oudtestamentische Studiën,* 17 (1972), 1-10; L. Bronner, *The Stories of Elijah and Elisha* (1968); R. E. Brown, *Perspective,* 12 (1971), 85-104; J. Gray, *I & II Kings* (*OTL,* 2nd ed. 1970); J. M. Miller, *JBL,* 85 (1966), 455-466 (presents a radical reconstruction of the history); H. Schweizer, *Elischa in den Kriegen* (1974); G. von Rad, *OT Theology,* II (1965), 25-32; R. S. Wallace, *Elijah and Elisha* (1968).

J. H. STEK

ELISHAH ē-lī'shə [Heb. *'ělîšâ*–'God saves'; Gk. *Elisa, Eleisai*]. Mentioned in Gen. 10:4; 1 Ch. 1:7 as the eldest son of Javan, and in Ezk. 27:7 as the source from which the Tyrians obtained their purple dyes. On the basis of this latter statement attempts have been made to identify it with southern Italy or northern Africa. Josephus (*Ant.* i.6.1) identified Elishah with the Aeolians. The Targum on Ezekiel gives "the province of Italy." A place known as Alashia was mentioned in cuneiform records from the Middle Euphrates region, Hattusas, and Tell el-Amarna between the 18th and 13th cents. B.C., and this is probably the OT Elishah. Some section of Cyprus is probably indicated by the references, though distinct from the territory described as Kittim (Cyprus) in Ezk. 27:6.

R. K. H.

ELISHAMA ē-lish'ə-mə [Heb. *'ělîšāmā'*–'God has heard'].

1. Grandfather of Joshua and son of Ammihud; leader of the tribe of Ephraim in the Exodus (Nu. 1:10; 2:18; 7:48, 53; 10:22; 1 Ch. 7:26).

2. A son of David, born in Jerusalem (2 S. 5:16; 1 Ch. 3:8; 14:7).

3. A textual corruption in 1 Ch. 3:6 for ELISHUA, another of David's sons; cf. 2 S. 5:15.

4. A scribe of Jehoiakim (Jer. 36:12, 20f.).

5. One "of the royal family," grandfather of Ishmael the slayer of Gedaliah (2 K. 25:25; Jer. 41:1).

6. A man of the tribe of Judah (1 Ch. 2:41).

7. One of the priests appointed by Jehoshaphat to teach the law (2 Ch. 17:8). F. K. FARR

ELISHAPHAT ē-lish'ə-fat [Heb. *'ělîšāpaṭ*–'God is judge']. One of the "commanders of hundreds" employed by Jehoiada the priest in the conspiracy against Athaliah, to make Joash king (2 Ch. 23:1).

ELISHEBA ē-lish'ə-bə [Heb. *'ělîšeḇa'*–'my God is fulness']. The daughter of Amminadab, sister of Nashon, wife of Aaron, and mother of Nadab, Abihu, Eleazar, and Ithamar; the founder, therefore, of the entire Levitical priesthood (Ex. 6:23).

ELISHUA el-i-shōō'ə, ē-lish'ōō-ə [Heb. *'ělîšû(a)'*–'God is salvation']. A son of David (2 S. 5:15; 1 Ch. 14:5); apparently called Elishama in 1 Ch. 3:6 through a misreading by the copyist.

ELISIMUS ē-lis'i-məs (AV 1 Esd. 9:28). *See* ELIASHIB **5.**

ELIU ē-lī'o͞o (AV Jth. 8:1). *See* ELIJAH **5.**

ELIUD ē-lī'əd [Gk. *Elioud*–'God my praise']. An ancestor of Jesus, four generations before Joseph (Mt. 1:14f.).

ELIZABETH ē-liz'ə-beth [Gk. *Elisabet* < Heb. *'ĕlîšeḇa'*–'God is (my) oath,' i.e., a worshiper of God]; AV ELISABETH. The wife of ZECHARIAH the priest and mother of JOHN THE BAPTIST (Lk. 1:5ff.). Elizabeth herself is described as being "of the daughters of Aaron," i.e., of priestly lineage. Although it was required of a priest only that he marry a virgin of Israel, it was preferable if he could marry the daughter of a priest (SB, II, 68-71). Luke also describes Elizabeth, along with her husband, as "righteous [Gk. *díkaios*] before God, walking in all the commandments and ordinances of the Lord blameless" (1:6). The language used is strongly influenced by the LXX and indicates that they were fully obedient to the will of God (*TDNT,* II, 189). Thus, Zechariah and Elizabeth possessed strong qualifications for being chosen as the parents of John the Baptist: not only in pure lineage but also as models of OT piety.

Elizabeth, however, was BARREN (Lk. 1:7) — the greatest misfortune that could befall a woman at that time. In this respect she stood in continuity with Sarah (Gen. 11:30), Rebekah (25:21), Rachel (29:31), Samson's mother (Jgs. 13:2f.), and Hannah (1 S. 1:2, 5). As in the case of each of these women, Elizabeth's barrenness set the stage for a miraculous intervention of God in which He blessed Israel with a special leader. The parallel with the story of Isaac's birth is especially close in that Elizabeth and Zechariah, like Sarah and Abraham, were both "advanced in years" (Lk. 1:7). Like Abraham (Gen. 17:17) and Sarah (18:12), Zechariah at first found the promise of a son too hard to believe (Lk. 1:18); but there is no record of doubt on Elizabeth's part (perhaps because Zechariah could not inform her of the angel's message) — only of gratitude, after the conception, that God had removed her barrenness (1:25; cf. v. 58; Ps. 113:9).

Luke calls Elizabeth a "kinswoman" of MARY **(6)** the mother of Jesus. The Gk. *syngenís* indicates that they were relatives, but not necessarily cousins; it may indicate that Mary also was of priestly descent. The angel Gabriel informed Mary of Elizabeth's pregnancy in order to assure her that with God nothing is impossible. When Elizabeth heard Mary's greeting, her baby "leaped for joy" in her womb (Lk. 1:41-44) and Elizabeth was inspired by the Holy Spirit to prophesy. Without anyone telling her she knew about the angel's visit to Mary, the messianic future of Mary's child (1:42f.), and Mary's response of faith (*TDNT,* VI, 835). Her tribute to Mary's faith (1:45) may be intended as a contrast to Zechariah's doubt (vv. 18, 20).

Bibliography.–I. H. Marshall, *Gospel of Luke* (1978); A. Plummer (*ICC,* 1900); SB, II, 68ff.; *TDNT,* II, *s.v.* δίκαιος (Schrenk).

N. J. O.

ELIZAPHAN el-i-zā'fən, ē-liz'ə-fan [Heb. *'ĕlîṣāpān*–'God has protected; Gk. *Eleisaphan, Elisaphan, Elisapha, Elisaphat*].

1. The son of Uzziel the son of Kohath, thus a leader of the Levitical class of the Kohathites (Nu. 3:30; 1 Ch. 15:8; 2 Ch. 29:13). But in 1 Ch. 15:8; 2 Ch. 29:13 he seems to head a class parallel to the Kohathites. He is called Elzaphan in Ex. 6:22; Lev. 10:4.

2. A leader of Zebulun, who represented that tribe in the division of the land (Nu. 34:25).

ELIZUR ē-lī'zər [Heb. *'ĕlîṣûr*–'my God is a rock'; Gk. *Eleiour, Elisour*]. A leader of the tribe of Reuben (Nu. 1:5; 2:10; 7:30, 35; 10:18).

ELKANAH el-kā'nə [Heb. *'elqānâ*–'God has possessed'].

1. An Ephraimite, the father of Samuel (1 S. 1:1-28; 2:11-20). Of his two wives, Hannah, the childless, was most beloved. At Shiloh she received through Eli the promise of a son. Elkanah and Hannah took the young Samuel to Shiloh when he was weaned, and left him with Eli as their offering to the Lord. They were blessed with three other sons and two daughters.

2. The second son of Korah (Ex. 6:24), who escaped the fate of Korah, Dathan, and Abiram (Nu. 26:11).

3. One "next in authority to the king" in Jerusalem in the time of Ahaz; slain by Zichri of Ephraim in a war with Pekah (2 Ch. 28:7).

4. One of the Korahites among David's "mighty men" (1 Ch. 12:6).

5. A Levite, possibly the same as **2** above (1 Ch. 6:23, 25, 36).

6. Another Levite of the same line (1 Ch. 6:26, 35).

7. Another Levite of the same line (1 Ch. 6:27, 34).

8. Another Levite, ancestor of Berechiah (1 Ch. 9:16).

9. Another Levite (if not the same as **4** above), one of the "gatekeepers for the ark" (1 Ch. 15:23).

F. K. FARR

ELKIAH el-kī'ə [Gk. *Elkia*]; AV ELCIA; NEB HELKIAS. An ancestor of Judith (Jth. 8:1).

ELKOSH el'kōsh, **(OF)** [Heb. *hā'elqōšî*; Gk. *Elkesaiou*]; AV, NEB, ELKOSHITE. A name occuring in Nah. 1:1 only, probably designating the home of the prophet. The site is unknown.

The tradition identifying Elkosh with el-Qôsh, about 50 km. (30 mi.) N of Mosul, a rather large village with a Nestorian monastery, is not traceable before the 16th cent. and is utterly improbable. According to Jerome in his commentary on Nahum, Elkosh is Helkeseï in Galilee, often identified with el-Qauze W of Tibnin (21 km., or 13 mi., SE of Tyre), but the identification is doubtful; moreover, it is more probable that Nahum was a Judean, as was assumed by Cyril of Alexandria.

Vitae Prophetarum, wrongly ascribed to Epiphanius, identifies Elkosh with Elkesi, which, according to the text as corrected by Nestle, should be looked for "the other side of Begobara." This last name Nestle identifies with Beit Jibrîn. If he is right, the indication of pseudo-Epiphanius is based on a confusion between Elkosh and Lachish (situated in Roman times at el-Qubeibeh); however, the *qoph* in Elkosh is an obstacle against such an identification. Basing on the uncorrected text, H. J. Schoeps (*Theologie und Geschichte des Judentums* [1949], pp. 326f.) compares Begobara with Gk. *Bēthabara* in numerous text witnesses of Jn. 1:28, a town just over the Jordan, SE of Jericho; in that case Nahum's town should be sought in the eastern Jordan Valley N of the Dead Sea and might be the same as the center of the sect of the Elchesaites in later times.

For the meaning of the name, cf. *lāqaš* in Job 24:6, "glean," or *leqeš* in Am. 7:1, "latter growth."

A. VAN SELMS

ELLASAR el-ā'sär [Heb. *'ellāsār*]. A city of Mesopotamia ruled by Arioch and other Babylonian kings (Gen. 14:1, 9). The Babylonian form of the name is *(âl) Larsa,* "the city Larsa." The Sumerian name is Ararwa, "abode of light."

At one time Ellasar was thought to be Asshur, ancient capital of Assyria. Others suggest it is located in northern

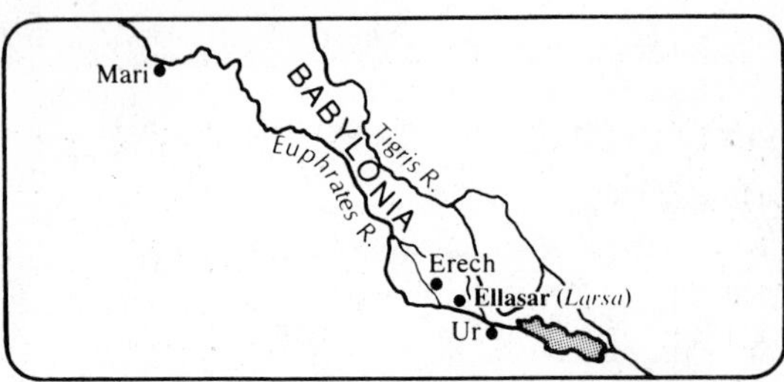

Mesopotamia at the town of Ilanzura of the Mari texts, a site between Carchemish and Haran. Most scholars accept H. Rawlinson's view that Ellasar is Larsa, ancient Babylonian city of the sun-god, whose ruins are seen at Senkereh in lower Babylon, on the east bank of the Euphrates midway between Erech (Uruk, Warka) and Ur of the Chaldees.

Its King Arioch, confederate of Chedorlaomer king of Elam, invaded Canaan, captured Sodom, and carried off Lot (Gen. 14:1,9). The Sumerian town flourished in the Mari period. The Elamite Kudur-Mabuk had set on the throne his son Warad-Sin, who was succeeded by his younger brother Rīm-Sin. The last ruler Rīm-Sin was defeated by Hammurabi, who made the town a capital of his Babylonian empire.

W. K. Loftus excavated Larsa in 1854. He discovered a cemetery there, but dated the finds incorrectly. He also found the ziggurat and temple of the old city. In 1922-1923 A. Parrot led an expedition, finding temples, palaces, and inscriptions that confirmed the importance of the ancient city in both Sumerian and Babylonian times. Tablets found indicate that the site was a noted center of Babylonian mathematical learning. Parts of walls and remains of homes were also uncovered.

The temples discovered reveal that the city was a seat of the worship of the sun-god Šamaš among the Babylonians. Like other important cities of Babylonia it boasted a great temple tower, known as the "house of the bond of heaven and earth." Its temple, named in honor of the sun-god, was called "House of Light." The sanctuary was restored by Hammurabi, Nebuchadrezzar, and Nabonidus.

Bibliography.–NBD; *EB*; *LAP*, p. 45; *HDB*.

C. L. FEINBERG

ELM. *See* TEREBINTH.

ELMADAM el-mā'dəm [Gk. *Elmadam* or *Elmōdam*]; AV ELMODAM. An ancestor of Jesus, according to Luke's genealogy, in the sixth generation before Zerubbabel (Lk. 3:28).

ELNAAM el-nā'əm [Heb. *'elna'am*–'God is delightfulness']. According to the MT the father of two of David's warriors (1 Ch. 11:46); according to the LXX himself one of the warriors.

ELNATHAN el-nā'thən [Heb. *'elnāṯān*–'God has given'; Gk. Apoc. *Elnatan, Ennatas*]; AV Apoc. ALNATHAN, EUNATAN; NEB Apoc. also ENNATAS.

1. The grandfather of Jehoiachin (2 K. 24:8). He was one of the princes present when Jeremiah's scroll was read by Baruch to Jehoiakim (Jer. 36:12). He was leader of the party sent to Egypt (Jer. 26:22) to extradite the prophet Uriah. The name Elnathan occurs in the third ostracon from Lachish as the father of the "commander of the host," but a positive identification of the two is difficult.

2, 3, 4. The name of two "chief men" — unless textual corruption has introduced the name at its second occurrence — and of one "teacher" sent for by Ezra from the camp at the river Ahava (Ezr. 8:16). If 1 Esd. 8:44 (LXX 43) is correct, only two persons should be named here.

R. K. H.

ELOAH e-lō'ə. *See* GOD, NAMES OF II.A.3.

ELOHIM e-lō'him, el'ō-hēm. *See* GOD, NAMES OF II.A.2.

ELOI ē'loi, ē-lō'ī **ELOI** (Mk. 15:34). *See* ELI, ELI, LAMA SABACHTHANI.

ELON ē'lon [Heb. *'êlôn, 'êlōn, 'ēlôn*–'terebinth'].

1. A Zebulunite who judged Israel ten years and was buried in Aijalon (Jgs. 12:11f.).

2. A son of Zebulun (Gen. 46:14; Nu. 26:26).

3. A Hittite whose daughter Esau wedded (Gen. 26:34; 36:2).

ELON ē'lon [Heb. *'êlôn*–'terebinth'; Gk. *Ailōn*]. An unidentified town in the territory of Dan (Josh. 19:43). *Westminster Dictionary of the Bible* (1944) and *IDB* conjecture that the site is either 'Alein, W of Beit Maḥṣir, or Khirbet Wâdī 'Alin, between Deir Aban and 'Ain Shems. It may be identical with ELONBETH-HANAN.

R. P. DUGAN

ELONBETH-HANAN ē-lon-beth-hā'nən [Heb. *'êlôn bêt ḥānān*–'terebinth of the house of Elon'] (1 K. 4:9). A town in the second district supplying food for Solomon's household; probably the same town as ELON.

ELONITES ē'lən-īts [Heb. *'ēlônî*]. NEB ELONITE FAMILY. Descendants of Elon (Nu. 26:26). *See* ELON **2.**

ELOQUENT [Heb. *'îš dᵉḇārîm*–'man of words'] (Ex. 4:10); NEB "ready speech"; [Gk. *lógios*] (Acts 18:24); [*sophía lógou*] ("eloquent wisdom," 1 Cor. 1:17); AV "wisdom of words"; NEB "worldly wisdom."

When God commanded Moses to go to Pharaoh and to lead the people out of Egypt, Moses protested and tried to escape by claiming that he was not a "man of words" or "good with words." This disclaimer became characteristic of the prophets (cf., e.g., Jer. 1:6; also Childs, pp. 49, 78). The NT use of *lógios* to describe the Jew Apollos from Alexandria can refer either to his great learning or to his skill in speaking. The first sense is similar to Josephus's use of the term (*Ant.* xvii.6.2) and to classical and more modern Greek descriptions of one well versed in the arts and literature, especially in history and the antiquities (Thayer, p. 379). On the other hand, the picture of Apollos from Acts 18:25ff.; 1 Cor. 1:12; 3:5ff. shows him to be well versed in the Scriptures and a bold speaker. The general description "a man of culture" may best convey the sense of Acts 18:24 (MM, p. 378).

In 1 Cor. 1:17 Paul declares that he has been sent to preach the gospel, but "not with eloquent wisdom, lest the cross of Christ be emptied of its power." Here there are several possibilities as to the meaning of "eloquent wisdom" (lit. "wisdom of speech" or "wisdom of the word"; *see* WISDOM). Similar phrases are found in 1 Cor. 2:1, where Paul writes, "I did not come proclaiming to you the testimony of God in lofty words (*hyperóchē lógou*) or wisdom (*sophía*)," and in 2:4, "my speech and my message were not in plausible (*peithós*) words of wisdom (*sophías lógoi*)." "Wisdom" probably means philosophical knowledge or style. Thus Paul contrasts his straightforward telling of the story of the Cross with the usual presentations of public teachers who used elaborate argument and stylish, masterful rhetoric. Ancient sophists were very artful in public speech, often consciously disguising the truth by presenting persuasive arguments calculated to influence people's minds by their appearance of rationality. Paul denounces the use of learned and fascinating "wisdom" to trick or charm the audience. The "power of God" and the "wisdom of God" (1:24) lie in the facts of His action and not in any man's dramatic presentations (see Orr and Walther, p. 152).

Some have seen in the Corinthian situation an influence of Jewish Gnosticism in which "a wisdom doctrine had replaced the cross" for some sects and "Wisdom" had become a title for the exalted Christ (*see TDNT,* VII, 520; Bultmann, I, 180, 327; II, 132). Paul counters this by calling it "worldly wisdom" (2:5; RSV "wisdom of men"), therefore "wisdom of the word."

A final suggestion is that "wisdom of speech" includes some of the more unusual and refined methods of OT interpretation, perhaps coming from Philo of Alexandria through his supposed pupil Apollos. However, there is no proof that Apollos' "excelling in the knowledge of the Scriptures" (*dynatós en graphaís*) had come as a result of methods of interpretation he had learned from Philo or one of Philo's pupils.

Bibliography.–MM; Thayer; *TDNT,* IV, *s.v.* λέγω (G. Kittel); VII, *s.v.* σοφία (U. Wilckens); F. F. Bruce, *Acts of the Apostles* (*NIC,* 1953); R. Bultmann, *Theology of the NT* (Eng. tr. 1970); B. Childs, *Exodus* (*OTL,* 1974); W. D. Davies, *Paul and Rabbinic Judaism* (2nd ed. 1955); W. F. Orr and J. A. Walther, *I Corinthians* (*AB,* 1976); W. C. Robinson, Jr., "Word and Power," in J. M. Richards, ed., *Soli Deo Gloria* (1968), pp. 68-82.

D. K. MCKIM

ELOTH ē'loth. *See* ELATH.

ELPAAL el-pā'əl [Heb. *'elpa'al*–'God has wrought']. The name of a descendant of Benjamin (1 Ch. 8:11f., 18).

ELPALET el-pā'let (AV 1 Ch. 14:5). *See* ELPELET.

EL-PARAN el-pâr'ən [Heb. *'êl pā'rān*] (Gen. 14:6). The southernmost point subdued by Chedorlaomer and his allies from the east. *See* PARAN.

ELPELET el'pē-lət [Heb. *'elpālet*]; AV ELPALET. The name of a son of David (1 Ch. 14:5).

ELTEKE el'tə-kē, **ELTEKEH** [Heb. *'eltᵉqēh* (Josh. 19:44), *'eltᵉqē'* (21:23); Gk. B *Alkathá,* A *Elkethṓ*]. A place in the territory of Dan named between Ekron and Gibbethon (Josh. 19:44), and again between Beth-horon and Gibbethon, as given to the Kohathite Levites (21:23). It is probably identical with the Assyrian *Altaku,* where Sennacherib (Oriental Institute Prism inscription) claims to have defeated the allied armies of the Philistines and the Egyptians. The site is unknown, but should probably be located either E of Ekron toward Timnah or to the north between Ekron and Gibbethon. W. W. BUEHLER

ELTEKON el'tə-kon [Heb. *'eltᵉqōn*] (Josh. 15:59). A village in the hill country of Judah, listed with Beth-zur and Beth-anoth, therefore in the area between Bethlehem and Hebron. F.-M. Abel (*GP,* II, 314) identifies it with Khirbet ed-Deir, about 3 km. (2 mi.) S of Ḥauṣan, and about 6½ km. (4 mi.) W of Bethlehem. W. S. L. S.

ELTOLAD el-tō'lad [Heb. *'eltôlad*]. A city in the inheritance of Judah (Josh. 15:30) or Simeon (19:4), probably a variant form of TOLAD (1 Ch. 4:29). The name could be translated as "El shall cause to bear," hence the suggestion that it was a shrine to which women went to pray for children; but this lacks objective support. F.-M. Abel (*GP,* II, 314) identifies the site with Khirbet Erqa Saqra, but this is uncertain. W. S. L. S.

ELUL ē'lul, e-lo͞ol' [Heb. *'ᵉlûl* (Neh. 6:15); Akk. *elulu, ululu*; Gk. *Eloul* (1 Macc. 14:27)]. The sixth month of the Hebrew year, corresponding to August/September. *See* CALENDAR II.A.2.

ELUZAI ē-lo͞o'zī [Heb. *'el'ûzay*–'God is my strength'; cf. UZZIEL]. A Benjaminite who deserted Saul to become one of David's "mighty men" (1 Ch. 12:5).

ELYMAIS el-ə-mā'əs [Gk. *Elymais*]. Mentioned in 1 Macc. 6:1 as a "city" (Gk. *pólis*) in Persia "famed for its wealth." No other reference to Elymais as a city occurs except in Josephus *Ant.* xii.9.1, which simply reflects the account in 1 Macc. 6:1; and even 1 Macc. 6:1 has variant textual readings. Tob. 2:10 simply states that Ahikar went "to" or "into" (Gk. *eis*) Elymais, without indicating whether this was a city or a region. References in Strabo and Ptolemy seem to indicate that Elymais, derived from ELAM, was the name of a region between Persia and Babylonia, essentially equivalent to the province Susiana, whose capital was Susa.

Bibliography.–Pauly-Wissowa, V, 2458-2467; Strabo *Geog.* xv.3.12, xvi.1.1; Ptolemy *Geog.* vi.3. W. S. L. S.

ELYMAS el'ə-məs [Gk. *Elymas*–'sorcerer'] (Acts 13:8). *See* BAR-JESUS.

ELYON el-yōn', ē-lī'ən. *See* GOD, NAMES OF.

ELZABAD el-zā'bad [Heb. *'elzāḇāḏ*–'God has given'; cf. ZABDIEL and ZEBADIAH].

1. The ninth of David's Gadite heroes who joined him in the wilderness (1 Ch. 12:12).

2. A Korahite gatekeeper (1 Ch. 26:7).

ELZAPHAN el-zā'fan [Heb. *'elṣāpān*]. One of the sons of Uzziel (Ex. 6:22) commissioned by Moses to remove from the camp the corpses of their priestly relatives who had offered "unholy fire" to the Lord (Lev. 10:4). *See* ELIZAPHAN **1.**

EMADABUN ē-mā'də-bun [Gk. *Ēmadaboun*] (1 Esd. 5:58); AV MADIABUN. The head of a family of Levites who superintended the repair of the temple; not named in Ezr. 3:9.

EMATHIS em'ə-this [Gk. *Emathis,* B *Emaththis,* A *Ematheis*]; AV AMATHEIS. One of the sons of Bebai (1 Esd. 9:29), called "Athlai" in Ezr. 10:28. *See* ATHLAI.

EMBALMING. *See* BURIAL II.B.

EMBASSY [Gk. *presbeía*] (Lk. 14:32; 19:14); AV AMBASSAGE; NEB ENVOYS, DELEGATION. A body of ambassadors with a message entrusted to them. The term *presbeía* is used by Jesus twice: (1) in the parable of the pounds, of the citizens who hated the nobleman and sent a delegation after him with the message that they refused to have him reign over them, thereby illustrating those who wilfully rejected Jesus' own kingdom (Lk. 19:14); (2) in the parable of a weak king who sends to a stronger ruler a delegation to ask conditions of peace (14:32). In 2 Macc. 4:11 *presbeía* is translated "mission" by the RSV

(NEB "treaty"; AV "ambassador").
See also MESSENGER. N. J. O.

EMBRACE [Heb. *ḥāḇaq*] (Gen. 29:13; 33:4; 48:10; 2 K. 4:16; Prov. 4:8; 5:20; Cant. 2:6; 8:3; Eccl. 3:5); NEB also "have in your arms" (2 K. 4:16), "was round me" (Cant. 2:6; 8:3); [*ḥêq*] (Gen. 16:5); AV BOSOM; NEB ARMS; [Gk. *epipíptō*] (Lk. 15:20; Acts 20:37); AV "fell on"; NEB "flung their arms around," "folded in their arms"; [*symperilambánō*] (Acts 20:10); NEB "seizing in his arms." The word has two distinct meanings in the OT: (1) to clasp and hold fondly in the arms, pointing to a common custom (Gen. 29:13; 33:4; 48:10; 2 K. 4:16; Cant. 2:6; 8:3; cf. Acts 20:10), and (2) to have sexual intercourse (Prov. 5:20; Eccl. 3:5). It seems to have acquired this technical sense in later Jewish usage.

EMBROIDERY [Heb. *riqmâ*; Gk. usually *poikilía, poíkilma*]. The AV usually has "broidered"; the NEB, besides "embroidered," uses "brocade," "striped," "patterned." How much ornamentation of cloth was in fact needlework, and how much was woven on the loom, is difficult to determine.

There is clearly a distinction between the work of the weaver (Heb. *'ōrēg*) and that of the embroiderer (*rōqēm*, Ex. 35:35). The embroiderer produced the colored work such as decorated the tabernacle hangings (Ex. 26:1, 31), the ephod, girdle, and breastplate of the high priest (Ex. 28:6, 8, 15), and the garments of those who served in the sanctuary (Ex. 39:1). The same explicit connection with colored work is seen again in Jgs. 5:30.

Fine embroidery depicted in a detail of a relief of Ashurnasirpal II (9th cent. B.C.) from Nimrûd (Trustees of the British Museum)

Embroidered garments were naturally a sign of luxury (Ps. 45:14, NEB; Ezk. 16:10; 26:16). Egypt (Ezk. 27:7) and Syria (Ezk. 27:16) are singled out as producers of embroidered work, though the art probably originated in Babylon (cf. the costly Babylonian mantle, Josh. 7:21).

The word is applied metaphorically to the plumage of an eagle (Ezk. 17:3), to variegated stones for the house of God (1 Ch. 29:2), and to an unborn child (Ps. 139:15).

Gold thread cut from thin plates of beaten gold (Ex. 39:3) was sometimes worked into the embroidered pattern by the inventive craftsmen (Heb. *ḥōšēḇ*, Ex. 36:8, 35), as in the design of cherubim for the tabernacle. This was probably done with the needle rather than woven in on the loom, in view of the complex pattern.

The colored pomegranates that, together with gold bells, decorated the high priest's robe (Ex. 28:33) were probably of appliqué work.

In contrast, Aaron's tunic was of checkered work (Heb. *keṯōneṯ tašbēṣ*, Ex. 28:4), perhaps woven in a checkered design, or with the pattern produced by threads sewn between two layers of cloth, as is still done in Syria. A similar pattern was fit for royal clothing (Ps. 45:13 [MT 14]). But here the reference may be to pearls in plaited settings of gold thread (reading Heb. *penînîm* for *penîmâ* [*BDB*]); this is parallel to the use elsewhere of Heb. *mišbeṣôṯ* for the settings of gems in the ephod (Ex. 28:11, 13) and in the breastplate (Ex. 39:13, 16). G. I. EMMERSON

EMEK-KEZIZ ē'mek-kē'ziz [Heb. *'ēmeq qeṣîṣ*; Gk. B *Amekasis*, A *Amekkasis*]; AV VALLEY OF KEZIZ. One of the cities of Benjamin, located near Jericho and Beth-hoglah (Josh. 18:21). The exact site is unknown, but it was probably located in the Jordan plain, S of Jericho.
K. G. JUNG

EMENDATIONS OF THE SCRIBES [Heb. *tiqqûnê hassôperîm*]. A list of eighteen words emended in the MT to remove anthropomorphism.

EMERALD. *See* STONES, PRECIOUS.

EMERODS em'ə-rodz. Archaic term used in the AV for "hemorrhoids." *See* TUMORS.

EMIM ē'mīm [Heb. *'êmîm*–'terrors'(?); Gk. *Ommaein* and variants]. A Moabite designation of a race of giant people whom the Moabites dispossessed (Dt. 2:10f.). Chedorlaomer defeated them during the time of Abraham at Shaveh-kiriathaim, a plain E of the Dead Sea (Gen. 14:5), identified with modern el-Qereiyât. Known to the Israelites generally as REPHAIM who occupied much of the land E of the Jordan, they are called Zuzim, Horites (by the Edomites), and Zamzummim (by the Ammonites); see Gen. 14:5 and Dt. 2:10f., 20-23. A great and powerful people with an advanced civilization, they are unknown outside the OT. D. B. PECOTA

EMINENT. Occurs twice in the RSV: in Lk. 14:8 (Gk. *entimóteros*, "more eminent") referring to social standing, and in Rom. 16:13 (*eklektós*, "select"), describing Rufus. The AV uses the term in Ezk. 16:24, 31, 39; 17:22 in the literal sense of physical elevation.

EMMANUEL ē-man'ū-el. *See* IMMANUEL.

EMMAUS e-mā'əs [Gk. *Emmaous*]. A village (Gk. *kṓmē*) in Judea, "60 stadia from Jerusalem" (Lk. 24:13). It was the destination of Cleopas and an unknown companion to whom Jesus appeared after His resurrection. He spoke

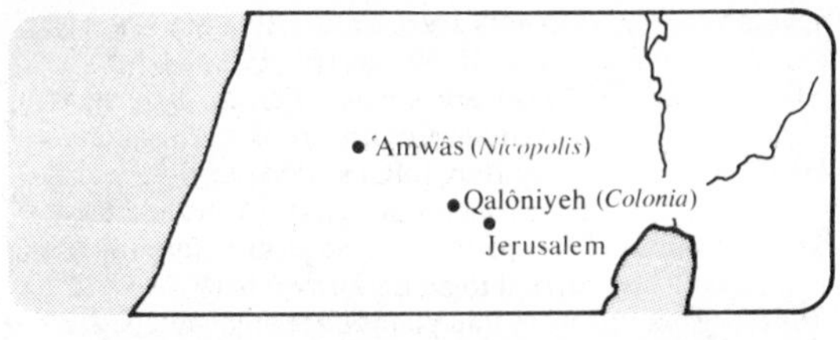

Road near el-Qubeibeh, the traditional site of Emmaus (W. S. LaSor)

and ate with them before vanishing as suddenly as He had appeared. Josephus says the name of this town "may be rendered 'a warm bath' for therein is a spring of warm water useful for healing" (*BJ* iv.i.3). The name may be derived from Heb. *ḥammaṯ*, "hot spring."

The exact site of Emmaus is unknown, and various towns have been suggested as the original location. The Crusaders located Emmaus at el-Qubeibeh, just 60 stadia (about 11 km., 7 mi.) NW of Jerusalem. In 1873 the Franciscans unearthed the ruins of a Crusader basilica. In one of the adjacent naves the ruins of a small house were found, which was believed to have been the house of Cleopas. A hospice and school attached to the rebuilt Franciscan Church of Saint Cleopas fortify the tradition.

Some have located Emmaus at Qalôniyeh (Colonia), about 34 stadia (about 6½ km., 4 mi.) W of Jerusalem. According to Josephus (*BJ* vii.6.6), Vespasian assigned a place called Emmaus for eight hundred dismissed men. This site, however, has no spring and is only half the distance recorded in Luke; it may be instead Heb. *ḥammoṣa* of Josh. 18:26, mentioned in the Talmud (*Sukkah* iv.5) as a *colonia*.

The site with the most external evidence and tradition supporting it is the village of ʿAmwâs. Early tradition identifies ʿAmwâs as the Emmaus where Judas Maccabeus defeated the Syrian Georgias (1 Macc. 4:1-5), a site that was "in the plain" (1 Macc. 3:40). Because Josephus describes Emmaus as a city rather than a village (*BJ* iii.3.5), some scholars have not acknowledged ʿAmwâs as the biblical Emmaus (cf. *WHAB*); Josephus, however, relates the utter destruction of Emmaus by Varus (*Ant.* xvii.10.9); it is quite possible, therefore, that it was only a village at the time of the postresurrection appearance but was later the seat of a toparchy. In the early Christian period ʿAmwâs was also famous for a spring of reputed healing qualities. In the 3rd cent. A.D. it was called Nicopolis and was an episcopal see. The Bordeaux Pilgrim, the Holy Paula, and Jerome, in agreement with Eusebius, accepted this site as the Lukan Emmaus. The main question in identifying ʿAmwâs with the biblical Emmaus is the distance involved. Instead of the Lukan 60 stadia, ʿAmwâs is 160 stadia (about 31 km., 19 mi.) from Jerusalem. Some MSS, however, including Codex Sinaiticus, do read "160."

See *EAEHL*, II, *s.v.* (M. Avi-Yonah). K. G. JUNG

EMMER em'ər (AV, NEB, 1 Esd. 9:21). *See* IMMER.

EMMERUTH em'ər-uth (NEB 1 Esd. 5:24). *See* IMMER.

EMMOR em'ôr (AV, NEB, Acts 7:16). *See* HAMOR.

EMPEROR [Gk. *ho sebastós*; Lat. *augustus*] (Acts 25:21, 25); AV AUGUSTUS; NEB also "His Imperial Majesty"; [Gk. *basileús*] (1 Pet. 2:13, 17); AV KING; NEB SOVEREIGN. A title, from Lat. *imperator* ("commander"), designating the rulers of the Roman empire. Originally *imperator* was a military term employed by the troops to salute a victorious general. Julius Caesar was the first to use the title continuously, and from the time of Octavian it was used regularly as an official title. Gk. *sebastós* (AUGUSTUS), likewise, was decreed an official title of the Roman ruler in 27 B.C., during the rule of Octavian, and it was so used by all the succeeding Roman emperors. Historians, however, have applied the designation "augustus" only to Octavian and have used "emperor" to designate the title of office. In Acts 25:21, 25 *sebastós* refers not to Augustus Caesar Octavian (who had died in A.D. 14) but to the one who then held the office; thus the RSV and NEB have substituted the title "emperor" to avoid confusion.

See also CAESAR; ROMAN EMPIRE AND CHRISTIANITY.

N. J. O.

EMPTY; EMPTINESS; EMPTY-HANDED [Heb. *rîq* (noun), *rêq* (adj.), *rêqām* (adv.), also *ʿārâ* (Gen. 24:20; 2 Ch. 24:11), *yāṣaq* (2 S. 13:9), *nāṯaḵ* (2 K. 22:9; 2 Ch. 34:17), *bāqaq* (Isa. 19:3; Jer. 51:2), *šāwᵉʾ* (Job 7:3; 15:31; 35:13; Ps. 41:6; Hos. 10:4; Zec. 10:2), *tōhû* (Isa. 29:21; 40:17; 41:29; 59:4), *pānâ* (Lev. 14:36), *pāqaḏ* (1 S. 20:18, 25, 27), *heḇel* (Job 21:34; 35:16; Eccl. 5:7; Isa. 30:7); Gk. *kenós, kenóō* (1 Cor. 1:17; Phil. 2:7), *battalogéō* ("heap up empty phrases," Mt. 6:7), *scholázō* (Mt. 12:44), *mataiológos* ("empty talker," Tit. 1:10)]; AV also VOID, VANITY, VAIN, etc.; NEB also FUTILE, VAIN, NOTHING, NONSENSE, etc. In Ezk. 24:10 the RSV ("empty out the broth") and NEB ("pour out all the broth") follow an emendation based on the LXX (Heb. *wᵉhārēq hēmmārāq*); the AV reads, with the MT, "spice it well."

The Hebrew verb stem *ryq* means "pour out," and so "empty"; thus the adjective means "empty" or "vain," the adverb "empty-handed," and the noun "that which is empty or worthless." An appearance at the sanctuary required a gift: no one was to appear "empty-handed" (Ex. 23:15; 34:20). Significantly, Hittite treaties also required annual appearances before the suzerain, probably for the purpose of bringing tribute (cf. Plastaras). In Ruth 1:21 *rêqām* is used opposite *mᵉlēʾâ* ("full") where Naomi says, "I went away full, and the Lord has brought me back empty." Here her emptiness refers especially to the loss of her husband and sons — in addition to her loss of property. Naomi's empty days are over when Boaz assumes the levirate (3:17; cf. Gesenius §100g). *See also* FULL. The remaining Hebrew verbs have a variety of meanings: "empty out" (*ʿārâ*), "pour out" (*nāṯaḵ*), "lay waste" (*bāqaq*), "clear out" (*pānâ*), etc. (cf. *CHAL*, pp. 46, 249, 282, 293).

In the NT the adjective *kenós* is used in both a literal and a figurative sense. Literally the term means "empty" or "devoid of content" — thus, "with empty hands" in

Mk. 12:3; Lk. 1:53; 20:10f. In Eph. 5:6 and Col. 2:8 Paul uses *kenós* figuratively of deceitful words and philosophy; here the emphasis is not only on the lack of content, but also on the futility of these false teachings (cf. *TDNT,* III, 659f.). This second, figurative meaning of futility and powerlessness is also present in the term *mataiológos,* a compound of *mataíos* ("idle," "empty") and *lógos* ("word"), in Tit. 1:10 (cf *mataiología,* 1 Tim. 1:6). For the difficult *battalogéō,* Bussby suggests an Aramaic root *bṭl,* which means "not legal" (p. 26); Delling, on the other hand, suggests that it has been "constructed in analogy with" a more commonly used term, *battarízō,* which means "stammer or stutter" (*TDNT,* I, 597; cf. also Bauer, p. 137; BDF § 40; MM, p. 107). On Phil. 2:7, *see* KENOSIS.

Bibliography.–F. Bussby, *Expos.T.,* 76 (1964), 26; W. Gesenius, E. Kautzsch, and E. Cowley, *Hebrew Grammar* (Eng. tr., 2nd ed. 1910); J. Plastaras, *God of the Exodus* (1966), p. 212; *TDNT,* III, *s.v.* κενός κτλ. (A. Oepke).

J. T. DENNISON, JR.
N. J. O.

EMULATION. Used by the AV and NEB in the sense of "jealousy" or "envious rivalry" in Rom. 11:14 for the verb *parazēlóō* (RSV "make jealous"), and by the AV in Gal. 5:20 for the verb *zēlóō* (RSV "jealousy"; NEB "envy").

EN [Heb. *ʿayin*; cf. Arab. *ʿAin*]. The Hebrew word for "spring" or "fountain" (Gen. 16:7; Nu. 33:9; Neh. 2:14; Prov. 8:28 [fem. pl.]). It occurs in numerous compound words, e.g., EN-GEDI, EN-HADDAH, EN-HAKKORE, EN-HAZOR, EN-RIMMON, EN-ROGEL, EN-SHEMESH. In the same way the word *ʿAin* is a very common component of modern Arabic place names throughout Palestine and Syria. Places with names compounded with *En-* were almost always located near a spring. *See* FOUNTAIN; WELL.

ENABLE [Gk. *dýnamai*] (Phil. 3:21); AV "(whereby) he is able." In 1 Tim. 1:12 the AV uses "enable" (Gk. *endynamóō*) in the sense of "strengthen" or "endue with strength."

ENAIM ē-nā'əm [Heb. *ʿênayim*–'two fountains' or 'double fountain'; Gk. *Ainan*] (Gen. 38:14, 21); AV "open place," "openly"; NEB "(where the road) forks." One of the fourteen cities of Judah in the Shephelah or low hill country between the mountains of Judah and the coastal plain. It is the same as Enam in Josh. 15:34, where it is mentioned along with Jarmuth, Adullam, Socoh, and Azekah in the territory assigned to Judah. The site has not been identified.

ENAM ē'nəm [Heb. *ʿênām*] (Josh. 15:34). *See* ENAIM.

ENAN ē'nən [Heb. *ʿênān*–'fountains'; Gk. *Ainan*]. The father of Ahira and leader of the tribe of Naphtali, who assisted in the first census of Israel (Nu. 1:15; 2:29; 7:78, 83; 10:27).

ENASIBUS ē-nas'ə-bəs (1 Esd. 9:34, AV, NEB). *See* ELIASHIB **6.**

ENCAMPMENT. *See* WAR.

ENCAMPMENT BY THE RED SEA. According to the version of the wanderings of Israel given in Nu. 33, they "encamped by the Red Sea" (v. 10) after leaving Elim and before entering the Wilderness of Sin. *See* WANDERINGS OF ISRAEL.

ENCHANT; ENCHANTER; ENCHANTMENT [Heb. *nāḥaš*] (Nu. 23:23); NEB DIVINATION; [*ḥôḇēr*] (Ps. 58:5 [MT 6]); AV CHARMING; NEB SPELL; [*ḥeḇer*] (Isa. 47:9, 12); NEB SPELLS; [*ʾaššāp*] (Dnl. 1:20; 2:2); AV ASTROLOGER; NEB EXORCIST; [Aram. *ʾāšap*] (Dnl. 2:10, 27; 4:7 [MT 4]; 5:7, 11, 15); AV ASTROLOGER; NEB EXORCIST. A practice of the pagan cults involving magic, divination, astrology, and exorcism. The OT has little information about such practices, since they were strictly forbidden (Dt. 18:10-14).

In Nu. 23:23 Balaam seems to be saying that magical practices are of no effect against Israel, although the Hebrew text is ambiguous and may mean that in Israel there is no use of such practices. In Syriac and postbiblical Hebrew/Aramaic the root *nḥš* means to divine or augur, which accords well with this context in Numbers.

In Ps. 58:5 the context clearly points to a vocal enchantment by one who casts spells (cf. v. 4). Akk. *abaru,* Syr. *ḥabbārāʾ,* postbiblical Heb. and Aram. *ḥabbār,* etc., all signify a charmer or one who casts spells. Isa. 47:9, 12 reflect God's attitude toward such practices, and also the importance of these practices in Babylonia (cf. 47:1).

Similarly, the passages in Daniel indicate the importance of enchanters as cultic officials or advisers and reflect the Babylonian setting of the book. Since "enchanters" occurs only in lists of these officials, their specific function is not clear, and commentators (e.g., S. R. Driver, *Daniel* [*Cambridge Bible,* 1901], pp. 15f.; E. J. Young, *Prophecy of Daniel* [1953], pp. 51, 57) have inferred that the author used these terms in a broad sense without knowing the specific function or duty of these officials (but cf. Davies, p. 84). In spite of the concurrence of Theodotion's use of Gk. *mágos* for Heb. *ʾaššāp* with the postbiblical Hebrew meaning of *ʾaššāp* ("astrologer"), the Akkadian cognate *āšipu* points to a different meaning and must be given full consideration, since the Hebrew term is a loanword from Akkadian. The Babylonian *āšipu* was an exorcist and diagnostician, but not an astrologer (cf. *CAD,* I/2, 431ff.). His function was to avert or exorcise evil spirits from any political or physical manifestations by means of apotropaic rituals and incantations. The decision about the meaning of *ʾaššāp* thus depends somewhat on one's opinion regarding the date of Daniel: if the book is late, then the evidence from Theodotion and postbiblical Hebrew is more likely correct; but if the book was written in the 6th cent. B.C., then the Akkadian evidence is decisive.

See also CHARM; MAGIC; DIVINATION.

See T. W. Davies, *Magic, Divination and Demonology among the Hebrews and Their Neighbors* (1898).

G. A. L.

ENCOURAGE; ENCOURAGEMENT [Heb. piel of *ḥāzaq*] (Dt. 1:38; 3:28; 2 S. 11:25; 2 Ch. 35:2; Isa. 41:7; Ezk. 13:22); AV also STRENGTHEN (Ezk. 13:22); NEB also URGE STRENGTHEN, "tell (him) to take heart"; [*ʿal lēḇ*] (2 Ch. 30:22; 32:6); AV COMFORTABLY; [Gk. *paráklēsis, parakaléō, symparakaléō* (Rom. 1:12)]; AV COMFORTED, EXHORTATION, CONSOLATION; NEB also EXHORTATION, STIR THE HEART, HEARTEN, etc.; [*paramythéō* (1 Thess. 5:14), *protrépomai* (Acts 18:27), *euthýmos* (Acts 27:36), *oikodoméō* (1 Cor. 8:10)]; AV COMFORTED, EXHORTING, "of good cheer," EMBOLDENED (1 Cor. 8:10); NEB also GIVE SUPPORT, PLUCK UP COURAGE (Acts 27:36), EMBOLDENED (1 Cor. 8:10).

The OT uses a piel verb form (*ḥizzaq*) meaning "strengthen" for expressing its concepts of encouragement. Leaders are to be encouraged by their followers (Dt. 1:38; 3:28; 2 S. 11:25), and fellow workers by each other (Isa. 41:7). This strengthening takes place within a person and thus has to do with the attitudes with which one faces life; cf. the adverbial uses in 2 Ch. 30:22; 32:6 (lit. "he spoke to their hearts"). In Ezk. 13:22 "encourage" (Heb. lit. "strengthening the hands") refers to the inner strengthening that enables one to work. In all of these uses of *ḥizzaq* the LXX also uses a verb for strengthening, usually Gk. *katischýō*.

In the NT "encouragement" usually translates Gk. *parakaléō* or a cognate. Unlike Heb. *ḥizzaq*, Gk. *parakaléō* in biblical writing usually means to "comfort," and only in a small percentage of its uses does it actually relate to encouragement. It is only a short step, however, from comfort in times of bereavement to encouragement in times of lesser troubles, a step taken most noticeably in the Apocrypha (esp. 1 Macc. 5:53; 12:5; 13:3; 2 Macc. 13:12; 3 Macc. 1:6; 3:8).

Two NT passages are of particular importance. Rom. 15:4-6 speaks of a situation in which a brother with a stronger conscience must allow for the conscience of the weaker brother. Encouragement is bound closely with hope in this passage. Paul says that divine aid is given to the community of believers through the exhortations and encouraging events of the Scriptures, which give the hope of final deliverance from the trials of this present life. In 1 Thess. 5:11-14 the idea of encouragement is closely related to exhortation. In v. 14 *paramythéō*, a synonym meaning "encourage" or "comfort" (cf. its use with *parakaléō* in 1 Cor. 14:3; Phil 2:1; 1 Thess. 2:11), calls for encouraging the weak, while *parakaléō*, translated "encourage" in 1 Thess. 5:11, is rendered "exhort" in v. 14. Thus exhortation becomes the means by which one gives strength to others. This function of exhortation was a part of early Christian worship (1 Cor. 14:3, 31).

In Acts 18:27 the AV differs significantly from the RSV and NEB. In the AV the objects of the encouragement are those brethren to whom the church in Ephesus wrote, while the RSV and NEB interpretation has Apollos receiving the encouragement. Both the context and the grammar (the verb normally takes an accusative object, not a dative) support the latter interpretation.

See *TDNT*, V, *s.v.* παρακαλέω, παράκλησις (Schmitz, Stählin).

D. W. WEAD

END [Heb. nouns *qēṣ*, *'aḥ^a^rîṯ*, *sôp*; verbs *kālâ*, *šāḇaṯ*, *sûp*, *gāmar*, etc.]; AV also AFTER, LAST or LATTER END (*'aḥ^a^rîṯ*), CONSUMED, CAUSE TO CEASE, etc.; NEB also AFTER, LATER, LAST DAYS (*'aḥ^a^rîṯ*), FINISHED, etc.; [Gk. *télos*]; NEB also FULL EXTENT (Jn. 13:1), etc.; [*ákron*–'peak']; AV, NEB, TIP (Lk. 16:24), etc.; [*éschatos*] (Acts 1:8; 1 Pet. 1:20); AV UTTERMOST PART, LAST; NEB ENDS, LAST; [*syntéleia*–'completion'] (He. 9:26); NEB CLIMAX; [*pímplēmi*–'fulfil'] (Lk. 2:21); AV WERE ACCOMPLISHED; NEB LATER; [*ekleípō*] (He. 1:12); AV FAIL; [part. of *teleutáō*–'die'] ("at the end of his life," He. 11:22); AV WHEN HE DIED; [*píptō*–'fall']; AV FAIL.

I. In the OT.–Numerous Hebrew words are translated "end." Only four (*qēṣ*, *'aḥ^a^rîṯ*, *kālâ*, *šāḇaṯ*), however, occur more than a few times. The term most frequently used is *qēṣ*, from the verb *qāṣaṣ*, "cut off." Often it refers to the end of a period of time, as in Nu. 13:25 where the spies end forty days of spying in the Promised Land (AV, NEB, "after forty days"). It can also refer to the physical end of something, e.g., in Gen. 23:9 the cave of Machpelah is at the end of the field. The term *'aḥ^a^rîṯ* means "that which comes after" and has several shades of derived meaning. In Dt. 8:16 it refers to the period after the wilderness wandering. In many places, however, it refers to the "outcome," as in Am. 8:10 where the outcome is like a bitter day. The verb *kālâ* means "be complete, at an end, finished." For the hiphil the RSV often translates "make a (full) end" (e.g., Ezk. 20:13) while the NEB simply translates "destroy." When used with another verb the NEB translates "finish" (e.g., "finished speaking," Ex. 31:18). The verb *šāḇaṯ*, from which is derived the word "sabbath," in the hiphil means "cause to cease" (the usual AV translation) or "put an end to." The NEB uses several good equivalents, e.g., "stop" (Jer. 48:35), "quell" (Ezk. 7:24). Two other roots with the meaning "end" occur infrequently. The verb *sûp* means "come to an end, cease" (Am. 3:15), while the related noun *sôp* seems to be a synonym for *qēṣ* in later parts of the OT (e.g., Ecclesiastes and Daniel). The verb *gāmar*, "end, come to an end, complete," occurs only in the Psalms, e.g., 7:9 (MT 10; NEB "do no man harm"); 77:8 (MT 9; NEB "unfulfilled").

Several verbs which in a derived sense mean "end" are sometimes so translated by the RSV. They include: *tāmam*, "be complete, finished" (e.g., Nu. 14:35; NEB "be consumed"), *bāla'*, "swallow, engulf" (Ps. 107:27; NEB "all in vain"), *šāḵaḥ*, "forget" (Lam. 2:6), *kāraṯ*, "cut off" (Zec. 9:6; NEB "uproot"), *šālēm*, "be complete" (e.g., Isa. 38:12f.; NEB "torment"), *mûš*, "depart, remove" (Nah. 3:1), *māhar*, "hasten" (Job 5:13), *pānâ*, "turn" (Ps. 90:9; NEB "go by").

The noun *tôṣā'â* (e.g., Nu. 34:8; NEB "limit"), derived from the verb *yāṣā'*, refers to borders or the extremities of a territory. Some nouns that do not normally mean "end" are occasionally so translated on the basis of their context: *rō'š*, "head" ("ends of the poles," 1 K. 8:8); *t^e^qûpâ*, "circuit" ("end of the year," Ex. 34:22; NEB "turn of the year"); *zeh*, "this" (in *mizzeh ûmizzeh*, "each end of a step," 1 K. 10:20); *peh*, "mouth" (in *peh lāpeh*, "one end to the other," 2 K. 10:21); *ballāhoṯ*, "calamity, destruction" ("dreadful end," Ezk. 26:21); *mēhabbayiṯ*, "from the house" ("at the inner end," Ezk. 40:7, 9; AV "within, inward"); *nēṣaḥ*, "everlastingness, perpetuity" ("to the end," Job 34:36, etc.; NEB "once and for all").

"End" in the sense of purpose is conveyed by *ba'^a^ḇûr* (Ps. 105:45), *l^e^ma'an* (Lev. 17:5), and Aram. *'aḏ-dibraṯ* (Dnl. 4:17 [MT 14]), all translated "to the end that." Consequence is expressed by *'ēqeḇ* (Ps. 119:33, 112), translated "to the end" (NEB "reward"), and by *lāḵēn* (Isa. 26:14), "to that end."

There are a few difficult passages. In Am. 8:4 *lašbîṯ* is a difficult construction and has occasioned several emendations, but the MT should be retained and understood as referring to the oppressive destruction of the poor (E. Hammershaimb, *Book of Amos* [2nd ed. 1958], pp. 121f.). In Isa. 33:1 *kann^e^lōṯ^e^ḵā* probably comes from *nlh*, "complete, finish," though this is the verb's only occurrence (E. J. Young, *Isaiah* [repr. 1977], II, 405). In Job 36:14 the RSV translation "ends in shame" is a paraphrase; the literal rendering "among the cult prostitutes" (RSV mg.) is preferable.

II. In the NT.–The most frequent word for "end" is Gk. *télos*. It is used in the senses of termination or cessation (e.g., 1 Pet. 4:7), last part or conclusion (e.g., Mt. 24:6), goal or outcome (e.g., He. 6:8), and to the last (e.g., 1 Cor. 1:8). In a few cases the preposition *eis* plus neuter pronouns indicate purpose and are translated "to this/that end" (e.g., 1 Tim. 4:10). Other terms translated "end" occur only once or twice each; these are summarized in the heading of this article.

See also ESCHATOLOGY.

Bibliography.–*TDOT,* I, *s.v.* "'acharith" (Seebass); *TDNT,* VIII, *s.v.* τέλος κτλ. (Delling); II, *s.v.* ἔσχατος (Kittel); VI, *s.v.* πίμπλημι κτλ. (Delling); πίπτω κτλ. (Michaelis).

J. C. MOYER

END OF THE WORLD. *See* ESCHATOLOGY.

ENDAMAGE. Archaic for "damage" in the AV of Ezr. 4:13.

ENDEAVOR [Gk. *zētéō*] (Gal. 2:17); AV, NEB, SEEK; [*spoudázō*] (1 Thess. 2:17); NEB BE ANXIOUS. This word has been weakened since the AV was translated. In the 17th cent. it implied utmost exertion and success; now it emphasizes the difficulty of the effort and suggests the possibility of failure. For the AV "endeavouring," "endeavour," the RSV reads "sought" in Acts 16:10 (NEB "set about"), "eager" in Eph. 4:3 (NEB "spare no effort"), "I will see to it" in 2 Pet. 1:15, and "deeds" in Ps. 28:4.

ENDIRONS. A corruption of the Middle English term "andirons." *See* HOOK.

ENDLESS [Gk. *apérantos*] (1 Tim. 1:4); NEB "interminable." "Endless" can refer to "myths" as well as to "genealogies." Whether the myths and genealogies be interpreted as gnostic, Jewish, or a combination of Judaism and Gnosticism, the use of *apérantos* here seems to imply that they are tiresome, a waste of time (cf. Bauer, *s.v.*; also Dibelius/Conzelmann, *The Pastoral Epistles* [*Hermeneia*; Eng. tr. 1972], p. 17).

EN-DOR en'dor [Heb. *'ên dōr*–'fountain of dwelling' (Josh. 17:11), *'ên dō'r* (Ps. 83:10 [MT 11]); Gk. *Dōr, Aendōr*]; **ENDOR** [Heb. *'ên dôr*; Gk. *Aendōr, Nēndōr, Ēndōr, Aeldōr*] (1 S. 28:7). A town in the territory assigned to western Manasseh (Josh. 17:11). It is identified with modern Endôr, a village on the northern slope of Jebel ed-Duhy, more commonly known as the hill Moreh or Little Hermon. It is about 11 km. (7 mi.) SE of Nazareth and 6 km. (4 mi.) S of Mt. Tabor.

Two other villages of biblical significance are on the slopes of the hill Moreh. The village of Nain is about 3 km. (2 mi.) SW of Endôr, and on the south slope stood Shunem.

Endor (or En-dor) is mentioned three times in the OT. It is first mentioned among the towns in the territory of Manasseh (Josh. 17:11). Ps. 83:10 says that here the fugitives of Sisera's army perished after their defeat at the Kishon River (Jgs. 4). It was the residence of the woman with a "familiar spirit" (AV, NEB) whom Saul consulted on the night before the battle of Gilboa (1 S. 28:7); *see* DIVINATION III.G; MEDIUM.

J. F. PREWITT

ENDOW; ENDOWED; ENDOWING [*zāḇaḏ*] (Gen. 30:20); AV ENDUE; [piel of *mālē'*] (Ex. 28:3); AV FILLED; [*yāḏa'*] (Dnl. 1:4); AV CUNNING; NEB "at home in all branches of"; [hiphil of *nāḥal*] (Prov. 8:21); AV "cause to inherit"; **ENDOWMENT** [Gk. *dósis*] (Jas. 1:17); AV GIFT; NEB GIVING; **ENDUED** [Heb. *yāḏa'*] (2 Ch. 2:12f.); NEB ENDOWED. "Endow" originally meant "provide with a dowry," while "endue" meant "clothe." The likeness of the literal meanings confused the metaphorical uses of the words despite their different origins, so that they are now used in a nearly synonymous fashion. Thus we find in the RSV phrases in which "endow" and "endue" are used interchangeably: "whom I have endowed with an able mind" (Ex. 28:3), "youths . . . endowed with knowledge" (Dnl. 1:4), "a wise son, endued with discretion and understanding" (2 Ch. 2:12), and "a skilled man, endued with understanding" (v. 13).

F. K. FARR

ENDS OF THE EARTH. *See* EARTH, CORNERS OF THE.

ENDURE [Heb. *ḥāyâ, 'āmaḏ* (e.g., Ex. 18:23; Ps. 102:26 [MT 27]; 111:3, 10; 112:3, 9; Ezk. 22:14; Dnl. 11:6), *qûm*–'arise' (e.g., Job 8:15), *yāḵōl* (e.g., Est. 8:6; Ps. 101:5; Isa. 1:13; Jer. 10:10), *yāšaḇ*–'sit down' (Ps. 102:12 [MT 13]); Gk. *ménō, hypoménō* (e.g., Mt. 10:22; 24:13), *phéro, hypophérō* (e.g., 2 Tim. 3:11), *makrothyméō* (He. 6:15), *stégō* (1 Cor. 9:12), *eimí* (Mt. 13:21 par. Mk. 4:17), *kakopathéō* (2 Tim. 4:5), *anéchomai* (e.g., 1 Cor. 4:12; 2 Tim. 4:3), *kateréō* (He. 11:27)]; **ENDURING** [Heb. *'êtān*–'lasting' (Nu. 24:21; Jer. 5:15; Mic. 6:2), *'āṯēq,* qal part. of *'āmaḏ* (Ps. 19:9 [MT 10]), *le'ôlām* (e.g., Eccl. 2:16); Aram. *qayyām* (Dnl. 6:26 [MT 27]); Gk. *anéchomai, hypomonḗ*]; **ENDURANCE** [Gk. *hypomonḗ*] (e.g., Lk. 21:19; Rom. 5:3f.; 4; 2 Cor. 6:4; Col. 1:11; He. 10:36).

The more common biblical terms are Heb. *ḥāyâ* and *'āmaḏ* and Gk. *hypoménō* and *hypomonḗ*. Sometimes the RSV inserts "endure" or "enduring," e.g., to render Heb. *'im šāmeš,* "like [=as long as] the sun" (Ps. 72:5), *le'ôlām ḥasdô,* "his steadfast love (is) forever" (Ps. 136), *ziḵrôn . . . le'ôlām,* "remembrance . . . forever" (Eccl. 2:16, AV; cf. Prov. 27:24; Lam. 5:19).

Basically "endure" has two meanings: (1) "last," "remain" (cf. Heb. *le'ôlām,* "forever" [Ps. 136]; Gk. *ménō,* "remain" [Jn. 6:27]); (2) "tolerate," "suffer" (cf. Gk. *phérō,* "bear [patiently]" [Rom. 9:22; He. 12:20], *hypomonḗ,* "patience" [2 Cor. 1:6]). In Job 8:15 the reference is to a house that does not hold up when leaned against (cf. Heb. *qûm,* "arise"; parallel to "stand").

(1) In the sense of "last" or "remain," "endure" is used of God. His years (Ps. 102:26), His glory (Ps. 104:31), His dominion (Ps. 45:6 [MT 7]; Lam. 5:19), His righteousness (Ps. 111:3), His faithfulness (Ps. 117:2), and His steadfast love (in Chronicles and frequently in the Psalms, esp. in Ps. 136) do not cease. In comparison with God's unending life, human life is brief (Ps. 102:24), and prayers are made that the king may live a long life (Ps. 61:6; 72:17; cf. 89:36). In the moral dimension, truthful lips (Prov. 12:19; in contrast with the lying tongue) and human righteousness (e.g., Ps. 112:3, 9; 2 Cor. 9:9, quoting Ps. 112:9) last.

(2) In the sense of "bear" or "tolerate," Paul tolerated all things in order that Christ's gospel would not be an obstacle to some (1 Cor. 9:12; cf. 2 Tim. 2:10), and stated forcefully that Christians bear all things in love (1 Cor. 13:7).

At times God's people must endure persecution (Ps. 119:84). In the NT particularly, believers accept persecution (1 Cor. 4:12; 2 Cor. 1:6; 2 Tim. 4:5; cf. Rev. 1:9) and are urged to bear divine discipline (He. 12:7). But they are reminded that suffering leads to endurance, which in turn produces character (Rom. 5:3f.) and in the end leads even to salvation (Mt. 10:22; 24:14 par. Mk. 13:13).

See *TDNT,* IV, *s.v.* μένω κτλ.: μένω, ὑπομένω, ὑπομονή (Hauck).

R. W. V.

EN-EGLAIM en-eg'lā-əm, en-əg-lā'əm [Heb. *'ên 'eglayim*–'spring of (the two) calves'; Gk. *Enagaleim*; Lat. *Engallim*]. Ezk. 47:10 says that in the new age a stream of water issuing forth from the temple mount will so purify the Dead Sea that "fishermen will stand beside the sea; from En-gedi to En-eglaim it will be a place for the spreading of nets."

Documents from the Judean wilderness dating to the Bar Cochba period refer to *meḥôz 'eglaṯayin,* "the harbor town of Eglatain." J. Starkey has suggested plausibly that this place be equated with En-eglaim. It is simply called *māḥôzā'* in the Aramaic texts from this collection and *Kōmē Maōza,* "the town of Maoza," in the Greek documents, which always specify a location in the vicinity of Zoar. A Hebrew deed concerns two residents of *hallûḥîṯ šebbimḥôz 'eglaṯayin,* "Luhith, which is in [the municipal district of] the harbor town of Eglatain." Luhith is associated with Zoar and Eglath-shelishiyah (Isa. 15:5; Jer. 48:34); the latter may be another form of the same Eglaim/Eglatain.

Clearly the site must have been on the southeastern shore of the Dead Sea (near ZOAR) and must have had a good water source (*'ên* = "spring"); in the Roman period it must have been a port for sea traffic on the Dead Sea. Thus the prophet was evidently speaking of a purification of the poisonous waters from one end of the sea to the other. Earlier attempts to locate En-eglaim at the northern end of the Dead Sea can no longer be sustained.

Bibliography.–H. B. Tristram, *Bible Places* (1884), pp. 94f.; *GP,* II, 316; J. Starkey, *RB,* 61 (1954), 167; W. R. Farmer, *BA,* 19 (1956), 17-21; Y. Yadin, *IEJ,* 12 (1962), 242, 251; H. J. Polotsky, *Eretz-Israel,* 8 (1967), 46, 50. A. F. RAINEY

ENEMESSAR en-ə-mes′är [Gk. *Enemessar, Enemessaros*] (AV, RSV mg., NEB mg., Tob. 1:2, 15, etc.). The name of an Assyrian king, generally considered (since H. Grotius, 17th cent.) to be a corruption (though sometimes defended as an alternative form) of the name of Shalmaneser who carried Israel captive to Nineveh, as related in 2 Kings. The writer of Tobit makes Sennacherib the son (1:15) as well as the successor of Enemessar, whereas according to the Assyrian inscriptions Sennacherib was the son of Sargon. This is only one of several serious historical difficulties in Tobit. J. HUTCHISON

ENEMY; FOE [Heb. *'ōyēḇ, ṣar (ṣār), ṣōrēr, śōnē', šôrēr* (Ps. 5:8 [MT 9]; 27:11; 54:5 [MT 7]; 56:2 [MT 3]; 59:10 [MT 11]; 92:11 [MT 12]), *'ār* (1 S. 28:16), *qāmîm* (Ex. 32:25), *'aḵzārî*–'cruel' (Jer. 30:14), *ṣîyîm*–'dwellers in the wilderness' (Ps. 72:9); Aram. *'ār* (Dnl. 4:19); Gk. *echthrós, antikeímenos* (1 Tim. 5:14)]; AV also ADVERSARY, "one who hates," "one who troubles" (Ps. 3:1 [MT 2]; 13:4 [MT 5]), TROUBLE (Ps. 108:12 [MT 13]; 60:11 [MT 13]), AFFLICTION (Zec. 8:10), CRUEL ONE (Jer. 30:14), "ones who dwell in the wilderness" (Ps. 72:9); NEB also ADVERSARY, "one who hates," "one who speaks evil" (Ps. 92:11), CAPTOR (1 K. 8:48), OPPRESSOR (Jer. 30:16), PERSECUTOR (Ps. 81:14 [MT 15]), ETHIOPIANS (Ps. 72:9), INVADER (Lam. 4:12), etc. The RSV also has "enemies" in 1 S. 10:1 and 2 Ch. 32:22, where it follows the LXX (AV omits). It supplies the term as suggested by the context in Gen. 14:11 (NEB "four kings"); 1 K. 5:3; Jer. 46:22 (AV "army"); Zec. 10:5. It emends MT *zārîm* (Isa. 29:5), literally "strangers" as AV renders it, to *ṣārîm,* and MT *ṣārâ* (Nah. 1:9), literally "affliction" (cf. AV), to *ṣar.*

In the OT "enemy" and "foe" most frequently refer to national enemies of Israel and her king (1 S. 29:8; Dt. 20:1; etc.), although they also indicate personal enemies (Ex. 23:22; Nu. 35:23; Est. 7:6; etc.). It is in the latter sense that the word frequently appears in the Psalms. Many of these references express intense hatred toward the enemies: "I hate them with perfect hatred; I count them my enemies" (Ps. 139:22). Since these enemies are described in general terms, their identity has been much debated by scholars. Some have suggested that they were wicked sorcerers, political opponents, rich extortionists, or criminals. Christoph Barth thinks that we should not view these references as "outbursts of personal desire for revenge," but that we should consider them elements of "liturgical prayers and formulas, which are directed against the enemies of God in general, and only in a secondary sense against particular adversaries" (*Intro. to the Psalms* [Eng. tr. 1966], p. 48).

In the traditions that characterize Yahweh as a "divine warrior," He is spoken of as the enemy of Israel's enemies (Ex. 23:22; Dt. 20:4; Isa. 42:13 etc.). In His judgment of Israel, however, Yahweh can also be understood as Israel's enemy (Lam. 2:5).

In the NT "enemy" and "foe" usually refer to personal enemies (Gal. 4:16; 2 Thess. 3:15; etc.), but "enemies" can also be used in the OT sense of the national enemies of God's people (Lk. 1:71, 74; 19:43; etc.). Anyone who is hostile to God and His Son is an enemy (Lk. 19:27; Phil. 3:18; and the passages that quote Ps. 110:1, e.g., Mk. 12:36 par.; Acts 2:35; 1 Cor. 15:25; He. 1:13). In the latter sense, it is the devil who is the enemy above all enemies (Mt. 13:39; Lk. 10:19; etc.). Paul refers to death as the last enemy to be destroyed (1 Cor. 15:26). Only in the NT is the command given to love one's enemies (Mt. 5:44); however, in many places in the OT kindness to one's enemies is encouraged (Ex. 23:4; Prov. 24:17; 25:21).

E. W. CONRAD

ENENIUS e-nē′ni-əs (AV, NEB, 1 Esd. 5:8). *See* BIGVAI **1.**

ENFLAME. *See* BURN.

EN-GADDI en-gad′i (Sir. 24:14, AV); RSV mg. "on the beaches." *See* EN-GEDI.

ENGAGE. In 2 Ch. 24:13 the Hebrew verb *'āśâ,* "labor," "make something," is used of the restoring of the house of the Lord. In Lk. 22:5 the Greek verb *syntíthēmi* occurs in the sense of "make a contract," "sign an agreement." In Phil. 1:30 the common verb *échō,* "have," is rendered "engaged" because of its association with the term "conflict."

EN-GANNIM en-gan′im [Heb. *'ên gannîm*–'spring of gardens'].

1. A town in the "valley" or Shephelah territory of Judah, named with Zanoah and Eshtaol (Josh. 15:34). Two places have been suggested as locations: one is Khirbet Umm Jina, very close to Beth-shemesh; the other is at Beit Jemâl about 3 km. (2 mi.) to the south.

2. A town in the territory allotted to Issachar (Josh. 19:21) assigned to the Gershonite Levites (21:29). In 1 Ch. 6:73 the name is replaced by Anem. It probably corresponds to the Ginnea of Josephus (*Ant.* xx.6.1; *BJ* iii.3.4) and may certainly be identified with the modern Jenîn on the southern edge of the plain of Esdraelon about 8 km. (5 mi.) SE of Megiddo and 11 km. (7 mi.) SW of Mt. Gilboa, on the road leading through Samaria to Jerusalem. The area is lush with beautiful gardens and fruitful orchards abundantly watered by local springs.

See A. Saarisalo, *Boundary Between Issachar and Naphtali* (1927), pp. 62f. J. F. PREWITT

EN-GEDI en-ge′dē, en′gə-dī [Heb. *'ên geḏî*–'fountain of the kid'; Gk. *Engad(d)ei(n), Ēngaddi*]; AV Apoc. EN-GADDI. An ancient settlement on the western shore of the Dead Sea. It bears the name of a perennial spring that gushes from a small promontory about 180 m. (600 ft.) above the lake; this name has been preserved in the Arabic 'Ain Jidi. The remarkable water supply in the midst of such a desolate region led to the creation of a small community at the oasis between the courses of the Wâdī Sudeir and the Wâdī 'Areijeh. *See* Plate 3.

I. Iron Age.–En-gedi was included, along with five other

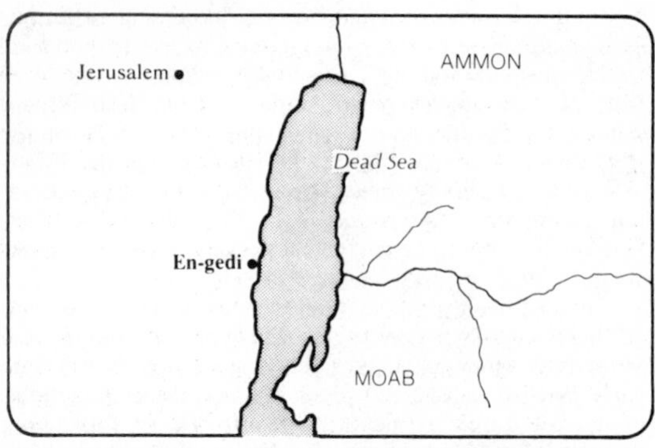

The spring of En-gedi with the mountains of Judah in the background (B. VanElderen)

settlements, in the "wilderness" district of the tribe of Judah (Josh. 15:62). During David's outlaw days the "strongholds of En-gedi" (1 S. 23:29 [MT 24:1]) in the "wilderness of En-gedi" (1 S. 24:1 [MT 2]) provided refuge from Saul and his armed search parties. The cave that figures so prominently in one of their encounters (1 S. 24) cannot be identified today, but investigators have noted several caverns in the ravines around En-gedi, especially the "Cave of the Pool" in the Wâdī Sudeir.

As a reprisal for the Judean and Israelite attack on Moab (1 K. 3), the Moabites, Ammonites, and Meunites crossed the Dead Sea (probably at the narrowest and shallowest point from the Lisân to the western bank) and encamped at En-gedi (2 Ch. 20:2; *see also* HAZAZON-TAMAR) in preparation for an invasion of Judah. Their alliance was not firmly established, however, and the would-be attackers soon fell to fighting among themselves and thus destroyed each other.

The prophet Ezekiel saw a vision of the Dead Sea being transformed by the life-giving waters from the Jerusalem temple. Fishermen would stand on the banks from En-gedi to En-eglaim, and their nets would bring in a multitude of different fish as if from the Great Sea (Ezk. 47:10).

The Song of Solomon also bears witness to the importance of En-gedi and its oasis: "My beloved is to me a cluster of henna blossoms in the vineyards of En-gedi" (Cant. 1:14). This is apparently a reference to the *Lausonia alba,* known for its small fragrant blossoms from which cosmetics were made.

There is no written record of En-gedi's destruction after the fall of Jerusalem (586 B.C.). Perhaps it can be ascribed to Edomite incursions against the hapless Judean settlements. The OT reflects the enmity provoked by this action (e.g., Ezk. 35:5, 10, 15; Ps. 137:7; Lam. 4:21). Mazar has suggested that this destruction took place *ca.* 582/581, when Nebuchadrezzar conducted a military campaign in Syria during which Ammon and Moab fell under his sway. Nebuzaradan deported additional members of the Judean population in that same year (Jer. 52:30).

Though archeological evidence has shown that a settlement arose at En-gedi during the 5th-4th cents. B.C., no references to it have been found in writings from the Persian period.

II. Hellenistic and Roman Periods.–The tall palm trees of En-gedi were still famous in the Hellenistic period (Sir. 24:14), as well as its balsam (Josephus *Ant.* ix.1.2). This latter, evidently the *commiphora opobalsamum,* produced a very precious resin used in the manufacture of perfume and medicine. Whether the settlement there in Ben Sira's day was Jewish or not is hard to say. Mazar assumes that En-gedi had been occupied by Edomites (Idumeans) who converted to Judaism upon the conquest of Idumea by John Hyrcanus (Josephus *Ant.* xiii.9.1). The Hasmoneans probably took over a Ptolemaic estate at En-gedi, which they in turn developed into a flourishing administrative center for the toparchy in that area (Josephus *BJ* iii.3.5). Some scholars think that Herodion became the capital of the toparchy under King Herod.

During the Jewish revolt against Rome, En-gedi suffered a cruel fate. The Sicarii (Zealots) who had seized Masada made a plundering raid during the Feast of Unleavened Bread, slaughtering the populace and looting the stores (Josephus *BJ* iv.7.2). Thus, after the Romans had quelled the rebellion, Pliny records that En-gedi was in ruins (*Nat. hist.* v.15 [73]).

At the beginning of the 2nd cent. A.D. En-gedi was rebuilt and assigned to the administrative district of which Jericho was the headquarters. The community consisted mainly of Jews plus a cohort of Thracian auxiliary troops. Much valuable information about the residents of En-gedi at this time is being gleaned from the MSS discovered in the "Cave of the Letters." These indicate that there was a very important commercial center, probably associated with a harbor, which had connections with other towns in the Dead Sea region. There are ample indications that the groves and vineyards were also flourishing. These documents add a new chapter to En-gedi's history.

The Second Jewish War with Rome clearly involved the Jewish population there. The leader of this new revolt, Simon Bar Cochba ("son of the star"), had representatives at En-gedi who governed in his name. In one of his letters he rebuked them for enjoying the benefits of the oasis without showing sufficient concern for their brethren on the battle line. Eventually, many of the residents had to flee to the caves high in the cliffs overlooking the desert canyons W of the Dead Sea. There they held out to the death against the Roman troops who encamped above them on the plateaus.

III. Byzantine Period.–Although historical sources do not describe the destruction or the rebuilding of En-gedi by the Romans, the geographer Ptolemy was aware of its existence in the middle of the 2nd cent. A.D. (*Geog.* v.15.5). Eusebius affirmed that a "very large village" was at En-gedi in his own day and indicated that it was attached to the Jericho administrative district; he also referred to the *opobalsamon* (*Onom.* 86.16-19). Stephanus Byzantius also mentioned this "large village" (170.10ff.). The decline of the settlement may have begun even prior to the Arab conquest. After that only bedouin or transhumants were in the area until the present kibbutz was founded after the establishment of the modern state of Israel.

Bibliography.–F.-M. Abel, *Une Croisière autour de la Mer*

Morte (1911), pp. 134-36; W. F. Albright, *BASOR*, 18 (Apr. 1925), 11-15; *EAEHL*, II, *s.v.* (D. Barag); B. Mazar, T. Dothan, and I. Dunayevsky, *IEJ*, 12 (1962), 145f.; 14 (1964), 121-130; J. Naveh, *IEJ*, 7 (1957), 264. A. F. RAINEY

ENGINE. *See* SIEGE.

ENGLISH VERSIONS. The English Bible in the form of the Authorized (or King James) Version has secured for itself an enduring place in the thought, piety, speech, and literature of the English-speaking world. It is not always appreciated, however, that this result was achieved only after a long effort and struggle dating back to the re-evangelization of Britain after the Roman withdrawal and the barbarian invasions. Nor is it always realized that the translation of the Bible into English did not stop in 1611, for with the discovery of new texts, the intensified examination of Scripture and its background, and changes in the English language, new renderings were continuously needed and attempted right up to the great outburst of translating in the later 19th and the 20th centuries. To give at least a summary of this larger story of the English Bible is the purpose of the present article.

I. Anglo-Saxon Versions
II. The Middle Ages
  A. Early Norman Period
  B. Middle English
  C. Wyclif
  D. Purvey
III. Reformation Bibles
  A. New Factors
    1. Renaissance
    2. Reformation
    3. Printing
  B. Tyndale
  C. Joye
  D. Coverdale
  E. Matthew's Bible
  F. Great Bible
  G. Opposition
  H. Other Versions
IV. Elizabethan Versions
  A. Geneva Bible
  B. Bishops' Bible
  C. Rheims-Douay Version
V. Authorized or King James Version
VI. Seventeenth- and Eighteenth-Century Contributions
VII. Revised and American Standard Versions
VIII. Other Nineteenth-Century Translations
IX. Twentieth-Century Translations
X. Revised Standard Version and New English Bible
XI. Roman Catholic and Jewish Versions
XII. Recent Translations

I. Anglo-Saxon Versions.–The original British churches lived within the Roman empire, so they could make intelligent use of the Latin Bible, which from the 4th cent. on meant Jerome's translation, the Vulgate. With the barbarian invasions, however, a new situation arose. Whereas the Vulgate could be studied, used, and copied in the circles of Celtic monasticism, the newcomers, who had first to be evangelized, brought with them no background of Latin language and culture. The need for translation into the vernacular arose, therefore, with the extensive evangelization and the growth of the Anglo-Saxon Church in the 6th century.

The beginnings of this work seem to have come in the latter part of the 7th cent., not so much through precise translation of the Bible as through the rendering of portions of it into Anglo-Saxon poetry. Accrding to Bede's *Ecclesiastical History* iv.24, the herdsman Caedmon led in this new development. Inspired by a dream, Caedmon sang of creation; and when Hilda took him into Whitby Abbey for further teaching, he put other parts of the Pentateuch — and also, it is said, stories from the NT — into verse. Others adopted the same method of popularizing the contents of Scripture, including the ninth-century Cynewulf, who composed a poetic version of the gospel story in his *Crist*.

Translation proper began shortly after Caedmon. Aldhelm, who studied under Theodore of Tarsus, did pioneering work with his rendering of the Psalter into early English around 700. Bede himself, the great scholar of Jarrow, took a considerable interest in promoting popular knowledge of Scripture. His pupil Cuthbert wrote in a letter that Bede had been translating John's Gospel when he died in 735, and had either finished the work or reached as far as 6:9. Unfortunately all of his work has perished.

Further information comes only with Alfred the Great (848-901), and here again the reports are fragmentary and obscure. The tradition agrees solidly that the Decalogue and portions of Ex. 21–23, along with Acts 15:23-29, were put into English at the head of the code of laws. A further account has it that Alfred was at work on a translation of the Psalms at the time of his death. Undoubtedly the king stimulated the growth of Anglo-Saxon culture, with an important biblical component.

The practice of glossing (writing interpretative comments) the Latin text became widespread in the later Anglo-Saxon period. Various manuscripts of the Psalms with such glosses are extant, and in the middle of the 10th cent. Aldred added an interlinear Anglo-Saxon rendering to the Latin text of the Gospels. From the same period, the Rushworth Gospels offer more or less the same glosses on three of the Gospels but have an independent gloss on Matthew by a priest called Farman.

Some translations from this period have also come down to us, although not of a complete testament, let alone the whole Bible. The Wessex Gospels are the first translation of all four Gospels in English without the Latin text. From around 1000 we have a rendering of parts of the Hexateuch by Abbot Aelfric of Eynsham, who in his homilies rendered portions from other OT and NT books as well. Thus by the time of the Norman Conquest in 1066, important steps had been taken in the direction of an Anglo-Saxon Bible.

II. The Middle Ages.–*A. Early Norman Period.* The Normans initiated many reforms in the English Church, and in many areas a higher standard of Christian life resulted. From the standpoint of the English Bible, however, the conquest had adverse effects, so that translation work into English came to lag behind that into many other European tongues. Two reasons can be advanced for this. More important, initially, was that the Normans did not speak English; hence they had little interest in promoting versions in the native tongue. The second reason is that Anglo-Saxon itself was gradually developing into Middle English with the fusion of the peoples. For a time Anglo-Saxon versions could be copied, improved, and put to use, but in time they became unintelligible, and only as Middle English began to develop into a literary language did new work on Bible translation begin.

B. Middle English. This new beginning came at the end of the 12th cent., and it arain took the form of a poetic version, this time of the Gospels and Acts. The author, an Augustinian monk named Orm, also included a commentary in his edition. By the middle of the 13th cent. poetical versions of Genesis and Exodus had appeared, and by the end of that century a poetical rendering of the Psalms.

The Psalms had their usual appeal, and two versions in prose followed in the 14th century. One is from the Midlands, while the other is the famous translation by Richard Rolle of Hampole near Doncaster in the North. Rolle's version was incorporated in a commentary and proved to be so successful that it was copied out in other dialects.

Work on the NT followed before the end of the 14th century. This time the Epistles came first, apparently in a version made for English monasteries. Later, Acts and the first chapters of Matthew were added, along with a prologue summarizing Genesis and Exodus.

C. Wyclif. The mentioned renderings thus far did not cover the whole Bible and seem to have been designed for monastic rather than for popular use. Yet during this same period — the end of the 14th cent. — a giant stride was made toward the attainment of a complete Bible for the whole people. The reforming scholar John Wyclif was undoubtedly the driving force behind this enterprise. The first edition of the so-called Wyclif Bible came out between 1380 and 1384, in the closing years of Wyclif's life. The early part, up to Baruch 3:20, is stated in some copies to be the work of a certain Nicholas of Hereford, an ardent disciple of Wyclif whose career was interrupted by the repressive measures of 1382. The rest is ascribed to "j. and other men." On the assumption that *j.* stands for John, some conclude that John Wyclif is meant, but it might equally well be John Purvey or some other John; it is quite certain, however, that it comes from the Wyclif circle.

This first edition used the Latin Vulgate as a basis and adopted an extremely literal method that preserved Latin construction and even word order. Much speculation has arisen about the reason for this method, since it can hardly have contributed to the value of the work for popular instruction. Possibly the version was meant not so much for the people at large, who would mostly be unable to read and who could not afford copies, but rather for lay leaders of the Wyclif movement, who could make better use of commentaries and glosses if the English kept close to the Latin, and who could themselves pass on the contents in idiomatic form.

Earlier Wycliffite Version of the Bible (15th cent., on vellum, Egerton MS 618), Mt. 6:7-15, including the Lord's Prayer (British Library)

D. Purvey. With the second edition, however, came a radical revision, especially of the part done by Nicholas of Hereford. John Purvey, who had been Wyclif's secretary, in 1396 prepared the new edition and affixed a prologue explaining his aims and principles. The general purpose was to make it possible for all English people to know the divine law. The principles included the establishment of a pure text (Nicholas of Lyra was studied to this end), careful examination of the meaning, translation by sentence rather than word for word, and a rendition into the speech of the common man. In spite of an attempt to suppress this translation at the Synod of Oxford in 1408, it apparently enjoyed considerable success, and, since there was nothing in the text to suggest a Lollard provenance, copies made without the prologue and glosses could easily be accepted as orthodox productions.

Purvey represents a highly important transition to the period of modern Bible translation. He understood the task of translation so well, and did his work so competently, that he contributed much to the great translations of the Reformation period and through them to those of more recent times. Possibly the impact of his work might have been greater still had printing been available to give it wider and more economical circulation. As it was, however, the spoken tongue was changing so fast as to date it badly; in addition, some new factors had begun to make necessary a fresh and even greater and more successful movement for an English version of the Scriptures that all people might read and understand.

III. Reformation Bibles.–*A. New Factors. 1. Renaissance.* The first among these factors is the Renaissance. This opened up in a new way the treasures of classical and patristic learning. It also revived and extended the study of Greek and Hebrew, thus making possible a consultation of Scripture in the original languages. It stimulated textual research with a view to the preparation of original editions. It brought a searching light to bear on the ignorance and corruption of the contemporary church and in so doing showed a need to return to the first springs. Finally, it gave a sense of the value of learning, which filled scholars like Erasmus with enthusiasm to make Scripture available to people of all ages, states, and countries.

2. Reformation. The Reformation is the second and related factor. Even more radically than the humanists, the Reformers measured the church life and teaching of their day by the standard of Holy Scripture. The discrepancies appalled them. They thus made it their task to get at the pure message of the Bible and to reconstruct the teaching and work of the Church in accordance with it. In carrying out their task the Reformers naturally drew on the resources placed at their disposal by the new learning, in which they were themselves ardent participants. So urgent did they consider the need for disseminating Scripture and its teaching that they were not prepared to wait for officialdom to act, but regarded it as both legitimate and necessary to take the initiative when circumstances compelled.

3. Printing. Finally, the invention of movable-type printing came just at the right time to circulate the translated Bible on a scale previously unthinkable. Speed and comparative cheapness resulted from this technical advance. Large-scale illiteracy still posed a problem, especially in rural areas; thus educational reforms were an essential part of the Reformation program. But even before these reforms were effected, Bibles could be placed in the hands of those who were already literate and these persons could then read to others or share their newly acquired knowledge of Scripture with them.

B. Tyndale. In England the Reformation came late. Even the impulses stirred by the new learning were

The gospell of S. Mathew.
The fyrst Chapter.

Thys ys the boke of the generació of Jesus Christ the sõne of David/The sonne also of Abraham. Abraham begatt Isaac: Isaac begatt Jacob: Jacob begatt Judas and hys brethren: Judas begat Phares: and Zaram of thamar: Phares begatt Esrom: Esrom begatt Aram: Aram begatt Aminadab: Aminadab begatt naassan: Naasson begatt Salmon: Salmon begatt boos of rahab: Boos begatt obed of ruth: Obed begatt Jesse: Jesse begatt david the kynge: David the kynge begatt Solomon/of her that was the wyfe of ury: Solomon begat roboam: Roboam begatt Abia: Abia begatt asa: Asa begatt iosaphat: Josaphat begatt Joram: Joram begatt Osias: Osias begatt Joatham: Joatham begatt Achas: Achas begatt Ezechias: Ezechias begatt Manasses: Manasses begatt Amon: Amon begatt Josias: Josias begatt Jechonias and his brethren about the tyme of the captivite of babilon After they were led captive to babilon/Jechonias begatt

* Abraham and David are fyrst rehearsid/ because that christe was chefly promysed vnto them.

Saynct mathew leveth out certeyne generacions/ & describeth Christes linage from solomõ/after the lawe of Moses/ but Lucas descributh it accordyng to nature/frõ nathan solomõs brother. For the lawe calleth them a mannes childrẽ which his broder begatt of his wyfe lefte behynde hym after his deth. deu. xxv. c.

Facsimile of William Tyndale's translation of the Bible (Cologne, 1525; repr. London, 1871), Mt. 1 and facing woodcut illustration of the Gospel writer and an assisting angel. Later translations and compilations, including Coverdale's, Matthew's, the Great, and the Geneva Bibles, made use of Tyndale's Bible (New York Public Library)

checked by fears of Lutheran heresy. Bible translation found an early champion, however, in William Tyndale. Educated at Oxford and later at Cambridge, Tyndale heard the call of Erasmus for Bibles in the common tongue, and the manifest ignorance of the clergy confirmed his desire to take biblical instruction directly to the people. When the cultured Cuthbert Tunstall (then Bishop of London) refused him patronage in 1523, he secured support from a London merchant. Convinced that he could not realize his ambition in England, he made his way to Germany in 1524 and lived out the rest of his life in various cities abroad. After an early visit to Wittenberg, where he probably met Luther, Tyndale finished his translation of the NT in 1525, and printing started at Cologne. The authorities interrupted the work, but Tyndale was able to escape to Worms with some of the sheets. There the first octavo edition of the NT appeared in 1526, followed by a notable revision in 1534 and another of less significance in 1535. Copies of the Cologne fragment in quarto, which contain only Matthew and the beginning of Mark but to which there is an important prologue, might well have reached England too, since at least one copy has survived.

This prologue follows that of Luther's 1522 NT. Since the contents page lists the books in the same way as Luther's, and since Tyndale's work in English is very similar to Luther's work in German, some have suggested that Tyndale displayed little originality but simply turned Luther's version into his own tongue. There is no doubt that he used Luther's work, as he also used the Vulgate, but careful study shows conclusively that he used Erasmus's Greek text as well. At many points his translation diverges from that of Luther, and in the main he emerges as a better Greek scholar. He broke free from subservience to the Vulgate, too, especially in his rejection of terms that had taken on a special ecclesiastical sense, such as "priest" for "elder" and "do penance" for "repent." Like Purvey, although in an English that had changed much since Purvey's day, he achieved a fresh and simple idiomatic translation that has laid its imprint on many subsequent versions.

The official reaction to Tyndale's NT was hostile. Those who bought copies were required to hand them in for destruction. The ports were watched to check imports. Thomas More initiated a violent attack on alleged mistranslations, the heart of the controversy being the ecclesiastical terms (cf. More's *Dialogue* of 1529). Tunstall apparently bought up as many copies as possible for burning. This action, however, encouraged printers to issue pirated editions. It also provided cash for Tyndale's own work of revising the NT and pressing on with the OT. He managed to publish his version of the Pentateuch in 1530 and of Jonah in 1531. After his execution in 1536 the Matthew's Bible appeared (1537), containing material from Joshua to 2 Chronicles which most scholars ascribe to Tyndale. The OT displays the same boldness and idiomatic freshness as the NT. It is a tribute to the quality of all of Tyndale's work, not only that it proved a model for later versions, but that at some points the RV went back to it where the AV had taken another course.

C. Joye. By 1530 Tyndale was no longer alone in the field. George Joye had also moved into exile, and worked for a while with Tyndale. Joye published his first version of the Psalms in 1530, Isaiah in 1531, and Jeremiah and Lamentations along with the Song of Moses and a second edition of the Psalms in 1534. In this same year he put out a new edition of Tyndale's NT with some annoying changes, especially the odd "life after this life" for "resurrection." This work, however, had the happy effect of stirring Tyndale to bring out his own 1534 edition, which B. F. Westcott described as his "noblest monument." Joye's further contribution consisted of another edition of the NT and some work on the OT, possibly including Proverbs and Ecclesiastes.

D. Coverdale. By 1534 the break with Rome and the cautious sponsorship of Thomas Cranmer, Archbishop of Canterbury, opened the way to less clandestine activity. Miles Coverdale, who had helped Tyndale in Hamburg

are of hym. After thys maner therfore shall
ye praye:
c.11.a O oure father which art in heauen, halowed be thy name. Thy kyngdome come.
Thy wyll be fulfilled vpon earth as it is in
heauen. Geue vs this daye oure dayly bred.
And forgeue vs oure dettes, as we also forgeue oure detters. And lede vs not in to tēp
tacion: but delyuer vs from euell. For thyne
is the kyngdome, and the power, and the
glorye for euer. Amen. For yf ye forgeue o-
ther men their treaspases, youre heauenly
t.18.d father shall also forgeue you. But and ye
rc.11.c wyll not forgeue mē their trespases, nomo-
re shall youre father forgeue you youre tres
pases.
l.58.a Moreouer when ye fast, be not sad as ye
t.9.b ypocrytes are. For they disfigure their faces, that they myght be sene of men to fast.
Verely I saye vnto you: they haue their re
warde. But thou, whē thou fastest, annoyn-
te thyne heed, and wash thy face, that it ap-
peare not vnto men, that thou fastest: but
vnto thy father which is in secrete: and thy
father which seyth in secrete, shal rewarde

They laboure not, nether spynne. And yet
for all that I saye vnto you, that euen Salo
mon in all his royalte was not arayed lyke
vnto one of these. Wherfore yf God so cloth
the grasse, which is to daye in the felde, and
to morowe shalbe cast in to the fornace: shal
he not moch more do the same vnto you, o ye
of lytle fayth?
Therfore take no thought, sayinge: what
shall we eate, or what shall we drinke? or
where with shall we be clothed? After all
soch thynges do the heithen seke. For youre heauenly father knoweth, that ye haue
nede of all these thynges. Seke ye fyrst the
kyngdome of heauen and the right eousnes
therof, so shal all these thynges be ministred
vnto you.
Care not then for the morow, for the morow shall care for it self: Euery daye hath
ynough of his owne trauayll.

The VII. Chapter.

Iudge not, that ye be not iudged:
For as ye iudge, so shal ye be iudged.

Miles Coverdale's Bible (Marburg?, 1535), Mt. 6–7, including the Lord's Prayer (New York Public Library)

and Antwerp, took advantage of the new situation to present his own rendering of the Bible for official approval. A graduate of Cambridge, Coverdale had translated the entire Bible while still abroad. Published in Europe (1535), the first complete printed English Bible soon reached England, furnished with a fulsome address to the king. Since no heresy could be found in it, Henry reportedly said: "Then in God's name let it go abroad among the people." A folio and a quarto edition appeared in 1537, and Coverdale added to his work in 1539 by publishing the Vulgate with an English translation in parallel columns.

Coverdale's work went more rapidly because he did not study the originals so closely as Tyndale. Indeed, he claims only to have translated from German ("Douche") and Latin versions using the Vulgate, the new Latin version of Pagninus, Luther, the Zurich Bible, and Tyndale where appropriate. Yet Coverdale brought excellent stylistic gifts to the task. If he relied heavily on Tyndale in the NT, he revealed his own talents in those parts of the OT that Tyndale never reached. His version of the Psalms, as he himself revised it for the Great Bible (1539), has become familiar to generations of Anglican worshipers through the Book of Common Prayer. If it is less accurate than the AV and later revisions, it has at many points both finer rhythms and more striking phrases.

E. Matthew's Bible. The year 1537 saw the appearance of an important English version bearing on the title page the name of a certain Thomas Matthew. No such person is known, and it seems probable that this was a pseudonym for John Rogers, a former assistant of Tyndale. Nor should Matthew or Rogers be called the translator, for in fact he was just an editor or compiler. His Bible consists of all of Tyndale's work supplemented by that of Coverdale, along with a rendering of the Prayer of Manasseh from Olivetan's French version. Yet this Bible is a significant one, for it quickly attracted the attention of Cranmer, who, by way of Thomas Cromwell, secured for it the approval of Henry VIII. A royal license was issued for it, so that by a stroke of irony Tyndale's work came out with official commendation only a year after his untimely death. The Bible of Richard Taverner, published in 1539, is simply a revision of Matthew's Bible, in which Taverner's fine Greek scholarship helps to attain greater accuracy in the NT.

F. Great Bible. The publication of Matthew's Bible opened the door for even greater accomplishments. In 1536, 1537, and 1538 diocesan and national injunctions were issued ordering the provision of English Bibles in all the churches. Little could be done as long as no approved version existed; but when the 1538 injunction called for "one book of the whole Bible of the largest volume in English," arrangements were also made to publish a new and larger edition of Matthew's Bible. Coverdale was entrusted with the task of revising it, and with the backing of Henry and Cromwell the printing was done in Paris. After some delays due to the Paris inquisition, what came to be known as the Great Bible was published in 1539. A revised edition followed in 1540 with a title page indicating that this was the Bible meant to be used in the churches, for it had royal approval and had sustained examination by two bishops, one of whom was Tyndale's former opponent Tunstall. Archbishop Cranmer contributed to this edition a preface which earned for it the name Cranmer's Bible. In it he recommended the use of Scripture and adduced passages from the church fathers to show that in it all people may "learn all things,

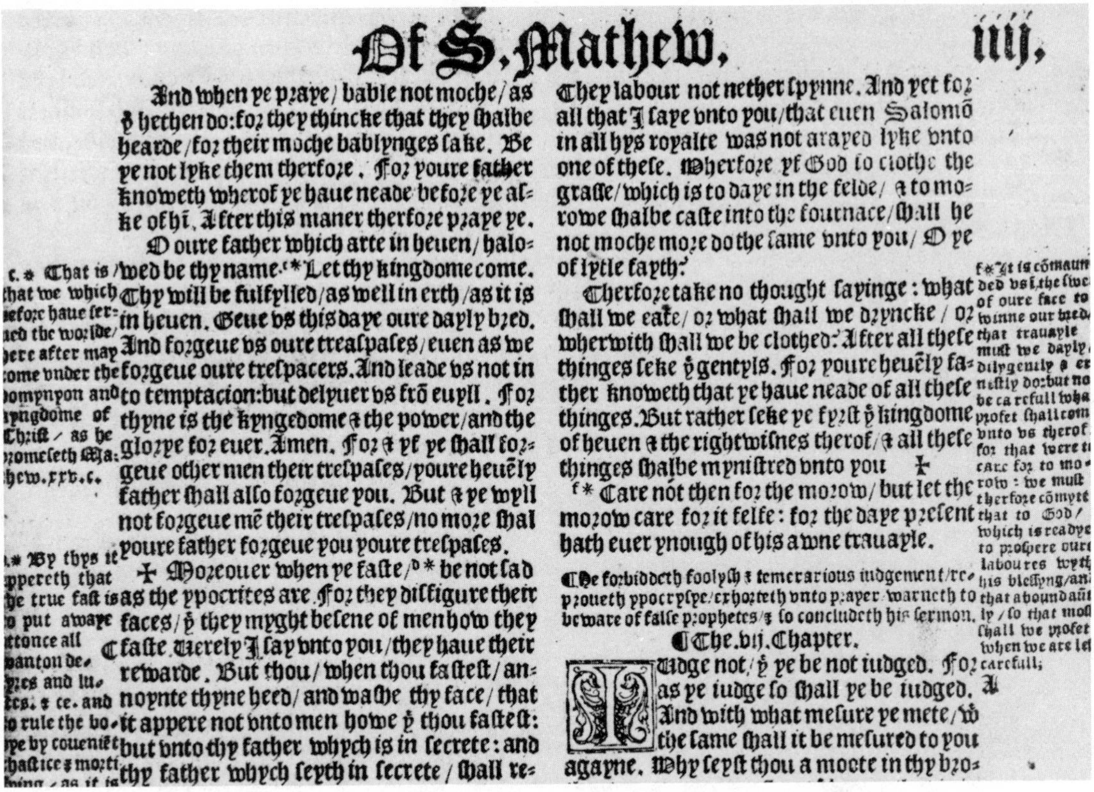

Thomas Matthew's Bible (Antwerp, 1537), Mt. 6–7, including the Lord's Prayer. This version is a compilation, probably by a Tyndale associate, of Tyndale's and Coverdale's Bibles (New York Public Library)

what they ought to think, what they ought to do, and what they should not do." Further editions followed rapidly in 1540 and 1541, and from all accounts it seems that in these early years at least, when English readings were no official part of the liturgy, considerable use was made of the church Bibles both by individuals and by groups. Indeed, an order had to be passed in 1539 checking reading out loud from the Bible while divine service was in progress.

G. Opposition. Opponents of the English Bible remained active. The 1542 convocation censured the Great Bible and tried to initiate revision and correction, which Cranmer stalled by passing on the task to the slow-moving universities. In 1543 Parliament condemned Tyndale's own work while retaining his contribution to the Great Bible; it also laid restrictions on both public and private reading. In 1545 the use of primers, which contained Scripture passages, came under closer control. At the same time, paradoxically, provision was made for reading chapters of the NT at the morning and evening services. Even Coverdale came under the ban in 1546, but the Great Bible remained openly in the churches. With Henry's death in 1547, however, the situation changed dramatically. Restrictions on Bibles and Bible readings were eased, and new editions of the Great Bible were called for in 1549 and 1553. Furthermore, translation of the liturgies in the 1549 and 1553 Books of Common Prayer allowed for the use of the Great Bible in lections, canticles, and Psalms.

H. Other Versions. Of interest during the brief reign of Edward VI are two new versions. First comes that of the illustrious scholar John Cheke, who in 1550 began a translation which, so far as possible, would be confined to words of English derivation. In this respect he took the opposite course to that advocated by Stephen Gardiner, who wanted a strongly latinate version. Cheke finished only the first Gospel and part of the second, and his work survived only in manuscript until printed in the 19th century. While the principle of translation has something to commend it, some of Cheke's terms sound very odd today (e.g., "freshman" for "proselyte") and the compounds he was forced to invent (e.g., "frosent" for "apostle") have no marked advantage. In contrast, Bishop Becke's Bible of 1551 is based essentially on Tyndale's NT and Taverner's OT. It contains a new rendering of 3 Maccabees, a dedication to the king, and copious notes which aroused no little opposition and were later dropped.

IV. Elizabethan Versions.—The reaction under Mary Tudor (1553-1558) put a brief halt to the dissemination of Scripture in English. The government, it seems, did not actively remove the Great Bible on a national scale; Edmund Bonner of London, an active persecutor, found it difficult, when challenged, to condemn a Bible that he himself had helped to promote. Yet according to John Foxe many Bibles were burned, while John Rogers was executed, and Coverdale prudently sought refuge abroad. Furthermore, no additional work of Bible translation was undertaken in England. Those who condemned and destroyed available versions did not take active steps to replace them with what they might regard as more orthodox or accurate renderings.

When Elizabeth succeeded her half sister in 1558, in an early set of injunctions she ordered again the setting up of "one book of the whole Bible in the largest volume in English in all parish churches." Parishes which still had the Great Bible in good condition could retain their copies. Others were to buy new copies, which apparently they did from unsold, but undestroyed, stocks of the 1553 edition.

1.Cor.11,9.

o Or, Mannes, because she cometh of man: for in Ebr Ish, is man, and Ishah the woman.

Mat.19,5. mar.10,7. 1 cor.6,16. ephes.5,31.

p So that mariage requireth a greater ductie of vs towarde ỹ wiues, thẽ otherwise we are bounde to shewe to our parents.

23 Then the man said, This now is bone
of my bones, and flesh of my flesh. She
shalbe called o woman, because she was taken out of man.
24 *Therefore shal man leaue p his father
and his mother, and shal cleaue to his wife,
and they shalbe one flesh.
25 And they were bothe naked, the man &
his wife, and were not q ashamed.

q For before sinne entred, all things were honest and comely.

THE SITVACION OF THE GARDEN OF EDEN.

La grand Armenie. *Or, Armenia the great.

Terre de Hauilah *Or, land of Hauilah.

La cheute d Euphrates. *Or, the fall of Euphrates.

La cheute de Tygris. Or, the fall of Tygris.

Le golf. de la mer Persique Or, the golfe of the Persian sea

Because mencion is made in the tenth verse of this seconde chapter of the riuer that watered the garden, we muste note that Euphrates and Tygris called in Ebrewe, Perath and Hiddekel, were called but one riuer where they ioyned together, als they had foure heades: that is, two at their springs, & two where they fel into the Persian sea. In this countrey and moste plentiful land Adam dwelt, and this was called Paradise: that is, a garden of pleasure, because of the frutefulnes and abundance thereof. And whereas it is said that Pishon compasseth the land of Hauilah, it is meant of Tygris, which in some place, as it passed by diuers places, was called by sundry names, as some time Diglitto, in other places Pasitygris, & of some Phasin or Pishon. Likewise Euphrates towarde the countrey of Cush or Ethiopia, or Arabia was called Gihon. So that Tygris and Euphrates (which were but two riuers and some time when they ioyned together, were called after one name) were according to diuers places called by these foure names, so that they might seme to haue bene foure diuers riuers.

CHAP. III.

1 The womã seduced by the serpẽt. 6 Entiseth her housbãd to sinne. 14 They thre are punished. 15 Christ is promised. 19 Man is dust. 22 Man is cast out of paradise.

Wisdo. 2,25

a As Satan cã change him selfe into an Angel of light, so did he abuse the wisdome of the serpent to deceaue man.

b God suffered Satan to make the serpent his instrument and to speake in him.

c In douting of Gods thretning, she yelded to Satan.

1 NOw *the serpent was more a subtil
then anie beast of the field, which ỹ
Lord God had made: and he b said to the
woman, Yea, hathe God in dede said, Ye
shal not eat of euerie tre of the garden?
2 And the woman said vnto the serpẽt, We
eat of the frute of the trees of the garden,
3 But of the frute of the tre, which is in the
middes of the garden, God hathe said, Ye
shal not eat of it, nether shal ye touche it,
c lest ye dye.
4 Then *the serpent said to the woman, Ye
shal not d dye at all,
5 But God doeth knowe, that when ye shal
eat thereof, your eyes shalbe opened, & ye
shalbe as gods, e knowing good and euil.
6 So the woman (seing that the tre was
good for meat, and that it was pleasant to
the eyes, & a tre to be desired to get knowledge) toke of the frute thereof, and did
* eat, and gaue also to her housband with
her, and he f did eat.
7 Then the eyes of them bothe were opened, & they g knewe that they were naked,
and they sewed figtre leaues together, and
made them selues "breeches.
8 ¶Afterwarde they heard the voyce of

2 Cor.11,3.

d This is Satans chiefest subtilties, to cause vs not to feare Gods threatnings.

e As thogh he shulde say, God doeth not forbid you to eat of the frute, saue that he knoweth that if you shulde eat thereof, you shulde be like to him.

Eccles 25,33. 1.tim.2,14.

f Not so muche to please his wife, as moued by ambicion at her persuasion.

g They began to fele their miserie, but they soght not to God for remedie.

"Or, things to girde about them

The Geneva Bible (Geneva, 1560) is also known as the "Breeches Bible" because of its rendering of Gen. 3:7: ". . . & they knewe that they were naked, and they sewed figtre leaues together, and made them selues breeches." The map shows the area of Eden (New York Public Library)

A. Geneva Bible. A significant event, however, had occurred during the reign of Mary. English exiles in Geneva had continued the work of translation and revision which had been going on steadily from the publication of the first edition of Tyndale's NT. In 1557 they produced a revised NT, the work of William Whittingham, who had married a relative of Calvin and later became Dean of Durham. For this revision of Matthew's Tyndale, Whittingham used Theodore Beza's Latin NT of 1556. He introduced the verse divisions, first found in Stephanus's Greek NT of 1551. He also used italics for supplementary words, went back to "church" instead of Tyndale's "congregation," and substituted "General Epistles" for the earlier "Catholic Epistles."

This 1557 translation was only the first part of a larger project which reached its culmination with the total Bible of 1560, normally called the Geneva Bible from its place of origin and also, perhaps, its theological slant. This version contains a dedicatory epistle to Elizabeth and a general address explaining the need for this revision. In particular it notes that the parts of the OT not done by Tyndale had never been directly translated from the Hebrew (and Aramaic). It also stresses that the presence of so many scholars in Geneva provided greater resources than could have been tapped in England. The books of the Apocrypha are included, although with warnings not to accord them the same authority as canonical writings. The polemical notes, which champion Calvinism and condemn Romanism, caused offence in some quarters, but for others they gave the Bible its strength; in fact, they are no stronger than was customary in annotated Bibles of the period.

During the reign of Elizabeth publication of the Geneva Bible went on unhindered. The work attained considerable popularity with the rise of various forms of Elizabethan Puritanism. A folio edition came out in 1561 and several editions followed, some printed in Geneva and others in England. In 1576 L. Tomson issued a revision of the NT which was often used in subsequent editions of the whole Bible. The Scottish edition of 1579 was the first Bible ever printed in Scotland, and even in later competition with the AV the Geneva Bible held its own for many years in Scotland. In England, too, editions of the Geneva Bible continued up to 1644.

B. Bishops' Bible. Even those who disliked Puritanism had to accept the superiority of the Geneva Bible over the Great Bible. In response, therefore, Archbishop Parker in 1561 advocated and promoted a revision of the Great Bible by the bishops with himself as chief editor. The revision was to be based primarily on Latin versions of the OT, which were themselves based directly on the Hebrew. Notes were not to be included, and some regard was to be had to matters of taste and style. Parker made no attempt to obstruct the Geneva Bible, which the revisers appear in fact to have used, but he did not want it as the version commended for public reading at worship. His colleagues completed the revision by 1568, and in 1571 convocation accepted it for public use. The second edition of 1569 included small changes, and the third edition of 1572 had a more thorough revision of the NT. To prevent confusion arising from the continued use of the Coverdale version of the Psalms for worship, some later editions either printed this version of the Psalms in parallel columns with that of the Bishops' Bible, or substituted it for that of the Bishops' Bible. The Bishops' Bible sold well but fell far short of the impressive figures achieved by the Geneva Bible in the period leading up to the accession of James and the proposal for a common version.

C. Rheims-Douay Version. As Mary's reign produced its exiles, so did Elizabeth's, and these Roman Catholic exiles produced their own translation of the Bible. This version emanated from the English College founded by William Allen and located first at Douay (1568), then at Rheims (1578), then back at Douay (1593). The work of translation was done mainly by Gregory Martin, formerly an Oxford scholar, who published the NT first at Rheims

The Bishops' Bible (London, 1st ed. 1568), a summary and the text of Ps. 23. Compare "for a long tyme" in v. 5b to the AV rendering (v. 6b), "for euer" (see picture of AV Psalms page in V below) (British Library)

¶ The argument of the.xxiij.Psalme.

Dauid resemblyng God to a sheepehearde and hym selfe to a sheepe, declareth that all commodities, plentie, quietnesse and prosperitie, ensueth them that be fully perswaded of Gods prouidence: for God feedeth, norisheth, defendeth, and gouerneth those that put their wholl trust in hym after a more ample sort then any sheepehearde doth his sheepe.

¶ A psalme of Dauid.

1 GOd is my sheephearde, therfore I
A can lacke nothyng: he wyll cause
me to repose my selfe in pasture full
of grasse, and he wyll leade me vnto
calme waters.
2 He wyll conuert my soule: he wyll
bring me foorth into the pathes of righteousnesse for his name sake.
3 Yea though I walke through the
valley of the shadowe of death, I wyll
feare no euyll: for thou art with me,
thy rodde and thy staffe be the thynges
that do comfort me.
4 Thou wylt prepare a table before me
in the presence of myne aduersaries:
thou hast annoynted my head with
oyle, and my cup shalbe brymme full.
5 Truely felicitie and mercie shal folowe
me all the dayes of my lyfe: and I wyll
dwell in the house of God for a long
tyme.

Rom.viii.d. *For your father knoweth, what
thynges ye haue nede of, before ye aske
of hym.
9 After this maner therfore pray ye.
Luke.xi.a. *O our father, which art in heauen,
halowed be thy name.
10 Let thy kyngdome come. Thy wyll
be done, as well in earth, as it is in
heauen.
11 Geue vs this day our dayly breade.
12 And forgeue vs our dettes, as we forgeue our detters.
13 And leade vs not into temptation,
but delyuer vs from euyll. For thyne is
the kyngdome, and the power, and the
glory, for euer. Amen.
Mat.xviii.b Mark.xi.d. 14 For, *yf ye forgeue men theyr trespasses, your heauenly father shall also for-
geue you.
15 But, yf ye forgeue not men theyr
trespasses: no more shall your father,
forgeue [you] your trespasses.
Esay.lvii.a. 16 Moreouer, *when ye fast, be not of

The Bishops' Bible (London, 1568), Mt. 6, including the Lord's Prayer. Archbishop Parker promoted this revision of the Great Bible (New York Public Library)

(1582) and then the OT at Douay (1609-1610). Allen and another colleague, Richard Bristowe, acted as consultants and revisers.

Four points call for notice regarding the Rheims-Douay version. First, the preface explains that the translators did not share the erroneous view that Bibles in the vernacular are always necessary or profitable. They undertook the work only because, according to "the present time, state, and condition of our country, . . . divers things are either necessary, or profitable, or medicinable now, that otherwise in the peace of the church were neither much requisite, nor perchance wholly tolerable." The work found its motive and justification in the need to counteract the mischievous translations of Protestants which had corrupted Scripture by "adding, detracting, altering etc."

Second, the translators took the Latin Vulgate as their original text. In this respect they remained loyal to the authoritative position of the Vulgate endorsed by the Council of Trent in 1546. At the same time they clearly did not ignore the Greek texts or even the Hebrew, as B. F. Westcott has convincingly shown (*History of the English Bible* [1868], p. 254). Thus they dealt well with the definite article, which Latin does not have. But by placing the apocryphal books in their Latin order, rather than grouping them separately in an appendix as the Reformation versions did, they confirmed their canonical status.

Third, the translators adopted the ecclesiastical and latinate style, which Gardiner had favored earlier, in place of the more idiomatic renderings championed by Tyndale and his successors. At difficult points they "presume not to modify the speeches or phrases but religiously keep them word for word." Some renderings come out oddly because of the general failure of the English language to follow this pattern. A commonly adduced example is Eph. 6:12: "Against the spirituals of wickedness in the celestials." In the Lord's Prayer supersubstantial bread is prayed for instead of daily bread, and the Good Samaritan is ready to pay back whatever the innkeeper will supererogate. "Do penance" is demanded by John the Baptist, while Paul and Barnabas ordain priests and in Gethsemane Jesus prays that the chalice will pass from him. At the same time, when no doctrine is at stake the Rheims-Douay Bible can be no less simple and direct than Tyndale. It has been observed that the AV took over a few of the terms of Latin origin (Westcott, p. 253) and by its greater influence brought them into regular English use.

Fourth, the translators provided extensive notes, partly to clear up problems but primarily to ensure that readers would understand what they read in accordance with the new orthodoxy of Trent. For this purpose positive interpretations accompany refutations of Reformation teaching. Allen bore chief responsibility for this part of the work as Martin did for the actual translation.

V. Authorized or King James Version.–When Elizabeth died in 1603, James VI of Scotland became also James I of England. Pressured immediately by the Puritans, he summoned a conference at Hampton Court early in 1604. The conference made only minor changes in the Puritan interest and it might indeed have been largely forgotten had it not reached an epoch-making decision when, with the enthusiastic support of the king, it accepted the proposal of Puritan leader John Reynolds: "That a translation be made of the whole Bible, as consonant as can be to the original Hebrew and Greek." For out of this decision came seven years later the so-called Authorized or King James Version (AV or KJV).

Arrangements were quickly set in hand to implement the decision. Responsibility for the OT devolved on three panels, for the NT on two, and for the Apocrypha on one. Fifty-four of the finest scholars of the day, both Anglican and Puritan, were chosen to serve on the panels, which met at Westminster, Oxford, and Cambridge. Each scholar on a panel made his own version of a passage and all the renderings were then discussed until agreement was reached. When a panel finished a whole book, it sent it to the other panels for approval or criticism. The drafts finally came under the scrutiny of a group of twelve composed of two representatives from each of the panels.

As the preface explains, the translators were not expected to begin with a clean slate. The aim was revision, not a fresh translation: "not to make a bad version good, but to make a good one better, or out of many good ones one principal good one." The Bishops' Bible provided the starting-point, but the revisers could also use Tyndale, Coverdale, Matthew's Bible, the Great Bible, and, of course, the Geneva Bible; in addition, they seem to have consulted at least the NT of Rheims-Douay. All these versions were checked against the tongues in which "God was pleased to speak to his Church by his Prophets and Apostles." In spite of the time involved, the companies also turned for help to other versions and commentaries in both ancient and modern tongues. The preface modestly admits that the precise meaning of many words has not been attained. It therefore makes a plea for an ongoing work of revision, perfection being beyond achievement in all human enterprises.

Certain rules governed the translation. First, change was not to be made merely for the sake of change. Second, biblical names were to correspond to popular usage and not to try to follow the Hebrew or Greek so closely as the Geneva and Bishops' Bibles had done. There are some unfortunate exceptions to this rule, Jesus for Joshua in the NT being a particularly bad example. Third, ecclesiastical terms such as "church" and "baptism" were to be retained, although "do penance" was not accepted as an accurate alternative for "repent." The AV tried to steer a middle course between Geneva, with its "congregation" and "washing," and Rheims-Douay, whose latinate expressions brought the AV's condemnation of "the obscurity of the Papists." Fourth, synonyms might freely be used, as by Tyndale, where the Hebrew or Greek word was the same. The preface offers a predominantly literary defense of this procedure: one should avoid discrimination between English words and not fall victim to pedantry ("niceness of words was always counted the next step to pedants"). It scoffs at the notion that "the kingdom of God is become words or syllables," yet in its application of this rule the AV tends at times to carry freedom to inordinate and unnecessary lengths. Fifth, notes were not to be included apart from alternative renderings in the margins. Most of the offense given by the Geneva Bible was due to the notes, which James found "very partial, untrue, seditious." An attempt to reach agreement on a new set of notes might well have wrecked the whole project; hence, the decision to drop them was wise. Sixth, the practice of indicating supplementary words by different type was to be continued. Seventh, chapter and verse divisions were to be employed, and chapter headings were to be provided. The latter might have aroused controversy; but the translators did the work well, offering factual headings for the most part, or agreed interpretations where some passages—especially in the Psalms and Prophets—were understood christologically.

When the first edition came out in 1611 it carried in its title the phrase "appointed to be read in Churches." This, along with official sponsorship and the known backing of the king, probably helped to give the new Bible in England the common name of Authorized Version, although in fact neither the king, parliament, nor convocation ever granted formal authorization. In America the title King James Version obviously derives from the important contribution that the sovereign made to the venture, which is acknowledged in excessively flattering terms in the dedicatory epistle.

Although many readers were attached to existing versions, especially the Geneva Bible, the AV met with a good reception. The only severe critic was Hugh Broughton, a distinguished scholar who, no doubt to his chagrin, had not been given a place on the panels, and who found the new version so distasteful that he called for it to be burned. In spite of his and other less fierce objections, three folio editions of the AV came out in 1611, including the so-called He and She versions named after the alternative renderings "he went" and "she went" in Ruth 3:15. Octavo editions followed in 1612 and many others in the succeeding decades and centuries, some with misprints which earned them such special titles as the Wicked Bible (1631; it left out "not" in the seventh commandment), the Vinegar Bible (1717; "vinegar" for "vineyard" in Lk. 20), and the Murderers' Bible (1795; "killed" for "filled" in Mk. 7:27). Across the years, publishers independently modified the spelling to reduce archaisms. In some Scottish editions the metrical version of the Psalter came to be added as an appendix for use in worship, just as the Bishops' Bible had included the Coverdale version, although the step was not taken of putting the metrical rendering in the main body of the text.

The AV undoubtedly merited the position it fairly quickly

Dedication to King James VI and I, who supported the translation of what came to be called the Authorized (King James) Version of the Bible (London, 1611) (New York Public Library)

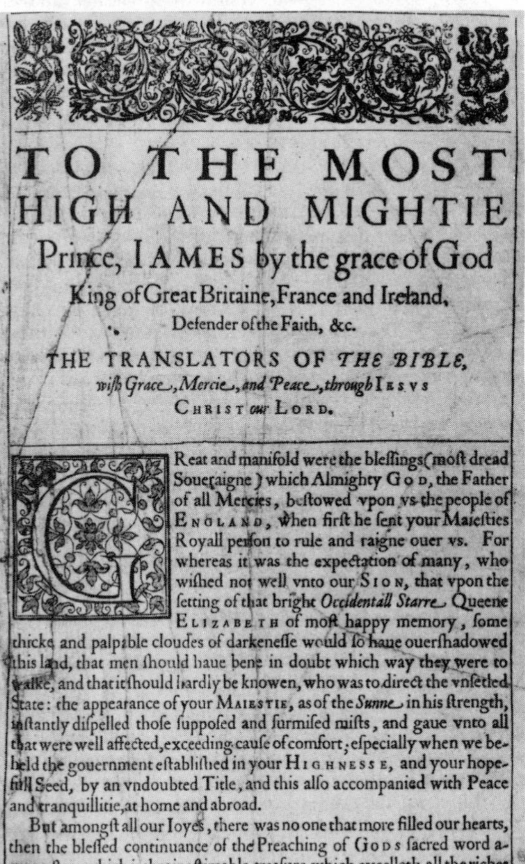

TO THE MOST HIGH AND MIGHTIE Prince, IAMES by the grace of God King of Great Britaine, France and Ireland, Defender of the Faith, &c.

THE TRANSLATORS OF THE BIBLE, wiſh Grace, Mercie, and Peace, through IESVS CHRIST our LORD.

GReat and manifold were the bleſſings (moſt dread Soueraigne) which Almighty GOD, the Father of all Mercies, beſtowed vpon vs the people of ENGLAND, when firſt he ſent your Maieſties Royall perſon to rule and raigne ouer vs. For whereas it was the expectation of many, who wiſhed not well vnto our SION, that vpon the ſetting of that bright *Occidentall Starre*, Queene ELIZABETH of moſt happy memory, ſome thicke and palpable cloudes of darkeneſſe would ſo haue ouerſhadowed this land, that men ſhould haue bene in doubt which way they were to walke, and that it ſhould hardly be knowen, who was to direct the vnſetled State: the appearance of your MAIESTIE, as of the *Sunne* in his ſtrength, inſtantly diſpelled thoſe ſuppoſed and ſurmiſed miſts, and gaue vnto all that were well affected, exceeding cauſe of comfort; eſpecially when we beheld the gouernment eſtabliſhed in your HIGHNESSE, and your hopefull Seed, by an vndoubted Title, and this alſo accompanied with Peace and tranquillitie, at home and abroad.

But amongſt all our Ioyes, there was no one that more filled our hearts, then the bleſſed continuance of the Preaching of GODS ſacred word amongſt vs, which is that ineſtimable treaſure, which excelleth all the riches of the earth, becauſe the fruit thereof extendeth it ſelfe, not onely to the time

Authorized (King James) Version of the Bible (London: Robert Barker, 1st ed. 1611), Pss. 23–25 (British Library)

Gods goodneſſe. Pſaln

PSAL. XXIII.

Dauids confidence in Gods grace.

¶ A Pſalme of Dauid.

The LORD is * my ſhep-
heard, I ſhall not want.
2 He maketh me to lie
downe in † greene pa-
ſtures: he leadeth mee be-
ſide the † ſtill waters.
3 He reſtoreth my ſoule: he leadeth
me in the pathes of righteouſnes, for
his names ſake.
4 Yea though I walke through the
valley of the ſhadowe of death, * I will
feare no euill: for thou art with me, thy
rod and thy ſtaffe, they comfort me.
5 Thou prepareſt a table before me,
in the preſence of mine enemies: thou
† anointeſt my head with oyle, my cuppe
runneth ouer.
6 Surely goodnes and mercie ſhall
followe me all the daies of my life: and
I will dwell in the houſe of the LORD
† for euer.

*Eſa. 40.11 Iere. 23.5. Ezech. 34.23. Ioh. 10.11. 1.Pet. 2.25. † Heb. paſtures of tender graſſe. † Heb. waters of quietneſſe. *Pſal. 3.6. & 118.6. † Heb. makeſt fat. † Heb. to length of dayes.

PSAL. XXIIII.

1 Gods Lordſhip in the world. 3 The citizens of his ſpirituall kingdome. 7 An exhorta-

ENGLISH VERSIONS

9 After this maner therefore pray
yee: *Our father which art in heauen, *Luke
hallowed be thy name.
10 Thy kingdome come. Thy will
be done, in earth, as it is in heauen.
11 Giue vs this day our daily bread.
12 And forgiue vs our debts, as we
forgiue our debters.
13 And lead vs not into temptation,
but deliuer vs from euill: For thine is
the kingdome, and the power, and the
glory, for euer, Amen.
14 *For, if yee forgiue men their tres- *Mark
passes, your heauenly father will also 25.
forgiue you.
15 But, if yee forgiue not men their
trespasses, neither will your father for-

Authorized (King James) Version of the Bible (London, 1611), Mt. 6:8-19, including the Lord's Prayer (New York Public Library)

came to occupy in the English-speaking Christian world. While not, unfortunately, based on the best texts, it achieved considerable accuracy as a result of the many years of work and experience that had preceded it. At the same time it achieved a literary quality which tends to be the despair of all who try to improve it or even to break away from it. Many factors contribute to this literary excellence: freshness, vigor, simplicity, and rhythms which make it particularly impressive in public reading. One might wonder how a group of committees could ever produce a masterpiece of this order. Analyses have shown, however, that as much as 60 percent of the AV comes from previous versions and that always the underlying genius is that of Tyndale and Coverdale, who not only provided a model for all who followed, but whose hands may still be traced clearly in this consummation of the Reformation effort.

VI. Seventeenth- and Eighteenth-Century Contributions.– The early users of the AV did not regard it as a final word in the way that many of its more recent admirers have come to do. For a time some continued to buy previous versions. Others worked steadily at improving the AV itself; e.g., over 300 corrections were made already in the 1613 edition. Others again attempted new translations either because better manuscripts were becoming available or because changes in vocabulary and style demanded more up-to-date renderings. H. Ainsworth, e.g., had published a new translation of the Pentateuch and Canticles by 1616 and 1623, and later his version of the Psalms came out posthumously.

The Puritan period raised a demand for more official action. The Long Parliament went so far as to appoint a commission, but nothing came of it. For the most part later Puritans took the path of paraphrase. Thus a paraphrase of the NT came out in 1652, a paraphrase of Paul's Epistles in 1675, and Richard Baxter's *NT with Paraphrase and Notes* in 1685. Presentation of the fifth-century Alexandrine Codex to Charles I had made possible at this time an extensive textual scrutiny, but for the time being no advantage was taken of the new opportunity this offered.

The pace quickened in the 18th century. Paraphrase still dominated the scene in the first decades. Whitby, Guyse, Clarke, Pyle, and Barlee all made contributions between 1703 and 1735. The normal method was not to do an independent paraphrase but to use the AV text (usually the NT or some part of it) with supplementary or explanatory material in brackets. In the strict sense, then, these works were not new versions as some modern paraphrases are.

E. Wells, however, took a slightly different course with his revision of the AV NT in *The Common Translation Corrected, with a Paraphrase and Notes* (1718). He was followed by D. Mace, who, using new manuscripts, published a Greek edition of the NT along with the AV corrected both critically, to make it conform to the better readings, and linguistically, to keep it idiomatic as the language was changing. Other translations of this period were the *Paraphrase and Version of the NT* by P. Doddridge, *Translation of the Gospels* by G. Campbell, and *Translation of All the Apostolical Epistles* by J. Macknight; these three translations were later put together in a new version of the entire NT published in 1818. W. Whiston, the translator of Josephus, made a further attempt to use better manuscripts in his *Primitive NT* of 1745. R. Wynne had the same interest (1764) and a little later W. Newcome worked along similar lines, using Griesbach's Greek NT.

Others showed a greater concern to keep the language up-to-date. J. Worsley's rendering of the NT in the "Present Idiom of the English Tongue" came out posthumously in 1770. But E. Harwood's *Liberal Translation of the NT* (1768) is the most striking example, with its strange transposition of biblical prose and poetry into the "elegant" speech of the later 18th century. In the same year J. Wesley put his varied talents to work in providing a revised AV for "plain unlettered men." Wesley's many alterations include few of any significance, but his division of the text into paragraphs calls for notice. Even more boldly in the same period, N. Scarlett expressed the dawning sense of the literary character of the Bible by putting some of its material in dramatic form. The Friends contributed a version by A. Purver, which came out after many years of work, in 1764.

The Roman Catholics, however, made perhaps the most significant advance of the century with an important revision of Rheims-Douay by Bishop R. Challoner. Challoner had apparently supervised the 1738 edition of the Rheims NT but realized that the version had become badly dated by that time. With the help of F. Blyth he thus undertook an extensive revision of the NT in five editions from 1749 to 1772 and of the OT in two editions in 1750 and 1763. While maintaining the ecclesiastical terminology of Rheims-Douay, Challoner discarded many latinate terms and allowed the influence of the AV in phrasing and rhythm. He also cut down significantly the excessive annotations of the timid translators of Douay-Rheims. Subsequent editions did not consistently follow Challoner but all borrowed from him to some extent. American Roman Catholics received permission to use the Douay-Rheims-Challoner Bible in 1810.

During the 18th cent. many developments took place which contributed strongly to the sense of a need for official revision of the AV. Textual study proliferated. A beginning was made in the literary and historical investigation of the Bible as we have come to know it today. More and more people were trying their hand either at more accurate or more modern translations. Changes in written and spoken English became increasingly obvious. At the same time interest in the Bible surged with the movements, both evangelistic and theological, which gave birth to the Bible societies for publication and distribution of Scripture at home and translation abroad. By the turn of the century the time was surely approaching when the AV would have to yield to a new version more up-to-date in both scholarship and expression.

VII. Revised and American Standard Versions.–The first half of the 19th cent. brought increasing pressure for a revision of the AV, but this had to face strong opposition. H. J. Todd published a *Vindication of the AV* in 1819, and the anonymous pamphlet *Remarks upon the Critical Principles . . .* (1820) has been called "the most masterly manifesto against change." Typical of the divided mind of the period is R. C. Trench, who in his *On the AV* acknowledged that change was inevitable but was less sure that the time for it had come.

E. H. Plumptre later took a line not dissimilar in spirit to that of Trench. Writing in the revised edition of W. Smith's *Bible Dictionary* (1870), he agreed that change must come but argued that "as little change as possible should be made in the language of the AV" and deplored the "emasculated elegance" of eighteenth-century attempts. "Some words," he confessed, "absolutely need change," because they had become obsolete or had shifted in sense. He also favored the elimination of chapter and page headings on the ground that they were interpretative.

J. B. Lightfoot in his *On a Fresh Revision* (1871) disputed the idea that the time had not yet come, at least so far as Greek scholarship was concerned. He believed that this scholarship "had never stood higher." There was not only "a sufficient body of scholars" to do the work but also of others able to submit their work to "minute and searching criticism." Indeed he feared that the present opportunity might not recur: "Greek scholarship has reached its height in England and henceforth it may be expected to decline" (p. 188).

Already in 1870 the discussion had come to a head with a motion in Canterbury Convocation to set up a committee to confer with York and report on the "desirableness of a revision of the AV." The report, quickly submitted in May of 1870, consisted of five resolutions supporting revision by emendations and marginal notes so long as all necessary changes followed "the style of the language employed in the existing version." A radically new translation was not contemplated.

The next step was an enunciation of eight principles. Some of these were procedural but others were of basic importance. The AV was to be altered as little as possible. In alterations the language of the AV and earlier versions was to be used as far as possible. When the text adopted differed from the AV, this was to be noted in the margin. Chapter headings were to be revised. Learned men "at home and abroad" might be consulted by scholars entrusted with the task of revision.

Two committees of eighteen members each were next formed, the one to revise the OT and the other the NT. Among the outstanding members of the OT panel were R. Payne Smith, T. K. Cheyne, A. B. Davidson, S. R. Driver, P. Fairbairn, J. J. S. Perowne, E. H. Plumptre, and W. Robertson Smith. The NT panel included C. J. Elliott, R. C. Trench, H. Alford, J. Angus, J. B. Lightfoot, E. Milligan, W. F. Moulton, and B. F. Westcott. The committees met for over eight years, usually at ten-day sessions four times a year.

The Revised Version of the NT was published in London and New York in May of 1881 and caused tremendous excitement. By the end of the first year a circulation of one million had been achieved. Readers found that chapter and page headings had been eliminated and that alterations had been made under five principal heads: (1) those required by the different text adopted (for the most part that of Westcott and Hort); (2) those adopted where the AV seemed to be incorrect or followed a less probable rendering; (3) clarifications of obscure or ambiguous translations; (4) changes for the sake of inner self-consistency; and (5) changes by consequence of other necessary alterations. It might be noted that the RV also followed "the rule of translating, as far as possible, the same Greek word by the same English word." Thus, in Mk. 1 the RV always has "straightway" for the same Greek term, whereas AV has "straightway" four times, "immediately" four times, and "forthwith" twice. Incidentally, the whole text of the NT is carefully broken up into paragraphs which are not necessarily controlled by the older chapter divisions.

When the OT followed, it adhered to the same principles but in the main the changes were not so noticeable. The constant use of "Jehovah" for "Lord" caused some adverse comment but many phrases were made more intelligible, e.g., "meal offering" for "meat offering." Sheol was translated "grave" or "pit" in the historical books but merely transliterated in the poetical works. In accordance with changed English usage the neuter possessive pronoun was altered from his to its, which was just coming into use in 1611 and which adds clarity at many points.

One NT change gave rise to a deep and prolonged controversy. In the opening clause of 2 Tim. 3:16 the RV supplied the verb "is" (missing in the typical Greek syntax here) at a point different from that in the AV, rendering "Every scripture inspired of God is also profitable . . .," instead of AV "All scripture is given by inspiration of God and is profitable. . . ." This seemed to many to leave open the possibility of Scripture that is not inspired of God, and, since the question of inspiration was sensitive at the time, theological criticism was quickly voiced. Indeed, even though the RV retained the AV in a marginal reading, many were prepared to denounce the RV and to oppose its use on this ground alone, regardless of any merits it might have in other respects.

The marginal notes in the RV were very important and much labor went into them. The notes fall into four groups: (1) those signifying different readings; (2) those indicating correct meanings which English idiom cannot reproduce literally; (3) those offering an explanation demanded by the original; (4) those giving alternatives at debatable points. Marginal biblical references were prepared separately and for these permission was secured to use the references in F. H. A. Scrivener's Paragraph Bible of 1873. Under the leadership of W. F. Moulton so vast a body of material was collected that a revision and selection had to be made when a reference edition finally came out in 1898. Eventually in 1910 a special edition was published which incorporated all the materials that Moulton had gathered with the assiduous help of J. H. Moulton and A. W. Greenup. The thoroughness of the treatment may be seen from the references given under Mk. 10:19, offering no less than ten OT quotations and thirty-two verses for comparison.

At the very outset the British revisers had invited American scholars to join in their enterprise, and by 1872 two American committees were at work, one on the OT and the other on the NT. Each committee consisted of fifteen scholars, representing nine denominations in one case and eight in the other. P. Schaff was the presiding genius of the total effort, and the NT committee included such illustrious figures as E. Abbott and T. Dwight.

Soon it became evident that, because of important differences of approach, a joint revision would not be possible. Cooperation continued until 1881, and the RV of that date listed preferred American renderings in an appendix. The American committees then set their own course, although agreeing not to publish for fourteen years.

They put out their NT in 1897, which was followed in 1901 by the whole Bible under the title *Standard Version*. Over the years the American version has enjoyed greater success than its British counterpart, and in many circles it has been regarded as a superior production. It benefited, of course, from the critical and constructive reactions to its predecessor.

Comparison of the ASV with the ERV is interesting. Indeed, the ASV itself appended a lengthy list of particulars in which the two differed. A few illustrations of the differences may be given. Page headings are included in the ASV. The spelling of geographical names is more consistent. To some extent the ASV agrees with the ERV in using the same English word for the same Greek word, e.g., "straightway" in Mk. 1. In relation to the AV, "demons" is substituted for "devils" and the error in Lk. 23:15 is properly corrected. In Acts 17:22, where the AV has "too superstitious," the ERV offers "somewhat superstitious," but the ASV strikes out on its own with "very religious." This is more felicitous, although the delicate shade of meaning in the comparative is obscured.

An unfortunate misunderstanding temporarily soured relations between the two groups. In 1898 a new edition of the ERV was published which put the American preferences in the text and the British alternatives in an appendix. The change was perfectly legal but it seems the American revisers had not been told of it in advance, and they were annoyed when people received the impression, due in part to retail advertising, that this was in fact their edition. Under pressure the misleading title of *American Revised Version* was withdrawn, and once the full ASV came out the misunderstanding was quickly cleared up. From this time on the two revisions could stand on their own feet and secure their own followings without fear of confusion.

VIII. Other Nineteenth-Century Translations.–During the 19th cent. attention naturally focused on the more official cooperative ventures. It should not be imagined, however, that individuals did not also try their hand at fresh translation, especially when reproducing the text in commentaries. A brief survey of some of the more important independent revisions will thus be given.

The early decades of the century brought the Unitarians on the translation scene. T. Belsham published Paul's Epistles in English in 1822 and C. Eyre covered the same ground in 1832. S. Sharpe worked over the whole of the NT in a revision of the AV based on Griesbach's text, and his edition came out in 1840. He then did similar work in the OT, publishing the results in 1865 with the title *Hebrew Scriptures Translated*.

In the middle of the century, when the campaign for revision was gathering force, many commentators, e.g., R. C. Moberly and H. Alford, offered their own renderings of the works on which they wrote, which included John's Gospel, Romans, and 1 and 2 Corinthians. In addition, W. J. Conybeare made a new translation of all Paul's Epistles in his *Life of St. Paul,* which he wrote in collaboration with J. S. Howson (1851). In 1864 this translation was published independently with elaborate footnotes.

During the decade before work on the RV and ASV began, R. Young, who is best known for his invaluable *Analytical Concordance to the Bible* (1873) attempted singlehandedly a new version of Scripture. This was the *Literal Translation* (1862), in which a word-for-word rendering of the Hebrew and Greek texts was given. Young's odd handling of the Hebrew tenses prevented the work from securing wide approval, but it was not without merit and it helped to stimulate demand for an official revision.

Two other translators from this period call for notice. First is H. Alford, who not only offered new renderings in his commentaries but also published a scholarly revision of the NT in 1869. Alford regarded this purely as an interim report. He did not believe that one man could "fulfil the requisites for an accepted Version," but he hoped to stir the Church at large to action. In this hope, as has been seen, he was not disappointed.

Second was the founder of the Plymouth Brethren, J. N. Darby. In a remarkable tour de force Darby had first put the Bible into both German and French. He then turned to English and finished the NT and much of the OT. After his death in 1882 the OT was completed from his German and French versions. Darby, who was no mean scholar, supplied excellent critical notes, but was less successful in turning the originals into good and effective English. The second and revised edition of the NT came out in 1871 and the OT in 1890.

Other translators of the NT who deserve brief notice fall mostly into two groups. First are those who tried to achieve greater accuracy on the basis of the textual work of J. J. Griesbach, C. Tischendorff, and S. P. Tregelles. Among them are G. W. Braineld (1863), R. Ainslie (1869), and J. Davidson (1875). Then there are those whose aim was to put the NT into the speech of their time. A. Norton did this for the Gospels in his 1855 edition and L. A. Sawyer for the whole of the NT in his translation of 1858.

A work which found more extensive use, and even achieved a reprint in the second half of the 20th cent. (1959), was the so-called *Emphasized Bible* of J. Rotherham. The NT came out in 1872, and the OT was issued in successive volumes from 1897 to 1902, the whole then being gathered into a single volume. The first two editions of the Greek text were based on Tregelles, the third on Westcott and Hort. Like Young, Rotherham attempted a strictly literal translation. The new factor which gained his work attention, however, is the stress on pronunciation and emphasis. Speeches and poetic parallelisms are set out with indentations. OT refrains are distinguished by the use of italics. Rotherham also added an important expository introduction, and throughout the work he provided elaborate section heads, footnotes, references, and appendices.

The RV itself gave rise to two interesting experiments in the early years of the 20th century. The first was the *Interlinear Bible* (1907), which offers a ready comparison between the AV and the RV. As the preface explains, the large type in this edition represents agreement of the two versions. Where they differ, the renderings are printed in small type, the one above the other, the RV in the upper line and the AV in the lower. The RV notes are at the foot of the page with the AV notes below them.

The second experiment was *The Modern Readers' Bible . . . Printed in Modern Literary Form* (1914). Edited by R. G. Moulton, this won considerable acclaim and achieved wide use in colleges and universities. It presented the RV in such a way as to bring out the literary genres, e.g., poetry and drama. Introductions were provided for the various books, which included the Apocrypha, and extensive notes contributed to the value of the work. In fact, the edition was planned as a series of twenty-one volumes which began to appear already in 1895. When these were put together, they made up a single volume of over 1700 pages, of which 150 were devoted to introductions and 200 to notes. So long as the RV remained in common use, this work proved to be of real worth in many circles.

Two special editions of the RV itself call for brief notice. The *Parallel NT,* in quarto size, came out in 1882. This contained the AV of 1611 (with a few minor changes in spelling, capitalization, etc.) with its marginal notes in the left-hand column, and the RV of 1881 with its marginal notes in the right-hand column. Three years later, in 1885, a quarto edition of the whole of the RV was published in five volumes — four for the OT and one for the NT. This special edition featured large type and wide margins but the text itself differed in no way from that of the ordinary edition.

IX. Twentieth-Century Translations.–Apart from publications that made use of the RV, some new ventures in translations also appeared in the early years of the 20th century. The first of these, catching the moment, grandiosely styled itself the *Twentieth Century NT.* Its first section had in fact come out in 1898, but the complete text was published in 1901 and a second edition in 1904. Although the translators remained anonymous, the work had many useful characteristics and E. H. Robertson could even call it "one of the most careful translations ever undertaken" (*New Translations of the Bible* [1959], p. 53). Each book was given a detailed table of contents and a short introduction. Longer quotations from the OT were put in modern form and shorter ones in quotation marks, while allusions were indicated by references at the foot of the page. Once all the contributors had died, their names were finally disclosed in 1955; none of them had any established reputation as a scholar (*BJRL*, 38 [1955]).

To a similar category belongs the *Holy Bible in Modern English* by F. Fenton, for Fenton was a businessman who had received no special training in Greek or Hebrew. He brought out the first part, Romans, in 1882, the Epistles in 1884, the full NT in 1895, and the whole Bible in 1903. In spite of an unfortunate solecism at the very start in Gen. 1:1 ("By periods God created. . . ."), Fenton offered a creditable rendering, fully furnished with introductions and notes. He followed the order of the Hebrew Bible in the OT but an odd order of his own in the NT. The poetry of the OT he set out as such, and in some places he achieved excellent rhythms in English. Some of Paul's arguments were put in dialogue form, e.g., a discussion between Paul and "the Jew" in Rom. 3:1-18. The version enjoyed some success, being reprinted as late as 1944. It shows that a translation can make a useful contribution even though it be the work of a person with no formal training.

Far different is the case with the next important translation, the work of the distinguished classicist A. S. Way, who had already translated and edited a number of Greek and Roman classics. In a first edition Way confined himself to the *Letters of St. Paul to Seven Churches and Three Friends.* A second edition in 1906 added Hebrews and involved revision to the extent of five hundred changes. A 5th edition was called for within twenty years. A mark of this version is that some texts are printed as hymns; reasons for this are given by the author. The text is clear, vivid, illuminating, and at times exquisitely beautiful.

Precisely while Way was at work, the first of a great triad of NT translations was in preparation: that of R. F. Weymouth. Weymouth was also a gifted classical scholar. For many years he devoted his spare time to textual study which led to his *Resultant Greek Text.* This came out in the year of his retirement from teaching (1886), and he dedicated his remaining years to philological study and the attempt at a new rendering of the NT. As he stated in his preface to the *NT in Modern Speech,* this was based upon more than sixty years' study of both the Greek and the English languages. Weymouth's final illness prevented him from seeing the work through press, but it appeared in the year of his death (1903) and underwent a later revision by J. H. Robertson.

Weymouth broke relatively new ground by trying to use modern idiom instead of the hallowed language of the past. He achieved a high degree of success, as A. T. Robertson acknowledged when he called the work "a modern translation of a high order in dignified vernacular that is reasonably faithful to the Greek text" (*Sunday School Times* [1924], p. 424). Yet Weymouth himself modestly saw that he was merely a pioneer in this field. He believed—prophetically — that "some day the attempt will be renewed to produce a satisfactory English Bible . . . even altogether to supersede both the AV and the RV." It might be added that his version included hundreds of footnotes, although some of these are highly interpretative in nature.

The second of the three epoch-making versions followed ten years later when J. Moffatt produced his *New Translation of the NT* (1913), a work which took the English-speaking world by storm. Influenced by A. B. Bruce at Glasgow, Moffatt had already in 1901 published his *Historical NT,* which included a translation of his own. As a parish minister in Scotland, he continued his studies and brought out his *Intro. to the Literature of the NT* in 1911. This led him to an academic career at Oxford, Glasgow, and New York.

Moffatt's *New Translation* achieved swifter popularity than any previous individual rendering. Within a quarter of a century it went through seventy printings, and it came into extensive use in Bible classes, personal devotions, and the pulpit. Moffatt constantly revised the text up to the final revision of 1935. Some of his translations brought severe criticism, e.g., Mt. 1:16: "Joseph (to whom the virgin Mary was betrothed), the father of Jesus . . . ," or 1 Pet. 3:19: "Enoch also went and preached to the imprisoned spirits." But at other points he achieved such a happy blend of clarity and beauty that the appeal of his work is readily understood. Emboldened by his success in the NT, Moffatt turned next to the OT. After many years of labor he published this work in 1924 and the combined Moffatt Bible in 1926. The OT translation, however, hardly enjoyed the same success as its NT predecessor, although it is not without its valuable features.

The third notable translation of the early 20th cent. was *The NT: An American Translation,* by E. J. Goodspeed (1923). Like Moffatt, Goodspeed caused considerable controversy (surveyed in his *As I Remember* [1953]), but he also met with instant success. Not only did the version sell over a million copies in twenty-five years, but it was also printed in full in several newspapers in the autumn of 1923. Like Moffatt, Goodspeed moved on to the OT, but put this in the hands of J. M. P. Smith (1935). He then took up the Apocrypha as well (1939), so that he could finally call his work "the first complete English Bible ever translated throughout from the 'original tongues.'" An unusual feature in the Amer. Tr. is the complete elimination of footnotes. In defence of this he argued that Moffatt's textual notes "are generally of little use to the reader." But his most telling argument was not in terms of utility, but simply, "there were none in the original NT."

The only woman singly responsible for an extended translation of the Bible into English was H. B. Montgomery, an excellent Greek scholar and cautious translator. Her *Centenary Translation of the NT* (1924) was published by the American Baptist Publication Society of Philadelphia to mark its 100th anniversary. Each book was furnished with a short introduction, and popular titles were provided for each chapter. Thus Philippians has the four headings: (1) A Great Voice out of Prison; (2) Weaving the Fair Pattern of the Gospel; (3) Real Religion and Formalism; (4) Paul's Recipe for a Life of Victory. Subtitles were also supplied for sections within the chapters. The work had some appeal but could not compete with its Weymouth and Moffatt rivals in either excellence or popularity.

Another version of the NT, which began to appear in 1921 and was completed in nine parts in 1926, bears an extraordinarily lengthy title but is usually referred to by the first three words: *The Concordant Version*. The editor was A. E. Knoch, a self-taught student of Greek, who with assistants had spent many years preparing a concordance of the Greek language. His bulky translation consists of the Greek text in uncials, a sublinear translation in English, and on the opposite page an idiomatic rendering, all accompanied by an enormous mass of notes and adding up to some eight hundred pages. An unusual feature of the work is that Knoch rejects all existing Greek texts and offers "a totally new text" of his own. The work also shows some peculiarities in translation. Thus he displays an anti-trinitarian bias by always using the lower case for Spirit. "Eternal" in Rom. 16:26 is rendered "aeonic," while Rev. 1:18 reads: "the keys of death and the unseen." Finally, "to rouse" consistently replaces "to raise" in 1 Cor. 15.

The success achieved by Moffatt was not repeated until J. B. Phillips issued his *Letters to Young Churches* in 1947. The enthusiastic response to this up-to-date rendering led Phillips to continue with the *Gospels* in 1952, the *Young Church in Action* (Acts) in 1955, then Revelation, and finally the complete NT. Phillips was an English vicar, a fine linguist, whose translation work began in London during air-raid days when the young people with whom he worked could make neither head nor tail of the Epistles which he himself found so helpful and inspiring. He solved the problem by beginning again from the Greek, and when C. S. Lewis warmly received a sample of his work he continued with all the Epistles and eventually with the whole Bible. In this task, according to his own account, he deliberately tried to blot out all existing versions and all that he had read about translating and interpreting. He could then look at the Greek documents "as something I had never seen before," receive their impact afresh, and try to convey it in modern idiom. This meant, of course, that in many places Phillips had to paraphrase instead of giving a more literal rendering, and his work is exposed to obvious criticism in consequence. Nevertheless, he was not trying to provide a translation for scholars or more highly sophisticated Christians but to unlock the living message of the Bible for those who knew little about it and who received no great help from existing versions. At this level Phillips succeeded magnificently and in so doing posed the question whether, at least for certain purposes, the literal rendering is in fact the true translation. Certainly many passages which in previous versions did not carry a very vital message were now throbbing with life, e.g., 2 Cor. 6:11-13: "Oh, our dear friends, in Corinth, we are hiding nothing from you and our hearts are absolutely open to you. Any stiffness between us must be on your part, for we assure you there is none on ours. Do reward me (I talk to you as though you were my own children) with the same complete candour."

K. W. Wuest, for many years a teacher of Greek at the Moody Bible Institute, brought out the *Expanded Version of the NT* in three volumes (1956, 1958, and 1959). This rendering includes not only the customary notes but also definitions of terms and a bibliography. The text is printed single column in paragraph form, and verse numbers are given only at the beginning of the paragraphs. All the books have brief introductions. The distinctive feature of the work, however, is that by expansion the editor tries to bring out fully the various nuances of the Greek and at the same time to express the theological truth of Scripture. A high degree of verbosity and interpretation often results, as may be seen from Jn. 1:14: "And the Word, entering a new mode of existence, became flesh, and lived in a tent (His physical body) among us. And we gazed with attentive and careful regard and spiritual perception at His glory, a glory such as that of a uniquely begotten Son from the Father, full of grace and truth."

A not dissimilar version which has enjoyed wide circulation came out in 1958, namely, the *Amplified NT.* Many scholars helped to prepare this work under the editorial supervision of F. E. Siewert and the sponsorship of the Lockman Foundation. Behind this translation lies the sound principle that single English words are not exact equivalents of the Greek words. The translators concluded that at more important points alternatives should be offered in order to convey the fuller sense to the reader. Thus in Acts 16:31 Paul and Silas reply: "Believe in *and* on the Lord Jesus *Christ* — that is, give yourself up to Him, take yourself out of your own keeping and entrust yourself into His keeping, and you will be saved. . . ." Obviously this procedure has some advantages for students with no access to Greek, but it has obvious disadvantages too. Formally it makes the use of standard concordances difficult. Materially it may confuse, or even lead astray, those with no independent power of discrimination, and it involves an interpretative element in spite of the statement in the preface that "this version is free from private interpretation." The *Amplified OT* followed in two volumes in 1962 and 1964.

The year 1950 saw the entry of Jehovah's Witnesses, or the International Bible Student's Association, on the translation scene with the *New World Translation of the Christian Greek Scriptures Rendered from the Original Languages by the New World Bible Translation Committee.* This version rests largely on the Greek text of Westcott and Hort supplemented by that of Nestle. Footnotes, aids, and maps formed part of the enterprise. In 1953 the OT followed in five volumes on the basis of the Hebrew text of the 7th edition of R. Kittel's *Biblica Hebraica.* A single volume comprising both OT and NT came out in 1960. As might be expected, some unusual renderings characterize this translation. In 237 instances of what is normally given as "Lord" in the NT, "Jehovah" appears as a replacement. Jn. 1:1 has the strange statement: "In the beginning the Word was, and the Word was with God, and the Word was a god." Jn. 3:8b speaks of "everyone that has been born from the spirit." B. M. Metzger (*Theology Today,* 10 [1953], 65-85) may be consulted for a careful analysis of this interesting version.

X. Revised Standard Version and New English Bible.–In 1928 the copyright of the ASV, which had been taken out to protect it against pirated editions, came into the hands of the International Council of Religious Education, on which were representatives of the Churches of the United States and Canada. This Council proceeded to set up a committee to look into the need for revision and, acting on its report, voted in 1937 in favor of a revision which should "embody the best results of modern scholarship as to the meaning of the Scriptures, and express the meaning in English which is designed for use in public and private worship and preserves those qualities which have given to the KJV a supreme place in English literature." Essentially, then, the principle underlying the RV and ASV remained in force: what was being attempted was yet another revision, not a new translation.

To carry out the resolution, a committee of thirteen scholars — later increased to thirty-two — was appointed in 1937. Moffatt served as executive secretary up to 1944, and Goodspeed also served on the committee. One group devoted itself to the OT and another to the NT, but each group submitted its work to the other and changes had to have the agreement of two-thirds of the whole. In addition, the committee kept in touch with an advisory board made up of fifty representatives of the cooperating denominations. The NT appeared first in 1946 and the OT followed in 1952. In 1951, by a vote of the National Council of the Christian Churches, publication of the Revised Standard Version secured official approval. With some changes in the NT of 1946, the whole Bible came out in 1952 and the Apocrypha followed in 1957.

The main reasons for change, as explained in the preface, are the great advances made in the previous decades in textual scholarship, and more especially in linguistic studies. With respect to the OT, the discovery of writings in Semitic languages "has greatly enlarged our knowledge of the vocabulary and grammar of biblical Hebrew and Aramaic." Regarding the NT, "we now possess many more ancient manuscripts." While this was also true, of course, for those who worked on the RV and ASV, "they lacked the resources which discoveries within the past eighty years have afforded for understanding the vocabulary, grammar, and idioms of the Greek NT." With respect to the whole Bible, the preface reaffirms the need to replace AV terms and usages that have become obsolete or archaic, and expressions that have changed their meaning since 1611 so that "they no longer say what the KJV translators meant them to say." In favor of revision as opposed to a fresh start, the preface quotes the AV preface: "We never thought . . . to make a new translation, nor yet to make of a bad one a good one . . . but to make a good one better." The committee reaffirmed these principles in 1959, when it studied various suggestions and criticisms and made a few changes, for the most part minor in nature.

Some of the new features in the RSV quickly commended themselves. The general elimination of the outdated "thou," "thee," and "thy," and of the verb-endings in *-eth* and *-th* is a case in point, although the retention of "thou," etc., in address to God can lead to problems. Some would argue for a complete elimination so as to prevent address to God being set in an archaic world of its own, whereas others who approve of the exception think it should, in some cases at least, be used in relation to Christ too, e.g., in Mt. 16:16. The abandonment of "Jehovah," in direct rebuttal to the ASV also met with little resistance, since "Jehovah" is a late medieval form and "Yahweh," while probably correct, is not specifically indicated in the Masoretic text and has never had for the Christian public the attraction it seems to have for some scholars and clergy. In the updating of language the RSV achieves for the most part a fine blend of added clarity with the original beauty of the AV. Many passages (e.g., in Job or the prophets) which have in the AV only a magnificent obscurity, are illuminated in a new and impressive way with no stylistic loss. At the same time the revisers are modest or honest enough to confess that they cannot always fix the meaning with certainty (they indicate problem passages and alternatives in the notes) and that they did not always attain unanimity in their rendering.

1 Kings 10:28 might be adduced as one example among many in which previous versions, even including the RV and the ASV, gave little information, but upon which the RSV — in this instance combining new geographical knowledge with the LXX rendering — sheds new and clarifying light. When it comes to coins in the NT, the RSV retains clarity by refusing to be too modern. Thus it stays with "denarius" in Jn. 12:5 or simply has "a coin" in Mt. 22:19 for the Roman coins which have been put into pence in the AV, shillings in the ASV, and quarters and dollars (not always too accurately) in the American versions of Phillips. Inflation quickly robs the exchange equivalents of any credible meaning, whether they be given in the text or indicated in notes or tables. An example of return from the RV and ASV to the AV, which has given much satisfaction in conservative circles, occurs in 2 Tim. 3:16, where the RSV renders: "All scripture is inspired by God and profitable. . . ."

Against the many advantages of the RSV, which have won for it wide use and approval, must be set some criticisms. The criticism that Jn. 7:53–8:11 and Mk. 16:9-20 have been removed from the body of the text, along with some smaller verses or phrases, carries little weight, since these have dubious manuscript support. More serious is the dropping of the practice of indicating in some way (traditionally italics) words that have been added, for even though such additions are often essential for grammatical, stylistic, or even material reasons, readers who cannot refer to the original for themselves ought to know when and where they are made.

With respect to individual renderings the RSV committee has not been inflexible. "Consecrate" for "sanctify" met with much opposition in the first edition, and "sanctify" has been largely restored—although oddly enough "consecrate" is kept at Jn. 17:19 when "sanctify" returns at 17:17. Earlier editions offered Moffatt's rendering of Mt. 1:16 in a footnote, but later editions, recognizing the weakness of the "ancient authorities" he cited, eliminated this. Another interesting case where the RSV committee has reversed its decision is in 1 Tim. 3:2. Here the first rendering was "married only once." Obviously this imposed on bishops a definite prohibition of second marriage. But commentators have always thought that other possibilities were open, e.g., the forbidding of polygamy or, more likely against the background of the time, of second marriage after divorce. At any rate, the less definite "husband of one wife" has been restored in more recent editions.

In other instances, however, the translators have stayed with their choices in spite of heavy criticism from some quarters. "Letters" for "epistles" can hardly be regarded as a serious problem. The use of "young woman" for "virgin" in Isa. 7:14 has provoked more prolonged and vehement objection. It is argued that this entails contradiction between the OT passage and the fulfillment of it perceived in Mt. 1:23, as though the NT author had misunderstood or possibly even distorted the Hebrew text. Some conservatives, however, allow that "young woman" more accurately reflects the Hebrew term, and there does not have to be contradiction with the more precise sense of the Greek word demanded by the messianic fulfillment. Again, at Rom. 3:25 and 1 Jn. 4:10 the familiar "propitiation" has been replaced by "expiation." Fortunately, this does not carry with it the elimination of an objective presentation of the atonement. On the other hand, it seems to many that the reason for the change is far more theological than linguistic. On the literary plane, lovers of the AV are disturbed and irritated when what seems to be a pendantic or unnecessary change ruins a familiar and perhaps even proverbial saying, e.g., in Mt. 6:28: "They neither toil nor spin"; 1 Cor. 13:13: "So faith, hope, love abide"; and He. 12:16: "Who sold his birthright for a single meal." This difficulty can hardly be avoided, of course, when what is attempted is not a fresh translation but the revision of a superb literary achievement like the AV.

On this point the British Churches proved to be more radical and innovative. They entered the field later, but when they did they voted for the bolder and freer course of a completely fresh start. The initiative came this time from the Church of Scotland, which in 1946 adopted an overture recommending the translation of the Bible into present-day speech. As a result, delegations from the Anglican, Scottish, Methodist, Baptist, and Congregationalist Churches met in conference in 1947, accepted the idea of fresh work on the Bible, and endorsed the preference for a new translation instead of a further revision. At a second conference the same year, steps were taken to form a joint committee, which extended the representation and set up four panels to do the work, one each on the OT, NT, and Apocrypha, and one for the literary revision of the work of the other three. The noted scholar C. H. Dodd served as director of the total enterprise. After many years of work the NT came out in 1961, and the OT and Apocrypha in 1970. The publication of the NT was accompanied by a strong advertising campaign which led to the demand for at least ten printings in the first three years.

Two of the reasons advanced for the new venture were substantially the same as those given for the RSV. First, the introduction draws attention to the progress in textual criticism not only since 1611 but even since the RV of 1881. Second, the better knowledge of Hebrew and Greek, enriched especially by new Semitic documents and papyri materials found after 1881, made possible a better grasp of the meaning of the text at many points. The translators, of course, preserved a due sense of modesty in both areas. They did not claim a perfect text, being "well aware that their judgement is at best provisional"; nor did they pretend that there had been "any far-reaching change in our understanding of the Greek of the NT period," only "a better appreciation of the finer shades of idiom." Nevertheless, it was felt, not without reason, that better tools were now available to enable scholars to do a more accurate job.

On a third point the NEB disagreed sharply with the RSV. It argued that the 1881 revision was hampered by the provisos that as little as possible should be changed and that changes should be adapted to the style of the AV. No such restrictions governed the new venture. Instead, as the introduction says, the AV has become archaic at an ever more rapid pace and the demand is "consistently to use the idiom of contemporary English to convey the meaning of the Greek." Word order, syntax, and vocabulary all came under searching review, and it was laid down that fidelity to the original need not involve "such irregularities of grammar as were indeed natural enough to authors writing in the easy idiom of popular Hellenistic Greek, but less natural when turned into English."

In this respect the committee consciously adopted "a different theory and practice of translation," which tried to reproduce, not an English word for a Hebrew or Greek word, but a set of terms that would "carry over the meaning of the sentence as a whole." On this theory the RV goal of using the same English term for the same Hebrew or Greek obviously proved to be undesirable. At the same time, care was taken to distinguish the new practice from paraphrasing. Paraphrase introduces "something which is not there, to elucidate the meaning which is there." That paraphrase occurs cannot be denied. It is indeed, justified on the ground that "every intelligent translation is in a sense a paraphrase." The plea is made, however, that this version, if not literal, is a faithful one "so far as we could compass it."

Not unexpectedly, the translation ran into heavy criticism. Some of the objections have been on literary grounds. Many sentences sound rough or crude. Readers outside Britain find that certain idioms are more enigmatic than helpful. A few passages are hardly distinguished for syntactical purity. Obviously the work as a whole does not measure up to the literary stature of the AV and dependent versions. Yet one wonders whether literary excellence is essential to Scripture or whether it might just be a happy by-product when it occurs. Furthermore, some striking and illuminating phrases can be found, and in the narrative portions especially the NEB often seems to catch the vigor and freshness of the original which the more venerable AV occasionally misses — at least for modern readers.

The main problems, of course, relate to specific renderings and the changes, omissions, additions, and delimitations one finds in them. It should be noted that, like the RSV, the NEB does not indicate supplementary words; it also removes Jn. 7:53–8:11 and Mk. 16:9-20 from the body of the text, in the former case printing it in isolation from its traditional context. Looking only at the NT, one finds a challenging reading already at Mt. 1:23: "The virgin will conceive." Lk. 22:19b-20 has been dropped from the main text. Jn. 1:1 has in the third clause the infelicitous and debatable, "What God was, the Word was." In Jn. 4:20 three new words are supplied: "Jews," "temple," and "God," and in 7:21 "sabbath" is inserted. The handling of the term "righteousness" in the early chapters of Romans raises questions. In 1:17 "God's way of righting a wrong" replaces "righteousness," and in 3:6, 21f., etc., "justice" stages a return. The concept of expiation partly covers that of propitiation in Rom. 3:25, but the weaker "remedy" replaces it in 1 Jn. 2:2. In Gal. 2:5 a phrase has been added: "I was determined. . . ." What is demanded of the leader or bishop in 1 Tim. 3:2, and the deacon in v. 12, is that he be "faithful to his one wife," with two alternatives in the notes: "married to one wife"; "married only once." Two interesting points arise at the important verses Jn. 3:16 and 2 Tim. 3:16. In the former "loved the world so much" restricts the meaning of "so," which might also mean "in such a way." In the latter "every inspired scripture" continues the ambiguity of the RV; moreover, all reference to God is eliminated, which is hard to understand in the light of the underlying Greek term. Page headings have been supplied for this version, and some of these raise questions. Thus in the NT four main subdivisions are helpfully suggested: The Gospel; Acts; Letters; and Revelation. But this being so, does it not cause confusion to entitle the first part of Romans (1–8) "the Gospel according to Paul"?

Beyond individual questions, perhaps the main difficulty with the NEB is that it tries to do too many things at once without excelling at any of them. Thus it seeks to be both scholarly and popular, and yet often the idiomatic English blunts the rendering academically without quite succeeding as the language of the people. Again, the desire to give the work sufficient dignity for use in public reading tends to be at odds with the aim of reaching people who will seldom if ever be in the pew. Thus the NEB finds itself caught in the middle. It cannot compete with the RSV liturgically nor with authentically popular versions evangelistically. Yet these drawbacks must not be exaggerated. The NEB undoubtedly has a solid scholarly base. It frequently achieves commendable idiomatic clarity. It has not proved unsuitable for use in public worship. It certainly demonstrates in practice that modern translators need not be held under the tyranny of the AV any more than the Reformers were under that of the Vulgate. Moreover, it raises the critical question that lies at the center of modern debate in this area, namely, that of the relation between literalness and fidelity in the translation of the Bible into other tongues.

XI. Roman Catholic and Jewish Versions.–The idea that the Roman Catholic Church in Britain and America has made little contribution to Bible translation apart from the Douay version has no substance. In fact many new versions came out in the first decades of the 19th cent.; those of Coyne in 1811, of Haydock in 1811-1814, of Syers in 1813, and of Gibson in 1816-1817, not to speak of renderings of the NT alone. Then the Roman Catholic Emancipation Act of 1829 released a fresh translation wave of which G. MacGregor says that "the output is so prolific and the variety of renderings so staggering that it would require immense research and several volumes to give a full bibliographical account of the astonishing story" (p. 206).

In the middle of the century N.P.S. Cardinal Wiseman published his own edition in 1847. J. C. Cardinal Newman came under pressure to try his hand but declined on the strange ground that the Douay-Challoner version met all requirements. In America F. P. Kenrick published a translation of the NT for which he used the Vulgate but compared it constantly with the original Greek. Entitled *The Four Gospels*, etc. (1849) this carried so many critical and explanatory notes that it added up to a large volume. The OT came out in 1860.

In the latter part of the 19th and the first half of the 20th cent. more versions followed. Among the more important is *Westminster Version* by the Jesuit C. Lattey and many American and British assistants. The *Confraternity Edition*, published in 1941, and used extensively by English-speaking Roman Catholics in World War II, also deserves mention. This translation received its name from its sponsorship by the Episcopal Committee of the Confraternity of Christian Doctrine. E. P. Arbez edited it, and it was approved by the Biblical Commission and scholars of the Catholic Biblical Association. Many reprintings were required.

Perhaps the most interesting and significant Roman Catholic version of the 20th cent., at least by an individual, is that of the gifted writer and scholar R. Knox. After making his name as the author of *Loose Stones* and then as Roman Catholic chaplain at Oxford, Knox in 1938 was granted official authorization to prepare a new translation of the NT from the Clementine Vulgate, i.e., the Latin Bible approved by Clement VIII in 1592. Announcement of the authorization in 1939 roused vociferous protest, but support from the hierarchy enabled Knox to press on with the task. He finished the NT in 1942, although for various reasons publication was delayed until 1949. In the meantime Knox learned Hebrew and on his own volition began the translation of the OT, which also came out in 1949. Knox found the work demanding; he devoted no less than nine months full time to the Psalms. But he also found it exciting, so much so that he regarded the translation as the one great work of his life. His reward came when the work sold far beyond expectations and became the only individual translation at this period to carry the imprimatur of the hierarchy.

Attention may be drawn to two points of interest in this rendering. The first is in the OT. Here in Ps. 119 Knox makes a valiant effort to reproduce in English the alphabetical structure of the Hebrew. Thus in the fourth section each of the eight verses of the English begins with a word whose initial letter is "d": Deep, Deign, Direct, Despair, Deliver, Deity, Disappoint, and Do. The first verse of the section (v. 25) runs: "Deep lies my soul in the dust, restore life to me as thou hast promised." Most translations make no attempt at all to preserve this ACROSTIC in English apart perhaps from indicating the Hebrew letters.

The second point of interest is in the NT. From the Reformation period to modern times Roman Catholics have argued strenuously that Gk. *metanoéō*, which in verb and noun form occurs fifty-eight times in the NT, should be rendered "do penance" ("penance"), not "repent" ("repentance"). Indeed, T. More castigated Tyndale severely for his ignorance or falsification on this and similar matters. Knox, however, allows his scholarship to override age-old prejudice and accepts "repent" and "repentance" in the vast majority of instances (forty-nine out of fifty-eight). Even where this is not used he has such varied alternatives as "relent" in Mt. 21:29, 32, "full of remorse" in Mt. 27:3, "be sorry" in Lk. 17:3f., "feel sorry" in 2 Cor. 7:8, "change of heart" in 2 Cor. 7:10 and He. 6:1, and "second chance" ("no second chance was given him") in He. 12:17. "Do penance" remains only twice, in Mt. 12:41 and Lk. 11:32. Here, then, the Roman Catholic Knox provides Tyndale with tardy vindication against the vituperation of More and in so doing helps to forward both a new use of the Bible and also a more fruitful ecumenical approach to its translation and dissemination.

A point not always remembered is that English-speaking Jews also have a stake in translations of the major part of the Bible, namely, the OT. Hence their renderings should also be taken into account. I. Leeser, who introduced preaching in English into American synagogues and who founded the first Jewish Congregational Sunday School to have many years of continuous existence, proved to be the pioneer in OT translation too. His English version of the OT came out in Philadelphia in 1853. He based it on the AV but also drew heavily on German versions. Some of his renderings are designed to refute the christological interpretation of key OT passages. For many decades Leeser's work remained the most widely accepted Jewish rendering of the OT in English, and synagogues in both the United States and Great Britain used it extensively.

In 1892 the Jewish Publication Society proposed a thorough revision of the Leeser version. As the work proceeded, however, it was felt that a completely new translation was needed. To this end a committee was appointed with the illustrious scholar M. Jastrow as its president. The first part of the new version to appear was Psalms in 1903. On Jastrow's death a committee of seven was set up to carry on the work. M. L. Margolis, a noted Hebrew expert who became editor of *JBL* (1914-1921) and *JAOS* (1922-1932), took over the post of editor-in-chief. The whole of the OT had come out by 1917 and it was so well received that by 1950 it had enjoyed twenty-four reprintings and almost half a million copies had been sold.

Some Jews, of course, have given themselves to NT study too, among them H. J. Schonfield, who used his specialized knowledge of the NT background in an independent translation which he calls *The Authentic NT* (1955). The title seems to promise more than is offered, for Schonfield is not demonstrating that either the texts used in previous versions or the actual renderings have been inauthentic. In fact, Schonfield has little to add in these areas, although he achieves a high level of competence in his translation. The extra element, if any, derives from his greater closeness to the Jewishness of the NT and its authors. This enables him to bring out its true flavor a little better than any Gentiles, even Christian Gentiles, can do.

XII. Recent Translations.–The more official RSV and NEB ventures were accompanied and have been followed by a great number of other translation attempts during the middle and later parts of the 20th century. These tend to conform to well-defined patterns. Some, for example, aim primarily at revision of the AV, the ASV, or the RV, often in a certain conscious rivalry with the RSV. Others try to strike out in new directions with the principal aim of making Scripture more understandable, more graphic, and perhaps more immediately appealing to the new age. Usually one finds a certain combination of the attempt to be more accurate on the one side and more contemporary on the other. A new feature is the readiness of different national or denominational groups to work together. Roman Catholics since Vatican II have done much to stimulate this cooperativeness and they showed their good intentions by putting out a special edition of the RSV for the use of Roman Catholic readers. The tension between more literal translation and the urge to modernize has also produced important discussion of what translation involves.

Among revisions of the ASV a first undertaking to call for notice is the Berkeley or Verkuyl Version. The first part of this came out in Berkeley in 1945, and the whole Bible was published in 1959. G. Verkuyl, the general editor, translated the NT. For the OT he enlisted the aid of several conservative scholars, although exercising tight editorial control. Not unjustly the work might be called the conservative alternative to the RSV.

It has many interesting features. Italics for supplementary words have been abandoned. Quotation marks are used in direct speech except when God speaks, for He, of course, is the speaker in and through all Scripture. In address to God "thou" is still used, but everywhere else "you." In the case of Christ we find a consistent but confusing pattern. Capitalization of pronouns referring to God represents a new departure. Capitals in general show which parts of the OT are taken messianically. Mostly Verkuyl follows the AV here, but surprisingly he does not adopt a typological understanding of Canticles. The assistant translators apparently followed their own judgment regarding the name of God in the OT, for "Yahweh," "Jehovah," and "the LORD" all occur.

The Berkeley Version provides in the main a sound and straightforward translation but it has perhaps a greater share of odd phrases and inappropriate idioms than most Bibles. F. F. Bruce in his *English Bible* (p. 223) points to "pattern after me" in 1 Cor. 1:11, "the left-overs shall be saved" in Rom. 9:27, "my facesaver and my God" in Ps. 42, and "my insides" in Jer. 4:19, while the notes have in Gen. 3:12 the tasteless slang phrase "passing the buck."

Materially the notes vary in quality. Some provide helpful information while others are moral comments. The dating of events after Gen. 14 has naturally caused controversy, especially when it comes to a highly debatable date for the Exodus. Opposition has also been aroused by the correction of the Hebrew text in 1 K. 10:28 on the ground that Egypt "was not a producer of horses." The attempt to provide equivalent values for Bible coins has fallen victim to accelerating inflation. Some useful corrections and revisions may be found in the 1970 edition.

Another alternative to the RSV has been advanced in the form of the New American Standard Version which came out in its entirety in 1963. The main criticism which has been brought against this more conservative revision of the ASV is that it is too pedantic and that it shows arbitrariness in its handling of the Greek tenses. Yet it has excellent qualities too. It aims at close fidelity to the originals. It has a keen sense of the need for grammatical correctness. Where necessary it keeps to the time-honored custom of offering alternatives in the margin. It stays with the use of italics to indicate necessary additions. At the same time it aims at clear contemporary language which will make Scripture more readily comprehensible and also dispel the idea that the Bible is an old-fashioned book. Many readers who not unjustly admired and profited from the ASV feel that this is its true modern successor rather than the much more radically altered RSV.

A notable new version which has tried to combine scholarship with simplicity and even at times a graphic or dramatic quality is the so-called *Jerusalem Bible* of the Roman Catholic Church. Edited by A. Jones, the first part of this came out in 1956, the complete Bible following in 1966. It was published in Liverpool and secured the approval of Cardinal Heenan, the leader of English Roman Catholics.

The name is derived from the fact that the French *Bible de Jérusalem,* the work of the Dominican School in Jerusalem, forms an important basis. At times the first draft was little more than a translation of the French version, although this was then checked by the originals. Sometimes, however, the procedure was reversed with translation done directly from the originals in consultation with the French. In the OT "Yahweh" is used as the divine name, but for the most part the version uses good idiomatic English as it is employed today. While this involves some freedom at the word level, this version does not give translation the more extended sense it bears in some circles, since it rejects any attempted updating of symbols and metaphors. Good supplementary materials are provided, particularly an index of biblical themes.

Among examples of cooperative work, which naturally includes the RSV and the NEB, the New International Version calls for notice. This interdenominational venture was set in motion by the New York Bible Society and drew on scholars of different countries from a wide range of churches apart from the Roman Catholic and Greek Orthodox. Teams were assembled for each book and the procedure was for the team to make a draft and then submit it successively to three editorial committees, the intermediate, the general, and then the final committee of translation. Literary consultants were also employed. The translation of the NT came out in 1973, and that of the OT in 1978. The NT follows an eclectic text. It does away with archaisms such as "thou" and "thee." Alternative renderings are provided in the notes. The thrust of the work is conservative in the theological sense but not at the expense of contemporaneity of language. In the evangelical world in particular this version has been highly rated and warmly received.

The most ambitious cooperative undertaking, however, is undoubtedly the *Anchor Bible*. Under the initial leadership of W. F. Albright and D. N. Freedman, this employs scholars of different nationalities and even of different faiths, since Jews are included as well as Protestants and Roman Catholics. The *Anchor Bible,* which is not rushing on to the NT first, offers not just a new and exact translation but also some extended exposition and an attempted reconstruction of the historical setting of the books which will, it is hoped, enhance the understanding and appreciation of the general reader. Genesis came out first in 1964 and contained some challenging readings. Thus the very first verse, following Moffatt, replaces the traditional "In the beginning God . . ." with "When God set about to create. . . ." Again, in v. 2 the familiar "And the Spirit of God . . ." yields to "Only an awesome wind swept over the water," while in v. 26 "I will make man" replaces "Let us make man." The expository section, of course, explains and supports changes of this kind, although the general reader, who does not find similar material in more common versions, may well be left in the confusion of a little knowledge if he is not prepared for wider investigation. When completed the *Anchor Bible* promises to be an important contribution to Bible translation and study, although it is unlikely to crowd out more established versions in either individual or public use.

Another group of modern versions focuses primarily on

increasing the clarity or effectiveness of the text for modern readers. In this regard the Penguin edition of the *Four Gospels* by E. V. Rieu (1952) and the *Acts of the Apostles* by C. H. Rieu (1957) forms an interesting point of departure, for apart from the merits of the rendering E. V. Rieu was an eminent classical scholar who devoted much thought to the aims and methods of translation. He helped to formulate the theory, found already in Moffatt, that beyond clarity and modernity of language a good translation should achieve an equivalent effect to that of the original. In some cases this might extend no little latitude in wording. Phillips, of course, operated on much the same principle, although it is interesting that in a famous radio discussion Rieu and Phillips disagreed a great deal on what an equivalent effect might be in specific instances. Thus Rieu did not like Phillips' rendering in Jn. 1:14, "The Expression of God became a human being," but Phillips thought that Rieu failed to make the right impact, especially in Matthew, by putting the observations on the fulfillment of OT prophecy in footnotes, since they are an integral part of the writer's message. The law of equivalent effect obviously leaves a good deal of play for the translator's subjective judgment on what the authors intended, how it struck the original readers, and how and to what readers can and should react today.

Among versions which are more concerned about simplicity an interesting example in E. Vernon's *Gospel of St. Mark* (1951). Vernon was trying here to embody his conviction that a proper translation of Scripture should not use any words that an average child of twelve could not understand. The *Basic English Bible* (NT 1940, whole Bible 1949) attempts something of the same. Accepting C. K. Ogden's list of 850 basic English words, along with 150 additional words permitted for and demanded by the project, it passes on the total message of the Bible in a vocabulary which is not beyond the grasp of readers with only a rudimentary knowledge of the language. The disadvantages of this type of restriction need not be labored, but under the able leadership of S. H. Hooke many of them were turned into at least partial assets as the translators necessarily discarded existing versions, worked from the originals, and considered every word and sentence with the utmost care in order to make the best possible use of their limited resources.

Shortly after the *Basic English Bible* came out in 1949, a *Plain English NT* followed (1952). Plain English, according to a London report of 1936, consists of 1500 "fundamental and common words" in ordinary use. The *Plain English Version* is the work of C. R. Williams, who had experience teaching English in India and Ghana, and who wished specifically to provide a copy of the NT in English for educated foreigners, while perhaps helping at the same time ordinary English readers of very limited vocabulary. Williams had to add some special words but he carefully explained the meaning of these in a glossary. Having at its disposal a greater range of English words than the *Basic English Bible,* his version enjoys many obvious advantages, although at many points *Basic English* offers a better rendering.

Incidentally another Williams, C. B., had much earlier, in 1937, published a similar sounding version, *The NT in the Language of the People*. Here, however, the main aim was to bring out the nuances of the Greek, especially the tenses, and this does not always produce sentences of a type that most people would speak. The version has, however, some effective renderings of individual statements and passages. The *NT in the Language of Today* is another work with much the same title. Produced by the Lutheran W. F. Beck, this strikes a good balance between fidelity to the original and modernity of expression.

The translation of Moffatt, and even more so the work of Phillips, raised with new acuteness the question whether what is in part a paraphrase might not be just as good a translation as, and possibly even a better one than, a more literal rendering. Experience in missionary translation helped to pinpoint the issue. Should the translator aim at a formal equivalent or at an effective or "dynamic equivalent" in which the content is forcefully presented even though individual words and even metaphors may be changed? On the latter view a translation is more than the reproduction in another tongue of the same terms and phrases as the original. It involves "translation" into another age and culture in order that what the original means and signifies for the writer and his first readers may make an equivalent impact on those who now read his work in a completely different time and setting.

Obviously the issue has a greater urgency among peoples who have no history of influence by Hebraic and Greek cultures. Yet it also has relevance to the evangelistic transmission of the biblical message to those in the Western world who have had little or no grounding in Christianity and its traditional idioms. Obviously, effective transmission in these circumstances entails the use of contemporary modes of thought and speech, as all modern versions allow. Does it also presuppose that, at least for certain purposes, careful paraphrase is the most authentic translation?

An example of the paraphrase translation is *Good News for Modern Man,* put out by the American Bible Society in 1966 with the subtitle *The NT in Today's English Version*. Very explicitly this version aims at those with little Christian background. Even the title is paraphrased to put across what the NT is all about. Line drawings are also provided as visual aids. Niceties of language and grammar are not allowed to stand in the way of simplicity, vigor, and relevance. The work is inexpensive and is admittedly introductory. There is even a preface showing in simple terms what the NT is. A word list explains more difficult technical terms and identifies some of the people and places mentioned in the text. An index enables the reader quickly to locate "the more important subjects, persons, places, and events in the NT." Christians moving on to fuller knowledge will need more literal versions, but for those who are only just finding their way to the Bible, or who are beginners in the faith, a version of this type serves a useful and necessary function. The OT was added in 1976 and the completed Bible bears the title *Today's English Version or The Good News Bible*.

The *Living Bible Paraphrased* (1972) has much the same goal as *Today's English Version*. K. Taylor, the translator, began this venture simply by paraphrasing the ASV for his own children. As the work proceeded and expanded, he enlisted the aid of scholars to check his version against the original and of literary consultants to examine and improve the style. Unable to find a publisher, Taylor founded his own publishing house to issue the NT and later the whole Bible. The work proved to be an astonishing success. After only three years some eighteen million copies in various editions had been sold and the *Living Bible* had captured almost half the total Bible sales in the crowded U.S. market.

The *Living Bible Paraphrased* obviously serves the purpose for which it was designed. It offers a translation, or rather, as Taylor freely admits in the preface, a paraphrase, which can be read easily by people of all ages and backgrounds. It has a particular sphere of mission among children and recent converts but even more so among those outside the churches who are easily discouraged even by contemporary versions, let alone the more formal AV, ASV, or RSV. In this sense the *Living Bible* might be regarded as predominantly a form of the spoken word rather than, in the stricter sense, the written word. It is the Bible as living word of proclamation. Proclamation is supremely the sphere of dynamic as distinct from formal equivalence.

Yet the *Living Bible* also illustrates the problems which inhere in paraphrase and which challenge the view that dynamic equivalence means authentic translation. Taylor himself realizes these problems, for in his preface he asks for help and has now appointed a Revisions Committee. If one leaves aside occasional stylistic weaknesses, these problems are basically threefold.

First, a large area of subjective judgment opens up when the translator adopts the double rule (1) of going by what he thinks the author means to say rather than precisely by what he does say, and (2) of deciding how best what he means to say can make its impact on readers of another age and language. Second, the possibility of exegetical mistakes and theological intrusions, which is present in all translation, increases rapidly with the increase of elasticity in rendering. The *Living Bible* has received severe criticism at this level, especially where passages which might be open to differing theological interpretations have been definitely, if unintentionally, steered in the direction of the translator's own position. Here the translator gets between author and reader instead of mediating between them. Third, the focus on the Bible as spoken word, while undeniably justifiable, can in this form impede the functioning of the Bible as a normative written word. Ultimately, of course, only the Hebrew and Greek originals can fulfill this function but for the vast majority of Christians versions have to serve as a working norm. If, however, translations take considerable liberties with the originals, introducing subjective judgments, dubious exegesis, and theological interpretation, the rule of faith and practice undergoes a relativization which impairs and finally destroys its true use.

The *Living Bible,* with its staggering popularity and circulation, might prove to be a critical point in the history of English versions. If the Bible as written word comes to be absorbed in the Bible as spoken word, as naive enthusiasm for dynamic equivalence might entail, then the churches can be betrayed into the paradox of becoming both more and less biblical at one and the same time. But there are alternatives. A better balance might be struck between literal and dynamic translation; Taylor himself seems to be seeking it. Again, a clear distinction between translation and paraphrase might be perceived, upheld, and explicitly stated; readers who are introduced to the Bible by paraphrase can be specifically referred to more literal versions for teaching the Christian faith and life. To avoid confusion, some contribution of the two alternatives might well prove to be the best option. With this safeguard, ventures like the *Living Bible* unquestionably have an important and constructive role to play in the ongoing provision of versions of the Bible in English.

Bibliography.–D. M. Beegle, *God's Word into English* (1960); F. F. Bruce, *The English Bible: A History of Translations* (1961); C. C. Butterworth, *Literary Lineage of the KJV* (1941); M. Deanesly, *Story of the Lollard Bible* (1951); H. Grierson, *English Bible* (1943) P. Levi, *The English Bible 1534 to 1850* (1974); G. MacGregor, *Literary History of the Bible* (1968); W. F. Moulton, ed., *History of the English Bible* (1911); J. F. Mozley, *William Tyndale* (1937); *Coverdale and His Bibles* (1953); E. A. Nida and C. R. Taber, *Theory and Practice of Translation* (1969); A. W. Pollard, *Records of the English Bible* (1911); H. Pope, *English Versions of the Bible* (1952); H. W. Robinson, ed., *Bible in Its Ancient and English Versions* (1940); B. F. Westcott, ed., *General View of the English Bible* (1927).

W. M. SMITH G. W. BROMILEY

ENGRAVING. *See* CARVING; CRAFTS.

EN-HADDAH en-had'ə [Heb. *ʿên-ḥaddâ*; Gk. B *Aimarek,* A *Ēnadda*]. One of the cities of Issachar (Josh. 19:21) mentioned with Remeth (*see* JARMUTH **2**). The exact site is unknown, but it is probably to be identified with el-Hadetheh, located about 10 km. (6 mi.) E of Mt. Tabor.

EN-HAKKORE en-hak'ə-rē [Heb. *ʿên haqqōrē*–'spring of the partridge' (or 'of the one who calls'; cf. LXX, Gk. *pēgḗ toú epikalouménou*)] (Jgs. 15:19). A spring at Lehi, miraculously provided by the Lord when Samson called upon him (hence the LXX translation). The site is unknown.

EN-HAZOR en-hā'zôr [Heb. *ʿên ḥāṣôr*; Gk. *pēgḗ Asor*]. A fortified city in Naphtali (Josh. 19:37). The site is usually identified as Khirbet Haṣîreh, on the slopes W of Kedesh near Ḥazzûr. Other geographers, however, attempt no identification.

ENJOIN [Heb. hiphil of *ʿûḏ*] (Dt. 32:46; Zec. 3:6); AV TESTIFY, PROTEST; NEB "solemnly give," "give . . . this solemn charge"; [piel of *qûm*] (Est. 9:21,31); AV PUNISH, STABLISH; NEB BIND, PRESCRIBE; [*pāqaḏ*] (Zeph. 3:7); AV PUNISH; NEB INSTRUCTIONS; [Gk. *kōlýō*] (1 Tim. 4:3); AV, NEB, FORBID. Its usual sense is "impose something," as a command, a charge, or a direction. In all the RSV references the matter enjoined is of a serious nature, demanding immediate attention and implicit observance. In some instances where the RSV renders "command," the AV and NEB have "enjoin" (for Gk. *epitássō,* Philem. 8, AV; *entéllō,* He. 9:20, AV, NEB).

ENJOY; ENJOYMENT [Heb. *rāṣâ*] (Lev. 26:34,43; 2 Ch. 36:21; Job 14:6); AV also ACCOMPLISH; NEB also "ran the full term," "counting the hours"; [*ḥālal*] (Dt. 20:6; Jer. 31:5); AV EAT; NEB USE, DEFILE; [*ʾāḵal*] (Dt. 20:14; Neh. 9:36; Eccl. 5:19 [MT 18]; 6:2; Jer. 2:7); AV EAT; NEB also EAT; [*rāʾâ*] (Ps. 34:12 [MT 13]; Eccl. 2:1,24; 6:6; 9:9); AV also SEE, BE FED; NEB also FIND, PROSPER; [*ʿāśâ ṭôḇ*] (Ps. 37:3; Eccl. 3:12); AV DO GOOD; NEB "live the best life he can"; [*śāmē(a)ḥ*] (Eccl. 3:22; 5:19 [MT 18]; 8:15); AV REJOICE, BE MERRY; NEB also REJOICE; [*śāḇaʿ*] (Eccl. 6:3); AV BE FILLED; NEB GET SATISFACTION FROM; [*bālâ*] (Isa. 65:22); [*ʿālas*] (Job 20:18); AV REJOICE; NEB "spew up undigested"; [*ḥûš*] (Eccl. 2:25); AV "hasten [to eat]"; NEB "be anxious"; [*śimḥâ*] (Eccl. 5:20 [MT 19]; 8:15; 9:7); AV MIRTH, JOY; [Gk. *tyncháno̅*] (Acts 24:2); [*apólausis*] (1 Tim. 6:17; He. 11:25); [*empímplēmi*–'have one's fill'; cf. Bauer, p. 255] (Rom. 15:24); AV BE FILLED. Heb. *rāʾâ* frequently occurs idiomatically with *ṭôḇ* and means, literally, "see (or seeing) good" (Ps. 34:12; Eccl. 2:1,24; 5:18 [MT 17]; cf. 6:6). Recent translations of Heb. *ḥûš* (Eccl. 2:25), implying "feel" or "perceive," thus "enjoy (with the senses)," reflect parallels in Aramaic, later Hebrew, and Ethiopic. Elsewhere the verb (or a similar form from a different root) is translated "hasten" (cf. AV; BDB, pp. 301f.).

Among those things from which one might take pleasure or satisfaction are the fruit and other "good gifts" of the Promised Land (Dt. 20:6; Neh. 9:36; Jer. 2:7; 31:5), wealth and possessions (Eccl. 5:19), the spoils of war (Dt. 20:14), work (Eccl. 3:22; Isa. 65:22) and the products of one's labors (Eccl. 2:21), the company of others (Rom. 15:24), or life in general ("enjoy oneself," Eccl. 2:1; 3:22; 8:15). One might also enjoy the "fleeting pleasures of sin" (He. 11:25).

Enjoyment might also entail possessing, or experiencing

with satisfaction, sabbaths (Lev. 26:34, 43; 2 Ch. 36:21), one's lifetime ("his day," Job 14:6), peace (Acts 24:2), security (Ps. 37:3), honor (Eccl. 6:2), God's favor (Prov. 14:9), and the good things of life (Ps. 34:12; Eccl. 6:7; 1 Tim. 6:17).

The references to "enjoyment" in Job and Ecclesiastes contrast the attitudes of the sinner and the righteous man, primarily toward their labors (Job 20:18; Eccl. 2:24f.; 5:18f.). Zophar says that the wicked man's pleasure turns bitter in his mouth (Job 20:12-15) and he will derive no pleasure from the fruits of his labor (v. 18). By contrast, the Preacher says that the righteous one may find enjoyment in his work, his food, or his life as a whole, because all are gifts from God.

In Lev. 26:34, 43; 2 Ch. 36:21, Heb. *rāṣâ* (lit. "make acceptable," "satisfy") means to pay off a debt (cf. RSV mg.), indicating that the sabbath dues of the subject land are to be paid off even while the people of Israel are in exile.

To enjoy the fruits of a vineyard (Dt. 20:6; Jer. 31:5) is to defile or profane it by rendering it "common" (Heb. *ḥālal*, lit. "pollute"; cf. BDB, p. 320).

See also JOY; PLEASURE. A. C. M.

ENLARGE [Heb. hiphil of *rāḥaḇ* (Ex. 34:24; Dt. 12:20; 19:8; 33:20; Isa. 5:14; 54:2; Am. 1:13), hiphil of *pāṯâ* (Gen. 9:27), *šāṭaḥ*–'spread out' (Job 12:23), piel of *rāḥaq* (Isa. 26:15), hiphil of *rāḇâ* (1 Ch. 4:10), *qāraʿ* (Jer. 4:30); Gk. *megalýnō* (2 Cor. 10:15)]; AV also "remove" (Isa. 26:15), "rent" (Jer. 4:30); NEB also EXTEND, WIDE, GREED FOR (Am. 1:13), etc.

As used by the RSV, "enlarge" usually refers to territorial expansion by a family (e.g., Dt. 33:20; 1 Ch. 4:10; Gen. 9:27, where *yapt* is a play on the name Japheth, Heb. *yepeṯ*) or a nation. God's covenant with Israel included the promise of extended borders (Ex. 34:24; Dt. 12:20; 19:8; cf. Ex. 23:27-31), and the prophet Isaiah looked forward to a time after the Exile when Israel's borders would once again be extended (Isa. 26:15; 54:2f.). But to describe the severity of God's judgment against Judah's wickedness, Isaiah pictured Sheol as a ravenous beast with gaping mouth (5:14). Amos warned that judgment would fall upon the Ammonites for the atrocities they committed while expanding their territory at Israel's expense (1:13). Job testified that God is omnipotent; it is He who enlarges some nations and leads others into captivity (12:23). In the NT "enlarge" appears only once, of the expansion of Paul's field of missionary activity (2 Cor. 10:15).

See also BORDER. N. J. O.

ENLIGHTENED [Gk. *epiginṓskō*] (Rom. 10:2); AV "according to knowledge"; NEB INFORMED; [*phōtízō*] (Eph. 1:18; He. 6:4; 10:32); AV also ILLUMINATED; NEB also ILLUMINED; **ENLIGHTENING** [Heb. *'ôr*] (Ps. 19:8 [MT 9]); NEB "shines clear"; **ENLIGHTENMENT** [Heb. *daʿaṯ*] (Isa. 40:14); AV "taught him knowledge"; NEB "gain discernment"; **ENLIGHTENS** [Gk. *phōtízō*] (Jn. 1:9); AV LIGHTETH.

Paul writes of those whose zeal for God is not "enlightened" in Rom. 10:2. The word *epiginṓskō* is used here to refer to a specifically theological knowledge of God, a higher and more perfect knowledge that recognizes the knowledge of God and of Christ to be the perfection of knowledge.

In Ephesians and Hebrews the term *phōtízō* is translated "enlightened." This refers to the knowledge of the truth, which, when received into their own lives (cf. Isa. 40:14), "enlightens" people by giving them life (Jn. 1:9, 4). This "illumination" in the early Christian communities took place in baptism, which was "the moment at which the individual passed out of the kingdom of darkness into the realm of light and hence the baptized were spoken of as 'the enlightened' [*phōtísthentes*, He. 6:4; 10:32; cf. Eph. 1:18]" (Richardson, pp. 338, 348). Justin Martyr (*Apol.* i.61; cf. *Dial.* 39.2) saw this illumination as the "illumination of the mind," though it should be noted that in the NT the word is not directly applied to baptism.

Bibliography.–R. Bultmann, *Theology of the NT*, I (Eng. tr. 1951), 143; *ERE*, VIII, 54f.; A. Richardson, *Intro. to the Theology of the NT* (1958); S. H. Turner, comm. on Hebrews (1852), pp. 72ff.

D. K. MCKIM

ENLIL en'lil. *See* RELIGIONS OF THE BIBLICAL WORLD: ASSYRIA AND BABYLONIA I, II.

EN-MISHPAT en-mish'pat. *See* KADESH 1.

ENMITY [Heb. *'êḇâ*] (Gen. 3:15; Nu. 35:21f.; Ezk. 25:15; 35:5); AV also HATRED (Ezk. 25:15; 35:5); NEB also ENEMY (Nu. 35:22), FEUD (Ezk. 35:5); [*śānē'*] (Dt. 4:42; 19:4, 6; Josh. 20:5); AV HATED; [*śāṭam*] (Ps. 55:3 [MT 4]); AV HATE; NEB REVILE; [Gk. *thymós*] (Gal. 5:20); AV WRATH; NEB "fits of rage"; [*échthra*] (Lk. 23:12; Jas. 4:4); NEB also FEUD (Lk. 23:12). Hostility or animosity directed toward God (Rom. 8:7; Jas. 4:4; cf. Rom. 1:30) and man.

The outward manifestation of enmity, whether vertical or horizontal, presupposes an inner disposition of hostility (cf. Mt. 15:19). The occurrence of the word in the fall narrative is significant; where God becomes man's enemy, enmity originates in man's sin (cf. the phrase "wrath of God" in Jn. 3:36; Rom. 1:18; Eph. 5:6; Col. 3:6). The tables must be turned; hence, the *protevangelium* (Gen. 3:15) proclaims victory and the cessation of hostilities (cf. Eph. 2:15f.).

The Heb. *śānē'* (Ugar. *šn'*) is equivalent to the Gk. *mísos*, while *'êḇâ* is equivalent to *echthrós* (*TDNT*, II, 811-15; Morris, pp. 220-25). *Thymós* differs little from *orgḗ* ("wrath," "anger"); *thymós* originally referred to violent movements of air, water, etc., and consequently came to mean "well up" or "boil up" (*TDNT*, III, 167f.).

According to the Pentateuch, the absence of enmity distinguishes unpremeditated from premeditated murder (cf. Ex. 21:12-14). The avenger of blood may not retrieve the manslayer, who kills accidentally, from the city of refuge. Thus, according to Scripture there is a type of killing that is not murder. In this connection, it must be noted that God Himself becomes the avenger of blood in the judgment oracles of Ezekiel (25:15-17; 35:5-9); He will pursue Philistia and Edom to destruction.

See also ENEMY; HATE.

Bibliography.–L. Morris, *Apostolic Preaching of the Cross* (1965); *TDNT*, II, *s.v.* ἐχθρός (W. Foerster); III, *s.v.* θυμός κτλ.: ζυμός (F. Büchsel).

J. T. DENNISON, JR.

ENNATAS en'a-tas (1 Esd. 8:44, NEB). *See* ELNATHAN 2.

ENOCH ē'nok [Heb. *ḥ^anôḵ*–'initiated'; Gk. *Henōch*].

1. The eldest son of Cain (Gen. 4:17f.).

2. The son of Jared and father of Methuselah, seventh in descent from Adam in the line of Seth (Jude 14; cf. 1 Ch. 1:3, AV HENOCH). He is said (Gen. 5:23) to have lived 365 years, but the brief record of his life is comprised in the words, "Enoch walked with God; and he was not, for God took him" (v. 24). The expression "walked with God" denotes a devout life, lived in close communion with God, while the reference to his end has always been understood, as by the writer of Hebrews, to mean that "by faith Enoch was taken up so that he should not see death; and he was not found, because God had taken him" (He. 11:5). *See also* APOCALYPTIC LITERATURE III.A.

A. C. GRANT

ENOCH. A city built by Cain in the land of Nod and named after his firstborn son (Gen. 4:17).

ENOCH, BOOK OF THE SECRETS OF. Also called 2 Enoch. *See* APOCALYPTIC LITERATURE III.F.

ENOCH, ETHIOPIC ē-thi-op'ik, **BOOK OF.** *See* APOCALYPTIC LITERATURE III.A.

ENOCH, SLAVONIC sla-von'ik, **BOOK OF.** *See* APOCALYPTIC LITERATURE III.F.

ENORMITY (Hos. 6:9, AV mg.). *See* VILLAINY.

ENOS ē'nos, **ENOSH** ē'nosh [Heb. *'ĕnôš*–'man,' 'mankind'; Gk. *Enōs*] (Gen. 4:26; 5:6-11; 1 Ch. 1:1; cf. Lk. 3:38); AV ENOS; RSV ENOS only in Lk. 3:38; NEB ENOSH. The son of Seth and grandson of Adam, in whose time a new religious development began, for "at that time men began to call upon the name of the Lord" (Gen. 4:26). There seems to be an implied contrast to Gen. 4:17-24 which records a development in another area of life, represented by Enoch the son of Cain.

S. F. HUNTER

ENQUIRE. This is an Old English word, now obsolescent, common in the AV. In the RSV it is usually replaced by the more modern "inquire." *See* INQUIRE.

EN-RIMMON en-rim'on [Heb. *'ên-rimmôn*–'fountain (or 'spring') of the pomegranate']. A city of Judah ascribed to Simeon, located S of Jerusalem. "Ain and Rimmon" in Josh. 15:32; 1 Ch. 4:32 should probably be Ain-rimmon or En-rimmon as in Josh. 19:7; Neh. 11:29. Nehemiah mentions it as a city resettled after the Captivity. Zechariah (14:10) speaks of it prophetically in connection with the future blessing that shall flow out from Jerusalem. The site usually accepted is Umm er-Ramāmîn, 14 km. (9 mi.) N of Beer-sheba.

J. F. PREWITT

EN-ROGEL en-rō'gel [Heb. *'ên rōgēl*–'spring of *rogel*'; *rogel*–uncertain, variously 'stream,' 'spies' or 'explorers,' 'treaders' and thus 'waterwheels,' 'fullers' or 'bleachers'; Josephus *Ant.* ix.10.4 (cf. Am. 1:1; Zec. 14:5) connects it by means of Gk. (LXX) *rhḗgnymi*– 'split,' with the earthquake in the time of Uzziah]. A spring (the *'ên* or *'ain*, "spring," has a visible and spontaneous flow of water) second only to Gihon in supplying water to Jerusalem. It was located at, or close to, the present Bîr Ayyûb ("Job's Well"), near the confluence of two deep valleys, Kidron and Hinnom, and in OT times a third, the Tyropoeon. By its geological location a steady flow of ground water is assured.

A *bîr* is a spring that is accessible through an artificial entrance. Bîr Ayyûb today is a well 38 m. (125 ft.) deep. Those who live nearby praise the quality of its water. Local tradition connects the well with the curing of Job's diseases, probably a confusion traceable to the appearance of Joab's name in 1 K. 1:9. En-rogel is about 168 m. (550 ft.) below the temple hill and about 27 m. (90 ft.) lower than Gihon, from which it is out of sight but within earshot.

According to Josh. 15:7; 18:16, En-rogel was on the border between the tribes of Benjamin and Judah, the point nearest Canaanite Jerusalem. At En-rogel spies received information from within the city walls for David at the time of Absolom's revolt (2 S. 17:17). It was also the site of Adonijah's premature celebration of his kingship (1 K. 1:9).

The "dragon well" (AV), "Jackal's Well" (RSV), or "Dragon Spring" (NEB) of Neh. 2:13, a well or spring with serpent associations, is often thought to be En-rogel. J. Simons (*GTTOT*) and others relate the "gate of the spring" (MT), "gate of the fountain" (AV), or "Fountain Gate" (RSV, NEB) of Neh. 3:15 to En-rogel, as the Water Gate of Neh. 3:26 is related to Gihon.

Bîr Ayyûb, the site of En-rogel (W. S. LaSor)

En-rogel has been called Nehemiah's well by legendary identification as the place where the fire was miraculously preserved during the Exile (2 Macc. 1:19).

See JERUSALEM II.C.2, F.2.f.

P. L. GARBER

ENROLLMENT; ENROLLED [Heb. *yāḥaś*, also *kāṯaḇ*; Gk. *apográphō, apographḗ* (Lk. 2:2), *synkatapsēphízomai* (Acts 1:26), *katalégomai* (1 Tim. 5:9)]; AV RECKONED, also GENEALOGY (2 Ch. 31:16-18), WRITTEN, TAXED (Lk. 2), TAXING (Lk. 2:2), NUMBERED (Acts 1:26), "taken into the number" (1 Tim. 5:9); NEB also REGISTERED, REGISTRATION, "entered in the roll" (Ezk. 13:9), "assigned a place" (Acts 1:26), "put on the roll" (1 Tim. 5:9), "citizens" (*apográphō*, He. 12:23). A listing or census of people according to family (tribal) relationship and/or occupation.

Although we have no details of how such enrollments were made or how and where such records were kept, there can be no doubt that the practice had a long history. In the Bible, for example, we find it from the wilderness period to the apostolic age.

Because of the great importance attached to keeping the tribal inheritance intact, family and tribal genealogical registers were kept. A "register of the house of Israel" is mentioned in Ezk. 13:9. A genealogical register seems to be preserved in 1 Ch. 1–8 (cf. 1 Ch. 9:1a, "So all Israel was enrolled by genealogies"). Josephus tells us that he has set down the genealogy of his family as he found it described in the public records (*Vita* 1). It is obvious that the Jewish marriage laws concerning prohibited degrees of consanguinity required a carefully kept system of genealogical records.

A specific use of genealogical registers pertained to the priests. In order to prove his right to serve as a priest and to receive support, a man had to be able to prove his descent from Levi (cf. Ezr. 2:61-63; Neh. 7:61-65). An enrollment (numbering) of the Levites was made by David (1 Ch. 23:3). Josephus, with indefensible hyperbole, says that the high-priestly record extended back over two thousand years (*CAp* i.36).

The use of the enrollment (numbering or census) for the purpose of raising an army — superficially similar to the "draft" — likewise is found. The first such enrollment was made by Moses at the command of God (Nu. 1:2f.). This seems to have been more for the purpose of maintaining order in the encampments and marches than for war. On this and other numberings, *see* CENSUS.

In the NT the Roman enrollment is mentioned in connection with the birth of Jesus (Lk. 2:2) and again in a passing reference to the revolt of Judas the Galilean (Acts 5:37). It appears that the Romans took a census every fourteen years for the purpose of levying taxes. On the problems of dating the census of Quirinius, *see* QUIRINIUS; CHRONOLOGY OF THE NT I.A.2.

It appears that the early Church also maintained some kind of register, for Paul cautions Timothy against enrolling younger widows (1 Tim. 5:9, 11). No other references to such enrollment are found, however.

The Greek word used in Acts 1:26 is a hapax legomenon meaning "count/reckon together with." It has no relationship to a census.

See also GENEALOGY. W. S. LASOR

ENSAMPLE. *See* EXAMPLE.

EN-SHEMESH en-she'mesh [Heb. *ʿên šemeš*–'spring of the sun'; Gk. *pēgḗ hēlíou* (Josh. 15:7), *pēgḗ Baithsamus* (Josh. 18:17)]. An important landmark on the border between Judah and Benjamin (Josh. 15:7; 18:17). It is usually identified with the little spring ʿAin el-Hôd just E of Bethany, on the road between Jerusalem and Jericho, the last spring before the Jordan Valley. Tradition dating from the 15th cent. relates that the apostles drank from this spring; since then ʿAin el-Hôd has been called the "Spring of the Apostles."

ENSIGN. *See* BANNER; STANDARD.

ENSUE. Used by the AV in the obsolete sense of "pursue" in 1 Pet. 3:11 (Gk. *diṓkō,* "follow after," "pursue").

ENTANGLE [Heb. *bûḵ*] (Ex. 14:3); NEB HEM IN; [*môqēš*] (Prov. 22:25; 2 S. 22:6; Ps. 18:5 [MT 6]); AV SNARE, COMPASS; NEB "catch in a trap," TIGHTEN ABOUT (AROUND); [*sāḇaḵ*] (Nah. 1:10); AV "fold together"; NEB TANGLE; [Gk. *pagideúō*] (Mt. 22:15); NEB TRAP; [*emplékō*] (2 Tim. 2:4; 2 Pet. 2:20); AV ENTANGLE (2 Pet. 2:20); NEB BE INVOLVED (2 Tim. 2:4). Various processes of frustration, including conversational or moral confusion (in addition to physical entrapment).

Physical entrapment is suggested by *bûḵ* in Ex. 14:3, which speaks of being lost in the desert. Moses had seemingly led the people on a foolish route, for Canaan lay to the northeast but the cloud led them southwest. Pharaoh would think them lost in the wilderness as in a maze; thus he could say they were "entangled in the land." Similarly, when *môqēš* is used symbolically in David's song (Ps. 18:5 par. 2 S. 22:6), the image is one of death closing in and engulfing him. Likewise, Prov. 22:25 suggests that involvement with anger catches us as if a trap had ensnared us. *Sāḇaḵ* suggests the actual intertwining of branches. *Pagideúō* is a bird-hunting term (cf. LXX Eccl. 9:12), used figuratively in Mt. 22:15 to indicate a conversational or mental snare.

A type of moral involvement can also be indicated. *Emplékō* means "entangle," or "become enchanted or involved with." Thus Paul alludes to soldiers whose first commitment is to soldiering and who cannot afford to become enmeshed or "involved in civilian affairs" (2 Tim. 2:4, NEB). Peter warns those who follow Christ never to become entangled again with the defilements of the nonbeliever (2 Pet. 2:20). Here the allusion to entrapment may suggest nets used not only for catching animals but also as weapons of combat.

The AV translates *enéchō* (Gal. 5:1) "entangled," while the NEB has "tied to the yoke," and the RSV has "submit again." The idea is that of yielding willingly rather than becoming entrapped or entangled.

See also SNARE; FOWLER. V. B. GILLESPIE

EN-TAPPUAH en-tap'ōō-ə, en-ta-pōō'ə [Heb. *ʿên tappû(a)ḥ*–'apple spring'; Gk. *pēgḗ Thaphthōth*]. A spring whose location is still disputed, but no doubt near Tappuah in Manasseh (Josh. 17:7f.), although it was possessed by Ephraim. On the border of Ephraim, it is probably to be identified with the spring at Yāsūf, about 13 km. (8 mi.) S of Shechem.

ENTERTAIN [Gk. *xenízō*] (Acts 28:7; He. 13:2); AV LODGE; **GUEST ROOM** [*katályma*] (Mk. 14:14; Lk. 22:11); AV GUEST CHAMBER; NEB "room reserved for me," ROOM; [*xenía*] (Philem. 22); AV LODGING; NEB ROOM; **HOSPITALITY** [*philoxenía*] (Rom. 12:13; He. 13:2; 1 Pet. 4:9); AV also ENTERTAIN; [*xenodochéō*] (1 Tim. 5:10); AV LODGE; **HOSPITABLE** [*philóxenos*] (1 Tim. 3:2; Tit. 1:8); AV HOSPITALITY; **HOSPITABLY** [*philophrónōs*] (Acts 28:7); AV COURTEOUSLY; **HOST** [*ho keklēkṓs*] (Lk. 14:10); AV "him that bade thee"; [*xénos*] (Rom. 16:23).

I. Hospitality in the Levant.–Throughout the Mediterranean world, hospitality toward strangers was recognized as a sacred duty. Among the Greeks hospitality was a decisive mark of culture. The civilized were "those who love strangers and fear the gods" (Homer *Od.* viii.576; ix.175). Zeus himself was the "Friend of Strangers" (2 Macc. 6:2; Homer *Il.* xiii.625; cf. Dt. 10:18). In Egypt the practice of hospitality assured a favorable existence in the next world. For the Romans entertaining strangers was considered a sacred obligation.

The emphasis upon entertaining guests probably originated in nomadic life. Travel was seldom, if ever, for pleasure but rather because of necessity. One never knew when he would be dependent upon the hospitality of others. Therefore a stranger had the right to expect hospitable treatment. A visitor had no need even to thank his host, since he was only receiving what was due him. The host would provide for his guest housing, protection, and food, if he arrived in time for the evening meal. (Many times, however, even if the visitor arrived too late and was not entitled to food, the host sought to provide for him [cf. Lk. 11:5f.].) A murderer would find protection in the tent of his host even if the host were the victim's own son. No expense or labor was too great for the traveler, who was treated as the master of the house. The host frequently prepared for his guest a luxurious banquet (Gen. 18:6-8; note how Abraham minimizes his gracious provision by referring to it in v. 5 as a "morsel of bread").

In time, villages began the practice of maintaining a room for sojourners, the expense being shared by the village. In Mk. 14:14 par. Lk. 22:11 the *katályma* probably means such a guest room, while in Lk. 2:7 a caravanserai is equally possible. Lk. 10:34 clearly refers to an inn. We know from Josephus (*BJ* ii.8.4) that the Essenes assigned someone in "every" town to care for strangers (cf. Cyprian *Epistula* 7, where Cyprian in his absence orders certain priests to supervise the entertainment of travelers).

II. Hospitality in Israel.–In Israel hospitality was encouraged. This was due in part to the command of Scripture (Lev. 19:33f.; Dt. 10:13f.; 24:17, 19), and in part to Israel's own experience of being aliens in Egypt (Ex. 22:21; 23:9;

Lev. 19:33f.; Dt. 10:19) and later in Babylon. It was not merely a courtesy but an obligation to care for strangers. Abraham, upon seeing strangers coming in his direction, runs out to greet them and pleads with them to stay in his home (Gen. 18:2f.), and Reuel is amazed that his daughters did not extend hospitality toward the stranger who assisted them in watering their flocks (Ex. 2:20). The extent to which a host felt responsibility toward his guests is illustrated in a number of ways. In Gen. 19:1-11, Lot seeks to protect his guests from sexual abuse by the hostile crowd by offering his virgin daughters to the crowd. A similar example is found in Jgs. 19:22f. Elijah is offered by his host, the widow at Zerephath, the last bit of food left in the house (1 Kgs. 17:10f.).

III. Breaches of Hospitality.–Breaches of such hospitality did occur in the ancient world. The Ammonites and Moabites are castigated for such discourtesy (Dt. 23:4), as are the Benjaminites (Jgs. 19:15, 18; cf. Josephus *Ant.* v.2.8), and the Sodomites, who are referred to as "haters of strangers" (Josephus *Ant.* i.11.1). Jael's murder of Sisera (Jgs. 4–5) must also be considered such an instance, even if it was a patriotic act. Nabal's lack of hospitality almost cost him his life, but he was saved by the actions of his wife Abigail (1 S. 25). James and John were so angry at the Samaritans in Lk. 9:54 largely because they had not extended to Jesus and His disciples the simplest hospitality to which every stranger was entitled (cf. Lk. 7:44f.). The OT mentions wicked men who hated and even killed strangers (Ps. 94:6; cf. Wisd. 19:13-15). At times Jewish exclusiveness resulted in a marked reserve toward strangers. (For violations of hospitality in the Greek world, cf. Homer *Od.* iv.535; xi.411; xxi.27).

Nevertheless, in general there existed throughout the Levant an emphasis on entertaining strangers, and a man's worth and piety was readily seen by his hospitality (Job 31:32; T. Zeb. 6:4f.). Furthermore, even as lack of hospitality brought condemnation, so its practice brought reward. According to 1 Clem. 10:7, Abraham was given a son because of his faith and his hospitality. Lot was spared from the destruction of Sodom and Gomorrah because of his hospitality (1 Clem. 11:1), as was "hospitable Rahab" from the destruction of Jericho (He. 11:31; Jas. 2:25; 1 Clem. 12:1-3). Because of their hospitality to Israel, the Kenites were excluded by Saul from the judgment brought upon the Amalekites (1 S. 15:6), and, despite his idolatry, Micah (Jgs. 17) was spared because of his hospitality (T.B. *Sanhedrin* 103b). Hospitality was especially extended to fellow Jews, and throughout the Diaspora a Jew could be assured of receiving such hospitality from his fellow Jews. To practice such hospitality toward the rabbis was particularly praiseworthy (T.B. *Berakoth* 63b).

IV. Jesus' Teaching Concerning Hospitality.–Our Lord frequently during His ministry experienced hospitality (Mt. 13:1, 36; Mk. 1:29f.; 7:24; 9:33; 11:11; 14:3f.; Lk. 7:36f.; 8:3; 10:38f.; 14:1f., 12f.; 19:5; Jn. 4:40; 12:1f.) and assumed that such courtesy would be offered Him (Lk. 9:51f.; cf. Jesus' use of this theme in the parables: Lk. 11:5f.; 14:12f., 15f.). The mission of the Twelve (Mk. 6:8-11 par.) and of the Seventy (Lk. 10:1-12) was based upon the assumption that such hospitality would be available. Both here and in the later mission which Jesus envisioned (Mt. 10:40; Jn. 13:20) one's destiny was bound up with the hospitality (or lack of hospitality) extended to Jesus' messengers. The reception afforded the messengers would ultimately bring eternal life or death. It might be argued that the sin here envisioned is not so much the lack of hospitality shown Jesus' messengers but the rejection of the gospel preached by them, but both are intimately connected. The reception of Christian strangers and messengers is in reality the reception of Christ Himself (Mt. 25:43).

V. Hospitality in the Early Church.–In the NT great emphasis is placed upon entertaining strangers. A bishop must have as one of his qualifications a hospitable nature and reputation (1 Tim. 3:2; Tit. 1:8), as must anyone seeking to be enrolled as a widow (1 Tim. 5:10). The practice of hospitality was enjoined upon the Church for several reasons. First, loving one another demanded being hospitable. One could not love strangers or visitors without caring for them and entertaining them. It should be noted that in Rom. 12:9-13; He. 13:1f.; and 1 Pet. 4:8f. the commands to love and to show hospitality are intimately connected. (Love and hospitality are also intimately associated by the rabbis. In T.B. *Kiddushin* 39b five acts are listed as bringing future reward: honoring parents, deeds of love, hospitality, establishing peace, and [the most important] studying the Torah. But some rabbis [T.B. *Shabbath* 127a] thought the practice of hospitality was more important than the study of the Torah.) Second, hospitality was essential for the propagation of the gospel. Itinerant missionaries were immensely aided in their labors, knowing that they would be received by fellow Christians and helped on their way. Furthermore, entertaining these missionaries made the host a "fellow worker in the truth" (3 Jn. 5-8; cf. Rom. 16:3f.) with the men he entertained.

Third, the possibility of angelic visitation (He. 13:2) prompted hospitality. No doubt the writer had in mind such OT passages as Gen. 18:1f.; 19:1f.; Jgs. 6:11.; 13:2f. (cf. Tob. 5:4f.). Mt. 25:31f. intensifies even this expectation by stressing that the unity of Christ with His Church is such that showing hospitality to a Christian is showing hospitality to Christ Himself (cf. Ign. Eph. 6:1, where receiving itinerant missionaries is equated with receiving the Lord). Fourth, one is to exercise the particular gift that the host has in this area (1 Pet. 4:9f.). The wherewithal to entertain is seen by Peter as a gift of the Lord. Faithful stewardship of such a gift required the practice of hospitality.

It is not surprising, therefore, that we find many examples of such hospitality in the life of the early Church. Paul's mission work was greatly aided by such hospitality (Acts 16:14f.; 17:5-7; 18:7, 27; 21:4-6, 8, 16; 28:7; Rom. 16:1f., 23; Philem. 22), as was the work of Peter (Acts 10:6, 18, 32, 48) and others (2 Jn. 10f.; 3 Jn. 5-8).

VI. Rules for Guests.–The danger of abuse of hospitality was recognized in Ps. 41:9 [MT 10], which assumed an obligation on the part of the guest as well as the host (cf. Job 19:15; Ps. 55:12f. [MT 13f.]; Jn. 13:18). Certain rules by which a guest should conduct himself are listed in T.B. *Berakoth* 58a (cf. the rules of hospitality by Ptaḥ-ḥetep in E. A. W. Budge, *History of Egypt* [1968], II, 149). That Jesus was sensitive with regard to this matter is evident from Mk. 6:10f. and Lk. 10:7b (cf. Mk. 12:39). His followers were not to presume upon the hospitality of one house after another. In the early Church care was also to be taken to discriminate between the true believers and deceivers, for the latter were not to be entertained in one's home (2 Jn. 10f.; cf. 1 Jn. 4:1), lest one find himself sharing in a deceiver's wicked work. In the Didache the treatment of itinerant missionaries is carefully described. These itinerant missionaries (called "apostles") were to be entertained for only two days. If they remained longer they were deceivers (Did. 11:5; among the Arabs one could usually remain three days according to R. de Vaux, *Ancient Israel* [1961], p. 10). Furthermore, they should be given bread for their journey and not money (Did. 11:6, 12; cf. Rom. 15:24). To aid believers in this regard, letters of recommendation were frequently sent along with these missionaries (Acts 18:27; Rom. 16:1f.; 2 Cor. 3:1). They were not always required, however, and the Christians tended to err on the side of generosity and to practice ungrudging hospitality toward one another (1 Pet. 4:9; cf. Aristides *Apologia* 15, where all Christians are portrayed as being hospitable).

See also GUEST; INN; INVITE.

Bibliography.–*ERE,* VI, *s.v.* "Hospitality (Semitic)" (W. Cruickshank); C. Phillipson, *International Law and Custom of Ancient Greece and Rome* (1911), pp. 122-135, 210-229; D. W. Riddle, *JBL,* 57 (1939), 141-154; *TDNT,* V, *s.v.* ξένος (G. Stählin).

R. H. STEIN

ENTHRONEMENT [Heb. *yāšaḇ*] (1 S. 4:4; 2 S. 6:2; 2 K. 19:15; 1 Ch. 13:6; Ps. 9:7 [MT 8]; 22:3 [MT 4]; 29:10; 33:14; etc.); AV DWELL, "endure," INHABIT, SIT, HABITATION, ABIDE; NEB also ROYAL SEAT (Ps. 29:10b), DWELLING-PLACE, DWELL, THRONE, omits in Ps. 29:10a.

The THRONE was symbolic of royal office and power; thus to say that a king was enthroned (i.e., took his seat upon the throne) meant that he began to reign (cf. 1 K. 16:11; 2 K. 13:13). In Israel all royal authority ultimately rested with Yahweh (cf. 1 Ch. 29:22f.). Apart from Ps. 61:7 (MT 8) the RSV uses "enthroned" exclusively of Yahweh, who is depicted as enthroned "on the praises of Israel" (22:3), "in the heavens" (123:1), "over the flood" (29:10), and "upon the cherubim" (e.g., 1 S. 4:4; 1 Ch. 13:6; Ps. 80:1 [MT 2]). The latter epithet should probably be understood as an allusion to the idea that Yahweh was enthroned upon the ark of the covenant, the symbol of God's presence among His people Israel (*see* ARK OF THE COVENANT, esp. VI). Thus the fact that the ark was carried at the head of the people (e.g., at the crossing of the Jordan [Josh. 3:3f.] and the conquest of Jericho [ch. 6]) symbolized that Yahweh was marching before His people and that the victory and the kingship belonged to Him.

Some scholars (e.g., S. Mowinckel) identify certain of the Psalms as enthronement Psalms that were used in a ritual reenthronement ceremony of Yahweh as King of Israel (cf. Pss. 47, 93, 95, etc.). That such a ceremony was ever celebrated in Israel is still, however, a matter of much debate. *See* PSALMS IV.C.

See also KING (esp. IV).

N. J. O.

ENTRAILS [Heb. *qereḇ*] (Ex. 29:13, 17, 22; Lev. 1:9, 13; 3:3f.; 4:8, 11; 7:3; 8:16f.; 9:14); AV INWARDS; [*kāḇer*] (Prov. 7:23); AV LIVER; NEB VITALS. The inner organs of sacrificial animals. In the case of the burnt offering they were burned, after cleansing, with the whole of the offering. For the sin offering only these parts were burned as a sacrifice and the rest of the animal was burned outside the camp, while for the peace offering these parts were burned and the rest was eaten by the priests and the people. The fat, as well as the blood, was considered Yahweh's portion of the sacrifice. *See also* SACRIFICES AND OFFERINGS IN THE OT V.D-H; LIVER; DIVINATION III.E.

ENTREAT; INTREAT (AV) [Heb. *pāga'* (Gen. 23:8; Ruth 1:16; Jer. 15:11), *'āṯar* (Ex. 8:8f., 28; 9:28; 10:17f.; Jgs. 13:8; 1 Ch. 5:20; 2 Ch. 33:13, 19; Ezr. 8:23), *ḥālâ* (1 S. 13:12; 1 K. 13:6; 2 Ch. 33:12; Ps. 119:58; Jer. 26:19; Dnl. 9:13; etc.), *bāqaš* (Est. 4:8), hithpael of *ḥānan* (2 K. 1:13); Gk. *parakaléō* (Lk. 15:28; Acts 9:38; 2 Cor. 6:1; 10:1; Phil. 4:2), *paraitéomai* (He. 12:19)]; AV usually INTREAT, also MAKE REQUEST, MAKE SUIT, BESEECH, PRAY, etc.; NEB also SPEAK, PRAY, URGE, SEEK, INTERCEDE, etc.; **ENTREATIES** [Heb. *taḥ^{a}nûnîm*] (Prov. 18:23); AV INTREATIES; NEB "tone of entreaty."

In 1611 the AV spelling was indifferently "intreat" or "entreat"; in the editions since 1760, however, "intreat" is used in the sense of "beg," and "entreat" in the sense of "deal with." As examples of "intreat" see Ex. 8:8, "intreat the Lord" (Heb. *ṣā'aq*); Ruth 1:16, "intreat me not to leave thee" (*pāga'*); 2 Cor. 8:4, "praying us with much intreaty" (Gk. *paráklēsis*). In Gen. 25:21 "intreat" indicates the success of a petition. For "entreat" see Gen. 12:16, "he entreated Abraham well"; Acts 27:3, "and Julius courteously entreated Paul" (Gk. *philanthrṓpōs chrēsámenos,* lit. "having used in a philanthropic way"); cf. also Jas. 3:17 where *eupeithḗs,* literally, "easily persuaded," is translated "easy to be entreated."

The RSV does not use "intreat"; instead it uses "entreat" or another word. The meanings of "entreat" in the RSV include "intercede" (Gen. 23:8), "beg" (Ruth 1:16; He. 12:19; etc.), "earnestly pray for" (Heb. *'āṯar, ḥālâ;* Gk. *parakaléō*), and "seek" or "request" (Est. 4:8).

R. B. MILLER
N. J. O.

ENTRUST [Heb. *'āman*] (Nu. 12:7); AV, NEB, FAITHFUL; [*nāṯan*] (Jer. 39:14); AV COMMIT; NEB HAND OVER; [Gk. *pisteúō*] (Lk. 16:11; Rom. 3:2; 1 Cor. 9:17; Gal. 2:7; 1 Thess. 2:4; 1 Tim. 1:11; Tit. 1:3); AV COMMIT, "commit to trust," "put in trust;" NEB also TRUST, "discharge a trust"; [*títhēmi*] (2 Cor. 5:19); AV COMMIT; [*paratíthēmi*] (2 Tim. 2:2; 1 Pet. 4:19); AV COMMIT; NEB COMMIT, "put into the charge of"; [*paradídōmi*] (Mt. 25:14); AV DELIVER; NEB "put into the hands of"; [*parathḗkē*–'deposit'] (2 Tim. 1:12); AV COMMIT; NEB "put into the charge of"; [*parakatathḗkē*–'deposit'] (1 Tim. 6:20; 2 Tim. 1:14); AV COMMIT, "commit to trust"; NEB also "in our charge."

After telling the parable of the unjust steward, Jesus asks, "If then you have not been faithful in the unrighteous mammon, who will entrust to you the true riches?" (Lk. 16:11). Here the word *pisteúō* has the sense of committing something to someone while trusting in that person's fidelity and faithfulness (cf. LXX Nu. 12:7; Wisd. 14:5; 1 Macc. 8:16; 4 Macc. 4:7). This is very similar to the meaning of *paratíthēmi,* which was used in classical Greek for anything deposited with a friend for the purpose of safekeeping (cf. 1 Cor. 9:17). The instruction in 1 Pet. 4:19 for those who are suffering and being persecuted is that they should "entrust their souls to a faithful Creator." God will keep them safe just as He will ultimately keep safe the transmission of His own truth. In the Pastorals there is special teaching regarding the apostolic tradition. That body of tradition which the apostles "delivered to the saints" (Jude 3) is called a "deposit" (*parathḗkē* in 1 Tim. 6:20; cf. 2 Tim. 1:12). The "instructions" or "proclamation" (*parangelía*) is handed over to Timothy (1 Tim. 1:18), who is twice urged to guard and keep safe the "deposit" entrusted to him (1 Tim. 6:20; 2 Tim. 1:14; cf. Gal. 2:7; Rom. 3:2). But Timothy must also hand this over to those who are faithful, able to teach others (2 Tim. 2:2). Thus the delivery of God's "good news" continues throughout the community and from generation to generation.

Bibliography.–Bauer, rev., pp. 623, 662; F. F. Bruce, *Tradition: Old and New* (1970); E. G. Selwyn, *First Epistle of Peter* (1946); *TDNT,* VIII, *s.v.* τίθημι (C. Maurer); *TDOT,* I, *s.v.* "'āman" (Jepsen).

D. K. MCKIM

ENVOY [Heb. *ṣîr*–'messenger' (Prov. 13:17; Isa. 57:9), *mal'āḵ* (2 Ch. 35:21; Isa. 30:4; 33:7), *mēlîṣ*–'interpreter'

(2 Ch. 32:31)]; AV AMBASSADOR, MESSENGER; NEB also "those sent to sue," PROCURER. In 2 K. 20:12 and Isa. 39:1 the RSV and NEB follow the LXX, which adds *kaí présbeis* ("and envoys"). An envoy is an official representative of a king or government, as of Pharaoh (Isa. 30:4); of the princes of Babylon (2 Ch. 32:31); of Neco king of Egypt (2 Ch. 35:21); of the messengers of peace sent by Hezekiah king of Judah to Sennacherib king of Assyria (Isa. 33:7). The same Hebrew term (*mal'āḵ*) is used of the messengers sent by Jacob to Esau (Gen. 32:3); by Moses to the king of Edom (Nu. 20:14); etc.

See also AMBASSADOR; MESSENGER.

ENVY; ENVIOUS [Heb. *qānā'*] (Gen. 26:14; 30:1; Ps. 37:1; 73:3; Prov. 3:31; 23:17; 24:1, 19; Ezk. 31:9); NEB also JEALOUS, EMULATE; [*rāṣaḏ*] (Ps. 68:16 [MT 17]); AV LEAP; [*qin'â*] (Eccl. 4:4; 9:6; Ezk. 35:11); NEB RIVALRY, JEALOUSY; [Gk. *phthónos*] (Mt. 27:18; Mk. 15:10; Rom. 1:29; Gal. 5:21; Phil. 1:15; 1 Tim. 6:4; Tit. 3:3; 1 Pet. 2:1); NEB also MALICE, JEALOUSY; [*ponēría*] (Mk. 7:22); AV "evil eye"; [*phthonéō*] (Gal. 5:26); NEB JEALOUS. The RSV also supplies "envious" in 1 S. 2:32.

The verb *rāṣaḏ* (piel) of Ps. 68:16 occurs nowhere else in the OT, but its meaning has been preserved in Arabic, where the related word means "watch as an enemy, lie in wait or view with envy," carrying the idea of hostility and ill will (Alexander, II, 113). In other OT passages "envy" is closely tied to jealousy, rivalry, and misplaced zeal.

Among NT references to envy, the Greek phrase used in the list of vices in Mk. 7:22 is *ophthalmós ponērós*, lit. "evil eye" (used also in Mt. 20:15; cf. RSV mg.). All other translations are of *phthónos* (or *phthonéō*), a classical word denoting an intense feeling and eager desire of ill will or malice (cf. Tit. 3:3). This means "the desire to deprive another of what he has" (Lightfoot, p. 212) and frequently occurs in catalogue lists of vices (Rom. 1:29; 1 Tim. 6:4; 1 Pet. 1:21). Sometimes the word is joined with *zḗlos* ("zeal" or "jealousy," cf. 1 Macc. 8:16; Gal. 5:20f.), though *zḗlos* may upon occasion be seen as good (Jn. 2:17; Rom. 10:2; 2 Cor. 9:2) while *phthónos* is "incapable of good [and] is used always and only in an evil signification" (Trench, p. 82). It was "out of envy" that the chief priests delivered Jesus up to be crucified (Mt. 27:18; Mk. 15:10; cf. 1 Clem. 5:2, where this is said to have been the cause of the martyrdom of Peter and Paul) and "out of envy" that some even preach Christ (Phil. 1:15).

Bibliography.–J. A. Alexander, *Psalms*, II (6th ed. 1853); Bauer, rev., pp. 690, 857; E. D. Burton, comm. on Galatians (*ICC*, 2nd ed. 1956), p. 310; J. B. Lightfoot, comm. on Galatians (repr. 1957); R. C. Trench, *Synonyms of the NT* (1950).

D. K. MCKIM

EPAENETUS ep-ē'nə-təs [Gk. *Epainetos*]. One of the Christians at Rome to whom Paul sent greetings (Rom. 16:5). All that is known of him is told here. Paul describes him as (1) "my beloved," (2) "who was the first convert in Asia for Christ." He was one of the first Christians in the Roman province of Asia.

This salutation raises the question of the destination of vv. 3-16. It has been argued that they are addressed to the church in Ephesus because Prisca and Aquila and Epaenetus are known to have dwelt in Asia. (For a summary, see H. Gamble, *Textual History of the Letter to the Romans* [1977], pp. 37-39.) On the other hand, more than twenty others in this list are not known to have spent any time in Asia. Prisca and Aquila had once dwelt in Rome (Acts 18:2), and there would be nothing unusual about an Ephesian dwelling in the capital of the empire. Of interest is a discovery made in Rome of an inscription bearing the name of Epenetus, an Ephesian (*CIL*, VI, 17171).

S. F. HUNTER

EPAPHRAS ep'ə-fras [Gk. *Epaphras*]. A contracted form of EPAPHRODITUS. He must not, however, be confused with the messenger of the Philippian community. He was with Paul during a part of his first Roman imprisonment, joining in Paul's greetings to Philemon (Philem. 23). Epaphras was the missionary by whom the Colossians had been converted to Christianity (Col. 1:7), and probably he had founded the other churches of the Lycus. In sending his salutation to the Colossians Paul testified, "He has worked hard for you and for those in Laodicea and in Hierapolis" (Col. 4:13). Epaphras had brought to Paul good news of the progress of the gospel among the Colossians, of their "faith in Christ Jesus," and of their love toward all the saints (1:4). Paul's regard for him is shown by his designating him "our beloved fellow servant," "a faithful minister of Christ" (1:7), and "a slave of Christ Jesus" (4:12 mg.). The last designation Paul uses several times of himself, but only once of another besides Epaphras (Phil. 1:1).

S. F. HUNTER

EPAPHRODITUS e-paf-rō-dī'təs [Gk. *Epaphroditos*]. Mentioned only in Phil. 2:25; 4:18. The name corresponds to the Lat. Venustus ("handsome") and was very common in the Roman period, appearing frequently in Greek and Latin inscriptions, sometimes in its contracted form "Epaphras" (see J. B. Lightfoot, *Philippians* [1896], p. 123). Epaphroditus was the delegate of the Christian community at Philippi, sent with their gift to Paul during his first Roman imprisonment. Paul calls him "my brother and fellow worker and fellow soldier." On his arrival at Rome, Epaphroditus devoted himself to "the work of Christ" (v. 30), both as Paul's attendant and as his assistant in missionary work. So assiduously did he labor that he lost his health and was "near to death" (v. 27). He recovered, however, and Paul sent him back to Philippi with this letter to quiet the alarm of his friends, who had heard of his serious illness. Paul sought for him an honorable and joyful reception by the church.

S. F. HUNTER

EPHAH ē'fa [Heb. *'êpâ*–'darkness'].

1. The son of Midian, descended from Abraham by his wife Keturah (Gen. 25:4 par. 1 Ch. 1:33), mentioned again in Isa. 60:6 as a tribe, transporting gold and frankincense from Sheba, thus bringing enlargement to Judah and praise to Yahweh. According to some scholars *'êpâ* is an abbreviation of *'Ayappa*, the Khayappa Arabs of the time of Tiglath-pileser III and Sargon.

2. A concubine of Caleb (1 Ch. 2:46).

3. The son of Jahdai, a descendant of Judah (1 Ch. 2:47).

C. B. WILLIAMS

EPHAH ē'fa [Heb. *'êpâ*]. A dry measure equal to one tenth of a homer, or about two thirds of a bushel. It corresponds to the bath in liquid measure and was the standard for measuring grain and similar articles, since it is classed with balances and weights (Lev. 19:36; Am. 8:5) in the injunctions regarding just dealing in trade. In Zec. 5:6-10 it is used for the measuring utensil itself. *See* WEIGHTS AND MEASURES.

EPHAI ē'fī, ē'fə-ī [Heb. *Q 'êpay, K 'ôpay*; Gk. *Iōphe, Ōphe*]. "The Netophathite," whose sons were numbered among "the captains of the forces" left in Judah after the carrying away to Babylon (Jer. 40:8). His sons assembled at Mizpah with Gedaliah, governor of the scattered Jews, and with him were slain by Ishmael, the son of Nethaniah (Jer. 41:3). The words "the sons of Ephai" are missing from the account in 2 K. 25:23.

EPHER ē'fər [Heb. *'ēper*–'young deer'; Gk. *Apher, Opher*].

1. The second son of Midian, descended from Abraham by his wife Keturah (Gen. 25:4; 1 Ch. 1:33).

2. The third son of Ezra, descended from the tribe of Judah (1 Ch. 4:17).

3. The first of five "heads of their fathers' houses," described as "mighty warriors, famous men" in the half-tribe of Manasseh, who dwelt between Bashan and Mt. Hermon (1 Ch. 5:23f.).

EPHES-DAMMIM ē-fes-dam'im [Heb. *'epes dammîm*]. A place in Judah (also called Pas-dammim in 1 Ch. 11:13) about 21 km. (13 mi.) SW of Jerusalem, where the Philistine armies drew their forces in preparation for battle with the Israelites (1 S. 17:1). It was here that David slew Goliath (17:50).

The meaning of the name is uncertain. The deep red color of the newly plowed earth in this area may have suggested blood (Heb. *dām*), so some scholars would interpret "end [or border] of blood."

EPHESIAN ə-fē'zhən [Gk. *Ephesios*]; **EPHESIANS** (Acts 19:28, 34f.; 21:29). *See* EPHESUS.

EPHESIANS, EPISTLE TO THE. This profound Epistle has been variously described as "the Switzerland of the New Testament," "the divinest composition of man," "the quintessence of Paulinism." The divergent texts and translations of the first verse in the RSV ("To the saints who are also faithful in Christ Jesus") and the NEB ("To God's people at Ephesus, believers incorporate in Christ Jesus") suggest the fluid state in the discussion concerning the historical circumstances surrounding the writing of Ephesians.

I. Contents
II. Authenticity
  A. Difficulties for Pauline Authorship
  B. Similarity of Ephesians and Colossians
  C. Style and Vocabulary
  D. Problem of the Addressees
III. Origin and Purpose
IV. Date
V. Text
VI. Theology

I. Contents.–The letter presents few personal data, concentrating rather on the unity of the Church. In what one may call his introductory chapter, the writer sends the customary greetings (1:1f.); states the purpose of God's redemptive plan, the summation of all things in Christ, with anticipation of the final installment of God's saving intention (1:3-14); and concludes with the prayer that his readers may appreciate the large and splendid scope of their new expectation as called saints (1:15-23).

In 2:1–3:13 the writer proceeds to expand on the theme of unity in terms of a common need. All are the children of wrath (2:3); and the Gentiles, who lacked all ability to locate God, find themselves the object of God's search, brought from death to life (2:1-10). Their common need introduces them to a common hope. This hope they share with their Jewish comrades, who also have access to God the Father through one Spirit on the basis of the cross of Jesus Christ, which breaks down all walls of partition (2:11-22). The apostolic and prophetic ministry of the early Christian Church, and especially that of Paul, who transferred his attentions from Jewish to gentile quarters, undergird the fact of the Church's unity in Christ. This ministry is part of God's plan (3:1-13). A prayer that the Church may see the significance of the common grace she enjoys in her common gospel paves the way (3:14-21) for a consideration of the second main portion of the letter, that the Church shares a common walk (4:1–6:20).

To ensure the success of her calling, the Church has been endowed with various instruments of edification, such as apostles, prophets, evangelists, shepherds, and teachers, so that through a common doctrine she might walk a common life (4:1-16). This common life is displayed in proper attitudes toward one another, for contrary patterns of behavior destroy the unity of the fellowship (4:17-32). Specifically, the Christian must shun the works of darkness and thus reflect his understanding of God's redemptive purpose (5:1-18). In their relations with one another — husbands with wives, parents with children, and masters with slaves — the members of Christ's body express their understanding of the unifying lordship of Jesus (5:19–6:9). United in her common arsenal (6:10-17), the Church enjoys her fellowship of prayer (6:18-20). A reminder of the unity between the apostles and the rest of the Church is signaled by the reference to Tychicus (6:21-22). The closing doxology impresses on the readers the supreme unifying force — love (6:23f.).

II. Authenticity.–Debate about the authenticity (Paul's authorship) of Ephesians was initiated in England by E. Evanson in 1792 and gained momentum in Germany under the searching criticism of W. M. L. de Wette and F. D. E. Schleiermacher. The trend continued on the Continent and in the United States; but British scholars, with the notable exception of J. Moffatt, have in the past largely supported Paul's authorship of Ephesians. At present, national lines in the discussion are largely blurred, and scholars from every quarter are urging reconsideration of both sides of the problem.

A. Difficulties for Pauline Authorship. Despite the evident affinities with Pauline theology, other aspects of thought in the Epistle have led to skepticism regarding its authenticity. C. L. Mitton (*Epistle to the Ephesians*), largely following E. J. Goodspeed, lists twelve such objections. The principal arguments are these:

(1) Such unquestionably Pauline letters as 1 and 2 Corinthians and Galatians specify individual congregations alongside discussion of the Church catholic. In Ephesians the Church appears as the "mystical" body of Christ, and all traces of a more fluid usage have vanished.

(2) The observation in Eph. 2:20 that the Church is "built upon the foundation of apostles and prophets" rings with a strange sound after the statement in 1 Cor. 3:11: "No other foundation can anyone lay than that which is laid, which is Jesus Christ." F. J. A. Hort, who strenuously defended the genuineness of Ephesians, admitted that this variation is embarrassing to the defense.

(3) Whereas in Paul's time the controversy between Jews and Gentiles can hardly be called settled, in Ephesians the position of the Gentiles is taken for granted. As Goodspeed observes, "There is no room for any Jewish Christianity in the picture. Christianity is now definitely a gentile religion" (*Key to Ephesians,* p. v). Ephesians, moreover, is unique in asserting that a principal object of Christ's redemptive work is the reconciliation of Jews and Gentiles.

(4) That the immediacy of the second coming of Jesus is a large factor in Paul's thought is evident from a cursory examination of his letters. Even Philippians, regarded by many as Paul's last Epistle, affirms that the Lord is near (4:5); and the earlier Thessalonian correspondence reflects the problem Paul had with his congregations on this subject. Ephesians, on the other hand, lacks the note of urgency sounded in Col. 3:4. The prospect of a long period of development is anticipated in the words, "To him be glory in the church and in Christ Jesus *to all generations,* for ever and ever. Amen." (Eph. 3:21).

(5) Connected with this approach to the Second Coming is the doctrine on marriage. In view of the expectation

of an early return of Jesus Christ, Paul was reluctant to see his Christians entangle themselves in the cares of life engendered by the responsibilities of marriage (see, e.g., 1 Cor. 7). In Ephesians marriage is elevated to such a position of honor that it becomes a symbol of the relationship between Christ and His Church. Mitton observes: "If the different attitudes towards the Second Coming can be reconciled as representing an earlier and a later stage in Paul's own experience, so probably can this change of attitude toward marriage. But many feel that the change is so great as to point to a different author rather than to a later phase in the life of the same author" (*Epistle to the Ephesians,* pp. 22f.).

(6) With respect to Eph. 6:4 Goodspeed writes, "The injunction of 6:4, to bring their children up with Christian training and instruction, is hardly like Paul; all he had to say on it in Col. 3:21 was, 'Do not irritate your children.' For Paul, expectations of the return of Jesus as the Messiah and of the establishment of God's kingdom are still too vivid and imminent to warrant the projection of long-term programs of religious education" (*Key to Ephesians,* p. vii). As Mitton observes, "The discipline of children would, of course, take on new importance as the expectation of an early end to all things diminished" (*Epistle to the Ephesians,* p. 23).

B. Similarity of Ephesians and Colossians. Those who favor the traditional authorship (see III below) attach great weight to the similarity of Ephesians and Colossians. As Percy admits, however, if both letters are Paul's, they must have been written within a very short time of one another. But this insistence poses difficulties, for, in answer to T. Zahn's challenge (*Intro. to the NT* [Eng. tr. 1909], I, 501), similar words and phrases are employed to express completely different concepts. In Col. 1:25 Gk. *oikonomía* is used in the sense of "assigned task"; in Eph. 1:10; 3:2, 9 of God's plan of redemption. Even more striking is the contrasting use of the Gk. *mystḗrion,* used in Eph. 1:9; 3:3f., 9; 6:19 (in view of the total context) with reference to the unity of Jews and Gentiles in benefits of salvation; in Col. 1:26f.; 2:2; 4:3, it is the mystery centered in "Christ, the hope of glory." Eph. 5:19f. appears to be a conflation of Col. 3:16f. If Paul had written Eph. 5:20 shortly after Col. 3:17, is he likely to have altered his own thought while retaining substantially the same wording? What occurs is exactly what might be expected from a writer who recalls a striking sentence or phrase without being very concerned about its context. Hence, he connects "giving of thanks" with *pánta,* which in Colossians properly goes with the clause immediately preceding. In Colossians angelic powers are in the main morally neutral, and Christians are cautioned not to substitute them for Jesus Christ as the means of contact with God; in Ephesians, however, they are an abiding source of evil.

The Gk. *apokatallássō* occurs only three times in the NT, in Col. 1:20, 22, and Eph. 2:16. Moffatt (p. 377) observes that in Colossians the word is used to describe the reconciliation of supernatural powers and of sinners to God, whereas in Ephesians the accent is on the new relation between Jews and Gentiles. Moreover, in Colossians God is the subject of the reconciliation, while in Ephesians it is Christ who takes the initiative.

A further impediment to common authorship of Colossians and Ephesians is posed by the divergent usage of the Gk. *plḗrōma,* found four times in Ephesians (1:10, 23; 3:19; 4:13), twice in Colossians (1:19; 2:9), and a total of six times in Romans (11:12, 25; 13:10; 15:29), 1 Corinthians (10:26), and Galatians (4:4). In Col. 1:19 and 2:9 the word gives expression to a solemn affirmation that the sum total of divine character inhabited the human personality of Jesus, to use Mitton's phrase. This usage represents a development over that in Romans, 1 Corinthians, and Galatians, and this fresh nuance should be reflected in Ephesians, a letter alleged to have been written so shortly after Colossians. Instead, Eph. 3:19 echoes the phrase in which the word occurs in Colossians but uses it in a different sense from Colossians. Indeed, three of the four uses of the word in Ephesians are strange to the reader of the other Pauline letters.

Finally, in Colossians the Christians are warned not to worship "principalities or authorities" (1:16; 2:10). These supernatural hosts become in Ephesians spiritual enemies against whom the Christian soldier must marshal his finest arsenal (1:21; 6:12). These differences between the thought and diction of Colossians and that of Ephesians are not in themselves decisive enough to establish the non-Pauline authorship of Ephesians, but many scholars feel that if Ephesians were written shortly after Colossians, these variations pose an almost insuperable obstacle to common authorship of these two Epistles.

C. Style and Vocabulary. Arguments based on style and vocabulary are apt to be deceptive in dealing with a mercurial personality like that of the apostle Paul (see esp. Cadbury). Yet there are impressions that cannot be ignored. W. R. Inge, according to A. M. Hunter, confessed that after reading the Epistle in English he was sure Paul wrote it, but when he read it in Greek his doubts began to awaken. One cannot gloss over the fact that Ephesians, when viewed in the light of familiar Pauline style, is like a duel with heavy swords compared with a contest of rapiers. Absent is what W. Sanday and A. C. Headlam call the "rapid, terse, and incisive" movement of the great letters. Paul is quick, agile, and nimbly allusive. Ephesians is massive and ponderous with the pressure of heaped synonyms, the piling of defining genitives, and frequent amplifications of individual words (e.g., 2:7; 3:12) and thoughts (1:17b is repeated in v. 18a; 1:22a repeats 1:20b-21). As a syntactical salmagundi, the marvelous spiral of Eph. 1:3-14 is probably without rival in Greek literature. But as K. G. Kuhn points out, it is not strange to the Qumrân texts, which also offer genitival constructions parallel to some in Ephesians (cf. Eph. 1:19 and 1QH 4:32).

Of the lexical phenomena, the occurrence of Gk. *diábolos* (4:27; 6:11) in place of the usual *satanás* is striking, although it should be noted that the two words are apparently quite often used interchangeably (e.g., Mt. 4:1-11). Nor should the peculiar transposition of Eph. 6:12 from the more usual "flesh and blood" to "blood and flesh" be cast into a main anchor for non-Pauline authorship. Percy may be right in suggesting that the writer here avoids collision of two *sigma*s. (Critics of this view usually ignore Percy's own footnote, which is at pains to state that 1 Cor. 6:16 and Eph. 5:31 indeed admit the conjunction of two *sigma*s, but in citations of the LXX [p. 184].) More to the point is the use of the Gk. *hágioi* (3:5). As a designation of the apostles, it is the typical usage of an age that is reassessing itself in the light of past authority (cf. 2 Pet. 3:2 and the shorter appendix to Mark's Gospel). The use of this adjective also involves in this passage a surprising modification of Col. 1:26, which states that the mystery is "now made manifest to his saints." Ephesians limits the saints to the "*holy* apostles and prophets." The Gk. *en toís epouraníois* (1:3, 20; 2:6; 3:10; 6:12) appears to be a mannerism with the writer.

D. Problem of the Addressees. Further difficulty in maintaining Pauline authorship for Ephesians is encountered when the attempt is made to locate the addressees in Paul's chief field of missionary labors on the "third missionary journey" as described in Acts. Few scholars are prepared to defend the variant reading *en Ephesǭ* in 1:1, for the tone of the letter is too impersonal. Paul spent from two to three years in Ephesus, and one would expect some personal greetings in a letter addressed to the congregations there. On the contrary, the recipients appear to be unknown to the writer of Ephesians (1:5; 2:11; 3:2; 4:21). The writer's statements might be interpreted as ironical, but the rest of the letter is so unlike the tone of the Corinthian correspondence, in which such irony finds a proper place.

Scholars writing in defense of the authenticity, therefore, usually follow Archbishop Ussher's view that Ephesians is an encyclical addressed to a circle of churches. According to J. Armitage Robinson, the opening sentence contained a space into which the name of each church in turn might be read. Unfortunately for this theory, several important MSS lack not merely the place name, but the preposition *en* as well. Others suggest that the apostle produced several copies, each with a blank in which the courier could write the name of the receiving congregation. As Percy points out, one must be on guard against reading modern practices into the ancient world. Paul had no duplicating machines and the various congregations would not have been pleased to receive form letters.

Robinson also espouses the popular view that Ephesus was one of the primary recipients, thus explaining the subsequent attachment of the title "To the Ephesians," and the reading "in Ephesus" (p. 11). Fatal to this view, again, is the lack of personal references, which would certainly be forthcoming even in a circular letter, especially to a well-known circle of readers. Moreover, one is forced to explain the absence of "in Ephesus" from such authoritative MSS as ***p***[46], B, and ℵ. Percy senses the difficulty; he locates the addressees in a circle of churches whose members had had no personal relations with the apostle because of their recent conversion and are being reminded to use the gifts they have received through their baptism. But the context of the letter does not lend support to this view, for advice to new converts on such topics as common meals between Jews and Gentiles and the holy eucharist is missing. The admonitions of the Epistle, especially 4:17-24, suggest that the writer is coming to grips with the moral relapses of Christians who are failing to consider sufficiently the meaning of the truths they have known for some time. Feine (p. 196) therefore takes refuge in the view that the letter is addressed to churches in the area around Ephesus, but that Ephesus was not one of the recipients. Yet on this view the Ephesians are ignored by the apostle (unless he sent them a letter of which we are totally ignorant), and the initial problem still remains: How may one explain the lack of personal concern in a letter addressed to an area where the apostle was so well known? Even Colossians, addressed to a congregation not mentioned in Acts, conveys a warmer note (cf. Col. 4:10-18).

Marcion's view that Ephesians is the letter to the Laodiceans mentioned in Col. 4:16 found support in A. Harnack, who suggested that the name Laodicean was very early expunged because of the indictment in Rev. 3:14-22. But the church at Ephesus also receives a serious indictment (Rev. 2:4-7), and it is difficult to conjecture what reasoning prompted the deletion of the one name in preference for the other. Ancient monarchs chiseled off the exploits of their predecessors, but where is the evidence for this type of erasure in the early Church? Masson's amplification of Marcion's view, including the interpolation of 4:16 in Colossians, lacks the credible grace of simplicity.

III. Origin and Purpose.–It is indeed possible to meet singly each of the objections to authenticity with a solid defense; yet one should recognize that the combined challenge presented by the divergences in theological thought, by the differences between Ephesians and Colossians (assuming that the latter epistle is Paul's), by the style and diction, and by the difficulties concerning the addressees, is indeed formidable; and a serious hearing at least must be given to views that attempt to account for the data in other ways.

The puzzling conjunction of Pauline terminology and Pauline thought, in a letter that bears so many non-Pauline marks, prompted E. J. Goodspeed to undertake a study in which the correspondence between Ephesians and the nine generally accepted Pauline letters was carefully documented. From his study Goodspeed concluded that in all probability Onesimus, former slave and perhaps bishop of Ephesus (A.D. 110-117), was inspired by the publication of Luke-Acts to begin a search for Paul's letters, and that as an introduction to this collection Onesimus wrote Ephesians, a kind of patchwork composed out of Paul's genuine letters. Goodspeed was anticipated by J. Weiss in this view that the collector of Paul's letters is also the composer of Ephesians.

Taken as a whole, Goodspeed's theory is unconvincing

This Chester Beatty papyrus (***p***[46]) is one of the earliest extant texts of Ephesians (*ca.* A.D. 200). Note that while the heading is *pros ephesious,* "to the Ephesians," in v. 1 the *en Ephesō,* "in Ephesus," of later MSS is missing (University of Michigan Library)

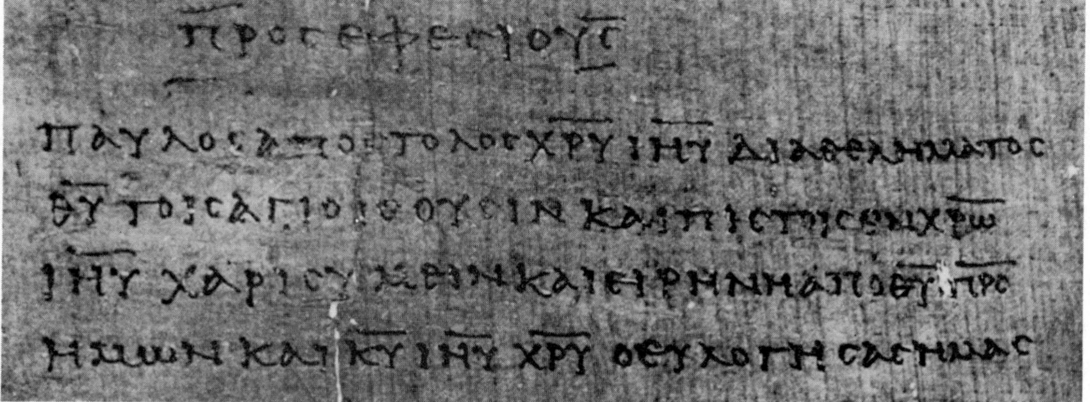

for the following reasons: (1) the connection proposed between Ephesians and Acts overemphasizes the influence of a book and ignores personal relationships; (2) it is highly improbable that the letters of so influential a teacher as Paul should have lain in disuse for several decades; (3) Ephesians includes too many non-Pauline elements to serve as an introduction to Pauline thought and practice; (4) all trace of the primacy of Ephesians in the sequence of Paul's letters is absent from the MS tradition; and (5) the writer does not depend nearly so heavily on the other Pauline letters as he does on Colossians, a fact obscured by Goodspeed's method of citing parallels. Yet, in its main points, Goodspeed's presentation supports the view that many scholars have endorsed.

The detailed chart of seventy-three pages that Goodspeed submits could, of course, be interpreted as evidence for Paul's echoing of his own writings; but the admixture of non-Pauline elements noted previously suggests to many a later Paulinist who has consciously modeled his presentation of the faith after the pattern of Paul's letter to the Colossians, and partly after the eight other generally accepted Pauline letters. If this is so, the author's aim is to make Paul's letter to the Colossians relevant to his own time. Hence he is not constrained to trace slavishly the theological contours of his master and in the manner of a homiletician offers fresh interpretation and application of his "text." Lack of reference to the eucharist in his model Colossians would help explain its absence in Ephesians. The perplexing fluctuation of 1st and 2nd person (see esp. 2:1-3) becomes explicable, and so does the change of emphasis from Paul's view of Christ as the foundation of the Church to the view of Ephesians that the apostles and prophets are its substructure. Assuming the validity of this view of a later authorship, the writer invokes the authority of the "holy apostles," including that of the apostle Paul, and thereby submerges his own identity. The addition of the phrase "Christ Jesus himself being the chief cornerstone" thus tips the writer's hand. Knowing full well what 1 Cor. 3:11 said, he is at pains to avoid what might appear to be a contradiction. That the writer includes almost verbatim the reference to Tychicus made in the first edition (Col. 4:7f.) need not be interpreted as an attempt to "lend *vraisemblance* to the writing" (Moffatt, p. 393). If this is a later Paulinist, it is his own signal that we are not dealing with an attempted "forgery" but a posthumous revision in the direction of a new type of early Christian literary genre.

If the question is raised concerning the admissibility of a pseudonymous writing in the sacred canon, it is well to note that the Holy Spirit's activity in the 1st cent. is not to be prejudged by contemporary canons of publication, which require more precise reference to sources and their contents. Sufficient precedents for pseudonymous authorship are at hand in such books as Daniel, the Testaments of the Twelve Patriarchs, Enoch, Epistle of Jeremiah, Epistle of Aristeas, and others. Luke himself reconstructs the kind of letter Claudius must have sent to Felix (Acts 23:26-30), thus indicating the literary freedom taken in antiquity. Neither the value nor the authority of the Epistle then is weakened by uncertainty concerning its authorship.

From the viewpoint of apostolic doctrine there is no hindrance to such a conclusion, for the Spirit's gifts are varied and His choice of instruments is not subject to human judgment. On the other hand, where false doctrine was an issue Paul warned his readers not to be taken in by a letter purporting to be his (2 Thess. 2:2; 3:17). For the recipients of Ephesians there would be no such problem. The apostle was already dead, and there could be no suggestion of underhanded methods, but rather a reaffirmation of Paul's instruction in accordance with the needs of the hour; hence the shifts in theological accent, but not conflict with apostolic doctrine.

The writer himself suggests the broader range of inspired channels in the early Church (Eph. 4:11) and perhaps in these words signs his own right to confront the Church of his time with the authoritative claims of the Head of the Church. That one who was capable of such high theological flight should have destroyed his identity for posterity is not inexplicable. Like the four Evangelists, like the author of Hebrews, he traded fame for nameless greatness. Precisely because of the Spirit's guidance, there is lacking both the inferior secondary increment often evident in a mere imitator's work and slavish adherence to the model under revision. That the letter should have been identified as Paul's without apparent dissenting vote is a proof not only of the writer's inspired orthodoxy, but a tribute to his understanding of the unity of the Church.

The many associations with Qumrân noted by K. G. Kuhn, the rabbinic treatment of Ps. 67:19 LXX (Eph. 4:8f.) and Isa. 57:19 (Eph. 2:13-17), and the direct address to the Gentiles in 2:11f. point to a Jewish convert. The writer's view of the universality of the new Israel of God and the fact that this new Israel is predominantly gentile would help further to account for the fluctuation between 1st and 2nd plural in 2:1-3.

Yet, when all is said, scrupulous scholarship must confess that the many lacunae in the history of early Christian literature admit of only tentative conclusions in the matter of Ephesians. The History of Religions school, which emphasized too strongly the influence of Hellenistic thought, has been compelled to learn from Qumrân. If the present state of evidence seems to favor the view that Ephesians is more probably post-Pauline, future discoveries and more detailed investigations yet to come may move the pointer more decisively in the opposite direction.

The best case for the traditional view of Pauline authorship is made by D. Guthrie (pp. 490-508).

(1) Linguistic and stylistic arguments. Guthrie cautions about dogmatizing on what expressions Paul could or could not have used and warns against the methodological hazard of conclusions based on questionable dating of "so-called later first-century books." The stylistic variations may be an indication of "Paul's versatility." If Ephesians is the work of someone else, the literary artistry displayed in the handling of Pauline themes is "extraordinary" (Guthrie, pp. 491f.).

(2) Literary arguments. Criteria of dissimilarity are not sufficiently refined to dissociate Ephesians from Paul. In fact, "a conscious imitator would have endeavoured to keep as close as possible to his model," but Ephesians displays both "spiritual and intellectual power" and "freedom from a slavish reproduction of Colossians" (p. 494). Furthermore, why should a later Paulinist have chosen Colossians, rather than another Epistle, as his base? Since both Epistles identify the body as the Church (Col. 1:18; Eph. 5:23), the alleged difference between Eph. 4:15f. and Col. 2:19 is untenable. Words like Gk. *mystḗrion* (see Rom. 16:25f.) and *oikonomía* could be used in various senses by the same person. The conflations are more probable on the assumption of Paul's authorship, for an imitator could easily have consulted Colossians. Mitton's two tests for discriminating between a writer and his imitator oversimplify literary data. Similarity in subject matter may well account for concentration of allusion to earlier writings into certain groups, and the reproduction of "striking and memorable phrases" is subject to a variety of factors. The personal references in Eph. 3:2, 4, 8 are not "theatrical," but accent Paul's dependence on the

grace of God; an imitator would hardly have made Paul, whom he admired so ardently, call himself "the least of the apostles" (Guthrie, pp. 492-502).

(3) Historical arguments. The theme of eliminating a spiritual barrier between Jews and Gentiles argues rather for Pauline authorship. After A.D. 70 a reference to the destruction of the temple would have borne much more force. The writer's self-identification as a "child of wrath" (2:3) does not rule out the apostle, who identifies himself in a universal expression with his readers and in v. 11 says "you Gentiles." Besides, both Jew and Greek are in "desperate need of God's mercy" (v. 4; Guthrie, pp. 502f.).

(4) Doctrinal arguments. A chain is as strong as its weakest link, and the support for non-Pauline authorship must be assessed analytically. Ephesians does not belabor the Christian ministry as a later "ecclesiastic" (Goodspeed) would have done. Eph. 2:20 is not out of harmony with Paul's frequent claims for apostolic authority. The description "holy" in 3:5 must not be confused with modern connotations. The term is also applied by Paul to believers in general, as in Col. 1:26. In addition, the term "prophets" suggests a more primitive period of the Church. Inconsistencies in expression of Christology are apparent also, e.g., in 1 Cor. 8:6. Goodspeed's argument based on Christ's descent into Hades founders on the questionable nature of his assumption that Rom. 10:6f. excludes the doctrine of Eph. 4:9. The doctrine of the unification of Jew and Gentile is less explicable in a later Paulinist who would be expected to stress the main Pauline themes of redemption rather than one of the subsidiary results of the death of Christ. Paul's high view of marriage in Ephesians is not inconsistent with his bachelor status. The admonition to fathers on rearing their children is scarcely indicative of "'a long-term policy of religious education' [Goodspeed]" (Guthrie, pp. 503-507).

(5) Conclusions. The self-testimony of the Epistles deserves greater consideration than is usually accorded it by exponents of pseudonymous authorship, insists Guthrie. Authorship by Paul rather than a later self-effacing Paulinist is more credible. It is improbable that the letter is to be traced to an amanuensis, for he would not have had access to all Pauline Epistles with which Ephesians has contacts; he would have adhered more closely to the phraseology of Colossians and would "hardly have enlarged upon the ethical sections as the author of Ephesians has done"; in addition, the author's references to himself become inexplicable, and "it is difficult to find an adequate motive for the apostle to adopt so unusual a procedure" (Guthrie, pp. 507f.; cf. van Roon, pp. 91-94).

IV. Date.–Allusions to this Epistle are indistinct in 1 Clement (36:2 [Eph. 4:18]; 59:3 [Eph. 1:18]; 46:6 [Eph. 4:4-6]), but more definite in Ignatius (Smyrn. 1:2 [Eph. 1:23; 2:16]; Polyc. 1:2 [Eph. 4:2f.]; 5:1 [Eph. 5:25]). In Polycarp the reproduction is even more precise; compare Eph. 2:8 with Polyc. Phil. 1:3, and 4:26 with Polyc. Phil. 12:1. If the letter is not Paul's, a date around A.D. 90 (perhaps a decade earlier if 1 Peter is dependent on the Epistle) would be perfectly plausible. The removal of the wall of partition between Jews and Gentiles (2:14) may be an allusion to the destruction of Jerusalem in A.D. 70. The Church has become predominantly gentile, and in place of fear of a relapse into Judaism (cf. Phil. 3, one of Paul's last letters) the temptation of the readers to fade back into pagan ways looms large. If the letter is from Paul's hand, its connection with Colossians and Philemon would point to Paul's imprisonment in Rome, *ca.* A.D. 61. (See Percy on the problems associated with the date and place of origin, pp. 467-474.)

V. Text.–The text of Ephesians has in general enjoyed an accurate transmission. The chief problem, as already noted, is in 1:1, the reading *en Ephesō̧*. Papyrus 46, the first hand in both Codices Vaticanus and Sinaiticus, 1739, and ancient codices known to Marcion and Origen omitted the words. The Gk. *toís hagíois toís oúsin kaí pistoís en Christō̧ Iēsou* is rendered by Moffatt, "to the saints who are faithful in Christ Jesus." The Epistle does not, however, stress faithfulness but unity in the faith. The association of Gk. *ekklēsía* with *hágioi* in Ps. 88:6 LXX suggests rather that the writer of Ephesians sees in the Christian an extension of the Israel of old. The members are saints, but they are qualified as believers in Jesus Christ. The Hebrew word underlying the LXX term is also applied to its community by the Qumrân sect (cf. 1QH 4:24f., where, however, angels may be meant; 11:11f.; and, if the restoration is correct, 6:13). The title "To the Ephesians" was probably added in the 2nd cent. through association of Tychicus with Ephesus (2 Tim. 4:12). Some place name was felt desirable, and the name Ephesus was chosen for reasons unknown.

VI. Theology.Beyond question this Epistle fits within boundaries largely familiar in other Pauline letters. In the following paragraphs the main parallels with other Pauline Epistles (except Colossians, because of the more obvious dependence) are listed.

The dominant note is God's design before the foundation of the world to work out a plan for men to share a family relationship with their Creator (Eph. 1:4f.; cf. 1QH 9:29-31; 15:13-15). The personal accent in this plan is also expressed in Rom. 8:28-30. God's own sovereign will is the determining factor (Eph. 1:5, 9, 11; cf. Rom. 9:19-26). Eph. 1:4, however, introduces the thought that election, which took place prior to creation, was *in Christ*. We are not the victims of an inscrutable fate; we are left not to the mercy of astral vagaries, but to the concern of the Father (1:2f). For the sovereign will of God is qualified by love, the principal motivating cause of man's redemption (Eph. 1:4f. [following Moffatt and RSV]; 1:7; 2:4). Such thought is customary in the Johannine writings; but also in Romans (5:8) Jesus' death is a demonstration of God's love, and according to Rom. 8:39 God's love in Christ Jesus undergirds the Christian's hope. Apart from God's controlling purpose the death of Jesus would lack significance. But because this death is God's way of demonstrating His kindness toward man, Jesus is the Christ and His blood may be said to be the effective means of redemption (Eph. 1:7). From the standpoint of OT religion, His death restores contact between God and especially the Gentiles (2:13); in Romans (3:25 and 5:9), too, Paul capitalizes on the apparent disaster of Jesus' death. The immediate goal of the death of Jesus is to unify Jews and Gentiles by eliminating the law as a criterion of a proper relationship with God (Eph. 2:16). Thus the writer moves on the plane of thought expressed in Rom. 5:10, where the accent is on man's reconciliation with God.

A further objective of the redemptive process in Jesus Christ is the praise of God (cf. 1QH 13:13; 15:13-15). Demonstration of God's extraordinary kindness in connection with Jesus Christ is to be made to succeeding ages (Eph. 2:7); this echoes the thought of Rom. 9:23. The praise of God is actualized as the Christian lives a life of good works. These good works are not an afterthought, nor a human contribution in return for the divine favor; they are integrally related to the redemptive design (God has prepared them beforehand, Eph. 2:10) and are viewed as divine conferments (cf. Phil. 2:13) — the Christian exercises the privilege of "walking in them" (Eph. 2:9f.). This new behavior is in contrast to the addressees' former way of life in "the lusts of the flesh," when they followed the dictates of their flesh and mind, i.e., their determination to live independently of divine direction (2:3f; cf. Gal. 5:16). It is made possible through union with Christ in His resurrection and enthronement (Eph. 2:6f.; cf. Rom. 8:10f.).

By thus reiterating the indicatives of redemption, the writer is able to present his practical ethical program inside a theological imperative. Union with God makes possible a fellowship guaranteed by "lowliness and meekness" (Eph. 4:2), honesty and respect for one another's property (Eph. 4:25-28; cf. 1 Thess. 4:1:1), and other desirable attitudes (4:29-32). The experience of God's love in Christ provides an objective criterion for strengthening proper impressions of the dignity and worth of fellow human beings, especially members of the opposite sex. Respect for personality rather than self-indulgence will indicate that one has learned to be an "imitator of God" (Eph. 5:1-20; cf. Gal. 5:19-23; 1 Cor. 6:9-11). Thus husbands and wives have a unique opportunity to indicate their understanding of the relation between Christ and His Church. Children are to obey their parents "in the Lord" (Eph. 6:1), and fathers are to bring up their children "in the discipline and instruction of the Lord" (6:4). Slaves are to serve their masters as though they were given their orders by Christ (6:6). In brief, the consciousness of an intimate connection with their heavenly Father is to trigger the Christians' responses to any social situation or demand. In the warnings against fellowship with the works of darkness (Eph. 5:7-14; cf. 2 Cor. 6:14) and the exhortation to reprove the guilty, we are perhaps justified in hearing echoes of 1QS 5:24–6:1; the same line of thought may underlie Eph. 4:26. In any event, the dualism light *v.* darkness is not cosmological but ethical, as at Qumrân (see esp. 1QS 3:13–4:26).

In competition with the objectives of God is the demonic world (Eph. 6:12; cf. 1 Thess. 3:5; 1 Cor. 7:5; 2 Cor. 2:11), whose headquarters are in the heavens (Eph. 2:2; 6:12; cf. Job 1:6; Zec. 3:1) and who govern the lives of unbelievers (Eph. 2:2). Against these celestial adversaries the Christian must fight valiantly (6:13-18; on the light shed from Qumrân on 6:10-20 see *TDNT,* V, 297-300 [Kuhn]). The outcome of the battle is never seriously in doubt, for Christ, as the Savior of the body (Eph. 5:23), is supreme over all rule, authority, power, and dominion (1:21; cf. Phil. 2:9); He is the head of all creation (Eph. 1:22). His achievements are ratified to the Christian's own satisfaction by the sealing of the Spirit, who is a pledge of the coming inheritance (1:13f.; cf. 2 Cor. 1:22; Gal. 3:2). He brings wisdom and insight into God's purpose (Eph. 1:17-19; cf. Rom. 9:23) so that the Christian's hope may remain alive. He supplies the Church with appropriate instruments of the revelation of His intent, namely apostles and prophets (Eph. 3:5), and fortifies the Christian to appreciate the greatness of God's redemption (3:16-19; cf. Rom. 9:23). Therefore the Christian must carefully avoid "grieving the Holy Spirit" (Eph. 4:30; cf. 1 Thess. 5:19). The Spirit prompts the Christian to proper worship (Eph. 5:18f.; cf. 1 Cor. 14:15) and equips him with a powerful offensive weapon, the Word of God (Eph. 6:17). The basic theme of election to unity is never left out of sight: that the Christian may not isolate himself he is reminded to pray "in the Spirit" and to make "supplication for *all* the saints" (6:18).

The Spirit makes possible the overarching unity of the Church through the missionary activity of the apostle Paul (3:1-13; cf. Rom. 12:5). The gentile Church is not a new or sectarian development but in continuity with Jewish history (Eph. 2:14f.; cf. 2 Cor. 8:1-7; Rom. 15:25-27). This Church is the body of Christ, the fulness of God, who has given Christ to the Church as the head of all things (Eph. 1:22f.). As God's new creation (2:15) it is the temple of the Spirit (2:22; cf. 1 Cor. 3:16) and the bride of Christ (Eph. 5:22-33; cf. 2 Cor. 11:2). At the same time the Church, being the *plḗrōma* or fulness of Jesus Christ, constitutes the Second Adam (Eph. 1:23; 2:15), who as God's creation is designed for good works (2:10; cf. 4:24; 2 Cor. 9:8). Thus ecclesiology becomes a function of Christology, and the Church's mission to the world is rooted in her understanding of the lordship of Christ.

The unity of the Church does not depend on resolutions of men; it is a gift of God, who gives one Lord, one faith, one baptism, and is Father to all who share the right of sonship (4:3-5; cf. 1 Cor. 8:6; 10:17; 12:13). The unity is to be maintained, not artificially created (Eph. 4:3). The peace of the Church is interrupted when Christians fail to exercise properly the gifts of service dispensed by Jesus Christ (4:1-3; cf. 1 Thess. 2:12). These gifts are designed for mutual edification and personal spiritual growth. Some, like the apostle Paul, who was given the opportunity (Gk. *cháris*) to preach the gospel to the Gentiles (3:7f.; cf. Gal. 1:16), are apostles, others prophets, others evangelists, and still others pastors and teachers (Eph. 4:11). William Tyndale has best caught the objective: "that the sainctes might have all thinges necessarie to worke and minister with all, to the edifyinge of the body of christ" (4:12; cf. 2 Cor. 12:19).

Mention of the holy eucharist is singularly absent from this letter. The sacrament of holy baptism, however, receives strong emphasis, in the reference to the sealing of the Spirit (Eph. 1:13; 4:30), and specifically in 4:5 and 5:26. Reitzenstein and Bultmann see in 5:14 a Gnostic call to the soul, but K. G. Kuhn (in *NTS*; cf. A. M. Hunter, *Paul and His Predecessors* [rev. ed. 1961], pp. 38f.) convincingly argues in favor of an early baptismal hymn and sees associations with Qumrân.

***Bibliography.–Comms.*:** T. K. Abbott (*ICC,* 1897); J. A. Allen (*Torch,* 1959); M. Barth (*AB,* 1974), esp. pp. 401-420; F. W. Beare (*IB,* 1953); F. F. Bruce (1961); H. Conzelmann (*NTD,* rev. ed. 1962); M. Dibelius (*HNT,* 3rd ed. 1953); F. Foulkes (*Tyndale,* 1963); W. Lock (*WC,* 1929); C. Masson (1953); C. L. Mitton (*New Century Bible,* 1977); J. A. Robinson (1903); H. Schlier (2nd ed. 1958); E. F. Scott (*MNTC,* 1930); E. K. Simpson, (*NICNT,* 1957); B. F. Westcott (1906).

Studies: E. Best, *One Body in Christ* (1955); H. J. Cadbury, *NTS,* 5 (1958/59), 91-102; L. Cerfaux, *Christ in the Theology of St. Paul* (Eng. tr. 1959); F. L. Cross, ed., *Studies in Ephesians* (1956); N. A. Dahl, *Theologische Zeitschrift,* 7 (1951), 241-264; "Cosmic Dimensions and Religious Knowledge (Eph. 3:18)," in E. E. Ellis and E. Grässer, eds., *Jesus und Paulus* (1975), pp. 57-75; E. J. Goodspeed, *Meaning of Ephesians* (1933); *Key to Ephesians* (1956); S. Hanson, *Unity of the Church in the NT* (1958); G. Johnston, *Doctrine of the Church in the NT* (1943), pp. 136-140 (critique of Goodspeed's theory); J. C. Kirby, *Ephesians, Baptism and Pentecost* (1968); J. Knox, *Philemon among the Letters of Paul* (rev. ed. 1959); K. G. Kuhn, *NTS,* 7 (1961), 334-346; R. J. McKelvey, *NTS,* 8 (1962), 352-59; C. L. Mitton, *Epistle to the Ephesians* (1951); *Formation of the Pauline Corpus of Letters* (1955); F. Mussner, *Christus das All und die Kirche* (1955); E. Percy, *Probleme der Kolosser-und Epheserbriefe* (1946); *RGG, s.v.* "Epheserbrief" (Käsemann); A. van Roon, *Authenticity of Ephesians* (1974); J. P. Sampley, *'And the Two Shall Become One Flesh': A Study of Traditions in Ephesians 5:21-33* (1971); G. Schille, *TLZ,* 82 (1957), cols. 325-334; H. Schlier, *Christus und die Kirche im Epheserbrief* (1930).

Intros.: P. Feine, J. Behm, and W. G. Kümmel, *Intro. to the NT* (14th rev. ed., Eng. tr. 1966), pp. 247-258; D. Guthrie, *NT Intro.* (3rd ed. 1970), pp. 479-521; W. G. Kümmel, *Intro. to the NT* (rev. ed., Eng. tr. 1975), pp. 350-366; A. H. McNeile, *Intro. to the NT* (2nd ed. 1953); J. Moffatt, *Intro. to the Literature of the NT* (3rd ed. 1918), pp. 373-395; A. Wikenhauser, *NT Intro.* (Eng. tr. 1958), pp. 421-430.

F. W. DANKER

EPHESUS ef′ə-səs [Gk. *Ephesos*–'desirable']. An important seaport city of the Roman province of Asia. In the NT it is mentioned in Acts 18:19-28; 19:1, 17-20; 20:16f.; 1 Cor. 15:32; 16:8; 1 Tim. 1:3; 2 Tim. 1:18; 4:12; Rev. 1:11; 2:1. Since some of the earliest MSS omit Gk. *en Ephesǭ* ("at Ephesus") in Eph. 1:3, the Epistle to the Ephesians may have been intended as a circular letter rather than specifically directed to the Ephesian church (*see* EPHESIANS, EPISTLE TO THE II.D).

The site of ancient Ephesus is S of the Caÿster River and about 5½ km. (3½ mi.) upstream from where it enters enters the Aegean Sea at the point opposite the island of Samos. Because of the sandy beaches it has been thought that Ephesus was situated on an inlet of the Aegean and that the coastline has receded. J. T. Wood in his archeological campaigns for the British Museum (1863-1872) discovered a continuous stone embankment along the river leading from the city to within a few hundred feet of the coast. This embankment undoubtedly was a part of the abortive plan of King Attalus Philadelphus to deepen the inland waterway (cf. Strabo *Geog.* xiv.1.24). Pliny's statement that "the sea used to wash up to the temple of Diana" (*Nat. hist.* ii.87[201]) may be nothing more than legend or may reflect a very early tradition reaching back several centuries before the Roman period.

The Caÿster is the smallest of four major rivers entering the Aegean from Asia Minor. As long as the inland harbor remained accessible, Ephesus was well situated to become the chief commercial center of western Asia Minor (Strabo, *loc. cit.*), for it had ideally positioned

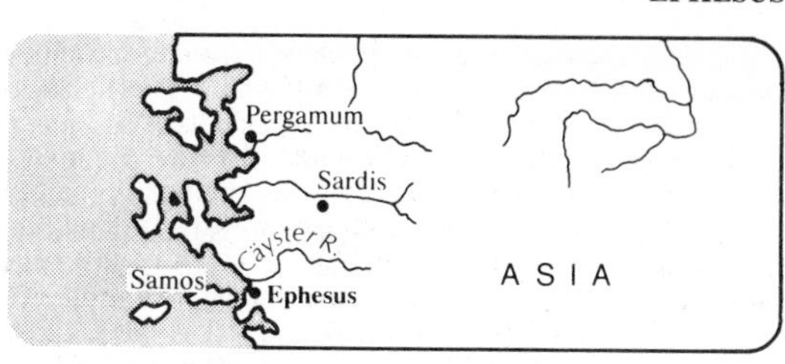

passes that gave immediate access for trade both N and S to the Hermus and Maeander river valleys. The presence of the temple of Artemis (Diana) added to the commercial importance of Ephesus, for two reasons. First, the temple was regarded as sacrosanct throughout the Mediterranean world and thus became the primary banking institution of Asia Minor. Second, pilgrims swelled the population and contributed substantially to Ephesian business, especially during the festivals of Artemis (March-April). So prominent was the city that during the early Christian period the population of Ephesus probably exceeded a quarter million.

Ephesus lay at the intersection of two ancient major overland routes: the coastal road that ran north through Smyrna and Pergamum to Troas (near ancient Troy); and the western route to Colossae, Hierapolis, Laodicea, and regions of Phygia and beyond. Ephesus can also be viewed as the starting-point of a type of postal route (cf. the order of the seven cities of Revelation 2–3) running north to Pergamum and southwest through Sardis to Laodicea.

Greek theater and the Arkadiane Way leading to the harbor at Ephesus (B. K. Condit)

The city was positioned between two mountainous ridges that run roughly northwest. The western ridge, composed of the Koressos and Astyages hills (also known as Bülbül), forms the background for the Ephesian harbor, while the eastern ridge, topped by the twin peaks of Mt. Pion (also known as Panayır), forms the foundation on which was constructed the theater (Acts 19:30). This theater held more than 24,000 people on sixty-six tiers of seats with a great stage measuring about 35 m. (115 ft.) by 21 m. (70 ft.). The facade was probably built in two periods, the first two levels apparently during the time of Domitian and the third level near the beginning of the 3rd century. Though the theater lies in ruins today, its acoustics are still superb.

Approximately ⅔ km. N of the theater lies the ruins of a great stadium, which probably served for various athletic events. The eastern end may also have been used for gladiatorial battles and wrestling matches with wild beasts.

The great marble main street of Ephesus, the Arkadiane, ran NW from the theater to the harbor and on both sides was flanked by an elaborate colonnade. Included in the remains are great baths, the once magnificent Fountain of Trajan, a second-century Temple of Hadrian, the Odeion or little theater, which served the city as a council chamber, a library linked with the name of Celsus (the opponent of the second-century Christian Apologists), and a great *agora* or marketplace (*see* picture in ACTS OF THE APOSTLES). Carved into the great sidewalk leading to a building on the marble street is the mark of a bare foot, the ancient sign of direction to a house of prostitution — a reminder that Ephesus was a port city with many visitors and sailors. Elsewhere, carved into the steps of the library, is a menorah, an indication of some Jewish presence in the city.

The temple of Artemis was situated about 1½ km. (1 mi.) NE of the city. Above the plain and overlooking the temple site in what is known as Aysaluk about 5 km. (3 mi.) from Ephesus was constructed the Basilica of St. John. John is supposed to be buried there. But Meinardus (p. 73) asks which John, since according to Eusebius (*HE* iii.3) Papias, the famed second-century bishop of Hierapolis, "asserts there were also two tombs in Ephesus, and that both are called John's even to this day." This church erected to the memory of John is not to be confused with the Church of the Virgin Mary in which the Council of Ephesus was held in A.D. 431, when Nestorius was condemned in the *Theotokos* issue. The Church of the Virgin was located slightly N of the Arkadiane and was built on the foundation of an earlier large building, probably used for a museum.

The early history of Ephesus is clouded by a legend involving the Amazons, who allegedly built the city because of its proximity to the birthplace of the mother goddess of earth. *Ca.* 1044 B.C., however, the Athenian King Androclus conquered the Asians (cf. Strabo *Geog.* xiv.1.4; 1.21) and established Ephesus as one of twelve cities in the Ionian Confederacy. As Pausanias indicates (vii.2.6), the oriental goddess native to the area was adopted by the Greeks and assumed the characteristics of Artemis. The Lydians under Croesus conquered Ephesus *ca.* 560 B.C. and dedicated the city to Artemis (Herodotus i.26). Croesus in turn was defeated by Cyrus (*ca.* 546 B.C.), and Ephesus fell under the rule of the Persians.

During the Ionian period the city developed on the slopes of the Koresos highland, while during the Persian period the population moved to the lowlands nearer the temple of Artemis, more in harmony with the Asiatic village orientation. Greek and oriental forces vied for Ephesus during the next two centuries, and it was not until Alexander the Great conquered the Persians in 334 B.C. that Ephesus fell under Macedonian influence. Apparently on the very night that Alexander was born (356 B.C.) the temple was burned. When Alexander reached maturity he offered to rebuild it at his own expense. The priests, who had already commissioned Dinocrates to rebuild the temple and who did not wish to be under greater obligation to Alexander, politely refused the offer, suggesting that it was not fitting for one god to build a temple to another (cf. Strabo *Geog.* xiv.1.22). M. Parvis notes an interesting shift in coinage after the period from the traditional bee, the symbol of Artemis, to the Greek type of image — the head of Artemis (p. 64).

Church of the Virgin Mary in Ephesus (B. K. Condit)

After the death of Alexander, Lysimachus, one of Alexander's generals, received Asia Minor and sought to move the city to a more defensible position on higher ground within a walled complex. The ruins of these upper fortifications are still evident today. The people refused, so he stopped the sewers during a great rain and flooded the city. The people moved (cf. Strabo xiv.1.21). Lysimachus also constructed a new harbor. He concluded a treaty with Ptolemy of Egypt, and thus an Egyptian influence was begun at Ephesus, especially in religion and the magical arts.

In 281 B.C. Lysimachus fell to Seleucus I, and Ephesus thus came under the control of the rulers who would govern Palestine. In 190 B.C. the Seleucid ruler Antiochus the Great was defeated by the Romans at the Battle of Magnesia with assistance from King Eumenes II of Pergamum. Pergamum was accordingly given control of Ephesus (Livy xxxvii.36-45). When in 133 B.C., by testimentary disposition of King Attalus III of Pergamum, Asia was given to Rome and thereby became a Roman province, Pergamum, not Ephesus, was made the capital. With the help of Mithradates of Pontus, Ephesus in 88 B.C. rebelled and slaughtered the Romans even in the hitherto inviolable precincts of the temple of Artemis. The rebellion was stopped by Sulla but Ephesus was not finally subjected until 41 B.C. by Mark Antony. During the reign of Caesar Augustus, Ephesus began to flourish. It continued to expand until the Goths sacked the city and burned the temple in the last half of the 3rd cent. A.D.

The temple of Artemis was first constructed under the direction of Chersiphron in the 6th cent. B.C. on the site of an earlier worship center. During the battle with Croesus the Ionians committed their city to Artemis and symbolically joined the walls to the temple by means of a holy cord, which was at least seven stadia in length (Herodotus i.26). Although the city fell, a tradition concerning Artemis began to develop which ultimately established the temple as the most sacrosanct in the eastern Mediterranean world. After the fire of 356 B.C. (allegedly set by Herostratus [Strabo,

Geog. xiv.1.22]), because of lack of funds and the Ephesians' proud refusal of Alexander's offer, the temple was not fully restored for over two centuries. This later temple, according to Wood's reconstruction, measured about 128 m. (420 ft.) long and 73 m. (240 ft.) wide. The roof was about 18 m. (60 ft.) high and was supported by 117 columns (not 127 as Pliny suggests). Its magnificence and beauty earned it a place among the seven wonders of the ancient world. The statue of Artemis was probably at least in part constructed from a fallen meteorite, which would explain the statement in Acts concerning "the sacred stone that fell from the sky" (Acts 20:35). Several statues of Artemis have been discovered that picture her as a female deity with many breasts, symbolic of her fruitfulness and wealth. Her temple was devastated by the Goths in A.D. 262 and, although apparently reestablished in a smaller temporary setting for a short time, it was finally demolished in the 4th century. The stones and pillars were used in the construction of both the great Basilica of St. Sophia at Constantinople and the early Church of St. John at Ephesus.

Paul first visited Ephesus on his second missionary journey (Acts 18:19-28) and on the third journey remained approximately two years, teaching first in the synagogue and then in the hall of Tyrannus (19:8-10). Apparently Paul established a fairly strong church at Ephesus, because in Revelation the church is commended for its earlier strength and exhorted to return to its former love (Rev. 2:1-7).

When it became evident that the gospel would gain an audience in Ephesus as it had elsewhere, Demetrius, a maker of Artemisian silver shrines, became concerned for his business (Acts 19:23-28). Some scholars have suggested that because no such silver images have been uncovered and because an inscription has been unearthed referring to a Demetrius who was "a temple warden" Luke must have been mistaken. But as Filson indicates (p. 77) archeologists have been investigating public buildings, not private homes where such shrines would be found. Moreover, silver items are among the first to be plundered and remolded. Also, the base of a statue that had been erected by the guild of silversmiths has been discovered in Curetes Street (Meinardus, p. 73).

The protest that arose against Paul here nearly reached riot proportions and was quelled only by the logic of the town clerk — a chief city officer (Acts 19:35-41). Some argue that there were at Ephesus a Roman *praetorium* and *collegia* of imperial freedmen and slaves who composed a company that could be called "Caesar's household" (Phil. 4:22). This argument seems to suggest incorrectly that the capital had already been moved to Ephesus, but such a theory runs counter to the text of Acts, according to which an *asiarch* — not a Roman proconsul — seems to be in charge of the city. One wonders whether a proconsul would absent himself from the scene if he was in the same city when a riot was taking place. Some also link this theory to an argument that Paul was imprisoned at Ephesus at the time he wrote the Epistle to the Philippians. This latter theory is based chiefly on the suggestion that 2 Cor. 11:23 implies that Paul suffered more than the imprisonments at Caesarea and Rome, and is supported by a statement in the apocryphal Acts of Paul concerning his imprisonment at Ephesus.

Christianity gradually made inroads into the city known as the "temple keeper of the great Artemis" (Acts 19:35), and according to the weight of tradition the city became the center for the labor of the beloved disciple John, whose memory was preserved in the building of a great church.

Although Ephesus lies in ruins today, the railway station nearby is called Ayasoluk, a corruption of Gk. *hágios Theológos*, "the holy theologian," a well-known reference in Eastern Christendom to the beloved Evangelist.

Bibliography.–J. T. Wood, *Modern Discoveries on the Site of Ancient Ephesus* (1890); M. M. Parvis, *BA*, 8 (1945), 61-73; F. V. Filson, *BA*, 8 (1945), 73-80; J. Keil, *Ephesos, Ein Führer durch die Ruinenstätte und ihre Geschichte* (3rd ed. 1955); O. F. A. Meinardus, *BA*, 37 (1974), 69-82.

G. L. BORCHERT

EPHLAL ef'lal [Heb. *'eplāl*]. A descendant of Judah (1 Ch. 2:37).

EPHOD ē'fod [Heb. *'ēpōḏ*]. Father of Hanniel, a leader of Manasseh (Nu. 34:23).

EPHOD ē'fod, e'fod [Heb. *'ēpôḏ, 'ēpōḏ, 'ᵃpuddâ* (Ex. 28:8; 39:5; Isa. 30:22); Akk. *epadu, epattum*; Ugar. *ipd*]. The name of a kind of garment, especially of the high priest, and perhaps of other coverings.

The references to the high priest's ephod in Ex. 28:4-40; 35:27; 39:2-30 describe a sleeveless vest, which fitted close to the body and may have extended somewhat below the hips. The feminine form of the word, Heb. *'ᵃpuddâ* (Isa. 30:22), also designates a closely fitting tunic. The high priest's ephod was made from choice, expensive materials including gold in the form of chains and perhaps also of thread or thin wire; purple, blue, and scarlet cloth; and finely woven linen. The ephod was fastened at the shoulder by clasps, to which were attached two onyx stones engraved with the names of the twelve tribes of Israel (Ex. 28:9-12). An elaborately woven girdle circling the waist held the ephod close to the body. Placed over the ephod on the chest of the priest was a breastpiece of the same materials, on which were set twelve precious stones in four rows. This breastpiece was arranged in a double fold (Ex. 28:16) so as to form a pocket or pouch, in which the URIM AND THUMMIM were placed. The latter seem to have been small flat or rounded objects which were cast as lots by the high priest to discover God's will on particular matters. (*See* DIVINATION III.B.) The nature of these objects is rather obscure, however, and some modern scholars, following the LXX, Josephus, and certain later Jewish traditions, have identified them with twelve stones attached to the breastpiece. Also associated with the ephod and worn underneath it was a blue robe that reached to the feet, a garment decorated at the bottom with golden bells and pomegranates.

An essential component of the high priest's vestments, the ephod was worn for ceremonies in the wilderness tent of meeting or at the altar of the holy place in the tabernacle. From the early monarchy the ephod figured prominently in all sacrificial rites involving the high priest. After the wilderness period persons other than the high priest wore ephods, particularly when ministering before the altar. Typical of such attire as worn by ordinary priests (1 S. 2:28; 14:3; 22:18) was the linen ephod that young Samuel wore as he assisted the aged priest Eli in ministering before the Lord (1 S. 2:18). David wore a linen ephod when he cavorted in the procession returning the ark of the covenant to Jerusalem (2 S. 6:14). The divinatory functions of the ephod were enlisted by David on two occasions (1 S. 23:9; 30:7) to ascertain God's will for the immediate future. Evidently Abiathar the high priest had removed this particular ephod from Nob; hence it represented for David God's presence and authority in Israel.

Some scholars have argued that ephods other than that described in Ex. 28–39 may have been images rather than garments. Thus the golden ephod that Gideon made for

Ophrah (Jgs. 8:27) has been considered either a gold idol or image (cf. Ex. 32:4) or a representation of deity upon which a golden ephod had been placed to symbolize authority. Since Isaiah condemned the Israelite idolatry that had encouraged "silver-covered graven images and . . . gold-plated molten images" (Isa. 30:22), the adornment of idols may have been current in Israel from the Settlement period, an apparent imitation of Canaanite cultic practices (cf. 2 K. 23:7). The text seems to indicate, however, that Gideon's ephod was in fact an imitation of the high priestly garment described in Exodus, fashioned from the gold and jewels taken by the Israelites from Midianite warriors slain in battle. In the case of Micah the Ephraimite (Jgs. 17:5; 18:14-20), the ephod was associated in worship with the silver graven image, the molten image, and teraphim (terra-cotta images of the household deities). A similar tradition apparently existed in the northern kingdom as late as Hosea's time (Hos. 3:4). Although the Hebrews were discouraged from using teraphim as early as the patriarchal period (cf. Gen. 35:2-4), terra-cotta images of deities, many examples of which have been recovered from Near Eastern archeological sites, continued in use intermittently until the Exile. Micah's ephod seems to have been independent of the images, and was most probably worn by Micah in his capacity as priest or diviner. The mention of the ark of the covenant in the MT of 1 S. 14:18 presents a problem of location, since the ark was then stationed at Kiriath-jearim. The problem is resolved by reading "ephod" instead of "ark," as does the LXX.

In all cases, the ephods appear to have been elaborately decorated, costly garments of various sizes and weights. They were worn by the high priest in his special ministrations, and later by other priests during cultic functions, including the determination of the divine will. Perhaps, when not in use, certain ephods were hung on a wall, or placed on a stand, possibly of roughly human shape, as may have been the case with Gideon's ephod. In such a situation, an image's clothing would have had coincidental rather than cultic significance. Ephods were used in worship in the northern kingdom as well as in the southern (cf. Hos. 3:4), though the extent to which they were patterned upon Aaron's garment is unknown. While the postexilic high priests most probably did continue to use ephods as part of their ceremonial regalia, in conformity with traditional Mosaic regulations, no evidence for this exists.

Bibliography.–W. R. Arnold, *Ephod and Ark* (1917); J. Morgenstern, *The Ark, the Ephod, and the "Tent of Meeting"* (1945); R. de Vaux, *Ancient Israel* (1961), pp. 349-352; H. M. Buck, *People of the Lord* (1966), pp. 93f.

R. K. HARRISON

EPHPHATHA ef'ə-thə, ef-ä'thə [Gk. *ephphathá* (transliteration of Aram.; cf. Heb. *pāṯaḥ*)]. An Aramaic word used by Christ in the healing of the deaf-mute (Mk. 7:34; cf. Isa. 35:5). Mark translates the term with Gk. *dianoíchtheti,* "be opened." This, with the corresponding act of the touch with the moistened finger, is the foundation of a corresponding ceremony in the Roman Catholic formula for baptism.

EPHRAEMI RESCRIPTUS. *See* TEXTS AND MSS OF THE NT I.A.2.c.

EPHRAIM ē'frē-əm, ē'frā-əm [Heb. *'eprayim* < either *pārâ*–'be fruitful' or *'ēper*–'earth'; Gk. *Ephraim*]. The name of the younger of the two sons of Joseph and Asenath, born in Egypt; and of the tribe named after him, its territory, and by extension, the northern kingdom.

Ephraim and his brother Manasseh were adopted by Jacob and ranked as his own sons, each becoming the ancestor of a tribe in Israel. In blessing his grandchildren, Jacob, despite their father's protest, preferred the younger, foreshadowing the future eminence of his descendants (Gen. 41:50-52; 48:17-20). In the Blessing of Jacob, however, the two are included under the name of Joseph (49:22-26).

At the first census after the tribes had left Egypt, Ephraim's men of war numbered 40,500, and at the second census 32,500 (Nu. 1:33; 26:37). In the wilderness march, with the standard of the tribe of Ephraim on the west side of the tabernacle were Manasseh and Benjamin (2:18).

The Ephraimite among the spies was Hoshea (i.e., Joshua) the son of Nun (Nu. 13:8). At the division of the land Ephraim was represented by Kemuel the son of Shiphtan (34:24). The future power of this tribe is again foreshadowed in the Blessing of Moses (Dt. 33:17). When Moses died, a member of the tribe, Joshua, whose faith and courage had distinguished him among the spies, succeeded to the chief place in Israel. It was natural that the scene of national assemblies and the center of the nation's worship should be chosen within the land occupied by the children of Joseph, at Shechem and Shiloh, respectively. Ephraim's leadership was further emphasized by the rule of Samuel. From the beginning of settlement in Palestine the Ephraimites enjoyed a certain prestige and were very sensitive on the point of honor (Jgs. 7:24; 8:1; 12:1). Their acceptance of, and loyalty to, Saul, the first king chosen over Israel, may be explained by his belonging to a Rachel tribe and by the close and tender relations existing between Rachel's children Joseph and Benjamin. But they were never reconciled to the passing of the scepter to Judah in the person of David (2 S. 2:8f.). That Israel would have submitted to the sovereignty of Absalom, any more than to that of David, is not to be believed; but his revolt furnished an opportunity to deal a shrewd blow at the power of the southern tribe (15:13). Solomon's lack of wisdom, and the crass folly of Rehoboam in the management of the northern tribes, fanned the smoldering discontent into a fierce flame. This made easy the work of the rebel Jeroboam; and from the day of the disruption till the fall of the northern kingdom there was none to dispute the supremacy of Ephraim, the names Ephraim and Israel being synonymous (cf. the book of Hosea where Ephraim represents Israel as the object of God's righteous judgment [e.g., 5:3-14] and also of His tender love [e.g., 11:1-4, 8f.]).

W. EWING

When settling in Palestine the children of Rachel occupied the central part of the mountain between Jerusalem and the Valley of Esdraelon. The southern part of it fell into the hands of the Benjaminites, while the larger and more important northern part was conquered by the house of Joseph (Ephraim and Manasseh). These two separate territories are described as one in Josh. 16:1-3, whereas Josh. 16:5-8; 17:7-11 may be a description of the boundaries between Ephraim and Manasseh. The settlement of the house of Joseph, referred to in 1 Ch. 7:28f., does not easily harmonize with the story in the book of Joshua.

Pythian-Adams believed that the boundary lists in the book of Joshua reflect the situation at the time of Ahab; most scholars now agree that they go back to the beginning of the period of the judges.

According to Josh. 15:16 the territory of the tribe of Ephraim was limited to the western half of the southern Mt. Ephraim.

The southern boundary started at a point SE of Jericho and passed westward toward Bethel, Beth-horon, and Gezer. The northern boundary passed from Michmethah and Taanath-shiloh (near Shechem) toward Tappuah and then ran along the southern bank of the river Kanah toward the sea. The eastern boundary passed N-S starting at Michmethah, forming a straight line to a point SE of Jericho. The western boundary is not as precisely known, for the biblical text included some land in Israelite territory although Canaanites continued to live there for a long time.

Yeivin believed that the tribes of the house of Joseph penetrated into western Palestine from the east (Jericho) and conquered the area of the central mountain that already had been occupied for long by old Israelite families (cf. the story of Dinah and the destruction of the city of Shechem). Possibly the tribe of Dan had previously settled in this area and was now pushed westward into new and insecure surroundings that they ultimately had to leave. At any rate, the tribe of Ephraim was fortunate in being surrounded by other Israelite tribes and therefore was not weakened in wars against the Canaanites and the Philistines, nor in fights against other Israelite tribes, as was the tribe of Benjamin. The tribe of Ephraim grew in strength and was finally able to spread northward and westward, taking possession of parts of the territories of Dan and Manasseh (Gen. 49:23).

Bibliography.–W. F. Pythian-Adams, *PEQ*, 1929, pp. 229ff.; M. Noth, *Beiträge zur Wissenschaft vom Alten und Neuen Testament*, 52 (1930), 122-132; K. Elliger, *ZDPV*, 53 (1930), 265-309; M. Noth, *ZDPV*, 58 (1935), 200-215; T. J. Meek, *BASOR*, 61 (Feb. 1936), 17-19; R. de Vaux, *RB*, 53 (1946), 263; S. Yeivin, *EB*, *s.v.*; Z. Kallai, *Northern Boundaries of Judah* (1960).

A. A. SAARISALO

EPHRAIM [Heb. *ʾeprayim*; Gk. *Ephraim*].

1. A town near Baal-hazor, Absalom's sheep farm on which he arranged to assassinate his half-brother Amnon, two years after Amnon's sin with his sister Tamar (2 S. 13:23). That it was located N of Jerusalem seems to be indicated by v. 34. It may be identical to the EPHRON of 2 Ch. 13:19 and the OPHRAH of Josh. 18:23. If it is to be identified with Ephron, then it was near Bethel. *See* **2** below.

2. The town near the wilderness to which Jesus retired after the raising of Lazarus (Jn. 11:54); probably the same town as **1** above. This may be the place named along with Bethel by Josephus (*BJ* iv.9.9). It is generally identified with modern eṭ-Ṭaiyibeh, about 21 km. (13 mi.) NNE of Jerusalem and 6½ km. (4 mi.) NE of Bethel. "Aphaerema," in the district of Samaria, may also refer to this city (1 Macc. 11:34; cf. Josephus *Ant.* xiii.4.9).

W. EWING R. J. HUGHES, III

EPHRAIM, FOREST OF [Heb. *yaʿar ʾeprayim*]; AV "wood of Ephraim"; NEB FOREST OF EPHRON (dubious, since it lacks textual support, though 1 Macc. 5:46 and 2 Macc. 12:27 mention an Ephron in Gilead [EPHRON **3**]). An unidentified region E of the Jordan in the mountainous country either N or S of the river Jabbok, apparently in the vicinity of Mahanaim (hence perhaps the LXX Lucian *Maainan* in 2 S. 18:6; cf. 2 S. 17:27). Here Absalom was defeated and killed by Joab (2 S.

Forest of oaks and pines in Jordan (ancient Gilead), perhaps to be identified with the Forest of Ephraim (D. Baly)

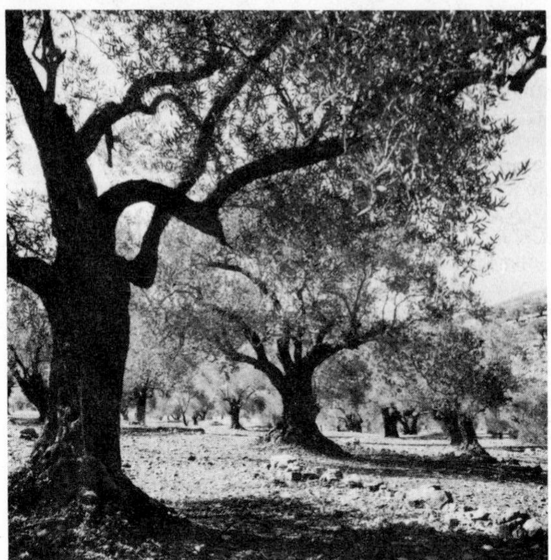

Olive grove in the hill country of Ephraim (D. Baly)

18:6-15). Although *ya'ar* can also mean open woodland, or even scrub, the area was probably thickly wooded, with oak, pine, cypress, arbutus, etc., since there is rich soil from the Cenomanian limestone and plentiful winter rainfall, averaging 70-75 cm. (28-30 in.). It was within the eastern half of the territory of Manasseh and the name may refer to the similarity of the landscape to that of the high hill country of the tribe of Ephraim W of the Jordan. It is also suggested that this area was at one time given to Ephraim (cf. Josh. 17:14-18) but later lost to the Gileadites (Jgs. 12:1-6). D. BALY

EPHRAIM, GATE OF. *See* JERUSALEM III.D.5.h, F.2.b′.

EPHRAIM, HILL COUNTRY OF [Heb. *har 'eprayim*]; AV MOUNT EPHRAIM. An expression used repeatedly to refer to that portion of the hill country of Canaan W of the Jordan Valley that was assigned to the tribe of Ephraim after the conquest under Joshua (Josh. 17:15; 19:50; etc.). The high plateau (900 m., 3000 ft.) was thickly forested at the time of the Conquest (17:15-18). As the Israelites settled there, the good soil and rainfall encouraged agricultural development. Today olive groves cover much of the area. The rocky gorges leading to this plateau were easily defended, so the area became a stronghold in wartime. Both Deborah (Jgs. 4:5) and Tola (10:1) lived there, and Samuel was born there (1 S. 1:1).

See also PALESTINE, GEOGRAPHY OF. G. A. L.

EPHRAIM, WOOD OF. *See* EPHRAIM, FOREST OF.

EPHRAIMITE ē'fra-im-īt [Heb. *'eprayim*, sing. *'eprāṯî*] (Josh. 16:5, 8f.; Jgs. 12:5f.; 1 S. 1:1; 1 K. 11:26; 1 Ch. 12:30; 27:20; 2 Ch. 25:7; Ps. 78:9); AV, NEB, also EPHRATHITE. A member of the tribe of EPHRAIM.

EPHRAIN ē'fra-in (2 Ch. 13:19, AV). *See* EPHRON **1**.

EPHRATH ef'rath, ē'frath [Heb. *'eprāṯ*; Gk. *Ephrath*]; **EPHRATHAH** ef'ra-tha, ef-rä'tha [Heb. *'eprāṯâ*; Gk. *Ephratha*]; AV EPHRATAH. The place of Benjamin's birth and Rachel's death (Gen. 35:16-20), the name either of Bethlehem itself or of a district in which Bethlehem was located. The designer of the mosaic Madeba Map has separated Ephrathah from Bethlehem; apparently he thought of Bethlehem as being in the territory of Ephrathah. The name occurs in the NEB at Josh. 15:59, based on the LXX (59a). A man of this place was called an Ephrathite (Ruth 1:2; 1 S. 17:12).

Some authorities hold that Ephrathah where Rachel was buried (Gen. 35:16; 48:7) was a city N of Jerusalem near Ramah in the territory of Benjamin, the words "the same is Bethlehem" being a late and erroneous gloss.

See also CALEB-EPHRATHAH (1 Ch. 2:24, AV). K. G. JUNG

EPHRATHITE ef'rath-īt, ē'frath-īt. *See* EPHRATH.

EPHRON ē'fron [Heb. *'eprôn*–'fawnlike']. The Hittite from whom Abraham bought the field and cave of Machpelah (Gen. 23:8f.; 25:9; 49:30) for four hundred shekels' weight of silver (cf. 33:19; 1 K. 16:24).

EPHRON ē'fron [Heb. *'eprôn*; Gk. *Ephrōn*].

1. A city captured along with its villages by Abijah king of Judah from Jeroboam son of Nebat, king of Israel (2 Ch. 13:19). Variant readings of this text and the apparent location lead many to identify this city with Ephraim (2 S. 13:23, so NEB), Ophrah (Josh. 18:23), and modern eṭ-Ṭaiyibeh, located about 21 km. (13 mi.) NNE of Jerusalem and 6½ km. (4 mi.) NE of Bethel. The RSV emends Josh. 18:15 also to read "to Ephron" (AV "on the west").

2. "The cities of Mount Ephron," a turning point in the boundary of the territory assigned to the tribe of Judah after the conquest of Canaan under Joshua (Josh. 15:9). The location remains undetermined.

3. A well-fortified city defeated by Judas Maccabeus (1 Macc. 5:46; 2 Macc. 12:27), located E of the Jordan, probably about 20 km. (12 mi.) SE of the Sea of Galilee. R. J. HUGHES, III

EPICUREANS ep-i-kū-rē'ənz [Gk. *Epikoureioi*] (Acts 17:18). Members of a philosophical movement initiated by Epicurus (341-270 B.C.) on Lesbos off the western coast of Asia Minor (311 B.C.) and taken to Athens (306 B.C.). The movement, which maintained the unaltered teachings of its founder, spread to Rome after 146 B.C. and during the 1st cent. B.C. became identified with hedonism. Its decline coincided with the decline of Rome, and it was no match for Christianity once the latter became an acceptable Roman religion (after A.D. 323).

*I. **Teachings**.–A. Individuality.* Epicurus and his followers devoted themselves primarily to the pursuit of personal, individual happiness. In contrast to classical Greek thought, Hellenistic thought gave ethics great importance. After the death of Alexander the Great (323 B.C.) many Greeks were unable to accept his notion of a "cosmopolitan culture" in which Greeks and non-Greeks would live together. When many Greeks were forced to abandon their secure existence within the city-state, they withdrew from active participation in a supranational culture and began to search inwardly for happiness. Though Epicurus advocated little involvement in social and political life and stressed individual happiness, he did not promote individualism. For the acquisition of friends was "the most important" means toward the securing of "happiness throughout the whole of life" (Diogenes x.148, *LCL*), and happiness included justice and other virtues (cf. DeWitt, *Epicurus*, ch. 14).

B. Pleasure. It is well known (even today) that Epicurus believed that human happiness consisted in pleasure (Gk. *hēdonḗ*). But to him pleasure was a substitute for the experience of pain, not an invitation to indulge in the

Epicurus (341-270 B.C.) (Trustees of the British Museum)

"pleasures of the flesh." According to his own testimony, Epicurus did not teach "the pleasures of the prodigal or the pleasures of sensuality, . . . [but] the absence of pain in the body and of trouble in the soul" (Diogenes x.131f.).

Although Epicurus warned against indulgence in physical things because pain will be increased, he did not deny moderate use of physical enjoyment. He even constructed a hierarchy of physical pleasures. Some are natural and necessary, such as food; some are natural but not necessary, such as sexual union. Some are neither natural nor necessary, such as fame; some are short-lived, and these are inferior to those that are long-lived (Diogenes x.149).

The bodily pleasures were not deemed evil in themselves, but the mental pleasures were preferred. The happy person was one who attained mental peace (Gk. *ataraxía,* "lack of disturbance"). Besides having peace of mind, the happy person would be just, wise, and temperate. If one "is not able to live wisely, though he lives well and justly, it is impossible for him to live a pleasant life" (Diogenes x.140). Clearly, then, the good life for Epicurus included the virtues of mental peace, justice, wisdom, and temperance, through which the individual achieved a maximum of pleasure and a minimum of pain.

C. Present Happiness. Epicurus aimed at a life-style in which the present was given more prominence than the future. For many of his contemporaries the future held the fears of death and divine punishment, but Epicurus taught that (1) there is no life after (physical) death, for death is the dissolution of the atoms of our bodily existence; (2) even if man were to live on, there would be no divine retribution, for the gods are not concerned with human life. This deliverance from fears of the future contributed to present human happiness.

D. Materialism. Epicurus's ethical teachings must be related to his thoughts on physics. He conceived of reality materialistically, with atoms as the basic components of the universe. Assuming that all of reality is material, Epicurus concluded that human souls and the deities likewise are material. Moreover, as life is the integration of atoms, so death is their disintegration. When death occurs, the person no longer perceives and ceases to be. Future life is nonexistent.

As Epicurus sought to avoid individualism in his social philosophy, so he tried to escape a thoroughgoing determinism in his natural philosophy. On the one hand, all atoms "act" according to natural laws, i.e., according to cause and effect. On the other hand, human actions are done in freedom: "necessity destroys responsibility . . .; whereas our actions are free, and it is to them that praise and blame naturally attach" (Diogenes x.133f.). (For a sympathetic treatment of Epicurus's attempt to reconcile human ethical freedom and physical determinism, see DeWitt, *Epicurus,* pp. 169, 171.)

E. Role of the Gods. Epicurus's materialism did not result in atheism (Diogenes x.123). For him deities were material beings who certainly did exist. For practical reasons, however, they did not play a crucial role in human life. The gods were eternal and felicitous and did not interfere with human actions because doing so would have detracted from their own blessedness. Thus they did not punish people for unethical deeds either in this life or in an afterlife (should there be one).

II. Epicurus and Scripture.*–A. Ecclesiastes.* The earlier scholarly attempts to show Epicurean influences on Qoheleth in the long run "could not prove convincing, and it transpired that the decisive parallels were to be sought less in Greece than in the Old Testament itself, in Egypt and in Babylonia" (M. Hengel, *Judaism and Hellenism* [Eng. tr. 1974], I, 115). There are striking similarities between the teachings of Epicurus and Qoheleth (cf. DeWitt, *Epicurus,* pp. 230, 182, 319, 199, etc.), but Qoheleth concluded his messages with "religious wisdom" (2:26; 12:13). He affirmed that keeping the law gives meaning to the life of the righteous (12:1, 13f.), and thus work and learning take on new significance. Life does not terminate in death (12:7). Without speculating about the nature of the immortal soul (see ESCHATOLOGY II), Qoheleth affirmed a future life and a future divine judgment (3:17; 11:9b; 12:14), which the righteous need not fear (8:12).

B. Paul. In Luke's summary of Paul's address on the Areopagus in Athens, Paul did not criticize the Epicureans for their stress on pleasure but for their denial of the Resurrection (Acts 17:31). Nowhere in his letters does Paul mention the Epicureans, not even in Col. 2:8 (though Colossae was "the sort of town where Epicureanism flourished" [DeWitt, *St. Paul,* p. 75]). But he was very much aware of their presence in many of the cities of his missionary journeys.

Paul used phrases similar to Epicurus's (e.g., "peace and safety," 1 Thess. 5:3) and possibly employed similar words (e.g., the uncommon NT words "eternal" [Rom. 1:20, Gk. *aídios*] and "atom" [1 Cor. 15:52, Gk. *atómos*; cf. DeWitt, *St. Paul,* pp. 13, 117]). Paul also voiced Epicurus's warning not to revel in physical pleasures (Gal. 5:13; 1 Cor. 5:1, 11).

But Paul's teachings differed from the teachings of Epicurus. Paul used the word "pleasure" sparingly (Tit. 3:3), for "no compromise with pleasure was conceivable" to him (DeWitt, *St. Paul,* p. 172). Personal pleasure became a rejoicing in the Lord (Phil. 4:4); "all the treasures of wisdom and knowledge" are hidden in God (1 Cor. 2:7) and not in nature; freedom is not merely a deliverance from fear, pain, and death but a positive putting into practice of divine love (Gal. 5:1, 13); the atoms are not eternal but God's power is (Rom. 1:20); mental peace is replaced by divine peace (1 Thess. 5:3).

The central thrust of Paul's theology contrasts with Epicureanism. (1) The universe is basically spiritual and not material (though the material realm is not negated), and man's spirit is a reflection of the divine Spirit. (2) God is blessed (Gk. *makários*, 1 Tim. 1:11) and eternal but does become actively involved in human affairs — notably in the Incarnation. (3) God's final judgment will be just — a warning to unbelievers and a comfort to believers. (4) Christ's death overcomes the "sting" of death, and a future life is affirmed. (5) True peace is found in the present life within the Christian community.

***Bibliography*.**–G. J. D. Aalders, *Paulus en de antieke Cultuurwereld* (1951), pp. 74-142; C. Bailey, *Greek Atomists and Epicurus* (1928, 1964); E. Bréhier, *Hellenistic and Roman Age* (Eng. tr. 1965), pp. 69-97, 138-143; N. W. DeWitt, *Epicurus and His Philosophy* (1954); *St. Paul and Epicurus* (1954); B. Farrington, *The Faith of Epicurus* (1967); A. J. Festugière, *Epicurus and His Gods* (Eng. tr. 1955); O. Gigon, *Epikur von der Überwindung der Furcht* (1949); *TDNT*, II, *s.v.* ἡδονή κτλ. (Stählin). R. W. VUNDERINK

EPILEPSY. The Greek term in Mt. 4:24 and 17:15 (the only two occurrences of "epileptic" in the RSV) is the verb (part. in 4:24) *selēniázomai*, which literally means to be moon-struck. The AV renders "lunatick," a literal translation, in both cases. The Greek term reflects a widespread ancient belief in a connection between certain phases of the moon and various mental and physical disorders among human beings. It is not known, however, whether such a belief was still held in NT times. The Synoptists all regard the ailment described here as caused by demon possession (Mt. 17:14-20; cf. Mk. 9:14-29; Lk. 9:37-43).

The choice of the term "epileptic" by the RSV and NEB is good, for the symptoms described in all three accounts point to such a nervous disorder: the victim had "a dumb spirit" (temporary aphasia), and "wherever it seizes him, it dashes him down; and he foams and grinds his teeth and becomes rigid" (Mk. 9:17f.); "often he falls into the fire, and often into the water" (Mt. 17:15); "the demon tore him and convulsed him" (Lk. 9:42).

See also DEMON, DEMONOLOGY; DISEASE IV.H.

N. J. O.

EPIPHANES. *See* ANTIOCHUS IV EPIPHANES.

EPIPHI ep'ə-fī [Gk. *Epiphi*]. Name of the eleventh month of the Egyptian calendar (June 25-July 24), mentioned in connection with Pachon in 3 Macc. 6:38.

EPISTLE ē-pis'əl [Gk. *epistolḗ*–'letter,' 'epistle'].

- I. Antiquity
- II. OT
- III. Greco-Roman Period
  - A. Kinds
  - B. Characteristics
  - C. Form
- IV. NT
- V. Paul
  - A. Context
  - B. Form
- VI. Conclusions

***I. Antiquity*.**–The term "epistle" indicates a form of written communication between two persons or parties, private or official. The epistle is among the oldest and most abundantly preserved types of texts from antiquity. Apart from ancient administrative records, inscriptions, and chronological annals, the earliest known writings are in epistolary form. Epistolographical study has emphasized the importance of these extant documents for historical, literary, and biblical research.

As early as 2275 B.C. Babylonian royalty and officials used epistolary communication, while a similarly extensive correspondence is evidenced by Egyptian remains from the 2nd millennium B.C. Akkadian letters have been preserved on potsherds and clay tablets; approximately fourteen thousand letters are extant from the Greco-Roman period, though many others have been lost due to the deterioration of the materials (waxed, wooden tablets) on which they were written. Other epistolary materials have survived from such places as Tell el-Amarna, Mari, and Lachish. The Elephantine papyri also provide a rich source for epistolary studies.

In the Roman period Cicero, Seneca, and Pliny typified the literary epistolary traditions, and their letters are generally long, stylized, and formal products. Other epistles are embedded in literary or historical works such as Josephus' *Vita* and 1 Maccabees, but questions of authenticity and interpolation often negate their value for studies of epistolary form. The publication of official, administrative letters was by public posting, proclamation, or inscription on stone or ostraca, and frequently the royal archives preserved this material. Literary epistles were generally used as paradigms of style to be copied and studied in circulation before being edited into collections (cf. Cicero).

***II. OT*.**–While none of the books of the OT can be classified as an epistle, there is ample evidence of epistolary activity throughout OT history. The following contain letters: 2 S. 11:14f. — David to Joab concerning Uriah; 1 K. 21:8f. — Jezebel to Jezreel officials concerning Naboth;

Papyri that have been rolled, bound, sealed, and addressed for dispatch (Staatliche Museen, Berlin)

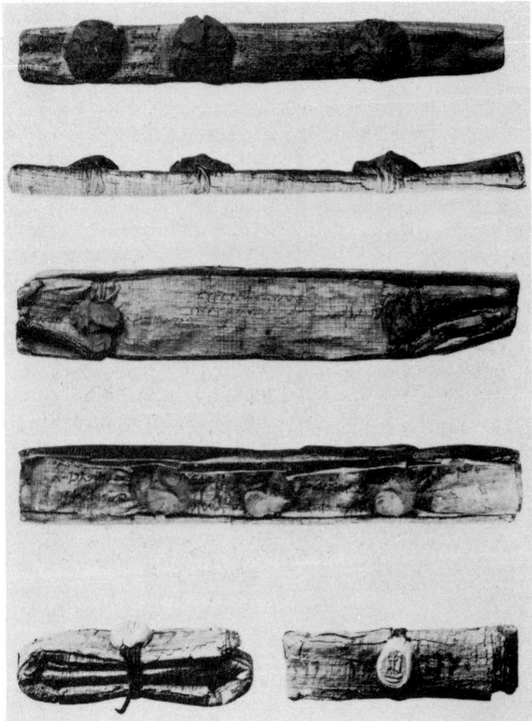

2 K. 5:5-7 — Benhadad king of Syria to Jehoram king of Israel; 2 K. 10:1f., 6f. — Jehu to Jezreel officials; 2 K. 19:14 (cf. Isa. 37:14; 2 Ch. 32:17) — Sennacherib to Hezekiah; 2 K. 20:12 (cf. Isa. 39:1) — Merodach-baladan to Hezekiah; Jer. 29:1, 4-32 — Jeremiah to the exiles (the closest OT approximation to NT epistolary polemic); Ezr. 4:7-23 — correspondence, in ARAMAIC, between enemies of the Jews and Artaxerxes; Ezr. 5:6-17 — Tattenai to Darius; Ezr. 7:11-28 — Artaxerxes to Ezra; Neh. 2:7f. — a request from Nehemiah to Artaxerxes for letters of recommendation; Neh. 6:17, 19 — correspondence among Tobiah, Nehemiah, and Jewish nobles. Additionally, Job 9:25 indicates the long-term existence of a mail courier system, particularly prominent in the Persian period. (See Est. 3:13, 15; 8:10, 14; and 2 Ch. 30:1, 6, 10.)

III. Greco-Roman Period.–*A. Kinds.* Several factors contributed to a surge of epistolary activity during this period: the increase of scribal learning and influence; the growing demands for carefully articulated verbal documents in the areas of commerce and travel; the need for official propaganda vehicles for which the letter form provided a tract/treatise base; the administrative concerns of the government, military, and legal and other professions; apologetic considerations; philosophical speculations; rhetorical practice (forensic, didactic, and epideictic). To these needs the responses came in the form of business letters, official communiqués, letters for public consumption and influence, discursive letter-essays, letters of introduction and commendation, poetic letters, epistles of consolation, encyclical documents, rhetorical paradigms, legal pleas, or "non-real" letters comprising representative compendia. Letters may also be classified according to form of preservation and writing materials used, the modes of dissemination indicated, stylistic intent, the particularity of an epistle and its context, or the distinction between personal (familiar) and ideological (negotiatory) missives. Other subclassifications might include reports, petitions, or "novelistic" epistles of pseudonymous or purportedly divine origin. For all these subcategories are found appropriate stock phrases and formal structures.

B. Characteristics. While the context and kind of a given epistle clearly influenced certain aspects of its format, definite characteristics were almost universally incorporated in the epistle beyond the rhetorical, stylistic, or situational demands. These included the establishment of a "friendly relationship" (*philophrónesis*) between sender and addressee; a sense of the author's "presence" (*parousía*); the facilitation of "dialogue" (*homilía*); clarity of expression, conventional courtesies, and adherence to "epistolary things" — a somewhat nebulous requirement. These factors correspond with the general intentions of epistles, which were basically to convey information, preserve communication, and facilitate requests. Both the opening and closing epistolary conventions and the flexible items, such as expressions of joy or third-party greetings, reflect these main purposes. Where an epistle goes beyond the simple paradigm to a more sophisticated, elaborate product, illustrative matter may be inserted in the form of personal experience, historical anecdotes and quotations, proverbial sayings and folk wisdom, or ethical paradigms (cf. Paul's epistles, *passim*).

C. Form. Where the rhetorical influence is strongest, as in the classical examples drawn from pedagogical exercises or in highly literary productions, the form of the epistle reflects a deliberately elaborate structure. The same effects hold true in letters of historical fiction written to express dialogical or ideological stances (cf. *Letter of Aristeas*, the fictional correspondence between Paul and Seneca, or the forensic portions of Romans and Galatians). Elsewhere, the basic, set form, also underlying the more hortatory letters, was as follows: first, the author's identity, along with the recipient's, in the form "A to B, greetings [*chaírein*]"; second, the main body of the epistle, followed by the closing greeting, which was nearly always a simple word (*érrōsō*) wishing the recipient good health (cf. Latin *vale*); last, the final signature of endorsement by the writer. This element authenticated the epistle, since frequently the epistle's contents were dictated to the scribe on a "thought" rather than verbal basis. At times, it is suggested, the amanuensis (scribe) may have played a significant part in a given epistle's actual literary formulation, for which the sender's signature would then have been an attestation of the accuracy and reliability of the contents. Additional information could be conveyed orally

Letter of Mnesiergus of Athens to his household, the oldest extant Greek letter. It was written on a leaden tablet and folded so that the contents were inside (left) and the address outside (right) (Antikenmuseum, Staatliche Museen, Berlin)

by the courier to circumvent possible forgery or distortion. These substantive oral instructions provided further corroboration and explication of the epistle's contents, often avoiding risks that volatile written material might entail (cf. also 2 Thess. 2:2; 3:17; 1 Cor. 4:17: cf. 2 S. 11:14f.; Rom. 16:1f.; Col. 4:7-9). Thus what probably began as a pattern in which written communication substantiated an oral message, was by the Hellenistic period a practice in which oral communications reinforced or informally expanded epistolary documents.

IV. NT.–Twenty-one NT writings are generally classified as letters, including the commonly acknowledged Pauline, the Pastoral, and the Johannine Epistles. The Epistle to the Hebrews appears to be a homily in contrived and artificial epistolary form, while that of James lacks significant epistolary features. The epistle of Jude and those of Peter also exhibit superficial epistolary form while using other modes (e.g., baptismal homily style or the device of a last will and testament). The book of Revelation provides an initial epistolary framework but more clearly belongs to the apocalyptic genre. Thus the epistle, written on a specific occasion to a particular person or circle for direct communication, without necessarily wider distribution, can double as a homiletic device (Hebrews, James, 1 Peter, 1 John), testament (2 Timothy, 2 Peter), or wisdom discourse (James). Alongside the "gospel" genre, therefore, the "epistle" alone carried equal importance in early Christian literature. With its formal but flexible dialogic quality the epistle supremely represented the early Church's "linguistic newness" (Doty). It became a uniquely appropriate and indispensible genre for the primitive Church's literary production and growth.

A. Deissmann first drew the distinction between the literary forms of letter and epistle, suggesting that the former is more particular, concrete, personal, and limited in scope than the latter, which he defined as a treatise or essay addressed to the general public and using the greeting as a merely literary device. (See Cicero *Ad Familiares,* xv.21.4 for private/public audience differentiation.) While this delineation has some validity, it should not be imposed on the NT writings mechanically or indiscriminately since often, due to exchange of letters (Col. 4:16), public readings (1 Thess. 5:27), and intercommunity cooperation (Gal. 1:2; 2 Cor. 1:1), what may have been intended as a personal communication could tend subconsciously toward an "official" text. Thus a double level of intentionality and reception probably operated quite early in the Christian community. (For more formal "epistles," literarily influenced, cf. Acts 9:2; 15:23-29; 18:27; 22:5; 23:25-30; 28:21).

V. Paul.–A. Context. For Paul the epistolary form was the extension of his presence, the embodiment of his person and the fellowship he shared with his addressees, as well as a vehicle by which to convey his apostolic authority and influence (cf. 2 Cor. 16:10). In structure his letters exhibit a familiar rather than negotiatory style, appealing consistently to the mutual experience and life-style he assumed he shared with the recipients. While retaining an appearance of studied casualness for private, specific consumption, Paul's letters were the result of his theological understanding and the formal implementation of the apostolic task. Background stylistic influences, such as Jewish epistolary materials, Hellenistic teacher-disciple modes (cf. Apollonius), or papyrological protocol, were subjugated to his overall aim of producing appropriate instruments for early Christian missionary work which reflected his personal, but also official, interest in the recipients. Thus the epistles came to have the stylistic flavor and features of oral missionary address — proclamation through worship, parenesis, preaching, witness, prophecy, credal hymns and formulas (cf. on this point Col. 1:15-20; Phil. 2:6-11; 1 Cor. 15:3-5; Rom. 1:3) — while using accepted literary types and features, e.g., thanksgiving (Phil. 1:3ff.; 4:10ff.), recommendation (Philemon; 2 Cor. 3:1-3; Rom. 16:1-2), apologetic (Romans *passim*; Gal. 1–2; 1 Cor. 1–4; 2 Cor. 10–13), philophronesis (2 Cor. 1–7), didactic (Rom. 1–11), parenesis (1 Thessalonians).

B. Form. A Pauline letter had certain typical elements. At the beginning were: an opening, which included name of sender, recipient, and greeting (cf. Rom. 1:1-7; Phil. 1:1-2); and a thanksgiving section, which may have included a prayer of intercession (Rom. 1:9f.) and an eschatological climax as transitional vehicles (1 Cor. 1:8f.; Phil. 1:10f.; Col. 1:5; cf. 1 Pet. 1:7). The body of the letter included formulary openings establishing relationship (Rom. 1:13-15; Phil. 1:12-18), eschatological digressions or conclusions (Gal. 6:7-10), travelogues (Phil. 2:19-24), formal disclosures or expressions of joy or disappointment (cf. Phil. 1:3-6; 1 Thess. 1:2-10; Gal. 3:1-5), expositional, theoretical arguments followed by practical parenesis (Gal. 5:13–6:10; cf. Rom. 1–8; 12–15), or an apostolic *parousía* (1 Cor. 4:14-21; 5:3; Col. 2:5). Typically the letter closed with a greeting, a doxology, and a benediction (cf. Phil. 4:21f.; 1 Cor. 16:20-24), with occasional references to public reading or circulation of the document (1 Thess. 5:27; Col. 4:16), and allusions to the amanuensis involved (Rom. 16:22). Personal signatures were also included (see Gal. 6:11ff.; 2 Thess. 3:17) to support veracity of authorship. Clearly the format was heavily influenced by the immediate context of a given Epistle, e.g., 1 Cor. 7:1; 1 Thess. 4:9; Rom. 1:13, in which the formal structures were used with considerable flexibility to meet situational demands. Even here conventional formulas indicated discrete intent. (See Philem. 8-10; Rom. 12:1 for *parakalō* formulas. Cf. "negative" philophronetic statements in Col. 1:6-9; 3:1-5; 4:8-11; 5:2; 6:17; and "liturgical" adaptation of epistolary formulas in, e.g., Philem. 1-7, 21-25, 1 Thess. 1–3; cf. 3 Jn. 4-6, 13-15.)

VI. Conclusions.–Post-Pauline epistolary production continued the basic Pauline letter type in and beyond the patristic period (cf. Ignatius, 1 Clement, Polycarp, Epistle of Diognetus). However, a more ecclesiastical and catholic style developed; increasingly, pseudonymous works were produced in which the literary creation of a sophisticated treatise-like letter often served merely to suggest orthodoxy by perpetuating tradition. Many of these and other "pseudo-epistles" were lost or suppressed, the fate also of many legitimate epistolary productions of the apostolic period (cf. 1 Cor. 5:9; 2 Cor. 10:9f.; Eph. 3:3; 2 Thess. 3:17; Col. 4:16; also Rev. 22:18f.).

Bibliography.–*Background Texts and Studies: ANET,* pp. 475-492; P. Benoit, J. T. Milik, and R. de Vaux, eds., *Les Grottes des Murabba'at* (*DJD,* 1, 1955), pp. 115-169; Deiss.*LAE,* pp. 146-251; J. A. Fitzmyer, *JBL,* 93 (1974), 201-225; H-S, II, 111f., 128-166; H. Koskenniemi, *Studien zur Idee und Phraseologie des Griechischen Briefes bis 400 n. Chr.* (1956); H. G. Meecham, *Light from Ancient Letters* (1923); A. L. Oppenheim, *Letters from Mesopotamia* (1967); Pauly-Wissowa, Supp. V, 199f.; J. G. Winter, *Life and Letters in the Papyri* (1933).

NT Studies: C. Andresen, *ZNW,* 56 (1965), 233-259; R. L. Archer, *Expos.T,* 63 (1951/52), 296-98; W. A. Beardslee, *Literary Criticism of the NT* (1970); K. Berger, *ZNW,* 65 (1974), 190-231; N. A. Dahl, "The Particularity of the Pauline Epistles as a Problem in the Ancient Church," in *Neotestamentica et Patristica* (*Nov.Test. Supp.,* 6, 1962), pp. 261-271; W. G. Doty, *CBQ,* 31 (1969), 185ff.; "Emphasis upon the Historical: Recent Evaluations of Primitive Christianity," in *Contemporary NT Interpretation* (1972), 89-104; F. X. J. Exler, "The Form of the Ancient Greek Letter" (Diss., Catholic University of America, 1923); F. O. Francis, *ZNW,* 61 (1970), 110-126; R. W. Funk, "The Apostolic

Parousia: Form and Significance," in W. R. Farmer, C. F. D. Moule, and R. R. Niebuhr, eds., *Christian History and Interpretation* (1967), pp. 249-268; *JBL*, 86 (1967), 424-430; *Language, Hermeneutic and Word of God* (1966), pp. 251-274; D. Greenwood, *JBL*, 89 (1970), 418-426; R. Jewett, *ATR*, 51 (1969), 18-34; E. Kamlah, *Die Form der Katalogischen Paränese im Neuen Testament* (1964); C. H. Kim, *Form and Structure of the Familiar Greek Letter of Recommendation* (1972); W. G. Kümmel, *Intro. to the NT* (Eng. tr., 2nd ed. 1975), pp. 247-252; T. Y. Mullins, *Andrews University Seminary Studies*, 15 (1977), 59-64; *Nov. Test.*, 7 (1964), 44-50; *JBL*, 87 (1968), 418-426; *Nov.Test.*, 5 (1962), 46-54; *RGG*, *s.v.* "Formeln," II; J. L. White, *Body of the Greek Letter* (1972); *Form and Structure of the Official Petition* (1972); A. N. Wilder, *Early Christian Rhetoric* (2nd ed. 1971).

Pauline Writings: G. J. Bahr, *CBQ*, 28 (1966), 465-477; *JBL*, 87 (1968), 27-41; H. D. Betz, *NTS*, 21 (1974/75), 353-379; C. J. Bjerkelund, *Parakalô* (1967); H. Boers, *NTS*, 22 (1975/76), 140-158; L. G. Champion, *Benedictions and Doxologies in the Epistles of Paul* (1934); N. A. Dahl, *Theologische Zeitschrift*, 7 (1951), 250ff.; R. Jewett, *Nov.Test.*, 12 (1970), 40-53; L. Mowry, *JBL*, 63 (1944), 73-86; *RGG*, *s.v.* "Paulusbriefe"; B. Rigaux, *Letters of St. Paul: Modern Studies* (Eng. tr. 1968); O. Roller, *Das Formular der paulinischen Briefe* (1933); J. T. Sanders, *JBL*, 81 (1962), 352f., 358-362; W. Schmithals, "Die Thessalonicherbriefe als Briefkompositionem," in E. Dinkler, ed., *Zeit und Geschichte* (1964), pp. 314f.; P. Schubert, *JR*, 19 (1939), 167; *Form and Function of the Pauline Thanksgivings* (*BZNW*, 20, 1939), pp. 17, 24-26; M. L. Stirewalt, "Paul's Evaluation of Letter-Writing," in J. M. Myers, *et al.*, eds., *Search the Scriptures* (1969), pp. 179-196; W. Wuellner, *JBL*, 89 (1970), 199-204.

J. S. LOWN

EPISTLES, CAPTIVITY. *See* PHILEMON, EPISTLE TO.

EPISTLES, PASTORAL. *See* PASTORAL EPISTLES.

EPISTLES, SPURIOUS. *See* APOCRYPHAL EPISTLES.

EQUAL; EQUALITY. "Equal" occurs ten times in the RSV of the OT, for various Hebrew terms. In Ex. 30:34, e.g., "an equal part" renders *baḏ b^{e}ḇaḏ* (lit. "part for part"); in Dt. 18:8 "equal portions" translates *ḥēleq k^{e}ḥēleq*. In Job 28:17 "equal" translates *ʿāraq*, here meaning "compare": gold and silver cannot compare in value with wisdom. The cognate *ʿēreḵ* appears in the phrase *ʾ^{ĕ}nôš k^{e}ʿerkî*, literally, "a man of my value" (Ps. 55:13 [MT 14]), which the RSV renders "my equal" (cf. NEB "a man of my own sort"; *AB* "a man of my rank"). "Liken" (piel of *dāmâ*), "make equal" (hiphil of *šāwâ*; cf. AV of Lam. 2:13), and "compare" (hiphil of *māšal*) occur as parallels in Isa. 46:5 to emphasize that God the Creator cannot be compared to any creature — therefore He is far superior to the idol gods of the heathen (cf. 40:18-31). In Ezk. 18:25, 29; 33:17, 20, the AV translates the niphal of *tāḵan* ("is weighed") with "is equal" in the obsolete sense of "is just or impartial."

In the NT, "equal" occurs six times and "equality" three. The Greek is *ísos* and cognates (*isótēs* in 2 Cor. 8:14; *isángeloi* in Lk. 20:36; *isótimos* in 2 Pet. 1:1) except in 1 Cor. 3:8, where the term is *heís*, "one." In Mt. 20:12 "made them equal" means "put them on the same footing," i.e., regarded their brief service as though it were the very same as long hours of toil. In Lk. 20:36 the context restricts the equality to a particular relation. The precise meaning of *ísos* in Jn. 5:18, "making himself equal with God," is clearly defined by the preceding clause; for Jesus' opponents said that He had "called God his Father" (Gk. *patéra ídion*, i.e., His Father in a peculiar and exclusive sense; cf. *idíou huioú* of Rom. 8:32, applying the same adjective to the Son in His relation to the Father). They correctly interpreted the language of Jesus as declaring that He was the Son of God in a way that put Him in equality with God. The charge against Him was not that He said that He was "like" (*hómoios*), but that He was "equal" (*ísos*), i.e., of the very same rank and authority.

In Phil. 2:6 "equality" occurs in a paraphrase of Gk. *tó eínai ísa theǭ*, "the being on an equality with God." In this passage *ísa*, according to a not unusual Attic idiom, is construed adverbially (see Bauer, p. 382). This passage has been interpreted in many different ways. Perhaps the most likely interpretation is that Christ did not appear to men in "the form of God" in order to force them out of wonderment to acknowledge His divinity, but "emptied himself, taking the form of a servant, being born in the likeness of men" (v. 7). H. E. JACOBS

N. J. O.

EQUIPMENT. In the OT, Heb *k^{e}lî* is a general term for equipment of a material kind, e.g., utensils or furnishings (Nu. 4:26, 32; 1 S. 8:12; 2 K. 7:15; 2 Ch. 4:16; AV "instruments," "vessels"). "Equipment" appears twice in the RSV of the NT, for Gk. *katartismós* in Eph. 4:12 (AV "perfecting") and for *hetoimasía* in 6:15.

In Eph. 4:12 the equipment is spiritual. The Spirit's gifts are distributed to equip the members of the Christian community for active ministry.

A variety of interpretations has been given to *hetoimasía* in Eph. 6:15 (its only NT occurrence): cf. "preparation" (AV), "firm footing" (NEB), "eagerness" (JB), "steadfast" (*AB*), "readiness" (Today's English Version). The verb *hetoimázō* generally means "make ready" or "prepare"; the most common translation of the noun is "preparation" or "readiness" (cf. Bauer, p. 316; *TDNT*, II, 706). Because of the reference to the "gospel of peace," some have seen in this passage an allusion to Isa. 52:7 (e.g., *TDNT*, V, 312 n. 9); this is unlikely, however, because (1) the context is one of military imagery, and (2) *hypodēsámenoi toús pódas* indicates that something is strapped on the feet, whereas the one who ran quickly to bring a victory-message would have worn nothing on his feet (Barth, pp. 798f.). The author of Ephesians is referring figuratively to the Lat. *caliga* (cf. Vulg. *et caliciati pedes in praeparatione evangelii pacis*), the heavily studded half-boot worn by the Roman soldier, which enabled him to have a "firm footing" (NEB) in battle. It is the "gospel of peace," therefore, that enables the Christian to remain "steadfast" (*AB*). *See also* FOOTWEAR.

Bibliography.–M. Barth, *Ephesians* (*AB*, 1974), pp. 770f., 797-99; *TDNT*, I, *s.v.* ἄρτιος κτλ.: καταρτισμός (Delling); II, *s.v.* ἕτοιμος κτλ. (Grundmann); V, *s.v.* ὅπλον κτλ.: ὑποδέω (Oepke).

N. J. O.

EQUITY [Heb. *ʾ^{ĕ}meṯ*] (Prov. 29:14); AV FAITHFULLY; NEB STEADFASTLY; [*ṣ^{e}ḏāqâ*] (2 S. 8:15; 1 Ch. 18:14); AV, NEB, JUSTICE; [*yāšār*] (Mic. 3:9); NEB STRAIGHT COURSE; [*mîšôr* (Ps. 45:6 [MT 7]; 67:4 [MT 5]; Isa. 11:4), *mêšārîm* (Ps. 9:8 [MT 9]; 75:2 [MT 3]; 96:10; 98:9; 99:4; Prov. 1:3, 2:9)]; AV also RIGHT, RIGHTEOUSLY, UPRIGHTLY, UPRIGHTNESS; NEB also RIGHTEOUSNESS, JUSTICE, FAIRLY, JUSTLY, PROBITY, "keep only."

The term *ʾ^{ĕ}meṯ* denotes firmness, faithfulness, and truth. The throne of the king with these characteristics will be established forever (Prov. 29:14); in contrast, the rulers of Israel condemned by Micah (3:9) were characterized by a lack of uprightness. David administered his kingdom with *ṣ^{e}ḏāqâ*, "righteousness." *Mîšôr* and *mêšārîm*, literally denoting "level ground," are used metaphorically to mean straightness, evenness, uprightness, in descriptions of the

Lord's judgment and that of His servant.

See *TDOT*, I, *s.v.* "'āman" (Jepsen), 309-316.

J. R. PRICE

ER âr [Heb. *'ēr*–'watcher'; Gk. *Er*].

1. The eldest son of Judah the son of Jacob, by Shua the Canaanite. Judah took for him a wife named Tamar. It is recorded that Er "was wicked in the sight of the Lord; and the Lord slew him" (Gen. 38:3, 6f.; 46:12; Nu. 26:19; 1 Ch. 2:3).

2. "Er the father of Lecah" is mentioned among "the sons of Shelah the son of Judah" (1 Ch. 4:21).

3. An ancestor of Jesus in Luke's genealogy in the seventh generation before Zerubbabel (Lk. 3:28).

ERAN ē'ran [Heb. *'ērān*; Gk. *Eden*]. The son of Ephraim's oldest son Shuthelah (Nu. 26:36). The Eramites were his descendants.

ERASTUS ə-ras'təs [Gk. *Erastos*–'beloved']. The name occurs three times, each time denoting a companion of Paul.

1. A Corinthian Christian who sent greetings to Rome (Rom. 16:23). He is given the title "city treasurer," and is probably the same Erastus mentioned in a Corinthian inscription as "procurator of public buildings" (cf. O. Broneer, *BA*, 14 [1951], 78-96, esp. p. 94; H. J. Cadbury, *JBL*, 50 [1931], 42-58; W. Miller, *Bibliotheca Sacra*, 88 [1931], 342-46; A. M. Woodward, *Journal of Hellenic Studies*, 49 [1929], 221).

2. One of Paul's helpers who accompanied Timothy from Ephesus to Macedonia (Acts 19:22).

3. One who "remained at Corinth" (2 Tim. 4:20).

Although Erastus was a common name, all three could be the same Erastus, since both **1** and **3** are connected with Corinth and **2** and **3** are connected with Timothy. The latter connection is strengthened by the absence of any qualifying description, which might be expected with so common a name if different individuals were meant.

G. A. L.

ERECH ē'rek, er'ek [Heb. *'erek*; Gk. *Orech*]. One of the cities founded by Nimrod, the others being Babel, Accad, and possibly Calneh (Gen. 10:10; cf. RSV, NEB). Erech was known to the Assyrians and Babylonians as Uruk, to the Hebrews as Erech, and to the Arabs as Warka. Its importance can be seen in that no fewer than eleven names have been given it.

The city is located on the left bank of the Euphrates, 55 km. (35 mi.) N of Tell el-Obeid and 65 km. (40 mi.) NW of Ur. An important Sumerian city, Erech is one of the most ancient Mesopotamian cities and was the home of the mythical hero Gilgamesh. It was occupied continuously for nearly four thousand years, until the Greek period. Its ruins, almost 10 km. (6 mi.) in circumference, compare in importance with those of Babylon. The antiquity of the city is attested by (1) the number of names the site bears in the inscriptions, (2) the mention of the city in a non-Semitic creation story, and (3) references in Strabo, Ptolemy, and Pliny.

In the Sumerian king list the city appears as the center of the 2nd Dynasty after the Flood. The great wall of Erech was built during the Ur Dynasty before the middle of the 3rd millennium B.C. The city was captured by the Elamites *ca.* 2280 B.C., and the statue of the goddess Nana was removed. It was later recovered for Erech by Ashurbanipal of Assyria *ca.* 635 B.C. The city was inhabited in later centuries, but never again attained its early importance.

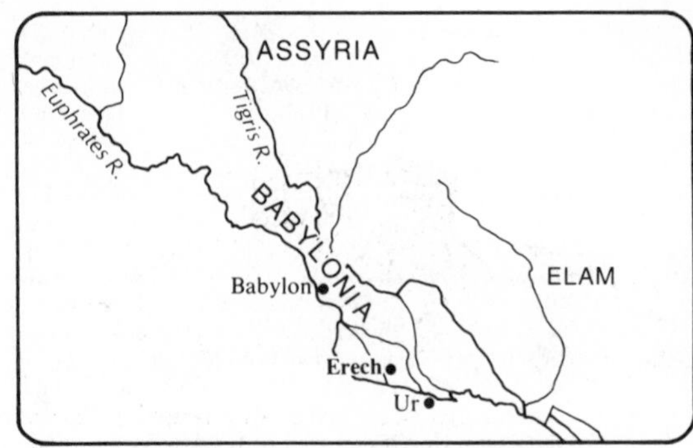

Earliest excavations of the site began in 1850 with W. K. Loftus; the German expedition under J. Jordan started thorough research in 1912. Interrupted by World War I, the work was resumed in 1928 and carried on until 1939. World War II caused another delay, but excavation began again in 1954 and continued until 1960. Eighteen levels of occupation were verified at one point.

The Mesopotamian ziggurat is first found at Erech. The Assyro-Babylonian word means "apex" or "top of a mountain." Thus the ziggurat was an artificially constructed mountain on whose summit stood the shrine of a god. Two ziggurats and several temples from the late 4th and early 3rd millennia B.C. were unearthed. The deities worshiped at Erech were Ishtar and Anu. The Ishtar temple is the great ziggurat of the site, rising to a height of about 28 m. (100 ft.) above the plain.

The excavated area yielded, in addition to the temples, the remains of buildings, walls, and gateways. Other finds included inscriptions of kings; tablets from the reigns of Nabopolassar, Nebuchadrezzar, Cyrus, Darius, and some Seleucids; many glazed earthenware coffins, and other receptacles for burials. Erech made distinctive pottery, the most important being the red ware, although other types were also found. The pottery, made on a spinning potter's wheel, was highly polished, but was unpainted. A rough limestone pavement in Erech is the oldest stone construction in Mesopotamia.

Erech's greatest contributions to the history of civilization were the cylinder seal and cuneiform script. A seal found in one of the temples is the first instance of such usage known to us. The seal was in the form of a small stone cylinder, with an incised design which left an impression when rolled across a soft surface. The use of such seals antedated the invention of writing. They were employed mainly to indicate ownership of property and to safeguard possessions. Such seals were used for more than three millennia, until displaced by the stamp seal in Persian times. The high quality of workmanship of the seals in Erech is seen in their animal figures, ornamental compositions, religious symbols, and illustrations of rituals.

Writing emerged soon after the appearance of the cylinder seal. Clay tablets have been unearthed at Erech bearing inscriptions in crude pictographic script, which is evidently the direct forerunner of the CUNEIFORM script used for the Sumerian language of Erech. The pictographs, in the interest of speed, were reduced to wedge-shaped writing or cuneiform, made by pressing a three-sided stylus into soft clay. This form of writing was used later by the Assyrians, Babylonians, Hittites, and Canaanites.

See also ARCHEVITES.

Bibliography.–*LAP*, pp. 19ff.; *HDB*; J. Jordan, *Uruk-Warka nach den Ausgrabungen durch die Orient-Gesellschaft* (1928); S. Lloyd, *Foundations in the Dust* (1947), p. 147; C. Pfeiffer and H. Vos, *Wycliffe Historical Geography of Bible Lands* (1967), pp. 11f.

C. L. FEINBERG

Drawing and model of the "white temple" (so called because of the lime plastering) that forms part of the Anu ziggurat at Uruk (Erech). An early type of cult building, the temple has a central hall with a small, stepped altar and side rooms (early 3rd millennium B.C.) (Staatliche Museen, Berlin)

ERI ē'rī; **ERITES** ē'rīts [Heb. *'ērî*–'watcher']. The fifth of the seven sons of Gad (Gen. 46:16; Nu. 26:16), after whom a clan in Gad was named (Nu. 26:16).

ERI-AKU er-ē-ä'kōō [the probable Sumerian reading of a known Babylonian name that includes characters meaning 'servant' and that stands for the moon-god Sin, the entire phrase meaning 'servant of the moon-god']. A king of Larsa (ELLASAR), generally identified with the ARIOCH of Gen. 14:1,9. A number of contract tablets mention Eri-Aku. The linguistic background of the name is Hurrian. The comparatively rare form is not attested after the middle of the 2nd millennium B.C. Thus its occurrence in Genesis presupposes an ancient tradition. As king of Ellasar, Arioch was an ally of Chedorlaomer of Elam and Amraphel of Shinar, who fought against Sodom and Gomorrah.

Inscriptions show that Eri-Aku belonged to an Elamite family that ruled Larsa. He was a son of Kudur-Mabuk, known as "the father of the land of the Amorites [=Syria]." Kudur-Mabuk, the Elamite, is considered to have ruled in a province in the eastern part of southern Babylonia adjacent to Elam, and to have lent his support to his son Eri-Aku, who governed Larsa and the surrounding parts of southern Babylonia. The rule of both was brought to an end by their defeat at the hands of Hammurabi.

According to one view Eri-Aku is to be identified with Rim-Sin king of Larsa, whose accession to the throne is dated *ca.* 2098 B.C. It has been suggested that his Semitic subjects changed the name to Rim-Sin. Another view proposes the equation Arioch=Eriagu=Warad-Sin, who is to be kept distinct from Rim-Sin. A firm consensus has not yet been achieved.

In the so-called Chedorlaomer texts, Arioch appears twice in the forms Eri-e-a-ku and Eri-e-ku-a, father of Dur-maḫ-ilani. Some older scholars identified Eri-eaku with Arioch king of Ellasar, reasoning that such a reading was possible if the signs were given Sumerian instead of Semitic values. However, the documents are in Semitic, so that possibility appears to be ruled out.

Bibliography.–W. F. Albright, *BASOR*, 88 (Dec. 1942), 28ff.; E. A. Speiser, Comm. on Genesis (*AB*, 1964).

C. L. FEINBERG

ERR; ERROR [Heb. *šāgâ*] (Nu. 15:22; 1 S. 26:21; Job 6:24; 19:4; Isa. 28:7; Ezk. 45:20); NEB also "(omit) through inadvertence" (Nu. 15:22), "in the wrong" (1 S. 26:21); [*šāgag*] (Lev. 5:18); AV IGNORANCE; [*šᵉgāgâ*] (Nu. 15:25f., 28; Eccl. 10:5); AV also IGNORANCE; NEB also OMISSION (Nu. 15:25), INADVERTENCE; [*šᵉgî'â*] (Ps. 19:12 [MT 13]); NEB "unwitting sins"; [*mᵉšûgâ*] (Job 19:4); [*tā'â*] (Ps. 58:3 [MT 4]; 95:10; Prov. 14:22; Isa. 29:24; 35:8; 63:17); AV also "go astray" (Ps. 58:3); NEB "taken to devious ways," ASTRAY, CONFUSED, TRESPASS, WANDER; [*tô'â*] (Isa. 32:6); NEB LIAR; [*tohᵒlâ*] (Job 4:18); AV FOLLY; NEB "find at fault"; [Aram. *šᵉḥāṯ*] (Dnl. 6:4); NEB "neglect of duty"; [Gk. *agnóēma*] (He. 9:7); NEB "sins of ignorance"; [*plánē*–'wandering'] (Rom. 1:27; 1 Thess. 2:3; Jas. 5:20; 2 Pet. 2:18; 3:17; 1 Jn. 4:6; Jude 11); AV also DECEIT (1 Thess. 2:3); NEB also PERVERSION, CROOKED, "heathen environment" (2 Pet. 2:18).

"Err" and "error" are in the OT mainly the translation of Heb. *šāgâ* and *tā'â* with their cognates. Both of these verbs mean literally "wander" or "go astray" and are used to refer to unintentional sins or sins of ignorance (note the contrast with presumptuous or "high-handed" sins, Nu. 15:30) for which atonement can be made. *Agnóēma* is the Greek equivalent to Heb. *šgh*, referring to a sin committed in ignorance (cf. *TDNT*, I, 115f.). *See also* IGNORANCE.

Greek *plánē* is frequently used in the LXX as a translation of *tā'â*, though is also occurs in Job 6:24 and 19:4 for Heb. *šgh*; in the OT it generally refers to Israel's disobedience, especially her following after and worshiping false gods. This LXX use is reflected in Rom. 1:27, where gentile idolatry is viewed as apostasy and is punished in the form of God's judicial abandonment. In 2 Pet 2:18 its meaning is broadened to include all gentile immorality. In 2 Pet. 3:17 and Jude 11 the term is used in description of false teachers who have abandoned the truth and "followed the way of Balaam, the son of Beor, who loved gain from wrongdoing" (2 Pet. 2:15), while in 1 Thess. 2:3 Paul declares that he (unlike the false teachers) did not preach from error.

In Prov. 12:28 the RSV, emending the MT to read *tô'ēḇâ* instead of *nᵉṯîḇâ*, translates "the way of error" (AV "in the pathway thereof"; NEB "there is a well-worn path"). Actually there is no need to emend the MT, as Dahood and Kidner have shown (M. Dahood, *Bibl.*, 41 [1960], 176-181; D. Kidner, *Proverbs* [1964], p. 100). Dahood notes (*Bibl.*, 50 [1969], 340) that Heb. *nāṯîḇ* ("path") is equivalent to Ugar. *ntb*.

J. T. DENNISON, JR.

ERUPTION [Heb. *sappaḥaṯ* (Lev. 13:2; 14:56), *mispaḥaṯ* (Lev. 13:6-8)]; AV SCAB; NEB PUSTULE. A redness, rash, or sore on the skin. The *mispaḥaṯ* of Lev. 13:6f. was harmless, but because such an eruption was one of the signs of leprosy, one had to be quarantined for fourteen days before it could be diagnosed as benign.

See also SCAB.

ESAIAS ē-zā'əs. *See* ISAIAH.

ESARHADDON ē-sər-had'ən [Heb. *'ēsarḥaddōn*; Assyr. *Aššur-aḫ^a-iddin*–'Ashur has given a brother'; Gk. *Asbasareth, Asbakaphath, Sacherdonos*]; AV Apoc. AZBAZARETH (1 Esd. 5:69 [LXX 66]), SARCHEDONOS (Tob. 1:21f.); NEB Apoc. ASBASARETH (1 Esd. 5:69). King of Assyria 681-669 B.C., son of Sennacherib and father of ASHURBANIPAL. The Bible mentions him only in connection with the assassination of his father, who was slain by his sons Adrammelech and Sharezer, "and Esarhaddon his son reigned in his stead" (2 K. 19:37; Isa. 37:38). Esarhaddon is sometimes identified with Osnapper (Ezr. 4:10), but this view is not generally accepted.

Sennacherib named Esarhaddon, who was still a youth, as his successor even though Esarhaddon was not the oldest son. (In his treaty with Baʿlu of Tyre, Esarhaddon refers to himself as "the oldest son of [Sennacherib]." A. L. Oppenheim, however, suggests that the name "Ashur has given a brother" implies that the child replaced "a lost son" [*IDB*, II, 124].) This caused his brothers to turn to deeds of violence (*ARAB*, II, §§ 500f.). When the sons slew Sennacherib the people backed the assassins, but the gods supported Esarhaddon (*ARAB*, II, §§ 503f.) and he pursued his brothers into Ḫanigalbat (*ARAB*, II, § 505; 2 K. 19:37 par. use the less precise term "Armenia"). Supporters of the brothers were slain or exiled, the people turned to Esarhaddon, and he took the throne to Nineveh (*ARAB*, II, §§ 505f.; *ANET*, pp. 288f.). His wife bore him twin sons, Ashurbanipal and Šamaš-šum-ukīn, whom he named crown princes of Assyria and Babylonia, respectively, doubtless in an effort to avoid the kind of internecine hostilities that had inaugurated his own reign. The plan failed, however.

Esarhaddon had problems on all frontiers. He began his reign by attempting to secure the northern frontier against the Cimmerians, the Manneans, and other peoples (*ARAB*, II, §§ 516f., 530-32). He reports controlling the Medes and other tribes beyond them (*ARAB*, II, §§ 519, 540) as well as the Elamites to the east (*ARAB*, II, § 524). To the south, he had numerous campaigns against the peoples of the Sea-Land (Chaldeans and others), whom he brought under control by putting Na'id-Marduk, brother of the defeated Elamite king, over their territory (*ARAB*, II, §§ 509f., 534f.). The kings of Arabia likewise received his attention (*ARAB*, II, §§ 518a, 536, 557). On the west Esarhaddon had a number of serious revolts by various kings of "Ḫatti" (Syria), doubtless instigated by Egypt (*ARAB*, II, §§ 511f., 527f.), and he resolved this problem by reorganizing the province, putting his official as governor over them, and increasing the amount of tribute required of them (*ARAB*, II, § 512). He reports in an inscription that he summoned twenty-two kings of the land of Ḫatti. Baʿlu king of Tyre and Manasseh king of Judah lead the list. This is probably the event recorded in 2 Ch. 33:11: Manasseh was taken to Babylon "bound with fetters of bronze." According to the biblical account Manasseh was later restored to his reign in Jerusalem. The restoration — and also the humiliating capture — may have taken place under ASHURBANIPAL. Sidon was destroyed after a three-year siege. Tyre also was attacked, but apparently it was too well defended by its island location. Esarhaddon records his treaty with the king of Tyre (*ARAB*, II, §§ 587-591).

Esarhaddon's most important campaign was his invasion of Egypt (*ARAB*, II, §§ 554, 557-565, 710). He had prepared for this through his policies on the other frontiers, particularly the settling of the Babylonian and Sea-Land region with the loyal Na'id-Marduk, and the stabilizing of the Syrian region and the treaty with Baʿlu of Tyre. He had also taken the city of Arzani "on the border of the Brook of Egypt" (the Wâdī el-ʿArîsh?) two years

Basalt stele of Esarhaddon (680-669 B.C.) from the outer city gate of Zenjirli (Sam'al). The king holds two prisoners by a rope, probably Ushanahuru son of Pharaoh Taharqa (kneeling) and Abdi-Milkuti prince of Sidon (or Baʿalu prince of Tyre) (Staatliche Museen, Berlin)

earlier. Esarhaddon invaded Egypt in 675. Taharqa (2 K. 19:9) fled to Nubia, and Esarhaddon sacked and destroyed Memphis. In his words, "Memphis, his royal city, in half a day, with mines, tunnels, assaults, I besieged, I captured, I destroyed, I devastated, I burned with fire" (*ARAB*, II, § 580). Esarhaddon claims to have conquered all of Egypt. On his stele, found at Zenjirli, he portrays himself holding ropes that pass through the lips of two men kneeling at his feet; one is probably Taharqa, and the other is perhaps Baʿlu of Tyre. We must accept his claims with caution, however. In one inscription Esarhaddon says, "I captured Tyre, which is in the midst of the sea" (*ARAB*, II, § 710); this does not appear to be supported by any other evidence, however, and Esarhaddon does not make the claim in other accounts of his campaign against Tyre. Taharqa, we know, continued to reign in Egypt, and led another revolt a few years later. Esarhaddon was in Haran, on his second campaign against Egypt, when he took ill and died (10 Araḫ-samnu 669). Ashurbanipal succeeded him.

Esarhaddon was proud of his building achievements

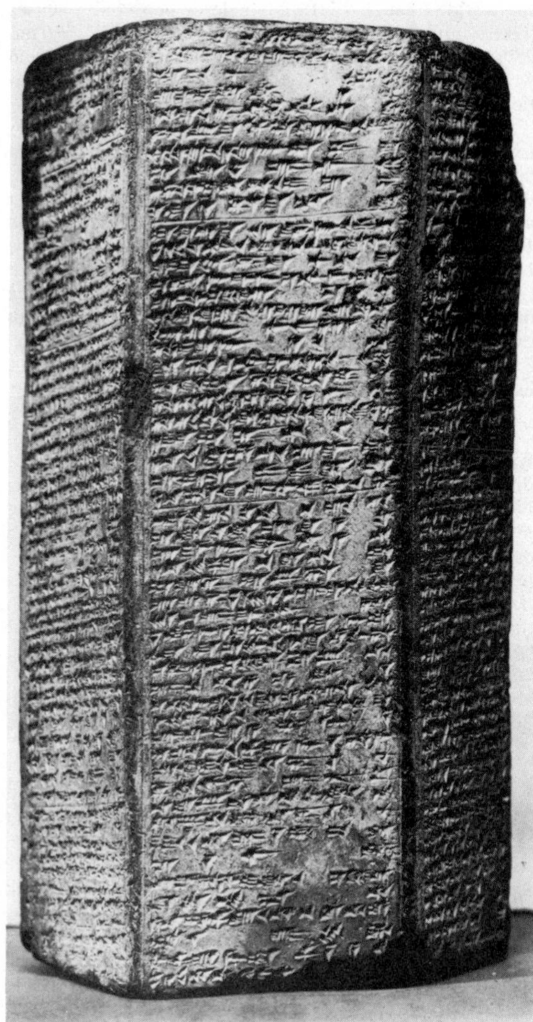

Historical records of Esarhaddon on Prism A, the best preserved of the king's annals (Trustees of the British Museum)

and has left many prisms, stelae, and building inscriptions. One of his first efforts was to rebuild Babylon, which his father had destroyed, and to restore the shrine Esagila (*ARAB,* II, §§ 641-676, 712). It has been suggested that the summoning of the kings of the Ḫatti lands to Babylon (cf. 2 Ch. 33:11) was in connection with this building campaign. Esarhaddon built a new palace at Kar-Esarhaddon ("Esarhaddonsburg") not far from Nineveh (*ARAB,* II, §§ 688-700, 721), and he restored the temple of Ashur which Shalmaneser I had built *ca.* 1250. Then he established its foundations and started work. "I built and completed it, I made it magnificent, to the astonishment of the peoples" (*ARAB,* II, § 702).

Esarhaddon, like so many of the kings of the Assyrian empire, was a cruel and powerful monarch. His dedication to the gods and goddesses of his land is recorded many times in his inscriptions, which may give us some idea of how religion can be used to foster excessive might. He claimed to rule the "universe": Egypt, Ethiopia, and the islands of the sea, including Ionia, and Knossus (possibly to be read "Tarshish"), as well as the lands adjacent to Assyria (*ARAB,* II, § 710). In the Zenjirli stele Esarhaddon says, "I am powerful, I am all powerful, I am a hero, I am gigantic, I am colossal, I am honored, I am magnified, I am without an equal among all kings, the chosen one of Assur, Nabû and Marduk, called of Sîn, favorite of Anu, beloved of the queen Ishtar, goddess of all (the world); unsparing weapon, which utterly destroys the enemy's land, am I" (*ARAB,* II, § 577). He also calls himself "the humble king" (*ARAB,* II, § 707). The personality traits of Esarhaddon, which may seem contradictory to modern man, in a way serve to illustrate the characteristics of the Assyrian empire.

Bibliography.–*ARAB,* II, §§ 497-761B; *ANET,* pp. 289-294; R. Borger, *Die Inschriften Asarhaddons, Königs von Assyrien* (1956); R. C. Thompson, *Prisms of Esarhaddon and Ashurbanipal* (1931); D. J. Wiseman, "The Vassal-Treaties of Esarhaddon," *Iraq,* 20 (1958), 1-99.

W. S. LASOR

ESAU ē'sô [Heb. *ʿēśāw*; Gk. *Ēsau*]. A son of Isaac and Rebekah, the older twin brother of Jacob (Gen. 25:24-26; 27:1, 32, 42). Esau's name ("hirsute") was given because of the presence of hair on his body at birth (25:25), and also because of his reddish appearance at delivery, from which his other designation, Edom or "red," was derived, in conjunction with the episode involving the lentil soup (25:30). Later Edomite peoples claimed Esau as their ancestor, and the name Seir, designating Edomite territory, may have been intended to preserve the memory of his name (*śāʿîr*–'hairy').

The birth narrative that mentioned the second child grasping the heel of the first foreshadowed the subordinate relationship of the Edomites to the offspring of Jacob (cf. Jer. 49:8; Ob. 6; Rom. 9:10-13). As a youth, Esau became an accomplished hunter, much as Ishmael had been; this way of life was a contrast with the semi-sedentary activities of his brother Jacob, and appears to mark the transition from nomadic to sedentary life in the patriarchal period.

The wild meats that Esau brought back pleased his father's tastes much more than the blander meats that Jacob provided from his own flocks; consequently Esau became the favored son. Returning on one occasion famished from an unsuccessful hunt, Esau traded his rights of primogeniture for food at his brother's instigation (Gen. 25:29-34). Archeological discoveries from Nuzi have shown that disposing of the birthright among members of the same family was not unknown.

Esau's apparent indifference to such valued possessions as the birthright was reflected in his marriage to two local women who were not of Abrahamic stock. This was a matter of great regret to Isaac and Rebekah (Gen. 26:35), and doubtless prompted the latter to instruct Jacob in ways of obtaining the patriarchal blessing that properly belonged to Esau (ch. 27). The successful deception prompted the prediction of a comparatively bleak future for Esau and his descendants, but with the assurance that one day they would be free from servitude to Jacob's seed (vv. 39f.). When he discovered the deception, Esau's anger was such that Rebekah advised Jacob to leave for Haran until Esau should be more amiably disposed to his fate. Two decades later Jacob appeased his brother successfully, helped by the fact that Esau had obviously forgiven the earlier act of treachery 33:4-16). Patriarchal blessings of the kind described in Genesis were a feature of Middle Bronze Age society in the Euphrates Valley, as indicated by archeological discoveries at Mari and Nuzi.

Historically the relationship between the Israelites and the Edomites followed the lines forecast by Isaac. In the time of David the Edomites were subjugated to the Israelites (2 S. 8:11-14; 1 Ch. 18:13) and remained under their control until the time of Jehoram of Judah (2 K. 8:20-22; 2 Ch. 21:8-10). They rebelled *ca.* 845 B.C.

and sacked Ezion-geber, becoming independent of Judah for a generation. They were reconquered under Amaziah (796-767 B.C.), but in 735 B.C. the Edomites regained their freedom, and never again came under the control of Judah.
See also EDOM. R. K. H.

ESAY ē'sā [Gk. *Ēsaias*] (AV, 2 Esd. 2:18; Sir. 48:22). *See* ISAIAH.

ESCAPE [Heb. *mālaṭ* (e.g., Gen. 19:20), *pālaṭ, pālîṭ, p^elêṭâ, yāṣā'*–'go out' (e.g., 1 S. 14:41), *mipp^enê*–'from the face of' (Gen. 7:7), *lûz* (Prov. 3:21; 4:21), *'ālâ*–'ascend' (Ex. 1:10), *mānôs*–'refuge' ("way of escape," Job 11:20), *sûr*–'turn aside' (Job 15:30), *tôṣā'ôṯ*–'out going' (Ps. 68:20 [MT 21]), *'āḇar*–'pass on' (Ps. 141:10), niphal of *nāṣal*–'be delivered' (Dt. 23:15), *š^e'ērîṯ*–'the rest' (2 Ch. 36:20), hiphil of *yāṯar*–'have remaining' (Ezk. 12:16), *bô'*–'come' (Jer. 26:21); Gk. *pheúgō, ekpheúgō* (e.g., Lk. 21:36), *diapheúgō* (Acts 27:42), *apopheúgō* (2 Pet. 1:4; 2:18, 20), *paraitéomai*–'avoid' ("seek to escape," Acts 25:11), *ékbasis*–'way out' ("way of escape," 1 Cor. 10:13), *ananḗphō*–'come to one's senses' (2 Tim. 2:26; cf. Bauer, p. 57; NEB), *exérchomai*–'go out' (Jn. 10:39), *lanthánō*–'hide' (Acts 26:26), *diasṓzō*–'bring safely through' (Acts 28:1, 4)]; AV also DEPART, FLEE (OUT), "the issues" (Ps. 68:20), etc.; NEB also SLIP FROM, ABANDON, "become masters of" (Ex. 1:10), "pass safely through," WAY OUT, etc.

Hebrew *mālaṭ* is the most common OT word for escape. It occurs along with Heb. *nûs*, "flee," in 1 S. 19:10 (cf. the parallelism in Jer. 46:6) and with *bāraḥ*, "flee," in 1 S. 19:18. The RSV sometimes translates Heb. *pālîṭ* ("the escaped one") and *p^elîṭâ* ("an escape") as verbs (Ezk. 7:16; Joel 2:3; Am. 9:1), and the latter at least once as "a remnant that has escaped" (Ezr. 9:15). The RSV has "Rock of Escape" for Heb. *sela' hammaḥl^eqôṯ* (lit. "rock of divisions," 1 S. 23:28; cf. AV, NEB; *see* ESCAPE, ROCK OF); in 2 S. 20:6 the RSV follows the Targum with "cause us trouble" rather than the MT *hiṣṣîl* (hiphil of *nāṣal*) *'ênēnû* (lit. "snatch away our eyes"; AV, NEB, "escape us"). In Prov. 3:21 both the RSV and the NEB have reversed the MT order of the parallelism.

The RSV has preserved only in part the Hebrew pleonasms: "any survivors escape" (Ezk. 7:16, Heb. *ûpāl^eṭû p^elîṭêhem*; AV "they that escape of them shall escape"; NEB "if any escape"), and "the survivors . . . who escaped" (Neh. 1:3, Heb. *hanniš'ārîm ^{'a}šer-niš'^{a}rû*; AV "the remnant that are left"; NEB "those . . . who had survived"); but cf. 1 S. 27:1; Am. 9:1.

"Escape" often occurs in the ordinary sense of escape from persons or dangers, e.g., Ehud escapes from the Moabites (Jgs. 3:26), David from Saul (1 S. 27:1). For some, however, there could be no escape: Zedekiah (Jer. 32:4), the Baal prophets (1 K. 18:40), the liar (Prov. 19:5), etc. Among the dangers from which people seek escape are a flood (Gen. 7:7), the sword (Lev. 26:37), a trap (Ps. 141:9f.), fire (Ezk. 15:7), and a stormy sea (Acts 28:1, 4).

A few times the term is used figuratively: cities cannot escape their destroyers (Jer. 48:8), the land of Egypt its defeat (Dnl. 11:42), nor the wicked person darkness (Job. 15:30); and one is urged not to let wisdom escape (Prov. 3:21). Since Yahweh is a God of salvation, to Him belongs escape from death (Ps. 68:20). Paul said he did not seek to escape death should he be convicted of injustice (Acts 25:11).

In some passages the moral sense of the term is shown: those who please God escape the ensnaring woman (Eccl. 7:26), and the righteous escape trouble (Prov. 12:13). The Christian must escape from the enslaving corruption of the world (2 Pet. 1:4; 2:18, 20) and "come to one's senses [Gk. *ananḗphō*] out of the snare of the devil" (2 Tim. 2:26; cf. NEB); Paul assured the Corinthians that God would always provide a way out (Gk. *ékbasis*) of temptations (1 Cor. 10:13).

In both the OT and the NT the term occurs with respect to divine judgment. For Israel there was no escape from divine punishment (Ezr. 9:14; Jer. 11:11; Ezk. 15:7; Am. 9:1). Many Israelites lost their lives in the Exile, but a remnant escaped death (cf. Ezr. 9:15; Ezk. 12:16); and Joel prophesied that those who call upon the name of the Lord will escape divine anger on the Day of the Lord (2:32 [MT 3:5]). In the NT, likewise, those who continue in their unbelief or evil ways are warned that they will not escape divine judgment (Mt. 23:33; Rom. 2:3; 1 Thess. 5:3; He. 12:25). The summons to receive strength to escape judgment continues to sound forth (Lk. 21:36).
R. W. V.

ESCAPE, ROCK OF [Heb. *sela' hammaḥl^eqôṯ*–'the rock of divisions' (1 S. 23:28)]; AV SELA-HAMMAHLEKOTH; NEB DIVIDING ROCK. The place in the wilderness of Maon where Saul had to forego his pursuit of David in order to go fight the Philistines (vv. 27f.). In this context the RSV rendering seems superior to both the AV's transliteration and the NEB's "Dividing Rock," although the primary sense of *ḥālaq* is "divide" (but cf. Akk. *ḫalāqu*, "escape," and a secondary meaning of Heb. *ḥālaq*, "be smooth, slippery," hence "slip away"; cf. also KD; BDB, p. 325). The place is perhaps to be identified with Wâdī el-Malâqi, about 20 km. (12 mi.) ESE of Hebron. G. A. L.

ESCHATOLOGY es-kə-tol'ə-jē [<Gk. *éschatos*–'last']. The doctrine of the last things. Included are two distinct but inseparable questions: the destiny of the individual — life, death, immortality, the intermediate state, and resurrection; and the destiny of history — the Day of the Lord, the end of the world, judgment, and the kingdom of God in the new world. Traditionally, eschatology has been concerned primarily with the destiny of the individual; but in biblical eschatology, individual destiny must be understood in connection with the destiny of history as a whole.

- I. Recent Criticism
- II. The OT Hope
  - A. General Features
  - B. Individual Hope
- III. The NT Hope
  - A. General Structure
  - B. Synoptic Gospels
  - C. Fourth Gospel
  - D. Acts
  - E. Paul
- IV. Coming of Christ
- V. Mystery of Lawlessness
- VI. Resurrection and the Rapture
- VII. Intermediate State
- VIII. Judgment
- IX. Future of Israel
- X. Consummation

I. Recent Criticism.–In modern times "eschatology" has come to mean much more than the events that will attend the end of the world; the basic stance of the interpreter will determine to a large degree his attitude toward eschatology. (1) Orthodox theologians have often regarded the Bible as a storehouse of texts whose proper interpretation and arrangement would lead to the correct program of the final events. One of the most vigorously debated questions among these theologians is whether the consummation will include an interval between the parousia of Christ and the final judgment (premillennialism) or whether the Parousia will be immediately followed by the judgment and the new world (amillennialism). The older view held by many orthodox theologians, that the gospel would so prevail in the world that the kingdom of God would be established within history through the effective agency of the Christian Church, has today few proponents (see R. Campbell, L. Boettner). *See* MILLENNIUM.

(2) One particular school within orthodox circles has exercised great influence, namely, dispensationalism. The heart of this system is not, as has often been supposed, seven dispensations; it is rather that there are two peoples of God, Israel and the Church, for whom God has different programs and different destinies. This basic premise rests upon a strictly literal interpretation of the OT. The OT promises that Israel will be God's people forever and the promises that the nation will be restored in Palestine to rule over the Gentiles are taken as the basic program for eschatology; the NT is interpreted in terms of this OT program. Therefore, Jesus' proclamation of the kingdom of the heavens was an offer of this earthly nationalistic kingdom to the nation Israel. The Sermon on the Mount is the new law for the earthly kingdom. The Olivet Discourse and the Revelation of John are largely concerned with the eschatology of the Jewish nation, not with the Church; for the Church belongs to the "Great Parenthesis" in God's program for Israel. In this system the millennium is quite essential, for only in this period can the promises of God to Israel be fulfilled.

(3) Albert Schweitzer's epoch-making *Von Reimarus zu Wrede* (1910; Eng. tr. *QHJ*) interpreted Jesus as a Jewish apocalyptist whose entire mission centered upon the proclamation of the imminent catastrophic end of the world and the inbreaking of the apocalyptic kingdom of God ("thoroughgoing" or "consistent eschatology"). Jesus died in disillusionment because the end did not come; but Paul and the early Church believed that in His death and resurrection the messianic age had indeed begun, and that the blessings of the eschatological era were actually experienced (A. Schweitzer, *Mysticism of Paul the Apostle* [Eng. tr. 1931]). Other scholars have accepted this thesis as the key to the understanding of Paul (H. J. Schoeps, *Paul* [Eng. tr. 1961]).

(4) C. H. Dodd moved "realized Eschatology" back from Paul to Jesus Himself and made it the central fact in NT theology. In the person and mission of Jesus the eschatological crisis was present; the kingdom of God *has come*. The apocalyptic language in which Jesus described this present crisis was only a symbolic representation of that which stands beyond history — the absolute, the "wholly other," which in His person has entered into time and space (*Parables*). The early Church at first misinterpreted Jesus' "realized eschatology" because of its familiarity with Jewish eschatology, thus making two days out of what had been for Jesus a single Day of crisis. Thus Paul's letters reflect a good bit of Jewish apocalyptic eschatology; but finally the Gospel of John recovers the "realized eschatology" of Jesus, and the crude apocalyptic notions are refined away (*Apostolic Preaching*).

(5) Eschatology becomes existentialism in the theology of Rudolf Bultmann. Eschatology, realistically conceived, is mythology and is alien to a modern world view. Historically, Jesus was an apocalyptic prophet; but His eschatological perspective was only the reflex of His intense God-consciousness, before which the world seemed to fall away and be at its end. Indeed, when confronted by the demand of God, the person who answers by responsible decision does enter into eschatological existence. He comes to the end of his old life — he is freed from his past; and he enters into newness of life — he is open to the future.

(6) An increasing number of scholars recognize that there is truth in both consistent and realized eschatology; that the OT hope is in some real sense fulfilled in the person and mission of Christ, while the consummation of the hope awaits an eschatological consummation (Kümmel; Cullmann; Schnackenburg; see Ladd, *Jesus and the Kingdom*). The present article is written from this perspective of *Heilsgeschichte* or "biblical realism"; its primary purpose is not to attempt a systematic structuring of eschatological teaching but to show the integral role of eschatology in the biblical teaching of redemption.

II. The OT Hope.–NT eschatology can be understood only when interpreted against its OT background. Furthermore, the relation between OT and NT eschatology can be best understood in the light of progressive revelation in the terms of *Heilsgeschichte*, "redemptive history." The OT hope is set forth primarily in terms of God's dealings with the nation Israel and the economy of the old covenant; the NT reinterprets Israel as the Church and provides a more refined description of the fulfillment of God's redemptive purpose. The OT, therefore, must be interpreted in terms of the NT fulfillment.

The OT does not predict the era of the Christian Church. Ezekiel provides the fullest program of the eschatological hope. Israel is to be restored to the land (Ezk. 34:11-16) under a Davidic prince (37:24), to be converted (36:26), and enjoy the blessings of a covenant of peace (34:25), with God's sanctuary established in their midst forever (37:28). After the restoration of Israel under the blessings of God's kingdom, there will occur a final eschatological war (38–39), which will be followed by the final state of blessedness as described in great detail in terms of the OT cult (40–48). The life-giving river flowing from the temple (Ezk. 47:12) is redefined in Revelation as the river of life flowing from the throne of God (Rev. 22:1f.). Similarly, Isaiah sees a new heaven and a new earth (Isa. 65:17; 66:22), but death and sin still exist (65:20). Here is a fundamental characteristic of biblical eschatology: the description of the future in terms of known human experience.

A. General Features. Several features characterize the OT hope. It is, first of all, a *dynamic* hope; i.e., it is a hope in God more than in the future. The most fundamental idea in OT eschatology is "the God who comes." God will finally visit His people in both judgment and salvation. Behind the eschatological hope is the historical experience of divine visitations. God came down to deliver Israel from Egypt and to make them His people (Dt. 33:2, 5); God comes in history to visit His people with judgment as well as deliverance (Mic. 1:3f.); God even comes to deliver His individual servant in times of trouble (Ps. 18:6-15 [MT 7-16]). This same God will finally visit His people to bring them into the fulness of His salvation (Zec. 14:3, 5; Isa. 29:6; 35:4; 59:20), to punish the wicked (Isa. 26:21; 2:21; 63:1-6; 64:1ff.; 66:15f.; Zeph. 3:8), and to bring salvation even to the Gentiles (Isa. 66:18ff.; Zec. 2:10f.). Thus Israel's eschatological hope was rooted in history, or rather in the God who comes in history.

The OT hope may properly be called *eschatological*. The definition of eschatology and the use of the term to designate the OT hope have been vigorously debated. Some have insisted that eschatology properly refers to a great drama of the end time in which the age of this world ends and a new eternal age of salvation is introduced, i.e., it must include the dualistic concept of the two ages (Mowinckel, p. 125). Allied with this view is the critical hypothesis that two very different kinds of hope are found in the OT: the prophetic and the apocalyptic (or eschatological; see Mowinckel; Bousset; Volz; Bultmann). The prophetic hope is entirely historical and earthly, centering upon the nationalistic hopes of Israel and her triumph over his enemies under the leadership of a Davidic king. This kingdom did not come to pass. Instead, after the restoration Israel found herself in Palestine, a small, weak nation, subjected to the rule of one pagan nation after another. Finally came the proscription of the Jewish religion by Antiochus Epiphanes, accompanied by fierce persecution and martyrdom. Under the burden of such experiences and the influence of Persian dualistic ideas, there emerged another kind of hope — the eschatological or apocalyptic, which despaired of history as the scene of God's kingdom and saw the kingdom coming only beyond history, in a transcendent order. Instead of a historical Davidic king, this dualistic hope posited a heavenly supernatural Son of Man as the messianic ruler. The prophetic hope expects a kingdom to arise within history; the apocalyptic hope expects the kingdom to come from outside of history. This distinction between the prophetic and apocalyptic kinds of hope has played a significant role in the contemporary discussion of eschatology.

Other scholars, however, recognize that the prophetic hope itself involves a divine breaking into history. "There is no eschatology without rupture" (Jacob, *Theology of the OT,* p. 318; see Frost; North; Vriezen). The sharp distinction between a prophetic historical hope and an apocalyptic transcendental hope is a structure of modern critical ideas about history which does not do justice to the biblical concepts (see C. C. McCown, *HTR,* 38 [1945], 151-175). The OT conceives of God as acting redemptively in history, and as finally bringing history to its consummation in the kingdom of God. History does not produce the kingdom; for evil has befallen both men and nature. Nothing less than a mighty inbreaking of God can avail to accomplish redemption.

Therefore the OT hope may properly be designated a *historical* hope, i.e., it has its setting within history and is viewed as the final term of God's acting in history. The biblical perspective does not allow for the sharp disjunction between "history" and "beyond history" that is often found in contemporary theology. The cleavage between history and eschatology in the OT is never radical, for the God who will reveal Himself by a grandiose theophany in the eschatological consummation has already manifested Himself and does not cease manifesting Himself in the course of history. Therefore all historical events in redemptive history are already charged with eternal significance (Jacob, p. 318).

That eschatological redemption means redemption of history is illustrated by the use of the expression, "the last (or latter) days" to designate the final redeemed state. This phrase in itself has no intrinsic eschatological significance but refers only to a period of time in the indeterminate future (Gen. 49:1; Nu. 24:14; Dt. 4:30; 31:29). It is used to designate the final period of time when God's kingdom of peace and blessedness will be realized (Isa. 2:2-4) and Israel will be redeemed under a Davidic king (Hos. 3:5). In Ezk. 38:16 it is used of the time of the eschatological war after Israel has been restored.

This view of the future, as including both the near and the far, involves what may be described as a tension between history and eschatology. This is illustrated by the fact that "the Day of the Lord" designates an imminent, purely historical judgment (Am. 5:18, 20, 27; Jer. 46:10) and also the eschatological event lying behind it (Isa. 2:12-22). A profound theology lies behind this phenomenon: the God who acts in history is also the God who will act at its eschatological consummation to accomplish a single redemptive purpose. In other words, the OT hope is not largely concerned about questions of chronology or sequence or the time of the consummation; it is concerned about God and His redemptive working. The purpose of prophecy is not to satisfy curiosity about the future, nor even to give to God's people a guaranteed future; it is rather to let the light of the future shine upon the present that God's people may be brought into conformity with His will.

This tension between history and eschatology explains an important characteristic of a number of prophecies: the immediate historical and the more remote eschatological are blended together as though they constituted a single event. The destruction of Babylon at the hands of the Medes is described in eschatological terms as though it constituted the end of the world (Isa. 13). Some unknown historical danger is described in Zephaniah in terms of a cosmic catastrophe. In Joel (1:4-7), the judgment of locusts and drought so blends into the eschatological judgment that it is impossible to be sure when one leaves off and the other begins. The critic fails to grasp the character of the OT hope when he analyzes such prophecies into two disparate types of expectation, or concludes that the historical is authentic and the eschatological a later accretion. The tension between history and eschatology is of the essence in the biblical hope, for hope is in God, not in the future.

The OT hope is *earthly* in character. The eschatological redemption includes the realm of nature and the world, for both man and the world are God's creation and both have suffered under the burden of evil. The evil that curses the world must be judged and cleansed (Isa. 51:6; 13:13; 34:4), and a new order of righteousness and blessedness created (Isa. 35:1-10; 11:6-9; Am. 9:13f.). This new order can be brought about only by the coming of God — a glorious theophany. But the new order that emerges is always earthly. Even the new heavens and the new earth of Isa. 65–66 are described in this worldly terms. The theology underlying this description is that man as creature stands in solidarity with the created world and even in the new age remains a creature.

This new order usually is seen as arising from the single eschatological visitation of God. In Ezekiel, the usual pattern is modified into two stages: first, Israel is restored to the land and enjoys the blessings of God's rule (Ezk. 34–37); then after the kingdom occurs an eschatological war with Gog and Magog (Ezk. 38–39), after which is seen, in very symbolic form, the final redemption when God forever dwells among His people, receiving their perfect worship (Ezk. 40–48). Seldom, however, are the prophets concerned about such sequences; their entire attention is focused upon the divine visitation for salvation and judgment. Questions that concerned later Judaism, such as the Days of the Messiah and the age to come, do not appear in the OT.

One reason for this is that the OT hope has above all an *ethical* concern. The prophets were not primarily concerned about the future but with God's people in the present. Prophets who promised peace instead of judgment were false prophets (Jer. 14:13-16). Indeed, Amos rebukes the popular hope of his day, that the Day of the Lord would bring certain salvation to Israel. Instead, that Day will be darkness and not light (Am. 5:18-20). The Day of the Lord will mean judgment for Israel as well as for the Gentiles; but beyond judgment is salvation both for Israel and the Gentiles. The prophetic announcements have as their main concern the divine demand for obedience and faithfulness in light of the total redemptive purpose of God.

Because of the ethical character of the OT hope, the

eschatological salvation of Israel is viewed not in particularistic terms but in terms of a converted *remnant*. Israel as a nation is sinful and doomed. The name of Hosea's son, Lo Ammi, illustrates that Israel as such is no longer God's people (Hos. 1:9). The Day of the Lord will mean national doom (Am. 5:18-20; 9:8a). "Never again, so far as we know, did a prophet seek to reform the state by direct political action" (J. Bright, *Kingdom of God* [1953], p. 66). Yet a remnant is to be saved (Am. 9:8b; Isa. 4:2-4; 10:20-22; 37:30-32), converted (Jer. 31:31-34; Ezk. 36:22-32; Joel 2), and restored to the land in righteousness. To the Gentiles is assigned a diverse destiny. Sometimes the prophets anticipate an eschatological war between converted Israel and the Gentiles (Mic. 4:11-13; Isa. 31:4-9; Ezk. 38–39; Joel 3:9-16; Zec. 12:1-9); sometimes the Gentiles will serve Israel (Am. 9:12; Mic. 5:9; 7:16; Isa. 45:14-16; 49:23; 60:12, 14); sometimes they are seen as converted and worshiping the God of Israel (Zeph. 3:9; 20; Isa. 2:2-4; 42:6f.; 60:1-14; Zec. 8:20-23; 14:16-19).

The OT prophets have diverse *messianic concepts*. The most common view is that of a Davidic messianic king who will reign in the eschatological kingdom of God (Pss. 2, 110; Isa. 9, 11). The king does not establish the kingdom but rules when the kingdom has been established by God. This figure plays an important role in later Jewish expectations as the Lord's Anointed, or Messiah (Ps. Sol. 17).

A second figure is the Suffering Servant of Isa. 52–53. The prophet describes an unidentified humble figure who comes to bring salvation through suffering and death. This figure is not identified with the messianic king, although Isa. 55:3f. may suggest such an identification. A humble king does appear in Zec. 9:9, and a smitten shepherd in Zec. 13:7-9. Later Judaism did not know how to relate this figure to that of the Messiah. J. Jeremias has attempted to prove that such an identification actually existed in Judaism (*Servant of God* [2nd ed. 1965]), but his evidence is tenuous.

A third messianic personage is the Son of man, or rather "one like a man" in Dnl. 7:13f. It is not altogether clear that this figure is to be identified as a distinct person in Daniel, for in the interpretation the "one like a man" disappears and the kingdom is given to the people of God. Thus the "one like a man" may be only a symbol for God's people; but since he comes to the throne of God to receive the kingdom, he is probably a supernatural heavenly being representing the people of God who on their behalf will receive the kingdom of God and reign in it. In any case, this heavenly figure became very important in Judaism as the supernatural agent of God's rule and judgment on earth (1 En. 37–71; 2 Esd. 13:3).

The OT does not conflate these messianic figures; they stand as three distinct concepts, without indication as to how they are related to each other or how there could be such diversity in the coming of God's kingdom.

B. Individual Hope. A question standing apart from the eschatology of God's people and the world is the fate of the individual. The OT pictures the dead as descending to Sheol (translated "grave," "hell," or "pit" in the AV). Sheol is pictured as a place beneath (Ps. 86:13; Prov. 15:24; Ezk. 26:20), a region of darkness (Job 10:22), the land of forgetfulness (Ps. 88:12 [MT 13]; 94:17; 115:17). Here the dead, who are gathered in tribes as in life (Ezk. 32:17-32), receive the dying (Isa. 14:9f.). The dead exist not as souls or spirits capable of existence apart from the body, but as "shades" (Ps. 88:10 [MT 11]; Prov. 9:18; Isa. 14:9). This shadowy, unsatisfying state of the dead is not meant to describe the geography of Sheol; it is rather the OT way, shared through general revelation with other ancient religions, of expressing the conviction that death does not terminate human existence. Sheol is not so much a place as the state of the dead (Jacob, p. 304). It is not nonexistence; but from the OT perspective, it is not life, for life can be enjoyed only in fellowship with God (Ps. 16:10f.). In a few places God gives the added revelation that since He is the living God, He will not abandon His people to Sheol but will bring them into the enjoyment of life in His presence (Ps. 16:9-11; 49:15 [MT 16]; 73:24; Job 19:25).

The concept of the resurrection of the body is found in only a few references, but it is a logical and necessary conclusion from the OT concept of humanity and God. A person does not consist of separate parts — flesh, soul, and spirit. Rather, these terms are different ways of viewing a single dynamic person. Both life and death involve the whole person. Therefore, while the concept is not developed, the OT anticipates ultimately the resurrection of the body (Isa. 25:8; 26:19) and the final participation of God's people in His kingdom (Dnl. 12:2). Belief in the resurrection is rooted in the confidence that God is the living God and therefore cannot abandon His people to death.

***III. The NT Hope.**–A. General Structure.* The OT hope that the kingdom of God cannot be produced by history but only by a glorious theophany, which will redeem a fallen order and issue in both a transformed society and a renovated world, was developed in Judaism in various directions. Sometimes the contrast between the present and the future is relatively small; sometimes it is so great that the future is viewed in altogether transcendental terms, having nothing to do with this world or human history. 1 En. 1–36 pictures the kingdom in very materialistic terms. Ps. Sol. 17–18 pictures a Davidic messiah arising from among mankind, supernaturally endowed to destroy his enemies and to inaugurate an earthly kingdom with Jerusalem as its capital and the Jews triumphant over their foes. On the other hand, 1 En. 37–71, which pictures a radically transformed earth (45:5; 51:4f.), develops the motif of Isa. 65–66. Some scholars find in these Similitudes of Enoch a completely transcendental hope; but the kingdom remains on earth, even though radically transformed. The messianic person of the Similitudes is a supernatural, preexistent Son of man who has been kept in heaven since creation and who will come to earth and sit on the throne of his glory (47:3; 51:3; 62:5) to judge the living and the resurrected dead (51:1-5). A completely transcendental eschatology is found in 1 En. 92–105, where the final redemption will witness a new heaven but not a new earth (91:16). The righteous will be raised from Sheol (92:3-5), but not in bodily form. The portals of heaven will be open to them (104:2), and they will become companions of the hosts of heaven (104:6) as disembodied spirits (103:4).

This brief survey suggests that different apocalypses (the term given to this type of writing) dwelt upon various OT pictures of the future, some emphasizing one aspect and some another. Some prophets had described the future in very earthly terms, while Isa. 65–66 looked for a new order so different it could be called a new heaven and a new earth. Some apocalyptists emphasized the earthly aspect of the OT hope, sometimes in very sensuous terms. Others, pondering the implication of a new heaven and a new earth, tried to picture what this transformed order would be like. Two first-century A.D. apocalypses combined the two ideas of a very earthly kingdom followed by the new creation (2 Esd. 7; 2 Bar. 29–30). Charles has said that these conceptions are in germ and principle as old as Isa. 65–66 (*Apocalypse of Baruch,* p. 81). These two forms of the kingdom are found also in rabbinic terminology and are called "the days of the Messiah" and "the age to come" (see Klausner, pp. 339, 354-365, 408-419).

The NT, like Judaism, does not abandon the centrality of the eschatological hope in its teaching of redemption. Indeed, the meaning of the person and work of Jesus is set within this *heilsgeschichtliche* perspective. But the NT, like Judaism, employs a terminology that goes beyond the OT, by which it expresses the same redemptive structure as that implicit in the OT. The present "historical" order and the eschatological redeemed order are set more sharply over against each other by the Greek terms *hoútos ho aiṓn, ho nýn aiṓn, ho enestṓs aiṓn,* "this age," "the present age" (Mt. 12:32; 13:22; Lk. 16:8; Rom. 12:2; 1 Cor. 1:20; 2:6, 8; 3:18; 2 Cor. 4:4; Gal. 1:4; Eph. 1:21; 2:2; 6:12; 1 Tim. 6:17; 2 Tim. 4:10; Tit. 2:12), and *ho aiṓn ekeínos, ho aiṓn méllōn, ho aiṓn erchómenos,* "that age," "the coming age" (Mt. 12:32; Lk. 18:30; 20:35; Eph. 2:7; He. 6:5). This terminology emerges at about the same time in Jewish literature (2 Esd. 7:50, 113; 8:1; 2 Bar. 14:13; 15:7; Mish. *Aboth* iv.1, 21f.; vi.4, 7) and appears in the rabbinic literature as *ʿôlām hazzeh* and *ʿōlām habbāʾ* (Klausner, pp. 408ff.; Volz, *Eschatologie der jüdischen Gemeinde,* p. 65). This terminology is implicit in 1 En. 16:1; 48:7; 71:15, but the earliest explicit references do not appear to be earlier than the last part of the 1st cent. A.D. While it is possible that a piece of Jewish theology has by divine revelation been incorporated into the NT teaching (Vos, p. 28), it is also possible, if the Gospels accurately represent Jesus' teachings, that He was the first to use this terminology. In any case, the same basic structure emerges at about the same time in the NT and in Jewish thought. Many scholars attribute this dualistic eschatology to Persian influence, but such a hypothesis is not necessary. The idea of the two ages separated by a glorious theophany is a natural development of the OT hope (W. D. Davies, *Setting of the Sermon on the Mount* [1964], p. 121), for it develops the dual idea of the earthly and the supramundane character of the eschatological Kingdom (Eichrodt, *Theology of the OT,* I, 491).

While the NT reflects the same basic eschatological structure as Judaism, at an all-important point it stands apart from Jewish thought. The prophets taught eschatology with the ethical purpose of confronting a disobedient and sinning people with the will of God seen from the perspective of His total redemptive purpose, which involved both judgment and salvation. Therefore, they viewed history in the light of eschatology, interpreting both in the light of God's redemptive acts in history.

Jewish apocalyptic thought lost the sense of God's acting in history. As never before in Israel's history, the people were obedient to the law; and in Maccabean times many chose torture and martyrdom rather than break the law. Here was a dark enigma: an obedient, righteous people enduring tragic, crushing evil. The apocalypses offer a solution to this problem of theodicy: God is no longer redemptively active in history to deliver His people but has surrendered this age to evil demonic powers (1 En. 9:11; 42:3; 89:58, 71, 75). God's righteous people (2 Esd. 6:55-59) are enduring evils that are inexplicable (2 Esd. 4:12; 7:66). The solution is found in the hope of God's imminent coming to end the corrupt age, to destroy the powers of evil, and to bring Israel into the blessedness of the kingdom. Eschatology is altogether severed from history; salvation is exclusively eschatological.

The most distinctive difference between NT and Jewish apocalyptic thought is that the NT, like the prophets, again roots the eschatological consummation in God's redemptive working in history. The mission of Jesus in history is seen as the fulfillment of the OT promise, which in turn makes possible the eschatological consummation.

O. Cullmann has structured this distinctive element by making Christ the new center of the redemptive time line (*Christ and Time*). Judaism placed the center at the eschatological transition point between the ages; the gospel retains this eschatological structure but changes the center to the person and work of Jesus in history. Long before Cullmann, Vos had expressed this idea even more vividly by saying that the redemption wrought in Christ had in fact set in motion the eschatological process so that the age to come had in principle become present. Vos described the redemptive realities in Pauline thought as "semi-eschatological" (p. 38).

This means that the OT promise of eschatological redemption is fulfilled in two redemptive acts: in the mission of Jesus in history and in His parousia at the end of the age. What is seen in the OT as a single great Day of the Lord has become two days. This idea has been widely accepted in modern biblical theology; it means that the age of the Church is a period "between the times," in which the two ages, as it were, overlap. Therefore, instead of speaking of a new center in the time line of redemptive history, it would be more accurate to say that there are two pivotal points: the Incarnation and the Parousia, which are interrelated and equally essential in the accomplishment of redemption. This structure of "realized-futuristic" eschatology is the unifying factor in the diversity of NT thought. It also renders all NT truth essentially eschatological in character.

B. Synoptic Gospels. The two central themes of the Synoptic Gospels are the kingdom of God and the messianic mission of Jesus. In these two themes is a pattern of fulfillment of the OT hope within the structure of eschatological dualism. In Jesus' mission, God is fulfilling the OT promises; yet the consummation of the promise awaits the age to come, which is always future. Fulfillment is the note with which Mark introduces his Gospel (Mk. 1:14f.); and Luke deliberately sets the sermon in Nazareth at the beginning of his Gospel to sound the note of fulfillment (Lk. 4:18-22). Jesus' disciples were witnessing the events that the OT saints had longed to see (Lk. 10:23f.). In response to the perplexity of John the Baptist, Jesus asserted that the promise of Isa. 35:5f. was being fulfilled. Yet the fulfillment occurs in this age; the consummation awaits the eschatological age to come.

Here is a new fact in redemptive history: the messianic hope, which the OT anticipated as a single great Day of the Lord, even though it had historical antecedents, is in fact fulfilled in two acts — one within history, the other at the consummation of history. This means that the historical event that occurred in the person and mission of Jesus is essentially eschatological, and that the eschatological is the consummation of the historical. Apart from the historical, the eschatological could never come to pass; but without the eschatological, the historical remains incomplete.

This is why the kingdom of God can be spoken of as both future and present — an idea which, although logically inconsistent, is the heart of Jesus' message. Jesus, like the prophets, looks forward to the perfect establishment of God's reign in a renewed world (Mt. 19:28), when God's people will enter into eternal life in the age to come (Mk. 10:17-31; Mt. 25:31-46). The eschatological coming of the kingdom will mean, positively, the gathering of the elect into salvation (Mk. 13:27) and, negatively, the destruction of Satan and all evil powers (Mt. 25:41) and the exclusion of the wicked from the blessings of the kingdom (Mt. 7:23; 25:12). Their destiny is described sometimes in terms of fire (Mt. 13:42, 50; 25:41) and sometimes in terms of darkness (Mt. 8:12; 22:13; 25:30), both apparently symbolic descriptions of banishment from the presence and blessings of God in His kingdom.

While Jesus proclaims the consummation of the redemptive working of God only in terms of the eschatological consummation in the age to come, it has often been pointed out that He has little to say about the form and character of the kingdom, but chose to refer to it in metaphorical language: the Shepherd will gather His sheep (Mt. 25:32); the pure in heart will see God (5:8); an inheritance is received (19:29); a treasure is accumulated (6:20); thrones and positions of authority are bestowed (19:28); the harvest is gathered into the barn (13:30); the Gentiles will join in a heavenly feast with the patriarchs (8:11) at the table of the Son of man (Lk. 22:29f.) and drink the wine of the new age (Mk. 14:25); the marriage feast is celebrated (Mt. 22:3; 25:10). All of these metaphors describe the restoration of perfect communion between God and mankind which had been broken by sin.

The Gospels also assert that the kingdom of God has become present in history in the person and mission of Jesus, in anticipation of the eschatological consummation. This is most clearly asserted in Mt. 12:28f., where the presence of the kingdom of God means a defeat of Satan (here described as the binding of a strong man), that his goods may be spoiled — i.e., that people held in his power may be delivered. The efforts of the school of "consistent eschatology" to prove that *éphthasen* means *ēngiken,* "has come near," forces that language to fit a theory. In advance of his eschatological destruction, Satan has already been defeated and bound. This spiritual victory is again reflected in Lk. 10:18, where the presence of the kingdom in the mission of Jesus' disciples is seen as toppling Satan from his heavenly place of power.

This means that in response to Jesus' mission, believers may enter into the enjoyment of the blessings of the kingdom before its eschatological consummation. This is why the Gospels speak of entering the kingdom in the present (Mt. 21:31; 23:15; Mk. 12:34). The messianic salvation present in Jesus' mission in fulfillment of Isa. 35:5f. is a new era which takes the place of the Law and the Prophets (Mt. 11:11-13). John was the last of the old era; with the message of Jesus, God's kingdom is working powerfully among people (Gk. *biázetai,* Mt. 11:12) and requires a strong response from its hearers. Because of the greatness of these messianic blessings, the "least" who is now in the kingdom, i.e., who has received the reign of God (Mk. 10:15) and entered into the blessings of His reign, is greater than the greatest of the prophets.

The presence of the kingdom means the gift of salvation. Salvation is both eschatological (Mk. 10:26) and present (Lk. 19:9f.). The parables of the lost sheep, the lost coin, and the lost son refer to a present salvation: the seeking of the lost and bringing them, like the prodigal, into restored fellowship with the Father. This anticipation of the eschatological salvation is set forth in the frequently acted parable of table fellowship. Jesus warmly received tax collectors and sinners at dinner (Mk. 2:15f.; cf. Lk. 15:1f.). There is joy in heaven over one sinner who repents (Lk. 15:7); but it is a joy that was anticipated on earth in the table fellowship of Jesus with repentant sinners. So typical was such fellowship that Jesus was accused of being a glutton and a drunkard (Mt. 11:19). Jesus did not observe the Jewish regulations about fasting because the presence of the bridegroom calls for joy, not fasting (Mk. 2:18f.).

Jesus' miracles of healing were a pledge of the resurrection life of the age to come (Lk. 20:35f.) and evidence of the presence of the messianic salvation (Mt. 11:4f.). Bodily healing and "spiritual" salvation, however, belong together. All ten lepers were cleansed and "healed" (Lk. 17:14f.); but to the Samaritan who returned to express gratitude Jesus said, "Your faith has saved you" (Lk. 17:19). The woman in the house of Simon received salvation apart from any miracle of healing (Lk. 7:50).

The presence of the messianic salvation also meant the gift of forgiveness. Forgiveness is a promise for the eschatological consummation (Isa. 33:24; Mic. 7:18-20; Jer. 31:31-34; Ezk. 36:22-28; Zec. 13:1). It was a prerogative belonging to God alone (Ps. 103:3; Isa. 43:25); there is no known Jewish source that expects the messiah on his own authority to forgive sins. This divine messianic forgiveness Jesus brought to mankind. His claim to possess such authority (Mk. 2:10) shocked the scribes (2:7). On their own presuppositions they were in the right; but Jesus forgave sins because He was the Son of man (2:10) in whom the blessings of the kingdom were present.

The messianic salvation meant, furthermore, the gift of righteousness. Righteousness in Judaism was a human activity, achieved by obedience to the law and by acts of mercy. The kingdom of God demands a greater righteousness than did Judaism (Mt. 5:20), but this very righteousness is itself the gift of God (Lk. 18:14; Mt. 5:6).

This emergence of the eschatological in history is the mystery of the kingdom (Mk. 4:11), which is illustrated by the parables of the kingdom (Mk. 4; Mt. 13). The kingdom is present, not in apocalyptic power but like a sower scattering seed; it demands a human response to be effective (the four soils). The kingdom is present without disrupting the course of this age, yet the apocalyptic separation will surely come (tares). The kingdom is present in an outwardly insignificant form (mustard seed, leaven), but eventually it will fill all the earth. Nevertheless, the kingdom even in its present hidden form is like a treasure or a pearl, to be acquired at all costs. In the present, the kingdom creates a mixed fellowship of people among whom are both good and bad; but at the consummation, there will be a separation even of those who profess the kingdom (draw net). In the parables, the present activity of the kingdom in Jesus' mission and the eschatological consummation are two inseparable aspects of a single redemptive work.

The union of history and eschatology is also seen in the nature of Jesus' messiahship. Jesus was the Messiah (Mt. 16:16f.; Mk. 14:61f.), the Son of David (Mk. 10:47; 11:10; Mt. 15:22; 20:30), but in a radically reinterpreted sense. Even as the mystery of the kingdom means the presence of the kingdom in a new and unexpected form, so Jesus' messianic mission did not involve eschatological judgment nor a political role. In fact, He firmly refused to play any political role (Jn. 6:15), for His mission was a spiritual one. Therefore He did not proclaim Himself Messiah, for such an announcement would have been misunderstood. His favorite self-designation was Son of man, derived from Dnl. 7. As Son of man, He has an eschatological mission at the consummation, when He will come in glory and power to destroy the powers of evil and to judge mankind (Mk. 13:26; 14:62; Mt. 13:41; 25:31). The eschatological Son of man, however, must first appear among mankind in history, in weakness and humiliation (Mt. 8:20) to fulfil a mission of suffering and dying in order to effect the messianic salvation (Mk. 8:31; 9:31; 10:45; 14:41). It was utterly unforeseen and unexpected that the eschatological Son of man should first fill the role of the Suffering Servant of Isa. 53 before coming as the heavenly judge. Indeed, the future destiny of men is determined by their reaction to Jesus as the lowly Son of man (Mk. 8:38). In some way not explained by the Gospels, the death of Jesus is an essential element in the coming of the eschatological kingdom (Mk. 14:25).

Jesus' reported teachings contain the so-called Olivet Discourse (Mk. 13; Mt. 24; Lk. 21:5-23). While this discourse obviously owes its present diverse form to the Evangelists, it does not contradict the teachings of Jesus as a whole, and it may be accepted as an accurate report of the substance of His eschatological teaching. Many scholars do not accept this conclusion but feel rather that the Evangelists embodied in part or in toto Jewish apocalyptic materials (see Beasley-Murray, *Jesus and the Future*). The "signs" of the end (Mk. 13:5-13) do not, however, provide a means of calculating the imminence of the end. In fact, they are not eschatological signs at all, for the discourse itself says that certain events will occur, "but the end is not yet" (Mk. 13:7). These are therefore signs of the delay of the end. They are only the "beginning of woes" (Mk. 13:8), which will mark the entire age until the end comes. Furthermore, the motif of these so-called signs is different from that of the messianic woes in the apocalypses (cf. 2 Esd. 4:52ff.; 6:18ff.; 8:63ff.; 1 En. 80:2ff.; 99:1ff.; Jub. 23:16ff.; Sib. Or. 2:199ff.; 2 Bar. 25:1ff.; 48:31ff.; 70:2ff.). The discourse also differs from the apocalypses in that it makes no use of pseudonymity, it is not based upon heavenly revelations or visions, and it does not rewrite history in the guise of prophecy. It is a prophecy of the future and in both form and language stands closer to the prophets than to the apocalyptists.

The central problem of the discourse is that it deals with two events: the destruction of the temple at the fall of Jerusalem, and the parousia of Christ at the eschatological consummation (Mk. 13:1-4; Mt. 24:1-3). The Evangelists, in compiling the discourse, have emphasized these two aspects differently. Mark and Matthew emphasize the eschatological aspect and Luke the historical (Lk. 21:20-23). In fact, Jesus views the future as did the prophets: He sees in the near future a historical judgment — the destruction of Jerusalem — that is an anticipation of the eschatological desolating sacrilege, or Antichrist. At this point, he again stands apart from the apocalyptists, who had lost the sense of God's acting in history. The two notes of time (Mk. 13:30-32) probably refer to these two facets of the future. "All these things" in Mk. 13:30, which are to occur within a generation, cannot include the end itself, for v. 29 has just used the same phrase to anticipate the end. To say, "When you see the Son of man coming, you know that he is near," is impossible. Therefore, the day and hour of the eschatological end is known only to the Father (Mk. 13:32); but the signs and events that are to precede the end, including the fall of Jerusalem, do not belong to the remote future but will begin to take place in the present generation (Cranfield, *SJT,* 6 [1953], 298).

The motif of Mk. 13:1-13 is that this age is to retain its evil character down to the very end. Evils will continue to occur in nature and in human society, and the disciples of Jesus will find themselves caught up in the same spiritual struggle in which Jesus Himself engaged, and will therefore suffer persecution and even martyrdom. God has not, however, abandoned the age of evil, as the apocalyptists thought; on the contrary, the good news of the kingdom is to be proclaimed in all the world before the end comes (Mk. 13:10; Mt. 24:14).

The evil that is to press heavily upon Jesus' disciples throughout the age will undergo a terrible intensification at the end. A desolating sacrilege (foreshadowed in the Roman intrusion into the temple in A.D. 66-70) will appear, which will bring persecution and martyrdom to a terrible climax (Mk. 13:9-20). The parousia of the Son of man will be attended by a cosmic catastrophe that will shake the established order (vv. 24-26), and the Son of man will appear in glory to gather His elect into the kingdom of God (v. 27). Nothing is said about resurrection or judgment, but these must be assumed.

Mark concludes the address (Mk. 13:33-37) with a motif, enlarged by Matthew with materials from Q (Mt. 24:37-51) and M (ch. 25), that again sets the Gospels apart from the apocalypses: a strong ethical emphasis, addressed to Jesus' disciples, that the eschatological consummation will mean judgment for those who are spiritually asleep. The apocalypses were written to encourage the righteous in persecution with the sure hope of imminent eschatological salvation; the Olivet Discourse challenges the Church with spiritual alertness lest the Day be one of judgment. This is particularly evident in the parable of the ten maidens (Mt. 25:1-13), which teaches that among Jesus' disciples (i.e., in the Church) are those who are spiritually unprepared for the Parousia and who will therefore be excluded from the wedding feast. The story of the talents (25:14-30) teaches that some among the professing servants of Christ will prove faithless and will be shown at the consummation not to have been servants at all. As in the prophets, eschatology has primarily an ethical orientation. It sheds the light of God's future upon His people in the present.

The Olivet Discourse in Matthew concludes with a prophetic parable of judgment (25:31-46). A common sight in Palestine is a small flock of sheep and goats mixed together, which are separated at night. Jesus announced that the eschatological consummation will witness a separation of all people on the principle of how they have treated His disciples as they go about preaching the gospel of the kingdom. The setting of this prophecy is the preaching missions of Jesus' disciples when they were dependent upon a friendly welcome both to get a hearing for their message and to find food and lodging (Mt. 10:9-15; Lk. 10). Jesus' disciples — His "brethren" (Mt. 25:40; cf. 12:48-50) — stand in such close relationship to Him that the treatment they receive is in effect treatment administered to Christ Himself (10:24, 40, 42). They will suffer maltreatment, they will be hungry, ill-clothed, sick, and imprisoned; but those who hear their message and receive the messengers in kindness and love will thereby show that they have responded to the message of the kingdom and will inherit this blessing in the eschatological judgment. This parable is designed not to provide a program of the future but to state in vivid terms the principle on which the final judgment will be carried out. The disciples of Jesus carry the destiny of the nations with them in their preaching of the gospel.

C. Fourth Gospel. The eschatology of the Gospel of John must be studied apart from the Synoptics because its entire emphasis is different and many scholars feel it has altogether lost the futuristic eschatology of the Synoptics. The difference in emphasis must be frankly admitted. The central theme of the Synoptics is the presence of the eschatological kingdom of God; John has almost nothing to say about this theme (3:3, 5). On the other hand, John's central theme is eternal life as a present possession (20:31; 3:36); the Synoptics say very little about eternal life, and that little refers to life as the eschatological blessing of the age to come (Mk. 10:17, 30; Mt. 25:46). It is a gross disservice to biblical studies to gloss over such distinctive differences.

This obvious difference of emphasis does not, however, mean that we have two contradictory theologies or that John has quite surrendered the futuristic eschatology of *Heilsgeschichte* in favor of a completely realized (Dodd) or existential (Bultmann) interpretation. That in John eternal life is still the life of the age to come is proven by 12:25. While the Gk. *aiṓn* does not here appear, *kósmos* is its equivalent (as is proved by comparing 1 Cor. 3:19; 5:10; 7:31; Eph. 2:2 with 1 Cor. 1:20; 3:18; 2:6). This saying reflects more distinctly the dualism of the two ages than does its parallel in the Synoptics (Mk. 8:35; Mt. 10:39; 16:25; Lk. 9:24; 17:33); and the eternal life in this verse belongs to the coming age. The eschatological character of eternal life is reflected also in Jn. 4:36; 5:39; 4:14; 6:27; 5:29.

This eschatological life has been brought to mankind in history in the person and mission of Jesus. That eternal life is now present does not empty the concept of its eschatological character, any more than the synoptic presence of the kingdom of God annuls its eschatological character. In fact, here is the analogous structure of futuristic-realized eschatology which gives the Synoptics and John the same underlying theology even though the form of expression is different. Both the kingdom of God and eternal life belong to the age to come, yet both have, by virtue of Jesus' mission, become objects of present experience. As Mk. 10:17, 25 equate eternal life with the future eschatological kingdom, Jesus' discourse with Nicodemus equates the kingdom of God with eternal life (Jn. 3:6; cf. v. 36). So in the Synoptics, to "inherit eternal life" and to "enter into the kingdom of God" seem to be interchangeable terms (cf. W. F. Howard, *Christianity According to St. John* [1946], p. 112).

Another Johannine illustration of the contemporizing of eschatology is quite lacking in the Synoptics. In spite of his strong emphasis upon realized eschatology, John has more to say about the Resurrection than do the Synoptics. The Resurrection continues to be an eschatological event at the "last day" (5:28f.; 6:39, 44, 54; 11:24; cf. 12:48). Although Bultmann's critical excision of such sayings is a desperate expedient (*Theology of the NT,* II, 39), resurrection in John is contemporized: it has become a present spiritual experience (5:25). But the present is linked with the future. Only those who have been spiritually raised will enter into life at the last day.

The eschatological judgment is also contemporized. Judgment is still an eschatological event at the last day (Jn. 12:48; 5:28f.), but the future judgment has reached back into the present because of the mission of Christ; and the eschatological judgment will be the execution of the sentence of condemnation that has in effect been determined on the basis of response to the person of Christ here and now (3:18f.; 5:24). While the language is different, the same idea that a person's future destiny depends upon his or her present relationship to Jesus appears in the Synoptics (Mt. 10:32f.; cf. Mk. 8:38; Lk. 12:8f.).

John has little to say about the Parousia. Many critics conclude that John deliberately substituted the long discourse in the upper room (chs. 14–17) for the Olivet Discourse, and in doing so meant to replace apocalyptic eschatology by an altogether realized eschatology. It must be recognized that John's emphasis is very different. John does describe the coming of the Holy Spirit as a coming of Christ to be with His bereft disciples (14:18, 28). However, Dodd's conclusion that "all that the Church hoped for in the second coming of Christ is already given in its present experience of Christ through the Spirit" (*Apostolic Preaching,* p. 174) ignores the force of such sayings as 21:22. The promise to come to His disciples (14:3) includes the Parousia as an integral element in the Johannine doctrine. The same realistic eschatology appears in 1 Jn. 2:28 (Dodd attributes the Epistles to a different author).

In conclusion, while John focuses attention upon the realized aspect of eschatology, he has the same basic tension between futuristic and realized eschatology as have the Synoptics. In both, the consummation of God's redemptive purpose will occur in the age to come; but the life and blessings of the consummation have entered into history in the person and mission of Jesus.

D. Acts. If the Gospels interpret the mission of Jesus and His proclamation of the kingdom of God as a fulfillment in history of the OT eschatological hope whose consummation awaits the age to come, Acts sees in Easter and Pentecost a new depth of meaning in the same eschatological fulfillment. Thus the eschatological tension appears but in a different form. Modern criticism has recognized that the resurrection of Jesus, His enthronement at the right hand of God, and the coming of the Holy Spirit are essentially eschatological events and mean that in some real sense the messianic age has begun (Schweitzer; Schoeps; Dodd; Davies). Dodd has gone too far, however. It is too much to say, as he does, that the *eschaton* has come. In the age to come, the present order of evil, death, and trouble will be transformed into perfect righteousness, life, and blessedness. Acts still awaits this new order at the coming of Christ (3:21; cf. 1:11), when all that God had promised through the prophets would be established. The kingdom of God in Acts is usually the eschatological new order (1:3; 8:12; 19:8; 20:25; 28:23, 31). The eschatological judgment remains (10:42; 17:31; 24:25), and resurrection is awaited at the end of the age (23:6; 24:15, 21). Such sayings cannot be contemporized; God's redemptive purpose will be consummated only in the age to come after the parousia of Christ, the resurrection, and final judgment.

Yet within this futuristic expectation is found an anticipation of the eschatological blessings. The resurrection of Jesus was not merely the restoration of a dead man to physical life; it was such that it placed the entire doctrine of the resurrection in a new light. The Sadducees were annoyed because the disciples preached in Jesus the resurrection of the dead (Acts 4:2). The Pharisees, too, believed in resurrection, but this did not greatly annoy the Sadducees; the idea of the resurrection of Jesus, however, was an entirely different matter. No longer was resurrection merely a hope for the future; the resurrection of Jesus was the assurance of the eschatological resurrection. He was "the first to rise from the dead" (26:23); i.e., others would rise as He had risen. Here is the same theology of Jesus' resurrection as the "firstfruits" or beginning of the eschatological resurrection that is found in Paul (1 Cor. 15:23). The resurrection of Christ has introduced a new eschatological reality into history.

This same structure is seen in the ascension and enthronement of Jesus. By His exaltation to God's right hand, He has entered into a new dimension of His messianic mission; God has made Him both Lord and Messiah (Acts 2:36). This does not mean that He became Messiah at the ascension, for it was as Messiah that He suffered in the flesh (3:18). However, He is no longer the Messiah who is to suffer as the servant but the King who has been seated upon the throne of David and has begun His messianic reign (2:30-35). Peter reinterprets the throne of David, viewing it no longer as a literal throne of a political sovereignty exercised in Jerusalem by an earthly ruler, as in Ps. 110:1f., but as a spiritual sovereignty exercised by the exalted Lord in heaven. Messiah and Lord in this context (Acts 2:36) designate the same function: heavenly rule. Jesus as exalted Lord reigns as the Davidic King over His kingdom; the messianic age has come in history.

This fact is again illustrated by the gift of the Holy Spirit at Pentecost. Peter interprets the meaning of this event by citing Joel 2:28-32 (MT 3:1-5), which in its OT setting is an eschatological promise for the kingdom of God. Peter asserts that this eschatological event has taken place in history. He illustrates this motif of messianic fulfillment further by a striking addition to his quotation of Joel. The prophet had said "afterward"; Peter reinterprets "in the last days" (Acts 2:17). In Isa. 2:2 "the last days" designates the time of the establishment of the kingdom of God; Peter asserts that this fulfillment has come in history before the age to come. The eschatological gift of the Spirit, in a way quite unforeseen in the OT, has occurred in the old age.

Because of these messianic blessings, "times of refreshing" come from the presence of the Lord while the consummation of the promises to the prophets awaits the return of Christ (Acts 3:19). Realized and realistic eschatology are both essential in Acts.

If Acts has the same basic tension of realized eschatology within the framework of futuristic eschatology as do the Gospels, is there any difference in their eschatological perspective? In other words, if the eschatological blessing of the kingdom of God was in some real sense present in the person and mission of Jesus, what redemptive need was there for the Resurrection and Pentecost? Why did the Christian kerygma not consist of the proclamation of the kingdom present in the Jesus of history, instead of His death and resurrection?

There is, in fact, a real difference between the theology of Acts (and the Epistles) and that of the Gospels. In the Gospels the presence of the kingdom is inseparable from the historical person of Jesus. Jesus' disciples did indeed preach the word and perform the works of the kingdom (Mt. 10; Lk. 10). They were, however, able to be instruments of the kingdom only when Jesus explicitly commissioned them so to be. The eschatological blessing was localized by Jesus' historical presence.

By virtue of Easter and Pentecost the eschatological blessings were experienced in a new depth of meaning; for by the indwelling of the Holy Spirit the life and blessings of the age to come were released from localization in a single historical personage and became the permanent possession of all God's people dwelling in the Church corporately and in believers individually. This probably explains why the primitive Christian kerygma centered in Jesus' resurrection rather than in His life and deeds. Redemptively, all that is included in the latter is present in the former — and far more.

E. Paul. The emphasis on realized eschatology in Acts has primarily a historical and collective reference. The proclamation of the resurrection of Jesus and the coming of the Spirit created in history the Church. In this sense, the Church is an eschatological fellowship of those who have experienced the powers of the age to come and who anticipate the consummation in the eschatological order. These motifs are made much more explicit in Paul and are developed with greater emphasis upon their personal dimension. Paul's entire theological structure must be understood in terms of eschatology. It would be profitable to begin with the Pauline themes of the present redemption in Christ and develop the eschatological dimension of each; but because of the large body of explicit eschatological material in the Pauline corpus, we must concentrate on these materials, showing that in each instance eschatology is the necessary consummation of redemptive realities already experienced in history.

This points up the perspective in which Pauline eschatology must be viewed. The events of the eschatological consummation are not merely detached events lying in the future about which Paul speculates. They are, rather, redemptive events that have already begun to unfold within history. The blessings of the age to come no longer belong exclusively to the future; they have become objects of present experience. The death of Christ is an eschatological event. By virtue of Christ's death the believer has already been delivered from this present evil age (Gal. 1:4). He has been transferred from the rule of darkness and now knows the life of the kingdom of Christ (Col. 1:13). In His cross, Christ has already defeated the powers of evil that have brought chaos into the world (Col. 2:14f.).

The resurrection of Christ is an eschatological event. The first act of the eschatological resurrection has been separated from the eschatological consummation and has taken place in history. Christ has already abolished death and displayed the life and the immortality of the age to come in an event that occurred within history (2 Tim. 1:10). Thus the light and the glory belonging to the age to come have already shined in this dark world in the person of Jesus Christ (2 Cor. 4:6).

Because of these eschatological events, the believer lives the life of the new age. The very phrase describing the status of the believer, "in Christ," is an eschatological term. To be "in Christ" means to be in the new age and to experience its life and powers. "If any one is in Christ, he is a new creation; the old has passed away, behold, the new has come" (2 Cor. 5:17). The believer has already experienced death and resurrection (Rom. 6:3f.). He has even been raised with Christ and exalted to heaven (Eph. 2:6), sharing the resurrection and ascension life of his Lord.

Yet the experience of this new life of the age to come is not a secular event of world history; it is known only to believers. All others are blinded so that they cannot behold it (2 Cor. 4:4). They are still in the darkness of the present evil age.

This new life of the believer therefore is an ambiguous experience, for he still lives in the old age. He has been delivered from the power of this age but must still live out his life in this age; yet he is not to be conformed to its life but is to experience the renewing powers of the new age (Rom. 12:1f.). The believer's new life is only "in the Spirit." He still has to make use of the world, but is no longer concerned to make full use of it (1 Cor. 7:31), for this world is transitory. Although Christ dwells in him, and his spirit has been made alive by the powers of the new age, his body is dying (Rom. 8:10).

Thus the transition from the sin and death of the old age to the life of the new age, although real, is as yet only partial. All that the new age means cannot be experienced in the old age; it must pass away and give place to the kingdom of God in the age to come when all that is mortal is swallowed up in life (2 Cor. 5:4). The believer lives in a tension of experienced and anticipated eschatology. He is already in the kingdom of Christ (Col. 1:13), but he awaits the coming of the kingdom of God (1 Cor. 15:50). He has already experienced the new life (2 Cor. 2:16), but he looks forward to the inheritance of eternal life (Gal. 6:8). He has already been saved (Eph. 2:5), but he is still awaiting his salvation (Rom. 13:11). He has been raised into newness of life (Rom. 6:4), yet he longs for the resurrection (2 Cor. 5:4).

The present ambiguity of the new life in Christ demands the return of Christ to complete the work of redemption already begun. The central theme of the Pauline eschatology is the consummation of God's saving work. Apart from the return of Christ and the age to come, God's saving purpose remains ambiguous and unfinished.

IV. Coming of Christ.–In the OT, "the Day of the Lord" could designate a day in the immediate historical future when God would visit His people in judgment (Am. 5:18; cf. Isa. 2:12ff.); and it could also designate the final visitation of God when He would establish His kingdom in the world, bringing salvation to His faithful people and judgment to the wicked (Zeph. 1:14-18; Joel 3:14-21). In the NT the term has become a technical expression for the day when God will visit the world to bring this age to its end to inaugurate the age to come. The term is not to be thought of as a single calendar day but as the entire period that will witness the final redemptive visitation of God in Christ.

The expression assumes different forms: the Day of the Lord (1 Thess. 5:2; 2 Thess. 2:2; cf. Acts 2:20; 2 Pet. 3:10), the Day of the Lord Jesus (1 Cor. 5:5; 2 Cor. 1:14), the Day of the Lord Jesus Christ (1 Cor. 1:8), the Day of Jesus Christ (Phil. 1:6), the Day of Christ (Phil. 1:10; 2:16), that Day (2 Thess. 1:10; 2 Tim. 1:18); cf. the Day of God (2 Pet. 3:12); the last time (1 Pet. 1:5). Since the exalted Christ is for Paul, as for the early Church, the Lord (Phil. 2:11; Rom. 10:9), it should be obvious that efforts to distinguish between the Day of the Lord and the Day of Christ, and to find in them two different eschatological programs, one for Israel and one for the Church, are misguided. The coming of Christ to gather His people, both living and dead, to Himself (1 Thess. 4:13-17) is called the Day of the Lord (1 Thess. 5:2), as is His coming to judge the man of lawlessness (2 Thess. 2:2).

Paul uses three words to describe the return of the Lord. The first is Gk. *parousía,* which may mean both "presence" (Phil. 2:12) and "arrival" (1 Cor. 16:17; 2 Cor. 7:7). The word was used in a semitechnical sense of the visit of persons of high rank, especially of kings and emperors visiting a province. Since His ascension, Christ is pictured seated at the right hand of God in heaven. He will visit the earth again in personal presence (Acts 1:11) at the end of the age (Mt. 24:3) in power and glory (24:30), to raise the dead in Christ (1 Cor. 15:23), to gather His people to Himself (2 Thess. 2:1; cf. Mt. 24:31), and to destroy evil (2 Thess. 2:8; cf. 1 Thess. 2:19; 3:13; 4:15; 5:23).

The coming of Christ will also be an *apokálypsis,* an "unveiling" or "disclosure." The power and glory that are now His by virtue of His exaltation and heavenly session must be disclosed to the world. Christ has already been elevated by His resurrection and exaltation to the right hand of God, where He has been given sovereignty over all spiritual foes (Eph. 1:20-23). He now bears the name that is above every name; He is now the exalted Lord (Phil. 2:9). He is now reigning as king at God's right hand (1 Cor. 15:25). However, His reign and His lordship are not evident to the world. His *apokálypsis* will be the revealing to the world of the glory and power that are now His (2 Thess. 1:7; 1 Cor. 1:7; cf. 1 Pet. 1:7, 13). Thus the second coming of Christ is inseparable from His ascension and heavenly session, for it will disclose His present lordship to the world and be the means by which every knee shall finally bow and every tongue acknowledge His lordship (Phil. 2:10f.).

A third term, *epipháneia,* "appearing," indicates the visibility of Christ's return. Although this term is limited largely to the Pastoral Epistles, Paul tells the Thessalonians that Christ will slay the man of lawlessness by the breath of His mouth and destroy him by the *epipháneia* of His *parousía* (2 Thess. 2:8). The return of the Lord will be no secret hidden event but a breaking into history of the glory of God.

The inseparable connection between the two acts in Christ's redemptive work is illustrated by the twofold use of *epipháneia* to designate both the Incarnation and the Parousia. God has already broken the power of death and displayed the reality of life and immortality within history through the appearing (*epipháneia*) of our Savior Christ Jesus in the flesh (2 Tim. 1:10). This, however, is not the final term of redemption. Hope still awaits us in the future in the "appearing [*epipháneia*] of the glory of our great God and Savior Jesus Christ" (Tit. 2:13). In view of this twofold usage, the objections sometimes made against speaking of a "second" coming of Christ are overly critical.

The background for this language of the coming of Christ in glory is the OT language of theophany. The OT conceives of God working in history to accomplish His redemptive purposes; but it also looks forward to a day of divine visitation when God will come in judgment and salvation to establish His kingdom. In the NT this divine theophany is fulfilled in two stages: (1) in the coming of Jesus, who has already accomplished a redemptive work in history; (2) in His glorious return to bring the consummation of salvation to His people (1 Thess. 5:8f.) and judgment upon the wicked (2 Thess. 1:7f.), and to establish the kingdom, which is already His, in the world (2 Tim. 4:1).

V. Mystery of Lawlessness.–The coming of Christ is to be preceded by certain eschatological events. In his first letter to the Thessalonians, Paul spoke only of the return of Christ to gather the saints, both dead and living, to be with Him (4:13-18). He wrote with earnest anticipation, admonishing the Thessalonians to live with an attitude of expectancy of that day so that they would not be taken by surprise (5:1-11). As a result, believers in Thessalonica became upset and excited, and some claimed to have revelations from God or a special word from Paul indicating that the end was upon them and the events of the day of the Lord had actually begun (2 Thess. 2:1f.). In his second letter Paul corrects this erroneous view of imminency by saying that before the end comes, there will appear an evil ruler, the man of lawlessness, who will arrogate to himself all authority, both secular and sacred, and will demand the total submission of men to his rule, including worship (2:3f.). The statement that he will take his seat in the temple of God is an OT metaphorical way of expressing his defiance of God (cf. Ezk. 28:2; Isa. 14:13f.). He will be satanically empowered to deceive people and turn them away from the truth (2 Thess. 2:9f.). The essence of his character is his "lawlessness"; he defies the law both of God and of man, insisting that his will alone is law.

The "revealing" (v. 3) of the man of lawlessness is not merely an eschatological event; it will be the final manifestation of a principle that was operative even in the days of Paul. "For the mystery of lawlessness is already at work" (v. 7). Paul saw in his own time the principle of the deification of the state, which demanded not only civil obedience but also religious worship. This principle of lawlessness will one day break forth in uncontrolled concentration in a final evil ruler; and his appearance will be accompanied by an apostasy (v. 3) or rebellion against God. Many will submit to the man of lawlessness and defy the law of God.

This lawlessness is, however, held in check by some unnamed restraining power. The Thessalonians knew what this restraining power was, for Paul had told them about these things when he had visited them (vv. 5f.). We cannot recover Paul's verbal instruction, which he here assumes, and therefore we cannot be dogmatic about the identity of this restraining power. The day will come, however, when the restraint will be removed, and then the man of lawlessness will be revealed in all his God-defying wickedness.

The best solution to this difficult passage finds its clue in the character of this evil personage; he is the man of *lawlessness,* one who defies all duly constituted law, whether human or divine. Because Paul elsewhere clearly teaches that human government is a divinely established ordinance (Rom. 13:1-7), we may conclude that the restraining power is the institution of duly constituted law and order, an instrument of God to restrain lawlessness. In Paul's day, God had invested this authority in the Roman empire and its head, the emperor. Paul sees a day when the rule of law will collapse, when political order will be swept away and be unable any longer to restrain the principle of lawlessness. Then, the last defenses that the Creator has erected against the powers of chaos will break down completely. This can well be understood in the principle of the deification of the state in defiance of the divine ordinance. The principles of both order and lawlessness can be at work at the same time, even in the same state. These two principles will be in conflict during the course of the age. At the very end, law and order will break down, demonic lawlessness will burst forth, and the Church will experience a brief period of terrible evil that will be quickly terminated by the return of Christ (v. 8).

VI. Resurrection and the Rapture.–The Pauline teaching of the eschatological resurrection is an extension of the resurrection of Jesus; or, better, the resurrection of Jesus is the beginning of the eschatological resurrection of the saints and demands it.

The same power that raised Christ will raise up His people (1 Cor. 6:14; 2 Cor. 4:14). In fact, Christ's resurrection is itself the first act of the final resurrection. It is the firstfruits of which the eschatological resurrection will be the harvest (1 Cor. 15:20). Therefore, the resurrection as Paul discusses it is concerned only with the resurrection of "the dead in Christ" (1 Thess. 4:16). Paul has no word in his Epistles concerning the resurrection of those who do not stand in solidarity with Christ — the unsaved. Luke quotes him in Acts 24:15 asserting resurrection of both the just and the unjust; and we may well believe this, for Paul does teach the judgment of all mankind (Rom. 2:6-11). But he says nothing about the time or the nature of the resurrection of any except Christians. Neither does Paul refer to the state of the unsaved after death. He does not even mention Hades in his letters (1 Cor. 15:55, AV, reflects the inferior reading of the TR).

The resurrection of those who belong to Christ is essential not only because Christ has been raised, but because the nature of mankind and of redemption requires it. Redemption means the redemption of the whole person, including the body (Rom. 8:23). Paul knows nothing of a blessed immortality of the spirit freed from its entanglement in the created order. Paul often contrasts the sufferings of earthly existence with the future glory (8:18), but he never considers bodily life in itself an evil thing from which he longs to be freed. Rather than being discarded, the body that often humiliates us is to be transformed and glorified (Phil. 3:21). The Holy Spirit who has quickened our spirits will also give fulness of life to our mortal bodies in the resurrection (Rom. 8:11). Paul's doctrine of bodily resurrection is grounded in his unitary view of the person.

The consummation of salvation and the full possession of inheritance at the resurrection (Eph. 1:14) await the return of Christ when "God will bring with him those who have fallen asleep" (1 Thess. 4:14). Then the spirits of the dead will be reunited with their bodies, but transformed, glorified. Paul knows nothing of glorified spirits apart from the body. The problem that called forth his long discussion of the resurrection was some sort of denial of the resurrection of the body (1 Cor. 15:12, 35). If Paul had taught a form of blessed immortality of the soul or resurrection of the spirit out of its entanglement in the world of matter into the realm of God, the Corinthians would have had no problem. Their difficulty was in accepting the idea of bodily resurrection. Paul's description of the resurrection body is one that transcends present historical experience. "Flesh and blood" (i.e., bodies constituted of mortal flesh) cannot inherit the kingdom of God, for they are perishable and the kingdom of God is the order of the imperishable (15:50). Therefore, a body suited for the life of the kingdom must be different from the bodies of this age. That there can logically be such a body Paul establishes by pointing to the difference between a kernel of grain and the shoot that comes from it (vv. 35-38). There are also different kinds of flesh — of humans, beasts, fish, birds (v. 39) — and there are different kinds of bodies — earthly and heavenly — which differ in their glory (vv. 40f.). Therefore it should not be surprising that God has a new and different kind of body adapted to the life of the age to come.

Paul does not attempt, however, to describe the nature of the resurrection body. He knows nothing of its constitution; but he can speak of some of the qualities which differentiate it from the body of "flesh and blood." The latter is perishable, dishonoring, and weak. The new body will be imperishable, glorious, and powerful (vv. 42f.). The contrast is summarized in the words *psychikón* (for which there is no adequate translation) and *pneumatikón* (v. 44).

The resurrection will occur instantaneously at the coming of Christ (1 Thess. 4:16; 1 Cor. 15:52). The change that will occur for the dead in Christ will also overtake those living in Christ (1 Cor. 15:51). Those "who are left until the coming of the Lord" will have no advantage over those who have fallen asleep (1 Thess. 4:15). The living will, as it were, put the new resurrection body on over the mortal body (*ependýsasthai*, 2 Cor. 5:4) without the dissolution of the latter. This is what Paul means by the so-called "rapture" of the Church. The "catching up" of living believers immediately after the resurrection, to meet the Lord in the air, is Paul's vivid way of expressing the sudden transformation of the living from the weak, corruptible bodies of this physical order to the powerful, incorruptible bodies which belong to the new order of the age to come. It is the sign of passing from the level of mortal existence to immortality. The important word is "so shall we always be with the Lord" (1 Thess. 4:17).

VII. Intermediate State.–If salvation includes the redemption of the body at the eschatological resurrection, an important question arises: What is the state of the dead between death and the resurrection? Paul has very little to say in answer to this question. He seems to deal with this question in 2 Cor. 5; but this is a notoriously difficult passage. Paul appears to shrink from death, because it is evidently a time of being unclothed (5:3f.). He does not know what will be the mode of existence between death and resurrection; God had not revealed this to him. Greek thought might find pleasure in the anticipation of the soul naked of the body, but not Paul. He longs for the resurrection body when mortality will be swallowed up by life (v. 4). He would prefer, indeed, to be alive when Christ comes, that he might have "the new [resurrection] body put on over" the mortal body without dying (v. 4, NEB). If he dies, he knows that a new body awaits him which will be suited to the new eternal order of the age to come (v. 1). The language of this passage has led some interpreters to feel Paul is here referring to an intermediate body, which already exists in heaven, to be put on at death; but the language is very similar to that of 1 Cor. 15:47-49 where Paul is discussing the resurrection body, even though he speaks of "those who are of heaven," who shall "bear the image of the man of heaven." Christ is now, as the last Adam, the man from heaven, bearing His resurrected glorified body; and Paul looks forward to sharing the heavenly likeness of his exalted Lord in the age to come.

Meanwhile, although he shrinks from the nakedness of death, Paul takes courage in the realization that even though he does not know the mode of his existence, he will be "at home with the Lord" (2 Cor. 5:8). This is all Paul has to say about the intermediate state. To depart is to be with Christ (Phil. 1:23); but it is enough.

VIII. Judgment.–The Pauline doctrine of an eschatological judgment is related to the historical fact of justification. Here is a vivid illustration of the tension between realized and futuristic eschatology. Justification is an eschatological fact that has occurred in history. It is the decision of the Judge of all mankind that a person is clear of guilt. In Judaism it meant acquittal at the Day of Judgment, and the NT does not surrender this eschatological dimension (cf. Mt. 12:36f.; Rom. 8:33f.; 5:19; Gal. 5:4f.). What sets the gospel apart from Judaism at this point is the conviction that by virtue of Jesus' death this eschatological event has already occurred. The believer has been justified; the eschatological Judge has declared the person of faith to be guiltless, i.e., righteous before God.

Yet judgment remains an eschatological event, both for believers and for unbelievers. While Paul nowhere develops this doctrine as he does the resurrection, it stands constantly in the background of his thinking. He speaks of those who store up wrath for themselves on the day of wrath when God's righteous judgment will be revealed (Rom. 2:5). In that day God will judge the secrets of mankind by Christ Jesus (2:16). Other passing references to judgment are found in Rom. 3:6; 13:2; 1 Cor. 4:5; 11:32; 2 Thess. 2:12; 2 Tim. 4:1. In some way not explained to us, the saints are to assist God in the judgment of the world, even to the point of judging angels (1 Cor. 6:2f.).

The most developed passage on judgment is Rom. 2. There will be a Day when God will judge all people according to their works (Rom. 2:5). To the righteous He will give eternal life, to the wicked wrath and fury (vv. 6-10). Furthermore, people will be judged by the light they have. All have the light of nature by which they should recognize the existence of the true God and worship Him alone (1:18-20). Jews will be judged by the law (2:12), and those who have not had the law will be judged by the law of God that is written on their hearts — by conscience (2:14-16). While these verses suggest theoretically that people could survive the Day of Judgment on the basis of good works, Paul states clearly that people have not lived up to their light. Gentiles have perverted the light of general revelation (1:21-23), and Jews have failed to keep the law (Gal. 3:10-12). God in His mercy, however, has provided a way of salvation in the redeeming work of Christ, and the final basis of judgment will be the gospel (Rom. 2:16; 2 Thess. 1:8). God's final judgment will be absolutely just and not arbitrary.

Judgment is also an eschatological fact for believers. The righteousness we hope for (Gal. 5:5) is acquittal at the final judgment. "We must all appear before the judgment seat of Christ" (2 Cor. 5:10), which is also the judgment seat of God (Rom. 14:10). Because of the justification in Christ, however, the Day of Judgment has lost its terror for the person in Christ (8:1, 33f.). Nevertheless, the believer will be judged for his or her works. Our life will be laid bare before the divine scrutiny, so that each one may receive the proper recompense for the things done through the life of the body, whether that life record is good or bad. This judgment is not a declaration of doom, but an assessment of worth, involving not condemnation or acquittal, but rewards or loss on the basis of the worth or worthlessness of the Christian's life.

The same principle of judgment is expounded in 1 Cor. 3:12-15. Paul is here speaking of the work of Christian leaders, but the principle is valid for all believers. The only foundation upon which anything permanent can be built is Jesus Christ; not all, however, build alike. Some erect beautiful structures with gold, silver, precious stones; others build worthless houses of wood, hay, stubble. Clearly, Paul is applying his metaphor rather loosely, for these materials were not normally used in ancient construction. He deliberately uses a radical metaphor to contrast great value with worthlessness. Some Christians live worthless lives; their works, like wood, hay, and stubble, will be consumed in the flames of judgment so that nothing remains as a result of their life on earth. While this does not mean the loss of salvation ("he himself will be saved"), it does mean the loss of the "well done, good and faithful servant." Those who have built faithfully and effectively, on the other hand, will be rewarded for their love and devotion — although Paul does not indicate what the reward will be. The principle involved in this judgment is that, while salvation is altogether of grace, the Christian is fully answerable to God for the quality of his present life in the body.

IX. Future of Israel.–NT eschatology is centered almost exclusively on the destiny of the Church. This raises a serious question about the continuity between the OT promise and the NT fulfillment. The OT hope is structured in terms of the nation Israel and its future in the land. Jesus offered the reinterpreted messianic blessings to Israel, the natural "sons of the kingdom" (Mt. 8:12). The fulfillment of the OT promise in Jesus' messianic mission did not include a national destiny for Israel; realization of the blessings of the Kingdom was found in personal fellowship with Jesus. He accepted into fellowship with Himself all who responded to His challenge of the Kingdom, and indicated that this new fellowship of the Kingdom would constitute His *ekklēsía* (Mt. 16:18), i.e., the new people of God (21:43), which may be called the new Israel. The old Israel was to suffer the historical judgment of destruction and war (Lk. 13:34f.; 19:41-44; 23:27-31; Mk. 13:1f.; Lk. 21:20-24), for this generation was evil (Mt. 11:16-19) and could not recognize the fulfillment of the OT hope in Jesus' mission.

If, then, the Church has taken the place of Israel as the people of God, has God proved unfaithful to His OT promises to Israel? This is the question that Paul treats in Rom. 9–11; and while the main points of his thought are clear, they leave many questions unanswered as to how the promises are to be fulfilled.

Paul points out that God has not forgotten His promises to Israel, for there is in fact a believing Jewish remnant in the Church (Rom. 11:5). The key to interpretation, however, is that Paul implicitly redefines "Israel," both intensively and extensively. He indicates, first, that the true Israel does not include all physical descendants of Abraham but is limited to a believing remnant (9:6-13). Then he indicates that the people of God, the true Israel, is also extended to include Gentiles (9:24); taking promises from Hosea (1:10; 2:23), which in their OT setting referred only to the future of the nation Israel, Paul applies them to the Church (Rom. 9:25f.). Those who were "not my people"— Gentiles — have now become "my people," "sons of the living God," by inclusion in the Church. In a real sense, then, the OT promises to Israel are fulfilled in this new definition of the people of God, the Church.

The question remains: Does this mean the final rejection of all but a small believing remnant of Jews? Is there no redemptive purpose in the unbelief and rejection of Israel? The answer to this question is summed up in the statement,

"Now if their [the Jews'] trespass means riches for the world, and if their failure means riches for the Gentiles, how much more will their full inclusion mean" (11:12). That is, God has used the unbelief and the rejection of Israel as a means of bringing salvation to the gentile world; but God will yet include the Jewish people in the people of God, which will in turn result in even greater blessings for the Gentiles. Paul clearly asserts that Israel is still a "holy" people (11:15f.), i.e., the special object of God's concern. Therefore, while the trespass of Israel means salvation for the Gentiles (v. 11), and their rejection results in reconciliation of the gentile world, the acceptance of Israel into the people of God will result in a tide of blessing for the Gentile world so great that Paul calls it "life from the dead" (v. 15). This future movement of *Heilsgeschichte* Paul summarizes in vv. 25-32: (1) a (large) part of Israel has been hardened; (2) this issued in the carrying out of God's full purpose for the salvation of the Gentiles; (3) in some unexplained way, however, this salvation of the Gentiles is designed to make Israel jealous (10:11, 14); and (4) "in this manner" (*hoútōs*), namely, through provocation by gentile salvation, "all Israel [the Jewish people] will be saved." When and how these events will take place is not indicated. The basic and central affirmation is, however, that in some form or other the Jewish people is yet to be included in the new people of God, the Church. Piper has suggested that Israel is yet to become a Christian nation (O. Piper, *Theology Today,* 18 [1961], 60-71). In any case, the consummation of God's redemptive purpose is to include the salvation of the Jews.

X. Consummation.–The goal of God's redemptive purpose is the restoration of order to a universe that has been disrupted by evil and sin. This includes the realm of human experience, the spiritual world (Eph. 1:10), and, as we shall see, even nature itself. God will finally reconcile all things to Himself through Christ (Col. 1:20). All things were originally created through Christ and for Him (v. 16), and He will finally enjoy the preeminence that is His due (v. 18). The very cosmos that has been rent by conflict and chaos will be restored to peace with its Creator. This eschatological reconciliation will be accomplished through the blood of the cross (v. 20). Paul sees in the death of Christ a triumph over evil spiritual powers (2:14f.), although he nowhere explains what this involves; and the final eschatological reconciliation is but the effective extension of the victory won on the cross.

This same emphasis of universal reconciliation is repeated elsewhere. In the great kenosis hymn (Phil. 2:5-11) Jesus is now exalted as Lord, and because of this every knee will yet bow and every tongue confess that Jesus Christ is Lord, to the glory of God the Father (vv. 10f.). No rebellious will can finally remain outside the sovereignty of Christ's lordship.

The final subjection of every hostile will is also asserted in 1 Cor. 15 as the extension of Christ's kingly rule in the universe. He is to reign as king (*basileúein*) until He has subdued every enemy, the last of which is death (v. 25). When He has subdued every hostile spiritual power, He will deliver the Kingdom to the Father (v. 24). In view of the Pauline emphasis that Jesus has been exalted and is now reigning as Lord at God's right hand (Eph. 1:20-23; Phil. 2:9), it is clear that this kingly reign began at the Ascension. Lord and King are interchangeable concepts expressing Christ's exalted sovereignty, a sovereignty grounded in His resurrection.

1 Corinthians 15 envisages three stages in the subjugation of Christ's enemies, of which death is the final foe. Christ's resurrection is the first stage (v. 20; cf. Phil. 2:9). A second stage will be manifested at His *parousía,* when those who belong to Him will be raised (1 Cor. 15:23). Only "after that" (*eíta*) comes the end (*télos*), when His triumph is made complete. As there is an interval between Christ's resurrection and parousia, so there is an undefined interval between the parousia and the *télos*; and during the entire period between resurrection and *télos* Christ is reigning as king. Paul explains neither necessity for this second intermediate period nor its duration; but for some reason in God's redemptive purpose Christ's rule is to be extended between the parousia and the *télos* to complete the divine conquest of evil. During this interval the reign of Christ and His saints will be made visible to the world (4:8; 2 Tim. 2:12), and it is probably to this period that Paul refers when he says that the saints will share Christ's judgment over the world (1 Cor. 6:2f.). It is not insignificant that the structure of this passage parallels that of Rev. 20, where there is an intermediate kingdom of Christ and His saints (lasting "a thousand years," vv. 4-6) between their resurrection and the final consummation — but here, too, only as an extension of Christ's present messianic reign.

Some interpreters have seen in the language of this final reconciliation a "universal homecoming," interpreted in terms of a universal salvation of all sentient creatures, both human and angelic. Such an interpretation can indeed be drawn from such verses as Col. 1:20, if they are taken out of the context of the total Pauline teaching. A universal reconciliation would mean that peace is everywhere restored. The universal acknowledgment of Christ's lordship (Phil. 2:10f.), however, is not synonymous with universal salvation. There is a stern element in Paul's eschatology that cannot be avoided. There remain recalcitrant wills which must be subdued and which will bow only unwillingly before Christ's rule. How Christ will deal with them Paul does not say except in very general terms.

The final restoration includes the material world. Creation awaits the disclosure of the children of God when they will experience the redemption of their bodies, for creation itself will be freed from the bondage to decay and will experience freedom from the evil to which it has been subjected (Rom. 8:19-23). Thus the redemption of the natural world from evil and decay is the corollary of the redemption of the body. While Paul does not develop this truth, it is built upon the same profound biblical theology that is found in the OT. The prophets constantly described the establishment of God's kingdom in terms of a redeemed world (Isa. 11:6-9; 65:17-25); the NT shares the same theology. Creation is never viewed as something evil that must be escaped. Man as body is a creature of God. A person is not sinful because he or she is a creature, but because he or she has rebelled against God. In the final consummation the whole person and the world of which he is a part will be delivered from the curse of evil.

Paul describes the final state of those who have not obeyed the gospel of Christ by saying they "shall suffer the punishment of eternal destruction and exclusion from the presence of the Lord and from the glory of his might" (2 Thess. 1:9; cf. 1 Thess. 5:3). The rebellious and impenitent store up for themselves wrath on the day of wrath when God's righteous judgment will be revealed (Rom. 2:5, 8; cf. 5:9; 1 Thess. 1:10; 5:9). Paul also describes the fate of the unsaved by the concept of perishing (Gk. *apóllymi*). This is both a present condition (1 Cor. 1:18; 2 Cor. 2:15; 4:3) and a future doom (Rom. 2:12; 2 Thess. 2:10). This eschatological doom is also destruction (*apṓleia,* Phil. 3:19; Rom. 9:22). It is also expressed as death. Death, in the full inclusiveness of the term, is the penalty of sin (Rom. 5:12; 6:16, 23). While this death is the death of the body (Rom. 8:38; 1 Cor. 3:22), the term designates much more. This is seen in that death is the opposite of eternal life (Rom. 6:23; 7:10; 8:6; 2 Cor. 2:16). It is both a present fact (Rom. 7:10f.; Eph. 2:1) and a future fate (Rom. 1:32; 6:16, 21, 23; 7:5). The central idea is exclusion from the presence of the Lord in His consummated kingdom (2 Thess. 1:9) and the subsequent loss of the blessings of life that come from the enjoyment of the divine presence. However, the terms Paul uses make it clear that the final judgment will issue in a fearful condemnation which is the just desert of sin and unbelief; but he nowhere describes what this doom involves.

For the eschatology of the book of Revelation, *see* REVELATION, BOOK OF.

Bibliography.–OT: Theologies by A. B. Davidson (1904); L. Koehler (Eng. tr. 1957); E. Jacob (Eng. tr. 1958); T. C. Vriezen (Eng. tr. 1958); W. Eichrodt (5th ed. 1961); R. H. Charles, *Critical History of the Doctrine of a Future Life in Israel, in Judaism, and in Christianity* (2nd ed. 1913); G. Hölscher, *Ursprunge der jüdischen Eschatologie* (1925); W. Bousset, *Religion des Judentums im späthellenistischen Zeitalter* (2nd ed. 1934); A. S. Peake, *Servant of Jahweh* (1931); P. Volz, *Eschatologie der jüdischen Gemeinde im NT Zeitalter* (2nd ed. 1934); "Der eschatologische Glaube im AT," in A. Weiser, ed., *Festschrift für G. Beer* (1945), pp. 73-87; C. R. North, *OT Interpretation of History* (1946); H. W. Robinson, *Inspiration and Revelation in the OT* (1946); G. Pidoux, *Le Dieu qui vient* (1947); S. B. Frost, *OT Apocalyptic* (1952); J. Bloch, *On the Apocalyptic in Judaism* (1952); T. C. Vriezen, "Prophecy and Eschatology," in *SVT,* 1 (1953), 199-229; J. Klausner, *Messianic Idea in Israel* (Eng. tr. 1955); S. Mowinckel, *He That Cometh* (Eng. tr. 1956); H. H. Rowley, *Faith of Israel* (1956); O. Plöger, *Theokratie und Eschatologie* (1959); R. Martin-Achard, *From Death to Life* (1960); G. Fohrer, *TLZ,* 85 (1960), 401-420; J. M. Schmidt, *Die jüdische Apocalyptic* (1969); P. D. Hanson, *Dawn of Apocalyptic* (1975); W. Schmithals, *Apocalyptic Movement: Introduction and Interpretation* (1975); C. E. Armerding and W. W. Gasque, eds., *Dreams, Visions, and Oracles* (1977).

NT: S. D. F. Salmond, *Christian Doctrine of Immortality* (4th ed. 1904); H. A. A. Kennedy, *St. Paul's Conception of the Last Things* (1904); W. O. E. Oesterley, *Doctrine of the Last Things* (1908); G. Vos, *Pauline Eschatology* (1930); H. D. Wendland, *Eschatologie des Reiches Gottes bei Jesus* (1931); A. N. Wilder, *JBL,* 50 (1931), 201-206; M. Goguel, *RHR,* 106 (1932), 383-434; C. H. Dodd, *Parables of the Kingdom* (1936); *Apostolic Preaching and Its Development* (1936); W. G. Kümmel, *Die Eschatologie der Evangelien* (1936); C. C. McCown, *JR,* 16 (1936), 30-46; F. C. Grant, *JR,* 22 (1942), 359-370; W. Michaelis, *Der Herr verzieht nicht die Verheissung* (1942); R. Otto, *Kingdom of God and the Son of Man* (1943); T. F. Glasson, *Second Advent* (1945); H. A. Guy, *NT Doctrine of the Last Things* (1948); C. C. McCown, *JR,* 28 (1948), 1-12; A. N. Wilder, *JR,* 28 (1948), 177-187; J. A. T. Robinson, *In the End, God* (1950); A. N. Wilder, *Eschatology and Ethics in the Teaching of Jesus* (2nd ed. 1950); C. H. Dodd, *Coming of Christ* (1951); G. E. Ladd, *Crucial Questions about the Kingdom of God* (1952); W. Manson, *et al., Eschatology* (*SJT Occasional Papers,* no. 2, 1952); E. Käsemann, *ZTK,* 49 (1952), 272-296; C. K. Barrett, *SJT,* 6 (1953), 136-155, 225-243; C. E. B. Cranfield, *SJT,* 6 (1953), 189-196, 287-303; 7 (1954), 284-303; R. Bultmann, *NTS,* 1 (1954), 5-16; G. R. Beasley-Murray, *Jesus and the Future* (1954); J. W. Bowman, *Theology Today,* 11 (1954/55), 160-178; E. Brunner, *Eternal Hope* (1954); P. E. Minear, *Christian Hope and the Second Coming* (1954); O. Cullmann, "Kingship of Christ and the Church in the NT" and "Return of Christ," in A. J. B. Higgins, ed., *The Early Church* (1956), pp. 105-141, 141-164; W. D. Davies and D. Daube, eds., *Background of the NT and Its Eschatology* (1956); G. R. Beasley-Murray, *Comm. on Mk. 13* (1957); E. Grässer, *Das Problem der Parusieverzögerung* (1957); W. G. Kümmel, *Promise and Fulfilment* (Eng. tr. 1957); G. E. Ladd, *JBL,* 76 (1957), 192-200; J. A. T. Robinson, *Jesus and His Coming* (1957); N. Q. Hamilton, *Holy Spirit and Eschatology in Paul* (1957); R. Bultmann, *History and Eschatology* (Eng. tr. 1957); O. Cullmann, *TLZ,* 83 (1958), 1-12; W. G. Kümmel, *NTS,* 5 (1958/59), 113-126; J. D. Pentecost, *Things To Come* (1958) (Dispensational); A. Corell, *Consummatum Est* (Eng. tr. 1958); E. Conzelmann, *RGG,* II, 665-671; D. E. Holwerda, *Holy Spirit and Eschatology in the Gospel of John* (1959); A. N. Wilder, *NTS,* 5 (1959), 509-536; A. J. McClain, *Greatness of the Kingdom* (1959) (Dispensational); J. E. Walvoord, *Millennial Kingdom* (1959) (Dispensational); H. Ridderbos, *Coming of the Kingdom* (1962); M. E. Dahl, *Resurrection of the Body* (1962); G. E. Ladd, *JBL,* 81 (1962), 230-38; H. H. Rowley, *Relevance of Apocalyptic* (rev. ed. 1963); N. Perrin, *Kingdom of God in the Teaching of Jesus* (1963); G. Lundström, *Kingdom of God in the Teaching of Jesus* (1963); R. Schnackenburg, *God's Rule and Kingdom* (1963); J. P. Martin, *Last Judgment* (1963); J. Jeremias, *Parables of Jesus* (rev. ed. 1963); O. Cullmann, *Christ and Time* (Eng. tr., 2nd ed. 1964); Dale Moody, *Hope of Glory* (1964); J. Moltmann, *Theology of Hope* (Eng. tr. 1965); A. L. Moore, *Parousia in the NT* (1966); G. E. Ladd, *Presence of the Future* (1974 = 2nd ed. of *Jesus and the Kingdom* [1964]); *The Last Things* (1977); R. G. Clouse, ed., *Meaning of the Millennium: Four Views* (1977); A. Hoekema, *The Bible and the Future* (1979).

G. E. LADD

ESDRAELON, PLAIN OF ez-drə-ē'lən, ez-drā'lon [Gk. *Esdrēlōn*] (Jth. 1:8; 3:9; 4:6; 7:3); AV also ESDRAELOM (Jth. 1:8; 7:3). The Greek name, derived from Jezreel (Heb. *yizr*$^{e'}$*e'l,* Josh. 17:16; Jgs. 6:33) for the central part of the lowland corridor extending from the modern bay of Haifa to Beth-shean. It is also called the "plain of Megiddo" (Zec. 12:11; AV "valley of Megiddon," NEB "vale of Megiddo"). *See* JEZREEL, VALLEY OF; Plate 16.

ESDRAS, BOOKS OF. Two books of the OT Apocrypha.

I. Literary Introduction
II. The Greek Ezra (1 Esdras)
III. The Apocalyptic or Latin Esdras (2 Esdras)
IV. Conclusion

I. Literary Introduction.–The Greek Ezra and the Apocalyptic or Latin Esdras are the unambiguous titles of the two apocryphal books here discussed. These are distinct from the canonical Ezra-Nehemiah, though much of the scriptural material is incorporated in the Greek Ezra. The bewildering confusion of version nomenclature may be seen from the table, which lists the preferred titles at the left.

	Eng. Bible	LXX	Lucian	Vulgate
Ezra	Ezra	2 Esdras	1 Esdras	1 Esdras
Nehemiah	Nehemiah			2 Esdras
Greek Ezra	1 Esdras	1 Esdras	2 Esdras	3 Esdras
Latin Esdras	2 Esdras	....	....	4 Esdras

The Greek Ezra contains most of the canonical Ezra with smaller sections of Chronicles and Nehemiah, as well as considerable interpolation. The Semitic original is lost, but the Greek offers a polished, idiomatic version. The apocryphal-canonical relationship may be studied in parallel columns of English in *APOT,* I, 21-29, 34-57. The Greek is in *OTG,* II, 129-161. See also *IOTG,* pp. 265ff.; *HDB*; *HJP,* II/3, 177-181; *HNTT,* pp. 233-257. Pfeiffer (*HNTT,* p. 249) suspects Alexandrian origin and a date for the present form of the book not later than 150 B.C.

The Apocalyptic Esdras, lacking Greek textual attestation, is often ignored, despite its greatly superior intrinsic interest and importance. There is a critical Latin text, edited by R. L. Bensly, with a lengthy introduction by M. R. James, in *Texts and Studies,* 3/2 (1895). The RV is followed in W. O. E. Oesterley's *II Esdras* (*WC,* 1933). The central chapters are independently rendered in G. H. Box, *The Ezra Apocalypse* (1912); cf. also *APOT,* II, 542-624. J. H. Lupton expounds both books in Wace, I, 1-148. (Cf. also *HDB*; *HJP,* II/3, 93-114; etc.) The main section, beginning in 3:1, may with high probability be dated A.D. 100. The other portions are likely to fall within twenty years of this date, either way, excepting chs.

15–16, which are from the 3rd cent. A.D. Most Latin MSS designate chs. 3–14 as 4 Esdras (whence the other common designation, 4 Ezra), regarding the remaining chapters as independent books; some versions designate chs. 1–2 as 2 Esdras or 5 Esdras and chs. 15–16 as 5 Esdras or 6 Esdras. For fuller discussion, see the literature cited.

II. The Greek Ezra (1 Esdras).*–*The Interpolation, 3:1–5:6. As the rest of the book is virtually scriptural, attention may be concentrated on the story of the Three Guardsmen, related also, with significant variation, in Josephus *Ant.* xi.3.2-7. R. H. Pfeiffer is convinced that the Greek Ezra text is translated from an Aramaic version, resting in its turn on a pagan Persian source, perhaps a "Zoroastrian popular homily" (p. 256), adapted to Jewish tastes. The Aramaic version he would date *ca.* 300 B.C., the Persian perhaps a century earlier (p. 255). He makes the yet more interesting speculation (pp. 253f.) that this story inspired the personification of wisdom in Prov. 8. The special Christian significance springs from the mention of Zerubbabel, doubly attested (Mt. 1:12f; Lk. 3:27) in the ancestry of Jesus Christ. Pfeiffer regards the proper names as fictitious importations into an already existing story skeleton (*HNTT*).

The story recounts that the king — Darius, according to the text and Josephus, though other editorial preferences have been expressed — makes a great feast. Afterward, while he sleeps, three of his guardsmen decide that the king will richly reward the one of their number who makes the wisest decision as to which thing in the world is strongest. They write their sentences, and these are placed under the king's pillow. The first chooses wine; the second the king; the third, women and truth, in juxtaposition (3:1-17). (According to Josephus, the king himself initiated the contest, prescribing the theses to be defended. This purges the story of one absurdity.)

The first guardsman discourses before the king and his governors on the potential of wine, particularly its harmfulness (3:18-24); the second on the strength and authority of the king (4:1-12). It is not clear why Zerubbabel, or whoever he was, should have a double chance. He disclaims first on women, particularly on their seductive power over men, making a personal and surprisingly unresented reference to the king's concubine. It is most unlikely that an oriental despot would tolerate such public impertinence, even from an intimate; this offends against verisimilitude (4:13-32). Zerubbabel then speaks with yet greater eloquence on truth (4:33-41). The king bids him not only receive the stipulated reward but ask what he will in addition. His Majesty is then urged to fulfil his vow to rebuild Jerusalem and restore the sacred vessels. All this is royally implemented (4:42–5:6).

On Pfeiffer's theory (*HNTT*), this finale is a Jewish *cauda* to a Persian tale. He bestows on the whole composition a praise (p. 256f.) that is perhaps excessive. A Persian original might account for the very un-Jewish view of women, and the lack of direct religious teaching. Probably some compiler perceived in the story of the Three Guardsmen a useful etiological tale to account for the restoration of the temple and fitted this at the appropriate point into a borrowed framework of scriptural history.

III. The Apocalyptic or Latin Esdras (2 Esdras).*–*Synopsis, Chs. 1–2. An addition by a Jewish-Christian hand, giving the genealogy of Ezra, pseudepigraphically borrowed, and his divine prophetic commission, in OT style. The interest has really shifted to the Christian Church, the successor-in-privilege of the OT covenant.

The Apocalypse Proper, Chs. 3–10

Synopsis of First Vision, 3:1–5:19. The seer muses on God and sin, Adam's transgression, the sin and suffering of Israel, and the impunity of greater national offenders. The archangel Uriel appears, discusses the seer's intellectual problems, and heralds the approaching end of the age.

3:1. For the identity of Salathiel or Esdras, cf. Box, pp. 1-3, 8; Oesterley, pp. xiiff., 18, etc. The supposed date is 556 B.C., with Babylonian wealth flaunted before captive Jewish poverty. But Babylon is a cryptogram for Rome, and the real date is A.D. 100. Box (pp. 41ff.) believes that the original text contained a dream vision, now lost, between vv. 1 and 2.

3:7. Talmud and Midrash largely reject the doctrine of original sin. (Cf. R. A. Stewart, *Rabbinic Theology* [1961], pp. 67-81.) Here and elsewhere in the present work the doctrine emerges with almost Christian clarity — cf. 4:30ff.; 7:11f., 48, 118; 8:31, 60. *Diligentia,* usually "carefulness, heed," means here the verbal commandment to Adam to abstain from the forbidden fruit (cf. 3:19).

3:8. It is taught that the heathen nations sinned against God by His permissive will. The thorny problems of God, man, sin, and freedom recur frequently, but remain unsolved. (Cf. Stewart, *passim,* esp. pp. 26-31, 89-92.)

3:10. The writer sets Fall and Flood in punitive parallel; final judgment may be added in series. (Cf. Mt. 24:37, etc.)

3:19. Here *lex* means the written, *diligentia* the oral, Torah.

3:20. The *cor malignum* (evil heart) introduces another key rabbinic concept, the "evil impulse." (Cf. Stewart, pp. 81-85; cf. 7:48, etc.; Rom. 7:18-23.)

3:21f. These almost Pauline verses contain one fallacy — if Adam's corrupt heart antedates his fall, God must have put it there and must therefore be the author of sin. The stark reality of original sin, and the impotence of the law to save, may be freely admitted (cf. Rom. 3:20).

3:33. The concept of the treasury of merits, more specific in 7:77, is here implied. (Cf. Stewart, pp. 127-133.)

4:3f. The etiology of corruption would certainly be a skeleton key to unlock the innermost secrets of hamartiology! For the form of the archangel's words, cf. Lk. 20:1-8.

4:12. Cf. T.B. *Erubin* 13b. In the excellent parable following, v. 17 may be compared with Jer. 5:22.

4:30. The *granum mali seminis* (grain of evil seed) is another term for the evil impulse. (See 3:20 above.)

4:36. According to a similar deterministic rabbinic teaching, the Messiah will not come till all the unborn souls have lived out their earthly lives (T.B. *Yebamoth* 63b; Midr. *Gen. Rabbah* xxiv.4; etc.). This chapter wavers between a mundane and supramundane theater for the life of the world to come. This may be either personal inconsistency or bad editing.

4:45, 50. Cf. 14:10ff., which is from a different hand.

4:52. Archangels are represented as limited in knowledge.

5:2. The Synoptic apocalypses, Mt. 24, Mk. 13, and Lk. 21, may be aptly compared with many echo passages in chs. 4–9.

Synopsis of Second Vision, 5:20–6:34. This is partly repetitive, but introduces new questions, such as the fate of those who die before the close of this world order.

5:23-30. In all this rich, varied symbolism of Israel's election, the vine image of v. 23 rests probably on Ps. 80. Verse 28 stresses the darker side of the Jewish Diaspora, ignoring its spiritual challenge and missionary potential.

5:35. Cf. Jer. 20:17f. Job 3:11 and 10:18f. visualize death following conception; the metaphor of Jeremiah and Esdras, the womb of a living mother becoming a grave, is biologically impossible, but forceful and striking.

5:41. Cf. 1 Thess. 4:13ff.

6:5. The key thoughts are: (1) Human-computed time is finite, created, and distinct from the eternal realm (see notes on 6:8 and 9:8). (2) Estrangement from God is the fruit of sin. (3) The treasury of merits is here interpreted in terms of faith, though this is not necessarily the exact equivalent of Pauline faith. (4) The sealing presupposes divine election. The splendor of the cosmological language of vv. 1-6 shines through the Latin translation.

6:6. In contrast to Prov. 8, Jn. 1, and the rabbinic literature, intermediaries in the divine act of creation — memra, wisdom, or logos — are here strongly rebutted. (Cf. Stewart, pp. 34-39.)

6:8ff. The usual rabbinic view of an earthly messianic era before the final consummation is here rejected. Jacob's hand gripped Esau's heel at their birth (Gen. 25:26), in symbol of continuity — so the world to come will be in immediate temporal succession to the present age. This cannot be true if, as v. 5 suggests, eternal and mundane time are different in kind. (See also note on 9:8.)

Synopsis of Third Vision, 6:35–9:25, including Bensly's Missing Fragment, 7:36-140. The seer discourses on the works of creation, the election of Israel, and the strange triumph of lesser and unchosen nations over her, with just a trace of proud particularism (6:35-59). There is worked out, in angelic parable and mortal objection, a fairly rigid doctrine of election and reprobation, with admission that the well-being of Israel is gravely compromised by Adam's sin. The seer is rebuked for judging too hastily the "unfairness" of God (7:1-25). A parenthetical and eschatological passage follows (7:26-44). Election and reprobation are further discussed at length, with angelic pronouncements on the future state of wicked and righteous. The seer will not be comforted by the bright hopes of the small minority or the bleak rewards of the many wicked — the perishing of the majority fills him with pity, sorrow, and questioning (7:45–9:25).

7:21. God's law has a universal reference.

7:28f. The original Jewish writer certainly referred only to the Son-Messiah, who became *filius meus Jesus* (my son Jesus), probably through the chain of associations *māšî(a)ḥ–Christos–Christus,* in the hands of a Christian copyist. Yet a Christian scribe would find it difficult to accept the notion of Christ dying, not on Calvary, but after four hundred years of interim terrestrial messianic reign. Box, p. 117, mentions the very significant alteration of *morietur* (shall die) to *adsumetur* (shall be taken up) in one Latin MS. The claim of assumption is much more likely, even from a Jewish standpoint.

7:32, 37. These are strong statements of corporeal resurrection.

7:36. Fiery torment and restful bliss, following the judgment of vv. 33-35. Oesterley, p. 74, suspects some confusion of thought; but surely there is adequate parallel in the parable of Dives and Lazarus and in the rabbinic teaching that paradise and Gehenna are adjacent (Midr. *Eccl. Rabbah* vii.14.3).

7:48. The seer's deep concern for the lost somewhat mitigates the particularism of certain other passages.

7:48. The evil impulse again (cf. 3:20 above), with almost universal corruption. Note the thoroughly Jewish reluctance to admit that man's depravity is total, despite the most obvious approximation.

7:52-61. If all glass beads are turned into diamonds, or all sinners into saints, the quality is cheapened so much that the article becomes worthless — therefore the spiritual fate of the myriads of the damned may be dismissed with a shrug. (The non sequitur, an archangelic one at least by attribution, is that a truth valid for diamonds is also necessarily valid for human beings. Admittedly sin keeps the saints few in number; but God is a righteous judge, not a diamond merchant concerned with extrinsic qualities. The teaching needs to be corrected with both halves of Mt. 3:9. Similar objections apply to vv. 54-57. The doctrine of God implied in v. 61 also needs amendment.)

7:62-69. Happy the grazing ox in the field, unreasoning and therefore unsinning, destined at death to oblivion and not to fiery torment! These somber verses lose much of their significance if they are understood only satirically. (Cf. 8:20-36, with note on 8:19 below.)

7:70. A somewhat rigid doctrine of determinism.

7:72. On the premises given, the deduction is at least logical.

7:75. The seer asks about the interim state between death and final judgment. The answer, extending to v. 115, is fascinating, though sometimes inconsistent. For general apocalyptic appraisal of the theme, see Oesterley, pp. 85f.; Box, pp. 141f.

7:78. When death occurs, unsaved and saved alike adore God. The seven special sorrows of the unsaved and special rests of the saved are next detailed.

7:88. The spirits of the righteous are separated at death *a vaso corruptibili,* from the corruptible vessel or body. This is somewhat like the Greek doctrine of *sṓma sē̂ma* (the body is a tomb), or the Pauline view of the flesh; it is very unlike the characteristic rabbinic acceptance of the body.

7:93. The frustration of the wicked on perceiving the bliss of the righteous in v. 83 may be inevitable and merited, but the converse satisfaction of the saints in the misery of the damned is very unpleasing. This strain crept into Judaism as a result of persecution. (Cf. Midr. *Lev. Rabbah* xxxii.1 and the references in note on 7:36 above.)

7:101. The "seven days" are carefully documented by Oesterley, pp. 90f., with Jewish, Iranian, and Mithraistic parallels.

7:102-115. In the final judgment, the fate of the individual is fixed absolutely by the quality of the life once lived in the flesh; no prayer by another is effective or even permitted. By implication, intercession for the dead seems to be excluded. This runs entirely counter to 2 Macc. 12:43-45 (*see* MACCABEES IV.D). Jerome fiercely repudiated the teaching of these verses. Indeed, they cut at the base of one of the pillars of the Roman Catholic Church. This is significantly part of Bensly's Missing Fragment; it may well have been suppressed for ecclesiastical reasons. Protestants have a clear-cut answer to the question involved. This cannot be said for the rabbinic literature and the Pseudepigrapha; see Oesterley, pp. 92f., and Box, pp. 153-56, for fuller discussion. The differing quality of earthly time and eternity is again hinted at in v. 113 (see notes on 6:5, 8 above, 9:8 below).

7:116. In the text available, the seer says: *hic sermo meus primus et novissimus, quoniam melius erat non dare terram Adam, vel cum iam dedisset coercere eum ut non peccaret.* (This is my first and last word, that it would have been better if the earth had not produced Adam, or else, when it had produced him, had restrained him from sinning [RSV].) The RSV takes the earth as the subject both of *dedisset* and of *coercere.* Yet some understand God as the implicit subject of *coercere,* which would come dangerously close to making Him the author of sin. This is heavily counterbalanced by the strong statements of original sin in v. 118 and of human freedom in vv. 122ff. Here and elsewhere, the writer cannot be exonerated from formal inconsistency; but apart from his prevailing pessimism, his heart is frequently in the right place. The passage 7:116-131 is a variant presentation of vv. 62-74 and has other parallels. This is Job 3, with the added interplay of volition and responsibility.

8:1-3. The rigid doctrine of limited election and widespread reprobation again. (Cf. note on 7:52 above; also 9:21f. below.)

8:6. The bounds of Judaism are outpassed in a stray note of universalistic concern for all mankind — but particularism returns in v. 15.

8:14. The writer asks what he cannot answer.

8:19. This evidently reflects a legend of Ezra's assumption, based on the argument from the silence of Scripture. The prayer following (vv. 20-36) is of great beauty, though the writer is torn between an almost Pauline insight into man's total depravity (vv. 31, 35) and an instinctive clinging to the concept of the treasury of merits (vv. 26-29, 33). This is the problem of Rom. 3:20-26; but the writer, earnest and honest as he is, possesses only a poor, legalistic substitute for the power of the risen Christ. Certainly there is contradiction, but it is the grappling of a sincere heart with problems beyond its reach.

8:28. A warning to hypocrites, who cannot deceive God, but may hoodwink their neighbors and even themselves. The writer's personal humility is seen in vv. 49ff.

8:38f. This representation of divine indifference to the fate of the unrighteous is contradicted in v. 47, which states emphatically that God's love for mankind exceeds people's love for each other — though the book as a whole fails to bring this out adequately. Oesterley aptly remarks that the seer, earnest but a little jaundiced, has grasped the enormity of sin without properly allowing for the potential of repentance.

9:7. A man is said to be saved *per opera sua vel per fidem in qua crediderit* (by his works or by faith in what he has believed). If the *vel* were changed to *et* (and), this would be Paul and James together in a nutshell. (Cf. 6:5; 13:23.)

9:18. The phrases *tempus erat saeculi* and *antequam fieret illis saeculum* are in formal contradiction. The first phrase, literally "the time within the age," refers to the eternal realm. The RSV renders the second "before the world was made for them," i.e., before time impinged into eternity. There are three popular definitions of eternity: "unending time," "timelessness," and "the transcending of time in infinity," of which the last is to be preferred (M. F. Cleugh, *Time and Its Importance in Modern Thought* [1937], p. 79). The creation of our solar system, involving the physical causation of our temporal divisions, occurred in the eternal realm — God's eternity is not therefore unending time into which our cosmic duration may be fitted as part of a greater whole; it belongs to a higher and entirely different plane of experience, poorly comprehended by mortals. Ps. 90:4 and 1 Pet. 3:8 are nearer the mark; so, in fairness, is 6:5 of this book.

Synopsis of Fourth Vision, 9:26–10:59. The seer has a vision of a woman mourning for the son of her old age, dead on his wedding night. This represents the heavenly Zion weeping for the earthly Jerusalem, destroyed in A.D. 70. The allegory contains many details not used in the interpretation, but this is not unusual.

9:31-37. The ground outlasts the seed sown therein, the sea the ships that sail thereon, the drinking vessel the particular draught for which it is used — so the law will outlast in honor its human transgressors. Yet the law cannot save; cf. v. 36 and 3:20, 22; 8:19, note; Rom. 3:20 and Rom. 7 *passim*.

9:45. Cf. Sarah, Hannah, the woman of Shunem, Elizabeth.

10:16. The hypothetical folktale here adapted might have related the birth of a second son or the restoration of the first to life. But the simple expectation of immortality affords a cogent enough explanation.

10:25ff. Cf. the transfiguration of Christ; also Rev. 21.

10:39, 57. The personal character of the seer is again commended.

10:54. Even the place of vision must be kept free from the works of human hands — a most interesting touch.

Chs. 11–12. The Eagle Vision. This is from a different author, political rather than religious in his interests. The eagle, a variant of the fourth beast of Dnl. 7, is a symbol for the Roman empire. A simple theory has been offered to explain difficulties and discrepancies. The chapters were first drafted *ca*. A.D. 96 as an apt and contemporary political allegory. About twenty-five years later circumstances had changed, and the document was manipulated to fit them, perhaps by a less skillful hand, with some resultant confusion. (For fuller discussion, see Box, pp. 244-280; Oesterley, pp. xviif.; 130-147.)

11:1. For the Jew, the sea, like the Roman empire, held predominantly evil associations (cf. Dnl. 7:3; Rev. 21:1; etc.). T.B. *Shabbath* 56b declares that Solomon's marriage into heathendom caused Gabriel to fix a reed in the sea, which gathered round it a sandbank on which Rome was built. This seems a flimsy foundation for the Imperial City, but the allegorical significance is clear. The three heads of the eagle have been widely interpreted as symbolizing Vespasian, Titus, and Domitian. This makes it difficult to equate the twelve wings with the twelve Caesars, though Oesterley, p. 145, applies three wings to aspirants who never actually became emperors. He cogently argues also that the eight smaller wings represent Roman governors in Palestine, which would account for the Jewish interest in them.

11:37. The Lion of Judah is the Messiah.

12:3. The downfall of Rome, in symbol.

12:11. It was customary at an earlier stage to take Daniel's fourth beast as signifying Greece, but interest and interpretation both shifted to Rome.

12:15. This is usually understood to mean Augustus.

12:37. A touch, perhaps, of pseudepigraphic embroidery.

Synopsis of Ch. 13. In vision the seer beholds a man, representing the preexistent Messiah, rise from the sea and ascend a mountain that has miraculously appeared. With the breath of his mouth he slays the multitude of his gentile foes. He then summons another multitude, the ten tribes of exiled Jews, some of whom accept his rule willingly, some unwillingly. This is probably an adaptation of a Babylonian creation epic, with Iranian elements, transmuted into a piece of Jewish eschatology, but not without the continued protrusion of discrepant elements. (See further Box, pp. 280-86; Oesterley, pp. 150-164.)

13:3. The sea and clouds are here incompatible, but so are other unresolved elements in the vision. The prejudice against the sea suggested in the last section has now disappeared; this chapter is from a different hand.

13:16-20, 22-24, 29-32. The thoughts are either parenthetic or interpolated.

13:40-50. The legend of the Lost Tribes.

Synopsis of Ch. 14. A controversial apologia for apocalyptic literature. After partaking of a cup divinely administered, Ezra with chosen assistants is divinely commissioned to restore to posterity the twenty-four lost books of the OT for open perusal, with seventy apocalyptic ones for esoteric use. On the supposed restoration of the forgotten Bible text, see *Jew.Enc.*, V, 323f., with the rabbinic references there. The clear purpose of the chapter is to assert the equal authority of apocalyptic with canonical Scripture — a claim that rabbinic and other strains of Judaism would repudiate. Noteworthy are the reference to the Messiah as the Son of God in 14:9 and the clear presupposition of the transition to Hebrew square characters for writing in 14:42.

Chapters 15–16, a late addition, contain a mixture of prophecy and eschatology, not equal in interest to the earlier sections. Oesterley gives the historical background, pp. 175-190. These chapters are to be dated probably in the second half of the third Christian century.

See also APOCALYPTIC LITERATURE III.G.

IV. Conclusion.–From the viewpoint of Apocrypha study, the interest of the Greek Ezra limits itself to the interpolation, though the rest of the book has its value for OT textual investigation. In the Latin Esdras, chs. 3–10 far outweigh the rest of the book in attractiveness and significance. The mind that produced them is somber but deeply pious, still Jewish, yet with a flavor more Christian than rabbinic in certain respects.

Bibliography.–G. H. Box, *Ezra-Apocalypse* (1912); L. Gry, *Les Dires prophétiques d'Esdras* (2 vols., 1938); B. M. Metzger, *JBL*, 76 (1957), 153-56; H. Montefiore, *IV Ezra — A Study in the Development of Universalism* (1929); W. O. E. Oesterley, *Intro. to the Books of the Apocrypha* (1935), pp. 133-160; *II Esdras* (*WC*, 1933); *RGG*, II, *s.v.* "Esrabücher" (Galling, *et al.*).

R. A. STEWART

ESDRIS ez'dris, es'dris [Gk. *Esdris*]; AV GORGIAS; NEB ESDRIAS. A leader of the troops of Gorgias, "put to flight" by Judas Maccabeus (2 Macc. 12:36). He is mentioned in the best texts and adopted in the RSV for "Gorgias" of the AV.

ESEBON es'ē-bon (Jth. 5:15, AV). *See* HESHBON.

ESEBRIAS es-ē-brī'əs, ə-sē'bri-əs (1 Esd. 8:54, AV). *See* SHEREBIAH **1.**

ESEK ē'sek [Heb. *'ēśeq*–'strife,' 'contention']. The name given by Isaac to a well dug by his servants, over which the herdsmen of Gerar contended until the patriarch was forced to abandon it and dig another well (Gen. 26:20). The location is not known but it must have been between Gerar and Beer-sheba.

ESHAN ē'shən [Heb. *'eš'ān*–'support'] (Josh. 15:52); AV ESHEAN esh'i-ən. A village in the hill country of Judah, part of that tribe's inheritance. Its location is uncertain, although the LXX B rendering *Soma* has led to conjecture that it may be Khirbet Sama'a, about 17 km. (10 mi.) SW of Hebron.

ESHBAAL esh'bā-əl (1 Ch. 8:33; 9:39). *See* ISHBOSHETH.

ESHBAN esh'ban [Heb. *'ešbān;* Gk. *Asban*]. A chief of the Horites (Gen. 36:26; 1 Ch. 1:41).

ESHCOL esh'kol [Heb. *'eškōl*–'cluster'; Gk. *Eschōl*]. The brother of Mamre and Aner, the Amorite allies of Abraham who took part with him in the pursuit and defeat of Chedorlaomer's forces (Gen. 14:13, 24). He lived in the neighborhood of Hebron (13:18) and may have given his name to the Valley of ESHCOL, which lay a little N of Hebron (Nu. 13:23).

ESHCOL esh'kol [Heb. *'eškōl*; Gk. *pháranx bótryos*–'cluster of grapes']. A valley near Hebron from which the spies brought back to Moses and Aaron a single cluster of grapes carried on a pole between two of them (Nu. 13:23f.; 32:9; Dt. 1:24). It is possibly located near Mamre, on the basis of Gen. 14:13 (so *GTTOT,* p. 255). The name is echoed in the (corrupted) form Burj Haskeh, about 3 km. (2 mi.) N of Hebron at the head of a vineyard-laden valley.

See also CLUSTER.

ESHEAN esh'ē-an, ē'shē-an. *See* ESHAN.

ESHEK ē'shek [Heb. *'ēšeq*–'oppressor']. A descendant of Jonathan son of Saul (1 Ch. 8:39).

ESHKALONITE esh'kə-lon-īt (Josh. 13:32, AV). *See* ASHKELON.

ESHTAOL esh'tä-ol [Heb. *'eštā'ôl*]. A town of the Danites located in the Shephelah of Judah, always referred to in connection with Zorah (Josh. 15:33; 19:41; Jgs. 13:25; 16:31; 18:2, 8, 11; 1 Ch. 2:53). Between Eshtaol and Zorah the Danites established their camp where the Spirit of the Lord began to arouse Samson (Jgs. 13:25) and where Samson later was buried (16:31). Five men of valor were sent forth as spies from these centers (18:2); and a contingent from Eshtaol formed part of the six hundred Danites who captured Laish, the modern Tell el-Qâḍī, in their thrust to the north (Jgs. 18). It is probably to be identified with Eshwa', about 2½ km. (1½ mi.) E of Zorah and about 21 km. (13 mi.) W of Jerusalem.

K. G. JUNG

ESHTAOLITES esh'tä-ol-īts [Heb. *hā'eštā'ulî*]; AV, NEB ESHTAULITES. Inhabitants of Eshtaol, named among the descendants of Shobal the son of Caleb (1 Ch. 2:53).

ESHTEMOA esh-tə-mō'ə [Heb. *'ešt^{e}mô(a)'*–'listening post'].

1. Son of Ishbah; a descendant of Caleb (1 Ch. 4:17). Another view is that Ishbah was "lord" of the city of Eshtemoa.

2. A Maacathite, son of Hodiah, of the tribe of Judah (1 Ch. 4:19).

ESHTEMOA [Heb. *'ešt^{e}mô(a)'*–'listening post']; **ESHTEMOH** esh'tə-mō [Heb. *'ešt^{e}mōh*] (Josh. 15:50). A mountain town of Judah about 15 km. (9 mi.) S of Hebron, assigned to the priests (Josh. 15:50; 21:14; 1 Ch. 6:57 [MT 42]). It is identified with es-Semû'.

According to 1 S. 30:28 David sent some of the booty taken in the recapture of Ziklag from the Amalekites to the elders of Eshtemoa, out of gratitude for their kindness to him and his army during his flights from Saul.

See *EAEHL*, II, *s.v.* (D. Barag). F. E. YOUNG

ESHTON esh'ton [Heb. *'eštôn*]. A name found in the genealogical table of Judah, probably that of a Calebite clan (1 Ch. 4:11f.).

ESLI es'lī [Gk. *Eslei, Esli*]. An ancestor of Jesus in Luke's genealogy, the tenth before Joseph the husband of Mary (Lk. 3:25).

ESORA ē-sō'rə (Jth. 4:4, AV). *See* AESORA.

ESPOUSAL; ESPOUSE. In the AV these words, following English usage that is now obsolete, are used to signify marriage or betrothal. The RSV renders "wedding" (Cant. 3:11), "bride" (Jer. 2:2; NEB "bridal"), and "betrothed" (2 S. 3:14; Mt. 1:18; Lk. 1:27; 2:5; 2 Cor. 11:2).

ESRIL es'ril, ez'ril. *See* AZAREL **4.**

ESROM es'rom, ez'rom (AV Mt. 1:3; Lk. 3:33). *See* HEZRON.

ESSENES es'ēnz [Gk. *Essēnoí*, *Essaíoi*–None of the numerous explanations of the name is more than merely plausible (see, e.g., Audet, pp. 373-380)]. Members of an important Jewish community that existed in Palestine during the ministry of Jesus.

I. Sources
II. Jewish Sects
III. Essene Economy
IV. Monasticism
V. Slavery
VI. Vows
VII. Divisions
VIII. Worship and Theology
IX. The Ossaeans
X. Therapeutae and Other Sects
XI. The Scrolls and the Essenes
XII. Essenes and Christianity

I. Sources.–The primary sources for an examination of the Essenes are the descriptions given by Philo, Josephus, Pliny, and Hippolytus. Supplementary sources to be used for comparison are Epiphanius *Haer.* and the Qumrân (Dead Sea) Scrolls.

A. Philo. The earliest sources for our knowledge of the Essenes (at least apart from the Qumrân Scrolls) were written by Philo of Alexandria, who lived before A.D. 50. His writings on the Essenes include *Apologia pro Iudaeis* 11 and *Quod omnis probus liber sit* 12 (75-87). He also wrote about the Therapeutae, a group some scholars identify with the Essenes, in *De vita contemplativa*. The differences between the Essenes and the Therapeutae, however, are too great to use the Therapeutae as source material for learning about the Essenes. Philo intrudes his own point of view more than Josephus or Hippolytus, and therefore his account especially must be examined critically.

B. Josephus. Josephus is the main source for Jewish history from the Hasmonean period to the end of the Jewish War (A.D. 73). His discussions of Essenes are found chiefly in *BJ* ii.8; *Ant.* xiii.5.9; xv.10.5; xvii.13.3; xviii.1.5.

Josephus's source of knowledge of the Essenes is an enigma. He professes to have begun his study of the Essenes at about the age of sixteen (*ca.* A.D. 54). Under great difficulties he went through all three sects of the Jews. He thereafter spent three years with a certain Banus, who was evidently a very scrupulous observer of purity and dietary rules. At the age of nineteen, Josephus returned to the city and followed the rules of the Pharisees. Although there is the suggestion that he had lived with and studied each of the three sects, he cannot have given much time to this research, since most of this time between sixteen and nineteen must have gone into the "three years" with Banus (see *Vita* 2). Accordingly Josephus may have "gone through" the sects in a purely academic manner. At any rate it is safest to treat the information Josephus gives of the Essenes as if it were obtained indirectly.

C. Hippolytus. Hippolytus was a schismatic bishop of Rome *ca.* A.D. 218-235. Although some scholars have doubted that Hippolytus wrote the passage on the Essenes (see M. Smith, *HUCA*), the value of the account for an examination of the Essene sect has become increasingly apparent. Some have also dismissed Hippolytus because his account is very much like that of Josephus, but Smith (*HUCA*) has convincingly shown that both Josephus and Hippolytus utilized a common Semitic source which they sometimes translated differently into Greek. This admits the use of Hippolytus as a basic source that includes some information omitted by Josephus. His account is found in *Ref.* ix.13-23.

D. Pliny. Gaius Plinius Secundus, best known as Pliny the Elder, was born in A.D. 23. His *Naturalis historia* was dedicated to Titus in A.D. 77. He is the earliest ancient writer to describe the Essenes as a sect living on the west coast of the Dead Sea (*Nat. hist.* v.15[73]). There is no assurance that Pliny's account is derived from firsthand observation; it probably reports hearsay from a considerably earlier period.

E. Epiphanius. For this study his important work is *Adversus lxxx haereses* (*Haer.*), a book intended to contain antidotes for heresies of Barbarism, Scythism, Hellenism, Samaritanism, Judaism, and various Christian heresies, primarily the Origenists. Among the Jewish sects are the Osseni or Ossaeans, and among the Samaritans the Esseni (10.1), who have been thought by some to be successors to the Essenes.

F. Qumrân Scrolls. Since 1947 a very important source for studying Jewish beliefs in Palestine prior to A.D. 70 has been the DEAD SEA SCROLLS. Although no document so far published has recorded the name "Essene," the scrolls provide the only material written in Palestine prior to the fall of Jerusalem that could not have been edited or altered by Jews or Christians outside of Palestine at a later date. For this reason they are invaluable for comparing, interpreting, and testing Jewish documents of a later date that are presumed to reflect earlier views. The most descriptive sectarian document in this collection is the Manual of Discipline (1QS). Fragments of another manual were found in Cairo in 1897, called the Zadokite Fragments or Damascus Document (CD).

The scrolls were found in various caves along the northwest shore of the Dead Sea near Qumrân. They include OT texts, commentaries, psalms, and rules of order. It is not certain that all these documents represent either the compositions or points of view of any one particular sect within Judaism, but they disclose opinions that were held in Palestine before the fall of Jerusalem.

II. Jewish Sects.–Sectarianism within Judaism has an ancient history. The books of Kings and most of the prophets record numerous conflicts that took place within a people who worshiped one God but differed in their understanding of the way He should be worshiped (see Smith, *NTS*). Part of the disagreement arose over the practices enjoined in the pentateuchal holiness rules. The ark of the covenant and the presence of the Lord were in the camp. Because the Lord is holy, the members of the congregation must be holy (Lev. 20:7; Nu. 5:1-3; 16:3; Dt. 7:6). Holiness was maintained by contributing the proper offerings (Ex. 25:1-8; 29:38-45; 30:22-38; Lev. 16; 19:23f.; 21–23; Nu. 15; 18f.; Dt. 26), observing sabbaths, feasts, and jubilees (Ex. 31:12-17; 35:1-3, 11; Lev. 25; Dt. 15), eating only prescribed food (*kāšēr*) (Lev. 7:19-27; 17; 22:10-16; Dt. 14), etc. Because Israelites had various views concerning the exact way in which these laws were to be fulfilled, and because they disagreed on the importance of the various rules, certain sects arose within Judaism.

During the Roman period, especially after Archelaus was banished and Roman procurators were introduced (A.D. 6-7), Jews were keenly aware that their generation did not possess the heritage God had promised the children of Abraham. This must mean that they had sinned and must change their ways before God would comfort His people by restoring to them the Promised Land. The various groups had conflicting ideas about God's demands. The Zealots, basing their policy on the story of Phinehas (Nu. 25) and the history of the Maccabees, took up the sword at every opportunity in an attempt to expel the Romans and Roman collaborators from the land by military force. Those represented by 2 Macc.

6:12-17 and 1QS 9:21-23 believed Israel must be punished for her sin. Therefore, Jews must voluntarily accept whatever afflictions were placed upon them, believing that this would help cancel the debt and also make the sins of the oppressing nation greater, so that on the Day of Vengeance God would vindicate the Jews and suppress the Romans (see Stendahl). Some, like John the Baptist, practiced righteousness, carefully observing all dietary laws and avoiding all contact with unrepentant sinners. On the other hand, many, like the tax collectors, took advantage of the existing situation, collaborated with the Romans, and made little pretense of observing the pentateuchal regulations. These were called "sinners." A more moderate position was that of some Pharisees who mingled with the Romans but carefully observed the stipulated tithes, bathed properly before eating, and were careful not to eat with those who were less careful than they. Sects also probably had differences which were not directly related to interpretation of the Torah, but which reflected economic, philosophical, or social attitudes. One of the sects that existed in NT times was the Essenes.

III. Essene Economy.–The effect of the close-knit structure of the Essene sect on its whole economic existence is shown by two features: (1) the common fund of the monastic order, and (2) the hospitality shown to other members of the sect.

A. The Common Fund. Philo, who evidently described only the monastic Essenes, said that the Essenes owned no private property, but that they had pooled all of their resources into a common fund that was distributed to the individual members as each had need. Members labored daily for wages that were contributed to the common treasurer to buy the necessary provisions for the group. Not only was food for the entire group purchased from the common fund, but also clothing, which continued to be the property of the group. In addition to the practicality of the economy, this plan permitted strict supervision to see that all foods were *kāšēr* and properly tithed and that all Essenes were dressed with garments made of only one kind of material (Lev. 19:19). Furthermore, those who were ill or aged were treated at the common expense and given the same thoughtful care that parents might expect of children. Hence it was possible for Essenes with no children to live to a comfortable old age.

The reason for the communistic administration is not given. Bauer, however, gives several other instances in classical literature where people have abandoned their goods because they believed material things to be the root of all evil; and he presumes the Essenes had the same motivation for their economy (Pauly-Wissowa, Suppl. IV, 410-14). A more likely possibility is suggested by the circumstances. Since cultures of the ancient Near East had no social security program or pension plan to care for the aged, the principal insurance against neglect and starvation in old age was the care that children would provide. Members of a celibate order, deprived of children, needed some community plan to fulfil the needs otherwise met by family members.

B. Essene Hospitality. Philo said that no Essene called his house his own in the sense that he was free to exclude other Essenes, but that the door was open to visitors from other localities who *shared his convictions*. This meant those who could be trusted to keep the same tithing, heave offering, dietary, and purity regulations. Josephus said further that Essene customs permitted them to travel without taking any provisions except weapons as protection against brigands, but that in every city an appointed person was responsible for providing visiting Essenes with clothing and other necessities. Hippolytus added that the person assigned to provide for traveling Essenes did so from funds put aside for that purpose.

The Essene program of hospitality seemed well planned, efficient, and also necessary for a sect so exclusive in its regulations that its members could not accept the food or other provisions supplied either by Gentiles or by other sects within Judaism.

IV. Monasticism.–Philo, Josephus, and Hippolytus all agreed that the Essenes did not marry. Although both Josephus and Hippolytus conceded that one order of Essenes did permit marriage, they maintained that those who married did so only for the propagation of the race. Hence no more sexual intercourse was permitted than was necessary to produce children. Like others seeking admission, prospective wives were first required to observe the three-year probation period and were required to have had at least three purification periods to show that they were mature enough to bear children.

The reason given for celibacy was not that the sect objected to children. Indeed, they were willing to raise children to whom others had given birth. But according to Hippolytus they wanted to avoid every deed of concupiscence, and they distrusted women altogether; Josephus said the Essenes thought that marriage led to unrighteousness, and that no woman was faithful. Philo expounded at greater length on the wiles of women and the way wives and children could unconsciously divert an Essene's attention from his primary concern.

Pliny stated that the Essenes had renounced the patterns of ordinary society because they were tired of life and were driven to their accepted way of living by the waves of fortune. Pliny's interpretation has probably led many to associate Essene monasticism with Greek asceticism. Indeed, Eduard Zeller singled out the Essenes as the sect on Palestinian soil showing the greatest degree of Hellenistic influence (*Outlines of the History of Greek Philosophy* [Eng. tr. 1955], pp. 278f.). Marks of Greek philosophy, he said, were to be seen in asceticism based on dualism, worship of the sun, belief in angels and in preexistence of the soul and its survival after death. Bauer claimed that their rejection of marriage could be paralleled only in Buddhism (Pauly-Wissowa, Suppl. IV, 428f.).

A. Biblical Regulations. Philo said that the Essenes observed sabbaths meticulously. They avoided work and gathered in synagogues to read the books (presumably the OT) and discuss their meaning. Josephus claimed that they were stricter than all other Jews in sabbath observance, preparing all of their food the day before, refusing to kindle a fire or even to yield to nature's demands for elimination on the sabbath day. Some Jews of the Greco-Roman period insisted that elimination take place at least 2000 cubits from the camp (1QM 7:7). But 2000 cubits was the extreme limit a Jew was permitted to walk on the sabbath, and some held that the limit was 1000 cubits (Mish. *Sotah* v.3; T.B. *Erubin* 51a; CD 10:21). Any Jew, then, who was zealous not to defile the camp or break the sabbath would find it necessary to schedule his consumption so that elimination on the sabbath was not necessary. Hippolytus maintained that some Essenes would not even get out of bed on the sabbath.

On other days, the Essenes followed the Deuteronomic (Dt. 23:12-14) prescription of taking care of elimination needs in deserted places, modestly covered with cloaks, and carefully covering up the excrement with earth and washing themselves afterwards as if excretion were polluting.

Philo said that the Essenes ate together, and Josephus testified that only the initiated were allowed to share the common meals and only after they had bathed and dressed in special linen garments. Hippolytus noted that no one of a different persuasion was permitted in the house while Essenes were eating. They kept such strict dietary laws that they were not at liberty to eat any other person's food. So rigidly were these rules imposed that any member excommunicated from the group was destined to die of starvation. Members would endure tortures or even death rather than eat food offered to idols.

The sectarians believed that oil was defiling, and if they accidentally came into contact with any they would scour themselves to be cleansed of this defilement. They were careful not to spit into the midst of the company or to the right.

Those who wanted to join the sect were not immediately received into the group but were given prescribed clothing and equipment and proper food to eat in separate quarters. Only after two (Hippolytus) or three (Josephus) years of probation, if the candidate was observed to be "worthy" (Gk. *áxios*), he was admitted to the inner circle. If a senior member accidentally touched a junior member, he would have to take a bath to remove the defilement, just as if he had touched a Gentile. Hippolytus told of an extremely scrupulous group of Essenes who considered themselves so much different from the "younger generation" of Essenes that if one of them happened to touch one of the less rigorous Essenes by mistake, he would bathe to remove the defilement.

The care with which Essenes are reported to have kept various regulations justifies the claim that they were known for their self-control and respect for the law, and that they were particularly concerned for the writings of the ancients dealing with the welfare of the soul and body — probably the ancient pentateuchal rules on cleanness and uncleanness. These were rules governing the attitude of the community toward leprosy, menstrual periods, childbirth, seminal discharges, and other conditions that rendered a member of the congregation unclean. If the holy army of Israel followed regulations specifically, it could expect with only a few men to overthrow an army (cf. 1 S. 14:6; Jgs. 7; 1 Macc. 3:18-22; 4:9f.; 2 Macc. 8:16-18). Before beginning a military campaign the soldiers of Israel had to be sanctified (Heb. *qᵉḏôšîm*; Josh. 3:5; 7:13-15). Those prepared or "sanctified" for war (Jer. 6:4; 51:27f.; Joel 3:9 [MT 4:9]) were ritually pure or "holy." The Israelites who were sanctified so that the Lord could appear at the giving of the Ten Commandments had stayed away from women for two days and had washed their garments (Ex. 19:10-15). David told Ahimelech that his soldiers' vessels were holy because the soldiers had kept themselves from women (1 S. 21:4-6). Uriah refused to lie with his wife while his fellow soldiers were at war (2 S. 11:11).

Later tradition held that after the commandments were given, Moses continually kept away from his wife. Since he never knew when God would speak to him, he had to be ritually pure every hour of every day. On the eve of the Day of Atonement the high priest was given short rations and kept awake all night to prevent a seminal discharge that would disqualify him for his function as high priest the following day (Mish. *Yoma* i.1, 4-8). The War Scroll gives instructions to prevent any type of defilement within the camp because holy angels were with their armies (1QM 7:3-7).

With so many regulations, and with so long a tradition underlying Israel's belief that ritual purity was necessary for holiness and that holiness was necessary for the Lord to be present in the congregation, it seems logical to suppose that a congregation could not be pure if men had free access to women. It is further reasonable to conjecture that the most scrupulous, pious Jews would find basis enough in holiness regulations to prompt them to form a celibate order. Only when Israel was in tents away from women was holy warfare possible. Since God could save the nation with only a small remnant of faithful covenanters, the monastic Essenes may have accepted the limitations necessary to be a holy congregation standing ready for God to act. The marrying order of the Essenes, then, observed the same rules as well as they could while still propagating the race.

B. "Trustworthiness." Josephus and Hippolytus referred to the Essenes who were finally accepted into full membership as "worthy" (Gk. *áxioi*). In rabbinic literature, a person who undertakes the responsibility of being "trustworthy" (Heb. *ne'ᵉmān*) keeps *kāšēr,* fulfilling all the dietary, purity, tithing, and heave offering regulations that his association (Heb. *ḥᵃḇûrâ*) demands. Although the term *ne'ᵉmān* generally means "trustworthy" in any sense, it also has the technical meaning of a person who remains *kāšēr*. The "trustworthy" person must tithe what he eats and what he sells and buys, and may not be a guest of an outsider. He enters the prescribed program by degrees: first he is accepted with regard to cleanness of hands and afterward for purities. The school of Hillel accepted members as "trustworthy" who had observed the regulations without default for thirty days. The school of Shammai prescribed thirty days for liquids; for clothing, twelve months.

There is a very close relationship among *áxios,* "worthy," *kāšēr,* "worthy" or "ritually permitted," and *ne'ᵉmān,* "one who is worthy of being trusted to stay within the ritually permitted limits." The contexts show that the use of *áxios* by Josephus and Hippolytus is similar to the pharisaic use of Heb. *ne'ᵉmān*; the only difference is in the particular qualifications required to achieve this standing. The Essenes required a longer probation period than the schools either of Hillel or Shammai, and they required all members of the monastic community to be "trustworthy," and possibly the marrying Essenes as well; whereas only very scrupulous Pharisees or Sadducees made any pretense of being "trustworthy."

Both Josephus and Hippolytus claimed that the Essenes believed no woman could be trusted. It seems unreasonable to believe that this lack of trust referred to marital loyalty. The text employed by Josephus and Hippolytus may have intended to say simply that the Essene sect differed from the pharisaic "association" in that it did not accept women as persons to be trusted with dietary rules, heave-offering and tithing rules, and purity regulations. Hippolytus seems to bear out this suggestion by his statement that Essenes did not even trust women who wished to devote themselves to the same polity. Since women were necessarily unclean at least one fourth of the time, it is not surprising that a meticulous group would not trust them with matters concerning defilement.

This does not mean that Essenes were misogynists. In fact, they were willing to rear children and even permitted these children to marry — a strange behavior, indeed, if the group really had strong feelings against the character of women. The monastic order avoided women for reasons of purity, and the sect in general apparently did not accept them as "trustworthy" (Heb. *ne'ĕmunôṯ*), but Philo's description of the Essene understanding of women's wiles probably reflects his own views as much as those of the Essenes. The Gk. terms *tēreín . . . pístin* (observing . . . trust) and *pisteúontes* (trusting) may reflect a mistranslation of the Heb. *ne'ĕmunôṯ* (trustworthy). To be sure, this is only a conjecture; but reason requires some interpretation other than general hatred for the female sex, and this suggestion is possible.

V. Slavery.–According to Philo, "Not a single slave is to be found among them, but all are free, exchanging services with each other, and they denounce the owners of slaves, not merely for their injustice in outraging the law of equality, but also for their impiety in annulling the statute of Nature, who mother-like has born and reared all men alike, and created them genuine brothers, not in mere name, but in very reality, though this kinship has been put to confusion by the triumph of malignant covetousness, which has wrought estrangement instead of affinity and enmity instead of friendship." One of the ways by which they show their love of men is "by benevolence and a sense of equality" (*Quod omnis probus* ix.79, 84).

Josephus said, "They neither enter into marriage nor practice slave holding, considering the one to lead to unrighteousness and the other to give way to the formation of insurrection, but they live by themselves, making use of one another in service" (*Ant.* xviii.1.5 [21]). Of the two social customs, marriage would be the one thought to lead to unrighteousness, because marriage would cause Jews to break Levitical rules of purity. Slavery, then, according to Josephus, was avoided because slaves could form a subversive movement of some kind within the group.

Although both Philo and Josephus agreed that the Essenes did not hold slaves, the reason given for this refusal is quite different in each case. Philo's reason was that the Essenes were convinced of the equality of all men and for this reason would not treat another man in a subordinate fashion. But the egalitarianism Philo attributes to the Essenes is contrary to their basic outlook on life. Philo himself noted that in their sabbath instruction they were ranked "in rows according to their ages, the younger below the older"; they did nothing without orders from their superiors, and were careful to obey their elders. Therefore Philo's quasi-philosophical explanation of their refusal to have slaves is to be dismissed as a projection of his own quasi-philosophy.

Jews in Palestine before A.D. 70 might have held Jewish slaves until sabbatical years, or gentile slaves permanently. All slavery would be excluded for the Essenes on the basis of ritual purity. If even junior members of the sect could not be touched by senior members, and if meals could not be eaten while there was a non-Essene in the house, then it would be virtually impossible to keep slaves of any kind. The Levitical rules, then, and not the Essene concern for egalitarianism, prevented the acquisition of slaves among the Essenes. Josephus may have been more nearly correct when he said that the Essenes feared that slaves would "give way to the formation of insurrection" — a practical consideration which probably bolstered the decision dictated by the concern for purity. The Levitical rules that prevented the Essenes from marrying also prevented their use of slaves. The communistic economy was necessary to provide for a people deprived of children, and an organized sharing of each other's work was necessary because they were deprived of slaves.

VI. Vows.–The Mishnaic tractate *Shebuóth* deals with oaths. According to the rabbis, a person who swore and broke his oath was obligated to bring an offering (iii.1-4), receive stripes (iii.7f., 10f.), or pay a fine (iv.6; v.4). They considered oath-taking a serious matter, since the curses imposed might prevent the coming of the kingdom. Philo presumed an oath would be taken in the name of God; therefore he warned anyone tempted to take an oath to be sure his soul was pure from lawlessness, his body from pollution, and his tongue from evil speaking so that he did not commit a sacrilege in pronouncing the holiest of names. Furthermore, he must carefully choose the place and the time so that the occasion would not profane the holy name (*De decalogo* 18 [84-95]).

2 Enoch 49:1 was more careful than the later rabbis in the use of oaths: "I swear to you, my children, but I swear not by any oath, neither by heaven nor by earth, nor by any other creature which God created. The Lord said: 'There is no oath in me, nor injustice, but truth.' If there is no truth in men, let them swear by the words 'yes, yes,' or else 'no, no.'"

This position was similar to that of the Essenes. Philo said one of the proofs of their religious purity was their abstinence from oaths. Josephus said, "Any word of theirs has more force than an oath; swearing they avoid, regarding it as worse than perjury, for they say that one who is not believed without an appeal to God stands condemned already."

Nonetheless, upon admission to the sect, Essenes were made to swear tremendous oaths regarding their loyalty to the group and its accepted discipline. An Essene was required to die rather than break one of these oaths.

The two attitudes of the Essenes toward oaths are not necessarily inconsistent. The required oaths were necessary to insure the scrupulous self-discipline and prescribed order required of the sect. The refusal to take oaths was a further mark of carefulness to do nothing that would prevent God from dwelling with a remnant of His people and restoring to them the land promised to the children of Abraham.

VII. Divisions.–In addition to the monastic and marrying Essenes, both Josephus and Hippolytus describe other divisions. Josephus said there were four grades, but he described only three: (1) new candidates who remained outside the fraternity for one year, (2) those who had successfully completed the first probationary period and were allowed to share the purer kind of water "for sanctification," and (3) those who, if found "worthy" after two years in the second stage, were fully admitted into the society. Some have held that the fourth degree was made up either of the children being reared or the officers of the sect, but this is only a conjecture. The four grades may also have been degrees of full initiates, divided according to the time of membership.

Hippolytus listed four divisions of Essenes according to differences of their practice rather than their stages of development, but he also described only three: (1) those who carried no coins with images nor walked through gates bearing statues, (2) those (called by some "zealots," by others "sicarii") who killed all uncircumcised men who discussed God or the law, unless they would accept circumcision, and (3) those who accepted death rather than confess any other Lord but God (*see* ZEALOT). Hippolytus added that those Essenes who held to the early rules of order considered themselves defiled if they accidentally touched any later (i.e., more liberal) types of Essenes.

It is likely that there were grades of membership such as Josephus described, since, though more exacting, these are very similar to the probationary steps necessary for admission as a "trustworthy" member into a pharisaic "association." It is also likely that there were sects within the sect something like the ones Hippolytus described. There is no probability, however, that the zealots or sicarii described by Josephus were varieties of Essenes. Hippolytus began by misunderstanding his text and expanded his misunderstanding by misinformation. But some elements of his account have historical background.

Josephus described the torture Essenes suffered during the war with Rome while holding fast to their convictions (see also Smith, *HUCA*, pp. 282f.).

VIII. Worship and Theology.–In addition to their purifications, legalistic practices, and sacred meals, the Essenes also sent gifts to the temple; but they did not sacrifice at the temple because of its uncleanness (Gk. *koinós*). Hence they offered their own sacrifices according to the special conditions of purity they observed.

Essenes also prayed every morning at dawn to the sun, according to Josephus, as if entreating it to rise. Hippolytus simply mentions a hymn to God without any reference to possible sun worship. This is consistent with the Jewish practice of reciting the Shema and benedictions.

Josephus said the Essenes believed in the immortality of souls, and he further explained this doctrine to Romans in terms of Greek theology. He was probably describing the same belief Hippolytus called resurrection of the body, which he associated with a final judgment. After God, they honored most the name of their lawgiver and punished with death anyone who blasphemed him.

One of the "tremendous oaths" Essenes were required to swear was that they would carefully preserve the books of the sect and the names of the angels. Following the discovery of a text in Qumrân dealing with angelology (Strugnell, *SVT*), many scholars are quite convinced of a belief in angels among the Essenes.

The Essenes, said Josephus, differed from the Pharisees and Sadducees concerning fate, by which he probably meant providence. Essenes believed that providence caused all things; Sadducees said that providence did not exist; but Pharisees held that some actions were the work of providence and some were the result of human effort.

IX. The Ossaeans.–During the time of Epiphanius (*ca.* A.D. 310-403), there existed a Samaritan sect of Essenes (Gk. *Essēnoi*) who observed circumcision, the sabbath, and other legalistic requirements very carefully.

Another sect, which Epiphanius classified among the Jewish sects, was called the Ossaeans (Gk. *Ossaioi*). These originated from the areas of Ituraea, Nabatea, Moab, Arielis (perhaps Jerusalem), and the regions near the Dead Sea. They followed Jewish customs of sabbath observance, circumcision, and the fulfillment of the law. This sect existed from before the time of Christ until the destruction of Jerusalem (A.D. 70). The sect of Ossaeans still survived in Nabatea and Peraea near Moab during Epiphanius' lifetime under the designation Sampsaions (Gk. *Sampsaioi*). Together with the Ebionites, the Nazorians, and the Nasarians, this sect followed the leadership of a certain Elxai. The Sampsaions called themselves Jews, but they reflected Greek and Christian influences as well.

There is enough similarity between Epiphanius' descriptions of the Essenes and of the Ossaeans to prompt some scholars to identify the two (*HJP*, p. 213). The names are sufficiently alike to be confused. Furthermore, though not detailed, the description of the Ossaeans before the influence of Elxai is similar to other accounts of the Essenes. But it is also similar in general to other Jewish sects. Sects have been known to develop, change, and even reverse positions over a period of time.

It is conceivable that the Sampsaions are a later development of the Ossaeans or Essenes; but if this is so, the insights gained from later descriptions of them are of little value for understanding the early sect of Essenes.

X. Therapeutae and Other Sects.–The Therapeutae were members of a group described in Philo's *De vita contemplativa*. They existed in many places in the inhabited world, but flourished in Egypt, especially around Alexandria, near Lake Mareotis.

Philo began his discussion of the Therapeutae by mentioning that he had "discussed the Essenes." Instead of concluding that by this Philo indicated that he was moving into a different subject, many scholars have identified the Therapeutae with the Essenes. In some ways they are similar. Like the Essenes, the Therapeutae heal diseases, forfeit wealth and family, pray at dawn, study scriptures, are instructed on the sabbath, stress self-control, eat simple food, have common meals, do not hold slaves, and help one another with their work. They also differ at many points. Instead of giving their wealth to a common fund, Therapeutae give it to relatives and friends; they do not migrate; their location is principally in Egypt; instead of physical labor, they spend six days a week in meditation, some eating only once or twice a week; they include women in their group; and they do not baptize.

Vermes attempted to strengthen the belief that Therapeutae were Essenes by deriving the name Essene from Aram. *ʾāsîn*, "healers." He was opposed by H. G. Schönfeld (*RQ*, 3 [1961], 219ff.), who claimed that Philo's use of Gk. *therapeútein* was restricted to "worshiping," and that "Essenes" could not be derived from *ʾāsîn*. Geoltrain says, "The Therapeutae are the Essenes of the Diaspora" (*Semitica*, 10 [1960], 28). Even if this were so, the relationship between the two groups is too remote and uncertain to use the description of the Therapeutae to learn anything about the Essenes.

Various scholars have postulated relationships between the Essenes and other sectarian Jewish groups, such as the Boethusians and Ebionites, that flourished in Palestine. Usually some similarities are adduced to justify the supposed connection. But it is a priori likely that sects of the same religion developing in the same area and at the same time should have many similarities, so none of these proposed relationships is worth discussion, except in the case of the Dead Sea sect.

XI. The Scrolls and the Essenes.–Among the Dead Sea Scrolls was found a book of regulations for some Jewish sect that has prompted many scholars to presume that the Essenes inhabited the quarters excavated at Qumrân and composed the documents found in the caves nearby. Strugnell (*JBL*) has suggested that the Scrolls be considered primary source material by which Josephus, Philo, and others should be corrected. This opinion, however, though now general, is not universally accepted. Rabin (*Qumran Studies*) said the Dead Sea sect was Pharisaic, and Habermann claimed it was Sadducean.

Without prejudging the case, we shall compare the unknown sect governed by the Manual of Discipline (1QS) with the Essenes already described. Then a second book of sectarian regulations, the Damascus Document (CD), will also be compared with the Essenes to learn the similarities and differences of some of the sectarian movements in Palestine before the fall of Jerusalem.

A. Manual of Discipline. The sect governed by 1QS is similar in many ways to the Essenes. Those who joined the sect had to contribute all their possessions to the community. Members within the order were ranked according to status and were required to obey superior members. This also was an exclusive sect, which required meticulous observance of the law and purity rules. Only those within the sect were considered pure. For all others, ablutions were useless. Those not cleansed might not have contact with pure possessions of the sect, and were to be kept separate from the sectarians. Like the Essenes, members were kept on varying degrees of probation for two years — more rigorous than the pharisaic "associations." Upon admission to the sect, members were bound by oaths to follow the prescribed order, and

Column 5 of the Manual of Discipline from Qumrân. Here the community members are commanded to avoid "men of deceit" and to obey the Torah and other rules of purity (Trustees of the British Museum; picture J. C. Trever)

failure to keep these oaths would bring upon them the assigned curses of the covenant. In addition, they might be fined or excommunicated. Like the Essenes, the Qumrân sect demanded very rigorous self-discipline, agreeing in such specific details as forbidding spitting into the midst of the session or to the right and punishing with death one who blasphemes the name of God.

Members of the Qumrân sect were to love all the sons of light (members of the sect) and hate all the sons of darkness (nonmembers), just as God loves one spirit and hates the other. Sectarians were not to hate one another. According to a man's spirit he should either be loved or hated, either accepted or rejected from the community "according to the cleanness of his hands."

Hippolytus said the Essene was required to vow to hate no one who wronged him or was an enemy to him, but this was apparently an attitude within the sect, or else hatred was given a different meaning, similar to 1QS 9:22f.: "[Let there be] eternal hatred toward the men of the pit in a spirit of secrecy, yielding to them wealth and manual labor as a servant to his master and the submission [fitting] toward one who rules him. But let each be zealous for the decree and its season — for the day of vengeance."

Although the discipline of the Essenes was not explained in terms of love and hatred, the attitude of acceptance or rejection based on a member's willingness to observe prescribed rules is descriptive of both groups. The Qumrân sect described rejection as hatred and acceptance as love.

Like the Essenes, the Qumrân sect based its existence on the Scriptures, which were to be read day and night and interpreted. Studying the Torah was the way sectarians prepared a highway for God in the desert. Anyone who transgressed a word from the Torah of Moses was to be banished from the council never to return.

B. Damascus Document. Like the Essenes and the Qumrân sect, the Covenanters called their group or special group within the sect "the many" (see Smith, *HUCA*, p. 291). They also ranked people according to status. Like the Essenes, they considered the sanctuary to be defiled, and like the Qumrân sect they held that there had to be a priest wherever ten men were present. They were meticulous in discriminating between the clean and unclean so as to observe ritual purity; they were strict sabbath observers; and they may have referred to their own group as a "trustworthy house" (Heb. *byt n'mn*). They identified hatred (*śn'*) with rejection (*m's*). They evidently enrolled their members by requiring them to take oaths, which if broken would impose upon the offenders the curses of the covenant; but they did not limit swearing to the oath of admission into the sect. Neither did the Covenanters prohibit slavery or marriage, but presumed a normal family existence in which members had children. They did object to bigamy, incest, and sexual intercourse in the holy city, and they excommunicated members who violated these rules. They gave offerings, as did the Essenes; but they had no communistic economy, although each member was taxed for charity.

It would not be surprising to discover similarities among many of the sects that existed in Palestine before the fall of Jerusalem. Agreements in belief and practice do not constitute enough evidence to conclude identity. The most convincing evidence that the Qumrân group was an Essene community was Pliny's statement that the Essenes lived on the west side of the Dead Sea above En-gedi. But this does not say whether "above" meant "to the north" or higher in altitude (see Audet; Burchard). Although there are striking similarities between CD and 1QS, there are important differences: The sect of CD had no monastic or communistic order and it permitted slavery. It was careful in its attempt to fulfil the law, but not so scrupulous as the Qumrân sect or the Essenes. The Qumrân sect is more like the Essene sect than any other known Jewish group, and Pliny's description is strongly in favor of identifying the Qumrân group with one community of Essenes; but it is more important to see the kind of movements that went on in Palestine before A.D. 70 than to identify the beliefs of a group with the name of a sect.

XII. Essenes and Christianity.*–A. Christianity and Communism.* There are obvious parallels among the practices

Two leaves of the Damascus (Zadokite) Document (CD 10:1-23; 11:1-23) outlining the strict Sabbath regulations of the sect. From the Cairo Genizah, 10th cent. A.D. (Cambridge University Library)

of the Essenes, the sect at Qumrân, the Zadokite Covenanters, and the early Christian Church. Some early Christians evidently practiced a form of communism similar, perhaps, to that of the marrying Essenes. Certainly men and women were both admitted into the economic community described in Acts 4:32ff., and they apparently were not required to contribute all their possessions to the group; but those who contributed under false pretenses, like Ananias and Sapphira, were severely punished.

There are also in the NT hints of a type of complete communism similar to that of the Essenes. The man who had kept the normal commandments was told that if he wanted to be "perfect" (a full member; see 1QS 1:8, 22; 3:3f.; 4:22; 8:1, 9f., 18-21), he must take all he had and give it to the poor (Mt. 19:21). By this Jesus may have been asking the man to contribute his resources into the common treasury of a group called the "poor," an economic policy similar to that of the Essenes and the sect at Qumrân. When confronted by Jesus, Zacchaeus volunteered, "'Behold, Lord, the half of my goods I give to the poor; and if I have defrauded any one of anything, I restore it fourfold'" (Lk. 19:8). This might mean complete surrender of wealth — one-half to repay his fraudulent acts in the past and one-half for the sect.

B. Monasticism. Jesus encouraged those interested in His teaching to break family ties and follow Him. He rejected His own family to accept a new one (Mt. 12:46-50; Mk. 3:31-35; Lk. 8:19-21). He said, "If any one comes to me and does not hate his own father and mother and wife and children and brothers and sisters, yes, and even his own life, he cannot be my disciple" (Lk. 14:25f.). In this instance the word "hate" means "reject" as in 1QS, CD, and Lk. 6:22. Likewise, would-be followers were not permitted to wait until their parents had died and were properly buried (Mt. 8:21f.; Lk. 9:59f.) nor even to say farewell to their families (Lk. 9:61f.). Jesus called people to take stands that would separate family members from one another. Those who had greater loyalty to their families than to Jesus could not be accepted into the movement. It was by losing one's life (so far as family was concerned) for Jesus' sake that one would find his life (so far as the group was concerned; cf. Mt. 10:35-39).

Paul also chose to be celibate, but he indicated that other apostles had married (1 Cor. 9:3-5). Mt. 19:27-29 implies, however, that the disciples of Jesus had left everything to follow Him. Paul recommended celibacy for others, but did not require it (1 Cor. 7:1-40). The 144,000 who were redeemed from the earth were celibates who had not defiled themselves with women (Rev. 14:3f.).

There is no indication that Christians rejected slaves on the grounds of ritualistic righteousness. This may be because the habits of monastic Christians were not described in detail in the NT.

C. Hospitality. Like the Essenes, Christians expected hospitality in every city in the homes of the "worthy." The twelve were sent out without gold, silver, or copper in their belts, no bags nor sandals, and with only one tunic each. They were told: "And whatever town or village you enter, find out one who is worthy in it, and stay with him until you depart. As you enter the house, salute it. And if the house is worthy, let your peace come upon it; but if it is not worthy, let your peace return to you" (Mt. 10:11-13). In conformity with the Essene type of hospitality, Christians were told not to give to dogs (Gentiles) that which was holy (Mt. 7:6), and to ask, seek, and knock, and be assured that their needs would be met (Mt. 7:7). Jesus said that the one who was more loyal to his family than to Him, and who would not take up his cross and follow Jesus, was not "worthy" so far as He was concerned (Mt. 10:37f.). The returning prodigal son who has been with "swine" and "harlots" (i.e., Gentiles, and Jews who mingled with Gentiles) knew he was no longer "worthy" (Lk. 15:19, 21.) Those commended for acceptance as fellow workers deserving hospitality, so that they could be sent on "in a manner worthy of God," had refused gentile hospitality for the sake of the Name (3 Jn. 5-8, NIV). Those who did not remain in the true doctrine were not to be admitted into the homes of the faithful, or even greeted by them (2 Jn. 7-11). Those in Sardis who had not "soiled their garments" were called "worthy" (Rev. 3:4). The one who could open the scroll and break its seals had to be "worthy" (Rev. 5:2, 4, 9, 12).

The Christians, as well as the Essenes and members of other sectarian "associations," belonged to a background of careful legalistic observances, followed similar hospitality practices, and called accepted members "worthy" or "trustworthy."

D. Antiexclusivism. Primitive Christianity, however, cannot be fully described in terms of monastic, communistic, exclusive sectarianism. Some of the earliest Synoptic sources depict Jesus as one who opposed Pharisees on the very point of ritual purity and dietary laws. Hence He was distinguished from John the Baptist. John practiced "righteousness" (Mt. 21:32), neither eating nor drinking (with those not "trustworthy"). But Jesus was called "an eater and a wine-drinker, a friend of tax collectors and sinners" (Mt. 11:18f.). The tax collectors and sinners were the Roman collaborators and those who did not observe the dietary and purity rules. Jesus taught that God accepted and forgave these nonobservant Jews (e.g., Mt. 9:10-15 par.; 15:1-3 par.; 18:21f. par.; 23:25 par.).

Paul, who represented a branch of Christianity that had broken away from ritualistic purity, was in constant conflict with those Christians who held to it (Gal. 2:1–5:25; Rom. 2:17-29; 3:19–6:23; 8:1-8; 15:7-18). Yet on occasion he modified or adapted his counsel to maintain order within the community (1 Cor. 6:12-20; 8:1-13; 9:19-23; 10:6-33).

E. Oaths. Like Essenes, Christians were forbidden to take any oath (Mt. 5:33-37), and Pharisees were criticized for upholding those who bound themselves by oaths to neglect their parents in their old age (Mt. 15:4-6; Mk. 7:10-12). The Pharisees feared the effects of the curses imposed in the oath more than the effects of neglected parents. (See Acts 23:12-15 for another example of an oath; cf. G. W. Buchanan, *HTR*, 58 [1965], 319-326.)

F. Theology. The Christian belief in providence reflected in the Gospels (Mt. 6:25-34; 7:7-11; Lk. 12:32) and in Paul's insistence that God controls all things (Rom. 1:18-32; 9:6-18) and acts without consulting anyone or needing justification (Rom. 9:19-29) is similar to that of the Essenes. Paul said it was God who foreknew, predestined, called, justified, and glorified (8:28-33). Like the Essenes and Pharisees, Christians believed in the resurrection of the dead (1 Cor. 15; Acts 23:6-10) and held that Christ was the first fruits of those who had died since He rose from the dead (1 Cor. 15:1-21).

Bibliography.–J.-P. Audet, *RB*, 68 (1961), 346-387; M. Black, *The Scrolls and Christian Origins* (1961); W. H. Brownlee, *Dead Sea Manual of Discipline* (1951); G. W. Buchanan, *Consequences of the Covenant* (1970); *Nov.Test.*, 7 (1964), 195-209; *Religion in Life*, 48 (1979), 136-142; *RQ*, 4 (1963), 397-406; 6 (1969), 553-58; 9 (1977), 241-43; *To the Hebrews* (*AB*, 1972); C. Burchard, *RB*, 69 (1962), 533-569; M. Burrows, *Dead Sea Scrolls* (1955); A. Dupont-Sommer, *Essene Writings from Qumran* (Eng. tr. 1961); A. Frank-Duquesne, *Syntheses*, 7 (1952), 361-375; J. Gnilka, *RQ*, 3 (1961), 185-207; M. Hengel, *Die Zeloten* (1961); *Jew.Enc.*, V, *s.v.* (M. Kayserling); H. Kosmala, *Hebräer-Essener-Christen* (1959); J. B. Lightfoot, *St. Paul's Epistles to the Colossians and to Philemon* (1875), pp. 82-95, 114-179; F. Nötscher, *RQ*, 2 (1959/60), 163-181, 313-344; Pauly-Wissowa, Suppl. IV, 386-430 (W. Bauer); C. Rabin, *Qumran Studies* (1957); *Zadokite Documents* (1954); B. J. Roberts, *NTS*, 3 (1956/57), 58-65; M. Smith, *NTS*, 7 (1960/61), 347-360; *HUCA*, 29 (1958), 273-313; K. Stendahl, *HTR*, 55 (1962), 343-355; J. Strugnell, *JBL*, 77 (1958), 106-115; "The Angelic Liturgy at Qumran — 4Q *Šěrek Šêrôt 'Ôlat Haššabbat*," in *SVT*, 7 (1960), 318-345; E. F. Sutcliffe, *RQ*, 2 (1959/60), 245-255; G. Vermes, *RQ*, 2 (1959/60), 427-443.

G. W. BUCHANAN

ESTABLISH [Heb. *kûn, qûm, ʿāmaḏ, śûm* or *śîm, ʾāman*, also *yāsaḏ* (1 Ch. 9:22; Hab. 1:12), *ḥāzaq* (2 Ch. 1:1; 21:4), *ʾāmēṣ* (Prov. 8:28), *yāṣag* (Am. 5:15), *sāmaḵ* (Ps. 111:8), *sāʿaḏ* (Isa. 9:7 [MT 6]); Aram. *tᵉqan* (Dnl. 4:36 [MT 33]); Gk. *stērízō, hístēmi*; also *synteléō* (He. 8:8), *bebaióō* (Col. 2:7; 2 Cor. 1:21); cf. *apokatástasis* (Acts 3:21)]; AV, NEB, also CONFIRM, PERFORM, MAKE, PREPARE, STRENGTHEN, APPOINT, STAND, SET (UP), FULFILL, CONSTITUTE, DETERMINE, etc. The Hebrew words may be translated by many synonyms of the English "establish," depending upon the context; in the RSV they appear as many as five hundred times with translations other than "establish" (cf. AV, NEB). Although it is not possible to draw too much significance from the roots, their basic meanings reflect the dual senses of the English "establish," namely, "make firm or stable" and "institute, bring into existence."

Six Hebrew words yield the first sense. The most frequently translated "establish" (sixty-eight times) is the verb *kûn*, "make firm," usually in the niphal or hiphil stems. This verb is usually connected with the idea of "kingdom," "throne," or "house (family)," especially in the historical books (cf. 2 S. 7:12f., 16, 26; 1 K. 2:12, 24, 45f.; 1 Ch. 14:2; 17:11f., 14; 22:10; 28:7; 1 K. 9:5 has *qûm*). A second word, *ʾāman*, "confirm, support," is translated "establish" four times (1 Ch. 17:23f.; 2 Ch. 20:20; Isa. 7:9). A third, *ḥāzaq*, "be (grow) firm, strong," is twice translated "establish" (2 Ch. 1:1; 21:4). The other three so translated are *ʾāmēṣ*, "be stout, strong," *sāmaḵ*, "lean, lay, rest, support," and *sāʿaḏ*, "support, sustain, stay."

The second basic sense of "establish" is reflected in five Hebrew words. Most frequent is the verb *qûm*, "arise, stand up, stand," usually translated "establish" in the hiphil (causative) stem. Its most important connection here is with the theme of covenant (and God's word) or covenant people, especially in the Pentateuch (Gen. 6:18; 9:9, 11, 17; 17:7, 19, 21; Ex. 6:4; Dt. 28:9; 29:13 [MT 12]; 1 S. 1:23; 1 K. 2:4; Ezk. 16:60, 62; cf. *kûn* in Dt. 32:6). A second word is similar: *ʿāmaḏ*, "to take one's stand, to stand," is translated "establish" in the hiphil stem (1 K. 15:4; 2 Ch. 9:8; Neh. 13:30; Ps. 30:7 [MT 8]; 148:6). This meaning also occurs with *śîm* or *śûm*, "put, place, set," (1 K. 20:34; Job 38:33; Ps. 89:29 [MT 30]; Isa. 42:4) and *yāṣag*, "set, place" (Am. 5:15). Finally, *yāsaḏ* has a basic meaning "establish, found, fix," and is perhaps the closest parallel to the English word "establish."

The contexts of the two basic words of each sense are of interest. *Qûm*, with the connotation "bringing into existence" what has not previously existed, is used in the original declarations of the covenant to Abraham and Moses; *kûn* is used of the promise of the kingdom to David, suggesting "making firm" an already existing situation.

The NT Greek verbs also reflect the dual sense of "establish." On the one hand, *stērízō* (1 Thess. 3:2, 13; 2 Thess. 2:17; Jas. 5:8; 1 Pet. 5:10; 2 Pet. 1:12) has the basic sense of "make fast" what already exists, as does *bebaióō*, "make firm, confirm, make sure" (2 Cor. 1:21; Col. 2:7). On the other hand, *hístēmi* (a frequent LXX translation of *qûm, ʿāmaḏ*, and *yāsaḏ*) in the transitive sense means "cause or make to stand; place, put, set" (Thayer).

The remaining two words are more complicated. In He. 8:8 the author uses *synteléō* instead of the LXX *diathḗsomai* (Jer. 31:31 [LXX 38:31]) of the OT quotation.

This reflects the new perspective of the NT that the covenant has been completed, "effected," or "accomplished" and not simply initiated or reaffirmed. The NEB "conclude" is perhaps better than the RSV "establish." In Acts 3:21, the RSV translates *apokatástasis,* "establishing," instead of the more correct "restoration" (cf. NEB; AV "restitution"). This is apparently on the theological grounds that "the fulfillment here is much wider in scope than the restoration of the Kingdom of Israel. . . ." (F. F. Bruce, *Acts* [*NICNT,* 1954], p. 51).

Bibliography.–Bauer; BDB; Thayer; *TDNT,* I, *s.v.* ἀποκαθίστημι, ἀποκατάστασις (Oepke); II, *s.v.* τέλος κτλ.: συντελέω (Delling); *TDOT,* I, 292-309; *s.v.* "'āmats" (Schreiner).

H. VAN BROEKHOVEN, JR.

ESTATE. The AV uses "estate" in the obsolescent sense of "state" or "condition" (cf. Col. 4:8) as well as for "position." The RSV uses it only in the latter sense and in the sense of "property."

ESTEEM [Heb. *'ênayim*] (Neh. 6:16); AV "eyes"; NEB "achievement"; [*qālâ*] ("lightly esteemed," 1 S. 2:30); NEB "treated with contempt"; [*lō' ḥāšab*] ("esteem not," Isa. 53:3f.); NEB "hold of no account"; [*yāqar*] (1 S. 18:30); NEB "won a great name"; [Gk. *exouthenéō*] ("least esteemed," 1 Cor. 6:4); NEB "count for nothing"; [*krínō*] (Rom. 14:5); NEB REGARD. In 2 S. 16:23 the RSV and NEB supply "esteem" to make the Hebrew construction understandable.

In the one instance of "esteem" as a noun (Neh. 6:16) it translates the plural of *'ayin* ("eye"), which often means "opinion"; *see* EYE. As a verb it is used in the RSV for the neutral terms *ḥāšab* ("account") and *krínō* ("judge"), for the negative terms *qālâ* ("dishonor") and *exouthenéō* ("despise"), and for the positive term *yāqar* ("be prized").

In Isa. 53:3f. "esteem" is used for Israel's response to the Suffering Servant. In 53:3 what disturbs the prophet most is that Israel "esteemed him not," i.e., it did not know Him or what He was doing. Verse 4 gives Israel's interpretation of His suffering; "Yet we esteemed him stricken, smitten by God, and afflicted." Like Job's comforters, Israel considered suffering a punishment from God.

Those designated as "least esteemed" in 1 Cor. 6:4 are the pagan judges who are outside the Church. Paul says that these people should have no right to judge the disputes which are dividing the Corinthian church.

The reference in Rom. 14:5 to one who "esteems one day as better than another" and to another who "esteems all days alike" presupposes two groups who are divided over the observation of special feast days. "Esteem" (Gk. *krínō*) here denotes the theological judgment of the two groups. In the first instance it means "prefer" and refers to those who set aside special feast days (cf. Gal. 4:10; Col. 2:16); in the second instance it means "not distinguish." The same Greek word is translated "judge" in Rom. 14:3, where Paul counsels against allowing different views on feast days to cause one to "pass judgment" on his neighbor. Thus, while brothers may "esteem" the question of foods differently (v. 5), this difference in view is no excuse for condemnation of the brother (v. 3).

Bibliography.–O. Michel, *Der Brief an die Römer* (12th ed. 1966), pp. 337f.; J. Muilenburg, *Isaiah* (*IB,* 1956), pp. 618-622.

J. W. THOMPSON

ESTHER es'tər [Heb. *'estēr*; akin to the Sanskrit *stṛi,* Gk. *astḗr*–'a star'; Gk. *Esthēr*]. According to the book of Esther, Esther was a Jewish orphan who became the queen of Ahasuerus (Xerxes) the Persian king. She was brought up at Susa by her cousin Mordecai, who seems to have held a position among the lower officials of the royal palace. After he had divorced Vashti, his former queen, Ahasuerus had the most beautiful virgins from all the provinces of the empire brought to the palace of Susa so that he might select her successor. He chose the Jewish maiden.

Soon after Esther's accession a great crisis threatened the entire Jewish people with destruction. The name of Esther is forever bound up with the record of their deliverance. By a course of action that gives her a distinguished place among the women of the Bible, Haman the great enemy of the Jews was destroyed and her people were delivered. Nothing more is known of her than is recorded in the book that Jewish gratitude has made to bear her name. *See* ESTHER, BOOK OF.

The change in the queen's name from Hadassah (Heb. *hadassâ,* "a myrtle") to Esther ("a star") reflects local usage. Hadassah was apparently her Jewish name, whereas Esther was used when she was given her official Persian title as queen. The narrative displays her as a woman of clear judgment, of magnificent self-control, and capable of the noblest self-sacrifice. J. URQUHART

ESTHER, ADDITIONS TO THE BOOK OF; AV, NEB, REST OF THE CHAPTERS OF THE BOOK OF ESTHER. Part of the OT Apocrypha.

The critical introduction to Esther and its additions bears some resemblance to a bog, with but a few firmer footpaths. The late and hesitant acceptance of the Hebrew text as canonical Scripture was eventually offset by its immense popularity in militant Judaism, once its propaganda value was discovered. No other book of the OT has been so freely translated or so copiously embellished as Esther, not only in the LXX, but also in Josephus, the Targum, the Talmud, and the Midrash. This article is confined to the LXX additions, which are the earliest in date.

I. Canon and Apocrypha.–The Greek text of Esther with the interpolations is preserved in two main forms:

(1) The ordinary Greek text, based on the famous uncial Codices Vaticanus, Alexandrinus, Sinaiticus, etc., and numerous minuscules. This text is followed in *OTG.*

(2) The rescension of Lucian, on which several further MSS are based. (See esp. A. E. Brooke, N. McLean, and H. St. J. Thackeray, *The OT in Greek,* III, [1906], v, vi, 1-42; also Paton, comm. on Esther [*ICC,* repr. 1951].)

These Greek traditions vary from the Hebrew and from each other. The Latin Vulgate, forsaking the good example of the LXX, placed the six main additions to the book of Esther in a disconnected and confused lump at the end; the English Apocrypha RV has segregated them further from the setting in which they are meaningful. The NEB Apocrypha, on the other hand, translates Swete's entire Greek text, with the apocryphal portions in brackets. The *ICC* translates all the interpolations from all the sources in their proper places, as is also done, with notes in another volume, in L. Ginzberg, *Legends of the Jews* (rev. ed. 1961). The English Bible and Apocrypha are sufficient for understanding, if the additions are read where they belong.

The exceptional discrepancies have led to several theories about the relationship between the Hebrew and Greek versions of Esther. Many Catholic exegetes maintain that the existing canonical Hebrew book is the abridgment of a once larger work containing all the apocryphal material. The hypothesis of C. C. Torrey (*HTR,* 37 [1944], 1-40) is broadly that both surviving versions were translated from an older and larger Semitic original, possibly Aramaic, which became represented more fully, and at an earlier date, in the Greek version. But the controversial issue as to whether the additions are translation Greek or original compositions, or some the one, some the other, affects both theories. A third and more common view is that the LXX translates the canonical Hebrew, but that it does so more freely than in the case of other OT books, and at the same time interpolates long passages in their first or Greek dress.

The Hebrew text of Esther not only avoids the name of God but almost lacks a discernible religious motif — which explains some of the difficulties over its canonicity. Several reasons have been suggested. The writer may not have been a deeply religious man. Or the Feast of Purim with which Esther is associated, a noisy, secular, and alcoholic affair, may have been felt to be an occasion ill suited to the use of the divine name. Or religious sentiments openly expressed may have been fraught with some contemporary political danger. Or this outwardly secular book may have a deeper allegorical meaning — though this has not been satisfactorily demonstrated. Some have regarded the interpolations as being themselves intended to supply the missing religious motif.

For the additions, several scholars suggest a date in the last quarter of the 2nd cent. B.C. But this is a matter open to variant opinion. (See *APOT,* I, 665-671; *HNTT*; C. C. Torrey, *Apocryphal Literature: A Brief Intro.* [1945]; W. O. E. Oesterley, *Intro. to the Books of the Apocrypha* [1935]; *Jew.Enc.*; *HDB*; *ICC*; *IOTG,* pp. 257ff.)

II. The Six Additions to Esther, A-F.–A. The RSV 11:2–12:6 should be read before the beginning of the Hebrew version. It is significant for Mordecai's dream (11:5-11), which is interpreted in Addition F (10:6-9), and for Mordecai's revelation of the treasonable plot of the two eunuchs against Ahasuerus, which earned the hatred of Haman (12:1-6). The Vulgate and the RV disastrously place the interpretation before the dream.

The MT of Esther opens, quite Hebraically, with *way^{e}hî,* which the LXX renders *kaí egéneto*; Joshua, Judges, Ruth, 1 Samuel, etc., conform in both languages. It is only to Western, not to Eastern, thinking that such an opening is strange. In Est. 1:1, the LXX significantly adds the words *metá toús lógous toútous,* which are not contained in the Hebrew. This clearly refers back to Addition A and treats it as an integral part of the text.

B. RSV 13:1-7 should be inserted in ch. 3, between vv. 13 and 14, where it appositely supplies the decree of Artaxerxes against the Jews, inspired by the hatred and craft of Haman. This passage is an early and interesting parody of anti-Semitic polemic.

C. RSV 13:8–14:15 should be inserted between chs. 4 and 5 in the Hebrew. It contains the prayers of Mordecai and Esther. Mordecai's self-justification for refusing to bow to Haman may possibly be pride, casuistry, or special pleading (13:12-17.; cf. Paton, *ICC,* pp. 193ff.). Esther's hatred of her regal splendor (14:15-18) is very noble from a Jewish viewpoint, though some regard it as the invention of a later age. Both prayers are fine, though particular phrases might arouse criticism. They supply a religious element.

D. RSV 14:1-16, subjoined to C and also preceding ch. 5, provides a fuller account of Esther's appearance before the king.

E. RSV 16:1-24 should be inserted at 8:12 in the Hebrew text. Artaxerxes revokes his decree against the Jews, denounces Haman, and utters some religious sentiments. Here, apparently, the laws of the Medes and Persians may be altered.

F. RSV 10:4–11:1, appended to the canonical book, includes an interpretation of Mordecai's dream, an account of the institution of Purim, and a superscription.

III. Conclusion.–For the contradiction in the Greek version, and for fuller theological evaluation, the reader must be referred to larger works. R. H. Pfeiffer (*HNTT,* p. 311) dismisses the Greek work as an "anti-Gentile tract," "a travesty of a noble religion," and so forth. His strictures are perhaps too harsh, but it cannot be claimed that Esther, Hebrew or Greek, has uniformly commended itself to Christians, though it has its lesson to teach. The canonical portion may conceivably, as the Word of God, answer the special needs of special periods or situations. R. A. STEWART

ESTHER, BOOK OF.

I. Contents
II. Additions
III. Position in the Bible
IV. Canonicity
V. Authorship
VI. Date
 A. Internal Evidence
 B. Maccabean Theory
VII. Nature and Purpose
VIII. Historicity
IX. Moral and Religious Problems

I. Contents.–The story is set in the Persian capital, Susa, during the reign of Ahasuerus (probably Xerxes I, 486-465 B.C.). The king, somewhat drunken during a state banquet, summoned Queen Vashti to his presence; but Vashti, insulted by his intention to make her a public spectacle, rebuffed him, and he in a fury divorced her. He then took steps to replace her, sending his courtiers to fetch all the beautiful, marriageable girls in the kingdom for his inspection. His final choice was Esther, a Jewish orphan, who had been adopted and reared by her cousin Mordecai. Shortly afterward, a plot to assassinate the king came to Mordecai's notice, and he was able to send a message to Esther, warning Ahasuerus. The plotters were duly executed, but Mordecai went unrewarded.

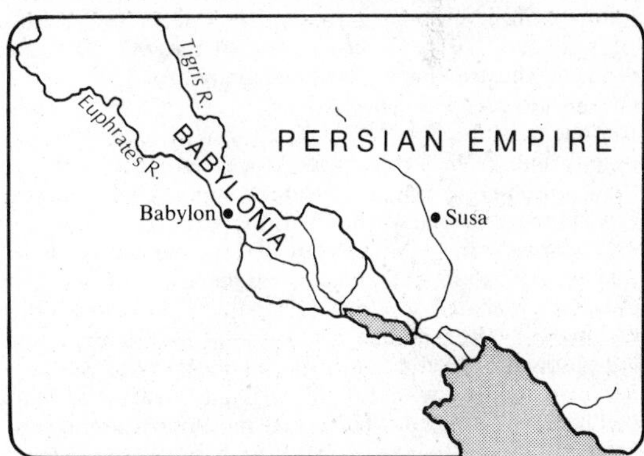

One of the king's chief nobles was called Haman. This man developed a violent dislike of Mordecai, who did not show him what he considered proper respect. Knowing Mordecai to be a Jew, he inveigled the king into issuing an edict authorizing the extermination of all the Jews in the Persian empire. Haman took pleasure in making his own arrangements for the death of Mordecai, even constructing gallows for the purpose. Frightened for her people, Esther (whose nationality had been kept secret) determined to approach the king and made arrangements to see him and Haman at a private banquet. At this juncture, the king chanced to read the court chronicles, where he was reminded of Mordecai's loyalty, and learned that he had never been rewarded for it. So the next day Haman, much to his chagrin, was ordered to parade Mordecai through the streets in royal array, as a mark of honor.

At her feast, Esther now pleaded for her own life and her people's, with such success that the king gave orders for the immediate execution of Haman, as the instigator of the edict. Mordecai was elevated to Haman's position, and the edict was in effect revoked, for the Jews received permission to take revenge on their enemies. This they were not slow to do, and the occasion ended in a joyous festival, which became an annual feast called Purim. The book ends with the Jews happy and secure, Mordecai in high office, and Esther retaining her position as queen.

SYNOPSIS

Ch.	1	Banquet of Ahasuerus; dismissal of Vashti
	2:1-18	Choice of Esther as queen
	2:19-23	Mordecai foils the assassins
	3	Haman's rise to power; the fateful edict
	4	Jewish mourning; Esther and Mordecai confer
	5	Esther prepares her banquet, Haman his gallows
	6	Ahasuerus remembers and honors Mordecai
	7	Esther's banquet; execution of Haman
	8	New, pro-Jewish edict
	9	Jewish vengeance; feast of Purim
	10	Conclusion

II. Additions.–The LXX version of Esther has over one hundred verses, distributed throughout the book, that are not found in the MT. It is certain that the extra material is not original to the book; it was added at a later date to give the book a more explicit religious tone. This extra material was extracted by Jerome and placed at the end of the book in his translation; in English versions it appears in the Apocrypha, as the Additions to the Book of Esther, or the Rest of Esther. (*See* ESTHER, ADDITIONS TO THE BOOK OF.)

III. Position in the Bible.–In the English Bible the book of Esther is appended to the historical books; it therefore follows Chronicles–Ezra–Nehemiah and precedes Job. This follows the LXX order. But in the MT the book is in the third division, the Hagiographa or "Writings," and is the last of the five Megilloth or "scrolls." These five books (Ruth, Song of Solomon, Ecclesiastes, Lamentations, and Esther) were placed together, since each was read annually to commemorate some occasion of the Jewish year. Esther was, and still is, read at Purim.

IV. Canonicity.–After the fall of Jerusalem in A.D. 70, a school of rabbis at Jamnia, near the coast of southern Palestine, debated the right of Esther and a few other OT books to be included in the canon. No doubt it was the absence of God's name that made the book suspect, perhaps coupled with Purim's being a festival without pentateuchal authority. However, the Jamnia rabbis confirmed its canonical status. In all probability, the debates merely served to confirm what had already been agreed on (by public opinion); they were thus more of an academic exercise than an open-minded discussion. The earliest Christian canon of the OT known to us, that of Melito of Sardis (*ca.* A.D. 170), does not include Esther, but the reason for the omission is uncertain. The canon of Origen (*ca.* A.D. 187-254) includes it, and the book found its place in the canon of both Jews and Christians. It has always had a strong appeal to Jewish minds. In the Mishnah it is called *Megillah,* "*the* Scroll" par excellence. Maimonides prized Esther so highly that he bracketed it with the Pentateuch. It has not always been similarly valued by Christian writers, however. Its lack of explicit religious sentiment and its somewhat bloodthirsty nationalistic ardor have offended many, notably Martin Luther (cf. H. Bornkamm, *Luther and the OT* [Eng. tr. 1969], p. 189).

V. Authorship.–There is no available evidence to enable us to decide who wrote Esther. The suggestion that Mordecai himself did so, which may have been prompted by 9:20, is without any good foundation. In fact, Mordecai probably died before the book was written, although 10:3 does not necessarily imply this.

VI. Date.–The outside limits are obviously the reign of Ahasuerus (if he was Xerxes I, then the first half of the 5th cent. B.C.) and the date of the first extant quotation from or allusion to the book. The *terminus ante quem* is not easily determined, however. Neither the Qumrân Scrolls (to date) nor the NT documents reveal any knowledge of Esther. Josephus, on the other hand, at the end of the 1st cent. A.D., knew the LXX form of the book well — including the additions, which obviously postdate the composition of the Hebrew original — and apparently thought it canonical. The Jamnia discussions too make it clear that the book had received general recognition by the end of the 1st cent. A.D. The earliest evidence of the existence of Esther is the LXX, which may give us a second-century B.C. date as the *terminus ante quem.* On the other hand, Sirach (Ecclesiasticus, early 2nd cent. B.C.) fails to mention Esther and Mordecai in its list of biblical heroes; but the value of such negative evidence is uncertain. *See* Plate 25.

A. Internal Evidence. The book itself strongly suggests that it was written before the fall of the Persian empire. The reference to the Persian royal chronicles in 10:2 certainly implies that they were still accessible. Whereas the reign of Ahasuerus was probably past, the book reveals no hint of knowledge of any but a Persian administration. It is also noteworthy that although Persian loanwords appear in the Hebrew text, there are no borrowings from Greek, nor do any Greek personal names appear. A date prior to the fall of the Persian empire to Alexander the Great (331 B.C.) is therefore strongly indicated.

B. Maccabean Theory. The strong nationalistic feelings of the author and the anti-Semitic situation described in Esther have led a considerable number of scholars (e.g., *PIOT,* pp. 740-42) to conclude that it cannot have been written till after the Maccabean revolt against Antiochus Epiphanes. Haman, on this view, is but a caricature of Antiochus. But the details of the story are totally different from the Maccabean situation; and it is probable that anti-Semitism and Jewish nationalism existed prior to the reign of Antiochus (175-163 B.C.).

VII. Nature and Purpose.–The book of Esther has been variously described as history, fiction, and mythology. Numerous scholars (e.g., L. E. Browne, *s.v., Peake's Comm. on the Bible* [rev. ed. 1962]) call it a historical novel or romance. However, there seems to be a growing tendency to believe that there is at least a historical basis for the story, even when some of the details are regarded as fictional embellishments (so, e.g., B. W. Anderson, *Understanding the OT* [1957], pp. 504-508). The purpose of the book may have been merely to tell a story (whether true or fictional); but most scholars are agreed that the main function was to explain the origin of the PURIM festival and to authorize its continued observance. R. H. Pfeiffer's view (*PIOT,* pp. 737-747) that Purim, together with the story as a whole, was invented by the author, has gained little support.

The view of it as mythological is based on the similarity of the names of the chief characters in Esther to the names of some Babylonian and Elamite deities. Mordecai is equated with the god of Babylon, Marduk, and Esther herself with the goddess Ishtar (who was Marduk's cousin), while Haman and Vashti are the Elamite deities Humman and Mashti (cf. L. P. Paton, *Esther* [*ICC*, 1905], p. 88). Furthermore H. Zimmern (*ZAW*, 11 [1891], 157-169) derived "Purim" from the Babylonian *puḫru*, the assembly of the gods. On this theory, the story of Esther represents the victory of Babylonian gods over the Elamite deities. The coincidence of the names is curious, but of course personal names were very often theophorous (cf. the name "Baal" for a man, 1 Ch. 5:5). In any case, the discovery of a cuneiform text (cf. A. Ungnad, *ZAW*, 58 [1940/41], 240-44; 59 [1942/43], 219) referring to a court official of Xerxes I called Mardukâ would seem to rule out the mythological approach. It seems clear that Mordecai was a real person.

This cuneiform text also confirms the identification of Ahasuerus (Heb. *ʾaḥašwērôš*) with Xerxes I, who reigned 486-465 B.C. The LXX renders the name "Artaxerxes," and following this hint some scholars (e.g., J. Hoschander) have identified Ahasuerus with Artaxerxes II (404-358 B.C.). It is just possible that there was another courtier named Marduka or Mordecai at the latter king's court, but the balance of probability must now support Xerxes I as the king of the book of Esther.

VIII. Historicity.–The discovery of a historical person named Mardukâ in the reign of Xerxes I is the most important evidence available for defending the book's historicity. It is true, moreover, that "the author possessed an amazingly accurate knowledge of Persian palaces and manners" (B. W. Anderson). It is also noteworthy that while Vashti was deposed in the third regnal year of Xerxes, it was his seventh year before Esther became his queen; during the intervening period Xerxes assembled a large army and naval force and invaded Greece, where he suffered heavy defeats at Thermopylae and Salamis in his sixth year (480 B.C.). The dates given by the book of Esther thus dovetail neatly with the known dates of events of his reign; it is improbable that this is just a coincidence.

On the other hand, to view the whole book as history raises certain problems. The first of these is that the only queen of Xerxes known to the contemporary Greek historian Herodotus (vii.61, 114) was named Amestris, and she was the daughter of a Persian general. In spite of an apparent similarity of name, it is difficult to equate her with Esther. This problem is the more serious, in that according to Herodotus (iii.34) the Persian king was not free to marry any but a Persian. Another difficulty is the age of Mordecai: 2:6 seems to state that he had been one of the exiles removed from Jerusalem by Nebuchadrezzar (in 597 or 587 B.C.). This is not certain, however; Mordecai's great-grandfather Kish may be the antecedent of the relative pronoun "who" in 2:6. Even if the chronological error were proved, that in itself would not necessarily reflect on the truth of the narrative as a whole. But most of the problems are of a more subjective nature; several scholars feel that the book has too many coincidences and improbabilities. In view of these difficulties, it may be best to treat the book as basically historical, while recognizing the possibility of fictional embellishments, the extent of which cannot be accurately evaluated until we are in a position to consult the Persian records to which the book refers the reader in 10:2. The fact is that our knowledge of the Jews in the eastern Persian empire is very slight.

IX. Moral and Religious Problems.–The lack of religious sentiment and the book's exultation in the Jewish slaughter of their enemies have made it repugnant to not a few Christians and moralists. The first deficiency was certainly felt at an early stage by Jews themselves, hence the pious additions in the LXX. But probably the writer saw the outworkings of divine providence in the elevation of Esther and Mordecai to positions where they could rescue their fellow Jews. And in view of the strong feelings inevitably roused by anti-Semitism, Jewish exultation in the downfall of their persecutors is not surprising; the book was penned long before Jesus uttered His revolutionary words, "Love your enemies and pray for those who persecute you" (Mt. 5:44). The universal interests of the latter part of Isaiah and the book of Jonah certainly seem far loftier to us today; but Israel could not channel God's blessing to the whole world while her own continued existence was threatened. Evidently the spirit of the book of Esther is due to the circumstances under which it was written, a time when the Jewish race was in jeopardy. (Cf. the similar tone of the book of Ezra, also written at a time when the Jewish faith was in jeopardy.) The missionary spirit could flourish only when the nation was secure.

Bibliography.–Comms. by B. W. Anderson (*IB*, 1954); H. Gunkel (1916); L. B. Paton (*ICC*, repr. 1951); C. A. Moore (*AB*, 1971); A. W. Streane (*CBSC*, 1907); J. Hoschander, *Book of Esther in the Light of History* (1923); R. Murphy, *Wisdom Literature* (*Forms of the OT Literature*, 1981), pp. 151-170.

D. F. PAYNE

ESTIMATE. *See* VALUATION.

ESYELUS ē-sī-ē'ləs [Gk. *Ēsyēl, Esyēlos*] (RSV mg., NEB, 1 Esd. 1:8). *See* JEHIEL **6.**

ETAM ē'tam [Heb. *ʿêṭām*].

1. A place mentioned along with Tekoa, Bethlehem, and other towns in northern Judah (2 Ch. 11:6; Josh. 15:59, LXX, NEB; the authenticity of this latter passage, though missing in the MT, is favored because the district focuses on Bethlehem). It was evidently named after an important member of the tribe of Judah (1 Ch. 4:3). In 2 Ch. 11:6 it occurs between Bethlehem and Tekoa as one of the cities fortified by Rehoboam. Thus it was designed to play an important role in the defensive network established at that time.

Josephus describes "a certain spot two *schoinoi* [about 14 km. (9 mi.)] distant from Jerusalem, which is called Étan [Gk. *Ētán*], delightful for, and abounding in, parks and flowing streams, and to this place he [Solomon] would make excursions, mounted high on his chariot" (*Ant.* vii.7.3[186], *LCL*). Mention of ʿAitān, described as the most elevated place in the land, occurs in T.B. *Zebahim* 54b, and T.P. *Yoma* iii.41 states that a conduit ran from ʿAtān to the temple. Traces of this conduit remain; it may also have provided the water for the Roman bathhouse excavated at Ramat Raḥel, located between ʿAin ʿAitān and the Old City of Jerusalem.

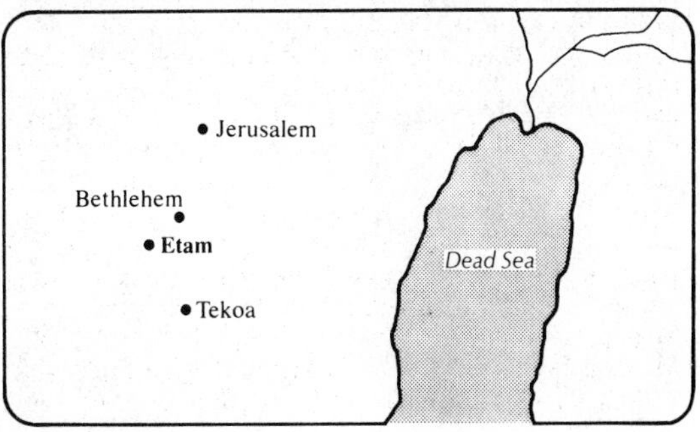

One of the five springs in the vicinity of present-day ʿArṭas still bears the name ʿAin ʿAitān; it is the lowest of the springs supplying the aqueduct leading to the so-called Pools of Solomon. These latter may very well date from the Herodian period; their location suits the description by Josephus. Their repair is attributed to Pontius Pilate (*Ant.* xviii.3.2; *BJ* ii.9.4). During Turkish rule, water from these pools was brought to Jerusalem via ten-centimeter (four-inch) pipes. After the capture of Jerusalem by Allenby in 1917, the British Army installed pumps for transferring the water to storage reservoirs in Jerusalem. Today ʿAin ʿAitān provides water for Bethlehem by pipeline.

During the Middle Ages the association of the pools with Solomon was bolstered by citing Eccl. 2:6. Opposite the upper pool are situated the ruins of a Turkish fort from the 17th or 18th cent., Qal ʿat el-Burak. Roman remains are also abundant in the vicinity of ʿArṭas. The OT town of Etam, however, is probably to be sought at Khirbet el-Khôkh.

2. A town assigned to Simeon (1 Ch. 4:32), though not mentioned in Simeon's inheritance according to Josh. 19. Its location is unknown.

3. The rock of Etam, where Samson took up his dwelling after smiting the Philistines "hip and thigh with great slaughter" (Jgs. 15:8, 11), was in Judah but apparently in the low hill country. The rocky hill on which lies the village of Beit ʿAtab, near Ṣarʿah (Zorah), was suggested by Conder, but unless **3** is really identical with **1**, which is quite possible, the cavern known as ʿArak Ismaʿin, described by Hanauer (*PEQ* [1886], p. 25), suits the requirements of the story better.

E. W. G. MASTERMAN A. F. RAINEY

ETERNAL [Heb. *ʿôlām* (Jer. 20:11; Eccl. 12:5), *qeḏem* (Dt. 33:27); Gk. *aiṓn* (Mt. 18:8; Mk. 3:29; Jn. 3:15; etc.), *aḯdios* (Rom. 1:20; Jude 6)]; AV also LONG (Eccl. 12:5), EVERLASTING; NEB also SHALL LONG BE (Jer. 20:11), AGE-LONG (Eph. 3:11), etc.; **EVERLASTING** [Heb. *ʿôlām* (Ps. 90:2; etc.), *ʿaḏ* (Isa. 9:5 [MT 4]), *qeḏem* (Hab. 1:12); Aram. *ʿālam* (Dnl. 7:14, 27; etc.)]; NEB also FROM OF OLD (Hab. 1:12); **FOR EVER** [Heb. *l*^{e}*ʿôlām* (Gen. 3:22; 6:3; etc.), *ʿaḏ* (Job 19:24; Ps. 9:18; etc.), *nēṣaḥ* (Ps. 13:1 [MT 2]; 74:10; etc.), *kol-hayyāmîm*–'all the days' (Gen. 43:9; Dt. 4:40; etc.); Gk. *aiṓn* (Lk. 1:33; Jn. 8:35; Eph. 3:21; etc.), *diēnekḗs* (He. 7:3)]; AV also FOR EVERMORE (Ps. 132:12); NEB also TO THE UTTERMOST (Isa. 28:28), BE ALWAYS (Ps. 9:18), etc.; **ALWAYS** [Heb. *kol-hayyāmîm* (Dt. 5:29; 1 K. 11:36; etc.), *tāmîḏ* (Ex. 25:30; 2 S. 9:7; etc.), *neṣaḥ* (Ps. 103:9; Isa. 57:16; etc.), *ʿôlām* (1 S. 27:12; Ps. 73:12), *t*^{e}*môl*–'before' (1 S. 21:5), *w*^{e}*lōʾ-yikkārēṯ*–'and it shall not be cut off' (Josh. 9:23); Gk. *pásas tás hēméras*–'all the days' (Mt. 28:20), *pántote* (Lk. 15:31; Jn. 6:34; etc.), *diá pantós* (Mt. 18:10), *en pásin* (2 Tim. 4:5), *aeí* (2 Cor. 4:11; Tit. 1:12; etc.)]; AV also ALWAY (Ex. 25:30; 2 S. 9:10; etc.), CONTINUALLY (2 S. 9:7, 13; Prov. 6:21), etc.; NEB also AT ALL TIMES (Dt. 6:24; 2 Tim. 4:5), "hitherto" (1 S. 21:5), "from year's end to year's end" (Dt. 11:12), etc. A duration of time, whether of time that endures without end, either of the past (Hab. 1:12) or future (Eccl. 12:5), or of time in a more limited sense, as of a lifetime (Dt. 15:17) or age (Gen. 49:26).

Terms often are repeated in the same phrase to express the concept of eternity, e.g., *ʿ*^{a}*ḏê-ʿaḏ* ("forever," Ps. 132:12), or synonyms are combined, e.g., *l*^{e}*ʿôlām wāʿeḏ* ("forever and ever," Ps. 9:5 [MT 6]; 10:16; etc.). Hebrew poetry often uses the terms in synonymous parallelism to achieve the same emphasis, e.g., in Gen. 49:26 and Hab. 3:6 the RSV translates *ʿaḏ* and *ʿôlām* as "eternal" and "everlasting."

In some cases, the NEB emends the MT, resulting in a different translation. In Dt. 33:27, e.g., "The eternal God is thy dwelling place" (RSV; MT *m*^{e}*ʿōnâ ʾ*^{e}*lōhê qeḏem*) becomes "who humbled the gods of old"; here the NEB reads Heb. *m*^{e}*ʿanneh,* the piel of *ʿānâ,* "be bowed down, afflicted, humble" (BDB, p. 776), and *ʾ*^{e}*lōhê* as referring not to the God of Israel but to pagan deities. The RSV "dwelling place" understands *m*^{e}*ʿōnâ* as a den or lair of wild beasts (BDB, p. 733); thus Israel ("Jeshurun") is compared to a wild animal (cf. 33:17, 20, 22, 27b). In Job 19:24 "graven in the rock forever" (RSV) becomes "to be a witness" in the NEB, based on the emendation of MT *lāʿaḏ* ("forever") to read *l*^{e}*ʿēḏ* ("for a witness") (cf. Theod.).

The use of *ʿôlām* and its synonyms in the OT provides the basis from which the later thought of intertestamental Judaism, Christianity, and rabbinic Judaism developed. The development in the use of such terms coincides with the development of eschatology in the postexilic and intertestamental period.

I. In the OT
  A. The Eternal God
  B. Destiny of the Righteous and the Wicked
II. In the Intertestamental Literature and the Dead Sea Scrolls
III. In the NT and Rabbinic Judaism
  A. In the Synoptic Gospels
  B. In the Johannine Tradition
  C. In the Pauline Epistles
  D. In Hebrews

***I. In the OT.**–A. The Eternal God.* The concept of God as an eternal being who has endured and will endure forever is a cornerstone for much OT thought. The psalmist ponders this idea and exclaims, "From everlasting to everlasting [*mēʿôlām ʿaḏ ʿôlām*] thou art God" (Ps. 90:2). For Isaiah, God is the "everlasting father" (*ʾ*^{a}*ḇî-ʿaḏ,* 9:5) and an "everlasting rock" (*ṣûr ʿôlāmîm,* 26:4). Habakkuk asks the rhetorical question, "Art thou not from everlasting?" (*miqqeḏem,* 1:12). The eternal nature of God and the transitory nature of man and other creatures are depicted in detail in Ps. 104. Because the God of Israel was believed to be eternal in nature, His decrees and attributes were also said to endure for ever. "His steadfast love endures for ever" (Ps. 136 *passim*). "The counsel of the Lord stands for ever" (33:11). The lamp outside the tent of meeting is to burn continuously (Ex. 27:20). This is a "statute for ever [*ḥuqqaṯ ʿôlām*] before the Lord" (v. 21; cf. Lev. 10:9; 16:29; etc.).

B. Destiny of the Righteous and the Wicked. The concept of a last judgment at which the fate of all humanity will be decided in regard to eternal life or resurrection is not clear in the earlier parts of the OT. In fact, some passages show a total lack of developed doctrine of the afterlife. The idea that God has any relationship with the dead is sometimes negated (e.g., Isa. 38:18; Ps. 88:11-13 [MT 12-14]; etc.).

Some passages, however, clearly imply a hope of fellowship with God after death: "But God will ransom my soul from the power of Sheol, for He will receive me" (Ps. 49:15 [MT 16]). The basis for an idea of the resurrection of the dead can be found in Isa. 26:19, even if the verse was originally intended to proclaim political restoration rather than physical revivification: "Thy dead shall live, their bodies shall rise. . . . For thy dew is a dew of light, and on the land of the shades thou wilt let it fall" (cf. Ps. 16:10; 73:24).

The idea of eternal punishment is likewise not thoroughly formulated in the OT. The story of the descent of Korah and his relatives into Sheol alive as a result of their rebellion against Moses certainly implies a retribution for evil deeds (Nu. 16:33). This passage led to rabbinic speculation about whether Korah and his family would be resurrected in the age to come (Mish. *Sanhedrin* x.3). Sheol, however, is not always seen as a place of repose for the wicked only. Job claims that the small and great are there, including infants who died at birth (Job 3:16-19). Certainly the wicked are to be the objects of God's wrath, both in this life and, implicitly, in the life hereafter: the Edomites are the objects of God's anger "for ever" (*'aḏ 'ôlām,* Mal. 1:4), Zophar reminds Job that the wicked "will perish for ever" (*lāneṣaḥ yō'ḇēḏ,* Job 20:7), etc.

The book of Daniel has a clearer view of the resurrection and afterlife. Although some (e.g., G. F. Moore, *Judaism* [1927], II, 295-99) have argued that such ideas were imported from Greek ideas of immortality common during the 3rd or 2nd cent. B.C., the book of Daniel may be dated *ca.* 400 B.C. (*see* ARAMAIC III; DANIEL, BOOK OF VIII). Dnl. 12:2 reads, "And many of those who sleep in the dust of the earth shall awake, some to everlasting life [*ḥayyê 'ôlām,* lit. "life of the age"] and some to everlasting contempt [*lᵉḏir'ôn 'ôlām*]." "Those who turn many to righteousness" will shine like the stars "for ever and ever" (*lᵉ'ôlām wā'eḏ,* 12:3). These are synonymous with "the saints of the most high" of 7:18, who will possess the kingdom "for ever, for ever and ever" (*'aḏ-'ālmā' wᵉ'aḏ 'ālam 'ālmayyā'*).

II. In the Intertestamental Literature and the Dead Sea Scrolls.–The use of "eternal," etc., in the intertestamental literature follows that of the OT, except that eternal destiny is much more sharply depicted. Thus in 1 En. 10:10 the "children of the watchers" and of fornicators hope to live an "eternal life" (Gk. *zōḗn aiṓnion*), but they will be destroyed. Other wicked individuals will be confined to an abyss of fire "for ever" (*aiṓnos,* 10:13). In contrast, martyrdom of the righteous Israelites results in resurrection: "The King of the universe will raise us up to an everlasting renewal of life" (*aiṓnion anabíosin zōḗs hēmás anastḗsei,* 2 Macc. 7:9). Wisd. 5:15 teaches, "The righteous will live for ever" (*eis tón aiṓna zṓsin*).

The intertestamental literature also shows the development of eschatological dualism: the differentiation between "this age" and "the age to come" (Ladd, *Presence of the Future,* p. 90). Thus 4 Ezra 7:50 teaches, "The most high has not made one age but two," and 7:113, "But the Day of Judgment shall be the end of this age and the beginning of the eternal age that is to come" (cf. 2 Bar. 14:13; 15:8; Mish. *Aboth* iv.1; vi.4). This concept of the two ages forms the basis of eschatology in the NT and rabbinic Judaism.

The Hebrew vocabulary for "eternal," etc., is used frequently in the Dead Sea Scrolls. The God of the Qumrân covenanters continues to be the eternal God of the OT, as in 1QH 13:13: "You will remain for ever and ever" (*lᵉ'ôlᵉmê 'aḏ*). Ex. 15:17 is quoted in 4QFlor 1:3: "Yahweh is king for ever and ever" (*'ôlām wā'eḏ*). The attributes of God and the benefits He bestows are eternal. His loving mercy is bestowed "from eternity to eternity" (*mē'ôlām wᵉ'aḏ 'ôlām,* CD 3:20). He is able to bestow "eternal knowledge" (*bᵉḏa'aṯ 'ôlāmîm,* 1QS 2:3). The fate of the righteous and the wicked is sharply defined. The "sons of light" are contrasted with the "sons of darkness." The "spirit of light" and the "spirit of darkness" characterize these groups (1QS 4:1). God loves the spirit of light "for all eternity" (*'ᵃḏē 'ôlāmîm*) and He takes pleasure in its deeds "for ever" (*lā'aḏ*). But he hates the ways of the spirit of darkness "for ever" (*lāneṣaḥ*). One of the blessings of the "sons of truth" is "everlasting life" (*ḥayê nēṣaḥ*). But the reward of "walking in a spirit of deceit" (1QS 4:12f.) is "eternal perdition" (*lᵉšaḥaṯ 'ôlāmîm*) and "everlasting terror" (*ḥerpaṯ 'aḏ*).

III. In the NT and Rabbinic Judaism.–Although the use of "eternal," etc., in the NT is derived primarily from OT material, it takes on a new significance since it is intimately related to the Christology and eschatology of primitive Christianity.

A. In the Synoptic Gospels. The Synoptic tradition reflects the influence of intertestamental Judaism, which developed the terminology of "this age" and "the age to come." In Lk. 18:18-30, e.g., the opening question, "What must I do to inherit eternal life?" demonstrates the desire among Jews to obtain the life of the age to come. Jesus' reply is that one must not only obey the Decalogue (18:20) but also follow Him in discipleship (18:22). The person who does so "will receive manifold more in this time [*en tǭ kairǭ toútǭ*] and, in the age to come, eternal life" (*en tǭ aiṓni tǭ erchoménǭ zōḗn aiṓnion,* 18:30). Obtaining the life of the age to come is synonymous with resurrection from the dead (cf. Mish. *Sanhedrin* x.1-3). The difference between rabbinic thought and the Synoptic tradition is the element of Christian discipleship: it is by following Jesus that one obtains the life of the age to come (cf. Mk. 10:17-31; Mt. 19:16-30; Lk. 10:25-28; 16:8f.).

The fate of the wicked is clearly demarcated in the NT. The wicked are destined for the "eternal fire" (*tó pýr tó aiṓnion*) along with the devil and his angels (Mt. 25:41; cf. 18:8f.). He who attributes the works of the Spirit of the God to Satan, blaspheming the Holy Spirit, assures himself of such a fate, for he becomes guilty of an "eternal sin" (*aiōníou hamartḗmatos,* Mk. 3:29). The Matthaean account more clearly illustrates the Synoptic eschatology (Mt. 12:22-32). Jesus' ability to cast out demons demonstrates that He is indeed the son of David (v. 23), the servant-messiah of OT promise (vv. 18-21). As the Messiah, Jesus is the emissary of the kingdom of God, i.e., God's rule in this present age. He casts out demons by the power of the Spirit of God, proving that the kingdom has arrived (v. 28). The person who attributes such power to the devil has forgiveness neither in this age (*en toútǭ tǭ aiṓni*) nor in the age to come (*en tǭ méllonti,* v. 32). It is possible that this pronouncement represents part of Jesus' Halakah concerning those who are to be excluded from the age to come, in a manner similar to Mish. *Sanhedrin* x.1-4 (e.g., those who deny the resurrection, who say that the law is not from heaven, etc.).

B. In the Johannine Tradition. The Johannine concept of eternal life differs from the Synoptic view. Here eternal life is a present possession that is received when one believes in Jesus as the Messiah, the Son of God (Jn. 20:31). In John eternal life is totally christocentric: "Whoever believes in him may have eternal life" (3:15); "he who believes in the Son has eternal life: he who does not obey the Son shall not see life, but the wrath of God rests upon him" (v. 36); "you refuse to come to me that you may have life" (5:40); etc. According to the Johannine eschatology eternal life and eternal damnation are already a reality in this age (3:18). John's eschatology, however, does not differ totally from that of the Synoptics. Other elements of the eschatology of Pharisaic Judaism remain unchanged. Jn. 5:28f. contains a clear allusion to Dnl. 12:2, used as a proof text of the resurrection in T.B. *Rosh ha-Shanah* 16b, where the interpretation is attributed to the house of Shamai (*ca.* A.D. 10-80; H. Danby, *Mishnah* [1933], p. 799), and T.B. *Sanhedrin* 92a, where it is attributed to Raba and Rabina (4th cent.). John's view of eternal life continues to include a future blessing. This is clear in Jn. 12:25: "He who loves his life loses it, and he who hates his life in this world will keep it for eternal life [*eis zōḗn aiṓnion*]." Here the Jewish concept of this age and the age to come, in which one can enjoy the "life of the age," is set forth even more clearly than in the Synoptics.

C. In the Pauline Epistles. The concept of eternal life in the Pauline tradition bears similarities both to the Synoptics and to the Johannine writings. Paul shares with the Synoptics the Jewish eschatological dualism of the two ages. Christ has been exalted above all other authority, "not only in this age [*en tǭ aiṓni toútǭ*] but also in that which is to come [*en tǭ méllonti*]" (Eph. 1:21). Although this is the only place the full idiom appears, Paul frequently uses the expression "this age" (1 Cor. 1:20; 2:6; 2 Cor. 4:4; etc.) and also the phrase "the day of the Lord" (1 Thess. 5:2; 2 Thess. 2:2; etc.), a common OT expression. "In this basic eschatological structure of the two ages, divided by the day of the Lord . . . Paul agrees with the Old Testament perspective as developed in apocalyptic Judaism and found also in the Gospels" (Ladd, *Theology*, p. 365). In Paul, as in John, eternal life is christocentric: "As in Adam all die, so also in Christ shall all be made alive" (1 Cor. 15:22). Eternal life is a present reality which endures into the age to come. The Christian has been brought out of death into life (Eph. 2:1), but looks forward to the inheritance of eternal life (Gal. 6:8). Those who disobey the gospel, however, shall suffer "eternal destruction and exclusion from the presence of the Lord" (2 Thess. 1:9).

D. In Hebrews. The writer to the Hebrews uses the concept "eternal" frequently, usually in the exposition of his Christology. Faced with an audience that was lapsing back into the practices of Judaism, the author develops the theme of the eternal salvation accomplished by Christ, in contrast to the OT covenant which was intended to be only temporal. Jesus through suffering became the source of "eternal salvation" (5:9). He entered into the heavenly holy place upon His ascension, securing an "eternal redemption" (9:12). Jesus was appointed high priest as was Melchizedek in the OT. The author refers to Ps. 110:4 three times (He. 5:6; 6:20; 7:17) to stress this point: "Thou art a priest for ever." The eternal priesthood of Jesus contrasts with that of the Levites, which was temporary (7:11-27). Jesus is exalted in the heavens and is equal to God Himself: "Thy throne, O God, is for ever and ever" (1:8); and He remains enthroned forever (13:8).

See also AGE; ESCHATOLOGY; ETERNITY.

Bibliography.–J. Barr, *Biblical Words for Time* (2nd ed. 1969); G. E. Ladd, *Presence of the Future* (1974 = 2nd ed. of *Jesus and the Kingdom*); *Theology of the NT* (1974); *TDNT*, I, *s.v.* αἰών, αἰώνιος (Sasse). R. J. W.

ETERNITY. For Christians eternity must be defined in accord with biblical and not philosophical categories. While philosophical reflection may clarify such notions as "time" and "infinity," only a careful attempt to understand the concept of eternity as it is used by the authors of Scripture will enable us to grasp the significance of eternity in a specifically Christian, i.e., biblical, sense. This is because only such an exegetical approach will allow us to understand eternity within the larger context of God's redemptive activity, which occurs within the space-time continuum of our universe. This larger context is accessible only through the study of the self-revelation of God contained in the Bible

It should first be noted that eternity is not simply an abstract term in the biblical writings. Rather, it refers to one aspect of God's multifaceted nature, that of the endless duration of His being or existence. At the same time, though not bound by time as are finite creatures, God nevertheless reveals Himself through His redemptive acts, which occur on the same spatio-temporal stage as the one on which we play out our own lives. God, who is thus the Lord of time, is able to act in time. Further, it is because of this very divine transcendence over time that the eternity of the divine being and the eternity of man are qualitatively the same. Man eschatologically and God ontologically experience an endless duration of time; both experience a non-terminating sequence of events; both participate in eternity.

Two distinctions, however, between God's eternity and man's eternity must also be acknowledged. (1) Quantitatively, a person's eternity is bounded on one side by its beginning at a point in time. The human experience of eternity begins at an as-yet-undefined moment between conception and birth. In a similar way the NT speaks soteriologically of "eternal life" beginning at the time of regeneration (cf. Tit. 3:5-7). In such passages eternity in the sense of eternal life, i.e., the life characteristic of the age to come, becomes an immediate possession even though a full and complete experience of that life, that eternity, awaits the coming of Jesus at the Parousia. (2) In this way the chronological, quantitative aspect of the terminology shifts to the qualitative. Eternal life is distinguished from the life of this age not only by its endless duration but even more significantly by the superlative character of the existence enjoyed by the redeemed. This qualitative distinction which eternity often connotes is discernible in those references in the text which speak of the eternity of God. Here eternity is sometimes used apart from its temporal meaning of "unending time" and instead represents the nontemporal idea of "God over all," i.e., His immutability and glory (Isa. 40:28). But here we should be wary of construing God's eternity as some sort of metaphysical timelessness.

I. Eternity in the Greek Philosophical Tradition.–In Platonic and Hellenistic thought eternity was often conceived of as timelessness. According to this tradition man's final goal is to seek to escape from time into timelessness, i.e., into eternity (cf. Plato *Phaedo* 79, 106e-108a; *Symposium* 208a; *Republic* 611a-b; *Timaeus* 27d-28a [contrast 37d]). Because this present life in time was conceived of as consisting of unbroken cycles of experience which afford no means of escape from the limitations of mortality and a life oppressed (cf. the Orphic tradition), redemption could be found only in a transcendent experience of eternity, which would be qualitatively superior to the experience of being in time. Since it was often held that time contained only reverberations of the eternal prototype or "idea," time could not be the stage upon which a redemptive act could occur. In this way a sharp distinction between time and eternity developed in Western thought. This dualism is generally accepted in contemporary philosophy.

From the biblical perspective such a dualism, which posits an exclusive and qualitative difference between time and eternity, is false. In the understanding of the writers of the OT and NT, eternity is not timelessness but endless time.

II. Eternity in the OT.–The OT has no special term for "eternity" that can be contrasted with a term denoting "temporality." The Hebrew word most often used to express "eternity" is *ʿôlām*. It is the same word that expresses duration of time, and it designates eternity only in such statements as "from *ʿôlām*" and "until *ʿôlām*" (Ps. 90:2). Its meaning also shifts from a quantitative/temporal sense of a long span of time to a qualitative sense conveying the idea of permanence or immutability (2 S. 23:5; Ps. 78:69). Use in this latter sense does not deny the essential temporal quality of all OT thought when *ʿôlām* is used. While this word can shift in meaning to the qualitative ideas of greatness, power, or transcendence when referring to God, it must be noted that these are qualities of God and are not implied in *ʿôlām* itself. Because the concept of God's uniqueness was established in the postexilic period, "eternity" became increasingly a synonym for "godliness" and soon became a symbol for God's world and His activity (Ps. 90:2; 102:12f., 25f.; Isa. 35:10; 60:15, 19f.; 61:7f.).

In the LXX the Gk. *aiṓn* translates the Heb. *ʿôlām*. *Aiṓn* conveys a number of meanings, ranging from "life" in Homer (e.g., *Od.* v.152) to "generation," "time," and "eternity" (cf. Pseudo-Demosthenes *Orationes* 60.6). The temporal idea is prominent. It refers to a period of time of either limited or unlimited duration. When unlimited duration is meant it should be translated "eternity." But even here no philosophically derived concept of eternity is connoted.

III. Eternity in the Intertestamental Literature.–The concept of eternity in the intertestamental Jewish literature quite closely parallels that of the OT. A prominent and characteristic feature of this literature is the dualism contrasting "this age" and the "coming age" (cf. 2 Esd. 7:50; 8:1; 2 Bar. 15:7). In this dualism both "this age" and "the coming age" are temporally conceived. The "coming age" may be eternity, but that is eternity in the sense of endless time (Sir. 18:9f.). Some writers of this literature even had difficulty imagining eternity as endless duration of time, rather than as a very long time. For example, 1 En. 10:10 represents eternal life as a span of five hundred years. About the time of Christ Greek influences penetrated this literature. The result was that the idea of an immediate escape from time into a timeless eternity was incorporated in certain writings (cf. 1 En. 37–71; 2 Enoch; Asm. M. 10:9ff.). In these writings a temporally oriented dualism of now and then is shifted to a metaphysical dualism of here and beyond.

IV. Eternity in the NT.–The NT, like the LXX, used Gk. *aiṓn* (translated "age") for eternity. This same word is used for a long but limited duration of time. The use of identical terms for both everlastingly continuing time and limited time emphasizes the notion of eternity as an endless succession of ages. Time is not demeaned in the NT, but rather exalted. The very terminology that refers to the mundane, earthly time of a limited duration also refers to the eternal God and the eternal experience of the Christian with God. The ultimate redemptive experience of which the NT knows, the eschatological consummation, is preserved and presented in a temporally oriented context. That is, Jesus appears at the close of "this age" and inaugurates the "age to come" on the plane of human history. This is so for a profound theological reason: God revealed Himself in time, not for the purpose of redeeming man from the evil of time, but rather to redeem man from the evil of this age or this world and from the evil of man's own life. Indeed, since time is not evil, time will not come to an end. (The well-known saying at Rev. 10:6 that there will be no more "time" [Gk. *chrónos*] does not refer to an era of timelessness. The context shows it means that there will be no more delay.) Time, then, did not first come into being in the fallen creation and so is not itself tinged with moral corruption. The NT representation is rather that God revealed Himself as a man limited to the fabric of created space and time so that man might be redeemed in time and not from time. (Apparently the view contrasting time and eternity, the view found in some intertestamental literature, never had a substantial impact on the NT.)

V. Eternity in Modern Philosophical Thought.–Basic to philosophical conceptions of eternity is the belief that the eternal belongs to another order of reality, that of timeless reality. Eternity is not to be defined in terms of time at all. God is the supratemporal *ens perfectissimum* (most perfect being); He experiences a mode of timeless self-existence as the Absolute Ground of the universe. To be sure, His timeless self-sufficiency and impassible aloofness are not such as to keep Him from being a source of strength and help in our temporal strivings — God's lordship over time is preserved. But the eternal cannot pass over into the temporal because an eternal Being who thinks all things as present and yet views the time sequence as a succession of states of consciousness is a self-contradiction. Thus for the Absolute Consciousness, time does not exist; the future cannot be thought of as beginning to be, nor the past as having ceased to be. For example, Spinoza used the term "eternity" to refer to God's infinite existence (*Ethica more geometrico,* propositions 8, 19, 21). Contingent or durational existence would not, in Spinoza's view, be eternal though it lasted forever. Neo-Kantian and neo-Hegelian philosophers follow this same conception by tending to regard metaphysical time conceptions as inappropriate categories for attempting to conceptualize the ultimate explanation of the universe. This fundamental qualitative distinction between time and eternity in modern philosophy harks back to the Platonic and Hellenistic conceptions that prevailed in classical and pagan philosophy before and during the formulation of the biblical texts.

VI. Summary Observations on Eternity.–Three summary observations must be made. (1) When viewed from the vantage point of the Bible, eternity is a term that includes temporal relations. Eternity is time stretching endlessly forward and backward, with the result that time itself must be regarded as a segment of eternity. Eternity may be best conceived of as a linear, goal-directed span of time that runs through this age, through the still-future events of the eschaton, and on into the coming age. ESCHATOLOGY is thus concerned not with the state of affairs subsequent to time but with the affairs and events connected with the termination of this age and the inauguration of the age to come. The entirety of redemptive history encompassing all of the ages can thus be located on a time line, the center point of which is Jesus Christ, who represents the ultimate validation of time and who Himself is the revelation of God in time, the *kairós* in the history of eternity (cf. Cullmann).

(2) This understanding of eternity is fundamentally important for grasping the biblical world view. To diverge from it is to diverge from the basic structure of redemptive history revealed in the Bible. Any nontemporal conception of eternity implies a docetism that results in a denigration of time and those events of redemptive significance that occurred in time, with a corollary emphasis on an eternity that becomes the exclusive and proper sphere for the life and redemptive work of God. It is beyond question that the biblical view of eternity as endless time is necessitated by, and intrinsic to, an incarnational theology. The divergence of this conception from Platonic and Hellenistic thought is not incidental or peripheral, but at the very heart of the biblical proclamation, and constitutes that miraculous and "new" thing that occurred in the 1st cent. A.D.: God became man in space and time.

(3) Finally it must be observed that while we may think philosophically about eternity if we so wish, we must do so cautiously. We are looking at these matters through darkened glasses. Everything divine, including God's eternity, can be seen only "from our point of view," i.e., from the revelation that came to us in Jesus Christ in the 1st cent. A.D. But "whatever ideas one may form concerning God's eternity 'in itself,' they must not destroy the characteristic perspective in which Primitive Christianity sees all revelation. This perspective is that of a point of time" (Cullmann, p. 66).

Human experience, human be-ing, is in time. However much we may try, we can only in small ways bring to understanding the unending time that characterizes the eternity of God. "From everlasting to everlasting thou art God" (Ps. 90:2). "I am the first and I am the last; besides me there is no god" (Isa. 44:6). "I am the first and the last, and the living one; I died, and behold I am alive for evermore" (Rev. 1:17f.).

Bibliography.–T. Boman, *Hebrew Thought Compared with Greek* (1960); F. H. Brabant, *Time and Eternity in Christian Thought* (1937); S. G. F. Brandon, *Time and Mankind* (1951); E. Brunner, *Das Ewige als Zukunft und Gegenwart* (1953), pp. 46-52; O. Cullmann, *Christ and Time* (Eng. tr. 1950); G. Delling, *Das Zeitverständnis im NT* (1940); M. Eliade, *Myth of the Eternal Return* (1954); J. Guitton, *Le Temps et l'éternité chez Plotin et Saint Augustin* (1933); E. Jenni, *ZAW,* 64 (1952), 197-248; 65 (1953), 1-35; J. Marsh, *Fulness of Time* (1952); *TDNT,* I, *s.v.* αἰών (H. Sasse).

C. R. SCHOONHOVEN

ETHAM ē'thəm [Heb. *'ēṯām*; Gk. *othṓm* (Ex. 13:20); *Bouthán* (Nu. 33:6f.); in 33:8 the LXX reads "in their wilderness," from another pointing for the word]. The name used to be explained as the Coptic *Atium,* "border of the Sea" (S. P. Tregelles, ed., *Gesenius' Hebrew and Chaldee Lexicon* [Eng. tr. 1846; repr. 1949], *s.v.*), which would agree with the MT in Nu. 33:8, where the "wilderness of Etham" is mentioned instead of that of Shur (Ex. 15:22) E of the Red Sea (*see* SHUR). At Etham (Ex. 13:20), the Hebrews camped on the "edge," or at "the end," of the desert W of the sea that they were to cross (*see* EXODUS, ROUTE OF THE). This camp was probably near the north end of the Bitter Lakes, not far from Succoth. H. Brugsch (*History of Egypt,* II [1879], 359) would compare Etham with the Egyptian *ḫetam* ("fort"), but the Hebrew word has no guttural. The word *ḫetam* is not the name of a place and more than one such "fort" seems to be mentioned. In the reign of Seti II a scribe's report (cf. *ANET,* p. 259) mentions the pursuit of two servants, apparently from Zoan, to the fortress of Ṯeku southward, reaching *ḫetam* on the third day; but if this was the *ḫetam* of Ramses II, or even that of Merneptah, it would not apparently suit the position of Etham.

C. R. CONDER

ETHAN ē'thən [Heb. *'êṯān*–'firm,' 'enduring'; Gk. *Haitham, Aitham, Aithan*].

1. A wise man with whom Solomon is compared (1 K. 4:31 [MT 5:11]). Called there "Ethan the Ezrahite," to whom the title of Ps. 89 (MT v. 1) ascribes the authorship of that Psalm.

2. A son of Kishi or of Kushaiah, of the Merari branch of the Levites; and, along with Heman and Asaph, placed by David over the service of song (1 Ch. 6:44 [MT 29]; 15:17, 19). *See* JEDUTHUN.

3. An ancestor of Asaph of the Gershomite branch of the Levites (1 Ch. 6:42).

4. A descendant of Zerah son of Judah, and ancestor of Azariah (1 Ch. 2:6, 8). His link with Heman and Calcol has led some (e.g., KD) to identify him with **1.**

5. (2 Esd. 14:24, NEB). *See* ETHANUS.

ETHANIM eth'ə-nim [Heb. *'ēṯānîm*]. The seventh month of the Jewish year (1 K. 8:2), later called Tishri. The word is of Phoenician origin and signifies "perennial," referring to the streams that still contained water during this dry month. It corresponds to September-October. *See* CALENDAR.

ETHANUS e-thā'nəs [Lat. *Echanus*]; AV ECANUS; NEB ETHAN. One of the scribes who wrote for forty days at the dictation of Ezra (2 Esd. 14:24).

ETHBAAL eth-bā'əl, eth'bə-al [Heb. *'eṯbaʿal*–'with Baal']. "King of the Sidonians" and father of Jezebel, whom Ahab king of Israel married (1 K. 16:31). According to Josephus (*CAp* i.18 [123]), Menander identified *Ithobalos* (his spelling of Ethbaal) as "the priest of Astarte," who assumed the throne by murdering the king, Pheles, and reigned over Tyre and Sidon for thirty-two years. Menander is also quoted as saying that "under him, there was a want of rain from the month Hyperberetaios till the month Hyperberetaios of the year following" (Josephus *Ant.* viii.13.2 [324]). This was the same drought that occurred during the reign of Ahab (1 K. 17).

ETHER ē'thər [Heb. *ʿeṯer*–'perfume'].

1. A place between Libnah and Beit Jibrîn, one of a group of nine cities in the plain of Judah (Josh. 15:42). Its location is perhaps modern Khirbet el-ʿAter, about 6 km. (4 mi.) N of Lachish (Tell ed-Duweir).

2. A village assigned to Simeon (Josh. 19:7), probably modern Khirbet ʿAttîr, about 13 km. (8 mi.) N of Beer-sheba.

ETHICS.

TERMINOLOGY
OT ETHICS
THE ETHIC OF JESUS
NT ETHICS
PHILOSOPHICAL ETHICS
ETHICS AND DOGMATICS
MODERN PROBLEMS

TERMINOLOGY

Ethics is a vast and comprehensive subject constituting one of the main branches of theological study. Nevertheless, it has a slender linguistic base in the Bible. The word "ethics" derives from Gk. *éthos,* which in ordinary Greek usage has two related senses: habit or custom, and cultic ordinance or law. These can, of course, cover the whole range of human behavior. Hence it is no surprise that when customs and ordinances come under academic scrutiny, "ethics" can take on the significance that it does in Greek and later thought, that of the science of conduct. Jewish usage contributes nothing essentially different. A link is made with the OT, however, when the LXX employs *éthos* for Jewish law in 2 Macc. 11:25. Josephus gives the term a more specifically cultic reference when he uses it for the OT sacrifices (*Ant.* xv.8.4 [288]).

The NT preserves the normal secular use at Acts 25:16, referring to a practice or custom in Roman law whereby an accused person must be confronted by his accusers and have the chance to answer them. The same may well be true at 1 Cor. 15:33, where Paul argues that "bad company ruins good manners." Some exegetes and translators (e.g., RSV) prefer "morals" to "manners" in this context.

The other NT instances all have a religious slant, whether with reference to the OT cults, the law in general, or the practice of individual piety.

Thus in the Lucan Infancy stories, with their OT background, the "customs" mentioned at 1:9 and 2:42 are those of the regulated cultic life of the Jewish community. Zacharias, the father of John the Baptist, fulfils his duties at the temple "according to the custom of the priesthood." The parents of Jesus go with him to Jerusalem to keep the Passover feast "according to the custom."

In various passages in Acts, where there is tension between expanding Christianity and Judaism, the word is then used for the (cultic) law as a whole. Stephen, for example, is said to have taught that Jesus would change the rites or customs established by Moses (6:14). The Judaizers in Antioch argue that believers cannot be saved unless they are circumcised "according to the custom of Moses" (15:1). Paul is warned that he is suspected of

ETHICS: OT ETHICS

advocating that the Jews forsake Moses, neglect circumcision, and not observe the customs (21:21). Paul himself, in his speech before Agrippa, attributes to the king expertise in all Jewish "customs and controversies" (26:3). At Philippi Paul and Silas, as Jews, are rather oddly accused of sponsoring "customs which it is not lawful for us Romans to accept or practice" (16:21). Finally, in his discussion with the Jewish leaders in Rome, Paul says that he has been accused, and sent as a prisoner to Rome, even though he has done nothing contrary to "the customs of the fathers" (28:17).

For more specific usage one might turn to Jn. 19:40. Here Joseph of Arimathea and Nicodemus behave "ethically" by binding the body of Jesus in linen cloths and with spices according to "the burial custom" of the Jews — a practice not without religious significance. In Lk. 22:39, when Jesus follows his "custom" of going to the Mt. of Olives to pray, he observes an individual practice of piety, although one that has its roots in the law. The custom of individuals may sometimes be a bad one. Thus He. 10:25 issues a warning against neglecting to meet together, as is "the habit of some." Different Greek words are used for "custom" at Mk. 10:1 (*éthō*; cf. Mt. 27:15), Lk. 4:16 and Acts 17:2 (*eiōthós*), and Jn. 18:39 (*synḗtheia*; cf. 1 Cor. 11:16), but they come from the same root and have essentially the same meaning.

The movement from the original meaning of "ethics" to its use for the study of human behavior does not take place in Scripture or, indeed, in the earliest Christian writings. From the OT and NT standpoint the things that believers should do are laid down by God and have their basis in His word and work. Customs and conduct may be the subject of theological reflection and in this sense one might properly speak of biblical ethics. In contrast, no place exists in Scripture for ethics in the sense of philosophical analysis and construction. G. W. B.

OT Ethics

- I. Introduction: Dangers of Oversimplification
  - A. The Scope of the Material
  - B. The Complexity of Israel's Society
  - C. The Perspective of Christian Faith
- II. Sources of Ethical Conviction
  - A. Worship
    1. Ethics of Response
    2. Ethics of Imitation
  - B. Law
    1. Law as Story
    2. Law as Statute
       - a. Decalogue
       - b. Covenant Code
       - c. Deuteronomic Code
       - d. Holiness Code
       - e. Prophetic Summaries
  - C. Wisdom
    1. Contrasts with Law
    2. Similarities to Law
    3. Unique Contributions
- III. Centrality of the Divine Relationship
  - A. Divine Will
  - B. Divine Enablement
  - C. Divine Sanction
  - D. Divine Mission
  - E. Divine Preparation
- IV. Limitations and Uniqueness
  - A. Limitations
    1. Social Structures
    2. Politics
    3. Law
    4. Motivation
  - B. Uniqueness
    1. One Will
    2. Communal Context
- V. Apocryphal and Apocalyptic Writings

I. Introduction: Dangers of Oversimplification.–Like other topics that span the OT, ethics tempts us to oversimplification. Several factors dictate the need for caution.

A. The Scope of the Material. The OT material presents both chronological and hermeneutical difficulties. Chronologically, questions arise in the dating of the law codes and the statutes within them — about seven hundred years are thought by some to be bridged in the development of the legal corpus. Similarly, though the wisdom books — Job, Proverbs, Ecclesiastes, Canticles — were perhaps composed in the exilic and postexilic periods, they contain ethical standards that reach back into Israel's antiquity. Hermeneutically, we face the problem of literary genres — narratives, various forms of laws (e.g., apodictic, casuistic) and proverbs (e.g., exhortations, descriptions, comparisons), oracles, visions of judgment, etc. — each of which has its peculiar way of conveying its ethical teaching. Moreover, it is not always possible to tell whether the ethical standards expressed in these various literary forms are to be understood as ideals toward which the people strove or as regulations that were enforced.

B. The Complexity of Israel's Society. Anthropologists warn against the oversimplification of OT tribal life and customs. To what extent a structure of social classes prevailed, with differing standards of conduct, is not clear. Though much of the teaching in Proverbs and Ecclesiastes seems to be directed toward a moneyed or landed class, the OT does not reflect the well-defined social layering of, e.g., Hammurabi's Code. Where class may be a factor, the OT seems to place a greater weight on the shoulders of the noble, powerful, and wealthy, who are made to bear the greater judgment for their ethical failures (Hos. 5:1; Am. 7:7-17).

C. The Perspective of Christian Faith. Often Christians puzzle over the application of OT ethical teachings. Have OT norms been completely superseded and thereby made obsolete by NT teachings? To what extent may one read NT teachings back into OT ethical instructions and thus claim them for Christian life?

These reminders of our distance in time and culture from the OT suggest humility and caution in approaching the basic questions: What factors governed the ethical practices of the people of God in the OT period? What contributions do these practices make to Christian conduct today? The complexity should neither be minimized nor allowed to paralyze us into silence. The subject can be pursued under three main headings: the sources of ethical conviction; the centrality of the divine relationship; the limitations and uniqueness of OT ethical instruction.

II. Sources of Ethical Conviction.–Basically, the OT has only one source of ethical teaching: the will of Yahweh for the people He has created and with whom He has made covenant. Yet that divine will is expressed in at least three significant ways: worship, law, and wisdom.

A. Worship. 1. Ethics of Response. In the OT, ethics is a response to the redeeming and creating work of Yahweh. Obedience to Yahweh is an act of gratitude and obligation for His providence and grace. The Decalogue sets the pattern. Yahweh announces His act of rescue and calls for the exclusive adoration and obedience of His people (Ex. 20:1-17; Dt. 5:6-21), summed up in the great commandment: "You shall love the Lord your God with all your heart, and with all your soul, and with all your might" (Dt. 6:5). Love is the ground of all other duties; "Love leads to fellowship and fellowship to service" (H. H. Rowley, *Faith of Israel* [1956], p. 135).

A cluster of literary forms demonstrates this ethics of response: covenant renewal ceremony (Josh. 24:1-28); ritual of firstfruits (Dt. 26); Psalms of entrance (15; 24); accusations or judgment speeches (Am. 2:9-16); divine complaints (Hos. 7:14-16; 10:11).

2. Ethics of Imitation. Israel's worship also called for an ethics of imitation: "God made man in His own image, and His essential law for man is that he shall reflect the image of God and become like Him in character" (H. H. Rowley, *Unity of the Bible* [1953], p. 77). Yahweh's holiness calls His people to holiness (Lev. 20:26); His attributes are to become theirs — love that fulfils its covenants (*ḥesed,* Ps. 136; Mic. 6:8), faithfulness that discharges its responsibilities (*'ᵉmûnâ,* Lam. 3:23; Prov. 28:20), truthfulness that is reliable (*'ᵉmet,* Ex. 34:6; Hos. 4:1). His social concerns are to be implemented in justice that both maintains a balanced order and seeks compassionately to correct abuses (*mišpāṭ,* Isa. 30:18; Mic. 6:8) and in righteousness that aims to conduct all its relationships with integrity and responsibility (*ṣeḏeq,* Ps. 35:24, 28; Dt. 1:16; *ṣᵉḏāqâ,* Mic. 7:9; Dt. 6:25). A sure test of covenant loyalty is whether God's people reflect His concerns for the neglected or exploited segments of society — the slave (Ex. 21:2-6; Dt. 15:12-18; Jer. 34:8-22), the poor (Isa. 29:19; Am. 2:7), the widow and orphan (Ps. 68:5 [MT 6]; Isa. 1:17), the resident alien (Ps. 146:9; Lev. 19:33f.).

Without this practice of imitation, worship is invalidated (Am. 5:21-24; Hos. 6:6): "the worth of worship, far from being absolute, is contingent upon moral living, and . . . when immorality prevails, worship is detestable" (A. Heschel, *The Prophets* [1962], p. 195).

Two other divine activities merit imitation: loving forgiveness of wrongs done by a neighbor (Ps. 103:8-18; Lev. 19:18), although the motivation for this is sometimes expressed more harshly (Prov. 25:21f.); willingness to suffer for a righteous cause (Isa. 50:4-10; Zec. 11). *"The God who suffers for the sake of men,* who was known to Hosea and Jeremiah, *is now balanced by the man who suffers in the service and commission of God"* (Eichrodt, *Theology,* p. 332).

Humility and delight become the experience of those who imitate Yahweh's holiness and character. God's awesome action in creation and history and His compelling compassion conspire to spark awed humility as well as gratitude. This humility is part of the required response to Yahweh's majestic grace (Mic. 6:8) and lies at the heart of the "fear of the Lord" that is "the beginning of wisdom" (Ps. 111:10). Simultaneously, God's joy (Ps. 104:31) kindles joy in His obedient people, who rejoice in His worship (Lev. 23:39f.) and delight in His law (Ps. 1:2; 119:111).

Gratitude and holiness are necessary results of worship; a supreme sin, then, is to *forget.* Both Hosea (2:13) and Jeremiah (2:32) brand forgetfulness as the source of other sins: "only because the present generation has forgotten God's deeds and gifts for Israel could such transgressions arise" (C. Westermann, *What Does the OT Say About God?* [1979], p. 55).

B. Law. The specific obligations of God's grace, which are themselves gracious, were a safeguard against such forgetfulness. In the broad sense of Torah (Heb. *tôrâ,* "instruction"), law includes both stories and statutes.

1. Law as Story. While the primary purpose of the patriarchal narratives is to depict God's saving deeds, they also convey ethical instruction — so they are *tôrâ* in the full sense of the word. They often illustrate upright behavior. Abraham is merciful to Lot, giving him the choice land (Gen. 13:8-13), compassionate toward Sodom's citizens despite their iniquity (18:22-33), humble and fair in his dealings with the Hittites (ch. 23), unselfish in his refusal of Amraphel's booty (14:21-24), and, finally, submissive to God's command to sacrifice Isaac (ch. 22). Joseph is resistant to the lures of Potiphar's wife, aware that adultery is "great wickedness . . . against God" (ch. 39). At the opposite extreme, human misconduct is also portrayed, as in the story of Jacob's dealings with Esau and Laban (chs. 27–31).

Similarly, the accounts of the establishment of the monarchy under Saul and David are alive with illustrations of good and bad conduct and the consequences of each (1–2 Samuel). Lesser known Israelites, e.g., Manoah and his wife (Jgs. 13), also serve as illustrations of ethical piety (Porteous, pp. 72f.).

2. Law as Statute. The statutes of the law were introduced into Israel's experience at the beginning of its existence as a nation. Prior to the Sinai encounter with God, the patriarchal families lived according to the tribal mores of their cultures except where their covenant with God dictated otherwise. Israel's establishment as a distinct political-religious entity under Moses called for legislation, setting the specific terms of their covenant with God and each other and stipulating appropriate penalties for transgressors.

The rugged terrain of Canaan made centralized authority difficult except under mighty monarchs like David and Solomon. The law, therefore, was the strongest force for building community. Justice was dispensed at the city gate, probably in the early morning (Am. 5:10, 15; Zeph. 3:5). Sharing in those deliberations was the pride of the respected elders (Job 29:7-25; cf. L. Köhler, pp. 125-149).

a. Decalogue. The most basic of law codes is the Decalogue (Ex. 20:1-17; Dt. 5:6-21). Its connection with Moses is well established. Its form is apodictic, a series of commands, usually negative, without much elaboration. Their force is highly personal — note the second person singular; their purpose is more to outlaw unacceptable conduct than to prescribe righteous acts; their scope is both religious and social — witnessing to the inextricable connection between OT religion and ethics: "Religion is not reduced to ethics. It is ethical religion because it expresses itself in ethical living, but it is religion because it springs from an experience of God and devotion to him" (H. H. Rowley, *Unity of the Bible* [1953], pp. 79f.). Flowing out of the exclusive worship of God — shunning idolatry and honoring His name and day — is the regard for human life, reputation, and property, summarized as love for neighbor (Lev. 19:18).

b. Covenant Code. The civil laws (e.g., Ex. 20:22–23:33, often called the Code of the Covenant) are generally casuistic in form, not apodictic. They propose representative cases, frequently introduced by "if" or "when." Where punishment is prescribed, it is commensurate to the crime — a form of *lex talionis,* which, though stern by modern standards, was a vast improvement over clan practices of excessive vengeance (e.g., Gen. 4:23f.). Designed for life in village and field, the laws protect the personal and property rights of society's every member by outlawing harm to the neighbor's family, goods, and animals.

c. Deuteronomic Code. Though some sets of statutes are clearly ceremonial (e.g., Ex. 34:17-26, "Ritual Decalogue") the Israelites made no clear distinction in law between the civil and the ceremonial. The Deuteronomic code (Dt. 12–26) mixes the two types of regulations with no discernible pattern: e.g., the call for judges who refuse bribes (16:18-20) is surrounded by regulations regarding feasts and a prohibition of pagan pillars; an outline of royal responsibility to enforce justice (17:14-20) is fol-

ETHICS: OT ETHICS

lowed by rules against divination; the barring of usury charges (23:19f.) is preceded by ritual laws for army life.

d. Holiness Code. Similarly, the Holiness Code (Lev. 17–26), among its stipulations of ritual purity, sets laws of reverence for parents (Lev. 19:3), of gleaning rights for poor and resident aliens (vv. 9f., 33f.), of abstinence from stealing, lying, oppression of neighbor, and abuse of deaf and blind (vv. 11-14), of justice without discrimination (vv. 15f.), of love for neighbor instead of revenge (vv. 17-19), of punishment for intercourse with a slave betrothed to another (vv. 20-22), of respect for aged persons (v. 32), of just weights and measures (vv. 35-37).

Again, the civil and ceremonial laws join in the Deuteronomic sabbath commands, where sabbath rest is extended to servants, sojourners, and animals as part of Israel's remembrance of Egyptian oppression (Dt. 5:12-15). In the various law codes, the one Lord, Sovereign of all of life, has laid down His demands for holiness, justice, and compassion. Though ritual law may label some areas of life as sacred and others as profane, Yahweh's dominion has no boundary.

e. Prophetic Summaries. The prophetic summaries of law (e.g., Am. 2:6-8; Hos. 4:2; Jer. 7:9) indicate Israel's accountability. Breach of these laws became the evidence for prophetic accusations against the people and the ground for announcements of judgment, which in effect invoked the curses threatened in Dt. 28:15-68 for violation of the covenant. The prophetic oracles of doom presuppose both Israel's knowledge of the law and its obligation to practice the law.

The expression of the will of the one God, Israel's law was an "unconditional obligation" (cf. W. Eichrodt, *Man in the OT* [Eng. tr., *SBT* 4, 1951], pp. 9-27), binding in every sphere, authoritative over every member — especially the most powerful, and beyond appeal to any court in heaven or earth. This obligation embraced motivation and action, attitude and deed, as the law against coveting (Ex. 20:17; Dt. 5:21) and the call to love God with the heart (Dt. 13:3) suggested. The prophets, in announcing God's judgment on Israel's failures, were not preaching novelty but reformation. Their cry was not "Go forward" but "Return." "They perceived . . . the glaring contrast between the way of life which God required of Israel and the way of life which resulted from compromise with the nature religion of Canaan" (Porteous, p. 56).

Tragically, the law was unevenly enforced throughout Israel's history. Kings (Ps. 72; 2 S. 12:5f.) and priests (Hos. 4:4-6; 5:1-4; 6:7-11) were particularly culpable, because of their responsibility to enforce and teach the law. The reforms of Jehoash (2 K. 12:1-16), Hezekiah (2 K. 18:1-8), and Josiah (2 K. 22:1–23:30) corrected that laxity in law enforcement.

C. Wisdom. Observation of order in creation and in experiences of society was another source of ethical conviction. The prophets were not unfamiliar with wisdom's methods (cf. Am. 3:3-8; 5:18-20; 6:12; Isa. 1:3; Jer. 8:4-7; 17:5-8, 11); but it is the wisdom books (Job, Proverbs, Ecclesiastes) that contain the main ethical teachings of Israel's sages.

1. Contrasts with Law. The contrasts between wisdom and law are apparent. Wisdom's moral dictates were dependent on observations of what actually happened in life, while law was ascribed to direct revelation. Wisdom's sanctions were blessings and woes that followed inevitably from good and bad conduct, whereas the sanctions of law were legal punishments that society imposed. Wisdom's focus was often twofold: both wise and foolish behaviors were described, with the contrast in results, i.e., "the two ways" of happiness or distress, whereas laws, whether positive or negative, did not regularly employ such a contrast (cf. Ex. 20:16 with Prov. 12:17).

2. Similarities to Law. Both law and wisdom used direct commands as a basic form; exhortations, both negative and positive (e.g., Prov. 24:1, 13, 15, 17, 27), resembled apodictic laws. There was also correspondence in ethical content: honor of father and mother (1:8; 19:26), refusal to bear false witness (6:19), abstention from adultery (6:20-35; 7:1-27), pursuit of just business practices (11:1), regard for the poor (13:23; 14:21, 31), consideration for animals (14:4), avoidance of bribery (15:27), proper use of power (16:12), justice in punishing wrong (17:26), reluctance to avenge (20:22), concern for the orphan (23:10f.), banning of usury (28:8), refusal to participate in bloodshed and theft (1:10-19).

Both wisdom and law stressed submission to God's will. For the sages that will was reflected chiefly in the orders of creation. They looked for patterns in society and nature that revealed Yahweh's demands and taught them as ethical norms but not mechanistically; they were open also to divine surprises: "A man's mind plans his way, but the Lord directs his steps" (Prov. 16:9). Such surprises call for submission, even when they carry loss, pain, and hardship, e.g., Job's experiences (cf. Pss. 49, 73).

3. Unique Contributions. As its contribution to the OT picture of the good life, wisdom made explicit the concern for personal dignity, humane values, and social stability implicit in the laws. Diligence in work (Prov. 10:4f.), refusal to hate (10:12), openness to correction (10:17), prudence in speech (10:31f.), humility of spirit (11:2), avoidance of gossip (11:12f.), generosity with wealth (11:24-26), commitment to truth-telling (12:19f., 22), discipline of children (13:24), patience of disposition (14:17), harmony in family life (17:1), comfort in friendship (18:24), temperance in drinking and eating (23:19-21), compassion for the grieving (25:20), and openness in personal relations (27:5f.) were among the virtues of those who showed their fear of God in all their dealings (1:7, 29-31; 2:1-5).

Part of that fear of Yahweh was the regard for the rights and abilities of women. Both adultery and lust were rejected (Job 31:1). The wise men's belief that "a prudent wife is from the Lord" (Prov. 19:14) became the theme played with variations in the ode to the devout and competent woman of Prov. 31:10-31, of which Eichrodt (*Theology,* p. 339) says: "If nothing like this is to be found anywhere else in the wisdom of the ancient Near East, then credit can only go to the Jewish belief in the Creator God, before whom man and woman stand in equal responsibility."

Worship, law, and wisdom all pledge allegiance to the will of the covenant Lord — the one true way to happiness. Any evolutionary approach to these three sources should be rejected; they represent three interrelated ways of discerning God's will, not three historical stages in its discovery.

III. Centrality of the Divine Relationship.–OT ethics can in no way be divorced from theology, because ethics is in the first place a statement about God — who He is, how He acts, what He values. Crucial, then, to obedience is fellowship with God: "ethical behaviour is a consequence of man's becoming fully personal through the realization of his immediate relationship to the will and purpose of God" (Porteous, p. 67).

Alien to the OT is any idea of abstract good, any imagined *summum bonum.* Good works are a response to God's personal authority as Creator (Gen. 1:26-28), King (Ps. 97:1), Husband (Hos. 2:16), Father (Hos. 11:1-4), Shepherd (Ps. 23:1), Judge (Gen. 18:25). These metaphors imply intimacy, as well as authority — intimacy that made possible the integrity of OT exemplars like Abraham and Joseph and that the prophets treasured as the knowledge (i.e., intimate fellowship; cf. Gen. 4:1) of God (Hos. 2:19f.; 4:1, 6; Jer. 2:8). So essential is this fellowship that it is frequently described with the most basic words possible: "life" or "live" (Dt. 5:33; 30:15, 19f.; 32:46f.; Am. 5:4, 6, 14). This ethic of relationship expresses itself in a variety of ways: the divine will, enablement, sanctions, mission, preparation.

A. Divine Will. The divine will aimed to bring unity to all of Israel's life. Israel's belief in one God (Dt. 6:4) spared it the fragmentation characteristic of pagan polytheism, which had various aspects of life under the vigilance of individual deities with narrowly specialized authority. Consequently, Israel's ethical obedience was to be a harmony of action and motive. Words alone were not enough (Am. 5:21-24; Isa. 29:13f.), for they had to be expressed in deeds; but deeds alone were not enough, for God wanted the allegiance of the heart by which the true issues of life were decided (Dt. 6:5f.; Prov. 4:23). Similarly, Israel's obedience embraced both communal and individual responsibilities, since the one Lord had formed both the community (Ps. 100:3) and the life of the person within it (Ps. 139:13-16). A common historical and spiritual destiny bound the nation together as a community accountable to God; at the same time each person was to be blessed or judged on the basis of covenantal loyalty (Ezk. 18; cf. Vriezen, pp. 382-87).

B. Divine Enablement. The divine enablement came first through the light of revelation, without which the people would founder in the tides of ethical confusion (Ps. 19:7-13 [MT 8-14]; 119). Beyond that, divine forgiveness and cleansing were essential if ethical perspective and power were to be restored to the one who had failed wretchedly (Ps. 51:6-11 [MT 8-13]). Moreover, a divinely renewed heart and spirit were required (Ps. 51:10-12 [MT 12-14]) — the kind of heart that God will give His people in the latter days (Jer. 31:31-34; Ezk. 36:26).

C. Divine Sanction. The divine sanction was indispensable: "for I will not acquit the wicked" (Ex. 23:7). At stake was God's holiness, the dignity of His name; the inevitable result of ethical transgression was punishment. The punishment, suited to the crime, took several forms: specific penalties to be exacted by the courts (e.g., Ex. 21:12-19); divine retribution in history for persons (2 K. 1:16), nations (Am. 1:3–2:3), or Israel (Jgs. 2:11-15), when God's law was violated — history being the arena of judgment (e.g., the Exile) as it was of redemption (e.g., the Exodus); harmful results of bad conduct, where the laws of creation, precious to the sages, overtake those who spurn the divine order (e.g., Prov. 8:35f.; 16:18; 24:30-34; Ps. 9:15f. [MT 16f.]; cf. G. von Rad, *Wisdom in Israel* [Eng. tr. 1972], pp. 124-137).

D. Divine Mission. The divine mission insisted on Israel's obedience. The Servant of the Lord, embodying what Israel was meant to be, was commissioned to establish justice as part of his mission to the world (Isa. 42:1-9), a reminder that Israel's righteous walk was not for her sake alone but that the world might know that Yahweh is God (cf. Köhler, p. 126).

E. Divine Preparation. The divine preparation for the NT is another role of OT ethics. The call to personal and social justice, the sanctity of family life, the submission to God's will, the imitation of His acts and attitudes, the esteem for the rights of all persons regardless of sex or station — all of these demands the NT made concrete Christian duties. Even more, they are all personified in the person of the incarnate Son, whose mission embraces the king's commitment to righteousness, the priest's skill in applying the law, the prophet's drive for renewal, the sage's use of wisdom, and the servant's willingness to suffer. Nowhere is the unity of the Bible more apparent than in the correspondence between the major themes of OT ethics and their enfleshment in Jesus.

IV. Limitations and Uniqueness.–*A. Limitations.* Limitations of OT ethical instruction are frequently pointed out in social structures, politics, law, and motivation.

1. Social Structures. The social limitations include the toleration of slavery and polygamy. The OT laws sought to control perversions of slavery prevalent in the cultures of Israel's neighbors: the covenant militated against the permanent enslaving of Israelites; a periodic pattern of emancipation was established (Ex. 21:1-4) though not always enforced (Jer. 34:8-22); foreign slaves may have been protected also; only for volunteers was lifelong servitude allowed (Ex. 21:5f.); special protection was afforded female slaves (Ex. 21:7-11). Despite these policies, slavery did exist without protest from law, prophecy, or wisdom. Polygamy was evidently at variance with the Edenic picture of partnership, which shared the image of God, exercised dominion over the creation (Gen. 1:26-30), and enjoyed the delights of love (Gen. 2:24f.); yet it seemed to be tolerated throughout the OT period. Both polygamy and slavery illustrate the ways that Israel's historical and cultural setting kept the people from applying their faith fully and consistently.

2. Politics. In the political sphere, while both neighbor and resident alien (sojourner or stranger) had their rights guarded in laws of love (Lev. 19:18, 33f.), political enemies, troops, or citizens of other nations were offered no such defense (cf. David's bloody victories in 2 S. 8; also imprecatory poems like Ps. 137). Yet even in warfare, certain humane prescriptions were to apply, e.g., in the treatment of female captives (Dt. 21:10-14). Further corrective to a crass nationalism was found in the stories of Ruth and Jonah, as well as in the universal concerns of Am. 1:3–2:3; 9:7.

3. Law. The dominant role of law in OT ethics made Israel susceptible to legalism, especially from Ezra's day onward. Laws, carefully codified and meticulously enforced, at times diverted Jewish attention from the living demands of the covenant Lord. Yet without such laws the Jews' uniqueness as God's people was prone to continual compromise.

One by-product of legalism was the temptation to casuistry — the tendency to "make the consciousness of sin an outward show" (Vriezen, p. 403). Because sinful acts are the chief basis of judgment, the attitude of the heart both in a firm commitment to righteousness and in a genuine contrition in repentance was sometimes overlooked, especially as ritualistic and cultic observations began to play a dominant role (cf. Isa. 29:13; Ps. 51).

4. Motivation. Two factors dealing with motivation should be noted. (1) The doctrine of rewards, especially in wisdom literature, often seems *eudaemonistic* — good deeds are done for the gain involved, not simply because they are right. (2) Commands to righteousness are viewed as *heteronomous* — their authority lies outside the person, who may be forced to behave in ways with which he does not inwardly concur. Though neither of these motivations may be ideal, each takes seriously the realities of human sin and the inevitable need for both incentive to and direction in righteous living. Two reminders: (1) though rewards are held out as encouragement to righteousness, *"in the last analysis, the fellowship with God granted in election and covenant-making was felt to be the goal of moral action more important than all individual goods"* (Eichrodt, *Theology,* p. 351); (2) the OT itself looks be-

ETHICS: THE ETHIC OF JESUS

yond the external demands of law to a time when "I will put my law within them, and I will write it upon their hearts. . . . And no longer shall each man teach his neighbor . . . for they shall all know me" (Jer. 31:33f.).

B. Uniqueness. Claims for uniqueness in OT ethics need careful stating, because in both content and sanction Israel's ethical standards often parallel those of its neighbors; cf., e.g., Mesopotamian and Hittite law codes and Egyptian wisdom literature.

1. One Will. The one will of Yahweh, the incomparable source of human values, was binding on every level of society from king to commoner. In a way not possible to polytheists, the people of Israel had to reckon with Yahweh's lordship over every area of life: the Creator is the Redeemer, who is the King, who is the Enabler, who is the Judge, who is the Rewarder.

2. Communal Context. The communal context is also part of the OT's ethical uniqueness. It was the immediacy of fellowship with the living God and the believing community that accounted for Israel's rich ethical contribution. Porteous (p. 60) has suggested that the prophets' ethical teaching could not have developed elsewhere, "because it is not just the communication of ideas, but it is rather the flowering of lives lived in conscious fellowship with God and within a human fellowship which had been created by Him as a special medium of His revelation."

V. Apocryphal and Apocalyptic Writings.–In the main, the approaches to ethics found in the Law, the Prophets, and the Writings are continued in the intertestamental period (cf. R. T. Herford, *Talmud and Apocrypha,* 1933). The same virtues are extolled and the same vices excoriated.

Yet a few discernible trends beyond those of the OT should be noted. Jesus ben Sira (Ecclesiasticus) links Wisdom to Torah (24:23) in a way unprecedented in the OT and thus strengthens the idea that the Israelites must reckon with the one will of God. Ben Sira also was the first to use the stories of OT heroes as ethical examples (44–50; cf. He. 11). Apocalyptic literature (e.g., 1 Enoch) drives the wisdom doctrine of the two ways to its relentless conclusion in the heavenly blessing of the righteous and the destruction of the wicked at the last day. The Testaments of the Twelve Patriarchs (T. Iss. 5:2; 7:6; T. Dan 5:3) join the two great commandments of love for God (Dt. 6:5) and neighbor (Lev. 19:18) in a manner that anticipates the words of Jesus (Mt. 22:37-40). The doctrines of resurrection and final judgment, hinted at (Pss. 49, 73) or briefly stated (Dnl. 12:1f.) in the OT, come into prominence in the Maccabean period and give the demands of morality an eternal dimension (2 Macc. 7:9, 14; 14:46; cf. also 2 Bar. 50–51; 2 Esd. 7; T. Jud. 25:1-4; T. Benj. 10:6-9; T. Zeb. 10:4; 1QH 6:29-34). In these matters as in so many others, the intertestamental writings prepare the way for the full revelation of Jesus and the apostles.

Bibliography.–J. Barton, *Journal for the Study of the OT,* 9 (1978), 44-64; R. E. Clements, *OT Theology* (1978), pp. 104-130; J. L. Crenshaw and J. T. Willis, eds., *Essays in OT Ethics* (1974); W. Eichrodt, *Theology of the OT,* II (Eng. tr. 1967), 316-379; J. Hempel, *Das Ethos des AT* (2nd ed. 1963); L. Köhler, *Hebrew Man* (Eng. tr. 1956); H. McKeating, *Journal for the Study of the OT,* 11 (1979), 57-72; N. W. Porteous, *Living the Mystery* (1967); P. van Imschoot, *Théologie de l'AT,* II (1956), 83-107; H. van Oyen, *Die Ethik des AT* (1967); T. C. Vriezen, *Outline of OT Theology* (Eng. tr., 2nd ed. 1970), pp. 377-404; H. W. Wolff, *Amos the Prophet — The Man and His Background* (1973); W. Zimmerli, *OT Theology in Outline* (Eng. tr. 1978), pp. 109-166. D. A. HUBBARD

THE ETHIC OF JESUS

I. Importance of Jesus' Ethic
II. Diversity of Interpretations
  A. Construing Jesus' Ethic
  B. Content of Jesus' Ethic
  C. Mode of Application
III. The Kingdom of God and Jesus' Ethic
  A. Apocalyptic Background
  B. Jesus' Revision of Apocalyptic
  C. An Ethic of Response
  D. Jesus and the Law
  E. The Politics of Jesus
IV. Validation of Jesus' Ethic

I. Importance of Jesus' Ethic.–The Church has always turned to the ethic of Jesus for moral guidance. Even before the NT was written, the sayings of Jesus circulated in the churches and shaped their moral life and thought. The authors of the Epistles and Gospels preserved existing traditions of Jesus' sayings and actively appropriated them, shaped them, and applied them in new contexts. Again and again in its history the Church has returned to the sayings of Jesus to discover in them the way of life worthy of the gospel.

II. Diversity of Interpretations.–While the importance of Jesus' ethic cannot be denied, neither can the diversity of interpretations it has received. Some order can be brought to this diversity by considering the variety of judgments about Jesus' teachings: (1) how to construe them, (2) their content, and (3) the mode and range of their application.

A. Construing Jesus' Ethic. Many construe Jesus' teachings as a new *law* that prescribes the conduct appropriate to the new covenant (e.g., H. Windisch, J. Knox, Thomas Jefferson, some Anabaptist writers). Many others construe Jesus' ethic as providing *ideals* to be sought rather than rules to be obeyed (e.g., N. Smyth, W. Rauschenbusch). Others insist that Jesus was concerned not so much with external acts as with the internal dispositions, the formation of *character* (e.g., L. H. Marshall, L. Dewar). Still others claim that "Jesus teaches no ethics at all" (R. Bultmann, *Jesus and the Word* [2nd ed. 1958], p. 66) in the sense of providing a morality, whether of precepts, ideals, or dispositions. Rather, He reveals a *reality* to which people must respond (e.g., H. R. Niebuhr, Bultmann).

B. Content of Jesus' Ethic. Those who share a certain judgment about how to construe Jesus' ethic may, nevertheless, differ significantly on the content of Jesus' moral teachings. Among those who construe Jesus' ethic as a new law, one finds, e.g., Jefferson's "sublime moral code," the prohibitions of violence, oaths, private property, etc., of some Anabaptists, and the identification of the new law with the love commandment (e.g., R. Niebuhr). Among those who agree that Jesus gives ideals, those ideals range from the ascetic (e.g., Thomas á Kempis), to personal moral development and consecration (Smyth), to an ideal social order (esp. Rauschenbusch). Those who take Jesus' ethic to be concerned with the formation of character do not always agree about which dispositions are to be formed. Finally, those who understand Jesus' teachings as the revelation of a reality can describe that reality quite differently. For Bultmann, for example, that reality is the individual person standing alone before the will of God and called to radical obedience in the crisis of decision. For H. R. Niebuhr, it is the one God who stands behind the law as Creator, Judge, and Redeemer.

C. Mode of Application. Already in the 2nd cent. a double standard was found within the teachings of Jesus, one standard being incumbent on all Christians, the second being only for those who sought a higher righteousness ("evangelical counsels"). Luther rejected this double standard, maintaining that Jesus' ethic is valid in its entirety for everyone; but for Luther it is valid only for private life. In Luther two realms with "two kinds of righteousness" remain, one for personal relations (the ethic of Jesus) and another for social relations (also, e.g., H. Cadbury). The Radical Reformers — and many others — rejected both monasticism's double standard and Luther's two realms and insisted that Jesus' teachings are applicable to the whole of life of all Christians.

More recently application has been affected by views of Jesus' eschatology. A. Schweitzer introduced the influential theory that Jesus taught a heroic "interim ethic" immediately applicable only on the mistaken assumption that the end of the world was imminent. According to some radical dispensationalists, Jesus' ethic applies to a future dispensation of the kingdom and only secondarily to the extended interim of this dispensation.

For some (e.g., Jefferson), Jesus' ethic, because of its apparent reasonableness, makes claims on the universal human community. Others think that His ethic makes no sense apart from loyalty to Him or from His loyalty to God, and thus it is applicable only to the Christian community. Finally, some see Jesus' ethic as intentionally impossible in order to reveal our sinfulness; thus, its application will ordinarily allow some form of compromise or approximation (e.g., R. Niebuhr).

III. The Kingdom of God and Jesus' Ethic.–The best starting-point for inquiry into Jesus' ethic is Mark's striking summary of Jesus' teaching, placed at the head of his account of Jesus' public ministry: "The time is fulfilled, and the kingdom of God is at hand; repent and believe the gospel" (Mk. 1:15).

A. Apocalyptic Background. Jesus' proclamation of the kingdom of God must be understood against the background of first-century Jewish apocalyptic (e.g., Perrin, pp. 158-206; Wilkens, pp. 72f.). Jesus announced to His contemporaries that the promised "age to come," the new age of God's undisputed sovereignty over all His creation, was "at hand."

Against this background, to interpret the kingdom as an ideal social order whose coming is contingent upon human striving is clearly a misunderstanding. The coming of the kingdom is contingent only on the apocalyptic, world-shattering, world-renewing act of God that brings both final judgment and final salvation. Its coming is not something human beings can either hasten or delay, but something for which they can only pray — as the Jews did in the Kaddish (see Jeremias, *NT Theology*), and as Jesus taught His disciples (cf. Lk. 11:2).

It is equally mistaken, however, to limit the kingdom to God's sovereignty in the mysterious region of the soul, for the coming act of God establishes His sovereignty over the whole cosmos. Jesus nowhere narrowed the scope of apocalyptic expectation to the mystical or pious or "existential" surrender of the heart to God. Surely repentance is demanded of individuals, but not only of individuals (cf., e.g., Mt. 11:20-24; 12:38-42; see III.E. below).

B. Jesus' Revision of Apocalyptic. Jesus came announcing that the kingdom of God was "at hand" and, indeed, already making its power felt. God's sovereignty was not merely future, but already having effect in Jesus' exorcisms and miracles — and also in His ethical teachings. Thus, both Schweitzer's "consistent eschatology," with its single focus on the imminent future of the kingdom of God, and C. H. Dodd's "realized eschatology," which emphasized the present reality of the kingdom to the point of dismissing Jesus' proclamation of the future act of God, are mistaken. Both the future act of God and its present impact are part of Jesus' teachings and of His ethic (see Perrin, pp. 74-78, 83f.; see also Kümmel).

Although the proclamation of the future act of God remains fundamental in Jesus' teaching, the present impact of the kingdom is critical, for it involves an important revision of apocalyptic thought. Apocalyptic typically divided history into two ages, of which this present evil age, although it is submissive to the powers of darkness, is nevertheless running its predetermined course to its eschatological end. Human action was therefore thought to be fruitless and inconsequential, and the apocalyptic seer was preoccupied simply with the discovery of epochs and the calculation of the end time. (*See* APOCALYPTIC LITERATURE II.) But Jesus did not indulge in such speculation and calculation (Lk. 17:20; Mk. 13:32 par.). Rather, He emphasized the suddenness of the end (e.g., Mt. 24:37-41 par.; Mk. 13:35 par.) and the present impact of God's sovereignty in His own ministry. His eschatological command to "watch" (Mk. 13:35 par.) has in the tradition a whole range of ethical cognates (Lk. 12:35-48; 21:34; Mt. 24:45–25:46; cf. 1 Thess. 5:2-8; 1 Pet. 5:1-10; see Minear, pp. 152-177). For Jesus the eschatological command to "watch" and His moral teachings have a common source in the coming sovereignty of God and His holy will. This kind of moral alertness is not required where casuistry on the basis of law neatly defines what is to be done and what left undone; it is required in ethics in which anger, lust, and pride are condemned with equal seriousness as murder and adultery.

Thus, while apocalyptic provides the background for Jesus' teaching, to reduce Jesus to an apocalyptic seer is a misunderstanding, for He broke through the pessimistic determinism of apocalyptic. While human action does not establish the kingdom, it is nevertheless called for as the eschatologically urgent response to the action of God which is at hand and already making its power felt. The ethic of Jesus is first of all, then, an ethic of response — response to God's apocalyptic action.

Jesus also revised the material content of apocalyptic expectation. He still expected the reign of God to bring liberation and security. He still expected a great reversal of the present age. But the nationalistic hope for Israel's lordship over the nations is strikingly absent (e.g., Lk. 4:16-29; Jeremias, *Jesus' Promise,* pp. 41-46). Moreover, the eschatological woes and blessings are pronounced upon the very people conventionally thought least likely to receive them: blessings are pronounced upon the poor, the hungry, those who weep and are despised (Lk. 6:20-22; cf. Mt. 5:1-12; Lk. 16:25); woes fall upon the rich and carefree (Lk. 6:24-26; cf. 16:25) and on the scribes and Pharisees who use religion to assert their reputations and financial interests (Mt. 23:13-36; Lk. 11:42-52; cf. Mk. 12:38-40; Mt. 6:16-18). In Jesus' ethic the "great reversal" of God's rule is condensed into axioms like "Many that are first will be last, and the last first" (Mk. 10:31; Lk. 13:30; Mt. 19:30; 20:8), and "Whoever exalts himself will be humbled, and whoever humbles himself will be exalted" (Mt. 23:12; Lk. 14:11; 18:14; cf. Mt. 18:4); thus it is clear that both the apocalyptic seer who dreamed of vengeance and the rabbi who insisted on the first seat in the synagogue (Lk. 11:43; Mk. 12:38-40 par.) belonged to the present evil age.

C. An Ethic of Response. The "great reversal" already made its power felt in Jesus. Blessings already began to fall on the poor, the weak, and the despised (e.g., Lk. 4:16-21; 7:22 par.; Mt. 10:7f.). Already those who were entrenched in power, privilege, and their own conventional righteousness began to be cast out (cf. Mk. 11:15-17). Jesus said, "Blessed is he who takes no offense at me" (Lk. 7:23; Mk. 11:6); that is, one's eschatological destiny hinges on one's response to God's rule as it is presently manifested in Jesus and His ministry (cf. Mk. 8:38 par.; Lk. 12:8 par.). The response called for is repentance (Mk.

ETHICS: THE ETHIC OF JESUS

1:15; etc.), a radical transformation of values and behavior. There were some who were scandalized by Jesus' reversal of values. They had no readiness to repent and so missed the eschatological blessing. But others, particularly among the outcasts and sinners, welcomed the proleptic presence of the kingdom in Jesus' ministry. These repented and were blessed. What repentance means concretely can be discovered only in the specific commands of Jesus that issue from His announcement of the kingdom, and from the kingdom's impact on His own behavior.

1. "Be Last of All." Repentance means to welcome the announcement of a kingdom where "many that are first will be last, and the last first." It means obedience to Jesus' concrete command of humble service: "If any would be first, he must be last of all and servant of all" (Mk. 9:35 par.; cf. 10:43f.). Such humble service does not assert its own rights and privileges but submits to the coming reign of God and pours itself out for the neighbor's good. One's response to this command is also a response to Jesus, who was among them both "as one who serves" (Lk. 22:27; cf. Jn. 13:2-17; Mt. 20:28; Mk. 10:45) and as the one in whom God's kingdom already exerts its power. This command takes a number of cognate forms, such as not insisting on titles of distinction (Mt. 23:8-10) or the most honorable seat (Lk. 14:7-11; cf. Jas. 2:2-4) and showing hospitality to "the poor, the lame, the blind" (Lk. 14:13, 21).

2. "Be Not Anxious." God's eschatological blessing falls on the poor, judgment on the rich. The response to this great reversal is a carefree disposition toward riches. Jesus' concrete instruction is "be not anxious" (Mt. 6:25, 31, 34; Lk. 12:22). Jesus Himself had "nowhere to lay His head" (Mt. 8:20 par. Lk. 9:58). His command forces a choice between the present age and the age to come, between serving mammon and serving God (Mt. 6:24; Lk. 16:13), between trusting the conventional patterns of privilege, prestige, power, and security, and trusting God (Mk. 10:23-25 par.). But to trust riches will soon be shown up as folly (Lk. 12:13-21), and to "be not anxious" is to lay up "treasures in heaven" (Mt. 6:20).

3. "Give Alms." This carefree attitude toward riches results in a readiness to give generously to help the poor — the other side of the response to the eschatological blessing on the poor. The concrete command is "Sell your possessions and give alms" (Lk. 12:33; Mk. 10:21 par.). This concrete command is not intended as legislation, as is made clear by the cognate command to lend to the poor (Lk. 6:34f.), which presupposes continuing possession, and also by the example of Zacchaeus (19:1-10); nevertheless, it does give concrete shape to repentance. To help the poor with self-forgetful generosity is to welcome God's coming rule (19:9), and not to do so is to expose oneself to His judgment (16:19-31; Mt. 25:31-36). Such generosity takes many concrete forms: feeding the hungry, giving the thirsty drink, practicing hospitality, clothing the naked, visiting the sick and imprisoned (Mt. 25:31-46).

Jesus' word, "You always have the poor with you" (Mk. 14:7; Mt. 26:11), does not compromise His concern for the poor. That "the poor will never cease out of the land" (Dt. 15:11) is caused by the refusal of the community to keep the covenant with its stipulations for the alleviation of poverty (15:1-11; cf. Lk. 16:29-31). Thus, Jesus rebuked the disciples for presumptuously singling out this woman and self-righteously judging her when the very presence of the poor was a judgment on the whole community.

4. "It Shall Not Be Taken from Her." The blessing on the poor and outcast extends to women. Against the background of the conventional depreciation of women in first-century Palestine (see P. Jewett, *Man as Male and Female* [1975], pp. 86-94), Jesus' behavior was indeed a great reversal. He broke convention simply by talking publicly with women (Jn. 4:1-26; Mk. 7:24-30; etc.) and by including them among His followers (Lk. 8:1-3; etc.). He commended women (e.g., Mk. 12:41 par.) and defended them (Lk. 7:39f.; Mk. 12:40 par.). Two women stand out: the sisters Mary and Martha (Lk. 10:38-42; Jn. 12:1-8). In each narrative Martha serves at table (itself a surprising departure from custom when a group of men are present), but Mary's behavior is shocking and offensive to conventional protocol regarding women. In John's narrative she lets down her hair to anoint Jesus' feet (cf. Lk. 7:38), and in Luke's she takes the posture of the disciple, sitting at Jesus' feet listening to His teachings (no rabbi would permit a woman to be taught). It is little wonder that women apparently heard Him gladly (cf. Lk. 11:27), or that it was women who remained faithful to Him at the hour of His death (Mk. 15:40f. par.; Jn. 19:25). While no explicit commands to welcome this aspect of the great reversal are preserved in Jesus' sayings (but cf. the protection of women by the prohibition of divorce, Mk. 10:11 par.), it is not unreasonable to assume that there were such; such a command may be echoed in the formulation, "the good portion . . .shall not be taken away from her" (Lk. 10:42). To respond to the coming kingdom and its present impact in Jesus means welcoming rather than resisting the good news for women.

5. "Forbid Them Not." The coming kingdom is also good news for children. The disciples' rebuke of the women who brought their children to Jesus was conventional; but Jesus welcomed the children and blessed them (Mk. 10:13-16 par.). "Forbid them not, for of such is the kingdom of God" (v. 14) is a concrete command that challenges both conventional expectations of the kingdom and customary rules of protocol. To care for and love little children is to welcome the coming kingdom and its present impact in Jesus (9:37 par.).

6. "Judge Not." Among the poor, finally, are to be numbered the "sinners." To include repentant sinners in the coming kingdom was scandalous, yet such is the great reversal Jesus announced: "I came not to call the righteous, but sinners" (Mk. 2:17 par.; cf. Mt. 21:31; Lk. 19:10). He was notorious as "the friend of the sinners" (Mt. 11:19; Lk. 7:34, 37, 39; 15:2; 19:7). He ate with them and (already!) forgave them (Mk. 2:5 par.; Lk. 7:48; cf. Jn. 5:21-27). But the "righteous" who refused to repent, who refused to welcome such a kingdom, were already judged, and that judgment was the announcement of the coming reversal itself (Mt. 21:31; Lk. 15:7; 18:9-14). The concrete meaning of welcoming such a kingdom is captured in the commands to "judge not" (Mt. 7:1; Lk. 6:37; cf. Mt. 7:24; Lk. 6:41f.; Mk. 4:24) and to "forgive" (Mt. 6:14f.; 18:21-35; Mk. 11:25; Lk. 17:3f.).

Jesus' prohibition of judging does not eliminate the need for discernment and mutual admonition. On the contrary, Jesus commanded His disciples, "If your brother sins, rebuke him" (Lk. 17:3; cf. Mt. 18:15-17). But such a rebuke is transformed from an attempt to find security in conventional righteousness into an effort to serve the coming kingdom and the sinner.

D. Jesus and the Law. While Jesus' ethic is fundamentally one of response rather than obedience to law, the question of His attitude to the law is of obvious importance to any description of His ethic. The question is complicated by the presence of apparent discrepancies in the tradition: some texts seem to disclose an almost rabbinic nomism (e.g., Mt. 5:17-19; 18:16; 23:2f.; Mk. 1:44; 7:9f.; 10:18f.; 12:28-34; Lk. 5:14; 16:27-31), others

ETHICS: THE ETHIC OF JESUS

a radical rejection of law (e.g., Mt. 5:31f., 38f.; Mk. 2:18–3:6; 7:14-23; 10:2-12; Lk. 6:37; 13:10-17; 14:1-16). It is little wonder that some interpretations represent Jesus as an exponent of the law who "exposits" it (sometimes, indeed, reaching new depths, penetrating behind the letter to the spiritual principle), while others view Him as an opponent of the law who abrogates it and disobeys it (see Banks, pp. 1-9). The Gospels themselves apparently interpret and communicate the attitude of Jesus to the law differently, relating it to their specific themes, intentions, and audiences (see Banks). But, while Mark may emphasize the "rejection" of the law and Matthew the "exposition" of the law, the apparently disparate attitudes of Jesus to the law may be found within both Gospels.

1. External Observance in Crisis. The key is again related to Jesus' proclamation that the kingdom is at hand and already making its power felt in His ministry. Because of this, observance that is merely external and legal is put in crisis. A casuistry which attempts merely to insure external observance is condemned, for it leaves the internal dispositions untouched (Mt. 15:17-20 par.; 23:25-28; Lk. 11:39-41). The coming kingdom forces something more radical than Halakah (the casuistic application of legal precepts), something more penetrating than certain limits set on the external expression of one's lust, lack of truthfulness, vengefulness, avarice, and pride. It demands the response of the whole person, and its proclamation uses the narratives of the Torah (especially of creation; see Mk. 10:2-12 and 2:27; Jn. 5:9f.), the Prophets, and the Writings — as well as mundane parables — to lay claim to and form the whole character. In Jewish categories, the announcement of the coming kingdom forces a shift of emphasis from Halakah to Haggadah — the homiletical, nonlegal part of the Talmud (see G. F. Moore, *Judaism,* I [1927], 161-173). Jesus upheld the law — not, however, by casuistry, but by bringing it to its eschatological fruition, so that the intentions of God in creation and in the Law and the Prophets are fulfilled.

2. Jesus' Authority. The coming kingdom already made its power felt in Jesus and His ministry. So the will of God was revealed finally not on the basis of ancient authorities but on the basis of the authority of Jesus' own words. His deeds expressed His consciousness of authority (explicit links are made between "authority" and His cleansing the temple [Mk. 11:28-33 par.], His exorcisms [Mk. 1:21-28, 39; Lk. 4:31-37], and His forgiving of sins [Mk. 2:10f.; Lk. 7:48]). His words were spoken with authority (cf. His use of *amḗn* and the emphatic *egṓ*). Indeed, it was this authority that amazed His hearers (Mk. 1:22 par.). Here was no pious interpreter of the law, but one who claimed to announce the will of God Himself. So Jesus set His own authority over against the authority of the law as the rabbis had interpreted it. His authority was connected with the apocalyptic sovereignty of God which was already making itself felt in Jesus' ministry, and with the apocalyptic revelation of God's will, which was now identified with Jesus Himself. Jesus' own words now took the place of the law (Lk. 16:16 par.) in providing the foundation for a life able to stand in the judgment of God (Mt. 7:24-27 par.). In all of this, however, Jesus did not destroy the law but fulfilled it (Mt. 5:17f.; Lk. 16:17). He brought it to its eschatological fruition.

3. Summary of the Law. It is love that fulfills the law. The double love commandment (Mk. 12:28-34 par.) was handed down in the tradition as a controversy saying in which Jesus put forth His own summary of the law. Such summaries were commonplace among the rabbis, but they were not Halakah. The purpose of these summaries was not to rank commandments for the sake of eliminating some or giving priority to others. They were "merely" Haggadah. But for Jesus it was legal observance that was put in crisis and Haggadah on which the emphasis fell. The commandments to love God and the neighbor are quotations of the Torah (Dt. 6:4; Lev. 19:18) and, it may be noted, they are "not ranked, but listed" (Furnish, p. 25f.; Luke makes of them one commandment). But they do allow other commandments to be ranked. In Mark the low ranking of the sacrificial system is explicit (12:33); the same point is made in Luke's parable of the Good Samaritan (Lk. 10:30-37). Matthew presents the summary of the law more on the model of the summaries of the rabbis, but he too uses love to rank and interpret the law (cf. Mt. 9:13; 12:7 with Hos. 6:6; see Furnish, pp. 74-84). Some of the controversies arose precisely because Jesus ranked acts of love higher than observance of the sabbath or purity regulations (e.g., Mk. 3:1-6 par.; 7:1-23 par.; Lk. 14:1-6; Jn. 5:2-18). Love, boundless and uncalculating, is the law for the new age. Love is, of course, no mere sentiment; it is a readiness for the concrete action which helps the neighbor (cf. the concrete command at the conclusion of the parable of the Good Samaritan, Lk. 10:37: "Go and do likewise").

The ethic of Jesus is, nevertheless, hardly an ethic of obedience to law, even the law of love. The love command is not used as a basic principle from which subsidiary rules are deduced. Jesus' ethic is rather an ethic of response to the coming kingdom of God and its present impact in Jesus. It is the recognition of what God is doing, rather than the love command as an ethical principle, which consistently shaped Jesus' moral discernment. Perhaps the clearest example is what happened to Lev. 19:18 in His teaching.

4. "Love Your Enemies." The commandment to love the neighbor had not been judged relevant to enemies; but now Jesus, without exegeting the text according to any rabbinic patterns, said on his own authority: "But *I* say to you, Love your enemies" (Mt. 5:44; cf. Lk. 6:27, 35). In justification of this command, Jesus appealed to the nature of God, who "is kind to the ungrateful and selfish" (Lk. 6:35; cf. Mt. 5:45). Implicit is the imminent rule of this God. Response to His coming kingdom is made concrete in the command to love the enemy. Repentance involves a radical turning from the conventional patterns of reciprocity, of loving those who are kind to us (Mt. 5:46; Lk. 6:32) and seeking the limit of lawful revenge against those who do us harm (Mt. 5:39-40, Lk. 6:29-30). Again the disposition to love is not merely sentiment. It makes one ready to do good to one's enemies, to pray for them, to bless them (Lk. 6:27f.). It penetrates to commonplace behavior like greeting them on the street (Mt. 5:47), not returning a blow (Mt. 5:36; Lk. 6:29), and lending (Mt. 5:42; Lk. 6:34). The power of the conventional pattern of reciprocity is broken only by trust in the coming rule of God. Those who follow the conventional pattern already have their reward, but those who welcome the new age shall receive the eschatological blessing (Lk. 6:35). So Jesus brings the commandment of love to its own eschatological fruition.

5. "Let Your 'Yes' Be 'Yes'." There was a well-developed casuistry with respect to oaths (echoed in Mt. 5:33-37; 23:16-22); but on His own authority Jesus simply demanded absolute truthfulness of His followers: "Let what you say be simply 'Yes' and 'No'" (Mt. 5:37; cf. Jas. 5:12). The integrity of one's words should not need the confirmation of oaths: "But I say to you, 'Do not swear at all'" (Mt. 5:34). The external regulations with respect to oaths could simply hide deceit, and could indeed be of use to the deceitful one who knew the law (Mt. 23:16-22;

Mk. 7:11-13 par.). But Jesus did not provide a legal pronouncement that there should be no oath-taking. Mt. 23 simply judges the casuistry which made it possible to swear some oaths "safely" or with impunity; it does not condemn oath-taking itself. The controversy over "Corban" demonstrates the same point (Mk. 7:9-13 par.). Jesus did not condemn oaths; He condemned a casuistry that made it possible to use oaths in self-seeking ways rather than in dutiful service. The emphasis is on the disposition of truthfulness (Mt. 12:34; Lk. 6:45). God's coming sovereignty means victory over Beelzebub, the father of lies (Jn. 8:44), and is already at work in Jesus' teaching. To welcome the kingdom is to accept the demand of absolute trustworthiness of speech; to resist such claims leaves one open to the judgment of God (Mt. 12:37).

The truthfulness Jesus required is not to be reduced to external conformity between words and the situation. It involves the whole person's response to the coming kingdom and therefore with seeking the neighbor's good. So truthfulness has its cognates in the prohibition of "careless words" (Mt. 12:36) and common insults (5:22). Thus Jesus brought to eschatological fruition God's intention in the commandment about false witness.

6. Other Commands. Everywhere the pattern is the same. Casuistry based on the sabbath legislation is put aside for the present impact of God's intentions of relief for the poor (Mk. 2:27). Casuistry about ritual cleanliness (and perhaps the laws themselves) is put aside for the fulfillment of God's desire for inward purity (Mk. 7:1-23; Mt. 15:1-20). Casuistry about divorce (cf. Dt. 24:1-4) is put aside for the fulfillment of God's initial and final purpose (Mk. 10:2-11 par.; *see* DIVORCE). External observance of even unquestionable stipulations of the law is put in crisis. So on His own authority Jesus commanded those who would welcome the kingdom not merely not to kill, but not to be angry and to be ready always to reconcile (Mt. 5:21-26); He prohibited not merely the external act of adultery but its inner motive of lust (Mt. 5:27f.).

7. Call to Discipleship. The call to discipleship is related to this simultaneous rejection and fruition of the law. The pupils of the rabbis gathered themselves around the teacher to study the law and its interpretation. They devoted themselves to the study of Torah. But the disciples responded to Jesus' call to follow Him, and they devoted themselves to *Him,* the one who spoke with authority. Rather than simply learning the old rules, they heard Jesus' words and were commanded to do them (Lk. 6:47; cf. Mk. 8:34-38). In His words and deeds they caught a glimpse of the coming kingdom, and they struggled to welcome it. To follow Him was costly; it meant an end to egotistical calculations and the comfortable old securities (Mt. 8:18-22 par.; Lk. 14:26-34).

E. The Politics of Jesus. As stated above (III.A), Jesus never announced a political program, as though the coming of the kingdom were contingent on human striving. On the other hand, the kingdom was not some secret sovereignty over souls but a cosmic sovereignty, and the repentance demanded (of cities and a generation as well as of individuals) was total. This total repentance in response to a cosmic kingdom may not be reduced to political dispositions and behavior, but it surely includes them.

Jesus rejected the vengeful nationalism of much contemporary apocalyptic expectation as well as the personal vengeful use of the law of retaliation. The zealot desire for vengeance surely belonged to the old age; Jesus was no zealot. But the implication is not a new law, namely, a total prohibition of political power and coercion. The implications seem rather to be a great reversal with respect to political power itself, and political dispositions which conform to that new reality. The pride of power is already judged and condemned: Herod Antipas ("that fox," Lk. 13:32) and the gentile rulers who "lord it over" those beneath them (Mk. 10:42) belong to the old age; authority in society is to be construed as a vocation to humble service (vv. 42-44 par.). Politically too, then, the kingdom is good news for the poor and oppressed. Even as He commended a pious sinner's wasteful use of ointment, Jesus called attention to the community's responsibility to the poor (Mk. 14:3-7 par.; IV.C.3 above).

Jesus was no Sadducean collaborator either. The temple cleansing (Mk. 11:15-18 par. Jn. 2:13-17) was surely — even if not merely — a political challenge to the priestly aristocracy. The famous but notoriously difficult saying of Jesus about the tribute money ("Render to Caesar the things that are Caesar's, and to God the things that are God's") was no zealot call to arms, but neither was it the sort of compartmentalization of "two realms" which would leave the Herodians, the Sadducees, and other collaborators with an easy conscience. In the context of Jesus' proclamation of God's cosmic sovereignty, there can be no question about what things do and do not belong to God. All things will belong to Him, the claims of Caesar notwithstanding, and Jesus' hearers were being called to welcome that coming sovereignty of God. The collaborators were being called to political (even if not merely political) repentance. Just what concrete commands gave shape to such repentance it is now impossible to say. But the great reversal of the kingdom affected political values, even while it could not be reduced to the kind of political reversal of fortunes that the apocalypticists and zealots envisioned.

IV. Validation of Jesus' Ethic.–It is not implausible that this Jesus should be considered dangerous by those who refused to repent. So He was put to death. But God raised Him up. And against the background of apocalyptic, the resurrection is the vindication of this man, including His teachings. It is the verification of His claim to speak with authority, the divine stamp of approval on Jesus and His ethic. Matthew summarizes it well in his account of the words of the risen Lord (28:18-20): "All authority . . . has been given to me. Go therefore and make disciples . . . teaching them to observe all that I have commanded you. . . ."

Bibliography.–R. J. Banks, *Jesus and the Law in the Synoptic Tradition* (1975); V. P. Furnish, *Love Commandment in the NT* (1972); J. Jeremias, *Jesus' Promise to the Nations* (1958); *NT Theology: The Proclamation of Jesus* (1971); W. G. Kümmel, *Promise and Fulfilment* (1961); T. W. Manson, *Teaching of Jesus* (2nd ed. 1935); P. Minear, *Commands of Christ* (1972); N. Perrin, *Kingdom of God in the Teaching of Jesus* (1963); A. Schweitzer, *Quest of the Historical Jesus* (1916); M. J. Suggs, "The Antitheses as Redactional Products," in L. Schottroff, ed., *Essays on the Love Commandment* (1978); U. Wilkens, "Development of the Concept of Revelation within the History of Primitive Christianity," in W. Pannenberg, ed., *Revelation as History* (1968), pp. 55-121; J. Yoder, *Politics of Jesus* (1972).

A. D. VERHEY

NT ETHICS

ETHICS: NT ETHICS

I. Introduction.–Because Jesus was raised from the dead, the early Church proclaimed that He was "both Lord and Christ" (Acts 2:36). The Resurrection thus became the basis and norm of all early Christian reflection, including reflection about the conduct and character "worthy of the gospel of Christ" (Phil. 1:27). The Resurrection was both the vindication of Jesus and the expectation of His return.

For this reason morality in the NT is not autonomous. It is an inalienably religious morality. To isolate the ethics of the NT from its religious basis is to distort both. The NT literature includes no work concerned with the self-conscious and systematic address to questions in ethical theory and no work concerned with providing a comprehensive code. The concern is always rather to bring the memory of Jesus and the expectation of God's final victory to bear upon concrete situations faced by the churches. Ethics in the NT is always, therefore, both religious and concrete.

The relationship between religious affirmations and concrete moral exhortations is mediated, of course, by the theological and ethical reflection of each of the NT writers. The NT presents no unitary and monolithic ethics, and we cannot speak of *the* NT ethics as though it did. The authors of the NT address different communities with different concrete problems; they have different pastoral objectives and different theological and ethical concerns; they are heirs of moral traditions besides the Christian tradition, and even if they see those traditions now through the prism of the Resurrection, they use the wisdom of other traditions in their own ways. The Hebrew Scriptures, for example, always played an important role in the moral discernment and judgment of the early Christian communities, but the precise place and use of the law was a matter of considerable debate in the early Church, and the NT authors themselves provide no unified perspective on that critically important ethical question. Other traditions, whether Jewish and rabbinic or Greek and philosophical, were also used and left an impression, both formally and materially, on the ethics of the NT.

The different situations, objectives, and traditions influenced and shaped the memories about Jesus, the expectation of His return, and surely the ways in which these were brought to bear on concrete moral questions. Because God had vindicated Jesus by raising Him from the dead, His memory was from the beginning normative for the moral discernment and judgment of the churches. But precisely because He had been raised, remembering Him could not follow the pattern of preserving the words of some famous, but dead, rabbi. He was not merely a figure of the past but also the present Lord who would come again as Judge, and the tradition about Him was not merely passively received but actively appropriated, constantly applied to new situations as the means by which the risen Lord continued to address His followers, also morally. The faith that the remembered Jesus had been raised allowed, and indeed called for, modification of the tradition to address new audiences concerning new situations.

The expectation of God's final victory had a double consequence for the life of the early Church. On the one hand, it forced a recognition of the distance between this world and the age of God's undisputed sovereignty. On the other hand, since it was the Creator's sovereignty over His own creation that was expected, it enabled a positive evaluation of the world God had made (e.g., 1 Cor. 10:26). This double consequence was susceptible, of course, to two different perversions, either denying the reality of the continuing power of sin or denying the goodness of the created world. The NT preserves the tension and balance, but its authors emphasize sometimes one consequence, sometimes the other.

The moral tradition which the NT receives, and of which it is the normative expression, is diverse and pluralistic, not simple and monolithic. To see and appreciate both the diversity of NT ethical thoughts and their convergence in loyalty to the risen Lord is the task undertaken here.

II. Synoptic Gospels.–*A. Mark.* Mark was probably the first Gospel to be written. After the death of Peter in Nero's persecution, A.D. 64/5, Mark wrote to preserve Peter's preaching and to encourage and exhort the Roman Christians. The primary focus of his encouragement was that Jesus Himself had suffered and died; the primary focus of his exhortation was the call to discipleship (Mk. 1:16-20; 2:14; 3:13; 8:34; 10:52).

In the central section of his Gospel, framed by Peter's confession and the Transfiguration, Mark placed the first prediction of the passion and its sequel, the call to discipleship, "If any man would come after me, let him deny himself and take up his cross and follow me" (Mk. 8:34, addressed to "the multitudes" as well as the disciples). The meaning is clear: to follow Jesus is to suffer with Him. But it was precisely that which the disciples could not or would not understand, according to Mark. In each of the three passion predictions Mark called attention to the failure of the disciples to understand (8:32 [Peter!]; 9:32; 10:32-35). Those failures climaxed in the garden when the disciples "all forsook him, and fled" (14:50), except for Peter, who followed Him to the courtyard of the high priest but then denied Him (14:66-72). Peter, of course, as Mark's readers knew, had learned and accepted that to follow Jesus is to suffer with Him; he had followed Jesus to the cross. Mark encouraged and exhorted his readers to a similar discipleship. (The references to martyrdom are most explicit in 10:38f. and 13:9-13.)

This heroic morality is essentially eschatological. It is enabled and required by the eschatological outlook called for in the command to "watch" (Mk. 13:33-37). Jesus had begun the great battle against the powers of darkness and by His patient endurance of suffering had carried the first stages of that battle to a victorious conclusion (3:23-27; note also Mark's interest in exorcisms, nature miracles, and, of course, the Resurrection in 8:31; 9:9, 31; 10:34; 14:28; 16:1-8). The departed Lord will return (within a generation; cf. 13:30; 9:1) to complete the victory and reveal His glory, but the watchers do not know "the day or the hour" (13:32f., 35). The period between His departure and His return, the "night," tests the loyalty and perseverance of His disciples.

Mark links the command to watch with his treatment of the disciples' failure to understand that to follow Jesus is to suffer with Him. The three exhortations to "watch" (13:33-37) are paralleled by the three failures of the disciples to "watch" in Gethsemane (14:32-40), and even as

Jesus accepted the will of the Father to drink the cup of His suffering, the disciples, including Peter, slept. But now the command to watch comes to "all" (13:37), and so all are encouraged and exhorted to a discipleship that is prepared to suffer with Jesus in the expectation of His final triumph.

Mark's eschatological ethic of watchful discipleship is applied to topics besides suffering, and illumines even the most mundane of them with the same moral heroism. The call of Levi the tax collector to discipleship (Mk. 2:14) and the table fellowship of Jesus with other sinners (2:15-17) provided the background for the first controversies about the law (2:18–3:6). These controversies are a strikingly recurrent motif in this Gospel. Whatever else discipleship required, it apparently provided significant freedom from punctilious observance of the law. Fasting (2:18-22), sabbath-observance (2:23–3:6), the distinction between "clean" and "unclean" (7:1-23), and the permission of divorce (10:2-12) belong to the past, not to the eschatological community oriented to the coming of the Son of man. The final norm is no longer the precepts of Moses but the Lord and His words (8:38). "The commandment of God" still holds, of course (7:8; cf. 10:19; and esp. the double love commandment, 12:28-34), but it is simply not identical with any manipulatable code or casuistry, even one based on the law.

The "vice list" (Mk. 7:21-23) is traditional, with echoes of Jewish morality, but Mark focuses on "the heart," the source of evil acts and traits. In Mark's address to the issues of a household, marriage, children, and possessions (10:1-31; the narratives compose a *Haustafel,* i.e., a table of rules for the household). Jesus and His words do not rely on the law or conventional righteousness; they call attention, rather, to God's intentions at the creation (10:6), to the coming kingdom of God (10:14f.), and to the cost of discipleship (10:21). The saying about paying taxes to Caesar (12:13-17) is not a casuistic apportioning of rights and obligations but an emphatic assertion of the total claims of God's sovereignty. Mark's eschatological ethic provided no code, but it did provide a moral posture that was both less rigid and more demanding than any code, a moral stance that, by its readiness for humble service and suffering, was contrasted with the ethos of both Jewish lawyers and gentile rulers (e.g., 10:42-45).

B. Matthew. The Gospel of Matthew contains almost all of Mark, but was written to a different audience, a largely Jewish Christian audience, facing a different crisis, namely, the conflict with the synagogue, with quite another ethical perspective, described below.

1. The Sermon on the Mount. Matthew followed Mark's order, but self-consciously imposed on it a pattern of alternating narrative and discourse sections (see the formula concluding each discourse section in Mt. 7:28; 11:1; 13:53; 19:1; 26:1). The first discourse section is the Sermon on the Mount (5:1–7:29), a collection and arrangement of originally independent sayings of Jesus. The sermon is the quintessence of Matthew's ethic, made easily accessible for instructing catechumens (Jeremias). The theme and outline of the sermon and, indeed, the focus of Matthew's ethic may be found in 5:20: "unless your righteousness exceeds that of the scribes and Pharisees, you will never enter the kingdom of heaven." Matthew exhorted the Church to righteousness (Gk. *dikaiosynē,* Mt. 3:15; 5:6, 10, 20; 6:1, 33; 21:32), a righteousness that does not fall below the standards of the synagogue but rather surpasses them.

Such a righteousness preserves the law of Moses as a normative standard. This was the teaching of Jesus Himself according to Matthew. He announced that He had not come to abolish the law, that the whole law, down to the very letters, remains in effect, and that even the least of the commandments ought to be taught and done (5:17-20; cf. 23:23). Even the oral law is preserved: "the scribes and Pharisees sit on Moses' seat" (23:1). It was not their teaching function itself but rather their self-righteous elitism and their pettifogging legalism which were excoriated in ch. 23. In the controversies about sabbath observance (12:1-14; cf. Mk. 2:23–3:6), Matthew added legal, "halakic," arguments to the Marcan material to show that Jesus was "guiltless" (Mt. 12:7) and that what He did was "lawful" (12:12). In the controversy about "clean" and "unclean" (15:1-20; cf. Mk. 7:1-23), Matthew omitted the Marcan interpretation that Jesus "declared all foods clean" (Mk. 7:19, which would abolish a large section of the written law) and focused the discussion instead on tradition's concern for external purity at the expense of a concern for internal purity (Mt. 15:20; cf. 23:25-28). In the controversy about divorce in Matthew (19:3-12), Jesus did not set aside Dt. 24:1ff. as belonging to the past (cf. Mk. 10:2-12), but rather used it as the basis of a strict legal judgment. The law holds, and its precepts, even the least of them, ought to be taught and done.

Matthew demanded a righteousness which "exceeds that of the scribes" (Mt. 5:20). The antitheses of 5:21-48 are both a judgment on the self-serving and legalistic interpretations of the scribes (cf. also ch. 23) and a demonstration of the fulfillment of the law in the surpassing righteousness that Jesus required. They do not provide "a new law." (Notice that Matthew omitted Mk. 1:27, which indeed described Jesus' teaching as "a new teaching.") They do not annul the law, but bring it to its own fruition. The surpassing righteousness is not something added but something transformed by its connection with the kingdom (6:33; the Beatitudes, 5:3-12; and especially 4:17, for the Sermon on the Mount was clearly intended as a development of this summary of Jesus' preaching in the first narrative section). The laws forbidding murder (5:21), adultery (v. 27), and false swearing (v. 33), restricting divorce (v. 31) and punishment (v. 38), and requiring love of the neighbor (v. 43) are not swept away. What is rejected, rather, is the scribal interpretation that placed only an external limit on the expressions of anger, lust, deceit, revenge, and self-centeredness. The scribal "righteousness" left the moral agent untouched, so that even the observance of the law was grudging and external. The righteousness of the Christian community was to exceed the righteousness of the scribes by making claims upon the moral agent himself, claims in line with both the intention of the lawgiver (e.g., 5:45) and the repentance required by the coming of His kingdom (4:17).

The righteousness required also "exceeds that . . . of the Pharisees" (Mt. 5:20; see 6:1-18). The contrast is simple: the righteous acts of the Pharisees, their almsgiving, praying, and fasting, were done "to be seen of men" (6:1f., 5, 16; 23:5, 28). These pious duties are not to be abandoned, but the self-righteousness with which they were performed must be.

Finally, Matthew undertook in the Sermon (6:19–7:27) to describe the righteousness without comparison or equal. To treasure "his kingdom and his righteousness" (6:33) gives and requires freedom from anxiety about earthly treasures or about food and clothes (6:19-34), calls for repentance and disallows self-righteous judgment (7:1-5), and prompts a life of prayer (vv. 7-11). A summary is provided by the Golden Rule (v. 12), and the conclusion is provided by a trio of contrasts, the two gates, the two trees, and the two houses (vv. 13-27), each reminding the congregation that it is not enough to call Jesus "Lord"

ETHICS: NT ETHICS

(v. 21), that it is necessary rather to "do" the surpassing righteousness He announced.

2. *Rules for Discipline and Discernment*. The fourth discourse (Mt. 18:1-35) is concerned with discipline and discernment in the community. Set among the exhortations to exercise patient and persevering concern for "the little ones who believe on me" (vv. 6-14) and to forgive "seventy times seven" (vv. 21-35) stand the rules for dealing with an offending brother (vv. 15-20). The rules insist both on the individual's responsibility for reconciliation and on the community's responsibility for mutual admonition and communal discernment. The authority to make judicial rulings and judgments "to bind and loose" was vested in the Church as a whole "gathered in his name" (vv. 18-20).

3. *"Works Righteousness" and Eschatology*. Matthew's ethic has often been described as a "works righteousness." There is surely some truth in the characterization. He made "entering the kingdom" (a phrase Matthew used more than any other NT author) contingent upon doing the righteousness required in the Sermon (5:20; 7:21; cf. 6:14f.). The rewards (e.g., 6:1-6, 16-18; 25:34) and punishments (e.g., 7:23; 13:42, 50; 22:13; 24:51; 25:30, 41) of the Final Judgment are consistently emphasized (cf., e.g., his treatment of Mk. 8:38, where Matthew adds to the coming of the Son of man in glory, "and then he will repay every man for what he has done" [Mt. 16:27; see also 12:36f.]).

But for all its persuasiveness, this characterization is deceptive. It overlooks the fact that the demands themselves were premised on Jesus' announcement of the kingdom and the proleptic demonstration of its saving power in His ministry (the first narrative; see the summary, Mt. 4:23-25). Matthew's perspective was thoroughly eschatological. In Jesus the times were fulfilled (the fulfillment of prophecy is a central motif in Matthew; cf. 1:22; 2:5, 15, 17, 23; 3:3; 4:14; 8:17; etc.). The new age, having made its power felt in Jesus' acts of healing and forgiveness and in His resurrection, is certain, and the new age can already mark the life of the community among whom He abides. The risen Lord abides with the community "always, to the close of the age"; that eschatological promise is the context for the continuing exhortation to "observe all that [Jesus had] commanded" (28:16-20; cf. v. 20 with 18:20). The message of God's gracious intervention retains its important priority. God's gracious intervention, however, also establishes the validity of His will. The present time, then, is a time of testing — not, however, as in Mark through suffering with Him, but rather through obedience to His righteousness. (See the series of parables used to close the apocalyptic discourse, 24:45–25:46.) So, in the parable of the unforgiving servant (18:23-35), the Lord's forgiveness is both gracious and demanding, the premise both for the requirement to forgive and for the judgment on not forgiving (cf. 18:35 with 6:15). In the parable of the marriage feast (22:1-14), the invitation to the joy of the eschatological banquet is indiscriminately given to "both bad and good," but with the invitation comes the demand for righteousness (and the guest with no wedding garment is cast out). At the beginning of the Sermon on the Mount stand announcements of the blessings of the kingdom (the Beatitudes, 5:3-12) and the glories of the eschatological community (5:13-16).

C. Luke-Acts. Luke, like Matthew, seems to have made use of Mark, but modified it and added to it from yet another ethical perspective, a perspective distinguished by its solicitude for the poor and oppressed and by its concern for the unity of Jewish and gentile Christians.

Both distinguishing characteristics are present in the episode which Luke, by a modification of Mark's order, put at the very beginning of Jesus' ministry. Jesus' sermon at Nazareth (Lk. 4:16-30; cf. Mk. 6:1-6) was made a preface to His ministry and took the place of Mark's summary of His preaching (Mk. 1:15, which Luke omitted). Jesus went to this synagogue "as his custom was" and used Isa. 61:1-2a to describe His own ministry: "the Spirit of the Lord God is upon me, because he has anointed me to preach good news to the poor . . ." (cf. 7:22). But He made no mention of "the day of vengeance of our God" (Isa. 61:2b). It was evidently this omission that prompted the ensuing discussion, with its reminder of the sympathy of Elijah and Elisha for Gentiles (Lk. 4:25-27). The form is narrative rather than hortative, but no one could claim loyalty to this Christ, this "anointed" one, and be unsympathetic toward the poor; no gentile Christian could claim loyalty to this Christ and repudiate the Jewish heritage of the gospel, and no Jewish Christian could repudiate the eschatological inclusion of the Gentiles.

1. *Care for the Poor and Oppressed*. From the very beginning Luke's story of Jesus emphasized His identification with the poor and the outcasts. It is Mary, not Joseph (cf. Mt. 1:20), who is visited by the angel. Mary's Magnificat (Lk. 1:46-55) rejoices in God's action to exalt the humble, the hungry, the poor, and to humble the exalted. The shepherds, not Magi, visit Jesus in an animal stall, not a house (cf. Mt. 2:1-12). John the Baptist exhorts the multitudes to share food and clothing, and tax collectors and soldiers not to abuse their power (Lk. 3:10-14). In Luke's Sermon on the Plain (6:20-49), Jesus makes no attempt to "spiritualize" the blessings on the poor and hungry (cf. Lk. 6:20f. with Mt. 5:3, 6); He includes corresponding "woes" on the rich (6:24-26), and He calls for a response to this eschatological reversal that focuses on the duties of love and mercy (cf. Lk. 6:26 with Mt. 5:48), including generosity, benevolence, lending without expecting a return, and almsgiving (Lk. 6:27-38). Luke's "travel narrative" (9:51–19:44), a long teaching section set in the form of a narrative of Jesus' journey to Jerusalem contains a number of hortatory parables: "the Good Samaritan," which explicates the love commandment in terms of mercy and concludes with Jesus' command, "Go and do likewise" (10:25-37); "the rich fool," with its judgment on the wealthy person's concern for his own ease (12:13-21); "the great supper," with its reminder of God's eschatological blessing on "the poor and maimed and blind and lame" (following an exhortation of solicitude toward the same in 14:12-24); "the unrighteous steward," with its exhortation to generosity, to "make friends . . . by unrighteous mammon" (16:1-13); and "the rich man and Lazarus," a parabolic announcement of the eschatological blessings on the poor and woes on the ungenerous rich (16:19-31). It includes biographical narratives like Mary's choice to sit at the Lord's feet as an equal among the disciples (10:38-42) and Zacchaeus's choice to do justice and mercy (19:1-10); both choices are commended by Jesus.

This focus continues into Acts. All the heroes give alms (Acts 3:1-10, Peter and John; 10:1-4, Cornelius; 11:27-30; 12:25; 24:17, Paul). The early Church itself "had all things in common . . . and distributed them to all, as any had need" (2:44f.; 4:32-35). The mission encounters resistance because it interferes with the "hope of gain" (16:19; 19:23-25).

The "great reversal" theme, first enunciated in the Magnificat, emphasized in the inaugural address, and displayed in Luke's whole portrait of Christ, is related, of course, to the key testimony text, Ps. 118:22, about the rejected stone being made the head of the corner (Lk. 21:17; Acts 4:11). The "great reversal" was important both morally and christologically for Luke. The God who

ETHICS: NT ETHICS

exalts the humble exalted Him. It is little wonder that at the end of Luke's Gospel, the risen Lord reminds them of the reversal (24:46) and exhorts them to preach repentance in His name (v. 47). There is no repentance in Luke that does not practice sympathy toward the poor and oppressed, no welcoming the saving act of God in Jesus Christ that does not do justice and kindness (19:1-10), no waiting for His return that does not expect and anticipate God's vindication of the humble poor (18:1-8).

2. Unity of Jew and Gentile. It is also little wonder that such repentance is to be preached "to all nations beginning from Jerusalem" (Lk. 24:47; cf. Acts 1:8). It was, of course, programmatic for the book of Acts, but also typical of Luke's insistence on both the Jewish origins of the gospel and the inclusion of the Gentiles.

The Jewish origins of the gospel are plain from the very beginning. Luke alone begins in the temple with the story of Zechariah, a devout and pious (1:5-13) old priest. Luke alone relates Jesus' circumcision (2:21; also that of John the Baptist, 1:59), His presentation in the temple "as it is written in the Law of the Lord" (2:22f.), and His annual Passover pilgrimage with His parents (2:41f.). In Luke's Gospel Jesus' ministry was conducted almost exclusively among Jews (he omitted Mark's narratives of Jesus' ministry in Tyre and Sidon and the Decapolis). The centurion's request for his slave was mediated by Jews (Lk. 7:1-10, esp. 3f.; cf. Mt. 8:5-13). In Luke the Resurrection appearances took place in Jerusalem, and the Gospel ends where it began, "in the temple."

The mission "to all nations" really begins in Acts (and there not until ch. 10). But from the beginning of Luke, alongside the emphasis on the Jewish origin of the Christian movement, were foreshadowings of the mission to come. The announcement to the shepherds was that the gospel would be "to all the people" (2:10). The song of the devout Simeon celebrated God's salvation of "all peoples" (2:25-32). John the Baptist, citing Isa. 40, described the coming of the Lord: "and all flesh shall see the salvation of God" (3:6; cf. also 13:29). The centurion's approach to Jesus was mediated by Jews, but he was nevertheless held up as a model of faith (7:9). In the beginning of Acts, long before the gentile mission began, Peter in his Pentecost sermon quoted Joel's saying that the Spirit would be poured out "upon all flesh" (2:17). In the narrative of Peter's visit with Cornelius, the real beginning of the gentile mission (9:32–11:18), Peter was hardly an eager evangelist, and the inclusion of uncircumcised Gentiles was plainly God's decision (15:7), not Peter's idea. By visions, heavenly messages, and the gift of the Spirit, God made it plain that He "shows no partiality" (10:34; cf. 11:12; 15:9) and that "what God has cleansed you must not call common" (10:15; 11:19; cf. 15:9). God's decision, however, did not apparently settle the issue in the Church; that awaited the Apostolic Council and its decision on Paul's case (ch. 15). Even then the controversy did not cease but marked the rest of the book of Acts (e.g., 21:19-21; 26:19-23) and, undoubtedly, the Christian communities to which Luke wrote.

To Jewish Christians and gentile Christians, these features of the narrative were not merely of historical interest, but fundamental to their relationship within the churches. The Jewish Christians ought to join Peter in welcoming, not judging, the Gentiles, and in acknowledging, not resisting, God's decision to include them *as Gentiles*: "What God has cleansed you must not call common" (Acts 10:15; 11:9). The gentile Christians ought to join the centurion in acknowledging that their access to God's saving power is through the Jews, repudiating neither the Jewish heritage of the gospel nor Jewish Christians, and in loving, not despising, the Jews (Lk. 7:5). This unity and harmony did not require uniformity. The Jewish Christians were to welcome the gentile Christians *as Gentiles*, demanding neither circumcision nor observance of the Jewish law. The gentile Christians were to love Jewish Christians *as Jews*, respecting their pious observance of the law.

Luke's treatment of the law is unique and clearly related to this distinctive concern. The law holds for Jews, but the duties of love and mercy take priority over ritual observance (Lk. 10:25-37; 6:1-11; 13:10-17; 14:1-6). And it also holds with respect to Gentiles, but in quite a different way! The Apostolic Council's "judgment" (Acts 15:19; Gk. *krínō*) was a legal ruling. The law simply does not require gentile observance; to accept God's decision to include them *as Gentiles* means legally not to require Jewish observance of the law from them. The council required only, as a *modus vivendi* to facilitate some degree of fellowship between Jews and Gentiles, that Gentiles "abstain from the pollutions of idols and from unchastity and from what is strangled and from blood" (15:20, 29). Luke surely intended to recommend such observance to gentile Christians, at least as a way of accommodating the Jewish Christians. The Gentiles need not observe the law, then, but they — like the Jews — were required "to repent and turn to God and perform deeds worthy of their repentance" (Acts 26:20).

***II. Paul and His Interpreters.**–A. Paul. 1. A Pastoral Ethic.* Before the Gospels put the memories of Jesus into writing, Paul was addressing pastoral letters to his churches. His letters were intimate and personal, relevant to the concrete problems of particular communities, not self-consciously addressed to a larger (or later) audience. He presented no "timeless truths" in the style of either a philosopher or a code maker, but rather the timely application of the gospel to the concrete situations faced by the churches. He always wrote as an apostle (e.g., Rom. 1:1; 1 Cor. 1:1; 2 Cor. 1:1; Gal. 1:1), and he always wrote to churches (even the letter to Philemon was addressed "to the church in your house," v. 2). The letters sent in the service of Paul's mission were the means by which he was present as an apostle even while he was absent (Col. 2:5). So he could write with apostolic authority to pronounce judgment in the name of the Lord (1 Cor. 5:3-5). But, although he could, he seldom commanded; he rather "appealed" to his readers' own judgment (Philem. 8f.; 1 Cor. 10:15). He used the language of polite request (Gk. *parakalō*, Rom. 12:1 *et passim*) rather than the language of command, and so conveyed to the churches a sense of their own freedom and responsibility in moral discernment. He respected and cultivated the churches as the communal context of moral discernment and judgment, as "full of goodness, filled with all knowledge, and able to instruct one another" (Rom. 15:14).

Paul's use of Gk. *parakalō* and *paráklēsis* in exhortation is informative in another way as well, for Paul used the same words to mean also the "comfort" and "encouragement" of the gospel (e.g., 2 Cor. 1:4-7). So in Phil. 2, the "encouragement [Gk. *paráklēsis*] in Christ" (v. 1) comes to expression as exhortation to "have this mind among yourselves, which you have in Christ Jesus" (v. 5). The word itself demonstrates the inseparable unity of the gift and the demand, the indicative and imperative, in Paul's ethical thought (see Furnish, *Ethics,* pp. 106-111). Paul's moral exhortations were of one piece with his preaching the gospel.

2. Indicative and Imperative. Paul's continual proclamation of the gospel, "the power of God for salvation to everyone who has faith" (Rom. 1:16), to his churches was expressed sometimes in the indicative mood (e.g., 1 Cor. 5:7b, "You really are unleavened") and sometimes in the imperative mood (e.g., 1 Cor. 5:7a, "Cleanse out the old leaven"). Indeed, frequently statements in the indicative have hortatory force; they function as subtle imperatives (e.g., Rom. 5:1-5). There is plainly, in Paul's thought, an intimate relation between the indicative and the imperative. There is, to be sure, an important priority to the indicative in Paul's thought, as his insistence on "justification by grace" makes clear (e.g., Rom. 3:21-30; cf. 1 Cor. 4:7). But the priority must not be understood in terms of the establishment of an ideal or principle which needs later and separately to be actualized or realized in decisions about character and conduct, for there is also an important "finality" to the indicative, as his persistent references to the promised future make equally clear (e.g., Phil. 3:20f.; Rom. 13:11-14). The relation must, then, be understood in terms of Paul's conviction that in the crucified and risen Christ God has acted eschatologically. In Christ God has acted to end the old age, which stood under the powers of sin and of death, and to begin the new age, the age of the undisputed sovereignty of God's transcendent power. The old age, however, continues; the powers of sin and death have not laid down their arms. They have been conquered but not destroyed; and they are, therefore, not yet ineffectual, not even against the believer. But the power of God stands in fundamental opposition to the powers of this age. And the one who receives the power of God is freed from their dominion to stand under the lordship of Christ. That "standing" is always *now* both gift and demand, both indicative and imperative (cf. Rom. 5:2 with 1 Cor. 10:12; 16:13; Eph. 6:14).

The juxtaposition of indicative and imperative is possible and, indeed, indispensable precisely because of the present coexistence of the old age and the age to come. The indicative describes the eschatological salvation of which Christians in the Spirit have the "first fruits" (Rom. 8:23) and "guarantee" (2 Cor. 5:5). But the imperative acknowledges that Christians are still threatened by the powers of the old age, though the doom of those powers is sure, and therefore that they are responsible for holding fast to the life given them in Christ against the powers of sin and death. "If we live by the Spirit, let us also walk by the Spirit" (Gal. 5:25).

3. Discernment. The ages have turned, and there is a corresponding change in discernment. So Paul admonished the Romans, "Be not conformed to this world [or age] but be transformed by the renewal of your mind, that you may prove [or discern] what is the will of God, what is good and acceptable and perfect" (Rom. 12:2). The Christians' discernment ought for Paul to be radically affected by God's eschatological action in Jesus Christ.

Their self-understanding as moral agents is to be determined by their incorporation into Christ (Gal. 2:20; Rom. 6:1-11; 2 Cor. 5:14f.). They "belong" to Christ (1 Cor. 6:19b-20) and freely offer themselves (Rom. 12:1). And this moral identity is important to discerning what they ought to be and do.

Their perspective on the world has also been determined by God's eschatological act. They understand that there is a "new creation," that "the old has passed away" and "the new has come" (2 Cor. 5:17), but also that there is a continuing conflict between the power of God and the "powers" (Eph. 6:12; Rom. 8:38), and they look for the day on which "the creation itself will be set free from its bondage to decay" (Rom. 8:21). This interpretation of the situation illumines the analysis of any particular situation and its moral requirements. Paul's own emphasis was relative to his audience and their situation. To the Corinthians, where the confidence of some that they were already fully in the new age led sometimes to libertinism (1 Cor. 5:12; 6:12), sometimes to asceticism (1 Cor. 7:1), and always to elitism, Paul consistently emphasized the "not yet" character of our existence (e.g., 5:3-5; 7:2; ch. 15). To the Colossians, however, tempted to submit again to the powers and their taboos (Col. 2:16-19), Paul emphasized that Christ had "already" achieved lordship over the powers and that their strength was already broken (v. 15).

This christological and eschatological perspective on the self and the world could be articulated by Paul in terms of some basic values. Those were not first carefully defined by Paul and then applied deductively and casuistically to concrete cases; Paul's discernment is more like the expression of the character and community formed by Christ. Yet there are articulated values, statements of principle, and indeed appeals to moral wisdom taken from a number of sources. Discernment as personal and historical response to what God has done, is doing, and will do in Christ surely involved for Paul rational discrimination.

Perhaps the most fundamental of the Christian values is freedom. "For freedom Christ has set us free; stand fast therefore, and do not submit again to a yoke of bondage" (Gal. 5:1; cf. 2 Cor. 3:17). This freedom is surely freedom from our bondage to sin and death, but it is also always freedom from the law (Gal. 5:2-4), and not only from the curse of the law but from the divisions established in and by the law, especially the division between Jew and Gentile, circumcised and uncircumcised (Gal. 5:5; 3:28). This gift and value took concrete shape when Paul insisted that the Galatians not yield to those who would compel them to be circumcised and to keep the law, when he judged the Corinthians free from scruples about food offered to idols (1 Cor. 8:4-8; but see v. 9 and below), and when he proclaimed to the Romans "the glorious liberty of the children of God" (8:21), which allows Jewish and gentile Christians their Jewish and gentle identities as long as they are subsumed to their Christian identity (Rom. 14).

If freedom is the most fundamental value, love is the most important. The two are related to each other because both are related to God's action in the cross and Resurrection. Christ frees us from our bondage to the powers of the old age to an eschatological existence whose distinguishing characteristic is love (1 Cor. 13:8-13; Rom. 5:5; also Gal. 5:22f. where love stands first in Paul's list of the "fruit of the Spirit"). The liberation God wins and grants in Christ is not license or independence but the freedom to love: "Do not use your freedom as an opportunity for the flesh, but through love be servants of one another" (Gal. 5:13; 1 Cor. 6:12; 10:23f.). Faith, by which we receive the liberation God has wrought, acts "through love" (Gal. 5:6). Indeed love is the characteristic that enables a new discernment; "It is my prayer," Paul says, "that your love may abound more and more, with knowledge and all discernment, so that you may approve what is excellent" (Phil. 1:9f.; cf. 1 Cor. 8:1f.). Love is the fulfillment of the law (Rom. 13:8-10; Gal. 5:14). This gift and value took concrete shape when Paul called for unity, peace, and love in churches composed of Jew and Gentile (Eph. 4:1-3; cf. Rom. 14:1–15:6), when he admonished some enthusiasts in Corinth against an elitism based on their "spiritual gifts" (1 Cor. 12–14), when he encouraged the Corinthians to give generously to the collection for the poor in Jerusalem (2 Cor. 8:8, 24), and when, dealing with role relationships, he required husbands to love their wives (Eph. 5:25, 28; Col. 3:19) and advised Philemon about his relationship to Onesimus (Philem. 7, 16). Paul described the concrete shape of love in the central section of 1 Cor. 13 with his list of the works of love (vv. 4-7; the Greek uses verbs, not predicate adjectives).

Paul's ethic of response to God's eschatological act in Jesus Christ was, then, an ethic of freedom and love that took concrete shape according to the situation of the readers. But it did not create new guidelines for character and conduct *ex nihilo.* Love's discernment made use of other sources, especially the teachings of Jesus, the Jewish law, and "natural" moral standards.

The tradition which Paul received and handed down surely included a collection of Jesus' sayings, and he did occasionally make use of these in moral argument (explicitly in 1 Cor. 7:10f.; 9:14). Moreover, when he did use them, it is plain that he considered them authoritative, for he took care to distinguish them from his own opinion (1 Cor. 7:12, 25). Still, they are surprisingly seldom used; the collection of Jesus' sayings did not apparently play a leading role in Paul's ethic, and surely did not provide a basis for "Christian Halakah" (Davies, *Paul and Rabbinic Judaism* [rev. ed. 1955]). The focus of Paul's discernment was the Christ-event, not the teachings of Jesus. (When Paul demanded "imitation of Christ," 1 Cor. 11:1; 1 Thess. 1:6, the focus was not on the "earthly Jesus" but on the cross.)

Paul frequently cited the Jewish Scriptures in contexts of moral exhortation, but never casuistically. Indeed, he cited the Prophets and Wisdom more often than the Torah, and when he did appeal to the Torah it was more often to narratives than to statutes. We have already mentioned Paul's insistence on freedom from the law. Paul acknowledged that the "law" and the "commandment" are "holy and just and good" (Rom. 7:12). But he insisted that the law is not eternal, but secondary, added after the promise (Gal. 3:17; Rom. 4:10). Moreover, in the old age, it was co-opted by the powers of sin and death; it was even "the power of sin" (1 Cor. 15:56). It led to sins being "counted" (Rom. 5:13) and provided an "opportunity" for sin (7:8, 10). It was a "custodian until Christ came" (Gal. 3:24-26). Then the promise is kept, and Christ is "the end of the law" (Rom. 10:4; cf. Gal. 3:25). With Christ we have died to the law (Rom. 7:4; Gal. 2:19) and are "discharged from the law . . . so that we serve not under the old written code but in the new life of the Spirit" (Rom. 7:6). The fault was not with the law itself, of course, but with "the flesh," with man's susceptibility to the powers of sin and death (Rom. 8:3). The promise is fulfilled in Jesus Christ, so that in Him "the just requirement of the law might be fulfilled in us" (Rom. 8:4; cf. 13:8-10). But there is no going back to the boasting self-righteousness, to the condemnations, to the old written code. There is no building up again the "dividing wall of hostility" (Eph. 2:14; cf. Gal. 2:18) between Jew and Gentile. So when Paul used the OT, he did not use it as a code to determine God's will. He used it in the light of Christ (2 Cor. 3:16) as narrative, promise, and wisdom to illuminate and persuade his readers with respect to the gift and claim of the new life in Christ.

Paul also used the "natural" moral wisdom of the Hellenistic street preachers and philosophers. Even pagans, after all, live in God's creation and can know something of God and His law (Rom. 1:19; 2:14-16); so Paul could and did use Hellenistic concepts like "conscience" (Gk. *syneídēsis*), Hellenistic terminology for certain moral qualities (see esp. Phil. 4:8), Hellenistic forms of moral argument (esp. the diatribe, e.g., 1 Cor. 6:12-20), the Hellenistic appeal to "nature" as a moral teacher (e.g., 1 Cor. 11:14), and the Hellenistic emphasis on role assignments in determining one's conduct (e.g., the *Haustafeln,* the tables of rules for the household in Col. 3:18–4:1; Eph. 5:21–6:9). It has often been suggested that Paul (or a later Paulinist) simply adopted the familiar standards of Hellenism when it became clear that an ethic based on the eschatological salvation in Christ did not enable a settled common life in the midst of the world. But the appeal to moral commonplaces was not inconsistent with Paul's eschatological and christological themes, for it was Paul's conviction that the new creation is the fulfillment of the original will of God the Creator. Moreover, these familiar standards were thoroughly transformed in the light of Christ. In the *Haustafeln,* for example, the model was no longer the aloof dignity of the philosopher but the patience and love of Christ; the focus was no longer the self but the neighbor; the basic principle was not provided by the roles themselves but by mutual subjection (Eph. 5:21) and equality (Eph. 6:9; Col. 3:25). By addressing women and slaves and children as moral agents along with the freemen (and first!) and by demanding the freemen's submission to Christ and love of the neighbor, the *Haustafeln* did not conform to this age but were transformed and became serviceable to discernment (cf. Rom. 12:1f.).

Paul provided no theory of discernment, but the pattern is plain. It is done always in view of God's eschatological action in Jesus Christ, His gift and demand of a new life. God's act established a new identity, a new perspective on the world, and certain characteristics of the eschatological existence like freedom and love. The new discernment did not, however, create new principles, guidelines, and rules *de novo*; it rather selected, assimilated, and transformed Jewish, Christian, and "natural" moral wisdom in order to discern the particular conduct and character demanded at any particular time. For Paul, these sources of wisdom were never normative in the same way that God's action in Jesus Christ was, and they remained constantly under the criticism and transforming power of the new life claimed in Christ for Christians and of Christians.

4. Concrete Problems. a. Jew and Gentile. Paul's concern for the relation of Jews and Gentiles in the churches has already been observed. In Galatians, Romans, and Ephesians this problem seems to have been the occasion for the letters. For Paul the unity and equality of Jew and Gentile was closely related to "the truth of the gospel" (Gal. 2:5, 14), the "obedience of faith" (Rom. 1:5; 16:25), and "the mystery of God's will" (Eph. 1:9f.; 3:4-6). It is an eschatological unity to be sure (Gal. 3:28), but it must already shape the social reality of the Church. Paul did not demand that Jewish Christians or gentile Christians repudiate their Jewish or gentile identity (and stood against those who would make such demands), but he did demand that they not repudiate each other either. Jew and Gentile are equally "under the power of sin" (Rom. 3:9, with an appeal to the Jewish Scripture; cf. Eph. 2:1-3), and they are equally "justified by his grace as a gift . . . to be received by faith' (Rom. 3:24-30; cf. Gal. 3:6-14; Eph. 2:8). So "there is no distinction" (Rom. 3:22); there is "life for all men" (Rom. 5:18). These indicatives claimed a harmonious pluralism marked by respect and love for those who were and remained different. They must "welcome each other" (Rom. 15:7) and be "eager to maintain the unity of the Spirit in the bond of peace" (Eph. 4:3).

b. Slave and Free. There is also an eschatological unity of slave and free (Gal. 3:28; Col. 3:11). That unity also did not demand uniformity; there remained slave and free. But the relationship stood under the norm of what God has done in Christ. So masters were reminded in their relations with slaves that they, too, had a master (Gk. *kýrios*) and that with Him "there is no partiality" (Eph.

ETHICS: NT ETHICS

6:9); and Philemon was instructed to receive Onesimus back "no longer as a slave but . . . as a beloved brother . . . both in the flesh and in the Lord" (Philem. 16). New relationships were established "in the Lord" and that unity and fraternity must also have some consequences "in the flesh," in the social realities of the Church. The unity is eschatological, but it is not docetic. Paul brought the existing role relationship of slave and master under the lordship of Christ in such a way that it transformed that relationship (and ultimately shattered it).

c. Male and Female. The eschatological unity of male and female (Gal. 3:28), too, did not demand uniformity (especially since 1 Cor. 11:8f. traces the distinction not just to the law but to the original creation; Gal. 3:28, however, uses the very language of Gen. 1:27 [Gk. *ársen kaí thēly*] to say "there is no 'male and female' "). The unity, however, did and must shape the new life in Christ. Paul counted Phoebe his "helper" and Prisca his "fellow worker" (Rom. 16:1-3). He brought the existing role relation of husband and wife under the lordship of Jesus Christ in such a way as to assimilate and transform that relationship. There is mutual subjection (Eph. 5:21), and "head" (v. 23) is defined in terms of Christ's love and sacrifice. This equality and mutuality in the marriage relationship is perhaps most striking in 1 Cor. 7:2b-4. Nevertheless, it was also in 1 Corinthians that Paul insisted that, when women pray and prophesy, they be veiled (11:3-16), and that women "be silent" (14:33b-35). The passages are difficult to reconcile with each other and to Paul's other behavior toward, and advice concerning, women (including the parenthetical 1 Cor. 11:11f.). However they are finally to be interpreted, the occasion for them was apparently that among the Corinthian enthusiasts, claiming on the basis of their "spiritual gifts" to be already and without remainder living in the new age, were women who disturbed the order and decorum of the church with their protestations of independence and their exercise of the gifts. Paul would, of course, be quite unsympathetic with both their eschatology and their concept of "freedom" (independence), and he made a wide variety of appeals, to the law, rabbinic teaching, church custom, and nature, to convince the Corinthians not to tolerate their excesses.

d. Sex and Marriage. Some of the same Corinthian enthusiasts thought that what they did in the body was a matter of indifference, since they lived already in the new age of the Spirit (1 Cor. 6:12-20). Some even boasted about their sexual libertinism (5:1f.). Against these Paul insisted on the resurrection of the body, so that the body, too, belongs to Christ. "The body is not meant for immorality, but for the Lord. . . . So glorify God in your body" (6:13, 20; cf. 1 Thess. 4:3-8).

Others among the enthusiasts at Corinth drew a quite different conclusion: because they were already in the age of the Spirit, they had to be ascetic and to refrain from sexual intercourse. ("It is well for a man not to touch a woman" is a Corinthian slogan which, while not rejected outright, is immediately qualified by Paul, 7:1f.) With them Paul affirmed that celibacy is a sign of a new age and that in the new age marriage is no longer a duty. But against them Paul insisted on the "not yet" character of our existence, recognized the temptation to immorality (7:2), and refused to make celibacy a duty either. Both marriage and celibacy are gifts (Gk. *chárisma,* 7:7). Within marriage sexual intercourse is not only allowed but encouraged (7:3-5; cf. Col. 2:20-23, where Paul again rejects asceticism, and Eph. 5:31f., where Paul draws an analogy between the sexual relation of husband and wife and the relation of Christ and the Church; on divorce, *see* DIVORCE: IN THE NT).

e. The State. Rom. 13:1-7 has often been misunderstood as requiring uncritical obedience to the state. The passage (written years before Nero's persecution in A.D. 64) has affinities with similar teaching of Hellenistic Judaism (e.g., Philo *De legatione ad Gaium*). Paul would seem to be instructing the Roman churches (especially the Jewish churches there) to keep to the tradition that had formed their political posture. Paul used the institutionally oriented advice of Hellenistic Judaism, that the rulers are appointed by God (13:1f.), that their legitimate function is to protect the innocent, promote the good, and punish the evil (vv. 3f.), and that those who desire a well-ordered community life ought to render the authorities appropriate taxes and honor (vv. 5-7). But Paul put that advice, that moral wisdom, in a new context, a transforming context. He set before it and behind it the duty to love (12:9; 13:8) and his reminders of the eschatological situation (12:2; 13:11f.). Submission to government was set in the context of the more urgent duty to love the neighbor while we await God's justice. To love the neighbor in a world still marked by selfishness and evil requires political responsibility. When Christians bring suit against each other, however, it signifies a failure to live the life that ought to mark their character and communities; it is a "defeat" (1 Cor. 6:1-8; also a clear indication of the presumption in the claims of the enthusiasts at Corinth). Love's politics, then, does not insist on one's own rights, is willing to "suffer wrong" (1 Cor. 6:7), but it does insist on government, on justice for the neighbor (Rom. 13).

f. The Collection. At the Apostolic Council Paul's mission among the Gentiles was approved by the elders at Jerusalem, and there they requested that he "remember the poor" (Gal. 2:10). Paul honored that request with the collection he conducted among his gentile churches for the poor in Jerusalem (e.g., 1 Cor. 16:1-4). It was an act of charity that was also to be instrumental in establishing the unity of Jewish and gentile Christians (Rom. 15:25-31; 2 Cor. 9:11-15). In exhorting the Corinthians to complete the collection Paul appealed to love (2 Cor. 8:8, 24) and the example of Christ (v. 9) as fundamental claims on their character (their "readiness," v. 12) and conduct. These took concrete shape not in inequitable burdens (vv. 12f.) but precisely in "equality" (v. 14 twice). That equality is explicated in terms of the distributive principle, "from each according to his ability, to each according to his need" (see 8:14).

In each case Paul's pattern of discernment is operative. The eschatological act of God in Jesus Christ provides a moral identity and a perspective on the world, and establishes certain fundamental values, but it does not create *ex nihilo* new rules, or roles, or institutions. To deal with concrete cases different traditional sources of moral wisdom are assimilated to, and transformed by, the new life given in Christ.

B. The Pastoral Epistles. The authorship of the Pastorals is disputed, but whether by Paul or a devoted student, the spirit of the ethic in them is indisputably more pedestrian and prosaic. To be sure, the gospel remains the eschatological act of God in Jesus Christ (1 Tim. 3:16; 6:11-16; 2 Tim. 1:8-10; 2:11-13; Tit. 2:11-14; 3:4-8), and it remains the basis of the morality (esp. Tit. 2:11-14). But the gospel that was entrusted to Paul (1 Tim. 1:11) and which he in turn entrusted to Timothy (1:18), charging him to guard it (6:20) and to entrust it to "faithful men who will be able to teach others also" (2 Tim. 2:2), gradually becomes identified with the tradition, with "sound doctrine" (1 Tim. 1:8).

Orthodoxy and morality are a matched set for the Pastorals (e.g., 1 Tim. 1:3-5; 3:9; 2 Tim. 2:14-19; Tit. 2:1ff.). The particular heresy (cf. 2 Tim. 1:15) opposed here seems to have been a Jewish gnostic form of Christianity (1 Tim. 1:7; Tit. 1:10, 14-16; 3:9). The heretics held that "the resurrection is past already" (2 Tim. 2:18) and, on the basis of their otherworldliness, demanded abstinence from marriage and "foods" (1 Tim. 4:3). Against them the Pastorals remember that His coming is "not yet" (e.g., 2 Tim. 4:8; Tit. 2:11-14) and that God is the Creator of this world (1 Tim. 4:3f., "everything created by God is good, and nothing is to be rejected if it is received with thanksgiving"). Against the speculative and ascetic morality of these heretics, it was necessary carefully to define and courageously to defend sound doctrine and morality. An antinomian reaction to this legalistic heresy on the part of some compounded the problem (1 Tim. 1:19); so the readers are exhorted to "wage the good warfare, holding faith and a good conscience" (1 Tim. 1:18f.).

In spite of this commendable resistance to gnostic, legalistic, speculative, and antinomian perversions of the Christian ethic, in the Pastorals "the gospel" exercised less critical and transformative power on the sources of moral wisdom and role definitions that it assimilated and used. (Perhaps precisely because of the necessity of resistance to gnostic and antinomian tendencies it was important soberly to reinforce mundane obligations taught in the law and acknowledged in this world.) Orthodoxy and morality are a matched set, but the determination of what is good and right depends more on the common moral assumptions of the readers than on any "new discernment." The virtues and vices listed (1 Tim. 1:9f.; 2:2-5; 2 Tim. 3:2-5; etc.) are largely commonplace for the time. The position on the law simply affirms it against the antinomians and protects it against the speculative and ascetic interpretations of gnostic Judaizers: "the law is good, if anyone uses it lawfully" (1 Tim. 1:8). Most strikingly and troublesomely, the traditional role assignments of women (1 Tim. 2:9-15; Tit. 2:3-5) and slaves (1 Tim. 6:1f.) are assimilated without being balanced by appeals to mutual submission. The exhortations to pray for (1 Tim. 2:2) and be submissive to (Tit. 3:1) rulers are commonplace to Hellenistic Judaism and are not here transformed by the duty of neighbor love in a still selfish world (as in Rom. 13). The treatment of riches is also traditional (1 Tim. 6:7-10), but the final exhortation (1 Tim. 6:17-19) uses the eschatological perspective both to stand against asceticism and to demand that the rich be "rich in good deeds, liberal and generous."

C. Hebrews. Hebrews describes itself as a "word of exhortation" (Gk. *paráklēsis,* 13:22), and so it is. The sustained and involved theological arguments are punctuated and climaxed by vibrant exhortations to acknowledge the truth and to act on it (2:1-4; 3:7–4:16; 5:11–6:12; 10:19-39; 12:1–13:19). The author is not interested in theological and exegetical elegance for its own sake, but for the sake of showing his readers their great privilege and the immeasurable loss that would be theirs if they were to let the passage of time, whether in hardship or in ease, weary them in their "struggle against sin" (12:5).

The theological focus is the covenant, the "second" covenant (8:7), which is "new" (8:8, 13; 9:15; 12:24) and "better" (7:22; 8:6) precisely because it is based on God's effective and "once for all" dealing with sin in Jesus Christ (7:27; 9:12, 26; 10:10). This new and better covenant is "eternal" (13:20); the old covenant is "obsolete" (8:13). The stipulations and sacrifices of the old covenant are obsolete, but a response of gratitude and worship is also required by the new covenant (12:28). In the benediction the author prays that the God who raised Jesus from the dead and so made "eternal covenant" may equip the readers "that you may do his will" (13:20f.; cf. 10:5-9). The covenant theology supports and calls for the general exhortations in the first twelve chapters, e.g., to "hold fast the confession of our hope without wavering" and "to stir up one another to love and good works" (10:23f.), which are given concrete content in ch. 13.

Chapter 13 intends to provide paradigms of new covenant gratitude and worship (12:28). The foci are brotherly love (13:1), hospitality to strangers (13:2), a sympathetic identification with the imprisoned and ill-treated (13:3; cf. 10:32-34), respect for marriage (13:4, a position contrary to both asceticism and adultery), and the freedom "from the love of money" that comes from trusting God (13:5). These duties are summarized again in 13:16, where they are identified as the "sacrifices" appropriate to the new covenant: "Do not neglect to do good and to share what you have, for such sacrifices are pleasing to God."

IV. Catholic Epistles.*–A. James.* The "letter" of James is really a parenesis, a collection of general moral instructions, often — as here — a miscellaneous collection without a single focus. James must be read and understood as such, but as such it defies systematization and summarization. The sayings are often linked merely by catchwords. The moral instructions themselves are eclectic, drawn from a variety of sources, including Greek philosophy (the parenetic form, the use of diatribe, e.g., 2:14-26 and the material in 1:13-15 and 4:12), the wisdom literature of Hellenistic Judaism, the Law and the Prophets, and the sayings of Jesus.

There is, of course, the famous polemic against "faith apart from works" (2:14-26). There can be little doubt that the author had the Pauline teaching in view (as it was used in a perverted "Paulinism," to be sure; see also 2 Pet. 3:14-17); he used the same example, Abraham, and explicitly Gen. 15:6, but the decisive evidence is linguistic — both Paul and James (and only they!) used the phrase "justified *by faith* [Gk. *ek písteōs*]." But James was hardly interested in defending a different theology of justification or a new concept of faith. Indeed, he acknowledged the important priority of God's gracious action (1:17f.). He was interested only in preventing avoidance of one's obvious duty through rationalizing. James, like Paul, wanted a faith that acts (2:22; cf. Gal. 5:6; see also Jas. 1:22-25; cf. Mt. 7:24-27). The ethical perspectives of James and Paul are neither altogether contradictory nor identical, but complementary.

The law, at least in its moral parts, was obligatory for James (1:25; 2:8-12; 4:11f.). But cultic obligations were thoroughly relativized by the overriding religious significance of morality (1:26f.). Love was a commandment "first among equals" (see 2:8-12; 4:11) and entailed impartiality (2:9).

The foci of the parenesis included admonitions to govern the tongue (1:26; 3:1-12, with echoes of instructions found in the sayings of Jesus, Hellenistic Judaism, and Stoicism; 5:12; cf. Mt. 5:7), a severe rebuke of "the rich" (1:11; 2:1-7; 5:1-6), and exhortations not to judge or boast (4:11-16).

James's interest was not a theological basis for morality or transformation of morality, but the author did identify himself as "a servant of God and of the Lord Jesus Christ" (1:1; cf. 2:1) and reminded his readers of "the coming of the Lord" (5:7f.). His coming grounds the exhortation to patience and marks the whole parenesis with urgency and stringency (cf. 1:7f., 21; 2:12f.; 4:4; 5:1, 9). If any theological focus is to be discerned, it seems to be Jesus' theme of "the great reversal" of the kingdom (cf. 2:5; 4:6-10, with its exhortations to repentance; 5:1).

B. 1 Peter. Some have identified 1 Peter with a baptismal homily. Such an identification overstates the case,

ETHICS: NT ETHICS

but the baptismal allusions are clear (see esp. 3:18-22) and leave their mark on the ethic of this Epistle. The readers are "newborn babes" (2:2); they have been "born anew to a living hope through the resurrection of Jesus Christ from the dead" (1:3; cf. 2:23). This is cause for great joy (1:6), but "now" (1:6; 3:21) it is also reason to "be sober, set your hope fully upon the grace that is coming to you at the revelation of Jesus Christ" (1:13). This jubilation and sobriety in response to God's eschatological action in Jesus Christ correspond to Paul's indicative and imperative. The newborn are exhorted to be "obedient children," not to be "conformed to the passions of your former ignorance" (1:14). They are incorporated into Christ and into a new society (2:4-10). This affects their identity and their perspective on the world (they are "aliens and exiles," 2:11). Their character and conduct are no longer to be marked by "the futile ways inherited from your fathers" (1:18) or "the passions of the flesh" (2:11; 4:1-3 — note the proximity of indicative and imperative), but by brotherly love (1:22 — again, proximity of indicative and imperative; 2:17; 3:8; 4:8).

The *Haustafel* is here set in an eschatological context (2:11) and makes "good conduct" serviceable to the missionary enterprise of the Church (2:12; cf. 2:15; 3:1f.). The traditional exhortation to be subject to civil authorities is balanced by the exhortation to freedom (2:16) and the recognition of God's greater authority (2:16f.). Similarly the exhortation to women (3:1-6; the advice about adornment and submission, vv. 3-6, is quite traditional) is balanced by an exhortation to men to treat "the weaker sex" with consideration and honor as "joint heirs" (3:7). The exhortation to slaves to be submissive is not balanced by any appeal to masters to recognize one impartial Master, but it is the occasion for introducing the important theme of the example of (and participation in) Christ's sufferings (2:21-24; see also 3:9; 4:1, 13, where it is used to encourage perseverance in the midst of persecution). That theme contains the expectation of vindication and blessing, and the slaves may, like Jesus, trust "him who judges justly" (2:23).

C. 2 Peter and Jude. These two Epistles both ardently defend orthodoxy and morality against the heretics who "promise freedom" (2 Pet. 2:19) but "pervert the grace of our God into licentiousness" (Jude 4) and scoff at "the promise of his coming" (2 Pet. 3:4). This abandonment of orthodoxy and morality only renders these heretics "creatures of instinct" (2 Pet. 2:12; Jude 10) and proves the imminence of the coming of the Lord (Jude 18). God's judgment is sure; that hope gives urgency to "lives of holiness and godliness" (2 Pet. 3:11-14).

***V. Johannine Literature.**–A. The Gospel and Epistles.* The Gospel of John has sometimes been accused of anti-Semitism, and indeed uses the term "the Jews" pejoratively (in many of its nearly seventy occurrences). But this Gospel never draws a contrast between "the Jews" and "the Gentiles" (indeed, Gk. *tá éthnē* never occurs in either the Gospel or the Epistles). The only Gentile who figures in the narrative is Pilate, and he is clearly an outsider (18:35; compare the Synoptic Gospels, in which Gentiles are continually pressing their way into the narrative). Nowhere is the heritage of the Jews given to the Gentiles (note the contrast in John's and Paul's treatments of the vine, an old image for Israel, Jn. 15:1-8; Rom. 11:17-24). "The Jews" are contrasted with "the Jews who had believed" (8:31; 11:45; 12:42; etc.), not non-Jews. If "the Jews" are criticized, they are criticized from within Judaism. Far from anti-Semitic, John's Gospel is perhaps the most Semitic of our Gospels. The crisis he addressed was a crisis within Judaism. For John, Jews stood at a choice between light and darkness, truth and falsehood, life and death; that choice was being made in their response to their Messiah.

The ethics must also be understood against this Jewish background. The law apparently still stands. But as the eschatological prophet (in John, Jesus is the prophet, not John the Baptist! [1:21, 25; 4:19; 7:40; 9:17]), Jesus renders final judgment about the requirements of the law. He discards the ritual requirements in favor of "worship in spirit and in truth" (4:19-24). He subordinates sabbath observance to His work of healing (5:9b-18; 7:22-24; 9:13-34). In all this Moses remains an authority, but not one to be used independently of, or in judgment against, Jesus (cf. also 5:39-47).

The focus of John's ethics, however, is not the law or its messianic interpretation. The focus is Christ and the "life in his name" (Jn. 20:31; 10:10; etc.). Christ is the great revelation of God's love (Jn. 3:16; 1 Jn. 4:9; etc.), as both a gift and a demand. John's narrative of the cross is unique and arresting in its description of Jesus' crucifixion as His exaltation (3:14; 8:28; 12:32, 34). He is exalted not after but precisely in the self-sacrificing love of the cross (e.g., 15:13). The narrative turns conventional judgments of glory upside down, and that glory of humble service and love is what is shared with His followers (17:22) as indicative and imperative. Christ Himself is exemplar (1 Jn. 2:6) and teacher (1 Jn. 3:24). But all of this, God's act of love in Christ, Christ's example (e.g., the footwashing, Jn. 13:14f.), and His teaching, is concentrated in a single command, "that you love one another" (Jn. 13:34; 15:12, 17; 1 Jn. 3:11, 23; 4:11f.; 2 Jn. 5f.; etc.). This commandment is "a new commandment" (Jn. 13:34; 1 Jn. 2:8) precisely because of the christological and eschatological basis, a basis signed in the addition "as I have loved you." In the Epistles, however, it is also emphasized that the commandment is "old" (1 Jn. 2:7; cf. 2 Jn. 5), precisely because the new community is not seen over against the old covenant but in continuity with it and its "commandments" (see esp. 2 Jn. 5f., but also 1 Jn. 2:3-8; 3:22-24; 4:21–5:3).

The commandment to love one another surely focuses on relations within the community, but a focus is not a restriction. 1 Jn. 3:11-18 makes it quite plain that the duty of love extends to those outside the community (the contrast in vv. 13f., e.g., would be quite unintelligible if love were restricted to members of one's own community) and to concrete deeds of service to people in need (vv. 17f.).

B. Revelation. The apocalyptic character of Revelation is unmistakable; it is not to be overlooked, however, that the apocalypse is put into the form of a letter (cf. the opening in 1:4-7 and the closing in 22:21). Revelation was concrete pastoral encouragement and exhortation to churches in Asia Minor who found themselves in persecution. The confidence that God has acted, is acting, and will act eschatologically in Jesus Christ was the basis of this encouragement and exhortation. The seven letters to the churches (2:1–3:22) demonstrate the pattern of Revelation's ethics. After being introduced by an identical command to write (2:1, 8, 12, 18; 3:1, 7, 14), each letter identifies the speaker, and although a great variety of images is used (each relevant to the particular encouragement and exhortation to follow), each identification of the speaker acknowledges the unlimited lordship of Christ. There follows in each case (2:2, 9, 13, 19; 3:1, 8, 15) Christ's discernment of the church's conduct and character, His verdict on it, and His command to it. These sections were each no doubt relevant to the concrete situation of the particular churches, but the encouragement and exhortation were also intended to be universally relevant (cf. the formula, "He who has an ear, let him hear what the Spirit says to the churches" in 2:7, 11, 17, 29; 3:6, 13, 22). The focus in each case is life in conformity with the work of Christ, especially "patient endurance" (2:2f., 13, 19; 3:10f.). The need for patient endurance arose because of persecutions by Roman emperor and Jewish synagogue (2:9; 3:9), temptations to immorality (2:14, 20f.; 3:4), and indeed the seductions of ease (3:17). There is, finally, in each of the letters, a promise of a share in Christ's victory (2:7, 11, 17, 26-28; 3:5, 12, 21; the images return in the last two chapters of Revelation). From the very beginning the criterion upon which the commendations and commands were based needed no defense; it was established in God's vindication of Christ's work and accepted by the churches in their worship of Him. With John they "share . . . in Jesus the tribulation and the kingdom and the patient endurance" (1:9).

The remainder of the book is a series of apocalyptic visions developing the promise of the victory already assured in the enthronement of the Lamb that was slain (chs. 4–5). This victory involved them then in martyrdom and agony (2:13; 6:9; 13:15; 17:6; 20:4), in conflict with the satanic power exercised in imperial might and its totalitarian and religious claims (ch. 13). Such power could be resisted only in the victory assured in the past and promised in the future and expressed even then in loyal endurance (13:10; 14:12; see also 14:13; 15:2-4). It is a victory that involved them then in a spiritual exodus from "Babylon," fallen and to fall (ch. 18). The immorality of "Babylon" was exercised in Roman cities, but the Lord had won a great victory and established a new kingdom. The certainty of Babylon's doom and the Lord's victory was both encouragement (the funeral dirge, ch. 18, becomes "alleluia" in 19:1) and exhortation ("Come out of her, my people," 18:4). The exodus required is from the demonic values, the pride of power (18:3, 9f.), and the greed (18:3, 11-19) that marked her life and justified her doom. That exodus could be undertaken only in the assurance of a new city, a holy city, new Jerusalem, where "they shall be his people" (21:2-4).

Bibliography.–V. P. Furnish, *Theology and Ethics in Paul* (1968); *The Love Command in the NT* (1972); *Moral Teaching of Paul* (1979); J. L. Houlden, *Ethics and the NT* (1973); J. Jeremias, *Sermon on the Mount* (Eng. tr. 1963); W. Lillie, *Studies in NT Ethics* (1961); L. H. Marshall, *Challenge of NT Ethics* (1947); P. Minear, *I Saw a New Earth* (1968); J. Murray, *Principles of Conduct* (1957); J. T. Sanders, *Ethics in the NT* (1975); R. Schnackenburg, *Moral Teaching of the NT* (2nd ed. 1965); W. Schrage, *Die konkreten Einzelgebote in der paulinischen Paränese* (1961); *IDB*, II, *s.v.*; J. H. Yoder, *Politics of Jesus* (1972).

A. D. VERHEY

Philosophical Ethics

I. Nature and Function
II. History
   A. Classical Period
   B. Patristic and Medieval Christianity
   C. Modern Period
III. Conclusion

I. Nature and Function.–All cultures and religions have customs, practices, traditions, and modes of conduct. In this sense ethics is universal. Nevertheless, while maxims and adages regarding the proper way to act are common, not everywhere has there been more detailed and scientific reflection on human behavior. When this happens, as it did in ancient Greece, the result is ethics in the narrower sense of a philosophical inquiry into conduct in the context of a corresponding philosophical system.

In Greece, of course, "ethics" originally had the general sense of customs. Latin *mos* (pl. *mores*, from which Eng. "morality" derives) bears a similar sense. When thoughtful people began to question traditional modes of behavior in the light of new situations, interests, and concerns, this questioning took three related forms, which have become normative in ethical discussion. First, what is the basis of the action? On what ground ought one to do this action and not do another? Second, what is the criterion of evaluation? Is there some absolute or only a relative rule or principle by which to judge? Third, what is the goal of human conduct? What end or ends should actions serve? The link between the three questions is apparent, for the basis, norm, and goal might easily be the same.

Since ethics deals with ends and norms, the propriety of its description as a science has sometimes been challenged. If the procedures of natural science are regarded as criteria which all intellectual disciplines must meet in order to earn the title of science, ethics can be quickly eliminated. Predictability is certainly not possible in view of the variable human factors, and verification by experiment is obviously ruled out. Nor can an evaluative factor be eliminated from ethics, for by its very nature it puts the question, not merely of what we do, but also of what we ought to do. To assign ethics a purely descriptive role is to empty it of its main interest and content. The volitional element (the "will"), which must certainly be presupposed or taken into account in ethical study, also militates against the "scientific" character of ethics in a narrower definition of the term science. Nevertheless, ethics as an intellectual discipline can meet two of the fundamental requirements of science in the broader sense: it can adopt the necessary academic rigor, and it can let itself be controlled by its object. Ethics may rightly be numbered among the humane sciences.

How far philosophical ethics has a valid function, at least in the Church, has been a matter of considerable debate. Undoubtedly Christian ethics with its distinctive theological foundation must take a different course. Yet even in so doing it must be aware that philosophy, too, is concerned about the question of human conduct and is pursuing its own line of investigation and recommendation. It may be that, both negatively and positively, certain things can be learned from this parallel discussion. It may be that some Christians should actively participate in philosophical ethics as they do in other branches of human learning and inquiry. It may be that all Christians should have some knowledge of philosophical, and more recently sociological and anthropological, developments insofar as these exert a strong and pervasive influence on contemporary thinking and conduct which even Christians cannot wholly escape. If the Church must avoid the temptation to commingle theological and philosophical ethics, it can hardly afford to turn a blind eye to philosophical ethics and treat it as nonexistent.

II. History.–*A. Classical Period. 1. Socrates.* The study of ethics originated in Greece during the 5th cent. B.C. with the protest of the Sophists against established habits and traditions (*ethiká*). The attack on these practices went hand in hand with the decay of the religious and poetic beliefs on which they rested and the accompanying change in intellectual and educational life. The Sophists themselves were unable to follow up their attack, for they talked in abstractions that had little practical application. Socrates seems to have been the thinker who tried to show, not only what form conduct should take, but also what the goal of action should be, and the means of effecting it. Ignorance, he believed, lies behind wrong conduct and gives rise to disputes concerning right and wrong. The exposure of ignorance is thus an essential ethical task. All people want the good, but they do not achieve it because they do not know it. Knowledge is the basis of right conduct. Knowledge of what? Not of moral rules but of the true nature of pleasure or happiness which, as Socrates sees it, is the goal of life, the good. All people want the good because they want happiness. But true happiness cannot be had without knowledge. Once it is known, the good will be both sought and done.

2. Plato. In his earlier period, when he was more strongly under the influence of Socrates, Plato accepted the thesis that pleasure constitutes the good. Hence right conduct will be that which brings pleasure and the art of ethics is discovering what this is. After Socrates' death, and with his Italian journey, Plato moved over to Pythagorean views which confirmed him in the belief in immortality and helped to give his thinking a broader social and cosmic aspect. As he now saw it, there are two worlds, the one the prototype of the other. Man belongs to both worlds, that of ideas and that of sense. What gives pleasure merely to the senses can no longer be regarded as the good, since sensation ties us to the lower world from which our higher being seeks to escape. Asceticism thus replaces an earlier hedonism. Plato, however, did not become a simple dualist. In his *Republic* he postulated a threefold division of the soul with desire at the lowest level, the affective element in the middle, and reason at the top. For each of the levels he found an appropriate virtue, temperance for the first, courage for the second, and wisdom for the third. Justice, somewhat in the sense of "to each his own," constitutes a fourth virtue, that of letting each division pursue its own end in such a way that harmony results. Evil arises not out of ignorance alone, but out of disorder, the disruption of inner harmony. This may be seen politically as well as individually, for Plato applied the three virtues to the three classes of merchants, soldiers, and philosopher-rulers, with justice again as the harmony of the three. Like Socrates, Plato saw no serious impediment to the willing of the good. Once it is truly known, to choose it should present no problem.

3. Aristotle. Aristotle, a pupil of Plato, did not show the same concern for immortality as his mentor did. He had a stronger interest in man in his distinctiveness as a social being. Ethics, then, had to do with social customs and conduct. The problem of ethics as he understood it was still that of the good that should inform such conduct and customs, but in order to discover this he engaged in a more exact and detailed investigation. For Aristotle the good is the ultimate purpose behind every lesser purpose in life. He accepted an equation of this purpose with happiness, but he rejected the simple equation of happiness and pleasure. Happiness relates to the nature and function of man, not that which he shares with other creatures, but that which is distinctive to him and consists in his rationality. The good may thus be defined as activity, or, more specifically, as "the activity of the soul in accordance with reason" (*Eth. Nic.* i.5).

In the moral sphere the means to attain the good is habit. Here as elsewhere, Aristotle believed, practice makes perfect. Habit produces character. In contrast to Luther's famous dictum, attention does not focus on the person doing the acts but on the acts constituting the person. The norm or goal of moral action is to be found in the mean between extremes. Each extreme has its opposite, and excess will always fall short of the good. Too much prudence, for example, is just as bad as too much rashness. The mean can be achieved by counterbalancing one's inclination to the extreme either on the right hand or the left.

In the intellectual sphere, which as that of reason is higher than the moral sphere, happiness is attained in the supreme activity of contemplation. This bears no necessary relation except to the self and it also constitutes an end in itself, not an end which might also be a means. It thus comes closest to what is immortal and divine.

Aristotle recognized that education and favorable circumstances are conducive to virtue. He also perceived that some actions are involuntary, whether through ignorance or coercion. He conceded that even voluntary actions do not always involve deliberation and choice. Nevertheless, he contended for an area in which man can exercise deliberate choice, namely, the area in which the moving principle is the agent himself. Since deliberation and choice relate to purpose, they play an important role in his conception of moral and intellectual virtue. They also imply the ability of some people at least to achieve such virtue, although by its very nature Aristotle's ethics, like his politics, is aristocratic, not democratic, in both its conception and execution.

4. Epicureans. Epicureanism is popularly associated with the pursuit of sensuous pleasure. In fact, Epicurus himself (342-270 B.C.) set out to correct the licentiousness of the Cyrenaics. He certainly adopted pleasure as the supreme good, but, as he saw it, true pleasure can be attained only by living prudently and honorably, reducing desire, and avoiding pain. The Epicurean attitude to religion, which does not postulate the non-existence of the gods but their practical irrelevance, is shaped by the belief that religion causes evil and unhappiness. Even though the Epicurean system might suggest materialistic determinism, a certain freedom is reserved in it for the moral will. The difficulty in defining pleasure is what leaves the door open for the association of Epicureanism and sensuous living. If enjoyment is thought to constitute the norm and goal of conduct, then anything may be done so long as it does not entail pain or disturbance.

5. Stoics. Founded by Zeno of Citium (*ca.* 336-264 B.C.), Stoicism, too, regarded happiness as the supreme end of conduct. It equated happiness with the realization of man's natural purpose and thus arrived at the definition of good conduct as living in accordance with one's rational nature, namely, the avoiding of what is harmful and the doing of what is appropriate. The Stoics believed that happiness results when what is fitting is done, and they viewed pleasure and pain as mere accidents or incidents which the wise person will meet with indifference. Living in accordance with reason, the truly wise will achieve self-mastery and independence of earthly desires. Since this sovereignty can rise above the accidents of circumstance, the Stoics regarded it as a universal possibility binding all humanity into a single brotherhood. Of all the ethical systems of antiquity, Stoicism made perhaps the greatest appeal to the early Church because of its emphasis on moral integrity, the necessity of virtue, the joys of the inner life, and common humanity.

B. Patristic and Medieval Christianity. 1. The Early Church. The Church began its mission against the background of Greek thought and teaching. Nevertheless, its early ethical instruction gave little evidence of association with classical moral philosophy. Christianity was certainly seen as a way of life, not just a set of beliefs. The customs and conduct of Christians, however, were drawn from a different source and had a basis, norm, and goal established by the divine revelation in Christ to which their faith was directed. Justin could compare the ethical teachings of Scripture to the best insights of the philosophers, but any similarities, he suggested, arose simply because the philosophers were influenced by Moses. GNOSTICISM, of course, introduced Hellenistic ideas with related ascetic or licentious practices, but these were strongly resisted by the Church. If asceticism prospered in some orthodox circles, too, a biblical rather than a philosophical reason was found for it. At most, Clement of Alexandria introduced classical precepts into his portrayal of Christian life in his *Paedagogus,* but even here the

ETHICS: PHILOSOPHICAL ETHICS

ultimate source seemed to be theological, not philosophical. Elsewhere, ethics denoted rules of Christian living either in the ecclesiastical world in general or in the monastic world in particular. Ambrose adopted some ideas of Cicero in his *On the Duties of the Clergy* (i.30, 50) but no need was seen for a specific philosophical investigation.

2. Augustine. In view of his evident Neo-Platonic leanings, Augustine has sometimes been presented as a bridge-builder between Christian theology and classical ethical inquiry. It can hardly be disputed that he appropriated many of the terms and concepts of philosophical ethics. Thus he referred consistently to the good as the supreme goal to which knowledge is subject. He found a progression from thought to action and from action to contemplation. Yet one should remember that Augustine did not address himself directly to the ethical question as such. If he spoke of the good, he always equated it, not with an abstraction, but with the known God of revelation. In contrast to the classical ethicists, he did not find in sinful man the freedom to achieve moral goodness by knowledge, choice, or practice. He identified love — the love of God graciously shed abroad in the heart by the Holy Spirit — as the motive power of true righteousness. For all the philosophical influences, Augustine seems to have been primarily a theologian. He might borrow thoughts and expressions from pagan ethicists but his own ethical reflections had finally a source in dogma.

3. Medieval Church. Legalism, not philosophical instruction, posed perhaps the most serious challenge to ethics in the Middle Ages. Original lists of customs and duties, partly collected already in the Apostolic Constitutions, achieved elaborate codification in Gratian's *Decretum* (*ca.* 1140). The developing church courts provided a powerful means of enforcement. While it was not intended that either theologically or personally the Christian way of life should be severed from its root, only too often this was the unhappy consequence. Ethics codified as law necessarily gave rise to "cases," and casuistry inevitably developed as an important and at times confusing branch of moral science with the possibility of rigid, moderate, or elastic interpretations.

Classical learning did not wither away, of course, even in the so-called Dark Ages. In the Carolingian renaissance Alcuin of York (735-804) included in his many works a significant treatise entitled *Virtues and Vices.* Abelard (1079-1142) contributed an ethical work and not merely his unsatisfactory ethical conduct to the twelfth-century scene. Under the title *Ethica,* or *Scito te ipsum* (*Know Thyself*), this work explored the importance of intention in moral acts. Lombard, too, has an ethical section in his famous *Sentences.*

4. Aquinas. Aquinas holds special interest because of his respect for Aristotle, his work in the development of a philosophical methodology in theological inquiry, and his influence on later Christian thinking. At three points he imported classical ideas into his substantially biblical presentation. First, he acknowledged a natural inclination to the good, or at least to individual goods, with a certain freedom of rational and volitional choice, although not to the point of a Pelagian freedom from the bondage of sin apart from special grace. Second, he accepted the place of habits, which, he believed, imply order in action and are necessary. Here again, however, he did not agree that habits can bring virtue unless they be the habits graciously implanted by God. Finally, he found a place for natural as distinct from both eternal and civil law. Natural law is a rule based on reason with the common good as its goal. It is natural inasmuch as the eternal law has been indelibly inscribed on the heart of man (cf. Rom. 1–2) and may be known by self-investigation. Aquinas did not conclude, however, that to know natural law is to know eternal law. As God's will cannot be done without grace, so it is not finally known without revelation. Thus the so-called theological virtues of faith, hope, and love, which form the apex of Christian morality, are known and given to us only by God's gracious word and work in Jesus Christ.

C. Modern Period. 1. British Hedonism. The Reformation brought with it a new surge of biblical and theological ethics, although not without a continuing philosophical interest in some thinkers. By the 17th cent. this surge had partly exhausted itself and in England especially a new attempt was made to put ethics on a scientific basis. In the work of Thomas Hobbes this led to a revival of the ancient idea that, since all people are motivated by self-interest, personal pleasure will have to be the norm and goal of action. Hobbes did not claim that this ought to be so but recognized that in fact it is. In his political theory he thus advocated authoritarianism on the ground that this offers the best safeguard for the achievement of pleasure.

2. Intuitionism. In reaction to both the teaching and the methodology of Hobbes many English moralists tried to find a higher principle of conduct and also a form of ethical imperative. Cudworth returned to the Platonic concept of ideas but the more common trend was toward a type of moral intuitionism. More, for example, argued that we instinctively know certain things to be right, and Shaftesbury and Hutcheson pointed out that variations in moral evaluation all rest on a general sense of what is good and bad. Butler related this intuition more specifically to conscience, although he tried to give it a more factual basis by arguing that observation will show that people everywhere have always distinguished between right and wrong. Partly in answer to hedonism, partly to find a legitimate place for it, he believed that following conscience even when it seems to be to one's disadvantage coincides with true self-interest. Yet even if it does not, conscience should still be followed; inequities will be balanced out at the last judgment, "the final distribution of things."

3. Natural Law. Even at the time of the Reformation the idea of natural law persisted. Melanchthon, in his discussion of law in the *Loci communes,* found three forms of law: divine, human, and natural. So long as natural law was equated in some sense with the knowledge of right and wrong described in Rom. 2, and thus seen as a form of eternal law, a distinctive Christian orientation could be maintained. By the 18th cent., however, an important reversal took place among the Deists and French Rationalists. Christian ethics now came to be viewed as either a republication of natural law or a mistaken divergence from it. Thinkers like Voltaire, adopting ideas parallel to those of the intuitionists, believed that all people know by nature that some things are right and others are wrong, although ignorance, superstition, and bad teaching can obscure and pervert this knowledge. Voltaire himself thought the requirements of natural law could be reduced to a few simple virtues and argued forcefully against the "unnatural" moral teaching of the Church, which confused matters and worked against genuine morality. Proponents of a secularized natural law in this sense experienced no difficulty in thinking that people can keep this law as well as know it, although they found little to their taste in the extreme naturalism of life and conduct rhetorically advocated by Rousseau in his famous essays.

4. The Categorical Imperative. In most of the moral thinking of the 17th and 18th cents. the results of acts, whether for the self or others, formed an important element in ethics. This is one reason why observation played a big part in the systems of such diverse moralists as Hobbes and Butler. Indeed, even intuitionists and advocates of natural law, in their positing of a general sense of right and wrong, tended to relate this in some way to the happiness which right actions would bring. In Immanuel Kant, however, a new stress came to be laid on the *a priori* character of the moral imperative. Good acts certainly should be beneficial to others. Nor did Kant oppose the legitimacy of the pursuit of happiness as a goal of life. With a stricter realism, however, he perceived that in this world personal happiness may often be incompatible with doing one's duty and in these circumstances duty must be done, i.e., the moral imperative is categorical. Like Butler, Kant believed one must postulate God and immortality in order that a right balance may finally be struck between duty and happiness. While he recognized that an evil inclination opposes the inclination toward the good, Kant, like most thinkers of his day, presupposed that the will has the power to obey the categorical ethical demand. In his *Religion Within the Limits of Reason Alone* he thus emerged as one of the most blatant Pelagians of the whole Christian epoch. Divine forgiveness, he argued, can be merited by the moral achievement of which we are capable. No thinking person can believe in vicarious atonement or free justification except perhaps as theoretical ecclesiastical doctrines. Theology can be tolerated only as it promotes virtue. For Kant the categorical imperative constituted the *a priori* which formed not only an unassailable ground of action but also the only possible basis of his minimal religion.

5. Utilitarianism. Kant undoubtedly made an impressive plea for duty but he failed to gain many adherents. Idealists like Hegel moved back quickly to the idea of personal self-development, conceived of in triadic fashion. In England the idea of happiness as the goal and norm of right action took a new form in the utilitarianism of Jeremy Bentham, John Stuart Mill, and Henry Sidgwick. Starting from the position that each individual seeks happiness, Bentham argued that there is also a general and collective happiness. Morality, then, seeks what is good not only for the individual or for other individuals but for the aggregate of all individuals. Its goal must be the greatest good for the greatest number. How is this determined? Bentham suggested certain criteria of happiness, e.g., intensity and purity, by which right action may be measured. How is it enforced? He found sanctions in the physical, political, social, and religious consequences of acts, along with the possibility of eternal punishments. As Bentham saw it, the happiness of the whole will carry with it that of the individuals who compose the whole. Empirically, however, this does not follow. For this reason Sidgwick proposed a new basis for utilitarianism in the universal view of things set before us by reason. He had to admit that without a doctrine of ultimate retribution few could be persuaded of the rationality of this collective outlook.

6. Relativism. The failure of philosophy to come up with a goal or standard whereby an act may be clearly defined as right or wrong led many ethicists into forms of relativism. John Dewey may be cited as an impressive example. For him standards of morality were like accepted weights and measures. These are convenient and necessary but they are also temporary and variable. They serve their turn and may then be discarded or replaced. No act is intrinsically good or bad. If it has a beneficial effect it is good. If it ceases to have such an effect it may no longer be regarded as good. In practice, of course, Dewey ran into difficulties when trying to work this out consistently. He obviously found it hard to think that certain acts could ever be good and thus he fell back to some degree on the old idea of human consensus. Taken strictly, his ethics would simply be a matter of conflicting opinions or even tastes, about which there can be no ultimate debate.

This seems in fact to be the position of a group of moralists of whom W. H. F. Barnes and A. J. Ayer are influential spokesmen. In their view, moral statements have only subjective validity. They do not express facts but indicate personal reactions. At the most they can aim only to win over others to one's own preference. Finally, then, they have no real basis and can have no compelling force.

Situational ethics betrays a similar relativism. Adopting only a very general principle like love, it leaves the ground clear for individual decisions about what is right, i.e., loving, in a given situation. A twofold relativism ensues. First, the general principle itself may be different for different people. Second, the situation decides to a considerable extent the course of action that may be called right according to the principle adopted. Thus what is good at one time may be bad at another and what is bad may sometimes be accepted as good. In these circumstances there can be no final arbitrament. According to his own view each will have done what is right and no criticism can have any objective or absolute validity. Ethical discussion may continue only as an exchange of views.

III. Conclusion.–In the last analysis the whole history of philosophical ethics may not incorrectly be described as a history of relativism. Many bases, standards, and goals have been proposed. Many of them carry a certain cogency. None, however, has objective authority or absolute force. Each can be a matter of debate and division. Nor indeed can any of the proposals solve the deeper problem, not only of knowing the right, but of having the power to do it. The existence of this power may be lightly assumed. The history of human ethics has lamentably failed to demonstrate it.

Bibliography.–*Enc.Brit.*, *s.v.* "Ethics"; *Encyclopedia of Philosophy* (1967), III, *s.v.* "History of Ethics" (R. Abelson and K. Nielsen); C. C. Brinton, *A History of Western Morals* (2 vols., 1919); O. Dittrich, *Geschichte der Ethik* (4 vols., 1926-1932); T. E. Hill, *Ethical Theories* (1950); W. E. H. Lecky, *History of European Morals* (2 vols., 1919); J. Macquarrie, *Twentieth Century Religious Thought* (1963); R. A. P. Rogers, *A Short History of Ethics* (1911); H. Sidgwick, *Outlines of the History of Ethics* (1886); E. Westermarck, *Origin and Development of Moral Ideas* (2 vols., 1908).

G. W. BROMILEY

ETHICS AND DOGMATICS

I. The Problem
II. Scripture
III. Historical Survey
  A. Early and Medieval Church
  B. The Reformation
  C. Post-Reformation Period
  D. Liberal Theology
  E. Contemporary Theology
IV. Theological Principles
V. Conclusion

I. The Problem.–On the surface ethics and dogmatics are so closely related in Christianity that they cannot be disjoined. Christians behave the way they do because they believe the way they do. Their life of action has its root in their life in Christ. The inner motivation of love for God and commitment to Christ impels them to love their neighbors and engage in practical discipleship. Even more detailed beliefs about God and His nature and work shape their lives positively and constructively. Insofar as Christians adopt a certain life-style, whether or not it conforms to that of contemporaries, it is because they are placed under obligation to do so by their Christian understanding of God, man, the world, and the future.

Yet is the matter quite that simple? First, ethics deals with visible acts and not just inner motivations. At this level a Christian may well do at many points precisely what a non-Christian does. Even if he does it for different reasons, the act itself can be studied independently of its motivation, and this opens the door for ethics as an autonomous discipline with its primary focus on behavior. Second, even the Christian beliefs which underlie Christian conduct do not differ totally from beliefs which underlie non-Christian ethical systems. Thus, a comparison of systems becomes possible and Christian ethics can be subsumed under general ethical and philosophical investigation. Third, Christian conduct does not consistently or absolutely express the revelation which provides its ultimate motivation but undergoes intellectual and cultural assimilation. At this level, too, ethics can break free from dogmatics and merge into a more general inquiry. Finally, the question can at least be raised whether faith does in fact provide motivation for conduct. Might it not be a subsequent rationalization of acts which are basically performed for other reasons? If so, a general anthropology can finally absorb not only ethics but biblical and dogmatic theology as well.

II. Scripture.–Scripture, of course, leaves no place for an isolation of ethics as an independent sphere of study. This comes out very clearly already in the OT. All the ethical injunctions or prohibitions in the OT are rooted in the redemptive acts of God. The preamble to the Decalogue brings this out forcefully. Israel is given these commandments by the God who has liberated it from Egypt. The covenant, too, embraces the divine initiative on the one side and the resultant and responsive human action on the other: "I will be your God and you shall be my people" (cf. Ezk. 34:30; 36:28). For the prophets, misconduct is not just ethical ignorance or weakness; it is unfaithfulness to God and His covenant. Similarly, righteousness is not a realization of human possibilities of thought and action; it is the promised covenant fulfillment. Human behavior can never be considered from any standpoint apart from the underlying and overarching relationship with God.

The NT makes the same point with equal clarity and force. Even linguistically it finds no place for an autonomous ethics in the sense of moral science. Where ethical instruction is given, as it often is, the context of the divine relationship is plain. John the Baptist calls for specific works as the fruit of repentance (Lk. 3:7-14). Jesus proclaims the ethics of the kingdom in the context of His claim to lordship and the summons to discipleship (*see* ETHICS: THE ETHICS OF JESUS). Paul opens the ethical section of Romans with a "therefore," a call to self-dedication, and a demand for transformation by the renewing of the mind (12:1f.). Ephesians grounds the manner of Christian life in the saving work of Christ and the ministry of the Spirit (chs. 4–6). As John succinctly puts it, love for God necessarily finds expression in love for neighbor, and love for God proceeds from God's love: "We love, because he first loved us" (1 Jn. 4:19).

III. Historical Survey.–*A. Early and Medieval Church.* The early Church took over the biblical understanding. This may be seen in the baptismal vows, where obedience came to be linked with repentance and faith. Catechetical instruction followed the same pattern; the ethical section dealt with living the new life in accordance with the revelation of God's will for His people. The Apologists, it is true, compared Christian moral teaching with that of the philosophers. Justin Martyr argued that nowhere was more lofty ethical instruction to be found. Yet, if there is any relation, it is because Plato and others originally took their teachings from Moses. Philosophical ethics, then, drew on the same source of revelation. Instead of a philosophizing of Christian ethics, the Apologists engaged in a theologizing of philosophical ethics.

The dogmaticians of the early and medieval Church were also informed by the biblical outlook and for the most part developed their ethical instruction in a dogmatic context. For early examples we may turn to the *Enchiridion* of Augustine and the *De fide orthodoxa* of John of Damascus, while Lombard's *Sentences* and Aquinas's *Summa Theologica* may be quoted from the Middle Ages. Ethics is not viewed as a separate branch of investigation and discussion, nor is it brought under a general discipline which embraces philosophical ethics on the one hand and biblical ethics on the other.

Yet, these Christian writers were not insensitive to the problems raised by the externality and visibility of Christian action and its consequent exposure to comparison with the ethical thought of pagan philosophy. An odd reflection of the former may be seen in Basil's use of the title "Ethics" for his monastic rule, although naturally the rule itself has dogmatic and biblical roots. More seriously, Gregory in his *Moralia* explored a general basis of ethics in which Aristotelian and Stoic anthropology figured prominently. Materially if not formally, a similar pattern may be found in other theologians. Thus Aquinas preserved the formal structure by including ethics within dogmatics. Yet what he had to say on the subject included a good deal of material drawn from nonbiblical sources (*see* ETHICS: PHILOSOPHICAL ETHICS II.B.4).

A separate question was raised at the same time by the increasing development, codification, and enforcement of church law (cf. Gratian's *Decretum* [*ca.* 1140]). Originally seen as an exposition of biblical law and still subordinate to it, church law tended to take on an authority of its own. It thus promoted a special type of moral theology in which detailed cases could be decided by the various ethical norms, and rules were thus set up for spiritual direction. This type of casuistry ultimately had a theological basis, but in practice it became a science of its own, drawing on various sources and modeling itself to a large extent on law rather than theology.

B. The Reformation. Reaction against theological distortions and casuistic perversions of the later Middle Ages led the sixteenth-century Reformers to a new stress on the interrelation of theology and ethics. Neither Luther nor Calvin specifically rejected the idea of an innate natural law, but the rethinking of justification and good works, along with the new understanding of renovation of life, necessarily brought Christian conduct into closer relation to Christian faith. Luther's *Sermon on Good Works,* Cranmer's *Homilies on Justification,* and the relevant sections in Calvin's *Institutes* (esp. iii.6-10, 19) offer clear illustrations. True works of righteousness derive from faith and, according to the third use of the law, may be learned only from Scripture. Christians need to learn the mind of Christ; they cannot act apart from the Word and the Spirit. Right behavior is thus inseparable from true faith. Authentically Christian ethics, then, arises only in the context of dogmatics. The development of an independent ethics could mean only (1) that salvation and the reconstruction of life may be achieved apart from faith, or (2) that faith is mere belief which, however necessary in its own place, has no life-changing effect.

Melanchthon with his humanistic leanings proved to be a partial exception to the general rule. In his *Loci communes* he showed the usual Reformation understanding; but in a later work, *Epitome of Moral Philosophy* (1538), he used Luther's old enemy Aristotle as a basis and set up an autonomous ethics, which also did duty as a proof of God. Melanchthon was not entirely alone in taking this course. Indeed, T. Venatorius had preceded him with a work on *Christian Virtue* in 1529. Yet Melanchthon probably bears a larger share of responsibility for the development which followed.

C. Post-Reformation Period. In the main both Reformed and Lutheran orthodoxy stayed close to the chief Reformers in the handling of ethics. L. Danaeus had a special work on *Christian Ethics* (1577) and B. Keckermann a *System of Ethics* (1577); predominantly, however, the theologians still dealt with ethics within the context of dogmatics. Even W. Amesius in his *Marrow of Theology* did not depart from this, although he took the strange and radical step of defining theology as the practice of God, thereby absorbing theology into ethics.

At the same time a tendency developed to divide theology, formally at least, into theoretical on the one side and practical on the other (e.g., Polanus, Wollebius, and Amesius). Although the division makes sense and may even claim the model of Paul's Epistles, a serious problem arose with the tendency to introduce natural ethics in some way into the ethical section of dogmatics, thereby weakening the grounding of ethics in Christian theology. G. Calixtus perhaps took a logical course when he presented a completely independent ethics, *The Epitome of Moral Theology* (1634), in which he seemed to see the Decalogue as a reaffirmation of natural law. He did, of course, equate natural law with the law of creation or general revelation; but even so he prepared the ground for the later stripping away from Christian ethics — and indeed from Christianity in general — of any element of special revelation, as in English Deism.

Puritanism made its own unusual contribution to the ultimate severance of ethics from theology. Largely, it seems, in an attempt to find verification of election in changed patterns of life, the Puritans came to focus increasingly on Christian action, whether introspectively in the searching of conscience or externally in the application of discipline. While the reasons for this development were primarily theological, the result in practice was an isolation of conduct from its theological root. Hand in hand with the concept of an original covenant of works and the developing orientation to natural law, this led to a decisive shift away from the Reformation's integration of theology and ethics, even though formally the crucial doctrines of the Reformation were still held and taught.

D. Liberal Theology. Three tributaries — the rationalist, empirical, and emotional — flowed together to form the mainstream of modern liberal theology. Each helped to dissociate ethics and dogmatics. Rationalism distrusted dogmatics, had a philosophical orientation, and tended to seek an ultimate criterion in rational conduct. Empiricism brought with it an anthropological and sociological interest which concentrated on human phenomena rather than theological origination. Emotionalism in its romantic form focused on the individual, had no primary concern for moral action, and made the religious *a priori* in man its point of departure; thus little place remained for dogmatics except in an anthropocentric sense.

Rational-empirical ethicism found its natural culmination in I. Kant's *Religion Within the Limits of Reason Alone.* Here dogmatic theology is allowed a place, but it proves to be completely irrelevant to true religion, which derives from the moral imperative and has a strictly ethical orientation. At most man needs only an example of right conduct and earned forgiveness for his mistakes on the way to moral perfection. For Kant ethics itself plays the role of an independent *a priori.* Being self-grounded, it obviously rests on nothing else. Intermingling ethics with dogmatics can lead only to unethical confusion and hampering of the ethical pursuit which is real religion. (*See* ETHICS: PHILOSOPHICAL ETHICS II.C.4.)

Romantic emotionalism as expressed by Schleiermacher offered the fine principle that "the doctrine of Christian ethics is the doctrine of faith," for "is not also Christian doctrine ethical doctrine?" (*Die christliche Sitte* [1843]). Schleiermacher offered primarily a religion of feeling rather than of thinking and doing. He saw, however, that feeling results in thinking and doing, and along these lines he found a relation between theology and ethics. Unfortunately, theology for him amounted to little more than a description of pious states. Piety, which is innate in us, forms the basis. In the larger sense, then, Christian conduct rests on an anthropocentric understanding rather than the revelation of God in word and work. Ethics stands related to religion. It even stands related to a type of theology. But it does not stand related to Christian theology in the strict sense.

The more purely ethical component found a representative in R. Rothe. Rothe boldly and logically developed what he regarded as a theological ethics. Yet in his presentation doctrine seems to be dissolved in cultural science. The primarily phenomenological approach leaves no place for authentic dogmatics. Thus, the interrelating of ethics and theology, while seriously meant, has no authenticity unless one accepts the liberal redefinition of theology.

Nineteenth-century theology retained an awareness of the problem and made various attempts at true unification, including those of J. C. Nitzsch (1828) and, in the early 20th cent., H. H. Wendt (1906). Perhaps the most impressive and effective effort along those lines was that of M. Kähler in his *Wissenschaft der christlichen Lehre* (1883). But even for Kähler, the center and starting-point is mankind, not the divine revelation in Jesus Christ. Thus, theological ethics is still the ethics of liberal theology; a true grounding of ethics in Christian dogmatics is not achieved.

E. Contemporary Theology. In his monumental *Church Dogmatics* (I/2 § 22, 3) Karl Barth began with the principle that dogmatics always involves ethics and vice versa. This led him to incisive criticism of the sixteenth- and seventeenth-century dogmaticians who prepared the way both for separation and for misunderstanding of dogmatics itself. In this regard he asked a series of probing questions. How could Venatorius first describe Christian faith as faith in Christ and then go on to speak, in a highly unbiblical sense, of Christian virtue? How could Polanus and Wollebius, while including ethics in dogmatics, effect a separation of discussion which so easily implies or entails material separation? Why was a door left open for the smuggling in of the principles and themes of philosophical ethics when what was supposedly being attempted was an orthodox theology of revelation?

When he turned to the 19th and early 20th cents. Barth's questions took on an even sharper edge. He asked C. Palmer (*Die Moral des Christentums* [1864]) how doctrine could be defined as what God has done and morality as what we must do. He asked A. Ritschl (*Rechtfertigung und Versöhnung,* III [1875]) how doctrine could be viewed as God's effectual working and ethics as a scheme of independent personal activity. He asked T. Häring (*Das christliche Leben* [1907]) how a distinction could be made between doctrine as a gift becoming a possession through faith and ethics as a task for which we have power in faith. He asked O. Kirn (*Grundriss der theologischen Ethik* [1906]) how doctrine as reception could be differentiated from ethics as spontaneity. Finally, he asked C. Stange (*Dogmatik* [1927]) how both doctrine and ethics could be brought into correspondence with religion in general, the former as its supposed essence and the latter as its supposed effects.

Obviously the detailed descriptions matter little here. The core of Barth's objection lay in the detachment of the Christian from Christ in ethical matters. Since the Christian life is, and has to be, life in Christ, at no point can what God does yield to what we do, nor gift lead simply to task. Such concepts as action, task, and spontaneity have a certain validity, but not when they entail isolation from the all-embracing act of divine salvation fulfilled by God through His Son and Spirit. The Christian life and our understanding of it must rest in the divine word and work which are the true theme of theology.

On the proper interrelating of ethics and dogmatics, Barth made three main points. First, the Christian can be the theme of neither theology nor ethics except as he is seen in Christ. This necessarily implies that ethics has a christological root and center. When this is changed the true basis of ethics is lost and another foundation has to be sought, i.e., in philosophical ethics. Second, theology focuses on the Word of God. Very explicitly, however, the Word itself demands doing as well as hearing. This applies not merely in matters of sin, law, and sanctification, but at every point. For the Christian, then, ethics arises within the context of the Word of God and the Church's resultant word about God. Ethics belongs necessarily to theology. Third, ethics is not merely bound up with theology; it is itself theology just as theology is ethics. Barth thought this would be brought out best by making ethics an integral part of dogmatic presentation. Yet it did not have to be this. A dogmatics might well be written with no explicit ethics or an ethics with no explicit theology. But, if authentic, the dogmatics would still be ethics too, and the ethics dogmatics.

Various attempts have been made at a truly theological ethics in recent decades. Brunner's *Divine Imperative* (Eng. tr. 1937) and Bonhoeffer's *Ethics* (1955) both try, in different ways, to solve the problem of natural law by bringing the related themes under the doctrine of creation. The concept of orders figures prominently in this understanding, although the question arises whether many of the orders should not be described as orders of the fall rather than of creation. Along similar lines, Dutch theologians in particular have explored the possibility of bringing all philosophical ethics under a theological rubric through the concept of common grace (e.g., A. Kuyper, *Calvinism* [1899]). On this view the truth in human systems does not derive from the unaided nature of fallen humanity but from the divine work, either in an original general revelation or in the common operation of the Spirit, even in those to whom revelation and salvation have not yet come. H. Thielicke has offered a detailed discussion of the whole question in his *Theological Ethics* (Eng. tr. 1966). In the Prolegomena he discusses issues such as the relation between indicative and imperative, the Lutheran view of spontaneity, the problematic nature of casuistry, the "two kingdoms" teaching of Luther, the scholastic approach to natural law, and the role of the Ten Commandments and the Sermon on the Mount in a fallen world. Later volumes illustrate the outworking of theological ethics in such varied fields as politics, aesthetics, and sex.

In America Reinhold Niebuhr, author of *Interpretation of Christian Ethics* (2nd ed. 1963), *Nature and Destiny of Man* (2nd ed. 1963-1964), and *The Children of Light and the Children of Darkness* (1944), presented ethics from a theological perspective. Like Barth, he objected to humanistic ethics and the separation of ethics from Christian faith. Jacques Ellul's *Ethics of Freedom* (1976) provides another example of ethics on a theological foundation.

Barth himself, although unable to finish his ethical chapters in *CD*, did at least develop his methodology and make an impressive material start in the early volumes. In the Prolegomena (I/1 and 2) he has his study of the place of ethics in theology. He also includes a brief ethical discussion in the great chapter on the trinity. Then in II/2, which deals with the divine election and command within the doctrine of God, he lays a theological basis for ethics by bringing both election and command together as twin aspects of the covenant of grace made and fulfilled in Jesus Christ. III/4 forms the ethical chapter of the doctrine of God the Creator, and here, with the Decalogue as a guide, Barth uses criteria from the theology of creation to bring out the Christian implications of love of God and love of neighbor in relation to pressing contemporary problems such as war, suicide, abortion, the family, and sex. Similar chapters were planned for the doctrine of reconciliation (Vol. IV) and the doctrine of redemption (Vol. V), but Barth did not live to complete IV/4 or to write any of V.

IV. Theological Principles.–In any theological development of ethics certain principles must be taken into account. They can be worked out in various ways, but they play a fundamental part in any authentically Christian ethics.

First, God Himself is the ground of right human action. He is this in His very being as God — the God in whose image we were created. He is this in His sovereign will for us, expressed in the covenant and expressly stated in His commandments. He is this as the Creator, who establishes human life and its nature and destiny; as the Redeemer, who brings men and women back to Himself in reconciliation and renewal; and as the Consummator, who is effecting our continuing renovation in the image of Christ and who will achieve its definitive fulfillment at the resurrection. He is known to us as the ground of our true being and conduct through His self-revelation in Jesus Christ, according to the inspired testimony of Holy Scripture.

Second, God Himself, as ground, is also the norm of right human action. Created in the image of God, we are to be as God is and to act as He acts (cf. Lev. 11:44; Mt. 5:43-48 par.; 1 Pet. 1:15). In order that we might have a sense of right and wrong, God wrote on our hearts what the law requires and gave us conscience as a witness (Rom. 2:15). When sin intervened, He gave us His law in the moral commandments, which bear testimony to what He demands from those whom He has redeemed (Ex. 20:1-17). Finally, He sent His Son, Jesus Christ, who radicalized the law by demanding purity of inner motivation (Mt. 5:21-48), and who at the same time provided a model of authentic humanity by fulfilling it. Christian ethics, then, is the ethics of transformation into the likeness of Christ (Rom. 8:29; 12:1f.), who, being Himself the express image of God (Col. 1:15; He. 1:3), came down for us in the likeness of man (Rom. 8:3; Phil. 2:7). Holy Scripture as the record of God's word and work constitutes the functioning norm whereby the will of God for us, both in His commandments and in His Son, is presented to us, and whereby our own acts may consequently be directed, evaluated, and corrected.

Third, God Himself, as ground and norm, is the power of right human action. Although systems of philosophical ethics may contain useful insights, they all break down at the decisive point of achievement. Their only alternative to devastating pessimism, expressed in attempted ethics of self-interest, is a naive and ungrounded optimism about human capability or even perfectibility. The gospel frankly admits — indeed, it proclaims — the impotence of human beings to fulfil the divine commandments. Nevertheless, it heralds a new beginning with the justification of sinners by Jesus Christ, the regenerative ministry of the Holy Spirit, the movement of repentance and faith from which spring authentic works of righteousness ordained by God, and the grateful love of believers which responds spontaneously to God's loving grace. The love of God "poured into our hearts through the Holy Spirit" (Rom. 5:5) achieves the necessary purification of motive; the new life given by God constitutes the driving force for the doing of what is right (cf. 1 Jn. 3:9); and Holy Scripture serves both as the Word of God by which renewal comes and as the guide by which the right that corresponds to God's sovereign will may be discerned.

Fourth, God Himself, as ground, norm, and power, is the goal and purpose of right human conduct. As we are from Him and by Him, so we are to Him. According to His self-revelation God is to be glorified in His creation. Thus the praise of God constitutes the ultimate ethical purpose. God is praised as His will is done. Obedience is thus the means to achieve the goal. Nevertheless, God's glory does not stand alone; for the glory of God means also the glorifying of the creature (Rom. 8:17, 30; cf. 2 Cor. 3:18). This glorifying is linked with the "spirit of sonship" that is given to all children of God who through right action are joined to Christ (Rom. 8:15-17). Human beings are thus brought into union with God both in being and in act — a union that embraces union with fellow believers (e.g., Eph. 4:4-16). In the obedient doing of the will of God is achieved the authentic humanity, or being in the divine image, which God planned for men and women in His creative work. Since the divine mandate at creation included also dominion over other creatures (Gen. 1:26), the proper ordering and curatorship of the physical environment forms part of theological ethics according to its goal in God (cf. Rom. 8:18-22). In relation to goal as well as to ground, norm, and power, Holy Scripture plays a key role, for it is only through the inspired record that God as the goal of human action may be known and accepted, with all that this implies for the direction of life, the course and validity of right action, and the destiny of those who commit themselves to God as their all in all.

V. Conclusion.–As we have seen, there is no biblical justification for a separation of ethics from dogmatics, especially when human philosophy takes the place that biblical theology should occupy, or when the moral teaching of Christianity is seen simply as a promulgation of natural law. Nor does the Bible leave any place for a two-tier structure in which philosophical ethics, even in the form of general revelation or a common work of the Spirit, forms the foundation and the ethics of special revelation the superstructure. Biblical ethics appears consistently as the ethics of special revelation, not of human ratiocination.

On the other hand, philosophical ethics is a fact, and one need not conclude that philosophical ethics and theological ethics stand in complete isolation from one another. Obviously, many of the recommended actions coincide, even if motives and reasons differ. Hence at the very least comparison and contrast are not to be ruled out. Beyond that, a theological interpretation of the existence and nature of philosophical ethics can hardly be viewed as illegitimate. From this standpoint there is room for investigation along the lines of the doctrines of creation, general revelation, and common grace. Danger arises, of course, when this type of work is done in such a way that an alliance is sought between philosophical and theological ethics or the latter is diminished or even dissolved altogether in the former. For this reason it is essential that the biblical norm be taken seriously and the integral relation between ethics and dogmatics not be forgotten. What is sought is an integration of philosophical ethics itself into a theological understanding.

G. W. BROMILEY

MODERN PROBLEMS

In Christian tradition the Bible is authoritative for morals as it is for faith. In situations that have no biblical precedent, however, it is not self-evident how the Bible's moral teachings are to be applied. The understanding of how the ancient biblical moral standards bear on uniquely modern problems is, therefore, a continuing task for the Christian community. The purpose of this article is to show how the Bible's moral teaching might be pertinent to one illustrative set of moral problems that has arisen in modern times, in the area of medical science.

I. Biblical Morality
II. The Bible and Medical Technology
  A. Life-prolonging Techniques
  B. Life-changing Techniques
  C. Life-determining Techniques
III. Summary

I. Biblical Morality.–Prior to a consideration of specific problems, some general comments on how the Bible teaches morality are in order. (1) The Bible's directions for the moral life are varied. The Bible contains clear moral precepts and norms, the Decalogue being the best known — but not the only — set of moral laws (Ex. 20, Dt. 5). But morality is also taught through living examples (unique among which is the life of Jesus Christ), through parables and stories (the parable of the Good Samaritan [Lk. 10:29-37] teaches a moral lesson more vividly than moral rules), and, to mention but one other, through the great and decisive events of redemption (the cross of Christ, when accepted analogously as one's own cross, has deep moral implications for the Christian's pilgrimage).

(2) The Bible writers expected Christian people to be led by the Spirit in their search for the morally right decision in a morally difficult situation. Paul prayed that the Colossian Christians would "be filled with the knowledge of his will in all spiritual wisdom and understanding, to lead a life worthy of the Lord . . ." (Col. 1:9f.). He prayed similarly for the Ephesian Christians that God would give them "a spirit of wisdom" (Eph. 1:17). The gift of the "spirit of wisdom" — in answer to prayer — suggests strongly that members of the believing community are expected not only to deduce the will of God from the texts but to pray and counsel together for spiritual understanding of moral issues and to expect guidance in their decisions. The need for spiritual wisdom suggests the need for insight into the realities of a new situation and an ability to calculate the moral importance of the various factors in the situation.

(3) The total biblical message of God's creation and redemption provides for the believer a certain way of looking at and evaluating what is at stake in moral problems. For instance, the belief that every person exists by virtue of God's care, is an image-bearer of God, and has an eternal destiny, compels the Christian to view every person's life as having such value that it demands respect, care, protection, and support from the human community. To view human life in this way provides a profound moral bias with respect to such issues as euthanasia, abortion, capital punishment, and war. That every person is called by Jesus Christ to enter the kingdom of God through faith likewise provides a perspective on persons: every person is seen as open to God's redemptive

healing. Indeed, redemption and healing are the believer's most pressing desires for other persons. This, too, compels a bias of moral significance. The Christian's relationships with other persons will be dominated, not by self-interest, not by consideration of gain, but by the redemptive desire for their salvation.

The Bible does not give clear instruction on how to reason from its moral imperatives to their application in every problem of real life. For instance, it does not apply the sixth commandment ("thou shalt not kill") to the question of whether defensive nuclear warfare might ever be justified (*see* HOMICIDE; KILL; MURDER). Nor does it state how the same commandment would apply to the question of when it is right to remove life-support mechanisms from a comatose patient whose brain has ceased to function. Having noted, then, that biblical direction for moral decisions comes in varied forms and with no explicit instructions for its application to modern moral problems, we will now consider a specific set of moral problems in the light of Scripture.

II. The Bible and Medical Technology.–Moral problems arise in the area of medical technology because we are now turning technology on ourselves (as we used to turn it mainly on nature) in ways that can determine life and death or change human beings at the core of their humanity. The moral question is whether we, as mere creatures, have a warrant to use our techniques to determine the lives of human beings. Moreover, ought we to encourage medical technologists to experiment with life-changing and life-determining techniques? How does the Bible speak to such problems?

Medical technology offers various possibilities, which may be divided into three types: life-prolonging, life-changing, and life-determining. Such devices as heart transplants and dialysis machines are life-prolonging. Psychosurgery and the use of chemicals for brain alteration are life-changing. Test-tube conception and cloning may be called life-determining.

To discover the Bible's direction in the use of life-affecting medical technology, we need much knowledge about what is actually happening in the various applications of technology. But the facts in cases entailing modern technology are sometimes very complex, involving not merely technical and medical data but also such matters as the possibilities for weal or woe in the experiments, the ability of the engineers to predict all the effects of their work, and the nature of the human person(s) being affected. Such facts are not easily ascertained or interpreted. How one interprets them will depend on how one views human life and human responsibility; and this depends not merely on clinical information but on one's deepest beliefs.

A. Life-prolonging Techniques. The biblical view of the value of human life gives us, to begin with, a strong bias toward using technology to save or prolong human life. The sixth commandment against killing (Heb. *rṣḥ*) implies a positive command to protect, nourish, and sustain human life; this seems to be the thrust of Paul's word that love is the fulfillment of the law (Rom. 13:8-10). Hence the biblical message constrains us to do all we can to sustain human life.

Moral problems arise in the use of techniques to prolong a life that without them would have ceased. The problems cluster around three typical sets of circumstances: (1) the life prolonged is only questionably human; (2) the extension of life brings indignity to the patient and great grief to loved ones; (3) the use of the techniques exacts an enormous price in both money and human resources. These circumstances raise the questions: is it morally required to use a machine to keep alive a comatose person whose brain is so irretrievably damaged that there remains no promise of any human activity? or to force a patient to exist biologically when his or her truly human selfhood is destroyed? or to continue to use the machine in such a case if its use taxes inordinately the financial and psychic resources of the loved ones? What does the Bible say?

The Bible teaches us to nourish and sustain human life, but there is still the question of what constitutes human life. Is the patient still human whose heart beats only as it is stimulated by a machine, or whose brain has all but ceased to function? There is much uncertainty, medically and often legally, about what constitutes normative humanity. Further, there is the question of whether we are morally obligated to sustain *all* human life at *any* cost. Are we obligated to keep alive an aged comatose patient who would have died had medical technology not invented its machines — just because a machine manages to make his heart beat? The Bible gives no precise answer to such questions. It does commend a bias toward life-support when uncertainty exists; but it does not give detailed medical information to help one determine whether a given patient is still a living human being who has a moral claim on others to support his or her life. In cases of painful uncertainty, we are called to prayer for "spiritual wisdom," for purity of motive, for courage, and for guidance from the Church, the Body of Christ. We act in the assurance of God's gracious forgiveness and the prevailing power of His providential will.

B. Life-changing Techniques. Another moral question is created by medical technology: when do human beings have the right to change or determine the lives of other human beings? In the light of scriptural data, we must rephrase the question to show that it has religious as well as moral dimensions: do mere creatures under God have the right to intervene in human lives in ways that are fitting only for God? Is there a biblical directive that tells us what we may or may not do?

There appears to be no biblical injunction against all interference into natural processes. While life is at God's disposal, to give or to take away (Ps. 90), it is also given into the care of human parents, human governors, and human physicians. Human beings have always exercised intervening care over one another as God's caretakers in the covenant responsibilities of God's family. Yet there is a limit. To intervene into the fundamental structure of a person, to determine his or her future, particularly without that person's consent, seems to be arrogating God's sovereign prerogatives. Two biblical teachings warn against aspiration for such control over other human beings, even if it is benevolent: (1) each individual, in the depths of his or her personhood, stands as the image of God against the will of other human beings to alter the person; (2) technologists also are sinners, whose hearts are as deceptively wicked as the hearts of all others, and whose judgment and ambition cannot be totally trusted in such profoundly person-changing endeavors.

Not even love sanctions all things. Love must respect the reality of the neighbor as God's image. Love must respect the will and consent of the neighbor. Love must be practiced in awareness of our sin-infected judgment and our penchant for controlling others in the name of love. The biblical warrant for asserting that love must respect certain limits is the example of God's respect for the individual reality and freedom of His creatures. Thus, love's consent to the use of technology for the support of life does not sanction any or all uses of technology for the changing life.

We may draw a general rule from the inviolable status of each person as God's image-bearer and the command of love to help one another. That rule might be: healing intervention into human life is limited by the responsible consent of the patient and also by the patient's uniquely human nature. This general rule leaves much room for the use of "spiritual wisdom." For there is no certain way to tell when a patient is indeed giving free and responsible consent, uninfluenced by the authority of the physician, the weakness of old age, or the debilitating effects of drugs. There is, further, no certain guide to indicate when one is intervening to alter the essentially human dimension of a person. The Bible does not provide precise guidance, for instance, as to whether it is right to change the personality of a violent person through brain- and personality-altering chemicals in order to render him more passive and, therefore, safer to himself and others. Clearly, the guidance of Scripture does not eliminate the necessity of prayer and the agony of coming to decisions without precise instructions.

C. Life-determining Techniques. Another set of moral problems is created by medical technology's ability to determine human life. In one instance, in what is popularly called test-tube conception, technology determines whether human life shall be born. In another instance, technology projects the possibility of determining the genetic structure of a human life through a process called cloning. We will confine our attention here to the Bible's guidance on whether it is morally allowable to conceive a child in a laboratory.

The process of "test-tube conception" requires surgical removal of ova from the woman. Several ova are removed, to improve the chances of success, and are placed in a fluid synthetically similar to the fluids of the uterus. The man's semen is then added to the fluid. Once an ovum has been fertilized and has gone through a short period of development, the zygote is surgically planted in the uterine chamber. In this way a married couple who would otherwise be barren may conceive a child.

Are there biblical guidelines that indicate the moral rightness or wrongness of conceiving a child in this way? The question is complex. First, is there a specific prohibition of test-tube conception? The Bible assumes that (except in the case of Jesus) children are conceived only through sexual union of a man and a woman and that sexual union produces offspring unless God wills otherwise. The Bible nowhere prohibits any other mode of conception, probably because its writers never imagined that any other way might be possible. May we, nonetheless, suppose that the *intention* of God is that the profound reality of the conception of a new life is properly associated only with the profoundly intimate sexual union of two people in a marriage covenant? Theologians have drawn such an inference, not from the Bible, but from natural law. Perhaps such an inference could be drawn from the Bible's silence, but it would surely lack convincing biblical authority.

The issues, however, are too complex to allow us to accept the legitimacy of test-tube conception on the basis of the Bible's silence on it. We might note that this procedure gives the medical technologist power to manipulate life at its genesis, a power the Bible is inclined to concede only to God, the giver and taker of life. Even if it is not explicitly prohibited, may it be *inappropriate* for human beings to exercise such power? This question has been asked many times in the face of modern technology; it can never be answered simply, once and for all. We do grant to medical science the power to *prolong* lives that otherwise would have died — and in effect postpone the day of God's taking a person. May we then refuse similar powers at the point of conception?

The question of appropriateness is intensified by the possibilities of irresponsible experimentation, especially in view of the secrecy in which such experiments are carried out. For example, there is the possibility that at an early stage the fertilized ovum may reveal a terrible deformation, such that the doctors would not place the ovum in the mother's uterus. But this would leave open the possibility of preserving the "monster" alive in the test tube for experimental purposes, and only later killing it. The biblical respect for even potential human life provides a strong motive for wanting to avoid such experiments. Thus, we must also face the question whether such experiments are likely accompaniments of test-tube conceptions.

The question of test-tube conception is also bound up with the question of abortion. The procedure calls for placing several ova in the laboratory dish. This means that several ova are likely to be fertilized. From among several fertilized ova, one is chosen for implanting in the uterus. The others are destroyed. In short, human zygotes are aborted. If the Bible speaks against all induced abortion, short of defense of the mother's life, it speaks against test-tube abortion. This feature can be removed only as technicians are able to confine the procedures to the use of only one ovum.

A basic biblical law that bears on the potential parents is the law of love. Test-tube conception offers barren couples the hope of having children. Love constrains us to act in order to fulfil their natural hope. The question, however, is whether the possibility of unknown evils and the likelihood that innumerable abortions will occur are sufficient reasons to deny the gift of procreation to childless couples.

The answer does not come to the believing community through a single text; nor will it come without agonizing reflection. The prayer of Paul for "spiritual wisdom" must be offered continually. There must be mutual help and counsel in the spirit of Christ. We deal here, as in other medical problems and, indeed, in many other moral problems, with the question of the right means to achieve a benevolently intended goal. The Bible provides general moral laws and calls us, in Christ, to discern the will of God in their light. Discernment calls for biblically informed understanding of the facts, a reasoned calculation of the consequences of our acts, a prayerful sensitivity to the Spirit's movement, and a sure persuasion that when a decision is made, it is made under the sustaining and forgiving grace of God.

III. Summary.–We will conclude this discussion with several summary observations regarding the Bible's guidance in moral problems not foreseen within the Bible.

(1) The Bible gives moral direction in various forms, including prescriptions, general principles, examples, and stories.

(2) Modern life presents moral problems not covered in the specific prescriptions of Scripture.

(3) The Bible's moral teachings are relevant, in a general sense, to all modern moral problems. The positive intent of the Decalogue, the law of love, and the goal of justice inform the moral agent in significant, if general, ways.

(4) The application of biblical guidance to moral problems requires a careful analysis of the facts of the case. Without analysis of the facts, moral guidance is aimless. All facts are viewed and interpreted, however, from a moral and religious bias; all facts touching human life, especially, ought to be interpreted in the light of the Bible's message concerning human values and human nature.

(5) In the crucible of life's moral challenges, we are not excused by the Bible from the agonies of decision making. Not every right act is outlined in advance on the pages of the Bible. Here we must turn to prayer for "spiritual wisdom," to the promise of guidance in the practice of godliness, and to the assurance of forgiveness when we fail.

Bibliography.–B. Birch and L. I. Rasmussen, *Bible and Ethics in the Christian Life* (1976); H. Brody, *Ethical Decisions in Medicine* (1976); J. F. Dedek, *Contemporary Medical Ethics* (1975); C. A. Frazer, *Is It Moral To Modify Man?* (1973); J. M. Gustafson, *Theology and Christian Ethics* (1974); B. Haring, *Medical Ethics* (1973); P. Ramsey, *Ethics of Fetal Research* (1974); K. Vaux, *Biomedical Ethics* (1974); *Encyclopedia of Bioethics* (4 vols., 1978).
L. B. SMEDES

ETHIOPIA ē-thi-ō'pē-ə [Heb. *kûš*; Gk. *Aithiopia*]; AV also CUSH (Isa. 11:11); NEB also CUSH, NUBIA. A geographical term derived ultimately either from Gk. *aíthops,* "red (face)," or from *aíthō* plus *óps,* "burnt face" (cf. Jer. 13:23). "Ethiopia(n)" in the RSV of the OT translates Heb. *kûš(î),* although *kûš(î)* is sometimes simply transliterated as "Cush(ite)" (cf. Gen. 2:13; 10:6-8 par. 1 Ch. 1:8-10; Nu. 12:1; 2 S. 18:21-32; Ezk. 38:5) or as the personal name "Cush(i)" (cf. Ps. 7 title [MT 7:1]; Jer. 36:14; Zeph. 1:1). In these last three passages the LXX also reads a personal name, *(ho) Chousi,* and probably also in Gen. 10:6-8 par. 1 Ch. 1:8-10 (*Chous*). In Ezk. 30:5 the LXX reads erroneously *Persai,* "Persians" (perhaps through contamination from Ezk. 38:5). Elsewhere in the LXX, *Aithiopia/Aithiops,* "Ethiopia(n)," translates Heb. *kûš(î),* as well as Heb. *kûšān,* a synonym for "Midian" in Hab. 3:7, and *ṣîyîm,* "desert creatures," in Ps. 72:9; 74:14.

I. Location and Extent.–Egyptian *K3s/š* (later *Kš*) — whence Assyr. *Kûsu,* Bab. *Kûšu,* Amarna *Kâšu,* Heb. *kûš* — designated, in its broadest sense, the countries of the upper Nile S of Egypt. More precisely, however, the southern border of Egypt proper was in the area of the First Cataract of the Nile; S of Egypt the land of Wawat stretched to the vicinity of the Second Cataract; still further south, reaching at least as far as the Fourth Cataract, was Cush in the narrower sense. Wawat and Cush together were called "Ethiopia" by the classical writers of Greece, although Homer (*Od.* i.22-24) could also use the term in its broader sense by referring to "the distant Ethiopians, the farthest outposts of mankind, half of whom live where the Sun goes down, and half where he rises." It is thus clear that "Ethiopia" could denote all southern peoples with dark skins, from Cush to India. Herodotus mentioned Asiatic Ethiopians during the reign of Darius (iii.94) and as part of the army of Xerxes (vii.70), thus differentiating them from African Ethiopians and demonstrating that "Ethiopian" could be employed as a broad generic term. Herodotus also used "Ethiopia" in its narrower sense, however, by identifying it with the kingdom of Meroë: "Ethiopians inhabit the country immediately above [= S of] Elephantine [at the First Cataract

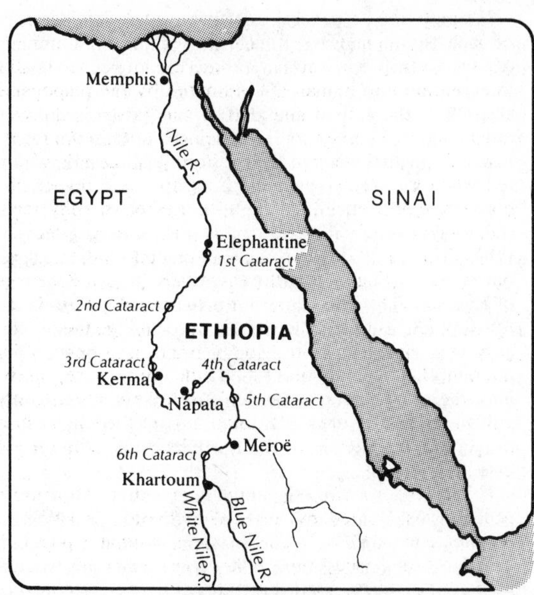

near Aswan, OT "Syene"; cf. Ezk. 29:10] and one half of the island; the other half is inhabited by Egyptians; . . . finally, you will arrive at a large city called Meroë: this city is said to be the capital of all Ethiopia" (ii.29). One of the terms used by Assyrian rulers of the 8th and 7th cent. B.C. to refer to the territories S of Egypt was *Meluḫḫa,* formerly believed by some to be identical to Meroë. The latter city, however, did not become historically significant until much later, and the origin of the name *Meluḫḫa* therefore remains obscure.

Like Egyp. *K3s/š* and Gk. *Aithiopia,* Heb. *kûš* is used in both a broad and a narrow sense (although only rarely does it include modern Ethiopia [= Abyssinia]). More frequently it corresponds roughly to the present northern *Sûdân,* a word meaning "black (country)," the equivalent of ancient "Nubia" (meaning "slave country"?), the earliest occurrence of which appears in the writings of Eratosthenes *ca.* 200 B.C. (Strabo *Geog.* xvii.1.2), who mentions the Noubai on the western side of the Nile "as far as the bends of the river."

The referent of *kûš* in Genesis is a vexing problem, however. In Gen. 2:13 it is rendered "Ethiopia" (cf. also the AV) by the LXX, which apparently understood Gihon to be another name for the Nile (cf. Jer. 2:18, LXX; also Josephus *Ant.* i.1.3). To this day Ethiopians refer to the Nile springs as "Giyon," the Ethiopic word for Gihon. But since the Garden of Eden narrative (Gen. 2:10-14) can hardly be understood as representing two ancient foci of civilization, it would seem best to seek the Cush of Gen. 2:13 in Mesopotamia, the region of the well-known Tigris and Euphrates Rivers (2:14). It would thus be equated with Akk. *Kaššû,* Gk. *Kossaioi, Kissioi,* the Kassite (Cossaean) rulers of Babylonia for about half a millennium down to the 12th cent. B.C. (cf. perhaps the personal name Cushan-rishathaim in Jgs. 3:8, 10).

The Cush of Gen. 10:6-8 (= 1 Ch. 1:8-10) is in some respects even more difficult to locate. With the exception of Canaan, the areas mentioned in the passage, as far as they can be identified, lie S of Egypt and on both sides of the Red Sea. The inclusion of Canaan may simply reflect the broader imperial interests of Egypt during much of her history, or there may be at least an incidental relationship to the presence of Cushite tribes in the Arabah mentioned in the nineteenth-century Egyptian Execration

Texts published by G. Posener. The problem is heightened, however, by the fact that the Cushite Nimrod's activities take place entirely in Mesopotamia according to Gen. 10:9-12 (a passage omitted by the Chronicler in his summary). While it is possible that Nimrod migrated from Nubia to Mesopotamia, it is also possible that the Cush of Gen. 10:6f. (= 1 Ch. 1:8f.) is Nubia, whereas the Cush of Gen. 10:8 (= 1 Ch. 1:10) is Mesopotamia (as is likely in Gen. 2:13) and that the compiler of the Table of Nations inserted the story of Nimrod because of the catchword "Cush" (LXX *Chous,* throughout this passage; Gen. 10:13 returns to a list of Egypt's relationships after the Nimrod interlude). Alternatively, the Cush of Gen. 2:13; 10:8 could refer to Kish, the storied Mesopotamian city that tradition states to have been the seat of the first Sumerian dynasty after the Flood.

The original location of the Nubian Cush was probably S of the Third Cataract at or near Kerma, the most important native kingdom in the northern Sudan. It seems likely that the pharaohs of the 11th Egyptian Dynasty (*ca.* 2133-1991 B.C.) permanently occupied the northern reaches of Nubia, attracted as they were by the possibilities of exploiting its riches. The material wealth of Nubia has tempted Middle Eastern rulers from time immemorial (cf., e.g., Job 28:19); Gudea of Lagash imported its black diorite stone; the Middle Kingdom pharaohs its spices, resins, fine wood, ostrich feathers, and black slaves; Darius of Persia its ivory; and everyone its gold.

A certain amount of intermarriage took place between Egyptians and Nubians, since the two peoples were ethnically related to each other. In fact, Amenemhet I, founder of the 12th Dynasty, may have had a Nubian mother. At the same time, Egyptians tended to regard Nubians with disdain. The Admonitions of Ipuwer, possibly antedating the 12th Dynasty, refer to the Nubians as "barbarians," as do inscriptions of Thutmose III and Amenhotep III centuries later.

II. History.**–*****A.*** *12th-17th Dynasties.* The earliest inscriptional references to "Cush" derive from the reign of Sesostris I (1971-1928 B.C.), who completed the conquest of Nubia that had been initiated by his father, Amenemhet I. After a peaceful interval of about eighty years, Sesostris III (1878-1843 B.C.) resumed military operations and Nubia was once again annexed to Egypt as far as the region of the Second Cataract at Wâdī Halfa. Sesostris himself became a sort of patron deity in Nubia and was worshiped there for centuries after his death. The Middle Kingdom pharaohs built a total of fourteen forts in Nubia during the period of their hegemony, and Egyptian trade penetrated even farther up the Nile than did political control. A fortified trading station called the "Walls of Amenemhet" was constructed at Kerma and a thriving mercantile colony was established there. The ushering in of the unsettled Second Intermediate period (13th-17th Dynasties, 1786-*ca.* 1550 B.C.) witnessed the end of effective Egyptian control over Nubia. It seems certain, however, that the Hyksos conquerors of Egypt were firmly entrenched in Nubia for a considerable time, occupying the area as far south as Kerma.

B. 18th Dynasty. After the expulsion of the Hyksos, the pharaohs of the 18th Dynasty reconquered Nubia with a vengeance, extending the frontier to Napata near modern Jebel Barkal S of the Fourth Cataract. A key figure in the program of expansion was Thutmose I (1525-1512 B.C.). The entire territory from Hierakonpolis (S of Thebes) to Napata was now put in charge of a viceroy, called the "King's 'Son' in Cush," appointed by, and directly responsible to, the pharaohs from Ahmose (at the beginning of the 18th Dynasty) to Herihor (at the beginning of the 21st Dynasty). Meroë, the capital of the Meroitic kingdom (descendants of the 25th Dynasty) from *ca.* 500 B.C. to *ca.* A.D. 350, may well have originated as an Eighteenth-Dynasty Egyptian post. After Thutmose III (1504-1450 B.C.) and well into the 19th Dynasty, expeditions to Nubia are mentioned frequently in the sources. Under a peaceful and efficient administration, the region prospered with the construction of irrigation works, the founding of new cities, and the erection of at least a dozen new temples, many of great size. The finest of the temples was built by Amenhotep III (1417-1379 B.C.) at Soleb; although reminiscent of his lovely temple at modern Luxor with its closed papyrus columns, it is sadly ruined today. One of the Amarna Tablets (Am.Tab. 287), probably dating from the early years of the reign of Amenhotep IV (Akhenaten, 1379-1362), mentions Cushite mercenaries garrisoned in Jerusalem. Four centuries later, during Shishak's invasion of Palestine, Cushite mercenaries, who were skilled warriors when properly trained (Jer. 46:9), would again make their appearance in Jerusalem (2 Ch. 12:2f.).

C. Moses. It is virtually certain that there were Nubian elements in the family of Moses. According to Ex. 6:25; 1 Ch. 6:3f., 50 (MT 5:29f.; 6:35); Ezr. 7:5, his brother Aaron had a grandson named Phinehas (Heb. *pînḥās* = Egyp. *p3-nḥsy,* "the Nubian"; cf. the various OT spellings of the Egyptian place name Tahpanhes, Egyp. *t3-ḥ(t)-p3nḥsy,* "the Fortress of the Nubian"). Moses himself had earlier (Nu. 12:1) married a Nubian (RSV "Cushite"; LXX, AV, "Ethiopian") woman, an action for which at that time he was criticized by Miriam and Aaron. It is possible that Moses' Nubian wife is to be equated with the Midianite Zipporah (Ex. 2:16-21; 18:1f.), since "Cushan" (Heb. *kûšān*; LXX *Aithiopōn*) appears in synonymous parallelism with "Midian" in Hab. 3:7. Although some early Jewish commentators were clearly embarrassed by the likelihood that Moses had married a Nubian slave girl, others made capital of the relationship by midrashically elevating her to the status of princess or queen and giving her various names, such as Tharbis (cf., e.g., Josephus *Ant.* ii.10.2) or Adoniah. (*See also* CUSHITE WOMAN.)

D. 19th-21st Dynasties. Ramses II (1304-1237 B.C.), the greatest builder of the 19th Dynasty, constructed six major temples in Nubia during his reign, locating them at Beit el-Wali, Gerf Husein, Wâdī es-Sabua, Derr, Abu Simbel, and Aksha. The temple of Abu Simbel, with its four sandstone colossi 20 m. (67 ft.) high, is the most famous and greatest of the six. Before completion of the High Dam at Aswan, engineers cut the Abu Simbel temple into huge blocks and then rebuilt it on higher ground to protect it from the backed-up waters of the Nile — a remarkable feat worthy of Ramses himself, who during his sixty-six-year reign remade Egypt and Nubia in his own image, effectively Egyptianizing the southern reaches of his vast empire. The riches of Nubia were bequeathed to the Twentieth-Dynasty pharaohs, the last of whom, Ramses III (1198-1166 B.C.), attempted to rival the vast building projects of his earlier namesake. The weaklings who followed him spawned nearly a century of power struggles and graft, at the end of which the "King's 'Son' in Cush," Herihor, intervened in the name of law and order and established the 21st (Tanite) Dynasty, the final years of which were contemporary with Israel's united monarchy under David and Solomon.

The unnamed messenger who informed David of Joab's victory over Absalom is called simply "the Cushite" (AV "Cushi"; 2 S. 18:21-32). That he was a foreigner in Israel is perhaps indicated by his ignorance of the shorter route taken by Ahimaaz, by the failure of the watchman to recognize him, and by his lack of familiarity with the emotional attachment that David had for his son. Some would equate him with the Benjaminite named "Cush(i)" in the title of Ps. 7, but without sufficient reason.

E. 22nd (Libyan)–25th (Cushite) Dynasties. The death of Solomon doubtless encouraged Sheshonq (Shishak) I (945-924 B.C.), the founder of the 22nd (Libyan) Dynasty, to test the defenses of Israel's divided monarchy in Rehoboam's fifth year. Nubian mercenaries were among the troops who attacked Jerusalem at that time (2 Ch. 12:2f.). Sheshonq's success is underscored by the account of his victory inscribed on a wall of the temple of Amon at Karnak in Upper Egypt. Not so fortunate was Zerah the Ethiopian who, according to 2 Ch. 14:9-13 (MT 8-12), was unable to defeat Asa of Judah in spite of his superior military strength (cf. also 16:7f.). Although some scholars would equate Zerah with Osorkon I, the son of Sheshonq, linguistic considerations make such an identification unlikely, and it is best to assume that the otherwise unknown Zerah was one of Osorkon's generals.

The lackluster 23rd and 24th Dynasties were partly contemporaneous with and almost completely overshadowed by the 22nd (Libyan) Dynasty and the 25th (Cushite) Dynasty. The latter was founded by Kashta, ruler of Cush at Napata, who obtained control of Upper Egypt, adopting Amon, the Theban king of the gods, as the national deity. Kashta's son, Piankhy (751-716 B.C.), completed the conquest of virtually the entire country. It was probably during the hegemony of the powerful Piankhy that Cush, now an independent kingdom, began to attract the attention and even the admiration of the writers of the OT (see Am. 9:7), who frequently referred to the territory as an exemplar of the remote and strange (cf. also Ps. 87:4; Zeph. 2:12). The Display Inscription of Sargon II (722-705 B.C.) similarly mentions Nubia as "a distant country, . . . an inapproachable region," and (referring as it does to his conquest of Ashdod) illumines the text of Isa. 20 and underscores the rivalry between Assyria and Cush.

Other Isaianic references reflecting the rising importance of Nubia are 7:18; 11:11; and 18. Some scholars identify "the rivers of Cush [RSV, AV, Ethiopia]" (18:1; cf. also 18:2, 7; Zeph. 3:10) as the White and Blue Niles (which converge at modern Khartoum) and the Atbara (which meets the Nile at a point between the Fifth and Sixth Cataracts). The "vessels of papyrus" (18:2) have their modern counterparts in the *tankwas* still used on Lake Tana in Abyssinia. The "fly which is at the sources of the streams of Egypt" (7:18) is a veiled allusion to Cush; whether it helps to interpret the "whirring wings" of 18:1 is a matter of conjecture. Particularly instructive for Isaiah's use of the term "Cush" is 11:11, which refers to *miṣrayim* (Lower or Northern Egypt), *paṯrôs* (Upper or Southern Egypt), and *kûš* in the same north-to-south geographical order as the *Muṣru–Pāturîsu–Kûsu* of the somewhat later Assyrian inscriptions of the prophet's contemporary (37:38), Esarhaddon (681-669 B.C.). In 11:11 Cush is represented once again as being a faraway place, as far to the southwest as Mesopotamia is to the northeast, in a manner reminiscent of one of the Jerusalem Amarna Tablets (Am.Tab. 288). During the reign of the Persian Xerxes (486-465 B.C.), the termini of his empire were "from India to Ethiopia" (Est. 1:1; 8:9; cf. similarly the Akkadian version of a Persepolis foundation tablet ordered by Xerxes, translated in *ANET*, pp. 316f.).

The brilliant work of G. A. Reisner in the Sudan brought into relative chronological order the rulers of the Cushite Dynasty and made possible a continuous history of the area from the 8th to 4th cents. B.C. Shabaka, Piankhy's

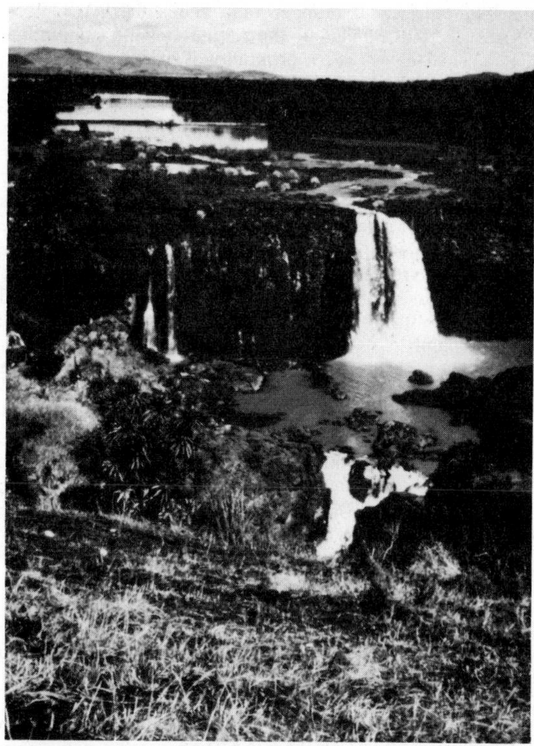

Tisisat Falls at Lake Tana in Ethiopia, the source of the Blue Nile (W. S. LaSor)

brother, strengthened the Cushite hold over all of Egypt and took the title of "King of Cush and Egypt." The names (though not necessarily the persons) of Shabaka and Shabataka (Piankhy's son) have been claimed by some to be reflected in Sabta(h) and Sabteca, two of the "sons of Cush" mentioned in Gen. 10:7 (= 1 Ch. 1:9).

The reign of Taharqa, the brother of Shabataka, has been brought into clearer relief by F. L. Griffith's excavations at Kawa near the Third Cataract. During the days of Hezekiah king of Judah, Taharqa was Assyria's archenemy. In Isa. 37:9 (= 1 K. 19:9) he is referred to as "Tirhakah king of Cush" (perhaps proleptically; for a reasoned treatment of the chronological issues involved cf. esp. K. A. Kitchen, *Ancient Orient and OT* [1966], pp. 82-84), exactly as in the royal inscriptions of Esarhaddon and Ashurbanipal, both of whom report Esarhaddon's destruction of Taharqa's Memphis *ca.* 671 B.C. Ruins of Taharqa's impressive building projects are visible throughout northern Sudan, and a fine column from his period of rule still stands at Karnak near the temple of Amon.

Ashurbanipal (669-627/6) records the Assyrian sack of Thebes during the reign of Tanutamun (Ta-net-Amon, whom Ashurbanipal calls Ur-damane), Taharqa's nephew, in 663 (cf. esp. Nah. 3:8-10). The Assyrian ruler thus brought the Cushite Dynasty to an end and inaugurated Egypt's 26th Dynasty under Psamtik I (663-610 B.C.), although the successors of Tanutamun continued to reign for another thousand years in Cush, first at Napata and later at Meroë. They no longer ruled Egypt, but Egyptian influence continued, however feebly, to make an impact on their culture to the end.

F. New Foreign Influences. During this millennium a new ethnic strain manifested itself in Nubia. Steady migrations westward across the Red Sea produced the amalgamation of a small number of Semites from southwest Arabia with the mass of the native Cushite population. 2 Ch. 21:16 alludes to the proximity of Arabs and Cushites, as does Isa. 43:3 and 45:14. Jer. 44:1 mentions Jews who had settled in both Lower and Upper Egypt; Zeph. 3:10 refers to a diaspora in Cush; and the Elephantine papyri demonstrate the existence of a Jewish colony near Aswan at least as early as the 5th cent. B.C. Undoubted Hebraic influences and practices still exist among the inhabitants of Abyssinia (modern Ethiopia), the cultural heirs of the ancient Cushites. For their part, the Cushites made an impact on Israel as well. There is good reason to believe that the prophet Zephaniah had some Cushite blood (Zeph. 1:1; cf. Jer. 36:14 for another occurrence of the proper name "Cushi"), and the prophet Jeremiah was befriended by Ebed-melech, a Cushite who held a responsible position in the court of King Zedekiah (Jer. 38:7-13; 39:15-18). Another prophet, Ezekiel, predicted doom for the Cushites of the future (Ezk. 30:4-9; 38:5; cf. also Dnl. 11:43), while the OT Apocrypha and Pseudepigrapha tended to portray Nubia as being remote and/or barbarous (cf. Jth. 1:10; Sib. Or. 3:319f.; 512-19).

G. Meroë, Aksum, and Ethiopian Christianity. Beginning with Queen Bartare (*ca.* 284-275 B.C.), female rule became increasingly important in the kingdom of Meroë. "Candace" is the Meroitic word for "queen (mother)" and was therefore a title rather than a name. The Candace of Acts 8:27 may be Amanitēre who perhaps survived her husband, Natakamun, ruling as queen mother in his place (see plate 16b in A. J. Arkell, *History of the Sudan*). Modern Ethiopians erroneously tend to equate her with the queen of Sheba on the basis of passages in the *Kebra Nagast,* the Ethiopian national saga.

The first known reference to Aksum, the ancient capital of the territory today called Ethiopia, is in the *Periplus Maris Erythraei,* an anonymous first-century A.D. account of travel and trade in the Indian Ocean. The kingdom of Meroë at that time was languishing, and Aksum stepped into the power vacuum. In *ca.* A.D. 350, Meroë was sacked by ʿEzānā, Aksum's greatest king, the kingdom of Meroë came to an inglorious end, and the ancient name of Cush ceased to be used for all practical purposes. A convert to Christianity, ʿEzānā made it the official religion of the Aksumite kingdom. An impressive series of obelisks was built during his reign.

H. Moslem Conquest and Solomonic Dynasty. The Moslem conquest in the 7th cent. A.D. temporarily severed Ethiopia from its spiritual source, the patriarchate of Alexandria. Isolated from the outside world for almost a thousand years, the people retired within their impregnable mountain fastnesses, and Ethiopian Christianity began to assimilate indigenous and even pagan elements. Because Ethiopia turned its attention southward, very little is definitely known of the thousand-year period. In A.D. 1270, however, the so-called Solomonic dynasty became dominant and reigned in Ethiopia until 1975. Proper historical documentation is available for it. The province of Amhara became Ethiopia's political center, and church and state were once again fused. In 1434 Zarʿa Yaʿqob, the greatest ruler Ethiopia had seen since ʿEzānā, became king. With the exceptions of Menelik II and Haile Selassie, none can be compared to him. He instituted religious and administrative reforms and enjoyed military successes against the Moslems. Only two or three MSS in Geʿez (the ancient Ethiopic language) antedate him, but many derive from his time and later. Although his successors were unable to stop further Moslem encroachment, the Portuguese helped them to remove the menace forever in the 16th century.

P. Rombulo, an Italian who arrived in Ethiopia in 1407, was the first modern reliable reporter of the Ethiopian scene. In the following century F. Alvarez, a Portuguese, produced a coherent and authoritative work on Ethiopia that excited considerable interest in Europe. In 1588 the Italian G. Gabriel became the first European to visit the source of the Blue Nile at Gish above Lake Tana, the largest of Ethiopia's lakes, about 3235 sq. km. (1250 sq. mi.). The eighteenth-century Scottish explorer J. Bruce traversed the length and breadth of Ethiopia in a manner unexcelled until his time and brought back a magnificent collection of Ethiopic MSS.

After the great Galla migrations from Ethiopia's coastlands (*ca.* 1550-1850) Ethiopia again emerged from her isolation. King Theodore (1855-1868) eliminated his rivals and was anointed *negusa nagast* ("King of Kings"). Menelik II rose to power in 1889 and moved the capital to Addis Ababa, ruling there till 1913. After a fourteen-year regency, Ras Tafari prevailed over his rivals and was crowned in 1930 as Emperor Haile Selassie ("Might of the Trinity") I in St. George's Cathedral there. Except for the Italian Fascist interlude (1936-1941), he reigned until deposed by a military coup in 1975.

III. Geography.–The modern country encompasses about 1,035,000 sq. km. (400,000 sq. mi.). Separated from Arabia (Asia) by the narrow Bâb el-Mandeb, Ethiopia is shaped like a triangle with its apex to the north. Its vast mountain massif, 2100-2400 m. (7000-8000 ft.) high, makes for astonishing contrasts in climate. The mountains are cleft by the great rift valley in a NE-SW direction. W of the mountains is the immense Nile Valley, fed by the Abbai (Blue Nile), which, a thousand miles from its source above Lake Tana, meets the White Nile at Khartoum in the Sudan. The Takkaze, Atbara, and Mareb rivers also flow westward toward the Nile, ultimately emptying their waters into the Mediterranean.

IV. Climate and Crops.–Ethiopia has three main climatic zones: the highlands (temperate), over 2100 m. (7000 ft.); the intermediate (once the main region for vine cultivation), 1500-2100 m. (5000-7000 ft.); and the lowlands (hot). The "small" rains last from March to May, the "big" rains from June to September. It is the alternation of Ethiopia's dry and rainy seasons that causes the annual flooding of the Nile. Planting of crops in Ethiopia takes place from March to June, and harvesting occurs immediately after the "big" rains. Needless to say, the nature, yield, and frequency of crops (and all plants) vary considerably depending on altitude. Domestic and wild animals and birds of all sorts abound.

V. Population and Language.–The population of Ethiopia numbers about ten million. Cushitic, Semitized Cushitic, and Nilotic are the three main ethnic groups. Amharic is the official language, although other dialects such as Tigre and Tigriña are widely used.

Serious investigation into the nature of the ancient Geʿez language of Ethiopia did not begin until the 16th century. The Italian scholar M. Victorius published the first grammar of Ethiopic in 1548. Ninety years later, J. Wemmers of Antwerp published the first Ethiopic dictionary. J. Ludolf, a seventeenth-century German, was the most brilliant and prolific of all the earlier Ethiopic scholars. In the 19th cent. A. Dillmann published a new grammar, dictionary, and chrestomathy. Other important names in the highly specialized modern field of Ethiopic studies are T. Nöldeke, F. Praetorius, C. C. Rossini, E. A. Wallis Budge, E. Littmann, H. J. Polotsky, W. Leslau, and E. Ullendorff.

VI. Abyssinian Church.–Geʿez serves the same purpose for the Abyssinian Church as did Latin for the Roman

Catholic Church. Monophysite Christianity as enshrined in the Ethiopian Orthodox Church is the official religion of Ethiopia. Before their conversion to Christianity under ʿEzānā, the Abyssinians were probably partly pagan, influenced by Cushite animism, and partly adherents of a form of Judaized religion brought by immigrants from south Arabia across the Bâb el-Mandeb. The Scripture of the Abyssinian Church consists of the OT and NT, plus a number of apocryphal books. The councils of Nicea (325), Constantinople (381), and Ephesus (431) are recognized, but not that of Chalcedon. Christ is believed to have only one nature (divine). Of the traditional seven sacraments, confirmation and extreme unction are not practiced. Trine immersion constitutes baptism. Magical practices and superstitions abound in Ethiopian Christianity, derived partly from old Cushitic pagan beliefs and partly from the ancient Semitic world. Feasts, fasts, and commemorative days are numerous, including thirty-three in honor of the Virgin Mary alone. Until very recently, close ties existed between the Abyssinian and the Coptic Church. Famous monasteries are located at Debra Libanos and Debra Damo. The most beautiful and oldest of the Ethiopian churches is the rectangular building at Debra Damo, dating back to the early Middle Ages. The eleven rock-hewn churches of the village of Lalibala are also outstanding in beauty and workmanship.

King Amda Sion (1314-1344) started a literary renaissance in Ethiopia. During his reign the foremost creation of Ethiopian literature, the *Kebra Nagast* ("Glory of the Kings"), came into being. The legend of the queen of Sheba is its *pièce de résistance,* telling how she visited King Solomon (cf. 1 K. 10:1-13), accepted his religion, and bore him a son (Menelik I), who later visited his father and abducted the ark of the covenant, taking it to Aksum, the new Zion. The basic elements of this legend were also enshrined in Article Two of the 1955 Constitution.

About half the populace of modern Ethiopia are adherents of the Ethiopian Church. Their favorite Bible verse is undoubtedly Ps. 68:31 (MT 32), which is frequently used as a motto or in heraldic devices. The verse represents Ethiopia (LXX *Aithiopia*) hastening "to stretch out her hands to God" and has become a proof text of much of the country's passionate adherence to Ethiopian Orthodox Christianity. Moslems and pagans make up most of the rest of the population. The Falashas are not the Jews of Ethiopia (as is often claimed) but rather indigenous Judaized tribesmen, non-Christianized remnants of the Aksumite kingdom. In recent years evangelical Christianity has experienced an upsurge in Ethiopia resulting in thousands of converts.

Bibliography.–C. Aldred, *The Egyptians* (1961); A. J. Arkell, *History of the Sudan* (2nd rev. ed. 1961); W. A. Fairservis, *Ancient Kingdoms of the Nile* (1962); G. Last and R. Pankhurst, *History of Ethiopia in Pictures* (1969); G. Steindorff and K. C. Seele, *When Egypt Ruled the East* (rev. ed. 1957); E. Ullendorff, *Ethiopia and the Bible* (1968); *The Ethiopians* (1960).

R. F. YOUNGBLOOD

ETHIOPIAN EUNUCH [Gk. *Aithiops eunoúchos*]. Acts 8:26-40 gives an account of Philip's evangelization of a eunuch returning home to Ethiopia after a visit to Jerusalem. This man was called a eunuch (*eunoúchos*) and a ruler (*dynástēs*) of the Ethiopian court. Probably he was a castrated man with authority in the court of the queen mother of Ethiopia, since eunuchs were most often used where queens were involved. Plutarch even records that Lysimachus resented being called a treasurer (which this Ethiopian was, cf. Acts 8:27) because treasurers were usually eunuchs (*Demetrius* 25.5). Usage during this time also permitted the application of *eunoúchos* to a high ruler with a military commission, not necessarily castrated (cf. *TDNT,* II, 766), or to one who by choice desired to abstain from marriage (Mt. 19:12).

The ETHIOPIA referred to here is not the modern country of the same name but the ancient kingdom of Meroë, which lay along the upper Nile S of Aswan to Khartoum in the Sudan. It appears that the king of this country was venerated as a child of the sun and regarded as too sacred a person to care for the duties of state; hence these duties were filled by the queen mother, who was regularly called "Candace," as the Egyptian ruler was called "Pharaoh."

The relation of the eunuch to Judaism is a problem. The text merely tells us that he was on a pilgrimage to Jerusalem. Dt. 23:1 and Lev. 21:20 indicate that eunuchs were not to be admitted to the congregation of Israel or allowed to minister in the sanctuary. This was perhaps because the divinely created state of man was thus destroyed or because mutilation of the male destroyed the patriarchal ideal of the early nation (cf. *TDNT,* II, 766). Isa. 56:3-5 seems to have provided a basis for the admission of the eunuch into the nation of Israel, although this cannot be certain. If this is so, the Ethiopian may have been a Jew or a Jewish proselyte; but it is more probable that he was a God-fearing Gentile (*see* DEVOUT; DISPERSION V.C.). This account must then be considered in relation to the general spreading of the gospel to the Gentiles. Luke intends this segment of the book of Acts to show the spread of the gospel to Africa and is not concerned with the question whether this was the first gentile conversion. The conversion of Cornelius was undoubtedly more important for the Jerusalem church because Cornelius was a prominent Gentile and his conversion took place in Palestine, where news of it would be widespread. This conversion of the Ethiopian was important as a fulfillment of the prophecies of Zeph. 3:10 and Ps. 68:31 (MT 32).

In Luke's account the angel of the Lord appeared to Philip and commanded him to go to the road to Gaza, a road which led from Jerusalem through the coastal plain and then along the Mediterranean to Egypt. As he went along this road Philip saw the eunuch in a wagon (perhaps covered). As it was usual for people in ancient times to read aloud, Philip would have had no trouble knowing that the man was reading the prophet Isaiah. Although Meroë had its own language and also used a form of Egyptian hieroglyphics, there seems to be little problem related to the eunuch's use of Greek. In answer to the eunuch's question as to the person about whom the prophet spoke, Philip told him that the Suffering Servant of Isa. 53 was Jesus Christ. Accepting the message about Jesus, the eunuch desired baptism in a body of water along the road. Many believe that this is the Wâdī Ḥesī NE of Gaza, although this cannot be known with certainty. After the baptism Philip was caught away and the eunuch proceeded to his homeland.

The eunuch's confession of faith (8:37) is omitted from the best Greek MSS and therefore is not found in our most reliable English translations. This confession appears earliest in Irenaeus and then in the later Western texts. Most scholars believe that such confessions were the usual practice before baptism. For this reason the verse was added to the text of Acts at a very early date.

Bibliography.–F. F. Bruce, *Acts* (*NICNT,* 1966), pp. 184-190; H. J. Cadbury, *Book of Acts in History* (1955), pp. 15-18; O. Cullmann, *Baptism in the NT* (Eng. tr. 1950), pp.71ff.; *TDNT,* II, *s.v.* εὐνοῦχος (J. Schneider).

D. W. WEAD

ETHIOPIC ē-thi-op′ik [Eth. *lesāna Geʿez*–'the tongue of Geʿez']. The language of Ethiopia, used in the inscriptions of the kings of the ancient Aksumite (Axumite) empire and in most of the literature of Christian Ethiopia. The Agʿazyan or "Geʿez" tribe must have dwelt in or near Aksum (Axum) in antiquity.

The names "Ethiopia" and "Ethiopians" have had a variety of uses in various stages and writings of history, and in ancient times designated something quite other than the Ethiopia of today. While to classical Greek historians (and hence in Bible translations; *see* CUSH) "Ethiopia" referred specifically to the land S of Egypt, to Nubia in what is now the Sudan, in Hellenistic times it covered all the land between the Red Sea and the Nile. To some historians "Ethiopian" and "Indian" became synonymous, and on some ancient maps Ethiopia spanned Africa to the Atlantic. Historically, as well as officially today, the Ethiopians themselves have preferred the name "Ethiopia" (*ʾItīōpiyā*) to "Abyssinia." Therefore, in the bilingual inscription of King Aeizanas (ʿĒzānā), Gk. *Aithiopia* is a rendering of the Semitic *Ḥābāšāt* (Abyssinia, but here referring more specifically to northern Ethiopia). Under the same king, *ca.* A.D. 350, Ethiopia became a Christian kingdom, and after the translation of the Bible into the Geʿez language the name "Ethiopia" came to be used widely and proudly.

The term "Ethiopic language" has come into accepted usage as an equivalent of *lesāna Geʿez* and must be understood to apply specifically to the ancient or classical language of Ethiopia. Ethiopic (Geʿez) was a highly evolved language, distinct from its south-Arabian origins, by the 4th cent. A.D. when Frumentius established a connection with the Christian church of Alexandria that was to open a new epoch in Ethiopian history; thus the language provided a ready vehicle for a body of both translated and indigenous Christian literature.

This language, closely allied to the languages of south Arabia, is the most extensive extant representative of that branch of Semitic languages. While Ethiopic has a great deal in common with the Arabic language, at the same time it preserves elements of ancient Semitic usage that at points align it more closely with Hebrew and even with Babylonian and Assyrian. The Semitic inhabitants of Ethiopia must have come from across the Red Sea. It is thought that Yemeni colonizers of the Red Sea coast of Africa became established during the 4th and 3rd cents. B.C., and that the Geʿez language, though only one of several dialects derived from South Arabic, had developed distinctively by the end of the 1st cent. A.D.

The two races of peoples that the Semitic conquerors of northern Ethiopia found were African aborigines and Cushites, a branch of the Hamitic family. While the Semites did not at first allow the several representatives of these varied linguistic groups to influence their own dialects very much, the local influence increased with time, as is evident in the modern Semitic languages of Ethiopia.

Many of the details of the stages of development remain obscure to us, but an outline of the history of the Ethiopic language can be made as follows. Its oldest monument known so far is the Semitic part of the bilingual inscription of King ʿĒzānā (*ca.* A.D. 325). Well before that time Ethiopic must have been spoken, if not written (Greek and Sabean were written). Although Sabean script was still used ornamentally, knowledge of that language was slight by ʿĒzānā's time. The Semitic part of the aforementioned inscription is true Ethiopic but is carved once in Sabean script and repeated in the Ethiopic script that had been derived from it. In the former version just a few Sabean words are employed for the Ethiopic equivalents. A few other ancient inscriptions of the same period have been found in the Aksum area.

Two features set the Ethiopic script apart from other Semitic writing systems. The first is its development into a quasi-syllabic system, in which a modification of the basic consonantal form of each letter yields a vowel sound in combination with it; the second is that the order of the alphabet differs from any of the other Semitic systems or their derivatives. A recent archeological discovery at the site of ancient Timnaʿ in Yemen reveals a sequence of Qatabanian consonants similar to that now seen only in Ethiopic.

Possibly also in the 4th cent. the translation of the Bible into Ethiopic was begun; this marks the beginning of Ethiopic literature. Probably the Psalms and Gospels were translated first, being most needed in church services. Apparently both Testaments were translated from the Greek by men whose mother tongue was Aramaic. This tradition is supported by the presence of Greek and Aramaic words and by the forms in which Hebrew names appear in the Ethiopic transliteration. Subsequent Ethiopian authors show dependence upon the style of these translations of the Scriptures.

The formative influences upon the Ethiopic language were, therefore: (1) Sabean, from which a number of technical terms may have been adopted by the ancient Aksumites even after Geʿez became their literary language; (2) African, i.e., Cushitic and native African, especially for local flora and fauna; (3) Aramaic, both Jewish and Christian, primarily the former, mostly words referring to religious or theological matters; and (4) Greek, appearing in the form of religious and technical borrowings,

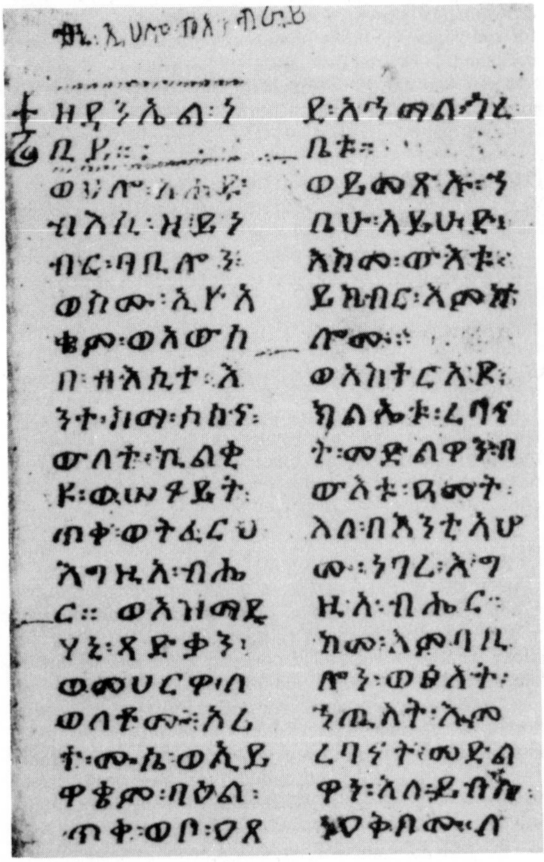

Ethiopic MS of Job and Daniel, 14th cent. A.D., showing part of Susanna, the apocryphal addition to Daniel (Deutsche Bibelstiftung, Stuttgart)

either transliterations or names for objects foreign to Ethiopian culture.

The Ethiopic language flourished during the time of the Aksumite empire (*see* ETHIOPIA II.G-H); but of the succeeding period, *ca.* A.D. 700-1300, we know very little. When, after a lapse, the Solomonic dynasty was restored in 1270, the seat of the empire was no longer Aksum, but Gondar N of Lake Ṭānā. Meanwhile, the literary language had become a dead language, new dialects having sprung up and taken its place in everyday conversation. But Geʿez continued to be the sacred language, the language of the Bible and of the Church; and when in the 14th and 15th cents. a revival of Ethiopian literature occurred, the literary language was still Geʿez. Yet it was influenced by new dialects, especially by Amharic, the language of the Amhara people of Gondar, where most of the books were written or translated. This influence affected the spelling of Geʿez in religious books, and in historical books many words were taken from Amharic, so that *lesāna tārīk,* "the tongue of the chronicles," often has the appearance of a mixed language.

When in the 16th and 17th cents. European missionaries used Amharic literature, attempting to attract the common people to Roman Catholicism, the defenders of the native Orthodox Church felt compelled to reply in kind, so that Amharic became a recognized literary language. But Geʿez has continued to be the real language of the Church, both in liturgy and in sacred studies. Amharic was apparently derived from a sister language of Ethiopic, the most widespread direct descendant of Geʿez being Tigriña, with the minor language called Tigre being the most closely related geographically.

Ethiopic study continues to shed as much light on other Semitic languages as it receives from them, so that both for comparative Semitic studies and for historical study of biblical, apocryphal, and church liturgic and dogmatic material written in Ethiopic, it holds no small place in biblical research.

Bibliography.–A. Dillmann, *Ethiopic Grammar* (Eng. tr. 1907), Intro.; E. Littmann, *Geschichte der äthiopischen Literatur* (1907); E. Ullendorff, *Semitic Languages of Ethiopia* (1955); A. M. Honeyman, *Africa* (Apr. 1952); S. G. Wright, *Enc.Brit., s.v.* "Ethiopian Literature."

E. LITTMANN
M. C. FISHER

ETHIOPIC VERSIONS. *See* VERSIONS.

ETHIOPIC WOMAN. *See* CUSHITE WOMAN.

ETH-KAZIN eth-kā'zin [Heb. *ʿittâ qāṣîn*]; AV, NEB, ITTAH-KAZIN. A town on the east border of Zebulun (Josh. 19:13). "Ittah" in the AV and NEB is due to a misunderstanding of the changed spelling that indicates direction (*he* locale). While the location is uncertain, the context may put it at Kefr Kennā.

ETHMA eth'mə (1 Esd. 9:35, AV). *See* NEBO **2.**

ETHNAN eth'nan [Heb. *'eṯnān*–'give' or 'hire'; Gk. *Ethnadi*]. A Judahite (1 Ch. 4:7), perhaps from the south Judean town of Ithnan, which may have been founded by one of his ancestors (cf. Josh. 15:23). R. K. H.

ETHNARCH eth'närk [Gk. *ethnárchēs*–'ruler of the people' < *éthnos*–'people' + *árchōn*–'ruler'] (1 Macc. 14:47; 15:1f.); AV GOVERNOR, PRINCE. A title used to designate a subordinate ruler. The precise meaning of the term varied throughout the centuries of its use.

The RSV uses this term only in 1 Maccabees, where Simon Maccabeus the high priest is called "commander and ethnarch of the Jews and priests" (14:47; cf. 15:1f.). Here the title denotes a representative of a subject people who has been given certain powers of control and discipline over his own people but is responsible to the foreign dominating power. The title appears several times with this meaning in the writings of Josephus. He reported that this title was granted by the Roman senate to Hyrcanus, "the high priest and ethnarch" of the Jewish people (*Ant.* xiv.8.5). Archelaus son of Herod was appointed ethnarch over half of his father's kingdom, while the other half was divided into two tetrarchies granted to Philip and Antipas (*BJ* ii.6.3; *Ant.* vii.11.4); thus, the office of ethnarch was greater than that of TETRARCH. The Jewish community in Alexandria is also reported to have had the privilege of being governed by an ethnarch of its own race (*Ant.* xiv.7.2; xix.5.2).

The Gk. *ethnárchēs* appears once in the NT, in 2 Cor. 11:32 (AV, RSV, "governor"; NEB "commissioner"). The nationality and function of this ethnarch are not certain, since scholars are divided about whether Damascus at this time was under Roman domination or under the full control of the Nabatean king Aretas IV (9 B.C.-A.D.40). (*See also* ARETAS **3**; DAMASCUS III.) The ethnarch was likely the leader of the Nabatean community in Damascus or its environs, responsible either to the Roman authority or to Aretas. It is also possible, however, that he was a Jew with some control over the large Jewish community in Damascus (cf. *BJ* ii.20.2; vii.8.7), similar to the Jewish ethnarch in Alexandria (see Hughes, p. 424). According to the Acts 9 account of Paul's escape from Damascus, it was the Jews who plotted to seize Paul (v. 24). Apparently the Jewish community enlisted the support of the ethnarch — whatever his ethnic identity — in this scheme.

Bibliography.–Comms. on 2 Corinthians by C. K. Barrett (1973), F. F. Bruce (*New Century Bible,* 1971), P. E. Hughes (*NICNT,* 1962), A. Plummer (*ICC,* 1915), and others; *HJP*[2], I, 581f.

N. J. O.

ETHNI eth'nī [Heb. *'eṯnî*–'gift']. An ancestor of Asaph, of the Gershomite branch of the Levites (1 Ch. 6:41 [MT 26]).

EUBULUS ū-bo͞o'ləs [Gk. *Euboulos*–'of good counsel'] (2 Tim. 4:21). A member of the church in Rome who remained loyal (cf. v. 16) at the time of Paul's second imprisonment in that city.

Nothing more is known in regard to Eubulus. As his name is Greek, he was probably a Gentile by birth. The name occurs frequently in inscriptions and papyri.

EUCHARIST ū'kə-rist. *See* LORD'S SUPPER.

EUERGETES ū-ûr'jə-tēz [Gk. *euergétēs*–'benefactor'] (Sir. Prologue). A title given in ancient times to those who had performed outstanding works of benevolence. The author of the Prologue to Sirach dates his writing by referring to his arrival in Egypt in the thirty-eighth year of Ptolemy VII Euergetes (132 B.C.). *See* PTOLEMY.

EUGNOSTOS, LETTER OF. *See* NAG HAMMADI LITERATURE II.

EUMENES II ū'me-nēz [Gk. *Eumenēs*–'well-disposed']. King of Pergamum (197 B.C.), son and successor of Attalus I. He is mentioned in the Apocrypha (1 Macc. 8:8) in connection with the league that Judas Maccabeus made with the Romans. As their ally in the war against Antiochus the Great and in recognition of his distinguished service at the decisive battle of Magnesia (190 B.C.), the Romans granted Eumenes extensive tracts of land so that he rose at once from comparative insignificance to sovereign of a great territory. The statement in 1 Maccabees of the territory granted to him differs from those of Livy (xxxviii.39), Polybius (xxi.45), and Appian (*Syr.* 44), and cannot be correct. The Romans are said to have taken "India and Media and Lydia" from Antiochus and to have given them to Eumenes. Antiochus never had any possessions in India, nor had any earlier king of Syria. He was obliged to give up only the countries on the side of Taurus toward Rome (cf. A. H. McDonald, *Journal of Roman Studies,* 57 [1967], 1-8). No alternative for the reading "India" in the narrative has met with acceptance (it may have been a copyist's error for "Ionia"; see Livy xxxvii.56). Eumenes cultivated the Roman alliance carefully but became suspect in connection with the affairs of Perseus, the last king of Macedonia. He never came to an open rupture with the Romans, however, and died in 159 B.C. after a reign of thirty-nine years.

J. HUTCHISON

EUNATAN ū-nā'tən (1 Esd. 8:44, AV). *See* ELNATHAN **3.**

EUNICE ū'nis [Gk. *Euníkē*–'good victory'] (2 Tim. 1:5). The mother of Timothy. Although her name was Greek, she was a Jewess (Acts 16:1). Her husband was a Gentile. Eunice was in all probability a daughter of Lois, Timothy's grandmother, for Paul mentions these Christian women together in highly commendable terms (2 Tim. 1:5).

Timothy had not been circumcised in childhood, probably because his father was a Gentile, but Eunice and Lois did everything in their power to train him in the fear of God and knowledge of the OT Scriptures (2 Tim. 3:15). Timothy's name, signifying "one who fears God," was evidently chosen not by his father but by Eunice. Apparently Eunice, along with Timothy and Lois, was converted during Paul's visit to LYSTRA on his first missionary journey. This is implied in the account of Paul's second missionary journey, where it is said that Paul found in Lystra "a disciple . . . named Timothy, the son of a Jewish woman who was a believer" (Acts 16:1). This conclusion is confirmed in 2 Tim. 3:11, where Paul reminds Timothy that he had witnessed the persecution the apostle had endured at Lystra. This persecution occurred on Paul's first visit to that city (Acts 14:8-22). Eunice was therefore among those who on that occasion became "disciples" (v. 21). Her faith in Christ stood the test of the "many tribulations" about which Paul warned them (v. 22). During Paul's next visit to Lystra she had the great joy of seeing her son chosen by the apostle to be his companion in his missionary work. Eunice is not afterward mentioned in the NT, though she may be included in what is said about widows and their children in 1 Tim. 5:4f.

See also TIMOTHY. J. RUTHERFURD

EUNUCH [Heb. *sārîs*]; AV also CHAMBERLAIN; [Gk. *eunoúchos*] (Mt. 19:12; Acts 8:27, etc.); NEB also INCAPABLE OF MARRIAGE; [part. of *eunouchízō*] ("made eunuchs," Mt. 19:12); NEB also RENOUNCE MARRIAGE. An emasculated human male.

I. In the Ancient World.–Exactly where and why human castration began is still uncertain. The tradition reported by the Byzantine historian Ammianus Marcellinus (*Rerum gestarum libri* xiv.6.17) — that it was instituted by the legendary Assyrian Queen Semiramis (Sammu-ramat, *ca.* 810-805 B.C.) — at least suggests Mesopotamia as its place of origin, though it is now known that the Assyrian practice of making men eunuchs actually antedates this queen by many centuries. Castration as a means of punishment was known in Assyria already in the 2nd millennium B.C. An example may be noted in the "Middle Assyrian Laws" (tablets from the time of Tiglath-pileser I, 12th cent. B.C., but laws and regulations which may actually derive from the 15th cent. B.C.): "if a seignior has caught a(nother) seignior with his wife . . . if the woman's husband puts his wife to death, he shall also put the seignior to death, but if he cuts off his wife's nose, he shall turn the seignior into a eunuch [*aīla*(LÚ) *ana ša rēšēn útâr*] and they shall mutilate his whole face" (Tablet A.15; tr. T. J. Meek, *ANET,* p. 181; text, R. Borger, *Lesestücke,* II, 51; III, plate 34).

Commonplace from early times in Mesopotamia was the employment of eunuchs as servants or supervisory officials in the women's quarters of royal households (see E. Weidner, pp. 264ff.). But eunuchs in ancient Mesopotamia were known not only as bodyguards or domestics, but also as palace officials, statesmen, and military generals (see, e.g., Borger, *Lesestücke,* I, lxxvi, *s.v. šūt rēši*).

Concerning the origin of eunuchs, it is generally assumed that human castration was first suggested by analogy with that of animals. Xenophon (*Cyropaedia* vii.5.60-65) reports that it was the belief of the Persian king Cyrus the Great that emasculation yielded more docile and easily managed slaves who, undistracted by family ties, were characterized by single-hearted loyalty (and in the harem by unquestioned fidelity). Thus Xenophon says of Cyrus, "Recognizing these facts, he selected eunuchs for every post of personal service to him, from the doorkeepers up" (*Cyropaedia* vii.5.65 [LCL]).

The use of eunuchs, both domestically and politically, became commonplace throughout the Persian empire under the Achaemenean kings (559-330 B.C.), during the Roman and (especially) Byzantine empires, and in the various Islamic caliphates after *ca.* A.D. 750. Nevertheless, the phenomenon was not unique to the Fertile Crescent or Mediterranean cultures, for eunuchs are known to have served royalty in China as political advisers already in the Chou period (*ca.* 1122-221 B.C.) (cf. *Enc.Brit.* [1974], III, 994). There is no clear evidence, however, of eunuchs in ancient Egypt (see G. Kadish, p. 61).

Through Near Eastern influence the custom of making men eunuchs was introduced to the ancient Greek world, although the concept of human castration was fundamentally alien to Greek thought (*TDNT,* II, 765). This influence was most prominently felt in hellenized Asia Minor, the land-bridge between the Near East and the Aegean sphere. There, particularly in the cults of Cybele, Attis, and Artemis, the institution of ritual castration and a corresponding eunuch priesthood flourished, probably motivated by a desire to be one physically with the deity (i.e., in transmundaneity) as well as spiritually (*ERE,* V, 580-82; *TDNT,* II, 765).

II. In Israel.–A. OT Teaching. Castration was prohibited in ancient Israel. In Dt. 23:1 eunuchs are excluded from the cultus. The rationale for this exclusion was multifaceted and in varying proportions included the following arguments: (1) emasculation is contrary to the divine order in creation; (2) it represents syncretistic accommodation to foreign influence; (3) the maimed or mutilated are considered unfit for priesthood, since by definition they constitute an affront to the God who made the world without blemish (cf. Lev. 21:20); and (4) the practice tends to undermine the natural patriarchal cultic order.

This prohibition notwithstanding, the eunuch is later considered admissible to the worship assembly (Isa. 56:3f.). This does not constitute the establishment of some new cultic norm, but rather the concrete application, to an especially problematic case, of the universalistic principles delineated by Isaiah in passages such as 44:5; 45:14, 23; 55:5, so that the unlimited nature of Yahweh's love may be manifested. With a skilful piece of prophetic *tôrâ,* the prophet counters the traditional objection to membership of eunuchs ("a dry tree," i.e., unproductive of offspring) with the instruction that the single most important thing is devoted loyalty to the covenant. The kind of perpetual memory gained by the eunuch's loyal deeds represents, in the prophet's eye, a more significant hope than the traditional one of a name perpetuated through numerous progeny. This teaching is reemphasized in Wisd. 3:14: "Blessed is the eunuch, if he has never done anything against the law" (cf. the first two categories of Mt. 19:12, those born eunuchs and those castrated involuntarily); sterility is no disgrace or impediment for the pure in heart, for he will find "a place in the Lord's temple" (NEB).

B. OT Terms. 1. Heb. sārîs. The Hebrew term *sārîs* appears forty-seven times in the OT (including four times in the title *raḇ-sārîs* and six in the title *śar-hassārîsîm,* both "chief eunuch"). In twenty-eight of these occurrences the RSV translates literally, "eunuch," but in the others it renders "(military) officer," "(political) official," or "chamberlain." (The NEB consistently translates "eunuch" for every occurrence of the term.) While in some instances *sārîs* clearly has the literal sense "emasculated male" (BDB, p. 710), especially in some of the later OT writings (cf. Dnl. 1; Est. 1–2 *et passim.*; Isa. 56:3f.; Sir. 30:20), elsewhere it appears to denote in a more general sense "courtier," "political official," or "military officer" in service to royalty. *See also* CHAMBERLAIN; OFFICER; OFFICIAL.

This usage in a more general sense occurs in 1 K. 22:9 par. 2 Ch. 18:8, where a *sārîs* functions as an emissary for Ahab, and in 2 K. 8:6, where another is appointed by the king to restore lost property to the woman of Shunem. Several *sārîsîm* throw Jezebel to her death from a palace window (2 K. 9:32f.). Describing the despotic character of Near Eastern kingships, Samuel warns that the royal servants and *sārîsîm* will be beneficiaries of the king's harvest and vintage tax (1 S. 8:15). *Sārîsîm* are listed among ranking dignitaries in Jer. 34:19: princes, priests, and *sārîsîm* (cf. LXX *dynástas,* "men in power"). The *sārîs* Nathan-melech is said to have had a room in the temple during the time of Josiah (2 K. 23:11). In Jer. 29:2 (cf. 2 K. 24:12, 15) *sārîsîm,* together with the queen mother, harem wives, princes, courtiers, nobles, craftsmen, and smiths, are taken into exile along with King Jehoiachin. At the fall of Jerusalem the Babylonians captured, among others, a *sārîs* who was "in command of the men of war" (Jer. 52:25; 2 K. 25:19).

The term is similarly applied in the OT to foreign dignitaries; e.g., Potiphar, the captain of Pharaoh's guard (Gen. 37:36; 39:1), is called a *sārîs,* as are Pharaoh's chief butler and chief baker (40:2). In military contexts, the Assyrian officials sent by Sennacherib to negotiate tribute from the besieged Hezekiah (2 K. 18:17) are the *tartān* (commander-in-chief), the *raḇ-sārîs,* and the *raḇ-šāqēh* (chief officer); and the Babylonian *raḇ-sārîs* of Nebuchadrezzar, Nebushazban, is named in Jer. 39:13 (cf. v. 3) along with a host of other military officers of the Babylonian king. It is not certain whether *sārîs* has the general or specific sense in Isa. 39:7 par. 2 K. 20:18 — Isaiah's warning to Hezekiah that "some of your own sons . . . shall be eunuchs in the palace of the king of Babylon" (but cf. LXX *spádōn,* "eunuch").

The literal sense of the term is exemplified particularly in Esther (twelve times), where the *sārîsîm* are regularly identified by their personal names and by such titles as "keeper of the women" (*šōmēr hannāšîm,* 2:3, 15), "keeper of the concubines" (*šōmēr happîlagšîm,* 2:14), "keepers of the door" (2:21; 6:2), all generally reflective of Persian custom. The *sārîsîm* in 2 K. 9:32 and Jer. 41:16 may also have functioned in connection with the harem.

The Heb. *sārîs* is now generally considered a loanword from Akk. *ša rēši (šarri),* "the one who is at the head [of the king]," i.e., "courtier" (first proposed by P. Jensen, 174 n.1; see also R. Borger, *Akkadische Zeichenliste* [1971], p. 31; *Lesestücke,* I, lxxvi; Bauer and Leander, p. 538; R. de Vaux, *Ancient Israel,* I, 121; K. A. Kitchen, p. 160; J. Fitzmyer, p. 108; BDB, p. 710). The term may have passed into Hebrew via Aramaic (cf. Sfire stele III.5; I.B.45; S. Kaufman, *Akkadian Influences on Aramaic* [1974], pp. 100, 147f., 152), and thence into Syriac and Arabic as well (cf. BDB, p. 710).

The Akkadian idiom *ša rēši* exhibits in the cuneiform literature the same double meaning as Heb. *sārîs.* Originally a generalized term for "courtier," "official," *ša rēši* underwent a specialization of meaning already before (cf. *ANET,* p. 181, where the term is used in the expression "turn into a eunuch"), but especially after the turn of the 1st millennium B.C. This semantic narrowing likely occurred as eunuchs increasingly were found to be the most reliable supervisory personnel in the harem. The same evolution of meaning may well explain the OT uses of the Hebrew counterpart, *sārîs,* since the specialized sense is clearly evident only in the later strata of the OT. Although scholarly consensus generally rests with the above explanation, two other opinions have been suggested: (1) two originally distinct Semitic homophones meaning "official" and "eunuch" have inextricably coalesced in Heb. *sārîs* (*Enc.Brit.* [1914], II, 247 [Cheyne]; cf. J. Gray, *I & II Kings* [*OTL,* 2nd rev. ed. 1970], pp. 449f.); (2) the meaning evolved from the specific to the general sense as eunuchs in domestic service for royalty merited ever more responsible positions for their reliability (*Enc. Brit.* [1911], IX, 890; this opinion, dependent on a suspect etymology of Gk. *eunoúchos* as "bed wardens," is rejected by L. Gray in *ERE,* V, 579).

2. LXX Usage. In the LXX *eunoúchos* is used almost exclusively to represent Heb. *sārîs* (thirty-one times, and seven times in Daniel in the compound *archieunoúchos*; cf. also *spádōn,* "eunuch," in Isa. 39:7). The peculiar LXX translation of *sārîsîm* as *dynástas,* "men in power," in Jer. 34:19 (LXX 41:19) suggests conscious accommodation to the Deuteronomic regulation excluding the castrated from the cultus. *Eunoúchos* is used in the LXX much as *sārîs* in the Hebrew OT, i.e., in the sense of a military or political official as well as in the more restricted sense of eunuch. In the Apocrypha the latter sense prevails (cf. Wisd. 3:14; Sir. 20:4; 30:20).

C. Judaism. That Herod the Great employed eunuchs in his court is reported by Josephus (*Ant.* xv.8.4.; xvi.8.1). Rabbinic Judaism approached the question of eunuchs from the viewpoint of creation, teaching that not to beget offspring was to disobey the divine command of Gen. 1:28 ("be fruitful and multiply"). A distinction was also made between the *s^e^rîs 'āḏām,* "man-made eunuch," and the *s^e^rîs ḥammâ,* "eunuch by nature" (Mish. *Yebamoth* viii.4-6; cf. Jesus' distinctions in Mt. 19:12; see *TDNT,* II, 767).

III. In the NT.–The Gk. *eunoúchos* appears infrequently in the NT: five times in Acts 8:27-39 and twice in Mt. 19:12; in addition, the cognate verb *eunouchízō,* "make a eunuch," appears twice (Mt. 19:12). In Acts 8 the eunuch of the Ethiopian queen Candace comes to faith in Jesus and is baptized. That this person is a eunuch is of greater significance than that he is an Ethiopian, for this event is a fulfillment of the prophetic saying in

Isa. 56:3-5. The eunuch (an outcast like the Samaritans in the preceding verses of Acts 8) is no longer excluded from the kingdom of God. *See* ETHIOPIAN EUNUCH.

Jesus' teaching goes beyond the rabbinic teaching in that He distinguishes three types of "eunuchs": those who are so by birth, those who have been involuntarily castrated, and those who have "made themselves eunuchs for the sake of the kingdom of heaven" (Mt. 19:12). The last category is often interpreted figuratively rather than literally, in the sense that those who for the sake of the kingdom forego the sexual life and marriage do so in order to focus their energies totally on a goal that reaches beyond the demands of existence — the goal of establishing the kingdom of God on earth (*TDNT,* II, 768). A contemporary example of this last group, familiar to Jesus, would have been the Qumrân Essenes for whom celibacy was a part of the community discipline.

IV. In the Early Church.–The attitude of the early Church to self-mutilation appears to have been ambivalent. The Mt. 19:12 saying wielded a strong influence and in early exegesis was frequently interpreted literally (*TDNT,* II, 768). Nevertheless, only a few early Christians (the great theologian and linguist Origen, A.D. 185-254, being the most celebrated example) took the drastic step of self-castration in hope of avoiding temptation or sexual sin. Canons were eventually adopted in the 4th cent. admitting into the Christian ministry those belonging to the first two categories of Mt. 19:12, but permanently barring from the ministry those who had emasculated themselves (Apos. Const. viii.21-24, 47; see *ERE,* V, 583; *TDNT,* II, 768; Quesnell, pp. 335-358; Blinzler, pp. 254-270).

See also CELIBACY.

Bibliography.–*ANET,* pp. 180-88; H. Bauer and P. Leander, *Historische Grammatik der hebräischen Sprache des AT* (1922), p. 538; J. Blinzler, *ZNW,* 49 (1957), 254-270; R. Borger, *Babylonisch-Assyrische Lesestücke* (1963), I-III; *Enc.Brit.*(1965), IX, 822; (1974), III, 994; *ERE,* V, 579-584; J. Fitzmyer, *Aramaic Inscriptions of Sefîre* (1967); P. Jensen, *Zeitschrift für Assyriologie und verwandte Gebiete,* 7 (1892), 174; G. Kadish, "Eunuchs in Ancient Egypt," in *Studies in Honor of John A. Wilson* (1970), pp. 55-62; K. A. Kitchen, *JEA,* 47 (1961), 158-164; Q. Quesnell, *CBQ,* 30 (1968), 335-358; *TDNT,* II, *s.v.* εὐνοῦχος, εὐνουχίζω (J. Schneider); R. de Vaux, *Ancient Israel* (Eng. tr. 1965), I, 121, 225; E. F. Weidner, *AfO,* 17 (1956), 264f.

D. G. BURKE

EUODIA ū-ō'dē-ə [Gk. *Euodia*–'prosperous journey'] (Phil. 4:2); AV EUODIAS. A Christian woman, one of the members of the church in Philippi. She and SYNTYCHE, who is named in the same verse, were evidently persons of note, prominent in the work of the church there. At Philippi the gospel was preached first to women (Acts 16:13) and the church was first formed among women, evidently in the house of Lydia (vv. 15, 40). Possibly, as J. B. Lightfoot (*Philippians* [1978], *in loc.*) has suggested, Euodia and Syntyche were deaconesses in the Philippian church; but whatever their position in this respect, differences had arisen between them. The dispute — the nature of which is not known — had become chronic, and news of it had reached Paul in his captivity in Rome.

The Christian life exemplified in the church at Philippi gave Paul almost complete satisfaction. Apparently the only thing that caused him uneasiness was the lack of harmony between Euodia and Syntyche. In Phil. 4:2, therefore, he appeals to them impartially (he repeats the verb *parakalō,* "I entreat") to give up their differences and to live at peace in the Lord. His motive is to bring about reconciliation between these two women who had "labored [Gk. *synēthlēsán,* 'struggled,' 'fought'] side by side with me in the gospel" (4:3). Paul asks a certain (unnamed) person, whom he terms "true yokefellow," to assist them. It is uncertain who is meant by "true yokefellow" (*see* YOKEFELLOW). He also asks Clement and all the other Christians at Philippi, his fellow workers, to aid in this work of reconciliation.

See comms. on Philippians.

J. RUTHERFURD

EUPATOR ū'pə-tor [Gk. *Eupatōr*–'of noble father']. The name given to Antiochus V (1 Macc. 3:32; 6:17). Epiphanes had appointed his friend and foster brother Philip as his son's guardian; but in Philip's absence Lysias continued his duty as guardian, set the king upon the throne, and named him Eupator (164 B.C.). Shortly after his accession Eupator collected a large army and, accompanied by Lysias, marched against Jerusalem for the relief of a Syrian garrison that was threatened by Judas Maccabeus (6:19f.). Judas was repulsed at Beth-zechariah, and after a severe struggle Beth-zur was captured (vv. 31-50). The Jewish force in the temple was hard pressed and reduced to the last extremity (v. 53), when Lysias, upon hearing that his rival Philip had returned from Persia and had made himself master of Antioch (Josephus *Ant.* xii.9.5f.), made a hasty peace and returned to meet Philip, whom he easily overpowered. In the following year (162 B.C.) Antiochus and Lysias were both put to death by Demetrius Soter, son of Seleucus, in requital of wrongs inflicted upon himself by Antiochus Epiphanes (1 Macc. 7:2-4; 2 Macc. 14:1f.; Josephus *Ant.* xii.10.1).

J. HUTCHISON

EUPHRATES ū-frā'tēz [Heb. *p^erāt*; Gk. *Euphratēs*; Akk. *purattu*]. The largest river in southwest Asia and one of the two main rivers in Mesopotamia. The upper course includes the streams of the Armenian mountains, which unite through two main branches to form the Euphrates N of Malatya. The northernmost of these main tributaries according to some maps still bears the name Firat, the Turkish form of Euphrates. After going through a narrow channel, generally southward, the river swings SW and enters the plain at Samsat, the ancient Samosata, about 80 km. (50 mi.) NW of the ancient site of Ḥarrân (Haran, Gen. 11:31). *See* Plate 45.

From this point, which is the beginning of the middle Euphrates, the river begins the "great bend" until at last it is flowing SE, continuing for 1100 km. (700 mi.) to the plain of ancient Babylonia. Approximately at the modern border between Turkey and Syria, just N of Jerablus, is the site of Carchemish, an important crossing, the capital of the kingdom of Mitanni, and one of the capitals of the Hittite empire and later of the Assyrian empire. At Carchemish in 605 B.C. Nebuchadrezzar II of Babylon defeated Neco of Egypt (2 K. 24:7). Farther south at ar-Raqqah the Balîkh River, one of the important tributaries, flows into the Euphrates from the north. Ḥarrân is on the Balîkh just N of the Turkish border. The Khābûr (Habor) River, the only other main tributary, empties into the Euphrates from the north at Bushayrah. The name Aram Naharaim ("Aram of the two rivers," the Mesopotamia of Gen. 24:10) originally belonged to the region between the Khābûr and the west bend of the Euphrates. Some 80 km. (50 mi.) SE of the junction of the Euphrates and the Khābûr is the site of Mari, an important city-state in the time of Hammurabi. A few miles to the northwest is Dura-Europus.

The lower Euphrates begins at Hit, where important bitumen (pitch) reservoirs were located that supplied the bonding material for much of the building in ancient southern Mesopotamia. The land from here south is very flat, and the lower Euphrates follows a circuitous route

through it before flowing into the Persian Gulf. This portion of the river overflows its banks every spring because of the melting snow in the mountains, and this flooding has caused much of the area to become marshland.

The river flows generally SE for 2860 km. (1780 mi.). In ancient times it emptied directly into the Persian Gulf, which according to some scholars extended over 160 km. (100 mi.) farther inland than it does today. This view has been challenged by other scholars, and discussion on the matter continues. It has been thought that the coast was built up through the centuries by the great amount of silt brought down by the Euphrates and Tigris rivers. Today these two streams are joined together and flow as one river, the Shaṭṭ el-Arab, 190 km. (120 mi.) to the gulf, where the water is deep enough for warships. In antiquity the course of the lower Euphrates was considerably different from its present location, as indicated by the locations of the ancient ruins. At that time it flowed considerably farther to the east than it does today, passing such sites as Kish, Nippur, Shuruppak, and then turning southward to Erech (Warka). From Erech the river continued SE, crossing the present course of the Euphrates,

The Euphrates winds through the Syrian countryside E of Aleppo (D. Baly)

The Euphrates flows through mountains in Anatolia (W. S. LaSor)

and touched Ubaid and Ur. If the theory of the extension of the Persian Gulf is accepted, Ur was close to the gulf at that time.

The Euphrates is the third most frequently mentioned river in the Bible. Only the Jordan and the Nile surpass it in scriptural notice. It is referred to by name twenty-one times and probably more often is simply called "the river" (in which cases it must be identified from the context). This designation is given to supply the location of the action being narrated or to limit the scope of a phrase denoting a geographical area. By this means, however, we learn two rather unusual details about the Euphrates River: It flowed in the vicinity of the Garden of Eden (Gen. 2:14), and in Revelation it is the scene of some phases of divine judgments that will fall on the earth during the tribulation period (Rev. 9:14; 16:12). This stream was too far away from the land of Canaan to appear prominently in the history of the ancient Hebrews. It was the largest river that flowed the year around, in contrast to the watercourses of their own land, which were torrents in the rainy season and dry beds the rest of the time.

The plain through which the Tigris and Euphrates rivers flowed was the home of one of the earliest civilizations, that of the Sumerians, so the Euphrates was one of the most famous waterways of ancient times. The literature of these people mentioned this river frequently as one of the elements of their daily lives. Many cities were erected on its banks, the most notable of which was Babylon. IRRIGATION was practiced, for although rainfall in the region was insufficient for crop growing, this use of the water from the river made the land very productive and able to support a dense concentration of people.

The Babylonians who succeeded the Sumerians in control of this region adopted and improved the irrigation system of their illustrious predecessors. It is recorded that one of the Babylonian kings had a tunnel dug under this stream to enable him to pass back and forth from his royal palace on one side to the temple of his god on the other bank of the river. The medieval and more recent inhabitants of the vicinity have not practiced irrigation. The soil that became barren, through neglect, can support only a very sparse population. In modern times some attempts are being made to remedy this unhappy situation.

The upper Euphrates formed a natural boundary. This is demonstrated by historical events. The ancient royal Egyptian conquerors never carried their arms beyond this waterway; it formed the dividing line between the Hittite empire on the west and the Assyrian domain on the east; and the forces of Rome were able to extend their realm eastward only as far as this stream. But most important from the biblical standpoint, the river marked the eastern limit of the Promised Land (see Gen. 15:18).

Bibliography.–J. J. Finkelstein, *JNES*, 21 (1962), 73-92; T. Jacobsen, "Waters of Ur," in *Toward the Image of Tammuz* (1970), pp. 231-243.

C. E. HARRINGTON
W. S. LASOR

EUPOLEMUS ū-pol'ə-məs [Gk. *Eupolemos*] (or Hakkoz, as he is called in Neh. 3:4, 21, etc.). Son of John the son of Accos; one of the two deputies sent by Judas Maccabeus (1 Macc. 8:17; 2 Macc. 4:11) to Rome *ca.* 161 B.C. to ask the help of the Romans against Demetrius. Eupolemus has been identified with the historian of the same name quoted by Eusebius (*Praep. ev.* ix.17ff.), but there is no evidence that the historian was of Jewish origin.

EUROCLYDON (Acts 27:14, AV). *See* NORTHEASTER.

EUTYCHUS ū'tə-kəs [Gk. *Eutychos*–'fortunate'] (Acts 20:9). The story of Eutychus occurs in the "we" section of Acts and is therefore related by an eyewitness of the incidents (Acts 20:7-12). On the first day of the week the Christians of Troas met for an evening service in an upper chamber, where they were joined by Paul and his company. Since he was to leave in the morning, Paul "prolonged his speech until midnight." The youth named Eutychus, sitting at the open window, was overcome by sleep because it was so late, and fell through the opening from the third story. He "was taken up dead." This direct statement is evaded by some scholars, who understand it as merely the judgment of those who took him up, translating "for dead" or "as though dead." This, however, is not the reading of the Greek. Luke the physician is giving his verdict, and he plainly believes that a miracle was wrought by Paul in restoring a corpse to life. According to his account, Paul went down and embraced the youth (cf. 1 K. 17:21; 2 K. 4:34) while comforting the lamenting crowd, "Do not be alarmed, for his life is in him." The interrupted meeting was resumed, the bread was broken, and the conversation continued till break of day. "And they took the lad away alive, and were not a little comforted."

S. F. HUNTER

EVANGELIST [Gk. *euangelistḗs*–'a bringer of good news' < *euangelízomai*–'announce good news'] (Acts 21:8; Eph. 4:11; 2 Tim. 4:5); NEB also "to spread the Gospel." Though the noun *euangelistḗs* occurs in the NT only three times, the verb occurs frequently. Jesus Christ was an evangelist, for He preached the gospel (Lk. 20:1); Paul was an evangelist as well as an apostle (Rom. 1:15); Philip the deacon was also an evangelist (Acts 21:8), as was Timothy the pastor (2 Tim. 4:5), and indeed all the early disciples who, upon being driven out of Jerusalem, "went about preaching the word" (Acts 8:4).

But Eph. 4:11 teaches that one particular order of the ministry, distinguished from every other, is singled out distinctly by the Head of the Church for this work. All may possess the gift of an evangelist in a measure and be obligated to exercise its privilege and duty, but some are specially endued with it. "And his gifts were that some should be apostles, some prophets, some evangelists, some pastors and teachers."

It will be seen that as an order in the ministry, the evangelist's work precedes that of the pastor and teacher, a fact that harmonizes with the character of the work each is still recognized as doing. The evangelist has no fixed place of residence, but moves about in different localities, preaching the gospel to those previously ignorant of it. As these are converted and united to Jesus Christ by faith, the work of the pastor and teacher begins, to instruct them further in the way of Christ and build them up in the faith.

At a later time the name of "Evangelist" was given the writers of the four Gospels because they tell the story of the gospel and because the effect of their promulgation at the beginning was very much like the work of the preaching evangelist. In character, the Gospels bear something of the same relation to the Epistles as evangelists bear to pastors and teachers.

J. M. GRAY

EVE [Heb. *ḥawwâ*; Gk. *Heua*]. The name given to the first woman by the first man after the fall. According to the popular etymology in Gen. 3:20, the name seems to be derived in some way from the verb *ḥayyâ*, to "live": "The man called his wife's name Eve, because she was the mother of all living."

It is interesting that this is the third name given to the first woman. When she was created and brought to the first man, he named her "woman" (Heb. *'iššâ*) to indicate that she was taken from man, made of the same bone and flesh, and therefore able to be his partner and to become one flesh with him (Gen. 2:23). This was her second name.

Her first name was given to her by God. It is the same name given to the first man. Together they are called *'āḏām* ("man," "mankind"), created by God in His own image to be fruitful, to fill the earth, and to rule over all living creatures (Gen. 1:26-28).

Each of these three names has its own significance and its own usage in Scripture. Heb. *'āḏām* is found explicitly as a name for Eve in Gen. 1:26-28 and 5:2. Thereafter, Eve is presumably included in the further references to "man" or "mankind." This is her primary name, assigned by God, signifying that she, with the man, is created in the image of God, blessed by God, named by God, and given by God the same responsibility to tend and have dominion over creation.

The second name, *'iššâ* ("woman" or "wife"), is used to refer to the first female human being in the stories of the creation of mankind and the fall (Gen. 2:20-25; 3:1-19; cf. Gk. *gynḗ* in 1 Cor. 11:8f.; 1 Tim. 2:14 [referring to the "curse" on the woman in Gen. 3:16]). This name, given to her by her husband, signifies her role as partner and wife, "of one flesh" with her husband.

The third name, Eve, occurs after the story of the fall (Gen. 3:20; 4:1). The first reference tells us that Adam gave her this name to signify that she was mother of all the living; the second occurs in telling of the conception of her first son.

In the NT there are only two references to the first female human being under the name of Eve. The first (2 Cor. 11:3) occurs in the context of a warning by Paul to the church in Corinth, recalling the seduction of Eve by the serpent and declaring that the church is in similar danger of being seduced into corrupt thinking and into losing her single-hearted devotion to Christ. The second (1 Tim. 2:13) occurs in a warning to a church in similar danger — the church in Ephesus, of which Timothy was bishop or elder — again recalling the creation and seduction of Eve, and instructing Timothy not to allow a woman to "be a teacher" or "domineer" over men in his church (2:8-15, NEB).

In the OT "Eve" has its primary significance in referring to the first woman as the mother of the human race. But in the NT a shift takes place. When Paul alludes to the creation and fall, he refers to the man Adam as the one in whom all die because of his sin (Rom. 5:12-19; 1 Cor. 15:21f.); but he refers to Eve as an illustration of the dangers of being seduced into evil (2 Cor. 11:3; 1 Tim. 2:13). The references to Adam are made in the context of a teaching about the condition of mankind lost in sin. The references to Eve appear in warning instructions to churches in specific danger of being seduced into false teaching.

Thus, whereas in the OT "Eve" simply signifies the role of the first woman as mother of the human race, NT usage also recalls the seduction of the first woman into evil, and Eve comes to serve as a warning — an example of what can happen when false teachings are heeded.

The influence of rabbinic theology of the intertestamental and early Christian eras in this shift is quite clear. In a typical passage from the Midrash, women are viewed as having qualities that make them unreliable and far from the ideal that God intended: "I will not create her from the eye, lest she be coquettish; nor from the ear, lest she be an eavesdropper; nor from the mouth, lest she be talkative; nor from the heart, lest she be of a jealous nature; nor from the hand, lest she be thievish; nor from the foot, lest she be a gadabout" (Midr. *Gen. Rabbah* xviii.2.; see Stewart, p. 71). The daughters of Eve, like herself, are thus seen as having the very qualities that God tried to avoid. This and many other rabbinic passages indicate that by NT times there was a significant body of teaching, with which Paul must have been familiar, that referred to Eve (and woman in general) in terms of her seductiveness and other undesirable qualities (cf. Stagg and Stagg, pp. 50-53).

It is not surprising, therefore, that Paul refers to Eve not simply as "mother of the living" but also with respect to her seduction into evil. Much traditional theology has concluded from this that in the NT passages Eve is not only an illustration but in her fallen nature is somehow representative of all women. Some early church fathers exegeted these NT passages to show that women are by nature weaker, more prone to evil, and the original cause of the fall; therefore they are unworthy to teach or hold positions of authority in the church or society (e.g., Tertullian, Basil of Ancyra, and St. Augustine; see Tavard, pp. 76, 115).

A more positive view of Eve is based on Eph. 5:22-33. Although Paul does not mention Eve by name in this passage, the quotation of Gen. 2:24 shows that the relationship of Adam and Eve (before the fall) is understood as symbolizing that of Christ and the Church. This positive view was so important that some of the church fathers could view Mary as the New Eve and Christ as the Second Adam.

In modern times conservative theologians often appeal to Eve's being created after Adam and to her being the first to fall into sin as arguments against allowing women to hold positions of ordained leadership within the church (although, interestingly, they no longer use these arguments with respect to leadership in society). Many other conservative, evangelical theologians, however, have come to interpret the references to Eve as purely illustrative. They point out that the old descriptions of the nature of all women, derived from Pauline references to Eve, are simply not borne out in experience, nor are they supported by exegetical material (cf. Wilson and De Jong, pp. 121-176). Some have traced carefully the influence of rabbinic theology in Paul's references to Eve (e.g., Jewett, pp. 86-94). Others have documented cultural factors that may have called for Paul's instructions (e.g., Stagg and Stagg, pp. 15-79, 162-187; Mollenkott, pp. 90-106). Still others have pointed out that in Ephesus, where Timothy was bishop, there was a special danger of heresy propagated by false teachers, some of whom may have been women, and that this may have prompted the instructions to keep women from teaching in that particular church (e.g., Spencer, pp. 215-222).

Finally, biblical scholars are now more aware that Paul's own practice of allowing women to prophesy in the Corinthian church, his use of women as fellow workers, and the examples of such women as Deborah, Huldah, Miriam, Anna, and Phoebe create real difficulties for the position that would limit the role of women on the basis of Paul's references to Eve (cf. Callahan, pp. 35-56).

Bibliography.–S. Callahan, *Illusion of Eve* (1965); H. Freedman and M. Simon, eds., *Midrash Rabbah* (1939); P. K. Jewett, *Man as Male and Female* (1975); V. R. Mollenkott, *Women, Men, and the Bible* (1977); A. D. B. Spencer, *JETS*, 17 (1974), 215-225; E. Stagg and F. Stagg, *Woman in the World of Jesus* (1978); R. A. Stewart, *Rabbinic Theology* (1961); G. Tavard, *Woman in Christian Tradition* (1978); D. Wilson and P. DeJong, *Husband and Wife* (1979).

M. V. RIENSTRA

EVE, GOSPEL OF. A Gnostic work mentioned by Epiphanius (*Haer.* 26.2ff.). It is possible that the subject of this work is Eve's discovery of *tó brōma tḗs gnṓseōs* ("the food of *gnṓsis*," or saving knowledge) through a revelation from the serpent (*Haer.* 26.2.6), and that this may account for its being called a "gospel" (see H-S, I, 241-43). *See also* APOCRYPHAL GOSPELS V.B.

EVENING [usually Heb. *ʿereḇ*; Gk. *opsía, opsé, hespéra*]; **EVENTIDE** [Heb. *ʿāraḇ*] (Isa. 24:11); AV, NEB, DARKENED. "Evening" is used by the RSV with slightly different meanings. In Lev. 15 it designates sunset, the beginning of the Hebrew day, as the time when a ceremonially unclean person became clean again. Gk. *hespéra* apparently designates sunset in Lk. 24:29. Gk. *opsé* is literally "late" (Mk. 11:19; 13:35). In Ezk. 12:4, 7 "evening" means the early part of the night, "in the dark" (vv. 6f.). In Prov. 7:9 and Jer. 6:4 ("the shadows of evening lengthen") it is twilight, the time of approaching darkness.

Twilight may also be the time designated by the Heb. *bên hāʿarbayim* (lit. "between the two evenings" [cf. Ex. 12:6, RSV mg.]; RSV "in the evening"). It is mentioned as the time when the lamps were lit and the evening incense burned (Ex. 30:8), when the evening portion of the daily burnt offering was made (Ex. 29:39, 41; Nu. 28:4), and when the Passover lamb was slain (Ex. 12:6; Nu. 9:3, 5, 11). The precise time of day it designated is not known. According to the Karaites and Samaritans it was a time between sunset and total darkness. Although the Mishnah allowed for slaughtering the Passover lamb in the afternoon, this may originally have occurred after sunset (see *IB*, I, 919; KD on Ex. 12:6).

H. PORTER N. J. O.

EVENT. Occurs in the plural only, translating *taúta eplērṓthē* (AV "after these things were ended"; NEB "when things had reached this stage") in Acts 19:21 and the phrase *perí tṓn mēdépō blepoménōn* (AV "of things not seen as yet"; NEB "the unseen future") in He. 11:7.

EVERGREEN CYPRESS [Heb. *beroš raʿanān*] (Hos. 14:8 [MT 9]); AV GREEN FIR TREE; NEB PINE-TREE. According to KoB (p. 148), Heb. *berôš* designates a Phoenician juniper. H. N. and A. L. Moldenke, however, take this passage as referring to the stone pine, or *Apinus pinea* (*MPB*, p. 46). The adjective *raʿanān* indicates that it was "luxuriant" or "full of leaves" (*CHAL*, p. 343). *See* CYPRESS; FLORA IV.D.

EVERLASTING. *See* ETERNITY.

EVI ē'vī [Heb. *ʾ^{e}wî*–'desire'; Gk. *Euei*]. One of the five kings or chiefs of the Midianites slain by Israel during their sojourn in the plains of Moab (Nu. 31:8; Josh. 13:21).

EVIDENCE; EVIDENTLY. In Jer. 32:10-16, 44, the AV uses "evidence" for Heb. *sēper* ("a writing") in the obsolete sense of a deed of purchase (cf. RSV, NEB). In Acts 10:3 the AV uses "evidently" in another obsolete sense to translate Gk. *phanerṓs* ("openly," "clearly," "manifestly"; cf. RSV, NEB, "clearly").

"Evidence" is also the AV's translation of Gk. *élenchos* in He. 11:1: "Now faith is . . . the evidence of things not seen." The Greek term denotes "putting to the test," "examining for the purpose of proof," "bringing to conviction." Thus, a well-grounded and assured CONVICTION (cf. RSV; NEB "makes us certain") of things not seen is the implied result of this putting to the test. See also *TDNT*, II, *s.v.* ἐλέγχω κτλ.: ἔλεγχος (Büchsel).

W. L. WALKER
N. J. O.

EVIL [Heb. *raʿ* (Gen. 2:9; Dt. 23:9; 2 Ch. 33:9; Est. 7:7; Ezk. 14:21; etc.), *rāʿaʿ* (Ex. 5:22; etc.), *rō(a)ʿ* (Dt. 28:20; 1 S. 17:28; Isa. 1:16; Jer. 21:12; 23:2, 22; 26:3; 44:22), *dibbâ*–'calumny' (Nu. 13:32; 14:36f.; Ezk. 36:3), *ʾāwen*–'trouble, deceit, nothing' (Job 15:35; Ps. 6:8 [MT 9]; 7:14 [MT 15]; 28:3; 53:4 [MT 5]; 59:2, 5 [MT 3, 6]; 92:11 [MT 12]; Isa. 29:20; Jer. 4:14f.), *zimmâ*–'evil plan' (Ps. 26:10; 119:150; Prov. 21:27; 30:32), *m^{e}zimmâ*–'plot' (Ps. 37:7; 139:20; Prov. 12:2), *rāšāʿ* (Ps. 140:8 [MT 9]), *rešaʿ* (Prov. 16:12), *ma^{ʿa}lāl*–'deed' (Jer. 11:18); Gk. *ponērós* (Mt. 5:11, 37; 7:17f.; Lk. 3:19; 6:22; Acts 28:21; 2 Tim. 4:18; He. 10:22; Jas. 2:4; 3 Jn. 1:10; Rev. 16:2; etc.), *ponēría* (Rom. 1:29; 1 Cor. 5:8), *kakós* (Mt. 27:23; Acts 23:5; Rom. 1:30; Col. 3:5; Tit. 1:12; etc.), *kakía* (1 Cor. 14:20; 1 Pet. 2:16), *kakopoiéō*–'do evil' (3 Jn. 11), *kakologéō*–'speak evil of' (Mt. 15:4; Mk. 7:10; 9:39; Acts 19:9), *phaúlos*–'worthless' (Jn. 3:20; 5:29; 2 Cor. 5:10; Tit. 2:8), *saprós*–'decayed, corrupt' (Eph. 4:29), *blasphēméō*–'speak evil against' (Rom. 14:16; Tit. 3:2), *katalaléō*–'speak evil of' (Jas. 4:11), *adikéō*–'injure, act unjustly' (Rev. 22:11)]; AV also WICKED, BAD, INIQUITY, VANITY, HARM, MISCHIEF, SLANDER, etc.; NEB also WRONG, WRONGDOING, HARM, MISCHIEF, CRUELTY, CALAMITY, RUIN, WICKEDNESS, MISDEED, FALSE, etc. *See also* EVIL-DOERS; EVIL-WORKERS.

"What is the meaning of evil?" can be taken as a semantic question, "What does the word 'evil' mean?" But it can also be taken — and must also be taken — as a human and existential question, "How can one account for, and how should one respond to, the reality of evil in our world?" The semantic question appropriately calls for our attention first.

I. The Meaning of "Evil." *–A. The Expressive Component.* The word "evil" can be analyzed as having both an expressive and a descriptive component. It is expressive of disapproval, whether of an action, or a state of affairs, or a person. The speaker reveals something about himself when he calls anything evil, namely, that he disapproves of it. Sometimes this expressive component dominates the meaning of the word, e.g., when it is used simply to express an immediate or spontaneous reaction of dislike. This seems to be the case when Jacob complains to Pharaoh that his life has been evil (Gen. 47:9); "evil" is used here to express Jacob's own emotive state rather than to describe his life.

The expressive component dominates the use of the word by the author of Ecclesiastes. When he says, "This also is vanity and a great evil" (Eccl. 2:21), and "There is a grievous evil" (5:13; cf. 5:16; 6:1; 9:3; 10:5), he expresses his emotive reaction to certain states of affairs. He does not give any criteria for this emotive response; he simply reports it or, better, expresses it.

B. The Descriptive Component. The expressive component is never dismissed; the word "evil" is always expressive of the speaker's emotive state. But the emotive state is not exhausted by being vented. Rather, people not only express their disapproval and dislike, but also direct them. To direct disapproval, to direct the acting and reacting that is associated with our emotive states, demands that "evil" be given some objective referent, some descriptive component.

1. Unhappiness. "Evil" in the Bible can refer to someone else's emotive state as well as express one's own. So when Judah appeals to Joseph to allow Benjamin to return with them, he says that he fears "to see the evil that would come upon my father" if Benjamin were not to return (Gen. 44:34). Judah is not only expressing his own dislike of what would come upon his father; he is also referring to his father's emotive state, his misery, if Benjamin stayed in Egypt. So the descriptive component of "evil" can be unhappiness. This is the meaning in Prov. 15:15, "All the days of the afflicted are evil." "Evil" there expresses the unhappiness and misery of the afflicted as well as expressing the author's own emotive state in response to that situation.

2. Harm or the Threat of Harm. The descriptive component, however, is not always equivalent to unhappiness. Sometimes what harms or threatens to harm one's life, self-esteem, reputation, or society's well-being is called "evil." This descriptive component is obvious when "evil" is used of animals that are considered dangerous (Lev. 26:6; Ezk. 14:21) or of places like Kadesh, where there was no water and the people of Israel thought they would die (Nu. 20:5), or even of situations that are full of danger, as when Pharaoh requires the same number of bricks without providing straw (Ex. 5:19). This is the meaning when "evil" is used of diseases (Dt. 7:15), sores (Rev. 16:2), spirits (e.g., Lk. 7:21), or men who harm (Ezk. 30:12). A name or epithet can be called "evil" when it is an accusation that harms a person's reputation (Dt. 22:14, 19; Neh. 6:13).

Harm or the threat of harm seems to be the descriptive component of "evil" in Jas. 3:8 in its description of the tongue as a "restless evil." That interpretation is confirmed by the next phrase, "full of deadly poison." Heb. *dibbâ* is to be interpreted as having this objective referent, but notice that while the "evil report" of the spies (Nu. 13:32; 14:36f.) was evil in the sense that it threatened harm to the people if they entered the land, the "evil gossip" of Ezk. 36:3 was evil in the sense that it was a threat to their reputation. With the words, "Evil is determined by him" (1 S. 20:7), Jonathan reports that his father Saul planned to harm David. Harm or the threat of harm is the descriptive component whenever God "brings evil" or "sends evil." Joshua warned the people of God that God would bring evil upon them until they perished if they transgressed the covenant (Josh. 23:15). In response to unfaithfulness God brings harm (e.g., 1 K. 14:10; 21:21,29; 2 K. 22:16,20; Jer. 4:6; 6:9).

3. Dysfunction. In the proverb "the bad tree bears evil fruit" (Mt. 7:17f.), the descriptive component of "evil" is simply some departure from commonly accepted standards. Similarly, Eccl. 10:1 calls the odor evil because it departs from the standard for perfumes and ointments.

4. Immorality and Unfaithfulness. "Evil" can also have either immorality or unfaithfulness as its descriptive component. This "moral sense" and this "religious sense" can be distinguished in Scripture, but they cannot be separated. In the refrain of 1 and 2 Kings, ". . . did what was evil in the sight of God," "evil" refers always to unfaithfulness and specifically to idolatry and apostasy (e.g., 1 K. 11:6). In Judges and Chronicles the phrase is identically used, always with reference to apostasy and idolatry (cf. also Nu. 32:13; Dt. 4:25; 9:18; 17:2). But in Samuel the phrase is used with reference to immorality; it is used of Saul when he disobeys God's concrete command by gathering the spoils of victory rather than destroying the enemy and its goods (1 S. 15:19), and of David when he kills Uriah and takes Bathsheba (2 S. 12:9).

In the phrase of Deuteronomy, "you shall purge the evil from the midst of you" (i.e., capitally punish), "evil" refers to apostasy and idolatry (Dt. 13:5; 17:7), to disobedience of authority (17:12), dishonoring parents (21:21), giving false testimony (19:19), harlotry (22:21), adultery (22:22,24), and stealing (24:7).

The intimacy of this relation between evil as immorality and evil as unfaithfulness comes into clearest focus with the prophets. The "evil" of Isa. 1:16, e.g., is at once that they have forsaken God and that they do not correct oppression. Isaiah defines (by means of parallelism) "did what was evil in my eyes" simply and comprehensively as "chose what I did not delight in" (Isa. 65:12; 66:4). That includes both unfaithfulness and immorality.

Not only actions can be called "evil" in these senses, however, for there are not only "evil doings" but an "evil way" (e.g., Jer. 23:22; 25:5). Indeed, evil doings and an evil way are but the concretization of evil dispositions. The wicked man "with perverted heart devises evil" (Prov. 6:14). "The soul of the wicked desires evil" (Prov. 21:10). Therefore, persons themselves can be called evil (e.g., Ezk. 30:12; Prov. 11:21; 12:13), and similarly the heart (Jer. 3:17; 7:24; 11:8; 18:12) and the will (Jer. 16:10) can be called evil with the use of synecdoche.

This movement in emphasis from external actions to internal dispositions reaches its climax in the NT. That is, of course, the point of the proverb about trees and their fruit (Mt. 7:17f.). Perhaps the clearest indication is Mt. 12:35 (cf. par. Lk. 6:45), "The evil man out of his evil treasure brings forth evil." The concern of Jesus — and the NT generally — is less with concrete acts of unfaithfulness and specific acts of disobedience than with the person from whom they issue. "For out of the heart come evil thoughts, murder, adultery, fornication, theft, false witness, slander" (Mt. 15:19 par. Mk. 7:21). Moreover, not only individuals and their dispositions but also groups can be called evil: family (Jer. 8:3), a people (Jer. 13:10), a generation (Dt. 1:35; Mt. 12:39,45; 16:4; Lk. 11:29). This movement from calling actions evil to calling individuals and groups evil seems to be licensed when people habitually do evil, when they stubbornly persist in evil, adamantly refusing education and repentance (cf. Jer. 3:17; 7:24; 11:8; 16:10).

This diversity of meaning is obviously important for interpretation. The diversity is already present in the Hebrew and Greek words; therefore, translations frequently represent some decision about the descriptive component. When Pilate, e.g., asks the people for a justification for their demand that Jesus be crucified ("Why, what evil [Gk. *kakós*] has he done?" [Mt. 27:23 par.]), is the descriptive component of "evil" harm, threat, immorality, or unfaithfulness? The NEB has made the decision that the descriptive component here is harm and translates *kakós* thus. The parallel in John, however, makes it clear that the Jews and Pilate were concerned about a crime Jesus had committed — some wrong, some disobedience to the law. The meaning is usually made clear from the context, but that does not allow one to ignore this diversity of meaning.

By providing a referent the descriptive component enables us to direct our expressions of dislike and disapproval. But it is also necessary to criticize our feelings of dislike and disapproval and to criticize our ways of thinking and acting associated with them. That critical task confronts us with the necessity of discerning what the status and meaning of evil really is. If "evil" really is an expletive for expressing the emotive state of dislike — and only that — then the critical task is impossible. Perhaps we can choose to ignore or change those feelings; but a reason for ignoring or changing them would have to come from some source other than the meaning of evil, for "evil" is then simply a word to use to vent those feelings. If evil really is unhappiness, then one must do all we can to promote happiness. The critically reflective process demands that we at least rank these descriptive components. Harm may be evil and not evil at the same time, and that is not a contradiction, nor even a paradox, but the result of using "evil" with two different descriptive components. It is clearly evil in the sense of evil in which the descriptive component is harm, but it may very well not be evil in the sense of evil in which the descriptive component is immorality or unfaithfulness. (Of course, sometimes something is both immoral and a threat of harm, e.g., the "evil woman" of Prov. 6:24.) It is therefore important to look beyond the semantics of "evil" to the theology of evil, to ask the question of the meaning of evil in the purposes of God.

II. Special Semantic Studies.*–*A. Evil One. Gk. *ho ponērós* may be translated "evil" or "the evil one." It clearly means "the evil one" in Mt. 13:19, because the Synoptic parallels have *satanás* (Mk. 4:15) and *diábolos* (Lk. 8:12). And these passages may also be used to define the use of *ho ponērós*: "the evil one" is a term for the devil, for Satan, for the spirit that opposes God and His people. It is a common term for the devil in 1 John. The dualism of the Epistle, which makes man the field for the battle between Christ and Satan, is reflected in this use of "the evil one" (2:13f.; 3:12; 5:18f.). Eph. 6:16 also is a fairly clear reference to the devil (cf. 6:11).

Other cases, however, are more dubious (Mt. 13:38; 5:37; Jn. 17:15; 2 Thess. 3:3). Probably the most important of the disputable cases is Mt. 6:13, where *toú ponēroú* occurs in the Lord's Prayer. The NEB translates it "the evil one," while the RSV translates it "evil" and gives "the evil one" as a marginal reading. The Eastern

Church has favored "the evil one," the Western Church, "evil." Calvin, in his commentary on the passage, leaves the question open. And that seems the prudent course, for whether one understands the whole of evil or the eminence of evil, the petition is for God's deliverance.

B. Knowledge of Good and Evil. Consideration of this phrase is important, not only because it contains the word "evil," but also because the tree of the knowledge of good and evil has figured importantly in theologies of the origin of evil. This phrase is, of course, most familiar in connection with the tree of the knowledge of good and evil, but it may be best to begin apart from that tree.

In Dt. 1:39, after God has told the Israelites that He will not permit them to enter the land of Canaan, He says, "Moreover your little ones, who you said would become a prey, and your children, who this day have no knowledge of good or evil, shall go in there." Is knowledge of good and evil here a mark of moral maturity? And is the children's lack of it their innocence, their inculpability for the unfaithful anxiety of the people about entering Canaan? An alternative interpretation would be to construe their lack as parallel to "would become a prey." "Have knowledge" (Heb. *yāḏaʿ*) can mean "have skill" or "have the power to do" (e.g., Gen. 25:27). And the expression "good and evil" can be understood as encompassing everything (Prov. 15:3; Lev. 5:4) — everything is either good or evil. Taking the two components together, then, the lack of the knowledge of good and evil would be equivalent to the children's complete lack of power in anything whatsoever, which would make them a prey to the Canaanites. But the context of this phrase — the judgment of God upon the people of Israel — and the apparent excusing (rather than justifying) of the children supports the first interpretation, that "knowledge of good and evil" is equivalent to moral maturity, a presupposition for moral culpability, as one assumes when excusing children by saying "they do not know any better yet."

Hebrews 5:14 picks up the Hebrew idiom with obvious reference to maturity. The parallel phrase, denoting that which children lack, is "the word [Gk. *lógos*] of righteousness." That the culpability theme is also present here is evident from 6:4f.

In 2 S. 14:17 the phrase "to discern good and evil" clearly refers to the omnipotence of David in the land, to his power to do anything. The woman sent by Joab may be insincere in flattering David with this phrase and with her likening of him to an angel of God on account of this power, but there is little doubt that this is what she meant by it (cf. v. 20).

The prayer of Solomon provides a third understanding of this phrase. His request for the knowledge of good and evil (1 K. 3:9) is clearly to be understood as moral and judicial discernment, the ability to discern what is right (cf. 1 K. 3:11, 28). God commends Solomon's request and desire for the knowledge of good and evil and rewards him with riches and honor.

In addition, the phrase seems to hint at sexual potency in 2 S. 19:35 (MT 36) and in the Rule of the Congregation of Qumrân (1QSa 1:10f.; cf. *New Catholic Encyclopedia*, XIV, 269).

The phrase, then, is open to different interpretations: moral maturity, cultural power, moral discernment, sexual maturity. The striking thing is that these references are positive. The meaning of knowing good and evil is positive; it is of some good for man. Indeed Sir. 17:7 quite appropriately says of God's creation of man that "He filled them with knowledge and understanding, and showed them good and evil."

What, then, of the tree of knowledge of good and evil? It has no close analogy in ancient Near Eastern texts — quite the reverse of the situation of the tree of life — so contemporary religions provide no guidance for interpretation. The tree of the knowledge of good and evil was created by God (Gen. 2:9), but of all the trees of the Garden only it was proscribed as a source of food (v. 17; the penalty was death). The serpent urged Eve to eat its fruit, for, he said, death would not come, but their eyes would be opened and they would be as God. Eve saw that the tree and its fruit were good; so she ate the fruit, as did Adam. "The eyes of both were opened"; they were ashamed of their nakedness and hid from God. God acknowledged (3:22) that by eating the fruit they had become as gods, and He removed them from the Garden and from ready access to the tree of life. This context provides no decisive basis for determining whether this tree is the tree of moral maturity, the tree of cultural power, the tree of moral discernment, or the tree of sexual maturity. Indeed, man possessed all of these without eating the fruit of the tree. In fact, the argument sometimes advanced against understanding the tree of the knowledge of good and evil as the source of sexual maturity, viz., that sexual maturity is presupposed in the institution of marriage before the Fall, can be used against each understanding. Adam and Eve had to possess moral maturity and discernment in order to understand the probationary command and to be culpable for not obeying it. Cultural knowledge and power was given with the cultural mandate and was disclosed in the naming of the animals. The knowledge of good and evil is good and is given to mankind. It was the serpent's insinuation, however, that God intended to keep good things from mankind. This insinuation was accepted by Eve. In that attitude of distrust of the One who had called her into being, she seized what properly could only be received. The evil or sin was not in the knowledge of good and evil but in the unfaithfulness to God and disobedience to His command. The root of evil is not knowledge of good and evil, nor power, nor sexuality, but unfaithfulness.

III. The Meaning of Evil.–The meaning of evil is an existential question with which the people of God — not least among them the authors of Scripture — have always struggled.

A. Monotheism. Basic to their struggle to find the meaning of evil is the rejection of dualism. Other peoples might hold the world of demons or the skilful magic of evil persons responsible for misfortunes large and small, but that solution was not open to the Israelites. Their radical monotheism demanded that even the most grievous harm be accounted for in terms of the power of the same God who called them out of Egypt. The gracious God by whom all good things came to them is the same God by whom all evil things came to them.

The monism of the OT is clearly seen in the mention of evil spirits that come from God, which comes close to attributing the demonic to God (e.g., 1 S. 16:14, "Now the Spirit of the Lord departed from Saul, and an evil spirit from the Lord tormented him"). The descriptive component of "evil" here seems to be unhappiness; the objective referent is Saul's melancholia. The point, however, is that Saul's depression, which led to fits of madness (cf. 18:10; 19:9), is ascribed to God. Consider also the "evil spirit" God sent between Abimelech and the men of Shechem (Jgs. 9:23; cf. 1 K. 22:19-23).

B. Covenant. It is not simply the radical monotheism of the Hebrews that forces the question, however; this one God is the God of the covenant. Other religions explain the harm and suffering of men as resulting from the wrath of a god or gods; thus it would be possible to ascribe to the same god both good things and evil things by attributing the evil to his capriciousness. But the God of Abraham, Isaac, and Jacob has proclaimed His will and shown His purposes; and thereby He breaks the mold of the capricious and arbitrary power in which other Near Eastern deities were cast. On this account the Israelites were confident that God never departs from His fundamental intention to save and to bless His people, and that conviction protects the Israelites from despair.

But the contradiction looms still larger. The very God who intends to save His people brings harm to them. Within their convictions that God is one and that He has covenanted with men, the authors of Scripture struggled with the meaning of evil. The covenant assured the people of God that harm is not arbitrarily distributed. Yahweh is the covenant God, not an arbitrary divinity. The possibility of an explanation must exist; the contradiction must not be ultimate. But Moses himself could still ask, "O Lord, why hast thou done evil to this people?" (Ex. 5:22). That there is an explanation is certain; but the biblical authors struggle to find and to say what the explanation is.

C. Explanations. 1. Retribution/Reciprocity. The first explanation is given in terms of the covenant itself. God's wrath and its consequence, harm and suffering of men, is due to righteous retribution. Evil is just return for evil. Evil, i.e., harm or the threat of harm, is righteously brought upon evil, i.e., unfaithfulness and immorality. Typical is the refrain in the book of Judges, "The people of Israel did what was evil in the sight of the Lord and served the Baals. . . . So the anger of the Lord was kindled against Israel, and . . . the hand of the Lord was against them for evil" (Jgs. 2:11-15; cf. 2 S. 12:9, 11; 1 K. 2:44; 14:9f.). God reciprocates; He brings evil for evil. In this way harm and suffering have a place and, therefore, an explanation in God's world. Evil is not the result of an equally ultimate destructive power or of meaningless (because arbitrary) fate. It is justice.

2. Deterrent/Chastisement. Moreover, it is positive. It has a place in God's saving intention. It is a deterrent to deliberate disobedience among God's people (cf. Dt. 17:13, "And all the people shall hear, and fear, and not act presumptuously again"; 19:20). God's reciprocation of evil for evil provides a warning and a call to repentance (cf. Jer. 36:3). Ezekiel, e.g., in the face of evil provides this consolation to the people and justification of God's bringing harm, that the sons and daughters, chastened and purified, will live faithfully (Ezk. 14:22; cf. 6:10). Education and purification put harm and suffering within the context of God's saving will.

3. Beyond Reciprocity: Mercy to the Unjust. The recognition of God's saving will forces the biblical authors to move beyond their account of evil in terms of simple reciprocity. God can "repent of the evil." Sometimes for the sake of His covenant will He bears the evil rather than returns evil. When Moses reminded God of what he had sworn to Abraham, Isaac, and Jacob, God "repented of the evil which he thought to do to his people" (Ex. 32:13f.). He is long-suffering and does not bring evil out of spite or revenge. His promise is that if the nation "turns from its evil, I will repent of the evil that I intended to do to it" (Jer. 18:8; cf. 26:3, 13, 19).

Jonah, after attempting to escape the presence and mission of God, proclaimed God's judgment upon Nineveh. But the Ninevites responded to the threat of harm in penitence and faith, and "when God saw what they did, how they turned from their evil way, God repented of the evil which he had said he would do to them" (Jonah 3:10). Then Jonah complained that God had justified his fears, for He had acted according to character; Jonah said, "That is why I made haste to flee to Tarshish; for I knew that thou art a gracious God and merciful, slow to anger, and abounding in steadfast love, and repentest of evil" (4:2). The covenant God may legitimately reciprocate evil for evil, but His intention is always to save. Therefore, He does not deal with mankind simply in terms of retribution, but also mercifully.

This move beyond reciprocity does not challenge that account of evil, but builds on it. The appropriate human reaction to evil, then, is first to turn from evil, i.e., to turn from immorality and unfaithfulness, and second, to accept evil contritely, i.e., to accept harm or the threat of harm in penitence and confession. Thus the OT Scriptures constantly urge their hearers to hate the evil, to turn from their evil ways, to repent of their evil works. The appropriate reaction to evil is neither sloth nor pride, but rather gratitude and humility.

4. Beyond Reciprocity: Suffering of the Innocent. The explanation of the reality of evil in terms of reciprocity, however, was soon to face a decisive challenge: the suffering of the righteous. As long as the individual's responsibility and destiny were seen as subordinate to those of the nation, the question did not press so desperately upon the consciousness of Israel (but consider 2 S. 24:17; 1 Ch. 21:17). But as the explanation in terms of reciprocation developed, the notion of corporate responsibility diminished. And soon the sufferings of the righteous man demanded an account. Both Jeremiah and Ezekiel reject the proverb, "The fathers have eaten sour grapes, and the children's teeth are set on edge" (Jer. 31:29; Ezk. 18:2; however, both prophets refuse to surrender the concept of corporate responsibility; cf. Jer. 32:18f.). When individual responsibility gains clarity and attention, the evils that befall the innocent cannot but call into question that very righteousness of God that had been the mainstay of Jewish life and theodicy. The account of evil in terms of reciprocity continued, now construed individually; cf., e.g., Prov. 1:33, "He who listens to me will dwell secure and will be at ease, without dread of evil." But the evil that comes upon the innocent contradicted that concept. The educational value of evil might mitigate the contradiction, but it could not finally account for the evils wrought on the innocent. Moreover, where the concepts of reciprocity and chastisement were hard-heartedly and bullheadedly held, this could only result in the conclusion that every person struck by some misfortune had been guilty of unfaithfulness or immorality.

Jesus stands against that conclusion (Lk. 13:1-5; Jn. 9:1-3). But already the OT writers, especially the wisdom teachers, stand in sharp opposition to the proud and clever attempts to save God's honor at the expense of innocent persons and in the face of the simple truth. The author of Ecclesiastes struggles with the problem. He acknowledges that sentence is executed tardily against evil men, but he does not let go of the righteousness of God (Eccl. 8:11f.). For the present, however, evil does indeed seem arbitrary; there is no way to "know . . . what evil may happen on earth" (11:2). And the author of Job also struggles with the problem. The cry of Job is simply, "When I looked for good, evil came" (30:26). The innocence of Job, that he is a man who "fears God, and turned away from evil" (1:1, 8; 2:3), is the stumbling block for any simple attempt to justify God's bringing of evil as reciprocation. Job will let go of neither his own innocence nor the righteousness of God, and it is clear finally that his friends' accusations do an injustice not only to him but also to God. The God of Job 38–42 is majestically awful, not prosaically awful. He calls mankind to stand humbly before its Creator, not fearsomely and desperately before its inquisitor (cf. ch. 7). This is not so much a positive answer to the evils that befall the innocent as a rejection of simple reciprocity.

5. Beyond Reciprocity: Mission of God. The positive explanation in the OT is occasionally that the disclosure of God's justice will take place some time in the future. When the people complain against God that the evil seems rewarded by Him (Mal. 2:17; 3:15), Malachi reminds them of their own sin and the consequent presumption of their complaint (3:7-9); but more to the point, he promises a day in which "all evildoers will be stubble" and in which "for you who fear my name the sun of righteousness shall rise, with healing in its wings" (Mal. 4:1f. [MT 3:19f.]).

But a profound shift occurs in the understanding of and reaction to evil, and the development of explanations for innocent suffering reaches its climax with the concept of vicarious suffering — when the life and suffering of the people of God is interpreted in terms of a Suffering Servant (cf. the Servant Songs of Isaiah, Isa. 42:1-9; 49:1-6; 50:4-11; 52:13–53:12). Perhaps the careers of the prophets themselves provided the impetus for this reinterpretation, for they endured the evil, the harm, and the threat of harm that their loyalty to God and His cause brought upon them. Their consolation was precisely their mission and their confidence in its ultimate vindication. To participate in the cause of God involves suffering in this present age. Jeremiah, e.g., experiencing harm and the threat of harm, has cause to complain, "Is evil a recompense for good?" (18:20), but he never loses hope. He endures the suffering involved in his mission for the sake of God's cause.

The view here, too, is toward the future, no longer in the sense that in the future reciprocity will finally be clear, but now rather in the sense that the future reveals the present community to be a humble interim community whose mission is precisely to prepare the way for, and to give way to, a new world order. There is suddenly a relation between God's activity and the evil that befalls the innocent. The Servant Songs of Isaiah prophesy a messianic figure, but they also declare how the innocent sufferer is to regard, and respond to, the evils that befall him. These evils do not mean that one is guilty before God, but rather that one is called to participate in God's mission.

The OT itself abrogates the painful and sometimes malicious calculating of reciprocation. The justification of God's actions upon mankind is finally cast in a different mold, a mold which prepares the way for the cross of Christ. There, precisely in the worst evil borne by the One whose claim to innocence is not pretentious — i.e., precisely in the cross of Christ — the Scriptures discover and declare that God is good.

And in the light of that cross and in the light of this Suffering One's vindication at the Resurrection, the NT urges a faith-full response to evil. The NT, as the OT, makes no compromise with evil: "Hate what is evil, hold fast to what is good" (Rom. 12:9); "Abstain from every form of evil" (1 Thess. 5:22; cf. 1 Pet. 3:10-12, quoting Ps. 34:12-16). But the uniqueness of the NT lies in its exhortation to the followers of Christ to mirror the cross-bearing of Christ by dismissing reciprocity and retributive calculations in their dealings with each other and their neighbors: "Repay no one evil for evil" (Rom. 12:17); "Do not be overcome by evil, but overcome evil with good" (Rom. 12:21; cf. 1 Thess. 5:15; 1 Pet. 3:9); "Do not resist one who is evil" (Mt. 5:39). The community that follows Christ bears the hurt, the harm, and the threat of harm for love's sake, for the sake of the mission of God. And that patient love is the climax of the struggle of God's people to direct their thinking about, and reacting to, evil.

D. Summary. Evil remains a mystery. Any attempt finally to explain evil must be an oversimplification and a falsification. Still, it is necessary to take this mystery seriously if anything like an adequate account of life is to be given. There are basically two directions in which reflection on evil may go. One direction is simply the agonized acknowledgment of the reality of evil. This may be heroic, but it frequently tears meaning from life. The opposite direction, then, is to hold fast to meaning. But frequently this response all too facilely ignores the reality of evil. Theologically, these two directions presuppose two generalizations: If evil is real, God is not good; and if God is good, evil is not real. The Bible takes neither of these directions and it rejects both of these hypothetical generalizations. It affirms both that the one covenant God is good and that evil is real. Indeed, precisely in the context of the worst evil, the Scriptures discover and announce that God is good — i.e., precisely in the cross of Christ. And precisely in this event the Scriptures discover and direct the people of God to a faith-full reaction to evil, that of patient love.

Bibliography.–W. M. Clark, *JBL,* 88 (1969), 266-278; W. Eichrodt, *Man in the OT* (Eng. tr., *SBT,* 1/4, 1951); C. S. Lewis, *Problem of Pain* (1962); A. Miller, "Evil," in M. Halverson, ed., *Handbook of Christian Theology* (1958); *New Catholic Encyclopedia,* XIV, *s.v.* "Tree of Knowledge" (I. Hunt); R. Niebuhr, "Honesty about Evil," in A. J. Bellinsoni, Jr., and T. V. Litzenburg, eds., *Intellectual Honesty and Religious Commitment* (1969); P. Ricoeur, *Symbolism of Evil* (1967); E. Sutcliffe, *Providence and Suffering in the Old and New Testaments* (1953); *TDNT,* III, *s.v.* κακός κτλ. (W. Grundman); VI, *s.v.* πονηρός, πονηρία (G. Harder).

A. D. VERHEY

EVIL EYE. A look or glance that reflects an unfavorable disposition toward a person. The phrase appears several times in the AV as a literal translation of the biblical text: in Prov. 23:6; 28:22 for Heb. *raʿ ʿayin* (RSV "stingy," "miserly"; NEB "miser"); in Dt. 15:9; 28:54, 56 for *ʿayin* with the verb *rāʿaʿ* (RSV "eye be hostile," "will grudge"; NEB "look askance," "will not share"); in Mt. 20:15; Mk. 7:22 for Gk. *ophthalmós ponērós* (RSV "begrudge," "envy"; NEB "jealous," "envy").

The discovery of the widespread and ancient popular belief in the power of an envious glance to inflict harm has aroused speculation that this belief may be referred to in the passages cited above. Although there is evidence that this superstition existed in ancient Judaism (see Jastrow), it is unlikely that these passages preserve any connection with magical practices. The RSV and NEB correctly translate the phrase as referring simply to an envious or miserly disposition.

In Gal 3:1, however, this superstition clearly lies behind the use of Gk. *baskaínō* (AV, RSV, NEB, "bewitch"). Paul uses the term figuratively to denote the Galatians' captivation by the falsehood into which the Judaizers had led them.

See also BEWITCH; EYE; MAGIC.

Bibliography.–Comms. on Deuteronomy, Proverbs, Matthew, and Mark; M. Jastrow, *Dictionary of the Targumim, the Talmud Babli and Yerushalmi, and the Midrashic Literature* (1903), II, *s.v.* עַיִן; MM, p. 106; *TDNT,* I, *s.v.* βασκαίνω (G. Delling).

N. J. O.

EVIL ONE. *See* EVIL II.A.

EVIL SPIRIT. *See* DEMON; SATAN.

EVIL THING [Heb. *rāʿ* (Ps. 140:2 [MT 3]; Prov. 15:28), *dāḇār rāʿ* (Dt. 17:5; 23:9; Josh. 23:15; Neh. 13:17); Gk. *tó ponērón* (Mk. 7:23; Lk. 3:19), *tó kakón* (Lk. 16:25)]; AV also MISCHIEF, WICKED THING, EVIL; NEB also WICKED SCHEME, MISCHIEF, WICKED DEED, FOULNESS, MISDEED, etc. "Evil things" may refer to thoughts, plans, or deeds of evil men; the things people suffer for their own errors; or the evils that result from the errors of others. The evil thing referred to in Dt. 17:5 is the breaking of the covenant with Yahweh and the pursuit of other gods; in Neh. 13:17 it is sabbath-breaking. According to Prov. 15:28, "The mouth of the wicked pours out evil things." In the proverb of the rich man and Lazarus (Lk. 16:19-31), the rich man had good things in his life but did not use them to the glory of God or the good of men. The poor man had evil things: sickness, nakedness, and hunger. The situation was reversed, however, after death. D. R. DUNGAN N. J. O.

EVIL-DOING [Heb. *rāʿâ*] (1 S. 25:39; Prov. 14:32; Eccl. 7:15); AV WICKEDNESS; NEB WICKEDNESS, WRONGDOING; **EVILDOER** [Heb. *ʿāśâ rāʿâ* (2 S. 3:39; Ps. 34:16 [MT 17]), *rāʿ* (Ps. 10:15), *ʿāśâ rišʿâ* (Mal. 3:15; 4:1 [MT 3:19]), *rāʿaʿ* (Ps. 22:16 [MT 17]; 27:2; Prov. 24:19; Isa. 1:4; 9:17 [MT 16]; etc.), *pāʿal ʾāwen* (Job 34:8, 22; Ps. 14:4; 36:12 [MT 13]; 64:2 [MT 3]; Prov. 10:29; 21:15; Hos. 6:8); Gk. *hoi ergazómenoi tḗn anomían* (Mt. 7:23), *hoi poioúntes tḗn anomían* (Mt. 13:41), *kakón poiṓn* (Jn. 18:30), *adikṓn* (Rev. 22:11)]; AV also WICKED, EVIL MEN, WORKER OF INIQUITY, DOER OF EVIL, MALEFACTOR, etc.; NEB also WRONGDOER, RUFFIANS, CRIMINAL (Jn. 18:30), etc.

The term "evil-doing" can refer to a personal injury, as in 1 S. 25:39, where it refers to Nabal's personal affront to David. In other instances it is used in a general sense of evil actions. The author of Eccl. 7:15 complains that people who perform such evil works are rewarded with long life (cf. Mal. 3:15).

The basic meaning of each of the Hebrew terms rendered "evildoer" is "one who causes evil." The Gk. *anomía* has the basic meaning of "lawlessness." The meaning of *kakón poiṓn* in Jn. 18:30 is "one who is a lawbreaker." *Adikṓn* in Rev. 22:11 is the normal Greek term for one who violates a divine or human law.

The Bible regularly assumes that a person has two possibilities: to do evil and to do good. It is within this framework that the "evildoer" is to be understood. In the OT, the historical literature has the term only once, 2 S. 3:39, for the murderous activity of the enemies of David; but in the Writings (Job, Psalms, Proverbs) and prophetic literature the subject receives considerable attention. It is usually assumed that the "evildoers" are those who neither call on the Lord (Ps. 14:4; Isa. 14:20; 31:2) nor keep God's law (Ps. 119:115). They are thus the opposite of those who are described as the "righteous" (Ps. 34:16; cf. 125:5; Prov. 10:29; Mal. 3:15; 4:1). Their arrogance and refusal to acknowledge the demands of God on their lives result in their failure to lead ethical lives. Thus they are known for their violence and mischief (Prov. 24:19), their adultery and lies (Jer. 23:14), and their lives of murder and oppression (Ps. 94:4, 16). The Psalms regularly give an indication of the continual struggle of the righteous against those "evildoers" who attempt to crush them (Ps. 22:16; 27:2; 119:115; 141:9). The OT expresses the conviction that although "evildoers" frequently prosper (Mal. 3:15), they will be crushed in the end (Ps. 92:7, 9 [MT 8, 10]).

In Matthew two descriptions of the last judgment mention the condemnation of "evildoers" (7:23; 13:41). These people are in each instance those within the community of believers who have failed to meet the requirements of discipleship. In Matthew's Gospel the Church is regarded as a mixture of the good and the evil (13:41; 25:31-46). In the final judgment these two groups will be separated and judged according to the criterion laid down in 7:21: the doing of God's will. The "evildoers" of 7:23 have been followers of Jesus and have carried on miraculous activity in the name of Jesus, but they have failed to meet the demands of discipleship laid down in v. 21. In Matthew discipleship involves bearing fruit (7:16) and the doing of good deeds (10:42; 25:40). To fail in this responsibility is to be an "evildoer." According to 7:23; 13:41 (cf. 25:31-46), these "evildoers" will be condemned in the final judgment.

In Jn. 18:30 Jesus is described by the Jews with the term *kakón poiṓn,* a general term for "criminal." The related term *kakopoiós* (RSV "wrongdoer") is used in 1 Pet. 2:12 for the claim of outsiders that the Church is a company of criminals. This claim provides the background for Peter's exhortation that the Church be known for doing good rather than for doing evil (1 Pet. 3:17; cf. 4:15).

Bibliography.–G. Bornkamm, *et al., Tradition and Interpretation in Matthew* (1963), pp. 58-62; *TDNT,* III, *s.v.* κακός (W. Grundmann). J. W. THOMPSON

EVIL-FAVOREDNESS (Dt. 17:1, AV). The word is the translation of the Heb. *dāḇār raʿ,* literally "evil thing" (RSV "defect"), and refers to the ritual unfitness for sacrifice of any animal that, though included in the class of clean beasts, yet possesses a blemish or otherwise lacks beauty of symmetry, or is lean-fleshed (cf. "ill blemish," Dt. 15:21, AV). *See* BLEMISH.

EVIL-MERODACH ē'vəl mer'ə-dak [Heb. *ʾᵉwîl-mᵉrōḏaḵ*; Bab. *Amēl-Marduk*–'man of Marduk']. King of the Neo-Babylonian empire, 562-560 B.C., son of Nebuchadrezzar II.

Nothing is known of the brief reign of this king from Babylonian annals. In 2 K. 25:27-30 par. Jer. 52:31-34 we read that Evil-merodach, in his accession year, freed Jehoiachin king of Judah from prison and elevated him above the other kings who were in Babylon; from then on Jehoiachin "dined regularly at the king's table." This almost incredible statement has received support from administrative tablets found at Babylon that contain lists of rations that were issued. Among those receiving rations is "*Ia-ku-ú-ki-nu,* the soṇ of the king of *Ia-ku-du*" (*ANET,* p. 308; "Jehoiachin" and "Judah" are rendered thus, since the writing system lacked *h*). In other tablets from the same period, the writing *Ia-ʾu-ki-nu* and *Ia-ḫu-du* also occur, demonstrating the inability of the Babylonian scribes to render the names with phonetic precision (cf. *DOTT,* p. 86).

According to Berossus (quoted by Josephus *CAp* i.20[146f.]), Evil-merodach conducted his reign in an illegal manner and was slain by his brother-in-law Neriglissar (*Nergal-šar-uṣur*), possibly the Nergal-sharezer of Jer. 39:3, 13. It is a curious fact that Nabonidus mentioned Nebuchadrezzar and Neriglissar as his predecessors but made no mention of Evil-merodach: "I am the real executor of the wills of Nebuchadnezzar and Neriglissar, my royal predecessors!" (*ANET,* p. 309).

W. S. L. S.

EVIL-SPEAKING. *See* SLANDER.

EVIL-WORKERS [Gk. *kakoí ergátai*] (Phil. 3:2); NEB "malpractices." The literal meaning is "malicious laborers." The noun *ergátai* is used frequently, almost technically, of Christian missionaries, the "laborers" whom God sends forth into His harvest (Mt. 9:38). Used of Jewish propagandists — probably an extremist party of Judaizers within the early Church — the phrase suggests that they are carrying on a parody of the Christian mission, working to bring harm to men rather than salvation. The adjective *kakós* is one of the broadest Greek words for "evil," "bad," but often has the particular sense of "malicious," "bent on doing evil to others." The reference in Phil. 3:2 (cf. 2 Cor. 11:13) is to opponents whose teaching includes certain Judaizing elements, the same group that Paul brands "dogs" and "those who mutilate the flesh."

See also EVIL-DOING.

Bibliography.–F. Beare, *Epistle to the Philippians* (1959), p. 104; D. Georgi, *Die Gegner des Paulus im 2. Korintherbrief* (1964), pp. 49f.; J. B. Lightfoot, *Saint Paul's Epistle to the Philippians* (1888), p. 144. J. W. THOMPSON

EVOLUTION [<Lat. *evolvere*–'unfold'].

I. Meaning and Usage
II. Evolution in Nature
III. Evolution in History
IV. Evolution in Religion
V. Evolution in Revelation

I. Meaning and Usage.–The term "evolution" in earlier biological use referred to the development of the embryo, and this was in accordance with the stricter etymological sense, for the intended meaning was not the developing of a new thing out of an older, but the continuing process of unfolding that which was implicit from the very first. In modern thought, however, the word has taken on a much more extended and general meaning which includes the possibility of completely new features emerging. Thus the root idea of "unfolding" can be retained only in the sense either of disclosure to view or of the development of possibilities rather than latent features. Construed thus, evolution can mean that things emerge *de novo*. This may be in terms of a simple historical process but it often carries the further implication that what is present has the power either to change into or to produce new things in certain conditions, that these things constitute on the whole an ascending scale, and that at some point within the process there may be a movement from the inorganic to the organic.

Within such an interpretation of evolution there is naturally a great deal of variation. Under the general concept of evolution it is possible to hold to the stricter construction, namely, that all developments are implicit in the world from the very first. It is also possible to think in terms of deistic evolution, namely, that God created the world in such a way that the process of cause and effect would give rise to all subsequent developments. It is also possible to understand evolution theistically, namely, that God commands and uses the process of evolution in the work of creation, perhaps intervening at specific points to introduce new turns, e.g., the specifically human element in man. In many cases, however, evolution is taken to be a self-contained cosmic process whereby all that is or can be is subsumed pantheistically or materialistically under the single factor of matter; and purpose, if there be such, is explained in terms of an immanent teleology of progress.

To add to the confusion, the word can be figuratively applied to developments in the human sphere: historical evolution, the evolution of ideas, the evolution of a literary form, or the evolution of a movement. In this usage the word is for the most part a loose equivalent of "development." It may equally well denote on the one hand the unfolding of incipient tendencies or implications and on the other the emergence of new things. Often it carries the sense of progress from the more primitive and simple to the more complicated and sophisticated, though this is not essential. In some cases its use is based on a grand interpretation of all dimensions of life in which the advancing achievements of the human spirit are regarded as a continuation of the creative evolution discerned first in the inorganic and then in the organic world.

This brief review of the meaning and use will be enough to show that "evolution" is in fact a very imprecise word, which can be used as the vehicle of ideas that differ very widely both in general and in detail. In a strictly scientific sense, the older usage stands on a solid basis; and it is also beyond question that the history of a species will manifest changes and that natural causes may sometimes have produced changes of a more radical character. On the other hand, the broader postulates, that lifeless matter develops into living, that simple mechanisms evolve into more complex, and that the changes will be necessarily advantageous, give rise to serious difficulties; and the general presupposition of some thinkers that eternal, self-existent matter has of itself some kind of inherent or random creative power is a speculation that does not lie in the sphere of true science. It is in fact a matter for serious regret that a word that had its own limited but precise scientific usage was ever exalted to its present status as the catchword of a whole interpretation or philosophy. Since this has happened, it is most important that the distinctions among strictly scientific, semiscientific, speculative, and figurative meanings should be kept clearly in view when the term is encountered or used, more particularly when the claim is made that evolution is a proved and accepted fact of science (which is of course true in a strict and limited sense).

II. Evolution in Nature.–The word "evolution" in the modern sense forms no part of the vocabulary of the Bible. On the one hand, the Bible has no particular occasion to mention or to describe the objective process of evolution, e.g., in the case of an embryo or a species. Ordinary physiological developments are obviously presupposed in Scripture, and it might be assumed that even the strictest teaching on creation allows for normal variations and mutations, whether for good or for bad. Such matters are of no particular interest in the biblical narrative except perhaps in terms of questions concerning, e.g., the apparently declining lifespan of man through the patriarchal period.

On the other hand, the Bible quite definitely opposes the fact of creation to concepts of creative evolution. In particular, it states that God commanded vegetation to come forth and that He created or made creatures that swim, the fowls of the air, the beasts of the field, and man. Two points may be noted in this connection. First, the Bible does not itself say that each species of plants or animals was individually created, unless this is the implication of the "after his (their) kind" in Gen. 1:11, 21, 24f. Second, the Bible does in fact seem to suggest something of a progression up through vegetation to man. If the days of creation are to be taken literally, what might otherwise seem to be the slow development of millennia is speeded up, as it were, in great creative acts. But there are many expositors who claim that the days stand for long periods of time and that specific creative acts are divine interventions in a slow natural process. What is plain in any case is that the divine self-witness decisively rejects any suggestion of an autonomous creativity of matter or of necessary progress by mutation. Even changes within a given species can be for the worse as well as for the better, and it is not proved that they must or will constantly lead on to higher stages of life. While the use of secondary causes is not excluded, decisive progression is attributed to the Creator alone. *See* CREATION; CREATOR.

Thoughtful consideration will show that the actual data of natural history are broadly parallel to such data as are given in the theological account of Scripture. There is, of course, a difference of purpose, for science aims to give a description and theology seeks to supply the ultimate interpretation. This leads to a difference of presentation, for science develops its own terminology and classification for the purpose of exact description, whereas theology used broad and simple terms which can convey the divine self-revelation to all sorts and conditions of persons. Once these points are grasped, however, it will be seen that there need be no quarrel about the actual data. The biblical creation narrative involves either a series of aeons or an acceleration which covers true scientific findings, and the biblical account of the early period of civilized or historical man is in agreement with available data from other sources. Where conflict arises is in the sphere of interpretation, for the theological data of the divine self-revelation as Creator cut sharply across the philosophical and pseudo-scientific hypotheses of uninformed mankind. At this level, however, science betrays its own ultimate inadequacy. It really has no data regarding the origin of nature; it can work only within a self-enclosed cosmos. Within closely defined limits, and where there is a modest awareness of limitation, this is, of course, valid. But when all the data are taken into account — those concerning the Creator and His relation to the cosmos as well as those concerning the cosmos — the very limitation of science obviously involves a final invalidity which is inescapable in the fallen state of mankind, or which can be escaped only when ignorance is dispelled by the divine self-revelation.

III. Evolution in History.–The Bible does not speak of evolution in history. It recognizes, of course, that there is change in people and nations. It recognizes that there is a rise of people and nations. It recognizes that people and nations are in a sense comparable to seeds — they contain already the harvest the future will unfold. It also recognizes, however, that there is a fall of people and nations as well as a rise. Nor is the fall merely a single step backward for the sake of two steps forward. No general line of progress is discerned in history. The first period of civilization is in general one of deterioration which moves irresistibly to the Flood. Since then, good and bad periods have followed or intermingled with one another, and the final movement at the end of the age will again be one of decline. The standard of judgment is theological. In the biblical view, then, advances in arts and sciences do not compensate in the long run for apostasy from God and injustices among people. Rising prosperity and population, even if they continue, do not indicate true human progress. Even knowledge is not necessarily a sign of advance, for greater knowledge, e.g., of literary or artistic technique, may go hand in hand with a decline in art and letters; and scientific knowledge, while it can do great good, can also work great mischief. According to the biblical story, human history is set under the judgment of God. This judgment is immanent, but it is also divinely directed. While not every individual sin is individually visited, there is a broad movement of judgment without which history is inexplicable.

This means that the real story of mankind in the Bible is not the story of autonomous and progressive mankind but the story of mankind under God. The bright side of this story of great expectations and great disappointments, of human upsurgence and divine judgment, is that it is not merely of the outworking of divine judgment, but also of the ongoing history of salvation. It has a teleological direction — good seed is sown and will grow along with the tares until the harvest. The age of final decline is the night before the dawn of the new age. In the parable of the seed growing secretly (Mk. 4:26-29), the emphasis is perhaps not on the element of growth. Hence, no doctrine of historical evolution can be derived from it. Yet God is secretly at work for good even when it appears that evil or neutral powers are dominant, and to that degree history is the story of fulfillment as well as judgment. The point is, however, that this is wholly God's work. Mankind contributes only confused and conflicting patterns in which the judgment of God on human achievement is manifest. The true hope of mankind is not in his own evolution, but in the saving work that God Himself accomplishes in, through, and in spite of human deeds.

The polemic of the Bible is sharper against historical evolution than against natural evolution (in the sense of a rising scale of life-forms) because in the former case there are no data to which to appeal and on which to find a measure of common ground. The most that can be said is that history involves progression in a nexus of events and that in some areas and ages there is a rising graph, though the graph falls again in others. For the rest of the term "evolution," unless it is taken rather colorlessly to mean the unfolding of all possibilities, can only be an interpretation and not a statement of facts. The biblical data show, however, that it is a false and imposed interpretation. Its criteria are inadequate, its speculations are ill-founded, and its philosophical framework is without substance. Except in a platitudinous sense, the word is quite inappropriate in this sphere. As history is theologically grounded and controlled, so it is to be theologically understood. As it is the sphere of the outworking of the divine purpose, so it is to be expounded in terms of the divine data of judgment and salvation.

IV. Evolution in Religion.–What is true of history in general is true of the history of religion in particular. Now it is true that the Bible is not itself the story of human religion or even a part of this story. It is also true that religion does show movement. Ideas originate, are developed, modified, perhaps purified, and make way for, or merge into, other ideas. In many cases a line of advance may be discerned. But the Bible, both as a record of the divine self-revelation and, incidentally, as a record of religious beliefs and practices, does not at all support the view that there is a real evolution of religion, e.g., from primitive animism to purified monotheism. Indeed, it shows that the very opposite is the truth. An original knowledge of God gave way to idolatry (Rom. 1:21-23). When knowledge was restored by revelation, the basic pattern remained the same. Primitive idolatry might have evolved into more sophisticated idolatry, but it was still idolatry. With regard to the true knowledge and worship of God, the clever thinkers of Greece had no advantage over the most primitive of savages. Within Israel the movement was one of decline and restoration, and if the religion of, e.g., the Pharisees was in many ways inestimably superior to that of the ordinary Israelites of the 8th cent. B.C., it was still not the religion of the majority, and it also contained within itself the same corruption. (Even today the Bible could give us little ground for supposing that the religious ideas and practices of most Christians show any real advance over those of Abraham, Moses, or Isaiah.) The history of religion, then, would appear on a graph as a fluctuating line, not a general upward rise.

Nor is it true that there is a steady unfolding of possibilities hitherto latent, for both on the good side and on the bad most of the possibilities have already been explored during the course of the centuries, and the only differences are in detail. Where there is decisive change, e.g., in the setting aside of the OT sacrifices, it is not by a process of religious evolution but in terms of a response to the new situation created by God's revealing and reconciling action. Indeed, it is interesting that even at a point like this the tendency of religion is to substitute new sacrificial forms in spite of the clear revelation that they are now redundant. This is characteristic of human religion as it is depicted in the Bible, for did not the early Israelites set about to transform Yahweh into the more familiar Baals? In fact, the Bible bears consistent testimony against the view that there is an evolution of religion. Its whole thesis is that the knowledge of God is by revelation from above, not by upward movement from below — that the movement below is a movement in the circle of ignorance and idolatry which will still manifest themselves only too easily even in the response to revelation. It might be contended that in the Bible as we now have it later redactors have altered the story to fit a thesis which differs widely from the actual facts. But to try to recover the so-called facts requires a drastic new work of redaction which is highly speculative, which necessarily denies the fundamental biblical principle of the divine self-revelation, and which still leaves so many loose ends that the idea of religious evolution obviously remains in the sphere of hypothesis. The Bible is in fact the story of revelation, not of evolving religion.

V. Evolution in Revelation.–Is there, then, an evolution of revelation? If God's self-revelation takes historical form, does this mean that here at least there is genuine evolution either in the sense of making explicit what is implicit, or in that of gradually introducing new things on an ascending scale, or perhaps in both? The ancient dictum that what is latent in the OT is patent in the NT seems at least to point in the direction of an unfolding, and in the age of the evolutionary hypothesis the concept of a progressive revelation has gained wide credence as the theological counterpart of theistic evolution in nature. What truth is there in this application of the term?

Certain points allow little questioning. There is no doubt that God reveals Himself in history. But history involves successiveness or progression. Even if there is no necessary advance from the lower to the higher, there is always movement. Movement is to be discerned in revelation too; the things of God are not all revealed at the same time, or at least not with the same emphasis or fulness at the same time (He. 1:1f.). If it is true that all the NT is present in essence in the OT, this does not mean that the NT is a mere repetition of the OT; and the same principle holds good of the various portions or books within both the OT and the NT. If things were different, there would be no need for the spread of revelation over so many centuries. The principle is particularly confirmed when we come to Jesus Christ the incarnate Word, for in Him God is bodily present and accomplishes salvation, so that a new point of reference is given for the proclamation of the old truths, and the truths themselves are set in a new light. Again, the movement of the Bible is in the main a movement from promise to fulfilment. This may not always be true in detail, e.g., in the movement from the Law to the Writings or from the Gospels to the Epistles, but it is certainly true in general, i.e., in the movement from the Law to the Gospel. And in the relation of the Prophets and the Writings to the Law, or the Epistles to the Gospels, there is unquestionably the basic element of explication and application, so that one could very well speak here of evolution in the sense of an unfolding or unrolling.

Nevertheless, there are other points which show that the indefinite word "evolution," and even the ambiguous "progressive," are to be used of the biblical revelation only with the greatest circumspection. The first point is that revelation is not an immanent process. If there is evolution, it is not from within the world or humanity itself. It is always by the act of God's unfolding. Revelation does not unroll itself; God unrolls it. God is here the acting subject in the history; the progression is that of God's own acts. The second point is that the object of revelation does not really change. For the object of revelation, like the subject, is God Himself. Certainly, revelation takes the form of specific acts and words which both advance the concrete history of salvation and also display or express this or that aspect of God. But the movement is not from a lower God to a higher, or from the bit of God to more bits of God and finally to the whole. If God reveals Himself, He does not first reveal Himself as it were in embryo and then through growth to maturity. The action goes forward, and God constantly reveals Himself in word and act until He takes the stage in person. But the subject, who is also the Subject, remains the same.

It must be emphasized as strongly as possible that the progression here is not from the lower to the higher, so the word "progressive" is suspect if it is used as the adjective of "progress" rather than of "progression." One might perhaps say that there is progression from the partial to the total, for the divine work of salvation and the divine self-manifestation are not really complete before the coming of the incarnate Son. On the other hand, this is hardly the best way in which to present the biblical data, for the Bible makes it plain that in a very true sense God is fully at work at every stage, but "at sundry times and in divers manners" (He. 1:1, AV). The categories used in the Bible seem to be rather those of promise (or prophecy) and fulfillment. God reveals Himself to the patriarchs and the prophets with great and gracious promises, which carry with them a first installment but which look and move forward to their fulfillment in the Word. God then reveals Himself to the Evangelists and apostles in the fulfillment of these promises in and through the incarnation of the Word. Since this is all worked out in history, it obviously entails movement or progression. The promise itself is given in various forms, and at every stage there is an installment which is also action moving to the fulfillment. Again, the divine record accompanies the various forms of promise and, bringing out the implications and making the applications, it moves with the divine action to the fulfillment and its meaning. While the element of movement is obvious, it may be doubted whether the upward line or curve of progress is really the right figure to express this progression; and the pedagogic concept of a teacher leading the class from elementary aspects of a subject to more complex is plainly inappropriate in relation to God's revelation of Himself in word and act from Abraham through Moses and the prophets to Paul and John. For pedagogically this is not in fact the order in which this subject is best learned, e.g., in the work of evangelization and instruction as it is now carried on in the Christian world.

The truth is, of course, that revelation is too big to be brought under the categories implied in such words as "evolution" or "progressive." As the revelation of the eternal God in time and history, revelation is unique. It merges into the stream of history, but it is never absorbed in it. It does not follow the pattern of rise and fall that may be discerned even in the religious life of its recipients. It cannot be described adequately by analogies from natural and historical life. If epithets are to be used, they are better taken from the divine side. This is not evolutionary or progressive revelation. It is God's revelation in history. It is incarnational revelation. It is revelation in salvation history. From the standpoint of the record, it is biblical revelation. This can allow for such elements of evolution (i.e., unfolding) or progression (movement) as may be rightly discerned. But it safeguards the divine work against the imposition of an alien and distorting principle of interpretation and leaves room for its primary and determinative understanding from within itself and in its own categories.

See also CREATION; SCIENCE AND THE BIBLE.

G. W. BROMILEY

EWE [Heb. *keḇeś*] (Gen. 21:28-30); NEB also LAMBS; [*kiḇśâ*] (Lev. 14:10; Nu. 6:14; 2 S. 12:3); [*rāḥēl*] (Gen. 31:38; 32:14; Cant. 6:6); AV also SHEEP; [*śeh*] (Lev. 22:28); NEB SHEEP; [*ʿûl*] (Ps. 78:71); [*qeṣûḇâ*] (Cant. 4:2); AV SHEEP; NEB "ewes just shorn." This term generally denotes a female sheep, though in Lev. 22:28 it could refer equally well to a female goat. *See* SHEEP.

EXACT (vb.) [Heb. *nāgaś*] (Dt. 15:2f.; 2 K. 23:35); NEB also "press for payment"; [*nāšā', nāšâ*] (Neh. 5:7, 11; Job 11:6); NEB also "holdings," "taking as pledges"; [*yāṣā'*] (2 K. 15:20); NEB "lay a levy"; [*śûm*] (Ex. 22:25); AV "lay usury upon"; [*ḥāḇal*] (Job 22:6; Ezk. 18:16); AV TAKE, WITHHOLD; NEB TAKE; [*terûmôṯ*] ("[one] who exacts gifts," Prov. 29:4); AV "(he) that receiveth gifts"; NEB "forced contributions." Used by the RSV with several shades of meaning: (1) establish or impose a tax (Ex. 22:25; 2 K. 15:20); (2) demand interest or secure it by force (Dt. 15:2f.; 2 K. 23:35; Neh. 5:7, 11); (3) take in pledge (Job 22:6; Ezk. 18:16); (4) demand (Job 11:6; Prov. 29:4). The Heb. *terûmâ* means "tribute," "gift," or "contribution"; thus Prov. 29:4 would read, literally, "a man of gifts" or "a man of exactions."

N. J. O.

EXACTION. The term is used three times by the RSV: (1) Heb. *maššā'* (Neh. 10:31 [MT 32]), a demand for money lent on pledge, which the Jews agreed to forego in the seventh year; (2) *maśʾēṯ*–"tribute," "tax" (Am. 5:11; NEB "levy taxes"), condemned by Amos as blatant exploitation of the poor; (3) Gk. *pleonexía*–"greed," "cupidity" (2 Cor. 9:5; NEB "extortion").

EXACTOR [Heb. *nôgēś*]; AV "raiser (of taxes)"; NEB "officer . . . to extort (tribute)." The verb *nāgaś* generally has an oppressive connotation, as the noun "taskmasters" in Ex. 3:7. In the RSV, "exactor" occurs only in Dnl. 11:20 to describe some government official who will levy tribute upon an otherwise unidentified kingdom.

EXALT; EXALTED [Heb. *gāḇah, gāḏal* (Josh. 4:14), *ʿelyôn* (2 Ch. 7:21), *zeḇul* (1 K. 8:13; 2 Ch. 6:2), *nāśā'*, *sālal* (Ex. 9:17), *ʿālâ* (Ps. 47:9 [MT 10]; 97:9), *rûm, rāmam* (Job 24:24; Ps. 118:16), *śāgaḇ*; Gk. *doxázō* (He. 5:5; 1 Pet. 1:8), *hyperaírō* (2 Thess. 2:4), *hyperypsóō* (Phil. 2:9), *hypsēlós* (Lk. 16:15; He. 7:26), *hypsóō*]; AV also EXCELLENT, GLORIFY, HIGH ABOVE, HIGHLY ESTEEMED, LIFT UP, MADE HIGHER, MAGNIFY, SET UP, "to dwell in" (1 K. 8:13), "of habitation" (2 Ch. 6:2), "set up the horn of" (Lam. 2:17), "full of glory" (1 Pet. 1:8); NEB also ARROGANT, BOAST, BUILD UP, CONFER GLORY, CONFIRM, DENOUNCE, ELATE, GREATER GLORY, GROW ARROGANT, HEIGHT, HIGH ABOVE, HOLD HIGH, INCREASE, YEARN, "held in high honor" (2 Ch. 32:23), "stand erect in their full height" (Ezk. 31:14), "too great for words" (1 Pet. 1:8), etc.; **EXALTATION** [Gk. *hýpsos*] (Jas. 1:9); NEB "that God lifts him up."

"Exalt" is most often used to translate Heb. *rûm*, "be high, exalted, rise." It is used with reference to humans exalting God (e.g., Ps. 34:3 [MT 4]), God exalting humans (Ps. 89:17), and humans exalting themselves (Dnl. 11:36). Other words used are: *gāḇah*, "be high, lofty, tall," used positively of God being exalted (Isa. 5:16), exalting kings (Job 36:7), and admonishing humility among men (Ezk. 21:26) (for its negative use, *see* ARROGANCE; HAUGHTY; PRIDE); *nāśā'*, the common word for "lift, carry, take" in the qal, "lift up, exalt" in the piel, "be lifted up, exalted" in the niphal; *gāḏal*, commonly having to do with "being great, lifted up, high," translated "exalt, exalted" four times (Josh. 3:7; 4:14; Ps. 138:2; Zec. 12:7); *sālal*, in the hithpolel meaning "exalt oneself, resist," used of pharaoh in Ex. 9:17; *ʿālâ*, the common term for "go up, ascend, climb," and in the niphal used twice of God being exalted (Ps. 47:9; 97:9); *rāmam*, the niphal of *rûm*, "be high, exalted" (Job 24:24; Ps. 118:16); *śāgaḇ*, "be inaccessibly high," is used only of God being exalted (Job 36:22; Ps. 148:13; Isa. 2:11, 17; 12:4; 33:5). The term *zeḇul* has a disputed rendering: the older lexicons translated it "habitation, residence," especially of God, thus the AV "habitation, dwelling, to dwell in"; this translation would also fit the poetic parallelism of the prayer of Solomon in the MT. Later studies, however, particularly of cuneiform inscriptions, produced the translation "elevation, height, lofty abode," from the Assyr. *bît zabal*, "lofty house," and Ugar. *zbl*, "exalt, honor"; thus the RSV translates *zeḇul* "exalted" in 1 K. 8:13 and 2 Ch. 6:2 (NEB "lofty"), while retaining "home" in Ps. 49:14 [MT 15] (NEB "honor") and "habitation" in Isa. 63:15; Hab. 3:11 (NEB "heights" and "course"), from the older rendering.

The RSV translates Heb. *ʿelyôn* in 2 Ch. 7:21, referring to the temple of Solomon, as "exalted"; two emendations, however, have been suggested: *šemāmâ*, "desolation," based on the Syriac, and *leʿiyîn*, "ruins, ruinous heaps," based on a LXX variant, from which the NEB translates "ruins."

In the NT "exalt" translates *hypsóō*, "lift up, raise high, elevate." It is used mainly of people, especially in the Gospels of exalting the lowly and humbling the lofty (Mt. 23:12; Lk. 14:11; 18:14), but also twice of Christ's being exalted to the right hand of God (Acts 2:33; 5:31). In Jas. 1:9 *hýpsos* is to be taken in the sense of exaltation of rank, following the usage of *hypsóō* in Mt. 23:12; Lk. 14:11; 18:14. See *TDNT*, VIII, *s.v.* ὕψος (Bertram).

Other NT terms are *doxázō*, usually "glorify" but twice "exalt" (He. 5:5; 1 Pet. 1:8); *hyperaírō*, "lift oneself up, exalt oneself" (2 Thess. 2:4); *hyperypsóō*, "exalted to the highest rank" (Phil. 2:9); and *hypsēlós*, used of Christ in the comparative sense of "raised to greater heights than the heavens" (He. 7:26) and used in the negative figurative sense of "haughty, proud" in Lk. 16:15 (Bauer, rev., pp. 849f.).

W. A. SHELL

EXALTATION OF CHRIST. After the completion of His earthly ministry of humiliation and suffering, culminating in His crucifixion, Christ was exalted to an estate of heavenly blessedness and installed in the glory of full lordship (Phil. 2:6-11). His earthly ministry was filled with intimations of His future exaltation. The steps in this exaltation are Christ's resurrection, His ascension, His enthronement at the right hand of God, and His parousia or coming in glory.

There are numerous anticipations of exaltation in Jesus' life of service. At His transfiguration, the voice out of heaven acclaimed Him "my beloved Son," as had occurred also at His baptism. Our Savior affirmed His former glory (Jn. 17:5), prophesied His future exaltation (Mk. 14:61f.), and avowed the unique reciprocal knowledge, authority, and revelation of the Son (Himself) and the Father (Mt. 11:25-27 par.) His exaltation is implied in the disciples' confession of Jesus as Messiah, Lord, and Son of God, and by the mighty miracles of His person and work. So greatly do these anticipations permeate the Gospel accounts that for G. Bertram (*TDNT,* VIII, *s.v.* ὑψόω) the concept of His exaltation is logically prior to that of His humiliation. Paul testifies that the rulers of this age crucified the Lord of Glory (1 Cor. 2:8).

I. Christ's Resurrection.–On Easter morning the disciples found Jesus' tomb empty except for His grave clothes. To them an angel announced, "Jesus who was crucified . . . is not here; for he has risen, as he said" (Mt. 28:5f.; Jn. 20:6f.).

A. Its Attestation. Over a period of forty days the risen Christ appeared several times to His disciples. Each of these appearances resulted, though not always immediately, in their recognition of Him. They saw Him with the scars of Calvary on His body; they heard His familiar voice; they touched Him with their hands; they ate with Him; He breathed upon them. They testified that He did not see corruption (Acts 2:27; 13:35). Moreover, the wisdom of the Risen One opened their minds to interpret the OT christologically. His lordship challenged their wills with the Great Commission. His love made their hearts burn with a new devotion. He blessed them spiritually with repentance, forgiveness, peace, and power for witnessing. His fellowship knit them together as the Church of God in Christ Jesus. The numerous impacts of the risen Lord established the objective character of the Resurrection as an event brought about by God, not by the disciples.

B. Its Glory. Like a great avalanche, sin and death swept over all men, but in raising Christ from the dead God broke that reign of death. Christ's resurrection (1) revealed His power over death (Rev. 1:18; Jn. 5:25f.; 1 Cor. 15:20-23); (2) confirmed His divine sonship (Rom. 1:4); (3) attested God's acceptance of His finished work of righteousness for the justification of His people (Rom. 3:21-24; 4:25; 10:4; Phil. 3:9); (4) is the beginning of the new creation that is life eternal, over which death has no power (Rom. 6:4-19; Col. 2:13; 2 Tim. 1:10); (5) is the entrance of the Son of God, the divine-human head of His body the Church, into the resurrection power and royal glory of His redemptive reign of grace (Eph. 1:19-21); (6) and is God's assurance that He has ordained Christ to judge the world on the day He has appointed (Acts 17:31).

C. Its Author. In the scriptural accounts Christ generally is spoken of as passive, while God is the active author of His resurrection, e.g., "This Jesus God raised up" (Acts 2:32; cf. 2:27, 31; Rom. 6:4; Eph. 1:19f.; 1 Pet. 1:3). In two passages, however, John represents Jesus as affirming His own action in this event: "I lay down my life, that I may take it again" (Jn. 10:17f.; 2:19). Nor is the Holy Spirit absent from the resurrection process. At His resurrection, Christ became a life-giving Spirit (1 Cor. 15:45). Through His Spirit God will give life to our mortal bodies (Rom. 8:11), i.e., raise them as spiritual bodies (1 Cor. 15:44), conformed to the body of His glory (Phil. 3:21).

II. Christ's Ascension.–"Ascension" means the transfer of Jesus to heaven, i.e., to the realm of the divine. The Ascension and sitting at the right hand of God are combined in 1 Pet. 3:22. More often the NT writers imply the Ascension in their references to Christ's exaltation to the right hand of the Father and, once, to His being received up in glory (1 Tim. 3:16). In Eph. 4:10 (cf. 1:20), Christ is described as ascending above all heavens.

A. Johannine Account. In Jn. 20:17 the risen Lord says to Mary, "Do not hold me, for I have not yet ascended to the Father; but go to my brethren and say to them, I am ascending to my Father and your Father, to my God and your God." This suggests an invisible Ascension on the day of the Resurrection and interprets the several appearances as returns of the risen Christ (*see* ASCENSION I). On this interpretation the Johannine accounts of the Resurrected One coming where the doors of the house were shut are best understood as His descending into the open court around which many first-century homes were built, thus bypassing the closed outer doors of the residence.

B. Public Event. Lk. 24:50f. and Acts 1:9-11 give accounts of Christ's public ascension. The latter details the witnessing of the event by His disciples, the cloud that received Him out of their sight, and the promise of His return in like manner.

C. Saving Significance. Christ's triumphal departure from this world demonstrated that He had accomplished the work that His Father had given Him to do (Jn. 17:4; 4:34; 19:30). As our representative He had perfectly obeyed the Father's will (Phil. 2:8f.; Rom. 5:19). As our substitute He had borne our sins in His body on the tree (1 Pet. 2:24; 2 Cor. 5:21). Now ascended to the right hand of God He is our righteousness (1 Cor. 1:30) and our Advocate near the ear of the Father (1 Jn. 2:1). Thence the ascended Lord sends from the Father the Holy Spirit to convince the world of righteousness because of His finished work (Jn. 16:7-11). Thus does the Spirit bear witness to and glorify Christ (Jn. 15:26).

Gnostic thinkers interpreted Christ's ascension as the finality of God's victory and taught that those united to Him by baptism had risen and ascended with Him and were thus exalted above the suffering and service of earthly life. In contrast to this claim, J. M. Robinson (*IDB, s.v.* "Ascension") shows Paul's position to be "that our ascension has not already happened so as to remove us from historical involvement, but rather that our future ascension does await us, thus giving meaning to that involvement (Phil. 3)."

III. Christ's Enthronement at God's Right Hand.–Based on Our Lord's application of Ps. 110:1 to the Messiah, the NT writers frequently present the ascended Christ as enthroned at the right hand of God and as sharing the throne of His Father. By His exaltation Christ was reinstalled in the primal glory that He had with the Father before the world was (Jn. 17:5,24; cf. 1:1-18 and Mk. 1:1-11, where He is already the beloved Son and heir when He comes to the vineyard). Yet the christological summaries present that exaltation as a reward for His incarnate ministry; His obedience even unto death (Phil. 2:6-11); His having made peace by the blood of His cross (Col. 1:15-20); and His purification of sins (He. 1:3). Thus it is as the Reconciler, the divine-human Person, that He is associated with God in power and glory. In Christ, "the dust of earth is on the throne of the universe." With the Father He is praised by the heavenly hosts (Rev. 1:6; 5:9-14). According to Pliny the Younger the primitive churches "sang antiphonally to Christ as to God" (*Ep.* x.96.7). Examples of these hymns have been identified in Jn. 1:1-18; Phil. 2:6-11; Col. 1:15-20. *See* Plate 35.

According to Acts 5:31, God has exalted the crucified Jesus to His right hand to be a Leader and a Savior to give repentance and forgiveness of sins. In Rev. 5, the sacrificed Lamb in the midst of the throne is opening the seals and applying the redemption He has won for mankind. Such passages led Justin Martyr to write, "The Lord entered His glory directly from His cross" (*Dial.* 73.1).

In His Great Commission, the resurrected Jesus affirmed, "All authority in heaven and on earth has been given to me. Go therefore and make disciples of all nations, baptizing them in the name of the Father and of the Son and of the Holy Spirit" (Mt. 28:18f.). Despite wars, tumults, and persecutions Christ is so reigning that disciples are being made in all nations. From His throne of grace, Christ rules His Church by His Spirit and Word and appoints ministers to proclaim His gospel and to maintain His lordship in His Church.

In the book of Revelation, Jesus Christ is the faithful witness whose name is the Word of God, even as in 1 John He is the Word of life and in Jn. 1:1-18 the eternal Word who reveals the Father. By the word of His mouth and by His Spirit the enthroned Christ speaks to His churches and sends forth His saving revelation to all the world (Rev. 2–3).

Hebrews presents Christ as our High Priest entering into heaven itself to appear before the face of God in our behalf (He. 9:24). His propitiation, His presence, and His intercession open the way for His people to the throne of grace (He. 2:17; 4:14-16; 10:19-22). Upon heaven's golden altar the fragrant incense of His intercession is added to the prayers of the saints (Rev. 8:3), so that as we pray in Christ's name He becomes both our merit and our mouth.

IV. Christ's Coming in Glory.–Referring to Dnl. 7:13, Our Lord prophesies the coming of the Son of man on the clouds with power and glory (Mk. 13:26; 14:62), coming with His holy angels (Mk. 8:38). His return will be like His ascension (Acts 1:11) and as sudden as lightning (Mt. 24:27). In the Epistles, this coming is the Day of the Lord (1 Cor. 1:8; 2 Pet. 3:10), the revelation of Jesus Christ (1 Cor. 1:7; 2 Thess. 1:7; 1 Pet. 4:13), and His appearing (1 Tim. 6:14; 2 Tim. 4:1; Tit. 2:13). By cataclysmic events Christ's reign of grace will be transformed into His reign of glory, and He will be revealed as:

A. Conqueror of Death. Bringing with Him "those who have fallen asleep," Christ will come to raise the dead and to bring the rapture of the living (1 Thess. 4:14; Jn. 5:25-29; 1 Cor. 15:22, 52). Indeed, He will destroy death itself, the last enemy (1 Cor. 15:25f.; 54-57; Rev. 21:4).

B. Judge of the Living and the Dead. We must all appear before the judgment seat of Christ (2 Cor. 5:10), for the King shall gather all nations before the throne of His glory and separate them as a shepherd separates the sheep from the goats (Mt. 25:31-46; Acts 17:31). He will vindicate His martyrs (2 Thess. 1:5-10) and bring into His everlasting fold those written in the Lamb's book of life (Rev. 20:11-15), for His verdicts are final (Mt. 7:23; 25:46).

C. Bridegroom of the Church. Having cleansed the Church "by the washing of water with the word," the Savior of the world will present to Himself the glorious Church without spot or wrinkle (Eph. 1:22f.; 5:23-27). And blessed are those who are bidden to the marriage feast of the Lamb (Rev. 19:7-9; 21:9).

D. King of Kings. The kingdom of the world will become "the kingdom of our Lord and of His Christ, and He shall reign forever" (Rev. 11:15; cf. 12:10). For in the end Jesus will put all enemies under His feet, abolish all rule and every authority and power, and then deliver up the kingdom to God the Father (1 Cor. 15:24).

E. Consummator of Creation. Christ returns to bring all God's purposes in creation to completion and all His precious promises to fulfillment. For the promises of God are all Yes and Amen in Christ (2 Cor. 1:20). His coming is the final act of world history in which the heavens and the earth shall be dissolved, and "new heavens and a new earth in which righteousness dwells" shall appear (2 Pet. 3:10-13; Rev. 21:1; Rom. 8:21).

See also JUDGMENT, LAST; PAROUSIA; RESURRECTION.

See G. C. Berkouwer, *Work of Christ* (Eng. tr. 1965), chs. 6-10.

W. C. ROBINSON

EXAMINE; MAKE EXAMINATION [Heb. *rā'â* (Lev. 13:3; 14:3; etc.), *ḥāqar* (Prov. 18:17; Lam. 3:40), *tûr* (Eccl. 9:1), *dāraš* (Ezr. 10:16), *bîn* (Jer. 2:10); Gk. *dokimázō* (Lk. 14:19; 1 Cor. 11:28), *anakrínō* (Lk. 23:14; Acts 4:9; 12:19; 17:11; 24:8; 25:26; 28:18; 1 Cor. 9:3), *anetázō* (Acts 22:24, 29), *peirázō* (2 Cor. 13:5)]; AV also SEE, LOOK, SEARCH, CONSIDER, PROVE; NEB also "make formal inquiry" (Ezr. 2:10), "cross-question" (Prov. 8:17), "consider well" (Jer. 2:10), "test himself" (1 Cor. 11:28), etc. "Examine" is used for a variety of Hebrew and Greek words with the meaning "look at" (*rā'â*, Lev. 13-14), "search" (*ḥāqar, dāraš*), "discern" (*bîn*), "make a judicial inquiry" (*anakrínō, anetázō*), or "put to the test" (*dokimázō, peirázō*).

The subject of Lev. 13–14 is physical examination for skin diseases. *Rā'â*, generally "see" or "look at," is used for the physical examination conducted by the priests to determine whether a skin disease was of such a nature that it rendered the person ritually unclean.

In other instances in the OT, "examine" is used for the act of discerning a truth. *Ḥāqar* is used in Prov. 18:17 for the investigation of a legal case; cf. Job 29:16 (RSV "search out") and Prov. 28:11 (RSV "find him out"). In Lam. 3:40 the term is used for rigorous self-examination; cf. Ps. 139:1 (RSV "thou hast searched me . . ."). Ezr. 10:16 employs *dāraš* for the inquiry conducted concerning the intermarriage of Israelites and other peoples. In Eccl. 9:1 the RSV emends the MT *bûr* (AV "declare") to *tûr*, "search out" (cf. Eccl. 1:13; 2:3; 7:25), indicating that the author is examining "how the righteous and the wise and their deeds are in the hand of God." Similarly, *bîn* occurs in Jer. 2:10 for an inquiry into religious matters.

In the NT Gk. *anakrínō* and *anetázō* are used regularly for the judicial interrogation of the accused; cf. the interrogation of Jesus (Lk. 23:14) and of the apostles (e.g., Acts 4:9; 22:24, 29). In 1 Cor. 4:3 *anakrínō* (RSV "judged") is used for a quasi-judicial investigation that the arrogant bring against Paul. In one exceptional case, the term is used in a nonjudicial text for "examining the Scriptures" (Acts 17:11); here the term may reflect the Heb. *dāraš* ("search"), a technical term for interpreting Scripture.

As the author of Lam. 3:40 uses Heb. *ḥāqar* to urge self-examination, so Paul in two NT texts encourages Christians to practice self-examination. In 1 Cor. 11:28 he uses *dokimázō* (lit. "put to the test") to encourage the Corinthian Christians to test themselves before partaking of the Lord's Supper. In vv. 21, 28, and 30 he indicates what is involved in failing to conduct this self-examination. To disregard one's brother (v. 21) is to disrupt the fellowship, or body, created by Christ (vv. 27, 29), and thus to act "in an unworthy manner" (v. 27) and bring judgment (v. 29) upon oneself. Both *dokimázō* (RSV "test") and *peirázō* are used in 2 Cor. 13:5 for the self-examination of the community. This exhortation is to be understood in the context of Paul's impending visit and his warning that he will not "spare" those who have been the source of trouble. The Corinthians have desired "proof" of Paul's genuineness as an emissary of Christ (v. 3). Paul therefore implies in 13:5, "You must give the proof, not I." To meet the test is to comply with Paul's demands before he arrives.

Bibliography.–H. Lietzmann, *An die Korinther* (*HNT*, 1949), pp. 58f., 160f.; M. Noth, *Leviticus* (Eng. tr., *OTL*, 1965), pp. 105f.; *TDNT*, III, *s.v.* κρίνω κτλ.: ἀνακρίνω (Büchsel).

J. W. THOMPSON

EXAMPLE [Gk. *hypódeigma*] (Jn. 13:15; Jas. 5:10; 2 Pet. 2:6); AV also ENSAMPLE; NEB also PATTERN, OBJECT LESSON; [*íchnos*] (Rom. 4:12); AV STEPS; NEB FOOTPRINTS; [*týpos*] (Phil. 3:17; 1 Thess. 1:7; 2 Thess.

3:9; 1 Tim. 4:12; 1 Pet. 5:3); AV also ENSAMPLE; NEB also MODEL; [*deigmatízō*] (Col. 2:15); AV SHEW; NEB SPECTACLE; [*hypotýpōsis*] (1 Tim. 1:16); AV PATTERN; NEB TYPICAL; [*hypogrammós*] (1 Pet. 2:21); [*deígma*] (Jude 7). "Example" is supplied by the RSV in Eccl. 9:13 and Gal. 3:15.

A number of Greek words are translated "example" in the RSV. Used in an ethical sense the word *týpos* — meaning "pattern" — is prominent. It is formed from *týptō* (to "strike"), and in classical Greek means a "blow" or the "mark" left by a blow. Thus it was a suitable term for describing the "impression" made on wax by a seal. This is the most common meaning and the one from which most of the others come. These other meanings fall under two classifications: (1) "pattern" or "model" and (2) "that which is formed" or the "image" (Lampe and Woolcombe, p. 61).

Paul always uses *týpos* in the sense of "pattern" or "model," e.g., when he marks himself as an "example" of living in the faith and a model to be "imitated" (*miméomai*) by others (Phil. 3:17). The Thessalonians are to emulate him as a *týpos* for their own walk as Christians (2 Thess. 3:9; cf. 1 Cor. 11:1). He urges Timothy to "set the believers an example" (1 Tim. 4:12) and praises the Thessalonians for having become a model for others (1 Thess. 1:7). Paul finds that their community of faith is a model that makes an impression "because it is moulded by God" (*TDNT,* VIII, 249; cf. 1 Thess. 1:4, 6). The same mighty grace of God that Paul experienced is to be the *hypotýpōsis* ("pattern" in the sense of prototype) for future believers (1 Tim. 1:16).

Another NT word for "example" is *hypogrammós,* derived from *gráphō* (to "write"). The term is rarely used but is found in Plato, where it refers to the "drawing of lines by the elementary teacher in order to guide children who are learning to write" (*TDNT,* I, 772); it can also be "an architectural outline or artist's sketch to be colored or filled in by others" (Selwyn, p. 179; cf. 2 Macc. 2:28). Hence it means a model or pattern to be copied, as in its only NT usage in 1 Pet. 2:21, which says that "Christ also suffered for you, leaving you an example, that you should follow in his steps." This means that Christ has left footprints through His sufferings, and that we must take these as models in the same way that a student learns by following the guiding lines of his teacher (*TDNT,* I, 773). The "footprint" image is also found in Rom. 4:12 in the use of the word *íchnos,* which literally means "footprint" but is used here in the figurative sense of following the example of Abraham's faith. Abraham, though dead, has left his "footprints" through his faith, the nature and reality of which we perceive and experience. These "tracks" that he left serve as markers for those to come, for both Jews and Gentiles. On the other hand, the graphic picture of judgment for lack of faith and for disbelief is found in the "example" (*deígma*) of Sodom and Gomorrah (Jude 7).

An "example" to be imitated is found in Jesus' words at the footwashing, "I have given you an example [*hypódeigma*], that you also should do as I have done to you" (Jn. 13:15). The "suffering and patience" of the prophets are the things to be imitated in Jas. 5:10, while in 2 Pet. 2:6 the destruction of Sodom and Gomorrah is again cited as a warning example of the results of disobedience.

In Col. 2:15 Christ is descibed as having "disarmed the principalities and powers and made a public example of them." Here the word *deigmatízō* (from *deíknymi*), meaning to "display in public boldly," signifies that Christ displays the conquered forces before the whole cosmos — possibly in the same way as the ancient victors displayed their captives as trophies in a triumphal procession before the people. Thus the true nature of inferiority and ultimate powerlessness of the conquered forces is exhibited.

Bibliography.–G. Lampe and K. Woolcombe, *Essays on Typology* (1957); E. G. Selwyn, *First Epistle of Peter* (1946); *TDNT,* I, *s.v.* γράφω (G. Schrenk); II, *s.v.* δείκνυμι (H. Schlier); III, *s.v.* ἴχνος (Stumpff); VIII, *s.v.* τύπος (L. Goppelt).

D. K. MCKIM

EXCEED; EXCEEDING; EXCEEDINGLY. The verb is used by the AV in the obsolete, intransitive sense of "overdo" in Job 36:9 for the hithpael of Heb. *gāḇar* (RSV "behaving arrogantly"; NEB "insolence and tyranny") and in 1 S. 20:41 for the hiphil of *gāḏal* (RSV "recovered himself"; NEB "was even greater than"). The versions differ in their interpretation of this term (*higdîl*). The usual meaning is to "make something (or someone) great"; the NEB takes it in a comparative sense in reference to David and Jonathan's grief while *CHAL* suggests "take courage" (p. 56). "Exceeding" (as an adverb with adjectives and rarely as an adjective) and "exceedingly" occur often as representing various expressions for the superlative in Hebrew and Greek.

EXCELLENT [Heb. *gāḏal*] (Isa. 28:29); NEB WONDERFUL; [Aram. *yattîr*] (Dnl. 5:12, 14; 6:3); NEB NOTABLE, PECULIAR, etc.; [Gk. *krátistos*] (Lk. 1:3; Acts 24:2; 26:25); AV MOST NOBLE; NEB EXCELLENCY; [*diaphérō*] (Rom. 2:18; Phil. 1:10); [*diáphoros*] (He. 1:4; 8:6); NEB FAR SUPERIOR; [*hyperbolḗ*] (1 Cor. 12:31); NEB SURPASSES; [*kalós*] (Tit. 3:8b); AV GOOD; **EXCELLENTLY** [Heb. *ḥayil*] (Prov. 31:29); AV VIRTUOUSLY; NEB CAPABLE.

Daniel is described as having an "excellent" spirit in him (Dnl. 5:12; 6:3) and being great or abundant in wisdom (5:14), as is also the Lord of hosts (Isa. 28:29).

In the NT *krátistos* is the official equivalent of the Latin phrase *vir egregius* ("most noble") and is used in addressing the procurator of Judea (Acts 24:2; 26:25). In Lk.1:3, however, "most excellent Theophilus" is a form of polite address used in dedications and has no official connotations implied (Bauer, p. 450).

In Rom. 2:18 and Phil. 1:10 Paul speaks of "approving what is excellent" (*diaphérō*), which in its absolute sense may mean "the things that really matter" as opposed to *adiáphora.* His audience in Corinth is shown a "far better way" (*hyperbolḗ*), one of "extraordinary quality," the way of love (1 Cor. 12:31–14:1). Christ has a more "excellent" name than the angels (He. 1:4) and His ministry far surpasses and is more outstanding (*diáphoros*) than any earthly ministry because of the superiority of the covenant He mediates (He. 8:6). The "good deeds" that Paul insists on in Tit. 3:8b are "excellent" in the sense of being morally good or beautiful, and they form a striking contrast to the senseless controversies and quarrels which are "unprofitable and futile" (*anōphelḗs* and *mátaios*) in Tit. 3:9.

The woman who does "excellently" in Prov. 31:29 is a woman of virtue who shows strength in mind and body.

D. K. MCKIM

EXCHANGE; EXCHANGER. *See* BANK; BANKING.

EXCITED [Gk. *throéō*] (2 Thess. 2:2); AV TROUBLED; NEB ALARM YOURSELF. The translation "excited" is acceptable if understood to mean "stirred by strong emotion" (*Oxford English Dictionary,* I [1971], 381), without, perhaps, the connotation of pleasurable anticipation. In the Synoptic Apocalypse (Mk. 13:3-37 par.), which has a number of similarities with Paul's caution in 2 Thess.

EXCOMMUNICATION

2:2f., *throéō* also appears (raising the question of Paul's familiarity with this material, or at least of a common background). There, the cause of this agitation is the rumor of war, justifying the translation "alarmed" (Mt. 24:6; Mk. 13:7; cf. Lk. 24:37, "startled," following var.).

The situation is more ambiguous in 2 Thess. 2:2f., depending somewhat on the meaning of "day of the Lord." If it means a complex of events, including wars, tribulation, and judgments, then fearful anxiety, alarm, or fright (cf. Bauer, p. 364) may be the dominant mood. If, however, it means primarily the parousia of the Lord (v. 1), then the believer might indeed have been beside himself with joy. The effect is the same, in any case: an unwarranted agitation of mind that interferes with the normal sobriety necessary for "standing firm" (v. 15) and distinguishing the real Christ from impostors (Mt. 24:5).

H. VAN BROEKHOVEN, JR.

EXCOMMUNICATION.

I. Definition.–Excommunication in its most general sense is the deliberate act whereby a group denies the privileges of its membership to those who were once members in good standing. As part of a broad range of social control that includes limited ostracism, temporary or permanent exclusion, and sometimes death, excommunication came in the Christian era to refer to an act of exclusion by which a religious community denies to offenders the sacraments, congregational worship, and possibly social contact of any kind. Such action is taken because of heresy, sin, or both. Although excommunication in its broadest sense is known from very early times, its purposes, penalties, procedures, and intended results within the Jewish and Christian religions have changed over the centuries. The distinct category of "excommunication" (Lat. *excommunicatio*) did not come into use until the era of the Christian Church.

II. Terms.–The OT includes no term specifically designating excommunication in its narrower sense. The OT vocabulary, however, does include many terms that would fall under the more general definition cited above: Heb. *ḥāram,* noun *ḥērem,* "banish, put to destruction" (e.g., Ex. 22:19; Lev. 27:28; Josh. 6:17), *'ālâ,* "curse" (Lam. 3:65), *kāraṯ,* "cut off" (Ex. 12:15, 19), *bā'ar,* "extirpate" (Dt. 13:6), *bāḏal,* "be excluded" (Ezr. 10:8), *'ārar,* "curse" (Mal. 2:2), *zā'am,* "curse" (Nu. 23:7f.), *nāḏa',* "cast out, banish" (Isa. 66:5), *qālal,* "declared cursed" (2 S. 16:5), *šammâ,* "desolation, thing of horror" (2 K. 22:19; Jer. 25:18).

The NT, likewise, contains not just one term for excommunication in the narrower sense, but a number of terms whose meanings fall within the larger sense of the term: Gk. *anáthema, anáthēma* (corresponding to Heb. *ḥērem*), "devoted, accursed" (Lk. 21:5), *katáthema,* "accursed thing" (Rev. 22:3), *katára, epikatáratos,* "curse," "accursed" (Gal. 3:10), *ará,* "curse" (Rom. 3:14; cf. Ps. 10:7), *aphorízō,* "exclude" (Lk. 6:22), *aposynagṓgos,* "expelled from the synagogue" (Jn. 16:2).

Because there is much overlapping of meaning in the original languages as well as in translation, extreme caution should be exercised in attempting to make distinctions on the basis of terminology alone. It is best to be content with determining the particular idea given in each specific context, rather than trying to draw distinct lines between excommunication and simple exclusion.

III. Rationale.–The basic rationale for excommunication was to protect the standards of the group: "a little leaven leavens the whole lump" (1 Cor. 5:6). This motive is clear in most biblical and extracanonical passages, but concern for the individual, even after expulsion, was the basis of Paul's pleas in 2 Cor. 2:7-10 and 2 Thess. 3:15 (but see also 1 Cor. 5:5).

IV. Causes.–Specific causes for excommunication fall into two categories: sin and heresy. Thirty-six OT offenses punishable by extirpation are summarized in the Mish. *Kerithoth* (<Heb. *kāraṯ,* "to cut off"). Examples include breaking the fast on the Day of Atonement (Ex. 12:15-19), sexual violations, and ritual impurities (Lev. 18:6-30). In the NT the author of 2 John authorized a limited form of ostracism for those who promulgated a heretical Christology (vv. 7, 9; cf. Gal. 1:8f.; 4:30), and the writer of 3 John was prepared to take action against Diotrephes, who not only was insubordinate and failed to practice hospitality, but was himself excommunicating those who did practice it (vv. 9f.). 1 Cor. 5:11 lists other reasons.

V. Procedures.–Procedures for excommunication within the various religious groups must have varied, but a general guideline was widely followed. Mt. 18:15-18, based on Jewish tradition, provided a series of steps the group was to employ before purging a recalcitrant sinner: personal confrontation, then two or three witnesses, then exposure before the congregation. Only if the offender acknowledged wrongdoing and still refused to repent was he or she to be excommunicated. Some NT writings allude to this cautious procedure (e.g., Lk. 17:3; Gal. 6:1; 1 Tim. 5:20; Tit. 3:10), but others suggest a speedier operation (Rom. 16:17; Gal. 1:8f.; Eph. 5:7). (The Qumrân community also followed the more cautious procedure [1QS 5:25–6:1].)

VI. Degrees of Punishment.–The Mishnah states that the court had the power to inflict four kinds of capital punishment: stoning, burning, decapitation, and strangulation (*Sanhedrin* vii.1). Stoning was the most common form in NT times (Jn. 7:58–8:11; Acts 7:58). Jesus was almost executed by being thrown off a cliff (Lk. 4:28-30). "Delivering to Satan" (1 Cor. 5:5; 1 Tim. 1:20) apparently involved some physical punishment, perhaps culminating in death (cf. Acts 5:5; 8:20; 13:11). The rigid OT penalties were later softened by the rabbis, who added conditions, exceptions, and degrees of punishments (see, e.g., *Kerithoth* i.2). Although "cutting off" could mean death, and is often so translated, the basic idea was separation from the community — as this term implies — rather than "execution." *See also* PUNISHMENTS.

Unless the offense was an unforgivable sin, usually blasphemy, excommunicants were expected to continue in piety and good deeds, with hope of restoration. (For a list of the procedures for restitution and unforgivable sins, see Buchanan, pp. 222-237). Paul (Gal. 6:1; 2 Thess. 3:15) and James (5:19f.) stressed a continuing concern for those put outside because of sin or false doctrine. Ignatius urged the Smyrnaeans to pray for those who should repent, but not to receive them (Smyrn. 4:1) until they did so.

VII. Authorization.–Numerous examples in the Torah, later Prophets, and Psalms show that God was the one who sent curses upon those who disobeyed the commandments (Dt. 27; Ps. 119:21) and otherwise broke the covenant (Mal. 2:2-9; 4:6 [MT 3:24]). But beginning in early times, the community assumed its responsibility for acting on God's behalf to reprimand or punish offenders within the group, sometimes by exclusion (see, e.g., Isa. 66:5; 1 Cor. 5:3). Balaam saw that his curses and denunciations were not automatically those that God would make: "How can I curse whom God has not cursed?" (Nu. 23:8). David, on the other hand, even though he was on the receiving end of Shimei's curses, assumed that the condemnations of his policies might well have come from the Lord; therefore he rebuked those who sought to silence Shimei (2 S. 16:5-14).

The authority to excommunicate was vested in the communiy and exercised by its leaders. Within normative Judaism the power was with the Sanhedrin in Jerusalem or with the elders of a local synagogue. At Qumrân the decision was made by the priests (1QS 5:25–6:1; Heb. *rabbim,* lit. "great ones"; the precise meaning, whether leaders only or all members in full standing, is debated). Jesus assigned the power of "binding and loosing" on earth and in heaven to Peter (Mt. 16:18f.) and the other disciples (18:18f.; Jn. 20:23). Paul assumed such authority among the churches he had established (Gal. 1:8f.; 2 Thess. 3:6, 14). He could also authorize a local church to excommunicate offenders in his absence (2 Cor. 6:10), but not all church leaders were so empowered. Timothy and Titus were not instructed to excommunicate, although both heretics and sinners were in their midst. They were simply to avoid controversy and lead exemplary lives.

VIII. In the Early Christian Community.–The early Christians knew of excommunication through their Jewish heritage before they themselves experienced such pressures from the synagogues (Lk. 6:22; Jn. 9:22; 12:42; 16:2). Whether such pressures were the direct result of Christian doctrine, or behavior resulting therefrom, is debated (see Hare, ch. 2). Later, Christians also struggled with the problem of sin after baptism and of the possibility of remaining in the community after a second offense (He. 6:4-6; Shep. Herm., esp. Vis. 2:2:5 and 3:5:4).

See also DISCIPLINE.

Bibliography.–G. Bornkamm, *TLZ,* 75 (1950), 227-230; G. W. Buchanan, *Consequences of the Covenant* (1970), pp. 305-313; G. Forkman, *Limits of the Christian Community* (1972); D. Daube, "*Repudium* in Deuteronomy," in E. E. Ellis and M. Wilcox, eds., *Neotestamentica et Semitica: Studies in Honour of Matthew Black* (1969), pp. 236-39; D. R. A. Hare, *Theme of Jewish Persecution of Christians in the Gospel According to St. Matthew* (1967), esp. ch. 2; J. Lawson, *Theological and Historical Intro. to the Apostolic Fathers* (1961). J. T. CLEMONS

EXCUSE [Gk. *próphasis*] (Jn. 15:22); AV "cloak"; [*paraitéomai*] (Lk. 14:18); NEB "please accept my apologies"; for the terms in Rom. 1:20; 2:1, 15, see below.

Statements in Luke (14:18f., 24), John (15:22; cf. 9:41), and Romans (1:20; 2:1, 15) together make it clear that people who reject God are judged to be without excuse. Such people cannot plead that they had received no invitation, for the invitation to the kingdom of God had come (Lk. 14:17); nor that the Son had not come to them, for He had both come and spoken (Jn. 15:22); nor that God was unknowable because He is invisible, for the fact of divine sovereignty (Gk. *dýnamis kaí theiótēs*) is clearly seen in God's works of creation (Rom. 1:20). Since none of these writings presupposes a comprehensive philosophy of religions, nor comparisons between religions, one is not justified in deducing from these early texts modern conclusions about "what happens to those who never heard of Christ." Rather, the function of each text in its context must be respected.

(1) The parable of the great supper (cf. Gospel of Thomas 64, perhaps closer to the earliest form of the parable) functions for both Luke (14:16-24) and Matthew (22:1-14) as a commentary on "the kingdom of God," as their introductions indicate. The invitation to come to the prepared banquet echoes Jesus' call to "repent, for the kingdom of God has drawn near" (Mk. 1:14).

The guests who were invited first (i.e., the "righteous" leaders) were excluded only by their own action of begging pardon for rejecting the invitation. The point of the parable is: the time of decision is now (Perrin), for God has made everything "ready," and that time cannot be deferred by trying to make excuses (Gk. *paraiteísthai*).

(2) In the upper-room discourse (Jn. 14–17) Jesus is presented as analyzing the world's hatred of both the Master and the servants (15:18-22). There is no *próphasis* for the sin of rejecting the light that came in the incarnate Word, or of unbelief in Jesus (cf. 16:9) "without a cause" (15:25; cf. Ps. 69:4 [MT 5]).

Because the Messiah had come and spoken to "them" (i.e., religious authorities who were hostile to Jesus), their subsequent "hatred" was in no way due to God. Both the making of excuses (the parable of the great supper) and the inability to find any valid excuse for rejecting the Messiah are, accordingly, part of the mystery of evil.

The consequent judgment comes, for the Fourth Gospel, not on Jews as Jews, but on any opposition to Jesus (Brown).

(3) In Romans the Greek expression *anapológētos eínai* ("be without excuse," "have no excuse") is used in 1:20; 2:1, and a form of *apologéomai* in 2:15 (AV "excusing" is better; cf. AV "we excuse ourselves" for *apologoúmetha* in 2 Cor. 12:19, where the RSV uses the concept of "defense" [as does the NEB in all three passages]).

Paul's charge of inexcusability provides no warrant for anti-Semitism. It is unrighteousness and ungodliness as such that are literally "without apology," for gentile (Rom. 1:20) and Jewish (2:1) opponents of God have acted alike (1:18; 2:1, 3).

What is inexcusable among non-Jews is stated in Rom. 1:21-23 (introduced by *dióti*): they did not glorify nor thank God, and they did make themselves out to be wise while actually concluding with empty thoughts, while exchanging the glory of God for shadowy images. But many non-Jews are doers of the law (2:14).

On the other hand, many Jews who have and hear God's law do not do it (Rom. 2:13, 17-24). So, when Jews follow falsehood rather than the truth and act with selfish ambition, their inexcusability likewise is met with God's wrath (2:8).

Why is there "no excuse"? There is no excuse for Jewish opponents because they have received the law and could have responded to God's will (Rom. 2:17f.). The reason that the gentile opponents have no excuse is less clear. Some interpreters have said it is because Gentiles have "natural theology" (Calvin, Brunner); but others have denied this (K. Barth, C. K. Barrett). Quite possibly this debate is about a false issue, arising from the premise, shared by Paul, of natural revelation. That revelation, no less than the law, has often been inexcusably misused.

Paul's thesis in the first main section of Romans (1:18–3:20) is, rather, that all people actually (objectively) are under God's sovereign will, whether or not they know it and respond to it. There is, as Lightfoot put it, "remarkable correspondence" between this part of Romans and Wisd. 13–15. The point established in Wisd. 13–15 is that idolatry is evil (in 13:1-9 the point is the uselessness of deifying nature). One would have to be a fool, one who does "not deserve to be excused" (13:8, NEB; LXX *oud' autoí syngnōstoí*), not to know the mere fact that God "really is" (13:1), and that He is "much better" and "much more powerful" than His works (13:3f.). Natural theology is not predicated thereby.

Paul similarly presupposes that there is, even outside the law given to Israel, an awareness of the God who "really is." There is, then, "no excuse" not to respond to this God, even though such awareness outside the law is never equated with the knowledge of God according to law. This Law shows what natural revelation does not, namely, God's kindness (Rom. 2:4), will (v. 18), knowledge and truth (v. 20), faithfulness (3:3), peace (v. 17), righteousness (v. 21), etc. Hence, Paul's mission continuously upheld the priority "to the Jew first and also to the Greek" (1:16; 3:2,29; 9:3-5; 11:1f., 17-24,29). But the inexcusability is shared by both those who have and those who have not received the law and who, in either case, reject God.

See also JUDGMENT, LAST.

Bibliography.–K. Barth, *Shorter Comm. on Romans* (1959), pp.24-41; C. K. Barrett, *Epistle to the Romans* (*HNTC*, 1957), pp.33-61; R. E. Brown, *Gospel According to John*, II (*AB*, 1970), 697f.; E. Brunner, *Revelation and Reason* (1946), pp.58-80; J. Calvin, *Comm. on the Epistle to the Romans* (new tr. 1960; repr. 1973); *Inst.* i.3f.; C. H. Dodd, *Parables of the Kingdom* (1936), pp.121f.; *Interpretation of the Fourth Gospel* (1953), pp.412-15; J. B. Lightfoot, *Notes on the Epistles of St. Paul* (1895; repr. 1957); N. Perrin, *Rediscovering the Teaching of Jesus* (1967), pp.110-14. J. G. GIBBS

EXECRATION [Heb. *ʾālâ*] (Nu. 5:21,27; Jer. 42:18; 44:12); AV also CURSE; NEB also ADJURATION. Though "execration" can refer to either a curse or the victim of a curse, it is used by the RSV only in the latter sense. Heb. *ʾālâ* is more often translated "curse." In Jeremiah "execration" is used to distinguish *ʾālâ* from another Hebrew word (*q^{e}lālâ*), translated "curse," which occurs in the same passage. *See* CURSE.

EXECUTE [Heb. *ʿāśâ* (Ex. 12:12; Nu. 5:30; 33:4; Dt. 10:18; 33:21; etc.), *nāqam* (Lev. 26:25; Nu. 31:3), *ḥāšaḇ* (2 Ch. 2:14), *šāpaṭ* (2 Ch. 20:12; 22:8; Ps. 75:7 [MT 8]; Isa. 66:16), *dîn* (Ps. 110:6; Jer. 21:12), *pāqaḏ* (Jer. 51:52), *ʿāḇaḏ* (Ezr. 7:26), *qûm* (Jer. 30:24); Gk. *poiéō* (Jn. 5:27; Rom. 9:28; Jude 15), *ékdikos* (Rom. 13:4)]; AV also AVENGE, DO, FIND OUT (2 Ch. 2:14), JUDGE, MAKE, PERFORM, etc.; NEB also "deal with," EXACT, MAINTAIN, JUDGE, PUNISH, etc. Used mainly of carrying out vengeance or justice. Heb. *ʿāśâ* and Gk. *poiéō* are very common verbs meaning "do" or "make"; the RSV renders *ʿāśâ* by "execute" about forty times. In 2 Ch. 2:14 the Hebrew term *ḥāšaḇ* refers to devising or inventing artistic designs. In Rom. 13:4 the rare noun *ékdikos*, "an avenger," is used of the governing authorities as they enforce the law.

EXECUTIONERS [Heb. *p^{e}quddôṯ*] (Ezk. 9:1); AV "them that have charge"; NEB "those appointed to punish." The OT has no special word for those who carry out a legal sentence of capital punishment. Ezk. 9:1 refers to officers in charge of the city who were appointed to carry out this sentence.

See also PUNISHMENTS.

EXEGESIS. *See* INTERPRETATION.

EXERCISE. As a verb this term is used ten times by the RSV with two different shades of meaning: (1) "to do," "to put into action," "to perform," as in Lev. 25:33 (Heb. *gāʾal*, "exercise the right of redemption"), Mt. 20:25 and Mk. 10:42 (Gk. *katakyrieúō*, "exercise authority"), Rev. 13:5 ("exercise [*dídōmi*] authority [*exousía*]"), etc.; (2) "to subject to training and discipline," as in 1 Cor. 7:9 and 9:25 (Gk. *enkrateúomai*, "exercise self-control").

The AV uses "exercise" in several ways that are now becoming obsolete; (1) to "take pains" (RSV), as in Acts 24:16 (Gk. *askéō*); (2) in the general sense of "to train," as, e.g., in 1 Tim. 4:7 (Gk. *gymnázō*).

EXHORT [Gk. *parakaléō*] (Acts 2:40; 11:23; 14:22; 15:32; 16:40; 20:1; Rom. 12:8; 1 Thess. 3:2; 4:1,10; 5:14; 1 Tim. 5:1; He. 3:13; etc.); AV also COMFORT, BESEECH, ENTREAT, omits in Acts 20:1; NEB also ENCOURAGE, APPEAL TO, URGE, etc.; **EXHORTATION** [Gk. *paráklēsis*] (Lk. 3:18; Acts 13:15; 15:31; Rom. 12:8; He. 12:5; 13:22); AV also CONSOLATION; NEB also ENCOURAGEMENT, STIRRING SPEECH, APPEALS.

The NT word for "exhort" is *parakaléō*, a word with various translations for its 103 uses in the NT (fifty-four in the writings of Paul). It can mean either "call" in the sense of "summon," "invite," "address," or "speak to" someone, the meaning then being dependent upon the nature of the call. This second sense is predominant in the NT with *parakaléō* meaning not only "exhort," but also "request" and "comfort." (*See* COMFORT.)

When the term is used for "exhorting," it refers to that urging and encouraging addressed to those of the community of faith which is "designed to lead them to conduct worthy of the Gospel" (*TDNT*, V, 795; cf. 1 Thess. 4:1, 10). It is more than just an appeal to morality, inasmuch as it has for its basis and presupposition the action of God in Jesus Christ for salvation. The acceptance of this offer of grace involves obligations for life and conduct. Paul's desire that his fellow workers be active in "exhorting" others (1 Tim. 5:1; Tit. 2:15) has led to speculation that perhaps there was even a *chárisma* ("gift") of pastoral exhortation in the early Church (cf. Rom. 12:8). Mutual exhortation in the community is desired also by the author of Hebrews (3:13). While some passages indicate no sharp, polemical, or critical sides to the exhortings (1 Thess. 3:2), other passages have surrounding terms and contexts that make it clear just how serious and urgent the exhorting is to be (1 Thess. 5:14; 2 Thess. 3:12; 1 Pet. 5:1).

That this exhorting played an important part in the life of the early Church is seen by the use of the word *paráklēsis*, meaning "exhortation." In Pisidian Antioch the rulers of the synagogue asked Paul and Barnabas if they had any "word of exhortation" for the congregation (Acts 13:15). The remarks that follow provide an example of the "word of exhortation," which was probably "a synagogue expression for the sermon which followed the Scripture lessons" (Bruce, *Acts*, p.261; cf. 1 Tim. 4:13). This is the same expression used by the author of Hebrews to describe the book's literary character (13:22), thus making it a kind of "homily in written form" (Bruce, *Hebrews*, p.413). The encouraging and comforting aspects of an "exhortation" are seen in the rejoicing of the congregation of Antioch when they received the letter from the Jerusalem Council (Acts 15:31) and in the words of wisdom of Prov. 3:11f. quoted in He. 12:5f.

Bibliography.–F. F. Bruce, comms. on Hebrews (*NICNT*, 1964), Acts of the Apostles (1951); *TDNT*, V, *s.v.* παρακαλέω (G. Stählin, O. Schmitz). D. K. MCKIM

EXILE. In the OT the most common term for "exile" is Heb. *gālâ* and its cognates (1 Ch. 5:22; Jer. 13:19; 29:1; Ezk. 12:3; etc.). One cognate is *gālûṯ* (2 K. 25:27; Ezk. 1:2; Am. 1:6; etc.), which has the same meaning as *gôlâ* and can refer either to exile (Ezk. 1:2; 12:11) or corporately to those who had been exiled (Jer. 29:20,22). In preexilic OT writings *gôlâ* is applied to peoples other than Israel and Judah (cf. Isa. 20:4; Jer. 48:7; Nah. 3:10; etc.), though it most commonly refers to Assyrian or Babylonian deportations. The verb *gālâ* refers only once to a non-Israelite people (Am. 1:5), otherwise alluding to Israel (2 K. 15:29; 17:11; etc.) or Judah (2 K. 24:14; Ezr. 2:1; etc.). Synonymous in meaning with *gālâ* is *šāḇâ*, "carry off captive" (Ezk. 6:9), while *$š^{e}$ḇî* and *šiḇyāṯ*, both meaning "captivity," "captives," are synonymous with *gôlâ* (Dt. 32:42; Ezr. 2:1; 35c). *See* CAPTIVITY. In Ezr. 6:16 Aram. *gālû* occurs in reference to "those taken into exile." In the LXX, Gk.

aichmalōtízein and *metoikízein* with their cognates are used to render *gālâ* and its cognates.

NT writers varied equally in their use of terms. *Metoikízein* occurs in Acts 7:43 ("take into exile"; NEB "banish"), while the concept of exile itself is rendered by such terms as *metoikesía* (Mt. 1:11f., 17; NEB "aliens"), *aichmatōsía* (Rev. 13:10; NEB "made prisoner"), and *paroikía* (1 Pet. 1:17; NEB "your time on earth"). An exile is designated in Acts 7:29 (NEB "settled") and 1 Pet. 2:11 (NEB "aliens") by the term *pároikos*. The dispersion consequent upon exile is referred to in Jn. 7:35; Jas. 1:1; 1 Pet. 1:1.

R. K. HARRISON

EXIT [Heb. *môṣā'*] (Ezk. 42:11; 43:11); AV GOING OUT; [*tôṣā'ôṯ*] (Ezk. 48:30); AV GOING OUT; NEB WAY OUT. An outlet from the temple (42:11; 43:11) or city (48:30) described in Ezekiel's vision. In 42:11 the RSV emends the MT *kōl môṣā'êhen* (AV "all their goings out") to read *k^e môṣā'êhen* (lit. "like their exits").

EXODUS, BOOK OF.

I. Introduction
  A. Name
  B. Outline of Contents
  C. Connection with Other Pentateuchal Books
II. Composition of Exodus
  A. Critical Theory
  B. Weaknesses of Graf-Wellhausen View
  C. Composition in the Light of Ancient Scribal Practices
  D. Authorship and Date
III. Historical Criticism of Exodus
  A. The Deliverance from Egypt
  B. The Covenant at Sinai
  C. The Wilderness Tabernacle

***I. Introduction.**–A. Name.* The second book of the PENTATEUCH was known to the Jews by the designation *w^e'ēlleh š^emôṯ* ("and these are the names"), sometimes abbreviated to *š^emôṯ*, taken from the opening words. This designation was familiar to Origen in the form *Oualesmoth*. The LXX, however, entitled the book according to its main theme (Ex. 19:1), this being followed by the Vulgate (*Exodus*) and the English versions.

B. Outline of Contents. The book is extremely valuable in preserving the link between the historical material of the Genesis narratives and the later history of the people of Israel. The sequence of events is of prime importance to the Hebrew concept of history, and Exodus is of fundamental significance for the manner in which it depicts the historical basis for the existence of Israel as the chosen people of God.

The contents can be broken down into three broad divisions:

I. Events Leading to the Exodus (chs. 1–11)
  A. Preliminary Genealogy (1:1-6)
  B. The Bondage in Egypt (1:7-22)
  C. Early Days of Moses (2:1-10)
  D. Later Life of Moses (2:11–4:26)
  E. Israel in Bondage (4:27–6:13)
  F. Genealogical Table (6:14-27)
  G. Moses and Aaron Encounter Pharaoh (6:28–7:25)
  H. The Ten Plagues (8:1–11:10)
II. The Exodus and the Journey to Sinai (chs. 13–19)
  A. The Passover Instituted (12:1-28, 43-50)
  B. The Tenth Plague and the Withdrawal from Egypt (12:29-42, 51)
  C. Regulations about Firstlings and Unleavened Bread (13:1-16)
  D. Preparations for Complete Withdrawal (13:17-22)
  E. The Exodus Accomplished (14:1-31)
  F. Song of Moses (15:1-21)
  G. The Wilderness of Shur (15:22-27)
  H. The Wilderness of Sin (16:1-33)
  I. Editorial Gloss (16:34-36)
  J. Occurrences at Rephidim (17:1-16)
  K. Jethro and Moses (18:1-27)
  L. Moses at Sinai (19:1-25; 20:18-21)
III. The Legislation at Sinai (chs. 20–40)
  A. The Decalogue (20:1-17)
  B. The Covenant Code (20:22–23:33)
  C. The ratification ceremony (24:1-8)
  D. Moses' return to Sinai (24:9-18)
  E. The tabernacle specifications (25:1–27:21)
  F. The Tabernacle Ministry and Ritual (28:1–31:11, 18)
  G. Sabbath enactment (31:12-17)
  H. The golden calf incident (32:1-35)
  I. God and Moses at Horeb (33:1-23)
  J. A second recording of the covenant (34:1-35)
  K. A brief sabbath enactment (35:1-3)
  L. Sanctuary offerings (35:4–36:38)
  M. Ark and tabernacle furniture constructed (37:1–38:31)
  N. Preparation of priestly garments (39:1-43)
  O. Erection of Tabernacle (40:1-33)
  P. The Guiding Cloud (40:34-38)

C. Connection with Other Pentateuchal Books. Ex. 1:1-7 connects the history of the people as found in Exodus with the family history of Genesis by narrating how the seventy descendants of Jacob who had migrated to Egypt (cf. Ex. 1:5; Gen. 46:27) had come to be the people of Israel, and that the God who offers Himself as a liberator to Moses and the people is also the God of those fathers of whom Genesis spoke (cf. Ex. 3:6, 13, 15f.; 4:5; 6:3). His covenant with the patriarchs and His promises to them are the reasons why He cares at all for Israel (2:24; 6:8; 33:1), and when Moses intercedes for the sinful people his most effective motive is found in God's promises made to the patriarchs (32:13).

As is the case with Genesis, Exodus stands in very close connection with the succeeding books of the Pentateuch. Israel is certainly not to remain at Sinai, but is to come into the Promised Land (3:17; 6:8; 23:20-26; 32:34; 33:1-3, 12-17; 34:11.; cf. also the many ordinances of the Books of the Covenant, 21–23; 34:11-26). In this way the narratives of the following books, which begin again in Nu. 10:11ff. with the story of the departure from Sinai, continue the history in Exodus. But the legislation in Leviticus also is a necessary continuation and supplement of the book of Exodus and is prepared for and pointed to in the latter. The erection of the altar of burnt offering (27:1-8; 38:1-8), as well as the mention of the different kinds of sacrifices, such as the sin offering and the burnt sacrifices (29:14, 18), and of the wave offering (29:28), point to the promulgation of a law of sacrifices such as we find in Lev. 1–7. The directions given in regard to the consecration of the priests (Ex. 29) are carried out in Lev. 8–9. The indefinite commands of 30:10 in reference to the atonement on the horns of the incense altar once every year render necessary the special ritual of the Day of Atonement in Lev. 16 as a supplement. The more complete enlargement in reference to the showbread mentioned in 25:30 is found in Lev. 24:5-9; and even the repetitions in references to the candlesticks (Ex. 25:31-40; Lev. 24:1-4; Nu. 8:1-4), as also the *tāmîḏ* ("continuous") sacrifices (cf. Nu. 28:3-8 with Ex. 29:38-42), point to a certain connection between Exodus and the following books. The close connection between Deuteronomy and Exodus, in regard both to the historical narratives and to their legal portions (cf. the Decalogue and the Books of the Covenant), will be examined subsequently.

II. Composition of Exodus.–A. *Critical Theory.* The literary criticism of Exodus has for long been linked with that of Genesis and the other pentateuchal writings (*see* PENTATEUCH; CRITICISM II). The criteria for such activity, as furnished by Astruc (1753) and developed with certain modifications by a succession of scholars including Eichhorn, Geddes, Hupfeld, Graf, and Wellhausen, consisted primarily of the variants of the divine name used in Genesis. In his attempts to resolve supposed chronological confusion in the MT and set the material in proper order, Astruc postulated several underlying literary sources or "documents." All passages that used the tetragrammaton YHWH were assigned to a J(ahwistic) document, while those in which the common designation Elohim occurred were credited in a similar manner to an E(lohistic) document. Subsequent literary-critical speculation produced a P(riestly Code) source (which at first was thought to be early but under the influence of Wellhausen was assigned to the postexilic period) and finally a D(euteronomistic) document, consisting predominantly of the canonical book of Deuteronomy. At this point it must be emphasized that J, E, and P are purely hypothetical "documents" whose existence has never been even remotely demonstrated by any adherent of the literary-critical theory. Astruc, in fact, had some reservations about the validity of his criteria, but despite whatever circulation these reservations were given, they were swept aside by nineteenth-century European scholars in their eagerness to develop an "evolutionary" hypothesis of pentateuchal literary growth. It is only recently that the erroneous postulates and methods employed in such source-analysis have been recognized and exposed for their inadequacy and inaccuracy. Consequently there are few contemporary liberal scholars who would care to identify themselves in every respect with the complexities of the literary analysis of Exodus as postulated in the heyday of the Graf-Wellhausen theory of pentateuchal origins. Indeed, even at that period, there was considerable difference of opinion as to where the alleged underlying "documents" began and ended, and this constituted a tacit recognition of the fact that, on any basis of literary criticism, the book of Exodus exhibits a remarkable compositional unity and is therefore considerably more difficult to analyze than might be the case for other pentateuchal material.

As late as 1956, however, Eissfeldt was insisting that there was at least one other documentary source for the Pentateuch that up to that time had eluded the best efforts of the literary critics to isolate. To meet this deficiency he gathered up all those fragments that had not already been marshalled into one "document" or another and claimed that they belonged to an L or Lay source. J. Morgenstern claimed to have found a less exotic source styled as the K(enite) document, which comprised the story of the life of Moses, containing details of the Sinai covenant and its supplementary legislation.

B. Weaknesses of the Graf-Wellhausen View. While these are discussed at greater length in the article PENTATEUCH, some of the more important deficiencies may be referred to here. Perhaps the most significant is that the entire literary-critical theory was based on a priori intellectual considerations, whereby it assumed without reference to objective criteria the validity of certain antecedent postulates and then proceeded to make the facts as contained in the MT agree with them. What was undoubtedly one of the more embarrassing results of this procedure was its description in nineteenth-century literature as "scientific."

Regrettably for the OT literary-critical speculators of nineteenth-century Europe, their activities gave no indication whatever of the basic knowledge or application of scientific method. Since they felt no need to concern themselves with external evidence, the followers of Astruc, Hupfeld, and Graf paid no attention whatever to the increasing corpus of archeological material that was being amassed by contemporary antiquarians. Instead of inquiring into the methods employed by ancient Near Eastern scribes in compiling their material, the Graf-Wellhausen school preferred to indulge in literary-critical speculations that had absolutely nothing in common with the Near Eastern methods of literary transmission but that, in accordance with the spirit of the age, were dominated by a strictly evolutionary character. One result of this view was the notion that all material passed through long interludes of oral transmission before being committed to writing, a view that leaned heavily upon theories of the origins of European literature. In contrast, more recent studies in Near Eastern scribal methods have shown that anything of significance was written down within a very short period after the event itself and that the primary use of oral tradition was for disseminating material that was already in written form.

Because of their a priori approach, the exponents of the documentary theory showed markedly little respect for the MT and felt at liberty to make whatever textual emendations and rearrangements were thought desirable to make the Hebrew text conform to their theories of origins. Some enterprising analysts would extract a few words from the middle of a verse already credited to one "document" and quite arbitrarily assign them to another of supposedly quite different provenance. Thus, not a little discredit accrued to the various analytical schemes because of the wide range of disagreement regarding the contents of the "documents," along with the fact that the various literary sources were incapable of the slightest degree of factual demonstration.

Probably the greatest weakness of the literary-critical approach, however, is its almost complete divorce from factual reality as experienced in the ancient Near Eastern life-setting, a fact that has been demonstrated amply by modern archeological discoveries. The criterion of the divine names (about which even Astruc entertained some doubts, as remarked above) has now been shown to be entirely invalid as a basis for postulating pentateuchal documentary sources. There *are* genuine literary sources for the pentateuchal writings, of course, but they are quite different in nature from those formulated by nineteenth-century European scholars (*see* GENESIS). The doublets and repetitions taken by the literary-critical school as indications of diverse documents are now known to have been a regular part of ancient Near Eastern compositional activity. Finally, form-critical studies in Genesis give clear indications that the bulk of the book consisted of ancient historiography, patterned along Mesopotamian lines and united with the Joseph narratives to form the completed canonical work. These studies, which are supported by archeological discoveries from Mari, Nuzi, and elsewhere, deal the death-blow to any European theory of subjective and rather fragmentary "documents" based upon the tightly-restricted use of one or other of the divine names and committed to writing many centuries after the events that they described.

C. Composition in the Light of Ancient Scribal Practices. It will be necessary in attempting to indicate the possible means by which Exodus was compiled to draw to some extent upon what is now known about literary and scribal practices in the 2nd millennium B.C. As indicated above, a great many Near Eastern literary sources such as annals

EXODUS, BOOK OF

and court histories show that events of any significance were recorded at the time they occurred or shortly thereafter. This was one result of the comparatively high degree of literacy in the ancient Near East, as contrasted with the virtual illiteracy of early European nations, which consequently had to depend to an embarrassing extent upon campfire bards for the preservation of national sagas and other topical material.

The assumption by Graf, and especially Wellhausen, that writing came into use only about 1000 B.C., at the beginning of the Iron Age, and was therefore not available to Moses, was one of the tragic results of ignoring already extant factual material in the form of ancient Near Eastern inscriptions. It is now known that writing was one indication of culture in the Orient from at least 3500 B.C. onward, and archeological discoveries in Canaan have shown that in the Late Bronze Age (*ca.* 1550-1200 B.C.) the native population employed a linear alphabetic script, an indigenous cuneiform language (Ugaritic), and a syllabic script used at Byblos in Phoenicia. In addition, Babylonian cuneiform was the *lingua franca* of the age, as demonstrated by the Amarna Tablets, while Egyptian hieroglyphic writing had also been in use in the ancient Near East for many centuries.

In the light of this evidence it is impossible on any basis of reasoning to deny the existence of writing in the Mosaic period or to doubt the validity of the Hebrew tradition which ascribed literary activity to Moses and other Hebrew personages in the Late Bronze Age. As far as contemporary writing materials are concerned, the most readily accessible for the wandering Hebrews, and by far the most permanent, would have been the hides of slaughtered animals, suitably prepared to receive writing. According to Jewish tradition the Torah was originally written on leather scrolls in an early angular Phoenician script, which was replaced only in the days of Ezra by the square or Aramaic script used in modern printed editions of the Hebrew Bible (cf. T.B. *Sanhedrin* 21b). It is certain that leather rolls would have been much more accessible during the wilderness wanderings than papyrus, which in any event would have disintegrated quickly once it was removed from the dry Egyptian climate, and would have been far more desirable than stone blocks, which would have been too cumbersome for easy handling or transporting. The Dead Sea Scrolls show how the scribes of antiquity stitched pieces of leather together in order to form a roll of suitable length.

While the actual mechanics of the compilation of Exodus are, of course, unknown, it may be possible in the light of current information concerning Near Eastern scribal practices to suggest the process by which the canonical work was composed. As a basis for the work the compiler would have access to the Decalogue (20:1-17) and the Book of the Covenant (20:22–23:33), the latter perhaps in a shortened form, as well as the songs composed by Moses and Miriam. In addition there would be available the various regulations relating to sabbath observance and the instructions for the fashioning of the tabernacle. The detailed nature of the various moral and ceremonial regulations would suggest that they were written down at, or shortly after, the time of their promulgation, in accordance with ancient Near Eastern scribal practice. Even if the songs of Moses and Miriam were still in oral form, they also would be in written form by the time the compiler had finished his work. Since, however, in the view of the present author the songs were delivered orally and committed to writing within the same generation, any time lapse between the two stages of transmission would be negligible.

The book was compiled against the background of its principal theme of deliverance, but enough historical material was introduced as a preface to the actual departure of the Hebrews from Egypt to preserve a proper sense of historical continuity. Since the sequence of events was the prime consideration in Hebrew historiography, questions of strict chronology or the identification of specific foreign personages such as the Egyptian pharaohs were relegated to a somewhat secondary position, to the disadvantage, unfortunately, of the modern student. However, the Exodus scroll began with 1:1-17, a section that linked the work with Genesis by the simple expedient of identifying the enslaved peoples. The insertion of a list dealing mainly with the ancestry of Moses and Aaron helped to ground these individuals firmly within Hebrew historical tradition, and at this point the first section (1:1–6:28) ended. A rather better chronological picture might have been preserved had the material of 6:14-27 been inserted after 4:26, but as indicated above, strict chronological considerations were not of paramount significance to Hebrew historians. The list of names is very similar to the Genesis genealogical tables, some of which may have been written on the back of the tablets that, in the view of the present writer, formed the original, genuine literary sources of that book (*see* GENESIS). Lists of this kind have been recovered in abundance from Mari, Nuzi, and other sites in Mesopotamia. While the Exodus material does not conform to the general pattern as closely as its Genesis counterparts, 6:26-28 is quite similar in character to the typical colophon of Mesopotamian tablets, in which the owner (or scribe) of the material was identified ("this Moses . . . this Aaron") and some scribal attempt at dating was generally made ("on the day when the Lord spoke to Moses in the land of Egypt"). Probably Ex. 6:10-13 and 6:28–7:7 indicate the end of one leather roll and the beginning of another, since the similarity of the two passages would enable the second to be read intelligently yet independently of the first. A similar relationship exists between 2 Ch. 36:22f. and Ezr. 1:1-3a, where the former is used as a rather lengthy "catch-line" in the traditional Mesopotamian manner, with the intention of ensuring the proper continuity of the narrative.

Any attempt to understand the processes of compilation of Exodus must necessarily be conjectural. But if it is legitimate to suppose that the book was written on leather, as suggested above, a new piece of scroll would have been added after 6:29. This would then carry the narrative material to 12:28, where there appears to be some dislocation of the text. In such an event, 12:43-50 may have come originally after 12:18 in order to preserve the general continuity. Ex. 13:1-16 is also somewhat displaced as far as the order of events is concerned, but would have been inserted at that point because of its priestly characteristics. Another portion of the scroll would commence at 13:17-22, where there is some overlapping with 12:37-41 similar to that noticed above in connection with 6:10-13 and 6:28–7:7. The narrative then continued to the events at Sinai and the Decalogue (20:1-17), but whether or not all this was contained on one piece of leather scroll is impossible to say. The Covenant Code (20:22–23:33) may well have had an independent existence at one point, or else was in circulation in conjunction with the Decalogue (20:1-17), if the remarks in 24:4 are a credible record of contemporary happenings. Ex. 20:18-21 would form the introduction to a new section of scroll that continued to 24:18.

At 25:1 occurs the beginning of a corpus of material dealing with the tabernacle and the regulations relating to its use. This was oral in form originally and, following

Exodus 29:41–30:23b in the oldest extant Torah codex (*ca.* A.D. 900) (Trustees of the British Museum)

ancient Near Eastern scribal practice, was committed to writing very soon after it was received, not least because of its fundamental importance for Israel's religious life. This material terminated at 31:11, 18, with vv. 12-17 perhaps constituting a dislocation from 31:1-3. The general historical narrative was resumed with 32:1 and carried on without interruption to 34:28. The remainder of the book was written on one piece of leather, since it is an unbroken account of how the instructions for the building of the tabernacle were implemented.

The entire roll was concluded somewhat in Mesopotamian fashion by a colophon, dealing with the finished tabernacle and the guiding cloud (40:36-38), a theme picked up later in Nu. 9:15-23. From 34:27 it would appear that the enactments of 34:11-26 may have had an independent existence at one period, and these, along with the Decalogue and Covenant Code, would comprise some of the original literary sources employed by the compiler in assembling the appropriate portions of the Exodus scroll. On any basis of literary criticism the delineation of sources in Exodus is an extremely difficult task, as scholars in an earlier generation discovered. While the foregoing suggestions are based upon current knowledge of scribal methods in the Amarna Age and later periods, it must not be imagined that they necessarily depict even approximately the method by which the book was originally compiled.

D. Authorship and Date. Liberal scholars generally have been unanimous in their repudiation of the traditional Mosaic authorship of Exodus, although in recent years increasing numbers of them have been prepared to allow the antiquity of specific elements in the "documents" that they regard as constituting the underlying sources of the work. Classic liberalism assigned little if any of Exodus directly to Moses himself, preferring to think instead of literary sources that, while going back in a general manner to the Mosaic period, actually appeared in writing no earlier than the 9th cent. B.C., and that were intermingled with postexilic priestly material to form the basis of the extant work.

That this position is by no means wholly uniform for contemporary liberals has been shown by the willingness of Albright and others to assign a date in the Late Bronze Age to the songs of Moses and Miriam (15:1-18, 21). Furthermore, archeological discoveries have demonstrated the antiquity of specific formal elements in the legal institutions of Israel, and this again has won acceptance in liberal circles. Thus, the Covenant Code (20:22–23:33) is now known to contain a legal tradition reflected in the Sumerian Code of Eshnunna, the legislation of Hammurabi, the Hittite law code, and the enactments from Assyria. While none of the above codes is characterized by exactly the same conditions of society as any other, there is a common element of jurisprudence in these Near Eastern codes, described by Alt as "casuistic" law, and this element occurs also in Exodus. This type of formulation commenced with a conditional clause, stated the case, and outlined the penalty to be described. Another characteristic element of Exodus that also has early Near Eastern parallels is the covenant, which as a theological compact must obviously have had some precursor in secular jurisprudence. This antecedent has now been discovered in the Hittite suzerainty treaties from the Late Bronze Age, the nature of which is discussed below. But even the demonstration of the antiquity of specific elements of Exodus has been insufficient to shake the faith of many liberals in the comparatively late date of the final form of Exodus.

In a reaction against the Graf-Wellhausen theory, Pedersen suggested that Ex. 1–15 comprised the nucleus of the whole Pentateuch, and that it was in effect cultic material forming a separate integrated unit that celebrated God's victory over Egypt at the Reed Sea (*ILC,* III-IV, 726ff.). While this view had the undoubted merit of relating the central theme of Exodus to the religious life of Israel, it seemed to ascribe its provenance to community rather than to individual activity and gave little indication concerning the time when the material achieved definite literary form. In the light of the oral-tradition concepts of the Uppsala school, it suggested that the text had experienced a prolonged history of transmission after having originated in cultic (presumably priestly) circles whose connection with Moses could not be established with certainty. Von Rad postulated a similar origin for Ex. 20–24 in his liturgical interpretation of that material (*Gesammelte Studien zum AT* [1958], pp. 9ff.). For him the Sinaitic tradition arose from a cultic festival that was marked by certain characteristic liturgical acts such as exhortation, the recitation of the law, and the promise of blessing. Again, certain anonymous cultic officiants were credited with originating and perpetuating this material, which in its final form was thought to be of comparatively late date. A rather incidental connecting of the Exodus event with the person of Moses was made by Noth (*History of Pentateuchal Traditions* [Eng. tr. 1972], pp. 38ff., 173f.) in an attempt to study Exodus by the "history of tradition" method. But even this was based upon the supposed literary sources for the book as adduced by earlier European scholars, and while certain fundamental themes were held to be enunciated in Exodus, the traditions were really viewed as the property of the amphictyonic Israelites during the judges period and consequently had little, if anything, to do with Moses and his age.

All such reconstructions of alleged sources imply some kind of oral transmission of the material involved. While this concept may well be true of certain isolated elements such as the songs of Moses and Miriam, it is by and large a remarkable assumption in the light of the fact that the MT repeatedly mentions writing and written records. It is even more curious that such oral transmission supposedly continued for many centuries before literary fixity was accomplished, despite clear Near Eastern evidence to the contrary. For those scholars who ascribed little, if anything, of Exodus to the activities of Moses, the extant composition was, in effect, a retrojection of later customs and traditions to the Mosaic age (S. R. Driver, *Book of Exodus* [*CBSC*, 1953 reprint], p. lxv). Enthusiastic nineteenth-century representatives of literary criticism were accustomed to claim that narrators in different generations embellished the narratives in an imaginative manner, so that by the time the compilers of the supposedly underlying "documents" came to their task, the oral tradition from which they worked had become heavily overlaid with miraculous material — much of it, as far as the book of Exodus was concerned, associated in a rather dubious manner with the man Moses. In many quarters serious doubts were entertained with respect to the historicity of Moses, and these have persisted in various forms to the present time (*see* MOSES). There are doubtless plausible reasons why liberal scholars have neglected to take the person of Moses seriously, but it is still true that, in the light of modern archeological knowledge of Egypt and Canaan in the Late Bronze Age, the man Moses is long overdue for historical rehabilitation.

Another institution described in Exodus that was relegated to a late date by Wellhausen and his followers was the tabernacle. This arbitrary position meant that any material dealing with this topic was necessarily of a late date also, since for many nineteenth-century critics the tabernacle as described in Exodus was unhistoric, being instead a simple retrojection to the Mosaic age, on the part of postexilic priests, of traditions connected first with the Solomonic temple. (This position will be discussed in greater detail below.) It seems, therefore, that whatever variations from nineteenth-century liberal orthodoxy have been entertained by later scholars, they have encompassed approximately the same conclusions regarding authorship and date as the earlier views. This has occurred because many writers have held the same assumptions regarding the alleged "documents" that underlie the finished composition.

Those scholars who espoused the Mosaic authorship of Exodus regarded the views of the literary critics as in effect postulating the essentially fraudulent nature of the composition. Conservative scholars were the first to make proper use of archeological evidence in substantiating their case for overall Mosaic authorship of Exodus, in contrast to the nineteenth-century critics who, ignoring archeological discoveries, preferred instead to appeal to late Arabic customs if possible. More recent conservative investigators have combined a knowledge of literary artifacts and scribal transmissional techniques current in the Bronze Age with form-critical studies of Genesis to isolate a series of tablets that give every appearance of comprising the genuine underlying literary sources of that book (*see* GENESIS). This kind of literary analysis absolutely precludes the existence of "documents" such as J, E, and P.

Conservative scholars have generally recognized that Exodus was not written originally as a continuous narrative and that there was probably some editorial activity brought to bear upon the material, possibly even in the immediate post-Mosaic age. It should be noted that the scribes of antiquity, with the exception of the Sumerians, regularly revised earlier literary material and made such changes in orthography, grammar, and syntax as would update it. Explanatory glosses and other relevant additions were frequently inserted by scribes without any prejudice at all to the integrity of the original authorship. Because the scribes of Near Eastern nations were uniformly some of the most responsible elements of the population and pursued their craft along accredited disciplinary lines, editorial activity of the kind mentioned could seldom do anything but enhance the original composition by making the ancient national traditions and literature meaningful for the current generation.

The view that Moses compiled or dictated the bulk of Exodus is based partly upon the biblical report that committing events directly to writing was a part of the regular activity of Moses. This again is in complete harmony with what is known about ancient scribal activity and is therefore an unexceptionable presupposition for authorship by the celebrated Hebrew leader of important sections of the extant Exodus. Moses is credited specifically with a brief document dealing with divine judgment on Amalek (17:14), which would have been in written form shortly after the occurrence if ancient scribal practices were being followed at the time. The resultant book (*sēper*) would then correspond to the "annals" written by the scribes of all the major Near Eastern nations, in which by ancient tradition all the memorable events of the particular period being surveyed, especially if they reflected favorably on the nation, were written down for posterity. Other documents in Exodus attributed directly to Moses are the Book of the Covenant (20:22–23:33; 24:4-8) and the material dealing with the restoration of the covenant (34:27; cf. 34:10-26). Elsewhere in the Pentateuch he is credited with the compilation of statutes (Dt. 30:10), legal enactments (Dt. 24:1), details of the Israelite wanderings (Nu. 33:2), and the words of the victory paean (Dt. 31:19, 22).

Persons other than Moses were also occupied in making records during this period, including priests who wrote down curses (Nu. 5:23) and names of objects (Nu. 17:3). Moses was helped in his literary activities by *šōṭerîm,* or literate officials (Nu. 11:16; AV, NEB, "officers") of recognized standing in the community. Because these men were able to record decisions, they played an important role in the entire judicial process (cf. Dt. 16:18; 1 Ch. 23:4) and probably recorded much of the material as Moses dictated it. With this kind of secretarial assistance and the existence of a basic source-residuum (consisting of the Decalogue and Covenant Code, the songs of Moses and Miriam, the enactments relating to sabbath observance, and the detailed specifications for the tabernacle), it would undoubtedly be possible for Moses, or some person such as Joshua or Eleazar under the direction of Moses, to have compiled Exodus in substantially its present form during Moses' lifetime or immediately after his death. The historiographic method employed, as noted above, preferred to cover the general trend of events rather than to depict a precise chronological sequence. Leather would probably be the material used for the purpose of containing the written record, and would certainly be the most readily available substance in the wilderness.

In the light of this general compositional procedure it will be readily recognized that post-Mosaic and even non-Mosaic additions could be present in the extant book. Since, however, it was considered a normal function of scribes who were editing and revising earlier material to explain, modify, and even supplement the text at hand without impairing the original authorship, it will be seen that the possibility of post-Mosaic insertions raises no real problems with regard to the Mosaic authorship of the extant composition. One commonly alleged post-Mosaic element is 6:26f., where it has been supposed that one would write in that fashion only of deceased persons. However, the verses in question follow a genealogy and comprise a colophon that means: "this is the genealogy of Moses and Aaron to whom God spoke." When 6:26 is compared with 6:14, it carries precisely the same force as v. 27 compared with v. 13, thus raising immediate doubts as to whether in fact 6:26f. is post-Mosaic. Ex. 16:33-35, which mentions the "testimony," is actually referring to the covenant tablets, which had not yet been given to the people if the strict succession of events is being followed. Despite this, there is nothing in the passage being considered that would preclude its insertion in the Exodus scroll during the lifetime of Moses, especially if the book were compiled at a later rather than at an earlier stage in his career. If later than Moses, however, it is possible that Ex. 16:33-36 comprised an editorial explanation of the manna phenomenon that was designed for the understanding of later generations. Even this, however, does not require a date later than the time of Samuel. The explanatory gloss represented by 16:36 has been thought to indicate a time of composition when the value of the comparatively rare word *ʿōmer* had been forgotten. The term occurs only in that chapter in the MT, but in such a manner as to make its significance as a measure and as a measured quantity immediately evident to anyone who understood the phenomena of the wilderness wanderings. Ex. 11:3 would appear *prima facie* to present greater difficulties, since Moses could hardly be expected to have described himself as being of impressive stature in Egyptian society. But even here little prevents this from being a typical marginal gloss that was incorporated into the text at a later stage.

Having regard to the nature of scribal activity in the ancient Near East, the greatest caution is necessary before authoritative pronouncements are made about supposedly non-Mosaic material in Exodus and other Pentateuchal books. It is no longer necessary to urge that the use of the third person militates against direct Mosaic authorship, since this procedure was common a millennium or more after the Mosaic era, occurring, e.g., in the writings of Xenophon and Caesar. The practice finds OT support in prophetical literature of persons such as Isaiah (20:1-4) and Ezekiel (24:24).

In view of the above considerations, then, the ancient tradition that credited Moses with a substantial amount of literary activity is supported by what is now known of scribal practices in the Bronze Age. Furthermore, the fact that certain characteristic Israelite institutions had significant elements in common with contemporary secular forms would seem to point to the coordinating activity of an outstanding leader of the people, which again is in accord with ancient Hebrew tradition. When the biblical data are reviewed in the light of the objective evidence now available, the most logical explanation of the provenance and date of Exodus is that the work is a product of the Late Bronze Age and was most likely compiled by Moses from contemporary written and oral sources with the assistance of certain priests and the *šôṭᵉrîm*. The finished product was, of course, amenable to the normal processes of later scribal revision, as mentioned above.

III. Historical Criticism of Exodus.–*A. The Deliverance from Egypt.* The function of historical criticism is to establish as far as possible the historicity of the events and personages under consideration in a given area of the biblical record. Where extrabiblical sources such as annals, inscriptions, and monuments testify directly or indirectly to the historic nature of the people and happenings mentioned in the OT, they obviously confirm the record of the MT and serve as valuable supplements to the biblical narratives.

While many OT books have been illumined in this manner, the general period covered by the age of Moses exhibits little in the way of specific correlation between secular Egyptian records and the scriptural text. That particular time was one of Egyptian preoccupation with the restoration of the national greatness of earlier days after the embarrassment of the Hyksos occupation during the Second Intermediate Period (*ca.* 1780-1570 B.C.). During this cultural renaissance known as the New Kingdom period (*ca.* 1570-1150 B.C.), in which Egypt once again exercised an important military, economic, and social influence in the Near East, the work of Moses can be placed with the greatest degree of historical accuracy. This assessment is based, among many other factors, on the interval of 430 years (Ex. 12:40; cf. Gen. 15:13) that occurred between the entry of Jacob and his family into Egypt at *ca.* 1700 B.C. and the rise of a pharaoh who "did not know" (Ex. 1:8) the achievements of Joseph during the Hyksos period (*see* CHRONOLOGY OF THE OT). Characteristic of the unnamed pharaoh was the cultural reaction of the New Kingdom period, which set about the deliberate physical and mental obliteration of anything connected with the hated Hyksos. This wave of nationalism, which reached its height in the 18th Dynasty in the later Amarna period, would naturally take no official cognizance in annals or inscriptions of a person such as Moses once his Hebrew ancestry was discovered. The absence of extrabiblical information about Moses has been one factor in the vagueness of many modern liberals about the historicity and work of Moses, but against this must be reckoned the uniform testimony of Hebrew tradition as concerning the towering stature and fundamental importance of this man as the founder of normative Hebrew law.

Egyptian archeology has yielded a vast amount of background information for the life of Moses without actually corroborating the biblical record about him at any specific point. There is ample evidence for the royal harems of the New Kingdom period, the educational system of that time, life in the Egyptian courts, and the social conditions existing in the 13th cent. B.C. The name "Moses" is evidently a play on the verb *māšâ*, "draw out," but may also have a superficial relationship to the Amarna-age word for "child" (*ms*[*w*]). Since the pun is Semitic rather than Egyptian in form, it suggests that the name was originally given by Moses' natural mother and not by one of the harem princesses who subsequently adopted him. Excavations at Tell el-Retabah uncovered what was believed to be the ancient city of Pithom, and the recovery from the massive brickwork there of "bricks without straw" such as were manufactured by the captive Israelites (Ex. 1:14; 5:7f.) seems to lend historical dimensions to the Hebrew account of the captivity in Egypt. The store-city known to the Hebrews as RAMESES (Ex. 1:11) was possibly ancient Tanis (Zoan). Rameses was the capital city of the 19th Dynasty and originally the capital of the Hyksos rulers also, which Ramses II enlarged considerably. Since Exodus uses the name by which the city was known only for a period of two centuries (*ca.* 1300-1100 B.C.), it is highly probable that the Hebrew tradition dated from this time. In passing it should be noted that the corporal punishment endured by the captive Hebrews adds an authentic if unfortunate touch to the situation, since this was standard procedure in ancient Egypt for encouraging progress in any kind of work (C. H. Gordon, *Intro. to OT Times* [1953], pp. 130f.) and was applied without discrimination to native peoples and foreigners.

According to Papyrus Anastasi III, it was not uncommon for the people of Rameses to present petitions to Pharaoh Ramses II (P. Montet, p. 71) and therefore not surprising that Moses should also be able to do this, particularly if the pharaoh of the Exodus were Ramses II. Egyptian ostraca recording the absences of workmen have also been recovered from this period (A. Erman, *Life in Ancient Egypt* [1894], pp. 124f.), one source mentioning certain workmen being away from their tasks in order to present offerings to their gods. That the Hebrews were able to make a similar request without arousing popular resentment (Ex. 8:26f.; 10:9, 25f.) is thus thoroughly in accord with the contemporary situation.

Historical criticism of the plagues in Egypt encounters the difficulties associated with the factual demonstration of any historic natural phenomenon. No account of the plagues has been recovered from Egyptian sources, so that the description in Exodus furnishes the only information about the situation. Recent studies have helped to confirm the actuality of the plagues and have shown the accuracy with which the phenomena were reported. The first nine plagues are now seen to have followed in sequences on the basis of an unusually high inundation of the Nile, commencing in July-August. The chronology of the Exodus account would point to the termination of the plagues the following March (G. Hort, *ZAW*, 69 [1957], 84-103; 70 [1958], 48-59). The final plague, being supernatural in nature, is naturally not amenable to historical demonstration.

The place where the actual departure from Egypt occurred is difficult to locate, if only because the construction of the Suez Canal altered the appearance of the landscape in the area of the papyrus marsh mentioned in Ex. 13:18. This locality, rendered "Red Sea" in many translations, is probably the "Papyrus Lake" mentioned in the Egyptian Anastasi III papyrus as the source of papyrus for the city of Rameses. Since papyrus is a freshwater plant, it is not found in the salty Gulf of Suez, nor for that matter in the brackish waters of the Bitter Lakes or Lake Timsah. Most likely the "Reed Sea" was located E of Rameses in an area that may now be covered by part of Lake Menzaleh (*see* RED SEA).

The date of these events is one of the most perplexing matters in OT chronology, and archeological discoveries have so far failed to resolve the problems presented by the two principal conflicting views (*see* CHRONOLOGY OF THE OT; EXODUS, DATE OF THE). The suggested dates differ by over 150 years and each can be supported to some extent by the OT records. The earlier date places the Exodus at the time of Thutmose III (*ca.* 1504-1450 B.C.), while the later one regards it as falling within the reign of Ramses II (*ca.* 1290-1224 B.C.). The fifteenth-century date rests in part on a chronological note in 1 K. 6:1, which mentions that the Solomonic temple was started in the 480th year after the Exodus. If Solomon is to be dated *ca.* 971-930 B.C., the Exodus would have occurred about 1441 B.C. Excavations undertaken by J. Garstang at Jericho purported to indicate that the city fell before 1400 B.C. (*Joshua-Judges* [1931], p. 146) and showed that diplomatic contact with Egypt ceased under Amenhotep III. According to Garstang the Exodus occurred in the time of Amenhotep II (*ca.* 1436-1422 B.C.). The mention of marauding Ḫabiru in the Amarna Tablets was equated by some other scholars with the conquests of the Hebrews under Joshua, and the disturbances reflected in the letters were regarded as a native Canaanite version of the Israelite conquest of Palestine.

A thirteenth-century-B.C. date was based in part on Ex. 1:11, which implies that the Hebrews were enslaved when Pithom and Rameses were being enlarged, thus making Seti I or Ramses II the pharaoh of the Israelite oppression. A stele recovered from Tanis and dated *ca.* 1320 B.C. states that the city had been founded four hundred years earlier. Since most scholars identify Pi-ramses with a site at or near ancient Tanis, the Hyksos capital, it is not difficult to associate the Exodus with the Avaris era on the basis of such references as Ex. 12:40 and Nu. 13:22. More recent archeological work at Jericho by K. Kenyon has compelled a modification of Garstang's conclusions by showing, among other things, that his "City D" went back to about 2300 B.C., and that the walls that he discovered had no relevance for Joshua's campaign (*see* JERICHO II). Unfortunately, the site (Tell es-Sulṭân) has been so denuded by a variety of agents that it is virtually impossible for archeologists to say anything accurate about Jericho during the 15th to 13th cents. B.C. A more critical study of the Amarna correspondence (see above) has shown that the Canaanite princes loyal to Egypt were appealing for help against the mercenary troops (Ḫabiru) employed by neighboring city-states as a means of self-aggrandizement. Since as few as fifty, and in one case ten, Egyptian soldiers were requested to strengthen Canaanite defensive forces, the repulsing of a concerted attack by large and determined forces of Hebrew invaders can scarcely have been envisaged. Furthermore, while the reference in 1 K. 6:1 when taken at face value would indicate a fifteenth-century-B.C. date, it may not be a factual number so much as a symbolic one, indicating a cycle of twelve generations consisting of forty years each and related consciously to the activities of the Hebrew tribes.

While these and other difficulties indicate the complexity of the problems associated with the date of the Exodus, it is quite possible that future discoveries in Egypt or Canaan will go far towards resolving one of the major issues in OT chronology.

B. The Covenant at Sinai. The mighty acts of God

demonstrated in the phenomena of the Exodus and the deliverance of the Israelites from captivity in Egypt formed a preliminary to the establishment of a spiritual covenant between God and the Hebrews (*see* COVENANT). This relationship elevated the Hebrew tribes to the status of an elect people, bound to the God with whom they had entered into a solemn agreement not merely by religious ties but by specific legal obligations. The idea of a pact or treaty binding contracting parties to agreed terms was familiar to the Hebrews (cf. Gen. 21:27; 26:28; 31:34; 1 S. 18:3; etc.), but the Sinai covenant was unusual in that it constituted a proposal initiated by a Divine Ruler who, in revealing Himself to a particular people, demanded their obedience to the terms that He was proposing and their continuing loyalty as His servants. This type of association has been greatly illumined by a study of second-millennium-B.C. suzerainty treaties as recovered principally from Boghazköy. So close are these secular treaties to the OT traditions of the Sinaitic covenant in their general form and more specific items of content that the parallels cannot possibly be accidental in nature. The Hittite suzerainty covenants were established between a great king and an inferior power on which he wished to impose a political alliance. A brief analysis of the overall form, accompanied by the appropriate Exodus references to indicate the characteristic internal elements common to both, will illustrate the similarities.

Suzerainty treaties of the 2nd millennium B.C. commenced with a title or preamble in which the instigator of the covenant was identified (cf. Ex. 20:1). This was followed by a historical prologue recapitulating any previous relations between the contracting parties in order to secure the vassal's acceptance and submission for the future (cf. 20:2). Then came the stipulations imposed by the overlord, of both a general (20:3-17, 22-26) and detailed (chs. 21–23; 25–31) nature. Hittite treaties required the deposit of a copy of the covenant in the chief shrine of the vassal (cf. 25:16) in order to guarantee its preservation. Lists of gods were regularly invoked in the secular international treaties as witnesses to the covenant, but because pagan deities were obviously precluded by the nature of the Sinai covenant, memorial stones could serve equally well (cf. 24:4). Blessings and curses invoked upon the vassal in the text of the secular covenants, to become operative according to whether the treaty was kept or broken, do not actually occur in Exodus, but are represented clearly in Dt. 28:1-14 (blessings) and 28:15-68 (curses). The book of Deuteronomy is itself, of course, a covenant-renewal document (*see* DEUTERONOMY). The solemn ratification and oath-taking ceremony prominent in Hittite treaties is paralleled by Ex. 24:1-11.

This type of covenant formulation differed from Hittite treaties of the 1st millennium B.C. in that in the latter the historical prologue was consistently omitted and the curses were not balanced by corresponding blessings. These and other factors indicate clearly that the form of the Sinaitic covenant corresponds to that of international treaties of the late 2nd millennium B.C., as Mendenhall (*BA*, 17 [1954], 56, 61) and others have shown, indicating that it could have originated in the 15th or 13th cent. B.C. (cf. K. A. Kitchen, *Ancient Orient and OT* [1966], pp. 90ff.).

The Sinai covenant furnished a nucleus about which Israelite historical tradition could develop, and for this reason it was of fundamental importance for all future national growth. It also provided the means of transmitting legal terminology into theological language, thereby providing the Israelites with an assured metaphysic of history. In conformity with secular treaties, which contained a clause regulating modes of procedure against rebellious vassals, the so-called controversy pattern of the Sinai covenant enabled God, through His spokesmen the prophets, to arraign His people in subsequent generations for breaking the provisions of the agreement. The entire relationship between God and Israel was based upon a free demonstration of divine grace that had ransomed captive Israel from bondage and promised protection, prosperity, and guidance for the future. As was fitting, the agreement was established upon a proper legal basis, the significance of which would be immediately apparent to all informed people in the 13th cent. B.C. Its acceptance by the Hebrews made them unique in antiquity for their endeavors to interpret all national life in terms of a solemn covenantal agreement with a single, living deity.

Brief mention should be made of the probable content of the Book of the Covenant read at Sinai by Moses when the divine agreement with Israel was ratified. Its description as a "book" (*sēper*) denotes its existence in written form, since that term was never used to describe oral tradition. Most likely it at first comprised only the Decalogue (Ex. 20:2-17), though in scholarly circles it has long been the practice to refer to Ex. 20:22–23:33 as the "Book of the Covenant." It is the oldest extant codification of Hebrew law, containing elements of civil and criminal legislation, humanitarian prescriptions, and ritual regulations. Its nature is such that it could easily have been modified or amended during the period immediately after the death of Moses as circumstances warranted, without doing the slightest violence to the concept of Mosaic authorship. Thus Ex. 22:18f., 31; 23:1 may be later scribal insertions that could conceivably date from the early judges period. The legislation included "precedents," which appeared as case-law, and "statutes," which assumed the form of prohibitions. As noted above, the case-law or casuistic form is the dominant one known from ancient Near Eastern law codes. In the Book of the Covenant it is expressed initially as a conditional clause that then states the case and concludes with the prescribed penalty. The "statutes," sometimes described by scholars as "categorical" or "apodictic" in nature, consist of specific prohibitions, which, however, do not carry any stated form of implementation. A related variety also occurring in the Book of the Covenant commences with an active participial form and concludes with the emphatic prescription "(he) shall surely be put to death."

Earlier critical scholars had imagined that the agricultural and community legislation in Exodus presupposed a date of origin not earlier than the time of Samuel. It is too often forgotten, however, that the Israelites at Sinai were already the inheritors of four centuries of agricultural and pastoral experience in a highly fertile area of the Nile delta and that they had never been a nomadic people in the sense of the modern bedouin Arabs. Such a situation would make a date of the 15th to 13 cent. B.C. for the Book of the Covenant eminently suitable, whereas a considerably later date would involve making conjectures or retrojections that would be out of harmony with the wilderness milieu of the book. In short, there was absolutely no need for the Hebrews to have been settled in Canaan for some centuries before such laws and regulations could have been promulgated.

The principle on which the laws in the Book of the Covenant were arranged is not clear. As noted earlier, the case-laws have points of contact with other Near Eastern bodies of jurisprudence, while at the same time pointing to a consistently less sophisticated life-style. Some scholars have suggested that the Covenant Code can be divided into ten sections, each of which has to do with the concerns of one of the commandments to comprise a "running midrash" to the Decalogue (cf. E. Robertson, *The OT Problem* [1950], p. 95), but this is at best uncertain.

C. The Wilderness Tabernacle. Chs. 25–31 deal with the regulations for constructing and equipping a portable shrine that would serve as the focus of congregational worship and the place where divine guidance could be received. The literary sources describing this structure were held by Wellhausen to have been nothing more than an idealization of the Solomonic temple and as such were historical fiction. The materials were regarded as the product of a postexilic priestly writer and thus did not emerge from the Mosaic age in any significant respect. Archeological discoveries have done much to modify this extreme view, however, by showing among other things the antiquity of portable tent-shrines in the Near East. Early prefabricated structures from Egypt include the magnificent portable bed canopy of Queen Hetepheres I (*ca.* 2600 B.C.), whose beams and rods were so fashioned as to enable rapid assembly and dismantling, as with the Hebrew tabernacle. The prevalence of such canopies in Egypt between 2850 and 2200 B.C. is indicated by the number of sculptures from the 4th to 6th Dynasties that displayed them, as well as by the recovery of fragments of canopy poles from a royal tomb of the 1st Dynasty at Saqqara (cf. K. A. Kitchen, *Tyndale House Bulletin,* 5-6 [1960], 8ff.). The cultic use of a tabernacle was familiar to the people of Ugarit, as indicated in one of the cuneiform texts (*Legend of Krt,* 159), which in an age of roofed houses spoke of the king as performing certain rituals in a tent, while the fragmentary Phoenician histories of Sanchuniathon (*ca.* 7th cent. B.C.) made reference to a portable shrine drawn by oxen. The concept of the tabernacle as a palladium was by no means restricted to the Hebrews, since the Egyptians regularly took on their military campaigns a sacred shrine that was stationed in the middle of the camp and was used for consultations with the deity. A bas-relief from the time of Ramses II, *ca.* 1285 B.C., depicts a scene in which the tent of the divine king is stationed in the middle of the Egyptian military encampment. Another interesting structure of an even older nature was the third-millennium B.C. Egyptian "Tent of Purification," where the corpses of deceased royalty and high government officials were deposited before and after embalming. Old Kingdom representations of these portable structures show that they were made from a framework of vertical pillars linked with horizontal bars and surrounded with hangings of cloth.

Although liberals have objected that the Hebrews of that age did not possess the skills necessary for constructing a tent of the kind described in Exodus, numerous Egyptian tomb scenes consistently depicted the Hebrews as skilled workers in precious metals (cf. D. J. Wiseman, *Illustrations from Biblical Archaeology* [1958], p. 34 fig. 29).

In view of this and other evidence it is entirely unwarranted to deny either the antiquity or the historicity of the Hebrew tabernacle or to assume that the tabernacle represented an end product of postexilic priestly cultic speculation. Instead, the wilderness tabernacle must now take its legitimate place as a genuine Hebrew cultic phenomenon of the 2nd millennium B.C., fulfilling the purposes and objectives described in connection with it by the narratives of Exodus.

Bibliography.–*Comms.:* B. Baentsch (1903); G. Beer and K. Galling (1939); B. S. Childs (*OTL,* 1974); S. R. Driver (1953 reprint); H. Holzinger (1900); A. H. McNeile (1908); M. Noth (*OTL,* 1962); J. C. Rylaarsdam (*IB,* 1952).

Intros.: A. Bentzen (1941); S. R. Driver (1912); R. K. Harrison (1969); R. H. Pfeiffer (1941); A. Weiser (1961); E. J. Young (1954).

Supplementary Literature: W. F. Albright, *BASOR,* 58 (Apr. 1935), 10-18; D. M. Beegle, *Moses, the Servant of Yahweh* (1972); M. Bietak, *Tell el-Dab'a II* (1975); J. J. Bimson, *Redating the Exodus and Conquest* (1978); F. M. Cross, *BA,* 10 (1947), 65ff.; J. Finegan, *Let My People Go* (1963); K. M. Kenyon, *Digging Up Jericho* (1957); *Archaeology in the Holy Land* (rev. ed. 1979); *Bible and Recent Archaeology* (1978); T. J. Meek, *Hebrew Origins* (1950); G. E. Mendenhall, *Law and Covenant in Israel and the Ancient Near East* (1955); P. Montet, *Egypt and the Bible* (Eng. tr. 1968); J. A. Motyer, *Revelation of the Divine Name* (1959); M. Noth, *Das System der zwölf Stämme Israels* (1930); *History of Pentateuchal Traditions* (Eng. tr. 1972); G. von Rad, *Moses* (1960); M. Reisel, *Mysterious Name of Y.H.W.H.* (1957); H. H. Rowley, *BJRL,* 34 (1952), 81ff.; C. de Wit, *Date and Route of the Exodus* (1960); *WBA.*

R. K. HARRISON

EXODUS, DATE OF THE.

- I. Introduction
- II. Egyptian Evidence for Thirteenth-Century Date
  - A. City of Raamses
    1. Tanis
    2. Qanṭîr
  - B. Political History of 19th Dynasty
    1. Ramses II's Wine-Jar Sealings
    2. Ramses II's Transjordan Campaign
    3. Ramses II's Hittite Treaty
    4. Form of Mosaic Covenant
  - C. Objections
    1. City of Raamses
    2. Political History of 19th Dynasty
       - a. Ramses II's Wine-Jar Sealings
       - b. Ramses II's Transjordan Campaign
       - c. Ramses II's Hittite Treaty
       - d. Form of Mosaic Covenant
    3. Historical Evidence
       - a. Ramses II and Merneptah
       - b. Seti I and Ramses II
- III. Fifteenth-Century Date
  - A. Biblical Evidence
  - B. Egyptian Evidence
    1. Thutmose I
    2. Hatshepsut
    3. Thutmose III
    4. Amenhotep II
    5. Thutmose Son of Amenhotep?
    6. 'Apiru
  - C. Objections
    1. Chronology
    2. City of Raamses
    3. Archeology

I. Introduction.–The date of the Exodus is one of the most debated topics in OT studies because of the ambiguous nature of the evidence. Although the biblical texts seem to require a date in the middle of the 15th cent. B.C., archeological evidence seems to point to a date in the 13th cent. B.C. (*see* CHRONOLOGY OF THE OT III.B; ISRAEL, HISTORY OF THE PEOPLE OF III). Merneptah's "Israel" stele (*ca.* 1220 B.C.) fixes a date before which the Exodus occurred, since it mentions Israel, as a people, among names that otherwise refer to places (cf. K. Kitchen, pp. 59f.; *see* picture in ISRAEL). Thus Israel was established in Canaan by at least 1220 B.C.

II. Egyptian Evidence for Thirteenth-Century Date.–*A. City of Raamses.* Exodus 1:11 indicates that the Israelites built Raamses (usually spelled "Rameses") for the pharaoh of the oppression. The stele of Merneptah indicates that Israel already was settled in Palestine early in his reign. Only two pharaohs preceding Merneptah bore the name of Ramses, and Ramses I was not very significant since he reigned less than two years. Ramses II, however, ruled Egypt from 1290 to 1224; he was a great builder whose

Granite statue of Ramses II (1301-1234 B.C.) wearing the double crown of Upper and Lower Egypt and holding the flail and scepter (Trustees of the British Museum)

monuments are known throughout Egypt. Papyrus Anastasi III describes his royal residence city of Pi-ramses, located in the delta. If the reference to this city in Ex. 1:11 is related to this information from Egypt in a straightforward manner, Ramses II should be connected in one way or another with the events of the oppression and the Exodus. Thus the archeology of this site might offer some assistance in deriving the date of the Exodus if the site has been located correctly and excavated.

1. Tanis. A sizable number of monuments from the Hyksos kings and Ramses II has been recovered at Tanis (P. Montet, *Les Nouvelles fouilles des Tanis* [1934]; *Le Drame d'Avaris* [1940]). It is generally agreed on the basis of Egyptian evidence that Pi-ramses occupied the site of the earlier Hyksos capital of Avaris, so Hyksos monuments are to be expected there (P. Montet, *RB,* 39 [1930], 1-28). The presence of such objects at Tanis does not confirm its identification with Pi-ramses, however, because not one of them was found in its original location; rather, they were taken from their original locations and brought to this site to be used as building materials. There is no archeological evidence *in situ* for the occupation of Tanis in the second half of the 2nd millennium B.C. before the time of the 21st Dynasty, *ca.* 1100 B.C. Inscriptions date the foundation of the inner wall of Tanis to the 21st Dynasty and its outer wall to the 22nd Dynasty. No palace has been found there yet and its excavator Montet admits that no evidence is available with which to date the temples of Tanis as early as Ramesside times.

Egyptian textual evidence concerning Pi-ramses indicates that it was situated on the waters of Ra, which have been identified with the Pelusiac or easternmost branch of the Nile. Tanis, however, was located on the Tanitic branch, the next branch W of the Pelusiac. Pi-ramses was also located "at the forefront of every foreign land." Tanis was an important port but it was poorly situated to serve as a place from which to leave for Asia by land. Papyrus Anastasi III praises the fertility of the fields around Pi-ramses, but the land around Tanis is low and often flooded from the sea, so that it consists primarily of infertile salt flats.

Thus the literary evidence relating to Pi-ramses does not accord well with Tanis, and there is no architectural and stratigraphic evidence for its existence prior to the 21st Dynasty. If the biblical Rameses was located at Tanis, then according to this archeological evidence the Exodus could not have taken place before the 21st Dynasty, more than a century after Merneptah's reference to Israel in Palestine.

There is also some biblical evidence that the Raamses of Ex. 1:11 was not located at Tanis. When the Israelites left Egypt they started out from "Rameses" (Ex. 12:37). No bridges crossed the branches of the Nile in the delta in ancient times. Therefore, if the Israelites traveled E from a Rameses located on the Tanitic branch, they still would have had to cross the Pelusiac branch. This would have posed a considerable problem for a sizable group of people accompanied by herds and flocks. Thus Tanis must be rejected as the site of the Egyptian Pi-ramses. The last reason for this rejection requires a site located on the east bank of the easternmost branch of the Nile. That leads to a consideration of Qanṭîr.

2. Qanṭîr. Since 1930 various studies have suggested that Qanṭîr was Pi-ramses (e.g., M. Hamza, *Annales du service des antiquités de l'Égypte,* 30 [1930], 31-68). Recent examinations of the literary evidence relating to Pi-ramses have concluded that it should be located in the vicinity of Qanṭîr (cf. J. Van Seters, E. Uphill [*JNES,* 27], and M. Bietak). The fertility of the fields around Qanṭîr, its location on both the land and sea routes to Asia, the existence of a palace of Ramses II there, and the geographical divisions of the city and its surrounding regions all correspond to the literary references to Pi-ramses.

Just S of Qanṭîr is Tell el-Dabʿa. The occupation of this site under the 12th and 13th Dynasties was brought to an end with a violent destruction. Three Hyksos strata or building phases follow this destruction and the city enlarged progressively through these three periods. The third and last Hyksos stratum was brought to an end with a violent destruction which has been connected with the conquest of Lower Egypt by the early 18th Dynasty. The 18th Dynasty appears to have left this site unoccupied (Bietak, p. 25), but it was rebuilt under the 19th Dynasty.

These archeological findings lend support to the reasons advanced above for identifying Qanṭîr and its immediate vicinity with the Hyksos capital of Avaris and with Pi-ramses, the delta residence of Ramses II. Since the 19th Dynasty is represented here and the 18th Dynasty is not, these findings seem to support a 19th-Dynasty (thirteenth-century) date for the Exodus.

B. Political History of the 19th Dynasty. 1. Ramses II's Wine-Jar Sealings. To support his date of *ca.* 1290 for the Exodus, W. F. Albright called attention to the sharp reduction in wine-jar sealings from this time found in the Ramesseum at Thebes (*Yahweh,* p. 156). Since earlier Egyptian tomb reliefs depict ʿApiru (Egyp. *ʿpr.*) or HABIRU working in the vineyards of the northeastern delta, and since these Ḫabiru have been connected in part with the biblical Hebrews, the departure of the large number of Hebrews could have left these vineyards largely untended and caused a sharp drop in the production of wine. Albright connected this departure with a revolt by Egypt's Asiatic dependencies which called for Ramses' campaign of Year 8.

2. Ramses II's Transjordanian Campaign. The only text of historical significance from the second decade of Ramses' reign is the stele from Beth-shean in Palestine that is dated to his 18th year (Schmidt, p. 36; *see* picture in INSCRIPTIONS). An inscription from the Karnak temple (cf. K. Kitchen, *JEA,* 50 [1964], 47-70) indicates that Ramses II campaigned in Moab. His previously known inscriptions indicate that he also campaigned in Edom, which he referred to as Seir in the land of the Shasu bedouin (cf. R. Giveon, *Les Bédouins Shosou des documents égyptiens* [1971]). Geographically his campaigns in Moab and Edom probably should be linked together as parts of the same campaign. This Transjordanian campaign is best dated to Year 18 because his targets on the preceding four campaigns from Year 4 through Year 10 were located in Lebanon and Syria. Ramses probably crossed the Sinai peninsula on the central route through Kadesh-barnea. If the Exodus occurred shortly before this time, that would have put Ramses II in the very territory where the Israelites were wandering before they went around Transjordan. Given this course for this campaign, one could regard part of this mission as a search for the escaped Israelite slaves.

3. Ramses II's Hittite Treaty. Support for dating the Exodus *ca.* 1290 might be drawn from an unusual feature of the covenant between Ramses II and the Hittite king Ḫattusilis III. This treaty was inscribed on the walls of both the Karnak temple and the Ramesseum. A Hittite copy of it is known, also (*ANET,* pp. 199-203). Of the four main stipulations in this treaty, the first, second, and fourth apply similarly to the Egyptian and Hittite kings.

The third stipulation incumbent upon Ramses II was that, in the event of an irregularity in the succession to the Hittite throne, he was to support — evidently by force of arms if necessary — the successor designated by Ḫattusilis. Ḫattusilis became king by deposing his nephew Mursilis III (Urkhi-Teshub) and installing himself upon the throne. He obviously wanted to insure that his designated successor would not have similar problems and enlisted the aid of Ramses toward that end. The third stipulation incumbent upon the Hittite king was that, in the event that Ramses' "own subjects" committed "another crime against him," the Hittite king would come to his aid in suppressing such a disorder.

This third stipulation is extraordinary and can be attributed to the exceptional conditions of that time. In the case of the Hittite king that condition was his own irregular accession to the throne. In the case of the Egyptian king that condition appears to have involved a recent "crime" committed by his subjects against him. The evident distinction between the foreign territories of the pharaoh in the second stipulation and "his own subjects" in Egypt in the third stipulation appears to be quite intentional. The use of the word "another" modifying the word for crime in the third stipulation also appears to be intentional (cf. J. Schmidt, p. 133).

This treaty dates to the twenty-first year of Ramses II. Ramses was preoccupied with Asia during the first decade of his reign, campaigning there in his fourth, fifth, eighth, and tenth years according to his dated inscriptions. Given the tendentious nature of royal inscriptions of ancient Egypt, no direct reference to the Exodus is to be expected from them. If the Exodus took place at this time, its setting can be sought only through veiled Egyptian references to events that correspond satisfactorily with those events described in the Bible. Unfortunately for such a search, the second decade of Ramses' reign is largely unknown (cf. Schmidt, p. 170).

In spite of this paucity of sources, the situation presupposed by the third stipulation of Ramses' treaty with the Hittites could be viewed as providing just such a veiled reference to these biblical events. The departure of the Israelite slaves could have been viewed by the pharaoh as a crime. The severity of the "crime" perpetrated by Ramses' subjects shortly before the treaty of Year 21 was of such a magnitude that he was willing to appeal to a foreign potentate for assistance to prevent a recurrence. The biblical description of the events surrounding the Exodus appears to reach this level of importance from the Egyptian point of view. At least it comes at the right time to accord with Albright's date for the Exodus.

4. Form of the Mosaic Covenant. A sociological point in the context of the Exodus can be made from the present knowledge of the Hittite treaty form used in Egypt at that time. This particular treaty refers to two previous Egyptian-Hittite treaties, the earlier of the two dating to the middle of the preceding century. These are parity treaties, in which the two great kings treated each other essentially as equals. The other type of covenant known from the Hittites is the suzerainty type, used by Hittite kings to make vassal treaties with the kings of smaller states. G. E. Mendenhall noted that there are a number of significant resemblances between the Mosaic covenant of the Bible and the suzerainty covenants of the Hittites (*BA,* 17 [1954], 24-46; 50-76; *see* COVENANT [OT]). These resemblances could be most easily explained if Moses was in Egypt during the 13th century.

C. Objections.–1. City of Raamses. The Bible does not employ the name of Ramses with the same chronological specificity with which it is employed in Egyptian texts. This is evident from Gen. 47:11, which refers to the "land of Rameses" as that part of Egypt in which Jacob and his descendants settled. Since no one dates the arrival of the biblical patriarchs in Egypt in the time of Ramses II of the 19th Dynasty, the use of the name Ramses here must represent the modernization or updating of an older name for that region. If the name of Rameses was used in this way in Gen. 47:11, it could have been used similarly in Ex. 1:11. Thus the mere presence of the name of Ramses in Ex. 1:11 cannot be the final arbiter of the date of the Exodus.

2. Political History of the 19th Dynasty. The political conditions cited above as a possible historical context for the Exodus early in the 13th cent. are not sufficiently specific to confirm that date for it. They only provide a potential historical situation for it.

a. Ramses II's Wine-Jar Sealings. The reduction in wine-jar sealings at Thebes may have occurred because the wine was shipped elsewhere. These sealings continued at a low rate there for the next four decades, and it seems improbable that the wine industry of Egypt did not recover for more than four decades after the Israelite workers in the vineyards were supposed to have departed.

b. Ramses II's Transjordanian Campaign. Ramses may have conducted his campaign through Transjordan and Sinai in order to pacify his eastern flank prior to concluding his treaty with the Hittites, not to pursue any escaped Israelite slaves.

c. Ramses II's Hittite Treaty. Ramses' allusion in the Hittite treaty to a crime by his subjects could just as well have referred to a conspiracy or revolt by native Egyptians as to an Exodus of Israelites.

d. Form of the Mosaic Covenant. Moses' knowledge of Hittite treaties is a general feature that could be applied to earlier times as well.

3. Historical Evidence. Beyond the nonspecific nature of the preceding suggestions, some problems with dating the Exodus in the 13th cent. arise when the history of this period is examined from the biblical point of view. These problems have to do with the pharaohs involved: the pharaoh of the oppression, who died while Moses was in exile (Ex. 2:23), and the pharaoh who died during the Exodus (Ex. 14:23-28; cf. Ex. 15:19; Ps. 136:15; and F. M. Cross and D. N. Freedman, *Studies in Ancient Yahwistic Poetry* [1975], p. 50, on Ex. 15:4).

The question here is how well the pharaohs of the 19th Dynasty fulfil these qualifications. Two sets of rulers are involved. Either Ramses II was the pharaoh of the oppression and Merneptah was the pharaoh of the Exodus (the older view), or Seti I was the pharaoh of the oppression and Ramses II was the pharaoh of the Exodus (the more recent view).

a. Ramses II and Merneptah. Ramses II corresponds to the pharaoh of the oppression well, employing state slaves on his many building projects, but Merneptah does not correspond to the pharaoh of the Exodus very well. If Merneptah was the pharaoh of the Exodus, the Exodus must have occurred early in his reign, because the Israelites already were in Palestine by the time his stele mentioning Israel was inscribed. But that does not allow sufficient time for Israel to wander in the wilderness, and in any case Merneptah did not die at the time of the Exodus.

b. Seti I and Ramses II. These difficulties with Merneptah lead to consideration of Seti I and Ramses II as the pharaohs of the oppression and the Exodus. Seti I reigned only eleven years, so he would not fit very well as pharaoh of the oppression if one takes seriously the biblical indications that Moses stayed in the wilderness a long time (Ex. 4:19; 7:7). Ramses II would not fit very well as pharaoh of the Exodus either, according to this scheme, for he did not die until *ca.* 1224, long after the latest possible date for the Exodus.

Thus there is no satisfactory way to harmonize the rulers of the 19th Dynasty with all that is stated or implied in the Bible about the pharaohs of the oppression and the Exodus. If the Exodus is to be dated at this time, then a pharaoh did not die while Moses was in the wilderness (Ex. 2:23), or a pharaoh did not die with his army at the time of the Exodus (Ex. 14–15; Ps. 136:15), or Moses did not spend a long time in exile (Ex. 4:19; 7:7), or the Israelites did not wander very long in the wilderness (Numbers–Deuteronomy), etc. The lack of satisfactory historical correlations with these elements in the biblical record casts some doubt upon dating the Exodus during the 19th Dynasty.

III. Fifteenth-Century Date.–*A. Biblical Evidence.* The main text is in 1 K. 6:1, which states that Solomon began to build the temple in the fourth year of his reign, 480 years after the Exodus. (Note that the month is also given; such specificity may give some weight to the literal understanding of these 480 years.) Since the dates for Solomon's reign are generally agreed to be *ca.* 971-931 (perhaps beginning earlier if a coregency with David is allowed), the Exodus would be dated *ca.* 1450 (*see* CHRONOLOGY OF THE OT IV.B).

One other text may be correlated roughly with this date. In Jgs. 11:26 Jephthah (*ca.* 1100) states that the Israelites had lived in Transjordan for three hundred years. Thus the Conquest would be dated *ca.* 1400, and the Exodus *ca.* 1440. Other texts (e.g., Gen. 15:13, 16; Ex. 12:40) that might appear relevant have other problems that lessen their value (*see* CHRONOLOGY OF THE OT III).

B. Egyptian Evidence. The pharaohs of this period must be dated as accurately as possible before the attempt is made to associate biblical events with them, because if they have been misdated then the correlations suggested by the biblical date for the Exodus will be incorrect. The chronology of the 18th Dynasty has been established by using three types of data: Sothic cycle dates, new moon dates, and the highest-numbered regnal years attested for each of the kings who ruled during this period (*see* EGYPT). Using these data the following correlations may be suggested.

1. Thutmose I. When Moses was born a decree was in effect which ordered that all male babies born to the Hebrews were to be killed (Ex. 1:22). Aaron does not appear to have been threatened by this decree, and he was only three years older than Moses (Ex. 7:7); hence this decree may have been proclaimed only a short time before Moses was born. Moses was eighty years old when he went to negotiate with pharaoh (Ex. 7:7). Adding these eighty years to the date of 1450 for the Exodus dates the birth of Moses in 1530. The Sothic cycle datum and the total number of regnal years known for Amenhotep I date his reign from 1553 to 1532. This would put Moses' birth, when the death decree was in effect, early in the reign of Thutmose I, and the birth of Aaron three years earlier, when the death decree was not in effect at the end of the reign of Amenhotep I. These considerations suggest identifying Thutmose I as the pharaoh who proclaimed the death decree.

In some respects the character of Thutmose I would fit that part very well. Prior to his time the 18th Dynasty had been mainly on a defensive footing after defeating the Hyksos. It was Thutmose I who set this dynasty on the road to an empire; he staked out the territory of that empire by campaigning all the way to the Euphrates and to the Fifth Cataract of the Nile. Some of his barbarity can be seen in his act of hanging the head of his executed Nubian enemy, as Amenhotep II did later, from the prow of his royal barge. He moved his court to Memphis, where the palace he built was still used by royalty 150 years later (Redford, *History,* p. 79), and it was here in the north that the daughter of the pharaoh who issued the death decree came in contact with the baby Moses (Ex. 2:1-10). All factors considered, therefore, Thutmose I fits reasonably well as the pharaoh of the death decree.

2. Hatshepsut. It is possible that she was the pharaoh's daughter who rescued the baby Moses (Ex. 2:1-10). If Moses was born *ca.* 1530, the pharaoh who decreed the death of all Hebrew male babies would have been Thutmose I, Hatshepsut's father. Moses would have grown up during the reigns of Thutmose I and Thutmose II (Hatshepsut's husband), and with Hatshepsut's sponsorship he could have attained the prominence that later tradition attributed to him (cf. Acts 7:22; Josephus *Ant.* ii.10). If Moses fled Egypt when he was forty (Acts 7:23), then it was late in the reign of Hatshepsut (1504-1482), and her

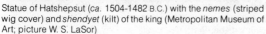

Statue of Hatshepsut (*ca.* 1504-1482 B.C.) with the *nemes* (striped wig cover) and *shendyet* (kilt) of the king (Metropolitan Museum of Art; picture W. S. LaSor)

Statue of Thutmose III (1504-1450 B.C.) (Service des musées, Cairo; picture W. S. LaSor)

coregent Thutmose III (1504-1450) may have begun to assert himself (note that *ca.* 1488 is the last reference to Senmut, Hatshepsut's prime minister; Thutmose may have disposed of him in order to gain full control of the throne).

According to this scheme, Hatshepsut also would have been the pharaoh who died while Moses was in exile (Ex. 2:23; the masculine reference here may be explained by Hatshepsut's adoption of all royal titles and prerogatives, including the masculine ones). During the reign she undertook building projects that would have required the kind of labor the Israelites could supply.

3. Thutmose III. Several characteristics of the pharaoh of the Exodus could be pointed out from the biblical references to him, but the most significant information about him is that he died in the Reed Sea at the time of the Exodus. No reference in Egyptian sources to his death need be expected; not only would such a reference be contrary to the propagandistic nature of the royal inscriptions of Egypt but it would also be contrary to the Egyptian theology of kingship. Pharaoh was a god, Horus incarnate. Gods, of course, do not die in the human sense of the term. In spite of this qualification, a few random dates of pharaohs' deaths have survived.

The date of Thutmose III's death has come down to us through the biography of Amenemhab, who served in the Egyptian navy under several pharaohs. That date is given as "the last day of the 3rd month of the 2nd season" (Breasted, III; 234).

The Egyptian calendar was divided into three seasons of four months each, so the third month of the second season was the seventh month of the year. These months had thirty days, so the date referred to here is VII/30. The Elephantine temple inscription from 1468 B.C. dated the mid-July rising of Sothis at the end of the eleventh Egyptian month. The rising of Sothis had moved only four days by 1450 when Thutmose III died at the end of the seventh month, four months before Sothis rose in mid-July. Thus the death of Thutmose was in mid-March, March 17 to be exact when more detailed calculations are carried out (Breasted, III, 234).

The pharaoh of the Exodus died shortly after Passover, according to Ex. 12–14. Passover — the celebration of which began with the Exodus — was celebrated in the middle of the first month of the Israelite lunar calendar, later called Nisan, which corresponds to March-April in the Julian calendar. Although one would thus expect the pharaoh's death to be in early April, the slightly later spring harvest in Palestine, coupled with the later omission of an intercalary month (which would have been added *ad hoc* at this early period), could account for this difference. Thus not only did Thutmose III die in the year of the Exodus according to the chronologies worked out above, but he also died at the right time of that year.

A mummy labeled with his name in the Cairo Museum warrants closer inspection. Occasionally it has been objected that neither Ramses II, Merneptah, Thutmose III, nor Amenhotep II could have been the pharaoh of the Exodus because their mummies have all been found, whereas the pharaoh of the Exodus drowned and his body should have been lost in the Reed Sea. His body could have washed ashore (Ex. 14:30), however, and been recovered by a search party that set out when it became evident that he and his troops were overdue. But further evidence needs to be considered. These mummies have been x-rayed recently to determine their ages at death, and the one labeled Thutmose III has been estimated to have been between forty and forty-five when he died (cf. R. Harris and K. Weeks, *X-raying the Pharaohs* [1978], p. 138). Since Thutmose III reigned fifty-four years, he presumably should have been at least sixty when he died. Thus it may be that another body was substituted for Thutmose III when his was not recovered from the Reed Sea.

It is important to note that the Israelites' oppression became worse at this time (Ex. 2:23). A fitting circumstance to explain this development is present in the history of the 18th Dynasty. Thutmose III was one of the great military pharaohs. He established Egypt's Asiatic empire by a series of some sixteen campaigns into Syro-Palestine, conducted almost annually from his twenty-third year, the year after Hatshepsut died, to his forty-second year.

From these conquests the booty and tribute, described in long lists of Thutmose III, flowed into Egypt's treasuries. It was also necessary to establish a base N of Memphis as a point of departure for these campaigns. The location of the later Rameses would have been a logical site for such a base. The cities of Pithom and Rameses that the Israelites built are described as "store-cities" (Heb. *ʿārê miškᵉnôṯ*). Elsewhere in the OT (1 K. 9:19; 2 Ch. 8:4, 6; 16:4; 17:12) this phrase refers to military bases with armories and supply depots, which were usually on the periphery or borders of the Hebrew kingdoms. This phrase should have a similar meaning in Ex. 1:11, and the Asiatic campaigns of Thutmose III provide an excellent explanation why construction on these delta projects would have become more pressing, since they served both as bases from which his troops and their supplies were sent into Asia, and as temporary sites for the storage of the booty and tribute brought back from those campaigns.

4. Amenhotep II. The coregency of Thutmose III and Amenhotep II should be taken into account here. Three main lines of evidence point to the existence of this coregency (Redford, *JEA*, pp. 108-122). General evidence for it comes from monuments on which their names appear together. Specific evidence for it comes first from Amenhotep II's accession date of IV/1, which should have been VIII/1, after the death of his father on VII/30, if a coregency was not involved here. The second specific line of evidence in support of this coregency comes from Amenhotep II's Syrian campaign of his third year (Amada and Elephantine stelae) and his seventh year (Memphis stele), both of which are called his "first victorious campaign." This was a specific and technical identification in Egyptian political terminology, not a general one, and thus two "first" campaigns present a problem. The best solution to this problem is to suppose that when Amenhotep II campaigned in his third year he still was coregent with his father, but when he campaigned in his seventh year he was sole ruler after his father's death, and that fact was indicated by the reuse of this term (Redford, *JEA*, p. 121).

The new-moon date of Amenhotep II, published recently, and the new-moon dates of Thutmose III together indicate that their reigns overlapped by three years regardless of which set of absolute Julian dates is selected for them (R. Parker, "Once"). This means the campaign of Amenhotep II was conducted during his third year, the last year of his coregency with his father Thutmose III, who died that same year. During his last dozen years Thutmose III did not campaign in Syro-Palestine. This absence led to a revolt among his vassals there and he dispatched Amenhotep II with the army to quell this revolt in the last year of his reign. When Amenhotep II returned to Egypt from that campaign, in the eleventh month according to the relevant stelae, he found that his father had died some three months earlier.

The existence of this coregency does not mean that Moses dealt with two pharaohs, because only one of them (Thutmose III) remained in Egypt, while the other (Amenhotep II) was away in Asia. This historical context provides a good reason why Thutmose III would have been resident in the delta where Moses consulted with the pharaoh, since it probably was from that area that he had sent his son on his first military expedition not long before this, and he may have remained there to await news of his son's success. The revolt in Syria could have strengthened Thutmose III's resolve not to let his Semitic slaves go to sacrifice in the wilderness (Ex. 5:2). From the Israelite point of view, however, this would have been an auspicious time to leave Egypt, since some of the troops were away. Of possibly greater importance could have been the effect this information had upon the route chosen for the Exodus. The coastal route had the risk not only of military engagements with the residents of southern Canaan (Ex. 13:17), but also of a possible encounter with the troops of Amenhotep II returning to Egypt.

Of importance in this connection was the reaction of Amenhotep II upon his return to Egypt. After giving the date of Thutmose III's death, the tomb biography of Amenemhab describes the coronation of Amenhotep II, and this description is remarkable in that it contains a reference to the execution by beheading of the foreign chiefs he brought back to Egypt with him as captives. As Breasted noted (III, 319), "Amenemhab doubtless refers to the sacrifice of the seven kings of Tikhsi." This region (Semitic Taḫši) was the target for the campaign of Amenhotep II's third year, and the execution of these captive princes in Egypt upon his return is also mentioned by the stelae which refer to that campaign.

Several reasons for this extraordinary course of action can be suggested when it is viewed from the standpoint of the events of the biblical Exodus. First, the rebellion raised by these princes took Amenhotep away from Egypt when he should have been there with his troops to defend his father, and this reflected upon his kingship. Second, the escaped Hebrew slaves who caused his father's death were Semites and the royal captives he executed were Semites, so he could have expressed his anger at the Semites as a group in this way. Third, the Hebrews had rebelled against pharaoh by escaping from Egypt. It was in the interests of Amenhotep to provide the strongest possible deterrent to prevent any other subjects, native or foreign, from attempting to follow their example. Executing these foreign princes and parading their heads up the Nile warned everyone else against such a course of action. From a biblical point of view, therefore, these actions of Amenhotep II fit very well with the actions of the enraged son of the pharaoh of the Exodus who returned to Egypt to find his father dead from circumstances caused by the Hebrews.

Two elements in the Egyptian texts mentioned above appear to be false, and this emphasizes the extraordinary nature of these events. Amenemhab introduced the description of Amenhotep II's coronation with the phrase, "when the morning brightened." This phrase has been understood by Egyptologists as indicating that Amenhotep II was crowned the day after his father died. But Amenhotep was away in Syria at the time; his coronation had taken place three years earlier when he was installed as coregent. At that time he "was established upon the throne of his father," and at that time he "assumed the royal titulary." Egyptian records do not describe any ceremony for a coregent coming to sole reign, because he already had been installed as king and assumed the royal titulary when he was enthroned as coregent. By identifying this occasion as Amenhotep's coronation, Amenemhab attempted to deny the coregency. The Amada and Elephantine stelae of Amenhotep indicate that the princes of Takhsi were executed at a public function, but it is unlikely that this function was Amenhotep's coronation as Amenemhab would have us believe.

The other example of falsification comes from the Memphis stele of Amenhotep II, in which he identified the campaign of his seventh year as his "first victorious campaign"; that designation, however, had already been applied to the campaign of his third year. This looks like a deliberate attempt to expunge the memory of the campaign of Year 3. Was some disgrace connected with it? For Amenhotep to have been out of the country when his father died under unusual circumstances could have brought some disgrace upon him. Thus Amenemhab's incorrect date for Amenhotep's pseudo-coronation and the contradictory system of numbering employed by Amenhotep for his own campaigns look like deliberate distortions in an attempt to cover up the truth of what really happened.

If Amenhotep held the Hebrews responsible for the death of his father, it would have been natural for him to seek revenge. It is interesting to note in this connection, therefore, that the first contemporary Egyptian reference to ʿApiru *outside* of Egypt comes from the Memphis stele's combined record of the campaigns of Amenhotep's seventh and ninth years, in which he claimed that he brought 3600 ʿApiru back to Egypt among the captives he took in Syro-Palestine (*ANET,* p. 247). This could have been a compensation for the escape of the Hebrews four years earlier. The loss of a sizable number of Hebrew slaves also depleted the ranks of the Egyptian work force. Amenhotep's claim to have brought a total of 90,000 captives back from these two campaigns could have been an attempt to replenish that depleted work force.

Finally, from the end of Amenhotep's reign comes a text that is so unusual that Egyptologists think he may have been drunk while dictating it. Basically, it expresses his hatred of Semites (cf. A. Gardiner, *Egypt,* p. 199). This inscription is dated fourteen years after the last of his Asiatic campaigns, that of Year 9, which shows that he still had the Semites on his mind, even when he was as far away from them as Nubia. The Hebrews are not mentioned by name in this inscription, but Takhsi, where Amenhotep campaigned in the proposed year of the Exodus, is. If Amenhotep held the Hebrews responsible for the death of his father at the Exodus, then he had good reason for the hatred of the Semites he expressed here. The reference to magicians is interesting, and although the Nubians may have been noted for their practice of the magic arts, the reference to that practice in this context might convey echoes of the contest in magic between Moses and the Egyptians which preceded the death of Thutmose III — if he is identified as the pharaoh of the Exodus. Taking all the factors discussed above into consideration, Amenhotep II fits very well as the pharaoh after the Exodus.

5. Thutmose Son of Amenhotep? Few texts are known from the end of the reign of Thutmose III; thus it is not surprising that no reference to the biblical plagues have been found in Egyptian sources. Even if more sources were available, it is unlikely they would mention such adverse events. Indirect evidence of the tenth plague, however, might be found among the members of the royal household. Amenhotep II was not the eldest son of Thutmose III, for he had an elder half brother named Amenemhet who died earlier in the reign of Thutmose (Redford, *JEA,* p. 108). Thus Thutmose III's firstborn son was not alive in 1450 when the tenth plague fell on Egypt. If the household of the pharaoh suffered the loss of a son in this plague, therefore, that son must be sought in the family of Amenhotep II.

In earlier presentations of the fifteenth-century Exodus, attention was called to the Dream Stele of Thutmose IV, which relates how he was told that he would become king even though he was not in line for the throne. This was taken as indirect evidence for Amenhotep II's firstborn son who was thought to have been lost in the tenth plague. This view must be revised now that the sons of Amenhotep II have been studied more carefully. The son of Amenhotep II who was in line for the throne before Thutmose IV was named Amenhotep. It has been estimated that he was born early in the reign of Amenhotep II, and he is known to have been the heir apparent until his father's twentieth year (Redford, *JEA,* p. 115). He apparently died around that time, which is the reason Thutmose IV came to the throne. But Amenhotep the son of Amenhotep II did not die until near the end of his father's reign; so he could not have been the son who was lost in the tenth plague at the beginning of his reign.

It has been noted, however, that it is somewhat unusual to have a king and eldest son by the same name. While this arrangement is not impossible, it seems more likely that the firstborn son of Amenhotep II would have been given a different name. Thutmose was the other royal nomen particularly favored by this dynasty. It has been proposed therefore, wholly apart from any consideration of the Exodus, that Amenhotep II had a son named Thutmose who was older than Amenhotep. Even though no inscriptional evidence for this son named Thutmose has been recovered, he has been suggested as the one who was originally first in line for the throne (cf. Redford, *JEA,* p. 114). If Amenhotep II did have such a son, he would have been born late in the reign of Thutmose III and would have died early in the reign of Amenhotep II, which would make him the best current candidate for the royal son who died in the tenth plague. This relationship could have given Thutmose III added cause to pursue the Hebrews.

6. ʿApiru. The first reference to ʿApiru in Egypt comes from a tomb painting which depicts them working in the vineyards of the eastern delta in Hatshepsut's time. On the basis of a 1450 Exodus date, this was around the time when the enslavement of the biblical Hebrews became especially oppressive. The dictum appears to apply here that the Hebrews were ʿApiru, but not all ʿApiru were Hebrews (*see* HABIRU). Thus these ʿApiru working in the Delta could have been Hebrews, but they could also have come from some other Semitic group.

The next contemporary Egyptian reference to ʿApiru comes from the Memphis Stele of Amenhotep II, which lists 3600 ʿApiru as captives he brought back to Egypt from the Asiatic campaigns of his seventh and ninth years. These probably were not biblical Hebrews, because they still were wandering in the wilderness when Amenhotep conducted these campaigns. These ʿApiru could have been taken captive, however, to compensate for the damage to Egypt and to Amenhotep's pride that occurred as a result of the Hebrew Exodus.

In some instances in the Amarna Letters, "Ḫabiru" is used to refer in a derogatory way to rival Canaanite rulers (*see* AMARNA TABLETS). In other instances these letters refer to Ḫabiru who are more like those known in texts from elsewhere in the ancient Near East. In still other instances the activities attributed to some Ḫabiru are consistent with activities of the biblical Hebrews early in the period of the judges — which is when these texts should be dated in terms of biblical history, according to a fifteenth-century date for the Exodus.

The stele of Seti I from Beth-shean (*see* picture in INSCRIPTIONS) refers to military contacts with ʿApiru. Since these operations took place in a region where the northern Israelite tribes settled, it is possible that some of these ʿApiru were Hebrews. Some of the ʿApiru depicted as state slaves in Egypt during the 19th Dynasty could have come from this campaign, but they may have come from other Semitic groups captured at other times.

C. Objections. 1. Chronology. The main objection to a fifteenth-century date for the Exodus is that the figure of 480 years presented by 1 K. 6:1 may have been derived from an inaccurate estimate, such as calculating twelve generations of forty years each. Since the length of time from the birth of one generation to the next was closer to twenty years, it is argued that this period should be shortened considerably. (The presence of the stock numbers twelve and forty may be indicative of an approximation, but there is no other indication in the text that the 480 is not literal.) The reference in Jgs. 11:26 may be a gloss based on the preceding chapters in Judges, which include a total of approximately three hundred years for the reigns of the judges up to that point.

From the lines of evidence discussed above, however, it is evident that the Israelites who lived at the end of the 2nd millennium and at the beginning of the 1st millennium B.C. held chronological views dating the Exodus in the 15th cent., and that corresponds to the only date given for it in the Bible. While it is possible that these data could have been corrupted in transmission, the most reasonable approach to them is to examine in more detail the historical context in which they date the Exodus. This biblical date for the Exodus has a reciprocal relationship with the events described in Exodus as related to Egyptian history. A pragmatic approach to this date suggests a period in Egyptian history that should be examined for a possible relationship to the biblical Exodus, and considerable agreement of the evidence from Egyptian and biblical sources pointing to that period supports the accuracy of the chronological datum (480 years) from which that search started.

2. City of Rameses. The problem that Rameses poses for the 18th-Dynasty (fifteenth-century) Exodus is not so much that it was named for a 19th-Dynasty (thirteenth-century) pharaoh as that archeological evidence for an 18th-Dynasty (fifteenth-century) occupation of the area with which Rameses is best identified has not been found yet. This is especially the case now with the excavations at Tell el-Dabʿa, which have revealed a gap in occupation from the end of the Hyksos settlement there down to the time when it was rebuilt by the 19th Dynasty (thirteenth century).

The first point that should be taken into account here is the extent and nature of the area involved. Including its suburbs or sectors, the city of Pi-ramses took in an extensive area that now includes a number of tells. J. Van Seters estimated its size as 3 km. (2 mi.) from north to south and 1.5 km. (1 mi.) from east to west, and he located six sites of antiquities within that area. E. Uphill has estimated this area as more than 3 km. (2 mi.) on a side, and he has located six sites of antiquities within that area. M. Bietak, the excavator of Tell El-Dabʿa, estimates it covered 3 square km. (1.2 square mi.), and he has mapped almost a dozen sites of antiquities within that area.

The Egyptian texts that describe the city of Rameses refer to the palace area in its center and four sectors of the city surrounding it. They also refer to its port and granaries, and some area within this complex must have been occupied by the troops of pharaoh, including his chariots. If Ramses' palace has been correctly located at Qantir, the excavators of Tell el-Dabʿa have been digging in the southern sector of the city. Hyksos remains have been found at both Tell el-Dabʿa and Ezbet Rushdi N of it. Remains from the 12th Dynasty have been found at Tell el-Dabʿa, Ezbet Rushdi, and Khataʿna S of Tell el-Dabʿa.

Thus, the city of Rameses took in a large area, and the more thorough study of that area by means of excavation has only begun. It is possible, therefore, that evidence for an 18th-Dynasty (fifteenth-century) occupation in this area will be found during subsequent explorations. A fragmentary inscription with the name of Haremhab, the last pharaoh of the 18th Dynasty, has already been found at Tell el-Dabʿa. Since the 18th-Dynasty pharaohs who ruled through the 15th cent. (Thutmose III, Amenhotep II, and Thutmose IV) conducted well over twenty campaigns into Asia, one would expect that they had a base of operations somewhere in this vicinity.

An alternate proposal to solve this problem has been to interpret Ex. 1:11 as referring to Israelite work on the sites involved under the Hyksos or the Egyptian rulers of the Middle Kingdom (J. Bimson, p. 244). Since evidence for the occupation of this area during both of these periods exists, this proposal satisfies the requirements of the archeological findings in the area. The context of Ex. 1:11 appears to connect the construction work of the Israelites more closely with the Exodus than it does with their entrance into Egypt, however, so this suggestion seems less likely at the present time. Further archeological developments from the region of Rameses can be expected, and they may well include the discovery of evidence for an 18th-Dynasty (fifteenth-century) occupation there.

3. Archeology. The major objection to the fifteenth-century date for the Exodus has come from the results of excavations in Palestine. Ai, Arad, Bethel, Debir, Gibeon, Hazor, Hebron, Heshbon, Hormah, Jarmuth, Jericho, Lachish, and Megiddo are among the more important sites that have relevance for the date of the Conquest, and hence the Exodus. The prevailing opinion among archeologists has been that a number of these sites show evidence of destruction and resettlement in the13th cent., presumably caused by the Israelite conquest, since the Bible mentions most of these towns in its account of the Conquest. As the excavations continue, however, new evidence comes to light that renders the earlier interpretations inconclusive. A brief summary of this evidence is given below; for a more detailed discussion, see the articles on the individual sites.

Several factors must be considered in evaluating the archeological evidence. First, according to the Bible only three towns were burned (Jericho, Josh. 6:24; Ai, 8:19;

Hazor, 11:13); thus destruction levels should not be expected at other sites, although evidence of occupation should be found. Second, other peoples, e.g., the Egyptians and sea-peoples, could be responsible for the destruction of some of these towns. Third, the tentative nature of archeological evidence must be remembered. Bimson's theory that the relative chronology should be revised downward, moving the end of M.B. II.C from 1550 to 1400, would help to harmonize the biblical account with archeological evidence, but his theory is not without problems.

Arad, Hebron, and Jarmuth yield no evidence of thirteenth-century occupation, and thus these towns do not support a late date for the Exodus. Similarly Ai, if it is identified with et-Tell, has no evidence of occupation from 2400 to *ca.* 1220. This fact can be harmonized with Josh. 7–8 in two ways: either the excavations need to be expanded to another part of the tell, or another site identification must be made. Albright followed the latter option and located Ai at Bethel, which had a thirteenth-century destruction level. This level, however, may be earlier in the 13th cent. than Albright supposed; but in any case, if that level is assigned to the Conquest, then the later destruction of Bethel (Jgs. 1:22-25) is not in evidence. It seems more plausible to locate Ai at et-Tell and assign Bethel's thirteenth-century destruction to the judges period.

Debir, which Albright incorrectly identified with Tell Beit Mirsim, has now been identified with Khirbet Rabûd, but it was apparently destroyed in the early 12th cent., too late to be relevant to the Exodus and Conquest. Gibeon has yielded no evidence of occupation in the 13th cent., although one would expect such evidence in view of Josh. 9–10. Hazor has destruction levels at the end of the 15th, 14th, and 13th cents., but the Early Iron Age occupation was only a small village, which hardly corresponds with Jgs. 4:2; hence it would seem that one of the earlier destructions was a result of the Conquest. The earliest occupation of Heshbon (modern Ḥesbân) was in the 12th cent. (L Geraty and R. Boraas, *Andrews University Seminary Studies,* 16 [1978], 1-17), and thus it is of no help; however, it is possible that Heshbon was earlier located elsewhere, perhaps at Jālûl, where there is evidence of Late Bronze Age occupation. Jericho has no evidence of thirteenth-century occupation or destruction, but some scarabs point to a fifteenth-century occupation (despite disclaimers) and there is Late Bronze Age pottery there; also, the Middle Bronze Age wall could have continued into the Late Bronze Age, and thus could have been the wall of Josh. 6. Lachish and Megiddo were destroyed early in the 12th cent., too late for a thirteenth-century Exodus and Conquest. Finally, N. Glueck's surface survey (*AASOR,* 14-15 [1934/35]; 18-19 [1939]; 25-28 [1951]) of Moab was inadequate, and thus his results showing no occupation until 1300 must be discarded (so J. M. Miller in "An Archaeological Survey of Central Moab," a report presented to the annual session of the American Schools of Oriental Research on Nov. 19, 1978).

In conclusion, the archeological evidence does not seem to support a thirteenth-century Exodus and Conquest; rather, much of it points to a fifteenth-century date.

Bibliography.–W. F. Albright, *JAOS,* 74 [1954], 222-233; *Yahweh and the Gods of Canaan* (1968); *BHI*; M. Bietak, *Tell el-Dab'a II* (1975); J. J. Bimson, *Redating the Exodus and Conquest* (1978); J. H. Breasted, *Ancient Records of Egypt,* vols. I-V (1906); E. Brugsch, *Zeitschrift für Ägyptische Sprache,* 10 (1872), 16-20; E. F. Campbell, *BA,* 23 (1960), 2-22; B. Couroyer, *RB,* 53 (1946), 75-98; A. H. Gardiner, *Egypt of the Pharaohs* (1966); *JEA,* 5 (1918), 127-138, 179-200, 242-271; 10 (1924), 87-96; 19 (1933), 122-28; L. Habachi, *Annales du service des antiquités de l'Égypte,* 52 (1954), 443-459; W. C. Hayes, *Metropolitan Museum of Art Papers,* 3 (1937), 5-8; F. Hommel, *Expos.T.* 10 (1898), 214-230; J. W. Jack, *Date of the Exodus* (1925); K. A. Kitchen, *Ancient Orient and OT* (1966); G. Lello, *JNES,* 37 (1978), 327-330; G. E. Mendenhall, *Tenth Generation: The Origins of the Biblical Tradition* (1973); *MNHK*; E. Naville, *JEA,* 10 (1924), 18-39; J. Orr, *Expos.,* 5th ser., 5 (1897), 161-177; R. A. Parker, *Calendars of Ancient Egypt* (1950); *JNES,* 16 (1957), 39f.; "Once Again the Coregency of Thutmose III and Amenhotep II," in *Studies in Honor of John A. Wilson* (1969); W. M. F. Petrie, *Hyksos and Israelite Cities* (1906); *Egypt and Israel* (1911); D. B. Redford, *History and Chronology of the Eighteenth Egyptian Dynasty: Seven Studies* (1967); *JEA,* 51 (1965), 108-122; J. D. Schmidt, *Ramesses II* (1973); E. P. Uphill, *JNES,* 27 (1968), 291-316; 28 (1969), 15-39; J. Van Seters, *The Hyksos: A New Investigation* (1966); G. A. Wainwright, *JEA,* 24 (1938), 213-19; *WBA*; E. F. Wente, *JNES,* 34 (1975), 265-272; C. de Wit, *Date and Route of the Exodus* (1960).

W. H. SHEA

EXODUS, ROUTE OF THE.

I. Introduction
II. Geography of the Sinai Peninsula
III. Beginnings of the Journey
IV. The Three Major Route Theories
    A. Northern Theory
        1. Extreme Northern Crossing
        2. Alternate Northern Route
    B. Central Theory
        1. Arabian Sinai
        2. Alternate Central Route
    C. Southern Theory
        1. Route to Jebel Mûsā
        2. Alternate Southern Route

I. Introduction.–Identification of the route of the Exodus must take into account significant geographical, topographical, and critical problems. Some understanding of these problems is necessary to appreciate the complexity of the task of identification. Further, because of the fragmentary and often tenuous nature of the evidence, all route suggestions must remain hypothetical.

Scholars differ in their evaluations of the historical aspects of the scriptural narrative. The traditio-historical approach of Noth posits that many of the geographical notations of Exodus and Numbers are secondary, intended to connect originally disparate traditions, although some lists within the narrative might be authentic (Noth, *Traditions,* pp. 220-27). Others, working from the traditional literary divisions (JEDP), suggest that several routes of the Exodus are preserved in the various strata (Haran, *IDB Supp.*). Some (e.g., de Vaux, pp. 374-76) have suggested a "double Exodus" theory, holding that one group took a northern route while another made its way south. However, some effort must be made to understand the present scriptural narrative in terms of the geography of the northeastern Nile Delta and the Sinai.

This in turn draws attention to a second set of problems. Although Exodus and Numbers are replete with geographic notations concerning the route, these are not as helpful as one might hope. Sinai's isolation and desolation throughout the centuries have destroyed the continuity of place names. When it is recalled that many sites in Palestine have been identified on the basis of identical, similar, or corrupted forms of the ancient names that are retained in the immediate area, the seriousness of such discontinuity in Sinai becomes apparent.

One factor that will be assumed in this discussion is the identification of Kadesh-barnea. This important site has been identified with near certainty at 'Ain Qudeirât (cf. *EAEHL,* III, *s.v.* "Kadesh-Barnea" [M. Dothan]). Also, some attention will be given to the possible locations of Mt. Sinai, since this would affect any route theory. Finally, since all travel in the Sinai is restricted to certain tracks, some attention is given to the ancient routes and geography.

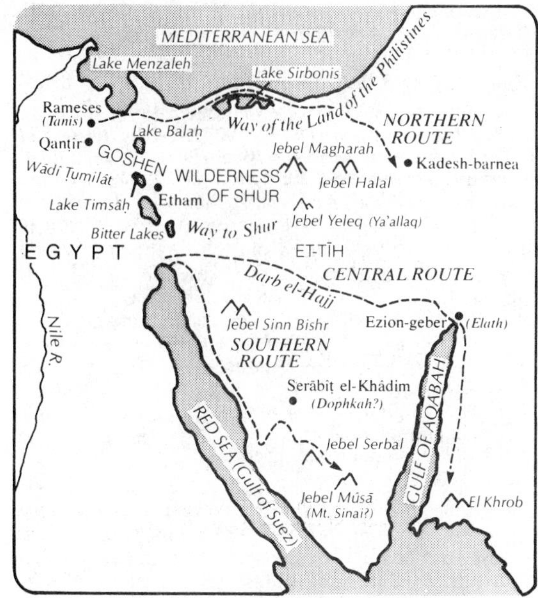

II. Geography of the Sinai Peninsula.–Sinai is a triangle of land measuring approximately 240 km. (150 mi.) across the top and 420 km. (260 mi.) along the sides. Two arms of the Red Sea, the Gulf of Suez and the Gulf of Aqabah, flank it on the SW and SE respectively. Geologically and geographically, this area of 60,115 sq. km. (23,220 sq. mi.) is divided into three distinct parts.

The northern sector of the peninsula consists of a sandy coastal plateau. Averaging 32 km. (20 mi.) in width and narrowing in the eastern extremity, this area is often characterized by sand dunes reaching 27 m. (90 ft.) in height. To the west the area opens out into the desert of Al-Jifar, probably the ancient wilderness of Shur (Ex. 15:22). The term "Shur" seems to be connected with a line of Egyptian fortresses built by the Middle Kingdom ruler Amenemhet I (1991-1962 B.C.). The line was built to control the influx of Asiatics who sought pasturage here in time of famine (cf. *ANET,* p. 259).

South of the coastal area a limestone plateau rises slowly from N to S and stretches across almost two-thirds of the peninsula. A series of low mountains jutting upward from the plain forms the plateau's northern limit. These mountains, rather unimpressive to the eye, range from 610 to 1070 m. (2000 to 3500 ft.) in height. From W to E the major peaks are Jebel Jiddi, Jebel Yeleq (Ya'allaq), Jebel Magharah, and Jebel Halal. The plateau's southern limit is much higher, culminating in Jebel ʿAjmah (1625 m. [5335 ft.]). In the center of the plateau lies an area known as Badiyat et-Tīh, "the desert of the wanderings." The characteristic bare, unending gravel plain of et-Tīh has virtually no water and little vegetation.

Southern Sinai differs radically geologically and geographically. Basically sedimentary material further north gives way to igneous masses forming peaks that reach over 2440 m. (8000 ft.) in height. Chief among these peaks are Jebel Katerīn (2636 m. [8651 ft.]), Jebel Umm Shomer (2584 m. [8482 ft.]), and Jebel Mûsā (2280 m. [7482 ft.]). The latter has been identified traditionally as Mt. Sinai since at least the 4th cent. A.D. Access to the area is by the Wâdī Feiran and Wâdī es-Sheikh. Southwest Sinai in particular interested the Egyptians from very ancient times down to the 20th Dynasty (*ca.* 1200 B.C.) because of turquoise and copper deposits in the area (Rothenberg, *PEQ*).

III. Beginnings of the Journey.–The biblical narrative consistently places the Hebrews prior to the Exodus in areas that have been identified with the northeastern delta (Gen. 47:27; Ex. 1:11; 13:17). The delta reaches out to the desert by two extensions. The northern extension protrudes to Qantarah while the southern extension begins near Zagazig and ends near Ismailia (Wâdī Ṭumilât); it has been suggested that this corresponds to the biblical Goshen, although Goshen appears in a general way to refer to the northeastern delta region. Both extensions were connected to lands further east by important routes. The "Way of Horus" (the biblical "way of the land of the Philistines") connected Egypt with Canaan. This route hugged the coast and was a major military highway (Gardiner, *JEA,* 6). God specifically forbade the Hebrews to take this route (Ex. 13:17). A second route began near Ismailia, crossed to Kadesh-barnea, and branched off to Canaan, the Arabah, and Ezion-geber. This route could be the "Way to Shur."

Between the Mediterranean and the Gulf of Suez several salt marshes and lakes separated the delta from

Sand dunes characteristic of the northern Sinai peninsula (D. Baly)

Al-Jifar. From N to S they were Lakes Menzaleh, Balaḥ, Timsâḥ, and the Bitter Lakes. Each of these, along with the more traditional Gulf of Suez, has been suggested as the "Reed Sea."

The biblical narratives locate the beginning of the journey at Rameses (Ex. 12:37; "Raamses" in Ex. 1:11). The exact location of Rameses is of considerable debate (*see* EXODUS, DATE OF THE II.A. and III.C; cf. Uphill). Two sites, Tanis and Qanṭîr (Tell el-Dabʿa) have been suggested, with scholarship increasingly favoring the latter. From Rameses the Hebrews journeyed southward to Succoth (Ex. 13:20), generally located at Tell el-Maskhûṭah, and to Etham. Here, apparently unable to move on, the Hebrews turned northward (Ex. 14:2; Nu. 33:7). Three sites are mentioned next: Baal-zephon, Migdol, and Pi-hahiroth. One should probably locate Baal-zephon on or near a body of water because its name is that of a deity with nautical associations. An inscription mentions Baal-zephon in association with Tahpanhes (Tell Defneh), which borders Lake Menzaleh (cf. Albright). Migdol probably is to be identified with Tell el-Ḥeir, NW of Qantarah.

Why did the Hebrews change directions? The reason may have involved their inability to penetrate the "Wall of Shur," traditionally thought of as a line of fortresses extending from Pelusium to Ismailia to keep check on migrating bedouin (Gardiner, *Egypt,* p. 131). A canal discovered in the eastern delta in the 1970s suggests that the "Wall" actually was a canal with fortresses stretched along its length (cf. Sneh, Weissbrod, and Perath; W. Shea, *BASOR,* 226 [Apr. 1977], 31-38). Such an obstacle would force the Hebrews to take a more northerly track and eventually "entangle" them in the salt marshes of the northern delta (cf. Ex. 14:3). It is interesting to note that the name Pi-hahiroth may come from the root *ḥrt,* "dig," suggesting a location on a canal (Albright, p. 16). The deliverance through the sea could be located in the north, perhaps on a southern extension of Lake Menzaleh. After crossing to the east any line of march would place the Hebrews in Al-Jifar. Instead of continuing east, however, they very likely turned south toward the southern Sinai to avoid further contacts with the Egyptians (see IV.C below).

***IV. The Three Major Route Theories.**–A. Northern Theory. 1. Extreme Northern Crossing.* One northern theory holds that the Hebrews crossed the narrow spit of land separating the Mediterranean Sea from Lake Sirbonis (Sabkhat Bardawil). The latter is a shallow clay pan that becomes filled with water when certain winds blow. After escaping the Egyptians, the Hebrews continued along the arm of land, crossed over through the coastal dunes, and reached Kadesh-barnea. Suggestions for Mt. Sinai in relation to this theory include Jebel Magharah, Jebel Yeleq (Ya'allaq), and Jebel Halal. The latter is particularly attractive because of its proximity to Kadesh-barnea.

Several arguments lend weight to this theory. Baal-zephon has been identified by some with either Mohammediyeh or, more likely, Ras Kasrun (cf. Cazelles and Eissfeldt). If the latter identification is correct, this route becomes a certainty since Ras Kasrun is located approximately halfway across the arm of land around Lake Sirbonis. A second argument suggests that the Hebrews' immediate objective was Kadesh-barnea (cf. Jgs. 11:16). This route is one of the shortest to that objective, yet still manages to avoid the Egyptian fortresses along the "Way of Horus." Further, the Hebrews encountered the Amalekites (Ex. 17:8), a people otherwise located in the Negeb and W of Kadesh-barnea. The request of Moses for a "three days' journey" (Ex. 3:18; 8:27) fits a Mt. Sinai located in the north. Again, the quail narrative (Ex. 16) points to a northern route; a similar phenomenon still occurs near el-ʿArîsh on the Mediterranean coast, where natives catch the migrating quail on their flight from Europe to Africa. Also, records of military catastrophes occurring in Lake Sirbonis recall the destruction of Pharaoh's army. Finally, it is interesting to note that Titus used this route in A.D. 68 on his way from Alexandria to Syria (E. Kraeling, *Rand McNally Bible Atlas* [1956], p. 105).

Serious objections to a northern route have been raised. First, the identification of Baal-zephon with Ras Kasrun is by no means certain (see III above). It is difficult to see how this route would avoid the Egyptian garrisons along the "Way of Horus." In any case, no natural route connects Lake Sirbonis with Kadesh-barnea. Nearly impassable dunes would prevent movement. One must also point out that Dt. 1:2 states that Mt. Horeb (Sinai) was eleven days' journey from Kadesh-barnea. This statement is impossible to harmonize with any Mt. Sinai in the north and argues for a more southerly location. Finally, Israel apparently very soon lost the precise location of Mt. Sinai. It is difficult to accept that this could occur if Mt. Sinai was located in the north, since Judah's borders included the area of Kadesh-barnea for much of its history.

2. Alternate Northern Route. Another proposal suggests that the Exodus followed the ancient track that connects the Wâdī Ṭumilât with Kadesh-barnea (the "Way to Shur"). The suggestion retains many of the strengths of the previous theory and avoids some of the pitfalls; but it is still susceptible to many of the above objections. Further, bedouins in search of pasturage undoubtedly used this route as a conduit to the delta. The Egyptians would keep a sharp watch over this route and it seems unlikely that a group of runaway slaves would be successful if they fled in this direction.

B. Central Theory. 1. Arabian Sinai. From the late 19th cent. until quite recently many scholars proposed locating Mt. Sinai in northwest Arabia on the strength of two primary arguments. First, the Sinai theophany (Ex. 19:16-20) was said to reflect an active volcano (Beke). But the Sinai Peninsula has had no active volcanos in historical memory; northwest Arabia represents the nearest area displaying that phenomenon. Second, it is noted that the biblical material connected Moses with the Midianites (Ex. 3:1; 18:1). Northwest Arabia generally is acknowledged as the homeland of the Midianites and this suggested that Mt. Sinai also should be located there.

A reconstructed line of march connects the Exodus with the ancient route that joined Egypt to Arabia, known today as the Darb el-Hajj, the modern Moslem pilgrim route. This route crosses the Sinai on a line from Suez to Elath (ancient Ezion-geber). From Ezion-geber the Hebrews turned south along the east side of the Gulf of Aqabah to the vicinity of El Khrob, where Mt. Sinai is to be located.

Objections to the two foundational arguments have seriously weakened this theory. Two counter-arguments militate against using Moses' connection with the Midianites. First, Moses also was connected with the Kenites (Jgs. 1:16; 4:11), whose relationship to the Midianites is unclear. Most interpreters suggest that the Kenites were a Midianite clan of trading smiths; their presence in the Sinai would not be surprising. Further, the Midianites were nomads; determining their sphere of influence is impossible. A near-fatal blow to an Arabian Mt. Sinai has been the recognition that the theophany of Ex. 19:16-20 is typical of other ancient theophanic descriptions which certainly do not presuppose volcanic activity (F. Cross, *Canaanite Myth and Hebrew Epic* [1973], pp. 156-177). Finally, Rothenberg's survey of southern Sinai raises serious questions concerning the identification of the

Jebel Mûsâ, the traditional Mt. Sinai in the southern Sinai peninsula (W. S. LaSor)

Darb el-Hajj with any biblical road or any connection with the biblical period (Rothenberg, *PEQ*, p. 13).

2. Alternate Central Route. Another theory postulates that the Hebrews utilized the track connecting Egypt with Arabia, but turned northeastward before crossing the Sinai. Either Jebel Sinn Bishr or Jebel Yeleq (Ya'allaq) would be a good suggestion for Mt. Sinai. Note should also be made that some locate Mt. Sinai in Edom. Several references seem to associate the mountain of God with Mt. Seir (see *NHI*, p. 132). Interestingly, two of Haran's reconstructed pentateuchal source routes (ED and J) follow this general track. However, in addition to the objections raised by Rothenberg's survey mentioned above, it is difficult to fit the stations of the Exodus along this route. Moreover, if it could be demonstrated that the Exodus route went further south, any more northerly route theory would be invalidated.

C. Southern Theory. 1. Route to Jebel Mûsā. This theory suggests that after leaving the delta the Hebrews entered Al-Jifar and headed south (see III above for initial stages). The route proceeded along the coastline of the Gulf of Suez where several stations have been identified tentatively. Among the more significant are: Marah (Ex. 15:23) with either ʿAin Ḥawârah or ʿAin Musa; Elim (Ex. 15:27; Nu. 33:9) with Wâdī Gharandel; and the encampment by the sea (Nu. 33:10) with el-Merkhah. Near modern Abu Zeneimeh the route headed southeast inland. The wilderness of Sin (Ex. 16:1) may be the sandy plain Debbet er-Ramleh while Serābîṭ el-Khâdim probably is the biblical Dophkah (Nu. 33:12). Two major wadis, Wâdī Shellal and Wâdī Feiran, connect the coast with the great granite peaks of the south, one of which is to be identified with Mt. Sinai. In addition to the traditional Jebel Mûsâ, Râs eṣ-Ṣafṣefeh and Jebel Katerīn are plausible candidates. The route to Kadesh-barnea is more difficult to determine but likely followed a series of valleys, passing near Ezion-geber (Nu. 33:35). *See* Plate 7.

Several factors make a southern route attractive. Although traditional identifications of sacred sites are often erroneous, it should be noted that this location goes against the early tendency to locate sacred places in areas readily accessible to pilgrims. Further, there may be some indication that the tradition was established prior to Christian penetration of southern Sinai (Rothenberg and Aharoni, *Wilderness*, p. 170). Again, Dt. 1:2, which placed Mt. Sinai (Horeb) an eleven-day journey from Kadesh-barnea, fits well a southern route. It should also be noted that the stations of the journey are much easier to locate along a southern route.

The existence of copper and turquoise mines in southwestern Sinai, although admittedly providing no direct link, may establish a context which lends support to a southern route. Cultural relationships between southern Sinai and Arad in the Early Bronze Age II (*ca.* 2850-2650 B.C.) suggest that miners, smiths, or traders, motivated by the presence of ore, sought out this area (R. Amiran, *IEJ*, 23 [1973], 197). Serābîṭ el-Khâdim, an Egyptian turquoise mining center, has been identified with Dophkah (Nu. 33:12) on the basis of the similarity of the Egyptian word for turquoise (*GTTOT*, § 428). Early alphabetic inscriptions (15th cent. B.C.), bearing affinities with the Semitic family of languages, suggest the use of Semitic labor. It seems clear that Semites from very early times were interested in southwestern Sinai. Moses' association with Kenites (wandering smiths) may have led him into this area, where he encountered the holy mountain.

That Israel early forgot the exact location of Mt. Sinai argues for a more remote area. It is also curious that many of the stations mentioned in the Exodus, including those in Nu. 33, are not found again either in the Bible or in extrabiblical documents, including the Karnak inscription of Sheshonq (Shishak) that lists many sites in the Negeb. It would appear that the Exodus sites were no longer normally accessible, a situation that suits the southern portion of the peninsula much better than the northern portion.

Work begun in 1956 has suggested that some of the stations mentioned before Ezion-geber should be located S of that site along the western shore of the gulf of Aqabah. Particularly striking are the identifications of Dizahab (Dt. 1:1) with Dhahab and Jotbathah (Nu. 33:33; Dt. 10:7) with Ṭabeh (Rothenberg and Aharoni, *Wilderness*, p. 167; *LBHG*, p. 183). If either identification is correct, this would argue strongly for a southern route. In addition to these specific identifications, there is some evidence that Paran, associated with Mt. Sinai (Dt. 33:2; Nu. 10:12; cf. Hab. 3:3), originally referred to the southern portion of the peninsula (*LBHG*, pp. 182f.).

Chief objections to a southern route include the assertion that the tradition is very late (4th cent. A.D.). Further, it is suggested that the locations of the initial stages presume a northern route (see III above) and that the immediate objective was Kadesh-barnea. As has been presented, the tradition may be more solid than is sometimes acknowledged, and a northern "Reed Sea" crossing does not rule out a southern route. It should also be noted that the immediate destination was the mountain of God, not Kadesh-barnea.

2. Alternate Southern Route. A few believe that Mt. Sinai should be located at Jebel Serbal, which adjoins Oasis Feiran NW of Jebel Mûsā. The identification rests upon the similarity between Feiran and Paran (see IV.C above).

Bibliography.–W. F. Albright, *BASOR*, 109 (Feb. 1948), 5-20; C. T. Beke, *Mt. Sinai a Volcano* (1873); *Sinai in Arabia and of Midian* (1878); H. Cazelles, *RB*, 62 (1955), 321-364; G. J. Davies, *The Way of the Wilderness. A Geographical Study of the Wilderness Itineraries in the OT* (1979); R. de Vaux, *Early History of Israel* (Eng. tr. 1978); O. Eissfeldt, *Baal Zaphon, Zeus Kasios und der Durchzug der Israeliten durchs Meer* (1932); *JEA*, 6 (1920), 99-116; *GP*, II, 208-216; S. Herrmann, *History of Israel in OT Times* (1975); *IDB Supp., s.v.* "Exodus, The," (M. Haran); C. S. Jarvis, *Desert and Delta* (1938); *Yesterday and Today in Sinai* (1931); *JEA*, 10 (1924); 18-39; M. Noth, *History of Pentateuchal Traditions* (1972); E. D. Oren, *IEJ*, 23 (1973), 198-204; W. M. Petrie, *Researches in Sinai* (1906); E. Robinson, *Biblical Researches*, I (11th ed., 1956); B. Rothenberg, *PEQ*, 102 (1970), 4-29; B. Rothenberg and Y. Aharoni, *God's Wilderness* (1961); A. Sneh, T. Weissbrod, I. Perath, *American Scientist*, 63 (1975), 542-48; E. P. Uphill, *JNES*, 28 (1969), 15-39.

T. V. BRISCO

EXORCISM. A word derived from the Gk. *exorkízein*, meaning "adjure," "charge (someone) under oath." The verb *exorkízein* occurs in the NT only in Mt. 26:63, where it is translated "adjure" (NEB: "charge"), and as a variant reading in Acts 19:13f. The prefixed preposition *ek* (normally "from," "out of") functions as an intensifier or perfectivizer (BDF, § 318) of the verb *orkízein*, which means "adjure" or "implore, entreat." The two uses of *orkízein* in the NT (Mk. 5:7; Acts 19:13) are translated "adjure" (NEB paraphrases "in God's name" in Mk. 5:7). The LXX uses *exorkízein* in Gen. 24:3 and 1 K. 22:16 to translate Heb. *šāḇaʿ* ("swear"), which the RSV renders "swear" and "adjure" respectively. The LXX also uses *exorkízein* to translate the verb *ʾālâ* ("to swear, curse") in Jgs. 17:2 (RSV, AV, "curse"). The verb *orkízein* is used twenty-eight times in the LXX, always as a translation of Heb. *šāḇaʿ*. The simple use of the Greek noun *exorkistḗs* in the NT is the plural form in Acts 19:13, translated "exorcists." "Exorcism" may be defined as the process of expelling an evil spirit or spirits from a possessed individual through the means of (magical) adjurations and rituals. Oaths are important in exorcism, and the invocation of a supernatural being or beings is almost always a central feature of exorcistic formulas.

I. Ancient Near East
II. OT
III. Postbiblical Judaism
IV. Greco-Roman World
V. Early Christianity
 A. Synoptic Gospels
 B. Acts of the Apostles
 C. Second-Century Christianity

I. Ancient Near East.–People throughout the ancient Near East believed that they could be subject to a variety of ill effects caused by malevolent supernatural beings ("demons"). Apotropaic techniques (used to ward off the evil effects of demonic influence) included the use of charms, amulets, and prescribed ritual procedures. When evil spirits had already succeeded in invading the personality, exorcistic techniques were used to expel the spirit and to restore the afflicted person to physical and mental health. The harmful effects of demons were thought to include physical and mental illnesses, reversals of fortune, various types of antisocial behavior, and even death. The ancient Egyptians believed that demons were among the root causes of sickness and disease, and held that such beings could be expelled by magical incantations (E. A. W. Budge, *Egyptian Magic* [1901], pp. 206-213), though this was not a major concern, for they were not preoccupied with the concept of evil (Frankfort, *Ancient Egyptian Religion* [1948], pp. 73-80). The belief in the destructive effects of evil spirits was much more pervasive in ancient Assyria and Babylonia. One result of this belief was the Akkadian conjuration-priest's practice of relieving an afflicted individual by fashioning a small figure of the demon and then destroying it in fire.

The demonological beliefs that later pervaded the Greco-Roman world derived from Persian religious traditions shaped by Zoroastrianism. One of the better-known examples was Aeshma Daeva, one of the seven chief demons under Ahriman the prince of darkness. (Aeshma Daeva appears as the demon Asmodeus in the apocryphal book of Tobit.) The *Vendidad*, a collection of books containing apotropaic and exorcistic lore regarding demons, came into existence after the 5th cent. B.C. in Persia. One object of central concern for Zoroastrians was the proper disposition of cut hair and nails, regarded as potentially useful to the daevas (demons) for their attacks on man. The fly, partially because of its predilection for filth, was regarded as the embodiment of the female demon Nasu, and elaborate cleansing rites were instituted to ward off her influence.

II. OT.–Evil spirits or demons were also familiar figures to the ancient Israelites, though surprisingly, rites of exorcism are practically unknown (*see* DEMON). Demons are referred to in Dt. 32:17 and Ps. 106:37, and elsewhere in the OT the RSV translates Heb. *śaʿîr* (lit. "hairy one") "satyr" in Lev. 17:7; 2 Ch. 11:15 (but NEB "demons," AV "devils"). Two of the more prominent demonic figures in the OT are Lilith the "night hag" (Isa. 34:14) and Azazel (Lev. 16:8, 10, 26). While the existence of malevolent evil spirits is unquestioned in the OT, they are not the object of superstitious preoccupation. In ancient Israel, as in the later rabbinic literature, evil spirits were regarded as subject to the authority of Yahweh. "Lying spirits" were regarded as commissioned by God (1 K. 22:21-23; 2 Ch.18:20-23). Satan himself was not regarded as an independent evil force, but as subject to divine authority and control (Job 1:11-13; 2:5f.). As in ancient Assyria, Babylonia, Persia, and Egypt, evil spirits were closely associated with the spread of illness and disease in Israel (Lev. 14:2-9; 2 S. 24:15-17; 2 K. 19:35; Job 2:7).

In view of the strong demonological traditions in Assyria, Babylonia, and Persia, it is noteworthy that the Israelite emphasis on the sovereignty of Yahweh did not encourage the development in the preexilic period of a consistent or complex demonology and the requisite techniques of apotropaism and exorcism. The single instance of exorcism found in the entire OT is in 1 S. 16:14-23. This passage tells how the Spirit of the Lord departed from Saul and was replaced by an evil spirit, which began to torment him. David functioned as an exorcist, for whenever the evil spirit from Yahweh troubled Saul, David would play the lyre and cause the spirit to depart from him, thereby bringing temporary relief. No magical incantations appear to have been involved, though later Jewish tradition supposed that certain Davidic psalms were particularly effective in exorcisms (see below).

In the postexilic period Judaism became more profoundly aware of the existence and effects of evil spirits, a development facilitated by the historical experience of oppression and subjugation to a series of foreign conquerors beginning with the Babylonians who conquered Judah and sacked Jerusalem in 586 B.C. Among the elements of the eschatological program formulated by the prophet Zechariah were the opening up of a fountain for cleansing from sin and uncleanness, the removal of idols, and the removal of the unclean spirit (Zec. 13:1-6). This latter act functions as a kind of national experience of exorcism that is a prerequisite for the arrival of the eschaton (cf. 1QS 4:19-21; 1QM 14:10; 1QH 3:18).

III. Postbiblical Judaism.–The elaborate demonological systems of Assyria, Babylonia, and particularly Persia had a significant influence on the development of defensive techniques — apotropaic and exorcistic incantations and rituals in Judaism. The first literary evidence for the practice of exorcism in Judaism is found in the apocryphal book of TOBIT, which may have originated as early as the 4th cent. B.C. (*see* DEMON III). Tobias the son of Tobit drove off the demon Asmodeus by burning the heart and liver of a fish. This act of exorcism probably reflected actual practice.

King Solomon was increasingly regarded in postbiblical Judaism as the exorcist and magician par excellence, and as the patron of exorcists (SB, IV, 510-13, 533f.). Solomon's phenomenal wisdom was extolled in 1 K. 4:29-34, which says not only that he composed three thousand proverbs and a thousand and five songs, but also that he "spoke of" various plants and animals. In Wisd. 7:15-22, composed during the 1st cent. B.C., Solomon's knowledge is expanded to include "the powers of spirits" and the "virtues of roots" (v. 20). By the end of the 1st cent. A.D. Solomon's reputation as a magician and exorcist had been further embellished. This is evident in the expansions of Josephus on 1 K. 4:29–32:45; "And God granted him [Solomon] knowledge of the art used against demons for the benefit and healing of men. He also composed incantations by which illnesses are relieved, and left behind forms of exorcisms with which those possessed by demons drive them out, never to return" (*Ant.* viii.2.5 [45], *LCL*). Josephus then described the technique of exorcism used by Eleazar, a contemporary Jewish exorcist. Eleazar would take a ring containing a root prescribed by Solomon and put it to the nose of the afflicted person. The odor would draw the demon out of the nose and Eleazar would then recite Solomon's name and various incantations to prevent the return of the demon. As proof that the demon had actually been expelled, Eleazar would place a container of water near the possessed person and command the demon to overturn it as he left. "When this was done," continues Josephus, "the understanding and wisdom of Solomon were clearly revealed" (*Ant.* viii.2.5).

The fullest development of the tradition of Solomon as exorcist and magician is reflected in the Testament of Solomon, a second- or third-century A.D. Jewish text, originally written in Greek, with some Christian interpolations. This document describes how Solomon built the temple in Jerusalem with the aid of demons by controlling them with a magic signet ring that he had received from the archangel Michael. Solomon interviewed a number of demons, each of whom was asked his name, the kind of malevolent activities in which he indulged, and the name of the angel who was able to control him. The demon Asmodeus, for example, was thwarted by the angel Raphael and by the burning of the liver and gall of a fish. Evidence of Solomon's influence on the magical traditions of the Greco-Roman period is the use of his name in several incantations in the magical papyri (Preisendanz, I, 102 [Pap. IV, 850, 853]; II, 218 [Pap. 10, 30]). The following adjuration is found in Preisendanz, I, 170 (Pap. IV, 3039-3041): "I adjure you by the seal which Solomon placed on the tongue of Jeremiah, and he spoke."

The practice of exorcism is also reflected in several documents among the DEAD SEA SCROLLS. In the Aramaic expansion of the Genesis account called the Genesis Apocryphon (1QapGen) 20:28f., Pharaoh asks Abraham to pray that an evil spirit may depart from his household. "So I [Abraham] prayed for that [ ] . . . and I laid my hands upon his head. The plague was removed from him and the evil spirit was commanded to depart [from him], and he was cured" (Fitzmyer, p. 67). This narrative is striking in that it is the first instance found in a Jewish source of the rite of healing by laying on of hands, which has no parallels in the OT or rabbinic literature (Flusser). Further, prayer is not associated with the laying on of hands in the NT, as it is in 1QapGen. In another document from Qumran called the Prayer of Nabonidus (4QPrNab), Nabonidus the Babylonian king says in 1:3f.: "But I prayed to the Most High God and an exorcist forgave my sins; it was a Jewish [man], one of [the exiles]," i.e., Daniel (Dupont-Sommer, p. 322). Further, in one of the apocryphal psalms found at Qumran (11QPs[a] 19:15f.), we read: "Let Satan not rule over me, nor an unclean spirit; neither let pain nor the evil inclination take possession of my bones" (Sanders, p. 121). According to 11QPs[a] 27:10 David composed four psalms for singing to the stricken, a fact that may be correlated with the rabbinic tradition that Ps. 91 was particularly suited for singing to those afflicted with demons or evil spirits (van der Ploeg). Similarly, in the *Liber Antiquitatum Biblicarum* of pseudo-Philo (a Jewish composition of the late 1st cent. A.D.), the author provides a haggadic midrash (i.e., a periphrastic interpretative expansion) of the biblical account from Genesis to the death of Saul. In 6:1-3, the author mentions David's use of the harp to drive the evil spirit from Saul and quotes an apocryphal psalm that David is supposed to have sung.

The practice of magic was generally prohibited in Judaism (Lev. 19:26, 31; 20:27; Dt. 18:9-14; 2 K. 17:17; *see* DIVINATION; MAGIC), yet evidence suggests that, while it may not have been practiced publicly, it was practiced privately and surreptitiously (Trachtenberg). References to Jewish exorcists are found within the NT (Mk. 9:38f. par. Lk. 9:49f.; Acts 19:13-16), and Jewish magicians and exorcists were highly regarded throughout the Greco-Roman world. Jewish exorcists used the name of the God of Israel in their exorcisms (Josephus *Ant.* ii.12.4 [275f.]; viii.2.5 [46-48]; Irenaeus *Adv. haer.* ii.4.6), sometimes in the formula "the God of Abraham, (the God of) Isaac, and (the God of) Jacob" (Justin *Dial.* 85.135; Origen *Contra Celsum* i.22; iv.33f.; v.45; Rist; Heitmüller, pp. 180-82). Various Hebrew names of the God of Israel, transliterated into Greek, are found in the incantations of the magical papyri, revealing the extensive influence of Jewish magic (Preisendanz, I, 114 [Pap. IV, 1230ff.]; II, 77 [Pap. XII, 287f.], 124 [Pap. XIII, 815f., 975f.]). Jewish exorcists also used angelic names in their incantations (Heitmüller, pp. 176-180), a fact attested by the third-century Jewish magical handbook entitled *Sepher ha-Razim* ("Book of Mysteries") published in 1966 by M. Margalioth. In a lengthy exorcism found in a magical papyrus entitled "The Stele of Ieu the Hieroglyphist," Jewish influence is obvious (Preisendanz, I, 184 [Pap. V, 97-120]): "I invoke you, Headless one, who created earth and heaven, who created night and day, you who created light and darkness . . . I am Moses your prophet to whom you have transmitted your mysteries celebrated by Israel. . . . Listen to me and turn away this demon."

In Babylonian Judaism of the 6th and 7th cents. A.D., the practice of apotropaic and exorcistic rites against demons is reflected by inscriptions preserved on Aramaic incantation bowls. Some of these Jewish exorcisms are structured in accordance with legal divorce terminology: "This day above any day, and generations of the world, I Kômêš bath Maḥlaphta have divorced, separated, dismissed thee, thou Lilith, Lilith of the Desert, Hag and Ghul . . . I have fenced you out by the ban which Joshua ben Peraḥiah sent against you" (Neusner and Smith, p. 335). This evidence indicates the continuous existence and practice of exorcism in Judaism from the later post-exilic period into the Talmudic period and beyond.

IV. Greco-Roman World.–Though there is evidence that the Greeks believed in supernatural possession from very early times, evidence for the practice of exorcism as the expulsion of evil spirits by magical means does not antedate the 2nd cent. A.D. (Smith, p. 409). Lucian of Samosata, a second-century A.D. Epicurean philosopher and satirist, is the first pagan author to describe an exorcism in detail (*Philopseudes* 16, *LCL*): "Everyone knows about the Syrian from Palestine, the adept in it [i.e., exorcism], how many he takes in hand who fall down in the light of the moon and roll their eyes and fill their mouths with foam; nevertheless, he restores them to health and sends them away normal in mind, delivering them from their straits for a large fee. When he stands beside them as they lie there and asks: 'When came you into this body?'

the patient himself is silent, but the spirit answers in Greek or in the language of whatever foreign country he comes from, telling how and when he entered into the man; whereupon, by adjuring the spirit and if he does not obey, threatening him, he drives him out. Indeed, I saw one coming out, black and smokey in colour." In this remarkable narrative, the therapeutic interview is presented as an essential element in exorcisms. A comparison with similar accounts (i.e., the practices of the Jewish exorcist Eleazar described in Josephus *Ant.* viii.2.5 [46-48], Apollonius of Tyana as described by Philostratus *Vita Apollonii* 3.38; 4.20, 25; and others), allows us to characterize the essential features of the therapeutic interview of the ancient exorcist: (1) the demon must speak, (2) the demon must reveal his name or his nature and his evil works, (3) the demon is commanded to leave, (4) the exorcist swears an oath in the nature of a curse making use of particularly powerful names, and (5) the demon marks his departure by an act of physical violence (Bonner, *HTR,* pp. 39-49; Smith, p. 409). Eleazar caused the demon to overturn a container of water (Josephus *Ant.* viii.2.5 [48]), while the one expelled by Apollonius overturned a statue (Philostratus *Vita Apollonii* 4.20).

From the 1st to the 4th cents. A.D., the belief in the malevolent influence of evil spirits encouraged the production of enormous numbers of magical amulets, worn to ward off the deleterious influences of demons (cf. Bonner, *Amulets, passim*). Some exorcistic formulas have been preserved in the magical papyri, among which is this short adjuration (Preisendanz, I, 114 [Pap. IV, 1239-1244]): "I adjure you, demon, whoever you are, by this god sabarbarbathioth sabarbarbathiouth sabarbarbathioneth sabarbarbaphai come out, demon, whoever you are, and keep away from so-and-so, right now! right now! quickly! quickly!"

V. Early Christianity.*–*A. Synoptic Gospels. In the NT exorcisms are primarily found in the Synoptic Gospels and Acts. Surprisingly, no exorcisms are referred to in the Gospel of John. Jesus is depicted as an exorcist in the Synoptic tradition, and He is able to delegate this ability to His disciples (Mk. 3:14f.; 6:7 [par. Mt. 10:1; Lk. 9:1; 10:17-20]; 9:18, 28 [par. Mt. 17:16, 19; Lk. 9:40]; 16:17f.). Exorcisms, which are acts of liberating afflicted persons from the malevolent influence of demons, are distinguished from other forms of cures involving the restoration to health of those whose disease or affliction was not regarded as having a demonic cause (Mk. 1:32-34 [par. Mt. 8:16; Lk. 4:40f.]; 1:39 [par. Mt. 4:24]; 3:10f. [par. Lk. 6:17f.]; Lk. 13:32; cf. Eitrem, pp. 34f.). Jesus' method of curing the sick usually involved the touch of His hand, but in performing exorcisms He avoided the use of His hand and focused on addressing the demon with short, authoritative commands. Six accounts of exorcisms performed by Jesus are preserved in the Synoptic Gospels (1) Mk. 1:21-28 par. Lk. 4:31-37; (2) Mk. 5:1-20 par. Mt. 8:28-34; Lk. 8:26-39; (3) Mk. 7:24-30 par. Mt. 15:21-28; (4) Mk. 9:14-29 par. Mt. 17:14-21; Lk. 9:37-43; (5) Mt. 9:32-34; (6) Mt. 12:22f. par. Lk. 11:14. That Jesus' ministry was characterized, among other things, by the performance of exorcisms, is indicated by a number of editorial summaries and comments by the Synoptic evangelists (Mk. 1:32-34 par. Mt. 8:16; Lk. 4:40f.; Mk. 1:39 par. Mt. 4:24; Mk. 3:10f. par. Lk. 6:17f.; Lk. 7:21; 8:2).

In two of the six exorcism stories of the Gospels, Mt. 9:32-34 and Mt. 12:22f. (par. Lk. 11:14), nothing is said of the technique used by Jesus. In three exorcism stories Jesus expels demons with short, succinct commands: "Jesus rebuked him, saying 'Be silent and come out of him!'" (Mk. 1:25 par. Lk. 4:35); "Come out of the man, you unclean spirit!" (Mk. 5:8 par. Lk. 8:29); "He rebuked the unclean spirit and said to it, 'I command you, come out of him and never enter him again!'" (Mk. 9:25 par. Mt. 17:18; Lk. 9:42). The brevity and authority of such commands and the absence of the invocation of divine or angelic names contrast with the lengthy adjurations and invocations that characterize formulas in the magical papyri (cf. the "Recipe of Pibeches" in Preisendanz, I, 170ff. [Pap. IV, 3007-3086]). That Jesus could confidently command demons and expect instant obedience indicates that He regarded Himself as in full possession of all the supernatural powers necessary for the performance of such acts. The dumbness caused by some afflicting demons depicted in the Gospels may be regarded as a way to keep the healer from starting the "therapeutic interview" (cf. Mt. 9:32; 12:22 par. Lk. 11:14; Mk. 9:17, 25). In one instance Jesus asked a demon for his name (Mk. 5:9 par. Lk. 8:30), and the occasional convulsions and collapse of the victim would provide visible proof of the expulsion of the demons (Mk. 9:26), while according to Mk. 5:13 (par. Mt. 8:32; Lk. 8:33) the demons abandoned the Gerasene demoniac for a herd of swine which then stampeded into the sea in an act of self-destruction.

In addition to the references to exorcisms performed by Jesus, three sayings of Jesus deal specifically with exorcisms. (1) In Mk. 3:19-27 (par. Mt. 12:25f., 29; Lk. 11:17f., 21f.), Jesus is accused by His enemies of performing exorcisms "by Beelzebul" (i.e., "in the name of Beelzebul"), an indirect way of charging Jesus with the practice of magic (cf. BEELZEBUL). Jesus, however, is not recorded as having invoked any supernatural being in the performance of exorcisms. (2) In Lk. 11:19f. (par. Mt. 12:27f.) it is clear that Jesus' primary purpose in performing exorcisms was not to relieve afflicted individuals (though the element of compassion is not unimportant), but to demonstrate the presence and power of the Kingdom of God through His activities and message. (3) Lk. 13:32 shows that Jesus' ministry of curing and exorcism was integral to His ministry, the goal of which was His last fateful trip to Jerusalem. Jesus' battle against demons should be viewed within the setting of the Jewish eschatological hope that the unclean spirit would finally and decisively be banished from Israel (Zec. 13:2; 1QS 4:19-21; 1QM 14:10; 1QH 3:18; Betz, pp. 116-137). Some have suggested that when Jesus was occasionally addressed as "Son of David," as by blind Bartimaeus in Mk. 10:47f., the reference is really to Son of David = Solomon, i.e., to Jesus as the heir to the therapeutic and healing abilities associated with Solomon (Fisher, Berger). Solomon is referred to as "Son of David" in such late texts as the Testament of Solomon 1:7; 20:1 and in the inscriptions on some Aramaic incantation bowls, but it is doubtful that the title "Son of David" can bear this meaning in the Gospels (Duling).

B. Acts of the Apostles. The Gospels themselves contain evidence that the name of Jesus was used during His lifetime by disciples in the performance of exorcisms (Mt. 7:22; Lk. 10:17; cf. Mk. 16:17), as well as by other Jewish exorcists not formally associated with Him (Mk. 9:38f. par. Lk. 9:49). In Acts it is primarily through the utterance of the name of Jesus that healings and exorcisms are effected (3:6, 16; 4:7, 10, 30; 9:34). The name of Jesus was regarded as so effective that it was also taken up by non-Christian exorcists (Acts 19:13; Eitrem, p. 8 n. 1). Origen noted that the name of Jesus was so powerful that it was even effective when used by evil men (*Contra Celsum* i.6).

In Acts there is a general emphasis on miracles, exorcisms, and magic, since the author wishes to demonstrate not only that the gospel proclaimed by the apostles was confirmed by supernatural demonstrations of power, but also that Jewish and pagan magic and exorcism was impotent by comparison. The occurrence of exorcisms is only generally referred to in Acts (5:16; 8:7; 19:12). The only exorcism specifically narrated in Acts (and in the entire NT apart from those performed by Jesus) is that performed by Paul in Acts 16:16-18. Irritated by a demon-possessed slave girl, he turned and said, "I charge you in the name of Jesus Christ to come out of her" (Acts 16:18).

C. Second-Century Christianity. The Church drew a sharp dividing line between Christian exorcists and pagan magicians. The second-century Christian apologist Justin Martyr contrasted successful Christian exorcists who used the name of Jesus with pagans who relied on incantations and drugs. Justin also claimed that Jewish exorcists who attempted to cast out demons in the names of Israelite kings (Solomon?), righteous men, prophets, or patriarchs would not be successful, while those who used the name of the God of Abraham, Isaac, and Jacob might succeed (*Dial.* 85). Origen, himself a firm believer in the power of magic, attributed the success of Jewish and pagan exorcisms to the use of the name of the God of the Jews (*Contra Celsum* iv.33f.). Christians too, observed Origen, used the name of the supreme God and that of Jesus to effect exorcisms and curing which non-Christian magicians found impossible (*Contra Celsum* iii.24). By the time of Justin (*ca.* 150 A.D.), the name of Jesus had been supplemented in exorcistic formulas by the phrase "crucified under Pontius Pilate" (*Apol.* ii.6; *Dial.* 30.3; 76.6; 85.2; Irenaeus *Adv. haer.* ii.49.3; *Epideixis* 97). This tendency is already observable in the MS tradition of the NT, where in addition to Peter's short statement in Acts 9:40, "Tabitha, rise," some Latin versions added the phrase "in nomine domini nostri Jesu Christi" ("in the name of our Lord Jesus Christ"). Such expansions were apparently influenced by the notion that it was the crucifixion of Jesus that spelled the potential destruction of demonic powers. The same formula also entered baptismal liturgies, which came to function as magical rituals that expelled demons from baptismal candidates (Justin *Apol.* i.61; Böcher, *Christus Exorcista,* pp. 166-180; Dölger).

Bibliography.–K. Berger, *NTS,* 20 (1973), 1-44; O. Betz, *Nov. Test.,* 2 (35 33 116-137; O. Böcher, *Christus Exorcista* (1972); *Dämonenfurcht und Dämonenabwehr* (1970); *Das NT und die dämonischen Mächte* (1972); C. Bonner, *Studies in Magical Amulets* (1950); *HTR,* 36 (1943), 39-49; F. J. Dölger, *Der Exorzismus im altchristlichen Taufritual* (1909); D. C. Duling, *HTR,* 68 (1975), 235-252; A. Dupont-Sommer, *Essene Writings from Qumran* (1962); S. Eitrem, *Some Notes on the Demonology in the New Testament* (2nd ed. 1966); L. Fisher, "Can This Be the Son of David?" in F. F. Trotter, ed., *Jesus and the Historian* (1968), pp. 82-97; J. A. Fitzmyer, *Genesis Apocryphon of Qumran Cave I* (2nd ed. 1971); D. Flusser, *IEJ,* 7 (1957), 107f.; W. Heitmüller, *Im Namen Jesu* (1903); A. Harnack, *Die Mission und Ausbreitung des Christentums* (4th ed. 1927), I, 151-170; J. M. Hull, *Hellenistic Magic and the Synoptic Tradition* (1974); S. V. McCasland, By the Finger of God (1951); C. C. McCown, *Testament of Solomon* (1922); J. Neusner and J. Z. Smith, "Archaeology and Babylonian Jewry," in J. A. Sanders, ed., *Near Eastern Archaeology in the Twentieth Century* (1970), pp. 331-347; J. P. M. van der Ploeg, "Un petit rouleau de psaumes apocryphes (11QPsAp[a])," in G. Jeremias, *et al.*, eds., *Tradition und Glaube. Festgabe für K. G. Kuhn* (1971), pp. 128-139; K. Preisendanz and A. Henrichs, eds., *Papyri Graecae Magicae. Die Griechischen Zauberpapyri* (2 vols., 2nd ed. 1973-1974); M. Rist, *JBL,* 57 (1938), 289-303; J. B. Russell, *The Devil* (1977); J. A. Sanders, *Dead Sea Psalms Scroll* (1967); K. Seligman, *Magic, Supernaturalism and Religion* (1971); W. D. Smith, *Transactions of the American Philological Association,* 96 (1965), 403-426; J. Trachtenberg, *Jewish Magic and Superstition* (1939).

D. E. AUNE

Relief on a bronze door of the Romanesque church (11th-12th cents.) of S. Zeno Maggiore, Verona, Italy, showing a bishop exorcising a demon from a woman (Rosenthal Art Slides)

EXPECT; EXPECTATION [Heb. *tiqwâ,* piel of *yāḥal* (Ezk. 13:6), *tôḥeleṯ, ʿālay śāmû* (1 K. 2:15); Gk. *prosdokáō, prosdokía, apokaradokía* ("eager expectation"; Phil. 1:20), *dokéō* (Mt. 24:44 par.), *ekdéchomai* (1 Cor. 16:11), *elpízō* (2 Cor. 8:5), *apelpízo* (Lk. 6:35)]; AV also HOPE, THINK, LOOK FOR, WAIT FOR, "set their faces on me" (1 K. 2:15), "he should have" (Acts 28:6); NEB also "was looking to me" (1 K. 2:15), "passionately hope" (Phil. 1:20).

According to its predominant OT use "expectation" is the common property of all persons, good and wicked alike. At issue is not the fact of expecting, but the realization of that which is expected, the fruition of one's desires. The hopes of the wicked are frustrated, while those of the good find fulfillment (Prov. 10:28; cf. 11:23, which contrasts good results with destructive ones). The ultimate frustration for the wicked is death, which brings an end to all their hopes. It is not clear what this expectation is, but it is clear that for the wicked any such hope is thwarted.

Theologically, it is Yahweh who is the source of the fulfilled expectation, and conversely, the cause of the thwarted hope. It is Yahweh who guarantees such an order in the affairs of the world. It is for this reason that the person who had known affliction and suffered defeat confesses the loss of any expectation from Yahweh (Lam. 3:18; but cf. 3:22-27). Closely related is the question of the fulfillment of the spoken, prophetic word. The person who proclaims a word that is not from Yahweh waits in vain for its fulfillment (Ezk. 13:6).

In the NT "expect" is often used in the sense of awaiting or anticipating the arrival of someone. Gk. *ekdéchomai* (1 Cor. 16:11) connotes awaiting, while *prosdokáō* suggests anticipation or preparation (Acts 10:24). Theologically, regarding expected salvation, the latter term is used in the parable of the true and untrue servant to describe the return of the master. He arrives at a time the servant does not anticipate, when the servant is unprepared to encounter him (Mt. 24:50 par.). In Lk. 3:15 the term is used in the context of a messianic expectation. Speaking of the unknown hour at which the Son of Man will come, *dokéō* (lit. "think," "believe") is employed (Mt. 24:44 par.).

One can also expect something — a gift (Acts 3:5) or interest (or possibly repayment) on a loan (Lk. 6:35). In the latter case, Gk. *apelpízō* (the opposite of *elpízō*), which normally means "despair," probably means "expecting nothing (in return)."

"Expect" can also be applied to an anticipated act or a consequent event (the normal consequence). Gk. *elpízo*

(2 Cor. 8:5) connotes hoping, counting upon something. In Acts 28:6 *prosdokáō* suggests that which a person has been taught or led to anticipate, the consequences that should normally or naturally follow (cf. "expecting" in 12:11, where it suggests that which one has planned or prepared). The noun *apokaradokía* of Phil. 1:20 occurs elsewhere in the NT only in Rom. 8:19, where the RSV renders it "eager longing." It means literally stretching the head forward or looking away from other objects. It is intensive, unreserved waiting or watching. It is a confident waiting and is closely related to the concept of hope. *See also* HOPE; WAIT.

Bibliography.–G. von Rad, *Wisdom in Israel* (Eng. tr. 1972); *THAT,* I, *s.v.* יחל (C. Westermann); *TDNT,* I, *s.v.* ἀποκαραδοκία (G. Delling); II, *s.v.* ἐλπίς κτλ. (Rengstorf, Bultmann); δοκέω (G. Kittel); δέχομαι κτλ.: ἐκδέχομαι (W. Grundmann); VI, *s.v.* προσδοκάω κτλ. (C. Maurer); C. Westermann, *Forschung am AT* (1964), pp. 219-265; W. Zimmerli, *Man and his Hope in the OT* (Eng. tr., *SBT,* 2/20, 1971). F. C. TIFFANY

EXPECTATION, MESSIANIC. *See* CHRISTS, FALSE; ESCHATOLOGY; JESUS CHRIST; MESSIAH.

EXPEDIENT [Gk. *symphérō*] (Mt. 19:10; Jn. 11:50; 18:14); AV also GOOD; NEB BETTER, "more to your interest." Gk. *symphérō* ("help" or "be useful, profitable") is used by the disciples when Jesus is talking about divorce. If a man commits adultery by marrying another woman after he has been divorced, the disciples ask then if it is "better not to marry" (Mt. 19:10, NEB).

The high priest Caiaphas uses the word in his "unconscious prophecy" of the salvific nature of Jesus' death when he says, "It is expedient for you that one man should die for the people, and that the whole nation should not perish" (Jn. 11:50; 18:14). This concept that "the sacrifice of an individual is never too high a price to pay for national security" has OT roots (2 S. 20:20-22; Jonah 1:12-15), and the death of Jesus was to Caiaphas and the Sanhedrin "a means by which the Jewish nation may be saved from disaster" at the hands of the Romans (Dodd, p. 62). Ironically, this death did not preserve either the temple of the Jewish people or their permanent nationhood. To John the Evangelist, however, the "expediency" of His death took on a much deeper dimension, as "Jesus was indeed to die for Israel [but] no doubt in a more profound sense than Caiaphas dreamed of" (Dodd, p. 63).

Bibliography.–R. E. Brown, comm. on John (*AB,* 2 vols., 1966, 1970); C. H. Dodd, *More NT Studies* (1968), pp. 58-69; J. Marsh, *Saint John* (*Pelican Comms.,* 1968). D. K. MCKIM

EXPERIENCE; EXPERIENCED [Heb. *yāḏaʿ*] (Dt. 1:13, 15; Jgs. 3:1); AV KNOW, KNOWN; NEB REPUTE, "take part in"; [*rāʾâ*] (Eccl. 1:16); NEB FAMILIAR; [Gk. *energéō*] (2 Cor. 1:6); AV EFFECTUAL; NEB STRENGTH; [*gínomai*] (2 Cor. 1:8); AV "come to (us)"; NEB "come upon (us)"; [*páschō*] (Gal. 3:4); AV SUFFER; [*páthēma*] ("experience of suffering," 1 Pet. 5:9); AV AFFLICTIONS; NEB "kinds of suffering." The RSV also supplies "experienced" in 1 Ch. 12:8.

Several shades of meaning are present in the RSV's use of this term. The Hebrew verb *yāḏaʿ* is a common term meaning "know," "be acquainted with," "understand"; thus the men referred to in Dt. 1:13, 15 were either men of insight and judgment, or (according to the NEB) men who were well known in Israel. The writer of Eccl. 1:16 says, "I have acquired great wisdom . . . my mind has had great experience of wisdom and knowledge." Here *rāʾâ harbēh* means "has seen abundantly," and the idea seems to be that of a wide outlook combined with actual trial of the things discovered or known.

In the NT the term is always used in connection with suffering. While *páschō* originally meant to experience any sort of treatment and *páthēma* simply denoted an experience, both terms came to denote the experiencing of ill treatment or suffering. N. J. O.

EXPERIMENT. The AV uses this word in the phrase "the experiment of this ministration" (2 Cor. 9:13; cf. RSV "the test of this service"). The Greek term *dokimḗ* denotes "approvedness" or "tried character"; thus, the apostle is saying that the liberal contribution was proof of the sincerity of the Corinthian congregation's profession.

EXPIATE; EXPIATION [Heb. *kipper, kippurîm, kappōreṯ, kōper*; Gk. *hiláskomai, exiláskomai, hilasmós, hilastḗrion*].

In the OT the NEB renders Heb. *kipper* most often by "make expiation," but also by "(secure) pardon," "blot out," "wipe away," "purge." In place of "expiate" the AV and RSV prefer "atone" or "make atonement," but also render "forgive," "appease," "be merciful," and "make reconciliation." The RSV has "expiate" in 1 S. 3:14; Isa. 27:9; 47:11; or "(make) expiation" in Nu. 8:7; 35:33; Dt. 32:43; 2 S. 21:3. In the NT the RSV has "expiate" or "expiation" in Rom. 3:25 (*hilastḗrion*; AV "a propitiation"; NEB "the means of expiating sin"); He. 2:17 (*hiláskomai*; AV "make reconciliation"); 1 Jn. 2:2; 4:10 (*hilasmós*; AV "propitiation"; NEB "remedy"). The NEB has "the place of expiation" for *hilastḗrion* in He. 9:5 (RSV "mercy seat").

"Expiation" focuses on the removal of sin, and "propitiation" on the appeasement of wrath. "Atonement" in Scripture encompasses both concepts. Expiation of sin is usually accomplished by sacrifice. The OT understands that expiation can be achieved also by intercession (Ex. 32:30), a burning coal from the heavenly altar (Isa. 6:6f.), the death of the members of a guilty family (2 S. 21:3-6), loyalty and faithfulness (Prov. 16:6), or the purging out of idolatry along with captivity (Isa. 27:8f.). Expiation results in the reconciliation of God and the sinner by removing the cause of God's wrath.

There is some debate among scholars about the emphasis of Scripture. One group of scholars argues that the meaning of atonement in the Bible is exclusively expiation. Some of them carry this idea far enough to remove all stigma of the concept of the wrath of God. Another group argues that although expiation is evident in atonement the primary emphasis is on propitiation. The influence of the former group on newer translations is extensive, as evidenced in selected passages in the RSV and especially in the general way of translating this class of words in the NEB.

To gain some insight into the debate, a consideration of the OT emphasis will be given, followed by the LXX word usage and a look at key NT passages.

I. OT.–In the OT the root *kāpar* is central to the cultic ritual of atonement. Some take it etymologically to mean "(to) cover" (Arab.). Others go to Assyrian and understand it as "wipe away." *CAD* defines *kapāru* as "wipe off, smear on, clean (objects), purify"; an example is cited where the root deals with purifying a temple (cf. Lev. 16:33). This word may connote "propitiate"; e.g., Jacob seeks to appease his offended brother with presents (Gen. 32:20 [MT 21]; cf. Prov. 16:14). When this root relates to the cultic ritual of atonement in P (the Priestly Code), however, some significant observations must be made. (1) The priest serves as the subject of "atone" (*kipper*). (2) Only things stand as direct objects of "atone," i.e., the temple (Lev. 16:11), the altar (Ezk. 43:20); however, the object may be preceded by a preposition (e.g., Ex. 29:37). (3) Frequently "atone" is followed by a person preceded by the preposition "on" (*ʿal*) or "in behalf of" (*baʿaḏ*). (4) Often a word for sin follows "atone" preceded by a preposition as "on" (*ʿal*) or "from" (*min*). (5) The ritual of atonement is to take place in the presence of Yahweh (Lev. 10:17; 14:29). (6) Atonement is made by blood since blood bears the life (*nepeš*; 17:11). (7) The result of atonement is forgiveness (4:20, 31, etc.). Therefore, concerning sacrificial atonement, both the person who sinned and the sin itself are affected by the sacrifice. The person is purged or cleansed (16:30), and the sin is covered or wiped out (4:26, 35). The extent of the sacrificial system, however, is limited to sins of inadvertence; deliberate sins are beyond its scope. Certain OT passages refer to sins that cannot be expiated at all (1 S. 3:14; Isa. 47:11; cf. Jer. 18:23). Along with the other observations, the very restricted nature of the sacrificial system explains the reason that wrath is not in the immediate context of *kipper* in P. In these passages "expiation" is a correct translation.

The place of ritual atonement, however, must be further considered within the context of the covenant. Atonement is needed only for maintaining or restoring an established relationship that is endangered or broken. Sin violates the covenant law, with the result that the unfaithful party becomes subject to a series of curses (cf. Lev. 26). The OT explicitly understands that these curses do not take effect automatically, but become active only through the intervention of Yahweh. The OT also pictures God as slow to anger, but He will definitely execute His wrath against sin (Ps. 103:8f.). Whoever violates the covenant is to take advantage of God's mercy immediately upon awareness of his sin through the proper use of the cult. Through the action of *kipper* he gains forgiveness and is rendered acceptable to God (Lev. 1:4; 4:35; cf. Ps. 65:3 [MT 4]; 79:9).

In other passages *kipper* appears in the context of wrath. Ps. 78:38 (NEB) says, "Yet he wiped out [*kipper*] their guilt and did not smother his own natural affection; often he restrained his wrath and did not rouse his anger to its height." Wrath, not yet executed, is avoided by God's expiating iniquity and granting forgiveness (cf. Ps. 65:3 [MT 4]; 79:9). Thus atonement, instead of appeasing wrath, is normally structured to avert wrath. In addition, there are a few incidences where *kipper* appears in a context in which ignited wrath is appeased. When Moses intercedes for the Israelites who had committed idolatry through worshiping the golden calf, he hopes that his intercessory prayer will make atonement for or expiate their sins and remove God's wrath (Ex. 32:30). Another incident is recorded in Nu. 25:1-13. God was executing His anger through a plague against those who had yoked themselves to Baal-peor. His wrath ceased with the slaying of a guilty couple by Phinehas, a priest. Unquestionably God was propitiated. The text affirms that Phinehas made atonement or propitiation (*kipper*; v. 13) for the people of Israel. The word *kipper,* therefore, can mean "propitiate," and it certainly bears this idea as part of its wider meaning, even in P. In summary, S. R. Driver defines the scope of *kipper* as "*make . . . harmless* or *inoperative* . . . with the attached ideas of *reinstating in His favour, freeing from sin,* and *restoring to holiness*" (p. 131).

II. LXX.–The translation of the NT forms related to *hiláskomai* as "expiate" is based upon the LXX translation of the various passages regarding atonement. To translate *kipper* the LXX most frequently uses words related to *hiláskomai,* which in classical Greek definitely means "propitiate." The verb *kipper* is also translated by other words, including *hagiázō* ("sanctify," Ex. 29:36), *athōióō* ("absolve," Jer. 18:23), *apokathaírō* ("clear off," Prov. 16:6 [LXX 15:27]), *aphairéō* ("remove," Isa. 27:9; 28:18), *aphíēmi* ("cancel," "pardon," Isa. 22:14), *gínomai katharós* ("become clean," Isa. 1:16; 47:11), *ekkatharízō* ("cleanse," Dt. 32:43), *perikatharízō* ("cleanse all around," Dt. 30:6).

Forms related to *hiláskomai* render several other Hebrew words, e.g., *ḥiṭṭēʾ* ("purify from sin" or "uncleanness"), *pillēl* ("interpose," Ps. 106 [LXX 105]:30), *ḥillâ* ("appease"), *ḥālîlâ* ("far be it"), *niḥam,* niphal of *nāḥam* ("be compassionate"), and *sālaḥ* ("forgive"). (For complete lists see Nicole.)

C. H. Dodd takes this evidence and concludes, "The LXX translators did not regard *kipper* (when used as a religious term) as conveying the sense of propitiating the Deity, but the sense of performing an act whereby guilt or defilement is removed, and accordingly rendered it by *hiláskesthai* in this sense" (p. 93). Therefore he understands that the *hiláskomai* word-group in the LXX means "expiate" with a human subject and "be gracious toward," "forgive" with a divine subject (p. 88). He further discovers that the pagan ideas of "propitiation" are preempted from this Greek root, and it in turn is filled with the uniqueness of the Hebraic view of the deity, namely, a gracious, not an angry, Being, willing to show his mercy in forgiveness.

R. Nicole and L. Morris have clearly shown that Dodd overstates his case. It is true that the view of God's wrath is radically different from the wrath of the fickle Greek gods. But both testaments give abundant testimony to the fact of God's wrath. Certain passages also make it clear that the LXX translators still understood some element of propitiation in this word-group, e.g., by using *exiláskomai* to render *ḥillâ* ("appease") in Zec. 7:2; 8:22; Mal. 1:9; and *pillēl* ("mediate," "interpose") in Ps. 106 (LXX 105):30. In conclusion, these related words take on new force and convey more strongly expiation and forgiveness than in classical Greek, and yet to the translators they surely signified some element of propitiation.

III. NT.–In the NT, He. 2:17; 1 Jn. 2:2; 4:10 reflect the idea of P's use of *kipper*. In these passages, especially He. 2:17, Christ's death expiated the sins of the people. Once Christ had expiated sin He was in a position to reconcile mankind to God. Again, God initiated the means of atonement (1 Jn. 4:10; cf. 2 Cor. 5:19). Although the immediate thrust of the verb appears to be expiation, it also includes propitiation. 1 Jn. 2:1 clearly substantiates this interpretation. The believer is promised that Jesus Christ is his advocate to the Father. An advocate is needed only when enmity exists between the parties.

The use of *hilastḗrion* in Rom. 3:25 is more complex. Büchsel takes this word as having its background in the "mercy seat" over the ark of the covenant (Heb. *kappōreṯ*; in He. 9:5 it definitely refers to the mercy seat). Christ then is a superior mercy seat sprinkled with His own blood, fully exposed and accessible to the public. Conversely, L. Morris strongly argues that it is a neuter noun that signifies "the means of propitiation." The substitutionary work of Christ has averted God's wrath and established men into a new relationship with God (pp. 185f., 202). The main thrust of Rom. 3:25 is that God has secured the remission of sin for the one who has faith in Christ. Justification was obtained by *hilastḗrion*. Although wrath is not in the immediate context of Rom. 3:21-31, it is certainly in the larger context. Rom. 1–3 is a tightly argued passage. Chs. 1–2 explicitly argue that both Gentile and Jew are subject to God's wrath (cf. 1:18; 2:5). The only remedy for the guilty is Christ's expiatory work that secures the removal of God's wrath. As in the OT, atonement in the NT is achieved by expiation, which results in propitiation. The difference in the NT is the superiority of the sacrifice and the priest, both of which are Jesus Christ.

In conclusion, sin is expiated by sacrifice, for that represents the basis of justice, life for life. Only by expiation is reconciliation possible. In pagan religion an irate god could be propitiated by a bribe or a gift. But no human means are available to propitiate Yahweh's wrath, as Isa. 47:11 clearly reveals. His wrath is fully rational and under His complete control (Jer. 30:23f.) True, He must execute it against sin unless expiation is made, but God decides when and how to accomplish proper judgment. In the meantime, He extends His mercy by providing the means of atonement. The thrust of atonement, however, centers on the cause of the wrath, not on the wrath itself. Since God, or His servant the priest, or Jesus Christ is the subject of "expiate," the emphasis is on the object of God's activity, namely the purging of sin and the cleansing of mankind. This explains why expiation is more central to *kipper* and *hiláskomai* than propitiation. As a result of expiation God is propitiated.

This emphasis on expiation reflects a strong scriptural view of sin. Sin once committed has profound effects on a person's relationship to God, to other people, to himself, and to nature. Expiation seeks to purge the enduring fact of its commitment, and it cleanses the person so that sin's hardening of the heart is ended. The process results in a renewed relationship with God, which has the potential of renewing all of mankind's other relationships. Too much emphasis on propitiation may overlook the seriousness of sin itself, and too much emphasis on expiation may ignore the importance of God's wrath. Since English is very inadequate in cultic language, the best translation for *kipper* and *hiláskomai* appears to be "atone" or "make atonement"; in that way both ideas, propitiation and expiation, are expressed.

See also ATONEMENT; PROPITIATE.

Bibliography.–C. H. Dodd, *Bible and the Greeks* (1954), pp. 82-95; T. W. Manson, *JTS*, 46 (1945), 1-10; L. Morris, *Apostolic Preaching of the Cross* (1965), pp. 144-213; *Expos.T.*, 62 (1950), 227-233; R. Nicole, *WTJ*, 17 (1955), 117-157; *HDB*, IV, *s.v.* "Propitiation" (S. R. Driver); *TDNT*, III, *s.v.* ἵλεως (Herrmann, Büchsel).

J. E. HARTLEY

EXPLAIN [Heb. *bā'ar* (Dt. 1:5), *nāgaḏ* (Gen. 41:24; 1 K. 10:3; 2 Ch. 9:2; Est. 4:8), *bîn* (Isa. 28:9), *dāḇar* (Josh. 20:4); Aram. *ḥ^{a}wâ* (Dnl. 5:12); Gk. *epilýō* (Mk. 4:34), *phrázō* (Mt. 13:36; 15:15), *ektíthēmi* (Acts 11:4), *dianoígō* (Acts 17:3), *hermēneúō* (He. 5:11)]; AV DECLARE, TELL, "make to understand," SHOW, EXPOUND, OPEN UP, UTTER; NEB also PROMULGATE, STATE, TELL, "make sense to," LAY BEFORE, EXPOUND.

"Explain" occurs in a wide variety of contexts: a man expressing feelings to a woman (Est. 4:8), a leader warning his followers (Dt. 1:5), refugees presenting their cases to city elders (Josh. 20:4), a prophet delving into something considered deeply important (Isa. 28:9), etc. Such broad usage suggests a verb of generalized intent, conveying the basic idea of "giving an account." In the one instance where "explain" occurs in direct parallel with another verb (*paratíthēmi*, Acts 17:3), it receives the particular coloring of "making plain or clear," "rendering intelligible."

See also EXPOUND.

C. G. CHRISTIANS

EXPOUND [Gk. *ektíthēmi*] (Acts 18:26; 28:23); NEB also "dealt at length"; cf. Acts 11:4, RSV "explain." The sense of *ektíthēmi* is accurately conveyed by the English verb "expound"—to set forth vigorously a case in some detail. Thus the RSV is inconsistent in rendering Acts 11:4 with the weaker "explain." *See* EXPLAIN.

In all three NT passages, *ektíthēmi* involves a similar situation: a knowledgeable authority going to passionate length to inform a person or group about specific aspects of the gospel. In each case the subject (Peter, Aquila and Priscilla, or Paul) expounds on Christian truth with painstaking thoroughness. Acts 11:4-18 informatively provides the entire exposition and the reaction of the listeners: "When they heard this, they were silenced" (v. 18). The "expounding" was necessary as a corrective in Acts 18:26, and carries the overtone of persuasive urgency in 28:23. "To expound" suggests an extended one-way presentation in 11:4 and 18:26, though heated discussion erupted (at which point is unclear) while Paul was elaborating the truths of Christianity to the Jews in Rome (28:23).

C. G. CHRISTIANS

EXPRESS. In the AV of He. 1:3 "express" means "exactly resembling the original," as the impress of a seal resembles the figure engraved upon the seal. Thus "express image" is a good translation of Gk. *charaktḗr*, lit. "engraving" and hence "impression"; cf. RSV "very stamp."

EXTINCT [Heb. niphal of *zāʿaḵ*–'extinguish']. In Job 17:1 "my days are extinct" implies that a state of existence is being brought to a close (cf. NEB "are numbered").

EXTORT; EXTORTION; EXTORTIONERS [Heb. *ʿāšaq*] (e.g., Ezk. 18:18); AV "cruelly oppress," "use oppression"; NEB "be guilty of oppression," "be bullies"; [*ʿōšeq*] (Ps. 62:10 [MT 11]; Ezk. 22:12); AV also ROBBERY; [Gk. *harpagḗ*] (Mt. 23:25; Lk. 11:39); AV RAVENING; NEB GREED; [*hárpax*] (Lk. 18:11); NEB GREEDY. The RSV translates Heb. *ʿāš^{e}qû ʿōšeq* as "[they] have practiced extortion" in Ezk. 22:29 but as "[he] suffers extortion" in v. 7 (Targum; MT *ʿāśû* instead of *ʿāš^{e}qû*).

Extortion is the acquisition of another's money or property through deceit or force or under cover of office and is closely associated with robbery (cf. Ps. 62:10 [MT 11]). The poor and the alien are easy prey for the extortioner (Ezk. 22:7, 12, 29; cf. Zec. 7:10), so Israel's law seeks to protect them (cf. Ex. 22:21-24 [MT 20-23]). Consequently, righteousness stands in antithetical parallelism to extortion (NEB Isa. 33:15; cf. 54:14). Even if a person is legally right, he cannot be righteous and take advantage of another person for his own profit (cf. Am. 2:6-8; 4:1).

God strongly exhorts His people not to set their hearts on riches, especially when they increase (cf. Dt. 6:10-13). Material things are never to become the object of trust. But he who enjoys riches, with the freedom of life-style and power that they bring, often is enticed to search for greater wealth (cf. Eccl. 5:10 [MT 9]). The anxiety may lead one to attempt to increase wealth by inappropriate means, including extortion, and to forget that power belongs to God, not to the rich (Ps. 62:10f. [MT 11f.]).

The extortioner, too, suffers for his greedy practice. A proverb in Eccl. 7:7 says, "Surely oppression makes the wise man foolish." God's judgment against whoever practices this evil is death (Ezk. 18:18). Jerusalem, too, came under God's condemnation by taking advantage of its neighbors through interest and gain by extortion (Ezk. 22:7, 12; cf. Jer. 6:6).

Jesus condemns the scribes and Pharisees for falling into this evil; they "cleanse the outside of the cup and of the plate, but inside they are full of extortion and rapacity" (Mt. 23:25). Paul unequivocally asserts that extortioners will not have a part in the kingdom of God (1 Cor. 6:10, AV). Therefore whoever wishes to walk in God's way personally avoids extortion, resists it at all levels, and seeks to help its victims.

See also LEND; OPPRESSION; INTEREST.

J. E. HARTLEY

EYE. In the OT the word "eye" generally renders Heb. *ʿayin*; there are, however, a few exceptions, e.g., *pānîm* ("face") in Ex. 20:20, *nāḇaṭ* ("look at," "obey") in Ps. 119:6, 15. In the NT the usual term is Gk. *ophthalmós*; some exceptions here are *ómma* ("eye") in Mk. 8:23 and, for "eye" of a needle, *trýpēma* ("hole," "that which is bored") in Mt. 19:24 and *trymaliá* ("hole") in Mk. 10:25 par. Lk. 18:25.

"Eye" usually occurs in Scripture in the literal sense of the physical organ of sight, one of the chief channels of information for humans. David is described as having beautiful eyes (1 S. 16:12), and in Canticles the lovers describe each other as having eyes like doves or pools (1:15; 4:1; 5:12; 7:4). Leah had "weak" eyes (Gen. 29:17), although the meaning of Heb. *raḵ* may be "delicate, tender" (cf. AV; *CHAL*, p. 339).

A cruel custom among heathen nations sanctioned the gouging out of the eyes of an enemy or rival because his power was thereby most effectively shattered (Jgs. 16:21; 2 K. 25:7; Jer. 39:7). Such blinding or putting out of the "right eye" was also considered a deep humiliation, as it robbed the victim of his beauty and made him unfit for military service (1 S. 11:2; Zec. 11:17).

The Israelites were instructed by Moses that, in the execution of Yahweh's judgment upon the nations (Dt. 7:16) and upon wrongdoers (19:13, 21; 25:12), their "eye shall not pity," i.e., be deflected from the dictates of God's law by feelings of sympathy. Similarly, Yahweh warned through His prophet Ezekiel (5:11; etc.) that "my eye will not spare, and I will have no pity." The *lex talionis* demanded "life for life, eye for eye, tooth for tooth, hand for hand, foot for foot" (Ex. 21:23-25; Lev. 24:20; Dt. 19:21).

The Bible also uses "eye" in several figurative senses, which illustrate the intimate relationship in Hebrew thought between spiritual and physical realities. Brightness of eyes is a sign of well-being (Ps. 38:10 [MT 11]; cf. 1 S. 14:27; Ps. 19:8 [MT 9]), while dimness of eyes signifies a lack of well-being (Dt. 28:65; Job 17:7; Ps. 69:3 [MT 4]; Lam. 5:17). The eye provides a concrete medium of expression for a variety of emotions or mental attitudes. The eyes may waste away with grief, or pour down tears (Ps. 6:7 [MT 8]; 31:9 [MT 10]; 88:9 [MT 10]; 119:136; Lam. 1:16; 2:11; 3:48f.). They can express mockery or hatred (Job 16:9; Ps. 35:19; Prov. 6:13; 10:10; 16:30; 30:17), haughtiness (Ps. 18:27 [MT 28]; Prov. 6:17; 21:4; 30:13), generosity (Prov. 22:9; cf. Mt. 6:22), pity (Dt. 7:16; 13:8; 19:13, 21; 25:12; etc.), greed (1 S. 2:29, 32), desire or lust (Ps. 73:7; Prov. 17:24; 27:20; Eccl. 2:10; 4:8; Ezk. 6:9; 2 Pet. 2:14; 1 Jn. 2:16; cf. Mt. 5:29), etc. To "lift up the eyes" (e.g., Gen. 13:10, 14; 18:2; 22:4, 13; 24:63f.) means to look around for information and often for help; to "close the eyes" or "hide the eyes" indicates carelessness or lack of sympathy (e.g., Prov. 28:27; Mt. 13:15); to "set eyes upon" (e.g., Gen. 44:21; Ezk. 20:24) or "fix eyes upon" (e.g., Ps. 119:6, 15; Lk. 4:20) is to turn attention to someone or something. *See also* EVIL EYE.

Often the eye represents the total process of perception and understanding (e.g., Gen. 3:5, 7). The eyes as organs of spiritual perception may be enlightened or opened (e.g., Ps. 119:18); this act is accomplished by the law of God (19:8) or by the Spirit of God (Eph. 1:18); or they may be "darkened" or "blinded" (Lk. 24:16; cf. Mt. 13:13; 2 Cor. 4:4). The psalmist ridicules the idols of the nations, for "they have eyes, but they see not" (135:16). Similar words are used by the prophet Isaiah, who is commanded to "make the heart of this people fat, and their ears heavy, and shut [Heb. hiphil of *šāʿaʿ*, "smear," "stick shut"] their eyes; lest they see with their eyes, and hear with their ears, and understand with their hearts, and turn and be healed" (6:10). The message is one of doom: since they have refused to respond to God's word, let them now persist in their insensitivity (v. 9). Isaiah is commanded to preach to them so that their hearts will become hardened and eventually they will become blind and deaf to God, incapable of responding to His message. Thus their sin becomes their punishment (*see also* HARDEN). The same charge of insensitivity to God's message and deeds is brought against the people of God in Dt. 29:4 and Jer. 5:21. Jesus Himself quotes this Isaiah passage (Mt. 13:13f.; Mk. 4:12) with reference to those in His day who would not respond to His divine message (cf. Mk. 8:18; Acts 28:26f.; Rom. 11:8).

All-seeing "eye idols" from the temple area of Tell Brak, Syria. The temple may have originally contained 20,000 or more of these idols (Trustees of the British Museum)

The OT frequently attributes eyes to God as a figurative expression of His omniscience (e.g., Job 28:10; Ps. 139:16; Prov. 15:3; cf. He. 4:13) and His watchfulness and loving care (e.g., Jgs. 18:6; Ezr. 5:5; Ps. 33:18; cf. 1 Pet. 3:12). Similarly, in the NT the seven eyes of the Lamb (Rev. 5:6) and the many eyes of the four living creatures (4:6; cf. Ezk. 1:18; 10:12) describe His unceasing watchfulness.

A common phrase in the OT (occurring only twice in the NT, Mt. 21:42; Mk. 12:11) is "in the eyes of" ("find favor in the eyes of," etc.), generally meaning "according to the judgment of" (e.g., Gen. 6:8; 20:16; 50:4; Ex. 15:26). To do "what is right in one's own eyes" is usually to do wrong, the expression denoting a stubborn unwillingness to heed the will of God (e.g., Dt. 12:8; Jgs. 17:6; 21:25). The righteous kings of Israel were those who did "what was right in the eyes of the Lord," as, e.g., King David (1 K. 15:5, 11; 2 K. 14:3; etc.).

See also APPLE OF THE EYE.

Bibliography.–*RTWB*, *s.v.* (E. C. Blackman); *TDNT*, V, *s.v.* ὁράω: ὀφθαλμός (W. Michaelis).

N. J. O.

EYELIDS [Heb. *ʿapʿappayim*, *ʿayin* (Ps. 77:4 [MT 5])]; AV also DAWNING (Job 3:9), EYES (Ps. 77:4); NEB also EYE(S), SHIMMER, etc. Eyes and eyelids in Hebrew are sometimes used synonymously, as in the parallelism of Prov. 4:25 (cf. 6:4; 30:13; Job 41:18; Ps. 11:4; Jer. 9:18 [MT 17]). Paint was frequently applied to the eyes and lids in antiquity, partly for hygienic — but also for cosmetic — purposes.

KoB (p. 723) suggests as a better translation "beams, glare, glance, beaming eyes"; cf. Job 3:9; 41:18 (MT 10).

EYEPAINT. *See* EYELIDS; KEREN-HAPPUCH; PAINT.

EYES, BLINDING OF THE. *See* EYE.

EYES, DISEASES OF THE. *See* BLINDNESS; DISEASE III.G; IV.C.

EYES, TENDER. *See* BLINDNESS.

EYESALVE (Rev. 3:18, AV). *See* SALVE.

EYESERVICE [Gk. *opthalmodouleía*]. A term coined by Paul to describe the conduct of slaves who work only when they are being watched. Their motive, therefore, is not fidelity to duty but the desire to avoid punishment or to gain reward from their masters (Eph. 6:6; Col. 3:22).

EYEWITNESS [Gk. *autóptēs*] (Lk. 1:2); [*epóptēs*] (2 Pet. 1:16); NEB also "saw with our own eyes."

Luke in his famous prologue speaks of the gospel materials as having been delivered by eyewitnesses to those who wrote down these accounts. He apparently does not know of any written accounts by these eyewitnesses themselves (cf. 2 Pet. 1:16). But those who in fact wrote down the various accounts with which Luke was familiar did so using the reports of the eyewitnesses (cf. He. 2:3). These traditions were handed down during the oral period by the eyewitnesses and ministers of the word, who served as the normative bearers of the tradition (cf. Eusebius *HE* iii.39).

The early Church greatly esteemed and valued the testimony of the eyewitnesses. The first official act of the Church was to select a replacement among the Twelve for Judas, with the one condition that the individual be an eyewitness of Jesus' life from His baptism to His resurrection (Acts 1:21f.). Further evidence that the testimony of the eyewitnesses was highly esteemed in the early Church is found in Acts 4:20; 10:39; 1 Cor. 15:6; Jn. 19:35; 21:24; 1 Jn. 1:1-3; 1 Pet. 5:1; and 2 Pet. 1:16. Some form critics have sought to minimize the importance of these eyewitnesses in the life of the early Church, arguing that the NT references are not as simple or straightforward as they first appear and that the early Church was more concerned with charismatic leadership than with a centrally organized collegium of eyewitnesses located in Jerusalem. This argument has brought Taylor's well-deserved comment (p. 41) that in the eyes of some form critics "the disciples must have been translated immediately after the resurrection." Luke clearly states that during this period of oral tradition it was the eyewitnesses who passed on the gospel traditions, thus witnessing to what they had seen with their own eyes, heard, and handled concerning the Word of Life.

Bibliography.–V. Taylor, *Formation of the Gospel Tradition* (1935); H. Riesenfeld, *Gospel Tradition* (1970); D. E. Nineham, *JTS*, 9 (1958), 13-25, 243-253; 11 (1960), 253-264; B. Gerhardsson, *Memory and Manuscript* (1961).

R. H. STEIN

EZAR ē'zar (1 Ch. 1:38, AV). *See* EZER.

EZBAI ez'bə-ī, ez'bī [Heb. *'ezbāy*–'shining,' 'blooming'; Gk. *Azōbai*]. The father of one of David's "mighty men" (1 Ch. 11:37). However, *'zby* appears to be a corruption of *'rby*, "Arbite" (2 S. 23:35).

EZBON ez'bon.

1. [Heb. *'eṣbōn*; Gk. *Thasoban*]. A son of Gad (Gen. 46:16), called OZNI in Nu. 26:16.

2. [Heb. *'eṣbōn*; Gk. *Asebon*]. A grandson of Benjamin (1 Ch. 7:7).

EZECHIAS ez-ə-kī'əs (1 Esd. 9:14, AV). *See* JAHZEIAH.

EZECIAS ez-ə-kī'əs (1 Esd. 9:43, AV). *See* HILKIAH.

EZEKIAS ez-ə-kī'əs (Mt. 1:9f., AV). *See* HEZEKIAH **1.**

EZEKIEL ē-zē'kyəl [Heb. *yᵉḥezqē'l*; Gk. *Iezekiēl*; Lat. *Ezechiel*]. A prophet at the time of the Babylonian Exile (Ezk. 1:1-3; 3:11, 15; 11:24), the son of the priest Buzi. In the Hebrew canon this book follows Isaiah and Jeremiah as the last of the three Major Prophets. The LXX and most versions insert Lamentations between Jeremiah and Ezekiel because of the attribution of Lamentations to Jeremiah.

I. Prophet's Name
II. History of Criticism
III. Locale of the Prophet
  A. Problems with Babylonian Locale
  B. Varied Solutions
  C. Ezekiel at Gilgal
  D. Ezekiel in the Diaspora
  E. From Egypt to Israel
IV. The Man and His Message
  A. Mystic and Visionary
  B. Member of the Elijah School
  C. Sound in Body and Mind
  D. Herald of Individualism
  E. Deuteronomic Reformer
  F. Priest
  G. Internationalist
  H. Herald of National Renewal
  I. Poet and Dramatist
  J. Prophet of the Word
V. Editing
  A. By Ezekiel
  B. By a Disciple
  C. Additions to Chs. 40–48
  D. Fifth-Century Additions
  E. Additions from the Time of Alexander
  F. Major Revision
  G. Summary
VI. Canonicity
VII. Rabbinic Speculations Concerning the Chariot
VIII. Ezekiel and the NT
IX. Alternative Views and Additional Information
  A. Authorship and Locale
  B. "Set Your Face" as a Messenger Formula
  C. Eschatology

I. Prophet's Name.–Ezekiel's name (identical with that of JEHEZKEL) may be interpreted variously. The book suggests three meanings: (1) "God is strong, prevails" — at his call, Yahweh's hand was "strong" upon him (3:14), overwhelming him with a sense of divine presence and commission; (2) "God makes strong" — hence God "will strengthen the arms of the king of Babylon" (30:25) and "strengthen the weak" of His own flock (34:16); (3) "God makes hard" — therefore He will make Ezekiel every whit as "hard-headed" as his opponents, so that unflinchingly he will proclaim God's word to them (3:8f.).

II. History of Criticism.–The book has been exposed to many serious challenges to its unity and authenticity for over fifty years. Even the locale of the prophet, his sanity, and his authorship of prose in the book have all been questioned. Yet serious criticism was not anticipated at the close of the last century, and had only modest beginings at the opening of the 20th century. The general viewpoint at the end of the 19th cent. was summed up by S. R. Driver (p. 261, 1891 ed. [= p. 279, 1956 ed.]): "No critical question arises in connection with the authorship of the Book, the whole from beginning to end bearing unmistakably the stamp of a single mind."

Yet scholars have observed numerous repetitions, doublets and illogical breaks in the text. In 1900 R. Kraetzschmar suggested that these were the consequence of late editorial combining of two different recensions of the text, one of which was in the first person, the other in the third person (cf. 24:24).

In 1908 and 1924, J. Herrmann endorsed Kraetzschmar's theory that Ezekiel is an edited work incorporating dual recensions; but these were not distinguished by differences of person. He insisted that Ezekiel, as his own editor, added dates to a number of oracles; but the prophet gave primary consideration to homiletical and topical arrangement, so that some passages are out of chronological order, and not a few duplicate passages are to be found. In his final editing, he expanded and reinterpreted some of his earlier oracles. Although nearly all the book is by Ezekiel, there are evidences of later editorial activity.

G. Hölscher made a radically new approach in 1924, arguing that the authentic writing by Ezekiel was to be confined to a small poetic nucleus, all of it composed in the 3+2 rhythm characteristic of *qînâ*, or dirge (*see* POETRY, HEBREW II). He omitted some oracles because they seemed to imply the prophet's presence in Palestine. He retained as authentic only fifteen short poetic oracles and a few brief prose statements necessary for locating the prophet geographically and historically, keeping in whole or in part only 170 verses out of a total of 1273. He held that the book received its final and fullest redaction sometime after the rebuilding of the temple and before the time of Nehemiah (*ca.* 500-450 B.C.).

Hölscher's view was to most scholars far too radical, especially to W. Kessler and R. Kittel, who attributed both prosaic and poetic oracles to the prophet. Yet even Kittel felt a certain discordance between the prophet's Babylonian locale and his preoccupation with Palestine, and between his priestly and his prophetic concerns — which he reconciled by asserting that Ezekiel had "two souls in one breast" (p. 146).

In 1930 C. C. Torrey published the most radical view of Ezekiel. According to him the prophecy is a late pseudepigraphon composed *ca.* 230 B.C. It consists of an imaginary prophecy by one of the unnamed prophets of Manasseh's reign (2 K. 21:10), *ca.* 692-639 B.C. As the book was originally written, this prophet was a Palestinian; and his oracles were dated to the reign of Manasseh, who alone of the last kings of Judah ruled as long as thirty years (Ezk. 1:1). Torrey's assumption that the Deuteronomic reform carried out by King Josiah was permanent prevented him from placing the beginning of Ezekiel's ministry as late as the reign of Zedekiah, for Ezekiel constantly denounces practices abolished by Josiah. Soon after its composition the book was edited into an apology for the Jewish temple and cult as opposed to the Samaritan. It is this editing that altered the time and place of the prophet's ministry.

Also in 1930, James Smith set forth views of Ezekiel similar to those of C. C. Torrey, except that for Smith the prophet was a historical figure living in the area of the former northern kingdom of Israel. Late in his career, he may have visited exiles from that kingdom in Assyria.

G. R. Berry, in a review of C. C. Torrey, at once argued that the Palestinian locale of Ezekiel was correct, but that his oracles are to be dated from the fifth year of King Jehoiachin's captivity (1:2), which is likewise the fifth year of Zedekiah's reign. The authentic oracles are messages of doom for Judah; all the other materials (promises of restoration, oracles against foreign peoples, and apocalyptic materials [chs. 38–39]) are later additions. The whole book was subject to a revision in the middle of the 3rd cent. B.C., to which Berry attributed most of the legal and priestly materials as well as the Babylonian locale.

Torrey's views provoked strong rebuttals from other American scholars such as Shalom Spiegel and W. F. Albright, who continued to argue for the traditional understanding of Ezekiel. Yet eventually Spiegel conceded (*JBL,* 54 [1935], 145-171) that some passages were addressed to Hebrews living in Palestine, not to Babylonian exiles. He suggested that Ezekiel prophesied in Judah late in the reign of King Jehoiakim, or even as late as the fourth year of Zedekiah's reign; but shortly thereafter he went to the exiles in Chaldea (1:2f.). In this Spiegel was anticipated by Oesterley and Robinson in 1934 (pp. 328f.).

In 1932, V. Herntrich espoused a view of Ezekiel similar to Berry's. He was the first to support the theory of the Palestinian locale by a detailed critical analysis of the whole book. He postulated an exilic redaction at about the time that traditional scholarship supposed that Ezekiel had edited his own book. This redaction was responsible for the following: the throne vision of ch. 1, the exilic frame of the prophet's call in chs. 2–3, the visionary framework of chs. 8–11, the interpolation of chs. 9–10, the Babylonian setting of the account of the refugee (33:21f.), the sacerdotal program of chs. 40–48, and numerous minor interpolations. Many passages are of doubtful origin, especially oracles against foreign nations. Instead of finding a solution to the problems of the book in the dual personality of the author (as Kittel had done), he attributed the book to two distinct sources: Ezekiel himself in Palestine, and a priestly redactor of the Babylonian captivity.

J. B. Harford, in 1935, rebutted the views of James Smith (who had assigned the prophet to the northern kingdom of Israel) by a careful study of the expression "house of Israel." Its primary reference, according to him, was to Judah and Jerusalem rather than to Israel and Samaria — and Ezekiel was a Judean prophet.

In 1936 A. Bertholet assigned the prophet two ministries — the first in Palestine, after his vision of the scroll (Ezk. 2:9–3:3), the second in Chaldea, following his vision of Yahweh on the throne chariot (ch. 1). The former is to be dated to the fifth year of Jehoiachin's captivity, according to 1:2 (593 B.C.); but the latter to the thirteenth year (his emendation of the thirtieth year of 1:1), i.e., 585 B.C. Between these two ministries was a brief transitional ministry outside Jerusalem, where he withdrew shortly before the fall of Jerusalem (the "another place" of 12:3), and where he remained until he received news of Jerusalem's fall (33:21).

I. G. Matthews, in 1939, espoused views similar to those of Herntrich, but he allowed that Ezekiel may have written some of the hopeful materials, especially the promises for spiritual renewal, whereas materialistic hopes, sacerdotal promises, and eschatological materials were probably from a later, postexilic editing, between 520 and 500 B.C.

In the same year O. R. Fischer completed his Boston University thesis, which became the basis of the views of R. H. Pfeiffer. Like Bertholet, he divided the ministry of Ezekiel between Palestine and Babylon; but the vision that sent him on his Palestinian mission was received in Babylon, and the vision that launched his Babylonian ministry was received in Judah. The prophet traveled back and forth between the two areas. The exaggerated language of 8:3 was Ezekiel's way of describing inspired travel on foot. The whole book was basically authentic, except for the apocalyptic section (chs. 38–39).

W. A. Irwin picked up another thread of criticism, namely Hölscher's concern for an originally poetic author. Freed from the presuppositions that Ezekiel's meter needed to be uniform and that Ezekiel must have been in the Exile, Irwin reconstructed more authentic poetry — yet not very much more. In his book of 1943 he denigrated Hölscher's work of reconstruction as "pure subjectivism" (p. 12); and, despite his own attempt at an inductive method, most reviewers have passed a similar judgment upon Irwin's limited restorations.

Recognition of Ezekiel as a Palestinian prophet became widespread. P. Auvray (1948), H. W. Robinson (1948), J. Steinmann (1953), and H. G. May (1956) divided the prophet's ministry between Judah and Chaldea. Erratic views which locate Ezekiel in Palestine, but in a late postexilic period, are those of N. Messel (1945) and L. E. Browne (1952) — the former dating the prophet to *ca.* 400 B.C., the latter in the next century, in the time of Alexander the Great. Torrey's view of the book as a late pseudepigraph was endorsed by A. van den Born (1947), who, however, dated the composition to the earlier period of Ezra and Nehemiah. In 1951 O. Eissfeldt reported: "The majority of scholars would restrict Ezekiel's share in his book to a minimum, and represent him as prophesying either solely or additionally in Jerusalem" (p. 153).

Yet some continued to defend the traditional view of Ezekiel, while having to deal with the problem that this poses for the prophet's personality. Thus G. A. Cooke defended the supposed absurdity of "a prophet in Babylonia hurling his denunciations at the inhabitants of Jerusalem across 700 miles of desert" (p. xxiii) by averring (p. xxiv) that "to a man of Ezekiel's temperament the unseen was more vividly present than the seen." Kittel's idea of Ezekiel's schizophrenia was developed to absurd lengths by E. C. Broome, and G. Widengren interpreted Ezekiel in the light of parapsychic experiences.

A new trend in criticism began with the publication of the dissertation of C. G. Howie (1950). He argued strenuously for the prophet's exilic locale. He placed great weight upon archeological indications of Ezekiel's Babylonian milieu, citing such data as the imagery of the vision in ch. 1, the ceramic map of 4:1, and Ezekiel's digging through a sun-dried clay brick wall (12:5). In the hill country of Judea at that time only stone walls were used. If 8:8 seems to indicate an exception, one must remember that Ezekiel's tour was in vision only and need not be historical. Even the report of the death of Pelatiah in Jerusalem under the impact of the prophet's preaching (11:13) is to be explained as an embellishment based upon an oral report reaching the prophet at a later time. Ezekiel did not need to be present in Jerusalem to denounce it, since, as in oracles against foreign nations, the prophet could hurl his anathemas from afar. Then, too, as Jer. 29 proves, travel and correspondence between Babylon and Jerusalem continued, so that indirectly the Judeans could learn of Ezekiel's prophecies. He explained the relevance of the prophet's proclamations of doom for Judah as one of disabusing the exiles of any idea of their early return from captivity.

In his 1952 discussion of the chief problems of Ezekiel G. Fohrer stressed the book's theological aspects, which in his view both added to the relevance of the prophet's message for the exiles and reinforced the substantial unity of the book. Yet his analysis stresses complexity in literary development.

In the wake of Howie and Fohrer, most scholars have acceded to the Babylonian locale and to the basic unity of the book, with the authenticity of only a few passages being questioned. This view gives a much larger place to the contributions of disciples and editors than the earliest criticism. Still the result is a modified traditional view, championed by such scholars as W. Zimmerli, W. Eichrodt, and J. W. Wevers, whose commentaries are standard reference works. P. Auvray and W. H. Brownlee have continued to uphold the Palestinian locale.

***III. Locale of the Prophet.**–A. Problems with Babylonian Locale.* The issues raised by the study of the book show the need to weigh the evidence for the prophet's locale. The difficulties that the book presents for the Babylonian locale of the prophet are as follows.

(1) "The house of Israel" is used everywhere before the fall of Jerusalem (587 B.C.) for the Judean kingdom, except where it is necessary to distinguish the northern kingdom from the southern. Twice, in order to include the exiles, the book speaks of "the whole house of Israel" (11:15; 37:11). When the exiles alone are in view, after 587, "house of Israel" can designate them (36:16-20).

(2) The address of Ezekiel's sermons to Judah and Jerusalem indicates more than apostrophe, for he must "*make known* to Jerusalem her abominations" (16:2; 22:2). The promises of restoration (11:17-20; 20:41-44; 34:11-31; 36–37) are addressed to Jews scattered in many lands, not specifically to Babylonian exiles.

(3) His implied presence in Palestine is pervasive, though sometimes subtle, as in calls to repentance in order to avert ruin and death (3:17-21; 18; 33:1-20). He is said to "dwell in the midst of a rebellious house" (12:2), which he is to warn of coming exile. In ch. 8 he witnesses the abominations practiced in the temple and discovers seventy elders in secret conclave, of whom he recognizes one. In ch. 11, he visits the east gate of the temple, where he finds twenty-five men in secret counsel, two of whom he knows by name. He accuses them of murder, and Pelatiah the son of Benaiah drops dead.

(4) He has intimate acquaintance with the moral, political, and military conditions in Judah. He even addresses the sentiments of the people in Palestine, answering them directly (11:15; 12:21-28; 20:32; 33:23-29). His oracles often echo themes in Jeremiah, which is natural if both men were in Judah.

(5) No distinctive information about the Babylonian exiles is given. Only upon the assumption that he is among them may one infer a little about the exiles. Since he had a house (Ezk. 3:24; 8:1) and a wife (24:15-18), one supposes that they followed Jeremiah's advice and built houses and married (Jer. 29:5f.). Since elders of Judah (Ezk. 8:1) and Israel (14:1; 20:1) visit him, some have inferred that the exiles had worked out their own social organizations; but others think these elders came to him from Palestine. Since false prophets in the Exile were predicting their early return to Judah (Jer. 29), some have interpreted his prophecies of further ruin for Judah as an indirect reply to them; but Ezekiel never mentions this hope of the exiles. Where Ezekiel addresses the moods and sayings of his auditors (e.g., 18:2; 33:10), the statements are just as appropriate for people in the motherland (Jer. 31:29f.). A late editor may have known of a Jewish settlement in Chaldea at Tel-abib by the river Chebar (1:1; 3:15); but this place, as will be seen below, may be Palestinian.

(6) Apostrophe would be insufficient to accomplish the prophetic mission. Some have argued that the magical power of the spoken prophecies was sufficient to bring doom upon Judah; but the mission of the prophet was one of warning the people so that they would repent and avoid ruin. The urgency of warning every soul (33:1-9) would not be satisfied by his reliance upon rumor to carry his message to Palestine. Josephus (*Ant.* x.7.2 [106]) suggested that Ezekiel wrote letters, but these are never mentioned in the biblical text.

(7) The supposed miraculous or visionary transport of the prophet to Jerusalem (8:3) supports the contention that his personality was abnormal. It is sometimes claimed

that he was so unhappy in the Exile that he escaped into imaginary flights. Thus by mental telepathy he saw Pelatiah die in Jerusalem (11:13). His alleged schizophrenia is supported by 4:4-8, where he is supposed to lie 390 days (190 in the LXX) on his left side without turning, and then to lie another forty days on his right side without shifting. This feat is so extraordinary that it has been interpreted as evidence for catalepsy, which is not an organic disease, but a symptom of aggravated schizophrenia. In brief trances of this kind, during which one may see visions, a few minutes may seem like days.

B. Varied Solutions. Varied solutions to the problem of locale have been noted (see II above).

(1) The prophet's unusual (if not abnormal) personality was capable of embracing a wide variety of literature and outlook. It is not necessary, therefore, to say that the moral and poetic prophet could not compose a program of restoration in prose (chs. 40–48).

(2) Through telepathic powers he knew the exact date that Nebuchadrezzar laid siege to Jerusalem (24:1f.) and witnessed events in the temple (chs. 8–11).

(3) He was not really preaching to Jerusalem (despite 16:2; 22:2; etc.), but to the exiles in Chaldea, seeking to disabuse them of their false hopes.

(4) Ezekiel was either solely or initially a Palestinian prophet, but later editing has confused the issue.

(5) Ezekiel's original messages were often poetic, and their careful reconstruction often brings into stronger focus the implied Palestinian locale of his announcements of doom for Judah.

The present author believes that there is some truth in (1), using the word "unusual," but not "abnormal." He sees no need to resort to (2), since numerous texts either imply or state the prophet's presence in Judah. Solution (3) is an improbable rationalization. Solution (4) is fundamentally the correct solution, but it is important to understand how and why the editing was achieved. Solution (5) contains much truth; perhaps half of the book was composed in poetry; but poetic reconstructions are too long to be undertaken here. Both Hölscher and Irwin pointed the way, but they failed to grasp the wide stylistic range of the poet and the basic genuineness of most of the book, including prose materials such as chs. 1, 8–11, and 40–48. Though glosses, textual corruptions, and interpolations seem to be more common than in the other prophets, most of the book is authentic. Most of the literary problems arise from conflations (interweaving) of originally separate oracles or of different versions of the same oracle that the prophet preached in different periods of his career.

C. Ezekiel at Gilgal. 1. Gôlâ (Exile) = Gilgal. The varied spellings of GILGAL, together with the geographic requirements of the book, suggest that references to the *gôlâ* ("exile") conceal original mentions of Gilgal, Ezekiel's hometown. In the original consonantal spelling, "to [or at] Gilgal" was written *hglglh,* whereas "the exile" was written *hglh* (or *hgwlh*). The former could easily be reduced to the latter, either through scribal error or through editorial verbal play (discussed below). Very suggestive here is a peculiar spelling of Gilgal as *Golgol* in the LXX of Dt. 11:30; from this pronunciation one would get the Hebrew of "to Gilgal" in expansive spelling as *haggôlgôlâ,* which compares closely with *haggôlâ* ("the exile"). An ending that was originally locative (*h* or *â*) may in popular usage have become accepted as part of the name (cf. Josh. 5:9, LXX: "He called the name of that place *Galgala*"). Other dialectical forms of the name are possible, such as *haggalgôlâ* and *haggalgûlâ.*

2. Gilgal near Jericho. The Gilgal located NE of Jericho satisfies the geographical requirements. (On identification of the town see J. Muilenburg, *BASOR,* 140 [Dec. 1955], 11-33; B. M. Bennett, *PEQ,* 1973, pp. 111-122; G. Landes, *Report on Archaeological Work at Suwwanet eth-Thaniya, Tananir, and Khirbet Minha (Munhata)* [*BASOR Supp. Studies,* 21, 1975], pp. 1-24.) It is situated near a plain (3:22f.) and close enough to Jerusalem that a fugitive could bring Ezekiel news of the city's destruction in one night's downhill flight (24:25-27; 33:22). The area was watered by three copious springs (ʿAin ed-Dûq, ʿAin en-Nuʿeima and ʿAin Dajani) that once made of the Wâdī en-Nuʿeima in this area a perpetual river (Heb. *nāhār*), whereas later irrigation control that removed the water from the river bed has made of it a dry wadi (Heb. *naḥal*) most of the year. However little or much the flow of water from these springs was controlled in Ezekiel's time, the abundant water supply can explain the reference to his vineyard in 19:10: "Your mother was like a vine of *your vineyard* [so to be read], planted beside the water."

References to Tel-abib and the river Chebar (1:3; 3:15; 10:20-22; 43:3) are so few and nonessential to the understanding of the book that some have found it reasonable to explain them as interpolations based upon traditional data concerning known circumstances of the exiles in Babylon. Of the three named tells in the OT, the two not mentioned in Ezk. 3:15, Tel-melah and Tel-harsha (Ezr. 2:59 par. Neh. 7:61), are places from which exiles returned to Judah. Tel-abib as a place of Jewish settlement in Babylonia would provide us with a triple strand difficult to break. Some Mesopotamian towns with the prefix tēl (Bab. *til*) were not settled by Jews, e.g., Til-Turahi (*ANET,* pp. 278f.) and Til-Zibar (Albright, pp. 100f.). The inference that Tel-abib was a Babylonian site may be reinforced by the observation that ancient ruins throughout Mesopotamia were often termed examples of *til-abūbi* ("mound of the flood"), a ruin so old that people believed that it was a city destroyed by the great Flood. It may even be that before Tel-melah and Tel-harsha were settled by the Jews, they also were classified as examples of the *til-abūbi.* Assuming that Jewish exiles settled at one such site, they may have punned this popular designation as *Tēl-ʾāḇîḇ,* "mound of young barley heads." For a river named Chebar, one refers to the Babylonian canal *Nāru Kabari* ("big canal"), whose existence is attested in the 5th cent. B.C. Perhaps Tel-abib was near this canal.

The question now arises, however, whether this speculative position should be replaced by another speculation; for Gilgal seems to have consisted of several small, neighboring settlements that bordered the Wâdī en-Nuweiʿmeh. One may suggest, but not prove, that one of these was specified by the Hebrew name Tel-abib (*tēl ʾāḇîḇ*), or simply *ʾĀḇîḇ,* and that the Wâdī en-Nuʿeima was then called the river Chebar (*nehar kebār*). For the sake of comparison one may note that another nearby wadi, the Wâdī Kelt, is known popularly in the area as *Wâdī Kabîr* ("big wadi").

Constructions in the area have always been made of sun-dried clay bricks, and excellent examples from the time of Ezekiel have been found (cf. 12:5, 7).

3. The Plain of Ezekiel's Visions. This is possibly "the plain of Jericho" (Dt. 34:3), at the edge of which Gilgal is situated. This makes vivid his going forth into the "valley" or "plain" (3:22f.; 37:1). There one could get an unobstructed view of any storm sweeping down from the north (1:4).

This is also a suitable location for the enacted pantomime of 21:18-23 (MT 23-28). The prophet is to go to an intersection and set up signs, one reading "To Rabbah" and the other "To Jerusalem." Several places in the lower Jordan Valley would be appropriate for such an action.

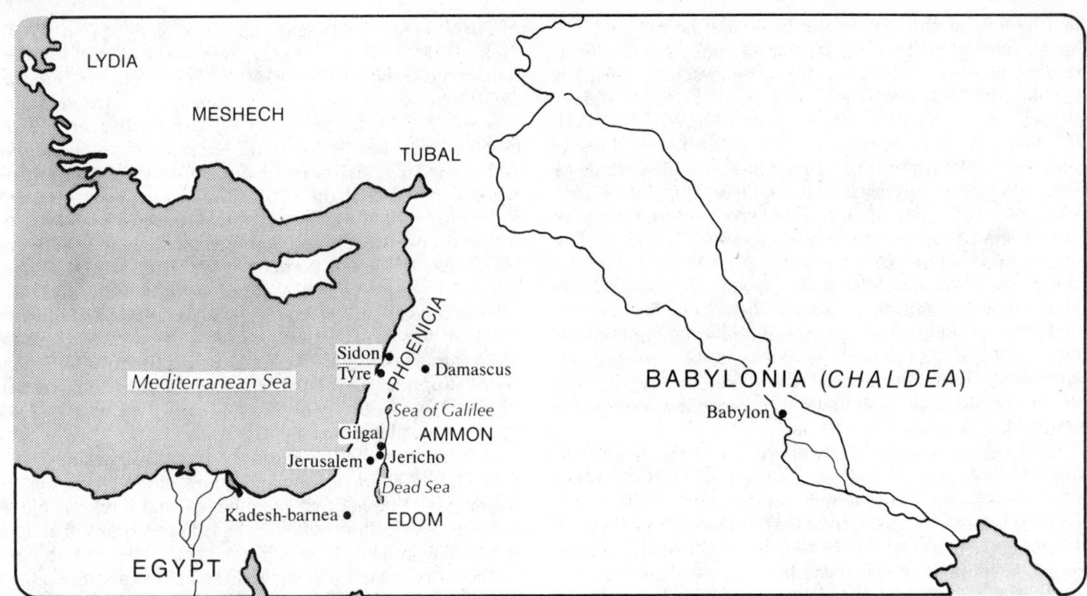

The bones of fallen warriors that Ezekiel in his old age saw in the plain (37:1-14) could be the remains of Zedekiah's army, which was defeated and dispersed there in July, 587 (2 K. 25:3-21; Ezk. 12:10-20). Herodotus (iii.12) has described a similar battlefield.

4. Religious Importance of Gilgal. The Gilgal near Jericho was important for the religious traditions that may have influenced Ezekiel. It figures in the story of conquest under Joshua, and remained an important center for national rallies and religious pilgrimages in later history. The priestly laws of Ezk. 40–48, which cannot all be reconciled with the priestly legislation of the Pentateuch, may stem from the traditions of this Gilgal. Elijah and Elisha established a school of prophets at Jericho and Gilgal (2 K. 2:5; 4:38). Even if this one were a different Gilgal, Jericho was so near Ezekiel's residence that any continuing influence of these "sons of the prophets" would be felt at the neighboring Gilgal.

5. Gilgal and Exile. The word *haggôlâ* is probably not the only corruption of the text. It is easy enough to explain "in the land of the Chaldeans" at 1:3 as a simple interpolation; but this may interpret an original "in Gilgal" (cf. 1:1) and be intended as a stylistic variation from the preceding *haggôlâ*. Similarly, at 11:24, the prophet possibly wrote: "And the Spirit lifted me up and brought me eastward [*qādîmâ*] to Gilgal." If so, this was revised to read: "and the Spirit lifted me up and brought me *in the vision by the Spirit of God into Chaldea [Kaśdîmâ] to the exiles.*"

The original reference to Gilgal in 11:24 is supported by the punning prophecy of Gilgal's imminent exile in the immediately following passage (12:1-9, 11). Such a pun is as ancient as Am. 5:5: "Gilgal [*hglgl*] shall surely go into exile [*glh yglh*]." The symbolic pantomime of digging through the wall at night does not represent captivity, but secret flight. This is an example of what the Qumrân commentary on Nahum calls "exile from fear of the enemy" (4QpNah 2:5). The case of Zedekiah (12:10, 12f.) is no exception, since before his capture he too was a fugitive. It is with the scattering of the people from the land, not with the captivity, that the prophet was constantly concerned (5:12; 11:16f.; 17:21; 20:34, 41; 28:25; 34:12; 36:19). Verses 6:8f. are exceptional in linking exile with captivity. Excavations at Gilgal (as also at nearby OT Jericho) reveal that all the constructions there were of a good quality of sun-dried clay bricks, which are the kind through which Ezekiel could dig.

D. Ezekiel in the Diaspora. 1. Idiom of Dispatch. An overlooked idiom in Ezekiel is "Set your face toward [place name, or personal name], and prophesy against [person or place], and say, 'Thus says Yahweh.'" In the literature of ancient Ugarit, whenever a god dispatches a messenger, he is told to set his face toward such and such divine person or place and to deliver such and such a message from the god sending him. This command is followed by a report of compliance, relating how the messenger actually went and delivered the message. (See J. C. L. Gibson, *Canaanite Myths and Legends* [2nd ed. 1978], e.g., Palace of Baal, 3F:vi:12ff. [p. 55]; Keret, 14: vi:301ff. [p. 90]; cf. also Gen. 31:21; Nu. 24:1; 2 K. 12:17; Jer. 44:12; Dnl. 11:17; Lk. 9:51.)

The same language occurs frequently in Ezekiel, but without the report of compliance, which may have seemed redundant. Thus the prophet does not often record his obedience in connection with symbolic actions (e.g., 4:1–5:4; 6:11; 12:17f.; 21:12-14, 18-20 [MT 17-19, 23-25]).

2. Messenger to the Nations. Interpreting the "set your face" passages as the language of dispatch (except for 4:7, where the Hebrew is different) makes Ezekiel visit "the mountains of Israel" (6:2), southern Judah (20:45f. [MT 21:1f.]), and Jerusalem (21:2 [MT 7]), and it also sends him home to rebuke the false prophetesses (13:17). More dramatically, it sends him forth into neighboring nations: Ammon (25:2), Phoenicia (28:21), Egypt (29:2), and Edom (35:2). Many scholars have noted Ezekiel's remarkable familiarity with Tyre: its island location, its resemblance to a ship, its seafaring, its commerce, and its mythology (26–28). Hence they have suggested his presence in Tyre at some time. If he actually visited these lands, his statements about what the peoples were saying are not all hearsay or literary convention (25:3, 8; 26:2; 27:3; 28:2; 29:3, 9; 35:10, 12; 36:2, 13) — even though the precise, poetic phrasing of their sentiments no doubt comes from the prophet. According to the MT of 2:3, the prophet was sent not only to Israel, but also "to nations that are rebellious" (ASV).

3. Ezekiel in Babylon? Did Ezekiel ever go to Babylon?

In the light of the above, one would like to affirm this. L. Finkelstein (*The Pharisees: The Sociological Background of Their Faith* [1938], I, 338) suggested that the cryptic meaning of 38:2 is: "Son of man, set your face toward Gog of the land of Babel" — reading *bbl* (Babel) for *mgg* (Magog). Ezekiel, he suggested, resorted to midrashic ciphers in order to conceal his message from the Babylonian authorities. Since, however, the prophet was frank and open toward other rulers and nations, this explanation seems less likely than a later editorial concealment of the prophet's presence outside "the land of Babel" until a late date in his career. The cryptic device would be first the spelling of Babel backwards (*lbb*) and then the substitution for each letter of the word the next letter of the Hebrew alphabet (*mgg* = Magog). As appealing as this suggestion is, it seems doubtful in view of the questionable genuineness of 38:1–39:16 (on which see below).

4. Ezekiel in Egypt, Interrupted by Visits Elsewhere. Ezekiel first went to Egypt on Jan. 7, 587, as the idiom of dispatch at 29:1f. indicates. This date corresponds to the lifting of the siege during the approach of Pharaoh Hophra's army (Jer. 37:5), when Jeremiah tried to return to Anathoth but was arrested (37:11-15). Ezekiel delivered three oracles in Egypt that spring (29:1-16; 30:20-26; 31). The other oracles against Egypt are later: (1) March 13, 586 (LXX) or March 3, 585 (MT) (32:1-16); (2) April 27, 586 (32:17-32); (3) April 26, 571 (29:17-20); and (4) probably 30:1-19, which is undated.

Other antiforeign oracles (chs. 25–28) lie between these two sets of dated messages to Egypt. The interval is sufficient to suggest that during the early summer of 587 Ezekiel returned to Gilgal, where his wife died (24:15-24) and he learned of Jerusalem's destruction on the day it happened, in agreement with 24:25-27. At 33:21f., one needs to correct the reading of the MT from the twelfth year/tenth month/fifth day to the eleventh year/fifth month/tenth day. With the MT date, it took the news seventeen months to reach the prophet in Babylon — which is far too long. One may reduce the time by a year by reading the eleventh year with the LXX, Syriac, and eight Hebrew MSS. Even so, Ezekiel would have been the last person in Babylonia to get the news! Ezra took only 108 days to make the journey with a considerable company (Ezr. 7:9; 8:31). Since Ezk. 24:25-27 requires that the news reach the prophet on the day of the temple's destruction, a transposition of the dates of the month and day is required; this corrected date (Aug. 28, 587) agrees with Jer. 52:12.

It was probably in late September or during October, after the assassination of Gedaliah (2 K. 25:24; Jer. 41–43), that Ezekiel went with other refugees to Transjordan (ch. 25) and after that, as early as November (?), to Phoenicia (chs. 26–28). His one dated oracle there, ch. 26 against Tyre, probably dates to the first day of the eleventh month of the eleventh year (the number of the month having fallen out), i.e., Feb. 13, 586.

Unfortunately, the idiom of dispatch is used only once in connection with the oracles against Egypt (29:2); but since this stands at the head of all the anti-Egyptian messages, it was probably regarded as sufficient to indicate that all these were delivered on the spot. At 32:2, the prophet is told to address a lamentation over the pharaoh "and say to him." In the light of Ezekiel's constant usage, this requires that the prophet at least attempt an audience with him. The date of either March 15, 586 or March 3, 585 (discussed above) would be the date the prophet received the command in Phoenicia to go to the pharaoh. A return to Egypt after his Phoenician ministry would put him in the company of Jeremiah and Baruch. This would help explain the continuing correlations of language and thought between the oracles of Ezekiel and Jeremiah.

E. From Egypt to Israel. 1. Vision of Restoration (chs. 40–48). Two years before Ezekiel's last dated oracle against Egypt (29:17) was his great vision of the restored cult and nation (chs. 40–48), dated to April 28, 573 (according to the spring reckoning of the year, as indicated by 45:21). The natural inference is that this great vision of restoration was received in Egypt. Between 586 (or 585) and 573, there are no dated oracles. One may infer that during this interval Ezekiel was engaged largely in his pastoral work among the Jewish exiles in Egypt and was even studying ideas for the restoration of the kingdom of Israel in the whole of the land. Many different ideas troubled his mind, until his vision of restoration brought clarity and cohesion to his thoughts.

His vision of the restored temple (40–43; 46:19–47:12) may be compared with Moses' vision of the tabernacle on Mt. Sinai (Ex. 25:8f.). His legislation concerning the future worship there (43:18–46:15) stands closest to legislation given Moses after his ascent of Mt. Abarim (Nu. 27:12–29:40). His program of land distribution (47:13–48:35) may be compared with that of Moses (Nu. 34–36) carried out under Joshua (Josh. 13–23). J. D. Levenson has recently stressed the Mosaic role of Ezekiel. Already a document of the 1st cent. A.D., *Lives of the Prophets*, published by C. C. Torrey (*JBL Monograph*, 1 [1946], pp. 23, 38), stated: "Also after the manner of Moses he foresaw the fashion of the temple, with its walls and its broad surroundings."

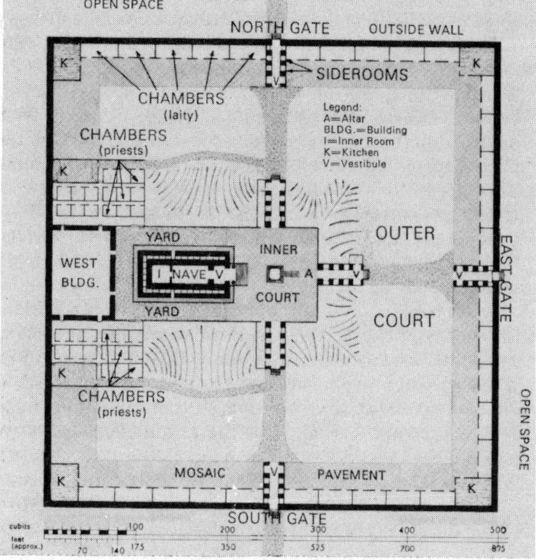

Floor plan of Ezekiel's envisioned ideal temple and temple grounds (interpretation W. H. Brownlee; drawing W. C. Loper)

The central place of the temple in the life of the restored nation must be viewed in relation to the total map of the area. The Mediterranean forms the western boundary as far north as Hethlon (47:15), N of Tripoli; and its northern boundary cuts E to a point NE of Damascus. The eastern boundary angles SW to the Sea of Galilee, S of which the Jordan River and the Dead Sea form the eastern boundary. The southern boundary runs SW from the southern end of the Dead Sea to Meribath-kadesh (47:19), which is Kadesh-barnea. Not far from there it follows the Brook of Egypt to the Mediterranean. This area does not correspond with any historical boundaries of ancient Israel, for it contains both too much and too little to reproduce the boundaries of the kingdom of Israel at their greatest expansion under David and Solomon. Phoenicia was not conquered by David or ruled by him. Hiram of Tyre was his ally, and we hear nothing of the area N of Sidon. But David did conquer Transjordan, which is entirely excluded by Ezekiel's ideal program. It seems that Ezekiel was drawing on ancient traditions that antedate the Conquest (described most fully in Nu. 34:1-12), which were never realized in the history of Israel.

This total area is to be divided into twelve strips for the twelve tribes, with the intention that each would receive a strip of equal size between parallel lines extending from east to west. The arrangements of the tribes are therefore totally different from those of the settlement period described in the traditions of Joshua and implied in subsequent history. The central portion, not assigned to any tribe, is 25,000 cubits wide (about 56 cm. [22 in.] here for each royal cubit), extending the total width of the country, from the Mediterranean to the Dead Sea. Seven tribes lie N of this strip and five S of it — Judah immediately to the north and Benjamin immediately to the south (the two tribes having changed places). In the middle of this sacral strip is a special holy portion, a square with sides of 25,000 cubits. This in turn is divided into three strips. The southernmost is 5000 cubits wide and has in its middle the capital city Yahweh Shammah (45:6; 48:30-35). North of this lie two strips, each 10,000 cubits wide (45:1-5), one strip for the priests and the other for the Levites. In the middle of the priestly strip is the temple, 500 cubits square (45:2). Since the temple is assumed to be in the middle of the holy portion, the priestly strip is generally supposed also to be the central strip, with the Levites bordering it to the north and the strip containing the capital lying immediately to the south of it. However, since the overall description in 47:15-29 proceeds from north to south and the sacral area is described in the midst of this (48:8-20), and since the priestly strip is mentioned before that of the Levites, it seems probable that the priestly strip lies along the north side of the holy portion, and that the Levitical strip lies between the priestly area and the strip containing the capital. With the temple to be placed at Jerusalem, the new capital Yahweh Shammah ("the Lord is there," 48:35) lies 7.7 km. (4.8 mi.) S of the temple, at Bethlehem; but according to the other arrangement, it lies only 2.6 km. (1.6 mi.) S of the temple, near Beth-hacherem (modern Ramat Raḥel), where excavations have discovered royal buildings from the late preexilic period. (For the arithmetic, see *Interpreter's One-Volume Comm.*, p. 435.)

All the land to the east and west of the holy portion is assigned to the prince, the reigning descendant of David (45:7f.; 48:21f.). He is thereby self-supporting, not needing to exact taxes (45:8f.). This will prevent any crimes like Ahab's seizure of Naboth's vineyard (1 K. 21). Also, all property rights of non-Jews living anywhere in Israel are protected and safeguarded, for they are counted equal to those born as sons of Israel (47:22f.). This rule prevents oppression of the sojourner (22:7).

Ezekiel was painfully aware of the desolation of the east half of the sacral portion, between Jerusalem and the Dead Sea. In his prophecy a holy spring in the temple area flows eastward to the Dead Sea, becoming a mighty river in the process and transforming the Judean wilderness into a paradise (47:1-12). Even the Dead Sea will be sweetened and become a great fishing area, with only a few salt marshes preserved for their salt production (47:8-11).

2. New Exodus. Only two years after Ezekiel's great vision of the restoration (i.e., in April, 571), he uttered a new prophecy predicting Nebuchadrezzar's invasion of Egypt (29:17-20). This did not begin until 568; but the invasion created new confidence in the prophet Ezekiel, so that at that time a group of Jewish exiles in Egypt "sprang forth" like "a horn to the house of Israel" (29:21). These are the people whom the prophet almost at once led back to the land of Israel.

The first movement is indicated by the anti-Edomite oracles (ch. 35), which are introduced by the idiom of dispatch (35:2). The designed antithesis between the mountains of Edom (ch. 35) and the mountains of Israel (ch. 36) indicates that Ezekiel returned to Israel via Edom, the route necessary to bypass the area of actual, or imminent, conflict. This route is also reminiscent of the Exodus, which also brought the Hebrews into contact with Edom (Nu. 20:14-22; 21:4). Here too Ezekiel is playing the role of the new Moses; he is leading a group of returning exiles who lay claim to the land by walking over it (36:12), while the prophet proclaims God's word, which wrests the land from its recent usurpers (35:10–36:5). At this point, then, Ezekiel has become a new Joshua.

3. Return to Gilgal. a. The Valley of Dry Bones. In ch. 37 the valley strewn with the dry bones of Zedekiah's fallen warriors is the setting of Ezekiel's vision of the resurrected nation. Since this is near Gilgal, it is inevitable that he would have returned there also. The passage that once said so was evidently 1:1, which should stand before 37:1: "In the thirtieth year, in the fourth month, on the fifth day of the month, I was in the midst of the *gôlâ* [or Gilgal?] by the river Chebar. The hand of Yahweh was upon me, and He brought me out into the midst of the plain, and it was full of bones." Since Gilgal lay in ruins, Ezekiel may have written *gôlâ* here (with reference to the returning exiles) rather than Gilgal, implicitly renewing the pun of ch. 12. The use of *gôlâ* for "[returned] exiles" appears also in Ezra 8:35; 9:4; 10:6-8, 16.

b. The Thirtieth Year of 1:1. This has been reckoned variously, but most notably: (1) from the year of King Josiah's reform, (2) from the year of the prophet's birth, (3) from the year of King Jehoiachin's captivity. The third reckoning is preferred, since this makes the dating consistent with the others. The era is not specified, since this is the last, not the earliest, dating of the book. Evidently the heading has been brought forward from ch. 37, which in the career of the prophet is later than chs. 40–48.

This solution has profound implications, for it means that Ezekiel has imitated Joshua in leading his people back to Gilgal, for a new settlement of the land. Also "the thirtieth year" at this point agrees with our inferences from 29:17-21 about the year of Ezekiel's exodus (568/567 B.C.)

c. The sprinkling of 36:25. As part of an exilic sermon, this sprinkling would have only a vaguely eschatological meaning; but once Ezekiel had led the exiles home, fulfillment had begun to take place. Under these circumstances, the prophet had to face the question of realization. Being a priest (1:3), there is no reason why he could not act as God's agent of purification. The call for "clean water" would be best satisfied by a river or spring (Lev. 14:5f., 51f.; 15:13). Any spring, such as Gihon at Jerusalem, would be suitable; but in view of the special significance of Gilgal, it may be that he led his little group of returning exiles to the river Chebar, whose perpetual spring would be a copious source of purifying water. Instead of holding a ceremony of circumcision (like Joshua), Ezekiel may have held a ceremony of lustral sprinkling, during which he proclaimed Yahweh's promise of the gift of the new heart. It is suggested, therefore, that upon first arriving at Gilgal, he repeated his old sermon of 36:16-36.

d. Symbolic Actions. Such actions (chs. 4–5) followed the accounts of the prophet's first visions; so also a symbolic action (37:15-20) followed his last vision. He joined two sticks labeled Joseph and Judah to indicate the reunion of the former northern and southern kingdoms in their own land. This action suggests that among the returning exiles (or refugees) were descendants of the former northern kingdom.

This theme of the reunited nation occurs in a balancing piece, 4:4-8. If this is dated to the time of ch. 4, Ezekiel's binding by the Lord (v. 8) would prevent him from preparing his own meals, as he is supposed to do in 4:9-17. More probably, the interest of 4:4-8 in the restoration of Israel and Judah reflects the final events in the prophet's life and his latest preaching (47:13–48:29). Just as he had given symbolic meaning to the death of his own wife (24:15-27), so his stroke of paralysis was interpreted as an atonement that made up for whatever was lacking in the sufferings of Israel and Judah, as needed for their restoration.

As a paralytic, Ezekiel could instruct his attendants to prop him up for 190 days (4:4f., LXX) on his left side to represent the number of years that Israel must suffer before being restored, and then order them to prop him up for forty days on his right side to represent the years of Judah's dispersion (4:6). The forty years of Judah would correspond with the forty years of the wilderness wandering with Moses (cf. 20:34f.). To be consistent with other dates in Ezekiel, this should be counted from Jehoiachin's captivity of 597 B.C., so that the exile of both former nations should terminate in the year 558/557.

From this line of reasoning, one should calculate the 190 years for the northern kingdom of Israel as the period between its first captivity mentioned in 2 K. 15:29 (that of Galilee) and the fortieth year of Jehoiachin's captivity. Scholars date this early exile from Israel (on the basis of ancient Near Eastern documents) to 734-732 B.C. Ezekiel, however, probably based his calculations on 2 Kings alone. Since the Galilean deportation is mentioned just before the reign of Jotham king of Judah, who began to rule in the second year of Pekah king of Israel, one would think that by adding up the reigns of the kings of Judah from Jotham to Jehoiachin he could obtain the total of 150 (190−40=150); but this yields 160+ years: 16+16+29+55+2+31+0.25+11+0.25 (2 K. 15:33; 16:2; 18:2; 21:1, 19; 22:1; 23:36; 24:8). An important synchronism at 17:1, which assigns the beginning of Pekah's successor to the twelfth year of King Ahaz of Judah, reduces the total to 150 years; for it allows only twenty-four years for the combined reigns of Pekah and Ahaz, whereas the total of the reigns of Jotham and Ahaz (with each assigned sixteen years [15:33; 16:2]), plus the nearly two years for the beginning of Pekah's reign (16:1), add up to thirty-four years. The inconsistency of ten years can be explained by a ten-year co-regency of Jotham with his aged father, King Azariah of Judah.

Although Ezekiel had already led a new exodus from Egypt during the thirtieth year of Jehoiachin's captivity, in 568 B.C., his group of people was too small to constitute the major event that 4:4-8 promises. Yet it was an important turning point in the history of Israel, a morning star heralding the dawn of the new day expected ten years later. It may be that Ezekiel's stroke occurred during the fortieth year itself, so that his exactitude in arithmetic was prompted by the timing of this significant event in his own life. One suspects that the original location of 4:4-6, 8 was immediately after ch. 37, and that this was followed by 39:25-29; and thus "*Now* I will restore the fortunes of Jacob and have mercy on *the whole house* of Israel" (v. 25) is Ezekiel's triumphant "It is finished!" after his 230 days of expiatory suffering, which by God's grace he had been enabled to endure.

IV. The Man and His Message.–*A. Mystic and Visionary.* Ezekiel's visions grew mostly out of concrete situations: (1) a storm cloud from the north (ch. 1), (2) the sight of apostasy at the temple (chs. 8–10), (3) the grim remains of an old battlefield (37:1-10). Only his vision of restoration (chs. 40–48) lacks this concreteness; it seems to be rooted rather in his past remembrances and his contemplations of the future.

B. Member of the Elijah School. His vision of the chariot throne of Yahweh may be partially inspired by speculations concerning the fiery chariot which took Elijah to heaven. The perfect mobility of Ezekiel's chariot (with wings, feet, and wheels) expressed Yahweh's freedom to intervene quickly at any time or place. Its manifestation at the temple (ch. 10) was proof that Yahweh perceives the people's most private sins (8:12), and that He is about to wreak judgment upon Jerusalem; for, as 43:3 states, He has come "to destroy the city." The halting of the celestial chariot on the Mt. of Olives (11:22f.) represents the hovering presence of God, awaiting the moment of real destruction through the Chaldeans. The descriptions of the hand of Yahweh coming upon Ezekiel and of his being lifted up and taken away (3:12-15, 22f.; 8:3; 11:1, 24; 37:1), are in language reminiscent of the accounts concerning Elijah and Elisha (1 K. 18:12, 46; 2 K. 3:15; cf. Isa. 8:11; Jer. 15:17; 1 S. 10:6).

C. Sound in Body and Mind. Ezekiel was not a sick man, insofar as we know, with two exceptions. After the death of his wife he suffered aphasia for a few weeks — a condition perhaps brought on by suppressed grief (24:15-24) and public threat to his safety by men who would bind him (3:25). From this he recovered when he perceived that his worst foreboding, the destruction of the temple, had been realized (24:25-27; 33:21f.). In his old age, as argued above, he suffered a stroke of paralysis which he marvelously transmuted into a redemptive experience. He was no recluse, with a mind wholly absorbed in faraway places; he lived and preached in Judah and neighboring lands. He was intimately acquainted with all aspects of public and private life, wherever he was. As "son of man," he claimed to be only a man among men.

D. Herald of Individualism. He called upon people to repent for their personal salvation (ch. 18), which was understood in historical terms (14:12-20) — a position actually compromised by experience (14:21-23). He himself felt a deep sense of personal responsibility for the salvation of each person (33:1-20). His implied rebuke of private persons is not recorded in the book; only general oracles denouncing the nation and its officials are noted. To apply these to persons would not require any special revelation, but it would consume much of his time. This pastoral ministry would be continued during his life as an exile in neighboring lands.

E. Deuteronomic Reformer. He emphasized the need for the people to worship solely at the temple in Jerusalem (20:27-31, 40f.; 6:1-7). He denounced the nation's rulers ("shepherds") for allowing the people to go astray upon the mountains, where occult shrines abounded (34:6a).

F. Priest. Ezekiel condemned the nation for despising "the holy things" of the temple; but these were not subordinated to the demands for justice and morality (22:6-12). Yet idolatrous practices in the temple (ch. 8) sealed the doom of Jerusalem more than anything else. His vision of the restored temple and of renewed sacrifices (chs. 40–48) is unique in prophetic literature.

EZEKIEL

G. Internationalist. He was not content to denounce foreign nations from afar, but he went to them and either spoke directly to the rulers (28:2, 12; 29:2; 31:2) or approached them as closely as possible. He denounced King Zedekiah for breaking an international treaty (17:11-21). In the future Israel, aliens were to have equal rights (47:21-23).

H. Herald of National Renewal. He traveled from land to land, proclaiming Yahweh's gracious intention of bringing back His dispersed people and of renewing them in heart and spirit (11:17-20; 34:11-16, 23-31; 36:16-38).

The new gift of the land, its marvelous new temple, and the new capital city Yahweh Shammah are not at all achievable by human intervention. They are to be wholly the gift of God. Since Ezekiel sees all this in a vision, it already exists in the mind of God and remains simply to be given. Thus, R. G. Hammerton-Kelly has argued that here is to be seen the origin of apocalyptic thought (*VT*, 20 [1970], 1-15). Others would emphasize chs. 38-39 as further proof that Ezekiel was the father of apocalyptic literature, since this material sets forth in its dramatic, cataclysmic judgment of Gog a further work of God in the salvation of Israel which makes no use of human instrumentality. There is also a new stress on the last days as the time of this salvation.

I. Poet and Dramatist. He had a large repertoire of literary forms and dramatic devices to make his message vivid. Symbolic pantomimes portrayed the coming doom (chs. 4–5; 12:1-7; 24:1-14) and the coming reunited nation (37:15-23). His vivid and colorful imagination found expression in poetry, especially in his allegories (chs. 15–17; 19; 23; 27). Many of his oracles were poetic and were probably chanted. Unfortunately some listened to him more out of aesthetic appreciation than out of moral concern (33:30-33).

J. Prophet of the Word. Ezekiel had had a vision of a scroll inscribed with words of "lamentation and mourning and woe" (2:10). He ate it and absorbed it into his very being. Therefore, his private experiences contain an omen for Israel: (1) the fear and sorrow with which he awaited the devastation of his country (12:17-20; 21:6f. [MT 11f.]), (2) the death of his wife (24:15-24), and (3) even the paralysis which preceded his own death (4:4-6, 8). This last passage has a remarkable affinity with Yahweh's Suffering Servant in Isa. 53.

V. Editing.–A. By Ezekiel. Individual oracles were probably repeated on many occasions, especially in view of the prophet's itinerant ministry. He was continually reshaping his oracles with new additions and adaptations. Thus the prediction of exile proclaimed to Gilgal (12:1-9, 11) was augmented in application to Zedekiah of Jerusalem (12:10, 12-16). An oracle of doom against the "shepherds of Israel" (34:1-10) was supplemented during Ezekiel's exilic ministry to assure the Diaspora of God's saving purpose for His scattered flock (34:11-16, 23-31).

Systematic arrangement of the oracles is based on mixed considerations of subject matter and chronology. The datings can come only from Ezekiel. He may himself have begun the process of grouping, but this task was completed by a disciple and altered by subsequent editings.

Ezekiel's editing is probably to be seen in some of the contents and arrangement of ch. 33, a summary of his preaching to the Egyptian Jews. He probably used the parable of the watchman in both chs. 3 and 33 (3:17-21; 33:1-9) because it expressed his consciousness of personal responsibility throughout his whole ministry. Chronologically 29:17-21 is the last of the anti-Egyptian oracles and should follow ch. 32. Placing this just before ch. 33 is illuminating, for it means that "the sons of your own people" in 33:2, 12, 17, 30 are naturally interpreted as "the horn for the house of Israel" (29:21) that has sprung forth. In its present (mildly expanded) form 33:1-6 portrays Ezekiel as the one whom "the people of the land" took "and made . . . their watchman." The same ministry is extended to these partisans of Ezekiel in 33:7-9, who are called upon as a corporate "son of man" to warn people of the sword coming upon Egypt. Verses 12-16 summarize ch. 18 and suggest that the theme of ch. 18 was important in Ezekiel's exilic ministry. Thus one can see that the prophet was still preaching doom to the Jews in Egypt. Those who "escape from the fire" of Jerusalem in 587 (15:7) face another fire (30:14, 16), so that 14:21-23 constitutes no contradiction of 14:12-20.

B. By a Disciple. This seems probable in 35:1–36:15. The passages are replete with introductory, transitional, and concluding formulas that are not always appropriate. Consequently it has been suggested that here is evidence for a series of editorial supplements, with stylistically inane results. More probably we have a condensation of several similar oracles. Identical verses were not repeated, but reverence for every word which the prophet uttered led to the preservation of the least consequential clauses in all their variations. It seems that Ezekiel was accompanied by a scribe on his return journey via Edom to Israel. This scribe recorded every speech of his master, even near duplicates, which he sought to amalgamate. Perhaps also other oracles existed in variant forms and were conflated.

If 4:4-6, 8 interpret Ezekiel's deathbed experience (as suggested above), its inclusion in the book would need to come from a disciple who completed the prophet's editing.

C. Additions to Chs. 40–48. These are problematic as to date. Praise for "the sons of Zadok" as those who were loyal to Yahweh in the former temple (44:15) can hardly come from Ezekiel, since this contradicts ch. 8. Perhaps Ezekiel distinguished between two classes of Levitical priests, the loyal and the disloyal, without distinguishing them as Zadokite and non-Zadokite. Yet the exclusion of the latter may contradict his doctrine of individualism (ch. 18). Pro-Zadokite material could have been inserted as early as Jeshua, the first chief priest of the postexilic community, or it could stem from the final editing of the book.

Inconsistencies indicate authors of divergent points of view. The prescription that the priests are to have no inheritance, but are to live solely from offerings (44:28-31), is in agreement with the priestly law of the Pentateuch (Lev. 2:3-10; 6:14-18 [MT 7-11]; 7; Nu. 18:8-32), but not with Ezk. 45:1-8. One supposes that the former is an orthodox correction, but by whom? There may be other supplements of various dates throughout these chapters.

D. Fifth-Century Additions. Some passages may be reminiscent of Nehemiah and his reforms. Among them 23:36-49 stands out. In the earlier part of the chapter, Oholah (Samaria) and Oholibah (Jerusalem) proved disloyal to Yahweh their husband by making alliances with foreign nations, instead of trusting in Yahweh alone for protection. In this new situation, they are accused of defiling the temple at Jerusalem. Earlier they were punished by Assyria and Chaldea, but in this section they are to be executed by "righteous men," who attack both cities and kill them with stones and swords. In contrast, the Chaldeans are described as "the most wicked of nations" (7:24; 28:7). This is reminiscent of the punishment of apostate cities prescribed by Dt. 13:12-16 (MT 13-17) and of the reforming zeal of King Josiah (2 K. 23:15-20). Cf. also the execution of adulterers and adulteresses with stones (Dt. 22:22-24). For Samaritans defiling the temple, see Neh. 13:28f., where Nehemiah expels from Jerusalem the priestly son-in-law of the governor of Samaria.

Yet 23:36-49 may be attributed to Ezekiel himself if it is

assigned to a time after his return from Egypt (after 568 B.C.). For people from Samaria worshiping at Jerusalem in this period, see Jer. 41:4f.; Ezr. 4:1f.

E. Additions from the Time of Alexander. According to some, these additions include all of ch. 26 (concerned with Tyre), since v. 8 suggests Alexander's stratagem of demolishing houses of the mainland to construct a land mole to the island city, so that siege weapons could be brought to bear against it. More probably (as the date of 26:1 suggests) we have here an oracle by Ezekiel which was later glossed with reference to Alexander.

The section 38:1–39:16, in its portrayal of God's judgment of the eschatological foe, Gog of the land of Magog, uses apocalyptic imagery not found elsewhere in the book. Its late stance is shown by its situation long after Israel has been restored to her land (38:8). Gog's invasion is in fulfillment of ancient prophecies (38:17; 39:8), but no such explicit predictions exist. An examination of the references in study editions of the ASV reveals that the phraseology of these chapters is borrowed largely from prophecies concerning Assyria and Chaldea, especially those of Isaiah, Jeremiah, and Ezekiel, which are here reapplied. (For a complete listing of these references, see G. Hölscher, pp. 177-189.)

Who is Gog? Some think that his name is derived from the ancient king Gyges of Lydia in northwestern Asia Minor. His portrayal as a foe from the north, and as chief ruler of Meshech and Tubal in the land of Magog, suggests the same general area (cf. Gen. 10:2f.). The fact that Gog must be turned around to be brought into Israel may suggest a conqueror who was headed toward another foe (such as Alexander toward Persia), but who was turned aside in order to be brought into Palestine. Alternatively, the foe has already passed through the land once and is to be brought back to his doom. C. C. Torrey and others have identified Gog with Alexander the Great, who came to Palestine from Macedonia after conquering the area of "Magog." (Late features of these chapters exclude Nebuchadrezzar as the enemy; see III.D.3 above.)

The idiom of dispatch in 38:2 (see III.D.1 above) suggests a historical figure and implies a prophetic journey to deliver the message. Either the apocalyptic author simply imitated the style of Ezekiel, or he actually visited the camp of Alexander in order to proclaim this hostile prophecy.

F. Major Revision. 1. Midrashic Methods. These were employed by the editors who transformed Ezekiel into a prophet of the Babylonian exile. (For reasons for this, see 3 below.) Simple verbal play could alter *hglglh* (Gilgal) to *hglh* (the exile) in 3:11, 15; 11:24f. (see III.C.1 above). The nearly identical headings of chs. 1 and 37 justified another rabbinic device (*gᵉzērâ šāwâ*), that of interpreting together passages with identical phrasing. This, one suggests, led to the moving of the heading of ch. 37 to 1:1 (see III.E.3.a, b above). Since in this verse Ezekiel himself probably wrote *hglh* with reference to the exiles he had brought back to Gilgal from Egypt, it served as proof that "Gilgal" everywhere in this book meant "the exile."

Unambiguous references to two ecstatic, but literal, journeys to Jerusalem (8:3; 11:1) could not be negated; but they were edited slightly in order to make of them one visionary round trip. (The composite character of Ch. 11 and the later insertion of most of this material is generally recognized.) In 8:3 Ezekiel's own words "in the visions of God" at 40:2 were cited. The fact that chs. 9–10 were vision made it plausible that ch. 8 and 11:1-13 were likewise vision. One conjectures that another verbal play in 11:24 interpreted *qāḏîmâ* ("to the east") to mean *Kaśdîmâ* ("to Chaldea"). (See III.C.5 above.) This interpretation could be supported by noting that "the east wind" (*qāḏîm*) was Ezekiel's allegorical term for Chaldea in 17:10; 19:12; 27:26. Hence *qāḏîmâ*, understood as "to the east wind," could be interpreted as "to Chaldea." There was nothing dishonest in this kind of midrash, for it rested upon the sincere conviction that the Scripture had hidden meanings which could be mined with cryptic tools.

2. New Structuring. This was achieved by rearrangements. The original answer to Ezekiel's cry of apprehension in 11:13 was 9:9f.; but these verses were replaced by an originally independent passage, 11:14-20, which not only substituted an optimistic answer for a pessimistic one, but which made chs. 8–11 relevant to the exiles. Such rearrangements are rather numerous.

The most dramatic restructuring builds upon Ezekiel's own correlation between chs. 3 and 33 by the dispersal of materials relating to the prophet's dumbness following the death of his wife. The original sequence was probably: (1) 24:15-24; (2) 3:24c-27 (the last clause of v. 24 to be inserted in v. 25, as the next to the last); (3) 24:25-27, (4) 33:21f. It is at first bewildering (esp. in the grandiose setting of 3:22f.) to discover Ezekiel confined and stricken with dumbness before he ever begins his ministry. The vision of 3:23b-24b harks back to chs. 1–2; and 3:22-23a was the original setting of that vision. The insertion of 3:22-27 here was not intended to halt the prophet's ministry before it began, but to interpret it by giving it a new dimension, that of redemptive suffering. Perhaps the editors were trying to identify Ezekiel with Yahweh's Suffering Servant, who also was "dumb" (Isa. 53:7) — though voluntarily so — and "bore the sin of many" (53:12). Their intention was not to declare that Ezekiel was dumb throughout chs. 4–24, etc., for their motivation was theological.

All this balanced structuring supports also a bisection of the book, according to an ancient custom supported in connection with Isaiah by the objective division of the great Isaiah Scroll of Qumrân into two parts. Viewed in this way, the divine judgments proclaimed against foreign nations (chs. 25–32) prepare the way for Israel's restoration (28:24-26). Hence God's punishment of His people dominates the first half (chs. 1–24) and His plan of gracious renewal dominates the second half (chs. 25–48).

3. Reasons for Major Revision. Some have already been adduced, but there are more.

a. Defense of the postexilic temple. This was achieved by a reinterpretation of Ezekiel's visions of the divine glory riding the celestial chariot. Originally, this represented Yahweh's descent from heaven to judge His nation (see IV.B above) and His coming to authenticate the future temple (44:4). Chs. 8–10 originally stressed the former, but a new dimension is suggested by the insertion of 11:14-20, for v. 16 declares that Yahweh will briefly become a sanctuary for the exiles in the lands to which they have gone. The reinterpretation made chs. 8–11 mean that the glory of Yahweh, which normally makes its abode in the most holy place of the temple, has departed (making possible the temple's destruction) and has taken up its abode among the Babylonian exiles, whence it will return to the new temple at Jerusalem. The destruction of Solomon's temple was not a repudiation of Jerusalem as the site of the true temple, but a judgment of purgation that removed past abominations (ch. 8) and prepared for the new, undefiled temple whither Yahweh's glory will return and abide forever (43:1-7a).

b. Defense of the Jerusalemite Priesthood. This is assured by the endorsement of the sons of Zadok (44:15-27), and it is reinforced by the manifestation of the divine glory to Ezekiel in Babylon by the river Chebar. One cannot say that Yahweh's exile of the leading priests to Babylon represented his repudiation of them, for the divine glory appeared to one of them in the plain near the river Chebar.

4. Occasion of Major Revision. This is to be defined in relation to the opposition party. Who objected to the Jerusalemite priesthood and temple? Who claimed that the Babylonian exile showed Yahweh's unalterable opposition to the leadership of the postexilic community? Are these people to be located already in the time of Jeshua and Zerubbabel? If so, the major revision of the book was much earlier in date than the additions mentioned under D and E. An opposition party with a rival temple and priesthood seems to be in view; it is suggested that they are the Samaritans.

According to Josephus (*Ant.* xi.8.4 [321-25]) the Samaritans built their rival temple at the time of Alexander the Great, and it stood two centuries before its destruction by John Hyrcanus in 128 B.C. (*Ant.* xiii.9.1 [254-56]). Therefore, the editing with which we are here concerned is probably from the late 4th century. Such a late date accords well with the advanced state of midrashic exegesis employed by this editing.

It is probably in relation to this editing that the figure of 390 days replaced the earlier reading of 190 days at 4:5. (For the interpretation of 190 which survived in the LXX, see III.E.3d above.) The 390 + 40 = 430 days represent 430 years of exile, corresponding with the 430 years of the Hebrew bondage in Egypt (Ex. 12:40). Counting 390 years from the fall of Samaria (722) brings us down to 332, the time of the conquest by Alexander the Great, at which time the Samaritans rebuilt the city of Shechem, the first capital of Israel. Allowing forty more years for the messianic fulfillments associated with Judah would be to anticipate a consummation at about 292 B.C. Consequently, the major revisions of the book seem to stem from an editing late in the 4th century.

G. Summary. This series of editings may serve to justify the rabbinic tradition (T.B. *Baba Bathra* 15a), that "the men of the Great Synagogue wrote Ezekiel." "Wrote" here probably means edited, and the activities of this assembly of sages is said to have begun with "Ezra and his companions" (Midr. *Lev. Rabbah* ii.11) and to have survived until the time of Simeon the Just (Mish. *Pirke Aboth* 1:1f.), roughly from the 5th to the 3rd cents. B.C. Despite all this editorial activity, the major contents of the book of Ezekiel are genuine, and whatever editing they later received serves to emphasize the prophet's greatness.

VI. Canonicity.–The Council of Jamnia (*ca.* A.D. 90), which apparently defined the final limits of the Hebrew Bible, found strong opposition to the book of Ezekiel. This is very surprising, since in all probability it had been recognized as inspired Scripture for centuries. The reason given (T.B. *Hagigah* 13a), "for its words contradict the words of the Torah," is, as Shalom Spiegel has stated (*HTR*, 24 (1931), 262), "a true statement of the Talmud which deserves full credence." Thus for the celebration of the new moon, Nu. 28:11 prescribed the sacrifice of two bulls, seven lambs, and one ram, while Ezekiel 46:6 requires only one bull, six lambs, and one ram. The Babylonian Talmud (*Menahoth* 45a) reconciles these numbers by stating that if one cannot find the larger numbers of animals, it is permissible to use the lesser. So numerous are the difficulties, however, that it is stated (T.B. *Hagigah* 13a) that Hananiah ben Hezekiah used 300 jars of midnight oil in an effort to harmonize the texts, and so the book was retained as Scripture. For an ultimate reconciliation, one must await the coming of Elijah.

VII. Rabbinic Speculations Concerning "The Chariot."–Even after the problem of canonicity was laid to rest, those who had not reached a mature age were forbidden to study the first chapter of the prophet. Special speculations that were current concerning the intricate vision of the celestial chariot were thereby discouraged. "The work of the chariot" (*maʿaśeh merkabâ*) could not be taught, but it could be discussed between two "sages" who had come to understand the mystery through their own unaided study (T.B. *Hagigah* 11b). Most scholars believe that all this concerns theosophical speculations concerning cosmogony and the angelic world, and one hymnic work from the Qumrân Scrolls (cf. J. Strugnell, "The Angelic Liturgy at Qumrân — 4Q *Serek Šîrôt ʿÔlat Haššabbât*," in *SVT*, 7 [1960], 318-345) shows that there were such speculations. Yet most aspects of the vision are repeated in 8:2 and ch. 10, on which there were no restrictions. C. C. Torrey (pp. 14-16) argued that the real reason for suppressing open study of ch. 1 was to prevent people from prying critically into the edited dates of 1:1f. and figuring out that Ezekiel was not really in the Babylonian exile at the time of Jehoiachin's captivity. Yet in the rabbinic Midrash *Mekilta* (*Pisha* 1.40ff.), one interpretation insinuates that Ezekiel's initial vision was "in the plain" of 3:22f., which it locates in the Holy Land. Even the Targum of Jonathan explains the repetitive text of 1:3, "The word of Yahweh *came came* [or, coming came; AV, expressly came] to Ezekiel" as meaning that the divine word came twice to the prophet: "The word of prophecy came from Yahweh's presence to Ezekiel the son of Buzi, the priest, in the land of Israel. Then it came back again and conversed with him in the province of the land of the Chaldeans."

The exact nature of the rabbinic interpretation of Ezk. 1 is not fully known, although the passage gave rise to a whole Jewish mystical tradition (cf. *Encyclopedia Judaica*, XI [1971], *s.v.* "Merkabah Mysticism" [G. Scholem]; G. Scholem, *Major Trends in Jewish Mysticism* [3rd rev. ed. 1954], pp. 40-79). The basis of the rabbinic interpretation was the identification of the chariot of Ezekiel's vision with God's throne; Ezekiel, having seen the throne, was supposed to be enlightened about the divine mysteries. Apparently later Jewish sages who had correctly understood and expounded Ezk. 1 were privileged with similar visions or at least some kind of mystical experience (cf., e.g., J. Neusner, *Life of Rabban Yohanan Ben Zakkai* [1962], pp. 97-103, esp. pp. 97f., where he quotes T. B. *Hagigah* 14b).

VIII. Ezekiel and the NT.–The frequent addresses to Ezekiel as "son of man" find an exact parallel only in Dnl. 8:17; but this expression is a frequent designation of Jesus in all four Gospels and rarely elsewhere (Acts 7:56; Rev. 1:13; 21:7). This title for Jesus may derive wholly from Dnl. 7:13f. and its lengthy interpretation in 1 En. 37–71, "the Similitudes [or Parables] of Enoch." Yet, in contrast with these sources, "son of man" in the Gospels sometimes designates Jesus as a lowly, suffering prophet (Mt. 8:20 par.; 17:12 par.). The son of man's mission "to seek and to save the lost" (Lk. 19:10) may be compared with Ezekiel's pastoral ministry of warning sinners (3:17-21 par. 33:7-9) out of conviction that Yahweh has "no pleasure in the death of the wicked" (33:11) and will Himself "seek the lost" (34:16). *See* SON OF MAN.

Jesus' role as the Good Shepherd (Jn. 10:1-18, 25-29) is reminiscent of Yahweh's work in this same capacity (Ezk. 34:11-16), especially since He and the Father are one (Jn. 10:30). "The one flock, one shepherd" (Jn. 10:16) accords with Ezekiel's emphasis upon the oneness of the restored nation (37:22), which will have but one royal shepherd (34:23; 37:24). A new element in Jn. 10 is the inclusion of Gentiles among the gathered flock (cf. v. 16a). Implicitly, Ezekiel's prophecy concerns the Church as the new Israel.

Among the hundreds of biblical allusions in the book of

Revelation, Ezekiel was not ignored. The "one like a son of man" (Rev. 1:13, exactly as in Dnl. 7:13) has a voice "like the sound of many waters" (Rev. 1:15), as the Almighty does in Ezekiel's vision (Ezk. 1:24). The "living creatures" of Rev. 4:6-9 are reminiscent of those in Ezk. 1; *see* CREATURE, LIVING. Most dramatically, "Gog and Magog" designate "the nations at the four corners of the earth" (Rev. 20:8), with allusion to the prophecies of Ezk. 38–39, which concern "Gog of the land of Magog" (38:2). Their siege of "the camp of the saints" in "the beloved city" (which in Sir. 24:11 designates Jerusalem) refers to the persecution of Christians, who alone in the NT are called "saints." The coming of these foes from "the four corners of the earth" (Rev. 20:8) stresses their universal character, in agreement with the depiction of the "many peoples" accompanying Gog in Ezk. 38:5f. who derive from every direction, and not just the north.

Like Ezekiel in 40:2, John in Rev. 21:10 was "carried away to a great, high mountain" where he saw "the holy city Jerusalem," but with a striking difference: Ezekiel saw there the new temple (Ezk. 40–47), whereas John's "new Jerusalem" had no temple in it, "for its temple is the Lord God the Almighty and the Lamb" (Rev. 21:22). In this respect, however, John's "holy city" is exactly like the future capital of Israel, the city of the reigning "prince" (Ezk. 45:7; 48:15-22). Although it will have no temple, it will be called Yahweh Shammah, "Yahweh is there" (48:30-35). Like this future capital, the new Jerusalem of Revelation will be foursquare (Rev. 21:16) and have twelve gates named after the twelve tribes of Israel (v. 12). It is important to note that Yahweh Shammah in Ezekiel is not a new Jerusalem, for the geographic arrangements of 47:13–48:29 make clear (as explained above) that this is at some distance south of the sanctuary, perhaps even at Bethlehem.

Bibliography.–*Commentaries:* P. Auvray, *Ézéchiel* (1947); A. Bertholet, *Hesekiel, mit einem Beitrag von Kurt Galling* (1936); W. H. Brownlee (*Interpreter's One-Volume Comm.*, 1971; with revisions in B printing); K. W. Carley, *Book of the Prophet Ezekiel* (1974); G. A. Cooke (*ICC*, 1936-37); *DBSup.*, VIII, *s.v.* (P. Auvray); W. Eichrodt (*OTL*, 1970); G. Fohrer, *Ezechiel, mit einem Beitrag von K. Galling* (1955); *IDB*, *s.v.* (C. G. Howie); R. Kraetzschmar (*HAT*, 1900); I. G. Matthews (*American Comm. on the OT*, 1939); H. G. May (*IB*, 1954); J. Muilenberg (*Peake's Comm. on the Bible*, rev. ed. 1962); J. Smith, *Book of the Prophet Ezekiel* (1930); A. van den Born, *Ezechiel uit de Grondtekst vertaald en uitgelegd* (*De Boeken van het Oude Testament*, 11, 1954); J. W. Wevers (*New Century Bible*, 1969); W. Zimmerli (*BKAT*, 2 vols., 1969; vol. I, Eng. tr., *Hermeneia*, 1979).

Other Books: L. E. Browne, *Ezekiel and Alexander* (1952); W. H. Brownlee, *Meaning of the Qumrân Scrolls for the Bible* (1964), esp. pp. 247-259; K. W. Carley, *Ezekiel Among the Prophets* (1975); S. R. Driver, *Intro. to the Literature of the OT* (1891 and 1956); O. Eissfeldt, *OT: An Intro.* (1965), pp. 365-382; H. L. Ellison, *Ezekiel, the Man and His Message* (1956); O. R. Fischer, "Unity of the Book of Ezekiel" (diss., Boston University, 1939); G. Fohrer, *Die Hauptprobleme des Buches Ezechiel* (*BZAW*, 72, 1952); J. B. Harford, *Studies in the Book of Ezekiel* (1935); V. Herntrich, *Ezechielprobleme* (*BZAW*, 61, 1932); J. Herrmann, *Ezechielstudien* (*Beiträge zur Wissenschaft vom AT*, 1908); G. Hölscher, *Hesekiel—der Dichter und das Buch* (*BZAW*, 39, 1924); C. G. Howie, *Date and Composition of Ezekiel* (*JBL Monograph*, 4, 1950); W. A. Irwin, *Problem of Ezekiel* (1943); W. Kessler, *Die innere Einheitlichkeit des Buches Ezechiel* (*Berichte des Theol. Seminar der Brüdergemeinde*, II, 1926); R. Kittel, *Geschichte des Volkes Israel*, III (1927), 144-180, 258-263; H. Lamparter, *Zum Wächter Bestellt* (1968); J. D. Levenson, *Theology of the Program of Restoration of Ezekiel 40–48* (1976); N. Messel, *Ezechielfragen* (*Skrifter utgitt av Det Norske Videnskaps*, 1945); W. O. E. Oesterley and T. H. Robinson, *Intro. to the Books of the OT* (1955), pp. 318-329; R. H. Pfeiffer, *Intro. to the OT* (3rd ed. 1941), pp. 518-565; H. W. Robinson, *Two Hebrew Prophets* (1948); J. Steinmann, *Le Prophète Ézéchiel et les débuts de l'exil* (1953); C. C. Torrey, *Pseudo-Ezekiel and the Original Prophecy* (1930); A. van den Born, *De historische Situatie van Ezechiels Prophetie* (1947); G. Widengren, *Literary and Psychological Aspects of the Hebrew Prophets* (1948).

Articles: W. F. Albright, *JBL*, 51 (1932), 77-106; P. Auvray, *RB*, 55 (1948), 503-519; G. R. Berry, *JBL*, 49 (1930), 83-93; 51 (1932), 54-57; 56 (1937), 115-17; 58 (1939), 163-175; W. H. Brownlee, "Ezekiel's Copper Cauldron and Blood on the Rock," in R. A. Coughenour, ed., *For Me to Live: Essays in Honor of James Leon Kelso* (1972), pp. 21-43; *HTR*, 51 (1958), 191-203; *JBL*, 89 (1970), 393-404; *RQ*, 13 (1963), 11-28; "Two Elegies on the Fall of Judah (Ezekiel 19)," in J. Bergman, ed., *Ex Orbe Religionum, Studia Geo Widengren Oblata* (1972), pp. 93-103; *VT*, 28 (1978), 392-408; O. Eissfeldt, "Prophetic Literature," in *OTMS*, pp. 153-58; M. Greenberg, *JBL*, 77 (1958), 101-105; "Prolegomenon," in M. Greenberg, ed., *Pseudo-Ezekiel and the Original Prophecy and Critical Articles by Shalom Spiegel and C. C. Torrey* (1970), pp. xi-xxix; W. A. Irwin, *VT*, 3 (1953), 54-66; H. H. Rowley, *BJRL*, 36 (1953/54), 146-190; S. Spiegel, *HTR*, 24 (1931), 245-321; *JBL*, 56 (1937), 403-408; C. C. Torrey, *JBL*, 53 (1934), 291-320.

W. H. BROWNLEE

IX. Alternative Views and Additional Information.–*A. Authorship and Locale.* The single-author view of the book can be demonstrated by several lines of evidence. The address "Son of man" is used ninety-three times in Ezekiel, always by Yahweh when addressing Ezekiel. Elsewhere in the OT it occurs as a form of address only in Dnl. 8:17, which according to Eichrodt (*Ezekiel* [Eng. tr., *OTL*, 1970], p. 61) is derived from Ezekiel. (The term *ben 'āḏām* is used in parallel strophes with *'āḏām*, "man," in Job 25:6; Ps. 8:4 [MT 5]). This address formula is found throughout Ezekiel (omitted only in chs. 1, 9–10, 18–19, 41–42, 45–46, 48) and often follows the phrase "the word of Yahweh came to me." The address first occurs in 2:1: "And he said to me, 'Son of man, stand upon your feet, and I will speak with you.'" It occurs in the language of commission, e.g., v. 3, "Son of man, I send you to the people of Israel . . . ," and 3:4, "Son of man, go, get you to the house of Israel, and speak with my words to them." Ezekiel describes the effect of the word in 2:2: "And when he spoke to me, the Spirit entered into me and set me upon my feet; and I heard him speaking to me." Similar phenomena throughout the book imply that Ezekiel was fully aware that Yahweh was speaking to him and even telling him what to say or do. To suppose that a later redactor has woven this formula into the account about ninety times requires more credulity than some scholars can muster. At face value it argues strongly for a single author.

The expression *'ᵃnî YHWH*, "I am Yahweh," occurs about sixty times in Ezekiel. Usually it follows some statement including the verb "know," such as "they shall know that I am Yahweh." According to BDB (p. 219, II.2.b), such expressions occur forty-nine times in Ezekiel and only nine times elsewhere. The expression *'ᵃnî YHWH* is therefore a hallmark of Ezekiel and is reminiscent of the same expression in Leviticus, where it occurs about fifty times. (For discussion of *yd'* passages as "proof sayings" in Ezekiel, and of *'ny yhwh* as self-introduction, cf. W. Zimmerli, *Ezekiel*, I [*Hermeneia*, 1979], 36-40.) This emphasis on Yahweh's being the one who is acting would be particularly significant to those exiled from the land that Yahweh had given them to a land that, according to popular belief, was the territory of Marduk and other gods. Thus the constant repetition of the words "that you/they shall know that I am Yahweh" supports not only the single authorship of Ezekiel, but also the foreign locale of the prophecies. The words would have had far less meaning to the defeated remnant in Judea, and probably just the opposite effect, i.e., they would have shown that Yahweh, after all, was powerless against the pagan gods.

The date formulas also support single authorship. Thirteen dates are given by day, month, and year, and each is connected with a revelation from Yahweh. These can be equated with our present calendar as follows:

Ezk.	subject	da mo yr	yr 1 = 597/6
1:2	Opening vision	5 4 5	Jul. 31, 593
8:1	Vision in the temple	5 6 6	Sep. 17, 592
20:1	Message to the elders	10 5 7	Aug. 14, 591
24:1	Report of siege of Jerusalem	10 10 9	Jan. 15, 588
26:1	Prophecy against Tyre	1 (1) 11	(Apr. 23) 587
*29:1	Prophecy against Pharaoh	12 10 10	Jan. 7, 587
*29:17	Prophecy to Babylon about Egypt	1 1 27	Apr. 26, 571
30:20	Prophecy against Pharaoh	7 1 11	Apr. 29, 587
31:1	Prophecy to Pharaoh	1 3 11	June 21, 587
*32:1	Lamentation over Pharaoh	1 12 12	Mar. 3, 585
33:21	Report of Jerusalem's fall	5 10 12	Jan. 8, 585
40:1	Vision of restored temple	10 1 25	Apr. 28, 573

*Obviously not in chronological sequence
(Dates calculated from tables in R. A. Parker and W. H. Dubberstein, *Babylonian Chronology 626 B.C.–A.D. 75* [1956], pp. 27f.)

Once again it is exceedingly difficult to accept the position that a later redactor carefully wove these date formulas into the work. Although it is possible to suppose that only the dated prophecies — with the dates — came from the original author, it seems more reasonable to suppose that the dates were intended to furnish some sort of sequence for the entire prophecy. The latter view is particularly significant because some of the dates are out of chronological order, which would be inconceivable for a later editor to have done. Again, the same evidence seems to support a Babylonian or at least a foreign locale.

B. "Set Your Face" as a Dispatch Formula. The suggestion that "set your face" is the language of dispatch (see III.D.1, 2 above) is most interesting and deserves careful evaluation. The formula "Son of man, set your face [*śîm pānêḵā*] to . . ." occurs nine times (6:2; 13:17; 20:46 [MT 21:2]; 21:1 [MT 7]; 25:2; 28:21; 29:2; 35:2; 38:2). Generally it is followed by *'el* but in 20:46 by *dereḵ*, and in 29:2 and 35:2 by *'al*. The formula is used with messages to "the mountains of Israel," "the daughters of your people," "the South," "Jerusalem," "the Ammonites," "Sidon," "Pharaoh king of Egypt," "Mount Seir," and "Gog of the land of Magog." With the exception of 29:1f., none of these occurs in connection with a date formula.

The expression "set (one's) face to" is found elsewhere in the Semitic world. In the Code of Hammurabi, for example, the idiom is *ana . . . panišu ištakan,* where the infinitive of the action follows the preposition *ana,* and the expression is translated "to [verb] his face he has set." The formula is found in such expressions as "has set his face to divorce" (§ 137), "has set her face to go out" (§ 141), "has set his face to disinherit his son" (§ 168). In these examples and throughout the code it is not a dispatch formula, but instead means "make up his/her mind" to do something. It should be noted, however, that the Babylonian examples are all in the indicative, but the *śîm pānêḵā* passages in Ezekiel are all in the imperative.

A similar idiom occurs in Ugaritic in the customary form *idk lttn pnm 'm . . .*, "then he/she set the face to/with . . ." (49.I.4; 49.IV.31f., *idk lttn pnm 'm nrt ilm špš,* "then she set her face toward the luminary of the gods Shipish"; 51.IV.20; 51.V.84; etc.). The verb is *ytn,* cognate with Hebrew *ntn,* "give, appoint, set." In context the expression seems to mean "go" or "make up the mind to go" and hence would lend support to the thesis in IV, V above.

While a study of cognate languages is an aid to understanding Hebrew (or any other language), ultimately the meaning of words must be determined from context. What did the author of Ezekiel intend when making use of the words *śîm pānêḵā*? A careful study of the numerous commands to Ezekiel to "prophesy," "speak," "say," "make known to," "raise a lamentation against," etc., does not indicate any special feature about the "set your face to" passages. When a dispatch formula is used, it contains *lēḵ,* "go," as in 3:1, 4, 11, and the recipients of the proposed message are always the exiles of Israel. A tentative conclusion is that "set your face against" is simply the language of commission, perhaps explained by 3:8, "I have made your face hard against their faces," to strengthen Ezekiel's determination to carry out the order. The idiom is similarly used in Lk. 9:51, where Jesus is said to have "set his face to go to Jerusalem," i.e., to have steadfastly determined to accomplish his appointed mission to be received up.

In the light of the facts adduced above, the single authorship of Ezekiel and the Babylonian locale of the prophet's work seem to be reasonable conclusions.

C. Eschatology. One of Ezekiel's great contributions to OT theology is his presentation of events relating to the end of the age. As is customary with the canonical prophets, the near and the distant are merged, so that it is impossible to mark out certain portions as dealing only with the latter days. Beginning with the prophecy against the "shepherds" (the spiritual and political leaders, cf. 34:2, 10), Ezekiel contains prophecies that have both gladdened the hearts of the people of God and filled them with foreboding. Yahweh identifies Himself as the true shepherd (34:11, 13) who seeks the lost (vv. 15f.; cf. Lk. 19:10). At the same time there is a merging of the shepherd's office, for "my servant David" is also the single shepherd (Ezk. 34:23). Ezekiel thus provides a basis for the ultimate identification of the Messiah with Yahweh Himself (cf. 37:24; Jn. 10:1-18).

Ezekiel makes it clear that Yahweh's purpose is not merely to punish some of His people while preserving a remnant. There is to be something new — a "new covenant," a "new heart," a "new spirit" — but the figures of speech used indicate that, although this program may be new, it will not be different. No new name replaces Israel, and no new king replaces David. The new law in the heart is still called Torah. Ezekiel added an element to the central truth: "It is not for your sake, O house of Israel, that I am about to act, but for the sake of my holy name, which you have profaned among the nations to which you came" (Ezk. 36:22; cf. v. 32). The vindication of God's character is an important point in Ezekiel. The concept of a tragic deity, caught in the vortex of history and unable to do anything about it, is foreign to Ezekiel. Yahweh is the Lord of history.

Chapter 37 does not portray the final resurrection although belief in the resurrection underlies its figures of speech. Rather, it is a prophecy of the reestablishment of the single nation: "These bones are the whole house of Israel" (v. 11). The "stick of Joseph" is joined to the "stick of Judah" to become "one stick" (vv. 19f.). "They shall be no longer two nations, and no longer divided into two kingdoms" (vv. 21f.). David is to be the king (v. 24), and the people shall dwell in the land which Yahweh gave to Jacob (v. 25).

Chapters 38–39 appear to teach that there will be a second attack on the nation after it has been reunited (38:8; cf. Rev. 20:8), an idea that is also found in Zec. 12:3. A power from the north comes against Israel "in the latter days" (Ezk. 38:14-16; cf. Rev. 19:17-21). There will be "a great shaking" in the land of Israel (Ezk. 38:19), but this time Yahweh does not call upon a Cyrus or a foreign power to deliver His people. He uses "every kind of terror" (v. 21) in a direct confrontation of God and Gog. The battle, described in gory detail (ch. 39), seems to represent the final judgment of the nations. It is a fitting introduction for the final section of the prophecy.

Chapters 40–48 are very difficult to interpret. It seems clear that Ezekiel has the messianic age in view (43:2-5, 7; 44:2; 47:7-12 [cf. Zec. 14:8; Rev. 22:1f.]; 48:35b). On the surface, Ezekiel seems to be foretelling the rebuilding of the temple, the reinstitution of the sacrificial system (45:18-25), and the reapportionment of the land among the twelve tribes. This interpretation, however, appears to be contrary to the prophetic view of the OT and to clear statements in the NT (cf. Mic. 6:6-8; Isa. 1:11; esp. He. 8–10). Since those who hold to the infallibility of Scripture will not concede that Ezekiel was mistaken, they must attempt to harmonize the OT and NT. Suggested solutions include: (1) a literal fulfillment, such as has been held by many Chiliasts and Premillennialists; and (2) a typico-symbolical fulfillment, which often fails to do justice to the many OT prophecies that bear on the subject and sometimes also fails to give serious consideration to Rom. 9–11; rather, it leans heavily on He. 8:13; 9:23–10:4. (3) A third suggestion is that in the messianic age, when Israel is gathered as a nation with the messianic king on the throne in Jerusalem, the temple and the sacrifices will be memorials (somewhat as many Christians in this age regard the Lord's Supper as a memorial), reminding the earthly Israel of their background.

The prophecy against Tyre (Ezk. 28) is also problematic. Who is this "prince of Tyre" who said, "I am a god, I sit in the seat of the gods," yet who was "but a man, and no god" (v. 2)? Yahweh says to him, "You were the signet of perfection, full of wisdom and perfect in beauty. You were in Eden, the garden of God.... You were blameless in your ways from the day you were created, till iniquity was found in you.... I cast you to the ground" (vv. 12-17). Like Isa. 14:12-21, these verses have often been taken as a prophecy concerning Satan. But how can such an interpretation be held in the light of grammatico-historical exegesis? The passage appears to be a taunt song, a characteristic of which is hyperbolic ridicule. In context it refers to the king of Tyre, perhaps Baʿli II. At the same time, scholars have found both in Ezk. 28 and Isa. 14 "reflections of Ugaritic mythology" (cf. H. G. May, *IB*, VI, 218; J. Morgenstern, *JBL*, 64 [1945], 29-37).

The king of Tyre (Ezk. 28), just like the king of Babylon (Isa. 14), has a satanic element. "Satan" means "adversary," and "satanic" means "opposed to God and His purpose." Tyre, with its Baal worship, its Jezebel-Elijah confrontation, and its determined efforts to replace Yahwism with Baalism, was satanic. All earthly kings represent the Edenic or existentialist Adamic experience that attempts to set personal choice above the will of the Creator. Like "Messiah," the term "Satan" later came to have a technical meaning. Every use of earthly power to oppose the purpose or people of God prefigures the satanic-messianic confrontation at the end of the age. Ezekiel, with his underlying emphasis on eschatology (cf. B. S. Childs, *Intro. to the OT as Scripture* [1979], pp. 366f.), must have intended this interpretation when he spoke at length on Tyre. W. S. LASOR

EZEL ē'zəl [Heb. *hāʾāzel*–'departure'] (1 S. 20:19). In the AV and RSV mg. the proper name of the stone at which David was to meet Jonathan.

The textual tradition is considerably confused at this point. The MT reads *ʾēṣel hāʾeḇen hāʾāzel,* literally, "beside the stone, Ezel." The LXX B reads *ergab ekeíno.* Driver conjectures that Gk. *ergab* is a transliteration of Heb. **hāʾargāḇ,* "mound, heap," apparently the word presupposed by the LXX B translator. If the letters of *hʾzl* are transposed and vocalized as *hāllāʾz* (lit. "this") the result is a coherent text presupposed by the LXX B: *ʾēṣel hāʾargāḇ hāllāʾz,* "beside this heap." This solution, although coherent, is not entirely satisfactory, since Symmachus and Theodotion read *líthon,* "stone," rather than *ergab,* and so agree with MT *hāʾeḇen.*

The textual difficulties are reflected in the various translations. The AV and RSV mg. follow the MT and render "the stone Ezel." The RSV "stone heap" follows the text presupposed by the LXX B and deletes *hāʾāzel.* The NEB follows the LXX B entirely: "the mound there."

Bibliography.–S. R. Driver, *Notes on the Hebrew Text and the Topography of the Books of Samuel* (2nd ed. 1913), pp. 167f.; *BH*; BDB, pp. 229, 918. R. J. W. G. A. L.

EZEM ē'zəm [Heb. *ʿāṣem* (Josh. 15:29; 19:3)]; AV AZEM; [*ʿeṣem* (1 Ch. 4:29)]. The Hebrew spelling with *ā* is a Masoretic pausal form, which the AV rendered literally. Ezem was a city of Simeon somewhere in the Negeb, perhaps to be identified with Umm el-ʿAzam, about 20 km. (12 m.) SE of Beer-sheba.

EZER ē'zər [Heb. *ʾēzer* (**1**); *ʿēzer*–'help'].

1. A Horite chief (Gen. 36:21, 27, 30; 1 Ch. 1:38, 42; AV EZAR).

2. A Judahite (1 Ch. 4:4).

3. An Ephraimite, slain by men of Gath (1 Ch. 7:21).

4. A Gadite who followed David while in exile on account of the wrath of Saul (1 Ch. 12:9 [MT 10]).

5. One of those who, under the direction of Nehemiah, repaired the wall of Jerusalem (Neh. 3:19).

6. A musician in one of the two great companies appointed by Nehemiah to give thanks at the dedication of the wall of Jerusalem (Neh. 12:42).

EZERIAS ez-ə-rī'əs (1 Esd. 8:1, AV, NEB). *See* AZARIAH **24**.

EZIAS ē-zī'əs (1 Esd. 8:2, AV). *See* UZZI **7**.

EZION-GEBER e'zē-ən gē'bər, e'zē-ən ge'bər [Heb. *ʿeṣyôn geḇer*]; AV also EZION-GABER (-gā'bər, -gä'bər). A port city of Edom on the north shore of the Gulf of Aqabah. It is mentioned as one of the cities on the route of the Exodus (Nu. 33:35; Dt. 2:8). It seems to have been an important commercial city in the time of Solomon, for he built there a fleet of ships, manned by Phoenician sailors, which he sent to Ophir for gold and other riches (1 K. 9:26-28; 10:11, 22; 2 Ch. 8:17). Jehoshaphat king of Judah joined with Ahaziah king of Israel to attempt a similar enterprise, but Jehoshaphat's fleet was destroyed in the port (1 K. 22:48; 2 Ch. 20:35-37).

ELATH may have been the later name for Ezion-geber, which was in the same general area.

See TELL EL-KHELEIFEH. E. K. VOGEL

EZNITE ez'nīt (2 S. 23:8, AV). *See* ADINO.

EZORA ē-zō'rə [Gk. *Ezōra*] (1 Esd. 9:34); AV OZORA. He and his six sons "pledged themselves to put away their wives" (v. 20; cf. "Machnadebai" of Ezr. 10:40).

EZRA ez'rə [Heb. *ʿezrāʾ*; Gk. *Esras*; *Esdras*; *Ezdras*; **EZRAH** [Heb. *ʿezrâ* (1 Ch. 4:17)]. Probably abbreviated forms of *ʿᵃzaryâ*–'Yah(weh) helps.'

1. A priest who returned from Babylonia with Zerubbabel (Neh. 12:1, 13). In Neh. 10:2 (MT 3) he is called Azariah.

2. A member of the tribe of Judah and father of Jether and three other sons (1 Ch. 4:17).

3. The author of the memoirs attributed to him in the canonical books of Ezra and Nehemiah (Ezr. 7–10; Neh. 8–10). His credentials are inherent in his genealogy (Ezr. 7:1-6), which traces his descent from Aaron, the first high priest of Israel. The genealogy is shortened by comparison with the list in 1 Ch. 6:4-14 (MT 5:30-40), six names being omitted in Ezr. 7:2-7 between Azariah and Meraioth, and one between Shallum and Ahitub. Ezra was a descendant of Seraiah, who was killed by Nebuchadrezzar at Riblah (2 K. 25:18-21), and whose son Jehozadak was the high priest taken in captivity to Babylonia (1 Ch. 6:14f. [MT 5:40f.]). The omission of Jehozadak's name from Ezra's genealogy might indicate his descent from a younger brother who was not a high priest.

In Jewish tradition Ezra was uniformly described as a "scribe" who was especially versed in the Torah. In his letter of instruction (Ezr. 7:6, 11), Artaxerxes designated him as "the scribe," indicating that he held a high position in the administration of the royal court. Ezra returned to Jerusalem with a group of repatriates and others in the seventh year of Artaxerxes, and depending upon whether the individual named was Artaxerxes I or Artaxerxes II, this would be either 458 B.C. or 397 B.C. (*see* CHRONOLOGY OF THE OT VI). Ezra had requested and received permission (Ezr. 7:11-26) to visit the returned exiles in an official capacity, and thus was acting as a crown commissioner. He received a grant from the royal treasury as well as freewill offerings from Jews living in Babylonia, and those he took to Palestine along with vessels for the service of the Lord's house. The royal decree afforded Ezra administrative privileges backed by civil authority.

When he arrived in Jerusalem he began his tour of inspection. He was shocked immediately to discover that the priests and Levites had intermarried with local pagan women, and that the civil leaders had been prominent in this actpvity also. He lamented and confessed the sin publicly, and in this act of contrition the people ultimately joined. As a result, the offenders agreed for the most part to divorce their pagan wives. At the Feast of Tabernacles (Neh. 7:73–8:12) Ezra read the "book of the law of Moses" and expounded it to the people, persuading the assembly to abide by its provisions. Consequently, mixed marriages were widely renounced, and promises were made to observe the sabbath and the sabbatical year. In addition, the people undertook to meet the administrative needs of the temple. Subsequent to this, Ezra apparently returned to Persia to report to the king; there are no further records of his life.

The Talmud enshrined various traditions regarding Ezra, one of which identified him with the prophet Malachi (T. B. *Megillah* 15a; Targum on Mal. 1:1). Exaggerated claims about his personality and role included the statement that he would have received the revealed Torah of God had Moses never existed (Tosefta *Sanhedrin* 4.7).

See also EZRA, BOOK OF; NEHEMIAH, BOOK OF.

R. K. HARRISON

EZRA, BOOK OF.

I. Name
II. Purpose
III. Sources
IV. Style
V. Languages
VI. Special Problems
   A. Edict of Cyrus
   B. Date of the Founding of the Temple
   C. Lists in Ezra 2 and Nehemiah 7
   D. Sheshbazzar and Zerubbabel
   E. Chronology of Ezra 4
   F. Date of Ezra's Coming to Jerusalem

I. Name.–The book of Ezra, like its companion Nehemiah, is named after the principal person mentioned in its pages. The two books are counted as one in the Talmud, in Josephus, and in the Canon of Melito (A.D. 171), and are so treated in the subscription of the MT. In the LXX Ezra-Nehemiah is called Esdras B, while an apocryphal book of Ezra is called Esdras A. The apocryphal Greek Ezra is usually in English versions called 2 Esdras or 3 Ezra following the Vulgate, which counts Ezra and Nehemiah as 1 and 2 Ezra. A later apocalyptic book is denominated 4 Ezra.

II. Purpose.–Ezra, with Nehemiah, completes the great postexilic history of Israel begun in 1 and 2 Chronicles. Although it incorporates a variety of sources, the book's function, in its present form, is clear from 2 Ch. 36:22 par. Ezr. 1:1-3. It was to show that God fulfilled His promise by the mouth of Jeremiah, that He would restore His exiled people to their inheritance in the land. To that end the Lord stirred up the spirit of great Persian monarchs (Cyrus, Darius, and Artaxerxes) on the one hand, and on the other hand the leaders of the community in Exile (Sheshbazzar, Joshua, Zerubbabel, Haggai and Zechariah, Ezra and Nehemiah). Historical details are clearly subordinate to the theological purpose, so that the structures and purity of the restored Israelite worship consistently overshadow details of political relationships of the period. The conviction of the author/editor(s) that the restored community must respond in pure forms is as basic to his book as his belief that God was working out His purpose. The object of the book is at once historical, theological, and polemical.

III. Sources.–The final editor of Ezra and Nehemiah is often considered to be the Chronicler; the larger question of when he wrote and how he used his sources remains a matter of dispute (*see* CHRONICLES, BOOKS OF). Support for a date considerably later than the events covered usually comes from the conclusion that certain names (e.g. Jaddua [Neh. 12:11, 22] and the later descendants of Zerubbabel [1 Ch. 3:19-24]) in these books represent later figures. In contrast, many scholars are quite ready to admit certain "marginal" additions and would retain a date for the bulk of the work closer to 400 B.C. In any case, if Ezra-Nehemiah is separated from the Chronicler's work (as has been argued) there is no reason to place the final form of the dual memoirs much after 400 B.C. (see VI below).

Four kinds of source material have been isolated in Ezra, though the provenance and genuineness of several of these sources has often been debated. Considered the most secure is the "Nehemiah Autobiography" (Neh. 1:1–7:5; 13:4-30). Of similar genre is the "Ezra Memoirs" section (Ezr. 7:27–9:15), a first-person account of the activities connected with Ezra's return under Artaxerxes, to which the third-person narratives of Ezr. 7:1-26 and Ezr. 10 may be added. The remainder of the work consists of Aramaic letters (4:8-22; 5:1–6:18; and 7:12-26), and various kinds of lists, the latter undoubtedly from temple records (Ezr. 2 par. Neh. 7; Ezr. 8:1-14; 10:18-43; Neh. 3; 10:1-27 [MT 2-28]; 11; 12:1-26). To this has been added the remaining narrative (Ezr. 1; 3:1–4:7; 4:23–5:6a; etc.), which forms an editorial framework for much of the source material cited.

Theories abound concerning the final arrangement of

EZRA, BOOK OF

Ezra-Nehemiah and its attendant purpose (cf. in R. W. Klein, pp. 368ff.). It is probably best to limit ourselves to the obvious purposes noted above, and examine the material and its arrangement from that standpoint.

IV. Style.–The diversified character of the style, languages, and other literary peculiarities of Ezra (and Nehemiah) may be explained by the large number and variety of the sources. Genealogical lists and diplomatic correspondence have their own well-documented style, for which the contents of Ezra and Nehemiah provide a rich source. The category of individual memoir is by no means so widespread in the ancient world; these books provide one of the earliest examples of this genre. As a means of related historical detail the third-person narrative is common not only in the biblical books but in such ancient historians as Herodotus and Thucydides as well. Nor is first-person narrative unknown — both the Babylonian monuments and the OT prophets employ it — but it is usually mixed with standard narrative. In Ezra and Nehemiah there is little mixing of the styles. Ezra begins with narrative, changes abruptly to a personal memoir (7:27, as a response to Artaxerxes' letter containing Ezra's commission), and reverts to the narrative third person (ch. 10), although the subject material remains largely the same. We must conclude that the preservation of the intact memoir sections came about because their presence and form gave a special authority to the entire book. More than anywhere else in the postexilic history these personal records breathe a sense of devotion and piety. The language of history has become the language of prayer, and the record of deeds done assumes the character of a holy crusade. Undoubtedly it was to capture something of this flavor that the final editor preserved the form as well as the content of such memoirs as he possessed.

V. Languages.–The language of the book is Hebrew, except 4:7–6:18 and 7:12-26, which are written in Aramaic. The Hebrew closely resembles that of Daniel, Haggai, and Chronicles, much more so than that of Sirach, written *ca.* 180 B.C. The Aramaic has been the subject of many contradictory claims, with frequent comparisons with the fifth-century Aramaic papyri of Elephantine in Egypt, and more recently with the first-century B.C. Genesis Apocryphon found at Qumrân. Differences between the language of Ezra (and Daniel) and the Palestinian first-century Genesis text have only begun to receive full scholarly attention. Again, the evidence is subject to quite varied interpretations, with G. L. Archer's claim to a clear separation (Archer, pp. 160-69) in contrast to H. H. Rowley's contention that both Daniel and the Genesis Apocryphon date from about the same period ("Notes on the Aramaic of the *Genesis Apocryphon,*" in D. W. Thomas and W. D. McHardy, eds., *Hebrew and Semitic Studies Presented to Godfrey Rolles Driver* [1963], pp. 116-129; cf. J. Fitzmyer, *Genesis Apocryphon of Qumran Cave 1: A Commentary* [2nd rev. ed. 1971], pp. 19-29). *See also* ARAMAIC.

VI. Special Problems.–The book of Ezra has more than its share of problems, which fall generally into the following (sometimes overlapping) categories: (1) problems of internal harmonization (e.g., variants of the Cyrus decree in chs. 1 and 6); (2) problems of harmonization with Nehemiah (e.g., the lists in Ezr. 2 and Neh. 7); (3) alleged conflicts with secular sources (e.g., the reference to Jehohanan in Ezr. 10:6, with the Elephantine papyri); and (4) problems of a literary nature (e.g., the role of the "Artaxerxes letter" of Ezr. 4:7-22). Many of these problems have made Ezra constantly the subject of critical attack, so they will be examined in turn.

A. Edict of Cyrus (538 B.C.). In addition to variant accounts of the edict within Ezra itself (Ezr. 1:1-4 par. 2 Ch. 36:22f.; Ezr. 6:3-5), we now have access to the Persian king's own records of his declarations regarding the return of captured peoples. In the famous Cyrus Cylinder (*ANET,* p. 315; *see* picture in CYRUS) Marduk is said to have declared that Cyrus would "become the ruler of all the world," in return for which Cyrus resettled (the statues of) all the gods in their sacred cities and endeavored to fortify (repair) their dwelling places. The language is not unlike that of Ezr. 1:1-4 (the Hebrew version), although of course Yahweh rather than Marduk called Cyrus to restore Jerusalem. The copy of the decree given in ch. 6 (the Aramaic version) omits the call to the captured peoples to return; instead it focuses on aspects of funding and supply. There is no reason to deny authenticity to either. In light of the similarities of both to contemporary documents it is difficult to understand claims that the historian was confused about the period.

B. Date of the Founding of the Temple. Perhaps more to the point is the contention that both Ezr. 5:1 and Hag. 2:18 date the founding of the temple to 520 B.C., whereas the edict of Cyrus and references in Ezr. 3:10 and 5:16 point to a founding in 536 B.C. It has been suggested (cf. *IDB,* II, 217) that if the great Cyrus really had issued such an order it could hardly have been ignored, and further that it is not possible for the temple foundations to have been laid twice. But the picture in Ezra is precisely that. Cyrus' decree was ignored when the exiles encountered some opposition (the fault lay with their timidity, not with the strength of the decree), and it was not until years later that the project was resumed. Ezra 5, the very passage alleged to support the 520 date, is very clear that in this year the abandoned task was recommenced. Furthermore, there seems no reason why, after such meager beginnings and such a long hiatus, the building activity of 520 would not be treated as something of a new beginning.

C. Lists in Ezra 2 and Nehemiah 7. Why Neh. 7 repeats almost verbatim the list of those returning under Zerubbabel (Ezr. 2) is explained in the text, and it is hardly fair to claim that the second list "is said . . . to be a list of the inhabitants of Judea in the time of Nehemiah a century later" (*IDB,* II, 217). The heading in Neh. 7:5f. makes it plain that no such idea was in the mind of the writer; rather, the earlier list provided a basis for the later genealogical reckoning.

D. Sheshbazzar and Zerubbabel. According to Ezr. 1:8-11, Cyrus originally committed the task of rebuilding to Sheshbazzar, or Shenazzar, a son of the exiled Judean monarch Jehoiachin or Jeconiah (1 Ch. 3:17f.). In v. 18 we find that Zerubbabel was a nephew of Sheshbazzar and a grandson of Shealtiel. Thus, when 3:2 and 4:2f. picture the latter as the secular head of the work force we should not be surprised. The younger man functioned as the executor of the plan initially given to his uncle. By 520 B.C., when the work recommenced, Sheshbazzar was probably dead (ch. 5), but the search for the decree would still have to be done in his name (5:14-17).

E. Chronology of Ezra 4. Ezr. 4:1-4 appears to be a continuation of the narrative that reports opposition to the building of the temple in 536/535 B.C. But v. 6 dates the writing of an accusation to the beginning of the reign of Ahasuerus (Xerxes I, 486-465 B.C.), while the correspondence of vv. 7-23 comes from "the days of Artaxerxes" (probably Artaxerxes I, 464-424 B.C.), and deals with rebuilding the walls (v. 12) rather than the temple. Finally, v. 24 returns to the "house of God" theme and closes with a reference to Darius (presumably Darius I, 522-486 B.C.) The whole section may have been misplaced, of course, but in light of the obvious nature of the conflict it is probably better to take the chapter as an episodal resumé of various attempts made by hostile forces to halt the work. However explained, it is a literary rather than a historical problem.

F. Date of Ezra's Coming to Jerusalem. Partly because of problems already alluded to and partly for other reasons, the statement in Ezr. 7:7 that dates the movement of Ezra from Babylon to the year 458 (the seventh year of Artaxerxes) has often been questioned. Since Nehemiah, whose arrival in Jerusalem is commonly dated to 444 B.C. (Neh. 1:1; 2:1), seems to know nothing of Ezra or his work before ch. 8, many have argued that the chronology of the two is confused or possibly reversed. Support for placing Ezra later than 458 is gained from Ezra 9:9 with its reference to a wall already in existence, as well as from Ezr. 4:12f. with its reference to the wall and opposition in the days of Artaxerxes prior to Ezra's coming. It is then contended that Nehemiah and his wall-building activities must have preceded Ezra's mission, whenever it was. Since the date for Nehemiah is considered firm, the easier course is to shift Ezra to a later period. A second problem is found in Ezr. 10:6 where Jehohanan the son of Eliashib is in the position of a high priest, presumably a contemporary of Ezra. For a detailed comment on the priestly lineage, *see* NEHEMIAH, BOOK OF; suffice it to say here that a reference in the Elephantine papyri to a "Johanan" as high priest in 408/407 B.C. is better harmonized with a later date for Ezra.

Three basic positions (and too many subpositions to mention) have emerged. The traditional date and order are still vigorously defended (J. S. Wright, *Date of Ezra's Coming to Jerusalem*), but perhaps the majority of contemporary scholars take the king of Ezr. 7:7 to be Artaxerxes II (Mnemon, 404-359 B.C.) rather than Artaxerxes I, thus dating the return at 398 B.C. A third position (cf. *BHI* [2nd ed. 1972], p. 363) emends Ezr. 7:7 to read the "thirty-seventh year," making the return at 428 and preserving the contemporaneity of Ezra and Nehemiah, though reversing their order. A few have even put both Ezra and Nehemiah in a later period (cf. R. W. Klein's article) though such radical solutions tend to create more problems than they solve.

The traditional dating leaves us with no more problems than its alternatives, and has the decided advantage of keeping the biblical order and the text of Ezr. 7:7 reasonably intact. Wright (pp. 17ff.) argues for an earlier wall, stopped forcibly under Artaxerxes I (Ezr. 4:7-23), and still a recent memory at the arrival of Nehemiah (Neh. 3:1).

The lineage of the high priest, likewise a knotty problem, can be solved by positing a second Jehohanan, the "son of Eliashib" (cf. Ezr. 10:6; Neh. 12:10) and thus uncle of the Jehohanan or Jonathan who, according to the Elephantine papyri, was high priest in 408 B.C. Since no date is attached to Ezr. 10, it could have occurred any time after Ezra's reforms of *ca.* 458. As neither Eliashib (known to be high priest in 444 [cf. Neh. 3:1]) nor Jehohanan is actually called high priest in Ezr. 10, the event can hardly be used to argue a detailed case. Alternative positions, particularly those which place Ezra's coming as late as 398 B.C., must either move the Chronicler (or whoever wrote Ezra and Nehemiah) to well after 300 B.C. or face the problem of how the true order could have been forgotten in such a short period.

Bibliography.–Comms. by L. W. Batten (*ICC*, 1913); W. Rudolph (*HAT*, 1949); C. W. Gilkey (*IB*, 1954); H. H. Grosheide (*Commentaar op het OT*, 1963); J. M. Myers (*AB*, 1965).

C. C. Torrey, *Ezra Studies* (1910, repr. 1970); J. S. Wright, *Date of Ezra's Coming to Jerusalem* (1947, repr. 1958); H. H. Rowley, *Servant of the Lord and Other Essays* (2nd rev. ed. 1965), pp. 135-168; J. S. Wright, *Building of the Second Temple* (1958); R. K. Harrison, *Intro. to the OT* (1969), pp. 1135-1151; G. L. Archer, "The Aramaic of the 'Genesis Apocryphon' Compared with the Aramaic of Daniel," in J. B. Payne, ed., *New Perspectives on the OT* (1970), pp. 160-69; R. W. Klein, "Ezra and Nehemiah in Recent Studies," in F. M. Cross, *et al.*, eds., *Magnalia Dei: The Mighty Acts of God* (1976), pp. 361-376.

C. E. ARMERDING

EZRAHITE ez'rə-hīt [Heb. *'ezrāḥî*; Gk. *Asebōn*]. Found in 1 K. 4:31 and in the titles of Pss. 88, 89; the clan of traditional Hebrew sages headed by Ethan and Heman, sons of the Judahite Zerah (1 Ch. 2:6). Interpretations based on Gk. *autóchthōn* favor the meaning "aborigine, native of the land" (W. F. Albright, *ARI* [5th ed. 1968], pp. 127, 210).

EZRI ez'rī [Heb. *'ezrî*–'my help'; Gk. *Ezrai* or *Ezdri*] (1 Ch. 27:26). "Ezri the son of Chelub," appointed by David to be superintendent of agriculture.

EZRIL ez'ril (1 Esd. 9:34, NEB). *See* AZAREL **4.**

FABLE. A parable-like story intended to teach truth in an interesting way.

Usually the characters in a fable are animals or plants that talk like human beings. Fables in the Bible include: Jotham's address to the people of Shechem (Jgs. 9:7-15); Jehoash's answer to Amaziah (2 K. 14:9); Isaiah's poem about the vineyard, which, although it did not speak, exercised its will against its owner (5:1-7; cf. Ezk. 19:2-9); and the debate among the members of the human body, told by Paul in 1 Cor. 12:14-26.

The term "fable," however, does not occur in the Bible. Although it appears in some English versions of the NT as a translation of Gk. *mýthos* (e.g., AV, ASV), it does so wrongly, based on the Vulg. *fabula.* It has subsequently been corrected to "myth" or "mythology" (RSV; NEB), "tale" (NEB), or "legend" (Good News Bible). *See* MYTH. G. F. HAWTHORNE

FABRICS. A word supplied by the RSV to fill out the meaning of 2 Ch. 2:7, 14; 3:14. The NEB employs "yarn." The AV has simply "purple, and crimson, and blue" without an additional noun. Dyes in the ancient Near East were obtained from such sources as the juice of crushed cochineal insects, mollusks, pomegranate rinds, and indigo plants. The skillful man sought by Solomon would, as the custom was, dye the threads and not the woven fabric.

FACE (noun) [Heb. usually *pānîm,* also *'ap*–'nose,' 'nostrils' (e.g., Gen. 3:19; 19:1; 48:12), *'ayin*–'eye' (e.g., Ex. 10:5, 15); Aram. *'anap* (Dnl. 2:46); Gk. usually *prósōpon,* also *ópsis* (Jn. 11:44), *stóma*–'mouth' (2 Jn. 12; 3 Jn. 14)]; NEB also SURFACE (e.g., Gen. 2:6; Acts 17:26), "(are) bent on" (Jer. 42:17), PRESENCE (Gen. 43:5), "made for" (Gen. 31:21), "(prostrated) himself" (Dnl. 2:46), "would have (nothing) to do with" (2 Ch. 29:6), SIGHT (Prov. 17:24), etc. (often not translated). Literally, the front part of the head of a human being or animal (e.g., Job. 41:14; Ezk. 41:19). The term is sometimes used figuratively in expressions such as "the face of" the deep (e.g., Gen. 1:2; Job. 38:30; Prov. 8:27), the waters (e.g., Gen. 1:2; 7:18; Job 24:18; 26:10), the ground (e.g., Gen. 2:6; 6:1, 7), the earth (e.g., Gen. 8:9; Ex. 32:12; Nu. 22:5; Jer. 25:26), the field (2 K. 9:37), the wilderness (Ex. 16:14), and even the moon (Job 26:9).

The human face was frequently regarded as representative of the person (e.g., Lam. 1:8; cf. the expression "face to face," Jer. 32:4; Acts 25:6; 1 Thess. 2:17), since personality is most clearly expressed through facial expressions. Often "my face" or "your face" is merely a circumlocution for "me" or "you" (cf. NEB Hos. 5:15; Ezk. 3:8; Mk. 1:2). Thus to seek someone's face (e.g., Ps. 24:6; 27:8; Hos. 5:15) was to make an effort to be in that person's presence (Ps. 105:4; Prov. 7:15; Acts 5:41; etc.), sometimes to obtain a favor (2 Ch. 7:14).

The range of emotions reflected in facial expressions includes determination (harden or "set" the face; cf. Isa. 50:7; Jer. 5:3; 42:17; Ezk. 3:8; Lk. 9:51); indifference, contempt, or rejection ("turn away the face," e.g., 2 Ch. 29:6); friendship or gracious favor (the face "shines" upon someone, e.g., Nu. 6:25); displeasure ("hide the face," e.g., Ps. 102:2; Ezk. 39:23); and hostility ("set the face against," e.g., Jer. 21:10). The face could also be averted out of an attitude of respect, fear, humility, or subservience (e.g., Ex. 3:6; 1 K. 19:13), while at a time of mourning (2 S. 19:4; Ezk. 12:6, 12) or imminent death (Est. 7:8) the face was completely covered. To "fall upon one's face" signified respect or submission, in which case the nose would touch the ground or be pressed into the earth by the foot of the conqueror (Gen. 19:1; 1 S. 5:4; etc.).

When applied to God, "face" often means God's presence (cf. Gen. 4:16; Mt. 18:10; 2 Thess. 1:9). (*See* ANTHROPOMORPHISM.) From the time of the wilderness wanderings the concept of "presence" was made specific in Hebrew worship through the use of the term "bread of the presence" (Heb. *leḥem pānîm,* lit. "bread of the face"; AV "shewbread"); *see* PRESENCE, BREAD OF THE. At times God hid His face from His people, showing indifference to their plight (cf. Dt. 31:17; Ps. 13:1 [MT 2]). When this happened prayers were made that God would again show His face (e.g., Dnl. 9:17). Moses was allowed to speak to God "face to face" (Ex. 33:11; cf. Dt. 34:10), but he was not permitted to see God's face, lest he die (Ex. 33:20, 23; on Gen. 32:30, *see* ANGEL II.C). To see God "face to face" is reserved for believers in the life to come (1 Cor. 13:12).

See also COUNTENANCE; PRESENCE.

Bibliography.–*RTWB,* pp. 173f.; *TDNT,* VI, *s.v.* πρόσωπον (Lohse). R. K. H.

FACETS [Heb. *'ênāyim*–'eyes'] (Zec. 3:9); AV, NEB, EYES. The small plane surfaces of a cut gem. A stone with seven facets will have an inscription engraved on it by Yahweh Himself, and it will then be given to the priest Joshua. (Cf. the use of *'ayin* for "surface" or "face" of the earth in Ex. 10:15; Nu. 22:5, 11.)

FACT. In 1 S. 24:11 the RSV renders a Hebrew infinitive periphrastically by inserting the term "fact." In several NT passages "fact" also occurs, either as a translation of the Greek particle *hóti* (Mt. 16:8; Mk. 8:17; Acts 13:34) or of *toúto* (2 Pet. 3:5, 8) or *nuní* (1 Cor. 15:20). The plural is used to render *tó asphalés* (AV "the certainty") in Acts 21:34.

FACTIONS [Gk. *hairéseis*] (1 Cor. 11:19); AV HERESIES; NEB DISSENSIONS; **FACTIOUS** [Gk. *eritheía*] (Rom. 2:8); AV CONTENTIOUS; NEB "governed by selfish ambition"; [*hairetikós*] (Tit. 3:10); AV, NEB, HERETIC. The term "factions" has various meanings in the NT. When used in a more neutral sense it connotes groups within a unified congregation. When used in its negative sense it denotes divisive persons or groups within a church.

The Gk. *haíresis* is from a root connoting a "free choice." Thus it becomes a term that describes the philosophical parties within Greek culture. This meaning is carried over into the NT to describe the Pharisees (Acts 15:5; 26:5) and the Sadducees (5:17). In these cases no negative connotation, such as the English "sect" carries, is implied; the meaning is closer to our word "party" (cf. RSV, NEB) in a political sense. Paul uses the Greek term in much the same way in 1 Cor. 11:19, where he says that "factions" (*hairéseis*) within the church are needed so that discussion may prove what is correct. These "factions" are different from the "divisions" (*schísmata*, v. 18) that Paul had earlier condemned (1:10f.); the *hairéseis* are groups that do not threaten the church's unity.

In other contexts *hairésis* takes on a negative connotation, as when Christianity is called the "sect of the Nazarenes" (Acts 24:5, 14; 28:22). This negative sense of the word became dominant in the patristic period (cf. the English term "heresy"). Thus the "factious man" is condemned in Tit. 3:10. The Christian is told not to have anything to do with such a man after one or two admonitions.

In Rom. 2:8 Paul denounces factiousness (Gk. *eritheía*) as a sin. *Eritheía* is used in classical Greek of one who seeks political office for the fulfillment of his selfish ambitions and for personal gain. Both *hairéseis* and *eritheía* appear in the catalog of sins in Gal. 5:20. The RSV renders *hairéseis* "party spirit" and *eritheía* "selfishness." This aptly shows the difference between the two words.

See also HERESY.

***Bibliography*.**–H. Ridderbos, comm. on 1 Corinthians (*NICNT*, 1953), pp. 34f., 266; *TDNT*, I, *s.v.* αἱρέομαι κτλ. (Schlier).

D. W. WEAD

FACULTIES [Gk. *aisthētḗrion*] (He. 5:14); AV SENSES; NEB PERCEPTIONS. A term denoting the "sense" that has the ability of moral discrimination (Bauer, rev., p. 25). Gk. *aisthētḗrion* occurs also in the LXX in Jer. 4:19 where Heb. *qîrôṯ libbî*, "walls of my heart," is rendered *tá aisthētḗria tḗs kardías mou*, "the senses of my heart." In He. 5:14 this internal sense of perceiving and judging is regarded as becoming perfected by use or exercise (cf. Eph. 4:12; 1 Tim. 4:7; 2 Pet. 3:18).

FADE. The concept of diminishing, dying out, or withering is expressed in the OT by Heb. *qāpaṣ* (Job 24:24; AV "taken out of the way"; NEB "wilt"), *mālal* (Ps. 37:2; 90:6; AV "be cut down"; NEB "wither," "is parched"), *nāḇēl* (Isa. 28:1, 4; 40:7f.; 64:6 [MT 5]; NEB also "flowering," "have withered"), the pulal of *'āmal* (Nah. 1:4; AV, NEB, "languish"), and *kālâ* (Job 7:9; AV "is consumed"; NEB "break up"). In the NT "fade" translates Gk. *maraínō* (Jas. 1:11; NEB "wither") and *katargéō* (2 Cor. 3:7, 11, 13; AV "abolish," "done away").

In 2 Cor. 3:7-18 the participle *katargouménos* means "transitory" (cf. Bauer, rev., p. 417). Paul contrasts the transitory splendor of the old covenant (mediated through Moses) with the greater splendor of the new covenant (mediated through Christ and the Spirit). The fading brightness of Moses' face (cf. Ex. 34:29-35) symbolizes the provisional character of the old order of Mosaic law.

N. J. O.

FAIENCE fā-ons'. A porous body of finely ground quartz held together by a glassy "connective tissue" and covered with a colored vitreous glaze. The surface is a hard glaze; the body remains relatively friable. This material may be modeled, or even thrown on a wheel like potter's clay, to achieve its final shape before firing. Although many objects were coated with a separate glaze by dipping or painting, several different techniques were probably used for making small faience objects in antiquity. Using contemporary Persian bead making as an analogous industry, Wulff has reported that faience donkey beads are made by mixing the quartz powder with some alkaline binder and forming the object, which is then placed in a tray filled with charcoal, potash, copper oxide, and lime. The entire unit is baked in a low-fired furnace of 900-1000° C for a day, so that a potassium silicate glaze is formed within the tray. This glaze migrates to the individual beads, whose surface is wetted by the alkaline binder, and a thin, relatively even glazing results. A similar technique must have been used to produce the millions of mummy beads preserved from antiquity.

***Bibliography*.**–H. E. Wulff, *Traditional Crafts of Persia* (1966); H. E. Wulff, *et al.*, *Archaeology*, 21 (1968), 100-102; A. L. Oppenheim, *et al.*, *Glass and Glassmaking in Ancient Mesopotamia* (1970).

S. M. GOLDSTEIN

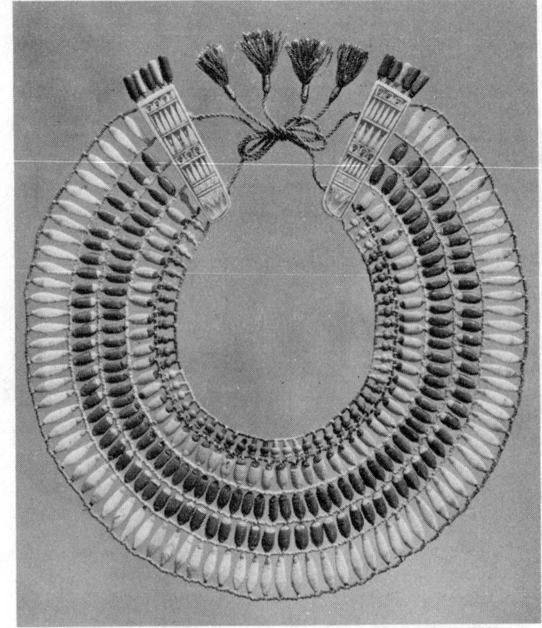

Broad collar of faience beads in the form of cornflowers, dates, and lotus petals. Egyptian, late 18th Dynasty (*ca.* 1400-1350 B.C.) (Metropolitan Museum of Art, Rogers Fund, 1940)

FAIL; FAILURE [Heb. *kālâ, rāpâ, kāraṯ, nāpal, ḥāsēr, yāṣā', kāšal, 'āḇaḏ* (Jer. 4:9), *'āzal* (Job 14:11), *'áyin* (Isa. 44:12), *bôš* (Joel 1:10, 12, 17), *gā'al* (Job 21:10), *ḥāḏal* (Job 19:14), *kāzaḇ* (Isa. 58:11), *kāhâ* (Isa. 42:4), *kāḥaš* (Hos. 9:2; Hab. 3:17), *nāšaṯ* (Jer. 51:30), *'āḏar* (Zeph. 3:5), *'āzaḇ* (Ps. 38:10 [MT 11]; 40:12 [MT 13]), *pārar* (Eccl. 12:5), *tam* (Ezk. 47:12); Aram. *šālû* (Ezr. 6:9); Gk. *ekleípō, anékleiptos* ("does not fail," Lk. 12:33), *hysteréō, adókimos, epileípō* (He. 11:32), *aníēmi* (He. 13:5), *asthénēma* (Rom. 15:1), *ekpíptō* (Rom. 9:6), *katalýō* (Acts 5:38), *ptaíō* (Jas. 2:10), *hēttēma* (Rom. 11:12)]; AV also FORSAKE, PERISH, FALL, BE CONSUMED, BE WITHERED, DECAY, BE DRIED UP, COME TO NOUGHT, BE REPROBATES (2 Cor. 13:5-7), etc.; NEB also STRAIN AFTER, LOSE HEART, LACK, WANT, DWINDLE, GROW DIM, DISOWN, BE UNSURE, BE BARREN, COLLAPSE, PROVE (or BE) UNEQUAL (2 Cor. 13:5f.), BE DISCREDITED (2 Cor. 13:7), PROVE FALSE, "tender scruples" (Rom. 15:1), etc. To be or become insufficient; to become extinct or break down; to neglect or forsake.

Of the twenty-two Hebrew roots translated "fail" in the RSV, the most common is *kālâ:* "come to an end, cease to function or exist," hence "fail." Its subject is most often "eyes" in the idiom "the eyes shall fail," meaning "to die" — an example of synecdoche (a part representing the whole). In most cases this event is to be understood literally and not simply as disappointment (see Dt. 28:65; Job 11:20; 17:5; 31:16; Jer. 14:6; Lam. 4:17; cf. Lev. 26:16; 1 S. 2:33); but a spiritual-emotional meaning occurs in Ps. 69:3 [MT 4]; Lam. 2:11. With other subjects this verb can refer to the physical destruction of plant life (Isa. 15:6) or a wine harvest (32:10), or a figurative dying of a human spirit (Ps. 143:7) or flesh and heart (73:26).

Hebrew *rāpâ* means "abandon, desert, forsake." The formula "he will not fail you" (Dt. 4:31; 31:6, 8; Josh. 1:5; 1 Ch. 28:20) affirms that God will not abandon His people but will be with them in every national crisis. This was confirmed by Israel's experience. When they prepared to occupy the Promised Land, when Solomon prepared to build the first temple, and when God's people longed to return from exile, they found their God to be faithful. In contrast, 2 S. 4:1 (MT; cf. AV) speaks literally of the failing of the warrior's hands, an idiom for the loss of courage in battle.

The faithfulness of God is also expressed in God's conditional promise concerning the royal line of David: "there shall not fail you a man on the throne of Israel" (1 K. 2:4; 1 K. 8:25 par. 2 Ch. 6:16; 1 K. 9:5 par. 2 Ch. 7:18). Here Heb. *kāraṯ* means "cut off," hence "be brought to an end" (cf. 1 K. 9:7). Another expression of God's faithfulness uses Heb. *nāpal,* literally, "fall down, be ineffective." God's promises do not "fall down"; God does not fail to fulfil His word (Josh. 21:45; 23:14; 1 K. 8:56). In contrast, human courage can fail (1 S. 17:32).

Hebrew *ḥāsēr* means "run out of, be without," and is used of oil (1 K. 17:14, 16) and bread (Isa. 51:14). Heb. *kāšal,* "stumble," is used figuratively for the failure of human strength and endurance (Neh. 4:10 [MT 4]; Ps. 31:10 [MT 11]; Lam. 1:14); men of violence will stumble in their plans (Dnl. 11:14).

In the NT, Gk. *ekleípō* means "cease, stop functioning." Its subject can be mammon (Lk. 16:9), the sun (23:45), or even human faith during a crisis (22:32).

Greek *hysteréō* means "come too late" or "come short, not far enough." In He. 4:1; 12:15, it expresses the failure of Christians to reach the goal of their faith, namely, God's rest. It also can mean "run short" or "run out" and is so used of wine in Jn. 2:3. The same word is translated "fall short" in Rom. 3:23.

Greek *adókimos,* "not standing the test," hence "unqualified, worthless," occurs in the context of endurance (2 Cor. 13:5-7). (*See* REPROBATE.) Faith must be proved by works; not to live the life one professes is to fail the test. (Cf. 1 Cor. 9:27; Tit. 1:16, where the same Greek word is used.) The opposite is to be approved (*dókimos,* Rom. 16:10; 2 Tim. 2:15; cf. Jas. 1:12).

Bibliography.–*TDNT,* II, *s.v.* δόκιμος κτλ. (Grundmann); VIII, *s.v.* ὕστερος κτλ.: ὑστερέω (Wilckens); *TDOT,* I, *s.v.* "ābhadh" (Otzen); II, *s.v.* "bôsh," III (Seebass); III, *s.v.* "gā'al" (Fuhs).

H. W. LAY

FAIN. Occurs twice in the AV, in the sense of "gladly": (1) in Job 27:22 as the rendering of Heb. *bārô(a)ḥ yiḇrāḥ:* "he would fain flee" (lit. as in AV mg., "in fleeing he would flee"; RSV "he flees . . . in headlong flight"); (2) in Lk. 15:16, as the translation of Gk. *epithyméō,* "fix the mind or desire on," in the clause: "he would fain have filled his belly" (RSV "he would gladly have fed on").

FAINT; FAINTHEARTED. These terms translate a number of words as follows.

(1) Heb. *ʿāyēp* denotes exhaustion after harassment by an enemy (Dt. 25:18; Jgs. 8:4f.; cf. Jer. 4:31) or following frustration (Isa. 29:8).

(2) *Yāʿap* is used in reference to exhausted troops (1 S. 14:28, 31; 2 S. 16:2; cf. adj. *yāʿēp* in Jgs. 8:15). In Isa. 40:28-31, God is said not to grow weary, giving strength to those who are weary (cf. 44:12).

(3) *Rāḵaḵ,* denoting loss of resilience, is used in prophetic warnings to the nation to remain resolute in the face of enemy opposition (Dt. 20:3; Isa. 7:4; Jer. 51:46). In Job 23:16 it refers to faintness before God. *Raḵ hallēḇāb* in Dt. 20:8 means faint of heart.

(4) *ʿĀṭap* indicates a general state of faintness, whether of body (Ps. 107:5; Lam. 2:11f., 19) or mind (Ps. 61:2 [MT 3]; 77:3 [MT 4]; 142:3 [MT 4]; 143:4; Jonah 2:7).

(5) *ʿĀlap* describes despondency (Isa. 51:20), physical faintness from heat (Jonah 4:8) or thirst (Am. 8:13); or it is used figuratively (Ezk. 31:15).

(6) *Kāhâ* (Ezk. 21:7) and adjective *kēhâ* (Isa. 61:3) denote faintness of spirit.

(7) *Māsas* describes melting in fear (Nah. 2:10).

(8) *Mûg* is a verb for melt or waver, in the niphal meaning "be disheartened," thus "fainthearted" in Josh. 2:24.

(9) *Ḥālâ* indicates exhaustion from a journey (Isa. 57:10).

(10) *Pûg* describes the numbness of Jacob upon hearing that Joseph was still alive (Gen. 45:26).

(11) *Kāmah* depicts David's intense longing for God (Ps. 63:1 [MT 2]).

(12) *Kālâ* is used to describe the psalmist's wasting away for desire of the courts of the Lord (Ps. 84:2 [MT 3]).

(13) *Dāwwāy* depicts the depletion of bodily reserves due to illness (Isa. 1:5) or calamity (Lam. 1:13, 22).

(14) *Rāpâ* indicates collapse in the face of adversity (Prov. 24:10).

(15) Gk. *eklýō* describes collapse from general physical exhaustion (Mt. 15:32; Mk. 8:3; He. 12:3).

(16) *Apopsýchō* is used for fainting from fear (Lk. 21:26).

(17) *Oligópsychos* means discouraged (1 Th. 5:14).

R. K. H.

FAIR. This adjective, along with its comparative, superlative, and adverbial forms, is used in two distinct senses:

(1) [Heb. *ṭôḇ* (Gen. 6:2; 24:16; 26:7; Nu. 24:5; etc.), *ṭûḇ* (Hos. 10:11), *yāpeh* (Job 42:15; Ps. 45:2 [MT 3]; Cant. 1:8; Jer. 11:16; Ezk. 31:3; etc.), *yāpâ* (Cant. 7:6 [MT 7]), *tip'ereṯ* (Ezk. 16:17, 39), *ḥēn* (Prov. 1:9; 4:9), *šiprâ* (Job 26:13); Aram. *šappîr* (Dnl. 4:12, 21 [MT 9, 18]); Gk. *eudía* ("fair weather," Mt. 16:2), *eulogía* ("fair words," Rom. 16:18)]; AV also GOODLY, BEAUTY, GRACE (Prov. 1:9; 4:9), "garnish" (Job 26:13); NEB also GOODLY, SPLENDID, BEAUTY, GRACE, etc. Good, fine, beautiful.

The broadest term is *ṭôḇ,* which in the above passages

refers to aesthetic goodness, or beauty. The adjective *yāp̄eh* and its cognate verb always indicate that something is "pleasing" or "beautiful"; the word occurs most frequently in Canticles (1:8; 2:10, 13; 4:7; 5:9; 6:1, 10; 7:6). *Ḥēn* usually means "grace" or "favor," but in Prov. 1:9 and 4:9 it denotes "charm" or "a pleasing quality" (*see also* GRACE).

Especially interesting is Rom. 16:18, where for the hendiadys *diá tḗs chrēstologías kaí eulogías* the RSV has "by fair and flattering words" (cf. AV "by good words and fair speeches"; NEB "with smooth and specious words"). This is the only NT use of *eulogía* (cf. English "eulogy"), "praise, blessing," in a negative sense, reminding believers that beauty — whether visible or audible — is indeed sometimes only skin-deep (cf. 1 S. 16:7; Jas. 3:5-10).

(2) [Gk. *kalós*] (Mt. 15:26); AV MEET; NEB RIGHT; [*isótēs*] (Col. 4:1); AV EQUAL. Unprejudiced, right, just. *Kalós,* like Heb. *ṭôḇ,* is an inclusive term for "good"; here it means "morally good." *Isótēs* denotes "equality of treatment."

See *TDNT,* II, *s.v.* εὐλογέω κτλ. (Beyer); III, *s.v.* καλός (Bertram). R. F. YOUNGBLOOD

FAIR HAVENS [Gk. *kaloí Limenes*]. A harbor on the south side of CRETE (Acts 27:8). It is now identified with a bay E of Cape Littinos. The harbor opens toward the east and is sheltered on the southwest by two small islands. In 1853 a naval officer, Captain T. A. B. Spratt, discovered on a hill overlooking the bay a chapel dedicated to Paul. He also noted that southeast winds blowing in winter would make the harbor unsafe (see T. A. B. Spratt, *Travels and Researches in Crete* [1865], II, 1-6). This hazard and the necessity (as some have thought) of obtaining supplies at LASEA 8 km. (5 mi.) away may be why the ship carrying Paul soon left Fair Havens for Rome (cf. vv. 8-12). R. EARLE

FAITH [Heb. *'ĕmûn*–'trustworthiness'; Gk. *pístis*].

I. The Term
II. Faithfulness
III. Mere Belief
IV. The Faith
V. Special Faith
VI. Trust
VII. Justifying Faith
VIII. In Theology

I. The Term.–This is the noun corresponding to the verb "believe." The Heb. *'ēmûn* has primarily the sense of faithfulness or trustworthiness, and *'ᵉmûnâ* normally refers to the faithfulness of God, though it can be used of man's response (Hab. 2:4). The LXX translation and NT equivalent, Gk. *pístis,* is very common in the NT, and bears the sense not of faithfulness alone, but of the reliance or trust that is the basis of man's faithfulness, i.e., the faithfulness that expresses confidence in the faithfulness of God. Incidentally, the English word "faith" is akin to the Lat. *fides,* and probably to the Sanskrit *bhidh,* "unite," "bind." An interesting feature of the NT usage is that Paul regularly has the noun whereas John prefers the verb, though with no essential difference of meaning. The AV once uses "faith" for *elpís,* which properly signifies "hope" (He. 10:23).

II. Faithfulness.–Before discussing the central meaning of the word in the NT we should take note of some of the subsidiary senses. The first is faithfulness, as in the OT. This is obviously the true sense in Rom. 3:3, where the reference is to the faithfulness of God. It is also very probably the meaning in Gal. 5:22, where the context suggests a quality that, like love, joy, peace, etc., is a gift of the Holy Spirit. Some commentators favor here a special faith rather beyond the general trust in God common to all believers. Mt. 23:23 is another instance in which the rendering "faithfulness" might be apposite, though this is not the normal usage on the lips of Jesus.

III. Mere Belief.–Another special use of the term is found in Jas. 2:14-26, where all that is denoted is an intellectual assent which carries no element either of true committal or of implied obedience. We are not to suppose that this is the only meaning of the term in James, since a fuller content seems to underlie 5:15. Again, there is no need to think that James is here arguing specifically against Paul, as though Paul were teaching that mere belief is enough to justify. Luther's hasty conclusion to this effect caused him to miss the real qualities of this epistle (cf. Tyndale's judicious correction of Luther on the matter); and the later thesis of a Paul-James controversy has hardly contributed to a proper understanding of the NT teaching on either faith or works. In fact, James is warning against the antinomian conclusion that mere assent is the justifying faith of Abraham and his believing successors; and in this James and Paul (cf. also He. 11) are wholly at one. While faith justifies, this faith is the faith which is demonstrated in works, which operates by love (Gal. 5:6), and which necessarily implies obedient action (He. 11).

IV. The Faith.–In a few verses in the NT the reference is fairly clearly not to faith itself but to "the faith" in the sense of the body of Christian truth implied in faith. This could be the meaning in Rom. 1:5, though some expositors prefer "the obedience of faith" (RSV) to "obedience to the faith" (AV). It is certainly the natural sense in Gal. 1:23; 1 Tim. 4:1, 6; and Jude 3. There is, of course, no conflict between faith as a body of beliefs and the living, personal reality of trust in God. For trust is no mere emotional and mystical experience; it has an intellectual element. Certain things are believed about the God in whom trust is placed, about His nature, word, and works, about His relation to man as Creator, Lord, Judge, and Savior. The gospel itself is believed when there is trust in Christ, and the gospel is the faith. This sense is thus legitimate in itself, though it tended to become too prominent after the NT; and in abstraction from the main sense it could easily come to be linked with the mere belief James finds so inadequate.

V. Special Faith.–The Lord Himself speaks of a faith that is so strong it can work miracles (Mt. 17:20f.) or cause the working of miracles (9:28f.). He Himself enjoyed this faith in full measure even to the point of raising the dead, and Peter and Paul are notable examples from the apostolic period. As noted, some have suggested that the faith of Gal. 5:22 belongs to this category, and certainly the spiritual gift of 1 Cor. 12:9 seems to do so. That this is not the faith all Christians must have for salvation is clear from the latter verse, for the whole point of 1 Cor. 12 is that the Holy Spirit distributes different gifts to different people, and the "faith" of v. 9 is one of these gifts. Conversely, not all who have the faith to work miracles necessarily have justifying faith; at least this seems to be implied in Mt. 7:22f.

VI. Trust.–The main sense of the word "faith" in the NT is that of trust or reliance. When this is the sense, the verbal form ("believe") is often accompanied by a preposition which brings out the meaning. Gk. *en* and *epí* with the dative express reliance on the thing or person in whom confidence is put, while the distinctively NT use of *eis* or *epí* with the accusative expresses the movement of confident committal to the object of faith. In very many cases it is a person on whom or toward whom there is faith, namely, God or Jesus Christ. This usage brings out very strongly the *fiducia* ("trust") aspect in faith, for this kind of reliance or committal signifies much more than intellectual belief. It is directed primarily not to facts or codified beliefs, but to God Himself in Jesus Christ.

Yet the intellectual element is included. A person is not an abstraction. Nor does a person exist merely as an existential object or concept. A person is and says and does things. To have faith in a person is to believe certain things about this person, his nature, word, and work. It is more than this, but it is certainly not less. One does not need to know everything, nor even everything that is knowable, but it is essential to know and believe something. One cannot really trust in Jesus Christ without believing that He is the Messiah, the incarnate Son, the crucified and risen Savior. The words and works, the essential being of Jesus, are all part of His person. It is not possible to have a vague attachment to a shadowy construct of one's own imagining and to say that this is faith in Jesus Christ. Or perhaps it is, for God's mercy is great and broad. But this can only be faith *per nefas*. True faith is confident attachment to the Jesus of the NT.

The content of faith is given in and by the Word of God. The Word of God is, of course, Jesus Himself. But it is also the word written and the word preached. This is why Paul says that sending and preaching and hearing are so important. "Faith comes from what is heard, and what is heard comes by the preaching of Christ" (Rom. 10:17). It is by receiving and believing the words and works recorded in Holy Scripture and proclaimed by ministers of the gospel that Jesus Himself is received and believed (Jn. 1:12; cf. 20:31). In this respect it should be noted that if there is no confidence in the testimony of Scripture it is hard to see how there can be real faith either in the God who gave the testimony (1 Cor. 2:13; 1 Thess. 2:13) or in the God to whose word and work testimony is given. As it is with Christ Himself (Jn. 3:11, 32ff.), so it is with the record that bears witness to Him (cf. Lk. 1:1,4).

Yet, while faith must include an intellectual element, i.e., the reception of the words and works fulfilled in Christ, recorded in Holy Scripture, and proclaimed in genuine preaching, a mere assent to the body of facts and truths herein contained is very much less than faith. For, in the first place, even to understand the facts and truths in their real significance an illumination is required that goes beyond ordinary comprehension (1 Cor. 2). This is the illumination that is effected by the Holy Spirit bearing His own witness along with that of the written and spoken word. Again, this illumination carries with it more than intellectual perception. It is a disclosure not only of facts and truths, but of the true nature of God in Jesus Christ and of the true nature of man as the lost sinner who has no hope of salvation except in God. As such, it carries with it also a redirection of the emotions and a liberation of the will, so that there can be true committal to God and a true reorientation of the whole life and person in this committal. If faith comes by hearing the word, it comes by hearing this word as the Word of God by the Holy Spirit. It comes through the operation of the illuminating and life-giving Spirit Himself (1 Thess. 1:5). Hence faith in the true sense is not a human possibility; it is the gift of God. While it may be true that the reference of Eph. 2:8b ("it is the gift of God") is not just to faith, it is also true that faith is consistently presented in Scripture as a divine gift or work. It is brought into the closest relation to regeneration in Jn. 3. To come to Christ one must be drawn by the Father (Jn. 6:44). It is given to Christians to believe and to suffer (Phil. 1:29). The Lord adds to the Church those that are saved (Acts 2:47). This is why faith is so confident: it is a trust in God evoked by God. This is why faith is so total and so powerful: it is the operation of God which claims and directs and energizes the whole man.

VII. Justifying Faith.–What, then, are the implications of faith in the NT sense? There are many different angles from which one might legitimately approach this question, but perhaps it will be best to bring out the features that are most prominent in Scripture itself. First, faith implies the honest recognition of one's own sinfulness. The faith that comes by hearing is acceptance of the truth about oneself. This is why repentance and faith are so closely connected (Acts 2:38-44; 17:30, 34; 26:20). Repentance, however, is more than recognition of sin. It is recognition that this sin is under the judgment of God. This is another aspect of what one might call faith on its negative side (Rom. 2:1-3). A sense, even a proper fear, of judgment is an essential ingredient in faith, for faith is faith in the righteous God, who neither can nor will relax His righteous demand nor overlook its unrighteous transgression. Repentance, however, takes no refuge in an illusory hope of meeting God's justice by amendment. This brings us to a third negative characteristic of faith: it is a recognition of helplessness, a renunciation of all other trust than trust in God. No works either under the law or apart from the law can avail for justification before God (Rom. 2:1-3; 3:19f.). There is nothing and no one else upon whom we can rely. Our trust must be in God alone.

But can we trust in God? This brings us to the positive and crucial aspect of faith. For faith is the movement not merely away from helpless self but toward God as the one who has in fact helped in Jesus Christ. The gospel is the news that God Himself has acted for our justification and that we can and should trust in Him. Faith is this committal to God. It is no blind committal, for the God in whom we trust is already revealed to faith. The action on which we rely has already taken place. Faith is thus acceptance. It is acceptance of the righteousness God has purchased for us by the death of Jesus Christ in our stead and on our behalf. It is committal to the God who is both just and the justifier of those who believe in Jesus, not in a puzzling intellectual paradox, but in the actual deed fulfilled in the incarnate Son. Faith is the conviction, grounded in the message of God Himself in the gospel, that though we are unrighteous in ourselves we are now righteous and accepted in Jesus. Faith is the humble recognition that sin is pardoned, its penalty borne, righteousness imputed. Faith is entry into the new relation of sonship established thereby. When there is no one else to trust, God is trusted, not as a last resort, but because in His revealing and reconciling action He shows Himself to be wholly worthy of trust. In this sense, i.e., because God has already acted, faith is justifying faith (cf. esp. Rom. 3–4). *See also* JUSTIFICATION.

It is important to note at this point that faith is not justifying faith because it is itself a work that avails as the ground of justification. Certainly, Abraham's faith was imputed to him for righteousness (Rom. 4:3). But behind faith is grace (Rom. 4:16; Eph. 2:8). The power of faith is the power of its object. Merely to believe does not help. One has to believe in God, in the promise, in Jesus Christ, in His word and work, in what God has done in Him. Faith is justifying faith, not because it justifies, but because it grasps the justification God Himself has effected. As Calvin finely observed, faith plays a passive role in justifying. It is necessary, but only as the empty hand which receives or the empty vessel which is filled. What really forgives is the atoning blood of Jesus Christ. What really justifies is the righteousness of Jesus Christ. Faith is the divinely appointed and divinely effected means whereby this forgiveness and righteousness are appropriated to us, whereby we are identified with Christ and enter into justification. It must be said, and said with force and conviction, that justification is by faith alone. But this can be said only because there stands behind it the even more fundamental truth that justification is by grace alone, i.e., by Christ alone.

Yet faith is not just passive. Divinely given, involving a total reorientation of life, it is also supremely active. Closely related to the regenerative work of the Holy Spirit, it is the dynamic behind the Christian life. To believe in Christ is in fact to have eternal life (Jn. 5:24). The Christian life is the life of faith. Faith is identification with Christ, not only in justification, but in sanctification. Faith means assurance of the resurrection (Jn. 11:25f.). It means the ability to do even greater works than those of Jesus (Jn. 14:12). With its certainty that the promises of God, fulfilled or not yet fulfilled, are all true, it is the knowledge of things not yet seen (He. 11:1). Faith is the seeing of life from the perspective of eternity. Faith is the inward compulsion, not only to trust God, but, trusting Him, to obey Him, to do exploits in His name, to bring forth fruits of righteousness, to find expression in faithfulness. Thus Abraham, believing in God, does things consistent with his faith. There is no cleavage between the faith that looks to God alone and the works which are the fruit and expression of obedient faith. Christians walk in faith (2 Cor. 5:7). They are strong in faith (cf. 1 Cor. 16:13). They rejoice in faith (Rom. 15:13). They are the household of faith (Gal. 6:10). They bear the shield of faith (Eph. 6:16). Their faith works by love (Gal. 5:6). Faith is one of the three things that abide (1 Cor. 13:13). The greatest of these is love; but the love for God, which is the very essence of love, is itself rooted and grounded in faith. It is the trusting response of love to Him who first loved us.

VIII. In Theology.–In the doctrinal presentation of faith, four main trends are to be observed corresponding to the four main epochs in the history of dogma: the patristic, the medieval (continued to a large degree in Roman Catholicism), the Reformation (represented today by orthodox Protestants), and the liberal Protestant. In a brief review it is impossible to do justice either to the details of, or variations within, the different movements. Nevertheless, it will be helpful to characterize the general tendencies, for thereby light is shed both on the pitfalls to be avoided and on the path to be followed in fidelity to the biblical and apostolic norm.

The patristic age, for all its magnificent achievements, quickly lost sight of the essential element in NT faith and tended to subsume faith under "the faith," or assent to the faith. This was not without reason, for the early Church had to face heresies that might easily have destroyed its message. There was need both to formulate the orthodox faith and to regard assent to it as an important element in true Christian profession. Nor should the development be seen out of proportion, for, in the first instance the creed was not just a statement of beliefs and facts but an expression of faith in God the Father, Son, and Holy Spirit. Furthermore, a transformation of life was expected as part of conversion to Christianity. Yet a trend toward intellectualization of faith is plainly to be seen, e.g., in Tertullian's concept of the rule of faith, or in the Alexandrian view of faith as little more than minimal assent to the rudiments. One of the reasons for this, and yet also a result of it, is failure properly to grasp the Pauline doctrine of justification, so that with the developing doctrine of baptismal regeneration, distorted emphasis on the problem of postbaptismal sin, and the excessive growth of monasticism in both theory and practice, faith and its role are increasingly misconceived and minimized in the early centuries.

The full results of this false development are to be seen in the Scholastic theology of the Middle Ages. Some fine notes were still sounded. Hardly anywhere could one find more magnificent expression of loving trust in God than in Bernard of Clairvaux. Lombard, followed by Aquinas, could still insist that unbelief or insincerity blocks the operation of grace in baptism. Yet the general dogmatic trend was toward an understanding of faith alone (*informata*) as the mere assent which may be very largely induced by reason and which in an adult opens the way to baptism and thus earns congruent grace, without which this faith is not adequate for justification. With baptismal grace the habit of virtue or love is then implanted, and faith is no longer alone. It is now formed faith (*formata*), the faith which is completed by love and which does in fact justify. This in turn brings further grace, the grace of condignity, so that unless grace is forfeited by mortal sin, final salvation is secure. But faith in itself has the significance only of a first and intrinsically not very important step in this whole process. It is essential, but alone it is not enough. A further reduction of faith is to be seen in the tendency toward an additional distinction between implicit faith and explicit faith. This distinction, already prepared in Scholasticism, is more fully worked out in later Roman Catholicism. It rested on the widespread ignorance of the laity and the alleged danger that instruction might open the way to heresy. The argument was that for ordinary people, who do not have the capacity for or the opportunity of instruction in the faith, and who may well be better without it, faith (implicit) is simply believing what the Church teaches, whether this be known or unknown. For the majority, no more is necessary for salvation. Even as assent, then, faith was robbed of any content except insofar as the Church itself now became the true object and content. In these circumstances, it is hardly surprising that Roman Catholicism has found it difficult to accept or even to understand the Reformation doctrine of justification by faith.

It was Martin Luther supremely who rediscovered the doctrine of justification by faith and therewith the rich signification and significance of faith in the biblical sense. His own lack of assurance and his intensive biblical study brought him to this epoch-making understanding, which had dogmatic and practical ramifications far beyond anything he himself had first envisaged. The heart of it all is that faith is no mere acceptance of facts and doctrines. It is trust in Christ and His accomplished work as the only but all-sufficient ground of salvation. Because of this orientation to Christ, faith alone is enough for justification. This does not mean that it alone is meritorious. Faith is a looking away from all human merit to the unique merit of Christ Himself. In this sense it is not a first step which must be followed by other steps if there is to be justification. It embraces the whole life of the Christian, so that there can be abiding assurance of forgiveness in spite of postbaptismal sin. Nor is faith merely a human response. It is the work of the life-giving Spirit, and as such it is itself a living and active thing which is naturally and necessarily accompanied by fruits of righteousness. These fruits are not a ground of justification. Justification and sanctification are not to be confused. On the other hand, the absence of these fruits is a sign that there is no true faith. Justification and sanctification are not to be separated. Calvin put this aspect of the matter finely in a single judicious sentence when he said that "it is faith alone which justifies, but the faith which justifies is not alone."

The beginnings of departure from the Reformation position are to be seen already in the 16th and 17th centuries. On the one hand, Osiander moved toward a new subjectivization with his doctrine of imparted righteousness. Antinomianism, on the other hand, attempted an impossible abstraction of faith from works. Arminianism, too, was responsible for a dangerous development with its implication that the free response of faith is the last stone, as it were, which we ourselves place in the edifice of salvation. The solid orthodoxy of the 17th cent. (both Lutheran and Reformed) was not free from the tendency to substitute right belief (including belief in the doctrine of justification by faith) for the true and living faith of the NT. The rise of liberal Protestantism brought even more serious departure from Reformation teaching, whether in the form of emotionalized psychological faith (Schleiermacher), moralism (Ritschl), faith mysticism (Schweitzer), or a new intellectualism (rational orthodoxy). The main trend has been toward a subjectivizing of faith, as though it were simply a human psychological factor which in some form accomplishes of itself a right relationship with God and the world. Existentialism as advocated by Bultmann and his disciples carries this subjectivism to the new point where it is the glory of the believer not to be concerned whether Jesus ever lived or died or rose again, but to commit himself to Jesus as the Christ who brings new light and life and to find the existential reality of His saving work by faith. Here the whole movement of liberal Protestantism reaches a climax. Not only is faith psychologized, it is completely divorced from any historically objective content (the message that evokes faith is also existential), so that faith in Christ is no longer real faith in the real person who has accomplished real work and who comes to us through the real Spirit in a real encounter. At one extreme this is as far from the faith of the NT as is the unformed or implicit faith of Roman Catholicism at the other.

Yet Luther's discovery has not been in vain. Orthodox Protestantism has continued to maintain its witness to biblical faith, with Pietism to prevent it from sinking into barren intellectualism. Continuing intensive linguistic and exegetical work has confirmed and deepened the exposition of the Reformers. Renewed interest in the theology of the Reformation has brought to light a wealth of dogmatic material. Karl Barth has attempted a solid restatement of the biblical and Protestant position. Roman Catholicism, too, has begun to show a new appreciation of the biblical teaching and the Reformation concern. An age of misunderstood faith has also become an age of diminished faith, and it is obvious that neither the new existentialism nor the new techniques and principles of communication, but only the NT faith in Christ which is the work of the Holy Spirit, can bring about any genuine restoration. This alone is faith, and there can be no substitute.

Bibliography.–K. Barth, *CD,* IV/1; L. Berkof, *Systematic Theology* (rev. ed. 1953), IV, viii; Calvin *Inst.* iii.2; T. Cranmer, *Homilies on Justification; DCG, s.v.; HDB, s.v.*; C. Hodge, *Systematic Theology* (1877), III, 41-113; Luther, *Catechisms; Galatians*; J. G. Machen, *What Is Faith?* (1925); *TDNT,* VI, *s.v.* πιστεύω κτλ. (Bultmann, Weiser); *TDOT,* I, *s.v.* "'āman" (Jepsen); B. B. Warfield, *Biblical and Theological Studies* (repr. 1962).

G. W. BROMILEY

FAITHFUL; FAITHFULNESS [Heb. *'āman, 'ᵉmûnâ, 'ēmûn, 'ᵉmeṯ*; Aram. *'ᵃman*]; AV also TRUTH, TRULY, STEADFAST (Ps. 78:8), ASSUREDLY (Jer. 32:41), "in their office of trust" (2 Ch. 31:15, 18); NEB LOYAL, TRUSTWORTHY, TRUE, TRUTH(FUL), SURE, CERTAIN, WELL-MEANT (Prov. 27:6), of steady character (Prov. 28:20), etc.; [Heb. *ḥāsîḏ, ḥeseḏ* (Jer. 31:3)]; AV HOLY ONES, SAINTS, LOVINGKINDNESS; NEB SAINTS, LOYAL SERVANTS, UNFAILING CARE; [*kēn*] (Jgs. 5:15); AV "so" (adverb), NEB "stood by"; [Gk. *pistós, pístis*]; NEB TRUSTY, TRUSTWORTHY, TRUST(ED), "keep faith," TRUE, "will not fail," FIDELITY, BELIEVER, FAITH; [*prosménō*] (Acts 11:23); AV CLEAVE; NEB "hold fast."

I. Vocabulary
II. Faithfulness of God
III. Faithfulness of God's People

I. Vocabulary.–The qal of the Heb. *'mn* stem, which is found only in the participle, refers to "carrying" a child (e.g., Nu. 11:12) or "caring for" a child (e.g., Isa. 49:23). Whether carrying or caring is the original sense is not clear, nor is that as important as the conjunction of the two — of the supporting activity and the intimate relationship. Indeed, both are probably developments from a more likely root meaning of "firmness, stability." Thus, in the niphal form the meaning is "show oneself firm," "be faithful." The hiphil form means "cause to be supported by, rely on, commit oneself to, believe." The substantives, Heb. *'ᵉmeṯ* and *'ᵉmûnâ,* represent the sense of the niphal, "faithfulness." It is noteworthy that the LXX renders these words mainly by Gk. *pistós* and *alḗtheia.*

II. Faithfulness of God.–The faithfulness of God can be defined as His "determined loyalty to a gracious covenant." This is disclosed first of all by the relation of "faithfulness" to "steadfast love" (Heb. *ḥeseḏ*, i.e., "love conforming to the covenant"; cf. Ps. 138). "Faithfulness" is frequently linked to "steadfast love" by means of a copula (e.g., Ps. 25:10; 40:10f. [MT 11f.]; 57:3 [MT 4]). Such a construction normally indicates that the terms thus joined are nearly synonymous or at least have some special bond. Likewise, "faithfulness" frequently parallels "steadfast love" in Hebrew poetry (e.g., Ps. 57:10 [MT 11]; 108:4 [MT 5]; 36:5 [MT 6]; *see* POETRY, HEBREW III). (The RSV once translates *ḥeseḏ* as "faithfulness" when referring to God, Jer. 31:3.)

There are other words to which "faithfulness" is sometimes joined or paralleled. It is joined to "thy saving help" (Heb. *tᵉšû'āṯᵉḵā,* Ps. 40:10 [MT 11]). It parallels "thy wonders" (Heb. *pil'ᵃḵā,* 89:5 [MT 6]). In Ps. 33:4 it parallels "upright," and in 111:8 it is joined to "uprightness" (Heb. *yāšār*). In 111:7 it is joined to "just" (Heb. *mišpāṭ*). In 119:138 and 143:1 it parallels "righteousness" (Heb. *ṣeḏeq*). These conjunctions and parallels, while occurring considerably less frequently than with *ḥeseḏ,* point also toward a determined loyalty to a gracious covenant.

This interpretation of faithfulness is beautifully confirmed in Hos. 2:19f. (MT 21f.), where God promises to betroth His unfaithful people forever in righteousness (*ṣeḏeq*), in justice (*mišpāṭ*), in steadfast love (*ḥeseḏ*), and in faithfulness (*'ᵉmûnâ*). That rich association of words itself points to God's determined loyalty to a gracious covenant, but the covenant reference is sealed when the Lord continues (2:23 [MT 25]): "and I will say to Not my people, 'You are my people'; and he shall say, 'Thou art my God'" (cf. Zec. 8:8). Dt. 7:9 affirms that God is faithful and explicates that affirmation in terms of God's keeping covenant (Heb. *bᵉrîṯ*) and His steadfast love (*ḥeseḏ*).

Faithfulness is seen as an attribute of God (Dt. 7:9; 32:4; Ex. 34:6; Ps. 31:5 [MT 6]; Isa. 49:6). And because God Himself is faithful, so are all His works faithful (and just, Ps. 111:7). His works are done in faithfulness (Ps. 33:4); His judgments have been appointed in faithfulness (119:138); His paths are faithfulness (25:10). The psalmist can even discern that afflictions are given in faithfulness (119:75). God gives men their recompense faithfully (Isa. 61:8); His plans are faithful (25:1).

The psalmists praise God for His covenant faithfulness (Ps. 33:4; 36:5 [MT 6]; 57:10 [MT 11]; 71:22; 92:2 [MT 3]; 98:3; 100:5; 108:4 [MT 5]; 117:2; 119:90; 138:2; cf. Gen. 24:27; Isa. 25:1) and witness to the congregation of His faithfulness (Ps. 40:10 [MT 11]; 91:4). Moreover, they base their appeals upon this faithfulness (Ps. 30:9 [MT 10]; 40:11 [MT 12]; 54:5 [MT 7]; 57:3 [MT 4]; 69:13 [MT 14]; 86:15; 88:11 [MT 12]; 115:1; 143:12; cf. Gen. 32:10, where Jacob appeals for safety from Esau on the basis of God's steadfast love and faithfulness even while he acknowledges that he is not worthy of it, and Lam. 3:23, where there is no overt appeal but whatever hopefulness remains is based upon God's faithfulness). Sometimes the appeal is not only based on God's faithfulness, but is specifically an appeal for God's faithfulness (Ps. 61:7 [MT 8]; cf. the bidding of David to Jabesh-gilead [2 S. 2:6] and to Ittai [15:20]: "May the Lord show steadfast love and faithfulness to you"). This sentiment is beautifully expressed in Ps. 85. The psalmist praises God for His gracious favor in the past, then appeals to God to manifest His favor in the present distress, and finally, with the assurance of hope, recites his vision of a time when steadfast love and faithfulness will meet, when righteousness and peace will kiss, when faithfulness will spring up from the ground and righteousness will look down from the sky.

Psalm 89 gives typical expression to these themes. It begins with praise for God's steadfast love and faithfulness, allowing faithfulness its connotations of both carrying and caring, both strength and love. The psalmist recalls God's covenant with David and the faithfulness and steadfast love with which God surrounded that covenant (vv. 24, 33 [MT 25, 34]); and on this basis (v. 49 [MT 50]) he appeals to God to grant His people victory. Similarly, Hezekiah's song includes both an appeal for health on the basis of God's faithfulness (Isa. 38:18) and praise and witness to His faithfulness: "the father makes known to the children thy faithfulness" (v. 19).

It is of God's covenant loyalty that the prophets assure His people, and it is on this assumption that they promise a restored Israel (Isa. 49:7; Hos. 2:20; Jer. 32:41). The conclusion of Micah (7:20) is typical: "Thou wilt show faithfulness to Jacob and steadfast love to Abraham, as thou has sworn to our fathers from the days of old."

The NT reaffirms this faithfulness of God, now powerfully and finally confirmed in Jesus Christ. "God is faithful [Gk. *pistós*]," Paul says, "by whom you were called into the fellowship of his Son, Jesus Christ our Lord" (1 Cor. 1:9). God's *pístis* surely continues to mean His determined loyalty to His gracious covenant. God has fully shown His caring and His carrying, His love and His strength, in the cross and resurrection of Jesus Christ (cf. 2 Cor. 1:18).

Because of that loyalty, Paul is confident that God will sustain the community even in temptation (1 Cor. 10:13; cf. 1 Thess. 5:24; 2 Thess. 3:3; He. 10:23; 11:11). Interestingly, in 1 Pet. 4:19 it is specifically the Creator who is called faithful (although this passage does not lose sight of the final revelation of God's covenant faithfulness in Jesus Christ). The one God who made heaven and earth can be entrusted with our souls because He has the strength and the love to carry and to care. Because God is faithful and just (Gk. *díkaios*; cf. Heb. *ṣeḏeq*), because He is loyal to His gracious covenant, He forgives our sins if we confess them (1 Jn. 1:9).

It should be observed that many times in the NT "truth" (Gk. *alḗtheia*) is to be understood against the background of "faithfulness." The LXX frequently translates *'ĕmeṯ* as *alḗtheia*. Consider, e.g., Jn. 1:17: grace and truth (Gk. *hē cháris kaí hē alḗtheia*; cf. Heb. *ḥeseḏ we'ĕmeṯ*) came through Jesus Christ.

III. Faithfulness of God's People.–God's loyalty to His covenant demands a response of loyalty from His people. God is faithful, says Moses in Dt. 7:9 (after reminding the people of the heart of the law, chs. 5–6), and therefore His people are required to respond with obedience to His commands.

When the Israelites were finally settled in Canaan, God renewed His covenant with them; Joshua's injunction was again that they serve the Lord in sincerity and faithfulness (Josh. 24:14). Similarly, Samuel recounted God's faithfulness and then demanded of the people that they serve Him faithfully with all their heart (1 S. 12:24).

It is striking that whereas "faithfulness" is most often linked with "steadfast love" when God is the subject, it is linked with other terms when the human response to God is described: with "righteousness" (Heb. *ṣeḏeq*, 1 S. 26:23; 1 K. 3:6). "uprightness" (Heb. *yāšār*, Ps. 111:8; 1 K. 3:6), "sincerity" (Heb. *tāmîm*, Josh. 24:14), and "with all your heart" (Heb. *kol-leḇaḇ*, 1 S. 12:24; Isa. 38:3; 1 K. 2:4; 2 K. 20:3; 2 Ch. 19:9). Human loyalty to God is plainly not a gracious act but rather a dutiful response.

It must, however, be mentioned here that *ḥāsîḏ*, a derivative of *ḥeseḏ*, is used of God only twice (Jer. 3:12; Ps. 145:17; possibly Job 39:13); for the rest it is used of man's loyalty with its disposition toward pious, humble service (e.g., Ps. 50:5; 1 S. 2:9; in Ps. 89:19 [MT 20] of David). *See* HASIDEANS; SAINTS.

The "way of faithfulness" (Heb. *dereḵ-'ĕmûnâ*) is the law of God (Ps. 119:30). The commands of God are to be performed in faithfulness and uprightness (Ps. 111:8), and disputed cases are to be judged in faithfulness (2 Ch. 19:9). God makes His claim upon both the dispositions and the actions of mankind; He claims a total response of faithfulness.

Such faithfulness brings reward (1 S. 26:23); the faithful are preserved (Ps. 31:23 [MT 24]). In Ezra's great confession he recites God's call to Abraham, Abraham's response of faithfulness, the promise of land, and its fulfillment (Neh. 9:8). Thus faithfulness brings the fulfillment of God's promises. David asks for vindication on the grounds that he has walked in faithfulness to God (Ps. 26:3), and Hezekiah protests God's decision with the claim that he has walked before Him "in faithfulness and with a whole heart, and . . . done what is good in thy sight" (Isa. 38:3; cf. 2 K. 20:3; 2 Ch. 31:20). It is clear, then, that faithfulness provides a basis of appeal before God.

The relation of faithfulness to both the law and the fulfillment of God's promises is assumed by David when he exhorts Solomon to follow the Mosaic law lest national ruin follow, and to be faithful to God so that his reign will be blessed (1 K. 2:4). It is in the context of this admonition that Solomon, seeing its truth in God's blessing upon his father David, asks for wisdom (1 K. 3:6).

But human beings are not faithful. God's faithfulness frequently stands in contrast to the unfaithfulness of men. "[He has] dealt faithfully and we have acted wickedly" (Neh. 9:33; cf. Ps. 78:8; cf. also 2 Tim. 2:13 and Rom. 3:3f. in the NT). Of this the psalmists lament and the prophets complain. Dt. 32:20 sees idolatry as lack of faithfulness, while Hosea cites "swearing, lying, killing, stealing, and committing adultery; they break all bounds" as evidence of a lack of faithfulness to God (Hos. 4:1f.; cf. Ps. 12:1 [MT 2]). Faithfulness to God's covenant entails, of course, the prohibition of idolatry; but beyond that what is required is not cultic purity so much as justice to, and care for, the neighbor. (Cf. the prophetic vision of a faithful city in Isa. 1:21, 26; Zec. 8:3.) *See also* FAITHLESS.

We have seen that faithfulness is not joined with steadfast love (*ḥeseḏ*) when man's faithfulness to God is in view (see II above). But when man's faithfulness to man is considered, once again faithfulness, as a human virtue, is typically joined with steadfast love. The spies tell

Rahab they will deal with her "kindly" (*ḥeseḏ*) and "faithfully" (*'ĕmeṯ*, Josh. 2:14). The wise man exhorts his son, "Let not loyalty and faithfulness forsake you; bind them about your neck, write them on the tablet of your heart" (Prov. 3:3). Human beings ought to form their characters toward steadfast love and faithfulness. These human virtues do good (Prov. 14:22) and cover evil (16:6); their effects in conduct are what God delights in (12:22).

These are especially virtues in a king (Prov. 20:28); one can rely on such a king. The promised king of Isa. 16:5 will rule in faithfulness, seeking justice and being swift to do righteousness. Faithfulness and righteousness are the panoply of the Messiah in 11:5. The promised servant will faithfully bring forth justice (42:3).

But faithfulness is a virtue for other roles as well: for the servant (1 S. 22:14; 2 S. 20:19), the messenger (Prov. 13:17; 25:13), the witness (Prov. 14:5; Jer. 42:5), the priest (1 S. 2:35; 2 Ch. 31:18), contributors (2 Ch. 31:12), administrators (31:15; Dnl. 6:4), workmen (2 Ch. 34:12), preachers (Jer. 23:28). Being counted faithful is reason for appointment to roles in Neh. 7:2 (charge over Jerusalem) and 13:13 (treasurer of the storehouse). Faithfulness here is role-relative; the priests, e.g., are faithful "in keeping themselves holy" (2 Ch. 31:18). Social expectations are attached to these roles, creating a kind of covenant, and thereby creating role obligations that must be met out of loyalty to the covenant.

The NT also refers to faithfulness as a human virtue. In Gal. 5:22, e.g., it is listed in a catalog of virtues. Here, too, it is a virtue relative to roles, a firm loyalty to the bond created by role expectations. In 1 Tim. 3:11 women are exhorted to be "faithful in all things," i.e., to fulfil the role obligations of women. It is used thus in Matthew's and Luke's references to faithful servants and faithful stewards (Mt. 24:45; 25:21, 23; Lk. 12:42; 16:10-12; 19:17). "Faithful" here is very much role-relative; but the point of the parables is not that the Christian should allow role expectations to determine totally his or her behavior, but that one be faithful to God and give that loyalty precedence over all others.

Faithfulness is applied to the roles of witness and minister (Tychichus, Eph. 6:21 and Col. 4:7; Epaphras, Col. 1:7), child (fig. of Timothy, 1 Cor. 4:17), brother (fig. of Onesimus, Col. 4:9, and of Silvanus, 1 Pet. 5:12), and even perhaps the role of martyr (Antipas, Rev. 2:13, where the role expectation is not to deny the faith). Paul gives as the reason for his appointment to his role, Christ's judgment that he was faithful (1 Tim. 1:12). Timothy is told to find faithful men and to appoint them to the role of teachers in the Church (2 Tim. 2:2). But in all these cases such faithfulness in a role meshes with faithfulness to the Lord, as can be seen by the frequent addition of a phrase such as "in Jesus Christ."

When the NT takes up the OT appeal for human faithfulness to God, Gk. *pistós* is generally translated "faith." (*See* FAITH I.) There are, nevertheless, a few occasions where "faithful" is used. The Christian community is frequently described as faithful (Eph. 1:1; Col. 1:2; cf. Rev. 17:14; Acts 16:15, with reference to Lydia). Acts 11:23 exhorts Christians to remain faithful (Gk. *prosménō*) to the Lord with a steadfast heart, while Rev. 2:10 promises a reward for faithfulness.

Finally, it must be noted that the NT describes Jesus as faithful. He is called a merciful and faithful (cf. Heb. *ḥeseḏ wᵉ'ĕmeṯ*) high priest. He fulfils that role finally and ultimately "in the service of God, to make expiation for the sins of the people" (He. 2:17). Similarly, He is faithful in Moses' role (3:2, 5f.); He surpasses and fulfils the faithfulness of Moses in building and ruling the house of God. He is the faithful witness (Rev. 1:5; 3:14, where Jesus is the "Amen" [Gk. *amḗn*; cf. Heb. root *'mn*], the faithful and true witness [Gk. *ho mártys ho pistós kaí alēthinós*]). In 19:11 the rider of the white horse is called faithful and true. This Jesus, then, is the consummation of God's determined loyalty to His gracious covenant. In Him God's grace and truth, His *ḥeseḏ* and *'ĕmeṯ*, fully are and are fully revealed.

See also COVENANT (OT) IV.

Bibliography.–C. H. Dodd, *The Bible and the Greeks* (1935), ch. 3; *TDNT*, I, *s.v.* ἀλήθεια κτλ. (Quell, Kittel, Bultmann); VI, *s.v.* πιστεύω κτλ. (Bultmann, Weiser).

A. D. VERHEY

FAITHFUL SAYINGS [Gk. *pistós ho lógos*]. The striking formula, "the saying is sure" (AV "this is a faithful saying"; NEB "here are words you may trust"), is found five times in the Pastoral Letters (1 Tim. 1:15; 3:1; 4:9; 2 Tim. 2:11; Tit. 3:8). Twice there is added, "and worthy of full acceptance" (1 Tim. 1:15; 4:9; NEB "words that merit full acceptance"). This formula either introduces or concludes a quotation borrowed from earlier preaching, liturgical forms, or church regulations. It also affirms that these sayings are efficacious and therefore constitute a reliable foundation for the life of Christians and the Church. The precise extent of the sayings cannot always be decided with certainty.

Two sayings highlight the work of Christ. 1 Tim. 1:15 affirms that "Christ Jesus came into the world to save sinners." This objective doctrinal statement is in essence a summary of the gospel and is in form similar to sayings in the Gospels. Tit. 3:4-7 seems to be a quotation from an existing confession in the early Church. Because of its stress on washing, the Holy Spirit, inner change, and the trinity, it is possible that this saying was originally a corporate baptismal confession.

Two sayings concern godly living. 1 Tim. 4:8 contains the familiar comparison between exercise for physical fitness and exercise for godliness. The former has only limited value, but the latter is valuable in every way because it contains the promise of true life now and in the age to come. Although some have interpreted bodily exercise in terms of asceticism, this saying is almost certainly a Christian antidote to the overemphasis on the gymnasium in the Hellenistic world.

The poetic structure of the saying in 2 Tim. 2:11-13 would seem to indicate that it is a fragment of an early Christian hymn. Because of the context (vv. 8-10), some view this hymn as a martyr song. Since, however, the first line almost exactly parallels Rom. 6:8, it is more likely that the reference is to a spiritual dying with, rather than a literal dying for, Christ. To those who have died with Christ and continue to endure, the hymn promises that they will live and reign with Him. Although denial merits Christ's denial, the hymn concludes with the assurance that Christ is faithful even when His people are not. Both the parallel with Rom. 6:8 and the content of the hymn suggest that originally this hymn may have been used in a baptismal setting.

The single saying concerning church order in 1 Tim. 3:1 is the source of much scholarly controversy. Some believe that the saying precedes the formula and is actually found in 2:15, "woman will be saved through bearing children." Several early scribes understood that the saying was contained in 3:1, but because of its content they felt it necessary to alter *pistós* ("sure") to *anthropínōs* ("human"; NEB "there is a popular saying"). The majority consider the faithful saying to be: "If anyone aspires to the office of bishop, he desires a noble task." For its life and well-being, the Church needs overseers or bishops.

This saying served not only to emphasize that need, but also to call qualified persons to that task.

A similar formula is found in Rev. 21:5; 22:6, "these words are trustworthy and true" (Gk. *hoi lógoi pistoí kaí alēthinoí*). This is not so much a formula designating a quotation as it is a formula of affirmation that underscores the complete reliability of the words of the ascended Lord.

***Bibliography*.**–Comms. on the Pastoral Epistles by M. Dibelius and H. Conzelmann (Eng. tr., *Hermeneia*, 1972); J. N. D. Kelly (*HNTC*, 1963); E. F. Scott (1936); G. W. Knight, *Faithful Sayings in the Pastoral Epistles* (1968). D. E. HOLWERDA

FAITHLESS; FAITHLESSLY; FAITHLESSNESS [Heb. *māʿal, maʿal, bāgaḏ, bōg^{e}ḏōṯ* (Zeph. 3:4), *m^{e}šûḇâ* (Jer. 3; Hos. 14:4 [MT 14:5]), *šôḇāḇ* (Jer. 3:14, 22), *šôḇēḇâ* (Jer. 31:22; 49:4), *z^{e}nûṯ* (Nu. 14:33); Gk. *apistéō* (2 Tim. 2:13), *ápistos, apistía* (Rom. 3:3), *asýnthetos* (Rom. 1:31)]; AV also TRANSGRESS, BACKSLIDE (esp. in Jeremiah), DEAL TREACHEROUSLY, TRESPASS, WHOREDOMS (Nu. 14:33), COVENANTBREAKERS (Rom. 1:31), UNBELIEF (Rom. 3:3), etc.; NEB also TRAITOR, TREACHERY, SCOUNDREL, APOSTATE, WAYWARD, UNBELIEVING, TREAT UNFAIRLY (Ex. 21:8), BREAK FAITH (Ezk. 14:13; 15:8), WANTON DISLOYALTY (Nu. 14:33), etc.; **UNFAITHFUL; UNFAITHFULLY; UNFAITHFULNESS** [Heb. *māʿal* and cognates, hiphil of *zānâ* (2 Ch. 21:11, 13); Gk. *apistéō, (moichoí kaí) moichalídes* ("unfaithful creatures," Jas. 4:4)]; AV also TRANSGRESSION, UNBELIEVERS (Lk. 12:46), NOT BELIEVE (Rom. 3:3), COMMIT FORNICATION (2 Ch. 21:13), WHOREDOMS (2 Ch. 21:13), etc.; NEB also DISLOYALTY (2 Ch. 12:2), SINS (1 Ch. 9:1), SEDUCE (2 Ch. 21:11, 13), etc.

While the English "faithless" is a privative form of "faith" (like Gk. *pist–*, which becomes *apist–*), the Hebrew terms rendered by "faithless" belong to a different set of words from those translated by "faith." The latter normally connote trust, confidence, and hope; the former describe a relationship—a *broken* relationship—between persons, between peoples, or between Yahweh and His people Israel. "Faithless" characterizes a lack of loyalty on the part of either or both parties in a relationship governed by covenant stipulations. It signifies a failure to adhere to the obligations of such a loyalty — a transgression of the covenant stipulations. Thus it is not so much an attitude as the actions expressive of that attitude.

Within the sphere of secular law, a marriage partner who committed adultery was "faithless" or "unfaithful" and therefore liable for divorce (Nu. 5:12, 27; cf. Ex. 21:8). The imagery and language of the broken marriage was used by the prophets in their announcements of judgment on Israel (and/or Judah). Israel had committed adultery in seeking other gods, in worshiping them, and in building altars to them. Thus Israel was liable for divorce from Yahweh, i.e., for the appropriate punishment (divorce, Jer. 3:8; servitude, 5:11ff.; desolation of the land, Ezk. 14:13; 15:8; Hos. 5:7). Particularly interesting is the language of Jer. 3:22, where the author plays with the root *šûḇ*, "turn," "return" (which was common treaty or covenant language; see Holladay, pp. 128-139, 152-54): "Return, turnable [faithless] children, and I shall heal your turnings [faithlessness]" (Holladay, p. 129). This verse illustrates that the prophets announced not only punishment for unfaithful Israel but also Yahweh's overriding desire to heal the relationship (cf. vv. 12, 14; Hos. 14:4; also Neh. 1:8).

Disloyalty was not restricted to legally established relationships. It could also define the rupture of "natural relations" (e.g., between a child and his or her parents, Jer. 31:22; 49:4), which also had their obligations. Thus kings (cf. 1 Ch. 10:13), prophets (Zeph. 3:4), and even the city of Jerusalem (2 Ch. 12:2) could be charged with "faithlessness." Extended to the international political realm, such a concept meant that certain demands of justice and world order were made of every state and nation. Thus even a foreign nation, a nation not party to the Yahweh-Israel covenant, could be called "faithless" (Hab. 1:13).

The OT proverbs also were concerned with faithlessness: (1) its consequences (Prov. 13:15; 21:18; 22:12); (2) one of its causes: the harlot (23:28); and (3) the attitude to be held toward the unfaithful person (25:19).

In the NT "faithless" sometimes designates disloyalty, but its range of meaning includes unbelief, distrust, and lack of confidence and hope. Jn. 20:27 contrasts "faithless" with believing in the resurrected Christ (cf. also Mk. 9:19 par.). In Lk. 12:46 the term probably refers to the "unbelievers," i.e., the "non-Christians" (*TDNT*, VI, 204f.). Rom. 3:3, which contrasts the faithlessness of the Jews with the faithfulness of God, carries the sense of covenant disloyalty (cf. 2 Tim. 2:13, where the contrasted faithfulness of God is that of His loyalty to the covenant; see M. Dibelius and H. Conzelmann, *Pastoral Epistles* [Eng. tr. 1972], p. 109). In Rom. 1:31 Gk. *asýnthetous* (lit. "breaking a covenant or agreement") occurs in a catalog of violations of relationships — with other persons generally, with parents, with God, or with oneself (cf. Rev. 21:8, Gk. *apístois*).

See also FAITHFUL, FAITHFULNESS.

***Bibliography*.**–W. L. Holladay, *Root šûbh in the OT* (1958); *TDOT*, I, *s.v.* "bāghadh" (Erlandsson); IV, *s.v.* "zānāh" (Erlandsson); *TDNT*, VI, *s.v.* πιστεύω κτλ.: ἄπιστος, ἀπιστία (Bultmann); *THAT*, I, *s.v.* בגד (M. A. Klopfenstein); זנה (J. Kühlewein); מעל (R. Knierim). F. C. TIFFANY

FALCON fô'kən, fôl'kən, fal'kun [Heb. *ʾayyâ* (Lev. 11:14; Job 28:7); LXX *iktínos, gýps*]; AV VULTURE, KITE. One of the members of the genus *Falco*, several species of which still survive in Palestine. The reference in Job alludes to the keen vision of these birds, which supports the identification with the *Falconidae*.

Sculpture from Tanis of the falcon-god Horus guarding Ramses II (Service des musées, Cairo)

FALL, THE. Although the term "fall" appears neither in Gen. 3 nor elsewhere in Scripture to designate the event recorded in Gen. 3, the term is apt, for it suggests mankind's loss of an earlier higher estate. Through the fall, humanity lost much of what it had been as created by God.

I. Philosophical Views
II. Biblical View
  A. Historicity
  B. Mystery
  C. Character

I. Philosophical Views.–Various views of the fall as an upward advance or a forward movement find no support either in Gen. 3 or elsewhere in the Bible. The Genesis account does not warrant the philosophical views of Kant (*Religion Within the Limits of Reason Alone* [Eng. tr. 1934], I), Hegel (*Lectures on the Philosophy of Religion* [Eng. tr. 1895], III, 46-56), and others that the fall was a sudden irruption of human self-consciousness. The divine command to till the ground, keep the garden, and have dominion over the earth all presuppose man's self-consciousness. An attempt to interpret the fall in terms of human sexuality, as has often been done (e.g., N. Berdyaev, *Destiny of Man* [Eng. tr. 1955], I, ch. 3, §3), also fails to comport with the biblical account. Sexual differentiation in the Genesis account is good, not evil; it reflects the image of God in which Adam and Eve were created, and the command to be fruitful and multiply and replenish the earth is issued by God before the fall. Nor does the account warrant the interpretation of those rationalistic theologians who regard the fall as the first post-creation forward step toward the realization of God's eternal purpose to have a populated heaven and hell. In biblical thought the fall is associated with sin, death, and a world whose history is spattered with blood and human agony; it is not, even for the heaven-bound Christian, something for which to be glad and thank God. It is a downward or retrogressive movement, not an upward or forward step.

Impression of the so-called Adam and Eve seal (*ca.* 3500 B.C.) from Tepe Gawra near Nineveh. It shows a man followed by a woman and a serpent in the upper field (University Museum, University of Pennsylvania)

II. Biblical View.–It is remarkable how infrequently the OT refers to the narrative of the fall. The Prophets, Psalms, and Proverbs never quote from it. At the most, Hos. 6:7 and Eccl. 7:29 may be allusions to it. Even Jesus and the NT apostles seldom allude to Gen. 3 (Jn. 8:44; Rom. 5:12; 2 Cor. 11:3; 1 Tim. 2:14). But it may be observed that the prophetic literature, Psalms, and Proverbs rarely mention past events and that even the apostles rarely quote the words of Jesus, and only seldom — and then only indirectly — refer to Jesus' virgin birth. But just as the NT pervasively assumes that the Incarnation was not a human achievement, so the whole of Scripture pervasively assumes that man has lost his original integrity, enters an abnormal world as a sinner, and from the moment of his entry is subject to death. The biblical significance of an event does not derive from the number of times it is explicitly mentioned.

A. Historicity. There is no general agreement, even among conservative scholars, about the literary form of the fall narrative or about the literal historicity of some of its details. Is the Genesis account to be regarded as symbolic, or is it prophetic (sermonic) historical writing, the specific form of which is determined by its religious purpose? Is it the type of historical writing found in Kings and Chronicles, or is it more like the prophetic historical writing of Revelation? The latter seems preferable and more faithful to the prophetic-religious intent of Scripture, for the intent and purpose of biblical historical writings is never simply to present an accurate historical account but to present a *redemptive* history.

Many conservative biblical theologians regard the Gen. 3 account of the fall — and even the Gen. 1 and 2 narratives of creation — as having received literary shape not from Israel's own inner religious perceptions, but from the divine disclosure of Israel's special status as a people created and chosen by God and placed in a covenantal relationship with Him. Israel understood the creation of the world through the perspective of her own creation as a nation by God, and similarly understood the nature of the fall through those very deeds by which Yahweh redeemed and recreated Israel as His own peculiar people. Thus Israel's inspired prophets and writers knew the reality and nature of the fall through the reality and nature of her redemption from it by Yahweh. Such a perspective comports with the fact that Israel understood and received the Law only after and within the context of the Covenant of Grace, and also with the fact that the reality and nature of sin are truly known only by those who know the grace of forgiveness. In biblical thought the fall is, no doubt, a historical event, something that occurred as surely as the historical reality of ancient Israel. Likewise, Israel's need for restoration within the historical world of space and time is as certain as mankind's historical fall.

Karl Barth regarded the fall not as myth, an event that never happened, but as a saga, an event that really occurred though it cannot be the subject of normal historical writing (*CD,* IV/1, p. 508). But because Barth regarded man as being eternally in Christ, he conceived of the fall also as an event in Christ, and of fallen man as eternally reconciled in Christ. Hence he regarded the fall, as well as the Resurrection, as an event of *Geschichte* and thus as an occurrence of *prae-historia,* a suprahistorical event rather than an event that can be recorded in terms of our space-time history.

Many other theologians, under the influence of existentialism, have defined the fall as everyman's act (cf. R. Niebuhr, *Nature and Destiny of Man* [repr. 1964], I, 260-64). Each of us falls and falls only for himself. As in Barth, this makes the fall a suprahistorical occurrence — something taking place outside of, and prior to, the experience of any of us. None of us has any experience of falling into sin and death, for none of us has any experience of having once lived in a sin-free, death-free world. Support for the view that each person effects his own fall is claimed in the consideration that Heb. *'āḏām* simply means man, not a particular man. Many biblical considerations, however, rule out such an interpretation: (1) it places the fall again outside our time-space history; (2) it undercuts the psalmist's claim of being born in sin and conceived in iniquity (Ps. 51:5 [MT 7]); (3) it rests on an unbiblical individualism which violates the biblical teaching of the parallelism between the first Adam and Christ; and (4) it cannot be squared with the Pauline teaching that all men living between Adam and Moses died even though they had not sinned in the same way as Adam, whose transgression brought death into the world (Rom. 5:14).

Moreover, in biblical thought sin is regarded not merely as a human act but as a destroying power that enters the *world* and does not wait on the fall of each individual. It was through one man's transgression that sin entered the world and with it death, just as it was through one man's obedience that man is made righteous (Rom. 5:17-21). This parallelism drawn by Paul between Adam and Christ breaks down completely where the fall is construed as an event that each person effects for himself alone. Such an exhaustive individualism leaves no room for God's judgment of all men through Adam's transgression and His redemption of all through Christ's obedience (Rom. 5). Sin and the death that comes with it are powers that stem from an original and unique fall and pervade the whole world from the moment of that fall.

B. Mystery. Much about the fall remains shrouded in mystery. How human beings created in God's image could succumb to sin is left unexplained. How a person created by God — not with a neutral, unqualified, but with a positive, authentic freedom, which subsists in obedience to God — could sin, not by coercion but freely, is something on which the Bible throws no light. How sin, though no part of God's creation, could enter the world from elsewhere through the successful temptation of a man created in possession of righteousness, holiness, and a true knowledge of God, is something human rationality cannot comprehend. Sin is a mystery; in biblical parlance it is the "mystery of lawlessness" (2 Thess. 2:7), something at which even Jesus "marveled" (Mk. 6:6). (*See also* EVIL III. C-D.)

Thus, sin lies beyond the reach of rational explanation. If a good and valid moral reason could be found for sin, it would not be immoral. If a good and valid rational explanation could be found for sin, it would not be irrational. Even God does not rationalize sin, but overcomes it, obliterates it, blots it out so that even He "will remember their sin no more" (Jer. 31:34). He knows that man cannot himself undo sin; therefore He "remembers that we are dust" (Ps. 103:14). The Bible summons us to respond to sin in a manner that comports with God's redemptive triumph over sin: to confess our sins, express our sorrow for them, and then through Christ be set free from them — free from even a guilty remembrance of them. Within this perspective, no one can make the fall lucid to either his moral or his rational consciousness any more than he can offer an exonerating explanation of any of his sins (cf. Augustine *Conf.* vii.5.7). It is only within these limitations that one can interpret the fact and nature of the fall recorded in Gen. 3.

C. Character. While we cannot, and the Bible does not, explain how the fall could occur, the Bible does in various ways describe the nature of the sin that constitutes the fall. Sin is described as a "transgression of the law," as that "offense" with which man reacts to the goodness and mercy of God (cf. Jonah 4), and to the right and freedom of God to dispose of His grace as He wills (Mt. 20:15), an offense which ultimately has Jesus as its target and prompted Him to say, "Blessed is he who takes no offense at me" (Lk. 7:23). Calvin defined sin as the absence of gratitude toward God for all His goodness (*Inst.* ii.1.4); Augustine saw pride as the essence of sin (*De natura et gratia* 33). Others have described sin as autonomy, man's claim to the right to rule himself.

However sin may be defined, it is clear that man was *tempted* to sin; i.e., the inducement that led to the fall was not made by a direct reference to the nature of sin. The inducement was via untruth about sin; sin was represented as a good and right thing.

According to Gen. 2:16, before creating Eve, God commanded the man, "You may freely eat of every tree of the garden; but of the tree of the knowledge of good and evil you shall not eat, for in the day that you eat of it you shall die." In Gen. 3 the serpent, identified later in Scripture as Satan, worked his strategy not upon the man but upon the woman. Since Scripture does not tell us why he chose this strategy, we ought to maintain a similar silence. Eve was asked an untruthful question: "Did God say, 'You shall not eat of any tree of the garden?'" (3:1). Eve's response was a mixture of truth and untruth: "We may eat of the fruit of the trees of the garden; but God said, 'You shall not eat of the fruit of the tree which is in the midst of the garden [true], neither shall you touch it [untrue], lest you die'" (vv. 2f.). From this less-than-truthful answer to his less-than-truthful question, the serpent moved strategically to the heart of the temptation: "For God knows that when you eat of it your eyes will be opened, and you will be like God, knowing good and evil" (v. 5). These words suggested — and were meant to suggest — to the woman that God's prohibitive command was a strategic protective device by which He sought unjustly to keep for Himself alone what belonged to man — the right to determine what is good and what evil.

The serpent told the woman that if she ate, her eyes would be opened (3:5); she looked at the tree and saw that it was "good for food," "a delight to the eyes" (v. 6). At this point the woman's eye reflected the evil inclination of her desire to be wise (v. 6). Then came the deed: she ate. She gave to her husband, and he ate. "Then the eyes of both were opened," and what they saw was their naked selves (v. 7). Once they had fallen they knew that while they had previously known the good, they now knew both good and evil, and what they now saw as evil was themselves. Hence they were ashamed, becoming aware of their nakedness. They wanted their nakedness to be seen neither by God, by each other, nor even by themselves. Thus they hid from each other by making for themselves garments of fig leaves, and from God by hiding in bushes (vv. 7f.). They attempted to hide from themselves in that neither admitted personal guilt: Adam blamed Eve — and even God for giving her to him — and Eve blamed the serpent. All these attempts to maintain innocence by transferring their guilt to someone else were attempts of the fallen, sinful creature to hide from itself what it had become.

The attempt of the creature to be like God his creator is not only unsuccessful, but an irrational act for which there is no explanation, an act in which the creature destructively acts against his own self. The Gen. 3 account of the fall is prophetic, sermonic. It presents the fall not in purely objective, historic factuality, but in terms of a summons to all men to admit their sin, guilt, and shame so that they may be saved. This it does admirably well. For as Herman Bavinck wrote, "There is a great deal of truth in the often-expressed thought, that we can give no account of the origin of sin, because it is not logical, and does not result as a conclusion drawn from two premises. But facts are brutal. What seems logically impossible often exists in reality. The laws of moral life are different from those of thought and from those of mechanical nature. The narrative of Gen. 3, in any case, is psychologically faithful in the highest degree. For the same way that it [sin] appears there in the first man, it repeatedly takes place among ourselves" (*ISBE* [1929], II, 1094).

The historical account of Gen. 3 was not written to satisfy the historical interest of historians, nor the scientific interest of scientists; it was written rather to show us the origin and nature of our sin, for the advancement of true religion. J. DAANE

FALLING STARS. *See* ASTRONOMY.

FALLOW. The term designates ground that has been plowed and then left uncultivated for a season. Jer. 4:3 and Hos. 10:12 read Heb. *nîrû . . . nîr,* literally, "freshly till the once-tilled [but fallow] ground." In Ex. 23:11 God commanded Israel to let the land "lie fallow" (Heb. *nṭš,* "leave") every seventh year, to permit the poor to eat from it. From Lev. 26:34f. it is clear that the Israelites did not adhere to this divine injunction. (*See* AGRARIAN LAWS III-V.)

The meaning of Prov. 13:23a, literally, "Much increased [will be] the fallow ground [*nîr*] of the poor," is uncertain. It has been interpreted that the fallow ground of the poor may produce a good crop if it be spared "injustice" (RSV, NEB) or "want of judgment" (AV). The LXX emends "the poor" to "the righteous" and reads the verse as a contrast between the happy life of the righteous and the unhappy life of the unrighteous (cf. *IB,* IV, 860). According to another emendation, the land of "chiefs" will not yield much because of lack of equity (W. McKane, *Proverbs* [*OTL,* 1970], pp. 462f.). R. W. V.

FALLOW DEER (Dt. 14:5; 1 K. 4:23, AV). The translation of Heb. *yaḥmûr,* which the RSV renders "roebuck" (cf. *CHAL,* p. 133). It belongs to the class of animals that Israel was allowed to eat and seems to indicate a member of the DEER family. *See* ROEBUCK.

FALSE APOSTLES [Gk. *pseudapóstoloi*] (2 Cor. 11:13); NEB SHAM-APOSTLES. Adversaries of Paul in Corinth, whom he opposes in 2 Cor. 10:1–13:10. Though little is said about their message, a few clues are given about their character. They were intruders who had invaded the territory marked out for Paul by divine commission (10:13-16) and were now attempting to undermine his apostolic authority (cf. the "false brethren" of 11:26). Their weapons included slander — charges of cowardice (2 Cor. 10:10; cf. 11:21) and guile (12:16f.) — and letters of recommendation (3:1). They were arrogant; they claimed for themselves the credit for having first brought the gospel to Corinth (10:13-18); in fact, they had gone so far in their boastful claims to apostolic authority that Paul twice refers to them sarcastically as "superlative apostles" (11:5; 12:11; cf. 11:12). They were also characterized by greed, being eager to accept financial support (11:7-12, 20) and showing no interest in collecting gifts for the needy Christians in Jerusalem.

Of their message, Paul simply says that they preach "another Jesus . . . a different gospel" (11:4). They are "false apostles, deceitful workmen, disguising themselves as apostles of Christ"; they are servants of Satan rather than "servants of righteousness" (11:13-15). Scholars do not agree on the content of the "gospel" they preached. Some suppose from the fact that they were Jews (11:22) that they were Judaizers (cf. 3:6-18; cf. also the "false brethren" of Gal. 2:4). Others have posited a Gnostic party that claimed special esoteric knowledge in opposition to the knowledge of God that is available to every person (cf. 2 Cor. 2:14; 4:6; 10:5; 11:6). These are conjectures; it is clear, however, that these opponents had succeeded in stirring up a rebellion against Paul in Corinth, and that their influence had resulted in selfishness and immorality (12:20f.).

See P. E. Hughes, comm. on 2 Corinthians (*NICNT,* 1962). N. J. O.

FALSE BRETHREN [Gk. *pseudadélphoi*] (2 Cor. 11:26; Gal. 2:4); NEB FALSE FRIENDS; SHAM-CHRISTIANS. Apparently the same persons whom Paul calls FALSE APOSTLES in 2 Cor. 11:13.

FALSE CHRISTS. *See* CHRISTS, FALSE.

FALSE PROPHETS. *See* PROPHECY, FALSE.

FALSE WITNESS. *See* CRIME; OATH.

FALSEHOOD. *See* CRIME; LIE.

FAME [Heb. *šēm*] (Dt. 26:19; 1 K. 4:31; 1 Ch. 14:17; 22:5; 2 Ch. 26:8, 15; Ps. 72:17); AV also NAME; NEB also RENOWNED, NAME; [*šēma'*] (Nu. 14:15; 1 K. 10:1; 2 Ch. 9:1); NEB also TALES, "heard of me" (Isa. 66:19); [*šōma'*] (Josh. 6:27; Est. 9:4); [*zēḵer*] (Ps. 145:7); AV MEMORY; NEB STORY; [Gk. *akoḗ*] (Mt. 4:24; 14:1; Mk. 1:28); NEB also REPORTS; [*diaphēmízō*] (Mt. 9:31); NEB "talked about him." "Fame" has a two-fold meaning: (1) report or rumor (now obsolete); (2) renown or reputation. In the OT it is not always easy to distinguish the two senses. *Šēm* means lit. "name" and thus would have the second meaning of renown or reputation. *Šēma'* (cf. *šāma',* "hear") probably means "report" in Nu. 14:15 but "renown" in the rest of its occurrences, while *šōma'* seems to indicate reputation. *Zēḵer,* in Ps. 145:7, seems to comprehend both meanings.

In the NT *akoḗ,* "hearing," means "report," while the verb *diaphēmízō,* "say throughout," "report publicly," seems to imply fame in the sense of reputation. In 1 Macc. 3:26 "fame" occurs in the sense of reputation: "His fame [Gk. *ónoma,* "name"] reached the king" (cf. "what was said," 3:41). W. L. WALKER

FAMILIAR. Of the OT occurrences in the RSV (1 K. 9:27; 2 K. 10:11; 2 Ch. 8:18; Ps. 55:13 [MT 14]; Jer. 20:10), all translate Heb. *yāḏa',* "know," in one form or another, except Jer. 20:10, where the Hebrew expression *'enôš šelômî,* "man of my peace," expresses the concept of familiarity. Gk. *gnṓstēs,* "knower," "expert," occurs only once in the NT (Acts 26:3).

The AV uses "familiar spirit" to render Heb. *'ôḇ*; *see* DIVINATION; MEDIUM.

FAMILY [Heb. *mišpāḥâ*]; AV also KIND (Gen. 18:19), KINDRED; NEB also CLAN, etc.; [*bayiṯ*] (Gen. 34:19; Josh. 22:14; Jgs. 6:15, 27; 8:27, 35; 16:31); AV, NEB, also HOUSE, HOUSEHOLD; [*'elep*] (Josh. 22:21, 30); AV THOUSAND; NEB CLAN; [*zera'*] (2 K. 11:1; 25:25; 2 Ch. 22:10; Jer. 41:1; Ezk. 43:19; Dnl. 1:3); AV SEED;

NEB also LINE, HOUSE, BLOOD; [*'āḇôṯ* < *'āḇ*–'father'] (2 Ch. 19:8; Ezr. 2:68); AV FATHERS; [*tôlēdôṯ*] ("history of the family," Gen. 37:2); AV GENERATIONS; NEB DESCENDANTS; [*'aḥîm* < *'āḥ*–'brother'] (Nu. 25:6); AV BRETHREN; [Gk. *oíkos*] (1 Tim. 5:4, 8; Tit. 1:11); AV HOUSE, HOME; NEB also HOUSEHOLD; [*patriá*] (Acts 3:25; Eph. 3:15); AV also KINDRED; [*génos*] (Acts 4:6; 7:13; 13:26); AV KINDRED, STOCK; NEB also STOCK. In Ezk. 45:15 the RSV and NEB emend MT *mašqeh,* literally "watering place" (cf. AV "fat pastures"), to *mišpāḥâ* on the basis of the LXX *patriá.*

- I. Terminology
  - A. In the OT
  - B. In the NT
- II. Scope of the Family
- III. Status and Role of Family Members
- IV. Figurative Use

***I. Terminology.**–A. In the OT.* No Hebrew term in the OT corresponds precisely to the modern Eng. "family." The term most frequently translated "family" is *mišpāḥâ,* which had a larger connotation than "family." It meant "clan" and could be applied, e.g., to six hundred Danites from two villages (Jgs. 18:11). The term closest in meaning to Eng. "family" is Heb. *bayiṯ* (lit. "house"). This may indicate a house either as a building or as the occupants of a building, i.e., a "household" or "family." So we read of Abram's trained men "born in his house" (Gen. 14:14; cf. 17:12f.). In Ex. 1:21 the word refers to "families" that God gave to the Egyptian midwives and in 1 Ch. 4:21 to a family of linen workers. It could be used not only of those who lived under the same roof (Ex. 12:4) but also of much larger groups, e.g., the house of Israel (Isa. 5:7), which included the whole nation. Quite frequently the word is applied to a family of descendants, e.g., in 1 K. 12:19, where it refers to the "house of David." The Hebrew terms *'elep, zera', 'āḇôṯ, 'aḥîm,* and *tôlēdôṯ* are translated literally by the AV, but more accurately in terms of the context by the RSV and NEB.

B. In the NT. The NT generally uses Gk. *oíkos,* "house," as the equivalent of Heb. *bayiṯ* and renders it "family" in 1 Tim. 5:4, 8; Tit. 1:11 (and "household," or a family of descendants, in Lk. 1:27, 69). Gk. *patriá* is the NT equivalent of Heb. *mišpāḥâ* and can mean: (1) the historical origin of a household, i.e., its patriarch rather than its present head (Lk. 2:4); (2) a tribe or even a nation (Acts 3:25, "the families of the earth"); (3) the whole human race in Eph. 3:14f. ("every family . . . on earth"), behind which is the universal fatherhood of God. The term *génos* refers to descendants of a common ancestor and can designate a family, race, or a nation. The RSV inserts "family" in Rom. 16:10f. (AV, NEB, "household"), and in Mk. 3:21 renders *hoi par' autoú* as "his family" (AV "friends"; NEB "family").

II. Scope of the Family.–Partly because of the acceptance of polygamy, in some instances the OT family could be quite extensive. Even where monogamy was practiced the family was large, including the father, mother, sons, daughters, brothers, sisters (until marriage), grandparents, and other kinsmen as well as servants, concubines, and sojourners. The Israelites were encouraged to have large families for economic as well as religious reasons. The solidarity of a large family was maintained by its organization around the father figure.

III. Status and Role of Family Members.–Implicit from the beginning was the equality of the sexes before God. EVE, "the mother of all living" (Gen. 3:20), is portrayed as distinctly as Adam in the picture of the first couple. She is the feminine representative (*'iššâ*) of the race as Adam is the masculine representative (*'îš*) (Gen. 2:23). Her personality is as complete as Adam's; she is as rational and accountable as he. After the fall the position of the wife and of the mother became less than equal (*see also* MARRIAGE II.D).

In OT times family life was father-centered. The family was a community of people related by ties of marriage and kinship, ruled by the authority of the father. The father might be a grandfather or a great-grandfather. He had the power to offer his son as a sacrifice (Gen. 22; but *see* SACRIFICE, HUMAN) and could destroy members of his family if they undermined his loyalty to God (Dt. 13:6-10). He also had the responsibility of teaching his sons (Prov. 1:8) and did pity them on occasion (Ps. 103:13).

In Semitic society the family was much more than a mere social organism. One of its highly significant features was its function as a religious community. It was through the family that the cult of the household and the tribal deities was practiced and perpetuated. The father of the house, by virtue of being the family head, was the priest of the household. As such he was responsible for the religious life of his family; he maintained the family altar and he offered sacrifices to the family gods. This situation is reflected in the stories of the Hebrew patriarchs (Abraham, Isaac, and Jacob; cf. also Job) who, living before the centralization of worship, offered sacrifices to Yahweh as the tribal or national deity. It goes far to explain records such as those in Gen. 31:53; 32:9 and the exceptional reverence that was paid to paternal sepulchres (1 S. 20:6).

Abraham was regarded as the father of the nation of Israel. The family continued to play a constructive and important role in the development of Hebrew thought and life, forming the basis for its social structure, merging gradually into wider tribal organisms, and vitally affecting the political and religious life of the nation of Israel. The solidarity of the family as institution was such that forces that threatened its security were vigorously combatted. Each member was urged to fight for the defense of his brothers, sons, daughters, wives, and home (Neh. 4:14). All members were obliged to protect the entire family through the correctness of their own behavior. During

Akhenaten (left), Nefertiti, and their three daughters. Painted limestone plaque (14th cent. B.C.) from a house chapel at Tell el-Amarna (Service des musées, Cairo)

economic crises, however, entire families might be sold for debt (Mt. 18:25).

See also FATHER.

In the NT the size of the family is little mentioned (but cf. Eph. 6:4-9), and some of the OT prerogatives of the father had vanished. Though Christ said little about the family (on Mk. 3:31-35 see W. L. Lane, comm. on Mark [*NICNT,* 1974], pp. 147f.; on Lk. 8:19-21 see I. H. Marshall, comm. on Luke [*New International Greek Testament Commentary,* 1978], pp. 330-32), He criticized moral impurity among members of a family. He reaffirmed the monogamic character of marriage (Mt. 19:11f.; Mk. 10:2-12) and the indissolubility of the family not only with regard to the parties involved but also in terms of the power of society. Christ, curiously, did not touch on children's obedience to their parents, though He Himself was obedient to Joseph and Mary (Lk. 2:51).

In his "household ethics" Paul stressed the mutual duties of the members of the family, those between husbands and wives, between parents and children, and between masters and slaves (Eph. 5:22–6:9; Col. 3:18-22). Unlike Christ he specifically restated the fifth commandment as applied to children's obedience to parents. Accepting other OT obligations, he stated that religion was to be taught in the home (1 Tim. 5:4), and (economic) provision had to be made for the members (v. 8).

IV. Figurative Use.–A religious metaphor is used in the description of the relation between Yahweh and His people. God remembered Israel as His "bride" (Jer. 2:1) and would call back His "children" (3:14), "betrothing" Himself forever in love to Israel (Hos. 2:19f. [MT 21f.]). In the NT this image is applied to Christ and the Church. Paul betrothed the Corinthian church as a "pure bride" to Christ (2 Cor. 11:2) and compared the conjugal love between husband and wife in Eph. 5:25-33 to the love Christ has for His Church. (Cf. similar images in Rev. 19:7, "the marriage of the lamb," and 21:2, the new Jerusalem as "the bride.")

In a related image, God's love for Israel (cf. Am. 3:1f.) was to include all "the families of the earth" (e.g., the promises to Abraham, Gen. 12:3; 28:14, will one day be fulfilled, Ps. 22:27 [MT 28]; cf. Zec. 14:18f.). In the NT believers from every nation are called "members of the household of God" (Eph. 2:19; cf. 3:15 where God is said to be the father of "every family . . . on earth"). Frequently the Christian Church is compared to "the household of God" (Gal. 6:10; 1 Tim. 3:15; 1 Pet. 4:17).

See also MARRIAGE; RELATIONSHIPS, FAMILY.

Bibliography.–E. B. Cross, *Hebrew Family* (1927); R. de Vaux, *Ancient Israel* (Eng. tr. 1961), I, part one; D. Jacobson, *Social Background of the OT* (1942); E. A. Judge, *Social Pattern of the Christian Groups in the First Century* (1960); T. G. Soares, *Social Institutions and Ideals of the Bible* (1915); *TDNT,* V, *s.v.* οἶκος κτλ.: οἶκος (Michel); V, *s.v.* πατήρ κτλ.: πατριά (Schrenk); *TDOT,* II, *s.v.* "bayith," VI (Hoffner); A. N. S. White, *Roman Society and Roman Law in the NT* (1963). L. HUNT

FAMILY RELATIONSHIPS. *See* RELATIONSHIPS, FAMILY.

FAMINE [Heb. *rāʿāḇ*–'hunger,' 'famine'; cf. Ugar. *rǵb*–'to be hungry'] (Gen. 12:10; 26:1; 41:27-54; etc.); AV also DEARTH; NEB also HUNGRY, etc.; [*reʿāḇôn*] (Gen. 42:19, 33; Ps. 37:19); NEB also HUNGRY; [*kāpān*] (Job 5:22); NEB STARVATION; [Gk. *limós*] (Mt. 24:7; Mk. 13:8; Lk. 4:25; 15:14; 21:11; Acts 7:11; 11:28; Rom. 8:35; Rev. 6:8; 18:8); AV also DEARTH, HUNGER; NEB also HUNGER.

I. Causes of Famines.–The Fertile Crescent with Palestine in its center is highly dependent upon rainfall. If little or no rain falls, drought with consequent famine results. This natural cause of famine is often referred to in the OT (Gen. 12:10; 26:1; 41:54; 2 S. 21:1; 1 K. 18:1f.; 2 K. 8:1; Am. 4:6f.; Hag. 1:1-11; Ruth 1:1). Jer. 14:1-6 depicts the dreaded results of the drought. Another natural cause of famine was the destruction of the crop through "blight and mildew" (Am. 4:9) and locusts (Joel 1:4-20; Am. 4:9). An extensive drought led also to the loss of livestock and thus to starvation (1 K. 18:5). Some of the most terrible famines were man-made. The siege of Samaria by Ben-hadad king of Syria brought a famine of such severity that children were eaten (2 K. 6:24-29). The siege of Jerusalem by Nebuchadrezzar in 586 B.C. also led to a very severe famine (2 K. 25:3), which was intensified by two seasons' use of the crops by the Babylonian army and by the latter's sealing off of the city so that no food supplies could reach it. A standard practice of ancient warfare by the Hittites, Egyptians, and Assyrians was to bring about starvation by cutting down grain, orchards, gardens, etc. in order to break political independence and prevent quick repopulation (*ANET,* pp. 239-241; Goetze, p. 127; *ARAB,* I, 230, 243, 279, etc.).

The Bible understands famine in terms of the God-man relationship. In opposition to the Canaanite fertility religion, in which the natural processes are deified and Baal, "the rider on the clouds," is the god of rain and fertility, the OT emphasizes that Yahweh, as Creator, possesses and controls the forces of nature, the order of the seasons, and the material support of human life (cf. Ps. 104). In this sense the OT affirms that God caused famines throughout Israel's history for certain purposes in His plan of salvation.

II. Famines in the Bible.–*A. In the OT.* Such early historical figures as Abraham (Gen. 12:10) and Isaac (26:1) were forced to migrate to other lands in order to escape local famines (cf. 2 K. 8:1-3). A protracted seven-year famine during Joseph's stay in Egypt (Gen. 41:27) affected Canaan (42:1) as well as Egypt and is said to have been "over all the earth" (41:57). Since Egypt was watered by the seasonal inundation of the Nile and Palestine by occasional rainfall, drought seldom occurred in the two areas simultaneously (cf. Gen. 12:10; 26:1f.). Egypt experienced famines from time to time. Records report famines so severe that the inhabitants resorted to cannibalism (Vandier, pp. 8f., 14f.; *ANET,* p. 31 n. 1). The Egyptian ruler's duties included the responsibility for providing enough food in times of famine to keep the population from starvation. One Egyptian biographical text reads: "When famine came for many years, I gave grain in my town in each famine" (Vandier, p. 115). An Egyptian relief from Saqqârah, dated to the 5th Dynasty (*ca.* 2500-2350 B.C.), pictures emaciated, starving people (*ANEP,* no. 102). Egyptian sources refer to numerous instances in which inhabitants from other nations, or even whole nations, sought help from Egypt during periods of famine (Janssen). Against this background the seven-year famine in Joseph's day has a ring of historical accuracy. It is beyond doubt that this famine had a significant role in salvation-history, for it threatened the life of the clan of Jacob. The touching scene in which Joseph reveals himself to his surprised brothers climaxes in his statement that God had sent him to preserve a remnant on earth (Gen. 45:5-7). God's providential guidance reunited estranged brothers and preserved the clan of Jacob as a remnant from which the nation Israel would emerge.

A famine in the time of the Judges led to the emigration of Elimelech and his family to Moab (Ruth 1:1). Later in the Davidic period mention is made of a three-year famine (2 S. 21:1), and one of seven (1 Ch. 21:12, LXX "three") years is threatened (24:13). In Ahab's day Elijah

An emaciated desert herdsman leads oxen in a procession of tributebearers to Ukh-hotep. Relief from Meir, Egypt (20th cent. B.C.) (photograph courtesy of Metropolitan Museum of Art)

announced a three-year famine (1 K. 17:1; 18:2; cf. Josephus *Ant.* viii.13.2 [319]), and two famines are mentioned during the days of Elisha (2 K. 4:38; 8:1). The Shunammite woman was forced to journey to the land of the Philistines to escape a seven-year famine (2 K. 8:1-6). The famine of Samaria caused by the siege of the Syrian forces (2 K. 6:25; 7:4) and the famine of Jerusalem caused by the Babylonian army (2 K. 25:3; Lam. 4:8-10) were so severe that some resorted to cannibalism (2 K. 6:28f.; Lam. 2:30f.; 4:10; cf. Dt. 28:56f.; Ezk. 5:10). Cannibalism under the stress of siege is recorded again for Jerusalem during the siege of the Romans in A.D. 70 (Josephus *BJ* vi.3.4 [207f.]).

The classical triad of major calamities in the form of sword, famine, and pestilence (Jer. 14:12; 21:7, 9; 24:10; 27:8, 13; 29:17f.; 32:24, 36; 34:17; 38:2; etc.; Ezk. 6:11f.; 7:15; 12:16) appears in more elaborate form in Lev. 26:3-33 and Am. 4:6-11. When David was confronted by God with a choice between famine, sword, or pestilence (2 S. 24:13-17), he chose the last, apparently because it was the calamity feared the least. The writer of Lamentations reflects the conviction that those who perish by the sword are better off than those who die of hunger (Lam. 4:9). This suggests that famine was the most terrible affliction on the scale of ancient scourges (Dt. 32:23; Ezk. 3:16).

Famines played an important role as "chastisements" sent by God for Israel's sins. Their aim was to lead the covenant people to obey God (Lev. 26:18-26). God warned that He would withhold the gift of rain, inevitably resulting in famine and death (Dt. 11:17), should Israel engage in idolatry. Lack of rain in the Promised Land would be experienced as God's curse for Israel's disobedience (Dt. 28:23). In the dedicatory prayer of the temple, Solomon referred to lack of rain (1 K. 8:35) and famine (v. 37), which came because of sin, and requested that they be removed if Israel repented. Amos proclaimed that what God had threatened in Lev. 26 and Dt. 28 had actually occurred (Am. 4:6-11). He exhorted in the tradition of 1 K. 8:33-40, that the calamities of insufficient rain and famine were designed to lead to repentance. The ultimate goal of these "natural" catastrophes was to bring Israel back to wholehearted obedience to the divine will. Release from the scourge of famine was to come through prayer and supplication (1 K. 8:37-40).

Wisdom literature teaches that the God who sends famine will redeem man from death by famine (Job 5:20). Those who fear the Lord and hope for His kindness are preserved in spite of famine (Ps. 33:18f.; 37:19). The sage knows that Yahweh does not let the righteous go hungry (Prov. 10:3). The inner appetite (Heb. *nepeš*) of the just will not lead to perpetual frustration but will be satisfied by complete fulfillment and total self-realization.

"Famine" appears in a metaphorical sense in Am. 8:11: "I will send a famine on the land; not a famine of bread, nor a thirst for water, but of hearing the words [LXX, Syriac, Vulgate, 'word'] of the Lord" (cf. 1 S. 3:1; 28:6; 2 Ch. 15:13; Ezk. 7:26). The truth is here affirmed (as Jesus taught later) that man does not live "by bread alone" (Dt. 8:3; Mt. 4:4; cf. Dt. 30:15f.; 32:46f.) but by the word of the Lord. Amos warned that sometime in the future would come the worst famine that can be experienced, namely, the inability to hear the word of the Lord.

B. In the NT. Two NT passages refer to famines mentioned in the OT: Jesus refers to the famine of Elijah's day (Lk. 4:25; cf. 1 K. 17:1, 8-16) and Stephen to the seven-year famine during the time of Joseph's stay in Egypt (Acts 7:11).

The famous general famine predicted by Agabus, the Jerusalem prophet (Acts 11:27f.), came in the reign of the Roman Emperor Claudius (A.D. 41-54). Classical writers reported famines at various times during the reign of Claudius (Suetonius *Claudius* 18; Tacitus *Ann.* xii.43; Dio Cassius *Hist.* lx.11; Orosius *Historiae* vii.6.17), while the Jewish historian Josephus recorded a great famine in Palestine in A.D. 44-48 when grain was imported from Egypt to relieve the great suffering (*Ant.* xx.2.5; 5.2 [51; 101]).

Jesus predicted that famines will be a part of the eschatological woes serving as signs of the last days, when the kingdom of God will be ushered in by the apocalyptic return of Jesus Christ (Mt. 24:7; Mk. 13:8; Lk. 21:11). These famines point to the end and are a pledge of it, just as the labor pains of a woman in childbirth are a promise of that which she has expectantly awaited. Thus these sufferings are a sign that the Parousia is near and a pledge that a new age will break in. Famine is a part of the triad of calamities in Rev. 6:8 (cf. 18:8) that together with death by wild beasts will bring widespread devastation. But once the new age of final salvation has begun, there will be no more hunger and famine (Rev. 7:16; cf. Ezk. 34:29).

See also HUNGER.

Bibliography.–*ARAB*, I, II; K. S. Gapp, *HTR*, 28 (1935), 258-265; J. Janssen, *Bibl.*, 20 (1939), 69-72; J. Vandier, *La Famine dans l'Égypte ancienne* (1936); A. Goetze, *Kleinasien* (1957); *TDNT*, VI, *s.v.* πεινάω (λιμός) (Goppelt); *Encyclopedia Judaica*, VI, *s.v.* "Famine and Drought."

G. F. HASEL

FAMISH. The RSV renders Heb. *rāzâ* ("make lean") as "famish" in Zeph. 2:11, describing the action of God against other deities. In Gen. 25:29f. *ʿāyēp* ("faint," "weary") depicts the condition of the exhausted and hungry Esau, while in 41:55 the seven-year famine of Egypt is portrayed by *rāʿēḇ* ("be hungry").

FAN; FANNER (AV Isa. 30:24; 41:16; Jer. 4:11; 15:7; 51:2; Mt. 3:12; Lk. 3:17). *See* FORK (3); WINNOWING.

FANCY. In Cant. 6:12 *nepeš*, "self," is translated "my fancy" by the RSV. The meaning of the MT is obscure, and the NEB "I did not know myself," while a literal rendering, does not particularly clarify the passage. In Dnl. 4:5 (MT 2) "fancies" renders Aram. *harhōrîn*, "dream-fantasies" (*CHAL*, p. 404).

FANGS [Heb. *maltᵉʿôṯ* (Ps. 58:6 [MT 7]), *mᵉṯallᵉʿôṯ* (Job 29:17; Joel 1:6)]; AV GREAT TEETH, JAWS, CHEEK TEETH; NEB also JAWS. The word is used figuratively, as a synonym of reckless strength and cruelty.

FAR. Used either as an adjective ("distant," "remote") or as an adverb ("widely removed"). It most frequently translates Heb. *rāḥôq* in the OT and Gk. *makrán* in the NT, but it also renders other Hebrew and Greek words. Heb. *ḥālîlâ* (cf. Gk. *mḗ génoito*; *see* FORBID), an exclamation of abhorrence or aversion, is rendered "far be it from me," "far be it from thee," etc. (Gen. 18:25; 44:7, 17; Josh. 22:29; 24:16; 1 S. 2:30; 12:23; 20:9; 2 S. 20:20; 23:17; 1 Ch. 11:19; Job 27:5; 34:10; cf. Gal. 6:14).

In addition to its literal sense, distance in a spiritual sense is expressed by "far," as in "Salvation is far from the wicked" (Ps. 119:155; cf. Prov. 15:29), "far from deliverance" (Isa. 46:12), "not far from the kingdom of God" (Mk. 12:34).

W. L. WALKER

FAR HOUSE [Heb. *bêṯ hammerḥāq*–'house (place) afar'] (2 S. 15:17, NEB); AV "a place that was far off"; RSV "at the last house"; cf. RV "Beth-merhak." A place mentioned in the account of David's flight from Absalom, probably not to be identified as a town.

FARE. "Fare" occurs in the RSV OT eleven times as a verb and three times as a noun. As a verb it generally means "go," "get along," or "succeed"; the AV often translates the Hebrew more literally with "be" (e.g., for Heb. *hāyâ*, Gen. 18:25). In 1 S. 17:18 "fare" translates the noun *šālôm*, "peace," "prosperity," "completeness." In Hag. 2:16 the RSV follows the LXX rather than the MT, which is translated literally by the AV "since those days were." In 1 K. 22:27 par. 2 Ch. 18:26 "scant fare" renders *laḥaṣ* literally, "affliction" (cf. AV), while in Jonah 1:3 the noun *śāḵār*, "hire," "reward," refers to the price Jonah paid for a voyage to Tarshish.

In the NT "fare" occurs only once, Rom. 9:29, for the Greek verb *gínomai*, "be," "become," or "be made."

N. J. O.

FAREWELL [Heb. *nāšaq*] ("kiss farewell," Gen. 31:28); AV, NEB, KISS; [Gk. *apotássomai*] ("say farewell," Lk. 9:61); NEB "say good-bye"; [*rhṓnnymi*] (Acts 15:29); AV "Fare ye well"; [*apaspázomai*] ("bid farewell," Acts 21:5); AV "take leave"; NEB "say good-bye"; [*chaírō*] (2 Cor. 13:11). Originally a wish at parting for those traveling (faring) forth.

The term occurs in the OT (RSV) only once, for Heb. *nāšaq* ("kiss"); the context indicates a farewell kiss. As a parting wish at the close of a NT letter it represents the Gk. *rhṓnnymi* ("make strong") and *chaírō* ("Rejoice!"). As equivalent to our saying "good-bye" (cf. NEB) it represents the Gk. *apaspázomai* and *apotássomai*.

W. L. WALKER

FARM [Gk. *agrós*] (Mt. 22:5); **FARMER** [Heb. *'ikkār*] (2 Ch. 26:10; Jer. 14:4; 31:24; 51:23; Am. 5:16); AV HUSBANDMAN, PLOWMAN; NEB also PLOUGHMAN; [Gk. *geōrgós*] (2 Tim. 2:6; Jas. 5:7); AV HUSBANDMAN. Mt. 22:5 is the only passage where Gk. *agrós* ("field," "ground") has been rendered "farm." Farms in the Western sense — isolated dwellings with their groups of outbuildings, surrounded by walls or hedges and overlooking the planted fields — were probably unknown in Palestine. For protection against wild beasts and human marauders, everyone lived in a village and went out to the fields, located perhaps miles away, only as occasion required.

The "farmer" in the RSV is not a landowner, but one who works the land, thus a serf or tenant farmer.

See also HUSBANDMAN.

J. A. PATCH

FARTHING. *See* MONEY.

FASHION [Heb. *yāṣar*] (Ps. 33:15; Isa. 44:10; 45:9; 54:17); AV also FORM; NEB also CAST METAL, MAKE; [*ṣûr*] (Ex. 32:4); NEB CAST; [*ʿāśâ*] (Isa. 44:13); AV FIT; NEB PLANE; [polel of *kûn*] (Job 31:15; Ps. 119:73); NEB CREATE, MAKE; [piel of *ʿāṣaḇ*] (Job 10:8); AV MAKE; NEB GIVE SHAPE. To create, shape, form; the work of a craftsman.

The root *yṣr* refers to the concrete act of making an object. The most common RSV translation is "to form." It refers most extensively to the act of pottery-making, and the noun "potter" is a form of this verb (*yôṣēr*). This meaning was extended to include the work of a metalsmith (Isa. 44:12 [RSV "shapes"; the word translated "fashions" is an emendation]). It is often used to refer to God's creative activity and has more concreteness than the verbs *ʿāśâ* ("make") and *bārā'* ("create") (cf. Gen. 2:7; Isa. 45:7, 18). Inherent in this concept is the sovereignty of the workman. The craftsman forms the object according to his own plans and desires. This concept is applied to God in Jer. 18:1-11. Jeremiah is sent to watch a potter (*yôṣēr*) at work, and God informs Jeremiah that this is the manner in which He is shaping Israel (cf. G. C. Berkouwer, *Divine Election* [Eng. tr. 1960], pp. 76-78).

The verb *kônēn* (polel of *kûn*) connotes firmness and stability. It is more commonly translated "establish" (Ps. 8:3 [MT 4]).

The RSV translates "fashion," meaning "way" or "manner," in 2 Ch. 32:15 (Heb. *kāzō'ṯ*; NEB "like this") and 2 Cor. 10:2 (Gk. *katá sárka*; lit. "in accordance with flesh"; cf. Bauer, p. 408, "on the physical plane"). In 2 K. 16:10 the AV renders Heb. *d^emûṯ* as "fashion," in the obsolete sense of "model" (NEB "sketch").

See also FORM. H. W. LAY

FAST. Deliberate and sustained ABSTINENCE from all food for a specific period of time. A fast may be associated with private acts of piety, the acknowledgment of disaster, emotional disturbance, mourning, or repentance, or it can form part of public devotion. The biblical writers accepted the social and religious concepts of fasts without discussing the origin of the custom.

Hebrew terms include *ṣûm* (verb) and *ṣôm* (noun), along with expressions such as *ʿānâ nepeš* (Lev. 16:29; Isa. 53:3, 5), "afflict oneself"; *lōʾ ʾāḵal leḥem* (1 S. 28:20), "not to eat bread"; and the niphal of *kānaʿ* (1 K. 21:29; cf. v. 27), "humble oneself." Heb. *taʿ^anîṯ* (later the name of tractates in the Mishnah, Talmud, etc., that deal with fasting) occurs only in Ezr. 9:5. The Aram. *ṭ^ewaṯ* (Dnl. 6:18 [MT 19]) describes part of Darius's anguished response to having to put Daniel in the lions' den. The LXX and NT verb for "fast," *nēsteúō* (Mt. 9:15; Lk. 5:33), usually denotes abstinence from food as a religious rite but also can mean simply hunger (Mt. 15:32; Mk. 8:3; 2 Cor. 6:5; 11:27). From early times the wearing of sackcloth and ashes accompanied by fasting indicated self-abnegation.

Moses fasted at Sinai while receiving the law from God (Ex. 34:28; Dt. 9:9) and again when he smashed the law tablets in front of the apostate Israelites (Dt. 9:17f.). In the law the tenth day of the seventh month was reserved for "afflicting one's soul" (Lev. 16:29), an activity that was entirely appropriate for the Day of Atonement.

At all periods in Israelite history fasts were proclaimed as a response to national emergency or distress (Jgs. 20:26; 1 S. 7:6; 2 Ch. 20:3; Ezr. 8:21-23; Neh. 1:4; Est. 4:16; Jer. 36:9), as an act of penitence (1 K. 21:27; Neh. 9:1), or as an accompaniment to earnest prayer, whether public or private (2 S. 12:16; Ps. 35:13). Fasting often accompanied periods of mourning (2 S. 1:12; 12:21; Isa. 31:13).

During and after the Exile certain fasts commemorated the Babylonian destruction of Jerusalem. The fasts were: the ninth day of the fourth month, for the fall of Jerusalem (2 K. 25:3f.); the tenth day of the fifth month, for the destruction of the temple (cf. Jer. 52:12f.); the second day of the seventh month, for the murder of Gedaliah (2 K. 25:23-25); and the tenth day of the tenth month, for the first attack on Jerusalem (2 K. 25:1). Zechariah prophesied (8:19) that these fasts would be transformed into times of joy.

Fasts varied in length from one day (1 S. 14:24; 2 S. 3:35) to one night (Dnl. 6:18), three complete days (Est. 4:16), seven days (1 S. 31:13; 2 S. 12:16-18), or forty days (Ex. 34:28; Dt. 9:9; 1 K. 19:8). In Nineveh the Assyrians made even the animals fast (Jonah 3:7), and Jth. 4:10-13 records this practice among the Jews. Isa. 58:5; Joel 2:13; Jer. 14:12 discourage ostentation in fasting.

In the Apocrypha, fasting was regarded as a meritorious religious exercise (Tob. 12:8). It figured prominently in the devotions of Judith (Jth. 8:6) and Ezra (2 Esd. 6:31). People also fasted in times of national danger (1 Macc. 3:47; 2 Macc. 13:12).

John the Baptist required his followers to fast, whereas Jesus imposed no such rule on His disciples. When asked about this divergence from Jewish tradition (Mt. 9:14; Mk. 2:18; Lk. 5:33), Jesus stated that His followers would indeed fast once the bridegroom had been taken from their midst, i.e., after the Ascension. This statement has been interpreted as making fasting a legitimate, though not obligatory, function of the Christian life. Jesus is recorded as having fasted before His temptation (cf. Mt. 4:2; Mk. 1:13), but this was evidently a necessity because of the barren locale. Elsewhere He agreed with the prophets in denouncing ostentatious fasting (Mt. 6:16-18; Lk. 18:9-14), but he did not condemn fasting itself, apparently expecting His listeners to fast voluntarily.

Paul fasted after his blinding vision (Acts 9:9), before his first missionary journey (13:2f.), and for fourteen days during the storm in the Mediterranean Sea (27:33). Certain Jerusalem Jews took a vow of fasting until death (23:12-14) in an attempt to ensure Paul's death. The Textus Receptus associated fasting with prayer in several NT passages (Mt. 17:21; Mk. 9:29; 1 Cor. 7:5), but scholars generally consider these to be inferior readings, since they do not occur in several early uncial manuscripts.

Bibliography.–DNTT, I, 611-13; *TDNT,* IV, *s.v.* νῆστις κτλ. (Behm). R. K. HARRISON

FAT. In the OT "fat" usually translates Heb. *ḥēleḇ* or *ḥeleḇ*. It designates the layer of subcutaneous fat and the compact suet surrounding the viscera and imbedded in the entrails, which like the blood were forbidden as food in the Mosaic code (Lev. 3:17). Fat was to be sacrificed to God by being burned upon the altar (3:16; 7:30) on the very day on which a beast had been slaughtered, to remove temptation from the Israelite to use it otherwise (Ex. 23:18). The law was probably a sanitary restriction, for at an early date leprosy, scrofula, and disfiguring cutaneous diseases were thought to result from eating fat. The law was, moreover, an important pedagogical provision teaching self-denial and the maxim that the richest and best meat of the edible animal belonged to the Lord. *See also* SACRIFICE IN THE OT V. On Mt. 22:4, *see* FATLING.

"Fat" is often used in figurative senses, e.g., abundant, fertile, robust, outwardly successful, insensitive, dull (see Dt. 32:15; Ps. 92:14 (MT 15), AV; 119:70; Prov. 11:25, AV; 13:4, AV; Isa. 6:10; Jer. 5:28; etc.). *See also* FATNESS.

In the AV of Joel 2:24, "fats" is an obsolete spelling of "vats." *See* WINE. H. L. E. LUERING R. K. H.

FATE [Heb. *p^equddâ*] (Nu. 16:29); AV VISITATION; [*ʿēṯ*–'time'] (Ps. 81:15 [MT 16]); AV TIME; NEB TROUBLES; [*dereḵ*–'way'] (Ps. 49:13 [MT 14]); AV WAY; [*miqreh*] (Eccl. 2:14; 3:19; 9:2f.); AV EVENT, "that which befalleth"; NEB also CHANCE; [*nāweh*] (Jer. 49:20; 50:45; Lam. 3:51); AV HABITATION, "because of." In the Bible fate is usually associated with the inevitability of death. But this is always seen as being determined by the sovereign will of God; thus the Hebrew notion of fate was not fatalistic, as was the Greek (cf. W. C. Greene, *Moira: Fate, Good and Evil* [repr. 1963]). This does not mean, however, that the concept of fate was not problematic for the Hebrews. The Preacher perceived that the same fate came to all men, whether wise or foolish (Eccl. 2:14), righteous or wicked, good or evil (3:19; 9:2f.). This appeared to him an evil, a vanity that renders all things vain. He concluded that, because this mystery could not be fathomed, one should enjoy life while it lasts by living as God wills (cf. 9:7-10; 12:13; etc.).

See DEATH II; ECCLESIASTES III.

G. WYPER N. J. O.

FATHER [Heb. *ʾāḇ* (cf. Akk. *abu*; Ugar. *ab*; etc.); Gk. *patḗr*].

I. Uses of the Term.–Along with its usual meaning (Ex. 20:12; Job 42:15; Jer. 47:3; etc.), Heb. *ʾāḇ* can also mean grandfather (Gen. 28:13; 32:9 [MT 10]; etc.), great-grandfather (1 K. 15:11, 24; etc.), or even the ancestral father of a tribe or people (Gen. 10:21; 17:4f.; 19:37f.; Dt. 26:5; etc.). Sometimes "the fathers" refers to the early generations of a people, i.e., the forefathers (Ex. 3:15; Nu. 20:15; Ps. 22:4 [MT 5]; etc.). On the expression "be gathered to one's fathers" *see* GATHER.

The Heb. *'āḇ* can also refer to the founder of an occupation or a life-style (e.g., Gen. 4:20f.; Jer. 35:6, 8). Sometimes a specific characteristic of a literal father is applied in a nonliteral way; thus the *'āḇ* may be a person who provides protection (Job 29:16; 31:18), acts as a counselor (Gen. 45:8; 1 Macc. 2:65; 11:32), or is worthy of honor or respect, e.g., a prophet (2 K. 2:12; 6:21; 8:9; 13:14) or a priest (Jgs. 17:10; 18:19). Cf. also Acts 7:2; 22:1; and the title of the Mishnaic tractate *Aboth,* which contains the sayings of the esteemed rabbis. To prevent excesses in this regard, Jesus exhorted His followers not to desire the title of "father," i.e., respected teacher (cf. vv. 8, 10, where Jesus similarly discouraged the desire for the titles "rabbi" and "master"). The use of "father" in 1 Jn. 2:13f. is problematic; it may refer to elders in the church (so B. F. Westcott, *Epistles of John* [repr. 1966], p. 60), although a reference to mature Christians seems more likely (cf. I. H. Marshall, *Epistles of John* [*NICNT,* 1978], pp. 137-140).

In an exchange with some Jewish followers, Jesus stated that they were of their "father the devil" (Jn. 8:44). The context indicates that Jesus was thereby referring to their spiritual heritage, which contrasted so vividly with His own (cf. vv. 37-43). Cf. also 1 Cor. 4:15, where Paul says that he became the spiritual father (Gk. *egénnēsa*) of the Corinthians.

For God as father, see III below and GOD THE FATHER.

II. Function of the Father in the Family.–In the OT, the father was the main figure who wielded authority and commanded respect. He was to be honored (Ex. 20:12; Dt. 5:16; Mal. 1:6; cf. Ex. 21:15, 17) and obeyed (Dt. 21:18; Prov. 23:22; cf. Isaac's obedience to Abraham in Gen. 22:1-14). He possessed almost unlimited power over the lives of the members of his family — he could sell his daughter into slavery (Ex. 21:7), have his son stoned if the son attempted to entice him away from Yahwism (Dt. 13:6-10) or if the son was a glutton or drunkard (Dt. 21:18-21; cf. Judah's pronouncement of the death sentence upon his daughter-in-law in Gen. 38:24), or take away the birthright of the eldest son for a serious offense (Gen. 35:22; 49:4; 1 Ch. 5:1; favoritism was prohibited, however, in Dt. 21:15-17; cf. deVaux, pp. 41f.). Along with this position of authority the father had certain responsibilities. He had to love, care for, and protect his children (Dt. 1:31; Ps. 103:13; cf. Job 1:5; Jer. 47:3; Hos. 11:1-3). He also had to train, educate (Dt. 4:9; 6:7; Prov. 1:8; 22:6) and discipline them (Prov. 13:24; 19:18; 23:13f.; Sir. 30:1-13; cf. deVaux, pp. 48-50).

In the NT, Jesus acknowledged the continuing validity of the command in Ex. 20:12 for children to honor their parents (Mk. 7:9-13; 10:19). Paul reiterated this (Eph. 6:2f.) and added that obedience to one's parents is also necessary (Eph. 6:1; Col. 3:20). He instructed fathers not to provoke their children to anger (Eph. 6:4a; Col. 3:21), but to discipline and instruct them (Eph. 6:4b).

III. Theological Concept of Father.–God, in biblical thought, is designated as the father of the second person of the trinity, of the world and of all things in it, of the individual believer, of the nation Israel, of Jesus of Bethlehem, and of all spiritual blessings and realities. Contingent on this meaning of father, and corresponding to it, the term son is applied in biblical thought to angels (Job 38:7), to the individual believer, to the nation of Israel, and to Jesus of Bethlehem as the eternal Son.

To childless Abram, husband of barren Sarai, God's promise to make him a prolific fountain was expressed in terms of fatherhood. Abram's seed will be in number like the stars of the heavens and the sands of the seashore. God will make him "exceedingly fruitful" (Gen. 17:6), so that his seed will be in number "as the dust of the earth" (Gen. 13:16), "as the stars of heaven and as the sand which is on the seashore" (22:17); "kings shall come forth from you" (17:6); Abram will become "the father of a multitude of nations" (17:5), "the father of all who believe" (Rom. 4:11), "the father of the circumcised" (v. 12), and "the father of us all" (v. 16). In each instance the promised fatherhood was a promise of becoming a source from which would flow that which was not Abram; yet in becoming such a source Abram would become what he had not been, and therefore he received a new name, Abraham. That Abram became the father of others, and through this what God willed him to be, only by faith and through the promise of God, indicates that God Himself is the father of the whole movement. God, accordingly, is the father of Israel (Jer. 31:9; Isa. 63:16; cf. Isa. 64). Similarly, the source-quality of God's fatherhood is expressed in the phrases "Father of glory" (Eph. 1:17), and "Father of lights" (Jas. 1:17).

Thus the concept of father, whether applied to God, man, the devil, or evil, and whether used biologically or spiritually, literally or figuratively, always expresses the notion of source or fountain of procession. The richness and beauty of the biblical concept of father lies in that, being a source of another, the father imparts and communicates himself to this other. This idea of self-impartation and self-communication is as definitive of the concept of father as is the notion of source. A father gives of himself to that which he fathers, so what proceeds from the source participates in the source. He who is a father communicates something of himself to that which he fathers in such a way that the other has not merely his source in the father, but also the nature of the father's reality. The other partakes of the nature of his father. This accounts for the close ties and deep affection between the source and that which proceeds from it.

This relationship between source and its issue must be distinguished from all pagan notions that conceive of reality as an emanation from or an overflow of the divine being. On the contrary, this relationship must be understood within the biblical categories of creation and re-creation.

Since the created world has its source in God the Creator, it shares in the power and glory of God and is thus a revelation of its Maker. Man, too, has his origin in God, and as the image of his Father he shares in the nature of his Father, as for example, in his sexuality and in his dominion over the earth (Gen. 1:26-28). A more expansive example of this truth is found in the teaching of the Heidelberg Catechism that man is created in the image of God in order that man may rightly "know" God, "love" Him, and "live with Him in eternal blessedness" (Lord's Day III). In this sharing in the life of God whence man came, man's life consists. Because God is man's origin, God is man's home, his "dwelling place in all generations" (Ps. 90:1), and man is restless until he rests in God; for the same reason, a human rejection of God and departure from Him is self-destructive, the way to death.

In this biblical idea of fatherhood, as a source that shares its nature with its issue, lies the basis for the distinctive feature of biblical epistemology. Knowledge, as biblically defined, depends on the willingness of the object to make itself known and on the willingness of the knower to participate in, and be identified with, the object of his knowledge. There is no essential dualism between the knower and the known. Adam "knows" his wife (Gen.

4:1), and in this knowing they become "one flesh" (2:24); the believer knows God, and in this knowing he shares God's life and has, thus, "eternal life" (Jn. 17:3). In the Bible nothing is to be found of that objective-subjective dualism that has characterized modern epistemology since Kant, in which the knower is alien and estranged from the object of his knowledge. In biblical thought both nature and man derive from God, and each in its own way mutually shares the nature of its origin. Thus there is no ontological estrangement between man and man, or between man and nature. The strange reality is only a matter of time, place, and circumstance, without ontological rootage. In biblical thought even the "ox knows its owner, and the ass its master's crib" (Isa. 1:3).

This self-communication of God as father that is expressed in creation comes to clearer expression in God's relationship to Israel. God is the source, the creator of Israel; He is therefore the father of Israel, and Israel is God's son. To Israel He gives Himself in His covenant, makes known His secret, and gives His name so that His people are called by His name (Jer. 14:9); and from Israel He takes His own name, a name that is His "name for ever," "to be remembered throughout all generations," when He declares Himself to be the God of Abraham, Isaac, and Jacob (Ex. 3:15). The unique and profound significance of this divine self-giving to Israel, through which each assumes and wills to be known by the name of the other, is expressed in the biblical concept of father and in the singularly rich meaning that a name has in biblical thought.

The full meaning of father, as the denotation of origin and also as self-impartation, comes to ultimate expression in the NT in that fatherly act of God in sending forth His only begotten Son into the world of sin, death, cross, and hell, that Israel and the world might be saved, and in that complementary act in which God sends forth His Spirit into the Church and into the hearts of its members. The sum of this action is variously described as a creation in Christ (Eph. 2:10), a new birth (Jn. 3:5f.), and a being begotten again by the Word of God (1 Pet. 1:23). Peter puts the whole purpose of God's fatherly redemptive action in bold theological shorthand when he says that mankind "may . . . become partakers of the divine nature" (2 Pet. 1:4).

The statement that God is Father and the statement that God is love are only two different ways of asserting what God *is*. God is father, not by independent decision, but in His very nature and being. God is not love because He loves; He loves because He is love. God is not a father because He has a son; He has a son because He is a father. In His free sovereign decision to father the world, Israel, Jesus of Bethlehem, and the Church, to be the God by whom every family on earth is named, God neither contradicts nor violates but only freely reveals what He in His nature and being necessarily is. Within the trinity God as Father gives and communicates Himself in His begetting of the Son and aspiration of the Spirit; and in His free works *ad extra* by which He makes Himself the source of that which is not-God, and gives Himself to that which He has willed to issue from Himself, He reveals in being-for-us what He is in Himself.

Because God as father is not only the source of man but a source that determines the nature of man, biblical thought regards it as wholly natural that the creature will honor its creator, and that the son will acknowledge, honor, and thank his Father, and that the Son, through whom, by whom, and unto whom all things were created, will be acknowledged when He comes to "his own" (Jn. 1:11). Where this occurs, the son finds himself in the father. Where this does not occur, sin is present, the son is rejecting his father, and thereby repudiating both whence he came and what he is. For what he is is determined by his origin, his father; and in repudiating his father he repudiates himself. Father and son are so related that if the son loses the father, he loses himself.

See also FAMILY; RELATIONSHIPS, FAMILY.

Bibliography.–R. de Vaux, *Ancient Israel* (Eng. tr. 1961); *TDNT*, V, *s.v.* πατήϱ κτλ. (Schrenk, Quell); *TDOT*, I, *s.v.* "'ābh" (Ringgren).

J. DAANE

FATHER, GOD THE. *See* GOD THE FATHER.

FATHER-IN-LAW. *See* RELATIONSHIPS, FAMILY.

FATHERLESS [Heb. *yāṯôm, 'ên 'āḇ*]; AV also POOR (Job 5:15); NEB also ORPHAN, DESTITUTE (Job 5:15), INNOCENT (Job 31:21), WITHOUT A FATHER (Lam. 5:3). The fatherless were one of the oppressed classes in Israelite society, together with the widow and sojourner (cf. Zec. 7:10). Because the husband or father was the primary legal defender in biblical times, the widow and her children often had no one to defend them. Consequently, in every instance in which the fatherless are mentioned, the context is one of helplessness in the face of oppression.

God is the Father of the fatherless and the Protector of widows (Job 5:15; Ps. 10:14; 68:5 [MT 6]; 146:9; Jer. 49:11), and He is the one who executes justice for them (Dt. 10:18; Ps. 10:18). The Covenant Code contains special provisions for their protection and welfare. The fatherless were entitled to receive a share of the produce of the field by gleaning (Dt. 24:19-21) and by sharing in the third year's tithe (14:29; 26:12f.). They were to be included in the feasts (16:11, 14) and had to be protected from all forms of injustice (Ex. 22:22-24 [MT 23-25]; Dt. 24:17; 27:19; Prov. 23:10; Ps. 82:3; 2 Esd. 2:20). Israel's duty to the fatherless was rooted in the Exodus (Dt. 24:18, 22). Because God had redeemed Israel from oppression, Israel was required to redeem the helpless in her society.

In spite of the Covenant Code, however, the fatherless frequently lived in a situation of terror (Ps. 10:18; 94:6); thus, the most terrible curse invoked on the wicked man is that his children be fatherless (Ps. 109:9, 12), and God's judgments on Israel could be described as an absence of His compassion on Israel's fatherless (Isa. 9:17). Consequently, oppression of the fatherless became a typical way of describing Israel's failure to keep the covenant. In the book of Job, the sinner is one who oppresses the fatherless (6:27; 22:9; 24:3, 9), and the righteous person is one who defends their cause (29:12; 31:17, 21). The prophets condemn Israel for breaking the covenant by oppressing the fatherless (Isa. 1:17, 23; 10:2; Jer. 5:28; Ezk. 22:7), and they announce that exile can be avoided only by doing justice and showing kindness to the fatherless (Jer. 7:6; 22:3; Zec. 7:10-14). In exile Israel became like the fatherless she had never defended (Lam. 5:3). Then the people of Israel experienced, as the fatherless had always known, that God alone could help her (Hos. 14:3, AV).

The fatherless, who necessarily depended on God for safety and salvation, became a type representing the people of God. Consequently, Israel's treatment of the fatherless revealed in a most unique way whether Israel itself understood what it meant to be the people of God.

See also JUSTICE; ORPHAN; WIDOW.

D. E. HOLWERDA

FATHER'S BROTHER. *See* RELATIONSHIPS, FAMILY.

FATHER'S HOUSE; FATHER'S HOUSEHOLD [Heb. *bêṯ hā'āḇ*, Gk. *hós oíkos toú patrós, en toís toú patrós* (Lk.

2:49)]; AV also FAMILY, "Father's house" (Jn. 14:2); NEB also FATHER'S FAMILY, FAMILY, FATHER'S LINE, TRIBE, CLAN, ANCESTRAL HOUSE. The idea of "house" is also elliptical in Heb. *rā'šê hā'āḇôṯ*, "head of the fathers' (houses)."

The father's house was the basic social unit within Israel. Israel was a tribal society in which kinship played the primary part. The phrase *bêṯ hā'āḇ* occurs most frequently in regard to genealogies and census taking; it apparently refers to the smallest unit used for these purposes. The relationship between a father's house and a family is vague. Such passages as Gen. 12:1 suggest that the family was a larger unit. There is, however, no clearcut line. The NEB translates the Hebrew with "family," "tribe," and "clan," thereby showing that the phrase could also refer to a very large unit. The number within a father's house could be large. Jerubbaal's house was composed of seventy-two sons (Jgs. 9:5); the house of Eleazar produced sixteen heads of fathers' houses (1 Ch. 24:4).

Fathers' houses played a crucial role in the organization of the nation. In the wilderness the camp was arranged by fathers' houses (here for tribes, cf. Nu. 2:2f.), each with its own ensigns (v. 2). During the kingdom the army was ordered according to fathers' houses (2 Ch. 25:5). At the time of King Uzziah there were numbered 2600 heads of fathers' houses who commanded an army of 307,500 (2 Ch. 26:12f.). Moses communicated instructions to the people through the heads of fathers' houses (Nu. 32:28). David did the same in regard to the priests (1 Ch. 15:11f.): he summoned two priests and six Levites as heads of fathers' houses to communicate a message to the entire tribe. Heads of fathers' houses were also present at important matters of state. At his enthronement, Solomon delivered an address in their presence (2 Ch. 1:2). Later they were present for the great occasion of bringing the ark into the temple built by Solomon (1 K. 8:1). Again they participated in the covenant when Joash was enthroned under the leadership of the high priest Jehoiada (2 Ch. 23:2f.). In Babylon after Cyrus assumed the rulership, God moved the spirits of the heads of fathers' houses to return to Jerusalem in order to rebuild the house of the Lord (Ezr. 1:5). Those who returned and could not prove that their fathers' houses belonged to Israel were excluded from the priesthood and holy food (2:59-63). In reestablishing the Jerusalem community, Ezra, in his desire to produce a far-reaching observation of the law, instructed the heads of fathers' houses (Neh. 8:13-19).

The head of each house bore responsibility for that house. He was to see that the members learned the law and observed it. His participation in the formal worship of Yahweh affected all of his family. He might confess the sins of the members of the household (Neh. 1:6; cf. Job 1:5). As long as the father was living, even his sons' families remained a part of his family. If a father was very important (e.g., in the case of Jacob or King David), all the members of that family continued to partake of that name as well as the name of their immediate father.

Women and children received their standing through the father's house. When a woman made a vow, her father — or her husband if she was married — had the right to negate it (Nu. 30). Inheritance of the father's house was through his sons (Gen. 31:14) or, if there were no sons, through the daughters (Nu. 36). A childless widow or divorcee returned to her father's house (Gen. 38:11; Lev. 22:13). At least one bride who became dissatisfied fled from her husband and returned to her father's house (Jgs. 19:2).

A member of the house could act in such a way as to bring blessing or condemnation on the entire house, as Rahab did in saving her whole family from the Israelite destruction of Jericho (Josh. 6:17,23). Similarly, Korah, Dathan, and Abiram, in wrongly challenging God's methods, brought destruction on their entire households (Nu. 16:16-33). An illegitimate son might be expelled from the household, as in the case of Jephthah (Jgs. 11:2).

In OT times the preservation of one's memory through his father's house was a great concern. Saul realized that David was destined by God to become king over Israel; therefore he had David take an oath that he would not destroy Saul's name from his father's house (1 S. 24:21). Brothers without many children could join together to become one father's house (1 Ch. 23:11). Levirate marriage was intended to insure the establishment of a father's house for the deceased brother (cf. *ILC*, I, 77-81).

In the NT the rich man in Hades asked that a messenger be sent to his father's house, which included five brothers (Lk. 16:27f.); the same concept is employed here as in the OT (cf. Acts 7:20). In the same manner the Philippian jailer brought salvation to his entire household through his own faith (Acts 16:31-34). The phrase took on a richer meaning, however, when Jesus referred to the temple as His Father's house (Jn. 2:16). After failing to accompany His parents on their homeward journey from Jerusalem, Jesus stated His reason for remaining behind: "I must be in my Father's house" (Lk. 2:49; lit. "about the things of my father"). Obviously "the things" refer to His ministry, which began at the temple and ended there. In Jn. 14:2 Jesus referred to heaven as His Father's house, where He was about to go to prepare "rooms" for His followers. Jesus belongs to God's household; and He makes all of His followers members of that household. J. E. HARTLEY

FATHOM [Gk. *orguiá*] (Acts 27:28). The literal meaning is the length of the outstretched arms, equal to 4 cubits or about 2 m. (6 ft.). *See* WEIGHTS AND MEASURES.

FATLING; FATTED ANIMAL. A domestic animal, generally young, well cared for, and fattened for sacrificial slaughter, although not restricted to such use (cf. 1 S. 28:24; Mt. 22:4; see also Prov. 15:17; Jer. 46:21).

The several terms so translated stress the animal's quality rather than its species. Most frequent is Heb. *m^erî'* (2 S. 6:13; 1 K. 1:9, 19, 25; Isa. 11:6; Ezk. 39:18; AV also "fat cattle"; NEB "buffaloes," "fat beasts," "calf"). Primarily used for cattle and listed with other sacrificial animals, in Ezk. 39:18 it is a general term for a variety of "princes of the earth" that are to be sacrificed. Similar in use is Heb. *mē(a)ḥ* (Ps. 66:15; Isa. 5:17), derived from the word for marrow. Heb. *bārî'* (Ezk. 34:3) is rendered "fat sheep" in Ezk. 34:20 (AV "fat cattle"). The AV translates Gk. *sitistós* in Mt. 22:4 as "fatlings" (RSV "fat calves").

Probably meaning "second offspring" and implying higher quality than firstlings, Heb. *(ham)mišneh* is generally emended to *hammašmannîm,* literally "fatted things," or *hašš^emēnîm,* literally "fat" (pl.) (cf. BDB, p. 1041).

Participial adjectives meaning "fatted" include Heb. *marbēq* (1 S. 28:24; Jer. 46:21, AV mg. "bullocks of the stall"; NEB "stall-fed") and Gk. *siteutós* (Lk. 15:23, 27, 30), referring to cattle, and Heb. *'āḇas,* applied to an ox (Prov. 15:17) and fowl (1 K. 4:23 [MT 5:3]). The plural of Heb. *m^erî',* "fatling," is translated "fatted beasts" in Am. 5:22.

See also CALF; CATTLE. A. C. M.

FATNESS. A term describing either animal tissue or the condition of the soil. Heb. *mišmān* denotes the fatness or fertile condition of the land (Gen. 27:28, 39; NEB "richness"). Heb. *dešen* points to the best part of a tree (Jgs. 9:9; NEB "rich oil"), the best food served (Job 36:16; NEB "unlimited plenty"), or the earth's abundant fruits (Ps. 65:11 [MT 12]; NEB "sweet juice"). Israel was not forbidden to enjoy the rich increase of the soil; in fact it would be theirs as long as they served the Lord (cf. Isa. 55:2; NEB "the fat of the land").

Hebrew *ḥēleḇ* refers to the fat of animals that covered their inner parts (*see* FAT). Its meaning in Ps. 73:7 is not clear. The context describes the proud and violent behavior of the arrogant (v. 6). In v. 7 the "fatness" of the eyes" parallels the "folly of the heart." One likely meaning is "gluttony" (*IB*, IV, 388), which is shown through the stretching of the eye. R. W. V.

FAULT [Heb. *ḥaṭṭā'ṯ*–'sin' (Ex. 5:16), *rîḇ* (Ex. 17:2), *me'ûmâ* (2 S. 29:3), *ḥēṭ'* (Gen. 41:9), *sēṯer*, *'āwōn* (2 S. 3:8; Ps. 59:4 [MT 5]); Aram. *šeḥaṯ*; Gk. *elénchō* (Mt. 18:15), *mémphomai* (Rom. 9:19; He. 8:8), *mōmáomai* (2 Cor. 6:3)]; AV also CHIDE, BLAME; NEB also DISPUTE WITH, "charge with disloyalty," MALPRACTICE, "take the matter up with" (Mt. 18:15), etc.; **FAULTFINDER** [Heb. *rîḇ*] (Job 40:2); AV CONTENDETH; NEB (A MAN WHO) DISPUTES; **FAULTFINDING** [Heb. *rîḇ*] (Ex. 17:7); AV CHIDING; NEB DISPUTED; **FAULTLESS** [Gk. *ámemptos*] (He. 8:7).

In Ps. 19:12 (MT 13) the RSV renders Heb. *sēṯer*, "hiding place," as "hidden faults" (NEB "secret faults"), parallel to "sin" (Heb. *šegî'â*, "sin [of ignorance]"). In Dnl. 6:4 (MT 5) Aram. *šeḥîṯâ* (part. of *šeḥaṯ*, "spoil") occurs in conjunction with *šālû*, "negligence." The Hebrew of Ps. 73:10, *ûmê mālē' yimmāṣû*, literally "and waters of fulness were drained out," is difficult. The AV rendering, "and waters of a full cup are wrung out of them" (cf. RSV mg.), is a literal though unintelligible translation. The RSV emendation, *ûme'ûmâ lō' yimṣā'û lehem*, "and find no fault in them" (cf. NEB), relates v. 10 to the preceding verses: people agree with violent men and accept their behavior. (Cf. M. Dahood, *Psalms*, II [*AB*, 1968], 186, 190.)

The OT words for "fault" point to wrong or error that results in the failure to reach a certain standard. Moses was accused by the Israelites of failing to meet their needs (Ex. 17:2); Abner had to defend himself against the charge of moral impurity (2 S. 3:8); and David had to face enemies who harassed him for no sin on his part (Ps. 59:4). In two instances, however, people were found blameless (1 S. 29:3, David; Dnl. 6:4, Daniel).

The NT deepens this OT concept. According to Mt. 18:15 the sinner must confess his fault to the one against whom he sinned. Human wrong, moreover, is seen as a failure to reach integrity with God. Thus the first covenant became faulty because of human unbelief, so God established a new covenant (He. 8:7f.; *see* COVENANT [OT] IV.D). In Rom. 9:19 Paul rebukes those who accuse God of unfairly finding fault with human beings (*see* ELECTION).

See also INIQUITY; RIGHTEOUSNESS.

V. B. GILLESPIE
R. W. V.

FAULTY. The AV translates Heb. *'āšēm* in 2 S. 14:13 in the obsolete sense of "guilty."

FAUNA. *See* ZOOLOGY.

FAVOR; FAVORABLE; FAVORABLY; FAVORITE [Heb. *ḥēn*, *ḥānan*, *teḥinnâ*, *rāṣâ*, *rāṣôn*, *ṭôḇ*, *ṭôḇâ*–'good,' *nō'am* (Ps. 90:17), *šālôm*–'peace' (Gen. 41:16), *ḥāpēṣ* (2 S. 20:11), *dereḵ*–'way' (Jer. 3:13), *diššēn*–'find (burnt-offering) fat' (Ps. 20:3 [MT 4])]; AV also GRACE, ACCEPT(ABLE), GOOD, GOOD WILL, BEAUTY, PEACE, WAYS, etc.; NEB also "delightful things," WELFARE, "are for" (2 S. 20:11), "promiscuous traffic" (Jer. 3:13), GRACIOUS, KINDNESS, PITY, ESTEEM, SUCCESS, WILL, etc.; [Gk. *cháris*, *charitóō* (Lk. 1:28), *peíthō* (Gal. 1:10), *prókima* (1 Tim. 5:21), *hessóomai* (2 Cor. 12:13)]; AV also GRACE, PERSUADE, PREFER, "be inferior" (2 Cor. 12:13); NEB also "canvass . . . for support" (Gal. 1:10), PRE-JUDGE, "be treated worse" (2 Cor. 12:13), etc. The term also occurs in such OT and NT phrases as "find favor in the sight of" (Heb. *māṣā' ḥēn be'ênê*, occurring frequently), "find favor" (*nāśā' ḥēn be'ênê*, Est. 2:15), "win favor" (*nāśā' ḥeseḏ lipnê*, Est. 2:9), "give favor" (*nāṯan ḥēn*), "grant [show] favor" (*nāśā' penê*–lit. "lift up the face of"), "entreat the favor of" (*ḥillâ penê*–lit. "make the face pleasant"), "look with favor on" (*'ênê be*–lit. "eyes on," Ps. 101:6), "in favor of" (Gk. *hypér*, 1 Cor. 4:6), "find favor" (*heurískō chárin*), "give favor" (*dídōmi chárin*, Acts 7:10), "do a favor" (*chárin katathésthai*, Acts 24:27; 25:9), etc.

"Favor" characterizes strong personal relationships. It is any free act of kindness toward another person. "To find favor" means to receive the attention and respect of another. Lot was granted deliverance from Sodom, for the messengers favored him (Gen. 19:15-23). Jacob sent all kinds of gifts to appease his brother and gain his favor (32:5). Joseph was successful, became greatly favored by his master, and was elevated to overseer of the household (39:4). These three examples indicate a type of relationship in which the party favored receives great benefits. Therefore, in making a request one entreats the favor of the other person (50:4f.).

To behold the FACE of someone or to be granted an audience, especially with regard to an important leader, is to receive his favor. Consequently, many phrases translated with "favor" have the word "face" as a component. "To lift up the face" is translated "to win the favor of" or "accept." "To make the face of one pleasant" is to entreat that person so that his hostility is turned to kindness. The same is true in prayer when the supplicants endeavor to gain the face or favor of God; i.e., they desire to be heard, and God's hearing His people implies that He will act on their behalf.

Thus favor is ultimately a divine quality, given to human beings as long as they live (Ps. 84:11 [MT 12]); by it people are firmly established (Ps. 30:5, 7 [MT 6, 8]). God grants His favor to help a person endure difficult circumstances (Gen. 39:21). It protects the righteous like a shield (Ps. 5:12 [MT 13]). Whoever has the favor of the Lord has great power in prayer. Moses had the favor of the Lord so he was able to intercede for the people (Ex. 32:7-14; 33:12-23). Finally, when God acts openly and dramatically for the salvation of humanity, the time is called "a time of favor" (Isa. 49:8; cf. 61:2).

God can also cause an enemy to be favorably disposed to His people, as the citizens of Egypt were to the Israelites to the extent that they provided them with all kinds of gifts at the time of the Exodus (Ex. 3:21f.; 11:2f.).

On "Favour and Union" (Zec. 11:7, 10, NEB) *see* GRACE AND UNION.

See also GRACE; MERCY. J. E. HARTLEY

FAWN. *See* DEER.

FAWNING, COME [Heb. *kāḥaš*] (Dt. 33:29); AV "be found liars"; NEB "come cringing." Heb. *kāḥaš*, properly "lie, deceive," here probably means "insincerely (or unwillingly) show homage."

FEAR

I. Introduction.–This article concentrates on the relationship between God and fear. This relationship may be viewed from three perspectives. Though these three points of view are interrelated and unavoidably overlap, it is helpful to treat them separately in order to delineate as fully as possible the nuances of each one. It must be stressed that the classification given below is suggestive, not absolute, and many texts listed under one category might well be included under another.

II. OT.–*A. Terms.* Although the root *yr'* is by far the most common Hebrew root related to "fear," other roots occur often enough to warrant consideration and more specifically elucidate the concept. The following is a list of these roots with their primary and/or significant (RSV) translations.

'ym, "terror, dread"
bhl, "dismay, terror"
bʿt, "terror"
gwr, "fear"
ḥyl, "anguish, trembling"
ḥrd, "trembling, fear"
ḥtt, "dismay, terror, ruin"
yr', "fear"
ʿrṣ, "ruthless, dread, terror"
pḥd, "dread, fear"
plṣ, "horror"
rgz, "tremble"
rʿd, "tremble"
rʿš, "quake, shake"

(For a complete list of related terms and a thorough treatment of this subject, see Becker.)

From this list it is apparent that the notion of fear ranges from terror, which may be evidenced by shaking or trembling, to awe or reverence, which induces love or worship rather than terror. That these extremes are not contradictory is suggested not only by instances of the same Hebrew word being translated by both extremes (e.g., niphal of *ḥāṯaṯ,* "stand in awe," Mal. 2:5, and "be terror-stricken," Isa. 30:31), but also by synonymous parallelism of two (or more) different Hebrew roots (e.g., Ps. 55:4f. [MT 5f.], *ḥîl,* "be in anguish," *'êmâ,* "terror," *yir'â,* "fear," *raʿaḏ,* "trembling," *pallāṣûṯ,* "horror"). Even in nonpoetic contexts the clear correlation of terms may indicate their synonymity (e.g., niphal of *ḥāṯaṯ,* "be dismayed," and *yārē',* "fear," in Dt. 1:21; Josh. 8:1; *ʿrṣ,* "be frightened," and the niphal of *ḥāṯaṯ,* "be dismayed," in Josh. 1:9—note the similarity of contexts).

B. Meaning. 1. Religion. One peculiar characteristic of the root *yr'* (and its derivatives) is that it frequently occurs as an equivalent for true religion. This characteristic is evidenced by those words or expressions with which it is associated. Most frequently this root is connected with God's ways or laws, for which several different expressions are used. Thus to fear God is to keep His commandments (Dt. 5:29; 6:2, 24; Eccl. 12:13; etc.) and His laws (Dt. 31:12f.; 28:58; cf. Jer. 44:10), obey His voice (1 S. 12:14; Hag. 1:12), walk after Him (Dt. 10:12) or in His ways (Dt. 8:6; 2 Ch. 6:31), or simply serve Him (Dt. 6:13; 10:20; Josh. 24:14). The fear of the Lord is parallel to the ordinances of the Lord in Ps. 19:9; in 86:11 the psalmist asks God to teach him His way that he may walk in His truth, and to unite his heart to fear God's name. In Dt. 10:20 the Israelites are told to fear God, serve Him, cleave to Him, and swear by His name (cf. 6:13); in 13:4 they are commanded to walk after Him, fear Him, keep His commandments, obey His voice, serve Him, and cleave to Him. It should be noted that such obedience is not a burden, but a delight (Ps. 112:1; Isa. 11:3).

The elements of loyalty (*ḥeseḏ*) and faithfulness (*'ĕmûnâ* or *'ĕmeṯ*) or belief (hiphil of *'mn*) are also associated with fearing God (Ex. 14:31; 2 Ch. 19:9; Prov. 16:6). Similarly, the fear of the Lord and the knowledge of Him are related (1 K. 8:43 par. 2 Ch. 6:33; Prov. 1:29; note the parallelism in Prov. 2:5 and 9:10; cf. also Isa. 11:2). Thus Eliphaz can charge Job with "doing away with the fear of God and hindering meditation before God" (Job 15:4; cf. Mal. 3:16), Zephaniah can parallel fearing God with accepting instruction (*mûsār*; cf. Prov. 15:33, "the fear of the Lord is instruction [*mûsār*] in wisdom"), and the Chronicler can speak of Zechariah instructing Uzziah "in the fear of God" (2 Ch. 26:5). This relation with knowledge or wisdom is most evident in that famous wisdom saying, "The fear of the Lord is the beginning of knowledge" (Prov. 1:7; with slight variation in Job 28:28; Ps. 111:10). The meaning of this saying has been debated; some (e.g., von Rad, p. 66) understand "beginning" (Heb. *rē'šîṯ*) as the starting point, i.e., the most basic level, but others (e.g., D. Kidner, *Proverbs* [*Tyndale OT Comms.,* 1964], p. 59) prefer to see it as the "first principle," i.e., an essential or chief factor.

The fear of the Lord, moreover, is connected with departing from evil (Job 1:1, 8; 2:3; 28:28; Prov. 3:7; cf. 8:13). Thus those in authority who fear God will rule justly (2 S. 23:3; 2 Ch. 19:7). To withhold kindness (*ḥeseḏ*) from a friend is to forsake the "fear of the Almighty" (Job 6:14). The fear of the Lord is contrasted to wickedness: it "prolongs life, but the years of the wicked will be short" (Prov. 10:27; cf. Eccl. 8:12f.). Thus believers should not envy sinners, but persevere in the "fear of the Lord" (Prov. 23:17; cf. 15:16).

Perhaps the most characteristic expression for religious persons is "those who fear him [God]" (*yᵉrē'āyw* or *yir'ê YHWH*). This expression occurs almost exclusively in the Psalms (elsewhere only Mal. 3:16; 4:2 [MT 3:20]) and is an indicator of the Psalms' use as cultic hymns in the temple. That the phrase is a synonym for the worshipers assembled in the temple is clear from its synonymous parallelism with various other terms for that congregation: sons of Jacob and sons of Israel (22:23 [MT 24]), great congregation (22:25), Israel and the house of Aaron (115:9-11; 118:2-4), etc. In other psalms the identification is perhaps less explicit, but equally clear. Thus it is several times tied to the covenant (the means by which God related to His people), either explicitly (Ps. 25:14; 111:5), or implicitly by mention of *ḥeseḏ* (RSV "steadfast love"), the covenant love (33:18; 103:11, 17; 147:11; on *ḥeseḏ* as covenant love, see N. Glueck, Ḥesed *in the Bible* [Eng. tr., repr. 1975]). In at least one case the cultic setting is clear from the context (66:16; cf. vv. 13-15; cf. also 34:9; 128:4f.).

Although the probable late date of most (or all) of these psalms and the undoubtedly late date of Malachi suggest that the identification of the fear of Yahweh with religion was a later development, many other texts with this identification do not admit of a late date (even if postexilic editing is allowed, it can hardly have been that extensive). According to W. Eichrodt (II, 268), this identification has in the OT a "remarkable regularity from earliest to latest times," as is clear from such passages as Gen. 20:11; Ex. 18:21; 2 K. 4:18. Thus it seems that this identification must have developed in preexilic times and been maintained along with the other senses of fear (i.e., reverence and terror). (For a general contrast of Israel and its ancient Near Eastern neighbors on this point, see Eichrodt, II, 272f., 275f.; cf. also R. Pfeiffer.)

This fear of God, this piety, has various effects, often resulting in some general good (Prov. 22:4; Eccl. 7:18; 8:12f.), social justice (2 K. 4:1; 2 Ch. 19:7 [*pāḥaḏ*, "fear"], 9; Neh. 5:15), personal longevity (Prov. 10:27; 14:27; 19:23), or family security (Prov. 14:26). It also aids instruction (Ps. 25:12; Prov. 1:7; 15:33) and prevents sin (Ex. 20:20; Prov. 16:16).

2. Reverence. The fear of God may also be understood as one important element in religion. This notion is most apparent in texts that conjoin or parallel two of the Hebrew synonyms listed above. In Ps. 33:8, e.g., "all the earth" is called upon to fear (*yr'*) the Lord, and the inhabitants of the earth to "stand in awe [*gûr*] of him" (cf. Ps. 22:3 [MT 4]; cf. also *pāḥaḏ* in Ps. 119:161). Here reverence for God is clearly in view, as it is in Mal. 2:5, where the prophet says Levi "feared" (*yr'*) God and "stood in awe" (niphal of *ḥāṯaṯ*) of Him. God is to be "held in awe [*nôrā'*, niphal part. of *yr'*] above all gods" (1 Ch. 16:25); the Israelites are to follow the law, that they may fear (*yārē'*) God's awful (*nôrā'*) name (Dt. 28:58).

The RSV uses "revere" only three times in reference to God. In Dt. 32:51 God rebukes His people for breaking faith with Him at Meribath-kadesh, for not revering Him as holy (piel of *qāḏaš*). In 1 K. 18:3, 12, Obadiah, who was over Ahab's household, is said to have revered ([*hāyâ*] *yārē'*) the Lord, as evidenced by his action of hiding God's prophets during Jezebel's purge (v. 4). (Cf. Ps. 130:4 for the relation between forgiveness and fear of God.) *See also* AWE; REVERENCE.

In many texts the fear of God is strongly linked with obedience and sometimes may be identified with it. (G. von Rad's thesis that one should interpret "'fear of God' simply as a term for obedience to the divine commands" [*Genesis* (*OTL*, rev. ed. 1972), p. 242; cf. also *OT Theology* (1965), II, 215; *Wisdom in Israel* (Eng. tr. 1972), p. 66] is an overstatement; cf., e.g., 2 Ch. 19:9; Jonah 1:9. For a more balanced view, see Brongers, pp. 161f.; Ringgren, pp. 126f.) Thus in Ps. 119:63 "all who fear thee [God]" is parallel to "those who keep thy precepts" (cf. v. 48; Dt. 5:29; 6:2, 24; 10:12; etc.). Prov. 24:21 states, "Fear the Lord and the king, and do not disobey either of them" (cf. Dt. 13:4; 1 S. 12:14; Hag. 1:12). A series of commands in Leviticus concludes with "and you shall fear your God" (19:14, 32; 25:17, 36, 43), clearly implying obedience.

As with the first sense of the fear of God, several effects may be attributed to reverence. Some of the same blessings accrue: general good (Dt. 5:29; Jer. 32:39), military victory (2 K. 17:39), political success (1 S. 12:14; Neh. 1:11), and family (Ps. 128). One of its purposes is to prevent people from turning away from God (Jer. 32:40).

3. Terror. A third aspect of "fear of God" is terror. God does inspire human beings to be in dread of him, sometimes unintentionally (in contexts of revelation or theophany, e.g., Ex. 3:6), sometimes intentionally. Thus He may rebuke the people for not fearing (*yr'*) or trembling (*ḥîl*) before Him (Jer. 5:22), and the psalmist exhorts: "Serve the Lord with fear [*yir'â*], with trembling [*r^e'āḏâ*] kiss his feet" (2:11f.). (The RSV here follows the traditional emendation, while the AV follows the MT; although the emendation seems preferable, it is not entirely satisfactory. See the comms.) Isaiah uses "terror" (Heb. *paḥaḏ*) in contexts of judgment. Three times in ch. 2 the prophet states that sinful people should hide from the "terror of the Lord" (vv. 10, 19, 21). In 24:17f. the prophet plays on the words "terror" (*paḥaḏ*), "pit" (*paḥaṯ*), and "snare" (*pāḥ*) to indicate the hopelessness of sinners on the Day of the Lord. Jeremiah may have borrowed this saying and applied it to Moab (48:43f.; cf. Lam. 3:47 for a similar play on words whose alliteration has not been lost in the RSV translation). He also states that God will bring terror on the Ammonites (49:5). (For a discussion of outward manifestations of fear, *see* HORROR; TREMBLE.)

But God also delivers His people from fear. The formula "Fear not" (or its equivalents) characterizes a great number of texts in which the objects of the fear are human enemies. The niphal of *ḥāṯaṯ*, "be dismayed," is frequently paired with *yr'* in contexts of impending battle, and usually God is exhorting His people not to fear, because He is with them (e.g., Dt. 1:21; 31:8; Josh. 8:1; 10:25; 2 Ch. 20:15, 17; 32:7; Jer. 30:10; 46:27; Ezk. 2:6; 3:9). *Yr'* also parallels *'āraṣ*, "be in dread," in similar contexts (Dt. 1:29; 31:6; cf. 7:21, where the Israelites are told not to be in dread of the Canaanites because God is great and terrible [*nôrā'*, niphal part. of *yr'*], and He is with the Israelites). Dt. 20:3 adds a third element: the Israelites need not fear, tremble (*ḥāpaz*), or be in dread. The root *ḥrd* is used several times when God promises peace for His people — no one shall make them afraid (Lev. 26:6; Jer. 30:10; 46:27; Ezk. 34:28; 39:26; Mic. 4:4; Zeph. 3:13).

To the believers this fear of God may become a problem. Since they (presumably) have been delivered by God from judgment, they should not have to experience the dread and terror that are usually associated with divine judgment. One solution to this problem is to regard this terror as a chastisement rather than a judgment (*see* EVIL III).

Job is the best example of one who has a great reverence for God (even God says so, 1:8; 2:3) but also an almost overwhelming terror of Him. (It is no solution to the problem to state that the prologue may have been part of an earlier and shorter story and the dialogues added later, and therefore the two different analyses of Job's relationship to God need not be reconciled. Whoever finally put the book together in its present form could not have been unaware of the problem, and must have thought of this tension as contradictory. It is the canonical form of the book that is important.) Job associated God with the thing that he feared (*paḥaḏ pāḥaḏ*) and dreaded (*yāgar*, 3:25). In 6:4 he claimed that the "terrors [*b^e'ûṯ*] of God" were arrayed against him. He became afraid (*yāgar*) of all his suffering, for which he held God responsible (9:28), and he appealed for the removal of the dread (*'êmâ*) of God that terrified (*bā'aṯ*) him (9:34; repeated in 13:21). Later he confessed that he was terrified (*bāhal*) at God's presence and in dread (*pāḥaḏ*) when he considered Him (23:15f.).

One final expression warrants examination here. "Fear" and "trembling" are twice used together with the sense of reverence, although their obvious meaning is the common one (cf. Ex. 20:18; Dt. 20:3; Jgs. 7:3; etc.). In Jer. 33:9 the nations will "fear and tremble" (*pāḥaḏ w^erāgaz*) at God's work in Zion; reverence seems to be the more likely connotation here. Reverence also seems clearly in view when Darius decrees that everyone "tremble and fear" (Aram. *zw'* and *dḥl*) before the God of Daniel (Dnl. 6:26 [MT 27]; cf. also Ps. 2:11; 119:120). It should also be noted here that the participle *ḥārēḏ*, "trembling," is used four times to describe the (pious) response to God's word (Ezr. 9:4; 10:3; Isa. 66:2, 5 — if scholars are correct in assigning this part of Isaiah to postexilic times, this expression may be a later, alternative expression for "fear of the Lord").

C. Fear of Isaac (Heb. *paḥaḏ yiṣḥāq*). The name or epithet of the deity by whom Jacob swore an oath as part of his covenant with Laban (Gen. 31:42; in v. 53 it is slightly altered to the "Fear of his father Isaac"). The name has been interpreted in three basic ways. Some scholars (cited in A. Alt, p. 33 n. 63) thought it meant the fear that proceeded from the deity Isaac. In rejecting this proposal, Alt successfully argued for what has become the most widely accepted analysis of this name — the name of a deity (perhaps the deity's main or most impressive characteristic) who terrified Isaac and whom Isaac therefore worshiped. This analysis could have as its background Isaac's experience in Gen. 22 (for an interesting interpretation of Gen. 22, see Kierkegaard). Alt further pointed out (pp. 33f.) that on his analysis the "Fear of Isaac" would parallel in form "God of Abraham" and "Mighty One of Jacob," the deities of the other patriarchs (cf. Gen. 49:24 for "Mighty One of Jacob").

On the basis of several Semitic cognates W. F. Albright proposed a new sense for *paḥaḏ* — "kinsman" (*FSAC*, pp. 248f., esp. n. 71). Though his proposal was emotionally more palatable than "fear" and was widely accepted, D. Hillers later offered a thorough criticism of Albright's philological arguments, and Albright's proposal should now be rejected.

Thus Alt's explanation of the basic meaning of *paḥaḏ yiṣḥāq* as "Fear of Isaac" seems preferable; his analysis need not be accepted in all its details, however. The main criticism of it is that it supposes that the "Fear of Isaac" was a deity distinct from the "God of Abraham," a distinction bound up in large part with the documentary hypothesis (cf. pp. 22f., 34, esp. n. 66, 60f., 65-70). (On the weaknesses of the documentary hypothesis, *see* CRITICISM II.D.) The plain sense of Gen. 31:42 is that the "God of my father," the "God of Abraham," and the "Fear of Isaac" are all identical; these were simply different names or titles of the one God. Jacob's use of this title in v. 52, following (the pagan) Laban's reference to the "God of Abraham" and the "God of Nahor," may have been intended to avoid identifying too closely his God with Laban's.

D. Conclusion. The role of fear in the OT must not be isolated from other major elements in OT religion, especially when the "fear of the Lord" is seen as the OT expression for religion. Some references to faith, obedience, and the covenant were pointed out above (cf. Eichrodt, II, 309f., for further discussion of fear and faith).

Love (Heb. *'hb*) is another element that should not be ignored. Especially in Deuteronomy the love and fear of God are closely related (so closely that Eichrodt, II, 299, states, *"The requirement of love is thus nothing other than a new clarification and a deeper understanding of the old commandment to fear God"*). Not only are they explicitly linked (10:12f.; cf. 13:3f.), but they are also implicitly related through texts that delineate each of them by similar or identical expressions. Thus love is associated with walking in God's ways and keeping His commandments (e.g., 11:22; 19:9; 30:16) and obeying His voice (30:20). Blessing is also associated with love (7:13). The response of love, therefore, may be seen as a primary characteristic of that OT piety called the "fear of the Lord" (cf. further B. J. Bamberger, *HUCA*, 6 [1929], 39-53; Becker, pp. 60-65; V. H. Kooy, "The Fear and Love of God in Deuteronomy," in J. I. Cook, ed., *Grace Upon Grace* [1975], pp. 106-116).

Both divine holiness and human sinfulness are also related to the fear of God. Obviously God's holiness requires the judgment of human sin, and people's awareness of this requirement often causes them to be in dread of Him (e.g., Gen. 3:10; Dt. 9:19; Ps. 76:8 [MT 9]). But the grace that characterizes God (cf. the formula in Ex. 34:6, repeated in Neh. 9:17; Ps. 103:8; 145:8; Jonah 4:2) and His forgiveness can change that dread into reverence (Ps. 130:4), so that His terrible (*nôrā' < yr'*) name may be praised (Ps. 99:3; 111:9; cf. Becker, pp. 42-46).

III. Intertestamental Period.–*A. Apocrypha and Pseudepigrapha.* Most of these references occur in Sirach, which has several extended passages on the topic. Fear is used only in the sense of religion, however (but cf. von Rad, *Wisdom*, pp. 242-45). Sirach uses exalted language in delineating this concept: it is glory (cf. 40:27), it causes gladness, and gives long life (vv. 11-13). Verses 14-20 relate the fear of the Lord to wisdom: "To fear the Lord is the beginning of wisdom," i.e., its "foundation" (cf. 19:20, where "All wisdom is the fear of the Lord"; and 21:11, where "wisdom is the fulfilment of the fear of the Lord"); it is wisdom's full measure, giving satisfaction (cf. 40:26); it is wisdom's crown, giving peace and health; finally, it is the root of wisdom and gives long life. (Some manuscripts add v. 21, "The fear of the Lord drives away sins; and where it abides, it will turn away all anger.") Thus the person who fears the Lord is greater than the nobleman, the judge, and the ruler (10:24); and the "God-fearing man who lacks intelligence" is better than "the highly prudent man who transgresses the law" (19:24).

Outside of Sirach "fear" occurs less frequently, e.g., in the Letter of Aristeas fear is related to keeping God's law (159, 189); in T.Benj. 3:3f. fear denotes both religion and reverence. For further discussion of these and other texts, see *TDNT*, IX, 204-207.

B. Qumrân. The DSS mention the fear of God several times, though as K. Romaniuk (p. 29) points out, this element is not as dominant in the DSS as it is in the OT. Some of the same Hebrew terms are used (e.g., forms of *yr'*, *pḥd*) in ways similar to OT usage. Thus the members of the community are called *yr'y 'l* ("those who fear God," 1QH 12:3; 1QSb 1:1; CD 10:2; 20:19f.). The only occurrence of *yr't 'l* (1QSb 5:25) corresponds to its use in Isa. 11:2f., as one would expect, since the Qumrân text is dependent on the OT passage.

Pāḥēḏ occurs once for "reverence" (of the Torah) (1QS 4:2); elsewhere *pḥd* expresses its more basic meaning of dread, e.g., which a believer feels when he has erred and he knows God's judgment or chastisement is imminent (1QH 10:34). *Pḥd* is also coupled with *'ymh* several times; in 1QS 1:17 the members of the community must be faithful regardless of the terror or dread that the enemy (Belial) might cause them to feel (cf. also 10:15).

Several other roots express this dread. God is described as "terrible" (*nôrā'*, 1QM 10:1; 12:7). Twice several terms are conjoined in exhortations not to fear (1QM 10:3f.; *yr', yrk, ḥpz, 'rṣ*; 15:8: *yr', ḥtt, 'rṣ*); elsewhere only one term occurs (*yr'* in 1QM 17:4; *ḥtt* in 1QH 2:35; 7:8).

Both Romaniuk and DeVries assert ties between the DSS and the Bible (OT and NT). Romaniuk links closely the Qumrân concept of the fear of God (which he claims is very primitive compared to that of the NT) with that of the OT. But DeVries calls it "a deterioration and a distortion" (p. 237) that reflects only later, more legalistic OT developments (except for 1QH 4:29-37, which "while coming short of expressing the fulness of New Testament salvation, surely stands upon its very threshold" [p. 236]; note the use in v. 33 of *r'd*, "trembling," and *rtt*, "shivering," to describe the believer's reaction to his sin). DeVries prefers to see the NT as directly related to the earlier and purer classical Yahwism.

IV. NT.–*A. Terms.* Though the relation between God

and fear is far less frequently treated in the NT than in the OT, it is by no means ignored and is quite similar to the OT conceptualizations. Fewer terms are involved, the dominating ones being *phobéō* and its cognate noun *phóbos*; these generally denote terror (cf. Eng. phobia).

B. Meaning. 1. Religion. In the Magnificat, which is composed of various OT phrases, Mary states, "His mercy is on those who fear him" (Lk. 1:50; cf. Ps. 103:13, 17). Acts 9:31 states that the church was built up and multiplied by "walking in the fear of the Lord and in the comfort of the Holy Spirit." In Col. 3:22f. Paul links fearing the Lord with obeying and serving one's earthly master; one should serve him "as serving the Lord." Peter commands: "Love the brotherhood. Fear God" (1 Pet. 2:17; cf. Lk. 18:2, 4 for a contrasting divine-human correlation). In Rev. 11:18 prophets, saints, and those who fear God are rewarded. In 14:6f. an angel proclaims the "eternal gospel": "Fear God and give him glory . . . and worship him" (cf. 15:4). In 19:5 God's servants are identified with those who fear him.

Another expression connoting this idea is "the ones who fear God," i.e., the God-fearers. These were the gentile adherents to the synagogue. Their status is most clearly seen in Acts 13:16, where Paul addresses the synagogue: "Men of Israel, and you that fear God" (cf. also v. 26). Thus Cornelius was "a devout man who feared God" (Acts 10:2; cf. v. 22), and Peter, when addressing Cornelius and his guests, states, "Anyone who fears him [God] and does what is right is acceptable to him" (10:35).

2. Reverence. Jesus' deeds often inspired awe or reverence (e.g., Mt. 17:6; Lk. 5:26). Paul warned the Roman Christians not to be proud but to stand in awe (Rom. 11:20). Reverence for Christ should cause believers to be subject to one another (Eph. 5:21). He. 5:7 states that Jesus' prayers were answered because of His "godly fear" (*eulábeia*). In 12:28 the author exhorts his readers to "offer to God acceptable worship, with reverence [*eulábeia*] and awe [*déos*]" (but note the element of terror that immediately follows — "for our God is a consuming fire").

Peter exhorts his readers not to fear their persecutors, but to reverence (*hagiázō*) Christ as Lord and defend the faith with "gentleness and reverence" (1 Pet. 3:14-16). He also encourages wives with non-Christian husbands to win them over by "reverent and chaste behavior" (3:2; cf. Tit. 2:3, where Paul instructs Titus to ask the older woman to "be reverent [*hieroprepḗs*] in behavior").

3. Terror. Like the OT, the NT mentions that people stand in dread of God's actions toward them. At times this dread is produced unintentionally by God (e.g., Mt. 17:7; 28:10; Lk. 5:10), though often He causes it intentionally as a sign of His judgment on sin (e.g., Lk. 12:5; Acts 5:5, 11; 1 Tim. 5:20). Perhaps the most famous statement relating terror and God is He. 10:31: "It is a fearful thing to fall into the hands of the living God." Here the context is clearly one of judgment (cf. vv. 27, 30).

But God encourages His followers not to fear their enemies, for He will deliver them either in this world or in the world to come. Thus in Mt. 10:26 Jesus exhorts His listeners to "have no fear" of those who might persecute them, for the persecutors can kill only the body and not the soul (v. 28; cf. v. 31). God used a vision to encourage Paul not to be afraid to speak the gospel, for He was with him (Acts 18:9f.). God later used an angel to reassure Paul that he would not die, even though the situation looked hopeless (27:24). No doubt these experiences enabled Paul to exhort the Philippians not to be frightened (Gk. *ptýrō*) by their opponents, for God would judge the opponents but save the believers (Phil. 1:28).

The idea that believers need not fear receives its most radical expression in 1 John. This Epistle, with its great emphasis on love and its fatherly tone, reassures its readers that on the day of judgment they need not fear, because fear has to do with punishment, and God's perfect love for them has removed that threat (4:17f.; cf. I. H. Marshall, *Epistles of John* [*NICNT,* 1978], pp. 222-25).

The expression "fear and trembling" (Gk. *phóbos kaí trómos*) may also be considered here. It occurs four times (1 Cor. 2:3; 2 Cor. 7:15; Eph. 6:5; Phil. 2:12). In 1 Cor. 2:3 it may denote only timidity (cf. "weakness"), but the context does allow a more religious connotation (cf. vv. 2, 4), i.e., that Paul did not live and preach by human ability or power but by his faith. Respect may be the meaning in 2 Cor. 7:15 — the Corinthians received Timothy with respect and obeyed him. But "fear and trembling" here may also be understood in reference to God; Timothy was impressed by their obedience and piety, which enabled them to receive him so graciously. In Eph. 6:5 obedience is again linked to "fear and trembling," here in regard to the slave-master relationship. While it is possible to see this as a reference to fearing punishment from the master, it may also be seen as a reference to piety. The service that slaves render to their masters should be done "as to Christ"; they should consider themselves "slaves of Christ" (RSV mg., v. 6) who do "the will of God from the heart." The enigmatic Phil. 2:12f. also links obedience with "fear and trembling." By itself v. 12 could be understood as an exhortation for the believers to live carefully, doing what is right in order to avoid judgment. But when it is taken with v. 13, such an interpretation seems unlikely. Instead, Paul seems to be exhorting his readers to continue to obey him, even though he is absent, and to continue to manifest the saving work of Christ in their lives, even though Paul is not there to help them — God is still with them, and He is the one who does the work.

V. Conclusion.–God and fear were thus integrally related throughout biblical times. In its more positive sense "the fear of God" could be the essence of biblical religion, or at least one aspect of it, reverence. God instilled this fear in people, who at the same time were both attracted and terrified by His awesomeness (Otto's *mysterium fascinans* and *tremendum*). Only those who had faith could perceive both elements. The unfaithful could only tremble at the coming judgment.

Bibliography.–A. Alt, "The God of the Fathers," in *Essays in OT History and Religion* (Eng. tr. 1966), pp. 1-100; J. Becker, *Gottesfurcht im AT* (1965); H. A. Brongers, "La Crainte du Seigneur," *Oudtestamentische Studiën,* 5 (1948), 151-173; S. J. DeVries, *RQ,* 5 (1965), 233-37; W. Eichrodt, *Theology of the OT* (2 vols., Eng. tr. 1961, 1967), esp. II, ch. 21; D. Hillers, *JBL,* 91 (1972), 90-92; *ILC,* III-IV (2nd ed. 1959; repr. 1963), 623-27; P. Joüon, *Bibl.,* 6 (1925), 174-79; S. Kierkegaard, *Fear and Trembling* (Eng. tr. 1954); G. F. Moore, *Judaism* (3 vols., 1927-1930); J. Murray, *Principles of Conduct* (1957), esp. ch. 10; R. Otto, *Idea of the Holy* (Eng. tr., 2nd ed. 1950); R. Pfeiffer, *IEJ,* 5 (1955), 41-48; H. Ringgren, *Israelite Religion* (Eng. tr. 1966); K. Romaniuk, *RQ,* 4 (1963), 29-38; J. C. Rylaarsdam, *Revelation in Jewish Wisdom Literature* (1946); *TDNT,* IX, *s.v.* φοβέω κτλ. (Balz, Wanke); *THAT,* I, *s.v.* ירא (H.-P. Stähli); G. von Rad, *Wisdom in Israel* (Eng. tr. 1972).

G. A. LEE

FEAR AND TREMBLE. *See* FEAR II.B.3; IV.B.3.

FEASTS [Heb. *môʿēḏ*–'an appointed matter,' either a place, as the tabernacle (Ex. 30:30), or a time, as the Hebrew feasts (= Heb. *miqrāʾ*–'what is called,' a convocation, Lev. 23:2), *ḥag*–'dancing, procession,' a pilgrimage feast; Gk. *heortḗ*–'feast'].

I. Nature of the Hebrew Feasts.–The sacred seasons of Israel stem directly from divine revelation and were designed to illustrate significant aspects of the eternal redemption that God had already ordained for His own under the OT. The Hebrew calendar of convocations is therefore not to be explained on the basis of natural phenomena, such as the phases of the moon or the Palestinian agricultural cycle, as proposed by liberal theology (cf. Eichrodt, I, 120-23). Neither may it be attributed to pre-Mosaic custom, whether Canaanite or nomadic (cf. Pfeiffer, p. 40). Israel's feasts served rather as divinely revealed expressions of the moral obligations of His people, as memorials of God's saving acts in the past, as sacraments of His sanctifying power in the present, and as types of His anticipated victory over sin in the forthcoming first and second advents of Jesus Christ. Parallels to the sacred calendars of the surrounding pagans may then be accounted for by a divine grace that was willing to grant to Israel certain forms that were already more or less familiar. For their secondary but still real purpose was that of expressing Israel's gratitude for God's providential sustaining of life in general throughout the year.

The sacred feasts of Israel were communal in nature, whether of the kind claimed by Moses for observance in the desert prior to the Exodus (Ex. 5:1), or those celebrated when the Israelites were in sedentary occupation of the land (Dt. 16:14; 1 S. 1:3). Even the way in which the Israelites worshiped the golden calf in the wilderness was described as a "feast" (Ex. 32:5-19) because of the religious associations involved, pagan though they were.

Feasts appear to have been times of rejoicing and excitement, with ceremonial dancing (Jgs. 21:21), songs (Isa. 30:29) and noisy processions going on their way to the temple (Ps. 42:4 [MT 5]). Where Canaanite traditions were in evidence on such occasions, drunkenness and other undesirable forms of behavior would be inevitable accompaniments to festal celebrations (cf. 1 S. 1:13f.; Am. 2:8).

In addition to communal feasts there were also times of private rejoicing in which a small social unit such as a family would be involved. These occasions included weddings (Gen. 29:22), weaning feasts, when a child began to eat solid food (Gen. 21:8), the visit of a guest (Gen. 19:13), or the celebration of someone's birthday (Gen. 40:20). Families recognized the beginning of the sheepshearing activities by holding a feast and sending a token offering of wool to the Lord's house (Dt. 18:4; 1 S. 25:4-11; etc.). The children of Job apparently entertained each other regularly in turn on a purely social basis (Job 1:4f.), and this fact indicates that it was not necessary for a specific occasion to arise for a feast to be enjoyed. Life in the ancient Near East was arduous for the great majority of people, and a feast was a welcome diversion from the rigors of workaday living.

II. Mosaic Festivals.–*A. The Sabbath and Its Extensions.* In addition to daily sacrifices, morning and evening (Ex. 29:38-42), God revealed through Moses a set of seasonal *mô‘ᵃḏîm,* "set feasts" (Lev. 23:2, RV; see esp. Ex. 23:10-17; Lev. 23 and 25; Nu. 28–29; Dt. 16). First in importance stood the weekly sabbath (Lev. 23:3), which originated in God's rest on the seventh day of creation and is reflected in certain Babylonian parallels, but which was reinstituted among the Hebrews by Moses (Neh. 9:14), though prior to Sinai (Ex. 16:23-26). Of similar character were the seven "convocation" sabbaths at the five annual feasts, Passover and Tabernacles having two each (Lev. 23:7f., 35f.); note the title of the last, *‘ᵃṣereṯ,* "restraint [of work]" (v. 36; cf. Jn. 7:37). A day of rest observed monthly was the New Moon (Nu. 10:10; 28:11-15). By analogy to the sabbath, moreover, every seventh year constituted a Sabbatical Year (Ex. 23:11; Lev. 25:1-7;

Pages from the Passover Haggadah (Moravia, A.D. 1732), which relates the Jewish ritual of the feast (Jewish Theological Seminary Library)

Title page of Ecclesiastes from a prayerbook (Italy, A.D. 1492). Ecclesiastes is traditionally read in the synagogue during the Feast of Sukkoth (Booths) (Jewish Theological Seminary Library)

Title page of the Ethics of the Fathers (a mishnaic tractate also called *Pirke Aboth*) from a prayerbook (Italy, A.D. 1452). Since the Ethics of the Fathers begins with the events at Mt. Sinai, it is customarily read during the seven weeks between Passover and Pentecost (Feast of Weeks). The latter feast celebrates the giving of the Torah (Jewish Theological Seminary Library)

Dt. 15:1); and every cycle of seven Sabbatical years terminated with a Jubilee Year (Lev. 25:8-18).

B. The Five Annual Feasts. The *mô'ᵃḏîm* in a stricter sense consisted of Moses' five annual feasts (Lev. 23:4). The three *ḥaggîm,* or pilgrimage festivals, were so designated because on them the Israelites gathered at Jerusalem to give joyful thanks to their God (Dt. 16:16). They were of agricultural significance as well as commemorative of national events. Thus the Passover, followed by the seven days of unleavened bread, is connected with the barley harvest (Ex. 12:6; Lev. 23:5-8; Nu. 28:16-25; Dt. 16:1-8); Pentecost, the Feast of Weeks, celebrates the wheat harvest (Ex. 34:26; Lev. 23:10-14; Nu. 28:26-31); and Tabernacles (Booths) is at the same time the Feast of Ingathering, the general harvest festival (Ex. 23:16; Lev. 23:33-36; Dt. 16:13-15). The Passover was described specifically as a "feast" only in Ex. 34:25, although its association with the observance of the Feast of Unleavened Bread left no doubt as to its festival character (*see* PASSOVER). The one-day Feast of Pentecost was celebrated on the fiftieth day after the Passover sabbath (Ex. 23:16; 34:22; Lev. 23:15-21; Nu. 28:26-31; Dt. 16:9-12). The Feast of Tabernacles occurred five days following the Day of Atonement, and lasted for a week. It was a time of general rejoicing (Lev. 23:33-43) that assumed a special character in the time of Ezra (Neh. 8:13-18), and continued to be observed in the time of Jesus. (*See* TABERNACLES, FEAST OF; *see also* PENTECOST, FEAST OF; APPOINTED FEAST.)

Trumpets (Lev. 23:23-25; Nu. 29:1-6) and the Day of Atonement (Lev. 16; 23:26-32; Nu. 29:7-11) may have marked the turning of the year according to the older calendar (cf. Ex. 12:2; 23:16) but found their primary significance in the inner life of the nation and the individual. The latter celebration was Israel's supreme type of the atoning work of Christ (He. 2:14f.; 6:19; 7:27; 9:24; 13:12) for those who would turn to God in sincere repentance, "afflicting their souls" (Lev. 16:29-31, AV) through prayer, sackcloth, fasting, etc. (Fasting, however, is never specifically legislated in Scripture, though this phrase came later to be so understood; cf. Ps. 35:15; Isa. 58:3-6; *see* FAST.) On each of the feasts special sacrifices prescribed for the occasion were offered (Nu. 28–29); trumpets were blown while the burnt offerings and peace offerings were being presented (10:10).

III. Exilic Fasts and Feasting.–A. Zechariah. In the exilic situation important historical events were made the basis for new observances. When the first temple was destroyed and the people were carried into captivity, "the sacrifice of the body and one's own fat and blood" came to be substituted for animal sacrifices (T.B. *Berakoth* 17a). Four new fasts were introduced: that of the fourth month commemorated the Babylonian breach of Jerusalem's walls (Zec. 8:19; Mish. *Taanith* iv.6), the fifth month recalled the burning of the temple (Zec. 7:3, 5; 8:19), the seventh marked the murder of Gedaliah the governor (Zec. 7:5; 8:19; *Seder Olam Rabbah* 26), and the tenth observed the beginning of the Babylonian siege (Zec. 8:19).

B. Esther. The only new observance that is known to have been enjoined by divine inspiration is the Feast of

PURIM (Est. 3:7; 9:24-32; 2 Macc. 15:36). Out of the total list of Israel's God-given festivals, some are noted in the NT as still celebrated by early Jewish Christians (cf. Acts 20:16); but the sabbath and the Passover have now become, respectively, the Lord's Day and the Lord's Supper, and have been explicitly continued with moral, sacramental, and typological force (He. 4:9; Acts 20:7; Mt. 26:26-28). Otherwise, however, the Hebrew feasts, including the seventh day of the week for the observance of sabbath, have been fulfilled in Christ and have been abrogated for Christians as far as their present observance is concerned (Gal. 4:10f.; Col. 2:16f.). But while the precise forms and times no longer possess relevance, the moral principles that lay behind the feasts — of gratitude toward God, of care for the poor, of submission to His providence, and of joy in His service — retain permanent validity (cf. Payne, Appendix E).

IV. Intertestamental Observances.–A. Added Days. During intertestamental times, Judaism incorporated two additional services, the Feast of Dedication, or "Lights" (1 Macc. 4:52-59; Jn. 10:22; Mish. *Taanith* ii.10; *Moed Katan* iii.9; Josephus *Ant.* xii.7; *CAp* ii.39) and the Fast of Esther (Est. 4:16f.; 9:31), which have been preserved by Jewish tradition to this day. Other fasts and feasts no doubt were instituted on similar occasions and received a local temporary observance, e.g., the Feast of Acra (1 Macc. 13:50-52; cf. 1:33) to celebrate the recapture of Acra ("the citadel") on 23 Iyar, 141 B.C., and the Feast of Nicanor in celebration of the victory over Nicanor on 13 Adar, 160 B.C. (1 Macc. 7:49).

Several other festivals are mentioned in the Talmud and other postbiblical writings that may have been of even greater antiquity. The Feast of Woodcarrying (Midsummer Day; Neh. 10:34; Josephus *BJ* ii.7.6; Mish. *Taanith*

Title page of the book of Esther (Cologne, A.D. 1843). Esther is traditionally read at the Feast of Purim (Jewish Theological Seminary Library)

The order of the lighting of the Hanukkah candles, from a prayer-book (Pforzheim, A.D. 1723) (Jewish Theological Seminary Library)

iv.8a), for example, is referred to as the greatest day of rejoicing of the Hebrews, ranking with Atonement Day. It was principally a picnic day to which a religious touch was given by making it the woodgatherers' festival for the temple. A New Year for trees is mentioned in the Mishnah (*Rosh ha-Shanah* i.1). The pious, according both to the Jewish tradition and the NT, observed many private or semipublic fasts, such as Mondays, Thursdays, and the Mondays after Nisan and Tishri (the festival months: Lk. 18:12; Mt. 9:14; 6:16; Mk. 2:18; Lk. 5:33; Acts 10:30; T.B. *Megillah* 31a; *Taanith* 12a; T.P. *Baba Kamma* viii.2). The day before Passover was a fast day for the firstborn (*Sopherim* xxi.3).

B. Added Meanings. In several instances the rabbis proceeded to connect the dates of the feasts and fasts with national events, other than those for which the days were primarily instituted. Pentecost was called *z^{e}man mattan tôrâ,* the "date of the giving of the law"; and this religious side has so completely overshadowed the agricultural that among modern Jews Pentecost has become "confirmation day." On the day of the fast of the fourth month it was held that the Israelites made the golden calf and Moses broke the tables of the law. On that of the fifth month, not simply was the first temple destroyed by Nebuchadrezzar, but also the second temple by Titus. In addition it is said that on this day Yahweh decreed that those who left Egypt should not enter the land of promise, and the day is also the anniversary of the capture of the city of Bether by the emperor Hadrian.

V. NT Feasts.–In NT times the sabbath was observed regularly, as was the Feast of the Passover and Unleavened Bread (Mt. 26:17; Mk. 14:1; Lk. 22:1; Jn. 7:2). After Jesus entered on His public ministry He may have participated in as many as four Passover celebrations (Jn. 4:45; 5:1; 6:4; 12:1). According to the custom of the day, Christ ate the Passover privately with His disciples. After the meal He initiated the Lord's Supper, a communion in which He gave sacramental significance to the bread and wine by associating them symbolically with His death on Calvary. This event also occurred during the Passover season (Jn. 13:1), and it may be that Christ was actually dying on the cross as the Passover lamb was being slain. Paul regarded Christ as the Passover lamb (1 Cor. 5:7) whose atoning death brought redemption and salvation to mankind (*see* PASSOVER).

The Feast of Tabernacles continued with unabated popularity in Christ's time, and the esteem in which it was held was noted also by Josephus *Ant.* viii.4.1). The feast acquired ceremonial accretions in the postexilic period, one of which involved a procession to the pool of Siloam and the drawing of a libation of water. Since Jesus attended this feast (Jn. 7:2-14) it is possible that His teaching about living water (vv. 37-39) was prompted by this particular ceremony.

The Feast of Dedication, mentioned only in the NT in Jn. 10:22, was otherwise known as the Feast of Hanukkah, described by Josephus as the Festival of Lights (*BJ* xii.7.7). It was a winter feast that lasted eight days, and commemorated Judas Maccabeus' discovery in 167 B.C. of a small container of oil that lasted surprisingly for eight days (cf. 1 Macc. 4:53-59; 2 Macc. 10:3; *Ant.* xii.7.6). In NT times it was observed, like Tabernacles, by means of feasting, singing, and processions with palms and tree branches. The Feast of Pentecost was the occasion when the Holy Spirit was poured out upon the disciples as they were assembled in Jerusalem (Acts 2:1-4).

Other feasts celebrated in NT times included the *agápē* or "love feast," when Christians met in fellowship and provided for the needs of the poor. It is not always easy to distinguish between the *agápē* and the Lord's Supper in the records of primitive Christian worship (cf. Acts 2:42, 46; 6:1f.; 1 Cor. 11:20-34). These occasions were open to certain abuses (cf. Jude 12), which probably included inebriation and false teaching. Paul permitted the Corinthian Christians to attend feasts held by unbelievers, but instructed them to ask no questions about the food for conscience's sake (1 Cor. 10:27). Christ sometimes accepted invitations to feasts (Lk. 5:29; Jn. 2:8), and occasionally used the imagery of a banquet or festival in His teaching (Mt. 22:2-14; Lk. 14:16-24, etc.).

In postbiblical times the Jews outside of Palestine doubled each of the following days: the opening and closing day of Passover, Tabernacles, and Pentecost, because of the *ṣāpēq,* or doubt as to the proper day to be observed, growing out of the delays in the transmission of the official decree of the Sanhedrin in each season. Differences in hours of sunrise and sunset between Palestine and other countries may have had something to do at least with the perpetuation of the custom. New Year's Day seems to have been doubled from time immemorial, the forty-eight hours counting as one "long day."

Many new modes of observance appear in postexilic times in connection with the old established festivals, especially in the high festival season of Tishri. Thus the *ṣimḥaṯ bēṯ haššō'ēḇâ,* "water-drawing festival," was celebrated during the week of Tabernacles with popular games and dances in which even the elders took part, and the streets were so brilliantly illuminated with torches that scarcely an eye was closed in Jerusalem during that week (T. B. *Hullin*).

The last day of Tabernacles was known in talmudic times as *Yom Hibbot Araboth* from the custom of beating willow branches, a custom clearly antedating the various symbolical explanations offered for it. Its festivities were connected with the dismantling of the booth. In later times the day was known as *Hoshanah Rabbah* from the liturgical passages beginning with the word *hôša'nā',* recited throughout the feast and "gathered" on that day. The day after Tabernacles has been made *Simḥath Torah,* the Feast of the Law, from the custom of ending on that day the cycle of fifty-two weekly portions read in the synagogues.

In general it may be said that although the actual observance has changed from time to time to meet new conditions, the synagogal calendar of today is made up of the same festivals as those observed in NT times.

Bibliography.–W. Eichrodt, *Theology of the OT* (Eng. tr. 1961), I, 119-133; E. Jenni, *Die theologische Begründung des Sabbatgebotes im AT* (1956); H.-J. Kraus, *Gottesdienst in Israel* (1962); W. G. Moorehead, *Studies in the Mosaic Institutions (ca.* 1895); G. Oehler, *Theology of the OT* (Eng. tr. 1883), pp. 323-352; J. B. Payne, *Theology of the Older Testament* (1962), ch. 28; R. H. Pfeiffer, *Religion in the OT* (Eng. tr. 1961), pp. 39-41, 92-95, 150, 167; H. Schauss, *Jewish Festivals* (1938); T. C. Vriezen, *Outline of OT Theology* (Eng. tr. 1958), pp. 284-88.

E. D. ISAACS J. B. PAYNE

FEATHERS [Heb. *nōṣâ*] (Lev. 1:16); NEB "contents." This term occurs only twice in the RSV: Lev. 1:16, relating to the sacrifice of a turtledove or pigeon; Dnl. 4:33 (MT 30), where the MT actually has no word for "feathers" but the concept of plumage is obviously necessary in order to preserve the figure of a bird.

FEEBLE KNEES. The expression occurs twice in the RSV: Job 4:4, "you have made firm the feeble knees" (Heb. *birkayim kōr$^{e'}$ôṯ,* lit. "bending knees"); Isa. 35:3, "make firm the feeble knees" (*birkayim kōš^{e}lôṯ,* lit. "tottering knees"). Weakness of the knees could be the result of fear, fasting, old age, or disease. It is used as a figure for general weakness or fear (cf. Ps. 109:24; Ezk. 7:17; 21:7; Dnl. 5:6; Nah. 2:10; He. 12:12).

FEEBLE-MINDED. Only in 1 Thess. 5:14, AV, for Gk. *oligópsychos,* in the obsolete sense of "fainthearted," as it is translated in the RSV. In the LXX this term is used as the equivalent of Heb. *kôšēl,* the tottering or feeble-kneed in Isa. 35:3; 54:6; Gk. *oligopsychía* occurs in the LXX twice (Ex. 6:9; Ps. 54:7 [MT 9]) for "anguish of spirit" and "trouble." The term refers to weakness of will and vacillation of purpose rather than to idiocy or morbid imbecility.

FEED. The term most often rendered "feed" by the RSV is Heb. *rā'â.* This verb usually occurs with reference to the feeding of animals, either transitively (e.g., Gen. 30:31, 36; 1 S. 17:15; Isa. 61:5) or intransitively (e.g., Gen. 41:2, 18; Ex. 34:3; Isa. 5:17; 11:7; Jonah 3:7). It frequently appears in figurative passages using the shepherding motif (see below). In Job 24:21 the AV ("evil entreateth") and NEB ("may have wronged") follow the Targum and LXX, reading Heb. *hēra'* in place of MT *rō'eh* (RSV "feed on"). When speaking of human beings, the OT frequently uses *'āḵal,* meaning "eat" in the qal (cf. "feed on," Hos. 4:8), "give to eat" or "feed" in the hiphil (Ex. 16:32; Dt. 8:3, 16; 1 K. 22:27; Ps. 80:5 [MT 6]; 81:16 [MT 17]; Isa. 58:14; Jer. 9:15; 23:15; etc.). The pilpel of *kûl* means "sustain, support, nourish" (BDB, p. 465). Yahweh sustained Elijah through the help of ravens and a widow (1 K. 17:4, 9); Obadiah kept a hundred prophets alive in a cave with bread and water (18:4, 13). Heb. *śāḇa',* "be sated" ("satisfy" in the hiphil), is rendered "fed to the full" in Hos. 13:6 (qal) and Jer. 5:7 (hiphil). In Ex. 22:5 (MT 4) the NEB renders the piel of *bā'ar* by its most common meaning, "burn" (but cf. mg.). The RSV and AV correctly interpret the verb to mean "graze" or "feed on"; cf. the cognate noun *be'îr,* "beast," used in the same verse (see *TDOT,* II, *s.v.* "bā'ar" [Ringgren]).

In the NT, Gk. *bóskō* is used either actively or passively of the feeding of animals (Mt. 8:30; Mk. 5:11; Lk. 8:32; 15:15; Jn. 21:15, 17). *Poimaínō,* likewise, means "tend" or "feed" a flock (Acts 20:28). *Chortázō* can be used of either human beings or animals and means "fill" or "satisfy" (Mt. 15:33; Mk. 7:27; 8:4; Lk. 16:21). In Lk. 15:16 the RSV renders "fed on" for Gk. *chortasthḗnai ek*; the AV and NEB follow a different textual tradition, reading *gemísai tḗn koilían autoú apó* ("filled his belly with"). *Tréphō* (Mt. 6:26; 25:37; Lk. 12:24) means "nourish," "provide with food." *Psōmízō* ("feed," Rom. 12:20) and *potízō* (lit. "give to drink," 1 Cor. 3:2) are each rendered "feed" once by the RSV.

The Bible emphasizes that it is God who supplies food for all His creatures (see Gen. 1:29f.; Ps. 104:14f., 27f.; 136:25; 145:15f.; etc.; cf. Mt. 6:26 par. Lk. 12:24). Yahweh, the covenant God, fed the Israelites in the wilderness with manna to teach them His providential care and their dependence on Him (Ex. 16; Dt. 8:3, 16; cf. Ps. 78:23-25). Jesus, the new Moses, satisfied the hunger of the multitudes (Mt. 14:15-21 par.; 15:32-38 par.) in order to teach them that He Himself was "the bread which came down from heaven," "the bread of life" (Jn. 6:30-59). *See also* BREAD V; MANNA.

Hebrew *rā'â* appears frequently in the prophetical literature in metaphorical passages depicting God's people as sheep and their ruler(s) as shepherd(s). Hosea warns that Yahweh cannot be expected to feed Israel, because Israel is a stubborn heifer rather than a docile lamb (Hos. 4:16). Isa. 40:11, however, prophesies of a day when God Himself "will feed his flock like a shepherd." Micah calls upon Yahweh to shepherd His people in fertile pasture lands (Mic. 7:14), and he looks forward to a time when God will feed His flock through a messianic shepherd (5:4). Jeremiah, likewise, prophesies that Israel will one day be restored to its pasture (Jer. 50:19) and that Yahweh will give Israel faithful shepherds who will "feed you with knowledge and understanding" (3:15). In the most extended passage, Ezekiel condemns the shepherds of Israel for feeding themselves instead of the sheep (Ezk. 34:1-10); Yahweh Himself will rescue His sheep and "feed them with good pasture" (vv. 11-16); He will judge between the sheep to see that each gets its fair share of pasture (vv. 17-22); finally, He will establish over them a messianic shepherd of the line of David, through whom He will rule and feed them (vv. 23f.; cf. Mic. 5:4). The same shepherding metaphor is used in the NT with reference to the Church. Jesus refers to Himself as the "Good Shepherd"— the messianic shepherd promised to Israel (Jn. 10). As representatives of Christ, church leaders are responsible for feeding His sheep (Jn. 21:15-17; Acts 10:28). (See *TDNT,* VI, *s.v.* ποιμήν κτλ. [J. Jeremias]; *see also* SHEEP.)

See also EAT; FULL; SATISFY. N. J. O.

FEEL [Heb. *mûš, bîn, yāḏa', māṣā', bāṭaḥ, kā'ēḇ*; Gk. *psēlapháō, zēlóō, phronéō, chaírō, peíthō*]; AV also "handle," "find," TRUST, "have pain" (Job 14:22), "think," "persuaded" (He. 6:9), etc.; NEB also "What of it?" (Prov. 23:35), "untroubled" (Am. 6:1), "become black" (Job 14:22), etc.

The RSV translation of Ps. 58:9 [MT 10], "Sooner than your pots can feel the heat of thorns" (Heb. *beṭerem yāḇînû sîrōṯêḵem 'āṭāḏ,* lit. "before your pots understand the thorny bush"), is unintelligible. The NEB emendation, "All unawares [=before they understand], may they be rooted up like [Heb. *yikkārᵉṯû kᵉmô* instead of *sîrōṯêḵem*] a thornbush," is to the point (cf. *IB,* IV, 305 and *Tyndale OT Comms., in loc.*). The wicked will be trodden down (v. 7), dissolved (v. 8), and finally rooted up (v. 9). The RSV rendering of Heb. *yimṣā'û* (lit. "they may find," Jer. 10:18) as "they may feel it" makes little sense. The AV translation "they may find it so" is better but still is unclear. J. Bright's emendation (*Jeremiah* [*AB,* 1965], p. 70), "they may be squeezed dry" (Heb. *yimmāṣû*; cf. NEB), makes this phrase parallel to the preceding one, "I will press hard upon them." God will (figuratively) uproot the inhabitants and increase their afflictions.

The RSV eliminates the Greek pleonasms in 2 Cor. 11:2 (Gk. *zēlō̂ . . . theoú zḗlǭ,* "I am jealous with a divine jealousy"; cf. AV, NEB), "I feel a divine jealousy," and in 1 Thess. 3:9 (Gk. *pásę̄ tę̄̂ charą̄̂ hę̄̂ chaíromen,* "with every joy in which we rejoice"; cf. the AV) "for all the joy which we feel."

"Feel" may mean: (1) external, physical contact with someone or something, "touch or be touched" (Heb. *mûš*). Jacob is touched by his father Isaac (Gen. 27:12, 21), Samson takes hold of the pillars supporting the Philistine temple (Jgs. 16:26), and the hands of an idol are lifeless and cannot feel anything (Ps. 115:7).

(2) The word may refer to internal, subjective experiences, such as "feel secure" (Am. 6:1), "feel about others" (Phil. 1:7, Gk. *phronéō,* "think or feel in a certain way," Bauer, rev., p. 866), "feel sure of" (He. 6:9, Gk. *peíthō,* "be convinced of," Bauer, rev. p. 640; cf. NEB). The phrase "feel after" in Acts 17:27 (Gk. *psēlapháō,* "grope after," Bauer, rev., p. 892; NEB "touch") refers to a spiritual search for the Creator.

In two passages the distinction between physical contact and inward experience disappears. In Prov. 23:35 the intoxicated person does not "feel" (Heb. *yāḏa'*, "know") the blows he received nor remember what happened to him. Job 14:22 mentions a person "feeling pain" (Heb. *kā'ēḇ*, "be in pain").

Bibliography.–TDNT, II, *s.v.* ζῆλος κτλ.: ζῆλος (Stumpff); VI, *s.v.* πείθω κτλ.: πεῖθομαι (Bultmann); IX, *s.v.* φρήν κτλ.: φρονέω (Bertram); χαίρω κτλ. D.3 (Conzelmann); *TDOT*, II, *s.v.* "bāṭach" (Jepsen); "bîn" (Ringgren).

H. W. LAY
R. W. V.

FEES [Heb. *qᵉsāmîm*–'divinations'] (Nu. 22:7); AV "rewards (of divination)." The context (Nu. 22:18) indicates that the emissaries from Balak brought fees to entice Balaam to curse Israel.

FEIGN [Heb. *hālal*] (1 S. 21:13 [MT 14]); NEB "act like." This term occurs only once in the RSV, where Heb. *hālal* is used reflexively to describe how David "played the part" of a madman.

FELIX fē'liks **ANTONIUS** an-tō'ni-əs [Gk. *Phēlix* < Lat. *felix*–'happy']. A Roman procurator of Judea, appointed by the emperor Claudius to succeed Cumanus.

The event that led to the introduction of Felix into the narrative of Acts was the riot at Jerusalem (Acts 21:27). There Paul, being attacked at the instigation of the Asian Jews for alleged false teaching and profanation of the temple, was rescued with difficulty by Lysias the chief captain. But Lysias, finding that Paul was a Roman citizen, and that therefore the secret plots against the life of his captive might entail serious consequences for himself, and finding also that Paul was charged on religious rather than on political grounds, sent him on to Felix at Caesarea for trial (Acts 21:31–23:34). On his arrival, Paul was presented to Felix and was then detained for five days in the judgment hall of Herod, till his accusers could also reach Caesarea (23:33-35).

The trial was begun, but after hearing the evidence of TERTULLUS and the speech of Paul in his own defense, Felix deferred judgment (24:1-22). The excuse he gave for delay was the continued absence of Lysias, but his real reason was to obtain bribes for the release of Paul. He therefore treated his prisoner at first with leniency and pretended along with DRUSILLA to take interest in his teaching. But these attempts to induce Paul to purchase his freedom failed ignominiously; Paul sought favor of neither Felix nor Drusilla and made the frequent interviews that he had with them an opportunity for preaching to them concerning righteousness, temperance, and the final judgment. The case dragged on for two years till Felix, upon his retirement, "desiring to do the Jews a favor . . . left Paul in prison" (24:27). (According to some MSS, the continued imprisonment of Paul was due to the desire of Felix to please Drusilla.)

Felix was the brother of Pallas, the infamous favorite of Claudius who, according to Tacitus (*Ann.* xiii.14), fell into disgrace in A.D. 55. Tacitus implies that Felix was joint procurator of Judea along with Cumanus before being appointed to the sole command, but Josephus is silent about this. Both Tacitus and Josephus refer to his succeeding Cumanus, Josephus stating that it was at the instigation of Jonathan the high priest. There is some doubt about the chronology of Felix's tenure of office. Harnack and Blass, following Eusebius and Jerome, place his accession in A.D. 51, and the imprisonment of Paul in 54-56; but most modern commentators incline to the dates 52 for his accession and *ca.* 58-60 for Paul's trial. Felix was succeeded, after Nero recalled him, by FESTUS. (*See also* CHRONOLOGY OF THE NT II.G.)

The testimony of Acts concerning the evil character of Felix is fully corroborated by the writings of Josephus (*BJ* ii.13.2-4 [252-261]; *Ant.* xx.8.5 [160-66]; cf. Tacitus *Ann.* xii.54). Although he suppressed the robbers and murderers who infested Judea, among them the "Egyptian" to whom Lysias refers (Acts 21:38), yet "he himself was more hurtful than them all." When occasion offered, he did not hesitate to employ the Sicarii (*see* ASSASSINS) for his own ends, including the murder of the high priest Jonathan (Josephus *Ant.* xx.8.5). Trading upon the influence of his brother at court, his cruelty and rapacity knew no bounds; during his rule revolts became continuous, marking a distinct stage in that seditious movement which culminated in the outbreak of A.D. 70 (cf. *HJP*, II/2, 174-182). His leaving Paul in bonds was but a final instance of one who sacrificed duty and justice for the sake of his own unscrupulous selfishness.

C. M. KERR

FELLOES (1 K. 7:33, AV). Archaic term used by the AV. *See* WHEEL.

FELLOW [Heb. *rē(a)'*–'companion' (Ex. 2:13; Jgs. 7:22; 1 S. 14:20; Isa. 34:14; Zec. 8:10; 14:13), *'îš*–'man, person' (1 S. 25:25; 29:4; 30:22; 2 S. 20:1; 1 K. 20:35; 2 K. 9:11; Isa. 3:5), *'āḥ*–'brother' (Dt. 18:7; 20:8; Ezr. 3:2; 6:20; Jer. 34:14; Ezk. 11:15; Hag. 2:22), *'ᵉnôš* (Dt. 13:13; Jgs. 9:4; 11:3; 18:25; 1 K. 21:13), *'eḥāḏ*–'one' (Gen. 19:9), *ḥāḇēr*–'companion' (Ps. 45:7 [MT 8]; Eccl. 4:10; Isa. 44:11), *bēn*–'son' (Jgs. 19:22; 20:13; 1 S. 10:27; 1 K. 21:10), *zeh*–'this' (1 S. 21:15; 25:21; 1 K. 22:27; 2 K. 9:11; 2 Ch. 18:26); Aram. *ḥaḇrâ* (Dnl. 7:20); Gk. *anḗr*–'man' (Acts 17:5; 24:5), *ánthrōpos*–'human being' (Jas. 2:20), *plēsíon*–'neighbor' (He. 8:11), *hoútos*–'this' (Mt. 26:61), *toioútos*–'of such a kind' (Acts 22:22), *syn*-(see below)]; AV also NEIGHBOR, BROTHER, MAN, ANOTHER, PERSON, SON, etc.; Gk. also NEIGHBOR, ANOTHER, MAN, COMPANION, COMRADE, BROTHER, etc.

Colloquially "fellow" can refer to any man (1 S. 29:4; 2 S. 16:7; Jas. 2:20); used as a noun, however, it usually denotes a "companion," "comrade," or "associate" (Eccl. 4:10; Hag. 2:22; Zec. 14:13). In the NT the term is usually used as an adjective to denote "accompaniment" and "association," the usual prefix *syn-* (meaning "with") forming the first part of the word. There are a variety of such words, each indicating different relationships.

Greek *sýndoulos* ("fellow servant") refers to the relationship between the oriental court official and his ruler (Mt. 18:28-34). It is used literally in Mt. 24:49, and it shows a relationship with the heavenly Lord when Paul designates certain Christians as his "fellow servants" in Col. 1:7; 4:7. In Revelation (6:11) the term means "fellow Christian" and is used by the angel himself in relation to the writer and his brothers (19:10; 22:9).

Thomas speaks to his *symmathētḗs* ("fellow disciples") in Jn. 11:16, and the term *synkleronómos* ("fellow heir") in Eph. 3:6 shows that both Gentiles and Jews inherit the promise in Jesus Christ. When a Gentile accepts the faith he becomes *sympolítēs* ("fellow citizen") with the saints as a citizen of God's kingdom (Eph. 2:19; cf. Rom. 8:17).

One who helped Paul spread the gospel is called his *synergós* ("fellow worker," e.g., Rom. 16:3, 9, 21; 1 Cor. 3:9) or *synstratiṓtēs* ("fellow soldier" or "fellow campaigner," Phil. 2:25; Philem. 2). Anyone who is a prisoner for the sake of the gospel is Paul's *synaichmálōtos* ("fellow prisoner," Rom. 16:7; Col. 4:10; Philem. 23).

In 1 Pet. 5:1 the plural of the term *sympresbýteros* ("fellow elder") may include "all who have any kind of authorized pastoral office and function" in the Church (Selwyn, p. 227).

Bibliography.–E. G. Selwyn, *First Epistle of Peter* (1946); *TDNT*, VII, *s.v.* σύν (Grundmann).

D. K. MCKIM

FELLOWSHIP. *See* COMMUNION.

FEMALE [Heb. *n*ᵉ*qēḇâ*; Gk. *thḗlys*]. The counterpart of the male of a species, either human or animal. In Gen. 7:2 Heb. *'iššâ* is translated "female" by the AV but "mate" by the RSV. Heb. *n*ᵉ*qēḇâ* is a cognate of the verb *nāqaḇ,* meaning "pierce" (cf. BDB, p. 666). Gk. *thḗlys,* literally "the one nursing" or "the one giving suck," is a cognate of the verb *thēlázō,* "suckle."

In the OT "female" is used of both man and animal; in the NT it refers solely to the human species. In both the OT and NT it has an original biological meaning, but while the Hebrew seems to refer to the female primarily as the sexual partner of the male, in the Greek the emphasis falls on her function as mother.

In the OT "female" occurs particularly in the accounts of Creation (Gen. 1:27; 5:2) and the Flood (6:19; 7:3, 9, 16), and in the passages describing the laws by which Israel was to live (Ex. 21:20, etc.; Lev. 3:1, 6; 4:28, 32; etc.). In the NT the term appears only three times: in Mt. 19:4 par. Mk. 10:6, in Jesus' discourse about marriage and divorce; and in Gal. 3:28, where Paul states that in Christ "there is neither male nor female."

It is striking that most of the references to "female" occur in the linguistic pair "male and female." The contexts of the NT references to "female" and of the Creation account cited by Jesus reinforce the impression given by the use of "female" with "male," namely, that the two are seen in Scripture as belonging together in a unity. This is stated clearly in the Gen. 1 account of the creation of man: "So God created man in his own image . . .; male and female he created them" (v. 27). Jesus explicitly forbade the parting asunder of the union of male and female in marriage (Mt. 19:4).

In Gal. 3:28 Paul declared that in Christ the old separations between male and female no longer hold, for all are one in Christ. The context clearly indicates that Paul was referring to the Law, which contained many provisions separating Jews and Gentiles, slave and free, male and female, both in social life and in liturgical practices. The Galatians were in danger of becoming enslaved again to such laws, after having been given new freedom in Christ. Paul's stern warning showed that "in Christ" the barriers people have created on the basis of class, race, and sex must give way to a unity that transcends these historic divisions. This reinforces the insight of the creation story, which sees male and female as two aspects of humanity. Thus, all that Gen. 1:26-28 says about the image of God and the responsibility for ruling and tending the creation applies equally to male and female.

See also WOMAN.

Bibliography.–E. Clark and H. Richardson, eds., *Women and Religion* (1977), pp. 26-30; E. Stagg and F. Stagg, *Woman in the World of Jesus* (1978); R. A. Stewart, *Rabbinic Theology* (1961), pp. 145-48, 155; G. H. Tavard, *Woman in Christian Tradition* (1973); *TDNT,* I, *s.v.* γυνή (Oepke). M. V. RIENSTRA

FENCE [Heb. *gāḏēr, g*ᵉ*ḏērâ*] (Ps. 62:3 [MT 4]; Nah. 3:17); AV also HEDGE; NEB WALL. The term occurs twice in the RSV to describe some kind of boundary or enclosure.

FENCED CITIES (AV Nu. 32:17, 36; Dt. 3:5; 9:1; 2 Ch. 8:5; 11:23; etc.). The AV uses "fenced" in the obsolete sense of "fortified" (cf. RSV "fortified cities"). *See* FORTIFICATION.

FERRET (Lev. 11:30, AV). A domesticated breed of polecat. "Ferret" is an incorrect translation of Heb. *'*ᵃ*nāqâ.* *See* LIZARD.

FERRY BOAT (2 S. 19:18, AV). *See* FORD.

FERTILITY CULTS. *See* ASHTORETH; RELIGIONS OF THE BIBLICAL WORLD: CANAANITE.

FERVENT; FERVENTLY. Each term occurs only once in the RSV. Acts 18:25 describes Apollos as "being fervent [Gk. *zéōn*–'burning'] in spirit," and Jas. 5:17 refers to Elijah as having "prayed fervently [Gk. *proseuchḗ*–'with prayer'; AV, NEB, "earnestly"] that it might not rain."

FESTAL GARMENTS [Heb. *ḥ*ᵃ*lip̄ôṯ ś*ᵉ*mālōṯ*–'changes of mantles'] (Gen. 45:22); AV "changes of raiment"; NEB "changes of clothing"; [*ḥ*ᵃ*lîp̄ôṯ b*ᵉ*gāḏîm*– 'changes of garments'] (Jgs. 14:12f., 19; 2 K. 5:5, 22f.); AV "changes of garments"; **FESTAL ROBES** [*maḥ*ᵃ*lāṣôṯ*] (Isa. 3:22); AV "changeable suits of apparel." The festal garment was a special item of clothing for occasions other then the ordinary. The connotation of the festal robe, though worn on similar occasions, was cleanness, purity, and whiteness (cf. Zec. 3:4).

FESTAL GATHERING [Gk. *panḗgyris*] (He. 12:22); AV GENERAL ASSEMBLY; NEB FULL CONCOURSE (the AV and NEB consider the word part of v. 23). The various readings of the passage in which this Greek term occurs are based on different punctuations of the Greek text. The AV and NEB take *panḗgyris* in close conjunction with *ekklēsía prōtotókōn,* "assembly of the first-born," while the RSV correctly takes it as a circumstantial dative with *myriás angélōn* (see F. F. Bruce, *Hebrews* [*NICNT,* 1964], p. 370 n. 131), with the alternate reading in the margin. Thus, the "festal gathering" refers to the angels while the "assembly of the first-born" refers to the whole Church of Christ, whose members have their names "enrolled in heaven." N. J. O.

FESTIVAL. *See* FEASTS.

FESTUS fes'təs **PORCIUS** pôr'shəs [Gk. *Porkios Phēstos*]. The Roman governor or procurator who succeeded FELIX ANTONIUS in the province of Judea (Acts 24:27). The only sources of information concerning Festus are the NT and Josephus.

Josephus' writings picture Festus as a prudent and honorable governor. Felix's maladministration bequeathed to Festus the impossible task of restoring order to a province embroiled in political strife and overrun by robbers. The Sicarii (*see* ASSASSINS), as the robbers were called on account of the small swords they carried, would come upon a village, plunder it, set it on fire, and murder whomever they wished. Through the use of an impostor, Festus succeeded in ridding the province of many of these criminals (*Ant.* xx.8.10 [185-88]). But his procuratorship was too short to undo the legacy of his predecessor, and under his successor, Albinus, the situation rapidly deteriorated once again (*BJ* ii.14.1 [271-76]).

One of the problems Festus inherited from Felix was the question of Paul's imprisonment. Attempting to exploit the new governor's inexperience, the Jews requested that Paul be sent to Jerusalem for trial, hoping to assassinate him on the way (Acts 25:3). Festus at first refused their request, and upon his return to Caesarea he himself examined Paul (v. 6). On finding that the evidence was conflicting, however, and desiring to please the Jews, he asked Paul if he were agreeable to making the journey to Jerusalem (vv. 7-9). But Paul, who knew well the nefarious use that the Jews would make of the favor Festus was willing to grant them, made his appeal to Caesar (vv. 10f.). To this request of a Roman citizen accused on a capital charge (cf. v. 16), Festus had to give his consent (v. 12).

When King Agrippa and Bernice arrived in Caesarea a few days later, Festus sought Agrippa's advice on this difficult case. (*See* HEROD VIII.) At Agrippa's request, Paul was brought before him for a private hearing. Festus' reaction to Paul's testimony betrayed his Roman mind and his ignorance concerning the Jewish and Christian religions (vv. 24-27). Festus' friendship with Agrippa is further illustrated by Josephus' account of a dispute between Agrippa and the Jewish priests (*Ant.* xx.8.11 [189-196]). When the priests discovered that Agrippa could observe the activities in the temple from his portico, they built a wall to obstruct his view. Agrippa objected to this, and Festus sided with him. The Jews therefore appealed to Rome, with the result that Nero permitted the wall to stand.

The exact dates of Festus' term in office are uncertain. Eusebius gives the date of his accession as A.D. 56, but this is too early. His term probably extended from 60 to 62.

See F. F. Bruce, *Paul: Apostle of the Heart Set Free* (1977), ch. 31. C. M. KERR N. J. O.

FETCH A COMPASS. Archaic in the AV for Heb. *sāḇaḇ* ("turn," "go around"; cf. RSV, NEB) in Nu. 34:5; Josh. 15:3; 2 S. 5:23; 2 K. 3:9, and for Gk. *periérchomai* ("make a circuit," "go around") in Acts 28:13.

FETTER [Heb. *neḥōšeṯ* (Jgs. 16:21; 2 S. 3:34; 2 K. 25:7 par.; 2 Ch. 33:11; 36:6), *ziqqîm, keḇel* (Ps. 105:18; 149:8), *'ēsûr, bêṯ pequddâ*–'guardhouse' (Jer. 52:11); Gk. *desmós, pédē* (Mk. 5:4)]; AV also BANDS, BONDS, CHAINS, etc.; NEB also IRONS, PRISON, "shut up." Except for 2 Tim. 2:9 (Gk. *déō*) the term occurs in the RSV in the plural. (In 2 S. 3:34 the RSV renders *linḥuštayim huggāšû*, "they will be put into fetters" as "[they] were . . . fettered" to preserve poetic parallelism.) Fetters of iron (Heb. *keḇel*; prob. Gk. *pédē*) or bronze (Heb. *neḥōšeṯ*) were frequently used for securing prisoners. (*See* CHAIN.) Paul's "fetters" in Acts 16:26 were stocks that "had more than two holes for the legs, which could be forced wide apart in such a way as to cause the utmost discomfort and cramping pain" (F. F. Bruce, *Acts* [*NICNT,* 1954], p. 336).

In Eccl. 7:26 the hands of the woman with evil intentions are figuratively compared to "fetters" (Heb. *'ēsûr*) which people can escape only through divine help (*see* WOMAN). The righteous may be "bound in fetters" (Heb. *ziqqîm,* Job 36:8; parallel to "caught in the cords of affliction"), but their punishment is for purification (*see* EVIL III.C).

At the end of his life Paul was confined in fetters (Gk. *desmós,* 2 Tim. 2:9; cf. Col. 4:18) for the sake of the gospel. Though according to outer appearance he was a criminal, he used his humiliating condition to further the gospel — the word of God "is not fettered" (Gk. *déō*).

See *TDNT,* II, *s.v.* δεσμός, δέσμιος (Kittel). R. W. V.

FEUD [Heb. *rîḇ*] (Jgs. 12:2); AV STRIFE. The term *rîḇ* generally denotes some sort of legal dispute or lawsuit. When the men of Ephraim demanded to know why Jephthah had not called for their assistance in the conflict against the Ammonites, Joshua answered that he and his people had a great *rîḇ* against the Ammonites, and that they were forced to fight the battle alone when Ephraim refused to respond to their request for help.

FEVER [Heb. *qaddaḥaṯ, dalleqeṯ, ḥarḥur, šaḥepeṯ*; Gk. *pyretós, dysentérion*]. A bodily condition (pyrexia) in which the temperature exceeds 37°C. (98.6°F.). Of the many forms of febrile disease, those mentioned in the Bible can usually be identified with reasonable certainty. As in antiquity, certain fevers are among the commonest of illnesses in Palestine today. Most frequent of all is malaria, which prevails wherever pools or marshes permit mosquitoes to breed. These conditions occur mainly in the north, the Shephelah, and the Jordan Valley.

The AV translates Heb. *qaddaḥaṯ* (LXX Gk. *íkteros*) in Lev. 26:16 as "burning ague" (RSV "fever"; NEB "recurrent fever"), linking it with Heb. *dalleqeṯ* (Gk. *rhígos,* "ague") in Dt. 28:22, where, however, the LXX renders Heb. *qaddaḥaṯ* by Gk. *pyretós.* The variation is interesting, since Galen employed the Gk. *rhigopýretos* to describe a common Palestinian fever. The LXX of Lev. 26:16 means "jaundice," a disease not otherwise mentioned in the Bible. This condition (icterus) results from a yellowish staining of the skin and other tissues with bile pigments and is symptomatic of organic liver disease. Toxemic jaundice is often associated with such infectious conditions as relapsing fever, yellow fever, and malaria. The two Hebrew terms may describe different stages of the same malarial condition. The attack commences with chill and severe shivering (Gk. *rhígos*), which are followed by a febrile stage and concomitant physical symptoms, terminating in a period of profuse perspiration. In tertian malaria the paroxysms recur every second day and in quartan malaria every third day (not reckoning the day of the paroxysms as the first).

Blackwater fever, a disease similar to malaria in which the urine contains hemoglobin, has been reported infrequently in Palestine, as has undulant (Malta) fever, which also presents characteristics similar to malaria. The AV "extreme burning" (RSV "fiery heat") of Dt. 28:22 (Heb. *ḥarḥur*; Gk. *erethismós*) may be a description of undulant fever. A differential diagnosis might include erysipelas or some other eruptive fever such as measles or scarlatina.

Hebrew *šaḥapeṯ* (Lev. 26:16; Dt. 28:22; Gk. *aporía*), translated "consumption" in most English versions, was a febrile disease with distressing aftereffects. Phthisis, however, is infrequent in Syria, so that the disease implied may perhaps be undulant fever. This condition is frequently accompanied by febrile paroxysms, anemia, and emaciation. It may have been referred to in the Ebers papyrus as a "fever of the gods" (46), or as a "burning of the heart" (102), an affliction sent by the "god of fever" and having sequelae affecting the eyes, stomach, heart, and other organs. Diseases such as typhoid and typhus almost certainly existed in the ancient Near East but cannot be identified from biblical references.

In the NT, "fever" is mentioned eight times. Where Gk. *pyretós* is employed it generally indicates malaria, a disease of frequent occurrence in Palestine. Peter's mother-in-law (Mt. 8:14 par.) and the nobleman's son at Capernaum (Jn. 4:52) were probably afflicted with this disease. The dysentery of Acts 28:8 (AV "bloody flux") was accompanied by a febrile condition, perhaps relapsing malarial fever. The serious nature of the condition might indicate acute gangrenous dysentery, which is usually fatal.

See also DISEASE III.H; IV.E. R. K. H.

FIELD [Heb. *śāḏeh, ḥelqâ* (e.g., 2 S. 14:30f.), *yegēḇîm* (Jer. 39:10), *šerēmôt* (Jer. 31:40), *śāḏay* (e.g., Dt. 32:13), *šeḏēmâ* (Dt. 32:32; Isa. 16:8), *ḥûṣ* (Job 5:10); Aram. *bar* (Dnl. 2:38); Gk. *agrós, chṓra* (Jn. 4:35; Jas. 5:4), *chōríon* (Acts 1:18), *geṓrgion* (1 Cor. 3:9), *kanṓn* (2 Cor. 10:15f.), vb. *agrauléō* ("were . . . in the field," Lk. 2:8)]. In Jer. 39:10 the NEB reads *yōgeḇîm,* "labourers," for MT *yegēḇîm,* "fields" (so RSV, AV) on the basis of similar texts in 2 K. 25:12 par. Jer. 52:16; the change, however, is unwarranted, since the MT makes sense as it stands (also note that the NEB rendering calls for another change, reading *kōrᵉmîm,* "vine-dressers," for MT *kᵉrāmîm,* "vineyards"). Heb. *šᵉrēmôṯ,* which occurs only in Jer. 31:40, is probably an error for *šᵉḏēmôṯ* (so *Q*; cf. KoB, p. 950; *BH*; on Ugar. *šdmt,* see M. Lehman, *VT,* 3 [1953], 361-371).

The most common biblical words for "field" are Heb. *śāḏeh* and Gk. *agrós.* A basic distinction exists between open fields (e.g., Nu. 19:16; 2 S. 11:11; Ezk. 29:5; 32:4; 33:27) and enclosed fields (e.g., Nu. 22:23f.; Prov. 24:30; cf. Dt. 27:17). An even more important distinction must be made between cultivated (Ruth 2:2; Ps. 107:37; Eccl. 5:9) and uncultivated fields. Fields could be owned by one family, or even by a nation (e.g., "country of Moab," Gen. 36:35); the fields of the fatherless were to be especially respected (Prov. 23:10).

Beside the literal use of "field," figurative uses include fields exulting (1 Ch. 16:32; Ps. 96:12) and languishing (Isa. 16:8). Human beings are likened to fields in Gen. 27:27 (the human smell is compared to the smell of the field), and in Isa. 1:8 Zion is represented as a "lodge in a cucumber field" (cf. Jer. 26:18). The Corinthian church is a field to be cultivated by the apostles (1 Cor. 3:9; cf. 2 Cor. 10:15). "Field" represents the world in Mt. 13:38, and in Jn. 4:35 the fields are "already white for [spiritual] harvest."

Fields were not only places of sowing, harvesting, and raising cattle but also arenas of battle (1 S. 4:2; 2 S. 18:6), murder (Gen. 4:8), and burial grounds (2 Ch. 26:23; but cf. 2 K. 9:37; Jer. 9:22). They provided an opportunity for meditation (Gen. 24:63; Jgs. 13:9). They could be dedicated to God (Lev. 27:17f.) or used for spiritual harlotry (Jer. 13:27). The fields became fruitful (Isa. 32:15, Heb. *karmel,* "orchard"; NEB "grassland") when blessed by God (Dt. 28:3; Isa. 29:17) but withered when cursed by Him (Dt. 28:16; Isa. 16:10; but cf. Hab. 3:17f.).

See also FULLER'S FIELD; POTTER'S FIELD.

R. W. V.

FIELD OF BLOOD (Acts 1:19). *See* AKELDAMA.

FIERCE [Heb. *ḥārôn, ḥᵒrî* (1 S. 20:34; 2 Ch. 25:10; Isa. 7:4; Lam. 2:3), *'aḵzār, 'āz*–'strong,' 'insolent' (Gen. 49:7; Ps. 59:3 [MT 4]; Isa. 19:4), *hāḏaḏ* (Hab. 1:8), *za'am*–'curse' (Lam. 2:6), *qāšâ*–'be hard' (2 S. 2:17; Isa. 27:8), *šaḥal*; Gk. *anḗmeros*–'untamed' (2 Tim. 3:3), *barýs, chalepós*–'dangerous' (Mt. 8:28)]; NEB also FURY, RAGE, CRUEL, BURNING (Zeph. 2:2), "fearfully" (Rev. 16:9), etc., and frequently omits; **FIERCENESS** [Heb. *ḥārôn* (Dt. 13:17; 2 K. 23:26), *ra'aš* (Job 39:24)]; NEB also "trembling" (Job 39:24), and omits (Dt. 13:17 [MT 18]); **FIERCELY** [piel of *mārar*–'irritate' ("fiercely attacked," Gen. 49:23), *nāḥar*–'snort' ("blow fiercely," Jer. 6:29)]; AV SORELY, "are burned" (Jer. 6:29); NEB SAVAGELY, PUFF AND BLOW.

The most common word for fierce(ness) is Heb. *ḥārôn,* which, like *ḥᵒrî,* means "heat, fervor." Frequently these occur with Heb. *'ap,* "anger," and denote the intensity of anger (e.g., Job 20:23; 2 Ch. 25:10). In Job 4:10 the NEB's rendering "cubs" (Heb. *šaḥal,* "[young] lion") is perhaps preferable to RSV, AV "fierce lion" (cf. *TDOT,* I, *s.v.* "'ᵃrî" [Botterweck]). In Job 39:24 Heb. *bᵉra'aš wᵉrōgez* may be translated either "with rattling and excitement" (cf. NEB) or "with fierceness and rage" (RSV, AV; see comms.). Heb. *'aḵzār* (elsewhere "cruel"; cf. KoB, p. 43) in Job 41:10 (MT 2) is best understood as "fierce" in the sense of "bold" (cf. Syr. *kᵉzîr*; *BH,* KD *in loc.*); see the context, especially v. 10b.

"Fierce" may denote the intensity of a battle (2 S. 2:17) or of a fire (Rev. 16:9). Animals can be fierce or menacing (e.g., Hab. 1:8). A few times "fierce" applies to humans, in the sense of being savage (NEB, Ps. 59:3), cruel (NEB, Isa. 19:4), and violent (NEB, Mt. 8:28). In 2 Tim. 3:3 fierceness is a vice; in the last days people will be "savage" or "brutal" (Bauer, rev., p. 66). Luke uses "fierce" (Gk. *barýs*) figuratively: those coming after Paul's departure are compared to "fierce wolves" (Acts 20:29).

Most often "fierce" occurs in the expression "fierce anger." In the Blessing of Jacob the anger of Simeon and Levi is denounced (Gen. 49:7); but note that the reaction of Jonathan to Saul's intention to kill Jonathan's best friend David appears to be condoned in 1 S. 20:34.

Scripture does not hesitate to ascribe intense anger to the holy God because of human sinfulness. His anger (e.g., Nu. 25:4), His wrath (e.g., Ex. 32:12), and His indignation (Lam. 2:6) are such that crops (Jer. 12:13), the land (Jer. 4:26), people (e.g., Jer. 49:37), and possibly the earth itself (Isa. 13:9) are or will be destroyed. But His fury is tempered by His love (Hos. 11:9). *See also* WRATH.

R. W. V.

FIERY HEAT [Heb. *ḥarḥur*] (Dt. 28:22); AV EXTREME BURNING; NEB ERUPTIONS. *See* FEVER.

FIERY ORDEAL [Gk. *pýrōsis*] (1 Pet. 4:12); AV FIERY TRIAL. The metallurgical associations of this word later were used in a vivid designation for sufferings, even persecutions, that tested faith. (Cf. the meaning of Heb. *kûr* in Dt. 4:20, 1 K. 8:51, Prov. 17:3; 27:21; etc.) *Pýrōsis* meant: (1) exposure to burning, as in cooking or surgery; (2) the place of burning, as a furnace (LXX Prov. 27:21); (3) the process of burning, which either caused destruction (cf. Josephus *Ant.* i.11.4 [203], referring to Sodom; Rev. 18:9, 18, referring to Babylon) or purified and refined metals (cf. LXX Ps. 66:10; Rev. 3:18); (4) metaphorically, the testing of faith.

The last is the meaning of Heb. *kûr* in the Manual of Discipline at Qumrân (1QS 1:17f., a close parallel to 1 Pet. 4:12) and of *pýrōsis* in an edited manual of church order from the 2nd cent. (Did. 16:5). 1 Pet. 4:12 refers back to 1:7, and both verses describe the protracted ("do not be surprised") crisis in which Christians were persecuted "for the Name" (cf. Mt. 5:10f.; Acts 4:7, 17; 5:28, 40f.; 9:14, 16), but a crisis filled with hope and eschatological meaning (1 Pet. 4:13-19; cf. the role of fire in apocalyptic expectations of the end, as in 1 En. 102:1; 108:3, 5). (*See also* PETER, FIRST EPISTLE OF IV.)

Bibliography.–J. N. D. Kelly, *Comm. on the Epistles of Peter and of Jude* (1969), pp. 184f.; E. T. Sander, "ΠΥΡΩΣΙΣ and the First Epistle of Peter 4:12" (Th.D. diss., Harvard University, 1967); E. G. Selwyn, *First Epistle of St. Peter* (2nd ed. 1947), pp. 53-56, 221; J. Strugnell, *CBQ,* 29 (1967), 580-82.

J. G. GIBBS

FIERY SERPENT. *See* SERPENT.

FIG; FIG TREE [Heb. *tᵉ'ēnâ, pag*; Gk. *sýkon, sykéa, sykḗ, olýnthos*]. The common fig, *Ficus carica* L., mentioned nearly sixty times in Scripture, is one of the most important Bible plants and was cultivated throughout Palestine, particularly in the mountainous regions. The wild fig was also commonly found as a shrub, but was generally barren. Its flowers contained insects that probably fertilized the cultivated fig. Am. 7:14 may refer to artificial fertilization of the fig. *See* Plate 10.

Usually growing to about 5 m. (15 ft.) in height, the fig tree sometimes attains a maximum of 8 m. (25 ft.). Its foliage is dense, providing welcome shade (e.g., Mic. 4:4; Zec. 3:10; Jn. 1:48). The fruit of the fig tree (a *syconium*) is peculiar, being an enlarged fleshy receptacle containing small gritty particles at maturity, which are the true fig seeds and fruit. As the flower develops, the axis closes upon the small internal blooms instead of expanding outward, ultimately leaving a minute aperture at the apex. The axis becomes pulpy and succulent, and the tree is fertilized by the presence of small hymenopterous insects.

Various stages in the development of the fruit are mentioned in the OT. Heb. *t*$^{e'}$*ēnîm* in Jer. 8:13, etc., describes figs ripe from the end of August; Heb. *pag* (LXX Gk. *ólynthos*) in Cant. 2:13, the green fig remaining on the tree during the winter; Heb. *bikkûrâ* (Gk. *okopós*) in Hos. 9:10, an early fig growing on the stock of the preceding year; Heb. *d*^{e}*ḇēlâ* (Gk. *paláthē*) in 1 S. 25:18, a cake of pressed dried figs kept for winter use. *See* Plate 13; *see also* EARLY.

There are several varieties of Palestinian figs, some of which are inferior (cf. Jer. 24:1f, 8; 29:17). Two crops are gathered; the first is ripe about June and grows from the midsummer shoots of the previous year, while the second, ripe about August, is produced from the new spring shoots. By December all figs in the mountainous areas have shed their leaves, and new leaf buds appear only in March (cf. Mt. 24:32 par.), when the tiny figs appear simultaneously in the leaf axils. The figs grow to about the size of a small cherry and then the majority fall off (cf. the "winter fruit" of Rev. 6:13; AV "untimely figs"). Known to the Arabs as *taksh,* this underdeveloped fruit is often gathered for sale in the markets. In April and May the fig leaves develop and the fruit reaches maturity about June (cf. Isa. 28:4; Jer. 24:2; Hos. 9:10), being then of delicate flavor (e.g., Mic. 7:1). Frequently, ripe winter figs can be found, hidden by leaves, when the summer figs are growing in August and September.

Christ's miracle (Mt. 21:18f. par.) during the Passover season (about April) can be understood in the light of these observations. When the young leaves are appearing in spring, every fertile fig will have some *taksh* on it, even though the season for edible figs (Mk. 11:13, AV) has not arrived. When the leaves are fully developed the fruit ought to be mature also. But if a tree with leaves has no fruit, it will be barren for the entire season. Thus the fig tree was cursed for its pretentiousness, predicting the fate of the fruitless Jewish nation (cf. W. L. Lane, *Mark* [*NICNT,* 1974], pp. 399f.).

Years of labor are required (cf. Lk. 13:7) before newly planted figs bear profitably, since the tree grows slowly. Thus the destruction of the fig (cf. Ps. 105:33; Jer. 5:17; Hos. 2:12; Am. 4:9) would have serious economic implications. Obversely, the state where the individual dwelt securely under his own fig tree was one of safety and prosperity (1 K. 4:25; cf. 2 K. 18:31; Isa. 36:16; Mic. 4:4; Zec. 3:10; 1 Macc. 14:12). Only a supreme faith in God could bring rejoicing in the absence of a flourishing fig tree (Hab. 3:17).

Dried figs were always a more important dietary item than fresh figs. Cakes were made by pressing the figs together (1 S. 30:12). Abigail gave David two hundred such cakes (1 S. 25:18); the people of northern Israel sent fig cakes with other gifts to the newly crowned David (1 Ch. 12:40). A poultice of figs was applied to Hezekiah's boil (Isa. 38:21 par.), following contemporary therapeutic practices.

See *TDNT,* VII, *s.v.* συκῆ κτλ. (Hunzinger).

R. K. HARRISON

Men and monkeys gather figs in a reconstruction of Egyptian wall paintings (Royal Ontario Museum, Toronto)

FIGHT. *See* WAR.

FIGURE [Heb. *semel, miqlaʿaṯ*]; [*m*^{e}*lîṣâ*] (Prov. 1:6); AV INTERPRETATION; NEB PARABLE; [*taḇnîṯ*] (Isa. 44:13); NEB SHAPE; [*k*^{e}*lî*] (1 S. 6:8, 15); AV JEWEL; NEB OFFERING; [*d*^{e}*mûṯ*] (2 Ch. 4:3); AV SIMILITUDE; NEB "what looked like"; [Gk. *paroimía*] (Jn. 10:6; 16:25, 29); AV PARABLE, PROVERB; NEB also PARABLE; [*týpos*] (Acts 7:43); NEB IMAGE. The term is employed in three different ways in the RSV; its basic meaning is "form," "shape," or "image."

(1) Frequently "figure" designates images used in worship. Heb. *semel* in Dt. 4:16 is the normal word for "statue" (cf. 2 Ch. 33:7, 15). *Taḇnîṯ* in Isa. 44:13 is the word ordinarily used for a "model" or "pattern" for construction; in Dt. 4:16f. it is translated "likeness." In Ex. 25:40 the term refers to the heavenly "pattern" that served as the model for the earthly tabernacle (cf. Josh. 22:28). In Am. 5:26 Amos condemns Israel's worship of "images" (LXX *týpos*) they had made for themselves. (*See* KAIWAN.)

Clearly evident in each of these texts is the distinctive Hebraic attitude toward the use of any form that humans can shape with their own hands. The ground given in Dt. 4:16 for the prohibition against figures is that at Sinai Israel had not seen God's form (4:15). Because God is above the creation, there is no form, shape, or likeness that human beings can construct to represent Him. Similarly, the prophet in Isa. 44:13 ridicules the notion that any shape or figure made out of material objects can represent the deity. Because God is Creator, no figure or likeness can represent Him (Isa. 40:12-18). (*See also* GOD II.D.2; IDOL.)

Stephen's accusation directed at Israel in Acts 7:43 sets the condemnation of Am. 5:25-27 in a new context. The rebellion of Israel in OT times included the use of the tent of MOLECH and the making of figures (*týpoi*) for worship. Stephen contrasts the pagan tent and figures (*týpoi*) to the true tent that was made according to the divine pattern (*týpos*). In this instance the contrast is between the purely material *týpoi* (Acts 7:43) that characterized pagan worship and the divine *týpos* that characterized the tabernacle (v. 44). The material figures, shaped by human hands, were not suitable for representing God because He is set apart from the creation. This is the basis for the condemnation of any material figures used to represent Him. (For *týpos* as "type" *see* TYPE.)

(2) Hebrew *miqlaʿaṯ* (<*qālaʿ*, "carve") refers to carved figures. The term is used in 1 Kings for the carvings

that adorned the temple. In 6:18 *miqlaʿat* (RSV "form") is used for the cedar carvings of gourds and flowers in the temple, and in v. 32 for the carvings of cherubim, palm trees, and open flowers.

(3) In a few instances obscure or enigmatic speech is designated as a "figure." Heb. *meliṣâ* ("satire," BDB, p. 539; cf. Hab. 2:6) denotes enigmatic speech (Prov. 1:6; *see* DARK SAYINGS). Similarly, Gk. *paroimía* expresses hidden or obscure speech. The Fourth Gospel, which never uses the more familiar *parabolḗ,* uses *paroimía* for the speech of Jesus that needed interpretation. Just as Jesus in Mk. 4:10-12 intentionally speaks in parables that are difficult to understand, so the Johannine Christ speaks "in figures" (*see* MYSTERY III; PARABLE). Thus Jn. 10:6 calls the shepherd speech (vv. 1-5) a "figure," and 16:25 describes all of Jesus' words up to the departing discourses as "figures" that can only imperfectly indicate divine truth in human words.

Bibliography.–L. Morris, comm. on John (*NICNT,* 1971), pp. 500f., 708f.; *RGG,* I, *s.v.* "Bild" (B. Gemser); *TDNT,* II, *s.v.* εἰκών (von Rad); V, *s.v.* παροιμία (Hauck); VIII, *s.v.* τύπος (Goppelt).

J. W. THOMPSON

FIGURED STONE [Heb. *ʾeḇen maśkîṯ*; Gk. *líthos skopós*]; AV IMAGE OF STONE (Lev. 26:1), PICTURES (Nu. 33:52); NEB also CARVED FIGURE (Nu. 33:52). An object used in pagan religious worship. It probably comprised a slab of stone decorated with some carved or painted idolatrous representation such as occurred on Egyptian temple walls or orthostats.

See also IDOL.

R. K. H.

FIGUREHEAD (Acts 28:11). *See* TWIN BROTHERS.

FILIGREE [Heb. *miśbeṣôṯ*]; AV OUCHES; NEB ROSETTES; [*milluʾâ*] (Ex. 28:20); AV INCLOSINGS; NEB ROSETTES. Ornamental work of fine wire, used in setting the two onyx stones on the high priest's EPHOD (Ex. 28:11; 39:6), the twelve stones on the BREASTPIECE (28:20; 39:13), and the cords that fastened the breastpiece to the shoulder-pieces of the ephod (28:13, 25; 39:16, 18). The use of *miśbeṣôṯ* in Ps. 45:13 (MT 14), where the princess is said to be dressed in "gold-woven" robes, indicates that the settings were not of solid gold but of woven wire. Ex. 39:3 tells how this wire was produced. A floral design such as the NEB suggests is a likely possibility.

R. K. H.

FILL. *See* FULL.

FILLET [Heb. *ḥāšûq*] (Ex. 27:10f.; 36:38; 38:10-28); NEB "bands on the posts." This word describes a metal band that enclosed the tops of pillars used in the construction of the tabernacle. From Ex. 26:32, 37 it seems that the veil and the screen were suspended from hooks attached to the fillets on the pillars, and this would preclude the older concept of a fillet as a rod that connected the pillars.

R. K. H.

FILTH; FILTHINESS; FILTHY [Heb. *ṣōʾâ*] (Isa. 4:4; 28:8; Prov. 30:12); [*ṣōʾî*] (Zec. 3:3f.); [*šiqqûṣ*] (Nah. 3:6); [*tumʾâ*] (Ezk. 22:15; 24:11, 13); NEB also DEFILEMENT, IMPURITY; [*niddâ*] (2 Ch. 29:5; Lam. 1:8, 17); AV also "menstruous woman," "removed"; NEB also POLLUTION; [Gk. *aischrótēs*] (Eph. 5:4); NEB COARSE; [*rhypaínō, rhypareúō, rhyparía, rhyparós*] (Jas. 1:21; Rev. 22:11); NEB also SORDID. Anything that defiles or soils in such a way as to be disgusting or revolting. In its literal sense filth may refer, for example, to vomit (Isa. 28:8), impurities in metal (Ezk. 24:11), or soiled clothing (Zec. 3:3f.). The word may be used figuratively in the sense of ceremonial uncleanness, such as idolatrous practices in the temple (2 Ch. 29:5), or in the sense of ethical uncleanness or immorality (Prov. 30:12; Ezk. 24:13; Eph. 5:4; Jas. 1:21; Rev. 22:11).

E. W. CONRAD

FIN. *See* FISH.

FINAL PUNISHMENT [Heb. *ʿēṯ ʿawōn qēṣ*–'time of punishment (iniquity) of the end'] (Ezk. 21:25, 29 [MT 30, 34]; 35:5); AV "iniquity shall have an end." Ezekiel is concerned with God's judgment of destruction upon a faithless king and people (Israel in 21:25 and 35:5, Ammon in 21:29), rather than a judgment day at the end of time (cf. Isa. 40:2).

FIND. Among the many words translated "find," Heb. *māṣāʾ* and Gk. *heurískō* are the most common. Aside from the obvious literal uses, "find" is used figuratively with an object or complement (e.g., "find favor"); often it is supplied where the original text has only the complement (e.g., in 2 Ch. 30:9 the RSV translates Heb. *leraḥamîm,* lit. "for compassion," as "will find compassion"). Sometimes the RSV simply supplies "find" (e.g., 1 Cor. 5:1). In Ps. 73:10 the RSV ("find no fault") and the NEB ("find nothing to blame") emend the MT *mê mālēʾ yimmāṣû* (cf. AV "waters of a full cup are wrung out") apparently to *meʾûmâ lōʾ yimmāṣeʾû*; there is little textual evidence, however, for this change, although it does improve the sense of the passage.

Our Lord's claim, "Seek, and you will find" (Mt. 7:7 par. Lk. 11:9) is a reassurance to those uncertain of God's existence (cf. I. H. Marshall, comm. on Luke [*New International Greek Testament Comm.,* 1978], p. 467). Jesus' enigmatic statement "He who finds his life will lose it, and he who loses his life for my sake will find it" (Mt. 10:39; 16:25; cf. Mk. 8:35; Lk. 9:24; 17:33; Jn. 12:25) seems to mean that the selfish person will forfeit eternal life, but the person who lives (and dies) for Christ will gain eternal life (cf. W. F. Albright and C. S. Mann, *Matthew* [*AB,* 1971], p. 133).

R. W. V.

FINE. An adjective that indicates superior quality. Only in a few instances does the English translation "fine" represent a separate word: (1) Heb. *ṭôḇ,* "good," qualifies gold (2 Ch. 3:5, 8, "fine gold"; cf. Gen. 2:12, "good") and copper (Ezr. 8:27, "fine bright bronze"); Aram. *ṭāḇ* (Dnl. 2:32, "fine gold"); (2) Heb. *yōšer* (emended from *yeṯer,* following the LXX), "uprightness," modifies "speech" (Prov. 17:7); (3) *ʿāṯîq,* "choice," describes clothing (Isa. 23:18); (4) *tipʾereṯ,* "beauty," qualifies jewels (Ezk. 23:26); (5) Gk. *kalós,* "good," describes pearls (Mt. 13:45); (6) *lamprós,* "shining," is used of clothing (Jas. 2:2f.).

In other places there is no separate word, but "fine" expresses a quality of the substantive: Heb. *keṯem,* "fine gold" (Job 31:24); *pāz,* meaning "refined gold" (Job 28:17; Ps. 19:10 [MT 11]; Prov. 8:19; Isa. 13:12; Lam. 4:2); *sōleṯ,* "flour," rendered "fine flour," rolled or crushed small (Lev. 2:1, 4f., 7; etc.); *qemaḥ sōleṯ,* "fine meal" (Gen. 18:6); *bûṣ,* "fine linen" (Ezk. 27:16, etc.); Gk. *býssos,* from Heb. *bûṣ* (LXX in 2 Ch. 2:14; 3:14), deemed very fine and precious, worn only by the rich (Lk. 16:19); Gk. *býssinos,* "made of fine linen" (LXX for *bûṣ* in 1 Ch. 15:27; Rev. 18:12, 16, "clothed in fine linen"; 19:8, 14); *semídalis,* "fine flour and wheat" (18:13).

In Job 28:1 the AV employs "fine" in the obsolescent sense of "refine."

W. L. WALKER
N. J. O.

FINER. (Prov. 25:4, AV). Obsolete for "refiner." *See* SMITH.

FINES [Heb. vb. *'ānaš* (Ex. 21:22; Dt. 22:19; Prov. 17:26; Am. 2:8)]; AV BE SURELY PUNISHED, AMERCE IN, PUNISH, CONDEMN. Monetary penalties, often added to other forms of punishment, were assessed in biblical times both as compensation for hurt, loss, or damage and as a deterrent to criminal behavior. As elsewhere in the ancient Near East, fines were paid to the victim, who was responsible for the execution of the court's verdict. No evidence has been attested of fines paid to the court or state, although some scholars so interpret goods and moneys contributed through guilt or sin offerings (cf. Am. 2:8; 2 K. 12:16 [MT 17]; Lev. 5:6-19); confiscation of property as a judicial punishment was permitted after the Exile (Ezr. 7:26; 10:8; cf. 1 K. 21:15f.).

Indemnification was to be made by one who caused a miscarriage, in an amount determined by the woman's husband and approved by judges (Ex. 21:22). For seduction of a virgin a man was to pay to her father her "marriage present" and make her his wife (Ex. 22:16f. [MT 15f.]; Dt. 22:29). False defamation of a virgin carried a fine of one hundred shekels (Dt. 22:19). An unspecified sum was assessed for seducing a betrothed slave woman (Lev. 19:20-22). Compensation for loss of time, as well as medical care, was to be given in cases of personal injury (Ex. 21:18f.). When an ox gored a person to death the deceased's kin could accept a ransom in place of the negligent owner's life (Ex. 21:30). Damages were to be paid for an ox or ass that fell into an open pit (Ex. 21:34). In the case of stolen property, fines could amount to several times the actual value, depending upon whether the goods were returned (Ex. 22:1-4, 9 [MT 21:37–22:3, 8]; cf. Lev. 6:5; 2 S. 12:6; Prov. 6:31; Lk. 19:8).

In contrast with earlier Israelite laws and Mesopotamian codes that accorded the death penalty for theft, the law of "eye for eye, tooth for tooth" (Ex. 21:22-24) reduced the punishment to restitution plus a fine, thus demonstrating the Hebrew concern for all members of the community.

See PUNISHMENTS. A. C. M.

FINGER [Heb. *'eṣba'*, *qōṭen*–'small thing' ("little finger," 1 K. 12:10 par. 2 Ch. 10:10); Gk. *dáktylos*]. In 1 K. 7:15 the RSV and NEB follow the LXX (cf. also Jer. 52:21), while the AV follows the MT.

In ancient as in modern times the fingers were frequently an important adjunct to conversation. Insulting, perhaps obscene, gestures are alluded to in Prov. 6:13 and Isa. 58:9 (*see* GESTURE III.A). The fingers were often decorated with valuable rings that needed careful safeguarding. In the same way the Hebrews were commanded to bind God's laws upon their fingers (Prov. 7:3; cf. Dt. 11:18). In 1 K. 12:10 and 2 Ch. 10:10 Rehoboam employs "finger" in a figurative sense.

Often the fingers were used in cultic ceremonies to sprinkle the blood of animals upon the horns of the altar (e.g., Ex. 29:12; Lev. 4:25), on or in front of the mercy seat (Lev. 16:14), and in front of the tent of meeting (Lev. 4:6; Nu. 19:4). In the administration of the guilt offering the priest was instructed to use his right finger (Lev. 14:16, 27). (*See also* SACRIFICES AND OFFERINGS IN THE OT.)

The "finger of God," a highly anthropomorphic phrase like the "hand of God," is synonymous with divine power. Pharaoh's magicians had to concede that God was responsible for the plagues, that human means could not produce them (Ex. 8:19 [MT 15]). In Ps. 8:3 (MT 4) the psalmist stands in awe of the vast universe made by the fingers of God. For Moses God wrote the law with His own finger (Ex. 31:18; Dt. 9:10; cf. Ex. 32:15), impressing upon His people the infallible evidence of its divine authorship. In contrast, human fingers create idols (Isa. 2:8; but cf. 17:8) and are full of bloodshed (59:3). The "fingers of a man's hand" in Dnl. 5:5 refer to God's dramatic intrusion in Belshazzar's feast.

In the NT Jesus cast out demons by the "finger of God" (Lk. 11:20; on the relation of this verse to Mt. 12:28, see I. H. Marshall, Comm. on Luke [*New International Greek Testament Comm.*, 1978], pp. 475f.; see also *TDNT*, II, 20), signifying the heavenly origin of His power. The resurrected Christ allowed Thomas to touch Him with his fingers (Jn. 20:27).

The phrase "they themselves will not move them with their finger" (Mt. 23:4) refers to the Pharisees' practice of not removing with their fingers (= erasing) the numerous requirements of the (ceremonial) laws placed as a heavy burden upon the common people (*IB*, VII, 529).

For "finger" or "digit" as a linear measurement (1 K. 7:15; Jer. 52:21 [LXX *dáktylos*; Josephus *Ant.* viii.3.4 (77)]), *see* WEIGHTS AND MEASURES.

See HAND. H. L. E. LUERING R. W. V.

FINING POT (AV Prov. 17:3; 27:21). *See* CRUCIBLE.

FINISH. The most common OT and NT verbs rendered "finish" by the RSV are Heb. *kālâ* and Gk. *teléō;* the usual sense is "complete" or "end." Gen. 2:2, e.g., reads that "on the seventh day God finished [*kālâ;* AV "ended"; NEB "completed"] his work." In 2 Tim. 4:7 Paul says, "I have fought the good fight, I have finished the race" (*teléō*); the term in Lk. 13:32, however, is *teleióō,* where Jesus says, "the third day I finish my course" (Bauer, rev., p. 809, "reach my goal").

The most significant scriptural example is the cry upon the cross, "It is finished" (*tetélestai,* Jn. 19:30; cf. v. 28). The surface meaning is that Jesus' life is ended. The more important meaning, however, is that His work is completed: God's plan of redemption has been brought to completion. Thus, in John's Gospel Jesus' last word on the cross is a cry of triumph (cf. R. E. Brown, comm. on John [*AB*, 1970], II; L. Morris, comm. on John [*NICNT,* 1971]). N. J. O.

FINISHER. *See* PERFECTER.

FIR TREE [Heb. *b*[e]*rôš*] (Ps. 104:17; Ezk. 27:5; 31:8); NEB also "tops" (Ps. 104:17), PINE (Ezk. 27:5). The true fir, *Abies cilicia* Carr., though well suited to regions such as Lebanon, is seldom found there and as an identification has generally been abandoned by botanists in favor of either the pine (cf. NEB, 1 K. 5:8, 10; etc.; 2 K. 19:23; 2 Ch. 2:8; 3:5; Isa. 14:8; etc.; Hos. 14:8; Zec. 11:2) or cypress (the RSV rendering of the foregoing references). The NEB translates *b*[e]*rôš* in Ezk. 27:5 by "pine" as against the RSV "fir."

The Heb. *tiḏhār* (Isa. 41:19f.; 60:13), a rare word rendered "pine" (AV) and "plane" (RSV), is probably correctly translated by the NEB "fir." Evidently one of the juniper species is meant, perhaps *Juniperus excelsa* Bieb., a tall, sturdy tree resembling the cedar in shape and producing durable timber.

The AV consistently translates *b*[e]*rôš* by "fir," but the confusion attending the identification of many Hebrew trees and shrubs makes such a uniform rendering improbable. In 2 S. 6:5, the RSV ("with songs") and the NEB ("singing") follow the LXX (and the par. 1 Ch. 13:8), assuming only a slight change in the MT (*bšyrym* for *brwšym*). In Nah. 2:3 (MT 4) the RSV has "chargers" and the NEB "squadrons of horse," following the versions and requiring only a slight change in the MT (*pršym* for *bršym*).

See also CYPRESS; PINE TREE; PLANE TREE.

R. K. H.

FIRE [Heb. *'ēš* (Ex. 3:2; 22:6 [MT 5]; Ps. 39:3 [MT 4]; Jer. 51:58; Hab. 2:13; etc.), *'iššeh* ("offering by fire," Lev. 3:3, 9, 14; 7:25, etc.), *'ûr* (Isa. 31:9; 44:16; 47:14; 50:11; Ezk. 5:2), *śᵉrēpâ* (2 Ch. 16:14; 21:19); piel of *lāhaṭ*–'devour, scorch' ("set on fire," Dt. 32:22; Isa. 42:25), hiphil (or niphal; cf. *BH*, KoB, p. 397) of *yāṣaṭ* ("be on fire," Jer. 51:30); Aram. *nûr* (Dnl. 3:22, 24-27; 7:10), *'eššā'* (Dnl. 7:11); Gk. *pýr* (Mt. 17:15; Lk. 17:29; 1 Cor. 3:13; etc.), *pyrá* (Lk. 22:55; Acts 28:2f.), *pýrinos* (Rev. 9:17), *kausóō* (2 Pet. 3:10, 12), *phlogízō* (Jas. 3:6)]; AV also VERY FIRE (Hab. 2:13), BURNING (2 Ch. 16:14; 21:19), BURNED (Jer. 51:30), BURNING FLAME (Dnl. 7:11), etc.; NEB also FEVER (Ps. 39:3 [MT 4]), "mere nothing" (Jer. 51:58; Hab. 2:13), GREAT FIRE (2 Ch. 16:14), FLAMES (Dnl. 7:11), "red-hot" (Jas. 3:6), etc. On the meaning of *'iššeh*, see Hoftijzer. In Jer. 6:29 the *K* of the MT (*m'štm*) is corrupt; following the LXX and *Q*, read *m's tm*, "is consumed by the fire" (cf. *BH*, comms.).

"Fire" in the Bible may be discussed under three headings — literal, metaphorical, and eschatological. These divisions are somewhat artificial, however, and especially in some eschatological contexts it is difficult to distinguish the literal from the figurative.

I. Literal Fire.–*A. Domestic Fire*. The method of making fire is not mentioned in the Bible, unless friction by wood is implied in Nu. 15:32f. (cf. Ex. 35:3) and 1 K. 17:12 (see also flint fire in 2 Macc. 10:3). The necessary preservation of fire in hot coals may stand behind Prov. 25:32. Incidental references to domestic fire are relatively infrequent: e.g., metalwork (Ex. 32:24; Isa. 44:12; 54:16), baking, cooking, and warmth (Isa. 44:15f.; Mk. 14:54 par.; Jn. 18:18; 21:9; Acts 28:2-5; etc.).

B. Ritual Fire. Altar fires are frequently mentioned. Of particular interest is the legislation for a perpetual altar fire (Lev. 6:9ff. [MT 2 ff.]; cf. 24:1f.). This legislation, contrasted with the "unholy fire" of Nadab and Abihu (Lev. 10:1-3; cf. Nu. 3:4; 26:61), indicates, according to some scholars, special veneration for a fire of heavenly origin (cf. Lev. 9:24). More probably, the perpetual flame is maintained as a symbol of God's presence and human preparedness for perpetual sacrifice (cf. Lev. 6:8-13). The "unholy fire" may refer to an improper ritual — due perhaps to drunkenness (cf. Lev. 10:8-11) — rather than to an inherently unholy origin or quality. There is no other hint that the Hebrew religion included the worship of fire as such. The OT also refers to funeral burnings (2 Ch. 16:14; 21:19) and the persistent sin of child sacrifice in fire (e.g., Lev. 18:21; Dt. 12:31; etc.; *see also* MOLECH; SACRIFICES AND OFFERINGS IN THE OT V.D).

C. Civil and Military Fire. Fire had both purgative and punitive use. It was used to combat the contagion of diseases (Lev. 13:52, 55), gross sexual sins (Lev. 20:14; 21:9), and false religions (Dt. 7:5, 25; 12:3). Of particular effect was the punishment by "divine fire" (e.g., Lev. 10:2; Nu. 11:1-3; 16:35).

In military campaigns, the purgative and preventive role of fire merges with the punitive, especially in the conquest of Canaanite cities under the ban (e.g., Nu. 31:10; Josh. 6:24; 8:8, 19; 11:11). But burning a city with fire was a basic principle of ancient total warfare (e.g., Jgs. 1:8; 9:49; 18:27; 20:48; 1 S. 30:1-4; 1 K. 9:16), and eventually the same fate fell upon the Holy City (2 Ch. 36:19), as Jeremiah had sadly prophesied (Jer. 17:27; 21:10; 22:7; 32:29; etc.). Not surprisingly, then, the vengeance prophesied for the nation's enemies often included the burning of cities (Jer. 43:12f.; 49:27; etc.), expressed with particular effect in Amos (1:4-14; 2:2, 5).

D. Theophany. The ancient Hebrews described lightning as fire (e.g., Ex. 9:23) and may have regarded the lightning as angels (cf. the MT and LXX in Dt. 33:2; Ps. 104:4). Similarly, God's presence was seen in fire (e.g., Gen. 15:18): the burning bush (Ex. 3:1f.; Acts 7:30); the pillar of fire (Ex. 9:24; 13:12, 22; 14:24; Nu. 9:15f.); above all, the theophany of Sinai (Ex. 19:18). Several eschatological visions use this imagery (Isa. 4:5; 66:15; Dnl. 7:9f.; Mic. 1:4; Mal. 3:2; cf. also Ezk. 1:13). In the NT this fire motif continues. Thus the descent of the Holy Spirit is accompanied by "tongues as of fire" (Acts 2:3), and in John's vision of Christ, He has eyes "like a flame of fire" (Rev. 1:14; 2:18; 19:12).

II. Metaphorical Fire.–*A. Of Individuals*. Human speech (Prov. 16:27; Jas. 3:5f.), jealousy or passion (Cant. 8:6), vexation (Ps. 39:3; cf. NEB "fever"; Jer. 20:9; Lam. 1:13), peril (Ps. 66:12; Isa. 43:2; Zec. 3:2; Jude 23; cf. Am. 4:11), personal disaster or decline of prosperity (Job 18:5; 20:26), adulterous activity (Job 31:12), and wickedness (Isa. 9:18) are likened to fire.

B. As a Judgment on Nations or Peoples. Israel is "on fire" (Isa. 42:25); Israel is compared to an olive tree on fire (Jer. 11:16), a vine on fire (Ps. 80:16 [MT 17]; Ezk. 15:4-7; 19:12-14), thorns on fire (Isa. 33:12). Jerusalem is a caldron on fire (Ezk. 24:10-12); Babylon will be burned as chaff (Isa. 47:14). In the NT, similar pictures are presented (eschatologically) of unbelievers (e.g., Mt. 3:12; 13:24-30, 37-42; Jn. 15:1-6) or of believers' works (1 Cor. 3:13ff.).

C. Of God. His jealous wrath (Zeph. 1:18; 3:8), His wrath (e.g., Ps. 89:46 [MT 47]; Jer. 4:4; Lam. 2:4; Ezk. 21:31), His tongue (Isa. 30:27), His words (e.g., Jer. 23:29), and His presence (Ps. 68:2 [MT 3]) can be described in terms of fire. The same metaphor extends to God's judgment (Ps. 11:6; 21:9 [MT 10]; 97:3; Isa. 30:30; Jer. 21:14; Lam. 2:3; Ezk. 20:47; Am. 7:4).

Perhaps the strongest metaphor is "God is a devouring fire" (Dt. 4:24; He. 12:29; cf. Ex. 24:17; Dt. 9:3; cf. also *TDOT*, I, 238f.) This statement seems to be added as a warning to the people about the seriousness of their covenant responsibilities.

III. Eschatological Fire.–Occasionally in the prophets and usually in the NT, fire is mentioned in an eschatological context. (For postbiblical Jewish literature, see *TDNT*, VI, 937ff.)

A. Final Judgment of the World. The fire of final judgment is mentioned frequently in the OT, especially in the prophetic literature (Isa. 66:15f.; Ezk. 38:22; 39:6; Zeph. 1:18; 3:8; Zec. 12:6; cf. Mal. 4:1 [MT 3:19]), and in the NT as well (2 Pet. 3:7, 10, 12; also Rev. 8:7f.; 9:17f.; 16:8; 18:8; 20:9).

B. Eternal Fire as Hell. The OT references to hell fire are rare and disputed (esp. Isa. 34:10; 66:24). It is this fire to which the NT most often refers: eternal fire (Mt. 18:8; 25:41; Jude 7); unquenchable fire (Mt. 3:12; Mk. 9:43; Lk. 3:17); hell of fire (Mt. 5:22; 18:9; for GEHENNA alone, cf. Mt. 5:29f.; 10:28; 23:15, 33; Mk. 9:43, 45, 47; Lk. 12:5; Jas. 3:6); the furnace of fire (Mt. 13:42, 50); lake of fire (Rev. 19:20; 20:10, 14f.; 21:8).

C. Fire as a Sign of the Day of the Lord. While by implication fiery judgment would signal the Day of the Lord, fire is explicitly mentioned as a sign in Joel 2:30 (MT 3:3). In apocalyptic imagery, the Lord and the Son of man are identifiable by their fire (e.g., Dnl. 7:9-11; 2 Thess. 1:7; Lk. 17:29f.; Rev. 1:14; 2:18; etc.).

As final eschatological victory has been anticipated in Christ, so also has been His judgment. Christ is introduced (Mt. 3:10f.; Lk. 3:16f.) as baptizing "with the Holy Spirit and with fire." "Fire" is sometimes seen as "purifying" to lessen its contrast to "Holy Spirit." But the contrast is intended, just as "wheat" is gathered to the granary and the "chaff" to the furnace. This baptism of fire is amplified in Lk. 12:49-51. Remarking that He came to cast fire upon the earth, Jesus continued to say that He must wait until His own baptism was accomplished. This was done at Calvary and the judgment thereby assured. Mk. 9:49 ("For every one will be salted with fire") is difficult but perhaps best explained from the OT sacrifice that was "salted" (Lev. 2:13; Ezk. 43:24). Each believer is a "sacrifice" to God, made suitable by the "fire" of self-imposed judgment (cf. Mk. 9:43f.) or perhaps of persecution.

Bibliography.–TDOT, I, *s.v.* "'ēsh" (Bergman, Krecher, Hamp); II, *s.v.* "b'r" (Ringgren); *Jew.Enc.,* V, *s.v.* "Fire" (E. G. Hirsch); *TDNT,* VI, *s.v.* πῦρ (Lang); P. D. Miller, *CBQ,* 27 (1965), 256-261; J. Morgenstern, *Fire upon the Altar* (1963); J. Hoftijzer, "Das sogenannte Feueropfer," in B. Hartmann, *et al.,* eds., *Hebräische Wortforschung* (*SVT,* 16; 1967), pp. 114-134.

H. VAN BROEKHOVEN, JR.

FIRE BAPTISM. *See* BAPTISM OF FIRE; MOLECH.

FIRE, LAKE OF. *See* LAKE OF FIRE.

FIRE, PILLAR OF. *See* PILLAR OF CLOUD AND PILLAR OF FIRE.

FIRE, STRANGE. *See* UNHOLY FIRE.

FIRE, UNQUENCHABLE. *See* UNQUENCHABLE FIRE.

FIREBRAND. The RSV uses this term only twice and in the plural form. In Prov. 26:18 Heb. *ziqqîm,* "sparks" (NEB "darts"), describes fiery torches in the hands of a madman, while in Isa. 7:4 *'ûḏîm* (NEB "firewood") is used figuratively of angry men.

FIREPAN [Heb. *maḥtâ*] (Nu. 4:14; 1 K. 7:50; 2 K. 25:15; 2 Ch. 4:22; Jer. 52:19); AV also CENSER. A vessel for carrying coals. Brazen firepans were part of the furnishings of the altar of burnt offerings (Nu. 4:14). In 1 K. 7:50; 2 K. 25:15; 2 Ch. 4:22; Jer. 52:19 the firepans were apparently of gold and were used in conjunction with the golden candlestick to receive the burnt ends of the wicks. A similar firepan is described by the same term but rendered "censer" (Lev. 10:1; 16:12; Nu. 16:6, 17f., 37-39); this was used to carry the glowing coals upon which the incense was thrown and burned. *See also* CENSER.

FIRKIN fûr'kin. The AV translation of Gk. *metrētḗs,* stone jars used for the Jewish rites of purification. The British firkin was one-fourth of a barrel. *See* GALLON; WEIGHTS AND MEASURES.

FIRM; FIRMLY; FIRMNESS [Heb. *ḥāzaq*–'be strong' (2 K. 14:5; 2 Ch. 25:3; piel, Isa. 33:23; hiphil, Dnl. 11:32); *kûn*–'be stable, secure' (niphal, 1 K. 2:12; 1 Ch. 16:30; Ps. 112:7; hiphil, Ps. 89:2 [MT 3]); *'āmaṣ*–'be strong' (piel, Job 4:4; Prov. 8:28; Isa. 35:3); *'āman*–'be lasting, sure' (niphal, Ps. 89:28, 37 [MT 29, 38]); *'ᵃmānâ*–'sure, firm' (Neh. 9:38 [MT 10:1]); *yāṣaḇ*–'stand' (hithpael, Ex. 14:13; niphal, Ps. 119:89); *yāṣaq*–'pour out, cast' (Job 41:23 [MT 15]); *ḥubbar lāh yāḥdāw*–'be bound firmly together' (Ps. 122:3); *nāṭa'*–'plant, infix' (Eccl. 12:11); *'āṭâ 'āṭōh*–'grasp firmly' (Isa. 22:17); *bᵉ'ēṯān*–'in perpetuity' (following *BH* emendation of MT *yittēn,* Prov. 12:12); Aram. *niṣbᵉṯā'*–'hardness' (Dnl. 2:41); Gk. *stḗkō*–'stand firm, be resolute, steadfast' (1 Cor. 16:13; Phil. 1:27; 4:1; 2 Thess. 2:15); *stereós*–'solid, firm' (1 Pet. 5:9); *steréōma*–'solidity, steadfastness' (Col. 2:5); *hístēmi*–'stand firm' (2 Cor. 1:24; 2 Tim. 2:19), *antéchō*–'hold on to firmly' (Tit. 1:9); *bébaios*–'steadfast' (He. 3:14); *pistóō*–'be assured of' (2 Tim. 3:14)]; AV also CONFIRM(ED), ESTABLISH(ED), WELL, STRONG, etc.; NEB also FAITHFUL, FIX(ED), STEADFAST, SECURE, etc.

In the OT the psalmist states that God's covenant with David "will stand firm for him" (Ps. 89:28), which means that, as promised (cf. 2 S. 7:12-16), David's dynasty will be perpetual (cf. A. Weiser, *Psalms* [Eng. tr., *OTL,* 1962], pp. 592f.). In another psalm Yahweh's word is said to be "firmly fixed in the heavens" (Ps. 119:89), which perhaps means that the precepts, statutes, etc. about which the psalmist has been speaking (e.g., vv. 4f.) have (in the language of personification) their permanent residence with God in heaven. Alternatively, it may mean that these precepts, etc. are as enduring as the heavens (emending *baššāmayim* to *kaššāmayim;* so NAB; cf. W. O. E. Oesterley, *Psalms* [1939], p. 494), or that they are more stable than the heavens (M. Dahood, *Psalms,* III [*AB,* 1970], 183f., who posits a comparative meaning for the preposition *b*). In the line of a psalm that the Chronicler attributes to Asaph and his brothers it is said that "the world stands firm, never to be moved" (1 Ch. 16:30; cf. Ps. 96:10). This is perhaps a poetic reference to the ancient notion that the world was constructed upon and supported by pillars (cf., e.g., 1 S. 2:8; Ps. 75:3 [MT 4]). Wisdom (personified) says that she was there when Yahweh "made firm the skies above" (Prov. 8:28), which is probably a reference to the creation of the heavenly dome or firmament (L. I. J. Stadelmann, *Hebrew Conception of the World* [*Analecta Biblica,* 1970], p. 100).

In the NT Paul encourages the Corinthians to "stand firm in [their] faith" (1 Cor. 16:13; cf. 2 Cor. 1:24), which means to maintain a persistent attitude of belief and obedience to the Lord and to the teachings/traditions delivered to them by Paul and his representatives (cf. 2 Thess. 2:15). He tells the Colossians of his joy "to see... the firmness of [their] faith in Christ" (2:5). This use of *steréōma,* "firmness," may contain an allusion to the Gnostic *steréōma,* which was the solid barrier between the upper and lower realms (H. Chadwick, *NTS,* 1 [1954/55], 272f.).

Bibliography.–TDNT, VI, *s.v.* πιστεύω κτλ. (Bultmann, Weiser); στερεός κτλ. (Bertram); *TDOT,* I, *s.v.* "'āman" (Jepsen).

J. E. H.

FIRMAMENT [Heb. *rāqî(a)'*] (NEB VAULT, VAULT OF HEAVEN). The expanse of the atmosphere or sky. This term is derived from *firmamentum,* the Vulg. rendering of the LXX *steréōma*. Although in classical Greek the latter denoted something solid, or a firm structure such as a foundation, its LXX usage was of the open sky, or the expanse stretching above the earth. This curious divergence of meaning is matched by the difficulty in translating the original Hebrew term *rāqî(a)'*. It is a cognate form of the verb *rq'*, "spread out" (Ps. 136:6; Isa. 42:5; 44:24), or "beat out" (Ex. 39:3; Nu. 17:4), the former usage referring to the expanse of the heavens at creation, and the latter to the beating out of metal into thin plates or sheets.

In Job 37:18 the existence of the vault of heaven is attributed to God's spreading it out, "hard as a molten mirror." From this poetic allusion some writers have assumed the existence of a primitive cosmology in which the universe was formed as a hollow, beaten-out sphere, using the analogy of the "brassy heaven" of Homer. A concept of this kind was never part of Greek cosmology, however, which like its Babylonian and Egyptian counterparts conceived of water encircling the cosmos both above and below it. Even Homer spoke of an all-encompassing river, Oceanus, which surrounded the universe (cf. *Iliad* xviii. 483-85; xxi. 194-97). The suggestion by T. H. Gaster (*IDB*, II, 270) that in Job 26:13 the sweep of the winds across the sky represented God breathing on the hard metallic surface of the firmament in order to polish it seems to overemphasize the poetic imagery of what is only a basic process of atmospheric self-renewal.

In Gen. 1:6 the firmament comprised an expanse that penetrated the mass of water vapor covering the earth and divided it into lower (or terrestrial) and upper (or atmospheric) levels. The expanse that was formed by the lifting of the water vapor constituted the atmosphere, which stretched around the earth and made possible the existence of subsequent plant and animal life. In Gen. 1:8, the expanse was given the name "heaven" (*šāmayim*), a better translation of which would be "sky" (cf. Ps. 85:11 [MT 12]; Prov. 30:19).

The word firmament occurs only in the OT, and always within the context of creation, of which the nine occurrences in Gen. 1 are representative. In Ps. 19:1 (MT 2) the sky and the firmament are parallel and synonymous terms used to symbolize the unanimity with which cosmic creation adulates its Creator. The brightness of the ethereal expanse above the earth was alluded to in Dnl. 12:3, when in the eschatological disclosure the wise were to shine like the brightness of the firmament. In certain OT passages the firmament was conceived of as God's sanctuary (Ps. 150:1) in which man could offer Him praise, or as forming the foundation of a celestial throne room (Ezk. 1:26) which contained the likeness of God's glory. In this passage the imagery is highly pictorial in nature, but it still manages to preserve, and even enhance, the general concept of brightness associated with the firmament by describing it as "shining like crystal" (Ezk. 1:22). The relationship of the firmament to the concept of heaven can be clarified if the firmament is identified with the troposphere, and then by thinking of the celestial heavens either as a topographic dimension beyond the firmament itself, or as the designated abode of God (cf. Ps. 33:13f.; Isa. 63:15; Lk. 16:9). R. K. H.

FIRST. The most common words for "first" are Heb. *ri'šôn, 'eḥāḏ,* and Gk. *prṓtos, prṓton*. Other words include Heb. *rē'šîṯ*–'beginning' (Nu. 15:20; 24:20; Neh. 10:37 [MT 38]; Am. 6:1); AV also FIRSTFRUITS, CHIEF; *qeḏem*–'in front,' 'before,' 'aforetime' (Prov. 8:22); AV, NEB, BEFORE; *rō'š*–'head,' 'top,' 'chief' (Prov. 8:23, 26); AV BEGINNING, HIGHEST PART; NEB BEGINNING; and Gk. *próteron*–'formerly' (2 Cor. 1:15; Gal. 4:13); AV BEFORE; *mía*–'one' (Mt. 28:1 par.; Rev. 9:12); AV also ONE; *archḗ*–'beginning,' 'ruler,' 'rule' (Jn. 2:11; 6:64; He. 2:3; 5:12); AV also BEGINNING; NEB also "all along."

Hebrew *ri'šôn* and *rē'šîṯ* differ in that the former generally means "first in order" (e.g., in a series), and (along with *'eḥāḏ*–'one') is thus always the word used in temporal references (cf. Gen. 8:5; Ex. 40:2; Nu. 9:1), whereas the latter means "first in importance," "choicest, " "best," and thus can mean FIRST FRUITS. Thus, Moses is commanded to cut two tablets of stone like the first ones (*ri'šōnîm*) that he had broken (Ex. 34:1, 4; cf. also Gen. 25:25), and Israel is called the "first [i.e., "best," "choicest," *rē'šîṯ*] of the nations" (Am. 6:1; cf. also Nu. 24:20, "Amalek was the first of the nations"). "At the first" (Gen. 13:4; Neh. 7:5; Isa. 1:26; 52:4) translates *bāri'šōnâ*.

Greek *prṓtos* can mean both first in order and first in rank. As "first in order," Acts 1:1 refers to the Gospel of Luke as the "first book," Paul speaks of his "first defense" (2 Tim. 4:16), and He. 9:1, 15, 18, etc., discuss the "first covenant." Likewise, Christ is called the "first to rise from the dead" (Acts 26:23), and He designates Himself "the first and the last" (Rev. 1:17; 2:8; 22:13), the same title which Yahweh gives to Himself in Isa. 44:6; 48:12 (Heb. *ri'šôn 'aḥ^a rôn*). Examples of *prṓtos* in the sense of "first in rank," "most important" are: Mt. 22:38, where Jesus calls the commandment to love God with one's whole being "the great and first commandment" (cf. Mk. 12:28f.); Mt. 20:27, "whoever would be first among you must be your slave" (cf. Mt. 19:30; 20:16 par.); and 1 Tim. 1:15, where Paul calls himself the "foremost of sinners." *En prṓtois* ("among the first, most important things") in 1 Cor. 15:3 is translated "as of first importance." The adverbial form *prṓton* has this twofold meaning, too, e.g., Mt. 13:30, "gather the weeds first"; Mt. 6:33, "But seek first [i.e., above all, especially] his kingdom"). Other NT words translated with "first" are *phthánō* (2 Cor. 10:14) and *prophthánō* (Mt. 17:25), meaning "come before," "precede"; *proelpízō,* "be the first to hope" (Eph. 1:12); and *philoprōteúō,* "wish to be first" (3 Jn. 9). "When we first believed" in Rom. 13:11 translates *hóte episteúsamen,* the aorist tense being understood in an inchoative sense. Christ's reply to the request that some of His disciples be first (i.e., the most important ones) in the kingdom of God is fitting: "whoever would be first . . . must be [a] slave" (Mt. 20:27; cf. Mt. 19:30 par.). Among believers preeminence becomes service.

For "first principles" in He. 5:12 *see* PRINCIPLES; for "first and second Adam," *see* ADAM (NT) III.

Bibliography.–*TDNT,* I, *s.v.* ἄρχω κτλ.: ἀρχή (Delling); VI, *s.v.* πρῶτος κτλ.: πρῶτος, πρῶτον (Michaelis); *TDOT,* I, *s.v.* "'echādh" (Lohfink, Bergman). R. C. TOGTMAN

FIRST FRUITS [Heb. *bikkûrîm, rē'šîṯ*; Gk. *aparchḗ*]. In acknowledgment of the fact that the land and all its products were the gift of Yahweh to Israel, and in thankfulness for His bounty, all the first fruits were offered to Him. These were offered in their natural state (e.g., cereals, tree fruits, grapes), or after preparation (e.g., musk, oil, flour, dough), after which the Israelites were at liberty to use the rest (Ex. 23:19; Nu. 15:20; 18:12; Dt. 26:2; Neh. 10:35, 37). No absolute distinction can be made between *rē'šîṯ* and *bikkûrîm,* but *rē'šîṯ* seems generally to mean what is prepared by human labor, and *bikkûrîm* the direct product of nature. The phrase "the first of the first fruits" (Ex. 23:19; 34:26; Ezk. 44:30, Heb. *rē'šîṯ bikkûrê'*) is not quite clear. It may mean the first ripe or the choicest of the first fruits. The *rē'šîṯ* offerings were individual, except that a *rē'šîṯ* of dough was to be offered as a heave offering (Nu. 15:17-21). The priest waved a *rē'šîṯ* of corn before the Lord on the morrow after the sabbath in the week of unleavened bread (Lev. 23:9-11). These offerings were given to the priests (Nu. 18:12). *Bikkûrîm* refers specially to things sown (Ex. 23:16; Lev. 2:14). At the Feast of Weeks, seven weeks after the offering of the sheaf, *bikkûrîm* of corn in the ear, parched with fire and bruised, were brought to the house of the Lord as a meal offering (Ex. 34:22–26; Lev. 2:14–16). The *bikkûrîm* also were meant for the priest, except a portion that was burned as a memorial (Lev. 2:8–10, 16). The beautiful ceremony of the offering of the *rē'šîṯ* in the house of God is described in Dt. 26:1–11 and is enlarged upon in the Talmud (Mish. *Bikkurim* iii.2). According to the Talmud (Mish. *Terumoth* iv.3) a sixtieth part of the first fruits in a prepared form was the minimum that could be offered; the more generous brought a fortieth part, and even a thirtieth. The fruits of newly planted trees were not to be gathered during the first three years; the fruits of the fourth year were consecrated to Yahweh and from the fifth year the fruits belonged to the owner of the trees (Lev. 19:23-25). According to Mish. *Orlah* i.10, even the shells of nuts and pomegranates could not be used during the first three years as coloring matter or for the lighting of fires. It is held by some scholars that the institution of the tithe (but *see* TITHE) is a later development from the first fruits.

In Jer. 2:3 Israel is called "the first fruits of his harvest." In the NT *aparchḗ* is applied figuratively to the first convert(s) in a particular place (Rom. 16:5; 1 Cor. 16:15); to the Christians of that age (Jas. 1:18; 2 Thess. 2:13), and to the 144,000 in heaven (Rev. 14:4); to Christ, as the first who rose from the dead (1 Cor. 15:20, 23); as well as to the blessings which we receive now through the Spirit, the earnest of greater blessings to come (Rom. 8:23).

P. LEVERTOFF

FIRST-BEGOTTEN. *See* FIRST-BORN.

FIRST-BORN; FIRSTLING [Heb. *bᵉḵōr*; Gk. *prōtótokos*]. The Hebrew word denotes the first-born of human beings as well as of animals (Ex. 11:5), while a word from the same root denotes first fruits (Ex. 23:16).

Some of the early Semitic tribes believed that the first-born belonged to the deity and had to be offered up sacrificially. Child burials uncovered at some Palestinian sites have been interpreted occasionally as the remains of such sacrifices, but direct evidence for this supposition, associated with Megiddo, Jericho, and elsewhere, is lacking. Thus the narrative of the Moabite war records that Mesha sacrificed the heir to the throne to Chemosh, the national god (2 K. 3:27). This barbarous custom must have become extinct at an early period in the religion of Israel (Gen. 22:12). It was probably due to the influence of surrounding nations that the cruel practice was revived toward the close of the monarchical period (2 K. 16:3; 17:17; 21:6; Jer. 7:31; Ezk. 16:20; 23:37; Mic. 6:7).

Already in the patriarchal period a ram was deemed an acceptable sacrificial substitute for the first-born (Gen. 22:13), but at the time of the EXODUS God renewed His claim to the first-born of humans and animals (Ex. 13:1-16). Since heathen practices involving child sacrifice were abhorrent to God, the first-born child was redeemed while corresponding animals were offered as a sacrificial offering. But even the firstling of an ass could be redeemed through the sacrifice of a kid. A special degree of sanctity was accorded to first-born male animals, and certain prohibitions were attached to them (Dt. 15:19).

The regulations governing the first-born were given spiritual significance by being connected with the miraculous departure of the Israelites from Egypt, and with the enactments concerning the Feast of Unleavened Bread (Ex. 13:1-10). It was also made incumbent upon the Israelites to observe these prescriptions once they were in sedentary occupation of the Promised Land (Ex. 13:11), as a reminder of God's saving power and also as a safeguard against the influence of heathen customs.

In the wilderness period there was instituted the practice of consecrating the Levites for service in the Lord's sanctuary as a substitute for the offering of the first-born (Nu. 3:11-13, 45). On the thirtieth day after birth the first-born was brought to the priest by the father, who paid five shekels for the child's redemption from service in the temple (cf. Lk. 2:27; Mish. *Berakoth* viii.8).

The first-born possessed definite privileges which were denied to other members of the family. The Law forbade the disinheriting of the first-born (Dt. 21:15-17). Such legislation, in polygamous times, was necessary to prevent a favorite wife from exercising undue influence over her husband in distributing his property, as in the case of Jacob (Gen. 25:23). The oldest son's share was twice as large as that of any other son. When Elisha prayed for a double portion of Elijah's spirit, he simply wished to be considered the first-born, i.e., the successor, of the dying prophet. Israel was Yahweh's first-born (Ex. 4:22; cf. Jer. 31:9 [Ephraim]). Israel, as compared with other nations, was entitled to special privileges. She occupied a unique position in virtue of the special relationship between Yahweh and the nation. In three passages (Rom. 8:29; Col. 1:15; He. 1:6), Jesus Christ is the first-born — among many brethren (Rom. 8:29) — of every creature (Col. 1:16).

It is important that the relationship between Jesus as first-born of Mary (Mt. 1:25; Lk. 2:7) and as the first-born of all creation (Col. 1:15) be understood correctly. The incarnate Christ is still truly God, while as "first-born" Jesus exercises complete preeminence over all created things. As first-born from the dead (Rev. 1:5) Christ demonstrates His power over death and the grave and initiates the new life in which all believers rejoice. The "assembly of the first-born" (Heb. 12:23) represents the corpus of those who have died in the Christian faith and are in the nearer presence of God. Because the believer is "in Christ," he shares the privileges of Christ's own relationship to God as first-born. A messianic interpretation of the term may also be derived from Ps. 89:27, in which the Davidic ruler is described as the Lord's first-born.

See CHILD II.B; CIRCUMCISION; PLAGUES OF EGYPT.

T. LEWIS
R. K. H.

FIRSTLING. *See* FIRST-BORN.

FISH [Heb. *dāg, dāḡâ, dā'g*; Gk. *ichthýs, ichthýdion, opsárion, prosphágion*].

Fishes abound in the inland waters of Palestine as well as in the Mediterranean. They are often mentioned or indirectly referred to both in the OT and in the NT, but it is remarkable that no particular kind is distinguished by name. In Lev. 11:9-12 and Dt. 14:9f. "whatever has fins and scales" is declared clean, while all that "have [not] fins and scales" are forbidden. This excluded not only reptiles and amphibians, but also, among fishes, siluroids and eels, sharks, rays, and lampreys.

The most remarkable feature of the fish fauna of the Jordan Valley is its relationship to that of the Nile and East Central Africa. Two Nile fishes, *Chromis nilotica*

Coptic stone relief (4th cent. A.D.) of fish and cross, two symbols of Christianity (Louvre)

Hasselquist, and *Clarias macracanthus* Gunth., are found in the Jordan Valley, and a number of other species found only in the Jordan Valley belong to genera (*Chromis* and *Hemichromis*) that are otherwise exclusively African. This seems to indicate that at some time, probably in the early Tertiary, there was some connection between the Palestinian and African river systems. No fish can live in the Dead Sea, and many perish after being carried down by the swift currents of the Jordan and other streams. There are, however, several kinds of small fish which live in salt springs on the borders of the Dead Sea. *Capoëta damascena* Cuv. and Val., a common fish of Syria and Palestine, also finds its way occasionally to the approaches of the Dead Sea.

There are three main varieties of fish in the Sea of Galilee, comprising *Cichlidae,* which include the Tilapia or "St. Peter's fish"; the *Cyprinidae* or carp family, ranging from the Barbel species to the small lake "sardine," and the *Siluridae* or catfish. Not indigenous to the Sea in Bible times, but of comparatively recent introduction, is the Gray Mullet (*Mugil cephalus*).

Fishes are mentioned indiscriminately in Scripture, and aside from being recognized as "clean" or "unclean" according to the Mosaic law there seems to have been no other form of differentiation or attempt at classification (cf. Gen. 1:26; 9:2; Nu. 11:22; Dt. 4:18; 1 K. 4:33; etc.).

Figuratively, the fish "declare" that God punished Job (12:8). That so many of Our Lord's disciples were fishermen lends a profound interest to their profession. Christ tells Simon and Andrew (Mt. 4:19 par.) that He will make them fishers of men (cf. W. H. Wuellner, *Meaning of "Fishers of Men"* [1967]). The kingdom of heaven (Mt. 13:47) is likened to a net that was cast into the sea. When it was filled, men gathered the good into vessels, but the bad they threw away. Such sorting processes are still common among fishermen in Galilee and elsewhere. In Jer. 16:16 God promised that foreign peoples would drag the apostate inhabitants of Judah out of their hiding places as a fisherman plucks a fish from the depths of the waters. Then they would be punished the way that freshly caught fish were treated, namely, by having sticks placed through their gills ready for being carried away (cf. Job 41:2).

In the vision of Ezekiel (47:9f.), the multitude of fish and the nets spread from En-gedi to En-eglaim are marks of the marvelous change wrought in the Dead Sea by the stream issuing from the temple. The same sign, i.e., of the spreading of nets (Ezk. 26:5, 14), marks the desolation of Tyre. It is a piece of broiled fish that the risen Lord eats with the Eleven in Jerusalem (Lk. 24:42), and by the Sea of Galilee (Jn. 21:13) He gives the disciples bread and fish. By NT times there was a thriving trade in fish caught in the Mediterranean and brought to ports such as Tyre and Sidon. The fish was preserved in salt and brought to Jerusalem, where some of it was sold at a specially named "Fish Gate" in the city (*see* JERUSALEM).

For the "great fish" in Jonah, *see* JONAH. A. E. DAY
R. K. H.

FISH GATE. *See* JERUSALEM.

FISHER; FISHERMAN [Heb. *dawwāg* (Jer. 16:16; Ezk. 47:10), *dayyāg* (Isa. 19:8); Gk. *halieús*]. Although the Bible makes few references to fishermen, these men and their vocation are brought into prominence by Jesus' call to certain Galilean fishermen to become His disciples (Mt. 4:18f. par.). Fishermen, then as now, formed a distinct class. The strenuousness of the work (Lk. 5:2-5) ruled out the weak and indolent. They were crude in manner, rough in speech and in their treatment of others (Lk. 9:49, 54; Jn. 18:10). James and John before they became tempered by Jesus' influence were nicknamed the "sons of thunder" (Mk. 3:17). The fishermen's exposure to all kinds of weather made them hardy and fearless. They were accustomed to bear with patience many trying circumstances. They often toiled for hours without success; yet they were always ready to try once more (Lk. 5:5; Jn. 21:3). Such men, when impelled by the same spirit as filled their Master, became indeed "fishers of men" (Mt. 4:19; Mk. 1:17; cf. Lk. 5:10). J. A. PATCH

FISHER'S COAT. This expression is found in the AV of Jn. 21:7 where the RSV has "clothes" and the NEB "coat." John here, after representing Peter as "naked" (Gk. *gymnós*), pictures him as girding on his "coat" (*ependýtēs*), literally "outer garment," and not specifically a "fisher's coat." *See* COAT; GARMENTS.

FISHHOOK [Heb. *ṣîr dûgâ*] (Am. 4:2); NEB FISH-BASKET; [*ḥakkâ*] (Job 41:1 [MT 40:25]); AV HOOK; NEB GAFF. The ancient Hebrews appear to have fished in order to feed themselves rather than for sport, and thus the net was preferred to the hook, which caught only one fish at a time. Reliefs from Egypt and Assyria depict individual fishermen catching fish by means of a fishhook, and the antiquity of the device is indicated by the presence of bone fishhooks at Natufian levels. Iron hooks from the Solomonic period have been found at Ezion-geber. The use by Amos of *sîr* might indicate that the original fishhook in Israel was a curved thorn. In Hebrew tradition the hook and line were familiar objects (cf. Isa. 19:8); but there is no mention of fishing rods, since these do not appear to have been used significantly in the ancient Near East. R. K. H.

An Assyrian, with a basket holding his catch on his back, fishes with a line in a mountain pool. Gypsum relief (7th cent. B.C.) from Kuyunjik (Nineveh) (Trustees of the British Museum)

FISHING. In the OT fishing is rarely mentioned and did not play an important role in economic life. The Mediterranean Sea was full of fish (Ezk. 47:10), but its shores were occupied by the Philistines and Phoenicians. The Dead Sea had no fish (cf. Ezk. 47:9f. to the contrary). The river Jordan and its main tributaries had some fish, but not enough for any considerable part of the population to live on. The Baḥret el-Kheit (the northernmost lake formed by the river Jordan) was called Semechonitis in Josephus' time and Samko in the Palestinian Talmud and therefore must have been a fishing place (cf. Arab. *samak*,

Fishing and fowling in the marshes. At right a man spears a fish. Painting of mural in tomb of Menna (18th Dynasty, 15th cent. B.C.) at Thebes (Oriental Institute, University of Chicago)

"fish"). Finally, there was Lake Tiberias, whose abundance of fish is mentioned only in the NT.

In most instances where fishing is mentioned in the OT, the reference is to countries outside Palestine, especially Egypt (cf. Nu. 11:5) and Phoenicia, which sent dried salted fish to Jerusalem (Neh. 13:16; cf. Zeph. 1:10). Fishing as a trade is mentioned in Isa. 19:8 (Egypt); Jer. 16:16 (metaphor for foreigners); and Ezk. 47:10 (in an ideal future). Lev. 11:9-12 and Dt. 14:9f. draw a line between inhabitants of the water that may be eaten and those that may not (*see* FISH).

Fish were caught in three ways: (1) by hook (without a rod), Heb. *ḥakkâ* (Isa. 19:8; Hab. 1:15; Job 41:1 [MT 40:25]), *sîrâ* (Am. 4:2), and *ḥāḥ* (Ezk. 29:4) or *ḥô(a)ḥ* (Job 41:2 [MT 40:26], perhaps rather a thorn put through the branchiae to carry the fish home; bronze hooks found in Tell el-ʿAjjûl look like modern ones); (2) by a fish spear or harpoon, frequently used in Egypt, Heb. *ṣilṣāl* and *śukkâ* (Job 41:7 [MT 40:31]); (3) by nets. *Meṣôḏâ* seems to be a general word for a "catching" net (Eccl. 9:12); *rešeṯ*, otherwise a hunting net, is mentioned in Ezk. 32:3 as a means to catch a sea monster; *mikmereṯ* (Hab. 1:15f.) or *mikmōreṯ* (Isa. 19:8) is a net cast from the shore, which falls flat on the water and sinks by means of leaden weights; *ḥerem* is a seine, leaded on one edge and provided with floats on the other; it is payed out from boats and gradually drawn in to the shore (Ezk. 26:5, 14; 32:3; Hab. 1:15-17). Most words used in connection with fishing are also familiar from hunting vocabulary.

In the NT, especially the Gospels, fishing as a trade is frequently mentioned. This is quite different from the OT and is probably the result of the shifting of the main scene from Judea to Galilee. There were several important centers of fishing and fish industry along the shore of Lake Tiberias, as attested by the names Bethsaida ("house of fishing"), Magdala (Migdal Nūnayā, "bulwark of the fishes"), and Tarichaea ("salting installation for fish," the Greek name of Magdala). Fish was a common dish, not only in Galilee (Mt. 7:10; 14:17 par.; 15:34 par.; Jn. 21:9) but also in Jerusalem (Lk. 24:42). Several of the disciples of Jesus were fishermen (Gk. *halieús,* Mt. 4:18 par.; Lk. 5:2), and after His resurrection Jesus appeared to seven of them while they were fishing (Jn. 21:2).

As in the OT, fishing is done with the help of a hook without rod (Gk. *ánkistron,* Mt. 17:27), with a net cast from the shore (*amphíblēstron,* Mt. 4:18 par.), and with nets payed out from boats. Here the NT distinguishes between the *sagḗnē* (Mt. 13:47), the seine, which is only a few feet high and is cast out in shallow water, and the *díktyon,* also a seine but six or more feet high (Mt. 4:20f. par.; Lk. 5:1-8; Jn. 21:1-11). This last net was not normally pulled to the shore, as the seine was, but was lifted into the ships (Lk. 5:7; Jn. 21:8 is an exception). One of the fishermen had to be ready to dive if the net should be caught on the rocks of the sea bottom (Jn. 21:7). The harpoon or fish spear is not mentioned in the NT. As the steering oar of the boats was on the right side, the *díktyon* was pushed out over the left board, lest it should be caught by the end of the steering oar. The command "Cast the net on the right side of the ship" (Jn. 21:6) required something quite unusual.

Egyptian funerary models made of papyrus (9th Dynasty): fishing boats and fish being caught in a net (Metropolitan Museum of Art, photograph by Egyptian Expedition)

Fishermen were the owners of their own ships, took hirelings into their service, and sometimes joined together to form companies (Mk. 1:20; Lk. 5:7). One should, therefore, regard the disciples as members of the lower middle class rather than a very low social class.

See also FISH.

Bibliography.–P. Montet, *Les Scènes de la vie privée dans les tombeaux Egyptiens de l'ancien empire* (1925), pp. 20-42; A. G. Barrois, *Manuel d'archéologie biblique*, I (1939), 347-49; G. Dalman, *Orte und Wege Jesu* (1924), pp. 142-46. A. VAN SELMS

FISHPOOLS (Cant. 7:4, AV). This is a mistranslation. The Heb. *b^e rēḵôṯ* simply means "pools" (RSV); "fish" is quite unwarrantably introduced in the AV. In Isa. 19:10, again, instead of "all that make sluices and ponds for fish" (AV), one should read with the RSV, "All who work for hire will be grieved."

FIST. *See* GESTURE; HAND.

FIT. The Hebrew phrase *ʿēzer k^e negdô* in Gen. 2:18, 20 is translated "a helper fit for him" (AV "help meet for him"; NEB "partner for him"). Literally the expression means "a helper according to what is in front of him," i.e., "corresponding to him," "his complement."

In 2 K. 10:3 the Heb. adjective *yāšār,* "straight, right," "just, upright," is used in the superlative degree in a discussion of throne succession to refer to the "fittest of your master's sons" (AV "meetest"; NEB "most suitable"), i.e., the "most right" for the job. *See also* MEET; RIGHT.

Hebrew *yāpeh,* "fair, beautiful," most commonly an attribute of women, is used in Eccl. 5:18 (MT 17) in evaluating certain actions as behavior that is good and "fitting" (AV "comely"; NEB "proper"). Also having reference to appropriate behavior is Aram. *'^a rîḵ,* "fitting, proper," in Ezr. 4:14 (AV "meet"; NEB "right"). *See also* PROPER.

In Prov. 25:11 praise is given for a word that is "fitly spoken" (NEB "spoken in season"). The sense of the Heb. *ʿal-'opnāw* is usually understood as "(spoken) at its times" or "in its circumstances," i.e., "appropriately." This meaning, however, is not at all certain, for **'ōpen* is a hapax legomenon in the OT. The term has traditionally been associated with the more common *'ôpan,* "wheel," and thus, supposedly, denoting "circumstance" as an abstraction from the root sense of "turning" (see BDB, p. 67). The suggestion has been made that the vowels have been mispointed and that the form should rather be *'ōpannāw* (dual of *'ôpan,* "wheel"). The underlying hypothesis is that the dual of "wheel" may have served as a technical term in wisdom poetry referring to the two balancing halves of a wisdom sentence, and that in the context of Prov. 25:11 it would mean "a compact elegance of expression" (see KoB, p. 78, and W. McKane, *Proverbs* [*OTL,* 1970], p. 584). Another etymological proposal relates this word to Arab. *fannu(n),* "manner, mode" with the sense "at the right moment" (see KoB, p. 78).

In Cant. 5:12 the bride alludes figuratively to the eyes of her lover: "His eyes are like doves/beside springs of water,/bathed in milk,/fitly set." The phrase "fitly set" (NEB "they sit where it [water] is drawn") is an attempt to render the obscure Heb. *yōš^e ḇôṯ ʿal-millē'ṯ*. The first part of the phrase is clear — the feminine plural participle, "those sitting," having reference to the doves. The second part is not so clear. The RSV "fitly" follows the AV "fitly set" and likewise assumes that this final phrase alludes to the setting of jewelry. This is suggested naturally by the fact that two Hebrew substantives, *millū'â* (cf. Ex. 28:17) and *millû'* (cf. Ex. 25:7), both very similar to the obscure hapax legomenon *millē'ṯ,* are used in the OT to designate the setting of jewels. In this light the phrase *yōš^e ḇôṯ ʿal-millē'ṯ* is construed as a redundancy — "sitting as a setting," i.e., "fitly set" (see BDB, p. 571).

But in view of the consistency of the imagery of bright-plumed birds sitting beside the shining milky waters (the irises and whites of the eyes), such an unexpected change at the very end of the verse to allude to jewelry is viewed with suspicion by some scholars. What is expected is a noun denoting "pool" or "watering place." Emendation has been proposed (see, e.g., KoB, p. 527; A. Harper, *Song of Solomon* [*CBSC,* 1902], pp. 39f.), but without confidence or success. Strong support for understanding *millē'ṯ* to mean "watering place," "water-filling place" comes from the Jewish Aramaic term *mlyṯ,* "watering place, place where water is drawn" (cf. LXX "sitting by pools [*plērōmata*]"; see E. Y. Kutscher, *SVT,* 16, 170 ["Schöpfstelle"]; R. Gordis, *Song of Songs* [1954], p. 90).

The Hebrew verb *šālaḇ,* "be bound, joined," occurs only twice in the OT. In both instances it appears as a pual (passive) participle, *m^e šullāḇōṯ,* and has reference to the twin tenons in each frame of the tabernacle that are used "for fitting together" (Ex. 26:17; AV "set in order"; NEB "joined"; Ex. 36:22; AV "equally distant"; NEB "joined").

The Hebrew verb *kûn,* "be firm," appears in an intensive form (polel, "make firm, set up") in Ps. 11:2 with reference to the fitting of arrows to the taut bowstring: "they have fitted their arrow to the string" (AV "made ready"). The expression "fit for war" appears three times in the OT: in 2 K. 24:16 for *ʿōśê milḥāmâ* (lit. "makers of warfare"; AV "apt for war"; NEB "skilled armorers"), and in 2 Ch. 25:5; 26:11 for *yôṣ^e 'ê ṣāḇā'* (lit. "those who go out to battle"; AV "able to go forth to war," "that went out to war"; NEB "ready for service"). These expressions denote warriors or soldiers who have been trained in the martial arts and are thus ready for battle (see also J. Greenfield, *Bibl.,* 45 [1964], 527-534).

Greek *eúthetos* (lit. "well-placed"), "fit, useful," has the sense "prepared, suitable (for the kingdom)" in Lk. 9:62. In Lk. 14:35 unsavory salt is said not to be fit for anything (cf. NEB "useless").

The Greek verb *prépō,* "be suitable," is translated four times in the NT as "fitting." In Mt. 3:15 Jesus replies to John that "it is fitting for us to fulfil all righteousness" (i.e., "appropriate" or "necessary"). The sense of appropriateness is also implied in the other occurrences: among believers immorality and covetousness are not "fitting" (Eph. 5:3); it was appropriate for God to make Christ the perfect pioneer of human salvation (He. 2:10), who fulfils the role of high priest (He. 7:26). Elsewhere Gk. *prépō* is applied to the behavior of women ("befits"; 1 Tim. 2:10), or to doctrine ("befits," Tit. 2:1).

The Greek verb *anḗkō,* whose primary sense is "refer, relate, belong to (something)," also has a secondary meaning in the NT — "be suitable, proper, fitting." In Col. 3:18 wives are urged to be subject to their husbands "as is fitting in the Lord," and in Eph. 5:4 filthy or silly talk is said not to be "fitting."

The Greek adjective *áxios,* "worthy, comparable," when used without a particular referent, as in 2 Thess. 1:3, has the meaning "(it is) worthwhile, fitting." The noun *chreía* usually has the sense "need, lack, necessity" (cf. the cognate *chráomai,* "use, make use of"). In a context of admonition about evil talk, it appears in the phrase *prós oikodomḗn tḗs chreías,* "for edifying, as fits the occasion" (Eph. 4:29; AV "to the use of edifying"; NEB "helpful to the occasion"), meaning the kind of talking that serves to build up "where it is necessary" (see Bauer, rev., p. 885).

At the end of the parable of the prodigal son the father responds to the eldest son's complaints with the advice, "It was fitting [Gk. *deí,* "is necessary"] to make merry" (Lk. 15:32). Here, as elsewhere, Gk. *deí* has the sense that whatever happened "had to happen" (e.g., Lk. 22:7; Acts 1:16).

The verb *dokimázō,* which commonly has the meaning "test, accept as tested, approve," is sometimes used with a following infinitive to mean "intend, wish (to)" (e.g., "see fit to," Rom. 1:28).

See also BECOME. D. G. BURKE

FITCHES. *Nigella sativa* L., an annual of the buttercup family, popularly named "nutmeg-flower," mentioned only in the AV (Isa. 28:25, 27; Ezk. 4:9). The seeds were used as a condiment in antiquity, having aromatic and carminative properties. As with other plants that yield their seed easily, the seeds were beaten out with rods. The contrast between the stouter staff for "fitches" and the lighter one for cummin is the more notable because of the similarity between the two kinds of seed.

See DILL; SPELT.

See *MPB,* pp. 152f. R. K. H.

FIVE [Heb. *ḥāmēš*; Gk. *pénte*]. *See* NUMBER.

FIVE SCROLLS. A designation of Canticles, Ruth, Lamentations, Ecclesiastes, and Esther. *See* CANON OF THE OT I.C.

FLAG. *See* REED (Job 8:11; Ex. 2:3, 5); RUSH (Isa. 19:6).

FLAGON [Heb. *nēḇel*] (Isa. 22:24); NEB POT; [*qaśwâ*] (Ex. 25:29; 37:16; Nu. 4:7); AV COVER. A large pitcher or jug, which in the tabernacle rituals was the container from which the drink offerings were poured out.

In 2 S. 6:19; 1 Ch. 16:3; Cant. 2:5; Hos. 3:1 the AV mistranslates *'ašîšâ* as "flagon." In all these passages the RSV correctly translates "raisins" or "cake of raisins."

FLAGSTAFF. *See* STANDARD.

FLAME. In the OT "flame" usually translates Heb. *lahaḇ* or a form from the same root. Other terms are *labbâ* (Ex. 3:2), *lāhaṭ* ("burn, scorch," Gen. 3:24; Ps. 104:4). Aram. *šeḇîḇ* in Dnl. 3:22 refers to an already burning fire bursting into flames (cf. "fiery flames" in 7:9). In Ps. 83:14 (MT 15); Isa. 5:24; 10:17, the imagery of flames is a symbol of divine wrath.

In the NT "flame" renders Gk. *phlóx* (Lk. 16:24; Acts 7:30; He. 1:7; etc.). In Revelation flames are used figuratively to describe the eyes of the glorified Christ (1:14; 2:18; 19:12).

FLASK [Heb. *paḵ*] (2 K. 9:1, 3); AV BOX; [*baqbuq*] (Jer. 19:1, 10); AV BOTTLE; NEB JAR; [Gk. *aggeíon*] (Mt. 25:4); AV VESSEL; [*alábastron*] (Lk. 7:37); AV ALABASTER BOX. The *paḵ* was a small perfume jug, while the *baqbuq* was a container for water and other liquids found in the wealthier homes. The *aggeíon* carried by the wise virgins was a small oil jug. The flask of perfume used by Mary (cf. Jn. 12:3) to anoint Jesus' feet is called an *alábastron* (cf. "alabaster jar," Mt. 26:7; Mk. 14:3). This was a jar with a long neck that was broken when the ointment was about to be used. *See* Plate 28.

FLAT CAKES [Heb. *ḥaḇittîm*] (1 Ch. 9:31); AV "things that were made in the pans"; NEB WAFERS. *See* BREAD IV.

Ointment flask (*ca.* 1400-1200 B.C.) from Lachish. A hollowed elephant tusk forms the torso of the human figure; the hole pierced through the head into the spoon (which is shaped like a hand) may have been a channel for liquid ointment (Israel Department of Antiquities and Museums)

FLAT NOSE (Lev. 21:18, AV). The AV translation of Heb. *ḥārum* (LXX *kolobórin*; RSV "mutilated face"; NEB "stunted"). The Hebrew term occurs only in Lev. 21:18 as the name of a deformity that disqualified a member of a priestly family from serving at the altar. It is not certain whether this deformity is congenital or the result of self-mutilation.

FLATTERY [Heb. *ḥālāq,* hiphil of *ḥālaq*] (Ps. 5:9 [MT 10]; 12:2f. [MT 3f.]; 36:2 [MT 3]; Prov. 26:28; 28:23; 29:5; Ezk. 12:24; Dnl. 11:21, 32, 34); NEB also SMOOTH, SMOOTH TALK, SPECIOUS, DISSIMULATION, PLAUSIBLE PROMISES, INSINCERE; [piel of *kānâ*] (Job 32:21f.); [piel of *pāṯâ*– 'deceive'] (Ps. 78:36); NEB BEGUILED;

[Gk. *thaumázō prósōpon*] (Jude 16); AV "have men's persons in admiration"; NEB "court favour"; [*eulogía*] (Rom. 16:18); AV FAIR SPEECHES; [*kolakeía*] (1 Thess. 2:5).

The term "flattery" as used by the RSV is always associated with deception. Elihu says that he would not "use flattery toward" any man (Job 32:21; cf. AV "give flattering titles"). In the next verse he says that his Maker would put an end to him if he spoke in such a manner. Gk. *thaumázō prósōpon,* "admire the face" of someone (Jude 16), has its source in many similar expressions used in the OT (cf. Bauer, rev., p. 352).

FLAX [Heb. *pešeṯ, pištâ*; Akk. *pištu*; Gk. *línon*]. The Hebrew terms are used to describe the plant in bloom (Ex. 9:31), the stalks placed on the roof to dry (Josh. 2:6), and the fibers used for illumination (Isa. 42:3; 43:17). Isa. 19:9 refers to "combed" flax, i.e., ready for spinning (Heb. *pištîm śerîqôṯ* cf. Hos. 2:5, 9; Prov. 31:13). The twisting of flax into ropes is mentioned in Jgs. 15:14, while in Jgs. 16:9 and Isa. 1:31 Heb. *neʿōreṯ* was the material shaken off from flax when beaten, i.e., "tow." The plural form was used of linen or linen garments (cf. Lev. 13:47f., 52, 59; Dt. 22:11; Jer. 13:1; Ezk. 44:17f.). Flax is the oldest known textile fiber, and in antiquity linen was the preferred fabric for clothes, especially in Egypt, where the priestly garments were of pure linen. (*See* picture of statue of Egyptian nobleman in GARMENTS.) Mummies were wrapped in linen strips (*see* LINEN); the Hebrews and Greeks also employed it for wrapping around the dead.

Flax is produced from the herbaceous plant *Linum usitatissimum* L., which grows up to 1.3 m. (4 ft.) in height and is probably native to Mesopotamia. The tough fibers of the stalks are separated from the soft, nonfibrous parts by prolonged soaking in water. When dried the fibers are removed by combing. Egyptian monuments contain pictures of the method. Linseed, linseed oil, and oilcake are produced from this plant.

See *MPB,* pp. 129-133. R. K. H.

FLAYING. *See* PUNISHMENTS IV.G.

FLEA [Heb. *parʿōš*; cf. Arab. *bargûṯ*–'flea'; Akk. *pāršuʾu*]. The only biblical reference to the flea is in 1 S. 24:14, as a symbol of insignificance. A wingless member of the species *Pulex* is indicated, perhaps *Pulex irritans, P. penetrans,* or *P. canis,* all of which are found in Palestine.

FLEE [Heb. *bāraḥ*] (Ex. 2:15); NEB "made good his escape"; [*nāḏaḏ*] (Isa. 22:3); NEB "are . . . in flight"; [*nûs*] (Prov. 28:1); NEB RUNS AWAY; [Gk. *pheúgō*] (Mk. 14:50 par. Mt. 26:56); NEB RAN AWAY; **FLIGHT** [Heb. *ḥippāzôn*] (Dt. 16:3); AV HASTE; NEB URGENT HASTE; [*menûsâ*] (Isa. 52:12); NEB LEAVE LIKE FUGITIVES; [Gk. *phygḗ*] (Mt. 24:20); NEB ESCAPE; **PUT TO FLIGHT** [hiphil of Heb. *nûs*] (Dt. 32:30); [Heb. *rāḏap*] (Josh. 23:10); [Gk. *klínō*] (He. 11:34); NEB "put to rout"; **IN FLIGHT** [Heb. *nāḏaḏ*] (Isa. 10:31); AV "is removed." The Heb. noun *mānôs,* "place of escape" (Jer. 25:35), is rendered "refuge" by the RSV, and "way to flee" by the AV. The Heb. noun *menûsâ* and verb. *nûs* occur together in Lev. 26:36; the two verbs *bāraḥ* and *nāḏaḏ* are parallel in Isa. 22:3, as are the two Heb. nouns *ḥippāzôn* and *menûsâ* in 52:12.

Metaphorically, waves are said to flee from the presence of God (Ps. 104:7, Heb. *nûs* in parallel position with Heb. *ḥāpaz*; AV "fled . . . hasted away"; NEB "ran . . . rushed away"; cf. Ps. 114:3), sleep has fled a person (Isa. 38:15; AV "I shall go softly all my years"; NEB "I wander to and fro all my life long"), the harvest will flee (Isa. 17:11), and "sorrow and sighing shall flee away" (Isa. 35:10 par. 51:11).

In a religious sense, a person cannot flee from the presence of God (Ps. 139:7f.), even though Jonah attempted to do so (Jonah 1:3, 10). It is, furthermore, futile to flee from the Day of the Lord (Am. 5:18-20; cf. Mt. 3:7 par. Lk. 3:7). Rather, people are to flee to the Lord for refuge (Ps. 143:9; cf. He. 6:18).

One interesting instance of "flight" is the holy family's flight into Egypt (Mt. 2:13; cf. Hos. 11:1). This is one of a number of parallels that Matthew draws between Jesus and Moses in order to show that Christ is greater and thus more authoritative than Moses (cf. P. F. Ellis, *Matthew: His Mind and His Message* [1974], pp. 29f.; J. D. Kingsbury, *Matthew: Structure, Christology, Kingdom* [1975], p. 12). As Moses was miraculously spared while many other male children perished (Ex. 1:15-20), so Christ was protected while the other male infants in Bethlehem were killed (Mt. 2:16-18).

See *TDOT,* II, *s.v.* "bārach" (Gamberoni).

R. W. V.

FLEECE. *See* GIDEON IV; WOOL.

FLEETING. In Ps. 39:4 (MT 5) Heb. *ḥāḏēl,* "transient," is used to convey the brevity of human life (*see* ETERNITY). "Fleeting" translates the niphal of *nāḏap,* "scatter," in Prov. 21:6. One plausible interpretation of this verse is that the accumulation of wealth through lying is something ephemeral which may cause death (cf. KD *in loc.*). In He. 11:25 it is stated that Moses would rather suffer with his fellow Hebrews than enjoy the "fleeting [Gk. *próskairos,* "transitory"] pleasures of sin" at the Egyptian court. Here the contrast is between a few years of personal prominence and prestige in Egypt and many years of hardship leading God's people out of slavery in Egypt into the Promised Land (cf. F. F. Bruce, comm. on Hebrews [*NICNT,* 1964], pp. 318-320). R. W. V.

FLESH [Heb. *bāśār, šeʾēr* (Ps. 73:26; 78:27; Mic. 3:2f.), *ṭerepâ* (Nah. 2:12 [MT 13]), *leḥûm* (Zeph. 1:17); Aram. *beśar* (Dnl. 2:11; 4:12; 7:5); Gk. *sárx, sarkikós* (1 Pet. 2:11), *katatomḗ*–'mutilation' (Phil. 3:2)]; AV also NAKEDNESS (Ex. 28:42), SKIN (Ps. 102:5 [MT 6]), NAVEL (Prov. 3:8), CARNAL/CARNALLY (Rom. 8:6f.; 1 Cor. 3:1, 3), CONCISION (Phil. 3:2); NEB also MEAT, BODY, MANKIND, MORTAL MAN, etc.

I. OT.–The term has a number of different meanings.

A. Literal Flesh. Heb. *bāśār* and less often *šeʾēr* mean the muscular part of the human or animal body. "Flesh" is sometimes mentioned with other body parts: bones and skin (Job 10:11; Lam. 3:4), blood (Isa. 49:26, etc.), fat (Isa. 17:4), etc.

B. Food or Sacrifice. As the muscular part of human or animal bodies — frequently translated "meat" in the RSV — flesh is also viewed as food or sacrifice. Animal flesh is food for humans (e.g., Gen. 9:4) and for wild animals (Ex. 22:31; here the flesh is killed prey and thus unclean). In Nah. 2:12 (MT 13) Heb. *ṭerēpâ* is "prey" (RSV, "torn flesh"). Animal flesh, moreover, is given as a sacrifice (e.g., Ex. 29:31), which, depending on the type of sacrifice, may then be eaten by the priests. Human flesh may be food for wild creatures (e.g., Gen. 40:19) or for people. In the latter usage it refers metaphorically to exploitation or oppression (Mic. 3:3, Heb. *šeʾēr*), folly ("eats his own flesh," Eccl. 4:5), or slander (Job 19:22). Cannibalism could be the result of a siege or, as in Lev. 26:29, of divine punishment.

C. Body. "Flesh" can mean simply "body" (Jgs. 8:7;

1 K. 21:27; 2 K. 4:34; etc.). Often where the AV has "flesh" for this meaning of Heb. *bāśār*, the RSV translates "body" (e.g., Ex. 30:32; Lev. 6:10 [MT 3]). (*See* BODY I.)

D. Euphemism. "Flesh" is a euphemism for the sexual organs (Ex. 28:42; cf. Gen. 17:14; Lev. 15:2f.).

E. Relationship. "Flesh" can denote a relationship in such phrases as "bone of my bones and flesh of my flesh," meaning kinsman (Gen. 2:23), "one flesh," i.e., husband and wife (Gen. 2:24), "my bone and my flesh," i.e., kinsman (Gen. 29:14).

F. The Whole Person. "Flesh" may denote the entire person, not just the physical aspects. Thus, "much study is a weariness of the flesh" (Eccl. 12:12) is an apt description of the toil humans go through to become wise. In several passages, "flesh" parallels "heart" (Heb. *lēḇ*, e.g., Prov. 4:21f.; cf. Ps. 73:26, "my heart and my flesh may fail") or "soul" (Heb. *nepeš*, Ps. 63:1 [MT 2]; 84:2 [MT 3]; etc.; cf. Job 14:22). This is a means of referring to human beings in their entirety. There is no hint here of a dualism, in which the mind or the soul is sharply distinguished from and superior to the flesh. Quite the contrary, the external and internal human aspects are closely tied together: "My soul longs, yea, faints for the courts of the Lord; my heart and my flesh sing for joy to the living God" (Ps. 84:2 [MT 3]). (*See also* BODY I; ANTHROPOLOGY III.E.) The phrase "all flesh" may denote all animals (Gen. 6:19; Ps. 145:21; etc.); all humans (e.g., Isa. 40:5f.); and all living beings, including humans (Gen. 6:17; 9:11; etc.).

G. Theological Significance. The use of the word "flesh" to designate both humans and animals suggests their common condition as creatures. God gives life to all flesh (Gen. 6:3; Job 10:11). As flesh, humans are mortal, weak, and limited (Isa. 40:6f.), compared with God, who is superior to "all flesh" (Jer. 32:27). In a number of passages the difference between mankind and God is expressed in terms of the antithetical pair "flesh" and "spirit" (e.g., Gen. 6:3; Isa. 31:3; God is spirit, not flesh, cf. *TDOT*, II, 330). The sometimes pejorative use of "flesh" or "all flesh" stems from this distinction. There is nothing sinful about flesh per se. Sin arises when a person ignores the difference between flesh (human) and spirit (divine). Jer. 17:5 puts this well: "Cursed is the man who trusts in man and makes flesh his arm, whose heart turns away from the Lord." To attribute to humans what is God's is sin. In Ps. 78:39 flesh and sin seem closely related. God checked His wrath against Israel in the wilderness because "He remembered that they were but flesh" (i.e., "weak and liable to sin"). (In later Judaism and in the theology of Paul the contrast between flesh and spirit would return; see III.B below.)

In His grace, however, God promises to give His people a "heart of flesh" and to remove their "heart of stone" (Ezk. 11:19; 36:26), so that they may respond obediently rather than disobediently as before. Some of the prophets look forward to the age in which "all flesh shall come to worship" before the Lord (Isa. 66:23; cf. Joel 2:28 [MT 3:1]).

II. Intertestamental Literature.*–*A. Qumrân. The usage of flesh (*bśr*) in the Qumrân texts reflects the OT usage. It includes the literal meaning (1QS 9:4), flesh as body (1QpHab 9:2; 1QSa 2:5f.), and the phrase "all flesh" (in 1QSb 3:28, not negative). In 1QS 3:8f. flesh denotes the total person.

Drawing on the OT meaning of flesh as limited, moreover, the Qumrân texts understand flesh as a synonym for human corruptibility (e.g., 1QH 4:29; 15:21) and the tendency toward sin (e.g., 1QM 4:3; 12:12). (See also *TDNT*, VII, 110-14.)

B. Apocrypha, Pseudepigrapha. To some extent, the OT usage is followed — the literal meaning of flesh occurs (e.g., Jub. 7:4), flesh as human body (7:28), as sexual organ (15:13f.), and commonly the term "all flesh." There is an evident development toward both a cosmic and an anthropological dualism here, which can be seen already in the LXX translation of Nu. 16:22; 27:16: "the God of the spirits [Heb. *l^eḵol-bāśār*; LXX *kai pásēs sarkós*] of all flesh" (see *TDNT*, VII, 110, 119-121).

III. NT.–A. Continuation of OT Uses. The principal NT word for "flesh" is Gk. *sárx*, which the LXX usually employs as a translation of Heb. *bāśār* (*TDNT*, VII, 108; cf. 1 Pet. 1:24, quoting Isa. 40:6; Acts 2:17, quoting Joel 2:28 [MT 3:1]). "Flesh" is (1) food (Jn. 6:52; Rev. 19:18; etc.), and can be considered for sacrificial purposes; (2) a synonym for the body in Eph. 5:29; He. 9:13 (cf. 2 Cor. 12:7); (3) a euphemism in Col. 2:13; Phil. 3:2; Gal. 6:13; Eph. 2:11 (for Phil. 3:2 *see* CIRCUMCISION III); (4) a relationship in Rom. 1:3 (the relation between David and Jesus); and (5) the whole person in Acts 2:26f. (a quote from Ps. 16:9f., LXX [Heb. *bāśār*]); Col. 1:24 (cf. Rom. 7:18, "my flesh" = "me").

Two NT expressions are not found in the OT. The expression "flesh and blood" may signify specific individuals, as in Gal. 1:16 and Eph. 6:12. In Mt. 16:17 it points to the human inability to know apart from revelation that Christ is the Son of the living God, while in 1 Cor. 15:50 humans cannot "inherit the kingdom of God" because of their mortal nature. The second expression, "according to the flesh," may mean "the merely natural" (e.g., Rom. 1:3), but often it refers to taking the natural as a norm in opposition to the spirit (e.g., Rom. 8:13; cf. Gal. 4:23, 29).

B. Theological Significance. In the NT, flesh represents the natural, created human aspect. As such it is not sinful — merely weak, limited, and temporal. Because of its limitation, it is liable to sin, e.g., to set up the natural and human as God, neglecting the true God, and thus can even be regarded as mankind's master (Gal. 5:17). It then becomes "sinful flesh," with passions, indulgences, or "zeal, boasting," etc. In 1 Pet. 2:11, e.g., the "passions of the flesh . . . wage war" against the soul, and the believers are exhorted to have a good conduct among the Gentiles. In 2 Pet. 2:18 the passions of the flesh are labeled "licentious" and can barely be escaped. For John (1 Jn. 2:16) "the lust of the flesh and the lust of the eyes" are not of the Father but of "the world," which is darkness, in opposition to the light, which is God.

The contrast between flesh and spirit reflects in part the OT idea of the distinction between God and mankind (e.g., Jn. 6:63: "It is the spirit that gives life, the flesh is of no avail") and is not always expressive of the contrast between sin and grace (e.g., Mk. 14:38, "The spirit indeed is willing, but the flesh is weak"). But for Paul the "flesh" can oppose the Spirit (e.g., Gal. 5:17, "For the desires of the flesh are against the Spirit"; cf. Rom. 8:8f.; Jn. 1:13; 3:6; 1 Pet. 4:6). Here flesh is the opposite of the Spirit, not because it is material but because it lives by its own standards. This contrast between spirit and flesh is reflected in Rom. 7:14 (see comms.), where Gk. *sárkinos* (adjective of *sárx*) is translated "carnal" (NEB, NIV, "unspiritual"). Unlike the Gnostics, for whom the flesh as such is identified with evil (*see* GNOSTICISM III, IV), Paul is aware of the distinction between the flesh as created and fallen (*see* BODY II; DESIRE). (The life "in the flesh" of Phil. 1:22-24 does not designate the sinful but the "weak, transitory nature of the physical body" [J. J. Müller, comm. (*NICNT* [1955]), p. 62].)

Though flesh and sin are closely related, Christ redeemed sinful human flesh. In the Incarnation Christ assumed human flesh (Jn. 1:14) and lived as a human being (e.g., He. 5:7; 1 Tim. 3:16). It is in His flesh that Christ suffered (1 Pet. 4:1). Against the Gnostics, John taught that the flesh as such is not sinful (*see* GNOSTICISM VIII.B; cf. VI.D). In fact, Christ's incarnation and death are the occasion for the believer's fellowship with Him in the "eating" of His flesh (Jn. 6:52; *see* LORD'S SUPPER VIII). As in the OT, the NT professes that one day "all flesh shall see the salvation of God" (Lk. 3:6; cf. Jn. 17:2).

See ANTHROPOLOGY.

Bibliography.–*ILC,* I, 99-106; *New Catholic Encyclopedia,* V, *s.v.* "Flesh (in the Bible)" (W. E. Lynch); *TDNT,* VII, *s.v.* σάρξ κτλ. (Schweitzer, Baumgärtel, Meyer); *TDOT,* II, *s.v.* "bāśār" (N.P. Bratsiosis); C. Tresmontant, *A Study of Hebrew Thought* (Eng. tr. 1960), pp. 83-124; H. W. Wolff, *Anthropology of the OT* (Eng. tr. 1974), pp. 26-31.

F. B. KNUTSON

FLESH AND BLOOD. *See* FLESH III.A.

FLESHHOOK (AV). *See* FORK.

FLESHPOT [Heb. *sîr habbāśār*–'kettle of meat']. One of the six kinds of cooking utensils spoken of as pots, pans, caldrons, or basins. These were probably made of bronze or earthenware. The only mention of fleshpots, specifically so named, is in Ex. 16:3, where the discontent Israelites recall the abundance of meat during their Egyptian servitude. *See* FOOD IV.

FLIES. *See* FLY.

FLINT; FLINTY (ROCK) [Heb. *ṣōr*] (Ex. 4:25; Josh. 5:2f.; Isa. 5:28; Ezk. 3:9); AV also SHARP (Josh. 5:2f.); NEB also "shooting stars" (Isa. 5:28); [*ḥallāmîš*] (Dt. 8:15; 32:13; Job 28:9; Ps. 114:8; Isa. 50:7); AV also ROCK; NEB also HARD, GRANITE. This substance, which is an imperfect type of quartz, is found in abundance in the limestone rocks of Syria, Palestine, and Egypt and is represented from the earliest occupational deposits there. Flint artifacts were prominent in the Neolithic period, being used for a wide variety of purposes. Even after the introduction of copper, bronze, and iron they continued to be used for specific purposes such as circumcision (Ex. 4:25; Josh. 5:2f.). In Ezk. 3:9 ADAMANT is regarded as even harder than flint.

Flint knife, 37 cm. (14 in.), of King Djer (Egyptian, early 1st Dynasty, *ca.* 3000 B.C.) with his name inscribed on the gold foil of the handle (Royal Ontario Museum, Toronto)

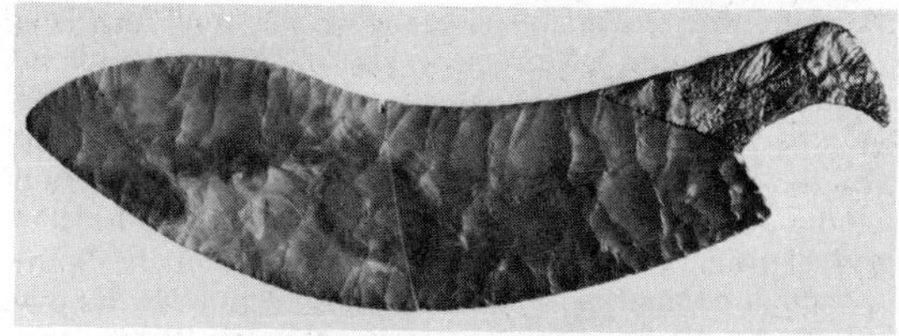

Figuratively, the impact of horses' hooves is likened to the hardness of flint (Isa. 5:28), and humans can harden their faces like flint (50:7; cf. Ezk. 3:9). The psalmist sings of God turning flint into "springs of water" (Ps. 114:18), an allusion to God's rescuing His people in the desert (Dt. 8:15; cf. 32:13).

See ROCK.

R. K. H.

FLOAT [Heb. *hālaḵ*–'go'] (Gen. 7:18); AV WENT; [hiphil of Heb. *ṣûp*] (2 K. 6:6); AV SWIM. *See* MIRACLE; SCIENCE AND CHRISTIANITY.

FLOCK. *See* CATTLE; SHEEP.

FLOG [hiphil of Heb. *nāḵâ*–'strike, smite'] (Prov. 17:26); AV STRIKE; NEB INFLICT BLOWS; [Heb. *mahᵃlumôṯ*–'strokes'] Prov. 18:6; 19:29); AV STROKES, STRIPES; NEB BLOWS; [Gk. *mastigóō*] (Mt. 10:17); AV SCOURGE.

In Prov. 17:26 Heb. *nāḵâ* may be rendered "flog" (cf. Dt. 25:2); like imposing a fine, flogging in the OT was considered a punishment for a crime (*see* PUNISHMENTS IV.A,B). According to H. Cohn, "floggings were administered with a whip made of calfskin on the bare upper body of the offender — one third of the lashes being given on the breast and the other two thirds on the back. The offender stood in a bowed position with the one administering the beating on a stone above him and the blows were accompanied by the recital of admonitory and consolatory verses from Scripture" (*Encyclopedia Judaica,* VI [1971], 1350). In Prov. 18:6 foolish talk leads to strife or quarreling (cf. 20:3) and thus may be punished by flogging (cf. 19:29), usually executed with rods (10:13; 26:3). This may be Proverbs' understanding of Dt. 25:1-3.

Flogging was also applied to children for correction (Prov. 23:13; cf. 13:24). In fact DISCIPLINE had been interwoven in the fabric of child-rearing as long as the Israelites had been in Palestine (Dt. 21:18).

Though the innocent were not supposed to be flogged, often they were. Jeremiah was flogged ("beat," hiphil of Heb. *nāḵâ,* Jer. 37:15; NEB "flogged") for no moral wrongdoing at all. The only NT reference to flogging is in Mt. 10:17 (NEB "flog"; cf. 23:34, "scourge"). Here our Lord warned His followers of the beatings that may be inflicted on them for the sake of the preaching of the gospel (and not because of unethical behavior; cf. Acts 5:40, "beaten," Gk. *dérō*). The reference is clearly to Dt. 25:1f.; their punishment will be executed legally in the synagogue. Paul was "beaten with rods" (Gk. *rhabdízō,* "beat with a rod") by the Roman officials (Acts 16:22f.; cf. 2 Cor. 11:24f.). The Romans used flogging to speed up the death of criminals by crucifixion (*see* CROSS VI.B); perhaps Christ was flogged for that reason (Mk. 15:15; W. L. Lane, comm. on Mark [*NICNT,* 1974], pp. 556f.; on Jn. 19:1, see R. E. Brown, comm. on John, I [*AB,* 1970], 874, 885-89).

See *TDNT,* IV, *s.v.* μαστιγόω (Carl Schneider).

R. W. V.

FLOOD [Heb. *mabbûl*] (Gen. 6:17; 7:6-17; 9:11, 15, 28; 10:1, 32; 11:10; Ps. 29:10); [*mayim*–'water'] (2 S. 5:20; 1 Ch. 14:11; Job 27:20; Ps. 88:17 [MT 18]; 124:4); AV WATER(S); NEB also RIVER, WATERS; [*nāhār*–'stream, river'] (Ps. 93:3; 98:8; Cant. 8:7; Jonah 2:3 [MT 4]); NEB OCEAN, RIVERS; [*šip'â*] (Job 22:11; 38:34); AV ABUNDANCE; NEB WEIGHT; [vb. *śāḥâ*] (Ps. 6:6 [MT 7]); AV "make to swim"; NEB SOAK; [*šibbōleṯ*] (Ps. 69:2, 15 [MT 3, 16]); [*šēṭep, šeṭep*] (Dnl. 9:26; Nah. 1:8); NEB also DELUGE; [*tᵉhôm*] (Ex. 15:5); AV DEPTHS; NEB WATERY ABYSS; [*nāzal*] (Ex. 15:8); NEB WATERS; [Gk. *kataklysmós*] (Mt. 24:38f.; Lk. 17:27; 2 Pet. 2:5); NEB also DELUGE; [*plḗmmyra*] (Lk. 6:48); [*potamós*–'river, stream'] (Mt. 7:25, 27; Rev. 12:15).

The word "flood" always brings to mind the flood at the time of Noah. Gen. 6–9 uses a special word for that flood, *mabbûl.* Its origin is only conjectured (cf. U. Cassuto, *From Noah to Abraham* [1964], pp. 66f.). However, it must have a meaning wider than "flood," for "waters of" generally appears before it and it appears frequently with the article. The NT supports this idea, for it refers to that flood as *kataklysmós,* from which comes the English "cataclysm." Frequently ancient documents date themselves by reference to some natural phenomenon; such is the case in Gen. 9–11, for events from the flood to the call of Abraham are classified as "after the flood." *See* FLOOD (GENESIS).

Numerous Hebrew phrases refer to the powerful force of water, particularly as a metaphor for any type of disaster, such as distress (Job 22:11) and the anger of enemies (Ps. 124:4). Love, however, can overcome all of these difficulties; "many waters cannot quench love, neither can floods drown it" (Cant. 8:7). Jonah figuratively describes his circumstances within the belly of the fish as "the flood was round about me" (Jonah 2:3). The Song of the Sea portrays the Egyptians as being overcome not by the sword but by the waters (deeps, floods) of the sea (Ex. 15:5). In Revelation the flood is one of the dragon's weapons in his attempt to overcome the woman (Rev. 12:15f.).

The Psalms particularly use "river" in the plural to signify the massive power of water. Rivers and oceans are often poetically visualized as primeval enemies of God. Ps. 93 observes that the mighty noises put forth by these waters are not powerful enough to drown out the voice of God. No natural force or mythological being is a threat to Him. In fact, the floods will even break forth in praise of God (Ps. 98:8), for "the Lord sits enthroned over the flood" (Ps. 29:10). No hostile force is adequate even to challenge His kingship.

Drawing from the past judgment of the Flood, Nahum (1:8) and Daniel (9:26) foresee God as destroying His enemies by a flood. That does not mean they anticipate another literal flood, but rather they use the same image to point out that God has complete authority and power to overcome His enemies totally by whatever means He chooses. Jesus also talks about the Final Judgment in terms of the Flood (Mt. 24:38f.).

See also ABYSS; DEEP; RIVER. J. E. HARTLEY

FLOOD (GENESIS). The concise and somewhat cryptic account of the Flood in the days of Noah (Gen. 6–9) would fill little more than 225 lines of a modern newspaper. Yet it has given rise to whole shelves of books, which seek to clarify and debate aspects of the Flood. Any attempt to interpret the biblical account introduces uncertainty, and all the efforts of modern scholarship have settled little. In faith the Genesis account is accepted as historical, but numerous unanswered questions remain.

- I. Biblical Account of the Flood
  - A. Reason
  - B. Size and Nature of the Ark
  - C. Causes
  - D. Duration
  - E. Theological Significance
- II. Extent of the Flood
- III. Date
- IV. Flood Geology
- V. Search for the Ark
- VI. Nonbiblical Flood Traditions

I. Biblical Account of the Flood.–*A. Reason.* God determined to destroy all living creatures with a flood because "the wickedness of man was great," "every imagination of the thoughts of his heart was only evil," and "all flesh had corrupted their way upon the earth" (Gen. 6:5, 12). Evidently the corruption of humanity was so great that God could find only one, Noah, who was "righteous," right with God, and of unimpeachable character. God commissioned him to be a "herald of righteousness" (2 Pet. 2:5) while he constructed an ark for the safety of himself, his wife, his three sons and their wives, and numerous animals (1 Pet. 3:20). The usual interpretation is that 120 years elapsed between God's announcement of the Flood and the occurrence of the catastrophe (Gen. 6:3).

If this was the case, Noah was 480 when God ordered him to build the ark and 600 when the Flood came (Gen. 7:6). Whether he did much preaching during that extended period of time or whether construction of the ark itself was viewed as an act of warning (He. 11:7) must be left undecided. It is also uncertain whether Noah hired a work force to help him, how he financed the project, how much ridicule he received, and whether he suffered sabotage or hate attacks that slowed construction.

B. Size and Nature of the Ark. According to Gen. 6:14-16 God commanded Noah to build an ark of gopher wood 300 cubits long, 50 cubits broad, and 30 cubits high. It was to have three stories divided into compartments, was to be covered with pitch on the inside and outside, and was to have a door and a window. GOPHER WOOD has not been identified. Some believe that it was a cypress or cedar and others oak, but there is no certainty on this point today.

Likewise, it is impossible to be dogmatic about the length of the CUBIT and thus about the size of the ark. The length of Babylonian, Egyptian, and Hebrew cubits differed; and the Hebrews themselves had two cubit measurements: a long cubit of 52 cm. (20.4 in.) and a common cubit of about 44.5 or 46 cm. (17.5 or 18 in.). If the shorter Hebrew cubit is used as a basis of computation, then the ark was about 135 m. by 22.5 m. by 13.5 m. (450 ft. by 75 ft. by 45 ft.), with a total volume of just over 41,000 cubic m. (150,000 cubic ft.). The use of a longer cubit would substantially increase the size of the ship. Computing on the basis of the shorter cubit, the ark was 185 m. (510 ft.) or almost half the length of the Queen Mary. And apparently no ship would have exceeded the length of the ark until the Cunard Line built the Eturia in 1884.

There is no need to debate whether Noah and his sons had the engineering skills to design such a great ship early in antiquity. It was probably a very large barge; nothing is said about its having a keel, oars, or rudder. Its function was only to serve as a houseboat for animals and people for the duration of the flood. Apparently long before Noah's day people had learned the art of making the metal tools necessary for such a massive undertaking (Gen. 4:22). Bitumen for caulking purposes was available in quantity in Mesopotamia; presumably that is where the ark was built.

The door was located in the side of the ark; but the nature of the window is uncertain. Frequently this is interpreted to have been an open area a cubit high under the eaves and running around the entire structure. Such an aperture would have been divided into segments by the supporting timbers of the roof, and lattice work could have been installed in places where birds were housed. The window could have provided light and ventilation for the lower decks only if a large area was open in the center of the ark.

Though compartments were to be constructed for the animals on the ark, their nature is unknown. It has been assumed that cages for small birds or mammals were stacked to make maximum use of deck space. Of course no one knows how many animals the ark housed. The Genesis account commands only that a single pair of unclean fauna and seven pairs of clean fauna should be taken aboard the ark. The reason for the larger number in the latter case was to provide food for Noah and his family. Evidently the distinction between clean and unclean existed long before the decrees of the Mosaic law. The problem of determining the number of animals involved is complicated by the difficulty of deciding whether only certain parent types (dog, cat, cow) or more numerous representations were involved. Some 4500 species of mammals and some 8,650 species of birds exist on earth today.

Various computations have been made to demonstrate that the ark was large enough to house the required number of species. On the generous side, LaHaye and Morris settled on a figure of 50,000 animals that would need to have been housed in the ark, averaging in size a little smaller than a sheep. They conclude that these would fill only about one-third of the capacity of the ark, leaving plenty of space for storage (p. 247). Though the various estimates do show the feasibility of protecting fauna against even a global flood, one need not be dogmatic about the way it was accomplished. Another unanswered question is how Noah rounded up all those animals and birds. It may be that God somehow compelled or impelled the fauna to move toward Noah and the ark in advance of boarding day (cf. Gen. 6:20).

See also ARK OF NOAH.

C. Causes. The Genesis account gives a twofold source of the waters responsible for the flood: "the sluice gates of heaven were opened" with the result that rain cascaded upon the earth; and "the fountains of the great deep burst forth" (Gen. 7:11). What is meant by the latter clause is not clear. Often it is taken to imply some terrestrial convulsion that released vast stores of subterranean waters, but no evidence of subterranean reserves on the required scale can be found. Nor is there evidence of any general and cataclysmic alteration of the earth's crust at a given time in the past when such reservoirs may have been eliminated by the collapse of geological structures above them.

D. Duration. According to popular opinion the flood lasted forty days because that was the length of time it rained. But a careful reading of the Genesis account reveals that Noah, his family, and the animals were shut up in the ark for a total of 371 days. This figure is calculated as follows. On the seventeenth day of the second month of Noah's six hundredth year, Noah, his family, and all the animals were safely in the ark and God shut the door (Gen. 7:11, 16). Then it poured for forty days and nights, during which time the waters rapidly covered the earth. Evidently it continued to rain lightly for another 110 days, making a total of 40 + 110 or 150 days of rain (7:24; cf. 8:4).

For the next 74 days (13 + 30 + 30 + 1, Gen. 8:5) the waters abated until the tops of the mountains could be seen. Then Noah waited forty days before opening the lattice on the window of the ark and releasing a raven (8:6f), which did not return because as a scavenger it was able to live off the land. Seven days later (deduced from the "other seven days" of v. 10 and the total of v. 14) Noah sent out a dove which found no resting place (v. 9). Seven days later he sent out a dove again; this time it returned with an olive leaf (v. 11). After another seven days Noah sent out the dove for the third time, and this time it did not return (v. 12). After a lapse of twenty-nine more days Noah removed the covering of the ark (v. 13). And after another fifty-seven days God commanded Noah to evacuate the ark (vv. 14-17), on the twenty-seventh day of the second month of his six hundred first year (vv. 13f.), 371 days after God shut the door at the beginning of the flood.

A consecutive reading of the whole Flood narrative shows a continuous progress from beginning to end, with only such repetitions for literary effect as commonly appear in oriental writings. There is no basis for asserting, as Wellhausen did, that Gen. 6–9 is a patchwork of J and P source materials (cf. *IDB*, II, 279). Not only does such a view contradict common literary practice and common sense, but it also runs counter to the Babylonian flood account, which includes supposed J and P elements side by side. Unity of authorship in the biblical narrative may be confidently assumed.

F. Theological Significance. A number of important religious truths may be derived from the historical event of the Flood. First among them is God's displeasure with sin and the certainty of His judgment against it. Flood waters inundated the earth because of humanity's complete corruption. Second, it shows His mercy and grace as He withheld judgment for many years — for more than a century — while He continued to call for repentance through the preaching and ark-building of Noah (cf. 1 Pet. 3:20 about God's patience). Third, the Flood demonstrates God's right to govern His creation and to interfere in its affairs in a cataclysmic way. Fourth, it portrays His sovereign power as He exercises absolute control over the forces of nature. Fifth, it indicates God's grace to Noah and his family by saving them (He. 11:7; 1 Pet. 3:20), the flood being a symbol of baptism (1 Pet. 3:21; *see* BAPTISM VII.A). Last, the Flood and conditions preceding it served as an example and warning of events at the end of time. Jesus Himself declared that just as people turned their backs on God in the days before the Flood and fell under the hand of God's judgment, so they will ignore Him at the end times and can just as certainly expect judgment by another cataclysmic event — the second coming of Christ (Mt. 24:36-42; Lk. 17:26f.).

II. Extent of the Flood.–A literal interpretation of the biblical account of the Flood leads to the conclusion that the Flood was universal. But numerous questions have been raised about this traditional position, and the tendency today is to posit a local flood (cf. *IDB*, II, 283).

Arguments for a local flood include the following. (1) The Genesis narrative does not use *tēḇēl* (the world as a whole) in the Hebrew text but *'ereṣ* ("earth, land"). Thus, statements which sound universal in the English Bible could have a local reference (see, e.g., 7:4, 10, 17-19). (2) In order to cover the highest mountains, eight times more water would be required than the earth now possesses. (3) The disappearance of such a tremendous quantity of water after the flood is hard to explain because neither the atmosphere nor subterranean cavities can hold more than a small fraction of it. (4) Probably most of the marine life would have been destroyed by the flood — crushed by the tremendous water pressure, starved by loss of feeding grounds, or killed by the dilution of the salt waters to which they were accustomed. (5) Most plant life would have been destroyed by submersion under salt water for over a year, even though the salt water was considerably diluted. (6) Some areas of the earth's surface show no evidence of submersion during a flood.

There are various arguments in defense of a universal flood. (1) It is asserted that the phrase "under the whole heaven" (Gen. 7:19) cannot be reduced to a local condition (but cf. Dt. 2:25). (2) The purpose of the Flood was to judge the sinfulness of the entire antediluvian population; a local flood would not have fulfilled this purpose. (3) The size of the ark makes a local flood impossible; in fact, the construction of an ark of any size would have been unnecessary because animals could have simply fled the Mesopotamian valley and returned when the flood was over. (4) Universality of flood legends seems to require a universal flood. (5) An overwhelming cosmic catastrophe seems to be in view in 2 Pet. 3:3-7. (6) A flood that would cover the Ararat Mountains (which rise to a height of 5163 m. [16,946 ft.]) for over a year could not be a local flood. Water seeks its own level and would flow over the entire earth to a depth of three miles. It would not stand in heaps over the Near East. (7) The promise never again to cut off all flesh or to destroy the earth with a flood (Gen. 9:11) has universal implications.

It should be clear from a study of the arguments for and against a universal flood that neither side has the preponderance of answers at the present stage of research. In fact, even if one were to grant the validity of only a local flood, great difficulties would remain. As already indicated, water seeks its own level. Mesopotamia is no watertight basin to be filled with flood waters; and certainly inhabitants could scurry up the slopes of the Zagros or other mountains flanking the lowlands. Moreover, if salty waters of the Persian Gulf had mixed with fresh water standing on land, at least the southern part of the region would have been rendered sterile after a year of inundation. As a matter of fact, the salinization of southern Mesopotamia did not begin to be serious until the 3rd cent. B.C., as a result of conditions that had nothing to do with any flood. Taking literally the various features of the Flood narrative (e.g., size of the ark, depth of flood waters), one would find it hard to accept a purely local flood. And if the Flood was designed to bring judgment on all mankind, it would have to be universal. Whatever is concluded about the extent of the Flood, the element of miracle should not be discounted. The Flood cannot be completely explained in terms of natural causes.

III. Date.–The date of the flood raises as many questions as do the extent and other aspects of this event. Flood layers found by L. Woolley at Ur and by other archeologists at various Mesopotamian sites can have no bearing on the question because they date to a wide range of periods, hundreds of years apart. Obviously they resulted from purely local floods which were often devastating in their own regions.

After the 6th or 5th millennium B.C., there is no break brought on by a flood or any other catastrophe in Near Eastern civilization. And in fact excavations at Jericho in Palestine and Jarmo in Iraq push undisturbed remains at those sites back into the 8th millennium B.C. Unfortunately, there is no basis for assigning any firm dates earlier than that time either (*see* CHRONOLOGY OF THE OT II) Thus, various popular handbooks that assign dates for the Flood should be read with care because they lack significant collections of evidence in support of their conclusions.

Regrettably, as new information becomes available the picture does not become any clearer. Anthropologists, e.g., are now claiming that human beings arrived in North America from Asia well before 20,000 B.C. An assertion that all mankind was judged by the Flood would require either that the flood was universal and may have occurred after the arrival of humans in North America or that it was local and came before they crossed the Bering Strait.

IV. Flood Geology.–Twentieth-century flood geology is an outgrowth of the nineteenth-century catastrophic school. Chief representatives in the earlier part of this century were G. M. Price, B. Nelson, A. M. Rehwinkel, and H. W. Clark (*New Diluvialism*). In 1961 J. C. Whitcomb, Jr. and H. M. Morris updated the flood geology argument in *The Genesis Flood*. Their work brought about a rebirth of flood geology in Christian circles and led to the establishment of such organizations as the Creation Research Society and the Creation Science Research Center, and the circulation of a great amount of literature propagating this position.

According to this view, the Flood was a truly catastrophic event, responsible for a tremendous amount of geologic work. In fact, the geologic formations as they now appear

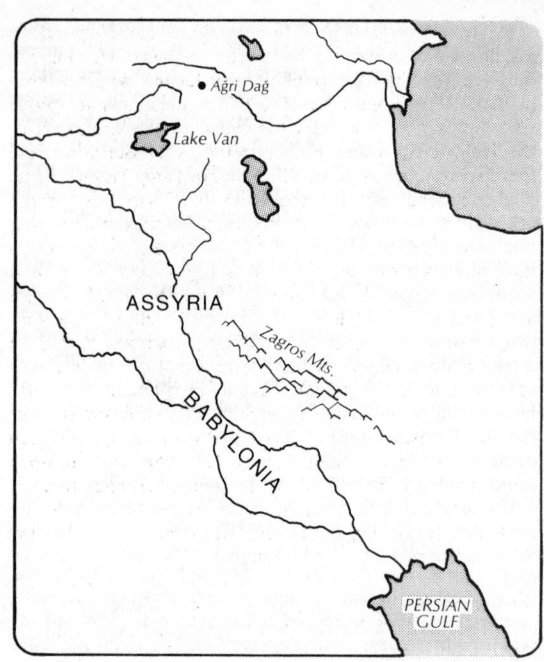

are essentially due to the Flood. The rates of erosion and sedimentation were speeded up during the Flood year. Even the radioactive decay process was increased so that rocks and minerals have a greater apparent age than is actually the case. Death did not occur until after the curse on Adam; so all fossils were entombed after the fall — most of them in sedimentary layers laid down during the Flood. Thus the earth is not as old as it appears to be and the position known as uniformitarianism is rejected.

The flood geology position has been discredited in university geology departments and is being rejected almost universally by evangelical geologists. This is true in part because it does not agree with scientific arguments according to which, e.g., many geologic features could not have been formed under water or in so short a time. (A survey of some of the arguments against flood geology may be found in B. Ramm, pp. 124-130; D. Young, pp. 176-210.)

Flood geology is also rejected because it does not tally very well with Scripture itself. Geography or topography, e.g., does not seem to have been changed greatly by the Flood. Mesopotamia with its great rivers appears to have been much the same after the Flood as before it. Even the generous supplies of pitch (bitumen), available for such projects as ark-building, were still there in quantity after the Flood. Furthermore, as Young has argued (pp. 121-25), "waters above the firmament" cannot be interpreted as a canopy that cascaded down on the earth during the Flood because Ps. 148:4, written long after the Flood, calls on the waters above the heavens to praise God. The waters above the firmament are still there and evidently are the clouds.

Those who oppose flood geology observe that the Flood was designed to be an event in redemption history, not in geological history. And as Young points out (p. 172), one can hold to a universal flood brought on by rains and tidal waves, which deposited surface materials such as gravels and silts, without holding to flood geology. Flood geology is an interpretation of the universal flood and its effects, but is not synonymous with a belief in a cataclysmic or even a universal flood.

V. Search for the Ark.–Many students of Scripture are not interested in looking for the ark because they believe the Genesis Flood account to be a legend with no basis in fact. At the opposite end of the spectrum are those who support such a search because they want to prove the historicity of the Flood and thus of Scripture and thereby bring many to the kingdom of God. Though some might, indeed, opt for the truth of Christianity if the ark were to be discovered, it should be remembered that one cannot be argued into the kingdom and that scoffers have always abounded. Most who knew Jesus Christ and witnessed His miracles refused to put their faith in Him and even to accept His resurrection. A more sober approach to a search for Noah's ark recognizes this to be a legitimate endeavor, which, if successful, would throw light on one of the greatest events of biblical and world history and would provide tremendous confirming support for the Christian faith. Christians who engage in such projects as this one should approach them with an open mind, willing to follow where the evidence leads them.

If one is going to search for the ark on Mt. Ararat, he must first locate the mountain. The Bible states that the ark came to rest on "the mountains of Ararat" (Gen. 8:4), and thus warns the modern reader against seizing too readily on any particular spot for the landing of the ark. (*See also* ARARAT I.) The traditional site is Ağri Dağ, the highest peak (5163 m., 16,946 ft.) of Ararat, located in eastern Turkey on the Russian border. Ancient traditions point to at least six other landing places. Most Christians prefer the traditional site, however, largely because it would have been the first peak to emerge from the receding flood waters. Clearly the identification is not absolute, so there is always the possibility that expeditions may be looking for the ark in the wrong places. Searchers have always concentrated on the traditional peak, however. *See* Plate 46.

Numerous popular books on the Flood and Noah's ark have reported sightings of the ark on Mt. Ararat during ancient, medieval, and early modern times. (Some of these appear in the bibliography.) A new "ark fever" has broken out since the 1950's, and the results of some expeditions require comment. Of special interest are the efforts of F. Navarra, a French industrialist, whose 1952 expedition to the traditional site claimed to have found the dark form of a ship under the ice at the 4100-m. (13,500-ft.) level. In 1955 he extracted a section of wood that he believed to be a piece of the ark. This was subjected to a variety of tests, such as lignite formation and fossilization, and was determined to be oak, hand-tooled and partly fossilized, about 5000 years old. When carbon-14 tests were made, they dated the wood to the 8th century A.D. If the earlier date is right, the wood apparently has no bearing on the ark because there is no evidence of a major break in civilization about 3000 B.C. If the later date is right, the wood certainly can have no connection with the ark. Specialists conclude that the various nonradiocarbon methods of dating are not very reliable in this case; and these radiocarbon tests do not suffer from conditions that make carbon-14 dating somewhat uncertain. Evidently this wood did not come from Noah's ark.

Moreover, individuals close to the Navarra expeditions claimed that he planted the wood or purchased it and perpetrated a hoax. Subsequently he seemed rather vague about where he had found the wood. Later, in 1969, Navarra served as a guide for an expedition of SEARCH, Inc., and secured additional pieces of wood encased in ice high on the mountain. Again cries of fraud arose, but too many people of excellent reputation were involved this time for the discoveries to be contrived. Finding some old wood on the traditional Mt. Ararat is not the same as finding Noah's ark, however. Carbon-14 tests on this wood dated it to the first half of the 7th cent. A.D.

In 1959 a report appeared in a Turkish magazine of the sighting of the ark by a Turkish airman in the foothills adjacent to Ararat. The Archaeological Research Foundation was formed to investigate what had been seen at a height of 2130 m. (7,000 ft.). Following the Turkish report, an issue of *Life* magazine (Sept. 5, 1960) printed an article on the ark and a photograph that stirred considerable interest. But the ARF expedition of 1960 showed that the supposed boat was merely a "freak of nature," a "clay up-push in a lava flow." Thus another case of ark fever came to an end.

A satellite photo of Ararat (taken July 13, 1973), was announced by Senator Frank E. Moss of Utah (Feb. 21, 1974) as possibly showing the ark. Later the possibility was completely discounted.

In 1974 a Palestine, Texas group claimed to have been on Mt. Ararat and to have seen the ark from a distance of 600 m. (2000 ft.). Some question that they ever ascended the mountain, and the CIA demonstrated that the photo they showed of the "ark" was retouched.

Numerous expeditions scrambled up Mt. Ararat in the 1960's and 1970's looking for Noah's ark. Their task was herculean, for they attacked one of the largest mountains in the world, the base of which covers approximately 12,950 sq. km. (5000 sq. mi.) and the ice cap 52 sq. km. (20 sq. mi.). The ark was not found, and exploration came to an end with worsening Turkish-American relations in the wake of the Cyprus dispute.

VI. Nonbiblical Flood Traditions.–Flood stories have been discovered among nearly all nations and tribes. Though most common on the Asian mainland and the islands immediately south of it and on the North American continent, they have been found on all the continents. Totals of the number of stories known run as high as about 270, of which more than 220 are definitely known to the writer of this article.

Although these traditions have been modified through the ages and some have taken on fantastic elements, most of them have certain basic elements in common. LaHaye and Morris concluded (p. 237) that 88 percent of them single out a favored individual or family; 70 percent point to survival due to a boat; 66 percent see the Flood coming as a result of human wickedness; 67 percent speak of animals saved along with human beings; 57 percent record that the survivors end up on a mountain; and 66 percent indicate that the hero or favored one receives warning of the coming catastrophe.

The universality of the flood accounts is usually taken as evidence for the universal destruction of humanity by a flood and the spread of the human race from one locale and even from one family. Though the traditions may not all refer to the same flood, apparently the vast majority do. The assertion that many of these flood stories came from contacts with missionaries will not stand up because most of them were gathered by anthropologists not interested in vindicating the Bible, and they are filled with fanciful and pagan elements evidently the result of transmission for extended periods of time in a pagan society. Moreover, some of the ancient accounts were written by people very much in opposition to the Hebrew-Christian tradition.

Most important of all the flood stories is the Babylonian account. Interest in it rises because it comes from the same Semitic context and the same geographical area as the Genesis narrative and because it is similar to the Genesis account in so many ways.

The Babylonian flood story was part of the library of King

Fragment of Tablet XI of the Gilgamesh Epic (the Babylonian flood account) written in Assyrian cuneiform. It details the building of the ship, the storm, and the landing on Mt. Nişir (Trustees of the British Museum)

Ashurbanipal of Assyria (668-*ca.* 627 B.C.) found during the British excavations at Nineveh in 1853 and 1873. The story was on the eleventh tablet of a twelve-tablet piece entitled the *Gilgamesh Epic,* an account of Gilgamesh's search for immortality. In the eleventh tablet Gilgamesh (king of Uruk, biblical Erech) interviewed Utnapishtim, the "Babylonian Noah," and learned from him the story of the flood and his securing of immortality. (*See* BABYLONIA IX.A.)

Subsequently an early Akkadian story of the flood, written in Mesopotamia about 1600 B.C. and known as the Atra-ḫasis Epic, and a Sumerian version of the Babylonian flood story (dating *ca.* 1700 B.C.) have come to light. The story in all these texts is similar and the flood hero is known variously as Ziusudra in Sumerian and Atra-ḫasis or Utnapishtim in Akkadian.

As the story goes, the god Enlil could not sleep because the increasing number of people on earth made too much noise, and he finally decided to destroy mankind by a flood. Another deity, Enki, partial to Utnapishtim or Atra-ḫasis, warned the hero and instructed him to build a boat and load it with his family and possessions, and with animals and birds. The flood lasted for seven days and seven nights, after which the boat landed on Mt. Nisir and the hero sent out three birds (a dove, a swallow, and a raven) to investigate the situation. Upon disembarking, Utnapishtim made an offering to the gods, after which he was granted immortality. (*See* RELIGIONS OF THE BIBLICAL WORLD: ASSYRIA AND BABYLONIA V.)

A comparison of the Genesis and Mesopotamian flood stories shows numerous similarities. Both accounts indicate that the flood was divinely planned and that the disaster was revealed to the flood hero. Both accounts assert that the hero was divinely instructed to build a boat of large proportions in which a limited number of persons embarked along with other living creatures, and that those on board were not destroyed. Both accounts also specify the physical causes of the flood, its duration, the landing place of the boat, and the sending out of birds. And in both accounts the heroes offer a sacrifice after the flood is over, receive a divine blessing, and are given some assurance that a similar catastrophe will never again overtake mankind.

But the differences are far greater than the similarities. Most significant among them is that the Babylonian and Assyrian stories are (grossly) polytheistic, while the Genesis narrative is characterized by (an exalted) monotheism. Second, the Mesopotamian deluge comes as a result of the caprice of the gods or because mankind was so noisy that Enlil could not sleep, whereas the Genesis account gives human sin as the cause of the Flood. Third, in the Babylonian account an effort is made to hide from mankind the coming of the flood, but the biblical account gives abundant opportunity to repent. Fourth, Utnapishtim's ship was cubical, had seven stories, and was some fifteen times larger than Noah's ark. Fifth, the duration of the flood (rain) was different; Utnapishtim endured a rain of only seven days and nights. Sixth, Utnapishtim was granted immortality while Noah was not. There were also minor differences in the birds that were sent out, those who went aboard the ark, and the landing places of the boats.

Though the differences in these accounts are very great, the similarities are still amazing. Some scholars (the protagonists of higher criticism) commonly tried to explain these similarities by concluding that the Hebrews borrowed the flood account from Babylonian sources and merely purified it of polytheistic elements. But many contemporary biblical scholars find this view increasingly unacceptable because it is overly simplistic in its failure to account for differences between the two. More appealing is the view that both descended from a common original. After all, Genesis gives Mesopotamia as the original home of the Hebrews, the place where civilization first began, and where it made a fresh start after the Flood. What would be more likely than that many accounts of an early tragedy of such magnitude would be preserved by peoples who lived in Mesopotamia or had migrated from there. In accepting such a conclusion, divine inspiration is not ruled out. Biblical writers did not always write without access to source materials (cf. Lk. 1:1-4), but God overruled and directed in the choice of such materials, guaranteeing accuracy of the finished product.

Accounts of other flood narratives may be found in several works listed in the bibliography. The most extensive collection appears in Frazer's book.

Bibliography.–G. L. Archer, Jr., *Survey of OT Intro.* (rev. ed. 1974); L. R. Bailey, *Where is Noah's Ark?* (1978); D. Balsinger and C. E. Sellier, Jr., *In Search of Noah's Ark* (1976); F. A. Filby, *The Flood Reconsidered* (1970); J. G. Frazer, *Folklore in the OT* (1919); A. Heidel, *Gilgamesh Epic and OT Parallels* (2nd ed. 1949); T. LaHaye and J. Morris, *The Ark on Ararat* (1976); W. G. Lambert and A. R. Millard, *Atra-Ḫasis* (1969); J. W. Montgomery, *Quest for Noah's Ark* (2nd ed. 1974); F. Navarra, *Noah's Ark: I Touched It* (1974); B. C. Nelson, *Deluge Story in Stone* (1931); B. Ramm, *Christian View of Science and Scripture* (1954, 1976); A. M. Rehwinkel, *The Flood* (1951); J. C. Whitcomb and H. M. Morris, *The Genesis Flood* (1961, 1976); D. A. Young, *Creation and the Flood* (1977).

H. F. VOS

FLOOR. *See* ARCHITECTURE; HOUSE; THRESHING FLOOR.

FLORA.

I. Diversity of Species
II. Fertility and Climate in Historic Times
III. Identification of Plants
IV. Plant Zones in Palestine
  A. Coastal Plains and Western Mountains
  B. Jordan Valley
  C. Desert Zones
  D. Northern Mountains
V. Humans and Plants

I. Diversity of Species.–The flora of Palestine is exceptionally rich in species relative to the limited extent of the area. The number of indigenous species amounts, according to informed estimates, to about 2400, most of them annuals, the rest perennial herbs, shrubs, and trees.

Among the reasons for this diversity are the following factors. (1) The climate of Palestine, though generally of the Mediterranean pattern, i.e., with the year divided into a rainy winter and a dry, hot summer, displays a number of variants. On the snowcapped Mt. Hermon the climate approaches arctic severity, while in the lower Jordan Valley it is decidedly tropical. A number of climatic variants between these extremes can be distinguished, from the sand dunes and meadows of the western coastal region to the inland hills of central Palestine and the elevated plateaus E of the Jordan. Plants flourish in the warm springtime, rest in the summer, and grow again in winter. Many die through lack of water during the long summer months, but adaptation to conditions of heat and shortage of moisture has brought into prominence drought-resistant plants. The depredations of earlier centuries have resulted in large areas of Palestine, Syria, and Transjordan becoming barren; in some areas reforestation is being attempted, in the hope that rainfall will increase moderately.

(2) Topography, too, is extremely diverse in this country. Altitudes range from about 400 m. (1300 ft.) below sea level in the Dead Sea region to 1675 m. (5500 ft.) above in the highlands. Surface configuration varies among low and high beaches, open plains, intermountain valleys, rough mountainous areas, deep depressions, etc.

(3) Rocks and soils similarly display an array of varieties, both in their chemical make-up and in their physical constitution. Bare rocks of varied lithological character occur side by side with deep alluvial soils, salt marshes, sand dunes, and variously colored mountain soils.

This diversity of physical conditions divides the country into countless habitats, each harboring a flora and vegetation of its own.

(4) Time has also largely contributed to the richness of the flora. Palestine emerged from the sea in the Early Tertiary Age and was long subject to several changes in its flora in accordance with the changes of its climate. Repeated invasions and retreats of various floras during this long geological past have left their traces in the make-up of the present flora. Retreats have never been complete; hence there are many relic species of the floras that occupied this country during different geological periods.

(5) Another important factor is human interference with the vegetal environment. Destructive activity during the millennia has not only altered the make-up of the flora but has created numerous new secondary sites for alien plants that entered this country long before history.

II. Fertility and Climate in Historic Times.–Authorities differ on the issue of climatic changes in the period of human history. Some believe that no significant changes in climatic conditions have occurred since the Ice Age ended (cf. W. F. Albright, *FSAC,* pp. 108-112), while others assert that the migrations of Near Eastern peoples at the beginning of the 2nd millennium B.C. resulted from climatic conditions marked by drought (cf. N. Winkless, III and I. Browning, *Climate and the Affairs of Men* [1975], pp. 140ff.). Two facts are important in this matter. (1) The climate of Syria-Palestine has remained virtually unchanged since the Middle Bronze Age (*ca.* 1900-1550 B.C.). References to the "former" and "latter" rains (Dt. 11:14; Jer. 5:24; Hos. 6:3), the frequent droughts (1 K. 17; Am. 4:6f.), and the welcome dew (Dt. 32:2; 2 S. 1:21; Mic. 5:7; etc.) accord with modern climatic estimates. Equally consonant are the most characteristic features of modern Palestinian flora — the olive, fig, vine, and almond, the oak and the terebinth. Additional confirmation is supplied by the widely distributed ruins of ancient hillside terraces and abandoned wells at sites where once cultivation flourished.

(2) The destruction of forests and thickets, abundant in ancient times, has been greatest during the last hundred years. With the removal of the trees the exposed land eroded, and the fertile topsoil was swept from the hillsides by the action of wind, rain, and animals such as the mountain goat. Neglect of the ancient terrace type of cultivation, which took greatest advantage of the natural contours of the land, contributed further to the erosion, which the modern inhabitants are trying desperately to remedy.

Since time immemorial much available wood has been used in the manufacture of charcoal. When clearing land for cultivation after the Arabs settled in Palestine, the fellahin invariably disposed of existing vegetation by burning it off, and such fires often burned far beyond the intended area (cf. Ps. 83:14 [MT 15]). Once erosion had begun, the rainfall swept over the denuded rocks to lower levels instead of trickling through the soil to replenish the springs beneath the surface. Consequently many underground water resources dried up, and streams began flowing into disease-breeding marshes. Even where soil erosion was less evident, the removal of vegetation increased the evaporation rate of the moisture in the soil, making the land infertile. By these means the gloomy predictions of the eighth-century B.C. prophets (Isa. 32:13; 33:9; Hos. 10:8) were fulfilled and have remained valid ever since. Despite the comparative stability of climatic conditions over the centuries, it is certain that the native vegetation of Palestine was far richer in antiquity than at present. This situation has presented serious problems for the modern state of Israel, and it will be many years before the efforts to reclaim and conserve natural resources will begin to redress the depredations of past centuries.

III. Identification of Plants.–A number of problems hinder the identification of biblical plants, and these are complicated by the introduction of some non-native species into Palestine during the last century or so. In a survey of the flora A. Eig estimated that only 115 plant species were truly native to Palestine. This compares with over 2000 types of plants growing there today. Moldenke (p. 5) has pointed out that it is fallacious to think that present plant species in Palestine have always existed there, or that one can identify biblical plants from existing flora. In the first place, as Linnaeus discovered, floras and faunas vary considerably, depending upon such factors as location, climate, and geological considerations. In the second, numbers of plants now thriving in Palestine are of comparatively recent introduction, such as the American locust (*Robinia pseudo-acacia* L.) and the American pricklypear cactus (*Opuntia ficus-indica* L. Mill.) Some nineteenth-century botanists thought that the pokeweed (*Phytolacca decandra* L.) was the hyssop mentioned in connection with the Passover (Ex. 12:22), unaware that it was actually an American species. In fact, the identification of "hyssop" is one of the most difficult botanical problems of Scripture. Several varieties of Australian eucalyptus trees have found climatic conditions in Palestine congenial. Apart from being attractive, quick-growing evergreens, they are of value in drying up marshes by absorbing great quantities of water through their roots. Other trees of recent introduction that flourish even better than the indigenous trees are the "Spanish pepper tree" (*Schinus molle*), the "pride of India" (*Melia azedaracht*), the Australian *Casuarina stricta,* and the *Ailanthus glandulosus,* a native of China.

IV. Plant Zones in Palestine.–Palestine is situated on the crossroads of four biogeographical regions: the Mediterranean, the Irano-Turanian, the Saharo-Arabian, and the Sudanian. Accordingly, Palestine has been divided by botanists into four plant-geographical territories, each with a flora and vegetation of its own, and each with its peculiar climatic conditions, soils, and even human culture.

A. Coastal Plains and Western Mountains. These have a distinctive Mediterranean flora. The maritime plain has a rich alluvial soil with abundant underground water resources. The annual mean temperature is 70°F, with considerable humidity, though less rainfall than in the uplands. Frost is extremely rare in this zone. Citrus groves flourish in the area, while vines and cereals are cultivated extensively, but the wild flora varies somewhat from that found in the mountains. The sycamore-fig (*Ficus sycomorus* L; AV "sycomore") grows abundantly in the lowlands around Jaffa, being unable to survive the temperature fluctuations of the mountains (cf. Ps. 78:47). In the Talmud one distinction between lower and upper Galilee was that the sycamore-fig flourished in the former and not in the latter. Like the common FIG (*Ficus carica* L.) it produces fruit several times each year. Sometimes known as "mulberry fig" or "fig mulberry," it is a sturdy evergreen growing to 9 or 12 m. (30 or 40 ft.) in height, with a trunk circumference of up to 6 m. (20 ft.). (*See also* SYCAMORE.) Another tree that reaches perfection in the warmer lowlands is the TAMARISK, of which there are several species. *Tamarix articulata* and *T. tetragyna* grow in sandy places such as deserts and beaches. They are gnarled and stunted in appearance, unlike the larger *T. pentendra* Pall., which grows in hill country and provides wood that can be used in building. *See* Plates 10, 13.

In the central mountain range and on Mt. Carmel the temperature varies from a few degrees of frost in the winter to periods in the summer when the heat is in excess of 27°C (80°F), though this is rather unusual. Even then a breeze usually blows inland from the Mediterranean. These conditions are favorable for the fig, vine, and olive, while in gardens and sheltered areas it is possible to grow trees such as peach, plum, pomegranate, walnut, apple, and almond. In various areas of the mountain uplands wheat and barley are grown, while districts such as the Dothan Valley still produce the grain crops for which they were known in antiquity. *See* Plates 8, 14. In wadis leading from Transjordan to the Jordan Valley, in the Jordan Valley itself, and around the Sea of Galilee and elsewhere are masses of oleander (*Nerium oleander* L.). It is a beautiful evergreen shrub which can grow to 12 feet in height and bears clusters of white or pink flowers. For all its beauty the plant is highly poisonous.

A massive tree that flourishes in watery habitats is the *Platanus orientalis* L., or PLANE TREE, found throughout Lebanon and Syria but only rarely in northern Palestine. It often reaches a height in excess of 18 m. (60 ft.) with a maximum trunk circumference of 12 m. (40 ft.). It is usually mentioned in Scripture along with willows and POPLARS, which thrive in a similar habitat. Some eight varieties of willow have been reported, along with one native poplar. The Lombardy poplar, an imported species, is widely cultivated, while the walnut (*Juglans regia* L.), originally from Persia and northern India, flourishes in the Damascus region and elsewhere.

The southern hackberry or nettle tree (*Celtis australis*), a member of the *Ulmaceae* closely related to the elm, is extensively planted. It attains a maximum height of 9 m. (30 ft.) and yields a finely grained wood which takes a high polish. The carob (*Ceratonia siliqua* L.), an attractive evergreen bearing dense glistening foliage, is conspicuous in Palestine, especially in the lower mountain region. Its long pods, the "husks" of Lk. 15:16, contain seeds similar to peas, embedded in pulp. The pods are used now, as in antiquity, for feeding horses and cattle.

According to Moldenke, some twenty-four kinds of *Quercus* occur in Palestine, including the *Q. calliprinos,* a small OAK infested by an insect *Coccus ilicis,* which secretes a scarlet dye (cf. Ex. 25:4; 26:1; etc.). Another widely distributed tree closely allied to the oak both in the OT and by modern interpreters — although botanically quite distinct — is the TEREBINTH, *Pistacia terebinthus* L. It generally grows in localities that are too warm for the oak, and from it is extracted the commercial Cyprus turpentine.

Several important shrubs are found on the limestone hills and in sandy areas. *Pistacia lentiscus* L., the lentisk or MASTIC tree, is commonly distributed throughout Palestine. A bushy evergreen, it yields a fragrant gum identified by some with the OT balm. The bay laurel (*Laurus nobilis* L.), a tall and compact evergreen, flourishes in the Mediterranean region. Laurel crowns adorned the heads of Greek and Roman heroes, priests, and poets, and denoted victory in the Pythian and Olympic games. To the psalmist its evergreen nature and spicy fragrance symbolized prosperity (Ps. 37:35, AV). The tree was conspicuous in classical mythology, being sacred to Apollo. The leaves, roots, and bark had a reputed medicinal value. The MYRTLE (*Myrtus communis* L.) is commonly found in Lebanon and Palestine as a straggling bush of a few feet in height that in favorable locations seldom exceeds 1 m. (3 ft.). Its dark, fragrant leaves and aromatic berries were used in antiquity to manufacture perfumes. Prominent in the original Feast of Tabernacles, the myrtle symbolized justice, peace, and joy. A small and now rather rare shrub, the butcher's broom (*Ruscus aculeatus* L.), has flattened leaflike branches which bear small greenish flowers and red berries in such a way that they appear to arise from the center of the midrib to the leaf. One attractive species of *Arbutus,* a shrub that often exceeds 8 m. (25 ft.) in height, is found in the coastal plain and in the highlands. The *A. andrachne* has a smooth red bark which peels off to reveal a red inner surface and bears small orange-colored edible berries. The OLEASTER (*Elaeagnus angustifolia* L.), a small graceful shrub with silvery leaves and fragrant white blossoms, is commonly found in Palestine, although it is not native to the country. "Oleaster" is a name associated with one variety of the olive tree, and in translations the name of the shrub is variously rendered "oil tree" (Isa. 41:19, AV), "oil" (Mic. 6:7), "olive tree" (1 K. 6:23, 31f.; 1 Ch. 27:28; Isa. 41:19, RSV), and "wild olive" (NEB). It is now evident that the true "oil tree" is the *Pinus halepensis* Mill., or *P. maritima* Mill., which is native to the Mediterranean area. Another attractive shrub is the styrax (*Styrax officinalis* L.), which bears beautiful white flowers similar to orange blossoms. The exudate obtained from the incised stems was highly prized as a perfume in antiquity. The storax of modern commerce is derived from an unrelated tree, *Liquidambar orientale.* The common caperberry (*Capparis sicula* Duham.) grows profusely also, often covering rocks and ruins in the manner of a creeper. The young buds were used from early times as a condiment. Their effect in stimulating hunger and thirst, which become less acute in old age through atrophy of the tastebuds, is referred to in Eccl. 12:5. The manner in which the ripe fruit hung down on long stalks suggested to the oriental mind the figure of a drooping, aged man. Several species of *Cistus* flourish on Palestinian mountains and hills. The commercial oleoresin ladanum has been extracted from one of these bushes and was probably the "myrrh" of Gen. 37:25; 43:11.

Widely distributed in Palestine are many varieties of prickly shrubs described in Scripture as "briers" and "thorns." Many commentators have supposed that the genus *Rubus* or Palestinian bramble is indicated in all instances, but this is incorrect. Thus the "bramble" of Jgs. 9:14 is probably *Lycium europaeum* L., the European boxthorn, while the reference in Isa. 34:13 may be to the Syrian thistle (*Notobasis syriaca* L.) or the spotted golden thistle (*Scolymus maculatus* L.). The "thorn" of Ps. 58:9 [MT 10] appears to be the species *Rhamnus palaestina* Boiss., or Palestinian buckthorn, while in Jgs. 8:7; Isa. 7:19; 55:13; Mt. 7:16, the reference is possibly to the shrub *Zizyphus spina-christi* or Syrian Christ-thorn. In Mt. 13:7 and He. 6:8 the species *Centaurea iberica* Trev. may be intended, while in Isa. 34:13 and Hos. 9:6 the allusion is probably to *Xanthium spinosum* L., a prickly burweed. *See* Plate 5; *see also* THORN.

Although the rose is commonly mentioned in English translations (e.g., AV Isa. 35:1), there has been much dispute regarding the exact nature of the species mentioned. The "rose of Sharon" (Cant. 2:1) has been variously identified with *Narcissus tazetta* L., *Anemone coronaria* L., *Cistus creticus* L., and others, the most probable one, however, being *Tulipa montana* Lindl., common in the mountains of Palestine. The reference in Isa. 35:1 (AV; RSV "crocus") is to a bulbous plant, of which the most logical is the *Narcissus tazetta* L. or polyanthus narcissus. This may perhaps be the "rose" of Sir. 50:8, whereas those mentioned in Sir. 24:14 and 39:13 may have been the oleander (*Nerium oleander* L.), a colorful shrub flourishing in Palestinian wadis and watercourses. Probably the "roses" of 2 Esd. 2:19 and Wisd. 2:8 were Phoenician roses (*Rosa phoenicia* Boiss.), commonly found in Palestine. Though now only two species of true roses grow in the Holy Land, they afford little help in identifying the biblical "roses."

Spring flowers bloom profusely in this area, beginning with the CROCUS and cyclamen, and followed by narcissi, several varieties of anemone, gladioli, irises, FLAX, mountain lilies (*see* LILY), ranunculuses, and many others. When the blooms have disappeared further color is provided by varieties of the thistles and the glossy leaves of some evergreens. *See* Plates 9, 12.

B. Jordan Valley. The flora here has affinities with that of Africa. Prominent are several species of acacia, which in desert areas are often the only surviving trees. According to many authorities, the "shittim wood" was one of the acacias, either *A. seyal* Delile or *A. tortilis* Hayne, since these species alone provide timber to any extent. They now grow in areas E of the Dead Sea, in the Sinai Peninsula, and elsewhere in barren regions. In favorable locations these species attain a height of 8 m. (25 ft.), but in the desert they are gnarled, stunted, and shrublike in appearance. The bark is used in tanning leather, and gum arabic is derived from *A. seyal* and *A. arabica*, neither of which, however, actually grows in Palestine.

Characteristic of the entire region are species of the

zizyphus ("thorns," RSV, e.g., Jgs. 8:7), the most common of which is the *Z. spina-christi* (L.) Willd. It bears greenish flowers and rounded fruit, and under favorable conditions attains a height of 5 m. (15 ft.) A related species, the jujube (*Z. vulgaris* Lam.), a native of the Orient, has an edible berry-like fruit similar to an olive. Also common is the Levantine LOTUS bush (*Z. lotus* [L.] Lam.), a shrub that bears pale green flowers and pea-sized fruit. This bush may be the "shady tree" of Job 40:21f. (so RSV). Another shrub widely distributed in this region is the Jericho balsam, *Balanites aegyptiaca* (L.) Delile. In antiquity the oil was extracted from the fruit for medicinal usage, and this substance has been identified by some with the BALM OF GILEAD in Jer. 8:22; 46:11; 51:8; and perhaps in Gen. 37:25. A nauseous plant commonly found in the Dead Sea region is the colocynth, *Citrullus colocynthis* (L.) Schrad. This "vine of Sodom" (Dt. 32:32) has long straggling tendrils bearing atttractive orange-colored fruits. These, however, contain merely a dusty powder surrounding the seeds and are extremely nauseous. The colocynth may have been envisaged when some OT writers spoke of "gall" or "poison" (cf. Dt. 29:18; Ps. 69:21 [MT 22]; Jer. 9:15; 23:15). The neighborhood of the Dead Sea is also notable for species of plants that flourish in the saline marshes, and these include several kinds of saltwort (*Salsola*). Of the latter there are twelve kinds in Palestine, and in biblical times some of these plants were burned to obtain the alkaline salts (potash) which were then mixed with olive oil to make soap (e.g., Jer. 2:22; Mic. 3:2, according to *MPB*, pp. 215f.).

In various parts of the Jordan Valley several species of WILLOW are to be found, including *Salix alba* and *S. acmophylla* Boiss., the latter being the most common willow. The Egyptian bulrush (*Cyperus papyrus* L.) also thrives in the Huleh swamps beside the Jordan, though it is extinct in many other parts of Palestine. PAPYRUS was the source of the earliest form of paper. The TAMARISK (*Tamarix articulata* Vahl, *T. deserti* Boiss., etc.) abounds on saline flats and sandy locations in this general area, and is a valuable source of wood and charcoal.

The OLIVE TREE (*Olea europaea* L.) is represented here as elsewhere, and another familiar biblical tree, the PALM TREE (*Phoenix dactylifera* L.), was as characteristic of ancient Palestine as of Egypt. Its fruit was a staple dietary item, while the leaves and wood were used in building. The ancient Babylonians made an intoxicating drink from date flowers, and this may have been the "honey" of certain OT passages (e.g., Gen. 43:11; 1 S. 14:25-30; Ps. 19:10 [MT 11]). *See* Plate 4.

C. Desert Zones. These are notable for the absence of trees and for the stunted, straggly appearance of the small shrubs that grow there. Species of thistles and thorny plants such as *Notobasis syriaca* (L.) Cass. and *Scolymus maculatus* L. are among the numerous kinds with which Palestine abounds. In such sandy areas as the eastern Negeb and Edom, as well as other places in Palestine, the *Retama raetam* (Forsk.) or white broom flourishes, to the delight of travelers. It is a small, compact bush with rather sparse foliage and clusters of fragrant white flowers. Other forms of sandy desert vegetation include species of *Salsola* or saltwort, *Zygophyllum, Haloxylon persicum,* and *H. salicornicum.* Saline desert vegetation includes species of tamarisk such as *Tamarix articulata* Vahl and *T. deserti* Boiss, *Atriplex,* and varieties of *Salsola.* The lack of an adequate water supply stunts the majority of species, which often grow larger in other regions. *See* Plate 19.

D. Northern Mountains. No reference to Palestinian flora would be complete without some mention of the FIR TREE. Where this attractive tree is alluded to in Scripture, the reference is most frequently to the Aleppo pine, (*Pinus halepensis* Mill.), which flourishes in Palestine and Lebanon. A native of the Mediterranean area, its wood is comparable to that of the Lebanon cedar. An even more elegant species is the stone pine, *Pinus pinea* L., which has a hemispheric top and horizontal lower branches that are frequently removed to produce an ornamental umbrella-like effect. This tree, the stone pine, may be the one referred to in Hos. 14:8, the "fruit" being an edible nutlike seed with an almond flavor. The most characteristic member of this order of trees is the CEDAR (*Cedrus libani* Loud., var. *Pinus cedrus* L.), by far the tallest and most massive tree in Palestine. It grows rapidly, attaining a maximum height of 37 m. (120 ft.), and often has a trunk diameter exceeding 2 m. (6 ft.) Once widely distributed in the Lebanon and elsewhere, it is now reportedly restricted to a few areas of the Lebanon Range. Two species of heather (*Erica orientalis* Dyer; *E. verticillata*) are said to grow here, and of two species of juniper occurring in Palestine, the brown-berried cedar (*Juniperus oxycedrus* L.) is rare in the northern mountain areas. *See* Plate 11.

Above the height of 2100 m. (7000 ft.) trees and shrubs disappear, vegetation thereafter consisting chiefly of low thorny plants such as the *Astragalus* (especially *A. tragacantha* and *A. gummifer*) and Cerasus (*C. prostata*) species. Even on the summit of Hermon many tiny flowers bloom in the late summer after the snow has melted.

*V. **Humans and Plants.***–Recent discoveries in Palestine and neighboring countries have cast much light on human antiquity in Southwest Asia. Excavations in the upper Jordan Valley have brought to light human habitations, artifacts, and animal remnants of the Villafranchen period of the Lower Pleistocene.

A very long span of time elapsed between that era and the better-known Mesolithic period. It is now fairly certain that *ca.* 10,000-8000 B.C. many relatively developed cultures occurred in this region. Among these the Natufian culture, which can be synchronized with the period of the invention of food production, was the most eminent. The early types of farming — formation of crop plants from local wild ancestors and domestication of animals — was no doubt not a speciality of the Jarmo population on the Western slopes of the Zagros Mountains, but started simultaneously or successively along the whole Fertile Crescent, which abounds with prehistoric sites from that period and possesses all those properties that have sponsored or favored food production in Jarmo.

From that period on, devastation of the vegetation for farming assumed ever increasing dimensions, while domestication of animals changed the composition of the primeval vegetation enormously. Besides producing food, humans continued destroying vegetation by collecting plants for fuel, industries, buildings, etc. Even today, wild plants are being used for a variety of purposes:

(1) Food for mankind. There are hundreds of species of plants among the local vegetation of which various parts

Nabatean floral ornamentation from Khirbet Brak near Petra (E. K. Vogel; picture N. Glueck)

are edible. These plants are still collected by peasants and bedouin and some are even sold in the markets. There were no doubt many more of them in the past.

(2) Pasture and forage. A tremendous number of pasture plants still occur in the local vegetation, despite thousands of years of uncontrolled grazing.

(3) Medicinal plants. Folk medicine is a very common feature in the Middle Eastern countries. Many plants are used in healing external and internal diseases, and drugs from local plants are also sold in the markets.

(4) Forest and fruit trees. Some of the local tree species have since ancient times been used in afforestation or taken into cultivation as fruit trees. Of indigenous trees one might mention the cypress, the pine, the carob, the almond, and the olive tree.

(5) Ornamentals. Many indigenous species are known as ornamental plants (e.g., the myrtle, cistus, lily, antirrhinum, and spartium). Ancestral strains of some cultivated cereals such as wheat, barley, and oats are still growing wild in this country. Of other cultivated plants (e.g., clovers, flax, carthamus, vetches, lentils) the ancestral stocks are probably indigenous to Palestine.

The introduction of alien plants from almost all the main regions of the world, noted earlier, is yet another way in which humans have changed the primeval landscape. It can be concluded that if changes occurred in the vegetation during the Pleistocene these were due less to fluctuations in climate than to the influence of mankind.

See Map II.

See also FOOD II; FRUIT.

Bibliography.–G. M. Crowfoot and L. Baldensperger, *From Cedar to Hyssop* (1932); A. Eig, *Agricultural Experiment Station (Tel Aviv) Bulletin,* 4 (1926); 7 (1927); *Palestine Journal of Botany,* J Series, 1 (1938), 4-12; R. K. Harrison, *EQ,* 26 (1954), 218-224; I. Löw, *Die Flora der Juden* (4 vols., 1924-1934); *MPB;* G. E. Post, *Flora of Syria, Palestine, and Sinai* (2 vols., 2nd ed. 1932-1933); A. A. Temple, *Flowers and Trees of Palestine* (2nd ed. 1929); H. B. Tristram, *Natural History of the Bible* (7th ed. 1883); W. Walker, *All the Plants of the Bible* (1957); M. Zohary, *Arboreal Flora of Israel and Transjordan* (1951).

E. W. G. MASTERMAN
R. K. H.

FLOUR. *See* BREAD III, IV; FOOD II.

FLOURISH. The RSV uses this term only in the OT. It translates several Hebrew verbs with various shades of meaning: (1) *pāraḥ* (cf. Akk. *parāḫu*), "sprout, break forth" (Ps. 72:7; 92:12f. [MT 13f.]; Prov. 11:28; 14:11; Isa. 66:14; Ezk. 17:24; Hos. 13:15, AV "be fruitful"; 14:7, AV "revive," NEB "grow"); (2) *ṣûṣ,* "blossom" (Ps. 90:6; 92:7 [MT 8]; 103:15); (3) *nûḇ,* "thrive" (Zec. 9:17 AV "cheerful," NEB "strengthen").

FLOW. This term translates several Hebrew and Greek words. Figuratively, Palestine is portrayed as a land "flowing [Heb. *zûḇ*] with milk and honey" (e.g., Ex. 3:8; Jer. 11:5; Ezk. 20:6; note the Ugaritic parallel in *UT* 49:iii: 6f., 12f.); its hills are covered with milk and its streams flow with water (Heb. *hālak,* Joel 3:18 [MT 4:18]). In Job 20:17 the NEB attempts to improve the sense and parallelism of MT *pᵉlaggôṯ nahᵃrê naḥᵃlê* (lit. "canals, rivers of, wadis of"; cf. AV) by taking the second term as a reference to "cream." (The RSV prefers a lesser emendation and translates the third term as a verb, although this verb does not occur in the OT.) M. Dahood's suggestion (*Bibl.,* 48 [1967], 437) to understand *nhr* as "oil," though not without its problems, accomplishes what others attempt by emendation, namely, improving the sense and parallelism (see comms.). In Am. 9:13 the RSV renders the hithpoel of *mûg* as "flow," apparently to enhance the parallelism; in its other occurrences (Ps. 107:26; Nah. 1:5) the RSV uses "melt" (so AV; cf. KD *in loc.).* But Palestine's mountains may also flow with human blood (niphal of Heb. *māsas,* Isa. 34:3; cf. *exérchomai,* Rev. 14:20; the RSV slightly emends Ezk. 32:6, changing MT *ṣāpāṯᵉḵā* [<**ṣāpâ,* a hapax legomenon] to **ṣāpôṯ,* fem. pl. part. of *ṣûp,* "flow").

Human sadness is expressed by eyes "flowing with tears" (*yāraḏ,* lit. "descend," Lam. 1:16; 3:48f.). God's care for the widow was such that the oil stopped flowing only when the need was met (Heb. *ʿāmaḏ,* "cease moving," 2 K. 4:6).

In eschatological visions people will flow like a river to God (Heb. *nāhar,* Isa. 2:2 par. Mic. 4:1) in contrast to those who now flock to Bel in Babylon (Heb. *nāhar,* Jer. 51:44).

For the expression "flow of blood" (Heb. *māqôr,* "well," Lev. 12:7; Gk. *rhýsis,* Mk. 5:25 par.) *see* DISEASE IV.G; for the symbolic meaning of flowing/living water(s) *see* WATER.

See RIVER. R. W. V.

FLOWER; BLOSSOM; BLOOM; etc. [Heb. *peraḥ, ṣîṣ, ṣîṣâ, niṣâ, niṣān, nēṣ, ʾēḇ,* vbs. *pāraḥ, nûṣ, ṣûṣ, ṣāmaḥ*; Gk. *ánthos*].

The Heb. *peraḥ* (from *pāraḥ,* "break forth") denotes an early stage of flowering (Isa. 5:24; cf. 35:1f.; Nah. 1:4). It is used in Ex. 25:31-34 for the flowers molded on the candlesticks. Flowers as architectural ornaments are mentioned in 1 K. 6 (*ṣîṣ*); the same word indicates actual flowers in Job 14:2; Ps. 103:15; Isa. 28:1; 40:6-8.

The beauty and profusion of the Palestinian spring flowers seem largely taken for granted in the OT (cf. Cant. 2:12), though mentioned by Christ (Mt. 6:28; Lk. 12:27). The dramatic manner in which the flowers burst into bloom for a few short weeks in spring and then fade into masses of withered leaves and stalks was regarded as an apt illustration of the evanescent nature of human life (Job 14:2; Ps. 103:15; Isa. 40:6; Jas. 1:10).

See also FLORA. R. K. H.

FLUTE [Heb. *ḥālîl* (e.g., 1 S. 10:5); Gk. *aulós* (1 Cor. 14:7)]. *See* MUSIC II.C.

FLUX. Archaic in the AV of Acts 28:8 for DYSENTERY.

FLY; FLIES [Heb. *ʿārōḇ*; Gk. *kynómuia*–'dogfly'] (Ex. 8:21f., 24,29,31; Ps. 78:45; 105:31); [Heb. *zᵉḇûḇ*; Gk. *muíai*–'flies'; cf. Akk. *zumbu*; Arab. *dhubâb*–'fly,' 'bee'] (Eccl. 10:1; Isa. 7:18). The term *ʿārōḇ* alludes to a mixture of different types of insects, hence a swarm. It was associated with the fourth Egyptian plague and could have included the common housefly (*Musca domestica*), the Tabanid fly (*Stomoxys calcitrans*), or the Barghash midge. The word *zᵉḇûḇ* has been interpreted as the common housefly, but Isa. 7:18 implies a more vicious species such as the horsefly (*Tabanus arenivagus*). The god of flies, Baal-zebub, was worshiped at Ekron (cf. 2 K. 1:2-16; Mt. 10:25; 12:24, 27; Lk. 11:15, 18f.). *See also* ZOOLOGY.

FLY (vb.); **FLY AWAY; FLYING** [Heb. *ʿûp*] (e.g., 2 S. 22:11; Prov. 23:5; 26:2; Isa. 14:29; 30:6; 60:8; Hos. 9:11; Hab. 1:8; Zec. 5:1f.); AV also FLEE (Nah. 3:16); NEB also SWEEPING, "quickly pass" (Ps. 90:10), "spread in flight" (Isa. 6:2); [*nāṣōʾ*] (Jer. 48:9); AV FLEE; [*dāʾâ*] (Dt. 28:49; Ps. 18:10 [MT 11]; Jer. 48:40; 49:22); NEB also SWOOP (Dt. 28:49), "swoop down" (Jer. 48:40; 49:22); [*ṣippôr*] (Ps. 148:10); NEB WINGED; [*nāḏaḏ*]

(Nah. 3:17); AV FLEE; NEB SCURRY; [Gk. *pétomai*] (Rev. 4:7; 8:13; etc.); NEB "in flight" (Rev. 4:7); [*pheúgō*] (Rev. 9:6); AV FLEE; NEB ELUDE.

There are two basic meanings of the terms: (1) to move through the air — generally of birds (e.g., Gen. 1:20; Dt. 4:17), but also of sparks (Job 5:7), angels (Rev. 14:6), seraphim (Isa. 6:2, 6), and arrows (Ps. 91:5); (2) to disappear (e.g., Job 20:8) or escape (e.g., Ps. 55:6 [MT 7]). *Ṣippôr* (Aram.-Syr. *ṣeprâ*) is usually taken to be a generic term for "bird"; but according to Driver and Thomas it means "sparrow" (cf. Ps. 84:3 [MT 4]; Prov. 26:2). *Dā'â* (Ug. *d'y*; cf. Dahood) is used of the eagle as a bird that swoops (*CHAL* and Driver), soars (*CHAL*), or pounces (KoB).

Bibliography.–G. R. Driver, *PEQ*, 1955, pp. 5-20, 129-140; D. Winton Thomas, *VT*, 14 (1964), 114-16; M. Dahood, *Bibl.*, 45 (1964), 393-412. J. T. DENNISON, JR.

FOAL. *See* COLT.

FOAM [Heb. *ḥāmar*] (Ps. 46:3 [MT 4]; 75:8 [MT 9]); AV "be troubled," "red"; NEB also "seethe with tumult"; [Gk. *aphrízō* (Mk. 9:18, 20), *epaphrízō* (Jude 13), *metá aphroú* (Lk. 9:39)]. The Hebrew verb has two basic meanings: "foam" or "ferment," and "be reddened" (KoB, p. 312); hence the AV rendering of Ps. 75:8 (MT 9). The term probably refers here to wine that is still fermenting.

The NT terms are all based on Gk. *aphrós,* a medical term for the foam that appears in the mouth during an epileptic seizure. In Jude Gk. *epaphrízō* is used figuratively of the evildoers who foam up shameful deeds as the sea tosses foam and refuse onto the beach. N. J. O.

FODDER. *See* PROVENDER.

FOE. *See* ENEMY; PSALMS, BOOK OF VI.A.

FOLD; SHEEPFOLD [Heb. *nāweh*] (Job 5:24; Jer. 23:3; 49:19f.; 50:44f.); AV also HABITATION; NEB HOME, PASTURE; [*mā'ôn*] (Jer. 25:30); AV HABITATION; NEB "the heavens, his home"; [*rēḇeṣ*] (Jer. 50:6); AV RESTING PLACE; [*marbēṣ*] (Ezk. 25:5); AV COUCHING PLACE; NEB SHEEP-WALK; [*dōḇer*] (Mic. 2:12); [*miḵlâ*] (Ps. 50:9; 78:70; Hab. 3:17); [*g^eḏērâ*] (Nu. 32:16, 24, 36; Zeph. 2:6); [*nā'â*] (Jer. 25:37); AV HABITATION; NEB HOMESTEAD; [*mišp^eṯayim*] (Gen. 49:14; Jgs. 5:16); AV also BURDENS; NEB CATTLE-PENS; [*š^epattayim*] (Ps. 68:13 [MT 14]); AV POTS; [*giḏrôt haṣṣō'n*] (1 S. 24:3 [MT 4]); AV SHEEPCOTE; [*'^awērôṯ*] (2 Ch. 32:28); AV COTES; [Gk. *aulḗ* (*tṓn probátōn*)] (Jn. 10:1, 16).

In the RSV "fold" and "sheepfold" are used for a number of OT terms with a variety of meanings. Heb. *g^eḏērâ* means literally a "wall" or "hedge" made of stones, which might be used for a defense or a fold. *Rēḇeṣ* and *marbēṣ,* on the other hand, denote "a place to lie down." *Mišp^eṯayim* occurs only twice (see above), and scholars are not certain of its meaning. KoB (p. 580) suggests "both saddlebags (of an ass of burden with which he likes to lie down stubbornly)"; similarly, for *š^epattayim* KoB (p. 1006) suggests "places where to set down things" or "pack-saddles." In 2 Ch. 32:28 *'^awērôṯ* may be an error for *'ûrāwôṯ* (KoB "stall" [p. 84]).

The setting of this concept is generally a place of habitation for sheep and goats. The fold is their home, their place of security (Mic. 2:12). Folds were an essential part of ancient community life. They were built along with the cities (Nu. 32:24, 36). The fold as well as the house was an essential part of a person's belongings. If this is true, "fold" (RSV) is the better translation in Job 5:24 than "home" (NEB), for it stands parallel to tent; i.e., the blessed man has security both in his own house or tent and with his valuables or fold.

"Fold" is used in a metaphorical sense for the habitation of the people of God (Jer. 23:2f.). They are the flock and Jesus is their shepherd (Jn. 10:1, 16); He is the only way into His sheepfold. Once in a while "fold" can refer to the flock itself (Jer. 25:30). The NEB, however, understands that text differently as the habitation of God; "(The Lord) roars across the heavens, his home." In the end of days God will restore Israel to "a good fold" (AV) on the mountains of Israel (Ezk. 34:14).

See also HABITATION; SHEEP. J. E. HARTLEY

FOLLOW [Heb. *yālaḵ 'aḥar* (Gen. 24:5, 8, 39, etc.), *'aḥ^arê-ḵēn* (Gen. 41:31), *rāḏap* (Gen. 44:4), *regel*–'at the foot of' (Ex. 11:8), *tûr* (Nu. 15:39), *'āśâ* (2 S. 17:23), *hālaḵ 'aḥar* (Gen. 32:19; Dt. 4:3), *'aḥar*–'after' (e.g., Nu. 14:24; 32:11; Dt. 12:30), *zā'aq 'aḥar* (Jgs. 6:34f.; lit. "be called together after"), *ḥāyâ 'aḥar* (1 S. 12:14), *māšaḵ* (Job 21:33), *yāṣā' 'aḥar* (2 S. 11:8), *dāḇēq*–'cling to' (Jer. 42:16)]; AV also PURSUE AFTER, COME AFTER, WALK AFTER, GATHER AFTER, DRAW AFTER, etc.; NEB also GO AFTER, PURSUE, IMITATE, etc.; [Gk. *akolouthéō, epakolouthéō, exakolouthéō* (2 Pet. 1:16; 2:2, 15), *katakolouthéō* (Lk. 23:55; Acts 16:17), *synakolouthéō* (Mk. 5:37; Lk. 23:49), *deúte opísō, diṓkō*–'pursue' (17:23), *katadiṓkō* (Mk. 1:36), *stoichéō toís íchnesín, échō*–'cling to' (Lk. 13:33; 2 Tim. 1:13), *peíthomai*–'believe,' 'obey' (Acts 5:36f.), *eími, peripatéō* (2 Jn. 6; 3 Jn. 3f.), *apérchomai opísō* (Mk. 1:20), *thaumázō opísō*–'wonder after' (Rev. 13:3), *gínomai* (Rev. 8:7)]; AV also COME AFTER, HOLD FAST, WALK AFTER, etc.; NEB also COME WITH, WALK IN, "keep before you," OBEY, etc.

A common OT meaning is that of "walking behind" or "going with" someone (Gen. 24:5; Josh. 3:3; 2 K. 6:19). It can also refer to "setting off after someone to catch him," often with hostile intentions (*rāḏap* in Gen. 44:4). Perhaps it was the remembrance of divine benevolence in the face of enemy persecution that led the psalmist to choose this word in Ps. 23:6. "Follow" is also used in the sense of adherence to a leader (Jgs. 8:5; 1 S. 25:27; 2 S. 20:11). Theologically, especially in the Deuteronomic writings and Jeremiah, it means adherence to a god or to God. It then becomes an almost technical term, describing the going after other gods and the apostasy of the people, which is their basic sin (*TDNT*, I, 211; cf. Dt. 16:20; 18:9; 1 K. 18:21; Jer. 3:17; 13:10; 18:12).

The NT never applies the phrase to "following after God," but the early Christian community initiated the expression "following after Christ." This referred to the life of Christian discipleship and is the figurative use of the verb *akolouthéō,* which literally means to "come after" (cf. Mk. 14:13; Lk. 22:10; Jn. 10:4f.). Except for Rev. 14:4, 13, this discipleship aspect of "follow" occurs only in the four Gospels. The command to "follow" is absolute (Mt. 8:22; Lk. 18:22); the disciples did what the rabbis' students did, only with an "internal attachment to Jesus." (The traditional master-student relationship involved the rabbis' going ahead, perhaps riding on an ass, with their pupils following behind at an appropriate distance [*TDNT*, I, 213].) Jesus gave this type of "following" a new content—Himself. Participation includes "personal surrender to his summons, and acceptance of his leadership" (Taylor, p. 169) and participation in His suffering and outcome (Mt. 8:19-22; Mk. 8:34; Jn. 12:25f.).

A related word, *synakolouthéō,* means to "accompany someone" (Jn. 13:36; Mk. 5:37), and in Lk. 23:49 has the connotation perhaps of "being a disciple." The forcefulness of the command "Follow!" is found in the imperative *deúte opísō* ("Follow me!" in Mt. 4:19; Mk. 1:17; cf. *deúro akolouthéō* in Mt. 19:21, etc.).

Ethical conduct is related to the other NT words for "follow." Jesus warned His disciples not "to run after" or "pursue" (*diṓkō*) those claiming to be the Son of man in Lk. 17:23. Paul exhorts his readers to be "drawn up in a line with" or to "keep in the footsteps of" the faith of Abraham (*stoichéō* in Rom. 4:12). This is also the meaning of *epakolouthéō* in 1 Pet. 2:21, where believers follow in the footsteps of the suffering of Christ (*see* EXAMPLE). *Exakolouthéō,* used figuratively in 2 Pet. 1:16, means to follow in the sense of obedience to an authority, here an impersonal authority (cf. Josephus *Ant.* i.22).

In the Epistles of John, Christ's "walk of life" is the norm for believers' conduct (2 Jn. 6a). The state in which they live or ought to live is what they should "follow" (*peripatéō*); they are commanded to follow love (2 Jn. 6b) and the truth (3 Jn. 3f.).

Timothy is urged to "keep" or "preserve" (*échō*) the example of sound teaching in 2 Tim. 1:13 while Gk. *to esómenon,* "what was going to happen," colloquially stands for "what would follow" (Lk. 22:49; cf. Sir. 48:25).

Bibliography.–J. A. Alexander, *Psalms* (6th ed. 1850), I, 197; V. Taylor, *Gospel According to St. Mark* (1953); *TDNT,* I, *s.v.* ἀκολευθέω κτλ. (Kittel).

D. K. MCKIM

FOLLOWER. *See* IMITATE.

FOLLY. *See* FOOL.

FONDLING [Heb. piel of *ṣāḥaq*] (Gen. 26:8); AV SPORTING; NEB LAUGH. In the qal, *ṣāḥaq* means to "laugh." In the piel it has the meaning of "play," "jest," "amuse oneself," etc. Used with the object Heb. *ʾištô* ("his wife"), the term probably refers to conjugal caresses. In any case, the behavior of Isaac and Rebekah indicated to Abimelech king of the Philistines that they were husband and wife.

FOOD [Heb. *ʾōḵel, ʾoḵlâ, leḥem, maʾᵃḵāl, makkōleṯ, māzôn, ṣayiḏ, ʾᵃḵîlâ, bûl, šeʾēr*; Gk. *brṓsis, diatrophḗ, trophḗ*].

I. Mineral Food
II. Vegetable Food
III. Animal Food
IV. Food Preparation
V. Food Regulations
VI. Food Supply

This article is limited to the foodstuffs used in Israel in biblical times, specifically to those kinds of food that are explicitly mentioned in the Bible, though it may be assumed confidently that there were many more. The Mishnah and Talmud mention many varieties of vegetable food that are not found in Scripture. The list could be supplemented further by comparing the Egyptian or Babylonian diet, but there is no reason to assume that every food known in these countries was also used in Israel. Even more caution is needed when comparing present-day conditions in the East with those of biblical times. Several very common kinds of food (e.g., rice, tomatoes, maize) were wholly unknown in biblical times.

I. Mineral Food.–In biblical times, as in other times, there were only two kinds of food that were not products of the animal or vegetable kingdom: water and salt. The first was obtained from rivers, lakes, springs, wells, and cisterns; the second was produced from the Mediterranean, but especially from the Dead Sea. Josh. 15:62 mentions "the City of Salt" (Heb. *ʿîr hammelaḥ*), which is possibly to be identified with Qumrân, where the Dead Sea Scrolls were found.

II. Vegetable Food.–Though some scholars infer from a comparison between Gen. 1:29f. and 9:3 that divine permission to eat the flesh of animals was first given after the Deluge, it is more probable that mankind from the beginning made use of both animal and vegetable food. The dominion given to humans over animals (Gen. 1:26) included the eating of them, as dominion over fish at least cannot mean anything else. Abel's sacrifice (4:4) supposed the eating of mutton: mankind offered to the Divinity what he himself ate. The distinction between clean and unclean animals in the ark has no meaning if meat was not eaten (7:2). Prehistoric findings point to primitive man as an omnivore. It is only after settling down as an agriculturist that humans became chiefly eaters of vegetable food. Seminomads like the patriarchs combined both categories (18:5-8). They were prepared to go on lengthy travels (42:1-3, etc.) or even to leave their accustomed abodes (12:10, etc.) in order to get their supply of grain.

After the conquest of Canaan, Israel gradually became an agricultural nation with bread as its staple food. This was made of cereals, which therefore are to be mentioned first among the foodstuffs of the Bible. The most important grains of the Bible were WHEAT and BARLEY; the latter, though mainly used as a fodder, was often eaten in expectation of the wheat harvest, frequently by the poor, and in general when wheat was scarce. Other grains were MILLET and SPELT (Ezk. 4:9; Ex. 9:32; Isa. 28:25). The most primitive way to eat grain was to pluck fresh ears, remove the husks by rubbing in the hands, and eat the grains raw (Lev. 23:14; Dt. 23:25; 2 K. 4:42; Mt. 12:1 par.). A slightly more advanced method was to roast fresh ears and eat the grain unground (e.g., Lev. 2:14, as a sacrificial gift); Lev. 23:14 means perhaps the same, though it is possible to understand here (as in 1 S. 17:17; 25:18; 2 S. 17:28) roasted grain that has been threshed beforehand. In Ruth 2:14, however, one could think of roasted ears, harvested and parched on the field. After being crushed in a mortar (Prov. 27:22), wheat groats could be cooked (cf. Nu. 11:8); according to Dalman (III, 269), Heb. *gereś* (Lev. 2:14, 16) refers to these groats (but *see* BREAD). Probably these groats played a larger role in the Israelite diet than is apparent from their mention only in Lev. 2. The most frequent way of dealing with cereal, however, was to grind it into flour (*qemaḥ*) or groats (*sōleṯ*) by rubbing the grains between two stones (*rēḥayim*); turning mills were introduced into Palestine in Hellenistic times.

Vegetables of different kinds are mentioned occasionally in the Bible but much more often in postbiblical Jewish literature. Vegetables in general (cereals included) are mentioned in Dnl. 1:12 (*zērōʿîm,* lit. "things sown"; cf. Dnl. 1:16; Isa. 61:11). LENTILS, white and red, the "red" (brown) thought to be the best variety, were considered very tasty and nutritious. Though sometimes ground (Ezk. 4:9), they were commonly cooked into a pottage (Gen. 25:29, 34). 2 S. 17:28 shows the importance of lentils as food for the army. Of all the different sorts of BEANS, only horsebeans were mentioned (2 S. 17:28; Ezk. 4:9).

In the desert the Israelites longed for the CUCUMBER, the MELONS, the LEEKS, the ONIONS, and the GARLIC of Egypt (Nu. 11:5). None of these occurs in other parts of the Bible; yet one may be sure from numerous indications in postbiblical literature that all these vegetables were grown in biblical times. Moreover, Isa. 1:8 mentions a field of cucumbers, large and important enough that a lookout for a watchman was built in it; according to Jer. 10:5 a scarecrow was erected in it. Cucumbers, leeks, and onions could be eaten raw, with bread, but they could also be cooked.

The "bitter herbs" of the Passover ritual (Ex. 12:8; Nu. 9:11) were probably wild lettuce or wild endive. These, together with chervil and an herb (identified by Dalman [I, 346] as an eryngo variety) are mentioned in Mish. *Pesahim* ii.6. Most of the vegetables were wild plants, accessible to the poor, who also "pick mallow and the leaves of bushes" (Job 30:4). The "vegetables" (*láchana*) of Rom. 14:2 comprised both wild and cultivated plants; the same word is also used for those plants that yield condiments, as CUMMIN, black cummin (Isa. 28:25, 27), dill (Mt. 23:23), mint (Lk. 11:42), MUSTARD (Mt. 13:31; 17:20; etc.), and rue (Lk. 11:42), though these were cultivated. Apart from these special dainties a "dinner of herbs" was considered a poor dish (Prov. 15:17). 2 K. 4:38-40 presents a graphic picture of poor people who in times of dearth gathered wild herbs and faced the risk of unknowingly introducing some toxic plants into their pottage.

Genesis 1:29f. considers grains and fruits proper human food and assigns "every green plant" to the animals. But in Gen. 9:3 these herbs are described as a well-known food for humans, and in Dt. 11:10 and 1 K. 21:2 vegetable gardens are mentioned, in the latter passage as supplying the royal kitchen. Here certainly a garden of plants that yield condiments must be assumed; nevertheless, the passage seems to imply that changing a vineyard into such a garden was an insult to the good soil.

This shows, as is evident in many places, that fruits were appreciated above vegetables. Egyptian sources show that fruit trees abounded in Palestine many centuries before it was occupied by the Israelites. So important were they for the economy of the land that to destroy fruit trees in war was forbidden (Dt. 20:19f.). The parable of Jotham in Jgs. 9:8-13 enumerated the most important fruit trees: olive, fig, and vine.

It is not without significance that Jgs. 9:8-13 mentions the OLIVE TREE first; it is the most important tree around the Mediterranean. Its fruits were eaten, though this is nowhere expressly stated in Scripture; more important was the oil pressed from the fruits. It was used for baking and was an ingredient for nearly every dish; it was used also as fuel for the oil lamps both in the home and in the sanctuary; and it was used as an unguent for wounds (Lk. 10:34) and in illness (Jas. 5:14). Finally, it formed the basis of ointments, which made the human skin fresh and supple.

Next in importance is the FIG, whose sweetness was praised in Jotham's parable and whose "first-ripe fig," i.e., the early fig which grew on the previous year's wood, was esteemed a delicacy and was often eaten while it was still green (Isa. 28:4; Jer. 24:2; Mic. 7:1; Mk. 11:13). Of the late figs large quantities were dried in the sun and stored for use out of season. Pressed in a mold, they formed the "cakes of figs" (Heb. *d^e^bēlâ*) mentioned as provisions for soldiers (1 S. 25:18; 30:12; etc.); these cakes also could be used as a plaster upon a boil (2 K. 20:7; Isa. 38:21). The same device is mentioned in an Ugaritic veterinary treatise (Ugar. *dblt*, e.g., *UT* 56:33).

The VINE and its products have always been much prized in oriental literature. Palestine, and especially the mountainous region of Judah, yielded excellent grapes (e.g., Nu. 13:23). Grapes were enjoyed both before their full ripeness (Heb. *bōser*, a dainty snack in the Orient; cf. Isa. 18:5; Jer. 31:29; etc.) and when ripe; and they were often dried in the sun (Nu. 6:3) and made into raisin cakes (Heb. *ṣimmûqîm*, "military provisions," 1 S. 25:18; 30:12; etc.; or *'ᵃšîšâ*, 2 S. 6:19; Hos. 3:1). The juice of grapes, drunk before the fermentation process set in (*mišrâ*), is mentioned only in Nu. 6:3. The same is perhaps meant by *'āsîs* in Isa. 16:7. Three Hebrew words are used to indicate the product after fermentation: *ḥemer* probably means wine that is still fermenting; the non-Semitic word *yayin* is of the same obscure origin as our word "wine"; *tîrôš* does not seem to indicate a special stage or kind, but is rather an archaic and poetical word, as is also the "blood of the grape" (Heb. *dam ʿēnāḇ*, Dt. 32:14; cf. Ugar. *dm ʿṣm*, "blood of trees").

Food and drink; reconstruction of Egyptian wall paintings (Royal Ontario Museum, Toronto)

Less prominent were the fruits of other trees: almonds of the tree that is the first to flower in spring and therefore is called "the wakeful one" (*šāqēḏ*); nuts (in Cant. 6:11 only); pistachio nuts (Gen. 43:11 only); the fruits of the sycamore-fig (Am. 7:14); the *tappû(a)ḥ*, probably not our apple, but rather a quince (according to some scholars the apricot). The POMEGRANATE (*rimmôn*) is frequently mentioned, especially in Canticles. The "fruit of goodly trees" (Lev. 23:40) according to Jewish tradition is the etrog, a citrus variety. Though growing in a few parts of Palestine only (Jericho, the shores of Lake Galilee), the date-palm is often mentioned. Its name became a proper name for several biblical women (Tamar). Only in the Canticles is it mentioned; but it must have had some importance in Israel's diet, especially because the word rendered by "honey" (*d^e^ḇaš*) in some instances is to be explained as a date syrup, like the corresponding Babylonian and Arabic words. In times of need the rather tasty pods of the carob tree were eaten (Lk. 15:16).

III. Animal Food.–Like most Semitic nations, the Hebrews passed through a nomadic stage, during which animal food (meat and milk products) was the mainstay of their diet. This stage, however, is not represented in the Bible. Even the patriarchs, from Abraham on, were not nomads but transhumants or "seminomads," i.e., though they had their flocks and often went far away in search of good pasture (Gen. 37:12-14), they also sowed and reaped their own grains (26:12). A mixed diet therefore was the rule with them. Abraham offered both animal and vegetable foods to his guests (18:6-8). After the settlement in Canaan, Israel became gradually an agricultural nation and vegetable food prevailed. With the common people, animal food was reserved to festival times, mostly in connection with sacrifices; meat was a negligible part of the poor man's diet. Solomon and his courtiers devoured a great quantity of animal food daily (1 K. 4:22f. [MT 5:2f.]), and his way of life was imitated by the wealthy classes of later times, to the indignation of the prophets (Am. 6:4).

Among the mammals SHEEP and goats (*see* GOAT) were reared in large numbers. As a meat the goat was less appreciated than the sheep; goat's flesh, mostly of the kids, was the cheapest form of meat (Lk. 15:29). Most of the Israelites' milk came from goats (cf. Prov. 27:27). Milk (Heb. *ḥālāḇ*) was consumed both fresh and after it had soured. Many scholars maintain that Heb. *ḥemʾâ* was soured, thick milk; according to Dalman and others this word denoted fresh butter, produced by swinging the soured milk in a goatskin. Cheese (*g^{e}ḇinnâ*) is mentioned in Job 10:10. In 1 S. 17:18 David gave *ḥ^{a}rîṣê heḥālāḇ* to a captain of a thousand men. If the Hebrew is rendered "milk cheeses," then *ḥālāḇ* here has the meaning of "cheese," since *ḥ^{a}rîṣê* simply means "slices." In 2 S. 17:29 *š^{e}pôṯ* is mentioned, which Dalman identifies with "curds." A preferable translation is "cheese" (from cow's milk), since this explains how the valley inside Jerusalem, at whose end the "ash gate" stood, became known as "the valley of cheesemakers" (Tyropoeon) in Josephus' time (*see* CURDS).

The sheep of Palestine were mainly of the fat-tailed species. In honor of a guest or at a festive occasion lambs were slaughtered (2 S. 12:4); less is said about the slaughtering of adult sheep. Calves supplied a highly appreciated meat; the "fatted calf" of Lk. 15:23, like its counterparts in the OT (1 S. 28:24; Jer. 46:21; Am. 6:4; Mal. 4:2 [MT 3:20]), was a calf kept in a stall; Abraham chose a calf from the herd, i.e., one that was not kept in a stall (Gen. 18:7). A stalled ox (lit. "kept at the manger") was part of a rich man's dinner (Prov. 15:17, AV). 1 K. 4:23 (MT 5:3) distinguishes between "fat oxen" and "pasture-fed cattle."

The king's court devoured an abundance of game — fallow buck, gazelles, and roebuck — hunted for this purpose; to the game eaten by the Israelites Dt. 14:5 adds the wild goat, the *dîšôn* (an antelope?), the wild sheep, and another kind of gazelle. That these four names do not occur elsewhere in the OT may serve as a proof that hunted game did not play a very important role in the average Israelite diet. In Sinuhe's time (20th cent. B.C.) game was plentiful in Palestine and Syria, and the same seems to be the case in the patriarchal period (Gen. 25:28; 27:4). With the increase of the population during the 1st millennium B.C. most of the game disappeared.

Neither wild nor domesticated swine were allowed to the Israelites; unlike the Arabs they abstained also from camel flesh. The smaller mammals such as the hare or rabbit were also forbidden (Dt. 14:7f.).

Although some birds (especially the birds of prey) were forbidden (Dt. 14:12-18), fowl were an important source of food. We do not know what kind is meant by the "fatted fowl" (Heb. *barbur*) of 1 K. 4:23 (MT 5:3); many scholars understand geese here, and geese were a very frequent dish in Egypt; but Koehler (KoB, p. 147) supposes that the word should be rendered "cuckoos." Nowhere in the OT are chickens mentioned (*see* CHICKEN; COCK); but since the discovery of two preexilic seals showing an engraving of a fighting cock it is probable that the Israelites from an early date knew domesticated chicken. Job 38:36 is to be rendered: "Who put wisdom in the ibis or who gave understanding to the cock?" A drawing on ivory from Tell el-Fârʿah in the Negeb shows attendants bringing in ducks, probably wild ones. 1 S. 26:20 and Jer. 17:11 mention partridges (*see* PARTRIDGE). Quails passed Palestine and the Sinaitic desert on their way to Africa. Pigeons are frequently mentioned and are still a common food among the Arabs; both the tame kind (Heb. *yônâ*) and the wild (*tôr*) are eaten. Of most of the birds enumerated here the eggs were eaten too.

FISH were especially important for the population in the vicinity of the Sea of Tiberias, but there was also a large import of dried and salted fish from the Tyrian coast to Jerusalem (Neh. 13:16; cf. Zeph. 1:10). Water animals without fins and scales were forbidden (Dt. 14:9f.). This excludes, apart from snakelike fish, all shellfish and the like. No special kinds of fishes used as food are mentioned in the Bible.

The only insects whose use as a food was allowed were

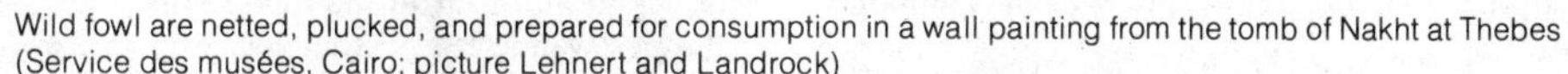

Wild fowl are netted, plucked, and prepared for consumption in a wall painting from the tomb of Nakht at Thebes (Service des musées, Cairo; picture Lehnert and Landrock)

locusts (Lev. 11:20-23). The Assyrians relished them, as is known from scenes from their reliefs; to this day one finds them sold in Arab markets. The most common way of preparing them is to remove the head, legs, and wings, to drop the bodies in meal, and then to fry them in oil or butter. One product of insects allowed to the Israelite was honey, if it was produced by bees and not from a date syrup. From the 2nd millennium on, bee farming occurs in Egyptian, Hittite, and Assyrian texts and drawings. It is therefore to be considered accidental that the Bible seems to mention "wild honey" only. The honeycomb (Heb. *ya'ar* or *ya'ᵃrâ*) is mentioned in Cant. 5:1 and 1 S. 14:27; perhaps Isa. 7:8 alludes to a custom of beekeepers. As sugar was unknown, honey was the best sweetening agency and was used in many dishes and dainties.

IV. Food Preparation.–In general, cooking or broiling took place in the open air, either outside the house (1 K. 19:6; Jn. 21:9) or inside, in the open courtyard. Ezk. 46:21-24 describes the four kitchens (Heb. *bêṯ hamᵉḇaššᵉlîm,* "house of those that cook") in the four corners of the outer temple court. The word rendered "vaulted" in v. 22, NEB, is rather to be understood as "without roof" (cf. T.B. *Middoth* 35a).

Food was prepared by the lady of the house (Gen. 18:6) and/or servants, both male (Gen. 18:7) and female (1 S. 8:13), but it was not considered undignified for a young man to prepare a special dish (Gen. 25:29-34) either for himself or for an honored guest (Jgs. 6:19). In the temple food was prepared by men.

Lentils, beans, all kinds of vegetables (Nu. 11:5), and herbs found in the fields (2 K. 4:39) were boiled in a cooking pot. 1 S. 2:14 mentions four different types of cooking pots, all made of clay. An iron griddle is mentioned in Ezk. 4:3, a copper pot in Ezk. 24:11. These utensils were also used for boiling meat. Boiling was the usual way of preparing flesh. Roasting of meat is seldom mentioned (1 S. 2:15; Isa. 44:16, 19); it was done on charcoal, probably with the help of a fork or a stick. A very special way of roasting by heaping charcoal and ashes all around the animal was prescribed for the paschal lamb, which was broiled with "head, shins, and entrails" (Ex. 12:9, NEB), as is still done by the Samaritans.

Fish was broiled (Jn. 21:9; Lk. 24:42; NEB "cooked"). The fish, brought by Tyrian merchants to Jerusalem (Neh. 13:16), was probably dried and salted (cf. Tob. 6:5). Salt and all kinds of herbal condiments were added to both vegetables and meat, and especially to broth or sauce (Heb. *māraq* [Jgs. 6:19f.; Isa. 65:4; cf. Ezk. 24:10]).

For the roasting of locusts, see III above; for the baking of bread, *see* BREAD IV. It is possible that grain was also used to make porridge, but this is never mentioned in Scripture.

V. Food Regulations.–The rules to distinguish between clean and unclean food were very strict. Since food goes into the body and therefore becomes part of the person, much caution was needed in order to prevent harmful influences from spreading through the body. As a rule mineral and vegetable foods were considered clean; but if water or food prepared with water was defiled by the carcass of a dead unclean animal, that water or food was considered unclean (Lev. 11:32-38, with the exception of water in a fountain or cistern). This shows already that the uncleanness of certain foodstuffs was in reality restricted to the animal kingdom. Of the mammals only those that part the hoof and chew the cud are allowed (Lev. 11:1-8; Dt. 14:6-8). It is difficult to see in which manner the combination of having cloven feet and chewing the cud could impart "cleanness"; it is probable that the rule is secondary only, discovered after clean mammals had been enumerated: cows, sheep, goats, and antelope. One should bear in mind that the meat of these animals was clean when they were slaughtered in the right way, i.e., after the blood had been removed. The consuming of blood was forbidden at least from Noah's time (Gen. 9:4). Since it could not be ascertained whether heathens had slaughtered in the right way, and there was a chance that the meat presented by them was part of a sacrifice, there was a taboo against partaking of food prepared by pagans (Acts 11:3; Gal. 2:12). If the Pharisees doubted that a person had presented the tithes of everything to the temple, they refused to eat with him. The rules about the "cleanness" and "uncleanness" of birds, fish, and insects are given in Lev. 11 and Dt. 14.

In the NT the food rules were reduced, at least for gentile Christians, to abstention from blood and things strangled (Acts 15:20). If meat was known to have been sacrificed to idols, it was not to be eaten; but Paul advised not to ask questions about the origin of the meat (1 Cor. 8; 10:23-33), though he warned against giving offense to more strict ("weaker") brethren (Rom. 14). In principle the teaching of Our Lord that "there is nothing outside a man which by going into him can defile him" (Mk. 7:14-23) meant the end of all OT food rules, though He Himself during His ministry on earth conformed to these rules. Peter could say, "Nothing common or unclean has ever entered my mouth" (Acts 11:8), but with the acceptance of former heathens into the Christian Church another attitude was indicated.

See also CLEAN AND UNCLEAN II.A; V.

VI. Food Supply.–The impression is given that in OT times as a rule every household provided food for its own wants. This is certainly true of nomadic life and generally also of the seminomadic life of the patriarchs. But even after Israel had settled and become an agricultural population, food was produced by every household for its own wants; every tiller of the soil had also some sheep and goats, and most had a few oxen. The towns were "the cities of our tillage" (Neh. 10:37 [MT 38], AV). An exception must be made for a royal settlement for industry and sea traffic like Ezion-geber, where it may be supposed that food was delivered from elsewhere by royal management.

In the main centers like Jerusalem or Samaria grain could be bought (e.g., 2 K. 7:1), but it is highly improbable that bread was for sale. (On Jer. 37:21 *see* BREAD IV.) Some condiments and other ingredients for more sophisticated dishes had to be bought from merchants. In Nehemiah's time, fish (dried and salted) was imported into Jerusalem by Tyrian merchants, and the Judean farmers used to bring grain and fruit to the metropolis (Neh. 13:15f.). In NT times wandering persons had to buy bread (Jn. 4:8), though we do not know who sold it. There was a meat market in Corinth (1 Cor. 10:25), and sparrows were sold in the Palestine markets (Mt. 10:29). Nevertheless, it is very probable that in general even in NT times most households were self-supporting, although a product like oil was then procured from professional shopkeepers (Mt. 25:9). Wine shops from Hellenistic times have been discovered in Marisa and Beth-zur.

Irregularities in nature could cause scarcity of food: too little rain or, less frequently, too much rain or rain in the wrong season might be the cause of "blight" or "mildew," respectively (Am. 4:9). In such times people tried to buy grain and sometimes wandered far to get supplies (Gen. 42:1f., etc.). They even changed their abodes in such cases — not only seminomads like Abraham and Isaac (Gen. 12:10; 26:1), but also farmers and town dwellers like Elimelech (Ruth 1:1) and the woman of Shunem (2 K. 8:1f.), returning sometimes after seven or more years. No mention is made of food imported by state measures, as from Egypt to Rome in the times of the Caesars.

On food as fellowship *see also* BREAD V.

See also BREAD; MEALS.

Bibliography.–A. G. Barrois, *Manuel d'archéologie biblique*, I (1939), 304-351; G. Dalman, *Arbeit und Sitte in Palästina*, II-IV (1932-35); M. Ebert, ed., *Reallexicon der Vorgeschichte*, *s.v.* "Jagd," "Rind," "Schaf," "Ziege"; R. J. Forbes, *Studies in Ancient Technology*, III (1955), 50-59; 84-104; *TDNT*, I, *s.v.* βρῶμα (J. Behm). A. VAN SELMS

FOOL; FOOLISH(LY); FOLLY.

I. In the OT.–*A. General.* Outside of wisdom literature the most common Hebrew words for "fool" and "folly" are *nāḇāl*, *nᵉḇālâ*, and *sāḵāl*. *Nāḇāl* denotes a wicked person, rather than merely a person who lacks sense. *Nᵉḇālâ* signifies "wickedness," "shameless impropriety" (cf. Isa. 32:6). Abigail described her husband Nabal as "this ill-natured fellow," for "as his name is, so is he" (1 S. 25:25), and his conduct confirms this judgment. Other occurrences of *nᵉḇālâ* are generally associated with some form of wickedness, often with base and unnatural lewdness (Gen. 34:7; Dt. 22:21; 2 S. 13:12, "wanton folly").

Sāḵāl, rendered "foolishly" or "foolishness" by the RSV, and its cognates *seḵel* and *siḵlûṯ* generally denote "thickheadedness." Though its use in 2 S. 15:31 does not imply moral condemnation (perhaps also in Gen. 31:28), *sāḵāl* usually implies sin and error (2 S. 24:10; 1 S. 26:21) or a lack of trust in God (2 Ch. 16:7-9; cf. Dt. 32:6, 21).

Other related words are **yā'al*, "be empty," "be or become foolish," rendered by the RSV "do foolishly" in Nu. 12:11 and "become fools" in Isa. 19:13 (parallel to *niššᵉ'û*, "are deluded") and Jer. 50:36, *'ĕwîl* (Isa. 19:11, parallel to *niḇ'ārâ*, "are stupid"; cf. *TDOT*, II, 204f.), which connotes a lack of understanding, and *kāsal*, "be foolish" (Jer. 10:8).

B. Wisdom Literature. In the wisdom literature "fool" and "folly" are frequent and distinctive words. Their significance is best seen in contrast with "wisdom," which was the outcome of careful observation and long pondering on actual life in the light of religion and divine revelation. Wisdom had its seat in God and was imparted to those who feared Him ("The fear of the Lord is the beginning [chief part] of knowledge," Prov. 1:7). Such wisdom was the essence of life, and to be without it was to walk in the way of death and destruction. Fools were thoughtless, careless, conceited, self-sufficient, indifferent to God and His will, and might even oppose and scoff at religion and wise instruction. *See* WISDOM.

Hebrew *'ĕwîl*, a frequently used word in the wisdom literature, denotes one who rejects instruction (Prov. 12:15; 15:5); is ready to speak and act without thinking (10:14); is quick to get angry, quarrel, and cause strife (12:16; 20:3; 29:9); is unrestrained in his anger (Job 5:2). He is associated with transgression (Ps. 107:17, RSV mg.) and sin (Prov. 24:9). The associated noun *'iwweleṯ*, "foolishness" (Ps. 38:5 [MT 6]; "fool," 69:5 [MT 6]; Prov. 13:16; etc.) occurs with *'ĕwîl* in Prov. 16:22; 27:22; and with *kᵉsîl* in 26:11. (In Prov. 14:24 the RSV and the NEB emend [with *BH*] the first occurrence of *'iwweleṯ* to *liwyaṯ*, "wreath," preserving the parallelism with "crown.")

Hebrew *kᵉsîl*, "stupid person" (cf. the related noun *kesel*, "stupidity"; Arab. *kasal*, "sluggishness") denotes one who is self-confident (Prov. 14:16; 28:26); ignorant (Eccl. 2:14); hates instruction (Prov. 1:22; 18:2); is thoughtless (10:23; 17:24); is angry and contentious (Prov. 18:6; 19:1; Eccl. 7:9); rages (Prov. 17:12); is indolent (Eccl. 4:5; Prov. 21:20); and engages in silly merriment (Eccl. 7:4-6). Such a one is also associated with slander (Prov. 10:18) and evil (13:19).

Hebrew *sāḵāl* and its derivatives occur in Ecclesiastes (e.g., 2:12; 7:25), but not in Proverbs. In Eccl. 7:25 Heb. *siḵlûṯ* is related to madness. Less frequent are *nāḇāl* (Prov. 17:7, 21; cf. Ps. 14:1; 53:1; Job 2:10), *nᵉḇālâ* (Job 42:8), and *hālal*, "make a fool of" (KoB, pp. 235f.) in Job 12:17.

II. In the Apocrypha.–Words for "fool" occur frequently in Wisdom and Sirach, Gk. *áphrōn*, "mindless," being the dominant term in the former and *mōrós*, "foolish," the dominant one in the latter. *Áphrōn*, like *mōrós* (Sir. 21:14; 22:7, 26), signifies lack of understanding (Sir. 22:13, parallel to *asýnetos*, "without sense") and is frequently associated with idolatry (Wisd. 12:24; 15:5). Some behavioral patterns of a fool may be excused (such as the raising of his voice when laughing, Sir. 21:20; his peculiar manner of lending money, 20:14f.; his inopportune speaking, 20:20), but he remains an ungodly person (22:12) and his folly should be hidden (20:13). In Wisd. 3:2 fools do not believe in divine protection and form a class of people opposite to that of the wise or righteous.

III. In the NT.–The RSV renders various Greek words by "fool," "foolish," or "folly" in the ordinary sense of being without sense or intelligence: *áphrōn*, "mindless" (Lk. 11:40; 12:20; 1 Cor. 15:36), *anóētos*, "without understanding" (e.g., Gal. 3:1-3), and *mōrós*, "foolish" (Mt. 7:26; 25:2; cf. 23:17 where it occurs with *týphlos*, "blind"). Other words have a decidedly moral connotation: *aphrosýnē*, "lack of sense," is a vice as are pride and slander in Mk. 7:22; *asýnetos*, "without sense," is ranked with being "faithless, heartless, and ruthless" in Rom. 1:31; *ánoia*, "without a mind," in 2 Tim. 3:8 is ascribed to men of "corrupt mind and counterfeit faith."

Greek *mōré* in Mt. 5:22 has been understood as: (1) a transliteration of the Hebrew-Aramaic term *mrh* or *mr'*, "bitter, rebellious"; (2) the vocative form of Gk. *mōrós*, "fool," which the rabbis borrowed and sometimes used in their debates; (3) Gk. *mōrós*, not as a loanword but simply as the equivalent of Aram. *šôṭeh*, "fool, blockhead"; (4) a translation into Greek idiom of Aram. *rêqâ*, "emptyhead," transliterated in the preceding clause in v. 22. This last explanation, however, would mean that there is no threefold progression of thought in v. 22, which is unlikely in view of the progressions in v. 25 (judge; guard; prison), vv. 34f. (heaven, throne; earth, footstool; Jerusalem, city of the king), and 7:7 (ask; seek; knock). Cf. *TDNT*, IV, 839-842.

In the Corinthian Epistles "foolishness" is a rich concept with at least three shades of meaning. (1) The message of the gospel is folly (Gk. *mōría*) to the Greeks, i.e., not in accord with their notion of wisdom (1 Cor. 1:18f.; cf. 2:14; *see* PHILOSOPHY). But God makes this so-called wisdom foolishness (Gk. *mōraínō*, 1 Cor. 1:20; 3:19; cf. Rom. 1:20) through the apparent "folly" of the gospel (1:21, 27). (2) Some of the Corinthian Christians are counseled to become fools, i.e., to behave as true Christians, which behavior the world would call foolish (3:18). (3) In 2 Cor. 11 Paul's own foolishness refers to his boasting in behalf of his church in response to the unwarranted bragging of intruders into the church (P. E. Hughes, comm. on 2nd Corinthians [*NICNT*, 1962], pp. 372f.).

For "fools for Christ's sake" (1 Cor. 4:10) see F. W. Grosheide, comm. on 1st Corinthians (*NICNT*, 1953), pp. 107f.

Bibliography.–A. Barucq, *Le Livre des Proverbes* (1964); T. Donald, *VT*, 13 (July, 1963), 285-293; *TDNT*, IV, *s.v.* μωρός κτλ. (Bertram), νοέω κτλ.: ἀνόητος, ἄνοια (Behm); *TDOT*, I, *s.v.* "'ᵉvîl" (Cazelles). W. L. WALKER R. W. V.

FOOT [Heb. *regel*]; NEB also "descendants" (Gen. 49:10), BODY (Isa. 7:20), "voyages" (Isa. 23:7), etc.; [*raglî, 'îš raglî, kap regel*–'sole of the foot,' *marg^{e}lōṯ, pa'am, taḥaṯ*–'under,' *qarsōl*–'ankle' (2 S. 22:37 par. Ps. 18:36 [MT 37])]; [Gk. *poús*]; NEB also (FOOT)STEPS (Acts 5:9; He. 12:13), GROUND (Acts 10:25), etc.; [*básis, hypopódion, pezḗ*] (Mt. 14:13 par. Mk. 6:33).

Both Heb. *regel* and Gk. *poús* mean "foot," and usually refer to the human foot (e.g., Ex. 21:24; Lev. 14:14; Lk. 7:38). As a euphemism for the pudenda the RSV renders Heb. *regel* "feet" in Ex. 4:25; Dt. 28:57, but in Jgs. 3:24 (AV "he covereth his feet"); 1 S. 24:3; 2 K. 18:27 par. Isa. 36:12 (AV mg. "the water of their feet" [*Q mêmê raglêhem*]); Ezk. 16:25 (AV "hast opened thy feet") the genital connotations are more explicit. (They may be implied in 2 S. 11:8; Cant. 5:3. See also *TDNT,* VI, 627.)

Hebrew *raglî*—translated "men on foot," "footmen," or "foot soldiers"—denotes an infantryman, armed with a spear, bow, sling, or sword. These men were apparently known for their speed and stamina, for Jeremiah's stamina is compared to theirs (Jer. 12:5).

Hebrew *marg^{e}lōṯ* ("legs" in Dnl. 10:6) means "the place of the feet." Ruth approaches the sleeping Boaz and uncovers his *marg^{e}lōṯ* (Ruth 3:4, 7). This was evidently a sign of (intention of) marriage (cf. Ezk. 16:8).

Hebrew *pa'am* is properly "foot." Like Heb. *regel* and Gk. *poús* it can stand for the whole person (Ps. 17:5; 140:4 [MT 5], RSV, NEB). The feet of the ark (Ex. 25:12; AV "corners") were probably short legs designed to keep the ark from resting directly on the ground.

Greek *básis* was commonly used for the base of a statue (MM, p. 106) and occurs only in Acts 3:7. *Hypopódion* (Jas. 2:3) is properly "footstool" (so AV, NEB; RSV "at my feet"). *Pezḗ* (Mt. 14:13 par. Mk. 6:33) means "by land," "on foot" in contrast to traveling by boat. In these two pericopes Jesus retreats by boat on the Sea of Galilee, but the crowd follows Him "on foot" along the shore.

Actions involving the feet are often rendered "trample, tread under foot" (e.g., Isa. 63:3; Dnl. 8:13; cf. Mt. 5:13; Lk. 8:5), "walk on foot" (Eccl. 10:7), "set upon [one's] feet" (Dnl. 8:18). The RSV and the AV interpret Heb. *yiḵbōš* (Mic. 7:19) as a form of *kāḇaš,* "tread down, subdue," (KoB, p. 423), keeping the parallelism with the next line "casting . . . into . . . the sea" (cf. LXX *katadýsei,* "he will make to go down"). The NEB translates "wash out" (piel of *kāḇas,* "wash out" [KoB, p. 422]). The various translations of Heb. *yard* (< *rdd* or *rdh*) (Isa. 41:2, "tramples . . . under foot"; AV "rule"; NEB "go down," from the root *yrd*) could all be correct and express dominance and conquest. The RSV understands the uncertain text of Ps. 68:30 (MT 31) to read *rāpas,* "kick" (KoB, p. 905), which is closer to the MT than the NEB's translation.

A common figure of speech, synecdoche, uses one part of the body to represent the total person. "Foot" is used this way, and accordingly the NEB often translates Heb. *regel* with a pronoun. The RSV does so less frequently (cf. RSV and NEB in Dt. 32:35; Job 31:5; Ps. 31:8 [MT 9]; Isa. 59:7). Likewise, Gk. *poús* is understood (though not translated) this way in, e.g., Lk. 1:79; Rom. 3:15; He. 12:13. The entire person is denoted by means of such expressions as "from the head to the foot" (e.g., Lev. 13:12), "from the sole of one's foot to the crown of one's head" (cf. 2 S. 14:25 and Job 2:7), "hand and foot" (Mt. 22:13).

Various expressions involving feet are found in the Bible. Roads in the Near East were dusty and dirty, so an act of hospitality was to supply visitors with water to wash their feet (Gen. 18:4; 19:2; 24:32; 43:24; Jgs. 19:21; 1 S. 25:41; Lk. 7:44). A sign of special welcome and devotion was for the host or hostess to do the washing (Jn. 12:3) or for oil to be used instead of water (Lk. 7:38; Jn. 12:3). Jesus Himself washed the feet of the disciples (Jn. 13:2-20) as an enacted parable of the meaning of His death (vv. 2-11) and of discipleship (vv. 12-20), thereby making loving service the highest Christian virtue. As a result, FOOT WASHING has been practiced in the Church since apostolic times and is mentioned as one of the duties of widows in 1 Tim. 5:10.

In the OT, washing the feet was a ritual of the priests preparatory to service at worship (Ex. 30:19, 21; 40:31). "Foot washing" may also refer to the preparation for conjugal love (2 S. 11:8; Cant. 5:3).

Placing one's feet on the neck of a person symbolized conquest and dominion (Josh. 10:24), as did placing someone under the feet of another (2 S. 22:39 par. Ps. 18:38; Ps. 8:6 [MT 7]; 47:3 [MT 4]). Ps. 110:1 speaks of God making the enemies of His people a footstool for the feet of the Davidic king. This Psalm took on messianic meaning during and after the Exile and is applied to Jesus Christ in the NT (Mt. 22:44 par. Mk. 12:36 par. Lk. 20:43; Acts 2:35; 1 Cor. 15:25; He. 1:13; 10:13).

After His resurrection Christ was understood by His disciples to have ascended to the right hand of God, from where He rules the universe until His enemies are subservient to Him at the end of the age (Acts 2:32-36; 1 Cor. 15:25; He. 10:12f.).

To sit at the feet of someone is to learn as a student from a master (Lk. 8:35; 10:39; Acts 22:3). To shake the dust from one's feet is a sign of repudiation and separation (Mt. 10:14; Lk. 9:5; 10:11; Acts 13:51). To bow before or hold the feet of someone is an act of supplication (Mk. 5:22 par. Lk. 8:41; Mk. 7:25; Jn. 11:32), thanksgiving (Lk. 17:16), submission (Rev. 3:9), and worship (Mt. 28:9; Acts 10:25; Rev. 19:10; 22:8).

In ethical contexts, feet may "run to evil" (Prov. 1:16), even "swiftly" (Prov. 6:18; cf. Rom. 3:15), in contrast to those who turn to God (Ps. 119:59). The feet of those bringing good tidings are beautiful (e.g., Nah. 1:15; cf. Rom. 10:15), and the feet of some are "shod" with the equipment of the gospel of peace (Eph. 6:15; *see* EQUIPMENT).

The "feet" of God are a symbol of the salvation of His people (Zec. 14:4). Clouds (Nah. 1:3) and darkness (2 S. 22:10 par. Ps. 18:9 [MT 10]) indicate His presence,

Fragment of a stele from Babylon (1st Dynasty, *ca.* 1800-1500 B.C.) showing victor with enemy underfoot (Louvre)

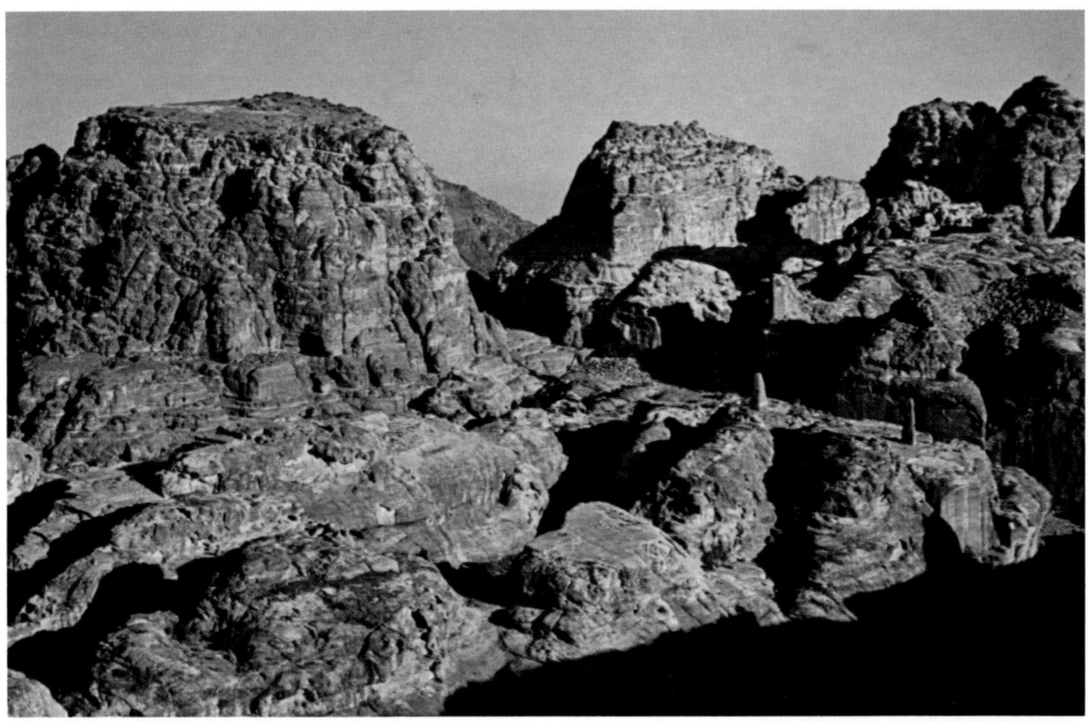

Plate 1. View west toward the three main heights at Petra: Sela, Robinson's High Place, and ed-Deir. Note the rugged terrain (L. T. Geraty)

Plate 2. West of Wâdī Mûsā are the sandstone mountains of Petra (L. T. Geraty)

Plate 3. Waterall at the oasis of En-gedi on the west bank of the Dead Sea (W. C. Williams)

Plate 4. Palms mark the site of water in the Middle East deserts (G. Nalbandian)

Plate 5. Akanthos ("thorn") plants (*Notobasis syriaca* L.) bloom in Jerusalem in the spring. These may be the thorns that Isaiah said would cover the ruined strongholds of Edom (Isa. 34:13) or that formed Jesus' crown (Mt. 27:29) (G. Nalbandian)

Plate 6. These desert plants in the Wâdī Qelt E of Jerusalem bloom only during the latter rains, in March (G. Nalbandian)

Plate 7. The Israelites of the Exodus may have stopped at the oasis Wâdī Feiran (the traditional Rephidim) near Jebel Mûsā if they had taken a southern route through the Sinai. At Rephidim Moses provided water for the complaining people by striking a rock with his rod (Ex. 17:1-7) (L. T. Geraty)

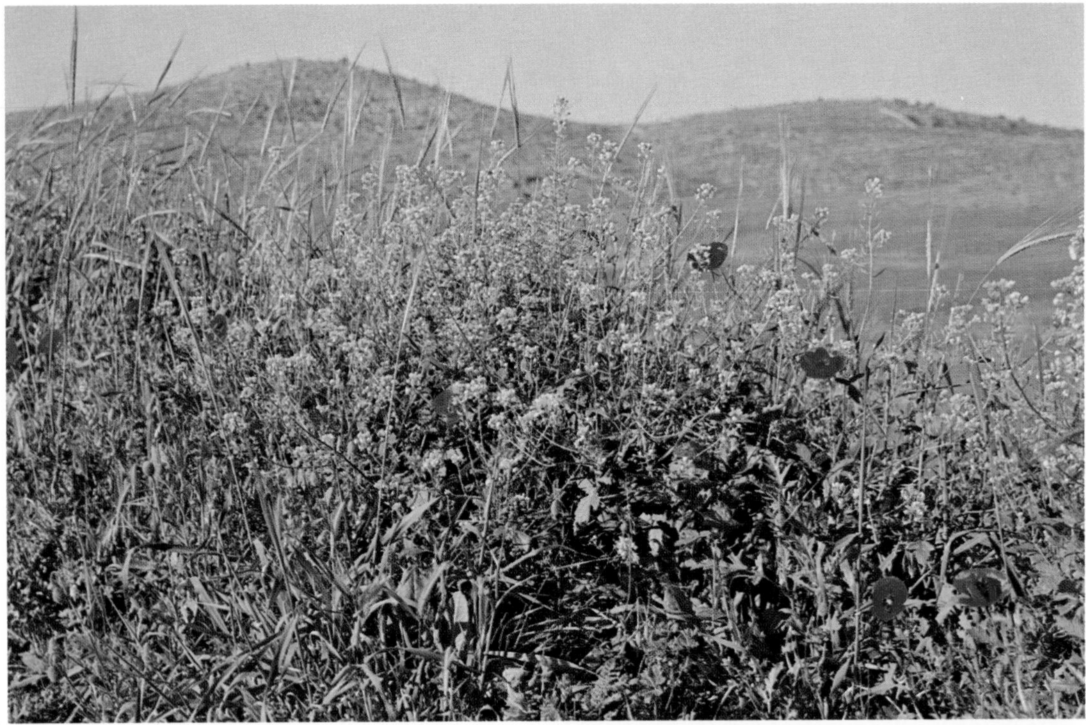

Plate 8. Barley, mustard, and poppies grow wild in the Vale of Elah. Tell ez-Zakarîyah is in the background (J. C. Trever)

Plate 9. Anemone blossoms near Jerusalem (J. C. Trever)

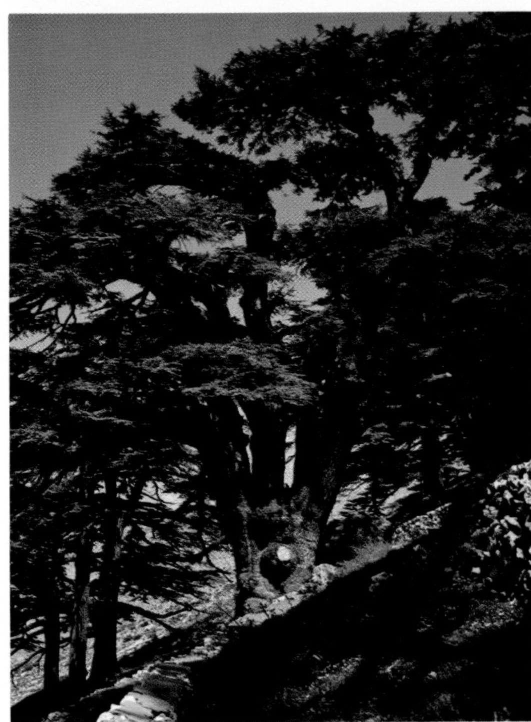

Plate 11. Cedars on a hillside above Tripoli in Lebanon (J. C. Trever)

Plate 10. Amos called himself "a dresser of sycamore trees" (7:14), trees perhaps similar to this sycamore-fig (*Ficus sycamorus* L.) near Ashkelon (J. C. Trever)

Plate 12. Plantain-leaved viper's bugloss (*Echium plantagineum* [?] L.) in a rocky field W of Tiberias (J. C. Trever)

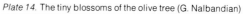

Plate 13. Fig branch with early fruit. The sweet, green figs are picked in early June and the mature, purplish figs from late August until early winter (G. Nalbandian)

Plate 14. The tiny blossoms of the olive tree (G. Nalbandian)

Plate 15. The plain of Gennesaret as seen from the traditional Mt. of Beatitudes near Capernaum (L. T. Geraty)

Plate 16. View southeast from Megiddo across the plain of Esdraelon. Mt. Moreh is on the left and Mt. Gilboa on the right (W. S. LaSor)

Plate 17. Pomegranate trees beside the Sea of Galilee. Mt. Hermon is in the background (W. S. LaSor)

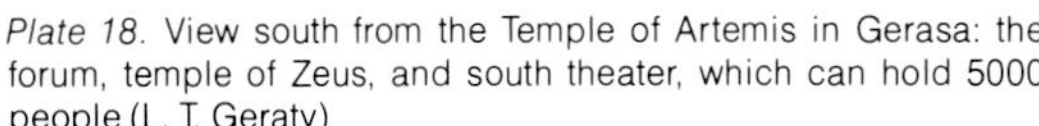

Plate 18. View south from the Temple of Artemis in Gerasa: the forum, temple of Zeus, and south theater, which can hold 5000 people (L. T. Geraty)

Plate 19. The Jordan River flows through the plain of Gennesaret into the northern end of the Sea of Galilee (L. T. Geraty)

Plate 20. Mt. Gilboa (known today as Jebel Fuqû'ah) is between Megiddo and Beth-shean and SE of Jezreel (D. Baly)

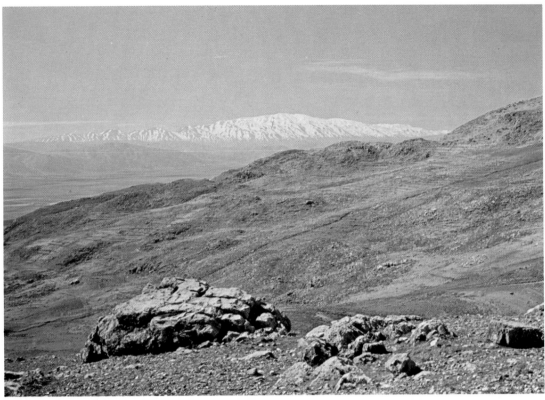

Plate 21. Snow-capped Mt. Hermon as seen from Lebanon (W. S. LaSor)

Plate 22. Reconstruction of a fortified gate and wall at Hazor (Institute of Archaeology, Hebrew University of Jerusalem)

King Darius (521-486 B.C.) sits on a throne with his feet on a footstool; behind him is Crown Prince Xerxes. Limestone relief from Persepolis (Oriental Institute, University of Chicago)

and His victory brings glory to the place of His feet, the temple (Isa. 60:13).

See GESTURE.

See *TDNT,* VI, *s.v.* πούς (Weiss).

H. W. LAY
R. W. V.

FOOT WASHING. In the Orient the wearing of open sandals on dusty roads made it necessary to wash the feet frequently; therefore a host would customarily provide water for his guests upon their arrival, so that they might wash their feet (cf. Gen. 18:4; 19:2; 24:32; 43:24; Jgs. 19:21). Sometimes a servant performed this service for the guests (1 S. 25:41). It was considered the most menial task a servant could perform (cf. Mk. 1:7 par.). Not washing one's own feet, on the other hand, was a sign of deep mourning (2 S. 19:24).

Luke records an incident in which Jesus rebukes Simon the Pharisee for not having shown the common courtesy of providing Him with water, while at the same time He commends the woman who has washed His feet with her tears, wiped them with her hair, and anointed them with ointment (7:36-50). Such an act of love prompts Jesus to declare that this woman, known as a "sinner," is forgiven.

John indicates that Jesus Himself performed this service for the disciples at the Last Supper (Jn. 13:1-17). None of the Synoptic accounts of the Supper includes the foot-washing incident; Luke, however, tells of a dispute that arose among the disciples at this time about which of them was the greatest. It may be that they were quarreling about which of them should perform this service for the others (22:26f.). As recorded in John's Gospel, this act of Jesus has a twofold significance. First, it is a symbolic prophecy of Jesus' atoning death, which would cleanse from sin and make it possible for His disciples to inherit eternal life with Him (13:8; cf. Lk. 22:28-30). Second, it is a lesson in humility. "It is a parable in action, setting out that great principle of lowly service which finds its supreme embodiment in the cross, setting out also the necessity for the disciple to take the Lord's way, not his own" (Morris, pp. 612f.). Some have also seen the foot washing as alluding to the sacraments of baptism and the Lord's Supper. Cullmann, e.g., believes that the intent of the Evangelist is to show the relationship between the two sacraments, baptism being that sacrament which is performed once for all and the Lord's Supper being that which is to be repeated (p. 109).

The NT contains one other reference to foot washing (1 Tim. 5:10), where Paul lists among the qualifications for enrollment as a widow that a woman must have "washed the feet of the saints." Hospitality was expected of all Christians, but particularly of widows, who were charged with accommodating travelers — of whom there were many, since the gospel was carried from village to village on foot. The reference to foot washing is probably both figurative and literal. Following the example of the Lord, the widow was to give evidence of her humility by performing even the most menial tasks.

In the early Church, foot washing came to be practiced as a rite. In its earliest form it was observed at the baptism service and involved the ceremonial washing of the feet of the newly baptized catechumens (cf. Augustine *Ep.* 119.18). This practice never gained universal acceptance, and no traces of it are left. The rite did come to be widely practiced, however, during the Maundy Thursday service in both the Western Church and the Eastern Church. At the Synod of Toledo in 694, Spain became the first European country to attest the practice; Rome first attested it in the 11th cent. (*Ordo Romanus* x). Called the *pedilavium,* this rite continues to be part of the Maundy Thursday observance in many churches. Among the Protestant churches and sects that have practiced foot washing are the Moravian Brethren, the Mennonites, and the Seventh-Day Adventists.

Bibliography.–Comms. on John by R. E. Brown, II (*AB,* 1970); R. Bultmann (Eng. tr. 1971); and L. Morris (*NICNT,* 1971); O. Cullmann, *Early Christian Worship* (1953), pp. 105-110; *ERE,* V, *s.v.* "Feet-washing" (G. A. F. Knight).

N. J. O.

FOOTMAN. *See* WAR.

FOOTSTOOL [Heb. *keḇeš* (2 Ch. 9:18), *hᵃḏôm regel* (1 Ch. 28:2; Ps. 99:5; 110:1; 132:7; Isa. 66:1; Lam. 2:1); Gk. *hypopódion tṓn podṓn* (Mt. 5:35; Acts 7:49)]. Of the nine RSV references, only one is literal in nature (2 Ch. 9:18), describing the golden footstool of Solomon's throne. In 1 Ch. 28:2 the allusion is to the ark, while in Ps. 99:5; 132:7; Lam. 2:1 the term is a metaphor for the Jerusalem temple. In Isa. 66:1 (quoted in Acts 7:49) it is used figuratively of the earth, in contrast to the heavens as God's throne. The concept of Davidic dominion as expressed in Ps. 110:1 is quoted by Christ in Mt. 22:44 par. 12:36; Lk. 20:43.

FOOTWEAR. *See* GARMENTS VII; SANDAL; SHOE.

FOR ALL; FOR THAT; FOR TO. Obsolete phrases used by the AV. In Jn. 21:11, e.g., "for all" occurs in the phrase "for all there were so many" (Gk. *tosoútōn óntōn*); the RSV correctly translates "although." "For that" renders Gk. *ei* (He. 7:15), *epeí* (He. 5:2), *epeidḗ* (2 Cor. 5:4), *epí* (Rom. 5:12), *hóti* (Jn. 12:18; 2 Cor. 1:24; 1 Tim. 1:12), etc. and generally means "since" or "because." "For to" is used for Heb. *lᵉmaʿan* (Jer. 43:3) and for Gk. *eis tó* (Rom. 11:11), *hína* (e.g., Mk. 3:10), *prós tó* (Mt. 23:5), etc. and means "in order that."

FOR EVER. *See* ETERNAL.

FORBEAR [Heb. *ḥāḏal*] (e.g., 1 K. 22:6; Job 16:6); NEB REFRAIN, BE SILENT; [Gk. *aníēmi*] (Eph. 6:9); NEB "give up"; **FORBEARING** [Gk. *anéchomai*] (Eph. 4:2; Col. 3:13); [*makrothyméō*] (2 Pet. 3:9); AV LONGSUFFERING; NEB VERY PATIENT; [*anexíkakos*] (2 Tim. 2:24); AV PATIENT; NEB KINDLY; **FORBEARANCE** [Heb. *'ereḵ 'ap*] (Jer. 15:15); AV LONGSUFFERING; NEB "be patient"; [Gk. *anochḗ*] (Rom. 2:4; 3:25); NEB TOLERANCE; [*epieikḗs*] (Phil. 4:5); AV MODERATION; NEB MAGNANIMITY; [*makrothymía*] (2 Cor. 6:6; 2 Pet. 3:15); AV LONGSUFFERING; NEB PATIENCE.

The usual meaning of Heb. *ḥāḏal* is "cease, come to an end, leave off," but in all the RSV uses it has the meaning of "desist from" (1 K. 22:6, 15; 2 Ch. 18:5, 14; Job 16:6). (*See also* REFUSE.) The AV translates Heb. *ḥāḏal* as "forbear" more frequently than the RSV, and unlike the RSV, the AV translates other Hebrew words in the same way. Heb. *'ereḵ 'ap,* "long of (concerning) anger," the RSV usually renders "slow to anger"; but in Jer. 15:15, where this translation would have been awkward, the RSV uses "forbearance."

In the NT *anéchomai* occurs fourteen times but is translated "forbearing" only twice. Although the usual meaning of the verb is "bear with, endure" (AV also "suffer"), in these two passages "forbearing one another" has a more positive meaning of Christian love in action. (*See* ENDURE; LOVE III.) The noun *anochḗ,* whose basic meaning is "a holding back" is used by Paul to speak of the restraint of God's wrath (see *TDNT,* I, 359f.).

The basic meaning of *aníēmi* is to "release from tension" (*TDNT,* I, 367), to "let go, relax, loosen," and metaphorically, to "desist from" in Eph. 6:9. *Epieikḗs* means "what is fitting, right, or equitable" (*TDNT,* II, 588), and except for its use as a noun in Phil. 4:5 it is translated "gentle" in all passages; the NEB renders it "considerate" (Jas. 3:17; 1 Pet. 2:18), and "forbearing" (1 Tim. 3:3; similarly Tit. 3:2). The RSV renders *makrothymía* "patience" in all but two instances. Only once is the verb *makrothyméō* rendered "forbearing"; *see* PATIENCE. The hapax legomenon *anexíkakos* means "tolerant of evil [things] or calamity," and calls the servant of Christ to be longsuffering toward those who would do him evil (cf. *TDNT,* III, 486f.).

Bibliography.–*RTWB, s.v.* "Forbear, Forbearance" (N. H. Snaith); *TDNT,* I, *s.v.* ἀνέχω (Schlier), ἀνίημι (Bultmann); II, *s.v.* ἐπιεικής (Preisker); III, *s.v.* κακός κτλ.: ἀνεξίκακος (Grundmann); IV, *s.v.* μακροθυμία (J. Horst). W. A. SHELL

FORBID; FORBIDDEN [Heb. *kālā'*–'restrain'] (Nu. 11:28); NEB STOP; [*ṣāwâ*–'command'] (Dt. 4:23; 17:3; Lam. 1:10); AV also COMMAND; [*ʿāral ʿorlâ*–'having a foreskin'] (Lev. 19:23); AV UNCIRCUMCISED; [*ḥālîlâ*] (1 S. 24:6 [MT 7]; 26:11; 1 K. 21:3); [Gk. *kōlýō*–'prevent'] (Mk. 9:39; Lk. 9:50; 23:2; Acts 10:47; 16:6; 1 Cor. 14:39; 1 Tim. 4:3); NEB also STOP, OPPOSE, WITHHOLD, PREVENT; [*híleōs soi*] (Mt. 16:22); AV "Be it far from thee"; [*mḗ génoito*] (Lk. 20:16).

The most significant use of "forbid" in the OT is in the phrase "the Lord forbid." The Hebrew phrase here is *ḥālîlâ* [denoting profanation or abhorrence; cf. the verb *ḥālal,* "be profaned"] *mēyahweh,* an interjection meaning "far be it from Yahweh." Elsewhere in the RSV *ḥālîlâ* is rendered "Far be it" (e.g., Gen. 18:25; Josh. 22:29; 24:16; 2 S. 23:17), "Far from it!" (1 S. 14:45; 20:2), or "No!" (1 S. 22:15). On Lev. 19:23, *see* UNCIRCUMCISED.

Greek *mḗ génoito* (lit. "let it not be") is one of the LXX renderings of *ḥālîlâ,* and it functions in the NT in much the same way. Whereas the RSV renders it "God forbid" only once and elsewhere gives "by no means!" (Rom. 3:4, 6, 31; 6:2, 15; 7:7, 13; 9:14; 11:1, 11), "Never!" (1 Cor. 6:15), "Certainly not!" (Gal. 2:17; 3:21), or "far be it from me" (Gal. 6:14), the AV renders "God forbid" in all these cases. According to Bauer (p. 376), *eíē ho theós* should be supplied in Mt. 16:22, giving a literal translation of "may God be gracious to you." The RSV correctly interprets the sense in which it was used.

N. J. O.

FORCE. The Hebrew, Greek, and Aramaic words that are rendered by the word "force" in the RSV contain either the idea of someone compelling or coercing another to do something against his will or the idea of sheer physical strength. The word has several distinct uses.

(1) [Heb. piel of *ʿānâ* (2 S. 13:12, 14, 22, 32), *'āpaq* (1 S. 13:12), *māraṣ* (Job 6:25), *kāḇaš* (Neh. 5:5); Gk. *angareúō* (Mt. 5:41; *see* COURIER), *anankázō* (2 Cor. 12:11), *kakóō*–'mistreat' (Acts 7:19), *ischýō* (He. 9:17)]; AV also COMPEL (Mt. 5:41; 2 Cor. 12:11), "bring into bondage" (Neh. 5:5), "evil entreated" (Acts 7:19), "strength" (He. 9:17); NEB also "dishonour(ed)" (2 S. 13:12-14), FELT COMPELLED (1 S. 13:12), MAKE GO (Mt. 5:41), DROVE TO (2 Cor. 12:11), "harsh" (Job 6:25). To force or compel. *ʿĀnâ* literally means to force someone to have sexual relations as Amnon forced his sister Tamar. *Kāḇaš* literally means to subdue or to bring into bondage.

(2) [Heb. *gāzal* (Gen. 31:31); Gk. *harpázō* (e.g., Mt. 11:12; Jn. 6:15)]; NEB also PULL OUT (Acts 23:10). To take or seize by force.

(3) [Heb. *ḥayil, maḥᵃneh*–'camp' (Josh. 10:5; 1 S. 28:1; 29:1), *zᵉrô(a)ʿ*–'arm' (Dnl. 11:15, 31), *memšālâ*–'dominion' (2 Ch. 32:9)]; AV also ARMY, HOST (Josh. 10:5), ARMS (Dnl. 11:15, 31), POWER (Est. 8:11; 2 Ch. 32:9); NEB ARMED BANDS, TROOPS (1 S. 29:1; 2 Ch. 17:2), ARMY (1 S. 28:1), ARMED FORCES (Dnl. 11:31); ARMED HORDE (Dnl. 11:10), "high command" (2 Ch. 32:9), strength (Est. 8:11). "Forces" in the sense of an army or band of warriors as an implement of force. The RSV also has "forces" for *ʿam,* "people," in Josh. 8:13, because of the context (NEB "army"). (In Gen. 14:3, 15; Josh. 11:5; 1 Ch. 19:17 the RSV adds the word "force" for a similar reason.)

(4) [Heb. *yāḏ*–'hand' (Nu. 20:20; Job 20:22), *ḥozqâ*–'strength' (1 S. 2:16; Ezk. 34:4), **lē(a)ḥ*–'moisture, freshness' (Dt. 34:7), **maʾᵃmāṣ* (Job 36:19); Aram. *'eḏrā'* (Ezr. 4:23)]; AV also HAND (Nu. 20:20; Job 20:22); NEB also HAND (Job 20:22), FULL STRENGTH (Nu. 20:20), VIGOUR (Dt. 34:7), "resources" (Job 36:19), etc. These terms all refer to force in the sense of physical strength. Though Dt. 34:7 is the only occurrence of the Heb. noun *lē(a)ḥ,* adjectival forms are found elsewhere describing freshness in rods (Gen. 30:37), grapes (Nu. 6:3), bowstrings (Jgs. 16:7f.), and trees (Ezk. 17:24; 20:47). (Cf. on Ugar. *lḥḥ,* "life-force, vigor," W. F. Albright, *BASOR,* 94 [1944], 32-35.) Moses, then, at the end of his long life, still possessed a physical vigor unusual for old men.

(5) **FORCED LABOR; FORCED LEVY** [Heb. *mas,*

sēbel (1 K. 11:28)]; AV TRIBUTE, TRIBUTARY, LEVY (1 K. 9:15), CHARGE (1 K. 11:28), "discomfited" (Isa. 31:8); NEB also LABOUR GANGS (1 K. 11:28). A body of workers coerced into labor, or (borrowed from the French) a corvée. Conquered populations were subjected to forced labor by Israel (Jgs. 1:30). Forced labor was used by David for his building projects (2 S. 20:24) and continued to be used under Solomon. Under Solomon the size of the group was reported to be thirty thousand men (1 K. 5:27). The biblical material is unclear as to whether Solomon's forced labor included Israelites (1 K. 5:13) or only the non-Israelite population of the old Canaanite city-states (1 K. 9:15a, 20-22).

See also LABOR; LEVY; SLAVE.

Bibliography.–*TDNT,* I, *s.v.* ἁρπάζω κτλ.: ἁρπάζω (Foerster); III, *s.v.* ἰσχύω κτλ. (Grundmann), κακός κτλ.: κακόω (Grundmann).

E. W. CONRAD

FORD [Heb. *maʿᵃbār* (Gen. 32:22 [MT 23]), *maʿbārâ* (Josh. 2:7; Jgs. 3:28; 12:5f.; Isa. 16:2; Jer. 51:32)]. In 2 S. 15:28 the RSV follows *K* *ʿᵃbrôt* (but cf. *Q* *ʿᵃrābôt* and the versions followed by AV "plain"). In three other passages the RSV slightly emends the MT: in 1 S. 13:7 "[they] crossed the ford" (presupposing *wayyaʿabᵉrû maʿbᵉrôt*) for MT *wᵉʿibrîm ʿābᵉrû,* "Hebrews crossed over" (so AV); in 2 S. 17:16, reading with 15:28 (*K*) and some MSS *ʿᵃbrôt,* "fords," for MT *ʿarᵉbôt,* "plains" (so AV); in 2 S. 19:18 (MT 19), reading "they crossed" (*wᵉʿābᵉrû* or *wayyaʿabᵉrû*) for MT *wᵉʿābᵉrâ,* "(it) crossed" (cf. AV), and understanding *hā-ʿᵃbārâ* as "ford" (as in the above passages, rather than "ferry boat," AV).

A location where one might "pass through" or "pass over" (cf. verb *ʿābar*) a body of water. In the OT the river crossed most frequently in this way was the Jordan (cf. Josh. 2:7; Jgs. 3:28; 12:5f.; 15:28; 19:18). The lower Jordan was between 27 and 30 m. (90 and 100 ft.) wide, and varied from 1 to 4 m. (5 to 12 ft.) in depth. Since in antiquity there were no bridges in Palestine, it was extremely important that there be areas of the river that could be crossed either by wading or swimming. In the Pentateuch allusions are made to the fords connected with the Zered and Arnon wadis (cf. Nu. 21:12f.; Dt. 2:24). The Jabbok is mentioned frequently, especially in connection with Jacob. It is now impossible to locate these ancient crossing points with any precision, although some have associated the fords of 2 S. 15:28; 17:16 with Maḥadat el-Hajilah and Maḥadat el-Henu, located at the southern end of the Jordan just N of the Dead Sea. The fords of Babylonia (Jer. 51:32) were evidently the many bridges across the rivers and irrigation canals of that country. Aenon near Salim, where John the Baptist was baptizing (Jn. 3:23), may have been a ford in the Jordan Valley, though some ancient traditions have located it in Perea beyond the Jordan.

R. K. H.

Drivers and laden donkeys ford the Jordan near Tell ed-Dâmiyeh (courtesy of E. K. Vogel)

FORECAST. Used by the AV in the obsolete sense of "devise" or "scheme" (Dnl. 11:24f.).

FOREFATHER. In the OT "forefather" renders Heb. *ʾāb riʾšôn* (lit. "preceding father," Jer. 11:10) or simply *riʾšôn* ("predecessor, ancestor," Lev. 26:45; Ps. 79:8). The NT terms are Gk. *propátōr* ("forefather," Rom. 4:1) and *patḗr* (lit. "father," often used in the sense of "ancestor"). *See* ANCESTOR.

FOREFRONT. A word occurring in the RSV only once, with reference to the planned death of Uriah (2 S. 11:15). The literal meaning of Heb. *mûl pānîm* is "over against the face," i.e., confronting (cf. NEB "opposite"). The AV uses "fore-front" in Ex. 26:9; 28:37; Lev. 8:9; 1 S. 14:5; 2 K. 16:14; Ezk. 40:19 (RSV "front"); in Ezk. 47:1 the RSV does not translate Heb. *pᵉnê* and in 2 Ch. 20:27 the RSV translates Heb. *rōʾš* literally, "head."

FOREGO. Occurs in the RSV for Heb. *nāṭaš* (Neh. 10:31 [MT 32]), referring to the practice of not tilling or sowing the fields in the seventh year (cf. Ex. 23:10f.).

FOREHEAD [Heb. *mēṣaḥ* (e.g., Ex. 28:38), *gibbē(a)ḥ* (Lev. 13:41-43), *pēʾâ* (Nu. 24:17; Jer. 48:45), *bên ʿênêkem*–'between your eyes' (Dt. 14:1); Gk. *métōpon* (e.g., Rev. 7:3)]; AV also BROW, "corner," "between your eyes", etc.; NEB also "squadrons" (Nu. 24:17), FORELOCK, etc.

The word occurs frequently in the literal sense. Every high priest was to wear on his forehead the golden frontlet having the engraved motto, "Holy to the Lord" (Ex. 28:36, 38). The condition of the forehead was an important criterion in the priest's diagnosis of leprosy (Lev. 13:42f.; 2 Ch. 26:20). (*See* LEPER.) It was in the forehead that brave young David smote Goliath with the stone from his sling (1 S. 17:49). While the cutting or tattooing of the body was strictly forbidden to the Israelites on account of the pagan associations of the custom (Lev. 19:28), frequent mention is made of markings on the forehead, which were especially used to designate slaves or devotees of a godhead (Lucian *De Syria Dea* lix). In 3 Macc. 2:29 it is stated that Ptolemy IV Philopator branded some Jews with the sign of an ivy leaf, marking them as devotees of Bacchus-Dionysos. Very clear is the passage Ezk. 9:4, 6 (and perhaps Job 31:35), where the word used for "mark" is *tāw,* the name of the last letter of the Hebrew alphabet, which in its earliest form has the shape of an upright cross (+) as in Egyptian hieroglyphic writing and the Sinaitic script (1500 B.C.), or the tilted cross (×) of the Iron Age Phoenician (*ca.* 1000 B.C.) and the Siloam Hebrew scripts (*ca.* 701 B.C.). The NT echoes Ezk. 9:4, 6, in the marking of the foreheads of the righteous (Rev. 7:3; 9:4; 14:1; 22:4). The godless followers of the beast are marked on the (right) hand and on the forehead (13:16; 14:9; 20:4), and the symbolic woman dressed in scarlet and purple has her name written on her forehead (17:5).

In a metaphorical sense the AV uses the expression "a whore's forehead" (Jer. 3:3; RSV, NEB "harlot's brow") to describe the shameless apostasy and faithlessness of Israel. Ezekiel speaks to the stiff-necked obstinacy and the persistent unwillingness of Israel to hear the message of the Lord: "All the house of Israel are of a hard forehead and of a stubborn heart" (3:7), and God makes

His prophet's "forehead hard . . . like adamant harder than flint," whereby an unflinching loyalty to God and a complete disregard of opposition is meant (vv. 8f.).

See *TDNT,* IV, *s.v.* μέτωπον (Carl Schneider).

H. L. E. LUERING
R. K. H.

FOREIGNER [Heb. *nēḵār, ben-nēḵār, noḵrî, zār* (Prov. 20:16; 27:13; Ezk. 7:21; 11:9; 28:10; 30:12; 31:12); Gk. *xénos* (Acts 17:21), *allogenḗs* (Lk. 17:18), *bárbaros* (1 Cor. 14:21)]; AV also STRANGER, ALIEN, BARBARIAN (1 Cor. 14:11), "other" (1 Cor. 14:21); NEB also STRANGER, ALIEN (Isa. 61:5), UNKNOWN PERSON, etc.

This term denotes one who is not a member of the people of Israel (Jgs. 19:12) and "comes from a far land" (Dt. 29:22; 1 K. 8:41). The foreigner is to be distinguished from the sojourner (*gēr*), the non-Israelite whose place of residence is in the land of Israel. The enemy who invades the land of Israel is referred to as a foreigner (Ezk. 7:21; 11:9; Ob. 11).

The OT includes legislation regarding Israel's relationship to the foreigner in both civil and cultic matters. There was special legislation regarding financial dealings with foreigners (Dt. 15:3; 23:20). Foreigners were forbidden to be kings over Israel (Dt. 17:15), to enter the temple (Ezk. 44:7), or to participate in the Passover (Ex. 12:43). Even animals bought from foreigners were not to be used in sacrifice (Lev. 22:25).

In the exilic and postexilic periods when the Israelites were living in increasing numbers in foreign lands, Israel was forced to reconsider its relationship to foreigners. In some contexts the foreigner's role in the religious life of Israel was viewed favorably (1 K. 8:41-43; cf. Isa. 56:3, 6, which refers to foreigners as Jewish proselytes); in others it was viewed critically (Neh. 9:2; Ezr. 10:2).

In the NT the word "foreigner" is used for the non-Jew only in Lk. 17:18, where it refers to the Samaritan who was the only leper of the ten healed by Jesus to offer Him thanks. At other places "foreigner" is used for the person who spoke a foreign language (1 Cor. 14:11) and for the non-Athenians who were present in Athens when Paul preached there (Acts 17:21).

See also STRANGE GODS; STRANGER (OT); SOJOURNING.

E. W. CONRAD

FOREKNOW [Gk. *proginṓskō*] (Rom. 8:29; 11:2); NEB KNEW BEFORE, "acknowledged of old as his own"; **FOREKNOWLEDGE** [Gk. *prógnōsis*] (Acts 2:23); NEB "plan." These Greek terms express the concept of knowing reality before it is real and events before they occur. In the NT these terms (used also in 1 Pet. 1:2, 20; RSV "destine") always refer to God's knowledge, except in Acts 26:5; 2 Pet. 3:17 (in which the human foreknowledge is the result of information received earlier or of revelation). In theology, therefore, "foreknowledge" refers to that aspect of God's omniscience whereby God not only knows all things and persons, but knows them before they are real or before they occur.

Scripture leaves little doubt about the all-comprehensive character of God's knowledge. God's eyes go "to and fro" through all the earth (2 Ch. 16:9) and are in every place beholding the evil and the good (Prov. 15:3); Sheol is naked before God's eyes (Prov. 15:11; Job 26:6); the night and darkness are light to Him, and darkness and light to God are both alike (Ps. 139:12). All animals and fowls are His and are known by Him (50:11), and as their Creator God knows all the hosts of the heavenly bodies (Ps. 147:4; Isa. 40:26). He knows the heart of man and his thoughts (1 S. 16:7; 1 K. 8:39; Ps. 7:9 [MT 10]; 94:11; 139:2; Jer. 11:20; 17:9f.; 20:12; Ezk. 11:5). Furthermore, God knows man entirely in all his ways (Ps. 139:1-5; Prov. 5:21), including evil and sin (Gen. 3:11; 6:5, 9, 13; 2 S. 7:20; Ps. 69:5 [MT 6]).

The NT similarly teaches that God knows all. Jesus taught that God knows the hidden secrets of man's heart (Lk. 16:15), and the apostles affirm God's omniscience (Acts 1:24; 15:8; 1 Cor. 3:20; 1 Thess. 2:4; Rev. 2:23). According to the Epistle to the Hebrews, everything is open to God, so that He is omniscient (He. 4:13).

Scripture also leaves no doubt that all of God's knowledge is of the nature of foreknowledge. Nothing future is ever hidden from His eyes (Isa. 41:23; 42:9; 44:6-8; 46:10). And what is true of God's knowledge of the future is also true of His knowledge of things past. God sees and knows us and our days when we and our years are not yet. This moved the psalmist to cry: "Wonderful are thy works! Thou knowest me right well; my frame was not hidden from thee, when I was being made in secret, intricately wrought in the depths of the earth. Thy eyes beheld my unformed substance; in thy book were written, every one of them, the days that were formed for me, when as yet there was none of them" (Ps. 139:14b-16). God's all-comprehensive knowledge is prescient, knowing reality before it is real, people before they exist, and days and events before they occur. God's knowledge, therefore, is not dependent on the object of His knowledge, nor contingent on the factuality of the event. God's is prescient knowledge for it is real before what is known is real.

This divine knowledge, which precedes the reality it knows, has caused theological difficulties, particularly in the area of human free will. Theologians have struggled with the problem of God's foreknowledge and human freedom — if human beings act freely, how can God foreknow their acts before they occur? Arminian theology, in all its variant forms, contends that God's foreknowledge is simply a prescient knowledge, a knowing in advance whether a given person will believe in Christ or reject him. God's election, therefore, is said to be simply God's choice unto salvation of those whom He knows in advance will choose to believe in Christ. God foresees the contingent free action of faith and, foreseeing who will believe in Christ, elects those because they do. But this is destructive of the biblical view of election. In biblical thought election means that God elects people, not that people elect God. In Scripture it is God who in Christ decides for us — not we who, by making a decision for Christ, decide for God.

Reformation theology has contended that the divine foreknowledge contains the ingredient of divine determination. The Reformers claimed that God indeed foreknows who will believe, because believing in Christ is not a human achievement, but a divine gift imparted to men by God's grace and Spirit. Thus God's foreknowledge is not merely prescience, but a knowledge that itself determines the event. That is, in Reformation thought what God foreknows He foreordains. This tradition also maintains that God could not foreknow an event if its occurrence were contingent on the free will of man, i.e., on a will that in its freedom might do one thing or might do its very opposite.

The argument that God could not foreknow the occurrence of faith had He not determined the believing response of faith itself may seem to be an argument based on a restrictive notion of what God can do. Does it rest on a faulty idea of divine possibility? If, indeed, the insistence that God can foreknow only what He Himself has determined lacked biblical support, the argument would be less than convincing. But there are biblical considerations that call into question the idea that God's foreknowledge is simply a prevision of purely contingent human actions and events.

There are, first, scriptural passages in which foreknowledge quite explicitly carries the meaning of foreordination. In Peter's speeches in Acts, what Peter says about the predestination of the crucifixion of Christ in 4:28 is almost identical with the meaning of *prógnōsis* in 2:23. What happened to Jesus, says Peter, took place according to "the definite plan and foreknowledge of God." Foreknowledge here echoes the idea of God's counsel or plan in 4:28, reflecting that foreknowledge is an ingredient of that determination which made the death of Christ certain. God foreknows the death of Christ because the crucifixion was His planned determination.

Similarly, in what 1 Pet. 1:2 says about an election which is "according to the foreknowledge of God," foreknowledge appears to be more than a mere divine prevision of faith. Foreknowledge here carries the notion of divine purpose (cf. RSV "destined by God"). If it meant a mere prevision of faith or of some other worthy quality in those characterized by Peter as "chosen," then Peter would be teaching a view of election quite contrary to the predominant scriptural emphasis that election does not rest on some worthy quality in the elect. It is clear that Peter teaches that the chosen (Gk. *eklektoís* in 1:1) are foreknown unto obedience and the sprinkling of the blood of Christ (1:2), but not because of some self-possessed worth observed by God and used by God as a reason for their being elect.

In Rom. 11:2 Paul, speaking of the Jews, says, "God has not rejected his people whom he foreknew." Given the context of this statement, which pointedly describes the unbelief and the spiritual hardness of Israel, it is quite impossible to hold that God's foreknowing of Israel is based on His prevision of some quality in Israel that prompted the divine choice.

That God's foreknowledge contains the idea of divine determination does not rest merely on a few biblical texts but reflects a truth about God that comes to expression in a variety of biblical concepts descriptive of the unique and mysterious character of God's actions. God's foreknowledge is itself a form of determination which accounts for the reality of that which is divinely foreknown. What God knows is real because He knows it. In biblical thought God calls the things that are not as though they were (Rom. 4:17), and then they are. God creates by uttering His word (Ps. 33:6). It is not only God's knowing and/or foreknowing that determines the reality that God knows. The uttering of His creative word determines that reality that we call the created universe. Thus God's speech shares in the mysterious character of His foreknowledge, indeed in the mysterious nature of God's entire relationship to the world. God calls Israel into existence and by that call Israel exists. God elects what is not and the elective divine call creates what it elects (Isa. 51:1f.). Jesus calls a dead, unhearing Lazarus, and His call gives hearing where there is none; His call determines the reality of the hearing (Jn. 11:43f.). The dead hear His voice (Jn. 5:25, 28). God causes His face to shine and men are saved (Ps. 80:19 [MT 20]). God *looks* upon the afflicted (Gen. 29:31-35; 2 S. 16:12), God *hears* Israel's groaning, God *remembers* His covenant with Abraham (Ex. 2:24f.), God *knows* Israel's sufferings (Ex. 3:7), God *turns to* the destitute (Ps. 102:17), and has *regard for* Abel's offering (Gen. 4:4; Ps. 119:132) — and these very divine actions impart deliverance and blessing. As in God's foreknowledge, all of these divine actions are reality-imparting, blessing-bestowing divine actions, which as such predetermine. He who creates (or recreates) by that very fact determines in advance. The inclusion of divine determination in divine foreknowledge is not essentially different from that determination that is reflected in God's creative, elective calling, looking, regarding, seeing, turning to, and remembering.

In view of what has befallen Israel, Paul asks whether God has rejected Israel. He answers emphatically that God has not rejected the people He foreknew (Rom. 11:1f.). God's foreknowing of Israel guarantees Israel's continuance. Similarly, God's calling and endowment of Israel guarantees that God will not repent of His calling and gifts (Rom. 11:29).

God's foreknowledge is far from mere prevision or prior intellectual awareness; even its ingredient of determination is an expression of blessing. In biblical usage God's foreknowledge does not relate to whatsoever comes to pass, to an all-comprehensive divine will. Foreknowledge relates to matters beneficent and salvific. In this it reflects and comports with the biblical idea that to be looked upon, regarded, remembered, and heard by God are all matters of blessing. The Bible uses the words "foreknow" and "predestinate" in a salvific context and with a salvific meaning. Israel as God's chosen people whom God foreknew is a clear example of the salvific character of God's foreknowledge. Scripture does not use the term "foreknowledge" to describe God's prescient knowledge of the Philistines, or the Moabites. This indicates how little foreknowledge can be limited to simple prevision or mere intellectual awareness.

But it must also be added that Scripture does not allow the drawing of the logical inference that none but the Jews are foreknown by God unto salvation. For it was to the church at Rome that Paul wrote, "For those he foreknew he also predestined to be conformed to the image of his Son" (8:29).

In biblical thought, divine foreknowledge includes the idea of foreordination to salvation and we may not enlarge the meaning of either term to include "whatsoever comes to pass." To give it a larger coverage is to include those whom the Bible describes as those whom God does not know, as in Jesus' disclaimer, "'I never knew you'" (Mt. 7:23).

See also OMNISCIENCE; PREDESTINATION.

J. DAANE

FOREMEN [Heb. *hōgᵉśîm*] (Ex. 5:6, 10, 14f., 19); AV TASKMASTERS. The overseers of forced labor gangs that are depicted on Egyptian reliefs carrying rods to insure the prompt completion of assigned tasks by those under them. The verb root on which the participle is based, *nāgaś*, means "oppress"; cf. "taskmaster," Ex. 3:7.

FOREORDAIN (1 Pet. 1:20, AV). *See* DESTINE; *see also* CHOOSE; ELECTION; FOREKNOW; PREDESTINATION.

FOREPART. Used by the AV in the obsolete sense of "bow" in Acts 27:41. *See* SHIPS.

FORERUNNER [Gk. *pródromos*]. This word occurs only once in the Bible (He. 6:20): "where Jesus has gone as a forerunner on our behalf." The word signifies one who comes in advance to a place where the rest are to follow, or one who is sent on before as a scout to make observations (cf. "pioneer" in 12:2). In this sense Christ is our forerunner, for He has gone into heaven to prepare for His people a place into which He will eventually lead them. The idea of a forerunner is peculiar to the NT. The OT high priest was a representative, not a forerunner: where he led, namely, into the holy of holies, the people could not follow. He was not the pioneer of the people; Christ is. Christ goes nowhere but where His people may follow. *See also* JOHN THE BAPTIST; RUNNER. W. EVANS

FORESAIL (Acts 27:40). *See* SHIPS.

FORESHIP (Acts 27:30, AV). Used by the AV in the obsolete sense of "bow." *See* SHIPS.

FORESKIN [Heb. *ʿorlâ*] (Gen. 17:11, 14, 23-25; Ex. 4:25; Lev. 12:3; etc.); NEB also "circumcise" (Jer. 4:4). The word is frequently mentioned in the literal sense. The rite of circumcision, practiced in Israel since the days of Abraham (Gen. 17:9-14), is also commonly attested among several other peoples of antiquity (and modern times). Among the Jews circumcision had to be performed by means of a flint or stone knife (Ex. 4:25; Josh. 5:2f.) on the eighth day after birth (Gen. 17:12; 21:4; Lev. 12:3; cf. Lk. 2:21; Phil. 3:5), even if this day were the sabbath (Jn. 7:23).

Very early the practice was one of which the descendants of Abraham became proud (Gen. 34:14); the Philistines, who did not practice the rite (1 S. 17:26; 18:25, 27), were scorned as "the UNCIRCUMCISED" (e.g., Jgs. 14:3; 15:18; 1 S. 14:6; 31:4; etc.). In the time of oppression under King Antiochus Epiphanes many Israelites suffered martyrdom rather than give up the distinctive sign of their people (1 Macc. 1:48, 60f.; 2 Macc. 6:10). Among the Arabs and all Moslems the custom of circumcision prevails from pre-Islamic times, for it is nowhere ordered in the Koran, and the appellation "uncircumcised" (Arab. *ghalaf*) is considered the greatest possible insult.

Metaphorically the word "foreskin" is used in the sense of "obstinacy," "opposition to God's law." The rite of circumcision meant submission under the law. While an outward form could not be identical with an inward attitude toward God, the use of the word "circumcision" was soon extended to that of purity and obedience of the heart (Dt. 10:16; Jer. 4:4; cf. Col. 2:11). The uselessness of outward circumcision that does not include obedience and purity is shown by Paul (Rom. 2:25; 1 Cor. 7:18; cf. Acts 7:51). *See* CIRCUMCISION. H. L. E. LUERING

FOREST; WOODS [Heb. *yaʿar, yaʿarâ, pardēs, ḥōreš, śāḏeh*; Gk. *drymós* (LXX), *hýlē* (Jas. 3:5)].

The Heb. *yaʿar* (cf. Ugar. *yʿr*) can mean a stony wasteland or a definite wooded tract (e.g., 1 S. 22:5; 1 K. 7:2f.). The root appears in "Kiriath-jearim" and "Mt. Jearim." See also Dt. 19:5; Ps. 96:12; Cant. 2:3; Mic. 7:14.

A moderately extensive growth of vegetation is indicated by Heb. *ḥōreš* (Ezk. 31:3; 2 Ch. 27:4). But in 1 S. 23:15-19 the RSV and NEB read *ḥōreš* as a proper name (*see* HORESH). In Isa. 17:9, the RSV and NEB follow the LXX by introducing "Hivites and Amorites" for the MT "the woodland (*ḥōreš*) and the elevated height." The Heb. *pardēs* (cf. Akk. *pardīsu*) can refer to a park (cf. Neh. 2:8, RV mg.; Eccl. 2:5, RV, RSV, NEB) or orchard (Neh. 2:8, AV; Cant. 4:12), but since it supplied timber it was no doubt meant to indicate a forest in Neh. 2:8 (NEB "forests").

Sometimes forests are intended by Heb. *sᵉḇāḵ, sᵉḇōḵ*, from a root meaning "be interwoven," and thus a "thicket," or "thicket of trees" (Gen. 22:13; Isa. 9:18; 10:34; Jer. 4:7; Ps. 74:5), but these two terms are infrequent in the MT. *See also* THICKET.

Palestinian forests and woodlands were much more extensive in antiquity than at present, several of them being mentioned by name in the OT. These included the celebrated Lebanon forest near Tyre, which was unquestionably the largest of its kind in Palestine, and produced pine and myrtle trees as well as the famous cedars. Another extent of woodland was the Carmel forest, which flourished on the top of the mountain (Cant. 7:5) from Neolithic times. The forest of Hereth in Judah stretched down to the edge of the Philistine plain, and at one period provided shelter for David after his departure from Moab (1 S. 22:5). An extensive forest of date palms is believed to have flourished in antiquity in the Jordan Valley N of the Dead Sea, and traces of it were still evident at Jericho in the time of Josephus (A.D. 37-95).

Forest of Gilead (D. Baly)

The expression "thickets in Arabia" (Isa. 21:13) does not appear to refer to a large woodlot so much as to shrubs and palm trees growing in the region of oases. Another phrase, "the House of the Forest of Lebanon" (1 K. 7:2f.), can also be misinterpreted, the actual reference being to a portion of the royal palace in Jerusalem in the Solomonic period. The name was derived from the Lebanese cedar used in the construction of the pillars and paneling.

Differences in soil and climate produced a wide variety of trees and shrubs in Palestine, although the woods and forests would consist principally of oaks, terebinths, cedars, Aleppo pines, and in the Dead Sea region would include tamarisk trees, willows, and poplars. Deciduous oak forests flourished in OT times in lower Galilee, Ephraim, Sharon, and Bashan. Woods and forests provided a home for animals of various kinds (2 K. 2:24; Ps. 50:10), and in the preexilic period the area known to the Arabs as the Zor, close to where the Jordan emptied into the Dead Sea, was luxuriant with trees and tropical vegetation. Asiatic lions were to be found there also, and it was deemed an outstanding feat of virility for a man to enter the area and kill a wild animal unaided (cf. 1 S. 17:35).

The indiscriminate felling of trees was prohibited in Dt. 20:19. Instead, they were to be conserved whenever possible, and like human beings were not to be regarded as disposable. The cutting down of trees causes the erosion of the soil and an alteration in the amount and frequency of rainfall. Taken together, these two conditions quickly bring about sizable areas of desert. The large expanses of woodland and forest that occurred in Palestine and Syria have disappeared for the most part, except in places that have been difficult of access, and belated attempts at reforestation have formed part of the national conservation programs of Israel and Jordan from the 1970's.

See also FLORA. R. K. H.

FOREST OF EPHRAIM. *See* EPHRAIM, FOREST OF.

FORETOLD [Heb. *dāḇar*] (2 K. 24:13); AV SAID; [Gk. *protangéllō*] (Acts 3:18); AV BEFORE SHEWED; [*semaínō* (Acts 11:28); AV SIGNIFIED; NEB PREDICT. In the OT the foretelling of future events is the prerogative of Yahweh (Isa. 41:22f.; 42:9; cf. Dt. 18:22; Acts 3:18). Though prophecy was believed to have ceased in Israel soon after the return from Exile, it reappeared with John the Baptist. In NT times a prophet named Agabus predicted a famine, which occurred in the reign of Claudius (Acts 11:28). *See* PROPHECY.

FORFEIT [Heb. niphal of *qāḏaš*–'be consecrated' (Dt. 22:9), *ḥāram*–'devote to the ban' (Ezr. 10:8), *ḥāṭā'*–'miss' (Prov. 20:2; Hab. 2:10), *taḥaṯ*–'instead of' (2 K. 10:24); Gk. *apóllymi*–'destroy' (Lk. 9:25), pass. of *zēmióō*–'inflict injury or punishment' (Bauer, rev., p. 338; Lk. 9:25 par.)]; AV also "be defiled," "sinneth against," "(his life shall be) for" (2 K. 10:24), LOSE (Mt. 16:26 par.); NEB also CONFISCATE, "is his own worst enemy" (Prov. 20:2), AT THE COST OF (Mt. 16:26 par.).

In the OT "forfeit" (from Lat. *forisfacere,* "act beyond") implies loss through transgression or nonobservance of some law or rule. One could forfeit, e.g., his crops when improperly sown (Dt. 23:9; *see* SOW). The most important instance of this term is Christ's referral to forfeiting one's life (Lk. 9:25 par.). Here Our Lord contrasts "the whole world" with human life (Gk. *psyché,* "soul"; cf. Heb. *nepeš,* "soul," in Prov. 20:2; 2 K. 10:24; Hab. 2:10) and "gain" with "forfeit." (In Luke Gk. *zēmióō* and *apóllymi* mean the same thing — "destroy.") Christ reminds His followers that earthly gains, such as the world's approval, are less important than the value of one's life, which here means one's fellowship with God and future eternal life. Those who deny Christ in this life Christ will deny ("be ashamed of") at the end of time (Lk. 9:26).

Bibliography.–W. L. Lane, comm. on Mark (*NICNT,* 1974); N. Geldenhuys, comm. on Luke (*NICNT,* 1951); *TDNT,* I, *s.v.* ἀπόλλυμι κτλ.: ἀπόλλημυ (Oepke); II, *s.v.* ζημία, ζημιόω (Stumpff).

R. W. V.

FORGE [Heb. *pā'al*] (Isa. 44:12); AV WORK; NEB SHAPE; FORGER [part. of *lāṭaš*] (Gen. 4:22); AV INSTRUCTOR; NEB MASTER. In Gen. 4:22 *lōṭēš,* "hammerer," describes Tubal-cain, "the forger of all instruments of bronze." The antiquity of this tradition has been demonstrated by Russian excavations at the foot of Mt. Ararat that uncovered an estimated two hundred amazingly sophisticated smelting furnaces. These were designed to produce different kinds of bronze, including alloys of copper with zinc and iron, as well as a variety of ceramics, glasses, and metallic paints. The location accords with the OT traditions relating to the contemporaries of Enoch and Methuselah. The activities of the forger are also referred to in Isa. 44:12.

R. K. H.

FORGET [often Heb. *šāḵaḥ*]; NEB also HEEDLESS (Ps. 44:24 [MT 25], IGNORE (Ps. 74:23), HOLD IN MIND (Ps. 78:7), etc.; [Heb. *šākē(a)ḥ*]; NEB also HEEDLESS (Ps. 9:17 [MT 18]); [*nāšâ* (Gen. 41:51; Job 39:17; Isa. 44:21)]; Gk. *epilanthánomai, eklanthánomai* (He. 12:5), *epilēsmonḗ*–'forgetfulness' (Jas. 1:25), *lḗthē*–'forgetfulness' (2 Pet. 1:9)]; AV also FORGETFUL (Jas. 1:25).

"Forgetting" as "loss of memory" has several closely related nuances. In Isa. 23:15f. Tyre is told that it will be forgotten as a harlot is forgotten (complete obliviousness of memory). In Gen. 40:23 the chief butler forgot (completely lost track of) Joseph, and the Egyptians in Gen. 41:30 are told that they will find their memory of the seven years of plenty obliviated by the misery of the seven-year famine. Jeremiah declared at the time of his beating at the hands of Pashhur that the "eternal dishonor" of his persecutors will never be obliviated (20:11). In Dt. 25:19 Israel is urged not to forget (NEB "not fail to") the treachery of Amalek (i.e., not to lose the freshness of memory). Similarly, in Job 11:16 to forget misery is to remember it as waters "that have passed away," and in Amos 8:7 Yahweh himself swears, "Surely I will never forget any of their deeds" (loss of fresh awareness).

This sense of "lose consciousness of" is prominent in the use of Heb. *šāḵaḥ* in connection with forgetting God and His mighty deeds (e.g., Ps. 78:7, 11; 106:13, 21; Hos. 2:13; 13:6), His name (Jer. 23:27), or the covenant with Him. Yet there can be a more concrete conception of how one forgets God, as the Deuteronomist makes clear: "Take heed lest you forget the Lord your God, by not keeping his commandments and his ordinances and his statutes" (Dt. 8:11; cf. also 26:13).

"Forget" approaches the meaning "unlearn" in such passages as Hos. 4:6, where the Lord accuses his people of having forgotten the law (parallel to "rejected knowledge"), Gen. 41:51, "God has made me forget all my hardship," and Lam. 3:17, "I have forgotten what happiness is."

But "forget" also has another range of meaning which does not really concern loss or obliviousness of memory; it may connote "overlook, neglect, care little for." The same Greek verb *epilanthánomai* is used in Jas. 1:24 to refer to the loss of memory of the features of one's own face, and in Mk. 8:14 (par. Mt. 16:5) to indicate the negligence of the disciples in forgetting to bring enough bread. (Cf. He. 6:10, "overlook," and NEB "forget.") Similarly, in Ps. 102:4 (MT 5) the distressed psalmist in his anxiety has even neglected eating ("I forget to eat my bread"; NEB "I cannot find the strength to eat"). The sense is "overlook" in Dt. 24:19: "When you reap your harvest in your field, and have forgotten a sheaf in the field, you shall not go back to get it; it shall be for the sojourner, the fatherless, and the widow." The ostrich in Job 39:15 overlooks an important fact in laying her eggs on the ground, "forgetting that a foot may crush them." (Cf. *šāḵaḥ* parallel to "forsake" in Isa. 49:14 and "hide [one's] face" in Ps. 44:24 [MT 25], etc; and *šākē(a)ḥ* parallel to "forsake" in Isa. 65:11.) God does not overlook the slightest detail according to Lk. 12:6, for not even a sparrow is "forgotten [NEB "overlooked"] before God."

In Dt. 32:18 the NEB uses this sense of overlooking when it renders "forgot the God who gave you birth" with "cared nothing for" (cf. Jer. 3:21 where NEB has "ignored . . . God" for "forgotten . . . God"). This sense is also present in the plaintive cry that echoes throughout the Psalms of Lament: "How long, O Lord? Wilt thou forget me forever?" (Ps. 13:1 [MT 2]), or "Arise, O Lord . . . forget not the afflicted" (Ps. 10:12), "Has God forgotten to be gracious?" (Ps. 77:9 [MT 10]). (Note also the ironic parallel in Am. 8:7 in language borrowed directly from the plaintive Psalms of Lament: "I will never forget any of their deeds.")

Psalm 137 is a community lament that reflects the agony of those people who painfully made the adjustment to the grim reality of exile and destruction and had to realize the implications of defeat for the power of Yahweh and of superior authority for Babylonian deities. They sat and wept when they remembered Zion. Could Yahweh still be worshiped in a strange land where other gods appeared to be in control? Ps. 137 captures the poignant despair that permeated the exilic community, but it also reflects in vv. 5f. the absolute determination to keep fresh and vibrant the memory of Jerusalem and what had been done to its proud temple and walls. These verses constitute a passionate self-imprecation aimed at safeguarding any forgetfulness or loss of fresh consciousness. The psalmist here looks both with hope for recovery of what was, and for the requital of Babylon for the wanton destruction that it wreaked on Jerusalem and its environs. In the context of the Exile, to remember what had happened was essential to Israel's continuity and survival as a people.

In Isa. 44:21f. Yahweh assures His despondent people that they "will not be forgotten," for He cast away their sins and redeemed them. Though seemingly God had forsaken His people, God's love for the despairing city of Zion is more secure than the love of a mother for her child — God "will not forget" (49:14f.).

A unique use of "forget" appears in Job 39:17. There it is said that God caused the ostrich to forget (hiphil of *nāšâ*; AV "deprived"; NEB "denied") wisdom, meaning that God had not endowed the ostrich with much wisdom when He created it. In Mic. 6:10 the RSV translation assumes the emendation *ha'eššeh,* "can I forget?" (NEB "overlook") for the obscure MT *ha'iš* (AV "is there?"). In Ezk. 39:26 the RSV and NEB follow the *qere* *wenāšû,* "they shall forget," rather than the *kethib* *wenāše' û* (AV "they have borne").

See also FORSAKE; REMEMBER. D. G. BURKE

FORGETFULNESS, LAND OF [Heb. *'ereṣ nešîyâ*] (Ps. 88:12 [MT 13]); NEB LAND OF OBLIVION. This expression is a poetic designation for SHEOL. In Ps. 88:11f. (MT 12f.) this is the fourth such circumlocution for Sheol in a parallel series: "the grave" (*haqqeḇer*) par. "Abaddon" (*'aḇaddôn*) and "the darkness" (*haḥōšeḵ*) par. "land of forgetfulness" (*'ereṣ nešîyâ*). (*See also* ABADDON.) Ps. 88:5, 10-12 (MT 6, 11-13), and the expression "land of forgetfulness" itself, suggest that the dead are beyond the care of God; but His presence even there with the dead is affirmed elsewhere (cf. Job. 26:6; Ps. 139:8; Prov. 15:11).

FORGIVENESS [Heb. *kāpar*–'cover,' *nāśā'*–'take away,' 'forgive' (Gen. 18:24, 26; Isa. 2:9), *sālaḥ*–'forgive,' *selîḥâ*–'forgiveness,' *sallāḥ*–'pardon,' 'forgiveness,' *kāsâ*–'cover,' 'conceal,' *māḥâ*–'wipe out']; AV also COVER (Ps. 85:2 [MT 3]; cf. 32:1); NEB also PUT AWAY; [Gk. *aphíēmi* (Mt. 6:12ff.; Mk. 2:7, 10; Jn. 20:23; 1 Jn. 1:9; etc.), *apolýō* (Lk. 6:37), *charízomai* (2 Cor. 2:7, 10; 12:13; Col. 3:13), *áphēsis* (Mk. 3:39; Acts 5:31; 13:38; 26:18)]; AV also REMIT (Jn. 20:23).

I. Terms
II. Forgiveness in the Ancient Near East
III. The Teaching of Christ
IV. Conditions of Forgiveness
V. The Offended Party
VI. Divine and Human Forgiveness
VII. Forgiveness and Justification
VIII. OT Teaching
IX. Limitations of Forgiveness
X. Christ's Power to Forgive Sins
XI. Need of an Atonement
XII. NT Doctrine of Atonement

I. Terms.–The Hebrew verb *kāpar* is the word commonly used for atonement, in which sins were "covered" by offering a sacrifice as a substitute for the life of the sinner. In this sense *kāpar* obviously refers only to God's forgiveness of the transgressor (Dt. 21:8; Ps. 78:38; Jer. 18:23). *Nāśā'* is forgiveness in terms of guilt being taken away, atoned for, or borne, resulting in divine pardon (Ex. 28:43; 32:32; Lev. 5:1, 7; Nu. 14:19, 34; 18:1; Josh. 24:19; Ps. 85:3; etc.), and also of human forgiveness (Gen. 50:17; Ex. 10:17; 1 S. 25:28). The cognates of *sālaḥ* always refer to an act or function of forgiveness on the part of God to mankind (cf. Nu. 30:5, 8, 12; 1 K. 8:30, 34, 36, 39, 50; 2 K. 24:4; Am. 7:2; Ps. 86:5; 130:4; Dnl. 9:9; Neh. 12:7, 20). *Māḥâ,* "wipe away," expresses the concept of forgiveness in Ps. 51:1, 7; Isa. 43:25; 44:22. *Kāsâ* has the general sense of covering or concealing, and from the idea of covering a person came that of covering sins (Neh. 4:5; Ps. 32:1; 85:2).

In the LXX Greek words expressing forgiveness are *euïlateúō,* "show mercy," used to translate both *nāśā'* and *sālaḥ,* while *epikalýptō, kalýptō,* and *krýptō,* "cover, conceal," serve as the equivalents of *kāsâ*. *Sālaḥ* is also occasionally rendered by *híleōs,* while the infrequent *māḥâ* is translated exactly by *exaleíphō,* "wipe away." The noun for "atonement" (*hilasmós*) appropriately renders the rare word *selîḥâ* in Ps. 130:4; Dnl. 9:9, and increases the dimension and spiritual depth of the concept of forgiveness by making specific the ideas of propitiation and atonement found elsewhere (Ex. 29:36; 30:10; Lev. 16:20; Ezk. 43:20; etc.).

In the NT the Greek terms used for forgiveness are the verbs *apolýō, aphíēmi, charízomai, kalýptō* (RSV "cover," 1 Pet. 4:8; Jas. 5:20), and *epikalýptō* (Rom. 4:7), and the nouns *áphesis* and *páresis*. *Apolýō* (Lk. 6:37) is used because of the analogy of sin to debt, and denotes the release from it. It has the meaning "forgiveness" in 2 Macc. 12:45 also, in which passage the word for sin is expressed. In Rom. 3:25 Paul uses *páresis* instead of the usual *áphesis*. The former means "passing over," the latter "putting away" completely and unreservedly. "Passing over" simply means that God had not executed the full measure of the retribution due to sin, that He exercised forbearance and longsuffering (cf. Acts 14:16; 17:30). This passing over of sins tended to destroy mankind's conception of God's righteousness, and in order to avert this Christ was set forth as a propitiation.

Charízomai is not found outside of the writings of Luke and Paul, and in the sense "forgive sins" is peculiarly Pauline (2 Cor. 2:7; 12:13; Eph. 4:32; Col. 2:13; 3:13). It expresses, as no other of these words does, Paul's conception of the graciousness of God's pardon. Remission (Mt. 26:28; Mk. 1:4; Lk. 1:77; 24:47; Acts 2:38; 10:43; He. 9:22; 10:18) and blotting out (Ps. 51:1, 9 [MT 3, 11]; Isa. 43:25; Jer. 18:23; Acts 3:19) are synonyms of forgiveness, and to understand the concept fully such words as "save," "justify," "reconcile," and "atonement" should also be considered. Forgiveness is thus an activity that is characteristic of a merciful and loving God who does not take pleasure in the death of the sinner, and who is ready to pardon him once proper confession and atonement have been made. Forgiveness is preceded by the covering of the sin so that it is obscured from God's sight. Consequent upon this, God undertakes to remember it no more (cf. Isa. 43:25; Jer. 31:34), so that there can be no further claim against the sinner for recompense by a God whose holiness has been violated by iniquity. Nor can any state of resentment continue against the transgressor for past misdeeds, since all demands have been met through the act of atonement. Forgiveness is always a matter of divine privilege rather than human right, for the price of sin must first be paid before the conditions can exist for forgiveness to become a reality. Thus, when under the New Covenant the vicarious atonement of Christ on Calvary is appropriated personally by penitence and faith, the blood of Christ cleanses from all sin, and results in pardon, peace, and the restoration of spiritual fellowship with God.

Forgiveness is necessary in the first instance because mankind is separated from God by the sins committed as a result of our fallen nature. This transgression may be deliberate or accidental, but in any event it is a consistent mark of human beings (Isa. 64:6). Those who would be God's followers have imposed upon them the demands of obedience (Dt. 13:4; Jer. 26:13; etc.) and holiness (Lev. 11:44), among other spiritual responsibilities, and the ethical nature of God is such that He cannot look with equanimity upon violations of His law (Ex. 20:5; Lev. 20:7). The sacrificial provisions of the Sinai covenant enabled the penitent sinner in Israel to obtain cleansing and forgiveness through divine mercy. By this means the spiritual integrity of the individual as a member of a holy nation was restored, the penal death of the ungodly was averted, and the complete removal of sin (Isa. 30:17) was accompanied by the assurance of a renewal of fellowship between God and the repentant sinner. The latter could thus take his place once again as a member of a nation of God's priests, pursue the ideal of a holy life, and experience the blessing of God in whatever he undertook. This rich spiritual relationship, like forgiveness itself, was a free gift of divine grace, and was available to all who in penitence and faith submitted to the overlordship of the one true God. *See* ATONEMENT; SACRIFICE.

II. Forgiveness in the Ancient Near East.–In the unremitting struggle for survival that characterized the lives of most persons in the ancient world, individual interest was a predominant concern. This expressed itself most satisfactorily in power and wealth, which went far toward allaying the widespread feelings of personal insecurity. Because of this, any threat to personal well-being was considered to be a most serious affair, so crimes committed against individuals or groups were dealt with according to current concepts of justice. Where codes of law existed, it was possible for the offender to be brought to trial, and if convicted, to be punished according to the penalty prescribed. Where such codes were ignored or did not exist, summary justice when opportune rather than a magnanimous act of forgiveness seems to have been the usual procedure righting wrongs.

Among the Hebrews a person's forgiveness of his fellow is only mentioned infrequently, and in each instance the one requesting pardon is in a position of subservience, and is petitioning for that to which he has no just or natural right (Gen. 50:17; Ex. 10:17; 1 S. 15:25; 25:28). Otherwise forgiveness is spoken of in relation to sin against God, where divine pardon is sought (Nu. 14:19; 1 K. 8:34; Am. 7:2; etc.). If the forgiveness of individuals was not considered especially virtuous, that of the nation's enemies was even less so. War in the ancient Near East was fundamentally a conflict between deities, fought by the peoples who owed allegiance to the gods in question. Victory was always the objective of such a struggle, and for one pagan deity to pardon another was unthinkable. Among the Israelites the imprecatory psalms attest that the pardoning of enemies was not esteemed as a virtue. This is not to say that the Hebrews were being vindictive or sadistic when they prayed that the young children of the enemy might be dashed against the rocks (Ps. 137:9). They were supplicating for the extinction of God's enemies, represented by a generation that might well live to rise against Him in the future, a contingency that would not occur were they to be exterminated forthwith. The Torah discouraged the Hebrews from seeking either the peace or prosperity of their enemies (Dt. 23:6), lest these conditions should lead the Hebrews to imagine that following a pagan way of life would make them equally prosperous also. The law thus made it legitimate for a follower of the covenant ethic to hate rather than to forgive his enemy.

III. The Teaching of Christ.–Jesus summed up this attitude broadly by contrasting the love of one's friends with the hatred of one's enemies (Mt. 5:43). In expounding the ethic of the New Covenant, Christ taught that forgiveness is a duty. No limit can be set to the extent of forgiveness (Lk. 17:4), and it must be granted without reserve. Jesus will not admit that there is any wrong so gross nor so often repeated that it is beyond forgiveness. To Him, having an unforgiving spirit is one of the most heinous of sins. Jesus sought to displace the pagan spirit of implacability by a generous, forgiving spirit. It is so far the essence of His teaching that in popular language "a Christian spirit" is not inappropriately understood to be synonymous with a forgiving disposition. His answer to Peter that one should forgive not merely seven times in a day but seventy times seven (Mt. 18:21f.) not only shows that He thought of no limit to one's forgiveness, but shows also that the principle could not be reduced to a definite formula.

IV. Conditions of Forgiveness.–Jesus recognized that there are conditions to be fulfilled before forgiveness can be granted. Forgiveness is part of a mutual relationship; the other part is the repentance of the offender. God does not forgive without repentance, nor is it required of mankind. The effect of forgiveness is to restore to its former state the relationship that was broken by sin. Such a restoration requires the cooperation of both parties. There must be both a granting and an acceptance of the forgiveness. Sincere, deep-felt sorrow for the wrong, which works repentance (2 Cor. 7:10), is the condition of mind that insures the acceptance of the forgiveness. Hence Jesus commands forgiveness when the offender turns again, saying, "I repent" (Lk. 17:3f.). It was this state of mind that led the father joyfully to welcome the Prodigal before he even gave utterance to his newly formed purpose (15:21).

V. The Offended Party.–It is not to be supposed, however, that failure to repent on the part of the offender releases the offended from all obligation to extend forgiveness. Without the repentance of the one who has wronged him he can have a forgiving state of mind. This Jesus requires, as is implied by, "if you do not forgive your brother from your heart" (Mt. 18:35). It is also implied by the past tense in the Lord's Prayer: "as we also have forgiven our debtors" (6:12). It is this forgiving spirit that conditions God's forgiveness of our sins (Mk. 11:25; Mt. 6:14f.). In such a case the unforgiving spirit is essentially unrepentance (Mt. 18:23-35).

The offended is to go even farther and is to seek to bring the wrongdoer to repentance. This is the purpose of the rebuking commanded in Lk. 17:3. More explicitly Jesus says, "If your brother sins against you, go and tell him his fault, between you and him alone" (Mt. 18:15-17). He is to carry his pursuit to the point of making every reasonable effort to win the wrongdoer, and only when he has exhausted every effort may he abandon it. The object is the gaining of his brother. Only when this is obviously unattainable is all effort to cease.

The power of binding and loosing, which means forbidding and allowing, was granted to Peter (Mt. 16:19) and to the Christian community (18:18; Jn. 20:23). It clearly implies the possession of the power to forgive sins. In the case of Peter's power it was exercised when he used the keys of the kingdom of heaven (Mt. 16:19). This consisted in the proclamation of the gospel and especially of the conditions upon which men might enter into relationship with God (Acts 2:38; 10:34ff.). It was not limited to Peter only, but was shared by the other apostles (Mt. 16:19; 18:18).

VI. Divine and Human Forgiveness.–That there is a close analogy between human and divine forgiveness is clearly implied (Mt. 5:23f.; 6:12; Mk. 11:25; Lk. 6:37; Col. 1:14;

3:13). God's forgiveness is conditional upon a person's forgiveness of the wrongs done him, not because God forgives grudgingly, but because forgiveness alone indicates that disposition of mind which will humbly accept the divine pardon. Repentance is a necessary ingredient of the fully developed forgiveness. There is no essential difference between the human and the divine pardon, though the latter is necessarily more complete. It results in the complete removal of all estrangement and alienation between God and mankind. It restores completely the relationship that existed prior to the sin. The total removal of the sin as a result of the divine forgiveness is variously expressed in the Scriptures: "for thou hast cast all my sins behind thy back" (Isa. 38:17); "Thou wilt cast all our sins into the depths of the sea" (Mic. 7:19); "I will forgive their iniquity, and I will remember their sin no more" (Jer. 31:34); "I, I am He who blots out your transgressions for my own sake, and I will not remember your sins" (Isa. 43:25); "as far as the east is from the west, so far does he remove our transgressions from us" (Ps. 103:12).

Ideally the same result is attained in human forgiveness, but actually the memory of the sin remains with both parties as a barrier between them, and even when there is a complete restoration of amity the former state of alienation cannot entirely be removed from memory. When God forgives, however, He restores a person to the condition of former favor. Release from punishment is involved, though divine forgiveness is more than this. In most cases the consequences, which in some instances are spoken of as punishment, are not removed, but they lose all penal character and become disciplinary. Nor does the forgiveness remove from the human mind the consciousness of sin and the guilt which that involved, but it does remove the mistrust that was the ground of the alienation. Mistrust is changed into trust, and this produces peace (Ps. 32:5-7; Rom. 5:1), and consciousness of the divine love and mercy (Ps. 103:2ff.); it removes fear of punishment (2 S. 12:13), and awakens love to God.

VII. Forgiveness and Justification.–Paul rarely uses the term "forgiveness," but in its place prefers "justification." They are to his understanding practically synonymous (G. B. Stevens, *Theology of the NT* [1902], p. 418). He preferred the latter, however, because it was better fitted to express the idea of secure, present, and permanent acceptance in the sight of God. It connoted both a complete and a permanent state of grace. In popular thought forgiveness is not so comprehensive, but in the biblical sense it means no less than this. It removes all of the guilt and cause of alienation from the past, it assures a state of grace for the present, and it promises divine mercy and aid for the future. Its fulness cannot adequately be conveyed by any one term or formula.

Divine, like human, forgiveness is always contingent upon the fulfillment of conditions. It must be preceded by repentance and a firmly fixed intention not to repeat the offense. In addition to this, one was required to conform to certain legal or formal acts before the assurance of pardon was his. These acts, expressive of the sinner's state of mind, consisted of certain kinds of sacrifice in the pre-Christian times and of baptism during the ministry of John the Baptist (Mk. 1:4; Lk. 3:3) and under Christ (Acts 2:38; 22:16). These acts are never regarded as in any sense a *quid pro quo* in return for which the benefit of forgiveness is granted. Forgiveness is an act of pure grace on God's part, and the human acts are required as expressions of the person's attitude toward God. The state of mind required in order to obtain the gift of forgiveness is that to which the Prodigal Son came (Lk. 15:17-19), and that of the sinner who went to his house justified rather than the Pharisee (18:9-14), because he realized that forgiveness was to him an act of pure favor.

VIII. OT Teaching.–There was real and actual forgiveness of sins in the OT times as well as since Christ. Certain passages have been construed to teach that the law provided only for a passing over or rolling back of sins, and that there was not then an actual forgiveness. The sacrifices prescribed by the law were not adequate atonements, so that there was constant necessity of yearly remembrance of sin (He. 10:3; cf. Lev. 16:21). The atonement of Christ is, however, of permanent adequacy, and became retroactive in the sense that it unified in Christ the divine arrangement for saving mankind in all ages (He. 11:40). No expression in the OT suggests any inadequacy of the forgiveness extended to Israel, but many passages may be quoted to show how rich and full it was deemed to be (Pss. 32, 103; Mic. 7:19; Isa. 38:17; Jer. 31:34).

IX. Limitations of Forgiveness.–Two passages seem to limit God's forgiveness. They are Christ's discussion of the unpardonable sin (Mt. 12:31f.; Mk. 3:28-30; Lk. 12:10), and the one that mentions the sin unto death (1 Jn. 5:16; cf. He. 6:4-6). In the former passage there is mentioned a sin that has no forgiveness, and in the latter, one on behalf of which the apostle cannot enjoin prayer that it be forgiven — though he does not prohibit it. In both cases the sin is excluded from the customary forgiveness that is extended to sins of all other classes.

The act of the Pharisees in attributing to Satan a good deed wrought by Jesus through the Spirit of God (Mt. 12:28) may have been what led Jesus to speak of the unpardonable sin. No one could do such a thing unless his moral nature was completely warped and the fundamental distinctions between good and evil were obliterated. He is beyond the hope of forgiveness, not because God has set an arbitrary line of sinfulness beyond which His grace of forgiveness will not reach, but because the person has put himself beyond the possibility of attaining that state of mind which is the essential condition of divine forgiveness. *See* BLASPHEMY.

There is no possible way of determining what specific sin, if any, John refers to. Probably the same principle applies in this case as in that of the unpardonable sin. God's forgiveness is limited solely by the condition that a person must accept it in the proper spirit.

X. Christ's Power to Forgive Sins.–Some passages seem to imply that forgiveness was the principal messianic task. This is suggested by the name given to the Messiah during His earthly career (Mt. 1:21) and by the fact that He was the Savior. The remission of sins was the preparation for the advent of the Messiah (Lk. 1:77), and repentance and remission of sins were the prerequisites to a state of preparation for the kingdom.

It is not surprising, therefore, that we find Jesus laying claim to the power to forgive sins. This provoked a bitter controversy with the Jews, for it was axiomatic with them that no one could forgive sins but God only (Mk. 2:7; Lk. 5:21; 7:49). This Jesus did not question, but He would have them infer from His power to forgive sins that He was the possessor of divine power. Jesus asserted His possession of this power on two occasions only, though it has been insufficiently inferred from Jn. 5:14; 8:11 that He was accustomed to pronounce absolution upon all of those He healed. On one of these occasions He not merely asserted that He possessed the power, but demonstrated it by showing Himself to be the possessor of the divine gift of healing. The impostor might claim some such intangible power as the authority to forgive sins, but he would never assert the possession of such easily disproved power as the ability to heal the sick. Jesus claimed both and based

His claim to be the possessor of the former on the demonstration that He possessed the latter. God would not support an impostor, so His aid in healing the paralytic proved that Jesus could forgive sins. The multitude accepted this logic and "glorified God, who had given such authority to men" (Mt. 9:2-9; cf. Mk. 2:3-12; Lk. 5:18-26).

On the other occasion when His possession of this power was under discussion (Lk. 7:36-50), He offered no other proof than the forgiven woman's deep gratitude and love. One expression that He uses, however, has raised some discussion about the relative order in time of her love and forgiveness (v. 47). Did she love because she was forgiven, or vice versa? Manifestly the forgiveness precedes the love, even though the first part of v. 47 seems to assert the opposite. This is supported by the parable of the two debtors (vv. 41-43) and the latter part of v. 47. It is clear that she had previously repented and had been accepted, and her anointing of Jesus was an outpouring of her gratitude. The phrase of v. 47, "for she *loved much,*" is proof of the greatness of her sin rather than a reason why she was forgiven. In both cases where Jesus forgave sins, He did so because the state of mind of the person forgiven was consonant with the blessing. To this as a condition of forgiveness there is no exception. Christ's prayer on the cross (Lk. 23:34) would not avail to secure the pardon of His murderers without their repentance.

XI. Need of an Atonement.–Though forgiveness is on God's part an act of pure grace prompted by His love and mercy, and though He forgives freely all those who comply with the condition of repentance and abandonment of sin, atonement is still necessary. The parable of the Prodigal Son was spoken to teach the freedom of God's forgiveness and acceptance of returning sinners, and the duty of men to assume the same attitude toward them. This much it teaches, but it fails to set forth entirely God's attitude toward sin. With reference to the sinner God is love and mercy, but with reference to sin He is righteous, and this element of God's nature is no less essential to Him than His love, and must be considered in any effort to set forth completely the doctrine of God's forgiveness of sinners. The atonement of Christ and the many atonements of the law were manifestations of this aspect of God's nature.

XII. NT Doctrine of Atonement.–The idea of an atonement is fundamental in the teachings of the NT (Rom. 5:10; 2 Cor. 5:18-21; Col. 1:21). It is very clearly implied in such terms as reconciliation and propitiation and is no less present in pardon, remission, and forgiveness. The doctrine of the atonement is not developed by Jesus, but it is strongly hinted at and is unmistakably implied in the language of Mt. 20:28; 26:28; Mk. 10:45; Lk. 24:46f. John the Baptist's salute, "Behold, the Lamb of God, who takes away the sin of the world!" (Jn. 1:29), also implies it. In the writings of the apostles it is repeatedly and clearly affirmed that our forgiveness and reconciliation to God are based upon the death of Christ. "And there is salvation in no one else" (Acts 4:12); through Him is the redemption (Rom. 3:24); God set Him forth to be a propitiation (v. 25); through Him "we have now received our reconciliation" (5:11); "God was in Christ reconciling the world to himself" (2 Cor. 5:19); "For our sake he made him to be sin who knew no sin" (v. 21); and "Christ redeemed us from the curse of the law, having become a curse for us" (Gal. 3:13). Such citations might be greatly multiplied. That which was so perfectly accomplished by the offering of Christ was in an analogous though imperfect way accomplished by the sacrifices required by the law. It was "a shadow of the good things to come" (He. 10:1).

The unvarying effect of sin is to produce an estrangement between the injurer and the wronged. The nature of God is such and the relationship between Him and mankind is of such a character that sin brings about an alienation between them. It is this presupposition of an estrangement between them that renders the atonement necessary before forgiveness can be extended to mankind. This estrangement must be removed and the alienation be transformed into a reconciliation. In what, then, does the alienation consist?

The sin of mankind produces a changed attitude toward each other on the part of both God and mankind. God holds no personal pique against a person because of his sin. The NT language is very carefully chosen to avoid any statement that would seem to convey such a conception. Yet God's holy righteousness is such that He cannot be indifferent to sin. His wrath must rest upon the disobedient (Jn. 3:36; Rom. 1:18). It is not merely impersonal. It is not enough to say He hates the sin. Man's unrighteousness has not merely alienated him from God, but also God from him. The word "enemies" (Gk. *echthroí*) of Rom. 5:10 is passive, and means the object of God's enmity (W. Sanday and A. C. Headlam, comm. on Romans [*ICC*, 14th ed. 1913], *ad loc.*). It was because of this fact that God set forth Christ to be a propitiation, to show His righteousness because of the passing over of sins done aforetime (3:25f.). God's passing over the sins of pre-Christian times, without inflicting punishment, was liable to obscure His righteousness and expose Him to the charge of tolerating sin. God could not be true to Himself while He tolerated such an imputation, and so instead of visiting punishment upon all who sinned — which would have been one way of showing His righteousness — He set forth Christ to death ("in his blood"), and in this way placed Himself beyond the imputation of unrighteousness while enabling Him to show mercy to sinners. The effect of sin upon man was to estrange him from God, to lead him farther and farther away from his Maker. Each successive sin produced a greater barrier between the two. Now the atonement was designed to remove the cause of this estrangement and restore the former relationship between God and mankind. This too, it has been observed, is the purpose of forgiveness, so that the atonement finds its completion in forgiveness. It should be noted that the reconciliation originates with God and not with mankind (Rom. 3:25; 2 Cor. 5:19). God woos a person before the person seeks God. The effect of the atonement is the removal of God's alienation from mankind. The recognition of the love and grace of God manifest in this reconciliation, and the experience of forgiveness flowing from it, evoke the response of love and win the hearts of people. "We love, because he first loved us." At the same time the atonement is such a complete expression of both the love and the righteousness of God that, while on the one hand it exhibits His yearning for mankind, on the other it shows that He is not tolerant toward sin. In the atonement of Christ, therefore, is the meeting place and the reconcilement of God's holy horror of sin and the free bestowal of forgiveness upon penitent believers.

See also JUSTIFICATION.

Bibliography.–H. R. Mackintosh, *Christian Experience of Forgiveness* (1927); E. B. Redlich, *Forgiveness of Sins* (1937); *ILC*, III-IV, 299-375; F. H. Wales, *Forgiveness of Sins* (1940); V. Taylor, *Forgiveness and Reconciliation* (1941); E. Brunner, *Divine-Human Encounter* (1943); R. Bultmann, *Theology of the NT,* I (1951), 22-26, 33-40, 72-74, 114-121, 135-144, 270-285; P. Tillich, *Systematic Theology,* I (1951), 286-89; A. Richardson, *Intro. to the Theology of the NT* (1958), 348-350; W. Telfer, *Forgiveness of Sins* (1959); J. G. S. S. Thompson, *The Praying Christ* (1959); J. Lowe, *Lord's Prayer* (1962), pp. 37-42; W. Lüthi, *Lord's Prayer* (1962), pp. 46-52; P. Tillich, *Systematic Theology,* III (1963), 217-

245; *TDNT*, I, *s.v.* αφίημι κτλ. (Bultmann); E. Lohmeyer, *The Lord's Prayer* (1965), pp. 160-190; E. M. B. Green, *Meaning of Salvation* (1965); W. Eichrodt, *Theology of the OT*, II (Eng. tr. 1967), 380-395; J. Jeremias, *Prayers of Jesus* (1967); H. Thyen, *Studien zur Sündenvergebung im NT* (*FRLANT*, 96, 1970); "ΒΑΠΤΙΣΜΑ ΜΕΤΑΝΟΙΑΣ ΕΙΣ ΑΦΕΣΙΝ ΑΜΑΡΤΙΩΝ," in J. M. Robinson, ed., *Future of Our Religious Past* (1971), 131-168; R. P. Martin, "Reconciliation and Forgiveness in Colossians," in R. J. Banks, ed., *Reconciliation and Hope* (1974), 104-124; *DNTT*, I, 697-703.

W. C. MORRO
R. K. H.

FORK. Renders several biblical terms with a variety of meanings.

(1) [Heb. *mazlēg*]; AV FLESHHOOK. A three-pronged sacrificial implement used by a priest to extract his portion of sacrifice (1 S. 2:13f.).

(2) [Heb. *mizlāgâ*]; AV FLESHHOOK; NEB also TOSSING-BOWL. An altar implement in the tabernacle (Ex. 27:3; 38:3; Nu. 4:14) and in the temple an implement of gold (1 Ch. 28:17) or bronze (2 Ch. 4:16).

(3) [Heb. *mizreh*]; AV FAN. A pitchfork with six prongs used in winnowing provender (Isa. 30:24), used figuratively of winnowing, i.e., chastising, the people (Jer. 15:7).

(4) [Gk. *ptýon*]; AV FAN; NEB SHOVEL. An implement used to separate chaff from grain, also used figuratively of God winnowing His people (Mt. 3:12; Lk. 3:17).

See also WINNOWING. J. R. PRICE

FORM [Heb. *tᵉmûnâ* (Nu. 12:28; Dt. 4:12, 15f., 23, 25; Job 4:16; Ps. 17:15), *miqlaʿaṯ, qeṣeḇ, yāṣar* (e.g., Gen. 2:19; Ps. 94:9; 104:26; 139:16; Isa. 27:11; 29:16; 43:1, 7, 10, 21; 45:7, 18; Jer. 33:2; Am. 4:13; 7:1; Zec. 12:1), *dᵉmûṯ, taḇnîṯ* (Ezk. 8:3; 10:8), *ḥāšaḇ, ṣîr* (Ps. 49:14 [MT 15]), *sāḵaḵ* (Ps. 139:13), *tōʾar, qiẓrâ* (Lam. 4:7), *marʾeh* (Ezk. 1:26; 10:1), *ṣûrâ* (Ezk. 43:11), *ʿāraḵ, sîm* (Job 1:17), *qāraṣ* (Job 33:6), *ḥîl* (Ps. 90:2), *kûn* (Ezk. 16:17), *ʿāśâ* (Dt. 31:21); Gk. *eídos* (Lk. 3:22; Jn. 5:37; 1 Thess. 5:22), *eikṓn* (He. 10:1), *schḗma, morphḗ, mórphōsis* (2 Tim. 3:5), *morphóō, plássō, synístēmi*]; AV also IMAGE, SIMILITUDE, LIKENESS, APPEARANCE, etc.; NEB also FIGURE, SHAPE, FACE, etc.

Various terms are used in the Hebrew Bible to express the concept of "form" both as a noun and a verb. In Gen. 1:2 the noun *tōhû*, elsewhere used for a "deserted" city (Isa. 24:10; RSV "city of chaos") or an "empty" plea (in court, Isa. 29:21), means "that which is waste and void and empty" (*CD*, p. 104), and thus the earth is said to be "without form." By His act of creating, God ordered this formless chaos. *Tᵉmûnâ,* sometimes used of an artistic image or representation (Dt. 4:25), is also used for the "shape" or "likeness" of Yahweh (Nu. 12:8), while *dᵉmûṯ* is used for the human "shape" or "likeness" (Ezk. 1:5; 8:2). In 1 K. 6:18 *miqlaʿaṯ* denotes the form of a carved figure or wood carving, while "size" or "shape" is denoted by *qeṣeḇ* in 1 K. 6:25 and 7:37. When "form" in the sense of "appearance" is meant, either human (Ezk. 1:26) or otherwise (10:1), the word *marʾeh* is used. In the Servant Songs of Isaiah, God's servant is said to have a "marred" appearance, a "form" (*tōʾar*) that was "beyond that of the sons of men" (52:14), and "no form [*tōʾar*] or comeliness that we should look at him" (53:2), meaning that his appearance was not one of dignity (cf. 1 S. 16:18, where the RSV translates *tōʾar* as "good presence").

The action of "forming" in the sense of "creating" is usually expressed by the Heb. verb *yāṣar* with God as the subject. It was the Lord God who "formed" man (Gen. 2:7f.) and every beast. He is the Creator who "brought to birth" (*ḥîl*) the created world (Ps. 90:2), who "formed" the earth (Isa. 45:18), the mountains (Am. 4:13), and the seas (Ps. 95:5). He is the Creator of all things (Jer. 10:16; 51:19). He is the eternal God and the only God; for "before me no god was formed, nor shall there be any after me" (Isa. 43:10). The Lord God "formed" for Himself a people named Israel to be His servant (Isa. 43:21; 44:21). He has been intimately connected with them, "forming" them from the womb (Isa. 44:2, 24), as He has also created the inward parts (Ps. 139:13) and "formed" from the womb (Jer. 1:5) individuals to be His servants (Isa. 49:5).

Other verbs expressing the same concept include *ḥāšaḇ* with its sense of devising a purpose against someone, as when Nebuchadnezzar "forms a purpose" against the inhabitants of Hazor (Jer. 49:30) or when God forms plans against the inhabitants of Teman (v. 20) and the land of the Chaldeans (50:45). The term *ʿāraḵ,* meaning to "draw up in battle order" in the sense of forming the battle line, describes the scene where the Israelites fight the Benjaminites (Jgs. 20:22).

In the NT "form" renders a number of Greek words, all of which are similar in meaning. Two of these are *morphḗ* and *schḗma*. In their strictest senses, *morphḗ* is connected with the essence of a thing while *schḗma* has to do with its qualities (Trench, p. 261f.). Both words are derived from the visual realm and are concerned with appearance. *Morphḗ* may represent "all those sensible qualities, which striking the eye lead to the conviction that we see such and such a thing," i.e., the inward reality (Lightfoot, *Philippians,* p. 127). *Schḗma,* however, "always denotes the outward form or structure perceptible to the senses and never the inward principle of order accessible only to "thought" (*TDNT,* VII, 954). "The *morphḗ* of a definite thing as such, for instance of a lion or a tree, is one only, while its *schḗma* may change every minute" (Lightfoot, *Philippians,* p. 127).

In the LXX, however, *morphḗ* denotes the "appearance, look or likeness of some one, that by which those beholding him would judge him" (cf. Job 4:16; Dnl. 5:6; Wisd. 18:1; 4 Macc. 15:4). In later Greek the term apparently lost the accurate, metaphysical content that belonged to it in writers like Plato and Aristotle, receiving instead a "vague, general meaning" (*Expos.G.T.,* III, 435; cf. *TDNT,* IV, 745). Thus "the meaning must not be overpressed in the NT occurrences" (MM, p. 417), nor should firm boundaries be established between the terms (*TDNT,* IV, 742).

Both terms are found in the "Christ-hymn" of Phil. 2. Christ was in "the form [*morphḗ*] of God" (v. 6); He took "the form [*morphḗ*] of a servant (v. 7), and was "found in human form" (*schḗma,* v. 8). These verses show that Christ is divine, since *morphḗ* "always signifies a form which truly and fully expresses the being which underlies it" (*Expos.G.T.,* III, 436), and that His "shape" or "form" is not "in contrast to His essence, but precisely as the expression thereof" (R. Bultmann, *Theology of the NT,* I [Eng. tr. 1951, 1970], 193). Thus, according to Bultmann, "the 'form of God' in which the pre-existent Christ existed is not mere form but the divine mode of being just as much as the 'form of a servant' is the mode of being a servant (Phil. 2:6f.) The same is true of *schḗma*. He who 'was found in human form' (Phil. 2:8) did not merely look like a man but really was a man 'obedient unto death'" (p. 193; cf. *TDNT,* VII, 955). Likewise, Christ's "servant form" designates "not only the outward form and shape in contrast to his nature but his nature itself [and] also shows that the 'form of a servant' is not a role that he plays, but the very nature he assumes" (Bornkamm, p. 115).

The only other use of *schḗma* is in 1 Cor. 7:31, where Paul warns not to become too attached to the world, "for the form of this world is passing away." Paul means here that the world itself, not just its form, is in the process of passing away (Bultmann, p. 193). The derivative *mórphōsis* (from *morphḗ*) is used in 2 Tim. 3:5 for those "holding the form of religion but denying the power of it." This verbal noun has the sense of "appear to be" and is used of those who hold to the external appearance of Christian life but who have no inner power. They have the mere mask of pious conduct "without the corresponding reality which derives from inner piety" (*TDNT,* IV, 755). "Religion is not entirely denied, but amounts to no more than an empty shell" (Guthrie, p. 158).

The verb *morphóō* finds its only NT use in Gal. 4:19, where Paul writes that he is "in travail until Christ be formed in you." The passage pictures the process of becoming a Christian in terms of a birth. Christ must take shape or develop (figuratively) in a life as a child develops in its mother's womb. The idea of creation is present in 1 Tim. 2:13, which states (following the existing Jewish-Hellenistic tradition) that "Adam was formed [Gk. *plássō* for Heb. *yāṣar*] first, then Eve"; and also in 2 Pet. 3:5, where the earth is said to have been "formed [*synístēmi*] . . . out of water and by means of water."

Greek *eikṓn* has a very important theological history in the Arian controversy and in the discussion about the "image" and "likeness" of God in Gen. 1:26 (see Trench, pp. 9-53; Lightfoot, *Colossians,* pp. 144ff.). It is used in the LXX mostly for Heb. *ṣelem,* meaning an image, model, or drawing. In Greek it is linked with *tíkō* ("be similar," "appear") and in its strict sense is used of artistic representations such as paintings, statues, or impressions on coins. In He. 10:1 it is used in contrast to *skiá* ("shadow"): "law has but a shadow of the good things to come instead of the true form [*eikṓn*] of these realities," for the law's continual sacrifices can never make perfect those who draw near. "In the NT the original is always present in the image" (*TDNT,* II, 395). Hence the image (*eikṓn*) is superior to the shadows (*skiá*; and also to the "copies" or "patterns" of 9:23f.), and in the same way Christ's high-priestly work is superior to the Levitical ceremonial law, which was only a "shadow of the good things to come."

Greek *eídos,* which has a rich history in Greek philosophy (Lightfoot, *Philippians,* p. 128), is the LXX rendering of Heb. *mar'eh* and *tō'ar,* meaning "that which strikes the eye or is exposed to view." This is the sense of Lk. 3:22 where the Holy Spirit is said to have descended upon Jesus "in bodily form, as a dove." *Eídos* can also refer to God, as in Jn. 5:37 where Jesus tells the Jews that they have never heard the Father's voice nor seen "his form." This context of seeing and hearing is reminiscent of Nu. 12:8, though it may instead refer to "the popular tradition about seeing and hearing God at Mt. Sinai" (Brown, p. 225; cf. Ex. 19:11; Dt. 4:12, 15). The use of *eídos* in the papyri supports the meaning "of every kind" or "manner" for the rendering "abstain from every form of evil" (1 Thess. 5:22; MM, p. 182).

Bibliography.*–*CD, III/1; G. Bornkamm, *Early Christian Experience* (Eng. tr. 1970); R. E. Brown, *Gospel According to John I-XII* (*AB,* 1966); F. F. Bruce, *Hebrews* (*NICNT,* 1964); D. Guthrie, *Pastoral Epistles* (1957); J. B. Lightfoot, *Colossians and Philemon* (1957); *Philippians* (1957); *TDNT,* II, *s.v.* εἶδος (Kittel), εἰκών (Kittel); IV, *s.v.* μορφή (Behm); VI, *s.v.* πλάσσω κτλ.: πλάσσω (Braun); VII, *s.v.* συνίστημι κτλ. (Kasch), σχῆμα κτλ.: σχῆμα (J. Schneider); R. C. Trench, *Synonyms of the NT* (1953, 1975), pp. 261-67.

D. K. MCKIM

FORM CRITICISM. *See* CRITICISM III; PETER, FIRST EPISTLE OF: SPECIAL APPENDIX.

FORMER. This word occurs only as an adjective in the sense of preceding in the order of time. In the OT Heb. *ri'šôn* and its derivatives are commonly used (Nu. 21:26; Dt. 24:4; Isa. 48:3; etc.). In the NT Gk. *próteros* occurs in Eph. 4:22; He. 10:32; *prṓtos* in Rev. 21:4; *próteron* in 1 Pet. 1:14, etc. The preposition *pró* compounded with verbs also expresses the concept of "former" (e.g., Rom. 15:4; He. 7:18; etc.).

FORNICATION [Gk. *porneía*–'unchastity,' *porneúō* ("commit fornication," Rev. 17:2; 18:3, 9)]; NEB also BASE-BORN (Jn. 8:41); **FORNICATOR** [Gk. *pórnos*] (Rev. 21:8; 22:15). Illicit (and immoral) sexual relations are strictly forbidden by Scripture (Gal. 5:19; Eph. 5:3; Col. 3:5; *see* MARRIAGE VI) and are considered a crime (*see* CRIME). According to Our Lord fornication proceeds from the heart and defiles a person (Mt. 15:19f. par. Mk. 7:21f.). In Revelation Babylon is symbolically portrayed as the great harlot leading the nations astray with her immoral behavior (*see* HARLOT).

The Jews' reply to Jesus' defense of His Sonship and His accusation that they were children of the devil is interesting. Clearly they were claiming their legitimate Abrahamic lineage: " 'we are not born of fornication . . .' " (Jn. 8:41). According to some commentators (R. E. Brown, comm. on John, I [*AB,* 1966], 357; L. Morris, comm. on John [*NICNT,* 1971], pp. 461f.), however, their words contained an implicit questioning of the legitimacy of Christ's own birth. (*See* VIRGIN BIRTH.)

See ETHICS: NT; IMMORAL.

See J. Jensen, *Nov.Test.,* 20 (1978), 161-184.

R. W. V.

FORSAKE; FORSAKEN; FORSOOK; etc. [Heb. *nāṭaš* (Dt. 32:15; Jer. 7:29), *'āzaḇ* (1 K. 12:8); Gk. *aphíēmi* (Mt. 26:56 par. Mk. 14:50), *(eg)kataleípō* (Mt. 27:46 par. Mk. 15:34)]. Heb. *nāṭaš* usually means abandon, and connotes cessation of activity, e.g., leaving a field fallow or debts unclaimed (Neh. 10:31 [MT 32]), ceasing to be concerned about animals (1 S. 10:2), abandoning quarrels (Prov. 17:14). Heb. *'āzaḇ* emphasizes being remote, departing from, or leaving behind some entity, e.g., a man leaving his parents (Gen. 2:24), forsaking counsel (1 K. 12:8, RSV, AV; NEB "he rejected the advice"), forsaking the God who made him (Dt. 28:20), abandoning one's cities (1 S. 31:7, NEB; RSV, AV, FORSAKE). Gk. *aphíēmi* is translated "forsook" only in Mt. 26:56 par. Mk. 14:50; where the AV has "forsaken" or "forsook" (Mt. 19:27, 29; Mk. 1:18; Lk. 5:11), the RSV has "left" (cf. *TDNT,* I, *s.v.,* ἀφίημι κτλ. [Bultmann]). Gk. *(eg)kataleípō* is rendered "forsake(n)" only in Mt. 27:46 par. Mk. 15:34; 2 Cor. 4:9; He. 13:5; 2 Pet. 2:15; the other AV passages (2 Tim. 4:10, 16; He. 10:25; 11:27) the RSV translates "deserted," "neglecting," and "left."

Sometimes the AV translation of "forsake(n)" is better rendered "left widowed" (Heb. *'almān,* Jer. 51:5, NEB; RSV = AV), "leave" (Heb. *ḥāḏal,* Jgs. 9:11, RSV, NEB), "fail" (Heb. *rāpâ,* Dt. 4:31, RSV, NEB), "leave not unfinished" (Heb. *rāpâ,* Ps. 138:8, NEB; RSV = AV), "left solitary" (Heb. *šālaḥ,* Isa. 27:10, NEB; RSV = AV), "turn their backs on" (Gk. *apostasía apó,* Acts 21:21, NEB; RSV = AV), or "renounce" (Gk. *apotássomai,* Lk. 14:33, RSV; NEB "parting with").

At times Heb. *'āzaḇ* and *nāṭaš* occur in parallelism (Jer. 12:7, "forsaken . . . abandoned"). Usually Heb. *'āzaḇ* is used when human beings are forsaking God; but cf. *nāṭaš* in Dt. 32:15.

There are several uses of forsake: (1) Things may (or may not) be forsaken: figurative paths (of righteousness) or ways (Prov. 2:13; 15:10; Isa. 55:7; 2 Pet. 2:15), teaching and wisdom (1 K. 12:8, 13; 2 Ch. 10:13; Prov. 4:2, 6; 6:20), idols (Ezk. 20:8; Jonah 2:8 [MT 9]), brothers (Josh. 22:3), a city (1 Ch. 10:7; Jer. 49:25), etc.

(2) Occasionally humans are described as not forsaking God (Josh. 24:16, the peoples' answer to the confession of faith at Shechem; 2 Ch. 13:10; Ps. 119:87, the psalmist himself).

(3) The majority of instances mention that people do forsake God: Dt. 28:20, Israel forsaking God in the wilderness; Dt. 31:16, the prediction of future forsaking; Josh. 24:20, Joshua's last warning to the people not to forsake; Jgs. 2:12f.; 10:10, the forsaking during the period of the judges; 2 K. 22:7, during Josiah's reform; Isa. 1:4, 28; Jer. 1:16; Hos. 4:10, the prophetic interpretation of Israel's history of forsaking God. Finally, in the NT the disciples forsook the Lord in the garden (Mt. 26:56 par. Mk. 14:50), in direct contrast to the forsaking of their nets to follow Him (Mk. 1:18). Similarly, people forsake God's law (Jer. 9:13; 2 Ch. 24:18), His commands (2 K. 17:16), His covenant (1 K. 19:10, 14; Dt. 29:25), His worship and His Levites (Dt. 14:27).

A major theme in the (late seventh-century B.C.) Deuteronomic theology of history (cf. esp. Jgs. 2:6–3:6) is that the Israelites forsook Yahweh, who brought them out of Egypt, and that they entered instead into the Canaanite nature cult with its worship of Baal. Israel's apostasy is placed in sharp contrast to "the God of faithfulness" (Heb. *'ĕmûnâ*, Dt. 32:4). The major purpose of Deuteronomy, then, is the recall of Israel to renew the covenant with Yahweh (Anderson, Bright). Jeremiah (early 6th cent. B.C.) reiterates God's call that Israel return (Heb. *šûḇ*, Jer. 35:15; cf. Am. 5:4; Hos. 11:8f.; cf. Rowley).

(4) Sometimes God forsakes people, their land, or their place of worship (Dt. 31:17; 2 Ch. 15:2; Ps. 78:60; Isa. 2:6; 49:14; etc.). But none of these texts describes that divine forsaking as God's final action toward His people. Deuteronomic theology, e.g., with all its confession of national guilt, emphasizes Yahweh's word of promise and forgiveness that follows upon His word of judgment (Hayes; cf. Isa. 54:7f.).

(5) God is frequently depicted as not forsaking people (e.g., Dt. 31:6, 8; Josh. 1:5; 1 K. 6:13; Ezr. 9:9; Ps. 94:14). Indeed, God's assurance that He will "never fail you nor forsake you" becomes the basis for rejecting materialism (He. 13:5, quoting Dt. 31:6, 8; Josh. 1:5). Consciousness of one's sin or need may prompt petitions to God not to be forsaken by Him (1 K. 8:57; Ps. 27:9; 38:21 [MT 22]; etc.).

(6) One of the most discussed occurrences of the term is Jesus' so-called cry of dereliction from the cross: "My God, my God, why hast thou forsaken me?" (Mk. 15:34, representing an Aramaic original; Mt. 27:46, a Hebrew parallel except for the Aramaic last word; cf. Metzger). This statement has long been a difficulty for some Christians: Luke has omitted it (23:44-49) and the Gospel of Peter 19 rendered it as "my strength, my strength."

Some have emphasized that Ps. 22:1 (which is here quoted, and not v. 20 as Bowman argued) (MT 22) ends in affirmation of faith (Trudinger). There appears to be indirect testimony in the Matthaean version, moreover, that Jesus is the Son of God, for Matthew interpolated Mark's text and made an explicit reference to the "Son of God" in 27:43, thereby confirming Jesus' response in 26:64, *sý eípas*. According to Matthew, Jesus remains obedient to the Father's will even though God is delivering Him up to death, with the result that God accomplishes through Jesus' obedience the forgiveness of sins (Kingsbury).

Although Jesus' question does not express loss of faith in God, and may even hint at the ultimate triumph to which the end of Ps. 22 points, it does express the loneliness of God-forsakenness. "It is no fiction or playacting," as Calvin put it, "that prompts His complaint, that He is forsaken by the Father" (*Harmony of the Gospels*, III [Eng. tr. 1972], 208).

The humanity of Jesus speaks here, the same humanity that "learned obedience through what he suffered" (He. 5:8) and that experienced the long descent of humiliation and emptying (Phil. 2:7f.), which ended when He was "crucified in weakness" (2 Cor. 13:4). After Christ's resurrection Christians found in this mortal cry, this "elementary crying in which the final reserves of man are concentrated" (*TDNT*, I, 627), at once the first cry of a new humanity that no longer cries out to be helped but now cries out for God Himself (cf. Rom. 8:16, 26; 2 Cor. 13:4; Gal. 4:4-6).

See also SEVEN LAST WORDS OF CHRIST.

***Bibliography*.**–B. W. Anderson, *Understanding the OT* (1957, 1975), pp. 138f., 348-359; T. Boman, *Studia Theologica*, 17 (1963), 103-119; *BHI* (2nd ed. 1972), pp. 332f., cf. pp. 318-321; J. Hayes, *Intro. to the Bible* (1971), pp. 81f., 230-36; J. D. Kingsbury, *Matthew: Structure, Christology, Kingdom* (1975), pp. 74ff.; B. M. Metzger, *Textual Commentary on the Greek NT* (1971), pp. 70, 119f.; H. H. Rowley, *Biblical Doctrine of Election* (1950), pp. 50-54; *TDNT*, I, *s.v.* βοάω (Stauffer); L. P. Trudinger, *Journal of the Evangelical Theological Society*, 17 (1974), 235-38.

J. G. GIBBS

FORTH. An adverb signifying movement (1) forward, (2) out of, (3) beyond a certain boundary. It frequently occurs as an expletive of various verbs, e.g., "go forth," "come forth," "set forth" (cf. Gen. 31:13; Nu. 26:4; Josh. 9:12; etc.). In the Fourth Gospel it is the translation of Gk. *éxō*, "without," "outside," in 11:43; 15:6; 19:4; etc.

FORTIFICATION. A structure built to defend a place or a position. Two basic types of fortifications developed, temporary and permanent. Temporary defenses thrown up in the field while combatants are facing the enemy or when contact is near are called field fortifications. Field fortifications, e.g., baggage piled around a defensive position or a parapet of earth and stone thrown up for protection, may be expanded under favorable conditions into major defensive systems. But normally they are abandoned when the arena of combat shifts or hostilities cease.

Permanent fortifications are usually built in times of peace to protect a place (i.e., a permanent settlement, rather than a temporarily defensible position) against sudden attack. Permanent fortifications are thus more substantial than field fortifications. In the ancient Near East they were normally constructed of masonry and/or mud brick. Such defensive works allowed an army to obtain maximum advantage of its weaponry and strength while impeding the advance of an enemy and the effective use of his resources. A major danger to an armed force within a fortified position, however, was the possibility of a siege if surrounded by a superior force.

Biblical writers refer to permanent rather than field fortifications, although the Israelite camp of Saul that David visited may have had temporary defensive works (1 S. 17); no field fortifications from biblical times have survived. Other information about fortifications in the biblical world is obtainable only through archeological research. Together the Bible and archeology provide a fairly comprehensive picture of the ancient search for physical security.

E. Late Bronze Age
F. Iron Age I
G. Iron Age II
H. Persian Period
I. Hellenistic-Early Roman Periods
IV. Fortification Terminology as Symbol
A. In the OT
B. In the NT

I. Biblical Terminology.–*A. Fortified Settlements.* The basic word used in the OT to designate a permanent fortified settlement is *ʿîr,* "city" (in the LXX chiefly Gk. *pólis*). The initial occurrence (Gen. 4:17) refers to a city built by Cain; thereafter the word appears some 1090 times in the OT. Its range of meaning includes a walled permanent settlement, a fortified area within such a settlement (citadel), an isolated smaller fortress (e.g., the Judean fortress at Arad, dating from the 10th to the 7th cents. B.C. or, infrequently, the population of a city (e.g., 1 S. 4:13).

A synonym of *ʿîr* is *qiryâ* (e.g., 1 K. 1:41), derived from Heb. *qîr,* which normally referred to the wall of a house but was also used to designate a city wall (e.g., Nu. 35:4; cf. Phoen. *qr*; Moabite *qr* means "town"). An allied, archaic form, *qereṯ* (cf. Ugar. *qrt*), occurs less frequently in the Bible (Job 29:7; Prov. 8:3; 9:3, 14; 11:11).

B. Nomenclature of Fortifications. As a reference to a permanent, walled settlement, *ʿîr* is frequently modified by *miḇṣār,* "fortified [place]" (KoB, p. 492). The word is derived from *bāṣar,* "to be inaccessible," an appropriate designation for a high-walled city. (The AV usually renders this word as "fenced" [Nu. 32:17] or "defenced" [Isa. 25:2].) Such a city was frequently located on a steep hill (e.g., Hazor, Lachish, and Jerusalem), and was viewed with awe by the Israelite spies (Nu. 13:28; Dt. 1:28).

Two other words derived from the same root are *beṣûrâ,* "fortified (wall)" (e.g., Isa. 2:15; AV "fenced," NEB "sheer") and *biṣṣārôn,* "stronghold" (Zec. 9:12).

The usual word for the wall of a city is *ḥômâ,* "(defensive) wall" (e.g., Dt. 3:5; Josh. 2:15; 1 S. 31:10; Am. 1:7). (The development of city fortifications will be discussed below.)

The Heb. *ḥēl/ḥêl,* "rampart" (AV "trench," e.g., 2 S. 20:15; Ps. 48:13 [MT 14]), usually connotes a steep embankment (glacis) thrown up against an inner core wall, often with a dry moat at its base.

The Heb. *šaʿar,* "gate," is used, e.g., in the description of the rebuilding of the Valley Gate in Jerusalem (Neh. 3:13), which mentions the basic parts: *delāṯôṯ,* "doors," *manʿulîm,* "bolts," and *berîḥîm,* "bars." In the construction of a gate *qôrôṯ,* "beams," were also used. The gate was a part of a defensive complex built around the *peṯaḥ,* "entrance," into the city through the wall.

An important word is *migdāl,* "tower" (e.g., 2 K. 9:17, NEB "watchtower"; Isa. 2:15). The "tower" of Gen. 11:4 is usually understood as a ziggurat, while that of Shechem (Jgs. 9:46-49) was the fortified citadel of the city, including the temple fortress (cf. R. Boling, *Judges* [*AB,* 1975], pp. 180f.). Frequently *migdāl* refers to towers or bastions built into the city walls (cf. Jer. 31:38; 2 Ch. 14:7 [MT 6]; 2 Ch. 26:9; Neh. 3:1). These functioned both as guard towers at the city gates and as firing stations along the walls. In the latter use they were spaced so that archers could cover the distance between towers. King Uzziah is credited with building towers in the wilderness (2 Ch. 26:10), a practice also pursued by his son and successor, Jotham (2 Ch. 27:4). These were "forts" (Heb. *bîrâ*), established at strategic points within Judah (cf. the ruins found in the lowest level of occupation at Qumrân by de Vaux).

The Heb. *ʾarmôn* (Gk. *ákra*) is variously translated as "castle" (Prov. 18:19), "citadel" (2 K. 15:25; AV "palace"), "palace" (Jer. 6:5), and "stronghold" (Am. 1:12; AV, NEB "palace"). In Hos. 8:14 it is synonymous with "palaces" (Heb. *hêḵāl*) and fortified dwelling places or cities (Heb. *ʿārîm beṣurôṯ*); however, in Ps. 122:7 it is rendered "towers" and is parallel to "walls" (Heb. *ḥēl*). Heb. *ʾalmānôṯ* appears in Isa. 13:22 (parallel to "palaces," Heb. *hêḵāl*) and Ezk. 19:7 (parallel to "cities," Heb. *ʿārîm*).

The Heb. *bîrâ* ("citadel, acropolis," KoB) appears only in the later books, Chronicles, Nehemiah, Daniel, and Esther, and may be a substitute for the earlier *migdāl,* "tower" (see below), although its plural, *bîrānîyôṯ,* is paired with *migdālîm* (pl. of *migdāl*) in 2 Ch. 27:4 as "forts and towers." *Bîrâ* is consistently translated "capital" in Esther and Daniel. The RSV renders it "fortress" (Neh. 2:8; AV "palace," NEB "citadel"), "castle" (Neh. 7:2), and "palace" (1 Ch. 29:1). The latter reference is to the temple complex. The temple complex, royal quarters, and major governmental buildings were the most important components of the citadel of a city. Citadels frequently occupied the heights of the city and could be encircled by a separate wall within the major defensive wall.

The Heb. *miśgāḇ,* derived from *śāgaḇ,* "to be (inaccessibly) high," may be rendered variously as "high" (Isa. 25:12), "place of defense" (Isa. 33:16), and "sure defense" (Ps. 48:3 [MT 4]; AV "refuge," NEB "tower of strength").

The Heb. *māʿôz,* which denotes a mountain stronghold or place of refuge, is rendered "fortress" in Dnl. 11:10 (NEB "stronghold"). The plural occurs in 11:39 (AV "strongholds"). The word is translated "stronghold" in Jgs. 6:26 (AV "rock"; NEB "earthwork") and in Isa. 23:14 (AV "strength," NEB "haven").

The Heb. *meṣûḏâ* normally refers to a mountain stronghold (KoB), but the references in 2 S. 5:7, 9 to "the stronghold (of Jebus)" obviously refer to the citadel of the city (AV "fort," v. 9).

The Heb. *māṣôr/meṣûrâ* is usually "rampart(s)," e.g., Zec. 9:3 (AV "stronghold"), Nah. 2:1 (AV "munition," NEB "bastions"); however, in 2 Ch. 11:5 *ʿārîm lemāṣôr* are "cities for defense," and *ʿārê meṣûrôṯ* is rendered "fortified cities" (AV "fenced cities") in v. 10 while *ham-meṣûrôṯ* in v. 11 is translated "fortresses" (AV "fenced cities," NEB "fortifications"). The variations in translation for *māṣôr* are seen by comparing the above uses with Dt. 20:20, "siegeworks" (AV "bulwarks"); Ezk. 4:2, "siegeworks" (AV, NEB "siege"); 4:3, "state of siege" (AV, NEB "besieged"); and 4:7, "siege."

Rarer words for elements of fortifications include *baḥan,* "watchtower" (Isa. 32:14, AV "tower"; cf. *migdāl,* "tower," in Neh. 3:27); *pinnâ,* "battlement" (Zeph. 1:16; 3:6; AV "tower"), although the word usually connotes "corner"; *miṣpeh,* "watchtower" (Isa. 21:8; 2 Ch. 20:24); *ṣerî(a)ḥ,* "stronghold" (Jgs. 9:46, 49; AV "hold," NEB "great hall"); *muṣṣāḇ,* "towers" (Isa. 29:3; AV "mount," NEB "outposts"); *ʾagam,* "bulwark" (Jer. 51:32; AV "reed," NEB "guard-tower"); *ʾošyâ,* "bulwark" (Jer. 50:15; AV "foundation," NEB "bastion"), is more properly "tower" (cf. H. Cohen, *Biblical Hapax Legomena in the Light of Akkadian and Ugaritic* [1978], pp. 46f., 89f.); and *ʿōz,* "bulwark" (Ps. 8:2 [MT 3]; AV "strength," NEB "the mighty").

C. Act of Fortifying. The usual verb for fortifying is *bānâ,* "build," but also, "build, refurbish, or expand the fortifications," e.g., Josh. 6:26; Am. 9:14; Isa. 45:13 (NEB "rebuild"); 58:12 (AV "build," NEB "restored"); this rebuilding may include walls (1 K. 3:1), gates (2 K. 15:35; NEB "constructed"), and towers (2 Ch. 26:10).

The piel of *bāṣar,* "cut off, make inaccessible, fortify," occurs in Isa. 22:10 (NEB "make [the wall] inaccessible") and Jer. 51:53 (NEB "make [her high towers] inaccessible"). Both the feminine singular (*beṣûrâ*) and plural

($b^e ṣurôṯ$) passive participles are used adjectivally, e.g., Nu. 13:28 ("fortified") and Dt. 1:28.

The piel of *ḥāzaq,* "make strong, fortify," occurs frequently in later texts, e.g., Nah. 3:14, "strengthen [your forts]" (AV "fortify"); Ps. 147:13 (NEB "put new bars on your gates"); 2 Ch. 11:11, "made [the fortresses] strong" (AV "fortified," NEB "strengthened"); and 26:9. The hiphil stem is also used with the same meaning in Nehemiah for the refortification of Jerusalem's walls, e.g., "repair," 3:4.

The Heb. *gāḏar,* "build a wall, repair breaches," occurs rarely and is used in a figurative sense, e.g., Ezk. 13:5 (AV "made up the hedge," NEB "repair the broken wall [around the Israelites]"); cf. Hos. 2:6 (MT 8); Am. 9:11. The participle *gōḏēr* usually means "mason," but in Ezk. 22:30 it functions verbally, "[a man who . . .] should build up the wall" (AV "make up the hedge," NEB "build up a barricade").

II. Basic Elements.–In the ancient Near East defensible cities required a wall system with its associated components and a supply of water. A simple "curtain" wall functioned as a passive barrier to delay the entrance of an enemy. An opening in the wall for entrance and exit was closed with a simple swinging gate locked with a bar. Such simple walls were easily scaled or breached and did not provide adequate protection against siege.

The need for more adequate defense led to the development of a thicker and higher wall that provided the defenders with protection from the missiles of attackers and a firing platform from which to retaliate. Walls measuring as much as 7.5 m. (25 ft.) in breadth have been discovered in the ruins of biblical cities. They were usually built 10.5-12 m. (35-40 ft.) high in order to discourage scaling and were strengthened by thick buttresses at regular intervals. Attackers discovered that even thick walls were vulnerable to tunneling by sappers and to the destructive effects of battering rams, so further protective measures were developed. The foundations of walls were laid deep and broad, and frequently a protective glacis was thrown up against the base at a 45° angle. This battered earth (*terre pisée*) construction was then sealed with a thick layer of crushed and beaten limestone. Often a retaining wall at the base of the glacis helped to stabilize this thick protective device. As a further deterrent to both scaling and sapping operations, a moat (fosse) was sometimes excavated at the perimeter of the glacis.

Typical Middle Bronze fortifications: (1) fosse (moat), (2) glacis, (3) layers of stones or crushed, beaten limestone, (4) layers of beaten earth (*terre pisée*), (5) retaining wall, (6) natural slope of mound, and (7) city wall.

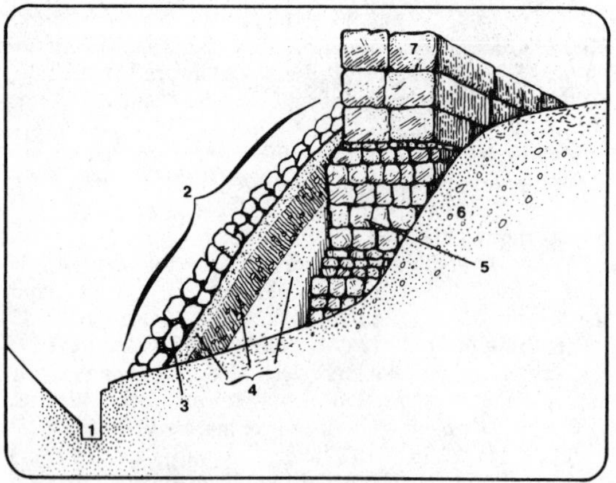

Atop the wall added features enabled the defenders to fire at the enemy frontally or toward either side while at the same time protecting the defenders from enemy fire. Battlements, consisting of parapets with crenelations, were developed. The caps or merlons that extended above the top of the parapet shielded the protectors of the wall from the missiles of attackers while the crenels, the openings between the merlons, provided space for firing down upon the enemy. In addition, towers or bastions — usually square or semicircular in shape — were often built into the wall at regular intervals within bow-range of one another, permitting the defenders to shoot directly along the base of the wall. Balconies were built from them and from the wall with holes in the floors that permitted firing at targets directly below. Another (though less effective) method of broadening the range of defensive fire from the wall was the building of the wall along an inset-offset line.

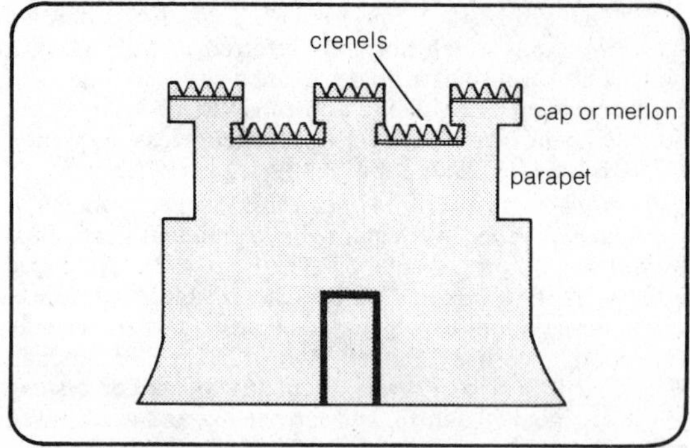

Another technique employed in defensive fortifications was the construction of an outer wall, with its own bastions and battlements, down the slope from the main wall. This wall was an alternative to the construction of a fosse, but some cities were exceptionally fortified with an outer wall, a fosse, and a glacis.

Like the walls, the city gate underwent development as siege tactics and equipment changed. The gate was essentially a hole through the wall and the weakest point in the line of defense. Extraordinary care was taken, therefore, to strengthen it. Towers were normally built on either side of the gateway, and the entire construction might extend from the line of the wall as much as 15-18 m. (50-60 ft.) into the city. Along this length chambers were formed by a series of paired pilasters on either side of the passageway. The space where the passageway passed between the pilasters could be closed with secondary gates, hindering the capture of the city should the main gate be penetrated. The popularity of one-, two-, and three-bay gates varied from time to time. The two leaves of the gate were constructed of heavy timbers, often plated with metal for protection from the axes or the fires of the foe. They were attached to heavy doorposts that turned in stone sockets. These doors of the entrance were closed at the center of the opening and barred with a heavy beam inserted in slots on either side of the gateway. The base of the doors rested against a doorstop when closed, and blocking against the interior bottom further strengthened them when closed against an enemy. For even greater protection, a strong outer gate with towers and a walled courtyard connected to the city walls and the main gate could be built.

Since most walled cities were located on elevations, a ramp was built leading from the base of the site to the gateway. Builders normally constructed these approaches along the wall to the right of the gate in order to leave the unshielded right arm of enemy soldiers open to attack from the wall. The passageway of the gate could have either direct access or the more popular indirect access. With the latter, two 45° turns, to the right and then to the left or vice versa, were required to enter the city. All of these features had the practical purpose of halting or slowing the entrance of an attacking force into the city. Even after penetrating the city beyond the major gate and wall system, the attacker still faced a heavily fortified citadel with its own walls, towers, and gates.

A heavily protected city could sometimes be defended for years, if sufficient food and especially water were available. Plastered underground cisterns provided one means of storing water. Another method was to dig a water shaft with a tunnel leading down to ground water level, thus providing a natural well or spring. Late in the Bronze Age and during the Iron Age impressive water

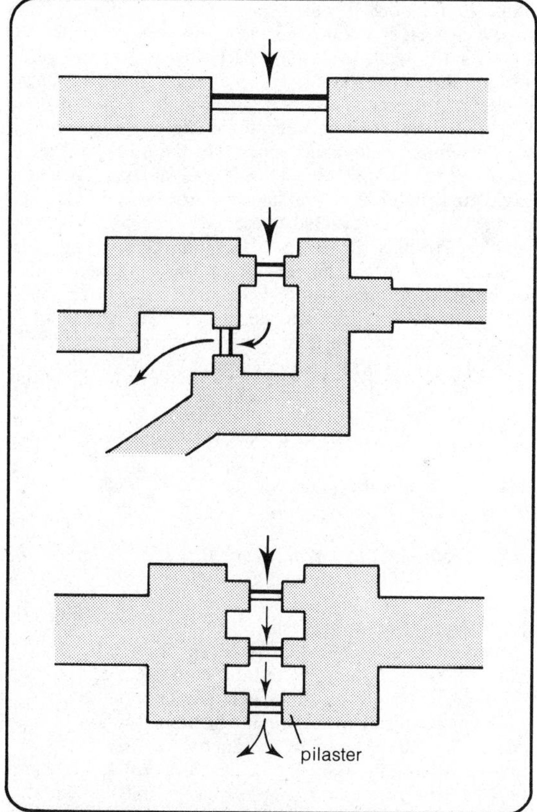

shafts were constructed at such sites as Gibeon, Gezer, Hazor, and Megiddo.

III. Archeological Evidence.–*A. Neolithic Age* (*ca.* 8000-4000 B.C.). The earliest known permanent fortifications of the ancient world were discovered at Jericho. The inhabitants of the Prepottery Neolithic A city had constructed a free-standing stone wall by 8000 B.C. The wall, which encircled a city of approximately 4 ha. (10 acres), was constructed of undressed stone. It was over 1.8 m. (6 ft.) thick and when excavated still stood over 7 m. (23 ft.) high.

Outside the wall a dry moat (fosse) 2.7 m. (9 ft.) deep and 8 m. (27 ft.) wide had been cut into the bedrock, an amazing achievement by builders who apparently worked with only flint tools. On the inside of the western part of the wall, a circular stone tower had been constructed. It measured 8.5 m. (28 ft.) in diameter and still stands 9 m. (30 ft.) high. Within the tower a stairway of twenty-two steps led to the top.

The Neolithic A wall had a long history, but eventually the site was abandoned so that it suffered from the effects of erosion, collapsing in places and being covered by debris. During the 7th millennium the site was reoccupied by Prepottery Neolithic B people who also built a defensive wall, but its use was of much shorter duration than the earliest wall of Jericho. These defensive structures at Jericho predate by some four thousand years other known fortifications.

B. Chalcolithic Age (*ca.* 4000-3100 B.C.). Although the earliest fortified city-states in southern Mesopotamia (Sumer) were being founded by the middle of the 4th millennium, open villages rather than fortified settlements dominated this period.

C. Early Bronze Age (*ca.* 3100-2000 B.C.). The close of the 4th and the beginning of the 3rd millennium witnessed the development of fortified cities in many regions of the ancient Near East. Urban centers developed in the two great riverine civilizations, Mesopotamia and Egypt, setting the stage and providing the stimulus for the development of cities in Syria and Palestine. Several factors contributed to the development of cities from unwalled villages in this period: the accumulation of wealth due to agricultural surplus and widespread trade activity; the development of the city-state with concomitant expansionist tendencies, including tendencies toward empires in Mesopotamia and Egypt; and the threat of nomadic tribes, who were always lurking on the fringes of cultivated lands and awaiting the opportunity to plunder the unprotected villages.

Even though a number of sites have been excavated that were occupied in the Early Bronze period (e.g., Jericho, Megiddo, Ai, Tell el-Fârʿah (N), Taanach, Beth-yerah, Beth-shean, and Dan), evidence for E.B. fortifications systems is sketchy because the E.B. remains are beneath a thick accumulation of debris. Archeological research has tended to explore the more accessible upper levels of sites in the Near East so that the lower E.B. levels have been reached only in restricted areas. The site of Arad is, however, an exception.

Just beneath the modern surface of Arad, Ruth Amiran uncovered the ruins of a major E.B. II (*ca.* 2900-2700) walled city. The evidence indicates an unbroken development from an early village to a major walled city. The wall, encircling an area of some 10 ha. (25 acres) and built on bedrock, was constructed of large stones along the outer courses with a rubble fill between. The width varies from 2.1 to 2.4 m. (7 to 8 ft.), and in places it still stands to a height of about 1 m. (3 to 4 ft.). A number of semicircular towers were built into the Arad city wall at intervals of 18-23 m. (60-75 ft.). The towers have interior diameters of 2.4 to 3 m. (8 to 10 ft.) and a passage to the inside of the city about 1 m. (3 ft.) across. No major city gate has been excavated at the site.

The E.B. II defenses of Arad are typical of contemporary Canaanite cities, although each site is unique. Some of the sites exhibit the earliest phases of mud brick, but these walls were soon strengthened or replaced by stone, usually small and undressed. At Megiddo the earliest wall was built of stone. Originally 4.5 m. (15 ft.) thick, it was later enlarged to 8 m. (26 ft.). Beth-yerah, located along the southwest shore of the Sea of Galilee, was protected by the lake on the east and north so that a wall was needed only along the west and south. A massive mud brick wall 7.5 m. (25 ft.) thick was built, consisting of a central core and steeply sloping walls on both sides. A gate on the south side of the tell was constructed of basalt stone. At Tell el-Fârʿah North, about 11 km. (7 mi.) NE of Shechem, R. de Vaux found a wall of mud brick 2.7 m. (9 ft.) thick, built on three courses of stone base and strengthened by towers and projecting bastions. Later additions to this wall included a stone wall 3 m. (10 ft.) thick and a glacis 9 m. (30 ft.) thick in places at the base. Such sloping embankments in this period were probably constructed to counteract the internal pressures against the wall caused by accumulated debris. The city consisted of an opening with two projecting rectangular towers, one on each side. At Ai a walled citadel stood atop the acropolis within an area of 11 ha. (27 acres), the city proper. The entire site was surrounded by a wall 5.5 m. (18 ft.) thick that underwent subsequent rebuilding to a width of 7.5 m. (25 ft.). A semicircular tower also strengthened the wall of Ai.

Many of the E.B. sites give evidence of frequent repairs, rebuilding, and the expansion of fortifications. The walls of Jericho, e.g., in this period exhibited seventeen different phases.

D. Middle Bronze Age (*ca.* 2000-1550 B.C.). The major urban centers of Palestine were by and large destroyed and left uninhabited by *ca.* 2300 B.C. Most scholars connect this disruption, which affected Egypt and Mesopotamia as well as the Canaanite world, with the movements of nomadic peoples called the Amorites. The ensuing Middle Bronze I period (*ca.* 2000-1800) in Palestine reflects a seminomadic population living in rural and unwalled settlements.

Middle Bronze IIA marked the resurgence in Palestine of sedentary life and the reestablishment of fortified cities. At Megiddo the first fortifications of the period consisted of a flimsy wall but in the succeeding phase a new city wall 1.5 m. (5 ft.) thick was constructed of mud brick on a stone foundation. A city gate was built so that a stepped approach led into a tower which contained both an outer and an inner gate. These were set at right angles to each other, with the inner gate chamber parallel to the city wall. Such a plan indicates that only foot traffic could use the gate.

A major change in city planning and fortifications ushered in the Middle Bronze IIB period (*ca.* 1750-1550 B.C.). Huge, steeply sloping mounds of earth were cast up around the cities. Atop these glacis were erected the city walls, frequently constructed of mud brick laid upon a stone foundation. Concurrent with this change was a redesigned city gate with a direct entrance, in contrast to the earlier indirect entrance.

The new fortifications have been associated with the HYKSOS who ruled the Canaanite city-states in this period. The Hyksos introduced a revolutionary war implement in the Middle East, the light chariot with four-spoked wheels. This development and that of the battering ram were apparently the causes for the change in the design of fortifications. The identification of the battered earth ramparts with the Hyksos period occurred early in this century when Flinders Petrie excavated Tell el-Yehûdîyeh, a site some 32 km. (20 mi.) N of Cairo. He found a camp surrounded by a huge glacis about 450 m. (1500 ft.) square. The embankment measured 24 by 42.5 m. (80 by 140 ft.) at the top with a base 40-60 m. (130-200 ft.) wide. The rampart had been built by heaping up sand and then covering it with bricks and plaster. The interior of the camp measured about 365 m. (400 yds.) square, and it has been estimated that forty thousand people could have taken refuge within it. A sloping ramp on the east side, guarded by two towers, was apparently an access route by which chariots could be brought into the city.

The mightiest Hyksos city in Palestine was Hazor. A description of the fortifications of Hazor in this period provides an insight into similar constructions discovered at such sites as Dan, Jericho, Megiddo, Taanach, Dothan, Shechem, Bethel, Jerusalem, Beth-zur, Beth-shemesh, Gezer, Lachish, Tell Beit Mirsim, Tell Jerîsheh, Joppa, Ashkelon, Tell en-Nagilah, and Tell el-ʿAjjûl in Palestine, as well as at sites to the north such as Qatna, Carchemish, and Tell Mardikh in Syria.

Hazor consisted of an upper city, the tell proper, covering 10 ha. (25 acres) and rising about 43 m. (140 ft.) above the surrounding landscape, and a lower city that covered some 71 ha. (175 acres) of the tell. The upper city, which began to be occupied in the Early Bronze Age, was unwalled. In the E.B. IV phase it lay deserted. In the M.B. IIB period a brick wall 7 m. (23 ft.) wide was built on a stone foundation. It was strengthened with towers, and on the eastern end of the tell a glacis of stone provided the base for the wall. (*See* Plate 22.) Adjacent to the glacis was a deep, narrow moat. This wall protected the tell, the citadel of the city. The lower city was built on a plateau which on the east had a steep slope that was strengthened with retaining walls and a glacis. To the north and west, however, the builders dug a deep, wide moat and used the excavated material to build a rampart. In one area a cut through the glacis revealed a core wall of mud brick against which earth was thrown in alternating layers with plastered surfaces intervening. Sealed in this sandwiched construction were quantities of E.B. and M.B. pottery, indicating that the rampart was constructed later rather than earlier in the M.B. period.

During the Hyksos period improvements in the construction of glacis were made at some sites. At Shechem, e.g., a glacis was constructed of stone. At Tell Dan the Hyksos period rampart is unique, with a huge core wall of stone that measures 6 m. (20 ft.) wide in places. Against this core, both within and without, the builders cast up a glacis so that the inner surface of the tell has a concave shape.

The glacis of this period were thrown up against the sloping sides of tells that had known long periods of occupation so that the slopes were soft and easily dislodged by the first crude battering rams. The Hyksos glacis was a response to this defensive problem. The walls, with towers, battlements, and gates, were built atop the glacis.

The Hyksos introduced the light war chariot, an innovation that required a change in the construction of city gates. The sharply angled entrance of earlier gates was now eliminated in favor of a design that provided a wider direct entry, but since the gate was the most vulnerable part of a city's fortifications, the passageway was lengthened and strengthened. The new gates, 15-18 m. (50-60 ft.) long, were divided by pilasters, three to each side, to which three doors could be fixed. Large towers were usually built on each side of the passage. When the gate was built high on a tell, a ramp was constructed from the base of the tell to the gate, with an area before the gate wide enough for turning a chariot. When feasible, the approach moved parallel to the wall from the right of the gate, leaving the unshielded arm of attacking troops who used the ramp open to fire from the adjacent wall.

E. Late Bronze Age (*ca.* 1550-1200 B.C.). Fortifications during this period changed little from those of the Middle Bronze period. The massive constructions of the Hyksos seem to have been used continuously during the L.B. period, or reconstruction took place along the same defensive lines. At Gezer a new wall about 3.5 m. (12 ft.)

Shechem's East Gate and steps leading down into the city. Originally built *ca.* 1600 B.C., it was destroyed by the Egyptians *ca.* 1550. New guard rooms were added in the Late Bronze Age, and Jeroboam I repaired and strengthened the gate. It was again destroyed in the 8th cent. B.C. (W. S. LaSor)

thick and strengthened by a glacis was erected early in this period. The wall was further strengthened with several rectangular bastions protruding from both sides. A number of the bastions were built at the same time as the wall, while others were added later. At Shechem the eastern gate was constructed with a broad entrance between two pilasters on each side strengthened by adjacent towers.

Sometime during the L.B. period the inhabitants of Gezer dug a huge shaft down through the tell and the subterranean limestone to ground water level. This assured the city of an adequate water supply within its fortifications in case of siege.

F. Iron Age I (*ca.* 1200-900 B.C.). The Late Bronze Age witnessed the decline of the major empires of the period — Egypt, the Hittites in Anatolia, and the Mitanni on the Middle Euphrates. By *ca.* 1200 B.C. the migrating seapeoples had ended the Hittite empire, destroyed the major cities along the Syro-Palestinian coast, and were threatening Egypt. Also during this period the Israelites conquered a part of Canaan while an Aramean kingdom was being established around Damascus.

These factors help to explain the decline in the quality of the Canaanite fortifications in the period of the judges and the united monarchy (Iron Age I). The conquering Israelites initially built no fortifications on the captured tells. The earliest phases of their occupation were characteristically villages and campsites with associated stone-lined storage pits. The earliest recognizable Israelite fortification is probably the flimsy wall of rubble stone about a meter (3 ft.) thick built at Tell en-Naṣbeh (biblical Mizpah). Double-chambered towers were set into this wall at strategic locations, but such a weak defensive structure could not sustain a long siege. The towers, however, gave a vantage point from which to identify an approaching hostile force, permitting the inhabitants either to flee into the surrounding countryside for safety or to send out their own troops to ambush the enemy or to engage them in open combat.

The establishment of the monarchy in Israel led to the refortification of the major cities and to the building of fortresses at strategic locations. At Tell en-Naṣbeh the earlier wall was replaced by a casemate wall 4 m. (13 ft.) thick, built perhaps during either Saul's or David's reign. It was about 800 m. (½ mi.) long and surrounded an area of 3.2 ha. (8 acres). Small stones were used to level the bedrock and were topped by large boulders. The wall itself, built of stone blocks, was erected on this base and plastered on the outside. It was further strengthened by ten projecting towers spaced irregularly along its perimeter and by a huge retaining wall at the base. The stone wall was probably surmounted by a brick wall. The gate, situated in the northeast section of the wall, had a direct approach and a double jamb. It was protected by a massive tower. Similar early Israelite casemate wall systems were discovered at Tell Beit Mirsim and Beth-shemesh.

During Solomon's reign major defensive works were built at Jerusalem, Hazor, Megiddo, and Gezer (1 K.

The Solomonic gate of Megiddo showing the typical triple piers. Rubble filling the spaces between the pillars later sealed off the guardrooms (Oriental Institute, University of Chicago)

Header-and-stretcher Israelite wall at Samaria (Israel Department of Antiquities and Museums)

9:15). The distinctive Solomonic casemate walls and gates have been uncovered at all of these sites except Jerusalem, where later rebuilding and continuing occupation make discovery of the Solomonic structures unlikely. The three known Solomonic gates have similar dimensions and are all built on the same plan: a six-chambered main gate built into the casemate wall and extending about 20 m. (65 ft.) into the city with an outer gate structure. The six chambers were formed by three piers on each side of the passageway. The piers were about 2 m. (6 ft.) thick, and the guard rooms measured 3 by 5 m. (10 by 17 ft.). The width of the passageway between the piers measured about 4 m. (14 ft.).

Two solid stone towers were built at the line of the wall. They were faced with well-cut ashlar masonry with nicely drafted margins. Beyond the main gate and set at a right angle to it was an outer gate with two piers and an enclosed courtyard large enough to permit a chariot to turn into the inner gate. A ramp led up the slope of the tell to the outer gate. Similar indirect approach gates have been found in Iron Age II levels at Tell en-Naṣbeh, Tell el-Fârʿah North, Tell Beit Mirsim, and Lachish.

G. Iron Age II (*ca.* 900-600 B.C.). The widespread use of the casemate wall in the early period of the Israelite monarchy was followed in the northern kingdom by new, solid walls, apparently erected in Ahab's reign (cf. 1 K. 22:39). These changes were probably made to defend against the more sophisticated battering ram that the Assyrians had developed. At Megiddo a solid wall with salients and recesses was built, and similar walls have been uncovered at Hazor, Beth-shemesh, and Tell en-Naṣbeh. A new gate design that reduced the space allocated to it within the city replaced the earlier Solomonic structure. It contained two piers on each side of the passage. Earlier, Omri had built a solid wall 1.5 m. (5 ft.) thick around the crest of the hill of Samaria that was superbly crafted with fine ashlar exterior stones laid in the header-and-stretcher fashion. Phoenician craftsmanship may be reflected in the marginal bossing and the tight fit that required no mortar. The inner wall was filled with stones about one meter (3 ft.) long chinked with smaller stones. Later an outer wall was built, in casemate fashion, around the earlier wall. It varied in width from 5 to 10 m. (16 to 33 ft.) with cross-walls nearly one meter (3 ft.) thick, spaced every 2 to 3 m. (7 to 10 ft.). This wall underwent several phases in the reigns of both Jehu and Jeroboam II.

Excavations at Tell el-Qâḍî (biblical Dan) have revealed massive fortifications datable to this period. There is no evidence of Danite defensive constructions following the conquest of Laish (Jgs. 18), but along the southern edge of the mound an Israelite gate structure and a massive wall at the base of the M.B. IIB rampart have been uncovered. Two major phases, attributable to Jeroboam I and Ahab, with possible additional modifications in the time of Jeroboam II, have been uncovered. The complex included a wall at the base of the rampart that is 3.6 m. (12 ft.) thick and probably once stood 7.6 to 9.1 m. (25 to 30 ft.) high, a beautifully cobbled street leading into a two-chambered gate structure and then up the rampart, and a second gate structure and wall system atop the rampart. A similar double-walled defensive system from this period at Lachish is graphically depicted on reliefs found in the ruins of Sennacherib's palace in Nineveh (cf. *ANEP,* nos. 372f.)

Apart from fortifications constructed around cities, royal Judean fortresses were built at strategic locations, particularly in the Negeb, during this period. The early fortress of Saul at Gibeah has been mentioned above. It was abandoned until the last decades of Iron Age II when it was again strongly fortified on the original plan.

Three basic types of fortresses were built: rectangular

forts, about 40 by 50 m. (130 by 160 ft.), with projecting towers; irregularly shaped fortresses without towers; and a smaller (about 20 m. [70 ft.] sq.) fortress without towers. Arad provides an excellent example of these structures, which were obviously built to control both military threats along the border and the incursions of nomadic elements (cf. the raids of the Amalekites, 1 S. 30:1ff.). The Arad fortress passed through six phases from the 10th to the early 6th cents. B.C. The first had a casemate wall. The second wall was solid and strengthened with a glacis. It was rebuilt and reused except during the last phase when a casemate wall was again constructed. A feature of extraordinary interest in the Arad fortress was a Judahite sanctuary.

Under King Uzziah, additional fortresses were built (2 Ch. 26:10). The earliest phase of Khirbet Qumrân, where the Dead Sea Scroll community later lived, was possibly one of Uzziah's forts.

H. Persian Period (*ca.* 600-330 B.C.). Benevolent Persian control may have reduced the necessity for fortified cities; thus few fortified sites of this period have been found in Palestine. At Tel Megadim, S of Haifa, a rectangular casemate wall in this period surrounded a 1.5 ha. (4 acre) site, presumably Phoenician. A few large administrative buildings have been discovered, of which the governor's palace at Lachish is the best preserved. The sparse population seems to have lived in small villages. Excavations in Jerusalem, however, have produced fragments of the walls built by Nehemiah on the east crest of Ophel.

I. Hellenistic-Early Roman Periods (*ca.* 330 B.C.-A.D. 70). The conquests of Alexander the Great brought a resurgence of urban life to the older locations in Palestine and led to the establishment of several new Greek cities (the Pentapolis). Examples of fortifications for cities in this period have been unearthed at such sites as Gezer, Jerusalem, Mareshah, and particularly Samaria.

In the early Hellenistic phase at Samaria, the old walls of the acropolis were reused with the addition of huge, round towers built on the earlier square Israelite foundations. One tower measured 19 m. (63 ft.) in diameter and still stood to a height of 8 m. (27 ft.) when it was discovered. John Hyrcanus, the Hasmonean ruler, destroyed Samaria in 107 B.C. It was rebuilt *ca.* 60 B.C. with an acropolis wall 4 m. (14 ft.) thick and a series of rectangular towers.

During the Roman period a wall encircled the entire city of about 70 ha. (170 acres). The city gate on the west boasted two huge, round towers, 14 m. (46 ft.) in diameter, which sat on earlier Hellenistic foundations. Herod the Great built a number of monumental buildings in the city and erected a 4-km. (2½-mi.) wall around it with imposing gates and towers.

Mareshah was a major Idumean city in the Hellenistic period, laid out on the Hippodamian plan, i.e., with streets intersecting at right angles. The city wall enclosed an almost square area, 158 m. (520 ft.) measured at the widest point from east to west, and 152 m. (500 ft.) from north to south. The gates were not definitely identified in the excavations.

The high priest Simon was noted (cf. Sir. 50:1-4) for repairing the walls of Jerusalem *ca.* 200 B.C. Apparently he refurbished the walls constructed by Nehemiah. In 168 B.C. Antiochus IV built a fortress within Jerusalem's walls in an effort to control the recalcitrant Jews, who rejected his demands to hellenize their ways. That fort, the Acra, is known from Josephus (*BJ* i.1.4 [39]; *Ant.* xii.5.4 [252]), but its location has not been identified. The two choices are: (1) on the slope of the Upper City to the west of the Temple Mount, and (2) to the south of the Temple enclosure. The latter location agrees with the account in Josephus.

In the Hasmonean phase of this period, the walls of Jerusalem were extended to the west and north to incorporate the western hill, the "Upper City." Beneath the Citadel of modern Jerusalem at Jaffa Gate (the Tower of David), remains of a Hasmonean tower have been uncovered. The wall extended eastward from this point to the Temple Mount near Wilson's Arch. Parts of this First Wall have been traced around Mt. Zion along the Valley of Hinnom to the Kidron Valley. Herod the Great not only erected monumental buildings, but also expanded the defenses of Jerusalem. The Second Wall was built to connect the First Wall with the new Damascus Gate to the north. The wall then turned southward to join with the Antonia fortress at the northwest corner of the Temple area (cf. Acts 21:34, 37, "barracks"). Little evidence remains of this fortress, so one must turn to Josephus for a description of it (cf. *BJ* v.5.8 [238-245]). The major remaining fortification from Herod's time is the Tower of David, actually a remnant of three towers that fortified his palace on the ridge of the Upper City. Here characteristic Herodian masonry with flat bosses and wide margins form the base of a tower 18 m. (60 ft.) square and still preserved to a height of 20 m. (66 ft.).

Herod also built fortress retreats in the desert, of which the two most striking are MASADA and the Herodium (*see* HEROD). At Masada a casemate wall 4 m. (13 ft.) thick with four gates and strengthened by thirty towers surrounded the summit. The walls and towers were coated with white plaster. The Herodium is located 5 km. (3 mi.) SE of Bethlehem. Herod artificially heightened a hill into a gigantic conical base upon which he constructed a fortress with a double circular wall. Four towers were built facing the four points of the compass, three semicircular in design and the eastern one round. The outer diameter of the complex is 55 m. (180 ft.) while the inner diameter is 45 m.

Qasr Abu el-Kharaq, a Moabite border fortress (E. K. Vogel; picture N. Glueck)

View of the Herodium showing its conical shape (L. T. Geraty)

Ruins at the top of the Herodium, a palace-fortress built by Herod the Great (37-4 B.C.). It is located about 6 km. (4 mi.) SE of Bethlehem (B. VanElderen)

(150 ft.). The interior was divided into palatial rooms and courts. Herod was buried in this fortress, but his coffin has not been discovered; it may lie hidden in the unexcavated east tower.

IV. Fortification Terminology as Symbol.–Although defensive walls never adequately protected city dwellers in biblical times, they did represent the most powerful physical means of security. Both biblical poets and prophets, therefore, used fortification terminology to express the spiritual (and frequently the physical) security of the believer in God.

A. In the OT. The psalmist notes in his thanksgiving (9:9 [MT 10]) that the Lord is "a stronghold [*miśgāḇ*; AV "refuge," NEB "tower of strength"] for the oppressed." The opening lines of Ps. 18 (v. 2 [MT 3] par. 2 S. 22:3) characterize God with a series of metaphors including *m*ᵉ*ṣûḏāṯî*, "my fortress," and *miśgabbî*, "my stronghold" (AV "my high tower," NEB "my strong tower"). In Ps. 46:7 (MT 8), the presence of the Lord of hosts is a "refuge" (*miśgāḇ*, NEB "high stronghold"). In Ps. 31:2 (MT 3) *ṣûr-mā*ʿ*ôz*, "rock of refuge" (AV "strong rock") parallels *bêṯ m*ᵉ*ṣûḏôṯ*, "a strong fortress" (AV "house of defence," NEB "strong hold"), and therefore the psalmist can trust in the Lord to save him from his troubles. That this protection by God was not merely spiritual is apparent from the account of Assyria's attack (and continued threats) on Jerusalem (1 K. 18–20 par. Isa. 36–38); God promised to "defend" (Heb. *gānan*; cf. *māgēn*, "shield") the city (19:34; 20:16), and He did (19:35f.). In describing both the beauty and chastity of a woman, Cant. 8:9 refers to her as a wall (Heb. *ḥômâ*) fortified (Heb. *bānâ*) with a silver battlement (Heb. *ṭîrâ*; AV "palace," NEB "parapet"; cf. M. Pope, *Song of Songs* [*AB*, 1978], pp. 679-683).

The prophets, too, use this imagery. God has made Jeremiah (1:18) "a fortified city" (ʿ*îr miḇṣār*, AV "defenced city") and "bronze [AV "brasen"] walls," so that he may speak fearlessly the word of God in the face of "all the tribes of the kingdoms of the north" (1:15). Zechariah perceived an eschatological vision of Jerusalem with no need for walls, for the Lord would be a "wall of fire" (*ḥômaṯ* '*ēš*) around the city (2:5 [MT 9]). The poem in Isa. 60 foresaw a time when war would cease in the Holy Land and the inhabitants would "call your walls Salvation [NEB "Deliverance"] and your gates Praise" (v. 18). So Nahum, to echo the thoughts of the psalmists, testified that "the Lord is . . . a stronghold [*mā*ʿ*ôz*, NEB "sure refuge"] in the day of trouble" (1:7).

B. In the NT. The writers of the NT were well acquainted with the cities, walls, and gates of their time, yet they employed fortification terminology very sparingly. Matthew recorded the statement of Jesus that "the powers of death" (AV "gates of hell") would not prevail against His Church (16:18), metaphorically referring to death occupying a fortress city under siege whose downfall was certain. Paul in 2 Cor. 10:3-5 wrote of a spiritual warfare in which "strongholds" (Gk. *ochýrōma*, which often in the LXX translates Heb. *miḇṣār*) are destroyed, implying siege warfare, but the more usual symbolism of Christian conflict is that of personal, hand-to-hand combat (cf. Eph. 6:10-17; 1 Thess. 5:8). In a spiritual conflict the Christian is to be on the offensive in the field rather than on the defensive within protective walls. Nevertheless, the book of Revelation (21:10-27) pictures the New Jerusalem fortified with a great wall and with twelve gates, marvelous in height and beauty. The visionary author was a child of his times and saw the eternal city in spiritualized terms of the walled cities of the first century. One important feature separated the heavenly from the earthly, however — the gates of the New Jerusalem would never close, for its sure defense was not in the walls but in the presence of the Lord God the Almighty and the Lamb.

Bibliography.–C. Herzog and M. Gichon, *Battles of the Bible* (1978); Y. Yadin, *Art of Warfare in Biblical Lands* (1963).

K. N. SCHOVILLE

FORTUNATUS fôr-to͞o-nä'-təs [Gk. *Phortounátos* < Lat. *Fortunatus*–'blessed,' 'fortunate']. Found only once in Scripture (1 Cor. 16:17). Fortunatus, with Stephanus and Achaius, was a member of the Corinthian church, whose presence at Ephesus refreshed the spirit of the apostle Paul. It is possible that these men carried the letter to Corinth (cf. the subscription of the TR).

FORTUNE [Heb. *gaḏ*] (Isa. 65:11); AV "troop," mg. GAD; NEB THE GOD OF FATE; **GOOD FORTUNE** [*K bāgāḏ, Q bā' gāḏ*] (Gen. 30:11); AV "a troop cometh"; NEB "good fortune has come." The different translations of Gen. 30:11 go back to variants in the Hebrew tradition. The *kethibh* reads literally "with fortune," thus "good fortune," "how propitious," etc., while the *qere* reads *bā' gāḏ*, "good fortune comes." (The AV's understanding of *gaḏ* in the sense of *g*ᵉ*ḏûḏ*, "raiding party," "troops," is based on popular wordplay in Gen. 49:19 [see S. R. Driver, *Expos.*, 2 (1885), 8f.].) The intention is to explain the origin of the name Gad (cf. E. A. Speiser, *Genesis* [*AB*, 1964], p. 229). The name Gad is also attested in the place names Baal-gad (Josh. 11:17; 12:7; 13:5) and Migdal-gad (Josh. 15:37).

In Isa. 65:11 Gad (Fortune) is parallel to the deity Meni (Destiny); thus Gad here may be the name of a specific deity. The reference is to the idolatrous practice of offering food to the gods (cf. R. de Vaux, *Ancient Israel* [Eng. tr. 1961], II, 413, 435; A. L. Oppenheim, *Ancient Mesopotamia* [1964], pp. 183-198).

Gad, or Fortune, was a West Semitic deity. Occurrences of the name, alone or in theophorous combination, are found in Punic, Nabatean, and Palmyrene texts, as well as those from Hatra. The word is also found in Palmyrene texts as a common noun meaning "fortune" or "destiny" (cf. Jean and Hoftijzer, p. 47; *IP*, pp. 126f.).

There is ambiguity about the gender of the deity. Jean and Hoftijzer refer to Gad as a goddess; yet the name is generally taken to be masculine. Meni, the other deity mentioned in Isa. 65:11, is also masculine in form, but is often equated with Manât, a goddess of fortune (cf. KD, *in loc.*). Both gods were apparently astral deities, as Gad is often identified with Jupiter and Meni with Venus.

G. Fohrer has suggested that Isa. 65:11 was composed in the 4th cent. B.C. when Israel came under the influence of the Nabateans. As a rule, he maintains, Gad was not the proper name of a specific god but was applied to various male and female deities in Syria-Palestine; it became the name of a specific deity in the 4th cent. B.C. among the Nabateans.

Bibliography.–C. F. Jean and J. Hoftijzer, *Dictionnaire des inscriptions sémitiques de l'ouest* (1965), p. 47; E. Sellin and G. Fohrer, *Intro. to the OT* (Eng. tr. 1968), p. 387; *TDOT,* II, *s.v.* "gadh" (Schunck); also comms. on Isaiah by T. K. Cheyne (1890), II, 117-19; G. Fohrer (1964), III, 264f.; J. Muilenberg (*IB,* 1956), pp. 751f.; C. Westermann (*OTL,* 1969), p. 405. A. F. CAMPBELL

FORTUNES [Heb. *šeḇûṯ, šeḇîṯ*] (e.g., Dt. 30:3; Ps. 14:7; 126:1, 4; Jer. 30:3, 18; Ezk. 29:14 etc.); AV CAPTIVITY; NEB also PROSPERITY. The phrase *hēšîḇ 'eṯ-šeḇûṯ* or *šāḇ 'eṯ-šeḇûṯ* occurs frequently, usually with God as its subject, and means to bring an end to captivity or imprisonment for debt, and thus to turn one's fortune for the better. Israel's fortunes will be restored (i.e., Israel will have material prosperity and forgiveness of sins) when the Lord brings the Israelites back from captivity to their homeland (e.g., Ezk. 39:25-29). Their return is contingent upon obedience to God (Jer. 29:12-14). Similarly, Job, who had been held captive by misfortune and disease, received again the status and possessions he had lost (Job 42:10).

FORTY [Heb. *'arbā'îm*; Gk. *tessarákonta*]. *See* NUMBER IV.

FORTY LASHES (1 Cor. 11:24). *See* PUNISHMENTS IV.A.

FORUM OF APPIUS (Acts 28:15). *See* APPIUS, FORUM OF.

FORWARD. This adverb implies an onward movement in time or space or in the conduct of affairs. It frequently modifies a verb, e.g., "go forward" (Ex. 14:15; 2 K. 20:9; etc.), "come forward" (e.g., Dt. 20:2). The Hebrew expression *lepānîm,* "forward," occurs in Jer. 7:24, while in Ezk. 1:9, 12; 10:22 the phrase *'el 'ēḇer pānāw* is rendered "straight forward." In Ezk. 39:22 *hāle'â,* "onward," denotes distance in time, while *ma'al,* "above," is used similarly in 1 S. 16:13; 30:25. The Greek particle *prós* occurs in such compound NT forms as *prosérchomai* (Mt. 8:5; 25:20; etc.), while *pró-* is found with *títhēmi* (Rom. 3:25) and *bállō* (Acts 19:33).

The AV also uses "forward, forwardness" in the sense of "eager" (e.g., 2 Cor. 8:10, 17; Gal. 2:10).

FOUL [Heb. *bā'aš*]; AV, NEB, STINK; [*bo'šâ*] (Job 31:40); AV COCKLE; NEB omits; [*zānaḥ*] (Isa. 19:6); AV "turn far away"; NEB STINK; [*piggûl*] (Ezk. 4:14); AV ABOMINABLE; NEB TAINTED; [*rāpaś*] NEB FOULING, TRAMPLE DOWN; [*be'ōš*] (Joel 2:20); AV STINK; NEB STENCH; [Gk. *aischrología*] (Col. 3:8); AV, NEB, FILTHY; [*kakós*] (Rev. 16:2); AV NOISOME; [*akáthartos*] (Rev. 16:13; 18:2); AV also UNCLEAN; NEB also UNCLEAN.

In the OT various things "became foul" (Heb. *bā'aš*): the Nile because of the dead fish (Ex. 7:18, 21), the manna that was left until the following morning in the wilderness (Ex. 16:20; cf. v. 24), and the wounds of the psalmist (Ps. 38:5 [MT 6]; cf. Joel 2:20; Job 31:40; Isa. 19:6). Meat from the peace offering sacrifice becomes "abominable" or "tainted" (*piggûl*) if not eaten within a specified time (Lev. 7:18; 19:7), and it is this "foul flesh" that Ezekiel claims had never "come into my mouth" (4:14). Making water muddy and thus undrinkable (*rāpaś*) by trampling through it is mentioned in Ezk. 32:2 and 34:18.

"Foul talk" (*aischrología,* from *aischýnō,* "shame" or "bring shame" in classical Greek) is condemned by Paul. This term is taken to mean "evil speech in the sense of obscene speech" (Bauer, rev., p. 25), or beyond that, "every kind of abusive language" (Lohse, p. 140; cf. Lightfoot, p. 214). "Foul and evil sores" (*hélkos kakós kai ponērós*) erupt upon the people who bear the mark of the beast and worship it in Rev. 16:2 (cf. Ex. 9:10; Dt. 28:27, 35; Job 2:7).

"Foul spirits" are mentioned twice in Revelation, once as "three foul spirits like frogs" (16:13) and once as inhabitants of fallen Babylon (18:2). *Pneúma akátharta* ("foul spirits") is used in Matthew, Mark, Luke, Acts, and Revelation to denote demons. In this moral sense, then, it means "evil spirits" (cf. Rev. 16:14; Mt. 10:1; Mk. 1:26; etc.). The reference to frogs in 16:13 may be an allusion to the plague in Ex. 8:1-7 and Ps. 78:45; and thus the "spirits" (or "breath") issuing from the mouth of the dragon, the beast, and the false prophet have the quality of evil, being "froglike," like a plague (Barclay, p. 169). These three spirits deceive (cf. Rev. 13:14) the "kings of the whole world" into waging battle against the Lord Almighty, a battle which leads to their doom.

In Rev. 18:2 "foul spirit" is again to be seen in its moral sense of being "evil." To say that the fallen Babylon is a "haunt of every foul and hateful bird" is using the term in its cultic sense, meaning "that which may not be brought into contact with the divinity" (Bauer, rev., p. 29). The double usage of *akáthartos* in this verse provides a contrast to the holy city which nothing unclean can enter (21:27). The context of 18:2 is the angelic proclamation of the doom of Babylon and is in the form of other "Doom Songs" found often in the prophetic literature (Isa. 13:19-22; 34:11-15; Jer. 50:39; 51:37; Zeph. 2:15) that portray unclean birds and wild beasts dwelling in the ruins of once great cities.

Bibliography.–W. Barclay, *Revelation of John* (1961), II; J. B. Lightfoot, *St. Paul's Epistle to the Colossians and Philemon* (1957); E. Lohse, *Colossians and Philemon* (Eng. tr., *Hermeneia,* 1971). D. K. MCKIM

FOUND [Heb. *yāsaḏ*] (e.g., Ps. 24:2; 78:69; 89:11 [MT 12]; 119:152; Prov. 3:19; Isa. 14:32; Zec. 12:1); AV also ESTABLISH, ORDAIN, "lay the foundation"; NEB also "first beginnings" (Ex. 9:18), "rebuke" (Ps. 8:2 [MT 3]), FIX, ARCH (Am. 9:6), etc.; [*yesûḏâ*] (Ps. 87:1); AV, NEB, FOUNDATION; [*kûn*] (Hab. 2:12); AV STABLISH; [Gk. *themelióō*] (Mt. 7:25); NEB FOUNDATIONS. The Hebrew cosmogony saw the world as resting on foundations. The psalmist, writing against a background of ancient Near Eastern creation myths, poetically depicts Yahweh as defeating the chaotic monsters of the DEEP (*see also* CHAOS) and establishing firm foundations for an ordered world (cf. Gen. 1:2, 9f.; Ps. 89:10-12 [MT 11-13]; 104:5f.; etc.). The author of Prov. 3:19 says that it was by wisdom that God founded the world, implying that man's life should be directed by this same wisdom in order that he might live in harmony with the world around him.

See also FOUNDATION. N. J. O.

FOUNDATION. ***I. In the OT.***–Hebrew *yāsaḏ* originally meant "support, lean against, firm up," thus by extension more commonly "found, establish, lay the foundation of." It appears most frequently in the literal sense in connection with the construction of buildings or cities (esp. the first and second temples in Jerusalem, e.g., 1 K. 5:17 [MT 31]; 6:37; Ezr. 3:6, 10-12; Isa. 44:28; Hag. 2:18; Zec. 4:9; 8:9; for cities cf. Josh. 6:26; 1 K. 16:34; Isa.

54:11) but also occasionally in the cosmological imagery of Yahweh establishing or laying the foundations of the earth (e.g., Ps. 102:25 [MT 26]; Isa. 51:13, 16). The RSV translates this verb with either active or passive variants of "lay (=set) the foundation(s) of" in nearly half its OT occurrences.

Several substantives are cognates of *yāsaḏ*. *Yᵉsôḏ*, "foundation," may refer to the foundation of a city wall (Mic. 1:6; Ps. 137:7), of Zion (Lam. 4:11), of one of the temple gates (known as the "Gate of the Foundation," 2 Ch. 23:5), or of a defense wall (fig. for false prophecies, Ezk. 13:24). Figuratively, it represents a national government (the "foundations" of Egypt, Ezk. 30:4), and human origins and human life (Job 4:19; 22:16).

Hebrew *mûsāḏ* occurs twice in the OT: as a figurative cornerstone in Zion in Isa. 28:16, and as the foundation of the Solomonic temple in 2 Ch. 8:16. Heb. *mûsāḏâ*, "foundation," occurs in Ezekiel's description of his temple vision (*Q*, Ezk. 41:8). *Môsāḏôṯ*, "foundations," is usually cosmological in meaning: the foundations of the earth (e.g., Ps. 82:5; Isa. 24:18; Mic. 6:2), of the world (2 S. 22:16; Ps. 18:15 [MT 16]), of the heavens (2 S. 22:8 par. Ps. 18:7 [MT 8]), and of the mountains (Dt. 32:22). It is also used temporally ("from the foundations of the earth," Isa. 40:21) and literally (for the cities of Judah, Isa. 58:12; and for Babylon, Jer. 51:26). *Massaḏ*, "foundation," occurs only in 1 K. 7:9.

Hebrew *māḵôn*, "fixed place," "site" (< *kûn*, "be firm," "make firm," "fix," "establish") is three times translated "foundation(s)." In Ps. 104:5 the phrase *yāsaḏ ʾereṣ ʿal-mᵉḵôneyhā* is rendered, "Thou didst set the earth on its foundations." Both of the other occurrences have an ethical connotation and appear in the phrase "righteousness and justice are the foundation of thy/his throne" (Ps. 89:14 [MT 15]; 97:2). In Ps. 11:3 the plural of *šaṯ* (< *šîṯ*, "set, put, constitute") is usually understood figuratively for the established laws of the land. The obscure first word in the phrase *ʾammôṯ hassippîm*, "foundations of the thresholds," in Isa. 6:4 is rendered largely from context, for its etymology is uncertain.

The plural of the Aram. *ʾuššayyāʾ*, "foundation," occurs twice in the Aramaic portion of Ezra (4:12; 5:16). In the context of the rebuilding of Jerusalem the first instance refers to the city itself, the second to the reconstructed temple.

II. In the NT.–The NT has two terms that are translated "foundations": Gk. *themélios* (sixteen times) and *katabolḗ* (ten times). The essential meaning of *themélios* is the "basic stone" or "foundation". Its only NT occurrence in a literal sense is in Acts 16:26, where the earthquake shakes the foundations of the Philippian prison, allowing Paul and Silas to escape. The other occurrences are figurative. Jesus Christ Himself is the foundation for all mission work and for the new life of the Church as the household of God (1 Cor. 3:10-12; Rom. 15:20). Indeed, He is the chief cornerstone that anchors the foundation of the apostles and prophets (Eph. 2:20) or of the apostolic teaching (2 Tim. 2:19). In He. 6:1 "foundation" is figurative for elementary doctrines, and in 1 Tim. 6:19 a reservoir of good and generous deeds is said to be "a good foundation for the future."

While *themélios* refers to city-wall foundations in Rev. 21:14, 19, and to city foundations in He. 11:10, that the city referred to in each case is the heavenly city (the New Jerusalem) indicates the metaphorical (and ecclesiological) nature of these passages. Similarly, in Lk. 6:48f. the house built with or without foundations is symbolic of a faithful or unfaithful life style; cf. Lk. 14:29 where the foundations are laid for a tower that is itself a figure for the life of commitment to Christ.

Greek *katabolḗ*, lit. "casting down, laying down," and thus "foundation," occurs ten times in the NT in the phrase *apó/pró katabolḗs kósmou*, "from/before the foundation of the world." (The only other appearance of this NT term is in the expression *eis katabolḗn spérmatos*, a technical term for the "casting or sowing of seed" [see *TDNT*, III, 621], in He. 11:11 [RSV "conceive"].) In most cases the phrase *apó/pró katabolḗs kósmou* has a temporal sense, and usually occurs within the context of salvation-history (Mt. 13:35; here *katabolḗ* is used absolutely without *kósmou* in B while the other codices have *kósmou*; see Aland, p. 50; Metzger, pp. 33f.; Lk. 11:50; He. 4:3; 9:26). Rev. 13:8 and 17:8 refer to those dwellers of earth "whose names have not been written in the book of life from the foundation of the world." These passages together with Mt. 25:34 stress the eternal verity of God's salvation plan. The pretemporal existence of God's love for Jesus (Jn. 17:24), His pretemporal election (1 Pet. 1:20), and as well the pretemporal election of believers in Christ (Eph. 1:4), are all expressed by the same phrase, *pró katabolḗs kósmou*.

See also FOUND.

Bibliography.–K. Aland, *et al.*, eds., *Greek NT* (2nd ed. 1968); B. M. Metzger, *Textual Comm. on the Greek NT* (1971); *TDNT*, III, *s.v.* καταβολή (F. Hauck).

D. G. BURKE

FOUNDATION, GATE OF [Heb. *šaʿar haysôḏ*] (2 Ch. 23:5). A gate in Jerusalem mentioned in connection with the plot to assassinate Athaliah. Exactly what gate is meant is problematic since the LXX has "middle [Gk. *mésos*] gate" (cf. Jer. 39:3) instead of "foundation," and the parallel passage in 2 K. 11:6 reads "the gate Sur" (Heb. *šaʿar sûr*).

FOUNDER (AV Jgs. 17:4; Jer. 6:29; 10:9, 14; 51:17). *See* GOLDSMITH; SILVERSMITH.

FOUNTAIN [Heb. *ʾāpîq*] (Ezk. 34:13); AV RIVER; NEB STREAM; [*mabbû(a)ʿ*] (Eccl. 12:6); NEB SPRING; [*maʿyān*] (e.g., Gen. 7:11; 8:2; Cant. 4:12, 15); NEB also SPRING, WELL; [*māqôr*]; AV also SPRING, WELL, WELL SPRING; NEB also ASSEMBLE, DISCHARGE, SPRING, WATERS, WELL; [*ʿayin*–'eye'] (Dt. 8:7; 33:28; 1 S. 29:1; Neh. 2:14; 3:15; 12:37; Prov. 8:28); NEB also SPRING, TRIBE, EN-HAROD; [Gk. *pēgḗ*] (Rev. 8:10; 14:7; 16:4; 21:6); NEB also SPRING, WATER-SPRING.

These OT and NT terms for a spring or source of water are used in various figurative senses. In eschatological visions a fountain is given as a sign of the Lord's favor (Isa. 41:18; Joel 3:18 [MT 4:18]), while dry fountains are described as a sign of His disapproval. The term *māqôr* is used in a variety of ways. (1) It is used for the source of a woman's menstrual discharge (Lev. 20:18). (2) It is also used for the source of life (Ps. 36:9 [MT 10]; Prov. 5:18), the mouth of the righteous (Prov. 10:11), the teaching of the wise (Prov. 13:14), the fear of the Lord (14:27), and wisdom (16:22; 18:4). (3) The Lord is called the fountain of Israel (Ps. 68:26 [MT 27]) and of living waters (Jer. 2:13; 17:13). (4) The eyes are a fountain of tears (Jer. 9:1). (5) The righteous giving way to the wicked is like a polluted fountain (Prov. 25:26); and (6) a source of true cleansing will become available in the final days (Zec. 13:1).

In 1 S. 29:1 the NEB, following the LXX reading *Aendōr*, renders "En-harod." In Dt. 33:28 "fountain of Jacob" means Jacob's descendants (cf. NEB "tribe").

For "fountains of the . . . deep" (Gen. 7:11) *see* FLOOD (GENESIS) I.C.

J. R. PRICE

FOUNTAIN GATE. *See* JERUSALEM VI.

FOUR; FOUR HUNDRED; FOUR THOUSAND; FOURTEEN; FOURTH PART. *See* NUMBER.

FOURFOLD [Heb. *'arba'tāyim* (2 S. 12:6); Gk. *tetraploún* (Lk. 19:8)]. Fourfold the amount stolen was the restoration that Roman law required of a thief. This was the extreme penalty the Jewish law imposed for destructive robbery (Ex. 22:1 [MT 21:37]). In some cases double the amount was to be restored (Ex. 22:4, 7 [MT 3, 6]); in others, a fifth of its value was added to the thing restored (Lev. 6:5 [MT 5:24]).

FOURSCORE [Heb. *šᵉmōnîm*; Gk. *ogdoḗkonta*] (Ps. 90:10). In modern versions, as in Hebrew and Greek, simply "eighty."

FOURSQUARE [pual part. of Heb. *rb'* (Ezk. 40:47); Gk. *tetrágōnos* (Rev. 21:16)]. Foursquare, meaning equal in length and breadth, is derived in both Hebrew and Greek from the word "four," i.e., having four equal sides. In some modern translations, e.g., NEB, "foursquare" has become, following contemporary usage, simply "square."

FOWL [Heb. *'ôp, ṣippôr, barburîm*]. Since the 16th cent. the word "fowl" has undergone a change in meaning. Then it meant any winged animal, domesticated or wild. Since then its meaning has been restricted to domesticated birds, and "birds" replaced "fowls." Accordingly, the RSV has retained only three of the eighty-five AV references to "fowls" and translated most other instances as "birds." The RSV also uses "winged insect," "winged things" (Dt. 14:20; Ps. 78:27), or "birds of prey" (e.g., Gen. 15:11; Job 28:7; Isa. 18:6; *see* BIRDS OF PREY) for AV "fowl."

It is not certain when the domesticated bird was introduced into Palestine. The "fatted fowl" (Heb. *barburîm 'ᵃḇûsîm*) of 1 K. 4:23 (MT 5:3) has been a subject of

A housemaid brings a fowl to the cook and baker in a reconstruction of Egyptian wall paintings (Royal Ontario Museum, Toronto)

much debate but with little conclusive evidence (cf. J. Gray, comm. on Kings [*OTL*, 2nd rev. ed. 1970], p. 143). These birds could have been guineas or pigeons. The young of ostriches were delicious food, and no doubt when Solomon's ships brought peafowl they also brought word that they were a delicacy for a king's table. The domesticated fowl were not common early in Palestine, but they may have been brought by Solomon with other imports from the East.

If this is a plausible assumption, then the RSV "fowls" (Heb. *ṣippôr*, < *ṣāpar*, "twitter, chirp") in Neh. 5:18 is an appropriate rendering. According to this translation (cf. NEB "fowls") fowl was part of the Jews' diet while Nehemiah was governor (*ca.* 430 B.C.). Lev. 7:26 forbids the eating of the blood of fowls or animals, probably because the life of the animal was thought to be (symbol-

Egyptians wearing the collar necklaces of royalty hurl throwsticks, handed to them by slaves, at wild fowl. Wall painting from the tomb of Nakht at Thebes (28th Dynasty) (Metropolitan Museum of Art, photograph by Egyptian Expedition)

ized) in the blood (cf. Gen. 9:4; Lev. 17:10-14; Dt. 12:23-25).
See also BIRDS; CHICKEN.

W. L. WALKER R. W. V.

FOWL, FATTED [Heb. *barburîm ʾᵃḇûsîm*] (1 K. 4:23). *See* BIRDS IV; FOWL.

FOWLER foul'ər [Heb. *yāqôš, yāqûš, yôqēš*]. A bird-catcher. The fowler was very common in the ancient Near East. In Egypt, e.g., "fowling was one of the great amusements of all classes" (J. G. Wilkinson, *Manners and Customs of the Ancient Egyptians* [rev. ed. 1878], I, 234); and in Israel there were both professionals and amateurs. The fowlers supplied the demand for birds used as caged pets, in sacrifice, and for food.

Many methods of birdcatching were used; one was the bow and sling; the net, of which there were at least four kinds, was probably the most common (Prov. 1:17; Hos. 7:12; Ezk. 12:13; 17:20; 32:3). In addition there were snares, also very common; springy twigs; clap-boards; and decoy birds (cf. Sir. 11:30, "like a decoy partridge in a cage, so is the mind of a proud man"), whose cry attracted others, which were then caught with the aid of birdlime, a sticky substance smeared on a stick to which the birds adhered. Another common piece of equipment was the throwstick. This was a small piece of wood thrown at the legs of birds; it was especially effective when thrown into flocks of ground birds. Jeremiah mentions the crates into which birds were put (5:27).

The five references to the fowler in the OT have a metaphorical sense. Deliverance from evil plans is promised (Ps. 91:3); the joy of the freed person is compared to the delight of the escaped bird (Ps. 124:7). A man must free himself from a pledge to a neighbor just as the bird struggles to escape from the snare of the fowler (Prov. 6:5). The work of wicked men in ensnaring their fellows is compared to the work of the fowler (Jer. 5:26); the prophet is in constant danger of being trapped: "a fowler's snare is on all his ways" (Hos. 9:8).

See also HUNTING.

J. A. BALCHIN

FOX [Heb. *šûʿāl*; cf. Arab. *thaʿlab* (Jgs. 15:4; Neh. 4:3; Cant. 2:15; Ezk. 13:4); Gk. *alṓpēx* (Mt. 8:20; Lk. 9:58; 13:32)]; NEB also JACKAL. In Ps. 63:10 (MT 11) and Lam. 5:18 the RSV and NEB read "jackal" for Heb. *šûʿāl* (AV "fox"); it is probable that "jackals" should also be used in Jgs. 15:4, since they were much more common than foxes.

In Cant. 2:15 there is an allusion to the fondness of the fox for grapes, while Mt. 8:20; Lk. 9:58 indicate the preference of the *Canidae* for a burrow as a lair. If they do not actually excavate these themselves, they will often take over the burrow of another animal such as the badger. The use of "fox" in reference to Herod (Lk. 13:32) indicated his low cunning and comparative worthlessness (cf. Neh. 4:3 for the insignificance of this animal). Ezekiel compared Israel's prophets to foxes; they care for themselves but show little concern for Israel's relation to God (13:4f.).

R. K. H.

FRACTURE [Heb. *šeḇer*] (Lev. 24:20); AV BREACH. The Hebrew noun comes from the verb *šāḇar*, to "break"; cf. "injury," Lev. 21:19. The law of personal retribution for both the native Israelite and the resident alien was to be the *lex talionis*. The loss of a tooth or the breaking of an arm, e.g., would be punished, respectively, by the loss of a tooth or a fractured arm in the body of the assailant — no less and also no more.

FRAGMENTS. The term "fragments" occurs four times in the RSV. In Isa. 30:14 the plural of Heb. *mᵉḵittâ* (a hapax legomenon) denotes the smashed pieces of an earthenware jar, collectively a symbol of effective divine judgment. The cognate verb (a form of which also occurs in this

A fowler hidden by a blind tugs a rope to trap marsh birds in a cagelike net. Relief from the tomb of Kagemni (6th Dynasty, 2350-2200 B.C.) at Saqqârah (Service des musées, Cairo; picture Lehnert and Landrock)

verse), is *kāṯaṯ,* "beat, smash." Again in Am. 6:11 divine judgment is symbolized by destruction; in this instance the picture is of houses reduced (perhaps by earthquake) to rubble, regardless of their size. The translation of *rᵉsîsîm* is not entirely certain, but it is usually rendered "fragments" in the light of postbiblical Heb. *rāsas,* meaning "break." Earthquake imagery is reinforced by the fact that *rᵉsîsîm* stands in poetic parallelism with *bᵉqîʿîm,* "cracks, fissures" (AV "breaches"; cf. Isa. 22:9).

In the NT the plural of Gk. *klásma,* "fragment, piece, crumb (of bread)," occurs twice in John's narration of the feeding of the five thousand (6:12f.). In the Synoptic parallels *klásma* is consistently translated as "broken pieces" (Mt. 14:20 par.; cf. Mt. 15:37 par.). (In the LXX of Ezk. 13:19 *klásma* also refers to scraps of bread.) The cognate noun *klásis* (Lk. 24:35; Acts 2:42) and the cognate verb *kláō* are likewise used in the NT only for the breaking of bread. The custom in the ancient Near East was not to cut bread for eating but to break it into pieces. It is significant that *klásma* is the term used in Did. 9:3f. for the eucharistic bread. (For a detailed comparison of the Didache's eucharistic prayer over the bread and the Johannine feeding narrative, see C. F. D. Moule, *JTS,* 6 [1955], 240-43.)

See also BREAD V.

See *TDNT,* III, *s.v.* κλάω (Behm). D. G. BURKE

FRAGRANCE [Heb. *rê(a)ḥ*] (Cant. 1:12; 2:13; 4:10; 7:13; Hos. 14:6); AV SMELL; NEB SCENT, SWEETER, PERFUME, FRAGRANT; [*beśem*] (Cant. 4:16; 5:13); AV SPICES; NEB PERFUMES; [*zēḵer*–'mention, memorial'] (Hos. 14:7); AV SCENT; NEB "be famous as"; [*ʾᵃḇāqâ*] ("fragrant powders," Cant. 3:6); [Gk. *osmḗ*] (Jn. 12:3; 2 Cor. 2:14, 16); AV ODOUR, SAVOUR; **FRAGRANT INCENSE** [Heb. *qᵉṭōreṯ sammîm*] (e.g., Ex. 25:6; 30:7; Lev. 4:7; Nu. 4:16); AV SWEET INCENSE; **FRAGRANT** [Gk. *euodía*] (Eph. 5:2; Phil. 4:18). AV SWEET-SMELLING, ODOUR. The RSV and NEB supply "fragrant" in Ps. 45:8 (MT 9) (AV "smell"). The difficult text of Cant. 1:3a is perhaps best understood as parallel to v. 2b: "For your love is better than wine, (better) than the fragrance [*rē(a)ḥ*] of your precious oil" (see M. Pope, comm. on Cant. [*AB,* 1977], *in loc.*; cf. NEB mg.).

Egyptian ladies present fragrant incense in a relief from the tomb of Meserhat, high priest under Thutmose I (*ca.* 1526-1512 B.C.) (Service des musées, Cairo; picture Lehnert and Landrock)

The love of the lover and the beloved in Canticles makes them sensitive to the fragrance of the flowers of the garden (2:13; 7:13) and of the oils they are wearing (1:12; 4:10) to the extent that the beloved is perceived in metaphors of fragrance. Likewise, when the Lord promises to heal the faithlessness of Israel, the resultant fellowship between the Lord and His people will be as a pleasant garden (Hos. 14:6f.). In the NT the love and adoration of Mary for the Lord Jesus is symbolized in the aroma of costly ointment that filled the house (Jn. 12:3). Paul's reference (2 Cor. 2:14, 16), however, is not to the fragrance of love but to the odor of incense burned by the priests in the triumphal procession of a conqueror, an odor that was highly agreeable to the victors but full of foreboding to the captives (*see* TRIUMPH).

Fragrant incense was manufactured by blending stacte, onycha, galbanum, frankincense, and a seasoning of salt (Ex. 30:34-38). Used for sacred purposes only, it was to be burned on the altar located before the curtain veiling the holy of holies.

See also INCENSE; ODOR; OINTMENT; PERFUME.

G. WYPER

FRAME. Several different and unrelated Hebrew words are rendered by the word "frame" in the RSV.

(1) [Heb. *qereš*] (e.g., Ex. 26:15-29; 35:11; 36:20-34); AV also BOARD; NEB PLANK. The individual vertical panels of the wooden framework over which the curtains of the tabernacle were spread. Scholarly opinion is divided as to whether the *qᵉrāšîm* were open framelike panels that would make the inner curtain visible from within the tent (reflected in the RSV's translation) or solid boards or planks (reflected in the translation of the AV and NEB). *See* TABERNACLE.

(2) [Heb. *misgereṯ*] (Ex. 25:25, 27; 37:12, 14; 2 K. 16:17); AV BORDER; NEB RIM, etc. A brace that gave support to the legs of the table for the bread of the Presence. According to the representation of the table taken from Herod's temple on the Arch of Titus in Rome, the frame was located about halfway between the top and bottom of the legs. In 2 K. 16:17 *misgereṯ* refers to a cross section of the stands that support the lavers in the temple (*see* LAVER).

(3) [Heb. *šālāḇ*–'cross-bar'] (1 K. 7:28); AV LEDGES. The cross sections of the stands that support the lavers in the temple.

(4) [Heb. *šeqep, šᵉqûp*] (1 K. 6:4; 7:4); AV LIGHT, WINDOW; NEB also EMBRASURES. The enclosing framework of windows and doors.

(5) [Heb. *môṭ*] (Nu. 4:10, 12); AV BAR; NEB POLE. The apparatus for carrying the lamps and utensils of the tabernacle.

(6) [Heb. *ʿēreḵ*] (Job 41:12 [MT 4]); AV PROPORTION; [*ʿeṣem*] (Ps. 139:15); AV SUBSTANCE; NEB BODY; [*yēṣer*] (Ps. 103:14); NEB "how we were made." In these passages "frame" refers to the human body.

(7) [Heb. *yāṣar*] (Ps. 94:20); NEB CONTRIVE; [*ṣāmaḏ*] (Ps. 50:19); NEB HARNESS. As a verb, "frame" is used figuratively. In Ps. 94:20, the wicked rulers frame mischief by statute, and in Ps. 50:19, the tongue of the wicked is said to frame deceit. E. W. CONRAD

FRANKINCENSE [Heb. *l^eḇōnâ*; Gk. *líbanos* (Mt. 2:11; Rev. 18:13)]; AV, NEB, also INCENSE. A substance referred to in, e.g., Ex. 30:34; Lev. 2:1f., 15f.; Neh. 13:5, 9; Isa. 66:3. The Hebrew term, from a root meaning "whiteness," refers to the milky color of the fresh juice. The English term comes from the Old French *franc encens*, "pure incense."

The references are to the true frankincense, derived from three species of the genus *Boswellia: B. carterii, B. papyrifera*, and *B. thurifera*. These trees grow in southern Arabia, India, and elsewhere and are related to the terebinth and the shrubs yielding balsam and myrrh. The gum is exuded from the incised bark in pale glittering drops. It is bitter in flavor and has a strong balsamic odor when heated. It was highly valued by the Egyptians for fumigation and embalming and was used ceremonially among the Hebrews. A refined variety was presented with the showbread (Lev. 24:7). It was often associated with myrrh (Cant. 3:6; 4:6) and was offered to the infant Jesus (Mt. 2:11).

See also INCENSE. R. K. H.

FRANKLY. Occurs once in the AV in the archaic sense of "freely," "graciously," as a partial translation of Gk. *charízomai*, "forgive" (Lk. 7:42, NEB "let off," NIV "cancel the debt").

FRAUD [Heb. *mirmâ*] (Ps. 55:11 [MT 12]; Zeph. 1:9); AV GUILE, DECEIT; NEB also SPITE; [Gk. *plánē*–'wandering'] (Mt. 27:64); AV ERROR; NEB DECEPTION; [*aposteréō*] (Jas. 5:4); NEB "(wages) never paid"; **DEFRAUD** [Heb. *ʿāšaq*] (1 S. 12:3f.); NEB WRONGED; [Gk. *aposteréō*] (Mk. 10:19; 1 Cor. 6:7f.); NEB ROB; [Gk. *sykophantéō*] (Lk. 19:8); AV FALSE ACCUSATION; NEB CHEATED. An act of deceit, treachery, extortion, or robbery in which something is taken unjustly from someone to whom it rightfully belongs.

Fraud was a sin with which Samuel as judge could not be charged (1 S. 12:3f.); but this was one of the sins for which the prophets later — under the kings — arraigned Israel (Zeph. 1:9). Paul charged the Corinthian Christians with defrauding even their own Christian brothers; and James accused the rich of robbing the workers of their wages. Zacchaeus promised to restore fourfold for any extortion of which he was guilty (Lk. 19:8). The term *plánē* is used in the Epistles especially of the error or delusion of the ungodly, in radical contrast to the truth of God (cf. Rom. 1:27; Eph. 4:14; 2 Thess. 2:11; 2 Pet. 2:18; 1 Jn. 4:6; *see* ERR, ERROR). R. J. HUGHES, III

FRAY. The AV translation of the hiphil of Heb. *ḥāraḏ*, "make afraid," in the archaic sense of "scare, frighten away" (Dt. 28:26; Jer. 7:33; Zec. 1:21 [MT 2:4]; cf. RSV "frighten," "terrify").

FRECKLED SPOT (Lev. 13:39, AV). *See* DISEASE III.I; TETTER.

FREE; FREEDOM. *See* CHOOSE; LIBERTY; WILL.

FREE WOMAN [Gk. *eleuthéra*] (Gal. 4:22f., 30f.); NEB also FREEBORN WIFE. In vv. 22f., 30 it refers to Sarah, the free woman and true wife of Abraham, in contrast with Hagar, the Egyptian slave who became his concubine (Gen. 16:1-6). In v. 31 the term is applied metaphorically to the Christians who are the children of the promise, of freedom, of the spirit, the children of the free woman, in contrast with the Jews who are the children of the letter, of bondage, of the slave woman.

FREEDMAN [Gk. *apeleútheros*] (1 Cor. 7:22). The Greek term, denoting one who was born a slave and has received freedom, is used only once in the NT. The freedom referred to here is spiritual freedom: he who was in bondage to sin has been presented with spiritual freedom by the Lord. This new freedom does not involve autonomy, however, but slavery to one's Lord (v. 22b).

See also LIBERTY; SLAVE.

FREEDMEN, SYNAGOGUE OF THE. According to Acts 6:9, Stephen incurred hostility from different groups, including members of a "synagogue of freedmen." The Greek word *libertínos* is Luke's transliteration of the Latin *libertinus*, which in turn appears in the older English versions as "libertine." The loanword means people who had been manumitted (Chantraine, p. 1 n. 2).

It was customary in antiquity for people of similar backgrounds and interests to form clubs or associations, often with a component of religious ceremony. The so-called synagogue of freedmen might well have owed its origin to Jews who had been taken as prisoners of war to Rome in the time of Pompey (63 B.C.). After their liberation they formed a colony on the banks of the Tiber (Philo *De legatione ad Gaium* 155). Tacitus relates that the Senate decreed (A.D. 19) that a number of Jewish freedmen should be transported to Sardinia and that the rest should leave Italy, unless they renounced, before a certain day, their profane customs (*Ann.* ii.85; cf. Josephus *Ant.* xvii.3.5; *HJP* II/2, 275f.). Many would naturally have sought refuge in Jerusalem and formed a synagogue there. Deissmann, however, correctly cautions against ready identification of the meeting place of this group with the building referred to in an inscription predating A.D. 70 (*LAE*, pp. 439-441; cf. *BC*, IV, 67f.). Similarly, Jackson and Lake (*BC*, IV, 67) reject G. B. de Rossi's attempt to interpret *CIL*, IV, 117 as a reference to an alleged synagogue of freedmen in Pompeii.

In large commercial and religious centers it was not uncommon for tradespeople to form or join associations that catered to citizens of specific cities, such as Cyrene and Alexandria (cf. Poland, *passim*). Memberships might range from a dozen to thirty or more, and it is highly probable that Luke means to designate the Cyrenians and Alexandrians as constituting two other synagogues (on Jews in Cyrene, cf. *HJP* II/2, 245f.; Safrai-Stern, I, 487-89; on Alexandrian Jews, cf. *HJP* II/2, 226-230; *HJP*[2] II, 445 n. 80).

Linguistic considerations also substantiate the foregoing interpretation. Throughout his twofold work Luke is at pains to avoid terms that require translation. Apart from Acts 4:36 (Barnabas = Son of Exhortation) and 13:8 (on the significance of Elymas' function in the narrative), 6:9 contains the only instance of Luke's overt concern over a foreign term. Precisely because the synagogue in question bore a Latin name, Luke did not use the Greek term *apeleútheros*; he alerted his auditors to the datum by using the qualification *legoménē* ("as it is termed"). Also, the application, for the sake of brevity, of the term *synagōgḗ* to two more groups, Cyrenians and Alexandrians, would have been quite acceptable. Indeed, the addition of a qualifying phrase, e.g., "and synagogues of," could have been taken as an insult to his auditors' intelligence. Moreover, in the three other instances in Acts (11:20; 15:24; 17:4),

Luke's use of *tines ek* consistently refers to defined groups. Conversely, Luke's use of the phrase *tines (tṓn) apó . . .* , which occurs only two other times in Acts in connection with geographical point of origin (10:23; 24:19), suggests that in 6:9b Luke thought primarily of people's shift in locale rather than of societal factors. In brief, the people from Cilicia and Asia sympathized with the members of the aforementioned synagogues.

Luke's overall literary interests are a primary factor in his choice of geographical terms at 6:9. In a general way he displays Stephen as a victim of international hostility from followers of Moses. The specific reference to Cyrene anticipates 11:20 and 13:1, which show the reversal of the attitude cited at 6:9. Similarly 18:24 displays Apollos as a converted Jew from Alexandria. Since Tarsus was the capital of Cilicia, with a large Jewish population, Luke's reference to the province would provide a backdrop for Paul's emphasis on his Jewishness (22:3; on the Jewish population, cf. Ramsay, 169-186). Despite the hostility generated in "Asia," 19:10 informs Luke's public that Jews and non-Jews of all Asia are hearing God's word (on Asian Jews, cf. *HJP* II/2, 226).

The exegetical literature on Acts 6:9 has, in general, failed to give adequate consideration to the literary and linguistic-semantic factors, and commentators for the most part ignore epigraphical evidence, as cited by Poland (cf. pp. 115, 125, 130f.), relating to clubs and associations (but see *HJP* II/2, 244-251). Among the older commentators, Calvin concluded that Luke referred to one synagogue (so also Beza, Bengel, and later Haenchen and Conzelmann); Wendt and Zahn, followed by Strathmann, allotted one to the three mentioned in v. 9a and one to the Cilicians and Asians; Alford apportioned three: one to the Freedmen, one to the Cyrenians and Alexandrians, and one to the Cilicians and Asians; B. Weiss, and Schürer (*HJP*², II, 76, 428. n. 8), designated five. In view of Luke's carefully chosen diction and syntax, Beza's conjectural emendation *Libystinōn,* with support from an Armenian catena (on Chrysostom's authority, Goodspeed, p. 128), is to be rejected (cf. Jackson and Lake, *BC,* III, 58).

Bibliography.–H. Chantraine, *Freigelassene und Sklaven im Dienst der Römischen Kaiser* (1967); A. Deissmann, *LAE*; E. J. Goodspeed, *Problems of NT Translation* (1945); F. J. Foakes Jackson and K. Lake, *BC,* III (1926); IV (1933); Pauly-Wissowa, XIII/1, 104-110; F. Poland, *Geschichte des Griechischen Vereinswesens* (1909); W. Ramsay, *The Cities of St. Paul* (1907); S. Safrai and M. Stern, *The Jewish People in the First Century,* I (1974); *TDNT,* IV, *s.v.* Λιβεϱτῖνοι (H. Strathmann).

F. W. DANKER

FREELY. The term occurs in three senses.

(1) The obsolete sense of "gratis, for nothing," in the AV of Nu. 11:5 (Heb. *ḥinnām*); Mt. 10:8 (Gk. *dōréan*); Rom. 3:24; 2 Cor. 11:7; Rev. 21:6; 22:17.

(2) "Willingly, spontaneously" for Heb. *nāḏaḇ* ("volunteer, offer voluntarily") in 1 Ch. 29:9, 17; Ezr. 1:6; 7:13, 15; Ps. 110:3; *n*ᵉ*ḏāḇâ* ("voluntary gift") in Hos. 14:4.

(3) "Without hindrance or restraint" in Gen. 2:16 and 1 S. 14:30 ("eat freely," Heb. *'āḵōl 'āḵal*); Dt. 15:10 ("give freely," Heb. *nāṯōn nāṯan*); 1 Ch. 12:1 ("not move about freely," Heb. *'āṣar*); Ps. 112:9 and Prov. 11:24 ("distribute or give freely," Heb. *pāzar*); Mk. 1:45 ("talk freely," Gk. *kēr̄ýssō pollá*); Jn. 2:10 ("drink freely," Gk. *methýō*); Acts 26:26 ("speak freely," Gk. *parrhēsiázomai*); Eph. 1:6 ("freely bestow," Gk. *charitóō*). W. L. WALKER

FREEWILL OFFERING. *See* SACRIFICES AND OFFERINGS IN THE OT.

FRESH. Several OT and NT terms are rendered "fresh": Heb. *laḥ*–'moist,' 'green' (Gen. 30:37; Nu. 6:3; Jgs. 16:7f.), *karmel*–'fresh grain' (Lev. 2:14; 23:14; 2 K. 4:42), *ṭārî* (Jgs. 15:15), *ḥāḏāš*–'new' (Job 29:20), *ra'ᵃnān* (Ps. 92:10 [MT 11]), *ṭārāp*–'newly plucked' (Ezk. 17:9), *rāpā'*–'restore,' 'make drinkable' (Ezk. 47:8f., 11); Gk. *néos*–'new' (Mt. 9:17 par.; 1 Cor. 5:7), *glykýs*–'sweet' (Jas. 3:11f.). In Job 33:25 Heb. *ruṭᵃpaš* is a hapax legomenon; the RSV emends the MT to read *yirṭaḇ*. The term "fresh" does not represent any specific Hebrew word in Job 10:17; Isa. 29:19; Jer. 6:7; and Ezk. 47:12.

FRESHETS [Heb. *'ᵃpîq n*ᵉ*ḥālîm*] (Job 6:15); AV "stream of brooks"; NEB "channel of streams." Job tells his friends that they have been as treacherous as the flash floods that sweep down the normally dry wadis after the snow has melted on the mountains, and as faithless as such a torrent, which vanishes when it is most needed (cf. Jer. 15:18).

FRET. The term comes from the Old English *fretan,* "devour." The RSV uses it only in the sense of "being vexed or agitated" for the hithpael of Heb. *ḥārâ* in Ps. 37:1, 7f.; Prov. 24:19. "Fretful" (*ka'as*) occurs in the sense of "irritable" in Prov. 21:19. The AV uses "fretting" in the sense of "eating away, consuming" (*mā'ar,* "be sharp, painful") of leprosy in Lev. 13:51f.; 14:44.

FRIEND [Heb. *'ōhēḇ, 'allup, m*ᵉ*yuddā', mōdā'* (Prov. 7:4), *mērē', rē(a)', rē'eh, rē'â, rō'eh, 'îš šālôm, šōlēm, m*ᵉ*ṯê sôḏ* ("intimate friends," Job 19:19), *yakkîr* ("they are friends," Job 24:17), *'ᵉnôš š*ᵉ*lômî* ("my familiar friends," Jer. 20:10), *'anšê š*ᵉ*lōmekā* ("your trusted friends," Jer. 38:22; Ob. 7); Gk. *hetaíros, phílos, 'ísthi eunoṓn* ("make friends," Mt. 5:25), *toús soús* ("your friends," Mk. 5:19), *toús idíous* ("their friends," Acts 4:23), *tṓn idíōn autoú* ("his friends," Acts 24:33)]; AV also COMPANION, "him that was at peace with me" (Ps. 7:4 [MT 5]; 55:20 [MT 21]), NEIGHBOR, "consentedst," (Ps. 50:18), ACQUAINTANCE, etc.; NEB also "another" (Ex. 33:11), "him" (2 S. 16:17), DARLING (Cant. 5:16), etc.; **FRIENDLY** [Heb. *š*ᵉ*lēmîm* (Gen. 34:21); Gk. *met' eirḗnēs* (Heb. 11:31)]; AV PEACEABLE (Gen. 34:21); WITH PEACE (He. 11:31); NEB KINDLY (He. 11:31); **FRIENDSHIP** [Heb. *šālôm* (1 Ch. 12:17 [MT 18]), *sôḏ* (Job 29:4; Ps. 25:14), *rā'ā'* (Prov. 22:24); Gk. *philía* (Jas. 4:4)]; AV also PEACEABLY (1 Ch. 12:17), "secret" (Job 29:4; Ps. 25:14); NEB also FRIENDS (1 Ch. 12:17), "protected" (Job 29:4), "confides his purposes" (Ps. 25:14); **COMPANION** [Heb. *'aḥ*] (Jer. 41:8), *'allup, ḥāḇēr, mērē', rē(a)', rā'â* (Ex. 32:27; Jgs. 14:20; 15:2, 6; Job 30:29, etc.); Gk. *synékdēmos* (Acts 19:29)]; AV also GUIDE (Ps. 55:13 [MT 14]; Prov. 2:17), FELLOWS (Jgs. 11:37), FRIENDS (Ps. 38:11 [MT 12]), etc.; NEB also FRIEND (Ex. 32:27; Jgs. 14:20; Ps. 88:8 [MT 9], Cant. 8:13), GROOMSMAN (Jgs. 15:2, 6), COMRADE (Ps. 55:13 [MT 14]), etc.

The semantic notion of "friend" includes a commitment, whether in business (e.g., Mt. 20:13) or marriage (e.g., Mal. 2:14). Thus "friend" has a broad semantic range, from casual acquaintance to the most intimate of personal relationships.

I. OT.–*A. Characteristics.* Central to the idea of "friendship" is loyalty. Through both good and bad times of life, friends are bound together (Job 17:5; Ps. 122:8; Prov. 16:28; 17:17; 18:24). This loyalty bridges even the generation gap, as Abner pointed out to Ishbosheth (2 S. 3:8; cf. Prov. 27:10). Because of this loyalty, one does not slander or otherwise harm a friend (Ps. 7:4; 15:3). It is just this characteristic that caused Absalom to suspect Hushai, a known "friend" of David (2 S. 16:16f.; *see* FRIEND OF THE

KING) and that motivated Hushai to act as David's spy (2 S. 15:32ff.). Job's loyalty to his friends enabled him to intercede for them in the end (42:8f.).

Concomitant with this loyalty is the sharing or participation that marks a friendship. Judah's friend Hirah traveled with him (Gen. 38:12), and then went to Tamar for the exchange of payment for pledge (38:20). Perhaps primarily because of loyalty, when a king was overthrown, his family and friends shared his fate (1 K. 16:11; 2 K. 10:11; Jer. 41:8; cf. Jer. 6:21; 20:4, 6). Daniel and his friends were to share the fate of their colleagues (Dnl. 2:13, 18); when Daniel mollified Nebuchadnezzar, all the wise men received a reprieve and Daniel shared his prominence with his three friends (Dnl. 2:48f.). Similarly Haman rejoiced with his friends over his apparent success (Est. 5:10), the lover called his friends to feast with him (Cant. 5:1), the royal bride was accompanied by her friends (Ps. 45:14 [MT 15]), and David shared the spoils of war (1 S. 30:26). Sharing the burden of grief is also common (Jgs. 11:37f.; Job 2:11ff.).

These ideas of loyalty and sharing are underlined in several texts which link friendship with covenant (Ps. 25:14; 55:20; Prov. 2:17; Mal. 2:14); hence the seriousness with which the betrayal of friendship is treated (Ps. 88:18 [MT 19]; Jer. 20:10; Ob. 7, etc.). Job frequently accused his friends of breaking their covenant of friendship by laughing at him (12:4), scorning him (16:20), failing him (19:14), and abhorring him (19:19). Proverbs contains several warnings about friends, because those who appear friendly may not turn out to be so (13:20; 22:24; 28:7; cf. Ex. 32:27; Dt. 13:6 [MT 7]; Mic. 7:5). This is especially true when wealth is either abundant or lacking (Prov. 14:20; 19:4, 6f.).

B. Special Classes. The "king's friend" was apparently an official in the royal court acting in some advisory capacity (e.g., 2 S. 15:37; 1 K. 4:5; 1 Ch. 27:33; *see* FRIEND OF THE KING).

For a select few (at least in preexilic times) another title was reserved — "friend of God." Moses was implicitly so called (Ex. 33:4), and Abraham was so designated (2 Ch. 20:7; Isa. 41:8), especially by later generations (2 Esd. 3:14f.; Jub. 19:9; Jas. 2:23). Job lamented the loss of the "friendship of God" (29:4). In more general terms God's friends are contrasted with His enemies (Jgs. 5:31) and Jeremiah quoted the nation calling itself God's friend (3:4). A similar generalization occurs in later Jewish literature (e.g., Wisd. 7:27, Philo, *Quis rerum divinarum heres* 21; *Quod omnis probus liber sit* 42).

C. Examples. Classic examples of friendship in the OT are David and Jonathan's (2 S. 1:26; cf. 1 S. 18:1; Mish. *Aboth* v. 19) and Ruth and Naomi's. Ruth's famous statement of commitment to Naomi epitomizes the depth of their relationship: ". . . where you go I will go, and where you lodge I will lodge; your people shall be my people, and your God my God; where you die I will die, and there will I be buried. May the Lord do so to me and more also if even death parts me from you" (Ruth 1:16f.).

D. Problem Texts. Four passages require brief comment. In Ruth 4:1 the RSV translates *p*[e]*lōnî 'almōnî* as "friend," but AV "such a one" and NEB "calling him by name" more accurately express the indefiniteness intended by the Hebrew phrase. In Ps. 55:20 the RSV unaccountably supplies "my companion"; NEB "such men" is slightly better, and AV "he" is most accurate. Prov. 27:6 makes little sense as it stands, but the contrast seems to be between a friend who faithfully speaks the truth, though it hurts, and one who appears friendly but really is an enemy (cf. the AV, NEB). Jer. 13:21 is a notoriously difficult passage (J. Bright, *Jeremiah* [*AB,* 1965], p. 95, does not attempt to make sense of it, but simply refers his readers to the other commentaries), but the sense seems to be one of betrayal, or at least a reversal in authority — one's former pupil now rules over his teacher; a further complication is that *'allupîm,* RSV "friends," may mean "chiefs"; cf. AV "captains," NEB "leaders."

II. NT.–A. Characteristics. The same characteristics outlined above may be seen here. Loyalty motivated Paul's friends to visit him in prison (Acts 24:23) and to voice concern for his safety (Acts 19:31). James stresses that God demands loyal friends — friendship with the world means enmity with God (4:4). Friends share their joy (Lk. 15:6, 9, 29; Jn. 3:29), their faith and experiences (Mk. 5:19; Acts 4:23; 10:24), as well as care for each other (Lk. 11:6; Acts 27:3). When they share a common experience, even enemies can become friends (Lk. 23:12); Jesus seemed to recognize this possibility when He exhorted His followers to "make friends quickly" to avoid jail (Mt. 5:25). Friends are entrusted with important errands (Lk. 7:6). Jesus also warned about betrayal by friends (Lk. 21:26).

B. Special Classes. In several passages Jesus used "friend" as an introductory greeting which appears to be casual; however, there may be a deeper significance to this use. In Mt. 20:13; 22:12; 26:50, W. F. Albright and C. S. Mann (*Matthew* [*AB,* 1971], p. 237) see an implied rebuke to the one so addressed; there seems at least to be a reminder of the mutual obligation that exists between the parties involved. "Friend" has similar connotations in Lukan parables (11:5ff.; cf. 14:10).

There is also mention of the "friend of Caesar" (Jn. 19:12), an official title that A. Deissman (*LAE,* pp. 377f.) traces back to Alexander's time. Echoes of this title also occur in intertestamental literature (1 Macc. 2:18; 3:38; 10:65; cf. Spicq, III, 167).

"Friends" (Gk. *phíloi*) apparently took on the special sense of "Christians" later in the 1st cent.; thus John concluded his third epistle: "The friends greet you. Greet the friends, every one of them" (v. 15; Stählin, *TDNT,* IX, 162f., 166, observes a similar tendency in Luke). It may be that such use was based on Jesus' own declarations to His followers, especially as recorded by John (15:13ff.; cf. Mt. 11:19; Lk. 7:34; 12:4).

C. Examples. Two great examples of friendship in the NT are Jesus and Lazarus's, and Paul and Timothy's. Jesus' love for Lazarus and his sisters is repeatedly mentioned (Jn. 11:3, 5, 36); it is in this context that the Bible's shortest and very powerful verse — "Jesus wept" — dramatizes Jesus' love for His friend (Jn. 11:35). The relationship between Paul and Timothy is like that of father and son (1 Tim. 1:2, 18; 2 Tim. 1:2; 2:1; 1 Cor. 4:17; Phil. 2:22), and the personal notes scattered throughout Paul's epistles indicate the depth of their relationship (e.g., 1 Cor. 16:10; 2 Cor. 1:19; Rom. 16:21; Phil. 2:19ff.).

D. Problem Texts. Two texts in Luke seem on the surface to be problematic. In 14:12 Jesus exhorted His followers not to invite friends and relatives to a banquet. But consideration of the context and of the verb "invite" clarifies Jesus' meaning: do not keep inviting only your friends and relatives, who you know will repay the favor. In 16:9 Jesus seemed to advocate buying friendship; but again the context makes clear that Jesus was telling His followers to make good use of their wealth; W. Manson, *Luke* (*MNTC,* 1930), p. 184, and A. Plummer, *Luke* (*ICC,* 1900), p. 385, suggest that Jesus is referring to giving to the poor, who will in turn bless them in prayer.

Bibliography.–H. Donner, *ZAW,* 73 (1961), 269-277; *ILC,* I-II, 57ff., 285ff.; C. Spicq, *Agapé dans le NT* (1958), I-III; *TDNT,* II, *s.v.* ἑταῖρος (Rengstorf); IV, *s.v.* φιλέω κτλ.: φίλος (Stählin); *TDOT,* I, *s.v.* "'āhabh" (Bergman, Haldar, Wallis).

G. A. LEE

FRIEND OF THE KING [Heb. *rēʿeh hammeleḵ*] (1 K. 4:5; 1 Ch. 27:33); AV also KING'S COMPANION; [Gk. *phíloi toú basiléōs*] (1 Macc. 2:18; 3:38; 6:10; 10:65). An intimate adviser or royal companion high in the hierarchy of palace officials. In Gen. 26:26 Ahuzzath appears to have been such an "adviser" (RSV, Heb. *rēʿeh*) to King Abimelech. The devotion of Hushai, who is repeatedly referred to as the friend of David, is a notable example of the affection of a subordinate for his superior (cf. 2 S. 15:32-37; 16:16ff.; 17; 1 Ch. 27:33).

A similar office is mentioned in Egyptian texts, the Amarna Letters, and the Akkadian documents from Ugarit (cf. E. A. Speiser, *JAOS*, 75 [1955], 154-165), although in all these texts the office is not exclusive, whereas in the OT only one man holds the office during the king's reign. From this fact and on the basis of other evidence A. van Selms (*JNES*, 16 [1957], 118-123) argued convincingly for a distinctively Canaanite office with this title. He traced the origins of the office to the best man (the "friend" of the bridegroom, e.g., Jgs. 14:20) at the king's wedding; since political marriages were frequent in OT times, a marriage adviser would have been necessary, especially to Solomon! (Cf. Prov. 22:11 for what appears to be a nontechnical use of the term.)

In 1 Maccabees these privileged advisers had become a distinct class. In view of the appointment of one of them as regent of Antiochus's empire and the consequent power of that position (6:14), the temptation of status and prestige presented to Mattathias was intended to be a powerful one (2:18).

N. J. O. G. A. L.

FRINGES [Gk. *kráspedon*] (Mt. 9:20; 14:36; 23:5; Mk. 6:56; Lk. 8:44); AV HEM, BORDER; NEB EDGE, TASSELS.

In OT times fringes consisted of tassels (Heb. *ṣîṣiṯ*) or twisted threads (Heb. *geḏilîm*) and were worn by the Israelites on the four corners of their garments to remind them of God's commandments (cf. Nu. 15:37-41; Dt. 22:12). Originally they contained a violet thread, but this was subsequently replaced by dark blue lines dyed on the borders of the garments on which the fringes were sewn. In Jewish tradition any garment having four corners was adorned by means of fringes, and this practice was still observed in NT times. The later Jews, after adopting the garments of the Diaspora, in order to observe the *ṣîṣiṯ* commandment began to use two extra four-cornered fringed garments: the large *ṭallîṯ* while at prayer, and the small *ṭallîṯ* as an undergarment during the day. Their tradition prescribed the exact manner in which each tassel was to be made and gave a symbolic meaning to the numbers of windings and knots. The main aim seems to have been the association of the fringes with the Law in the mind of the wearer.

The hemorrhaging woman who touched the fringe of Jesus' garment (Mt. 9:20f. par.) probably accepted the common idea that a person's clothes retained a person's power (cf. W. L. Lane, *Mark* [*NICNT*, 1974], p. 142); whatever her reason, the Lord honored her faith, and she was healed.

See GARMENTS.

E. D. ISAACS
R. K. H.

FROG [Heb. *ṣepardēa(a)ʿ*; cf. Arab. *ḍafdaʿ* (Ex. 8:2ff.; Ps. 78:45; 105:30); Gk. *bátrachos* (Rev. 16:13; cf. Wisd. 19:10)]. The references in the Psalms, as well as in Exodus, are to the plague of frogs. Rev. 16:13 refers to "three foul spirits like frogs," indicating the uncleanness of the animal (cf. Lev. 11:10, 41). The word *ṣepardē(a)ʿ* probably referred both to frogs and to toads, as does the

Ivory relief plaque from Nimrûd (Assyrian period) showing a man wearing a fringed cut-away coat (Royal Ontario Museum, Toronto)

Arab. *ḍafdaʿ*. In Palestine and Syria *Rana esculenta, Bufo viridis*, and *Hyla arborea* are common. The species found most frequently in Egypt are *Rana mascariensis* and *Bufo regularis*. *Rana esculenta, Bufo viridis*, and *Bufo vittatus* are also found, but are much less common.

A. E. DAY

FRONTIER. The term occurs four times in the RSV for three Hebrew words: *mûl*–'before, opposite' (Dt. 2:19; Josh. 22:11), *geḇûl*–'boundary' (2 K. 3:21), *qāṣeh* (Ezk. 25:9). The Hebrew conveys the sense of "territorial boundary."

FRONTLETS [Heb. *ṭôṭāpôṯ*, from *ṭûp*–'bind'] (Ex. 13:16; Dt. 6:8; 11:18; cf. Ex. 13:9); NEB PHYLACTERY. Ornaments worn on the forehead, particularly phylacteries, which were also worn on the arms. *See* PHYLACTERY.

FROST [Heb. *ḥanāmāl*] (Ps. 78:47); NEB RAIN; [*qîṭôr*] (Ps. 148:8); AV VAPOUR; NEB ICE; [*qeraḥ*] (Jer. 36:30); [*K yeqippāʾôn, Q weqippāʾôn*] (Zec. 14:6); AV DARK. A temperature of freezing or lower is called frost. Dew forms when the temperature is decreased; and if below freezing, the dew takes the form of a white film or covering over rocks and leaves. This white covering is called hoarfrost or frost. Like dew it is the result of condensation of the moisture of the air on objects that radiate their heat quickly. In order that condensation may take place, the atmosphere must be saturated. Frost may be expected on clear, still nights when the radiation is sufficient to reduce the temperature below the freezing point.

In Syria and Palestine frost is a very rare occurrence at sea level; but on the hills and elevated plains it is usual in the winter, beginning in November, and on the highest elevations throughout the year. Late spring frosts in March or early April do great damage to fruit. In clear weather there is often a great variation in the temperature of the day and the night, especially on the inland plains (Jer. 36:30). The reference in Jer. 36:30 night suggest that Jehoiakim's corpse was left unburied. Perhaps Heb. *ḥ*ª*nāmāl* in Ps. 78:47 would be better rendered "devastating flood" (cf. NEB "torrents of rain").

See also ICE.

A. H. JOY
R. K. H.

FROWARDNESS. Archaic term used by the AV for "perverseness" in Prov. 2:14; 6:14; 10:32.

FRUIT [Heb. *p*ᵉ*rî,* also *bikkûrîm, bikkûrâ, rē'šîṯ, qayiṣ, t*ᵉ*nûḇâ, y*ᵉ*ḇûl* (Dt. 11:17), *la*ʿª*nâ, rō'š, ma'*ª*ḵāl*–'food' (Neh. 9:25), *leḥem, pōrîyâ, 'ōsep, zimrâ, meged, yāgāʿ* ("fruit of toil," Job 20:18), *y*ᵉ*gî(a)*ʿ ("fruit of labor/toil," e.g., Ps. 78:46), *nîḇ, nûḇ, bāḵar, ḥālal*; Aram. *'ēḇ*; Gk. *karpós,* also *génēma, aparchḗ, ólynthos, opṓra, karpophoréō, telesphoréō*]; **FRUITFUL** [Heb. *pārâ, p*ᵉ*rî, pōrîyâ, karmel*; Gk. *karpós, karpophóros*]; **FRUITLESS** [Gk. *ákarpos*] (Jude 12); **UNFRUITFUL** [Heb. *m*ᵉ*šakkāleṯ*–'causing miscarriages' (2 K. 2:19); Gk. *ákarpos*].

I. Biblical Terms
 A. In the OT
 B. In the NT
II. Fruit Products

I. Biblical Terms.–*A. In the OT.* By far the most common Hebrew term translated "fruit," either independently or in combination, is *p*ᵉ*rî*. This general term denotes the edible product of a tree or woody plant, i.e., the succulent tissue that envelops the seeds (e.g., of fruit trees, Gen. 3:2f., 6; Ex. 10:15; Lev. 26:4; of grape vines, 2 K. 19:29). On occasion *p*ᵉ*rî* is also used to refer to vegetables or general produce as the "fruit of the ground" (Gen. 4:3, *p*ᵉ*rî hā'*ª*dāmâ*) or "fruit of the land" (Nu. 13:20, 26, *p*ᵉ*rî hā'āreṣ*).

More frequently *p*ᵉ*rî* has an extended symbolic sense. As the "product" or issue of human fertility, children are called "fruit of the womb" (*p*ᵉ*rî-ḇeṭen,* Gen. 30:2; Ps. 127:3; Isa. 13:18; cf. Lk. 1:42) or "fruit of your body" (*p*ᵉ*rî-ḇiṭn*ᵉ*ḵā,* Dt. 7:13; 28:4; etc.). Similarly, animal offspring are designated "fruit of your beasts/cattle" (*p*ᵉ*rî ḇ*ᵉ*hemt*ᵉ*ḵā,* Dt. 28:4, 11; 30:9). The phrase *pārîm ś*ᵉ*pāṯênû* in Hos. 14:2 (MT 3) is rendered "fruit of our lips" by the RSV, but "calves of our lips" by the AV and "cattle from our pens" by the NEB. The RSV assumes that the unpointed Hebrew text read *p*ᵉ*rî,* "fruit," rather than the MT *pārîm,* "bulls," for what follows is the worshipers' prayer, "the fruit of their lips" (i.e., their promise to renounce all false allegiances; cf. Prov. 12:14; 13:2; 18:20; Isa. 57:18; He. 13:15; 1QH 1:28; Ps. Sol. 15:3; LXX *karpón cheiléōn*; cf. also JB "our words of praise"). The final *m* may be satisfactorily explained as an archaic Canaanite case ending (see H. W. Wolff, *Hosea* [Eng. tr., *Hermeneia,* 1974], p. 231), or as a case of incorrect separation of words — the prefixed preposition *min-* misplaced at the end of the preceding word (i.e., *p*ᵉ*rî miśś*ᵉ*pāṯênû,* "fruit from our lips"; see also W. Rudolph, *Hosea* [1966], p. 248; S. Holm-Nielsen, *Hodayot: Psalms from Qumran* [1960], p. 29.)

*P*ᵉ*rî* also refers frequently to the results or consequences of one's actions. Thus in Ps. 104:13 the earth is said to be "satisfied with the fruit of thy work," the fruit being the manifest creativity of Yahweh in the natural realm. In many instances *p*ᵉ*rî* represents the divine judgment merited by human actions. In Jer. 17:10 the Lord is said to give to each person "according to the fruit of his doings" (cf. 32:19). Thus both the wicked (cf. Prov. 1:31; 14:14; Hos. 10:13; Mic. 7:13) and the righteous (cf. Prov. 12:14; 18:20) will eat the fruit of their deeds.

The phrase *bēn pōrāṯ* in Gen. 49:22 has traditionally been rendered "fruitful bough" (AV, RSV) by identifying *prt* as a form of the feminine participle of *pārâ* (see BDB, p. 826) and by assuming that the "son of a fruit-bearer/tree" is a "fruit branch or bough" (cf. Ezk. 19:10, where Israel is depicted as a "fruitful vine"). This identification of *prt* with *pārâ* is hardly certain, however, and it has been challenged. Observing that similar metaphors in the Testament of Jacob have to do with fauna and not flora (cf. Gen. 49:9, 14, 17, 21, 27), some have suggested that *prt* is rather the feminine form of *pere'*, "wild ass" (cf. Gen. 16:12), and that *bn prt* is thus a "wild ass colt" (see E. Speiser, *Genesis* [*AB,* 1964], pp. 367f.).

Another very common Hebrew term for "fruit" is *bikkûrîm,* "first fruits," i.e., that portion of the grain or fruit crop that ripened first and was harvested to be offered ritually to God. The very similar *bikkûrâ,* "early fig," usually translated "first-ripe fig" (Isa. 28:4; Jer. 24:2; Mic. 7:1), is rendered "first fruit on the fig tree" in Hos. 9:10 (*see* FIG). The term *rē'šîṯ*, "beginning" or "chief," also has the technical sense "first fruits" in the cultic vocabulary. *See* FIRST FRUITS.

The translation of Heb. *qayiṣ* (Am. 8:1f.; Mic. 7:1) as "summer fruit" is the secondary meaning of "summer, heat of summer" (cf. Aram. and Syr. *qyṣ'*; Ugar. *qẓ,* "summer"). Thus this term specifies whatever comes ripe in the heat of summer.

Hebrew *t*ᵉ*ḇû'â* most frequently designates the "yield" or "produce" of the earth (Ex. 23:10; 2 K. 8:6; etc.). It bears this meaning also in the four instances that it is rendered "fruit" in the RSV: Lev. 25:3 (NEB "harvest"); 25:21 (NEB "crop"); Dt. 33:14; Josh. 5:12 (NEB "produce"). *See also* HARVEST.

Another general term for "fruit" or "produce" is *t*ᵉ*nûḇâ,* derived from the little-used verb *nûḇ,* "bear fruit." The cognate noun *nîḇ (Q), nôḇ (K),* also meaning "fruit," connotes thanksgiving in the phrase "fruit of the lips" (Isa. 57:18).

The general term *'ōsep,* "gathering" (< *'āsap,* "gather, collect"), is rendered "fruit harvest" (parallel to *bāṣîr,* "vintage") in Isa. 32:10 (cf. AV "gathering"; NEB "produce"). *Leḥem,* "bread, food," appears to be uniquely applied to the product of a tree in Jer. 11:19, where schemers propose to destroy "the tree with its fruit [= bread, *ʿēṣ b*ᵉ*laḥmô*]." The RSV assumes that *leḥem* has reference to the produce of the tree. Emendation to *b*ᵉ*lēḥô,* "in its sap," has long been suggested (see *BH*), but such is probably unnecessary if the problematic *m* is an enclitic between the noun and its suffix (i.e., *lē(a)ḥ* + *m* + suffix; cf. KoB [3rd ed.], p. 499; M. Dahood, *Bibl.,* 47 [1966], p. 409; J. Bright, *Jeremiah* [*AB,* 1965], p. 84). The NEB follows the latter course, translating "sap" (cf. Ps. 92:14 [MT 15], where *dāšēn,* "fat," is used to designate the sap of a tree).

In nine instances Heb. *karmel* is translated "fruitful

field" (Isa. 16:10; 29:17; 32:15f.) or "fruitful land" (Isa. 10:18; Jer. 4:26; 48:33). Elsewhere *karmel* may be found as "garden land" (Mic. 7:14). *See also* GARDEN.

The obscure hapax legomenon *zimrâ* in Gen. 43:11 has customarily been translated "choice fruits" (AV "best fruits"; NEB "produce . . . famous") from the context and from an assumed association with *zmr,* "be strong" (cf. Ugar. and Arab. *ḏmr*; see also KoB [3rd ed.], p. 263). Thus from the literal sense "strength of the land" the meaning "best produce of the land" is derived. Another etymological possibility has been suggested, namely, derivation from *zmr,* "wonder at, admire" (Syr. *d^emîrā',* "wonder, admirable thing"; see BDB, p. 275).

In Dt. 29:18 "bitter fruit" renders Heb. *la'^anâ,* traditionally "wormwood" (cf. AV, NEB; but note AV "hemlock" in Am. 6:12). Wormwood is the popular term for a bitter and aromatic herb known botanically as *Artemisia absinthium L.* The Hebrew term is always used figuratively of things that are experienced as bitterness (e.g., Dt. 29:18, the consequences of idolatry; Am. 5:7; 6:12, the perversion of justice). (Note the parallel with *rō'š,* "poison," in Am. 6:12; Dt. 29:18; Jer. 9:14; 23:15; see also R. S. Cripps, *Critical and Exegetical Comm. on the Book of Amos* [1969], p. 183).

The plural of *meged* is translated "choice fruits" in Cant. 7:13 (cf. *p^erî m^egādîm,* "choicest fruits," 4:13, 16). Arabic cognates for this term suggest the sense of "excellence, glory," but the Syriac and postbiblical Hebrew equivalents mean "fruit" (BDB, p. 550); thus "choice fruits" accommodates both. (*Meged* also appears five times in Dt. 33, always with reference to the excellent benefits of nature.)

Several Hebrew verbs are translated with the terms "fruit," "fruitful." The divine command to "be fruitful" (i.e., reproductive) is expressed by the verb *pārâ* ("be fruitful"; hiphil "make fruitful") in the creation story (Gen. 1:22, 28) and after the Flood (Gen. 8:17; 9:1, 7). One prominent feature of God's promise to His chosen people was that He would "make them fruitful" (e.g., Gen. 17:6; 28:3; 48:4). *Pōrîyâ,* the feminine participle of *pārâ,* is translated in Isa. 17:6 as "fruit tree" (NEB "fruiting tree") by virtue of its literal sense, "fruit-bearer." The same term is rendered "fruitful" in the phrase *gepen pōrîyâ* (RSV "fruitful vine"; figurative for Israel in Isa. 32:12 and for a wife in Ps. 128:3). The rare verb *nûḇ,* "bear fruit," is applied to the majestic cedars of Lebanon in Ps. 92:14 (MT 15), for, like the righteous, they still "bring forth fruit" in old age (NEB "vigorous in old age"). *Bāḵar,* along with its Arabic, Aramaic, and Syriac cognates, has the basic meaning of "early," "do (something) early" (cf. the related noun *b^eḵôr,* "first-born"). In Ezk. 47:12 this verb is applied to fruit trees that will "bear fresh fruit" (NEB "bear early").

The verb *ḥālal,* "treat as common, profane, defile," sometimes has a specialized sense with regard to vineyards: "enjoy [use] the fruit of" (Dt. 20:6; 28:30; Jer. 31:5; cf. AV, NEB). That enjoying the fruit of a vineyard can be connoted by the term for "profaning" is based on the principle that the first produce of the vineyard is reserved as sacred. According to the Torah the fruit is taboo for the first three years, and in the fourth it is consecrated to Yahweh; thereafter, beginning with the fifth year, the sanctity is removed and the fruit is free for common use (Lev. 19:23-25). Thus, to enjoy the fruit of a vineyard for the first time may be conceptualized as profaning that vineyard, reducing its status from sacrosanct to common.

The Aramaic substantive *'ēḇ* (cf. Akk. *inbu,* "fruit") occurs three times in Daniel (4:12, 14, 21) as "fruit." In each instance it refers to the fruit of the great symbolic tree in Nebuchadnezzar's dream vision.

B. In the NT. The NT equivalent of *p^erî* is Gk. *karpós,* "fruit." Its meaning may be literal, e.g., fruit of a fig tree (Mt. 21:19 par.), of a vineyard (Mt. 21:34-43), and of the earth (Jas. 5:7). But more often it too is symbolical. A child is the "fruit of the womb" (Lk. 1:42); praise is the "fruit of the lips" (He. 13:15). The image of bearing fruit is used often in the NT to indicate the results of the obedient or disobedient life: the yield may be "good fruit" (e.g., Mt. 3:8; 7:17-19; 12:33; 21:43) or "bad fruit" (Mt. 3:10; 7:17f.; 12:33; Lk. 6:43). This imagery figures prominently in Jesus' analogy of the "true vine" (Jn. 15:2-11); it is only the branch that "lives" in the vine that bears fruit. The symbolism of the tree (Rev. 22:2) and of the grain of wheat (Jn. 12:24) similarly expresses the productive quality of the life of a servant people. In Phil. 1:22 Paul applies this imagery to his own ministry when he says that for him "life in the flesh" means "fruitful labor" (*karpós érgou,* lit. "fruit of labor"; cf. AV) on behalf of the churches.

In Gal. 5:22f. Paul catalogs the components of the "fruit of the Spirit" as "love, joy, peace, patience, kindness, goodness, faithfulness, gentleness, self-control." Similarly, in Eph. 5:9 the "fruit of light" is found in "all that is good and right and true." Contrasted with this are "the unfruitful [*ákarpos*] works of darkness" (v. 11), the "fruitless trees" of heretical teachings (Jude 12), and the unfruitful results of faith (Mt. 13:22 par.). One of the characteristics of the "wisdom from above" is that it is "full of mercy and good fruits" (Jas. 3:17; cf. 2 Pet. 1:8). The cognate verb *karpophoréō,* "bear fruit," is used figuratively for the exemplary conduct yielded by a life in Christ (Mt. 13:23 par.; Rom. 7:4; Col. 1:6, 10; cf. Wisd. 10:7). The hapax legomenon *karpophóros* (Acts 14:17) refers to the "fruitful" seasons that give constant testimony to God's beneficence.

Greek *génēma,* "product, fruit, yield," is used consistently in the Synoptic accounts of the Last Supper to refer to wine as the "fruit of the vine" (Mt. 26:29 par.; cf. the LXX translation of "fruitful vine" in Isa. 32:12). *Aparchḗ,* "first fruits," is a technical term from the sacrificial vocabulary, representing that initial portion of the harvest, yield, or (animal) offspring that is sacred to God and must therefore be consecrated to Him before the remainder may be used. Sometimes it is used of the first converts in an area (Rom. 16:5; 1 Cor. 16:15; on 2 Thess. 2:13, see B. Metzger, *Textual Comm. on the Greek NT* [1971], pp. 636f.). (*See* FIRST FRUITS.)

Three other Greek terms are hapax legomena in the NT. *Ólynthos* denotes the fruit of the fig tree (*sykḗ*) as "winter fruit" (Rev. 6:13; AV "untimely figs"; NEB "figs"). The verb *telesphoréō* has the meaning "bring or bear fruit to maturity" (Lk. 8:14). The meaning of *opṓra* as fruit (Rev. 18:14) is a secondary development in Greek usage. The term originally denoted the time of year that begins with the ascendancy of the star Sirius; because it coincided with the time that fruit ripened, *opṓra* by extension came into use for the fruit itself.

II. Fruit Products.–Fruit constituted an essential part of the diet in ancient Palestine, a country that was known for the abundance of its fruit trees. Fruit trees were so important to the economy that Israel was forbidden to destroy them, even in time of war (Dt. 20:19f.). The three most basic fruits of Israel's economy were the olive (*see* OLIVE TREE), the grape (*see* VINE), and the FIG. Their importance is illustrated by Jotham's parable of the olive tree, the fig tree, the vine, and the bramble (Jgs. 9:7-15), and by the fact that Israel itself could be symbolized by an

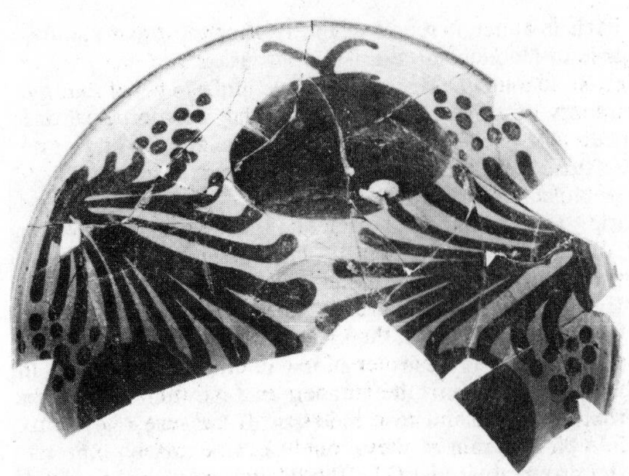

Pomegranate, palm-leaf, and date or grape designs, in reddish-brown paint on a buff background, on a partially reconstructed Nabatean bowl from Khirbet et-Tannur (SE of the Dead Sea) (E. K. Vogel; picture American Schools of Oriental Research)

olive tree (Jer. 11:16; Rom. 11:17-24), by a vine or vineyard (Ps. 80:8-11 [MT 9-12]; Isa. 5:1-7; Jer. 2:21; 12:10), or by a fig tree (Lk. 13:6-9; cf. Mt. 21:18f.; Mk. 11:12-14, 20f.).

Among the other fruits mentioned in the Bible are dates (*see* PALM TREE), the POMEGRANATE, MELONS, the APPLE (probably an apricot), the MULBERRY, the ALMOND, the pistachio nut and walnut, and SYCAMORE figs.

See also FLORA; FOOD; ORCHARD.

Bibliography.–*DNTT,* I, 721-23; III, 415-17; *TDNT,* I, *s.v.* ἄρχω κτλ.: ἀπαρχή (Delling); III, *s.v.* καρπός (Hauck).

D. G. BURKE

FRUSTRATE [hiphil of Heb. **pārar*] (Ezr. 4:5; Neh. 4:15 [MT 9]; Job 5:12; Ps. 33:10; Isa. 44:25); AV also "bring to nought," DISAPPOINT, "make of none effect"; NEB also DEFEAT, "bring to nothing"; **FRUSTRATION** [Heb. *migʿereṯ*] (Dt. 28:20); AV REBUKE; NEB "dysentery." The sense of the verb is to "make void, bring to nothing" human plans or intentions.

FUEL [Heb. *'oḵlâ* (Ezk. 15:4, 6; 21:32 [MT 37]), *ma'ᵃḵōleṯ* (Isa. 9:5, 19), piel of *bāʿar* (Isa. 40:16; 44:15)]; AV also BURN. Its general literal meaning is "food of fire" and might include any sort of combustible material. The common forms of fuel were wood of various sorts (even thorns, Ps. 58:9 [MT 10]; 118:12; Eccl. 7:6), dried stalks of flowers or grass (Mt. 6:30), charred wood as charcoal (Lev. 16:12; Isa. 44:19; etc.), and dried dung (Ezk. 4:12, 15).

Figuratively, the Israelites were like fuel consumed by God's anger for lack of brotherly love (Isa. 9:19). In Ezk. 21:32 this metaphor is even more apt. L. W. DOOLAN

FUGITIVE [Heb. *nû(a)ʿ*–'wander,' 'be unstable'] (Gen. 4:12, 14); NEB VAGRANT; [*pālîṭ, pālēṭ*–'escaped one'] (Nu. 21:29; Jgs. 12:4f.; Jer. 44:14; Ezk. 24:26f.; 33:22; Ob. 14); AV (HE THAT) ESCAPED; NEB also ESCAPE (omits in Jgs. 12:4); [*nûs*–'flee,' 'escape'] (Prov. 28:17; Jer. 48:45); AV FLEE; NEB also ESCAPE; [*nāṣâ*] (Lam. 4:15); AV FLED AWAY; NEB HASTENED AWAY; [*bārî(a)ḥ*] (Isa. 15:5); NEB NOBLES; [*nāḏaḏ*] (Isa. 16:3; 21:14; Jer. 49:5); AV HIM THAT WANDERETH; HIM THAT FLED. One who flees to escape danger; one who has no home; a refugee.

The dangers that a fugitive might seek to escape include retaliation for a crime committed intentionally or unintentionally (cf. Prov. 28:17; *see also* REFUGE, CITIES OF) and the ravages of war. Cain's punishment for murdering his brother was condemnation to a life of homelessness, wandering (Heb. *nāḏ*, parallel to *nāʿ*) in the land of NOD (Heb. *nôḏ*; cf. RSV mg. "Wandering"). The earth that had drunk his brother's blood would no longer provide a home for him (Gen. 4:10-16). The unfaithful prophets and priests of Judah shared Cain's fate when Jerusalem fell (Lam. 4:15). Like lepers, they were unwelcome among all the peoples; they were denied even the rights of sojourners (v. 15b).

In ancient as in modern times, one of the consequences of war was the displacement of many persons who fled their homeland to seek refuge in another country. At the time of Judah's collapse, many Jews fled to Egypt despite Jeremiah's warning that this would only bring suffering upon them (Jer. 41:17–44:30). Others sought refuge in Moab, Ammon, and Edom (40:11; cf. Ob. 14). The suffering of refugees was likewise a part of the catastrophe that was to befall Judah's neighbors (e.g., Moab, Isa. 15:5; 16:3; Jer. 48:45; Ammon, Jer. 49:5; Dedan, Isa. 21:14). Isaiah urged the Israelites to show compassion toward the Moabite refugees (16:3f.). Edom was castigated for its extreme cruelty in handing over Jewish refugees to the Chaldeans (Ob. 14). *See also* WAR.

N. J. O.

FULFIL [Heb. *mālē'*, *kālâ, qûm*; Aram. **mᵉlā'*, *kᵉlal, qûm*; Gk. *plēróō, anaplēróō, ekplēróō, plḗrōma, plērophoréō, teléō, teleióō, synteléō, pímplēmi*].

I. Terminology
II. Fulfillment of Prophecy
  A. Basic Concepts
  B. Time of Fulfillment
    1. In the OT
    2. In the NT
    3. In the Future
  C. Critical Theories
III. Fulfillment of the Law
IV. Other Uses

I. Terminology.–The most important theological meanings of the Hebrew, Aramaic, and Greek terms behind "fulfil" are "obey, observe, or meet the requirements of" and "bring to pass a prediction" (cf. the occasional translation "accomplish"). Dalman attempted to trace primary NT usage back to Heb. *qûm* ("stand," and thus causatively "confirm by fulfillment") rather than to *mālē'* ("fill," and thus "fulfil by bringing to pass") (G. Dalman, *Jesus-Jeshua* [Eng. tr. 1929], pp. 56ff.; but cf. *TDNT,* VI, *s.v.* πληρόω [Delling]; and W. D. Davies, in *Mélanges Bibliques . . . Robert* [1957], p. 429). In the LXX, however, Heb. *qûm* is represented mainly by Gk. *hístēmi* and its cognates; and the Mishnah rarely uses *qûm* to introduce scriptural quotations and never to indicate fulfilled prophecy. B. M. Metzger notes that W. Bacher (*Die exegetische Terminologie der jüdischen Traditionsliteratur*) cites only one example from later rabbinical literature (*Seder Olam* c. 27 *fin*) of *qûm* for the fulfillment of predictive prophecy through historical event (in *JBL,* 70 [1951], 301, 307). M. Black, on the other hand, has suggested that the ithpaal of Aram. *kᵉlal* with the meaning "be completed" stands behind Gk. *plērōthḗ* in the NT (*An Aramaic Approach to the Gospels and Acts* [2nd ed. 1954], pp. 168f.). The OT use of Heb. *kālâ* in 2 Ch. 36:22 = Ezr. 1:1 for fulfillment of prediction supports Black's suggestion. But the idea of completeness lies close to the idea of fulness, and it is probably *mālē'* that provides the primary rationale underlying the concept of fulfillment. A prediction by itself is only half full: the historical event fills up the prediction. Similarly, a command or precept not carried out is only half full: obedience fills it up. Fulfillment, then, is a figurative filling by means of actualization.

In the NT Gk. *plēróō* ("fill") and its cognates (cf. also *pímplēmi*) correspond most closely to Heb. *mālē'*, but Gk. *teléō* ("bring to an end" and thus "to completion"; cf. *synteléō*) carries a similar thought. The AV renders *plēróō* as "complete" in Col. 2:10; 4:12. Cf. the LXX use of Gk. *teleióō* and *teleíōsis* for Heb. *mālē'* (HR).

II. Fulfillment of Prophecy.–*A. Basic Concepts.* Particularly instructive on the synonymy and interchange of the Greek and Hebrew terms for fulfillment of prophetic prediction are 2 Ch. 36:21 (Heb. *mālē'*; LXX *plēróō*), 22 (Heb. *kālâ*; LXX *pleróō*), and the repetition of v. 22 in Ezr. 1:1 with *teléō* substituted for *plēróō* in the LXX. The type of expression that occurs in 1 K. 2:27 stands behind NT fulfillment formulas and concepts: "in order to fulfil the word of the Lord which he had spoken concerning the house of Eli in Shiloh." (*See* B. Gärtner, *ST,* 8 [1955], 14.)

This concept of fulfillment implies the unity of time and events in a history directed by God. Thus time itself is fulfilled (Mk. 1:15; cf. Gal. 4:4; Eph. 1:10) according to a divine timetable that makes events appropriate (Jn. 2:4; 7:30; 13:1; Lk. 21:24; 2 Thess. 2:6; 1 Tim. 6:15; Rev. 11:18). Fulfillment does not mean that history repeats itself in successive epochs (the cyclical view of history), but implies that the fulfilling event belongs to the same piece of fabric as the prediction. The prophetic word potently effects its own fulfillment; it is causative as well as descriptive, for it comes from the Lord of history. Moreover, typology receives its rationale, for in the single fabric of history God intends predictive symbolism in early events, persons, and institutions, and then causes the realization of that symbolism with the result that affinity of content overcomes temporal gaps as history develops into unified wholeness under divine direction. See B. S. Childs, *Interp.,* 12 (1958), 265ff.; O. Cullmann, *Christ and Time* (Eng. tr., 2nd ed. 1964). With Heb. *mālē'* instead of *qûm* behind the NT terms for fulfillment, then, fulfillment in the first instance is a matter of completion, not just confirmation.

Confirmation must not be excluded from the concept of fulfillment, however. For even *mālē'* occurs in the sense "to confirm" (1 K. 1:14); and the Gk. conjunctions *hína* and *hópōs* which frequently introduce fulfillment formulas in the NT, clearly convey the idea of the divine purpose being worked out for people to see, be convinced, and believe. See especially the latter half of Isaiah and the fulfillment citations in Matthew, each introduced by "This was to fulfil what was spoken by the prophet, saying . . . " or almost identical words (1:22; 2:15, 23; 4:14; 8:17; 12:17; 13:35; 21:4; cf. 2:5, 17; 26:56; Mk. 4:11f.; Jn. 12:37-43; 19:24, 28).

It has sometimes been debated whether the Gk. *hína* of fulfillment formulas is telic, indicating a deterministic purpose behind the fulfillment, or ecbatic, merely indicating a result whether deterministically accomplished or not. Lexicographically, *hína* usually is telic; and the occasional substitution of *hópōs* favors the telic idea. Conceptually, however, purpose and result merged in biblical thinking, so that the tension between divine determination and human freedom and responsibility was not keenly felt. For example, "The Son of man must [Gk. *deí* of predestination] be lifted up [crucified]" (Jn. 3:14; 12:34; cf. Mk. 8:31 par.) in no way contradicts "I lay down my life. . . . No one takes it from me, but I lay it down of my own accord" (Jn. 10:17f.). Even less specific expressions such as "it is written" frequently connote fulfillment (e.g., Mk. 1:2; 14:27 par.).

The Mishnah fails to use the fulfillment formulas so frequent in the NT, because there was nothing in mainstream Jewish theology comparable to the Christian belief that the ministry of Jesus had inaugurated the eschatological age in which the OT revelation was reaching completion and receiving confirmation. The writings from Qumrân, however, offer closer parallels to the NT. The Qumrân sectaries believed that the eschatological age of fulfillment had dawned or was about to dawn. But for the Qumrân writers the decisive fulfillments lay in the future; for the NT writers they had already taken place in the career of Jesus. Furthermore, the Qumrân Teacher of Righteousness was more a revealer of eschatological meanings in the OT than himself the embodiment and fulfiller of such meanings, as in the case of Jesus. To be sure, the Qumrân writers thought they could see the career of their leader foretold in the OT. But NT writers saw the career of Jesus predicted and prefigured in the OT far more extensively, so that Jesus occupied a position of far greater importance by fulfilling in deeds as well as by explaining in words the central events of the eschaton. Yet further, the imminent fulfillment expected at Qumrân was a carrying forward of the OT economy by way of purification and restoration. NT fulfillment exhausted and abrogated the OT economy and thereby necessitated a new beginning, related to the old but still new: "The law and the prophets were until John; since then the good news of the kingdom of God is preached" (Lk. 16:16 par.). (*See also* DEAD SEA SCROLLS II.H, I.)

As already noted, the biblical concept of fulfillment included typological fulfillment as well as the bringing to pass of conscious predictions (cf. Rom. 5:14; 1 Cor. 10:6; He. 9:24). The NT writers regarded OT historical events, persons, and institutions as divinely intended to be prefigurative by way of similarity or (occasionally) contrast between the OT type and the NT antitype (fulfillment of the type). As distinct from ALLEGORY, typological fulfillment does not overlook the historical meaning of the OT text. Indeed, the very historicity of the types in their contextual meaning gives them their worth as pointers toward a future culmination.

B. Time of Fulfillment. 1. In the OT. Already in the OT we see fulfillments. 1 K. 2:27 notes the fulfillment of the prophecy concerning the house of Eli (1 S. 3:11-18). So also 1 K. 12:15 notes the fulfillment of Ahijah's prophecy that Jeroboam would rule ten of the tribes of Israel (1 K. 11:29-39), and the Chronicler notes the fulfillment of Jeremiah's prophecy concerning the seventy years of Babylonian Exile (2 Ch. 36:21; Jer. 29:10). Daniel's prophecy of Nebuchadrezzar's madness was fulfilled (Dnl. 4:33 [MT 30]); and the near completion of Jeremiah's prophecy concerning the seventy years of Babylonian Exile prompted Daniel to pray for the restoration of Jerusalem and the temple (Dnl. 9:1-19). The Lord responded with the famous revelation of seventy weeks (Dnl. 9:20-27); thus the fulfillment of one prophecy led to the giving of another.

2. In the NT. In the NT the theme of fulfillment is more prominent. Since it is not always possible to determine whether the NT writer thought of the fulfilled OT text in terms of conscious prediction or unconscious typology, these two aspects of fulfillment may be lumped together and summarized under the following main themes accompanied by representative passages where the themes occur: Jesus fulfilled the activities of Yahweh Himself (Mt. 1:21; 3:3f. par.; 11:5 par.; 13:41; 24:31 par.; 27:9f.). He was the messianic King (Mt. 1:23; 2:6, 23; 3:17 par.; 4:15f.; 21:5; 22:44 par.; 26:64 par.), the Isaianic Servant of the Lord (Mt. 3:17 par.; 8:17; 11:5 par.; 12:18-21; 1 Pet.

2:22-24), and the Danielic Son of man (Mt. 24:30 par.; 26:64 par.; 28:18). He was the culmination of the line of OT prophets from Moses onward (Mt. 12:39f. par.; 13:13-15 par., 35; 17:5 par.; 1 Cor. 10:2; 2 Cor. 3:7f.; He. 3:1f.), of the succession of OT righteous sufferers (Mt. 21:42 par.; 27:34f. par., 39 par., 43, 46 par., 48 par.), and of the Davidic dynasty (Mt. 12:42 par.). He reversed the work of Adam (Mt. 4:1-11 par.; Rom. 5:12; 1 Cor. 15:21f., 45-48; He. 2:6-10; cf. Lk. 3:38), fulfilled the promise to Abraham (Gal. 3:16), and recapitulated the history of Israel (Mt. 2:15, 18; 4:4, 7, 10 par.).

Melchizedek prefigured His priesthood (He. 7:1-10), as did also (in an inferior and sometimes contrasting way) the Aaronic priesthood (He. 8–10). The paschal lamb and other sacrifices symbolized His redemptive death (1 Cor. 5:7; Eph. 5:2; He. 9–10; Rom. 3:25; 1 Pet. 1:19-21; Rev. 5:6) — and secondarily, Christian service (Rom. 12:1; 15:16; Phil. 2:17). He was life-giving bread like the manna (Jn. 6:35; 1 Cor. 10:3), the rocklike source of living water (1 Cor. 10:4; cf. Jn. 7:37), the serpent lifted up in the wilderness (Jn. 3:14), and the tabernacle-temple abode of God on earth (Jn. 1:14; 2:19-22; cf. Col. 1:19).

John the Baptist was the predicted prophetic forerunner (Mk. 1:2f. par.). Jesus inaugurated the foretold eschatological period of salvation (Jn. 6:45) and the new covenant (He. 8:8-12; 10:16f.). Judas Iscariot fulfilled the role of the wicked opponents of OT righteous sufferers (Acts 1:20). The Church is (or individual Christians are) the new creation (2 Cor. 5:17; Gal. 6:15; Col. 3:10), the spiritual seed of Abraham by incorporation into Christ (Gal. 3:29; 4:24-31; Rom. 4:1-12; 9:6-13; Phil. 3:3), the true Israel (Rom. 9:6-13; 11:17-21; 2 Cor. 6:16; 1 Pet. 2:9f.), and the new temple (1 Cor. 3:16; 6:19; 2 Cor. 6:16; Eph. 2:20-22). The Mosaic law prefigured grace both positively and negatively (Jn. 1:17; Col. 2:17; Galatians). The Deluge stood for the last judgment (Mt. 24:37-39) and for baptism (1 Pet. 3:20f.). Both the passage through the Reed Sea and circumcision also pictured baptism (1 Cor. 10:2; Col. 2:11f.). Jerusalem stood for the celestial city (He. 12:22; Rev. 21:2; Gal. 4:26). Entrance into Canaan prefigured the entrance of Christians into spiritual rest (He. 3:18–4:13). And proclamation of the gospel to all mankind fulfilled the promise to Abraham and prophetic predictions of worldwide salvation (Acts 3:25; 13:47; 15:16-18; Rom. 15:9-12, 21).

3. In the Future. Not even in the NT, however, are all prophecies considered fulfilled. Indeed, the NT itself offers a considerable amount of predictive prophecy that awaits fulfillment in the return of Jesus and attendant events (Mk. 13 par.; 2 Thess. 2:1-12; Rev. 6–22, esp. 10:7; 17:17). The very distinction between two comings of Christ rests on recognition that not all messianic prophecies reached fulfillment in the earthly ministry of Jesus (cf. His stopping short of the phrase "and the day of vengeance of our God" when reading Isa. 61:1-2 in the synagogue at Nazareth, Lk. 4:16-21). *See also* PROPHECY.

C. Critical Theories. For modern theological scholarship, however, fulfillment poses a problem that has received various answers. (For the following see the articles collected in C. Westermann, ed., *Essays on OT Hermeneutics* [Eng. tr. 1963], and other literature cited there.) The rise of critical thinking has called into question the legitimacy of the way in which NT writers cited the OT as fulfilled. R. Bultmann, W. Zimmerli, F. Baumgärtel, C. Westermann, and others have all denied that NT events fulfilled specific OT predictions, for OT scholarship has shown that the OT "predictions" did not at all mean what NT writers took them to mean when writing about their "fulfillment." Bultmann claims that the NT not only followed Jewish tradition in referring the OT to the eschatological age of salvation, but also followed Hellenistic tradition when reading into authoritative texts meanings not originally intended (cf. Philonic exegesis). Thus, fulfillment of predictive prophecy and typology is a fiction. One can speak of OT promise and NT fulfillment only in the negative sense that the miscarriage of history in the failure of OT legalism held the promise of justification by faith.

Zimmerli strives to save the concept of fulfillment by arguing that prophetic prediction has an opaqueness, which God reserves the right to clarify through His fulfillment. Thus it really does not matter that NT fulfillment does not correspond to the letter of the OT text.

Baumgärtel argues emphatically that historical-critical investigation not only explodes fulfillment of predictive prophecy, but also excludes typological and christological ways of understanding the OT: (1) the this-worldliness of the OT and the other-worldliness of the NT contrast so sharply that any correspondence between the two Testaments on the historical level is imaginary; (2) what the NT regarded as salvation-history in the OT has been proved to be historically distorted and false, so that typological fulfillment rests on an unhistorical base. Baumgärtel then tries to rescue the idea of fulfillment by distinguishing prophecy, which he defines as a humanly conditioned and therefore fallible attempt to understand the workings of God in history, from promise, which he defines as the central OT affirmation "I am the Lord thy God." It is only the promise which OT and NT really have in common, so that we may speak of *promise* and fulfillment but not *prophecy* and fulfillment. The OT expected by faith the realization of "I am the Lord thy God"; the NT knew by faith that in Jesus Christ the promise has been realized. With similar presuppositions A. A. van Ruler seems to ignore fulfillment and finds the value of the OT in its this-worldly emphases on creation, humanity, culture, society, and the state.

The salvation-history school of thought attempts to retain the idea of fulfillment and at the same time to acknowledge the higher-critical loss of detailed, long-range predictive prophecy by viewing prophecy as history itself rather than verbal prediction. Thus prophecy is the movement of historical events toward the goal of Jesus Christ and the redemption accomplished by Him. See J. C. K. Von Hofmann, *Weissagung und Erfüllung* (1841-1844); and O. Cullmann, *Christ and Time; Salvation in History* (Eng. tr. 1967). Cullmann speaks of *preparation* and fulfillment. Closely related is the revival of typological interpretation (W. Eichrodt, G. von Rad, J. Coppens, W. F. Pythian-Adams, G. W. H. Lampe and K. J. Woollcombe, W. Vischer, *et al.*).

Denial of verbal prediction in the OT and its *quid pro quo* fulfillment in the NT, however, leaves both salvation-history and typological fulfillment devoid of solid foundation. Without real and specific fulfillments of real and specific predictions, both the reconstruction of salvation-history and all typological interpretations lie open to the charge that they are purely speculative. Only NT fulfillment of conscious, detailed predictions in the OT can justify the addition of the broader typological and salvation-history approaches. To be valid, the concept of fulfillment must rest first of all on bona fide messianic predictions in the OT and their actual coming to pass in NT history.

III. Fulfillment of the Law.–A special question arises in connection with the fulfillment of the OT law. On the one hand the NT has indications that the fulfilling of the law established its validity as enduring forever: Mt. 5:17, 19, "I have come not to abolish . . . but to fulfil. . . .

Whoever then relaxes one of the least of these commandments and teaches men so, shall be called least in the kingdom of heaven; but he who does them and teaches them shall be called great in the kingdom of heaven"; Rom. 8:4, "in order that the just requirement of the law might be fulfilled in us"; 13:8, "he who loves his neighbor has fulfilled the law"; Gal. 5:14, "For the whole law is fulfilled in one word, 'You shall love your neighbor as yourself.'" On the other hand the NT also has indications that the new covenant abrogated the OT law: Mk. 7:18f., "Thus he declared all foods clean"; Mt. 5:31f., 38-42 (a contrast between OT statements and Jesus' teaching); Mk. 10:2-9 par. (Jesus' restricting the Mosaic law of divorce); Lk. 16:16 par., "The law and the prophets were until John"; Rom. 6–8; 10:4; Galatians; 2 Cor. 3. Perhaps it is best to say that the ministry of Jesus formed a transitional period during which He exhausted the demands of the OT law and thus outmoded it as a whole, but at the same time restated and intensified for the eschaton the timeless ethical demands embedded within the law. Cf. "Fulfill the law of Christ" (Gal. 6:2) and "not being without law toward God but under the law of Christ" (1 Cor. 9:21). *See also* ETHICS: THE ETHIC OF JESUS III.D; LAW IN THE NT.

IV. Other Uses.–Not all fulfillment deals with predictive prophecy. Besides obvious literal meanings, biblical words for fulfillment convey such notions as spending time ("complete," Gen. 29:27f.; "ended," Lk. 2:43), completing a term of pregnancy (Gen. 25:24), living out a lifespan (2 S. 7:12; 1 Ch. 17:11), doing a task ("complete," Ex. 5:13-14; Acts 12:25; 14:26; Col. 4:17; 2 Tim. 4:5), answering prayer (Ps. 20:5 [MT 6]), and bringing joy (Jn. 3:29; Phil. 2:2; 2 Thess. 1:11).

Bibliography.–S. Amsler, *L'AT dans l'Église* (1960); F. Baumgärtel, *Verheissung. Zur Frage des evangelischen Verständnisses des AT* (1952); F. F. Bruce, *Biblical Exegesis in the Qumran Texts* (1959); J. Coppens, *Les Harmonies des deux Testaments* (1949); *Vom Christlichen Verständnis des AT* (1952); J. Daniélou, *Sacramentum futuri* (1950); C. H. Dodd, *According to the Scriptures* (1952); P. Fairbairn, *Typology of Scripture* (1845, repr. 1952); L. Goppelt, *Typos* (1939; Eng. tr. 1982); P. Grelot, *Sens Chrétien de l'AT* (1962); H. Ljungman, *Das Gesetz erfüllen* (1954); H. H. Rowley, *Unity of the Bible* (1953); *TDNT*, VI, *s.v.* πίμπλημι κτλ.: πίμπλημι (Delling); πλήρης κτλ.: πληρόω (Delling).

R. H. GUNDRY

FULL. The term "full" appears approximately 270 times in the RSV, translating in the OT about six words and fifteen idioms and in the NT about seven words and ten expressions.

The most generally used OT word for "full" is Heb. *mālē'*, which in various forms is translated "full" about a hundred times by the RSV, with many variations in the AV and NEB. It is used to refer to various containers as being full (Lev. 16:12; Nu. 7:13f.; 2 K. 4:4; etc.), to a complete price (Gen. 23:9), to an excellent grain harvest (Gen. 41:7), to an abundance of the Lord's blessing (Dt. 33:23), to great wisdom (Dt. 34:9), to a man with plenty to say (Job 32:18), to hearts of evil men (Eccl. 9:3), to hands shedding much blood (Isa. 1:15), to a city enjoying prosperity as indicated by the presence of many children (Zec. 8:5), etc. In literal and figurative expressions the term refers to an abundance that allows little or nothing to be added to the supply (cf. "fill," Gen. 42:25; Ex. 10:6).

Hebrew *śāḇa'* usually includes the idea of "satisfaction" or "all that is wanted," e.g., of satisfying the appetite with foods (Ex. 16:3) until one is grown fat (Dt. 31:20; "eat your fill," Lev. 25:19; Dt. 23:24). A long and satisfying life is described as one full of days or years (Gen. 25:8; 35:29; 1 Ch. 23:1; 29:28; 2 Ch. 24:15; Job 42:17). But "full" is also used of Job's restlessness (7:4) and limitless trouble (14:1; "fills with bitterness," 9:18), and the psalmist refers to a soul that is "full of troubles" (88:3 [MT 4]). The author of Proverbs warns that the condition of being satisfied by abundance may cause one to leave God (30:9 [MT 10]).

Hebrew *šālēm* has the meaning of "complete," "sound," "safe," "at peace." In Dt. 25:15 it means that weights are to be true. Ruth was wished a perfect or "full" reward for her goodness to Naomi (Ruth 2:12). In 1 Ch. 12:38 *šālēm* denotes the unanimity of the warriors of Israel in their determination to make David king of all Israel (1 Ch. 12:38).

Hebrew *tāmîm* refers to that which is "sound" or "complete." It is used of time periods being complete (Lev. 23:15; 25:29f.) and of transgressors reaching their peak, which will set the stage for a bold and mighty king to arise with great power to do evil (Dnl. 8:23).

Hebrew *kālâ* ("be complete, at an end") refers to a final end intended for various kingdoms: Assyria (Isa. 10:23), Nineveh (Nah. 1:8f.), all the nations (Jer. 30:11; cf. Zeph. 1:18); but Israel, though severely punished, will have a remnant preserved (Jer. 4:27; 5:10, 18; 30:11; Ezk. 20:13, 17; cf. Lam. 4:11).

Numerous Hebrew expressions convey the implication of completion, perfection, precision, clarity, greatness, maturity, etc.: e.g., *yeraḥ yāmîm,* "a month of days" (RSV "a full month," Dt. 21:13), *šenāṯayim yāmîm,* "two years of days" (RSV "two full years," 2 S. 13:23; 14:28), *šelōšâ šāḇu'îm yāmîm,* "three weeks of days" (RSV "full three weeks," Dnl. 10:2f.). *Be'ĕrōt be'ĕrōṯ,* "wells, wells" (RSV "full of wells," Gen. 14:10) and *gēḇîm gēḇîm,* "pools, pools" (RSV "full of pools," 2 K. 3:16) indicate an area full of these depressions. In Ezr. 7:23 "in full" renders *'aḏrazdā',* "exactly," while *kol,* meaning "all," is rendered "full" in reference to authority (Est. 9:29), spirit (Prov. 29:11), and tithes (Mal. 3:10). *Pārāšâ,* "clear marking," is rendered "full account" in Est. 10:2.

In the NT the Greek root most frequently rendered "full" is *plēróō,* which in its various forms (*plēróō, plérēs, plérōma plērophoría*) is translated "full" about twenty-eight times in the RSV. It occurs in reference to nets stretched with fish (Mt. 13:48), baskets weighted with scraps (Mt. 14:20; 15:7; Mk. 6:43; 8:19, 20), persons rejoicing (Jn. 3:29; 15:11; 16:24) or being glad (Acts 2:28), Our Lord displaying grace and truth (Jn. 1:14; cf. "fill all things," Eph. 4:10). It is used to describe people characterized positively by the control of the Holy Spirit, and by wisdom, faith, grace, power, and good works (Lk. 4:1; Acts 6:3, 5, 8; 7:55; 9:36; 11:24), or negatively by envy, murders, etc. (Rom. 1:29), or by deceit and villainy (Acts 13:10). These characteristics have control of the person; they describe the dominant expression of the life, strength, or detriment that the individual asserts in society or in the church. The positive graces are usually in context related to the divine activity of the Holy Spirit, whereas the iniquities are related to godlessness, sinfulness, and domination by the Evil One. This root is also used in combination (Gk. *plērophoría*) to emphasize the degree of conviction, certainty, and assurance with which Paul preached the gospel (1 Thess. 1:5) and with which Christians are to hold their faith and hope (He. 6:11; 10:22).

About eighteen times the RSV renders Gk. *pímplēmi* "filled." Literally, a wedding hall is filled with guests (Mt. 22:10) and boats with fish (Lk. 5:7). Figuratively, people are filled with the Spirit (e.g., Lk. 1:41, 67; Acts 2:4), awe (Lk. 5:26), and wrath (4:28).

Twelve occurrences of "full" in the RSV translate Gk. *gémō* (Mt. 23:25, 27; Mk. 15:36; Lk. 11:39; Rom. 3:14;

Rev. 4:6, 8; 5:8; 15:7; 17:3f.; 21:9). Most of these uses are either figurative or describe an object in a vision. The emphasis is again on that which obviously dominates the scene, leaving room for little else.

Eight NT references to "full" translate Gk. *mestós,* which like *gémō* has both literal and figurative uses. A bowl of vinegar and a sponge (Jn. 19:29) and a net of fish (21:11) are literally full, while Pharisees known for hypocrisy (Mt. 23:28), Romans full of goodness (Rom. 15:14), the great capability of the tongue for evil (Jas. 3:8), godly wisdom producing always mercy and good fruits (Jas. 8:17), and men with eyes only for adultery (2 Pet. 2:14) give a figurative expression to this term.

Greek *pás* ("all," "every") is rendered as "full" courage in Phil. 1:20, payment in Phil. 4:18, and acceptance in 1 Tim. 1:15; 4:9. Gk. *téleios,* meaning "complete," "mature," "perfect," is behind the "full" effect steadfastness is to have in Jas. 1:4. The term *hólos* is used of the complete illumination or lack of it provided by healthy or unsound eyes (Mt. 6:22f.; Lk. 11:34, 36) and of the "full" moon turning to blood (Rev. 6:12). Luke uses the participle of the verb *empíplēmi* to refer to those who have enough to eat and are satisfied. The RSV also supplies "full" to translate several NT words or expressions in which this concept is implied (Mk. 8:8; Lk. 16:20; Acts 17:16; 1 Cor. 9:18; Phil. 2:2).

For Ruth 1:21 *see* EMPTY. *See also* FULNESS.

Bibliography.–TDNT, VI, *s.v.* πίμπλημι κτλ.: πίμπλημι (Delling), πλήρης κτλ.: πλήρης, πληρόω, πλήρωμα (Delling).

R. J. HUGHES, III

FULLER [Heb. *kāḇas* (2 K. 18:17; Isa. 7:3; 36:2; Mal. 3:2); Gk. *gnapheús* (Mk. 9:3)]; NEB also BLEACHER (Mk. 9:3). The fuller was usually the dyer since before the woven cloth could be properly dyed it had to be freed from the oily and gummy substances naturally found on the raw fiber. Many different substances were used for cleansing. Among them were white clay, putrid urine, and the ashes of certain desert plants (Arab. *qali* ["soap," Mal. 3:2]). The fuller's shop was usually outside the city (2 K. 18:17; Isa. 7:3; 36:2) for two reasons: first, because of his need for space to spread out his cloth for drying and sunning; and second, because of the offensive odors sometimes produced by his processes. The Syrian indigo dyer still uses a cleaning process closely related to that pictured on the Egyptian monuments. The unbleached cotton is soaked in water and then sprinkled with the powdered ashes of the *ishnan,* locally called *qali,* and then beaten in heaps on a flat stone either with another stone or with a large wooden paddle. To wash the cloth free from the alkali, small boys tread on it either in a running stream or in many changes of clean water (cf. *En-rogel,* lit. "foot fountain," but translated also "fuller's fountain" because of the fullers' method of washing their cloth). God's purifying activity has been compared to "fuller's soap" (Mal. 3:2), and Mark described Jesus' garments at the time of His transfiguration as being whiter than any fuller on earth could whiten them (Mk. 9:3).

J. A. PATCH

A dyeing plant with two cylindrical stone vats (2nd cent. B.C.) at Tirat Yehuda, about 18 km. (11 mi.) SE of Joppa (Israel Department of Antiquities and Museums)

FULLER'S FIELD [Heb. *śᵉḏēh ḵôḇēs*]. A well-known landmark at Jerusalem in the time of the monarchy, mentioned three times in the OT with similar phraseology: "the conduit of the upper pool, on the highway to the Fuller's Field." Here stood the Assyrian general in his interview with Eliakim and others on the wall (2 K. 18:17 par. Isa. 36:2); clearly the highway was within easy earshot of the walls. Here Isaiah met Ahaz by command of Yahweh (Isa. 7:3).

The biblical data do not suffice to locate the Fuller's Field with certainty or precision; the termini of the conduit can only be guessed at (though Isa. 7:3 suggests that at least one of them lay outside the city), and the same is true of the highway. The "upper pool," one of the conduit's termini, has been variously located. One common view is that it was the pool at the spring GIHON, the present "Virgin's Fount," which was perhaps known as the "upper spring" (2 Ch. 32:30). In this neighborhood — or lower down the valley near En-rogel, which is supposed by some to mean "the spring of the fuller" — is the natural place to expect "fulling." On the other hand, no known highway ran down toward En-rogel, and it seems unlikely that the Assyrian spokesman would have chosen this area SE of the city, down in the Kidron Ravine, for a parley. On the north side of Jerusalem, however, the terrain is of higher altitude than the city itself, and this is the side where armies more naturally mustered to attack Jerusalem. Furthermore, Josephus (*BJ* v.4.2 [142-155]) in his description of the walls placed a "Monument of the Fuller" at the northeast corner, and the name "fuller" survived in connection with the north wall till the 7th century.

See J. Gray, *I & II Kings* (*OTL,* 2nd ed. 1970), pp. 679-682.

D. F. PAYNE

FULLER'S FOUNTAIN. *See* EN-ROGEL.

FULNESS [Heb. *bᵉḵôr*] (Ex. 22:29 [MT 28]); AV, NEB, FIRST; [*mᵉlēʾâ*] (Nu. 18:27); [*mᵉlōʾ*] (Dt. 33:16; Ps. 24:1); NEB also ALL; [*mālēʾ*] (Job 20:22); NEB FULL FORCE; [*śōḇaʿ*] (Ps. 16:11); [Gk. *plḗrōma*]; NEB also RIPE, FULL, COMPLETE, etc.; [*plēróō*] (Col. 2:10); AV COMPLETE; NEB COMPLETION. *See also* FULL.

"Fulness" is an important theological concept that has been the focus of considerable study (see Lightfoot, pp. 257-273; Robinson, pp. 255-260). The usual biblical sense is "that which fills." This is the case in Ps. 24:1 (cf. Dt. 33:16), which says, "The earth is the Lord's and the fulness thereof." All that is in the earth is the Lord's. At other times "fulness" means "the state of being full," or "abundance," e.g., in God's presence there is "fulness of joy" (Ps. 16:11; cf. Job 20:22). The "full yield" of the wine press (Nu. 18:27) and the "first fruit" of the harvest (Ex. 22:29) are subsidiary OT renderings.

In the NT Gk. *plḗrōma* expresses the same ideas. Similar to the adjectival usage in the AV ("full of faith," etc.) is the phrase in Jn. 1:16: "from his fulness have we all received, grace upon grace." Christ, who is "full of grace and truth" (1:14), possesses this grace in "full measure" and in "completeness," and He imparts it to others. Similarly, in Col. 1:19 and 2:9 it is said that in Christ dwells the whole "fulness" of God, meaning that Christ is the complete incarnation of God Himself. In Him exists "the totality of the Divine powers and attributes" (Lightfoot, p. 159); Christians "come to fulness of life," i.e., they find completeness, by virtue of their incorporation into His body, the Church (Moule, p. 94).

That *plḗrōma* may be applied in some sense to the Church as well as to Christ is substantiated by several passages in Ephesians. Eph. 1:22f. clearly links the Church and the fulness of Christ, but it is not certain how the participle *plērouménou* should be understood. If it is taken to be passive, then the meaning is that "the Church is to be the completion (*plḗrōma*) of Christ who will (as the Church grows) be totally ('all in all') completed" (Moule, p. 167). If the participle is in the middle voice and is taken in the active sense, the Church is seen as the completion of Christ: "the fulness of him who fills all in all" (RSV). Taking the participle as active but *plḗrōma* (v. 22) as a passive noun gives the meaning that the Church is "that which is filled by the all-filling Christ" (Moule, p. 167). Or, again taking the participle as active with *plḗrōma* in apposition to "Christ" instead of "the Church," the meaning is that "God has appointed Christ both to be head of the church and to be God's own full representative" (*IDB*, III, 827; cf. Col. 1:19; 2:9).

Ephesians 3:19 ("the fulness of God"; cf. Col. 2:10) and 4:12f. ("fulness of Christ") describe the future condition of Christians: "they are to be 'filled up to the full maturity intended by God'" (Moule, p. 169). "The fulness of God is that excellence, says Chrysostom, of which God himself is full" (Hodge, p. 190). In Eph. 1:10 Christ is said to have been sent forth by God "as a plan for the fulness of time" (cf. Gal. 4:4). The underlying concept here is of God's predetermined plan unfolding in history. When according to God's plan the time had become fully ripe, He sent His Son (see Ridderbos, p. 155). This act of God was "not just an end point, but the dawning of a new period in which God's promise and law (that is, even all that is said in the Scriptures) are fulfilled" (M. Barth, p. 88; cf. pp. 200-210).

Bibliography.–M. Barth, *Ephesians 1-3* (*AB*, 1974); C. Hodge, *Ephesians* (1950); *IDB*, III, *s.v.* "Pleroma" (C. F. D. Moule); J. B. Lightfoot, *Colossians and Philemon* (1957); C. F. D. Moule, *Colossians and Philemon* (1957); H. N. Ridderbos, comm. on Galatians (*NICNT*, 1953); J. A. Robinson, *St. Paul's Epistle to the Ephesians* (2nd ed. 1904); *RTWB*, *s.v.* "Full, Fullness" (J. Y. Campbell); *TDNT*, VI, *s.v.* πλήρης κτλ.: πλήρωμα (Delling).

D. K. MCKIM

FUNERAL. *See* BURIAL III.

FURLONG [Gk. *stádion*] (Mt. 14:24); AV "in the midst of the sea." In Lk. 24:13; Jn. 6:19; 11:18; Rev. 14:20; 21:16 the AV uses "furlong" for Gk. *stádion,* while the RSV uses "stadia" or translates into miles. The *stádion* is a Greek measure of length, being 600 Gk. ft., or 100 *orguiaí* equal to 185 m. (607 ft.) and thus somewhat less than a furlong, which is 201 m. (660 ft.). *See* WEIGHTS AND MEASURES.

FURNACE. The word is used to translate six terms in the OT and one in the NT. The OT refers to four general types: (1) a furnace or oven for baking bread; (2) a furnace or kiln for pottery; (3) a furnace or smelter for metals (rare because of the lack of metals in Palestine, thus mostly used metaphorically); and (4) a furnace used as an instrument of execution.

The Aram. *'attûn* (Dnl. 3), a loanword from Akk. *utūnu, atūnu,* meaning "oven," for baking bricks or smelting metals (S. Kaufman, *Akkadian Influences on Aramaic* [1974], p. 110), was Nebuchadrezzar's instrument for the attempted execution of those who would not worship his image.

The Heb. *kiḇšān* (Gen. 19:28; NEB "lime-kiln") is used metaphorically to describe the smoke of Sodom and Gomorrah. It denotes a kiln for firing pottery or reducing lime to the desired form. The AV translated it thus in Ex. 9:8, 10 and used it metaphorically for the smoke of Mt. Sinai in Ex. 19:18 ("kiln" in RSV and NEB).

The Heb. *kûr,* a smelting pot or furnace for metals, is often used metaphorically: God has redeemed His people Israel out of an iron furnace (Dt. 4:20; 1 K. 8:51; Isa. 48:10; Jer. 11:4); God will consume the dross of Israel in the furnace (Ezk. 22:18, 20, 22; NEB "crucible"); it is used literally of a furnace for smelting gold in Prov. 17:3; 27:21.

Hebrew *môqēḏ,* literally "hearth," is translated "furnace" in Ps. 102:3 (MT 4) (AV "hearth"; NEB "oven") as a figure of judgment; otherwise it is rendered "burning" (Isa. 33:14, also metaphorical) and "hearth" (Lev. 6:9).

The Heb. *'ᵃlîl,* used only in Ps. 12:6 (MT 7; NEB "crucible"), is a metaphor of God's words that are as silver refined in a furnace.

The most common term, Heb. *tannûr,* is translated once as "furnace" by all three versions (Isa. 31:9), once metaphorically in the AV of God's presence (Gen. 15:17; RSV "fire pot"; NEB "brazier"), and all other times as "oven."

The Gk. *káminos,* used metaphorically of the fires of hell (Mt. 13:42, 50; Rev. 9:2) and of the appearance of Christ's feet (Rev. 1:15), is the common LXX term for Aram. *'attûn* and Heb. *kiḇšān* and *kûr.*

See also BREAD IV; CRUCIBLE; METALLURGY; POTTER, POTTERY; REFINER.

W. A. SHELL

FURNACES, TOWER OF THE. This is the AV rendering (cf. NEB mg.) of Heb. *migdal hattannûrîm* in Neh. 3:11 and 12:38; it is rendered "Tower of the Ovens" in the RSV and NEB. *See* JERUSALEM; OVENS, TOWER OF THE.

FURNISH. To furnish is to supply with what is useful or necessary, to provide, equip. It translates one Hebrew and two Greek words: the hiphil (infinitive followed by the imperfect) of Heb. *'ānaq,* "supply literally" (Dt. 15:14, NEB "give lavishly"); Gk. *strṓnnymi,* "spread" (Mk. 14:15; Lk. 22:12; NEB "set out"); *paréchō,* "provide" (1 Tim. 6:17; AV "give," NEB "endow"). "Furnish" is supplied in Ezk. 45:17.

FURNISHINGS [Heb. *kēlîm*] (Ex. 31:7; Nu. 1:50; 3:8; 4:15; 7:1; 19:18); AV also VESSELS, INSTRUMENTS; NEB also EQUIPMENT, VESSELS. *Kēlîm* is a very broad term; it can refer to vessels (e.g., Gen. 31:37), utensils of various sorts (e.g., Gen. 49:5), weapons (e.g., 2 K. 7:15), etc. The reference in the above passages is to cultic objects in the tabernacle. *See* FURNITURE; TABERNACLE.

FURNITURE [Heb. *kēlîm,* Gk. *skeuḗ*]. The Hebrew term, from a root *klh,* "be complete," refers in general to manufactured articles and objects. It is used particularly in connection with the furnishings of the wilderness tabernacle (Ex. 29:9; 40:9). In Ex. 31:7; 39:33, the AV reads "furniture" where the RSV has "furnishings" and "utensils" respectively. In 1 Ch. 9:29 the word occurs in connection with the Davidic organization of tabernacle worship, when certain Levites were made responsible for attending to the furniture (AV "vessels") in the shrine. In Neh. 13:8 the reference is to the household utensils and furnishings being thrown out of Tobiah's room in the temple precincts by Nehemiah, the governor.

The AV renders Heb. *kār* in Gen. 31:34 by "furniture,"

Model couch from an Iron Age tomb at Lachish (Israel Department of Antiquities and Museums)

Bronze stool of the Persian period, reconstructed with wooden connecting pieces, from Sharuhen (Tell el-Fârʿah South) (Israel Department of Antiquities and Museums)

but the RSV "saddle" conveys more properly the concept of a camel saddle.

See also TABERNACLE; TEMPLE IV. H. W. PERKIN

FURROW [Heb. *telem* (Job 31:38; 39:10; Hos. 10:4; 12:11), *g^e*ḏûḏ (Ps. 65:10 [MT 11]), *maʿ^anâ, maʿ^anîṯ* (1 S. 14:14; Ps. 129:3)]; AV also ACRE; NEB also PLOUGHED. In these passages the fields are pictured as they were in the springtime or late autumn. When the showers had softened the earth, the seed was sown and the soil turned over with the plow and left in furrows, not harrowed and pulverized as in our modern farming. The Syrian farmer today follows the custom of his ancient predecessors.

Hebrew *g^e*ḏûḏ probably refers to the ridges along the edge of the furrow rather than the furrow itself. *Maʿ^anâ* denotes the length of a furrow in 1 S. 14:14, and is used figuratively (*Q maʿ^anîṯ*) in Ps. 129:3.

See AGRICULTURE III.A.1; PLOW.

FURY; FURIOUS; FURIOUSLY [Heb. *ḥēmâ, b^eḥēmâ* (Ezk. 23:25), *ḥārôn* (Ex. 15:7), *ʿeḇrâ* (Ps. 7:6 [MT 7]; Prov. 22:8), *zaʿam* (Isa. 10:5; Hab. 3:12), *zaʿap* (Isa. 30:30), *nāqām* (Isa. 59:17), *b^ešiggāʿôn* (2 K. 9:20), *maḏhēḇâ* (Isa. 14:4), *qinʾâ* (Isa. 42:13); Aram. *q^eṣap* (Dnl. 2:12), *ḥ^amâ* (Dnl. 3:13, 19); Gk. *thymós* (Rev. 16:19; 19:15), *ánoia* (Lk. 6:11), *emmaínomai* (Acts 26:11), *orgḗ* (Rom. 2:8), *zḗlos*–'envy' (He. 10:27), *lían*–'exceedingly' (Mt. 2:16)]; AV also WRATH, JEALOUSY, "golden city" (Isa. 14:4), EXCEEDING (Mt. 2:16), etc.; NEB also INFURIATED, THREATS (Hab. 3:12), FIERCE, etc.

Most frequent is Heb. *ḥēmâ,* which basically means "heat" (see below); the AV frequently renders it "fury," while the RSV more often uses "wrath." The basic meaning of *zāʿap,* "to storm," is carried over in Isa. 30:30 to mean "furious (= raging) anger." In 2 K. 9:20 Jehu is decribed as one who "drives furiously" (lit. "with madness"; see below). The NEB follows the LXX in Prov. 22:8, reading *ʿ^aḇōḏāṯô* ("his work") instead of MT *ʿeḇrāṯô* ("his fury"), while in Isa. 14:4 the RSV, along with most modern translations, emends to *marhēḇâ,* supported by several versions and 1QIsa[a]; the AV interprets MT *maḏhēḇâ* on the basis of Aram. *d^ehaḇ,* "gold," hence "golden city'

Fury is often paralleled with the words "anger" and "wrath." It emphasizes the intensity of the anger. Many of the Hebrew words for "fury" literally mean "heat" or "burning." Intense anger overpowers a person; both facial features and inner sensations support the image of burning. Examples of men who experienced great fury are Haman against Mordecai (Est. 3:5), Nebuchadrezzar against the three Hebrew slaves (Dnl. 3:19; cf. 2:12), and the scribes and Pharisees against Jesus (Lk. 6:11). It may even become a part of one's disposition; the RSV renders *baʿal ḥēmâ* as "a man given to anger," and the NEB translates the verse "a hot-head is always doing wrong" (Prov. 29:22). Human fury can get out of control and cause a person to behave irrationally; hence sometimes a word with the underlying meaning of "madness" appears in English as "fury" (2 K. 9:20; Lk. 6:11).

In reference to God, the emphasis is definitely on the intensity of His anger rather than on any inability to control it. The sins of His people arouse God's fury (Lev. 26:28; Rom. 2:8), and His enemies are consumed by it (Ex. 15:7). His fury is visualized as being poured out like fire (Lam. 2:4; Jer. 7:20, AV); it justly punishes the wicked. The judgment of the Lord is full of fury, as the prophets Isaiah, Jeremiah, and Ezekiel frequently tell us (Isa. 66:15; Jer. 21:5; Ezk. 24:13). In the same manner, Rev. 16:19 and 19:15 build up words to indicate how intense the "fury of his wrath" will be during the final judgment. But God's fury is not continuous; it becomes satisfied and ceases (Ezk. 16:42; 21:17; 24:13).

A definite relationship exists between anger and jealousy. Jealousy is the basis for both human (Prov. 6:34) and divine (Ezk. 5:13b; cf. 16:42) fury. Three times the RSV translates as "fury" the basic word for jealousy (Isa. 42:13; 59:17; He. 10:27; cf. NEB "jealous anger," Isa. 59:17).

See also ANGER; INDIGNANT; JEALOUS; WRATH.

Bibliography.–*TDNT,* III, *s.v.* θυμός κτλ.: θυμός (Büchsel); IV, *s.v.* νοέω κτλ.: ἄνοια (Behm); V, *s.v.* ὀργή κτλ.: ὀργή (Kleinknecht, Grether-Fichtner, Stählin). J. E. HARTLEY

FUTILE [Gk. *mataióō*] (Rom. 1:21); AV VAIN; [*mátaios*] (1 Cor. 3:20; 15:17; Tit. 3:9; 1 Pet. 1:18); AV VAIN; NEB also NOTHING, EMPTY, POINTLESS; **FUTILITY** [*mataiótēs*] (Rom. 8:20; Eph. 4:17); AV VANITY; NEB FRUSTRATION, GOOD-FOR-NOTHING;

"Futile" in the RSV is restricted to Gk. *mátaios* and its two cognates, rendered "vain" or "vanity" by the AV. While there is a strong semantic bond between *mátaios* and *kenós* (usually rendered "vain" in the AV and RSV), the two words are not fully synonymous (*see* VAIN). The term *mátaios* indicates that something is "worthless" because it is "deceptive" or "ineffectual." It appears to be what it is not, or lays claim to causing something when it has actually had no effect.

Bibliography.–*DNTT,* I, 549-552; *TDNT,* IV, *s.v.* μάταιος κτλ. (Bauernfeind). G. H. HOVEE

FUTURE. *See* ESCHATOLOGY.

GAAL gā'əl [Heb. *gaʿal*–'scarab']. A man of whose antecedents nothing is known, except that his father's name was Ebed. He fomented and led an unsuccessful rebellion by the inhabitants of Shechem against Abimelech son of Gideon (Jgs. 9:26-45). *See also* ABIMELECH **4.**

GAASH gā'ash [Heb. *gaʿaš*]. A mountain first mentioned in connection with the burial place of Joshua, "in his own inheritance at Timnath-serah, which is in the hill country of Ephraim, north of the mountain of Gaash" (Josh. 24:30; cf. Jgs. 2:9). The wadis ("brooks") of Gaash are mentioned as the native place of Hiddai (2 S. 23:30), or Hurai (1 Ch. 11:32), one of David's heroes. Though its location is unknown, the mountain might have been about 30 km. (20 mi.) SW of Shechem. *See also* TIMNATH-SERAH.

GABA gā'bə [Heb. *gāḇaʿ*].

1. (AV Josh. 18:24; Ezr. 2:26 par. Neh. 7:30). *See* GEBA.

2. (NEB 1 Esd. 5:30). *See* HAGAB.

GABAEL gab'ə-el [Gk. *Gabaēl*; Lat. *Gabelus*].

1. An ancestor of Tobit (Tob. 1:1).

2. A poor Jew of Rages, a city of Media, to whom Tobit lent ten talents of silver (1:14). The money was restored to Tobit in the time of his distress through his son Tobias, whom the angel Raphael led to Gabael at Rages (1:14; 4:1, 20; 5:6; 6:9; 10:2).

GABATHA gab'ə-thə [Gk. *Gabatha*]. A eunuch of Artaxerxes the Great (Ad. Est. 12:1).

GABBAI gab'ī [Heb. *gabbay*; LXX Gk. *Gēbē*]. One of the chiefs of the Benjaminites in Jerusalem after the return from Exile in Babylonia (Neh. 11:8). Some (e.g., KoB, p. 106; *BH*) suggest reading *gibbōrê ḥayil,* "mighty men," on the basis of v. 14 and 1 Ch. 9:8f.; but cf. J. Myers, comm. on Nehemiah (*AB,* 1965), p. 184.

GABBATHA gab'ə-thə [Gk. *Gabbatha,* prob. < Aram. *gabbᵉṯāʾ*–'height,' or *gabbaḥtāʾ*–'open space'] (Jn. 19:13). Another name of the special pavement (Gk. *lithóstrōton*) where Pilate judged Jesus.

The excavations by L.-H. Vincent at the site of Herod's fortress, Antonia, include a massive Roman pavement, of which the central area is about 2000 sq. m. (2400 sq. yds.) and the blocks 1.2 by 1 by 0.6 m. (4 by 3.5 by 2 ft.). Some of these blocks have Roman games scratched on them (cf. Jn. 19:24f.). Theodosius (A.D. 530) called Antonia "the house of Pilate," and Vincent's discovery of this pavement supports this identification. Some think the pavement over the cisterns of Antonia dates to *ca.* A.D. 135. The so-called Ecce Homo Arch spanning the traditional Via Dolorosa at the west end of the pavement, the central arch of a triple triumphal arch, is also of Hadrianic construction.

Related data in Philo and Josephus indicate that Gabbatha was more likely located E of Herod's Palace, the so-called Tower of David near the Jaffa Gate (but *see* JERUSALEM III.H.10). The *sella curulis,* the judgment seat of the Romans, however, was a portable chair.

Bibliography.–M. Burrows, *BA,* 1 (1938), 17-19; C. C. Torrey, *ZAW,* 65 (1953), 232f.

D. J. WIEAND

GABDES gab'dēs (1 Esd. 5:20, AV). *See* GEBA.

GABRIAS gā'brē-əs [Gk. *Gabrias*]. In Tob. 1:14 he is described as the brother of GABAEL, but in 4:20 as Gabael's father.

GABRIEL gā'brē-əl [Heb. *gaḇrîʾēl*–'God is powerful,' 'man of God' (?); Gk. *Gabriēl*].

A celestial being or personage who is mentioned by name only four times in Scripture. In Dnl. 8:16 he is described as "one having the appearance of a man," who was directed by "a man's voice" to make clear to Daniel the significance of the vision that he had just seen but could not comprehend. In discharging this function the being indicated that the vision had eschatological significance.

In Dnl. 9:21 he was spoken of as "the man Gabriel," who appeared to Daniel while the latter was praying at the time of the evening sacrifice. On this occasion the stated purpose of his mission was to impart to Daniel "wisdom and understanding" because Daniel was "greatly beloved" of God.

These two incidents are the only mention of Gabriel in the OT, and neither of them accords him the status of an "angel," or preferably, "messenger." Since Gabriel clearly bears divine authority for his mission and message, however, it is legitimate to regard him as a "messenger" of God. Thus by implication he is a surrogate for God, since in the OT where God's messengers appeared God Himself was present (cf. Ex. 3:2).

His supernatural capacities also included the power to revive Daniel from his trance (8:18) and to appear to him "in swift flight" (9:21) before interpreting the vision of the seventy weeks. While Daniel was terrified by Gabriel's appearance on the first occasion, he was able to regard him as a "man" on the second. Whether or not Gabriel was the personage mentioned in 10:18 is unknown.

In the NT Gabriel was sent on a mission of annunciation on two occasions. In Lk. 1:11 he appeared to Zechariah the priest as an angel standing beside the altar of incense to announce the coming birth of a son. He subsequently revealed himself as one who stood in God's presence, and furnished his name. In a later appearance to Mary he announced the impending conception and birth of Jesus (1:31), and on that occasion was described simply as "the angel Gabriel." In contrast to the awe and fright that he inspired in Daniel, his function in NT annunciations was to reassure and comfort the one to whom he appeared, as well as to proclaim a demonstration of the power of God among people.

Gabriel may have been included among those beings who stood in the presence of God in Rev. 8:2, but this is at best uncertain since none of the angels is named. It is significant that each of the four biblical appearances of Gabriel was connected in some way with the implementing of the promise concerning the Messiah.

Gabriel figured prominently in the pseudepigraphal literature of the intertestamental and later periods. His status was raised to that of an archangel in 1 and 2 Enoch, and his activities were defined in terms of current Jewish folklore. Thus in 1 En. 40:3 he was represented as one of the four presences that looked down from heaven upon mankind. He was venerated as supreme over all powers (40:9), and was included among the Lord's glorious ones. In 1 En. 9:1-11 he was one of the four angels who took to God's presence the prayers of the martyrs as they appealed to God for an end to the lawlessness upon earth. In the narrative of 2 En. 24:1 Gabriel was described as one seated at the right hand of God in a position of supreme power. This function was indicated by the role he followed in avenging God by casting the wicked into the furnace (1 En. 54:6), which constitutes an interesting reflection on the book of Daniel. By this period Gabriel had become both intercessor and judge, thereby assuming functions that in the NT were accorded to Christ (cf. He. 7:25; Rom. 14:10).

The Jewish Targums elaborated on the role of Gabriel and attributed to his activities certain events that occurred in the earlier period of OT life. Thus he was credited with leading Joseph to his brothers (Gen. 37:15), participating with another archangel, Michael (cf. Dnl. 10:13, 21; 12:1), in the burial of Moses (cf. Dt. 34:6), and being sent by God to destroy the armies of Sennacherib (cf. 2 Ch. 32:21). In the cabalistic literature he participated in further exploits, along with Michael, Uriel, and Raphael.

L. HUNT

GAD gad [Heb. *gāḏ*–'fortune'; Gk. *Gad*].

1. The seventh son of Jacob, the first by Leah's maid Zilpah (Gen. 30:11); and the tribe named for him. His birth was welcomed by Leah with the cry, "Good fortune" (*Q bā' gāḏ,* "fortune came"; cf. the Pesh., Tgs.; *K* b^e*gāḏ,* "with fortune"; cf. the LXX), and thus he was named. Some have sought to connect the name with that of the pagan deity Gad, of which traces are found in the names Baal-gad, Migdal-gad, etc. *See* FORTUNE.

The Blessing of Jacob (Gen. 49:19) first plays upon the name as if it meant "troop" or "marauding band" (cf. *gāḏaḏ* and its related noun g^e*ḏûḏ*). This is doubtless a reference to the high spirit and valor that characterized the descendants of Gad. The enemy who attacked them exposed himself to grave peril. The Blessing of Moses describes Gad: "couches like a lion, he tears the arm, and the crown of the head" (Dt. 33:20). Leonine qualities are also ascribed to the Gadites, mighty men of valor, who joined David. Their faces were like the "faces of lions," and they were "swift as the gazelles upon the mountains" (1 Ch. 12:8). Among their captains "the least was equal to a hundred, and the greatest to a thousand" (v. 14).

Of the patriarch Gad almost nothing is recorded. Seven sons went down with him into Egypt when Jacob accepted Joseph's invitation (Gen. 46:16). At the beginning of the desert march after leaving Egypt the tribe Gad numbered 45,650 "from twenty years old and upward, all that were able to go forth to war" (Nu. 1:24f.). In the plains of Moab its number had fallen to 40,500 (26:18), tenth in size among the tribes. Gad's place was with the standard of the camp of Reuben on the south side of the tabernacle (2:14). The prince of the tribe was Eliasaph son of Deuel (1:14) or Reuel (2:14). Among the spies Gad was represented by Geuel son of Machi (13:15).

The biblical information regarding the tribes in eastern Palestine is scant compared with the details given in the genealogical and geographical lists of the tribes settled in western Palestine. These lists say very little that could shed light on the families, their lands, and the history of Gad; this information can be inferred (with difficulty) only from outside documents. Although archeological research has been carried out in this area no less than in other areas in eastern Palestine, with the exception of Dhībân (*see* DIBON 2) no systematic archeological excavations have added to our knowledge of the biblical period. Yeivin (*EB*, II, 423-29) believed that two waves of Israelite immigration into eastern Palestine took place at two different periods. Analysis of documents seems to show, in his opinion, that the first wave of Israelite tribes preceded the foundation of the kingdom of Sihon, and apparently also the consolidation of the kingdom of Moab, although Edomite and Moabite permanent settlements could have existed there before. The second wave, at the end of the 13th cent. B.C., led to a settlement in eastern Palestine. According to Yeivin the Gadites seem to have been among this second wave.

The Gadites established eight settlements upon entering their territory (Nu. 32:34-36), which consisted of two parts, one the territory between the brook Heshbon and the river Jabbok, the other a strip lying SE of this area bordered by the Arnon River in the south and in the west by the watershed. Most of the place names have been identified, and their examination proves that all of them were founded anew at the beginning of the Israelite period after their destruction in the 13th cent. B.C. It is not clear, however, whether the Gadites founded these new settlements or whether they settled there after the Moabites and the Amorites. According to Josh. 13:24-28, the kingdom of Sihon was divided between the Reubenites (13:21), who inherited most of it, and the Gadites, who took possession of a smaller part.

The identification of the boundaries of the territory of Gad depends on the place name RAMATH-MIZPEH, which Glueck identified with Khirbet Umm-dananir, in which case the territory bounded by the secondary watershed of the southern Gilead mountains lay between the brooks that flow into the Jordan from the west and those that flow into the southern course of the Jabbok from the east, from Heshbon to Ramath-mizpeh (Josh. 13:26). Another strip jutted out from the above-mentioned territory toward the southeast between Moab S of the Arnon, the territory of Reuben, and the area that later was conquered by the Ammonites. Possibly another area, consisting of the city of Dibon, was in their hands; but this may be the description of the situation at a later time, when the tribe of Reuben was weakened by border strife and Gad had taken possession of parts of Reuben's territory (Nu. 33:45).

The northern border reached Mahanaim (near ʿAjlûn) and, to the northeast, Lo-debar; from here it passed through the Jordan Valley to the Sea of Galilee (Josh. 13:27); its western border was the Jordan. The southern border is not mentioned; but apparently it went through the brook Heshbon toward the east, and from the city of Heshbon it turned SE to the Arnon.

Reuben and Gad were absent from the muster against Sisera (Jgs. 5:15-17), but they united with their brethren in taking vengeance on Benjamin; Jabesh-gilead, from which no contingent was sent, was destroyed (21:8-12). Jephthah was probably from this tribe, since his house at Mizpah (Jgs. 11:34) was apparently within its territory (Josh. 13:26). Gad furnished a refuge for some of the Hebrews during the Philistine oppression (1 S. 13:7). Certain Gadites attached themselves to David while he was hiding from Saul at Ziklag (1 Ch. 12:8-15). A company of them also joined in making him king at Hebron (12:38). In Gad the adherents of the house of Saul gathered around Ish-bosheth (2 S. 2:8-10). David went there in his flight from Absalom (17:24). Gad fell to Jeroboam at the disruption of the kingdom, and Penuel, apparently within its borders, was first fortified by Jeroboam (1 K. 12:25). It appears from the Moabite Stone (*ca.* 830 B.C.) that part of the territory afterward passed into the hands of Moab. (Note that according to line 10 Gadites had occupied Ataroth [cf. Nu. 32:34] *mʿlm,* "from of old," i.e., for a long time.) Under Omri this was recovered; but Moab again asserted its supremacy. Elijah probably belonged to this district, and the brook Cherith must be sought in one of its glens.

Gad formed the main theater of the long struggle between Israel and Syria. At Ramoth-gilead Ahab received his death wound (1 K. 22). Under Jeroboam II this country was once more an integral part of the land of Israel. In 734 B.C., however, Tiglath-pileser appeared and conquered all eastern Palestine, carrying its inhabitants captive (2 K. 15:29; 1 Ch. 5:26). This seems to have furnished the occasion for Ammon to occupy the country (Jer. 49:1). In Ezekiel's ideal picture (48:27, 34) Gad was allotted the southernmost of the tribal portions. Obadiah seems to have forgotten the tribe, and its territory was assigned to Benjamin (Obad. 19). In Rev. 7:5, however, Gad is placed among the tribes of Israel.

See Vol. I, Map VI.

Bibliography.–M. Noth, *ZDPV,* 58 (1935), 230ff.; A. Bergman, *JPOS,* 16 (1936), 247ff.; *GP,* II, 67ff., 77, 82, 103, 123, 138; N. Glueck, *AASOR,* 18-19 (1937-1939), 150-53, 250f.; 25-28 (1945-49), 103; *ARI,* p. 218.

W. EWING A. A. SAARISALO

2. David's seer (*ḥōzeh,* 1 Ch. 21:9; 29:29; 2 Ch. 29:25), or prophet (*nāḇîʾ*; cf. 1 S. 22:5; 2 S. 24:11). He appears (1) to advise David, when David was an outlaw fleeing before Saul, to return to the land of Judah (1 S. 22:5); (2) to rebuke David and give him his choice of punishments when, in spite of the advice of Joab and the traditional objections (cf. Ex. 30:11-16), he numbered the people of Israel (2 S. 24:11; 1 Ch. 21:9f.); (3) to instruct David to erect an altar on the threshing floor of Araunah when the plague that had descended on Israel ceased (2 S. 24:18; 1 Ch. 21:18); and (4) to assist in the arrangement of Levitical music with cymbals, psalteries, and harps (cf. 2 Ch. 29:25). Of his writings none is known, though he is said to have written a history of a part of David's reign (1 Ch. 29:29)

E. D. ISAACS

GAD ABOUT [Heb. *ʾāzal*] (Jer. 2:36); NEB omits; [Gk. *periérchomai*] (1 Tim. 5:13); AV WANDER ABOUT; NEB GO AROUND. Jeremiah asks the people of Judah why they are going about seeking alliances — first with Assyria and now with Egypt. God will shame them for disloyalty to Him by breaking the power of Egypt as well as that of Assyria. In the NT Paul warns Timothy that widows who make a practice of going about from house to house learn to be idlers, gossipers, and busybodies.

GAD, RIVER OF (AV 2 S. 24:5). The AV follows the MT, which reads *naḥal haggāḏ,* while the RSV ("valley, toward Gad") and the NEB ("gorge, proceeding towards Gad"), following Lucian, emend to *naḥal ʾel-haggāḏî.* The valley is probably the Arnon.

GADARA gad'er-ə [Gk. *Gadara*]; **GADARENES** gad'ə-rēnz [Gk. *Gadarenoi*]. Gadara was one of the more important cities of the DECAPOLIS (Polybius v.71.3; Pliny *Nat. hist.* v.74; Josephus *Ant.* xvii.11.4 [320]). The Gadarenes were the inhabitants of the city and the attached territory (*Ant.* xv.10.2f. [351, 354-59]). The designation "territory of the Gadarenes" (Gk. *hē chṓra tṓn Gadarēnōn*) occurs as the accepted reading only in Mt. 8:28. Variant readings include "Gergesenes" and "Gerasenes." In Mark (5:1) and Luke (8:26, 37) "Gerasenes" has the best support. "Gadarenes" and "Gergesenes" are the variant readings. The textual tradition reflects confusion over the story's proper locale ("opposite Galilee" according to Lk. 8:26; *see* GERASA I). *See also* GALILEE VI.

Gadara was already a well-established and significant fortress when Antiochus III subdued it (218 B.C.) and later occupied it (198 B.C.) after his victory over Scopas at Paneas (Polybius xvi.39.3, quoted in *Ant.* xii.3.3 [136]). Alexander Janneus captured the city during the Maccabean period (*Ant.* xiii.13.3 [356]; *BJ* i.4.2 [86]) and it remained in Jewish territory until it was annexed to the province of Syria by Pompey (*Ant.* xiv.4.4 [74-76]; *BJ* i.7.7 [155f.]). The passages in Josephus (*Ant.* xiv.5.4 [89-91]; *BJ* i.8.5 [170]) that are frequently used to show that Gadara functioned as the seat of one of the five councils (Gk. *synédria*) probably refer instead to Adora (Dûrā) in Idumea or Gazara (Tell Jezer) in Judea (cf. *HJP*², II, 134f.; Thackeray, *Josephus* [*LCL*], II, 78f. n. b; VIII, 494f. n. d).

In 30 B.C. Augustus gave Gadara to Herod the Great, whose oppressive policies the Gadarenes protested several times (*Ant.* xv.10.2 [351]; xv.10.3 [354-59]). After Herod's death in 4 B.C., Gadara was again annexed to the province of Syria (*Ant.* xvii.11.4 [320]; *BJ* ii.6.3 [97]) and was later sacked by Jews during the second revolt (A.D. 66). This resulted in the slaughter and imprisonment of Jews by the Gadarenes and the inhabitants of neighboring Hippos (cf. *BJ* ii.18.1 [457-460]; ii.18.5 [477f.]). Josephus refers to a Gadara occupied by Vespasian "on the fourth of the month Dystrus" (*ca.* March 21) A.D. 68, but this town is probably to be identified with Gedor (Tell Jedûr) in Perea (see Thackeray, *Josephus* [*LCL*], III, 120f. n. b; *HJP*², II, 134).

A fragmentary inscription ("col[onia] Valen[tia] Gadara"; *CIL,* III, 181) discovered by E. Renan (*Mission de Phénicie* [1864-1874], p. 191) indicates that Gadara was probably a Roman colony later in the imperial period. By the 2nd cent. A.D. the large Christian community there had developed into a bishopric. In A.D. 325, a bishop representing Gadara participated in the Council of Nicea (see Honigmann, pp. 429-439).

The ruins of Muqeis (or Umm Qeis) have long been identified as the remains of the ancient city of Gadara.

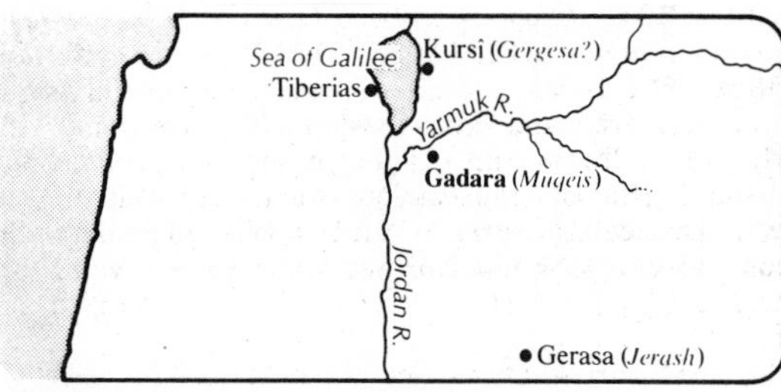

Eastern shore of the Sea of Galilee, possibly to be identified with Gadara (W. S. LaSor)

The city was strategically situated on a headland reaching westward into the Jordan Valley, protected on the north by the Nahr Yarmûk, and on the south by the Wâdī ʿArab, and located about 10 km. (6 mi.) SE of the Sea of Galilee. In 1974 Ute Wagner-Lux directed a survey of Muqeis, which was followed by archeological campaigns under the aegis of Das Deutsche Evangelische Institut in 1976 and 1977 (reported in *ZDPV,* 94 [1978], 135-144, 161-63). The remains demonstrate that Gadara was indeed a significant and vital Greek *pólis* (*Ant.* xvii.11.4 [320]; *BJ* ii.6.3 [97]) containing temples, theaters, a hippodrome, an aqueduct, etc. The epitaph of a Gadarene named Apion refers to Gadara as a *chrēstomousía* ("city of culture"). Philodemus the Epicurean, Meleager the epigrammatic poet, Menippus the Cynic and satirist, and Theodorus the orator were all sons of Gadara (Strabo *Geog.* xvi.2.29 [758]), as were the Cynic Oenomaus (D. R. Dubley, *History of Cynicism* [1937], pp. 162-170) and the rhetorician Apsines (F. Miller, *Journal of Roman Studies,* 59 [1969], 16).

The territory of Gadara extended at least as far north as the Nahr Yarmûk (Pliny *Nat. hist.* v.16.74) and probably included the renowned hot springs of Ematha (Tell el Ḥammeh; Eusebius *Onom.* 22.26); it probably extended as far south as the Wâdī et-Taiyibe; toward the east, it stretched at least as far as el Khureibe, where the city aqueduct originated; its western boundary was the valley of the Jordan (*BJ* iii.3.1 [37]) and perhaps the Sea of Galilee (Mt. 8:28; *Vita* 9 [42]).

Bibliography.–T. Baarda, "Gadarenes, Gerasenes, Gergesenes, and the 'Diatessaron' Traditions," in E. E. Ellis and M. Wilcox, eds., *Neotestamentica et Semitica: Studies in Honour of Matthew Black* (1969), pp. 181-197; *HJP*², II, 49f., 132-36; E. Honigmann, *Byzantion,* 9 (1936), 429-449; B. M. Metzger, *Textual Comm. on the Greek NT* (1971), pp. 23f., 84, 145; U. Wagner-Lux, *ZDPV,* 94 (1978), 135-144, 161-63.

J. J. C. COX

GADDI gad'ī [Heb. *gaddî*–'my fortune'; Gk. *Gaddi*].

1. One of the twelve spies, son of Susi, and a leader of Manasseh (Nu. 13:11).

2. [Gk. Apoc. *Gaddis, Kaddis*] (1 Macc. 2:2); AV CADDIS; NEB GADDIS. Surname of John, the eldest brother of Judas Maccabeus.

GADDIEL gad'i-əl [Heb. *gaddî'ēl*–'blest of God']. One of the twelve men sent by Moses from the wilderness of Paran to spy out the land of Canaan. He represented the tribe of Zebulun (Nu. 13:10).

GADFLY [Heb. *qereṣ*] (Jer. 46:20); AV DESTRUCTION. An insect that nips, stings, or pinches, perhaps either the horsefly (*Tabanidae* fampily) or the botfly (*Oestridae*) whose larvae are parasitic on horses and other animals. The mosquito is also suggested (KoB, p. 857). Since the beautiful heifer of Egypt has turned and fled because of the painful sting of Nebuchadrezzar, it would seem that the metaphor intended is that of the gadfly and not the mosquito, which might have been more annoying than painful.

GADI gā'dī [Heb. *gāḏî*–'fortunate']. The father of Menahem, one of the kings of Israel who reached the throne through murder (2 K. 15:14, 17).

GADITES gad'īts [Heb. *haggāḏî*]. Members of the tribe of Gad (Dt. 3:12, 16; 4:43; etc.).

GAHAM gā'ham [Heb. *gāḥām*]. A son of Nahor, brother of Abraham, by his concubine Reumah (Gen. 22:24).

GAHAR gā'här [Heb. *gaḥar*; Gk. *Gaer, Gaar,* Apoc. *Geddour*]; AV Apoc., NEB Apoc., GEDDUR. A family name of temple servants who came up with Zerubbabel to Jerusalem (Ezr. 2:47; Neh. 7:49; 1 Esd. 5:30).

GAIN. In the OT various idiomatic and periphrastic constructions express the verb "gain"; sometimes the RSV supplies "gain" from the context (e.g., Prov. 10:2; 20:17), thus translating the sense of the Hebrew rather than the literal words. Most frequently the root *bṣʿ* underlies the RSV's rendering (cf. *TDOT,* II, *s.v.* "bṣʿ" III [D. Kellermann]). The use of the participle with the cognate accusative (*bōṣē(a)ʿ bāṣaʿ*; cf. W. Gesenius, E. Kautzsch, A. E. Cowley, *Hebrew Grammar* [1910], § 117 p-r) describes robbers or plunderers, who "get gain" by violence (Prov. 1:19; Hab. 2:9). Jeremiah uses the same construction in denouncing the people of Judah, all of whom are "greedy for unjust gain" (6:13; 8:10; cf. also Ezk. 22:27).

In Job 30:2 and Jer. 2:18 the RSV renders the Hebrew idiom *mâ* ("what") + *lᵉ* + pronominal suffix ("to/for me/you"; cf. the American idiom "what's in it for you") as "what could I gain," "what do you gain." Related expressions with *yiṯrôn,* "profit," occur in Eccl. 1:3, where the RSV renders Heb. *mah yiṯrôn lā'āḏām* by "what does man gain" (cf. 3:9; 5:16 [MT 15]). In Eccl. 2:11 the RSV translates *'ên yiṯrôn* (lit. "there is no profit") as "there is nothing to be gained."

In the remaining occurrences various Hebrew words are translated "gain" on the basis of context. Heb. *gāḏēl* (lit. "great") describes Isaac's accumulation of wealth (Gen. 26:13); *rāḵaš* (lit. "gather property") describes Jacob's accumulation of livestock (31:18; 46:6), as does *ʿāśâ* (lit. "do, make") in 31:1. In 47:27 *'āḥaz* (lit. "seize, grasp") describes Jacob's prosperous growth while in Egypt.

"Gain" is not limited to a materialistic sense, however. We thus read that the enemy "gained [*gāḇar,* "be superior"] an advantage" in battle (2 S. 11:23) and the wise men were trying to "gain [Aram. *zᵉḇan,* "buy"] time," i.e., delay (Dnl. 2:8). *Māṣā'* (lit. "find") occurs in reference not only to material growth (Hos. 12:8 [MT 9]), but also to spiritual or religious growth (Prov. 16:31). *Qānâ* (lit. "acquire") can refer to the acquisition of knowledge (Prov. 15:32), as can *lāqaḥ* (lit. "take"; Prov. 21:11). In Proverbs the father instructs the son to "gain insight" (Heb. *lāḏaʿaṯ bînâ,* lit. "to know insight") by listening to the father's instruction (4:1); the wisdom teacher instructs his pupil to listen and accept instruction that he may "gain wisdom" (Heb. *hāḵam,* lit. "be wise"; 19:20); the man of understanding will "gain [*bîn,* "understand"] knowledge" when he is reproved (19:25).

As a noun "gain" usually has a negative connotation. *Beṣaʿ* is most frequent, and is sometimes translated "dishonest gain" (Jer. 22:17; Ezk. 22:13). Thus Samuel's sons "turned aside after gain," taking bribes and perverting justice (1 S. 8:3; cf. Prov. 15:27). Similarly Isaiah denounces the leaders because they went after their own gain (56:11). In several texts the upright or pious person is contrasted with those who go after gain (Ps. 119:36; Prov. 28:16; Isa. 33:15; Ezk. 33:31).

Only in three passages is "gain" used in a neutral sense. Eliphaz denies that God benefits from anyone's piety (Job 22:3). In Mic. 4:13 the wealth of conquered enemies will be given to the Lord. In Jer. 20:5 it is just the reverse: the wealth and all the "gains" (*yᵉgîʿā*) of Judah will be given to Babylon.

In Prov. 3:14 Heb. *saḥar* is used first positively, of the benefit of acquiring wisdom, and then negatively, of gain from silver. In Prov. 31:11 Heb. *šālāl* (usually a negative word meaning "booty"; cf. W. McKane, Proverbs [*OTL,* 1970], pp. 666f.) means the profit that the good wife is able to provide for her husband. The remaining occurrences are negative. Heb. *tᵉḇûʾâ* (lit. "what is brought in"), a neutral word, is clearly pejorative in Prov. 10:16 and Eccl. 5:10 (MT 9). Heb. *kišrôn* ("skill"), used elsewhere in Ecclesiastes positively (2:21; 4:4), has a neutral or negative connotation in 5:11 (MT 10).

In the NT the situation is similar. Of the verbs, Gk. *kerdaínō* occurs most frequently. It is used of material gain in Mt. 16:26 par., where Jesus contrasts the value of material possessions with the value of one's life (cf. also Jas. 4:13). One may, however, "gain" a brother (Mt. 18:15) through reconciliation, and Paul strives to gain Christ as his sole possession (Phil. 3:8; see *TDNT,* III, 673). Similarly, Gk. *ōpheléō* can refer to material gain (Mt. 15:5 par.), but also to personal advantage of a political (Mt. 27:24) or spiritual nature (1 Cor. 13:3). Gk. *peripoiéō* can mean "leave alive, preserve" (Lk. 17:33) and also "acquire" (1 Tim. 3:13). Gk. *ktáomai* refers to winning eternal life by perseverance through persecution (Lk. 21:19). Material gain is clearly in view in Lk. 19:15 (*diapragmatéuomia,* "gain by trading, earn") and in Rev. 18:15 (*ploutéō,* "be rich"). In 2 Cor. Paul uses "gain" (*symphérō*) in its general sense; cf. 2:11 where he explains that forgiveness is essential "to keep Satan from gaining advantage" (*pleonektéō*).

In Jude 4 ungodly people have "secretly gained admission" (*pareisdú[n]o*) to the church. In 1 Cor. 7:21 Paul tells slaves to "gain their freedom" (*eleútheros gínomai,* lit. "become free") if they are given the opportunity.

Two of these verbs have cognate nouns. Thus *kérdos* occurs in conjunction with *kerdaínō* in Phil. 3:7f. (cf. also Phil. 1:21), and *ōphéleia* (see *ōpheléō* above) occurs in Jude 16 in a pejorative sense of boasters who flatter people to "gain advantage." Other pejorative nouns are *ergasia,* which is used of the commercial profit from a slave girl's soothsaying (Acts 16:16, 19); *misthós,* which describes Balaam's love for profit from wrongdoing (2 Pet. 2:15; Jude 11); *aischrokerdés,* "greedy for gain," which neither deacons (1 Tim. 3:8) nor bishops (Tit. 1:7) are supposed to be (cf. also *aischrokerdṓs,* "shameful gain" in 1 Pet. 5:2), and *aiskroú kérdous,* "base gain," in Tit. 1:11). Gk. *porismós* is apparently a neutral word, for in 1 Tim. 6:5 it is used disparagingly, but in v. 6 it is admitted that there is "great gain in godliness with contentment." Gk. *óphelos* is another general word for benefit (1 Cor. 15:32).

G. A. L.

GAINSAY. Archaic term used in the AV for Gk. *antilégō* (Rom. 10:21, RSV "contrary"; Tit. 1:9, RSV "contradict"), *anteípon* (Lk. 21:15, RSV "contradict"), *antilogía* (Jude 11, RSV "rebellion"), *anantirrhḗtōs* (Acts 10:29, RSV "without objection").

GAIUS gā'yəs [Gk. *Gaïos*].

1. The Gaius to whom 3 John is addressed. He is spoken of as "the beloved" (3 Jn. 1f., 5, 11) and is commended for "the truth of [his] life" and his hospitality (vv. 3, 5f.).

2. Gaius of Macedonia, one of Paul's "companions in travel" (Acts 19:29). He was one of those who were seized by Demetrius and the other silversmiths in the riot at Ephesus during Paul's third missionary journey.

3. Gaius of Derbe, who was among those who awaited Paul at Troas and accompanied him on his return to Jerusalem on his third missionary journey (Acts 20:4). It is possible here that "of Derbe" should be taken with Timothy and that Gaius should be classed with the Thessalonians. According to the Western reading he was not from Derbe but "of Doberus," another Macedonian town.

4. Gaius, the host of Paul when he wrote the Epistle to the Romans (Rom. 16:23). As Paul wrote this Epistle from Corinth, it is probable that this Gaius is identical with **5.**

5. Gaius, whom Paul baptized at Corinth (1 Cor. 1:14). See **4** above.

GALAAD gal'ə-ad (AV Jth. 1:8; 1 Macc. 5:9, 55). *See* GILEAD.

GALAL gā'lal [Heb. *gālāl*]. The name of two Levites, one mentioned in 1 Ch. 9:15, the other in 1 Ch. 9:16 and Neh. 11:17.

GALATIA gə-lā'shə [Gk. *Galatia*]; **GALATIANS** [Gk. *Galátai*] (Gal. 3:1).

I. Two Senses of the Name
II. Origin of the Name
III. Luke's Narrative
IV. Paul's Use of "Galatians"

I. Two Senses of the Name.–"Galatia" was a name used in two different senses during the 1st cent. A.D.: (1) geographically, to designate a country in the northern part of the central plateau of Asia Minor, touching Paphlagonia and Bithynia on the north, Phrygia to the west and south, Cappadocia and Pontus to the southeast and east, and situated about the headwaters of the Sangarius and the middle course of the Halys; (2) politically, to designate a large province of the Roman empire, including not merely the country Galatia but parts of Paphlagonia, Pontus, Phrygia, Pisidia, Lycaonia, and Isauria. The name occurs in 1 Cor. 16:1; Gal. 1:2; 1 Pet. 1:1; and perhaps 2 Tim. 4:10 (*see* GAULS). Some writers assume that Galatia is also mentioned in Acts 16:6 and 18:23, but the Greek there has the phrase *hē Galatikḗ chṓra,* "Galatic region" or "territory." Although the RV has "Galatia," it must not be assumed without proof that "Galatic region" is synonymous with "Galatia." (To cross "British territory"

means something different from crossing "Britain.") So "Galatic region" must have had a distinct connotation, and the writer had some reason for using that term, even if it were geographically equivalent to Galatia (but see *SPT,* pp. 104, 194).

Two questions must be answered. (1) In which of the two senses is "Galatia" used by Paul and Peter? (2) What did Luke mean by "Galatic region" or "territory"? These questions have not merely geographical import; they bear most closely, and exercise determining influence, upon many points in the biography, chronology, and missionary work and methods of Paul.

II. Origin of the Name.–The name "Galatia" was introduced into Asia after 278 B.C., when a large body of migrating Gauls (Gk. *Galátai*) crossed from Europe at the invitation of Nicomedes I of Bithynia; after ravaging much of western Asia Minor they were gradually confined to a district, and boundaries were fixed for them after 232 B.C. Thus originated the independent state of Galatia, inhabited by three Gaulish tribes, Tolistobogii, Tectosages, and Trocmi, with three city centers, Pessinus, Ancyra (modern Ankara), and Tavium. They had brought their families, and therefore continued to be a distinct Gaulish ethnic community. The Gaulish language was apparently imposed on the former inhabitants, who remained in the country as an inferior caste. The Galatai soon adopted the religion of the country but retained also their own, at least until the 2nd cent. A.D.; it was politically important for them to maintain and exercise the powers of the old priesthood, as at Pessinus, where they shared the office with the old priestly families.

The Galatian state of the three tribes lasted until 25 B.C., governed first by a council and by tetrarchs or chiefs of the twelve divisions of the people (four to each tribe), and, after 63 B.C., by tribal kings. Deiotarus established himself as sole king by murdering the other two kings, and after his death in 40 B.C. his power passed to Castor and then to Amyntas (36-25 B.C.). Amyntas bequeathed his kingdom to Rome, and it was made a Roman province (Dio Cassius *Hist.* xlviii.33.5; Strabo *Geog.* xii.5.1 omits Castor). Amyntas had ruled also parts of Phrygia, Pisidia, Lycaonia, and Isauria. The new province included these parts, and to it were added Inner Paphlagonia in 6 B.C., part of Pontus in 2 B.C. (called Pontus Galaticus in distinction from Eastern Pontus, which was governed by King Polemo and styled Polemoniacus), and in A.D. 64 also Pontus Polemoniacus. Part of Lycaonia was non-Roman and was governed by King Antiochus; from A.D. 41 to 72 Laranda (Karaman) belonged to this district, which was distinguished as "Antiochiana regio" from the Roman "regio Lycaonia" called "Galatica."

This large province was divided into *regiones* for administrative purposes; and the *regiones* coincided roughly with the old national divisions of Pisidia, Phrygia (including Pisidian Antioch, Iconium, Apollonia), Lycaonia (including Derbe, Lystra, and a district organized on the village system), etc. The Romans called this province "Galatia," the kingdom of Amyntas. The extent of the application of names like Asia and Galatia, in the Roman language, varied with the shifting boundaries of each province. The name Galatia is used to indicate the contemporary province by Ptolemy, Pliny (*Nat. hist.* v.42 [146]), and Tacitus (*Hist.* ii.9; *Ann.* xiii.35), by later chroniclers when using the term in a sense no longer customary, and in inscriptions (*CIL,* III, 254, 272; VI, 332, 1408f.; VIII, 11,028, 18,270, etc.). These are almost all Roman sources, and express a purely Roman view. If Paul used the name "Galatia" to indicate the province, then he consistently and naturally took a Roman view, used names in a Roman connotation, and grouped his churches according to Roman provincial divisions; and that view is characteristic of the apostle, who looked forward from Asia to Rome (Acts 19:21), aimed at imperial conquest for Christ, and crossed the empire from province to province. Macedonia, Achaia, and Asia were always provinces to Paul. On the other hand, in the Greco-Asiatic world the tendency was to speak of the province either as the Galatic Eparchia (as at Iconium in A.D. 54, *CIG,* 3991) or by enumerating its *regiones* (or a selection of them). The latter method was followed in a number of inscriptions found in the province (*CIL,* III, *passim*).

III. Luke's Narrative.–Applying these contemporary facts to Luke's interpretation of the narrative, the evangelization of the province began in Acts 13:14. The stages were: (1) the audience in the synagogue at Pisidian Antioch, 13:14-43; (2) almost the whole city, 13:44; (3) the whole region, i.e., a large district that was affected from the capital (as the whole of Asia was affected from Ephesus, Acts 19:10); (4) Iconium, another city of this region — in 13:51 no boundary is mentioned; (5) a new region Lycaonia with two cities and a surrounding district, 14:6; (6) return journey to organize the churches in (a) Lystra, (b) Iconium, and (c) Pisidian Antioch (14:21-23, adopting the secondary reading of B. F. Westcott and F. J. A. Hort, *The NT in the Original Greek* [1886], Gk. *kaí eis Ikónion kaí Antiócheian,* and distinguishing the two regions Lycaonia and Iconium-Antioch); (7) progress across the region Pisidia, where no churches were founded (14:24; Pisidian Antioch is not in this region, which lies between Antioch and Pamphylia).

Again (in 16:1-6) Paul revisited the two *regiones*: (1) Derbe and Lystra, i.e., "regio Lycaonia Galatica"; (2) the Phrygian and Galatic region, i.e., the region that was racially Phrygian and politically Galatic. Paul traversed both regions, making no new churches but only strengthening the existing disciples and churches. In 18:23 he again visited the two *regiones,* and they are briefly enumerated: (1) the Galatic region (so called briefly by a traveler who had just crossed Antiochiana and distinguished Roman Lycaonia from it as Galatica); (2) Phrygia. On this occasion he specially appealed to individual disciples. It was a final visit before Paul went to Rome and the west. The contribution to the poor of Jerusalem was evidently instituted on this occasion, and the proceeds later were carried by Gaius of Derbe and Timothy (Acts 20:4; 24:17; 1 Cor. 16:1). This was a device to bind the new churches to the original center of the faith.

According to Lukan usage, these four churches always belong to two *regiones,* Phrygia and Lycaonia; and each *regio* is in one case described as Galatic, i.e., part of the province of Galatia. Luke did not follow the Roman custom, as Paul did; he kept the custom of the Greeks and Asiatic peoples, and styled the province by enumerating its *regiones,* using the expression "Galatic" (as in "Pontus Galaticus" and at Iconium, *CIG,* 3991) to indicate the supreme unity of the province. By using this adjective about both *regiones* he made it clear that for him all four churches were included in that unity.

From Paul's references we gather that he regarded the churches of Galatia as one group, converted together (Gal. 4:13), exposed to the same influences and changing together (1:6, 8; 3:1; 4:9), naturally visited at one time by a traveler (1:8; 4:14). He never thought of churches of Phrygia or of Lycaonia, only of the province Galatia (as of provinces Asia, Macedonia, Achaia). Paul did not include in one class all the churches of one journey; he classed the churches of Macedonia separately from those of Achaia. Troas, Laodicea, and Colossae he classed with Asia (as Luke did Troas, Acts 20:4f.), Philippi with Macedonia, Corinth with Achaia. These classifications are true only of the Roman usage, not of the early Greek usage. The practice (later universal) of classifying churches by provinces was derived from the usage of the apostles, according to Theodore of Mopsuestia on 1 Tim. 3:8 (Swete, *OTG,* II, 121; cf. A. von Harnack, *Mission and Expansion of Christianity in the First Three Centuries,* I [repr. 1962], 446f.; II [1904-1905], 96). His churches then belonged to four provinces, Asia, Galatia, Achaia, and Macedonia. There were no other Pauline churches; all united in the gift of money that was carried to Jerusalem (Acts 20:4; 24:17).

IV. Paul's Use of "Galatians."–The people of the province of Galatia, consisting of many diverse ethnic groups, when summed up together were called *Galatae,* e.g., by Tacitus (*Ann.* xv.6). An inscription of Apollonia Phrygiae also called the people of the city *Galatae.* If Paul spoke to an individual church at Philippi or Corinth, he addressed the members as Philippians or Corinthians (Phil. 4:15; 2 Cor. 6:11), not as Macedonians or Achaeans; but when he addressed a group of several churches (as Antioch, Iconium, Derbe, and Lystra) he could use only the term for the province.

All attempts to find in Paul's letter to the Galatians any allusions that reveal the distinctive character of the Gauls or Galatai have failed. The Gauls were an aristocracy in the land they had conquered. They clung stubbornly to their own Celtic religion long after the time of Paul, even though they also acknowledged the power of the old goddess of the country. They spoke their own Celtic tongue. They were proud, even boastful, and independent. They kept their native law under the empire. The "Galatians" to whom Paul wrote had changed very quickly to a new form of religion, not out of fickleness, but out of a certain propensity to a more oriental form of religion that exacted of them more sacrifice of a ritual type. They needed to be called to freedom; they were submissive rather than arrogant. They spoke Greek. They were accustomed to the Greco-Asiatic law: the law of adoption and inheritance which Paul mentioned in his letter. (This law is not Roman, but Greco-Asiatic.)

On 1 and 2 Maccabees *see* GAULS.

Bibliography.–W. M. Ramsay, comm. on Galatians (1900); *CRE; SPT; CERP; Monumenta Asiae Minoris Antiqua* (1928ff.); *Anatolian Studies*; F. F. Bruce, "Galatian Problems," five articles in *BJRL,* 51-55 (1968/69-1972/73); C. J. Hemer, *JTS,* N.S. 27 (1976), 122-26; *Themelios,* N.S. 2 (1976/77), 81-88; *Expos.T.,* 89 (1977/78), 239-243.

W. M. RAMSAY
C. J. HEMER

GALATIANS gə-lā'shənz. *See* GALATIA.

GALATIANS, EPISTLE TO THE.

I. General Theme
II. Addressees
III. Location of the Congregations of Galatia
IV. Occasion and Purpose
V. Date
VI. Content
  A. Paul's Defense of His Apostolic Qualifications
  B. Gospel of Justification by Faith Alone Upheld
  C. New Life Through the Holy Spirit
VII. Authenticity

I. General Theme.–The Epistle to the Galatians is perhaps, in its personal and emotional quality, the most characteristic letter that we possess from the hand of Paul. In the context of an antithesis between faith and Judaizing (under the influence of which the congregations in Galatia were beginning to observe Jewish practices and ceremonies), Paul presented an explication of the gospel and of the meaning of the law that, in its polemical radicalness and boldness of thought, in its emotional tone, and in its pastoral concern for the congregation, is scarcely equalled by any other Epistle.

II. Addressees.–Although a well-known controversy exists over the reference of the term "Galatia" in 1:2 (see below), we can, from the contents of the Epistle, deduce a few things concerning the relationship that existed between Paul and his readers. The churches of Galatia had been founded by Paul himself (1:8; 4:19). His first preaching of the gospel to them occurred as a result of (or while he was suffering from) a physical infirmity or sickness (4:13). Perhaps, due to illness, he had been compelled to remain with them for a period of time. If "Galatia" referred to the Roman province of that name, his infirmity may have been a result of physical suffering inflicted upon him when he preached the gospel in that area for the first time (Acts 13:50f.; 14:5-7; cf. 2 Tim. 3:11). Whatever it may have been, those who responded to his preaching did not despise him on account of his infirmity, but rather received him as an angel of God. Thus a close bond existed between Paul and these congregations, and Paul made an emotional appeal to this old and intimate relationship now that others had come between him and them (cf. esp. the moving pericope of 4:12-20). We can infer from 1:8 that others had accompanied Paul in the preaching of the gospel to the Galatians. The identification of these companions depends upon the meaning of "Galatia" in 1:2. If it referred to the northern geographical territory of that name, then they may well have been Silas and Timothy, Paul's companions on his second missionary journey. If the Roman province was intended, the most likely candidate is Barnabas.

It can also be inferred from 4:13 that Paul had already visited these congregations more than once, for in this verse he used the expression "when I preached the gospel to you for the first time" (Gk. *tó próteron*; RSV "at first"). It is true that *tó próteron* can be translated as "formerly" (cf. NEB mg.), in which case more than one visit was not implied. "The first time" is the preferable reading, however, since "formerly" would be somewhat superfluous in this context. "The first time," then, implies that Paul had already preached the gospel in Galatia on two different occasions (namely, "the first time," 4:13, and again very recently, cf. 1:6) before writing this Epistle. Thus it is more likely that "Galatia" referred to the province than to the territory, for it is not certain that Paul preached the gospel in the latter upon two different occasions (see III below). The interpretation of *tó próteron* in 4:13 also has great importance for the dating of the Epistle.

Finally, it is to be noted that the apostle apparently addressed himself to Christians of pagan background. He told in 2:5 how at Jerusalem he contended for the freedom of the gentile Christians, and how he was thus serving the interests of the Galatians. He reminded them in 4:8 of the time when they served idols and he warned them more than once not to allow themselves to be circumcised (5:2; 6:12). All of these considerations indicate the pagan origin of the Galatian congregations. It is true that Paul assumed on the part of his readers more than a mere passing acquaintance with the Jewish religion and the OT (cf. 3:6-22; 4:21-31). Perhaps many proselytes were among the members of the congregations. The Judaizing influences that were threatening the congregations, however, also confronted them with the Jewish religion. Finally, direct proof from the OT belonged to the heart of Paul's method of presenting the gospel. Thus the gentile congregations were in need of some knowledge about the OT, and they must have been instructed therein.

III. Location of the Congregations of Galatia.–We must here choose between the so-called North Galatian and South Galatian hypotheses (also known as the territorial and provincial hypotheses, respectively).

North Galatia, or the geographical territory of Galatia, referred to an area in the heart of Asia Minor, bounded on the north by Pontus and Bithynia, on the southwest by Phrygia, and on the east by Cappadocia. The Tectosages, Tolistobogii, and Trocmi, Celtic tribes that had infiltrated from Macedonia and Thessaly in the 3rd cent. B.C., gave it its name. Its principal cities were Ancyra, Pessinus, and Tavium. The inhabitants of this territory, in distinction from the West European Celts, were called the Gallogrecians. They constituted a heterogeneous element among the Asiatic peoples and for a long time preserved their own customs and peculiarities. Even after centuries had passed, a deep gulf separated them from the surrounding peoples. Shortly before the beginning of the Christian era, Rome took over the kingdom of Galatia and made it into a province with Ancyra as capital. In addition to the original regions of Galatia, however, this province now comprised the territory of Pisidia and parts of Lycaonia, Phrygia, and Cappadocia.

Whereas formerly scholars assumed that "Galatia" in 1:2 referred to the original landscape, since the middle of the 18th cent. the South Galatian hypothesis has been defended, especially under the influence of such scholars as T. Zahn and W. M. Ramsay. According to this theory, Paul was not addressing this Epistle to the North Galatians, but rather to the congregations in the more southern cities of Antioch, Iconium, Lystra, and Derbe, whose founding the book of Acts so vividly describes. Even today the South Galatian theory has many adherents, e.g., Goodspeed, T. W. Manson, McNeile-Williams, Michaelis, Guthrie, and Klijn. Other important spokesmen (e.g., Schürer, Behm, Greijdanus, Kümmel, and Stählin) still adhere to the North Galatian theory.

The most important arguments for and against the theory are the following five:

(1) For: Paul always, or at least nearly always, used the names of the Roman provinces, not those of the original territories.

Against: Important exceptions to the above statement suggest it cannot be considered a rule. Several times (Gal. 1:22; 1 Thess. 2:14; 2 Cor. 1:16) Paul referred to Judea in the old territorial sense, and he did not use an official name in the reference to Arabia in Gal. 1:17.

This counterargument does not carry much weight. It is not strange that Paul, a native Jew, should continue to refer to Judea in the original, territorial sense rather than in the official sense, and this can hardly be used as an argument against the general rule of using a provincial name. Concerning the reference to Arabia, though it is true that Paul did not intend the entire Arabian peninsula, but merely the Nabatean Kingdom (the capital of which was Petra) that lay in the northern part of the peninsula, in view of the geographical relationships, it would be difficult to use this fact as a touchstone for drawing conclusions about Paul's general usage. We can say with confidence that, as a rule, where there are no important reasons to do otherwise, Paul used the names of the Roman provinces.

(2) For: This Epistle assumes more contact with and knowledge of Judaism on the part of its readers than is likely to have been present in the remote areas of North Galatia. In contrast, we know from Acts 13–14 that the churches of South Galatia were from the outset exposed to heavy Jewish pressure. Acts 16:1-5 expressly mentions the cities of Lystra, Derbe, and Iconium as the places to which Paul conveyed the decisions of the apostolic council of Jerusalem.

Against: We know far too little about the situation in North Galatia to attach much weight to this argument. Moreover, the North Galatians' greater unfamiliarity with Judaism may have been precisely the reason that they were so quickly drawn away from the gospel (1:6-9.).

Although this does not constitute a decisive argument, in terms of the available evidence we can better account for the Galatians' familiarity with Judaism by means of the South Galatian hypothesis.

(3) Another argument in favor of the South Galatian hypothesis is that we actually know nothing of the foundation or existence of churches in the northern territory. These churches must have arisen during Paul's second or third missionary journey. Although Acts generally gives a clear picture of the churches that Paul founded on his journeys, it reports nothing concerning the foundation of churches in North Galatia. We read only that on his second missionary journey Paul went through the regions of Phrygia and Galatia with his coworkers, and that they were forbidden by the Holy Spirit to speak the word in Asia (Acts 16:6).

Regarding the third missionary journey, Acts 18:23 states that Paul, after remaining in Antioch (Syria) for a time, traveled successively through Galatia and Phrygia, strengthening all the disciples. Acts 16 gives more negative than positive indications with respect to the foundations of North Galatian churches. Thus we can more legitimately ask whether "all the disciples" in Acts 18:23 referred to congregations in the territory of Galatia, or whether Luke here (esp. in view of the sequence: Antioch [Syria], Galatia, Phrygia) had in mind the many congregations that lay to the south. In addition, if Paul did travel to the Celtic cities of North Galatia, he would have been required to make a detour of dozens of miles each time, whereas Acts 16 and 18 give the impression that he was merely passing through these regions en route to somewhere else. All of this can hardly be the background for the formation of congregations in North Galatia.

In opposition to this argument one could well maintain that Luke gave only a very summary report and that one must not attempt to read more into it than what is given (cf., e.g., A. Oepke, *Der Brief des Paulus an die Galater* [1957], p. 7). The question, however, is whether there is *any indication at all* of the foundation of churches in North Galatia. In any case, the possibility that the North Galatian hypothesis concerns itself with fictitious congregations cannot be ruled out.

(4) Paul's statement in Gal. 2:5 that he opposed the

false brethren in Jerusalem so "that the truth of the gospel might be preserved [Gk. *diameínēi*] for you" appears to have great importance in this connection. If we assume that Paul was here speaking of the apostolic council of Jerusalem (Acts 15), then the situation referred to in Gal. 2:5 occurred before Paul could have made his first visit to the territory of Galatia (Acts 16:6), and thus he could not at this time in Jerusalem have been defending the interests of congregations in North Galatia. He had every reason, however, to come forward for the congregations that he had just established in the southern parts of the province of Galatia. Thus Gal. 2:5 cannot be understood in terms of the North Galatian hypothesis.

(5) Over against these arguments in favor of the provincial hypothesis, to which a few of lesser importance could yet be added (e.g., the repeated mention of Barnabas [2:1, 9, 13], Paul's co-worker in the establishment of the South Galatian congregations; the comparison of 1 Cor. 16:1 with Acts 20:4, from which it could appear that Gaius of Derbe and Timothy of Lystra represented the congregations of Galatia on the journey to Jerusalem), the arguments that have been advanced in favor of the North Galatian hypothesis are of less significance. W. G. Kümmel (*Intro. to the NT,* p. 297) offers two arguments:

First, if the Epistle were addressed to the congregations of the so-called first missionary journey, Paul would not have said in 1:21, "then I went into the regions of Syria and Cilicia," but rather, "then I went to Syria and *to you.*"

Second, it is impossible that Paul would have addressed Christians from Lycaonia and Pisidia as "O . . . Galatians" (3:1), especially since such an expression occurs nowhere else in Paul's writings.

Concerning the former argument, however, Paul is not speaking at all in 1:21 about his first missionary journey, but about a journey that had taken place long before (cf. Acts 9:30) in which he did not come at all into the region of the South Galatian congregations. Regarding the latter argument it must not be overlooked that Paul was here writing to a *group* of congregations that could only be addressed with the collective name "Galatians." It may be true that such an expression never occurs in the (relatively few) sources that are now available, but this in no way proves the impossibility of Paul's having addressed the inhabitants of South Galatia in such a way.

We conclude as follows: though we must exercise much caution and reserve in judging a matter that involves so many historical factors that are not completely transparent, the greater part of the evidence seems to favor the South Galatian hypothesis. Thus we view the Epistle as sent to the churches that Paul founded (Acts 13–14) and again visited (Acts 16) after the Apostolic Council of Jerusalem (Acts 15). These churches were among the first that Paul founded, and it is thus no wonder that their welfare lay particularly close to his heart. His first visit to them took place, due to the enmity of the Jews, under very difficult circumstances; and it is understandable that Paul was greatly disturbed by the thought that of all his congregations, *these* might finally fall prey to Judaism: "My little children, with whom I am again in travail until Christ be formed in you" (4:19).

IV. Occasion and Purpose.–We can ascertain the following concerning the occasion and purpose of the Epistle to the Galatians and the false doctrine that it combated. Since Paul's recent visit to the Galatians (1:6), men had arisen among them who presented a doctrine other than Paul's and tried to question his authority. It appears that they were Christians. They at least claimed that their teaching was the gospel, although Paul declared that it was no gospel at all (1:6f.). They taught that circumcision was necessary for salvation (5:2; 6:12f.) and they demanded that the ceremonial law of Moses be maintained, at least in the observance of "days, and months, and seasons, and years" (4:10). Paul ascribed false motives to them in these matters. Although they wanted to subject the congregation to themselves, drawing them away from Paul (4:17), they did not themselves fulfil the law that they commended; on the contrary, they were driven by selfish ambition (6:13) and sought to escape from the offense of the cross of Christ (6:12).

From the way in which Paul defended his apostolic office, we can infer that these false teachers had cast doubt upon, or even denied, the legitimacy and genuineness of his calling. Over against their contentions Paul maintained that he was seeking to please God and not men (1:10) and that he was called not by men but by God Himself (1:1, 12) in a very direct and extraordinary way (1:13-17). In addition, he had received his knowledge of the gospel from the Lord Himself and not from the other apostles. Later, when he came into contact with the other apostles, he maintained his independence from them; e.g., he took his co-worker Titus with him to Jerusalem without first circumcising him (2:1-10), and later in Antioch, he openly opposed Peter for taking an indecisive stand with regard to the gentile Christians (2:11-21). Paul showed, however, in the same connection that there was no discord between him and the other apostles (the "pillars," 2:9). Rather, they were in full agreement about the conditions with which gentile Christians would have to comply, as appears from the solemn compact that they made in Jerusalem (2:7-10).

All of the evidence indicates that these false teachers were Jewish Christians who tried to combine the gospel with the observance of the Jewish ceremonies, above all with circumcision. Paul had met such people in Jerusalem; he referred to them there as "false brethren" who formed a threat to the freedom that had been given in Christ (2:4). It is quite possible that the false teachers in Galatia had connections with this Jerusalem faction, though we have little proof. Paul did speak in 4:21-31 of Jerusalem as the mother or center of enslavement under the law. It is certain that various influences in opposition to the freedom preached by Paul came from Jerusalem. But the available evidence gives no accurate information concerning the circumstances under which these false teachers appeared among the Galatian congregations. Some have wanted to infer from 5:10 that one distinct person of especial importance had the leadership in this group. The expression which Paul used here can be construed in more than one way, however, and it may carry a more rhetorical character. In any event, this verse offers no support to the (old Tübingen) contention that Paul's adversaries were the leaders of the congregation in Jerusalem (Peter and James). The way in which Paul spoke of these leaders in Gal. 2 is the most solid proof that he was in fundamental agreement with them, and it was on this basis that he could reprimand Peter when the latter in a moment of weakness tried to avoid the consequences of their agreement.

There are other conceptions concerning these false teachers of the Galatians. Some have argued that Paul's adversaries were themselves of pagan origin, pagans who had received the Jewish circumcision and who were attempting to win others over to it. Advocates of this position appeal, among other things, to the present tense of the verb in 6:13, saying that Paul thereby indicated that they were not Jews who had been circumcised from birth. They appeal, moreover, to Paul's reproach that these people did not keep the (whole) law themselves (6:13), and to his sharp word in 5:12 that they had better mutilate (castrate) themselves as the heathen did. This conception (as advanced, e.g., by E. Hirsch in *ZNW*, 29 [1930], 192ff., and later, in modified form, by J. Munck, in *Paul and the Salvation of Mankind* [Eng. tr. 1959], pp. 86ff.) is, however, hardly acceptable. For the present tense in 6:13 ("who receive circumcision") need not be taken in a temporal sense; what is more, it is open to question whether the variant reading, the perfect tense, which appears in p^{46} B and elsewhere, is not to be preferred. That these false teachers did not themselves observe the demands that they imposed upon others is not necessarily an argument against their Jewish origin (cf. Mt. 23:3f.; Lk. 11:46). Leaving aside these incidental expressions that have no decisive force, the entire tendency of Paul's argumentation in Galatians refutes this conception. Paul was not merely opposing the circumcision of gentile believers; he also gave a penetrating analysis of what the promise, the law, and the fatherhood of Abraham meant for the Jews. The antithesis, therefore, was directed against Judaism itself, not merely against the influence of Jewish proselytism.

Others, such as W. Lütgert (*Gesetz und Geist: Eine Untersuchung zur Vorgeschichte des Galaterbriefes* [*Beiträge zur Förderung christlicher Theologie,* 22/6, 1919]) and J. H. Ropes (*The Singular Problem of the Epistle to the Galatians* [*Harvard Theological Studies,* 14, 1929]) have thought that Paul was taking issue in Galatians not only with Judaism, but also with a spiritualistic libertinism. They appeal for support to Paul's pronouncements in Gal. 5 against the misuse of the freedom that had been given in Christ. Thus Paul is seen as fighting a battle on two fronts. W. Schmithals (*ZNW,* 47 [1956], 25ff.) went even further, contending that Paul is here (as in many of his other Epistles) involved in a struggle with Gnosticism. The circumcision that the false doctrine required is then not that of the Judaizers but one conceived from the standpoint of Gnostic dualism. "The elemental spirits of the universe" of which Paul spoke in 4:3, 9 in connection with the observance of days, months, seasons, and years, are seen as having reference to Gnostic ideas. Finally, Paul's warning to the Galatians (5:3) that he who allowed himself to be circumcised was obliged to keep the whole law indicates that the false teachers had *not* imposed this requirement and thus could not have been Judaizers.

This entire conception, however, misses the actual scope of the Epistle, for Paul was undoubtedly concerned with the relationship of the Galatians to Judaism (the promise to Abraham, the seed of Abraham, the law as pedagogue, etc.). The "Gnostic" interpretation of the circumcision mentioned in Galatians is therefore pure fancy, while the claim that the *stoicheía* ("the elements") have reference to angel-spirits cannot be substantiated (cf. A. J. Bandstra, *The Law and the Elements of the World* [1964]). For the same reason, Gal. 5:3 cannot be used to support this conception, but is best understood as an integral part of Paul's polemic against the Judaizers (see above). Finally, Paul's warning against the misuse of freedom need not be seen as directed against a libertine group. It can be well understood as a warning against a mistaken conception of freedom on the part of the congregation itself, or even as Paul's self-defense against criticism coming from the Judaizers that his doctrine of justification by faith would give free rein to sinfulness (cf. Rom. 3:8; 6:1). All in all, it cannot be said that these new conceptions offer a better vantage point for understanding the Epistle. On the contrary, they can only strengthen the conviction that Paul's polemic in Galatians was directed against Judaizers.

V. Date.–The question of the time and place of the writing of the Epistle to the Galatians is closely connected with the above discussion. If we accept the South Galatian hypothesis, then the Epistle must have been sent shortly after Paul's second visit to these congregations (cf. 1:6), for 4:13 speaks of a *second* visit, if we accept the interpretation of Gk. *tó próteron* given above. If we compare this evidence with what is given in the book of Acts, then there is much in favor of the view that Paul wrote this Epistle during his so-called second missionary journey, perhaps in Corinth, where he stayed for a considerable length of time (Acts 18). If we take into account the chronological information concerning Gallio's proconsulship in Achaia that can be deduced from the inscription on the stone fragment found at Delphi (cf., e.g., A. Deissmann, *St. Paul* [1912], pp. 213ff.), the date comes to A.D. 50/51 (*see also* CHRONOLOGY OF THE NT II.F). Galatians would then be one of the oldest, if not the oldest, Pauline letter that has been preserved.

The frequently discussed question of whether the trip to Jerusalem (Gal. 2) is identical to the Apostolic Council (Acts 15) has great importance for the dating of the Epistle. For more than one reason, this is a complicated matter. First, some are of the opinion that the information that is given in Galatians disallows the identification of Gal. 2 and Acts 15. Second, it is maintained that this identification would conflict with what is given in Acts; for according to Acts, the Apostolic Council occurred on Paul's third stay in Jerusalem after his conversion (cf. Acts 9:26; 11:30), whereas Galatians speaks of only two trips (1:18; 2:1), of which the second would then be the Apostolic Council.

It is difficult to deny that Gal. 2 and Acts 15 describe the same event, although it may be that they do so in different ways and from different points of view. In both reports the same matter was at stake — namely, to what extent gentile believers must subject themselves to the law of Moses, and especially whether they should be circumcised. Both reports show Paul and the leaders of the Jerusalem church (Peter, John, and James) arriving at a common viewpoint and adopting a common policy. That the same matter should be dealt with upon two different occasions under almost the same circumstances is highly unlikely.

As has been said, however, two objections against this identification have been entered. (1) On the basis of the information in Galatians, the following questions have been raised. If the Apostolic Council of Acts 15 preceded the Epistle to the Galatians, how could it be that Jewish Christians in Galatia were yet demanding the circumcision of gentile believers? And why then did not Paul in his letter simply refer to the clear pronouncements of the Apostolic Council instead of entering anew into a thoroughgoing argument against Judaism? Why did he not cite the utterances of James and Peter in order to terminate the attempts of the Judaizers to set him in opposition to the leaders at Jerusalem? How can Peter's conduct at Antioch (Gal. 2:11-14) be explained if the Apostolic Council had occurred just shortly before? These objections, which have been presented in various forms, are not too difficult to answer. To be sure, whatever the objections brought against the identification of the agreement in Gal. 2 with that of the Apostolic Council, one cannot deny that Paul in this Epistle presupposed this agreement. In Gal. 2 he referred to such an agreement at length. That all Jewish Christians (e.g., those in Galatia) did not adhere to the agreement that had been reached can hardly serve as an argument against the identification of Gal. 2 with Acts 15. Judaism was no minor problem among Christian congregations even *after* the Apostolic Council, as can be seen, e.g., from Romans and Philippians. It is not difficult to understand, moreover, why Paul in this letter did not, in a formal way, refer to or reproduce the decisions of the Apostolic Council; he had surely already done so before he wrote the Epistle (cf. Acts 16:4). Thus he was amazed that his readers were already departing from his injunctions (Gal. 1:6). Further, he was not content merely to demonstrate his conformity with the Jerusalem leaders. He asserted his independence of them and showed that it was in his independent position that Peter and James accepted him. Thus he did not content himself with an appeal to these "pillars" (2:9), but rather set himself the task of explaining to the Galatians his own insights into divine purposes in the history of salvation. Finally, with regard to Peter, his weakness at Antioch was not that he rejected the decisions of the Apostolic Council; rather, he did not draw the correct conclusions from them *for himself* in his intercourse with gentile Christians, and thus he indirectly put the gentile Christians back into an isolated position. Hence none of the above arguments constitutes a serious objection to the identification of Gal. 2 with Acts 15. (But *see* ACTS OF THE APOSTLES VIII.)

(2) At first sight, that Paul seemed to be speaking in Gal. 2:1 about his second trip to Jerusalem presents greater difficulties. For this reason several scholars think that what is reported in Gal. 2 must be identified with Paul's trip to Jerusalem described in Acts 11:30; 12:25 (the so-called collection journey). Calvin (comm. on Galatians [repr. 1965], p. 24) thought that Paul was speaking in Gal. 2:1 about the event recorded in Acts 11:30. If this were the case, then Paul could have visited the Galatians only once before he wrote his Epistle, and 4:13 would have to be interpreted accordingly (although one would still distinguish between Paul's journey [Acts 13:1–14:20] ending in Derbe, and his return journey [14:21], through the same cities of Galatia). De Zwaan, Guthrie, Klijn, and others have defended this position. It remains, however, a major problem for this concept that the same matter should have been decided by the same individuals on two different occasions, and that Gk. *tó próteron* in 4:13 would have to be interpreted unnaturally.

In addition, nothing in Acts 11:30 (cf. also 12:25) lends support to the notion that Paul went to Jerusalem on this occasion for any reason beyond the delivery of the collection money. This objection carries greater weight, since in accordance with Gal. 2:1 this unmentioned reason would actually have been the main business of the journey. Conversely, Gal. 2:1 says nothing about this collection as the first motivation for the journey. Thus there is more to favor the identification of Gal. 2 with Acts 15 than with Acts 11:30 and 12:25.

Must we then suppose that Luke erred in the report of Paul's journeys — either that the journey mentioned in 15:1-4 was identical to that of 11:30 and was incorrectly described as a later event, or that 11:30 was mistaken? The former position is held, e.g., by P. Bonnard (*L'Épître de Saint Paul aux Galates* [1953], pp. 46ff., who also gives an overview of all the alternative solutions to this problem), the latter by Kümmel (pp. 301f.).

It is our opinion, however, that all of these suppositions are based on a false premise, namely, that Paul in Gal. 1–2 enumerated all of his trips to Jerusalem and thus cannot have omitted the one recorded in Acts 11:30. This premise poses a dilemma: either Gal. 2 and Acts 11:30 must refer to the same event, or Acts 11 or 15 must be in error. A closer consideration of the chain of reasoning in Gal. 1:16–2:1, however, brings us to a different point of view. Paul was concerned here merely to show, first, that he was independent as an apostle, and second, that he was in agreement with the apostles in Jerusalem. For this reason, he said first (Gal. 1:17-24) that he did not go directly to Jerusalem after his conversion; he went there three years later for a fifteen-day period, at which time he had contact only with Peter. Thus he showed that he had received his commission and his gospel not from men, but from God. When he continued in 2:1, "Then after fourteen years I went up again to Jerusalem," his argument is not the same as in 1:17-24. He had no more need of demonstrating his independence and he was not concerned to enumerate his (few) journeys to Jerusalem. His concern, rather, is now to show how, on the matter of circumcision, he not only stood his ground in the presence of the Jerusalem leaders, but also met with their concurrence on every point. The matter that is at issue here is thus his quarrel with opponents in Galatia, and the attitude of the apostles with regard to it. It is therefore no surprise that he did not mention the collection journey of Acts 11:30, nor need this be regarded as a suppression of the truth (cf. 1:20). That journey was entirely beside the point here, having no relation to the conflict between Paul and his opponents.

Once we have set aside the notion that Paul is giving a review in Gal. 1f. of all his journeys to Jerusalem and of all his contacts with the other apostles, no difficulty remains in understanding both Gal. 2 and Acts 15 as speaking of the same meeting (the Apostolic Council). The issue at stake was the same in both reports. The differences between the two accounts could be discussed further, but they are hardly so great that one cannot regard the two as speaking of the same event.

Once this identity is established, the difficulties of dating the letter are essentially removed. Some think that since the terminology and contents of Galatians and Romans have so much in common, both Epistles must have been written during the same period. Others argue that the same applies to 2 Corinthians. Yet one cannot consider such comparisons of much value in dating Galatians. Romans and 2 Corinthians were written shortly after one another, but they are not significantly similar. Galatians is undoubtedly more akin to Romans than 2 Corinthians is. Yet closer consideration reveals Romans to be more balanced and thorough than Galatians (*see* ROMANS, EPISTLE OF VI, VII). Romans is most naturally understood as Paul's concluding summary of the position that he had developed as a result of his many disputations in many different places, including those with the Jews. Paul's reflections on one's relationship to Judaism, the law, justification, and the Spirit were not merely occasional concerns in his apostolic preaching and other activities. They were rather his constant preoccupation. Thus one may assume without difficulty that what Paul had treated in Galatians in terms of a very specific situation he took up again six or seven years later (when this phase of his activity had come to a close, cf. Rom. 15:23), expounding it in a larger context and with much less local color.

VI. Content.–The content and the theological character of the letter can be described as follows. The very brief and sober *exordium* and salutation (1:1-5), in which Paul immediately and with great power defended the unassailability of his apostolic calling, was *not* followed, as in all the other Epistles that we possess from the hand of Paul, by a thanksgiving for the recipients of the letter. Instead, he at once expressed his amazement that the Galatians had so quickly allowed themselves to be led astray by another gospel. He directly mentioned his opponents, denied that what they preached was worthy of the name "gospel," and pronounced an *anathema* against anyone who preached a gospel other than the one the Galatians had heard from him (1:6-9).

The remainder of the Epistle is essentially divided into three parts.

A. Paul's Defense of His Apostolic Qualifications (1:10–

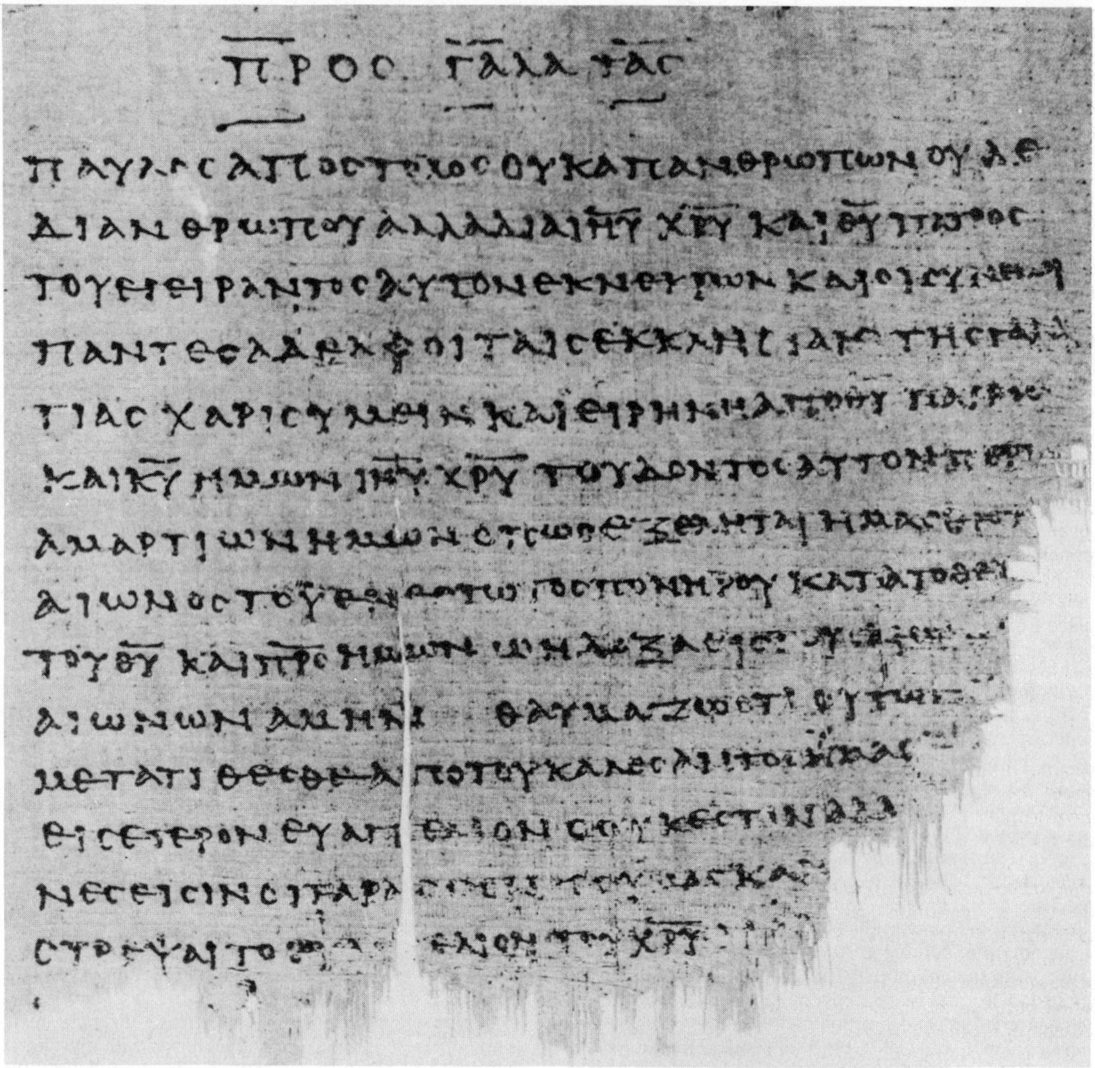

Chester Beatty papyrus (***p***[46]) showing Gal. 1:1-7 (University of Michigan Library)

2:21). The gospel that he preached was no human invention. He was at one time himself an enemy of the gospel, when in his zeal for the ancestral traditions he persecuted the Church. He had received his commission not from men but from God Himself. It was only later that he came into contact with a few of the apostles, and then only for a short time. He was personally unknown to the members of the Judean churches. All of this (as described in 1:10-24) indicates how little he was dependent upon people for his apostolic calling. He had also preserved his independence in the exercise of his calling. When he returned to Jerusalem fourteen years after his first visit (since his conversion), he presented his gospel with restraint to the leaders there, having Titus, a gentile believer who had not been circumcised, present with him. He had come to full agreement with them without conceding an inch to those who begrudged the gentile Christians their freedom in Christ (2:1-10). Later, in Antioch, he openly opposed Peter and Barnabas, when out of fear before certain men from Jerusalem they did not comply with the obligation that the agreement in Jerusalem had laid upon them (2:11-21). This passage at the same time forms a transition to the second section of the Epistle, for what was at stake in this conflict between Peter and Paul was the manner in which mankind is justified.

B. Gospel of Justification by Faith Alone Upheld (3:1–5:12). In this section, the apostle defended the contents of his gospel with great power and deep emotion. He rebuked the Galatians sharply. Had they been bewitched? Had they forgotten their experience of the gospel with all the blessings that it brought? Paul proceeded with a detailed argument from the OT, undoubtedly directed against the pretensions of the Judaizers. Abraham himself was justified, not by circumcision but on the basis of his faith, and it is *as one who had faith* that he became the father of many nations. In contrast, as Scripture makes plain, the law cannot secure the fulfillment of the promise, for the law brings a curse upon the transgressor. This curse has been borne by Christ in order that the fulfillment of the promise might come through faith rather than through the works of the law.

This issue brought the apostle to a profound contemplation of the relationship between the promise and the law (3:15-22). Here he made some of his most characteristic utterances concerning the law: the law, in the sinful situation in which it functions, can only increase sin; it bars the way to salvation, throwing mankind into prison; and thus it was, in the negative sense, mankind's pedagogue or disciplinarian until Christ came. Only with the coming of faith in Christ does mankind again have access to the promise, and it is only on this basis that all of those who are in Christ may call themselves children of Abraham and heirs of the promise (3:23-29).

This argumentation was continued in ch. 4, again in terms of mankind's enslavement under the law and the freedom that is in Christ. It is not the law but the Spirit who brings freedom (4:1-7). How then could the Galatians fall back into their former servitude (4:8-11)? This was followed by the apostle's most poignant emotional appeal to his relationship with the congregations, and his denunciation of those who would interpose themselves between him and them (4:12-20). He concluded with the profound allegory of Hagar and Sarah. In this allegory Paul pointed to the fundamental two-sided principle that was already manifest in the family of Abraham and that, via the law given at Sinai, had continued into the present — the principle, namely, of the earthly Jerusalem, the center of the law and of slavery, on the one hand, and on the other hand the heavenly Jerusalem, where Christ is, the place from which freedom is imparted in accordance with the Spirit and the promise and not in accordance with the flesh and the law (4:21-31). This section closed with the demand that the Galatians therefore make their choice — it is a question of all or nothing (5:1-12).

C. New Life Through the Holy Spirit (5:13–6:10). Proceeding from what had been said in the previous section about the Spirit (in opposition to the law), the apostle gave a fuller explication of the life that comes through the Spirit. It is a life in freedom — not a freedom that is in service of the flesh, but rather a freedom that is able to subdue active enslavement to the flesh. He placed the two in opposition to each other, here in terms of their manifestation in the works of the flesh and the fruit of the Spirit (5:13-25), and he continued with a series of separate exhortations (5:26–6:10). To the end, the opposition between the flesh and the Spirit formed the background of his presentation.

The postscript, written with Paul's own hand, warned once more against the self-seeking false teacher; it contains no further personal information or greetings, but closes with yet another personal appeal and with the apostolic blessing (6:11-18).

The great theological significance of this epistle lies in its central theme of justification by faith alone. This theme is then developed in terms of the *negative* role, so characteristic of his theology, that Paul accorded to the law in the history of redemption. The conception of the promise with which Paul operated here also has great significance. In contrast to the law, which is dependent upon human cooperation for fulfillment, the promise functions here as the overpowering, life-giving word of God. It is in this context that the Spirit enters into the picture, the new principle of life given in Christ, who alone has the power to give life to mankind, and to deliver from the bondage to sin and the flesh.

It is evident that the same thoughts were developed in a more thorough and perhaps more balanced manner in the Epistle to the Romans. A chapter such as 2 Cor. 3 also contains the same basic outlines of the Pauline gospel. The Epistle to the Galatians, although it is more abrupt and less systematic, has a great appeal in that in addition to being a document of deep theological insight, it gives a picture of Paul's great humanity and emotion in one of the most critical moments of his apostolic activity.

*VII. **Authenticity**.*–On the basis of the above considerations, we may say that the genuineness of this Epistle is self-evident. It has nevertheless at times been the object of certain hypercritical tendencies in the history of NT scholarship. Whereas the so-called Tübingen school chose for Galatians in the question of the alleged disparity between Acts and Galatians, the so-called radical Dutch school of the 19th cent. preferred to regard Acts as the authentic document, and Galatians as a second-century product of non-Pauline origin. Other arguments have been leveled against the authenticity of Galatians, e.g., its elevated Christology, which supposedly betrays a later origin. This radical criticism, introduced by Evanson (1792) and especially by B. Bauer (1850), was taken up by such scholars of the Dutch school as Loman, Pierson, Naber, and van Manen, who were followed by Steck of Switzerland. Others, for whom this radical criticism went too far, have sought to win support for the conception of an originally Pauline Epistle to which all sorts of insertions and interpolations were later added (Weiss, Baljon, Cramer, Völter, *et. al.).* Yet none of this criticism has been able to hold its ground. There is scarcely another Epistle of which the integrity and authenticity are now so generally accepted as that of Galatians. The arbitrary nature of this hypercriticism has been more and more acknowledged. The Epistle to the Galatians was accepted in the Christian Church from the beginning (cf. Polyc. Phil. 3:3; 5:1), and it is one of the most valuable documents that we possess for the understanding both of Paul's powerful personality and of the specific character of his gospel.

Bibliography.–Practically all the comms. contain a discussion of the problems dealt with above. For a list of the most important comms. on Galatians in recent years, see D. Guthrie, *NT Intro.* (1970), pp. 1027f., and W. G. Kümmel, *Intro. to the NT* (1975), p. 558.

For specific studies in Galatians, besides those mentioned in the article itself and listed by W. G. Kümmel, *Intro. to the NT* (1975), p. 294, see J. Becker, comm on Galatians (*NTD*, 8, 1976), p. 7; H. D. Betz, *Galatians* (*Hermeneia*, 1980); J. van Bruggen, "Na Veertien Jaren: de Datering van het in Galaten 2 genoemde Overleg te Jeruzalem" (Ph.D. diss., Kampen, 1973), esp. pp. 240-260 for an extensive bibliography.

H. N. RIDDERBOS

GALBANUM gal-ba'nəm [Heb. *ḥelbᵉnâ*; Gk. *chalbánē*] (Ex. 30:34; Sir. 24:15); NEB Apoc. GALBAN. A fetid yellowish resin derived from species of *Ferula*, probably *F. galbaniflua* (a plant in the carrot family), and apparently imported from Persia or India. When burned it emitted a disagreeable odor, and in antiquity was of some value as a fumigant. As the biblical texts indicate, however, it could be mixed with more fragrant spices and gums for a pleasant effect, since it enhanced and maintained those more pleasing aromas.

GALEED gal'ē-əd [Heb. *galʿēḏ*–'witness heap'] (Gen. 31:47f.); NEB GAL-ED. Its meaning is "cairn" or "heap of witness," corresponding to Aram. *yᵉgar śāhᵃḏûṯā'* (Gen. 31:47). It is applied to the stones piled up by Jacob and Laban to preserve the memory of their covenant, which was sealed by a common meal beside this cairn. The ancient custom of associating events with inanimate objects as witnesses is often illustrated in Hebrew history (e.g., Josh. 4:4ff.). This narrative may contain a suggestion of how the name "Gilead" came to be applied to that country. *See* GILEAD.

W. EWING

GALGALA gal'gal-ə [Gk. Galgala] (1 Macc. 9:2, AV). Equivalent to GILGAL, but it is uncertain which Gilgal is meant (cf. Josephus *Ant.* xii.11.1 [421]).

GALILEAN gal-ə-lē'ən. *See* GALILEE.

GALILEE gal'ə-lē [Heb. *gālîl*–'circuit, district, cylinder,' in construct 'the region of'; Gk. *galilaía*]. The northern portion of Palestine, scene of most of the earthly ministry of Jesus.

I. Name
II. Location
III. Physical Features
  A. Coastal Plain
  B. Upper Galilee
  C. Lower Galilee
  D. Plain of Esdraelon
  E. Galilee Rift
IV. Galilee in the OT
V. Galilee in the Apocrypha
VI. Galilee in the NT
VII. Galilee in Early Judaism

I. Name.–The modern Hebrew name *g^{e}lîl,* according to its vowel pattern, is in construct and requires another term to follow it in the genitive (cf. the plural *g^{e}lîlê kesep̱,* "rings of silver" [Est. 1:6] and *g^{e}lîlê zāhāḇ,* "cylinders of gold" [Cant. 5:14]). Such a phrase occurs in Isa. 9:1 (MT 8:23), *g^{e}lîl haggôyîm,* "the region of the gentiles/nations." The word became a proper name, however; cf. *qeḏeš baggālîl,* "Qadesh in (the) Galilee" (Josh. 20:7; 21:32; 1 Ch. 6:76 [MT 61]) and *b^{e}'ereṣ haggālîl,* "in the land of (the) Galilee" (1 K. 9:11), always written with the definite article. The feminine forms of the word, *g^{e}lîlâ,* pl. *g^{e}lîlôṯ,* also occur, used of the region of the Philistines (Josh. 13:2), of the regions of the Jordan (Josh. 22:10f.), and once of Galilee (2 K. 15:29). This last reference, as accented, appears to be with the *-â* directive ("toward the Galilee"), but the presence of the *'eṯ* of the direct object almost certainly requires the form to be a feminine singular with an erroneous accent. In the Greek of Josephus and the NT, the word *Galilaía* occurs regularly as a proper noun. It is reasonable to infer that the origin of the term is indicated in Isa. 9:1 — that "Galilee" was at first a pejorative term or at least descriptive of the fact that it was occupied or traversed by a large number of foreigners, and that "the Region" ("the Galil") subsequently became a proper name.

It is possible that *Gôyim* was originally the name of a people, for in Gen. 14:1 it appears in a list of kings of Shinar, Ellasar, Elam, etc., as "Tidal king of Goiim," and it would make little sense to speak of a "king of nations." If so, Harosheth-ha-Goyim in Jgs. 4:2 could also be understood as "the wooded hills of the Goyim." Later, because of gentile traffic in the region, *gôyim* came to be understood as meaning "gentiles."

II. Location.–In the OT, Galilee was "in the hill country of Naphtali" (Josh. 20:7). Likewise in Josh. 21:32 and 1 Ch. 6:76 Qedesh in Galilee is a portion of Naphtali. In Isa. 9:1 "Galilee of the nations" is associated with "the land of Zebulun and the land of Naphtali," but because of the structure of the passage it is not clear that identification is intended. ("The land beyond the Jordan" occurs in the same verse, immediately before the reference to Galilee.) According to 2 K. 15:29 Tiglath-pileser captured "Ijon and Abel-beth-maacah and Janoah and Kedesh and Hazor and Gilead and Galilee — all the land of Naphtali." The repetition of the conjunction "and" is significant, for it connects the first seven names and sets them apart from the next phrase; in other words, it names them as constituting "all the land of Naphtali." This, however, creates another problem, for while it places Galilee in Naphtali, as do the other texts mentioned above, it also places Gilead in Naphtali — which is not in accord with the boundaries of Naphtali given in Josh. 19:32-34. The northern border of Naphtali is not given, but it lay W of the Upper Jordan system (including lakes Huleh and Galilee) and was bounded

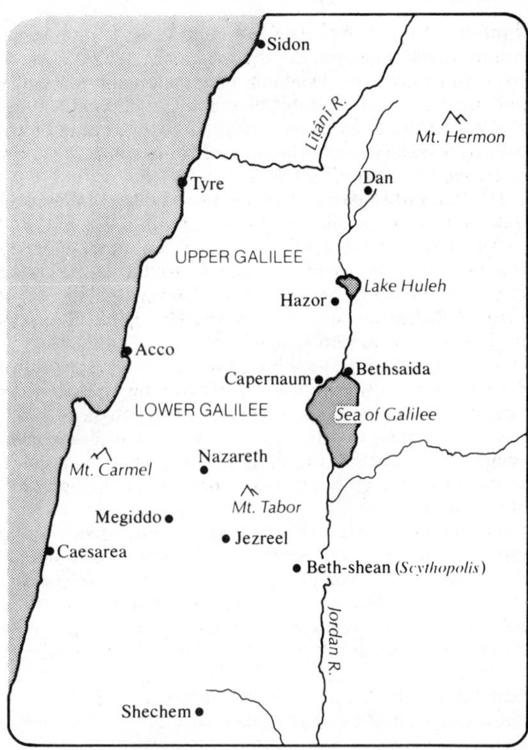

on the west, southwest, and south by the tribal portions of Asher, Zebulun, and Issachar. The southern boundary was approximately from the southern end of the Sea of Galilee to (but not including) Mt. Tabor, and therefore did not include Nazareth. Nor did it include the Valley of Jezreel, which belonged to Issachar.

In the Hellenistic and Roman periods Syrophoenicia included the coastal strip which was the tribal allotment of Asher. Indeed, there is little if any evidence that Asher ever fully occupied this region. The kingdom of Herod the Great did not include the coastal region N of Caesarea, nor did the tetrarchy of Herod Antipas. The plain of Esdraelon (Jezreel) was apparently included in Galilee during this period, but the eastern end, including Beth-shean (Scythopolis) was part of the Decapolis.

It is reasonable, therefore, to describe Galilee in NT times as consisting of Upper Galilee, Lower Galilee, and the plain of Esdraelon. Thus it stretched from the Jordan system (the source rivers, Lake Huleh, the Upper Jordan, and the Sea of Galilee) westward to, but probably not including, the maritime plain.

There is some evidence that a portion of the land E of the Jordan system was also included in Galilee. As we have seen, "beyond the Jordan" is mentioned in Isa. 9:1, and Gilead is mentioned along with Galilee in 2 K. 15:29. According to Josephus, "Judas the Galilean" (cf. Acts 5:37), who stirred up a revolt against the Romans (*BJ* ii.8.1 [118]), was from Gamala in Gaulonitis (*Ant.* xviii.1.1 [4]). Accordingly, G. A. Smith states that "the eastern shores of Lake Gennesaret also fell within the province," adding in a footnote that under the Turks it was part of Kada Tubariya, and that Palestine included a stretch along the eastern shore of the lake "from a minimum of 10 meters parallel with high-water mark to a maximum of about 2000" (*HGHL*, p. 271). The territory established by the United Nations (1947) for the Jewish state likewise includes such a strip.

It is not certain when the valley of Esdraelon was first

considered a part of Galilee. Josephus described the western frontiers of Galilee as "the outlying territory of Ptolemais and Carmel, a mountain once belonging to Galilee and now to Tyre" (*BJ* iii.3.1 [35]). G. A. Smith states that the valley became part of Galilee at the time of the Samaritan schism, but his reference to Josephus (*BJ* ii.3.4) is erroneous (*HGHL*, p. 247).

III. Physical Features.–Historically, Galilee has been divided into Upper Galilee and Lower Galilee (Josephus *BJ* iii.3.1 [35]), but for our purposes this oversimplifies the region. It is better to divide Galilee into five areas: (1) the coastal plain, (2) Upper Galilee, (3) Lower Galilee, (4) the plain of Esdraelon (Jezreel), and (5) the adjacent portions of the Rift (the Jordan system).

A. Coastal Plain. The tribal allotment of Asher included Carmel (Josh. 19:26) and extended "as far as Sidon the Great" (19:29). While it appears that Asher never controlled the coastal plain (cf. Jgs. 1:31), the limits mentioned cover roughly the same distance as is included in the other divisions we shall consider; hence this is a suitable starting-point.

The region is, generally speaking, a coastal plain, cut by numerous streams and wadis that drain the highlands on the east. One notable exception to this general description is the point where the mountains come right to the sea, between Naqûrā and Ras en-Naqûrā (Rōsh ha-Niqrāh), known from ancient times as "the Ladder of Tyre" (1 Macc. 11:59; Josephus *BJ* ii.10.2 [188]). Josephus located the Ladder 100 stadia (18.5 km., 11.5 mi.) N of Ptolemais (which he included in Galilee) — remarkably close to the actual distance from Acco to Rōsh ha-Niqrāh. The outer limits of Great Sidon would possibly be the mouth of the Litani gorge and may have been an "ideal" boundary, much as was "the entrance of Hamath," part of the "very much land" that remained to be possessed (Josh. 13:1). South of the Ladder of Tyre, the coastal plain is about 11 km. (7 mi.) wide, becoming much wider at the entrance to the plain of Esdraelon E of the Gulf of Haifa. This region is known today as *ʿĒmeq Zᵉvûlûn*, "the plain of Zebulun." The steep flank of Mt. Carmel forms a natural southern boundary and also interrupts the coastal plain. Most of the cities included in Asher's allotment are on the slopes of the Galilean hills. Significant exceptions are Carmel and Acco (emending "Ummah" in Josh. 19:30, following LXX; cf. Jgs. 1:31).

B. Upper Galilee. The division between Upper and Lower Galilee can be made roughly by drawing a line from Acco to Rōsh Pinnāh, 10 km. (6 mi.) N of the Sea of Galilee. Upper Galilee is a distinctive region of high hills and numerous narrow valleys; in fact, the highest point in all Palestine, Jebel Jarmāq (Har Mêrôn, 1208 m. or 3962 ft.), lies in this region. D. Baly divides Upper Galilee into the western and eastern regions. The Great Rift, which runs from the Syro-Turkic region to the southern part of Africa, divides somewhat at the southern end of the Beqʿa (between the Lebanon and the Anti-Lebanon), one part (the Lebanon Rift) being the valley of the Līṭānī River, the other (the Jordan Rift) draining the western slopes of Mt. Hermon into the Bereighith and Ḥasbânī rivers and ultimately into the Upper Jordan. The dividing line is approximately at the modern border of Israel and Lebanon, where a slight rise of about 200 m. (660 ft.), less than 4 km. (2.5 mi.) in width, divides the Bereighith from the Līṭânī. The western part of this rift can be traced southward through Wâdī Dubbeh, E of the mountains of Meron and Hillel, W of the Horns of Ḥattin, to where it joins the plain of Esdraelon E of Mt. Tabor. A modern road runs almost the entire length of this depression.

The northern limits of Upper Galilee, as we have seen, are not clearly defined. A case could be made for taking the Litani gorge as the edge of Galilee. Baly suggests a line running from Tyre to Tibnine as another possibility, noting that all land above 1000 m. (3300 ft.) lies S of this line. Much the same could be said if we used the northern boundary of the modern State of Israel as the northern limits of Upper Galilee. The highest peaks lie in the western part of Upper Galilee: Jebel Jarmāq (Har Mêrôm, 1208 m., 3962 ft.), Jebel ʿArûs (Har Hillēl, 1071 m., 3513 ft.), Jebel Haider (Har Haʾărî, 1048 m., 3437 ft.), and Jebel ʿAdathir (Har ʿAddîr, 1008 m., 3307 ft.). A cleft runs northwestward (*ʿĒmeq Peqîʿin*) from Har Haʾărî and then turns westward to empty into the coastal plain N of Nahariyya. The eastern part of Upper Galilee is less rugged but more irregular, as the tortuous road from Pārôd to Rōsh Pinnāh by the way of Mêrôn and Safed clearly indicates.

C. Lower Galilee. The northern limits of this region are fairly clearly defined, marked by the scarp of esh-Shagûr which begins about 10 km. (6 mi.) E of Acco and runs eastward to the Ghor near Rōsh Pinnāh. It consists of Har Gāmāl, Har Shēzôr, Har Hûd, Har Haʿărî, Har Kefîr, and Har Shimʿei in the western part of Lower Galilee, and Har ʿAkbārā (626 m., 2054 ft.) and several Ramoth (hills) in the eastern part. The highway from Acco to Parod by way of Biqʿat Beit Kerem closely traces much of this northern border. The southern limits of Lower Galilee are less well defined, but for our purposes we may take the plain of Esdraelon as the boundary. In some works, this plain is included in Lower Galilee. No mountains in Lower Galilee are higher than 600 m. (2000 ft.). Moreover, the valleys and depressions in Lower Galilee are broader, providing for numerous roads. The most important of these valleys are Biqʿat Beit Kerem (the basin of esh-Shagûr), Biqʿat Beit Nᵉṭôphāh (Sahl al-Baṭṭauf, the Baṭṭōf depression), Biqʿat Tirʿān through which the road runs from Nazareth to Tiberias, and Biqʿat Yabneʾēl in the hills above Tiberias. The road from Afula to Ṣômet Ḥanāniāh serves to mark the division between eastern and western Lower Galilee.

D. Plain of Esdraelon. The plain of Esdraelon (Valley of Jezreel) is bounded on the north by the foothills of Lower Galilee, and on the south by Mt. Carmel, the hills of Samaria, and the mountains of Gilboa. With the exception of the hill of Moreh (Gibʿat ha-Môrêh or Jebel Daḥī, 515 m., 1690 ft.), it is quite flat, rising from where it merges into the coastal plain between Mt. Carmel and Tel Meʿammēr to where it drops suddenly into the Ghor E of ʿÊn Ḥarôḏ; it is rarely more than 100 m. (330 ft.) above sea level.

The name "Valley of Jezreel" is sometimes used for the eastern part and "plain of Esdraelon" for the western (cf. *GB* [2nd ed. 1974], p. 147), but this is a somewhat artificial distinction. The western part, near Megiddo, was also the Valley of Jezreel in the OT, and "Esdraelon" was the Greek equivalent (Jth. 3:9, here actually used of the eastern portion). Josephus uses the term "the Great Plain" (*Vita* 24 [115]; *BJ* ii.10.2 [188]; here he states that Ptolemais was "built at the entrance to the Great Plain"; *Ant.*xx.6.1 [118]; etc.). A far more meaningful distinction would be the use of *Biqʿaṯ Mᵉgiddô*, "the broad valley of Megiddo" cf. 2 Ch. 35:22), and *ʿĒmeq Yizrᵉʿel*, "the deep valley of Jezreel" (cf. Josh. 17:16), the former to refer to the western portion and the latter to the eastern, as do the texts cited.

The western portion is drained by the Kishon River, which originates somewhere S of Afula (the wadi at this point is seasonally dry, hence the indefinite statement). In the rainy season in times past the Kishon flooded the flat plain, and until systematic cultivation of the region by Jewish pioneers at the end of the 19th and the beginning of the 20th cents., there were extensive marshes, hence the Arabic name *Merj ibn ʿAmr*, "the meadow of Amr's son."

This portion is roughly triangular in shape, the southwestern side extending along the foot of Mt. Carmel from N of Jokneam to Jenin, a distance of 36 km. (22 mi.), the eastern side from Jenin to Tel ʿAdashim just below Nazareth, a distance of 22 km. (13.7 mi.), and the northern side closing the triangle, a distance of 18 km. (11 mi.). An extension of this plain spreads eastward about 12 km. (7½ mi.) between the hill of Moreh and Mt. Tabor, so that the plain is often described as Y-shaped. The mountains of Gilboa extend northward in the area from Jenin to Jezreel and drop off sharply into the eastern part of the Valley of Jezreel and the Jordan Ghor.

The eastern portion (the true *ʿĒmeq Yizreʿel,* although modern Israeli maps use this name only for the broad plain), begins around Afula (biblical Ophrah?) and runs ESE for about 20 km. (12.4 mi.) to Beth-shean. It is drained by Nahal Harod (hence the modern name *ʿĒmeq Ḥarôḏ*), and is quite narrow (3 km., 2 mi.) where it begins its decline, reaching sea level in the vicinity of ʿAin Ḥarôḏ, dropping to 150 m. (500 ft.) below sea level at Beth-shean, and then falling suddenly to the Ghor, which is about 300 m. (1000 ft.) below sea level at that point.

This eastern portion, ʿĒmeq Ḥarôḏ, is well watered by the many springs from the mountains of Gilboa, and, at this writing, is filled with fish ponds for the raising of protein food supplies. The biblical Beth-shean is identified with Tell el-Ḥuṣn, a short distance N of the modern city. Biblical Jezreel is identified with Zerʿin, E of modern Jezreel.

E. Galilee Rift. We have already seen that the Great Rift divides at the lower end of the Beqʿa to form the Lebanon Rift and the Jordan Rift. The Jordan Rift (Arab. *Ghôr*) develops into much the greater trough; hence the name "rift" properly belongs to it from the region of Mt. Hermon southward. The streams and underground springs fed by Mt. Hermon furnish a copious amount of water, which develops into four sources of the Jordan River. The well-watered meadows around Merj ʿAyûn ("the meadow of the springs") at the southern end of the Lebanon Beqʿa are drained by the Wâdī Bereighith. In former times this river joined the other sources of the Jordan around Lake Huleh, but at present it is part of the drainage system of the Huleh basin. The longest of the sources is the Ḥasbânī (Nahal Shenir) which rises in the western part of the foot of Hermon. The other sources, which spring from the southern part of the foot of Hermon, are the Leddan (Nahal Dan), and the Bâniyâs (Nahal Hermon). These three join near the modern village of Śdêh Nehemyāh and become another part of the drainage system.

The upper end of the Jordan Rift has often been a meeting place of nations. In OT times, Phoenicia, Syria, and Israel met here (Dan, the northern limit expressed in the phrase "from Dan to Beer-sheba," was located at the source of the Leddan). In NT times, the Tetrarchy of Herod Antipas, the Tetrarchy of Philip (who built Caesarea at Bâniyâs, the source of the Bâniyâs River), and Phoenicia met in this region. More recently, it was the meeting point of Lebanon, Syria, and Israel.

Biblical maps include a turnip-shaped lake, Lake Huleh or Lake Semechonitis, N of the Sea of Galilee. In 1952 traces of the lake were still visible in the marshy valley, but since then it has entirely disappeared, the result of the drainage system installed by the Israeli government to create a rich agricultural region. In the biblical period the lake was about 5½ km. (3½ mi.) long and 4½ km. (2¾ mi.) wide, situated in the Huleh basin, a flat, low-lying region between the hills of Upper Galilee and the plateau of Gaulanitis (Jaulan, Golan). Neither "Huleh" nor "Semechonitis" occurs in the Bible, nor has any term been positively identified with the lake or the basin. In Josephus, the term Semechonitis (Semachonitis in *Ant.* v.5.1 [199]) is used of the lake above the "Lake of Gennesar" (the Sea of Galilee; cf. *BJ* iii.10.8 [515]; iv.1.1 [2f.]). Josephus described the region as one of marshes and lagoons, and gave the dimensions of Lake Semechonitis as 30 stadia (5½ km., 3½ mi.) in breadth and 60 stadia (11½ km., 7 mi.) in length — considerably larger than its measurements in more recent times. Josephus also stated that the marshes extended as far as Daphne, "a delightful spot with springs which feed the so-called Little Jordan, beneath the temple of the golden cow" (*BJ* iv.1.1 [3]), obviously referring to the Leddan and the temple at Dan. In some works, the marshes of the Huleh basin are identified as the waters of Merom (Josh. 11:5f.), but marshland is not suited to warfare such as is described in Josh. 11:1-9, and more recent scholars locate the waters of Merom near the village of Meron, WNW of Safed.

The elevation of Lake Huleh (from the Arabic name *Baḥret el-Ḥûleh,* "the little sea of Huleh") has been a matter of considerable confusion, some atlases recording it as 2 m. (7 ft.) below sea level, others as 2 m. (7 ft.) above sea level. The modern survey map indicates that the elevation is 73 m. (240 ft.) above sea level, and because of the basalt plug at the bottom of the basin, it could never have been much lower. Just S of Lake Huleh there was an important ford across the Upper Jordan, which came to be known in the Middle Ages as "the Bridge of the Daughters of Jacob" (*Jisr Banât Yaʿqûb;* the name has no reference to the patriarch Jacob, but was taken from a convent of the Daughters of St. James located near this place in Crusader times). From just S of this crossing the Upper Jordan plunges through a basalt gorge, descending about 270 m. (885 ft.) in the next 12 km. (7½ mi.), then spreading out over a grassy plain near the site of Bethsaida Julias (called simply Julias in *BJ* iii.10.7 [515]; Josephus gave the length of this portion of the Jordan as 120 stadia [22 km., 14 mi.]), and emptying into the freshwater Sea of Galilee.

The Sea of Galilee is a harp-shaped lake, 21 km. (13 mi.) long by 12 km. (7½ mi.) wide, lying at an altitude of 210 m. (689 ft.) below sea level (1976). In the OT it is called "the Sea of Chinnereth" (Nu. 34:11; etc., whence the modern Israeli name *Yam Kinneret*) and "the Sea of Chinneroth" (Josh. 12:3; etc.). In the NT it is called "the Sea of Galilee" (Mt. 4:18; etc.), "the lake of Gennesaret" (Lk. 5:1), "the sea of Tiberias" (Jn. 21:1; cf. the modern Arabic name Baḥr Ṭabarîyeh), "the lake" (Lk. 5:1; etc.), and "the sea" (Jn. 6:16, etc.). The name "sea of Gennesar" occurs in 1 Macc. 11:67, and "Lake of Gennesar" in Josephus (*BJ* iii.10.8 [515], etc.); Josephus also used the name "lake of Tiberias" (*BJ* iii.3.5 [57], etc.), and variants "Gennesaret" and "Gennesaritis" also occur.

Except for the northwestern area and the southern end, the Sea of Galilee is surrounded by high hills, the Golan Heights on the east being higher and the shoreline steeper than the hills of Lower Galilee on the west. Thus when the wind is from the west, as customarily, it generates a

Southern end of the Sea of Galilee (D. Baly)

high-pressure area over the lake and the water is calm; but when the wind shifts and blows from the east, it creates a venturi effect, resulting in a low-pressure area, and sudden and severe storms come up on the lake.

The northwestern shore is the plain of Gennesaret (Biqʿat Ginnesar), a well-watered and extremely fertile plain. The subtropical climate, caused by the altitude and the protection of the surrounding hills, enables almost continuous production of agricultural products in this plain. In an oft-quoted passage, Josephus described this region with a touch of hyperbole: "There is not a plant which its fertile soil refuses to produce, and its cultivators in fact grow every species" (*BJ* iii.10.8 [516]). The tetrarch Herod built a capital on the western shore of the lake about 5 km. (3 mi.) S of this plain, naming it Tiberias in honor of Tiberius Caesar (*Ant.* xviii.2.3 [36]; cf. Jn. 6:23). *See* Plate 15.

The Sea of Galilee empties into the Jordan River at the southwestern end, where the Jordan Ghor is broad. About 11 km. (7 mi.) S of that point, the Yarmuk enters the Jordan from the east, and about 15 km. (9 mi.) further south the Jezreel Valley empties into the Jordan Ghor from the west. In this region the Jordan system is entirely fresh water, salts being picked up from the soil as it progresses southward.

IV. Galilee in the OT.–The route of Abraham (then known as Abram) from Haran to Shechem is not clearly traced (Gen. 12:4-6). If Eliezer was indeed from Damascus (Gen. 15:2, a problem text; see comms.), the route was probably by the way of Ebla, Hamath, Damascus, and then along the southeastern flank of Mt. Hermon, across the ford where the Bridge of the Daughters of Jacob is located, through Lower Galilee, across the plain of Esdraelon, past Dothan to Shechem. Later, when the coalition of kings captured Sodom and Gomorrah, taking Lot with them, Abram pursued the enemy "as far as Dan" (Gen. 14:14), and indeed even to Hobah "north of Damascus" (14:15).

When Moses sent the twelve "spies" to survey the land of the Canaanites, they traveled "to Rehob, near the entrance of Hamath" (Nu. 13:21). The route is not described in detail N of the Valley of Eschol in Judea, but we may assume that they journeyed by the direct route, traversing Galilee from the plain of Esdraelon to its northern limits.

After Joshua had conquered the southern part of the land, Jabin king of Hazor formed a coalition of kings of the region which can roughly be described as Galilee (cf. Josh. 11:2f.), and Joshua engaged them in battle "by the waters of Merom" (11:7). The following locations are of interest: "the northern hill country" (v. 2) is probably Upper Galilee, "the Arabah south of Chinneroth" (v. 2) is the broad Ghor of the Jordan just S of the Sea of Galilee; "the lowland" (v. 2) is possibly the plain of Jezreel; "the land of Mizpah" which is "under Hermon" (v. 3) is possibly the region around Merj ʿAyûn; Misrephoth-maim (v. 8), which is connected in the context with Great Sidon and the valley of Mizpeh, may well be the Līṭânī gorge (cf. *LBHG*, p. 216); Hazor, which was formerly "the head of all those kingdoms" (v. 10), guarded the main road which went from Acco to the Bridge of the Daughters of Jacob and on to Damascus, as well as the north-south road through Upper Galilee; Hazor is N of the Sea of Galilee, overlooking the Huleh basin. The names in Josh. 12:7-24 could be studied with profit in this connection.

In the tribal allotment, Galilee was divided among the tribes of Asher, Zebulun, Naphtali, and Issachar. Later the tribe of Dan moved from its original location in Philistine country to the northern end of Galilee (Josh. 19:40-47).

The battle with Sisera, described in Jgs. 4–5, took place in the plain of Jezreel in the vicinity of Mt. Tabor (Jgs. 4:6f.). Deborah was from Ephraim (= Samaria), but Barak was from Kedesh in Naphtali (4:5f.). Sisera, the commander of the army of Jabin of Hazor, "dwelt" (Heb. *yôšēḇ*, perhaps meaning "had his headquarters") in Harosheth-ha-goiim (4:2). No such city is known, and the suggestion has been made that the term means "the wooded hills of the Goyim," synonymous with "Galilee of the Gentiles," referring to Lower Galilee. The battle began at Taanach "by the waters of Megiddo" (Jgs. 5:19), and moved toward Tabor. "The stars" (Heb. *hakkôḵāḇîm,* 5:20) fought Sisera, probably meaning rain (cf. J. Blenkinsopp, *Bibl.*, 42 [1961], 73f., for a Canaanite parallel) which caused the Kishon to flood and trap Sisera's army (5:21). Sisera fled on foot, and took refuge in the house of Heber (4:17), located near Kedesh. Aharoni locates Kedesh-Naphtali in the plain of Jabneel in the hills above the southwestern shore of the Sea of Galilee (*LBHG,* Map 16, p. 202), to be distinguished from Tell Qades in Upper Galilee (p. 204). The description of Sisera's flight on foot makes more sense if we accept such a location.

In the 11th cent. B.C. the "Midianites," tribes from E of the Jordan, were making raids on the Israelites. Finally, Gideon was called to put a stop to these harassments (Jgs. 6:7, 11-16). He assembled an army from Asher, Zebulun, Naphtali, and Manasseh, and probably also from Issachar, for that is where he was located (6:11). The Midianites came up the deep Valley of Jezreel (6:33), i.e., from the direction of Beth-shean, and camped by the Hill of Moreh, N of Gideon's band at the spring of Harod (7:1). Gideon and his three hundred put the Midianites to flight, and men from Naphtali and Asher joined in the rout, pursuing the Midianites "beyond the Jordan" (7:23, 25).

When Saul united the tribes into his kingdom, he apparently took control of the Via Maris ("the way of the sea"), the highway that connected Damascus with Acco and also, by way of Wâdī ʿAra next to Megiddo, with the Philistine region and Egypt. Such a situation would explain the Philistine attempt to seize the plain of Esdraelon. The Philistine army moved, it would seem, from Aphek in the Sharon plain (1 S. 29:1) via Wâdī ʿAra to Shunem at the base of the hill of Moreh (1 S. 28:4). Saul had visited the medium at EN-DOR, identified with the modern Ṣafṣefoth, 6 km. (4 mi.) S of Mt. Tabor, not far from the hill of Moreh (1 S. 28:7-19). Saul's forces were in the mountains of Gilboa when the Philistines attacked. Saul and his three sons fell in the battle (1 S. 31:1-8), and their bodies were hung on the wall of Beth-shean (31:10, 12).

David subdued the Philistines, regaining the plain of Jezreel, but in his campaign to Damascus and the north, it appears that he marched through Transjordan (1 Ch. 19:7-19). There can be no doubt, however, that David controlled Galilee and beyond. The census conducted by Joab included "Kadesh in the land of the Hittites" (2 S. 24:6, which would be Qadesh on the Orontes), Dan-jaan (24:6 [MT], possibly Ijon N of Dan in the vicinity of Merj ʿAyûn), Sidon, the fortress of Tyre (the mainland city, not the island), and "all the cities of the Hivites and Canaanites" (24:7, probably referring to the Phoenician coast from Tyre to Acco; cf. *LBHG*, pp. 264f.).

Solomon fortified Megiddo and Hazor, important and strategic points on the Damascus-Gaza route (the Via Maris) along with Gezer (1 K. 9:15). His fifth, eighth, ninth, and tenth administrative districts were in the region that we have defined as Galilee (1 K. 4:7-19). He ceded twenty cities in Galilee to Hiram of Tyre, seemingly to pay for materials used in his building program (1 K. 9:10f.). According to modern consensus the cities were in the coastal plain and foothills of Galilee.

When the monarchy was divided, Galilee became part of the kingdom of Israel under Jeroboam (cf. 1 K. 12:20), who built altars and erected golden calves, one at Bethel and the other at Dan (12:29). Dan was known as Laish (Jgs. 18:29) or Leshem (Josh. 19:47); cf. Lus(i) in Egyptian texts of the 19th cent. B.C.

Shishak (Sheshonq) of Egypt invaded Palestine in the fifth year of Rehoboam (*ca.* 926 B.C.; cf. 1 K. 14:25). According to Shishak's list, he also invaded the northern kingdom, naming among other places the Emeq, Rehob, Beth-shean, Shunem, Taanach, and Megiddo (*LBHG,* p. 285). A fragment of a stele erected by Shishak has been recovered at Megiddo.

Ben-hadad of Damascus, responding to a payment by Asa of Judah, invaded Galilee in the days of Baasha (*ca.* 885 B.C.), conquering Ijon, Dan, Abel-beth-maacah, all Chinneroth, and all the land of Naphtali (1 K. 15:18-20). The growing strength of the Aramean city-states, allied with Ahab of Israel, led to the confrontation with Shalmaneser III at Qarqar in 853 B.C. Elijah the prophet came from Tishbe, which has sometimes been identified with a place in Naphtali, but 1 K. 17:1 clearly locates it in Gilead. (In the light of Jn. 7:52 it is hard to believe that there was any Jewish tradition that Elijah came from Galilee!) His ministry, however, included locations in Galilee. The miracle at Zarephath took place near Sidon (1 K. 17:9). The contest with the prophets of Baal took place on Mt. Carmel (18:20-40), which, as we have seen, was at one time attributed to Galilee. The death penalty on the false prophets was exacted at the river Kishon in the plain of Esdraelon (18:40). Naboth's vineyard was in Jezreel, beside the palace of Ahab (1 K. 21:1), and it was there that Elijah rebuked the king. It was at Naboth's property that Jehu put to death Joram king of Israel (2 K. 9:21, 24). Jehu shot Ahaziah king of Judah with an arrow at the ascent of Gur near Ibleam, but the king died at Megiddo (9:27). At Jezreel Jehu caused the death of Jezebel (9:30-37). The prophet Elisha also performed part of his ministry in Galilee: the episode with the Shunammite woman (2 K. 4:8-37) took place at Shunem in the plain of Esdraelon.

Shalmaneser III continued his campaigns against the Arameans, defeating Hazael at Mt. Senir, possibly Mt. Hermon (cf. Dt. 3:9; but in Cant. 4:8 and 1 Ch. 5:23 the two names seem to refer to different places), probably destroying Hazor at that time (Level VIII), and reaching the mountain Ba'li-ra'si (= Baal Rosh, or Mt. Carmel), where he set up a monument (*ANET,* p. 280).

Tiglath-pileser III captured much of Galilee *ca.* 732 B.C., as described in 2 K. 15:29. The route apparently was down the Lebanon Beqʿa and into the upper Jordan Valley, but Tiglath-pileser's own account is devoid of details, stating simply, "...the wide land of (Naphta)li, in its entire extent, I united with Assyria" (*ANET,* p. 283; *ARAB,* I, § 815). The region that we know as Galilee became the Assyrian province of Megiddo. (Y. Aharoni, in *Macmillan Bible Atlas,* p. 95, takes the phrases in Isa. 9:1 to refer to the three Assyrian provinces, "the Way of the Sea" = Dor, "Galilee of the Nations" = Megiddo, and "Beyond the Jordan" = Gilead.) After the capture of Samaria, the province of Dor was incorporated into the province of Samaria.

When Pharaoh Neco went to the aid of Aššur-uballiṭ at Carchemish (609 B.C.), Josiah of Judah attempted to intercept him and was killed at Megiddo (2 K. 23:29). Neco probably continued through the Lebanon Beqʿa to Riblah (where he appointed Jehoiakim king of Judah, 23:33f.), then to Hamath, Aleppo, and Carchemish.

V. Galilee in the Apocrypha.–Simon the Maccabee (*ca.* 163 B.C.) led a band against enemies from Ptolemais, Tyre, and Sidon who had attacked the Jews in Galilee (1 Macc. 5:14-23). In 161 B.C. Demetrius I sent Bacchides at the head of an army to Judea and, passing through Galilee, he punished the Jews of Arbela near the Sea of Galilee (1 Macc. 9:1-4; *Ant.* xii.11.1 [420-22]). In 144 B.C. Jonathan defeated the forces of Demetrius at Cadasa near Hazor (1 Macc. 11:63f.; *Ant.* xiii.5.7 [158-162]). Tryphon marched against Jonathan in 143 B.C. from Damascus, and the two forces met at Beth-shean. By a series of ruses, Tryphon led Jonathan to Ptolemais, where Jonathan was captured (1 Macc. 12:39f.; 13:1-30; *Ant.* xiii.6.1-6 [187-212]).

In 104 B.C. Aristobulus conquered Galilee, making it a Jewish land and putting most of Galilee under the Maccabeans. In a very short time Sepphoris and Asochis were Jewish cities (*Ant.* xiii.11.3 [319]; *BJ* i.3.3 [76]). The coastal plain remained outside the Maccabean kingdom. In 63 B.C. Pompey conquered Palestine for Rome, "liberated" the cities that had been taken by the Jews, and established the Decapolis, including Scythopolis (Beth-shean). An attempt was made to partition Judea into five *synedria,* but this was short-lived. Galilee and Judea (except for a large coastal portion), together with Perea, formed the new Judea. Herod was made king of the Jews by Caesar Augustus and gradually accumulated almost all of Palestine as well as large portions of Transjordan. On the death of Herod in 4 B.C. Galilee and Perea were made the Tetrarchy of Herod Antipas (*Ant.* xvii.11.4 [317-321]; *BJ* ii.6.3 [93-98]).

VI. Galilee in the NT.–Since the major part of the ministry of Jesus was conducted in Galilee, it is not possible to review all of the NT references to Galilee. In general we should note that Jesus' boyhood and the opening of His ministry took place in Nazareth in Lower Galilee, and much of the rest of His public ministry took place at the northern end of the Sea of Galilee. A number of locations should be singled out for special mention.

Cana of Galilee, where the first miracle occurred (Jn. 2:1, 11), according to most modern scholars was not at the modern site of Kefr Kenna on the road from Nazareth to Tiberias, but more likely at Khirbet Qânā N of Nazareth on the far side of Biqʿat Beit Neṭofa; the old road would have gone through Sepphoris. On the other hand, Jesus' "second visit" to Cana (Jn. 4:46), in context, would appear to be on the Nazareth-Capernaum road, which would favor Kefr Kenna.

The call of the disciples took place on the shore of Galilee near Capernaum (Mk. 1:16, 21, 29). The site of Capernaum was formerly hotly debated, but since World War II scholars are generally agreed on the modern Kefr Nahum, where excavations have uncovered foundations of a house believed to be that of Simon Peter's family.

The raising of the widow's son occurred in the village of Nain, on the northern foot of the hill of Moreh, SE of Nazareth. The "hill of precipitation," to which Jesus was

Synagogue at Capernaum, built on the site of the synagogue where Jesus worshiped (W. S. LaSor)

taken by an unruly mob that would have lynched him (Lk. 4:29), would seem to be nearer to Nazareth than the precipice that today marks the traditional site. Perhaps it was at this time that Jesus withdrew from Nazareth and relocated at Capernaum.

His ministry around the lake involved a number of locations. The "Sermon on the Mount" (the envelope-pattern context of Mt. 4:25 and 8:1 suggests that it was a specific event at a specific place) probably occurred on the slopes above Capernaum. The feeding of the 5000 (Jn. 6; Mt. 14:13-21 par.) took place on "the other side of the Sea of Galilee" (Jn. 6:1), which probably means on the east side of the Upper Jordan, where there is a large, gentle, grassy slope, and not at Tabgha, where the modern site is located. Bethsaida presents a problem, for Bethsaida Julius was E of the Upper Jordan, but Mk. 6:45 suggests that the disciples were sent from a place E of the Jordan "to the other side, to Bethsaida" (6:45), to which a further note indicates that they were proceeding toward the plain of Gennesaret (6:53). It has therefore been proposed that there were two Bethsaidas, the second a "Bethsaida of Galilee" (Jn. 12:21) perhaps W of Capernaum. The woes pronounced against Capernaum, Bethsaida, and Chorazin (which is 4 km. [2½ mi.] N of Capernaum) would seem to require a Bethsaida near the other two cities (Mt. 11:21-23).

The drowning of the swine, caused by exorcising demons, is difficult to locate due to the textual problems (various readings are "Gadarenes," "Gergesenes," and "Gerasenes"; see Mt. 8:28). Gergasa was on the east side of the lake, N of Hippos, where the slope is not too steep to fit the story. Gerasa has been identified with Jerash, and is thus out of the question. Gadara is SE of the Sea of Galilee, on the slopes of the Yarmuk River. *See* GERASA.

The Gospels report that Jesus visited the region of Tyre and Sidon (Mk. 7:24; Mt. 15:21), but the expression does not necessarily imply that Jesus actually visited those cities. The border of Sidon, we have seen, may have been at the Litani gorge, which could also have been the northern border of the region of Tyre. It would therefore be possible to interpret the statement by proposing that Jesus traveled from the region of the sources of the Jordan along the Litani to an unknown place, or even to assume that the regions of Tyre and Sidon extended eastward to the vicinity of Merj ʿAyûn. After healing the Syrophoenician woman, Jesus returned to the Sea of Galilee through the region of the Decapolis (Mk. 7:31), which may simply indicate the eastern side of the Sea of Galilee.

At a critical point in His ministry, Jesus took His disciples to Caesarea Philippi (Mt. 16:13; again, since "the region of" is used, it is not necessary to understand that they actually went into that city). There Peter made his great profession of faith. A week later Jesus took Peter, James, and John and "led them up a high mountain" (Mt. 17:1), where the Transfiguration occurred. The traditional site of the Transfiguration is Mt. Tabor or "Little Hermon," E of Nazareth. But this is by no stretch of the imagination "an unusually high mountain" (*óros hypsēlón*); nor is it likely that Jesus could have found the necessary solitude so close to Nazareth. Caesarea Philippi is on the southern side of Mt. Hermon, near the source of the Bâniyâs, one of the tributaries of the Jordan. Mt. Hermon, furthermore, rises to an elevation of 2814 m. (9235 ft.), and in comparison with the mountains in Galilee, which are never above 1208 m. (3964 ft.), this is exceptionally high. Mt. Tabor, by way of contrast, is only 580 m. (1903 ft.), a little sugarloaf hill scarcely higher than the hills of Nazareth a short distance to the west.

There is no mention of evangelizing Galilee after the Resurrection, and Galilee is not mentioned in Jesus' parting instructions (Acts 1:8).

VII. Galilee in Early Judaism.–Since Josephus was a general of Jewish forces located in "both Galilees" (*BJ* ii.20.4 [568]), we could easily lose our objective if we were to track down his many references. Furthermore, for this article it would serve no useful purpose. Suffice it to say that Vespasian quickly conquered Galilee, taking Josephus prisoner in the process. Jotapata, Sepphoris, and Gischala were already important Jewish cities. After the destruction of Jerusalem in A.D. 70, the religion of the Jews might have come to an end. But Johanan ben Zakkai escaped from Jerusalem, according to tradition smuggling a copy of the Holy Scriptures with him, and obtained permission from Vespasian to set up an academy at Jabneh (Jamnia, the OT Jabneel in the Sharon plain). He organized a Beth Din to take the place of the Sanhedrin, which had ceased to exist. After the defeat of Bar Cochba in A.D. 135 the council moved to Sikhnin N of Jotapata, and due to the persecution under Hadrian other schools that had developed moved to Galilee, with locations at Usha, Peqiʿin, Sepphoris, Beth-shearim, and Tiberias. Galilee thenceforth became a strong center of Judaism. The teachings of the Tanna'im were gathered, the codification of the Mishnah was accomplished by Judah ha-Naśi', and the traditional pronunciation of the Hebrew Bible was preserved by the Tiberian masoretic pointing. Thus the foundations of modern Judaism were securely laid — in Galilee of the Gentiles.

Bibliography.–*GB* (rev. ed. 1974), esp. pp. 152-163; S. Freyne, *Galilee from Alexander The Great to Hadrian, 323 B.C.E. to 135 C.E.* (1979); N. Glueck, *The River Jordan* (1946), pp. 1-59; *GP,* I, 27-30; II, 13-18, 60-67; E. Hoade, *Guide to the Holy Land* (7th ed. 1973), pp. 823-954; *HGHL,* pp. 413-436; *LBHG, passim.*

W. S. LASOR

GALILEE, MOUNTAIN OF. *See* HILL III.C.3.

GALILEE, SEA OF [Gk. *hē thálassa tḗs Galilaias*]. The most common name in the Gospels for that lake where so much of Jesus' ministry took place, taken from the district in which it was located (Mt. 4:18; 15:29; Mk. 1:16; 7:31; Jn. 6:1). It was also named for the fertile plain at the northwest shore, i.e., "the waters of Gennesaret" (1 Macc. 11:67), and thus once in the NT it is called "the lake of Gennesaret" (Lk. 5:1). Josephus consistently uses "Genesar." In addition it was called the "Sea of Tiberias" (Jn. 6:1; 21:1), a name derived in NT times from the capital city built by Herod Antipas on the western shore. Sometimes it is simply called "the sea" (Gk. *thálassa,* e.g., Jn. 6:16) or "the lake" (Gk. *límnē,* e.g., Lk. 5:2). The Arabic name used today is Baḥr Ṭabarîyeh.

In the OT it is called "the Sea of Chinnereth" (Heb. *yam-kinneret̠,* Nu. 34:11; Josh. 13:27) and "the Sea of Chinneroth" (Heb. *yam-kinn*[e]*rôt̠,* Josh. 12:3). In Hebrew and Aramaic *yam* can mean both lake and sea, as is the case also with Gk. *thálassa.* The name appears to have been taken from an ancient Canaanite town (Josh. 11:2; 19:35; 1 K. 15:20), which has been identified with Tell el-ʿOreimeh, near the northwest shore. The lake formed a part of the boundary of the Promised Land (Nu. 34:11) and of the territory of the Gadites (Dt. 3:12; Josh. 13:27) and was mentioned in connection with the borders of the conquered Amorites (Josh. 12:3). Chinnereth means "harp" or "lyre" and perhaps is derived from the hill of Tell el-ʿOreimeh, which resembles an ancient harp. This is more likely than the notion that the town took its name from the lake, which itself is shaped roughly like a harp. (*See also* CHINNERETH.)

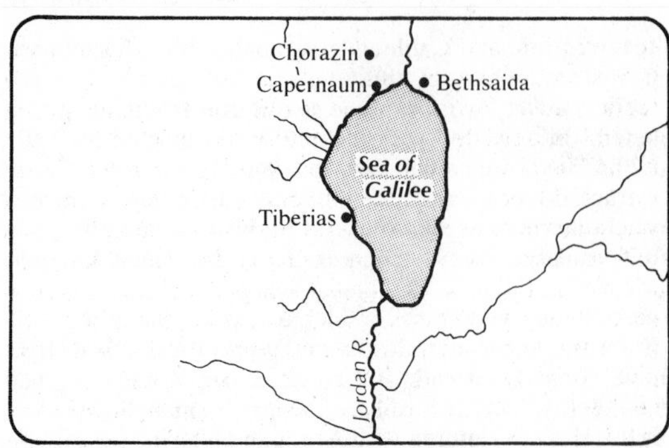

I. General Description.–The lake is 21 km. (13 mi.) long and about 13 km. (8 mi.) wide at the point of greatest breadth. It is pear-shaped, with the narrow end pointing south and a decided bulge to the northwest. The sea lies in the deep trough of the Jordan Valley with its surface 212 m. (696 ft.) below sea level. Due to this position it is for the most part surrounded by only a narrow ribbon of plain. Its greatest depth is over 46 m. (150 ft.). The lake is fed by the Jordan River flowing down from Lake Huleh in the north, as well as by underground streams. The water is clear and sweet, and fish abound.

The north end of the lake is open, with the hills about 3 km. (2 mi.) distant and green slopes stretching down to the water. On the northwest shore is the plain of Gennesaret. To the south, beginning in the vicinity of Tiberias, there are dark cliffs with only a narrow coast. At the south end the coast widens and the area becomes open once again. The east side of the sea is characterized by a wall of sharply rising hills that form the edge of the Jaulan Plateau (Gaulanitis). The main formation is limestone covered by a layer of basalt. The coast running along the east side is about 1 km. (½ mi.) wide and well watered. This plateau, about 610 m. (2000 ft.) above the lake, caused most of the life and activity to be confined to the west side. For those living on the east shore, commerce was easier with the towns across the lake than with the villages on the plateau. The shore on both sides is fertile, and water for irrigation is available from springs. There is large-scale agricultural activity around the lake now, although in previous years barrenness and desolation marked the area. Thus today the country is taking on more of the appearance of Jesus' time, when it was the center of industry and commerce in Galilee. *See* Plate 17.

The climate is semitropical. In the winter the hills and shores surrounding the lake are green, but during the summer the district becomes arid. During May and June the temperature rises as high as 40°C (104°F) in the shade, and by August the heat can become unbearable. The difference in temperature between the surface of the sea and the high surrounding mountains makes it liable to sudden and violent storms, as the cool air from the uplands sweeps down the gorges and upon the surface of the water. The Gospels mention two such storms (Mt. 8:24 par.; 14:24 par.).

II. Cities and Industry.–In the NT period cities of considerable size and importance surrounded the lake. The Gospels do not mention two of the busiest centers, Tarichea and Tiberias. Tarichea means "preserving" or "pickling," and its salted fish were known throughout the Roman world. In Pliny's time the whole lake was named for this city (*Nat. hist.* v.15 [71]), and Josephus credited it with a population of forty thousand and a fishing fleet of 230 boats (*BJ* ii.21.4, 8 [608, 635]). These boats were of good size, for from four to six thousand inhabitants of Tarichea were able to take refuge in them when pursued by the Romans (*BJ* iii.10.5 [499]). Some have placed the city at the southwest corner of the lake, but it is more probably to be identified with Magdala (present-day Mejdel), about 5 km. (3 mi.) N of Tiberias.

The name BETHSAIDA, "home of fishing," also reflects the fishing industry. This city, the home of Peter, Andrew, and Philip (Jn. 1:44), was located at the north end of the sea, possibly 3 km. (2 mi.) from the coast at et-Tell but more likely on the shore at el-ʿAraj. In NT times agriculture, dyeing, and tanning were also important industries in the lake region; but by far the most important was fishing, with the related occupations of boat building and fish curing. The Gospels themselves hint at this great fishing activity and its economic importance. At least four of the disciples—Peter, Andrew, James, and John—were fishermen, and there is no reason to believe that they were poor men. Mark intimated that the family of Zebedee was one of substance when he mentioned the hired servants left to help the father when James and John departed to follow Jesus (Mk. 1:20). That John was acquainted with the household of the high priest in Jerusalem also indicates that his family was one of some means and influence (Jn. 18:15; but cf. L. Morris, comm. on John [*NICNT,* 1971], pp. 752f.).

Hot springs located about 1.6 km. (1 mi.) S of Tiberias supplied baths, which were famous in the ancient world. They were mentioned by Pliny (*Nat. hist.* v.15 [71]) and appeared on a coin of Tiberias issued in the reign of Trajan.

CAPERNAUM, at the northwest corner of the lake, was a commercial center where the customs station was located from which Matthew was called (Mt. 9:9 par.). About 3 km. (2 mi.) to the north lay Chorazin (Khirbet Kerâzeh). The principal cities on the east side of the sea were Hippos and Gadara, both of which were much larger in the NT period than today.

III. Jesus' Ministry.–Jesus' entire ministry was limited to the northern half of the lake. There is no record of His traveling to the south or southwest shore, and apart from the feeding miracle on "the other side of the sea" (Jn. 6:1) and the meeting with the demoniac at Gergesa (Lk. 8:26 par.), the east side of the lake played no part in His life. The northern third of this area was predominantly Jewish, but the territory to the south was gentile. The location of Gergesa is uncertain, but the narrative points to a heathen district. The most likely spot is the vicinity of a small place named Kersa on the east shore.

Jesus moved to Capernaum at the beginning of His ministry (Mt. 4:13), and it became the center of His Galilean activity. The actual location of the city was long in doubt, but it has now been identified with Tell Ḥûm. Tradition has placed the site of the Sermon on the Mount in the surrounding mountain region.

TIBERIAS was one of the most important cities, yet Jesus and His disciples seem to have avoided it. This may have been due to the circumstances surrounding its construction. When it was built by Herod Antipas, he was forced to fill it with a gentile population because it was found to be resting upon the site of an old cemetery and thus the Jews considered it unclean. The Jewish attitude toward the city changed in later years, and after the destruction of Jerusalem in A.D. 135 it became a center of Jewish learning.

Bibliography.–*GP*; *LBHG,* pp. 30f.; N. Glueck, *River Jordan* (1946), pp. 33-59; *HGHL,* pp. 439-463.
W. W. BUEHLER

GALL [Heb. *mᵉrērâ, mᵉrōrâ, rō'š*; Gk. *cholḗ*] (Job 16:13; 20:14; 20:25; Lam. 3:19; Mt. 27:34; Acts 8:23).

The RSV used "gall" to translate Heb. *rō'š* (*rôš* in Dt. 32:32) only in Lam. 3:19, rendering "bitterness" in Lam.

3:5 and "poison," "poisoned," or "poisonous" for the other instances where the AV has "gall" (Dt. 29:18; Ps. 69:21 [MT 22]; Jer. 8:14; 9:15; 23:15; Am. 6:12). Probably the references are to the colocynth, *Cucumis colocynthis* L., a trailing vine bearing orange-colored fruit having drastic cathartic qualities. Hemlock is a less probable alternative.

The Heb. *m^erērâ* (Job. 16:13), *m^erōrâ* (Job 20:25), is human bile, but in Job 20:14 *m^erōrâ* is serpent venom. The poison of serpents was held to reside in their bile.

The Gk. *cholḗ* in Mt. 27:34 is a reference to the LXX of Ps. 69:21. In Mk. 15:23, "wine mingled with myrrh" indicates that the bitter ingredient of the analgesic potion was myrrh (cf. Pliny *Nat. hist.* xx.18 [36]; Seneca *Epistulae morales* 83.27). The "gall of bitterness" of Acts 8:23 may mean the "'bitter gall-root' of superstition and magic" (F. F. Bruce, comm. on Acts [*NICNT,* 1954], p. 184).

See also POISON. R. K. H.

GALLERY [Heb. *'attîq*; LXX *peristylon*–'colonnade' (Ezk. 42:3, 5); NEB CORRIDOR. A word of doubtful meaning. K. Galling (in G. Fohrer, *Ezechiel* [1955]) rendered it "terrace," which suggests a derivation from *nāṯaq,* "cut off, tear away." G. R. Driver (*JTS,* 32 [1931], 363) related it to Akk. *etēqu,* "to pass along," hence "corridor." But neither *etēqu* nor any of its derivative nouns means "corridor" in Akkadian, and since Heb. *'āṯaq,* "move forward," is clearly related to Akk. *etēqu,* Driver's suggestion should be rejected (contra KoB, p. 101). In addition, in 41:15 C. H. Cornill's emendation (comm. on Ezekiel [1886]), viz., "and the walls thereof" (cf. RSV, "and its walls") is textually unsupported (except for the minor detail of *w* [*K*] for *y* [*Q*], the MT makes as much sense and should be retained; cf. AV, NEB). That they were woodpaneled in 41:16 suggests that some form of interior corridor is intended.

Its use here must be interpreted by our understanding of the priests' chambers (*see* TEMPLE). Probably the building rose in three steps or terraces corresponding to the rise in the ground. If this is so, it will explain why only the upper story (42:6) was narrower; owing to the hillside the actual depth of the first and second stories will have been the same. The "gallery against gallery" (42:3) may refer to the symmetrical parallelism of the chambers to the north and south. Since the terraces presumably gave admission to the upper stories, it can easily be seen why the same word should be used with respect to corridors within the temple block itself.

See also RAFTER; TRESS; WALL. H. L. ELLISON

GALLEY [Heb. *'onî*] (Isa. 33:21). *See* SHIPS.

GALLIM gal'im [Heb. *gallîm*–'heaps']. Two sites, one N and the other S of Jerusalem.

1. A town in the hill country of Judah, listed among eleven towns in the LXX of Josh. 15:59 that are not found in the MT. It is mentioned between Karem (ʿAin Kârim) and Bether (Bittîr) and is probably to be identified with Beit Jalā, WNW of Bethlehem.

2. A town in Benjamin, mentioned along with Laishah and Anathoth (Isa. 10:30), on the route that the Assyrians would take in their advance to Jerusalem according to Isaiah's prophecy (Isa. 10:24-34). It was the home of Palti the son of Laish, to whom Saul had given his daughter Michal, David's wife (1 S. 25:44). It has been identified with the modern Khirbet Kaʿkûl, about 1 km. (0.6 mi.) W of Anathoth (ʿAnâtâ). W. S. L. S.

GALLIO gal'i-ō [Gk. *Galliōn*]. The Roman deputy or PROCONSUL of Achaia before whom Paul was brought by his Jewish accusers on his first visit to Corinth, during his second missionary journey (Acts 18:12-17). The trial was not of long duration. Although Gallio extended his protection to the Jewish religion as one of the religions recognized by the state, he contemptuously rejected the claim of the Jews that their law was binding upon all. In the eyes of the proconsul, the only law universally applicable was that of the Roman code and social morality, and under neither was the prisoner chargeable; therefore, without even waiting to hear Paul's speech in his own defense, he summarily ordered his accusers to clear the court. Even the subsequent treatment meted out to Sosthenes, ruler of the synagogue, was to him a matter of indifference. Gallio has often been described as typical of one who is careless or indifferent to religion; yet in the account given of him in Acts, he merely displayed an attitude characteristic of that with which Roman governors regarded the religious disputes of the time (*see also* LYSIAS; FELIX; FESTUS). He refused to adjudicate the squabbles of what he regarded as an obscure religious sect, whose law was to him a subtle quibbling with "words and names."

According to extracanonical sources the original name of Gallio was Marcus Annaeus Novatus, but this was changed when he was adopted by the rhetorician Lucius Junius Gallio. He was born at Cordova, but came to Rome during the reign of Tiberius. He was the son of Seneca the rhetorician and brother of Seneca the philosopher, by whom, as also by Statius, reference is made to his affable nature. An inscription from Delphi makes it probable that he acceded to the office of proconsul of Achaia *ca.* A.D. 52. (*See also* CHRONOLOGY OF THE NT II.F.) Early in Nero's reign he returned to Rome, having been granted a substitute consulate. He and his brother (who had earlier been Nero's tutor) lost their lives as a result of their participation in a conspiracy against Nero.

C. M. KERR

GALLON. The AV "two or three firkins" (Gk. *metrētḗs*) in Jn. 2:6 is rendered in the RSV and NEB "twenty to thirty gallons," an approximate equivalent. *See* FIRKIN.

GALLOWS. *See* HANG; PUNISHMENTS.

GAMAD, MEN OF gā'mad [Heb. *gammāḏîm*] (Ezk. 27:11); AV GAMMADIMS; NEB MEN OF GAMMAD. Gammad is the name of an unknown place near Tyre, the inhabitants of which were in Tyre's army. (The JB has "kept watch," following the LXX *phýlakes*.) Some have identified it with the Kumidi of the Amarna Letters.

GAMAEL gam'ə-el [Gk. *Gamaēl*]. Chief of the family of Ithamar who went up from Babylon with Ezra (1 Esd. 8:29); called Daniel in Ezr. 8:2.

GAMALIEL gə-mā'lē-əl [Heb. *gamlî'ēl*–'God is my recompense/reward,' indicating the loss of one or more earlier children in the family; Gk. *Gamaliēl*].

1. Gamaliel son of Pedahzur, leader of the tribe of Manasseh during the census of the Israelites in the desert of Sinai (Nu. 1:10; 2:20; 7:54, 59; 10:23).

2. Rabbi Gamaliel I, son of Simon and grandson (according to the Talmud) of Rabbi Hillel (founder of the more liberal of the two main schools of the Pharisees, Shammai being the other). Although an alternate tradition makes Gamaliel the son of Hillel, the Talmud is surely to be preferred on this point. A member of the Sanhedrin and a teacher of the law (Acts 5:34), he was known in rabbinical writings as Gamaliel the Elder to distinguish him from his grandson, Gamaliel II. He was the first of seven successive leaders of the school of Hillel to be honored with the title *Rabban* ("Our Rabbi/Master").

Illustration from the *Pollak-Pratto Haggadah* (Spain, *ca.* A.D. 1300) showing Gamaliel instructing two pupils (Jewish Theological Seminary Library)

While believing the law of God to be divinely inspired, Gamaliel tended to emphasize its human elements. He recommended that sabbath observance be less rigorous and burdensome, regulated current custom with respect to divorce in order to protect women, and urged kindness toward Gentiles. Scholarly, urbane, a man of great intellect, he studied Greek literature avidly. What we know of his tolerance and cautious spirit is entirely in keeping with the account of his appeal in the Sanhedrin to spare the lives of Peter and his companions (Acts 5:33-39).

T.B. *Shabbath* 30b mentions a student of Gamaliel who displayed "impudence in matters of learning," a young man identified by some as the apostle Paul. Paul himself says, "Under Gamaliel, I was thoroughly trained in the law of our fathers and was just as zealous for God as any of you are today" (Acts 22:3, NIV). Several indications from elsewhere in the NT tend to corroborate Paul's claim as recorded by Luke.

(1) Although Paul usually quotes from the LXX when referring to OT passages, he sometimes clearly makes use of the Hebrew text (Job 41:3 in Rom. 11:35; Job 5:12f. in 1 Cor. 3:19; Ex. 16:18 in 2 Cor. 8:15; Nu. 16:5 in 2 Tim. 2:19).

(2) In Gal. 1:14 Paul mentions a period of advanced and specialized study of the very kind that one might expect under a teacher of Gamaliel's stature, and he does so in language strongly reminiscent of Acts 22:3: "I was advancing in Judaism beyond many Jews of my own age and was extremely zealous for the traditions of my fathers" (NIV).

(3) In Phil. 3:6f. Paul asserts that before his conversion to faith in Christ he was faultless as far as legalistic righteousness is concerned. In accordance with the Judaism of his day, Paul had earlier believed in the possibility of salvation through works, but after exercising faith in Christ he came to realize that only through Him could the righteous requirements of the law be fully met in redeemed sinners like himself (Rom. 8:3f.).

(4) Paul made use of five of the seven hermeneutical principles usually associated with Gamaliel's grandfather Hillel. This is understandable in the light of the fact that Gamaliel consistently and faithfully perpetuated the teachings and methodology of his grandfather. For example, Paul uses the hermeneutical principle of arguing from the lesser to the greater in 1 Cor. 9:9-12, which begins as follows: "Do not muzzle an ox while it is treading out the grain." After thus quoting Dt. 25:4, the apostle makes application — in typical Halakic fashion — by stating that if God is concerned about oxen He is all the more concerned that His faithful human servants receive the support they deserve and need.

(5) In 1 Cor. 14:21 Paul quotes Isa. 28:11f. as a citation from "the law" — a statement entirely fitting for a student of Gamaliel.

Luke's characteristic restraint in his references to Gamaliel in Acts may be contrasted with two later passages that also mention him. According to Clement *Recognitions* i.65, the apostle Peter states that Gamaliel was "our brother in the faith," and Photius (*Bibliothecae codices* 171 [*PG,* p. 199]) asserts that he was baptized by Peter and Paul. But both of these traditions are now universally rejected as spurious.

Gamaliel's reputation as one of the greatest teachers in the annals of Judaism, however, remains untarnished and is perhaps best exemplified in Mish. *Sotah* ix.15: "Since Rabban Gamaliel the Elder died there has been no more reverence for the law, and purity and abstinence [*p^{e}rîšûṯ,* cf. "Pharisee"] died out at the same time."

Bibliography.–J. Jeremias, "Paulus als Hillelite," in E. E. Ellis and M. Wilcox, eds., *Neotestamentica et Semitica* (1969), pp. 88-94; E. F. Harrison, "Acts 22:3 — A Test Case for Luke's Reliability," in R. N. Longenecker and M. C. Tenney, eds., *New Dimensions in NT Study* (1974), pp. 251-260.

R. F. YOUNGBLOOD

GAME [Heb. *ṣayiḏ*] AV, NEB, VENISON. The RSV references to game occur in Gen. 25:28; 27:3-33 only, and refer to the wild beasts of the chase that were regarded as suitable for food. The list of provisions for Solomon's table (1 K. 4:23), including "harts, gazelles, roebucks and fatted fowl," represents the variety of game in the ancient Near East.

See also HUNTING.

GAMES. The Bible contains little information about amusements in the form of games, but archeology and history provide an invaluable background for the frequent indirect allusions to them.

- I. Games in Antiquity
  - A. In the Ancient Near East
  - B. In Greece and Rome
- II. Games in the Bible
  - A. In the OT
  - B. In the NT

I. Games in Antiquity.–*A. In the Ancient Near East.* From the vantage point of the history of religion, the various forms of secular games in antiquity seem to derive from original engagements that expressed magical intentions. The players, reenacting mythical scenes, represented deities and often carried masks. The purpose of these ritual enactments was to secure the existence of the world, the life cycle, or the victory of the positive principle over the antagonistic one (chaos, dragon). An illustration may be found in the fake battles fought between the followers of Osiris and those of Seth, god of battles, in the cult of Osiris (Herodotus ii.63f.). The name "sacer

Relief showing, from left, a runner, two wrestlers, and a javelin thrower (National Archaeological Museum, Athens)

ludus" has been suggested (G. van der Leeuw) for this form of the holy games from which drama developed (Montet, p. 297).

One of the Egyptian tomb paintings at Beni-hasan (*ca.* 1900 B.C.) shows young women or teenage girls playing ball. They show their skill by keeping two of four balls in the air at once. Another picture from the same tomb shows a player on his knees while two others, unseen by him, thump or pretend to thump his back with their fists (J. G. Wilkinson, *Ancient Egyptians* [1878], II, 61). This seems to have been the type of game known by the Greek name "Kollabismos," of which Pollux said that one player covered his eyes with the palms of his hands while another hit him and asked him which hand dealt the blow (Pollux *Onomasticon* ix.129). Egyptian paintings show boys or young men playing team games and tug of war, while girls practiced juggling or ball games, including catch played with younger girls sitting on older girls' backs (Montet, p. 101 fig.).

In Egypt married couples played checkers on a rectangular board, divided into thirty or thirty-three squares with black and white pieces much like the pawns in modern chess. The moves were governed by throwing dice, unlike the free moves of today (Hayes, pp. 249-251). Examples of dice have been found at Beth-shean and Tell Beit Mirsim (17th cent. B.C.) with playing pieces (Albright, p. 117 plate 21). A teetotum was spun, and the number of holes on the side that fell uppermost determined a player's moves. An ivory gaming board with the playing pieces was also found at Tell Beit Mirsim and further gaming boards have been recovered from excavations at Beth-shemesh (one from stratum V, *ca.* 1700-1500 B.C. and another from stratum IV, *ca.* 1500-1200 B.C.) and Tell el-ʿAjjûl in Palestine. These gaming boards from Palestine are presumably for a game that originated in Mesopotamia, where the Sumerians played on a board of twenty squares (van Buren, pp. 11ff.). From there it spread also to Egypt (Albright, p. 49). An elaborate game board made of ivory and ebony veneer with ten carved ivory pins having heads of dogs and jackals has been preserved in Egypt; the pins were moved according to the throwing of knucklebones.

Excavations at Megiddo in Palestine have brought to light an ivory game board (*ca.* 1350-1150 B.C.) for the "game of 58 holes," and one made of stones has been found at Gezer (*ca.* 1200 B.C.). Some ivory game pieces from Megiddo (*ca.* 1200 B.C.) include a circular disc with an animal and a tree incised on its face, and conical pieces with a knob at the top, not unlike the "halma" men of today. Pyramidical or conical game pieces and counters and "halma" men were also discovered at Lachish near Jerusalem.

At Umm el-Bayyârah (biblical Sela), the great mountain city that dominated the basin in which the Nabatean city of Petra was built, game boards were discovered carved

Queen Nefertari, wife of Ramses II, playing checkers in a painting from her tomb in the Valley of the Queens at Thebes (*ca.* 1292 B.C.) (Service des musées, Cairo; picture Lehnert and Landrock)

Two Egyptian games of checkers from the tomb of Tutankhamen (Egyptian Museum, Cairo; picture Lehnert and Landrock)

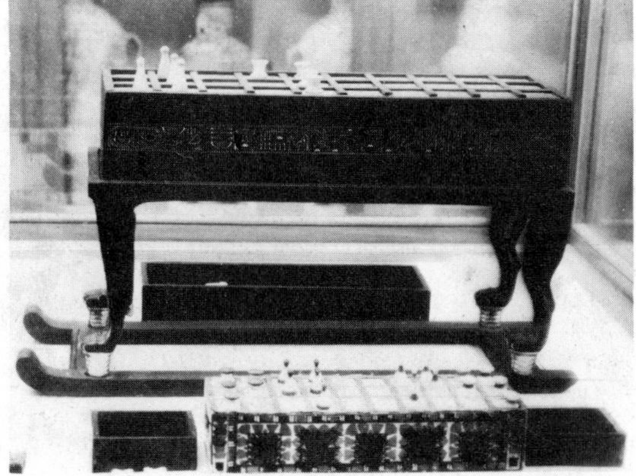

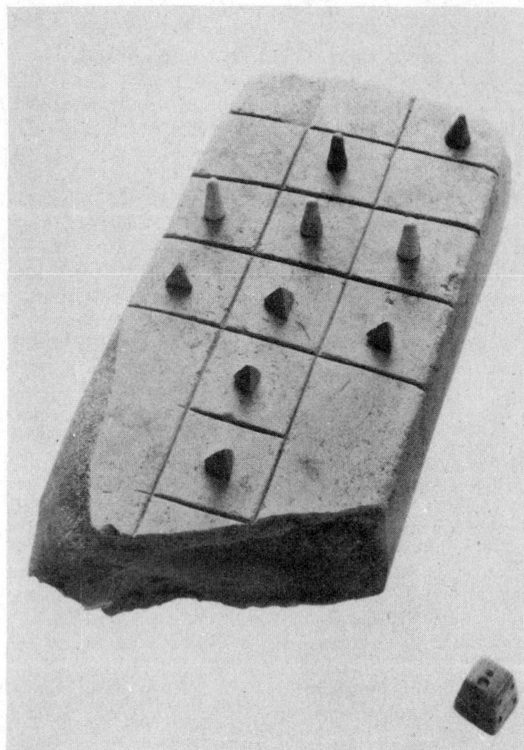

Game board from Beth Shemesh, with five pyramid-shaped and five conical pieces of blue faience from Tell Beit Mirsim. The object at lower right is ivory and looks like a die — note the varying number of holes on its four sides — and was perhaps thrown to determine the moves. All game parts are Middle Bronze (Israel Department of Antiquities and Museums)

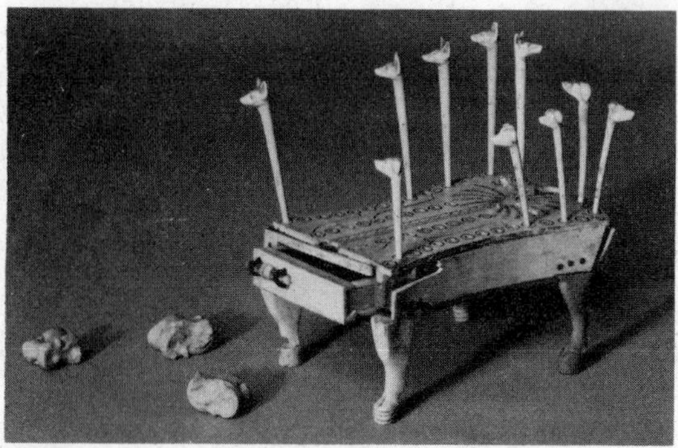

Hounds-and-jackals game made of ivory and ebony, from the tomb of Ren Seneb (*ca.* 1800 B.C.). The pegs were moved on the board according to the throw of the knucklebones (Metropolitan Museum of Art, Carnarvon Collection, gift of Edward S. Harkness, 1926)

Inlaid game board originally hollowed to contain the fourteen playing pieces, which are made of black shale inlaid with white shell, or of shell with lapis-inlaid spots. From a grave at Ur (25th cent. B.C.) (Trustees of the British Museum)

Ivory game board (*ca.* 13th cent. B.C.) with gold and blue paste inlays, found with twenty-six gold-leaf studs at Megiddo (Oriental Institute, University of Chicago)

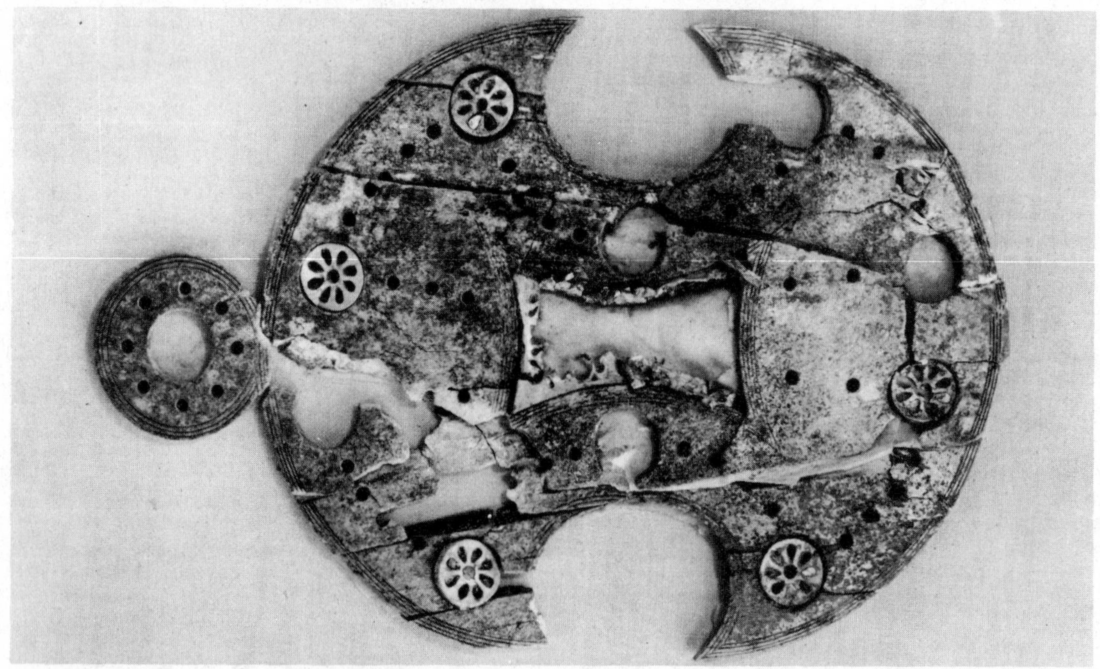

in rock. These game boards are made up of three rectangles within which are parallel rows of nine to eleven smaller rectangles (Morton, p. 35 fig. 6). It is believed that the game played on these boards may have been an ancient Nabatean or possibly pre-Nabatean version of the modern "mancala" game (Matson, p. 139), which is still played by the bedouin of the district (Morton, pp. 33f.). Another game played on a game board was chess, known to have been played in Babylonia and Elam from the 3rd millennium B.C. and possibly known in Palestine as well. Excavations at numerous Palestinian sites have brought to light what must be considered toys of the young, such as rattles, marbles, animals (with wheels), chariots, whistles, dolls, etc. These have survived because they were made of baked clay.

Although archeology has provided much information concerning games that were known in biblical times, information on the rules that governed their playing is still lacking.

B. In Greece and Rome. It is known that in the Hellenistic period many Jews readily adopted Greek games, and the gymnasium and theater became popular, largely through the influence of the Seleucid rulers. Early in the reign of ANTIOCHUS IV EPIPHANES (175-164 B.C.) a gymnasium was built in Jerusalem (1 Macc. 1:14; cf. 2 Macc. 4:9, 12). Reportedly even priests were such enthusiastic spectators at the athletic fields that they would leave the altar and run to the arena when they heard "the call to the discus" (2 Macc. 4:14). The Tobias family, which was the leader of a new aristocracy of wealth, was responsible for converting Jerusalem from an obscure city into a town of prominence. To hellenize Jerusalem they succeeded in building the above-mentioned gymnasium and formed bodies of (Gk.) *éphēboi,* i.e., corps of young men associated with this central institution of a Hellenistic city. Judean youths and priests were nude during the athletic games (1 Macc. 1:12-15). After the Maccabean revolt (167 B.C.) the athletic games fell into general disrepute among the Jewish population of Palestine (Josephus *Ant.* xv.8.2 [277]). Nevertheless, Hellenistic games were familiar to most in Jerusalem and elsewhere during the later Herodian and Roman periods. Herod the Great built a theater, amphitheater, stadium, and hippodrome in Caesarea, where games were to be held every fifth year. He also built a theater in Jerusalem and an amphitheater nearby (*Ant.* xv.8.1 [268]). Jericho reportedly was also provided with a theater, amphitheater, and hippodrome. Thus, Greek and Roman games appear to have been widely known in Palestine, and an acquaintance with them will facilitate a better understanding of a number of NT passages.

The public games of Greece (Gk. *agṓnes*) and Rome (Lat. *ludi*) consisted of a variety of athletic games and contests. The athletes were trained in the Greek gymnasium, which was the central market where poets, artists, and merchants brought their goods. The exhibitions of the later Roman amphitheater and circus never matched the glory of the ancient Greek games; they were at best a shadow and later nothing more than a farcical imitation.

The Olympic games were the earliest and remained the most celebrated of the four national festivals of Greece. The foot race (*drómos*) of a single lap of the stadium (*stádion*), which was about 180 m. (200 yds.) long, was at first the only contest. Later (14th Olympiad) the double lap and others were added. The goal of the foot race was a square pillar that the runner kept in view to redouble his exertion. Wrestling was introduced at the 18th Olympiad. Plutarch called wrestling the most artistic and cunning of all athletic games. The wrestler's limbs were oiled and sprinkled with sand. Otherwise wrestling differed little from that of today. No struggling was allowed on the ground, however, and the third throw decided the victory (cf. 2 Macc. 4:14). Boxing was carried on much as it is today, with leather thongs bound round the boxer's fists and wrists. The Greek boxers did not hit out straight from the shoulder but fought in a windmill fashion. A Roman development of boxing involved a weighting of the leather thongs with lead, iron, or metal studs, which produced grave injuries to the boxers. The chief strategy of the boxers was therefore evasion. Discus throwing was carried on with a round plate of stone or metal 30 cm. (12 in.) in diameter (2 Macc. 4:14). Pausanius enumerated twenty-four Olympic contests, though it must not be supposed that all were exhibited at any one festival. At first the games lasted one day; later they were extended to five.

Roman theater in Amman (W. S. LaSor)

The Pythian games, as a chronological era, dated from 527 B.C. and were especially devoted to musical competitions. The Pythiads were also held at the end of every fourth year. The Nemean games were biennial and dated from 516 B.C. The contests were like the Olympiads. The Isthmian games began in 523 B.C. and were held at the first and third years of each Olympiad. These games were managed by the Corinthians on the Corinthian Isthmus. They included gymnastics, horsemanship, and musical contests. A herald (Gk. *kḗryx*) announced the name and country of each competitor and the name, country, and father of each victor. The victors were rewarded at the great games by a wreath or crown consisting in the NT period of wild olive (Olympiads), laurel (Pythiads), wild celery (Nemeads), and pine or wild celery (Isthmiads).

The Romans introduced the *venatio,* i.e., the baiting of wild animals that were pitted against each other or against men who could be either captives, criminals, or trained hunters called *bestiarii.* This type of exhibition was carried on in the amphitheater. Herod the Great followed the custom of the Roman proconsuls and generals in supplying his arenas with lions and other wild beasts of rare or unusual strength in order to have condemned men fight them or have these animals fight each other (Josephus *Ant.* xv.8.1). The special show of the amphitheater was the *manus gladiatorium* or gladiatorial combat. These brutal shows clearly exhibit the vein of coarseness and inhumanity running through the character of mankind. It is known that Herod the Great had condemned criminals thrown to wild animals in his amphitheater near Jerusalem in order to afford "delight to spectators" (*Ant.* xv.8.1). After the fall of Jerusalem in A.D. 70, Titus had a great number of captives either thrown to wild beasts or forced to kill one another as if they were animals (Josephus *BJ* vii.2.1 [24]).

II. Games in the Bible.–The Bible gives only scattered indications of games and play. But the ancient Hebrews had their games as the various archeological finds indicate (see I.A above).

A. In the OT. Though there is not a single direct reference in the OT to toys for children, the finds of whistles, rattles, marbles, dolls, animals (at times with wheels), and other objects on numerous sites in Palestine give some indication of the type of toys with which the Israelite young played.

The first reference to playing is Gen. 21:9, where Ishmael was "playing" (Heb. *m^e^ṣaḥēq*) with Isaac (AV "mocking"; NEB "laughing at him"). The Hebrew word is the intensive form (piel) of the verb *ṣāḥaq,* a wordplay on the name "Isaac." Some interpreters suggest that the meaning "mocking" would require the Hebrew preposition *b-* to designate the object. Others point out that in the majority of instances this intensive form of the verb is used in the sense of behaving wantonly with someone, viz., taunting, jesting, making sport of someone (Gen. 19:14; 39:14-17; Ex. 32:6; Jgs. 16:25). On this basis the seventeen-year-old Ishmael appears to have maliciously laughed at this three-year-old brother Isaac (cf. Gen. 16:16; 21:5). This "playing" with Isaac would mean something much different than that the older brother was merely trying to "amuse" his little brother.

Yahweh's question to Job, "Will you play with him [Leviathan = crocodile] as with a bird, or will you put him on leash for your maidens?" (Job 41:5 [MT 40:29]), suggests that Hebrew children, especially girls, made pets of birds. Job 21:11f. makes reference to children engaged in carefree singing and dancing (*ANEP,* no. 216). In Zec. 8:5 the aged of the restored city are envisaged as enjoying days of leisure when boys and girls will be playing in the streets. The nature of their games is not indicated, but reliefs from Egypt that depict girls dancing or playing games (no. 216) and boys engaged in tug of war and other games (no. 217) may provide a background. Playing ball is alluded to in Isa. 22:18: "He will . . . whirl you round and round, and throw you like a ball into a wide land." The Hebrew verbs (from *ṣnp*) underlying the initial phrase imply a winding up of cloth into the shape of a ball that can roll freely.

Jacob's long bout of wrestling at Penuel seems to presuppose some prior practice of this type of fighting, for the struggle was indecisive for a long period of time (Gen. 32:24). Jacob's opponent won the upper hand when Jacob's hip socket was wrenched at the sciatic muscle during the struggle (vv. 25, 33). It is not impossible that both wrestlers were acquainted with the rules and tricks of fighting. The proverbial expression "hip and thigh" (lit. "thigh upon hip"), used in connection with Samson's victory over the Philistines (Jgs. 15:8), is taken by some interpreters to be a technical term that ultimately derives from wrestling.

The meeting between Saul's men and those of David at Gibeon, where Abner and Joab agreed to let them "arise and play before us" (2 S. 2:14 [Heb. *śiḥaq*]; NEB "join in a single combat"), seems to refer to a tournament or a group combat with wrestling. Wrestling by grasping the belt of an opponent was an ancient form of engagement in combat (*ANEP,* no. 219). In any case the group combat of the young men at Gibeon soon degenerated into a fierce battle (vv. 15-32).

Running evidently was practiced at least from the time of the monarchy. Saul and Jonathan (2 S. 1:23), Asahel (2:18), Ahimaaz (18:23, 27), and some of the Gadite warriors in David's service (1 Ch. 12:8) were famous for their swiftness, which must have been the result of exercise and training. The feats of those who ran before the king or prince (1 S. 8:11; 2 S. 15:1; 1 K. 1:5; 18:46) could not have been achieved without practice. The figure of speech of the sun rejoicing like a strong man to run his course seems to have its origin in competitive games (Ps. 19:5b [MT 6b]); for a similar metaphor, cf. the one who will "run the course" of God's commandments (Ps. 119:32, NEB).

Archery could be a game of skill with the shooting of an arrow at a fixed target (1 S. 20:20, 35-38). Job's complaint that "he set me up as his target, his archers surround me" (Job 16:12b-13a) reflects archery (cf. Lam. 3:12). Assyrian reliefs depict archery as both a game of skill and a warlike art. (*See also* ARCHER, ARCHERY.)

The custom of using a sling for projecting stones must also be mentioned. The sling was used among the Hebrews by shepherds (1 S. 17:34-36, 40, 49) and warriors (2 K. 3:25; 2 Ch. 26:14). But it must not be supposed that the use of the sling was in OT times restricted to these groups; doubtless it was also a game of skill. Stone-slinging as a formidable weapon of war was used not only by the Israelites but also by the Assyrians, Egyptians, and Babylonians. The Benjaminites had an elite group of seven hundred left-handed stone-slingers who could sling a stone at a hair and not miss (Jgs. 20:16; cf. 1 Ch. 12:2). Archeologists have discovered round stone balls of two or three inches in diameter at numerous Palestinian sites and have usually identified these as slingstones. According to estimates, a slingstone weighing up to 453 gm. (1 lb.) can be catapulted with a sling at a speed up to 140 km. (90 mi.) per hour and hit its target with great accuracy.

The Israelites also participated in another sort of "play." They spoiled the cult in the wilderness in that they "sat down to eat and drink, and rose up to play" (Ex. 32:6). Special emphasis is here placed upon extravagant celebrations. The eating and drinking refer to a sacred meal. But this cultic festival had its final aim in the rising up "to play," which "doubtless refers to sexual orgies (see Gen. 26:8) such as played a part in the Canaanite fertility cults" (M. Noth, *Exodus* [Eng. tr., *OTL,* 1962], p. 248).

B. In the NT. The NT references to games are fairly frequent but never direct. With rare exceptions they are used in drawing spiritual lessons.

An indirect reference to the games children played in the streets and town squares is provided by Jesus in quoting a saying that they called to their playmates (Mt. 11:17; Lk. 7:32). It reveals that these youngsters copied their elders in playing weddings and funerals. This may mean by implication that the children of Jesus' day copied other customs and rites of everyday life for their games.

Spiritual lessons could be easily drawn from the various known Greek and Roman games. In 1 Cor. 9:24-27, Paul, who may have witnessed the Isthmian Games in A.D. 51 (Broneer, pp. 185-87), called the attention of the Corinthian believers to the vigorous training of the athletes (a metaphor also used by the Greek poet Epictetus). The athletes exercised "self-control in all things" (v. 25; cf. 1 Tim. 4:7; 2 Tim. 2:5), which reflects the Greek custom that athletes observe a severe period of training under very specific rules and exercise self-denial in watching their weight. The race in which all the runners competed (v. 24) referred to the foot race (see I above). Paul did "not run aimlessly" (v. 26), because like the runners in the foot race of the Greek games he had his eyes fixed upon the goal. As the victor received the "prize" (v. 24) in the form of "a perishable wreath" (v. 25), viz., the wreath of wild celery of the Corinthian Isthmian games that withers quickly, so the Christian will receive a wreath. But his wreath or crown of victory is "imperishable" (v. 25; cf. 2 Tim. 2:5; 4:8; cf. 1 Pet. 1:4; 5:4). Phil. 4:1; 1 Thess. 2:19; He. 2:7-9; Jas. 1:12; Rev. 2:10; 3:11 also allude to the wreath or crown. The palm-bearing multitude of Rev. 7:9 is possibly reminiscent of the carrying of palm branches by victors at the games.

The phrase "I do not box as one beating the air" (1 Cor. 9:26) depicts a boxing contest in which the hands were bound with studded leather that inflicted grave injury. The boxers, therefore, used a technique of evasion rather than one of parrying — hence the phrase "beating the air." Paul concluded this passage by comparing himself to the "herald" (*kḗryx*) who called others to the contest but was himself disqualified from competing (v. 27; cf. 1 Tim. 2:7; 2 Tim. 1:11). These pictures drawn from the Greek games were particularly meaningful metaphors for the Corinthian readers of this letter, since the Isthmian games were a Corinthian festival.

Several NT epistles compare the Christian life to a foot race. The writer of the letter to the Hebrews stressed that the successful runner of the Christian's race had to lay aside everything that was a hindrance (sin) and had to persevere in order to win (He. 12:1). In addition, the runner's eye had to be fixed upon the goal, Jesus (v. 2), as the eye of the runner in the games was fixed on the square pillar that he must reach. Paul employed the picture of the runner a number of times. He wanted to make absolutely sure that the course that he was pursuing or had pursued was not in vain (Gal. 2:2). The fruit of the Philippian believers proved to Paul that he had not run the race in vain (Phil. 2:16). Paul's whole attention in the race that he was running was on the finish line in order to win the prize that God had in store, viz., life on high with Jesus Christ, his Lord (Phil. 3:14). But the wreath or crown of the winner could not be received unless one had kept the rules of the athletic contest (2 Tim. 2:5).

A reference to wrestling (Gk. *pálē*) is found in Eph. 6:12, where the Christian is told that he is engaged in an all-out wrestling match not against flesh and blood but against principalities and powers and world rulers of the present aeon of darkness.

Philippians 3:13f. may refer to a chariot race. In NT times hippodromes existed in many cities of the Roman empire, and Philippi was a Roman colony. Paul seemed to picture himself as a charioteer who in the decisive state of the chariot race was "straining forward to what lies ahead" (v. 13). In such intense pressing on "toward the goal for the prize" (v. 14) at high speed a glance at "what lies behind" (v. 13) would be fatal. Thus, Christians must "forget" that which they have achieved already, and with newly bestowed powers they must strain forward and press on with all their might to reach the goal and gain the prize of victory.

The judges who sat near the goal and had been carefully prepared for their task (at least at the early Olympiads) are employed in a metaphor in 2 Tim. 4:8: "The crown of righteousness, which the Lord, the righteous judge, will award to me on that Day. . . ." The emphasis on the "righteous" nature of the judge may likely be due to the deterioration of the games, as was illustrated by Nero's announcement of his own infamous victory at Olympia (A.D. 67).

In the Synoptic account of Jesus' "mockery" (*empaízō*, Mt. 27:29-31 par.) Jesus among other things was reported "blindfolded" (*perikalýptō*, Mk. 14:65 par. Lk. 22:64), "struck" (*kolaphízō*, Mt. 26:67; Mk. 14:65; *dérō*, Lk. 22:63), and also commanded to guess who was the source of the physical abuse by the specific demand, "Who is it that struck you?" (Mt. 26:68; Lk. 22:64). The mockery referred to the playing of blindman's buff with Jesus. This game, called *chalkḗ myía* by Pollux (*Onomasticon* ix.123), had a rich mythological and religious history and background (cf. Miller, pp. 309-311). A possible site of the events indicated in the accounts of Jesus' mockery is the court of the Fortress Antonia in Jerusalem. At the base of the northeastern stairway of the court archeologists have discovered games incised into the flagstone pavement (Aline de Sion, plate 45) underneath the convent of "Notre Dame de Sion." These game tables indicate the range of games: knucklebones, dice games, and capture games or tic-tac-toe board games. At three places in the flagstones a "B" was incised, symbolizing the Greek *basileús* (king) or the Roman *basilicus,* the latter being the best roll of dice and possibly implying that the "king's command" (Gk. *basilínda*) was played here. This game is related to the modern "dare, double dare" (Opie, p. 266). Pollux reported that in the ancient form of this game a king was elected by lot and all others had to obey his commands (*Onomasticon* ix.110). This game has been connected to the cruel practices of certain saturnalian festivals during which a scapegoat was elected by lot as a mock king, abused for the festival period, and killed at the end. This game may have been related to the parody of royalty imposed on Jesus during His passion (Mk. 15:16-20 par.).

See also DANCE; RIDDLE.

***Bibliography*.**–G. E. Matson, *National Geographic,* 67 (Feb., 1935), 139; E. D. van Buren, *Iraq,* 4 (1937), 11-15; W. F. Albright, *AASOR,* 17 (1936/37), 48f.; Pauly-Wissowa Supp., V, *s.v.* "Ludi publici" (J. Habel); VII, *s.v.* "Ludi circens" (J. Regner); W. M. Hayes, *Scepter of Egypt* (1953), pp. 249-251; M. A. de Sion, *La Forteresse Antonia à Jérusalem et la question du prétoire* (1955), pp. 44-48, 119-142; W. H. Morton, *BA,* 19 (1956), 33-35; P. Montet, *Everyday Life in Egypt in the Days of Ramses the Great* (Eng. tr. 1958), pp. 99-102; I. and P. Opie, *Children's Games in Street and Playground* (1969), pp. 266f.; O. Broneer, *HTR,* 64 (1971), 169-187; D. L. Miller, *JBL,* 90 (1971), 309-313.

G. F. HASEL

GAMMADIM gam'a-dim (Ezk. 27:11, AV). *See* GAMAD, MEN OF.

GAMUL gā'məl [Heb. *gāmûl*]. The head of the twenty-second of the twenty-four divisions of priests inaugurated by David (1 Ch. 24:17).

GANGRENE [Gk. *gángraina*] (2 Tim. 2:17); AV CANKER. A Greek medical term used since the time of Hippocrates for a spreading ulcer. Paul compares the corrupting influence of profane talk to this disease. The old English word "cankers" (cf. AV) was used by sixteenth- and seventeenth-century authors as the name of a caterpillar that eats into a bud.

GAR gar (1 Esd. 5:34, AV). *See* GAS.

GARB, HER CAPTIVE'S [Heb. *śimlaṯ šiḇyāh*] (Dt. 21:13); AV "raiment of her captivity"; NEB "clothes which she had when captured." The clothing worn by a woman of an enemy people at the time she was taken captive was to be shed when she was taken into the house of an Israelite as a wife. This act was perhaps symbolic of her crossing over to a new way of life.

GARDEN [Heb. *gan, gannâ, karmel*; Gk. *kḗpos*]. An enclosure or surrounded area of land, such as a fenced plot that could be used for various purposes. In different locations the fence could be made from thorns, stones, or mud bricks.

Gardens were a prominent part of the irrigation economies of both Mesopotamia and Egypt; and in the case of wealthy or influential persons the garden was quite ex-

Funerary model of a garden from the tomb of Meket-Re (11th Dynasty, *ca.* 2000 B.C.) at Thebes (Metropolitan Museum of Art, Museum Excavation, 1919-1920; Rogers Fund, supplemented by contribution of Edward S. Harkness)

Painting of the garden of a private estate with ornamental water, from the tomb of Nebamen at Thebes (*ca.* 1400 B.C.) (Trustees of the British Museum)

tensive and usually adjoined the residence. In ancient Mesopotamia the royal palace normally had adjacent courts where gardens were cultivated, the most celebrated being the so-called hanging gardens of Babylon. Actually, these "gardens" were elevated masonry terraces supposedly built in the form of a square of which the sides were about 120 m. (400 ft.) in length, and raised on arches to a height of 23 m. (75 ft.), so that the trees they contained were visible above the roofs of other buildings. When Babylon was enlarged under Nebuchadrezzar II it spread out on either side of the Euphrates, and according to Herodotus (i.178) enclosed an area of 525 sq. km. (200 sq. mi.), about nine-tenths of which comprised parks, fields, and gardens.

The ancient Egyptians, too, cultivated gardens, orchards, and parks, and wealthy families frequently maintained country estates where the owners could relax amid a profusion of flowers, fruit trees, and artificial ponds. Excavations at Râs Shamrah (Ugarit) have shown that a garden once occupied a large court inside the well-appointed palace of the kings of Ugarit in the 14th and 13th cents. B.C.

The gardens referred to in biblical times were generally walled enclosures that were frequently irrigated (Isa. 58:11); they sometimes contained a shelter or arbor in which the owner could sit and enjoy the fragrance of the herbs and flowers. Such gardens are mentioned in Eccl. 2:5f.; cf. the figurative use in Cant. 4:12-16; and the mention of "Eden the garden of God" in Ezek. 28:13; 31:8f.; Joel 2:3. If they belonged to kings or to people of wealth, they would probably include an orchard and a private park as well as a flower or herb garden (cf. 2 K. 25:4). The gardens mentioned in the Bible allowed various uses, since they were not merely cultivated for their produce but were often intended to serve as outdoor living areas in the summer, when the houses were hot and stuffy. The gardens in which trees were planted were favorite places for walking or for outdoor banqueting, or, if a pool had been installed, for bathing (Sus. 4, 7, 15-18). *See* picture in EAT.

The most common use of gardens was for the cultivation of vegetables, herbs, and flowers (Cant. 5:1; 6:2), while some gardens contained fruit and olive trees as well as grape vines. The Garden of Gethsemane, for example, was a private olive grove that would have its own vat for extracting the olive oil. In the case of large estates it was common for the family graves to be located in a garden (cf. 2 K. 21:18, 26; Jn. 19:41), while in preexilic times the seclusion of such places permitted unhindered indulgence in pagan rites that were most likely connected with the depraved fertility cults of the Canaanites (Isa. 1:29; 65:3; 66:17).

From the time of the Exile the Persian term *pairi-daēza* (Heb. *pardēs*; Gk. *parádeisos*) appeared in Hebrew literature to denote more extensive parks or gardens. In Eccl. 2:5 and Cant. 4:13, the AV translates the word "orchards," while in Gen. 2:8 the LXX translates the phrase *gan ʿēḏen* ("garden of Eden") by *parádeisos*. The word *pardēs* was nowhere used in Hebrew in an eschatological sense, unlike its occurrence in the NT, though in the pre-Christian period it was employed to describe the bliss of primeval times (*see* EDEN). Figuratively, the RSV translates Heb. *karmel* ("vineyard") as "garden land" in Mic. 7:14 (AV "Carmel"; NEB "meadows"), depicting the Jews' return to prosperity after the Exile.

A fruitful garden was synonymous with prosperity (Job 8:16; Isa. 51:3; Jer. 29:5, 28). The life of God's redeemed was likened to a watered fertile garden (Isa. 58:11; Jer. 31:12). In contrast, the destruction of gardens indicated desolation (Am. 4:9).

See also KING'S GARDEN.

See *TDNT,* V, *s.v.* παράδεισος (J. Jeremias).

R. K. HARRISON

GARDEN HOUSE [Heb. *bêṯ haggān*–'house of the garden']. The AV for RSV and NEB BETH-HAGGAN in 2 K. 9:27.

GARDENER [Gk. *kḗpouros*] (Jn. 20:15). "Gardener" occurs once in the RSV as the translation of *kḗros,* "garden," and *oúros,* "warden" or "keeper." The man referred to was probably the watchman or keeper (Arab. *naṭûr*; Heb. *nōṣēr*), corresponding to those mentioned in 2 K. 17:9; 18:8; Job 27:18; etc., and not one who did the manual work. It was the common practice in biblical times to set a watchman over a garden during its productive season. *See* WATCHMAN.

GAREB gār'eb [Heb. *gārēḇ*–'scabby'].

1. An Ithrite who was one of David's "mighty men" (2 S. 23:38; cf. 1 Ch. 11:40).

2. The prophet envisioned that Jerusalem should extend to a hill of this name (Jer. 31:39). The site is unknown, but the context (vv. 38-40, suggesting a northwest to southeast progression) points to an area W of the Tyropoeon Valley, possibly to the southwestern hill or the "upper city" of postexilic times.

GARIZIM gar'i-zim. *See* GERIZIM, MOUNT.

GARLAND [Heb. *liwyâ*] (Prov. 1:9; 4:9); AV ORNAMENT; [*'iwweleṯ*–'folly'] (Prov. 14:24); AV "folly"; NEB CHIEF ORNAMENT; [*pe'ēr*] (Isa. 61:3, 10); AV BEAUTY, ORNAMENTS; [Gk. *stémma*] (Acts 14:13). The RSV emends *'iwweleṯ* in Prov. 14:24 to read *liwyâ*.

A wreath to be worn on the head as an ornament for festive occasions; a chaplet. Its use in the OT is primarily figurative. In Proverbs the instruction of parents (1:9) and the work of wisdom (4:9) are to be worn on the head as a garland; they are to be worn as beautiful ornaments and not borne as a burden. The prophet in Isa. 61 uses "garland" (perhaps "turban"), an ornament worn at wedding festivities (v. 10), as a symbol of the joy and festivity that will characterize the salvation he announces.

In Acts 14:13, because the people believed Paul and Barnabas to be gods, a priest of Zeus brought garlands and oxen in preparation for a sacrifice with the people. These garlands were woolen fillets used to decorate animals to be offered in sacrifice. E. W. CONRAD

GARLIC [Heb. *šûm*; cf. Arab. *ṯûm*]. One of the Egyptian delicacies that the wandering Israelites longed for (Nu. 11:5). The common garlic, *Allium sativum* L., was cultivated in the ancient Near East for culinary purposes. It has stomachic, diuretic, antispasmodic, and anthelmintic (worming) properties. A bulb of garlic placed near a door was thought to be a powerful charm against evil influences.

GARMENTS. Ever since the fall humans have made and worn clothing (Gen. 3:7, 21) for modesty, protection, and status. Although this study of the biblical words for clothing covers a period of more than a thousand years, it is made easier because fashions in the ancient world did not change constantly, as in the modern world. This study can thus be organized according to the following outline.

- I. Materials
- II. Garments for Both Men and Women
  - A. Undergarments
  - B. Outer Garments
    - 1. General Terms for Clothing
    - 2. Specific Terms
- III. Garments for Men
  - A. Undergarments
  - B. Outer Garments
- IV. Garments for Women
- V. Girdles, Belts, Sashes
- VI. Headgear
- VII. Footwear
- VIII. Priests' Garments
  - A. Undergarments
  - G. Outer Garments
- IX. Ornaments
- X. Gestures and Figurative Uses

I. Materials.–The earliest common materials were animal skins: leather (Heb. *'ôr,* Gen. 3:21) and goatskins (*taḥaš,* Ex. 25:5; Nu. 4:6, 25); cf. Gk. *mēlōtḗ,* "pelt," any rough woolly skin, "skins of sheep and goats" that the ancient suffering heroes wore (He. 11:37; cf. the metaphoric usage referring to false prophets in Mt. 7:15; *see also* LEATHER). Wool (Heb. *ṣemer,* e.g., Lev. 13:47; Gk. *érion,* e.g., Rev. 1:14) was later produced and made into clothing in Palestine, especially in Judea; it was spun from fleece (*gēz,* Job 31:20) and woven into cloth. Hair (*śē'ār,* Zec. 13:4, "hairy mantle"; NEB "robe of coarse hair") from goats or camels was woven into coarse cloth (cf. *trichṓn kamḗlou,* the CAMEL'S HAIR garment of John the Baptist, Mt. 3:4). Linen (*baḏ,* e.g., Lev. 16:4) was woven from the fibers of flax (*pištâ,* e.g., Ex. 9:31; later produced mainly in Galilee and the Jordan Valley). The Hebrews were forbidden to wear *ša'aṭnēz,* garments of mixed fibers of wool and flax (Lev. 19:19; Dt. 22:11). Sackcloth (*śaq,* lit. "sack"; e.g., Gen. 37:34) refers to very coarse material from which a basic garment was made and worn in mourning and repentance (2 S. 3:31; Jonah 3:5); the corresponding Gk. *sákkos* is a coarse cloth of hair, especially goat's hair (Mt. 11:21; Rev. 11:3), that could be dark in color (Rev. 6:12; cf. Isa. 50:3).

Hebrew *bûṣ* was fine white Egyptian linen (Est. 8:15), known from very ancient times; Gk. *býssos, býssinos*

Wooden statue (*ca.* 1400 B.C.) of a high-ranking Egyptian nobleman wearing a tight, pleated, wide-skirted linen garment (Trustees of the British Museum)

(Isa. 3:23, LXX; Rev. 18:12, 16; 19:8, 14) referred to fine linen. Heb. *šēš*, translated "silk" in the AV (Prov. 31:22), should doubtless be translated "fine white linen" (cf. RSV, NEB, "fine linen"; LXX *býssos*).

Cotton was apparently an important Egyptian product in Isaiah's time (*ḥôrāy*, Isa. 19:9) and was later used for curtains in the palace at Susa (*karpas*, Est. 1:6; the LXX uses *býssos* in both instances).

The meaning of Heb. *mešî* (Ezk. 16:10, 13) is uncertain, though translated "silk" in the AV and RSV, "lawn" in the NEB. The LXX *tríchapta* indicates a "fine veil of hair" (LSJ, *s.v.* τρίχαπτον, p. 1824). Gk. *sirikós* (or *sērikós*, Rev. 18:12) does mean silk or a silken garment.

Variegated material (Heb. *riqmâ*) was evidently highly prized; thus it was worn by a princess at the marriage ceremony (Ps. 45:14 [MT 15], "many-colored robes"; AV "raiment of needlework"; NEB "richly embroidered"), and by a prince (Ezk. 26:16, "embroidered" garments; NEB "brocaded" robes), and it was a valued trade item (Ezk. 27:16, 24, "embroidered work"; NEB "brocade"). *See also* EMBROIDERY.

Various words for colors also mean cloth or clothing of those colors. Three common ones occur in Ex. 25:4 and 2 Ch. 2:7, 14 (MT 6, 13): purple (Heb. *ʾargᵉwān*/*ʾargᵉmān*, equivalent to Gk. *porphýra*), used for outer garments of kings and others of royal or priestly rank (cf. Ex. 26:1; Rev. 17:4; 18:12, 16); scarlet (Heb. *šānî*; probably the same as *karmîl*, "crimson," both of which were included in Gk. *kókkinos*; cf. Rev. 17:4; 18:12, 16); blue (Heb. *tᵉḵēleṯ*, Gk. *hyákinthos*; cf. Ex. 26:1; 28:31; Rev. 9:17 — of blue precious stones). The Beni-hasan tomb painting (from Egypt *ca.* 1900 B.C.) shows figured garments of red, blue, and white, on both men and women (*ANEP*, no. 3). *See also* COLOR; DYE; picture of faience tile depicting prisoner in HITTITE.

II. Garments for Both Men and Women.–*A. Undergarments.* Hebrew *kᵉṯōneṯ*, *kuttōneṯ*, "garment, coat" (Gen. 3:21, with *ʿôr*; 37:3, 23, 31-33; 2 S. 13:18f., with *passîm*) was a shirtlike or long tuniclike garment, with or without sleeves, usually of linen, worn next to the skin. It corresponded to the Gk. *chitṓn*, "coat, tunic," which early was used only of a man's undergarment, a woman's being *péplos*, but later was used of both (LSJ, *s.v.* χιτών, p. 1993). It is used for a man's garment (e.g., 2 S. 15:32), for a woman's (Cant. 5:3), for a princess' (2 S. 13:18f.), for a priest's (Ex. 29:8), and for the high priest's (Lev. 16:4). Jesus' garment was seamless; thus the Roman soldiers cast lots for it rather than dividing it (Jn. 19:23f.). Joseph's coat (Gen. 37:3, 23, 32) was evidently of great value or status, although it is uncertain whether it was "of many colors" (cf. the LXX and AV), or long with sleeves (cf. the RSV and NEB), or of many pieces (cf. KoB, p. 768), or ornamented (cf. E. Speiser, *Genesis* [*AB*, 1964], pp. 289f.). *See also* COAT.

B. Outer Garments. 1. General Terms. A number of words mean "clothes, clothing" in general. Heb. *beged* occurs 200 times and refers to items from bedclothes (1 K. 1:1) to the covering of the ark (Nu. 4:6-9) to kings' robes (1 K. 22:10). From the verb *lāḇaš*, "clothe," come the nouns *lᵉḇûš*, "raiment" (Ps. 102:26 [MT 27]; AV "vesture"; NEB "cloak"; LXX *peribólaion*); *malbûš*, "clothing" (1 K. 10:5; AV "apparel"; NEB "livery"; LXX *himatismós*); and *tilbōšeṯ*, "garments" (Isa. 59:17; LXX *himátion*). From the verb *kāsâ*, "cover," come the nouns *kᵉsûṯ*, "cloak" (Dt. 22:12, of men; AV "vesture"), and *mᵉḵasseh*, "clothing" (Isa. 23:18, as a garment of a metaphorical harlot, a city; NEB "attire"). Heb. *šîṯ* (from the verb *šîṯ*, "put"), "garment" is something put on (Ps. 73:6, of men; NEB "robe"; in Prov. 7:10 the RSV and NEB translate it as a verb, "dressed," but the AV uses the noun "attire"; the reference is to a harlot's clothing). From the verb *ʿāṭâ*, "wrap," comes *maʿᵃṭeh*, "mantle" (Isa. 61:3; AV, NEB "garment"). Though Dt. 22:5 forbids one sex to wear garments pertaining to the other, many of the outer garments looked very similar; probably distinctive headgear or sashes, or other differences such as in embroidery, made the distinction obvious.

Smith-god Vulcan (Hephaistos) wearing the workman's *chitṓn* (Trustees of the British Museum)

General Greek terms for clothing are *himatismós*, "apparel" (e.g., Acts 20:33; NEB "clothes"); *himátion*, "mantle" (Mt. 24:18; AV "clothes"; NEB "coat"), a length of cloth draped around the body, sometimes specifically worn over a *chitṓn* (cf. Mt. 5:40, which implies that legally only the less expensive inner garment could be claimed, since the outer garment was the poor person's cover at night; in Lk. 6:29 the order is reversed in a case of robbery); *peribólaion*, "covering" (1 Cor. 11:15) or "mantle" (He. 1:12; AV "vesture"; NEB "cloak"), literally "something thrown around one"; *amphíasis*, "clothing" (Job 22:6, translating *beged*; 24:7, translating *k*^{e}*sûṯ*) or "garment" (Job 38:9, translating *l*^{e}*ḇûš*). The *stolḗ* was a large, flowing robe of rank, used by men (Mk. 12:38, scribes; Lk. 15:22, the prodigal son on his return); by angels (Mk. 16:5); by multitudes including both men and women (Rev. 6:11; 7:9,13f.; 22:14). Garments that were wrapped around the body rather than being made with sleeves were held by a clasp or buckle. *See also* ROBE.

2. Specific Terms. Heb. *śimlâ* (sometimes *śalmâ* by metathesis) was a square cloth used by both men and women as a wrapper or mantle, and also as a cover for sleeping (Gen. 9:23, "garment"; NEB "cloak"; LXX *himátion*; *see also* GARB, HER CAPTIVE'S). A *sāḏîn* is a linen sheet or garment (Jgs. 14:12f.; Prov. 31:24; Isa. 3:23, a luxury item for women, but see IX below). The LXX uses *sindṓn* in these verses, except the last, which has *hyakínthinos,* elsewhere meaning "fine leather" (Ex. 25:5) or "blue color" (Ex. 26:4). *Sindṓn* occurs also in Mt. 27:59 of the "shroud" or winding-sheet used for Jesus' body (in nonbiblical Greek the word meant surgeons' or mummies' bandages, napkins, ships' sails, flags, and other things made of fine cloth, usually linen [LSJ, *s.v.* σινδών, p. 1600]). In Mk. 14:51f., it was the "linen cloth" on the unnamed young man, who fled without it.

The Hebrew word for an outer garment with the most status, used by both sexes, was *m*^{eʿ}*îl,* a (sleeveless) coat or mantle or robe of rank (Ezr. 9:3, 5; Job 1:20). It was worn by a king or a prince (1 S. 18:4; 24:4 [MT 5]), a princess (2 S. 13:18), the high priest (Ex. 28:4, 31), and a prophet (1 S. 15:27; 28:14).

The *šûl* or *kānāp̱* (lit. "wing") usually denotes the skirt of a garment. It was large enough to carry goods (Hag. 2:12), and in Isa. 6:1 God's "train" (*šûl*; NEB "skirt of his robe") is so long that it fills the temple. *Kānāp̱* by itself may mean "robe" (Zec. 8:23; AV "skirt") or "skirt" (Dt. 22:30 [MT 23:1]; 27:20; AV, RSV mg.). In the latter passages *kānāp̱* probably is a euphemism; to "cover with the skirt" was evidently a sign of (intention of) marriage (Ruth 3:9; Ezk. 16:8), and to "uncover the skirt" meant an invasion of sexual privacy (cf. the similar use of *šûl* in Jer. 13:22, 26; Nah. 3:5).

Hebrew *ḥ*^{a}*ṯullâ* is the "swaddling band" in which babies were wrapped (Job 38:9, used figuratively; cf. the LXX, which uses a verb, *sparganóō,* "wrap in swaddling cloths"; the same word is used of the baby Jesus in Lk. 2:7, 12).

III. Garments for Men.–*A. Undergarments.* Besides the tunic or shirt, the common primitive article of clothing, especially for slaves, was Heb. *ʾēzôr,* "girdle, waistcloth," which might be of skin (2 K. 1:8; NEB "leather apron") or of linen (Jer. 13:1; NEB "linen girdle"). It was the "waistcloth" worn by Assyrian warriors (Isa. 5:27) and the "belt" worn by Chaldeans (Ezk. 23:15); metaphorically it was the "girdle" of righteousness and faithfulness (Isa. 11:5). Rather than being a mere belt, when it was the sole garment it was a short wrapped skirt, as in Egyptian and Assyrian scenes (*ANEP,* nos. 1, 2, 8, etc.). Breeches apparently were reserved for the priests.

B. Outer Garments. Heb. *ʾaddereṯ* was a wide, sometimes magnificent cloak or robe, the garment of distinction worn by kings (Jonah 3:6; LXX *stolḗ*) and prophets (1 K. 19:13; 2 K. 2:8, 13f.); it was also part of the booty taken by Achan (Josh. 7:21, 24). It could be of fur or woven hair (Gen. 25:25; Zec. 13:4; goat's hair according to Dalman, V, 248). A related word is *ʾeḏer,* "robe" (Mic. 2:8; NEB "cloak"). Another rare word, *māḏû* (or *maḏweh*), names the long, probably stately "garments" worn by David's servants on a mission to the Ammonite capital, where for an insult the garments were "cut off . . . in the middle, at their hips" (2 S. 10:4 par. 1 Ch. 19:4). In Ezk. 27:24 "clothes" translates *g*^{e}*lôm,* apparently some kind of wrap or mantle (cf. postbiblical Heb. and Aram. *glm,* "to roll, wrap up"). *Sûṯ,* "vesture" (Gen. 49:11; AV "clothes"; NEB "robes"; LXX *peribolḗ*), may be a mantle (cf. postbiblical Heb. *sûṯ,* "dress, cloak," and F. Cross and D. Freedman, *Studies in Ancient Yahwistic Poetry* [1975], p. 84). *Taḵrîḵ* is a "mantle" of fine linen worn by Mordecai (Est. 8:15; AV "garment"; NEB "cloak"; cf. postbiblical Hebrew and Aramaic; but cf. the LXX *diádēma,* "fillet").

Hebrew words for warriors' armor are *mad(dîm),* "armor" (NEB "tunic"; LXX *mandýa,* "woolen cloak") of Saul, put on David, and *širyôn,* "coat of mail" (1 S. 17:38). The outfit was completed by the *qôḇaʿ,* a metal helmet (see VI below). Other words are: *ḥ*^{a}*lîṣâ,* "spoil" (NEB "belt"), stripped off defeated foes (Jgs. 14:19; 2 S. 2:21); *ḥ*^{a}*gôrâ,* "girdle, belt" (KoB, p. 276; cf. 2 S. 18:11; 1 K. 2:5; Isa. 3:24).

Greek words are *hópla,* used metaphorically of "armor" (Rom. 13:12) and "weapons" (2 Cor. 6:7). *Panoplía* is "armor" (Lk. 11:22) and "whole armor" (Eph. 6:11, metaphorically), which includes *thṓraka,* "breastplate," *thureós,* "shield," and *perikephalaía,* "helmet" (Eph. 6:11-17). *See also* WEAPONS OF WAR.

Greek terms for men's outer garments are: *chlamýs,* "robe" (Mt. 27:28, 31; NEB "mantle"; the parallel passages, Mk. 15:17, 20, and Jn. 19:2, 5, use *himátion,* "robe"), in classical usage a short mantle worn by horsemen, generals, kings, and also civilians (cf. LSJ, *s.v.* χλαμύς, p. 1993).

Esthḗs is usually used of apparently elegant clothing (cf. the "gorgeous apparel" Herod put on Jesus, Lk. 23:11; the "dazzling apparel" of the angels after the Resurrection, Lk. 24:4; cf. Acts 1:10; the "royal robes" of Herod, 12:21; cf. 10:30), but Jas. 2:2f. makes it clear that *esthḗs,* "clothing," could be either "fine" or "shabby."

Éndyma (e.g., Mt. 3:4, used only in Matthew) and *ependýtes* (both < *endýō*; "clothe, put on") mean simply something worn. The former is used for clothes from John the Baptist's garment of camel's hair to the "wedding garment" (Mt. 22:11f.) and the "raiment" of an angel (Mt. 28:3); in the LXX it is used of the "vestments" of the priests of Baal (2 K. 10:22). The latter is used of Peter's

Brickmakers wear short wrapped skirts in a reconstruction of Egyptian wall paintings (Royal Ontario Museum, Toronto)

"clothes" (Jn. 21:7; AV "fisher's coat"; NEB "coat"; *see also* FISHER'S COAT), and in the LXX of Jonathan's "robe" (1 S. 18:4).

Podḗrēs is a "long robe" that goes down to the feet, as its etymology indicates (cf. LSJ, *s.v.* ποδηνεκής, p. 1426; Ex. 28:31; Rev. 1:13). The "soft raiment" (*tá malaká*, Mt. 11:8; Lk. 7:25) that Jesus said was on those in kings' houses rather than on John the Baptist could refer to fine clothing of women as well as of male courtiers or royal family members. *Diploís*, "mantle" (lit. "double cloak"), occurs only in the LXX, e.g., Ps. 109:29 (LXX 108:29); in 1 S. 2:19 it is Samuel's "little robe," and in 1 S. 24:4, 11 (MT 5, 12) it is Saul's "robe." Paul's "cloak" (*phailónēs* rather than *phelónēs*, transposed from *phainólēs*; cf. Lat. *paenula*) left at Troas (2 Tim. 4:13), was a traveling coat. *See also* CLOAK; MANTLE; ROBE.

King Barrakib of Sam'al wears a pointed cap on his curled hair and a long, fringed garment; the beardless scribe has a plainer robe and a cap covering his hair. Relief from Zenjirli, *ca.* 730 B.C. (Staatliche Museen, Berlin)

Kore from Keratea, Attica, *ca.* 580-570 B.C. The woman wears a long pleated robe, fringed mantle, necklace, and bracelets and holds a pomegranate (Pergamon Museum, Berlin; picture Rosenthal Art Slides)

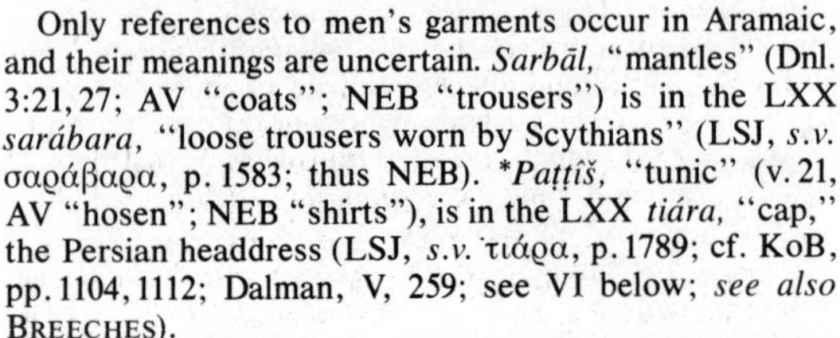

Only references to men's garments occur in Aramaic, and their meanings are uncertain. *Sarbāl*, "mantles" (Dnl. 3:21, 27; AV "coats"; NEB "trousers") is in the LXX *sarábara*, "loose trousers worn by Scythians" (LSJ, *s.v.* σαράβαρα, p. 1583; thus NEB). **Paṭṭîš*, "tunic" (v. 21, AV "hosen"; NEB "shirts"), is in the LXX *tiára*, "cap," the Persian headdress (LSJ, *s.v.* τιάρα, p. 1789; cf. KoB, pp. 1104, 1112; Dalman, V, 259; see VI below; *see also* BREECHES).

IV. Garments for Women.–Outer garments for women, aside from those listed for both sexes, include: Heb. *miṭpaḥaṯ*, "mantle" (Ruth 3:15; AV "vail"; NEB "cloak"; LXX *perízōma*), large enough to carry six measures of barley, or "cloak" (Isa. 3:22; AV "wimple"). Two words for "veil" are *ṣāʿîp* (Gen. 24:65; 38:14, 19) and *reḏîḏ* (Isa. 3:23; "mantle" in Cant. 5:7). The LXX has *théristron*, "light summer garment" (LSJ, *s.v.* θέριστρον, p. 793), for both words. The *qiššurîm*, "sashes" (Isa. 3:20; AV "headbands"; NEB "necklaces") or "attire" (Jer. 2:32; NEB "ribbons"), seem to be something a maiden or a bride puts on.

V. Girdles, Belts, Sashes.–Adam and Eve sewed fig leaves together to make the first garment, a *ḥagôrâ* (Gen. 3:7); these "aprons" (NEB "loincloths") were in other cases a "girdle" (1 S. 18:4; 2 S. 18:11; NEB "belt"; LXX *zṓnē, parazṓnē*), usually a woven piece of wool or linen cloth, folded and wrapped several times around the waist, such that its folds could be used for pockets or a purse in which to carry objects (e.g., a sword, 2 S. 20:8) or money (e.g., Mt. 10:9, *zṓnē*; *see also* APRON; BAG). The similar *ʾēzôr* (probably wider) could be of leather (e.g., the "girdle" of Elijah, 2 K. 1:8) or of cloth, e.g., linen (Jer. 13:1-11, "linen waistcloth"; AV "linen girdle"), and was worn next to the skin (Jer. 13:2, 4, 11).

The *mēzaḥ* (Ps. 109:19), of leather and also worn next to the skin (KoB, p. 509), and the *meziʿ(a)ḥ* (Job 12:21), were also belts. The *ʾaḇnēṭ*, "girdle" (NEB "sash") of the priests, was of fine linen, blue, purple, and scarlet (linen or embroidery; Ex. 28:4; 39:29); it was also worn by Shebna the steward (Isa. 22:21; NEB "sash"). The *ḥēšeḇ* was the "band" (AV "curious girdle"; NEB "waistband"; Ex. 28:8, 27f.) of the ephod (see VIII below).

The common LXX *zṓnē* is in the NT a girdle or belt; John the Baptist's was of leather (Mt. 3:4), and the risen Christ's was golden (Rev. 1:13). The loose *chitṓn* needed to be held around the waist by a belt, and its hem or folds could be tucked up into it so the person was "girded up" for work or rapid movement (cf. 1 K. 18:46). The loose outer garments, except stately, gorgeous robes left flowing, were also held in by a second belt or sash (Acts 21:11; Rev. 1:13; 15:6).

VI. Headgear.–Heb. *peʾēr*, "turban," was a headdress

for men (Ezk. 24:17), and possibly also for women (Ezk. 24:23; Isa. 3:20; cf. "garland" in Isa. 61:3); evidently it was of some distinction, since it was worn by priests (Ex. 39:28; Ezk. 44:18) and by a bridegroom ("garland," Isa. 61:10). According to Dalman (V, 331) the *pᵉʾēr* and the *ṣᵉnîpâ,* "turban" (possibly for women, Isa. 3:23; for men, Job 29:14; Zec. 3:5; "diadem" in Isa. 62:3 *Q*) were wound around the head (the root *ṣnp* means to "wrap"). Other words for a woman's veil (*rᵉḏîḏ* and *ṣāʿîp,* see IV above) mean cloth simply thrown over the head to hang down before the face, sometimes almost reaching the feet. The queen's headdress or "royal crown" (Est. 1:11; 2:17) was *keṯer malkûṯ* — also used for a horse's head ornament or "royal crown" (Est. 6:8).

Statue of Princess Washfari (or Sapphira), daughter of the ruler of Hatra, wearing an ornate headdress, long robe, and several necklaces or collars (1st-2nd cents. A.D.) (State Antiquities Organization, Republic of Iraq)

Moses' veil, used to hide the divine splendor reflected in his face, was called *masweh* (Ex. 34:33-35; LXX *kálymma,* which is used also in 2 Cor. 3:13-16 to refer first to Moses' veil and then metaphorically to the "veil over their minds"). The *kôḇaʿ* (1 S. 17:5; Isa. 59:17; etc.) or *qôḇaʿ* (1 S. 17:38; Ezk. 23:24) was a helmet (Goliath's was bronze); it is used metaphorically in Isa. 59:17 (cf. Eph. 6:17). It is apparently a foreign word, related to Hittite *kupaḫi* (KoB, p. 425). The LXX regularly has *perikephalaía,* literally something "around the head" (cf. Eph. 6:17). Aram. *karbᵉlâ* (Dnl. 3:21) was probably a cap or hat, related to Late Bab. *karballatu,* a word for the high pointed caps of the Kimmerians and Persians (KoB, p. 1087).

Greek *soudárion,* "handkerchief," may have been a headband (Acts 19:12; cf. Lat. *sudor,* "perspiration," and *sudarium*; *see also* HANDKERCHIEF). For the priests' headgear, see VIII below. *See also* CROWN; HAT.

VII. Footwear.–The general Hebrew word for shoe or sandal is *naʿal* (e.g., Ex. 3:5; LXX *hypódēma*), and its lace or thong is *śᵉrôḵ-naʿal* (Gen. 14:23; Isa. 5:27; LXX *sphairōtḗr* and *himás,* respectively). *Minʿāl,* AV "shoes," is better translated "bars" (RSV) or "bolts" (NEB) in Dt. 33:25 (but note LXX *hypódēma*). Shoes generally had soles of hard leather, and if they had uppers, these were of finer, softer leather (Ezk. 16:10, *taḥaš*). In the Beni-hasan tomb painting the men (except the two Egyptians, the barefoot leader, and the next man leading the gazelle) wear sandals; the women and the boy have higher shoes covering the ankles (*ANEP,* no. 3). For reverence (Ex. 3:5) or sorrow (Ezk. 24:17, 23) one went barefoot, and therefore the priests did so in the tabernacle and temple (cf. the Muslim custom today in the mosques). Removal of the shoes apparently also symbolized the renunciation of levirate responsibility (Dt. 25:9; Ruth 4:7f.).

Greek words are *hypódēma,* "sandals" (Mt. 3:11) or "shoes" (Lk. 15:22) and *sandálion,* "sandals" (Mk. 6:9; Acts 12:8). *Himás* is a sandal-thong (Mk. 1:7).

See also BOOT; SANDAL; SHOE.

VIII. Priests' Garments.–*A. Undergarments.* The *miḵnāsayim,* "breeches" (NEB "drawers"; LXX *periskelía*) were worn only by the priests. They were made of linen, as all the priests' garments were, except the outer mantle, which might have been of wool (Ex. 28:42f.; 39:28; Lev. 6:10 [MT 3]; 16:4; Ezk. 44:18). According to Josephus, "this garment is cut short above the waist and terminates at the thighs, around which it is drawn tight" (*Ant.* iii.7.1 [152]). The high priest also wore a "coat of checker work" (*kᵉṯōneṯ tašbēṣ,* Ex. 28:4; AV "broidered coat"; NEB "chequered tunic"; LXX *chitṓn kosymbōtós,* a fringed or tasseled *chitṓn* [LSJ, p. 985]), a "tunic descending to the ankles, enveloping the body and with long sleeves tightly laced round the arms" (Josephus *Ant.* iii.7.2 [153]). It was held by a "girdle," *ʾaḇnēṭ* (NEB "sash"), which was "embroidered with needlework" (Ex. 28:39, LXX *érgon poikiltoú*; cf. Josephus *Ant.* iii.7.2 [154]).

B. Outer Garments. A special garment for the high priest was the ephod, *ʾēpôḏ* (cf. Akk. *epattu,* Ugar. *ʾpd*; W. F. Albright, *BASOR,* 83 [Oct. 1941], 40 n.10), with its "breastpiece," *ḥōšen* (Ex. 28:4). The ephod was a sleeveless linen waistcoat (but cf. Josephus *Ant.* iii.7.5 [162]), with its front and back panels held together by shoulder pieces on which were set in gold two onyx stones engraved with the names, six on each, of the sons of Israel. It was worn over the robe (Lev. 8:7). Other priests wore plain linen ephods (e.g., 1 S. 2:18), but the high priest's was "of gold, of blue and purple and scarlet stuff, and of fine twined linen, skilfully worked" (Ex. 28:6). Its woven bottom "band," *ḥēšeḇ,* formed a belt, tying the garment once around the waist (Ex. 28:8, 27f.). The breastpiece was held in place by golden rings and chains (Ex. 28:15-30).

The *m^{e}ʿîl,* "robe" (NEB "mantle"), was long, apparently reaching to the feet (cf. LXX *hypodýtēn podḗrē,* Ex. 28:31), with "skirts" (*šûl,* Ex. 28:33f.) made of blue material; "fine linen" is not mentioned in connection with the robe, so it alone may have been of wool, especially for winter wear. It was woven in one piece, hem to hem, with a bound opening in the middle for the head, and the hem was decorated with alternate gold bells and pomegranates of the three colors (cf. Josephus *Ant.* iii.7.4 [160]).

Presumably all the priests were barefoot while serving. The common priests wore "caps," *migbāʿôṯ* (AV "bonnets"; NEB "tall head-dresses"; LXX *kídaris,* pl. *kidáreis*; Ex. 28:40; 29:9; 39:28; Lev. 8:13), but the high priest wore a "turban," *miṣnepeṯ* (AV "mitre") of fine linen, with a gold plate laced to its front engraved "Holy to the Lord" (Ex. 28:36, 39). The purpose of these special priestly garments is expressed in Ex. 28:40: "for glory and beauty" (NEB "to give them [the priests] dignity and grandeur").

IX. Ornaments.–Both men and women in the ancient world used gold, silver, and various semiprecious stones as ornamentation. Heb. *nezem* means a man's earring (Jgs. 8:24), a woman's earring (Ex. 32:2f.) or nose ring (Gen. 24:47; the LXX uses *enṓtion* in all three texts). Another word for earring is *n^{e}ṭîpâ,* "pendant," worn by Midianite kings (Jgs. 8:26; AV "collars") and perhaps by women (Isa. 3:19; AV "chains").

Abraham's steward gave Rebekah a "gold ring," *nezem zāhāḇ,* and two "bracelets," *ṣāmîḏ*; these are commonly found in Palestinian tombs, along with the "armlet," *ʾeṣʿāḏâ* (2 S. 1:10). "Crescents," *śah^{a}rōnîm,* were worn by kings and their camels (Jgs. 8:21, 26), and perhaps also by women (Isa. 3:18).

The "signet" or "signet ring," *ḥôṯām,* was worn on a cord around the neck (Gen. 38:18; LXX *daktýlios,* "finger ring"), or on the hand (Jer. 22:24; LXX *aposphrágisma,* "seal"). A "signet ring," *ṭabbaʿaṯ,* signified rank (e.g., Gen. 41:42; Est. 3:10) or was simply an ornament (Ex. 35:22; LXX *daktýlios*; cf. Lk. 15:22); the same word was used for the rings for the carrying poles of the ark (e.g., Ex. 25:12). A "magic band," *keseṯ,* was worn on the wrist (Ezk. 13:18, 20; AV "pillows"; see comms.; *see also* BAND).

P^{e}nînîm were "jewels" (Prov. 8:11) or "corals" (Lam. 4:7; AV "rubies"; NEB "coral" in both texts), evidently of great value. *Ḥ^{a}lî* was some kind of golden "ornament" (Prov. 25:12; NEB "necklace") or "jewel" (Cant. 7:1 [MT 2]); a related form *ḥelyâ,* "jewelry" (NEB "necklaces") appears in Hos. 2:13 (MT 15). A "brooch," *ḥāḥ,* similar to a safety pin but often ornamented, was used to hold together, e.g., the neck opening of a garment, and is a common archeological find (Ex. 35:22; AV "bracelets"; NEB "clasps"; it usually means the "hook" used to lead animals or captives on a rope, e.g., 2 K. 19:28; cf. KoB, p. 288).

Only some of the jewels in such lists as the stones in the high priest's breastpiece, Ex. 28:17-21; 39:10-14; Job 28:12-19; Isa. 54:11f.; and Ezk. 28:12-19 are well known. *See also* ORNAMENT; STONES, PRECIOUS.

Two terms for ornaments in general are *k^{e}lî* and *ʿ^{a}ḏî. K^{e}lî* is a common term for various objects, including vessels and equipment. It is used of gold and silver "jewelry" (Gen. 24:53; NEB "ornaments"; Ex. 3:22); such "jewels" were also part of the bride's attire (Isa. 61:10; Ezk. 16:17; in this last text NEB "ornaments" is preferable, since they are of gold and silver). *ʿ^{a}ḏi* is also used of a bride's "ornament" (Jer. 2:32), something bound on (Isa. 49:18). Such "ornaments" of gold are also worn by courtesans (Jer. 4:30; cf. Ezk. 23:40; NEB "finery"), and have been otherwise misused by Israel (Ezk. 7:20; NEB "jewels").

The description in Isa. 3:18-23 has often been used as a basis for sermons against women's supposed vanity, although in ancient times wealthy, proud men wore as much ostentatious adornment. Some of the terms are quite unknown; for others, archeology has brought understanding. It is now being recognized that many of the terms in the Isaiah list pertain to men rather than, or as well as, to women, both as ornaments and especially as insignia of official position. E. E. Platt threw light on the meanings of the twenty-one words in the list, and summarized them conveniently, as in the table below. Though

THE JEWELRY CATALOG OF ISA. 3:18-23

		RSV	HEBREW	SUGGESTIONS
v. 18		In that day the Lord		
		will take away the finery of	*tip̱ʾereṯ*	the insignia of office:
	(1)	the anklets,	*hāʿ^{a}ḵāsîm*	the ankle bangles,
	(2)	the headbands,	*w^{e}haššᵉḇîsîm*	and the sun- or star-disks,
	(3)	and the crescents;	*w^{e}haśśah^{a}rōnîm*	and the crescents;
v. 19	(4)	the pendants,	*hann^{e}ṭîpôṯ*	the drop pendants,
	(5)	the bracelets,	*w^{e}haššêrôṯ*	and the necklace cords,
	(6)	and the scarfs;	*w^{e}hār^{e}ʿālôṯ*	and the beads;
v. 20	(7)	the headdresses,	*happ^{e}ʾērîm*	the garland crowns,
	(8)	the armlets,	*w^{e}haṣṣ^{e}ʿāḏôṯ*	and the armlets (or foot jewelry),
	(9)	the sashes,	*w^{e}haqqiššurîm*	and the sashes (or girdles),
	(10)	the perfume boxes,	*ûḇātê hannepeš*	and the tubular "soul" cases,
	(11)	and the amulets;	*w^{e}hall^{e}ḥāšîm*	and the snake charms;
v. 21	(12)	the signet rings,	*haṭṭabbāʿôṯ*	the signet rings;
	(13)	and the nose rings;	*w^{e}nizmê hāʾāp*	and the nose rings;
v. 22	(14)	the festal robes,	*hammaḥ^{a}lāṣôṯ*	the loin cloths,
	(15)	the mantles,	*w^{e}hammaʿ^{a}ṭāpôṯ*	and the enveloping capes,
	(16)	the cloaks,	*w^{e}hammiṭpāḥôṯ*	and the mantles,
	(17)	and the handbags;	*w^{e}hāḥ^{a}rîṭîm*	and the wallets;
v. 23	(18)	the garments of gauze,	*w^{e}haggilyōnîm*	and the thin garments,
	(19)	the linen garments,	*w^{e}hass^{e}ḏînîm*	and the warriors' belts,
	(20)	the turbans,	*w^{e}haṣṣ^{e}nîpôṯ*	and the turbans,
	(21)	and the veils.	*w^{e}hār^{e}ḏîḏîm*	and the outer cloaks.

the helpful explanations and supporting archeological and linguistic evidence are impossible to summarize in the space available, only items 1, 9, 16, and 21 are shown to be exclusively women's articles; several were used by both sexes and the rest apparently only by men. Platt concludes (p. 83):

> Isa. 3 gives a collection of oracles that denounce *both* the men and women *aristocrats*. The choice of the symbols of office in jewelry, garments and cosmetics reflects the societal positions of both men and women. More items belonging to men are mentioned because Jerusalem was a predominantly "patriarchal" society in political structure. The injustices of the society are being condemned by denouncing the symbols of those officers who have transgressed their authority and taken advantage of the poor by virtue of power positions. The catalog in vss. 18-23 especially reflects this with its predominance of identifiable articles from other biblical contexts.

For garment decorations, *see* EMBROIDERY; FRINGES; TASSEL.

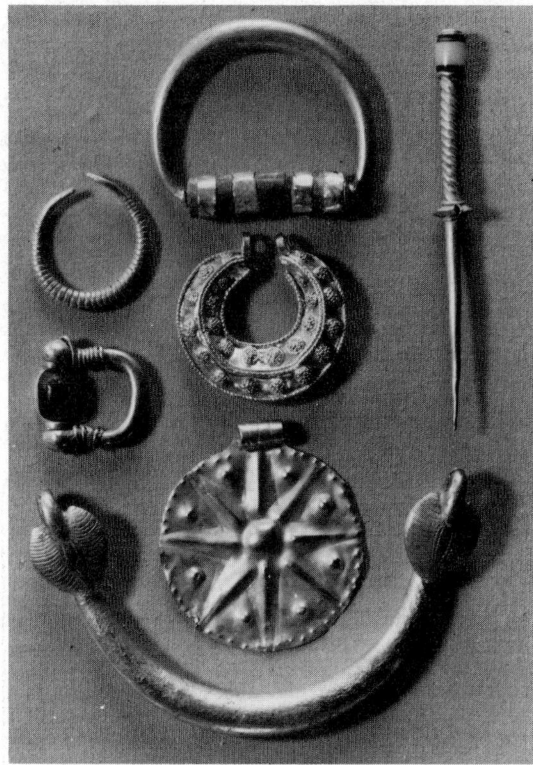

Gold and electrum jewelry of the Late Bronze Age from Tell el-ʿAjjûl (Israel Department of Antiquities and Museums)

X. Gestures and Figurative Uses.–Several gestures are associated with garments. In 2 K. 9:13 (cf. Josephus *Ant.* ix.6.2 [111]) men placed their garments (Heb. *beged*) on the steps of a house so that Jehu might walk on them; cf. the similar action of the people who spread their garments (Gk. *himátion*) before Jesus when He entered Jerusalem on a donkey (Mt. 21:8). In contrast to this gesture of respect are two other gestures. (1) Shaking out one's garments, as Paul did in Acts 18:6, was a Jewish practice that "signified the breaking off of all intercourse, and among Jews was tantamount to calling a man a heathen" (F. F. Bruce, comm. on Acts [*NICNT,* 1954], p. 284 n. 74). (2) Tearing or throwing a garment was an expression of horror caused by apparent blasphemy (Mk. 14:63; Acts 22:23). This act was also part of the mourning ritual, preparatory to putting on sackcloth (note Joel 2:12f., which emphasizes the importance of inner change accompanying the outward demonstration). To cover one's garment with violence (Mal. 2:16), moreover, may refer to the gesture of the bethrothal rite (see II.B.2 above), or figuratively to general acts of "injustice which, like the blood of a murdered victim, leave their mark" (J. Baldwin, *Haggai, Zechariah, Malachi* [*Tyndale OT Comms.*, 1972], p. 241). *See also* GESTURE VII.

A figurative use involving nature is Job 38:9, where God made clouds the garment (*lᵉbûš*) of the sea (cf. Ps. 104:4; Prov. 30:4). Ps. 104:2 describes God as covered with light "as with a garment [*śalmâ*]" (cf. Mt. 17:2 par.). In Isa. 59:17 God puts on "garments [*beged*] of vengeance" to judge the earth. Violence (Ps. 73:6) and curses (Ps. 109:19) cover the wicked like garments (*šîṯ* and *beged* respectively). Leviathan's thick skin is likened to a garment (*lᵉbûš*, Job 41:13 [MT 5]). The impermanent nature of garments is the image in Ps. 102:26 (MT 27), where enemies will wear out like a garment (*beged*). Several texts mention white, festive garments (Eccl. 9:8; R. Gordis, *Koheleth — The Man and His World* [3rd ed. 1968], p. 306, noted parallels in Rev. 3:4f.; 7:9; T.B. *Shabbat* 114a; cf. also Isa. 52:1; 61:10; Zec. 3:3f.; Rev. 3:18; 4:4).

Jesus used garment imagery to explain why His disciples were not fasting (Mt. 9:16 par.). His own garment was the medium of healing to the hemorrhaging woman (Mt. 9:20), perhaps due to the common idea that clothing retained the power of its wearer (cf. Acts 19:12; cf. W. L. Lane, *Mark* [*NICNT,* 1974], p. 192, n. 47, who points out that Lev. 15:27; 17:15; Mish. *Hagigah* ii.7 discuss the negative effects of sin on garments; cf. also Jude 23).

Bibliography.–A. C. Bouquet, *Everyday Life in NT Times* (1954), pp. 56-66; G. Dalman, *Arbeit und Sitte in Palästina,* V (1964), 199-356 and plates in "Bilderanhang"; H. Daniel-Rops, *Daily Life in Palestine at the Time of Christ* (Eng. tr. 1962), pp. 198, 211-18, 239, 379f., 431; A. Edersheim, *Sketches of Jewish Social Life in the Days of Christ* (1876, 1978), pp. 155, 216-225; *HJP,* II/2, 43-45, 256, 260, 276f.; *Seventh-Day Adventist Bible Dictionary* (1960), *s.v.* "Clothing" (S. H. Horn); *IDB,* I, *s.v.* "Dress and Ornaments" (J. M. Myers); *Living Bible Encyclopedia in Story and Pictures* (1968), V, *s.v.* "Dress" (G. F. Owen and S. Barabas); E. E. Platt, *Andrews University Seminary Studies,* 17 (1979), 71-84, 189-201; M. Radin, *Life of the People in Biblical Times* (1948), pp. 125-141.

L. G. RUNNING

GARMITE gär′mīt [Heb. *garmî*]. A gentilic name applied to Keilah in 1 Ch. 4:19, perhaps alluding to his physique (cf. *gerem,* "bone").

GARNER. The verb "garner" occurs once in the RSV, for Heb. *'āsap,* "gather" (Isa. 62:9; AV "gather"; NEB "bring in"). "Garner" as a noun is found in Ps. 144:13 and renders the hapax legomenon *māzû* (NEB "barns"; cf. KoB, p. 509).

GARNISH. The word is not used by the RSV, but it occurs in the AV twice in the OT and four times in the NT. In 2 Ch. 3:6, the piel of Heb. *ṣāpâ* means to "overlay, plate." Solomon overlaid or studded God's house with precious stones, and so adorned and beautified it. In Job 26:13, *šiprâ* is a feminine noun meaning "fairness, beauty, brilliancy." In the NT the Gk. *kosméō* means "set in order, make ready, adorn" (RSV "put in order," Mt. 12:44 and Lk. 11:25; "adorn," Mt. 23:29 and Rev. 21:19).

GARRISON. *See* WAR.

GAS [Gk. *Gas*]; AV GAR. Named among the "sons of Solomon's servants" (1 Esd. 5:34); not mentioned in the lists of Ezra and Nehemiah.

GASH [Heb. *gāḏaḏ*] (Jer. 41:5; 47:5; 48:37); AV CUT, CUTTINGS; [*gûr*] (Hos. 7:14); AV ASSEMBLE. Cutting oneself was practiced as a sign of grief and mourning or as a part of the ecstatic worship of pagan gods. The RSV and NEB follow the LXX (Gk. *katatémnō*) in Hos. 7:14, reading *yiṯgôḏāḏû* (hithpoel of *gāḏaḏ*, "show oneself sharp") for MT *yiṯgôrārû* (hithpolel of *gûr*, "loaf about").

See also CUTTINGS IN THE FLESH; GESTURE III.

GASHMU gash'mōō (Neh. 6:6, AV, NEB, RSV mg.). The name GESHEM (RSV) occurs in Neh. 6:6 for Heb. *gašmû*.

GASPAR gas'pər. One of the three Magi of late Western tradition, supposedly a king of India. The other two kings were BALTHASAR and MELCHIOR. The relics of these three that are possessed by the cathedral of Cologne can be traced to twelfth-century A.D. Milan. The names are from the 8th century. Neither the names, the number, nor the specific point of origin of the WISE MEN is mentioned in the NT.

GATAM gā'təm [Heb. *gaʿtām*]. An Edomite chief, grandson of Esau (Gen. 36:11, 16; 1 Ch. 1:36).

GATE [Heb. *šaʿar, deleṯ*–'door,' *peṯaḥ*–'doorway'; Aram. *teraʿ*; Gk. *pylṓn*–'gateway,' *pýlē, thýra*–'door' (Mt. 24:33 par.; Acts 3:2; 21:30]. Frequently an entrance to a city, but also to Israel's camp in the wilderness (Ex. 32:26), the tabernacle (Ex. 27:14-16), and the temple (Ezk. 40–48).

The gate of a house was separated from the house or complex of houses by a court (Lk. 16:20; Acts 10:17; 12:14; cf. *TDNT,* VI, 921), as was the "king's gate" (Heb. *šaʿar hammeleḵ*, Est. 2:19, 21, etc.; KoB, p. 1138; cf. Aram. *teraʿ malkāʾ*, "court," Dnl. 2:49). The "gate of the guards" (*šaʿar hārāṣîm*, 2 K. 11:19) seems to have been one of the palace gates; the "Gate of the Guard" (*šaʿar hammaṭṭārâ*, Neh. 12:39; AV "prison gate"; NEB "Gate of the Guardhouse") was apparently near the temple, though its location is disputed (cf. KD *in loc.*). In Jgs. 5:8 the NEB reads *lāḥēm śeʿîrîm*, "they consorted with demons," for MT *lāḥem šeʿārîm* (lit. "bread of the gates"; cf. LXX A), which the RSV and AV translate as "war [< *lḥm*, "to fight"] was in the gates" (cf. LXX B). Various other interpretations and emendations have been proposed (cf. *BH*), but none is satisfactory (see the comms.).

I. Means of Defense.–The usual gateway was provided with double doors, swung on projections that fitted into sockets in the sill and lintel. Ordinarily the material was wood (Neh. 2:3, 17), but greater strength and protection against fire was given by plating with metal ("doors of bronze"; AV "gates of brass," Ps. 107:16; Isa. 45:2). Josephus (*BJ* v.5.3 [201]) spoke of the *solid* metal doors of the Beautiful Gate (Acts 3:2) as a very exceptional thing. Some doors were solid slabs of stone, from which the imagery of single jewels (Isa. 54:12; Rev. 21:21) was derived. When closed, the doors were secured with a bar (usually of wood, Nah. 3:13, but sometimes of metal, 1 K. 4:13, "bronze bars"; Ps. 107:16; Isa. 45:2), which fitted into clamps on the doors and sockets in the post, uniting the whole firmly (Jgs. 16:3). Sometimes, perhaps, a portcullis was used, but Ps. 24:7 refers to the enlargement or enrichment of the gates. As the gate was especially subject to attack (Ezk. 21:15, 22), and as to "possess the gate" was to possess the city (Gen. 22:17; 24:60), it was protected by a tower (2 S. 18:24, 33; 2 Ch. 14:7; 26:9), often, doubtless, overhanging and with flanking projections. Sometimes an inner gate was added (2 S. 18:24).

For the specific towers of Jerusalem *see* JERUSALEM. *See also* FORTIFICATION.

II. Other Uses.–As even farm laborers slept in the cities, most of the men passed through the gate every day, and the gate was the place for meeting others (Gen. 19:1; Ruth 4:1; 2 S. 15:2) and for assemblages. For the latter purpose "broad" or open places (distinguished from the "streets" in Prov. 7:12) were provided (1 K. 22:10; Neh. 8:1), and these were the centers of the public life. Here the markets were held (2 K. 7:1), and other business was transacted (Gen. 23:10, 18; Ruth 4:1); the special commodities sold there gave names to the gates (Neh. 3:1, 3, 28). In particular, the "gate" was the place of the legal tribunals (Dt. 21:19; 22:15; 25:7; etc.), so that a seat "among the elders" "in the gates" (Prov. 31:23) was a high honor, while "oppression in the gates" was a synonym for judicial corruption (Prov. 22:22; Isa. 29:21; Am. 5:10; cf. 2 S. 3:27 for Joab's atrocious crime). The king held public audiences in the gate (2 S. 19:8; 1 K. 22:10; Jer. 38:7; cf. Jer. 39:3). To the gates, as the place of throngs, prophets and teachers went with their message (1 K. 22:10; Jer. 17:19; Prov. 1:21; 8:3; 31:31), while on the other hand the gates were the resort of the town good-for-nothings (Ps. 69:12 [MT 13]; cf. 1 S. 21:13).

The NT mentions gates only in passing. In Jn. 5:2-9 Jesus healed the paralytic near the Sheep Gate. Prayer was held outside the gate in Acts 16:13, and in 14:13 sacrifices were about to be given near the gates of the city of Lystra. In accordance with the OT and with Roman law crucifixions were held outside the city gate (Jn. 19:20; He. 13:12; cf. Mk. 15:20 par.; *TDNT,* VI, 921f.).

III. Symbolism.–The gate of a city was a symbol of defense and safety (Ps. 127:5; Isa. 28:6; cf. Jer. 49:31; Ezk. 38:11). The "gates of righteousness" (Ps. 118:19f.) perhaps referred to the temple gates (see the comms.). The loss of city gates denoted utter destruction (Neh. 1:3; 2:3; Lam. 1:4), which was sometimes dramatized by personifying the gates as wailing (Isa. 14:31), lamenting and mourning (Isa. 3:26), and languishing (Jer. 14:2). Nehemiah allowed the city gates to be open only during the middle of the day (7:3), but the prophets predicted a period in which the gates would remain open forever (Isa. 60:11; cf. Rev. 21:25, where the gates of the new Jerusalem will never be shut).

Our Lord used gate imagery to illustrate the difficulty of entering the kingdom (Mt. 7:13f.; in Lk. 13:24 the image is that of a door, Gk. *thýra*; cf. *TDNT,* VI, 922f.). In Mt. 16:18f., the AV more literally translates Gk. *pýlai hádou* as "gates of hell [Hades]"; the RSV and NEB translate as "powers of death," and thus indicate the (nonliteral) meaning of the expression more clearly. The background for this expression may be found in the OT (e.g., Isa. 38:10) and in intertestamental literature (e.g., Wisd. 16:13; cf. *TDNT,* VI, 924f. for further discussion of these parallels). Throughout the ancient Near East the underworld was portrayed as a kingdom (see Tromp), and in the OT that kingdom was a rival to God's kingdom (e.g., Ps. 107:18f.; Isa. 38:10f.).

Bibliography.–R. de Vaux, *Ancient Israel* (Eng. tr. 1961), I, 152f., 155, 166f., 233f.; *Jew.Enc.*, V, *s.v.* (E. G. Hirsch); *New Catholic Encyclopedia*, VI, *s.v.* "Gates of Hell" (F. A. Sullivan); *TDNT,* VI, *s.v.* πύλη (J. Jeremias); N. J. Tromp, *Primitive Conceptions of Death and the Nether World in the OT* (1969), pp. 129-176.

B. S. EASTON R. W. V.

GATE, BEAUTIFUL [Gk. *hē hōraía pýlē*]. A gate of Herod's temple mentioned in the narrative of the healing of the lame man by Peter and John (Acts 3:2, 10). The

Jerusalem Temple Model showing the Nicanor Gate, which some consider the Beautiful Gate (W. S. LaSor)

traditional view places this gate at the east side of the whole temple area, equating it with the Susa (or Shushan) Gate. Majority opinion, however, now locates this gate at the east side of the Court of the Women (i.e., leading from the Court of the Gentiles). This location is consistent with the NT usage of Gk. *tó hierón,* "the temple," and would probably have been an ideal position for a beggar.

Neither Josephus nor the Mishnah mentioned the Beautiful Gate, but Josephus (*BJ* v.5.3 [201]) spoke of a gate "of Corinthian bronze" outside the sanctuary; this may be equated with the Beautiful Gate with reasonable certainty. A problem arises, however, from the Mishnah (*Middoth* ii.3), which spoke of "Nicanor's Gate" as the only gate not of gold, and seemed to locate it at the west side of the Court of the Women, i.e., leading to the Court of Israel. It is probable that either the Mishnah is in error about the location or else Nicanor's Gate must be distinguished from the Beautiful Gate. It is less likely that the Corinthian Gate is to be placed at the west side of the Court of the Women and in this way equated with Nicanor's Gate.

Both the Corinthian Gate and Nicanor's Gate were especially magnificent. That the Beautiful Gate was probably neither of gold nor of silver may bear on Peter's remark in Acts 3:6. *See* TEMPLE.

Bibliography.–*BC,* V, 479-486; E. Stauffer, *ZNW,* 44 (1952-1953), 44-66; comms. *in loc.* D. F. PAYNE

GATE BETWEEN THE TWO WALLS [Heb. *šaʿar bên haḥōmōṯāyim*] (Jer. 39:4). *See* JERUSALEM.

GATE, CORNER, FOUNTAIN, HORSE, VALLEY, etc. *See* JERUSALEM.

GATE, EAST. The eastern gate of Ezekiel's ideal temple (Ezk. 43:1, 4). This gate was patterned after the gate of the tabernacle, which also was entered from the east (Ex. 27:13). Although the orientation of Solomon's temple is not specified, it was probably the same. The main gate of the second temple, known as the "Beautiful Gate" and described in detail by Josephus (*BJ* v.5.3 [201]), also faced the east (*see* GATE, BEAUTIFUL).

In Ezekiel's vision of the ideal temple the glory of God came from the east, passed through this eastern gate, and filled the temple (Ezk. 43:1-4). This gate was 13 cubits (about 6 m., 20 ft.) wide (40:11). Inside the gate on either side were three rooms. In several areas of the Middle East archeologists recently uncovered ruins of ancient temples that show this same tripartite construction of main gates. Ezekiel described gates of similar size and construction reserved for the use of priests on the north and south of the court. The eastern gate was the most important; it was reserved for "the prince," for royalty, for the Lord (44:1-3). This gate was to be closed to preserve its unique sanctity, since the Lord had used it for entry and exit. The inner portion of the east gate, however, was to be opened each sabbath and on each new moon (46:1).

Ezekiel earlier had reported seeing in a vision the temple of Solomon in Jerusalem, with similar structures. The north gate was being used as a seat of idolatrous worship, but toward the "door of the east gate" he saw the glory of God (10:19). From the east gate the glory of the Lord moved out to the Mt. of Olives on the east side of the city and disappeared (11:1, 23). But Ezekiel witnessed the Lord's return in his vision of the new temple (43:1-5). Also, from the south side of the "outer gate that faces toward the east" the prophet saw fresh water emerge. The water increased in volume until the Dead Sea area became teeming with new life: fish in the water and vegetation along the banks (Ezk. 47:1-12; cf. Rev. 22:1f.).

Today the most elaborate among the eight gates in the walls of the Old City of Jerusalem is the "Golden Gate" facing east from the temple area. It is of sixth-century Byzantine construction (Justinian), the only one designed more for ornament than for defense; it has been closed for centuries. Some think its closure is a fulfillment of the prophecy that the eastern gate will be closed until the return of the "prince" (at the Second Coming) as glimpsed in Ezk. 44:2.

On the East Gate of Jer. 19:2 (AV), *see* POTSHERD GATE. G. A. TURNER

GATEKEEPER [Heb. *šôʿēr*] (2 K. 7:10f.; 1 Ch. 9:17-26; 15:18; etc.); AV PORTER, DOORKEEPER (1 Ch. 15:23f.); NEB also DOOR-KEEPER, "watch (at the city gate)"; [Gk. *thyrōrós*] (Jn. 10:3); AV PORTER; NEB DOORKEEPER; **DOORKEEPER** [Heb. *sāpap*] (Ps. 84:10 [MT 11]); NEB "linger by the threshold"; [Aram. *tārāʿ*] (Ezr. 7:24); AV PORTER; [Gk. *thyrōrós*] (Mk. 13:34); AV PORTER; **GUARD THE THRESHOLD** [Heb. *šōmēr hassap*] (2 K. 12:9 [MT 10]; Est. 2:21; 6:2); AV also KEPT THE DOOR; NEB "on duty at the entrance" (2 K. 12:9); **KEEPER(S) OF THE THRESHOLD** [*šōmēr hassap*] (e.g., 2 K. 22:4; Jer. 35:4); AV also KEEPER OF THE DOOR; NEB also "on duty at the entrance" (2 K. 22:4; Jer. 52:24), "on guard at the threshold gates" (2 Ch. 23:4), "on duty at the threshold" (2 Ch. 34:9).

In the ancient Near East the entrances to both city and temple resembled the doorways of houses, the gates themselves being like doors; thus, one who guarded the entrance could be called either "doorkeeper" or "gatekeeper."

I. City Gatekeepers.–Their position was of some importance, requiring loyal and trustworthy men to ensure the safety of the entire city. Obviously their main responsibility was to admit or to refuse entrance (2 K. 7:10f.). On one occasion they had the additional duty of guarding the king's palace, but apparently this protective measure was due to special circumstances and was not part of their normal functions (2 K. 11:4-9).

II. Temple Gatekeepers.–Much more information is given about the temple gatekeepers, who had more duties than just guarding the temple entrances. In preexilic works it is mentioned (briefly and infrequently) that the "priests who guarded the threshold" gathered the worshipers' monetary offerings (2 K. 12:9; 22:4), and that a "keeper of the threshold" had a room in the temple complex (Jer. 35:4). During Josiah's reform the "keepers of the threshold" along with the high priest and the priests of the second order were commanded to rid the temple of the idols and pagan objects that had been desecrating it (2 K. 23:4). Thus the gatekeepers were apparently a third class of priests, who were somehow responsible for the care of the temple and perhaps were occasionally given a room in the complex for their own use.

It is in the postexilic writings of Ezra, Nehemiah, and Chronicles that the gatekeepers receive much more attention. They seem to have been organized into a sacred guild, as were the temple singers and servants (1 Ch. 9:10-33; Ezr. 2:36-43; Neh. 7:39-46). David and Samuel were credited with establishing the gatekeepers in their office (1 Ch. 9:22; cf. 15:16-18; 23:2-5), and Solomon likewise appointed sacred officers, including gatekeepers, during his reign (2 Ch. 8:14). Thus, although the office of gatekeeper could be traced back to Moses' time (1 Ch. 9:20), and could be hereditary (1 Ch. 9:19, 23), the king had the authority to appoint and establish his own staff. Apparently the only limitation of this royal authority was that temple personnel had to be Levites; cf. 1 Ch. 9:26; 15:23; 23:5; 2 Ch. 23:4; 34:13, for the identification of gatekeepers as Levites. (Although the RSV and NEB in Ezra 2:70 distinguish gatekeepers from Levites, this reading is based only on 1 Esd. 5:46; the AV follows the MT and makes no such distinction. Other texts [e.g., 2 Ch. 8:14; Ezr. 2:42; Neh. 7:1; etc.], which may be interpreted as maintaining this distinction, may also be construed as merely differentiating the subgroup of gatekeepers within the larger group of Levites. This explanation seems best, not only because of the unmistakable identification of gatekeepers as Levites in the texts mentioned above, but also because such an explanation accounts for the gatekeepers receiving portions like the priests and Levites [Neh. 12:47; 13:5].)

Aside from watching the temple entrances (1 Ch. 9:23-27; 2 Ch. 23:19), the gatekeepers cared for the ark (1 Ch. 15:23f.), oversaw and distributed the freewill offerings (2 Ch. 31:14), helped perform a service of purification (Neh. 12:45), and guarded the storehouses located at the gates (v. 25). They were given their gates by lot (1 Ch. 26:13-16). Their number varied from 4000 in David's time (1 Ch. 23:5) to 172 in Nehemiah's day (Neh. 11:19) — probably due to the great differences in the number of available Levites and in temple size.

III. Other Gatekeepers.–Est. 2:21; 6:2 mention "those who guarded the threshold" at the court of King Ahasuerus in Susa; these were "eunuchs" (AV "chamberlains"), probably serving as the king's bodyguards.

Only four other OT passages remain to be discussed, each with its own special problem. In Ps. 84:10 the RSV and AV render the hapax legomenon *histōpēp* as "doorkeeper," but the NEB translates "linger by the threshold," apparently on the basis of the LXX (*pararriptéisthai*). While this latter translation seems to fit the context, which could be interpreted as requiring a humble position to contrast with the dwelling in the tents of wickedness, the heading of the psalm should also be noticed, for it attributes the psalm to the "sons of Korah," who were gatekeepers (1 Ch. 9:19). Thus a reference to their office would be natural in this psalm, and the needed contrast in v. 10 could be seen in the difference between one serving in Another's house and one dwelling in tents.

The NEB's use of the LXX in Job 38:17 seems unwarranted, for the context and parallelism favor the MT, especially since elsewhere the gates of the netherworld are mentioned but not its gatekeepers (Isa. 38:10; Ps. 9:13 [MT 14]; 107:18).

In 2 S. 4:6, however, the LXX does read more smoothly, avoiding the awkward Hebrew phrasing and repetition. If it is accepted it would be the only OT reference to a woman doorkeeper in a private household.

1 Samuel 3:15 has been thought by some (e.g., L. Batten *Ezra-Nehemiah* [*ICC*, 1913], p. 85) to portray Samuel as a gatekeeper at the Shiloh sanctuary. Although it is clear that Samuel indeed served in some sense as a doorkeeper, he was probably too young (cf. v. 1) to serve in the full capacity of gatekeeper; and, as stated above, that office was not yet fully developed.

The NT has no references to either temple or city gatekeepers but does have several references to gatekeepers of private houses. Thus Jesus spoke of a "doorkeeper" who was to watch over the household while the master was away (Mk. 13:34). Another parable features the "gatekeeper" of a sheepfold (Jn. 10:3). Finally, it was a "maid who kept the door" at the house of the high priest who recognized Peter during Jesus' trial (Jn. 18:16f.).

Bibliography.–A. Cody, *History of OT Priesthood* (1969); *ILC*; R. de Vaux, *Ancient Israel* (Eng. tr. 1961). G. A. LEE

GATEWAY [Heb. *šaʿar*] (Ezk. 8:3; 11:1; 40:3, 6, 8, 11, 14, 16); AV GATE; NEB also GATE; [Gk. *pylṓn*] (Acts 12:13); AV GATE; NEB "outer (door)"; [*proaúlion*] (Mk. 14:68); AV, NEB, PORCH; RSV mg. "fore-court." In Ezekiel's vision of the temple the RSV uses "gateway" when the context clearly implies the opening rather than the gates themselves. Otherwise in Ezk. 40 the RSV uses "gate," while the NEB uses "gateway" thirty-five times and "gate" only six. The AV uses "gate" consistently throughout the chapter.

In Acts 12:13 the RSV has "door of the gateway," since *pylṓn* is the opening in which the door (*thýra*) is hung (cf. AV "door of the gate"). The word *pylṓn* is often used of a gate separated from the house by a courtyard, thus the NEB rendering "outer door." Mk. 14:68 parallels Mt. 26:71, where *pylṓn* is used (AV, RSV, "porch"; NEB "gateway"). *Proaúlion* is the space between the outer gate (*pylṓn*) and the house proper. The two Greek words are used imprecisely by Matthew and Mark to speak of the general courtyard area.

See also GATE; HOUSE III. G. A. VAN ALSTINE

GATH gath [Heb. *gaṯ*–'winepress'; LXX usually Gk. *Geth*, also *Gaith* (1 Ch. 7:21), *Gettha* (1 S. 5:8); cf. *Gitta* (Josephus *Ant.* vi.1.2 [8])]. Widely used as a place name in the Levant. Some of the Greek transcriptions, as well as Lat. *Getta* (Pliny *Nat. hist.* v.17 [75]) agree with the Hebrew gentilic form *gittî*, "Gittite," in showing gemination of the last consonant (cf. the related form GITTAIM; Akk. *gin-ti, gin-ti-e-ti* [*ANET*, p. 286]; Egyp. *k-n-ṯ, k-n-t, ḳ-ṯ, ḏ-d*); the gemination is also preserved in the Arabic reflex *Jatt*, frequently found as the name of modern Arab villages on or near the sites of the ancient Gaths.

I. Explanation
II. Gath (Philistia)
  A. Location
  B. History
III. Gath(-padalla)

I. Explanation.–Hebrew *gaṯ* usually means "winepress" (cf. LXX *lēnós*), although a more common word for winepress is *yeqeḇ*; in Joel 3:14 (MT 4:14) several of these latter "winepresses" are associated with Heb. *gaṯ*. While there are some allusions to "treading" the *gaṯ* (Isa. 63:2; Lam. 1:15), other agricultural activities could be carried out there as well (Jgs. 6:11; Neh. 13:15).

Ugaritic *gt* appears numerous times in geographical names on Ugaritic administrative tablets, e.g., *gt glʿd*, "Gath-gilead" (no relation to the biblical region) and *gt ʿṯtrt*, "Gath-ashtoreth." It is strongly reminiscent of Akk. *dimtu*, "tower," used in conjunction with another element to denote local districts or rural administrative centers (especially at Nuzi). The *dimtu* at Ugarit appears to have been more than just a tower, probably a complex of several agricultural and defensive installations located among the fields, vineyards, and orchards of an estate; cf. the familiar inclusion of a tower (Heb. *migdāl*) among the installations required for a well-planned vineyard (Isa. 5:1f.; Mt. 5:33). Although winepresses would naturally be found at a *gaṯ*, the term may have been somewhat broader in meaning. Therefore, as a geographical name, Gath probably signified a fortified complex where agricultural products were brought for processing and storage.

In the OT, Heb. *gaṯ* often appears with a second element, usually an ethnic designation; the respective clan or tribe must have used its own *gaṯ* as a central rallying point. Without such qualifying terms, it is sometimes difficult to decide which biblical Gath is meant, though the most prominent Gath was that of the Philistines. The Bible also records a Gath-hepher (Josh. 19:13; 2 K. 14:25) and two Gath-rimmons (the first, Josh. 19:45; 21:24; 1 Ch. 6:69; the second, Josh. 21:25). Gittaim, bearing the locative sufformative *-aim,* might be referred to simply as Gath. Such was apparently the case with Moresheth-gath, evidently the Gath intended in the list of Rehoboam's fortified cities (2 Ch. 11:8).

At least two other Gaths are known from the topographical lists of Thutmose III. The first can be identified with the Ginti-ashna of the Amarna correspondence and may be identical with the Gath-rimmon located in the same area near the plain of Jezreel (Josh. 21:25). The other town, perhaps the Gintēti or Ginti-ʾeti mentioned in Am.Tab. 295, was evidently in northwestern Galilee, and probably corresponds to the Gath-asher captured by Ramses II. The name of this Gath has been preserved in the modern Druze village of Jett.

II. Gath (Philistia).–A. *Location.* Perhaps the most debated issue in Palestinian geography is the location of Philistine Gath. Because a qualifying appelative is absent in many biblical passages, it is frequently difficult to ascertain just which Gath is intended. The early destruction of Philistine Gath (probably in the late 8th cent. B.C.) would account for the confusion in Roman-Byzantine sources about its location. The Madeba Map identifies Philistine *Geth* with Gitta, a contemporary town S and slightly W of Lydda (Lod) that corresponds with modern Ramle. Medieval Jewish tradition strongly identified Ramle with "Gath." The original Jewish inhabitants moved from Tell Râs Abū Hamid to the newly founded Ramle in the mid-18th cent. A.D. and carried with them the name of their former village. References in Eusebius' *Onomasticon* reveal that the relatively insignificant Gittaim (probably Râs Abū Hamid; 2 S. 4:3; Neh. 11:31, 33) had long since usurped in local tradition the place rightfully held by the extinct Gath of the Philistines. Concerning Gettha, to which the ark was brought from Ashdod, Eusebius says, "Even now there is a very large village which is called *Gitthám,* midway as one goes from Antipatris to Iamnia [Jamnia]. And there is also another *Gettheím*" (Klostermann, p. 72). The latter may have been the subject of a separate entry concerning 2 S. 4:3 that has subsequently dropped out of Eusebius' text. In any case, he does not equate the two places, although his description of Gittham coincides with the position of Gitta on the Madeba Map. Perhaps he had no suggestion for the site of Gittaim. With regard to Geth in Josh. 11:22, Eusebius noted, "Even unto the present time it is a village near the 5th milestone from Eleutheropolis [Beit Jibrîn = Beth Guvrin] as one passes along from Eleutheropolis towards Diospolis [Lydda]" (Klostermann, p. 68). He also described "Another Gethremmon [Gath-rimmon]; in the

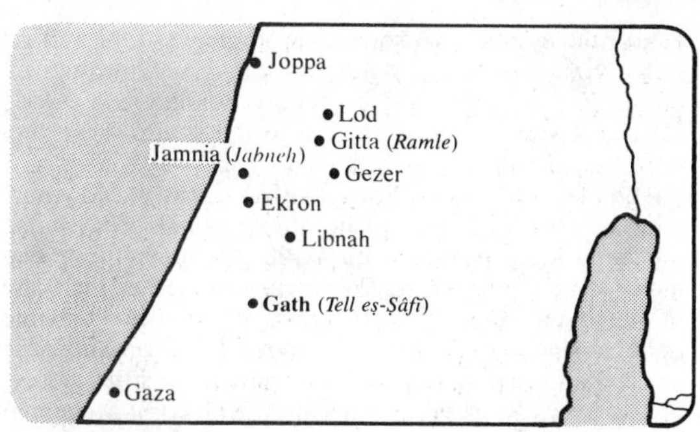

inheritance of Dan, set apart for the Levites" (Josh. 19:45). He said it was "a very large village, twelve miles from Diospolis as one goes towards Eleutheropolis" (Klostermann, p. 70). Jerome, in his Latin translation of Eusebius' work, reversed the direction slightly; he placed this town "twelve miles from Diospolis, as one goes towards it from Eleutheropolis" (p. 71). Elsewhere (*Comm. on Micah* 1:10), Jerome indicated that Geth "is one of the five cities of Philistia, close to the boundary of Judea, from Eleutheropolis when going towards Gaza (Gazam)."

Mainly on the basis of Jerome's commentary and the assumption that 1 S. 7:14 requires Gath to stand at the opposite end of Philistia from Ekron (cf. below), W. F. Albright proposed to identify Philistine Gath with Tell ʿArâq el-Menshîyeh (also known as Tell Sheikh Aḥmed eḷ-ʿAreini). This opinion soon gained acceptance in many quarters, and the site was named "Tel Gat" on Israeli maps. Excavations by S. Yeivin, however, have now shown that a city of such importance as Philistine Gath could not have occupied this tell on which the Iron Age town was limited to the small upper citadel. Although B. Mazar and others suggested that the most likely candidate for Gath was Tell en-Najīla, no Philistine ware was ever found at this site, and R. Amiran's excavations showed that it was not even a town in the Iron Age.

Noting that Josephus apparently placed Gath at the opposite extremity of Philistia from Gaza (*Ant.* ix.13.3 [275]; cf. 2 K. 18:8) — as part of the Danite inheritance near Jamnia and Ekron (*Ant.* v.1.22 [87]) — C. R. Conder suggested a textual error in Jerome's commentary on Mic. 1:10, which located Gath between Eleutheropolis and Gaza; the original statement may have concerned Gezer instead of Gaza, i.e., Gazam should be corrected to Gazaram (cf. 1 Macc. 13:43, which states that Simon Maccabeus besieged Gaza; Josephus shows that the attack was really against Gazara, Joppa, and Jamnia [*Ant.* xiii.6.7 (215)]).

Evidence from the Late Bronze Age through the Roman-Byzantine period clearly indicates that Gath was thought to be in the northern reaches of Philistia. Unless it originally had been relatively close to Gittaim, the two hardly would have been confused in such a manner. A reference to *Catharocastrum* located "on the mountain called Telesaphion or Telesaphy" apparently alludes to a Latin "Camp of Gath," no doubt Tell eṣ-Ṣâfī, which appears on the Madeba Map as Saphitha, just W of Bethzachar. The obviously Aramaic form Sapitha may mean "lamp" or something similar; it militates strongly against the assumption that the tell's Arabic name reflects the Hebrew place name LIBNAH, "white." Known as Lobna in the Byzantine period, Libnah was located in the immediate region of Eleutheropolis (Eusebius *Onom.,* in Klostermann, p. 120) and may be identified with Tell Bornāt. Tell eṣ-Ṣâfī is undoubtedly the most prominent site within the entire northeastern Philistine plain; it effectively guards the mouth of a major defile leading into the Judean hills, viz., the Wâdī ʿAjjūr, which is a continuation of the Vale of Elah, and it literally dominates a rolling plain that spreads out at its feet to the south, west, and north for a radius of about 11 km. (7 mi.).

The identification of Ekron with Khirbet el-Muqennaʿ 8 km. (5 mi.) N of Tell eṣ-Ṣâfī in no way militates against the latter's association with Gath. Although these two major Philistine cities would be closer together than any of the other three, perfect symmetry in the Philistine political divisions is not necessary. Their proximity is more intelligible if Tell eṣ-Ṣâfī were a mighty fortress before the Philistines founded Ekron. Khirbet el-Muqennaʿ was no doubt selected for its rich water supply, which was too far removed to serve Tell eṣ-Ṣâfī, yet provided a strong attraction for would-be town builders. Furthermore, Khirbet el-Muqennaʿ, situated just S of "the shoulder" (Josh. 15:11) that shielded it from the Wâdī eṣ-Ṣarâr (the valley of Sorek), was in a position to guard that strategic valley without being exposed, and it provided a vital link with the Philistine city of Timnah (clearly associated with Tell el-Baṭṭashi). Ekron hardly would have been founded as a regional center so close to such a powerfully situated city unless Gath were already enjoying extra prestige as the capital of *all* Philistia. Ekron also would have served as both a buffer and a connecting link between Gath and Gezer. Finally, certain biblical passages demand that Ekron and Gath be fairly close together, and the Amarna Letters strongly suggest a reasonable proximity to Gezer.

B. History. 1. Late Bronze Age. Of the Gaths occurring in Late Bronze Age sources, none of those listed by Thutmose III seems to correspond to the later Gath of the Philistines, and the Gittam in a cuneiform letter from Gezer probably is biblical Gittaim. A city called Gimti/Ginti in Am.Tab. 290 (*ANET,* p. 489) played a sufficiently important role in the history of that period to warrant consideration. Furthermore, regardless of its identification, Tell eṣ-Ṣâfī was one of the three dominant cities on the western border of the Shephelah during that period, between Gezer on the north and Lachish on the south. The question is whether the association of this Gimti/Ginti with Gath, and of Gath with Tell eṣ-Ṣâfī can be harmonized to produce an intelligible historical interpretation.

In the relevant epistle (Am.Tab. 290), ARAD-Ḫepa (*ANET* "ʿAbdu-Heba") king of Jerusalem complains to Pharaoh that Milkilu of Gezer and Šuwardata, ruler of the Hebron district, had "rushed troops of Gezer, troops of Gimti, and troops of Keilah [Khirbet Qîlā] in order to seize the territory of Rubute [probably biblical Rabbah; Josh. 15:60]." He also indicated that a town belonging to Jerusalem called Bīt-NINIB (perhaps Beth-horon; *ANET* "Bit-*Lahmi*") had transferred its allegiance to Keilah, thereby aligning itself with Šuwardata, master of Keilah. Previously Šuwardata had accused ARAD-Ḫepa of bringing Keilah to join him (Am.Tab. 280; *ANET,* p. 487), and requested Pharaoh's assistance because the town was in jeopardy (Am.Tab. 279). He was only too happy to comply with the ensuing Egyptian instruction that he retrieve Keilah by force (Am.Tab. 280:9-15; *ANET,* p. 487). Suffering along with Milkilu from pressure by the ʿApiru (Am.Tab. 271:9-16; *ANET,* pp. 486f.), their joint operation against ARAD-Ḫepa's town of Rubute (Am.Tab. 290; *ANET,* p. 489) is not surprising, and the use of troops from Gezer and from Keilah is perfectly understandable. The fact that soldiers from Gimti/Ginti also participated suggests that the latter was actually Šuwardata's capital city (cf. Aharoni). Locating Šuwardata's principal city at Tell eṣ-Ṣâfī permits a very logical reconstruction of the relationship among Gezer, Jerusalem, Keilah, and the other towns in the area. Later, Šuwardata fought alongside ARAD-Ḫepa against the ʿApiru (Am.Tab. 290a), perhaps after Milkilu's death; the situation had become so serious that it warranted their cry for assistance from Acco and Achshaph.

See picture in DISH.

2. Iron Age. The Israelite invasion drove the "giants" from the hill country, but they held fast in the low country at Gath, GAZA, and Ashdod (Josh. 11:22). Of the three major cities in the eastern coastal plain that stood at the edge of the Shephelah in the Late Bronze Age, Gezer remained in Canaanite hands (Josh. 16:10; Jgs. 1:29), while Lachish fell to the Israelites (Josh. 10:31f.; 12:11). Therefore only Tell eṣ-Ṣâfī was open to the Philistines, and it must have become the principal Philistine stronghold facing the hill country. At the same time Gath appeared as one of the five Philistine capitals (Josh. 13:3, 1 S. 6:17). That another, Ekron, was only 8 km. (5 mi.) north can be explained in terms of each site's topographical relation to the approaches to the hill country. The Philistine intrusion created a political situation that also called for certain precautions on the north side of Tell eṣ-Ṣâfī. A town at this site had already enjoyed a long history during the Late Bronze Age, probably as an ally of Gezer. With this new hostile situation, the Philistines had to reinforce their defenses on the northeast, both against the Canaanites at Gezer and the Israelites in the Aijalon-Zorah region. Therefore the choice of Khirbet el-Muqennaʿ within the territory of the mother city at Tell eṣ-Ṣâfī is logical and does not affect the latter's identification with Gath. In fact, some passages seem to require that Gath and Ekron be closer to each other than to the other Philistine cities. The captured ark of Israel's God was taken first to Ashdod, then to Gath, and finally to Ekron, from which it was returned via the valley of Sorek (1 S. 5:6-10; 6:9-12). Later, when the prophet Samuel succeeded in relieving the foreign pressure against his people, "the cities which the Philistines had taken from Israel were restored to Israel, from Ekron to Gath" (1 S. 7:14); Samuel's concern was to drive the Philistines out of the hill country and to secure the Israelite frontier against their incursions. Albright assumed that Gath must be in the south and Ekron at the opposite end of Philistia; but if the area between Ekron and Tell eṣ-Ṣâfī were intended, obviously no Israelite towns could have intruded within the 8 km. (5 mi.) between them. Also, the biblical phrase may refer to towns in the Sorek and Elah valleys that had fallen under Philistine control. An alternate explanation is that this is an additional allusion to Gittaim, or more likely, to the Gath in the plain of Sharon (see III below). In any event, the towns returned to Israel were in the northern areas of contact between the Philistines and their neighbors in the hill country. The Benjamites from Aijalon "who put to flight the inhabitants of Gath" (1 Ch. 8:13) may have been associated with this action under Samuel's leadership. At least their contact with people from Gath points to a northern location for that city (though Gittaim or Gath in the plain of Sharon might be meant).

The encounter between David and Goliath is singularly illustrative of the close association between Gath and Ekron. Goliath, evidently a descendant of the Bronze Age population absorbed when the Philistines occupied Gath (1 S. 17:4, 23), was one of at least four such warriors who fell before Israelite prowess (2 S. 21:18-22; 1 Ch. 20:4-8). The Philistine retreat can be explained only by Ekron's proximity to Gath. According to the MT the Israelites "pursued the Philistines to the entrance of the valley [Heb. *gay*ʾ; LXX *Geth*] and to the gates of Ekron; and the Philistine casualties fell on the road to Shaaraim, and as far as Gath and Ekron" (1 S. 17:52). Thus the retreating Philistines evacuated the valley of Elah, turned northward through the pass E of Azekeh (Tell ez-Zakarîyah), which put them on the "road to Shaaraim"; next they swerved left toward Tell eṣ-Ṣâfī, which they reached via Wâdī ʿAjjūr (MT *gay'*). Some sought refuge at Gath (Tell eṣ-Ṣâfī), while others turned northward to Ekron (Khirbet el-Muqennaʿ).

David's first attempt to find refuge at Gath (1 S. 21:10-15 [MT 11-16]) brought only suspicion from the servants of Achish, so he was obliged to flee (cf. superscriptions to Pss. 34, 56). Later when the warrior's alienation from Saul was obvious even to the Philistines, David returned to Achish and was well received (1 S. 27). David's appointment over Ziklag and his conduct there seemed to presuppose Gath in the north and Ziklag in the south. David viewed Gath as the "royal city" (1 S. 27:5) and requested his own town somewhere in Philistine territory. While at Ziklag, he reported regularly to Achish, claiming raids on Judean-occupied territory (v. 10) while actually assisting the southern Judean clans by attacking their enemies who dwelt in the desert to the south and east. Therefore Ziklag must have been in the south, in the "Negeb of the Cherethites" (1 S. 30:14), WNW of Beersheba (perhaps Tell esh-Sherîʿah). Yet if Ziklag were too close to the Judean foothills, David could not with impunity have pretended to attack the Israelites (this rules out Tell el-Khuweilfeh). Furthermore, if Gath were in southern Philistia, then the king could have noted the direction in which David headed on his campaigns. Therefore Gath must have been in the north, far removed from David's actions.

Gath's position as the "royal city" is demonstrated in 1 S. 29:1-10, where Achish is called "king" (Heb. *meleḵ*; 1 S. 21:10; 27:2), while the "lords" are ranked only as "commanders" (*śārîm*; 1 S. 29:3f.; only in 1 S. 29 is the Philistine loanword *seranîm* given its Hebrew equivalent, "prince, minister"). Achish's relation to the other Philistine lords was as "first among equals." Therefore David's position at Ziklag was as vassal to the senior Philistine ruler.

If the capital were in the north, e.g., at Tell eṣ-Ṣâfī, then clearly Achish was seeking to strengthen Philistine security by placing an allegedly loyal chieftain on his exposed southwestern frontier with Judah. David's practice of slaying all victims in his desert raids lest someone "bring tidings to Gath" (1 S. 27:11) may have become proverbial (cf. 2 S. 1:20; Mic. 1:10).

When David became king over all Israel, he waged a long and bitter struggle against his former Philistine masters. In his drive toward the sea and the resulting skirmishes along the Philistines' eastern frontier, David "took Metheg-ammah [lit., "the bridle of the forearm," perhaps an allusion to the Philistine capital's authority] out of the hand of the Philistines" (1 S. 8:1); the parallel 1 Ch. 18:1 substitutes "Gath and its villages." Apparently during this conflict the famed heroes of Gath tried their mettle several times against David's own men (2 S. 21:18-22; 1 Ch. 20:6-8). Eventually David's military prowess attracted a force of Gittite warriors to his banner (2 S. 15:18-23).

Early in Solomon's reign, Achish was still ruling at Gath, although somewhat overshadowed by the united Israelite monarchy (1 K. 2:39-41). His kingdom must have been separate, however, for Shimei's runaway slaves thought refuge could be found there.

The Gath listed among Rehoboam's fortified cities (2 Ch. 11:5-12) should be understood as Moresheth-gath (probably Tell el-Judeideh), following Aharoni and assuming scribal omission of the first element "Moresheth-" either because of confusion with the following Mareshah or more likely by a desire not to confuse the two places. The network of forts thus represented would be a defensive system quite suitable to the topography of the Shephelah and Judean hill country.

During the latter part of the 9th cent. B.C. Hazael king of Syria conducted a campaign against Jerusalem and western Palestine in which one of the principal objectives was the conquest of Gath (2 K. 12:17f.). This campaign, a part of Hazael's effort to gain control of the main commercial routes across the Palestinian land bridge, also serves as an indication that Gath was located in northern Philistia.

Gath's association with Jabneh (Yebnā) and Ashdod (Esdûd) as the target of Uzziah's military activities on the northern Philistine plain (2 Ch. 26:6) is the most important witness concerning its identification. Apparently this Judean attack in the mid-8th cent. B.C. brought about Gath's downfall as a major Philistine city. Royal stamp seals at Tell eṣ-Ṣâfī bearing the typical Heb. *lmlk* ("for the king") point to a temporary Judean occupation of the site during the late 8th or early 7th cent. B.C. Amos referred to Gath as an example of a mighty stronghold that was taken by siege (Am. 6:2), and he did not include it in his oracle against the leading towns of Philistia (1:6-8). Nevertheless, Gath (*Gimti*) appears alongside several towns in northern Philistia as one of the campaign objectives of Sargon II in 712 B.C. (*ANET,* p. 286). Micah's satirical reference (1:10) suggests that such a proverb as "Tell it not in Gath" had long since taken root in Israelite culture, possibly meaning that Gath was destined to suffer yet another attack, this time at the hands of Sennacherib (701 B.C.). Sennacherib, however, did not mention the city in the detailed account of his actions against Ekron and Timnah (cf. *ANET,* pp. 287f.), though Tell eṣ-Ṣâfī was probably included among the forty-six walled cities taken from Hezekiah.

Later references to the Philistine cities ignore Gath altogether (Jer. 25:20; Zeph. 2:4; Zec. 9:4-7). The Philistine hegemony had passed to Ashdod, which could provide for the new Assyrian provincial administration a center nearer to both the commercial trunk route and the sea. Gath eventually, if not suddenly at the end of the 8th cent. B.C., lost its former significance and apparently even its name. By the Greco-Roman and Byzantine periods the exact site of Philistine Gath had been irrevocably lost, and only the tradition of its northern location remained.

Bibliography.–Y. Aharoni, *Land of Israel in Biblical Times* (1962); W. F. Albright, *AASOR,* 2f. (1923), 1-17; *BASOR,* 15 (Oct. 1924), 2-11; R. Amiran, *IEJ,* 13 (1963), 143-45, 333f.; M. Avi-Yonah, *Madaba Mosaic Map* (1954); C. R. Conder, *PEF,* quarterly statement (1875), 138-152; *EAEHL,* IV, *s.v.* "Eṣ-Ṣafi, Tell" (E. Stern); Israel Department of Antiquities, *IEJ,* 9 (1959), 269-271; 10 (1960), 122f.; *RB,* 67 (1960), 391-94; H. E. Kassis, *JBL,* 84 (1965), 259-271; E. Klostermann, ed. *Eusebius Onomasticon der biblischen Ortsnamen* (1904); B. Mazar, *IEJ,* 4 (1954), 227-235; A. F. Rainey, *Eretz Israel,* 12 (1975), 63-76; *HGHL,* pp. 191-94; S. Yeivin, *IEJ,* 10 (1960), 193-203; *IEJ,* 11 (1961), 191; *First Preliminary Report on the Excavations at Tel "Gat" (Tell Sheykh Aḥmed el-ʿAreyny) Seasons 1956-1958* (1961); *Oriens Antiquus,* 2 (1963), 205-213; G. E. Wright, *BA,* 29 (1966), 78-86.

II. Gath(-padalla).–At least one biblical reference suggests a Gath located on the Ephraimite border. Two of Ephraim's sons, Ezer and Elead, were slain by "the men of Gath who were born in the land" in retaliation for cattle rustling (1 Ch. 7:21). Though the Ephraimites tried to take Gezer, and therefore were pushing toward Philistine Gath, their efforts were unsuccessful (Josh. 16:10; Jgs. 1:29). Most likely, the Gath whose residents resisted the Ephraimite incursions was located at modern Jett on the eastern edge of the plain of Sharon at the foot of the Ephraimite hill country. This Gath is first mentioned in Thutmose III's list (written *k-n-ṯ*) where its position on the traditional highway across Palestine is after Aphek (Râs el-ʿAin), Socoh (1 K. 4:10; Khirbet Shuweikeh), and Yaham (Khirbet Yammah), but before Megiddo (Tell el-Mutesellim). This was hardly the Gintikirmil (Gath-carmel) referred to by ARAD-Ḫepa king of Jerusalem, a town somewhere in the northern part of the country (Am.Tab. 288); its ruler, Tagi, was somehow in league with Milkilu of Gezer and also had a garrison at Beth-shean (Am.Tab. 289). Pliny mentioned a Getta N of the Carmel headland (*Nat. hist.* v. 17 [75]); this is most likely the Gath-carmel of the Amarna Letters, and thus should not be identified with Gath-padalla. In any case, Jett on the plain of Sharon was definitely known as Gath-padalla (cf. the Shishak reference below); a certain official, probably the ruler of this Gath (his name meant "Baal [the Storm God] is a warrior"), reported to Pharaoh that the princes of Shechem (Tell Balâṭah) were angry because he had put Gath-padalla under Egyptian aegis although it had formerly been subject to their father, the infamous Lab'aya king of Shechem (Am.Tab. 250). They evidently wished him to join them in their conflict with certain principalities in the Valley of Jezreel. The identification of Jett on the plain of Sharon with Gath-padalla is confirmed by its appearance in the list of Pharaoh Sheshonq (Shishak) (*ca.* 923 B.C.), situated between Borim (Khirbet Būrīn) and Yaḥam.

Justin Martyr claimed that Simon Magus (Acts 8:5-24) was a Samaritan from the town of Gitta (in the genitive, Gittōn *Apol.* i.26.56; *Dial.* 120; called Gitthōn in Eusebius *HE* ii.13.14 and Gitthṓn in Epiphanius *Haer.* 21.1.2). Stephanus Byzantius quoted an extinct portion of Polybius (xvi.40[41].2) concerning the Palestinian city of Gitta (*Ethnika,* ed. A. Meinemii, p. 208).

Bibliography.–W. F. Albright, *BASOR,* 19 (Oct. 1925), 5-19; 35 (1929), 1-14; A. F. Rainey, *IEJ,* 18 (1968), 1-14.

A. F. RAINEY

GATHER. Of the significant or unusual uses of the term, perhaps most interesting is its use in contexts of death. Most frequent in these contexts is the expression "to be gathered [Heb. *ne'ĕsap̱,* lit. "to be added"] to one's people." This expression is used of Abraham (Gen. 25:8), Ishmael (25:17), Isaac (35:29), Jacob (49:29, 33), Moses (Nu. 27:13; 31:2; Dt. 32:50), and Aaron (Nu. 20:24; Dt. 32:50); perhaps it was intentionally restricted to this select group. A similar expression, "to be gathered to one's fathers," occurs only in Jgs. 2:10 and 2 K. 22:20 (par. 2 Ch. 34:28); the former passage concerns all of Joshua's generation, who "served the Lord" (v. 7), and the latter passage is about Josiah (note that this passage adds the phrase "be gathered to your grave in peace"; for the significance of this and other apparent references to burial see below).

The qal of *'āsap̱* is used in apparently abbreviated forms of these expressions (Jgs. 18:25; 1 S. 15:6; Job 34:14; Ps. 26:9; 104:29; cf. Nu. 20:26, where the niphal of *'āsap̱* occurs alone, with apparently the same meaning as the fuller expression; cf. also Isa. 57:1).

The meaning of these expressions is debated. Archeologists have found family graves with evidence of secondary burial and have concluded that these expressions refer to such group interment (see Kenyon, p. 263). This idea finds biblical support in several passages that mention the "gathering" (Heb. *'sp̱*) of bodies or bones (Jer. 8:1f.; 25:33; Ezk. 29:5). Some, e.g., Meyers, add that the expression "to be gathered to one's people" reflects not only a family burial but also a belief in the afterlife — in SHEOL the whole family of Israel is assembled (*see also* BURIAL IV). Tromp (p. 168) holds that this sense of reunion in Sheol developed from the practice of family burials, and that this development occurred before the biblical texts were written. For Heidel and others the expression refers only to the afterlife; it cannot refer to burial because other terms for burial occur in the context (cf., e.g., Gen. 25:8f.; 2 K. 22:20) or the burial is clearly a later event (cf. Gen. 49:33 and 50:3-13). That the expression is used of those who were not buried in an ancestral grave, e.g., Abraham, Moses, and Aaron, seems a telling point (on these points see Alfrink; but cf. J. Skinner, comm. on Genesis [*ICC,* 1910], p. 352).

Another significant use of "gather" occurs in eschatological contexts. Thus God will gather all nations to see His glory (Heb. *qāḇaṣ,* Isa. 66:18), to do battle with them (Heb. *qāḇaṣ,* Joel 3:11 [MT 4:11]; Mic. 4:12; Heb. *'āsap̱,* Zech. 14:2; Gk. *synágō,* Rev. 19:19; 20:8; cf. 16:14, 16), and to judge them (Heb. *qāḇaṣ,* Joel 3:2 [MT 4:2]; LXX *synágō*). The agricultural associations of Gk. *synágō* are explicit in the imagery of Mt. 3:12 (cf. Lk. 3:17), where the Messiah will "gather his wheat into the granary," and in 13:30, where the "reapers" will gather first the "weeds," to be burned (cf. a similar use of Gk. *syllégō* in Mt. 13:28-30, 40f.; and *trygō* in Rev. 14:18f.), and then the wheat, to be saved. Gk. *episynágō* refers to the gathering of the elect in Mt. 24:31 (par. Mk. 13:27).

In Jn. 4:36 Jesus speaks of gathering "fruit for eternal life," apparently a reference to the results of evangelism (cf. v. 35; C. H. Dodd, *Interpretation of the Fourth Gospel* [1970], p. 146, noted the interesting parallel to Tosefta *Peah* 4:18).

Bibliography.–B. Alfrink, "L'expression נֶאֱסַף אֶל־עַמָּיו," *Oudtestamentische Studiën,* 5 (1948), 118-131; A. Heidel, *Gilgamesh Epic and OT Parallels* (1949), esp. pp. 187-89; K. Kenyon, *Excavations at Jericho,* I (1960); E. M. Meyers, *BA,* 33 (1970), 2-29, esp. pp. 15-17; *DNTT,* II (1976), *s.v.* "Gather, Scatter" (A. A. Trites); N. J. Tromp, *Primitive Conceptions of Death and the Nether World in the OT* (1969).

G. A. L.

GATH-HEPHER gath-hē'fər [Heb. *gaṯ haḥēper*–'winepress of the well']; AV also GITTAH-HEPHER (Josh. 19:13). A border town in the territory assigned to Zebulun after the Conquest (Josh. 19:13); also the hometown of the prophet Jonah (2 K. 14:25). Probably to be identified with modern Khirbet ez-Zurrâʿ, the city was located 5 km. (3 mi.) NE of Nazareth, 22 km. (14 mi.) W of the south coast of the Sea of Galilee. El-Meshad, located a short distance N of ez-Zurrâʿ, is the traditional site of Jonah's tomb.

GATH-RIMMON gath-rim'ən [Heb. *gaṯ rimmôn*–'winepress by the pomegranate'].

1. A city assigned by Joshua to the tribe of Dan (Josh. 19:45); one of the cities from Dan allotted to the Kohathites of the tribe of Levi (21:24). Gath-rimmon was located in the territory that Dan was unable to hold against the incursions of the Canaanites and that later became part of Ephraim. This explains the statement in 1 Ch. 6:69 [MT 54] that it was one of the cities from the hill country of Ephraim that were assigned to the Kohathites. It has been identified with Tell ej-Jerîsheh on the south bank of the river Yarkon about 8 km. (5 mi.) NE of Joppa.

2. A city in the territory of Manasseh W of the Jordan

that was assigned to the Kohathites of the tribe of Levi (Josh. 21:25). In this passage Gath-rimmon may have been copied incorrectly from v.24 (cf. 1 Ch. 6:70 [MT 55] and the LXX); perhaps the correct reading would be "Ibleam." *See* IBLEAM.

See *EAEHL,* II, *s.v.* "Jerishe, Tell" (N. Arigad).

D. H. MADVIG

GAULANITIS gôl-ə-nī′tis. *See* GOLAN.

GAULS [Gk. *Galatai*]; AV GALATIANS. The people of Galatia (1 Macc. 8:2). Celtic tribes from Gallia (Gaul) first entered Asia in 278 B.C. at the invitation of Nicomedes I of Bithynia. They plundered other peoples extensively until confined within the borders of Galatia by Attalus I of Pergamum *ca.* 232 B.C.

Galatia is literally the Gaul of the East: the peoples of both lands were called *Galli* by earlier Roman writers, and *Galatai* by the Greeks until the 2nd cent. A.D. The Gk. *eis Gallian* (א, etc.) for *eis Galatian* in 2 Tim. 4:10 reflects later usage and the belief that the words alluded to Gaul. Paul presumably wrote "Galatia"; and Timothy, in Ephesus, would naturally understand him to mean Asiatic Galatia, since he did not qualify the term. The tradition that Crescens founded the churches at Mainz and Vienne in Gaul is probably derived from this passage and is thus without independent value.

It is difficult to say whether 1 Macc. 8:2 refers to victories over the Gauls of Europe or those of Asia Minor. The Romans under Scipio Nasica subjugated the Boii in northern Italy in 191 B.C. and formed the province of Cisalpine Gaul; but in 189 B.C. Manlius Vulso subdued the Galatians who had assisted Antiochus III at Magnesia. T. Mommsen and others argue that the reference is to the Gauls of northern Italy, since they are here mentioned as tributary to Rome, and in connection with the Roman conquests in Spain. Not much can be based on the last point, however, for the defeat of Antiochus in Asia is also mentioned in this passage.

Although the occasion is uncertain, 2 Macc. 8:20 doubtless refers to the Asiatic Gauls. Possibly the victorious eight thousand, evidently Jews, were fighting for Antiochus III against Galatian mercenaries of his rebel satrap Molo in 220 B.C. Livy says that the Galatians never had more than twenty thousand warriors in the field.

See also GALATIA.

C. J. HEMER

GAUZE, GARMENTS OF [Heb. *gilyōnîm*] (Isa. 3:23). Traditionally scholars have assumed that Heb. *gilyōnîm* is the pl. of *gillāyôn* ("tablet," Isa. 8:1), and is thus derived from *gālâ,* "uncover, reveal." Since the cognate Arab. *jalā* can mean to clean or polish, some scholars hold that *gillāyôn* means "polished (metal) object," i.e., "mirror" (cf. AV, RV); others, however, retain the basic sense of "clarify, reveal," and thus see here a reference to delicate or sheer garments (cf. RSV, NEB; LXX *býssinos,* "[fine] linen"). While either of these suggestions seems preferable to *CHAL*'s "papyrus garments" (p. 61), this mention of papyrus points up the fundamental problem — in Isa. 8:1 *gillāyôn* clearly means a writing surface, which may have been metal, wood (cf. G. R. Driver, *Semitic Writing* [rev. ed. 1976], p. 80), or papyrus (cf. postbiblical Heb. *gillāyôn,* which means the blank part or margin of a page).

In view of this meaning of *gillāyôn,* E. J. Young's suggestion (comm. on Isaiah, I [*NICOT,* 2nd ed. 1972], p. 166) that Heb. *gilyōnîm* is related to Akk. *gulēnu,* "coat," seems preferable. If this is accepted, then Heb.

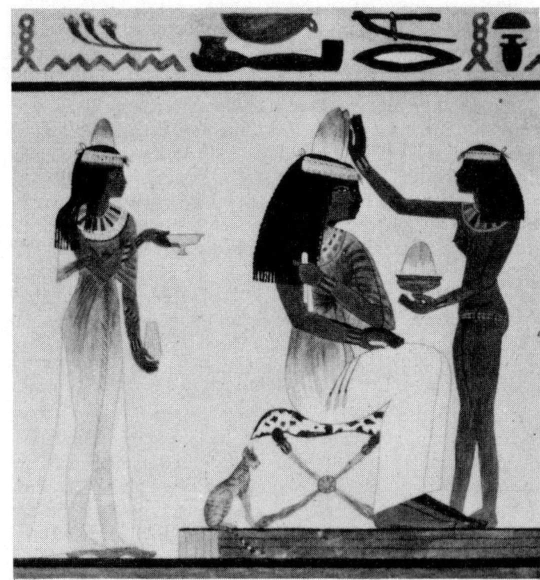

The maidservant at left offers unguent and wine to two seated guests; the three are clad in transparent garments. Reconstruction of Egyptian wall paintings (Royal Ontario Museum, Toronto)

gilyōnîm is probably related to Heb. g^e*lôm,* "mantle" (cf. *gālam,* "wrap"; *gālal,* "roll"; cf. also *CAD,* V, 127; H. Cohen, *Biblical Hapax Legomena in the Light of Akkadian and Ugaritic* [1978], p. 93 n. 253).

G. A. L.

GAZA gä′zə, gā′zə [Heb. *ʿazzâ*; Gk. *Gaza* (Acts 8:26)]; AV also AZZAH (Dt. 2:23; 1 K. 4:24; Jer. 25:20). One of the five chief cities of the Philistines.

- I. Location
- II. History
  - A. Early History
  - B. Iron Age
  - C. Persian Period
  - D. Hellenistic Period
  - E. Roman Period and Later
- III. Excavations

I. Location.–The ancient tell of Gaza is located at the site of modern Ghazzeh and consists of a hill rising from 18 to 61 m. (60 to 200 ft.) above the surrounding plain. It is separated from the sea, about 4 km. (2.5 mi.) away, by sand dunes. The plain around Gaza, especially on the east, is very fertile and dotted with numerous wells. Its greatest importance, however, stems from its location on the vital highway connecting Egypt with Syria and Mesopotamia. Recognition of this strategic position finds expression in the Bible. Gaza was known as the southernmost limit of the land of Canaan on the one hand (Gen. 10:19), and as the northernmost limit of the desert region separating Palestine from Egypt (Josh. 10:41; Jgs. 6:4) on the other.

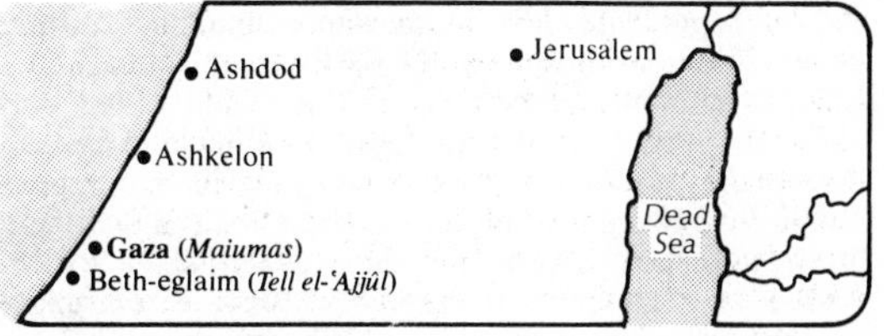

II. History.–A. Early History. The first appearance of Gaza in ancient records is the reference to it as "that-which-the-ruler-seized" (or "the holding of a ruler") by Thutmose III. He had marched to Gaza from Egypt on his first campaign in western Asia. Perhaps Gaza was still within the Egyptian "holdings" on Palestinian soil; it apparently served as the main staging area for the invasion of Palestine (cf. *ANET,* p.235; Am.Tab. 314:4; 315:3).

In a letter sent from Taanach (no. 6; cf. W. F. Albright, *BASOR* 94 [Apr. 1944]; 12-27) to Gaza by a certain Amenhotep, the writer appears to be displeased that he had not been met by the local official or his representative at Gaza. It has been (cogently) suggested that this letter (*ca.* 15th cent. B.C.) may reflect correspondence between the commander at Taanach and Pharaoh Amenhotep II on the eve of the latter's second campaign in Palestine. In any case, that an important personage with a manifestly Egyptian name should appear to be using Gaza as a base of operations conforms to the prior situation under Thutmose III as well as to that represented in the Amarna Letters. During the so-called Amarna age (*ca.* 14th cent. B.C.) Egyptian-occupied territory was organized into a province called "Canaan," which was divided into three districts, of which Palestine was the southernmost. Gaza appears to have been the headquarters of a district governor, and may also have served as the capital for the whole province. Its administrative importance is underlined by three references to it in a letter to Pharaoh from the king of Jerusalem (Am.Tab. 289; *ANET,* p.489). Since it was located at the southern extremity of Canaan (Gen. 10:19), Gaza maintained its prominence during the ensuing Ramesside dynasty.

According to the Bible, the original inhabitants of the region around Gaza were called the AVVIM and were subjected to an invasion by "the Caphtorim, who came from Caphtor" (a term for Crete or part of the Aegean area) and destroyed the indigenous population in order to settle in their stead (Dt. 2:23).

B. Iron Age. During the Iron Age Gaza and its territory were assigned to Judah in the biblical division of the land (Josh. 15:47). But its inclusion in the land that remained to be conquered after the initial invasion (Josh. 13:2f.; cf. Jgs. 3:3) demonstrates that the LXX of Jgs. 1:18 is probably correct, contra the MT. If so, then the verse must be translated: "Judah did *not* take Gaza with its territory. . . ." This harmonizes with the next verse, which clearly indicates that Judah did not drive out the inhabitants of the plain because of their iron chariots. It is also commensurate with the city's new role in the Philistine occupation by which it became one of their five major cities (Josh. 13:3; 1 S. 6:17; Jer. 25:20). As such it figured prominently in the adventures of Samson. During one of his amorous escapades there, he avoided an ambush by the citizens and carried away the doors of its gate (Jgs. 16:1-3). After his final capture by the Philistines, he was blinded and taken to Gaza as a prisoner and forced to grind at the prison mill (16:21). The account of his heroic death provides the earliest reference to a temple at Gaza devoted to the worship of the god Dagon (16:23-31).

Gaza represented the southernmost limit of the area under Solomon's aegis (1 K. 4:24). In this instance it is noted as a boundary point in the region called "beyond the river" (i.e., the Euphrates), which later became the official title of the Persian province in that region. The history of the relationship between Philistia and Israel during the monarchy is not clearly delineated by the sources. Gezer seems to have been on the recognized border between the two realms. In the fifth year of Rehoboam an invasion was carried out by Pharaoh Sheshonq (Shishak, 1 K. 14:25f.; 2 Ch. 12:2-9). Entry no. 11 on Sheshonq's list of "conquered" towns may perhaps be a reference to Gaza, though some scholars have rejected this reading.

The Assyrian king Adadnirari III (810-783 B.C.) claimed that Philistia had paid him tribute (*ANET,* p.281), but the implications of this boast for the history of Gaza are not clear. During the 8th cent. B.C. Gaza was, however, known for her active slave trading with the Edomites (Am. 1:6f.). This conforms to the general picture of the Philistines' role as middlemen between Phoenicia and the interior (cf., e.g., Joel 3:4-8 [MT 4:4-8], where it is stated that Judah will usurp this function). With the appearance of Tiglath-pileser III (745-727 B.C.), Gaza became an important buffer state on the border of Assyria's empire. In 734 B.C. Tiglath-pileser made a foray into Philistia, forcing Khanno king of Gaza to flee to Egypt. The Assyrian conqueror set up his own images in Gaza and thus established his authority over it. He also appointed an official to guard the frontier with Egypt (*ANET,* pp. 282-84). Khanno evidently returned after Tiglath-pileser's death and probably had a part in the rebellion against Assyrian authority that brought about the final downfall of Samaria (2 K. 17:4-6). In 720 B.C. Sargon II (722-705), after seeing to the final deportations of the Israelites, turned south and recaptured Gaza (*ANET,* pp. 284f.).

When Sennacherib succeeded Sargon II (705 B.C.), Gaza seemingly did not join in the general revolt against Assyrian authority. This left the city exposed to attack by Hezekiah king of Judah, who was one of the leading partners in the anti-Assyrian alliance (2 K. 18:7f.). After Sennacherib (705-681 B.C.) had defeated the Egyptians at Eltekeh and crushed all Judean resistance in the Shephelah, he transferred many of Hezekiah's towns to the jurisdiction of Ṣilli-Bēl king of Gaza, as well as to the rulers of Ashdod and Ekron (*ANET,* pp. 287f.). Thus was Gaza rewarded for her loyalty. It was probably this same king (Ṣilli-Bēl) who was ordered to Mesopotamia by Esarhaddon (681-669 B.C.) to do corvée work (*ANET,* p.291) along with Manasseh of Judah (2 Ch. 33:11). Ṣilli-Bēl was required by Ashurbanipal (669-*ca.* 627 B.C.) to assist in the second Assyrian invasion of Egypt (669 B.C.) in which Thebes (MT No-amon, Nah. 3:8) was destroyed (*ANET,* p.294).

It is not clear what position Gaza may have taken in regard to Pharaoh Neco's attempt to aid the Assyrians against the combined forces of Media and Babylon (609 B.C., 2 Ch. 35:20). Jeremiah pronounced an oracle against the Philistines "before Pharaoh smote Gaza" (Jer. 47). Therefore, the people of Gaza may have sought to prevent Neco's advance; perhaps Neco had to subdue Gaza before his encounter at Megiddo with the hapless Josiah (2 Ch. 35:20-24). Neco's failure and the consequent rise of Nebuchadrezzar II (605-562 B.C.) to power, however, was envisioned by Jeremiah as a time of impending judgment upon the whole Middle East, in particular on Gaza and her commercial associates of long standing (Jer. 25:20-22). After Syria and Palestine became firmly established in Babylonian hands, a king of Gaza may have been taken captive as was Jehoiachin (2 K. 24:10-16; 2 Ch. 36:9f.); this seems to be indicated by the reference to a ruler of Gaza on a prism from the Babylonian court (*ANET,* p.308; cf. the oracle against Gaza in Zec. 9:5).

C. Persian Period. Herodotus, who at one time must have paid a personal visit to Gaza, was quite impressed by its size and importance — it was "not much smaller than Sardis" (iii.5; cf. also ii.159). In the same passage, however, he made it clear that Gaza (Kadytes) was no longer reckoned as part of Philistia. Instead, the entire strip of coast from Gaza to another port, Ienysos (as yet unidentified), was under the control of a "king of Arabia" (probably a king of Kedar). Cambyses exempted this "Arabian territory" from taxes for services rendered during his invasion of Egypt (525 B.C.; iii.9). Herodotus' silence concerning any resistance met by Cambyses at Gaza weighs against a later allusion by Polybius (xvi.22a.4) to a stand taken by the people of Gaza against the Persians (perhaps this latter is a reference to some Persian campaign to regain Egypt during the middle or late 4th cent. B.C.). It was to Persia's advantage that this district be preserved under friendly, local control. The Arabians were better able to maintain the famous watering stations on the route to Egypt (cf. the itinerary of Seti above); furthermore, they were masters of the trade routes connecting the Mediterranean coast with the Arabian peninsula. Gaza was especially important as the outlet for the precious commodities transported from south Arabia via the caravan routes. In the course of time, Persia transformed Gaza into a major royal seaport and fortress; Greek merchants, in stiff competition with the Phoenicians who controlled most of the coastal towns farther north, flocked to Gaza as a ready outlet for their wares. Gaza was the first town in Palestine to mint coins on the Attic standard.

D. Hellenistic Period. Alexander the Great found Gaza strongly fortified and defended by a trustworthy Persian "eunuch" named Batis. The account of the Macedonian siege serves to underline the strength of the city's position. After a two-month siege, including the erection of ramparts and the undermining of the city walls, Alexander finally took the city but sustained a personal injury (Arrian *Anabasis* ii.25-27). The slaughter of the population was greater than in Tyre, and the women and children were sold into slavery. Henceforth Gaza became a Macedonian garrison.

During the strife that followed Alexander's death, Gaza changed masters several times. At first it was under the aegis of Ptolemy I, who had seized power in Egypt (*ca.* 320 B.C.; Appian *Syr.* 52); but in 315/314 B.C. it passed into the hands of Antigonus, who was striving for mastery over the entire empire (Diodorus xix.59; Appian *Syr.* 69). Ptolemy made a play to retake Palestine in 312 and fought a pitched battle at Gaza against Antigonus' famous son Demetrius (Diodorus xix.82-84, 90-93). Although Ptolemy's superior forces gave him a decisive advantage, it was only after a valiant charge by Demetrius' elephants had spent itself against his own palisade that victory was won for the Egyptians. Shortly after that, Ptolemy retreated to Egypt and ceded the territory to Antigonus (311 B.C.; Diodorus xx.73). Nevertheless, Palestine changed hands another five times until 301 B.C. when Ptolemy refused to give it up to his former ally Seleucus. Gaza, along with several other coastal towns, became an independent Hellenistic city with the right to mint its own coins.

Antiochus III tried several times to take Palestine away from the Ptolemies. He was severely defeated in a fierce battle near Raphia, but finally won a decisive victory at Paneion (later Caesarea Philippi) that gave him mastery over the country as far as Gaza (198 B.C.). Under Seleucid rule, Gaza enjoyed autonomy as a Hellenistic city. Its great importance as a world market is illustrated by the lists of cult prostitutes on inscriptions from Maʿîn. While there were eight such women devoted to the local shrine from Egypt and nine from Dedan, there were twenty-seven from Gaza, which was doubtless a major source for the purchase of such women.

During the Maccabean struggle for power, Gaza resisted Jonathan's attempt to seize the city. But after he had burned the suburbs, the townspeople finally came to terms and surrendered hostages to him (1 Macc. 11:61f.; Josephus *Ant.* xiii.5.5 [150-53]). Although Simon is said to have subdued it (1 Macc. 13:43-48, LXX, AV), the reference is contradicted by Josephus (*Ant.* xiii.6.7 [215]) and therefore is probably an error for Gezer (RSV and NEB Gazara). Sometime between 112 and 103 B.C. the phrase "the Seleucid citizenry of Gaza," which had been the expression of its ties with the Syrians, disappeared from its coins.

Alexander Janneus brought Gaza under Jewish control (*ca.* 96 B.C.), but only after it had been abandoned by Ptolemy VIII Lathyrus. Ptolemy had been driven from Egypt by his mother, Cleopatra III (*ca.* 107 B.C.), and had established himself in Cyprus. He invaded Palestine hoping to gain a land base with the support of several coastal cities, including Gaza, from which to attack Egypt. Ptolemy's severe defeat of Alexander Janneus drove him to invite Cleopatra's intervention. Then Alexander secured Raphia and Anthedon to the south, and Ptolemy decided to leave Gaza to its fate. During the night the people of Gaza attacked Janneus' camp and achieved a temporary success because the Jews thought that Ptolemy himself was against them. The following morning they realized that the city was actually standing alone. Nevertheless, Gaza continued to offer stiff resistance under their commander Apollodotus. Its close associations with Arabia are again illustrated by the offer of support that came at this time from Aretas king of the Nabateans. But before the promised assistance from Nabatea could arrive, Apollodotus' own brother Lysimachus slew the commander out of jealousy and betrayed the city. After gaining entrance to the city, Alexander Janneus pretended at first to offer them easy terms; a short time later he loosed his troops on the populace, and a terrible slaughter ensued. This siege lasted the better part of a year (Josephus *Ant.* xiii.13.2f. [352-364]; *BJ* i.4.2 [86f.]).

E. Roman Period and Later. Pompey declared Gaza a free city (62 B.C.; Josephus *Ant.* xiv.4.4). Gabinius, the Roman governor of Syria, rebuilt Gaza (57 B.C.). According to certain ancient authors this new town was somewhat S of the old town (cf. Strabo *Geog.* xvi.2.30; Appian *Syr.* 51 [also 54]; Josephus *Ant.* xiv.5.3), but this is contradicted by others (Diodorus xvii.49; Arrian *Anabasis* ii.26, etc.). To some commentators the desert Gaza of Acts 8:26 referred to the older site; it seems more likely, however, that this expression, like several others, was used to distinguish the old Gaza from the "new town" that existed on the seacoast and was more commonly known by the name Maiumas. On the other hand, the Greeks referred to Beth-eglaim (Tell el-ʿAjjûl) as "Old Gaza" to distinguish it from the other two (Diodorus xix.80).

After Octavian's victory at Actium (31 B.C.) he became convinced of Herod's trustworthiness and awarded him a number of coastal towns that Cleopatra VII had induced Antony to give her (Josephus *Ant.* xv.4.1 [95]); in addition Gaza was placed under Herod's jurisdiction, and henceforth it enjoyed the status of an autonomous city within his realm (Josephus *Ant.* xv.7.3 [217]; *BJ* i.20.3 [396]). When Herod's kingdom was divided after his death, Caesar returned Gaza to the direct control of the governor in Syria (*Ant.* xvii.11.4 [320]; *BJ* ii.6.3 [97]). With the outbreak of the Jewish War, the Jews sacked Gaza (*BJ* ii.18.1 [460]); but the numismatic evidence, namely, coins in honor of Titus and Vespasian, indicates that the city soon revived after the revolt was quelled.

Subsequently, Gaza continued to thrive as a center of

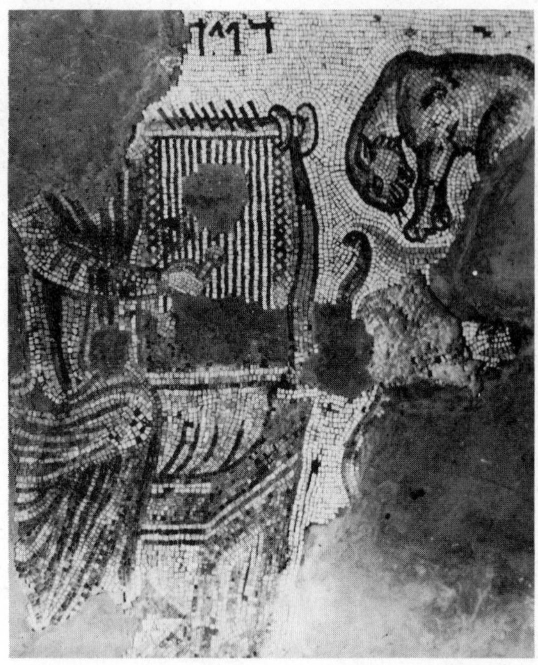

David plays the harp, above which is his name in Hebrew, and a lion cub listens in a fragment of the sixth-century-A.D. mosaic in Gaza (Israel Department of Antiquities and Museums)

Part of the Gaza mosaic showing a lioness and suckling cub, zebra, tigress, giraffe, peacock, and other animals, surrounded by grapes and flowers, and the synagogue dedication in Greek (Israel Department of Antiquities and Museums)

Greco-Roman culture and a market of world renown. The captives of the Bar Cochba revolt were sold there as slaves. Nevertheless, the late Roman Period saw a thriving Jewish community there, even though the city was, like other parts of Palestine, considered by rabbinic authorities to be out of the bounds of the "Holy Land" and therefore not subject to all relevant commandments. During the Byzantine period, when Jews were forbidden to enter Jerusalem, those who lived in the southern parts of Palestine assembled at Gaza for their convocations. Sozomenus (*HE* v.3) relates that under Constantine the seaport of Maiumus was granted status as an independent Christian town apart from Gaza, which was predominantly pagan. The emperor Julian, however, ordered them to be united into one town. When Julian announced the plan to rebuild the temple at Jerusalem and to turn Palestine over to the Jews, the pagan mob at Gaza persecuted the local Christians and burned their churches. Eventually, however, Gaza itself became the seat of a bishopric. During the 4th cent. A.D. there was also an important Samaritan community at Gaza, which continued its existence until conquered by Napoleon Bonaparte.

Gaza was conquered by the Muslims after they had defeated the Byzantines led by Sergius, patrician of Palestine, in the Arabah S of the Dead Sea. When Sergius retreated toward Gaza, his forces were overtaken and nearly annihilated. The Arab commander, Amr ibn-al-As, took Gaza in A.D. 634.

III. Excavations.–W. J. Pythian-Adams excavated part of the mound in 1922, and A. Ovadiah resumed excavation there in 1967 after a mosaic pavement (*ca.* A.D. 500) was discovered in 1965. This mosaic, the only surviving remains of a Jewish synagogue, "depicts King David as Orpheus, dressed in Byzantine royal garments and playing a lyre" while surrounded by various animals (*EAEHL*, II, 412). A section of an industrial complex, probably dye works, dates to *ca.* A.D. 420.

See also AYYAH.

Bibliography.–W. F. Albright, *AJSL*, 55 (1938), 337-359; Baly, *GB*, pp. 112-17, 138-142, 264; T. G. Dowling, *Gaza, A City of Many Battles* (1913); *EAEHL*, III, *s.v.* (A. Ovadiah); M. A. Meyer, *History of the City of Gaza* (1907); W. M. F. Petrie, *Ancient Egypt* (1932), pp. 1-9, 41-46, 97-103; (1934), pp. 1-6; *Ancient Gaza* (4 vols., 1931-1934); V. Rappaport, *IEJ*, 20 (1970), 75-80.

A. F. RAINEY

GAZARA gə-zā'rə [Gk. *Gazara, Gazēra*]; AV also GAZERA (1 Macc. 4:15; 7:45). A strong fortress in Judea that figures often in the Maccabean wars (1 Macc. 4:15; 7:45; 9:52; 13:53; 14:7, 34; 15:28, 35; 16:1, 19, 21; 2 Macc. 10:32; cf. Josephus *Ant.* xii.7.4 [308]; xiv.5.4 [91]; *BJ* i.8.5 [170]). In 1 Macc. 13:43, the LXX and AV Gaza should probably read Gazara (so RSV, NEB).

Judas pursued Gorgias to Gazara. It was fortified by the Greek general Bacchides. In 142 B.C. it was captured by Simon Maccabeus, who expelled the pro-Syrians, strengthened the fortifications, and built a palace for himself. (A Greek graffito by Pampras is said to read, "To blazes with Simon's palace.") Simon appointed his son John commander of his army (1 Macc. 13:53).

Seven boundary stones *ca.* A.D. 100 read in Greek *Alkiou,* "belonging to Alkios"; the other line is in Hebrew and reads, "the boundary of Gezer" — which may mean the boundary of Alkios' estate worked by laborers from Gezer (cf. *WBA,* p. 44a; *BA,* 30 [1967], 47).

The city is identical with Tell Jezer, the ancient GEZER. Part of Macalister's so-called Maccabean castle is now held to be a Solomonic gate (W. G. Dever, *BA,* 30 [1967], 49).

D. J. WIEAND

GAZATHITES gā'zə-thīts. The AV in Josh. 13:3 for Heb. *hā'azzāṯî,* RSV "those of Gaza." The Hebrew form is a gentilic singular (collective), lit. "the Gazite [= Gazathite]"; the form in Jgs. 16:2 is a gentilic plural, "the Gazites

Gazelles captured in the chase are led by the horns in a relief from the tomb of Ptahhotep at Saqqârah (Service des musées, Cairo; Lehnert and Landrock)

[= Gazathites]." No distinction between the use of the two terms is apparent. W. S. L. S.

GAZELLE gə-zel' [Heb. *ṣᵉḇî, ṣᵉḇîyâ*; Gk. *Dorkas*–'the one seeing clearly'(?)]; AV ROEBUCK, ROE. The gazelle is an antelope belonging to the bovine family of the even-toed ruminants. There are more than twenty species of gazelle, all belonging to Asia and Africa. The species found in Syria and Palestine are the Dorcas gazelle, *Gazella dorcas* (cf. RSV mg., NEB, Acts 9:36) and *Gazella arabica*. Both species are about 60 cm. (2 ft.) high at the shoulders, and about 1 m. (3 ft.) long. Both sexes have unbranded, lyrate, ringed horns, which may be 30 cm. (1 ft.) long. The *Gazella dorcas* is tawny and the *Gazella arabica* is grey, though both are creamy white below and on the rump, with a narrow white line from above the eye to the nostril. Several varieties have been distinguished, but they will not bear elevation to the rank of species — except perhaps *G. merilli*, which has been captured in the Judean hills and found to have horns distinctly different from those of the common gazelle. The gazelle is found singly or in small groups on the interior plains and the uplands, but not in the high mountains. It is a marvel of lightness and grace, and when alarmed a herd makes off with great rapidity over the roughest country (cf. Prov. 6:5). The skin is used for floor coverings, pouches, or shoes, and the flesh is eaten, though not highly esteemed. A. E. DAY

The gazelle and hart were among the clean animals that the Israelites were permitted to eat (Dt. 14:5). They were known for their speed (2 S. 2:18) and their beauty (Cant. 2:9; 4:5; 7:3). But the gazelle is also one of the more timid animals. Thus Isaiah described the Day of Judgment as a time when "like a hunted gazelle . . . every man will turn to his own people . . . and flee to his own land" (Isa. 13:14).

Relief of a gazelle with reverted head surrounded by acanthus. From Qasr er-Rabbah in Transjordan (2nd cent. A.D.) (E. K. Vogel; picture American Schools of Oriental Research)

The oath formula "I adjure you . . . by the gazelles or hinds of the field" (Cant. 2:7; 3:5) may be interpreted in two ways. Some scholars, e.g., M. H. Pope (*Song of Songs* [*AB*, 1978]), discuss the appropriateness of the gazelle's known "amative properties" for the contexts in Canticles. The LXX and Tg., however, suggest references to deities (cf. NEB). R. Gordis combines these two views; he sees the expression as a euphemism using the words for animals in place of divine names, which would have been thought inappropriate in those contexts (*Song of Songs and Lamentations* [rev. ed. 1974], pp. 26-29).

See also DEER. R. W. V.

GAZER gā'zər (AV 2 S. 5:25; 1 Ch. 14:16). *See* GEZER.

GAZERA gə-zē'rə [Gk. *Gazēra*].

1. (1 Esdr. 5:31, AV, NEB). *See* GAZZAM.

2. A fortress in Judea (AV 1 Macc. 4:15; 7:45). *See* GAZARA.

GAZEZ gā'ziz [Heb. *gāzēz*–'shearer'] (1 Ch. 2:46). Two individuals, one the son of Caleb's concubine Ephah, and brother of Haran and Moza, and the other Haran's son, thus nephew of the first Gazez. Although the repetition of the name (which is otherwise unknown) seems suspicious, the textual tradition strongly supports the MT (only a few minor LXX MSS have variant readings).

GAZINGSTOCK [Heb. *rᵒ'î*–'seeing'] (Nah. 3:6); NEB "excrement." An obsolete word, probably meaning a spectacle. Elsewhere Heb. *rᵒ'î* does not have the negative connotation (Gen. 16:13; 1 S. 16:12; Job 7:8; 33:21). The AV also translates Gk. *theatrízō* "gazing stock" in He. 10:33 (RSV "publicly exposed," NEB "public show"). The reference here may be literally to a public show, for in antiquity people delighted in observing the suffering of slaves, criminals, and captives; or the term may be used figuratively, as Paul uses *théatron gínomai* in 1 Cor. 4:9 to compare himself and the other apostles to men condemned to death who are exhibited as a spectacle before the world, angels, and men. W. L. WALKER

GAZITES gāz'īts [Heb. *'azzātîm* (Jgs. 16:2). Inhabitants of Gaza.

See also GAZATHITES.

GAZZAM gaz'am [Heb. *gazzām*; Gk. Apoc. *Gazēra*]; AV Apoc., NEB Apoc., GAZERA. Head of a family of temple servants who returned from exile (Ezr. 2:48; Neh. 7:51; 1 Esd. 5:31).

GEAR [Gk. *skeúos*] (Acts 27:17); AV SAIL; NEB MAINSAIL. Scholars disagree about the precise meaning of this term, which elsewhere in the NT ranges in meaning from a thing or object, e.g., a bowl (Jn. 19:29), to a metaphor for the human body ("vessel" in 2 Cor. 4:7). From the context it is clear that *skeúos* here refers to an object on the ship that, when lowered, would reduce the danger of running on the sands of the Great Syrtis. Some, e.g., Bauer (rev., p. 754) and E. Haenchen (comm. on Acts [Eng. tr. 1971], pp. 703f. n. 2) suggest "drift-anchor," which would lessen the storm's effect on the ship, and thus enable it to navigate more safely. Others, e.g., F. F. Bruce (comm. on Acts [*NICNT,* 1954], pp. 505 n. 24, 510), suggest the gear connected with one or more of the sails that, when partially lowered, would reduce the wind's effect but still allow the sailors to navigate. Perhaps in view of the use of *skeúos* ("tackle") in v. 19, this latter suggestion is preferable. G. A. L.

GEBA gē'bə [Heb. *geḇa'*–'height'; Gk. *Gaba, Gabaa, Gabee*], AV also GABA (Josh. 18:24; Ezr. 2:26 par. Neh. 7:30), GIBEAH (Jgs. 20:33; 1 S. 13:16; 14:5), GABDES (1 Esd. 5:20); NEB also GIBEAH (Jgs. 20:33; 1 S. 13:16), GABBES (1 Esd. 5:20). In Jgs. 20:10 read Gibeah (so RSV, AV, NEB, contra MT Geba'); so again probably in 1 S. 13:3 (cf. LXX, Tg.); in 2 S. 5:25 read Gibeon with the LXX and 1 Ch. 14:16. On the other hand it is probable that in 1 S. 14:2 Geba is meant (cf. 13:16; 14:5). A Levitical town (Josh. 21:17; 1 Ch. 6:60) in Benjamin (Josh. 18:24), identical with present-day Jeba', 9 km. (5.5 mi.) N of Jerusalem. Thus far no excavations have been carried out. The name means "height," as do Gibeah and Gibeon, two other towns of Benjamin which have often been confused with Geba, not only in the versions but also in the MSS of the MT.

Because of textual uncertainty in Jgs. 20:33 (cf. LXX *Maraagabe*) the scene of the decisive battle between Benjamin and the other tribes is not quite clear; Driver (*Welt des Orients,* 1 [1947], 30), followed by KoB, p. 550, translates "in the vicinity of Geba." Here Saul had his camp before his first battle against the Philistines (1 S. 13:16), who themselves encamped at Michmash, 3 km. (2 mi.) NE of Geba. Between the two localities lies the deep gorge of Wâdī Ṣuweinît, the pass described graphically in 1 S. 14:4f.

Asa fortified the town as a boundary fortress against the northern kingdom (1 K. 15:22; 2 Ch. 16:6), and so it was an indication of the northern boundary of the kingdom of Judah (2 K. 23:8; cf. also Zec. 14:10). It protected a secondary road to Jerusalem, the main road following the watershed. The Assyrian invasion as visualized by Isaiah followed this secondary road (Isa. 10:29). After the Exile it was again inhabited (Ezr. 2:26 par. Neh. 7:30) by Benjaminites (Neh. 11:31) and Levitical singers (12:29). Perhaps 1 Ch. 8:6f. throws some light on the early history of Geba: the father of judge Ehud and his uncles carried the original inhabitants, Canaanites, into exile to Manahath (5 km. [3 mi.] WSW of Jerusalem); from that time on the town was Benjaminite.

Bibliography.–A. Alt, *PJ,* 23 (1927), 17-20; A. Demsky, *BASOR,* 212 (Dec. 1973), 26-31. A. VAN SELMS

GEBAL gē'bəl; **GEBALITES** gē'bəl-īts [Heb. *geḇāl*–'border,' *giḇlî, giḇlîm*]; AV also "stone-squarers" (1 K. 5:18 [MT 32]), GIBLITES.

1. An ancient Phoenician city — the modern Jebeil, situated on a bluff of the foothills of Lebanon, overlooking the Mediterranean about 32 km. (20 mi.) N of Beirut — and its inhabitants. It was one of the principal seaports of Phoenicia and had a good harbor for small ships. The brisk trade between Egypt and Gebal in ancient times brought such a large volume of papyrus into the port that its Greek name "Byblos" came to be synonymous with papyrus, or book (our word "Bible" ["the book"] perpetuates the name of the ancient port). Josh. 13:5 mentions the town with its dependent territory as the land of the Gebalites; later the Gebalites aided in the construction of Solomon's temple (1 K. 5:18). The "elders" and the "wise men" of Gebal were among the workmen employed on Tyrian ships (Ezk. 27:9). "The land of the Gebalites" was given to Israel as part of its future territory (Josh. 13:5), but the Israelites never occupied it.

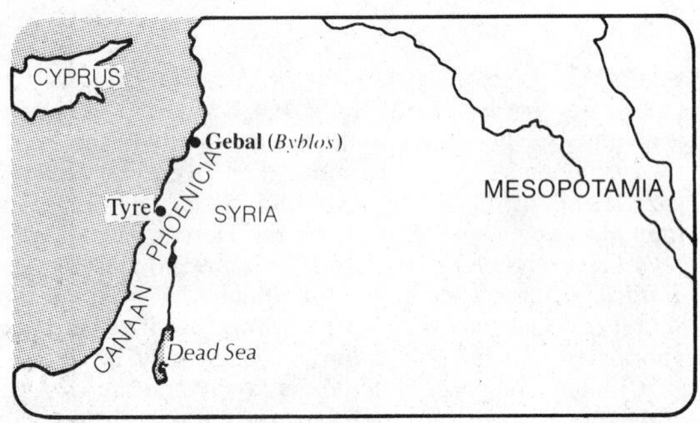

E. Renan conducted preliminary archeological work at Gebal in 1860. P. Montet undertook systematic excavations there from 1920 to 1924. Since then the Lebanese government has taken over the work, and put it under the leadership of M. Dunand.

Gebal was regarded as a holy city by the ancients. According to tradition the god 'El, whom the Greeks identified with Kronos, established himself there at the beginning of time and surrounded his house with a rampart. Excavations found that the earliest occupation of the site dated to *ca.* 5000 B.C. By 3000 B.C. real urbanization had occurred, and evidence of trade with Egypt, Mesopotamia, Sudan, Cyprus, and the Caucasus region multiplied. Trade relations with Egypt were especially extensive during the Egyptian Old Kingdom (*ca.* 2700-2200 B.C.). A famous temple dedicated to the goddess Baalat was built near the end of the 4th millennium; Egyptian pharaohs sent gifts there during the entire Old Kingdom period.

Five hundred years of peace terminated sometime before 2100 B.C. when the end of the Egyptian Old Kingdom coincided with Amorite conquest. The Amorites brought a new era to Mesopotamia (where they put an end to Sumerian power), Syria, Phoenicia, and Canaan, and even threatened Egypt. After a semblance of peace settled over the land again, Gebal enjoyed a new era of prosperity. Culturally it gave evidence of closer ties with Western Asia; economically and politically it fell under the dominance of the Egyptian Middle Kingdom. The temple of Resheph, god of destruction (*ca.* 2000 B.C.), contained about twenty stone pillars cut in the general form of obe-

Walls from seven civilizations at Gebal (A. C. Myers)

Stele of Yehawmilk king of Gebal (5th-4th cents. B.C.) describing his offerings to his goddess, the Lady of Gebal, who is seated and holds a scepter. The double-horned crown is the symbol of Hathor, the Egyptian goddess of the sky and love, whom the Egyptians had identified with the Lady of Gebal since the 15th cent. B.C. (Louvre)

lisks, the famous *maṣṣēḇôṯ*, perhaps representing the god (later an abomination in the OT).

As the Egyptian Middle Kingdom declined *ca.* 1800 B.C., Egypt lost its grip on outposts in Phoenicia and Syria. The Hyksos moved in to control not only the whole region of Syria and Palestine but even the delta of Egypt. Gebal at this time enjoyed great population density, and armaments excavated demonstrate the military capabilities of the Hyksos. The Egyptians chased out their conquerors after 1600 and moved rapidly northward to establish military control over Phoenicia (perhaps their earlier control had been only economic and cultural). During the Amarna age (*ca.* 1400 B.C.) Egyptian power again waned. Pressure of the Hittites and local rulers built up against all Egyptian strongholds in Phoenicia. Rib-Addi of Gebal sent some fifty fruitless appeals to Amenhotep IV of Egypt for help (e.g., Am.Tab. 137; cf. *ANET,* pp. 483f.), but soon Egyptian power crumbled all along the coast. Restoration of Egyptian control under Ramses II (after 1300) did not last long and Phoenicia entered her period of independence by 1200. Thus *ca.* 1100 Wen-Amon, an Egyptian official sent to Gebal to buy lumber, received abrupt and cavalier treatment there (*ANET,* pp. 25-29). By that time the Arameans had occupied Syria, the Hebrews the highlands of Palestine, and the Philistines the southwest coast of Palestine.

One of the most interesting finds unearthed at Gebal is the tenth-century sarcophagus of King Ahiram. This sarcophagus bears an alphabetic inscription that includes a typical curse for disturbing a sarcophagus and is of special interest as one of the oldest Canaanite inscriptions (cf. *ANET,* p. 661; *ANEP,* nos. 456-59 and notes p. 302).

Gebal lapsed into eclipse under the rising sun of Tyre. Gebal could still assemble a considerable force to contribute to the coalition that met the Assyrian invasion of Syria in 853, but Tyre was destined to dominate the area for several centuries. During the Persian, Hellenistic, Roman, and Byzantine periods Gebal remained quite prosperous, but archeologists found no remains at the site after the Moslem conquest in 636.

2. A district SE of the Dead Sea, referred to in Ps. 83:7 (MT 8) in connection with Moab, Ammon, Amalek, and others, as making a covenant together against Israel. E. Robinson (*Biblical Researches,* II [1856], 154) found the name Jebal still applied to this region, and Josephus (*Ant.* ii.1.2 [6]) spoke of a Gobolitis as forming part of Idumea. H. F. VOS

GEBER gē′ber [Heb. *geḇer*–'strongman'].

1. The last named individual in the list of Solomon's commissariat officers (1 K. 4:19). His district was E of the Jordan, in Gilead.

2. (1 K. 4:13, AV). *See* BEN-GEBER.

GEBIM gē′bim [Heb. *gēḇîm*–'trenches']. A city N of Jerusalem whose inhabitants fled at the approach of the Assyrian invaders (Isa. 10:31). Its place in the order of names, after Anathoth and before Nob, seems to point to some position not far from Jerusalem, though its precise location is unknown.

GECKO. *See* LIZARD.

GEDALIAH ged-a-lī′ə [*g*ᵉ*ḏalyâ, g*ᵉ*ḏalyāhû*–'Yahweh is great'].

1. Son of Ahikam (the friend and protector of Jeremiah) and grandson of Shaphan (the scribe during the reign of Josiah) (2 K. 25:22-25; Jer. 39:14; 40:5-16; 41:1-18).

After destroying Jerusalem and sending many captive Jews to Babylon (586 B.C.), Nebuchadrezzar appointed Gedaliah governor over the poor Jews who had been left in the land to be vinedressers and plowmen (2 K. 25:12, 22). To his charge were committed also some royal princesses (Jer. 43:6) and courtiers (41:16) who had been allowed to remain as unlikely to cause any trouble. Gedaliah fixed his residence at Mizpah, about 11 km. (7 mi.) NW of Jerusalem. Here he was joined by Jeremiah (40:6).

The Jewish soldiers who had escaped capture, having heard that the Chaldeans had departed and that Gedaliah, one of their own nation, had been appointed governor in Judah, came with Ishmael, Johanan, and other officers to Gedaliah at Mizpah (2 K. 25:23f.; Jer. 40:7-10). The governor assured them that they need not fear vengeance from their conquerors, and under oath promised them protection and security, if they would remain and cultivate the land and become peaceful subjects of the king of Babylon. This assurance led to a general gathering around Gedaliah of refugees from all the neighboring countries (Jer. 40:11f.). For two months (some think longer) Gedaliah's beneficent and wise rule did much to consolidate affairs in Judah and to inspire the feeble remnant of the Jews with heart and hope.

But evil forces were at work against him. Baalis king of Ammon was determined to take his life (Jer. 40:13-16). The peaceful and popular rule that was being established by the good governor stood in the way of any plan of conquest Baalis entertained. Baalis found a ready instrument for his murderous design in Ishmael who, as one of royal birth and among the chief officers of the king (41:1), was doubtless jealous of the man who had been chosen governor in preference to himself. Gedaliah was informed by Johanan and the other captains of the plot to assassinate him, and Johanan at a private interview expressed to him a strong desire to go himself and slay Ishmael secretly, declaring that the safety of the Jews depended upon the life of the governor. But Gedaliah refused to allow Johanan to anticipate his enemy, believing, in the generosity of his heart, that Ishmael was not capable of such an act of treachery. He soon found, however, that his confidence had been sadly misplaced. Ishmael, with ten of his companions, came on a visit to him to Mizpah, and after they had been hospitably entertained they fell upon their good host and murdered him, along with all the Jewish and the Chaldean soldiers he had with him for order and protection (2 K. 25:25; Jer. 41:1-3). They then cast the bodies of their victims into the cistern that Asa had made (v. 9). Ishmael was pursued and overtaken by Johanan, but he succeeded in escaping to the Ammonites (vv. 11-15). Then Johanan and the other captains, afraid lest the Chaldeans should avenge upon them the murder of the governor (vv. 16-18), and against the earnest entreaties of Jeremiah (ch. 42), fled to Egypt, taking the prophet and the Jewish remnant with them (43:5-7). In memory of the date of Gedaliah's assassination the Jews kept a fast (which is still retained in the Jewish calendar) on the third day of the seventh month, Tishri (Zec. 7:5; 8:19).

The narratives reveal Gedaliah in a very attractive light, as one who possessed the confidence both of his own people and their conquerors; a man of rare wisdom and tact, and of upright, transparent character, whose kindly nature and generous disposition would not allow him to think evil of a brother; a man altogether worthy of the esteem in which he was held by succeeding generations of Jews.

2. [*g^e^ḏalyāhû*]. Son of Jeduthun, and instrumental leader of the second of the twenty-four choirs in the Levitical orchestra (1 Ch. 25:3, 9).

3. A priest of the sons of Jeshua, during Ezra's time, who had married a foreign woman (Ezr. 10:18).

4. [*g^e^ḏalyāhû*]. Son of Pashhur (who beat Jeremiah and put him in the stocks, Jer. 20:1-6) and one of the chiefs of Jerusalem who, with the sanction of the King Zedekiah, took Jeremiah and let him down with cords into a cistern where he sank in the mud (38:1, 4-6).

5. Grandfather of Zephaniah the prophet and grandson of Hezekiah, probably the king (Zeph. 1:1).

J. CRICHTON

GEDDER ged'ər (1 Esd. 5:30, AV, NEB). *See* GAHAR.

GEDEON ged'ē-on (He. 11:32, AV). *See* GIDEON.

GEDER gē'dər [Heb. *geḏer*] (Josh. 12:13). A royal city of the Canaanites conquered by Joshua. It may be the BETH-GADER in 1 Ch. 2:51 and the birthplace of Baal-hanan, the custodian of David's orchards in the Shephelah (1 Ch. 27:28). Its location is unidentified, but it is listed together with the cities of the Shephelah and upper Negeb taken by Joshua (Josh. 12:11-14).

GEDERAH gə-dir'ə [Heb. *g^e^ḏērâ*–'enclosure']; AV also "hedges" (1 Ch. 4:23); **GEDERATHITE** gə-dir'ə-thīt [Heb. *g^e^ḏērāṯî*] (1 Ch. 12:4, AV); RSV, NEB, "of Gederah." A town of the Shephelah in the allotment to Judah (Josh, 15:36). Certain of the posterity of Judah are listed as dwelling in a town by this name and in the neighboring Netaim (1 Ch. 4:23). This town is probably to be identified with Gedera, about 19 km. (12 mi.) SW of Lod. "Gederathite," applied to Jozabad (1 Ch. 12:4), means an inhabitant of Gederah.

GEDERITE gē'dər-īt [Heb. *g^e^ḏērî*]. An inhabitant of GEDER. Baal-hanan, the custodian of David's orchards in the Shephelah, was a Gederite (1 Ch. 27:28).

GEDEROTH gə-dir'oth [Heb. *g^e^ḏērôṯ*]. A town in the Shephelah of Judah (Josh. 15:41). It is mentioned along with Beth-shemesh, Aijalon, and Soco, as taken by the Philistines during the reign of Ahaz (2 Ch. 28:18). It has been identified with modern Qaṭrā, a site about 18 km. (11 mi.) SW of Lod on the Ramle-Al Mughar road.

GEDEROTHAIM ged-ə-rō-thī'əm [Heb. *g^e^ḏērōṯayim*–'enclosures' or 'sheepfolds'] (Josh. 15:36); NEB "namely both parts of Gederah." This term stands fifteenth in a list that professes to give the names of only fourteen cities in the Judean Shephelah. Many modern scholars suggest that it be read "and her sheepfolds" instead of "and Gederothaim"; this would agree with the LXX, which reads "and its cattle shelters." Thus rendered the term is a further description of the previously mentioned GEDERAH, and the number of places are reduced to fourteen as the text states.

J. F. PREWITT

GEDOR gē'dôr [Heb. *g^e^ḏôr*–perhaps 'wall' or 'pockmarked'].

1. A personal or family name of Judah (1 Ch. 4:4 [but see **2** below]) and Benjamin (8:31; 9:37).

2. A town in the hill country of Judah, named with Halhul and Beth-zur (Josh. 15:58), possibly Khirbet Jedûr about 12 km. (7.5 mi.) N of Hebron. If 1 Ch. 4:4 refers to the same town, Penuel, who is called the "father" of Gedor, may be its founder.

3. A Calebite town in Judah mentioned with Soco and Zanoah (1 Ch. 4:18) and founded by Jered; site uncertain but possibly S of Hebron. Some would equate this with **1.**

4. In 1 Ch. 4:39f. the pasture lands of Simeon extend

to the east side of the valley of Gedor. Here the LXX reads "Gerar" (Tell Abū Hureirah) and is probably correct.

5. Joelah and Zebadiah, two of David's followers, came from this place in Benjamin (1 Ch. 12:7). The site is uncertain but possibly Khirbet el-Gudeirah, 10 km. (6 mi.) W of Gibeon (cf. 1 Ch. 9:35; cf. also *GP,* p. 330).

Bibliography.–Y. Aharoni, *IEJ,* 6 (1956), 26-32; J. E. Pritchard, *BA,* 23 (1960), 25.

D. J. WIEAND

GE-HARASHIM gə-har'ə-shim [Heb. *gê' ḥ^a^rāšîm*–'valley of craftsmen' (1 Ch. 4:14); AV "valley of Charashim." Cf. Neh. 11:35, where it is rendered "valley of craftsmen" and placed in the vicinity of Lod and Ono, which would be in the southern part of the Plain of Sharon. Joab of the tribe of Judah was the founder of this community of craftsmen (1 Ch. 4:14). Following the return from Babylon it was resettled by Benjaminites.

GEHAZI gə-hā'zī [Heb. *gêḥ^a^zî*–'valley of vision']. The confidential servant of Elisha. Various words are used to denote his relation to his master. He is generally called Elisha's "boy" (Heb. *na'ar*), servant, or personal attendant; he calls himself (2 K. 5:25) his master's servant or slave (Heb. *'eḇeḏ*); and if the reference is to him in 4:43 (cf. RV mg.), he receives the designation "minister" (Heb. *m^e^šārēṯ*), or chief servant of Elisha. He is mentioned by name in three narratives: 2 K. 4, 5, and 8.

He is introduced in the story of the wealthy Shunammite who provided in her house special accommodation for Elisha (2 K. 4:8-37). Having failed to determine what she might desire as repayment for her kindness, Elisha asked Gehazi what should be done for her. Gehazi had the insight to recognize her great wish and told Elisha of her secret desire for a son. Elisha promised that this wish would be granted. Later when the child died, in her grief she clutched at the prophet's feet, and Gehazi thrust her away, probably in a desire to protect his master but nevertheless exhibiting a lack of the finer feelings so apparent in Elisha. Gehazi was directed to hasten to Shunem and lay the prophet's staff on the child. In this narrative he appears in general as a willing, efficient, and practical man.

In the incident connected with the healing of Naaman (2 K. 5:20-27) the moral character of Gehazi is revealed in its sordid covetousness. Elisha's integrity in refusing the gifts of Naaman sharply contrasts with the baseness of Gehazi's action. To him, Elisha's refusal of the Syrian's wealth was incomprehensible. The careless repetition of Elisha's oath, the glibness with which he lied to Naaman, and the coolness with which he subsequently appeared before Elisha indicate that such actions were characteristic of him. His deception of Naaman was in itself worthy of punishment, but his guilt was magnified because his actions gave the Syrians occasion to impugn Yahweh's servant and thus Yahweh Himself. Although the story told by Gehazi about the fictitious guests who had come unexpectedly to Elisha was credible, the Syrians would undoubtedly have interpreted the request as a measure of covetousness on the part of Elisha. Gehazi's punishment was immediate and permanent leprosy, extending even to his descendants.

Gehazi is mentioned only once more by name, in 2 K. 8:1-6, where he appears in a more favorable light. King Jehoram summoned him into his presence to recount the wonderful deeds of Elisha. The truthfulness with which he told about his master's deeds, along with the retention of his title "the servant of the man of God," would seem to indicate a lack of vindictiveness for his severe sentence and a probable penitence. When the Shunammite entered the presence of the king during Gehazi's recital, he identified her as the woman whose son Elisha had restored, and the king secured her inheritance for her. Although no positive word is given concerning Gehazi it would appear that his chastening, though for the moment grievous, yielded the peaceable fruit of righteousness (cf. He. 12:1-11).

Although the conversation between Jehoram and Gehazi has raised some questions, conversation between lepers and others was not forbidden. The leprosy (Heb. *ṣāra'aṯ*) of Gehazi was not necessarily the disease now known as leprosy (*see* DISEASE III.I). It is also possible that the sentence of perpetual leprosy was not carried out if Gehazi was indeed penitent, for the judgments of God, though apparently unconditional, are often withdrawn when the judged person repents (cf. 2 K. 20:1-11).

M. A. MACLEOD

GEHENNA gə-hen'nə [Gk. *géenna* < Aram. *gêhinnām* < Heb. *gê-hinnōm*–'valley of Hinnom' (Josh. 15:8) < *gê ben-hinnōm*–'valley of the son of Hinnom' (Josh. 15:8; 18:16; 2 Ch. 28:3; etc.) or *gê b^e^nê hinnōm*–'valley of the sons of Hinnom' (2 K. 23:10)]. The English transliteration of the Gk. *géenna,* which the RSV, AV, and NEB translate as "hell" (RSV mg. "Gehenna"; in Mk. 9:47 the AV has "hell fire," apparently on the basis of some MSS that add *toú pyrós,* "of fire," which occurs with *géenna* in Mt. 5:22; 18:9).

The idea of Gehenna originated in the OT. The Valley of Hinnom (Wâdī er-Rabâbeh, S of Jerusalem) was infamous for the pagan rites, especially child sacrifice, that were offered there (2 K. 16:3; 23:10), and Jeremiah prophesied that God's judgment would fall there (e.g., Jer. 19:6f.; *see* HINNOM, VALLEY OF). As the concept of the afterlife developed in the intertestamental period, the Valley of Hinnom came to represent the eschatological place of judgment (1 En. 27:1f.; 54:1-6; 90:25-27; etc.) or hell itself (2 Esd. 7:36; 2 Bar. 85:13). It is not necessary to see Iranian influence in this development, since the purpose of the Zoroastrian molten fire was purgatorial rather than penal (*Yasna* 51:9; but cf. one early rabbinic tradition that Gehenna was a purgatory for those whose merits and sins balanced each other [Tosefta *Sanhedrin* xiii.3]).

The NT seems to distinguish Gehenna from Hades: Gehenna is the place of final judgment, and Hades is the intermediate place where the ungodly await their final judgment (cf. Rev. 20:14, where Death and Hades are cast into the lake of fire at the last judgment). As the place of final punishment, Gehenna receives both body and soul (Mt. 10:28 par. Lk. 12:5), whereas Hades receives only the soul (Acts 2:27, 31; but *see* HADES). Thus Jesus urged His listeners to avoid Gehenna at all costs (Mt. 5:29f.; 18:9; Mk. 9:43, 45, 47), for it is the place where "the fire is not quenched" (Mk. 9:48). Those who call their brothers "fools" (Mt. 5:22) and the "scribes and Pharisees, hypocrites" (Mt. 23:29, 33) are liable to Gehenna (the rabbis similarly consigned various groups to Gehenna, e.g., physicians [Mish. *Kiddushin* iv.14], those who talk much with women [Mish. *Aboth* i.5], disciples of Balaam [*Aboth* v.19], the shameless [*Aboth* v.20]). Like the rabbis, Jesus used the term "child of hell" (Gk. *huiós geénnēs,* Mt. 23:15) as an epithet for the ungodly (cf. *b^e^nê gêhinnām,* T.B. *Rosh ha-Shanah* 17b).

The only other NT reference to Gehenna is in Jas. 3:6. Here James warns his readers about the dangers of the tongue, which can cause great destruction if one allows it to be "set on fire by Gehenna," i.e., motivated by the evil powers that are consigned to Gehenna.

See also HELL.

Bibliography.–*DNTT,* II, 208f. (H. Bietenhard); SB, IV, 1002-1118; *TDNT,* I, *s.v.* γέεννα (J. Jeremias).

G. A. L.

GELASIAN DECREE. *See* APOCRYPHA II.E.

GELILOTH gē-lī'loth [Heb. *g*[e]*lîlôṯ*]. This term is used only in Josh. 18:17 as a place name. Geliloth lay on the boundary between Judah and Benjamin which passed En-shemesh (probably ʿAin el-Hôd, about 3 km. [2 mi.] E of Jerusalem), "thence goes to Geliloth, which is opposite the ascent of Adummim." From this point it "goes down" toward the plain. The place cannot therefore be identified with Gilgal in the Jordan Valley. Some point on the road leading from Jericho to Talʿat ed-Damm, about 10 km. (6 mi.) from Jerusalem, was probably intended, but no identification is possible. W. EWING

GEMALLI gə-mal'ī [Heb. *g*[e]*mallî*–'camel owner'(?)]. Father of the spy Ammiel from the tribe of Dan (Nu. 13:12), who was one of those sent by Moses to spy out the land of Canaan.

GEMARA gə-mä'rə. *See* TALMUD I.

GEMARIAH gem'ə-rī'ə [Heb. *g*[e]*maryāhû, g*[e]*maryâ*–'Yahweh has accomplished']. The name occurs in Lachish Ostracon I (*ca.* 590 B.C.; cf. *DOTT,* p. 213), and is perhaps the same as "Gemariah" in one of the Elephantine Aramaic papyri (cf. *ANET,* p. 491).

1. A son of Shaphan the scribe, one of the princes, from whose chamber Baruch read Jeremiah's prophecies to the people. He, with others, sought to dissuade Jehoiakim from burning the roll (Jer. 36:10-12, 25).

2. A son of Hilkiah, one of Zedekiah's ambassadors to Babylon, by whom Jeremiah sent his letter to the captives (Jer. 29:3).

GENDER. Used by the AV as a verb in the obsolete sense of "engender" (Lev. 19:19; Job 21:10; 38:29; Gal. 4:24; 2 Tim. 2:23).

GENEALOGY jē-nē-äl'ə-jē [Heb. *yaḥaś*; *tôlēḏôṯ*; Gk. *genealogía*]. A record or catalog of an individual's descent from ancestors according to generations. Whereas in modern genealogical records the lines of descent are traced generation by generation, in the ancient Near East it was not uncommon for individuals to be omitted from such records for a variety of reasons. OT genealogies traced inheritance lines both forward (cf. Ruth 4:18-22) and backward (cf. Ezr. 7:1-5) for a nation, tribe, family, or individual. Such records were compiled to authenticate hereditary succession and inheritance rights, biological descent, and geographical or ethnological relationships. Because of the patriarchal nature of Semitic society, lineage was normally traced through the males of a family, but females were mentioned occasionally too, particularly where property inheritance was involved (cf. Nu. 26:33; 27:1-11).

I. Terminology
II. In the Ancient Near East
III. Purpose and Use
IV. Problems

I. Terminology.–Hebrew *yaḥaś* may originally have signified "people" in a general sense, without any attempt to do more than suggest some ethnic or social group. Because of the strong sense of family and tribal kinship among the ancient Semitic peoples, the term ultimately came to be used in a more specific sense involving legitimate descent. By the postexilic period it had acquired the technical meaning of a genealogical register (Ezr. 8:1; 1 Ch. 4:33; etc.), or the process by which one's line of descent was recognized officially (Ezr. 2:62; Neh. 7:5; etc.).

Whereas *yaḥaś* was used technically at a comparatively late period in Israelite life, the term *tôl*[e]*ḏôṯ* appeared in the earliest historical records. The word is commonly translated "generations," and only once in the RSV as "genealogies" (Gen. 10:32). It also means "succession," "narrative," and "family history," and in the first thirty-seven chapters of Genesis it occurs in a particular formula translated in the AV and RV by "these are the generations of," which the RSV uses along with "descendants." The NEB renders *tôl*[e]*ḏôṯ* by "story" or "record." This expression occurs at the end of eleven sections of narrative material, some of which include genealogies while others do not (Gen. 2:4; 5:1; 6:9a; 10:1; 11:10a, 27a; 25:12, 19a; 36:1, 9; 37:2). As such it serves to mark the ending of a specific section of the text in a manner comparable to the colophon of Mesopotamian tablets. If the formula in which *tôl*[e]*ḏôṯ* occurs is taken in this way rather than being regarded as a heading for subsequent material, it will be seen to refer specifically to whatever precedes it. Since persons are usually named in connection with the word *tôl*[e]*ḏôṯ,* the narratives may well have been written or commissioned by the individual mentioned, and at the very least were undoubtedly the personal property of that man and his family. Where these narratives contain actual genealogies, it would appear that attempts were being made to trace the lines of descent of historical families or peoples. When the eleven sections of narrative are assembled in general chronological order, they furnish a connected history of life from the time of its origin to the period of Joseph, with special reference to the line of descent through Noah and the patriarchs. While other peoples are mentioned, such notices are incidental to the purpose of indicating precisely how the twelve tribes later came into existence. Within such a context it is thus proper to take the word *tôl*[e]*ḏôṯ* as a description of a form of historiography that was comparable to the rather terse historiographical compositions of ancient Mesopotamia. (*See also* GENESIS II.D.1-2.)

In the NT the word *genealogía* occurs in 1 Tim. 1:4 and Tit. 3:9 in connection with the formulation or discussion of pedigrees, while the cognate verb is found only once to describe Melchizedek king of Salem as a person without recorded ancestry (He. 7:6).

II. In the Ancient Near East.–In the 3rd millennium B.C. the Sumerians compiled records dealing with the dynastic descent or succession to office of the early rulers of Mesopotamia. One such early list cataloged eight kings whose reigns were centered in five different Sumerian cities for a total of 241,000 years. Another Sumerian king list was found by Woolley at Tell el-Ubaid, and was dated *ca.* 2700 B.C. This tablet listed the four kings who together made up the First Dynasty of Ur, and who reigned for a total of 177 years. This particular record also gave evidence of a tendency that was to become more prominent in subsequent periods, namely, that of occasionally omitting names from lists of successors or descendants. It showed that Mes-Anne-pada had founded the First Dynasty, but equally significantly that his son and successor, A-Anne-pada, had apparently been dropped from the list. His regnal years, however, had evidently been added to those of his father, making a total of 80 years, as compared with 36 years for Meskiag-Nanna, 25 for Elulu, and 36 for Balulu. Why the name of A-Anne-pada had been omitted is impossible to say, since it was included with that of his father in a foundation deposit of contemporary date at Tell el-Ubaid. In later Hittite and Israelite genealogies names were omitted perhaps because the person was considered unimportant or regarded as an individual from whom a claim of descent might not have been an honor.

The list of early kings recovered from Ebla (Tell Mardikh) has proved to be an important record of succession in Syria when the Sumerians still dominated Mesopotamia. Beginning with Gumalum, who may have ruled *ca.* 2400 B.C., it preserved the list (though it may have gaps) of Eblaic kings to the time of Dubuhu-Ada, who was a contemporary of Naram-Sin of Akkad (*ca.* 2250 B.C.).

The early Mesopotamians also began the tradition of using the terms "son" or "daughter" to mean simply "descendant," without specifying a particular interval in the descent. As far as ancient royalty was concerned, the interest was mainly in the succession itself rather than in the actual lineal relationship of individuals. Thus the Egyptian Pharaoh Tarhaqa (OT Tirhakah) (*ca.* 685 B.C.) could speak quite correctly of his ancestor Sesostris III, who lived *ca.* 1850 B.C., as his "father." From Kassite times in Babylonia the terms "son" and "daughter" were also used to indicate a grandson or a granddaughter. Family trees written on the backs of cuneiform tablets dealing with personal or business matters have been recovered from NUZI, and if the sections of Genesis that form criticism can isolate on the basis of the incidence of *tôl^{e}ḏôṯ* were in fact ancient historiographical material, then the genealogical passages that they contain could also have been written on the backs of tablets dealing with narrative or other types of material and incorporated into the text when the ancient sources were edited to form, with the Joseph narratives, the extant book of Genesis.

While ancient scribes made official genealogical tables, and individuals preserved their own family pedigrees (at least in part) down to Roman times, nothing quite like the biblical genealogies of Genesis and 1 Ch. 1–9 has been found elsewhere in antiquity. While it was by no means impossible for detailed records to have been kept by other nations, none is extant. The Hebrew practice of collecting and preserving complicated genealogical records was taken up once more with the extension of Islam, and has remained a permanent feature of that tradition. A number of Western scholars have reported an intense interest in genealogies among Arab peoples, especially tribal nomads, and have listened with some surprise as individuals have spent an hour reciting from memory the names of ancestors who went back several centuries. Some contemporary Jews are also able to trace their ancestry back to very early times, even to such a remote person historically as Aaron, though in the writer's experience written rather than oral material was always used for the exercise.

III. Purpose and Use.–Records of descent were an extremely important part of Hebrew tradition from the very beginning, and no fewer than three of the earliest were concerned with the posterity of Adam (Gen. 4:1f., 17-22, 25f.; 5:1-32). If the Genesis sources were originally in tablet form as suggested above, these genealogies are among the most primitive of their kind. For the Hebrews, such catalogs of descent served various purposes, the first of which (Gen. 4:1f., 17-22) indicated that considerations of biological succession by generations was but one function of such records. Although the line of Cain was traced for seven generations, an equally important emphasis in this chapter was placed upon recording new cultural or technological events. Thus, the occupations of Cain (agriculturalist and city builder), Abel (shepherd), and Jabal (cattleman) represented the agrarian aspect of early Mesopotamian life, which was enriched almost contemporaneously by such developments as music (Jubal) and metallurgy (Tubal-cain).

The second genealogy (Gen. 4:25f.), dealing with the offspring of Seth, has more in common with a pedigree, but also serves the purpose of contrasting the fidelity to God of Seth's offspring with the behavior of Cain's apostate descendants. The third of these early sources (Gen. 5:10-32; cf. 1 Ch. 1:1-4) traced the posterity of Adam through Seth down to Noah and his sons and stopped at a point just before the Flood. The background of this material is obviously Mesopotamian in character, and if the sources were transmitted originally on tablets the lists would have been inscribed most probably in an ancient form of Mesopotamian script on the reverse side of one or more of the tablets.

At the beginning of the patriarchal period when God promised a specific amount of territory to Abraham and his descendants, the importance of maintaining personal genealogies became more obvious. When the Israelite tribes came into existence after Jacob, the recording of family and community relationships assumed a new importance in the light of the necessity for establishing and maintaining the allotment of the land by tribal divisions. Once sedentary occupation of Palestine had taken place under Joshua and the land had been apportioned to the various tribes, the genealogical records were adduced as evidence of a legitimate title or claim to the property of one's ancestors.

Genealogies also served a fundamentally important purpose when the hereditary Aaronic priesthood was established. Pentateuchal tradition uniformly regarded the priesthood as restricted to the tribe of Levi and the house of Aaron in particular, and one had to meet these conditions to be eligible for the priestly service of the sanctuary in the tabernacle and the later temples. To be able to trace one's descent from Aaron was therefore mandatory for the Levitical priests, and in the time of Josephus every priest was expected to be able to prove such a descent.

Genealogical records were used, furthermore, to establish and maintain the right of royal succession in the southern kingdom. Here descent from the house of David was the important consideration, and when the prophets began to teach that the Messiah would emerge from that stock (cf. Isa. 11:1-5), such genealogies immediately became far more significant than before. As a result, it is hardly surprising that in the NT great care was taken to establish Jesus' lineal descent from David.

Membership of families and tribes was emphasized during the period of the wilderness wanderings, when the very position that was occupied in the camp and on the march was determined on that basis (Nu. 2:2, 17; 10:1-28). During that time the military organization of the Israelites was also governed by genealogy (Nu. 1:2-4), and this included the priests and Levites (Nu. 3:11-39). Taxes and offerings (Nu. 7:11-89) for the support of the sanctuary (Nu. 3:40-51) were also based on such records. Where communities were organized in terms of a general tribal structure, the genealogy of an individual served the purpose of identifying him and locating him within the community.

The great stress laid upon the need for the congregation of Israel to be pure (cf. Dt. 7:1-4; 23:1-8) naturally tended to enhance the keeping of records in order to prevent the possible intrusion of foreign, and therefore pagan, elements into Israel. This issue became one of great concern in the postexilic period, when many foreign wives managed to find their way into the families of the nation (Neh. 13:23). For Ezra, the presence of such foreign elements was incompatible with the theocratic ideal, and with Nehemiah he insisted upon separating all foreign women from the mainstream of Jewish life (Ezr. 2:59-63; 10:9-44; Neh. 13:23-28). Written evidence of purity of descent became a requisite for admission to the priesthood, and those who could not document their claims by reference to genealogical records were excluded from priestly functions because they were deemed ceremonially unclean (Neh. 7:61-64). With the incursion of subversive Greek cultural elements into traditional Jewish faith during the Hellenistic period, the compiling of genealogies became a matter of great concern for the orthodox Jews. The covenant nation, whether in the preexilic or postexilic period, was always conscious that the blessings of God were transmitted from one member of a family to his progeny (Gen. 48:15f.). Obversely, in defense of His own rights, God could visit the iniquity of the fathers upon the children up to the third or fourth generation of those who rejected His sovereignty (Ex. 20:5).

*IV. **Problems.***–OT genealogies clearly served a variety of interests, with some early lists being as much ethnic or geographic in character as personal. With Wellhausen, many literary-critical scholars came to think of the lists in terms of groups rather than as pedigrees of individuals. Thus for them the marriages that were mentioned represented the union of groups rather than persons, the names being regarded as eponymous in character. This view encounters difficulties in that it fails to define the nature of a "group," or to distinguish between such a "group" and a "family" as one unit of a clan or tribe. As a result, this view is in danger of assuming that far more "groups" than families or clans existed.

That the OT pedigrees describe individuals rather than "groups" (except where "groups" resulting from an eponymous ancestor are mentioned) seems borne out by the evidence of Mesopotamian and Eblaic king lists, where there is no question that the names mentioned are those of individuals. Perhaps the most difficult problem that literary-critical adherents have yet to resolve is the determination of the stage at which "group" genealogies began to assume an individual character. Some scholars who support the literary-critical position have adopted the view that the genealogies from the Middle Bronze Age onward deal specifically with persons, a contention that receives ample support from the family trees inscribed on tablets recovered from Nuzi.

The interval of time covered by a GENERATION is a different problem. In Semitic usage "generation" generally designated the period between a person's birth and that of his first son (cf. KoB). In a corporate sense it also designated the people who were living during that interval (cf. Ps. 24:6; 78:8; etc.). The average length of a generation has been assumed to be forty years (cf. Ps. 95:10), based on the life span of those who died in the wilderness (Dt. 2:14). Here, however, the reference seems to be to persons who were already young adults, making for an average life span of some sixty years. It is probably more correct to assume that the interval between a man's birth and that of his firstborn would be closer to thirty years or less. Though persons such as David (1 K. 2:11) and Solomon (1 K. 11:42) were credited with forty-year reigns, it is important to note that the Hebrew text does not equate this period with a generation. This term is used on one occasion only for a thirty-eight-year interval (Dt. 2:14).

The principal OT genealogical records are as follows:

(1) The line from Cain through seven generations (Gen. 4:17-22).

(2) The descendants of Seth (Gen. 4:25f; 5:6f.), of unspecified number.

(3) The line from Adam to Noah (Gen. 5:1-32), comprising ten names in all. There is some variation among the MT, LXX, and Samaritan Pentateuch regarding the life span of certain individuals. Thus according to the MT and the LXX, Methuselah lived 969 years, but 720 years according to the Samaritan Pentateuch. According to the MT, Lamech lived 777 years, but the LXX has 753 years, and the Samaritan Pentateuch 635 years. These divergent figures may be based on ancient manuscript traditions other than those of the MT, and should not necessarily be understood to have resulted from errors in copying. The ten names in this list have been seen as reminiscent of an ancient Sumerian king list which named ten "great men" who ruled in antediluvian times.

(4) Noah's descendants (Gen. 10; cf. 1 Ch. 1:1-23). This is the so-called Table of Nations. The names seem to have been originally those of individuals that were applied subsequently to their descendants or to the territory in which they lived. Attempts to identify the various peoples have not met with complete success, but allowances must be made for changes in the significance of names due to conquest, migration, and other movements of peoples. If at least some of these names bore different meanings at different times, then they could describe linguistic, social, and geographical entities without particular consistency and still be correct for given periods of time or special circumstances (*see* TABLE OF NATIONS).

(5) The line from Shem to Abraham (Gen. 11:10-26; cf. 1 Ch. 1:24-27), comprising ten names. Again there are divergences between the MT, LXX, and the Samaritan Pentateuch, where in most instances the MT and the Samaritan Pentateuch agree against the LXX. Thus the LXX assigned Terah 145 years of life, whereas the MT and the Samaritan Pentateuch credited him with 205 years (Gen. 11:32).

(6) Lot's descendants (Gen. 19:37f.).

(7) Descendants of Nahor (Gen. 22:20-24).

(8) Abraham's offspring by Keturah (Gen. 25:1-4; cf. 1 Ch. 1:32f.), who became the ancestors of various north Arabian tribes.

(9) Ishmael's descendants (Gen. 25:12-18; cf. 1 Ch. 1:29-31).

(10) Offspring of Jacob (Gen. 46:8-27) by Leah (8-15), Zilpah (16-18), Rachel (19-22), and Bilhah (23-25).

(11) Reuben's genealogy (Gen. 46:9; Ex. 6:14; Nu. 26:5-11; cf. 1 Ch. 5:1-10).

(12) Simeon's descendants (Gen. 46:10; Ex. 6:15; Nu. 26:12-14; cf. 1 Ch. 4:24-43).

(13) Levi's offspring (Gen. 46:11; Ex. 6:16-25; cf. 1 Ch. 6:1-53 [MT 5:27–6:38]). This was the line from which the priests descended. Aaron's ancestry is condensed in Ex. 6:16-20, and all subsequent high priests claimed him as their ancestor.

(14) Judah's lineage (Gen. 46:12; Nu. 26:19-22; cf. 1 Ch. 2:3f.; 9:4), from which David and the preexilic kings of Judah from Solomon to Josiah descended (1 Ch. 3:10-15).

(15) Issachar's descent (Gen. 46:13; Nu. 26:23-25; cf. 1 Ch. 7:1-5).

(16) Zebulun's descent (Gen. 46:14; Nu. 26:26f.).

(17) Gad's offspring (Gen. 46:16; Nu. 26:15-18; cf. 1 Ch. 5:11-17).

(18) Asher's descendants (Gen. 46:17; Nu. 26:44-47; cf. 1 Ch. 7:30-40).

(19) Joseph's descent (Gen. 46:20; Nu. 26:28-37; cf. 1 Ch. 7:14-27). Joseph's two sons, Ephraim and Manasseh, were sometimes known as the "tribe of Joseph," the "house of Joseph," or the "sons of Joseph," and were adopted by Jacob as his own sons (i.e., descendants) in Gen. 48:5, 16.

(20) Benjamin's descent (Gen. 46:21; Nu. 26:38-41; cf. 1 Ch. 7:6-12; 8:1-40; 9:7, 35-44).

(21) Dan's descent (Gen. 46:23; Nu. 26:42f.).

(22) Naphtali's offspring (Gen. 46:24; Nu. 26:48-50; cf. 1 Ch. 7:13).

(23) A comprehensive genealogy of persons from Adam to Saul (1 Ch. 1–9), the most lengthy of its kind in the

Bible; it stresses the importance of purity of descent in the postexilic times.

The above records were supplemented by a number of registers of individuals, families, or periods as follows:

(24) Levitical registers dating from the periods of David (1 Ch. 15:5-24), Jehoshaphat (2 Ch. 17:8), Hezekiah (2 Ch. 29:12-14; 31:12-17), Josiah (2 Ch. 34:12f.; 35:8f.), Zerubbabel (Neh. 12:1-24), and Nehemiah (Neh. 10:9-13 [MT 10-14]).

(25) Registers and lists of David's soldiers (2 S. 23:8-39; 1 Ch. 11:11-47; 12:3-13,20), tribal supervisors (1 Ch. 27:16-22), and administrative officials (1 Ch. 27:25-31).

(26) Lists of individuals and families in the postexilic community from the time of Zerubbabel (Ezr. 2:2-61; Neh. 7:7-63) and Ezra (Ezra. 8:2-14), along with the roster of those who built the wall around Jerusalem (Neh. 3), those who had married foreign women (Ezr. 10:18-43), the signatories to the covenant (Neh. 10:1-27 [MT 2-28]), and the register of persons resident in Jerusalem (Neh. 11:4-19; 1 Ch. 9:3-17).

The NT has only two genealogies of any significance. Both of these trace the descent of Jesus Christ the Messiah from the house of David, one of them (Mt. 1:1-17) beginning with Abraham, and the other (Lk. 3:23-38) tracing the pedigree back to "Adam, the son of God."

In the Western practice of drawing up family trees, great care is taken that the genealogical record is as complete as possible for each generation. This procedure contrasts notably with ancient Near Eastern custom, where it was not considered necessary for pedigrees to be complete. Variations in designation from the modern pattern were also entertained in a manner that is not always easily recognized. The term "father," e.g., could be applied to a superior who was not a relative, and this is reminiscent of the "schoolfather" (i.e., school principal) of the Sumerians. People could also be considered brothers merely by being associated with one another in a treaty (cf. Am. 1:9). The word "son" could be used almost as widely as it is in modern Western society, and the same was generally true for "mother" and "daughter" as well.

The aim of such genealogies was to establish the general line of descent from given ancestors, and this objective was in no way impaired by the omission of certain generations as long as the line was being traced properly. For purposes of ancient Near Eastern genealogies, all members of a particular line were not necessarily equal in importance, and because of that principle, as well as for other reasons, certain names and generations could be omitted from family lists without prejudice to either the intent or the accuracy of content of the genealogy. Thus the Levitical pedigree of Moses (Ex. 6:16-20) records four generations between Levi and Moses, i.e., over four hundred years (cf. Ex. 12:40). In this list Kohath appears as one of Levi's sons and the leader of a Levitical clan. Amram was descended from Kohath after an unknown interval. It seems quite clear that some generations were omitted in the compilation, if only because the Levites numbered 22,000 males alone in the days of Moses (Nu. 3:39). The purpose of establishing Moses' descent from the family of Levi was accomplished, despite what appear to be obvious omissions from the list.

In the same manner, the genealogy of Ezra (Ezr. 7:1-5) cataloged only five generations of ancestors from *ca.* 458 B.C., when Ezra came to Judea, back to the high priest Zadok (*ca.* 966 B.C.). Obviously this is a condensed record of the family line, but still it achieved its objective of demonstrating Ezra's descent from Zadokite stock, which was Ezekiel's ideal of priestly ministry for the postexilic theocracy. Mt. 1:1 is a similar, though even shorter, genealogy — just three links from Christ to Abraham were recorded. The fuller form of Christ's ancestry (Mt. 1:2-17) was still incomplete (omitting Ahaziah, Joash, Amaziah, and Jehoiakim) when compared with OT records of royal descent.

Schematic patterns can be discerned periodically in Scripture, notably in Gen. 5 and 11. The genealogies in both these chapters consist of ten units in which the age of the parent at the birth of his firstborn was recorded, as were the remaining years of his life. Both lists also concluded with the names of three male siblings in a manner that can hardly be accidental. While these genealogies are no doubt genuine and ancient, they seem to have been arranged in such a manner as to permit easy memorization of the chief descendants of the ancestral stock.

The NT genealogies of Jesus Christ exhibit similar internal patterns. The period covered by Mt. 1:1-17 is divided among forty-two generations, and consists of three blocks of fourteen generations each. This schematic arrangement, involving a multiple of the sacred number seven, was obviously formed by processes of selection and omission. Such a list can hardly be considered an official, detailed pedigree, but once again the purpose of the compiler had been achieved, namely that of authenticating the descent of Christ from the Davidic line through Joseph, his putative father. (*See also* GENEALOGY OF JESUS II.A.). Multiples of seven characterize the series of names listed in Lk. 3:23-38, where each series normally comprises twenty-one names. Fourteen generations occupy the period between the time of David and the Exile in the Matthaean account, while the Lukan genealogy has almost double the number of names that represent twenty-one generations.

The period from the Exile to the time of Christ is covered by another fourteen generations in Matthew, and by twenty-one generations in Luke. A further complication is the wide dissimilarity in the names of persons from the time of David to the period of the birth of Christ. This discrepancy has been explained by the supposition that both lists belonged to Joseph, but were based upon different principles of compilation. Some scholars have suggested that Luke's list was actually the lineage of Mary, not Joseph, since she also most probably belonged to the Davidic house (cf. 1:32). For some writers Luke's list reflects the prophetic office of Jesus, and his extension of Christ's pedigree beyond Abraham to Adam emphasized the universality of Jesus' messianic mission. (*See also* GENEALOGY OF JESUS IV.B.)

Considering the difficulties inherent in the recording and transmission of Hebrew names, it is remarkable that so many genealogies have survived in the Scriptures. So many names in antiquity either sounded or were spelled alike that written records would be a necessity for establishing and maintaining proper identity, however tenacious oral tradition might have been. While "all Israel" was believed to have been enrolled by genealogies in a register (1 Ch. 9:1), there can be no doubt that many names would have been forgotten or omitted on other grounds, while some would be reduplications in one way or another of already existing names. Thus Elihu was also known as Eliab and Eliel (1 S. 1:1; 1 Ch. 6:27,34), while Nahath had the names Tohu and Toah at various times in his life (1 S. 1:1; 1 Ch. 6:26,34). The removal of the pagan theophoric element "baal" from Hebrew names resulted in Merib-baal becoming known as Mephibosheth (2 S. 4:4), a circumstance that can cause some confusion for the unwary. Certain names were regarded as general family property for the males, and as such were shared by one or more generations (see the prologue to Sirach), as is occasionally the case today. For reasons not apparent from the text, the name of a father could be replaced by that of a more distant ancestor (cf. Josh. 7:1,24).

The eclectic principles upon which the compilation of so many Scriptural genealogies are based should be a sufficient caution against using them for anything more than the most general of chronological purposes (cf. 1 Tim. 1:4; Tit. 3:9). Quite obviously a person such as Archbishop Ussher, who assumed that the Genesis genealogies were complete and proceeded to date terrestrial creation in 4004 B.C., was totally unaware of the rationale of ancient techniques of genealogical compilation, and the consequent pitfalls awaiting uninstructed occidental investigators. Nevertheless, it must not be forgotten that such records, whether written or oral, comprised history for those who utilized them, and consequently it is of the greatest importance for modern students to understand such lists as far as possible from the point of view of the original compilers before drawing conclusions from them.

Bibliography.–E. L. Curtis and A. A. Madsen, *Chronicles* (*ICC,* 1910); W. F. Albright, *JBL,* 57 (1938), 230f.; 58 (1939), 95-97; W. Rudolph, *Chronikbücher* (1955); J. M. Myers, *I and II Chronicles* (*AB,* 1965); R. K. Harrison, *Intro. to the OT* (1969), pp.147-152. R. K. HARRISON

GENEALOGY OF JESUS. A record (compilation) of Jesus' purported descent, found in extensive form only in Mt. 1:1-17 and Lk. 3:23-38.

I. Setting in Judaism
  A. Concern for Genealogical Purity
  B. Speculation on the Ancestry of the Messiah
II. Purpose of Matthew's Genealogy
  A. Structure
  B. Details
  C. Relation to Matthew's Gospel
III. Lukan Genealogy
IV. Comparison of the Two Lists
  A. Differences
  B. Harmonizing Attempts
V. Conclusion

I. Setting in Judaism.–While interest in genealogical relationships, especially among clans and tribes, can be traced back to the oldest written sources of the OT, it is clear that after the Babylonian exile the function of the genealogical form changed and its importance increased. The priestly writings in the OT — especially Ezra, Nehemiah, and 1-2 Chronicles — as well as later Jewish writings (Apocrypha, Pseudepigrapha, Dead Sea Scrolls, and rabbinic materials) demonstrate that interest in genealogies centered on the following two functions:

A. Concern for Genealogical Purity. The books of Ezra and Nehemiah as a whole present the idea of genealogical purity more explicitly than any other OT material. The author warns against any mixing of "the holy seed" (Ezr. 9:2) with the peoples of the land, implying that all returning exiles were required to prove descent from a preexilic Israelite family (Ezr. 2:59,62); the motivation here is to demonstrate and preserve a continuity between preexilic and postexilic Israel. Moreover, the list of returning exiles includes five categories: people of Israel (noncultic), priests, Levites, temple servants, and king's servants (Ezr. 2:2-58 par. Neh. 7:7-60; 11:3). Of these the first three were considered to represent the core of Israel (Ezr. 9:1; 10:18-25). These categories provided the basis for later rabbinic classifications of degrees of purity in the Mishnah (*Kiddushin* iv.1; *Horayoth* iii.8), except that the latter became more precise with regard to the position of those with doubtful or impaired ancestry. The distinction between full Israelites and those of doubtful descent was particularly important for the regulation of marriage, but it included also the whole question of social position and civil liberties (Jeremias, pp.271-344). The rabbinic sources, however, also reflected the difficulty of obtaining genealogical information and frequently revealed recourse to midrashic exegesis of biblical texts in the attempt to establish genealogical relationships (Johnson, pp.99-115). The motivation for the composition — though not the *manner* of composition — of the two genealogies of Jesus within Jewish-Christian circles therefore can be seen as the necessity to show Jesus' status as a full Israelite, without genealogical impairment.

B. Speculation on the Ancestry of the Messiah. It was not the unanimous Jewish opinion in the early Christian period that the Messiah would stem from David. On the basis of the OT concept of the perpetuity of the priesthood alongside the office of king (1 S. 2:35; Jer. 33:17-22; Zec. 4:14; cf. Sir. 45:6f., 15, 23-25; 1 Macc. 2:54), the expectation of a priestly Messiah came to be reflected in various Jewish sources, e.g., the Testaments of the Twelve Patriarchs, the Dead Sea Scrolls, and rabbinic materials. Rabbinic sources have clear and numerous traces of discussions between the partisans of each expectation. It was argued that the Davidic line was tainted by the illegal marriage of Judah and Tamar, the gentile status of Ruth, the Bathsheba affair, and the fact that the mother of Rehoboam was Naamah the Ammonitess (1 K. 14:31). The rabbinic writings were generally concerned with explaining these difficulties and at the same time charging that the priestly line was tainted in similar ways (Johnson, pp.115-138). Thus the purpose of Mt. 1:1-17 and Lk. 3:23-38, the only extant genealogies written from the point of view of messianic fulfillment (i.e., from the conviction that the Messiah had already come), also may have been to provide the proper credentials for Jesus as the Messiah and so reflect contemporary Jewish speculation on the ancestry of the Messiah.

II. Purpose of Matthew's Genealogy.–The Matthaean genealogy is composed of OT (LXX) data for the names from Abraham to Zerubbabel (vv.2-12; cf. Ruth 4:18-22; 1 Ch. 2:5-15; 3:10-15; Ezr. 3:2,8; 5:2; Neh. 12:1; Hag. 1:1, 12; 2:2) with some deletions in the list of kings (between Joram and Uzziah) and a few apparent discrepancies (cf. 1 Ch. 3:19; Mt. 1:12). The derivation of the nine names between Zerubbabel and Joseph is unknown. The intention of the compiler of the Matthaean genealogy can be determined only by accounting for the deliberate 3x14 structure, the details added to the succession of names in the list, and the relation of the genealogy to the subsequent material in Matthew.

A. Structure. In Mt. 1:17 the compiler of the genealogy emphasized that he found three groups of fourteen generations each in the ancestry of Jesus, beginning with Abraham. This emphasis transforms the genealogy at once into a periodization of Israel's history: fourteen generations from Abraham to David, fourteen from David to the Exile, and fourteen from the Exile to the Messiah. What was the intention of this structure? A commonly accepted view is that the number fourteen was reached by *gematria,* i.e., from the numerical value of the Hebrew letters in the name David (*daleth-waw-daleth,* 4+6+4), thus triply emphasizing the Davidic descent of Jesus. This view, however, is weakened by the probability that the genealogy was originally composed in Greek. W. D. Davies (pp.302-304) suggested that the number fourteen was a conscious reaction to the Pharisaic chain of tradition that may have included fourteen members or groups from Moses to Hillel and Shammai. According to this view the Matthaean genealogy constituted the credentials of the Messiah in opposition to the credentials of the rabbinic oral law. Yet the two lists have a different tone; while the rabbinic chain shows how past events have been transmitted to the present, the Matthaean genealogy shows how the historical process has reached a fulfillment in the coming of the Messiah. Moreover, the most numerous parallels to the structure of Mt. 1:1-17 are found in the periodizations of history that were common in Jewish apocalyptic (Daniel; 2 Bar. 53–74; 1 En. 91, 93; 2 En. 33:1f.) and that occur also in rabbinic writings. According to the apocalyptic structuring of history, a fixed number of equal periods would elapse before the beginning of the age of fulfillment. Thus, the original readers of this genealogy would probably have understood its structure to have eschatological significance: history is in order with its symmetrical periods, the time is fulfilled, and the messianic age has dawned.

B. Details. In addition to the climactic v. 17, the author included several phrases that were not essential to the pedigree of Joseph. "The book of the genealogy [Gk. *bíblos genéseōs*] of Jesus Christ" (1:1) is reminiscent of Gen. 2:4a and 5:1 and carries the connotation of a new beginning. "The Son of David, the son of Abraham" (1:1) recalls the central position of these two figures in the genealogical memory of the rabbis (SB, I, 13f.). The phrase "and his brothers" (v. 2) acknowledges that Jacob was the father of the twelve tribes, while the same phrase in v. 11 recalls the departure from the father-to-son succession of kings at the end of the monarchy.

Certainly the most curious feature of the Matthaean genealogy is the mention of the four women, a rare feature in Jewish genealogies. This is especially striking since Tamar and Rahab were harlots, Bathsheba was an adulteress, Ruth was a Moabitess, and all four were probably considered Gentiles in the Jewish tradition contemporary with Matthew. Many ancient and some modern scholars have considered this the result of Matthew's desire to anticipate Jesus' concern for sinners and Gentiles (a motif stronger in Luke). Others find their function to be a demonstration that God can use even the humble and despised to accomplish His purpose. Still others find the four women to be "types of Mary," or more explicitly, a refutation of Jewish calumnies on the nature of Jesus' birth.

It is not often recognized, however, that each of these four women was in the Jewish tradition a subject of polemical controversy related to the question of the legitimacy of the descent of David. The Pharisaic tradition, which held to the expectation of the Davidic Messiah, exonerated and in fact glorified the four women, and by the end of the 1st cent. B.C. these four had a traditional place in the Pharisaic speculation on the ancestry of the Messiah. It is therefore probable that Matthew included the four women in Jesus' genealogy to show that in every respect the Pharisaic expectation of the Messiah has been fulfilled in Jesus of Nazareth, who was the son of David and therefore a descendant of the four women (Johnson, pp. 153-179).

C. Relation to Matthew's Gospel. Many contend that the account of the Virgin Birth (Mt. 1:18-25) is irreconcilable with a genealogy of Jesus that traces descent through Joseph, and that therefore the genealogy is not the work of the Evangelist himself. Against this view it can be argued that the distinctive features of the genealogy — its numerical structure, its dependence on data from the LXX, its "son of David" Christology, its eschatological tone — are consistent features of Matthew as a whole. A purpose can be seen behind the startling juxtaposition of genealogy and virgin birth: both describe who and what Jesus is on the basis of His ancestry; both use the title "son of David" (the genealogy applying it to Jesus, and 1:18-25 to Joseph); and the Virgin Birth account already presupposes the genealogy (Pesch, *BZ,* 10 [1966], 220-245). The genealogy centers on the Davidic sonship of Jesus, while 1:18-25 centers on His divine sonship. The whole of Mt. 1 may be considered a midrash on these two titles, possibly suggested by the terms "Christ, Son of God" in Mk. 1:1, which Matthew had as a source (Johnson, pp. 224-26). We may therefore conclude that the whole of Mt. 1 is composed by the author of the Gospel of Matthew and is not merely an incorporation of earlier materials.

III. Lukan Genealogy.–After the introductory remark that Jesus was about thirty years of age when He began His ministry, Lk. 3:23-38 consists of a bare list of names with the genitive article, going from Joseph back to Adam or, more precisely, to God. The names from Abraham back to Adam (vv. 34-38) are derived from Gen. 5; 11:10-27 (1 Ch. 1:1-4, 24-26), with Cainan added from the LXX of Gen. 10:24; 11:12f. From Nathan to Abraham (vv. 31-34) the list follows Gen. 25:19-26 and Ruth 4:18-22 except that Arni and Admin in Lk. 3:33 replace Ram (LXX "Arran") in Ruth 4:19. The only other identifiable names are Salathiel and Zerubbabel (v. 27) until Joseph. The remaining names are striking in two respects. There are several repetitions (five variations of Mattathias, two of Simeon, two of Levi, two of Melchi, three of Joseph, and two of Jesus). Moreover, Jeremias (p. 296) showed that use of the names of the twelve tribal fathers of Israel as personal names cannot elsewhere be traced to preexilic times; yet in his preexilic section Luke lists the names Levi, Simeon, Judah, and Joseph. These duplications and anachronisms not only necessitate caution with regard to the historical authenticity of Luke's list, but also suggest a pre-Lukan origin for at least some of his data.

Among the special features of the Lukan genealogy, the following should be noted:

(1) In 3:23 the author remarked that Jesus was the "son (as was supposed) [Gk. *hōs enomízeto*] of Joseph. . . ." This phrase may be an editorial remark by Luke indicating his awareness of the difficulty of tracing Jesus' descent from Joseph while at the same time holding to the tradition of the Virgin Birth. Others think the phrase indicates that Luke was recording a tradition different from that of Matthew while being aware that the latter list was the correct one. The phrase, however, can be read equally well as an indication that the genealogy of Jesus was already a matter of polemics and that Luke has some uncertainty regarding the historical authenticity of the list itself. In any case, this phrase is another indication of the pre-Lukan origin of some data in the list.

(2) Some attempts have been made to find a significance in the total number of names in Lk. 3:23-38, i.e., seventy-seven. This number may be seen as eleven "world-weeks" at the end of which the messianic week begins. But nothing here is comparable to Mt. 1:17, which draws attention to the symmetrical pattern there. Moreover, the Lukan list has much textual variation. Several MSS testify to seventy-two names, as does Irenaeus, who believed that this corresponds to the number of names in Gen. 10, "implying that it is He [Jesus] who has summed up in Himself all nations dispersed from Adam downwards . . ." (*Adv. haer.* iii.22.3). It seems impossible to demonstrate any special meaning in the total number of names in the Lukan list.

(3) Lk. 3:23-38 traces Jesus' ancestral line back to "Adam, the son of God," unlike Matthew, who goes back only to Abraham and therefore is limited to Israelite

history. It is often rightly held that this illustrates Luke's general concern to portray the universal character of Jesus' ministry. But attempts to find here an Adam/Christ typology must realize that this Pauline motif is nowhere explicit in Luke-Acts. Moreover, the genealogy does not end with Adam but with the phrase, "Adam, son of God." If Luke intended a typological significance between the beginning and the end of his list, it would seem more appropriate to find it in the designation of Jesus as the Son of God.

(4) Unlike Matthew, who began his Gospel with the genealogy, Luke inserted his list into a pre-Lukan context (i.e., between the baptism of Jesus and the temptation) in such a way that the sequence was disturbed (4:1 refers to 3:21f.). This fact has often been linked with the "Proto-Luke" theory, according to which the first edition of Luke began at 3:1. Certainly the position of the genealogy in Luke is a curious one, whether seen from the "Proto-Luke" perspective or not. It is, moreover, striking that the only motif common both to the baptism account (3:21f.) and the genealogy (3:23-38) is the mention of sonship from God. The genealogy runs *backward* from Jesus to God (no other known biblical or Jewish genealogy culminates in the naming of God). Perhaps Luke saw in the genealogy one way of understanding the ascription of divine sonship to Jesus: He is Son of God through the line of OT patriarchs and subsequent historical figures. He inaugurates a new epoch and yet derives significance from his historical continuity with the redemptive history of the OT and of Judaism.

(5) The most striking feature of Luke's genealogy of Jesus is the rejection of the royal line of Judah in favor of proceeding from David to his son Nathan (2 S. 5:14; 1 Ch. 3:5; 14:4) and from him through a series of unknown names to Shealtiel and Zerubbabel. Why Luke (or his source) avoided the royal line cannot adequately be explained by appealing to his desire to avoid political overtones in connection with Jesus' messiahship. It is more probable that the Lukan genealogy reflects an awareness of esoteric Jewish tradition found in several sources (Johnson, pp. 240-45), according to which David's son Nathan was identified with the prophet Nathan and was considered to be an ancestor of the Messiah. Eusebius (*Quaestiones ad Stephanus* iii.2) suggested that the explanation for Nathan's position in Luke's genealogy was to be found in the Jewish disagreements over the ancestry of the Messiah. Perhaps, then, the Lukan genealogy reflects postbiblical Jewish data, or Luke himself, in line with his predilection to picture Jesus as a prophet (Lk. 7:16, 39; 13:33; 24:19), desired to include a prophet in the lineage of Jesus.

IV. Comparison of the Two Lists.–*A. Differences.* (1) Matthew followed the royal line from David to Jechoniah, while Luke traced Jesus' descent from David's son Nathan through a series of different and unknown names; both lists meet again in Salathiel, who is given different fathers in the two lists (Mt. 1:12; Lk. 3:27). (2) From Zerubbabel to Joseph both lists are composed of unknown names, those in one list differing from those in the other until they meet again in Joseph. Thus Joseph's father in Mt. 1:16 is Jacob; in Lk. 3:23, Heli. (3) Matthew has thirteen names from the Exile to Jesus (in spite of his assertion in 1:17 that he has fourteen); Luke has twenty-two for the same period — a more probable number for six centuries, though Matthew's is not impossible, as is often contended. (4) Matthew included an introduction (1:1), references to brothers of Judah and Jechoniah (1:2, 11), the four women (1:3, 5f.), and a deliberate 3x14 scheme (1:17). (5) Matthew has an ascending order, Luke a descending one; in Matthew the formula is "N was the father of N," while Luke has the genitive article with the name. (6) Matthew goes back to Abraham, Luke to Adam. Besides these differences there are minor variations in orthography and form among those names that the two lists have in common.

B. Harmonizing Attempts. It is especially the first two differences mentioned above that have caused numerous attempts to harmonize the two lists. Briefly stated, the most frequently recurring hypotheses have been the following: (1) Both lists are genealogies of Joseph, but Matthew traced the biological ancestry, Luke the legal. The earliest extant harmonizing attempt, that of Africanus (*ca.* A.D. 200), was of this sort. He presupposed that the custom of levirate marriage was the key: Matthan, grandfather of Joseph in Matthew's list, married Estha and fathered Jacob. After Matthan's death, Melchi (unrelated to Matthan), grandfather of Joseph in Luke's list, married Estha and begat Heli; hence Jacob and Heli were half-brothers. Heli married and died childless; his half-brother Jacob married the widow in a levirate marriage and fathered Joseph. Thus Matthew gave the physical ancestry of Joseph, Luke the legal. In diagram form this argument can be seen more clearly:

Matthew *Luke*

Matthan Estha Melchi

Jacob widow Heli

Joseph

Jesus

(2) More frequently suggested in modern times is the theory that Matthew gave the legal line of descent and Luke the natural. (3) Annius of Viterbo (*ca.* 1490), Luther, and Bengel have been followed by several modern scholars in considering the Matthaean list a genealogy of Joseph and the Lukan list a genealogy of Mary. This view is usually linked to the assumption that the phrase, "as was supposed" (Lk. 3:23), applied only to Joseph. (4) Tertullian and a few modern scholars reversed the preceding view and held that Matthew gave the genealogy of Mary and Luke that of Joseph.

Certainly none of these attempts has proved to be totally convincing. While one may argue that a study of Luke's list reveals a more accurate use of historical information than that of Matthew (Jeremias, pp. 292-97), it would be rash to treat the genealogies of Jesus as pure reflections of accurate genealogical information concerning Jesus' ancestry, especially in view of the midrashic exegesis that usually accompanied rabbinic messianic speculation.

V. Conclusion.–The two genealogies of Jesus are probably examples of the tendency to historicize traditional motifs in the Gospel material. They, along with all early Christian literature, presuppose the Davidic ancestry of Jesus. But the genealogies probably arose in Jewish-Christian circles from the need to historicize this item of belief. On this view both lists fall into the category of midrash, the Jewish method of exegesis that expounded Scripture in such a way as to comfort, exhort, edify, and strengthen faith. No NT materials are more closely connected with Jewish forms and thought than these two passages; yet both are apologetic attempts to express more fully the Christian conviction that Jesus is the fulfillment of the hope of Israel.

Bibliography.–See esp. M. D. Johnson, *Purpose of the Biblical Genealogies* (1969), pp. 85-256; A. Vögtle, *Messias und Gottessohn* (1971), ch. 1.

See also E. L. Abel, *NTS*, 20 (1973/74), 203-210; H. A. Blair, "Mt. 1:16 and the Matthean Genealogy," and M. J. Moreton, "Genealogy of Jesus," both in *SE*, II (*TU*, 87, 1964), 149-154,

176ff.; M. M. Bourke, *CBQ*, 22 (1960), 160-175; R. E. Brown, *Birth of the Messiah* (1977); W. D. Davies, *Setting of the Sermon on the Mount* (1964), pp. 67-77; J. M. Gibbs, *NTS*, 10 (1963/64), 446-464; A. J. B. Higgins, *NTS*, 13 (1966/67), 211-239; R. T. Hood, "The Genealogies of Jesus," in A. Wikgren, ed., *Early Christian Origins* (1961), pp. 1-13; J. Jeremias, *Jerusalem in the Time of Jesus* (1969), pp. 271-344; R. Pesch, *Bibl.*, 48 (1967), 409f.; *BZ*, 10 (1966), 220-245; 11 (1967), 79-97; E. Rasco, "Mt. I-II; Structure, Meaning, Reality," in *SE*, IV (*TU*, 102, 1968), 214-230; A. Vögtle, *BZ*, 8 (1964), 45-58, 239-262; 9 (1965), 32-49; H. C. Waetjen, *JBL*, 95 [1976], 205-230. M. D. JOHNSON

GENERAL [Heb. *śar*] (Jgs. 4:7); AV CAPTAIN; NEB COMMANDER; (cf. AV 1 Ch. 27:34; RSV, NEB, "commander"); [Gk. *stratēgós*] (1 Macc. 10:65); AV DUKE; [*chilíarchos*] (Rev. 6:15); AV CHIEF CAPTAIN; NEB MARSHAL. In the OT both Sisera and Joab held the rank of *śar* in the sense of "general." The title of the officer noted in 1 Maccabees might be given to either a military or civil official. A chiliarch was technically the commander of a thousand men, but the Roman tribune of NT times actually led only about six hundred. Rev. 6:15, however, has in view a broader high military designation than that of tribune.

See also CHIEF; COMMANDER; TRIBUNE.

GENERATION [Heb. *dôr, tôlēḏôṯ*; Aram. *dār* (Dnl. 4:3, 34); Gk. *geneá*]; AV also AGE (Eph. 3:5, 21), TIME (Acts 14:16; 15:21), "nation" (Phil. 2:15); NEB also TIME, DESCENDANTS, AGE, TRIBAL LISTS, etc. The AV, RSV, and NEB also supply "generation" when the Hebrew, in speaking about the future, refers to the third and fourth generation but uses only the words "third" (*šillēšîm*) and "fourth" (*ribbēʿîm*) (Gen. 50:23; Ex. 20:5; 34:7; Nu. 14:18; Dt. 5:9; 2 K. 10:30; 15:12; cf. Jgs. 1:14). In 2 S. 7:19 the RSV emends the MT, partially on the basis of the LXX in the par. 1 Ch. 17:17 (on these difficult verses cf. KD *in loc.*; S. R. Driver, *Notes on the Hebrew Text and Topography of the Books of Samuel* [1913], pp. 276f.; J. M. Myers, *I Chronicles* [*AB*, 1965], p. 129).

Hebrew *dôr*, Aram. *dār*, and Gk. *geneá* refer to a period of time loosely defined as the time between a parent's prime and that of his child. These terms may be used to speak about past ages (Isa. 51:9; Col. 1:26) or about the ages or times to come (Isa. 34:17; Lk. 1:48). Those living at a given time in history are referred to as a generation (Jer. 2:31; Mt. 11:16), and can be characterized as a whole, e.g., as a "perverse and crooked generation" (Dt. 32:5), as a "faithless and perverse generation" (Lk. 9:41), or as "the generation of the righteous" (Ps. 14:5). Cf. *TDOT*, III, *s.v.* "dôr" (Freedman-Lundbom, Botterweck).

Hebrew *tôlēḏôṯ*, which is found only in the plural, is used in genealogical lists and refers to the successive generations of families (Nu. 1:20-42). In some instances the word has the sense of an account of a man and his descendants (Gen. 2:4; 6:9; NEB "story"). (*See also* GENESIS II.D.1-2.)

In the AV of Mt. 3:7 "generation" is used in the obsolete sense of "offspring" (RSV, NEB "brood," Gk. *génnēma*).

See *DNTT*, II, 35-39. E. W. CONRAD

GENEROSITY; GENEROUS [Heb. *nāḏîḇ*] (Ex. 35:5; Prov. 19:6); AV WILLING, "prince"; NEB WISH, "the great"; [*ḥānan*] (Ps. 37:21; 112:5); AV "sheweth mercy," "sheweth favour"; NEB also "be gracious"; [Gk. *agathós*] (Mt. 20:15); AV GOOD; [*haplṓs, haplótēs*] (2 Cor. 9:11, 13; Jas. 1:5); AV BOUNTIFULNESS, "liberal distribution," LIBERALLY; NEB also "liberal"; [*aphelótēs*] (Acts 2:46); AV "singleness of heart"; NEB "unaffected joy"; [*koinōnikós*] (1 Tim. 6:18); AV "willing to communicate"; NEB "ready to give away."

The man with a "generous heart" (*neḏîḇ libbô*) of Ex. 35:5 is one who gives willingly, and Heb. *ḥānan* means especially to deal graciously with the needy but undeserving. Whereas the NT term *agathós* can be used for any good characteristic, *koinōnikós* specifically denotes giving what is one's own, and *aphelótēs, haplṓs,* and *haplótēs* emphasize sincerity in giving. R. J. HUGHES, III

GENESIS jen'ə-sis.

I. General Data
  A. The Name
  B. Survey of Contents
  C. Connection with Succeeding Books
II. Composition
  A. Literary-critical Theories of Authorship and Date
  B. Early Opponents of These Theories
  C. Weaknesses of the Literary-critical Approach
    1. General
    2. Specific
  D. Form-criticism and the Origin of Genesis
    1. *Tōleḏōṯ* as Indicative of a Colophon
    2. Structure of the Eleven Proposed Underlying Tablets
    3. Joseph Narratives
    4. Authorship and Editorial Activity
    5. Translation Problems
III. Archeology
  A. Genesis and Sumerian Historiography
  B. Genesis and Near Eastern Archeology

***I. General Data.**–A. The Name.* The first book of Moses is named by the Jews from the first word, namely, Heb. *berēʾšîṯ*, preferably translated "by way of beginning" (cf. the Gk. *Brēsith* of Origen). In the LXX it is called *Genesis,* because it recounts the beginnings of the world and of mankind. This name has passed over into the Vulgate (*Liber Genesis*). As a matter of fact, the name is based only on the beginning of the book.

B. Survey of Contents. The book opens with the story of the creation of the world and of the first human beings (ch. 1). It tells of Paradise and the fall (chs. 2–3), Adam's and Eve's descendants and Cain's murder of Abel (chs. 4–6), the Deluge and Noah and his descendants (5:28–10:32; 11:10-26), and the construction of the tower of Babel (11:1-9). It also contains the lineage and histories of the patriarchs and their households: Abraham (11:27–25:18), Isaac and Jacob (25:19–37:2), and Joseph (37:3–50:26). The first part of the book (1:1–11:26) is the history of mankind. The second part (11:27–50:26) is the history of families and the introduction to the history of the chosen people, which begins in Ex. 1. The promise made to Abraham (Gen. 12:1-3) declares that God, even if He originally set apart one man and his family (chs. 12–50) and then a single nation (Ex. 1–2), nevertheless intends salvation eventually to include all mankind.

C. Connection with Succeeding Books. By the statements just made it has already been indicated in what close connection Genesis stands with the subsequent books of Scripture. The history of the chosen people, which begins with Ex. 1–2, at the very outset and with a clear purpose refers back to the history as found in Genesis (cf. Ex. 1:1-6, 8 with Gen. 46:27; 50:24-26), although hundreds of years had elapsed between these events. To Abraham in Gen. 12:1-3 the promise had been given, not only that he was to be the father of a mighty nation that would recognize him as their founder (the earliest history of which is reported in Exodus and the following books of the Pentateuch), but also that he would receive the Promised Land. In this respect the book of Joshua, which gives the story of the capture of this land, is also a continuation of the historical development begun in Genesis. The blessing of God pronounced over Abraham, however, continued to be efficacious also in later times among the people who had descended from him. In this way Genesis is an introduction to all the succeeding OT books that in any way have to do with the fate of this people. But insofar as this blessing of God was to extend to all the nations of the earth (12:3), the promises given can be entirely fulfilled only in Christ, and can expand only in the work and success of Christian missions and in the blessings that are found within Christianity. Accordingly, this book treats first of beginnings and origins, in which is contained, as in a kernel, the entire development of the kingdom of God down to its consummation.

II. Composition.–Jewish and early Christian traditions (as well as the rest of the Torah) ascribed the composition of Genesis to Moses. Sporadic criticism of Genesis during the 10th and 11th cent. cast some doubt on Mosaic authorship, but it was only in the 16th and later cents. that the traditional views of composition began to be seriously questioned. In 1753 Astruc published a treatise on Genesis which, while ascribing the compilation of the book to Moses, purported to discover "duplicate" narratives of events such as the creation and the Flood. More important was his recognition of the use of two names for God, namely, Yahweh and 'Elohim, in Genesis and parts of Exodus, and these he employed as "criteria" for the recovery of what he imagined to be the corresponding underlying literary sources. With disarming simplicity he suggested that all passages that used the name Yahweh belonged to one source document, while those in which 'Elohim occurred belonged to another. The Elohistic document was for him the original source for the contents of Genesis, but it stood parallel to the Yahwistic document. In addition, he purported to have discovered numerous repetitions which, along with supposedly non-Israelite material, made up four literary "columns" from which Moses had compiled Genesis.

A. Literary-critical Theories of Authorship and Date. The age of rationalism was reflected in the work of Eichhorn, who in 1780 published the first of what ultimately proved to be a lengthy series of modern introductions to the OT. He extended the "criteria" suggested by Astruc by including considerations of literary style and phraseology as an additional means whereby alleged underlying sources could be differentiated. In 1792 and 1800 Geddes published two works in which he assigned the Pentateuch to the age of Solomon and attributed its compilation to a redactor. He agreed with Astruc's suggestion that the incidence of the divine names could be used to cover two underlying sources, but rejected the Yahwistic and Elohistic documents as they had been reconstructed by Astruc and Eichhorn, preferring instead to think of two series of fragmentary sources. A developed fragmentary hypothesis of pentateuchal origins was formulated by J. S. Vater, for whom there may have been as many as forty separate fragmentary sources, some of which were held to be older than the time of Moses. Astruc and Eichhorn found a degree of support in the writings of de Wette, who thought that their documentary hypothesis was superior to the fragmentary theory advanced by Geddes. De Wette therefore argued that Genesis depended for its origins on an Elohistic document, and that much of this material was in fact like epic poetry.

In 1823 Ewald strongly attacked the fragmentary theory and supported the view that an Elohistic type of source, supplemented by earlier sections such as the Decalogue, underlay the final form of Genesis. This supplementary theory was favored by de Wette in 1840, who advanced the view that the augmenting had actually been made from a Yahwistic source. In his *Komm. über die Genesis* (1838) Tuch argued that the basic source (*Grundschrift*) of the entire Pentateuch was the Elohistic document, and that it had been supplemented by portions of the Yahwistic material that he himself dated in the early monarchy.

In his study of the sources of Genesis (1853), Hupfeld argued that the *Grundschrift* was not the literary unity maintained by earlier writers, but in fact the product of two persons, both of whom had used 'Elohim as the name of God, and who could be differentiated by means of certain linguistic peculiarities. Redactors or editors, always of an anonymous character, were adduced as necessary elements in the process of compilation, and passages that presented problems for the various theories were frequently credited to the activities of these persons.

For Genesis, therefore, there were by now three alleged documentary sources which had been used in the process of compilation: a Yahwistic (J) source, an Elohistic (E) document, and a postexilic Priestly (P) source, the latter formerly thought to have been part of the *Grundschrift*.

K. H. Graf followed Vatke in the view that the *Grundschrift* was one of the latest, rather than the earliest, sources of Genesis and the other pentateuchal writings, and assigned it to a postexilic period. Although his criteria for these options could not be demonstrated objectively, and even though he was challenged seriously by some of his contemporaries, he nevertheless clung to his position. Colenso agreed with Graf that the basic documentary source claimed by earlier scholars was late in date, thereby giving impetus to an interpretation of the significance of ancient priestly writings from the Near East that was totally contrary to the actual facts of the case. Kuenen, who was influenced by Colenso, supported Graf in the view that the J source was basic to all pentateuchal writings and that it had been supplemented by portions of the E source. Wellhausen, a student of Ewald, leaned heavily and uncritically upon the views of Graf in developing an evolutionary reconstruction of the Hebrew religion. His theory regarding the literary sources behind the Pentateuch came to be recognized as the classical literary-critical theory of pentateuchal origins (*see* PENTATEUCH). As far as the composition of Genesis was concerned, Wellhausen regarded it as a compilation of material obtained from the supposed documents P (dated to the 5th cent. B.C.), J (assigned to the 9th cent. B.C.), and E (dated approximately to the 8th cent. B.C.). While these conclusions added virtually nothing to the views expressed by Graf, they did succeed in bringing all earlier literary-critical speculation to a climax. So completely did the theory meet the intellectual and emotional needs of most European scholars of that time that within a very short period it had swept all other competitors aside and gained dominance of the field. Soon it spread to Britain and the USA.

Some attempts will now be made to convey at least part of the content of each of the hypothetical documents, although scholars seldom agreed precisely — or sometimes even in broad detail — about the content of individual sources, due to the rather subjective nature of the accepted analytical method. The majority of scholars during the time of Wellhausen, however, would have credited the supposed J source with many of the following portions of Genesis: 12:1-4a, 7-9; 12:10-20; 13:1f., 4f., 7a, 8-10a; 16:1f., 4-7a, 8, 11-14; 18:1-33; 19:27f.; 21:1a,

2a, 7, 33; 24; 25:21-26a, 27-34; 26:1-33; 28:10, 13-16, 19a; 41:14a, 21a, 29-31, 35b, 36b, 42a, 43b, 45b, 49, 54, 56a, 57. The supposed P source was thought by its proponents to have included parts of the following sections: 1:1–2:4a, 5; 6:5–9:19, 28f.; 10; 11:10-27, 31f.; 12:4b-5; 13:6, 11b-12a; 16:1a, 3, 15f.; 17; 19:29; 21:2b-5; 23; 25:7-10, 12-17, 19f., 26b; 26:34f.; 27:46; 28:1-9; 29:24, 28b-29; 30:4a, 9b; 31:18b; 33:18a; 35:6a, 9-13, 15, 22b-29; 36:1-2a, 6-8, 40-43; 37:1f.; 41:4a; 46:6-27; 47:5-11, 27f.; 48:3-7; 49:1, 28-33; 50:12f. The E document was credited by most literary-critical speculators with at least the following: 15:1-3, 5f., 11-12a, 13f., 16; 20:1-17; 21:6a, 8-24, 27, 31; 22:1-13, 19; 28:11f., 17f., 20-22; 29:1, 15-18; 30:1-3, 4b-8, 17-20a, 21, 22b-23, 26, 28; 31:2, 4-11, 13-17, 19-25a, 26a, 28-31a, 33-35, 36b-37, 41-43, 45, 47, 49f., 54f.; 32:13b-21, 23a, 24a, 26b, 27f., 31f.; 35:5, 11a, 18a, b, 19f.; 36:1-4, 6b-8, 14, 16-20; 37:5a-11, 19f., 22, 24, 28-30, 32-34a, 35b, 36; 40:2-3a, 4-5a, 6-15a, 16-23, 41; 45:1b, 3, 5b, 7a, 8-9a, 13, 15-18, 20, 24b, 25-27; 46:2-5a; 47:7; 48:1-2a, 7-9, 11f., 15f., 20-22; 50:15-26. It must be emphasized that the apparent precision of the foregoing is illusory, and is in fact dependent to a very large extent upon the literary-critical whim of the individual analyst. In time it came to be recognized that certain parts of the text of Genesis defied any attempts at separation into documents, particularly some sections in which there was thought to be a mixture of J and E documents. The general theory was therefore adjusted to accommodate this embarrassment, and accordingly a source dubbed JE was postulated. Depending upon the views of the individual critic, this consisted of a minimum of chs. 27; 29:2-14, 26, 31-35; 30–32; 33:1-17.

For a more extensive treatment of the Wellhausen hypothesis, see *ISBE* (1929), II, 754-760.

B. Early Opponents of These Theories. It must be recognized that this evolutionary hypothesis of origins was never without its serious critics, and this situation has persisted to the present time. The fragmentary theory of Geddes, developed by Vater, came in for strong criticism by Ewald in 1823, who in a work on the composition of Genesis presented strong arguments for the unity of the composition on philological and other grounds without, however, actually giving support to the traditional view of Mosaic authorship. In 1846, J. H. Kurtz in a commentary on Genesis inquired why Elohistic passages, supposedly earlier than the time when the Yahwistic supplementer began his work, still presupposed or alluded to the contents of the Yahwistic sections of Genesis. Supporters of the supplementary hypothesis could not answer this question and never resolved the problem that had provoked it. Another outstanding opponent of the various literary-critical views was the orthodox scholar E. W. Hengstenberg (1802-1869), who in a professional lifetime of literary activity made many devastating criticisms of the liberal movement; his criticisms, however, seemed to have had little effect upon those whose views he was opposing. Others who stood in the same general conservative tradition included M. Drechsier, H. C. Havernick, and C. F. Keil.

In a discerning OT intro. published in 1889, E. Riehm condemned the theory that priestly material was of a later date than any other of the pentateuchal sources. In this stance he was supported by R. Kittel, who ascribed a lengthy pre-history to priestly writings, taking them to be documents that had been restricted primarily to priestly circles and only made public subsequently through force of circumstances. F. Delitzsch made a frontal assault on the entire Wellhausen scheme in 1887 in a commentary on Genesis, arguing among other things for an early date for priestly materials in Genesis. A. Klostermann also rejected the developmental hypothesis and in its place suggested a modification of Ewald's views, which involved dating priestly sources in the preexilic period.

In Britain, E. C. Bissell castigated the basic presuppositions of the Wellhausen school and its critical method in 1885, while in 1906 an impressive theological appraisal of contemporary literary criticism was made by J. Orr. Orr exposed some of the basic weaknesses of Wellhausen's system, and so devastating was his approach that his arguments were never accorded the courtesy of an answer. Much the same result occurred in the case of Baxter, whose *Sanctuary and Sacrifice* (1895) argued strongly for an early date for priestly material. The distinguished scholar A. H. Sayce was the first to bring archeological discoveries to bear upon the theories of the Wellhausen school, one result of which was that Sayce himself abandoned his earlier liberal opinions and lent massive intellectual support to more traditional views. Further pointed attacks upon the criteria employed by exponents of literary criticism were made in 1903 by J. Dahse, and in 1912 by H. M. Wiener. Both men indicated the wide degree of divergence between the traditional Hebrew text and the LXX, and suggested that the extent of this inconsistency made the divine names totally unsuitable as criteria for the recovery of underlying sources. B. D. Eerdmans enlarged on this approach between 1908 and 1914, rejecting entirely the view that the divine names could be employed as valid criteria. In the USA one of the most outstanding nineteenth-century opponents of the Graf-Wellhausen theory was W. H. Green of Princeton Theological Seminary, who in a number of publications leveled fundamental charges against the procedures adopted by the exponents of literary criticism.

C. Weaknesses of the Literary-critical Approach. 1. General. Despite the great weight of academic respectability that the developmental theory was commanding at the end of the 19th cent., its critics were correct in pointing to many areas in which the procedures and the resultant conclusions were either gravely deficient or absolutely incorrect. Scholars such as Bruston, Smend, Eichrodt, and others, however, continued to propose even greater fragmentation of supposedly underlying sources than their predecessors had done. Typical of this activity were the efforts of Eissfeldt, who produced an entirely new document described as a "Lay" source or "L document." Characteristic of this material in Genesis was its "antique flavor," as he described it. It comprised most of the fragments of verses left over from the attempts of others to formulate underlying documents. His source seems to have contained the following sections of Genesis: 2:4b–3:24; 4:1, 17a, 18-24; 6:1-4; 9:21-27; 11:1-9; 12:1-4a, 6-8; 13:2, 5, 7-11a, 12b-18; 18–19; 25:1-6, 11b, 21-26a, 29-34; 26:1-2a, 3a, 6-23, 25b-33; 29:1–30:24, 25-43; 31:1, 3, 19-54; 32:24b-33; 33:18f.; 34; 35:5, 21-22b; 36:2b-5, 9-39; 38; 49:1-7.

It was in fact this very kind of unrestrained speculation that brought discredit upon the method in the judgment of observers such as Möller and König, and led Kittel and Gressmann to declare, shortly after World War I, that the minutiae of literary-critical research had attained the limits of their usefulness. It had become evident that from the beginning opinions about the contents of the supposed pentateuchal "documents" diverged widely, and this lack of unanimity in a crucial area did nothing to increase the confidence of those who were already dubious about the methodology. Unfortunately, many exponents of the developmental theory of pentateuchal origins were already heirs to two intellectual disadvantages. The first partook of the character of ancient Greek life, in which speculation, wholly unverified by an reference to external or objective phenomena, was allowed to serve as an acceptable substitute for critical ratiocination. The second was that, for the nineteenth-century scholars, the evolutionary zeitgeist appeared to be the only rational, scientific explanation of biological existence, and it was but a small step to transfer that principle from the descriptive sciences to literary criticism in the misguided belief that the latter would then become scientific. The developmental hypothesis was the very antithesis of all that can be described as scientific, and this unfortunate situation has proved to be the greatest weakness of the literary-critical approach. In the laboratories of Europe, scientific investigators were following a proper method of approach known technically as a posteriori, in which the investigator first examines relevant factual evidence and argues cautiously from what he has found to some possible explanation of the phenomena under consideration. In contrast, the literary-critical speculators were following the a priori approach, in which the investigator begins with a preconceived explanation of the materials that he is studying and is concerned to find evidence that will justify (even partially) his intellectual position. Because so much of the general evidence available even at that period militated against the position represented by the developmental view, European scholars had to resort to such measures as the emendation of the text, the reconstruction and rewriting of the history, the invoking of anonymous redactors or editors to help in awkward situations in which the theory was threatened, and the assigning of specific passages which controverted the theory to a different author in a much later period. At best, any OT material was held to be comparatively late rather than early in origin, and replete with myth, legend, and folklore, and narratives of dubious accuracy. At worst it was deemed valueless for serious historical study and in need of wholesale reconstruction by modern literary-critical methods before it could be of the slightest use to scholars. The abandon with which the European savants indulged in their speculations was never clouded by any reference to specific facets of ancient Near Eastern life which might have been inferred from monuments and inscriptions known at that time; the closest that Wellhausen himself ever came to this sort of explanation was the occasional recognition of parallels between some biblical passages or incidents and a few late Arabic institutions. The latter obviously postdated the OT by many centuries, however, and are thus of no significant value for purposes of comparison.

Another weakness of the literary-critical approach was that it reflected the skeptical and positivistic outlook typical of Hegelian philosophy. The contemporary rationalistic prejudices against supernatural phenomena made for the immediate relegation to the realm of myth and legend of any OT material that could not be interpreted strictly along positivistic lines. As far as Genesis was concerned, the sections dealing with the creation of mankind and the fall were dismissed as mythological simply because they were not understood from the standpoint of the ancient Near Eastern mind. The tower of Babel incident and the Flood were regarded similarly as long-remembered traditions that have claimed only a vague and rather confused historicity at best, while the names of Abraham and the patriarchs usually were understood as probable tribal designations that were only later attached to individuals (and at that under quite dubious historical circumstances).

From the foregoing general remarks it will have become apparent that the development theory was a microcosm of the evolutionary, positivistic, rationalistic, and doctrinaire intellectual movements of nineteenth-century Europe, and that its weaknesses were compounded by inadequate methodologies.

2. Specific. Some of the more serious weaknesses can now be examined in greater detail. The earliest criterion used for the separation of the alleged underlying documents in Genesis, namely that of the variant usage of the divine names YHWH and 'Elohim, appeared disarmingly simple and effective, but even its originator Astruc realized that it was inadequate by itself for purposes of analysis. In fact, the criterion was entirely erroneous and misleading and had no validity as a means of determining the presence or absence of source material in Genesis. This position can be substantiated quite readily when subjective considerations are relinquished in favor of an examination of the objective data furnished by archeology. Of the many religious documents recovered from various sites in the Near East, not one of them can be shown to have been compiled in the manner described by nineteenth-century literary critics and their successors for the book of Genesis. Were one to take a characteristic Mesopotamian composition such as the Epic of Gilgamesh, which is known to have incorporated older sources, and analyze it into underlying documents with the aid of Astruc's criterion, one would be able to formulate as many hypothetical documents as the number of deities named in the Epic.

Clearly, such a result can have no relevance for the composition of the Gilgamesh Epic, or, for that matter, for any other documents from the ancient Near East. Not even a considerably later body of Semitic literature, the Koran, can be reduced to underlying documents by utilizing the analytical system of Graf and his successors. R. Dick Wilson studied the incidence of the divine names in the Koran (cf. *Princeton Theological Review,* 17 [1919], 644ff.) and showed that in some suras God was spoken of as Allah and in others as Rab, just as YHWH was used in some parts of Genesis and 'Elohim in others. But even though Astruc's criterion can be seen to exist in the Koran, Islamic scholars are united in their denial that the Koran was compiled along the lines suggested by literary criticism for Genesis. Again, it is possible, as K. A. Kitchen has pointed out (*Ancient Orient and OT* [1966], p. 125), to take monumental inscriptions from the Near East that were composed and executed as literary units under the direction of one person and purport to discover underlying documentary sources. Thus a biography of Uni, an Egyptian official who lived *ca.* 2400 B.C., contained flowing narrative of a J or E variety, alternating with summary statements of a P type, a paean of victory (H or hymnal material), and two different refrains (editorial additions?). Although all the elements basic to classical literary-critical speculation are present in this particular inscription, no one questions that it was an integrated compositional unit with no oral or literary pre-history, executed over a short period within the lifetime of the individual who commissioned it, and entirely independent of any underlying documentary sources. Other rock inscriptions of this general kind can be adduced to show the essential falsity of the literary-critical criteria entertained by eighteenth- and nineteenth-century speculation. If the scholars concerned had been conversant with the practices adopted by Near Eastern scribes for perpetuating literary traditions, they might not have resorted to their own a priori criteria.

If the situation is demonstrably false where single names for deity were employed, it is even more so when compound forms such as YHWH-'Elohim occur, as in Gen. 2:4–3:24. Liberal scholars tried to explain away this difficulty by regarding it as a conflation of J and E sources into JE. The precise meaning of JE is far from clear, because it ran completely counter to the theoretical use of the criterion by combining the same divine names that by their independent occurrence were supposed to help identify the documents from which Genesis and other pentateuchal writings were compiled. The discovery that the LXX contained many more examples of compound names for deity than the MT made the situation even more awkward. Because the scholarly speculators were unaware of the nature of literary forms and usages in the ancient Near East, however, they were reduced to all sorts of desperate expedients to sustain a basically erroneous theoretical approach to source-analysis.

More recent studies have shown that in Greek, Ugaritic, Babylonian, and Egyptian literature compound names of deity occur frequently. In the code of Hammurabi one god was known as Nintu and Mama; in the Babylonian Creation Epic, Ea was also described by the name Nudimmud, while at Ugarit Kothar was named Hayyin in some of the texts. In Egypt the most familiar compound name for deity resulted from the fusion of Amon and Re during the 18th Dynasty. Second-millennium B.C. literature has many other examples of this tendency, all of which show how commonplace it was for deities to have compound names. Attempts to delineate underlying documents by employing the occurrence of double names for persons, places, tribes, etc., are equally fallacious. Out of many possible Near Eastern examples it may suffice to point out that Hittite kings sometimes had double names (cf. H. G. Güterbock, *JCS,* 10 [1956], 120-22), while in the Amarna correspondence the Mitanni kingdom was known as Ḫanigalbat and the Mitanni people also described as Hurrians (I. J. Gelb, *Hurrians and Subarians* [1944], pp. 72ff.). For Jacob to be known alternately as Israel, or for Jethro also to be called Reuel, was thus a perfectly normal procedure in the 2nd millennium B.C., and had this been known and acknowledged by nineteenth-century literary critics, some of their criteria would have been shown to be wrong from the start.

So-called duplicate narratives in Genesis (e.g., 1:1–2:4a and 2:4b-25; 15 and 17; 16 and 21; 21:22-34 and 26:12-22; 28:10-22 and 35:15; etc.) were also erroneously accepted as an indication that the same material had survived from two different documentary sources. In the first instances the narratives are never duplicates in the strictest sense of the term, as a glance at the material will show. Thus, the first chapter of Genesis deals with the creation of the cosmos and the appearance of organic life on the earth, while Gen. 2:4b-25 localizes the terrestrial situation and against a specific topographical background treats of the creation of *homo sapiens*. It is quite clear that each passage describes different activities and therefore the real issue is a matter of correct interpretation rather than the presence of alleged underlying documents. Similar considerations should be remembered regarding the supposition that the Joseph narrative contains irreconcilable statements about the sale of Joseph into Egypt (cf. K. A. Kitchen, *Ancient Orient and OT* [1966], p. 119f.). Furthermore, a wider acquaintance with ancient Near Eastern literature on the part of modern scholars now makes it evident that duplication and repetition in a looser sense were actually accepted features of literary style in the 2nd millennium B.C. and later. Babylonian, Ugaritic and Greek literary works all contain such repetitions, while the Koran, a much later composition, is replete with repetitions of the traditional Semitic style. Apparently such forms had pedagogic as well as a literary or artistic value, and occasionally one narrative would appear in both prose and poetic forms, as in Jgs. 4 and 5.

Early literary-critical scholars argued a great deal about such matters as variations in literary style and the incidence of differing theological conceptions. Unfortunately even from the beginning this particular facet of criticism was so subjective in nature that it had little value. All too frequently the alleged changes in style were the result of a difference in subject matter within the same narrative, but because arbitrary characteristics had already been assigned to the various documents, the unity and continuity of particular narratives were shattered in the interests of shoring up entirely hypothetical postulates whose validity has still not been demonstrated. In the light of more recent information about ancient scribal techniques and the way in which information was transmitted at that time, it is now clear that stylistic variations were governed by the character of the personages or events being described, and that in every case they were compatible with the accepted ideas of literary suitability (cf. C. H. Gordon, *Ugaritic Literature* [1949], p. 6).

The foregoing criticisms will have made clear some of the graver weaknesses of the Graf-Wellhausen view of the origins of Genesis. From the very first the theory was ill-founded, being a priori in nature and characterized by a monolinear view of evolution (*see* PENTATEUCH; CRITICISM II). The error of this approach was compounded by a misinformed concept of what was actually scientific, leading to the questionable practice of manipulating the OT text in order to make it conform to the demands of the theory. When genuine literary evidence from the ancient Near East is considered, this theory can be shown to be erroneous and misleading.

D. Form-criticism and the Origin of Genesis. The vast majority of compositions, both ancient and modern, draw upon various kinds of source material, and Genesis is no exception to this principle. In the light of the conspicuous failure of European literary criticism of the Graf-Wellhausen variety to elicit accredited and realistic sources, however, it is clearly necessary to adopt some other approach that will accommodate itself much more readily to relevant, objective evidence. For this purpose the most satisfactory analytical tool available is that of form-criticism, through the exercise of which specific units of the book can be recognized and classified according to their form.

This is no arbitrary or subjective procedure of the Graf-Wellhausen variety, however, for to be valid it must necessarily take account of data relating to ancient life as furnished by Near Eastern archeological discoveries. In this instance the data involve, among other things, the literary form of many clay tablets unearthed at Mesopotamian sites. Those artifacts varied considerably in size and contained a wide range of material, including contracts, invoices, business ledgers, letters, genealogical information, diplomatic correspondence, and epic poetry. Tablets containing communications normally commenced with a title, continued with the text of the document, and concluded with a colophon. The colophon contained all that one would expect to find today on the title page of a book, though the modern use of the term "colophon" is restricted to the publisher's imprint at the foot of the title page. In an ancient colophon the title was sometimes repeated, the scribe or owner of the tablet was often identified, and it was not unusual for a date to be given. Certain tablets were rendered more personal by the imprint of the owner's button- or stamp-seal, as well as by the occasional recording of his family tree on the back of the tablet. If the length of the particular communication required more than one tablet, the proper order of the text was preserved by a system of numbering, as well as by titles and catch lines. The latter involved the repetition of the first word or two of the succeeding tablet at the bottom of its precursor, a practice still followed in the printed Hebrew Bible. If a tablet formed part of a series, the colophon usually furnished a serial number and noted whether that particular tablet concluded the series. The object of all this was intelligibility and ease of reading, and the method can be attested readily from a great many Mesopotamian tablets.

1. Tōlᵉḏôṯ *as Indicative of a Colophon.* All commentators on Genesis, both liberal and conservative, have recognized the recurrence of a distinctive expression, translated in many English versions as "these are the generations of." While some scholars have observed that the phrase was intimately connected with the structure of Genesis, few knew how to proceed further because of their ignorance of the literary form of many Mesopotamian tablets. On the assumption that most of the separate sections in Genesis began with a genealogy, as sometimes occurred in ancient cuneiform texts, scholars supposed that the phrase actually comprised a preface or heading that related to what followed. Thus, for S. R. Driver (*Book of Genesis* [*WC,* 1904], p. ii; *Intro. to the Literature of the OT* [1912], pp. 6f.), it indicated that the principal person mentioned, along with his offspring, would form the basis of consideration in the section following the phrase until some other prominent individual was discussed in the narrative. That this principle of interpretation was faulty in at least one vital respect is shown in the case of Abraham, who though being the most widely described individual in Genesis, was never once mentioned by name in the phrase "these are the generations of." A careful study of the text shows, in contrast, that the preponderance of information given in relation to the person mentioned in the phrase comes before, not after, the expression "these are the generations of." Thus, following the notation about Adam in Gen. 5:1, nothing else is said concerning him except a statement of his age at death. Again, after the mention of Jacob in Gen. 37:2, the only other references to him are of a rather incidental character, with Joseph being the principal person under consideration. Quite clearly, therefore, the phrase "these are the generations of" cannot legitimately constitute a heading for a subsequent section. Thus it is legitimate to ask if this distinctive phrase points to the *conclusion,* rather than to the commencement, of a division in the MT. The word *dôr,* not *tōlᵉḏôṯ,* is the common word for "generation," and it can refer to a past (Isa. 51:9) or future (Ex. 3:15) period. Since the time of Gesenius, lexicographers have given the meaning of "history," "narrative," or "genealogical record" to the word *tōlᵉḏôṯ,* and it seems clear from the special use of the term on ten occasions in Genesis that it describes family history in its origins. If the term is held to be part of a phrase that concludes a section of the narrative material and thus points back to its beginnings, as is obvious in Gen. 2:4, it is possible to isolate eleven passages as comprising genuine literary sources for the book. When these eleven units are examined carefully, they can be seen to exhibit clearly a definite form-critical character which coincides with that demonstrated from a vast number of clay tablets from Mesopotamia. The term "book" in Gen. 5:1 can refer only to such a clay tablet, and in the light of what is now known about ancient Near Eastern practices of writing history, personal and other, it seems clear that this type of tablet record was in the nature of ancient historiography. It might also be noted, following Mesopotamian usage, that the person mentioned in connection with the term *tōlᵉḏôṯ* could have been either the writer of the tablet, the owner, or both. In Gen. 10:1 the allusion to the sons of Noah can be taken to mean that the preceding account of family history was in their actual possession, a practice that can be documented at great length from family archives uncovered at Mari, Nuzi, and other sites in Mesopotamia.

2. Structure of the Eleven Proposed Underlying Tablets. If *tōlᵉḏôṯ* indicates a colophon, it is possible to identify eleven literary units or tablets characterized by this form. The first tablet (Gen. 1:1–2:4), describing the origins of the cosmos, would have as its title "God created the cosmos" (regarding the MT "heavens and the earth" as a *merismus* form for "cosmos," "universe"). This title is repeated in the colophon (2:4), unless that verse is to be divided in half with the latter portion constituting the title of the second tablet. If not, the second proposed tablet (2:5–5:2), dealing with the origins of mankind, would have its own title which was lost either in transmission through tablet damage, as commonly occurred in the ancient Near East, or through editorial deletion. The recording scribe or scribes attempted to convey the antiquity of this material by the phrases "when they were created" (2:4), "when God created man" (5:1), and "when they were created" (5:2). Whereas the colophon of tablet one contained no hint of ownership, that of tablet two (5:2) spoke of this ancient historiography in terms of the Adamite family. Tablet three (5:3–6:9a), containing the Noachian histories, had as its title "when Adam"; it narrated his descent and mentioned Noah in the colophon (6:9a), perhaps as owner of the material. Tablet four, treating the histories of Noah's sons (6:9b–10:1), had as its probable title "Shem, Ham, and Japheth." This tablet ended with the colophon in 10:1, which repeated the title in a manner familiar from other Mesopotamian texts. The reference to the period "after the flood" may perhaps be a scribal attempt at dating the material.

Tablet five (10:2–11:10a) is a rather short source entitled (apparently) "the sons of Japheth"; it dealt with the Table of Nations and the incident in the land of Shinar. The colophon shows that it was in the possession of Shem. Another brief source, tablet six (11:10b–27a), containing the genealogical table of Terah, probably bore the title "Shem," and the mention of Terah's age (11:26) may be a scribal attempt at dating. Tablet seven, consisting of family histories in the possession of Ishmael (11:27b–25:12), dealt in considerable detail with the activities of Abraham. Its title was apparently "Abram, Nahor, and Haran," and the reference to Isaac living at Beer-lahai-roi (25:11) may be an attempt by the scribe to date the material, following a Mesopotamian tradition. This section seems closely linked to the contents of tablet eight, a small document (25:13-19a) originally written by Isaac. The occurrences recorded in these two tablets ended just prior to Isaac's death. He seems to have survived Ishmael by well over fifty years, according to the MT, and presumably gained possession of the family histories when Ishmael died. Tablet nine (25:19b–36:1), apparently entitled "Abraham begat Isaac," dealt in some detail with Esau and Jacob, concluding with the death and burial of Isaac. These narratives were of Edomite origin, as the colophon in 36:1 makes clear. Another rather fragmentary record, also from Edomite sources, comprised tablet ten (36:2-9), which preserved a record of the descendants of Esau. A scribal attempt at dating in the colophon may perhaps be seen in the statement that, at the time, Esau was living in the area of Mt. Seir (36:8). An explanatory gloss, obviously a later scribal addition, equated Esau and Edom. The final postulated source, tablet eleven (36:10–37:2), also seems to have come from an Edomite background, with Gen. 36:31 appearing to comprise a post-Mosaic scribal comment that may have originated in the early monarchy. An attempt at dating by the scribe who compiled this source may be seen in the statement (coming immediately before the colophon) that Jacob was then living in the land of Canaan (37:1). It was not long after this that Jacob migrated to Egypt, but when the narrative closed he was still residing in the area of Hebron.

If these eleven literary units are genuine underlying literary sources for Genesis, as form-critical study would suggest, then it is apparent that they have been edited in such a way as to minimize interference with the texts of the various tablets. As is now known, it was common for Babylonian and Egyptian scribes to insert explanatory glosses, update grammatical and syntactical forms, and replace ancient place names with their more modern counterparts, without impugning the integrity of the original authorship. The tactful nature of the editorial changes in Genesis might well point to the compiler's high degree of veneration for the sources because of their origin and antiquity. An attempt to link certain of the tablets in series, following Mesopotamian tradition, may be seen in 6:9; 11:10; 11:27; 25:19; and 36:1, in which the last word of a suggested tablet is the same as the first word of its successor, excluding the obvious gloss in 36:1. If this was a genuine attempt to preserve continuity and a rough chronological sequence, it would constitute a primitive form of what at a later time came to be the more highly developed catch lines, by which Mesopotamian tablets were linked in series. As a means of emphasizing the ancient historiographic character of the material (over against any mythical or legendary estimate), it should be noted that none of the tablets contains any information that could not have been known to the individuals mentioned in the colophons as scribes or owners of the various sources. Ancient Near Eastern literary traditions furnish ample support for the composition of Genesis on the basis of the foregoing proposed tablets, with the addition of the Joseph narratives, but deny any credibility whatever to a book of origins compiled on the basis of eighteenth- and nineteenth-century literary-critical speculation. It is thus regrettable that eminent orientalists such as E. A. Speiser and T. J. Meek, who were thoroughly conversant with Near Eastern tablet material, were so committed to the traditions of European documentary speculation that either they were unaware of the real nature of the sources in Genesis, or were unwilling to go in the direction indicated by all the evidence. Unfortunately scholarship of this kind has not abandoned the a priori character of the Graf-Wellhausen school.

3. Joseph Narratives. This portion of material (Gen. 37:2b–50:26) completes the book of Genesis. Egyptological research has done much to illumine the cultural background of these narratives (cf. P. Montet, *Egypt and the Bible* [Eng. tr. 1968]; J. Vergote, *Joseph en Égypte* [1959]; K. A. Kitchen, *Tyndale House Bulletin,* 5-6 [1960], 4ff.; etc.), and consequently only a few matters will be noted here. The best indications at present are that Joseph and his brothers were settled in Egypt during the Hyksos period (*ca.* 1715-1570 B.C.), perhaps *ca.* 1700 B.C. The Hyksos were Semites who employed the iron-fitted, horse-drawn chariot and compound Asiatic bow to conquer Egypt and establish their own regime there. Only during a period of foreign conquest would it have been possible for a non-Egyptian such as Joseph to succeed to high office and promote ambitious schemes that included the nationalizing of the land (Gen. 47:13), since under native Egyptian leadership all foreigners would have been excluded from important positions in government. While there were many Semites working as servants in Egyptian households during the Middle Bronze Age (*ca.* 1950-1550 B.C.), as indicated by Albright (*JAOS,* 74 [1954], 222ff.), comparatively few became household stewards, as Joseph did under Potiphar (G. Posener, *Syria,* 34 [1957], 145ff.), or rose to the position of grand vizier of Egypt (Gen. 41:40; 45:8). A mural from the time of Seti I (*ca.* 1308-1290 B.C.) has depicted the way in which the grand vizier was formally invested with his golden collar of office. Only high state officials normally rode in chariots and merited the command to passersby to "stand to attention" (Gen. 41:43; NEB, incorrectly, "Make way!"). The incidence of periodic famines in Egypt was noted by inscriptions on the walls of tombs at Beni-hasan as early as 1980 B.C., and also from a later period at El Kab.

Contrary to earlier assertions, the narrative dealing with the attempted seduction of Joseph by Potiphar's wife (Gen. 39:7-23) contains no other parallels with the *Tale of the Two Brothers* (A. Erman and A. M. Blackman, *Literature of the Ancient Egyptians* [1927], pp. 150ff.) aside from indicating that such an occurrence was not an isolated incident. Pharaoh's command to Joseph's family to leave their possessions behind in Palestine and settle in Egypt (Gen. 45:17, 21; 46:5) was matched by the instructions of an earlier pharaoh to Sinuhe, a fugitive Egyptian living in Syria *ca.* 1900 B.C. Among other evidence, a final touch of veracity is added by the last verse in Genesis (50:26), which spoke of Joseph dying at the age of 110 and being embalmed before being placed in an anthropoid coffin. In ancient Egypt, to credit the deceased with a life span of 110 years was tantamount to saying that he had lived an ideal, productive, and blessed life. Embalming had been practiced from the beginning of the Old Kingdom period (*ca.* 2700 B.C.) as part of a well-developed eschatology and proved to be one of the most characteristic of Egyptian mortuary customs.

4. Authorship and Editorial Activity. Whether the Joseph stories were in written form by Moses' time is uncertain, although if Near Eastern scribal practices were being followed, Joseph's achievements would most probably have been recorded as they occurred. It is quite probable that Moses had a hand in producing the elegant literary form in which they are extant in Hebrew. If it is correct to assume that the first thirty-six chapters of Genesis had originally had an independent existence as cuneiform tablets, it would have been a comparatively easy matter for a talented person such as Moses to compile the canonical book by arranging the tablets in a rough chronological order, adding the material relating to Joseph, and transcribing the entire corpus on a leather or papyrus roll. As opposed to the Graf-Wellhausen contention that writing was unknown during the time of Moses, numerous archeological discoveries have demonstrated that several literary means of communication were available in the Mosaic age. Thus, the Amarna texts show that Babylonian cuneiform was the diplomatic language of the day, while Egyptian hieroglyphic script had been in existence for many centuries. In addition, excavations at Râs Shamrah have recovered tablets containing the native cuneiform language (Ugaritic), to which can be added the syllabic script used at Byblos in Phoenicia and the linear alphabetic form of writing also employed in Canaan during the Late Bronze Age (*ca.* 1550-1200 B.C.). Supplementing these was the "proto-Sinaitic" script (*ca.* 1500 B.C.), in which certain inscriptions recovered from the turquoise mines of Serābîṭ el-Khâdim had been written. A person like Moses, who was by tradition educated in all the wisdom of the Egyptians (Acts 7:22), would thus have had ample means for recording his sources in the language of his choice. Perhaps at this time leather began to be used in preference to papyrus or clay tablets as a more durable material, and this would seem to be implied by the passage in Nu. 5:23f.

Once all this material had been transcribed, it would then have achieved the kind of literary fixity characteristic of Near Eastern annalistic and historiographic sources, and from that time onward would be subject only to the kind of modification current in ancient oriental scribal circles. Extant literature shows that in Babylonia and the Near East generally, apart from Sumer, such modification included the modernizing of archaic grammatical forms, sometimes on a thoroughgoing basis, as well as the updating of ancient names of places and persons by successive generations of scribes, and the insertion of explanatory glosses for the guidance of the reader. All this was done strictly in the interests of intelligibility and contemporaneity. This modest degree of literary freedom was forbidden to Sumerian scribes, however, who for generations reproduced without alteration the texts as they had received them. Modern comparative historiographic studies have made it clear that, along with the Hittites, the Hebrews were the most careful recorders of history in the ancient Near East, and this tradition of scribal scrupulosity would obviously extend to other than purely historiographic material. Yet no evidence indicates that these scribes thought their activities infringed upon or compromised the literary integrity of the original composition, or usurped the place or function of the attributive author. On such a basis of scribal operation one can explain the later additions or anachronisms in Genesis, e.g., the earlier waves of sea-peoples would be known by their later name of Philistines (cf. Gen. 21:34; 26:14).

5. Translation Problems. On the whole, English translations of the first dozen or so chapters of Genesis are so literal that they betray the translators' ignorance of the Mesopotamian background that Genesis so faithfully reflects. Even translators who are versed in Mesopotamian studies are so frequently stultified in their efforts by the dead hand of past literary-critical tradition that their versions prove to be just as inadequate as others'. Even when such influences are not immediately present, other factors combine to furnish a rendering that is less than satisfactory in the light of modern linguistic knowledge. For example, most modern English renderings of Genesis (including the NEB) translate the very first word of the Hebrew Bible incorrectly, giving it the meaning "in the beginning," when there is quite clearly no definite article in the MT. A more accurate rendering would be "by way of beginning," "to start with," a translation that has the merit of removing an absolute temporal beginning from the fact of God's creative activity. Or, as Augustine expressed it (*Conf.* xii), *Non in tempore sed cum tempore deus finxit mundum* ("Not in time but with time God created [lit. shaped] the world"). The same verse contains what seems to be one of the most ancient of literary expressions, the significance of which was not generally known or appreciated until recently. Familiar to modern scholars as *merismus,* it was a means of expressing the totality of a concept through the use of words paired in an antonymic relationship. It originated with the Sumerians, was subsequently adopted by the Egyptians, and became current in the Near East, where in the writings of the Hebrews it occurred in phrases such as "evening and morning," "young and old," "from the greatest to the least," to express different kinds of totality. The Sumerian phrase *an-ki* ("heaven-earth") meant "cosmos," and therefore its counterpart in Gen. 1:1; 2:1, 4 should also be translated in that manner, and not in the literal sense of all English versions. Translators are slowly becoming aware of the fact that the AV "spirit of God" in Gen. 1:2 should actually be rendered "an awesome gale," using *'ĕlōhîm* as an adjective, following the pattern of 1 S. 14:15; Jonah 3:3; etc. The "evening-morning" *merismus* of Gen. 1:8 should be more accurately rendered "this was the second complete phase of the entire cycle" in order to capture the meaning as understood by the original author. This procedure should obviously be adopted *pari passu* throughout the chapter in the relevant verses.

In Gen. 2:6 the term "mist" (NEB; RSV mg. "flood") is an erroneous translation for "river," "canal," which when rectified points to the irrigation culture characteristic of early Near Eastern civilizations. The four-branched "river" in Eden clearly consisted of two rivers that would be recognized as such at the present day, i.e., the Tigris and Euphrates, and two major irrigation canals, Pishon and Gihon, which have long since disappeared from the area. That Babylonian had no separate words for "irrigation canal" and "river" accounts for the confusion in modern translations, which, of course, would not be present in the mind of the original author. On such a basis of interpretation it is obviously unnecessary to consider countries such as India and Ethiopia as possible locations of Pishon and Gihon.

Again, the time-honored translation of *ṣelāʿ* as "rib" in Gen. 2:21 is as arbitrary as it is incorrect, for the context makes it clear that the term describes part of the essence of the original man's totality, not just an organ or a portion of bony tissue. When viewed in this context, the ancient comment in Gen. 2:24 has much to say about the manner in which a compatible monogamous union reflects the primal integration of human personality. Gen. 6:16, which deals with the construction of the ark, is another difficult passage for the translators, and not least where the word *ṣōhar* is involved. Both the RSV and NEB render it "roof," with the former reading "window" in the margin. The NEB translation suggests a roof having a pitch of one cubit, but this would make the ark an entirely closed box without any light inside. Since it had to have three decks, it would obviously have a roof in any event, so that probably the best way to render *ṣōhar* would be to commence the verse: "You shall make a peripheral window for the ark, and you shall take it to within a cubit of the top. . . ."

Other points of interest to translators include a rare grammatical expression in 40:10, which should be translated, ". . . just as it was on the point of budding, its blossoms shot up . . . ," instead of the RSV, NEB rendering, ". . . as soon as it budded. . . ." The command given by the Egyptian outriders in Gen. 41:43, translated "Bow the knee" by the RSV and "Make way!" in the NEB, seems to have been a characteristic Egyptian order meaning literally, "Heart to thee!" and more properly rendered by "Stand to attention!" or some similar expression. In the blessing of Jacob (Gen. 49), verse 14 should begin, "Issachar is an alien donkey-herder camping between the sheepfolds . . . ," a rendering which involves a slight alteration in one word of the MT. These and numerous other instances show that advances still have to be made before it is possible for modern readers to appreciate the significance of the text as the original authors envisaged it.

III. Archeology.–A. *Genesis and Sumerian Historiography.* The Sumerians were evidently the first Near Eastern people to write as well as make history. They had a dynamic appreciation for life and kept records of all manner of happenings in both the past and present. Some of these sources have survived in the form of king lists, official inscriptions commemorating the building of palaces and temples, court annals, chronicles, epic compositions (often based on historical personages and events, which had subsequently become overlaid with legend and myth), and a number of other nonliterary sources. Like most of the ancient Near Eastern peoples, the Sumerians were profoundly superstitious, and their great sense of inferiority virtually demanded that the course of events in the cosmos should be governed by decisions that came from superhuman beings. This feature was a prominent element in their myths and legends and indicated that, for them, history was primarily theocratic. The deities venerated by the Sumerians were originally the forces of nature as experienced personally; thus the metaphysical force that activated history had a distinctively elemental character to it and partook of reality in this special manner. The Sumerians began the Mesopotamian tradition of writing history against a cosmic background, presenting in their narratives what can best be described as a world view. In their cosmological material they represented themselves as one member-group of the human race that inhabited one of the four regions into which they had divided the world. The Sumerians had had a "golden age" in their history, when "there was no fear, no terror. Man had no rival" (S. N. Kramer, *The Sumerians* [1970], p. 262). But because the gods had planned unethical, immoral, and criminal behavior as part of human conduct, this state of bliss was short-lived. One Sumerian composition even spoke of the creation of woman against the background of the paradiselike land of Dilmun, located E of Sumer. In the story, a goddess healed one of the god

Akkadian (originally Sumerian) account of the gods Marduk and Aruru creating the world. Babylonian cuneiform tablet (6th cent. B.C.) from Sippar (Trustees of the British Museum)

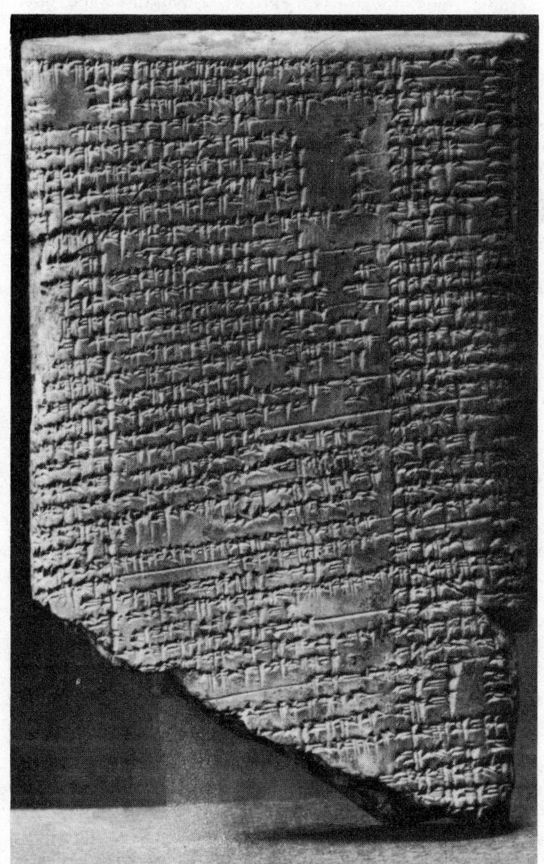

Enki's diseased organs, which proved to be a rib. Consequently the goddess came to be known as "the lady of the rib," or, as an alternative translation, "the lady who makes live." While this narrative clearly has little in common with that in Gen. 2, it makes the latter much more intelligible if envisaged against a Sumerian literary background rather than one involving the second temple and a postexilic date, as nineteenth-century literary criticism would have had its adherents imagine.

When the gods of Sumer, angered by human clamor, planned to engulf them by means of a devastating flood, they brought about a deluge that in effect destroyed the Sumerian world. This cataclysmic event was perpetuated in subsequent Babylonian tradition, even though its scope was confined to southern Mesopotamia. Again, it is hardly surprising that the biblical account of a similar deluge described an occurrence of "world" proportions, particularly if that narrative, too, came from a Mesopotamia cultural milieu. Once this is understood it will be apparent that the Noachian flood involved the Mesopotamian world only, and not the entire earth.

Extant compositions indicate that the Sumerians were far more interested in composing religious epics and mythological texts than they were in historiography. Despite this they devised dating schemes for their historical records, and this procedure involved the naming of the years in relation to important political and religious events. Even more precisely, the Sumerians scribes began to list all the year names in a given regnal period, or in a succession of such reigns. The compilers of the celebrated king list (cf. S. N. Kramer, *The Sumerians*, pp. 328-331) apparently used this system of date formulas, containing as it did a record of the majority of the Sumerian rulers with the computed length of their reigns. While the material presents certain problems for the historian, it is of interest for Genesis because of the large numbers credited to the regnal years of many rulers in the earlier dynasties. Some scholars have accused both the ancient Sumerian scribes and their Genesis counterparts of mixing fact with fancy in exaggerating the longevity of specific individuals. It would appear, however, that a common numerical tradition underlies both types of material, and therefore it is important for modern scholars to try to discover the basis upon which the computations were made. It is possible that a precursor of the traditional Chinese method of reckoning ages was used, or alternatively, that the numbers were pictorial in character and described the relative importance of the individual to the authors. As far as Genesis is concerned, the reference to Joseph (50:26) falls into this latter category, as observed above, although this, of course, is Egyptian, not Mesopotamian, in provenance (cf. J. W. Wenham, *Tyndale House Bulletin*, n. 18 [1967], 2-36). Because the literary and other problems presented by the first six proposed tablets underlying Genesis, i.e., 1:1–11:27, have so much in common with some that occur in Sumerian and other Near Eastern writings, it seems only legitimate and appropriate to evaluate them against what is now known of life and culture in that early phase of human history.

See also SUMER; SUMERIANS.

B. Genesis and Near Eastern Archeology. To what extent the earliest chapters of Genesis can be related to specific phases of Sumerian history is uncertain. It seems clear, however, that the background of Gen. 2–3 is in harmony with the river- and irrigation-culture that the Sumerians apparently originated and certainly developed. One of the most significant archeological discoveries concerning early biblical traditions occurred in 1966, when some Russian excavators working at the foot of Mt. Ararat

The main source of the Sumerian king list, which records most of the Sumerian monarchs and the length of their reigns from the beginning of the empire until the fall of Isin (*ca.* 1800 B.C.). The text also mentions a flood "that swept over (the land)" early in Sumerian history (Ashmolean Museum, Oxford)

unearthed what they claimed to be the oldest known astronomical observatory and iron smeltery in the Near East. An estimated two hundred smelting furnaces employing a surprisingly sophisticated technique for producing alloys of copper with tin, iron, zinc, and arsenic were uncovered. Other smelters were designed in order to produce a variety of glasses, metallic paints, and ceramic ware. The site, located near the joint boundaries of Iran, Turkey, and the U.S.S.R., seems to accord very well with the activities of the sons of Lamech (Gen. 4:22), and shows the amazingly advanced civilization in that area toward the close of the Chalcolithic Age (4000-3200 B.C.). The technology associated with the smelting of iron was apparently rediscovered by the Hittites at an early period in the Middle Bronze Age (*ca.* 1950-1550 B.C.) and manufactured iron tools have been recovered from Early Dynastic III levels (*ca.* 2600 B.C.) at some Sumerian sites (cf. *CAH* [3rd ed.], I/2). By the Early Iron Age ore smelting was being promoted by the Philistines at various Canaanite sites. The discoveries at the foot of Mt. Ararat, however, throw interesting light on the Genesis tradition relating to the origin of metallurgical activity.

The Noachian Deluge, described in Genesis by the rare word *mabbûl* (cf. Ps. 29:10), was evidently a flood of stupendous proportions (cf. Gk. *kataklysmós* in Mt. 24:38f.; Lk. 17:27; 2 Pet. 2:5). On the assumption that the biblical Flood might have left identifiable traces behind, attempts have been made to associate one or more of the alluvial layers discovered in Mesopotamia with that catastrophic event. From time immemorial that part of the world has been subjected to sudden inundations, and the tradition of a vast flood established itself in Sumerian literature during the early dynastic period. Some texts even located the main inundation at Shuruppak, and a fragmentary Sumerian tablet from the 3rd millennium B.C. described the event in six columns of text. A later poem from Babylonia, the celebrated Gilgamesh Epic, leaned considerably upon Sumerian tradition in furnishing a Babylonian account of a devastating flood at Shuruppak from which a godly man was preserved by means of an ark. When late Jemdet Nasr levels at Shuruppak were explored, a large deposit of alluvial clay was revealed. At Kish, an analogous stratum discovered by Langdon measured 46 cm. (18 in.) in depth, while at Ur, Woolley found a 2.5-m. (8-ft.) alluvial layer dating from the middle Ubaid period. Both Langdon and Woolley claimed their discoveries as the material remains of the biblical Flood, but problems arose when the two layers were found to have originated at different periods in the chronology. Nor do similar levels at Uruk and Lagash correspond with the suggested dating of the Ur stratum. At Kish, Watelin uncovered a number of alluvial levels, two of the larger ones being separated by a 6-m. (19-ft.) section of debris, while at Tell el-Ubaid, 6 km. (4 mi.) from Ur, there were no indications of water-laid clay when Woolley excavated the site. Since it is in the nature of alluvial deposits to be virtually free from any form of positive identification, attempts at dating have to be related to associated levels. When several water-laid deposits are at a given site, separated by numerous layers of debris, the problem of deciding which one of them, if any, represents the biblical Deluge becomes correspondingly difficult. Indeed, not a few scholars have maintained that positive identification of the Noachian Flood level is not only improbable but virtually impossible in the present state of the evidence, whether the Deluge was local or not. Despite this pessimism, however, it is not too much to hope that further discoveries will help to resolve at least some of the more pressing difficulties in this area.

Since 1856, more than two hundred persons have claimed to have seen some sort of structure on Mt. Ararat resembling an ancient vessel. This has been taken as an indication that the remains of the celebrated ark built by Noah to escape destruction during the Flood have somehow been preserved under the ice covering the mountain. It is possible to identify the mountains of Ararat (Gen. 8:4), the traditional resting place of the ark, with the *Urarṭu* of Assyrian records and modern Armenia. Ararat was a country in the general district of Armenia, with Lake Van as its geographical center. The particular object claimed by many as constituting the remains of Noah's ark is located at the 4300-m. (14,000-ft.) level of Mt. Ararat, and for some time has been the focus of antiquarian and archeological interest (cf. Violet Cummings, *Noah's Ark: Fact or Fable?* [1972]; J. Warwick Montgomery, *Quest for Noah's Ark* [1972]). Explorers have recovered pieces of hand-tooled lumber from the area, some of which have been estimated to be between four and five thousand years old, though others have been dated at only *ca.* 1500 years, using carbon-14 calculation.

While it seems clear that some sort of ancient structure is involved, a number of difficulties remain for the claim that it is in fact a vessel and the one used by Noah and his family. In the 1960's and 1970's topographical and political difficulties have conspired to hinder the excavation of the artifact, whatever it might be, and even if these are resolved it will not be possible to identify the structure with certainty as Noah's ark unless it is in fact a vessel, and if other associated artifacts (such as tablets demonstrating ownership) are also present at the site. If the material is excavated and found to have come from some sort of medieval shrine on the mountain, as some have imagined might be the case, there would seem to be little point in searching for any other ark in the location. The same would apply if the ancient timber were proved to have been part of an ark reconstructed for purposes of Christian piety either before or after the Crusades. In either of these two cases, however, definite proof concerning the nature of the artifact would need to be furnished. Were an ancient vessel to be found, it would be by no means impossible for inscribed tablets demonstrating ownership to be recovered from the site, too, since materials of the later variety have been recovered in quantity from third-millennium B.C. sites in Mesopotamia.

See also FLOOD (GENESIS).

The excavations of Woolley at Ur of the Chaldees have provided a rich background of information regarding the history of that city. The Sumerian king list has claimed that Mes-Anne-pada was the founder of the 1st Dynasty, and this was confirmed dramatically when a tablet was found at Tell el-Ubaid. Dated *ca.* 2700 B.C. it read as follows: "A-Anni-pad-da King of Ur, son of Mes-Anni-pad-da King of Ur, has built this for his Lady Nin-kharsag" (C. L. Woolley, *Ur of the Chaldees* [1950], p. 73). The artifacts unearthed showed graphically the advanced nature of the culture of Ur during the 1st Dynasty. Temples and other structures revealed the presence of elaborate mosaic work and elegantly decorated columns, while a number of copper bulls were recovered in fragmentary condition. From the lower levels of a burial area outside the walls of the early city came the celebrated "royal tombs" of Ur. Though some have suggested that these burial places contained the bodies of priestly persons sacrificed in fertility rites rather than the remains of royalty (cf. S. Smith, *Journal of the Royal Asiatic Society* [1928], pp. 862f.; E. A. Speiser, *Antiquity*, VII [1934], 451; H. Frankfort, *Kingship and the Gods* [1948], p. 400 n.12), they were clearly the tombs of important individuals in the state, if only because they were constructed principally from limestone blocks that would have to be imported from a considerable distance. Artifacts recovered from the site included a lapis lazuli cylinder, objects and vessels of gold, silver, and semi-precious stones, jewelry, weapons, and some funerary objects. Among the latter were one or two exquisitely inlaid harps and two statues of goats standing erect before a bush (C. L. Woolley, *Ur of the Chaldees*, plates 5[a], 6).

The high standard of workmanship at this time is adequately illustrated by the superb golden helmet recovered from the grave of "Mes-kalam-dug, hero of the Good Land." It had been hammered into the form of a wig from a sheet of solid gold, and on the surface were locks of hair in relief, with the individual hairs engraved in delicate symmetrical lines. From the same site came the so-called Standard of Ur, a wooden panel 56 cm. (22 in.) long and 23 cm. (9 in.) wide, with triangular end pieces. When restored, one side of the panel depicted the theme of war, with soldiers and military equipment fashioned skillfully from shell and set into a lapis lazuli background. On the other side, the panel expressed the activities of peace in terms of a lavish regal feast at which musicians performed in the presence of the king and his guests. In conformity with the Sumerian literary device of *merismus*, in which opposite concepts were paired to describe the totality of a given situation, the mosaic panel would thus symbolize all life activities at Ur.

A significant renewal of culture occurred during the magnificent 3rd Dynasty (*ca.* 2070-1960 B.C.), whose first ruler was Ur-Nammu. This pious and energetic king erected a massive ziggurat or staged temple some 21 m. (70 ft.) high. It was unique in having no straight lines in its structure, but instead employed curves and slopes to convey the effect of lightness and strength. One of the workshops associated with this temple produced a dozen varieties of woolen cloth. Several tablets recovered from the ruins contained the names of the weavers, their rations of food, and an inventory of supplies and finished products (*LAP*, p. 44). Abraham apparently was born at Ur during this period, as can be deduced from archeological discoveries in the area of Bâb edh-Dhrâʿ, SE of El Lisan, located E of the Dead Sea. This site, apparently a place of festival and pilgrimage between *ca.* 2300 and 1900 B.C., was no longer patronized after Sodom, Gomorrah, and the other cities of the plain were destroyed *ca.* 1900 B.C. Since Abraham was in Palestine at that period (Gen. 19), his birth would seem to have occurred at the end of the 20th cent. B.C. *See also* ARCHEOLOGY OF MESOPOTAMIA III.G.

Excavations at Mari, Nuzi, and Alalakh have enriched our understanding of many aspects of the patriarchal narratives, which can now be placed confidently against a background of Middle Bronze Age culture. To mention just a few examples, the names of Abraham, Isaac, Jacob, Laban, and Joseph were in common use during the 2nd millennium B.C., while in the Balîkh valley S of Haran the names of some patriarchs were perpetuated in the designation of such sites as Serug, Peleg, and Terah (*FSAC*, pp. 236f.). From the Horite city of Nuzi (Yorgan Tepe) came some twenty thousand tablets, dated mostly in the 15th cent. B.C., that dealt among other things with the practice of adoption. Very often, it seems, this procedure was used as a device to mask the transfer of land, which was divine property and could not legally be bought or sold. The adopted person was expected to bring a filial gift amounting to the value of the property involved, and came into possession of it when the adopting parents died. Genuine adoptions by childless couples were also common, and even slaves could be adopted for this purpose. Possession of the terra-cotta household gods or teraphim was an indication of the rights of inheritance, but if they were originally the property of an adopted son, they were forfeited when a natural son was born to the adopting couple.

The birthright or right of primogeniture could be negotiated under Nuzi law, and this is paralleled by the transaction occurring between Esau and Jacob (Gen. 25:31-34). Birthrights do not seem to have been transferred to people other than members of the same family, since they were after all the property of specific family units. Quite frequently Mesopotamian marriage contracts obliged a sterile or infertile wife to give her handmaid to her husband as a concubine in order to preserve the family line (C. H. Gordon, *BA*, 3 [1940], 3), a fact which clarifies the situation relating to Abraham and Sarah (Gen. 16:2). An important provision of Nuzi law made it mandatory for the offspring of a concubine to remain in the family, and attempts to expel the mother and child were regarded in a very serious light (cf. Gen. 21:11). Mesopotamian adoption traditions seem to throw light on the relations between Jacob and Laban, the latter apparently having no male heir when he adopted Jacob. As was customary, Laban gave his daughters to his heir as wives after a suitable period of service had been completed, and the agreement included a provision to the effect that Jacob would forfeit his inheritance rights if he married any other women. From the way in which Laban behaved as a patriarch it would seem that Jacob was regarded in every sense as an adopted son, so that his wives were still Laban's property and thus not free to leave Laban's household. Rachel's flight may have been prompted by the birth of Laban's natural sons, who would have taken over Jacob's rights of primogeniture. Her theft of the household gods (Gen. 31:19) was evidently meant to secure her husband's privileges in this regard. At Nuzi, impending death furnished an opportunity for the bestowing of patriarchal blessings on members of the family (cf. Gen. 27:27-29; 49:3-27). Such pronouncements were in the nature of a last will and testament on the part of the dying person, and were regarded as legally binding on all those involved (cf. Gen. 27:33). In one Nuzi text a dying father willed a certain young woman in marriage to his bachelor son, and subsequently a court ruling upheld the latter's right to proceed with the marriage.

Archeological discoveries have now shown clearly that references to domesticated camels in Genesis are by no means anachronistic, as some earlier scholars supposed. While camel caravans seem to have been used regularly only from the Late Bronze Age onward, archeologists have found numerous bones of domesticated camels. Thus when Parrot was excavating Mari, he found camel bones in the ruins of a house dated in the pre-Sargonic period (*ca.* 2400 B.C.). An eighteenth-century-B.C. relief from Byblos pictured a camel in a kneeling position, and a socket on the back showed that the animal's hump and its load had been attached separately. In accord with patriarchal traditions, cylinder seals from Middle Bronze Age Mesopotamia showed riders seated upon camels. Excavations on the island of Bahrain (cf. G. Bibby, *Looking for Dilmun* [1970], pp. 303ff.) have revealed the existence of camel bones that may go as far back as the 4th millennium B.C., while other evidence for the early domestication of the camel has been recovered from the Indus valley (cf. J. Marshall, *Mohenjo-daro and the Indus Civilization* [1931], I, 28; II, 660), and in southeast Persia (cf. S. Piggott, *Ancient India* [1948], p. 36).

At Alalakh, texts were found at Levels VII (*ca.* 1900-1780 B.C.) and Level IV (15th cent. B.C.) that proved to be even closer topographically and chronologically to the patriarchal period than most of those coming from Assyrian sites. Among the social customs at Alalakh that bore on patriarchal traditions were those wherein the father had the privilege of disregarding the rights of primogeniture and choosing an heir from among his sons. In the light of this practice it is possible to see new significance in the events relating to Manasseh and Ephraim (Gen. 48:13-20), the repudiation of Reuben (49:3f.), and the status accorded to Joseph (48:22). Other traditions of Alalakh society illumine some Hebrew practices in the Late Bronze Age and Early Iron Age. Discoveries at Boghazköy in Turkey, the site of the ancient Hittite capital of Hattusas, have thrown light upon the transaction that resulted in Abraham's acquiring the cave of Machpelah. One who purchased a complete unit of property was required, under contemporary Hittite law, to render certain feudal services of a still uncertain nature to the vendor. If only a portion of the property was sold, however, such duties were no longer mandatory for the purchaser. With the latter situation doubtless in mind, Abraham wished to purchase only a part of the entire holding (Gen. 23:9), but Ephron was unwilling, thus compelling Abraham to become legally feudatory. The sale was ratified in public, according to local custom, and the price was paid in weighed amounts of silver. The mention of trees in the transaction (Gen. 23:17) reflected the Hittite practice of listing the precise number of trees growing on every piece of property sold.

Some indication of what the Hebrew patriarchs must have looked like has been afforded by a tableau in relief from a tomb at Beni-hasan in Egypt (*ca.* 1900 B.C.) (*ANEP,* no. 3). It depicts a group of Semitic seminomads on their way to an Egyptian city, dressed in multicolored clothing and carrying their wares on donkeys. While the men wore short skirts and sandals, the women were attired in long dresses, fastened at the shoulder with a clasp, and shoes. This kind of clothing may well have appeared rustic to the fastidious Egyptian townspeople, but it was by no means primitive, and was practical in nature.

The Egyptian background of the JOSEPH narratives (*see* EGYPT) has been well attested by archeological discoveries, as has been noted earlier. The rise to power of a Semite like Joseph is best associated with the period of the Semitic-Asiatic Hyksos rulers, and the location of their capital, Avaris, accords well with conditions occurring at the end of Genesis and the beginning of Exodus. The phrase "overseer of his house" (Gen. 39:4) is a direct rendering of a title used of officers in Egyptian noble houses, while Egyptian inscriptions contain the familiar designations "chief of the butlers" and "chief of the bakers" (Gen. 40:2). These titles appear to be very ancient, and it is probable that by Joseph's time the original functions of the office had changed drastically while the archaic title still survived. The royal birthday celebrations in Egypt normally included the pardoning of prisoners (Gen. 40:20), while the place given to magic, the general attitude adopted toward Asiatic seminomads (Gen. 46:34; cf. 43:32), the 110 years of Joseph as a symbol of a fruitful, creative, and blessed life, along with the embalming of Jacob and Joseph, are all readily attestable indications of genuine background of Egyptian culture for the Joseph narratives.

See pictures of Genesis Apocryphon in DEAD SEA SCROLLS.

***Bibliography.**–Comms.*: F. C. Cook, *Speaker's Commentary* (1877); F. Delitzsch (1887); M. Dods (*Expos.B.*, 1888); A. Dillmann (*Kurzer Hand-Commentar zum AT,* 1892 ed.); H. L. Strack (*Kurzgefasster Kommentar zu den heiligen Schriften,* 1905 ed.); W. H. Griffith Thomas (1907); H. Gunkel (*Handkommentar zum AT,* 1910); O. Procksch (*KAT,* 1924 ed.); J. H. Hertz (*Soncino Comm.*, 1929); P. Heinisch, *Das Buch Genesis* (1930); J. Skinner (*ICC,* 1930); W. H. Bennett (*Century Bible,* n.d.); S. R. Driver (*WC,* 1948); J. Chaine, *Le Livre de la Genèse* (1948); R. de Vaux (*La Sainte Bible,* 1951); A. Clamer, *La Genèse* (1953); C. A. Simpson and W. R. Bowie (*IB,* 1952); B. Vawter, *Path Through Genesis* (1956); E. A. Speiser (*AB,* 1964); D. Kidner (*Tyndale OT Comms.*, 1967); G. von Rad (*OTL,* rev. ed. 1972); B. Vawter, *On Genesis* (1977).

Modern Intros.: E. J. Young (1949); *PIOT*; A. Weiser (1961 ed.); G. L. Archer (1964); O. Eissfeldt (Eng. tr. 1965); E. Sellin and G. Fohrer (Eng. tr. 1968); R. K. Harrison (1969).

General Studies: W. H. Green, *Unity of the Book of Genesis* (1897); H. Gunkel, *Legends of Genesis* (1964); E. Meyer, *Die Israeliten und ihre Nachbarstämme* (1906); A. R. Gordon, *Early Traditions of Genesis* (1907); B. D. Eerdmans, *Die Komposition der Genesis* (1908); J. Orr, *Problem of the OT* (1909); H. Gunkel, *Zeitschrift des deutschen morgenländishen Gesellschaft,* 76 (1922); P. Dhorme, *RB,* 37 (1928), 67-85, 481-511; 40 (1931), 364-374, 503-518; A. Alt, *Der Gott der Väter* (1929); F. M. Th. Böhl, *Das Zeitalter Abrahams* (1930); U. Cassuto, *La Questione della Genesi* (1934); C. A. Simpson, *Early Traditions of Genesis* (1944); J. S. Wright, *How Moses Compiled Genesis* (1946); R. de Vaux, *RB,* 53 (1946), 321-348; 55 (1948), 321-347; 56 (1949), 5-36; A. Heidel, *Babylonian Genesis* (1951); *KS,* I (1953); G. von Rad, "Josephgeschichte und ältere Chokma," in *SVT,* 1 (1953), 120-27; *Die Josephgeschichte* (1956); D. J. Wiseman, *Alalakh Tablets* (1953);

G. Castellino, "Les Origines de la civilisation selon les textes bibliques et les textes cunéiformes," in *SVT,* 4 (1957), 116-137; J. Vergote, *Joseph en Égypte* (1959); K. A. Kitchen, *Tyndale House Bulletin,* 5-6 (1960), 4-18; D. F. Payne, *Genesis One Reconsidered* (1964).

R. K. HARRISON

GENEVA BIBLE. *See* ENGLISH VERSIONS IV.A.

GENNAEUS gə-nē'əs [Gk. *Gennaios*] (2 Macc. 12:2); AV GENNEUS. Father of APOLLONIUS, one of the Syrian generals who troubled the Jews while Lysias was governor for Antiochus Eupator. The description is added to distinguish the Apollonius here mentioned from several others of the same name.

GENNESARET gə-nes'ə-ret, **LAKE OF.** *See* GALILEE, SEA OF.

GENNESARET gə-nes'ə-ret, **LAND OF** [Gk. *Gennēsaret*]; AV Apoc. GENNESAR. The fertile plain on the northwest bank of the Sea of Galilee, which in Jesus' time enjoyed a reputation of fabulous fertility and was heavily populated. The name, which occurs twice in the Gospels (Mt. 14:34 par. Mk. 6:53), is a lengthened form of Gennesar (cf. AV 1 Macc. 11:67, Gk. *Gennēsar*; Josephus *BJ* iii.10.7f. [506, 516]). Some scholars, following the Targums, identify the name with Chinnereth of the OT (Nu. 34:11; Dt. 3:17; Josh. 11:2; 12:3; 13:27; 19:35; 1 K. 15:20), while others treat it as a compound of Heb. *gan* (garden) with a proper name, or even Heb. *gan ha-śar,* "garden of the prince." The modern designation is el-Ghuweir, "the little valley."

Gennesaret is a coastal plain about 5 km. (3 mi.) long and 1.5 km. (1 mi.) wide, extending from Magdala to just S of Capernaum. Sheltered from the wind by mountains

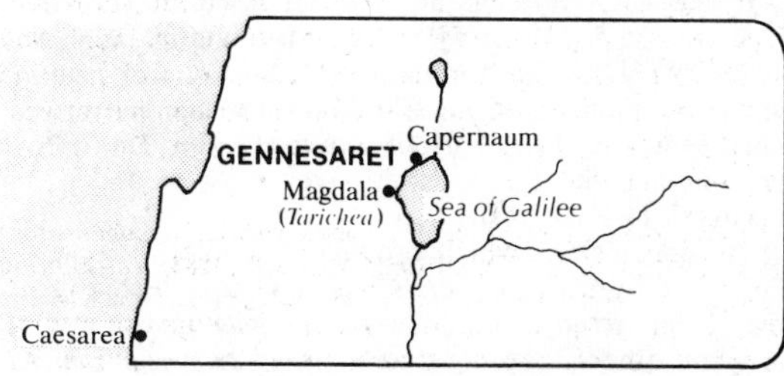

and lying 210 m. (682 ft.) below sea level, it consists of well-watered alluvial soil and enjoys a subtropical climate. (*See* Plate 15.) Josephus (*BJ* iii.10 [516]) described it as an area in which "there is not a plant which its fertile soil refuses to produce," with a climate "so well-tempered that it suits the most opposite varieties." The vigorous agricultural activity by the present Israeli state has brought to the plain once again the verdant qualities it had in the NT period. In addition to the walnuts, figs, olives, and grapes mentioned by Josephus, modern irrigation methods have brought forth products such as citrus fruits, bananas, peppers, and tomatoes.

The plain of Gennesaret was an integral part of the commercial complex that characterized the northwest side of the lake in Jesus' day. Not only was it a rich agricultural center, but the area also played an active role in the great fishing industry. Magdala (Tarichea), the chief city on the plain, had a population of forty thousand and a fishing fleet of 230 boats (Josephus *BJ* ii.21.4,8 [608, 635]). Capernaum, at the north end of the plain, was an important military post and toll station on the great caravan route from Damascus to the seaport of Caesarea. This road, the *Via Maris,* traversed Gennesaret.

View southwest from the hill above Capernaum across the plain of Gennesaret. At left is the Sea of Galilee (D. Baly)

The district with its dense population afforded Jesus a fruitful area for ministry, while its fishing and agriculture provided the setting for many of His parables. Because the region to the south was gentile, Jesus limited His Galilean activity largely to the plain of Gennesaret and the northern half of the lake.

W. W. BUEHLER

GENTILE [Heb. *gôy,* pl. *gôyim*; Sabean, Phoen., *gw–* '(the whole) community' (cf. G. A. Cooke, *Textbook of North-Semitic Inscriptions* [1903], no. 33); Gk. *éthnos, Hellēn*]. Non-Jewish (non-Hebrew, non-Israelite) person(s) or peoples. The Heb. *gôy* is rendered "Gentiles" in the AV in some thirty passages, but much more frequently "heathen," and still more often "nation," which is the usual rendering in later versions; but it is commonly used for a non-Israelite people, and thus corresponds to the meaning of "Gentiles." It also occurs, however, in passages referring to the Israelites, as in Gen. 12:2; Dt. 32:28; Josh. 3:17; 4:1; 10:13; 2 S. 7:23; Isa. 1:4; Zeph. 2:9; but Heb. *ʿam* is the term commonly used for the people of God, and in some of the texts quoted Heb. *gôy* is used for Israel as a rebuke or in a slighting way. The relation between the two words may be seen in Zec. 2:11 (MT 15). In the NT Gk. *éthnos* is the word corresponding to *gôy* (usually rendered "Gentiles" by the English versions), while Gk. *laós* is the word corresponding to *ʿam.* The AV also renders Gk. *Hellēnes* "Gentiles" in six passages, but the RV renders "Greeks" throughout. In Gen. 14:1, 9; Josh. 12:23; Jgs. 4:2, 13, 16 *gôyim* is a proper name (cf. Isa. 9:1 [MT 8:23], where *gôyim* is translated "nations," but may be a proper name).

Antagonism against the Gentiles was present far more in NT times than in OT times. The book of Genesis reports no barrier between the patriarchs and their Canaanite surroundings. Though Isaac and Jacob avoided marrying Canaanite wives, Jacob's sons as far as we know married the daughters of Canaanites (or in Joseph's case, of Egyptians). It is true that the conquest of Canaan saw some instances of complete massacres of the indigenous population, but this was not the case in Gibeon and the neighboring towns, nor in those towns that remained Canaanite until the time of the first kings (Jgs. 1:27-36). What happened in Jerusalem probably was typical: after the conquest by David the non-Israelite Araunah lived there in full possession of his ancestral domain (2 S. 24:16-24). Notwithstanding injunctions like Ex. 34:15f., we may assume that in the course of the centuries intermarriage took place frequently. In any case no one objected to marrying women conquered in war (Dt. 21:10-14) or from neighboring nations; cf. Boaz's marriage to Ruth and several of David's marriages. Solomon's defection, however, is traced to the influence of his foreign wives (1 K. 11:1-4), and even more dangerous was the influence of gentile women like Jezebel and Athaliah.

A systematic opposition to marriages with non-Jewish women appears only after the Exile (cf. Ezr. 9f.; Neh. 13:23-30; and figuratively Mal. 2:11-16). This did not mean, however, that foreign-born people were excluded from Israel. There were many living as protected *gērîm* ("strangers") in Israel (one should not, however, assume that every *gēr* was a non-Israelite; cf. Jgs. 19:1). In any case a *gēr* was supposed to conform to the Hebrew way of life (cf. Ex. 12:43-49). It was otherwise with the *nokrî,* the foreigner living (mainly as a trader) in Israel without conforming to the religious laws. Prov. 2:16-19; 5:3-23; 6:24-35; 7:1-27 warn against such foreign women (RSV "adventuress"; for this sense cf. W. McKane, *Proverbs* [*OTL,* 1970], pp. 285f., and D. Kidner, *Proverbs* [1964], p. 62). Gentiles were allowed to visit the outer precinct of the temple, up to the low wall; inscriptions in Greek warned them to go no further if they did not want to be the cause of their own death. The costs of sacrifices could be borne by strangers, even if they remained pagans (Josephus *BJ* ii.17.2-4; *Ant.* xi.8.5; etc.); and for the pagan Persian kings and their Greek and Roman successors sacrifices and prayers were offered (Ezr. 6:10; 1 Macc. 7:33; etc.).

Even in NT times pious Jewish women married gentile husbands; cf. Acts 16:1. The general tendency, however, was one of increasing hostility toward Gentiles. They and their countries were considered unclean (Am. 7:17) even before the Exile, and the harsh treatment meted out to the Jews by Antiochus IV and later by tactless Roman administrators strengthened this tendency, which finally led to the terrible rebellion of A.D. 66-70.

Some elements in the oldest Christian community shared the common Jewish aversion to Gentiles. Peter was the first to break through the barrier (Acts 10f.), though at a later moment he wavered again (Gal. 2:11-14). It was Paul who drew the full consequences from the gospel of salvation by grace and not by the works of the law; he even suffered for the Gentiles (Acts 21). The mother church in Jerusalem accepted a compromise, requiring gentile Christians to abstain at least from some of the most offending pagan customs (Acts 15:23-29). One part of the Church in Palestine maintained a rather exclusive attitude against the Gentiles, namely, the Ebionites, who at the end of the 2nd cent. were considered a sect by the Church as a whole and gradually disappeared during the next century.

See NATIONS.

Bibliography.–*TDNT,* II, *s.v.* ἔθνος (Bertram, K. L. Schmidt); A. Bertholet, *Die Stellung der Israeliten und Juden zu den Fremden* (1896); L. Rost, *Die Bezeichnungen für Land und Volk im AT,* Festschrift Procksch (1934), pp. 125-148. A. VAN SELMS

GENTILE NATIONS. *See* NATIONS.

GENTILES, COURT OF THE. *See* TEMPLE (HEROD'S).

GENTILES, ISLES OF THE. *See* ISLAND.

GENTLE [Heb. *marpē'*] (Prov. 15:4); AV WHOLESOME; NEB SOOTHING; [*'allûp*] (Jer. 11:19); AV "ox"; NEB "obedient"; [**śā'îr*] ("gentle rain," Dt. 32:2); AV "small rain"; NEB "fine rain"; [Gk. *praÿs*] (Mt. 11:29; 1 Pet. 3:4); AV MEEK; [*ḗpios*] (1 Thess. 2:7); [*epieikḗs*] (1 Tim. 3:3; Tit. 3:2; Jas. 3:17; 1 Pet. 2:18); AV also PATIENT; NEB FORBEARING, CONSIDERATE; **GENTLENESS** [Gk. *praÿtēs*] (1 Cor. 4:21; Gal. 5:23; 6:1; 2 Tim. 2:25; 1 Pet. 3:15); AV also MEEKNESS; NEB also MODESTY; *praÿpathía* (1 Tim. 6:11); [*epieíkeia*] (2 Cor. 10:1); NEB MAGNANIMITY; **GENTLY** [Heb. *l*^e*'aṭ*–'for gentleness'] (Isa. 8:6); AV, NEB SOFTLY; ("deal gently," 2 S. 18:5; Job 15:11); AV also "secret thing"; NEB also "whispered quietly"; [*nāhal*] ("gently lead," Isa. 40:11); NEB "lead to water"; [Gk. *metriopathéō*] ("deal gently," He. 5:2); AV "have compassion"; NEB "bear patiently"; [*hypopnéō*] ("blow gently," Acts 27:13); AV BLOW SOFTLY; NEB "spring up."

Two major Greek words are translated "gentle" or "gentleness" in the English versions. *Epieikḗs* is prominent in the highly developed ethical thought of the Greeks and broadly means "'that which is the general conception of life,' and therefore 'what is fitting, right, or equitable'" (*TDNT,* II, 588). The notions of equity and fairness present in the Greek cannot be adequately expressed in one word by either Latin (*clementia, aequitas,* or *modestia*) or English. The word was originally connected with *eikós,* meaning "what is fit and reasonable," but later became associated also with *eíkō* ("yield"), thus indicating "one ready to give way" (Eng. "meek"; Mayor, p. 131). The understanding is of "that moderation which recognizes the impossibility cleaving to all formal law, of anticipating and providing for all cases that will emerge, and present themselves to it for decision" (Trench, p. 154). Aristotle contrasted the man who stands up for his legal rights in strict justice with the one who is willing to give way and be "reasonable" (*Eth. Nic.* v.10). This same "yieldingness" is the quality of character possessed by the individual with "heavenly wisdom" in Jas. 3:17 who is *epieikḗs* and peaceful, not always insisting on standing upon his own rights.

In the LXX this characteristic is found supremely in God (Ps. 85:5 [MT 86:5], *sālaḥ,* "forgiving"; cf. "mildness," Wisd. 12:18; "forbearance," 2 Macc. 10:4). In Tit. 3:2 it is enjoined on all Christians in general, while it must especially be a mark of bishops (1 Tim. 3:3). Slaves are commanded to be submissive to "kind and gentle masters" (1 Pet. 2:18).

The inner spirit which produces "gentle" behavior is described by the term *praÿtēs.* The Greeks highly prized the social virtue of "mildness" or "friendliness in dealing with others," seeing it as opposed to roughness, bad temper, or sudden outbursts of anger. *Praÿtēs* has the sense of "quiet and friendly composure which does not become embittered or angry at what is unpleasant, whether in the form of people . . . or fate. This is an active attitude and deliberate acceptance, not just passive submission" (*TDNT,* VI, 645). Such an attitude is reflected in Tit. 3:2, where the RSV translates *praÿtēs* by "courtesy."

"Gentleness" is one of the self-predications of Jesus (Mt. 11:29) and was an established disposition describing Him at the time of Paul (2 Cor. 10:1). The spirit of the "gentleness of Christ" is one rooted and grounded in Christian love which "cannot think in terms of harsh punishment even in relation to the disobedient" (*TDNT,* VI, 650; cf. 1 Cor. 4:21). Thus because of its basis, Christian "gentleness" is distinct from Greek "virtue" and is one of the gifts of the Spirit (Gal. 5:23). This gift enables believers to correct an erring brother (Gal. 6:1) or an opponent (2 Tim. 2:25) without arrogance, anger, or impatience; it is also a dominant attitude when believers must make a defense for the hope that is within them (1 Pet. 3:15). This kind of gentle and quiet spirit is called an "imperishable jewel" (1 Pet. 3:4).

In the OT, King David directly ordered his commanders to "deal gently for my sake with the young man Absalom"

(2 S. 18:5), an order later broken (v. 14). In the book of Isaiah the Lord God is portrayed as feeding His flock like a shepherd and gently leading the sheep with young (40:11). Every high priest appointed by this same Lord God has the inward feelings that are in keeping with his sacred work of offering sacrifice, which is to "deal gently [*metriopathéō*] with the ignorant and the wayward" (He. 5:2). This too is the disposition of the "gentle" Jesus Christ who is the "great high priest" (4:14).

Bibliography.–E. D. Burton, *Galatians* (*ICC*, 1921), p. 317; J. B. Mayor, *James* (3rd ed. 1913); *TDNT*, II, *s.v.* ἐπιεικής (Priesker); VI, *s.v.* πραΰς, πραΰτης (F. Hauck and S. Schulz); R. C. Trench, *Synonyms of the NT* (1953).

D. K. MCKIM

GENUBATH gə-nōō'bəth [Heb. *g^e^nubat*– 'weaned'(?)]. Son of Hadad, the fugitive Edomite prince; born and brought up at the court of Egypt, to which Hadad had fled when David conquered Edom (1 K. 11:20). His mother was a sister of Tahpenes, queen of the pharaoh who ruled Egypt at that time, and who belonged to the notoriously weak and uninfluential 21st Dynasty.

GENUINE [Gk. *anypókritos*] (Rom. 12:9; 2 Cor. 6:6); AV "without dissimulation," UNFEIGNED; NEB SINCERE; [*dókimos*] (1 Cor. 11:19); AV APPROVED; NEB SOUND; [*gnḗsios*] (2 Cor. 8:8); AV SINCERITY; NEB "put to the test"; **GENUINELY** (CARE) [*gnēsíōs*] (Phil. 2:20); AV NATURALLY (CARE); NEB (TAKE A) GENUINE (INTEREST); **GENUINENESS** [*dokímion*] (1 Pet. 1:7); AV TRIAL; NEB "which has stood the test."

Anypókritos is a negative adjective related to *hypokritḗs* and refers to a nonhypocritical love (Rom. 12:9; 2 Cor. 6:6), as well as to "sincere" faith (1 Tim. 1:5; 2 Tim. 1:5), wisdom (Jas. 3:17), and brotherly love (1 Pet. 1:22). *Gnḗsios* comes from *gnētós*, which means "born in wedlock," or "legitimate." It is used figuratively of a spiritual relationship that the writer believes is legitimate and true. Paul used this term of Timothy (1 Tim. 1:2), Titus (Tit. 1:4), and an unnamed person in Phil. 4:3, perhaps because Paul not only was assured of their genuine faith but also felt that he was their spiritual father (cf. Phil. 2:22; 1 Tim. 1:18; 2 Tim. 2:1).

The root *dokim-* is used in technical terms for the testing of something or someone. In the LXX it is used in reference to precious metals (Gen. 23:16; 1 Ch. 28:18; 29:4; 2 Ch. 9:17; Prov. 8:10) that had passed the test and were therefore pure. Since the Bible, and especially the NT, sees God testing all of human existence (Mt. 25:14-30; 1 Cor. 3:13; 9:27; 1 Thess. 2:4; Jas. 1:12; etc.), it is not surprising to find this root frequently used for the divine examination of mankind. (Rom. 14:18, which speaks of being "approved by men," is an exception.) Although the final judgment still lies in the future, in a sense certain people such as Apelles (Rom. 16:10), some Corinthians (1 Cor. 11:19), and Paul (2 Cor. 13:6f.) have passed the test already in this life, and Paul urged Timothy (2 Tim. 2:15) and the Corinthians (2 Cor. 10:18) to seek this approval in their lives and service for God.

Bibliography.–*TDNT*, I, *s.v.* γνήσιος (Büchsel); II, *s.v.* δόκιμος κτλ. (Grundmann); VIII, *s.v.* ὑποκρίνομαι κτλ.: ἀνυπόκριτος (Wilckens).

R. H. STEIN

GEOGRAPHY. *See* PALESTINE; TABLE OF NATIONS; WORLD.

GEOGRAPHY, BIBLICAL. The study of the characteristics of particular places on the surface of the planet Earth as it relates to an understanding of the Bible. Of the several categories into which geography has been divided, historical geography is of primary importance for biblical studies; physical and political geography are also meaningful.

The study of geography is an essential part of biblical exegesis. It is not generally recognized that the Bible is the only book of the religions of the world that puts any emphasis on geography. The Koran, e.g., hardly includes geographical data, and scholars of the Koran have to decide only whether a Sura (chapter) originated in Mecca or Medina. The Bhagavad-Gita is timeless and placeless, and students of this Hindu work have first of all to realize that it does not deal with time or place. But in the Bible almost every event is anchored in a specific location, and although the chronological details in the earlier portions (and even some in the later portions) are not sufficient for the scholar seeking an absolute chronology (i.e., to the day, month, and/or year) or even a relative chronology (i.e., relating the event to other data that can be absolutely or approximately dated), these data are everywhere present.

From Abana to Zuzim there are about two thousand place names in the Bible, including regions and countries, cities and villages, mountains and valleys, seas and rivers. The atlases, geographies, and similar reference works for the Bible far outnumber those available for other religions. The Bible, as G. E. Wright pointed out, "is primarily a historical literature, which tells how God confronted men at particular times and places. Geography, history, and religion are so inextricably bound together in it that the religious message cannot be truly understood without attention to the setting and conditions of the revelation" (*WHAB*, p. 5).

Physical geography deals with the physical details of the earth: mountains, river valleys, rock and soil structure, winds and weather, etc. In the Bible physical geography is an elemental part of God's creation and providence. He formed the mountains and causes the rivers to flow to the seas. He sends the rain, the blasting east wind, and the drought. Physical geography affects lives of human beings, for forest, rocks, and clay determine the types of housing they build; rainfall and the seasons cause them to move with their flocks or to collect and store water for agricultural needs. Almost every page of the Bible reports some details of physical geography. The parables of Jesus and the journeys of Paul, like the migration of Abraham and the questions God put to Job, cannot be understood without some knowledge of the physical details of this earth.

Political geography deals with the organization of groups of peoples. The earliest form encountered in the Bible is the city-state, a petty kingdom ruled by a king, or an equivalent governmental form. Later in biblical history kingdoms were larger, more powerful, and generally more cruel. The "kingdom of God" becomes the term for the eternal reign of God and for His ultimate kingdom on earth. The vision granted to John of a "great multitude, which no man could number, from every nation" (Rev. 7:9) indicates that the kingdom of God comes into existence not by destroying the peoples of other kingdoms but by redeeming men and women "from all tribes and peoples and tongues" to sing praises "to our God who sits upon the throne, and to the Lamb" (v. 10).

Historical geography, the broadest category, deals with the historical development of peoples in place and time. This discipline, even more than those previously mentioned, is an essential characteristic of biblical studies. The Bible is the record of how, where, and when God revealed Himself and His purpose to His chosen men and women, who lived at specific places and times. This revelatory activity progresses historically, continually referring to previous revelatory acts. It begins in prehistory, before the garden of Eden, and its teleological consummation is beyond history, in the new heavens and the new earth. But between the first chapters of Genesis and the last chapters of Revelation, revelation always occurs in space and time. Thus scholars can make such statements as "God entered into history," and theologians can speak of "God incarnate." The ultimate demonstration of the significance of historical geography in the study of biblical revelation is the Incarnation, which took place "in the days of Caesar Augustus" in a city of Judah called "Bethlehem" to Joseph and Mary, who had come from "Nazareth." It achieved its purpose in "Jerusalem," where Jesus was crucified by "Pontius Pilate," was buried in a tomb belonging to "Joseph," was raised from the dead, and departed to heaven from "the Mount of Olives." Bible students ever since have traced and retraced the footsteps of Jesus, and pilgrims have visited every site, real or imaginary, identified with the Gospel record.

An existentialist may say that it does not matter where, when, or even if the events recorded in the Bible actually occurred; what matters is the divine encounter, the meeting between God and those who read about these events. Part of that statement is a great basic truth, for it is indeed the divine encounter that matters. "Now these things happened to them as examples and were written down as warnings for us" (1 Cor. 10:11, NIV). There is also a greater truth to take into consideration: if "these things" had not happened to the men and women of the Bible — if God had not encountered them in time and space — there would be no divine encounter in reading the stories. It is precisely because God has entered into history that He meets us in the Bible. The study of the historical and geographical details of each biblical account makes God's revelation personally meaningful.

Bibliography.–"Geography," *Enc. Brit.* (1970), X, 144-160; *GAB; GB; GP; GTTOT; HGHL; WHAB*, pp. 5-14; M. A. Beek, *Atlas of Mesopotamia* (1962); A. A. M. van der Heyden and H. H. Scullard, *Atlas of the Classical World* (1963); F. van der Meer and C. Mohrmann, *Atlas of the Early Christian World* (1958).

W. S. LASOR

GEOLOGY OF PALESTINE. *See* PALESTINE, GEOLOGY OF.

GEON gē'on (Sir. 24:27, AV). *See* GIHON **1.**

GEORGIAN VERSION. *See* VERSIONS V.

GERA gē'rə [Heb. *gērā'*]. A family name of the tribe of Benjamin; thus **3** and **4** are not necessarily separate persons.

1. A son of Benjamin (Gen. 46:21).

2. According to 1 Ch. 8:3, 5, 7, a son of Bela and grandson of Benjamin. The name is repeated (v. 5) in the list of Bela's sons.

3. Father, or ancestor, of the judge Ehud (Jgs. 3:15).

4. Father, or ancestor, of Shimei, the Benjaminite who cursed David when David fled from Absalom (2 S. 16:5; 19:16, 18; 1 K. 2:8).

GERAH gē'ra [Heb. *gērâ*–'grain, kernel']. A weight, the twentieth part of a shekel (Ex. 30:13; Lev. 27:25; Nu. 3:47; 18:16; Ezk. 45:12). *See* WEIGHTS AND MEASURES.

GERAR gē'rär [Heb. *g^erār*–meaning unknown]. A town in the western Negeb. Gen. 10:19 states, "The territory of the Canaanites extended from Sidon, all the way to Gerar,

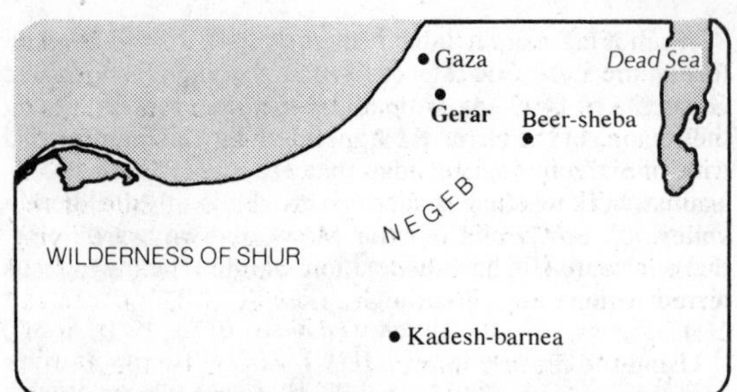

near Gaza" (after Ginsberg). According to this reading Gerar was in the southern extremity of the land of Canaan.

The patriarchs Abraham and Isaac each spent an extended period of time in the territory of Gerar. "Abraham journeyed . . . toward the territory of the Negeb, and dwelt between Kadesh [-barnea] and Shur [the Egyptian defense "wall" which guarded the eastern delta], and [then] he sojourned in [became a resident of] Gerar" (Gen. 20:1). He was apparently seeking the status of a resident alien in the kingdom of Gerar; this was awarded to him after the episode between Sarah and the local king (Gen. 20:15). When the rest of the land was suffering a famine, Isaac also sought resident status at Gerar (Gen. 26:1, 6). The account of his own troubles over Rebekah (Gen. 26:7-11) requires an urban setting. Later he lived outside the city in the "valley [brook] of Gerar" (Gen. 26:17). After various troubles with the local inhabitants, both Abraham and Isaac were obliged to remove their entourage to the very margin of Gerar's territory, i.e., as far as Beer-sheba; but they were still within the hegemony of Gerar's ruler (Gen. 21:31-34; 26:26) and entered into treaty relationships with him.

The king of Gerar bore the Semitic name Abimelech (Gen. 20:2) in the passages concerning the two patriarchs. He is also called "king of the Philistines" (Gen. 26:1, 8), and the term Philistine is used of the people (Gen. 26:14f.) as well as the land (Gen. 21:34). This association with the sea-peoples is related to the statement that the original inhabitants of this same region, the Avvim, were displaced by the Caphtorim (Dt. 2:23; *see also* CAPHTOR). The prophets preserved the recollection that the Philistines came from Caphtor (Am. 9:7; Jer. 47:4). Furthermore, the same area was also called "the Negeb of the Cherethites" (1 S. 30:14; cf. Ezk. 25:16; Zeph. 2:5).

Nevertheless, Gerar was not counted among the principal Philistine cities (Josh. 13:3). It is absent from the list of towns conquered by the Israelites (Aharoni emends the Geder of Josh. 12:13 to Gerar, but this is unlikely) because all the Philistine territory, including that of the Avvim, was still unsubdued by Israel at the end of Joshua's career (Josh. 13:1-4).

Tell esh-Shariyeh, the possible site of Gerar (W. S. LaSor)

When King Asa of Judah routed the invading Ethiopian forces under Zerah, his troops pursued the enemy as far as Gerar (2 Ch. 14:13-15) and plundered all the settlements in the region. In the reign of Hezekiah, many clans from the tribe of Simeon "journeyed to the entrance of Gerar [LXX against MT, which has Gedor], to the east side of the valley..." and drove out the Meunim, who were living there in tents (1 Ch. 4:39-41). The valley [Heb. *gāy'*] referred to here is evidently the "valley of Gerar" (Gen. 26:17).

Using the meager information provided by the written sources, various scholars have sought to identify Gerar with one of the ancient sites in the region between Beer-sheba and Gaza. More recently, however, Tell Abū Hureirah has become a serious candidate. The Madeba Map and other Byzantine evidence support the existence of a real town called Gerara within the Geraritike district; the most natural assumption from the patriarchal narratives is that Gerar was a city in that time also. Assuming that the Wâdī esh-Sherî'ah is the "valley of Gerar," Tell Abū Hureireh stands on the western bank, for the stream bed actually takes a NE-SW course at this point. The Simeonites who intruded into Gerar's territory during Hezekiah's reign are said to have remained on the eastern side of the valley; the tell is also reasonably close to Beer-sheba, but probably was outside the original Simeonite inheritance (Josh. 19:1-9). (Cf. also Eusebius *Onom.* 60.7.)

Antiochus Eupator appointed Hegemonides governor of the district "from Ptolemais to Gerar [Gk. *Gerrēnōn*]" (AV "Gerrhenians," NEB "Gerra," 2 Macc. 13:24).

Bibliography.–Y. Aharoni, *IEJ*, 6 (1956), 26-32; 8 (1958), 26-38; K. Galling, *ZDPV*, 52 (1929), 242-250; H. L. Ginsberg, *BASOR*, 122 (Apr. 1951), 13; W. M. F. Petrie, *Gerar* (1928).

A. F. RAINEY

GERASA ger'ə-sə [Gk. *Gerasa*]; **GERASENES** ger'ə-sēnz [Gk. *Gerasēnoi*]. Gerasa was one of the significant cities of the DECAPOLIS (Pliny *Nat. hist.* v. 74). The Gerasenes were the inhabitants of the city and its surroundings (Josephus *Ant.* xiii.15.5 [398]). The ancient city has been identified with modern Jerash, about 36 km. (22 mi.) N of Amman, 30 km. (19 mi.) E of the Jordan, and 60 km. (37 mi.) SE of the Sea of Galilee. The identification is based on the similarity between the ancient and modern names and on inscriptions which describe the ancient residents as "the first Gerasenes" (Gk. *tōn próteron Gerasēnōn*; see *EAEHL*, II, 417).

The Bible does not refer to the city itself but to "the territory of the Gerasenes." "Gerasenes" is the reading of the RSV in Mk. 5:1 (also NEB; AV "Gadarenes"), Lk. 8:26 (AV "Gadarenes"; NEB "Gergesenes"), and Lk. 8:37 (AV "Gadarenes"; NEB "Gergesene district"). In Mt. 8:28 the RSV reads "Gadarenes" (also NEB; AV "Gergesenes").

I. Text Criticism.–In three instances (Mk. 5:1; Lk. 8:26, 37), the reading *tōn Gerasēnōn* ("of the Gerasenes") accords with the best MS evidence, early witnesses "of both Alexandrian and Western types of text" (Metzger, pp. 84, 145). The variant *Gadarēnōn* ("Gadarenes") is regarded as the work of a scribe who changed the text to agree with the text of Mt. 8:28. The variant *Gergesēnōn* may be a correction inspired by Origen (comm. on John vi.24), who argued that Gergesa (*see* GERGESENES) was the most suitable site for the destruction of the swine, for GADARA (Muqeis or Umm Qeis) and Gerasa were too far from the Sea of Galilee (Metzger, pp. 23f.).

II. History.–Greek traditions attribute the founding of the Hellenistic city of Gerasa to Alexander the Great, though excavations in the vicinity have revealed sites dating as far back as the Stone Age (*EAEHL*, II, 417). One tradition claims that Alexander founded the city for his veterans (Gk. *gérontes*); another states that Alexander killed all the young men in the area, leaving only the elderly (Gk. *gérontes*). An inscription on a coin from the reign of Commodus (A.D. 180-192) reads *Alex[andros] mak[edon] kti[stēs] Gerasōn* ("Alexander the Macedonian, founder of Gerasa"; see H. Seyrig, *Syria*, 42 [1965], 25-28). A statue of Perdiccus, one of Alexander's generals, has also been discovered at Gerasa, suggesting that he was related to the founding of the city (*EAEHL*, II, 419).

Probably the city was well established by 143/2 B.C. This can be inferred from an inscription on a lead weight from the Seleucid era (*ca.* 170 B.C.) that refers to the inhabitants of Gerasa as "the Antiochenes by the Chrysorhaas" (see Kraeling, p. 461; H. Seyrig, *Numismatic Notes and Monographs*, 119 [1950], 33, n. 45).

According to Josephus, the city was conquered by Alexander Jannaeus (*Ant.* xiii.15.3 [393]; *BJ* i.4.8 [104]) toward the end of his career (*Ant.* xiii.15.5 [398]). It remained under Jewish rule until Pompey took it for Rome in 63 B.C. Thereafter Gerasa was included among the cities of the Decapolis and reckoned its continuing history from that date. The inscriptions of Gerasa are frequently dated according to the Pompeian era (see Kraeling, p. 358; C. C. McCown, *Transactions of the American Philological Association*, 64 [1933], 81-88). One inscription dates the dedication of the southern theater to the year 153, i.e., A.D. 90/91 (see B. VanElderen, *American Schools of Oriental Research Newsletter*, 4 [1974], 2). During the Roman period Gerasa enjoyed increasing prosperity.

At the outbreak of the First Jewish Revolt (A.D. 66-74) Gerasa and the neighboring cities of Philadelphia and Heshbon were attacked by Jewish rebels (*BJ* ii.18.1 [458]), and, although the inhabitants of the other cities retaliated, the Gerasenes "not only abstained from maltreating the Jews who remained with them, but escorted to the frontier any who chose to emigrate" (*BJ* ii.18.5 [480]). The Gerasa captured and destroyed by Lucius Annius under the command of Vespasian (*BJ* iv.9.1 [486-89]) can hardly have been this one (cf. *HJP*², II, 149-155; K. H. Rengstorf, *Complete Concordance to Flavius Josephus*, supp. I: *Namenwörterbuch zu Flavius Josephus, s.v.* "Gerasa, 2").

Like the other cities of the Decapolis, Gerasa belonged originally to the province of Syria. This is indicated by an inscription from Pergamum (R. Caguat, *et al.*, *Inscriptiones Graecae ad Res Romanas Pertinentes*, IV, 374) and by the observations of the geographer Ptolemy (v.74.18). By the end of the first decade of the 2nd cent. A.D., however, Gerasa had become one of the three chief cities of the province of Arabia. Its importance is attested by the visit of the emperor Hadrian in 129.

After a period of decline, the city revived under Diocletian and became an important ecclesiastical center. Another period of decay had set in by the 6th cent., and the city was captured first by the Persians (614-628) and then by the Moslems (635). The city was eventually deserted about the 12th century. J. J. C. COX

III. Excavation.–The excavation of Jerash was a joint venture begun in 1925 by J. Garstang, then director of the Department of Antiquities of Palestine and the British School of Archaeology in Jerusalem. The Department of Antiquities, the British School, Yale University, and the American Schools of Oriental Research joined in the excavations, which lasted from 1925 to 1940. Further clearance and restoration work has been conducted by the Jordan Department of Antiquities since 1953.

An excellent example of city planning, Jerash was laid

The Gerasa forum and colonnaded way as seen from the temple of Zeus (L. T. Geraty)

out with a single main street intersected at right angles by two cross streets. The main street was just over 0.8 km. (0.5 mi.) in length and was flanked by 260 Ionic and Corinthian columns on either side. The side streets likewise were colonnaded, and a drainage system ran under the middle of the streets. All the principal buildings and the best shops had their entrances from the main street, which ran N-S. To the west of the main street on the highest point in town rose the second-century temple of Artemis, patron deity of the municipality, with Corinthian columns 14 m. (45 ft.) high. East of the street stood two bath complexes and in the north part of town was a theater.

At the south end of the street stood a first-century circular forum, unique in the Greco-Roman world. From the forum a great flight of steps led up to the temple of Zeus, begun in A.D. 22. Next to it stood the south theater (1st cent.) capable of accommodating about 5000 people. At the south entrance of the city was a great triumphal arch, commemorating Hadrian's visit to the city in A.D. 129, and next to that sprawled the hippodrome. Ruins of thirteen churches appeared in the excavations. *See* Plate 18.

H. F. VOS

For further description of the buildings and other ruins excavated at Gerasa, see *EAEHL,* II, 423-28.

Bibliography.–M. Avi-Yonah, *Gazetteer of Roman Palestine, Qedem: Monographs of the Institute of Archaeology, The Hebrew University of Jerusalem* (1976), pp. 58, 61; A. Detweiler, *BASOR,* 87 (Oct. 1942), 10-17; N. Glueck, *BASOR,* 75 (Oct. 1939), 22-30; G. L. Harding, *PEQ,* 1949, pp. 12-20; J. Iliffe, *QDAP,* 11 (1944), 1-26; D. Kirkbride, *Bulletin of the Archaeological Institute of London,* 1 (1958), 9-20; *ADAJ,* 4-5 (1960), 123-27; C. H. Kraeling, ed., *Gerasa, City of the Decapolis* (1938); B. M. Metzger, *Textual Comm. on the Greek NT* (1971), pp. 23f., 84, 145; A. Negev, ed., *Archaeological Encyclopedia of the Holy Land* (1972), pp. 123f.

GERGESENES ger'gə-sēnz [Gk. *Gergesēnoi*]. Residents of a town (and its territory) on the east coast of the Sea of Galilee identified by Origen (comm. on John vi.24) and certain NT MSS (mostly later than the 4th cent.; ℵ² L Θ, etc.) as the locale of the healing of a demoniac and the subsequent drowning of a herd of swine in the sea (Mt. 8:28-34 par. Mk. 5:1-13; Lk. 8:26-39). The ruins of a cliff town are found near the modern village of Kursî, but the Greek and Arabic names are not exact equivalents, leaving the identification uncertain.

See GADARA; GERASA I.

GERIZIM ger'ə-zim, **MOUNT.** [Heb. *har gᵉrizîm*]; AV also GARIZIM (2 Macc. 5:23; 6:2). Modern Jebel eṭ-Ṭôr, about 3 km. (2 mi.) NW of Shechem.

Mt. Gerizim (868 m., 2849 ft.) stands almost exactly in the center of Palestine W of the Jordan. Together with Mt. Ebal to the north, it commands the Nâblus Valley, which gives the only E-W access into the hill country of Ephraim. Its location on the N-S road also gave it strategic importance from earliest times. Jacob's well (Jn. 4:6) lay in the valley at the northeastern foot of the mountain. Abram built his first altar nearby after arriving in Canaan from Mesopotamia (Gen. 12:6f.).

In obedience to Moses' command, the great ceremony of rehearsing the law took place here after the Hebrews entered Canaan. The ark and the Levites stood in the valley between the two mountains. The people arranged themselves on the slopes of the mountains and responded antiphonally to what was read — those on Mt. Ebal responding to the cursings and those on Mt. Gerizim to the blessings (Josh. 8:30-35; cf. Dt. 11:29; 27:11-13).

During the days of the judges Jotham uttered his taunting parables from a spur of Mt. Gerizim (Jgs. 9:7). Jgs. 9:37 apparently refers to Mt. Gerizim as the *tabbûr hā'āreṣ,* a phrase of uncertain meaning. Although some (e.g., R. Boling, *Judges* [*AB,* 1975], pp. 178f.) follow the LXX *ómphalos tēs gēs,* "navel of the earth" (so JB), and thus accept the postbiblical Hebrew and Aramaic meaning of *tabbûr,* others (e.g., *TDOT,* III, 438) derive the meaning "plateau, height" (cf. NEB "central ridge") from the context (cf. L. Stadelmann, *Hebrew Conception of the World* [1970], pp. 148f., 154). After the Babylonian captivity a separate Samaritan sect arose when the Jews under the leadership of Ezra and Nehemiah insisted on Jewish ethnic purity. This cleavage became complete with the construction of a Samaritan temple on Mt. Gerizim, probably during the 4th cent. B.C. Mt. Gerizim became the spiritual center of the Samaritans. In NT times this fact is reflected in Jesus' conversation with the Samaritan woman at Jacob's well (Jn. 4, esp. v. 20).

The Samaritans have suffered at the hands of pagans, Jews, and Christians. Antiochus IV Epiphanes desecrated the Samaritan temple and dedicated it to Zeus Helios (2 Macc. 6:2). A few decades later, in 128 B.C., the Jewish king John Hyrcanus destroyed the Samaritan temple completely. Then, just before the destruction of Jerusalem in A.D. 70, the Romans surrounded Mt. Gerizim and massacred 11,600 Samaritans there (Josephus *BJ* iii.7.32 [307-315]). Early in the 2nd cent. the emperor Hadrian built a temple to Zeus over the ruins of the Samaritan temple and constructed a monumental access stairway to it. In a struggle between Samaritans and Christians during the 5th cent. the emperor Zeno drove the Samaritans from Mt. Gerizim and commanded that a church be built on the highest point and dedicated to Mary as the mother of God (486). The Samaritans destroyed this church, but Justinian later built another on the spot and fortified it (*ca.* 530). This was destroyed during the Arab conquest (7th cent.).

A. M. Schneider of Göttingen excavated the ruins of Justinian's octagonal church and the protecting enclosure in 1928. In 1964 R. J. Bull of Drew University excavated at Tell er-Râs, a spur on the northern slope of Mr. Gerizim. There he found remains of the temple of Zeus, confirmed by an inscription "to Zeus Olympius." The temple itself measured 20 by 14 m. (65 by 45 ft.) and stood on a platform 6.7 m. (22 ft.) high measuring 65 by 45 m. (213 by 148 ft.). Remains of a monumental stairway were located on the slope nearby. Under the temple of Zeus were remains of a Hellenistic structure 21 by 20 m. (68 by 65 ft.), which may belong to the Samaritan temple destroyed by John Hyrcanus.

A third area of Mt. Gerizim received archeological attention in 1968 when R. G. Boling led an American Schools of Oriental Research dig at Tananir on the lower north slope about 300 m. (1000 ft.) from ancient Shechem.

The structure he excavated, probably a temple, went through four building phases (1650-1540). It had rooms grouped around a central courtyard in which was a sacred pillar. Scholars have suggested that it was on the ruins of this building that Jotham stood when he uttered his condemnation (Jgs. 9:7-20).

The Samaritan community that maintains a synagogue in nearby Nâblus still celebrates the feasts of Passover, Pentecost, and Tabernacles on Mt. Gerizim every year.

See SAMARITAN.

Bibliography.–R. G. Boling, *BA*, 32 (1969), 82-103; R. J. Bull, *AJA*, 71 (1967), 387-393; *BA*, 31 (1968), 58-72; *BASOR*, 190 (1968), 4-19; *EAEHL*, IV, *s.v.* "Er-Ras, Tell" (R. J. Bull). H. F. VOS

GERRHENIANS gə-rē'ni-ənz (AV, 2 Macc. 13:24). *See* GERAR.

GERSHOM gûr'shəm [Heb. *gērᵉšōm*]. Derived, according to the etymology in Ex. 2:22; 18:3 from *gûr*, "be a sojourner."

1. Firstborn son of Moses and Zipporah. The only details of his life contained in the Pentateuch are the account of his circumcision (Ex. 4:25), and his remaining under the care of Jethro while Moses was in Egypt leading the Exodus. His descendants were numbered among the tribes of Levi (1 Ch. 23:14). One of them apparently was the Jonathan who officiated as priest of the idolatrous sanctuary at Dan, and whose descendants held the office until the captivity. Another descendant was Shebuel, a ruler over the treasuries of David.

2. A son of Levi, so called in 1 Ch. 6:1, 16f., 20, 43, 62, 71 (MT 1f., 5, 28, 47, 56); 15:7; 23:6; elsewhere GERSHON.

3. A descendant of Phinehas, the head of a father's house, who journeyed with Ezra from Babylon to Jerusalem during the reign of Artaxerxes (Ezr. 8:2; 1 Esd. 8:29; Gk. *Gērsōn*). E. D. ISAACS

GERSHON gûr'shən [Heb. *gēršôn, gērᵉšôm*]; **GERSHONITES** gûr'shən-īts [*gēršunnî*]. Firstborn of the three sons of Levi (Ex. 6:16; Nu. 3:17; *see also* GERSHOM **2**). He had two sons, Libni, also known as Ladan (1 Ch. 23:7 mg.; 26:21), and Shimei (Ex. 6:17; Nu. 3:18), and consequently two groups of descendants, enumerated in the censuses taken in the Wilderness of Sinai (Nu. 3:21ff.) and in the plains of Moab (Nu. 26:57). In the distribution of functions among the Levites, the Gershonites were charged with the carrying of the curtains, coverings, screens, hangings, cords, and instruments of the tabernacle and the tent of meeting on the journeys in the wilderness, under the supervision of Ithamar the son of Aaron. Their function was thus more exalted than that of the Merarites, who carried the boards, but less than that of the Kohathites, who carried the most holy utensils and symbols. The Gershonites were given two wagons with four oxen — half as many as the Merarites, according to their service (Nu. 7:7). Thirteen cities were assigned to the Gershonites in northern Palestine by Eleazar and Joshua (Josh. 21:6, 27-33 par. 1 Ch. 6:62, 71-76 [MT 47, 56-61]).

Among the Gershonites who achieved distinction in later biblical times was the family of Asaph, the singers from the time of David to the days of the second temple (1 Ch. 6:31-47; 25:1-7; 15:7, 17, 19; 16:5, 7; 2 Ch. 35:15; Ezr. 2:41; 3:10; Neh. 11:17, 22; 12:35; 1 Ch. 9:15). Other Gershonites named are the heads of the fathers' houses in the days of David in connection with the dividing of the Levites into divisions (1 Ch. 23:7-11); the superintendents of the treasuries of the house of the Lord at the same time (1 Ch. 26:21f.; 29:8); and, finally, Gershonites are mentioned among those who cleansed the house of the Lord in the days of Hezekiah (2 Ch. 29:12f.). E. D. ISAACS

GERSON gûr'sən (1 Esd. 8:29, AV). *See* GERSHOM **3.**

GERUTH CHIMHAM gē'ro͞oth kim'ham [Heb. *gērûṯ kimhām Q*] (Jer. 41:17); AV "habitation of Chimham"; NEB "Kimham's holding." If the reading *gērûṯ* is correct, a "lodging-place" or "khan" on the highway to Egypt may be meant. It may have been built by CHIMHAM son of Barzillai; or it may have been named after him as owner of the land on which it stood. It was in the general area of Bethlehem, but to date the location has not been identified. Perhaps this was the "inn" to which Joseph and Mary were refused admittance (Lk. 2:7).

GESHAN gē'shən [Heb. *gêšān*–'firm,' 'strong']. A descendant of Judah through Caleb (1 Ch. 2:47). The AV has "Gesham," but not in the original 1611 edition.

GESHEM ge'shəm [Heb. *gešem, gašmû*; Gk. *Gēsam*, 'rain storm']. An Arab, probably chief of an Arabian tribe that either settled in southern Palestine during the Exile in Babylon or was settled in or near Samaria by Sargon (Neh. 2:19; 6:1f., 6). He was a confederate of Sanballat and Tobiah and strenuously opposed the building of the wall under Nehemiah. He with the others mocked at the first efforts to build the wall and afterward repeatedly sought to entice Nehemiah to the plains of Ono. The name also occurs in the form *Gašmû*, perhaps an Assyrian form of the same name Geshem. J. J. REEVE

GESHUR gesh'ər [Heb. *gᵉšûr*–'bridge']; **GESHURITES** [Heb. *gᵉšûrî*]; AV also GESHURI.

1. A small Aramean kingdom (2 S. 15:8), known extrabiblically also as Gessur, located N of Bashan (Dt. 3:14; Josh. 12:5; 13:11) and NE of the Sea of Galilee on what is now the southwest border of Syria. Geshur was an independent kingdom within Israel (Josh. 13:13), for the half-tribe of Manasseh never expelled the Geshurites.

David made an alliance with Geshur by marrying Maacah, who was the daughter of Talmai its king and the mother of Absalom (2 S. 3:3); and it was to Talmai that Absalom fled after killing Amnon (2 S. 13:37; 14:23). Later, during the reign of Solomon, Geshur became subordinate to the kingdom of Israel, but with the division of the Israelite kingdom Geshur joined Aram in raiding the area of Bashan, capturing the cities of Jair from the Israelites (1 Ch. 2:22f.). Geshur then probably became part of the kingdom of Damascus, sharing Damascus' fate in 732 B.C.

According to some scholars "Geshurites" should be read for "ASHURITES" in 2 S. 2:9 (cf. Pesh., Vulg.). The Targum, followed by the NEB, reads "Asherites" (cf. Jgs. 1:32), keeping the same consonants as "Ashurites," which appears nowhere else in the Bible.

2. "Geshurites" also appears as a tribe bordering the Philistines on the south (Josh. 13:2); while David was in exile he raided them and other old inhabitants of the land (1 S. 27:8). P. C. HUGHES

GESHURITES gesh'ə-rīts [Heb. *gᵉšûrî*]. *See* GESHUR **2.**

GESTAS. A name given to the unrepentant thief (Lk. 23:39-43). *See* APOCRYPHAL GOSPELS III.B.

GESTURE. The word is derived from the Latin *se gerere*, "comport or behave oneself," and *gestus*, "carriage of the body." Near Eastern peoples, both ancient and modern, make extensive use of gestures to express emotion, to emphasize words, or to communicate nonverbally. Almost every available part of the body is employed in gesture; however, the freest body parts are the most naturally used — the hands, feet, head, and face.

Gestures in general may be categorized as autistic (highly personalized and very predictable movements, especially of the hand or face in speaking), "instinctive" or universal (transcultural), technical (true substitutes for speech, e.g., a sign-language system), culture induced, and semiotic (folk gestures). The bulk of the gestures illustrated in the Bible fall into the last two categories.

I. Hands
II. Other Appendages
  A. Finger
  B. Arm
  C. Foot
  D. Thigh
  E. Knee
III. Breast
IV. Whole Body
V. Head
  A. Face
  B. Eye
  C. Mouth
  D. Nose
  E. Ear
  F. Neck
  G. Beard
VI. Clothes

I. Hands.–Predictably, the hands are most frequently involved in gesture. As a liturgical gesture the hands are "spread forth" (NEB "spread out") toward heaven, both to accompany verbal prayer and to enact or symbolize its nature as an appeal. In 1 K. 8:22 Solomon literally "divided his palms heavenward" (Heb. *wayyiprōś kappāyw haššāmāyim*) at the outset of his great temple prayer. The suppliant probably makes this gesture by placing his palms together (cf. examples in Mesopotamian sculpture of this "attitude of adoration" in *ANEP,* nos. 431, 433, 435, and 436) and then raising his arms and spreading out his hands (cf. 2 Ch. 6:12f.; Ezr. 9:5) to enact the rising of the prayer to heaven. Interestingly, the same word combination (Heb. *pāraś* + *yad*) is applied with a quite different sense to Yahweh in Isa. 65:2. In this instance it is a gesture of entreaty with which a very available Yahweh sadly demonstrates His loyal concern for a people more interested in superstitious cults.

Sargon II (center), pointing his finger in supplication and holding a mace, and an officer (right) with folded hands stand before a god, who holds symbols of authority, the rod and ring. Reconstruction of a wall painting at the Khorsabad citadel of Sargon II (721-705 B.C.) (Oriental Institute, University of Chicago)

The "lifting up" (Heb. *nāśā'*) of the hands is so naturally and integrally the gesture of prayer in the Bible that reference to the gesture itself often suffices to express the act of praying. In Lam. 2:19 the besieged and desperate mother Jerusalem is urged: "Lift your hands to him [*śᵉʾî ʾēlāyw kappayiḵ*] for the lives of your children, / who faint for hunger at the head of every street." In Ps. 141:2 the gesture parallels the verbal prayer: "Let my prayer be counted as incense before thee, / and the lifting up of my hands as an evening sacrifice!" (Cf. 1 Tim. 2:8, "I desire then that in every place the men should pray, lifting holy hands" [Gk. *epaírō* + *cheír*]; Neh. 8:6; Ps. 28:2; 63:4 [MT 5]; and 1 Clem. 2:3, "you stretched out your hands to Almighty God . . . beseeching him. . . .") For visual examples of the hand raised in prayer, see the relief on the Syrian funerary stele of Sen-zer-ibni (*see* picture in INSCRIPTIONS), as well as several Mesopotamian statuettes (Gray, pp. 56f.). The force of this gesture is to underscore the psychosomatic character of prayer — it is an experience involving the total self, and the physical comportment of the body in the act of praying is important.

Carved ivory casket from Hazor depicting a man with outstretched arms kneeling in prayer (9th-8th cents. B.C.) (Institute of Archaeology, Hebrew University of Jerusalem)

Holding the hands at shoulder level with the palms forward, simultaneously turning the head slightly to one side, is a gesture of surrender throughout the contemporary Arab world (Barakat, p. 778 no. 104). This gesture is illustrated in a Theban tomb painting in which five submissive foreigners, with hands up and palms out, are portrayed enclosed in a platform that serves as a footstool for Pharaoh Amenhotep III (*ANEP,* no. 4; cf. Ps. 110:1, and the discussion of foot gestures below; similarly, cf. *ANEP,* nos. 46f.).

Nubian tribute bearers. Painting of wall painting in the tomb of Ḥuy (18th Dynasty), Thebes (Oriental Institute, University of Chicago)

The hand placed upon one's mouth is a universal gesture for silence. This gesture becomes even more forcefully a sign of respect to a superior, as Job recalled an earlier preeminence when

the young men saw me and withdrew,
and the aged rose and stood;
the princes refrained from talking,
and laid their hand on their mouth

(Job 29:8f.). Contemporary Arabic cultures employ a similar semiotic gesture — touching the tips of the right forefinger, second finger and thumb to the mouth and bowing slightly while so doing — for precisely the same purpose of showing respect to the person addressed (Barakat, p. 773 no. 24). To cease talking in the presence of a superior is to show proper respect; the hand-over-mouth gesture thus signifies both the cessation of speech and the acknowledgment of respect. This gesture is clearly portrayed in a Persepolis relief featuring a Median dignitary with his right hand raised to his mouth out of respect for King Darius before whom he stands (*ANEP,* no. 463).

The right hand placed upon the head of another signifies the blessing of that other person. This gesture indicates physically that one has "touched" the other with the hand of authority, and that a transfer of power or authority has occurred. In Gen. 48:14f. the dying patriarch Israel/Jacob blessed (Heb. *bārak̠*) Joseph and his Egyptian-born sons by putting his hands on the heads of the two sons (deliberately crisscrossed so as to suggest the later preeminence of the second born, Ephraim). The gesture of placing one's hand on the head of a person being blessed is so integral to the concept of blessing that blessings can be spoken of as being "on the head of" someone (Gen. 49:26; Prov. 10:6; cf. also Rev. 1:17; Mk. 10:16). (For the "laying on of hands" in healing, baptism, investiture of office, etc. [e.g., Lk. 4:40; Acts 28:8; 8:17f.; 6:6], *see* HANDS, LAYING ON OF.) A related gesture is the laying or resting (Heb. *sāmak̠*) of the hand on the head of the burnt offering (Lev. 1:4) or the scapegoat (Lev. 16:21); this action symbolized the transfer of sin from the guilty person(s) to the substitutionary sacrifice.

The hand(s) may also simply be "lifted up" for the act of blessing, e.g., of the people by Aaron (Lev. 9:22), of the disciples by Jesus (Lk. 24:50), and of God by the people (Neh. 8:6; Ps. 134:2). Ancient Near Eastern art provides ample illustration of the hand raised in blessing, e.g., by a deity (*ANEP,* nos. 535, 537; *see* picture of relief showing Sargon II and deity) or by a king (*ANEP,* no. 460; Gray, pp. 71, 68). The lifting up (and shaking) of the hand or fist may also be a gesture of defiance (Isa. 10:32) or contempt (Zeph. 2:15). Rebellion against the Davidic monarchy is twice described as men having "raised/lifted their hand" against the king (2 S. 18:28; 20:21). For the so-called brandishing gesture illustrated on an exorcism amulet see *ANEP,* no. 660.

A very common gesture is the raising of the hand in the solemn act of swearing an oath: "For I lift up my hand to heaven, and swear, As I live for ever" (Dt. 32:40). The phrase "to heaven" indicates that the hand was pointed up in the direction of God, in whose name the oath was sworn. The semiotic gesture of contemporary Arabic cultures for oath taking is similar — the right hand is held up before the right shoulder with the palm facing out (Barakat, p. 772 no. 10; cf. modern practice: "Raise your right hand and repeat [the oath] after me"). In Ps. 106:26 this hand gesture also accompanied the verbal act of oath taking, but in other instances the gesture itself sufficed to convey the entire action so that the literal phrase "lift up the hand" can be translated as "swear" (cf., e.g., Gen. 14:22 where Heb. *hᵃrîmōṯî yāḏî ʾel-YHWH* is rendered by the AV, "I have lift up mine hand unto the Lord," by the RSV, "I have sworn to the Lord," and in composite fashion by the NEB, "I lift my hand and swear by the Lord"; cf. Ezk. 20:5f., 15, 23, 28, 42).

Closely related as an oath-taking gesture is the placing of the right hand "under the thigh" (Heb. *taḥaṯ yᵉrēḵî*) of another when taking a solemn oath. In the two biblical instances of this practice (Gen. 24:2; 47:29) the last request of a dying superior (Abraham, Jacob) is that the inferior (the servant, Joseph) make a final oath of loyalty while holding his hand on or near the genitals of the superior. The usual meaning of the contact with the genital organ in oath taking is to render the oath as inviolable as possible, i.e., if the oath is broken may the same happen to the object touched. A similar gesture may be observed in Saudi Arabia when a sheikh or judge places his right hand on or near the genital organ of a man being questioned. That man is thus threatened with sterility and lack of posterity if he lies (Barakat, pp. 761, 784). In Roman custom a man swearing to tell the truth placed his forefinger on his own testicles, with the same threat implicit in that gesture (Barakat, p. 761). The striking feature of the biblical examples is that the procedure is the opposite of that described above; if anyone's genital organ (his virility) is here being placed under threat it is not that of the oath taker but rather that of the dying oath imposer. The significance in these instances may be that failure to comply with the request of the dying patriarch would mean dire consequences for the very important line of patriarchal descent to which Yahweh's promises were attached. Or, it may be that another oath-taking pattern is involved — that of placing one's hand on a sacred object while swearing the oath, with the threat coming from the power of the sacred object.

A pledge of SURETY was concluded between an intervening bail lender and an insolvent debtor by the symbolic gesture of "striking the hands" (Heb. *tāqaʿ* + *kap̱*), i.e., a vigorous handshake (cf. Prov. 6:1; 17:18; 22:26; Job 17:3). In these instances the gesture itself (always in poetic parallelism with *ʿāraḇ,* "intervene, go surety") suffices to denote the pledge of surety and is so translated (RSV "give pledges"; AV "strike hands") in the above passages. (The same Hebrew expression can mean simply "clap," as a sign of joy [Ps. 47:1 (MT 2)].)

Without the legal aspects of the above example the "giving of the hand" (Heb. *nāṯan* + *yaḏ*) may also be a gesture that signifies an agreement or unity between persons (2 K. 10:15). Further, in a society in which the clasping together of right hands was immediately recognized as a sign of agreement such a simple phrase as "hand to hand" (Heb. *yaḏ lᵉyaḏ*) came naturally into idiomatic use as an affirmation: "indeed, surely" ("be assured," Prov. 11:21; AV "though hand join in hand"; NEB "depend upon it").

The clapping of hands (Heb. *nāḵâ* + *kap̱*) appears as a sign of acclamation in the Hebrew coronation rite (by the citizens for King Joash in 2 K. 11:12), and as a figurative gesture of rejoicing in Yahweh (Heb. *māḥāʾ* + *kap̱*; by the floods in Ps. 98:8; and by the trees in Isa. 55:12). By the addition of the preposition *ʿal,* "against," "at," the clapping of hands becomes sinister — a derisive gesture of malicious glee directed at someone suffering misfortune (e.g., the passersby at Jerusalem in Lam. 2:15 [Heb. *sāp̄aq* + *kap̱* + *ʿal*], all who hear of Assyria's demise in Nah. 3:19 [Heb. *tāqaʿ* + *kap̱* + *ʿal*], and, figuratively, the east wind at the wicked in Job 27:23 [Heb. *śāp̄aq* + *kap̱* + *ʿal*]).

In Isa. 49:22 the upraised hand (Heb. *nāśāʾ* + *yaḏ*) appears as a gesture of Yahweh, "I will lift up my hand" (parallel to "raise my signal"), done to indicate (NEB "beckon") to the nations that the ingathering of scattered Israel must now begin. The lifting up of the hands (Heb. *nāśāʾ* + *yaḏ*) may also be a gesture of homage (figuratively, of the deep to Yahweh in Hab. 3:10; but cf. the NEB, which divides vv. 10f. differently and conjectures, "The sun forgets to turn in his course" [lit. "The sun raised the height of his hands"]). (For illustrations of this gesture see *ANEP,* nos. 132, 246 [the Hammurabi stele], 325, 460, 700.)

Black-marble inscribed stone of the Babylonian king Merodach-baladan (722-711 B.C.), holding a staff in his left hand and lifting his right as he grants land to an official (right), who also holds a staff and lifts his right hand to show respect. Above are emblems of several deities who thus give their sanction to the grant (Staatliche Museen, Berlin)

To "wave the hand" (Heb. niphal of *nûp* + *yaḏ*) has several connotations. In 2 K. 5:11 the disappointed Naaman declares that he surely had expected the holy man, Elisha, to "come out to me, and stand, and call on the name of the Lord his God, and wave his hand over the place [*ʾel-hammāqôm*], and cure the leper." This is either a gesture of invocation accompanying healing ("over the place") or a beckoning hand signal directing Naaman ("to the place"). This same Hebrew idiom (niphal *nûp* + *yaḏ*) is used for the menacing gesture of the hand poised to strike that accompanies or effects Yahweh's drying up of the Euphrates in Isa. 11:15, and in Isa. 19:16 and Zec. 2:9 (MT 13) it signals impending disaster when Yahweh "shakes his hand." In Job 31:21 the phrase "If I have raised my hand against the fatherless" refers to exploiting or taking advantage of the defenseless. To "shake the fist" is yet more intensely accented with menace in Isa. 10:32 and Zeph. 2:15. In the first instance it is the defiant gesture of the Assyrian general about to set Jerusalem under siege — his "shaking of the fist" (polel of Heb. *nûp* + *yaḏ*) conveys in a gesture the full menace of his army's devastating progress through the land to the very environs of Jerusalem. In the second it is the same gesture (though here translating the hiphil of Heb. *nû*[*a*]*ʿ* + *yaḏ*) of defiance and doom still being hurled at the now deserted and ruined Nineveh by passersby, whose recollection of Assyrian terror is still strong enough to elicit such gestures of contempt even after the fact of destruction. Nevertheless, depending on context, the wave of the hand may be simply an innocent gesture of direction, as in Isa. 13:2.

In Acts 12:17; 13:16; 19:33; 21:40, the Greek verb *kataseíō,* "motion, signal" (lit. "shake at") is employed in combination with *cheír,* "hand," to represent the gesture a public speaker uses either to gain the crowd's attention or quiet it down before beginning his speech. The RSV translates in each instance "motioning/-ed with his hand" (cf. NEB "with a movement of the hand he signed" [Acts 12:17], "made a gesture with his hand" [13:16]). The same motion is described by the Greek verb *ekteínō,* "extend, stretch out," in combination with *cheír* in Acts 26:1: "Then Paul stretched out his hand and made his defense."

The washing of the hands as a symbolic gesture is a declaration of innocence or noncomplicity (Dt. 21:6 [Heb. *rāḥaṣ* + *yaḏ*]; Mt. 27:24 [Gk. *aponíptō* (from *aponízō*) + *cheír*]; cf. also Ps. 26:6; 73:13).

To "catch/lay hold of [Heb. *ḥāzaq, ʾāḥaz*] the horns of the altar" is a public and political gesture of sanctuary (1 K. 1:50f.; 2:28). The drooping or weakening of the hands is a spontaneous or instinctive gesture triggered by utter terror (Heb. *rāpâ* + *yaḏ*; 2 S. 4:1; Jer. 6:24; 38:4; 50:43; Isa. 35:3; cf. He. 12:12), expressing the sheer helplessness engendered by fear (cf. hand wringing in Wolff, p. 45). Holding the hands on the loins or abdomen is a natural gesture indicating birth pains and thus also, by extension, expressing terror and fear (Jer. 30:6). In Lk. 1:22 the aged priest Zechariah, suddenly mute, "made signs" (Gk. *dianeúō*; AV "beckoned") to communicate. This hardly represents technical gesture (i.e., a sign-language system), for he would have had little prior need to learn one; his signs were more likely a matter of spontaneous invention (*see* BECKON).

See also HAND.

II. Other Appendages.–A. Finger. Gestures with the finger(s) appear less frequently in the Bible. The bad habits of the scoundrel or mischief-maker (Heb. *beliyyaʿal*) cataloged in Prov. 6:13 are that he: "winks with his eyes, scrapes with his feet, points with his finger" (Heb. *mōreh beʾeṣbeʿōṯāyw*). Together these amount to a kind of duplicitous sign language that correlates closely to the scoundrel's malevolent mind and interior orientation toward evil (cf. AV "teacheth with his fingers"; NEB "a sign with the fingers"). In Isa. 58:9 the "pointing of the finger" (Heb. *šelaḥ ʾeṣbaʿ*) is a menacing gesture linked with such politically freighted symbols as "the yoke" (oppression) and "speaking wickedness" (AV "speaking vanity"; cf. AV "the putting forth of the finger"; NEB "to point the accusing finger"; and McKenzie, p. 165, "insulting gesture"). Contemporary Arabic cultures have a threatening or angry gesture that consists of extending the right forefinger from the fist and pointing it steadily at someone (Barakat, p. 773 no. 22). While appealing to the compassion of those who had caught a woman in the act of adultery (Jn. 8:6, 8), Jesus "wrote with his finger on the ground" (Gk. *tǭ daktylǭ katégraphen eis tḗn gḗn*). In healing the deaf-mute in the Decapolis region Jesus "put his fingers into his [i.e., the deaf-mute's] ears" (Mk. 7:33).

B. Arm. Gestures made with the arms are mostly embraces. In Mk. 9:36 Jesus extended His arms (Gk. *enankalízomai*) to embrace a small child as He announced: "Whoever receives one such child in my name receives me" (v. 37, cf. 10:16). In Gen. 33:4 the repentant Jacob, approaching Esau with ample bowing and prostration, is surprised to be warmly embraced (*ḥāḇaq*) by his forgiving brother (cf. NEB "threw his arms round him"; cf. Gen. 48:10). The use of the Greek verb *kataneúō,* "signal, motion," in Lk. 5:7 with regard to the fishermen who "beckoned to their partners in the other boat to come and help them," strongly implies a vigorous arm gesture.

C. Foot. A very ancient foot gesture is placing one's foot on the neck of the slain or prostrate foe to symbolize conquest or subjugation. In Josh. 10:24, after the five captured Amorite rulers were paraded before the Israelite army, Joshua summoned his "chiefs of the men of war" to "put [their] feet upon the necks [*śîmû ʾeṯ-raḡlêḵem ʿal-ṣawweʾrê*] of these kings" to signify their victory and superiority. The same gesture appears in Bar. 4:25 where exiled Israel is urged to wait patiently: "Your enemy has hunted you down, but you will soon see him destroyed, and will put your foot on his neck" (NEB; cf. Gen. 49:8; Dt. 33:29 [LXX]; 1QM 12:11). The same gesture is the working image of 1 Cor. 15:25 — "For he must reign until he has put all his enemies under his feet" (cf. Ps. 110:1, and the surrender gesture above).

Tiglath-pileser III (745-727 B.C.) rests his foot on the neck of a prostrate king. Relief from Calah (Nimrûd) (Trustees of the British Museum)

"Shaking off" (Gk. *ektinássō*) the dust from one's feet is a NT gesture indicating the severance of the connection with, or responsibility to, others. In Mt. 10:14 among His instructions to the disciples Jesus stated, "And if any one will not receive you or listen to your words, shake off the dust from your feet as you leave that house or town." This gesture appears also in Acts 13:51; as Paul and Barnabas were being driven from Pisidian Antioch, "they shook off the dust from their feet against them" (*ep' autoús*). The simple addition of the prepositional phrase adds force to the gesture; thus NEB "they shook the dust off their feet in protest against them" (cf. JB "in defiance"). It is also clear from this passage that the gesture is directed *at* someone.

Uncovering one's feet is a gesture of grief and repentance in 2 S. 15:30 as the king himself, head covered and weeping, walked barefoot (Heb. *yāḥēp*). Isaiah went barefoot (as well as naked) for three years (Isa. 20:2, 4) to dramatize the stark threat of Assyrian exile.

Uncovering the feet of another may also in some contexts be a sign of willingness to marry. The young widow Ruth followed the instructions of her mother-in-law Naomi to "uncover the feet" (*wegillîṯ margelōṯāyw*) of Boaz as he slept (Ruth 3:4, 7). (Heb. **margelôṯ* means "legs" in Dnl. 10:6 and is closely related to *raglayim,* "feet," which can be a euphemism for the genitals, e.g., Jgs. 3:24, etc.) Thus in the light of commands against uncovering another's "skirt" (*kānāp*) (Dt. 22:30 [MT 23:1]; 27:20), and a context rife with sexual connotations (e.g., the verbs *šāḵaḇ,* "lie down"; *yāḏa',* "know"; *bô',* "go in"), a few interpreters have considered Ruth's action part of a deliberate seduction of the potential *gô'ēl* ("redeemer"), Boaz. Such an interpretation, however, is inconsistent with the character of Ruth and Naomi revealed throughout the story. Although Naomi's plan does leave itself open to misunderstanding (indeed, the deliberate ambiguity is a sign of the narrator's craft in heightening the suspense; cf. E. F. Campbell, *Ruth* [*AB,* 1975], pp. 130-32), it really only intends a symbolic act, a mimed invitation to marriage. The ambiguity begins to clear up at v. 13 with Boaz's use of Heb. *lûn/lîn,* "lodge," which has no sexual connotations. This was not a sexual encounter after all; Boaz did not take advantage of the young widow, and his measuring out of grain is evidence of his determination to care for the two widows as custom and generosity dictate.

The expression "covering his feet" is a well-known euphemism for relieving oneself (e.g., Jgs. 3:24, *mēsîḵ hû' 'eṯ-raglāyw*).

In Jn. 13:5-12 Jesus washed (Gk. *níptō*) the feet of His disciples as a symbolic gesture of humble service, thereby delineating the authentic character of authority: "If I then, your Lord and Teacher, have washed your feet, you also ought to wash one another's feet" (13:14). To "lift the heel against" another, as used in Ps. 41:9 (MT 10) and quoted in Jn. 13:18, is a gesture (or at least a figure of speech with its roots in gesture) for opposition (cf. NEB "has turned against me").

In Prov. 6:13 the scoundrel is said to have several signals ready when he desires to communicate covertly; in addition to winking and finger gesture he "scrapes [Heb. *môlēl,* lit. "speaks"; RSV mg. "taps"] with his feet" (cf. AV "he speaketh with his feet"; NEB "a touch with the foot"). This may have taken the form of tracing patterns or signs in the dust with the foot (see McKane, p. 325).

See also FOOT.

D. Thigh. In Jer. 31:18f. Ephraim figuratively recalls how as a youth he had to be chastened "like an untrained calf" by Yahweh, and adds:

For after I had turned away I repented;
and after I was instructed, I smote upon my thigh;
I was ashamed, and I was confounded,
because I bore the disgrace of my youth.

In the context the smiting of the thigh appears to be a gesture of remorse or shame, but following an experience of insight or instruction it may well be a gesture of coming to one's senses or of suddenly recalling something important. In contemporary Arabic cultures hitting the right thigh with the right palm indicates surprise, joy, or the recollection of something (Barakat, p. 774 no. 30).

E. Knee. Knees (Heb. *birkayim*; Gk. *góny*) are bowed (Heb. *kāra'*; Gk. *kámpō*) in homage (1 K. 19:18; Isa. 45:23; Rom. 14:11; Phil. 2:10) or in prayer (Ezr. 9:5; cf. also 2 Ch. 6:13). See illustration in Gray, p. 56. (*See also* KNEE.)

III. Breast.–The "beating of the BREAST" (Gk. *týptō*

Inscribed alabaster cult socket of Tukulti-Ninurta I (1243-1207 B.C.) from Asshur. The king is shown twice, first standing and then kneeling, holding a mace and pointing his index finger at the shield of the fire-god Nusku (Staatliche Museen, Berlin)

tó stēthos) appears twice in the NT as a gesture of remorse or contrition: on the part of the tax collector in the temple (Lk. 18:13) and the crowd at the crucifixion (23:48). Mourning women in the ancient Near East lacerated their breasts to express their grief (Ezk. 23:24). Figures slash their breasts and pull out their hair (see below) on the sarcophagus of King Ahiram of Byblos (see *ANEP*, no. 459; Gray, p. 87). In addition to shaving off their hair and beard, tearing their clothing, and putting on sackcloth, mourners were known to lacerate their bodies as a public gesture of grief — "cut himself" (Jer. 16:6), "their bodies gashed" (41:5), and "upon all the hands are gashes" (48:37). *See also* CUTTINGS IN THE FLESH.

IV. The Whole Body.–The whole body is bowed to the ground (Heb. *šāḥâ* + *'ārṣâ*) in greeting, and to indicate deference to a superior (Gen. 18:2; 19:1). In some instances protocol demanded a fixed number of such bows (seven times in Gen. 33:3, 7, and in Am.Tab. 137, 147, 234, etc.; three times in 1 S. 20:41). Similarly, "bowing, doing obeisance to" (*šāḥâ* + *l*[e]-) someone is a sign of deference to a superior (Gen. 23:7; 42:6; 2 S. 9:6, 8; 1 K. 1:31, 53; 2:19), of obedience (2 S. 18:21), or of worship (2 K. 5:18; 2 Ch. 29:29). To stand upright (Heb. *qûm*) in the presence of the elderly is a gesture of respect and honor for the aged. Such action is commanded in Lev. 19:32. Thus, so highly esteemed was Job before the onset of all his calamities that even "the aged rose and stood" (Heb. *qûm* + *'āmaḏ*) in his presence (Job 29:8)! This same gesture of respect is also practiced in contemporary Arabic cultures whenever an esteemed person enters the house or tent (Barakat, p. 783 no. 181).

V. Head.–The head is bowed (*qāḏaḏ*) for prayer (Gen. 24:26). The lifting up of one's head (Heb. *nāśā'* or *rûm* + *rō'š*) is a gesture signifying rebellion (Ps. 83:2 [MT 3]; Jgs. 8:28), resistance or opposition (Zec. 1:21 [MT 2:4]). It may also indicate victory: "my head shall be lifted up above my enemies" (Ps. 27:6; cf. Ps. 110:7). Thus this phrase, *nāśā'* + *rō'š*, may also be idiomatic for "free" or "release from captivity" as in 2 K. 25:27, "Evil-merodach king of Babylon . . . graciously freed Jehoiachin" (AV "did lift up the head of Jehoiachin"; NEB "showed favor to Jehoiachin . . . brought him out").

Covering (Heb. *ḥāpâ*) the head is a gesture of grief (2 S. 15:30), mourning (Est. 6:12), or shame (Jer. 14:3f.). Grief or remorse is also indicated by the gesture of putting on dust (*'āpār*, Josh. 7:6), earth (*'ᵃḏāmâ*, 1 S. 4:12; 2 S. 1:2), or ashes (*'ēper*, 2 S. 13:19; Est. 4:1). This gesture is usually accompanied by the rending of one's garment(s) (2 S. 13:19), and at times the donning of sackcloth (Est. 4:1). Tamar, after her cruel mistreatment at the hands of Amnon, not only put ashes on her head and rent her robe, but also "laid her hand on her head" (Heb. *wattāśem yāḏāh 'al-rō'šāh*) in a gesture of shame as she went away crying. Likewise the people will march ignominiously into exile with their hands on their heads (Jer. 2:37; cf. the Egyptian relief from Abusir of a procession of prisoners [*ANEP*, no. 1]).

A common head gesture is the "wagging" or "shaking" of the head to indicate contempt, reproach, or horror. Job wished that he could "shake" (Heb. **nû(a)'*) his head in reproach at his advisers just as they had been doing to him (Job 16:4). Jeremiah envisioned passersby "shak-

Lachish residents (extreme left) bow before Sennacherib as he receives tribute. Relief from Kuyunjik (Nineveh) *ca.* 700 B.C. (Trustees of the British Museum)

ing" (Heb. *nûḏ*) their heads at the coming ruin of Israel (Jer. 18:16). And so did they "wag" (Heb. **nû(a)ʿ*) their heads over the plight of fallen Jerusalem (Lam. 2:15). In addition, in both these instances the passersby also hissed contemptuously. The personified Jerusalem in 2 K. 19:21 (= Isa. 37:22) wagged her head behind the arrogant Sennacherib to signify her contempt of his might. Heads were "wagged" (Heb. **nû(a)ʿ*) also in derision and reproach of the sufferer in Ps. 22:7 (MT 8), 109:25; cf. Sir. 12:18. Similarly, at the crucifixion taunting onlookers "wagged" (Gk. *kinéō*) their heads at Jesus (Mt. 27:39 par.). Thus, since the gesture of head wagging suffices in itself to indicate derision, the phrase *menôḏ-rōʾš* may be idiomatic for "laughingstock" (Ps. 44:14 [MT 15]; RSV mg., AV "a shaking of the head"; NEB "shake their heads").

The head is "nodded" (Gk. *neúō*) in order to signal another person (Jn. 13:24; RSV, AV, "beckon"; NEB "nodded"). The "wagging" or "shaking" of the head may also be a genuine gesture of sympathy in a context of grief or dismay. The Hebrew verb *nûḏ*, "move to and fro," frequently appears in the extended sense of "commiserate, express sympathy" as in Job 2:11 ("condole") and 42:11 ("showed . . . sympathy"). (Cf. also Jer. 18:16.) *See also* HEAD.

A. Face. Covering the face is a gesture of solitary mourning in 2 S. 19:4 (MT 5) where David "covered his face" (Heb. *lāʿaṭ ʾeṯ-pānāyw*; NEB "hid his face") while grieving deeply over Absalom's death.

B. Eye. The most obvious gesture with the eyes is winking, and in Prov. 6:13 one aspect of the scoundrel's sinister sign language is that he "winks with his eyes" (*qōrēṣ beʿênāw*) for no good purpose. That the wink is a duplicitous gesture is confirmed by Sir. 27:22, "A man who winks is plotting mischief" (NEB), and Prov. 10:10, "he who winks the eye causes trouble." Looking upward prior to or during prayer is a gesture obviously directing the prayer to God. In Lk. 18:13 the tax collector considered himself so unworthy to enter into the divine presence that he "would not even lift up his eyes to heaven" (Gk. *oudé toús ophthalmoús epárai eis tón ouranón*). In Lk. 9:16, before blessing and breaking the five loaves and two fishes, Jesus "looked up to heaven" (Gk. *anablépsas eis tón ouranón*). It is the same eye gesture in each instance; the first is simply described differently through a semitism.

In another context, however, lifting the eyelids, and thus the eyes, becomes the obvious gesture of self-righteous pride that looks down on others:

> There are those who are pure in their own eyes
> but are not cleansed of their filth.
> There are those — how lofty are their eyes,
> how high their eyelids lift!

(Heb. *weʿapʿappāyw yinnāśēʾû*, Prov. 30:12f.; NEB "how disdainful their glances"; see McKane, p. 311, for "glances").

C. Mouth. The sufferer in Ps. 22:7 (MT 8) lamented that "all who see me mock at me,/they make mouths at me,/they wag their heads." The literal meaning of the Hebrew phrase *yapṭîrû beśāpâ* is "they cause the lips to separate." The verb *pāṭar* is also used to describe the opening up of a flower (1 K. 6:18); "to make mouths at" (RSV, NEB; cf. AV "shoot out the lip") is thus to gape at another in mock horror or derision. The mouth was used in a very common gesture of greeting and salutation — the kiss (Heb. *nāšaq*; Gen. 45:15; 48:10; Ex. 18:7; 1 S. 20:41; Gk. *kataphiléō*; Mt. 26:49; Lk. 15:20). Jesus spat in connection with His healing of both the deaf-mute (Mk. 7:33) and the blind man (8:23). Spitting in someone's face was a way to shame him. Thus the brother-in-law who refused to act on his leviratic obligation, in the presence of the elders, had to face the solitary widow who by law was required to remove his sandal and spit in his face (Heb. *weyāreqâ bepānāyw*, Dt. 25:9); cf. Nu. 12:14; Isa. 50:6, "I hid not my face from shame and spitting" (Heb. *rōq*). This gesture has the same import in the NT where it appeared in Jesus' humiliation (Gk. *emptýō*; Mt. 26:67 par.; 27:30 par.). Spitting in the face of another person, or at his feet, is still a contemporary Arab expression of shame or insult (Barakat, p. 783 no. 185). *See also* MOUTH.

D. Nose. The NOSE is the focus of an obscure gesture mentioned in Ezk. 8:17 — in a vision twenty-five idolatrous sun worshipers are observed by Ezekiel to "put the branch to their nose" (Heb. *šōleḥîm ʾeṯ-hazzemôrâ ʾel-ʾappām*). This gesture has been understood, on the one hand, to be one of appeasement (cf. NEB "even while they seek to appease me"), and one of extreme offensiveness on the other. (Cf. Today's English Version, "they insult me in the most offensive way possible." T. H. Gaster, following older Jewish interpretation that suspects Persian influence involving the smelling of aromatic plants, proposes: "They were inhaling the fragrance of vine-branches (lit. sending the vine-branches to their nose)" [p. 309]. The LXX has *myktērízontes*, "turning up the nose" [i.e., sneezing]. H. Saggs suggests [pp. 318ff.] that Mesopotamian parallels point to phallic fertility-cult associations with the stick or vine branch; cf. Isa. 10:17.) It seems clear that in a context of progressive abominations this final one, whatever it is, should be the worst. Thus, as traditional Jewish exegesis has generally concluded, it may be that this gesture was obscene. Such a conclusion is supported by the fact that this passage contains one of the eighteen textual emendations (*tiqqûn sôperîm*) made by the ancient scribes for the sake of maintaining proper reverence for God. In the original text the offense had been directed at Yahweh Himself — "to *my* nose." Thus Eichrodt, conjecturing the sense of "stink" for *zemôrâ*, "branch, tendril," renders the passage: "forcing their stink up my nostrils," in reference to their blasphemous rituals (see Eichrodt, pp. 106, 108, 127f.). It may also have been that the act of putting a branch to someone's nose was an ordinary and obvious gesture of provocation whose meaning and origin were subsequently lost. Thus Gordis (p. 287) contends that this idiom, whatever its origin, functions with the meaning "harass, irritate."

E. Ear. To "incline the ear" (i.e., "bend" or "lean near," Heb. *nāṭâ* + *ʾōzen*) is a common gesture of attentiveness in the OT (cf. Ps. 45:10 [MT 11]; 86:1; Jer. 7:26; NEB "hear my words," "turn," "paid heed"). *See also* EAR.

F. Neck. "Stiffening of the NECK (Heb. *qāšâ* + *ʿōrep*) appears as a gesture of obduracy in Prov. 29:1 (AV "hardeneth his neck"; NEB "still stubborn"); Jer. 7:26 (NEB "were obstinate"); 17:23; 19:15; and Neh. 9:16f. (NEB "were/remained stubborn"). To "fall upon the neck" (Heb. *nāpal* + *ʿal-* + *ṣawwāʾr*; Gk. *epipíptō* + *epí* + *tráchēlos*) of someone (i.e., embrace with arms encircling the neck) is a gesture of warm welcome (Gen. 33:4; 45:14; 46:29; AV Lk. 15:20; Acts 20:37). Walking "with outstretched necks" (Heb. *neṭûwōṯ gārôn*) is a gesture of haughtiness that Isaiah found distasteful in the conduct of the daughters of Zion (Isa. 3:16). One of Jeremiah's symbolic actions was to fashion a yoke and put it on his own neck (Jer. 27:2).

G. Beard. In contemporary Arab societies it is customary for the victorious in battle to cut off the BEARD of those conquered, a victory gesture implying that the defeated men have lost the virility that the beard represents (see Barakat, p. 782 no. 174). Thus Ezekiel in one of his symbolic actions shaved his beard (and head) as a gesture that signified what sort of dire consequences might be expected to follow the siege of Jerusalem (Ezk. 5:1; cf. Isa. 15:2). Again, when Ammon's new king Hanun had half the beard of each of King David's ambassadors cut off, they were too ashamed to return home until the hair was regrown, so strongly did this act imply that they were each thereby only half a man (2 S. 10:1-5). The act of shaving the beard (except in cases of leprosy; cf. Lev. 14:9) became then a desperate public gesture of shame and loss of potency (Jer. 41:5). In Isa. 7:20 Yahweh is envisioned as using the rapacious Assyrian war machine as a "razor" that will "shave" (fig.) not only the beard of Judah but also all the hair on its body — complete devastation and loss of virility. "Plucking out" (Heb. *māraṭ*) the hair of one's own beard or head is a gesture of consternation and anger, as illustrated by Ezra's reaction to troubling news (Ezr. 9:3).

VI. Clothes.–A dramatic gesture expressing grief, horror, or anguish is the tearing of one's garments (e.g., Heb. *qāraʿ + beged*, Nu. 14:6; Jgs. 11:35; 2 S. 1:2; Ezr. 9:3, 5; Gk. *diaréssō* or *diarrēgnymi + himátion, chitṓn*, Mt. 26:65; Mk. 14:63; Acts 14:14; Jth. 14:19). That the external gesture of sorrow can never replace the need for internal reorientation or repentance is clear from Joel 2:13: "rend your hearts and not your garments." Another gesture involving garments is illustrated in Acts 18:6 where Paul, after being reviled, symbolically "shook out his garments" to indicate a severance of connection with, or obligation to, those who were rejecting him. *See also* GARMENTS.

See also POSTURES.

Bibliography.–R. A. Barakat, *Journal of Popular Culture*, 6 (1973), 749-787; W. Eichrodt, *Ezekiel: A Commentary (OTL*, 1970); T. H. Gaster, *JBL*, 60 (1941), 289-310; R. Gordis, *JTS*, 37 (1936), 284-88; J. Gray, *Near Eastern Mythology* (1969); M. I. Gruber, *Aspects of Nonverbal Communication in the Ancient East* (1980); W. McKane, *Proverbs (OTL*, 1970); J. L. McKenzie, *Second Isaiah (AB*, 1968); H. W. F. Saggs, *JTS*, N.S. 11 (1960). 318-329; C. Wolff, *Psychology of Gestures* (1972); W. Wundt, *Language of Gestures* (1973).

D. G. BURKE

GET. Many Hebrew and Greek verbs are rendered "get" and have various shades of meaning.

(1) Literally, "get" is used in the sense of "acquire" or "obtain," e.g., property (Gen. 34:10, niphal of *'āḥaz*), wealth or riches (Dt. 8:17, *ʿāśâ*, "do," "make"; Prov. 11:16b, *tāmaḵ*, "grasp, lay hold of"), cities (2 S. 20:6, *māṣā'*, "find"). Metaphorically, one is to "gain" understanding (Job. 11:12, niphal of **lāḇaḇ*, "be made intelligent"; Ps. 119:104, hithpolel of *bîn*, "pay attention to"), wisdom and understanding (Prov. 16:16, *qānâ*, "obtain"), a new heart (Ezk. 18:31, *ʿāśâ*), honor (Prov. 11:16a, *tāmaḵ*), etc.

(2) At times "get" is equivalent to "fetch," as in Jer. 36:21 ("get [a scroll]," *lāqaḥ*, "take"), Lam. 5:6 ("get enough [bread]," *śāḇaʿ*, "be sated with"), Mk. 12:2 ("get [fruit]," Gk. *lambánō*, "take"), 2 Tim. 4:11 ("get [Mark]," *analambánō*, "take up").

(3) Often "get" occurs in compounds and signifies "go" (e.g., "get out," *yāṣā' min*, Gen. 19:14, "get away from me," *lēḵ mēʿālāy*, Ex. 10:28), or "become" (e.g., "get warm," 1 K. 1:1 [*ḥāmam*], "get drunk," Lk. 12:45 [*methýskō*]). Of interest is Our Lord's rebuke to Peter, "Get behind me, Satan!" (*hýpage opísō mou, sataná*, Mk. 8:33 par.). It may mean that Christ, who would not yield to the temptation to forego His sufferings on the cross, implied that Peter should "return to [his] rank" as a true believer of Christ (W. L. Lane, comm. on Mark [*NICNT*, 1974], p. 295 n. 77). On the other hand, it may simply mean, "Get out of my way," i.e., do not try to block my determination to accomplish my mission. R. W. V.

GETHER gē'thər [Heb. *geṯer*]. In Gen. 10:23 named as one of the four sons of Aram. In 1 Ch. 1:17 mentioned simply among the sons of Shem.

GETHSEMANE geth-sem'ə-nē [Gk. *Gethsēmani* < Aram. or Heb. *gaṯ šᵉmānîm*–'oil press']. The place where Jesus agonized in prayer on the night of His betrayal.

I. Location.–The name is mentioned in Matthew (26:36) and Mark (14:32) as the piece of land or field (*chōríon*) to which Jesus and His disciples retired following the Last Supper. In Jn. 18:1 it is described as a garden (*kēpos*), from which comes the traditional designation "Garden of Gethsemane," while Lk. 22:40 has simply "place" (*tópos*). From Jn. 18:1 it is evident that it was across the Kidron, and from Lk. 22:39, that it was on the slope of the Mt. of Olives. It was a place where Jesus frequently went with His disciples (Lk. 22:39f.; Jn. 18:2). Its name suggests a grove of olive trees, as does its location on the Mt. of Olives. The language of John's Gospel seems to imply a walled garden ("entered," 18:1).

II. Event.–The terms in which the experience of Gethsemane is described in the Gospels speak of deepest sorrow and suffering. Lk. 22:44 used the word "agony" (Gk. *agōnía*) to speak of Our Lord's experience, thus implying a great strain or struggle (cf. Mt. 26:37 par. Mk. 14:33). And it is Luke who gave the physical description: "his sweat became like great drops of blood falling down upon the ground" (Lk. 22:44, RSV mg.). Jesus' words of warning to His disciples (Mt. 26:41; cf. Lk. 22:40, 46) and His prayer (Mt. 26:39 par.) imply that He regarded the event in terms of a temptation (cf. He. 5:7f.), from which He emerged victoriously (cf. I. H. Marshall, comm. on Luke [*New International Greek Testament Commentary*, 1978], p. 831).

III. Meaning.–The exact meaning of the event has been a subject of theological controversy from earliest times. But certainly there seems to be an anticipation of the cross, where the Son of God Himself was to experience man's

Rembrandt van Rijn, *Agony in the Garden*, a seventeenth-century etching showing Christ (right), an angel, and sleeping disciples (left) (Metropolitan Museum of Art, Harris Brisbane Dick Fund, 1923)

greatest inhumanity to man and also abandonment by God and man in fulfillment of the role of the Servant of Yahweh, who voluntarily suffered an atoning death for the sins of mankind. Some would see in the event an intended contrast with the experience of Adam in the Garden of Eden: here the Second Adam prevailed, by prayer and inward submission to the will of God, over temptation.

*IV. **Tradition**.*–The site on the slopes of the Mt. of Olives where the Franciscans maintain the Grotto of the Agony dates back at least to the 5th cent. and has as good a claim as any place to be the location of Gethsemane, but one cannot be certain. Several other spots vie for the honor of being the location of the event mentioned in the Gospels. Although the olive trees in the present Garden are very old, they cannot, in spite of claims to the contrary, go back to the 1st century. *See* Plate 42.

See *DBSup.*, III (1938), 631-659. W. W. GASQUE

GEUEL gū'el, gə-ū'el [Heb. *ge'ûʾēl*–'majesty of God' (?)]. The man from the tribe of Gad (Nu. 13:15), sent by Moses to spy out the land of Canaan.

GEZER gē'zər [Heb. *gezer*; LXX Gk. *Gazera, Gazēra, Gazer, Gader*]; AV GAZER (2 S. 5:25; 1 Ch. 14:16), GAZERA (1 Macc. 4:15; 7:45), or GAZARA. An important city in the northern Shephelah, the modern Tell Jezer.

*I. **Location**.*–Gezer is situated on the northwestern extension of that intermediary line of hills (the Shephelah) separating the Judean hill country from the Philistine plain. Its significance stems from its proximity to the great N-S trunk line (Via Maris) that runs along the coast to Jabneel (Jamnia) and turns eastward across the plain of Ono to reach Aphek (Râs el-ʿAin); and equally significant, Gezer guards the junction of the Via Maris with the principal highway going laterally into the hill country via the ascent of Beth-horon.

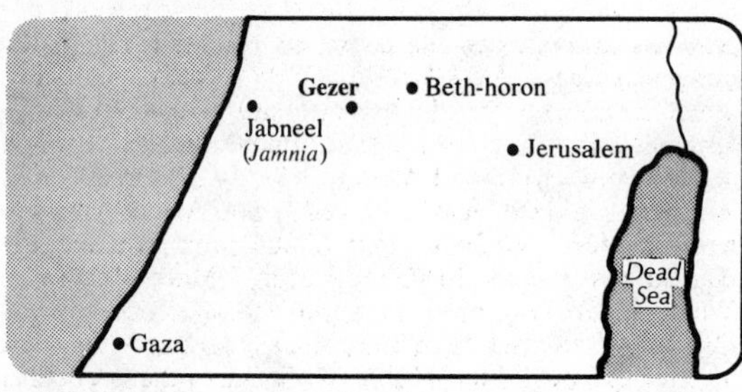

*II. **Excavation**.*–The site was discovered by C. Clermont-Ganneau in 1871. R. A. S. Macalister conducted two major campaigns at Tell Jezer between 1902 and 1905 and again between 1907 and 1909. From 1964 to 1974 the Hebrew Union College Biblical and Archaeological School in Jerusalem conducted a series of excavations directed by G. E. Wright, W. G. Dever, and J. D. Seger.

One problem that troubled scholars after the publication of Macalister's work was the apparent absence of a stratum from the period of the Israelite monarchy. Y. Yadin, by comparing the ground plan of the tenth-century city gate and casemate wall discovered at Hazor, demonstrated that a so-called Maccabean palace in Macalister's drawings had practically the same dimensions as half the gate at Hazor; the adjoining casemate wall was of exactly the same measurements (1958). Such a coincidence is hardly likely unless the two structures were contemporary.

Part of a row of ten monoliths (some of which are over 3 m. [10 ft.] high) at the so-called Gezer high place (17th cent. B.C.). These stones are now thought to have been connected with covenant ceremonies among the neighboring peoples (cf. Ex. 24:4) (D. Baly)

*III. **History**.–A. Bronze Age.* The first recorded reference to Gezer is in the topographical lists of Thutmose III, where it appears as no. 104 (written *g-ḏ-r*). This would indicate that it was conquered by that pharaoh during his first campaign to Canaan; his march from Gaza to Yaḥm was considerably impeded by the resistance he encountered from Gezer and her neighbors. Along with all of Canaan, Gezer seems to have remained loyal to Egypt throughout the reign of Thutmose III and Amenhotep II. Thutmose IV may have had to take punitive action there, however, for on a stele in his mortuary temple he mentions Khurru (Horite) captives from Gez[er] who have been installed in Egypt (*ANET*, p. 248). A cuneiform tablet discovered on the surface at Tell Jezer appears to be a request from a high-ranking Egyptian that the ruler of Gezer bring him seven oxen at the town of Gittim (Gath, or perhaps Gittaim). It has been suggested that the tablet was sent by Thutmose IV during some campaign to Canaan and that failure to comply with the request resulted in the capture of the city.

Gezer and its rulers figure prominently in the Egyptian archives from Tell el-Amarna. The course of events pertaining to the city and its neighbors as reflected in these texts has been the subject of several recent studies (cf. bibliography). These texts mention the ʿApiru (outlaws, renegade soldiers, or even political rivals to the Egyptians; *see also* HABIRU), who were exerting strong pressure on Gezer and on a neighboring ruler, Šuwardata (from Gath, or Hebron[?]); Milkilu, ruler of Gezer, called to Pharaoh for a chariot force that would rescue him and Šuwardata (Am.Tab. 271). Later Abdu-Ḫeba, prince of Jerusalem, confirmed an alliance between Gezer and Shechem (289); Milkilu and Šuwardata (290), supported by Tagu (289), had seized Rubutu (=Rabbah, Josh. 15:60), a town that belonged to Jerusalem. In another letter Abdu-Ḫeba blamed Gezer, Ashkelon, and Lachish for furnishing supplies to his enemies (287); but the king of Gezer (here called Ilimilku) seems to have been the prime mover behind the ʿApiru attempt to seize the territory loyal to Pharaoh (286).

How the new coalition under Milkilu's leadership fared is not stated in any of the Amarna Letters, but its failure seems to be implied by certain hints that have been preserved. Amenhotep IV (Akhenaten) is known to have planned an expedition to Canaan, probably directed against his recalcitrant vassal in the north, Amurru. Though the campaign was evidently cancelled at the last minute, the impending show of force may have caused the partners to fall out with one another. The death of Milkilu may have been a decisive factor, though that event is not recorded. What does seem clear is the replacement of Gezer's prince by his sons. The princess of Zaphon in the Jordan Valley reported that Pharaoh's land was falling away to the ʿApiru, who had attacked Aijalon and Zorah; during this encounter the sons of Milkilu escaped being smitten only by a "finger's breadth" (273). One of these sons was probably Yapaḫu, a subsequent ruler of Gezer. Yapaḫu affirmed his own loyalty in the face of pressure from the ʿApiru (299). His younger brother (unnamed) is said to have entered Muḫḫazu and to have aligned himself with the ʿApiru (298).

Gezer does not appear in the extant records of the later pharaohs of the 18th Dynasty, nor is it mentioned by members of the 19th Dynasty until the reign of Merneptah (*ca.* 1223-1211 B.C.), who called himself "the reducer of Gezer" and whose victory stele boasts that Gezer was captured (*ANET,* p. 378). The political circumstances that brought on this Egyptian attack are unknown; besides Gezer the same text gloats over Canaan, Ashkelon, Yanoam, and the people of Israel.

B. Iron Age. During the conquest of the land by Israel, Horam king of Gezer came to the aid of Lachish but was defeated in the field (Josh. 10:33; the LXX has Gk. *Gaza,* a common scribal error for Gazara in Greek sources). Thus Horam appears in the list of conquered Canaanite kings (Josh. 12:12). Gezer's location on the border of the territory allotted to the sons of Joseph after Lower Beth-horon (Josh. 16:3) was a helpful guide to the eventual discovery of the ancient site at Tell Jezer. Although the town was assigned to the tribe of Ephraim (1 Ch. 7:28), the Ephraimites did not succeed in driving out the Canaanite population (Josh. 16:10; Jgs. 1:29); when Israel became strong, the Canaanites were subjected to forced labor. The Kohathites (Levites) who settled in Ephraim's territory were allotted Gezer as one of their cities (Josh. 21:21; 1 Ch. 6:67 [MT 52]).

During the early stages of David's conflict with the Philistines, when he repulsed their intrusions into the hill country, he pursued them as far as Gezer (2 S. 5:25; 1 Ch. 14:16). Subsequently, David carried the war down to the region of Gezer itself (1 Ch. 20:4). It seems unlikely that David would have left Gezer untouched as a Canaanite enclave within his kingdom; nevertheless, the town was conquered and ravaged by the pharaoh of Egypt during the reign of Solomon (1 K. 9:15-17). Either the Egyptians had begun hostilities against Israel and later became reconciled to Solomon's power, or Gezer had somehow rebelled and regained its independence for a brief time in the early years of Solomon's reign. Whatever the situation, Solomon incorporated Gezer into his network of military stations along with Hazor, Megiddo, Beth-horon, and others (1 K. 9:15-17). (*See* Map VII.) As noted above, almost identical gates and casemate walls existed at Gezer and Hazor.

Perhaps the Philistines had gained control of Gezer before Pharaoh's deed. His drive across Philistia seems to reflect a renewed Egyptian suzerainty over that area. Such a situation apparently prevailed somewhat later, because Pharaoh Sheshonq (Shishak) was able to march across the Philistine plain from Gaza (no. 11 in his list) to Gezer (no. 12) without meeting resistance. Gezer itself did fall in his line of fire, however, and its reduction was essential for Shishak to penetrate the hill country via the Beth-horon route and threaten Jerusalem (1 K. 14:25-28; 2 Ch. 12:1-12).

During the period of the divided monarchy, it is not certain to whom Gezer belonged. In fact, Gezer does not figure in the biblical text at all. Only from a relief depicting its conquest by Tiglath-pileser III (*ANEP,* no. 369) was it learned that the city had suffered during his conquest of Philistia (734 B.C.) or of Israel (733 B.C.).

The discovery of two Assyrian cuneiform tablets in the excavations at Tell Jezer suggests an Assyrian colony there following the fall of the Israelite kingdom. The presence at Gezer of stamped jar handles and a shekel weight marked "for the king," however, indicate that Gezer was attached to the Judean monarchy during the late 8th cent. B.C.

In the postexilic period Gezer may have been attached to the Judean province, as evidenced by the stamped jar handles with the "Yehud" and "Yerushalem" inscriptions. But the situation is far from clear. After the Egyptians broke away from the Persian empire they may have maintained a foothold for some time in Palestine; a stone slab and a scarab bearing the name of Neferites, founder of the 29th Dynasty (398-393 B.C.), was found at Gezer.

C. Hellenistic Age. Before the rise of the Hasmonean kingdom Gezer was evidently a gentile fortress (Avi-Yonah suggests that the Andronicus of 2 Macc. 5:23 was stationed at Gezer rather than [Gk.] *Garizin*). Thus it served as a refuge for the fleeing Syrians after Judas Maccabeus had routed them near Emmaus (1 Macc. 4:15; Josephus *Ant.* xii.7.4 [308]; 165 B.C.). The same was true for the shattered remnants of Nicanor's army, whom the Judean villagers harrassed as they desperately sought to reach the safety of Gezer from the heights near Jerusalem (1 Macc. 7:45; 161 B.C.). After Bacchides' victory over Judas in 161, he began to surround central Judea with new fortresses, and Beth-zur and Gezer were strengthened at the same time (1 Macc. 9:52; Josephus *Ant.* xiii.1.3 [15f.]).

Twenty years later Simon Maccabeus took advantage of the dynastic struggle for the Seleucid throne to extend his authority to the coast; an essential link in the chain was Gezer (AV, Gk. "Gaza"; RSV, NEB "Gazara"), which he reduced by the use of a siege engine (1 Macc. 13:43-48). It was at Gezer that Simon stationed his son John with a garrison (1 Macc. 13:53; 14:34). In 137 B.C. Antiochus Sidetes had achieved a position of strength and therefore demanded that Simon return to him the coastal possessions, including Gezer (1 Macc. 15:28-35). When the Jews refused, he appointed an officer named Cendebeus to open hostilities against Judea; John went up from Gezer to inform his father Simon of the impending threat (1 Macc. 16:1); he was given command of a field army that repelled the Syrians (1 Macc. 16:4-10). Afterward, John (Hyrcanus I) remained at his post in Gezer until the murder of his father by Ptolemy son of Abubus. When the latter sent men to Gezer to slay John as well, they were caught by him and executed.

Once John Hyrcanus had become high priest in his father's place, Antiochus Sidetes came against him again (133/132 B.C.) and by besieging Jerusalem forced John to surrender the coastal cities (Josephus *BJ* i.2.5 [61]; *Ant.* xiii.8.3 [245-48]). After Antiochus' death, Hyrcanus regained Gezer and the other towns on the plain (129 B.C.); in this he had the support of the Roman senate (*Ant.* xiii.9.2 [259-266]). Though not included in Josephus' list of cities in Jewish hands during the reign of Alexander Janneus (*Ant.* xiii.15.4 [395-97]), Gezer was clearly still a Hasmonean fortress.

During the Roman period, Gezer had become merely

a village; it was by then overshadowed by the nearby town of Emmaus-Nicopolis (Eusebius *Onom.* 66.19–68.2).

See also GAZARA.

Bibliography.–W. F. Albright, *BASOR,* 92 (Dec. 1943), 16-26, 28-30; M. Avi-Yonah, *The Holy Land* (1966), pp. 22, 48f.; W. G. Dever, *BA,* 30 (1967), 47-62; *RB,* 75 (1968), 381-87; *Jerusalem Through the Ages* (1968), pp. 26-32; *PEQ,* 1973, pp. 61-70; W. G. Dever, H. D. Lance, G. E. Wright, *Gezer I: Preliminary Report of the 1964-66 Seasons* (1970); W. G. Dever, *et al., Gezer II: Preliminary Report of the 1967-70 Seasons, Fields I and II* (1974); *BA,* 34 (1971), 94-132; *EAEHL,* II, *s.v.* "Gezer" (W. G. Dever); H. D. Lance, *BA,* 30 (1967), 34-47; R. A. S. Macalister, *Biblical Sidelights from the Mound of Gezer* (1907); *Excavation of Gezer, 1902-1905 and 1907-1909* (3 vols., 1912); A. Malamat, *Studies in the Bible* (*Scripta Hierosolymitana,* 8, 1961), pp. 228-231; J. F. Ross, *BA,* 30 (1967), 62-70. A. F. RAINEY

GEZER CALENDAR. A listing of agricultural events in a twelve-month year, inscribed on a small piece of limestone excavated at Gezer in 1908 by R. A. S. Macalister (see *ANEP,* no. 272). It is undoubtedly a copy and may have been used for teaching or as a schoolboy's exercise (*see* EDUCATION II). A small hole in the tablet indicates that it may once have hung on a wall. It is important because it attests an early stage of both Hebrew orthography (spelling), which is valuable for tracing the development of the language, and paleography (the development of scripts), which is helpful (sometimes vital) for dating written material. It is also of sociological value, because it begins its calendrical reckoning in the fall rather than in the spring, contrary to OT practice. (*See* CALENDAR II.B.)

Bibliography.–W. F. Albright, *BASOR,* 92 (Dec. 1943), 16-26; *ANET,* p. 320; F. M. Cross and D. N. Freedman, *Early Hebrew Orthography* (1952), pp. 45-47; *DOTT,* pp. 201-203; J. C. L. Gibson, *Textbook of Syrian Semitic Inscriptions,* I (1971), 1-4; *KAI*; R. A. S. Macalister, *Excavation of Gezer,* II (1912), 24-28; *Palestine Exploration Fund Quarterly Statement* (1909), pp. 87-92.

H. W. PERKIN
G. A. L.

GEZRITES gez'rīts (1 S. 27:8, AV). *See* GIRZITES.

GHOR. *See* JORDAN.

GHOST [Heb. *'ôḇ*] (Isa. 29:4); AV FAMILIAR SPIRIT; [Gk. *phántasma*] (Mt. 14:26 par. Mk. 6:49); AV SPIRIT. The term "ghost" is the Middle English word for "breath," "spirit," and signifies the life-principle. The biblical references, however, seem to suggest some form of specter or apparition from the realm of the dead.

See also SPIRIT. R. K. H.

GHOST, HOLY. *See* HOLY SPIRIT.

GIAH gē'ə [Heb. *gî(a)ḥ*]. An unidentified place mentioned in 2 S. 2:24, though the text may be corrupt. The passage speaks of "the hill of Ammah, which lies before Giah on the way to the wilderness of Gibeon." Ammah has not been identified as either a place or a person, and there is no wilderness in the vicinity of GIBEON. The LXX renders *gî(a)ḥ* as Gk. *Gai,* suggesting Heb. *gay',* "valley." On the basis of the context, Simon (*GTTOT* §§ 745f.) suggests a location in the wilderness E of Gibeon (cf. Jgs. 20:42-45). Others suggest GEBA (cf. S. R. Driver, *Notes on the Hebrew Text and Topography of the Books of Samuel* [2nd ed. 1913], p. 244). Geba, Gibeah, and Gibeon are in the same general region, so it is rather pointless to attempt a more precise location.

W. S. L. S.

GIANTS [Heb. *rāpā', rāpâ*] (2 S. 21:16, 18, 20, 22; 1 Ch. 20:4, 6, 8). The RSV references are unquestionably to people of immense physical stature. The NEB uses "giants" and "Rephaim" interchangeably, making the latter the race from which the giants came. At present little archeological supports the existence of an ancient race of giants in Palestine, although one such skeleton has been found. It has been attributed to the period of the Crusades, though from what is known of the stature of medieval peoples it would appear that such a dating is open to considerable doubt.

People who exhibit gigantic stature usually have either genetic abnormalities or some disease. That 2 S. 21:20 mentions a giant who had six fingers on each hand and six toes on each foot seems to indicate that the individual concerned was the product of genetic mutation. Where disease is a factor, the usual cause is hypertrophy of the anterior pituitary lobe of young persons, often the result of a tumor. Perhaps Goliath of Gath was the victim of this kind of disease. Another form of gigantism, which is also the product of anterior pituitary hypertrophy, involves species as they approach familial extinction. Here the pathology is not fatal, but because it is frequently accompanied by sterility it eventually secures the demise of the species involved.

See also NEPHILIM; REPHAIM. R. K. H.

GIANTS, VALLEY OF THE (Josh. 15:18; 18:16, AV). *See* REPHAIM, VALLEY OF.

GIBBAR gib'är [Heb. *gibbār*–'hero']. In Ezr. 2:20 the "sons of Gibbar" are mentioned among those who returned with Zerubbabel. The parallel passage (Neh. 7:25) has "sons of Gibeon." It has been suggested that Gibbar might be a corruption of Gibeon, but this is uncertain.

GIBBETHON gib'bə-thon [Heb. *gibbᵉtôn*]. A city in the tribal allotment of Dan before Dan moved northward (Josh. 19:44). In the allocation of certain portions of land to the Levites, Gibbethon was assigned to the Kohathites (Josh. 21:23). In the context it is joined with Elteke, Aijalon, and Gathrimmon, all of which soon fell into the hands of the Philistines. Baasha the son of Ahijah assassinated Nadab as he was attempting to capture Gibbethon (1 K. 15:27). Twenty-five years later, Elah, who had succeeded his father Baasha as king of Israel the previous year, was assassinated by Zimri at Tirzah. When news of this coup reached the Israelite troops (who under Omri were attempting once more to capture Gibbethon), Omri was made king, and marched from Gibbethon to Tirzah (1 K. 16:15-17). The site of Gibbethon is possibly to be located at the modern Tell el-Melât, about 5 km. (3 mi.) E of Gezer, 22 km. (14 mi.) SSE of Joppa. W. S. L. S.

GIBEA gib'i-ə [Heb. *giḇ'ā'*–'hill']. A grandson of Caleb (1 Ch. 2:49). His father was Sheva, whose mother was Maacah, Caleb's concubine (v. 48).

GIBEAH gib'ē-ə [Heb. *giḇ'â*–'hill']. Along with its literal meaning, in which it is distinguished from *har,* "mountain," Heb. *giḇ'â* is sometimes used as a place name.

1. A city in Judah, named in a list of ten cities allotted to Judah (Josh. 15:57). It has been identified with el-Jebaʿ, 12½ km. (7½ mi.) WSW of Bethlehem, but since it is listed with "cities" further to the south, it is possibly to be located SE of Hebron. It is perhaps the Gibeah of 2 Ch. 13:2.

2. A town given to Phinehas. It was located somewhere in the hill country of Ephraim. There Eleazar the son of Aaron was buried (Josh. 24:33; cf. Josephus *Ant.* v.1.29 [119]), and, according to an addition in the LXX, there also Phinehas was buried. The Samaritan tradition that the location is at Awertah, 6 km. (4 mi.) SE of Nablus, is without support; its location remains unknown.

3. A city in Benjamin, called "Gibeah, which belongs to Benjamin" (Jgs. 19:14; 20:4), "Gibeah of Benjamin" (Jgs. 20:10; 1 S. 13:2, 15; 14:16), "Gibeah of the Benjamites" (2 S. 23:29; 1 Ch. 11:31), "Gibeath" (MT, AV Josh. 18:28; RSV Gibeah), and "Gibeah of Saul" (1 S. 11:4; 15:34; Isa. 10:29). It is possibly to be identified also with GIBEATH-ELOHIM, "Gibeah of God" (but cf. *LBHG,* p. 254 n. 2).

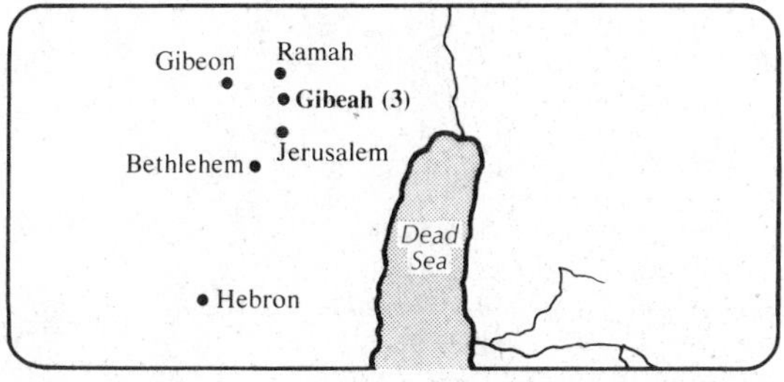

The first reference to Gibeah is in connection with the story of the Levite and his concubine (Jgs. 19–21). An old man from Gibeah provided a night's hospitality for a Levite, and certain men of the city, "base fellows," demanded to have the Levite to commit homosexual acts with him. The concubine was thrown out to them, and they "abused her all night." This led to action of the tribes against Benjamin resulting in a great slaughter of Benjaminites. The story is told to indicate conditions in the days when "there was no king in Israel" (Jgs. 19:1; 21:25), possibly to show the need for a king (see KD *in loc.*).

Gibeah was the home of Saul, who became the first king of Israel (1 S. 10:26). After he was anointed by Samuel, Saul met a band of prophets at Gibeath-elohim (10:5, called simply Gibeah in 10:10), and the spirit of God "came mightily upon him." Simons (*GTTOT,* §§ 669f.) would read Geba in both passages. From Gibeah Saul summoned the tribes of Israel to deliver Jabesh-gilead from the Ammonites (11:1-11). Gibeah was the site of Saul's war with the Philistines (13:2; 14:2, 16), apparently having become Saul's capital (15:34; 22:6; 23:19). Certain Ziphites came to Gibeah to inform Saul of David's hiding place (23:19; 26:1). David drew three of his "thirty" mighty men from Gibeah: Ittai the son of Ribai of Gibeah (2 S. 23:29), and the sons of Shemaah of Gibeah (1 Ch. 12:3). It is likely that these men were formerly associated in some way with Saul's court. According to the MT, seven sons of Saul were slain by the Gibeonites and were "exposed to Yahweh" at Gibeah of Saul (2 S. 21:6, RSV mg.), but this is generally emended to Gibeon in the light of the context and with the support of the LXX. Micaiah the mother of Abijah king of Judah is described as "the daughter of Uriel of Gibeah" (2 Ch. 13:2).

In Isaiah's prophecy of the Assyrian advance on Jerusalem, Gibeah of Saul is one of the places named (Isa. 10:29). Hosea mentioned the corruption of Gibeah, no doubt referring to the incident of the Levite's concubine and the sin of the city, and he prophesied that war would overtake Israel in Gibeah (Hos. 9:9; 10:9).

The location of Gibeah can be rather closely established from the OT passages: N of Jerusalem in the hill country of Benjamin, not far from Gibeon and S of Ramah. Josephus (*BJ,* v.2.1 [51] located "Gabath Saul, which means 'Saul's hill,'" thirty stadia (about 5.5 km., 3.4 mi.) from Jerusalem. The site of Tell el-Fûl ("mound of beans"), about 5 km. (3 mi.) from the old city of Jerusalem, just E of the main N-S road (where King Hussein began to erect a royal building before 1967), is generally accepted as the location of Gibeah of Saul. Excavations were conducted there in 1922/23 and in 1933, revealing a twelfth-century-B.C. village and the remains of a fortress of the late 11th cent. B.C., believed to be Saul's citadel. New excavations were undertaken in 1964 by Paul Lapp, to seek solutions to problems that had arisen from the earlier work. The plan of the structure proposed by Albright could not be fully supported, and a casemate wall of the late 7th and early 6th cents. was identified. A rebuilt city of the middle 6th cent. and a Hellenistic town of the latter part of the 2nd cent. were uncovered. The basic conclusions of earlier excavators, however, were not greatly altered.

Bibliography.–W. F. Albright, *AASOR,* 4 (1924), 1-89; *EAEHL,* II, *s.v.* "Gibeah" (L. A. Sinclair); L. A. Sinclair, *AASOR,* 34-35 (1960), 1-52; P. Lapp, *BA,* 28 (1965), 2-10.

W. S. L. S.

Northwest corner of the fortress at Tell el-Fûl from the time of Saul (Pittsburgh Theological Seminary; picture P. W. Lapp)

GIBEATH (Josh. 18:28, AV). *See* GIBEAH **3.**

GIBEATH-ELOHIM gi′bē-əth ə-lō-hēm′ [Heb. *giḇʿaṯ hāʾělōhîm*–'hill of God']; AV, RSV mg., NEB, "hill of God." The place where Saul, after leaving Samuel, met the company of prophets and prophesied with them (1 S. 10:5; note that in v. 10 it is simply called "Gibeah"). It is defined as the place "where there is a garrison [or "governor," "pillar"] of the Philistines." This may be intended to distinguish it from Gibeah of Saul, with which it is often identified. The site is probably the same as GEBA (13:3), where Jonathan defeated the Philistine garrison. The identification with Mizpah-Gibeon, Ram-Allah, or Bethel is unlikely.

Bibliography.–*GTTOT,* pp. 311-13; E. G. Kraeling, *Rand McNally Bible Atlas* (1956), pp. 178-180; *LBHG,* p. 254 n. 2.

D. J. WIEAND

GIBEATH-HAARALOTH gi'bē-əth hā-ar'ə-lōth [Heb. *giḇʿat hāʿarālôṯ*–'hill of the foreskins']; AV "hill of the foreskins," mg. GIBEAH-HAARALOTH. A place at or near Gilgal between the Jordan River and Jericho. Here the Israelites who grew up in the wilderness were circumcised after the passage through the Jordan (Josh. 5:3). The name was obviously given to the place from this event and is not otherwise a proper name. The site has not been identified. D. J. WIEAND W. S. L. S.

GIBEATHITE gib'ē-əth-īt (1 Ch. 12:3). *See* SHEMAAH.

GIBEON gib'ē-ən [Heb. *giḇʿôn*]. A city about 8 km. (5 mi.) NW of Jerusalem. It is first mentioned in the Bible in connection with the Israelite Conquest (Josh. 9:3). Following the Conquest, Gibeon became a levitical city in the tribal territory of Benjamin. The name *giḇʿôn* suggests a height, and the site is atop a limestone outcropping in the Judean hills at the eastern end of the Valley of Aijalon. Currently an Arab village occupies the northern slope of the tell. Its name, el-Jîb, retains a part of the ancient designation for the place.

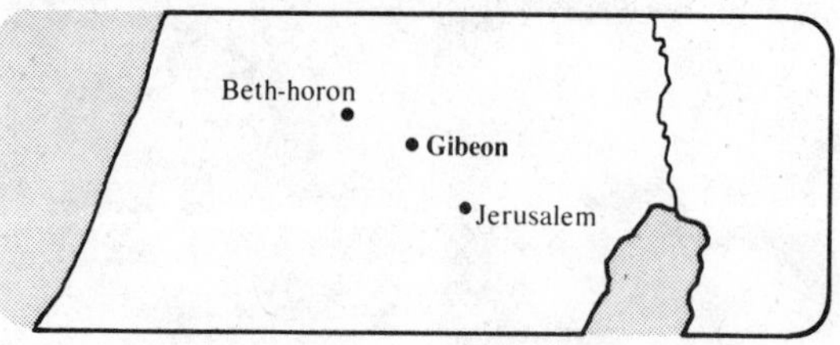

I. Gibeon in the Bible.–Josh. 9 recounts the successful ploy of the Gibeonites by which the invading Israelites were tricked into signing a treaty with the city. The Gibeonites were consigned to the role of "hewers of wood and drawers of water" in Israelite society (Josh. 9:21, 23, 27). When the Gibeonites were attacked by Adoni-zedek, the Amorite king of Jerusalem, because they had made peace with Israel, they called on Joshua for help. He remained true to his covenant vow and relieved the besieged city, pursuing the attackers down the ascent of Beth-horon and winning decisively (*see* BETH-HORON, THE BATTLE OF).

Gibeon is not mentioned again in the Bible until the time of David. 2 S. 2:12-17 reports the contest between the young warriors of Abner and those of Joab "at the pool of Gibeon." On another occasion, Joab treacherously disemboweled Amasa at the "great stone which is in Gibeon" (2 S. 20:8). In a strange case of blood revenge, David handed over to the Gibeonites seven of Saul's sons, who were hung "at Gibeon on the mountain of the Lord" (2 S. 21:6). This expression suggests the existence of a sacred place in conjunction with Gibeon. Solomon sacrificed at the high place at Gibeon and had his famous dream there (1 K. 3:4f.). 2 Ch. 1:3, 13 indicates that the tent of meeting was located at Gibeon, and this is confirmed by 1 Ch. 16:39; 21:29.

A certain Hananiah, a prophet from Gibeon, was soundly denounced by Jeremiah for lying to the people (Jer. 28). The book of Jeremiah also reports that in the troubled last days of the Judean state a rebel leader named Ishmael murdered Gedaliah, the governor who had been appointed over the remnant of the Jews by Nebuchadrezzar. His flight was stopped "at the great pool which is in Gibeon" (Jer. 41:12).

The Bible reveals nothing about the fate of the city during the Babylonian conquest, but scattered references from postexilic sources indicate that Gibeonites were among the people who returned from Exile (Neh. 7:25). Men from Gibeon helped rebuild the temple (Neh. 3:7), and, surprisingly, Gibeonites are connected with the house of Saul in a genealogical list in 1 Ch. 8:29; 9:35.

II. Gibeon in Extrabiblical Sources.–The earliest extrabiblical reference to Gibeon is in the list of Asian cities captured by Pharaoh Shishak (Sheshonq I, *ca.* 940-915 B.C.). He invaded the region in the fifth year of the reign of King Rehoboam (1 K. 14:25), and upon his return to Egypt he had his exploits engraved on the south wall of the temple of Amon at Karnak.

Josephus, the Jewish historian who wrote near the end of the 1st cent. A.D., recorded an incident that occurred in A.D. 66 and involved Gibeon. Cestius, the Roman governor of Syria, had marched toward Jerusalem to besiege the city, encamping en route at Gibeon (Gabao). Failing to capture Jerusalem, he retreated to Gibeon and remained in the area for three days before fleeing to the west from the attacking Jews (*BJ* ii.19.1 [515f.]).

III. Exploration and Excavation of Gibeon.–An early Arab geographer, Yakut, mentioned el-Jîb in the 13th cent., but the explorations of E. Robinson in 1838 first brought the attention of Westerners to the site and its identification with ancient Gibeon. Robinson's suggestion was based on both the location of the site and the similarity in sound between the modern Arab name of the village and the ancient name Gibeon. In 1926 A. Alt argued strongly against the identification of el-Jîb with Gibeon, convincing many of his peers that Gibeon was to be found at some other site. Only with the excavations that were begun in 1956 was the location of ancient Gibeon at el-Jîb confirmed by archeological evidence.

Excavations at el-Jîb were carried out during four summers in 1956, 1957, 1959, and 1960 by a team of archeologists under the direction of J. B. Pritchard. Their most spectacular discovery was the "pool." Located just inside the city wall on the northeast side of the city, this cylindrical shaft is 11.3 m. (37 ft.) in diameter and 10.6 m. (35 ft.) deep, with a balustraded spiral stairway cut out of the rock. An estimated 3000 tons of limestone had been excavated in the cutting of this shaft. (The stone was probably used in the construction of the adjacent city wall.) Beneath this great shaft a narrow tunnel slants downward for another 13.7 m. (45 ft.) to a water chamber that had been hewn out at groundwater level. The great pool apparently provided a catch basin for rainwater, which supplemented the groundwater. This was no doubt the pool mentioned in the Bible. It went out of use at the close of the Judean kingdom period, according to the ceramic evidence. Huge stones had been cast down from above to close the entrance to the tunnel, and sealed within the water chamber were two jars datable to the early 6th cent. B.C. Pritchard dated the construction of the pool to the 12th/11th cents. B.C., so it remained in use for over a half a millennium. It had been completely filled with debris and was indistinguishable until the expedition chanced upon its rim in 1956.

The water system described above was apparently insufficient to meet the needs of ancient Gibeon, however, for a tunnel system dated to the united monarchy in the 10th cent. B.C. was also discovered. It led from inside the city wall, also constructed in this period, down the slope of the hill to a spring chamber hidden from view within the hill. This spring has a copious flow of water; along with the water systems that were discovered, it illuminates the reference to "many waters [Heb. *mayim rabbîm*] that are in Gibeon" (Jer. 41:12).

The wealth of ancient Gibeon was apparently based on the cultivation of grapes and winemaking. An area of more

The tunnel's ninety-three steps lead from the city to the spring (University Museum, University of Pennsylvania)

The pool at Gibeon with its spiral staircase (University Museum, University of Pennsylvania)

than 920 sq. m. (1100 sq. yds.) which had been devoted to this work was discovered. The evidence supporting this view consisted of wine presses, plastered channels, settling basins, storage tanks, ceramic funnels, and jars with narrow mouths and stoppers obviously used for storing liquids. Large pits with small openings were cut into the limestone, profiding wine cellars with a constant temperature of 18° C (65° F). The jars had a capacity of 37 l. (9¾ gals.) each, and the entire complex could store an estimated 95,000 l. (25,000 gals.) of wine. It is presumed that the population of Gibeon did not consume this amount annually but carried on an extensive trade in wine.

Some of the jar handles were inscribed with the name of Gibeon itself, along with the word *gdr,* apparently another place. Several handles had personal names written upon them, such as Hananiah, Azariah, Amariah — names common in the Bible — and rarer names, Shebuel and Domla. These obviously Hebrew names confirm what is implied in the Bible, that the Gibeonites were thoroughly assimilated into the nation Israel before the Babylonian Exile and were worthy to be counted in the book of the genealogy "of those who came up at the first" (Neh. 7:5, 25).

Bibliography.–A. Alt, *PJ,* 22 (1926), 11f.; D. Cole, *Biblical Archaeology Review,* 6/2 (1980), 8-29; *EAEHL,* II, 446-450; J. B. Pritchard, *Gibeon: Where the Sun Stood Still* (1962).

K. N. SCHOVILLE

Jar handle inscribed *gbʿn gdr* (University Museum, University of Pennsylvania)

GIBEONITES gib'ē-ən-īts. Inhabitants of GIBEON.

GIBLITES gib'līts (Josh. 13:5, AV). *See* GEBAL.

GIDDALTI gi-dal'tī [Heb. *giddaltî*–'I magnify (God)']. A son of Heman (1 Ch. 25:4, 29), one of David's musicians. *See also* JOSHBEKASHAH.

GIDDEL gid'əl [Heb. *giddēl*–'very great,' 'stout'].

1. The name of the head of a family of temple servants (Ezr. 2:47 par. Neh. 7:49); it occurs as "Cathua" in 1 Esd. 5:30.

2. The name of the head of a family of Solomon's servants (Ezr. 2:56 par. Neh. 7:58); it occurs as "Isdael" in 1 Esd. 5:33.

GIDEON gid'ē-ən [Heb. *giḏʿôn*–'cutter down,' 'feller,' or 'hewer'; Gk. *Gedeōn* (He. 11:32)]; AV also GEDEON (He. 11:32). Also named Jerubbaal (Jgs. 6:32, etc.) and Jerubbesheth (2 S. 11:21), the youngest son of Joash, of the family of Abiezer in the tribe of Manasseh. His home was at Ophrah, and his family an obscure one. He became the chief leader of Manasseh and the fifth recorded judge of Israel. The record of his life is found in Jgs. 6–8.

I. Midianite Oppression.–Joash was an idolater, and sacrifices to Baal were common among the entire clan. Gideon held this worship in contempt and pondered the causes of Israel's reverses and the injuries heaped upon his family by the Midianites (camel-riding bedouin).

The Midianites under Zebah and Zalmunna, their two great chiefs, accompanied by other tribes of the eastern desert, gradually encroached on Israel's territory in central Palestine. They came first as marauders and pillagers at the time of the harvests, but later they forcibly took possession of lands, inflicting permanent injury and loss, especially upon Manasseh and Ephraim. The conflicts became so numerous and the appropriation of the land so flagrant that sustenance became a serious problem and defense difficult (Jgs. 6:4). The Israelites, lacking a sense of national unity, took to dens, caves, and rocky strongholds for safety (6:2). After seven years of such invasion and suffering, Gideon came upon the scene.

II. Call of Gideon.–Probably Gideon had already distinguished himself in Israel's resistance to the Midianites (Jgs. 6:12), but he now received divine commission to assume the leadership against them. Having hid his own little harvest in a secret place for threshing that it might escape the greed of the Midianites, he was surprised while at work by a visit from an angel of the Lord (6:11-24). There can be no question of the divine origin of Gideon's call or of the authenticity of God's voice. The brooding over the death of his brothers at Tabor (8:18f.) and the patriotic impulses surging in his soul cannot account for his assumption of leadership. Neither did the populace choose him as a leader. The call came to him as a surprise, and found him distrustful both of himself (6:15) and of his people (v. 13). Only his conviction that it was a divine command persuaded him to assume leadership. This attests to the accuracy of the essential facts of the account. After Gideon's demand for a sign (v. 17) was answered, and the food offered to the messenger was consumed by fire at the touch of his staff, Gideon acknowledged the divine commission of his visitor and built an altar to Yahweh (vv. 19-24).

III. His First Commission.–The call and the first commission of Gideon were closely united. He was commanded to destroy at once the altars of Baal set up by his father at Ophrah, to build an altar to Yahweh, and to offer one of his father's bullocks as a sacrifice there (Jgs. 6:25f.). So Gideon's call followed the usual command to God's prophets and reformers to begin their work at home. Taking ten men, under the cover of darkness Gideon obeyed his instructions (v. 27). The morning revealed his work, and in their wrath the people of Ophrah demanded Gideon's death. The answer of Joash his father is an ironical but valid defense of Gideon. Why should the people plead for Baal? A god should be able to plead his own cause (vv. 28-31). This defense gained for Gideon the name of Jerubbaal ("let Baal plead," 6:32).

The subsequent events of the story are somewhat confused but the difficulties are not irreconcilable. The narrative of Gideon's victory over the Midianites is probably preserved in two forms: an earlier (Jgs. 8:4-21) and a later (6:1–8:3) account.

IV. Gideon's Army.–When the allied invaders encamped on the plain of Jezreel, Gideon recruited the Abiezrites, sent messengers to the various tribes of Israel (Jgs. 6:34f.), and pitched his camp near the Midianites. Locating the various camps of Gideon is difficult, and his method of recruiting the tribes raises further problems (cf. 6:35 with 7:23). Evidently at the preliminary encampment, the rallying place, he further tested his commission by the dry and wet fleece (6:37-40; cf. Boling, p. 141). Now, convinced of God's purpose to save Israel by his leadership, Gideon moved his camp to the southeast edge of the plain of Jezreel, close to the Harod spring. From this vantage point he could look down on the tents of Midian. Neither of the tests by which he reduced his large army from 32,000 to 300 is unnatural, and the first was not unusual (cf. Dt. 20:1-8). Gideon, at God's command, first excused all the fearful, leaving himself with ten thousand men. Then this number was further reduced to three hundred by a test of their method of drinking water, leaving him only the courageous, eager, and discerning soldiers ready for battle (7:2-7).

V. Defeat of the Midianites.–Gideon, with a servant, went under cover of darkness to the edge of the camp of his enemy, and there heard the relating and interpreting of a dream, which greatly encouraged him and led him to strike an immediate blow (Jgs. 7:9-22). Dividing the remnant of his band into three equal parts, Gideon ordered that with trumpets, with lights concealed in pitchers, and with the cry, "The sword of Yahweh and of Gideon!" they should charge the Midianites simultaneously from three sides. This strategy of concealing his numbers and terrifying the enemy succeeded, and the Midianites and their confused allies fled in disorder toward the Jordan (7:18-22). The rout was complete, and victory was ensured when the enemy turned their swords against one another in the darkness.

One part of the fleeing enemy, under Zebah and Zalmunna, evidently crossed the Jordan to Succoth. The superior force followed the river farther S toward the ford of Beth-barah. Gideon sent messengers to the Ephraimites (Jgs. 7:24), probably before the first attack, requesting them to intercept the Midianites should they attempt to escape by the fords in Ephraim's territory. Ephraim defeated the enemy at Beth-barah and slew the princes Oreb and Zeeb ("the raven" and "the wolf"). As proof of their victory and valor they brought the heads of the princes to Gideon, and they accused Gideon of having discounted their bravery by not calling them earlier in the fight. But Gideon, being a diplomat and a strategist, won Ephraim's friendship by extolling their feat in comparison with his own (8:1-3).

Gideon then pursued Zebah and Zalmunna on the east side of the river. The people on this side were still in great fear of the Midianites and refused even to feed his army. At Succoth they complained, "Are Zebah and Zalmunna already in your hand, that we should give bread to your army?" (Jgs. 8:6). He met with the same refusal at Penuel (8:8). Promising to deal with Succoth and Penuel when he had completed his present task, Gideon pushed on with his half-famished but courageous men, overtook the Midianites, defeated them, and captured Zebah and Zalmunna. Upon his return he fulfilled his promise to both Succoth and Penuel (8:7, 9, 13-17).

Thus the power of the Midianites and of the desert hordes was broken in Canaan, and forty years of peace came to Israel. The two kings of Midian now had to meet their fate as defeated warriors. Because Gideon's brothers had perished in battle at Tabor fighting them, Gideon commanded his young son Jether to slay them, as though they were not worthy of an honorable death at a warrior's hand (8:20). But the youth feared the task and so Gideon slew them (8:21).

VI. Gideon's Ephod.–The people clamored to make Gideon king; but he refused — Yahweh was their king (8:22f.). (His son Abimelech did rule, however; *see* ABIMELECH **4.**) He requested only the jewelry captured in the battle (8:24-27), and with it he made an ephod (weighing about 30 kgs. [65 lbs.]) and placed it in the house of Yahweh at Ophrah. Some contend that this was an image of Yahweh, which later led Israel to idolatry; but it probably was a surrogate for an "ark" or sacred box used by the priests in divining (see W. R. Arnold, *Ephod and Ark* [1917], pp. 125, 128).

The narrative proper closes with 8:28; vv. 29-35, which include the account of Gideon's family and death (8:30-32) and the incidents immediately subsequent to Gideon's death (8:33-35), are probably taken from other secondary sources.

Bibliography.–R. G. Boling, comm. on Judges (*AB*, 1975), pp. 121-164; R. K. Harrison, *Intro. to the OT* (1969), pp. 688, 690-93.

C. E. SCHENK
D. W. DEERE

GIDEONI gid-i-ō'nē [Heb. *giḏʿōnî*]. The father of Abidan who was prince of Benjamin, mentioned only in connection with the son (Nu. 1:11; 2:22; 7:60, 65; 10:24).

GIDOM gi'dəm [Heb. *giḏʿōm*–'a cutting off or desolation'] (Jgs. 20:45); NEB "cut down." The terminus of Israel's pursuit of Benjamin in their civil war, located near the rock of Rimmon in the wilderness E of Gibeah.

GIER EAGLE. *See* CARRION VULTURE.

GIFT.
I. Terminology
  A. In the OT
  B. In the NT
II. Patterns of Giving Gifts

I. Terminology.–*A. In the OT.* The Hebrew terms *mattān, mattānâ,* and *mattāṯ* are all derived from the verb *nāṯan,* "give." *Mattān* refers to a marriage gift in Gen. 34:12, and to the priest's due in Nu. 18:11. In Proverbs, however, it has a pejorative sense: a bribe that makes friends (19:6) or spreads influence (18:16) or buys silence (21:14, par. *šōḥaḏ*). *Mattāṯ* characterizes a person's enjoyment of life as a gift of God (Eccl. 3:13; 5:19). In Prov. 25:14 it is used of ungiven gifts (i.e., promised but never delivered), in 1 K. 13:7 of the reward that the king is able to bestow. *Mattānâ* has a wide range of application. It characterizes Levitical and priestly service as a gift of God (Nu. 18:6f.), but it also denotes human sacrifice to idols (Ezk. 20:26, 31, 39). It represents the parting gifts of a father (Gen. 25:6) as well as the property inheritance of a ruler's sons (Ezk. 46:16f.; 2 Ch. 21:3). It may also be simply an offering to God (Ex. 28:38; Nu. 18:29) or charity to the poor (Est. 9:22). The Aramaic cognate *mattᵉnā'* refers to royal largesse in Dnl. 2:6, 48; 5:17.

The Hebrew *qōḏeš,* "holiness, sacredness," is applied in Kings and Chronicles to "votive" or "dedicated gifts." These constitute some of the temple treasuries (1 Ch. 26:26) and frequently are gotten as spoils of conquest (1 Ch. 26:27 [the hiphil stem of the vb. *qāḏaš* denotes the act of dedication]) and occasionally lost in the same manner (2 K. 12:18).

Hebrew *qorbān,* usually "offering," is thrice rendered "gift" by the RSV (Lev. 1:10; 17:4; Nu. 6:14; AV, NEB, always "offering"), apparently only for stylistic reasons. In these passages it refers to an animal though it may refer also to grain (Lev. 2:1), silver (Nu. 7:13), or gold (Nu. 31:50). In the NT Jesus' use of this same term transliterated in the Greek of Mk. 7:11 (*korbán*) referred to a current method of sidestepping the obligations of the law regarding the support of parents. The procedure was to dedicate one's money to God, declaring it to be *qorbān,* and thus legally (albeit uncharitably) retaining possession of it. Confirmation that *qorbān* was practiced in Jesus' day comes from a first-century-A.D. ossuary inscription that is a dedicatory formula offering the contents within to God, thereby prohibiting any profane use of them (see Fitzmyer, pp. 60, 65; *TDNT,* III, 860-66). *See* CORBAN. *Minḥâ,* usually rendered "offering," is used of the "gifts" that people brought to the Lord after Jerusalem's narrow escape from Sennacherib (2 Ch. 32:23) and of "gifts" to royalty designed to win favor (Ps. 45:12). *See* SACRIFICES AND OFFERINGS IN THE OT IV.A; V.E.

Maś'ēṯ (for **maśśᵉ'ēṯ*, from *nāśā'*, "lift"), literally "a lifting-up," is twice rendered "gift." In one instance it refers to royal largesse (Est. 2:18); in the other it is simply an offering to Yahweh (Ezk. 20:40). It can have other connotations such as exactions (Am. 5:11), lifting up (of the hands in prayer [Ps. 141:2]), and portions (Gen. 43:34). The obscure *niśśē'ṯ* in 2 S. 19:42 is usually understood to be a participial form from *nāśā'*. While it is rendered "gift," it may have the sense of "portion" or may be a mistake for *maś'ēṯ* (the LXX features a doublet, "gift" and "portion").

Hebrew *ṭûḇ,* "good things," is twice rendered "gifts" in the RSV: "choice gifts" to be presented to distant kinfolk (Gen. 24:10) and "good gifts" in reference to the produce of the land (Neh. 9:36). *Meḡeḏ,* "choiceness, excellence," referring in Dt. 33:13, 16 to divine provision, is translated "choice gifts" and "best gifts" ("abundance," Dt. 33:15). *Bᵉrāḵâ* is usually "blessing," but in one instance (Gen. 33:11) the RSV translates "gift" (cf. AV "blessing") because the reference is to a peace offering made by the returning Jacob to his swindled brother Esau. *Šay,* "tribute," is translated "gifts" (Ps. 68:29 [MT 30]; 76:11 [MT 12]; Isa. 18:7; cf. NEB "tribute"). Always used in combination with the verb *yāḇal,* "bear, carry," the sense of *šay* is that of tribute brought by vassals to a superior. In Ps. 68:29 (MT 30) it is kings who "bear gifts" to God.

Hebrew *'eškār* is a noun of uncertain etymology that occurs only in Ps. 72:10 (again "gifts" brought to God by kings) and in Ezk. 27:15 (referring to the seafaring merchant empire of Tyre), where the RSV has "payment." *Šōḥaḏ* is properly "bribe" but once is rendered "gifts" in the RSV (Prov. 6:35). Even in this instance the sense is clearly "hush-money"; the "gifts" spoken of are said to be incapable of appeasing the anger of a cuckolded husband. The plural of *šalmōn* is a hapax legomenon in Isa. 1:23. It is translated "gifts" by the RSV largely from context, but that it connotes a financial inducement or payoff is clear from its position in poetic parallelism with *šōḥaḏ,* "bribe." Isaiah thus characterized Judah's government officials: "Every one loves a bribe and runs after gifts."

Since the literal sense of *tᵉrûmâ* is "a raising-up," it is expectedly a common OT term for "offering" (cf. RSV Ex. 25:2; Lev. 22:12; etc.). In Prov. 29:4 the RSV translates the phrase *'îš tᵉrûmôṯ* (lit. "a man of raisings") as "one who exacts gifts" (cf. NEB "forced contributions"). Whereas a just king brings his land stability, the exacter of gifts is said to bring his land to ruin.

The terms *nēḏeh* and *nāḏān* in Ezk. 16:33 occur only in this passage and each denotes the fee given to a harlot. Jerusalem is here metaphorically characterized by Ezekiel as a wanton who, not content to receive such fees or gifts for her adulterous liaisons, even gives out such gifts to solicit further unfaithfulness. *Ḥᵃmûḏâ,* "preciousness," occurs only in the plural. In Dnl. 11:38 it is rendered "costly gifts" (elsewhere "precious things" [e.g., 11:43] or "greatly beloved" [9:23]).

Šillûḥîm, from the verb *šālaḥ,* "send away," may by extension connote "parting gifts" or "send-off presents." This is clearly the sense in 1 K. 9:16 ("dowry"; NEB "marriage gift"), and in Mic. 1:14 ("parting gifts"; but the NEB translates in the primary sense of "dismissal"). *See* DOWRY.

B. In the NT. The Gk. *dṓron,* "gift" (< *dídōmi,* "give"), is used variously in the NT. In Mt. 2:11 it refers to the material gifts of homage presented by the Magi. Most frequently, however, it points to sacrificial offerings (He. 5:1; 8:3f.; 9:9; 11:4) or money offerings (Lk. 21:1). In Eph. 2:8 God's gift of salvation by faith is a *dṓron*. The cognate *dōreá* differs from *dṓron* in that originally it appears to have had a more pronounced legal sense, denoting formal endowments (see *TDNT,* II, 167). Thus it is significant that in the NT it is always used for gifts of God (cf. Jn. 4:10). Justification by grace is the "gift" of God in Rom. 3:24, righteousness His "free gift" in 5:17. The Holy Spirit is consistently characterized in Acts as God's *dōreá* (2:38; 8:20; 10:45; 11:17; cf. He. 6:4). Elsewhere in the Pauline corpus the term appears generally for God's (or Christ's) gifts (2 Cor. 9:15; Eph. 3:7; 4:7; "free gift," Rom. 5:15). *Dṓrēma* similarly refers to God's gifts in its NT use. Paul declares the grace that is God's work in Jesus a "free gift" in Rom. 5:16, and according to Jas. 1:17, "every perfect gift is from above, coming down from the Father of lights. . . ." *Dóma,* "gift," is also used of God's gifts (Eph. 4:8 quoting Ps. 68:18 [MT 19; LXX 67:18, *dóma*]). The ability of imperfect human parents to provide good gifts to children suggests that God is all the more able to "give the Holy Spirit to those who ask him" (Lk. 11:13). In Phil. 4:17 *dóma* has the sense of "reward."

Cognate to *chaírō,* "rejoice," *cháris* in the classical literature denotes "what delights." In the LXX it almost exclusively translates Heb. *ḥēn,* "favor" (thirty-one times in Sirach alone; see *TDNT,* IX, 389); in the NT *cháris* usually has the meaning "grace, favor." In Rom. 4:4 the phrase *katá chárin* (lit. "according to grace, as a favor") is rendered "as a gift," and in 1 Cor. 16:3, in reference to the collection for the Jerusalem church, *cháris* represents a deed of grace or benefaction (thus a "gift"). *Chárisma* means a gift or favor bestowed freely and graciously. In the NT it always has reference to God's gifts of grace (Rom. 11:29; 12:6; 1 Pet. 4:10). Righteousness in Christ (Rom. 5:15ff.) and eternal life in Christ (6:23) are each said to be God's "free gift"; in 1 Cor. 1:7 the RSV translates "spiritual gift" (cf. Rom. 1:11, *chárisma pneumatikón*). Paul says in 1 Cor. 12:4 that there are "varieties of gifts" (*diairéseis charismátōn*) but the same Spirit. One of the Spirit's gifts is healing (1 Cor. 12:9, 30). Immediately preceding the love hymn in 1 Cor. 13 Paul admonished his readers, "Earnestly desire the higher gifts" (*tá charísmata tá meízona,* 12:31). Among the "gifts" Paul included sexual continence (1 Cor. 7:7). He also understood ecclesiastical office bestowed by the laying on of hands as a "gift" of God (1 Tim. 4:14; 2 Tim. 1:6). Paul's inclusion of officebearing and acts of ministry (1 Cor. 12) among the *charísmata* signaled the onset of a major tension in the early Church — that between Spirit and office (law), between charismatic and officebearer (see *TDNT,* IX, 406; Conzelmann, *1 Corinthians,* pp. 207ff.). In 1 Pet. 4:10 any serving deed that enacts the commandment of love is a *chárisma.* *See also* GRACE III.H.

Greek *hadrótēs,* "abundance," is a NT hapax legomenon used by Paul in reference to the collection for Jerusalem in 2 Cor. 8:20, where the RSV translates "liberal gift" (cf. AV "abundance"; NEB "generous gift"). *Eulogía* (lit. "a good word") is usually translated "praise, blessing" in the NT. The latter meaning allows for the connotation "bounty" and thus, again in reference to the Jerusalem collection, it is rendered in 2 Cor. 9:5 "a willing gift" (cf. NEB "bounty"). *Timḗ,* "honor, respect," when used in Acts 28:10 with its cognate verb (*pollaís timaís etímēsan*) has the sense of "confer honors." Since in context these honors appear to take the material form of parting gifts, however, the RSV renders "they presented many gifts." The plural of *merismós,* "division, distribution" (<*merízō,* "divide"), is once translated "gifts" in He. 2:4 in the phrase *pneúmatos hagíou merismoís,* "gifts of [lit. "distributions of"] the Holy Spirit."

The RSV supplies "gift" in Rom. 11:35 to translate more smoothly the verb *prodídōmi,* "give first, give in advance." Similarly, since the absolute use of the definite article in 1 Cor. 2:14 and Phil. 4:18 has as its antecedent something which has been given, it is rendered "gifts" in the RSV (but cf. AV and NEB). *Pneumatikós,* an adjective meaning "of the Spirit, spiritual," is used a few times in the NT as a substantive (i.e., *tá pneumatiká* are "spiritual things"). In 1 Cor. 12:1 and 14:1 the RSV translates "spiritual gifts" (cf. Rom. 15:27; 1 Cor. 9:11; 15:46).

II. Patterns of Giving Gifts.–Gifts were expected to accompany acts of worship in the cultus of ancient Israel; they were the material support of the priests and Levites as well as tokens of the worshiper's self-dedication (cf. Ex. 23:15; 34:20). Gifts were also requisite when soliciting an oracle or ministration from a prophet (2 K. 8:9, Heb. *minḥâ*; Dnl. 5:17, Aram. *mattᵉnā*'; cf. also 2 K. 5:5, 15-19; 1 S. 9:7). Kings expected homage in the form of gifts (Ps. 45:12 [MT 13]; 72:10), particularly from vassals (1 K. 4:21). The depiction of vassal rulers presenting their "gifts" to their overlords is a prominent motif in ancient Near Eastern monumental art. (*See* picture in JEHU; picture of tribute bearers in GESTURE.)

The OT model for the giving of gifts is the generous example of God Himself who bestows a countless variety of gifts. The application of this divine pattern of generosity to human society was particularly incumbent upon the king. Ps. 72, e.g., details a shepherding kind of concern for even the lowliest of subjects; the king is so to give of himself and of personal and national resources as to defend the defenseless, sustain the poor and needy, and provide justice for the oppressed. While the king regularly expected gifts from vassals and subjects, he was also expected to give generously in return (cf. Gen. 43:34; 2 S. 11:8; Est. 2:18; Jer. 40:5).

Nevertheless, the giving of gifts among people (royalty and commoners alike) often followed a lower standard, so that what is described as a "gift" in some OT passages may be difficult to distinguish from a "bribe" or "payoff." Prov. 18:16 indicates the fine line between gift and bribe and the selfish abuse of giving: "A man's gift makes room for him and brings him before great men." The numerous injunctions in the OT against the taking of bribes suggests that such abuse was well known (e.g., Ex. 23:8). In Sir. 18:17 the sage suggests that "a word is better than a gift."

"Gift" in the NT is used mostly to characterize all that God has given to humankind — life, His grace as a free gift, the Holy Spirit (and His manifestations), and especially Jesus Christ Himself. Paul referred to Jesus in 2 Cor. 9:15 when he exclaimed: "Thanks be to God for his inexpressible gift!" As in the OT, the pattern for human giving is the divine example of self-giving, now incarnated in Jesus, "who though he was in the form of God, did not count equality with God a thing to be grasped, but emptied himself, taking the form of a servant, being born in the likeness of men. And being found in human form he humbled himself and became obedient unto death, even death on a cross" (Phil. 2:6-8). Thus it is for humans "more blessed [i.e., more godly] to give than to receive" (Acts 20:35).

In the Gospels (cf. Mt. 6:1ff.; Lk. 6:30) Jesus affirmed charitable giving (giving of alms), but reoriented the practice away from all thought of thereby seeking favor with God or esteem from peers, toward a charitable social posture motivated by love for the other rather than self-interest. For Paul this self-giving, serving posture toward others is mandated for the believer by his new identity in Christ (cf. Gal. 5; Rom. 6, 12; etc.).

In the liturgies of the Church the offering of gifts has always been significant, not as influence on God, but rather as homage to God and a token of the volitional self-offering of the believer's life according to the Pauline dictum: "Present your bodies as a living sacrifice, holy and acceptable to God, which is your spiritual worship" (Rom. 12:1). The model, the mandate, and the fulfillment of this kind of self-giving are all to be found in Jesus.

See also GIVE.

Bibliography.–H. Conzelmann, *1 Corinthians* (Eng. tr., *Hermeneia*, 1975); J. A. Fitzmyer, *JBL*, 78 (1959), 60-65; *TDNT*, II, *s.v.* δίδωμι κτλ. (Büchsel); III, *s.v.* κορβᾶν, κορβανᾶς (Rengstorf); IX, *s.v.* χαίρω κτλ.: χάρις κτλ.: χάρισμα (Conzelmann, Zimmerli). D. G. BURKE

GIFT OF TONGUES. *See* TONGUES, GIFT OF.

GIFTS OF HEALING. *See* HEALING, GIFTS OF.

GIFTS, SPIRITUAL. *See* SPIRITUAL GIFTS.

GIHON gī'hon [Heb. *gîḥôn*–'stream'].

1. One of the four rivers of the Garden of EDEN, described as the "one which flows around the whole land of Cush" (Gen. 2:13). Assuming that CUSH referred to Ethiopia, some scholars identified it with the Nile; but it seems certain now that the Cush referred to here was the area of Mesopotamia from which the Kassites subsequently emerged. More plausibly some river descending into Mesopotamia from the eastern mountains has been suggested, such as the Kerkha or the Diyala. But there is no linguistic distinction in Babylonian between "river" and "irrigation canal," and the "river" Gihon was most probably a major irrigation ditch which can no longer be located. In Sir. 24:27 (AV Geon) it is used figuratively in reference to wisdom. R. K. H.

2. A spring in Jerusalem, evidently sacred, and for that reason selected as the scene of Solomon's coronation (1 K. 1:38). Ps. 110:7 may suggest that it became customary for a new king to drink of Gihon's waters during his coronation ceremony. It is the spring known to the Moslems as ʿAin Umm ed-Deraj ("the spring of the steps") and to the Christians as ʿAin Sittī Maryam ("the spring of the lady Mary"), or commonly as "the Virgin's Fount." It is the nearer and more important of the only two true springs of Jerusalem, and was the site's original source of attraction to the early settlers. It is situated in the Kidron Valley on the east side of Ophel, and due S of the temple area. The spring is intermittent in character, "bursting up" at intervals. This may account for the name Gihon, and for popular belief in its sacred character. Its position is clearly defined in the OT. Manasseh "built an outer wall to the city of David west of Gihon, in the valley" (Heb. *nahal*, i.e., the Kidron, 2 Ch. 33:14).

The eastern entrance of Hezekiah's tunnel as seen from the natural cave out of which the Gihon spring flows (G. Nalbandian)

The importance of Gihon to Jerusalem needs no stressing; but it has never been within the city walls, and this fact posed a problem in times of warfare and siege. During the Jebusite occupation of Jerusalem, several underground shafts enabled the inhabitants to reach the spring unobserved, and one tunnel served to bring water into the city itself. One such shaft may well have played a part in the capture of Jerusalem by David's men (2 S. 5:8), if indeed Heb. *ṣinnôr* does mean "water shaft." During the early monarchy the waters were collected in a pool (the upper pool?) at the spring mouth, and thence conveyed by an open channel S along a ridge to another pool (the old pool[?], modern Birket el-Ḥamra). This aqueduct was used for irrigation of the adjoining valleys. But Hezekiah, at the threat of Assyrian invasion, embarked on a more ambitious project, an underground aqueduct bringing the waters to a pool inside the city (2 Ch. 32:30; cf. 2 K. 20:20). This aqueduct is the famous SILOAM tunnel. Its construction, together with the damming up of previous outlets, must have emptied the older pool, unless perhaps the new pool overflowed into it.

Gihon is approached by a steep descent, the water rising deep underground; the condition is due to the vast accumulation of rubbish — the result of the many destructions of the city — that now fills the valley bed. Originally the water flowed down the open valley.

Bibliography.–R. Amiran, "Water Supply at Ancient Jerusalem," in Y. Yadin, ed., *Jerusalem Revealed* (1975), pp. 75-78; J. J. Simons, *Jerusalem in the OT* (1952), pp. 157-194; H. Vincent, *Jerusalem de l'AT* (1954), I, 260-64. D. F. PAYNE

GILALAI gə-lā'lī [Heb. *gil^{a}lay*]. A musician in the procession at the dedication of the wall, son of a priest (Neh. 12:36).

GILBOA gil-bō'ə, **MOUNT** [Heb. *har haggilbōa(a)ʿ*–'mount of the bubbling fountain']. A chain of mountains in the territory of Issachar rising from the eastern edge of the plain of Esdraelon, the southern edge of the Valley of Jezreel, to a height of 520 m. (1696 ft.) above sea level. On this mountain Saul camped against the Philistines (1 S. 28:4) and later died with three of his sons, including Jonathan, when the Philistines defeated Israel (1 S. 31:1, 8; 2 S. 1:6, 21; 21:12; 1 Ch. 10:1, 8).

Though the location is not named, apparently from this height GIDEON descended to rout the Midianites and their allies who were camped in the Valley of Jezreel (Jgs. 6:33), near the hill of Moreh, which is 6½ km. (4 mi.) N, across the valley from Gilboa (Jgs. 7:1f.).

Modern Jebel Fuqûʿah, about 11 km. (7 mi.) W of Beth-shean and 5 km. (3 mi.) SE of Jezreel, represents the location today. The village of Jelbôn on the southern slope perpetuates the ancient name. *See* Plate 20.

R. J. HUGHES, III

GILEAD gil'ē-əd [Heb. *gilʿāḏ,* possibly 'mound of stones' or 'stronghold'].

1. The grandson of Manasseh and son of Machir (Nu. 26:29). Gilead is described as the progenitor of "the family of the Gileadites," and their clans are mentioned in 26:30-33; Josh. 17:3-6.

2. The father of Jephthah (Jgs. 11:1f.). Since Jephthah is described as "the Gileadite" (11:1) and later was made the leader of the Gileadites in the war with Ammon (11:8, 11), it is possible to consider Gilead here as a patronymic, but the details in 11:1f. appear to contradict this view.

3. A descendant of Gad and ancestor of one of the clans of the Gadites (1 Ch. 5:14; cf. vv. 11-16). Again it is possible to consider Gilead as a patronymic or eponym, since the clan dwelt "in Gilead, in Bashan and in its towns" (5:16), but the name occurs in a genealogy: "These were the sons of Abihail the son of Huri, son of Jaroah, son of Gilead, son of Michael," *et al.* (5:14), and it is difficult to separate the name Gilead from this list and make it the patronymic of the entire clan. W. S. L. S.

GILEAD gil'ē-əd [Heb. *gilʿāḏ,* possibly 'mound of stones' or 'stronghold']. A place name.

I. Name.–According to Genesis 31:47f., it is derived from *gal ʿēḏ,* "a heap of [=for] witness," the Hebrew equivalent (written as a single word in the MT) of the Aramaic name Jegar-sahadutha. The tradition that Jacob gave the Hebrew and Laban the Aramaic name to the place is generally taken by modern scholars to be a folk etymology. The Arabic word *jalʿad* has the meaning "strong, sturdy," and is used of camels, particularly of camel humps; thus it has been suggested as an explanation of the word (cf. BDB, p. 166), but this could be challenged on phonemic grounds in the light of the Assyrian form of the word (*Gal'aza*).

II. Limits of the Region.–"Gilead," as used in the OT, is a rather imprecise term. In the narrowest sense, it is a "city" (Hos. 6:8), the place of the encampment of the Ammonites while the Israelites camped at Mizpah (Jgs. 10:17). At the other extreme, the term seems to be used for all of Transjordanian Israel (Jgs. 20:1; cf. 2 K. 10:33; Jer. 50:19; Zec. 10:10).

The term "Gilead" is most closely associated with the region around the JABBOK, a river formed by many tributaries that rise in the interior N of Amman, watering a broad area, draining into the deep gorge of the Jabbok (the modern Zerqâ), and emptying into the Jordan River S of Deir ʿallā. The Jabbok system thus forms a large loop, flowing first northeastward, then westward, and finally southwestward. The region within this bend has sometimes been considered to be Gilead proper, but this lacks substantial support. Baly (*GB,* rev. ed.; p. 220 map 69) suggests that the region occupied the triangular area from the Yarmuk to the Zarqā' Māʿîn, and from the Jordan extending back to Mafraq, but excluding Ammon and the surrounding region of the Ammonites. Thus Gilead is divided into two parts by the Jabbok, northern Gilead, the modern ʿAjlūn, extending northward from the Jabbok to the Yarmuk, and southern Gilead, the modern Belqā, extending southward more or less from the Jabbok to the Arnon. This general description can serve as a working basis for the present discussion, but it must be remembered that the southern boundary of Gilead is far from definite, and the Ammonites and the Moabites at times in history extended into this area. It must also be kept in mind that Gilead sometimes appears to extend northward in what is called "Bashan and Gilead" (Mic. 7:14), "Gilead and Bashan" (Josh. 17:5; 2 K. 10:33), and possibly "Gilead in Bashan" (1 Ch. 5:16).

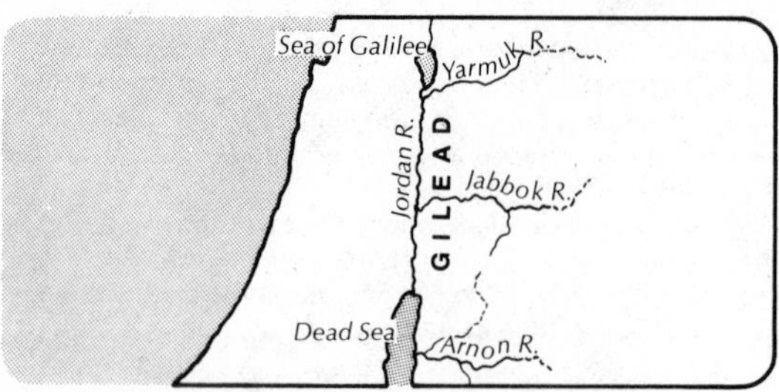

III. Physical Geography.–Because of the Jordan Valley, which is part of the Great Rift, and political boundaries, we are accustomed to think of Cisjordan and Transjordan as separate entities. As Baly makes clear, however, the "Dome of Gilead [is] a continuation structurally of the hill country of Judah" (*GB,* rev. ed., pp. 12, 219). It is formed principally of Cenomanian limestone, and the main lines of relief run SW-NE, which is at right angles to those of Bashan. The Transjordan plateau lies at an altitude of between 500 and 600 m. (1650 and 2000 ft.) above sea level, sloping gently downward toward the desert in the east. The term "plateau" is somewhat misleading, for Transjordan is cut by several deep river valleys, and there are a number of high points with elevations up to 1050 m. (3450 ft.), so that a person traveling the length of the region would only occasionally describe it as a plateau. (For a profile, see *GB,* rev. ed., p. 213 diagram 67.)

The Etesian winds that blow from the west through most of the year (from the northwest in winter and from the southwest in summer) bring rainfall to Palestine and Transjordan, but this rainfall is precipitated mainly on the western slopes, i.e., on the western part of Palestine and on the western part of Transjordan. It is this rainfall, together with springs, that waters Transjordan and forms the many tributaries of the large rivers that cut the plateau. The four main rivers, from north to south, are: the Yarmuk, traditionally the border between Bashan and Gilead; the Jabbok, on both banks of which lies Gilead; the Arnon (modern Wâdī Môjib), often the northern boundary of Moab (but *see* MOAB); and the Zered (modern Wâdī el-Ḥesā), the traditional boundary between Moab and Edom. Other river valleys in Transjordan are also significant and from time to time served as boundaries between peoples. Because the land slopes gently downward to the east, the rains form numerous streams that flow generally eastward. At the same time, the rains cut ravines in the scarp that rises above the Jordan, and the small streams converge to flow into these ravines, forming the rivers mentioned above.

Gilead is therefore more rugged than either the portion of BASHAN to the north or of Moab to the south. It is also more densely wooded, particularly in the higher portions, with scrub oak, carob, and pine. These regions are sometimes compared to the forests of Lebanon (cf. Jer. 22:6; Zec. 10:10), though no trees in Gilead compare to the famous cedars of Lebanon. There are spots of exquisite beauty, with phlox, lotus, narcissus, cane brake, oleander, tamarisk, white broom, arbutus, or hawthorn, sometimes in abundance along the streams. The medicinal "BALM OF GILEAD" (Jer. 8:22; 46:11) was exported to Tyre (perhaps Ezk. 27:17) and to Egypt (cf. Gen. 37:25). In the flatter portions of Gilead, olive trees and grape vines are plentiful, and in some areas wheat is grown; thus the staples of life, "the grain, the wine, and the oil" (Hos. 2:8), could be produced in Gilead. The rugged character of the land, however, is not to be overlooked, and it was a place of refuge as well as of encounters with God. In

A farm in the highlands of Gilead built on a rocky outcrop to conserve arable land. The grainfields are in the valley bottom and the olive orchards on the slopes (D. Baly)

Gilead Jacob sought refuge from Laban (Gen. 31:21). There the Israelites in the days of Saul sought escape from the Philistines (1 S. 13:7). When David was anointed king in Hebron, Saul's son Ishbosheth was established as king-in-exile in Gilead (2 S. 2:8f.). And when Absalom revolted against David, David fled to Gilead (2 S. 17:22-24; cf. v. 26). It was in Gilead by the river Jabbok that Jacob had his great experience with God and was called "Israel" (Gen. 32:22-30 [MT 23-31]). Elijah the prophet was of Tishbe in Gilead (1 K. 17:1), possibly receiving his prophetic call in that region. It was in the southern portion of Gilead (here called Moab) that Moses received his final message from the Lord (Dt. 32:48-52; 34:1-6), and it was in this same region that Joshua received his commission from Yahweh to cross the Jordan and take the Promised Land (Josh. 1:1-9).

IV. History of Gilead.–The early history of Transjordan is still somewhat of a problem. Early Bronze settlements have been found in a very few places. Middle Bronze sedentary populations have been established for Bashan and Ammon, but not for other parts of Transjordan. Glueck's view that Transjordan was largely unsettled during most of the 2nd millennium, though disputed, has not been completely refuted, and sedentary populations seem to be dated after the 13th cent. B.C. In the light of the Tell Mardikh (Ebla) materials so far published, it would not be surprising to find mercantile outlets in established cities all along the trade routes, with cities going back to Early Bronze III or IV, but no such evidence has yet come to light.

It is therefore with the Israelite journeyings from the wilderness of Sinai to the crossing of the Jordan that we begin the history of the region. Since the Israelites moved from south to north, the descriptions are given in this order, progressing from Edom to Moab, Gilead, and Bashan. The Ammonites entered the picture at this point only incidentally. The tribes of Reuben and Gad were immediately impressed with the land, and wanted to settle there (Nu. 32:1-5), but Moses insisted that first they should help their brothers in the conquest of Canaan, and afterwards inherit Gilead (32:28-32). The description set forth in Dt. 3:12-17 includes the words: "I gave to the Reubenites and the Gadites the territory beginning at Aroer, which is on the edge of the valley of the Arnon, and half the hill country of Gilead with its cities; the rest of Gilead, and all Bashan, the kingdom of Og, that is, all the region of Argob, I gave to the half-tribe of Manasseh." The tribe of Reuben occupied the southern part, from the Arnon in the south to a line extending from the northern end of the Dead Sea to Heshbon (cf. Josh. 13:15-23). A natural boundary would be Wâdī Ḥesbân or Wâdī el-Kefrein, which join to form the Wâdī Abū Gharrûbbâ, 5 km. (3 mi.) before emptying into the Jordan. At a time before the Mesha Inscription (or Moabite Stone, *ca.* 830 B.C.; cf. *ANET,* pp. 320f.), the territory of Reuben had been taken over by the Moabites; Gad is mentioned in the Mesha Inscription (line 10), but Reuben is not, and henceforth disappears from history. In fact, we think of this portion of Transjordan as Moab and not as Gilead. The tribe of Gad occupied the territory from the northern boundary of the Reubenites to the Jabbok. The half-tribe of Manasseh occupied the land north of the Jabbok, including "all Bashan" (Josh. 13:29-31).

In the time of Solomon, the nation was divided into twelve administrative districts (cf. 1 K. 4:7-19). Two of these were in Transjordan: that of Ben-geber in Ramoth-gilead, who had "the villages of Jair the son of Manasseh, which are in Gilead, and he had the region of Argob, which is in Bashan, sixty great cities with walls and bronze bars" (4:13); and that of Geber the son of Uri "in the land of Gilead, the country of Sihon king of the Amorites and of Og king of Bashan" (4:19).

During the last half of the 9th and the early 8th cents., the Aramean city-state of Damascus repeatedly attacked Gilead; in the words of Amos, "they have threshed Gilead with threshing sledges of iron" (Am. 1:3). From then until the Assyrian invasion, Gilead seems to have been a hotbed of rebellion. In the days of Ahab (874-853), the Syrians "filled the country" in the region around Aphek (modern Fîq), and Ahab won a victory (1 K. 20:23-43); but apparently it was not decisive, for three years later Ahab complained to Jehoshaphat of Judah that the Syrians held Ramoth-gilead. In the attempt to take the city, Ahab was killed (1 K. 22:1-4, 29-40). After the death of Ahab, Moab rebelled against Israel (2 K. 1:1), and although it seemed that victory was in sight for the Israelites, they withdrew without defeating the Moabites (2 K. 3:26f.). Ahaziah of Judah (841 B.C.) allied himself with Joram the son of Ahab in another attempt on the Syrians at Ramoth-gilead (2 K. 8:28). Joram was wounded and returned to Jezreel, and Jehu (841-814) was anointed by Elisha to be king of Israel (2 K. 9:1-10). In 2 K. 13:22 we read that Hazael king of Syria oppressed Israel all the days of Jehoahaz (814-796).

One of the knotty problems of Israelite chronology concerns Pekah, whose reign of twenty years (752-732; 2 K. 15:27) had to overlap the reigns of Menahem (752-743) and Pekahiah (741-740). Of all the suggested solutions to the problem, the most probable is the theory that Pekah had set up a rival government in Gilead when Menahem took the throne in Samaria. Menahem had assassinated Shallum (2 K. 15:14) and had waged bitter warfare on the cities of Israel. When Tiglath-pileser (or Pulu, the Pul of 2 K. 15:19), marched on Israel, Menahem paid tribute in order to avoid defeat. It was about this same time that Tiglath-pileser occupied Gilead; thus it is reasonable to suppose that Pekah was supported by Tiglath-pileser, in case Menahem should attempt a revolt.

When Tiglath-pileser III occupied Galilee, he established three provinces on the borders of Bīt Humria (the House of Omri, i.e., what was left of the northern kingdom), one at Dor, one at Megiddo, and one in Gilead (Assyr. *Gal'aza*; cf. 2 K. 15:29; *ANET,* p. 283; *ARAB,* I §815). According to Aharoni, Ezekiel had the Assyrian provinces in mind when he described the borders (Ezk. 47:17f.; cf. *LBHG,* p. 333 and map 31), but there is considerable time difference between Tiglath-pileser's campaign in 733 B.C. and Ezekiel's prophecy, and there is no evidence that these same districts continued under the Babylonians. Since Israelites had been taken captive from Gilead, Zechariah foretold that exiles would be returned to Gilead (Zec. 10:10; cf. Mic. 7:14; Ob. 19).

In the days of Judas Maccabeus, "the Gentiles in Gilead" plotted against Israelites who lived in the territory. The Israelites sent for help, and Judas and his brother Jonathan went to their aid (cf. 1 Macc. 5:9-51, AV "Galaad"). About seventy years later, Alexander Janneus subdued the people of Gilead and Moab (Josephus *BJ* i.4.3 [89]), but when he attacked the king of Arabia, he fell into an ambush and was forced to give up his gains (*BJ* i.4.4 [90]; *Ant.* xiii.14.2 [382]).

In the Greco-Roman period, the cities of the DECAPOLIS were developed, most of them in Gilead (cf. Pliny *Nat. hist.* v. 16 [74]). Best preserved of all these cities is Gerasa (Jerash). Other remains can be seen at Pella (Khirbet Faḥil), Gadara (Um Qeis or Muqeis), and Hippos or Susitha (Qalʿat el-Ḥuṣn). Philadelphia (modern ʿAmmân) lies outside Gilead, as does Scythopolis (Beisan).

During the Crusades, Baldwin I (A.D. 1118) and Baldwin II (A.D. 1121) attempted to control this region, and Crusader remains can be seen at Qalʿat er-Rabad, 3 km. (2 mi.) NW of ʿAjlūn, and at es-Salṭ.

See Vol. I, Map VI.

Bibliography.–M. Ottossen, *Gilead: Tradition and History* (Eng. tr. 1969); *GB*, rev. ed., pp. 210-225; N. Glueck, *AASOR*, 18-19 (1939); 25-28 (1951).

W. S. LASOR

GILEAD, BALM OF. *See* BALM OF GILEAD.

GILEAD, MOUNT. The AV rendering in Jgs. 7:3 "let him . . . depart early from mount Gilead" (Heb. *wᵉyiṣpōr mēhar haggilʿāḏ*; cf. LXX Gk. *ekchōreítō apó órous Galaad*) is questionable because there is no specific mountain in Gilead (though the terrain is hilly with several high and low points; *see* GILEAD III), and the terrain of Gilead is E (not W) of the Jordan. (The slight emendation *gilbō(a)ʿ*, cf. KD *in loc.* and *IB*, II, 737, fits the general geographical area W of the Jordan but is textually unsupported.) The RSV translation "and Gideon tested them" (*wayyiṣrᵉpēm gidʿôn*; cf. KoB, pp. 185, 817) eliminates the location E of the Jordan, but it requires too much emendation, none of which is textually supported. The NEB gives the most appealing solution: "is to leave Mount Galud." The area may be identified with ʿAin Jālûd, W of the Jordan and S of the Valley of Jezreel; thus no emendation is needed (cf. R. G. Boling, comm. on Judges [*AB*, 1975], p. 145).

R. W. V.

GILEADITES gil'ē-ə-dīts [Heb. *gilʿāḏî*].

1. A branch of the tribe of Manasseh (Nu. 26:29).

2. Natives of the district of GILEAD (Jgs. 12:4f.; 2 K. 15:25).

GILGAL gil'gal [Heb. *haggilgāl(â)*; Gk. *Galgal(a)* (usually declined as a pl.), *Golgol* (LXX, Dt. 11:30); Heb. also *galgûlâ* in the personal name of Yeshua ben Galgoula of the Bar Cochba documents].

The meaning is uncertain, but the use of the Hebrew article (*hag-*) indicates a common noun. *Gilgāl* as an ordinary noun occurs only in Isa. 28:28, where it means "wheel." This is the usual sense of the common *galgal* (e.g., Isa. 5:28; Jer. 47:3; Ezk. 10:2, 6, 13 [RSV "whirling wheels"]). The cognate verb *gālal* (reduplicated as *glgl*) means "roll" or "roll away" (e.g., Josh. 5:9). One would expect the noun to refer to something that rolls, whirls, or has been subjected to this motion. Yet it is commonly believed that *haggilgal* means "the stone circle of sacred pillars," a meaning derivable from the shape of the wheel. If the stones set up at Gilgal (Josh. 4:8) were sacred pillars (*maṣṣēḇôṯ*), they were very small, since each could be carried by one man (Josh. 4:2). Moreover, excavations of other sanctuaries in Canaan reveal pillars arranged in rows. One may consider another round shape, "the dome," the meaning which M. Dahood (*Psalms*, II [*AB*, 1968], 224, 232) gives *galgal* in Ps. 77:18 (MT 19). One may also consider the related term *gal*, "heap," in the pun of Hos. 12:11 (MT 12). Not all Gilgals need derive their original (probably forgotten) meaning from the same usage.

1. Gilgal near Jericho. ***I. History.***–The history of this Gilgal begins with the first military encampment of the Hebrews in the land of Canaan. From here they launched the Conquest (Josh. 5:13-15; 9:6; 10:6f., 15, 43; 14:6). It was the first place of sanctuary and altar (Josh. 9:23, 27) and an important place of sacrifice (1 S. 10:8; Hos. 12:11; Am. 4:4). The appearance of Yahweh's angel as commander of His army (Josh. 5:13-15) authenticated Gilgal as the site of the official sanctuary of the Israelite tribal alliance. The movement of this angel from Gilgal to Bochim (Bethel) in Jgs. 2:1 was probably due to the capture of the former by Eglon king of Moab (Jgs. 3:15-23), which required the removal of the ark of the covenant to Bethel. The "sculptured stones [*pᵉsîlîm*] near Gilgal" (3:19) may have been sacred pillars, but the ordinary meaning of the word is "idols."

Eclipsed for a long time by other cultic centers, Gilgal came into prominence again in the days of Samuel and Saul, after the demise of the sanctuary of Shiloh (1 S. 4; Jer. 7:12; 26:6). Though Gilgal was but one of three centers where Samuel sat as judge (1 S. 7:16), it was the spiritual capital where all the people rallied (1 S. 10:8; 13:4, 7, 15b-18; 15:10-33). Saul was made king there (1 S. 11:14f.), and David was welcomed back as king to Gilgal after his victory over Absalom (2 S. 19:15, 40).

The eighth-century prophets refer to Gilgal as a center of pilgrimage and they castigate it for apostasy (Hos. 4:15; 9:15; 12:11; Am. 4:4; 5:4f.). In the early 6th cent. (it is suggested), Ezekiel arose there as the last great preexilic prophet (*see* EZEKIEL III.C).

II. Cultic Celebration at Gilgal.–The cultic instruction and deeds of Josh. 3–6 sound like the prescriptions and acts of an elaborate liturgy, beginning at Shittim (Josh. 3:1), about 14 km. (8 mi.) E of the Jordan, with a movement across the Jordan to Gilgal and Jericho. When Micah called upon the people to "remember . . . what happened from Shittim to Gilgal, that you may know the saving acts of the Lord" (Mic. 6:5), he was referring, some scholars think, to a real liturgy performed there annually, which celebrated the Conquest and the formation of the twelve-tribe league. E. Otto argues for the intertwining of two parallel narratives, one of them written by the Yahwist (a tenth-century-B.C. historian) and the other by the Deuteronomic historian (6th cent. B.C.), both drawing upon an eleventh-century source. (There are other, often more complicated theories of composition.) Gilgal, having come into prominence just before and after the establishment of the Hebrew monarchy, served (many scholars believe) as the cult center where Israel's earliest historical and cultic traditions were brought together. The cultic celebration would begin with self-purification (Josh. 3:5) and be carried out with a processional crossing of the Jordan (Josh. 3–4), the erection of memorial stones (Josh. 4:1-9), the circumcising of the Hebrew males (Josh. 5:2-9), the celebration of a feast at Gilgal (Josh. 5:10-12), and the trumpeting processions about Jericho (Josh. 6) (but cf. J. R. Porter).

The dramatizing of history in the cult seems to have given everything a double meaning. The crossing of the Jordan recalled the previous crossing of the Red Sea at the Exodus from Egypt (Josh. 4:23f.; Ps. 66:6; 114:3, 5). The encamping at Gilgal was reminiscent of earlier encampments in the Wilderness of Sinai (Hos. 12:9 [MT 10]). Processions around Jericho represented the taking of numerous walled cities in Canaan. This dramatization of salvation history was probably completed by a covenanting ceremony reminiscent of the Sinaitic covenant (Ex. 24:1-11). This may have attracted to itself a reenactment also of the covenant first observed at Mts. Gerizim and Ebal (Dt. 27:2-8, 11-13; Josh. 8:30-35; 24). As performed anew, surrogate mountains with another diviner's oak (Oak of Moreh) were found in the vicinity of Gilgal (Dt. 11:29f.). Rabbi Eleazar (2nd cent. A.D.) identified these mountains with artificially constructed stone heaps set up at Gilgal (T.P. *Sotah* vii.21c): "They made two rock piles and called one Mount Gerizim and the other Mount Ebal." Even though this interpretation was used in disputation against the Samaritans and was contrary to that of Rabbi Judah, it was probably based on old tradition: the stones in the annual ceremony of crossing the Jordan were thrown into memorial heaps (Gen. 31:46-49), which grew larger every year until they were taken over to represent the mountains Gerizim and Ebal. The early church fathers were content to argue simply that these sacred mountains were near Jericho (cf. *GP,* I, 361f.).

The community at Qumrân performed an annual liturgy of covenant renewal; its Rule (1QS 1–2) prescribed a "crossing over into the covenant" (1:16) and a "crossing over" (the Jordan?) in military ranks (2:19-22), in a public ceremony concluding with a liturgy of blessings and curses (2:2-18) reminiscent of Dt. 27:11–28:68. This ceremony, which is ultimately derivable from that of Gilgal, was celebrated at the Feast of Weeks (W. H. Brownlee, *BASOR,* 123 [Oct. 1951], 30-32).

Scholars have disputed whether the ancient festival of Gilgal was celebrated at the Feast of Unleavened Bread, dated to the new moon of the month Abib (H. Wildberger; E. Otto) or to mid-month (H.-J. Kraus); at Passover, the 14th of Abib (J. A. Soggin; J. A. Wilcoxen); or at the Feast of Weeks, falling seven weeks later (von Rad); for though Josh. 5:10 refers to the Passover, "the unleavened cakes" of 5:11 may refer to an originally separate festival; and "parched grain" occurs elsewhere in the context of ordinary "bread" (Lev. 23:14). Even though the first celebration was held at Passover, the flooding Jordan was overcome only by an act of God (Josh. 3:15f.). The memorial celebration was best held at the Feast of Weeks, when the Jordan was low, as observed also by the people of Qumrân.

III. Location.–Gilgal's location is defined most explicitly in Josh. 4:19: "on the east border of [the territory of] Jericho." "Jericho" here refers to the entire oasis, and not just to the city proper on the mound W of Elisha's Fountain. This gusher of a spring, which gave water to Jericho and most of its fields, was next to the city itself, where it was easily defended against invading Israelites. There were two other major sources of water. One was the Wâdī Qelt, which flowed past Jericho on the south, emptying its perennial spring water to the southeast. The other was the Wâdī en-Nuʿeima (Nuʿeimeh), which augmented the oasis to the northeast with a perennial stream fed by copious springs (ʿAin ed-Dûq, ʿAin en-Nuʿeima, and ʿAin Dajani). Since Roman times these waters have been lifted out of the wadis in controlled irrigation.

No satisfactory location for Gilgal has been proposed

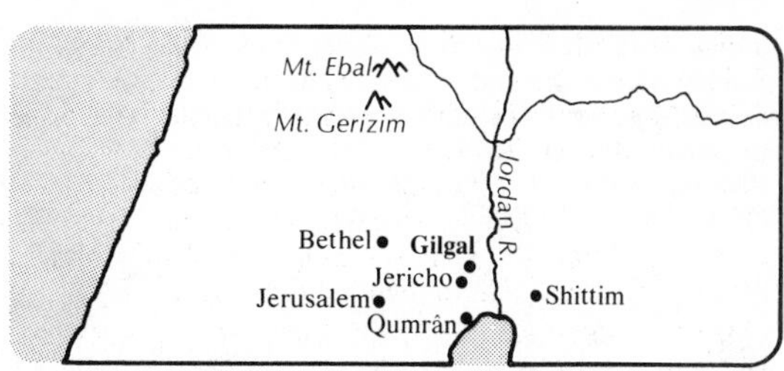

either E or SE of Jericho, since no archeological remains earlier than Byzantine have been found there. To the northeast, however, in the vicinity of Khirbet el-Mefjer, several small sites have disclosed the presence of pottery datable to the period *ca.* 1200 to 600 B.C. One of those areas, known as Suwwānet eth-Thaniye ("the flint rock of the winding road") lies immediately to the west of Mefjer, where the Wâdī en-Nuʿeima cuts through the ridge known as Dhaharet eth-Thaniye ("the ridge of the winding road"), which extends east from Jebel Qaranṭal ("the mount of temptation") to Mefjer. The very name of this spot, excavated by B. M. Bennett and G. M. Landes, calls attention to an outcropping of flint rock, which may have been the source of the flint knives at Gilgal (Josh. 5:2f.).

The distances of Gilgal from the ford of the Jordan and from Jericho as attested by ancient Christian pilgrims agree closely with those of Khirbet el-Mefjer. An older witness is Josephus (*Ant.* v.1.4 [20]): "These [invading Israelites] advanced fifty stades [from the Jordan], pitched their camp [Gilgal] at a distance of ten stades from Jericho." J. Muilenburg (p. 18) counted the actual distances from a spot just N of Mefjer (where he found preexilic pottery) as being 50.09 and 10.87 stades (9.3 and 2 km., 5.8 and 1.25 mi.), respectively.

2. The Gilgal of Elijah and Elisha has been identified by some scholars with **1**; but the description of the journey of these prophets to Transjordan by way of Bethel and Jericho (2 K. 2:1-8) suggests the existence of another Gilgal in the hill country above Bethel. Today a Jiljilieh does exist, about 13 km. (8 mi.) N of Bethel, not to be confused with Jiljulieh in the Shephelah to the west.

3. Joshua 15:7 mentions a Gilgal near the ascent of Adummim, about halfway from Jerusalem to Jericho; but 18:17 gives the name as Geliloth (cf. also the Pesh. of 15:7). Despite the error of the MT, it may be that it records the postexilic name of the place, at a time when the Gilgal near Jericho no longer existed. This gives us a place for Beth Gilgal (Neh. 12:29) within the tiny province of postexilic Judah.

The site, though commonly identified with Khan el-Aḥmar (the so-called Good Samaritan Inn), might be identified with nearby ʿArâq ed-Deir (R. Boling). Any hamlet in this arid region would consist mainly of huts for herdsmen and folds for their flocks. Perhaps the latter (like the sheepfolds of the area today) were circular stone corrals, hence called *g^elîlôṯ* ("circles").

4. Some suppose that Dt. 11:30 supports the existence of another Gilgal near Shechem; but on this verse see **1.** II above.

5. Joshua 12:23 refers to "King of Goiim in [or at] Gilgal"; but most scholars follow the LXX in reading *glyl* (*gālîl,* Galilee) for *glgl* (Gilgal). If Goiim is to be identified with Harosheth-ha-goiim (Jgs. 4:2), this place (or area) would be in Galilee. 1 Macc. 9:2, in its best-attested reading, refers to a northern Gilgal; but Josephus (*Ant.* xii.11.1 [421]) reads Galilee.

6. "Gilgal [*Galgala*] of the Jordan" occurs in some LXX MSS at Josh. 22:10, but the Hebrew text reads

"g^{e}lîlôṯ of the Jordan" as in 22:11, where the LXX reads "Gilead [Galaad] of the Jordan." The context favors reading g^{e}lîlôṯ with the MT and interpreting this as "the region about the Jordan" (RSV).

Bibliography.–B. M. Bennett, *PEQ,* 1973, pp. 111f.; "The Israelite Shrine of Gilgal: Its Location, History and Function, an Archaeological and Literary Investigation" (Diss., General Theological Seminary, 1969); R. G. Boling, *ASOR Newsletter,* 1-2 (July-Aug. 1976), 8; W. H. Brownlee, "The Ceremony of Crossing the Jordan in the Annual Covenanting at Qumran," in W. C. Delsman, *et al.*, eds., *Von Kanaan bis Kerala* (1981), *EAEHL,* III, *s.v.* "Al-Mafjar, Khirbet" (R. W. Hamilton); K. Galling, *ZDPV,* 66 (1943), 140-155; 67 (1944), 21-43; H.-J. Kraus, *VT,* 1 (1951), 181-191; G. Landes, *Report on Archaeological Work at Suwwānet eth-Thaniye, Tananir and Khirbet Minḥa* (*BASOR Supp.*, 21, 1975), pp. 1-24; E. Langlamet, *Gilgal et les récits de la traversée du Jourdain* (1969); J. Muilenburg, *BASOR,* 140 (Dec. 1955), 11-33; E. W. Nicholson, *Exodus and Sinai in History and Tradition* (1973), pp. 1-11; E. Otto, *Das Mazzotfest in Gilgal* (1975); J. R. Porter, *Svensk Exegetisk Årsbok,* 26 (1972), 5-23; P. P. Saydon, *CBQ,* 12 (1950), 194-207; J. A. Soggin, "Gilgal, Passah und Landnahme: Eine neue Untersuchung des kultischen Zusammenhangs der Kap. iii-vi des Josuabuches," in *SVT,* 15 (1968), 263-277; G. von Rad, "The Form-Critical Problem of the Hexateuch," in *The Problem of the Hexateuch and Other Essays* (Eng. tr. 1966), esp. pp. 33-39; J. A. Wilcoxen, "Narrative Structure and Cult Legend: A Study of Joshua 1–6," in J. C. Rylaarsdam, ed., *Transitions in Biblical Scholarship* (1968), pp. 43-70; H. Wildberger, *Yahwes Eigentumsvolk* (1960); J. N. M. Wijngaards, *Dramatization of Salvific History in the Deuteronomic Schools* (*OTS,* 16, 1969).

W. H. BROWNLEE

GILGAMESH gil'gə-mesh or gil-gā'məsh. *See* BABYLON IV.B; IX.A; RELIGIONS OF THE BIBLICAL WORLD: ASSYRIA AND BABYLONIA V.

GILOH gī'lō [Heb. *gilōh*]. A town in the hill country of the territory allotted to the tribe of Judah (Josh. 15:51). It was the home of Ahithophel (the "Gilonite," Heb. *haggîlōnî,* 2 S. 15:12; in 23:34 the RSV renders *haggilōnî* "of Gilo"; cf. AV, NEB), one of David's counselors (cf. 1 Ch. 27:33) who joined Absalom in his revolt (2 S. 15:12). The identification with Khirbet Jala, about 8 km. (5 mi.) NNW of Hebron, would seem to contradict Josh. 15:48-51, which suggests a location about 20 km. (12½ mi.) SSW of Hebron (cf. Y. Aharoni and M. Avi-Yonah, *Macmillan Bible Atlas* [rev. ed. 1977], map 130).

GILONITE gī'lō-nīt (2 S. 15:12). *See* GILOH.

GIMEL gim'əl [ג, ג]. The third letter of the Hebrew alphabet; used as such to designate the third part of Ps. 119; transliterated in this encyclopedia with the dagesh as *g,* and without as *g* (aspirated *g*). It came also to be used for the number three and with the diaeresis for three thousand. *See* WRITING.

GIMZO gim'zō [Heb. *gimzô*]. A city of Judah in the Shephelah near the Philistine plain that was captured by the Philistines in the days of Ahaz (2 Ch. 28:18). It is the modern Jimzū about 5 km. (3 mi.) SE of Lod off the Jerusalem road.

GIN. *See* TRAP.

GINATH gī'nath [Heb. *gînaṯ*]. Father of Tibni, the unsuccessful rival of Omri (1 K. 16:21f.).

GINNETHOI gin'ə-thoi [Heb. *ginn^{e}ṯôy*] (Neh. 12:4); AV GINNETHO; NEB GINNETHON; **GINNETHON** gin'ə-thon [Heb. *ginn^{e}ṯôn*] (Neh. 10:6 [MT 7]; 12:16). The head of a priestly family.

GIRDLE. *See* GARMENTS III.A; IV; VIII.A.

GIRGASHITE gûr'gə-shīt [Heb. *girgāšî*; Gk. *Gergesaios*]. One of the tribes of western Palestine descended from Canaan (Gen. 10:16; 1 Ch. 1:14), listed in the Abrahamic promise (Gen. 15:21), and dispossessed by Israel (Dt. 7:1; Josh. 3:10; 24:11; Neh. 9:8). Some identify them with the Qaraqisha of Hittite and Egyptian records. The name has been linked with the personal names Grgshy, Grgsh, and Grgshm found in Punic texts, and *grgš* and *bn grgš* in Ugaritic. This link suggests that the tribe was related to the Phoenicians. Maisler holds that their name is theophorous and means "client of Ges [the Sumerian god of light]," that his worship was introduced into Phoenicia and Palestine *ca.* 2000 B.C., and that "Gergesenes" ("Gerasenes," AV, RSV mg.) in Mt. 8:28; Mk. 5:1; Lk. 8:26, 37 may be the same name.

Bibliography.–*UT,* p. 381; P. Maisler, *ZAW,* 50 (1932), 86f.

D. J. WIEAND

GIRL [Heb. *ʿalmâ* (Ex. 2:8), *yaldâ* (Joel 3:3 [MT 4:3]; Zec. 8:5), *na^{ʿa}râ* (Jgs. 19:3-6, 8f.); Gk. *korásion* (Mt. 9:24f.; 14:11; Mk. 5:41f.; 6:22, 28), *paidískē* ("slave girl," Acts 16:16), *parthénos* (1 Cor. 7:28, 34)]; AV also MAID, DAMSEL, VIRGIN (1 Cor. 7:28, 34); NEB also CHILD (Mk. 5:41), VIRGIN (1 Cor. 7:28), CELIBATE WOMAN (1 Cor. 7:34); **YOUNG GIRLS** [Heb. *ṭap bannāšîm*] (Nu. 31:18); AV WOMEN CHILDREN; NEB WOMAN.

Except for the use of *yaldâ* in Zec. 8:5, the OT renderings refer to girls in late adolescence rather than childhood. The word *ṭap* denotes those of the tribe who are unfit to march, including women and children (KoB, p. 355), while *nāšîm* means "women." The NT terms range in meaning from "child" (*korásion*) to "unmarried woman of marriageable age" (*parthénos*). *Paidískē* always refers to a slave girl. In Mk. 5:41 *korásion* is used to translate the Aram. *ṭ^{e}lîṯâ,* "maiden" (transliterated in the Greek as *talithá*).

See also DAUGHTER; MAID.

N. J. O.

GIRZITES gûr'zīts. In 1 S. 27:8, the *kethibh* has *girzî,* whereas the *qere* reads *gizrî.* The RSV follows the *kethibh,* while the AV ("Gezrites") and NEB ("Gizrites") follow the *qere.* This in the only mention of an otherwise unknown people living between Philistia and the Egyptian border, who with the Amalekites and Geshurites were in brief conflict with David when he was at Ziklag. Attempts to associate the *qere* with the inhabitants of Gezer should be avoided, if only on topographical grounds.

R. K. H.

GISHPA gish'pə [Heb. *gišpāʾ*] (Neh. 11:21); AV GISPA. An officer of the temple servants. A comparison with Ezr. 2:43 makes it probable that he is to be identified with Hasupha, and quite possible that this word is a corruption of "Hasupha."

GITTAH-HEPHER git-ə-hē'fər (Josh. 19:13, AV); RSV, NEB GATH-HEPHER. "Gittah" is correctly "Gath" with *h* locale, meaning "toward Gath." *See* GATH-HEPHER.

GITTAIM git'ā-əm [Heb. **gittayim*–'double winepress']. The town to which the Beerothites fled for refuge from the persecution of Saul (2 S. 4:3). This town may be identical with the one named with Hazor and Ramah in Neh. 11:33, where returning Benjaminites settled after the Exile.

GITTITES git'īts [Heb. *gittîm*]. The inhabitants of Gath, one of the five chief Philistine cities, previously occupied by the formidable Anakim (Josh. 11:22).

Gath was the scene of an outbreak of bubonic plague (1 S. 5:6-12), which devastated its inhabitants. The Gittites were apparently men of great stature (cf. 2 S. 21:19-22; 1 Ch. 20:5-8), and the giant Goliath (1 S. 17:4-7) killed by David was one of them. David subsequently had Gittite friends in his retinue (2 S. 6:10f.; 15:19-22) and Gittite troops among his mercenaries (2 S. 15:18). One Gittite warrior had a congenital deformity of the hands and feet (2 S. 21:20; 1 Ch. 20:6). Twice David fled from Saul to Achish, king of Gath (1 S. 21:10-15; 27–28). The Gittites were successively subjugated by Rehoboam (2 Ch. 11:8), Hazael (2 K. 12:17), and Uzziah (2 Ch. 26:6), though in Am. 6:2 Gath is described as Philistine. R. K. H.

GITTITH git'ith [Heb. *gittîṯ*] (headings of Pss. 8, 81, 84). *See* PSALMS, BOOK OF II.C.

GIVE. I. Terminology–*A. Common Verbs.* In the OT "give" most frequently represents the common Hebrew verb *nāṯan* (more than 900 occurrences). The later synonym **yāhaḇ* (whose cognate *y^ehaḇ* exclusively denotes "give" in biblical Aramaic) is far less frequent and occurs only in the imperative. Used independently these two verbs denote simply "give": volitional transference of a thing or benefit from one to another. Sometimes these verbs occur in idiomatic combination with a substantive, e.g., *nāṯan qôl,* "utter a voice" (Am. 1:2; 2 S. 22:14), *nāṯan b^eyaḏ,* "give into the hand of" (i.e., "hand over to," Nu. 21:2; Dt. 1:27; etc.), *nāṯan b^enepeš,* "give up to the will of" (Ps. 27:12), *nāṯan lēḇ,* "give heed" (Eccl. 7:21).

In the NT the Greek verb *dídōmi* is by far the most frequently represented term (more than 300 occurrences), used either in independent form or in cognate forms in which prepositional prefixes add nuances to the verbal root. Examples of the latter are *apodídōmi,* "give back" (Lk. 9:42), *prodídōmi* (lit. "give first"), "give a gift" (Rom. 11:35), *metadídōmi* (lit. "share"), "contribute" (Rom. 12:8), *epidídōmi,* "give way" (Acts 27:15), *paradídōmi,* "give up" (Rom. 1:26, 28; etc.).

The RSV does not limit its translation of Heb. *nāṯan* or Gk. *dídōmi* to "give." *Nāṯan* is also translated as "put" (e.g., Ex. 25:16), "yield" (e.g., Lev. 26:4), "allow" (Dt. 18:14), "set" (2 K. 18:23), "bring" (1 S. 9:23), "bestow" (Ex. 32:29), etc. *Dídōmi* is likewise variously rendered as "offered" (Mt. 27:34), "put" (Bar. 3:7; Mk. 13:34), "assign" (1 Cor. 3:5), "make" (Eph. 1:22), "commit" (Rev. 20:4), etc.

B. Causative Verb Forms. In the OT "give" translates the hiphil form of many Hebrew verbs, e.g., the hiphil of *nāgaḏ,* "give account of" (Job 31:37), *zāhar,* "give warning" (Ezk. 3:17; 33:7), *yāṣāʾ,* "give vent to" (Prov. 29:11), *yārâ,* "give revelation" (Hab. 2:19), of *gāmāʾ,* "give to drink" (Gen. 24:17), of *kāʿas,* "give provocation" (Hos. 12:14 [MT 15]), of *yāḏâ,* "give thanks" (Ps. 7:17 [MT 18]), etc.

C. Specific Verbs. In addition, the RSV frequently renders many other Hebrew, Aramaic, and Greek verbs by expressions that use "give" as an auxiliary. Heb. *yālaḏ* (1 S. 4:19b) and *ḥûl* (Dt. 32:18), and Gk. *gennáō* (Lk. 1:57) and *tíktō* (Lk. 2:7) are rendered "give birth."

Many verbs for speaking and commanding are rendered with "give": Heb. *ʿānâ,* "give answer" (Gen. 41:16), *yāʿaṣ,* "give counsel" (Ex. 18:19), *ʾāmar,* "give command" (1 Ch. 14:12), "give orders" (Est. 6:1), *ṣîwwâ,* "give in commandment" (Ex. 25:22), *ʿāzaḇ,* "give free utterance" (Job 10:1), *pāṯar,* "give interpretation" (Gen. 41:12), niphal of *šāḇaʿ,* "give an oath" (2 S. 19:23 [MT 24]), etc.; Gk. *apokrínomai,* "give answer" (Mt. 27:14), *symbouleúō,* "give counsel" (Jn. 18:14), *parakaléō,* "give encouragement" (Acts 20:2), *keleúō,* "give orders" (Mt. 8:18), *diatássō,* "give directions" (1 Cor. 11:34), *diastéllomai,* "give instructions" (Acts 15:24), *parakaléō,* "give instruction" (Tit. 1:9), *emphanízō,* "give information" (Acts 25:15), etc.

Certain verbs expressing gratitude and praise are also rendered with "give." "Give praise" renders Heb. *hālal* (Jer. 31:7) and Gk. *exomologéō* (Rom. 14:11); "give glory," Heb. *śîm kāḇôḏ* (Josh. 7:19) and Gk. *doxázō* (Mt. 5:16); "give thanks," Gk. *eucharistéō* (Lk. 17:16; etc.).

The English idioms "give oneself," "give up," and "give away" represent a variety of terms with a range of meanings. "Give up" can mean deliver in the sense of handing someone over (e.g., hiphil of Heb. *sāgar* in Dt. 23:15 [MT 16]; Josh. 20:5; Gk. *paradídōmi* in Rom. 1:26, 28; *charízomai* in Acts 25:11, 16), or abandon, cease, neglect (e.g., Heb. *ʿāzaḇ* in Ps. 16:10; Gk. *kataleípō* in Acts 6:2; *aphíēmi* in Rom. 1:27; *katargéō* in 1 Cor. 13:11; cf. "give up worshiping," *mḗ proskynéō* in Rev. 9:20). The RSV renders "give themselves to" for hiphil of Heb. *ḥāzaq b^e,* with the meaning "devote themselves to" (2 Ch. 31:4). In 1 S. 11:3, 10 "give ourselves up" (Heb. *yāṣāʾ*) denotes surrender, as does "give way" (Gk. *epidídōmi*) in Acts 27:15. (Cf. also references to Jesus "giving himself [up]," discussed under II below.)

D. Nouns. "Given to" sometimes translates the Hebrew noun *baʿal* (lit. "possessor" or "master") in construct with a noun describing a human proclivity: *baʿal nepeš,* "a man given to appetite" (Prov. 23:2), *baʿal ʾāp,* "a man given to anger" (Prov. 22:24), *baʿal ḥēmâ,* "a man given to anger" (Prov. 29:22), *baʿal rešaʿ,* "those who are given to [wickedness]" (Eccl. 8:8).

E. As a Translational Facilitation. In some instances the appearances of "give" in the RSV are merely an aid to facilitate translation. In Nu. 11:12; 14:16, 23, e.g., the literal "swore to their fathers" becomes in the RSV "swore to give to their fathers." In Jn. 7:39 the literal "for the Spirit was not yet" is rendered "for as yet the Spirit had not been given" (but cf. the undoubtedly secondary Greek variant *dedoménou,* "given," that is represented in a number of Syriac, Coptic, and Latin MSS as well as citations by some church fathers). In Gal. 3:15 "to give a human example" renders Gk. *katá ánthrōpon légō* (cf. AV "I speak after the manner of man"). Cf. also Dt. 33:8; 1 Ch. 6:61 (MT 46); Jer. 43:11; Rom. 2:7; 5:13; 15:8.

II. Concept.–In the OT the concept of giving is significant and multifaceted. The model is God Himself who is ever giving generously of Himself and His own bounty. The land of promise, the covenants, the tablets, the Torah, the kingship, peace, power, justice, deliverance from the enemy, the phenomena of nature, provision, and sustenance are but some of the many gifts that the OT attributes to God's own gracious giving. It is God alone who gives salvation, but as Lord of history He is also viewed as giving peoples "into the hands of" (Nu. 21:2) or "over to" (Dt. 7:16) enemies.

God also gives people signs (2 Ch. 32:24), answers (Gen. 41:16), and blessings (Gen. 28:4). In contrast, the handcrafted idol cannot "give revelation" (Hab. 2:19).

In the OT human beings also give to God. They give Him thanks (Ps. 7:17 [MT 18]) and praise (Ps. 66:2). They promise and are urged to give Him their tithes and offerings (Gen. 28:22; Ex. 30:14). Freewill offerings for the furbishing of the Solomonic temple were "given willingly" (1 Ch. 29:9) by the people of Israel. The underlying rationale for this giving to God is clearly stated in 1 Ch. 29:14: "For all things come from thee, and of thy own have we given thee." The model is always God's own prior generosity; the goal is to show gratitude by emulation of that model in the human sphere. *See* TITHE.

The same elevated concept of giving may also be perceived in the Apocrypha. Tobit, affirming that "the Lord himself gives all good things" (4:19), indeed life itself (5:19), urged by both word and example (1:7f., 17, etc.) that human comportment model itself after God's own generosity: "Give of your bread to the hungry, and of your clothing to the naked. Give all your surplus to charity, and do not let your eye begrudge the gift when you make it" (4:16). "It is better to give alms than to treasure up gold" (12:8). The sage Sirach, however, advocated a more circumscribed posture of benevolence:

Give to the godly man,
but do not help the sinner.
Do good to the humble,
but do not give to the ungodly (12:4f., 7).

He reasoned that just as wicked people are odious to God, so must they be to the faithful. No distinction is made here between sin and the sinner; indeed, the righteous are to share in the retributive attitude that is ascribed to God vis-à-vis the unrighteous. In 1 Macc. 6:44 the concept of giving for the sake of others is extended even to the giving up of one's life: "he [Eleazar] gave his life to save his people" (cf. 2:50).

The NT particularly accents God's giving nature. In John's Gospel Jesus' own works (5:36) are attributed to God's giving. Indeed, "God so loved the world that he gave his only Son" (3:16), and the Father "has given all things into his [the Son's] hand" (3:35). Jesus Himself taught the maxim that it is "more blessed to give than to receive" (Acts 20:35), thereby extending to the sphere of human relations the divine example of giving freely of oneself for the well-being of others. This may include tithing but should not be construed in terms of "external magnitude" but on the basis of "the internal state of the giver's heart" (P. E. Hughes, comm. on 2nd Corinthians [*NICNT,* 1962], p. 330).

Consonant with divine giving is the "new commandment" that Jesus gives his followers in Jn. 13:34, "even as I have loved you, that you also love one another." By His life of total self-giving, humbling Himself and becoming obedient unto death, Jesus made the perfect offering of obedience to God and set an example for all to emulate. Using the traditional language for martyrdom (cf. 1 Macc. 6:44 above) the NT describes Jesus' death as an act of love in which He "gave Himself" (Gal. 1:4; 2:20; Eph. 5:25; 1 Tim. 2:6; Tit. 2:14). "Therefore," urged Paul, "be imitators of God, as beloved children. And walk in love, as Christ loved us and gave Himself up for us, a fragrant offering and sacrifice to God" (Eph. 5:1f.). (See M. Barth, comm. on Ephesians [*AB,* 1974], p. 556f.; *see also* LOVE III.)

This God, then, whose very nature it is to give and whose preeminent gift to humankind is Jesus (Jn. 3:16), calls all to a life of trust in His ability to give what is necessary for life. "He who did not spare his own Son but gave him up for us all, will he not also give us all things with him?" (Rom. 8:32).

See also ALMS; GIFT II.

Bibliography.–TDNT, II, *s.v.* δίδωμι κτλ. (Büchsel); IV, *s.v.* μέτρον κτλ. (Deissner).

D. G. BURKE

GIZONITE gī'zən-īt [Heb. *gizōnî*]. This gentile name in 1 Ch. 11:34, "Hashem the Gizonite," is probably an error for "Gunite" (cf. Nu. 26:48), and the passage should then be corrected, after 2 S. 23:32, "Jashen the Gunite." Other authorities emend to read "from Gimzo" (cf. 2 Ch. 28:18).

GIZRITES giz'rīts (1 S. 27:8, NEB). *See* GIRZITES.

GLAD [Heb. *śāmaḥ* (Ex. 4:14; 1 S. 11:9; 1 Ch. 16:31; Ps. 31:7 [MT 8]; etc.), *ṭûḇ/yāṭaḇ/ṭôḇ* (Jgs. 18:20; 1 K. 8:66 par. 2 Ch. 7:10; Est. 5:9; Eccl. 7:3), *gîl* (Prov. 24:17; Isa. 25:9; 66:10; Joel 2:21, 23), *śûś, śîś* (Job 3:22; Isa. 35:1; 65:18f.; Lam. 1:21), piel of *ḥāḏâ* (Ps. 21:6 [MT 7]), *bāśar* ("told the glad news," Ps. 40:9 [MT 10]), *rinnâ* (Ps. 42:4 [MT 5]; 118:15); Aram. *ṭeʾēḇ* (Dnl. 6:23 [MT 24]); Gk. *agalliáomai* (Mt. 5:12; 1 Pet. 4:13), *chaírō*–'rejoice' (Mk. 14:11; Lk. 15:32; 22:5; etc.), *thélō*–'will, wish' (Jn. 6:21), *euphraínō* (Acts 2:26; 2 Cor. 2:2)]; AV also REJOICE, PREACH (Ps. 40:9), JOY, MERRY, "is made better" (Eccl. 7:3), WILLINGLY (Jn. 6:21), etc.; NEB also PLEASED, "take heart" (1 S. 11:9), REJOICE, EXULT, etc.; **GLADNESS** [Heb. *śimḥâ* (Nu. 10:10; 1 Ch. 29:22; 2 Ch. 29:30; 30:21, 23; etc.), *ṭûḇ* (Dt. 28:47; Isa. 65:14), *śāśôn* (Ps. 45:7 [MT 8]); Isa. 61:3; Joel 1:12), hiphil of *bālag* ("know gladness," Ps. 39:13 [MT 14]), *rinnâ* ("shouts of gladness," Prov. 11:10), *māśôś* (Isa. 24:11), *śāmaḥ* ("give gladness," Jer. 31:13), *gîl* (Joel 1:16); Gk. *agallíasis* (Lk. 1:14; He. 1:9), *euphrosýnē* (Acts 2:28; 14:17)]; AV also JOY, "recover strength" (Ps. 39:13), SHOUTING (Prov. 11:10), MIRTH (Isa. 24:11), MAKE REJOICE (Jer. 31:13); NEB also FESTAL, REJOICING, JOY, JOYFULLY, SMILE (Ps. 39:13), etc.; **GLADLY** [Gk. *asménōs*] (Acts 21:17); [*hēdéōs*–'pleasantly'] (e.g., Mk. 6:20); NEB also LIKEN TO, EAGERLY, PREFER TO; [*epithyméō*–'desire'] ("would gladly," Lk. 15:16); NEB GLAD.

In 2 S. 18:11; Philem. 13 the RSV supplies "gladly" (AV, NEB, "I would have given"). Usually the RSV keeps the expression "gladness of heart" (e.g., Dt. 28:47; Cant. 3:11; Isa. 30:29), though it changes it in Acts 2:46 to "glad . . . hearts" (Gk. *en agalliásei . . . kardías*).

In Est. 9:19, 22, gladness is part of a larger context of "feasting and holiday-making," of sending "choice portions to one another" and "gifts to the poor." In Zeph. 3:17 it parallels love (Heb. *ʾahaḇâ*). Thus for the Hebrews "gladness" was more than mere gratification of a physical pleasure (as in Herod's case, Lk. 23:8). Often it is interchanged with "joy" (e.g., Ps. 14:7; cf. "rejoice and be glad" in Ps. 31:7; Mt. 5:12), finding its "seat" in the heart (Ex. 4:14; 1 K. 8:66; Prov. 27:11; Ps. 16:9 = Acts 2:26).

Gladness is expressed at the birth of a son (Lk. 1:14; but cf. Jer. 20:15), at a reunion of relatives (Ex. 4:14), and at a son's show of wisdom before his father (Prov. 10:1; 15:20; 23:24; 29:3). It is a contrast to sadness, lamenting ("mourning," Est. 9:22), and sorrow (Prov. 15:13; but cf. Jer. 31:13). Only rarely does one face death with gladness (Job 3:22; but cf. Ps. 39:13). But to Paul there can be gladness in pain and weakness (2 Cor. 2:2; 12:9; 13:9), and Peter linked gladness to suffering for the Lord (1 Pet. 4:13). It is unacceptable to rejoice at the calamity of one's enemy (Prov. 17:5; cf. 24:17), though this injunction had been violated (Lam. 1:21). (For other nonreligious occurrences of "gladness," see TDNT, II, 774.)

In the Psalms gladness refers to cultic celebration ("with glad shouts," cf. Ps. 42:4) of the great acts of divine deliverance (cf. Ps. 107:30, 42) and to a general joy in God. (See *TDOT,* II, 475; cf. p. 474 for the "secular" use of Heb. *gîl.*) To the psalmist God is the source of human joy (Ps. 118:14), which is associated with the stringed instruments (Ps. 45:8 [MT 9]), the flute (cf. Isa. 30:29), and the divine anointing with the "oil of gladness" (Ps. 45:7 = He. 1:9; Isa. 61:3; Prov. 27:9) or "superabundant joy" (KD *in loc.* on Ps. 45; cf. F. F. Bruce, comm. on Hebrews [*NICNT,* 1964], p. 20). The relation between gladness and wine is ambiguous; wine may cause merriment (at harvest time, Ps. 104:15; Eccl. 10:19; cf. Jer. 48:33; Zec. 10:7) or much misery (Isa. 22:13; see *DNTT,* III, 919, 922).

Metaphorically, "gladness" can be attributed to a nation (Ps. 106:5), to dry land (Isa. 35:1), to the heavens (1 Ch. 16:31; Ps. 96:11), etc. In Ps. 46:4 "streams make glad the city of God," while Isa. 65:17-19 gives a glimpse of an eternal jubilation. On Ps. 40:9 (Heb. *bāśar*) *see* GOOD NEWS; PREACH.

See JOY.

Bibliography.–*TDNT,* I, *s.v.* ἀγαλλιάομαι (Bultmann); II, *s.v.* εὐφραίνω κτλ. (Bultmann); IX, *s.v.* χαίρω κτλ.: χαίρω (Conzelmann); *TDOT,* II, *s.v.* "gyl" (Bergman-Ringgren, Barth).

N. J. O. R. W. V.

GLAD TIDINGS. Occurs in the AV translation of the Greek verb *euangelízō,* "tell the good news" (Lk. 1:19; 8:1; Acts 13:32; Rom. 10:15). The verb is also frequently translated "preach the gospel" (< Anglo-Saxon *godspell,* "good tidings"). The AV adopted "glad tidings" from Tyndale's version, which was the first English Bible to use the phrase. The RSV uses "good tidings" (only in the OT), "good news," and "gospel."

See GOOD NEWS; GOSPEL.

GLASS [Heb. *zᵉḵôḵîṯ* (Job 28:17); AV, NEB, CRYSTAL; Gk. *hýalos* (Rev. 21:18, 21)]. A homogeneous material that has a random liquid-like (noncrystalline) molecular structure, composed primarily of silica or sand mixed with soda and lime. The manufacturing process for glass requires that the raw materials be heated and reacted so as to form a completely fused melt, which is then cooled rapidly so that it becomes rigid without crystallizing.

I. Techniques.–Three basic techniques were used to fashion vessels: casting, mosaic, and core-forming. The casting of vessels was probably done in molds similar to those used in casting early metals. Usually some final cutting and polishing were needed after removal from the mold.

The more sophisticated mosaic glass technique is the same as that used today to make paperweights. By heating small amounts of glass and drawing them into thin rods, a design could be built with multiple rods, which were heated to form a solid cane. The cane could be heated again and pulled out like taffy to miniaturize the design. The resulting cane was cut into sections, which were used to make beads or arranged in a mold to form a vessel. Excavations at Tell er-Rimah in Iraq confirm a fifteenth-century B.C. date for this sophisticated technique.

In core-forming a rod or tool was dipped into a pot of molten glass and trailed onto a core that was made of clay and dung and supported on a metal rod. (The high viscosity of early glass would have made dipping the core directly into a pot very difficult.) Then the glass was reheated and smoothed by marvering, rolling the hot form on a flat stone surface. Characteristic of this technique are trail decorations in contrasting colors wound over the marvered form. With a single point or a comblike tool these trails were dragged up and down into elaborate feather or festoon patterns, a technique easily accomplished in glass but nearly impossible in any other medium. After the handles, feet, and rim were fashioned, the core-formed object was removed from the supporting rod and the core material was scraped out. Most of the extant bottles and jars from the middle of the 2nd millennium were fashioned by core-forming, although the three techniques were contemporary.

II. History.–Pliny's account of the accidental discovery of glass by Phoenician sailors at the Syro-Palestinian coast (*Nat. hist.* xxxvi.65 [191]) is quaint but anachronistic. The origin of glass was farther east and probably associated with the metal-working or faience industries, which required intense heat and used similar raw materials. Small objects, such as beads and pendants, were probably made of glass well before 1500 B.C. Shortly after the middle of the 2nd millennium glass vessels were made in western Asia by the three basic techniques mentioned above. With the expansion of Egypt under Thutmose III, glassmaking technology was brought back to Egypt where it flourished from the 18th through the 20th Dynasties. Job (28:17) equates the value of glass with gold and rubies; the vessels inscribed with the name of Thutmose III and found in the tombs of his minor wives confirm the high value of glass and suggest Asian glassworkers were eager to extol their new patron. After the 20th Dynasty, Egypt was not a glassmaking center again until the establishment of Alexandria in the late 4th cent. B.C. Near Eastern centers continued to produce glass objects after the 1st millennium B.C. Casting vessels seem to be the craftsman's tour de force. At the Anatolian site of Gordion, a Phrygian center, a colorless fluted bowl was discovered in a ninth-century-B.C. context. It is the first of a series of colorless glass objects which culminate in the shallow phiale that imitated rock crystals and precious metal forms at the Persian court of the 5th cent. B.C. These vessels are among the finest technological achievements in glassmaking before the invention of glassblowing.

Phiale of colorless glass, cast and cut in Persia during the Achaemenian period (450-400 B.C.) (Corning Museum of Glass)

Aristophanes (*Acharnians* 74) mentioned the haughty ambassadors at the Persian court drinking from goblets of glass and gold. At Nimrûd, vessels associated with Sargon II (722-705 B.C.) were excavated from the northwest palace. The most important of this group was an alabastrom with the king's name inscribed on the side. Several vessels, some without excavated context, relate to this early group, such as the large, yellow-green, footed vase now in Corning, New York.

Glass production between the 6th and 4th cents. was limited to small core-formed unguent containers (*see* Plate 29) made in the eastern Mediterranean. The vessels were as precious as their contents and were usually fashioned as miniature Greek ceramic forms such as the alabastron, aryballos, or amphoriskos.

The Hellenistic period is remarkable for its luxury vessels. Quantities of mosaic glass were made in Egypt, Rome, and Syro-Palestine. Pliny and Strabo mentioned the importance of Alexandria as a major glassmaking center, but little material has come from the site itself. Glass imitated costly minerals, especially *murrhine,* the fabulous material highly prized by wealthy Romans.

A formidable technique employed in the Hellenistic period was that of sandwiching a cutout design of gold leaf or foil between two colorless glass surfaces (*see* Vol. I, Plate 11). Even after the invention of glassblowing, this

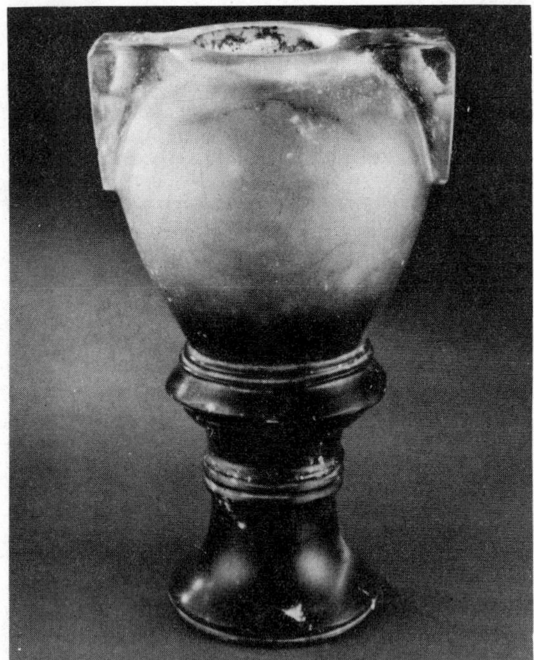

Footed vase of yellow-green glass, cast and cut in Assyria or Syria (750-700 B.C.) (Corning Museum of Glass)

technique continued to be used for decoration (see III below).

A transitional drinking vessel, the ribbed bowl, was produced between the 2nd cent. B.C. and the 1st cent. A.D. in both western and eastern glassmaking centers (see Weinberg). These bowls were mold-pressed; glass was forced into ribbed molds by some method not yet fully understood.

III. Glassblowing.–Somewhere along the Syro-Palestinian coast shortly after 50 B.C. the discovery was made that glass could be worked by gathering it on the end of a hollow pipe and blowing it; this remains the single greatest discovery since glass was first worked 3500 years ago. Excavations in Israel (see Avigad) have helped confirm both the location and date mentioned by authors such as Strabo and Pliny (see Grose for textual evidence).

Blown tablewares (*see* Plate 30) and mold-blown vessels were soon being manufactured at an increased rate. The numerous bottles, similar to test tubes, found as grave goods have often been called tear flasks or lacrimonia (see Scheiber), but most scholars think that these vessels contained scented unguents or perfume rather than tears of mourners collected at the funeral. (They should not be related to Ps. 56:8 [MT 9], where RSV, AV, "bottle" is misleading anyway, since Heb. *nō'd* is a container made of animal skins.)

Centers such as Tyre and Sidon became famous for the quantities of glass produced. Both Pliny (*Nat. hist.* v. 17 [75]) and Josephus (*BJ* ii.10.2 [189-191]) mentioned the Belus River near Acre as a source for excellent glassmaking sands. Many mold-blown vessels, some with religious symbols among the designs, are described as "Sidonian." Among these are the works of Ennion, a first-century A.D. glassmaker who signed his elegant vessels by cutting his name in the mold.

Glassmaking quickly spread throughout the empire and centers were established near many major cities. As the empire grew, glass was used for shipping and storage as well as table service. During the 3rd and 4th cents. numerous cups and bowls had gold-glass bases (see Morey). These bases often depicted OT or NT scenes, though some were individual or family portraits. The bases, often plastered on the catacomb wall, identified the deceased. It has been suggested that the vessels were used during the life of the individual and ceremonially broken at the funeral. Many gold-glass bases and wheel-cut vessels of this later period bear inscriptions such as "PIE ZESES" ("long life") or "DULCIS ANIMA VIVAS" ("sweet soul, may you live").

Base of a bowl made of colorless blown glass and gold glass with a scene of the Good Shepherd. Probably from Rome, 4th cent. A.D. (Corning Museum of Glass)

Pitcher of yellow-green glass, mold blown, with Christian symbols. From the Syro-Palestinian coast, late 6th-early 7th cents. A.D. (Corning Museum of Glass)

Although production declined with the Western Roman Empire, the Syro-Palestinian coast continued to produce glasses in the later Byzantine period. Mold-blown and wheel-cut decorations on fourth- and fifth-century vessels frequently depicted religious motifs. A series of sixth- and seventh-century hexagonal flasks were mold-blown with Jewish or Christian symbols (see Barag). Apparently the same workshops were supplying vessels filled with water, oil, or earth from Jerusalem to both Jewish and Christian pilgrims. These workshops and their counterparts farther east may have provided the basis for continuing glass production in the Islamic world.

On Rev. 4:6, etc., *see* GLASS, SEA OF.

See also FAIENCE; MIRROR.

Bibliography.–N. Avigad, *IEJ,* 22 (1972), 198-200, plates 45f.; D. Barag, *Journal of Glass Studies,* 12 (1970), 35-63; 13 (1971), 45-63; S. Goldstein, *Pre-Roman and Early Roman Glass in the Corning Museum of Glass* (1979); D. F. Grose, *Journal of Glass Studies,* 19 (1977), 9-29; D. B. Harden, "Glass and Glazes," in C. Singer *et al.,* eds., *History of Technology,* II (1956), 311-346; C. R. Morey, *The Gold-Glass Collections of the Vatican Library* (1959); A. L. Oppenheim, *Glass and Glassmaking in Ancient Mesopotamia* (1970); A. Scheiber, *IEJ,* 25 (1975), 152f.; G. D. Weinberg, *Journal of Glass Studies,* 12 (1970), 17-27.

S. M. GOLDSTEIN

GLASS, SEA OF [Gk. *thálassa hyalínē*] (Rev. 4:6; 15:2). In the vision of heaven in these two apocalyptic passages the likeness of a "glassy sea" is seen before the throne of God. The pure translucency of the sea is indicated in the former reference by the words "like crystal"; its fiery appearance is suggested in the latter passage by the words "mingled with fire." Beside the sea stood the victorious martyrs, with harps in their hands, singing the song of Moses and of the Lamb (15:2-4).

The background for this imagery is found in the OT. On Mt. Sinai the elders of Israel saw a vision of "the God of Israel; and there was under his feet as it were a pavement of sapphire stone, like the very heaven for clearness" (Ex. 24:10). Ezekiel also saw a vision markedly similar to John's: "Over the heads of the living creatures there was the likeness of a firmament, shining like crystal.... And above the firmament... there was the likeness of a throne, in appearance like sapphire" (Ezk. 1:22, 26). (Cf. also Solomon's molten sea [1 K. 7:23-26].) The "song of Moses" obviously points to the song of victory sung by Moses and the Israelites after their passage through the Red Sea (Ex. 15:1-18). Some would therefore see the "sea of glass" as a symbolic Red Sea through which the martyrs have safely passed in order to escape their persecutors. Others, however, simply see it as picturing the majesty, holiness, and purity of God.

J. ORR

GLAZE; GLAZING [Heb. *kesep sîgîm*–'silver of dross'] (Prov. 26:23); AV SILVER DROSS; [Gk. *chrísma*] (Sir. 38:30). Palestinian potters, unlike those of Egypt, did not glaze their products, but rather rubbed their surfaces with a tool, small stone, or shell. Sir. 38:30 may also have in view the smearing of an item with paint. The RSV, influenced by Ugar. *spsg* (*UT,* 2 Aqht 6:36; cf. H. L. Ginsberg, *BASOR,* 98 [Apr. 1945], 21 n. 55), combines the two words in Proverbs, which gives the meaning "like a glaze" (*kᵉsapsāgîm*; cf. D. Kidner, *Proverbs* [1964], p. 164).

GLEAMING BRONZE. *See* ELECTRUM.

GLEANING [Heb. *lāqaṭ* (Ruth 2:2-23; Isa. 17:5), *leqeṭ* (Lev. 19:9; 23:22), *ʿālal* (Dt. 24:21; Jer. 6:9), *ʿōlēlôṯ* (Jgs. 8:2; Isa. 17:6; 24:13; Jer. 49:9; Ob. 5; Mic. 7:1), *lāqaš* (Job 24:6)]; AV also GATHER, "some grapes" (Ob. 5); NEB also "stripped" (Isa. 24:13), "filch" (Job 24:6). Hebrew law required that the poor, the orphan, the widow, and the stranger be allowed to glean the grain, grapes, and olives left behind during the harvest. The owner was prohibited from harvesting the corners of his field and from stripping bare his fields, vineyards, and orchards (Lev. 19:9f.; 23:22; Dt. 24:19-21). In this way provision was made for those who had no property of their own. This practice is illustrated by the story of Ruth (2:2-23). The generosity of the owner determined the value of the gleanings; in Ruth's case it was beyond the commonly accepted bounds (2:16; cf. KD *in loc.*). Sometimes the poor were hired to glean the vineyard while others gathered the grapes (Job 24:6; cf. KD *in loc.*).

The prophets used the imagery of "gleaning" to depict destruction. According to Jeremiah (the remnant of) Israel is to be gleaned "thoroughly as a vine" (6:9; cf. the sharp contrast with Jgs. 8:2 where the "gleaning of the grapes of Ephraim" means Ephraim's victory over the Midianites; see KD *in loc.*), for it is "gleaned" of justice; only injustice is left (Mic. 7:1). Isaiah described divine doom as a gleaning of the ears of grain (17:5); but Israel will not be totally annihilated, for some gleanings will remain (v. 6). In Jer. 49:9; Ob. 5, the figurative gleaning of Edom is more thorough than the usual agricultural gleaning.

N. J. O. R. W. V.

GLEDE (Dt. 14:13, AV). *See* BUZZARD.

GLEN [Heb. *mᵉṣulâ*] (Zec. 1:8); AV BOTTOM; NEB HOLLOW. The Hebrew noun is from the root *ṣālal,* which can mean either "sink" or "grow dark, shadowy"; thus the idea of a low, shady place. The reference is probably to a valley in the neighborhood of Jerusalem.

GLISTERING. A poetic term meaning "glistening," used by the AV in 1 Ch. 29:2 and Lk. 9:29. *See* ANTIMONY; TRANSFIGURATION.

GLOOM [Heb. *ʿᵃrāpel*] (Dt. 4:11); AV THICK DARKNESS; NEB THICK MIST; [*ḥōšek*] (Job 3:5; 10:21; 34:22); AV DARKNESS; NEB also BLACKNESS, DARK; [*ʿêpâ*] (Job 10:22); AV DARKNESS; NEB GATHERING SHADOWS; [*ʾōpel, ʾāpel, ʾᵃpēlâ*] (Job 28:3; Isa. 29:18; 58:10; 59:9; Joel 2:2; Am. 5:20; Zeph. 1:15); AV DARKNESS, DARK, OBSCURITY, GLOOMINESS, VERY DARK; NEB also DARKNESS, DEEP GLOOM, DUSK; [*ṣalmāwet*] (Ps. 107:10, 14; Jer. 13:16); AV "shadow of death"; NEB "dark as death," DEEP GLOOM; [*māʿûp*] (Isa. 8:22); AV DIMNESS; NEB "constraint"; [*mûʿāp*] (Isa. 9:1 [MT 8:23]); AV DIMNESS; NEB "escape"; [*qāḏar*] ("clothe in gloom," Ezk. 31:15); AV "caused to mourn"; NEB "put in mourning"; [Gk. *zóphos*] (He. 12:18; 2 Pet. 2:4, 17; Jude 6, 13); AV MIST, DARKNESS, BLACKNESS; NEB also DARK, DARKNESS, BLACKEST. The "nether gloom" of 2 Pet. 2:4, 17 and Jude 6, 13 is synonymous with the HELL reserved for fallen angels and the heretical teachers who follow their sinful example. Elsewhere the term is employed literally (Dt. 4:11) or figuratively (Am. 5:20) of darkness (cf. Ps. 107:10, 14), and of the abode of the dead (Job 10:21f.).

See also DARK; DEATH III.B.

GLORIFY. *See* GLORY.

GLORIOUS. The word occurs in the obsolete sense of "boastful" in the AV of Ad. Est. 16:4. For its use in the RSV, *see* GLORY.

GLORY [Heb. *ʾaddereṯ* (Zec. 11:3); *tip̄ʾārâ* (Isa. 4:2;

28:5; Est. 1:4; Ps. 96:6; Zec. 12:7; etc.); *ṣᵉḇî*–'glory,' 'beauty' (2 S. 1:19; Isa. 13:19; 24:16; Ezk. 20:6; etc.); *kāḇôḏ,* from *kāḇēḏ*–'to be heavy,' hence 'wealth, honor, dignity, power,' etc.; Aram. *yᵉqār* (Dnl. 7:14); *yᵉqārā'* (Dnl. 2:37); Gk. *dóxa*– 'reputation, fame, splendor, honor, praise, majesty,' etc.]. A comprehensive term applicable to both men and God, reflecting such qualities as esteem, reputation, essential worth, prestige, fame, and honor. As used of God, it is deemed particularly appropriate for describing His moral uniqueness and grandeur as Lord of the universe.

I. OT and Intertestamental Background
II. Human and Natural Glory
III. Glory of God
IV. Glory of Christ
V. Glory of the Holy Spirit
VI. Glory of the People of God
VII. Special Uses
VIII. Theology of Glory
IX. Related Words

I. OT and Intertestamental Background.–In the OT, glory was an attribute that was applied, along with beauty and splendor, to such intricately contrived cultic objects as the priests' vestments (Ex. 28:40), or such architectural marvels as the Solomonic temple (1 Ch. 22:5). When glory was used of persons, it reflected noteworthy elements such as dignity of character, position (cf. Gen. 45:13), wealth (Gen. 31:1; Ps. 49:16 [MT 17]), or power. Thus the king's glory consisted in the multitude of his people (Prov. 14:28), but by contrast the glory and pomp of the rebellious people would receive its reward by being banished to Sheol (Isa. 5:14).

The common use of Heb. *kāḇôḏ* to describe human dignity occurs in Isa. 22:23, which depicts Eliakim as a symbol of the splendor and honor of his father's house. References to the glory of nations include the mention of Ephraim (Hos. 9:11), Moab (Isa. 16:14), and Kedar (Isa. 21:16). The species *homo sapiens* was described in Ps. 8:5 (MT 6) as crowned by his Creator with glory and honor because he represented the height of God's creative activity. In Ps. 49:16f. the word *kāḇôḏ* referred to the wealth of a rich man as "glory" without specification as to the means by which that wealth had been acquired. In Sir. 9:11, however, the glory of the sinner that is not to be envied appeared to be wealth obtained by dubious means. A loss of glory occurred when the Israelites were deprived of their sacred ark at the hands of the Philistines (1 S. 4:21f.). By its capture the covenant people lost their most distinctive religious symbol. In Job 29:20 the use of glory most probably indicates selfhood or life, as with certain passages in which *kāḇôḏ* is paralleled with, or substituted for, either *nepeš* or *lēḇ* (cf. Gen. 49:6; Ps. 4:2 [MT 3]; 7:5 [MT 6]; 16:9; 30:12 [MT 13]; 57:8 [MT 9]; 108:1 [MT 2]).

The concept of glory is employed supremely in the OT as a characteristic attribute and possession of God (cf. 1 Ch. 29:11). Because it is pervasive in nature, it is imparted to those persons or objects that come into close association with Him. God's glory implies His power, and consequently Isaiah saw God's self-manifestation in glory as bringing judgment upon human pride and power (Isa. 2:10,19,21). But whatever the consequences, it was through this type of revelation that divine glory became a factor in human consciousness. The earliest account of this phenomenon is in Ex. 33:18-23, where in a personal reminiscence of theophany Moses described his experience, momentary though it was, of God's glory in something resembling physical form. This type of manifestation appeared again, this time in visionary form to Isaiah (6:1-5), who saw the enthroned God attended by seraphim. There is no other indication of what Isaiah saw, or how he recognized the presiding figure as God. The experience of divine glory, however, was undeniable, since it was connected with his prophetic call. The concept of God's glory filling the earth occurs in Ps. 19:1 (MT 2), and is paralleled in Ps. 8:1 [MT 2]; 29:1-3,9; 57:5 [MT 6]; 108:5 [MT 6]; and 113:4.

The manifestation of divine glory was an essential element of the proceedings not merely at the time when the law was given on Mt. Sinai (Dt. 5:24), but also when Solomon's temple was dedicated (1 K. 8:10f.; 2 Ch. 5:14), where the cloud was identified with God's glory. Other cloud manifestations were recorded in Ex. 16:7, 10 (cf. 24:16f.); 40:34f.; Lev. 9:6,23; Nu. 14:21f.; 16:19,42; 20:6. Cf. Sir. 17:13; 45:3. The divine glory that Ezekiel saw was not identified with storm clouds or angelic beings, but was something peculiar to God Himself that exhibited certain human appearances or characteristics (Ezk. 1:28; 3:12,23; 8:4; 9:3; 10:4,18; 11:22f.). In each vision Ezekiel is careful to distinguish between the glory of God and its attendant circumstances.

Isaiah represented faithful Israel as an important aspect of divine glory (Isa. 40:5; 43:7; 60:1f.), which would be manifested by the restoration of the faithful to the land of their ancestors. There the presence of the Lord will bring grace and glory (Ps. 84:11 [MT 12]), and His saving of the remnant causes glory to dwell in the land (Ps. 85:9 [MT 10]). In this respect God's glory carries an ethical significance, relating to the holiness that must always characterize a priestly people (cf. Lev. 11:44). To recognize God's glory is thus to acknowledge Him as the supreme moral ruler.

In the Apocrypha, "glory" is the normal translation of the Greek noun *dóxa,* which generally appears to represent the thought underlying the Heb. *kāḇôḏ*. Glory also refers to human honor and splendor (1 Esd. 1:33; Wisd. 10:14; Jth. 15:9) as well as to the adornment of the temple (2 Macc. 5:16,20). Glory as an invariable accompaniment of God was referred to in 2 Esd. 3:19, where the Sinai theophany was mentioned. The glory of the messianic kingdom was probably being alluded to in 1 Esd. 5:61, whereas an apocalyptic realm inhabited by the saints in glory seems intended in 2 Esd. 2:36; 7:52; 8:51; 10:50. In general, however, the apocryphal use of glory is that of the blaze of light and splendor characterizing the expression of the Lord's holy majesty. Occasionally the term glory is used as a surrogate for deity (cf. 2 Esd. 8:30; 16:53; Tob. 12:15; 13:14; Wisd. 7:25). R. K. H.

In order to grasp the NT significance of *dóxa* it is necessary to survey its role in the LXX. Derived from Gk. *dókein,* denoting in classical usage "think" or "seem," *dóxa* has basically two meanings: opinion (what one thinks), or reputation (how one is thought of by others, how one appears in their estimation). Usually when the word denoted reputation it carried a favorable sense, which opened the way for such meanings as fame and glory. A major shift occurred in the LXX. On the one hand the word ceased to be used for opinion; on the other hand it acquired a cluster of meanings absent from classical usage. Of the 285 occurrences of *dóxa* in the OT, approximately 175 render *kāḇôḏ*. Since *dóxa* could be used legitimately to translate *kāḇôḏ* in the areas of reputation and honor, only a slight step was required to make it a blanket term for rendering other meanings of *kāḇôḏ* that had not belonged to *dóxa* in its classical Greek setting. Once *dóxa* had become established as a translation for *kāḇôḏ* in the sense of majesty or splendor, which was something of a departure from native Greek usage, apparently this was sufficient precedent to go further and employ *dóxa* to render a whole group of Hebrew words involving the notion of beauty or adornment. This group accounts for more than forty occurrences of *dóxa*. These Hebrew terms include *hāḏār, hôḏ, ṣᵉḇî,* and *tipᵉʼereṯ*. A few additional words were translated by *dóxa,* but in most cases these are restricted to a single occurrence and are of minor significance.

Of greatest importance among the *kāḇôḏ/dóxa* passages are those that portray a manifestation of the deity in terms of glowing light. This acquired force of *dóxa* carries over into the NT and becomes the medium for expressing the uniqueness and sublimity of God.

II. Human and Natural Glory.–As the handiwork of God, nature exhibits a beauty and order that constitute its glory, but God has crowned mankind with glory and honor in a manner exceeding that of the material creation (Ps. 8:5-8 [MT 6-9]). Made in God's image, mankind is set apart to rule over the earth. To the male element has been given a special prerogative of headship within the family (1 Cor. 11:7). Yet in contrast to God and even to the natural order, humans are weak and transient, likened to the grass that perishes (Isa. 40:6; 1 Pet. 1:24). Nevertheless, because the soul outlasts the body, it can be called his glory (Ps. 16:9). Similarly, in Gen. 49:6 "my spirit" is literally "my glory" (Heb. *kᵉḇōḏî*; cf. RSV mg.).

Some people, notably rulers, attain the glory that attaches to high station (2 S. 1:19; Ps. 21:5 [MT 6]). Joseph's exalted rank in Egypt is called his "splendor" (Heb. *kāḇôḏ,* Gen. 45:13). The magnificence of Solomon's reign was widely recognized (Mt. 6:29). The magnificence of royal tombs witnesses that death does not extinguish the prestige thus acquired (Isa. 14:18). The kingdoms of this world have sufficient splendor to serve as inducement in Satan's temptation of Our Lord (Mt. 4:8). A sovereign's military might, as represented by his army, can be designated as his glory (Isa. 8:7). One's wealth and prosperity bear this label also (Heb. *kāḇôḏ,* Gen. 31:1; cf. Isa. 61:6). The same term serves to summarize the beauty and stateliness of Solomon's temple (Hag. 2:3). Glory expresses one's good reputation, the honor in which one is held by one's peers, in contrast to shame or disrepute (Ps. 4:2 [MT 3]; Hab. 2:16). The finer traits of character set apart those who possess them and constitute their glory in the eyes of society (Prov. 19:11). Divine appointment to a position of leadership and responsibility bestows the glory of authority (Nu. 27:20). Scripture warns against conceit (Gk. *kenodoxía,* lit. "empty glory") that is fostered by the lack of perspective that humility can provide (Phil. 2:3; Gal. 5:26; cf. Jer. 9:23). The pride involved in human glory is an offense to God, inviting judgment (Isa. 23:9).

III. Glory of God.–In the ultimate sense, no subject is more important than this. Yet there is difficulty in trying to analyze God's glory because of its many aspects. No facile answer can be given to the question, Wherein does that glory consist? The answer must come in multiple terms. Only then can the comprehensiveness of the concept be appreciated.

Whereas it is the tendency of mankind to seek eminence and recognition, on God's part one finds no trace of ambition or naked claim unsupported by intrinsic worth. His is the right of preeminence by virtue of being God — the Creator, the Redeemer, the All in all. His glory has intrinsic worth and permanence. Through the prophet He announces, "My glory I give to no other" (Isa. 42:8; 48:11). What is involved here is the divine uniqueness, the right to be acknowledged as supreme. This lies at the heart of the biblical concept. In view of His uniqueness, profound indeed is the pathos of Judah's unfaithfulness. "Has a nation changed its gods, even though they are no gods? But my people have changed their glory for that which does not profit" (Jer. 2:11). That glory is personal — God Himself. He occupies a solitary throne that allows no place for a rival. Idolatry disputes this and by so doing invites the revelation of His wrath (Rom. 1:18-25). The attempt to worship what human hands have made is an affront to the deity because it not only repudiates His aseity but also His spirituality, an essential element of His glory (Ps. 106:20).

He does not leave His creatures without witness. The heavens declare the glory of God both by day and by night (Ps. 19:1-6 [MT 2-7]). Likewise the elements, thunder and lightning, are pictured as acting in His service (Ps. 29). His voice is heard in the thunder, His splendor seen in the lightning. In nature God presents in tangible form a demonstration of His own power, beauty, and order. These are ingredients of His glory. Things celestial and things terrestrial exhibit the magnificent tapestry that the Creator has woven into His handiwork (1 Cor. 15:40f.).

The manifestation of the deity by means of light could serve as a reminder that He is the One who brought light into being (Gen. 1:3). But the very intensity of the light on various occasions (Ex. 34:29; 1 K. 8:10f.) betokens something more, namely, the personal presence of One who is greater than His works. In connection with the Exodus God is represented as taking up His station in a pillar of cloud by day and of fire by night (Ex. 13:21), the cloud concealing the mystery of His being and the fire revealing His presence. As the account of the Exodus continues, this phenomenon is associated with the glory of the Lord (Ex. 16:10). What is denoted in both passages is God's might, in the one case designed to stress His protection of Israel and in the other His readiness to judge for their disobedience the very people He has rescued (cf. Nu. 14:10-19). He is the righteous judge as well as the mighty deliverer. This emphasis on the power element in glory reappears in the NT use of the word in connection with God's raising the dead (Jn. 11:40; Rom. 6:4).

When the tabernacle in the wilderness was completed, the glory cloud settled on it, preventing human entrance (Ex. 40:34f.). This was repeated at the dedication of Solomon's temple (1 K. 8:11). Here the emphasis falls on the holiness of God, a significant aspect of His glory (cf. Isa. 6:1-3).

In Ezekiel's prophecy the imagery of the glory of God becomes somewhat complicated (Ezk. 1:1–3:15), but a later vision, this time in Jerusalem rather than by the river Chebar, discloses the glory departing from the Lord's house (10:15-19). This separation of the divine presence from the sanctuary was due to the iniquity of the inhabitants of the city, and parallels the withdrawal of Yahweh into the wilderness after the worship of the golden calf (Ex. 33:3-7). In Ezk. 39:21-29 God's glory appears to be treated as something underlined by His judgment. In the same vein, His glory is revealed not only by restoring His people from captivity and dispersion but also by permitting captivity as a vindication of His righteousness.

A further manifestation of the divine glory emphasizes God's mercy. This provides a balance to the judgmental aspect. When in communion with God on the mount, Moses, weighed down by the responsibility of bringing Israel into the Promised Land, made two requests. "Show me now thy ways" (Ex. 33:13) was a plea growing out of his leadership role. He needed divine wisdom. "Show me thy glory" (v. 18) was a prayer that had its source in a personal longing. He did not have in view the bright cloud in making this request, nor yet the luminous pavement that he and the elders of Israel had seen (Ex. 24:10). Rather, he wanted to know God in His essence. This nuance is captured in the LXX by the rendering of Codex Vaticanus, which has *emphánisón moi seautón,* "Show me thyself," a perceptive rendering and one that is perfectly feasible for *kāḇôḏ/dóxa*.

But if "show me thy glory" is preferred, even so the context compels us to think in terms of internal, invisible factors. God Himself explains the glory in terms of goodness (Heb. *ṭûḇ,* goodliness or beauty), which means, as A. H. McNeile construed it, "a spectacle of outward beauty as a visible sign of His moral perfection" (*Book of Exodus* [*WC,* 1931], p. 215). The self-revelation of the glory continues: "I will be gracious . . . I will show mercy." This is reassuring, for the divine perfection has no existential significance of a positive nature for sinful mankind unless it is accompanied by the welcome adjunct that the Judge of all mankind is actually gracious and merciful. Surely there is a broad hint here that the Creator cannot afford to permit the marring and alienating effects of sin to continue indefinitely. He will accept the challenge so that the original purpose of creation may be realized. His honor is at stake.

Moses could not see God's face (His glory epitomized) but God allowed His goodness to pass before His servant. The glory of God on this occasion expresses His uniqueness, His perfect holiness, and consequently His detachment from the world, but also His deliberate intention to disclose Himself to mankind. This duality in the *kāḇôḏ/dóxa* concept may be illustrated by the veil that separated the holy of holies from the holy place. On the one side it was in contact with the ineffable glory of the most holy One and on the other side with the desperate need of sinful mankind.

God's glory will be most openly displayed in the consummation, whether depicted as a golden age on earth (Hab. 2:14; Isa. 4:5) or given a heavenly setting (Ps. 73:24). This eschatological use is more prominent in the NT than in the OT. The believer rejoices in his hope of sharing the glory of God (Rom. 5:2). It is the goal of the Christian's calling to salvation (1 Thess. 2:12; 1 Pet. 5:10). The New Jerusalem, the future home of the saints, is pictured in terms of radiance and splendor (Rev. 21:10f.). No artificial illumination is needed there, for the glory of God is its light (Rev. 21:23).

The expression "glory to God" in Lk. 2:14 must also be examined. It is the acclaim by the angelic host on the occasion of the birth of God's Son. Clearly it denotes praise. Similarly it becomes an established usage in Christian worship and in the doxologies that are a regular feature of NT letters (Eph. 3:21; Phil. 4:20). Paul cannot resist breaking forth into praise to God as he gives Him credit for the entire sweep of His redemptive purpose — the planning, the execution, and the consummation (Rom. 11:36). To God belongs the kingdom (His right to rule), the power (His ability to rule), and the glory (recognition by His subjects). This doxological use is common to humans and angels alike. It pervades the present age and the age to come.

In the captivity letters of Paul most of the references to God's *dóxa* are related to the gospel, which is something so characterized by the plenitude of wisdom, grace, and power that it reflects more fully than any other work of God the wealth of His glory (Eph. 3:16).

In a few passages the interpretation of glory is uncertain. Paul declares, "All have sinned and fall short of the glory of God" (Rom. 3:23). God's approval in the form of praise is possible here, but this force of the word is rare in Paul except in doxologies. Eschatological glory is unlikely also, although the present tense of the verb could be interpreted futuristically. Some understand here a reference to the image of God imparted at the creation and then lost through sin. According to 1 Cor. 11:7, however, that glory is not wholly lacking now, in spite of sin. Perhaps the best conclusion is that because of man's disobedience he lacks communion with God. He is deprived of access to His presence except as a child of God through faith in Christ (cf. Rom. 5:2).

The meaning of *dóxa* in Phil. 4:19 is not easily grasped. Some (e.g., NIV) take "in glory" to mean glorious, but this is somewhat awkward. Glory may be a synonym here for heaven, indicating that the divine resources will prove ample to meet the needs of God's pilgrim people.

In 2 Pet. 1:17 the "Majestic Glory" is probably best understood as a surrogate for God Himself.

IV. Glory of Christ.–By virtue of being the Son, Christ shares the glory of God (He. 1:3), not merely as a reflection but as the manifestation or radiance of that glory. Through Him the knowledge of God's glory (His essential being) is made available to mankind (2 Cor. 4:6). Before the world was created He shared that glory in fellowship with the Father (Jn. 1:1; 17:5).

The Incarnation made it possible for those with spiritual understanding to discern His glory, which consisted in being the unique Son of God, full of grace and truth (Jn. 1:14). The divine nature loses nothing of its essential character by being yoked with humanity, and the human nature is not so overshadowed by the divine as to cease to be truly human. This glory could be seen (apprehended) by true believers.

Jesus' humanity veiled the glory of oneness with the Father (Jn. 10:30) but the signs that He wrought manifested a phase of His glory, the divine power that He possessed (Jn. 2:11; 11:40-44).

On only one occasion did His inherent glory break through the veil and become visible, and then only to a select group of disciples on the mount of transfiguration (Lk. 9:28-36). This disclosure was accompanied by a cloud, the combination serving to provide a linkage with various manifestations in OT times. Coming only a few days after Jesus' solemn declaration about the death that awaited Him, this display was doubtless intended to be a pledge that despite the suffering in store for the Son of man there would be a glorious vindication at His return (Lk. 9:26; 2 Pet. 1:16-19). The splendor was an earnest of the coming of the kingdom of Christ. It is this splendor that makes improbable any attempt to explain the transfiguration as a reading back of Jesus' resurrection glory into His precross ministry, since the reports of the resurrection appearances lack any indication of heavenly radiance such as was seen on the mount.

In view of the distinct separation of Jesus' glory from His suffering in the representations of Scripture (e.g., Lk. 24:26) one is hardly prepared for the emphasis peculiar to one Gospel that links glorification with His death (Jn. 12:23; 13:31). This emphasis can be accounted for in part by the association of the Incarnation and the public ministry (specifically the miracles) with glory. Also, if we look forward from the public ministry to its close, we get the impression that John comprehends the totality of acts that embrace the winning of redemption into one, each phase having its share in the glorification, whether it be death, Resurrection, or Ascension.

Other NT writers make room for the element of glory in Jesus' ministry prior to the Resurrection. James describes Jesus as the Lord of glory (Jas. 2:1). Judging by the context, James is thinking of the great condescension involved in His coming to live among mankind, matching and even exceeding the condescension inherent in the dwelling of God among His people in the Shekinah. Paul notes that the rulers of this age, by crucifying the Lord of glory, gave evidence of their spiritual blindness, failing to perceive in Him and His mission the wisdom of God that centered in the very cross that took His life. There redemption was secured (1 Cor. 2:8).

The Ascension was anticipated by the Lord Jesus in His request that the Father glorify Him with the glory He had in the presence of the Father before the world was created (Jn. 17:5). In Peter's second address in Acts the apostle affirms that God did indeed glorify Jesus (3:13). A creedlike statement centering on Our Lord concludes with the words "believed on in the world, taken up in glory" (1 Tim. 3:16). Here the pairing of world and glory suggests that the latter is intended to denote heaven. That the present state of the ascended Lord is one of splendor is suggested by the vision of Stephen (Acts 7:55f.) and by the narrative of the conversion of Saul of Tarsus (Acts 9:3; 26:13).

Christ's resurrection body, which He continues to possess during this age, will be the pattern for the glorious resurrection bodies of the saints (Phil. 3:21). The same truth is suggested by the statement that Christ is a life-giving spirit (1 Cor. 15:45). According to 2 Cor. 3:18, as believers contemplate the glory of Christ they are being transformed into His (moral) likeness in preparation for the bodily transformation of which Phil. 3:21 speaks.

During His earthly ministry Jesus explicitly taught that He would return to this world. The Synoptics unanimously report His declarations of a coming in glory (Mt. 24:30; Mk. 13:26; Lk. 21:27). The certainty of this great event is affirmed in the Epistles also (e.g., Col. 3:4). Of special interest is the statement of the blessed hope of believers as being "the appearing of the glory of our great God and Savior Jesus Christ" (Tit. 2:13). Many gods and lords were honored as divine in the world of the apostolic age (1 Cor. 8:5). Some were hailed as saviors. Caesar was worshiped as lord. The Titus passage amounts to a challenge to the imperial cult. No Caesar returned, but Christians confidently affirm that Christ will honor His promise.

In His great prayer Jesus looked beyond His death, resurrection, and exaltation to the time when His followers would be with Him in the heavenly home. He prayed that they would then behold His glory — surely with greater understanding and appreciation than they had shown in the days of His flesh (Jn. 17:24; cf. 1:14). Meanwhile, as believers await His coming, they unite in praising Him by ascribing glory to Him just as they do to the Father (2 Pet. 3:18).

See also EXALTATION OF CHRIST.

V. Glory of the Holy Spirit.–Peter writes, "If you are reproached for the name of Christ, you are blessed, because the spirit of glory and of God rests upon you" (1 Pet. 4:14). Probably "spirit" should be capitalized here, despite the AV and RSV (cf. NEB, NIV). Otherwise the sense is virtually impossible to grasp. Even when understood of the Holy Spirit, the passage is difficult, as the history of the transmission of the text in the early centuries demonstrates by the emergence of variant readings. The latter half of the verse rather clearly reflects the influence of Isa. 11:2, a messianic prediction. Even as the Spirit rested on Jesus, so He rests on those who belong to Him, a source of comfort and strength when opposition confronts the believer. The glory is the divine presence whether that presence is indicated by a transfigured countenance, as with Stephen (Acts 6:15), or simply by the impartation of inner strength.

The severely limited use of *dóxa* in connection with the Spirit can be explained in the light of His customary role of subordination both to the Father and to the Son. Even so, the dispensation of the Spirit involves glory (2 Cor. 3:8) and His operation within the believer likewise (2 Cor. 3:18).

VI. Glory of the People of God.–In line with the tenor of biblical teaching, the saints do not find reason to glory in themselves but in God who is the fountain of all blessings. David exclaimed, "But thou, O Lord, art a shield about me, my glory, and the lifter of my head" (Ps. 3:3 [MT 4]). He found in God his sufficiency in every situation. This should also have been the confession of the nation Israel, but often this was not so (Jer. 2:11).

Simeon saw in the infant Jesus God's promised salvation, a light for revelation to the Gentiles and for glory to God's people Israel (Lk. 2:25-32). The Savior would be Israel's crowning token of God's favor.

In His great prayer on the threshold of His Passion Jesus made this observation regarding the disciples: "The glory which thou hast given me I have given to them" (Jn. 17:22). Here *dóxa* probably refers to the distinction of being permitted to represent God in the world. The apostles were to carry on the witness that Jesus initiated (Jn. 20:21).

Paul did not shrink from calling the Thessalonian believers his glory and joy (1 Thess. 2:20). He was proud of these people who had made so much progress in the faith in so short a time.

Sanctification is linked with glory in 2 Cor. 3:17-18. The passage has as its background the experience of Moses in his desire to behold the glory of God (Ex. 33). At length, in the Incarnation, the answer to Moses' prayer was given (Jn. 1:14). Even more fully was it given in the glorification of Christ wherein the contemplation of the Lord, mediated by the Spirit, accomplishes an increasing conformity to the exalted Savior. The Spirit is the key to this process, affording liberty to the saints to keep Christ before them and grow up into Him in all things (2 Cor. 3:18; Eph. 4:15). Meanwhile the Christ who indwells the believer by the Spirit constitutes the hope of glory (Col. 1:27), anticipating the time when the veil will not merely be penetrated but removed. The presence of the Lord with His people will be finalized.

This eschatological goal is characteristically described in terms of glory. Though rare in the OT (possibly Ps. 73:24, but cf. the NEB), the allusions in the NT are fairly numerous. Christ's earthly mission results "in bringing many sons to glory," a clear reference to heaven (He. 2:10). The future glory is frequently set forth by way of contrast to the present condition of trial and suffering (Rom. 8:18; 2 Cor. 4:17; 1 Pet. 5:10), affording a parallel to the experience of Christ (1 Pet. 1:11). A mark of the finality of this future blessing is the possession of the resurrection body that is portrayed in terms of glory (1 Cor. 15:43; Phil. 3:21). The reward for faithful service will be the unfading crown of glory (1 Pet. 5:4).

VII. Special Uses.–Not to be confused with that use of glory which denotes praise is the specialized expression "give glory to God" in a judicial interrogation (Josh. 7:19; Jn. 9:24). Here it amounts to an adjuration to tell the truth, a reminder that what is said will not escape the attention of the heavenly Judge.

In Jude 8 (cf. 2 Pet. 2:10) the plural of *dóxa* is used in what is evidently a reference to persons, either human dignitaries or angelic beings. The false teachers revile these "glorious ones." Jude's familiarity with apocalyptic imagery is thought by some to favor the identification with angels. However, a good case can be made out for the other view. In the OT *kāḇôḏ/dóxa* is used several times in a collective sense of leaders, the noblemen of the nation (Mic. 1:15; Isa. 5:13; etc.). It is possible that in Jude 8 what "authority" expresses in the abstract is then made concrete by the plural of *dóxa*. The latter term could denote those who stand for truth and decency, whether in society or in the Church, and are for that reason the target of these abusive libertines.

VIII. Theology of Glory.–Something of the significance of this biblical concept can be ascertained by noting the various terms with which it is combined. We have observed the pairing of glory with light and with holiness. Others deserve attention at this point.

Glory is frequently linked with honor. These terms can have both current application and future reference. To some extent they are synonyms, but *dóxa*, "glory," has a wider range of meaning. It is possible to ascribe honor to God (1 Tim. 1:17), but honor is not used of something God has, and it cannot serve to express His being in terms of perfection. As a species of honor, reward is sometimes involved in the use of glory. For example, Paul asserts that "this slight momentary affliction is preparing for us an eternal weight of glory beyond all comparison" (2 Cor. 4:17). Glory is pictured here as an expression of God's appreciation for the faithful endurance of suffering by His servants.

Glory is correlated with life when life is presented from the eschatological perspective. Eternal life is qualitative and is the present possession of the redeemed. But even in John's Gospel, where this emphasis is so strong, life is nevertheless associated at times with the resurrection and the age to come (Jn. 5:28f.; 11:25f.). The same is true in the teaching of Jesus (Mk. 10:30). Paul likewise links life with glory as though they were part of one great experience (Rom. 2:7). In his Captivity Epistles he treats their relationship most precisely (e.g., Col. 3:3f.). Christ dwells in Christians as their life and as their hope of glory. At present their life is hidden with Christ in God. When the Savior comes again, He will still be their life, but then the relationship will no longer be a hidden one. Right at this point Paul introduces the word *dóxa* to express this manifested phase of the relationship.

Quite naturally glory is closely associated with joy. The two elements mingle in the experience of the shepherds at the birth of Jesus (Lk. 2:9f., 20) and in the acclaim given Him at the triumphal entry into Jerusalem (Lk. 19:38), as well as in the Savior's expectation of return to the Father (He. 12:2). Likewise the prospect of future glory evokes in the saints the response of joy (Rom. 5:2; 1 Pet. 4:13; Jude 24).

Fulness *(plḗrōma)* has some affinity to *dóxa*. If Christ has (or is) the fulness of God (Col. 2:9), this could be another way of saying that He has the *dóxa* of God and imparts this to His people insofar as it can be shared with them. What *plḗrōma* expresses under the concept of completeness *dóxa* expresses through its emphasis on power and splendor.

Again, *dóxa* and *pneúma* are intimately related. The believer has the Spirit of Christ as the earnest of full redemption (Rom. 8:10f., 23). His operations are presently confined largely to the inner man, shaping the desires of the heart and molding the life in accordance with the divine will. But eventually His operations will reach the stage of external manifestation, for the "clothing" of the Christian in the eternal state is described as a "spiritual" body (1 Cor. 15:44). Whereas Christ as *pneúma* effects a present glory in His people (2 Cor. 3:18), He will accomplish a corresponding communication of external, bodily glory in terms of resurrection. Throughout these operations He is a life-giving *pneúma* (1 Cor. 15:45).

Dóxa as beauty illumines the concept of God. For some, God is little more than an idea. For others, He is conceded to be the Eternal One. But unending existence is scarcely able of itself to enhance the prospects of the saints. Eternity could be a dull experience. But it will not be, for it will involve fellowship with One who is the epitome of all that is good and beautiful in profound depth and ever enlarging revelation of Himself to His people during the coming ages.

In keeping with this prospect we can sense a degree of development in the disclosure of glory during the course of redemption history. In the OT the element of glory is basically concentrated on God. In the NT the glory is shared by the Son of God, yet not in such a way that the glory of the Father is diminished, for He is the end and goal of all things. In the OT the people of God characteristically experience His glory as a matter of seeing, whereas in the NT the glory is shared with believers on the basis of their relationship with the Son. No passage expounds the contrast to better advantage than the Pauline exposition of the two covenants (2 Cor. 3). The old is symbolized by the glory on the face of Moses, a glory that faded. The new is expressed in terms of a glory that is a permanent element and also permits of increasing participation by the saints. External glory marking a dispensation of condemnation gives way to a dispensation of righteousness that is both fixed as a standing (2 Cor. 5:21) and progressing as a state (2 Cor. 3:18). This work of the Spirit in the area of glory is a species of realized eschatology.

Finally, it is noteworthy that everything and everybody surrounding God is pictured as partaking of His glory — the cherubim of the sanctuary (He. 9:5), the angelic host (Lk. 2:9; 9:26; Rev. 18:1), and the holy city, the New Jerusalem (Rev. 21:11). No darkness (the symbol of ignorance and sin) characterizes the eternal city. The glory of God illumines it continually.

IX. Related Words.–*A. Glorious.* In the OT various forms of *kāḇēḏ* (vb. or adj.) are so rendered, as are some other terms denoting honorable, splendid, etc. God promises to do marvelous things in the eyes of Israel (Ex. 34:10). Samuel was held in honor (1 S. 9:6) and David also (1 S. 22:14). Glorious things are spoken of Zion (Ps. 87:3).

In the NT the adjective *endóxos* is used only four times, including a description of the works of healing wrought by Jesus (Lk. 13:17) and concerning the Church in the future as the bride of Christ (Eph. 5:27). More frequent is the use of the noun *dóxa* in various constructions that are capable of being rendered adjectivally. The gospel is glorious (1 Tim. 1:11), as are the resurrection body of the Savior (Phil. 3:21) and the future liberty of the children of God (Rom. 8:21). Occasionally such an adjectival rendering of the noun by translators is open to question, as when the RSV pictures the Lord at His return as seated on "his glorious throne" (Mt. 25:31). This calls attention to the throne rather than to the majesty of the One who occupies it. Here the AV ("throne of his glory") is preferable.

B. Glory (vb.). Used in a favorable sense this can mean to exult, as in the psalmist's injunction, "Let the righteous rejoice in the Lord, and take refuge in him! Let all the upright in heart glory!" (Ps. 64:10 [MT 11]). Occasionally the favorable and unfavorable connotations are juxtaposed (e.g., Jer. 9:23f.). In the preponderance of passages the force of the word is "boast," and modern versions tend to substitute this term for "glory."

Paul answers his detractors at Corinth by allowing himself to boast of his labors and sufferings in the service of Christ (2 Cor. 11:21–12:13). Yet he is aware that such boasting is valuable only for shutting the mouths of the opposition. The kind of boasting that needs no apology is boasting in the Lord (2 Cor. 10:17) and in His cross (Gal. 6:14). Secondarily the apostle considers it legitimate to boast on occasion in his converts (2 Thess. 1:4).

C. Glorify. Various situations involving God's action in judgment have had the result that He was glorified, presumably because He demonstrated His holiness and power in the face of those who acted unrighteously or rebelled against Him (Lev. 10:3; Ezk. 28:22; 39:13). At other times He is represented as acting on behalf of His people Israel to restore and transform them, with the result that He is glorified, i.e., that He is seen in the loveliness of His person and fidelity to His purpose (Isa. 60:21; 61:3). When God delivers His people out of their troubles, He expects them to glorify Him with appropriate praise and thanksgiving (Ps. 50:15).

On occasion the miracles of Jesus caused the assembled crowds to glorify (praise) God for the results achieved (Mt. 15:31; Mk. 2:12). His teaching in the synagogues of Galilee led to His being glorified (praised) by all (Lk. 4:15).

Of the fourteen occurrences of *doxázein* in the Synoptics, one refers to the desire of men (hypocrites) to be glorified by their fellows (Mt. 6:2). Only one involves praise rendered to Jesus (Lk. 4:15). The remaining instances record ascriptions of praise to God. On these occasions the Savior made no complaint that He was being overlooked. The Servant-Messiah would not have it otherwise.

In the Fourth Gospel the glorification of the Lord Jesus receives much more attention than in the Synoptics, but not in detachment from corresponding praise to God the Father. The purpose of it is that the Father may be glorified in the Son (Jn. 14:13). An additional emphasis in some cases is the inclusion of the redeemed in the acknowledgment of the Father. Since the Son has glorified the Father by accomplishing the work the Father has given Him to do (Jn. 17:4), it is fitting that those who belong to the Son should glorify the Father by their fruitful works (Jn. 15:8).

The Epistles have a modest contribution to make on this subject. Believers are enjoined to glorify God in their bodies (1 Cor. 6:20) and in the exercise of spiritual gifts (1 Pet. 4:11). By a daring use of language Paul asserts that those whom God has called and justified he *has* also glorified (Rom. 8:30).

D. Glorification. This form occurs once (1 Cor. 2:7). The allusion is apparently to the experience of full and final glory on the part of the redeemed in contrast to what is reserved for the rulers of this age who rejected Christ (v. 6).

See also HONOR.

Bibliography.–I. Abrahams, *Glory of God* (1973); L. H. Brockington, *Expos.T.*, 57 (1945), 21-25; G. B. Caird, *NTS*, 15 (1968-1969), 265-277; M. Carrez, *De la souffrance à la gloire; de la DOXA dans la pensée paulinienne* (1964); G. H. Davies, *IDB*, II, 401-403; A. von Gall, *Die Herrlichkeit Gottes* (1900); G. Kittel, *Die Religionsgeschichte und das Urchristentum* (1931), pp. 80-90; H. Kittel, *Die Herrlichkeit Gottes* (1934); R. D. Middleton, *JQR*, 29 (1938-1939), 101-133; E. C. E. Owen, *JTS*, 33 (1932), 132-150, 265-279; A. M. Ramsey, *The Glory of God and the Transfiguration of Christ* (1949); J. Schneider, *DOXA* (1932); *TDNT*, II, *s.v.* δοκέω κτλ. (von Rad, Kittel).

E. F. HARRISON

GLOSSOLALIA. *See* TONGUES, GIFT OF.

GLUTTON; GLUTTONOUS [Heb. *zālal*–'squander, be frivolous'] (Dt. 21:20; Prov. 23:20f.; 28:7); AV also RIOTOUS (MEN); NEB also RIOTOUS, GREED, GREEDY, WASTREL; [Gk. *phágos*] (Mt. 11:19; Lk. 7:34); [*gastḗr*] (Tit. 1:12); AV BELLY. In Dt. 21:20 and Prov. 28:7 the term may mean a prodigal or squanderer. The term "glutton" was applied to Jesus because of His freedom from the ascetic life-style of John the Baptist (Mt. 11:19; Lk. 7:34). Fasting was not an appropriate form of behavior when the Kingdom was being manifested in the works of Jesus (cf. Mt. 9:14f.). Gk. *gastḗr* means literally "belly," but is used figuratively here of gluttony.

W. L. WALKER
N. J. O.

GNASH [Heb. *ḥāraq*] (Job 16:9; Ps. 35:16; 37:12; 112:10; Lam. 2:16); NEB GRIND, GROUND (Ps. 35:16); [Gk. *brygmós*]; (Mt. 8:12; 13:42, 50; 22:13; 24:51; 25:30; Lk. 13:28); NEB GRINDING.

The Heb. *ḥāraq* occurs always in connection with *šēn*, "tooth" (or its plural). That it means "gnash" or "grind" (the teeth) is supported by other Semitic cognates (Syr. *ḥ^{e}rēq* [pael] may mean either "sharpen" or "gnash teeth"; postbiblical Heb., Aram. *ḥrq*; Arab. *ḥaraqa*). In four of the five occurrences the gnashing of teeth is a malicious gesture with which the wicked taunt the righteous ("gnashing the teeth at . . ." in Job 16:9; Ps. 35:16; 37:12), in one instance accompanied by railing and hissing (Lam. 2:16). Ps. 112:10 suggests that this action may also be one of despair or envy. (The LXX translates each occurrence with *brýchō* [*toús odóntas*], a Gk. vb. used initially by Hippocrates to connote "gnash" [i.e., as symptomatic of chills; see *TDNT*, I, 641].) The same Greek verb appears once in the NT with the very same form and sense. In Acts 7:54 the reaction of Stephen's adversaries is one of malice bent on destruction: "Now when they heard these things they were enraged, and they ground their teeth against him" (*ébrychon toús odóntas ep' autón*). This gesture on the part of Stephen's tormentors corresponds so closely to that of the psalmist's adversaries in Ps. 35:16 that it suggests deliberate allusion.

The Gk. *brygmós* is a cognate of *brýchō* and is in all seven occurrences found in the formulaic statement *ekeí éstai ho klauthmós kaí ho brygmós tṓn odóntōn*, lit. "there will be weeping and gnashing of teeth" (RSV "There men will weep and gnash their teeth"). In both form and sense this now differs markedly from the OT (and other Greek) usage mentioned above. This saying of Jesus describes the state of those who through their own faithlessness have in effect placed themselves outside the Kingdom (i.e., in the "outer darkness" [Mt. 8:12; 22:13; 25:30], in the "furnace of fire" [Mt. 13:42, 50], or "with the hypocrites" [Mt. 24:51]). Contrary to the usual OT pattern there is here no sense in which "the gnashing of teeth" is a gesture of malicious taunting. Rather, significantly always coupled in this phrase with "weeping" (*klauthmós*), it is symptomatic of the desperate hopelessness of such a status beyond the Kingdom. (1 En. 103:8 features this place of darkness as a place of grievous judgment for sinners; cf. 2 En. 40:12; Ps. Sol. 14:6; 15:11.)

The phrase *brygmós tṓn odóntōn* occurs also in the Apocrypha (Sir. 51:3 [Gk. text only]) in the usual OT taunting sense. The NT use of the phrase statistically appears to be peculiarly Matthaean, but the lone exception (Lk. 13:28) makes that uncertain. In Mk. 9:18 the verb *trízō*, "grind" (+ *toús odóntas*), expresses one of the manifestations of a seizure — the youth "grinds his teeth."

Bibliography.–BDB, p. 359; B. Schwank, *BZ*, 16 (1971), 121f.; *TDNT*, I, *s.v.* βρύχω, βρυγμός (Rengstorf).

D. G. BURKE

GNAT [Heb. **kēn*, pl. *kinnîm*] (Ex. 8:16-18 [MT 12-14]; Ps. 105:31; Isa. 51:6); AV LICE, "in like manner" (Isa. 51:6); NEB MAGGOTS; [Gk. *kṓnōps*] (Mt. 23:24); NEB MIDGE.

The third plague of Egypt (Ex. 8:16-18; Ps. 105:31) was brought about through gnats (*kinnîm*) and not "lice" as rendered by the AV, which follows Josephus *Ant.* ii.14.3 [300] and the Talmud, a tradition without linguistic basis.

The precise species of gnat is difficult to identify. The most common suggestion is that it was the *barghaš* midge (*Chironomidae*), a tiny gnat barely visible to the eye, but according to Philo and Origen its sting caused a most painful irritation of the skin. This gnat is said to creep into the eyes, nose, and ears. The Heb. *kinnîm* of Ex. 8:16-18 is probably derived from the Egyptian *chenemeś*, meaning "gnats" or "mosquitoes." It has also been supposed that the insect could be the dengue fever-carrying sand fly (*Psychodidae*) or the malaria-carrying Anopheles mosquito. But it is more likely that the fourth plague (Ex. 8:20-24) refers to such larger flies or mosquitoes.

Isa. 51:6 is problematic. The AV, following the LXX, reads "in like manner" for Heb. *kᵉmô-ḵēn*. But this Hebrew expression is redundant and of questionable sense. Thus *kēn* is usually either taken as the sing. of *kinnîm*, or the text is emended to read the pl. (cf. *BH*). There is no textual evidence for such a change, however, and the sing. of *kinnîm* should be *kinnâ*/*kînnâ* (cf. postbiblical Hebrew/Aramaic). Thus it seems that either *kēn* is an anomalous form, or a slight textual emendation is necessary (cf. also J. Reider, *ZAW*, 12 [1935], 270f.).

The hapax legomenon *kṓnōps* in Mt. 23:24 is believed to designate a "gnat" or "mosquito," though Aristotle employs this word for a certain worm found in wine (*Historia Animalium* v. 19). A typographical error crept into the AV and RV that read "strain at." It should have been rendered "strain out" as in the RSV and NAB or "strain off" as in the NEB. Jesus' accusation that the Pharisees drink water through a straining cloth to avoid swallowing an insect regarded as unclean, but meanwhile swallow a camel, emphasizes the contradiction between the scrupulous observation of the smallest detail of every religious rule and the disregard for weightier and more essential matters (Mt. 23:24).

Bibliography.–Pauly-Wissowa, XVI, 450-54; A. Dalman, *Arbeit und Sitte in Palästina* (1928), I, 267f.; SB, I, 933f.; G. Hort, *ZAW*, 69 (1957), 84-103; 70 (1958), 49-59. G. F. HASEL

GNOSTICISM nos'ti-siz-əm.

I. General Definition
II. Revived Interest in Gnosticism
III. Sources
  A. Alexandrian Philosophy
  B. Zoroastrianism
  C. Buddhism
  D. Dead Sea Scrolls
IV. Characteristics
V. Harnack's View of Gnosticism
VI. Gnosticism in the Early Christian Church
  A. Colossians
  B. 1 Corinthians: "Knowledge"
  C. Pastoral Epistles
  D. 1 John
  E. Revelation: "To Know the Depths"
VII. Christian Antithesis
  A. God and the World
  B. Evil
    1. Christian Doctrine of Sin
    2. Sin and the Moral Law
    3. Christ and Redemption
VIII. Influence and Development
  A. Cerinthus
  B. Gospel of John
  C. Various Sects
    1. Ophites
    2. Valentinians
    3. Basilideans
    4. Saturninians
    5. Marcionites
  D. Relation to the OT
  E. Influence on Theology
IX. Modern Gnosticism

Gnosticism was a heresy far more subtle and dangerous than any that had appeared during the early years of the church. It became so widespread that by the beginning of the 3rd cent. A.D. most of the intellectual Christian congregations throughout the Roman empire were to some degree infected by it. Except perhaps in 1 Tim. 6:20, where Paul warned Timothy against "what is falsely called knowledge [*gnōsis*]," it is not mentioned in the NT. The leaven was at work, however, and very soon its baneful influence became only too apparent. In the 2nd cent. the movement "spread with the swiftness of an epidemic over the Church from Syria to Gaul" (Law, p. 26). It is not easy to give a proper and complete account of this potent anti-Christian influence, for Gnosticism was not a homogeneous system of either religion or philosophy, but embraced many widely diversified sects holding opinions drawn from a great variety of sources.

I. General Definition.–"Gnosticism," according to Gwatkin, "may be provisionally described as a number of schools of philosophy, oriental in general character, but taking in the idea of a redemption through Christ, and further modified in different sects by a third element, which may be Judaism, Hellenism, or Christianity. . . . The Gnostics took over only the idea of a redemption through Christ, not the full Christian doctrine, for they made it rather a redemption of the philosophers from matter, than a redemption of mankind from sin" (II, 20).

James Orr viewed Gnosticism as "the fantastic product of the blending of certain Christian ideas . . . with speculations and imaginings derived from a medley of sources (Greek, Jewish, Parsic; philosophies, religions, theosophies, mysteries) in a period when the human mind was in a kind of ferment. . . . It involves, as the name denotes, a claim to *'knowledge,'* knowledge of a kind of which the ordinary believer was incapable, and in the possession of which 'salvation' in the full sense consisted" (*Early Church*, p. 71).

Neander, a Greek philosopher of the 2nd cent., described Gnosticism as "the first notable attempt to introduce into Christianity the existing elements of mental culture, and to render it more complete on the hitherto rather neglected side of theoretical knowledge; it was an attempt of the mind of the ancient world in its yearning after knowledge, and in its dissatisfaction with the present, to bring within its grasp and to appropriate the treasures of this kind which Christianity presented" (*Antignostikus*, Intro., 199).

Gnosticism accordingly comprehended in itself many previously existing tendencies; it is an amalgam into which quite a number of different elements have been infused. A heretical system of thought, at once subtle, speculative, and elaborate, it endeavored to introduce into Christianity a so-called higher knowledge, which was grounded partly on the philosophical creed in which Greeks and Romans had taken refuge consequent to the gradual decay and disintegration of their own religions, partly, as will be shown, on the philosophies of Plato and of Philo, and still more on the philosophies, theosophies, and religions of the East, especially those of Persia and India.

Though usually regarded as a heresy, Gnosticism was at first not really such; it was not the perverting of Christian truth but instead came from outside. Having worked its way into the Christian Church it then became intensely heretical.

II. Revived Interest in Gnosticism.–In recent times several original Gnostic writings have been discovered such as *Pistis Sophia,* written in Coptic and discovered in Egypt. A most important find was made in 1896 when a codex containing the *Gospel of Mary,* the *Apocryphon of John,* and the *Sophia of Jesus Christ,* all of them Gnostic, was discovered in the same country. Strangely enough, it was not published until 1955.

A more valuable discovery was made in 1945 by some peasants near the little town of Nag Hammadi in Upper Egypt. They found a large jar containing a collection of Coptic Gnostic books and documents dating from the 4th cent. A.D. Altogether there were forty-eight treatises — Gnostic gospels, epistles, etc. They were found near the site of one of the monasteries founded by Pachomius *ca.* A.D. 320, at Chenoboskion, and it is suggested that instead of calling them the Nag Hammadi Library they should be called the Chenoboskion Library. This exceedingly valuable collection, with the exception of one volume, the *Gospel of Truth,* is in possession of the Coptic Museum in Cairo. The *Gospel of Truth* (tr. and ed. by K. Grobel, 1960) was the first to be published. This book is thought to be by Valentinus or one of his contemporaries. It is thus of great importance as it gives a clearer idea than ever before of the views of the original Valentinian Gnostics — the most erudite Gnostic sect. Hitherto only the representations of later generations of Valentinians were known among whom the views of the founder had become adulterated.

With the examination of a large amount of new Gnostic literature, and the possibility of further important finds, the study of Gnosticism is probably about to enter upon a new phase when its origins, teachings, and developments will be better understood. While we are indebted to people like J. Doresse, R. M. Grant, H. Jonas, and R. M. Wilson for their careful examination of the new situation that has arisen, nothing has so far been brought to light that has shaken the main conclusions of authorities on Gnosticism at the beginning of this century.

See NAG HAMMADI LITERATURE.

III. Sources.–Mansel (p. 32) summed up the principal sources of Gnosticism in these three: Platonism, the Persian religion, and the Buddhism of India. To Platonism it owed much of its philosophical form and tendencies. From the dualism of the Persian religion it derived its speculations regarding the origin of evil, and much of what it taught about emanations. To Buddhism, Mansel believed, it owed the doctrine of the antagonism between matter and spirit, and the unreality of derived existence — the germ of Docetism.

A. Alexandrian Philosophy. Alexandrian philosophy endeavored to unite Greek philosophy and Hebrew religion. PHILO JUDAEUS, the great Jewish commentator of Alexandria (1st cent. A.D.), had tried to interpret the Jewish Scriptures by the aid of Greek philosophy, to expound the OT in terms of Platonic thought, and to discover allegorical meanings where they were not intended. Philo drew a sharp line between God and the material world: with him God cannot exert any action upon the world of matter except through intermediate agencies, the Jewish angels and the heathen demons. While Philo, like the gospel, said much about the Logos, his conception was very different. For him the Logos was merely an impersonal power of God, although He is the only firstborn of God, the chief of the angels, the viceroy of God, and the representative of mankind (*see* LOGOS).

According to Philo the creation of the universe was a gradual molding out of matter; thus evil arose. He also taught the preexistence of the soul, which is now imprisoned in the flesh. To secure salvation, therefore, mankind must break the thraldom of the flesh and rise by a sort of ecstasy to the immediate vision of God. It is clear that the various Gnostic sects were deeply indebted to Philo.

B. Zoroastrianism. The Zoroastrian or Persian system was based on the assumption that there existed two original and independent powers of good and evil, of light and darkness, Ormuzd (Ahura-Mazda) the wise Lord, and Ahriman (Angra-Mainyu) the wicked spirit. These powers were believed to be equal and each supreme in his own domain. The earth, which was created by Ormuzd, became the battlefield of the two powers. Ahriman led away the first man and woman from their allegiance to Ormuzd, and all evils to mankind resulted. From some angles Gnosticism might be regarded as a combination of spirit and matter; this combination could have resulted in its pessimism and asceticism.

C. Buddhism. Mansel's view that Gnosticism owed a great deal to the Buddhism of India has been strongly opposed by the greatest authorities. At the same time it is difficult to escape the conclusion that the hopelessness of the East and the intense asceticism so characteristic of India must have exercised a profound influence upon Persia, Iraq, and Syria in the early ages. It is now well known that ideas then spread with surprising rapidity, and while Gnosticism may not have owed a direct debt to Buddhism it was certainly influenced indirectly.

R. M. Grant proffered the theory that Gnosticism had its rise chiefly in the disillusionment and pessimism engendered among the Jews by the overthrow of their apocalyptic-eschatological hopes through the destruction of Jerusalem in A.D. 70 and the events following. This thesis is much too simple and does not take cognizance of all the complicated factors. A. M. RENWICK

D. Dead Sea Scrolls. The discovery of the Dead Sea Scrolls, beginning in 1947, opened up a new discussion of the origins of Gnosticism. In some respects there was more confusion than clarification, for the words "know," "knowledge," and "secret" were used, often in a prooftext methodology, to argue that the Qumrânians were "Gnostics." At the same time, the discussion evoked a number of studies that pointed toward, if they did not completely support, certain conclusions. These may be summarized as follows: (1) Zoroastrian origins of Gnosticism have been overstated; (2) Hellenistic Gnosticism — the type best known and most frequently discussed — almost certainly had an earlier and possibly non-Hellenistic basis; and (3) so-called Jewish Gnosticism, lacking at least one of the basic elements of true Gnosticism, namely cosmological dualism, must be clearly distinguished from Gnosticism. In this last category should be included the "Gnostic" elements of NT writings, since they sprang from Judaism rather than from a non-Judaic Hellenism.

(1) A number of scholars have argued strongly for a Zoroastrian background for the Qumrân sectarian beliefs. K. G. Kuhn, for example, wrote: "This Gnostic structure of the new text [i.e., Qumrân materials] can scarcely have sprung up from Jewish tradition — there the presuppositions for it would be lacking; while they would be genuinely present in this sect. But it agrees surprisingly with the original preaching of Zoroaster, and thereby is set forth anew the old question of the Parsee influence on Judaism" (*ZTK,* 47 [1950], 211). But this statement is not supported by what is known about Zoroastrianism. Zoroaster was born *ca.* 569 B.C. (E. Herzfeld, *Zoroaster and His World* [1947], I, 19, 29). The religion named after him underwent subsequent change. The dualism of Zoroastrianism passed from an ethical dualism in the Gathas (the earlier poems, generally attributed to Zoroaster) to a cosmological dualism in the later writings. According to

Herzfeld (p. 316), the doctrine that Ahriman is the creator of evil is not found until 1500 years after Zoroaster — a date, of course, much too late to be the source of ideas in either the NT or Qumrân literature. It is to be admitted that the forces that led to the development in Zoroastrian doctrine were at work for some time before the doctrine appeared in the Parsee scriptures. This, however, raises a further question: were such ideas indigenous to the Parsees, or did they come from outside this religion? If from outside, then we must still look for a possible common source of such ideas that may have been influential in Judaism, at least to the extent that it can be found in the DSS and/or the NT.

The suggestion, sometimes presented as an affirmed conclusion, that there is a true dualism in Qumrân must also be challenged. Careful study of the doctrines expressed in the DSS will lead to the conviction that the underlying philosophy was monistic. The God of Israel is creator of all beings and things, including evil and the beings connected with it. God "made Belial" (1QM 13:10f.). The angelology and satanology of Qumrân are basically that of Judaism. The dualism of Qumrân is ethical rather than cosmological.

(2) The Qumrân studies led a number of scholars to conclude that the rise of Gnosticism must be placed two or more centuries earlier than had been commonly held. Elements of Hellenistic Gnosticism have been found, as will be discussed below, in the Fourth Gospel, Colossians, and elsewhere in the NT. Critical scholars of the past have sometimes dated such portions of the NT in the middle of the 2nd cent., since they could find no earlier traces of Gnosticism. But with the advent of Qumrân studies, this was changed. Some scholars were dating the Fourth Gospel to the first half of the 1st cent. (e.g., W. F. Albright). Terms such as "pre-Christian Jewish Gnosticism" were used, and the term "Hellenism" was expanded to include non-Hellenistic ideas (cf. O. Cullmann, *JBL*, 74 [1955], 213-226). Other scholars protested against the confusion created by calling such pre-Gnostic non-Hellenistic concepts by the name "Gnosticism" (cf. W. S. LaSor, *Dead Sea Scrolls and the NT* [1972], p. 92 n. 5; R. M. Grant, ed., *Gnosticism: An Anthology* [1961]). The fact remains, however, that something like Gnosticism is found in the Judaism of the 1st cent. B.C. and 1st cent. A.D., and possibly earlier. More precise definition of terms is needed, and exegesis of the Qumrân, NT, and gnostic texts must be more carefully controlled. It is not satisfactory to seize upon a few key words, such as "knowledge," "mysteries," and "secrets," or to speak of "dualism" without further qualifying it, and to label the result "Gnosticism." The texts from Nag Hammadi must also be brought into the discussion. But once again, the methodology must be to recognize that these texts are later, and therefore the earlier elements that they contain must be carefully separated from the later developments that characterize them.

(3) Jewish "Gnosticism" likewise needs more carefully controlled study. It can be readily admitted that the concepts of Satan, angels, the two "spirits," and related ideas are more fully developed in Qumrân than in the OT. It can also be admitted that similar ideas and doctrines can be found in the NT. But the "mysteries" or "secrets" spoken of in Qumrân literature are clearly defined: they are to be found in the Jewish Scriptures (the Christian OT), as interpreted by Qumrânian exegetes. The Qumrânians were sectarian Jews — but they *were* Jews, and they drew their theology, anthropology, pneumatology, and eschatology from the OT. Other influences were and had been at work on them and their predecessors. It is part of the Judeo-Christian system to consider the God of Israel as using even the thoughts and acts of pagan peoples to shape the thoughts and actions, and even the destiny, of His own people. Nevertheless, the Judaism of Qumrân, like that of Christ and the apostles, is basically monistic. There is only one God, and beside Him there is none other. He is the Creator and Sustainer of all things visible and invisible. The gods of the nations are nothing — and the same could be said of the Demiurge and the emanations of Gnosticism or its ancestor. There is a kingdom of evil, headed by Satan (or Mastema or Belial), and there is a struggle within every person between the spirit of light and the spirit of darkness. But in Qumrân, as in the NT, the outcome is never in doubt. This is not an eternal struggle. In Qumrân, Michael at last overcomes the leader of evil, just as in the NT Jesus ultimately overcomes Satan. Further studies of "Jewish Gnosticism" are needed, but nothing will be gained by obscuring the clear distinctions between "Jewish Gnosticism" and the Gnosticism that developed in the Hellenistic world after the 1st cent. A.D.

The two essential elements of Gnosticism are (a) cosmological dualism consisting of matter and spirit, the one evil and therefore not created directly by a good spirit, and the other good; and (b) esoteric knowledge, limited to those who are initiated into the gnosis, by which they are able to be "saved," i.e., freed from evil material existence to enter into pure spiritual life. Both elements have seeming relationships with the Judeo-Christian Scriptures. Both, however, come into basic conflict with biblical doctrine. Matter is not evil in the Bible, but is God's creation, and the "new earth" exists in the age to come alongside the "new heaven." The body, likewise, is not evil, and salvation is not an escape from it. There is a resurrection body, as eternal as the soul. Jewish eschatology, like its Christian counterpart, knows nothing of salvation *from* the body, but rather of redemption *of* the body (cf. 1QM 12:9-15).

W. S. LASOR

IV. Characteristics.–"Gnosticism," stated Gwatkin, "is Christianity perverted by learning and speculation" (II, 73). The intellectual pride of the Gnostics changed the gospel into a philosophy. The clue to the understanding of Gnosticism is found in the Greek word from which its name is derived — *gnōsis,* "knowledge." The Gnostics claimed to be the elite, the wise, the philosophers, to whom was revealed a secret knowledge which the overwhelming mass of mankind could never know.

To the Gnostics the great question was not the intensely practical one, "What must I do to be saved from sin?" but "What is the origin of evil?" "How is the primitive order of the universe to be restored?" In the knowledge of these and of similar questions, and in the answers given to these questions, lay redemption as the Gnostic understood it.

The following may be regarded as the chief points in the Gnostic systems: (1) a claim on the part of the initiated to a special knowledge of the truth; a tendency to regard knowledge as superior to faith and as the special possession of the more enlightened, for ordinary Christians did not possess this secret and higher doctrine; (2) the essential separation of matter and spirit, matter being intrinsically evil and the source from which all evil has arisen; (3) an attempt to solve the problems of creation and the origin of evil by postulating a demiurge, i.e., a creator or artificer of the world distinct from the deity, and emanations extending between God and the visible universe (the demiurge for the Gnostics being the God of the OT, an inferior being infinitely remote from the Supreme Being who can have nothing to do with anything material); (4) a denial of the true humanity of Christ; a docetic Christology which considered the earthly life of Christ and especially His sufferings on the cross to be unreal; (5) the denial of the personality of the Supreme God, and also the denial of the free will of mankind; (6) the teaching, on the one hand, of asceticism as the means of attaining spiritual communion with God, and, on the other hand, of an indifference that led directly to licentiousness; (7) a syncretistic tendency that combined certain more or less misunderstood Christian doctrines and various elements from oriental, Jewish, Greek, and other sources; (8) ascription of the OT to the demiurge or inferior creator of the world. Some of these ideas are more obvious in one and some of them in another of the Gnostic systems.

V. Harnack's View of Gnosticism.–Harnack laid the chief emphasis on its Judeo-Hellenistic side. He described well how, when Christianity appeared, an extensive spiritualizing or allegorizing of the OT had already taken place. He maintained that this allegorizing was "the outcome of a lasting influence of Greek philosophy, and of the Greek spirit generally, upon Judaism. In consequence of this, all facts and sayings of the OT in which one could not find his way were allegorized. Nothing was what it seemed, but was only the symbol of something invisible. The history of the OT was here sublimated to a history of the emancipation of reason from passion" (*History of Dogma* [Eng. tr. 1958], I, 223). Harnack's insistence that the Greek element in Gnosticism was the predominant one has been challenged by many eminent scholars. It is obvious, however, that this element was very important, though by no means the only one.

VI. Gnosticism in the Early Christian Church.–The germ of Gnosticism made its appearance in the apostolic age. (On its presence in James, *see* JAMES, EPISTLE OF I.B.4.)

A. Colossians. Much is said of a false teaching, apparently a theosophist doctrine that was alienating Christians in Colossae from the gospel and leading them to worship of angels contrary to the worship of Christ. The esoteric exclusiveness and asceticism of its adherents were injurious to Christian freedom and derogatory to the human body as indwelt by the Holy Spirit. These tendencies were identical with the more fully developed Gnosticism of later days. Already present was the great Gnostic error that God had no connection with matter. From this theoretical basis arose the error that, as sin is inherent in the material substance of the body, the only way to perfection is to punish the body by pain and mortification of the flesh so that the soul may be saved. This ascetic attitude prevailed in many parts of the world, particularly among the pagans of the East, long before the advent of Christianity. The Epistle to the Colossians reveals the existence of ascetic practices inculcated by false teachers. Their words are quoted — "Do not handle, Do not taste, Do not touch" (Col. 2:21). Contrary to Christian teaching, they sought spiritual deliverance by "self-abasement and severity to the body" (Col. 2:21-23). These tendencies were worse later on, for Paul complained in 1 Tim. 4:3 of those who "forbid marriage and enjoin abstinence from foods." Such ascetic practices became very common among Gnostics. Paul set himself to correct these errors among the Colossians by presenting to them the person and work of Christ — Christ the Creator, possessing all the fulness of the Godhead bodily, Christ in whom all matter and all creatures "hold together" (*see* COLOSSIANS II, III.).

B. 1 Corinthians: "Knowledge." Even as early as 1 Corinthians Paul rebuked some who claimed to have "knowledge" which others did not possess, a claim the apostle met with stern resistance. They were given to disputing and professed that they "all had knowledge," but it only puffed them up and did not make them sympathetic (1 Cor. 8:1, 7-11). Even if they could "understand all mysteries and all knowledge," this of itself was worthless (1 Cor. 13:2).

C. Pastoral Epistles. In 1 Tim. 6:20f. Paul referred to "what is falsely called knowledge [*gnōsis*]." In 1 Tim. 1:4 he warned against "myths and endless genealogies which promote speculations rather than the divine training that is in faith." Philo had popularized allegorical interpretations of the OT. This, coupled with the teaching of the genealogies of the Gnostic aeons, would leave no place for the Redeemer. The ascetic teaching on marriage and abstention from certain foods was supposed to be most meritorious. Paul condemned it as unnatural and contrary to the constitution of the world (1 Tim. 4:3). Believers must not treat the Creator's good gifts as "common or unclean."

Those who favored unnatural asceticism often fell into the opposite sin of shocking licentiousness. As body and soul are entirely distinct in their nature, the soul cannot be defiled by anything, however carnal and gross, that the body can do. Let the soul go its way on the wings of spiritual thought, and the body indulge its fleshly desires. Such was the reasoning of this class of Gnostics. Many traces of this antinomianism are found in the Pastoral Epistles and 2 Peter and Jude; e.g., Paul warned against the Gnostics in 2 Tim. 3:2-5. They were "lovers of self, lovers of money . . . arrogant . . . unholy, inhuman . . . lovers of pleasure rather than lovers of God; holding the form of religion but denying the power of it." Ignatius of Antioch at the beginning of the 2nd cent. applied somewhat similar words to people in the area to which he addressed his letters.

Though they professed that they knew God, by their works they denied Him, being "detestable, disobedient, unfit for any good deed" (Tit. 1:16). They enticed others into sins of impurity (2 Tim. 3:6f.). Exactly the same kind of charges are made against this class in 2 Pet. 2:12-18 and throughout the vigorous little Epistle of Jude (cf. vv. 4, 8, 11, 19).

D. 1 John. Nowhere is the tendency to Gnosticism more clearly or emphatically condemned than in 1 John, the Epistle of the apostle of love. John referred reprovingly to the "spirit of error" (1 Jn. 4:6); "many false prophets" (4:1); they were "the antichrist" (2:22) and "the deceiver and the antichrist" (2 Jn. 7). Many claimed "I know God," "I abide in Christ," "I am in the light," even when they did not love their brethren on earth, did not obey Christ, and were destitute of love. John showed how the Christ of history is the Christ of experience. "And we know that the Son of God has come and has given us understanding, to know him who is true; and we are in him who is true, in his Son Jesus Christ. This is the true God and eternal life" (1 Jn. 5:20). This knowledge of God and communion with Him are attained not by Gnostic speculation, but by the obedience of faith, the outcome of which is love for one another and a life in which Christians walk even as Christ did. This is the test of Christian profession (cf. 2:7-11; 2:29; 3:10).

Gnosticism was distinguished by an unethical, loveless intellectualism. John described vividly this dry knowledge devoid of love and pity. In Gnosticism knowledge was the supreme end and purpose of life, but Gnostics were left in a loveless state.

On Gnostic principles God could have no immediate contact with matter. Thus the Incarnation was inconceivable, and it was denied that Christ's body was a real body. For John, the antichrist was docetic Gnosticism. John knew personally the historical Jesus; He was the divine Being. "Who is the liar but he who denies that Jesus is the Christ?" (2:22). "Every spirit which confesses that Jesus Christ has come in the flesh is of God: and every spirit which does not confess Jesus is not of God. This is the spirit of antichrist" (4:2f.).

Again and again John condemned antinomianism, which was so characteristic of certain sects of the Gnostics. "All wrongdoing is sin" (5:17). "No one born of God commits sin" (3:9; cf. 3:4, 7f., 10, which presuppose a situation where false teachers were proclaiming that morals were different so long as a person was "spiritual" through having Gnostic knowledge). (*See* JOHN, EPISTLES OF I.)

E. Revelation: "To Know the Depths." As time went on the Gnostics made greater and greater claims for themselves. A favorite claim was that they alone "knew the depths," and the Ophites in particular claimed this. According to John, the depths which they knew were not of God, but were rather "the deep things of Satan," because their works were so evil (Rev. 2:20-24). (See also R. H. Mounce, comm. on Revelation [*NICNT,* 1977], pp. 105f.)

Mansel (p. 71) and others believed that the NICOLAITANS mentioned in Rev. 2:6, 15 were antinomian Gnostics of the licentious type. While they certainly had the characteristics of this class of Gnostics it would be rash to conclude that they actually belonged to the Gnostic school.

VII. Christian Antithesis.–We now shall summarize briefly the difference between Gnosticism and Christian teaching.

A. God and the World. For the Gnostics God is the ultimate, nameless, unknowable being called the "Abyss." He is perfect, but the material world is alien to the divine nature. How, then, does it come to exist at all? What is the source of its imperfections and evils?

The Gnostic answer is that the FULNESS (Gk. *plḗrōma*) of the deity could flow out in no other way than in emanations or aeons or angels, all of which are necessarily imperfect, the highest of them being more spiritual than the grade immediately below. Of these aeons there is a gradation so numerous that at length the lowest of them is almost wholly corporeal, the spiritual element having been gradually diminished or eliminated until at last the world of mankind and of matter is reached, the abode of evil. In this way the gulf is bridged between God and mankind. The highest aeons approximate closely to the divine nature, so spiritual are they and so free from matter. These form the highest hierarchy of angels, and these with many other grades of angelic hosts are to be worshiped.

In opposition to this view, Christian faith worships God as the free self-sufficient Creator, infinitely good and wise and powerful and holy, the Author of all things, and affirms creation as an incomprehensible fact which is revealed to faith and which rises above the grasp of the understanding (cf. He. 11:3).

B. Evil. The doctrine of evil follows directly from the above account of the relation of God to the world. According to Gnosticism the manifestation of God is possible only through self-limitation on His part, for in His essence God is the unfathomable abyss. Through this self-limitation are evolved, first, the divine powers or attributes, which previously were hidden in the abyss of His being. These divine powers (the *plḗrōma*) become the principles of all further developments of life, which continues to unfold in such a way that its successive grades sink farther and farther from the purity of God. Life becomes feebler the nearer they come to matter, with which at length they blend. Such according to Gnosticism is the origin of evil.

Whenever people are not content with acknowledging evil to be the act of their own free will which has chosen to forsake its absolute dependence upon God, one of two results follows. They either limit the holiness of God, and find the cause of evil in God Himself, thus annihilating all distinction between good and evil — which is monism; or they limit the power of God by granting the existence of an eternal evil power beyond the control of God — which is dualism. In avoiding monism, Gnosticism accepted the dualistic solution, ascribing to evil an eternal self-subsistent nature. As absolute self-subsistence can be affirmed of none but God, the eternally self-subsistent evil of dualism must be God, which it cannot possibly be, because it is not good. Here is the self-contradiction in which dualistic Gnosticism was entangled.

1. Christian Doctrine of Sin. Directly contrary to this is the Christian doctrine, according to which evil is the refusal of the creature to lean absolutely and utterly upon God, on His care and love and upholding grace. Sin is defiance of God; it is moral transgression; its magnitude cannot be exaggerated — it would dethrone God if it could. It has defied His righteousness, holiness, wisdom, and even His grace. It is, therefore, dealt with by God in two ways, either by direct punishment or by redemption, which is effected by the Lamb of God who takes away the sin of the world. The question "What is sin?" is no mere academic or philosophical discussion in which one opinion may be as good as another. "Here, certainly, if anywhere, Christian theology must fight *for our altars and our hearths*" (Julius Müller, quoted in J. Orr, *Sin as a Problem of Today* [1911], p. 6).

2. Sin and the Moral Law. The universality of sin, its persistence, its gravity, its power to destroy and to deprave — these can hardly be exaggerated. To view sin aright, it is impossible to leave out of sight its relation to moral law, to God, and to His kingdom. It is the resolve of the sinful will to make itself independent of God and to renounce His authority. Sin is self-will, false independence, freedom which ends in bondage and misery.

But in Gnosticism sin is something quite different; it is only a physical fact or quality inherent in the body and in matter everywhere. Redemption, therefore, does not consist in the work of Jesus Christ for us on the cross, and the applying of the benefits of that work by the Holy Spirit in the renewal of human moral nature. Redemption is simply each person's efforts to secure emancipation from the flesh — from physical evil.

3. Christ and Redemption. A system of this kind has no need of Christ and leaves no place for redemption in the Christian sense of that term. Redemption in this scheme of thought is not deliverance from sin; it is not removal of guilt and renewal of the mind. It is something quite different. It consists in the restoration of the cosmic order and the illumination of the mind of the select few through knowledge. Christ is not the Savior who saves His people from their sins, and who gives them unceasingly, through union with Himself, deliverance from the power of sin. He is only one of the aeons, though the highest of them. He is an originated being, not God. Thus Gnosticism has no place either for the creation of the universe by God, or for the incarnation and work of Christ. Once the essential evil of matter is granted, the possibility of Christ's having assumed a true human nature is excluded, simply for the reason that the world and human nature are originally and necessarily evil. Thus, as already seen, a form of Docetism is being espoused.

The Christology of the Gnostics assumed two forms. "One class of early Gnostics separated the spiritual being Christ from the man Jesus; they supposed that the Christ entered Jesus at the time of His baptism, and left Him at the moment of His crucifixion. Thus the Christ was neither born as a man nor suffered as a man. In this way they obviated the difficulty, inseparable to the gnostic mind, of conceiving the connection between the highest spiritual agency and gross corporeal matter, which was involved in the Catholic doctrine of the Incarnation and Passion, and which Gnostics of another type more effectively set aside by the doctrine of Docetism, i.e., by assuming that the human body of Our Lord was only a phantom body, and not real flesh and blood" (J. B. Lightfoot, comm. on Colossians [1900], p. 264). We have already seen how strenuously this doctrine was combated by John and Paul.

VIII. Influence and Development.–Gnosticism is peculiarly (though not solely) the heresy of the 2nd cent. and in itself a proof of the extent to which a knowledge of the Christian faith had, at that early period, penetrated into literary and philosophical circles. Though it is true that Christianity at first influenced chiefly the humbler classes, yet it was not among these that the various Gnostic heresies arose. As Orr has pointed out, it presupposed a speculative bent of mind. Its appeal as a religion of *gnosis* was to intellectuals. Its rise was due to the impact of the gospel of redemption upon the educated classes (cf. Orr, *Neglected Factors,* p. 196).

A. Cerinthus. The earliest Gnostic known by name is Cerinthus, the antagonist of the apostle John. On the authority of Irenaeus, who quoted Polycarp the disciple of John, there is little doubt that the two met in Ephesus. Cerinthus was a Jew who seemed to have stood between the EBIONITES and Gnostics. From the accounts that have been preserved of Cerinthus and his teaching, it can be gathered that he taught that the world was created not by the Supreme God, but by an inferior power; he also taught a docetic theory of the Incarnation. Caius of Rome, a disciple of Irenaeus, recorded that Cerinthus held there would be a millennium of unrestrained sensuality. Dionysius of Alexandria (*ca.* A.D. 260) confirmed this (R. Law, p. 37). There is the testimony of Irenaeus, that the Gospel of John was written to oppose that form of Gnosticism taught by Cerinthus and, before him, by the Nicolaitans. According to Irenaeus, Cerinthus maintained that the world was made not by the sovereign Power but by some inferior being who was ignorant of the supreme God. He taught that Jesus was not born of a virgin but was the son of Joseph and Mary, born after the manner of other people. After His baptism the Spirit in the form of a dove descended on Him, and before His crucifixion the Spirit left Him. Thus, while the man Jesus suffered and rose again, the Christ remained impassible as a spiritual being (cf. Mansel, p. 74).

B. Gospel of John. Some regard Jn. 19:34f. as a personal protest against Gnosticism. After describing the piercing of Christ's side by the soldier's spear, and how "at once there came out blood and water," the apostle adds, "He who saw it has borne witness — his testimony is true, and he knows that he tells the truth — that you also may believe." Other passages seem to be directed against Docetism, e.g., "And the Word became flesh and dwelt among us . . . we have beheld his glory" (1:14). This is, perhaps, the most convincing statement of all (cf. also 4:6 and 20:27). It would be a mistake, however, to hold with Jerome that John wrote his Gospel in response to Gnostic attacks. He had much wider aims.

C. Various Sects. Generally the forms in which Gnosticism appeared varied greatly in different periods. Some departed farther than others from the Christian faith, but even in its mildest form Gnosticism was a danger to the Church.

Some communities, such as the Encratites, laid the greatest stress on the necessity of asceticism; other communities were wholly docetic. The Carpocratians taught the philosophy of Plato. One of these, Epiphanes son of Carpocrates, taught a pure form of communism. Although only seventeen when he died, he was honored as a god. Furthermore, there were impostors of all varieties: magicians, soothsayers, jugglers, and other deceivers, "who appeared using mighty words with a host of unintelligible formulae and taking up with scandalous ceremonies in order to rob men of their money" (Harnack, I, 239), and having even viler purposes.

1. Ophites. These represented the earlier manifestations of Gnosticism and stood for a number of coteries rather than a definite school. Their distinctive ideas were of pagan origin, and they derived their name from Gk. *óphis,* "serpent," which they honored as the highest intelligence. This worship of the serpent was widespread in the ancient world. The Ophite Gnostics held that the creator of the world was an ignorant and imperfect being, Ialdabaoth the Son of Chaos, and that it was a meritorious act when the serpent persuaded Adam and Eve to disobey him. Several Ophite sects, such as the Cainites, altered the Bible's moral standards and chose as their heroes those condemned in Scripture, e.g., Cain, Pharaoh, the men of Sodom, and Korah.

2. Valentinians. By the time of Justin Martyr (*ca.* A.D. 150) Gnosticism was represented by various sects or schools: Valentinians, Basilideans, Saturninians, and Marcionites.

Valentinus was born evidently on the Egyptian coast soon after A.D. 100. He was educated in Alexandria, receiving a thorough Hellenistic education. He moved to Rome *ca.* 136 and worked there for at least twenty years. When he became a Christian is unknown, but for a time he had very close relations with the church in Rome. It is held by some that his character and power were so clearly recognized in the church that he was on the verge of becoming a bishop when his heresy disqualified him. Even his archcritic Tertullian acknowledged that "both as to talent and eloquence he was an able man" (*De praescr. haer.* 30). He has long been regarded as the greatest of the Gnostics — an acute thinker with a touch of mysticism and a philosopher's delight in contemplating things *sub specie aeternitatis* (Gwatkin, II, 36). By common consent Valentinianism has been acknowledged as the most impressive of all the Gnostic systems.

Hitherto scholars had to depend very largely on Irenaeus' *Adv. haer.* (*ca.* A.D. 185) for an account of the work of Valentinus. It is now clear that what Irenaeus took to be teachings of Valentinus were in reality the version of Valentinianism taught by his disciples and successors at least three steps removed from the master. The *Gospel of Truth* makes this very clear (cf. Grobel, ed., Intro., p. 14). It shows that Valentinus must have been the nearest of the great Gnostics whose writings are known to the teachings of the Church. There is little doubt that the *Gospel of Truth* was written either by Valentinus himself or by a disciple who was his contemporary. According to Grobel,

> Deity, far from being a thirtyfold complex à la Irenaeus, consists of the Father, the Son, and the Holy Spirit. "God" as an explicit word . . . occurs twice; once in the most Hebraic passage of the whole work (37:33), and the context leaves us no doubt that the Hebrew-Christian God is meant, God whose will is supreme and who, Himself — not some Demiurge — is the creator of the universe. . . . Several of the other attributes and epithets of God from which the thirty Eons of the Pleroma bore their names in the system of Ptolemy's disciples occur either in transparent Coptic translation or are left as Greek, but they occur *as attributes* and *epithets* of *God,* not as independent mythological per-

> sons. There is but one Son, not a whole genealogy of several generations of Eons — the Father's beloved Son (30:31) who pre-existed as the Father's secret, His Word . . . , upon whom he conferred his name, whom the Father revealed, and who thereupon revealed the Father, thus bestowing saving knowledge of Him, salvation (Intro., pp. 21f.).

The difference between this kind of teaching and that given by the successors of Valentinus is amazing. The later Valentinians confound our imaginations with their aeons and their mythological persons — thirty aeons — Bythos and Sige, Word and Life, Horus, Achamoth, etc., so very different from the simple teaching of the original Valentinus.

3. Basilideans. Basilides, an Egyptian like Valentinus, taught at Alexandria during the time of Hadrian (117-138) and was a man of powerful intellect. It is clear that, as in the case of Valentinus, there was an earlier and a later form of Basilidean teaching. Clement of Alexandria and Hippolytus gave the earlier form of the teaching — a form strongly pantheistic and Greek. Irenaeus gave an account of the Basilidean movement as it existed in Gaul fifty years later when it had become dualistic.

A distinctive feature of Basilides' own teaching is that the world is continuously evolved from a *pansperma* or germinal "seed of the world" in which originally all things were potentially contained.

> Thus a not-being God made a not-being world of things that were not. From the seed came a triple Sonship, whereof one was light, which flew straight up to the not-being God, whom all things desire. A second was gross, and flew up too, taking the Holy Spirit as wings. The third Sonship (Divine element) needed purification, and remained in the seed. From this seed came forth the Great Archon, in power and beauty inexpressible. Then from the seed arose another Archon, less than the first but inexpressible too. These two Archons subserve the designs of the Supreme. The highest light descends through the successive spheres till it rests on Jesus of Nazareth. The process is complete when the Divine element (Sonship) is finally drawn out from the material and restored to God. Oblivion then falls on lower intelligence — the great mass of mankind (Gwatkin, II, 52f.).

All this is typical of the varieties with which the Gnostics built up their religious philosophy.

4. Saturninians. The Gnostic leader Saturninus flourished in Syria about the same time as Basilides in Alexandria. He was a disciple of Menander, who in turn is said to have been a disciple of SIMON MAGUS. His views were similar to those of Cerinthus with the mythology much more developed. He was not chiliastic like Cerinthus, but was strongly dualistic and a gloomy ascetic. For him the God of the Jews was only an angel, and the Savior had only the appearance of a body. He condemned marriage as a base adultery and abstained from animal food. The Assyrian church father, Tatian, became a member of this Gnostic sect and exercised very great influence in the Middle East, teaching the usual theory of aeons and the demiurge.

5. Marcionites. Marcion was a native of Pontus, where he was a prosperous shipmaster. He taught in Rome A.D. 140-155. He distinguished absolutely between the God of the OT, who was regarded as merely great, harsh, and rigorous, and the good God of the NT, who was wholly love. He also held to the usual Gnostic Docetism and dualism. He drew up a canon of Scripture that contained only one Gospel (Luke in a mutilated form) and ten Epistles of Paul. He cut out of the Gospel of Luke everything that connected Christ with nature and history. He was a rigorous ascetic, refusing baptism to married persons and using water, not wine, in the Lord's Supper. He was, perhaps, a greater danger to the Church than any of the other Gnostics (cf. P. Schaff, *History of the Christian Church* [1910], II, 482f.).

D. Relation to the OT. All the Gnostics regarded the OT and NT as revelations of two different deities. They looked upon the God of the Jews as far inferior to the Supreme Being, called by them the Abyss. The God of the OT was the creator of the world, often referred to as the demiurge. Some sects regarded him as being altogether alien from and opposed to the supreme God; others considered him merely as a subordinate power, inferior but not hostile to the supreme God and acting as His unconscious organ (cf. Mansel, p. 45).

E. Influence on Theology. The rise of Gnosticism compelled Christian thinkers to face up to and think out the problems of theology. This led to the rise of systematic theology and the anti-Gnostic works of the ancient catholic fathers (of Irenaeus, *Adv. Haer.*, Tertullian, *Adv. Marc.*, Hippolytus, *Ref.*, in particular). Gnosticism also gave a powerful impetus to the formation of a NT canon of Scripture, for the Gnostics claimed to have authoritative gospels and epistles of their own and it was necessary for the Church to distinguish between spurious and genuine Scriptures.

IX. Modern Gnosticism.–The ancient form of Gnosticism passed away completely in the 5th cent., but its spirit has reappeared from time to time in modern days. Gnosticism, as already seen, is not one aspect of thought alone, but many, and it surfaced again and again in one form or another. The denial of Jesus' Virgin Birth, e.g., is related to that form of Gnosticism that taught that the man Jesus became the divine Christ only at His baptism, when the Holy Spirit descended upon Him from heaven.

Aspects of Gnostic teaching are reproduced in modern pantheistic philosophies, and in forms of religious doctrine that deny an objective atonement.

It is easily seen how teaching of this sort strikes at the root of all religion and morality. The personality of God, the personality and free will of human beings, the existence of moral evil, the incarnation of Our Lord Jesus Christ, the redemption He accomplished for the world, His resurrection, the whole significance of His person and His work — all this is denied. This is the spirit of Gnosticism.

Bibliography.–F. C. Burkitt, *Church and Gnosis* (1932); E. de Faye, *Gnostiques et Gnosticisme* (1925); J. Doresse, *Secret Books of the Egyptian Gnostics* (Eng. tr. 1960); R. M. Grant, *Gnosticism and Early Christianity,* (2nd ed. 1966); H. M. Gwatkin, *Early Church History* (2nd ed. 1909), II; H. Jonas, *Gnostic Religion* (2nd ed. 1963); R. Law, *Tests of Life* (repr. 1978); H. L. Mansel, *Gnostic Heresies of the First and Second Centuries* (1875); G. R. S. Mead, *Pistis sophia* (1896); G. Murray, *Five Stages of Greek Religion* (1925); *New Catholic Encyclopedia* (1967), VI, *s.v.* "Gnosis, Christian," "Gnosticism" (G. W. MacRae); J. Orr, *Early Church* (2nd ed. 1903); *Neglected Factors in the Study of the Early Progress of Christianity* (1899); *Progress of Dogma* (1897); *TDNT,* I, *s.v.* γινώσκω κτλ.: γινώσκω, γνῶσις, ἐπιγινώσκω, ἐπίγνωσις (Bultmann); K. W. Tröger, *Gnosis und NT* (1973); A. von Harnack, *Marcion das Evangelium von fremden Gott* (2nd ed. 1924, 1960); R. M. Wilson, *Gnostic Problem* (1964); R. S. Wilson, *Marcion* (1933); E. Yamauchi, *Pre-Christian Gnosticism* (1973).

A. M. RENWICK

GO. "Go" ("went," etc.) occurs very frequently in Scripture and is the translation of a great many different Hebrew and Greek words. Since the word implies *movement* of all kinds, physical and mental, it has many applications.

I. In the OT.–In the OT Heb. *hālaḵ* is among the commonest words, meaning to "go" in its original sense of "walk" but also in the most varied senses — according to the verbal conjugation, the preposition attached, the context, etc. *Hālak* is often used figuratively (translated "walk," etc.) for "live" in the sense of pursuing a way of life, e.g., "walking ever in his ways" (NEB "conforming," Dt. 19:9; cf. Ps. 15:2; 89:30 [MT 31]; 1 K. 2:3f.; 3:3; etc.), and for "die," e.g., "He departed [lit. "went"] with no one's regret" (2 Ch. 21:20). *Bô'*, properly "go/come in, enter" (e.g., Gen. 7:9), is very common, and *yāṣā'*, "go/come out, exit," also occurs frequently, often with the meaning "go forth," e.g., Gen. 8:18, "So Noah went forth" (NEB "came out"). Other frequent words are *yāraḏ*, "go down" (Gen. 11:7; etc.); *ʿālâ*, "go up, come up" (NEB "used to rise," Gen. 2:6, etc.; Isa. 15:5, "go it up," AV), used also figuratively for "rise up, surpass" (e.g., Prov. 31:29, AV, NEB, "excel"), "come into mind, be remembered," (Isa. 65:17, NEB "be called to mind"; Jer. 3:16, NEB "think"; etc.); *ʿāḇar*, "go" or "pass over," "cross" (AV "get over," Dt. 2:13, etc.), also used figuratively for "fall into disuse" (e.g., Est. 9:28; AV "fail"), etc; *šûḇ*, "go again" (NEB "go back," Gen. 43:2, etc.); *nāsaʿ*, "move, go forward, set out" (Ex. 14:15, NEB "strike camp," 19; Nu. 2:24, NEB "march"; etc.); Aram. *ʾᵃzal*, "go" (Ezr. 4:23, AV "went up," NEB omits; Dnl. 2:17; etc.). Many other Hebrew words occur once or twice, e.g., *ʾāraḥ*, "go" (NEB "chooses to share," Job 34:8); *ʾāšar*, "walk" (AV "go," NEB "follow," Prov. 4:14; 9:6, AV "go," NEB "grow"); *dāraḵ*, "go" (NEB "walk," Isa. 59:8); *dāḏâ*, "led in procession" (Ps. 42:4 [MT 5], AV "went," NEB "the great"); *rāgal*, "taught to walk" (AV "taught to go," Hos. 11:3).

The AV uses two obsolete expressions in the OT: "go to" (derived from Tyndale) is the translation of *yāhaḇ* (BDB, p. 396; KoB, *CHAL, s.v. hab*; cf. Aram. *yᵉhaḇ*), "give," in Gen. 11:3f., 7; 38:16; but "come on" in Ex. 1:10; of *hālak* in 2 K. 5:5, and of the particle *nā'* in Jgs. 7:3; Isa. 5:5; Jer. 18:11 (omitted in RSV; NEB "go"). "Go aside" translates *śāṭâ* (NEB "go astray") in Nu. 5:12 (RSV "go astray"), 19f. (RSV "turn aside"), 29 (RSV "go astray"), and *sûr* in Dt. 28:14 (RSV "turn aside," NEB "turn neither to the right nor to the left").

II. In the NT.–In the NT, Gk. *anabaínō*, "go up," occurs in Mt. 3:16; 5:1; etc.; *érchomai*, "go on," in Mt. 12:9, etc.; *apérchomai*, "go off or away," in Mt. 2:22, etc.; *poreúomai*, "go, travel," in Mt. 2:8, 20, etc. (also used figuratively for "live" in the same sense as Heb. *hālaḵ* [see above] in 1 Pet. 4:3, etc.; *hypágō*, "go away," in Mt. 5:41; 8:32; etc.). Other combinations have different shades of meaning, e.g., *eisérchomai*, "go into," in Mt. 15:11, etc.; *proporeúomai*, "go before," in Lk. 1:76; Acts 7:40. *Ágō* (*ágōmen*) is rendered "let us go" in Mt. 26:46; Jn. 14:31; etc. "Go on" renders *phérō* in He. 6:1, while "go down" renders *epidýō*, "sink," in Eph. 4:26.

The AV uses "go" in several obsolete expressions in the NT: "go to" for *áge* in Jas. 4:13; 5:1 (RSV "come"); "go about" for *zētéō*, "seek" in Jn. 7:19, for *peirázo*, "try, attempt," in Acts 24:6, for *peiráomai* (RSV "try") in 26:21, and for *epicheiréō* (RSV "seek") in 9:29; "go beyond" for *hyperbaínō*, "transgress," in 1 Thess. 4:6.

Bibliography.–*TDNT*, I, *s.v.* βαίνω κτλ. (Schneider); II, *s.v.* ἔρχομαι κτλ. (Schneider); *TDOT*, II, *s.v.* "bô'" (Preuss); III, *s.v.* "halakh" (Helfmeyer).

W. L. WALKER

GOAD [Heb. *dorḇān*] (1 S. 13:21); [*dorḇōnôṯ*] (Eccl. 12:11); [Gk. *kéntron*] (Acts 26:14); AV PRICK; **OXGOAD** [Heb. *malmāḏ*–'learn'] (Jgs. 3:31). The goad used by the Syrian farmer is usually a straight branch of oak or other strong wood from which the bark has been stripped, and which has at one end a pointed spike and at the other a flat, chisel-shaped iron. The pointed end is to prod the oxen while plowing. The flattened iron at the other end is to scrape off the earth which clogs the plowshare. The ancient goad was probably similar to this instrument. It could do villainous work in the hands of an experienced fighter (Jgs. 3:31). If 1 S. 13:21 is correctly translated (cf. RSV, NEB mgs.), the goads were sharpened by files.

The term is used figuratively in Eccl. 12:11: "The sayings of the wise are like goads," meaning that they were as effective as goads. The only reference to goads in the NT is the familiar passage, "It hurts you to kick against the goads" (Acts 26:14). It was as useless for Saul to persist in the wrong way as for a fractious ox to attempt to leave the furrow. He would surely be brought back with a prick of the goad.

J. A. PATCH

GOAH gō'ə [Heb. **gōʿâ*–'lowing']; AV, NEB, GOATH gō'ath. (The RSV form is based on the standard analysis of Heb. *gōʿāṯâ*, a base form *gōʿâ* plus the directive *â* suffix, which preserves the original feminine ending *t* [cf. W. Gesenius, E. Kautzsch, A. Cowley, *Hebrew Grammar* (1910), § 90i]. This is the original form reflected in the AV, NEB "Goath.") Part of the restored city of Jerusalem envisaged in Jer. 31:39 and mentioned with the hill of GAREB, extending possibly to the south of the latter and eastward toward the Tyropoeon Valley.

GOAL (Phil. 3:14). *See* GAMES.

GOAT.

I. Terms.–The common generic word for "goat" is Heb. *ʿēz* (cf. Arab. *ʿanz*, "she-goat"; Gk. *aíx*), sometimes used for "she-goat" (Gen. 15:9; 30:35; etc.), also with Heb. *gᵉḏî*, "kid," as *gᵉḏî ʿizzîm*, "kid from the flock" (Gen. 38:17), with *śāʿîr*, "he-goat," as *śᵉʿîr ʿizzîm*, "kid from the flock" or "he-goat," or translated simply "goats," as in 1 K. 20:27, "The people of Israel encamped before them like two little flocks of goats." Next frequently used is Heb. *śāʿîr*, literally "hairy" (cf. Arab. *shaʿr*, "hair"; Gk. *chḗr*, "hedgehog"; Lat. *hircus*, "goat"; *hirtus*, "hairy"; also Ger. *Haar*; Eng. "hair"), like *ʿēz* and *ʿattûḏ* used of goats for offerings. The goat which is sent into the wilderness bearing the sins of the people is *śāʿîr* (Lev. 16:7-22). (*See also* AZAZEL.) Cf. also *śᵉʿîraṯ ʿizzîm*, "a female from the flock" (Lev. 5:6). The male or leader of the flock is *ʿattûḏ*; Arab. *ʿatûd*, "yearling he-goat"; figuratively "leaders" (Isa. 14:9; cf. Jer. 50:8). A later word for "he-goat," used also figuratively, is Heb. *ṣāpîr* (2 Ch. 29:21; Ezr. 8:35; Dnl. 8:5, 8, 21). In Prov. 30:31, one of the four things "which are stately in their stride" is the he-goat, *tayiš* (Arab. *tais*, "he-goat"), also mentioned in Gen. 30:35; 32:14 among the possessions of Laban and Jacob, and in 2 Ch. 17:11 among the animals given as tribute by the Arabians to Jehoshaphat. In He. 9:12f., 19; 10:4, we have *trágos*, the ordinary Greek word for "goat"; in Mt. 25:32f., *ériphos*, and its diminutive *eríphion*; in He. 11:37 *dérma aígeion*, "goatskin," from *aíx* (see above). "Kid" is Heb. *gᵉḏî* (cf. En-gedi [1 S. 23:29], etc.), fem. *gᵉḏîyâ* (Cant. 1:8), but also *ʿēz*, *gᵉḏî ʿizzîm*, *śᵉʿîr ʿizzîm*, *śᵉʿîraṯ ʿizzîm*, *bᵉnê ʿizzîm*, and Gk. *ériphos*. There remain Heb. *yāʿēl* (1 S. 24:2, RSV, NEB "wild goat"; Job 39:1, RSV, NEB "mountain goats"; Ps. 104:18, RSV "wild goats"; NEB "mountain-goat"); *ʾaqqô* (Dt. 14:5); and *zemer* (Dt. 14:5, RSV "mountain sheep"; NEB "rock-goat"). Heb. *yaʿᵃlâ* (Prov. 5:19) is more likely a (female) mountain goat (KoB, p. 389; BDB, p. 418).

II. Origin.–The goat is a hollow-horned ruminant that is lighter and more agile than the sheep. Perhaps the original species from which the Neolithic herds of Mesopotamian domesticated goats came was the Persian wild goat (*Capra aegagrus*), which can still be found in some upland areas of the Near East and the Aegean, as well as in southern Europe.

III. Domestic Goats.–Domestic goats differ greatly among themselves in the color and length of their hair, in the size and shape of their ears, and in the size and shape of their horns, which are usually larger in the males, but in some breeds may be absent in both sexes. A very constant feature in both wild and domestic goats is the bearded chin of the male. The goats of Palestine and Syria are usually black (Cant. 4:1), though sometimes partly or entirely white or brown. Their hair is usually long, hanging down from their bodies. The horns are commonly curved outward and backward, but in one very handsome breed they extend nearly outward with slight but graceful curves, sometimes attaining a span of 60 cm. (2 ft.) or more in the old males. The profile of the face is distinctly convex. They are herded in the largest numbers in the mountainous or hilly districts, and vie with their wild congeners in climbing into apparently inaccessible places. They feed not only on herbs, but also on shrubs and small trees, to which they are most destructive. They reach up the trees to the height of a man, holding themselves nearly or quite erect, and even walk out on low branches.

IV. Economy.–Their flesh is valuable for food and available when neither mutton nor beef can be found. Their milk is drunk or made into cheese and *semn,* a sort of clarified butter much used in cooking. Their hair is woven into tents, carpets, cloaks, sacks, slings, and various camel, horse, and mule trappings. Their skins are made into bottles (Heb. *nōʾḏ*; Gk. *askós*; Arab. *qirbeh*) for water, oil, *semn,* and other liquids (cf. also He. 11:37). According to 2 Ch. 17:11, Jehoshaphat received a gift of 7700 he-goats. From Ezk. 27:21 it appears that Tyre traded with Arabia in sheep and goats.

V. Religious and Figurative.–Just as the kid was often slaughtered for an honored guest (Jgs. 6:19; 13:19), so the kid or goat was frequently taken for sacrifice (Lev. 4:23; 9:15; 16:7; Nu. 15:24; Ezr. 8:35; Ezk. 45:23; He. 9:12). A goat was one of the clean animals (*śēh ʿizzîm,* Dt. 14:4). In Daniel, the powerful king out of the West is typified as a goat with a single horn (8:5). One of the older goats is the leader of the flock, reflecting the ancient custom whereby some male goats were trained to be leaders of the flock. Human leaders were typified as such in Isa. 14:9; Jer. 50:8; Ezk. 34:17, 23; and Zec. 10:3.

The scene of final judgment depicted in Mt. 25:32 represented the righteous and wicked in terms of sheep and goats (cf. Ezk. 34:17-22). While it is not unusual for sheep and goats to graze together on mountainsides, they are normally herded into separate folds. A. E. DAY

R. K. H.

Goats at Khirbet el-Kerak SE of the Dead Sea (D. Baly)

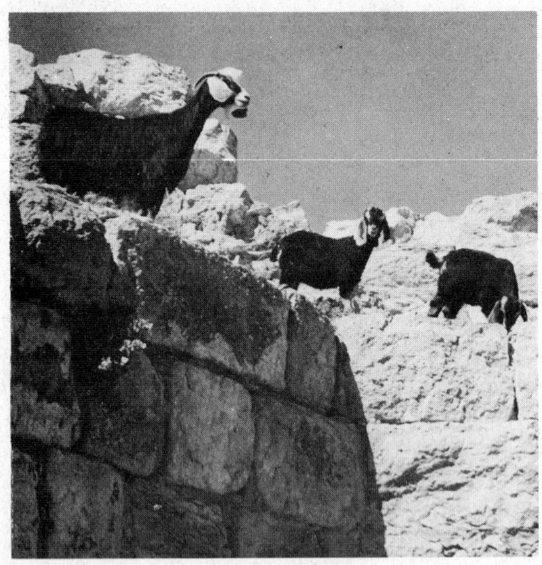

GOATH (Jer. 31:39, AV). *See* GOAH.

GOATS' HAIR. The word for goat (Heb. *ʿēz*) is used elliptically to mean goats' hair, which was used in the tabernacle furnishings in the form of curtains (Ex. 26:7; 36:14). Spun goats' hair was probably used in the Midianite and Israelite camps in making tent ropes, rugs, provision sacks, and saddlebags (cf. Nu. 31:20). A strip of the cloth rolled up furnished a bolster for the head while sleeping (cf. 1 S. 19:13, 16). Goats' hair cloth is admirably suited to stand the hard usage of a frequently shifting encampment. The Israelites appreciated its utility, even for the tabernacle, where according to most modern standards it would have been out of place, matched against scarlet and fine linen (Ex. 25:4; 35:6, 26).

See also HAIR; WEAVING. J. A. PATCH

GOATSKINS [Heb. *taḥaš, ʿôr taḥaš*] (Ex. 25:5; 26:14; 35:7, 23; 36:19; 39:34; Nu. 4:6, 8, 10-12, 14, 25); AV BADGERS' SKINS; NEB PORPOISE-HIDE, mg. "hide of sea-cow"; [Gk. *aígeion dérma*] (He. 11:37).

Taḥaš seems to designate some sort of animal whose skin was used as a covering for the tabernacle, ark of the covenant, and other sacred objects. The LXX understood *taḥaš* to be referring to the color of the skins. Scholars today agree that it refers to an animal, but they do not agree as to which animal. Both "badger" (AV) and "goat" (RSV) lack philological grounds. Arab. *tuḥas,* "dolphin" or "dugong," has been suggested as a cognate, and marine animals such as the dugong have been found in the Red Sea; thus the NEB rendering is possibly correct. But the only other occurrence of *taḥaš* refers to footwear, for which leather was the common material (Ezk. 16:10). *See also* LEATHER.

Goatskins are referred to only once in the NT (He. 11:37), where the wearing of goatskins indicates extreme poverty. Ascetics of various sects in Syria and Palestine, especially of Moslem sects, have frequently worn sheepskins or goatskins as a sign of their renunciation of all worldly things. N. J. O.

GOB [Heb. *gōḇ, gôḇ*–'pit' or 'cistern']. The scene of two of David's battles with the Philistines (2 S. 21:18f.). The parallel account in 1 Ch. 20:4f. identifies the place as Gezer, a fortified city with a long history, located 29 km. (18 mi.) NW of Jerusalem in the Shephelah, overlooking the coastal plain.

GOBLET [Heb. *k^{e}lî*] (Est. 1:7); AV VESSEL; NEB CUP. *K^{e}lî* is a very general term which can be used of various sorts of containers and other implements. At the seven-day banquet of Ahasuerus drink was served in golden vessels of different kinds. The quality and variety of these goblets indicated the great wealth of the king.

Gold drinking vessel (*rhyton*) reputedly from Ecbatana (Hamadân), 5th cent. B.C. (Metropolitan Museum of Art, Harris Brisbane Dick Fund, 1954)

"Nestor's cup," found in a Mycenaean grave circle, so called because it resembles the huge goblet described in the *Iliad*. It was hammered from a single sheet of gold and has a bird on each handle at the rim (National Archaeological Museum, Athens)

GOD [Heb. *ʾĕlōhîm, ʾēl ʿelyôn, ʾēl šaddāy, YHWH*; Gk. *theós*].

- I. Introduction
  - A. Description
    1. General
    2. Specific
  - B. Knowledge of God
    1. In Natural Theology
    2. In Biblical Theology
  - C. Human Concepts of God
  - D. Self-Revelation of God
- II. God in the OT
  - A. Forms of Manifestation
  - B. Names of God
    1. General
    2. Qualifying
    3. Personal
  - C. God in the Preprophetic Period
    1. God of Israel
    2. Israel's Response
    3. Biblical Witness
  - D. God in the Prophetic Period
    1. Righteousness
    2. Holiness
    3. Lordship
    4. Unity
    5. Faithfulness
    6. Salvation Through Suffering
    7. Messiah
- III. God in the NT
  - A. Relation to the OT
  - B. God as Father
  - C. God as King
  - D. God as Love
  - E. Christ as God
  - F. Spirit of God

***I. Introduction.**–A. Description.* Descriptions of God are as varied as the religious ideas and experiences of mankind. In principle, however, they may be divided into two classes. On the one hand are those which rest on human apprehension, on the other those which derive from the divine self-revelation. This does not mean that there is not a mediating group. Many descriptions, however inadequate or distorted, may finally spring from the primitive revelation of God whereby His "eternal power and deity" may be understood from the things which are made (Rom. 1:20). Again, many descriptions which derive from the specific self-revelation of God may incorporate elements that come from other sources. Nevertheless, a distinction is still to be made in principle between general religious or philosophical descriptions on the one side and biblical or theological descriptions on the other.

1. General. E. Caird, in his *Evolution of Religion* (3rd ed. 1899), I, 40, 64, offered a very general suggestion that God is "the unity which is pre-supposed in the difference of the self and not-self." H. Spencer (*First Principles*, V [1862], 31) took an equally abstract but more pessimistically agnostic line when he described God as "an inscrutable power manifested in and through all phenomena." (This is, incidentally, a strong confirmation of Paul's argument in Rom. 1:20, which condemns mankind for failing to see the things of God which are clearly manifested in creation.) Equally general descriptions, but with a little more content, are those of M. Arnold ("a power not ourselves making for righteousness"), E. B. Tylor ("spiritual beings"), A. Menzies ("a higher power"), Lotze ("a supersensible being or beings"), H. N. Wieman ("that character of events to which man must adjust himself in order to attain the greatest good and avoid the greatest ills"), and W. Adams Brown ("an unseen being, real or supposed, to whom an individual or a social group is united by voluntary ties of reverence or service," *Christian Theology in Outline* [1906], p. 30). In terms of experience rather than thought, a popular attempt has been made more recently to describe God in terms of the awe or reverence evoked by the sense of the unknown. God is the numinous element, the *mysterium tremendum* (R. Otto, *Idea of the Holy* [Eng. tr., 2nd ed. 1958]), which is not strictly definable, but which is sensed by all men, whether it be by the religious man in his worship, the poet in his awareness and expression of beauty, or the scientist impressed by the grandeur and complexity of the cosmos. Tillich's "ground of being" (*Systematic Theology,* I [1951], 235, 238) perpetuates the line of metaphysical definition; it is hard to see why something so commonplace should still find enthusiastic adherents, unless it be that human nature will always snatch at the offerings of natural theology.

Apart from their vagueness, such descriptions bear three obvious defects. First, they assume that there is a general category "God" or the "divine" of which the God of the Bible is an example, or perhaps the only example, and in terms of which He then has to be described. Second, they have no specific reference. Dealing with a generalized abstraction, they are themselves abstract. Third, they are thus reduced to the position that either they will have no content or they will take such content as they have from human ideas or experiences, not from God Himself. Thus, they are fundamentally anthropocentric in either the negative or the positive sense. Strictly, they are not descriptions of God at all; they are descriptions of what mankind thinks or senses the divine to be.

2. Specific. In sharp contrast are the specific theological descriptions which take their content from divine self-revelation. It is true that some of these, e.g., in the mediating theology of the 19th cent., are little more than general descriptions. Thus Schleiermacher, in the first edition of the *Speeches* (1799), was even prepared to substitute the term *Universum* for God (anticipating Tillich). Thomasius interjected a little more content with his description of God as the "absolute personality." Others went even further. W. N. Clarke (*Outline of Christian Theology* [1898], p. 66) called God "the personal Spirit, who in holy love creates, sustains and orders all." It is in the great doctrinal statements and credal definitions, however, that the most specific and pregnant descriptions of God are to be found. Melanchthon defined God as "a spiritual essence, intelligent, eternal, true, good, pure, just, merciful, most free, and of infinite power and wisdom." In the Thirty-nine Articles (Art. I) God is "the one living and true God, everlasting, without body, parts, or passions; of infinite power, wisdom, and goodness; the Maker and Preserver of all things both visible and invisible. And in unity of this Godhead there be three persons, of one substance, power, and eternity; the Father, the Son, and the Holy Ghost." The Westminster Confession is similar and even fuller (Art. II): "There is but one only living and true God, who is infinite in being, a most pure spirit, invisible, without body, parts, or passions; immutable, immense, eternal, incomprehensible, almighty, most wise, most holy, most free, most absolute; . . . most loving, gracious, merciful, longsuffering, abundant in goodness and truth, forgiving iniquity, transgression, and sin. . . . God hath all life, glory, goodness, blessedness, in and of Himself. . . . In the unity of the Godhead there be three persons, of one substance, power, and eternity." Descriptions of this kind could easily be multiplied, not only from Reformation and post-Reformation confessions and theologies, but also from patristic, medieval, and Roman Catholic writers.

The chief characteristics of these specific descriptions are as follows. They have no general category of God or the divine which must be described first in broad and comprehensive terms; they have from the very outset a specific reference. They are thus descriptive rather than speculative or abstract. They are theocentric, not anthropocentric; objective, not subjective. From the standpoint of a general definition it might be objected that they are simply defining the biblical view of God, not God. But this is the whole point. They deny that there is an abstract category of the divine. They deny that the biblical presentation is simply the biblical view of God. They claim that God is self-revealed in Scripture and that thus the definitions are not of a "divine," which may take different forms according to different human developments, but of God as He is. They take their content not from general ideas or experiences or aspirations, but from the data of God's self-revelation. Thus they are not definitions of human ideas of God, or of abstractions of God. They are in the strict sense descriptions of God Himself.

B. Knowledge of God. To be able to speak of such a definition it is essential that God be known. But a problem arises here, for God is obviously not in Himself an object of ordinary perception in the way that creation is. "No one has ever seen God" (Jn. 1:18) is not merely a statement of fact. It points to an intrinsic characteristic of God, namely, that in Himself He cannot be seen. He is no doubt an object to Himself but He is not an object to us. All genuine human knowledge, however, is by way of objectivity. It may thus be asked whether there can be any knowledge of God at all, and, if so, whether it will be a knowledge that is so clear and sure that specific definitions can be based on it.

Just as there are general and specific definitions of God, so there are general and specific approaches to the knowledge of God. One approach is that of natural theology and another that of theology based on revelation. To be sure, the distinction is not always clear cut. Much natural theology may be a confused development of the natural revelation to which Paul refers in Rom. 1:20. Again, much theology which is based on revelation makes use of elements taken from natural theology and in varying degrees and proportions and combinations works them into its theological presentation, perhaps as a preamble or supporting argument, perhaps even as a basic constituent. There is nonetheless a plain distinction in principle between the two approaches.

1. In Natural Theology. Natural theology assumes that in some way man can know God of and by himself. One may simply build on one's sense of the numinous; one may face the riddle of the universe and presume that there must be a transcendent cause. One may be conscious that there are powers, not merely of matter but of will and intelligence, beyond oneself and the cosmos. One may see evidences in life or history of a higher ordination or teleology. One may be impressed by the almost universal conviction that there is a divine being or beings. One may appeal to the religious instinct of mankind, the impulse to worship. One may be moved by the existence of an ethical sense, of awareness of an imperative for which there is no apparent basis in human or cosmic reality as such. One may tackle the question philosophically and argue that cosmological, ontological, or teleological considerations demand the existence of God as a first cause, a necessary postulate, or a final telos. One may advance elaborate arguments such as Aquinas's "five ways" or Descartes' ontological argument. In all these ways an idea or experience of God may be evolved which, even though it cannot claim the factuality of empirical knowledge, is not to be dismissed as mere imagination. The God thus postulated or experienced may then be endowed with various attributes, whether by extension of these discerned in the universe or mankind, or by abstraction from them, or by the *via negativa* of their opposites. If a conflict arises, as it will, between the results of such activity, the highest concept may then be selected as at least the nearest approximation to the God in whom one should believe and whose direction one should obey. In "pure" natural theology the Jewish and Christian views of God will be taken into account along with others. In a mixture of natural and revealed theology a jump will be made at some point from the highest concept of mankind to the God of revelation.

The characteristics of the knowledge of God by way of natural theology are plain to see. It is an anthropocentric knowledge, moving from mankind upward to God. It is a comparative and evolving, or at least changing, knowledge, for different people and groups reach different conclusions, and these conclusions are always open to revision as insights are gained or ideas are found to be groundless. It is an uncertain knowledge, for it has a shifting basis, its data are ultimately subjective, its arguments are all vulnerable, and even its best conclusions are far from adequate. Were it not that natural theology has some remote basis in natural revelation, in the original disclosure of God in nature and conscience, one might even pass the harsh judgment that it can lead only to illusion and confusion, to human ideas about God and not in any sense whatever to God Himself. Certainly, it does lead only to human concepts, though these may contain genuine elements of truth. For this is knowledge with neither the true subject nor the true object. It is knowledge of the Creator in which mankind is the subject and mankind, or the cosmos, the object. God Himself, who ought to be both subject and object, is given a place only as the final deduction. Thus the only truly scientific study that can result from natural theology is comparative religion, i.e., the study of religious ideas, beliefs, and practices. Natural theology has necessarily carried with it the replacement of exegetical and dogmatic theology and is finally the enemy of theology in its strict sense, namely, the study of God.

2. In Biblical Theology. Theology grounded in revelation forms a sharp contrast. It admits from the very outset that it can know God only from and by God. Since mankind is not God, it is not possible to proceed from mankind to God. Since nature is not God, it is not possible to proceed from nature to God. No doubt both these processes were possible before the fall, for then God Himself not only revealed Himself but was truly discerned internally in conscience and externally in nature. But we live after the fall. The invisible things of God are still revealed in the things that are seen, but they are not perceived because man is now vain in his imaginations and his foolish heart is darkened (Eph. 4:18). Left to himself, he now worships and serves the creature rather than the Creator (Rom. 1:20-25). He makes conscience and nature the object of his study and himself the subject, so that it is no longer God who is here speaking to him about Himself. If one is to know not a postulate of God but God Himself, one must learn from a new act in which God is both subject and object. Revelational theology begins with the claim that this act has taken place. It derives its knowledge of God from this divine self-manifestation. *God Himself* makes Himself known. He is the true subject of the act. He teaches what mankind can no longer find out for itself. But God makes *Himself* known. He is also the object of the act. He becomes an object of human knowledge, so that man can have a reference outside himself, so that he can have controlling external data and not just variable internal ideas, experiences, or arguments. This objectification of God involves historical acts which culminate in the incarnation of the Son, so that God's works may be the object of empirical study and even God Himself may be seen, heard, and handled in a historical person and a historical life. It also involves the written documentation of these acts of God, i.e., the records of Scripture, which are given in order that the objective revelation may still be there for those who live in other times and places. It is to be noted, however, that although the revelation takes the form of words, deeds, and records, these data do not merely add to our stock of historical, literary, or religious knowledge. They are data of revelation; God Himself is here the subject and the object of knowledge. The knowledge that may be acquired is truly knowledge of God; God Himself in His self-revelation is its basis.

This knowledge does not begin with mankind — its insights, experiences, emotions, needs, or genius; it begins with God. It is theocentric, not anthropocentric. The data are just as objective for mankind as are the data of natural science or history. The results are not comparative except insofar as there is variation in the exposition of the data. Just as the exact description of, e.g., a tree cannot be compared with abstract subjective conceptions of what a tree might be, so the exact description of God should not be relativized by abstract conceptions of what God might be. The knowledge also has solidity. It is based on the object itself, which provides an unchanging foundation. People may have varying ideas, needs, and experiences in their search for the divine. But here they all come under the constraint of the one object, God Himself. If it be argued that we cannot know that this is a real object, there is, of course, no answer to the absolute skepticism that destroys all knowledge, and in so doing destroys itself. Knowledge of every kind involves a measure of trust, even if it is only the trust that phenomena really are as they appear to be. The knowledge of God also demands trust. It demands commitment to the data presented. Either we learn from God, or we cannot know at all. There can be no knowledge of a nonexistent object. If we are prepared to learn from God, however, we can be quickly satisfied that it is in fact God who teaches us about Himself. And the truth learned rests neither on our perception nor indeed on our choice. It rests on the reality of the God who teaches us, on the data of self-revelation from which we learn.

C. Human Concepts of God. A brief enumeration of the most important human concepts of God may emphasize the biblical witness to the divine self-revelation. The fuller study of these concepts, both in general and in detail, is the proper business of comparative religion or the philosophy of religion, not of theology in the strict sense.

(1) Animism is relatively one of the lowest forms of human belief. It assumes the presence of spiritual beings or disembodied spirits which affect human life for good or ill and which are to be revered or placated. Some attempts have been made to construct an evolutionary ladder of religion with animism as one of the lowest rungs, but this is historically debatable.

(2) Fetishism has been defined as the view that the fruits of the earth, and phenomena in general, are divine, or are animated by powerful spirits (J. G. Frazer, *Adonis, Attis, Osiris* [3rd ed. 1961], p. 234). More specifically, it is the belief that spirits "take up their abode, either temporarily or permanently, in some object... then worshipped" (C. P. Tiele, *Outlines of the History of Religion,* p. 9).

(3) Idolatry occurs when a natural or artistically fashioned object is regarded as the habitation of deity, the artistic workmanship being designed to make it a more adequate representation of the god. The object itself is not strictly the god; it is the abode of the god. Nevertheless, the god is thought to bear at least some similarity to the object (cf. Acts 17:29).

(4) Polytheism is the belief in many gods. It may go

hand in hand with (1), (2), or (3), or it may be independent of them. It involves the worship of many more or less well-defined deities associated with natural objects (e.g., planets or mountains) or people (heroes/heroines), or regarded as pure spirits, and usually symbolized in images which express something of their character. It is clearly understood, e.g., in India or Greece, that the images are not the gods, which dwell in a higher sphere.

(5) Henotheism is a tendency to set one god above the rest, e.g., Zeus in Greece, and perhaps even to confine worship to this one god. Henotheistic or monolatrous tendencies may be perceived in Babylonia, Egypt, India, and China as well as in Greece. This may be due to varied causes such as rational reflection, ethical or personal considerations, sociological or political demands. It may even be due to the surviving influence of an original monotheism, for the idea that monotheism is a higher stage in upward development is not very firmly supported by the evidence.

(6) Pantheism means that the one god is so supreme that he absorbs all the others, who are simply forms of his manifestation; cf. the Indian Brahma. Indeed, this one god absorbs the universe as well, so that the deity is the totality of things (God is all) and the totality of things is the deity (all is God). Pantheism can easily embrace other forms of belief, for if the deity is all things, then he can be worshiped in all things. It can also be adapted to such diverse philosophies as idealism or materialism. In pure materialism, e.g., the cosmos itself may easily be regarded as the eternal and self-existent deity, and an element of immanent teleological direction may be ascribed to it.

(7) Deism restores the element of transcendence. It is belief in a single transcendent being who is the author of the universe but who is so high above that he has no living relation to it. Incipient deistic tendencies may be seen, e.g., in the Greek concept of necessity; but deism came into its own in the horologically inclined 18th cent., which depicted God as the clockmaker who has created and wound up a perfect clock and who now leaves it to tick away happily and irresistibly on its own. The deistic God is a remote and impersonal absentee, and may well be defined in such abstract terms as the first cause, the infinite, the supreme power, etc.

(8) Theism is a more personal deism. Borrowing in many cases from the biblical revelation, it postulates a personal and a more specifically moral relation between God and the world. God is the sole God, as in monolatry or pantheism. He is also the transcendent author of all things, as in deism. But He stands in continuing relation to the world, especially to mankind, so that He can be clothed with personal and ethical qualities. God in His self-revelation does in fact give us the basic materials of theism. It should be emphasized, however, that there is a difference between God Himself and a theistic conception of God. A theistic conception is not a preparatory stage on the way to true knowledge of God. If theism is no doubt the highest and comparatively the truest human concept, it is still a human concept. It is not knowledge.

D. Self-Revelation of God. Attention has been drawn already to the original self-revelation of God in nature and conscience. It is to be noted, however, that this does not form the substance of the biblical presentation. The reason is that sin has blinded the eyes and minds and hearts of mankind to this revelation. Due to the fall, it has become unprofitable. In fact, as Paul pointed out, it serves only to leave sinners without excuse. By virtue of this revelation humans might have known God, but in fact they do not. Restoration of this knowledge now requires a different route which allows for the sin and ignorance of mankind. The story of the Bible is the story of this new self-revelation, which is also reconciliation. It is the story of God's revealing and reconciling action for the restoration of mankind to knowledge and fellowship. Four aspects call for brief mention.

(1) It is revelation in historical acts. God enters human history and both reveals Himself and works out His saving purpose there. The record of this historical intervention is to be found in the biblical narrative from Abraham to Jesus and the apostolic mission.

(2) It is revelation in words which accompany and interpret the action. God speaks to people, telling them what He will do, presenting His own character in His action, making clear what He demands of mankind, interpreting His action as it takes place, and leaving a written record for all future generations.

(3) It is revelation through persons, and supremely in and through the person of the incarnate Son. Patriarchs, prophets, kings, priests, and apostles succeed one another as the people of God in and by whom God works and speaks. But finally God Himself enters the human stage to speak and act in person. He who cannot be seen or heard makes Himself the object of human seeing and hearing. The fulness of deity is present bodily (Col. 2:9) to work out reconciliation and to make God known both by teaching and by action and presence.

(4) It is revelation by the Holy Spirit, who guides the chosen instruments of God, who fills the incarnate Son, who inspires the sacred records, and who bears His accompanying witness, so that the inward eyes and ears of people are opened to the God who is here made known, and reconciliation is brought to its objective fulfillment in repentance and faith.

Two points may be emphasized. God Himself has the initiative and superintends the whole process. He is thus the subject of this knowledge. But God also gives Himself concrete embodiment in acts and words and records, and supremely in the incarnate Word. He is thus the object of this knowledge. In His self-revelation God is known as He presents Himself. He presents Himself in such a way that data are given by which He is accessible to us. He is thus known as the data are assessed and expounded. But by the Holy Spirit He Himself still remains the subject even in this exposition, so that what we have is not just true knowledge about God. It is in the ultimate sense knowledge of God.

***II. God in the OT.**–A. Forms of Manifestation.* In the OT various terms are used to indicate the direct action of God in the midst of His people. A certain measure of legitimate anthropomorphism is involved in these terms, but in some cases there can be little doubt that they involve sensual phenomena which indicate the divine presence. The underlying point in each case is that God Himself is present and active in such a way that there may be accompanying knowledge.

(1) Thus we read in many verses of the FACE or countenance (Heb. *pānîm*) of God. The place where He is seen is Peniel (lit. "the face of God," Gen. 32:30). With His face He brings up Israel out of Egypt, and His face goes with them to Canaan (Ex. 33:14, "presence" is lit. "face") and is their blessing (Nu. 6:25f.). Alienation from God is the hiding of (Dt. 31:17), or being hidden from (Gen. 4:14), His face. In these cases face is a metaphorical term for presence.

(2) The voice (Heb. *qôl*) and WORD (*dāḇār*) of God are also media of His action. They may include the direct voice of God, as at the burning bush or at Sinai, or they may be the indirect declaration of His will through the prophets (Isa. 2:1, etc.).

(3) The GLORY of God (Heb. *kāḇôḏ*) is also a phenom-

enon by which the direct presence of God is known. It is like a devouring fire (Ex. 24:17). It fills the tent (Ex. 29:43) and later the temple (cf. Ezk. 10). It is also reflected on the face of Moses (Ex. 34:29; cf. 2 Cor. 3:12-18). The divine glory figures prominently in the visions at the calls of Isaiah and Ezekiel. The glory of God is provoked (Isa. 3:8). In the final sense it fills the whole earth (Isa. 6:3), and this will finally be revealed. Behind the physical manifestation is God Himself, not merely in His transcendent immanence, but in His word and work.

(4) The ANGEL (Heb. *mal'āḵ*) of God or Yahweh is another mode of theophany. In itself the term angel is quite general and might be used for any divine messenger. But in many instances the angel is identified with God Himself in visible and audible form (cf. Gen. 16:7-14; 22:15-18; Ex. 3:2, 4-6), though usually with some degree of differentiation in order to make it clear that God Himself does not have such a form (Gen. 24:40; Ex. 23:20f.). The identity of the angel of the Lord (as distinct from angels in general) has been much discussed, and some scholars have seen here a reference to the Son who was to become incarnate. This is unlikely, however, in view of the role of the angel of the Lord in Lk. 2:9. The angel is the angel of God's presence, and this perhaps helps us to understand better the use of "face" (1) for the divine presence, at least in some instances. *See* ANGEL II.C.

(5) The name (Heb. *šēm*) of God is a common form of manifestation. The name stands for the person and it is also something visible and audible in terms of which He may be revealed and known. God's self-revelation is a proclamation of His name (Ex. 6:3; 33:19; 34:5f.). His servants derive their authority from His name (Ex. 3:13, 15; 1 S. 17:45). To worship God is to call on His name (Gen. 12:8; 13:4; 21:33; 26:25; 1 K. 18:24-26), to fear it (Dt. 28:58), to praise it (2 S. 22:50; Ps. 7:17 [MT 18]; 54:6 [MT 8]), to glorify it (Ps. 86:9). It is wickedness to take it in vain (Ex. 20:7), to profane and blaspheme it (Lev. 24:16). God dwells where He chooses to cause His name to dwell (Dt. 12:11, 21; 2 S. 7:13; 1 K. 3:2; 5:3, 5 [MT 17, 19]; 8:16-19; 18:32). God's name defends His people (Ps. 20:1 [MT 2]; Isa. 30:27). For His name's sake He will not leave them (1 S. 12:22). The point of this emphasis on the name is that God is the specific God who makes Himself known to His people and whose revelation is given concrete expression in the name.

B. Names of God. God bears many names in OT revelation, and since all these names are significant, they are of considerable importance in relation to human knowledge of God. Only a brief survey will be given here; for a fuller account *see* GOD, NAMES OF.

1. General. There are, of course, general names for God, of which the most common is *'elōhîm*. This word can, in fact, be used for other gods (Gen. 31:30) and even for men (cf. Ex. 4:16; 7:1; cf. BDB, p. 43). This does not mean, however, that God is brought under a general category, for the whole point of OT revelation is that Yahweh is *'elōhîm* in the strict sense. That is, *'elōhîm* is finally defined in terms of Yahweh, and all others who bear the name are then brought into relation to Him. The plural form has given rise to much discussion, and various explanations have been advanced, especially an underlying polytheism, a plural of majesty, or even an intimation of the trinity. The derivation is obscure, but the implied sense seems to be that of strength or authority. The singular *'elô(a)h* is found in poetry, mostly in Job. Another general term which occurs some 200 times is *'ēl*. Although not from the same root as *'elōhîm*, this, too, is a general word for God signifying ultimate supremacy.

2. Qualifying. The name *'ēl* in particular is often qualified in order to bring out the distinctive nature and person of God. God is not just *'ēl*, as in the last resort other gods might be. He is *'ēl 'elyôn*, the "Most High," or *'ēl šadday*, "God Almighty," or *'ēl-ro'î*, "a God of seeing" (Gen. 16:13). In addition to these compound forms there are many other qualifying names which bring out particular aspects of God. Thus He is Rock, Strong One, King, Lord, etc. These descriptive names are of great importance. They again make it clear that there is no such thing as God as an abstract concept; God is all these things in particular even though a generic name may often be used. Again, they specifically show that God stands in a personal relationship to mankind. Furthermore, they all indicate that God has the initiative in this relationship. Finally, they are not just poetic attributes; they are all based on actual dealings of God with His people. It is not that mankind has an idea of God and then selects and heaps up suitable epithets. Nor is it that mankind has certain experiences of what he takes to be the divine and then puts these experiences into words. God Himself provides both acts and words. He is this God, whether we experience Him as such or not. He acts and manifests Himself thus. Beside Him there is none else.

3. Personal. In addition to the general names and qualifying names, God also bears a qualifying name that is His OT name par excellence, that characterizes Him as the living God of revelation and reconciliation in a particular way, and that thus comes to have the nature of a proper name. This is the name Yahweh (Jehovah), which consists basically of the consonants *YHWH*, and which is connected in Ex. 3:13-15 with Heb. *hāyâ* ("to be") to give the interpretation "I am that I am," or "I will be that I will be." Several questions arise in connection with this name. The linguistic derivation is undoubtedly obscure. The meaning given in Ex. 3:13-15 can hardly bear the metaphysical sense that has sometimes been read into it, namely, that of self-existence (cf. Aquinas *Summa Theol.* i.2.3), but seems to imply rather the abiding faithfulness of God. Whether the name was already known and used by other groups, e.g., the Kenites, cannot be determined. In any case, its distinctive significance for Israel is undoubtedly given with the theophany at the burning bush. Whether the name was really new to Israel (Ex. 3:13f.; 6:2f.) must also be a matter of conjecture in view of its earlier use in the patriarchal stories. Two possibilities are: (a) that the name had in fact been used but had dropped out during the period in Egypt, or (b) that it was given for the first time with the new step of the divine deliverance from Egypt, and was then quite correctly read back into the earlier stories in order to bring out the continuity of God's saving action through Israel. The alternation of the divine names in the pentateuchal records underlies a good deal of modern source criticism, but the analysis is complicated and there might well be genuine theological reasons for the distinction. The existence of all these questions should not be allowed to divert our attention from the clear implications of the name Yahweh and from its outstanding importance in OT revelation. God is named; this in itself is of the utmost significance. God is not an abstraction; He is the living God. But this Yahweh, who is God, is *'elōhîm*, the God of creation, the Lord of the cosmos. He is not just a tribal deity like the deities of the nations. Yet He is in fact the God of Israel. He is the God who works in history, the God who has chosen this people as both the first object and the agent of His revealing and reconciling action. As the God of this people He is the covenant God, the God of relationship, the God who establishes a relationship of faithfulness and obedience, the God of a mutual relationship of love. The whole of the OT revelation, and the whole of the NT revelation as well, is already implicit in these four simple letters which are so puzzling and yet also so luminous and revealing. To say Yahweh is to say God; to say God is to say Yahweh.

C. God in the Preprophetic Period. The revelation of God in the preprophetic period might very well be regarded as the drawing out of the first implications of the name Yahweh both for the divine actions and for the required but sluggish response of the people. Already in the particular stories, the story of the Exodus, the law, the entry into the Promised Land, and the episodes of Judges, the main aspects of God and His word and work may be clearly discerned.

1. God of Israel. From the days of Abraham God is the one who has particularly chosen this family and people to be associated with Him in His action. He is the God of the patriarchs, who led Abraham from Ur to Canaan, who gave him the temporal and the spiritual promise, and who made Himself known in a particular way to Isaac and Jacob. He is the covenant God of Israel, who constituted Himself its King and Lord, manifested Himself to Moses, gave Israel the promise, delivered it in a mighty act of liberation from Egypt, declared to it the law, instituted its cultic life, brought it into the Promised Land, and there executed His righteous judgments and mercies in its relations to the surrounding peoples. This covenant God is the God of sovereignty, election, faithfulness, righteousness, mercy, and love. He is the God of creation, and He rules over the nations according to His sovereign will and power. Yet His sovereignty is the sovereignty of righteousness, and He demands righteousness from His people.

2. Israel's Response. That all the essential characteristics of God are revealed already in the early period admits of little question unless the evidence is readjusted to suit a different theory. It is no less incontestable, however, that then, as now and always, the response of the people moves on a different plane. Not only does Israel revolt against the teachings of Moses and his prophetic successors, but in many different ways, some more explicit than others, inadequate and erroneous ideas and practices are in continual conflict with divine self-revelation. The story of Israel's religion is in fact a very different one from the story of God's own action in self-revelation.

Thus it is evident that for many people Yahweh was just one of many national gods (1 S. 4:8). As such, He was thought to have a geographical restriction, first perhaps at Sinai (Jgs. 5:4), then in Canaan (1 S. 26:19f.). In addition, several superstitious practices continued, e.g., the use of teraphim (RSV mg., 1 S. 19:13, 16), the practice of necromancy (1 S. 28:7-19), and especially worship at the shrines of Baal with all the accompanying cultic ceremonies (Jgs. 2:13; 3:7; 8:33; etc.). Foreign worship was also established in Jerusalem by Solomon (1 K. 11:5-8), and worship of Yahweh Himself was transformed into idol worship, e.g., by Jeroboam with his golden calves (1 K. 12:26-33). Indeed, the setting up of different sanctuaries for Yahweh probably led to His localization, so that for the people He was Himself the equivalent of the earlier Baal. But this is still idolatry and apostasy, for it involves the substitution of a concept of Yahweh for Yahweh Himself; and the prophetic witness is raised up from the time of the judges onward to bear witness to God Himself in the face of all false ideas about God. As a final abomination human sacrifices seem to have been offered on occasion, though it seems to have been mainly in the prophetic period that this became customary (cf. 2 K. 16:3; Jer. 7:31; Ezk. 16:20).

3. Biblical Witness. A naturalistic interpretation of the Bible seizes on these inadequacies in the response of the people and tries to draw from them a scheme of gradual progress to true conceptions of God such as those enunciated by the great prophets from Elijah to the Exile. In fact, however, it is difficult to deduce any such scheme even from the religious data, for at many points it seems as though there is a progressive decline rather than a progressive advance. Even more important, the inadequacies are always portrayed in Scripture as a failure to be taught by the clear revelation which has already been given in word and work. Even through the so-called preprophetic period, and increasingly so in the age of the prophets, the Bible has another strand, that of revelation — the continuing acts and words of God through His chosen leaders and spokespeople. God bears constant witness to Himself, so that there is knowledge of God even in and in spite of the continuing false conceptions, superstitious practices, and blatant idolatries.

He bears witness to Himself in both the acts by which He judges and delivers Israel and the declarations of those whom He raises up to speak on His behalf. He manifests Himself as the God of the whole earth, who overrules, e.g., Syria or Egypt as well as Israel. He displays His power in the deliverance at the Red Sea and also in the great liberations of the judges period. He displays His righteousness in the great declarations of the law, in its administration by Moses, in the promises and threats of the Deuteronomic exhortation, and in the outworking of these threats in the lives of tribes and individuals. He also makes known His faithfulness, both in the great promises of the Exodus and in His refusal to abandon even a rebellious and apostate people. His faithfulness merges at this point into His mercy and grace. He is always ready to pardon His people and to deliver them again from oppression. If God has the sternness of justice and judgment, He has also the tenderness of pity and forbearance. The Davidic Psalms in particular cast a wholly new light on God at this early period. They bring out the intensely personal aspects of His dealings with Israel and Israelites — aspects that are only too easily lost in the lightnings and thunderings of Sinai, in the complicated ritual of the sanctuary, or in the story of the people's superstition and apostasy. God is the personal God of His people, who manifests His goodness to individuals as well as to the nation. One might properly say that all the essentials of the knowledge of God are present from the very first, for God Himself, not just an idea of God, is present from the very first. The task of the later prophets and psalmists is to make these essentials explicit in the varying situations of Israel's history, as God continues to work out His purpose and as the people continue to meet His self-revelation with different degrees of ignorance and apostasy.

D. God in the Prophetic Period. All that is true in the preprophetic period from the patriarchs to the judges and the early monarchy is no less true in the days of the later monarchy, the Exile, and the postexilic period, when the great prophets bore their distinctive witness to God in inspired interpretation of His dealings with Israel and the nations. New facets of God, of His sovereignty and love, were constantly brought out as the people moved more deeply into disobedience, came under catastrophic judgments in the form of defeat, occupation, and exile, and displayed continuing reluctance to walk in faith and discipleship even after their restoration. God was even more vividly self-revealed as the sovereign, righteous, and merciful God, ruling the universe and nations, faithful to the covenant promises to Israel, requiring righteousness of His people, visiting them with drastic judgments for their failures, yet always ready to pardon, to help, to heal, to restore, and to establish where there was penitence and faith. Indeed, there was a growing realization at this period that God had revealed Himself to be Israel's God, not for Israel's sake alone, but for the sake of all nations, to whom salvation was to be extended and to whom the Servant of the Lord was to be a light and witness.

As noted, this was again a period of widespread ignorance, apostasy, and disobedience. The idolatry and moral decline of the Ahab period were vigorously exposed and resisted by Elijah. The sins and social injustices of the later kingdoms were then graphically depicted and denounced by Amos, Hosea, Isaiah, and Micah. The worship of Israel had become so debased, so divorced from the reality of knowledge and service of God, that it was offensive rather than pleasing to God (Am. 2:6-8; 5:21-23; Hos. 3:1; Isa. 30:22). Prosperity had led to the pursuit of luxury and the spread of licentiousness, and increasing wealth to insatiable rapacity (Isa. 5:8-12). Against a fluctuating but threatening international background, the aggression of Syria and the Philistines, the internecine strife of the kingdoms, the ominous expansion of Assyria and the final upsurge of Babylon, Israel lacked confidence in God and futilely and disobediently resorted to diplomacy and alliances. God was not really accepted as the sovereign and righteous Lord. Profession had become a hollow mockery, sacrifice a sham, prophecy itself a professional business, and the expression of trust an empty self-reassurance.

1. Righteousness. In the face of this deteriorating situation the first prophetic emphasis was on God as the God of RIGHTEOUSNESS both in the sense that He is righteous and in the sense that He demands righteousness. In illustration, quotations could easily be multiplied from all the prophets, whether positively in the form of statements and exhortations or negatively in the form of threats and condemnations. What God requires is that people act justly (Mic. 6:8). He wants "justice [to] roll down like waters, and righteousness like an ever-flowing stream" (Am. 5:24). Zion is to be the city of righteousness (Isa. 1:26f.). Closely associated with the righteousness of God is His righteous judgment, which falls on Israel, too (cf. esp. Amos, Isaiah, Jeremiah, and Ezekiel). But it falls no less on the nations which do not realize that in their victories over Israel they are the rod of God's anger, and that God will bring down similar judgments on their own sins, cruelties, and pride (Isa. 10–13; Ezk. 25–32). Though judgment is collective, God deals with individuals as well. A righteous remnant is preserved (Isa. 4). The children are not to suffer for the sins of the fathers but each is to be individually responsible to God (Ezk. 18; cf. Jer. 31:29-34). Since this cannot always work out in terms of this life and its material blessings, the way is thus opened up for the truth of a final judgment of righteousness that is to come (cf. the problem of Job, the restoration after the Exile, and finally Dnl. 12:1). The final revelation is that righteousness is not just a demand. It is something that is itself revealed (Isa. 56:1), for God Himself is righteousness (Jer. 23:6).

2. Holiness. Closely associated with God's righteousness is His HOLINESS. If the original orientation of holiness is to separation or transcendence, this is increasingly revealed as the separation of the righteous God from sinful mankind. God is high and lifted up in power, majesty, and glory (Isa. 6:1; 8:13). But the real reason why one must shrink before Him is not because one is puny; it is because one is unclean (Isa. 6:5). God's holiness is profaned by the sin of His people. He vindicates His holiness by righteous dealing among the nations (Ezk. 36:23). He is finally sanctified in the obedience of His people (cf. Hag. 2:11-19). If He is the "high and lofty One who inhabits eternity, whose name is Holy," He dwells not merely in the high and holy place, but also with "him who is of a contrite and humble spirit" (Isa. 57:15). The lesson of God's holiness is brought home by ritual requirements. But it is only in popular misunderstanding that this can take the form of taboo or priestly externalism. For the God of holiness is the holy God. Separation for Him is the true holiness which He seeks. To be holy as He is holy is to be righteous as He is righteous.

3. Lordship. In the face of the attacks of the nations God reveals Himself clearly as the LORD of the nations. They are no less under His sovereignty than Israel. He uses them as the instruments of His judgment and mercy. Amos pronounces judgment on all the nations, including Israel (Am. 1–3). Isaiah recognizes that Assyria is the rod of God's anger (10:5), and Cyrus the chosen vessel of restoration (45:1). The gods of the nations are things of nought. Isaiah in particular scorns the idols of Babylon (46:1f.). Yet God's purpose for the nations is also positive. Jonah had a mission to Nineveh, which repented and was spared. Egypt and Assyria are to be won to true faith and worship (Isa. 19:24f.). All nations are to go up to the house of the Lord established on the top of the mountains (Isa. 2:2-4; Mic. 4:1-3). Israel has a holy mission to be God's witness (Isa. 43:10). It is the task of the servant to be a light to the Gentiles, God's salvation to the end of the earth (Isa. 45:6). The earth shall be "full of the knowledge of the Lord as the waters cover the sea" (Isa. 11:9).

4. Unity. This implies that God is God alone, and in His acts and declarations the message that only one God exists is carried to the people. This is the supreme revelation of Isa. 40. God is Creator, King of the cosmos, Ruler of the nations, the Lord to whom past, present, and future are all one. Rival deities are confidently challenged (Isa. 41:21-29); idols are dismissed with contempt (Isa. 44:20, 25). Some of the Psalms make the same point. If God is God of gods, this does not mean that other gods are real. The Lord God omnipotent reigns, and the earth is to rejoice, the multitude of isles to be glad (Ps. 97:1). Idols have mouths, eyes, and ears, but they cannot speak or see or hear (Ps. 115:4-8). God comes, the one God, and He shall judge the whole world with "righteousness, and the peoples with his truth" (Ps. 96:13). This is no new revelation; it is implied in the identity of Yahweh with the Creator. It finds expression in the great confession: "The Lord our God is one Lord" (Dt. 6:4). But it is now driven home with new power and emphasis: "Is there a God besides me? There is no Rock; I know not any" (Isa. 44:8). "I am the Lord, and there is no other" (Isa. 45:5).

5. Faithfulness. If, however, Israel is to be restored and light is to be brought to the Gentiles, then God must exercise His grace and loving faithfulness. God is FAITHFUL to Israel even though it is unfaithful to Him and has come under His judgment. He is like the husband who remains faithful to the unfaithful wife and redeems her when she has fallen (Hos. 1–3). This is the point of the restoration of Israel time and again during its history and supremely after the Exile. Israel has not been faithful, but God has formed it for Himself and therefore He redeems it just the same (Isa. 43:21–44:6). This obviously greatly transcends ordinary loyalty; it is a pardoning loyalty. God's message to Israel is: "Though your sins are like scarlet, they shall be as white as snow" (1:18). "I, I am He who blots out your transgressions for my own sake" (43:25). His dealings even with pagan Nineveh include the sparing of a penitent city, for He is "a gracious God and merciful, slow to anger, and abounding in steadfast love" (Jonah 4:2). This is also faithfulness, for the original covenant promise included the blessing of the nations in the seed of Abraham. It serves to enhance, however, the sweep and grandeur of the divine forgiveness, for the Gentiles are even further from God than Israel. God's faithfulness is also a saving faithfulness. This is illustrated especially in the deliverance of Jerusalem from the Assyrians and in the bringing back of Judah to new national life after the Exile: "Behold, God is my salvation; I will trust, and will not be afraid" (Isa. 12:2); "I am the Lord your God, the Holy One of Israel, your Savior" (Isa. 43:3). It is illustrated again in the final salvation of the nations: "That my salvation may reach to the end of the earth" (Isa. 49:6). Finally, it is the faithfulness of loving-kindness, of love. Even though Israel is unworthy and sinful, God loves His people. "And the Lord said to me, 'Go again, love a woman who is beloved of a paramour'" (Hos. 3:1). It was out of gracious love that at the very first He chose this foundling child (Ezk. 16:3-5) to be His own bride. Thus, He can appeal to the love of the wilderness marriage, and in the message of the new promise He can declare: "I have loved you with an everlasting love; therefore I have continued my faithfulness to you" (Jer. 31:3). The Psalms in particular are full of this thought of the gracious and loving faithfulness of God. Not only does God surround Israel with the constancy of the mountains (Ps. 125:2), but even when it falls from Him, it can still hope. "For with the Lord there is steadfast love, and with him is plenteous redemption" (Ps. 130:7). Thus He is to be praised for His loving-kindness and for His truth (Ps. 138:2).

6. Salvation Through Suffering. The salvation of the people of God is not without suffering. Already in the OT God is revealed as the one who overrules suffering, and ultimately His own suffering, as a means of blessing. This is apparent in His dealings with the prophets. From Moses down through Elijah to Jeremiah and beyond, the prophets suffer because of their fidelity to God and His message. When judgment falls on the people, righteous Israel suffers along with the guilty. Indeed, it seems at times that the righteous suffer more than the wicked (cf. Pss. 37, 73). Certainly they have the sense that the degree of their suffering is unmerited.

Out of this situation arises the great protest of Job. Yet the book of Job is also a revelation of God's dealings, for it shows that God is staking His own honor on the integrity of His tempted servant, that He is finally with and above Job in all the period of affliction, that out of the suffering He is forging a tested discipleship. The lesson of Job is not just that things will finally be redressed either in this world or in the world to come, though this is also true. The real point is that in a sinful and rebellious world no one can claim exemption from suffering, that God uses even affliction to test and strengthen righteousness, with a final hint that the one who comes through the test can make intercession and atonement for others (Job 42:8). As we learn from the prologue, Job suffered just because of his faith (1:8), and it is finally seen that he served God only for God's sake and not for concomitant blessings (1:9). As the psalmist puts it, "It is good for me that I was afflicted, that I might learn thy statutes" (Ps. 119:71).

Consistently, however, the servant of God suffers for the good of others too. What is hinted at in the case of Job is plainly seen in many of the prophets, whose sufferings were really the sufferings of their people, and who by their sufferings finally brought spiritual blessing to the people at large. This truth of the vicarious power of suffering comes to magnificent expression in the Servant Songs of Isaiah, especially Isa. 53. Here God, the God of grace, loving-kindness, and faithfulness, lays suffering on His faithful and righteous Servant in order that the Servant may bear the griefs and carry the sorrows of others. In imposing this suffering, God imposes the iniquity of us all, so that what seems to be heartless from the standpoint of the Servant is in fact gracious and pardoning love from the wider standpoint of the "all." It pleases God to put the Servant to grief, not in senseless sadism, but in fulfillment of the great purpose of intercession and redemption. Nor is God a mere spectator here, who leaves the burden to be carried by the Servant. For in truth it is He Himself who in the greatness of His love takes up the burden and carries it for His people. The suffering of the righteous, not merely in confirmation of his own righteousness, but on behalf of others, is a token that God Himself suffers, and that it is by His suffering that salvation is finally wrought.

In all their affliction he was afflicted,
and the angel of his presence saved them;
in his love and in his pity he redeemed them;
he lifted them up, and carried them all the days of old. (Isa. 63:9)

7. Messiah. In fulfillment of His gracious purpose, not merely in the sense of historical deliverance but in the wider sense of salvation, God is to raise up the root of David, the Messiah. Various representations are given, not all of which may originally have had the same figure in view from the standpoint of the authors and readers. The Messiah is the Davidic king who will reign in righteousness (Isa. 9:7 [MT 6]). He is the Son of man who is given dominion, glory, and a kingdom (Dnl. 7:13f.). He is the Suffering Servant, for, while Isa. 53 may have had an immediate reference to some figure of the time, or to righteous Israel, it obviously points beyond these to a deeper fulfillment (Calvin, comm. on Isaiah, *in loc.*; KD, *in loc.*). Thus the Messiah is also to be the one who will gather up the tribes of Israel and be a light to the Gentiles. He is finally the child, the son, who is given the significant name Immanuel, and who bears the tremendous titles "Wonderful Counselor, Mighty God, Everlasting Father, Prince of Peace" (Isa. 7:14; 9:6). The Messiah is in a very direct sense God Himself at work among and on behalf of His people. "Behold, the days are coming, says the Lord, when I will raise up for David a righteous Branch, and he shall reign as King and deal wisely. . . . And this is the name by which he will be called: 'The Lord is our righteousness'" (Jer. 23:5f.).

III. God in the NT.–A. Relation to the OT. The revelation of God in the NT is wholly consonant with His revelation in the OT. While certain terms may be adopted and adapted from current discussion (e.g., *logos*), there is no infiltration of the religious or philosophical concepts of the Hellenistic world. Nor is any attempt made, not even for the sake of the gentile mission, to introduce general theistic proofs of God as a preamble to faith in the God of revelation. Paul certainly claimed that God is the Creator of the earth and the one in whom "we live and move and have our being" (Acts 17:28). But he did not initiate a chain of reasoning that leads from a general concept of God to the God of Christianity. The NT does not deal with ideas or experiences of God any more than the OT. It is a declaration, a self-revelation of God. God Himself tells mankind about Himself; He reveals Himself in word and work. If there is a new feature as compared with the OT, it is that Jesus Christ is this word and work of God. But the element of self-declaration remains the same. The apostles are not preaching the idea of God either as it is found in the OT or as it is advanced by Jesus. They are preaching God Himself, the God of the OT, revealed in Jesus.

This God has all the attributes disclosed and emphasized already in the OT. He is the one God, the Creator of all things, the Lord of heaven and earth, the supreme King of people and nations. He is the covenant

God who has bound Himself to Israel, and through Israel to all nations, and who has thus bound Israel and all nations to Himself. He is the God of grace, faithfulness, mercy, and love. He demands righteousness and exercises judgment. Yet He is also the righteousness and salvation of His people, and He is this supremely in and by righteous and vicarious suffering, the suffering of Jesus. The writers of the NT quoted copiously from the OT. Jesus Himself claimed that He was fulfilling the Law and the Prophets, and He expounded to His disciples in all the Scriptures the things concerning Himself. Both Peter and Paul saw in the NT revelation a fulfillment of the OT covenant and promise (cf. Acts 2:14-36; Gal. 3:7-29; 1 Pet. 1:10-12). The God of Jesus is the God of the fathers. The God of Christians is the God of Abraham, the father of all who believe. No attempt whatever is made to revise or to correct the OT presentation. Nor, in the strict sense, is any attempt made to amplify it. "Thou shalt love the Lord thy God" is the great commandment both in the Law and in the Gospels, and this God is one and the same God: "The Lord our God is one Lord" (Dt. 6:4; Mk. 12:29).

B. God as Father. Yet, while it is the same God who is self-revealed, and while the substance of this self-revelation is not changed, the NT has certain new emphases. The first of these is that God is now more specifically and expressly self-revealed as Father. God is, of course, the Father of Israel in the OT. He pities those who fear Him as a father pities his children (Ps. 103:13). He chastens Israel as a man chastens his son (Dt. 8:5). He calls His son out of Egypt (Hos. 11:1).

In the NT, however, the fatherhood of God is shown to have a far deeper significance. Jesus constantly refers to God as the Father. He is "my Father," "your Father," "the heavenly Father," also the father in the parables. In relation to people generally this implies that He is the author of their being, that He distributes His gifts impartially (Mt. 5:45), that He watches over them with providential care (Acts 14:17), and that He is willing to forgive and restore the disobedient (Lk. 15:18-32). But beyond this, God is in a wholly specific sense the Father of Jesus. Jesus must be about His Father's business (Lk. 2:49, AV). He and the Father are one (Jn. 10:30). He is sent by the Father (Jn. 17:18), and He speaks the words and does the works of the Father (Jn. 14:10). He is loved by the Father and keeps His commandments (Jn. 15:9f.). He is acknowledged by the Father (Mt. 3:17) and disclosed to be the Son of the living God by Him (Mt. 16:17). He glorifies the Father and asks to be glorified by Him (Jn. 17:4f.). He commits His spirit into the hands of the Father (Lk. 23:46) and goes to the Father to prepare a place for His disciples (Jn. 14:2f., 12). All power is given to Him by the Father (Mt. 28:18; Jn. 17:2). He is the only One who truly knows the Father, and no one comes to the Father but by Him (Jn. 14:6). To know Him is to know the Father (Jn. 14:7). He is in fact the only-begotten Son who stands in a unique relationship to the Father (Jn. 3:16; Mk. 1:1; 1 Jn. 4:9f.).

Yet this relationship is in a secondary sense extended also to believers by regeneration or adoption. Believers, too, can call God their Father in a special way. They are the children of God through faith in Jesus Christ (Gal. 3:26). They have received the Spirit of adoption whereby they cry, "Abba! Father!" (Rom. 8:14f.). They are to pray: "Our Father . . ." (Mt. 6:9). They are heirs with Christ of the kingdom of God (Rom. 8:17). They have the glorious liberty of the children of God (Rom. 8:21). They are assured of a glorious destiny in virtue of their sonship (He. 2:10). Indeed, in a bold phrase it can even be said that they are made "partakers [*koinōnoí*] of the divine nature [*phýsis*]" (2 Pet. 1:4) — so significant is their union with the only begotten Son, and so real is the Fatherhood of God in Him.

C. God as King. Another NT emphasis is on God as the KING, or, more specifically, on the KINGDOM OF GOD. Once again, the basis is to be found in the OT, both in the truth that God is the real King of Israel (1 S. 8:7) and in the promise of the everlasting kingdom which God Himself is to establish (2 S. 7:13; Ps. 145:13; Dnl. 2:44; 7:14). In the NT, however, the kingdom fills the picture in a new way, for the time of temporal foreshadowing and promise now yields before the fulfillment. The kingdom is at hand (Mk. 1:15); it is indeed present (Mt. 12:28; Lk. 17:21). Repentance is demanded in face of it, for entry into the kingdom is only by conversion and regeneration (Mt. 18:3; Jn. 3:3). It is a kingly rule which is not of this world but which is present in this world, which will finally be brought to a great consummation (Mt. 25:31-46) and for which prayer is now made (Mt. 6:10). It is to be sought above all things (Mt. 6:33). It may be compared with the sowing of a seed. As humans sow the seed and wait for the harvest, so the seed of the kingdom is sown and God brings it to fruition (Mt. 13:3-30).

God the Father is the King in this kingdom (Lk. 12:32). He it is to whom we pray for the coming of the kingdom (Mt. 6:10). Yet Jesus is also King. He is to come in His kingdom (Mt. 16:28). As Judge, He is also King (cf. Mt. 25:31-46). He accepts the title "King" from Pilate (Jn. 18:37). The kingdom is present among people because He Himself, the King, is present among them, and it will come in manifest glory when He Himself comes again in power. Already He claims the allegiance of people as King, and the day is coming when every knee shall bow before Him and every tongue confess that He is Lord (Phil. 2:10f.). The kingdom may thus be related both to God and to Christ (Eph. 5:5). Christ subdues all things to Himself; but at the end He delivers up the kingdom to God, even the Father, that God may be all in all (1 Cor. 15:24-28).

D. God as Love. That the kingdom is a kingdom of LOVE as well as righteousness is a reminder that the love of God also receives a new emphasis in the NT. Here again there is no innovation. Quotations could easily be accumulated from the OT to show that the God of Israel is declared supremely to be a God of love. The idea that a stern OT God stands in contrast to the merciful and loving God of the NT is a travesty hardly deserving notice. Indeed, the NT itself in no way minimizes the emphasis on the righteousness of God, on the severity of His judgment. God is no feeble sentimentalist. The revelation of the gospel, of God's righteousness in the gospel, is also a revelation of the wrath of God (Rom. 1:17f.).

Nevertheless, the NT is primarily and finally gospel; and the revelation of righteous wrath only serves to enhance the revelation of justifying righteousness (Rom. 3:21-26). What is intimated largely in type and promise in the OT is brought to full and clear expression in the word and work of the NT. The central declaration of the NT is that God loves. He loves the Son (Jn. 5:20). He loves believers, for they are accepted in the Beloved (Eph. 1:6). In the Beloved, however, God also loves the world. This is why He sent the Son into the world (Jn. 3:16f.). The love of God in Christ is fully manifested as an initiative of grace, the initiative intimated already in Hosea and ultimately in the whole of the OT. God commends His love toward us "in that while we were yet sinners Christ died for us" (Rom. 5:8). Love is not "that we loved God but that he loved us" (1 Jn. 4:10). This love involved the achievement of reconciliation by the self-offering of the Son, i.e., by His dying for us, laying down His life for sinners. In full actualization of the gracious and saving involvement of God in the afflictions of His people, He became the atonement for our sins and reconciled us by His death and passion. God was prepared to go to the extreme length of love by causing His righteous Son to be the Suffering Servant who poured out His soul an offering for sin, the Lamb of God who bore the sin of the world.

God loves also in the sense that He pours His love into our hearts by the Holy Spirit (Rom. 5:5). He evokes the responsive chord of love so that we love Him as He first loved us (1 Jn. 4:19). So fully is love a divine perfection that in the last analysis one may go even further than the statement that God loves or that God is loving, and say quite categorically that "God is love [*agápē*]" (1 Jn. 4:8, 16). This is not, of course, a metaphysical identification. It could not be reversed and made into the abstraction that love is God. That God is love implies at once words and works of love, for God is the living as well as the loving God. The fact remains, however, that love is of the very essence of God. "His nature and His name is love" (Charles Wesley).

E. Christ as God. These NT emphases are all striking and significant. Yet they are not in the last resort the genuinely new thing in the NT declaration. The genuinely new thing is that all that can be said of God is also said of Christ. In Christ is fulfilled the messianic prophecy of the King, the Son of man, the Servant, the Immanuel, in whom God will be directly present and active among and on behalf of His people. But this active presence goes beyond the previous activity of God in and through chosen leaders and messengers. Jesus Himself comes with an immediacy of authority far above that of the prophets or even of Moses, as may be seen supremely in His use of the "I am." He quotes Ps. 110 to show that, even as David's son, He is also David's Lord (Mt. 22:44). He claims that all power is given to Him in heaven and on earth (Mt. 28:18). He endorses the confession of Peter that He is the Son of the living God (Mt. 16:17), and by His answer to the question of the high priest He makes it plain that He is indeed the Christ, the Son of God (Mt. 26:63f.).

The apostolic witness brings this identification out in terms which could hardly be more explicit. The risen Christ is exalted at the right hand of God (Acts 2:33). He is the incarnate Word who in the beginning was with God and was God (Jn. 1:1, 14). He is the express image of God, the One by whom all things hold together (Col. 1:15-20). In Him dwells all the fulness of the Godhead bodily (Col. 2:9). Hebrews, comparing Jesus with angels, demonstrated from the OT that He is the Son who is begotten of the Father, whose throne is for ever and ever, and who in the beginning laid the foundation of the earth (He. 1:1-13). As kingship, power, righteousness, and love belong to God, so they belong with the same fulness to Christ. God was in Christ reconciling the world to Himself (2 Cor. 5:19). In the vision of Rev. 21 the new Jerusalem has no temple, but the Lord God Almighty and the Lamb are the temple; and there is no sun or moon, for "the glory of God is its light, and its lamp is the Lamb" (v. 23). Christ is Himself "the Alpha and Omega, the first and the last, the beginning and the end" (Rev. 22:13). The name Immanuel, which had previously indicated the fact of God's presence, is now brought to its most literal fulfillment, for God is directly with His people in Jesus. Christ Himself is God. *See also* JESUS CHRIST.

F. Spirit of God. Less fully, yet hardly less plainly, the Holy Spirit is declared to be God. It is not just that the NT refers generally to the spirit of God, as the OT does. Nor is it merely that God Himself is Spirit (Jn. 4:24), though this is an important declaration which sums up in a simple phrase what has been implicit from the very first. Beyond this the NT speaks of the Holy Spirit in a distinction-in-unity from the Father and the Son. The Holy Spirit is the Comforter "who proceeds [*ekporeúetai*] from the Father" (Jn. 15:26), who is given by the Father (14:16) and sent by the Son (16:7), and who plays His own distinctive role in the divine work of revelation, reconciliation, regeneration, and redemption. (*See also* HOLY SPIRIT.) Hence trinitarian formulae already begin to appear in the NT. Baptism is to be in the name of the Father, Son, and Holy Spirit (Mt. 28:19). The fellowship of the Spirit is associated with the love of God and the grace of Christ (2 Cor. 13:14). If grace and peace are from the Father and the Son (1 Thess. 1:1, etc.), the gospel comes in the Holy Spirit (1 Thess. 1:5f.). The new birth is of God, Christ came by water and blood, and the Spirit bears witness, so that one who has eternal life from God in the Son has also the witness in oneself (1 Jn. 5:1-12). Father, Son, and Holy Spirit all have their part in the outworking of the one divine purpose of sovereignty, righteousness, and love.

The self-revelation of God as Himself a trinity of persons with a divine life of inner relationship is a distinctive element in the NT witness. The intimations of it in the OT take on new significance in the light of the fulfillment. The OT makes no express declarations. Nevertheless, it should be noted that no change in essential testimony is involved. God has not suddenly become different, so that after all we are still in the sphere of shifting human concepts or experiences. All that is said of God in the OT is still said of God in the NT. The only point is that it is now said of the Son and the Holy Spirit as well as of the Father. Even the unity of God is still maintained with vigor. Jesus Himself repeated the Shema: "The Lord our God, the Lord is one" (Mk. 12:29). Paul insisted that the God who justifies the circumcision by faith and the uncircumcision through faith is one Lord (Rom. 3:30). In respect of idol-meats he stated that to us there is but one God, and if he added that there is one Lord, Jesus Christ, it was not to set a second God alongside the first (1 Cor. 8:6). There is one God and Father of all (Eph. 4:6).

The Word was in the beginning with God, but the Word is not alongside God, for the Word is God (Jn. 1:1). No suggestion of polytheism is to be found in the NT, and tendencies in this direction were always sharply resisted in the early Church when it tried to grapple with the trinitarian question. There is one God; and the Father, the Son, and the Holy Spirit is God. In other words, the one God is not an isolated and abstract monad. He has His own rich life in which the Father loves the Son, the Son loves the Father, and the Holy Spirit is the bond of love (cf. Augustine *De trin.* v.11; vi.5).

How this can be said, and what it implies, is to involve not only conflict with Judaism, which will not agree that this is the self-revelation of God, but also much doctrinal effort and contention in the Church. But the fulness of Christian belief is that, quite irrespective of the element of mystery, this, too, is part of what God has revealed concerning Himself in His revealing and reconciling word and work, so that knowledge and exposition of the true and living God must also be knowledge and exposition of God in His triunity, the one God — Father, Son, and Holy Spirit.

See also DEITY; TRINITY.

***Bibliography.**–Biblical: DNTT,* II, 66-82; W. Eichrodt, *Theology of the OT,* II (*OTL,* Eng. tr. 1967), 15-92; *Encyclopaedia Judaica* (1971), VII, *s.v.* "God" (I. Arb); E. Jacob, *Theology of the OT* (Eng. tr. 1958), part 1; *New Catholic Encyclopedia* (1967), VI, *s.v.* "God" (R. T. A. Murphy, J. R. Gillis, and R. J. Buschmiller); *TDNT,* III, *s.v.* θεός κτλ.: θεός (Kleinknecht, Stauffer, Kuhn); *TDOT,* I, *s.v.* "'ēl" (Cross), "'ᵉlōhîm" (Ringgren); G. von Rad, *OT Theology* (Eng. tr. 1962, 1965); T. C. Vriezen, *Outline of OT Theology* (Eng. tr. 1958), pp. 128-198.

Historical-theological: Aquinas *Summa Theol.* i.1-43; Calvin *Inst.* i.1f., 13; F. Schleiermacher, *Christian Faith* (Eng. tr., Harper Torch ed. 1963), I, 194-232, 325-354; II, 723-751; C. Hodge, *Systematic Theology* (1877; repr. n.d.), I, 366-534; W. G. T. Shedd, *Dogmatic Theology*, I (1889), 151-546; S. Harris, *Self-revelation of God* (3rd ed. 1893); P. Schaff, *Creeds of Christendom* (1877, 1919); *CD*, I/1; II/1; E. Brunner, *Dogmatics*, I, *Christian Doctrine of God* (Eng. tr. 1949); H. Bavinck, *Doctrine of God* (Eng. tr. 1951); K. Rahner, *Trinity* (Eng. tr. 1970); H. Küng, *On Being a Christian* (Eng. tr. 1976), 57-88; C. F. H. Henry, *God, Revelation and Authority*, II (1976), chs. 4, 9, 13-15.

G. W. BROMILEY

GOD, ASCRIPTIONS TO. The term "ascription" is borrowed from ecclesiastical nomenclature and is used to identify some of the ways in which God is referred to or addressed. It does not appear in the Bible with this meaning. Grammatically, an ascription to God is an adjectival clause that comes after, or stands in place of, the divine name, as in "Our Father, who art in heaven," or "God who said, 'Let light shine out of darkness.'" Although easily identifiable as a literary form and significant for biblical interpretation, ascriptions have not received the scholarly attention afforded other forms.

I. Ascriptions in Nonbiblical Religious Literature.–As early as the 25th cent. B.C. religious writers used ascriptions to specify aspects of the nature, location, or function of their gods that were not specified in the divine names themselves. For example, an Egyptian text from this period addresses a god as the "Eye of Horus, who art glorious, unharmed, and youthful in peace." Nine centuries later, Egyptians referred to "Ptah who is upon the Great Throne . . . who made all and brought all gods into being." Similar elaborations on the divine names are found in the religious literature of later Hittites, Akkadians, Assyrians, Jews, Greeks, and Syriac-speaking Christians.

II. Biblical Uses.–*A. OT.* Ascriptions to God appear in many books of the OT, especially in the Pentateuch, the later chapters of Isaiah, and Psalms. Some examples are: "I am the Lord your God, who brought you forth out of the land of Egypt" (Lev. 25:38); "your God, who pleads the cause of his people" (Isa. 51:22); and "the God who gave me vengeance" (Ps. 18:47 [MT 48]). The Aramaic portions of Daniel, Ezra, and Jeremiah also contain divine ascriptions, each offering some specific aspect of God's nature or function.

B. NT. 1. Forms. Most English translations of NT ascriptions to God are adjectival clauses beginning with the pronoun "who," as in "God who," "the Father who," "the Lord who," "He who," etc. The original Greek forms of these ascriptions appear in two basic grammatical constructions, using either a relative pronoun and a verb (e.g., *toú theoú hós hikanṓsen hḗmas,* "the God who has qualified us") or a participle (*ho pémpsas me patḗr,* "the Father who sent me").

2. Types. Like earlier religious literature, the NT contains ascriptions that (1) assert God's existence (Mt. 6:6a); (2) locate God in a place, usually heaven (5:16); (3) attribute a quality to God (Lk. 1:49); and (4) describe an activity of God (1 Cor. 4:4).

3. Distribution and Function. Among the Gospels, Mark has only one ascription (11:25; v. 26 is a repetition) and Luke only four (1:49; 9:48; 10:16; 12:5). Matthew has twenty-nine, over half of which simply locate the "Father . . . in heaven." John has thirty-two, seventeen of which are spoken by Jesus to identify the "Father who sent me," a theme in keeping with this Gospel's unique christological emphasis. The repetition of these highly stylized ascriptions in Matthew and John strongly suggests that they were used in liturgical contexts.

Paul was by far the most prolific and creative user of ascriptions. In the first four Epistles, he referred to God forty-six times in this way. Not at all interested in merely making an assertion about God's existence or location (see II.B.2 above), and only slightly concerned with ascribing some static attribute to the divine (only Rom. 1:25; 9:5; 16:25; 2 Cor. 11:31; Gal. 1:5), Paul was most eager to express a wide range of God's activities (type 4 in II.B.2 above; forty-one occurrences).

A list of some of the Pauline ascriptions shows how the apostle saw God at work on cosmic, social, and personal levels. He referred to God as the One who justifies (Rom. 3:30; 4:5; 8:33), makes alive and calls things into being (4:17), raises the dead (4:24; 8:11; 2 Cor. 1:9; 4:14; Gal. 1:1), subjects things to Himself (Rom. 8:20; 1 Cor. 15:27f.), searches hearts (Rom. 8:27), loves us (8:37), gives the growth (1 Cor. 3:7; 2 Cor. 8:16), judges us (1 Cor. 4:4), enlightens and reveals the dark things (4:5), energizes us (1 Cor. 12:6; Gal. 2:8), gives us the victory (1 Cor. 15:57), establishes us (2 Cor. 1:21), calls us (2 Cor. 1:21; Gal. 1:6, 15), comforts us (2 Cor. 1:4; 7:6), always leads us (2:14), speaks (4:6a), prepares life for us (5:5a), has given us the Spirit as a guarantee (5:5b), reconciles us and gives us the service of reconciliation (5:18), and sets us apart (Gal. 1:15).

When Paul did occasionally use the attributive type of ascription, he usually added an "Amen," suggesting that he was in those rare instances repeating an ascription already well established in Christian liturgy. But his own understanding of God was that of a God who acts to enable, energize, and empower the Christian individual and community to bear witness that they were now justified, reconciled, and set apart for ministry.

III. Significance.–*A. Literary and Form-Critical.* Literary analysis of Scripture continues to yield new insights, especially in the areas of form and structure. Whereas earlier form critics worked primarily on larger units or segments (pericopes) of Scripture, especially in the Gospels, later scholars have given attention to smaller units of the Gospels and the Epistles, such as the greeting, thanksgiving, judgment, and benediction. Use of form-critical methodology on the ascriptions reveals that, far from being mere liturgical baggage, they were, especially for Paul, devices deliberately contrived and intentionally used in given contexts. As such, they not only describe God, but also give added or more precise meaning to the contexts in which they occur.

B. Theological. The purpose of critical study is to enable the informed reader to make a more responsible judgment whenever two or more interpretations of a text are possible. Also, such study can, as in the present analysis, provide broader perspectives and deeper insights into the author's mind, into his or her way of thinking about God. By noting the forms and uses of the ascriptions, readers can better understand the situation in which the words were used, their development within the tradition, and the theological dimensions of God that were intended by the writer to be uppermost in the reader's mind.

An example of this theological significance may be seen in Paul's use of two ascriptions in 2 Cor. 4:6. The first is simply an introductory formula, "God who said," for an OT quotation, "Let light shine out of darkness" (cf. Gen. 1:3). The references to light and darkness were deliberately chosen, tying in with references to Moses' veil in 2 Cor. 3:7, 13-18 and 4:4. Paul could easily have stopped there and still have made a good point. But by adding a second, and uniquely Christian, ascription he showed that this is the same active God who has more recently "*shone* in our hearts to give *light* of the *knowledge* of the *glory* of God in the *face* of Jesus Christ" (the italicized words relate to the Mosaic episode in Ex. 34:29f. and to Gen. 1:3). This intentional addendum in the second ascription provides a unique insight into Paul's literary skills and into the way he went about theologizing his gospel.

See CRITICISM III.B.; GOD, NAMES OF.

J. T. CLEMONS

GOD, CHILDREN OF. *See* CHILDREN OF GOD.

GOD, IMAGE OF. *See* IMAGE OF GOD.

GOD, NAMES OF.

- I. Significance of God's Names
  - A. Expressive of His Person
  - B. Gift of Revelation
  - C. Symbol of Authority
- II. OT Names
  - A. General
    1. 'El
    2. 'Elohim
    3. 'Eloah
  - B. "'El" Compounds
    1. 'El Shaddai
    2. 'El 'Elyon
    3. 'El 'Olam
    4. 'El Ro'i
    5. 'El Bethel
  - C. The Covenant Name: Yahweh
  - D. 'Adon, 'Adonai
  - E. Other Descriptive Terms
    1. Rock
    2. Holy One
    3. King
- III. NT Names

I. Significance of God's Names.–In contemporary Western culture personal names are little more than labels that distinguish one person from another. The pride often associated with having or giving a certain family name and the common use of character nicknames, however, are pale reflections of earlier periods of history, notably biblical times, in which a person's name had much deeper significance.

The importance of the personal name finds clear expression in the OT in the stories concerning the giving or changing of names. The name represented the whole person; it could be said that the name was the person. Thus a change in a person's character, destiny, or status could be marked by a change of name, e.g., Abram to Abraham (Gen. 17:4f.); Jacob to Israel (32:28); cf. Simon to Peter (Mt. 16:17f.). Names could be given prophetically and assume theological meaning, as did the names of the children of Hosea (Hos. 1:6, 9) and of Isaiah (Isa. 7:3; 8:3). Thus, if human names are important, it is to be expected that the names and titles of God carry great significance.

A. Expressive of His Person. God's person, presence, and character — none of which can be fully comprehended by the human mind — are all concentrated in His name. Therefore a certain mysterious quality attaches to that name. Yahweh's angel refers to this quality in his question to Manoah, "Why do you ask my name, seeing it is wonderful?" (Jgs. 13:18; cf. Gen. 32:29). In accordance with the coupling of God and His name, the intense reverence for it in Israel (witness the capital sanction of the law protecting it in Ex. 20:7) is really awe for the presence and power of God Himself.

An important early use of the name occurs in Ex. 23:20f., where the angel who was to lead the Israelites into the Promised Land bore God's name. He thereby not only embodied God's presence with His people but also possessed full divine authority to demand obedience and judge sins. Only the name, however, not the totality of God's being, was in the angel; the two appear to have been in some sense separable. Thus, after the people's apostasy of making the golden calf, God repeated His promise to provide an angel to go with them but refused to accompany them Himself (33:2f.). Only the persistent intercession of Moses secured the continued presence of God Himself with His people (vv. 12-16).

That the name signified the personal presence of God and yet was not in itself the "whole of God" was used by Deuteronomy and the "Deuteronomic" historical writers to express what a modern theologian would call the immanence and transcendence of God. God Himself dwells in heaven and cannot be contained by any place or structure (Dt. 26:15; 1 K. 8:27), but He condescends to choose a place where His name will be remembered (Ex. 20:24), dwell (Dt. 12:11; 14:23; etc.), and be set (12:5; 14:24). Solomon's prayer identified the temple as the place built "for the name of the Lord" (1 K. 8:20, 29). The rest of his prayer thus envisaged people praying and calling on God's name "toward this place," where His "eyes and heart" were (9:3), even though God Himself would hear in heaven, His dwelling-place (8:30).

Because the name represented the person of God, "calling upon the name of the Lord" was a means of entering into a personal relationship with Him. This relationship was the goal of cultic worship, so often described by that phrase (e.g., Gen. 12:8; 1 K. 18:24; Zeph. 3:9). The personal relationship thus established through the name of God was a means of salvation and assistance (e.g., Ps. 54:1 [MT 3], where God's name and saving might are paralleled). The third commandment strictly forbade any attempt to use the power of God's name for magical or selfish ends (Ex. 20:7), precisely because the name was considered so powerful. To attempt to manipulate God's power to one's own ends is to abuse the person and sovereignty of God Himself and is therefore similar to idolatry. The third commandment is thus a logical development from the first two.

It is interesting that one of the earliest descriptions of the Christian community was "those who call on this [i.e., Jesus'] name" (Acts 9:21), a phrase witnessing to the personal and saving relationship with God that they experienced through the person of Jesus Christ.

B. Gift of Revelation. "The revelation of the Name of God stands in the centre of the Biblical witness to revelation" (Brunner, p. 119). God Himself is known where His name is made known. The initiative of revelation thus lies clearly with God. The gift of knowledge of His name is an act of grace. It is appropriate, therefore, that the places where He makes His name known are places for worshiping response to His grace. Those who know God's grace, through knowing His name, are thereby led into a relationship of trust and confidence in Him (e.g., Ps. 9:10 [MT 11]; 91:14). When the priest invoked God's blessing of grace and peace he "put [God's] name upon the people" (Nu. 6:23-27); the revealed character of God guaranteed the blessing.

In the OT God's acts not only reveal His character but are also often marked by a particular mention of a divine name or title. In Gen. 17:1 the title 'El Shaddai was revealed when the covenant of promise with Abram was renewed. (Significantly, Abram's name was changed at the same time.) A fresh revelation of the name of Yahweh preceded the great redemptive act of the Exodus (Ex. 3:13-15; 6:2-8; see II.C below). The name of God was similarly stressed in Isa. 40–55 in expectation of God's new act of deliverance from Exile (cf. 42:8). No new name was actually given, but titles like "Your Savior," "Your Redeemer," "Holy One of Israel," "Lord of hosts," and "Mighty One of Jacob" occur frequently. Indeed, a glad appropriation of God's name by His people would mark the restoration (43:7; 44:5).

Since God's revelation of His name was an act of grace and enabled personal communion between Him and those to whom He revealed it, the name was closely associated with the covenant. Moses' intercession with God on behalf of the people (Ex. 33, esp. v. 19) and the remaking of the covenant, which followed the proclamation of the name — and character — of Yahweh (34:5f.), clearly show this association. Likewise, a prime feature of the covenant foretold by Jeremiah will be that God's people will know Him (Jer. 31:34).

In keeping with this, Jesus described the whole of His revelatory ministry in the words "I have manifested thy [God's] name" (Jn. 17:6, 26). His disclosure of the person, character, and saving work of God could all be summed up in the disclosure of "the name," and the saying is significantly put in the deeply covenantal setting of Jesus' last meal with His disciples before the crucifixion. Furthermore, the name of Christ as Lord (Gk. *kýrios*) takes over for the NT all that is contained in the titles, descriptions, and especially the covenant name of God in the OT.

C. Symbol of Authority. The angel of Ex. 23:20 exercised God's authority because he bore God's name. This coupling of God's authority with His name occurred often in Israel's history. Perhaps the most important example was the prophetic claim to speak in the name of the Lord, i.e., by His authority or commission. This was clearly the essential characteristic of the prophet mentioned in Dt. 18:18f. One who claimed, however, to speak in God's name without being commissioned and sent by Him not only committed a serious offence (cf. Dt. 18:20) but also could badly confuse God's people and His true prophets (cf. Jer. 14:13f.; 23:25-32; 29:8f.).

Many other things were said and done in the Lord's name in the sense of claiming His power or support. Battles were fought and won in His name (Ps. 20:7 [MT 8]; 44:5 [MT 6]; 118:10, 12), and David claimed personal protection and victory over Goliath (1 S. 17:45). Likewise, an oath in His name was binding (Dt. 6:13). Linked with this idea are passages where God acted "for the sake of his name," i.e., to vindicate His authority and power or to defend His character as Savior (e.g., Ps. 79:9f.; 143:11; Isa. 48:9-11; Ezk. 20:9, 22, 44; 36:21-23). Some of these passages refer to the honor that the nations of the world will pay to God's name (cf. Ps. 8:1 [MT 2]; 48:10 [MT 11]; Jer. 10:6f.; Mal. 1:11, 14), pointing not only to God's glory as universal Creator (Am. 4:13) but also to His sovereignty. His name is higher than any other; indeed, it is the only name (Isa. 45:21f.).

The NT transfers this concept of the authority of the name to Jesus Christ. He is both Lord and Christ (Acts 2:36). God has given Him the name that is above every name (Phil. 2:9 [alluding to Isa. 45:23]). His commission and authority, therefore, lay behind all that the apostles did in His name (cf. Acts 3:6, 16).

II. OT Names.–*A. General. 1. 'El* [Heb. *'ēl*]. This basic word for deity is found in various forms throughout the ancient Semitic languages. Although various opinions are held regarding its etymology, it probably derives from a root meaning "power" or "preeminence." Occasional adjectival use of the word to denote might or majesty (e.g., "cedars of 'El" = mighty cedars [Ps. 80:10 (MT 11)], "mountains of 'El" = majestic mountains [Ps. 36:6 (MT 7)], "in the 'El of one's hand" = within one's power [Gen. 31:29; Dt. 28:32; Mic. 2:1]) supports this derivation.

The word *'el* was also used as a proper noun to refer to the supreme god of the Canaanite pantheon, as is known from Ugaritic texts (14th cent. B.C.) that extol him as "father of men" and "god of gods." The name is commonly compounded with other descriptive titles in OT patriarchal narratives (mid-second millennium B.C.) (see II.B below). Of course the OT tradition treated all these as name of the one God, the God of Israel ("'El, the God of Israel," as He is actually called in Gen. 33:20). But probably separate names of possibly separate deities, or names associated with separate centers of worship of one deity, became identified with Yahweh, the personal name of the God of Israel. A great deal of uncertainty must surround any attempt to delineate the historical stages of this assimilation, however, and such a task is unproductive. Although the OT does witness to the strains of early Israel's polytheistic environment — and the polytheism in its own ancestry (Josh. 24:14f.) — from the perspective of the history of revelation it mainly witnesses to the various revelations of the one living God to the patriarchs against the cultural background of their time. Through those revelations He created that relationship of promise upon which the nation and its faith were founded.

In the postpatriarchal literature the name 'El is clearly interchangeable with Yahweh. It occurs more frequently in poetic literature (particularly in Psalms and Job), which preserves ancient literary forms and usage. It is commonly compounded with words describing the characteristics of Yahweh. In these compounds 'El can be in the construct state, e.g., "God ['El] of glory" (Ps. 29:3), "God of knowledge" (1 S. 2:3), "God of salvation" (Isa. 12:2), etc.; or it may be qualified by an adjective or participle, e.g., Yahweh is a great (Dt. 7:21), compassionate (Ex. 34:6), forgiving (Ps. 99:8), jealous (Ex. 20:5), living (Josh. 3:10) God (*'ēl*).

"'El" was also frequently used to form personal names (theophorous names), e.g., Eliezer, "God is help" (Gen. 15:2). In some cases it was an alternative to the use of "Yahweh" (Ja-, Je-, Jeho-, Jo-) in names, e.g., Elnathan = Jonathan, "God/Yahweh has given." Elijah's name, "Yahweh is my God," summed up his life's work.

2. 'Elohim [Heb. *'ᵉlōhîm*]. This word is plural in form, and although it most frequently means "God" it can be used in a plural sense. Thus it can refer to other gods (Ex. 20:3; Josh. 24:16), foreign gods (Jer. 5:7), gods of the nations (Isa. 36:18), etc. Sometimes it appears to mean beings with divine qualities or authority — either angelic or human (Ps. 8:5; 82:1, 6; 138:1).

The use of the plural form with singular meaning is not unique to Israel. Similar forms occur in pre-Israelite Babylonian and Canaanite texts in which a worshiper wishes to exalt a particular god above others. This form has been called the "plural of majesty" or the "intensive plural" because it implies that all the fulness of deity is concentrated in the one god. 'Elohim's being the most common word for God in the OT thus conveys this idea. Some have also thought that the frequent use of 'Elohim emphasizes that God is not intrinsically monistic but includes within Himself plurality of powers, attributes, and personhood.

'Elohim was frequently used by itself, much in the same way that modern speakers refer to Yahweh as "God." Like 'El it is often coupled with descriptive adjectives or genitives as a means of characterizing Yahweh (cf. BDB, p. 44). Frequently in Deuteronomy and related literature 'Elohim with a personal pronominal suffix occurs with Yahweh, e.g., "Yahweh your God" (*YHWH 'ᵉlōheyḵā*). The constant repetition underlies that intensely personal and possessive relationship between Israel and their God that was the essence of the covenant.

3. 'Eloah [Heb. *'ᵉlô(a)h*]. It is uncertain whether this form is an original singular, of which 'Elohim is the plural, or has been formed by inference from the latter. Nor is its etymology any clearer than that of 'El and 'Elohim.

Its use is confined almost entirely to poetry, and its appearance in very early Israelite poetry (Dt. 32:15, 17; Ps. 18:31 [MT 32]; Hab. 3:3 — usually regarded as an ancient hymn used by Habakkuk [cf. Dt. 33:1-5; Jgs. 5:4f.]), suggests that it was an ancient title of God. It appears to be synonymous with 'Elohim and can also be used synonymously with Yahweh (Ps. 18:31; 50:22f.; Isa. 44:8 [cf. v. 6]). It occurs more often in Job (42 times) than in the rest of the OT (15 times). Whether its use in Job was theologically motivated (i.e., intended to maintain a certain detachment from the historical connections of the God of Israel), was a deliberate archaism, or evinces an early date for the book, is a matter for the critics. (The Aramaic form of 'Eloah, *'ᵉlāh,* occurs frequently in Ezra [e.g., 5:2] and Daniel [6:7 (MT 8)].)

B. "'El" Compounds. 1. 'El Shaddai [Heb. *'ēl šadday*]. This title first appears in Gen. 17:1, where God identifies Himself thus when renewing the covenant with Abram. It recurs in 28:3; 35:11; 43:14; 48:3; 49:25 and appears to be the most common title of the deity known and worshiped by the patriarchs (cf. Ex. 6:3; see II.C below).

The antiquity of the title, however, seems likely to defeat all attempts to uncover its etymology. It has been derived from various roots that suggest that it means "sufficient," "lord," "rain-god," or "mountain-god." Most recently the meaning "all-knowing" has been suggested on the basis of an Akkadian name of the god Marduk (see Walker). In the postpatriarchal period, however, a connection seems to have been made in the popular mind between the title and the verb *šāḏaḏ,* "devastate, destroy." This meaning certainly fits contexts like Ruth 1:20f.; Job 5:17; 6:4; Ps. 68:14 [MT 15]; Isa. 13:6; and Joel 1:15, but is probably paronomasia rather than the true etymology. It has, however, influenced the Greek and Latin translations, which most often render the word respectively by *pantokrátōr* and *omnipotens,* "all-powerful," and have in turn produced the rendering "the Almighty" uniformly used by the AV, RSV, and NEB.

2. 'El 'Elyon [Heb. *'ēl 'elyôn*]. The second word of this title is a superlative (cf. W. Genesius, E. Kautzsch, and A. E. Cowley, *Hebrew Grammar* [2nd ed. 1910], § 133g) derived from *'ālâ,* "go up," and is often used, apart from its use as a divine title, as an adjective meaning "high, uppermost, exalted" (cf. Dt. 26:19; 2 Ch. 7:21). As a title for God, therefore, it obviously means "Most High," "Exalted One" (cf. Ugar. *'ly,* "Most High").

It first occurs in Gen. 14:18-21 in the encounter between Abram and Melchizedek king of (Jeru)Salem. Since Melchizedek was a "priest of 'El 'Elyon" and blessed Abram by that god, many scholars believe that 'Elyon was the deity worshiped at the Jerusalem cultic center in pre-Israelite times. Melchizedek called him "maker [or possessor] of heaven and earth," which Fisher, on the basis of Akkadian and Ugaritic comparisons, has interpreted as "parent of all gods in heaven and earth." This exalted status fits well with the occurrence of the title in the very ancient Israelite poem in Dt. 32:8, in which 'Elyon has preeminence over all the nations on earth.

In subsequent Israelite tradition the title was entirely appropriated and assimilated by Yahweh. Thus Abram in Gen. 14:22 spoke of "Yahweh, 'El 'Elyon." In the rest of the OT it occurs for the most part in poetry, especially in Psalms, is always synonymous with Yahweh, and is uniformly translated "the Most High." Ps. 91:1f. combines 'Elyon, 'El Shaddai, and Yahweh in one confession of trust in God. The same grouping appears in the oracles of Balaam (Nu. 24:16). 'Elyon also occurs several times in the exalted language of Dnl. 7, where the people of God are described as "saints of the Most High" (vv. 18, 22, 25, 27).

The following are other "'El" compounds occurring in Genesis that in the view of its narrator were synonymous with Yahweh but in the view of many contemporary scholars were originally particular names or titles by which the high god 'El was worshiped at different sites.

3. 'El 'Olam [Heb. *'ēl 'ôlām*]. Yahweh was invoked under this title, "the everlasting God," at Beer-sheba (Gen. 21:33). The title is not found in this form again (but cf. Isa. 40:28: "the Lord is the everlasting God" [*'ᵉlōhê 'ôlām YHWH*]; Ps. 90:2: "from everlasting to everlasting thou art God" [*'ôlām . . . 'ēl*]). Its meaning, however, lives on in the frequent description of Yahweh as "the living God" (cf. Josh. 3:10; Ps. 42:2 [MT 3]; 84:2 [MT 3]; Hos. 1:10 [MT 2:1]; etc.) and in the attaching of *'ôlām* to many of His attributes (e.g., His love [Jer. 31:3], mercy [Isa. 54:8], glory [Ps. 104:31], faithfulness [Ps. 117:2]).

4. 'El Ro'i [Heb. *'ēl rō'î*]. This expression appears only in Gen. 16:13, which tells how Hagar finds protection and sustenance in the desert at the spring Beer-lahai-roi. She addressed Yahweh with this title, which probably means "God of seeing" or "God who sees me."

5. 'El Bethel [Heb. *'ēl bêṯ 'ēl*]. This expression occurs in Gen. 31:13, where God thus identified Himself to Jacob, and again in Gen. 35:7, where Jacob built an altar at Bethel in memory of his earlier experience there (Gen. 28:10-22). The ELEPHANTINE PAPYRI mention this divine title.

C. The Covenant Name: Yahweh. Yahweh is the only truly personal name of God in Israel's faith; the others are titular or descriptive expressions. References to "the name" or "in the name" of God indicate this name.

The name consists of four consonants, YHWH (known as the tetragrammaton). Shorter forms also occur: *Yāh* (Ex. 15:2; the exclamation *hallᵉlûyāh,* "praise Yah," is frequent in the Psalms); *Yāhû* and *Yô,* both used in the formation of personal names (e.g., Joel [*yô'ēl*–'Yo is God'] and Elijah [*'ēlîyāhû*–'Yahu is God'). But these are probably abbreviations of the tetragrammaton rather than more original forms of the name, as some scholars have thought.

Recently archeologists unearthed what some scholars regard as early non-Israelite occurrences of the divine name. *Yw* as a name of Baal has appeared in a text from UGARIT, but the reading has been disputed. The Ebla tablets (*see* TELL MARDIKH) reportedly contain the name in the forms *-Ya* and *-Yau*. Unfortunately the reading is far from certain, and since the element forms the ending of a word, it may merely represent a common Akkadian hypocoristic or diminutive form. This phenomenon seems to have been preserved to some extent in Hebrew and can be illustrated by the name Abijah, commonly rendered "Yah is my father." The name, however, may mean nothing more than "little father," or something similar.

It would thus seem precarious to argue from early Ebla renderings that a deity named Ya(u) was worshiped there.

The pronunciation of YHWH in the OT can never be certain, since the original Hebrew text used only consonants. The vowel points added in the MT are not those of the name itself (see below), which had come to be considered too holy to pronounce (cf. Ex. 20:7; Lev. 24:11). But the early Greek transliterations of the name by Clement of Alexandria and Theodoret, respectively *iaoue* and *iabe* (*b* pronounced as an English *v*), have led scholars to the view that "Yahweh" is probably the closest equivalent to the original pronunciation.

The English form "Jehovah" arose by a latinized combination of the four consonants (YHWH) with the vowel points that the Masoretes used to show that they meant the reader to say "'Adonai" (see II.D below) when reading the tetragrammaton. That is, they left the consonants for "Yahweh" in the text but put with them the vowels for "Adonai" — *ᵃ, ō, ā*. Though the older English versions sometimes used this hybrid form with compound names (such as "Jehovah-Jireh" [Gen. 22:14]), usually the divine name has been rendered by "the LORD," following the ancient Greek translations of the OT, which commonly rendered Yahweh by *kýrios*.

Scholars have also disputed the linguistic root and meaning of YHWH, though, as H. H. Rowley pointed out, "Etymology is not finally important here for OT theology since not etymology but experience filled the term with meaning" (p. 55). Scholars now generally agree, however, that the name is connected with the verb *hāwâ,* itself an archaic form of *hāyâ,* "be, become, happen." What is in doubt, however, is the form of the verb. Some scholars have seen it as simply a combination of the root *hwh* plus prefixed *y* to make a personal name. Much more common is the view that it is the qal (simple) conjugation of the verb, with either a present sense — "He who is," "the self-existent one" — or an imperfect, future sense — "He who will continue to be (present with His people)." Another common view is that it is the hiphil (causative) conjugation: "He who causes to be, who brings into existence," i.e., "the Creator." Although this last explanation is attractive and has had much support, it is doubtful for two reasons. First, there is no known example of *hāyâ* in the hiphil. Second, on the only occasion where an apparent attempt is made to explain the name (Ex. 3:14f.), Yahweh's character and acts as Israel's redeeming, covenant God, not His role as Creator, are indicated.

In Ex. 3:14f. God declares that His name is *'ehyeh 'ᵃšer 'ehyeh*. The verb *'ehyeh* is imperfect qal and is obviously linked to the tetragrammaton, as vv. 14f. make plain. Of the two possible senses for it, "I am who/what I am" and "I will be who/what I will be," the latter is preferable but not because the idea of God as a self-existent, unique, transcendent being is "foreign to Hebrew thought," as has often been said (cf. Isa. 40–55, which describe Yahweh in exalted language that implies all those things). Rather, it is preferable because the verb *hāyâ* has a more dynamic sense of being — not pure existence, but becoming, happening, being present — and because the historical and theological context of these early chapters of Exodus shows that God is revealing to Moses, and subsequently to the whole people, not the inner nature of His being, but His active, redemptive intentions on their behalf. He "will be" to them "what" His deeds will show Him "to be."

It is especially made clear that He will be "with" them. In the context of the call of Moses and the revelation of the significance of the divine name, the promise "I will be with you/your mouth" occurs three times (Ex. 3:12; 4:12, 15). The presence of God is then realized in the covenant, of which the vital preface is God's proclaiming Himself as a redeeming (20:2) and forgiving (34:6) God. "It is this assurance of the presence of the Saviour God with his covenant people which is embodied in the name Yahweh" (Abba, p. 325).

Attempts to find extra-Israelite origins of the name have been entirely unconvincing. The view that Moses adopted the name from the Kenites (Midianites) during his stay with Jethro — apparently a priest of Yahweh (Ex. 18) — has at least some slight biblical basis (*IDB*, II, 409f.) but a totally new dimension of meaning was attached to the name at the Exodus.

More important is whether YHWH was known to the patriarchs or was first made known to Moses. Some scholars interpret Ex. 6:3 to mean that the patriarchs had not known the name Yahweh, and, regarding this passage as conflicting with passages in Genesis where the patriarchs apparently knew and worshiped God under this name (Gen. 15:7; 28:13; etc.), attribute the discrepancy to the existence of different documentary sources woven together in the text. According to this view, the J source had for theological reasons employed the name Yahweh anachronistically from the start, whereas the E and P sources had on the whole avoided it until the Exodus period. More careful exegesis of Ex. 6:3, however, shows that this passage concerns the character and content of the respective names 'El Shaddai and Yahweh, not simply knowledge of the names themselves. It should accordingly be translated: "I appeared to Abraham . . . in the character of 'El Shaddai, but as to the character of my name Yahweh I did not make myself known" (cf. Motyer, pp. 11ff.; Abba, p. 323). Therefore one need not doubt the biblical tradition that the use of this name was already very ancient by the time of Moses (cf. Gen. 4:26; 9:26; cf. the abbreviation *yô* in the name of Moses' mother Jochebed [*yôḵeḇeḏ,* Ex. 6:20]), so that God could in truth be called "the God of your fathers" (Ex. 3:15). What was new at the call of Moses and the Exodus was not the revelation of the name itself but a new experience of its meaning, bound up with God's faithfulness to His covenant promises and redemptive acts on behalf of His people (cf. Jacob, pp. 49f.).

The divine name also occurs in the compound "Lord of hosts" (Heb. *YHWH ṣᵉḇā'ôṯ*; sometimes found in the fuller form "Yahweh, God [*'ĕlōhîm*] of hosts"). This title is absent from the Pentateuch but occurs occasionally in Samuel, Kings, Chronicles, and Psalms. It is very common in the prophets, especially Isaiah, Jeremiah, and the postexilic trio Haggai, Zechariah, and Malachi.

Scholars hold various views concerning the identification of these "hosts." In the earlier passages the title occurs in connection with the ark of the covenant (2 S. 6:2, 18; 7:2, 8, 26f.; cf. 1 Ch. 17:7), and since the ark was a kind of war shrine (cf. Nu. 10:35), it is thought that the "hosts" were originally the armies of Israel (cf. 1 S. 17:45). This meaning, however, is not found in the prophets, where the title is used in nonmilitary contexts (e.g., Isa. 47:4; Jer. 5:14; Hos. 12:5; Am. 3:13; 6:14). Therefore some regard the "hosts" as heavenly, angelic beings (cf. Ps. 103:21; 148:2) or possibly astral divinities over whom Yahweh was supreme (cf. Isa. 40:26).

Probably all of these senses are combined in the title, which clearly is used to exalt Yahweh as all-powerful sovereign and controller of all human and superhuman forces. (For the view that *YHWH ṣᵉḇā'ôṯ* is a sentence-name meaning "he creates the [divine] hosts," see Cross, pp. 65f.)

D. 'Adon, 'Adonai [Heb. *'āḏôn, 'ᵃḏōnāy*]. This word is

of uncertain origin, but its basic meaning in Hebrew is "lord, master, sir." It is thus commonly applied to a human overlord (cf. esp. the phrase "my lord, the king" [e.g., 1 S. 26:19]), a husband (Gen. 18:12), a slave's master (Ex. 21:5), and other persons in authority (cf. BDB, pp. 10f.). Its application to God clearly implies dignity and dominion (cf. Ps. 2:4; Isa. 7:7).

'Adonai occurs most frequently with the name Yahweh. (It is thus usually translated in the English versions as "the Lord GOD" [e.g., Isa. 61:1] to distinguish it from "the LORD God," which is "Yahweh 'Elohim" [e.g., Ezr. 9:15].) This usage is widespread throughout the OT. It occurs less frequently with 'Elohim (e.g., Ps. 35:22f. [where Yahweh, 'Elohim, and 'Adonai all occur]; 86:12).

Eventually reverence for the divine name YHWH led to its being replaced by 'Adonai not only in oral reading but probably also in the written copying of the text (in several places). In the Masoretic pointing, the final vowel *a* was lengthened to *ā* to distinguish the divine title from *'ᵃḏōnay*, which denotes the human plural "my lords."

E. Other Descriptive Terms. The character and acts of God were so rich and many-sided that Israelite piety employed a wide variety of metaphors and epithets in trying to convey what He meant to them. Such terms were not strictly names, but a few were used so frequently that they almost became names.

1. Rock [Heb. *ṣûr*]. This title occurs frequently in poetic literature (Dt. 32:4, 15, 18; Ps. 18:2, 31, 46 [MT 3, 32, 47]; 19:14 [MT 15]; 89:26 [MT 27]; Isa. 17:10; 26:4; 44:8; Hab. 1:12) and obviously symbolizes Yahweh's steadfast, enduring strength and protection.

2. Holy One [Heb. *qāḏôš*]. Holiness is such an essential attribute of God that "holy" becomes a descriptive name (cf. Isa. 57:15). Most frequently it occurs in the phrase "the Holy One of Israel," which emphasizes that God's holiness is closely related to the holiness He demands of Israel (Lev. 19:2). It is a favorite title throughout the book of Isaiah (e.g., 1:4; 12:6; 40:25; 43:3; 60:9; cf. esp. 6:3), but it often occurs elsewhere (e.g., 2 K. 19:22; Job 6:10; Jer. 50:29; Hos. 11:9; Hab. 3:3).

3. King [Heb. *meleḵ*]. This title expresses the sovereignty of God. Although it derived from the institution of monarchy, it was nevertheless even used in premonarchial Israel, as certain early texts show (Ex. 15:18; Nu. 23:21; 24:7; Dt. 33:5). It is particularly frequent in the Psalms (5:2 [MT 3]; 44:4 [MT 5]; 68:24 [MT 25]; 74:12; 84:3 [MT 4]; etc.). It does not often appear elsewhere in the preexilic period, perhaps because of the existence of a foreign deity known as *mlk* (*see* MOLECH), whose cult appears at times to have infected Israel and to have included child sacrifice (cf. Lev. 20:2). But the title bursts forth in Deutero-Isaiah as part of his proclamation of the universal sovereignty of Yahweh (Isa. 41:21; 43:15; 44:6; 52:7).

C. J. H. WRIGHT

III. NT Names.–Greek *theós* occurs hundreds of times in the NT and is thus the most common NT name for God. *Theós* usually translates Heb. *'ᵉlōhîm* in the LXX, though it occasionally translates *YHWH, šadday*, etc. (HR, I, 630-648). "God" usually denotes the God of Israel (Acts 2:30; Rom. 11:1; etc.), the "Father who is in heaven" (Mt. 6:1 par.; 7:11 par.; 10:32 par.; etc.), the One who has sent the Son to redeem the world (Jn. 3:16). *Theós*, however, also denotes Jesus the divine Son in the Johannine tradition (Jn. 1:1, 18; 20:28), as well as the deities of the pagan pantheon (e.g., Acts 28:6; 1 Cor. 8:5; cf. Ps. 81:6 [LXX] = Jn. 10:34f.). The assimilation of the words of Jesus into Greek from their original Semitic languages is shown in Matthew (27:46) and Mark (15:34), who translate Heb. *'ēlî* and Aram. *'ᵉlāhî* ("my God") as Gk. *theé mou* (vocative of *theós*) and *ho theós mou*, respectively (cf. B. M. Metzger, *Textual Comm. on the Greek NT* [1971], pp. 70, 119).

Greek *kýrios* is usually translated "Lord" in the English versions and is the equivalent of Heb. *YHWH* in the LXX (e.g., Isa. 40:3; HR, II, 800-839). "Lord" may denote God (the Father; Mt. 5:33; Lk. 1:6; etc.) or deities of the Greco-Roman world (1 Cor. 8:5). Usually, however, *kýrios* is a title of the exalted Jesus, applied to Him by virtue of His resurrection and session at the right hand of God the Father (Acts 2:36; Rom. 10:9; cf. Phil. 2:11; Mk. 12:36 par.). The acknowledgment of Jesus as Lord was the earliest confession of faith in the Church (V. H. Neufeld, *Earliest Christian Confessions* [*NT Tools and Studies*, 5, 1963], pp. 51-60).

Other names for God in the NT are used infrequently. Gk. *hósios* most frequently translates Heb. *ḥāsîḏ* ("pious," "loyal") in the LXX (HR, II, 1018). *Hósios* usually means "devout," "holy" (e.g., 1 Tim. 2:8; Tit. 1:8) but denotes God, the "Holy One" in Rev. 16:5, and Jesus, the "Holy One" of God in Acts 2:27; 13:35 (= Ps. 15:10). Gk. *hágios* ("holy") corresponds to Heb. *qōḏeš* (HR, I, 12-15) and occurs most frequently as an adjective, but its use as a substantive in 1 Jn. 2:20 probably refers to God as the "Holy One," though it could refer to Jesus (cf. Jn. 6:69; see Bauer, rev., p. 10; R. Bultmann, *Johannine Epistles* [Eng. tr., *Hermeneia*, 1975], p. 37). The Greek term *despótēs* ("lord," "master") often denotes a slave owner (1 Tim. 6:1; Tit. 2:9; etc.) but also refers to God (see "Lord," Lk. 2:29; "Sovereign Lord," Acts 4:24; Rev. 6:10). Gk. *despótēs* is the usual equivalent of Heb. *'ᵃḏōnāy* ("master," "lord") in the LXX. Gk. *hýpsistos* usually translates Heb. *ʿelyôn* ("most high") in the LXX (HR, II, 1420f.). In the NT the term is used only of God the Father (Mk. 5:7; Lk. 1:32, 35, 76; 6:35; 8:28; Acts 7:48; He. 7:1). Gk. *pantokrátōr* is used extensively in the LXX to translate Heb. *ṣᵉḇā'ôṯ* ("hosts") in expressions such as "God of Hosts" (*kýrios pantokrátōr*, 2 S. 5:10), "Lord God the God of Hosts" (*kýrios ho theós ho pantokrátōr*, Am. 3:13), etc. (HR, II, 1053f.). In the NT *pantokrátōr* occurs ten times, with nine occurrences in the book of Revelation, and is always translated "Almighty." With the exception of Rev. 1:8, *pantokrátōr* appears with other names for God. Thus the RSV translates *kýrios pantokrátōr* in 2 Cor. 6:18 as "Lord Almighty," and *kýrie ho theós ho pantokrátōr* as "Lord God Almighty" in Rev. 16:7. The term is applied both to the risen Christ (Rev. 1:8) and to God (4:8; 11:17; etc.). Gk. *sōtḗr* ("savior," "deliverer") is a widely attested term for divinities in the Greco-Roman world as well as the title of deified rulers (Bauer, rev., pp. 800f.). The Hebrew root *yšʿ* ("save," "deliver") is the most frequent antecedent of *sōtḗr* in the LXX (HR, II, 1331). *Sōtḗr* is used as a name for God (Lk. 1:47; 1 Tim. 1:1; 2:3; 4:10; Tit. 1:3; 2:10; 3:4; Jude 25) as well as for Jesus (Jn. 4:42; Acts 13:23; Tit. 2:13; 1 Jn. 4:14; etc.). Gk. *basileús* ("king") is used of God, the "King of the ages" (1 Tim. 1:17; Rev. 15:3). The title "King of kings," denoting absolute authority rather than divinity per se, is used of God and Christ in the NT (always with "Lord of lords": 1 Tim. 6:15; Rev. 17:14; 19:16). Its use was a response by both Jews and Christians to the practice of deifying earthly political rulers (M. Dibelius and H. Conzelmann, *Pastoral Epistles* [Eng. tr., *Hermeneia*, 1972], pp. 89f.; H. B. Swete, *Apocalypse of St. John* [1906], pp. 7, 220).

R. J. W.

See also GOD; GOD THE FATHER; GOD, ASCRIPTIONS TO; FATHER; LORD.

Bibliography.–R. Abba, *JBL*, 80 (1961), 320-28; E. Brunner, *Christian Doctrine of God* (Eng. tr. 1949), pp. 117-127; F. M.

Cross, *Canaanite Myth and Hebrew Epic* (1973), pp. 3-75; O. Eissfeldt, "Renaming in the OT," in P. R. Ackroyd and B. Lindars, eds., *Words and Meanings: Essays Presented to David Winton Thomas* (1968), pp. 69-80; L. R. Fisher, *JBL*, 81 (1962), 264-270; D. N. Freedman, *JBL*, 79 (1960), 151-56; E. Jacob, *Theology of the OT* (Eng. tr. 1958), pp. 43-64; E. C. B. Maclaurin, *VT*, 12 (1962), 439-463; J. A. Motyer, *Revelation of the Divine Name* (1959); G. von Rad, *Studies in Deuteronomy* (*SBT*, 9, 1953), 37-44; *OT Theology*, I (Eng. tr. 1962), 179-187; H. Ringgren, *Israelite Religion* (Eng. tr. 1966), pp. 19-23, 31-34, 66-69; H. H. Rowley, *Faith of Israel* (1956), pp. 48-56; *TDNT*, III, *s.v.* κύριος κτλ. (Quell, Foerster); V, *s.v.* ὄνομα (Bietenhard); *TDOT*, I, *s.v.* "'ādhôn" (Eissfeldt), "'ēl" (Cross), "'ᵉlōhîm" (Ringgren); N. Walker, *ZAW*, 72 (1960), 64-66; F. Zimmerman, *VT*, 12 (1962), 190-95.

GOD, SON(S) OF. *See* SONS OF GOD (OT); SONS OF GOD (NT).

GOD SPEED. Occurs only in 2 Jn. 10f., AV, as the translation of Gk. *chaírein,* the infinitive of *chaírō,* and is rendered in the RSV "greet, greeting," in the NEB "give a greeting." It means "rejoice, be of good cheer, be it well with you"; *chaíre, chaírete, chaírein* were common forms of greeting and farewell, expressive of good will and desire for the person's prosperity, translated in the Gospels as "Hail!" (Mt. 26:49; 27:29; 28:9; etc.; it was transliterated *kêrî* in rabbinic Hebrew with the same meaning, "hail"; cf. M. Jastrow, *Dictionary of the Targumim, The Talmud Babli and Yerushalmi, and the Midrashic Literature* [repr. 1967], p. 63b), and "greeting" in Acts 15:23; 23:26; Jas. 1:1; cf. 2 Macc. 1:10. Thus it is similar to Heb. *šālôm,* "peace," which is used for a greeting in the OT (e.g., 1 S. 25:5f.; cf. Jn. 20:21). "Godspeed" first appears in Tyndale's version; Wyclif had "heil!" and Rheims, "God save you."

The author of 2 John warned against showing any form of hospitality toward those "who will not acknowledge the coming of Jesus Christ in the flesh" (v. 7). The people in view here were not merely heretics: "such a one is the deceiver and the antichrist" (v. 7). Extending Christian hospitality to such propagandists would enable them to lead more people astray. W. L. WALKER

GOD THE FATHER.

OLD TESTAMENT

I. Derivation of the Concept
II. Yahweh as Father
III. Yahweh's Son
IV. Meaning of Divine Fatherhood

I. Derivation of the Concept.–Israel's heritage from its neighbors included the concept of God as "father of the gods," but the references are fleeting and in no way constitutive for theology. In Semitic mythology paternity was understood literally and metaphysically. The other gods were seen as the offspring of God. Tribes and families traced their origin to God and expressed this in theophoric names. Israel would not disagree in essence but found other means such as the idea of "creation" to express their understanding of their debt to God. But some reflections of their neighbors' ways of thinking remain in the OT.

The term "sons of God" (Heb. *bᵉnê 'ēlîm*) in Ps. 29:1 and 82:6 (MT 7) (RSV mg.) probably means only "divine or supernatural beings," e.g., the members of the heavenly court (cf. Ps. 82:6f.; Dt. 32:8 [LXX]). On the difficult Gen. 6:2, where the sons of God (Heb. *bᵉnê hā'ᵉlōhîm*) marry "the daughters of men," see the comms.; elsewhere *bᵉnê hā'ᵉlōhîm* clearly denotes angels, heavenly beings (Job 1:6; 2:1; 38:7; cf. Aram. *bar 'ᵉlāhîn,* "a son of the gods," in Dnl. 3:25). Otherwise, OT references to God as "Father" speak of His relation to human beings.

Northwest Semitic literature shows that it was common to have names with *'āḇ,* "father," as an element. Most of them may be understood as theophoric, claiming God (or a god) as father. Such names are familiar in the OT. They may recall God as the father of the family or clan, but this is doubtful for most Israelite names. Others claim a particular god, as do Heb. *'ᵃḇî'ēl,* "My Father is El" (1 S. 9:1; 14:51); *'ᵉlîāḇ,* "My God is Father"; *'ᵃḇîmeleḵ,* "My Father is King"; and *'ᵃḇîšālôm,* "My Father is Peace." The name "Joab" testifies to Yahweh as Father, as does Heb. *'ᵃḇîyāhû.*

II. Yahweh as Father.–Yahweh is called the "Father of Israel." In Ex. 4:22 He calls Israel His "first-born son." He thus establishes His right to act on Israel's behalf. Dt. 32:6 asks, "Is not he your father, who created you, who made you . . .?" Paternity is used along with verbs usually associated with creation (cf. v. 18:1, "the Rock that begot you . . . the God who gave you birth"). In this verse, as in passages stressing the compassion or protection of God, masculine and feminine implications mingle. This should be enough to warn against using the father imagery as a sign of God's masculinity. Sex identification plays no part in the OT understanding of God. Only the origin of the metaphors or symbols that are used to portray His person or His role brings such an identification to the OT.

Hosea 11:1 states that Yahweh called His son from Egypt and cared for him, and Isa. 1:2 says that Yahweh has raised sons. These passages, along with Jer. 3:19, lament the lack of a response worthy of the relation. Jer. 31:9 supports the promise of God's providential care with "for I am a father to Israel, and Ephraim is my first-born."

References to God as Father stress His authority over Israel and His responsibility to care for her. In Isa. 45:9-11 the figure is paired with that of the potter who exercises his will freely over the pot. The same relation applies in Isa. 64:8: "O Lord, thou art our Father; we are the clay, and thou art our potter." Isa. 63:16 calls on Yahweh as Father at a moment when neither Abraham nor Israel can be called upon. Here Father and Redeemer are parallel concepts. Mal. 2:10 combines the Father and Creator concepts: "Have we not all one father? Has not one God created us?" One other use (Mal. 1:6) complains of a lack of appropriate response to God as father.

Interpreters agree that these references do not document a basic concept for OT doctrine. Fatherhood is one of many figures used by the OT to communicate a picture of God's relation to Israel.

III. Yahweh's Son.–Yahweh recognized the king as His son. The classic example is Ps. 2:7: "You are my son, today I have begotten you." This recognition testifies to an adoption ceremony and is based on the promise to David in 2 S. 7:14 and 1 Ch. 28:6: "I have chosen him to be my son, and I will be his Father." Ps. 89:26f. prescribes the names the king must use for God as "Father, God, and the Rock of his help." In return God will name him His firstborn and make him the greatest of the kings.

All the references fit a picture of adoption and support the authority of the king by this close association with God. Being recognized as "son" of God is a guarantee of the king's power and authority in Zion. Thus being "son" and "servant" of Yahweh is a basic concept of Davidic kingship in the OT and of messianic teaching which builds on Davidic promises and ideals.

IV. Meaning of Divine Fatherhood.–The OT is very restrained in its use of the father-son relation for God.

Only once is Israel called "the sons of the Lord" (Dt. 14:1), while Hosea reserves the title "'Sons of the living God'" (1:10 [MT 2:1]) for the last days. Yet Israel could think of God as they would of a father. By Hellenistic times one could even address Him as "Father" (Sir. 23:1).

The basic idea of God as Father was one of authority over His people, or of authority exercised through the king or the messiah. But the use of the father-child figure softened the picture, always lending it a touch of the love and tenderness which Hosea stressed so effectively.

When the idea of Father is combined with that of Creator, the groundwork is laid for a universal concept of God as Father. Quell's development of this idea (pp. 972f.) goes beyond the evidence. But Jeremiah's description (3:19) of Israel being set down among God's children with the hope that they would call God "Father" points in that direction. Other passages support the growing breadth of the concept.

The OT concept of God as Father is thin and underdeveloped, perhaps deliberately so in order to avoid association with pagan ideas of divine fatherhood in the sense of procreation. Nevertheless, the OT concept is the foundation for the NT doctrine.

Bibliography.–*TDNT,* IV, *s.v.* πατήρ (Quell); *TDOT,* I, *s.v.* "'ābh" (Ringgren); M. J. Lagrange, *RB,* 5 (1908), 481-499; B. Colless, *Biblia Revuo,* 4/4 (1968), 5-19; J. Hempel, *Gott und Mensch im AT* (1936), pp. 170-78; *IP,* p. 10.

J. D. W. WATTS

New Testament

I. Uses of the Term
II. God as the Father of Jesus
III. Limited Scope of Divine Fatherhood
IV. Comfort of Divine Fatherhood

I. Uses of the Term.–The most interesting and important term in the Gospels reflecting how Jesus thought about God is the simple word "Father." In the OT, God is occasionally thought of as Father, but the term is usually used of God's relationship to Israel as a people, not of His relationship to the individual. God is the Creator and Lord of His people; He can be called their Father.

In intertestamental Judaism, "Father" appears only infrequently: "because he is our Lord and God,/he is our Father for ever" (Tob. 13:4), "I praised the Lord: Thou art my Father" (Sir. 41:10), "O Lord, Father and Ruler of my life" (23:1), "O Lord, Father and God of my life" (23:4). The last two references are a translation of the Greek, but the Hebrew original has "God of my Father." In one reference (Jub. 1:24: "I will be their Father and they shall be My children"), the relationship is eschatological.

All the above instances come from the literature of Palestinian Judaism. Nowhere in this literature is God addressed in prayer as "Father" or "my Father."

The term occurs more frequently in the literature of the diaspora of Hellenistic Judaism. God is addressed in prayer as Father in 3 Macc. 6:4, 8 and He is called Father in the same work (5:7; 7:6), but here He is the Father of His people. We should conclude that this is also the meaning of 6:4, 8. In Wisd. 2:16; 11:10 God is called the Father of righteous men, and is addressed in prayer as Father (14:3). At Qumrân the term is rare (*Prayer for Intercession* 3:5-8; 1QH 9:35). In rabbinic literature God is called "our heavenly Father" by Johanan ben Zakkai (*ca.* A.D. 50-80; cf. J. Jeremias, *Prayers of Jesus,* p. 16), and this became a common designation in later rabbinic writings.

The term occurs four times in Mark, eight times in Q, thirty-six times in Matthew, and one hundred times in John. The most important of these are the expressions "my Father" (seventeen times) and "your Father" (nineteen times). Jesus teaches His disciples to pray "our Father," but Jesus never uses "Our Father" to designate God at the same time and in the same way as the Father of Himself and of His disciples. It is true that many of these expressions seem to be editorial on the part of the Evangelist Matthew, but this appears nevertheless to be a sound tradition reflecting Jesus' usage. This is especially true of the expression "heavenly Father" or "Father in heaven," which is found almost exclusively in Matthew (cf. Lk. 11:13 par. Mt. 7:11).

II. God as the Father of Jesus.–The distinction between "my Father" and "your Father" suggests that Jesus sustained a different relationship to God. This is supported by two exegetical facts. John seems to reflect a solid tradition when he quotes Jesus as saying, "I am ascending to my Father and your Father, to my God and your God" (20:17).

More crucial, however, is the Q passage in Mt. 11:27 (par. Lk. 10:22): "All things have been delivered to me by my Father; and no one knows the Son except the Father, and no one knows the Father except the Son and anyone to whom the Son chooses to reveal him." This passage contains such a "high" Christology that critics have often suggested that it cannot be an authentic saying of Jesus. But more conservative critics have recognized its authenticity (see A. M. Hunter, pp. 241-48). This is a decisive passage, for it puts Jesus' knowledge of God on a different level from that of His disciples. The Son knows the Father as the *Father knows the Son.* It is self-evident that the Father's knowledge of the Son is that of a direct, intuitive, innate, and unmediated knowledge. The Son knows the Father in the same way the Father knows the Son — by way of a *direct, intuitive, innate, unmediated knowledge.* Jesus sustains a mutual relationship with the Father that He can share with no other. The knowledge of God which people may come to possess is not an innate knowledge; it is not something they already possess. Christ possesses this innate knowledge of God because He is God's Son. Other people do not share this knowledge. They may come to a knowledge of God only secondhand, by way of mediation through the Son. This is not an innate knowledge, but is one that is experienced as people become disciples of Jesus. The Son knows the Father because He is by nature the Son; other people must become children through the mediation of Christ.

Another fact of great importance is His use of Father. It is brought out in His prayer in Mk. 14:36. Facing His agony of suffering and death, Jesus prayed, "Abba, Father, all things are possible to thee; remove this cup from me; yet not what I will, but what thou wilt." We are here indebted to the researches of J. Jeremias. He has thoroughly investigated the rabbinic literature of the time, and has come to the following conclusions which have been widely accepted. *'Abba* is an Aramaic word for father, an intimate word used by children when addressing their father, and by adults as well in the intimacy of the family relationship. Furthermore, Jeremias has discovered that the Jew avoided applying the word *'Abba* to God, even outside of prayers. "*We do not have a single example* of God being addressed as *'abbā* in Judaism but Jesus *always* addressed God in this way in his prayers" (Jeremias, *Theology,* p. 66). Furthermore, Jesus taught His disciples to call God "Abba, Father." This is proved by two passages (Rom. 8:15 and Gal. 4:6) where Paul reflects the early Christian practice of prayer, according to which God is addressed as "Abba." Here is an instance of an Aramaic word so imbedding itself in the Christian vocabulary that it can be merely transliterated into Greek. This represents the attitude Christians are to have toward

God. They are to approach Him with all the openness and confidence and affection of small children.

III. Limited Scope of Divine Fatherhood.–At one point, NT criticism has experienced a radical change. This is on the question whether Jesus saw the Fatherhood of God as limited to His disciples or as a relationship that exists for all mankind, i.e., the universal Fatherhood of God. Some of the "old liberal" scholars held that God was the universal Father because God is and remains what He ought to be, but people have relinquished their kinship through sin. Even the first edition of *ISBE* carries the statement, "Every man is born a child of God and heir of His kingdom" (T. Rees, *ISBE,* II, 1261). The ideas of the universal Fatherhood of God and the universal brotherhood of man became two of the chief elements in the theology of Old Liberalism (A. Harnack, *What Is Christianity?* [Eng. tr. 1900], pp. 69ff.). It is now commonly recognized, however, that this is an erroneous interpretation (cf. H. F. D. Sparks, p. 260). This more recent conclusion is based on two exegetical facts: (1) Jesus never grouped Himself together with His disciples as the sons of God, since His messianic sonship is different from the sonship of His disciples; (2) Jesus never applied the category of sonship to any but His disciples. People became children of God by recognizing His messianic sonship (see C. F. D. Moule, p. 560).

A universal Fatherhood of God has been seen in Jesus' saying, "Love your enemies and pray for those who persecute you, so that you may be sons of your Father who is in heaven; for he makes his sun rise on the evil and on the good, and sends rain on the just and on the unjust" (Mt. 5:44). This saying has been interpreted to mean that love for one's enemies is required because God is the universal Father and Jesus' disciples must love all mankind because God loves all people as His children. This interpretation reads something into the saying. Actually God is viewed only as the Father of Jesus' disciples. The goodness of God in sending rain to all mankind, good and evil alike, is not to be confused with the divine Fatherhood. The same exegesis should govern our understanding of another passage: "Look at the birds of the air; they neither sow nor reap nor gather into barns, and yet your heavenly Father feeds them" (6:26). It is not as Father that God cares for the birds, and it is not as Father that God bestows His creaturely blessings on those who are not His children. The Fatherhood of God belongs to those who have responded to the divine love and have submitted themselves to God's kingdom. God seeks people, not because He is their Father, but because He would become their Father.

The universal Fatherhood of God has also been seen in the parable of the Prodigal Son. The prodigal has been interpreted to mean that every person is by nature a child of God and needs only to return to where he belongs. (Cf. "The prodigal son may become unworthy to be called a son but the father always remains a father" [*ISBE,* II, 1262]). This ignores the fact that a parable is a story drawn from daily life whose purpose is to set forth a basic truth and whose details cannot be pressed. It is improper exegesis to say that this parable teaches that all people are by nature children of God, just as it would be to say that dumb beasts are also sons of God (Lk. 15:1-7). The central truth is not about a sheep nor a coin nor a son; the central truth is about the shepherd and the woman and the father. It is that God yearns for the lost and in Jesus' mission is like a shepherd seeking his lost sheep, or a woman searching for a lost coin, or a father weeping for the return of the prodigal, and *unconditionally* welcoming him when he returns home. The prodigal is a parable about the father, not about the son. The one element all three parables embody about the lost is belonging — the lost sheep belongs to the fold; the lost coin belongs to the housewife's possessions; the son belongs in his father's house. People, although lost, find their proper place in the house of their father.

God's Fatherhood is a gift of God's kingdom. God, in Jesus' mission, is seeking out sinners and inviting them to submit to His reign that He may become their Father. An inseparable relationship exists between the kingdom of God and the Fatherhood of God, and it is particularly notable that the affinity between the two concepts appears most frequently in an eschatological setting. In the eschatological salvation the righteous will enter the kingdom of their Father (Mt. 13:43). It is the Father who has prepared for the blessed the eschatological inheritance of the kingdom (Mt. 25:34). It is the Father who will bestow on Jesus' disciples the gift of the kingdom (Lk. 12:32). The highest gift of God's Fatherhood is participation in God's sovereignty which is to be exercised over all the world. In that day Jesus will enjoy a renewed fellowship with His disciples in the Father's kingdom (Mt. 26:29). Since the greatest joy of the children of God is that of sharing the blessings of the kingdom, Jesus taught His disciples to pray, "Our Father who art in heaven . . . Thy kingdom come" (Mt. 6:9, 10). Clearly kingship and Fatherhood are closely related concepts.

These eschatological sayings illustrate one important fact about God's Fatherhood. It is a blessing and a relationship which cannot be enjoyed by all people by some innate right, but only by those who are to enter the eschatological kingdom. The concept of Fatherhood is qualified by that of the kingdom. It is as the Father that God will grant entrance into the eschatological kingdom; and it follows that those who do not enter the kingdom will not enjoy the relationship to God as their Father.

IV. Comfort of Divine Fatherhood.–The gift of Fatherhood belongs not only to the eschatological consummation; it is also a present gift. That Jesus taught His disciples to call God Abba, Father, and look upon Him as such, indicates that the future blessing of the kingdom is dependent upon a present relationship. But even in this present relationship, Fatherhood is inseparable from the kingdom. Those who know God as their Father are those for whom the highest good is life in the kingdom of God and its righteousness.

Accepting the Fatherhood of God not only means eschatological salvation; it means also security in everyday life in view of the fact that God will care for Jesus' disciples as a father cares for his children. As Father, God knows what His children need (Mt. 6:8, 32; Lk. 12:30). The Father's goodness and care are boundless (Mt. 5:45). Nothing is too insignificant to escape His attention. The rabbis explicitly prohibited prayers that God's mercy should extend "even to a bird's nest" (J. Jeremias, *Theology,* p. 182). It was considered disrespectful to associate God with something as small as a tiny bird. By way of contrast, Jesus says that God's care embraces even sparrows. Although two of them can be bought for a "penny" (Gk. *assárion,* a tiny, worthless copper coin, Mt. 10:29f.), God extends His special protection even to the smallest animals. In the heavenly world, angels who encircle the divine throne, standing in the innermost circle immediately before God, guard the little children (18:10).

The certainty of participating in the eschatological salvation and the security granted by knowing God's fatherly care give the disciples courage to submit to the unpredictable elements in the divine will. The riddles of life remain. It is difficult to understand why the gospel should be rejected by the wise and learned (Mt. 11:25f.), why so much

GOD THE FATHER

of the Sower's work is in vain (Mk. 4:4-7). Jesus never attempts to vindicate God or prove His existence — the word "Father" suffices.

In particular, suffering appears in a new light when people are conscious of being children of God. At this point, Judaism had a cruel theology: all suffering is a punishment for particular individual sins. That was the firm conviction of the time (Jn. 9:2). God watches to see that guilt and punishment correspond exactly, measure for measure. If one meets a person who is maimed, lame, blind, or leprous, it is a pious duty to murmur, "Praise be the reliable judge" (J. Jeremias, *Theology,* p. 183). If a small child dies, the parents must have committed particular sins which God is punishing. This suffering is seen as the scourge of God.

Jesus strictly forbids such calculations. In Lk. 13:1-5 He attacks the dogma that misfortune is a punishment for the definite sins of a particular people. Rather, suffering is a call for repentance, a call which goes out to all. Whereas His contemporaries ask, "What is the cause of suffering?" the disciples of Jesus are to ask, "What is the purpose of suffering?"

In addition to God's purpose of summoning to repentance, Jesus knows of another purpose for which God uses suffering: some suffering serves God's glory. This purpose is not only clear in John (9:3; 11:4), but it is also implicitly contained in the statements of all four Gospels that deal with Jesus' way of suffering and the persecution of the disciples. Suffering for Jesus' sake is our occasion for joy because it serves to glorify God and is therefore recompensed by God (Mt. 5:11f.; Lk. 6:23).

When one knows God as one's Father and thus becomes a child of God, even death appears in a different light. Thus in Mt. 10:29-31, no sparrow dies without God's will; He has a hand even in that (v. 29). He has counted the hairs on His disciples' heads; His concern for His people includes even the most insignificant detail (v. 30). Then Jesus draws the logical conclusion, "You are of much more value than many sparrows" (v. 31). If no sparrow falls without God's permission, how much more is it the case that He holds the life and death of His people in His hands? This certainty frees them from anxiety, so Jesus can demand "Fear not" (v. 31).

In another saying, Jesus affirmed that God is not God of the dead but of the living (Mt. 22:32 par.). In the remarkable brevity of this saying, Jesus declares that faith in God includes the certainty of conquering death. Where one knows God as one's Father, the eternally unfathomable riddle of evil is left in God's hands. Even the devil's action is bounded by God's will. Satan has to request to be permitted to sift His disciples as one who sifts wheat (Lk. 22:31f.). Nothing happens without God. Jesus teaches that unconditionally. Stronger than all questions, riddles, and anxieties is the one word *abba*.

In the Pauline letters the description of God as Father occurs forty times, normally in liturgical formulas of blessings (Rom. 1:27; 1 Cor. 1:3; 2 Cor. 1:2), doxologies (Rom. 15:6; 2 Cor. 1:3; Eph. 1:3), creeds (1 Cor. 8:6; Eph. 4:5), and prayers (Eph. 5:20; Col. 1:12). When Paul uses, in addition to God the "Father" and "God our Father," the phrase "the God and Father of our Lord Jesus Christ," as he frequently does (Rom. 15:6; 2 Cor. 1:3; 11:31), he is emphasizing that God has revealed Himself as Father in Jesus Christ and can hence be recognized only in Him. The Fatherhood of God is not a part of nature, but an eschatological miracle (Rom. 8:14-17; Gal. 4:1-7).

Only on three occasions in the NT does the concept of God's Fatherhood appear without a christological context. In Eph. 3:14f., God in His capacity as Creator of the world is called "The Father . . . [of] every family in heaven and on earth." In He. 12:9 in His capacity as the Creator of people's souls He is called the "Father of spirits." In Jas. 1:17 as Creator of the stars, He is called the "Father of lights." It is possible that in these passages we see a trace of the doctrine of the universal Fatherhood of God which rests in creation, not redemption. This doctrine is expounded without referring to God as Father in Acts 17:27f.

Bibliography.–G. Dalman, *Words of Jesus* (1902), pp. 189-194; G. F. Moore, *Judaism* (1927), II, 201ff.; T. W. Manson, *Teaching of Jesus* (2nd ed. 1935), pp. 89ff.; *IDB,* I, *s.v.* "Children of God" (Moule); II, *s.v.* "God, NT" (Moule); H. F. D. Sparks, "The Doctrine of the Divine Fatherhood in the Gospels," in D. E. Nineham, ed., *Studies in the Gospels* (1955), pp. 241-262; H. W. Montefiore, *NTS,* 3 (1956/7), 31ff.; T. M. Taylor, *SJT,* 11 (1958), 62-71; A. M. Hunter, *NTS,* 8 (1962), 241-48; *TDNT,* I, *s.v.* ἀββά (Kittel); V, *s.v.* πατήρ (Schrenk); J. Jeremias, *Central Message of the NT* (1965), pp. 9ff.; *Prayers of Jesus* (1967); F. Hahn, *Titles of Jesus in Christology* (1969), pp. 307-317; H. Conzelmann, *An Outline of the Theology of the NT* (1969), pp. 102-106; J. Jeremias, *NT Theology* (1971), I, 36f., 61ff.; G. E. Ladd, *A Theology of the NT* (1974), pp. 84-87; O. Hofius, "Father," *DNTT* (1976), I, 614-621.

G. E. LADD

History of the Doctrine

I. The Early Period.–*A. The Creeds.* The creeds of the early Church offer testimony that, in line with Mt. 28:19, an expression of belief in God the Father, the Son, and the Holy Spirit soon came to form the essence of the baptismal confession. Thus a second-century creed contains a simple statement of faith "in (the Father), the ruler of the universe," in "Jesus Christ (our Redeemer)," in "the Holy Spirit (the Paraclete)" (*The Epistle of the Apostles,* 5). Another confession refers more familiarly to "God the Father Almighty, His only-begotten Son our Lord Jesus Christ, and the Holy Spirit" (the *Dêr Balyzeh Papyrus*). The baptismal office in the Hippolytan rite (*ca.* 200) poses the threefold question: "Dost thou believe in God the Father Almighty, Christ Jesus, the Son of God . . . , and the Holy Spirit?" (Hippolytus *Traditio apostolica* 21f.). From the very outset, then, belief in God the Father, along with the Son and Spirit, is an integral and constitutive part of being a Christian and making a Christian confession.

B. Early Writings. The confessional statements obviously coincide with those of the first Christian writings. One need only cite two examples, the church order known as the Didache, and Justin in his first Apology. In both these texts we learn that baptism was ordinarily given in or into the name of the Father, the Son, and the Holy Spirit.

C. The Gnostic Problem. The early confession involves

an identification of God the Father as the Creator of heaven and earth. This direct equation was opposed by Gnostic teachers and their schools in the 2nd century. As they saw it, the true God is undoubtedly the supreme Father, the author of all things, but only indirectly — through a series of emanations — is He the Creator of the present world. The real creator of this world is a demiurge who may certainly be seen as the God of the OT but who is not the same as the transcendent and ineffable Father who sent forth Christ and the Spirit. For the present world, as a world of matter, is evil, and the soul, which is from the true God, has to be redeemed out of it. Evil comes from the demiurge, not from the true God and Father.

D. The Orthodox Reply. Taught by Scripture, the Church firmly resisted this separation of Father and Creator. Hermas tells us that God "created and established all things" (Shep. Herm. Mand. 1). Clement describes God as the "Creator of the entire cosmos" (1 Clem. 19:2). The apologist Aristides identifies Him as "the creator and demiurge of all things" (15). Justin specifically dismisses any distinction between God and the demiurge (*Apol.* i.58). Irenaeus argues that in relation to origins one cannot stop at a subsidiary cause or a supposedly lesser god. All things go back to the first cause and this cause, the source and father of all things, is God (*Adv. haer.* ii.1.4; 6.1).

E. The Father as God. It should be noted that in the earliest thinking of the Church the tendency when speaking of God the Father is to conceive of Him first, not as the Father of Jesus Christ, but as the source of all being. Hence God the Father is, as it were, God par excellence. To Him belong such descriptions as unoriginate, immortal, immutable, ineffable, invisible, and ingenerate. It is He who has made all things, including the very stuff of creation, out of nothing. If He has the Son and the Spirit eternally in Himself, it is He who generates the Son and sends forth the Spirit for the purposes of creation, revelation, and redemption. Godhead and Fatherhood are coterminous.

This might seem to suggest that the Father alone is properly God and the Son and Spirit are only secondarily so. Many early statements appear to support this. Hermas gives a lower place to the Son and Spirit, whom he also tends to confuse. Justin, too, refers to veneration of the Son and Spirit in the second and third ranks. Yet one must not read too much into these less precise expressions of emerging trinitarian theology. The existence of Word and Spirit in and with God is clearly recognized. The reason why they are seen as second and third in order is not because they are so eternally in God but because their generation and procession are economic in time, i.e., for the purpose of God's dealings with what is outside Himself, not essential in eternity, i.e., in God's being in Himself. No inferiority in deity is thus involved. As Irenaeus puts it, "the Father is God and the Son is God, for whatever is begotten of God is God" (*Demonstration* 47).

***II. The Trinitarian Period.**–A. Modalism.* Modalism, of course, could not accept an eternal distinction of Father, Son, and Spirit. Noetus equated God specifically with the Father and argued that if Christ is God then He must be the same as the Father. For this reason he embraced the idea of the suffering Father (patripassianism). What Christ endures, the Father endures, even to the death and passion. On this view the term Father has meaning only in the sense of the fount of all being. It has no trinitarian content. As Hippolytus pointed out, the terms "Father and Son can be used interchangeably as the situation suggests" (*Ref.* 9f.). Praxeas took a similar line, so that, as Tertullian put it, he might just as well speak of the incarnation of the Father (*Adv. Prax.* 10). The equation does not extend to Jesus, however, so that illogically Jesus as the Christ would become His own father! Sabellius gave modalism a more sensible and consistent shape by developing the intrinsically orthodox doctrine of an economic trinity. In his three major external works God manifested Himself in three modes: in creation as Father, in redemption as Son, in imparting grace as Spirit. For particular purposes the Son and Spirit came forth from the Father and then returned. They have, however, no eternal being of their own in God, who is intrinsically and eternally single as the one God.

B. Tertullian and Hippolytus. Two fathers in particular, Tertullian and Hippolytus, exposed the modalistic error and in so doing advanced trinitarian understanding. For them God in Himself, while solitary in relation to everything outside Himself, is eternally accompanied by the Word and Wisdom, each of which constitutes God a second or third time (Tertullian *Adv. Prax.* 5). It is this eternal "threeness" of God which comes to manifestation in the outside works of creation and so forth in which the Son and the Spirit act alongside the Father. On this view God the Father is the fount of deity but the Word is light from light, God a second time but not a second God, and certainly not a creature. In the more restricted sense God the Word becomes the Son only as He comes forth in God's external works, so that God the specific Father of the Son as distinct from the Father of all things assumes importance only at the economic level (*Adv. Prax.* 7). To be sure, God is essentially a trinity in unity within which the Father is the source of deity. Only economically, however, does this come to expression in the more specific relation in which God the Father begets the Word and the Word begotten by the Father is designated God the Son.

C. Novatian and Origen. Thus far the divine generation had been linked to God's external work either in creation or the Incarnation. By the middle of the 3rd cent., however, the momentous step was taken of presenting the generation itself as eternal and essential. Novatian took this step in the West. In his work *On the Trinity* (*ca.* 250) he could still call the one God the Father of all being. He could also reason, however, that since God has always been Father there must always have been a Son. This Son, deriving His being uniquely from the Father, cannot be called ingenerate as the Father is. In this sense He is subordinate to the Father as the original Godhead. Yet, being generated in eternity, and sharing the nature of the Father who begot Him, He is no less God. Origen of Alexandria took a similar step in the East. For him, as for Novatian, the Father is strictly God. But outside time, He eternally generates the Son as also God (Preface, *De prin.* 4). Since the generation is eternal the Father is essentially and not just economically the Father of the Son. A similar relation arises in the case of the Spirit too. Thus the Father, Son, and Spirit may in their eternal distinctiveness be called three hypostases (individual subsistences), although, since the deity of the Son and Spirit is by participation, this does not rule out a unity of substance (*De prin.* iv.4.1).

D. Adoptionism. Failure to keep pace with this development seems to underlie the more refined forms of adoptionism or dynamic monarchianism. Basically the adoptionists, rejecting a true Incarnation, viewed Jesus as a man upon whom the Word of Christ descended, so that he was adopted into the deity. The Word was apparently divine but impersonal, while Jesus might be called Son of God but was not God in the true sense. The Father alone was God, the Son being man upon whom the Word came, and the Spirit being the grace that dwelt in the apostles. It is to deny that the Word has a distinct being that Paul of Samosata describes it as "of one substance with the Father." This is why a term that later came to be the touchstone of orthodoxy was condemned as heretical at Antioch in 268. The one God, the Father, embraces the Word. He becomes the Father of the Son only when the Word alights upon Jesus and Jesus is thus adopted, not generated, as the Son.

E. Arianism. While not specifically adoptionist, Arianism agrees with adoptionism in viewing the Father alone as God in the strict and proper sense. The *Thalia* of Arius show this when they say that the Father is "foreign in essence from the Son, since he alone is without beginning." Thus even when the Son was not, the Father was God. Arius builds his case on the uniqueness of God the Father. Ingenerate, He cannot communicate His own essence. Even the Son cannot also be ingenerate. Thus the Son and all other beings derive their existence from Him and exist at His will. The logic of generation supports this. Even if generation be before time, He who generates precedes Him who is generated. It follows, then, that "there was when the Son was not" — the primary Arian thesis. It also follows that the Son, not being ingenerate, is a creature, even if He is the most excellent of all creatures. As creature, he cannot be equal to God. He is not of one substance with the Father. He does not fully know the Father, for "God is ineffable to his Son." In principle, if not in fact, he is mutable. If he is called Word or Wisdom, he is not identical with, but only participates in, the Word and Wisdom that belong essentially to God. At this point the adoptionist element surfaces. Although the Son is created in eternity, it is only in virtue of his unique creation and participation that he may be called, improperly, the Son of God or even God. The Father alone, the unoriginated origin of all else, is truly God.

F. The Nicene Answer. Against Arianism, although not without a good deal of preliminary confusion, the theses were formulated that became the orthodox trinitarian teaching. The first of these acknowledges that the Father is the fount of deity, for the Son is from the substance of the Father. It is denied, however, that generation means creation: He is begotten, not made. Nor does generation impose an alien substance: He is of one substance with the Father. Furthermore, the Son can Himself be described as the Creator, for while God is still equated with the Creator of heaven and earth, and of all things visible and invisible, it is also stated of the Son that by Him all things were made.

The ultimate implication of these theses in relation to the Father is an important one. The Father is still, within the Godhead, the source of being of the Son and the Spirit. Substantially, however, the Son and the Spirit are no less God than the Father. This means that when we speak of God as the source of all being outside Himself, we do not speak exclusively of the Father but also of the Son and the Spirit. In relation to the created order the source and origin is the one God as Father, Son, and Spirit, or Father, Son, and Spirit as the one God. When we refer to God the Father, then, the primary reference must be an inner trinitarian one to the Father as the Father of the Son or the Source of the Spirit. When we speak of God the Father as the Author of all creation, we have to think of the triune God and not of God the Father as distinct from God the Son or God the Holy Spirit.

G. Augustine and Cyril of Jerusalem. This implication may be seen in Augustine's work *De trinitate.* For Augustine the one God is the triune God within whom each of the persons is consubstantial and co-inherent with the others. The distinction of persons arises only within the one Godhead. The Father is Father because He begets the Son and the Son is Son because He is begotten by the Father, and the Spirit is distinguished as proceeding from the Father and the Son. Augustine sees that the word "person" is inadequate to describe the Father, Son, and Spirit, and he finds it hard to distinguish between the generation of the Son and the procession of the Spirit, for the Father is the primary fount of divine being of both the Son and the Spirit. The problem, however, is one of human language, not of the reality it denotes. If Father, Son, and Spirit are distinguished within the trinity, the unity of God must be stressed in relation to the outward works. Creation cannot be viewed as exclusively the work of the Father, nor atonement as exclusively the work of the Son, nor regeneration and charismatic endowment as exclusively the work of the Spirit. All God's external works are works of the whole trinity; it is only by appropriation that creation is related more specifically to the Father or reconciliation to the Son. Within these works, however, the roles of the persons vary, so that while one can say that God suffered on the cross in the person of the Son one could not say that He did so in the person of the Father. The reconciling work of the Father consists in His giving of the Son, not in the giving of Himself. On the other hand, even in His death, the Son does not act without the Father and the Spirit.

If the outward works of God are works of the whole trinity, this means that God is no longer seen first as the Father in His capacity as the source of all created being. He is primarily and properly the Father within the one triune God. This is clearly expressed in the *Catecheses* of Cyril of Jerusalem. Dealing with the first article of the Creed, Cyril states plainly that God is properly Father as the Father of the Only-begotten. Then, by adoption, He is Father of those who believe in the Son. Only in an extended and figurative sense is He then Father of all created things, and this designation applies to the whole Godhead and only by appropriation to the person of God the Father. The Fatherhood of God is not just a fatherhood in relation to creation. Nor, within the trinity, is it merely an economic fatherhood. It is an eternal and essential fatherhood irrespective of any external works. This fatherhood is graciously enlarged, as it were, when human creatures of God are enabled, by regeneration/adoption, to participate in the sonship of Christ and to become fellow-children and fellow-heirs of the Father in Him. In the ultimate sense, however, within the Godhead which is the source of all other being, there is only one Son. It is in virtue of this exclusive sonship, into which we are privileged to be adopted by grace and faith, that God is God the Father, and that we know and confess Him as such.

III. The Modern Period.*–*A. Orthodoxy. Throughout the 4th-16th cents. the understanding of God the Father that was achieved in reply to Arianism remained for the most part uncontested. The schoolmen examined this teaching along with all teaching, but since it seemed so plainly to derive from revelation they raised no rational objections. Similarly the reformers, while they questioned much else in the medieval tradition, saw no reason for reforming activity in this area of Christian doctrine. Indeed, even after the Reformation orthodox statements may be found in the seventeenth-century dogmaticians, and as late as the early 20th cent. a brilliant restatement of Nicene orthodoxy may be found in the *Church Dogmatics* (I/1) of Karl Barth. Discussing the Father, Barth moves from God as Creator (§ 10, 1) to the eternal Father (§ 10, 2), and argues, as Cyril did, that "God alone as He is who He is by Himself, and therefore as the eternal Father of His eternal Son, is properly and adequately to be called Father" (p. 393).

B. Unitarianism. At the same time the modern age has spawned a host of questions and alternatives, mainly on the ground that the developed doctrine either exceeds what we learn from Scripture or involves irrational enigmas. For the most part these criticisms and reconstructions have introduced nothing new but have simply led to various forms of unitarianism such as one finds in the early centuries. The principal feature is that in some way God is Father, not specifically as the Father of the Son, but more generally as the source and origin of all being.

Deism, e.g., advances a natural theology and a natural law in which God is pictured as the Creator — the celestial clockmaker — who makes the universe, imposes its laws, and leaves it to its own operation. Christ comes forward as the teacher of natural religion, but the Church has unfortunately changed His simple teaching into complicated dogmas, laws, and ceremonies. Pantheism brings an even greater simplification in which God is equated with the totality of being (i.e., reality as a whole is self-existent or self-generating) and Christ may have at best only a mediatorial role between the one, represented by God, and the many, represented by individual beings. Idealism can find a place for the trinity but only as the ultimate form of the triad that is the structure of all reality; thus Father, Son, and Spirit are merely terms for other realities, or, more properly, for abstractions, e.g., the Father as idea, the Son as opposing objectification, the Spirit as the union of the two. Unitarianism in the narrower sense can retain a high regard for the Son and the Spirit but strictly and properly only the Father is God and He is the Father of Jesus only in a quantitatively, not a qualitatively, different way. Liberal Protestantism, even when it is not expressly unitarian, focuses similarly on the extended Fatherhood of God. Harnack, e.g., says bluntly in his *What is Christianity?* that the gospel is that of the Father and not of the Son. Jesus, he thinks, taught us to see in the Father, not just His own Father, nor in fact the general Father of all creatures, but the Father of men and women. Hence the divine Fatherhood has for him a predominantly human reference.

C. The Liberal View and the Early View. Superficially the modern reinterpretation seems to be a return to the early Christian thinking which started with the concept of God as the unoriginated origin of all things and thus made the more specific equation of God and Father. Nevertheless, two important differences should be noted. First, the early Church, even if only in a rudimentary way, tried to do justice to the biblical demand that Christ and the Spirit be also accepted and confessed as God. Second, they did this not only by associating the Word and Wisdom eternally with the Father but also by discerning a specific generation of the Son (and procession of the Spirit) in relation to God's external work. For all the apparent likeness, then, the undeveloped trinitarianism of the early Church stands in marked contrast to the developed unitarianism of the modern period.

D. Women's Liberation. A more recent challenge to the confession of God the Father has come from the women's liberation movement, which dislikes the sex discrimination implied in the term father. This criticism may take extreme forms, as in a refusal to use the address in the Lord's Prayer, or in the wilder and counter-discriminatory substitution of Mother for Father. On the other hand the criticism has some healthy aspects. It has brought into focus the fact that in Scripture God can be presented as the mother of His people as well as their father. In so doing it has issued both a warning and a reminder. We are warned against a misrepresentation of the Fatherhood of God in which God is modeled on man and therefore understood as a male. We are reminded that the male-female distinction, even if it reflects the unity-in-distinction of the trinity, still belongs to man and not to God, so that the Fatherhood of God as the one who begets the Son undoubtedly embraces more than the fatherhood of the human male as a joint-progenitor of human offspring. Along these lines the criticism also plays a useful role by never allowing us to forget the inadequacy of our human language when we speak of God. Like all our terms, the word father is analogical. It points to a similarity in spite of obvious dissimilarity. It must not be taken to mean that we know what God is from what man is. If we use for God a term that applies to man we do so with a definite recollection of the difference.

For all that, the term father is valid for two reasons. First, if God is not like man, man (male and female) is like God. God has made man, if not as a replica of Himself, at any rate in His image and likeness. In human parenthood there is thus a likeness of the divine Fatherhood. Human fatherhood as an image points authentically to divine Fatherhood as the original. Second, God Himself validates the term by choosing it in the inspired writings. He validates mother as well as father, but in the intratrinitarian relation it is Father/Son, not Mother/Daughter, that is selected and used. This does not mean, as we have seen, that the Father and the Son are males, for the male/female distinction cannot be read back into God. It also does not mean, however, that God in His revelation is the victim of a male-oriented culture. In the divine likeness in Gen. 1–2, Adam's role with respect to Eve corresponds to the Father's role with respect to the Son and the Spirit — although naturally within a common and equal humanity (cf. 1 Cor. 11:2-16). It is with aptness, then, that in giving us an analogical vocabulary by which to express the divine being, God should have Himself described, not as Mother, nor neutrally as Parent, but more specifically as Father. The Son and Spirit share in creating all the being outside God, as Adam and Eve share in giving life to their descendants. But the Father is the source of the Son and the Spirit even though they be equally God, and similarly Adam is the source of Eve even though she be equally man. The term father is human, but it derives its content from the divine reality that is imaged in the human.

Bibliography.–*CD*, I/1, esp. § 10; J. F. Bethune-Baker, *Intro. to the Early History of Christian Doctrine* (1938); J. N. D. Kelly, *Early Christian Doctrines* (1960); G. L. Prestige, *God in Patristic Thought* (1952); A. E. J. Rawlinson, ed., *Essays on the Trinity and the Incarnation* (1928); H. Thielicke, *Evangelical Faith*, II (1977).

G. W. BROMILEY

GOD, UNKNOWN. *See* UNKNOWN GOD.

GODDESS. There is no separate Hebrew word for goddess in the OT. In the only occurrence of the word in the OT of the RSV (1 K. 11:5, 33, Heb. *'ĕlōhîm*), the gender is determined by name: "Ashtoreth the goddess [lit. god] of the Sidonians." In the NT the Greek term *theá*, "goddess," is applied to Diana of Ephesus (Acts 19:27, 37).

GOD-FEARER. *See* DEVOUT; DISPERSION V.C; FEAR.

GODHEAD. *See* DEITY.

GODLESS (MEN) [Heb. *ḥānēp̱*] (Job 8:13; 13:16; 15:34; 17:8; 20:5; 27:8; 34:30; 36:13; Prov. 11:9; Isa. 9:17 [MT 16];

10:6; 33:14); AV HYPOCRITE; NEB also "my plight" (Job 17:8), PROUD MEN (Job 36:13); [*zēḏ*] (Ps. 119:51, 69, 78, 85, 122); AV, NEB, PROUD; [*beliya'al*] (2 S. 23:6); AV "sons of Belial"; NEB UNGODLY; [*'ônîm*] (Prov. 11:7); AV UNJUST MEN; NEB "affluence"; [Gk. *bébēlos*] (1 Tim. 4:7; 6:20; 2 Tim. 2:16); AV PROFANE; NEB also WORLDLY.

I. In the OT.–In the OT "godless" usually renders *ḥānēp*, which means "alienated from God" (KoB, p. 317). The root *ḥnp* also includes the idea of pollution or defilement. *Zēḏ*, "insolent, arrogant," is rendered "godless" only in Ps. 119. *Beliya'al* usually occurs in combination with "sons of," "man of," etc. Its meaning is uncertain; though the AV renders it as a proper name, in the OT it generally denotes wickedness (cf. *TDOT,* II, *s.v.* "beliyya'al" [Otzen]). In Prov. 11:7 the AV and RSV apparently take *'ônîm* to be the plural of *'āwen* ("wickedness"), following the LXX *tṓn asebṓn* ("the impious, irreligious"). The NEB seems to read it as the plural of *'ôn*, "strength, riches" (cf. W. McKane, *Proverbs* [*OTL,* 1970], pp. 439f.).

The "godless" are not merely without God but assume an attitude of opposition toward God. The godless person is not merely atheistic, unbelieving, or even irreligious, but openly impious, wicked, and profane. It is hardly correct to claim that the idea of hypocrisy is involved (cf. AV "hypocrite" for Heb. *ḥānēp*), for the godless person is not one who professes one thing and lives another, but one who openly avows not only disbelief in God, but also open opposition to God.

II. In the NT.–In the NT the term is used not of persons but of Gnostic teachings. The basic meaning of *bébēlos* is "profane" as opposed to "holy." "In opposition to their claim to offer an inward truth of religion inaccessible to others, the Gnostic statements concerning God are actually seen to be outside the sphere of the holy God and His Gospel" (*TDNT,* I, 605).

W. EVANS
N. J. O.

GODLINESS [Gk. *eusebeía*] (1 Tim. 4:7f.; 6:3, 5f., 11; Tit. 1:1; 2 Pet. 1:3, 6f.; 3:11); NEB RELIGION, RELIGIOUS, TRUE RELIGION, PIETY, DEDICATED; **GODLY** [Heb. *ḥāsîḏ*] (Dt. 33:8; Ps. 4:3 [MT 4]; 12:1 [MT 2]; 16:10; 32:6; 52:9 [MT 11]; 86:2; Mic. 7:2); AV also HOLY (ONE), SAINTS, GOOD MAN; NEB "loyal servant" (Dt. 33:8), "marvellous love" (Ps. 4:3), "loyalty" (Ps. 12:1), "faithful servant" (Ps. 16:10), etc.; [*'ĕlōhîm*] (Mal. 2:15); [Gk. *theoú*] (2 Cor. 1:12); [*katá theón*] (2 Cor. 7:9-11); NEB "as God would have you bear it," "borne in God's way"; [*eusebeía*] (1 Tim. 2:2); NEB RELIGION; [*eusebṓs*] (2 Tim. 3:12; Tit. 2:12); NEB also GODLINESS (Tit. 2:12); [*eusebḗs*] (2 Pet. 2:9); [*eulabeía*] ("godly fear," He. 5:7); AV FEAR; NEB "humble submission." In Ps. 52:1 (MT 3) the RSV emends the MT *ḥeseḏ 'ēl* (AV lit. "goodness of God") to read *'el-ḥāsîḏ*, "against the godly," following the Syriac (cf. the NEB "against God's loyal servant").

In the OT the usual term is *ḥāsîḏ*, often rendered "holy" by the AV. *Ḥāsîḏ* literally means "one who has come under the bond of *ḥeseḏ*," then "one who practices *ḥeseḏ*," a term denoting loyalty, faithfulness, kindness, and thus devoutness if used of one's relationship to God. In 2 Cor. 7:9-11 the phrase *katá theón* occurs three times, referring to the kind of grief that is according to the will or pleasure of God. The *euseb-* group is used to describe the Christian life only in the Pastorals and 2 Peter. Its general meaning is "piety" as the sort of conduct that honors God. The author of the Pastorals "uses it to denote respect for the divinely created orders which his opponents [the Gnostics] despise" (*TDNT,* VII, 183). Here the problem is a movement that considers creation to be evil, advocates asceticism, and despises all the established orders and standards. In 2 Peter, on the other hand, the term is used for the moral life in contrast with the ungodly sort of conduct practiced by the libertines.

See also FEAR; SAINT.

See *TDNT,* VII, *s.v.* σέβομαι κτλ.: σέβομαι, εὐσεβής (Foerster).

N. J. O.

GODS [Heb. *'ĕlōhîm*; Gk. *theoí*]. Beings of superhuman qualities and powers conceived as dominating nature or some part of nature, whom, through proper worship, people can appease, or from whom help can be obtained.

I. OT Terms.–The English versions usually translate Heb. *'ĕlōhîm* (pl.) as "God." This plural form means the one deity who possesses all divine powers; this usage is sometimes called "the plural of majesty." Thus, *'ĕlōhîm* is to be worshiped as the one God: "Hear, O Israel: The Lord [Yahweh] our God is one Lord" (Dt. 6:4); cf. "Yahweh is greater than all gods" (Ex. 18:11); "Our God [*'ĕlōhîm*] is greater than all gods [*'ĕlōhîm*]" (2 Ch. 2:5 [MT 4]); Yahweh is "God [*'ĕlōhîm*] of gods [*'ĕlōhîm*]" (Ps. 136:2); all other gods are "not gods" (Isa. 37:19; Jer. 5:7; 16:20).

Usually the English translation of *'ĕlōhîm* is "God," but where the context demands it *'ĕlōhîm* can be translated as "gods," e.g., "Thou shalt have no other gods [*'ĕlōhîm*] before me" (Ex. 20:3; cf. "the gods [*'ĕlōhîm*] of Egypt," Ex. 12:12). Occasionally problems arise in translating *'ĕlōhîm,* e.g., Ps. 8:5 (MT 6) where the AV translates it as "angel," the RSV as "God," and the NEB as "a god." Often the Hebrew writers add various adjectives to make explicit that *'ĕlōhîm* is used as "gods," e.g., "other," as "you shall have no other gods [*'ĕlōhîm*] before me" (Ex. 20:3; Dt. 5:7); "their" (118 times in RSV), as "you shall not bow down to their gods" (Ex. 23:24); "strange" or "foreign" (Josh. 24:20, 23); "new" (Jgs. 5:8); or, flatly, "no gods" (Jer. 5:7). Identification is also accomplished by reference to alien peoples or nations, as to the gods of Egypt, Babylonia, Assyria, Phoenicia, Syria, Moab, Edom, Tyre, the Philistines, and the Amorites.

"To bring to God [*'ĕlōhîm*]" (Ex. 21:6; 22:8) is an expression for a juridical oath or a serious sort of religious test, "a common feature of the Nuzu trials" (Gordon).

Hebrew *'ĕlōhîm* may be translated "the gods" when it refers to Yahweh's divine council (Ps. 82:1), the host gathered about Him (1 K. 22:19; Job 1–2; Ps. 89:6f.; Isa. 40:1f.). As members of an earthly king's council come "into the king's presence" (1 K. 1:28), the *'ĕlōhîm* of Yahweh's court share His counsel (1 K. 22:19), are associated with His rule (perhaps reflected in "us" of Gen. 1:26), may be sent as His messengers (*see* ANGEL), can serve as single warriors for Yahweh ("commander of the army of Yahweh," Josh. 5:14), or make up God's army (Gen. 32:1f.). The context of this meaning of *'ĕlōhîm* may be seen in "heavenly beings" (Ps. 29:1), "sons of gods" (Ps. 29:1, RSV mg.; 89:6, RSV mg.; Ps. 97:7), and "the sons of God" (Job 38:7). (*See also* SONS OF GOD.)

II. NT Terms.–Greek *theoí* refers to deities other than God, e.g., those of the Greco-Roman pantheon. In Acts 19:27, 35-37, Diana is called by her followers "the great goddess" and "our goddess" (*see* ARTEMIS). Acts 14:11f. tell how at Lystra the crowds mistook Barnabas for Zeus and Paul for Hermes. In 17:18 Luke reports that Paul's Athenian listeners thought he was a preacher of "foreign [Asiatic?] deities" (AV "strange gods"). The Gk. *daimónion,* translated "deities" or "gods," is derived from Gk.

daímōn (cf. Eng. "demon") and is the common NT word for demon, evil spirit, or devil. In Rev. 13, the sea beast, often taken as a symbol of emperor worship with deified Caesars, is said in v. 2 to have been given "his power and his throne and great authority" by "the dragon," the author's designation of the devil or Satan. *See* RELIGIONS OF THE BIBLICAL WORLD: GRECO-ROMAN.

Paul wrote, "What pagans sacrifice, they offer to demons, and not to God" (1 Cor. 10:20). Devotees of the gods are unable to share the kingdom of God now or ever (Gal. 5:21; Eph. 5:5). One text consigns idolaters to be burned "with fire and brimstone" (Rev. 21:8). In another, the idolaters have a place only outside the new Jerusalem (Rev. 22:15).

"Although there may be so-called gods in heaven or on earth — as indeed there are many 'gods' and many 'lords' — yet for us [Christians] there is one God, the Father, . . . and one Lord, Jesus . . ." (1 Cor. 8:5f.). For the NT, pagan deities were "beings that by nature are no gods" (Gal. 4:8). He who turns to God from the gods has turned away from what is deadly and false "to serve a living and true God" (1 Thess. 1:9).

See also IDOL; IDOLATRY.

Bibliography.–C. H. Gordon, *BA*, 3 (1940), 11; M. Noth, *Exodus* (Eng. tr., *OTL*, 1962), pp. 178-184; R. de Vaux, *Ancient Israel* (1961), pp. 157f.; W. F. Albright, *Yahweh and the Gods of Canaan* (1968), pp. 191-93; U. Cassuto, *The Goddess Anath* (Eng. tr. 1971); F. M. Cross, *Canaanite Myth and Hebrew Epic* (1973); *TDOT*, I, *s.v.* "ᵉlōhîm" (Ringgren). P. L. GARBER

III. Ancient Near Eastern Gods.–The Sumerians first identified and listed deities, thereby setting a pattern for other Near Eastern cultures. For the Sumerians the gods were initially the forces of nature as experienced personally, but in due course acquired an overlay of mythology. The principal beneficent deities of the pantheon who supervised the cosmos were An, the sky-god, Enlil, the air-deity, Enki, lord of the abyss, Ninḫursag, a creating goddess and perhaps the consort of An, Nanna, the moon-god, the daughter of Nanna, a deity named Inanna, familiar to the Semites as Ishtar, and her husband Dumuzi (Tammuz).

The pantheon was thought to govern like an assembly under the leadership of a king. All gods were regarded as specifically human in form and activity, but possessing characteristic attributes of invisibility and immortality. Evil demons from the underworld were assumed to be the agents of misfortune, sickness, and death, bringing hapless people to the nether world from which they did not return. The Sumerians honored the members of the pantheon creatively and imaginatively in lengthy mythological texts, cultic rituals, and ceremonies, carried on in association with the worship in the early temples and later ziggurats.

The Babylonians adopted the Sumerian religious traditions and accommodated them to their own ethos. The deity that ultimately emerged as leader of the pantheon was Marduk, although Ea (Sum. Enki), the powerful water-deity, was also prominent and had his own cult center as far back as the 3rd millennium B.C., and perhaps even earlier. In the magical texts Ea and his "son" Marduk commonly cooperated in insuring the efficacy of the incantations or spells.

The mother goddess Ninḫursag (also known as Damkina, Ninki, etc.) was associated with Ea or Enlil in creating human beings, following the general Sumerian tradition. The Babylonian gods were worshiped by a variety of rituals in elaborate temples, which were controlled by a highly regulated priestly hierarchy. An important difference between Babylonian and Assyrian religion is that, in the pantheon of the latter, the war-goddess Ishtar claimed equal status with Ashur, the local deity of the Assyrian capital in the 1st millennium B.C.

King Akhenaten (1370-1353 B.C.) and Queen Nefertiti (left) make offerings to the sun-god Aten. Limestone relief on balustrade at Tell el-Amarna (photograph courtesy of Metropolitan Museum of Art)

In ancient Egypt in the 4th millennium B.C., the worship of specific deities arose in different localities. At Heliopolis, the god Atum was held to have emerged from primeval chaos, after which he created the god Shu (Show) and the goddess Tefnut, who subsequently procreated the other deities of the pantheon. The cosmogony of Hermopolis described the initial chaos in terms of a primeval ocean, Nun, who was assigned a counterpart named Naunet. Thoth, son of the falcon-deity Horus, was credited with creating the world and bringing culture to mankind. During the First Intermediate Period (*ca.* 2250-2000 B.C.) the cosmogony of Hermopolis was assimilated to that current in Heliopolis, where the sun-deity Re was honored. His cult members believed that he had created all the other gods, and that he had also given life to the world and mankind. He was immensely influential in Egyptian religion, and his worship overshadowed that of all other cults.

At an early period the pharaoh was proclaimed a son of Re, or at times even the sun-deity himself, and the cultic priests devised complicated liturgies that involved the pharaoh himself. Egyptian deities had their totem animals, so that the vulture, e.g., was associated with the goddess Nekhbet, the ibis with Thoth, the cow with Hathor, the cat with Bastet, etc. Some deities were normally depicted with a human body but having the head of the appropriate cult animal. Thus Horus had the head of a falcon, and Anubis that of a dog. Ptah and Atum, by contrast, always appeared in fully human form.

The falcon-headed Egyptian god Horus on horseback. Sandstone relief, 4th cent. B.C. (Louvre)

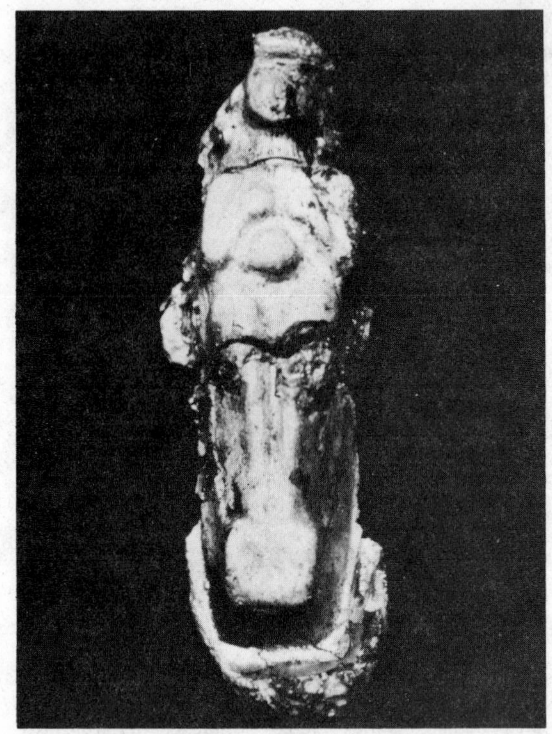

Mold-pressed glass figure of Astarte. Possibly from Syria or Mesopotamia, *ca.* 1400 B.C. (Corning Museum of Glass)

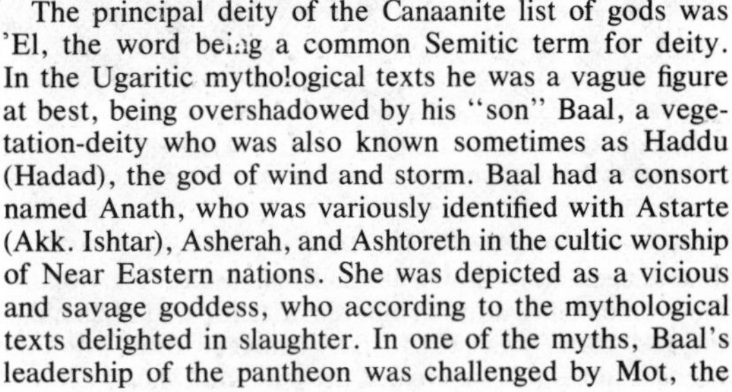

The principal deity of the Canaanite list of gods was 'El, the word being a common Semitic term for deity. In the Ugaritic mythological texts he was a vague figure at best, being overshadowed by his "son" Baal, a vegetation-deity who was also known sometimes as Haddu (Hadad), the god of wind and storm. Baal had a consort named Anath, who was variously identified with Astarte (Akk. Ishtar), Asherah, and Ashtoreth in the cultic worship of Near Eastern nations. She was depicted as a vicious and savage goddess, who according to the mythological texts delighted in slaughter. In one of the myths, Baal's leadership of the pantheon was challenged by Mot, the god of misfortune who lived in the underworld and who brought about Baal's death. The process by which Baal was revived was reminiscent of the Isis and Osiris cultic rituals in Egypt, and was linked to the cycle of seasons. Baal was worshiped in various Canaanite communities either under his own name or as Hadad.

Hittite religion, rather like that of Egypt, was distributed among a number of cults, but in general the chief deity of the pantheon was Tešub, the weather-god, who had a consort named Hebat. According to Hittite mythology they produced a "son" Sharruma, who also occupied an important place in the pantheon. Prominent in cultic

Reliefs from Khirbet et-Tannur (SE of the Dead Sea) of Atargatis as grain goddess (left) and dolphin goddess (right). This Aramean deity (was Hadad's consort; her attributes are like those of the Babylonian goddess Ishtar and Phoenician goddess Astarte (E. K. Vogel; picture American Schools of Oriental Research)

Procession of twelve unidentified Hittite gods. From Yazilikaya, near Boghazköy in central Anatolia (B. K. Condit)

worship was the goddess Shaushka, commonly identified with Ishtar. All of these were Hurrian deities, and along with such familiar Mesopotamian gods as Anu, Enlil, Ea, and Damkina, found a ready place in the syncretistic religion of the Hittites.

Gods of the indigenous Hatti that were venerated included the sun-goddess Wurusemu, along with her "daughters" Mezulla and Hulla, as well as an agriculture-deity named Telipinu. The official state pantheon was based on the identities of gods venerated at local shrines; Wurusemu was the principal deity at Arinna, "Queen of the land of Hatti," the great Hittite religious center. Her consort was Taru, the weather-god of Hatti, described as "King of Heaven," and he was also a god of war who represented Hittite interests in treaties with foreign powers.

In ancient cultic worship the gods were often represented as exhibiting rather fluid personalities, so that it was not always possible for them to be described consistently. Furthermore, the identification of deities with certain comparable gods from other nations was also common, so that a goddess such as Ishtar could be worshiped across the ancient Near East under a variety of names.

For a more thorough treatment, *see* RELIGIONS OF THE BIBLICAL WORLD. R. K. H.

GODS, STRANGE. *See* STRANGE GODS.

GOEL. *See* AVENGER; REDEEMER.

GOG gog [Heb. *gôg*; Gk. *Goug*].

1. A son of Joel and descendant of the tribe of Reuben (1 Ch. 5:4).

2. The chief prince of Meshech and Tubal (Ezk. 38:2f.; 39:1-16). His territory was known as the land of Magog, and he was the chief of those northern hordes who were to make a final onslaught upon Israel while the latter was enjoying the blessings of the messianic age. He has been identified with Gugu, known in his own land of Lydia as Gyges, and mentioned in the records of Ashurbanipal. The phonetic similarity is too uncertain for positive identification, however.

According to Ezekiel's account Gog's vast army included men from Persia, Cush, Put, Gomer (or the Cimmerians), and Togarmah, all from the extreme north, completely equipped for war. They were to come upon the mountains of Israel and cover the land like a cloud. Their purpose was plunder, for the people of Israel were rich and dwelt in towns and villages without walls. Gog's coming, which had been prophesied by the seers of Israel, was to be accompanied by a theophany and great convulsions in nature. A panic would seize the hosts of Gog; rain, hailstones, pestilence, fire, and brimstone would consume them. Their bodies would be food for the birds, their weapons would serve as firewood for seven years, and their bones would be buried E of the Jordan in Hamon-gog and thus not defile the holy land.

Perhaps Ezekiel had in mind something of the eschatology of Zec. 14, in which the nations that represented "the ends of the earth" would rise against Jerusalem in a final, desperate battle in which God will intervene by returning to earth.

See also EZEKIEL V.E.

3. In Rev. 20:7 Satan is let loose and goes to the nations at the four corners of the earth, Gog and Magog, to muster his hosts for the final struggle against God. In Ezekiel the invasion of Gog occurs during the messianic age, while in Revelation it occurs just at the close of the millennium. In Ezekiel Gog and Magog are gathered by Yahweh for their destruction; in Revelation they are gathered by Satan. In both cases the number is vast; the destruction, by supernatural means, is complete and final. *See* MAGOG.

J. J. REEVE R. K. H.

GOIIM goi'im [Heb. *gôyim*]. This term occurs only in Gen. 14:1, 9 and Josh. 12:23 in the RSV, replacing the "nations," "heathen," or "Gentiles" of most English versions. The Genesis references indicate a Mesopotamian nation or tribal group, perhaps non-Semitic in character. An identification with early Hittites on the basis of some similarity between the name Tidal and a royal Hittite personage named Tudḫalias has been suggested with some plausibility. The people mentioned in Josh. 12:23 (NEB "Gaiam") have been related by some scholars to the Philistines. The RSV and NEB follow the LXX in referring to "Galilee," whereas the MT has "nations to Gilgal." This latter might thus refer to some group located in the region of Aphek.

Bibliography.–W. F. Albright, *BASOR,* 11 (Feb. 1923), 8; *GAB,* Index, p. 164.

R. K. H.

GOLAN gō'lan [Heb. *gôlān*–possibly 'dust and sand'; Gk. *Gaulōn*]. A city in the territory allotted to Manasseh in Bashan. The surrounding region to which it gave its name is Gaulanitis, mentioned often in Josephus.

Golan was one of the CITIES OF REFUGE, the most northerly of those in Transjordan (Dt. 4:43; Josh. 20:8). It was assigned to the Gershonites, one of the families of the Levites (Josh. 21:27; 1 Ch. 6:71). The city was known to Josephus, who listed it among the cities taken by Alexander Janneus in Transjordan (*Ant.* xiii.15.3 [393]). The site of Golan has not been identified positively, but Abel (*GP,* II, 73) and others suggested Saḥem el-Jōlân as a possibility. This site, located about 16 km. (10 mi.) NW of Derʿā and 27 km. (17 mi.) E of the Sea of Galilee, would seem to be too far E to be located in the territory of Gaulanitis, or the modern Jōlân.

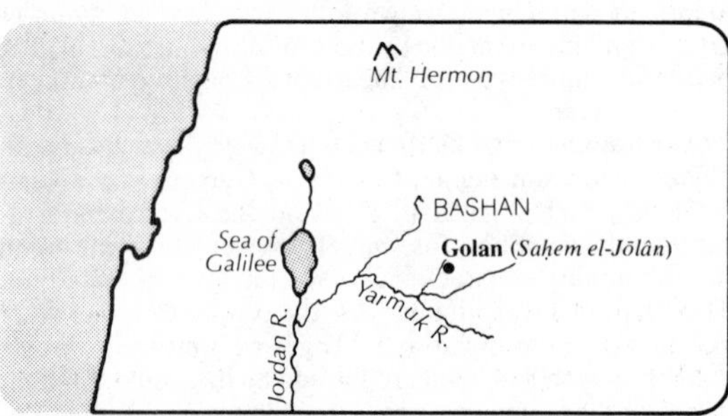

Gaulanitis (also spelled Gaulonitis), as the Greek word suggests, was the region belonging to Gaulan or Golan. (The Greek form *Gaulanitis* indicates that the original vocalization of the Hebrew was *Gawlān*.) Josephus made frequent use of this term; thus it is relatively easy to identify its location. Gaulanitis formed the east boundary of Galilee and was part of the tetrarchy of Philip (*Ant.* xvii.8.1 [189]; xviii.4.6 [106]; cf. Lk. 3:1). If we may judge from the boundaries of modern Jōlân, Gaulanitis extended from the foot of Mt. Hermon in the north to the Yarmuk River in the south. The east boundary is not clearly marked but may have been the Nahr er-Ruqqâd or the Nahr el-ʿAllan; if we are to identify Saḥem el-Jōlân with Golan, then we must push the boundary E of the Nahr el-ʿAllan. The territory, about 70 km. (45 mi.) long, is chiefly a plateau sloping N-S. The elevation at el-Quneitra is 1010 m. (3323 ft.), and at Khifsîn is 478 m. (1570 ft.) (see *GP,* I, 14). Along the west, numerous wadis cut their way into the upper Jordan River and the Sea of Galilee. A line of volcanic cones, rising 150-210 m. (500-700 ft.) above the surface of the plateau, runs in a NNW-SSE direction in northern Jōlân, just W of Wâdī er-Ruqqâd. Northern Jōlân is rather arid, but the south is well irrigated, with many springs (according to Abel seventy-five springs or groups of springs in addition to wells and reservoirs; *GP,* I, 153). The area has always provided excellent pastureland for nomads, and in addition produced wheat and some olives. There are traces of ancient forests, but today the region is practically without trees.

See Vol. I, Map VI.

W. S. L. S.

GOLD. This highly prized metal is mentioned 385 times in the Bible, more often than any other metal. In spite of its frequent mention it was not native to Palestine. It had to be imported from OPHIR, Havilah (Gen. 2:11f.), Sheba (1 K. 10:2 par. 2 Ch. 9:10, 14), Raamah (Ezk. 27:22), and Uphaz (Jer. 10:9; Dnl. 10:5). The location of these areas remains uncertain (cf. *TDOT,* IV, 36).

The most frequently used OT word for "gold" is Heb. *zāhāḇ*, rendered at times "pure gold" (*zāhāḇ sāgûr,* 1 K. 6:20; 2 Ch. 4:20; etc., and *zāhāḇ ṭāhôr,* Ex. 25:11; 2 Ch. 3:4; etc.), "refined gold" (*zāhāḇ mᵉzuqqāq,* 1 Ch. 28:18), "fine gold" (*zāhāḇ ṭôḇ,* 2 Ch. 3:5), "finest gold" (*K zāhāḇ mûpaz,* 1 K. 10:18), etc. It occurs with silver and other metals and has a wide range of application. Less frequent

Statuette of the god Amon, found near the Great Temple of Amon at Karnak (Metropolitan Museum of Art, Carnarvon Collection, gift of Edward S. Harkness, 1926)

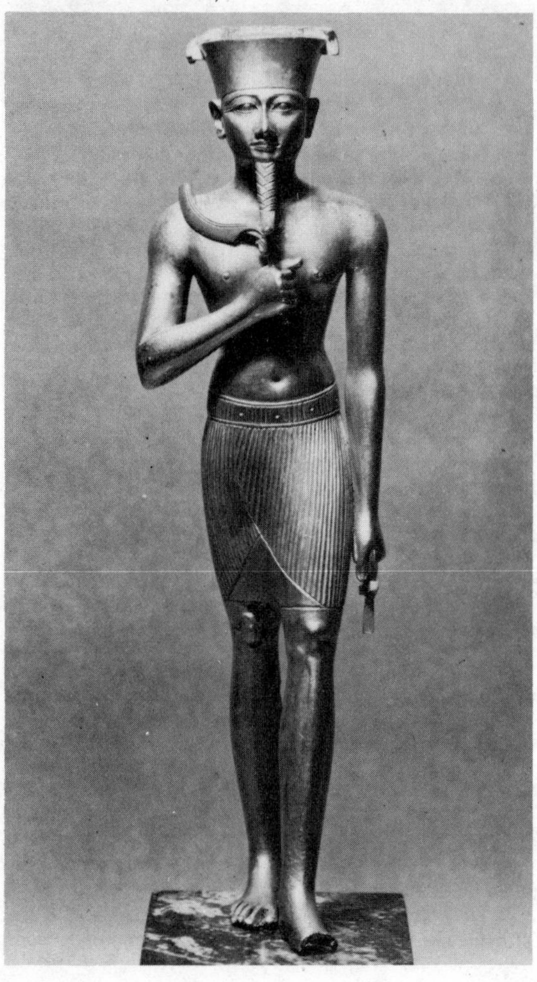

Bowl with relief of lion demons and gazelles from northwest Iran (12th-11th cents. B.C.) (Louvre)

Late Bronze pendant from Beth-shean showing a goddess holding a scepter (Israel Department of Antiquities and Museums)

Vessel from Bubastis, New Kingdom (19th Dynasty, *ca.* 1250 B.C.) (Egyptian Museum, Cairo)

are Heb. *paz, ḥārûṣ* (rendered "green gold," *yᵉraqraq ḥārûṣ,* in Ps. 68:13 [MT 14]; AV, NEB, "yellow gold"), *keṯem* and *sᵉgôr* (or *sāgûr*; cf. *BH,* Job 28:15), and Aram. *dᵉhaḇ*. Many of these terms occur only in wisdom literature; *dᵉhaḇ* is found only in Ezra (chs. 5, 7) and Daniel (chs. 2, 5) and refers to inanimate objects. *Paz* seems to have been the most precious gold (cf. Isa. 13:12), valued above *zāhāḇ* (Ps. 19:10 [MT 11]; 119:127) and *ḥārûṣ* (Prov. 8:19).

While *bāṣer* in Job 22:24 ("gold," RSV, AV) may refer to gold ore (*TDOT,* IV, 34), *bᵉṣār* in Job 36:19 should not be related to gold (AV, cf. NEB) but to *ṣār,* "distress" (RSV), *lō' bᵉṣār* meaning "not with affliction" (cf. KD, *in loc.*). The AV mg. follows MT *zāhāḇ* in Job 37:22; the RSV ("golden splendor") and the NEB ("golden glow") are based on the emendation to *zōhar,* "brightness"; *TDOT,* IV, 37 favors the MT, while KoB, p. 252 favors the emendation. On the interpretation of Isa. 14:4 *see* GOLDEN CITY.

The NT words for gold are *chrysíon,* and cognates *chrysós, chrysoús* (2 Tim. 2:20; Rev. 9:20; 21:15), and *chrysodaktýlios,* "gold-fingered" ("with gold rings," Jas. 2:2). "Pure gold" renders Gk. *chrysíon katharón* (Rev. 21:18, 21), while "golden" is *chrysoús.*

Gold was very important in public worship. The calf fashioned by Aaron and worshiped by the Israelites was made of gold contributed by the congregation (Ex. 32:2-4, 24). It was made by melting gold and later engraving the casting; thus it appeared to have been both a molten image (v. 24) and a graven image (v. 4). Gold was used lavishly in the construction of the tabernacle. The wooden ark was to be covered with gold within and without (Ex. 25:11). Most of the furniture of the building was gold-plated. The vessels and utensils were of "pure gold." The accoutrements of the high priest, including his crown, ephod, and breastplate, were also of gold (Ex. 39:2-30).

The offerings for worship in the wilderness included golden dishes totaling 120 shekels in weight (Nu. 7:86; *see also* WEIGHTS AND MEASURES). Gold was used even more lavishly in the temple of Solomon (1 K. 6:20-28; 2 Ch. 3:4–4:22; cf. 1 Ch. 29:2-7).

Gold acquired great importance in commercial exchanges. The annual importation of gold during the "golden age" of Solomon was said to total more than 666 talents (1 K. 10:14), some of which was made into "beaten gold" (MT *zāhāḇ šāḥûṭ*, lit. "slaughtered [i.e., hammered"] gold," so BDB, p. 1006; cf. J. Gray, *I & II Kings* [*OTL*, 2nd ed. 1970], p. 265) for ornamental shields (1 K. 10:16f. par. 2 Ch. 9:15f.). Gold was used almost exclusively in temple and palace since silver "was not considered as anything in the days of Solomon" (1 K. 10:21). Hiram of Tyre gave Solomon 120 talents of gold, although it is not stated on what basis (1 K. 9:14; KD, *in loc.*, suggests it was a loan).

The twofold use of gold among the Hebrews caused a twofold sin. (1) In wisdom literature the excessive preoccupation with the accumulation of gold was condemned and gold was valued below wisdom (Job 28:15, 17; Prov. 3:14; 8:10, 19; 16:16) and (religious) knowledge (Ps. 19:10 [MT 11]; 119:72, 127; Prov. 20:15; cf. 1 Pet. 1:7, where faith is valued above gold). Job resolved not to place his trust in gold (Job 31:24). Later it became a "stumbling block of their iniquity" (Ezk. 7:19), and though they were devoted to it as to a god, it could not avert God's judgment (Zeph. 1:18). (2) The worshiping of golden images (e.g., Ps. 115:4; Isa. 2:20; 31:7; Hos. 8:4) began in the wilderness wanderings and intensified at the beginning of the separation of Israel from Judah (1 K. 12:28f.). It became a substitute for the true worship of Yahweh but was declared to be of no value to the Hebrews (Isa. 46:6; Ps. 135:15; cf. Hos. 8:4).

But gold also retained its (positive) value. In Isa. 60:6 the possession of gold and the worship of Yahweh are compatible, and God will give gold instead of bronze (v. 17) for the rebuilding of the temple. Since gold belongs to God (Hag. 2:8), He can dispense it to His people (Hos. 2:8; cf. Ezk. 28:13, alluding to creation, and Isa. 13:12, possibly referring to judgment; cf. also its use in imagery in Prov. 25:11f.; Cant. 5:11, 14f.; Lam. 4:2).

The same ambiguity toward gold persisted in the NT. It was deemed "perishable" (1 Pet. 1:18; cf. Jas. 5:3). The apostles considered the possession of gold unnecessary (Mt. 10:9; Acts 3:6). The wearing of gold was not to be considered an indication of worth (Jas. 2:2); indeed, such ornamentation was expressly forbidden by Paul and Peter (1 Tim. 2:9; 1 Pet. 3:3).

On the positive side, the church at Laodicea was admonished to purchase "gold" (Rev. 3:18), i.e., "spiritual wealth that has passed through the refiner's fire and has been found to be totally trustworthy" (R. H. Mounce, comm. on Revelation [*NICNT*, 1977], p. 127). The wise men brought gold to the infant Jesus (Mt. 2:11), and the Holy City (Jerusalem) will consist of "pure gold, clear as glass" (Rev. 21:18). But mixed feelings remained: the elders wore "golden crowns" (Rev. 4:4), but the "great harlot" was "bedecked with gold" (17:4; cf. 18:16) too. It represented real wealth and served as a standard by which to measure wealth (1 Pet. 1:18); it also could be deceptive and worse than useless if it obscured higher moral and spiritual values (1 Tim. 6:9f.).

Gold ornament on a fine gold chain from prince's palace at Megiddo (14th cent. B.C.) (Oriental Institute, University of Chicago)

Of interest is the image of testing in 1 Cor. 3:12f., an image that has a long OT history (cf. Prov. 17:3; 27:21; Zec. 13:9; Mal. 3:3). If the believer builds his life with Christ as the foundation, his golden works will endure the testing by fire on the Day of Judgment (F. W. Grosheide, comm. on 1 Corinthians [*NICNT*, 1953], pp. 85-87).

See also METALLURGY.

See *TDOT*, IV, *s.v.* "zāhābh" (Kedar-Kopfstein).

G. A. TURNER R. W. V.

GOLDEN CALF. *See* CALF, GOLDEN.

GOLDEN CITY. The translation "golden city" (AV, Isa. 14:4) is an attempt to render the TR Heb. *maḏhēḇâ*, but can hardly be justified. (But cf. KD *in loc.*) Almost all the ancient versions read Heb. *marhēḇâ*, a word which connotes unrest and insolence, fitting the context well (cf. RSV "insolent fury"; NEB "frenzy").

GOLDEN RULE. A title commonly applied to the saying of Jesus in Mt. 7:12: "So whatever you wish that men would do to you, do so to them; for this is the law and the prophets" (cf. Lk. 6:31: "And as you wish that men would do to you, do so to them"). In the context of Matthew's Sermon on the Mount, it sums up the conduct demanded of Jesus' disciples (Mt. 5:2–7:27). The "golden rule" is a summary statement of the moral exhortations of the Law and the Prophets, given by Jesus to guide His followers. Thus, He claimed to fulfil the Law and the Prophets and demanded that the disciples, in their conduct, do the same.

The "golden rule" is not to be understood, however, as a new legal precept, but rather as a simplified reassertion of what the Decalogue taught concerning behavior toward others (Ex. 20:13-17; Dt. 5:17-21). In Matthew's Gospel, the triad of the "golden rule" and the twofold commandment of loving God above all and one's neighbor as oneself reflected Jesus' understanding of the law (Davies, p. 93). The twofold commandment is also said to be a summation of the Law and the Prophets (Mt. 22:37-40); Jesus is teaching the essence of the Law, not a new law.

The "golden rule" as it appears in Luke is found in abbreviated form, lacking the statement concerning the Law and the Prophets. Here the saying is not a summary statement, but part of a section of teaching that concerns itself with the ideal response of the disciples to persecutors and enemies, a response of merciful and generous love (Lk. 6:20-38; cf. Marshall, pp. 243-45; 261f.).

The general principle of reciprocity embodied in the "golden rule" is not unique to Jesus' teaching. Among the Greeks, Isocrates stated a similar principle: "You should be such in your dealings with others as you expect me to be in my dealings with you" (*Nicocles or The Cyprians* 49). Similar maxims are found in the Apocrypha and Pseudepigrapha that antedate the ministry of Jesus. "As you wish that no evil should befall you, but to be a partaker of all good things, so you should act on the same principle towards your subjects and offenders" (Letter of Aristeas 207). "Just as a man asks [something] for his own soul from God, so let him do to every living soul" (2 En. 61:1; cf. Tob. 4:15). None of these sources considers this principle to be a summation of the Law and the Prophets. This idea is, however, found in the story of Rabbi Hillel's advice to a proselyte who asked him to explain the whole law while the proselyte stood on one foot. Hillel is reported to have replied, "That which displeases you do not do to another. This is the whole law; the rest is commentary" (T. B. *Shabbath* 31a). The concluding remarks are similar to those of Mt. 7:12, indicating that there was a belief in first-century (A.D.) Judaism that the revelation of God in the OT could be taught in a single principle.

Some have concluded (e.g., R. G. Hammerton-Kelly, *IDB Supp.*, p. 369) that the "golden rule" originated in the Sophist movement in Greece (5th cent. B.C.), was taken over by Hellenistic Judaism, and from there found its way into early Christian teaching. It is incontestable that Christianity derived this principle from Judaism, but an ultimate origin in Stoicism may be doubted since the rule is also found in the distant writings of Confucius: "Tzu Kung asked: 'Is there any one word that can serve as a principle for the conduct of life?' Confucius said: 'Perhaps the word "reciprocity"; Do not do to others what you would not want others to do to you'" (*Analects* xv. 23). It may be that the embodiment of the principle of reciprocity in a single maxim was an attempt in several cultures to distill the essence of ethical teaching.

The "golden rule" appeared many times in later Christian literature. It is found in a negative form in the Did. 1:2. Tertullian, while attacking Marcion's concept of God, gave both the positive and negative forms of this precept (*Adv. Marc.* iv.16).

The "golden rule" in both Mt. 7:12 and Lk. 6:31 is applied specifically to the community of those who are disciples of Jesus (Mt. 5:1; Lk. 6:20), who are expected to suffer on His behalf (Mt. 5:11; Lk. 6:22). This removes the "golden rule" from the realm of a general ethical teaching for mankind and places it in a special relationship between Jesus and the Church.

Bibliography.–*APOT*; G. Barth, "Matthew's Understanding of the Law," in Barth, *et al.*, *Tradition and Interpretation in Matthew* (1963), pp. 75-105; W. T. de Bary, *et al.*, eds., *Sources of Chinese Tradition*, I (1960), 25f.; S. G. F. Brandon, ed., *Dictionary of Comparative Religion* (1970), *s.v.*; W. D. Davies, *Setting of the Sermon on the Mount* (1964); A. Dihle, *Die Goldene Regel* (1962); D. Hill, *Gospel of Matthew* (*New Century Bible*, 1972; repr. 1981); G. R. King, *JR*, 8 (1928), 268-279; I. H. Marshall, *Comm. on Luke* (*New International Greek Testament Comm.*, 1978).

R. J. WYATT.

GOLD-PLATED [Heb. *'ᵃpuddaṯ zāhāḇ*–lit. 'ephod of gold'] (Isa. 30:22); AV ORNAMENT OF GOLD; NEB SHEATHED IN GOLD; **GOLD-WOVEN** [Heb. *mimmiš-bᵉṣôṯ zāhāḇ*] (Ps. 45:13 [MT 14]); AV WROUGHT GOLD; NEB CLOTH-OF-GOLD. The manufacture of golden images was one of many ways in which the Hebrew GOLDSMITH used his skill (cf. Jgs. 8:26f.; Jer. 10:14). Special clothing was also ornamented with gold, either brocade or filigree, e.g., the priests' garments in Ex. 28:5-38.

See GOLD.

GOLDSMITH [Heb. *ṣōrēp*]. The only biblical references to the activities of this skilled craftsman are in the OT, alluding to the goldsmith as the one who fashioned elegant and costly idols (e.g., Jer. 10:9, 14; 51:17; AV "founder").

Superb examples of the goldsmith's art have been recovered from numerous early Sumerian levels, one of the more significant artifacts being the celebrated golden helmet from Ur, found in a first-dynasty burial pit. This object had been fashioned from solid gold in the form of a wig, on which the locks of hair had been hammered in relief and the individual hairs engraved with great delicacy and skill. A new decorating technique known as granulation appeared in the Middle Bronze Age; this consisted of tiny spheres of gold arranged in pattern form and then brazed onto the golden surface.

Like other peoples, the Hebrews employed the art of the goldsmith in their environment of worship, both in the tabernacle (cf. Ex. 31:4; 35:32) and the Solomonic temple (cf. 1 K. 6:20-35). In the postexilic period the guilds of goldsmiths were involved in the repair and restoration of Jerusalem (Neh. 3:8, 31f.; AV "goldsmiths"). Most large Near Eastern cities had a specific area in which the goldsmiths plied their craft. R. K. H.

GOLGOTHA gol'gə-thə [Gk. *Golgotha* < Aram. *gûl-galtā'*–'the skull' (cf. Heb. *gulgōleṯ*, Jgs. 9:53; 2 K. 9:35)]. In three references (Mt. 27:33; Mk. 15:22; Jn. 19:17) it is interpreted to mean (Gk.) *kraníou tópos*, "the place of a skull." In Lk. 23:33, AV, it is called "Calvary" (from Vulg. *calvaria*, "skull"), but in the RSV and NEB simply "The Skull." From the NT we may gather that it

Goldsmith at work; detail from N. Davies' painting of a mural in the tomb of Nebamen and Ipuki (late 20th Dynasty) at Thebes (Oriental Institute, University of Chicago)

Helmet from Ur made from a single sheet of gold (*ca.* 2500 B.C.) (State Antiquities Organization, Republic of Iraq)

was outside the city (He. 13:12), but close to it (Jn. 19:20), apparently near some public thoroughfare (Mt. 27:39). It was a spot visible from afar (Mk. 15:40; Lk. 23:49); this is the only possible biblical basis for calling Calvary a hill.

I. The Name.–Three reasons have been suggested for the name Golgotha or "skull." (1) It was a spot where skulls were to be found lying about and probably therefore a public place of execution. This tradition apparently originated with Jerome (*ca.* A.D. 347-420). (2) The name was due to the skull-like shape of the hill — a modern popular view. None of the church fathers suggested such an idea, and the NT offers no evidence that the crucifixion occurred on a raised place at all. (The tradition embodied in the name *Mons Calvary* appeared as early as the 4th cent., materialized in the traditional site of the crucifixion in the Church of the Holy Sepulchre.) (3) The name was due to an ancient pre-Christian tradition that the skull of Adam was found there. The first mention of this came from Origen (*ca.* 185-254), who himself lived in Palestine many years. This is by far the most ancient explanation of the name Golgotha, and may, in spite of the absurdity of the original tradition about Adam, be the true one.

II. The Site.–The NT gives no indication whatever about the position of Calvary and the tomb; indeed, by those who abandon tradition, sites have been suggested on all sides of the city. Two views dominate today: (1) the site of the crucifixion, or at any rate that of the tomb, is included within the precincts of the Church of the Holy Sepulchre; (2) a prominent, rounded, grassy hill above the so-called "Grotto of Jeremiah," NE of the modern Damascus Gate, is probably the true site. Both lie on the northeast side of ancient Jerusalem.

The Church of the Holy Sepulchre has the support of traditions going back to the 4th cent. The historian Eusebius (A.D. 263-339) stated that on the site stood a temple to Aphrodite (*Vita Constantini* iii.26). The church itself was erected on the same spot during the reign of Constantine and dedicated in A.D. 335. The tradition known to Eusebius may well be correct, but we cannot trace it back any further. The real question to be faced is whether the true site was forgotten when Jerusalem fell to the Roman armies in A.D. 70 and again in 135; the latter capture resulted in a drastic rebuilding of the city that may well have obliterated the true site. The traditional site has also been opposed in the past on the grounds that it may have lain within the city walls of Our Lord's time; but the latest excavations in Jerusalem have shown that the city wall must almost certainly have run to the south of the site of the church. See K. M. Kenyon, *BA*, 26 (1964), 34-52; she concludes, "The site of the Church. . . . may be based on an authentic tradition surviving to the time of Queen Helena [Constantine's mother]" (p. 50). *See* Plate 40.

The so-called skull hill appears to have appealed first to Otto Thenius (1842), but received its greatest support through the advocacy of Colonel Conder and General Gordon (thus the site is often called "Gordon's Calvary"). Two main arguments for this site are: (1) Its conspicuous and elevated position must impress every reverent pilgrim as strikingly suitable for an imaginary reconstruction of the scene. The very greenness of the hill may influence the subconsciousness of those who have been brought up from childhood to think of the "green hill far away," as the popular hymn puts it. But an imaginary reconstruction is not evidence. (2) The supposed resemblance to a human skull strikes many people, but it may be stated without hesitation that the most arresting points of the resemblance, the "eyeholes" and the rounded top, are not ancient; the former are due to artificial excavations going back perhaps a couple of centuries. Probably the whole formation of the hill is an entirely new condition since NT times.

Gordon's Calvary, one of the traditional sites of Golgotha (W. S. LaSor)

Thus probability favors the traditional site, though there can be no certainty. If it is not the true site, however, there are still no grounds for accepting "Gordon's Calvary" either.

Bibliography.–A. Parrot, *Golgotha and the Church of the Holy Sepulchre* (*Cahiers d'archéologie biblique*, no. 6 [1957]); K. M. Kenyon, *Jerusalem: Excavating 3000 Years of History* (1968), pp. 146-154; *Digging Up Jerusalem* (1974), pp. 226-234, 261-67; L. E. C. Evans, *PEQ*, 1968, pp. 112-136. D. F. PAYNE

GOLIATH gə-lī'əth [Heb. *golyāṯ*; Gk. *Goliath*].

1. The giant of Gath, and champion of the Philistine army (1 S. 17:4-23; 21:9; 22:10; 2 S. 21:19; 1 Ch. 20:5ff.). He defied the armies of Israel, challenging anyone to meet him in single combat while the two armies faced each other at Ephesdammim. He was slain by the youthful David.

It is probable that Goliath was not actually of Philistine stock, but instead was a descendant of an aboriginal group such as the Rephaim, Anakim, or Awim. These peoples may have served as combat troops in the Philistine forces, and some of them were certainly living in the area of Gath at the time of Saul (cf. 2 S. 21:22; 1 Ch. 20:8). The stature of Goliath was unusual, and if the cubit is taken at 45 cm. (18 in.), he would have been almost 3 m. (9 ft.) in height. (*See* DISEASE III.F; GIANTS.) The details of his encounter with David are in complete accord with the traditions of combat between two champions in the Near East.

2. The reference in 2 S. 21:19 to a Goliath slain by Elhanan seems to be the result of a transcriptional error in the text. When read in the light of 1 Ch. 20:5 it becomes clear that it was the brother of Goliath, not Goliath himself, who was killed by Elhanan.

See also ELHANAN **1.** R. K. H.

GOMER gō'mər [Heb. *gōmer*; Assyr. *Gimirrai*; Gk. *Kimmerioi*].

1. A nomadic people descended from Japheth and known also as Cimmerians. In the ancient geographical list of Gen. 10:2f.; 1 Ch. 1:5f. (*see* TABLE OF NATIONS)

Gomer appears among the Indo-European Japhethites, closely related to the Medes, Ionians, and certain peoples of Anatolia, and the Scythians (Ashkenaz). A similar association is implied in Ezk. 38:6, where Gomer supplies a part of the force of Gog, beside the Persians and other nations. These are the only biblical references to the Cimmerians.

The information of the OT can be supplemented with historical allusions from Akkadian sources and references in various classical writers, together with a certain amount of archeological evidence. The Cimmerians were nomadic herdsmen, apparently unacquainted with the horse as a mount, and distinguished for their archery (Babylonian texts of the 6th cent. B.C. list numbers of Cimmerian bows and arrows, after the Cimmerians as a people had ceased to exist). The few personal names preserved suggest that they were of Iranian stock, related to the Scythians, but this is disputed by some scholars.

Late in the 2nd millennium B.C. they were driven from their homeland N of the Caucasus into those mountains and into the Crimea by the Scythians, when their attempted expansion eastward into China was repulsed. The horse-riding Scythians continued to press the Cimmerians across the Caucasus and into Azerbaijan (Mannai), Armenia, Anatolia, and Eastern Europe. By the end of the 8th cent. B.C. the influx of Cimmerians was felt in all the peripheral states N and E of the Fertile Crescent. The power of Urartu was severely curtailed and the Assyrian king Sargon II was probably killed in a battle that prevented them from penetrating S of Lake Van (705 B.C.). The governors of Esarhaddon of Assyria defeated another attack in the Taurus Mountains in 679 B.C., though the Cimmerians continued their penetration by serving as mercenaries in the Assyrian army. By 670 the Cimmerians had taken control of central Anatolia, overrunning the Phrygians (Meshech) and their king Midas.

Their first assault upon the Lydians was defeated when Gyges gained Assyrian aid *ca.* 663 B.C.; but they took Sardis in 652 B.C., after Gyges had rebelled against Assyria, and held it until Alyattes drove them out in 626 B.C. Until that date they constantly threatened to break through into Assyrian territory, but thereafter the Scythians gradually subjected the Cimmerians, who were absorbed into the local populations and disappeared from history, leaving only their name as the Armenian term for Cappadocia, Gamirkʿ.

See Vol. I, Map X.

Bibliography.–*CAH* (3rd ed.), II/2, 425f.; T. Sulimirski, *Bulletin of the Institute of Archaeology* (of the Univ. of London), 2 (1959), 45-66.

A. R. MILLARD

2. Wife of Hosea. Hosea married Gomer according to divine appointment, and this was the beginning of God's word to him (Hos. 1:3; 3:1-4). She was to be a wife of whoredom and they were to have children of whoredom.

This fact has been accounted for by the suggestion that Gomer was a temple prostitute before her marriage; but unfortunately very little is known about the women who acted as prostitutes in the Baal fertility cults, and even less about such persons in a possible relationship to the Jerusalem cultus. Some scholars have adopted various interpretative devices to make Gomer rather more reputable, but the text leaves little doubt that Gomer was a practicing harlot before her marriage to Hosea, and that subsequently she went deeper into sin. She seems to have left him and become the slave of her paramour (3:1). Hosea is then commanded by Yahweh to buy her back, paying the price of the ordinary slave. The prophet kept her in confinement and without a husband for some time.

This experience of the prophet was typical of Israel's unfaithfulness, of Israel's exile, and of God bringing her back after the punishment of the Exile.

See HOSEA I.C.

J. J. REEVE
R. K. H.

GOMORRAH gə-môr'ə [Heb. *ʿᵃmōrâ*; Gk. *Gomorra*]. One of the CITIES OF THE VALLEY, destroyed by fire for its wickedness in the days of Lot (Gen. 19:23-29).

Good topographic and geographic factors indicate that the "cities of the valley" were not the Middle Bronze Age communities lying on the eastern side of the Ghor terrace of the Jordan River, but were situated in an extension of the Circle of the Jordan at the south end of the Dead Sea, immediately S of the peninsula known as el-Lisan (*see* Plate 7). Soundings in this locality indicate that the water is far shallower S of the promontory than N of it (*see also* DEAD SEA). Whereas Sodom was probably situated W of where the stream Seil en-Numeirah enters the Dead Sea, Gomorrah was probably located near the mouth of the Seil ʿEsal, a little farther to the north. The conflagration probably resulted from an explosion of petroleum gases in the area.

It is incorrect to identify Gomorrah with Khirbet Qumrân, despite superficial resemblances.

See Vol. I, Map V.

R. K. H.

GONG [Gk. *chalkós*–'(brass) gong'] (1 Cor. 13:1). *See* MUSIC II.D.

GOOD.

I. Terminology.–The 650 uses of "good" in the RSV translate a variety of Hebrew and Greek terms. By far the most common are Heb. *ṭôḇ* and Gk. *agathós*. Other frequent words are Heb. *ṭûḇ* ("good thing," Dt. 6:11; "the good," Isa. 1:19), the hiphil of *yāṭaḇ* ("do good," e.g., Gen. 32:12 [MT 13]; Zeph. 1:12), and Gk. *kalós* (e.g., Mt. 3:10; Jn. 10:11).

Hebrew *ṭôḇ* contains all the moral and nonmoral nuances mentioned under II below. Gk. *agathós* has basically a moral meaning. Gk. *kalós* can mean "beautiful" (Bauer, rev., p. 400), is sometimes synonymous with *agathós*, as in Jn. 10:32 ("good works") and Tit. 2:7 ("good deeds"), and expresses the quality of goodness in Mt. 3:10 and Lk. 3:9 ("good fruit").

The RSV uses "good" in translating various phrases. Thus in 2 Tim. 2:14 the RSV translates Gk. *ep' oudén chrḗsimon* as "does no good," in Lk. 13:9 *eis tó méllon* as "well and good," in 1 Cor. 9:11 *tá pneumatiká* as "spiritual good," in 10:24 *tó heautoú* as "his own good," and in He. 11:12 *taúta nenekrōménou* as "as good as dead." The RSV retains the AV rendering of *eudokía* as "good pleasure" in Phil. 2:13 (cf. Lk. 12:32), but changes it to "purpose" in Eph. 1:9. The RSV's "good news" sometimes replaces the AV's "gospel," "good tidings," and "glad tidings" (*see* GOOD NEWS).

II. Uses.–The term "good" has many nuances, both nonmoral and moral. (1) Useful for the accomplishment of some end or purpose: "the waistcloth was . . . good for nothing" (Jer. 13:7, 10), "good for edifying" (Eph. 4:29). (2) Pleasing, agreeable: "good-looking" (Gen. 39:6), "good fruit" (Jgs. 9:11), "good wine" (Jn. 2:10). (3) Advantageous, profitable: "it is vain to serve God. What is the good of our keeping his charge . . . ?" (Mal. 3:14), "to each is given the manifestation of the Spirit for the common good [Gk. *symphéron*]" (1 Cor. 12:7). (4) Fitting, appropriate: "we have sinned; do to us whatever seems good to thee" (Jgs. 10:15), "your boasting is not good" (1 Cor. 5:6). (5) Abundant, full measure: "good success" (Josh. 1:7), "a good old age" (e.g., Gen. 15:15). (6) Generous, benevolent: "My generosity" (Mt. 20:15; AV "good"; NEB "kind"), "kind and gentle" (1 Pet. 2:18; AV "good and gentle"). (7) Free from defects, sound, fine (usually Gk. *kalós* in contrast to *saprós,* "decayed," "rotten," or *ponērós,* "in poor condition," "sick"): "good fish" (Mt. 13:48), "either make the tree good, and its fruit good . . ." (Mt. 12:33), "good fruit" (7:17f.). (8) In every respect unobjectionable, excellent: "a good wife" (Prov. 31:10), "you will be a good minister of Jesus Christ" (1 Tim. 4:6). (9) Morally upright, righteous: "and you shall do what is right and good in the sight of the Lord" (Dt. 6:18), "a good man" (Jn. 7:12), "good deeds" (1 Tim. 5:10). (10) Just: "learn to do good; seek justice, correct oppression" (Isa. 1:17), "for rulers are not a terror to good conduct, but to bad" (Rom. 13:3).

Greek *agathḗ syneídēsis* ("good conscience," Acts 23:1; 1 Tim. 1:5, 19) designates a "clear [Gk. *kalós*] conscience" (He. 13:18), cleansed by Christ's sacrifice from "dead works" unto service of the "living God" (He. 9:14). According to Prov. 19:11 it is a mark of "good sense" (Heb. *śēḵel,* "insight, prudence," KoB, p. 922; NEB "intelligence") to restrain one's anger (cf. Jas. 1:19). To say "neither good nor bad" (Gen. 24:50; 31:24; 2 S. 13:22) signifies that nothing can be added or altered. The phrase "no knowledge of good and evil" (e.g., Dt. 1:39) may be a Hebrew way of saying no knowledge whatsoever (*see also* EVIL II.B), or it may refer to an inability to discern (cf. P. C. Craigie, comm. on Deuteronomy [*NICOT,* 1976], p. 105); its obverse, "the knowledge of good and evil" (Gen. 2:9, 17), may denote all possible knowledge (cf. G. von Rad, *Genesis* [Eng. tr., *OTL,* rev. ed. 1972], p. 78), or simply knowledge in general (cf. E. A. Speiser, *Genesis* [*AB,* 1964], p. 26; B. Vawter, *On Genesis* [1977], pp. 70f.). On "good fortune" (Gen. 30:11) *see* FORTUNE.

III. Theological Significance.–In biblical thought, the most profound and absolute sense of "good" is predicated of God alone. Thus, though "good" is used freely in all of the above-mentioned senses (and others), though everything created by God is good (1 Tim. 4:4), and though there are good and bad individuals (e.g., Mt. 5:45), Jesus affirms that God alone is good (Mk. 10:18 par.). The original creation was good, not due to its own intrinsic nature, but because it was created by God who is good (Gen. 1).

God's dealings with His people are good because they are the revelation and expression of His goodness. Yahweh's redemptive plan for Israel, His promises to the patriarchs (Gen. 32:12), His deliverance of His people from Egypt, and His continued preservation of them (Ex. 18:9; Nu. 10:29) — all these are called "good." God's law, delivered through Moses, is good and is the source for human knowledge about the good (Neh. 9:13; Ps. 119:39; cf. Rom. 7:7-20).

But after the fall the OT declares, "there is none that does good, no, not one" (Ps. 14:3; cf. Eccl. 7:20). Though God in His holy law has offered the good to His creatures, they are bound by the law of sin, which, according to Paul, is "working death . . . through what is good [i.e., God's law]" (Rom. 7:13). Thus "nothing good dwells within" them (v. 18). Because the law is powerless to accomplish the good in the face of human sin, God offers the good to Israel, not by pointing them back to the Mosaic law, but by the way of promise (Jer. 24:4-7; 32:36-41), which is fulfilled in the redemptive work of Christ. God's good for mankind, His gift of salvation, is freely offered a second time in a new covenant in Christ, who is the "high priest of the good things that have come" (He. 9:11). The OT (good) law, when viewed from the redemptive perspective of fulfillment, contained "but a shadow of the good things to come" (He. 10:1), which are now given freely to people in Christ. Thus with the accomplished redemptive work of Christ in view, Paul can say that "we are his [God's] workmanship, created in Christ Jesus for good works, which God prepared beforehand, that we should walk in them" (Eph. 2:10), and he can pray that the Colossians "lead a life worthy of the Lord, fully pleasing to him, bearing fruit in every good work and increasing in the knowledge of God" (Col. 1:10).

IV. Unresolved Questions.–Since God is good, what is the relation between God and the standard of human morality? To the Greek dilemma whether things are good because the gods say so or because of their participation in an objective standard of goodness (e.g., Plato *Euthyphro* 10a), the Scripture would reply that God Himself is that standard. Christians have always been closer to Plato's affirmation of an objective standard of morality (e.g., *Res publica* vii.517; cf. Harkness, p. 189; Bourke, p. 20) than to the Epicurean adage that morality is subjective (in this case based on pleasure; *see also* EPICUREANS). This identification permits an objective ethics on the one hand, and on the other hand insures that the standard is not merely abstract but one upheld by a personal God (see Henry, ch. 8). Christianity is perhaps more explicit on the content of the good than Plato. Morality implies worship (Ps. 16:2), praise (Ps. 92:1; 147:1), and justice (Am. 5:14f.). As Micah so succinctly asked, "What does the Lord require of you but to do justice, and to love kindness, and to walk humbly with your God?" (6:8). (*See also* ETHICS: OT; ETHICS: NT.)

It is difficult to harmonize the claim that after the fall no one can render any good with the exhortations of the prophets to *do* good (e.g., Am. 5:14f.; Isa. 1:17). For if no human being can do good, then moral injunctions are meaningless, and the Bible seems to be deceptive with its promise that divine blessings accompany good deeds (e.g., Dt. 6:18, 24; 12:28). Problems arise when we read that the OT expressly ascribes goodness and good deeds to some OT kings, e.g., to Asa (2 Ch. 14:2 [MT 1]), to Jehoshaphat (19:3), and to Hezekiah (31:20; 32:32; cf. Isa. 38:3). The doctrine of common grace, according to which God gives a measure of grace to all people (Mt. 5:45; cf. Ps. 145:9; Acts 14:17) to allow them to do some good, may be a partial solution. (See Calvin *Inst.* iii.14.2f.) In addition, God is of course directly at work in Israel to bring people to repentance, faith, and obedience.

An equally vexing problem is the interplay between God (who is good) and evil. Scripture clearly confers the attribute of goodness on God (e.g., 1 Ch. 16:34; 2 Ch. 5:13; Ps. 136:1). It is God who gives good gifts to people (Mt. 7:11; Jas. 1:17). The complaint that "the Lord will not do good" (Zeph. 1:12) is understandable particularly in adversity, but it is not Scripture's last word. God may punish sinners with physical evil (Jer. 21:10; Am. 9:4), but He will turn physical evil into good for His faithful, both the community (Jer. 32:40, 42; 33:9) and individuals (cf. Joseph, Gen. 50:20; Job, Job 42:10-17; and Jeremiah, Jer. 39:11-14; 40:4). Sometimes God's use of evil may be a means of testing His people's loyalties (Dt. 8:16; Ps. 119:71; He. 12:10). In the end Scripture portrays the eschatological triumph of the good (God) over evil (Satan). (*See also* EVIL III.)

Bibliography.–V. Bourke, *History of Ethics* (1968), pp. 11-45; C. Brinton, *History of Western Morals* (1959), chs. 3-7; *Encyclopedia Judaica,* VII, *s.v.* "Good and Evil"; G. Harkness, *Sources of Western Morality* (1954), chs. 5-9; C. Henry, *Christian Personal Ethics* (1957); *New Catholic Encyclopedia,* VI, *s.v.* "Good" (E. G. Salmon); *TDNT,* I, *s.v.* ἀγαθός (Grundmann); III, *s.v.* καλός (Bertram); *TDOT,* V, *s.v.* "ṭôbh" (Höver-Johag); G. F. Thomas, "Christian Ethics and Moral Philosophy," in W. R. Durland and W. H. Bruening, eds., *Ethical Issues* (1975), pp. 61-73.

R. C. TOGTMAN R. W. V.

GOOD, CHIEF. *See* GOOD.

GOOD NEWS; PREACH GOOD NEWS; etc. [Heb. *bāśar*] (1 S. 31:9; 2 S. 4:10; 1 K. 1:42; 1 Ch. 10:9); AV PUBLISH, TIDINGS, GOOD TIDINGS; [*beśôrâ*] (2 S. 18:27; 2 K. 7:9); AV GOOD TIDINGS; [*šemûʿâ ṭôḇâ*] (Prov. 15:30; 25:25); AV also GOOD REPORT (25:25); [Gk. *euangelízō, euangelízomai, euangélion*] (Mt. 11:5; Lk. 1:19; 3:18; 4:18; etc.); AV GOSPEL, GLAD TIDINGS, GOOD TIDINGS, PREACH, etc.; NEB also GOSPEL (1 Pet. 1:12, 25).

In the OT good news usually concerns victory in battle, though in 1 K. 1:42 political victory is the subject of the news. The texts in Proverbs seem to refer more generally to anything good that is heard, and to the refreshing effect such news has on the hearer. The "glad news of deliverance" of Ps. 40:9 (MT 10) may be the OT counterpart of the NT good news, proclaimed here among fellow believers. (For more general and more theological meanings of Heb. *bśr,* cf. *TDOT,* II, *s.v.* "bśr" [Schilling]; cf. also *TDNT,* II, *s.v.* εὐαγγελίζομαι κτλ. [Friedrich]; M. Burrows, *JBL,* 44 [1925], 21-33.)

The variety of ways in which *euangelízō* is translated in the English versions is due to a great extent to the fact that this verb is used both absolutely (e.g., "gospel," 1 Cor. 1:17; 9:16), and with other terms, such as "the kingdom of God" (Lk. 4:43; 8:1), "Jesus as the Christ" (Acts 5:42), "Jesus" (8:35), "the Lord Jesus" (11:20), "Jesus and the resurrection" (17:18), "the word" (8:4), "peace" (10:36; Eph. 2:17), "the gospel" (1 Cor. 15:1; Gal. 1:11), etc. Uniformity in translation is difficult since no common English verb such as "gospelize" is available to translate *euangelízō.* At times the immediate context also requires the verb to be translated in a way that does not permit uniformity (cf. Rev. 10:7).

The terms "good news," "gospel" (from Anglo-Saxon *god-spell,* which means "good tidings"), Lat. *evangelium,* and Gk. *euangélion* are literal equivalents. For the theological significance of these NT terms *see* GOSPEL.

R. H. STEIN

GOODLINESS (Isa. 40:6, AV). *See* BEAUTY.

GOODLY [Heb. *ṭôḇ*] (Ex. 2:2; Dt. 3:25; 6:10; 8:12; Ps. 21:3 [MT 4]; 45:1 [MT 2]; Prov. 28:10); AV also GOODNESS (Ps. 21:3), GOOD (Ps. 45:1; Prov. 28:10); NEB also FINE, PROSPERITY (Ps. 21:3), NOBLE (Ps. 45:1), "a fortune" (Prov. 28:10); [*ḥîn*] (Job 41:12 [MT 4]); AV COMELY; NEB GRACE; [*šāpār*] (Ps. 16:6); NEB "well content"; [*tōʾar*] (Jer. 11:16); NEB FAIR; **GOODLY TREES** [*ʿēṣ hāḏār*] (Lev. 23:40); NEB CITRUS-TREE.

Hebrew *ṭôḇ* often refers to a physically pleasing attractiveness, an appeal to the senses; but it also may have a more general meaning of pleasing or agreeable (cf. Ps. 23:1; Prov. 28:10; *see also* GOOD). Heb. *tōʾar* clearly refers to the physical form, usually with a positive connotation (cf. 1 S. 16:18 for a similar use). Heb. *šāpār* means "to be pleasing, beautiful" in a general sense (cf. postbiblical Heb., Aram. *špr*). Heb. *ḥîn,* a hapax legomenon, appears to be related to Heb. *ḥānan,* "to show favor, be gracious," but such a meaning hardly fits the context (cf. the comms., and BDB, p. 336).

Hebrew *hāḏār* usually means splendor or majesty, and thus here it probably referred to the beauty of these trees. It was one of four species of plants used in the Feast of Tabernacles. The Talmud (T.B. *Sukkah* 35a) spoke of this as the "Holy Citron," or etrog, a tradition going back to Maccabean times. Josephus (*Ant.* xiii.13.5 [372]) recorded that infuriated Jews threw citrons at Alexander Janneus while he served at the altar during this feast. The reference is probably to the *Citrus medica* var. *lageriformis* Roem., which may have been imported from Babylon by returning exiles.

R. K. H.

GOODMAN. The word occurs only once in the OT as the obsolete AV translation of the ordinary word for "man," Heb. *ʾîš* (Prov. 7:19): "the goodman *is* not at home." The RSV, along with the Geneva, Douay, and Wyclif versions, has "my husband is not at home," while the NEB has "the man of the house is away." In the NT the AV uses "goodman" five times for Gk. *oikodespótēs* (Mt. 20:11; 24:43; Mk. 14:14; Lk. 12:39; 22:11). The Greek term occurs twelve times in the Synoptics; the RSV and NEB generally render it "householder" or "master of the house," as does the AV in Mt. 10:25; 13:27, 52; 20:1; 21:33; Lk. 13:25; 14:21. (See also *TDNT,* II, 49.) The adjective was a mark of respect and was used somewhat as our word "Mr.," as an appellative of respect or civility. Relationship by marriage was distinguished by this epithet, as "good-father," "good-sister," both in England and Scotland. Later the adjective lost its distinguishing force and was replaced by the noun goodman.

J. J. REEVE

GOODNESS [Heb. *ṭôḇ*–'good'] (2 Ch. 6:41; Ps. 23:6; 68:10 [MT 11]); NEB also PROSPERITY (1 K. 8:66; 2 Ch. 6:41); [*ṭôḇâ*–'good things'] (1 K. 8:66 par. 2 Ch. 7:10); NEB PROSPERITY; [*ṭûḇ*] (Ex. 33:19; Neh. 9:25, 35; Ps. 27:13; 31:19 [MT 20]; 65:4 [MT 5]; 145:7; Isa. 63:7; Jer. 31:12, 14; Hos. 3:5); NEB also PROSPERITY (Neh. 9:35), BLESSING (Ps. 65:4), BOUNTY (Jer. 31:12, 14; Hos. 3:5); [Gk. adjective *agathós*] (Philem. 14); AV BENEFIT, NEB KINDNESS; [*agathōsýnē*] (Rom. 15:14; Gal. 5:22); [*kalós*–'beautiful, good'] (He. 6:5); AV GOOD; [*philanthrōpía*–'love for mankind'] (Tit. 3:4); AV, NEB, KINDNESS; **GOODNESS' SAKE** [Heb. *ṭûḇ*] (Ps. 25:7; cf. NEB v. 5); **LOVER OF GOODNESS** [Gk. *philágathos*] (Tit. 1:8); AV LOVER OF GOOD MEN; NEB "right-minded."

In the OT, God is always the source of goodness, which may be seen in the physical, earthly aspects of life as well as the spiritual and eternal. Thus He provides land and food (Neh. 9:25, 35; Ps. 68:10; Jer. 31:12), political deliverance (Ps. 145:7; Isa. 63:7), personal deliverance (Ps. 27:13) and protection (23:6; 31:19), a temple (1 K. 8:66; 2 Ch. 6:41) where one may be spiritually satisfied (Ps. 65:4; cf. Jer. 31:14 for another instance of the satisfying nature of His goodness), and forgiveness (Ps. 25:7; Hos. 3:5). God's character is described as goodness in Ex. 33:19 (cf. NEB mg., and Ps. 25:7).

In the NT, goodness is used in a more general sense, though still with God as the source, as the contexts imply in Rom. 15:14; Gal. 5:22; Tit. 1:8 (but cf. Philem. 14). In Tit. 3:4 the goodness of God, as evidenced in Christ, is contrasted with the evil of human life without God (cf. Gal. 5:19-23 and Tit. 1:7-10 for a similar contrast; cf. also Bauer, p. 866; MM, pp. 668f.). In He. 6:5 the "goodness of the word of God" is probably synonymous with the gospel (but cf. B. F. Westcott, *Epistle to the Hebrews* [repr. 1973], p. 149).

See also GOOD. G. A. L.

GOODS [Heb. *r^ekuš* or *r^ekûš, k^elî* (Gen. 31:37; 45:20; Ex. 22:7 [MT 6]), *m^elā'kâ* (Ex. 22:8 [MT 7]; Nu. 16:32), *ḥayil* (Nu. 31:9; Ob. 13; Zeph. 1:13), *k^ebûdâ* (Jgs. 18:21), *ṭûb* (2 K. 8:9), *ṭôb* (Eccl. 5:11 [MT 10]), *šālāl* (Est. 3:13; 8:11), *p^equddâ* (Ps. 109:8), *hôn* (Prov. 1:13; 6:31), *ma'^aśeh* (Ezk. 27:16, 18), *qinyān* (Ezk. 38:12f.); Aram. *n^ekas* (Ezr. 7:26); Gk. *skeúos* (Mt. 12:29; Mk. 3:27; Lk. 17:31), *tá hypárchonta* (Lk. 11:21; 16:1; 19:8), *hypárxis* (Acts 2:45), *katéchō*–'hold ("have no goods," 1 Cor. 7:30), *agathá* (Lk. 12:18f.), *tá sá* (Lk. 6:30), *bíos*–'life' (1 Jn. 3:17)]; AV also RICHES, SUBSTANCE, STUFF, VESSELS, TO TAKE SPOILS, CARRIAGE (Jgs. 18:21), OFFICE (Ps. 109:8), etc.; NEB also HERDS, PROPERTY, POSSESSIONS, CHATTELS, TREASURE, WEALTH, etc.; **SELLER OF PURPLE GOODS** [Gk. *porphyrópōlis*] (Acts 16:14); AV "seller of purple"; NEB "dealer in purple fabric." Material possessions of various kinds, often used of that which is plundered, stolen, or confiscated.

Both Heb. *hôn* (occurring only in poetry) and Heb. *ḥayil* speak of wealth in general; except for Prov. 6:31, all of the above-mentioned occurrences of these two words concern the seizure or plunder of such wealth. Heb. *r^ekuš* is a general term for possessions (cf. Ezr. 8:21; texts which refer to plundering are Gen. 14:11f., 16, 21; 2 Ch. 20:25; Dnl. 11:24), being linked with silver, gold, and animals in Gen. 46:6; Ezr. 1:4, 6. Similarly, Heb. *k^elî* and Heb. *m^elā'kâ* are general terms for possessions, with some overlap in meaning apparent in Ex. 22:7f. Heb. *ma'^aśeh* (< Heb. *'āśâ,* "do, make") probably refers to man-made or processed goods of all kinds (cf. Ezk. 27:18, where Heb. *hôn* further defines Heb. *ma'^aśeh*). Heb. (Aram.? cf. BDB, p. 889) *qinyān* refers to purchased property (cf. Heb. *qānâ* "get, acquire"); note the context in Ezk. 38:12 is again one of plunder. Heb. *šālāl,* a common word for booty or plunder, is probably translated as "goods" in Esther to avoid awkwardness. Although Heb. *p^equddâ* usually means "charge" or "visitation" (cf. BDB, p. 824), it may also mean what is in one's charge (cf. Isa. 15:7); note again the context of seizing another's property. Heb. *k^ebûdâ* occurs in a plunder context; but the spectrum of meaning associated with Heb. *kbd* (cf. BDB, pp. 457-59) makes it uncertain whether it is the splendor (NEB "valuables"; cf. G. F. Moore, *Judges* [*ICC,* 1901], pp. 397f.) or the weight (AV "carriage"; cf. R. Boling, *Judges* [*AB,* 1975], p. 264) which is meant; perhaps both. Aram. *n^ekas* (cf. Heb. *n^ekāsîm*) is another general term for possessions, common in Egyptian Aramaic (cf. A. Cowley, *Aramaic Papyri of the Fifth Century B.C.* [1923], pp. 20, 38, 42, etc.).

In the NT the meaning of the words is more obvious. Four speak of "possession": Gk. *tá sá* (lit. "what is your"), *ta hypárchonta,* and *hypárxis* ("what one has"), as well as *katéchō* ("to possess"). Gk. *bíos,* referring to earthly life or manner of life, emphasizes the "means of living" generally on a subsistence level (cf. Mk. 12:44; Lk. 8:43 [variant reading]; 15:12, 30; 21:4). Gk. *porphyrópōlis* (Acts 16:14) is a dealer in purple fabrics or goods (*see also* PURPLE).

See *TDOT,* III, *s.v.* "hôn" (Kutsch).

H. VAN BROEKHOVEN, JR.
G. A. L.

GOPHER WOOD [Heb. *'^aṣê-gōper*; Gk. *tetragōnía*]; NEB RIBS OF CYPRESS (Gen. 6:14). The Hebrew term has not been attested in cognate languages, and a connection with the Akk. *kuprītu,* "brimstone," seems improbable. Equally unlikely is the attempt to relate it to the modern Arabic *kufa* or boat made from interwoven willow branches and palm leaves coated with bitumen. Probably some resinous wood is implied; most botanical authorities favor the evergreen cypress, *Cupressus sempervirens,* an extremely durable species found throughout ancient Palestine and used by the Egyptians for making coffins.

R. K. H.

GORE [Heb. *nāgaḥ*] (Ex. 21:28f., 31f., 36); AV also PUSH; NEB also "be vicious." The basic meaning of the verb is "push," as indicated by the AV in Ex. 21:29, 32, 36.

GORGEOUS; GORGEOUSLY. This adjective and adverb occur once each in the RSV, both times to describe apparel befitting a king or his court. In Lk. 23:11 Gk. *lamprós* ("bright, shining"; cf. Acts 10:30) describes the kingly apparel in which Herod and his soldiers mockingly arrayed Jesus. In 7:25 Jesus told the crowds that "those who are gorgeously [Gk. *éndoxos,* "splendid, glorious"] appareled . . . are in kings' courts" — they are not to be found among the prophets.

GORGIAS gôr'gē-əs [Gk. *Gorgias*]. A general in the service of Antiochus Epiphanes (1 Macc. 3:38; 2 Macc. 8:9). Lysias, who had been left as regent during the absence of Antiochus in Persia, appointed Gorgias to take the command against Judea in 166 B.C. In 1 Macc. 4:1-24 is recorded a night attack by Gorgias with five thousand infantry and one thousand cavalry upon the camp of Judas Maccabeus near Emmaus, in which Judas was completely victorious. The victory was all the more striking as Judas's force was considerably smaller in number (1 Macc. 4:6). Later (164 B.C.) he held a garrison in Jamnia, and gained a victory over the forces of Joseph and Azarias who, envying the glory of Judas and Jonathan, in direct disobedience to the orders of Judas, attacked Gorgias and were defeated.

Jamnia, as given in Josephus *Ant.* xii.8.6 (350), is probably the correct reading for Idumea in 2 Macc. 12:32. The doings of Gorgias in 2 Maccabees are recorded with some confusion. He was regarded with special hostility by the Jews. In 2 Macc. 12:35 he is described as "the accursed man." J. HUTCHISON

GORTYNA gôr-tī'nə [Gk. *Gortyna*]. A city in south central Crete, second only to Knossus in importance. About 139 B.C. the Romans sent to it letters favoring the Jews (1 Macc. 15:23). R. EARLE

GOSHEN gō'shən [Heb. *gōšen*]. Attempts to derive "Goshen" from one or another Egyptian root are probably misdirected. It is most likely of Semitic origin (though the root is uncertain), since it designated a city and a region in southern Judah (see **1** and **2** below), as well as an area in Egypt.

1. Josh. 15:51 mentions a city by this name in a list of eleven cities in the hill country of Judah. It is preceded in the list by Anim and followed by Holon. The mention of Debir in the same context gives the general location. Some believe it is to be identified with modern Ẓâharîyeh, about 19 km. (12 mi.) SW of Hebron.

2. A district of Goshen — possibly the territory surrounding the city by the same name — is mentioned as one of the regions conquered by Joshua (Josh. 10:41; 11:16).

3. The region in which the Israelites settled during the lifetime of Joseph and in which they still lived at the time of the Exodus (cf. Ex. 8:22 [MT 18]; 9:26). The Israelites particularly desired this region because it was near enough to Joseph that he could look after them during the famine and apparently also because it would provide good grazing for their animals (cf. Gen. 45:9-11; 46:31–47:6). From the perspective of Joseph's own residence Goshen apparently lay in the direction of Canaan, for Joseph went up there to meet his father coming down from Canaan (Gen. 46:28f.).

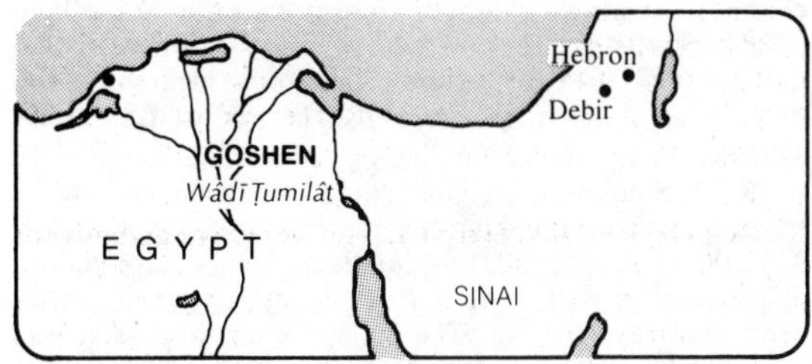

Added evidence for the identification of this region comes from the LXX, which usually translates Heb. *gōšen* as *Gesem Arabias,* "Gesem of Arabia" (45:10; 46:34; 47:1, 4, 27; 50:8). This rendering appears to identify Goshen with the later Egyptian nome of Arabia, which was located in the Wâdī Ṭumilât area. In 46:28b the LXX has *gḗ Ramessē,* "land of Ramses," apparently another name for the same area (cf. 47:11). And in 46:28a, 29 the LXX has *Hērṓōn pólis,* "city of heroes," i.e., Hierapolis, which was also located in this area. The practice of allowing shepherds within the Egyptian domain was not unknown (cf. J. Skinner, comm. on Genesis [*ICC,* 1910], p. 497); some even identify one area where such shepherds were as Goshen (*ANET,* p. 259 n. 4).

Bibliography.–W. F. Albright, *BASOR,* 140 (Dec. 1955), 30f.; A. H. Gardiner, *JEA,* 5 (1918), 218-223; 10 (1924), 94f.; E. Naville, *JEA,* 10 (1924), 18-39.

E. D. WELCH

GOSPEL [Gk. *euangélion*]; NEB also GOOD NEWS (Mt. 9:35; Mk. 16:15; Rom. 10:16; Eph. 1:13; 1 Thess. 2:9), "purpose" (Eph. 6:19), "mission" (Phil. 4:15); **PREACH THE GOSPEL** [Gk. *euangelízomai*]; NEB also TELL THE GOOD NEWS (Lk. 9:6; 20:1), BRING THE GOOD NEWS (Acts 8:25; 14:21; 16:10), PREACH (Acts 8:40; 1 Cor. 9:16), SPREAD THE GOOD NEWS (Acts 14:7), BRING THE GOSPEL (Rom. 15:20), CARRY THE GOSPEL (2 Cor. 10:16); **PREACH BEFOREHAND THE GOSPEL** [Gk. *proeuangelízomai*] (Gal. 3:8). In several texts the RSV supplies "gospel" where the Greek text has only a pronoun referring to *euangélion* (Rom. 1:3; Gal. 1:7; Eph. 3:7; 2 Tim. 1:11; 2:9) or an elliptical construction (Gal. 1:11b; 2:7b).

I. Derivation of the Term.–The family of Greek words rendered "gospel" or "proclaim" derives from the noun *ángelos* ("messenger"), and the verb *angéllō* ("announce, proclaim, publish news"). Basically the term "gospel," meaning "good news," is the content of what is preached, while the activity is characterized in the phrase "proclaim the good news" (Gk. *euangelízomai*). The epithet "good" is supplied to translate the prefix in *euangélion.* In the NT period *euangelízomai* was the activity of public or private speaking or else believing or receiving, but not writing or reading. The use of the word in the sense of written documents (e.g., the four Gospels) was much later, first found in Justin's description of a liturgical service at which the "memoirs of the apostles . . . called gospels" were read out to the congregation (*Apol.* i.66). In fact, the plural "gospels" was not a NT usage (*see* GOSPELS, SYNOPTIC).

Related terms are the verb *kērýssō,* "preach," and the noun *kḗrygma,* "preaching," both deriving from *kḗryx,* "herald." There is no apparent distinction in meaning between *euangélion* and *kḗrygma* (*see* PREACH).

II. Origin and Background.–The noun form *euangélion* meant originally the reward offered to a messenger who brought news of victory in battle or escape from danger. By a natural transference it came to mean the content of the message he brought, i.e., not simply news but good news. The immediate reaction on receiving the news was the offering of sacrifice to the gods as a token of gratitude. (*See* GOOD NEWS.)

The religious connotation gathered around the noun *euangélion* through the cult of the Roman emperor (cf. H-S, I, 71-73; *TDNT,* II, 724f.; P. Stuhlmacher, *Das paulinische Euangelium,* I [FRLANT, 95, 1968], 196-206 [critical of Schneemelcher]). Of special interest is the enthronement inscription from Priene in Asia Minor, dated 9 B.C., in which the birthday of the emperor Augustus was hailed as "the beginning of the joyful news [*euangélia*] for the world." The parallel with the NT announcement of "good news" through the coming of Jesus the Lord (as in Lk. 2:10f.) is impressive since the phrase in the imperial cult associated with Augustus' new age not only heralded that era but actually brought it about. "The proclamation is itself the *euangelion,* since the salvation it proclaims is already present in it" (*DNTT,* II, 108). But the general attitude of the NT writers to the veneration of the Roman emperor was at best neutral (1 Pet. 2:17; 1 Tim. 2:2) and sometimes definitely hostile (cf. comms. on Rev. 13, 17). It is therefore unlikely that Christians would borrow this term from a pagan source, especially since its religious overtones, setting up a competitive allegiance, were considerable.

More relevant is the background provided by the OT. To be sure, J. Schniewind denies any connection between the LXX and the NT use (*Euangelion: Ursprung und erste Gestalt des Begriffs Evangelium,* I [1927], 78). He correctly observes that the noun *euangélion* is absent from the LXX, but it is difficult to justify his contention that "the idea of a messenger of good news" is missing too. Especially in Isa. 40:9; 52:7-10; 60:6; 61:1 the herald of good news (Heb. *mᵉḇaśśēr,* rendered *euangelizómenos* in the LXX; *see* GOOD NEWS) played a prominent role. He announced a new age in which Yahweh is king and His rule is inaugurated. Gk. *euangelízomai* parallels *kērýssō,* "proclaim" (often a synonym in the NT), in Ps. Sol. 11:1f. (*ca.* 50 B.C.).

The influence of the Isaiah passages in later Judaism was considerable, especially at Qumrân (cf. 1QM 18:14: "a messenger . . . of Thy goodness; that to the humble he might bring glad tidings of Thy great mercy, [proclaiming salvation]," G. Vermes, *Dead Sea Scrolls in English* [1962],

p. 200) and among the rabbis, who used the participle *m^{e}baśśēr* for the herald of the messianic era of joy. The omission of the noun has caused some difficulty, but rather than conclude that early Christianity borrowed it from Greek usage, one might suggest that, with the precedent of the verb form the first Christians boldly appropriated a newly coined noun to express their conviction that the Jews' eschatological expectation had indeed arrived in history with the advent, ministry, passion, and triumph of Israel's messiah and the Church's Lord (see W. K. L. Clarke, "What Is the Gospel?" in *Divine Humanity* [1936], pp. 87-100; *TDOT,* II, 316).

III. Distribution.–An interesting statistical analysis yields the following result (drawn from R. Morgenthaler, *Statistik des NT Wortschatzes* [1958], p. 101): Both verb (twenty-one times, including Ephesians) and noun (sixty times, including four times in Ephesians and four times in the Pastorals) are most frequent in Paul. The Johannine literature (Gospel and Epistles) lacks both the verb and the noun, preferring parallel terms such as "witness" or "truth," with corresponding verbs. Luke favored the verb (twenty-five times in Luke-Acts) to the almost complete exclusion of the noun (only in Acts 15:7; 20:24), while Matthew had *euangelízomai* once (11:5) and amplified the noun with the description "of the kingdom" (4:23; 9:35), as though to give an extra dimension to the gospel's content in contrast to Mark. Mark preferred the noun (seven or eight times) to the verb (which is not found) and often used the noun in passages that are usually regarded as showing his own redactional handiwork (R. P. Martin, *Mark: Evangelist and Theologian* [1972], pp. 24-28). He alone of the Evangelists used *euangélion* as a technical term on its own, and in this respect he followed closely the pattern set by Paul, who provided the fullest exposition of what "gospel" meant and who used the unqualified term *euangélion* some twenty-three times.

IV. Meaning.–*A. In Paul.* The way Paul used the term without qualification ("the gospel") and without further explanation of its meaning has suggested to most scholars that he was drawing on a term borrowed or inherited from pre-Pauline Christianity. This is evident in Rom. 1:1-4, which incorporated a pre-Pauline creedal formulary (cf. K. Wengst, *Christologische Formeln und Lieder des Urchristentums* [1972], pp. 112ff.; M. Hengel, *The Son of God* [Eng. tr. 1976], pp. 59-66, tracing the section back to the first Jewish-Christian community in Jerusalem, even if Paul adapted it to conform to his theology of the Lord's preexistence), and in 1 Cor. 15:3-5. The latter is the oldest testimony to Jesus' resurrection; it was probably a Palestinian credo reformulated in a Jewish-Hellenistic milieu and used in proclaiming the gospel with a later adaptation as a baptismal confession like Rom. 6:3f.; Col. 2:12 (so J. Kloppenborg, *CBQ,* 40 [1978], 351-367). These statements in Rom. 1 and 1 Cor. 15 carry literary marks of their pre-Pauline origin (e.g., non-Pauline vocabulary) and a poetic or rhythmical arrangement of the lines that suggests a liturgical origin. More importantly, they relate the good news of Christ's person to His atoning and saving work, emphasize the centrality of His resurrection from the dead, and make it clear that these events of incarnation, death, and vindication occurred in accordance with the OT Scriptures (cf. C. H. Dodd, *According to the Scriptures* [1952]; F. F. Bruce, *NT Development of OT Themes* [1968]). These items form the heart of Paul's message centered in Christ's person as Son of God (2 Cor. 1:19) and risen Lord. Paul was called and commissioned as "apostle to the Gentiles" (1 Cor. 1:17; Rom. 10:14-17; Gal. 1:15f.) to preach this kerygma that leads to salvation (1 Cor. 15:1f., 11; 2 Thess. 2:13f.). "Gospel" and "apostleship" were intimately bound together in Paul's view; his whole missionary activity can be summed up in the one verb *euangelízomai* (1 Cor. 1:17). He saw his vocation to be the specially chosen herald of the "mystery" of God's plan for the Gentiles (Col. 1:24-29; Eph. 3:2-7), which he called not surprisingly "my gospel" (Rom. 2:16; 16:25) or "our gospel" (2 Cor. 4:3).

Among several reasons for this personal description, one was Paul's unique consciousness of being "an eschatological apostle" (A. Fridrichsen, *The Apostle and His Message* [1947]; J. Munck, *Paul and the Salvation of Mankind* [Eng. tr. 1959], pp. 40-49, 119-122, stressing how, according to his self-understanding, Paul's conversion led to his becoming "the central figure in the story of salvation" [p. 49]). Second, this destiny was seen as the fulfillment of the OT forecast of "a herald" who would proclaim God's kingly rule; Paul interpreted this in the light of his role as the servant who was to be a light to the nations (Gal. 1:15-17; 2 Cor. 6:1-4; Rom. 15:21; cf. Acts 13:47f.; see L. Cerfaux, *Recueil,* 2 [1954], 447f.).

Third, Paul's understanding of "preaching the gospel" — and the noun *euangélion* could also mean the act or service implied in making the gospel known (as in 1 Cor. 9:14, 18; Phil. 1:5; 2:22) — involved much more than a dispassionate recital of bare facts relating to Christ's death and resurrection. The apostle's whole person was included (cf. 1 Thess. 2:8). But more importantly Paul's rehearsing of the good news was no mere human statement. It was the activity of an apostle "entrusted with the gospel" (1 Thess. 2:4), which he conveyed "not as the word of men but as what it really is, the word of God" (1 Thess. 2:13). In fact, Paul's proclamation was nothing less than "God making his appeal through us" (2 Cor. 5:20; cf. 6:1, "working together with him [God]"; cf. J. Murphy-O'Connor, *Paul on Preaching* [1964], p. 75: "The preachers co-operate with God because they speak for him, or rather, because he uses them to convey his message to men"). The conclusion to be drawn from this statement is striking: "To proclaim the gospel" in Paul's missionary theology was to make actual and available the reality of God's salvation in Christ that is announced. "The gospel does not merely bear witness to salvation history; it is itself salvation history" (*TDNT,* II, 731). Paul could therefore use "gospel" to include the sphere of human life that is drawn into God's saving design, i.e., the Church (e.g., 2 Cor. 8:18, where "in the gospel" and "in all the churches" are parallel phrases). And he could employ "gospel" to mean the ethical standard required of those who are saved, as in Phil. 1:27, and possibly Gal. 2:14.

Finally, Paul called his message "my/our gospel" in distinction from a message "peddled" (cf. 2 Cor. 2:17) by other preachers in the early communities. Sometimes the variant message had only a change of emphasis; Paul regretted this but did not oppose it since "Christ is being proclaimed; and in that I rejoice" (Phil. 1:12-18; on the identity of these rival preachers, see R. P. Martin, *Philippians* [*New Century Bible,* 1976], pp. 72-74). More seriously, there were in Galatia (Gal. 1:1-11) and at Corinth (2 Cor. 11:4) — and probably elsewhere (Philippi, Thessalonica, Ephesus [1 Tim. 4; 2 Tim. 2:17f.]) — those whom Paul labeled "false apostles" (2 Cor. 11:13) and Satan's servants (11:15). They preached "another Jesus" and "a different [*héteros*] gospel from the one you accepted." In Galatia the alien gospel was a mixture of legalistic Judaism (as in Rom. 2–4; 2 Cor. 10–13; Phil. 3) and a species of Hellenistic Gnosticism (see R. Jewett, *NTS,* 17 [1970/71], 198-212). The deviant teaching that invaded the Corinthian church was chiefly christological (cf. 1 Cor. 12:3 — probably this refers, in the cry "Jesus be cursed," to a docetic denial of the earthly Jesus and an undue exalting of the heavenly aeon Christ), and was related to a false conception of salvation that denied all future hope of a bodily resurrection (1 Cor. 15:12; J. H. Wilson, *ZNW*, 59 [1968], 90-107; but cf. D. J. Doughty, *ZNW*, 66 [1975], 61-90; A. C. Thistleton, *NTS*, 24 [1978], 510-526).

Paul treated errors regarding the person of Jesus Christ (mainly by reducing Him to one intermediary in a gnostic system, as at Colossae) and the way of salvation (which for Paul and his disciples is "by grace alone, through faith alone" [Eph. 2:1-10] with no addition of legalistic merit [Gal. 2:21; Phil. 3:9]) as subversive of his gospel, thus needing (and receiving) clear refutation. No less disastrous was an antinomian disregard for the strict demands of a holy life by the Spirit, and Paul's call to his people to remain loyal to the gospel they had received included a summons to live in a manner pleasing to God and in conscious social responsibility for their neighbors (Col. 1:5f.). In this way a Christian's personal and corporate life becomes "worthy of the gospel" (Phil. 1:27; here "gospel" means the entire work of God in salvation; cf. 1 Thess. 2:12).

B. In Mark. Both in frequency of mention and in the significance attached to the term, Mark followed the path set by Paul. For this Evangelist Jesus' ministry was portrayed as a proclaiming of the good news by speech and deed; in this regard Matthew shared a common understanding (Mk. 1:14f. par. Mt. 4:7, 23). But Mark was clearly a writer closer to Paul in that (1) he used "gospel" as a technical expression for the kerygmatic announcement of God's salvation, whereas Matthew preferred to relate "gospel" to Jesus' teaching ministry; (2) he editorialized the tradition by adding *euangélion* at places where the other Evangelists did not choose to follow him (8:35; 10:29). This point suggests that Mark had a preference for "gospel" (as in 13:10, which is absent from parallel verses in Matthew and Luke); and this is seen especially in 1:1, where "gospel" is a title for his entire book (so W. Marxsen, *Mark the Evangelist* [Eng. tr. 1969], pp. 117-150; N. Perrin, *Expos.T.*, 82 [1970], 4-7), and in 1:14f. where "gospel" is the epitome of Jesus' message *both* in the sense of the message He preached *and* in the reality of God's rule He embodied. "Christology and the preaching of the kingdom" comprised two formulated centers of power that were held firmly together through the conception of the "gospel of God" (so G. Dautzenberg, *BZ*, 21 [1977], 219-234; 22 [1978], 76-91). Mark, therefore, was clearly an exponent of Paul's gospel who related the apostolic kerygma of a crucified and exalted Lord to some pressing needs in his day. These occasions may have been apologetic (to offer a rationale for some historical events, such as the fall of Jerusalem in A.D. 70), pastoral (to encourage persecuted and afflicted Christians in Rome in A.D. 65 when Nero's pogrom began), or christological (to refute an incipient Docetism by joining together precanonical miracle stories of Jesus as a wonder worker and the Passion narrative, thereby propounding and illustrating Paul's theme of Jesus' mission as one who was "crucified in weakness, but lives by the power of God" [2 Cor. 13:4; for this linkage of ideas see R. P. Martin, *Mark: Evangelist and Theologian* (1972), pp. 214-17; *Southwestern Journal of Theology*, 21 [1978], 23-36]). In the latter proposal, "gospel" for Mark was the fleshing out in historical detail of the substance of Paul's gospel of the Son of God, once rejected and crucified yet now risen, enthroned, and active in the Church.

C. In Matthew. Matthew's redaction of the Synoptic tradition is made fairly obvious by observing the direction of his pedagogical interests. So "gospel" became "gospel of the kingdom" (4:23; 9:35; 24:14) — a term that embodied the new life-style expected of Christians living in a Judeo-Hellenistic environment and needing a summons to the moral demands of the gospel (see W. D. Davies, *Setting of the Sermon on the Mount* [1964]). The process by which the kerygmatic gospel of Paul and Mark became adapted to *didachḗ* (teaching) in the later Church (e.g., the Didache [*ca.* A.D. 80-100], which draws extensively on Matthew's Gospel for its moralistic teaching) is seen to begin with Matthew's work (titled in 1:1 "the scroll of the origin of Jesus Christ") with its heavy emphasis on the new "law" (5:17-19), the higher righteousness (5:20), the call to perfection (5:48; 19:21), and obedience to Jesus' teaching (23:10; 28:20). These times are all set within the OT framework of "promise and fulfillment."

D. In Luke. As mentioned above (see III), Luke did not employ the noun *euangélion* in his Gospel, and it appears only twice in Acts (see H. Conzelmann, *Theology of St. Luke* [Eng. tr. 1960], p. 221 n. 1; *euangélion* is not found in Q either, except in Mt. 11:5 par. Luke 7:22). An interesting conclusion has been drawn from this datum, namely, that Luke deliberately avoided the noun since his purpose was to compose not a gospel but a "life of Jesus" with a paradigmatic value and related to the mission of the Church in Luke's day (W. Marxsen, *Mark the Evangelist* [Eng. tr. 1969], pp. 142-46). This conclusion is partly offset by the fact that the verb *euangelízomai* is frequent in Luke (ten times in the Gospel; fifteen times in Acts), though it covers a wide range of meanings (cf. 1:19; 2:10; 3:18). After the Baptist's death (16:16) the content of the gospel proclamation is given as the kingdom of God — a usage found in Acts (8:12; 20:25; 28:31) in a sense hardly different from "preaching the gospel."

What emerges from Luke's distinctive usage is his consistent emphasis on the act of preaching that is explained by the direct object that accompanies the verb; but the eschatological dimension has been lost in the use of the verb in the Birth stories and in reference to John the Baptist (3:8). Of all the Evangelists only Luke assumed the role of historian and set about the task of constructing a life of Jesus. "His Gospel is indeed the first 'life of Jesus'" (E. Käsemann, *Essays on NT Themes* [*SBT*, 41, 1964], p. 29; cf. R. P. Martin, *NT Foundations*, I [1975], 259f., with a reason sought in Luke's pastoral purpose. How far the term "gospel" here has assumed a biographical character is considered by G. N. Stanton, *Jesus of Nazareth in NT Preaching* [1974], pp. 31-66, and C. H. Talbert, *What Is a Gospel?* [1977]).

E. Elsewhere. Allusions and specific references in the remaining NT books do not alter the picture drawn above. Hebrews has the verb twice, used of the kerygmatic message the readers had received (4:6 refers back to 4:2 and parallels the use of the verb in Gal. 3:8). 1 Peter repeats this emphasis (1:12, 25 referring to the readers' new life in Christ), but in 4:6 has a tantalizing description of the gospel being proclaimed to the dead (see W. J. Dalton, *Christ's Proclamation to the Spirits* [1965], concluding with E. G. Selwyn, *First Epistle of St. Peter* [1946], and now J. N. D. Kelly, *Commentary on the Epistles of Peter and Jude* [*HNTC*, 1969], that the preaching was to Christians — since deceased — in their lifetime). The verb *kēryssō* in 1 Pet. 3:19 has to do with the doom of evil spirits [but cf. *TDNT*, III, 707]).

Revelation 14:6f. stands apart, since here the angel is the proclaimer of an "eternal gospel" (no definite article). This may be a verdict of judgment at the final Day (J. Jeremias, *Jesus' Promise to the Nations* [Eng. tr. 1958], p. 69), but an argument for taking *euangélion* in its unvarying NT sense of *good* news is cogent (*TDNT,* II, 735; G. B. Caird, comm. on Revelation [*HNTC,* 1966], p. 182).

V. Summary.–"Jesus Christ, risen from the dead, descended from David" (2 Tim. 2:8) may well stand as a summary of what the entire NT means by "gospel." It has to do with the person of Christ, though with an equal stress on Christ's saving work centered in the cross and Resurrection. The advent of salvation is depicted in the OT terms of promise and fulfillment (Rom. 3:21; 15:4-9; 1 Cor. 10:11). The present availability of that salvation is offered "by grace alone, through faith alone"; the work of reconciliation is both complete, i.e., God in Christ has effected the world's salvation (2 Cor. 5:19, 21), and incomplete, i.e., God has entrusted the gospel to His servants who as ambassadors for Christ call men and women to accept all that has been accomplished (5:20). "Gospel" is the link between these two ideas, meaning both all that has been done in Christ for human redemption (thus it is "good news"), and the offer freely extended to the hearers to "repent and believe the good news" by acceptance and obedience.

Bibliography.–*DNTT,* II, 107-115; *TDNT,* II, *s.v.* εὐαγγελίζομαι κτλ. (Friedrich); *TDOT,* II, *s.v.* "bśr" (Schilling).

R. P. MARTIN

GOSPEL ACCORDING TO THE HEBREWS. *See* APOCRYPHAL GOSPELS IV.C.

GOSPELS OF THE CHILDHOOD. *See* APOCRYPHAL GOSPELS II.

GOSPELS, SPURIOUS. *See* APOCRYPHAL GOSPELS.

GOSPELS, SYNOPTIC.

I. Introduction.–*A. The Gospels in Christian Literature.* The word "gospel" (Gk. *euangélion*), used earlier in Greek to mean "good news" or a reward for good tidings, was used by Jesus and His first followers to mean the good news that now, in Jesus Christ, God was acting to fulfil His promises and establish His kingdom. Since this action of God centered in the ministry, death, resurrection, and exaltation of Jesus Christ, this oral gospel was from the beginning a historical narrative with Jesus as the focal point. Only later did the Church begin to use the word "gospel" of the writings that told this story. The special word "gospel" was needed for such writings, for the biblical Gospels were a new literary form. They are not biographies or memoirs but the story of God's decisive action in Jesus Christ. No other literature has any real parallel to them; they are a distinctively Christian literary form. And while in later generations Christian writers tried to imitate the early Gospels, no later apocryphal gospel rivals the fourfold group of Gospels preserved in the NT. They are basic for the faith, life, worship, and witness of the Church in every generation.

B. Meaning of the Word "Synoptic." Among these four Gospels the first three — Matthew, Mark, and Luke — form a special group. To a considerable degree they share the same material in much the same order and in much the same wording. Yet each of the three has its own material, sequence, vocabulary, and style; none of the three is a mere copy of the others. The word "Synoptic," from Gk. *sýn* ("together") plus *ópsis* ("view"), means "giving a common view" of the Gospel story, and is used to refer to these three Gospels. The word emphasizes their agreements, but must not be allowed to obscure their differences; each Gospel has its own special content, outline, and style.

II. Synoptic Problem.–In order to understand what the Synoptic problem really is, some facts must be noted about the content of each Synoptic Gospel. (For comparison note that only 8 or 9 percent of John is paralleled in any of the Synoptic Gospels.) Of Mark's 661 verses, Matthew has a substantial parallel to more than 600 and Luke to over 350. Either Matthew or Luke or both follow Mark in the order of incidents, with only one exception; and Matthew and Luke never agree against Mark in the order of incidents. While each Gospel has its own special vocabulary and style, Matthew and Luke each parallel over half of the actual words used in Mark. In addition to the material in Mark that is paralleled by Matthew or Luke or both, about 200 verses that are not in Mark are found in both Matthew and Luke. These latter passages of Matthew and Luke consist mostly of sayings of Jesus; while parallel in content and to a greater or lesser extent in wording, their setting in the narrative outline and their order of appearance generally differ. Furthermore, each of the three Synoptic Gospels has material peculiar to itself. Mark has a few dozen verses not found in Matthew or Luke; Matthew has some 300 verses not found in Mark or Luke; Luke has some 520 verses not found in Matthew or Mark.

In addition to having a notable amount of material in common, with a great amount of agreement in the order of incidents, these three Gospels also have extensive agreement in wording. On the whole, the wording in the sayings of Jesus agrees most closely, but common narrative passages also show considerable agreement in actual wording. Yet rarely is the agreement complete; each Gospel writer has his own special vocabulary and points of style.

The problem raised by these data is this: how did it happen that these three Gospels were written with so much agreement in material, order, and wording, and yet with such differences that each writer remains an author and not a mere copyist of the Gospel tradition as recorded by others? Any solution of the problem must explain the similarities and agreements as well as the differences.

III. Languages of the Early Tradition.–*A. Aramaic.* In first-century Palestine and in the Roman empire three languages furnished the ordinary means of communication. One was Latin, the official language for Roman records. For our purpose it may be disregarded. It was little used in Roman provinces, and even first-century Rome was largely Greek-speaking. (Paul wrote to the Roman church in Greek; the Roman church *ca.* A.D. 95 wrote 1 Clement to Corinth in Greek.) Far more important was Aramaic. It was widely used in Palestine, Syria, and the Mesopotamian region, and was probably the daily tongue of the common people with whom Jesus talked. The survival in the Gospels of a few Aramaic words, e.g., *Abba, Rabbi, talitha cumi, ephphatha,* supports the conclusion, as G. Dalman argued in *Jesus-Jeshua* (Eng. tr. 1929), pp. 1-16, that Jesus Himself ordinarily spoke Aramaic; it also indicates that at least most of His first disciples did and that at first the Gospel tradition was mainly preserved in Aramaic form. It has been argued by H. Birkeland, *Language of Jesus* (1954), that Hebrew was a living language in Jesus' day. While this was no doubt true of certain groups, as the Qumrân Scrolls show, the common language for daily life in Palestine was more likely Aramaic.

B. Greek. The other language widely used during the 1st cent. A.D. was Greek. This was true even in Palestine, which had many Greek cities — not only the Decapolis but also a number of others, such as Samaria and Caesarea. In them Greek was the chief language. Even in other cities where Aramaic prevailed, dealings with the Romans and Herodians, and with traders and travelers, required at least some of the people to know Greek for use in business and government contacts. It seems highly probable that Jesus, coming from Galilee where Gentiles were rather numerous, could speak some Greek when occasion demanded (Dalman); and the Greek names of some of His disciples indicate that Greek background was not lacking in the life of such followers.

From the beginning, then, the apostolic Church probably included disciples who could speak only Greek, some who could speak only Aramaic, and some who could speak both Aramaic and Greek. The Hellenists named in Acts 6 attest the presence of Greek-speaking Christians in the earliest Church. The Semitic quality of our Greek Gospels shows that Aramaic was the prevailing language in the early Church. (C. C. Torrey, *The Four Gospels* [1933], even argued that the four canonical Gospels were written in Aramaic. A more balanced view is given by M. Black, *An Aramaic Approach to the Gospels and Acts* [3rd ed. 1967].) But some Greek was spoken from the first by Jewish disciples in the Jerusalem church, and this means — a most important point — that in the earliest years of the Church the Gospel tradition, while commonly used in Aramaic form, must also have been available in Greek for Greek-speaking Jewish Christians.

IV. Oral Gospel Tradition.–It is unlikely that the Gospel tradition was written down during the very first years of the Church. It is true that the Qumrân Scrolls show that a first-century Jewish sect dedicated to intensive study of their Scripture had a written Manual of Discipline and wrote down their interpretation of prophetic passages of Scripture. But the disciples in the earliest days of the Church, while they earnestly studied the Scripture and interpreted the coming and work of Jesus as the fulfillment of Scripture, were intent not so much on technical study as on urgent evangelistic appeal to their countrymen. Thus it is highly probable that for some years the Gospel tradition was preserved only in oral form.

A. Used in the Church. This account implies that the tradition was preserved and found daily use in the life, preaching, and teaching of the Church. It would be wrong to think that only a few key disciples with retentive memories treasured the Gospel tradition and then after many years wrote down their recollections or told them to another Christian who wrote them down. Those who knew the tradition continually passed it on. They told it as they remembered it to other believers; they spoke of it to unbelievers. The oral tradition was in constant use in the Church.

B. Role of Eyewitnesses. In those earliest years eyewitnesses played an important role. The disciples no doubt focused their attention on the fact of the resurrection and present lordship of Christ. But it was the Jesus who had lived, taught, and died who was now the exalted risen Lord; what He had done and said was an essential part of the gospel message. Thus those who had seen and heard Him during His ministry had a basic role in preserving and handing on the Gospel tradition, particularly in the first years, when the membership of the Church was small and most, if not all, new believers could know some who had seen and heard Jesus during His ministry.

C. Role of Christian Teachers. As time passed, teachers inevitably took an increasing role in preserving and handing on the Gospel tradition. The Church spread into places Jesus had never visited, places where the original disciples rarely or never came. In such places other evangelists and teachers played an important role. Those converted by evangelistic preaching needed instruction, and those who heard the message and were interested but had questions needed more detailed information about Jesus. The NT often speaks of teaching and teachers. The continual work of such teachers underlies the four canonical Gospels.

D. A Fixed Oral Tradition? The presence in the Synoptic Gospels of so many agreements not merely in content and order but especially in wording has led some to think that during the period when the Gospel story was preserved in oral form, this oral tradition was handed on in a fixed wording. This fixed oral tradition was then used by the Synoptic writers with such stylistic variations as each author chose to make. This idea of a fixed and carefully memorized tradition, which each new convert and especially each new teacher memorized and handed on, is too rigid to fit the facts. It might explain the agreements among the Gospels, but it hardly allows for the continual variation in wording that each Gospel exhibits. The idea of such an officially fixed oral tradition, handed on word for word, meets an added difficulty. The agreements we find in the Gospels are in Greek, and if an original oral tradition, handed on in Aramaic, was fixed and memorized by Aramaic-speaking Christians, it then must have been officially translated into Greek and its Greek form likewise strictly supervised to make sure it was handed on in accurate wording. No evidence exists for this complicated process, and the enthusiasm once felt for such a theory has practically disappeared.

E. Form Criticism. Since the 1920's the study of the oral period of Gospel tradition has been dominated by the method commonly known as form criticism. For this method extravagant claims have been made, but the extreme assertions by some of its advocates must not prevent us from seeing the contribution it can make to the understanding of the Gospels and the early Church. (*See* CRITICISM III.)

K. L. Schmidt (*RGJ*) argued that in the Gospel of Mark the chronological and narrative links between the units of tradition were provided by the writer of the Gospel. They do not preserve the actual historical order of events; the units of tradition had been preserved separately, without connecting links. Thus the actual order of events cannot be recovered. M. Dibelius (1919; Eng. tr., *From Tradition to Gospel* [1935]) emphasized that the Gospel writers used material that had been preserved in separate units and given literary form in church use. The Gospel tradition, he held, was remembered because the Church needed it in missionary work; and the original tradition about Jesus was preserved in church preaching. He singled out as literary types paradigms (concise narratives that climax in a saying of Jesus), individual stories that show Jesus as the marvelous wonder-worker, legends ("religious narratives of a saintly man in whose works and fate interest is taken"), and the Passion story. The last took form as a connected narrative in the very early days of the Church, sometime before the writing of any of the Gospels, and so was the one exception, Dibelius held, to the view that the oral Gospel tradition was preserved in unlinked, separate units. R. Bultmann in 1921 (Eng. tr., *HST*) divided the sayings material into apophthegms (including controversial and didactic sayings as well as biographical apophthegms) and sayings of the Lord (including logia or wisdom sayings, prophetic and apocalyptic sayings, legal sayings and community rules, and "I"-sayings). The narrative material he divided into miracle stories, historical narratives, and legends. His study is quite detailed, and the tendency among form critics to deny that we can know what Jesus said and did reached its most radical expression in him. For a more balanced view of the possibilities of form criticism see V. Taylor, *Formation of the Gospel Tradition* (1933), and L. J. McGinley, *Form-Criticism of the Synoptic Healing Narratives* (1944).

The form-critical method holds that the period between Jesus' death and the writing of the Gospels had a decisive role in shaping the Gospel tradition. This tradition was preserved only in oral form for the first two or three decades. It was used continually by the Church to meet its needs in worship, instruction of converts and immature believers, life guidance, and controversy. The material remembered and used for such purposes was chosen and its form was shaped to meet these church needs; we can discern and reconstruct with fair accuracy the situation in which the material was preserved and used. The early Church, in the view of extreme form critics, had no clear historical sense or interest; it was concerned to express its faith in the risen Christ its Lord. Therefore the Gospels resulting from this process are a direct witness to the faith and thought of the early Church rather than to the actual ministry and teaching of Jesus Himself. We really cannot know much about the historical Jesus; the Gospels attest only what the Church believed and taught about Him.

The form-critical method has real points of strength. It sees correctly that the first decades of the Church were of crucial importance; what happened to the Gospel tradition in those first years determined whether we can put any trust in the Gospels. Just when the Gospel material began to be written down is hard to say, but it may be accepted that the prevailing form of the tradition in the first two decades was oral. The material was continually used in the Church to meet the needs of its members; what Jesus had done and said was seen from the beginning as an aid to His followers. The selection and the form of the material were meant to serve these felt needs of Christians: an incident with a teaching point would be so told that the teaching point came as the climax of the story; and a healing story would be so told that the sickness was evident, the action and word of Jesus were clear, and the fact of the healing was in some way attested. The Gospel tradition does reflect the life of the Church; what the Church remembered, used, and applied to its needs tells much about its life, needs, and witness.

But it must be insisted that the attempt of form criticism to reconstruct the situation in the first two decades of the Church is difficult to carry out. Still more important, form criticism often underrates the historical sense of the early Church, and seems to trust its own hypothetical reconstructions more than the testimony of the first disciples. Their intention was to testify to what Jesus did and said; and while they centered their faith in the risen Christ their Lord, they were clear that He was the one who had lived, worked, taught, and died for them, and that only through knowing His earthly career could people know what His claim was and what His lordship meant. Moreover, some form critics tend to work with unexamined presuppositions, e.g., the assumption that most of the miraculous events told in the Gospel story could not have happened as reported.

*V. **Written Gospel Sources.***–The early period in which the Gospel tradition was preserved entirely or almost entirely in oral form did not last long. The more the Church spread and eyewitnesses died, the more the need of a written account made itself felt. The agreements among the Synoptic Gospels suggest that back of them lay written sources. Can anything trustworthy be said about such written sources?

A. Earlier Source Theories. Among views of the last two centuries three may be noted. One held that at first many brief fragments were written, each telling one incident or saying, or at most a few such items; the Synoptic Gospels were composed by combining many such fragments, with each Gospel writer making his own selection. A second theory was that before the writing of our Synoptic Gospels a large and comprehensive "Primitive Gospel" (now lost) had been written. From it each Synoptic writer drew the material that seemed most important to him, and thus produced a kind of "Reader's Digest" summary of the larger work. The third view, suggested in ancient times, held that two of the three Synoptic writers depended on the preceding author(s). Who wrote first and who next has been disputed, and every possible combination has been suggested, but the view most often defended was that Matthew was written first, Mark was a summary of Matthew, and Luke was dependent on Matthew and perhaps also on Mark. None of these theories has wide support today.

B. Two-Document Theory. For well over a century scholars have generally agreed that Mark is the earliest Synoptic Gospel and was used as a written source by the authors of Matthew and Luke. From this view developed the widely accepted Two-Document theory, which is that the writers of Matthew and Luke used as written sources both Mark and a second document, consisting mainly of sayings and commonly known as Q (*see* Q). In this view the writers of Matthew and Luke derived from Mark the bulk of their narrative material and from Q most of the sayings material they have in common.

C. Proto-Luke Theory. The Two-Document theory could claim to explain the source of most of Matthew's and Luke's material, but Matthew and Luke each contain material found in no other Gospel. Whence was it derived? Was Q in fact so extensive a document that it contained not only what Matthew and Luke have in common, but also much of the teaching of Jesus found in only one of them? This explanation might be used to account for the origin of part of the material peculiar to each of these two Gospels, but it pushes the theory too far to say that Q was the source of all such material. B. H. Streeter (*The Four Gospels* [1924]), followed by V. Taylor (*Behind the Third Gospel* [1926]), developed another theory to explain the origin of Luke. Instead of taking Mark as the basic source behind Luke, he suggested that Luke himself gathered a great deal of Gospel tradition; we may call this body of material L. Luke also knew Q. He combined Q with L to produce a gospel that we may call Proto-Luke. Later, when Luke had access to Mark, he inserted over half of Mark into his Proto-Luke, and this gave him what we know as the Gospel of Luke. Since everyone preferred the fuller Gospel, the earlier shorter draft fell into disuse and disappeared.

D. Four-Document Theory. Streeter soon took one more

step, to explain how Matthew came to its present form. He followed the Two-Document theory as far as it went; the author of Matthew used Mark as his narrative base and derived teachings of Jesus from Q. But now Streeter conjectured that in addition the author of Matthew had and used a written collection of Gospel material, which may be called M. Our Matthew is thus a combination of Mark, Q, and M. This M, like Q and Proto-Luke, disappeared because the Church preferred to use the more complete Gospel, Matthew. (That longer Gospels were favored is a fact; in ancient and medieval times Mark was copied much less often than Matthew and Luke. This lesser popularity of Mark in ancient times may be illustrated by the present ending of Mark. Mark as we now have it ends at 16:8; what follows in the AV was a later addition to the original Gospel; but it is hard to believe that Mark ended his Gospel at 16:8. That Mark survives only in a mutilated form shows how little interest it received in ancient times. Matthew and Luke were more valued because they were more complete.)

Thus Streeter arrived at his Four-Document theory. Matthew and Luke had four written sources; behind Matthew were Mark, Q, and M; while behind Luke lay L and Q, combined to form Proto-Luke, into which large portions of Mark were later inserted to produce our Gospel of Luke. Streeter held that in addition to these main written sources the author of Matthew had and used some minor items of "Antiochene tradition," while Luke had a written document as his source for Lk. 1–2. (Streeter assigned each source to a main center of the first-century Church: Mark was written at Rome, Q and L at Caesarea, M at Jerusalem, Matthew at Antioch, and Luke perhaps at Corinth.)

Critical scholars differ about the validity of Streeter's views. It is now generally agreed that the authors of Matthew and Luke used Mark as a source, and that they both used a now lost document Q, though a few scholars deny that Q existed and prefer to say that Luke knew the Gospel of Matthew and used it in writing his Gospel. That a document L was written and that Q was combined with L to form Proto-Luke is less widely accepted, and the existence of a written document M is still more debatable. Streeter did not claim finality for his results. He made an honest, resourceful attempt to explain how the Gospels were written and how Matthew and Luke came to show such similarities to one another and to Mark while at the same time each differed from the other in noteworthy respects.

E. Renewed Claim for the Priority of Matthew. Criticism of Streeter's views follows three main lines. Some scholars hold that he has not established the probability of the conjectured sources M and L. Others point out that form criticism, for which Streeter showed little interest, has made the problem of written sources relatively unimportant; what really counts is the study of the earlier stage of oral tradition; written sources no doubt existed, but at a relatively unimportant later stage in the origin of the Gospels. Still other scholars, including Roman Catholics and also a few Protestants, maintain that Matthew was the first of our Gospels to be written, as an ancient tradition asserted, or at least that even if the author of the present Greek Matthew used our Greek Mark as a source, an earlier (Aramaic or Hebrew) draft of Matthew was the first Gospel written (see B. C. Butler, *Originality of St. Matthew* [1951]; P. Parker, *The Gospel Before Mark* [1953]). Such reactions remind us that Streeter's views represent intelligent theories rather than established facts.

F. Conclusions. We now make a cautious attempt to sum up the results of generations of scholarly study of the Synoptic Gospels. The Gospel tradition was used in the Church from the earliest days, for worship, instruction, guidance for life, and controversy with opponents. At first it was used in oral form, and the selection and literary shaping of what was preserved occurred under the influence of the needs of the Church. This explanation does not deny to key eyewitnesses, such as Peter, a role in preserving the tradition, but it recognizes that many other eyewitnesses and teachers shared in the continual use of the Gospel material. Nor does it mean that as new needs arose the Church freely invented incidents and sayings; the Church rather met its needs by selecting and shaping remembered items of what Jesus had done and said. The writing down of such material began within two or three decades of Jesus' death; Lk. 1:1 speaks of a number of such earlier documents, though we may safely state that no gospel of the scope of the present Gospels was produced before Mark wrote the earliest canonical Gospel. It seems reasonably clear that Mark was the chief written source of Matthew and Luke, and it is almost as convincing that behind Matthew and Luke lay also some such document as Q, which we can never reconstruct with any finality. The writers of Matthew and Luke had access to other material, partly written but some still oral; yet the exact extent and source of such material eludes us. Each of the Gospels had an author of originality and skill and each possesses its own individuality. None of the Synoptists was a mere scribe, setting down what was already complete and fixed; each was an author, who showed remarkable skill in the selection and final phrasing of his material. Each Synoptic author aimed not only to honor Jesus Christ the risen Lord but also to record actual historical facts about Jesus of Nazareth, whose ministry, death, and resurrection are of the very essence of the gospel.

VI. Dating the Sources and Gospels.–Some books confidently give exact dates for the Gospels and profess to know just when their written sources were composed. But in fact we cannot determine exactly when any of the Gospels was written. The Gospels themselves contain no unmistakable testimony about their date of writing. This uncertainty results largely from our meager knowledge of the early generations of the Church. We know almost nothing about the stages of church life from A.D. 65 to the end of the 1st century.

In view of this uncertainty, two lines of approach may be followed. One is the ancient tradition of the Church about when the Gospels were written. This tradition is not entirely consistent. The earliest tradition (anti-Marcionite prologue; Irenaeus; Eusebius *HE* iii.39.15) indicates that Mark was written after Peter's death, which may be dated in A.D. 64. A later tradition suggests that Mark wrote while Peter was still alive. Probably the date after Peter's death should be preferred (A.D. 65-70). Then, if Mark was a written source for Matthew and Luke, these two Gospels must be dated some years after this date of Mark.

Another method of dating the Synoptic Gospels starts from the book of Acts. Acts ends with Paul spending two years in prison at Rome (28:30), *ca.* A.D. 61-63. If Luke wrote Acts while Paul was still in prison at Rome (one view is that Luke wrote Luke-Acts as a document for use by Paul in his trial before the emperor), then Luke would have to be dated before A.D. 63, for Acts 1:1 refers to Luke as already written. If Luke used Mark as a written source, Mark would have to be dated still earlier, in the 50's of the 1st century. If, however, as seems more likely, Luke and Acts were written after Paul's Roman imprisonment mentioned in Acts 28:30, and Mark was written after Peter's death, the dates assigned to the Synoptic Gospels will be a number of years later.

Tentatively and with the free admission that no certainty is possible (or necessary), we may follow the earliest tradition and date Mark after Peter's death, *ca.* A.D. 65-70. Since Matthew and Luke show use of Mark as a source, we must date them later than Mark. A date not later than A.D. 85 may be suggested for Matthew and a date not later than A.D. 80 or 85 for Luke; Acts then may be dated a very few years later than Luke (up to A.D. 85-90). (For an attempt to support early dates for all NT writings see J. A. T. Robinson, *Redating the NT* [1976].)

Bibliography.–R. Bultmann and K. Kundsin, *Form Criticism* (Eng. tr. 1934); B. S. Easton, *The Gospel Before the Gospels* (1928); F. V. Filson, *Origins of the Gospels* (1938); B. Gerhardsson, *Memory and Manuscript* (1961); F. C. Grant, *The Gospels: Their Origin and Growth* (1957); A. Harnack, *The Date of the Acts and of the Synoptic Gospels* (Eng. tr. 1911); J. Heuschen, ed., *La Formation des évangiles* (1957); A. H. McNeile, *Intro. to the Study of the NT* (rev. C. S. C. Williams, 1953), pp. 3-91; D. E. Nineham, ed., *Studies in the Gospels* (1955); V. H. Stanton, *Gospels as Historical Documents* (3 vols., 1903-1920); *SE* (1959); C. M. Talbert, *What is a Gospel?* (1977); T. Zahn, *Intro. to the NT* (Eng. tr., 2nd ed. 1917); A. Wikenhauser, *Intro. to the NT* (Eng. tr. 1958).

F. V. FILSON

GOSSIP [Heb. *rāḵîl*] (Prov. 20:19); AV TALEBEARER; [*dibbâ*] ("evil gossip," Ezk. 36:3); AV INFAMY; NEB COMMON TALK OF MEN; [Gk. *psithyrismós*] (2 Cor. 12:20); AV WHISPERINGS; [*psithyristḗs*] (Rom. 1:29); AV, NEB, WHISPERER; [*phlýaros*] (1 Tim. 5:13); AV TATTLER. In its biblical setting, "gossip" is used to designate the spreading of secrets or rumors, usually for the purpose of slander (which is the translation of *rāḵîl* in Lev. 19:16; Jer. 6:28; 9:3 [MT 2]). This designation is supported, e.g., by the literal meaning of the onomatopoeic term *psithyristḗs,* "whisperer." According to Prov. 20:19, the one who "goes about gossiping reveals secrets," and therefore no one should associate with one who "speaks foolishly" (cf. Prov. 11:13, where *rāḵîl* is translated "talebearer").

In the NT, Paul placed "gossip" in the midst of two separate lists of evil practices (2 Cor. 12:20; Rom. 1:29). The latter reference is part of a catalog of sins that characterized the pagan world in its opposition to God. Since people did not acknowledge God for what He is, "God gave them up to a base mind and to improper conduct" (v. 28). As a result, they were, among other things, gossips, slanderers, haters of God, and inventors of evil (Rom. 1:29-32). Paul also warned against enrolling younger widows for church ministry and support, since it was quite possible that they would desire to marry again. "Besides that," said Paul, "they learn to be idlers, gadding about from house to house, and not only idlers but gossips and busybodies, saying what they should not" (1 Tim. 5:13).

A. J. BIRKEY

GOTHIC VERSION. *See* VERSIONS VIII.

GOTHOLIAH goth-ə-lī'ə [Gk. *Gotholias*] (1 Esd. 8:33); AV, NEB, GOTHOLIAS. Father of Jeshaiah, one of the sons of Elam who returned from Babylon with Ezra. The name corresponds to Athaliah, the Gk. *gamma* being substituted for the Heb. guttural *ayin,* as in Gomorrah, Gaza, etc.

GOTHONIEL gō-thon'ī-əl [Gk. *Gothoniel*]. The same as Othniel father of Chabris, one of the governors of the city of Bethulia (Jth. 6:15).

GOUGE. *See* PUNISHMENTS IV.

GOURD. **1.** [Heb. *qîqāyôn*; Gk. *kolokýnthē*] ("plant," Jonah 4:6f., 9f.); AV mg. PALMCRIST; RV mg. PALMA CHRISTI. The Hebrew appears to be connected with the "kiki" oil derived by the Egyptians from the castor-oil plant *Ricinus communis* L. (cf. RSV mg., NEB mg.); the Vulgate "ivy" (*Hedera helix* L.) is incorrect. Widespread in the Orient, the shady castor-oil plant quickly attains a height of up to 4½ m. (15 ft.). The "bottle gourd" *(Cucurbita lagenaria)* has been suggested as an alternative, but it was unknown in Palestine at the time of Jonah.

See *MPB,* pp. 203f.

2. [Heb. *pᵉqāʿîm*] (1 K. 6:18; 7:24); AV KNOP; [Heb. *bāqār*–'ox'] (2 Ch. 4:3); AV "oxen." In 1 Kings, Heb. *pᵉqāʿîm* are gourdlike ornaments of the lining of Solomon's temple, and of the MOLTEN SEA. The RSV and NEB attempt to make the parallel description in 2 Ch. 4 more consistent with 1 Kings by reading "gourds" where the MT (and AV) has "oxen," taking *bᵉqārîm* as an error for *pᵉqāʿîm.*

3. WILD GOURD [Heb. *paqquʿōṯ śāḏeh*; Gk. *tolýpē agría*] (2 K. 4:39); NEB BITTER-APPLES. The Heb. root *pqʿ,* "split," has led some authorities to identify this gourd with the squirting cucumber (*Ecballium elaterium* [L.] Rich.), which at maturity discharges an irritating juice when touched or shaken. Its spiny appearance as well as its violent cathartic qualities preclude it as a dietary item. The traditional plant named by Linnaeus, the *Cucumis prophetarum* or globe cucumber, bears prickly, bitter fruit which is small and inedible. The most probable plant is the colocynth (*Citrullus colocynthis* [L.] Schrad.; cf. Syr. *paqôʾā*), a trailing, cucumber-like vine that bears round, orange-colored gourds containing a bitter, extremely poisonous pulp.

See *MPB,* pp. 78-80.

R. K. H.

GOVERNMENT. The biblical records give fragmentary information about political forms, institutions, and procedures for the governing of the body politic. Although they give detailed legislation, which may be classified as civil or judicial, for the nation of Israel itself, one must infer from meager and scattered references information about political administration and civil jurisprudence. Even when the information is explicit, all too often it reflects the theological, social, and political ideal, without necessarily coinciding with actual historical practice. (This is doubly problematic for those who would make practical application of these principles in our day and time, because much of the legislation was intended for Israel as a theocratic nation.) Nevertheless, the biblical data have been providentially verified by archeological and epigraphic materials discovered and published during the last half century. One must realize that in comparing biblical and extrabiblical sources, the Scriptures present all of life, including governmental, political, and judicial institutions, from a unique perspective, i.e., that God is the sovereign creator of the universe and that man stands in a privileged relationship with God. The conviction in ancient Israel that set it apart from all the surrounding nations and cultures was that it was specially chosen by the Creator to share His blessings in a unique covenantal relationship of redemption (*see* ELECTION; COVENANT). This relationship ultimately accounts for the canonical Scriptures of both OT and NT and must be considered the basic and normative principle, especially for Israelite government, political institutions, and administrative procedures. Hence, although Israel's political ideology and even specific legislation may have been shared or even borrowed from surrounding cultures, the sacred Scriptures present them transformed for the benefit of the covenant community.

I. Patriarchal Traditions

- A. Government in Ebla
- B. Mesopotamian Political Institutions
- C. Patriarchs
- D. Moses: Transition to Commonwealth
- E. Treaties, Covenants, and Law Codes

II. Theocratic Commonwealth
- A. Tribal Confederacy
  1. Territorial Allocation
  2. Cities of Refuge and Levitical Cities
  3. Decentralized Government
- B. Judges

III. Theocratic Monarchy
- A. Emergence of Monarchy
- B. Monarchy
  1. Office of King
  2. Civil Administration
  3. Foreign Relations and the Military
- C. Vassals of Assyria and Babylon

IV. Jewish Commonwealth
- A. Governors and Elders
- B. High Priest and Scribes
- C. Sanhedrin
- D. Synagogue

V. NT on Government
- A. Authority of the State
- B. Function of the State
- C. Responsibility of Citizenship
- D. Civil Disobedience

I. Patriarchal Traditions.–There is ample archeological evidence for the historicity of the patriarchal narratives in Genesis. It seems incontrovertible that the patriarchs exhibit the culture and customs of the ancient Near East, specifically the Mesopotamian and Syrian social structures and legal institutions that formed part of their ancestral background. (To a lesser degree the biblical sources reflect the Egyptian culture with which they came into contact as a result of famines and commercial enterprises.) This should surprise no one, for Abram lived in the Mesopotamian cities of Ur and Haran until the age of seventy-five (Gen. 11:31–12:4; cf. Dt. 26:5). The background is illustrated by government, political institutions, and administration in two major cities of northern Syria and Mesopotamia. The vast archives discovered at Mari (since 1933) and at Ebla (since 1974) gave us a wealth of information from which to make comparisons and draw conclusions.

A. Government in Ebla. In northern Syria, some 120 km. (75 mi.) from the Mediterranean Sea, the ancient empire of Ebla flourished during the second half of the 3rd millennium, reaching its zenith *ca.* 2300 B.C. It continued into the 2nd millennium, though in the shadow of other city-states, e.g., Aleppo. Ebla was an important commercial and agricultural center dealing in grain, vineyards, and cattle, as well as metalworking (gold, silver, copper), gems, textiles, woodworking, and pottery. Foreign trade, especially of textiles and metalware, was recorded on huge tablets, and ledgers were kept for the balance of payments. Trade was carried on under treaty arrangements in the empire of Akkad to the east, in the Anatolian plateau N of the Taurus Mountains, to the south in Palestine (already called Canaan) and even the Sinai peninsula. Many place names from the patriarchal narratives are mentioned in the Ebla tablets, either as part of the great empire or as cities and peoples with whom Ebla maintained commercial ties. It is a fair assumption that the patriarchs were familiar with the empire's kind of government and may even have benefited by its rule and protection. Furthermore, if the Eblaic language is correctly classified as Paleo-Canaanite it would strengthen the theory that even when the patriarchs did migrate south to Canaan they would have remained under a political government not unlike what they had experienced in northern Syria or upper Mesopotamia (Haran was only 200 km. [125 mi.] NE of Ebla).

The government of Ebla was centered in the acropolis and was ruled by a king and his royal family. The four major centers on the acropolis were the Palace of the King, the Palace of the City, the Stables, and the Palace of Service. The king's palace undoubtedly served as the central office for the administration of state and foreign affairs. The municipal affairs were handled in the second palace. The Stables may have governed the tremendous commercial enterprise of the empire, while the fourth may have been responsible for labor and related affairs of the state. In each of the first two palaces were ten officials, each with about six deputies under him. In each of the last two palaces there were some eighty leaders with almost one hundred subordinates — these last two groups having a lower status than those in the royal and city palaces. The records show that almost five thousand people worked in the acropolis, in a city of a quarter-million population. The bureaucratic activity points to considerable administrative sophistication for a third-millennium empire.

The lower city was divided into four quarters, each with a gate in the wall that surrounded Ebla. These districts were governed by a chief inspector with as many as twenty leaders and one hundred aides, or as few as ten officers with only thirty deputies. The Eblaic title for these officers was *nase* (cf. Heb. *nāśî'*, "leader, ruler, prince").

The king was called by the Sumerian title *en,* "lord," corresponding to Eblaic *malik,* "king" (cf. Heb. *melek̲*). Also sharing in matters of state was the queen (Eblaic *maliktum*). Their sons were also involved in the administration of the empire — the crown prince in home affairs and the second son in foreign affairs. These sovereigns called rulers of equal status *en* or *malik.* Officials of lower status they called *lugal* (Sumerian for "chief man, king") or *diku,* "judge" (cf. Heb. *šōpēṭ* and *dayyān,* "judge").

B. Mesopotamian Political Institutions. Although scholarly opinion is divided on the location of Ur of the Chaldees, the ancestral home of Abraham — either at the southeastern end of the Mesopotamian valley, i.e., near the confluence of the Tigris and Euphrates rivers, or near Haran in the northwest, as may be suggested by the Ebla tablets — it is significant that the cultural background of the patriarchs reflects Mesopotamian, if not Hurrian culture.

One of the great cultural and political centers of the 19th and 18th cents. B.C. was Mari, situated on the Euphrates approximately 325 km. (200 mi.) SE of Haran. Mari had already enjoyed a position of preeminence during the 3rd millennium. From its royal archive more than 200,000 tablets have been recovered, dealing with administrative, legal, economic, and religious matters from which the juridical, commercial, social, and political life of upper Mesopotamia and Syria can be studied. They also reflect contemporary ethnological movements. They provide some of the earliest insights into the complex relationships of suzerains and vassals, and diplomatic protocol, including the prominent role of women in the affairs of state. They reveal that the city-state was controlled by West Semitic peoples known as "Amorites." Although the place where these dynasties originated is not clearly indicated, the available evidence points to northern Syria. It is also significant that the cities of Nahor and Haran, the ancestral home of the patriarchs, were important centers dependent on and governed from Mari.

The archives reveal a tribal society very similar to the patriarchal society in organizational structure and institutions. The indigenous population was confronted by different kinds of tribal life. The tribes were at various stages of development, from fully nomadic to completely sedentary. Zimri-Lim's two titles, "king of the Haneans" and "king of the Akkadians," represented the two main population strata, the seminomadic tribe of Hana and the indigenous settled population of Akkadians. The term *hana* was applied not only to the land but also to a type of soldier and to a kind of wool, possibly reflecting their profession and trade, respectively. Furthermore, the Haneans had a broad tribal federation with the Yaminites, "the sons of the south," who were less settled and posed a threat to the government. The Yaminites, subdivided into subtribes, were scattered from the southern Mesopotamian valley to the northern extremities of the Euphrates, their major concentration being at the bend of the Euphrates. They had even extended themselves into the land of Amurru in southern Syria. Two other tribal groups are barely mentioned, the "sons of the north" who wandered in the Haran area, and the Sutu tribe, a fully nomadic people who become more prominent in later history. Tribal society, then, seems to be found in nomadic and urban forms, even at times combining both — habitation of the desert or steppe during the grazing season and urban settlement in "off" seasons. For example, the Haneans and the Yaminites lived in towns or villages (Akk. *ālāni,* "cities") and were engaged in cultivation as well as herding, or they lived in temporary camps (Akk. *nawûm,* "desert, uncultivated field"; cf. Heb. *nāweh,* "habitation, abode of shepherd") while tending flocks. Other groups established themselves in a settlement called a *ḥaṣārum* (cf. the application of Heb. *ḥ*ᵃ*ṣērîm* to a settlement of [Dt. 2:23]).

The family was the basic unit of patriarchal tribal organization. The tribal rulers (called *abū,* lit. "fathers," used as synonym for "tribal chiefs") were the family heads. Hence, the central governing institution seems to have been the council of elders, whose function was to decide on war and peace, to make treaties, and to represent the tribe before the governing authorities. The tribal hierarchy was led by a king (Akk. *šarru*), who seems to have been a military leader (cf. Heb. *śar,* "chieftain, captain, prince"). In some references, a group of "kings" seems to compose the collective tribal leadership, similar perhaps to the structure found among the Midianites (Nu. 31:8, Jgs. 8:12), the Edomites (Gen. 36:31-43), and the Arameans (1 Sam. 14:47).

Various tribal customs and institutions mentioned in the Mari archives have analogies in the patriarchal and Israelite tradition. For example, covenant making in Mari seems to have been concluded not so much by documents as by symbolic actions (contrast "the Book of the Covenant" in Exodus and Deuteronomy with the ritual sacrifice in Gen. 15:9f.), as in the case of the ritual killing of an ass-foal. An official in the Haran region relates to his king a peace treaty concluded between the Haneans and the land of Idamaraṣ and says, "They brought a whelp and a goat, but I obeyed my lord and did not allow a whelp and a goat. I caused the foal of a she-ass to be slaughtered" (*ARM,* II, 37:6-12).

Another example is the "patrimony" (Akk. *niḫlatum;* cf. Heb. *naḥ*ᵃ*lâ*), a possession or inheritance that could not be sold through an ordinary business transaction, but could be transferred only by inheritance within a quasi-familial framework (cf. Lev. 25:23). The law could be circumvented through the "adoption" of the purchaser. Even in the case of a man without progeny, the adoption procedure ensured the continuation of his line and patrimony. Indeed, some adoption contracts concerned the primogeniture of the eldest (i.e., the first adopted) son, stipulating that his inheritance benefits be a double portion (cf. the case of Abraham's heir, Eliezer of Damascus [Gen. 15:2; also Dt. 21:15-17]).

As a third example, a leader was denoted by the term "judge" (Akk. *šāpiṭum;* cf. Heb. *šōpēṭ*). This person was a prominent man of a tribe whose authority far exceeded that of merely administering justice. In fact, the primary connotation of the word and its derivatives is not so much judicial (denoted by Akk. *dayānu*) as of the broader concept of governor or ruler. One need only remember that the post-Conquest "judges" acquired such authority for ruling, even exercising military leadership, although in some cases they rendered judicial decisions.

One may further compare the materials from the Nuzi archives of the 15th cent. as well as legal and economic texts from Ugarit and Alalakh. The preceding evidence is sufficient, however, to demonstrate that many political practices of the late 3rd and early 2nd millennia continue to be reflected not only in the patriarchal period, but in some cases even in the periods of the commonwealth and monarchy.

C. Patriarchs. In light of the foregoing information one may make certain assessments of patriarchal life and institutions. It would be a serious mistake to assume that the patriarchs were nomadic keepers of flocks descending from the desert steppes, expressing the nomad's "aversion to the urban life" of the settled community (cf. *IDB,* II, 451). They were tribal, yes, but certainly not fully nomadic. The narratives of Genesis reflect the seminomadic life of transhumance, i.e., settlement in urban bases (e.g., Hebron, Beer-sheba, Gerar, Rehoboth, Shechem, Bethel) in the "off" months with migration in the spring and summer months to appropriate grazing lands (e.g., the migration of Joseph's brothers to the area around Shechem and Dothan [Gen. 37:12, 17]; cf. also Isaac's actions at Gerar [Gen. 26:12-17]). If one takes seriously the evaluation of a much later writer, Abraham set out on his nomadic journey precisely to receive as an inheritance a land in which to settle. He dwelt in tents yet looked for a city, not just any urban community, but far more, "the city whose builder and maker is God" (He. 11:10). Here we have an emerging covenantal concept of a theocratic nation. He and his descendants were willing to wait for the land promised by covenant (cf. Gen. 12:1, 7; 15:7, 18; 26:3; 28:13) while living in tents, yet purchasing property (e.g., Ephron's field near Hebron [Gen. 23:17-20]; the plot near Shechem [33:18-20]) as evidence of their faith. They not only raised flocks, but also cultivated crops (26:12-14). Furthermore, when they moved into Egypt they purchased lands (47:27) and evidently lived in a settled urban community. It was not until the Exodus that the Israelites may be considered nomadic — and then only for a relatively short period of forty years.

Regarding relations with other political units, one must observe that the patriarchs recognized the political authorities in Canaan and Egypt by abiding by the laws and customs of the land. Several examples are in order.

Official and legal transactions took place at the city gate — the place for public meetings or for the deliberation of the council of elders. The episode of Abraham's purchase of a burial site from the sons of Heth at the city gate (Gen. 23:3-20) offers a most illuminating example of careful legal procedures. The accurate description of the location for proper identification (v. 9), the fiscal references (vv. 9, 13, 15f.), and specific mention of trees (v. 17) reflect authentic judicial activity, as does the report of the burial on the property (v. 19), which constitutes the final stamp of transfer of ownership. Many Nuzi legal tablets conclude with the formula that the tablet was written "after the proclamation in the entrance of the gate." Whether the action recorded in Gen. 23 is best understood in terms of the Hittite law code or of the profound Mesopotamian influence via the Hurrians is open to question. What is indisputable is that the patriarchs as resident aliens acknowledge the local authority but also the law of the land (cf. Gen. 34:20, 24, and the prophetic concern that Israel establish justice in the gate [Amos 5:12, 15]).

Furthermore, as a distinct tribal group they acted within the limits of their sovereignty by making treaties. Parity treaties may have been made when Abraham led his military allies against the coalition of five kings under Chedorlaomer (Gen. 14). Another example is Abimelech's peace treaty with Isaac, sealed by an oath and ratified by a feast (26:26-31).

D. Moses: Transition to Commonwealth. Toward the end of the Egyptian bondage, leadership within the tribe was vested in the "elders" (*zᵉqēnîm,* variously referred to as "elders of Israel" or "elders of the people," Ex. 3:16; 4:29; etc.). They undoubtedly achieved this dignity by virtue of experience, and possibly by seniority. It was they who accepted the leadership of Moses and Aaron (Ex. 3:16; 4:29-31). Several years earlier Moses had assumed that, since he was in a position of leadership in Egypt, the Israelites should have accepted him. Their response, however, was "Who made you a prince [*śar*] or a judge [*šōpēṭ*] over us?" (Ex. 2:14), pointing to an established procedure. Furthermore, the foundation of this political superstructure (i.e., Moses/Aaron and the elders) was the congregation of Israel (*ʿēḏâ,* first used in Ex. 12:3). When assembled for a public meeting, it was called a *qāhāl,* "assembly" (LXX *ekklesía*), which therefore constituted the body politic of Israel as the people of God. The "people" (*ʿam*) of Israel were subdivided according to ancestry into the twelve "tribes" (*šēḇeṭ* [Gen. 49:28] or *maṭṭeh* [Ex. 32:2]), and these in turn were subdivided by families or "clans" (*mišpāḥâ* [Ex. 6:14; cf. Gen. 10:5]) with the basic unit being the "household" (*bayiṯ* [Ex. 1:1; cf. Gen. 7:1; 17:13, 27]) or "father's house" (*bêṯ ʾāḇ* [Ex. 12:3]). These terms sometimes overlap (e.g., cf. Ex. 12:3 with v. 21), and indeed sometimes go beyond the notion of mere consanguinity to include household servants (cf. Gen. 15:2f.; 17:27) or others who shared in the ideals of the community, i.e., their history, way of life, and destiny.

Another group was called the "leaders of the congregation" (*nᵉśîʾê hāʿēḏâ,* Ex. 16:22; Nu. 16:2; 32:2; sometimes rendered by "chief princes"). These may be officials serving at a lower level of administration, perhaps comparable to the *nase* officers of the lower city of Ebla.

The principle of representative government seems to have existed among the tribal communities even as early as the 3rd millennium. With the emergence of the city-state in ancient Mesopotamia, H. Frankfort claimed that "ultimate political power rested with a general assembly of all adult freemen. Normally the everyday affairs of the community were guided by a council of elders; but in times of crisis, for instance, when war threatened, the general assembly could confer absolute powers on one of its members and proclaim him king. Such kingship was an office held for a limited term; and as the assembly could confer it, so it could also revoke it when a crisis was past" (*Intellectual Adventure,* p. 141). Moses may well have failed to appreciate this when sitting to render administrative and judicial decisions (Ex. 18:13), but his father-in-law alerted him to this dangerous precedent, reminding him of the principle of representation and its corollary of delegation of authority (Ex. 18:17-27; cf. the later application of these principles in Dt. 16:18–17:20). It was through such representation that the assembly could carry out its deliberative, administrative, and judicial functions (cf. Ex. 24:1f.; Nu. 11:16; 27:1-4; contrast Dt. 31:28, 30 with Nu. 14:4, which reports the grumbling mob's desire to appoint a "leader" [*rōʾš,* "head"] and return to Egypt).

E. Treaties, Covenants, and Law Codes. A body politic is governed by an accepted standard, referred to in modern times as law. Such is the case with the social and political institutions in patriarchal times, as noted above (cf. Gen. 26:5). Valuable information about ancient laws comes from the well-known Code of Hammurabi and the older codes of Lipit-Ishtar, Ur-Nammu, and Eshnunna.

Far more significant, however, are the more than forty extant ancient Near Eastern treaties dating from the late 3rd millennium down to the late 1st millennium. Parity treaties were made between major city-state empires (e.g., Ebla and Assyria, Hatti and Egypt), as well as between tribal groups forming a confederacy (e.g., the tribes of Hana and Yamini; cf. also Gen. 14).

Suzerainty-vassal treaties were made between nations or tribes of unequal power. The special relationship established between two kings, the suzerain of the empire and the vassal king of the conquered people, may have served as a model for the unique covenant relationship between God, the Great King, and Abraham as vassal king (compare the numerous references in the treaties to the suzerain as the great king with Ps. 48:2 [MT 3]; 95:3). The pattern of the twenty-one reasonably preserved Hittite treaties of the 14th and 13th cents. B.C. generally follows the structure: (1) Title/Preamble; (2) Historical prologue; (3) Stipulations: (a) general, (b) specific; (4) Deposit and regular reading of the treaty; (5) Witnesses; and (6) Sanctions: (a) blessings, (b) curses. In addition, though not always in writing, the following items might be found: (7) Oath; (8) Solemn ceremony of ratification; and (9) A note of sanctions. This general formal framework coincides with the structure of Ex. 20–24 (the Book of the Covenant at Sinai; see Ex. 24:7), Deuteronomy (the covenant renewal at Moab), Josh. 24 (the covenant renewal at Gilgal), and 1 S. 11:14–12:25 (also at Gilgal). One may discern the same pattern in Gen. 15 and 17 (the Abrahamic covenant), and some of these elements are present even in the Adamic covenant of Gen. 2. In any case, the covenant that Yahweh the suzerain made with Israel the vassal — beginning with Abraham, renewed with Isaac (Gen. 26:3-5, 24) and Jacob (35:11f.), continued with Moses, and renewed before and after the Conquest — implanted a unique theocratic relationship in the consciousness of the people of Israel (cf. Ex. 19:4-6; Dt. 7:6; 26:19). It was this consciousness of a covenantal bond with Yahweh that would serve as a bond of union among Abraham's descendants. The rejection of that covenant relationship would in essence serve notice of separation and secession (as in the case of Esau [Gen. 28:6-9], and possibly Ishmael [21:12-21]). Conversely, acceptance of Yahweh and His covenant would serve to bind even non-Abrahamic people to the nation (e.g., Eliezer of Damascus, Rahab, Ruth the Moabitess, Uriah the Hittite, as well as the "mixed multitude" from Egypt; cf. Rom 2:28f.; Gal. 3:29).

II. Theocratic Commonwealth.–The transfer of leadership from Moses to Joshua was progressive. Shortly after the Exodus Joshua was appointed by Moses as his military adjutant (Ex. 17:9f.). Toward the end of the wilderness wanderings, God instructed Moses to commission Joshua before Eleazar the priest and the congregation of the people of Israel (Nu. 27:15-23). The ceremony of laying hands upon him, symbolizing the delegation of authority, probably followed the model of the priestly sacrifice, symbolizing the transference of sin and guilt to the animal (Ex. 29:10, 15, 19). The final transfer of authority is reported just before the death of Moses (Dt. 34:9). The narrative in Nu. 27 states that this was done at Moses' initiative as well as by the divine decree that Joshua be so commissioned. The people and elders of the council were essentially passive, possibly playing a consultative, corroborative, and permissive role. It could be argued, however, that the people had a more active participation through the elders, judging from the events reported in Josh. 1:12-18. During the period of the judges no leadership emerged merely by divine decree. The leadership arose when people recognized their extremities and acknowledged the capabilities of someone, who was called upon to serve the people as judge and military leader. (See II.A.3 below; cf. also Nu. 14:1-4; 2 K. 12.)

A. Tribal Confederacy. The biblical sources reveal that the Israelites in Egypt lived a sedentary life. After the Exodus they lived a nomadic or seminomadic life, but only for a relatively short period of thirty-eight or forty years. By the end of the desert period, the tribes of Reuben, Gad, and half of Manasseh were settling into Transjordan N of Amon and Moab. Through the military genius of Joshua, aided by miraculous events, the Israelites conquered the Canaanite territory W of the Jordan. However one correlates the chronology with the Amarna age, the evidence is clear that the Canaanite city-states, though nominally under Egyptian rule and protection, were themselves in a state of factious anarchy. This condition may well have lasted longer than the quarter of a century assigned to the Amarna period itself. Even so, it took Joshua's military leadership of the confederacy to break whatever coalitions developed against the incoming Israelites (*see* JOSHUA, BOOK OF).

The biblical narrative emphasizes that the bond of unity within the tribal confederacy was the covenant between God and His people. The crossing of the Jordan, the taking of Jericho, the final ratification of covenant renewal at Mt. Ebal, the defeat of the Amorites at Gibeon and Aijalon, the distribution of territory to the various tribes, and the covenant renewal at Shechem — all point to God as the suzerain and sovereign covenant Lord who acts out His benevolence on His obedient and faithful people. At the same time, the disobedience of Achan brought about the defeat at Ai, showing how seriously the covenant Lord takes His sanctions.

The covenant renewal documents of the ancient Near East provided for transition of leadership. Such was the book of Deuteronomy. It updated the historical benevolent activity of the suzerain Lord, but also considerably expanded the covenant stipulations, both general (chs. 5–11) and specific (chs. 12–26). The impending Conquest and Settlement in the land of promise called for such an amplification of the earlier Book of the Covenant (Ex. 20–24). Hence, this renewal document may be considered the basic constitution of the theocratic commonwealth. The provisions for governing, political institutions, and juridical processes given in Deuteronomy may be compared with their implementation or lack of implementation in the subsequent historical books. Several institutions need to be considered.

1. Territorial Allocation. The apportionment of the tribal territories to the remaining nine-and-a-half tribes as recorded in Josh. 13–22 is said to fulfil the arrangements made by Moses (Nu. 34:16-29). It is to be noted that the territory is not parceled out through arbitrary decisions of an autocratic leader. Joshua, together with Eleazar the high priest and one leader from each tribal group (*nāśî'*, equated with *rā'šê 'ᵃḇôt*–'heads of households/fathers') had the responsibility for the apportionment. In the case of land to be allocated for seven tribes, three surveyors from each of these tribes were appointed to write out a description of their survey (Josh. 18:4). These portions were then allocated by casting lots.

The distribution of territory apparently was not regarded as absolute, for the borders in some instances were rather vague. For example, in Joshua's time the mountain country of Judah and Ephraim was conquered, and most of that territory was rather clearly surveyed and allocated; but much of the Shephelah and the coastal plains were yet controlled by Canaanite strongholds of resistance. Even the Jebusite city Jerusalem, originally allocated to Benjamin (Josh. 18:28), was not taken until David's time, and then incorporated into Judah. The tribe of Dan, apparently unable to gain control of its inheritance in the coastal regions between Judah and Ephraim (Josh. 19:40-48), began seeking an inheritance elsewhere. Eventually the Danites settled at Laish, at the headwaters of the Jordan (Jgs. 18). Their migration may have been motivated by the promise to Abraham that his seed would dwell "from the river of Egypt to the . . . Euphrates" (Gen. 15:18) and by the provision for additional cities of refuge (Dt. 19:8-10). This flexibility may be the reason why Solomon felt free to reorganize the kingdom into twelve districts rather than preserve tribal lines (1 K. 4).

2. Cities of Refuge and Levitical Cities. The Levites did not receive a territorial inheritance (Dt. 18:1f.). Instead they were given forty-eight cities (including six cities of refuge) proportionately distributed throughout the land (Nu. 35:1-8; Josh. 21). The Levitical priests had not only religious functions, but educational and even juridical responsibilities, as may be surmised from their control of the cities of refuge (Dt. 19:1-10) and their involvement with the judges and officers in the administration of justice (Dt. 17:8-13; 19:17).

3. Decentralized Government. A central seat of government did not emerge until the Davidic monarchy in Jerusalem. Under the strong leadership of Joshua, the covenant renewal ratification took place at Shechem (Josh. 8:30), the tribe of Judah and Caleb went to Joshua at Gilgal to request their territorial allocation (Josh. 14:6), and later in Shiloh, where the tabernacle had been set up, Joshua allocated the territorial inheritance to the last group of tribes. This decentralization, even more apparent during the period of the judges, continued down to the time when Samuel emerged as a leader who unified the tribal confederacy to a large degree. Yet his leadership was exercised in an annual circuit of Bethel, Gilgal, Mizpah, and his hometown of Ramah (1 S. 7:15-17). Even the most unifying influence, the tabernacle itself, did not find a permanent home during the period of the theocratic commonwealth; indeed, it was not stationary until Solomon's temple was erected in Jerusalem in the 10th century. Historically, the ark of the covenant is mentioned as located at Shechem (Josh. 8:33; 24:26), at Shiloh (Josh. 18:1; 1 S. 1:3, 9; Jgs. 18:31), at Bethel (Jgs. 20:26f.), and at Kiriath-jearim (1 S. 7:1f.). The provision of Dt. 12:5 to seek the Lord "at the place which the Lord your God shall choose from all your tribes, to establish His name there for His dwelling" need not be understood as mandating a single central sanctuary. Rather, in contrast to the innumerable idolatrous Canaanite sites, it may be taken distributively, allowing for several such locations in accordance with the stipulations in Ex. 20:24, "in every place where I cause my name to be remembered." This may account for the ease with which Jeroboam the son of Nebat was able to institute (or possibly continue) Yahweh worship in Bethel and Dan.

With the settlement in the land there began to be a shift of the basic political unit from the genealogically related clan or family to the urban communities themselves. The urban communities that emerged were controlled by the elders, who administered the affairs of the city, both civil and judicial, at the gates of the city (cf. the provision for judges and officers in Dt. 16:18-20, and "the elders of his city, at the gate of the place where he lives" in 21:19). For example, the elders (*zᵉqēnîm*) of Gilead approached Jephtha, a valiant warrior (*gibbôr ḥayil*), asking him to become "head" (*rōʾš*) of all the inhabitants of Gilead in their struggle with the Ammonites (Jgs. 11:4-11). It is not clear whether these elders were representatives elected from each town in Gilead, or merely a group of leaders acclaimed by the people (cf. Jgs. 10:17f.). In Ruth 3:11 the expression "all the gate of my people" may reflect a pure democracy in which the whole community acted as a public assembly; or it may simply refer to the leadership of the elders at the gate. In some cases the elders were relatives in a single family or dominant clan, e.g., the Abiezer clan of Ophrah, Gideon's city (Jgs. 6:24); the thirty sons of Jair who controlled thirty cities of Gilead (10:3f.); and the people of Shechem, who through their leaders proclaimed Abimelech king over them (9:1-6), but learning of his treachery and conspiracy, were ready to replace him with Gaal the son of Ebed (9:26-29).

Only in response to a very critical situation does one find a modicum of concerted action. Even during Joshua's leadership, after seven years of united action to establish territorial claim, the tribes and their clans were set free to establish themselves in their territorial inheritance (cf. Josh. 14). The whole tribal confederacy was not involved in joint political and military action. Defense against foreign invaders was the responsibility of each tribe or clan until the dawn of the monarchy. On some occasions there was joint action among the tribes, e.g., Naphtali and Zebulun under the leadership of Deborah of the tribe of Ephraim (Jgs. 4–5); the people of Ephraim, Benjamin, Issachar, and possibly Reuben may have participated, but Asher, Dan, Gad, and perhaps Reuben and Manasseh failed to do so [5:15-17]).

Only one exception is recorded, when the whole assembly of the people of God, all the sons of Israel from Dan to Beer-sheba, met at Mizpah in order to make retribution for the heinous crime committed by men of Gibeah. Their fellow Benjaminites refused to hand them over for judicial process. This action so outraged Israel that for once they recognized the essence of covenantal responsibilities (Jgs. 20:1-11).

B. Judges. The expressed concern of Dt. 12:8 against potential anarchy was unfortunately realized in the next three hundred years (Jgs. 17:6; 21:25). The kind of leadership that Moses and Joshua typified apparently could not be replicated. Some leaders were successful, but none commanded the attention of the whole commonwealth. Perhaps the reason for this is more in the theological and moral spheres than in the political and social spheres. In any case, the kind of leadership that emerged was that of the so-called "judge" (*šōpēṭ*; *see* JUDGE). The term may be misleading, since the functions of the various judges may or may not have included judicial activities, but certainly involved public administration and even military leadership. It has already been noted that Deuteronomy uses the term judge (16:18) in juxtaposition with elder (19:12). More specifically, some leaders were called "deliverer" (*môšîᵃ(a)ʿ*) rather than judge, e.g., Ehud (Jgs. 3:15), Shamgar (3:31), and Gideon (6:14, 36). Others were simply called "judge," e.g., Jair (10:3-5), Ibzan (12:8-10), Elon (12:11f.), and Abdon (12:13-15); or it is said of them that they judged Israel, e.g., Deborah (Jgs. 4:4f.), Eli (1 S. 4:18), and Samuel (1 S. 7:15-17). It is noteworthy that Deborah was also called a prophetess, that Eli was a priest, and that Samuel was a prophet and a priest. Still others were referred to by both titles, judge and deliverer, e.g., Othniel (Jgs. 3:9f.), Tola (10:1f.), Jephthah (11:13; 12:7), and Samson (13:5; 15:18, 20).

It was the juridical function that kept alive the cohesion of the tribal alliance by considering problem cases in the light of the covenantal stipulations. The function of judging civil cases was one of many responsibilities of civil leaders throughout the history of Israel, including this period. The dominant role of the judges and the major concern of the people and elders, however, was defense against foreign aggression. It was precisely because of Jephtha's military prowess that the elders of Gilead called him to be "head and leader over them" (Jgs. 11:11; *qāṣîn*, "leader, chief, dictator," here bears the meaning "commander in war").

The biblical records point to the divine authority with which these judges were endowed. Insofar as this is mentioned, it came either as a direct revelation through a prophet (as with Barak [Jgs. 4:6-9]), or was granted through angelic mediation (as with Gideon [6:12-24] and Samuel [1 S. 3:4-9]), or through victory in battle (as with Jephthah [Jgs. 11:9]), or even through a special proclamation at birth (as with Samson [13:2-5]).

III. Theocratic Monarchy.–The possibility of a monarchy was already anticipated in the Deuteronomic constitution (Dt. 17:14-20). The warning there is against autocratic as opposed to theocratic government. It should be noted that since the monarchy was not mandated, but rather permitted, kingship was not considered antithetical to the founding principle of theocratic government; no specific form of government was demanded. Furthermore, it is clear that absolute monarchy was precluded, since the whole context envisions the continuation of other leaders in the theocracy, namely, judges and officers, priests and Levites, whose authority was covenantal rather than delegated by the king. In keeping with the treaty-covenant analogy, it was the suzerain's prerogative to oversee the vassal's choice of leadership; hence the concern that Israel have a king "whom the Lord your God shall choose" (Dt. 17:15). God's choice was revealed by a prophet (cf. 1 S. 10:24; 16:12f.; 1 Ch. 17:11-15; 22:8-10; 1 K. 19:15f.). The king was to be a fellow covenant servant; a foreigner was not to be considered. As a covenant vassal, he was to read regularly his own copy of the covenant document, the originals having been deposited in the ark of the covenant in the sanctuary (Dt. 17:18-20; Ex. 25:21 and Dt. 31:9; cf. 2 K. 11:12, where Joash was crowned and presented with the "testimony" [Heb. *ʿēḏûṯ*], i.e., the covenant stipulations). The restrictions enunciated for the Israelite monarchy were based on the covenant principle that Yahweh was king of Israel, in contrast to the typical Mesopotamian, Syrian, and Canaanite conceptualization of a king who was (or became) god; hence the concern for continual faith in Yahweh the covenant suzerain. Therefore, restrictions were placed on the king's personal, military, and economic aggrandizement, and even upon his harem, this last restriction because of its potential for syncretism and idolatry (Dt. 17:16f.; cf. Solomon's violations [1 K. 10:26–11:8] and the exhortation in Eccl. 5:10 [MT 9]). The possibility of dynastic succession was also envisioned (Dt. 17:20).

A. Emergence of Monarchy. The covenantal commonwealth had lasted for more than three hundred years. However, each tribal group had maintained a somewhat semiautonomous government and the confederacy was all the while deteriorating in power and unity. When some attempted to resolve the leadership crisis by choosing

Gideon (and his descendants) to rule over (*māšal bᵉ*) them, Gideon wisely refused because he perceived their concept of government to be inconsistent with the theocratic principle of the covenant (Jgs. 8:22f.). Similarly, Abimelech's attempt to establish himself as king over Shechem was based on the model of the Canaanite city-state, which was incongruous with the principle of covenant unity and hence doomed to failure (Jgs. 9). Samuel himself sought to perpetuate his judgeship by appointing (*śûm,* "set, place, establish") his two sons as judges (1 S. 8:1), though it may be debated whether he intended to make the office hereditary. Their ethical and legal corruption, however, made them unfit for public service. The elders of Israel therefore took the initiative and exercised their prerogative of seeking to consolidate their leadership in a king. That the elders were acting in a representative role may be deduced from the way God answered Samuel: "Listen to the voice of the people" (1 S. 8:7; cf. vv. 10, 19, 21). The scope of their representation is not clear, but it must have included at least the southern tribes (as far south as Beer-sheba) and the central tribes of Ephraim and Benjamin. They certainly had a legitimate claim for their request, based on the Deuteronomic covenant (Dt. 17:14f.). Whatever Samuel's own reasons for disappointment in their request, Yahweh's response clearly implies that their motive was improper when they asked for a king "like all the nations" (1 S. 8:5). In essence, they were rejecting the theocratic suzerainty of Yahweh, which clearly implied that, wittingly or unwittingly, they were rebelling in order to serve "other gods" (v. 8). The description of the arrogant, despotic kingship would have underscored the meaning of "like all the nations" (vv. 6-20). Saul became the first example of such an absolute monarch. The later kings of the northern kingdom were to follow that negative pattern. On the other hand, David set the standard (in spite of his lapse) for what Yahweh intended a theocratic king to be.

B. Monarchy. The monarchy was founded when Samuel anointed Saul as king over Israel (1 S. 10:1). The ceremony must be considered a public recognition of the gifts and authority of the king, being declaratory in nature rather than vesting authority upon the individual. It was the Spirit of the Lord who invested a person with power for service (1 S. 10:6; cf. the anointing of the priests [Ex. 40:9-15; Num. 3:3; etc.]), and when that Spirit was removed, the wisdom and power for governing was withdrawn (1 S. 16:14; 18:12; 28:15; cf. Zech. 4:6; 1 Cor. 9:26f.). Saul, however, did not turn out to be the king that the people had expected. Whether he had the necessary military and political sagacity may be debated. The biblical data point out the weakness of his spiritual and moral qualifications for the task (1 S. 13:13f.).

In contrast to Saul, it was David who, in spite of glaring weaknesses, was a man after God's own heart. He united the fractured confederacy. That he was crowned king in Hebron and only seven years later became king of the northern sector points to considerable independence among the tribal groups. This is shown also by the division of the kingdom in the days of Rehoboam and later in the days of Omri (1 K. 12; 16:21f.).

1. Office of King. In contrast to the Mesopotamian or Egyptian concept of kingship, in which the king was a human being who reflected the actions of the gods or was himself a god in human form, the Israelite kings were to reflect the theocratic character of the covenant, i.e., they were human beings who were to acknowledge the suzerainty of Yahweh as King over the people of God (cf. Pss. 93–100). David was therefore to be the vassal king. Likewise, Yahweh was the true Shepherd of Israel, but David was the under-shepherd serving as God's representative. This is quite explicit in Ezk. 34, where the last kings of Judah are excoriated as shepherds who miserably failed to carry out their responsibilities, forming the background for the magnificent Messianic prophecy that "My Servant David . . . will be their shepherd . . . will be prince among them."

Deuteronomy 17, anticipating the monarchy, limited the power of the king of Israel. The absolute, despotic authority of Near Eastern kings was not to be the model for the theocratic monarchy. For example, David himself was willing to pay the full price for Araunah's threshing floor (2 S. 24:24), recognizing the law of the covenant relating to family property. In contrast, a radical departure from this Israelite tradition took place in the northern kingdom in the next century. Ahab, though he was not willing to expropriate Naboth's vineyard, nevertheless allowed Jezebel his Phoenician-born queen to confiscate the property by having Naboth killed through judicial subterfuge (1 K. 21:1-16). This event marked a turning point in Israel's history as evidenced by the prophetic chorus of criticism against such arbitrary, unjust, selfish actions by kings (e.g., Hos. 5:10; Amos 5:10-13; Isa. 5:8; Mic. 2:1f.).

If Dt. 17 delimited the king's power, Ezk. 34 explicitly developed the duties and responsibilities of a theocratic monarch. He was responsible for the protection of his people from the nation's enemies (34:10, 22). He was responsible for consolidating the confederacy and maintaining the unity of the nation (34:11f., 16). He was also to be concerned for the general welfare of the people, administrating agricultural production as well as providing medical care (Ezk. 34:13-16a; cf. 2 S. 14:4 and 2 K. 6:26 — individuals appealed to him for help). Finally, he was responsible for justice in the land, which was to be carried out according to the principles of the covenant (34:16b-22; cf. 2 S. 15:1-5 and 2 K. 3:16-28 — people appealed to the king for justice). The humble attitude was to be a characteristic of the kingly vassal, since "God is the Judge, He puts down one and exalts another" (Ps. 75:7 [MT 8]; cf. 1 Pet. 5:2-4, where this principle is applied to church rulers).

The principle of dynastic succession was established with David (2 S. 7:15f.), it seems, primarily for the covenantal typology of a Davidic messiah, secondarily for the stabilizing influence that such continuity has politically. Solomon's kingdom was disrupted because of his disregard for convenantal stipulations (1 K. 11:8-13) and more immediately because of the irresponsible heavy taxation policy both of Solomon and his son Rehoboam (1 K. 12:1-11). In the northern kingdom, only two dynasties of any significance were established — the house of Omri, by which Israel was known throughout the ancient Near East (cf. Akk. *bit Ḫumri*), and Jehu's dynasty, which lasted almost a century. Otherwise, succession was based on violence, including the execution of the king and his heirs (cf. 1 K. 15:27-29; 16:2; 2 K. 9; 15:8-31).

2. Civil Administration. In carrying out his royal responsibilities, David proved himself a master administrator, delegating authority to functionaries generally designated "servants" (*ʿᵃḇāḏîm*). Throughout the monarchy this term was used for officials in the diplomatic corps (2 S. 10:2f.), the military (2 S. 2:12f.), the merchant marine (1 K. 9:26-28), and the investigative bureau (2 K. 22:12f.). More specifically, for the administration of public and domestic affairs the following "officials" (*śārîm*) are mentioned in the reigns of David and Solomon (2 S. 8:15-18; 1 K. 4:1-7).

(1) The "recorder" (*mazkîr* [1 Ch. 18:15; 2 S. 20:24; 2 K. 18:18, 37; 2 Ch. 34:8]) was not merely a historian or

archivist, but a record keeper of the most important affairs of the nation and the king; he reported the news to the king, served as spokesman for the king, and regulated royal audiences and royal protocol. His office was comparable to the royal herald of the Egyptian court, or the *waka nuvis* of the Persian court, or even the *magister memoria* of the Roman empire.

(2) The "secretary" (*sōpēr,* "scribe" [1 Ch. 18:16; 2 S. 20:25; 2 K. 12:10 [MT 11]; 22:3, 8-14; 25:19; Jer. 36:10; 37:15; etc.]) was the trained professional who, with a battery of scribes, kept official records and tabulations. In Jer. 36:10-12, the "secretary's chamber" was sufficiently large to accommodate a good-sized audience. It is not clear if the office was adopted from the Egyptian court, as might be suggested by the confusion in the spelling of the secretary's name (i.e., Seraiah, Shavsha, Sheva, or Shisha), which may be of Egyptian origin.

(3) The "priest" (*kōhēn* [1 Ch. 18:17; 2 S. 20:25f.; 1 K. 4:5]) need not be considered part of the cultic retinue serving as chaplain or spiritual adviser, but may well have served as the king's confidential advisor or ombudsman. His function may have been to represent the concerns of the people to the king, as a comparison of 2 S. 8:18b with 1 Ch. 18:17b suggests. In the former passage David's sons are called "priests," but in the latter "chiefs at the king's side" (lit. "first at the hand of the king"). In Solomon's list, the "priest" is further identified as "the friend of the king" (*rēʿeh hammelek̠* [2 S. 15:37; 1 K. 4:5]), a title also found in the Amarna correspondence.

In this connection, the biblical data mention the "counselor" (*yôʿēṣ* [2 S. 15:12; 16:20-23; 1 K. 12:6-10; 2 Ch. 22:3f.; Isa. 1:26]), who may not have had official standing but nevertheless played an important role in the kingdom. For example, Ahithophel the Gilonite was a priest who performed his sacerdotal functions, yet at the same time served as David's counselor, whose advice was "as if one inquired of the word of God" (2 S. 16:23).

(4) "The one in charge of corvée laborers" (*ʾašer ʿal hammas* [2 S. 20:24; 1 K. 5:14 (Mt. 28)]) was responsible for recruiting and overseeing the forced labor groups composed of war captives, Canaanites, and even some Israelites (1 K. 5:13 [MT 27; AV erroneously "tribute"]; 1 K. 9:20f.). This officer would not be a popular person, as shown in the case of Rehoboam's superintendent of the corvée, who was stoned to death (1 K. 12:18). Yet Jeroboam the son of Nebat had been such an official before becoming king in northern Israel (1 K. 11:28). This office was apparently established toward the end of David's reign.

(5) "The one over the house" (*ʾašer ʿal habbayiṯ* [1 K. 18:3, 6; 2 K. 18:18, 37; 19:2; Isa. 22:15, 20-22]) was the primary palace official. Instituted in Solomon's reign, this officer seems to have been the steward of the palace or of the king's household, although later he may have become the most prestigious official, judging from Isaiah's oracle against Shebna (Isa. 22:20-23).

(6) The one "over the deputies" (*ʿal hanniṣṣāḇîm* [1 K. 4:5, 7, 27 (MT 5:7)]) was the king's chief internal revenue officer. This office, too, must have been instituted during Solomon's reign, although one may presume that David developed a similar system for the collection of taxes and tributes. It is clear that Solomon reorganized his expanded empire into twelve administrative districts, each of which was to supply the king and his royal staff with food for one month out of the year. Each district had its own appointed "deputy" (*niṣṣāḇ*). This revenue system was perhaps the best administered program introduced during the monarchy. Jar handles and ostraca give archeological witness to the extensive use of the system.

The officials mentioned above represent the administration of the national monarchy, but it should be remembered that at the local level the authority of "the elders and the nobles" (*hazzᵉqēnîm wᵉhaḥōrîm* [1 K. 21:8, 11; Isa. 34:12; Jer. 27:20; 39:6]) continued. The same inference need not be drawn, however, respecting the "judges and officers" (*šōpᵉṭîm wᵉšōṭᵉrîm* [Dt. 16:18-20; 17:8-13]), since they are mentioned only in connection with the Levitical organization (1 Ch. 23:4; 26:29). The juridical function undoubtedly was taken over by the elders who sat at the gate of the city. Jehoshaphat, however, apparently reintroduced the judicial offices by appointing judges "in all the fortified cities" and assigning the Levites the responsibilities of the "officer" (2 Ch. 19:5-11; note the distinction that emerges between that which is cultic and "that which pertains to the king").

3. Foreign Relations and the Military. Astute leadership, then as now, was backed up by a strong military force. David recognized this, but not at the expense of his trust in Yahweh the God of the covenant (cf. 1 S. 17 with the bitter lesson of 2 S. 24). Military power was essential to fulfil the responsibility of defense (cf. 2 K. 13:5; 14:27). The king himself sometimes led the army in battle as supreme commander (cf. 2 S. 18:3; 21:15-17), even at the risk of dying, as did Saul, Ahab, and Josiah (1 S. 31:3; 1 K. 22:34-37; 2 K. 23:29). David's great organizational skill, much of it learned through his experience with Saul, enabled him to train an efficient military structure. The officers were generally designated "commanders" (*śārîm*), whether they were over thousands, hundreds, fifties, or tens (2 S. 18:1; 2 K. 1:9-14). The title of "commander of the army" (*śar haṣṣāḇāʾ* [1 S. 14:50; 17:55]) or "over the army" (*ʿal haṣṣāḇāʾ* [2 S. 8:16; 1 K. 4:4]) was given to the highest military officer under the king. The various units of David's army were his "mighty men" (*haggibbōrîm* [2 S. 10:7; 23:8-39]), "the choice men of Israel" (*bᵉḥûrê bîśrāʾēl* [10:9]), "the servants of David" (*ʿaḇᵉḏê dāwiḏ* [11:17]), and foreign mercenaries, e.g., the Gittites from Gath in Philistia (15:18), and the "Cherethites and Pelethites" (8:18) who may well have been his personal bodyguard. Carite mercenaries appear later, in the days of Jehoida's regency (2 K. 11:4, 19). Other military units were introduced on a large scale during Solomon's reign, i.e., the chariots and the cavalry (1 K. 9:19; 10:26; cf. David's earlier use of these components while seeking to observe the limitations of Dt. 17:16; cf. also 2 S. 8:4). The chariotry was a distinct unit from the foot soldiers, led by its own commanders (1 K. 9:22; 16:8). "The men armed for war" undoubtedly were the archers often seen on reliefs, sometimes described as "armed with bow and shield" (*nōšᵉqê qešeṯ ûmāgēn*; 2 Ch. 17:17f. [1 Ch. 12:8, 24, 34]).

Foreign diplomatic relations, often involving the display of military power, were employed both constructively and negatively. They were used to provoke hostilities (2 K. 14:8-10), to prevent hostilities (1 K. 15:18f.; 2 K. 12:17f. [MT 18f.]; 16:7-9; 18:14), to negotiate cease-fire agreements (1 K. 20:1-35), to establish coalitions (2 K. 3:6-8) and covenants or peace treaties (2 S. 3:12-16; 10:19), as well as to arrange for royal marriages consummating treaties (1 K. 3:1; 11:1-3; 16:31), to negotiate trade relations (2 S. 5:11; 1 K. 5:1-12 [MT 15-26]; 9:27f.; 20:34), and to handle protocol between visiting dignitaries (1 K. 9:10-14; 10:1-13; 2 K. 16:10; 20:12f.). Ambassadors or envoys (*ṣîr* [Isa. 18:2; 57:9; Jer. 49:14; Ob. 1; Prov. 13:17]) were appointed to carry on negotiations, though special delegations were also employed as messengers, i.e., representatives of the king (1 K. 20:2, 5, 9; 2 K. 14:8-10; 18:18).

C. Vassals of Assyria and Babylon. Although the theocratic monarchy continued in the north down to the fall of Samaria (722/721 B.C.) and in the south until the fall of Jerusalem (587/586 B.C.), neither Israel nor Judah enjoyed complete independence throughout the period. Territorial expansion or reduction depended on the relation of the military strength of Israel and/or Judah to that of the surrounding nations. Their rivalry was with the Aramean powers to the north, especially in the 9th cent., but the revival of the Assyrian empire and then of the Babylonian empire posed a greater threat (*see* ASSYRIA; BABYLON). When Tiglath-Pileser III came to power in 745 B.C., he imposed a heavy tribute tax on Menahem (2 K. 15:19f.), which caused an intensification of an existing climate of anarchy and brought about rebellion and final calamity on Samaria (2 K. 15:29f.; 17:2-6). Judah did not escape such pressures; Ahaz and his successors paid rather heavily to maintain their own independence (2 K. 16:7f.; 18:7, 13-16), and Manasseh ruled as a puppet king (2 K. 21; 2 Ch. 33:11-13). When the northern kingdom fell the Assyrians incorporated the territory, reorganizing it into the four provinces of Dor, Gilead, Megiddo, and Samaria, with a "governor" (Akk. *bêl paḫâti*) over each, under whom the "head of cities" (Akk. *rab alâni*) served as tribute collector.

The Assyrians had a policy of deporting peoples and replacing them with other conquered peoples, for better control of possible rebellions. The deportation of large numbers of Israelites and their replacement by Babylonians and Syrians (2 K. 17:24) had a continuing effect on the governing of the land down to the 1st cent. A.D.

With the rise of the Babylonians, Judah's independence was short-lived. The vassal king Zedekiah was replaced by Gedaliah, whom the king of Babylon appointed to rule over the province (2 K. 25:22f.; Jer. 40:5, 9). The Babylonians apparently did not replace the people whom they deported from Judah.

IV. Jewish Commonwealth.–The disastrous fall of Jerusalem under Nebuchadrezzar in 586 B.C. ended the monarchy and began a period of dependence under various world empires. The Babylonians appointed their own provincial governors or commissioners. The Persians who replaced them, however, adopted a benevolent policy with conquered peoples, allowing a measure of autonomous rule, while keeping a firm hand on the military power, thereby controlling the political destinies of the nations.

A. Governors and Elders. The Persians organized the conquered provinces into satrapies, with the satrap of Beyond the River (Aram. *paḥaṯ ʿaḇar naharâ* [Ezr. 5:6]) responsible for Syria and Palestine, and the provincial governors (*ʾaparseḵāyēʾ*) responsible with him to the king. Zerubbabel was one such "governor of the Jews" (Heb. *paḥaṯ yehûḏâ* [Hag. 1:1, 14; 2:2, 21]) who ruled in Jerusalem together with the "elders of the Jews" (Aram. *leśāḇê yehûḏāyēʾ* [Ezr. 5:9; 6:7]). These elders were responsible for the rebuilding of the second temple (Ezr. 6:14-18). Some seventy years later Nehemiah, who had enjoyed a high position as cupbearer in the Persian court, arrived in Jerusalem as the governor of the province of Judah (Neh. 5:14). He was permitted to rebuild the walls as well as the city of Jerusalem (Neh. 2:4-8). Jerusalem became the capital of Judah, a "province" (Heb. *meḏînâ* [Ezr. 5:8; Neh. 1:3; 7:6]) subdivided into districts (*peleḵ* [Neh. 3:9-18]), each ruled by a *śar* ("prince, ruler"). That Nehemiah enjoyed a measure of autonomy is further evidenced by his accomplishments: dealing with economic problems (5:1-15) and religious abuses (7:61-65; 13:4-28), instituting a genealogical registry (7:5) and a security force under the command of a "captain of the castle" (*śar habbîrâ* [7:2f.]). The political governor of the province continued to be an appointed official, as is evident from an Elephantine papyrus that refers to a certain Bagoas who was governor of Judea *ca.* 408 B.C.

B. High Priest and Scribes. The policy of allowing a large measure of autonomy led to a significant development of the influence of the high priest and also of "the scribe" (*hassôpēr*). The concern of the Jews in the Diaspora (*see* DISPERSION) to determine how to continue their religious culture following the destruction of the temple led to the renewed study of the Torah. This in turn brought about the development of the office of the scribe, who was to be "skilled in the Law of Moses" and teach "his statutes and ordinances in Israel" (Ezr. 7:6, 10). Furthermore, the Persian policy encouraging the restoration of the culture and religious practice of the subjected peoples gave additional impetus to the development of this profession. Toward the end of the biblical period the scribes were either Levites or priests (cf. 2 Ch. 34:13; Ezr. 7:21). The great importance attached to the Law of Moses for autocratic governing made the priests and scribes powerful political forces in the following centuries.

Regarding the high priest, one should remember that the Zadokite priests were reinstated in the temple service following the return from Exile (e.g., Jeshua ben Jozadak [Ezr. 3:2; 5:2]). The Zadokites gained greater authority during the Hellenistic period, when the Ptolemies and Seleucids recognized the high priest as the presiding officer of the elders, ascribing to him the title "ethnarch." He was responsible for the tribute payment and was thus empowered to levy taxes. When Onias was replaced by his brother Jason, who was more open to the hellenizing movement, the office became a political appointment rather than hereditary. Further intrigues brought about the rebellion, led by Mattathias of the Hasmonean family, against the Syrian Hellenistic pressures. Although not from Zadokite lineage, the Hasmonean priest Simon Maccabeus restored Judah to independence in 142 B.C. and continued as titular head of government. A grandson of Simon, Aristobulus I (104 B.C.) took the title "king," the first to do so since the Exile. These events led to serious difficulties for the more orthodox Jews, who looked for a Davidic king. Nevertheless, it is clear how powerful and important the office of priest was, especially since no Davidic political leader emerged after the collapse of the kingdom in 586.

C. Sanhedrin. One of the most powerful institutions of the second commonwealth period was the SANHEDRIN (Gk. *synédrion* [Mt. 26:59; Acts 5:21], sometimes translated "council"). Josephus mentions five Sanhedrins as the council that governed the five Roman districts of Judea (*Ant.* xiv.5.4 [91]). This council also had judicial authority; it was considered the supreme Jewish court (Mt. 26:59; Jn. 11:47; Acts 4:15; etc.). Its origin is not clear, but the elders of Ezr. 5:5, 9; 6:7, 14; 10:8; Neh. 2:16; 4:14, 19 [MT 8, 13]; 7:5 may have served as the prototype. During the Greek period a "senate" (Gk. *gerousía* [Josephus *Ant.* xii.3.3 [142]); 1 Macc. 12:3, 6; 14:20] was organized, with elders representing the nation. Under the Roman Gabinius this body was given considerable power, though Julius Caesar curtailed the territorial extent of its authority. Nevertheless, the internal governing of Judea was in its hands. There were local courts or councils (*synédria* or *boulaí* [Mt. 5:22; 10:17; Mk. 13:9; Josephus *Ant.* iv.8.14 (214)]), which reported to the central authority. These local courts consisted of at least seven elders, but in larger towns they had up to twenty-three elders. The Sanhedrin was abolished in A.D. 70 and replaced by the "Court of Judgment" (Heb. *bēṯ dîn*), which was composed only of scribes and had no political authority.

Originally the Sanhedrin was composed of the predominantly Sadducean priestly aristocracy. Queen Alexandra

(76-67 B.C.), however, included scribes and Pharisees whom she favored. By NT times the Great Sanhedrin was composed of the high priest, serving as the presiding officer, and former high priests, the elders, and the scribes (who were the legal authorities), all of them either Sadducees or Pharisees (cf. Mt. 26:3, 57, 59; Acts 4:1, 5; 5:17, 21, 34; 22:30; 23:6).

D. Synagogue. The basic meaning of Gk. *synagōgḗ* is "a place of meeting." The LXX often uses the word for the assembly of Israel (translating Heb. *qāhāl* or *ʿēḏâ*). As a Jewish institution, the origins of the synagogue (*see* SYNAGOGUE) go back to the Diaspora, the earliest testimonies coming from the 3rd cent. B.C., which mention synagogues in Egypt. Larger cities of the Roman empire seem to have had several places of Jewish worship, depending on the size of the Jewish community. In Palestine every town had its synagogue, where people worshiped, the Law was studied, and children were taught. The local Jewish congregation was governed by a board of directors consisting of three "elders" (Gk. *presbýteroi*). The *archisynágōgos* was the presiding officer. The instruction and discipline of the children was entrusted to the synagogue "attendant" or "servant," the only other official. Such instruction and discipline was to be in conformity with the law of Moses. Punishment was exercised by scourging or excommunication. As a school where the Law was studied, it was also called the "house of instruction." The synagogue became the center of community life, where people gathered to discuss community affairs.

V. NT on Government.–The *locus classicus* on civil government in the NT is Rom. 13:1-7. In making this statement, however, one should caution against looking only to these verses to understand the biblical teaching on civil government. They do not address themselves, e.g., to the question of what form this government should take, nor to the question of conscientious disobedience, nor to the question of whether Christians may participate in government. In considering government in the NT, due consideration must be given not only to Pauline theory and practice, but also to Christ's teaching and practice under Jewish autocratic rule and Roman imperial authority. For information on Roman law and civil administration which is helpful in formulating a clear and definitive background for NT teaching on government, *see* ROMAN EMPIRE AND CHRISTIANITY; ROMAN LAW. As mentioned at the outset, even though the biblical records give fragmentary information on political forms, institutions, and procedures for the governing of the body politic, there nevertheless emerges a clear and significant teaching in the NT on human government, i.e., the state as the body politic in the world, in contradistinction to the Church as the people or kingdom of God.

A. Authority of the State. The concise statement of Paul in Rom. 13:1 with respect to "governing authorities" (*exousíais hyperechoúsais*; NEB "supreme authorities") is that "there is no authority except from God, and those that exist have been instituted by God" (cf. 1 Pet. 2:14). All authority is ultimately derived from God, even though people may ignore Him or reject Him. God is sovereign over His creation, the world, and the people who live in it. The testimony of the OT agrees with this (cf. Gen. 9:5f.; Isa. 10:5; 45:1; Dnl. 4:34f. [MT 31f.]; Ps. 75:6f. [MT 7f.]). The judgments of the omnipotent God on the nations serve to underscore the truth of His sovereignty (cf. Ex. 7–12; Joel 3; Isa. 13–27; etc.). In the NT Christ acknowledged the authority of the Jewish Sanhedrin, the high priest, Herod the king, and Pilate the Roman procurator (cf. Mt. 26:59; 27:1f.; etc.); He even recognized the civil authority of Caesar (22:15-22). Eschatologically, God's final judgment on the empires of the world and the dragon that deceives the nations confirms the teaching that God is the ultimate authority from whom all other authority is derived (Rev. 17–20). It is then inconsistent with the Scriptures to consider that human governments derive their legitimate authority ultimately from a "social compact," or from "the consent of the governed," or even from "the will of the majority."

The state, then, may be considered an expression of God's common grace extended to all mankind. Hence, to resist the governing authorities is tantamount to resisting God (Rom. 13:2). Furthermore, the NT does not designate any particular form of civil government any more than the OT did (see III above, though it may be observed that the OT theocracy in whatever form was not designed as a pattern for all nations). Nor does the authority of the government depend on the moral character of its leadership. Whatever the character of a ruler in NT times, whether high priest or king, procurator or emperor, the authority vested in him was to be honored and respected. Paul's own practice under the autocratic Roman government was to acknowledge its authority. He frequently asserted his own obedient subjection to the laws of the empire, and even when imprisoned, his appeal to Caesar was a further recognition of the supreme authority whose laws he had obeyed and whose protection he sought. In this he followed the example of Christ, who was tried by Pilate, a man unworthy of his high office. Even though the trial proved to be a miscarriage of justice, Jesus firmly reminded him, "You would have no authority over me, unless it had been given you from above" (Jn. 19:11).

B. Function of the State. The governing authorities are vested with twofold responsibility: the administration of justice and the promotion of the general welfare. Regarding the first, Paul states that the government wields the sword as a "servant of God, an avenger who brings wrath upon the one who practices evil" (Rom. 13:4). It is thus responsible for restraining evil by punishing crime and violence. Furthermore, the justice meted out upon evil reflects to a greater or lesser degree the righteous judgment of God, the Judge of all the earth. The ministers of divine justice, therefore, must take appropriate measures that fairness, firmness, and mercy be exhibited. Only in this way will retribution function for the defense and encouragement of good people as well as for the punishment of criminals.

The second responsibility of government is the promotion of the general welfare (Rom. 13:4-7). The OT prophets, concerned about the needy, especially urged upon kings their responsibility to care for "the afflicted and needy," for "the orphan and the widow," and even for the resident alien (cf. Ps. 72:1-4, 12-14; Jer. 22:16; Ezk. 34:16). This general welfare was described by Paul in another connection. When urging Christians to pray "for kings and all who are in authority," he expressed the reason: "in order that you may lead a tranquil and quiet life" (1 Tim. 3:2). Without doubt, the general peace brought by the Romans (*pax Romana*) was one of the great blessings for the general well-being of the people in that period. Paul may already have had a premonition of times of distress and persecution, especially for Christians, in the decades ahead. Peter also acknowledged government's positive role of promoting the general good when he instructed believers to submit themselves to "governors as sent by Him for the punishment of evildoers and the praise of those who do right" (1 Pet. 2:14). The public recognition of those who do right is a tacit acknowledgment that government is responsible for promoting moral standards in the community and nation. There may be differences of opinion about how much government should do, but consideration should be given to maintaining programs of public health and education, to encouraging philanthropic activities, and to protecting the disadvantaged from abuses by the wealthy and powerful sectors of society.

C. Responsibility of Citizenship. Peter and Paul clearly called for submission to the powers that be (Rom. 13:1; 1 Pet. 2:13). Paul further admonished believers to pay taxes "to whom tax is due" (Rom. 13:6f.). In a very intriguing conversation between Peter and his Lord, one finds that Christ's own practice was to pay His taxes (Mt. 17:24-27). The principle seems to be that those who enjoy the benefits of the general protection and welfare of the state should share in the costs of maintaining that state. Citizens are to obey the laws of the land, to pray for civil authorities and all levels of government, and to give honor to whom it is due. Furthermore, the NT does not specifically forbid Christians to participate in government service — whether in military service or in judicial, executive, or legislative responsibilities. This is shown by the rather large number of converts who held public office without anyone calling them to renounce their position; e.g., the Ethiopian eunuch, Cornelius, Sergius Paulus, the Philippian jailer. Paul's references to "those in Caesar's household" possibly refer to persons holding official status in the government of the Roman empire. Again, this is in keeping with the positions of authority of certain OT believers, e.g., Joseph in Egypt, Daniel in Babylon, Mordecai in Persia, Naaman in Syria. The conclusion of most Christians is that they may participate in government as the political situation allows, not only by voting but also by serving as employees or as elected officials. In any case, believers exercise this prerogative as individual Christian citizens and not as representatives of the Church.

D. Civil Disobedience. Although human government is divinely instituted, it does not follow that its authority is unlimited. On the contrary, the Scriptures give ample evidence that when governments usurp the authority of God by demanding subjection to laws contrary to clear commands of Scripture, they have exceeded their authority. Acts 5:29 summarizes the concluding arguments of believers before the Sanhedrin: "We must obey God rather than men." No one may claim that he is entitled to disobey the laws merely because of his personal disagreement with them. In totalitarian societies some laws may be hard to accept, but Christians as well as all other citizens are responsible to obey them. No Christian, however, may be forced to declare "Caesar is Lord" as a recognition of Caesar's deity and as a denial of the Lordship of Christ. Furthermore, when governments oppress the righteous, reward evildoing, prevent justice, and subvert the ordinances of God, it may be necessary for Christians to resist them.

The major difficulty is arriving at a consensus about when such a government has gone too far. The nature of the opposition to be offered is also a debatable issue. Resistance, demonstrations, and propagandizing for a particular position within the law is one thing. Civil disobedience that goes beyond the law, such as advocating or participating in the violent overthrow of the government, is another. Such critical situations in the political affairs of government call for special periods of prayer "for kings and all who are in authority" (1 Tim. 2:1-4). This is not simply a pious platitude, but rather a sincere realization that "we wrestle not against flesh and blood" (Eph. 6:12) and that "the weapons of our warfare are not worldly" (2 Cor. 10:4).

David's experiences with Saul and other enemies amply illustrate this point. Hence, such prayers as Ps. 35:1; 43:1; 119:154; 129:1-4 may prove to be an encouragement. It is God who reigns and controls the destinies of the defiant rulers (Ps. 2:4; Rom. 9:14-24). In Rev. 6:10; 11:17f.; 15:2-4 the prayers of the saints persecuted and martyred by a demonically empowered world empire may hold the clue for Christians living under less severe conditions. Their trust is in a sovereign God who remains in control of political powers and who ultimately will vindicate the cause of the righteous.

Bibliography.–Calvin *Inst.* iv.20; H. Frankfort, *Intellectual Adventure of Ancient Man* (1946); *Kingship and the Gods* (1948); C. F. H. Henry, ed., *Aspects of Christian Social Ethics* (1964); *HJP*²; K. A. Kitchen, *Ancient Orient and OT* (1966); *Bible in Its World* (1977); M. G. Kline, *Treaty of the Great King* (1963); A. Malamat, *BA*, 28 (1965), 34-65; 34 (1971), 2-22; P. Matthiae, *BA*, 39 (1976), 94-113; H. Meeter, *Basic Ideas of Calvinism* (5th ed. 1967); G. E. Mendenhall; *Law and Covenant in Israel and the Ancient Near East* (1955); G. Pettinato, *BA*, 39 (1976), 44-52; A. N. Sherwin-White, *Roman Society and Roman Law in the NT* (1963); R. de Vaux, *Early History of Israel* (Eng. tr. 1978); D. J. Wiseman, "They Lived in Tents," in G. A. Tuttle, ed., *Biblical and Near Eastern Studies* (1978), pp. 195-200; J. H. Yoder, *Politics of Jesus* (1972).

P. R. GILCHRIST

GOVERNMENTS (1 Cor. 12:28, AV). *See* ADMINISTRATORS.

GOVERNOR [Heb. and Aram. *peḥâ*]; AV also PRINCE, DEPUTY; NEB also VICEROY; [Heb. hiphil of *pāqaḏ*–'appoint a governor']; AV also SET OVER; [part. of *māšal*] (2 Ch. 23:20); [*śar*]; AV also PRINCE, RULER; [*nāḡîḏ*]; AV also RULER; NEB also PRINCE; [*šallîṭ*] (Gen. 42:6); [*tiršāṯāʾ*] (Neh. 10:1 [MT 2]); [Aram. *ʾ^{a}pars^{e}ḵāy*] (Ezr. 5:6b; 6:6b); AV APHARSACHITE; NEB INSPECTOR; [*ʾ^{a}parsaṯḵāy*] (Ezr. 4:9); AV APHARSATHCHITE; NEB COMMISSIONER; [Gk. *hēgemṓn, hēgemoneúō*–'be governor,' *hēgéomai*–'lead']; AV also RULER; NEB also CHIEF ADMINISTRATOR; [*ethnárchēs*] (2 Cor. 11:32); NEB COMMISSIONER. (For Jas. 3:4, AV, *see* PILOT.)

The OT term most frequently rendered "governor" by the RSV is *peḥâ,* a loanword from Akk. *pīḫatu,* "governor." The hiphil of *pāqaḏ* is used in regard to Gedaliah (2 K. 25:22f.; Jer. 40:5, 7, 11). *Māšal* is a general term for rule; its participial form may indicate a sovereign. *Śar* (cf. Akk. *šarru,* "king") has a wide range of meaning, including the designation of rank; as "governor" it indicates the overseer of the sanctuary (1 Ch. 24:5, AV), the mayor of the capital (2 Ch. 34:8), and the officer over a district (1 K. 20:14f.). In Gen. 42:6 the term *šallîṭ* is used of Joseph, the appointed head over Egypt; here it indicates a very high-ranking official, perhaps vizier. Nehemiah bore the title of the Persian governor in Judah, *tiršāṯāʾ*. Dnl. 3:2 provides a list of the various officers of the Neo-Babylonian empire. The AV translates the second word on the list (Aram. *s^{e}ḡan*) as "governor" (RSV, NEB, "prefect"); the RSV assigns "governor" to the third word (*peḥâ,* AV "captain"; NEB "viceroy"); and the NEB renders "governor" for the summary word, **šilṭōn* (AV "ruler"; RSV "official"). In 2:48 Nebuchadrezzar appoints Daniel ruler (*š^{e}lēṭ*; NEB "regent") over all the province of Babylon and chief of the prefects (*s^{e}ḡan,* AV "governors") over all the wise men of Babylon. The AV renders *ʾ^{a}pars^{e}ḵāy* and *ʾ^{a}parsaṯḵāy* (Ezr. 4:9; 5:6; 6:6) as proper nouns, but many take these as the title of an office (cf. RSV, NEB); *see* APHARSACHITES, APHARSATHCHITES, APHARSITES.

The NT terms most frequently rendered "governor" are *hēgemṓn* and its cognates. These terms generally refer to a provincial governor, or procurator. The title *ethnárchēs* refers to the deputy of a king. The ethnarch who desired to capture Paul was head of Damascus and responsible to King Aretas of Nabatea. *See* ETHNARCH.

"Governor" is a general administrative term with wide range of use for a ruler with great responsibility, usually a king. Its use includes the head over a city, a province, or a territory. Translations use it quite freely: the AV widely employs it for God Himself but also for the captain or pilot of a boat. As a governmental title it varies drastically according to the numerous political systems that dominated Palestine. It is used most often for positions in foreign administrations.

Joseph is referred to as governor over Egypt (Gen. 42:6; AV 45:26). At the time of Ahab there were governors over districts who were responsible for supplying soldiers for the king's campaigns (1 K. 20:14-19). Each capital city of divided Israel had a governor; Amon was governor (*śar*) of Samaria at the time of Ahab (1 K. 22:26), and two governors of Jerusalem are mentioned during the reign of Josiah (Joshua and Maaseiah, 2 K. 23:8; 2 Ch. 34:8). After the fall of Jerusalem in 586 B.C., Nebuchadrezzar appointed Gedaliah governor over Judah at Mizpah (2 K. 25:22), but unfortunately he was assassinated (v. 25). During the postexilic period Nehemiah appointed Hananiah, who had been governor over the fortress in Jerusalem, head of that city (Neh. 7:2).

During the Persian period the OT mentions three governors of the province of Judah: Sheshbazzar under Cyrus (Ezr. 5:14; cf. 1:8, 11), Zerubbabel under Darius I (Hag. 1:1, 14), and Nehemiah under Artaxerxes I (Neh. 5:14). For Zerubbabel Ezr. 6:7 uses the title "governor of the Jews." These men were appointed by the Persian emperor. Nehemiah initially had to gain clearance for his journey to Jerusalem from the governor of the province Beyond the River (i.e., beyond the Euphrates, including Palestine and Syria) (Neh. 2:7-9). In the RSV of Ezr. 5:6; 6:6 both Tattenai, head of this province, and his associates are called "governor"; but two different Aramaic words are represented. According to J. M. Myers, Tattenai was assistant to Ushtani, the satrap of Babylon and Across (RSV "Beyond") the River (pp. 67f.). Tattenai challenged the work of rebuilding the temple, and as an unexpected result of his appeal to Darius he was commissioned by Darius to assist in the work (Ezr. 5f.).

Shortly before the birth of Christ, Augustus refined the administration of the Roman empire. Peaceful provinces came under the senate, which appointed a propraetor or a proconsul; other provinces were subject to the emperor, who as proconsul appointed a legate; more unruly provinces requiring a resident army were under a procurator responsible to the emperor — Egypt and Judea were famous in this regard. Quirinius was legate over Syria at the time of Jesus' birth (Lk. 2:2). The procurator over Judea resided at Caesarea, built for that purpose by King Herod. Pontius Pilate was procurator at the time of Jesus' death. Paul was imprisoned in Caesarea during portions of the terms of two procurators, FELIX and FESTUS (Acts 23:24; 24:27). As is evident from events in the lives of Jesus and Paul, the procurator was the judge in matters pertaining to disturbances.

The AV uses "governor" for the part. of Heb. *māšal* in reference to God and the Messiah. God is "the governor [RSV "he rules"] among the nations" (Ps. 22:28 [MT 29]). According to Jeremiah the Messiah is to be the governor (RSV "ruler") over restored Israel (30:21). In Matthew, Jesus is the one who comes to rule His people as governor (2:5f.).

The early Christians were exhorted to be subject to those in authority, including emperors and governors (1 Pet. 2:13f.). But they were also warned that they should expect to come under the state's suspicion and condemnation if they adhered to the teaching of Christ. During such a trial the Holy Spirit would guide them in giving a proper answer to the authorities (Mt. 10:17-21).

See also COMMANDER; DEPUTY; OFFICER; PRINCE; PROCONSUL; RULER.

Bibliography.–*BHI*; H. Mattingly, *Roman Imperial Civilization* (1957); J. M. Myers, *The World of Restoration* (1968).

J. E. HARTLEY

GOZAN gō'zan (Heb. *gôzān*; Akk. *Guzana*). A city or region in northern Mesopotamia. Sennacherib, the king of Assyria, boasted to Hezekiah that Gozan was among the "nations" that his fathers had destroyed (2 K. 19:12 par. Isa. 37:12). The "river of Gozan" is given as a descriptive name of the Habor (Ḫābûr), in an account of the places to which Israelites were taken captive when Samaria was destroyed (2 K. 17:6; 18:11; in 1 Ch. 5:26, however, the RSV translates "the river Gozan," where the MT reads "the river of Gozan"). Adadnirari II recorded, "The Habur I crossed; against Guzanu which Abisalamu, son of Bahiani held, I marched" (*ARAB*, I, § 373). Shalmaneser III referred to "Asu the Guzanite" (*ARAB*, I, § 598). In an eponym *(limmu-)* list, the eponym of Nergal-ilia contains the description "field marshal against Guzana" (*ARAB*, II, § 1198 no. 809). We should therefore take Guzana as a city-state through which the Habor River flowed. It has been identified with the Gauzanitis mentioned by Ptolemy (v. 18) and modern Tell Halâf (the site from which Halafian pottery drew its name), E of Haran. W. S. L. S.

GRABA grā'bə (1 Esd. 5:29, AV). *See* HAGABAH.

GRACE. In the OT, the RSV renders *ḥēn* by "grace" on four occasions only (Est. 2:17; Ps. 45:2 [MT 3]; Jer. 31:2; Zec. 4:7), while in two other instances (Zec. 11:7, 10) *nōʿam* (cf. Ugar. *nʿm*), "grace," "kindness," is used to convey the concept. *Ḥēn* is widely translated as "favor" in the RSV and NEB, where the AV reads "grace." The term carried some breadth of meaning for OT writers, beginning with the ordinary sense of that which brought approval, delight, and joy (Gen. 33:15; 1 S. 16:22) and also describing aesthetic experiences of loveliness and sweetness (Est. 2:9; 5:2). In a more developed form it signified goodwill toward a person, as between God and man (Gen. 6:8), and found special expression in the master-servant relationship (Gen. 39:4; Neh. 2:5). The common usage of "grace," "kindness" seems reflected in the term *nōʿam,* used by Zechariah in naming one of his two symbolic staffs (Zec. 11:7, 10; *see* GRACE AND UNION).

Grace or favor is the positive emotional reaction of approbation to some form of relationship, whether between man and nature, or something restricted to the level of human associations. Where God is involved in this relationship, it is He alone who bestows the estimate and consequences of favor and grace upon man (Prov. 12:2; Jer. 26:19). The term *ḥesed,* which is broadly descriptive of covenant love, is translated in the RSV by "favor" only in Est. 2:9 (AV "kindness"; NEB "special favor") and Dnl. 1:9 (AV "favor"; NEB "show kindness"), and in no instance by "grace." Apart from the six references involving *ḥēn* and *nōʿam,* the word "grace" does not appear in the RSV OT. R. K. H.

The word "grace" in its special Christian sense refers to the freedom of salvation in Jesus Christ. As used by Paul in particular, the word underscores the fact that salvation is freely given by God to undeserving sinners. This is its central meaning; it also has other meanings, some of them peripheral to the NT message of salvation.

The Greek term is *cháris,* a common word in secular Greek. The LXX uses *cháris* to translate OT Hebrew terms that often bear only a faint suggestion of the Pauline sense of *cháris*. NT writers other than Paul use the term, sometimes in a sense similar to Paul's, but none uses it consistently with its central Christian meaning, and a few do not use it at all. Once the Pauline sense of the word is grasped, however, we can recognize all the saving acts of God as acts of grace, even when the word is not used. Our primary objective will be to examine the uses of the word *cháris* in the Bible; but it must be kept in mind that, in the light of its most pregnant meaning, the reality of grace appears clearly wherever God is revealed in His redeeming purposes and actions as the God who saves freely, without obligation and without regard for merit.

I. Grace in Secular Greek
II. Grace in the LXX
III. Grace in the Letters of Paul
  A. Grace as God's Grace
  B. Freedom of Grace
  C. Grace in Justification
  D. Grace in Salvation
  E. Grace and Righteousness
  F. Grace and Faith
  G. Grace and Sin
  H. Grace as Power
  I. Grace and Office
  J. Grace Abounding
  K. Grace Irresistible
  L. Grace and Election
  M. Grace and Love
  N. Grace as Thanksgiving
  O. "Grace" in Greetings
  P. Acts of God in the Light of Grace
IV. Grace in Non-Pauline Writings
  A. Gospels
  B. Acts
  C. Hebrews
  D. Peter
  E. James
  F. Jude
  G. Revelation
V. Conclusion

I. Grace in Secular Greek.–*Cháris* is used to convey several meanings in secular Greek literature, some of which recommended the word to biblical writers. The first, and perhaps the original sense is the quality of anything that brings delight or pleasure, or that wins favor. A good wine and fine choice of words are examples of *cháris*. Persons have *cháris* when they are delicate, tactful, or artful; in this sense, Plutarch speaks of Homer's *cháris*. In this way, things or people win the *cháris* (favor) of others by having *cháris* (charm).

Cháris has an ethical as well as aesthetic side, for kindness and generosity are also graces. One shows *cháris* by displaying benevolence to inferiors. Aristotle speaks of the gods bestowing *cháris* on citizens. He also speaks of the moral quality of "helpfulness [*cháris*] toward someone in need, not... that the helper may get anything but for the sake of the person who is helped" (*Rhet.* ii.7). The gods have *cháris* in both the above senses.

In return for *cháris,* one ought to give thanks; and the word for thanks is *cháris*. To have *cháris* is to be thankful; to give *cháris* is to give thanks. Here *cháris* indicates both a delight in receiving the favor of a superior and the thanks one offers for it.

We have, then, three uses of *cháris* in classical Greek: (1) a charming quality that wins favor, (2) a quality of benevolence that gives favor to inferiors, and (3) a response of thankfulness for the favor given. As we shall see, it is the second sense that commends *cháris* for adoption into the NT vocabulary to indicate the benevolence of God toward sinners. The other senses are also taken over in biblical use, but are always peripheral to the central NT meaning.

It may be added that in later Greek *cháris* also had the sense of force or power. It could be a spell, or demonic force, affecting human life with supernatural influences. In Euripides, it was a power from the underworld that could convey the virtues of a dead hero to his living family or followers. This sense, too, though set in a new context, was used in the NT: grace became the power of God to enable Christians to live the new life in Christ.

Finally, in Hellenism, showing *cháris* to people came to suggest favoritism, or what the NT calls "respect of persons." To show *cháris* suggested an unfair bias toward those who ingratiated themselves, perhaps by bribery, with their superior.

II. Grace in the LXX.–The LXX used *cháris* to translate Heb. *ḥēn*. When translated as *cháris, ḥēn* refers to a quality that makes a favorable impression on someone, usually a superior. Grace, then, is not in the giver, not in the one impressed, but in the one receiving. Appeals to kings often begin with, "If now I have found favor [*ḥēn*] in your sight..." (Gen. 30:27; 1 S. 16:22; 2 S. 14:22; Prov. 18:22). In the same sense, people are said to find favor (*ḥēn*) in God's sight, as in the case of Noah and others (Gen. 6:8; Ex. 33:13; 2 S. 15:25). Jacob tried to win Esau's favor by plying him with gifts (Gen. 33:5). Joseph won approval (*ḥēn*) in Potiphar's house (Gen. 39:4). In such cases, grace is a personal quality that is recognized and rewarded. It is the sense commonly found in classical Greek, but bearing little resemblance to the deeper Christian sense given the word "grace" by Paul.

Sometimes, the quality of *ḥēn* is aesthetic. It refers to anything attractive or pleasant. An adornment is a *ḥēn* (Prov. 1:9; 3:22). Even a harlot's enticement is *ḥēn*. God promises to make the Israelites *ḥēn* (attractive) to the Egyptians, the better to help them make off with expensive objects (Ex. 3:21f.). So, too, the temple is *ḥēn,* or beautiful (Zec. 4:7). Here again, the translation of *ḥēn* by *cháris* manifests little sense of the central NT meaning of "grace."

The verb form *ḥānan* comes closer to the NT notion of *cháris*. *Ḥānan* usually denotes a superior's responding generously to inferiors. This form is found mostly in the Psalms, where God is invoked to hear prayer (4:1 [MT 2]), heal (6:2 [MT 3]), redeem (26:11), and forgive (51:1 [MT 3]) in connection with showing *ḥānan*. Though occasionally it is suggested that someone has a moral claim on *ḥānan* (26:11), the appeal is made mostly on the basis of need, the weakness (6:2), loneliness (25:16), or affliction (31:9) of the person seeking *ḥēn*.

Ḥānan demonstrates God's sovereign freedom: "I am gracious to whom I am gracious..." (Ex. 33:19). This, while harsh in sound, is said to indicate the freedom of God in electing Israel (cf. Rom. 9:14). In other instances, however, there appears a correlation between God's *ḥānan* and Israel's justice (cf. Am. 5:15).

The verb refers to a benevolent attitude that is expressed in concrete action. Yahweh shows *ḥēn* in giving Jacob children (Gen. 33:5). The righteous demonstrate their *ḥēn* to the poor and needy by giving generously (Ps. 37:21, 26). One does *ḥēn* also by sparing the lives of a defeated enemy (Dt. 7:2).

"Grace" is often paired with "mercy" (*ḥeseḏ*), as in Ex. 33:19, but most prominently in liturgical formulas (cf. Ex. 34:6; Josh. 2:13; 2 Ch. 30:9; Neh. 9:17; Ps. 11:4; 86:15; 103:8; Jonah 4:2). The words of Ex. 34:6 are a model: "The Lord, the Lord, a God merciful and gracious, slow to anger, and abounding in steadfast love and faithfulness. . . ."

The Heb. *ḥesed* comes closer than *ḥēn* to the NT concept of grace; but the LXX translates *ḥesed* with Gk. *éleos*. The English rendering of *ḥesed* is sometimes "mercy" (AV), but more adequately "steadfast love" (RSV) or equivalents. *Ḥesed* suggests, most often, Yahweh's freely given commitment to love. It is the character and conduct typical of God within the covenant He freely made with Israel. He shows "steadfast love to thousands of them that love me and keep my commandments" (Ex. 20:6; Dt. 5:10). "Know therefore that the Lord your God is God, the faithful God who keeps covenant and steadfast love . . ." (Dt. 7:9; cf. Jer. 9:24; 32:18). Within His covenant community, He abounds in *ḥesed* (Ps. 86:15; Ex. 34:9). The faithful know that "goodness and steadfast love" will follow them all the days of their lives (Ps. 23:6). The kind of spontaneous generosity with which He responds to the people of His covenant (e.g., 1 K. 8:23; Isa. 55:3; Ps. 89:29, 50; 106:45) is a harbinger of the grace that appeared bringing salvation to all people in Christ (Tit. 2:11).

In summary, the deep meaning Paul conveys with the word "grace" is hardly suggested by the Hebrew word *ḥēn*, which the LXX translated as *cháris*, "grace." The OT *ḥesed* — translated with *éleos* by the LXX — comes closer to Paul's "grace." It is not surprising that Paul never quotes from the OT in order to establish his use of the word "grace." Reading the OT in the light of the NT, however, we do not look merely to the word "grace" to discover the OT presentation of the reality of God's grace. All that God does in electing, saving, leading, forgiving, and preserving Israel is a revelation of His grace, whether the word "grace" is used or not.

III. Grace in the Letters of Paul.–The word "grace" was adopted by Paul to declare the ways of God with sinful people. He used it to point to the unique and unmerited acts of God to save sinners through Jesus Christ. Paul was not the only NT writer to use "grace" to indicate that salvation was wholly God's work. And Paul sometimes used the word in its older, weaker sense. But it is nonetheless true that in Paul's letters, as nowhere else, "grace" points to the several dimensions of God's loving act to bring salvation freely to those who cannot merit it.

The sheer number of times Paul uses the word suggests that it is integral to his theology of salvation. He uses it twice as often as all other NT writers. Only Luke, among the Synoptists, uses it at all. 1 John and 3 John do not use it, Jude and Revelation hardly ever. It occurs 51 times in books other than the Pauline letters, 27 of which are in Acts and 1 Peter. We find it 101 times in Paul.

A. Grace as God's Grace. Grace is uniquely God's to give; this is the special Pauline message. In all that he writes about the foundation and creation of the Christian life, he stresses one thing above all: that what comes to needy man comes as a gift from God. That it comes freely, as a result of God's decision and God's actions, is what is meant when Paul says it is of grace.

Paul does not distinguish precisely between the "grace of God" and the "grace of our Lord Jesus Christ." He almost always greets his readers with a variation of "Grace to you and peace from God our Father and the Lord Jesus Christ" (Rom. 1:7). Paul speaks of the "grace of our God and the Lord Jesus Christ" (2 Thess. 1:12; cf. 1 Cor. 1:3), and again of the "grace of God and the free gift in the grace of that one man Jesus Christ . . ." (Rom. 5:15). He refers grace to Jesus Christ rather frequently in his closing benedictions. It is found in the triune blessing of 2 Cor. 13:14: "The grace of the Lord Jesus Christ and the love of God and the fellowship of the Holy Spirit be with you all" (cf. also Rom. 16:20; 1 Cor. 16:23; Gal. 6:18; Phil. 4:23; 1 Thess. 5:23; 2 Thess. 3:18). Grace is also ascribed to God in His gifts to Paul (1 Cor. 15:10; Eph. 3:7) and to others (2 Cor. 6:1; 8:1; 9:14).

Grace is ascribed to both because God's decision to save people was effected in and through the incarnate Son of God, the man Christ Jesus. It was Christ, "the image of the invisible God" (Col. 1:15), through whom God reconciled the world to Himself and made believing sinners alive to God. And this fact, which is epitomized in the statement "by grace you have been saved" (Eph. 2:5), makes it reasonable to ascribe grace to both God the Father and Jesus Christ the Savior.

B. Freedom of Grace. The word "grace" conveys the truth that God is free in giving salvation to sinners through Christ. To say that grace is free is a tautology, since grace by definition indicates freedom. It indicates God's freedom. God is free in giving salvation because He is not obligated, nor constrained by some inner necessity or the moral merits of people who have earned salvation. Neither an inner necessity nor an external obligation accounts for what God has done for sinners. Only grace accounts for it; that is, only His free, loving will accounts for it. This is what is meant by the freedom of grace. Strictly speaking, no entity is given the label "grace"; therefore, grace is not a gift. Salvation is a gift; and Paul indicates its givenness by the word "grace."

Paul uses the word "grace" as shorthand for the entire event of Jesus Christ and His ministry. When he says, in Tit. 2:11, that the "grace of God has appeared for the salvation of all men," it can be understood as meaning that Christ has appeared, or that God's decision to save people freely has been enacted in Christ's appearance. When he says that we are saved by grace (Eph. 2:5), it can be taken to mean that we are saved by God's action in Christ, freely and divinely. In short, grace is not an *entity* which God and Christ dispense. Nor is it a moral *property* of the divine nature. It is a word that epitomizes the *freeness* of God's saving act on our behalf.

C. Grace in Justification. The act of justification demonstrates the freedom of grace. For it is in justifying sinners, rather than morally meritorious saints, that God's freedom to be gracious becomes abundantly apparent. Both Jews and Gentiles, none of whom could claim a merited favor with God as a right, are in fact justified through the free exercise of His grace (Rom. 3:23). Justification is clearly an act of God. And since it cannot be claimed as a right, it must be received as a gift (Gal. 2:17-21). Its givenness is what makes it an act of grace. Not even faith counts as a reason or basis for justification; we are not justified because we have faith, but are justified by grace *through* faith. The fact that it is by grace excludes the possibility of boasting or self-glory; the only proper boasting (1 Cor. 1:29, 31) or glorying (Gal. 6:14) is in the Lord and His cross.

D. Grace in Salvation. In Ephesians the great gift is called "salvation," which is a global term for all that God does for mankind in Christ (Eph. 2:1-10). Here Paul (we will assume he is the author) repeats with resounding clarity that salvation is by grace alone (Eph. 2:5, 8). "Salvation" is all that God gives to a person in Christ — the renewal of his life, rebirth from death to life, justification and sanctification, forgiveness, adoption, acceptance, glorification, all that can be swept into the meaning of being a new creature in Christ — and it is all a gift, and is therefore by grace.

E. Grace and Righteousness. The proclamation that people are justified by grace aroused the religious wrath of Judaism. To declare that God justified sinners seemed to make God a party to unrighteousness. For only just people may rightly be declared just; and just people are those who fulfil the law. Paul did not respond to this moral appeal to justice by setting NT grace in opposition to OT justice. Rather, he declared that God demonstrated His justice precisely in graciously declaring sinners just in Christ Jesus. "But now the righteousness of God has been manifested apart from the law . . ." (Rom. 3:21). Grace is a manifestation of evangelical righteousness or justice; in the act of grace God proves that He is indeed righteous (Rom. 3:26). Hence, the biblical ideal of the justice of God must be interpreted in the light of the grace of God; God's justice was satisfied in the judgment of the cross, but in His grace He freely apportions to sinners the liberating effect of that judgment.

F. Grace and Faith. The relationship between mankind's faith and God's grace has been the subject of long theological debate. The issue focuses on whether grace is given to mankind because of his faith or whether mankind's faith is the effect of God's grace. Whatever the disagreements in the Church's theology, Paul gave no sign that he felt a tension between faith and grace. We are saved by grace through faith (Eph. 2:8). We are justified by faith so that the promise will rest on grace alone (Rom. 4:16). Paul does not suggest that human faith is a cause or ground of God's grace. He says, rather, that faith is mankind's manner of receiving God's gift of grace. Indeed, it is in faith that a person is conscious that the gift is totally free (Rom. 3:24f.). Therefore it is most unlikely that faith could be construed as a Christian means of meriting grace. Faith and grace together form an antithesis to claims of merit. Faith excludes the claim of merit (Rom. 3:21-31) for the same reason that grace excludes it (Rom. 6:14; Gal. 2:21; 5:4).

In Galatians, Paul counters the Judaistic contention that mankind gains favor with God by moral and religious achievement with the declaration that mankind has status with God only through faith. His argument that justification is only through faith excludes all kinds of merit as the basis for mankind's status with God, including any merit that might be claimed for faith itself as an ersatz achievement. In other words, justification by faith eliminates merit of any sort, including the merit of believing; faith is precisely mankind's way of accepting salvation as a free and unearned gift of God, that is, as grace. To fall from the way of faith is to fall from the way of grace (Gal. 5:4).

G. Grace and Sin. Grace is the antithesis of sin. It denotes God's free act in Christ of overcoming sin and His free act of forgiving personal sin. The sin that Christ overcomes is not only personal sinfulness, but sin as the prevailing power of the old age. Sin manifests itself as a "law of sin and death" (Rom. 8:2) and as such reigns over human life until Christ's death and resurrection (Rom. 5:21). Since God's victory in Christ, grace has become the dominant power (Rom. 5:21). Thus, grace and sin are in conflict as the ruling forces of the two hostile kingdoms, the kingdom of darkness and the kingdom of grace. We can, in the light of this antithesis, see how grace can be a synonym for Christ and the Spirit. To be "in grace" (Rom. 5:2; cf. 1 Pet. 5:12) is the same as to be "in Christ" (Rom. 8:1; 2 Cor. 5:17) and "in the Spirit" (Rom. 8:9). Christ is the Lord of the new age, and the Spirit is the Lord at work in the Church (2 Cor. 3:17f.); and grace, as the typical way in which Christ rules, can be a synonym for Christ.

Grace is also the contradiction of sin in personal life. Some people interpreted the presence of grace as an invitation to sin; since God's free justification of sinners was not conditioned on moral merit, sin could not be a condition for rejection or condemnation. The more one sinned, in fact, the more the grace of acceptance abounded (Rom. 6:1, 15). Paul's answer is that it is grace that releases us from the dominion of sin; the law provokes people to sin and grace releases them from the necessity of sin (Rom. 5:14). To live in sin and in grace at the same time is unthinkable; it is to be loyal to two conflicting kingdoms. In grace, one is a "new creature in Christ" (2 Cor. 5:17) and is, through the Spirit, "alive because of righteousness" (Rom. 8:10).

H. Grace as Power. Grace is a renewing power as well as the free gift of pardon and acceptance. Grace present within the life of the Church is shown in the Church's overflow of generosity toward others (2 Cor. 8). In Tit. 2:11-13, Paul speaks of grace disciplining life unto sobriety, righteousness, and piety. Paul seems to be speaking of the power of grace within him when he says that what he is, he is by the grace of God; he works very hard, he says, but then is quick to credit his own achievements to "the grace of God which is with me" (1 Cor. 15:10). The promise that grace would be sufficient for him in his personal distress is probably also a promise of inner power through grace (2 Cor. 12:9).

Grace is sometimes personified. Paul speaks of grace reigning through righteousness (Rom. 5:20f.). It should be noted that he speaks of sin in the same way. Grace and sin, then, become the dominant powers of the new age and of the old age respectively. The grace-sin conflict is the same as the Spirit-flesh conflict (cf. Rom. 8:5-8). Grace and Spirit, then, stand for the dominant power of the new age. To live by grace, by the Spirit, and by Jesus Christ, come to one and the same thing; but when grace is mentioned, Paul probably wants to stress the surprising generosity in which the gift of power is given.

In this connection it may be mentioned that the Spirit gives grace-gifts (*charísmata*), which are, in effect, grace-powers. The one Spirit gives differing grace-gifts to individuals (1 Cor. 7:7; 1 Cor. 12). In Rom. 12:6, Paul speaks of gifts differing "according to the grace given us." But *charísmata* (grace-powers) and *pneumátika* (spirit-powers) are the same (cf. 1 Cor. 12:1; 14:1 and 1 Cor. 12:4; 1 Tim. 4:14). This suggests that Paul makes no sharp distinction between grace and the Spirit as the source of personal power in the Christian age.

I. Grace and Office. Paul saw his own apostolic office as a gift of grace. He had received "grace and apostleship" from the risen Christ to bring about the obedience of faith among the nations (Rom. 1:5). Though undeserving, he was commissioned by God Himself (Col. 3:10). His apostleship was not earned but given; it was of grace in this sense (Gal. 1:15f.; 1 Cor. 15:9). But he also spoke of the apostolic office as the result of a *chárisma*: "Are all apostles?" which is to say, "Do all have this grace-power?" (1 Cor. 12:29; cf. Rom. 12:3-8). No doubt the grace that the other apostles noted in Paul, convincing them that he was truly commissioned, was grace in the sense of power (Gal. 2:9). Others in the Church participate with him in his gift of ministry (Phil. 1:7); they are not apostles, but they share in the power of grace given to the apostles. God called him through grace (Gal. 1:15). The word "grace," then, stresses that (a) his office was not deserved but freely given, and (b) he was freely empowered to fulfil it; the strength and fruits of his efforts were attributable to God.

J. Grace Abounding. Paul exults in the abundance of grace (Rom. 5:15). Grace is multiplied to us (2 Cor. 4:15). It always exceeds our limited expectations (Eph. 2:7) as it comes in great richness (Eph. 1:7, 23). Disagreement exists as to whether Paul thinks of grace abounding only in an intensive sense, abounding to the persons who are in grace, or whether it abounds in an extensive sense, reaching those who are outside the believing community. In certain passages, its abundance suggests that it extends to all mankind; as Adam's sin led to the condemnation of all, so Christ's righteousness led to the acquittal of all (Rom. 5:18); to this, he added, as if by comment, the fact that "where sin increased, grace abounded all the more" (Rom. 5:20; cf. Rom. 11:32). In another passage (Tit. 2:11) Paul speaks ambiguously, saying, according to one translation, "For the grace of God has appeared for the salvation of all men" (RSV). But the passage is also translatable as, "For the grace of God that brings salvation has appeared to all men," leaving the extent of salvation unspecified, though grace is universally offered. To balance passages that universalize grace, one must recall Paul's dynamic coupling of grace with faith: we are saved by grace only through faith (Eph. 2:5). We must recall also his concern lest some might receive the grace of God in vain (2 Cor. 6:1). Paul's urgent summons to faith suggests that the extensive presence of grace should be understood in the light of the necessary correlation of faith and grace.

K. Grace Irresistible. Grace is the unqualified and unconditional gift of God, given freely, wholly apart from merit. It would seem, then, that grace would be irresistible; it is of God who gives it sovereignly. Yet, Paul worries that the Galatians might make void or nullify the grace of God (Gal. 2:11). He rebukes them for having fallen away from grace (Gal. 5:4). He pleads with others not to accept the grace of God in vain (2 Cor. 6:1). Paul does not systematically reconcile the sovereignty of grace with mankind's ability to deny or frustrate grace. He stresses the imperative of faith, the urgency of accepting grace and responding to it in the totality of one's life. Yet, when he turns to God in thanks, he is willing to concede that all that he is he owes to grace. The dynamic relationship between the objective work of grace and the subjective response to it is never precisely defined. Grace, in all its divine priority, cannot be taken for granted; yet, grace, in its abundance, can be wholly trusted as adequate for even the most unworthy and unfaithful.

L. Grace and Election. Divine election, according to Paul, is a divine act of grace. It is not as though God arbitrarily, apart from grace, chooses some people to whom He will give grace. It is rather that God's choice itself is a gracious choice. The remnant of Israel was "chosen by grace" (Rom. 11:5). Israel itself was elect, not "because of works, but because of his call" (Rom. 9:11). Paul does not use the word "grace" here, but his contrast between "works" and "call" is the same as the contrast between "works" and "grace." Israel owed its special role in history to electing grace. We are all, says Paul, chosen in Christ from before the foundation of the world (Eph. 1:4). This strongly suggests that God elects people for salvation in the same decision that He elected Christ as their Savior. This means, at least, that Christ, who is the gift of grace, the revelation of grace, and the medium of grace, in a sense contains us in Himself from the very beginning. Our election, therefore, is not only *unto* the receiving of grace, but is *in* grace from the beginning. Election is God's grace-filled decision to love and save sinners.

M. Grace and Love. No clear distinction is made between grace and love. *Agápē* (love) stresses God's personal disposition toward unworthy creatures, while grace stresses His freedom from obligation in saving them. But the distinction is not clearly nor consistently made. Both love and grace come to us through Christ (Rom. 5:8; Gal. 1:6). And both are unique in that they are undeserved. Both terms, *agápē* and *cháris,* are weak secular words adapted by the Bible to express the deepest dimensions of God's relation to mankind.

N. Grace as Thanksgiving. Grace refers to the Christian response to the free gift as well as to the gift itself. To "say grace" is to give thanks to the Lord (1 Tim. 1:12). The expression *cháris tǭ Theǭ,* "grace be to God," is translated as "thanks be to God," or its equivalent, in several places (Rom. 6:17; 1 Cor. 15:57; 2 Cor. 8:16; 2 Cor. 2:14). In such places, Paul is probably using the common secular expression, though the content is quite his own.

O. "Grace" in Greetings. In secular Greek usage, *chaíre* or *chaírete,* which means "rejoice," was a common form of greeting. Paul's greetings usually contain *cháris.* He is perhaps adapting the secular usage, informing it with a radical new significance. The letters usually open with a greeting of "grace and peace" from God the Father and/or the Lord Jesus Christ. They often close with a benediction that is one or another variant of "The grace of our Lord Jesus Christ be with you" (cf. Rom. 16:20; 1 Cor. 16:23; 2 Cor. 13:4; Gal. 6:18; Phil. 4:23; etc.). That his greetings and benedictions are not personal ones is suggested by the fact that he uses the same forms in letters to churches he has not personally visited, such as Rome and Colossae. They are not mere polite formulas. Paul evidently intends his greetings and farewells to be serious invocations of the grace that came, and continues to come, from the risen Lord Jesus.

P. Acts of God in the Light of Grace. By examining Paul's use of the word "grace" we see that all God's saving acts, even where the Bible does not use the word "grace," must be interpreted as acts of grace. We can overlook the weak LXX use of the word "grace" and recognize all the saving acts of God in the OT as truly gracious acts. God's covenant with Abraham is a covenant of grace. God's liberation of Israel from Egypt is a mighty act of grace. Indeed, even God's gift of the law witnesses to His grace (Rom. 3:21). His steadfast faithfulness to His covenant, during all of Israel's apostasy, was grace. The incarnation of His Son Jesus Christ was an act of grace, as was Christ's acceptance of poverty and humiliation (2 Cor. 8:9). Indeed, all of God's saving and forgiving, His calling and commissioning, His electing and justifying, are of grace. In the light of Paul's use of the word, we may say that "grace" refers to all that God is and does on behalf of His children, particularly to His free, utterly amazing decision to adopt, justify, forgive, renew, and glorify them as His new creation in Christ.

IV. Grace in the Non-Pauline Writings.*–*A. Gospels. Luke's is the only Synoptic Gospel where *cháris* occurs; it is used here in a variety of ways. Luke employs "grace" in the weak sense of Heb. *ḥēn,* as having favor or being pleasing. Mary found favor in God's sight (Lk. 1:30). Jesus found favor in the eyes of people as He grew up (Lk. 2:40, 52). Luke characterizes Jesus' words as "gracious words" (RSV) or "words of grace" (NEB). On four occasions, *cháris* is used for "thanks" (6:32-34; 17:9). Paul would see the entire Gospel of Luke as the story of God's acts of grace; but Luke does not use the word in this sense.

John uses the word "grace" only in his prologue, but then uses it four times, and very significantly. Grace comes into the world, along with truth, in the Word's incarnation (1:14). It is from Him that we receive grace, indeed "grace upon grace" (1:16). Herein lies the crucial difference between Jesus and Moses: Jesus brought grace to mankind; Moses gave only the law (1:17). The prologue to John's Gospel, then, seems to reflect Paul's Christ-centered definition of "grace."

B. Acts. The book of Acts uses "grace" in both its

special Christian sense and in a weaker, more general, sense. *Cháris* points to the salvation that appeared in Jesus Christ (Acts 15:11). The gospel is the word of grace (14:3). Miracles accompany the preaching of grace, perhaps demonstrating its power (6:8; 14:3). Grace enables Apollos to help believers (18:28). Paul commends the elders of Ephesus to the "word of his grace that has power to build you up . . ." (20:32), and the churches commend Paul and Barnabas to the grace of God for the work they did among them (14:26). The presence of grace marked the new believing community; the fellowship of unstinted love was the fruit of grace in the midst of the new communion (4:33; 11:23; 13:43; 15:40).

But *cháris* is also used to say that someone had favor in another's eyes: the early Church found *cháris* with "all the people" (2:47). Stephen recalls that Joseph found favor with Pharaoh (7:10), and David with God (7:46). The other places speak of someone doing another person a favor (24:27; 25:3, 9).

C. Hebrews. The writer of Hebrews uses "grace" in notably varied ways, some of them leaving unclear impressions. He says that Jesus became man "so that by the grace of God he might taste death for every man" (2:9). This probably means that the saving effects of Christ's death for sinners were a gift of God; it could also mean that Christ went to His death in the power of God's grace. Christians draw near to the "throne of grace" (4:16); this expression means, no doubt, that the exalted God receives petitioners and hears them out of His undeserved love. The writer also speaks vaguely of the Spirit of grace (10:29). In other places, he uses "grace" as meaning "thanks" (12:28, RSV), as a general reference to the help of God (12:15; 13:9), and in the benediction, "Grace be with all of you" (13:25).

D. Peter. In his first epistle Peter uses "grace" in association with the Christian life and ministry. He speaks of the "grace of life" (3:7) and outlines the kind of life that bespeaks "grace" or (as in RSV) God's "approval" (2:19f.). Grace is a "gift" that ought to be used for others (4:10). His readers are urged to "stand fast" in the "true grace of God" (5:12). Peter refers usually to the "grace of God" with reference to God's actions in Christ (1:10, 13; 5:10). Once he quotes Prov. 3:34: "God . . . gives grace to the humble" (5:5).

2 Peter uses the word "grace" in only one place other than the greeting (1:2). Here Peter challenges believers to "grow in the grace and knowledge of our Lord and Savior Jesus Christ" (3:18), probably having the sense of maturing in the kind of character Jesus Christ empowers one to have.

E. James. The epistle of "faith that works" uses the term "grace" only twice, both times to encourage submission to God's will. "He gives more grace," James says, somewhat vaguely, and then repeats (as 2 Peter does) the proverb: "God opposes the proud, but gives grace to the humble" (4:6).

F. Jude. Jude speaks of grace once, and there condemns people for perverting "the grace of our God into licentiousness" (v. 4). He is probably referring to people who supposed that since grace is freely given, it gives license to do as one pleases. (Cf. Paul's outrage against this attitude, Rom. 6:1.)

G. Revelation. "Grace" occurs in the Apocalypse only in the greeting and in the farewell. The same is true of 2 John. 1 and 3 John do not use the word.

V. Conclusion.–We have seen that the apostle Paul used a rather colorless Greek word, *cháris,* to signify the deepest truths about God's free and undeserved act of mercy to mankind. In secular Greek and in the LXX, *cháris* meant little more than to be approved of by a superior, to be found attractive or favorable. But in Paul's letters it became a word that vibrated with the amazing revelation that God's salvation came to sinful mankind freely, generously, and undeservedly. Used in many and varied contexts, and given several different nuances, the word "grace" always pointed to the reality of God's saving initiative. Paul did not use the word in this enormously full sense in every instance. And it must be recalled that not every NT writer used the word "grace" in the large Pauline sense. But in its vocabulary the Christian Church takes its cue from Paul and allows the word "grace" to speak to it of the broad range of God's sovereign gift of salvation. Taking the word from the pages of Paul's letters, the reader can use it as shorthand to describe the motive and manner of the whole program of redemption, from the beginning to the end, even where the word itself had not yet been put into Christian service. In this way, too, we confess that all that we have received and hope to receive, we receive not as a reward for services rendered, but as a gift, whose source is the God who became a servant to bring us salvation — which is to say, with Paul, that we are saved by grace.

Bibliography.–R. Bultmann, *Theology of the NT* (Eng. tr. 1952); E. J. Fortman, *Theology of Man and Grace: Commentary. Readings in the Theology of Grace* (1966); N. Glueck, *Ḥesed in the Bible* (Eng. tr. 1967); J. Moffatt, *Grace in the NT* (1932); R. Smith, *Bible Doctrine of Grace* (1956); *TDNT,* IX, *s.v.* χάρις κτλ. (Conzelmann, Zimmerli); T. F. Torrance, *Doctrine of Grace in the Apostolic Fathers* (1948); P. S. Watson, *Concept of Grace* (1959); W. T. Whitley, ed., *Doctrine of Grace* (1932).

L. B. SMEDES

GRACE AND UNION [Heb. *nōʿam*–'pleasantness, graciousness,' *ḥōḇᵉlîm*–'cords, ropes'] (Zec. 11:7, 10, 14); AV BEAUTY AND BANDS; NEB FAVOUR AND UNION. The names given to two symbolical staffs. (As R. C. Dentan [*IB,* VI, 1104] points out, an Ugaritic text [*UT* 68:11-19] offers an interesting, if remote, parallel. Here Baal is given two named clubs [Ugar. *ṣmd*] with which to vanquish his enemies.) Heb. *nōʿam* is characteristic of God (cf. "beauty" in Ps. 27:4; "favor" in Ps. 90:17), and here signifies Yahweh's Covenant of Grace with His people. Heb. *ḥōḇᵉlîm* may signify "union," i.e., the binding together of people (cf. 1 S. 10:5, 10, where *ḥeḇel* means "band" or "group"; cf. also Ugar. *ḥbl,* "flock of birds," "band of personages"); such union is "the intended outcome of gracious leadership" (J. Baldwin, *Haggai, Zechariah, Malachi* [*Tyndale OT Comms.,* 1972], p. 180). Thus the second staff represents the brotherhood of Judah and Israel (cf. Ezk. 37:16-23, where two sticks are joined to symbolize this unity). The breaking of the two staffs, then, symbolizes the breaking of Yahweh's covenant and of the union between Judah and Israel. G. A. L.

GRACIOUS [Heb. *ḥānan, ḥannûn, ḥēn* (Ruth 2:13; Prov. 11:16; 22:11), *ṭôḇ* (Zec. 1:13), *nāʿîm* (Ps. 135:3; 147:1); Gk. *eudokía* (Mt. 11:26; Lk. 10:21), *eúphēmos* (Phil. 4:8), *cháris* (Lk. 4:22; 2 Cor. 8:6f., 19; Col. 4:6)]; AV also SHOW, HAVE MERCY, MERCIFUL, FIND FAVOUR (Ruth 2:13), GOOD (Zec. 1:13; Mt. 11:26; Lk. 10:21), GRACE (Prov. 22:11; 2 Cor. 8:6f., 19; Col. 4:6), "of good report" (Phil. 4:8), "pleasant" (Ps. 135:3; 147:1); NEB also SHOW FAVOUR, "ask as a favour" (Ruth 2:13), "look with favour" (2 K. 13:23), "speak in favour" (Job 33:24), BENEFICENT (2 Cor. 8:19), GENEROUS (2 Cor. 8:7), etc. On the basis of one Hebrew MS, the LXX, and the Pesh., the RSV adds two lines to Ps. 145:13; "gracious" here translates Heb. *ḥāsîḏ* (the AV follows the MT; the NEB adds the lines to v. 14, and translates "unchanging"). **GRACIOUSLY** [Heb. *ḥānan* ("graciously given," Gen. 33:5; "dealt graciously," Gen. 33:11; "grant graciously," Jgs. 21:22; "graciously teach," Ps. 119:29; "speak graciously," Prov. 26:25), *nāśā' 'eṯ-rō'š* ("graciously freed," 2 K. 25:27); Gk. *kreíttōn* (He. 12:24)]; AV also "be favourable" (Jgs. 21:22), "grant graciously" (Ps. 119:29), "speak fair" (Prov. 26:25), "lift up the head" (2 K. 25:27), "better things" (He. 12:24); NEB also "be gracious" (Gen. 33:11; Prov. 26:25), "grant grace" (Ps. 119:29), "let us keep with approval" (Jgs. 21:22), "show favour" (2 K. 25:27), "better things" (He. 12:24).

Graciousness is a quality frequently attributed to God, particularly in the sense of a superior showing favor to the undeserving (for examples of this on a human level, cf. Ruth 2:13; 2 K. 25:27). One of the few recurring confessions about Yahweh affirms, "Thou, O Lord, art a God merciful and gracious, slow to anger and abounding in steadfast love and faithfulness" (Ex. 34:6; Neh. 9:17; Ps. 86:15; 103:8; 145:8; Joel 2:13; Jonah 4:2). God manifested His grace in redeeming Israel from Egypt (Ps. 111:4), and continued to manifest it during the kingdom by delivering Israel from her enemies (2 K. 13:23). He continually showed His graciousness by being faithful to the covenant (Ps. 111:5). Therefore, many petitions were made to Him "to be merciful" (e.g., Ps. 4:1 [MT 2]; 9:13 [MT 14]). When the psalmists were weak, lonely, afflicted, distressed, or when they had sinned against God, they sought His favor (Ps. 6:2 [MT 3]; 25:16; 31:9 [MT 10]; 41:4 [MT 5]). God extended His grace in meeting their needs and in forgiving their sins. God's bearing to mankind is one of grace and often He waits for the time when mankind will seek His favor so that He can demonstrate His grace (Isa. 30:18f.). Inspired by this God, the prophets call the people to repentance and base the reason for seeking God on the fact that He is gracious (Joel 2:13f.).

Graciousness may also be a human quality, especially in the sense of a kind, gentle personality. Prov. 11:16 says, "a gracious woman gets honor." To become gracious one needs to think on that which is gracious (Phil. 4:8). Gracious speech which finds its source in a pure heart is also a very desirable quality (Prov. 22:11; Col. 4:6). Luke records that the people marveled at the gracious speech of Jesus (Lk. 4:22). Gracious speech in itself is not sufficient, however; according to Prov. 26:25, the gracious speech of an enemy is never to be believed. In 2 Cor. 8:1-7, 19 Paul describes the work of sharing gifts for the relief of the saints, even out of poverty, as "this gracious work."

See also FAVOR; GRACE; MERCY.

See D. R. Ap-Thomas, *JSS*, 2 (1957), 128-145.

J. E. HARTLEY

GRAECIA grē'shə. *See* GREECE.

GRAFT [Gk. *enkentrízō*] (Rom. 11:17-24); AV GRAFF. The word occurs six times in Rom. 11. Paul assumed that those living about Rome were familiar with the process of grafting olive trees, for olive culture had been adopted by the Greeks and Romans in Paul's time. It is often pointed out that Paul's figure is not an accurate picture of how this grafting is actually done. Cultivated branches are grafted onto wild trees, not wild branches onto cultivated trees. The wild olive trees are cut back, slits made on the freshly sawed branch ends, and two or three grafts from a cultivated olive are inserted in such a way that the bark of the scion and of the branch coincide. The exposed ends are smeared with mud made from clay, and then bound with cloth or date straw, which is held by thongs made from the bark of young mulberry branches. Good fruit is thus obtained. J. Murray (*Epistle to the Romans* [*NICNT*, 1973 repr.], *loc. cit.*) and F. F. Bruce (comm. on Romans [*Tyndale NT Comms.*, 1963], pp. 217f.), however, point out that the grafting of a wild olive branch onto a cultivated olive tree was practiced occasionally (cf. Columella *De re rustica* v.9; W. Ramsay, *Expos.*, 6th ser., 9 [1905], 16-34, 152-160).

Although wild olives cannot be made cultivated olives by ingrafting, as Paul implies (v. 24), the meaning of his figure is clear. As a wild olive branch thus grafted would thrive, so Gentiles flourish spiritually when grafted onto the rich heritage of Israel. Paul warns the Gentiles, however, that as God did not spare the natural branches (the Jews), but for unbelief broke them off so that the Gentiles might be grafted in, so also He could break them off; and if God has grafted them, wild branches, onto the cultivated tree, how much more will He graft the natural branches back onto their own tree.

J. A. PATCH

GRAIN. A number of Hebrew words are used to describe the edible grains of certain cultivated crops. The AV employed the old English generic term "corn" to translate the various words, but the current association of corn with maize makes this undesirable.

The Heb. *bar, dāgān* (Ugar. *dgn*), and *šeḇer* were all used to describe types of grain, the Gk. counterparts being *kókkos* and *sítos*. Other terms include Heb. *gereś*, "crushed grain" (Lev. 2:14, 16), *karmel*, "fresh ears" (Lev. 2:14; 23:14; 2 K. 4:42), *ʿarēmâ*, "heap of grain" (Ruth 3:7; Neh. 13:15), *meʾlîlâ*, "ear" (of grain) (Dt. 23:25 [MT 26]), *qālî*, "parched grain" (Lev. 23:14; 1 S. 17:17; etc.), *qāmâ*, Gk. *spórima*, "standing grain" (Ex. 22:6 [MT 5]; Dt. 16:9; "grainfield," Mt. 12:1; etc.), *rîp̄ôṯ*, "grain" (2 S. 17:19; Prov. 27:22); and *šibbōleṯ*, Gk. *stáchys*, "ear of grain" (Ruth 2:2; Job 24:24; "head of grain," Mt. 12:1; etc.). The AV rendered the *bālîl* of Job 24:6 (RSV "fodder") as "corn."

The chief biblical grains were wheat, millet (Ezk. 4:9), barley, and spelt (*Triticum sativum* L.). Much of it was grown in the fertile Galilee valleys, the Shephelah and the Philistine plain, as well as on the plateau of Transjordan. Stalks of grain appeared early in the decorative motifs of Near Eastern art, occurring on cylinder seals and bas-reliefs from various sites and periods. The necessity for good crops stimulated fertility-cult worship, and one of the best-known grain deities was DAGON. His worship was well established in Mesopotamia during the Amorite period, and also flourished at Râs Shamrah (Ugarit).

Excavations at certain biblical sites in Palestine have disclosed the presence of storage jars containing amounts of carbonized grain. At Megiddo, a large grain-storage

Grain storage pits at Tanis (W. S. LaSor)

Workers (from top right to bottom left) break the ground with plow and hoe, scatter the seed, reap the grain, have cattle tread it out on a circular threshing floor, and separate grain from chaff. Reconstruction of Egyptian wall paintings (Royal Ontario Museum, Toronto)

pit with a pair of winding stairs was uncovered at level III (*ca.* 780-650 B.C.). The cultivation of grain was mentioned on the Gezer Calendar, a late tenth-century-B.C. limestone plaque that listed certain agricultural pursuits. The Feast of Weeks (Pentecost) occurred at the completion of the wheat harvest (Lev. 23:15f.; Dt. 16:9f.), and was a time of celebration.

Grain cultivation supplied imagery for certain parables of Jesus, such as the sower (Mt. 13:3-23 par. Mk. 4:3-20), the wheat and the weeds (Mt. 13:24-30), and the farmer and his barns (Lk. 12:16-21). The analogy of sown seed was also used by Paul in connection with the resurrection body (1 Cor. 15:35-44).

See also AGRICULTURE III.A. R. K. H.

GRANARY. *See* STOREHOUSES.

GRANDCHILDREN; GRANDSON; GRANDDAUGHTER [Heb. *bēn*] (Gen. 31:55 [MT 32:1]; 2 Ch. 22:9); AV, NEB, SON; [*ben benô*] (Gen. 11:31; Jgs. 8:22); AV [HIS] SON'S SON; [*benê bānîm*] (Jgs. 12:14; 1 Ch. 8:40; Prov. 17:6; Jer. 27:7); AV NEPHEWS, SON'S SONS, CHILDREN'S CHILDREN; [*baṯ*] (2 K. 8:26; 2 Ch. 22:2); AV DAUGHTER; [Gk. *ékgonos*–'descendant'] (1 Tim. 5:4); AV NEPHEWS. Grandchildren — especially grandsons — were regarded as a great blessing (Ruth 4:13-15; Prov. 17:6; cf. W. McKane, *Proverbs* [*OTL*, 1975], p. 503). Children were taught a sense of duty toward their own family (1 Tim. 5:4).

See also SEED.

GRAPE [Heb. *ʿēnāḇ*, *beʾušîm* (Isa. 5:2, 4), *bēser* (Job 15:33), *bōser* (Isa. 18:5; Jer. 31:29f.; Ezk. 18:2), *pereṭ* ("fallen grape," Lev. 19:10), *tîrôš* (Mic. 6:15), *ʿōlēlôṯ* ("gleaning of the grapes," Jgs. 8:2); Gk. *staphylḗ* (Mt. 7:16; Lk. 6:44; Rev. 14:18)]; AV also "sweet wine" (Mic. 6:15); NEB also BERRY (Isa. 18:5), "gleanings" (Jgs. 8:2), CLUSTERS (Rev. 14:18).

"Wild grapes" seem to be intended by Heb. *beʿušîm*; "sour" or unripe grapes are Heb. *bōser*; "unripe grapes" are also called *bēser* (Job 15:33). Partly formed grape clusters may be intended by Heb. *niṣṣâ*, "blossom, flower," in Gen. 40:10; Isa. 18:5. A "cluster" of ripe grapes is called *ʾeškōl* (e.g., Gen. 40:10; Cant. 7:7f.; Mic. 7:1), and Gk.

Painted limestone wall sculpture of festooned grapes and flowers. Originally from Tell el-Amarna, but reused by Ramses II at Hermopolis (*ca.* 1300 B.C.) (Royal Ontario Museum, Toronto)

Workers harvest grapes and tread them in a stone vat to make wine, which is then bottled and recorded. Reconstruction of a wall painting in the tomb of Nakht, Thebes (15th cent. B.C.) (Royal Ontario Museum, Toronto)

bótrys (Rev. 14:18); *see* ESHCOL. The "seeds" of grapes are Heb. *ḥarṣannîm,* the "skins," *zāg* in Nu. 6:4 (AV "kernels" and "husk"; NEB "shoot" and "berry").

In 2 Esdras are found Lat. *botrus* (9:21) and *racemus* (16:30) for "cluster," *acinium* (9:21) and *uva* (16:26) for "grape."

See also VINE. R. K. H.

GRAPE-GATHERER [part. of Heb. *bāṣar*–'gather grapes'] (Jer. 6:9; 49:9; Ob. 5); NEB VINTAGER. Grapes were harvested in August and September to be eaten as fresh fruit, dried, boiled to a thick syrup, or made into wine. Vintagers gathered the grapes and pressed them in the sun with their bare feet. Jeremiah is to search through Israel for a righteous man just as a grape-gatherer looks for grapes (6:9).

GRAPES, WILD. *See* GRAPE; VINE.

GRASP [Heb. *kap*–'palm'] (Ps. 71:4; Jer. 15:21); AV HAND; NEB CLUTCHES, omits in Jer. 15:21; [*qārā'*–'encounter, meet'] (Prov. 27:16); AV BEWRAY; NEB "pick up"; [*lāpaṯ*] (Jgs. 16:29); AV "take hold"; NEB "put arms round"; [*ḥāzaq*] (Isa. 45:1); AV HOLD; NEB TAKE; [*tāpaś*] (Ezk. 29:7); AV "take hold"; [Gk. *ginṓskō*–'know, understand'] (Lk. 18:34); AV KNOW; [*harpagmós*] ("a thing to be grasped," Phil. 2:6); AV ROBBERY; NEB "snatch at." By derivation the term may denote either an act of seizing or the result of the action. In Lk. 18:34 the reference is to grasping with the intellect, or comprehending.

Greek *harpagmós* occurs rarely in secular Greek, not at all in the LXX, and only once in the NT. The term has been interpreted in many different ways. The AV renders it "robbery"; the meaning here is that Christ, "being in the form of God," in fact always possessed equality with God and would not have needed to seize it. The RSV renders it "a thing to be grasped," perhaps referring to a prize, booty, or windfall (cf. Bauer, rev., pp. 108f.). W. Foerster suggests a third meaning for the phrase *harpágmon hygḗsato*: "to take up an attitude to something as one does to what presents itself as a prey to be grasped, a chance discovery, or a gift of fate, i.e., appropriating and using it, treating it as something desired and won" (*TDNT,* I, 473). The sense of Phil. 2:6b would then be that "Jesus did not regard equality with God as a gain to be utilised" (*op. cit.,* p. 474; but cf. *Expos.G.T.,* III, 436f.). In any case, Paul's point in this passage is that Christ was willing for our sakes to lay aside His equality with God, rather than treating it as a treasure to be held and utilized for Himself. *See also* KENOSIS.

See TDNT, I, *s.v.* ἁρπαγμός (Foerster). N. J. O.

GRASS [Heb. *deše',* *ḥāṣîr, yereq, 'ēśeḇ, 'āḥû, gēz, ḥ^ašaš,* vb. *dāšā'*; Aram. *deṯe', '^aśaḇ*; Gk. *chórtos*]; AV also HERB(S), HAY, CHAFF, MEADOW, etc.; NEB also REEDS, PASTURE, GREEN PLANT, HERBAGE, HERBS, CROPS, "heat" (Isa. 5:24), GREEN, etc.

The Heb. *'ēśeḇ* is a general term for "vegetation" and is so rendered by the RSV in Zec. 10:1. Besides "grass" (e.g., Dt. 11:15; Job 5:25; Ps. 72:16; 92:7 [MT 8]; Prov. 19:12; Am. 7:2; Mic. 5:7 [MT 6]), the RSV translates it "herb" (e.g., Dt. 32:2), "herbage" (Jer. 14:6), and "plants" (Gen. 1:11f.; 2 K. 19:26; Isa. 37:27). The Aramaic form occurs in Dnl. 4:15, 25, 32f. (MT 12, 22, 29f.); 5:21. Another general term is *ḥāṣîr* (e.g., 1 K. 18:5; 2 K. 19:26; Job 40:15), rendered "hay" in Prov. 27:25, AV.

The Heb. *deše'* is rendered "vegetation" by the RSV in Gen. 1:11f., "tender grass" in Dt. 32:2; 2 K. 19:26; Isa. 37:27, and "grass" in Job 6:5; 38:27; Isa. 66:14; Jer. 14:5; the AV often has "herbs." The Aramaic form occurs in Dnl. 4:15, 23 (MT 12, 20), "tender grass." The verb form in Jer. 50:11 (Heb. *dāšâ*), a heifer "at grass," is in the NEB a heifer "after threshing."

The RSV has "reed grass" (for *'āḥû*) in Gen. 41:2, 18, where the NEB has "reeds" and the AV "meadow"; in Job 8:11 the RSV and the NEB have "reeds" (AV "flag"). Other terms are *yereq* (Nu. 22:4), *gēz* ("mown grass," Ps. 72:6; cf. Am. 7:1), *ḥ^ašaš* ("dry grass," Isa. 5:24; AV "chaff"; NEB "heat"; cf. 33:11).

The NT word is Gk. *chórtos* (Mt. 6:30; 14:19; Mk. 6:39; Lk. 12:28; Jn. 6:10; etc.), which is "hay" in 1 Cor. 3:12, "blade" in Mk. 4:28, and "plants" in Mt. 13:26.

Grass was not sown artificially in antiquity, and no distinction was made between the true grasses (N.O. *Gramineae*) and other herbs. The rooftop grass (Ps. 129:6; Isa. 37:27) consisted of seeds germinating in the mud roofs. They withered quickly under the hot sun. Dew or rain on grass is mentioned in Dt. 32:6; Ps. 72:6; Prov. 19:12; Mic. 5:7.

Although human beings are concerned with abundance of grass for their cattle, it is God who ultimately makes the grass grow (Dt. 11:15; cf. Job 38:27), and He can punish His people by letting the grass wither (Dt. 29:23; Jer. 12:4). Metaphorically, grass may be a symbol of abundance (Job 5:25, parallel to "many"; Ps. 72:16; 92:7); more frequently, it symbolizes the brevity of life (Isa. 51:12, parallel to "death"). This theme runs through the Psalms (37:2; 90:5f.; 102:11 [MT 12]; 103:15f.) and is dramatized in Isa. 40:6-8 (cf. 37:27): only God is eternal; people are temporal and mortal. Isaiah's summary may have been a "catechetical source" for the NT (J. Adamson, comm. on James [*NICNT,* 1976], p. 63). James (1:10) and Peter (1 Pet. 1:24) quoted Isaiah to remind their readers that human life apart from faith does not go on forever. Our Lord combined this theme with that of the beauty of the flora to point to God's providential care (Mt. 6:30 par. Lk. 12:28).

See also FLORA; HERB; REED.

R. K. H.
R. W. V.

GRASSHOPPER. *See* LOCUST.

GRATING [Heb. *miḵbār*] (Ex. 27:4; 35:16; 38:4f., 30; 39:39); AV GRATE. A "network of bronze" (Ex. 27:4; 38:4) on the altar of burnt offering in the court of the tabernacle. The grating was situated under the ledge of the altar, and extended halfway down the side. At its four corners were rings through which poles were inserted for carrying the altar.

GRATITUDE. *See* THANK.

GRAVE. *See* BURIAL III.

GRAVE; GRAVING. *See* CARVING; CRAFTS.

GRAVEL. The term occurs twice in the RSV (Prov. 20:17; NEB "grit"; Lam. 3:16) for Heb. *ḥāṣāṣ,* from the verb *ḥāṣaṣ,* "divide." These passages suggest the frequent occurrence of grit in the coarse bread. The source of the grit may have been the grindstones themselves, or perhaps smaller stones originally mixed with the grain at threshing time and ground even smaller when the flour was being made. The teeth of some Egyptian mummies are worn level with the gums due to the incidence of grit and gravel in foodstuffs, bread, and confections.

GRAVEN IMAGE. *See* IDOL.

GRAVITY. In the RSV this term occurs only in Tit. 2:7 (NEB "high principle"), where it renders Gk. *semnótēs.* In his teaching Titus is to set an example of the type of dignity and seriousness that compels the respect even of opponents (cf. v. 8).

GRAY. *See* COLOR IV.D.

GREASE (Ps. 119:70, AV). *See* GROSS.

GREAT. "Great" translates a wide variety of Hebrew and Greek terms. In the OT it most often renders Heb. *gāḏôl* (also *gāḏal*–'be or become great') and *raḇ* (also *rāḇâ*–'be or become numerous, great'). Heb. *gāḏôl* can indicate both quantitative and qualitative greatness. In the quantitative sense of "much, large" (in dimensions, extent, intensity, etc.) it occurs as "great lights" (Gen. 1:16), "great darkness" (15:12), "great nation" (17:20), "great plenty" (41:29), "Great Sea" (Nu. 34:7), "great slaughter" (1 S. 4:10), etc. Expressing qualitative greatness of significance, excellence, importance, etc., it appears as "great sight" (Ex. 3:3, in reference to the burning bush), "great acts of judgment" (6:6), "great and terrible God" (Dt. 7:21), "great signs" (Josh. 24:17), "Great is the Lord" (Ps. 145:3), etc. Heb. *gāḏal* and its derivatives *gāḏôl* and *gōḏel* are the terms most frequently used to express the greatness of God, of His name, and of His actions and expressions of Himself on behalf of Israel. Thus, God is great (2 S. 7:22; 1 Ch. 16:25), He accomplishes "great and terrible things" (Dt. 10:21), His name is great (Josh. 7:9; 1 S. 12:22), His wrath is great (2 K. 22:13; 23:26), as are His power (Neh. 1:10), love (Ps. 57:10 [MT 11]; 86:13), and goodness (Neh. 9:25).

The other common OT terms, Heb. *raḇ* and *rōḇ,* mean "many, numerous, abundant," and designate mainly greatness of quantity. Thus, "the wickedness of man was great in the earth" (Gen. 6:5), "great household" (26:14), "his mercy is great" (2 S. 24:14), "the number of your days is great" (Job 38:21), etc. But it is also used for "great" in other senses, e.g., "greatness of God's majesty (Ex. 15:7), "great and noble Osnappar" (Ezr. 4:10), "great God" (5:8), "great king" (5:11), "I will divide him a portion with the great" (Isa. 53:12).

One interesting Hebrew expression for "great" involves the use of *ʾᵉlōhîm,* "gods." In 1 S. 14:15 the battle caused "a very great panic" (Heb. *ḥerdaṯ ʾᵉlōhîm,* lit. "trembling of the gods," i.e., it was enough to make the gods tremble). And in Jonah 3:3, Nineveh was an "exceedingly great city" (Heb. *ʿîr gᵉḏôlâ lēʾlōhîm,* lit. "a large city for the gods," i.e., the city would seem large even to the gods). The NEB follows many modern commentators (e.g., E. A. Speiser [*AB,* 1964], pp. 3, 5; B. Vawter, *On Genesis* [1977], pp. 40f.) in understanding the *rûa(a)ḥ ʾᵉlōhîm* of Gen. 1:2 as a great or "mighty wind" (but cf. E. J. Young, *Studies in Genesis One* [1976], pp. 36-42); cf. the similar understanding in Gen. 23:6 ("mighty prince," Heb. *nᵉśîʾ ʾᵉlōhîm*); Ps. 68:15 (MT 16) ("mighty mountain," Heb. *har-ʾᵉlōhîm*); and the same use of *ʾel,* "god," in Ps. 80:10 (MT 11) ("mighty cedars," Heb. *ʾarzê-ʾēl*); for other possible examples see BDB, pp. 42f.

In the OT "greatly" is sometimes expressed by means of pleonasms. Thus, e.g., God says "I will greatly multiply" (Heb. *harbâ ʾarbeh*) Hagar's descendants (Gen. 16:10); Laban tells Jacob "you longed greatly [Heb. *niḵsōp niḵsaptâ*] for your father's house" (Gen. 31:30); David rejoiced greatly" (Heb. *śāmaḥ śimḥâ gᵉḏôlâ,* lit. "he rejoiced a great joy") when the people gave their freewill offerings (1 Ch. 29:9); the father of the righteous "will greatly rejoice" (*Q gîl yāgîl, K gôl yāgûl*; Prov. 23:24) as did Isaiah (*śôś ʾāśîś,* 61:10).

The much more common way of expressing "greatly" is the use of the adverb *mᵉʾōḏ,* "very." Thus the phrase "he [God] is greatly to be praised" is Heb. *mᵉhullāl mᵉʾōḏ* (1 Ch. 16:25 par. Ps. 96:4; Ps. 48:1 [MT 2]; 145:3). Heb. *mᵉʾōḏ* also modifies bless (Gen. 24:35), fear (Gen. 32:7 [MT 8]; Josh. 9:24; 10:2; etc.), rejoice (1 S. 11:15; 1 K. 5:7 [MT 21]; Zech. 9:9), etc.

The most common NT words translated as "great" are Gk. *mégas* (comparative, *meízōn,* e.g., Mt. 18:1; 1 Cor. 13:13; superlative *mégistos,* 2 Pet. 1:4, "very great") and *polýs* (comparative, *pleíon,* Mt. 12:41f. par. Lk. 11:31f.; Acts 15:28), which the LXX uses to translate Heb. *gāḏôl* and *raḇ* respectively. Gk. *mégas,* like its Hebrew counterpart, can express greatness in both a quantitative and a qualitative sense. Quantitatively, it can indicate greatness of extension in space ("great stone," Mt. 27:60; "great mountain," Rev. 8:8), of number ("great herd of swine," Mk. 5:11), of age ("small and great," Acts 26:22; Rev. 11:18), of magnitude ("great reward," He. 10:35), of intensity ("great joy," Mt. 2:10; "great power," Acts 4:33; "great clamor," 23:9; "great lamentation," 8:2; "great storm," Mk. 4:37), etc. Qualitatively, it can express greatness of significance, excellence, dignity, and importance: "great signs and wonders" (Mt. 24:24; Acts 6:8), "greater [*meízō*] things than these" (Jn. 1:50), "great God and Savior" (Tit. 2:13, said of Christ [see *TDNT,* IV, 538]), "great prophet" (Lk. 7:16), "great mystery" (Eph. 5:32 [AV]; 1 Tim. 3:16), "great and first commandment" (Mt. 22:38). The Day of Judgment is called "the great day" (Gk. *hē hēméra hē megálē,* Acts 2:20; Jude 6; Rev. 6:17; 16:14; cf. Heb. *yôm-yhwh haggāḏôl,* "the great day of the Lord," Zeph. 1:14; Mal. 4:5 [MT 3:23]). Gk. *polýs,* like Heb. *raḇ,* has primarily a quantitative, numerical sense, and can mean "many, numerous, much, extensive": "great crowds" (Mt. 4:25; 8:1), "great possessions" (Mt. 19:22), "great learning" (Acts 26:24), "great opposition" (1 Thess. 2:2), "great glory" (Mt. 24:30), "great love" (Eph. 2:4).

"Greatly" renders Gk. *lían,* "much" (Mt. 27:14; 2 Jn. 4; 3 Jn. 3), *méga* (Rev. 17:6), *megálōs,* "greatly" (Phil. 4:10), *polýs,* "much" (Acts 18:27), *sphódra,* "very much" (e.g., Mt. 17:23), etc. John's Jewish background may be reflected in his use of pleonasm to express "greatly" in Jn. 3:29. Here Jesus states that the friend of the bridegroom "rejoices greatly" (Gk. *chará chaírei*; cf. L. Morris, comm. on John [*NICNT,* 1971], p. 241 n. 109). The only NT occurrence of "greatness" (*mégethos,* Eph. 1:19) refers to the "immeasurable greatness of [God's] power" in believers.

On Acts 8:10, "'This man is that power of God which is called Great,'" see *TDNT,* IV, 540f. *See also* SIMON MAGUS.

Bibliography.–TDNT, IV, *s.v.* μέγας κτλ.: μέγας (Grundmann); *TDOT,* II, *s.v.* "gādhal" (Bergmann-Ringgren, Mosis).

R. C. TOGTMAN
G. A. L.

GREAT BIBLE. *See* ENGLISH VERSIONS III.F.

GREAT KING (Hos. 5:13; 10:6, RSV, NEB). *See* JAREB.

GREAT SEA. *See* MEDITERRANEAN SEA.

GREAVES. *See* WEAPONS OF WAR.

GRECIA; GRECIANS. AV terms for GREECE (Dnl. 8:21; 10:20; 11:2; and Apocrypha) and GREEKS (e.g., Joel 3:6 [MT 4:6]); *see also* HELLENIST.

GREECE [Heb. *yāwān*; Gk. *Hellas*]. A region or federation of city-states in the lower Balkan peninsula, apparently approximately the same area as modern Greece (though not politically united for most of the biblical period).

- I. Name
- II. Geography
  - A. Location and Area
  - B. Mountains
  - C. Rivers and Lakes
  - D. Geology
  - E. Divisions
  - F. Climate
- III. Early Civilizations (6100-1200 B.C.)
  - A. Pre-Minoan
  - B. Minoan
  - C. Mycenaean
- IV. The Great Migrations (1200-850 B.C.)
  - A. Troy
  - B. Dorians
  - C. Aeolians and Ionians
- V. Rise of the Greek City-States (850-546 B.C.)
  - A. Cultural and Political Revival
  - B. Colonial Expansion
  - C. Warfare (750-550 B.C.)
  - D. Tyranny
  - E. Athens and the Rise of Democracy
  - F. Religion
- VI. Triumph of Greece (546-466 B.C.)
  - A. Persia *v.* Athens
  - B. Spartan Alliance
  - C. Ionian Revolt and Battle of Marathon
  - D. Persian Invasion of Mainland Greece
  - E. Athenian Alliance
  - F. Western Greeks
  - G. Literature, Philosophy, and Art
- VII. Crisis of the Fifth Century: Peloponnesian Wars
- VIII. Transition of the Fourth Century B.C.
- IX. Alexander and His Successors (336-217 B.C.)
- X. Coming of Rome (229-146 B.C.)
- XI. Rule of Rome (146 B.C.-A.D. 100)
- XII. Biblical References

I. Name.–In earliest times no single name was universally and exclusively used either of the people or of the land of Greece. In Homer, three appellations—*Achaioi, Danaoi,* and *Argeioi* — were with no apparent discrimination applied to all the Greeks. The Hebrews called them Ionians (see IV.C below; *see also* JAVAN). The name *Hellēnes,* which in historical times came into general use as a collective appellation, was applied in Homer to a small tribe in Thessaly. But the corresponding name *Hellas* was not primarily a geographical term but designated wherever the Hellenes had their own states or cities. In the 4th cent. B.C. many felt, as did Isocrates, that even "Hellene" stood not so much for a distinction in race as for preeminence of culture, in contrast to the despised "barbarian." Hence there was much dispute over whether certain peoples, e.g., the Epirotes, Macedonians, and even the Thessalians, should be considered Hellenes and included in Hellas. Aristotle said that the word *Graikoi* (Lat. *Graeci*) was an older name for those who were later called Hellenes. The meaning and truth of this statement are alike in doubt, but he probably referred only to the tribe living near Dodona in Epirus. At any rate, *Graeci* and *Graecia* practically owed their introduction to the Romans after their contact with the Greeks in the war with Pyrrhus; consequently the terms included Epirus and Macedonia (which "Hellenes" and "Hellas" did not).

II. Geography.–*A. Location and Area.* Hellas as the land of the Hellenes was used in a broad sense to include not only Greece proper but also the islands of the Ionian and Aegean seas; the seaboards of the Hellespont, Pontus, and Asia Minor; the flourishing colonial regions of Magna Graecia, Sicily, and Crete; and occasionally Cyprus, Cyrene, and the scattered colonies dotting the shore of the Mediterranean, almost to the Pillars of Hercules. Graecia, however, was restricted to continental Greece, which forms the southern extremity of the Balkan peninsula. While the Romans included Macedonia and Epirus, it is preferable to limit Greece to the territory lying roughly below 40° and extending almost to 36° North Latitude, and ranging between 17° and 23° East Longitude. If, as is proper, one includes the immediately adjacent islands, its greatest length, from Mt. Olympus in the north to Cythera in the south, is about 450 km. (280 mi.); its greatest breadth, from Cephallenia in the west to Euboea in the east, is about 390 km. (240 mi.). The area, however, owing to the great irregularity of its contour, is far less than one might expect, amounting to about 78,000 sq. km. (30,000 sq. mi.). With an area, therefore, considerably less than that of Portugal, Greece has a coastline longer than those of Spain and Portugal combined.

B. Mountains. The northern boundary of Greece is

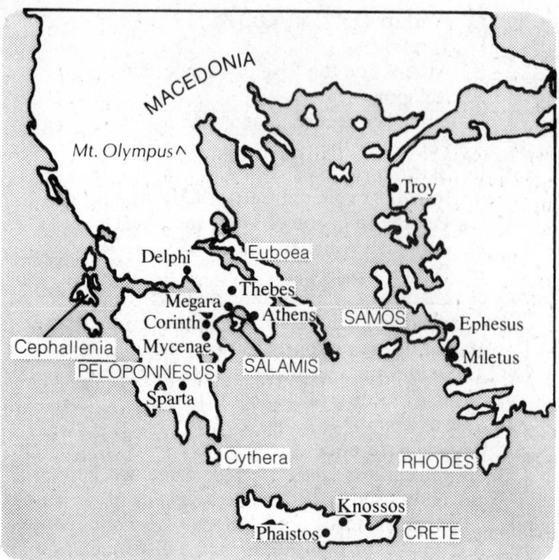

formed by an irregular series of mountain chains, beginning on the west with the Aeroceraunian range and ending in Mt. Olympus (2920 m. [9570 ft.]) on the east. Intersecting this line, the lofty Pindus range, forming the backbone of northern Greece, extends southward to Mt. Tymphrestus (2320 m. [7610 ft.]) in Aetolia, where spurs radiate through central Greece. The highest peaks are Mt. Corax (2490 m. [8180 ft.]) in Aetolia, Mt. Oeta (2150 m. [7060 ft.]), Parnassus (2500 m. [8200 ft.]), Helicon (1790 m. [5870 ft.]), Cithaeron (1410 m. [4630 ft.]) on the boundary between Boeotia and Attica, Mt. Geranea (1370 m. [4500 ft.]) N of the Isthmus, and, in Attica, Parnes (1410 m. [4640 ft.]), Pentelicon (1110 m. [3640 ft.]), and Hymettus (1030 m. [3370 ft.]). Along the eastern coast extends a broken range of mountains, the highest peaks of which are Ossa (1950 m. [6400 ft.]), Pelion (1620 m. [5310 ft.]), and, in Euboea, which virtually belongs to this range, Dirphys (1750 m. [5730 ft.]) and Ocha (1410 m. [4610 ft.]). Southern Greece, or the Peloponnesus, is united to central Greece only by a narrow isthmus (now cut by a canal 6 km. [4 mi.] long), with a minimum altitude of about 76 m. (250 ft.). In the northern portion, a confused mass of mountains rises to great heights: Cyllene (2380 m. [7790 ft.]), Erymanthus (2230 m. [7300 ft.]), Maenalus (1980 m. [6500 ft.]), all in Arcadia, Panachaicus (1930 m. [6320 ft.]) in Achaia, and, running southward through Laconia, the two important ranges called Taÿgetus (2410 m. [7900 ft.]) and Parnon (1960 m. [6430 ft.]). Minor ranges jut seaward in Argolis, Laconia, and Messenia.

C. Rivers and Lakes. The rainfall in Greece is not abundant and is confined largely to late autumn and winter. Whether the present rainfall differs much in amount from that of antiquity is disputed, although presumably the progressive denudation of the mountains since the 5th cent. A.D. has resulted in a corresponding loss in humidity. Even in antiquity, however, the rivers of Greece were much like the arroyos of the southwestern portion of the United States, which are in winter raging mountain torrents, and in summer dry channels. Because the sea is near all points in Greece, the rivers are short, and the scarcity of springs makes them dependent upon direct rainfall. The more considerable rivers include, in northern Greece (Thessaly), the Peneius, with its tributaries; in central Greece (Aetolia), the Achelous and the Evenus; the Spercheius, flowing between Oeta and Othrys into the Maliac Gulf; the storied, but actually insignificant, Ilyssus and Cephissus of the Attic plain; in southern Greece, the Alpheius, rising in Arcadia and flowing westward through Elis, and the Eurotas, which drains Laconia. In eastern Greece a series of basins become lakes in winter and are pestilent marshes in summer unless nature or man has afforded an outlet. The former is the case with the Peneius, which has cut a channel through the celebrated Vale of Tempe. Lake Copais in Boeotia affords an example of human activity. The prehistoric Minyae are credited with first enlarging the natural outlets and so draining the basin for a time. Similar basins occur at Lake Boebeis in Thessaly and Lake Stymphalus in Arcadia. The relatively few such basins in western Greece include Lake Pambotis in Epirus and Lake Trichonis in Aetolia. Often if no surface outlet to these basins exists, subterranean channels (called katavothrae by the Greeks) are formed in the calcareous rock, through which the waters drain and occasionally are again brought to the surface at a lower level.

D. Geology. The western half of Greece, in which the mountain ranges run generally from north to south, consists of a formation of greyish and yellowish-white compact limestone, while the eastern half—Macedonia, Thessaly, Euboea, Cyllene, and the mountains from Artemision to Cape Malea and Taygetus — together with the greater part of Attica and of the Cyclades, consists of mica-schist and crystalline-granular limestone (marble). Tertiary formations occur in narrow strips on the northern and northwestern slope of the ranges in the Peloponnesus and in the valley of the Eurotas in Boeotia and Euboea. The parallel elevations of similar or contemporary formation and the earthquakes frequent in all ages, especially in southern and central Greece and the islands of the Aegean, evince volcanic action. Perennially active volcanoes are nowhere found in Greece, but new formations due to volcanic action are most clearly seen on the island of Thera among the Cyclades, where they have occurred within the last half-century. The solfatara between Megara and Corinth, the abundant hot springs at widely scattered points in Greece, bear witness to the volcanic character of the region and the ruined temples of many ancient sites venerated for their sanctity in antiquity, like Delphi and Olympia. History records repeated instances of cities engulfed by tidal waves of appalling height.

E. Divisions. Mention has already been made of the sinuous coastline of Greece, and the land has been spoken of as consisting of three divisions. Northern Greece, to which Epirus and Thessaly belong, is marked off from central Greece by the deep indentations of the Ambracian Gulf on the west and the Maliac Gulf on the east. The Pegasaean Gulf, virtually continued by Lake Boebeis, reaches far into Thessaly and divides it from Magnesia, which lies to the east. The land of the Dolopians really belongs to northern Greece. Central Greece consists of Acarnania and Aetolia on the west and Phocis, Boeotia, and Attica (with the adjacent island of Euboea) on the east, separated by a group of lesser states — Aenis, Oetaea, Doris, Locris, and Phocis. Southern Greece is separated from central Greece by the Corinthian and Saronic gulfs, which almost meet at the Isthmus of Corinth and are now, after repeated efforts dating from the time of Julius Caesar, united by a sea-level canal. Megaris, which by its position belongs to central Greece, is here in accordance with its political affinities and predilections classed with Corinth, the keeper of the isthmus, as belonging to southern Greece. Facing the Corinthian Gulf, Achaia forms the northern division of the Peloponnesus, touching Elis, Arcadia, and Argolis, which belt the peninsula in this order from west to east. Arcadia is the only political division that does not have access to the sea; it occupies the great central plateau intersected by lesser ranges of varying height. The southernmost divisions, Messenia and Laconia, are deeply indented by the Messeniac and Laconic gulfs, and Laconia is separated from the peninsula of Argolis by the Argolic Gulf, all of which head in a somewhat northwesterly direction. Of the subjacent islands, which a reasonable view must include in the boundaries of Greece, Euboea has already been mentioned; but one should add the group of great islands lying in the Ionian Sea, namely Corcyra, Leukas, Ithaca, Cephallenia, Zacynthus, and Cythera at the mouth of the Laconic Gulf, as well as Salamis and Aegina in the Saronic Gulf.

F. Climate. The climate of Greece has probably changed little from ancient times, except that it may have been more salubrious when the land was more thickly populated and better cultivated. Herodotus said that of all countries, Greece possessed the most happily tempered seasons; Hippocrates and Aristotle commended its absence of extremes of heat and cold as favorable for intelligence and energy. But because of extreme variations in the land's altitude, the climate varies greatly in different districts. In the highlands of the interior the winter is often cold and severe, the snow lying on the ground until late in the spring, while in the lowlands near the sea there is rarely any severe weather and snow is almost unknown. The following data for Athens may be taken as a basis for comparison: humidity, 41 percent; rainfall, 33.5 cm. (13.2 in.), distributed over 100 days; mean temperature, January, 9° C. (48° F.), July, 27° C. (81° F.). Greece lies open to the northern winds that during certain seasons give a bracing quality to the air not always present in places of the same latitude.

W. A. HEIDEL

***III. Early Civilizations* (6100-1200 B.C.)**.–*A. Pre-Minoan*. Ordinarily historians identify the earliest settlements with the Early Neolithic I (6100-5100 B.C.) villages in the Aegean isles. These settlements are known at Knossos (Cnossus) and elsewhere and dated by carbon-14 to *ca.* 6100 B.C. The settlers built flat-roofed houses of fired brick. They imported obsidian from the island of Melos, which indicates a seagoing trade network. Evidence for religion includes anthropomorphic figurines, which can be interpreted in terms of ancestor worship, or, more generally, a fertility cult.

By the Neolithic II period (5100-3000 B.C.) regular town planning, indicating a complex social structure, is evident. Houses consisted of clusters of rooms with pebbled courtyards.

During the Early Bronze period (3000-2000 B.C.) waves of immigrants from Asia Minor settled in the Cyclades islands and in east and central Crete. These people founded the Minoan culture.

B. Minoan. At the beginning of the second phase of the Early Bronze Age a new people appeared in the plain of Phaistos (Phaestus). Perhaps their most striking innovation was a large, circular, thatched charnel house measuring up to 13 m. (42 ft.) in diameter. Several hundred skeletons have been found in one charnel house, suggesting long use by the extended family.

The early Minoan people used copper extensively, revealing great skill in metallurgy. They cast tools, weapons, and the famous votive double axes that appear to have played a vital role in Minoan religion. They also worked gold into jewelry with great craftsmanship. Their villages and towns yield faience, steatite, and fine Egyptian stone wares.

From 2000 to 1600 B.C. Minoan civilization was at its height. Their material culture and city planning were impressive. Their trade network extended from Egypt to mainland Greece and eastward to Anatolia and Syria. Economic success seems to have required invention of a writing system, pictographic in its earliest stages. The most famous and perhaps earliest extant example of this picture writing is the Phaistos Disk, on which the text was impressed in a spiral with dies while the clay was still soft. Scribes eventually developed a cursive script. Some scholars have proposed that this native language was Semitic and that the early Minoans were therefore a Semitic people (cf. C. H. Gordon, *Forgotten Scripts* [1971]).

Knossos and Phaistos, cities about 40 km. (25 mi.) apart on Crete, were the centers of Minoan civilization. Other traces of this civilization are found on a number of the Aegean islands, most dramatically on Thera (modern Santorini), 100 km. (60 mi.) N of Crete.

Minoan civilization at Knossos and Phaistos is generally dated 1900-1700 B.C. These centers traded briskly with cities to the north and west. The elaborate palace at Knossos occupied about 1½ ha. (3¾ acres). Masterful wall paintings, weaving, numerous examples of bronze smelting, and skillful ceramics and masonry provide further evidence of their civilization.

The possible eastern origins of this civilization may be enshrined in the Europa myth. The story is set in Canaan or Phoenicia (Tyre), where Europa and her five brothers are born to Agenor and Telephassa. Zeus falls in love with the beautiful Europa and appears in her father's herd as a snow-white bull. He carries her on his back to Crete, where as an eagle he ravishes her. Europa bears Zeus three sons: Rhadamanthys, Sarpedon, and Minos, who founded and ruled respectively Phaistos, Mallia, and

Minoan octopus vase. The dark coloration on a light background and the marine motif were typical of this period (*ca.* 1450 B.C.) (National Museum, Athens; picture Rosenthal Art Slides)

Knossos. From Minos comes the name of the Minoan civilization.

Religion in the Minoan realm apparently concentrated on worship of the Great Mother, a feature it held in common with Anatolian religion. The Great Mother had many names on Crete, especially Hellotis. (She was best known on the Greek mainland as Demeter.) She appeared in Minoan art as the lady of the snakes and later as a huntress. Sometimes she was flanked by lions, at other times by doves. Her consort was a younger male deity whom she overshadowed in importance. This pairing calls to mind Cybele and Attis, Tammuz and Ishtar, Adonis and Astarte, Demeter and Hades, or even ʾEl and Asherah at Ugarit. Her worship evidently included a reenactment of a sacred marriage to Zeus.

The destruction of Knossos and other centers of Minoan civilization is usually attributed to earthquakes *ca.* 1700 B.C. These civilizations, however, were too vigorous to disappear; the palace at Knossos, for instance, was rebuilt and the city flourished again. The date of the true end of the Minoans is still debated. One of the most popular theories is that the violent eruption of Thera (modern Santorini) destroyed all of Crete *ca.* 1450. Yet excavations reveal that no such disaster overtook Knossos, which seems inexplicable. Another view is that mainland Greeks seized Knossos *ca.* 1400 and the city continued as a prosperous, but now Mycenaean, city-state until the Dorians invaded and demolished it *ca.* 1180. In any case, after *ca.* 1600 the rising Middle and Late Helladic (Mycenaean) peoples gradually eclipsed the Minoans. Most Minoan palaces were violently destroyed *ca.* 1400.

C. Mycenaean. It is this civilization that figures in the myths of Homer and Greek memories of the Heroic Age. The names of Mycenaean centers appear in Homer, e.g., as the birthplaces of heroes, and probably represent genuine memories of the glories of Mycenae.

The destruction of Minoan civilization or its decline and displacement allowed the development of new centers of power in the mainland cities. These centers had been occupied as early as 6200 B.C. (at Nea Nikomedia in Macedonia), but not until the Minoan power was broken did these peoples advance in power and influence. In the Middle and Late Bronze (Helladic) Ages the tide of immigration turned from the east to the north, and Greek-speaking peoples occupied the mainland. These peoples produced a vigorous art, invested prodigious energies in building grave circles for their heroes, prospered mightily in trade, and vanquished neighbors through exceptional skill in war. Their art was distinctive and highly developed. Their gold-foil death masks and gold-inlay hunting scenes on bronze daggers are rightly famous. *See* Plate 23.

The grave circles of Mycenae are very unusual. Grave Circle B, e.g., was laid out 27.5 m. (90 ft.) in diameter. It contained twenty-four graves of heroes buried with exten-

Mycenean grave circle (Rosenthal Art Slides)

sive weaponry and often with the gold-foil death masks mentioned above. The grave goods resemble those of Albania of the same period, leading some scholars to suggest that the Mycenaeans owed their origins to central Albania (cf. R. A. Crossland and A. Birchall, eds., *Bronze Age Migrations in the Aegean* [1974], pp. 189-197).

About 1450 B.C. a Greek dynasty came to power at Knossos and ruled Crete. Its scribes developed a script now called "Linear B" (cf. J. Chadwick, *Decipherment of Linear B* [1958]), to record their form of Greek for administrative and economic texts. Perhaps more importantly for the social historian, the texts reveal an extensive bureaucracy that administered every aspect of the national life.

The principle figures of Mycenaean religion have long been known from the stanzas of Homer and Hesiod, but a coherent picture of beliefs and cultic acts has not emerged. Excavations within the citadel at Mycenae, however, brought to light a temple complex built about 1250 B.C. and destroyed near the end of that century. It contained a room furnished with platforms, a storeroom harboring nineteen idols with arms raised and extended outward (in blessing?), and a collection of seventeen broken clay snakes modeled naturalistically. One tablet from Pylos mentions offerings to seven Greek deities, among them Poseidon, Hermes, and Hera. The offerings included gold cups, bowls, and male and female slaves.

At least at Pylos a large body of religious functionaries was distinguishable from the civil bureaucrats. The king was central to the religious society. Possibly the elaborate burials of Mycenae indicate that Mycenaean religion involved ancestor worship. Such beliefs were well known in classical times, e.g., in the dramas of Aeschylus.

The Mycenaeans lived side by side with other great powers of the period, particularly the Egyptians, Phoenicians, Hittites, and smaller Anatolian kingdoms. They traded extensively with these lands for goods not naturally

Part of an inventory of vessels and furniture found in 1952 at Pylos on the southwestern coast of the Peloponnesus. This palm-leaf-shaped tablet was invaluable as a conclusive check on the decipherment of Linear B (National Archaeological Museum, Athens)

available in mainland Greece or Crete, e.g., gold, rope, papyrus, and linen from Egypt, silver from Asia Minor, copper from Syria, Cyprus, and the Sinai, and tin from Cirrha near Delphi. In return Mycenae exported timber, hides, dyes, wine, and olive oil to its trading partners, which included Troy, Italy, and Sicily.

In military matters Mycenae enjoyed success. Mycenaean warriors fought from horse-drawn chariots beginning in the 16th cent. B.C. Hittite records mention the sack of Cyprus *ca.* 1225 B.C., perhaps by Arteus, king of Mycenae and father of Agamemnon. The Egyptians had to repulse Achaian invaders in 1221.

These advances far outside the Greek confines of Mycenae were not signs of health, however, but of decline. Serious warfare on the Greek mainland, disruption of trade routes, and the massive displacements of peoples during the 12th cent. B.C. document the demise of Greek Mycenaean civilization.

***IV. The Great Migrations* (1200-850 B.C.).**–*A. Troy.* Although Troy was already a large city in the Early Bronze Age, its greatness is usually dated *ca.* 1900-1300 B.C. (Troy VI). An earthquake destroyed this city *ca.* 1300, but its citizens rebuilt it immediately. The new city (Troy VIIA) resembled a Mycenaean stronghold, complete with giant fortification walls. It and its predecessor controlled trade between Asia and Europe and therefore accumulated considerable wealth. Yet even greater economic power could not stop the hordes that shifted west from ancient Phrygia in central Asia Minor; they attacked and destroyed not only Troy but also Tarsus and Mirsin in southern Asia Minor and even the mighty Hittite empire. It is often said that other displaced peoples from southwestern Asia Minor and the Greek islands (the sea-peoples) played a major role in this widespread destruction (cf. R. A. Crossland and A. Birchall, eds., *Bronze Age Migrations in the Aegean* [1974]). Not even the legendary Troy could escape an advancing holocaust from these migratory tribes.

B. Dorians. Archeology documents a violent end to Greek civilization about the close of the 13th cent. B.C. The citadel at Mycenae was breached and burned to the ground. The city of Tiryns was leveled and turned into a cemetery. Virtually all the settlements of central Macedonia were destroyed and not reoccupied. The great trade and communications network of Mycenaean civilization vanished with nothing to replace it.

The invaders, according to their material remains, were not a single group. They apparently lived as nomads and had no urban traditions. Their utensils were wood, as were their idols. They seem to have had no developed art, at least in an imperishable medium.

Greek traditions remember the main group as Dorians, Greek-speaking tribes whose last point of departure before attacking the Greek mainland was Doris, a small district to the north bordering on Mycenae. The tradition (Hestod fragment 7) records that their leaders were an Achaian clan. The Greek histories by Herodotus (i.56; ix.26) and others suggest that the Dorians originated in northwestern Greece (Epirus), where they learned seamanship. They brought with them Northwest Greek, Doric, and the cult of Apollo-Karneios, likely a syncretism of their original ram-god and the indigenous Apollo.

The Dorian invaders held sway in the southern Peloponnesus from this time forward. Although at first hard taskmasters over their conquered cousins, they were gradually absorbed. Their descendants formed royal houses in Greece through classical times.

C. Aeolians and Ionians. The clash of the Dorians with local populations resulted, predictably, in displacement of certain local tribes. These refugees, Aeolians from Thessaly, Phocis, Locris, and Boeotia, sailed away to Thrace, Asia Minor, and the Greek islands. Here, of course, they met resistance from the indigenous Greeks but managed over several successive waves of migration to mingle with the local peoples. Nevertheless, memories of bitter fighting between the migrants and the indigenous populations of the Peloponnesus survive in the writings of Pausanias.

The oldest Greek dialect is usually thought to be that of the Ionians. During the Late Helladic (Bronze III) Period it was spoken in Attica (cf. Homer *Il.* xiii.685). Historians usually designate Ionian as the language of the first Greek-speaking settlers. The Ionians felt the shock of the Dorian advance in Achaia and fled to Attica, where the royal house of Pylos had already taken refuge. Other Ionians settled in Samos and introduced the cult of Hera.

From the list of Athenian kings it is possible to deduce that a main body of Ionian migrants settled in Attica *ca.* 1020 B.C. According to another tradition, the Ionian migration began four generations after the Aeolian. Either way, historians ordinarily identify the Ionians with the people who introduced proto-Geometric pottery into Athens during the first quarter of the 11th cent. B.C.

The Ionians' accomplishments imprinted their names indelibly on history. They continued their migrations east and by the 10th cent. B.C. occupied twelve cities on the coast of Asia Minor, including Miletus, Priene, Ephesus, Colophon, and the islands of Chios and Samos. They adopted a common name, *iaones* (<*iawov*), which appears in the Hebrew Bible (applied to all Greeks) as *yāwān*. The Ionians in Asia considered Athens their home city and Attica their homeland. The ties between the eastern and mainland Greeks remained strong for centuries.

It is Ionia that is reflected in the *Iliad,* which was recited in the Ionian dialect. Thus this poem described and codified the received traditions of the Ionians.

***V. Rise of the Greek City-States* (850-546 B.C.).**–*A. Cultural and Political Revival.* The composition of the *Iliad* and the *Odyssey* in Ionia during the 9th cent. B.C. may be a barometer of the renewed vigor of the Greek city-states in this period. Greek art flourished in the Dorian cities, Crete, Corinth, and Sparta. Hesiod composed the *Works and Days, Theogony,* and *Catalogues* in Boeotia. The production of literature was encouraged by the emergence of a stable system of tiny city-states in the Greek world, none of which was the kind of threat that the Mycenaean states had been.

On the mainland and in the south the gradually emerging city-states were on the same small order, but in a somewhat more settled condition. As a result of contact with the powerful emerging Iron Age civilizations of the Near East, the Greeks adopted the Phoenician alphabet, perhaps *ca.* 825 B.C. Carved ivories from Syria and Phoenicia dated 850-750 have been found in Crete, Rhodes, Samos, Sparta, and Athens, indicating renewed trade. Hesiod's celebration of law and order in his poems implies that chaos in the affairs of men had receded but was still an acrid memory.

Greek tradition places the adoption of constitutions on Crete in this period. The idea of a constitution is fundamental and far-reaching, orienting the individual citizens to the state rather than to the family. The polis, or independent Greek city-state, which Aristotle (*Pol.* i.2 [8]) called a cooperation of several villages, emerged in Crete and mainland Greece as the answer to the political fragmentation and instability of the previous centuries.

B. Colonial Expansion. Five Spartan villages united under one king *ca.* 800 B.C. and began to conquer the surrounding villages. By 720 Sparta ruled Messenia and had become the richest and most powerful state in Greece.

The Spartan example inspired other Dorians. In the Megarid the Dorian state of Megara appeared and fought with Corinth. The Megarans also started foreign colonies. The Corinthians united other villages into the single polis of Corinth. This pattern appeared repeatedly, even at Thebes; the polis became virtually the hallmark of Hellenic civilization, eventually honored even by the Romans, who gave special privileges to the conquered Greek city-states.

The expansion of the city-state into international trade followed the logic of its internal development. Each city-state recognized the value of setting up trading colonies in areas of rich markets. The mother city, after proper consultation with Apollo or Zeus, sent whole families from all classes and trades, for the new colony was to be self-supporting but loyal to the mother city. Thus Miletus set up colonies around the Black Sea, exploiting the amber trade. Lesbos sent colonists to the rich agricultural lands on the European side of the Hellespont. Chalcis and Eretria founded colonies in Sicily and Italy. Greek colonies appeared also in Spain, Gaul, Illyria, Corsica, North Africa, and Egypt. The Greeks had to contend with the hostility of the Phoenicians in their efforts to expand their trade, but the Phoenicians were curtailed by the Assyrian sack of Tyre in 701 and the Babylonian sack of Sidon in 677 (cf. J. Katzenstein, *History of Tyre* [1973]).

Thus from 750 to 550 the trade networks of the previous Greek civilizations reappeared, but with the added complication of colonization. Colonization increased warfare (see III.D below), but the commercial benefits were enormous. By 610 Ionia was fabulously wealthy. The Ionian fleets ruled the seas off the coast of Asia Minor and in the southeastern Mediterranean. Ionian mercenaries found employment far and wide. Ionian art, politics, philosophy, and poetry flourished in a commercial and artistic golden age.

C. Warfare (750-550 B.C.). In the competition between city-states for markets, territory, and position, warfare was inevitable. As noted above, the Spartans enslaved the Messenians (740-720 B.C.). Likewise Corinth and Megara warred over the southern territory of Megara. The victory of Corinth left it a commercial center second to none. Much later (600-540) the Athenians attacked Megara over the island of Salamis, which Megara also lost. Colonies also fought one another, sometimes because their mother cities were at war, sometimes because of competition for the same market, and sometimes in a struggle for general military supremacy.

Sparta lost decisively to Argos in 669 B.C. and for a while declined in prestige and power. Various colonies revolted from *ca.* 640 until 546, when Sparta defeated the Argos in the battle of the "Three Hundred Champions" of each side and reemerged as the most powerful military state in the Peloponnesus.

In central Greece the Phocan states of Delphi and Crisa fought the First Sacred War (595-586 B.C.), a local dispute in which Delphi utterly razed Crisa, vindicating the oracle in the eyes of many. Then the forces of Thessaly, in which Delphi lay, invaded Boeotia but were defeated.

None of these and other developments in war can be understood apart from certain Greek ideals, particularly the elevation of success in warfare as the highest aspiration of a young man. Defeat in battle meant death or enslavement, i.e., noncombatants were enslaved, while wounded or disarmed soldiers were simply killed. Thus war involved great strength, skill, and courage, as well as training — a considerable investment of men and intelligence, reflecting Greek ideals and values.

D. Tyranny. The main problem faced by the city-states was establishing a stable government. Stability could be achieved under the traditional king, but with the development of an inner unity as opposed to an imposed unity, kingship declined. For example, the new city-states in the eastern Aegean were republics. Aegina and Megara understood themselves to be founded by the god Apollo, not by a leader or king. It was Sparta that retained the traditional king in the sense of an absolute monarch. Nevertheless, the constitutional monarch became the overarching ideal in many cases. This king's authority was sanctioned either by an unwritten constitution of religion and custom or by an actual written constitution dividing authority between political institutions and the king. The king's council and court limited royal power in Argos, Athens, Corinth, and Ephesus.

On occasion city-states could not establish a stable government. Into the vacuum stepped a "tyrant" (Gk. *týrannos,* possibly a loanword from Lydian), who did not need to be an aristocrat or to have any special claim to power except brute force. In periods of tension between the traditional aristocracy of birth and the new nonaristocratic oligarchy of rapidly accumulated wealth, an interloper could all too easily seize power. Thus tyrannies emerged at Corinth, Sicyon, and Megara, powerful commercial centers. Tyrants generally held their powers by suppressing personal rights and political freedom. Therefore they always suffered from the ill will of citizens and feared revolt. So strongly did the Corinthians hate Psammetichus, tyrant of Corinth, that when he was assassinated in 582 B.C. they threw his corpse and the bones of his ancestors outside the city.

E. Athens and the Rise of Democracy. A quite different state of affairs existed in Athens during this period. This city-state had once (10th-7th cents. B.C.) been the most powerful on the mainland, but gradually others surpassed it in wealth, power, and commerce. Athens still depended on its tribal organization for political stability, while the new Dorian city-states developed small, compact structures that enabled them to move decisively in time of threat.

Athens operated on a constitution that recognized the "natural" groups of clan and tribe. There were four tribes, each divided into three brotherhoods. The brotherhoods in turn were composed of "thirds" and of clansmen and guildsmen. The clansmen owned and worked the land, and the guildsmen engaged in trades and handicrafts. Every adult male was admitted either into a clan or a guild, an event of considerable religious seriousness.

After the demise of kingship in Athens, power was divided among three magistrates. The duties of the king were administered by the royal archon, the duties of the army by the military archon, and the civil duties by the eponymous archon. Eventually Athens instituted the Areopagus Council, consisting of nine archons or magistrates.

The strength of the constitution lay in its long tradition and therefore in the awe in which it was held. Its weakness lay in the undiminished power of the clans. In 632 B.C. the followers of Cylon, who had attempted to seize power, took refuge at the altar of Athena but were slaughtered by the clan of the Alcemonidae. About 600 a jury of three hundred chosen by their birth found them guilty, banished the living members of the clan, and cast out the bones of their ancestors.

The massacre amounted to a crisis of conscience in Athens, and into this tense situation stepped a reformer, Draco, who instituted legal reforms that effectively strengthened the state at the expense of the individual, family, or other blood group.

Draco's reforms increased civil tensions rather than lessened them, and virtual civil war broke out. Then Solon, eponymous archon of 594/593 B.C., instituted reforms in debt penalties, law, and currency; his constitutional reforms were the most extensive. The new constitution's recognition of four "classes" defined by wealth, each eligible for various state offices, enabled citizens of lowly birth to participate in government.

Under Solon there were two legislative bodies: the traditional Council of the Areopagus, formed of ex-archons, and the new "Council of Four Hundred," composed of one hundred members from each tribe. The most radical departure from tradition was the institution of the Assembly, a judicial body elected by lot from the population at large. Aristotle labeled this body "democratic," since it was composed of the people (*dēmos*).

The ideals of Solon, as discussed by Aristotle, are now often considered the best in ancient Greece. It is true that Solon placed the state first, forced citizens to participate in government, and required the people to take a stand on political issues. He was also a religious reformer, requiring every citizen to take an oath of obedience to the state under the vengeful eye of Zeus. He lived his ideals as he programmed them into the new state constitution.

F. Religion. Religion remained a controlling factor during the city-states' rise to power. Families worshiped Hestia, goddess of the hearth, Zeus as protector of the courtyard, and their own gods and heroes. Every man was expected to maintain the family shrines, honor his ancestors in their tombs, invoke the familial Apollo, and revere his parents.

Every political group within the state was also a religious entity. Therefore each tribe, brotherhood, clan, and guild worshiped in its assemblies and gatherings. Every meeting of the council or assembly included homage to the appropriate deities.

Each state worshiped Hestia and also the god credited with its founding. Therefore Athenians worshiped Athena, but Spartans venerated Zeus. Every state meeting included time for public worship.

Regional centers provided a loose sense of identity among the Greeks. Greek pilgrims assembled continually at such centers as Delphi and Delos. Panhellenic festivals were held at Olympia, Delphi, Isthmus, and Nemea. All states consulted the oracles of the gods at Delphi, Dodona, and Didyma, but none of the priests at these centers held power over the states.

Alongside family religion, tribal and clan religion, and regional observance gradually emerged alternative religious expressions, notably the worship of Demeter the mother goddess, and also Dionysus, whose origins are usually traced to Bronze Age Thrace. Dionysus was worshiped sometimes in orgiastic frenzy, though the priests at Delphi adopted his worship in a more dignified mode. His attributes that guaranteed fertility closely parallel those of Demeter, who also seems to have controlled agricultural cycles. The worship of Demeter originated at Eleusis and may have included use of hallucinogens. The rites were called the "Eleusinian Mysteries" because the secrets of eternal life were promised to the initiates.

Another mystery religion (well portrayed in Euripides' *Bacchae*) was Orphism. Adherents experienced ecstatic frenzies, as in the worship of Dionysus and Demeter. Orphism also developed its own cosmogony, which gave it a philosophical facade. All three of the mysteries so far mentioned depended strongly on a well-developed myth and particularly attracted women.

Greeks in this period produced a wide range not only of religious prose but also of music and poetry. The musical and poetic genres included myth, elegy, hymn, processional song, personal poetry, triumph song, and satire. Sparta and Corinth became renowned as centers of music, dance, and poetry, most of which was associated with religious ceremony.

See RELIGIONS OF THE BIBLICAL WORLD: GRECO-ROMAN.

VI. Triumph of Greece **(546-466** B.C.**).**–*A. Persia v. Athens.* In the same year that Sparta emerged as the most powerful city-state in Greece (546 B.C.), Cyrus king of Persia defeated Croesus king of Lydia, an ally of Sparta, in Asia Minor. Sparta sent envoys to warn Cyrus not to advance on the Greek city-states in Asia, but sent no troops. Cyrus ignored Sparta and the other mainland states and proceeded to overrun the Asian Greek city-states. Persia turned its attention southward briefly, reaching as far as Egypt by 525 B.C., during the reign of Cambyses, successor to Cyrus.

Subsequently Darius I (522-486 B.C.) consolidated a vast empire that stretched from the Mediterranean to the Indus and from the Caucasus Mountains to the Persian Gulf. Persia commanded the mightiest army between Greece and China and used the Phoenician navy. Darius built roads from his capital at Susa, one of which terminated at Ephesus on the Ionian coast. He reigned as an absolute despot, though with twenty satraps or governors administering territories in his empire. Capital in the form of gold and silver flowed to Susa rather than to the Aegean.

Darius continued a policy of expansion and thereby threatened the Greek city-states. He annexed Arabia, Cyrenaica, Samos, and Barca. In a foolish gesture of power he ordered his largely Greek eastern troops to attack the Scythians on the north coast of the Black Sea. He lost that engagement, but by 500 B.C. he controlled all but peninsular Greece, his next target.

Meanwhile Athens had suffered thirty-six years of continuous tyranny (546-510 B.C.) at the hand of Pesistratus, former polemarch (military archon). He died in 528/527, but his descendants held power until Athens revolted in 510. In the turbulent months that followed, Athens actually sent envoys to Persia to seek protection from Sparta, which had been severely bruised by Athens under Pesistratus. Persia demanded no less than submission to the Persian yoke, which Athens rejected. Civil war broke out in Athens, but the city shortly regained inner stability. In fact, it now was the center of Greek power and the most important Greek rival to Persia.

B. Spartan Alliance. At this time Sparta was implacably hostile to all things Persian. The Spartans attacked Samos (an ally of Persia) *ca.* 524 B.C. and began collecting allies. By 510 the alliance included Boeotia, Phocis, Athens, and perhaps Chalcis. This group implemented a governing body of two equal and independent houses: the Assembly of Spartiates and the Congress of Allies. The purpose of the body was to develop a common policy against Persia. The Congress of Allies in effect acknowledged the military leadership of Sparta.

C. Ionian Revolt and Battle of Marathon. The Ionian city-states overthrew and expelled pro-Persian tyrants in Ionia *ca.* 500 B.C. and asked Sparta's support. But King Cleomenes decided not to risk direct confrontation when he learned that Persia could deploy armies a three-months' march away from Persia. Ionia turned to Athens. The Athenian assembly sent a portion of their fleet to Ionia, thus notifying the Persians of their hostile intent. The revolt spread to the Greek city-states of the Hellespont and the Bosporus. Darius sent Histiaeus, tyrant of Myrcinus and his agent in the area, and Athens withdrew.

By 497 B.C. Greeks friendly to Persia had sacked many Ionian coastal cities. In fact, by the summer of 493 Persia had regained all the rebellious city-states.

Darius sent a well-equipped punitive force against Eretria and Athens early in 490 B.C. On the way to Athens he subdued four large Euboian city-states. The Persian fleet anchored in the bay of Marathon NE of Athens. The planned deployment of troops in the plain of Marathon gave the edge to the Persian cavalry. But this calculation went awry, and the Athenians routed the Persians brilliantly under their general Miltiades. The Persians withdrew to their ships and then sailed around the point to attack Athens by surprise off Phalerum. But the Athenians foiled Darius again; the Persians withdrew to Asia Minor to regroup and await the arrival of the army.

D. Persian Invasion of Mainland Greece. Unfortunately Miltiades' aggressive policy died with him from a wound suffered at Paros. Now the initiative lay with Persia, which lost no time. Squadrons of Persian ships anchored off Doriscus, supplied by the Persian allies and subjugated peoples of Phoenicia, Egypt, Cyprus, and Greece. Xerxes, now leading Persia, delayed in Macedonia to construct a safe supply route. A sudden gale smashed part of his fleet, but the remainder was still so gigantic that the Greeks grew faint when they caught sight of it at Artemesium.

The Persian assault on the pass at Thermopylae was a disaster for them. The Greek general Leonidas held the pass, which narrowed to 2 m. (6½ ft.) wide. The Persians streamed fearlessly through to a veritable slaughter but finally overwhelmed the Greeks through sheer numbers. Meanwhile, in the first engagement of the Persian and Greek fleets, the odds were with the Persians, who nonetheless suffered worse in the conflict. In two more engagements the Persians finally emerged victorious but at a fearful cost. Now Xerxes was the victor in two land assaults and three naval battles, though the Greeks had distinguished themselves as superior soldiers and sailors.

Xerxes continued to wage war, assembling a huge fleet off Salamis, where the Greek fleet lay anchored. The Persians outnumbered the Greeks three to one but still lost the sea battle because of superior Greek tactics at every turn.

In 479 B.C., the following year, the war went much worse for the mainland Greeks. The Persian commander Mardonius actually burned Athens, though its population had withdrawn to Salamis under the protection of their fleet. Furthermore, the Greek alliance stood ever in danger of splitting because each group (Spartans, Athenians, Megarans, Plataeans, etc.) acted in its own interest first. Nevertheless, in the great collisions of Greek and Persian forces at Plataea and Mycale the Greeks managed to carry the day, even slaying Mardonius early in the conflict. Thus were the Persians stayed.

E. Athenian Alliance. By the close of Xerxes' and Mardonius's attack against mainland Greece, Athens was clearly the leading naval power and second only to Sparta in total military power. Increasing friction between Athens and Sparta led to Sparta's withdrawal from active command of the Greek League late in 478 B.C.

Athens, now in control of the league, reorganized the system of command according to Athenian ideals. This new Athenian Alliance ruled the Aegean seas, putting an end to piracy, expelling pro-Persian governors, and stimulating sea-borne trade. It is often called a "thalassocracy" because it ruled the seas until the death of Xerxes in 466 B.C.

F. Western Greeks. The Greeks in Sicily and the West found Carthage a much greater threat than Persia. Gelon had become tyrant of Gela on the south shores of Sicily and eventually controlled almost all the south coast. He and his descendants first fought Carthage in 481 B.C. and crushed it; they ruled in Sicily until 461.

Tyranny strengthened Hellenism in the West. The aggressive policies of the tyrants suppressed local ethnic groups and cleared the way for commercial expansion. The western Greek city-states grew strong economically and thus attracted immigrants from the Greek islands, Ionia, and the Greek mainland. At the very time that separatism was the rule in the Greek homeland, unity prevailed among the western Greeks.

G. Literature, Philosophy, and Art. The period from 546 to 466 B.C. is recognized as one of the most creative in Greek history. As prosperity increased, so did an educated aristocracy that shared freely their ideals in religion, statecraft, education, and art. In fact, a kind of Panhellenism was afoot, which came to expression in the Greek festivals at Olympia, Delphi, Corinth, and Nemea. The center of common worship for the Greek world was Olympia, where Zeus, king of the gods, was honored.

Pindar, a Dorian of Thebes, wrote his choral lyric poetry between 498 and 446 B.C. Pindar celebrated victories of his contemporaries, setting them in the context of Greek heroes and deities from the mythic past.

Meanwhile Ionian philosophers and dramatists, principally Aeschylus, Pythagoras, and Parmenides of Elea (an Ionian colony in Italy) were gaining prominence.

Aeschylus is usually dated *ca.* 525-456 B.C., precisely during the darkest threats from Persia. He fought at Marathon and Salamis; this experience is sometimes understood as the reason for the piety in his plays, in which the will of the gods, not the skills of men, determines history.

Pythagoras fled Samos when the tyrant Polycrates came to power. He found asylum in Croton in Italy, where he and his followers engaged not only in philosophical debate but also in political activity *ca.* 530-510 B.C. At Croton he founded a religious fraternity designed to bring mankind into proper relationship with the divine. His cosmogony is not well understood today, but some still invoke two of his principles: *harmonia* and *philosophia*.

By the beginning of the 5th cent. Heraclitus of Ephesus had bitterly attacked the ideas of Pythagoras. Since all things flow and change, said Heraclitus, it is pointless to speak of a harmonizing principle in the human soul and in nature. Parmenides of Elea (*ca.* 485-450 B.C.) also rejected most of Pythagoras's ideas and defined pure reason as that which apprehends truth.

Most Greek thinkers wrote in prose, eschewing poetry as fit for religion, not rational discourse. Their prose works in geography, history, and medicine were epitomes of rational expression. For example, Hecataeus of Miletus (*ca.* 500 B.C.) produced a veritable handbook of the world, including descriptions of peoples, customs, flora and fauna, and place names, so thorough that Alexander the Great used it in his sorties toward India.

Painting on pottery grew into one of the most cultivated of the arts. Athens became the center for this art, which attracted artists from all over the Greek world. These artists painted their figures black on red-fired ceramics. By 530 B.C. they outlined their figures in white on lustrous black wares. In other words, the red-fired clay of the vessel formed the figures, for which the artist provided detail in white lines. The black glaze provided the background. *See* Plate 24. Some artists signed their works.

Many other thinkers and artists were active in this period, e.g., the Ionian poet Xenophanes, the historian Cadmus of Miletus, and the writer of comedy Epicharmus of Syracuse. Others remained anonymous, or nearly so:

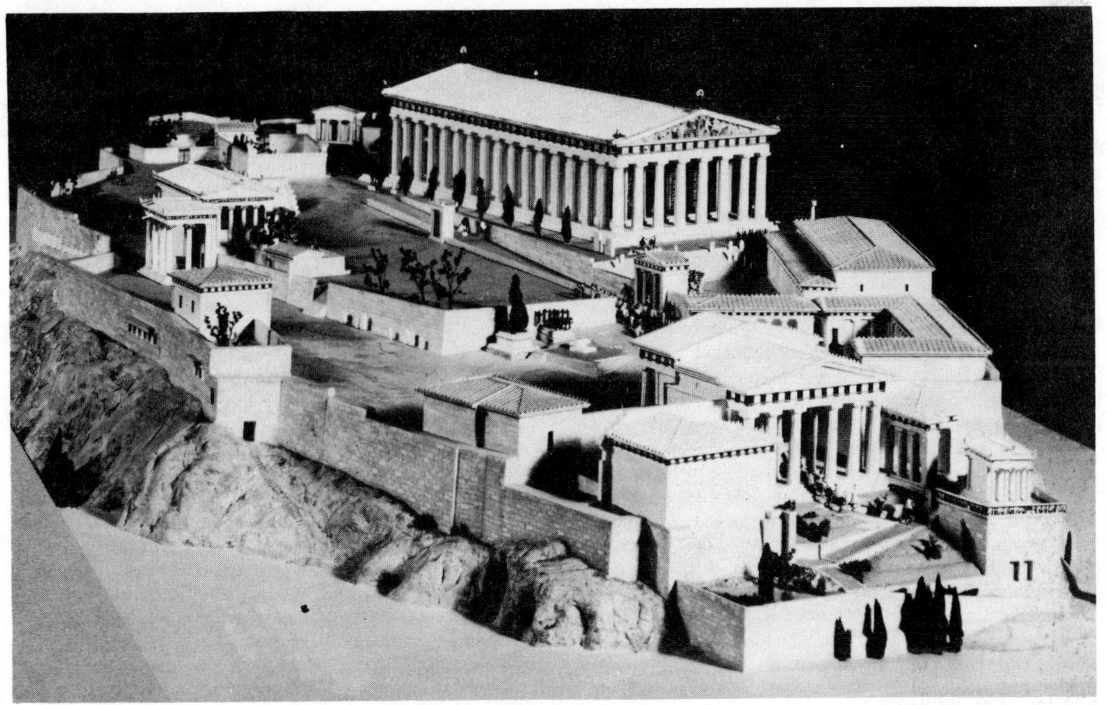

Reconstruction of the Acropolis, Athens' central fortress and sanctuary, which Pericles rebuilt after the Persians destroyed it in 479 B.C. Work began with the Parthenon (center), the temple of Athena Parthenos (Maiden), in 447. View from the northwest (Royal Ontario Museum, Toronto)

Athenian painters, architects of splendid temples and other public buildings, and fine engravers of coin-dies — themselves fine works of art.

VII. Crisis of the Fifth Century: Peloponnesian Wars.– When Persia was defeated after the assassination of Xerxes in 465 B.C., the outside threat that had held Greece together was dispelled, at least temporarily. As a consequence the internal tensions growing toward disruption of the alliance gained momentum. Leaders of the democratic party grasped power in Athens. They deposed the Areopagus, imposed their will on the allies of Athens, and finally broke with Sparta. Ephialtes and Pericles led the democratic opposition to the old aristocracy. They vigorously promoted Athenian interests above those of others in the alliance, even at the expense of Sparta. By 460 B.C. Athens was at war both with Sparta and with Persia. Pericles commanded the western fleet against the Peloponnesus (Sparta).

The years 460-455 were given to victory and expansion. By 454, however, Athens had lost so heavily in military campaigns even in Egypt that other states in the alliance revolted. Fighting finally ceased in 446, mainly because of the exhaustion of Athens and Sparta and their allies.

For fifteen years peace reigned in the Aegean and on the mainland, though Thucydides (i.18.3) reports that Sparta and Athens were preparing for war. When new hostilities broke out in 431 among the Greek city-states, Athens stood at the head of an empire. Wealth in the form of tribute from subjugated states and reparations from subdued rebel states had poured into the Athenian coffers. In turn Athens had protected these perhaps three hundred subject states from pirates, so that their trade prospered. Yet Athens had gained power through an imperialistic policy that seemed ill-conceived in terms of its own idealistic history. Furthermore, certain policies of war and economics overloaded the Athenian state with slaves, who had to be supported. The acknowledged leadership of Pericles did guarantee some form of stability to Athens and its empire. This stability, however, depended on the good will, nationalism, and integrity of Pericles, not upon the inner strength of the political institutions of Athenian democracy.

The first part of the Peloponnesian War (431-421 B.C.), resulted in Sparta's defeat of Athens. In the last engagement at Amphipolis the Athenian general Cleon was killed and Athens sued for peace. This peace lasted only until 416. War raged from 416 to 404, at the end of which Athens lay in total defeat, all its institutions and ideals in shambles.

The Peloponnesian Wars brought a cultural crisis to Athens. The young were attracted to sophists, who spoke elegantly but not always sensibly. Although Socrates (469-399 B.C.) had a strong following, his good sense and clear dialectics did not save him from disgrace and death. The violence of war seems to have polarized the citizens, so that either they advanced what amounted to superstition as an intellectual art or simply advocated a type of primitive revolutionary life. Extremism ruled the day rather than the old virtues of prudence and moderation.

Nevertheless, this century did produce the great dramatists Euripides (*ca.* 485-406 B.C.) and Aristophanes (*ca.* 450-385), the historian Thucydides (*ca.* 460-400), the orator Antiphon (*ca.* 480-411), the physician Hippocrates of Cos (*ca.* 460-400), the philosopher Democritus of Abdera (*ca.* 460-370), and others. Although the society was in many ways in crisis from the protracted wars, culture flourished.

VIII. Transition of the Fourth Century.–After defeating Athens, Sparta became the most powerful city-state in the Greek homeland. Persia and Carthage both threatened Greece, and most of the remaining Greek states were de-

GREECE

moralized and bankrupt. But Sparta was also corrupted by the war and could not provide sustained leadership. Furthermore, internal economic problems sapped its energies. For forty years it remained the most dominant state in Greece, but its repressive policies betrayed its inner struggles.

The rest of the century is a melancholy record of wars and rumors of wars. Civil war shook Attica. Sparta went to war against Persia. An anti-Spartan confederacy fomented wars from 395 B.C. and opened the Corinthian War in 394. Hannibal attacked Sicily, and during the ensuing wars Dionysius ruled Syracuse with an iron hand. Fighting at Thebes drew in many Greek states, culminating in the collapse of Sparta in 368.

The rest of the century saw the collapse of the other Greek states, the decline of the new Athenian Alliance, and the disintegration of the Boeotian Coalition. Sicily moved toward anarchy. Finally Philip of Macedon came to power. He was immensely popular with his army and the citizens and is often credited with creating one of the first national territorial states not based on the autonomy of a city. He distinguished himself in war, diplomacy, and culture, setting precedents that his son Alexander could scarcely surpass.

IX. Alexander and His Successors **(336-217** B.C.).– Political stability in Greece was apparently guaranteed by the League of Corinth in 337 B.C. This congress had allied itself with "Philip and his successors" for all time, which meant that most Greek states (except Sparta) now looked to a Macedonian, Alexander the Great, for leadership. Alexander immediately revealed his leadership qualities at the two revolts of Thebes in 336 and 335. The first rebellion he forgave, but at the second he destroyed the city and enslaved its inhabitants.

Alexander immediately set off on his world conquests (334), which encouraged Achaia, Sparta, Elis, and part of Arcadia to revolt in 331. As soon as they armed themselves, however, Antigonus, Alexander's regent in Macedonia, defeated them. To the ignominy of defeat were added the horrors of seven years of famine.

The internal instability of the mainland cities resulted in an endless stream of distinguished citizens being sent into exile. In 324 Alexander interfered directly by decreeing that all exiles must be repatriated. He also stirred up shocked animosity by requesting deification. Athens declared him a son of Dionysus but did so with contempt. Other states followed suit.

By 323 Alexander was dead. At the first confirmation of the news Athens led a new revolt against Macedonia called the "Greek Wars" by Greek historians. Even though almost all of Greece fanned the flames of revolt, it was all over by the next year. The Athenian navy was utterly destroyed, and Athens surrendered unconditionally. Demosthenes of Athens committed suicide. Athens and all the Peloponnesian states became protectorates of Macedonia.

For the rest of the 4th cent. the political situation was far from settled, though mainland Greece managed to stay clear of other international wars. The Near East was wracked from 320 to 275 B.C. by the Diodochi (Successor) Wars among Alexander's generals. The attacks of Pyrrhus of Epirus on Macedonian allies beginning in 292 marred the partial peace.

Rampant piracy was a major threat to security and economic stability in the 3rd century. Unchecked looting, kidnapping of wealthy citizens, and burning of coastal cities continued from 280 to 221. The Greeks responded to this and other threats by refounding city leagues. In 280 the old Achaian League was reformed; by 228 most of the Peloponnese had joined. The Aetolian League and the new Macedonian king, Antigonus Gonatas, succeeded in beating off the ferocious invasions of the Celts (Gauls) in 278.

Macedon still asserted its will to rule over Greece. In the Chremonidean Wars of 267-262 the Macedonian states were pitted against Athens, Sparta, and Ptolemy II Philadelphus of Egypt. Macedon finally prevailed.

Macedon held effective control of mainland Greece until 224, when the Aetolian League defeated the Boeotian League. Almost all central Greece became independent of Macedon. The Macedonians struggled from 224 to 205 to hold on to Greece, having success in the field at Sellasia in the southern Peloponnesus in 222, where the Spartans were defeated for the first time in history. The Macedonian king Antigonus died in 221; his successor was Philip V.

The so-called Social War against the Aetolian League occupied the new Greek League from 220 to 217. The outcome was indecisive, except that Macedon lost nothing.

X. Coming of Rome **(229-146** B.C.).–By 229 Rome controlled the Illyrian coast and the island of Corcyra off the coast of Epirus. The next year friendly Roman envoys appeared at the Isthmian Games at the invitation of Corinth. Rome, however, played no active military role in Greece until 215 B.C., when Philip V of Macedon allied himself with Carthage against Rome after the latter's stinging defeats by Hannibal during the Second Punic War. Yet Philip could not dislodge the Romans from Illyria. Rome used Elis, Sparta, Messenia, and the Aetolian League to hold Philip at bay. This conflict continued until 205 B.C. with no clear advantage to either side.

Rome's strategy of divide and rule became clear only after 197 B.C. The Romans, at the invitation of Pergamum and Athens, finally defeated Philip at Cynocephalae NW of Athens, thus confining him to Macedon. Subsequently Rome treated Philip lightly to wean him from Antiochus III ("the Great") of Syria and treated its Aetolian allies rather shabbily. The Romans officially proclaimed the independence of the Greek cities and promptly withdrew.

The somewhat miffed Aetolians invited Antiochus III into Greece. Antiochus obliged, but the Roman general Cato routed him at Thermopylae in 191. The war continued at sea and in Asia, with thousands of Roman sailors manning transport ships to Samos. As a result Rome defeated Antiochus at Magnesia in Asia in 190/89, deprived him of Asia west of the Taurus Mountains, and effectively boxed in Greece.

The Romans took the precaution of quieting the just fears of the Greeks by proclaiming the freedom of the Greek cities at the peace of Apamea in 188. Athens enjoyed the best return on the investment of good will in the Roman cause; it became virtually a center of Roman pilgrimage during the first third of the 2nd cent. B.C.

Philip's son Perseus, who became king in Macedonia in 179, had dreams of power that did not go unnoticed by the Romans. Finally, in 171 the Romans ordered him to disband his newly formed coalition army. He refused, and Rome attacked.

This, the Third Macedonian War, appeared to go badly for Rome and its allies at first. The campaigns of 171, 170, and 169 demanded much in men and materiel from Rome and its Greek allies. Athens had supplied huge levies of grain from its sparse stores.

The war ended in Rome's favor at the Battle of Pydna in Macedon in 168. Rome annihilated the Macedonian armies. Athens was given the city of Haliartus, the island of Lemnos, and the coveted port of Delos as a reward for unswerving loyalty. Now Rome, though it had annexed no Greek territory, was functionally the master of Greece. The Roman Senate became the body to which Greek city-states appealed their disputes. Roman fleets controlled the high seas and routed pirates. Roman armies enforced fines and levies.

By 148 Rome had annexed Macedon as Provincia Macedonia. In 146 the Romans intervened between Athens and the Achaian League in a dispute over the territory of Oropus. Rome dissolved the Achaian League and put these cities directly under the Macedonian proconsul. Corinth was utterly and brutally destroyed, probably as an object lesson to the other Greek cities. The Roman Senate declared the territories of Corinth and Thebes, and probably Boeotia, Chalcis, and the remainder of Euboea, properties of the Roman people. Athens and Sparta were allowed to remain free cities.

***XI. Rule of Rome* (146 B.C.-A.D. 100).**–The widespread destruction of the wars, heavy conscriptions, and oppressive taxations of the Romans depleted Greece severely. Thracians invaded the relatively unstable land in 135. Slave revolts caught the citizens of Attica off guard in 134 and again in 104-100. Piracy and brigandage were such a problem that Rome finally sent M. Antonius in 103 to restore order at sea and establish a permanent military presence in the heart of the troubles, Cilicia. During Antonius's visit to Athens a revolt occurred in which democracy was overthrown in favor of oligarchy.

Mithradates VI Eupator, who gained and consolidated territories in Asia, including Cappadocia, emerged as a new threat to Greece, and therefore to Rome. Rome faced Mithradates down in 100-95, but by 88 war had broken out. Mithradates had success at first and attracted Greek allies to his side. By 85, however, Rome had carried the day, though anti-Roman pirate bands continued to plunder coastal towns for almost twenty years.

The Roman general Pompey crushed the pirates in 67, but the Roman civil wars prevented peace. Julius Caesar decisively defeated Pompey on Greek soil at Pharsalus in 48. After Caesar's assassination many Greeks supported Brutus. Octavian (Augustus), victorious in the civil wars, incorporated Thessaly into Macedonia and organized the rest of Greece into the Roman senatorial province of Achaia. Athens and Sparta remained free states.

Greece spent the years to 15 A.D. reviving economically and demographically. In that year the Greeks successfully petitioned the emperor Tiberius to place them under a Roman legate rather than the Senate. In A.D. 44 Claudius restored Greece to the Roman Senate. Nero freed Greece for a few months, but Vespasian quickly rescinded what he regarded as a madman's order. Otherwise the provinces of Macedonia and Achaia lived in relative quiet under firm Roman control, engaging in commerce and the arts and remembering the past.

XII. Biblical References.–Greece is specifically mentioned four times in the OT (Heb. *yāwān*; Dnl. 8:21; 10:20; 11:2; Zec. 9:13; see IV.C above) and once in 1 Maccabees (1:1, Gk. *Hellas*), while Greeks are mentioned once (Joel 3:6 [MT 4:6]). Other more obscure references that are usually interpreted to mean Greece or the Greek people are Javan the fourth son of Japheth (Gen. 10:2, 4; 1 Ch. 1:5, 7; Isa. 66:19; Ezk. 27:13), the Dodanim (Gen. 10:4; 1 Ch. 1:7), Gog and Magog (Ezk. 38–39), the Philistines (Jgs. 14–15; 1 S. 17–18; etc.), and the "islands" (Ps. 72:10; Isa. 40:15; etc. — Cyprus, Crete, and the Aegean islands?).

In the NT the name occurs only once (Acts 20:2, Gk. *Hellas*), where it is distinguished from Macedonia; in this passage it is used as a popular synonym for Achaia, the Roman name of the territory. Reference to Greeks, however, is frequent (Jn. 12:20; Acts 11:20; 16:1; Rom. 1:14; 1 Cor. 1:22; etc.; as applied to the Syrophoenician woman in Mk. 7:26 the term Greek means Greek-speaking, Greek in culture, or possibly Gentile, pagan). The cities of Greece which Paul visited on his missionary journeys include Neapolis, Philippi, Amphipolis, Apollonia, Thessalonica, Beroea, Athens, Corinth, and Cenchreae (Acts 16–18; 20; *see* Vol. I, Maps XIX-XX).

See also GREEK LANGUAGE OF THE NT; HELLENISM; HELLENIST; JAVAN.

Bibliography.–M. Cary, *History of the Greek World from 323 to 146* B.C. (2nd ed. 1951); W. S. Ferguson, *Hellenistic Athens, An Historical Essay* (repr. 1969); W. K. C. Guthrie, *History of Greek Philosophy* (3 vols., 1971); M. Hadas, *Hellenistic Culture, Fusion and Diffusion* (1959); N. G. L. Hammond and H. H. Scullard, eds., *Oxford Classical Dictionary* (2nd ed. 1970); T. Mommsen, *Provinces of the Roman Empire from Caesar to Diocletian* (2 vols., 1909); G. E. Mylonas, *Mycenae and the Mycenaean Age* (1966); B. Niese, *Geschichte der Griechischen und Makedonischen Staaten* (3 vols., 1893); M. Rostovzeff, *Social and Economic History of the Hellenistic World* (3 vols., 1941); *Social and Economic History of the Roman Empire* (2 vols., 1957); R. Stillwell, ed., *Princeton Encyclopedia of Classical Sites* (1976); W. W. Tarn, *Alexander the Great* (2 vols., 1979); W. W. Tarn and G. T. Griffith, *Hellenistic Civilization* (1904); V. Tcherikover, *Hellenistic Civilization and the Jews* (1961).

J. F. STRANGE

GREECE, RELIGION IN ANCIENT. *See* RELIGIONS OF THE BIBLICAL WORLD: GRECO-ROMAN.

GREED [Heb. *nepeš*, *beṭen*–'inner most part' (Job 20:20); Gk. *pleonexía*–'desire to have more' (1 Thess. 2:5; 2 Pet. 2:3, 14), *pleonéktēs* ("guilty of . . . greed," 1 Cor. 5:11)]; AV COVETOUSNESS, DESIRE (Hab. 2:5), "will" (Ezk. 16:27), etc.; NEB also APPETITE (Job 20:20), "mouth" (Hab. 2:5), etc.; **GREEDY** (adjective) [Heb. *rᵉḥaḇ nepeš* (Prov. 28:25), *bāṣa'* (Ps. 10:3), *bāṣa' beṣa'*, *nāśā' nepeš*–'lift up the soul' (Hos. 4:8); Gk. *pleonexía* (Eph. 4:19), *aischrokerdḗs*–'fond of dishonest gain' ("greedy for gain," 1 Tim. 3:8; Tit. 1:7)]; AV OF A PROUD HEART (Prov. 28:25), COVETOUS, etc.; NEB SELF-IMPORTANT (Prov. 28:25), "stop at nothing" (Eph. 4:19), "given to filthy lucre" (Tit. 1:17), etc.; (noun) [*pleonéktēs* (1 Cor. 5:10; 6:10)]; **GREEDILY** (DEVOUR) [Heb. *lāhaṭ* (Ps. 57:4 [MT 5])].

Hebrew *nepeš*, rendered usually "soul," is translated "greed" in Ezk. 16:27; Hab. 2:5. The NEB's renderings "women who hate you" and "opens his mouth as wide as" (preserving the spatial image of Sheol and the parallelism with the next line) are to be preferred. The compound term *rᵉḥaḇ nepeš*, "broad soul," does have the meaning of "being greedy" in Prov. 28:25.

The Hebrew pleonasm *bāṣa' beṣa'*, "be greedy with greed" (Prov. 15:27; Jer. 6:13; 8:10) means "acquire excessive gain." Originally *bāṣa'* meant "cut off" and referred to a ready-woven piece of material that was cut off from the thrum (*TDOT*, II, 206). Later on it acquired the connotation of cutting off someone's profit. The RSV is as correct in its translation of *bōṣē(a)' bērēḵ* in Ps. 10:3 (following *K*) as the AV or NEB.

In Ps. 57:4 the RSV interprets MT *lōhᵃṭîm* as "greedily devour" (cf. KoB, pp. 474f.) instead of AV "set on fire," RSV mg. "are aflame." It may be that two roots overlap in meaning (cf. *'āḵal*, which can refer to humans eating or to fire consuming; cf. also *CHAL*, p. 173). The RSV also emends *tiḇ'ᵃṭû* (< *b't*, "kick"; cf. AV, RSV mg.) of 1 S. 2:29 to *tabbîṭ* (< *nāḇaṭ*, "look at"; cf. KoB, p. 137; cf. LXX *epéblepsas*). The mg. has "treat with scorn," which is a better rendering and could be based on *b't*, "kick" (cf. AV, NEB; cf. also *CHAL*, p. 43).

The most often used Greek word is *pleonexía*, which the LXX used to translate *beṣa'*. Another important word is *pleonéktēs*.

In the OT greed may range from an insatiable appetite

(Job 20:20f.) to an excessive urge to acquire military power (Hab. 2:5), "unjust gain" (Prov. 15:27; Jer. 6:13 par. 8:10), and religious evil (Hos. 4:8). In Ps. 57:4 greed is likened to a lion devouring people; in Prov. 28:25 greed leads to strife.

In both the OT and NT greed is condemned as a vice among the wicked (e.g., Ps. 10:3, "and renounces the Lord"), among the people "of the world" (1 Cor. 5:10), and among the Gentiles (Eph. 4:19). For Paul, greed will not permit a person to inherit the kingdom of God; he considered it a vice like immorality, idolatry, drunkenness, etc. (1 Cor. 5:11). Unjust gain is a "trouble for a household" the opposite of honest dealings (Prov. 15:27). Wealth as such is not subject to strictures, but the unlawful pursuit of it is (cf. *TDOT,* II, 207f.). The bishops and deacons should fulfil their office without considering (unlawful) gain (1 Tim. 3:8; Tit. 1:7). Those who trust the Lord will receive material and spiritual riches (Prov. 28:25).

Peter related greed to false teachers who eagerly exploited the religiously naive (2 Pet. 2:3). For him, greed is located in the human heart (v. 14), which may be similar to the OT notion of *nepeš* (cf. Prov. 28:25).

See also COVET, COVETOUSNESS.

Bibliography.–*TDNT,* VI, *s.v.* πλεονέκτης κτλ. (Delling); *TDOT,* II, *s.v.* "bṣʿ" (D. Kellermann).

E. D. WELCH R. W. V.

GREEK LANGUAGE OF THE NT. The Greek used in the NT is the Koine ("common dialect"), the stage in the development of the language from the classical Attic to the modern idiom; it prevailed from *ca.* 300 B.C. to the 6th cent. A.D. Koine is the form of the language used when Greek had attained its greatest territorial expansion as the lingua franca of the Mediterranean world. Greek colonies had been founded in Sicily, southern Italy, and Marseilles in Gaul, and there were other colonies as far west as Spain, as well as in the east: Asia Minor, Palestine, Syria, and upper Mesopotamia. The deliberate hellenizing of the lands conquered by Alexander the Great increased the use of Greek even further. It was widely used in Rome itself, and the services of the Roman Church were in Greek till the middle of the 3rd century.

Since most school grammars have been based on the classical Attic, descriptions of the NT language usually are in terms of the changes that occurred between the Attic of the 5th cent. B.C. and the language of the 1st cent. A.D. The differences in pronunciation, grammar, and vocabulary are noteworthy.

I. Pronunciation
   A. Vowels
   B. Consonants
II. Parts of Speech
   A. Nouns
   B. Verbs
   C. Prepositions
   D. Conjunctions and Particles
III. Syntax
IV. Vocabulary
V. Semitism
VI. Language of Individual Books

I. Pronunciation.–*A. Vowels.* The most noticeable changes in pronunciation, it seems, affected vowels and diphthongs. Throughout the history of the Greek language α, ε, ι, ο seem to have been pronounced somewhat as they are today, i.e., approximately as the Latin *a, e, i, o.* The letter υ, however, had long before the 1st cent. A.D. ceased to be pronounced like the Latin *u,* so Latins had adopted the uniform practice, except in diphthongs, of transliterating υ by *y,* adding *y* to their own alphabet because no Latin vowel corresponded in sound. The sound of υ seems in Koine to have been something like the German *ü* or French *u*. Also, υ was often confused with οι, the latter apparently no longer representing a diphthong but a sound like *ü*.

Some distinctions in vowel quantity seem to have been lost, so that ο and ω were pronounced alike (B. F. Westcott and F. J. A. Hort, *NT in the Original Greek* [1886], II, 309), as they have been ever since. But ε and η were not confused. Although literary Latin always transliterated both by *e,* since the original distinction was one of quantity, a difference in quality had developed. Attic η already had the sound of ι in the 2nd cent. B.C. (for history of sounds cf. Schwyzer, I, 174-414, esp. the table on p. 233), but ι and η are not often confused in the papyri till about three centuries later.

The confusion of αι and ε, though attested in the 2nd cent. B.C., does not seem to have become general until two centuries or more later, after which it has remained constant. Confusion in NT MSS to some extent reflects the pronunciation of later centuries.

The pronunciation of αυ seems to have varied between *a* and *aw,* the latter eventually developing into *av* and *af,* as at present. In the papyri of the 1st cent. A.D. it seems still to have been a true diphthong. It continued to be transliterated by *au* because standards of transliteration had become fixed, ceasing to reflect changes in pronunciation, except in the writing of the semiliterate. Even in the 2nd cent. B.C. instances of αυ = *av* occur.

The evidence for ευ = *ev* and *ef* is a few centuries later, so that in the 1st cent. A.D. ευ seems still to have been pronounced *e* + *u*.

By the beginning of the Koine period ει and ι were pronounced alike. In view of the abundant evidence from the 4th cent. B.C. on, it is mere carelessness not to pronounce ει as ι, the equation that has prevailed for over twenty-three centuries. (Cf. W. W. Goodwin and C. B. Gulick, *Greek Grammar* [1930], p. 10.)

The diphthong ου was regularly transliterated by Latin *u*. This means that even at the beginning of the Koine period ου had this sound, and that this sound was no longer represented by υ.

The diphthong υι had become equivalent to υ late in the classical period, though for some centuries a few still pronounced the ι, simply because it was written.

In summary, it seems that the prevailing pronunciation of the vowels and diphthongs in the 1st cent. A.D. was as follows:

α=a in arm	αι=ai in aisle, or e in met
ε=e in met	αυ=a+w, or a+wh, or av, or ow in owl
η=i in machine(?)	
ι=i in machine	ει=i in machine
ο=o in smoke	οι=German ü
υ=German ü	ου=oo in boot
ω=o in smoke	υι=German ü

As a result of the changes listed above, and others during the following centuries, substandard orthography in Koine documents and NT MSS much resembles the spelling of semiliterate Greeks today.

B. Consonants. Several features of consonant pronunciation should next be noted. By the Koine period φ and χ were changing from the aspirated "mutes" (stops) that had given rise to the Latin transliterations *ph* and *ch* into the continuants represented by *f* and German *ch*. The θ seems still to have been an aspirated stop, i.e., differing from τ somewhat as *t* in *tick* does from *t* in *stick,* and not yet to have acquired the sound represented in English by *th* in "thin," which it has had in later centuries.

The rough breathing (ʽ), represented in English by *h,* was no longer pronounced, though it has continued to be written down to the present day, even by the most avowed colloquial writers, because of the extreme conservatism of Greek orthography. It seems that some still pronounced it in the 1st cent. just because it was written, as most Americans now pronounce the *h* of "humble" and "forehead," and some are beginning to pronounce the *h* of "herb," all of which were previously silent. This phenomenon of recomposition is found in all written languages, especially when a historical orthography lags far behind changes in pronunciation.

The nonassimilation of ν before κ, γ, χ seems to have been common in the 1st century. There was also confusion of κ and γ, δ and τ, β and π, κ and χ, λ and ϱ, π and φ — some probably due to foreign influences. There were both omission and insertion of γ (e.g., ὀλίος for ὀλίγος and μναγιαῖον for μναϊαῖον), because γ was being pronounced as *gh* and *y* as early as the beginning of the Koine period.

The pronunciation of β was perhaps the most variable, ranging from *b* through *w* to *v* until the Christian era, when it settled down to *v*. The standard Latin transliteration for β has been *b* from early times, but there is considerable evidence that, as in Hebrew, the letter had more than one pronunciation (cf. LSJ, derivations under B, *passim*). The sound *v*, or *w*, is shown in the LXX Δαβιδ (*Dabid*) for David and in Λειβία (*Leibía*) for Livia, at the beginning of the Christian era; later in such spellings as *Bergílios* and *Bereníkē* for Vergil and Veronica (Schwyzer, I, 207ff., 829).

During the entire Hellenistic period δ was occasionally pronounced *dh* (as *th* in *this*), which has been its regular pronunciation through most of the Christian era.

In the combinations μβ, γγ, νδ, the consonants β, γ, δ have always been voiced stops, i.e., *b, g, d*.

The rough breathing on initial ῥ indicates some now unknown peculiarity in its ancient pronunciation.

The occasional confusion of λ and ϱ, e.g., φϱαγελλῶ (*phragellṓ*), from Lat. *flagello,* is a phenomenon common to other languages.

The σ before β, γ, δ, μ had been vocalized since early Hellenistic times, as it still is today, e.g., *Smýrnē*, pronounced *zmirni*, cf. Turkish *Izmir*.

The ζ had definitely become *z*, instead of *sd*, or possible *ds*.

Evidence for the statements above is well known to students of the papyri and inscriptions. Vast collections of papyri, as well as thousands of inscriptions and ostraca, have now been published. Convenient illustrative selections from this wealth of testimony may be studied in two small volumes: G. Milligan, *Greek Papyri* (1910); and R. Helbing, *Auswahl aus griechischen Inschriften* (1912). Deiss.*LAE* also offers numerous examples.

II. Parts of Speech.–A. *Nouns.* In common with other Indo-European languages, Greek in the historical period has tended to lose case forms and to depend more and more on prepositions and word order. The drift in Greek, however, has not been as rapid as in certain other languages, e.g., the Romance group.

The dual number, moribund in Attic, is completely absent from the NT. Luke once puts a dative plural on *dýo*. The dative case form, soon to die, had a final burst of extensive use in Koine. The Attic 2nd declension survives only in the relic *híleōs*.

Except for the dual, the first two declensions in their common forms are preserved intact, though the vocative case form is not always used.

The 3rd declension shows considerable loss, some of it made possible by the spread of the *-ion* ending, e.g., *thēríon, kynárion, ichthýdion, daimónion,* instead of *thḗr, kýōn, ichthýs, daímōn* (cf. D. C. Swanson, *JBL*, 77 [1958], 134-151). Others are replaced by second-declension nouns of different roots, e.g., *ónar, phréar, hýs, oís* by *enýpnion, pēgḗ, choíros, próbaton*. The NT often exhibits this phenomenon in process, having both old and new forms, e.g., *kýlix* and *potḗrion, phréar* and *pēgḗ*. Although *oús* was on the way out, neither *ōtárion* nor *ōtíon* proved satisfactory substitutes; all three occur in the NT. Long before the Koine period, *hēméra* had replaced *ḗmar*, as *nerón* was to replace *hýdōr* and *ánoixis éar*, then *ánoixē* replaced *ánoixis* and so on as the 3rd declension eroded further.

Third-declension accusative singulars in α sometimes received a ν on the analogy of the 1st declension, e.g., *astéran, cheíran, eikónan, mḗnan*. In view of the character of the MS evidence it is probable that *astéran* (Mt. 2:10) and *cheíran* (Jn. 20:25) are the original forms. (Copyists are usually "correctors.") Third-declension plurals in ς were changing to ας, e.g., *bóas, ichthýas*. The change of accusative plurals in ας to ες is extremely rare in NT MSS, *tésseres* being the only example, but on very good authority.

The treatment of the Semitic names *Iēsous, Ioudas, Leuis, Satanas,* making no changes except to add ς in the nominative and ν in the accusative, points in the direction of the modern colloquial masculine declension that has developed from the ancient 1st and 3rd, using the ancient accusative stem throughout, but adding ς to the nominative singular. Classical Lesbian and Doric masculine genitive singulars in α may possibly have aided the process. Subscript ι in the dative is purely orthographic.

Most Semitic names are treated in the NT as indeclinables, e.g., those in the genealogies of Matthew and Luke: *Abraam, Isaak, Iakōb, Rhouth, Adam, Sēth, Enōs*.

B. Verbs. In verb inflection the general Indo-European drift from synthetic to analytic forms is evident, not so much in the appearance of new analytic phrases as by the disappearance of certain synthetic forms, e.g., future perfect, future participle, and optative. This apparent impoverishment of the language, and actual impoverishment of the written language, is due to a reluctance to write new forms, even though they were in common use in the spoken language.

The Attic infinitive was in the process of being displaced by a new analytic infinitive, consisting of *hína* +subjunctive, usually in the aorist, e.g., *hína lýsē* instead of *lýsai*. This involved specification of person and number, e.g., *thélomen hína poiḗsēs*, "we want you to do"; *parḗngeilen autoís hína mēdén aírōsin*, "he ordered them to take nothing"; *hína ginṓskōsi tṓn theón*, "for *them* to know God." Note that this periphrasis does not involve the writing of a new form. This *hína* survives in modern Greek in the form *ná*.

Non-Attic forms of certain words do occur, however, such as the imperfects *edídoun, etíthoun, ḗmēn* (*ēn*), *ḗmetha* (*ḗmen*), the aorists *kráxas* (*kragṓn*), *ēnoígēsan* (*aneṓchthēsan*), *kerdḗsai* (*kerdánai*), *epeínasen* (*epeínēsen*), *eípas* (*eipōn*), perfects *oídate* (*íste*), *gégonan* (*gegónasi*), and the new presents *katharízō* (*katháirō*), *stḗkō* (from *héstēka*), the subjunctives *gnoí, doís, doí, dṓē* (*gnṓ, dṓs, dṓ*), and the optative *dṓē* (*doíē*).

The optative was almost dead, occurring mainly in the Lucan and Pauline books, and in these only rarely and in more or less set phrases. Of the sixty-seven optatives in the NT all but four are in the 3rd person; fourteen of the thirty-four Pauline optatives are the one word *génoito;* twelve of Luke's are the word *eíē*, which is the only optative form of *eimí* in the NT. Almost all of Luke's optatives follow expressions of inquiry. Both 1 Peter and Jude have two optatives and Mark, Hebrews, and 2 Peter one each. The optative *génoito* is still used in the modern language in the expression *génoito ho lógos,* more or less equivalent to "amen." No optative of a contract verb occurs.

In ο contracts there was a tendency to level the subjunctive to the same form as the indicative, e.g., *zēloúte* (Gal. 4:17), *physioústhe* (1 Cor. 4:6). Some confusion of indicative and subjunctive was due to the loss of quantitative distinction between ω and ο, and identity in the sound of ει and η.

The invasion of the 2nd aorist by the 1st aorist α, though found in Attic, is more prevalent in the NT, and was on the way to complete occupation.

The three Attic aorists in κα by NT times had the κα in the plural as well as the singular of the indicative, e.g., *aphḗkamen, edṓkate, éthēkan.* Whereas the 3rd plural sometimes had κα in classical Greek, Koine sometimes shows the older form.

The new infinitive, *hína* + subjunctive, was sometimes used as a substitute for the 3rd person imperative, a use that was to increase, along with *ás* + subjunctive, until the 3rd person imperative forms became extinct, e.g., *hē dé gynḗ hína phobḗtai tón ándra,* "and let the wife respect her husband" (Eph. 5:33).

The Koine pluperfect had lost the augment, and in the active voice has ει in all persons and numbers; NT examples are *pepoiḗkeisan, ḗdeisan.* An analytic paraphrase, such as *ḗn endedyménas,* is sometimes used instead of the pluperfect. Although the pluperfect was to become obsolete in later centuries, it shows no special signs of weakness in the NT. The perfect also was to disappear, except for the middle and passive participles, but was in full use in the NT.

C. Prepositions. The Attic prepositions *amphí* and *aná* do not occur; *metá* and *perí* no longer take the dative; *prós* is moribund and limited almost entirely to the accusative. The instrumental use of *en,* rare in Attic, was greatly expanded, though the preposition was soon to die with its case. *Eis* is occasionally used to express location, a use that was to become normal with the extinction of the dative. As in Attic, *ex* sometimes expresses location, e.g., *ho patḗr hēmṓn ex ouranṓn,* "our father in heaven"; *éti ek koilías mētrós,* "still in his mother's womb" (cf. J. M. Rife, *Bibliotheca Sacra,* 80 [Apr. 1931], 220). (Cf. also *DNTT,* III, 1171-1215.)

D. Conjunctions and Particles. Certain characteristic Attic conjunctions and particles are rare and were soon to disappear, at least from the spoken language and from natural writing, though Atticists long continued their use; e.g., *mén, dé, te, oún, ge,* were in varying stages of obsolescence at the beginning of the Christian era, though the first two still appear in atticizing composition today. As suggested above, the decline of the classical particles does not mean that the language was at any stage denuded of particles, but rather that the written language was impoverished due to prejudice against writing non-Attic forms. This development is an inevitable phenomenon in any written language, and the more serious the subject, the more archaizing and artificial the language.

III. Syntax.–Some of the departures from Attic verb syntax that appear in the NT are: *hótan* with the indicative, e.g., *hótan stḗkete proseuchómenoi* (Mk. 11:25); *hótan* with a past tense, *hótan opsé egéneto* (Mk. 11:19); *hína* with the indicative, *hína hymás katadoulṓsousin* (Gal. 2:4); *eán* for *án* with the subjunctive in quasi-conditional clauses, *hópou eán eisélthēte* (Mk. 6:10), one of the phenomena peculiar to Koine, i.e., not found in the later language; *eán* beginning to replace *ei* (which was to survive in later centuries only in the expression *ei mḗ*), *eán hymeís stḗkete* (1 Thess. 3:8); extension of the use of *mḗ* to everything but the indicative, *mḗ dynámenoi* (Mk. 2:4), *anástasin mḗ eínai* (Mk. 12:18); the future indicative used as an imperative, *ópsesthe autoí,* "see to it yourselves" (Acts 18:15); the increasing use of plural verbs with neuter plural subjects, which was to become regular in later centuries; the rarity of the future participle and the rare use of the participle in indirect discourse, these last two being among the learned survivals in the NT.

Non-Attic developments in the use of pronouns include the interrogative use of the relative, e.g., *eph' hó párei?,* "What are you here for?" (Mt. 26:50); the use of the 3rd person of the reflexive for all persons, *martyreíte heautoís,* "You testify against yourselves" (Mt. 23:31), *en heautoís stenázomen,* "We groan within ourselves" (Rom. 8:23). The regular classical position of *tis,* after the noun it qualiies, is found mainly in the Lukan writings, where it averages almost once a chapter, but only once per book in John, 1 Corinthians, James, and 2 Peter. As might be expected, it occurs more frequently in Hebrews, five times.

The retreat of adjective comparison to two degrees is almost complete, so that usually the comparative does duty for the superlative as well, e.g., Mk. 4:32, *meízon pántōn tōn lachánōn,* where "greater than all" equals "greatest of all" (cf. 1 Cor. 13:13). Most of the surviving superlatives in the NT are used in the elative sense, e.g., *krátiste Phēlix* (Acts 24:3) means "very excellent Felix," not that Felix is the most excellent of all men.

The changes illustrated above are treated exhaustively in Schwyzer, and very interestingly in J. H. Moulton, I, *Prolegomena.* W. F. Moulton and A. S. Geden, *Concordance to the Greek NT* (5th ed. 1978), is an indispensable convenience for investigating NT usage. BDF is very useful. Other useful historical treatments are L. von Radermacher, Jannaris, Costas, Kühner and Gerth, A. T. Robertson. Good descriptive grammars of the modern colloquial and literary languages respectively are K. Petraris, *Lehrbuch der Neugriechischen Volks- und Umgangssprache* (1914); and K. Petraris and A. Maltos, *Neugriechische Konversations-Grammatik* (1914). The last work is cited especially because most writers, in using modern Greek as an aid to understanding the language of the NT, seem oblivious to the fact that Greeks read and write as well as talk. As in the case of every civilized people, the written and spoken forms constantly influence each other. The writings of Hatzidakis are useful reminders of this fact.

IV. Vocabulary.–For three millennia a core of basic words has persisted in written Greek with the same spelling, and no doubt with somewhat similar pronunciation, e.g., *theós, ánthrōpos, thálassa, gḗ, pólis, potamós, ouranós, kaí, pṓs, blépō, lógos, diá, katá, metá, ónoma, ḗlthe, eíde, éphage, ángelos, éthnos, epískopos, zōḗ, phōs.* Changes of course took place, both in the choice of words and in their meanings. Certain words were adapted first to Jewish and then to Christian usage, and their older meanings were lost, e.g., *ekklēsía* in pre-Christian Greek was "town meeting," but throughout the Christian era has meant "church"; *daímōn* in pre-Jewish usage was any supernatural spirit, but by Jews and Christians has been applied only to evil spirits; the common nouns *diákonos, presbýteros, epískopos* became titles of church officials; *ángelos* was no longer "messenger," but "angel"; *graphḗ,* "writing," became "scripture"; *éthnos,* "nation," acquired the additional meanings "heathen" and "Gentile," as did *Héllēn* in some contexts; *euangelízō* became "preach the gospel," instead of "bring good news"; *eucharistía,* "gratitude," became "communion service." For detailed discussion of certain words see D. Hill, *Greek Words and Hebrew Meanings* (1967).

The extreme conservatism of the language is illustrated by the following: of approximately 1300 words in the first book of Xenophon's *Anabasis,* the NT contains about 900 and the roots of over 300 others, in spite of the wide difference in subject matter. Hatzidakis (quoted in Schwyzer, p. 40) said, "Of about 4900 NT words, one half are still in use, and of the other half, only 400 are no longer intelligible."

Linguistic conservatism in Greek is mainly Atticism. Due to the dominance of Athens in the 5th cent. B.C., and its intellectual dominance for some centuries afterward, most writers of Greek ever since have rather closely followed Attic models. Only during the past century has it been customary for writers of poetry and fiction to use the colloquial language, though even this is never entirely free from atticizing. (Colloquialism certainly is no bar to eloquence, as evidenced by some of Paul's outstanding passages.) Varying with schooling, linguistic ability, and taste, the amount of atticizing in the 1st cent. A.D. ranges all the way from the artless note of an Egyptian schoolboy to the stilted archaism of Josephus in his attempts to make OT history and Judaism respectable in the eyes of cultured pedants of his day.

Among the Gospels, Mark shows the least evidence of formal schooling, and Luke the most. Of all NT books Revelation seems least affected by the schools. Paul's Greek is more or less colloquial, but that may be partly due to his amanuenses. Opinions differ about which NT books most nearly approach Attic standards. Hebrews, James, and 2 Peter have each been mentioned for this distinction. It seems clear that Christians early became sensitive to the plebeian language of some of their writers. The Catholic Epistles and Apostolic Fathers show a marked increase of atticizing, 2 Peter being an outstanding example, both in vocabulary and sentence structure.

Atticism not only influenced the original writers but also had considerable influence on the transmission of the text. Educated copyists tend to "correct" the matter they are copying. Hence, e.g., Codex Borgianus (T) and the ecclesiastical text (i.e., the form used by Greek Orthodox Christians in their public and private devotions) of the Lord's Prayer have *elthétō* and *aphíemen* instead of *elthátō* and *aphḗkamen.* Thus, during the fourteen centuries of hand copying, the Greek text of the NT was a variable moving toward Attic standards.

The chief non-Attic influence in the development of the Koine was Ionic, the dialect of Ionia on the west coast of Asia Minor, closely related to the dialect of Attica, Euboea, and most of the Aegean Islands. Ionic had gone through some centuries of more or less independent development until the rise of the Athenian empire in the 5th cent. B.C. again brought close relations. As Attic developed into an international language its peculiar ττ gave way, in most words, to the σσ of other dialects, e.g., *thálassa.* Such Ionic vocabulary as *basílissa, tésseres, nossós,* and *eleúsomai* became standard; noun endings in μα and ας increased, e.g., *Dēmas, Epapras, Hermas, Kēphas, Thōmas*; ρσ was substituted for ρρ; third-declension forms of *noús* were used; etc. (For further details cf. Bauer, rev., pp. xiii-xiv.)

One of the most obvious changes in vocabulary was in the length of words due to: prefixes, as in *apophthéngomai*; compound prefixes, as in *apekdéchomai*; the spread of various suffixes, as in *himatismós hagíasma*; and the compounding of root elements, as in *oikodespótēs.* These increases in length refer to the written language. It is probable that many of these long words had shorter synonyms in the spoken language, as a Greek today might tell an inquiring foreigner that the word for pawnshop is *enechyrodaneistḗrion,* but in speaking use the folk etymology *pansophí,* or as in American schools one hears abbreviations like "lab" and "exam" more often than the longer, more formal words.

The NT contains a number of Latin words, such as *praitṓrion, kḗnsos, spekoulátōr, mílion, sandálion, kaísar, soudárion.* The suffix *-ianós,* as in *Christianós,* is a Latin borrowing; and *-ḗsios* in *Philippḗsios,* an ending like the classical *Ithakḗsios,* is thought to have been influenced by Latin *-enses.* Aside from vocabulary items, there seems to to be little if any Latin influence on the language of the NT.

*V. **Semitism.***–With regard to the Gospels in particular, but also for the rest of the NT, the claim has sometimes been made that its Greek is a Jewish dialect. In fact, this view was widely accepted until less than a century ago when the massive evidence of the papyri began to accumulate, showing that the Greek in general use by Gentiles in the Koine period was the same as that in which the NT was written. The major credit for scholarly realization of this fact is given to A. Deissman. His two works most often cited in this connection are *Bibelstudien* and *Licht vom Osten.* The former first appeared in 1895, and *Neue Bibelstudien* in 1897 (Eng. tr. A. Deissmann, *Bible Studies* [2nd ed. 1909], including both German works). *Licht vom Osten* first appeared in 1908 (4th ed. Eng. tr. Deiss.*LAE*).

Some or all of the Gospels have often been considered translations from Aramaic originals. This idea is as old as the statement of Papias that Matthew wrote his *logia* in the Hebrew dialect, and each one interpreted them as best he could. By "Hebrew dialect" he doubtless meant Aramaic. This same Papias wrote that "Mark, since he had been Peter's interpreter, wrote accurately, though not in order, as much as he could remember of the things said or done by Christ; for he himself had neither heard the Lord nor followed him" (quoted in Eusebius *HE* iii.39.15). As a matter of fact, Matthew shows less evidence of being a translation from a Semitic original than does Mark.

Christianity does, of course, have a Jewish background. It is rather generally agreed that Jesus and His disciples spoke Aramaic, though some have argued that they spoke Greek in Jewish Palestine. The chief considerations are: all Palestinian Jews knew Aramaic; upper-class Jews like Josephus had a Greek education; the government did not maintain a public educational system; those who had dealings with the government knew Greek more or less; Greek cities were established in Palestine, especially the Decapolis; there is no reason to suppose that the peasants, the Jewish masses, knew Greek; the language of Palestinian Christianity was Aramaic.

The most convincing testimony is found in the NT quotations of Aramaic, Mk. 5:41; 14:36; 15:34; Rom. 8:15; 1 Cor. 16:22 (see RSV mg.); Gal. 4:6; and the statements in Acts 21:40; 22:2 that Paul addressed the crowd at Jerusalem in Hebrew (Aramaic). That no interpreters are mentioned in certain situations is of no weight. It is a common practice to report bilingual conversations without mention of interpreters. In Papias's account of Mark and Peter, the interpreter is an essential feature of the statement.

That Jesus spoke Aramaic seems certain. Whether He used any Greek cannot be determined.

Papias's account of Mark and Peter seems to be at least partially true. Some of the early Christians were undoubtedly bilingual, e.g., Mark, since his family had moved to Jerusalem from Cyprus, a part of the Greek world. Paul was evidently another, for in Jerusalem he used Greek or Aramaic as the occasion demanded. Bilingual people who hear something in one of their languages often report it in the other language without conscious attention to idiom. This process, like Mark's alleged writing in Greek what he heard Peter say in Aramaic without even following the same word order, is quite different from translating a book. The most reasonable view is that the writers of the Gospels were either themselves bilingual, or obtained their information from people who were.

In view of the above facts and probabilities, and also inasmuch as the language of the LXX (the Bible of the early Church), which is mainly a translation from Semitic originals, was familiar to NT writers and extensively quoted by them, it would have been impossible to keep all Semitic coloring out of their Greek. No matter how many languages the NT passes through in translation, Christians still keep the Semitic words amen, hallelujah, hosannah, abba, and maranatha. But there seems to be no decisive evidence that any of the NT books is a translation from a Semitic original.

Attempts to prove that this or that Gospel is a translation have usually taken the form of claiming that certain expressions were Semitic idioms not native to Greek. (Cf. C. F. Burney, *Aramaic Origin of the Fourth Gospel* [1922]; J. A. Montgomery, *Origin of the Gospel According to St. John* [1923]; C. C. Torrey, *HTR,* 16 [1923], 305-344.) Such claims have been shown almost entirely groundless by demonstration that the idioms in question can be found in Greek that is free composition (cf. E. C. Colwell, *Greek of the Fourth Gospel* [1931]; M. Burrows, *JBL,* 49 [1930], 95ff.; J. C. Doudna, *Greek of the Gospel of Mark* [*JBL* Monograph Series, 12, 1961]).

Certain difficult passages are also claimed to be mistranslations. Even if they are, it is no proof that the whole book is a translation. Furthermore, the Semitic originals of the alleged translations and mistranslations are purely hypothetical. (Cf. M. Black, *An Aramaic Approach to the Gospels and Acts* [3rd ed. 1967].)

A more decisive criterion by which to detect translation Greek is word order. Greek, like Latin, has a comparatively flexible word order. Semitic languages have a relatively rigid word order for various sentence elements. The order in translation Greek tends to follow that of the Semitic original. This tendency can be endlessly illustrated by its regular occurrence in the LXX. Insofar as this test has been applied to NT books, the indications are that none is a translation from Aramaic (cf. J. M. Rife, *JBL,* 52 [1933]).

VI. Language of Individual Books.–The language of Matthew and Mark is often contrasted. Mark is less premeditated and more vigorous. In Matthew at the baptism the skies are "opened," but in Mark they are "split"; the voice from the sky speaks directly in the 2nd person in Mark and Luke, but more impersonally in the 3rd person in Matthew. At the healing of the leper Mark (1:41) says Jesus was "moved with pity" for him, but Matthew (8:3) and Luke (5:13) omit this detail. In Mark (6:39f.) at the feeding of the five thousand it is said that the multitude was seated "in picnic groups on the green grass, like one flower bed after another," three colorful details omitted by Matthew and Luke.

It seems quite possible that considerations of space may explain the comparative briefness of Matthew and Luke in some passages, or in many. A papyrus scroll longer than the length of Matthew's Gospel would probably be inconvenient to handle. Luke filled two rolls of this length; Mark had room to spare because he recorded fewer incidents.

At any rate, Mark is not as polished a production. The opening is comparatively abrupt, the transitions rougher, the sentence structure paratactic. These facts have been recognized from ancient times. There are, however, compensating features of vividness and vigor. Mark's Greek is literary in the sense that it is not illiterate. It shows constant though not total conformity to grammatical standards; e.g., he is one of the NT writers who strictly adhere to the rule for cases used with *akoúō*. Parataxis of itself does not necessarily destroy unity of thought or logical subordination of clauses or high literary effect. Outstanding examples of these truths are Ps. 23 and Isa. 40:12. J. A. Kleist, who long made a special study of Mark, wrote, "Mark is graphic and sure of his Greek" (*Gospel of St. Mark* [1936], p. 205, and similar observations *passim*).

Luke, who apparently followed written sources, seems to have refrained from demonstrating his own literary attainments when quoting; but when composing freely, as in the preface to his first volume, he reached a literary level in sentence structure not found elsewhere in the Gospels. As can be seen in any Greek harmony of the Gospels, both Matthew and Luke frequently used vocabulary and sentence structure considered more elegant than Mark's.

Matthew's preference for neat symmetrical arrangement appears in: the three divisions of his genealogy; his five concentrations of discourse material marked with opening and closing formulas; the poetic parallelism of his Beatitudes; the stanza-like structure of his paragraphs on the spiritual fulfillment of the law (5:17-47); the six on charity, prayer, and fasting; the seven woes pronounced on scholars and Pharisees (23:14-27); the concluding lament over Jerusalem; the unforgettable little rhyme in 21:41, *kakoús kakṓs apolései autoús;* and the classic form of his Lord's Prayer.

It seems fair to say that Luke is the most beautiful of the four Gospels. This impression is largely due to the first two chapters, in which Hebraic parallelism plays such a prominent part in the canticles; but the impression is strengthened throughout the Gospel. This seems, however, due less to diction and sentence structure than to the scenes he chose to represent.

John is really the most colloquial of the Gospels, the easiest for a modern Greek to understand, either by reading or hearing, on account of its vocabulary, the simple sentence structure, and the great amount of repetition. It has a core vocabulary, words used everywhere and always by Greeks, or sometimes, as in the case of *trṓgō,* the modern word instead of the classical or more prevalent Koine. Here again, the ideas combine with the form of language to produce the almost unrivaled devotional atmosphere of the book.

In Acts one finds more learned language than in any of the Gospels, even Luke. Vocabulary, sentence structure, and inflectional forms are less common (*koiné*), nearer the classical, but occasionally Luke uses a construction or a meaning that seems more colloquial than anything in Mark.

It is the subject matter of the Epistles that makes them harder reading even than Acts. By its nature, narrative is easier reading than discussion of ideas. Most narrative is necessarily concrete, while the ideas of the NT Epistles largely concern the intangible and abstract. Romans makes a strong impression of profundity, but the reader does not feel that Paul has been to school as much as Luke. The book has become a Christian classic of the first rank due to Paul's natural eloquence and intensity of feeling, rather than because of his advanced Greek schooling. Yet one may well ponder the statement of a native Greek classical scholar that "Paul . . . follows a middle course writing the language of an educated gentleman of his time" (Costas, p. 55).

The foregoing statements apply to the Pauline writings in general, but special mention should be made of a type of sentence of which two examples appear in Col. 1. It is well known that the long sentence of vv. 3-5 follows an elastic pattern that Paul used in other letters, i.e., a somewhat formal expression of warmhearted appreciation and confidence, varied to suit the occasion, and no doubt developed by repeated use. The much longer sentence of vv. 9-20 must be the result of similar practice in summing up the various phases of his gospel in one majestic period. A similar impression is made by the extensive summary of Eph. 1:3-14, as well as by the grandly flowing sentences of the rest of the latter Epistle. Written in the popular Greek of its time, it is of a style comparable to the art and beauty of the Greek Orthodox liturgy, in which it is quite at home.

Also worth mentioning are the irresistibly diplomatic appeal in Philemon and the repeated puns on the meaning of the name Onesimus: *áchrēstos, eúchrēstos, opheílei, prosopheíleis, onaímēn, xenían.* Was not an ironic pun also intended in connection with the names Euodia ("good journey, success") and Syntyche ("[good] luck, success") in Phil. 4:2?

Hebrews has a markedly different kind of language. It was only after the difference had been obscured by translation into Latin that attentive readers could fail to see the divergences from Paul's language. Clement of Alexandria, the earliest extant writer to discuss the matter, clearly recognized the difference from Paul's Greek. Hebrews is a masterpiece of impressive rhetoric. It is hard to say which is more striking, the distinguished character of the vocabulary, or the refined art of sentence building. Clement of Alexandria saw a similarity to Luke (quoted in Eusebius HE vi.14). Schwyzer called it a work of polished art ("das erste Denkmal christlicher Kunstprosa," p. 126); Moulton stated that Luke was "the only NT writer except the author of Hebrews to show any conscious attention to Greek ideas of style" (p. 18).

In the Catholic Epistles one finds a certain elegance of language, and in two or three of them considerable atticizing, indicating that the authors, or their amanuenses, had read more Greek literature than other NT writers, except Luke and the author of Hebrews. Renan said, "The Greek of James is pure and almost classic" (*L'Antichrist,* p. 47); he considered 1 Peter more like Paul's writing (p. 115). Judgments vary with regard to some of these books. Certainly there is more atticizing in Jude and 2 Peter than in the other Catholic Epistles. The language of the Johannine Epistles is clearly of the same kind as that of the Gospel (see above).

The Greek of Revelation is the least schooled of any book in the NT, but as a work of art it is the finest flower of apocalyptic literature. Its author used language of an elementary character, and it is the easiest Greek in the NT for a beginner to read. This is due to the concreteness of the imagery, the simplicity of sentence structure, the prevalence of action, the everyday nature of the vocabulary, and the minimum of Greek syntax involved. Its variety is of visualized things rather than of ideas.

The differences in language in different NT books are largely obliterated in translations. An ideal NT translation would make each book correspond to the literary character of its Greek.

Bibliography.–Bauer; BDF; C. N. Brown, *English-Greek, Greek-English Dictionary* (1924); P. S. Costas, *Outline of the History of the Greek Language* (1937); G. N. Hatzidakis, *Einl. in die Neugriechische Grammatik* (1892); *Die Sprachfrage im Griechenland* (1905); A. N. Jannaris, *Historical Greek Grammar* (1897); *Modern Greek Dictionary* (1895); R. Kühner and B. Gerth, *Ausführliche Grammatik der griechischen Sprache* (2 vols., 4th ed. 1955); H. Lietzmann, *Griechische Papyri* (1924); C. F. D. Moule, *Idiom Book of NT Greek* (2nd ed. 1959); J. H. Moulton, *Grammar of NT Greek* (3 vols., 1929-1962); MM; A. G. S. Papanastephanou, *Divine Liturgy of St. John Chrysostom* (1928); J. T. Pring, *Oxford Dictionary of Modern Greek* (1975); L. von Radermacher, *NT Grammatik* (1925); A. T. Robertson, *Grammar of the Greek NT* (1923); E. Schwyzer, *Griechische Grammatik* (3 vols., 1950-53); *SQE*; T. Zahn, *Intro. to the NT* (3rd ed. Eng. tr. 1909), I.

J. M. RIFE

GREEK VERSIONS. *See* SEPTUAGINT; VERSIONS.

GREEKS grēks; **GRECIANS** grē'shənz [Heb. *b^e^nê hay-y^e^wānîm*] (Joel 3:6 [MT 4:6], AV); [Gk. *Hellēn, Hellēnis*] (Jn. 12:20; Acts 14:1; Rom. 1:14; etc.); AV also GRECIANS. The word for Greeks occurs only once in the OT. (For references to Greece in the OT *see* GREECE XII; JAVAN.) In the AV of the Apocrypha "Grecians" and "Greeks" are used without distinction, e.g., 1 Macc. 6:2; 8:9; 2 Macc. 4:15, 36. Thus in 1 Macc. 1:1, Alexander the Great is spoken of as king of Greece, and in 1 Macc. 1:10 the Macedonian empire is called "the kingdom of the Greeks" (Gk. *basileías Hellēnōn*). In 2 Macc. 13:2 the army of Antiochus king of Syria is called "Grecian" (*dýnamin Hellēnikēn*), and in 2 Macc. 6:8 the "cities of the heathen" (*Hellēnidas póleis*) are Macedonian colonies. In 2 Macc. 6:1 an aged Athenian is sent by Antiochus the king and charged with the duty of Hellenizing the Jews; in 2 Macc. 9:15 Antiochus vows that he will make the Jews equal to the Athenians; in 1 Macc. 12–14 reference is made to negotiations of Jonathan the high priest with the Spartans, whom he calls brethren, seeking the renewal of a treaty of alliance and amity against the Syrians. With the spread of Greek power and influence, everything not specifically Jewish was called Greek; thus in 2 Macc. 4:36; 11:2; 3 Macc. 3:8, the "Greeks" contrasted with the Jews are simply non-Jews, so called because of the prevalence of Greek institutions and culture. "Greek" even came to be used in the sense of "anti-Jewish" (2 Macc. 4:10, 15; 6:9; 11:24).

In Isa. 9:12 (MT, LXX 11) the LXX reads *toús Hellēnas* for Heb. *p^e^lištîm,* "Philistines"; but we are not therefore justified in assuming a racial connection between the PHILISTINES and the Greeks. Further light on the ethnography of the Mediterranean basin may in time show that there was actually such a connection; but the rendering in question proves nothing, since "the sword of the oppressor" of Jer. 46:16 (LXX 26:16) and 50:16 (LXX 27:16) is likewise rendered in the LXX with "the sword of the Greeks" (*machaíras Hellēnikēs*). In all these cases the translators were influenced by the conditions existing in their own day, and were certainly not disclosing obscure relations long forgotten and newly discovered.

In the NT the AV, RSV, and NEB attempt to distinguish between Gk. *Hellēnes* and *Hellēnistai.* The AV and RSV generally render "Greeks" for *Hellēnes* (but cf. Jn. 7:35, AV; in Acts 11:20 the AV follows a textual tradition that reads *Hellēnistai*) while the NEB uses "Greeks" or "Gentiles." For *Hellēnistai* (Acts 6:1; 9:29) the AV gives "Grecians," the RSV "Hellenists, and the NEB "those who spoke Greek," "Greek-speaking Jews" (mg. "Hellenists"). These latter were Jews of the Dispersion who spoke Greek (*see* HELLENISM; HELLENIST), as distinguished from Palestinian Jews; but since many of the latter also spoke Greek by preference, the distinction could in no sense be absolute. In Jn. 7:35, e.g., *Hellēnes* can hardly refer to any but Greek-speaking Jews, and in Jn. 12:20 the "Greeks" (*Hellēnes*) who went up to worship at the FEAST of the Passover were almost certainly in the same category.

This difficulty is aggravated by the application of the term *Hellēnes* not only to those of Hellenic descent, but also to all those who had appropriated the language of Greece and the ideals and customs collectively known as Hellenism. These people were thus in the strict sense Hellenists, differing from the "Hellenists" (*Hellēnistai*) of the RSV only in that they were not of Jewish descent. In other words, *Hellēnes* (except perhaps in Jn. 7:35 and 12:20, as noted above) is in general equivalent to *tá éthnē,* "Gentiles" (*see* GENTILE). The various readings of the MSS (and thus the difference between AV [and NEB] and RSV) in 1 Cor. 1:23 well illustrate this.

Consequently there is much confusion, and in some cases it is quite impossible, with our limited knowledge of the facts, to clear up this confusion. In general, it would seem probable that where "Greeks" are comprehensively contrasted with "Jews," the reference is actually to "Gentiles," as in Acts 14:1; 17:4; 18:4; 19:10, 17; 20:21; Rom. 1:16; 10:12; 1 Cor. 1:22-24 (RSV "Gentiles," Gk. *éthnesin*); Gal. 3:28; Col. 3:11. In Mk. 7:26 the woman of Tyre, called "a Greek [NEB "Gentile"], a Syrophoenician by birth," was clearly not of Hellenic descent. Whether Titus (Gal. 2:3) and the father of Timothy (Acts 16:1, 3) were in the strict sense "Greeks," we have no means of knowing. Rom. 1:14, "I am under obligation both to Greeks and to barbarians," undoubtedly refers to Greeks strictly so called; possibly, though by no means certainly, the "Greeks" of Acts 21:28, alluding to Trophimus the Ephesian (v. 29), are to be taken in the same sense. In Acts 11:20 the MSS vary between *Hellēnistas* and *Hellēnas* (AV "Grecians"; RSV "Greeks"; NEB "Gentiles"). Even if one adopts the reading *Hellēnas,* however, it is not clear whether true Greeks or Gentiles are intended. *See* HELLENIST.

W. A. HEIDEL

GREEN; GREENISH. *See* COLOR.

GREET; GREETING [Heb. *šā'al leššālôm*] (1 S. 10:4; 17:22: 25:5; 2 S. 8:10; 1 Ch. 18:10); AV also SALUTE, "enquire of his welfare" (1 Ch. 18:10); [*bāraḵ*] (2 K. 10:15); AV SALUTE; [Aram. *šelām*] (Ezr. 4:17); AV "Peace"; [Gk. *aspázomai*] (Mk. 9:15; Lk. 1:40; Acts 18:22; 21:7, 19; etc.); AV also SALUTE, EMBRACE (He. 11:13); NEB also WELCOME (Mk. 9:15), "pay respects" (Acts 18:22), HAIL (He. 11:13), etc.; [*aspasmós*] (Lk. 1:29, 41, 44; 1 Cor. 16:21; Col. 4:18; 2 Thess. 3:17); AV SALUTATION; [*chaírō*] (Acts 15:23; 23:26; Jas. 1:1; 2 Jn. 10f.); AV also BID GOD SPEED (2 Jn. 10f.); NEB omits in Acts 23:26. (In Isa. 14:9 the RSV supplies "greet," the NEB "meet"; the AV "for thee" is to be preferred; in Ezr. 4:11 the RSV supplies "send greeting.")

The OT has no word for "greet" or "greeting." *Bāraḵ* means "bless." The expression *šā'al lešālôm,* however, was a form of greeting. *Šā'al* means to "ask" and *šālôm* denotes "peace, prosperity, well-being"; thus *šā'al lešālôm* means to "inquire about one's welfare." Elsewhere the RSV translates this expression literally, e.g., Gen. 43:27; Ex. 18:7; 2 S. 11:7. Other OT greetings are: "Is it well with you, my brother?" (Heb. *hašālôm 'attâ 'āḥî,* 2 S. 20:9), "The Lord be with you!" (*YHWH 'immāḵem,* Ruth 2:4), "The Lord bless you!" (*yeḇāreḵeḵā YHWH,* Ruth 2:4), "The blessing of the Lord be upon you!" (*birkaṯ-YHWH 'alêḵem,* Ps. 129:8), etc. For the king the greeting was "Long live the king!" (*yeḥî hammeleḵ,* 1 S. 10:24, etc.; cf. 1 K. 1:31, "May my lord King David live for ever!").

In the NT the usual word for "greeting" is *aspasmós* (cf. vb. *aspázomai*). A frequent form of greeting is *chaírō* ("rejoice"); the infinitive, *chaírein,* and imperative, *chaíre, chaírete* (lit. "Rejoice!" "Joy to you!"), are frequently translated "Hail!" or "All Hail!" (Mt. 26:49; 27:29; 28:9; Mk. 15:18; Lk. 1:28; Jn. 19:3). (Cf. *TDNT,* IX, 367.) When Jesus sent forth His disciples they were to "salute" the house they came to (Mt. 10:12), saying, "Peace [*eirḗnē*] be to this house!" (Lk. 10:5). After His resurrection Jesus greeted His disciples saying, "Peace be with you" (*eirḗnē hymín,* Jn. 20:19, 21, 26). He left His "peace" (*eirḗnē*) with them — "not as the world gives," in merely a formal way — as His parting blessing (Jn. 14:27). As used in these NT greetings, *eirḗnē* has a far broader meaning than our Eng. "peace." This Greek term was used in the LXX to translate Heb. *šālôm* and thus it took on the meaning of that term. In greetings it generally denotes well-being or salvation (*TDNT,* II, 411-17).

Epistolary greetings are found in the OT, the Apocrypha, and the NT. The Aram. *šelām* (cognate of Heb. *šālôm*) occurs in Ezr. 4:17; 5:7; Dnl. 4:1 (MT 3:31); 6:25 (MT 26). In the Apocrypha *chaírō* is frequent (1 Esd. 6:8; 8:9; 1 Macc. 10:18; etc.). The same form is used in Acts 15:23; 23:26. 3 John closes with "Peace [*eirḗnē*] be to you. The friends greet [*aspázomai*] you" (v. 15). Paul opened most of his letters with the special Christian greeting, "Grace to you and peace from God our Father and the Lord Jesus Christ" (Rom. 1:7; 1 Cor. 1:3; 2 Cor. 1:2; etc.); most of them close with "The grace of the Lord Jesus (Christ) be with you" (1 Cor. 16:23; 2 Cor. 13:14; etc.). He also sent greetings from those who were with him and directed that greetings be given to various persons (Rom. 16:3-23; 1 Cor. 16:19f.; 2 Cor. 13:12f.; Phil. 4:21f.; Col. 4:10-15; etc.). In these cases the word is *aspázomai.*

See also EPISTLE; GOD SPEED; KISS; SALUTATION.

See *TDNT,* II, *s.v.* εἰρήνη (Foerster).

W. L. WALKER

GREYHOUND (Prov. 30:31, AV). *See* COCK.

GRIDDLE [Heb. *maḥaḇaṯ*] (Lev. 2:5; 6:21 [MT 14]; 7:9); AV PAN. A thick plate of pottery or metal, used for frying the cereal offering. Cf. the use of *maḥaḇaṯ* ("iron plate") in Ezk. 4:3. *See* BREAD IV.

GRIEF; GRIEVE [Heb. *ka'as* (Ps. 6:7 [MT 8]; 31:9 [MT 10]; Prov. 17:25), *ka'aś* (Job 17:7), *tûgâ* (Prov. 14:13; 17:21), *ḥolî* (Isa. 53:3f.), *ḥālâ* (Ps. 77:10 [MT 11]; Isa. 17:11; 53:10; Am. 6:6), *pûqâ* ("cause of grief," 1 S. 25:31), *yāgôn* (Jer. 8:18), hiphil and piel of *yāgâ* (Lam. 3:32f.), *merîrûṯ* ("bitter grief," Ezk. 21:6 [MT 11]), hiphil of *'āḏaḇ* (1 S. 2:33), hithpael of *'āḇal* (1 S. 15:35; 16:1), *'āṣaḇ* (Gen. 6:6; 1 S. 20:3, 34; 2 S. 19:2 [MT 3]; Neh. 8:10f.; Ps. 78:40; Isa. 54:6; 63:10), *'āgam* (Job 30:25), *'āgēm* (Isa. 19:10); Gk. *lypḗ* (2 Cor. 7:10), *lypéō* (Jn. 21:17; 2 Cor. 7:8f., 11; Eph. 4:30; 1 Thess. 4:13), *syllypéō* (Mk. 3:5)]; AV also SORROW, INFIRMITY, HEAVINESS (Prov. 14:13), MOURN, SORRY, VEX (Isa. 63:10); NEB also SORROW, SUFFERING, BANE, "stumble" (1 S. 25:31), "exasperate" (Prov. 17:25), WOUND, HURT, etc. The RSV supplies "grieved" in Ps. 35:14 (cf. the AV); "grief" in Lam. 2:11 to translate Heb. *lā'āreṣ* (AV lit. "to the ground"; NEB "on the earth"); "cause grief" in 3:51 to translate *'ālal lenepeš* (AV lit. "affect [my] heart"; NEB "torment"); and "grief" in Eccl. 5:17, following the LXX (cf. NEB "gnawing anxiety") *contra* the MT (cf. the AV). The AV takes *'agmê* in Isa. 19:10 to represent the noun *'agam,* "pond" or "pool"; cf. Ex. 7:19.

The RSV uses "grief" to refer to sorrow, pain, and suffering, which may be physical and/or mental in nature. The Suffering Servant is reported to be "acquainted with grief" and to have "borne our griefs." "Grief" in these expressions literally means "sickness" or "disease" but may be used here for "suffering" in a more general sense (Isa. 53:3f.; cf. Isa. 17:11; Ps. 77:10). The psalmist who complains that his "eye wastes away because of grief" (6:7) is petitioning Yahweh to deliver him from grave illness which has caused such grief that his eyes are wasting away with weeping. Yet it is improper to draw too sharp a distinction between mental and physical suffering in Hebrew thought, which understood a person as a whole rather than as a composite of body and mind. Physical, mental, and even spiritual suffering are interrelated (Ps. 31:9).

Grief is the opposite or surcease of joy (Prov. 14:13) and may result when one is demoralized, as when Jeremiah pondered the fate of Judah (Jer. 8:18). One may experience grief when one has "pangs of conscience" or when one is annoyed or irritated (Prov. 17:21, 25). In 2 Cor. 7:10 Paul made a distinction between a "godly grief" — a deep sorrow that leads to repentance and opens the eyes to the gift of salvation — and a worldly grief that shrinks from guilt. This "worldly grief" blinds a person to the forgiveness offered in Christ and leads him only to deeper and deeper sorrow and finally to death (cf. P. E. Hughes, comm. on 2nd Corinthians [*NICNT*, 1962], pp. 271-73).

To "grieve" is to be (or cause someone to be) sad, troubled, irritated, distressed, or mournful. It is characteristic of the OT to attribute human emotions to Yahweh. The OT reports that Yahweh was grieved by the rebellion of Israel in the wilderness period (Ps. 78:40; cf. Isa. 63:10). Mankind caused Yahweh so much distress and trouble that He was grieved that He even made them (Gen. 6:6). Israel experienced grief during the Exile, when the prophet said that Yahweh called Israel as a wife "forsaken and grieved in spirit" (Isa. 54:6). Though Yahweh was the cause of the grief Israel experienced during the Exile, He will also have compassion on Israel (Lam. 3:32). Both the OT and the NT speak of grieving the Holy Spirit (Isa. 63:10; Eph. 4:30). To grieve means also to mourn the dead, as Samuel mourned the death of Saul (1 S. 15:35) and as David mourned Absalom (2 S. 19:2; cf. 1 Thess. 4:13). Jesus was grieved and angry at the hardness of heart of those around Him when they disapproved of His healing on the sabbath the man who had a withered hand (Mk. 3:5). Peter was grieved when Jesus asked him for the third time, ". . . do you love me?" (Jn. 21:17).

Bibliography.–*TDNT*, IV, *s.v.* λύπη κτλ.: λύπη, λυπέω (Bultmann); *TDOT*, I, *s.v.* "'abhal" (Baumann). E. W. CONRAD

GRIEVANCE. Occurs in the RSV only in 1 Cor. 6:1, where the Gk. *prágma* (AV "matter"; NEB "dispute") is used in a forensic sense, meaning "lawsuit." This usage is common in the papyri (cf. MM, p. 532). The AV uses it only in Hab. 1:3, for Heb. *ʿāmāl* (RSV "trouble"; NEB "wrongdoing").

GRIEVOUS [Heb. *raʿ*–'evil' (Dt. 6:22; 28:35, 59; Eccl. 2:17), *ḥālâ* (Eccl. 5:13, 16 [MT 12, 15]; Jer. 10:19; 14:17; 30:12; Nah. 3:19), niphal of *māraṣ*–'be sick' (1 K. 2:8; Mic. 2:10), *kāḇēḏ*–'heavy' (Gen. 41:31; 50:11)]; AV also SORE; NEB CRUEL, MALIGNANT, "singular," SEVERE, MORTAL, BITTERLY, "disaster" (Dt. 6:22), "trouble" (Eccl. 2:17). "Grievous" is used of something severe or intense. The word is frequently used to describe physical sickness (e.g., Dt. 28:59) or wounds (e.g., Jer. 30:12), but may be used to describe famines (Gen. 41:31), curses (1 K. 2:8), etc. "Grievously" does not translate a Hebrew term but is a translation device in the RSV for the emphatic use of the infinitive absolute in Ezk. 25:12 (*'āšam*, "be guilty"), and Zec. 12:3 (*śāraṭ*, "make incisions"); in Lam. 1:8 it is the use of the direct object (*ḥēṭ'*) with its cognate verb (*ḥāṭā'*, "sin"; cf. W. Gesenius, E. Kautzsch, and A. E. Cowley, *Hebrew Grammar* [1910], §§ 113o-r, 117). E. W. CONRAD

GRIND [Heb. *ṭāḥan* (Job 31:10; Isa. 47:2; Lam. 5:13), *gāras* (Lam. 3:16); Gk. *brýchō* (Acts 7:54), *trízō* (Mk. 9:18)]; AV also HAS BROKEN (Lam. 3:16); NEB also "be [a] slave" (Job 31:10), HAS BROKEN (Lam. 3:16); **GRINDERS** [Heb. *ṭōḥᵃnôṯ*] (Eccl. 12:3); **GRINDING** (part.) [Heb. *ṭāḥan* (Dt. 9:21; Isa. 3:15); Gk. *alḗthō* (Mt. 24:41 par. Lk. 17:35)]; (noun) [Heb. *ṭaḥᵃnâ* (Eccl. 12:4), *qôl*–'voice' (Jer. 25:10)]; AV, NEB, also SOUND (Jer. 25:10).

The grinding of flour was usually done at the MILL (Isa. 47:2; cf. Dt. 9:21 for the idea of pulverizing). Normally it was the work of women (Ex. 11:5; Isa. 47:2), though men did it too (Jgs. 16:21; Lam. 5:13). The cessation of grinding at the mill was a sign of desolation or loss of prosperity (Jer. 25:10; cf. Rev. 18:22). The grinders of Eccl. 12:3 are human teeth (Heb. *ṭōḥᵃnôṯ*, "grinding ones, molar teeth," KoB, p. 351), which in old age are few in number and no longer capable of fulfilling their task. Likewise, the "sound of . . . grinding" in v. 4 may have expressed the inability to speak (E. W. Hengstenberg, comm. on Ecclesiastes [repr. 1977], pp. 246f.; R. Gordis, *Koheleth – The Man and His World* [3rd ed. 1968], pp. 342f.).

The "grinding of the teeth" may mean a literal grinding in Mk. 9:18 (the result of a seizure), or it may be physical evidence of extreme anger (Acts 7:54; *see* GNASH). "Grinding gravel" in Lam. 3:16 may refer to lack of food, or oppression (parallel to the next line; cf. Isa. 3:15). (In Prov. 20:17 Heb. *ḥāṣaṣ*, "gravel," has a negative connotation too; cf. W. McKane, *Proverbs* [*OTL*, 1970], pp. 539f.; but *see* GRAVEL.) The idea of sexual molesting seems implied in Job 31:10 (paralleling the next line; cf. KoB, p. 351; M. Pope, *Job* [*AB*, 1973], p. 231; but cf. KD *in loc.*), and perhaps in Lam. 5:13. The MT in Lam. 5:13 is *ṭᵉḥôn nāśā'û*, which may be understood as "they lifted up the handmill" (cf. KD *in loc.*), or "they took [young men] to grind" (cf. D. R. Hillers, *Lamentations* [*AB*, 1972], p. 99). The sexual connotation is supported by the Vulg., but does not seem to fit the context.

Our Lord used the scene of two women grinding together at a mill (Mt. 24:41 par. Lk. 17:35) as one example of what will happen when He returns in glory.

R. W. V.

GRISLED (Gen. 31:10, 12; Zec. 6:36, AV). *See* DAPPLED.

GROAN [Heb. *'ānaḥ*, *'ᵃnāḥâ*, *'ānaq*, *'ᵃnāqâ*, *nā'aq*, *nᵉ'āqâ*, *šā'ag* (Ps. 38:8 [MT 9]), *šᵉ'āgâ*, *nāham*, *hāgîg* (Ps. 5:1 [MT 2]), *gî(a)ḥ* (Mic. 4:10); Gk. *stenázō* (Rom. 8:23; 2 Cor. 5:2), *stenagmós* (Acts 7:34), *sustenázō* (Rom. 8:22)]; AV also SIGH, MOURN, CRY, "meditation" (Ps. 5:1 [MT 2]), "labour to bring forth" (Mic. 4:10); NEB also SIGH, MOAN, LAMENT, "starve" (Prov. 5:11), "exhaust" (Joel 1:18), "trouble" (Job 23:2), "inmost thoughts" (Ps. 5:1), "labour" (Jer. 45:3). In Lam. 1:4, the NEB adds "and sigh" to "groan," thus conflating the RSV and the AV. In Jer. 22:23 MT *nēḥant* may be from *'ānaḥ*, "groan" (so RSV, NEB; cf. W. Gesenius, E. Kautzsch, A. E. Cowley, *Hebrew Grammar* [1910], p. 80 n. 1); the AV "be gracious" assumes that *ḥnn* is the root, but that root occurs nowhere else in the niphal, whereas *'ānaḥ* always occurs in the niphal (cf. also the LXX *katastenázō*, which elsewhere translates only *'nḥ*).

"Groaning" expresses strong pain or very deep distress in unintelligible sounds. The mortally wounded in battle groan (Jer. 51:52). Job bore his great physical and emotional distress by pouring forth his groaning like water (Job 3:24). The physical suffering resulting from the emotional stress over sinning is expressed in "groaning all day long" (Ps. 32:3; cf. Ezk. 30:24). He who succumbs to a harlot ends his life in groaning as his "flesh and body are consumed" (Prov. 5:11). Beasts that are deprived of food and water groan (Joel 1:18).

The community, like the individual, may groan under strenuous circumstances. One proverb stated: "When the wicked rule, the people groan" (Prov. 29:2). During the bondage in Egypt, which Pharaoh intensified in order to keep the Hebrews under control, the people of Israel groaned (Ex. 2:23). During the period of the judges, whenever a foreign nation oppressed Israel, the people groaned on account of their affliction (Jgs. 2:18). Jerusalem is personified as groaning intensely after it was decimated and the people taken captive (Lam. 1:4, 8, 11, 21f.; cf. Mic. 4:10). God hears the groaning of His people, however, and He intervenes to relieve His people's distress. This truth was uniquely demonstrated through the Exodus (Ex. 2:24; 6:5; Acts 7:34; cf. Ps. 102:20 [MT 21]).

The righteous are not afraid to present their groans before Yahweh. Yahweh opposes the wicked who boast against the upright, and He will come to His people's aid (Ps. 5:1f.). When the righteous see the disintegration of the community on account of its abominations, they groan and weep for its conversion. Yet on the Day of Judgment only they are delivered (Ezk. 9:4; cf. 14:16, 18, 20).

In the NT groaning occurs on three levels: nature desiring to be restored, the believer desiring to leave the burdens and limitations of the present body for the new resurrection body, and the Christian earnestly praying in the Spirit to God, troubled beyond words over the sin and corruption of this present world (Rom. 8:22f., 26; 2 Cor. 5:2, 4).

The use of "groan" in Jn. 11:33, 38 (AV; RSV "was deeply moved") is variously understood. When Jesus was confronted by Mary and the weeping crowds at Lazarus's death, He was deeply moved in His innermost being (His spirit). The Greek verb *embrimáomai* means with animals "snort in rage" and with people "be indignant." (In Mk. 1:43, the RSV renders it "charge sternly.") Commentators disagree whether Jesus was angry, or full of grief, or deeply distressed. No doubt Jesus' deep emotions here are complex, but this word probably denotes at least a strong element of anger — anger at death itself which Jesus was about to battle in His own death, and anger at the inadequate manner of coping with death in the surrounding crowds. Jesus' whole being was involved in His redemptive mission, especially His miracles, for they expressed the creative power of the new order overcoming the old, cursed order (Mt. 8:16f.). The greatest enemy of the old order is death. Thus in His inner preparation to overcome it by raising Lazarus Jesus was very deeply troubled.

Bibliography.–R. Brown, *John I-XII* (*AB*, 1966); L. Morris, *John* (*NICNT*, 1971); B. F. Westcott, *John* (1924); *TDNT*, VII, *s.v.* στενάζω κτλ. (Schneider). J. E. HARTLEY

GROSS. Used once by the RSV to translate Heb. *ṭāpaš* ("be insensitive") in Ps. 119:70, "their heart is gross like fat" (AV "fat as grease"; NEB "thick and gross"). The AV twice uses "wax gross" (RSV "grow dull"; NEB "become gross") of the heart in translating Gk. *pachýnō*, "make fat" (Mt. 13:15; Acts 28:27). *See* DULLNESS (OF HEART); FAT.

GROUND [Heb. *ʾᵃḏāmâ, ʾereṣ, yabbāšâ* ("dry ground," Ex. 4:9; Josh. 4:22), *māqôm, mîšôr*–'plain' ("level ground," e.g., Ps. 26:12), *nîr* ("fallow ground," Prov. 13:23; Jer. 4:3; Hos. 10:12), *ʿāpār*–'dust, ground,' *ʿāqōḇ* ("uneven ground," Isa. 40:4), *pāneh*–'face' (Prov. 24:31), *ṣāmāʾ* ("parched ground," Jer. 48:18), *ṣîyâ* ("desolate ground," Job 30:3), *ṣimmāʾôn* ("thirsty ground," cf. Ps. 107:33), *śāḏeh*; Gk. *gḗ, chamaí* ("on the ground," Jn. 9:6; 18:6), *édaphos*–'ground' (Acts 22:7), *edaphízō* ("dash . . . to the ground," Lk. 19:44), *petrṓdēs* ("rocky ground," Mt. 13:5, 20 par. Mk. 4:5, 16)]; AV also LAND, EARTH, DUST, FACE (Prov. 24:31), etc.; NEB also LAND, SOIL, COUNTRY, FIELD, DOWNWARDS, BATTLEFIELD (Ps. 83:10 [MT 11]), etc.

I. Terminology and Use.–The RSV renders the Heb. *ḥᵃrōš ḥᵃrîšô*, "plow his plowing," as "plow his ground" (1 S. 8:12). Although the text of Job 30:3 is corrupt (cf. *BH* and comms.), the meaning of Heb. *ṣîyâ*, "desolate ground," is clear (AV "wilderness"; NEB "desert"). Though the RSV's translation "punishment" (following the emendation to *mûsārōh*, "chastening"; cf. KoB, p. 503; *BH*; cf. also NEB "chastisement") is appropriate in Isa. 30:32, the AV's rendering "grounded (staff)" (following MT *mûsāḏâ*, "foundation") could be retained when understood as "(rod of) decree" (KD *in loc.*) or "appointment" (E. J. Young, comm. on Isaiah [1969], II, 368; he also points out that 1QIsa[a] agrees with the MT).

The most frequently used OT words for "ground" are Heb. *ʾᵃḏāmâ* and *ʾereṣ*. *ʾᵃḏāmâ* often means the cultivated land, property, or a region, but it can also mean simply dirt or humus (cf. *TDOT*, I, 90-94). Thus *ʾᵃḏāmâ* usually refers to a particular piece or area of ground and less often to the world or earth as a whole (cf. Stadelmann, pp. 128f.). On the other hand, *ʾereṣ* usually expresses "ground" in general, i.e., the land, the earth, etc. Thus it is a contrast to heaven, the sea, and the underworld (*TDOT*, I, 393, 399f.; note, however, that it can also refer to the underworld [cf. Stadelmann, pp. 167f., 170-73; *TDOT*, I, 399f.], like its Ugaritic and Akkadian cognates), and is never used, e.g., for a handful of dirt. The most common NT word is Gk. *gḗ*, which combines the meaning of *ʾᵃḏāmâ* and *ʾereṣ* (Bauer, rev., p. 157).

"Ground" occurs often in a variety of expressions in the OT. (1) To bow (with one's face) to the ground indicates respect (e.g., Gen. 42:6; 1 S. 28:14; 2 S. 1:2; 1 Ch. 21:21) or an act of worship (Neh. 8:6; Job 1:20; Dnl. 10:9). (*See also* GESTURE IV.) (2) One sits "on the ground" to lament (Jer. 14:2; Lam. 2:10; Ezk. 26:16), possibly because of the association of burial with a grave in the ground (for the significance of grave *see* BURIAL I). To sit on the ground can also signify humiliation (e.g., Isa. 47:1; cf. Ps. 89:44 [MT 45]) or sharing in human misery (Job 2:13). (3) To "clear the ground" signifies taking possession (Josh. 17:15) or preparing for cultivation (Ps. 80:9 [MT 10]). (4) To "smite," "strike," "level" (Jer. 51:58), etc., to the ground means to beat severely, kill, or destroy. In 2 K. 13:18f. Elisha tells Joash to strike arrows on the ground three times in order to symbolize the future war with Syria (cf. J. Gray, *I & II Kings* [*OTL*, rev. ed. 1972], pp. 599f.). (5) Words not "fallen to the ground" (1 S. 3:19; 2 K. 10:10) are apparently prophecies that have been fulfilled; the truth "cast to the ground" points at truth trampled down and disregarded (Dnl. 8:12). (6) To "give one's ground" to someone else (lit. "give the place," *nāṯan māqôm*, Jgs. 20:36) shows that one is yielding. (7) In the sense of "reason" or "cause" one may have "ground" for complaint (Dnl. 6:4f. [MT 5f.], Aram. *ʿillâ* [cf. Syr. *ʿeltāʾ*; postbiblical Heb. and Aram. *ʿîlâ*]; cf. "ground for boasting," 1 Cor. 9:15f., Gk. *kaúchēmá*). (8) "On ground of" in the sense of "because of" renders Heb. *ʿal* in Dnl. 9:18 (cf. KoB, p. 704) (cf. Gk. *diá, ek, hóti* in Rom. 3:30; 1 Cor. 10:25-27; 1 Tim. 6:2).

The NT does not have some of these expressions, and others are less frequent. The expression "fall on the ground" in prayer occurs only in Mk. 14:35, and "dash . . . to the ground" in the sense of severe beating only in Lk. 19:44. To "sit on the ground" does not carry any negative connotations (Mt. 15:35; Mk. 8:6). Divine providence is expressed with "not one of [your] hairs will fall to the ground" (Mt. 10:29, quoting 1 S. 14:45; cf. 2 S. 14:11). Jesus' writing with His finger on the ground (Jn. 8:6, 8) is enigmatic (cf. comms., esp. R. E. Brown, I [*AB*, 1966], 333f.).

II. Theology of the Earth.–When God created the universe, he created human beings (Gen. 2:7), trees (v. 9), and animals (v. 19) from the ground. Subsequently, He cared for the ground (v. 6). All this intimates that human beings are tied to the ground and continue to be dependent on it for sustenance (cf. v. 15). It also indicates that the physical aspect of creation is not in opposition to the spiritual aspect nor an expression of evil and sin. (*See* DUST.)

Sin did, however, enter into the human heart and, according to Gen. 3, the ground is cursed because of the fall. The ground will now produce "thorns and thistles" and turn work into labor. It will also be linked with death — we must return to it (3:17-19). In ch. 4 the soil "drinks" the shed blood of Abel, and Cain is no longer able to "till" the ground.

But God promised to bless the land with an abundance of crops (e.g., Dt. 7:12f.; 26:2; 28:1-14), in response to which the Israelites were to render the firstfruits of their increase to their Maker (Ex. 23:19; 34:26; cf. Neh. 10:35). Israel's frequent religious and cultic lapses affected God's dealings with His people: He not only threatened that locusts would consume the harvest (Dt. 28:15, 42; Jer. 7:20), but also sent them (Amos. 7:1). At times the nations became so deeply involved in licentious adultery that the ground "vomited" them out; the same could happen to Israel if it disobeyed the Lord (Lev. 18:24-28). To the prophets the curse of the land was frightfully real (Isa. 24:5-13).

Although Israel refused to be faithful to its Protector, God remained faithful and renewed the ground (Ps. 104:30). Even human work loses part of the curse of labor (Gen. 5:29; 8:21). The prophets looked for a time of abundance of rain and fruition (Isa. 30:23f.; Ezk. 36:33-36; Zec. 8:12). The final restoration of all things in the NT includes the ground. In Rev. 22 the curse is completely lifted from the ground, and nature will again yield its increase as before the fall.

III. Metaphors.–The ground can "open its mouth" (Gen. 4:11; Nu. 16:30), "mourn" (Joel 1:10), "be dismayed" (Jer. 14:4), or "thirsty" (cf. Ps. 107:33; cf. Isa. 44:3 for the symbol of "abundant water"). Faithfulness can spring up out of the ground (Ps. 85:11 [MT 12]). The "face of the earth" (AV) is rendered the "face of the ground" by the RSV. The heart is pictured as soil, which must be broken up, i.e., surrendered to God in true repentance (Jer. 4:3). In the parable of the sower, the various kinds of ground signify the various responses to the word of God sown in the human heart (Mt. 13:3-8 par. Mk. 4:3-20). In Eph. 3:17 love is compared to a foundation ("rooted and grounded in love") through which believers may comprehend the scope of divine love. The Suffering Servant "grew up" as a root "out of dry ground" (Isa. 53:2), i.e., among miserable circumstances and corruption (KD *in loc.*).

On "holy ground" (Ex. 3:5; Acts 7:33) *see* HOLY, HOLINESS.

Bibliography.–L. I. J. Stadelmann, *Hebrew Conception of the World* (1970); *TDNT,* I, *s.v.* γῆ κτλ. (Sasse); *TDOT,* I, *s.v.* "'ᵃdhāmāh" (Ploeger); "'erets" (Ottoson).

J. E. HARTLEY R. W. V.

GROUPINGS [Heb. *pᵉluggâ*] (2 Ch. 35:5); [*miplaggâ*] (2 Ch. 35:12); AV DIVISIONS; NEB GROUPS. Both terms are based on the verb *pālag,* "divide." They refer to divisions of priests (v. 5) and of laymen (v. 12), according to the families who traced their lineage from a common forefather. *See also* CLAN.

GROUPS [Gk. *prasiá*] (Mk. 6:40); AV RANKS; NEB ROWS. Literally a garden plot (cf. Sir. 24:31). The term *prasiá* is repeated in Mk. 6:40 (*prasiaí prasiaí*) and therefore carries with it a distributive effect (cf. repetition in Mk. 6:7, 39). The groups consisting of hundreds and fifties looked like garden plots distributed throughout and contrasting with the green grass (v. 39).

GROVE (Gen. 21:33; Ex. 34:13, AV). *See* ASHERAH; TAMARISK.

GRUDGE [Heb. *nāṭar*] ("bear a grudge," Lev. 19:18); NEB CHERISH ANGER; [hiphil of *rʿʿ* + *ʿayin*–'eye'] (Dt. 28:54, 56); AV "eye shall be evil"; NEB "will not share"; [Gk. *enéchō*] ("have a grudge," Mk. 6:19); AV HAVE A QUARREL; NEB NURSE A GRUDGE; **GRUDGING** [qal of Heb. *rʿʿ*–'look with displeasure at'] (Dt. 15:10); AV "be grieved." In the RSV "grudge" occurs as a verb only in Dt. 28:54, 56, where it means to do or give something unwillingly (*see* EVIL EYE). In earlier versions it was used frequently as a verb with the obsolete meaning of "murmur" or "grumble," e.g., Wyclif has in Lk. 15:2, "The farisies and scribis grucchiden seiyenge. . . ." The AV employs it in this sense in Ps. 59:15 (MT 16) and Jas. 5:9.

"Grudge" occurs twice as a noun in the RSV in the phrase "bear a grudge" or "have a grudge" (Lev. 19:18; Mk. 6:19). In each case the verb translated has reference to the nursing of feelings of ill will and resentment. According to Dt. 15:10 the creditors were to loan freely to the poor even when the year of release was near, without any grudge (P. C. Craigie, comm. on Deuteronomy [*NICOT,* 1976], p. 237).

GRUMBLE. *See* MURMUR.

GUARANTEE. The Greek term *arrabṓn* occurs three times in the NT (2 Cor. 1:22; 5:5; Eph. 1:14), translated in each case by "guarantee" in the RSV, "earnest" in the AV, and "pledge" in the NEB. It has an equivalent in Heb. *ʿērāḇôn* (Gen. 38:17f., 20), in Lat. *arrabo,* in French *arrhes,* and in Old English *arles.* The term is mercantile and comes originally from the Phoenicians. Its general meaning is that of a pledge or token given as the assurance of the fulfillment of a bargain or promise. It also carries with it the idea of forfeit, such as is now common in land deals, only from the obverse side. In other words, the one promising to convey property, wages, or blessing, binds the promise with an advance gift or pledge partaking of the quality of the benefit to be bestowed. If the agreement is about wages, then a part of the wages is advanced; if it is about land, then a clod given to the purchaser or beneficiary may stand as the pledge of final and complete conveyance of the property.

In the spiritual sense, as used in the passages above named, the reference is to the work of the Spirit of God in our hearts being a token and pledge of a perfect redemption and a heavenly inheritance. There is more than the idea of security in the word as used, for it clearly implies the continuity and identity of the blessing.

See also PLEDGE. C. E. SCHENK

GUARD (vb.) [Heb. *šāmar* (Gen. 3:24; Ex. 23:20; 1 S. 2:9; etc.), *nāṣar* (Prov. 2:11; 4:6, 13; 5:2; etc.), *šāqaḏ* (Ezr. 8:29); Gk. *phylássō, diaphylássō* (Lk. 4:10), *phrouréō* (2 Cor. 11:32; 1 Pet. 1:5), *tēréō* (Acts 12:6)]; AV also KEEP, "keep the watch," WATCH (Ezr. 8:29), "keep the ward" (Neh. 12:25), PRESERVE (Ps. 12:7 [MT 8]), WAIT (Prov. 27:18), "keep bound" (Lk. 8:29); NEB also "be on duty," "be on guard," WATCH, PROTECT, DEFEND, "keep safe," KEEP, etc.; (noun) [Heb. part. of *rûṣ, ṭabbāḥîm, maṭṭārâ, mišmār, šomrâ* (Ps. 141:3), *miṣṣāḇâ* (Zec. 9:8); Aram. *ṭabbāḥayyā'* (Dnl. 2:14); Gk. *koustōdía, hypērétēs, spekoulátor* (Mk. 6:27), *phylakḗ* (Acts 12:10), part. of *tēréō* (Mt. 28:4)]; AV also WATCH, WARD, PRISON, FOOTMAN (1 S. 22:17), ARMY (Zec. 9:8), SERVANT, KEEPER (Mt. 28:4), OFFICER (Mt. 5:25), EXECUTIONER (Mk. 6:27); NEB also BODYGUARD, ESCORT, OUTRUNNER, GUARDHOUSE, WATCH, GARRISON (Zec. 9:8), ATTENDANT (Mt. 26:58; Mk. 14:54), CONSTABLE (Mt. 5:25), GUARD-POST (Acts 12:10), "High Priest's men" (Mk. 14:65); **REAR GUARD** [Heb. *'āsap*–'gather' (Josh. 6:9, 13; Isa. 52:12; 58:8), *'āqēḇ* (Josh. 8:13)]; AV also REREWARD, LIERS IN WAIT (Josh. 8:13).

The verb means to protect, defend, watch (Eccl. 5:1). It occurs frequently in both the OT and the NT in the sense of guarding prisoners or captives (Josh. 10:18; Acts 12:4; 23:35; etc.). The word also means to protect someone or something from danger (1 S. 25:21; Neh. 4:22). God Himself guards His people (1 S. 2:9; Ps. 104:4; Jn. 17:12; 1 Pet. 1:5) or sends an angel to guard them (Ex. 23:20; Ps. 91:11; Lk. 4:10). When the psalmist said that he would guard his ways in order that he would not sin (Ps. 39:1 [MT 2]), he meant that he would restrain himself or keep himself within bounds. In wisdom literature the expression "guard one's mouth" means to be prudent of speech (Prov. 5:2; Ps. 141:3; cf. Mic. 7:5). In Prov. 2:11; 4:6 "understanding will guard" a person; conversely one should guard instruction (Prov. 4:13) and knowledge (1 Tim. 6:20; 2 Tim. 1:14).

The noun "guard" refers to an individual or a group of men who are responsible for guarding a person or a place; also to a place of confinement, a prison.

Ṭabbāḥîm is used for the special bodyguard of both the Egyptian pharaoh (Gen. 37:6; 39:1; 40:3f.; 2 K. 25:8-20) and the Babylonian king (Jer. 39:9–52:30; Dnl. 2:14). It occurs only in the phrase "captain of the guard." The literal or original meaning of the Hebrew term is "butchers" or "cooks," but it lost this meaning. The reason the royal bodyguard possessed this title is not known. An oriental monarch's bodyguard consisted of picked men attached to his person and ready to fulfil his pleasure in important and confidential concerns.

The royal guard or escort of the Israelite king, however, is designated by the term *rāṣîm* (lit. "runners"). These men acted as royal messengers or couriers from the time of Saul onward (2 K. 10:25; 11:6); and this designation connects them with the couriers of the kings of Persia (Est. 3:13, 15; 8:14).

The men of the royal bodyguard were usually foreigners like the janissaries of oriental monarchs down to modern times, who preferred to have around themselves warriors uninfluenced by family connection with the people of the land. Ramses II had such a bodyguard whose commanders ranked with the great officers of the crown. David's bodyguard of six hundred, known also as the *gibbōrîm* or "mighty men," consisted of Cherethites, Pelethites, and Gittites (2 S. 15:18; 20:23), and we read of Carites (2 K. 11:19), who may have been Carians or Cretans, as forming part of the guard at the coronation of King Jehoash.

It was the responsibility of these officers to guard the palace and the guardroom which housed the royal treasures (1 K. 14:27f.). That this guard had duties in connection with the temple as well as the king's house seems clear. They accompanied King Rehoboam when he visited the temple (v. 28). Jehoiada employed their captains to put Athaliah to death and to exterminate the worshipers of Baal who had fled to the temple precincts (2 K. 11:4-19); the temple gate leading to the palace was called "the gate of the guards" (v. 19). For this occasion, at least, the royal bodyguards were the temple guards. The temple in Ezekiel's vision apparently had guardrooms (*see* GUARDROOM).

Mišmār literally means "prison." Only in late OT writings did it come to mean one who guards or keeps watch (1 Ch. 9:23; Neh. 4:22f. [MT 16f.]; 7:3).

A prison is denoted by the word *maṭṭārâ* and with this sense it always occurs in one of two phrases: (1) *ḥ^aṣar hammaṭṭārâ* ("court of the guard"; cf. Jer. 32:2, 8, 12; 33:7; 37:21; 38:6, 13, 28; 39:14f.; Neh. 3:25; 12:39), referring to a place in the palace complex for detaining prisoners. It was here that Jeremiah was held prisoner in the closing days of Judah's existence. Jeremiah apparently had enough freedom to continue to prophesy and even to purchase a field from his cousin at Anathoth (Jer. 32:6-25). (2) *Ša'ar hammaṭṭārâ* ("gate of the guard," Neh. 12:39). The location of this gate is disputed. It may have been either a gate of the palace compound or one of the city gates.

In the NT *koustōdía* is used for the guard assigned to watch over Jesus' grave (Mt. 27:65f.; 28:11). A Latin loanword, it probably refers to soldiers of the Roman army, although they may have been Jewish. *Spekoulátōr* (Mk. 6:27) is also a Latin loanword (<*speculari*, "look, watch"), which could mean "executioner" (AV), but here refers to the bodyguard of Herod Antipas. *Hypērétēs* in Mt. 5:25; 26:58; Mk. 14:54, 65 refers to the servants of a court. According to Mk. 14:44 Judas instructed the crowd to lead Jesus to trial as a prisoner ("under guard"; cf. JB "well guarded"); the AV and NEB convey more the idea of protection, which may be closer to the meaning of Gk. *asphalṓs* ("securely," MM, p. 88).

T. NICOL E. W. CONRAD

GUARDIAN [Heb. *'ōmēn*] (2 K. 10:1, 5); AV "them that brought up," "bringers up"; NEB TUTOR; [*sôḵēḵ*] (Ezk. 28:14, 16); AV "that covereth," "covering"; [Gk. *epískopos*] (Acts 20:28; 1 Pet. 2:25); AV OVERSEER, BISHOP; NEB also "give charge"; [*epítropos*] (Gal. 4:2; 2 Macc. 11:1; 13:2; 14:2); AV TUTOR, PROTECTOR (Apoc.).

In the OT, Heb. *'ōmēn* (part. of the vb. *'āman*, "be faithful," "be entrusted with"; cf. Nu. 12:7) denotes one who was put in charge of training the children (*see* NURSE; cf. *TDOT*, I, 294). *Sôḵēḵ* is a participle of *sāḵaḵ*, "cover," "block off" (in order to protect). The AV follows the MT in Ezk. 28:14, 16, taking the king of Tyre to be the guardian cherub. The RSV and NEB (following the LXX and Syriac) read *'et*, "with," instead of *'at*, "you," in v. 14; and in v. 16 they read the consonants *w'bdk* as *w^e'ibbaḏkā*, "and he drove you out," rather than *wā'abbeḏkā*, "and I will destroy you." (Cf. *IB*, VI, 221.) The RSV and NEB readings have been adopted by most expositors. The function of the guardian cherub seems to parallel that of the CHERUBIM placed in the garden of Eden (cf. Gen. 3:24).

In the NT "guardian" is used twice by the RSV to render *epískipos*, a cognate of the verbs *episképtomai*, "look at, examine, inspect," and *episkopéō,* "look at, care for, watch over, oversee" (Bauer, rev., pp. 298f.). The LXX uses *epískopos* with reference to God as the one who sees all things, even what is hidden in the heart (cf. Wisd. 1:6), and in reference to men who are appointed as overseers (cf. Neh. 11:9, 14, 22). The term is frequently associated with the idea of shepherding (*poimaínō*), thus denoting "one who keeps watch over the flock" (*TDNT,* II, 615). It has this sense in both Acts 20:28, which refers to elders as guardians of "the flock," and 1 Pet. 2:25, which speaks of Christ as the "Shepherd and Guardian of your souls" (cf. 1 Pet. 5:2-4). While the term *epískopos* soon came to be used for "bishop" (cf. 1 Pet. 2:25, AV; *see* BISHOP) as the highest ecclesiastical office, this is not the case in these two passages. Peter uses the term to emphasize Jesus' intimate knowledge of the souls over which He is watching. In Acts 20:28 Paul is speaking to the Ephesian elders (*presbýteroi*); thus *presbýteros* and *epískopos* are used of the same people, *presbýteros* referring to the office and *epískopos* to an aspect of the elder's responsibility.

Epítropos is a common Greek term for one to whom is entrusted the entire care of a minor. Such was the responsibility of Lysias to the youthful Antiochus Eupator (cf. 1 Macc. 3:32f.; 6:15-17). Paul used the guardian as a figure for the law (Gal. 4:2) in order to make the point that those who through Christ have been adopted as children of God have reached maturity, and therefore are no longer under the supervision of the law (cf. 3:24; *see also* CUSTODIAN).

See *TDNT,* II, *s.v.* ἐπισκέπτομαι κτλ.: ἐπισκέπτομαι, ἐπισκοπέω, ἐπίσκοπος (Beyer). N. J. O.

GUARDROOM [Heb. *tā' hārāṣîm*–'room of the runners'] (1 K. 14:28 par. 2 Ch. 12:11); AV GUARD CHAMBER. Rooms in Solomon's temple where the golden shields and other treasures were stored. The "side rooms" (Ezk. 40:7-36, Heb. *tā'*) in Ezekiel's vision of the temple may have been in the same location or have served a similar function.

GUDGODAH gud-gō'də [Heb. *guḏgōḏâ*]. A place of encampment in the wilderness journeyings, listed between Moserah, where Aaron died, and Jotbatah (Dt. 10:7). It is called HOR-HAGGIDGAD in Nu. 33:32f. In the LXX the name occurs as *Gadgad* in both passages. W. S. L. S.

GUEST. In the OT "guest" generally translates some form of the Hebrew verb *qārā',* literally "call." The noun *gēr,* "sojourner," and verb *gûr,* "stay as a *gēr,*" are used of one who leaves his own tribe or village and lives elsewhere as an alien (cf. *TDOT,* II, *s.v.* "gûr" [D. Kellermann]). The usual words in the NT are Gk. *anakeímenos,* "one reclining at table" (Mt. 22:10f.; Mk. 6:26), and the cognate *synanakeímenos,* "one reclining at table with" (Mt. 14:9; Mk. 6:22). All three Synoptists recorded the saying of Jesus, "Can the wedding guests [*hoi huioí toú nymphṓnos*; AV lit. "children of the bridechamber"] fast [or mourn] while the bridegroom is with them?" In Acts 10:23 the word translated is *xenízo,* "receive as a guest."

Oriental customs growing out of a nomadic life demand a greater abandon and freedom with respect to the relation of host and guest than are permitted by the conventionalities of Western life. A householder is expected to entertain a traveler, and in turn the traveler may accept with perfect ease the hospitality shown without any obligation to pay. (*See* ENTERTAIN.) The significance of the Hebrew word is that of one who is called or invited. A certain sacredness, unknown to modern Western society, was attached to the guest, so that a special apartment was set aside for the guests. (*See* GUEST ROOM.)

The relation between host and guest is strikingly illustrated by the attitudes of Jesus on various occasions. Notable among these are the hospitality of Matthew (Lk. 5:29-32), Jesus' relation to Martha and Mary (10:38), and His entrance into the home of Zacchaeus (Lk. 19:1-10). Likewise, Jesus spoke frequently of the relation that should exist between the guest and his host (see Lk. 7:44-46; Mt. 25:35). W. G. CLIPPINGER

GUEST ROOM [Gk. *katályma*] (Mk. 14:14; Lk. 22:11); AV GUEST-CHAMBER; NEB ROOM; [*xenía*] (Philem. 22); AV LODGING; NEB ROOM. The Gk. *katályma* is derived from *katalýō,* "slacken, loosen," referring to the ropes of the beasts of burden, and hence "rest, find lodging." While in Mk. 14:14 it alludes to the room borrowed for the Last Supper, the normal usage was in connection with a single room in which travelers could stay overnight. In classical literature *xenía* meant "hospitality, entertainment," but in Philem. 22 it is used by metonymy of the place of entertainment itself. *See also* ENTERTAIN.

GUIDANCE [Heb. *taḥbulōṯ*] (Job 37:12; Prov. 11:14; "wise guidance," 20:18; 24:6); AV COUNSEL(S), WISE COUNSEL (Prov. 24:6), GOOD ADVICE (Prov. 20:18); NEB "guiding hand" (Job 37:12), "skilful strategy"; [*dāraš*] ("seek guidance," 1 Ch. 10:13f.); AV ENQUIRE. *Taḥbulōṯ* comes from *ḥebel,* "rope," "measuring line," and seems originally to have been a nautical term for "steering" or "guiding" a ship. It occurs only in Proverbs and Job, where it is used in the general sense of "steering, skilful direction" (KoB, p. 1025). *Dāraš* is a common word for "seek, inquire."

See also COUNSEL; SKILL.

GUIDE (vb.) [Heb. *nāḥâ* (Job 31:18; 38:32; Ps. 67:4 [MT 5]; 73:24; 78:72; Prov. 11:3; Isa. 58:11), *nāhal* (Ex. 15:13; Ps. 31:3 [MT 4]; Isa. 49:10; 51:18), *nāhag* (Ps. 78:52), *dāraḵ* (Isa. 42:16); Gk. *hodēgéō* (Jn. 16:13; Acts 8:31; Rev. 7:17), *metágō* (Jas. 3:3f.), *kateuthýnō* (Lk. 1:79)]; AV also LEAD, GOVERN, ACQUAINT (Eccl. 2:3), TURN ABOUT (Jas. 3:3f.); NEB also TAKE (Isa. 49:10), DIRECT, "give the clue" (Acts 8:31); (noun) [Heb. *nāhag* (Ps. 48:14 [MT 15]); Gk. *hodēgós* (Mt. 15:14; 23:16, 24; Acts 1:16; Rom. 2:19), *paidagōgós* (1 Cor. 4:15)]; AV also LEADER, INSTRUCTOR; NEB also TUTOR.

The word often occurs with Yahweh as the one who guides His people (Ps. 48:14; Ex. 15:13). The root *nhl* literally means to lead or guide to a watering place and to give rest there; thus the imagery is that of a shepherd guiding or leading his flock (Isa. 49:10; Ps. 78:52). Such imagery is appropriate for Yahweh, who will guide His people from exile (Isa. 49:10). In Rev. 17:7 the paradoxical picture is presented of the Lamb who, as a shepherd, will lead God's people to springs of living water.

People also guide or conduct, as Job guided the life of an orphan from birth (Job 31:18); and in the Benedictus it is said that John the Baptist will "guide our feet into the way of peace" (Lk. 1:79). The Ethiopian eunuch who was reading the prophet Isaiah needed to be guided so that he might understand (Acts 8:31).

In Acts 1:16 Judas is described as the one "who was guide to those who arrested Jesus," and in Mt. 15:14 and 23:16, 24 the scribes and Pharisees are described as "blind guides." The *paidagōgós* (lit. "boy-leader") was the slave who cared for a child when he was not in school. Paul used this word (1 Cor. 4:15) for other teachers in the church; they are related to the Corinthians as a *paidagōgós,* while Paul considered himself to be more intimately related to them as a father (cf. F. W. Grosheide, comm. on 1st Corinthians [*NICNT,* 1960], p. 112).

E. W. CONRAD

GUIDEPOSTS [Heb. *tamrûrîm*] (Jer. 31:21); AV HIGH HEAPS; NEB SIGN-POSTS. The Hebrew word is synonymous in the parallel structure of the verse with WAYMARK. Perhaps the object was formed of a heap of stones (cf. *tîmārâ,* Joel 2:30 [MT 3:3]; "column," Cant. 3:6; *tōmer,* "scarecrow," Jer. 10:5). Jeremiah may be using the term in a figurative sense; i.e., he may be telling the Israelites to note the mistakes that had led them into captivity in order that they will know the way to restoration and not repeat their past mistakes.

GUILE [Heb. *mirmâ*] (Gen. 27:35); AV SUBTILTY; NEB TREACHEROUSLY; [*šeqer*] (Ps. 119:78); AV PERVERSELY; NEB LIES; [*maššā'ôn*] (Prov. 26:26); AV DECEIT; NEB DISSIMULATION; [Gk. *dólos*] (Jn. 1:47; 2 Cor. 12:16; 1 Thess. 2:3; 1 Pet. 2:1, 22; 3:10); NEB FALSE, TRICK, DECEIVE, DECEIT, FALSEHOOD; **GUILELESS** [Gk. *akéraios*] (Rom. 16:19); AV SIMPLE; NEB SIMPLETONS. The basic meaning of each of the Hebrew and Greek terms is that of deceit, fraud, or dissimulation. Heb. *mirmâ* is frequently used for deceptive balances (Hos. 12:7 [MT 8]; Am. 8:5), but most often for treacherous or crafty speech in general (cf. Gen. 34:13; Ps. 17:1; 52:4 [MT 6]). Heb. *šeqer* often occurs in connection with the practice of fraud (Hos. 7:1; Jer. 6:13; 2 S. 18:13), a false oath (Zec. 8:17; Jer. 5:2), and false prophecy (Jer. 14:14; 23:25f.). Gk. *dolóō,* the verb form of *dólos,* was sometimes used for the deceit involved in the adulteration of wine (Bauer, rev., p. 203).

Guile is regularly understood as a particularly reprehensible sin. It is the godless, according to Ps. 119:78, who use guile to conceal their true intent (Prov. 26:26). In Gen. 27:35 Isaac relates the bitter news to Esau that his brother has come with guile and fraudulently taken his blessing. Significantly, the same Hebrew word used for the guile of Jacob is used in the "Suffering Servant" passage in Isa. 53:9, "there was no deceit [*mirmâ*] in his mouth." The biblical demand for truthfulness and honesty carries with it the implication that all fraudulent behavior is to be condemned and that the true representative of Israel (Isa. 53:10) should be without deceit.

In the NT the same judgment on guile is to be found. To be "without guile" is the ideal, as the reference to Nathanael indicates (Jn. 1:47). Part of the apostle Paul's defense of his own work was the claim that it had been without guile. In Paul's day it was inevitable that some might compare him to the wandering orators who went from city to city, many of whom were charlatans and deceived their hearers (cf. Dio Chrysostom *Orations* 32). Such comparisons probably evoked Paul's statement in 1 Thess. 2:3 that his appeal had not been made with guile. Paul found it necessary in 2 Cor. 12:16 to defend himself against opponents who had claimed that he was "crafty" and had deceived the church. Similar charges seem to lie behind Paul's defense in 2 Cor. 4:2, where he used the verb *dolóō* to say that he had not "tamper[ed] with" (or "adulterated") the Word of God (cf. 7:2). Whereas Paul insisted that his work had been without guile (2 Cor. 12:16), he charged that his opponents had used "cunning" (*panourgía*) to lead the church astray (2 Cor. 11:3).

In NT ethical teaching, guile is considered a reprehensible sin that is to be put away by every Christian. In Mk. 7:22; Rom. 1:29, *dólos* (RSV "deceit") is mentioned in lists of sins. In 1 Pet. 2:1; 3:10, the community is encouraged to put away guile. The basis of this exhortation is, as 1 Pet. 2:22 indicates, christological. Jesus, as the Suffering Servant of Isa. 53:9, was without guile; consequently the community, which follows "in his steps" (1 Pet. 2:21), is also to live without guile (Rom. 16:19).

Bibliography.–D. Georgi, *Die Gegner des Paulus im 2. Korintherbrief* (*WMANT,* 11, 1964), pp. 240f.; P. E. Hughes, comm. on 2nd Corinthians (*NICNT,* 1962), pp. 122f., 260f., 375f., 464f.; A. J. Malherbe, *Nov.Test.* 12 (1970), 203-217.

J. W. THOMPSON

GUILT; GUILTY [Heb. *'āšam, 'āšēm, 'āšām, 'ašmâ*]; AV also TRESPASS, SIN, OFFEND, OFFENCE, DESTROY, "be desolate" (Isa. 24:6), "become desolate" (Hos. 13:16 [MT 14:1]), ACKNOWLEDGE THEIR OFFENCE (Hos. 5:15); NEB PAY, PUNISH, DISMAY, LIABLE TO RETRIBUTION, OFFENCE, WICKEDNESS, TRANSGRESSION, BRING RUIN, "become desolate" (Hos. 13:16 [MT 14:1]), IN HORROR (5:15), "stand aghast" (Isa. 24:6); [Heb. *'āwōn*]; NEB also SIN, INIQUITY, OFFENCE, WRONG, WRONGDOING, WILFUL SIN, WICKEDNESS, EVIL DEEDS, PENALTY, BLAMES, BEHAVED DISGRACEFULLY (2 S. 19:19 [MT 20]); [Heb. *nāqâ*]; AV also ACQUIT (THE WICKED) (Nah. 1:3); NEB also CLEAR THE GUILTY (Nah. 1:3); [Heb. *rāšā'*]; AV also WICKED, WORTHY TO BE BEATEN; [Heb. *rā'â*]; [Heb. *dāmîm*]; AV "blood," "innocent blood," "bloody house"; NEB BLOOD-GUILT; [Gk. *énochos*]; AV also "in danger" (Mk. 3:29); [Gk. *hamartía*]; AV SIN; [Gk. *aítios*]; AV FAULT; NEB SUPPORT YOUR CHARGES (Lk. 23:14).

Guilt is both the legal and moral condition that results from breaking God's law. A number of terms are used in the Bible to communicate this concept. Most of these, however, tend to include the concepts of sin and punishment (cf. *TDNT,* I, 279f., 297f.; *see* SIN V). Newer translations have sought to express the nuances reflected in modern English usage. Consequently "guilt" is used much more frequently in the RSV and the NEB.

I. In the OT.–One of the most frequent Hebrew roots connected with guilt is *'šm,* which as a verb means "commit an offense" (e.g., 2 Ch. 19:10: ". . . you shall warn them to commit no offence against the Lord . . ." [NEB]). An extension of this meaning is "be guilty" (e.g., Lev. 5:3f.). Here someone commits the offense unwittingly, but when he knows of it, then he shall be guilty. Very closely related to this is the idea of being held guilty for something: "Do not slander a servant to his master, lest he curse you, and you be held guilty" (Prov. 30:10). In other cases the idea is that of bearing guilt, e.g., Hos. 13:16, "Samaria shall bear her guilt, because she has rebelled against her God." In Hos. 4:15 and 10:2 the NEB unnecessarily emends the text (cf. H. H. Wolff, *Hosea* [Eng. tr. 1974], pp. 72, 89, 170). Textual problems in Hab. 1:11 lead some (e.g., *TDOT,* I, 435) to replace "guilty" (Heb. *'āšām*) with "and he set" (Heb. *yāśîm*). The NEB apparently emends to some form of *šāmam,* "be dismayed, appalled," as in Isa. 24:6, where it followed the Targum and translated "stand aghast." The Hebrew nouns *'āšām* and *'ašmâ,* however, include both the iniquitous act and the guilt associated with that act; thus the emendations may be unnecessary. (*See also* SACRIFICES AND OFFERINGS IN THE OT V.H.)

Another common Hebrew term is *'āwōn,* which also combines the ideas of iniquity, the guilt accompanying iniquity, and the punishment for the iniquity. Differences in the translations are frequent. Usually, when the RSV translates Heb. *'āwōn* as "guilt" the AV has "iniquity" (e.g., Ex. 28:38, 43; 1 S. 20:8). The NEB sometimes has "guilt" along with numerous synonyms for "iniquity." Ezk. 21:23 (MT 28) is typical of this diversity: "he brings their guilt [AV "iniquity"; NEB "wrongdoing"] to remembrance, that they may be captured." A careful study of the context is the only way to determine the various shades of meanings for both Heb. *ʿāwōn* and *ʾāšām*.

Other terms for "guilt" occur less frequently. On three occasions the RSV translates *nāqâ* as "clear the guilty" (Ex. 34:7; Joel 3:21 [MT 4:21]; Nah. 1:3). (On Joel 3:21 see L. C. Allen, comm. on Joel [*NICOT*, 1976], p. 117 n. 47.) The Hebrew root *ršʿ*, which often refers to wickedness (e.g., 2 Ch. 22:3), points also to one guilty of a crime (Dt. 25:1). In the hiphil the verb *rāšāʿ* can mean "condemn as guilty" (KoB, p. 910). The common Hebrew word for "evil," *raʿâ*, is translated "guilt" in 1 S. 26:18 (AV "evil"; NEB "mischief"). Several times the plural of "blood" (Heb. *dāmîm*) is translated "bloodguilt" (e.g., Ex. 22:2) or "guilt of blood" (Dt. 22:8). In Dt. 19:10 the shedding of innocent blood also leads to "guilt of blood." The RSV and AV interpret Ps. 51:14 (MT 16) as referring to bloodguiltiness (NEB "bloodshed"; M. Dahood [*Psalms* (*AB*, 1968), II, 8] proposes *dammîm*, "tears of death," but cf. A. Weiser, *Psalms* [*OTL*, 1962], pp. 408f.; *TDOT*, III, 243-45).

Sometimes the RSV translation is not based on any word for guilt but is an attempt to achieve equivalent effect. In Jer. 3:11 the AV has "backsliding Israel hath justified herself more than treacherous Judah." The MT uses the verb "justify" with the comparative, but the RSV translates "Faithless Israel has shown herself less guilty than false Judah." In Ezk. 18:24 the RSV changes the pleonasm retained in the AV's "in his trespass that he hath trespassed" (Heb. *bemaʿalô ʾašer-māʿal*) to "for the treachery of which he is guilty."

Several passages are difficult to interpret and have occasioned textual changes. In Ezk. 35:6 both the RSV and NEB follow the LXX and translate "guilty of blood." The AV and the RSV mg. follow the MT and read "hate blood," but this is less likely in light of the context (cf. *BH*; *TDOT*, I, 436, also follows the LXX). Prov. 21:8 is difficult because the meaning of Heb. *wāzār* (a hapax legomenon) is uncertain. The RSV and NEB follow KD in relating it to Arab. *wazara*, "carry a burden" "commit a sin" (cf. also C. H. Toy, comm. on Proverbs [*ICC*, 1899], p. 402); the related Arab. noun *wizr* can also mean "crime" (cf. W. McKane, *Proverbs* [*OTL*, 1970], p. 562). The AV "strange" reflects the common meaning of Heb. *zār* (the *wā* is understood as the conjunction "and"). Others (e.g., *BH*; *CHAL*, p. 85) suggest deleting it as a dittography of the word following it (Heb. *wezak*). The reference to "guilt" in 1 S. 14:41 is based on a valuable addition of the LXX (followed by both the RSV and NEB).

II. In the NT.–The words "guilt" or "guilty" are used rarely in the NT. Gk. *énochos* is used in the legal sense of "liable, answerable" or "guilty." To break one law is to be guilty of (breaking) the whole law (Jas. 2:10). Eating the bread or drinking the cup unworthily is to be guilty of (desecrating) the Lord's body and blood (1 Cor. 11:27). To slander the Holy Spirit makes one guilty of eternal sin (Mk. 3:29). The common word for sin, Gk. *hamartía*, is used to refer to the guilt resulting from the sin of the Pharisees (Jn. 9:41). In Lk. 23:14 Pilate does not find Jesus guilty (Gk. *aítios*) of any of the charges brought against Him. Although there is no Greek word for "guilty" in 1 Cor. 5:11, the RSV achieves equivalent effect by translating "if [anyone] is guilty of immorality," instead of "if any man . . . be a fornicator" (AV).

For the religious significance of "guilt" and "guilty" *see* SIN VI-IX.

Bibliography.–*DNTT*, II, 138, 142f.; *TDOT*, I, *s.v.* "ʾāshām" (D. Kellermann); III, *s.v.* "dām" (Bergman, Kedar-Kopfstein); *TDNT*, I, *s.v.* ἁμαρτάνω κτλ. (Quell, etc.); L. Morris, *EQ*, 30 (1958), 196-210.

J. C. MOYER

GUILT OFFERING. *See* SACRIFICES AND OFFERINGS IN THE OT V.G, H.

GUILTLESS [Heb. *nāqâ*, *nāqî*; Gk. *anaítios*, *anénklētos*, *hagnós*]; AV also BLAMELESS, INNOCENT, QUIT OF THINE OATH (Josh. 2:20), APPROVED YOURSELVES TO BE CLEAR (2 Cor. 7:11); NEB BLAMELESS, INNOCENT, QUIT OF THE OATH (Josh. 2:19f.), BE RELEASED (Josh. 2:17), NOT HELD AGAINST THEM (Mt. 12:5), WITHOUT REPROACH (1 Cor. 1:8), CLEARED YOURSELVES OF BLAME (2 Cor. 7:11).

The Hebrew root *nqh* is primarily associated with cleanness. The verb *nāqâ* in the niphal means to "be clean," "free from guilt," "innocent," "free from punishment." After Jeremiah had accused the inhabitants of Jerusalem of killing the guiltless poor (Jer. 2:34), they protested that they were innocent (2:35a) and reiterated it with the parallel expression that they had not sinned (*lōʾ ḥāṭāʾ*, 2:35b). In 1 S. 26:9f. David said that no one who killed the Lord's anointed would be free from punishment. In the piel the meaning is to "hold guiltless," "acquit," "leave unpunished." The Lord will not hold the person guiltless who misuses His name (Ex. 20:7 par. Dt. 5:11), and David told Solomon not to leave Shimei unpunished (1 K. 2:9). Five times the adjective *nāqî* is translated "guiltless." On three occasions it refers to a freedom from obligations (Josh. 2:17, 19f., referring to the oath of Rahab). The other two references are to innocence (2 S. 3:28; 14:9).

In the NT Gk. *anaítios*, "without a reason, guilt," occurs in Mt. 12:5, 7 where, under certain conditions, priests who break the sabbath are still counted guiltless. (The LXX translates the phrase "innocent blood," Heb. *dām nāqî* [e.g., Dt. 19:10], with *anaítios*.) In 1 Cor. 1:8 the reference is to Christians whom Jesus will establish as guiltless or blameless (*anénklētos*) in the Day of the Lord. The word *hagnós* means "pure" or "holy," but the RSV translates it "guiltless" in 2 Cor. 7:11 (cf. NEB "you have cleared yourselves of blame").

Bibliography.–*TDNT*, I, *s.v.* ἁγνός (Hauck); ἀνέγκλητος (Grundmann); *THAT*, II, *s.v.* נקה (C. van Leeuwen).

J. C. MOYER

GULF. The AV rendering (RSV, NEB, "chasm") of Gk. *chásma* (<*chaínō*, "gape, yawn"), which occurs only in Lk. 16:26, "between us and you a great chasm has been fixed" (cf. "far off" in v. 23). This is very different from, though it probably reflects, the rabbinic conception of the separation between the two compartments of Hades (Sheol) by "a hand's breadth," "a wall," or even, later, "a chasm," for the parable can be given here only a figurative significance, and is of purely ethical import. The fundamental difference between the rich man and Lazarus lies not in their conditions but in their characters. For "besides all this" (v. 26) RV mg. gives "in all these things," thus implying that the moral distinctions that exist in this life (v. 25) become more pronounced ("fixed") in the next world, and the "gulf" is impassable in the sense that a change of condition will not necessarily produce a change of soul. *See also* ABRAHAM'S BOSOM.

M. O. EVANS

GUM [Heb. *nekōʾṯ*; LXX *thymíama*–'incense'] (Gen. 37:25; 43:11); AV SPICERY, SPICES; NEB GUM TRAGACANTH. Some have suggested "storax," the gum resin exuded by the *Styrax officinalis*. This plant is found in the Levant, but the identification is unlikely (*MPB*, p. 52). More likely is the application of Heb. *n^e^ḵō'ṯ* to the gum-tragacanth (cf. Arab. *naka'at*, "gum tragacanth"), probably the *Astragalus tragacantha* or the *Astragalus gummifer*. The latter shrub naturally exudes a nonaromatic gum from its stem and branches (*MPB*, p. 52). Such resins, along with oil, spices, nuts, etc., were an important article of trade in the ancient Near East.

GUNI gōō'nī [Heb. *gûnî*]; **GUNITES** gōō'nīts [*haggûnî*].

1. The name of a Naphtalite clan (Gen. 46:24; Nu. 26:48; 1 Ch. 7:13).

2. The head of a Gadite family (1 Ch. 5:15).

GUR gûr [Heb. *gûr*]. An ascent near Ibleam where Ahaziah of Judah was wounded by Jehu's archers (2 K. 9:27). Aharoni identified it with the Gurra near Taanach, mentioned in the Taanach Tablets (*LBHG*, p. 157).

W. S. L. S.

GURBAAL gûr-bā'al [Heb. *gûr-ba'al*]. A small colony town of Arabs, against which Uzziah king of Judah was given divine aid (2 Ch. 26:7). It remains unidentified, but probably was somewhere in Edom. Its mention immediately after the Philistines may have suggested the "Gerar" of the Targum, but association with the Meunim (elsewhere called Mehunim) points to the east. Jebel Nebī Hārūn, near Petra, has always been crowned by a sanctuary. This may have been "the dwelling place of Baal"; or, accepting the reading of the LXX (Gk. *pétra*) and the Vulg., it may be *ṣ/ṭûr ba'al*, the "rock" or "mountain of Baal."

D. B. PECOTA

GUTI; GUTIANS gōō'tē, gōō'tē-əns [Akk. *gu-ti-um*, *g/qu-tū*]. A people who dominated part of Babylonia in the 22nd cent. B.C.

The powerful dynasty of Akkad in Babylonia (*ca.* 2370-2200 B.C.) was faced constantly by threat of attack from the wild mountaineers of the Zagros. Prominent among these were the Guti, whose homeland was the area of Persian Kurdistan. They spread from there across northern Mesopotamia, it appears, sacking the city of Asshur and mixing with the West Semitic tribes of the mid-Euphrates region. In due course they spread southward and overthrew the rule of Akkad. As so often happened, they could not replace what they had destroyed, and confusion resulted. Their suzerainty left little mark upon the history of Babylonia; rather they became partly civilized, and their few royal inscriptions attest devotion to the gods of the cities they had conquered. After a few decades of supremacy the invaders were driven out by Utu-hegal king of Uruk (*ca.* 2120 B.C.).

Despite so meager a record, the period of Gutian rule left a lasting impression on the Babylonian mind. The invasion was reckoned a punishment for impious behavior on the part of an Akkadian king, and counted an era in history. The Sumerian king list gives almost a century for their dynasty and a score or so kings; but it is clear that the period was largely concurrent with the Akkad dynasty, and many of the kings may have been contemporaries. At about the same time as the fall of Akkad, the Guti also overwhelmed Elam, inaugurating a century of decline.

The toponym Gutu continued in use until the Persian period as a rather vague district name, but nothing is certain about the population of the area in this age. The ethnic relation of the third-millennium Guti is generally sought with the adjacent Lullubi, Elamites, etc. Certain names have distinctive form, e.g., Tirikan and Sargalab. The area passed through the control of the Elamites, Kassites, and Assyrians before the Persian empire inherited it from the Babylonians.

Some contend that Guti appeared under the banner of Nebuchadrezzar as Koa (Heb. *qô(a)'*; Gk. *Koue*), a contingent in the army attacking Jerusalem (Ezk. 23:23, where Shoa is Akk. Suhi of the Syrian desert, Shuah in Gen. 25:2). It has been suggested that the Guti survived as the Kurds.

See Vol. I, Map III.

Bibliography.–CAH (3rd ed.), I/2 (1971), 454-463; J. J. Finkelstein, *JCS*, 20 (1966), 106-111.

A. R. MILLARD

GUTTER (Gen. 30:38, 41, AV). *See* RUNNEL.

GYMNASIUM [Gk. *gymnásion*] (1 Macc. 1:14; 2 Macc. 4:9, 12). The gymnasium was an athletics ground used primarily for training the male youth of ancient Greece to run, wrestle, throw the javelin or discus, etc. It was usually located in a grove by a stream outside the city, where the shade and water could benefit its patrons. It most often had a *palaístra*, a building with rooms for undressing and dressing, bathing, powdering the body, etc. The word *gymnásion* first meant "an exercise performed while naked" but later was applied to the place where such exercise was done.

Ruins of the gymnasium at Olympia, Greece (Rosenthal Art Slides)

In Maccabean times Antiochus IV Epiphanes permitted hellenizing Jews to establish a gynmasium in Jerusalem (1 Macc. 1:14). The Jews who exercised there "covered over" their circumcision (ostensibly by undergoing some kind of operation) in order to imitate the Greeks more completely (Josephus *Ant.* xii.v.1 [241]; 1 Macc. 1:15).

In the NT Paul used some of the activities of the gymnasium as metaphors for Christian experience — running (1 Cor. 9:24-27; Gal. 2:2; Phil. 2:16), boxing (1 Cor. 9:26), and wrestling (Eph. 6:12, AV; RSV "contending"). Gk. *gymnasía*, "exercise (in a gymnasium)," occurs in 1 Tim. 4:8, where such activity is acknowledged to have some value for the body.

See also GAMES.

Bibliography.–J. Delorme, *Gymnasion* (1960); E. N. Gardiner, *Athletics of the Ancient World* (1930), pp. 72-98; H. A. Harris, *Greek Athletes and Athletics* (1964).

J. E. H.

H. Abbreviation for the "Law of Holiness" or "Holiness Code." *See* CRITICISM II.D.5; LEVITICUS III.

HA (Job 39:25, AV). *See* AH.

HAAHASHTARI hā-ə-hash'tə-rī [Heb. *hā'ᵃḥaštārî*] (1 Ch. 4:6). The Ahashtarites were a family belonging to the tribe of Judah. Apart from this nothing is known about them.

HABAIAH hə-bā'yə [Heb. *ḥᵒḇāyyâ*–'Yahweh has hidden'] (Ezr. 2:61); NEB HOBAIAH; [Gk. Apoc. A *Obdia,* B *Obbeia*] (1 Esd. 5:38); AV, NEB, OBDIA; **HOBAIAH** hō-bā'yə (Neh. 7:63); AV HABAIAH. A postexilic priestly family that was unable to establish its pedigree, and thus was not permitted to serve in the priestly office.

HABAKKUK hə-bak'ək [Heb. *ḥᵃbaqqûq*–'embrace' or 'embracer,' or according to Jerome 'wrestler'; LXX *Ambakoum* (Th. *Ambakouk*) presupposes Heb. *ḥabbāqûq*. A similar word, *ḫambaqūqu,* occurs in Assyr. as the name of a garden plant]. A prophet of Judah in the late 7th cent., and the book bearing his name.

I. The Prophet
  A. Name
  B. Life
II. The Book
  A. Content
  B. Unity
  C. Date
  D. Canonicity
  E. Text
  F. Form and Style
III. Theology

I. The Prophet.–A. Name. Some of the ancient rabbis, imagining that the prophet was the son of the Shunammite woman of 2 K. 4:16, assumed that the name came from the promise given, "You shall embrace [Heb. *ḥōḇaq*] a son." Jerome and others thought the name meant "wrestler," and reflected the prophet's spiritual struggle with God.

B. Life. Practically nothing is known of Habakkuk. The book bearing his name casts little light upon his life except by inference and the rest of the OT is silent concerning him, although numerous legends have grown up around his name. The identification of the prophet with the son of the Shunammite woman is one example, although biblical chronology renders it impossible by over a hundred years. Another example, equally anachronistic, connects Isa. 21:6 with Hab. 2:1 and makes Habakkuk the watchman set by Isaiah to watch for the fall of Babylon. One of the recensions of the LXX text of Bel and the Dragon declares that the story was taken "from the prophecy of Habakkuk the son of Jesus of the tribe of Levi." This may refer to an unknown apocryphal book ascribed to our prophet. The authority for calling his father Jesus is unknown. But the claim that he was of the tribe of Levi has usually been based on the presence of the musical notation at the end of the psalm (3:19). According to the *Lives of the Prophets* (ascribed erroneously to Epiphanius, Bishop of Salamis during the late 4th cent. A.D.), he belonged to Beth Zohar of the tribe of Simeon. Another interesting though equally anachronistic story is found in Bel 33-39. In this tale Habakkuk, while on his way to the field with a bowl of pottage, was taken by an angel to Babylon, placed in the lions' den where Daniel ate the pottage, and afterward returned to his own place. None of these legends has much historical value.

II. The Book.–A. Content. The book is generally divided into five sections comprising chs. 1 and 2, followed by ch. 3, the prayer or psalm of Habakkuk.

1. The Prophet's First Complaint (1:1-4). Following the traditional interpretation, this section forms the prophet's first lament to God concerning the violence and lawlessness rampant in the community of Judea surrounding him. According to this interpretation of the book, these verses describe conditions existing shortly before the destruction of Judah by the Babylonian invader in the early 6th century.

2. Yahweh's First Reply (1:5-11). God's reply to the prophet indicates that he should expect the unknown as a response to his prayer for justice. The unknown in this case is the raising up of the Chaldean horde to whom will be given the task of meting out divine justice to the wicked citizens of Judah. The suggestion in v. 5 that the arrival of the Chaldeans would be something unexpected suggests that the prophecy should be dated either shortly before or after the fall of the Assyrian capital Nineveh to the Babylonians in 612 B.C. Various scholars, following Wellhausen, have omitted these verses as a secondary addition and identified the violent, wicked men of 1:2-4 with the Chaldeans and the righteous men with the Judeans. The lament is then understood to be continued in vv. 12-17 (see O. Eissfeldt, *The OT: An Intro.* [Eng. tr., 3rd ed. 1968], p. 418).

3. The Prophet's Second Complaint (1:12-17). These verses form a response to the divine oracle concerning the Chaldeans in 1:5-11. In this section the prophet is perplexed and cannot understand how a righteous God can use these barbarians to execute judgment upon a people more righteous than they. He considers even the wicked among the Jews better than the Chaldeans. The section ends with the prophet's poignant question, "Is he then to keep on emptying his net and mercilessly slaying nations forever?"

4. Yahweh's Second Reply (2:1-4). In this section, which begins with the prophet stationed on his watchtower to await God's reply, an indication is given that the exaltation of the Chaldeans will only be temporary; in the end they will meet their doom, while the righteous will live by their faith (or alternatively, by God's faithfulness). The vision of God's direction for history is hastening toward its appointed time, and the prophet is asked to await its coming.

5. The Taunt Song Against Babylon (2:5-20). This section consists of five woe oracles, following similar but slightly varying form, directed against the Chaldean oppressor. Each woe is cast in the mouth of a nation that has suffered at the hand of Babylon and, with the exception of the fifth woe which opposes idolatry, deals with a nation arrogantly building its own power at the expense of its less able neighbors. The five taunting songs are punctuated by a vision of universal knowledge of God's glory (v. 14) and climaxed by a call for reverent submission to the Lord of history, who through all the vicissitudes of history remains seated in His holy temple (v. 20).

6. The Prayer of Habakkuk (3:1-19). This final section, which is often separated from the remainder of the book, comes to us replete with musical directions (vv. 1, 19b) and functions in its context as the prophet's reply to all that has been revealed in the opening two chapters. The divine revelation of ch. 2 is bypassed in favor of the timeless pictures of God's power in theophanies, allusions to which cover the entire expanse of Israel's history with its redeemer. The purpose of God's anger — the salvation of His people — is struck as a keynote in v. 13, while the section closes with the prophet's personal response in vv. 16-19. This final response, one of the great statements of faith in God in the face of adversity, lends its tone to the entire book and is probably the reason Habakkuk is preeminent among the minor prophets.

B. Unity. The question of the unity of Hab. 1 and 2 is closely tied to the question of its interpretation. As mentioned above, Wellhausen together with Giesebrecht deleted 1:5-11 and attempted to create a continuous lament with the remaining verses of ch. 1. Others, finding different objects for the lament in 1:2-4, rearrange and in some cases delete various verses within the opening chapters (Eissfeldt, pp. 417-420). If, however, the traditional interpretation is assumed, the first two chapters contain a distinct unity of theme and can be related to a sequence of events in the prophet's struggle with God during the closing days of the Assyrian empire and the rapid rise of Babylon in its place.

The psalm of ch. 3 presents additional problems. Stylistically distinct from the remainder of the book, the psalm has been subject to continued scrutiny and attack from scholars of a variety of persuasions. Many have found in the musical directions an indication of a second temple provenance, an argument which turns, however, on the question of dating not merely Hab. 3 but the Psalms in general (cf. G. L. Archer, *Survey of OT Intro.* [rev. ed. 1974], pp. 356f.). Apart from such considerations, one may conclude that the psalm was either composed by the author of chs. 1 and 2 or added to the prophecy by the same individual, who perhaps drew from a variety of sources. Certainly in its canonical form the third chapter is necessary to complete the thought of the book. Reference has been made to the absence of the third chapter in the Habakkuk commentary from Qumrân, but several reasons may account for this absence. For example, it has often been noted that the Qumrân commentaries lack the kind of systematic chapter-by-chapter exposition expected in a modern series.

C. Date. With the exception of questions surrounding the style of ch. 3, matters of dating are closely related to those of interpretation. Budde, and more recently Mowinckel, on the theory that the oppressors in 1:2-4 are the Assyrians rather than the wicked Jews, date the prophecy in the period before the destruction of Nineveh (621-612 B.C.). Scholars such as Wellhausen and Giesebrecht, who see in 1:2-4, 12-17 a lament concerning the mistreatment of Judah by the Chaldeans, would date the prophet to the time of the Neo-Babylonian empire (612-538 B.C.). Neither of the above seems necessary if we maintain the traditional interpretation.

If 1:2-4 is interpreted as referring to the oppression of Jews by Jews and 1:5-11 as a threat that Yahweh will raise up the Chaldeans already known as a nation thirsting for blood, then the dating of the prophecy becomes much more specific. Verses 5-11 would seem to indicate that, although the Babylonians had already given exhibitions of the cruel character of their warfare, they had not yet come into any direct contact with Judah. This would tend to place the prophecy in the period just before or after the destruction of Nineveh by the Babylonians and their allies in 612 B.C. It was not until 605 B.C. at the earliest that Judah was to feel the full force of Babylonian power, although by that time the coming of the Babylonians or Chaldeans would hardly be unbelievable. For this reason scholars generally prefer to date the prophecy closer to the time of Nineveh's destruction, perhaps just before that event, when Assyrian rather than Chaldean power would still be the expected source of an invasion.

D. Canonicity. Habakkuk was early grouped with the other so-called minor prophets in the Book of the Twelve, the acceptance of which was never questioned in either Jewish or Christian circles. Disputes about the unity of the book are essentially modern — there is no ancient record of a dispute over ch. 3 — and do not seem to have affected its acceptance.

E. Text. The text of Habakkuk is generally considered to be in a better state of preservation than has traditionally been supposed. Modern scholars tend less than their predecessors to attribute obscurities in an ancient text to copyists' errors. One textual emendation of substance proposed by Duhm in an earlier generation changed the name "Chaldean" (Heb. *hakkaśdîm*) to "Greeks" (*hakkittîm*). This emendation, considered precarious by Duhm's contemporaries, is rendered completely unacceptable by the Habakkuk commentary from the Dead Sea. In that document the original *hakkaśdîm* is neither excised nor changed into *hakkittîm*. Instead, the Dead Sea sectaries left the word for Chaldeans in the text but argued that they were to be identified with the *kittim* (the Seleucid or Roman forces). This was clearly not an emendation but an interpretation. *See* Vol. I, Plate 16; picture of 1 QpHab in COMMENTARIES, HEBREW.

The text of ch. 3 has suffered much under the hands of many interpreters, including W. F. Albright, who proposed "some 38 corrections of the Masoretic text" ("The Psalm of Habakkuk," in H. H. Rowley, ed., *Studies in OT Prophecy Presented to T. H. Robinson* [1950], pp. 1-18). When all is said and done, the many attempts to emend the text of ch. 3 have created as many difficulties as they have removed; thus the original remains preferable, if somewhat obscure.

F. Form and Style. Much has been said about the liter-

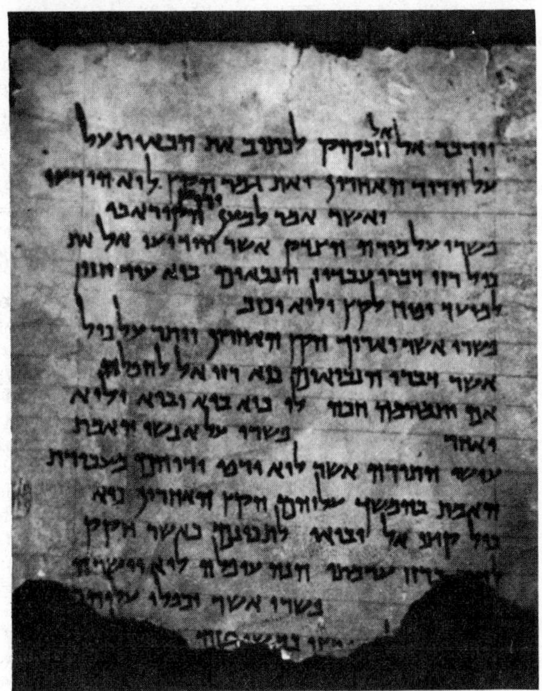

Column 7 of the *pēšer* (commentary) on Habakkuk from Qumrân (1QpHab) (J. C. Trever)

ary form of Habakkuk, but a word should be added about the book's literary power. The book is full of force, the descriptions are graphic and powerful, the thought and expression are alike poetic. Habakkuk is a master of terse, parallelistic, pregnant, classical style; and if ch. 3 is to be attributed to the same author, he is, moreover, a lyric poet of high order. The grand imagery and rhythmic flow of this psalm will bear comparison with some of the finest productions of the Hebrew muse.

Taking the first two chapters as traditionally interpreted, Habakkuk is stylistically unique among the prophets of Israel. Whereas most prophetic writings give the oracles of God as proclaimed through the prophet, this short book offers a glimpse of the theological and philosophical inner life of the poet dressed in the form of a short but gripping dialogue. The counterpoint of lament (or complaint) and judgment oracle in ch. 1 is matched by the taunt song as a response to the lament in ch. 2. Although elements of these forms are clearly part of the common stock of Hebrew prophetic literature (cf. 2:12 with Mic. 3:10; v. 13 with Jer. 51:58; v. 14 with Isa. 11:9; v. 16b with Jer. 25:15f.; vv. 18-20 with Isa. 44:9ff.; 46:6f.; Jer. 10:1-16), the general character of the first two chapters is unique.

Chapter 3, which combines personal affirmation with theophany and historical retrospect, is like certain of the Psalms or passages from the book of Job.

III. Theology.–Habakkuk's message, the core of which is found in 2:4, forms a basic point in OT theology and is cited as pivotal in three NT books. Paul, in Rom. 1:17, introduces his gospel as one of salvation by faith as opposed to salvation by works and cites Hab. 2:4, "the righteous shall live by faith," as OT support for his argument. Gal. 3:11ff. sets forth faith as the antithesis of law or legal salvation and again Hab. 2:4 serves as a supporting text. Finally, in the intriguing passage He. 10:37f., Hab. 2:3f. is again quoted, but the context focuses on the pending fulfillment of the vision and the identification of the Hebrews with those who have faith and thus persevere under pressure.

But the theological value of Habakkuk cannot be limited to a few NT quotations. The prophet asks some of the most penetrating questions in all literature, and the answers given are basic to a proper view of God and His relation to history. If God's initial response (1:5-11) sounded the death knell for any strictly nationalistic theology of Judah, his second reply (2:2-20) outlines in a positive sense that all history is hastening to a conclusion which is as certain as it is satisfying. For Habakkuk that conclusion was prefigured by the coming day when the Chaldeans themselves would receive just judgment for their violent deeds. For the NT writer of Hebrews the climax of history was to be found not in the destruction of any one temporal power but in the coming of the Lord Jesus Christ, whose return is merely prefigured in both the judgments on the nation and tribulations of the people of God.

In the interim, while history is still awaiting its conclusion (and Habakkuk is not told when the end will come), the righteous ones are to live by faith. The faith prescribed (or faithfulness, as many have argued that Heb. *'ᵉmûnâ* should be translated) is still called for as a basic response to the unanswered questions in today's universe. This theology for life both then and now stands as Habakkuk's most basic contribution. That this faith or faithfulness is related in NT theology to the objective salvation provided by the work of Christ is both to be expected and a natural development in the progress of revelation from the dark days of the late 7th cent. before Christ to the full light of God's coming in the person of His Son.

Bibliography.–Comms. by A. B. Davidson (*CBSC,* 1920); D. D. Garland (*Broadman Bible Comm.,* VII, 1972); D. E. Gowan (1976); J. M. P. Smith (*ICC,* 1911); L. E. H. Stephens-Hodge (*NBC,* rev. ed. 1970), pp. 767-772; C. L. Taylor, Jr. (*IB,* VI, 1956); W. Vischer (1958); G. W. Wade and G. G. Stonehouse (*WC,* 1929).

Comms. on Minor Prophets by J. Calvin (n.d.); J. Coppens (1950); S. R. Driver (*Century Bible,* 1906); K. Elliger (*ATD,* 4th ed. 1959); C. L. Feinberg (1976); KD; T. Laetsch (1956); E. B. Pusey (n.d.); G. A. Smith (*Expos.B.,* 2nd ed. 1928).

Other Books on Habakkuk: W. H. Brownlee, *Midrash Pesher of Habakkuk* (1978); F. F. Bruce, *Biblical Exegesis in the Qumran Texts* (1959); *The Teacher of Righteousness in the Qumran Scrolls* (1956); M. Delcor, *Les Manuscrits de la Mer Morte; essai sur le Midrash d'Habacuc* (1951); F. E. Gaebelein, *Four Minor Prophets: Obadiah, Jonah, Habakkuk and Haggai* (1970); E. M. Good, *Texts and Versions of Habakkuk 3* (1958); D. E. Gowan, *The Triumph of Faith in Habakkuk* (1976); P. Humbert, *Problèmes du livre d'Habacuc* (1944); P. Jöcken, *Das Buch Habakuk* (1977); D. M. Lloyd-Jones, *From Fear to Faith: Studies in the Book of Habakkuk* (1953); A. T. Pearson, *Problem of Unity and Date in Habakkuk* (1953); H. H. Rowley, *Zadokite Fragments and the Dead Sea Scrolls* (1952); D. Stokes, *Diversity and Unity in Habakkuk* (1976).

Articles on Habakkuk, Except Those Referring to Qumrân: F. C. Burkitt, *JTS,* 16 (1915), 62-85; W. Cannon, *ZAW,* 43 (1925), 62-90; H. H. Walker and N. Lund, *JBL,* 53 (1934), 355-370; G. R. Driver, *JTS,* 39 (1938), 394-98; W. Irwin, *JNES,* 1 (1942), 10-40; H. Schmidt, *ZAW,* 62 (1949), 52-63; M. Stenzl, *Bibl.,* 33 (1952), 506-510; S. Mowinckel, *Theologische Zeitschrift,* 9 (1953), 1-23; E. Nielsen, *ST,* 6 (1953), 54-78; P. Beguirie, "Le Psaume d'Habacuc," in *Études sur les prophetes d'Israel* (1954), 53-84; *VT,* 5 (1955), 13-33; J. E. Evans, *Bibliotheca Sacra,* 12 (1955), 62-67, 164-69; W. A. Irwin, *JNES,* 15 (1956), 47-50; E. M. Good, *VT,* 9 (1959), 11-30; W. H. Brownlee, *JBL,* 82 (1963), 319-325; J. H. Eaton, *ZAW,* 76 (1964), 144-171; J. M. Holt, *JBL,* 83 (1964), 298-302; W. Baars, *VT,* 15 (1965), 381f.; D. E. Gowan, *Perspective,* 9 (1968), 157-166; P. J. M. Southwell, *JTS,* 19 (1968), 614-17; M. Bosshard, *VT,* 19 (1969), 48-52; A. S. Vanderwoude, *ZAW,* 82 (1970), 281f.; B. Margulis, *ZAW,* 82 (1970), 409-442; S. L. Johnson, *Bibliotheca Sacra,* 28 (1971), 327-340; J. L. Crenshaw, *CBQ,* 34 (1972), 39-53; G. A. Tuttle, *Studia biblica et theologica,* 3 (1973), 3-14; C. A. Keller, *ZAW,* 85 (1973), 156-167; J. G. Harris, *EQ,* 45 (1973), 21-29; S. Schreiner, *ZAW,* 86 (1974), 538-542; C. F. Whitley, *JQR,* 66 (1976), 143-47;

E. Otto, *ZAW,* 89 (1977), 73-107; J. A. Emerton, *JTS,* 28 (1977), 1-18; H. C. C. Cavallin, *ST,* 32 (1978), 33-43.

Articles on Habakkuk Referring to Qumrân: W. H. Brownlee, *BASOR,* 112 (Dec. 1948), 8-18; 114 (Apr. 1949), 9f.; 126 (Apr. 1952), 10-20; M. Delcor, *RHR,* 142 (1952), 129-146; H. H. Rowley, *BJRL,* 40 (1957), 114-147; C. Roth, *VT,* 11 (1961), 451-55; L. H. Silberman, *RQ,* 3 (1961), 325-364; G. W. Buchanan, *RQ,* 6 (1969), 553-58; H. G. Williamson, *RQ,* 9 (1977), 263-65.

C. E. ARMERDING

HABAZINIAH (Jer. 35:3, AV). *See* HABAZZINIAH.

HABAZZINIAH hab-ə-zi-nī'ə [Heb. *ḥ*ª*ḇaṣṣinyâ*] (Jer. 35:3); AV, NEB, HABAZINIAH. The grandfather of Jaazaniah, the leader of the Rechabites, whom Jeremiah tested (Jer. 35:3-10).

HABERGEON hab'ər-jan. A medieval coat of mail. The AV uses this term for Heb. *taḥrā'* (Ex. 28:32; 39:23; RSV "garment"), *širyôn* (2 Ch. 26:14; Neh. 4:16 [MT 10]; RSV "coat of mail"), and *širyâ* (Job 41:26 [MT 18]; RSV "javelin"). *See* WEAPONS OF WAR.

HABIRU hä'bi-ro͞o, hä-bē'ro͞o [more correctly HAPIRU or ʿAPIRU; to conform to standard conventions, the form *Ḫapiru* will be adopted henceforth]. A term used in cuneiform and Egyptian literature of the 21st to 12th cents. B.C. to designate disparate groups of peoples. These peoples were apparently ubiquitous, appearing in the texts from sites in modern Iran (Susa), Iraq (Larsa, Nuzi, Babylon, Asshur), Turkey (Alishar, Boghazköy), Syria (Mari, Tell Brak, Alalakh, Ugarit), Lebanon (Kumidi), Palestine (Beth-shean), and Egypt (Memphis, Thebes, Heliopolis, Amarna).

- I. Name
  - A. In Cuneiform
    - 1. Ideographic Writing
    - 2. Phonetic Writing
    - 3. Alphabetic Writing
  - B. In Egyptian
  - C. Root and Etymology
- II. Historical Survey of the Evidence
  - A. Ur III
  - B. Larsa
  - C. Alishar
  - D. Mari
  - E. Alalakh
  - F. Boghazköy
  - G. Nuzi
  - H. Ugarit
  - I. Amarna
  - J. Egyptian Documents
- III. Ḫapiru as Designation
  - A. Ethnic
  - B. Socio-Legal
- IV. Impossibility of Equation of Ḫapiru and Hebrews in Biblical Studies
  - A. Impossibility of General Equation
  - B. Equation of Amarna Ḫapiru and Biblical Hebrews
    - 1. Philologically
    - 2. Ethno-Socially
    - 3. Onomastically
    - 4. Historically

***I. Name.**–A. In Cuneiform. 1. Ideographic Writing:* SA.GAZ. Although it sometimes appears in the agglutinated forms SA.GAZ.E (with subject element), SA.GAZ.ZA (with genitive element), and SA.GAZ.ŠÈ (with terminative element), SA.GAZ (or its variant SAG.GAZ) has no clear Sumerian meaning and appears to have been a pseudo-ideograph for the Akk. *šaggāšu,* "murderer, aggressor, marauder," or for the West Sem. *šgš,* "to be restive." The Akkadian lexical equivalent to SA.GAZ is *ḫabbātu,* "robber, brigand" or "wanderer, migrant," a word used occasionally as an Akkadian synonym for *ḫapiru* (cf. C. Schaeffer, ed., *Palais Royal d'Ugarit,* III, 16.03, $^{\text{lú.meš}}$SA.GAZ^{ru}).

2. Phonetic Writing: ḫa-pí-ru/a₄-pí-ru. The exact phonetic value of the Akkadian form is uncertain because the labial may be read either *bi* or *pí*; moreover, the Akk. *ḫ,* while regularly reflecting Proto-Semitic **ḫ* (= Arab. *ḫ,* not *ḥ*), may in proper names of foreign origin reflect *ḥ* or ʿ. Though two men bearing Kassite names and called *ḫa-bir-aya* are related by some with the Ḫapiru, the gentilic *-aya* may suggest that these men came from the otherwise attested second-millennium Mesopotamian town *Ḫa-bi-ri*^{ki}, coincidentally similar to Ḫapiru. One may legitimately theorize the SA.GAZ = *Ḫapiru* equation on the basis of Hittite god lists from Boghazköy, in which DINGIR.MEŠ ^{lú}SA.GAZ and DINGIR.MEŠ *Ḫa-pí-ri* freely alternate.

3. Alphabetic Writing: ʿ*pr,* (pl.) ʿ*prm.* Three tax lists from the king of Ugarit, one in Akkadian syllabic and two in Ugaritic alphabetic scripts, detail a registry of localities subject to the Ugaritic monarch. A city named Ḫalbi (probably Aleppo) is listed in four parallel entries, with the syllabic ^{uru}*Ḫal-bi* $^{\text{lú.meš}}$SAG.GAZ parallel to the alphabetic *Ḫlb* ʿ*prm.* This supplies the equation SA.GAZ = ʿ*pr,* and, combined with the Hittite evidence cited above, the equation SA.GAZ = *Ḫapiru* = ʿ*pr* obtains. In an effort to preserve a connection with the root ʿ*br,* some scholars appeal to the *b/p* interchange in Akkadian to argue that an original Sem. *b* shifted to *p* in the Ugaritic dialect. But as Astour has shown, whereas Akkadian exhibits an ambiguous *b/p,* in Ugaritic *b* can shift to *p* only rarely (by regressive assimilation in direct contact with an unvoiced consonant). Further, Ugaritic possessed the lexeme ʿ*br* (*UT,* p. 453), so there is no reason to suppose that Ugaritic scribes regularly spelled this word with a *p*. Again, appeal to a Hurrian influence is doomed to failure, owing to the presence of initial ʿ, which, if Hurrian, would have been lost.

B. In Egyptian: ʿ*pr,* (pl.) ʿ*pr.w.* Attempts to explain the *p* as the Egyptian rendering of an original Sem. *b* because it is followed by the liquid *r* are no longer tenable linguistically. Egyptian transcription of Semitic names containing the labial *b* always preserves the original *b* when it is found in an intervocalic position (as would be the case if the form were **Ḫa-bi-ru*).

C. Root and Etymology. Consonantal evidence from Ugarit and Egypt is uniform, mutually corroborating, and philologically unambiguous, so it is safe to assert that the root in question is ʿ*pr.* Akkadian evidence suggests that the intermediate vowels respectively are *a* and *i* (possibly **e*), producing the hypothetical form ***ʿ*apiru.* (Vowel quantity cannot yet be absolutely determined orthographically.) The initial pharyngeal ʿ justifies the West Semitic origin of the root ʿ*pr.* Thus, theories connecting ʿ*pr* with non-Semitic Sum. gabiri, "desert," Hitt. *ḫappariya,* "transfer, sale," or Hurrian *ipri,* "lord, aristocrat," are dubious at best. Moreover, etymological speculation dependent upon the Semitic root *ḥbr,* "bind, join" — e.g., "a confederate, ally" (cf. *ḥ*ª*ḇērîm*) — must be excluded. Additionally, etymologies predicated upon the root ʿ*br,* "cross over" — e.g., "a wanderer, nomad, boundary jumper" (cf. ʿ*iḇrî*) — are rendered untenable linguistically. Another unattractive theory sees in ʿ*pr* the West Semitic cognate of Akk. *epēru,* "dust" — e.g., "one covered with dust after long journeys, one who lives in tents." Semantics and lexicography argue against this latter theory. No Ḫapiru citations clearly place them in a "dusty" context, although one could counter that such an original meaning had already been lost by the time the form was used as a standard social designation. In no West Semitic text, however, does *ʿpr* mean "dust." A more plausible etymology sees in *epēru,* "work for a livelihood, provide with food," a reflex of West Semitic *ʿpr*. After all, Ḫapiru texts are full of references to their working in order to receive food, equipment, and living quarters. But the corresponding West Semitic root, as shown by Ugaritic, is *ḥpr,* not *ʿpr*. To argue that *ʿpr* means "outlaw" is to rely too heavily upon Amarna evidence and English etymology, in the absence of Semitic lexicography. One can conclude only that the problem of the etymology of *ʿpr* remains unresolved.

II. Historical Survey of the Evidence.–A. *Ur III* (21st-20th cents.). Documentation from this period includes two court depositions about persons called sa-gaz. In one of these texts the sa-gaz is the claimant, and in the other the sa-gaz may be the defendant. The tablets are somewhat fragmentary, however, and difficult to interpret. Another tablet, a Sumerian literary text, states that the sa-gaz people roam the steppe, destroy everything, and refuse to obey King Šulgi. A second tablet suggests that another king finds it necessary to punish the sa-gaz.

B. Larsa (19th cent.). Official court records from the reigns of Warad-Sin and Rīm-Sin detail monthly rations of small animals or clothing consigned by the king to the sa-gaz (in one case, to the Ḫapiru). One of these documents explicitly mentions that these people represent a contingent of state-supported troops.

C. Alishar (18th cent.). An Old Assyrian text speaks of a group of Ḫapiru who were attached to the palace of an enterprising Assyrian merchant near Alishar. The text goes on to imply that the Ḫapiru were dependent as well upon Alishar officials.

D. Mari (18th cent.). Ḫapiru occupy a dual role according to the Mari texts. On the one hand, they are loyal mercenaries allied with the forces of local kings. As such, they own land and donkeys and are among the settled population. Though their numbers are normally of moderate size, a large contingent of two thousand march under the command of one northern Mesopotamian monarch. On the other hand, the Ḫapiru represent independent groups of raiders. Ranging from Ḫarran on the upper Balīkh River to Larsa in southern Mesopotamia, an obvious reflection of their disparate character, Ḫapiru are constantly reported as raiding and seizing towns and carrying off booty. Like the Amarna Age pharaohs, King Zimri-Lim receives appeals from his vassals for protection against the Ḫapiru. At one place, an apparently influential local king enters into an alliance with a band of Ḫapiru so that he can raid a neighboring town.

E. Alalakh (18th, 15th cents.). Attesting to the importance of Ḫapiru at Alalakh is an economic document (18th cent.) concluding with the following date formula: "The year in which Irkabtum the king made peace with Šemuma and the *Ḫapiru* soldiers." The significance of this event may be measured by its serving to date the entire year.

Ḫapiru of the 15th cent. display a striking heterogeneity. Geographically, census lists supply names of individual Ḫapiru and more than forty localities from which they have come. They are always associated with towns; thus their place of origin is urban, not desert. Further, one should observe that a Ḫapiru's place of origin is almost always other than the town in which he is currently found. Ethnically, the names of Alalakh Ḫapiru reflect several linguistic backgrounds. Vocationally, those called Ḫapiru are shepherds, priests, city administrators, charioteers,

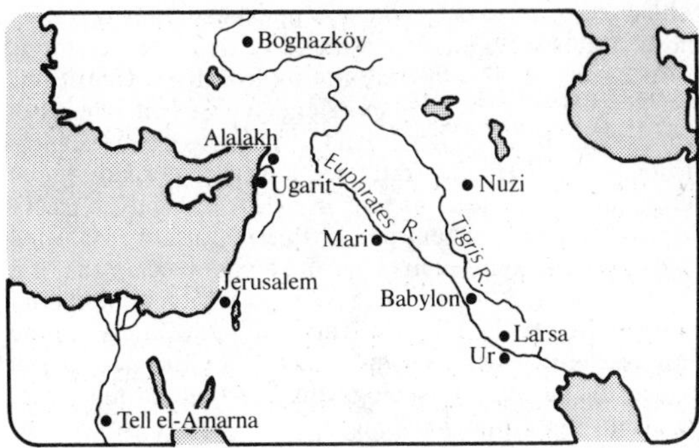

messengers, slaves, and several categories of soldiers. Some of these professions connote recognized positions of leadership within existing society, whereas others imply highly sophisticated training. Their hospitality to strangers is illustrated by Idrimi's autobiographical inscription. This king, fleeing from his native Alalakh, found refuge for seven years with a Ḫapiru colony near the Syrian coast, after which he was able to recover his kingdom with their military assistance.

F. Boghazköy (16th-13th cents.). Two documents from the Old Kingdom era tell of a treaty concluded between Hittite and Ḫapiru troops. Consistent with this notice is a tablet that speaks of Ḫapiru as a component of the Hittite army. A force of three thousand Ḫapiru mercenaries were deployed by a Hittite monarch to man a royal garrison against Hurrian insurgents. More than a dozen treaty texts from the Empire period of this central Anatolian archive mention, among those official deities invoked as divine witnesses and guarantors, the gods of the SA.GAZ and the gods of the Ḫapiru. This datum strongly suggests that Ḫapiru were a recognized stratum within society. An exorcism text specifically delineates various classes within Hittite society, including the Ḫapiru class between the children of nobility and commoners. Compatible evidence emerges from tablets that mention two female SA.GAZ who serve as official court singers and a SA.GAZ named Tette who achieved the high level of king in the Syrian town of Parqa near Ebla. Elsewhere six hundred SA.GAZ, presumably prisoners, are assigned service in Hittite temples. Ḫapiru urbanization is reflected in a document that speaks of their own settlement.

G. Nuzi (15th cent.). Memoranda from the private sector of Nuzi disclose that male and female Ḫapiru often made labor contracts with rich citizens, apparently with the right to end the agreement upon furnishing proper compensation. Ḫapiru would voluntarily enter this service, in return for which they received food and clothing. The occasional inclusion of patronymics, which would be highly unusual were these ordinary slaves, suggests that only to a certain degree were the Ḫapiru socially indigent. Only in cases of contract default did a Ḫapiru sink to the status of absolute slave. One tablet clearly indicates that a Ḫapiru parent had the right to arrange for his children to enter this voluntary service; at times parent and offspring entered together.

Public documents describe consignments of food or clothing to Ḫapiru. It is again reasonable to assume that these consignments were made to people serving as palace mercenaries, since mention is sometimes made of the distribution of barley for horses owned by Ḫapiru, and included among Ḫapiru professions were the hipponomist and military officer. Other Ḫapiru vocations included the carpenter, stone engraver, fisherman, and the enigmatic *ubbūtu*. Nuzi Ḫapiru seem to have emigrated from other settled regions and occasionally appear as family units, although remarkable ethnic dissimilarity characterizes them.

H. Ugarit (14th-13th cents.). Tax lists from Ugarit (cf. I.A.3) suggest that the Ḫapiru enclave at Ḫalbi had become normalized enough to lend its name to a geographical region. In fact, Ḫapiru settlements were accorded official recognition as fugitive havens in a Hittite-Ugaritic treaty discovered at Râs Shamrah. In this important text King Hattusilis III promised his Ugaritic contemporary that if a Ugaritic fugitive fled to the SA.GAZ territory, he would be extradited to the king of Ugarit. This text attests to the refugee element within Ḫapiru ranks (cf. Idrimi, Amarna evidence), yet its phraseology implies that, in this case, the Ḫapiru were dependent upon a Hittite sovereign. Moreover, the document specifies a definable SA.GAZ territory, again suggesting recognition within the bounds of society. The same picture seems to be mirrored in an Ugaritic royal grant which exempts the grantee from having to house SA.GAZ. Instead, such a one was to be quartered at the state's bidding. Some have suggested that Ḫapiru served in the Ugaritic navy at the time of the invasion of the Sea-peoples.

I. Amarna (14th cent.). The largest number of SA.GAZ/Ḫapiru references is to be found in the Amarna correspondence. Normally referred to in uncongenial circumstances and very often as a powerful military force, they represent one of a number of Syro-Palestinian population groups poised to exploit a moment of political weakness. They were mercenaries at the disposal of the seditionary ʿAbdi-Aširta, founder of Amurru, who is himself called one of them, and they were partially responsible for capturing vast areas of the Phoenician coast and parts of Syria. After ʿAbdi-Aširta's death, Ḫapiru formed part of the menacing forces under the aegis of his two sons. Often Palestinian Ḫapiru are described as small, marauding bands of men who seize, loot, and burn towns and generally ravage the landscape. At other times they form alliances with towns. The king of Megiddo complained that the sons of Lab'ayu king of Shechem had hired Ḫapiru to fight him. And the king of Jerusalem related that Lab'ayu had established a private Ḫapiru garrison at Shechem. Citizens of Lachish are said to have defected from Egypt to become Ḫapiru, as did the kings of Hazor and Tushulti. Elsewhere, the Ḫapiru are supported by the towns of Gezer and Ashkelon. Yet in three tablets Ḫapiru act in concert with Egyptian loyalists. An Egyptian commissioner numbers a contingent of Ḫapiru among his troops; in one case he bequeaths cities to the Ḫapiru. And the loyal governor of Byblos finds a Ḫapiru who is willing to transmit a message to a neighboring town. Though the Amarna Ḫapiru seem to be composed of diverse ethnic elements from various localities, they rather consistently represent an unrespectable element of society. They are associated with robbers (cf. 299:26, ^{lú}SA.GAZ$^{\text{meš-tu}_4}$, where phonetic complement suggests the reading *ḫabbātu*) and are twice called "dogs."

J. Egyptian Documents (15th-12th cents.). The *ʿpr.w* appear in Egyptian documents between the reigns of Thutmose III (or perhaps Hatshepsut) and Ramses IV in a consistently menial role, serving as quarry workers, wine pressers, bowmen(?), and stone haulers. Most likely Syro-Palestinian natives, they were perceived to be foreigners, as is sometimes indicated by a foreigner determinative written with *ʿpr.w*. Documents from two pharaohs that describe Egyptian encounters with the *ʿpr.w* in Palestine portray them as a disruptive element. A general in the army of Thutmose III requests princes near Joppa to permit horses to be stabled inside the city, lest the *ʿpr.w* pass by and steal them. A stele of Seti I states that warring *ʿpr.w* from Mt. Yarmut, in the Galilean highlands, were roundly defeated by Egyptian forces. A commemorative stele includes 3600 *ʿpr.w* among the booty brought to Egypt at the conclusion of the second campaign of Amenhotep II into Syro-Palestine. Their servile status is also reflected in letters discovered at Kumidi and dictated by an Amarna pharaoh, who instructed his vassals near Damascus to send certain Ḫapiru to Egypt in order that they might be resettled in Nubia. Ramses II forced the *ʿpr.w* to haul stones in conjunction with his building enterprise near Memphis. Some *ʿpr.w* are included in a list of items dedicated by Ramses III to a temple at Heliopolis. Ramses IV dispatched them as unskilled laborers to the turquoise mines in Wâdī Ḥammāmāt. The status of servitude ascribed to the *ʿpr.w* in Egypt resulted from their having been taken prisoner; thus their position there says nothing about their original status in Syro-Palestine.

III. Ḫapiru as Designation.–A. *Ethnic.* Following the publication of the Amarna Tablets, many scholars regarded "Ḫapiru" as an ethnic designation; now, however, the ethnic heterogeneity of the Ḫapiru has contributed to a change of thought. In the Old Babylonian period most Ḫapiru bore Akkadian names, while a few from Mari were West Semites. Alalakh Ḫapiru bore mostly non-Semitic names, and some were recognizably Hurrian. Though the majority of the Nuzi population was Hurrian, a full two-thirds of the Ḫapiru were Akkadians while others were varieties of non-Semites. Though no Nuzi Ḫapiru bore West Semitic names, Amarna Ḫapiru were largely West Semites. Ḫapiru names certainly suggest a mixed ethnic composition, often similar in stock to the local population. To such heterogeneity must be added geographic diversity. Ḫapiru are said to have been natives of towns in Babylonia, Assyria, Anatolia, Syria, Lebanon, Phoenicia, and Palestine. As a result of political exigencies, individuals or entire towns could become Ḫapiru overnight. And if Ḫapiru were an ethnic term at Ugarit, like other ethnica, it would have been written **ʿprym,* not *ʿprm.*

B. Socio-Legal. Texts describe Ḫapiru as having a predilection for military service, showing a tendency to remain in enclaves, possessing an economic status spanning the entire economic spectrum, displaying a great vocational variety, and exhibiting a warm hospitality (especially to fugitives). They frequently owned their own property, including houses, horses, donkeys, and land, and their origin was consistently urban, not desert fringe. Though united by a sense of foreignness, Ḫapiru were largely part of organized society. As such, they appear to have been uprooted persons who found a means of subsistence for themselves by entering a state of dependence to individuals or city-states. One should note in passing that their first appearance in Mesopotamia coincides with the cataclysmic upheavals and mass migrations at the end of the Early Bronze Age and that they no longer appear in literature after the advent of Aramean expansionism. Ḫapiru served various levels of need within a local society in exchange for supplies and shelter. Only in times of weak political authority (e.g., Mari, Boghazköy Old Kingdom[?], Alalakh VII [?], Amarna) do Ḫapiru abandon their status and become somewhat or absolutely independent. For this reason Greenberg argues that SA.GAZ originally derives not from *šaggāšu,* "murderer," but from West Semitic *šgš,* "be restive." Accordingly, *ḫabbātu* became the Akkadian lexical equivalent to SA.GAZ because it functioned as the semantic approximate of *šgš* (see I.A.1 above). In times of political disarray, however, by analogic extension the inoffensive SA.GAZ = *šgš,* "restive one, migrant," developed into the pejorative SA.GAZ = *šaggāšu,* "murderer."

IV. Impossibility of Equation of Ḫapiru and Hebrews in Biblical Studies. *– A. Impossibility of General Equation.* Beyond its ancillary role in questions pertaining to patriarchal antiquity, the equation Hebrews = Ḫapiru is applied in a critical way to biblical studies at two points: (1) the manner of the biblical Conquest, and (2) the date of the Hebrew Exodus from Egypt. To be sure, the Hebrews were too limited geographically, chronologically, and ethnically to permit their outright equation with the farflung and heterogeneous Ḫapiru. For this reason, advocates of the sociological approach to the biblical Conquest or the fifteenth-century date of the Exodus somewhat arbitrarily restrict their equation to the Ḫapiru of the Amarna Tablets.

B. Equation of Amarna Ḫapiru and Biblical Hebrews. Adherents of the sociological model for the Conquest see in the Hebrews = Ḫapiru an oppressed element of the native population of Palestine which, for religious reasons, willingly withdrew from all societal obligations and, in a manner reminiscent of the German Peasants' Revolt, established for themselves a counter sociopolitical system revolving around a covenant with Yahweh. The Conquest is thus viewed as a religious revolt against the ruling class, and its success is attested in the astonishing numerical growth of the Hebrews from seventy to more than one million — these were religious devotees. Accordingly, the Hebrews' basis of solidarity at the point of the Conquest was religion. Adherents of the fifteenth-century Exodus rely heavily upon the Hebrews = Ḫapiru equation both because, when taken in connection with the notice of 1 K. 6:1, a corroborative fixed chronological point exists, and because one then obtains an extrabiblical contemporary record of the Conquest. But this equation is confronted by a number of obstacles, which are problematic if not irreconcilable.

1. Philologically. The lexemes *ʿapiru* (Ḫapiru) and *ʿiḇrî* (Hebrew) are unrelated in derivation, morphology, and semantics. As already shown (see I.C above), whereas *ʿiḇrî* derives from the root *ʿbr*, *ʿapiru* incontestably derives from the root *ʿpr*. To suggest that the latter form can be explained as a phonetic variant of **ʿabiru* requires an unprecedented consonantal transformation in Ugaritic (see I.A.3 above) and Egyptian (see I.B above). Though Albright had theorized to the contrary, citing what he considered to be an example of Akk. *malik-* shifting to *milk-* in first-millennium Canaanite, the required vocalic shift from *ʿapir-* to *ʿibr-* is equally untenable. *Milk-* forms, now attested in cuneiform names as early as the Ur III period, show themselves to be parallel to *malik-* forms. Morphologically *ʿapiru* exhibits the adjectival *qaṭil* pattern whereas *ʿiḇrî* follows the *qiṭl* plus gentilic substantive model. Semantically, *ʿiḇrî* is an ethnicon and preserves no trace of social implications while *ʿapiru* refers to a socio-legal entity without indicating ethnic overtones.

2. Ethno-Socially. Aside from the fact that both the Ḫapiru and the Hebrews are depicted as militaristic groups, they are incompatible ethno-socially. "Ḫapiru" is an appellation denoting social status and referring to ethnically heterogeneous groups that show no discernible tribal structure and are usually politically subordinate. Their actions in no way reflect that they were part of a mass movement of peoples from outside Palestine. Though one could join their ranks voluntarily, various groups in their number do not seem to be united by a common cause, and their activities are sporadic and dissociated. On the other hand, "Hebrew" is an ethnic designation used to refer to the ancestors of the Israelite nation, beginning with Abraham, if not with Eber. (Does Hebrew equal Eberite?) This ethnically homogeneous group is uniformly bound by familial ties and tribal strictures, and appears to have been politically autonomous. The Hebrews' solidarity revolved around an ethnic, not a religious, axis and the biblical narratives contain no hint that one voluntarily became a Hebrew. The Joshua account shows that the Hebrews came from territories outside Palestine and that their conquest was strategically and tactically conceived and executed in a systematic, coherent, and purposeful manner.

3. Onomastically. The names of cities and kings specifically mentioned both in conjunction with the biblical Conquest under Joshua and with the Ḫapiru upheavals in the Amarna Tablets may be diagrammed as follows:

Place Name	King According to Joshua Account	King According to Amarna Tablets
Jerusalem	Adoni-zedek (10:1)	Abdi-Ḫeba (285-290)
Lachish	Japhia (10:3)	Yabni-Ilu (328) Zimredda (329) Šipti-baʿal (330-332)
Gezer	Horam (10:33)	Milki-Ilu (267-271, 369) Yapaḫu (298-300, 378)
Hazor	Jabin (11:1)	Abdi-Tirshi (228)
Hebron	Hoham (10:3)	Šuwardata(?) (278-284, 366)

If the Joshua account and the Amarna Letters described the same events, at least some of these personal names should be identical or analogous, especially in cases where more than one king from a given city faced the Ḫapiru dilemma. But no cases exist in which the names bear even a slight resemblance. Further, in one instance (possibly two) the corresponding names derive from dissimilar ethnic origins, which would normally imply a dynastic succession.

4. Historically. Historical discrepancies between the circumstances of the Ḫapiru and the Hebrews exist at several levels. First, the vast preponderance of Amarna texts that mention the Ḫapiru derive from exactly those cities and regions which, according to the Conquest narratives, Israel never attempted to capture. Alternatively, it is circular to reason, with Meyer and Böhl, that places like Shiloh, Bethel, Gibeon, and Hebron are not represented in the Amarna Letters because they had already fallen to the Hebrews. Leaving aside the possible representation of Hebron in the correspondence, such a contention would leave unexplained the fact that Lachish and Gezer, mentioned in the Conquest narrative precisely in conjunction with the liberation of Gibeon, *are* attested in Amarna documents as allies, not enemies, of the Ḫapiru. Further, one would then have to explain the Hebrew antagonism to the king of Hazor when according to the Amarna texts this king was a colleague of the Ḫapiru. The alleged equation also cannot offer an adequate explanation of the Ḫapiru loyalty to native governors or Egyptian emissaries sometimes attested in Amarna literature, when the Conquest account uniformly portrays Hebrew antipathy toward the local population. Additionally, Israel did not use chariot warfare in the Conquest (Josh. 11:6, 9; 2 S. 8:4), so it was unable to conquer the maritime and Esdraelon plains. Amarna Ḫapiru, however, were quite adept at this kind of warfare.

Second, in considering Egypt's political involvement in Syro-Palestinian affairs, one notices a conspicuous absence of reference to Egypt or an Egyptian hegemony in the Joshua-Judges narrative — suggesting that Egypt was politically passive at the time of the Conquest. Yet the Amarna Letters contain numerous requests for Egyptian assistance against the Ḫapiru, and the Kumidi tablets speak of Egyptian attempts to thwart Ḫapiru incursions — suggesting that Egypt was politically active at the time of the correspondence.

Third, historical discrepancies surface when discussing the manner and mission of the Conquest vis-à-vis the aim of the Ḫapiru. The biblical accounts agree that the Conquest, for however long its process continued, was tribal and that large groups of people, united by a sense of blood kinship, were motivated in their organized conquest and killing by a desire to acquire land for tribal occupation. On the other hand, the Ḫapiru are characterized as marauding plunderers. Engaging in sporadic forays in which they looted and burned towns only to withdraw quickly with their booty, the small, fragmented bands of Ḫapiru displayed no interest in mass depopulation and resettlement of an area. These data have the cumulative effect of evoking the greatest doubt regarding the proposed equation Ḫapiru = Hebrew.

Bibliography.–J. Bottéro, *Le Problème des Ḫabiru, à la 4e rencontre assyriologique internationale* (1954); *Reallexikon der Assyriologie und vorderasiatischen Archäologie,* IV/1 (1972), *s.v.*; M. Greenberg, *The Ḫab/piru* (1955); "Hab/piru and Hebrews," in B. Mazar, ed., *World History of the Jewish People,* II (1970), pp. 188-200; M. Weippert, *Settlement of the Israelite Tribes in Palestine* (*SBT,* 2/21, 1971); H. Cazelles, "The Hebrews," in D. J. Wiseman, ed., *Peoples of OT Times* (1973), pp. 1-28; R. de Vaux, *JNES,* 27 (1968), 221-28; M. Gray, *HUCA,* 29 (1958), 135-202.

B. J. BEITZEL

HABITATION [Heb. *môšāḇ*] (Ex. 35:3; Lev. 13:46; Ps. 132:13; Ezk. 6:14); NEB HOME, SETTLEMENT, etc.; [*šāḵan*] (Dt. 12:5; Ps. 104:12); NEB DWELL, NEST; [*māʿôn*] (Dt. 26:15; 2 Ch. 30:27; Ps. 26:8; 68:5 [MT 6]; 91:9; Jer. 21:13; 25:30); AV also DWELLING PLACE; NEB DWELLING-PLACE, "beauty," REFUGE, LAIR; [*nāweh*] (2 S. 15:25; Job 18:15; Ps. 79:7; Isa. 27:10; Jer. 10:25; etc.); AV also DWELLING PLACE; NEB DWELLING-PLACE, HOME, etc.; [*miškān*] (2 Ch. 29:6; Ps. 46:4 [MT 5]; 78:28; Isa. 22:16; 54:2; Hab. 1:6); NEB DWELLING-PLACE, RESTING-PLACE, etc.; [*zeḇûl*] (Isa. 63:15; Hab. 3:11); NEB ZENITH, "heights where thou dwellest"; [Gk. *épaulis*] (Acts 1:20); NEB HOMESTEAD; [*skḗnōma*] (Acts 7:46); AV TABERNACLE; NEB DWELLING-PLACE; [*katoikía*] (Acts 17:26); NEB TERRITORY; [*skēnḗ*] (Lk. 16:9); NEB HOME; **ABODE** [Heb. *yāšaḇ, šeḇeṯ*] (Ex. 15:17; Ju. 20:47; Ps. 68:16 [MT 17]); AV also DWELL; NEB DWELLING-PLACE, REMAIN, DWELL; [*šāḵan, miškān*] (Ex. 40:35; Lev. 26:11); AV also TABERNACLE; NEB SETTLE, TABERNACLE; [*nāweh*] (Ex. 15:13; Prov. 3:33); AV HABITATION; NEB DWELLING-PLACE, HOME; [*ḥāṣîr*–'grass'] (Isa. 34:13); AV HABITATION; NEB HAUNT; [*sōḵ*–'hut'] (Ps. 76:2 [MT 3]); AV TABERNACLE; NEB TENT; [*ʿalîyâ*–'upper room'] (Ps. 104:13); AV CHAMBER; NEB HIGH PAVILION.

The terms signify a place of dwelling. Human dwelling places consisted of tents (Ex. 35:3; Lev. 13:46), caves (Isa. 22:16), or permanent homes (Hab. 1:6). Frequently, the terms refer specifically to God's dwelling place in both its transcendent and immanent aspects. Cross made a distinction between Yahweh dwelling in heaven and Yahweh dwelling among His people, expressed by the verbs *yāšaḇ,* "sit," "dwell" (Ugar. *yṯb;* Akk. [*w*]*ašābu*) and *šāḵan,* "settle," "inhabit" (Ugar. *škn;* Akk. *šakānu*). The former term points to the occupation of heaven (*māʿôn* also clearly refers to the heavenly nature of God's dwelling place in Dt. 26:15; 2 Ch. 30:27; and Jer. 25:30); the latter indicates Yahweh's dwelling upon earth (cf. Woudstra, pp. 68-77). God's taking up residence (*miškān;* Ugar. *mšknt*) with His people, either in a temporary dwelling (tabernacle) or a permanent dwelling (temple), is indicative of His affection for, His condescension to, and His identification with, His people (cf. Fairbairn and Vos). In this connection, note the significance of Jn. 1:14: "The Word became flesh and dwelt [*eskḗnōsen,* lit. "tabernacled"] among us."

The Akk. *nawūm* is similar to Heb. *nāweh*. In the Mari documents, *nawūm* means "encampment" (Malamat). This sense would cover all pastoral associations of the Hebrew cognates. The combination of *nāweh* and *ṣeḏeq* (Job 8:6) is translated "an abode befitting you" by Holladay (*CHAL,* p. 231). Ugar. *zbl* (cf. Heb. *zeḇul*) means "ruler" or "lord" as a noun, and "exalt" or "elevate" as a verb (cf. Held and Ward). The exalted nature of God's heavenly abode is apparent in Isa. 63:15; and the fact that the sun and moon were appointed "rulers" at the creation (Gen. 1:16) may shed light on the very difficult Hab. 3:11.

Bibliography.–F. M. Cross, *Biblical Archaeologist Reader* I, (1961), 225-28; P. Fairbairn, *Typology of Scripture* (1854), II, 220ff.; M. Held, *JAOS,* 88 (1968), 90-96; A. Malamat, *JAOS,* 82 (1962), 143-150; G. Vos, *Biblical Theology* (repr. 1959), pp. 164-172; W. A. Ward, *Orientalia,* N.S. 32 (1963), 413-436; M. H. Woudstra, *Ark of the Covenant From Conquest to Kingship* (1965).

J. T. DENNISON, JR.

HABOR hā'bōr [Heb. *ḥāḇôr*; Gk. *habōr*]. A tributary of the Euphrates, called "the river of Gozan" (2 K. 17:6) from the region through which it flows (*see* GOZAN). It originates in the general vicinity of Haran, flows southeastward and then southward, and empties into the Euphrates not far above Mari. The name occurs in Assyrian inscriptions as *ḫabûr* and continues in use today as Ḫabûr (Khābûr). Tiglath-pileser (1 Ch. 5:26) and "the king of Assyria," either Shalmaneser or Sargon (2 K. 17:6; 18:11), settled some of the Israelite exiles in regions along the Habor.

W. S. L. S.

HACALIAH hak'ə-lī'ə [Heb. *ḥaḵalyâ*] (Neh. 1:1; 10:1 [MT 2]); AV HACHALIAH. Father of Nehemiah.

HACHILAH hə-kī'lə, hak'i-lə, **HILL OF** [Heb. *ḥaḵîlâ*]. A hill in the wilderness of Judah, associated with the wanderings of David. It is stated to be S of Jeshimon (1 S. 23:19) and "on the east of Jeshimon" (1 S. 26:1). It was near Ziph and Maon, but the site has not been identified.

HACHMONI hak'mō-nī; **HACHMONITE** hak'mō-nīt [Heb. *ḥaḵmônî*–'wise']. In 1 Ch. 11:11 the family of JASHOBEAM, one of David's heroes. The reference to him in 2 S. 23:8 as a "Tahchemonite" has resulted from textual corruption, and should agree with 1 Ch. 11:11 in form. In 1 Ch. 27:32 "Hachmonite" is the preferred reading.

HADAD hā'dad.

1. [Heb. *ḥaḏaḏ*] (Gen. 25:15 par. 1 Ch. 1:30); AV also HADAR. One of the twelve sons of Ishmael.

2. [Heb. *haḏaḏ*] (Gen. 36:35f. par. 1 Ch. 1:46f.). A king of Edom, son of Bedad, "who defeated Midian in the country of Moab," and whose "city was Avith."

3. Another king of Edom, written *haḏar,* "Hadar," in Gen. 36:39 by a copyist's mistake, but *haḏaḏ* in the parallel passage in 1 Ch. 1:50f. His city was Pau or Pai.

4. A member of the royal family of Edom during David's time, who as a child escaped Joab's slaughter of the Edomites and fled to Egypt. On David's death he returned to Edom, where he made trouble for Solomon by stirring up the Edomites against the rule of Israel (1 K. 11:14-22, 25).

5. An alternative name for Baal, the head of the Canaanite pantheon, whose worship was expressed in fer-

Head of Hadad from Khirbet et-Tannur SE of the Dead Sea, possibly showing Hellenistic-Parthian influences (E. K. Vogel; picture American Schools of Oriental Research)

tility rites. (*See* BAAL I; UGARIT.) The storm-god Hadad is mentioned in Assyrian inscriptions, and called on the monolith of Shalmaneser "the god of Aleppo." In the Assyrian inscriptions he is identified with the air-god Rimmon. The union of the two names in Zec. 12:11 suggests this identity. G. R. HOVEY R. K. H.

HADADEZER hā-dad-ē'zər, had-ə-dē'zər [Heb. *hᵃdaḏʿezer*] (2 S. 8:3-12; 1 K. 11:23); [*hᵃdarʿezer*] (2 S. 10:16, 19; 1 Ch. 18:3-11; 19:16, 19); AV HADAREZER. Mentioned in connection with David's wars of conquests, Hadadezer was king of Zobah in Syria. The exact position and size of this Syrian principality are uncertain, but it seems to have extended in David's time southward toward Ammon and eastward to the Euphrates.

When the Ammonites had put themselves in the wrong with David by the insult done to his ambassadors (2 S. 10:1-5), they summoned to their aid against the incensed king of Israel the Syrians of various adjoining principalities, among them the Syrians of Zobah under Hadadezer, the son of Rehob. The strategy of Joab, who arrayed the force under the command of his brother Abishai against the Ammonites and himself attacked the Syrian allies, won for Israel a decisive victory. Not content with this result, Hadadezer gathered together another Syrian force, summoning this time also "the Syrians who were beyond the Euphrates" (2 S. 10:16), with Shobach the captain of his host at their head. On this occasion David himself took command of the Israelite forces, and again defeated the Syrians near Helam, Shobach being left dead on the field. Hadadezer and his Syrian vassals, finding resistance hopeless, "made peace with Israel, and became subject to them" (2 S. 10:19). For the name Hadad- or Hadarezer, *see* BENHADAD.

Bibliography.–T. H. Robinson, *History of Israel*, I (1951), 201, 237f.; *WBA*, p. 123; M. F. Unger, *Israel and the Aramaeans of Damascus* (1957), pp. 42-48. T. NICOL

HADADRIMMON hā-dad-rim'on, hä-dad-rim'on [Heb. *hᵃdaḏ-rimmôn*]. A name mentioned in Zec. 12:11 of uncertain designation. The term seems to be a compound name for Baal composed by combining the Aramean Hadad, "thunderer," with the Akkadian Rammân, "thunderer."

The two major views of its reference in Zec. 12:11 are: (1) The term refers to a place near Megiddo at which mourning for Josiah took place after his death in battle against Pharaoh Neco (2 K. 23:29f.; 2 Ch. 35:20-25). (2) The reference is to ceremonies in the worship of Baal held near Megiddo. In either case, "the mourning of Hadadrimmon" was so famous that it could be used to illustrate the mourning to be exercised in Jerusalem when they "look on him whom they have pierced," which according to Jn. 19:37 refers to viewing the crucified Christ, whose side had been pierced by the soldier's spear.

See HADAD **5**. R. J. HUGHES, III

HADAR hā'där (Gen. 36:39). *See* HADAD **3**.

HADAREZER had-ər-ē'zər (AV 2 S. 10:16, 19; 1 Ch. 18; 19:16, 19). *See* HADADEZER.

HADASHAH hə-dash'ə [Heb. *ḥᵃdāšâ*–'new']. A town of Judah (Josh. 15:37) in the lowlands. The Mishnah (*Erubin* v. 6) claims it had only fifty inhabitants. It was possibly located between Gath and Lachish, but the exact site is unknown.

HADASSAH hə-das'ə [Heb. *hᵃdassâ*] (Est. 2:7). The Hebrew name formerly borne by ESTHER. If derived from Akk. *ḫadaššatu*, "bride," it would be one of the goddess Ishtar's titles that had been conferred on Esther (2:7). Otherwise it would be the Hebrew-Aramaic name of an evergreen shrub bearing white or pink flowers, and used by the Jews in the Feast of Tabernacles (Neh. 8:15).

R. K. H.

HADATTAH hə-dat'ə (Josh. 15:25, AV). *See* HAZOR-HADATTAH.

HADES hā'dēz [Gk. *hą́dēs*]; AV HELL; NEB also DEATH (Mt. 16:18; Acts 2:27, 31), DEPTHS (Mt. 11:23; Lk. 10:15), DEATH'S DOMAIN (Rev. 1:18). The underworld or realm of the dead.

In Greek mythology Hades was originally the proper name of the god of the underworld (Homer *Il.* xv.188), and the underworld was called "the house of Hades" (*Il.* vii.330; xxiii.389; xxiv.593). The regular use of Hades as the name of the place of the dead may have originated with Homer (*Il.* xxiii.244; cf. LSJ, p. 21). The LXX used Hades almost exclusively to translate Heb. *šᵉʾôl*, the most common OT term for the realm of the dead. The OT says little about SHEOL; it was apparently a gloomy underworld (Isa. 7:11) where all the dead went (Gen. 42:38; Eccl. 9:10).

In the intertestamental period the idea of the afterlife underwent some development. In Jewish apocalyptic literature Hades was an intermediate place (1 En. 51:1) where all the souls of the dead awaited judgment (22:3f.). The dead were separated into compartments, the righteous staying in an apparently pleasant place (v. 9) and various classes of sinners undergoing punishments in other compartments (vv. 10-13). The Pharisees also believed that the righteous were rewarded and the wicked punished (Josephus *Ant.* xviii.1.3 [14]; Ps. Sol. 14:6f.; 15:11f.).

The NT description of Hades resembles that of the OT and intertestamental portrayals. The depths of Hades are contrasted with the heights of heaven (Mt. 11:23 par. Lk. 10:15; cf. Isa. 7:11). Like the Babylonian (*ANET,* pp. 107-110) and Greek (Homer *Il.* v.646) mythologies, the NT Hades has gates like a city (RSV mg., Mt. 16:18; cf. Isa. 38:10; Job 38:17), although as Jeremias points out, this is figurative language, and the gates represent the "ungodly powers of the underworld" (*TDNT,* VI, 927). Thus the RSV's "powers of death," though not a literal translation, conveys the sense of the passage. In the book of Revelation Hades and Death are always paired and personified (1:18; 6:8; 20:13f.; an exception to this personification may occur in 1:18 if the genitives are understood as objective; cf. R. H. Charles, comm. on Revelation [*ICC,* 1920], I, 32). Christ has the keys of Death and Hades (1:18; Jeremias, *TDNT,* III, 746f., notes the rabbinic parallel in T.B. *Taanith* 2a). In 6:8 the personified Death and Hades seem to represent the ungodly powers of the underworld as they are loosed on the earth after the opening of the fourth seal.

The other NT passages that mention Hades are the focus of a debate about the NT view of the occupants of Hades. For Jeremias (*TDNT,* I, 148f.) Acts 2:27, 31 imply that all the dead are in Hades, whereas Lk. 16:19-31 and Rev. 20:13f. point to only the ungodly being in Hades. Bietenhard (*DNTT,* II, 207) claims that both Lk. 16 and Acts 2 regard Hades as the repository of all the dead, but Rev. 20 places only the ungodly in Hades. M. Rist (*IB,* XII, 520, 524f.) claims that Rev. 20 has all the dead (except the martyrs; cf. v. 5) in Hades. The reason for such conflicting interpretations seems to be that the NT presents an incomplete (though not necessarily inconsistent) picture of the afterlife, and each of these scholars tries to complete that picture without sufficient evidence.

The parable of the rich man and Lazarus (Lk. 16:19-31) should not be used as a definitive statement about the afterlife, since parables were told to illustrate a point, not to give a systematic account of any doctrine. Thus Jesus intended not to describe Hades, but to warn His listeners about their hardheartedness. Also, the text nowhere states that both Lazarus and the rich man were in Hades; Lazarus is clearly placed in "ABRAHAM'S BOSOM," a place "far off" (v. 23) from Hades and separated from it by "a great chasm" (v. 26).

As E. Haenchen pointed out, Acts 2:27, 31 may mean that Jesus "was not delivered into Hades" (comm. on Acts [Eng. tr. 1971], pp. 181f.), an interpretation that accords well with the psalmist's intent (cf. A. Weiser, *Psalms* [Eng. tr., *OTL,* 1962], pp. 176-78). A related, widely held view is that these verses teach that only the soul is in Hades. The parallelism, however, suggests that the whole person is referred to; this is especially clear in Hebrew, where *nepeš,* "soul" (the word used in Ps. 16:10, which Peter quotes here), is often used for a person (*CHAL,* pp. 242f.) and as a substitute for the personal pronoun (e.g., 1 K. 20:32; cf. H. W. Wolff, *Anthropology of the OT* [Eng. tr. 1974], pp. 10-25; *TDNT,* IX, 620). For the Hebrews a person was a unity, not to be divided into body, soul, and spirit as the Greeks did. Gk. *psychē* also can mean the whole person (Bauer, rev., p. 894; *TDNT,* IX, 639f.). Thus Acts 2:27, 31 offer little help in understanding the afterlife.

Rev. 20:13f. must be considered ambiguous. Although vv. 12 and 15 suggest that all the dead were in Hades, vv. 4-6 imply that believers had already been resurrected (cf. G. E. Ladd, comm. on Revelation [1972], pp. 263-68, 273f.). In the face of such conflicting evidence, it is better to suspend judgment than force an interpretation onto the texts. For a cautious but sensible treatment of this problem, see G. E. Ladd, *Last Things* (1978), pp. 33-39.

See DEATH.

G. A. L.

HADID hā'did [Heb. *ḥāḏîḏ*–'sharp'; Gk. *Hadida*]. A town of Benjamin (Neh. 11:33f.) which, along with Lod and Ono, was a home of exiles returning from Babylon (Ezr. 2:33; Neh. 7:37). It was located at the mouth of the valley of Aijalon NE of the coastal plain. It is included in the Karnak list of Thutmose III and also in the Mishnah (*Arakhin* ix.6) as existing as a walled city since Joshua. Hadid was rebuilt and fortified by Simon Maccabeus (1 Macc. 12:38; *see* ADIDA) and by Vespasian (Josephus *BJ* iv.9.1 [486]). It is probably to be identified with modern el-Ḥadîtheh, 5 km. (3 mi.) ENE of Lod (*WHAB*).

D. W. BAKER

HADLAI had'lī [Heb. *ḥaḏlāy*]. An Ephraimite (2 Ch. 28:12), father of Amasa, who was one of the heads of the tribe in the time of Pekah king of Israel.

HADORAM hə-dôr'əm [Heb. *hᵃḏōrām*].

1. Son of Joktan and apparently sixth in descent from Noah (Gen. 10:27 par. 1 Ch. 1:21).

2. Son of Tou king of Hamath, sent by his father with presents to King David (1 Ch. 18:10). In 2 S. 8:9f., written probably incorrectly "Joram," son of "Toi."

3. Rehoboam's superintendent of the forced labor department (2 Ch. 10:18), called ADORAM in 1 K. 12:18, a contraction of ADONIRAM. He was sent by Rehoboam as messenger to Israel at the time of the revolt of the ten tribes and was stoned to death by them.

G. R. HOVEY

HADRACH had'rak [Heb. *ḥaḏrāḵ*]. A place, probably a city-state, in northern Syria. "The land of Hadrach" is mentioned in Zec. 9:1, along with Damascus, in connection with a prophecy concerning "the cities of Aram." It is almost certainly to be identified with Ḫatarikka in Assyrian texts. Tiglath-pileser III named "the city of Hatarikka" in his annals as one of the "nineteen districts of Hamath" that had gone over to support Azariah of Judah (or Azriyau of Ya'udi, cf. *ARAB,* I, § 770; §§ 815, 821). Sennacherib referred to the "eponymy of Gahilu, governor of Ḫatarikka," in the Taylor Prism (*ARAB,* II, § 428). It has been identified with Tell Āfis, about 45 km. (28 mi.) SW of Aleppo, where the stele of Zakir (*ca.* 800 B.C.) was found (cf. *DOTT,* pp. 242-250). In Old Aramaic the name is written *ḥzrk,* suggesting an original **ḥḏrk* (or Hadhrak), but this raises a problem with the identification with Assyr. Ḫatarikka, for *ḏ* should be reflected by *z* in Assyrian.

W. S. L. S.

HA-ELEPH hā-ē'lef [Heb. *hā'elep̱*]; AV, NEB, ELEPH. One of the cities of Benjamin, in the vicinity of Jerusalem (Josh. 18:28). The name is omitted from the LXX B; in A it is joined to the preceding word (Heb. *ṣēlaʿ*), reading Gk. *Sēlaleph.* The exact site is unknown, but it is perhaps to be identified with Liftā, NW of Jerusalem (*HDB*; BDB, p. 49), though this has also been identified as (Me-)Nephtoah.

K. G. JUNG

HAEMORRHOIDS. *See* TUMORS.

HAG. *See* NIGHT HAG.

HAGAB hā'gab [Heb. *ḥagaḇ*–'locust'; Gk. Apoc. *Agaba*]; AV Apoc. AGABA; NEB Apoc. GABA. Ancestor of some of the Nethinim who returned from the Babylonian captivity with Zerubbabel and Nehemiah. The name occurs in Ezr. 2:46; 1 Esd. 5:30, but is omitted entirely from the parallel list of Neh. 7:48.

HAGABA hag'ə-bä [Heb. *ḥ^agāḇā'*]. *See* HAGABAH.

HAGABAH hag'ə-bä [Heb. *ḥ^agāḇâ*–'locust']; AV GRABA; NEB AGGABA (1 Esd. 5:29). Like Hagab, an ancestor of some of the temple servants who returned from Babylon with Zerubbabel (Ezr. 2:45); spelled "Hagaba" in the parallel passage (Neh. 7:48).

HAGAR hā'gär [Heb. *hāgār*–'emigration,' 'flight'; Gk. *Hagar*]. An Egyptian woman, the handmaid or slave of Sarai; a present, perhaps, from Pharaoh when Abram dissembled to him in Egypt (Gen. 12:16). Mention is made of her in two passages (Gen. 16; 21:8-21).

In the first narrative (Gen. 16) it is related that Sarai, despairing at her age of having children, gave Hagar to Abram as a concubine. As Hagar was not an ordinary household slave but the peculiar property of her mistress (cf. 29:24, 29), any offspring which she might bear to Abram would be reckoned as Sarai's (cf. 30:3–9). In the prospect of becoming a mother, Hagar, forgetting her position, seems to have become insolent toward her childless mistress. Sarai felt keenly the contempt shown her by her handmaid, and in angry tones brought her conduct before Abram. Now that her plan was not working out smoothly, she unfairly blamed her husband for what originated with herself, and appealed to God to redress her grievance. Abram refused to interfere in the domestic quarrel and, renouncing his rights over his concubine and her claims on him, put her entirely at Sarai's disposal. Under the harsh treatment of her mistress Hagar's life became intolerable, and she fled into the wilderness, turning her steps naturally toward Egypt, her native land.

But the angel of the Lord (who is here introduced for the first time as the medium of the theophany) appeared to her as she was resting by a spring and commanded her to return and submit herself to her mistress, promising her an innumerable seed through her unborn son, concerning whom he uttered a striking prediction (*see* ISHMAEL). To the angel (who is now said to be the Lord Himself) Hagar gave the name "Thou art a God of seeing" (16:13).

Obedient to the heavenly vision Hagar returned, as the narrative implies, to her mistress and gave birth to Ishmael, Abram being then eighty-six years old.

The other narrative (Gen. 21:8–21) relates what occurred in connection with the weaning of Isaac. The presence and conduct of Ishmael during the family feast held on the occasion roused the anger and jealousy of Sarah who, fearing that Ishmael would share the inheritance with Isaac, peremptorily demanded the expulsion of the slave-mother and her son. But Abraham's fatherly heart recoiled from such a cruel course, and it was only after the revelation was made to him that the ejection of Hagar

Jean Baptiste Corot, *Hagar in the Wilderness* (A.D. 1835). This oil painting shows the angel coming to encourage Hagar and Ishmael (Metropolitan Museum of Art, Rogers Fund, 1938)

and her son would be in the line of the divine purpose — for Isaac was his real seed, while Ishmael would be made a nation, too — that he was led to forego his natural feelings and accede to Sarah's demand. So next morning the bondwoman and her son were sent forth with the bare provision of bread and a skin of water into the wilderness of Beer-sheba. When the water was spent, Hagar, unable to bear the sight of her boy dying from thirst, laid him under a shrub and withdrew the distance of a bowshot to weep out her sorrow. But the angel of God, calling to her out of heaven, comforted her with the assurance that God had heard the voice of the lad and that there was a great future before him. Then her eyes were opened to discover a well of water; she filled the skin and gave her son a drink. With God's blessing the lad grew up amid the desert's hardships, distinguished for his skill with the bow. He made his home in the wilderness of Paran, and his mother took a wife for him out of her own country.

In Gal. 4:21-31 Paul makes an allegorical use of this episode in the history of Ishmael and Isaac to support his argument for the transitory character of the Jewish ritual and the final triumph of Christian freedom over all Judaizing tendencies. In elaborating his reference, the apostle institutes a series of contrasts. Hagar, the bondwoman, represents the old covenant which was given from Mt. Sinai; and as Ishmael was Abraham's son after the flesh, so the Judaizing Christians, who wish to remain in bondage to the law, are Hagar's children. On the other hand, Sarah, the freewoman, represents the new covenant instituted by Christ; and as Isaac was born to Abraham in virtue of the promise, so the Christians who have freed themselves entirely from the law of carnal ordinances and live by faith are Sarah's children. Thus Hagar corresponds to "the Jerusalem that now is," that is, the Jewish state which is in spiritual bondage with her children; while Sarah represents "the Jerusalem that is above," "our mother" (RSV), the mother of us Christians, that free spiritual city to which Christians even now belong (Phil. 3:20). By this allegory the apostle would warn the Galatian Christians of the danger which beset them from their Judaizing brethren, of their subjection to the covenant of works and their ultimate expulsion from the household of faith.

To us Paul's reference does not appeal with the same force as it would do to those to whom he was writing. The incident taken by itself, indeed, does not contain any suggestion of such a hidden meaning. Yet the history of the Hebrew nation is but typical of the history of the Church in all ages, and the apostle's familiarity with rabbinical modes of interpretation may have led him to adopt this method of confirming the truth which he had already proved from the law itself.

See *TDNT,* I, *s.v.* Ἄγαρ (Kittel). J. CRICHTON

HAGARENES hā'gär-ēnz (Ps. 83:6, AV); **HAGARITES** hā'gär-īts. *See* HAGRITES.

HAGERITE. *See* HAGRITES.

HAGGADAH hə-gä'də, hä-gə-dä'. *See* TALMUD.

HAGGAI hag'ē-ī, hag'ī [Heb. *ḥaggay*; LXX *haggaios*]; AV also AGGEUS (1 Esd. 6:1; 7:3; 2 Esd. 1:40). A prophet of the 6th cent. B.C. and the tenth book of the Minor Prophets. Haggai was written before the other two postexilic prophets Zechariah and Malachi.

I. Name
II. Personal Ministry
III. Historical Background
IV. Date and Structure
V. Message
 A. The Challenge (1:1-15)
 B. The Encouragement (2:1-9)
 C. The Reversal of Fortunes (2:10f.)
 D. The Promise (2:20-23)
VI. Style
VII. Text

I. Name.–The name means "festal," coming from the word *ḥag,* "feast, festival," usually linked with the pilgrimage feasts of Passover (Unleavened Bread), Pentecost (Weeks), and Tabernacles. Perhaps Haggai was born close to the time one of those feasts was being observed.

II. Personal Ministry.–Haggai was probably born to a humble family, since the name of his father is unknown. He may have been about eighty years old when he prophesied, because Hag. 2:3 implies that he had seen Solomon's temple prior to the exile. His age could explain the brevity of his ministry.

According to Ezr. 5:1 and 6:14 Haggai was a contemporary of the prophet Zechariah, and together the two men encouraged the rebuilding of the temple. Ezr. 5:2 mentions their valuable assistance in the building project. Haggai and Zechariah are linked together again in headings to several psalms found in major versions. For example, the Vulgate mentions them in the titles to Pss. 111 and 145, while the LXX lists the two in the headings of Pss. 137 and 145-148. This tradition — not found in the MT — may reveal the involvement of the two prophets in the worship of the temple they helped to rebuild.

Haggai, like Malachi, is called "the messenger of the Lord," a title that can refer to prophets (2 Ch. 36:15) or priests (Mal. 2:7). Although his ministry was short, no prophet was more successful.

III. Historical Background.–After Cyrus King of Persia captured Babylon in 539 B.C. he made a decree that allowed the Jews to return to Palestine and rebuild the temple, destroyed forty-seven years earlier by Nebuchadrezzar and his Chaldean armies. Under Zerubbabel and other leaders, about fifty thousand Jews did return to the Jerusalem area in 538 B.C. They soon began work on the temple and, with the help of skilled Phoenicians, the foundation was laid in 536 B.C. amid great rejoicing and thanksgiving (Ezr. 3:8-10). Unhappily their efforts were stalled by the opposition of the Samaritans, a mixed race of Jews and Gentiles who had been living in Palestine since the seventh century. They asked Cyrus and his successor, Cambyses, to stop the work on the temple, pointing to the number of times Judah rebelled before the exile. Apparently the Persians heeded the Samaritan complaints and intervened, because little additional work was done on the temple between 536 and 520 B.C.

In the year 521 B.C., however, Darius the Great came to power and, after quelling a series of revolts, adopted a policy of supporting religious activity throughout his empire. It should have brought a quick response from the Jews, but instead they made no effort to resume building. They seemed content to live without a temple, although the temple had been the focal point of the life of the nation. It was to awake them from this lethargy that Haggai began to preach his short but powerful sermons. The people were convinced and work on the temple began in 520 B.C. By 516 B.C. the task was completed and worship was fully restored.

IV. Date and Structure.–The book of Haggai consists of a series of four messages firmly dated in a four-month span during the second year (520 B.C.) of Darius the Great. The first message was given on the first day of the sixth month, which overlapped August and September. This was followed by a second message on the twenty-first day of the seventh month (September-October), the last day of the Feast of Tabernacles, the final religious festival of the year (Lev. 23:33). Both messages were addressed to Zerubbabel, governor of Judah, and Joshua, the high priest. The final two messages were given on the twenty-fourth day of the ninth month (November-December). The third message began with a legal question directed to the priests, while the fourth was a word of encouragement addressed to Zerubbabel alone.

*V. **Message**.–A. The Challenge (1:1-15).* The first message (1:1-11) presents a scathing attack on a nation that had neglected to finish the temple while at the same time individuals beautified their own homes. Their selfish attitude resulted in economic woes, for crops had failed and animals were diseased amid a severe drought sent by the Lord. The punishment was in line with the curse Moses had predicted in Dt. 28:38-40. Yet, through Haggai, the Lord challenged the people to resume the rebuilding of the temple so that He might bless them.

Led by Zerubbabel and Joshua, the nation responded wholeheartedly to the Lord's rebuke. They began to respect and fear God rather than the hostile neighbors who opposed their work. The Lord in turn "stirred up" the spirit of the people, just as he had done eighteen years earlier when he brought the remnant back from exile (Ezr. 1:5).

B. The Encouragement (2:1-9). After the work had resumed, a question arose as to how the new temple would compare with Solomon's. It was clear that the new building could not match the splendor of Solomon's temple, so the people were somewhat discouraged. In his second message (2:1-9) Haggai told the nation to "be strong" and "work," for God was with them. The same words were used by David when he challenged Solomon to complete the building of the first temple (1 Ch. 28:10, 20). Their material resources could not match Solomon's, but the same powerful God would help them. He would protect them as He did during the Exodus, and He would "shake all nations" and "fill this house with glory" (2:6f.).

The "shaking of nations" may have two aspects. It could refer to a "turnover" of resources — the financial help given to the temple by King Darius (Ezr. 6:8f.; cf. Isa. 60:5). The shaking also includes the overthrow of nations (see 2:21f.), perhaps referring to the fall of the Persian empire to the Greeks. He. 12:26f. quotes Hag. 2:6 in an eschatological setting. When Christ returns to earth He will defeat all the nations of the world (Joel 3:16 [MT 4:16]).

Another phrase with messianic overtones is "the desire (desired) of nations" in 2:7. The word "desire" can refer to material wealth or "valuables" (2 Ch. 32:27; cf. Isa. 60:5), a meaning that fits the silver and gold of 2:8. But "desire" (or "preciousness") can also refer to individuals who are highly esteemed. Three times Daniel is called a man of "high esteem" (Dnl. 9:23; 10:11, 19; cf. also 11:37). Perhaps Haggai wanted the word to refer not only to material wealth or "glory" but also to the glory of the presence of God. When Christ entered the temple, the building was filled with glory (cf. Lk. 2:32). In the OT the only glory that "fills the temple" (2:7) is the cloud that signifies the presence of God (Ex. 40:34f.; 1 K. 8:10f.). But not even Solomon's temple saw the glory of the incarnate Christ (2:9). At his second coming Christ will bring peace to "this place," that is, to Jerusalem and all mankind (cf. Isa. 60:17f.).

C. The Reversal of Fortunes (2:10f.). More than two months later Haggai presented his third message (2:10-19). He began with a question addressed to the priests as to how holiness and uncleanness are transmitted. The priests rightly answered that it is much easier to become unclean than clean (cf. Lev. 6:27). Because of their sin the nation had polluted the land and even the crops had suffered. In vv. 16f. Haggai reviewed the meager harvests they had experienced prior to resuming work on the temple. They still suffered from the effects of their sin because there had not been time for new harvests in the intervening few months. But if the people remained faithful in their resolve to rebuild the temple, the Lord promised that future harvests would be plentiful.

D. The Promise (2:20-23). The final message (2:20-23) also was given on that same twenty-fourth day of the ninth month. This time Zerubbabel alone is addressed, as Haggai brings the book to a climax. Verses 21 and 22 return to the theme of the overthrow of nations discussed in vv. 6 and 7. Parallel passages are found in Ezk. 38:19-23 and Zec. 14:13f. On that day of victory Zerubbabel will be exalted. The governor is called "my servant" and "chosen" one, two titles that sometimes have a messianic connotation (Isa. 42:1; 52:13). This does not mean that Haggai thought that Zerubbabel himself was the Messiah. But Zerubbabel was part of the messianic line (cf. Mt. 1:12) and his rise to power in Judah was a sign that one day the Messiah would come. In Jer. 22:24 the Lord said that King Jehoiachin was set aside as one would pull off a signet ring. Now Zerubbabel is compared to a signet ring, thus indicating that the line of David has been reinstated.

*VI. **Style**.*–The book of Haggai is rare among the prophetic books because it has no poetic lines. Yet its clarity and abruptness combine to make a powerful impact. Haggai's authority is derived from the fact that he was declaring the word of the Lord. In 1:1, 3 and 2:1 the Lord spoke "through" (literally "by the hand of") Haggai and in 2:10 and 20 the word "came to" the prophet. He delivered the "message of the Lord" (1:13) and "thus says the Lord" occurs in 1:2, 7, 13; 2:4, 6-9, 11, 14, 23.

Repetition of key words and ideas is skillfully used. Several times Zerubbabel the governor, Joshua the high priest, and the remnant are mentioned in the same verse (1:12, 14; 2:2, 4). The idiom "set your heart" or "consider" is found in 1:5, 7 and 2:15, 18. In ch. 1 Haggai twice speaks of the Lord's house being "desolate" or "in ruins" (vv. 4, 9) and 2:6, 21 repeat the prophetic line "I will shake the heavens and the earth."

A number of rhetorical questions are effectively used. The Lord directs probing questions to the people in 1:4, 9 and again in 2:3, 19. In 2:12f. Haggai was instructed to ask the priests an important question. Malachi, another postexilic prophet, employs rhetorical questions with even greater frequency and power.

Haggai also alludes frequently to earlier books. Hag. 1:6 reflects Dt. 28:38-40 and Hag. 2:17 refers to the "blight and mildew" of Dt. 28:22. The prophet uses these brief allusions to remind the people that the curses predicted by Moses had indeed come true. In Hag. 2:4 the thrice repeated phrase "Take courage" is identical to its more famous counterpart in Josh. 1:9. This time another Joshua — son of Jehozadak and the high priest — is the recipient of the exhortation.

*VII. **Text**.*–Haggai is relatively free from textual controversy, but some scholars reject 1:7b and 13 as later interpolations and on the basis of the ancient versions accept minor revisions in 1:9 and 12. The date formula in 1:15 is suspect because elsewhere the date tells when the word of the Lord came to Haggai (1:1; 2:1, 10, 20) and usually comes first in the sentence (except 2:20). Moreover, the time notation of 2:1 immediately follows 1:15, although each date makes good sense as it stands.

The LXX omits the first part of 2:5, adds a dozen words to 2:9, and expands 2:14 using Am. 5:10. The charge that 2:17 is dependent on Am. 4:9 fails to realize that both passages go back to Dt. 28:22 (see VI above).

Bibliography.–E. B. Pusey, *The Minor Prophets,* II (1885); H. G. Mitchell, comm. on Haggai (*ICC,* 1912); T. Laetsch, *Minor Prophets* (1956); R. T. Siebeneck, *CBQ,* 19 (1957), 312-328; R. Wolff, *Book of Haggai* (1967); H. G. May, *VT,* 18 (1968), 190-97; J. G. Baldwin, *Haggai, Zechariah, Malachi* (*Tyndale OT Comms.,* 1972); H. Wolf, *Haggai and Malachi* (1976); H. Wolf, *JETS,* 19 (1976), 97-102.

H. WOLF

HAGGEDOLIM hag-ə-dō'lēm [Heb. *hagg^e^ḏôlîm*] (Neh. 11:14); AV "one of the great men." According to the RSV and NEB, the father of the priest Zabdiel. The term may be better rendered by the AV. (Cf. the LXX, of which some texts omit the entire clause, while others read *tṓn megálōn,* "the great men.")

HAGGERI hag'ə-rī (AV, NEB, 1 Ch. 11:38). *See* HAGRI.

HAGGI hag'ī [Heb. *haggî*–'festive']. The second son of Gad (Gen. 46:16; Nu. 26:15). The latter passage refers to his descendants as Haggites, of whom nothing else is known.

HAGGIAH ha-gī'ə [Heb. *ḥaggîyâ*]. Named in 1 Ch. 6:30 as among the descendants of Levi. See *IP,* p. 222.

HAGGITES hag'īts. *See* HAGGI.

HAGGITH hag'ith [Heb. *ḥaggîṯ*–'festal']. According to 2 S. 3:4; 1 K. 1:5, 11; 2:13; 1 Ch. 3:2, the fifth wife of David and the mother of his fourth son, Adonijah. Adonijah was born in Hebron while David's capital was there (2 S. 3:4f.).

HAGIA hā'gi-ə (1 Esd. 5:34, AV). *See* HATTIL.

HAGIOGRAPHA hag'ē-og-rə-fə [Gk. *hagiographa*–'holy writings']. The third division of the Hebrew Bible, also known as the Writings (Heb. *k^e^ṯûḇîm*), comprising Psalms, Proverbs, Job, Canticles, Ruth, Lamentations, Ecclesiastes, Esther, Daniel, Ezra, Nehemiah, 1 and 2 Chronicles. *See* BIBLE III.A.1, 2; IV.A.3; CANON OF THE OT I.C.

HAGRI hag'rī [Heb. *hagrî*] (1 Ch. 11:38); AV, NEB, HAGGERI. The father of Mibhar, one of the "mighty men" who rallied round David during his foreign wars. He is mentioned only in 1 Ch. 11:38; the parallel passage (2 S. 23:36) gives instead the name "Bani the Gadite."

HAGRITES hag'rīts [Heb. *hagrî'îm*] (1 Ch. 5:10, 19f.; 27, 30; Ps. 83:6 [MT 7]); AV, NEB, HAGARITES, HAGERITE, HAGARENES. An Arab tribe, or confederation of tribes, against which the Reubenites fought in the days of Saul. Along with such traditional enemies of Israel as the Moabites, Edomites, and Ishmaelites, the Hagrites lived in Transjordan. In the early monarchy the Reubenites absorbed the Hagrites by conquest (1 Ch. 5:10, 19-22); and under David, Jazaz the Hagrite became an overseer of the flocks (1 Ch. 27:30). The extent to which the Hagrites were related to Hagar the mother of Ishmael (Gen. 16) has yet to be determined. R. K. H.

HA-HIROTH ha-hī'roth. *See* PI-HAHIROTH.

HAI hā'ī (AV Gen. 12:8; 13:3). *See* AI.

HAIL [Heb. *bārāḏ* (Ex. 9–10; Job 38:22; Ps. 78:47f.; etc.); Gk. *chálaza* (Rev. 8:7; 11:19; 16:21]; **HAILSTONES** [Heb. *bārāḏ* (Ps. 18:12f. [MT 13f.]), *'eḇen bārāḏ* (Josh. 10:11; Isa. 30:30), *'eḇen 'elgāḇîš* (Ezk. 13:11, 13; 38:22); Gk. *chálaza* (Rev. 16:21)]; AV also HAIL.

Hailstorms are not unknown in Syria and Palestine and when they occur may be of great severity. They occasionally take place in Egypt.

The plague of hail (Ex. 9:23f.; Ps. 78:47) was a local storm, as is usual, falling on the Egyptians and not striking the people of Israel in Goshen. It was of great severity, "such as had never been in all the land of Egypt since it became a nation" (Ex. 9:24). It took place in January, for the barley "was in the ear, and the flax was in bud" (v. 31), and it caused great damage to the crops. After Israel's battle with the Amorites at Gibeon there was a great hailstorm, which killed more Amorites than the Israelites killed in battle (Josh. 10:11).

Hail is often spoken of as a means of punishing the wicked: "like a storm of hail . . . he will cast down to the earth with violence" (Isa. 28:2); "and hail will sweep away the refuge of lies" (v. 17). It is used as a symbol of God's anger: "there shall be . . . great hailstones in wrath" (Ezk. 13:13; cf. Isa. 30:30; Hag. 2:17; Rev. 8:7; 11:19; 16:21).

God's power and wisdom are also shown in controlling the hail: "Have you seen the storehouses of the hail . . . ?" (Job 38:22); "fire and hail, snow and frost, fulfilling his command" (Ps. 148:8). A. H. JOY

HAIL. This interjection, found only in the Gospels as the translation of Gk. *chaíre, chaírete* (imperative of *chaírō,* "rejoice") is used as a greeting or salutation. The word "hail" is Old English and was formerly an adjective used with the verb "be," meaning "well, sound, hale," e.g., "Hale be thou." Wyclif has "heil" without the verb, followed by other English versions, except that the Geneva Bible has "God save thee" in Mt. 26:49; 28:9. The word occurs in Mt. 26:49; 27:29; 28:9 (NEB "greeting"); Mk. 15:18; Lk. 1:28 (NEB "greetings"); Jn. 19:3. *See* GODSPEED; GREETING.

HAIR [Heb. *śē'ār* (Lev. 13:3f., 10, 20, etc.; Jgs. 16:22; 2 S. 14:26; etc.), *śa'^a^râ*–'(single) hair' (Jgs. 20:16; 1 S. 14:45; Ps. 40:12 [MT 13]; etc.), *māraṭ*–'pluck hair,' 'grow bald' (Lev. 13:40f.; Neh. 13:25), *miqšeh*–'set hair' (Isa. 3:24), *nēzer*– 'unshorn, consecrated hair' (Jer. 7:29); Aram. *ś^e^'ar* (Dnl. 3:27; 4:33 [MT 30]; 7:9); Gk. *thríx* (Mt. 3:4; 5:36; Lk. 7:38; Jn. 11:2; Rev. 1:14; etc.), *kómē* (1 Cor. 11:15), *komáō*–'wear long hair' (1 Cor. 11:14f.), *plégma*–'woven, braided' (1 Tim. 2:9)]; **HAIRY** [Heb. *śā'ir* (Gen. 27:11, 23), *śē'ār* (Gen. 25:25; Ps. 68:21 [MT 22]; Zec. 13:4)]; AV also "rough" (Dnl. 8:21; Zec. 13:4); NEB also COARSE HAIR (Zec. 13:4). The Heb. *p^e'^aṯ rō'š^e^ḵem* of Lev. 19:27 is translated literally by the AV as "corners of your head." The RSV has the more idiomatic "hair on your temples," and the NEB renders "side to side" (cf. Jer. 9:26 [MT 25]). The Heb. *ṣammâ* (Cant. 4:3; 6:7; Isa. 47:2) is translated "locks" in the AV, although "veil" (RSV, NEB) is to be preferred (see M. Pope, *Song of Songs* [*AB,* 1977], p. 457).

I. Hair Fashions.–Hair was worn in various fashions by the peoples of biblical times, and not always in the same way among the same people at different periods. We know from Egyptian literature and monuments, as well as from the writings of Greek authors (esp. Herodotus), that the dwellers on the Nile had their heads shaved in early youth, leaving only a side lock until maturity was attained, when this mark of childhood was taken away. Priests and warriors kept their heads closely shaved; nothing but the exigencies of arduous warfare was allowed to interfere with this custom. On the other hand, the Hebrew people, like their Babylonian neighbors (Herodotus i.195), kept long, well-cared-for, bushy curls of hair as emblems of manly beauty. References are frequent in the

Hittite head of a man with short curled hair and beard (Louvre)

Scriptures and elsewhere. Absalom's long, luxuriant hair is specially mentioned (2 S. 14:26). The "seven locks" of Samson's never-shaven head (Jgs. 16:13f., 19) may have been plaits of hair resembling those of modern young bedouin warriors. The Shulammite sang of the locks of her beloved that were "wavy" (AV "bushy") and "black as a raven" (Cant. 5:11). The hair of the beloved "is like a flock of goats, moving down the slopes of Gilead" (4:1). The "flowing locks" (Heb. *dallâ*) of 7:5 signify the thin threads that represent the unfinished web in the loom (cf. Isa. 38:12), and thus the flowing hair of women. The Hebrew word *r*ᵉ*hāṭîm* means literally the "gutters" at which the flocks were watered (e.g., Gen. 30:38, 41) and figuratively women's long plaits (RSV, NEB, "tresses"; AV "galleries"), which charm men (Pope, p. 629). Josephus (*Ant.* viii.7.3 [185]) reported that Solomon's bodyguard was distinguished by youthful beauty and "hair hang[ing] down to a very great length."

II. Hair in Idol Worship.–It is well known that among the gentile nations that surrounded Israel the hair of childhood or youth was often shaved and consecrated at idolatrous shrines (cf. Herodotus ii.65 for Egypt). Frequently this custom marked an initiatory rite into the service of a divinity (e.g., that of Orotal [Bacchus] in Arabia, Herodotus iii.8). To the Jew it was therefore an abomination of the Gentiles (see Lev. 19:27; Jer. 9:26; 25:23; 49:32). The Syriac version of the latter passage renders, "You shall not let your hair grow long" (i.e., in order to cut it as a religious rite in honor of an idol). It is, however, probable that among the Jews, as still among many Moslems, the periodic cropping of the hair, when it had become too cumbersome, was connected with some small festivity during which the hair was weighed and its weight in silver was given in charity to the poor. At least, the weighing of Absalom's hair (2 S. 14:26) may be related to some such custom, which is paralleled in other countries. The use of balances in connection with the shaving-off of the hair in Ezk. 5:1 is probably common (W. Eichrodt, *Ezekiel* [Eng. tr., *OTL*, 1970], p. 87).

III. The Nazirite Vow.–The shaving of the head of the Nazirites may be compared to these gentile practices, though the resemblance is superficial. The man who made a vow to God was responsible to Him with his whole body and being. Not even a hair was to be injured wilfully during the entire period of the vow, for all belonged to God. The conclusion of the Nazirite vow was marked by sacrifices and the shaving of the head at the door of the sanctuary (Nu. 6:1-21), indicative of a new beginning of life. (Cf. Acts 18:18; F. F. Bruce, comm. on Acts [*NICNT,* repr. 1960], p. 377.) The long, untouched hair was therefore considered the emblem of personal devotion (or devotedness) to the God of all strength. Thus it was easily inferred that Samson's strength was in his hair (Jgs. 16:17, 20).

IV. Later Fashions.–In NT times, especially in the Diaspora, the Jews frequently adopted the fashion of the Romans in cropping the hair closely (1 Cor. 11:14); still the fear of being tainted by the idolatrous practice of the Gentiles, which is specially forbidden in Lev. 21:5, was so great that the side locks remained untouched and were permitted to grow freely. This is still the custom among the Jews of Eastern Europe and the Orient.

Long hair was a custom that Paul (1 Cor. 11:15) linked to "nature" (Gk. *phýsis*) or "general [human] consciousness" (F. W. Grosheide, comm. on 1 Corinthians [*NICNT,* 1953], p. 260). The reference to the "covering" of hair (cf. v. 13, "uncovered," Gk. *akatakálypton*) is an allusion to the OT practice according to which married women had their hair "covered," i.e., "bound up" (W. F. Orr and J. A. Walter, comm. on 1 Corinthians [*AB,* 1976], p. 260) or "orderly" (Grosheide, p. 260). Long, covered hair was a mark that distinguished the Corinthian Christian woman from the Corinthian prostitute whose hair was cut (Grosheide, p. 254).

Paul's warning against braided hair (1 Tim. 2:9) is not directed against the practice of braiding (an accepted custom in 2 K. 9:30; Jth. 10:3) but perhaps against the identification with prostitutes (M. Dibelius and H. Conzelmann, comm. on 1 Timothy [Eng. tr., *Hermeneia,* 1976], p. 46). For Peter (1 Pet. 3:3) inward purity is the "glory" of women, not outward "braiding of hair" (an emphasis echoed by Tertullian, distinguishing between Christian and Roman life-styles, esp. in *De cultu muliarum* ii.11; see also ii.6-8).

V. Hair Color and Symbolism.–The "flowing locks . . . like purple" in Cant. 7:5 (MT 6) are possibly a color achieved through dyeing (Heb. *karmîl,* "red," a play on the word "Carmel," the mountains N of Palestine (Pope, pp. 629f.). Black hair could signify health and youth in contrast to white hair, the color of sickness and decay (Lev. 13:3f., 10, 29-37; Cant. 5:11 [see Pope, pp. 536f.]). Gray hairs (Heb. *śêḇâ,* "gray-headedness," Prov. 20:29; 2 Macc. 6:23) and the hoary white of old age (Prov. 16:31; cf. Lev. 19:32) were highly honored by the Jews. They express old age (Dt. 32:25; Ps. 71:18; Isa. 46:4) and wisdom (Wisd. 4:9). Sometimes white hair is the emblem of a glorious, divine presence (Dnl. 7:9; 2 Macc. 15:13; Rev. 1:14). Calamity befalling the gray-headed was doubly terrible (Gen. 42:38; 44:29). The "hair of the flesh" is said to "stand up" (Job 4:15; Sir. 27:14) when sudden terror or fear takes hold of a person. The symbolic language of Isa. 7:20 compares Judah to a human body of which the head and the "hair of the feet" (a euphemism) will be shaved; Judah will be depopulated (KD *in loc.*). The expression "to sling a stone at a hair and not miss" (Jgs. 20:16) signifies an accurate aim.

God has numbered the very hairs of the head (Mt. 10:30 par. Lk. 12:7), which convey the idea of innumerableness (Ps. 40:12 [MT 13]; 69:4 [MT 5]). What God can number, He can also protect, so that not even a hair of the head might "fall to the ground" or "perish." These phrases express complete safety (1 S. 14:45; 2 S. 14:11; 1 K. 1:52; Lk. 21:18; Acts 27:34).

Sumerian statuette (3rd millennium B.C.) of a woman whose hair, adorned only by a ribbon, flows loosely down her back (Trustees of the British Museum)

Statue of a minor goddess with a large headdress and hair falling to her shoulders (early 2nd millennium B.C.) (Direction générale des antiquités et des musées, Damascus, Syria)

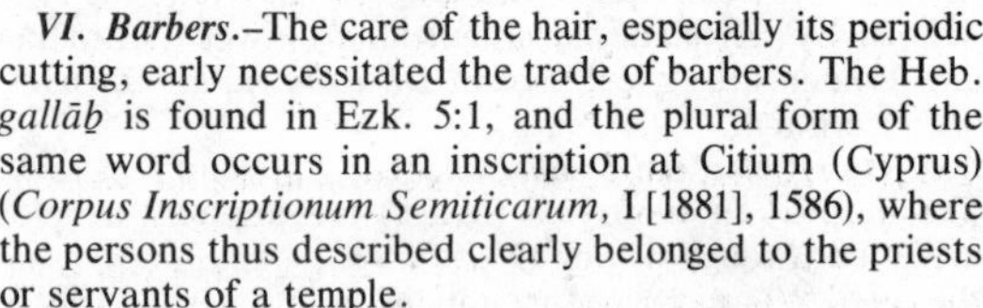

*VI. **Barbers.***–The care of the hair, especially its periodic cutting, early necessitated the trade of barbers. The Heb. *gallāḇ* is found in Ezk. 5:1, and the plural form of the same word occurs in an inscription at Citium (Cyprus) (*Corpus Inscriptionum Semiticarum,* I [1881], 1586), where the persons thus described clearly belonged to the priests or servants of a temple.

*VII. **Ointments.***–Numerous were the cosmetics and ointments applied to the hair (Eccl. 9:8; Mt. 6:17; perhaps Ruth 3:3), but some, reserved for sacramental purposes, were prohibited for profane use (Ex. 30:32; Ps. 133:2). Such a distinction is also found in Egypt, where the walls of temple laboratories were inscribed with extensive recipes of such holy oils, while the medical papyri (see esp. Papyrus Ebers, plates 64-67) contain numerous ointments for the hair. Even Greek and Roman medical authors have transmitted to us the knowledge of some such prescriptions compounded, it is said, by Queen Cleopatra VI of Egypt, the frivolous friend of Caesar and Antony (see H. L. E. Luering, *Die über die medicinischen Kenntnisse der alten Aegypter berichtenden Papyri,* etc. [1888], pp. 121-132). According to Josephus (*Ant.* xvi.8.1 [233]), Herod the Great, in his old age, dyed his hair black, a custom, however, which does not appear to be specifically Jewish, as hair dyes as well as means for bleaching the hair were well known in Greece and Rome. It is certain that the words in Mt. 5:36 would not have been spoken had this been a common custom in the days of Our Lord. A special luxury is mentioned by Josephus (*Ant.* viii.7.3 [185]), who stated that the young men who formed the bodyguard of King Solomon were in the habit, on festive occasions, of sprinkling their long hair with gold dust.

Barber at work in ancient Egypt. Tempera copy of a wall painting (*ca.* 1430 B.C.) in the tomb of the royal scribe User-het, Thebes (Metropolitan Museum of Art)

For the Jews the anointing of the head was synonymous with joy and prosperity (e.g., Ps. 23:5; 92:10 [MT 11]; He. 1:9; cf. also "oil of gladness" in Isa. 61:3; Ps. 45:7 [MT 8]). It was also, like the washing of feet, a token of hospitality (Ps. 23:5; Lk. 7:46).

But it was the custom in times of personal or national affliction and mourning to wear the hair unanointed and disheveled, or to cover the head with dust and ashes (2 S. 14:2; Josh. 7:6; Job 2:12), or to tear the hair or cut it off (Ezr. 9:3; Neh. 13:25; Jer. 7:29). Lepers were required to have their hair cut (Lev. 14:8f.), but natural baldness was not considered a stigma. *See also* BALDNESS.

See also CAMEL'S HAIR; GOAT'S HAIR.

H. L. E. LUERING
R. W. V.

HAIR, PLUCKING OF. *See* PUNISHMENTS IV.L.

HAIRCLOTH. In 2 K. 1:8 the RSV interprets Heb. *baʿal śēʿār* (lit. "a hairy man"; cf. AV, NEB) as a reference to Elijah's garments (cf. J. Gray, *I & II Kings* [*OTL*, 2nd ed. 1970], p. 464), which could be understood as typical garb of a prophet (cf. Zech. 13:4; Mk. 1:6 par. Mt. 3:4). *See* CAMEL'S HAIR.

HAKKATAN hak'ə-tan [Heb. Gk. *haqqāṭān*–'the little one'; Apoc. Gk. *Akatan*] (Ezr. 8:12; 1 Esd. 8:38); AV Apoc. ACATAN; NEB Apoc. HACATAN. The father of Johanan, who returned with Ezra to Jerusalem.

HAKKOZ hak'oz [Heb. *haqqôṣ*; Apoc. Gk. *Akkōs*] (1 Ch. 24:10; Ezr. 2:61; Neh. 3:4, 21; 7:63; 1 Esd. 5:38); AV also KOZ, Apoc. ACCOZ; NEB Apoc. ACCOS.

A priest and chief of the seventh division of Aaron's sons selected by David (1 Ch. 24:10) whose descendants returned with Zerubbabel from the captivity. The family was denied the privileges of priestly ministry at that time because they could not substantiate their claim to priestly rank. In 1 Macc. 8:17 the name is given as ACCOS.

HAKUPHA hə-ko͞o'fə [Heb. *ḥᵃqûpā'*; Gk. *Akipha* (Ezr. 2:51), *Achipha* (Neh. 7:53), *Achiba* (1 Esd. 5:31)]; AV Apoc. ACIPHA; NEB Apoc. ACHIPHA. A family name of some of the temple servants who returned with Zerubbabel from Babylon.

HALAH hā'lə [Heb. *ḥalaḥ*; Gk. *Halae*, *Hallae*, *Chaach*, *Chalach*, *Chala*]. A place in "Assyria" to which the "king of Assyria" exiled Israelites (2 K. 18:11). Because of the close association of Halah with the river HABOR in all three texts (2 K. 17:6; 18:11; 1 Ch. 5:26), scholars have tended to locate Halah near Habor. The suggested identification with Calah (Assyr. *Kalaḫ*, Nimrûd; cf. Gen. 10:11) presents geographical and philological difficulties. In the passages in Kings (but not Chronicles), however, the phrase "and in the cities of the Medes" is added, somewhat complicating the geographical problem. W. S. L. S.

HALAK hā'lək, **MOUNT** [Heb. *hāhār heḥālāq*–'the bald mountain']. A mountain in the Negeb that was one of the landmarks used to describe the southern limit of the conquests by Joshua (Josh. 11:17; 12:7). The mountain is described as "going up (to) Seir," but the context indicates that the area is W of the Arabah (*see* SEIR). In Nu. 34:4; Josh. 15:3, the southern boundary is described with reference to "the ascent of Akrabbim"; hence Mt. Halak is probably to be located in that general area. Modern Jebel Halâq, about 42 km. (26 mi.) S of Beer-sheba, may preserve both the site and the name.

W. S. L. S.

HALAKAH hə-lä'kə [Heb. *hᵃlāḵâ*]. *See* TALMUD I.

HALE; HALING. An obsolete English term (from Old English *halen*) meaning "pull" or "drag," used by the AV to translate Gk. *sýrō* in Acts 8:3 and *katasýrō* in Lk. 12:58. The RSV uses "drag" in both instances. A more frequent modern form is "haul."

HALF [Heb. *ḥᵃsî*, *ḥēṣî* (Ex. 24:6; 25:10; etc.); Gk. *hḗmisys* (Mk. 6:23; Lk. 19:8; etc.)]. For Dnl. 7:25; 12:7; Rev. 12:14, *see* TIME, TIMES AND A HALF.

HALF A SHEKEL; HALF-SHEKEL [Heb. *maḥᵃṣîṯ haššeqel* (Ex. 30:13, 15; 38:26), Gk. *dídrachmon* (Mt. 17:24)]; AV also TRIBUTE MONEY (Mt. 17:24), NEB also TEMPLE TAX (Mt. 17:24). An annual payment of the atonement money (Ex. 30:13, 15; 38:26) or of the temple tax (Mt. 17:24). Both were paid by males over nineteen years of age. The atonement money required of male Israelites was "an offering to the Lord" (Ex. 30:13), whereas the half-shekel of Mt. 17:24 was payment by Jewish males for the upkeep of the temple cult in Jerusalem. The atonement money of the OT served as the basis for this later temple tax.

The Gk. *dídrachmon* literally means "two drachmas," a coin worth two Attic drachmas. It was equivalent in value to the half-shekel of the Jews (Bauer, rev., p. 192). The coin from the fish's mouth (Mt. 17:27) was the Gk. *statḗr,* a silver coin worth four drachmas, thus translated "shekel" in the RSV (Bauer, rev., p. 764).

See MONEY; TAX.

HALF-TRIBE [Heb. *ḥᵃṣî šēḇeṭ* (Nu. 32:33; 34:13-15; Dt. 3:13; 29:8; Josh. 1:12; 12:6; 13:29; 21:5f.; etc.); NEB also HALF. The designation always refers to a portion of the Israelite tribe of Manasseh. Permission was granted to Reuben, Gad, and one-half of Manasseh to settle E of the Jordan River if they would help in the conquest of the land on the west. The remainder of Manasseh settled within the Promised Land itself (Josh. 17:5-12). *See* MANASSEH **1**.

HALHUL hal'hul [Heb. *ḥalḥûl*]. A town in the hill country of Judah (Josh. 15:58), the modern Ḥalḥûl about 6 km. (4 mi.) N of Hebron and SE of Beth-zur. In the war with Rome it was called Alurus, where the Idumeans assembled in the campaign of A.D. 68 (Josephus *BJ* iv.9.6 [522]).

HALI hā'lī [Heb. *ḥᵃlî*–'ornament'; Gk. A *Tholi*, B *Aleph*]. One of the twenty-two cities, with their villages, assigned to the tribe of Asher when the land of Canaan was divided among the tribes of Israel after the conquest under Joshua (Josh. 19:25). It has not yet been definitely located.

HALICARNASSUS hal'ə-kär-nas'əs [Gk. *Halikarnassos*] (1 Macc. 15:23). The largest and strongest city of the ancient country of CARIA in Asia Minor, situated on the shore of a bay, about 90 km. (55 mi.) S of Ephesus. Its site was beautiful, its climate temperate; the soil of the surrounding country was unusually fertile and noted for its abundance of fig, orange, lemon, olive, and almond trees.

When the ancient country fell into the possession of the Persians, the kings of Caria were still permitted to rule. One of the rulers was the famous queen Artemisia who fought at the battle of Salamis (490 B.C.). The most famous of the rulers, however, was Mausolus (d. *ca.* 353 B.C.), whose tomb (the Mausoleum) was long considered one of the wonders of the ancient world. Pliny described the tomb as a circular structure, 43 m. (140 ft.) high, 125 m. (410 ft.) in circumference, and surrounded by thirty-six columns; it was covered with a pyramidal dome. The ancient writer Vitruvius, in his description of the city, said that the agora was along the shore; behind it was the Mausoleum, and still farther away was the temple of Mars. To the right of the agora were the temples of Venus and Mercury, and to the left was the palace of Mausolus.

In 334 B.C. Alexander the Great destroyed the city after a long siege, though he was unable to take the acropolis. The city never quite recovered; yet it was later distinguished as the supposed birthplace of Herodotus and Dionysius. That a number of Jews lived there is evident from 1 Macc. 15:23, which states that in the year 139 B.C. a letter was written by the Roman senate in their behalf. In the 1st cent. B.C. a decree was issued granting to the Jews in Halicarnassus liberty to worship "according to the Jewish laws, and to make their *prosendrae* [place of prayer] at the seaside, according to the customs of their forefathers" (Josephus *Ant.* xiv.10.23 [258]).

The modern town of Bodrum represents the ancient Halicarnassus and covers a part of its site. The site was excavated by C. T. Newton in 1857/58.

Bibliography.–C. T. Newton and R. P. Pullan, *History of Discoveries at Halicarnassus, Cnidus, and Branchidae* (2 vols., 1862-1863); D. Magie, *Roman Rule in Asia Minor* (1950).

E. J. BANKS

HALL [Heb. *liškâ* (1 S. 9:22), *'ûlām* or *'ulām* (1 K. 7:6-8), *bayiṯ* (Est. 5:1); Aram. *bayiṯ* (Dnl. 5:10); Gk. *gámos* (Mt. 22:10), *scholḗ* (Acts 19:9), *akroatḗrion* (Acts 25:23)]; AV also PARLOR, PORCH, HOUSE, etc.; NEB also COLONNADE, CHAMBER, etc. In 1 S. 9:22 *liškâ* refers to a room adjacent to a shrine, where a meal could be eaten. In 1 K. 7 Heb. *'ûlām,* or *'ulām,* points to porches or vestibules in Solomon's palace. The word *bayiṯ* also applies to parts of a king's palace.

In Mt. 22:10 Gk. *gámos* occurs in a figurative sense and refers to the hall where the wedding banquet was held rather than to the wedding itself. (A few manuscripts read Gk. *nymphṓn* rather than Gk. *gámos.*) In Acts 19:9 Gk. *scholḗ* is used to describe the place where Paul preached to the residents of Corinth. A *scholḗ* was a place where students and teachers met. Paul was heard by Agrippa and Bernice in an *akroatḗrion,* a place that was used by a procurator to meet his subjects in somewhat private sessions (cf. Bauer, rev., p. 33).

See also TYRANNUS. P. L. BREMER

HALL OF JUDGEMENT (Jn. 18:28, AV). *See* PRAETORIUM.

HALLEL ha-lāl', hal'əl [from the Hebrew root *hll*–'praise']. In the fifth book of the Psalms (107–150) there are several groups of Hallelujah Psalms: 104–106; 111–118; 135; 146–150. In the worship of the synagogue Pss. 135–136 and 146–150 were used in the daily morning service. Pss. 113–118 were called the "Egyptian Hallel" and were sung at the feasts of the Passover, Pentecost, Tabernacles, and Dedication. At the Passover, Pss. 113 and 114 (according to the school of Shammai only Ps. 113) were sung before the feast, and Pss. 115–118 after drinking the last cup. The song used by Our Lord and the disciples on the night of the betrayal (Mt. 26:30), just before the departure for the Mt. of Olives, probably included Pss. 115–118. *See* HALLELUJAH.

J. R. SAMPEY

HALLELUJAH hal'ə-lo͞o'yə [Heb. *halᵉlû-yâ*–'praise ye the Lord'; Gk. *allēlouiá*]; AV, NEB, also ALLELUIA (Rev. 19:1, 3f., 6). The philology of this expression presents certain problems. Intensive and reflexive forms of the verb *hālal* occur in the OT (cf. 2 S. 14:25; 2 Ch. 23:12; 1 K. 20:11; Ps. 97:7; etc.), and while the expression has the particle "yah" (evidently a shortened form of the tetragrammaton *YHWH*) attached by means of a hyphen, it never occurred as a compound form in the MT, unlike the LXX and some other versions. Opposed to this interpretation is the Jewish tradition that "hallelujah" was a very ancient acclamation containing no reference to the divine name at all. It is unknown whether the expression originated in secular or cultic circles.

In the Psalter it occurs twenty-four times as one of several calls to praise. In some Psalms "hallelujah" is an integral part of the song (Ps. 135:3), but in others it simply serves as a liturgical interjection found either at the beginning (Ps. 111) or at the close (Ps. 104) of the Psalms, or both (Ps. 146). The Hallelujah Psalms are found in several groups: 104–106; 111–113; 115–117; 135; 146–150. In the first group "hallelujah" is found at the close of the Psalm as a liturgical interjection (106:1 is an integral part of the Psalm). In the second group "hallelujah" is found at the beginning (113:9 is an integral part of the Psalm depending on the adjective "joyful"). In the last two groups "hallelujah" is found both at the beginning and at the close of the Psalm. In Pss. 115–117 "hallelujah" seems to be an integral part of the Psalm. These groups were probably taken from an older collection of Psalms like the group Pss. 120–134. In the NT "hallelujah" is found as part of the song of the heavenly host (Rev. 19:1-6). The word is preserved as a liturgical interjection by the Christian Church. A. L. BRESLICH R. K. H.

HALLOHESH ha-lō'hesh [Heb. *hallôḥēš*–'the whisperer'] (Neh. 3:12; 10:24 [MT 25]); AV also HALOHESH. A postexilic chief whose son Shallum assisted in repairing the walls of Jerusalem. He was also one of the leaders who signed the national covenant.

HALLOW; HALLOWED [Heb. *qāḏēš, qōḏeš, miqdāš*]; AV also SANCTIFIED (Gen. 2:3); NEB also HOLY, "make holy," "declare holy," "keep holy," etc.; [Gk. *hagiázō*] (Mt. 6:9 par. Lk. 11:2). The usual meaning of the Hebrew and Greek terms is "holy" and "holiness." The translation "hallow," "hallowed" appears twelve times in the RSV as compared with thirty-seven times in the AV. The RSV, NEB, and other contemporary translations often employ "holy," "sacred," "consecrate," and "sanctify" for "hallow" and "hallowed."

I. In the OT.–Basic to the Hebrew concept of holiness is the idea of separation. God alone is "the Holy One" (Isa. 1:4; 47:4; Ezk. 39:7; cf. 1 S. 2:2; Ps. 99:9; Isa. 6:3). God's holiness is unique to His being, except when He imparts it to another person or thing. In this sense holiness is a relational concept, for it issues from, and is related to, the most elemental quality of God. It denotes on the one hand the awesomeness and unapproachability of God, the inscrutable mystery and otherness of God, and even His fearfulness when offended. On the other hand it signifies the kindly God who has chosen Israel in love and grace (Dt. 7:6-9) and who has mercy upon His people.

Leviticus 22:32 states that Yahweh's "holy name" shall not be "profaned." The Hebrew verbal root *ḥll,* "profane, pollute," is the most emphatic antonym to holiness. Unusual significance is placed upon the holiness of the name of God, because His name is an expression of His personal essence (cf. Ex. 3:5; Josh. 5:15). Yahweh "will be hallowed among the people" (Lev. 22:32). The people's hallowing of Yahweh grew out of a recognition of His holiness (Lev. 11:44; 19:2; 20:26; 21:8; Ps. 99:3, 5, 9; Isa. 6:3; 40:25). It is only God who can make mankind holy (Lev. 22:32) and who is able to restore Israel's holiness

(Ezk. 20:21; 37:28). God's holiness becomes the measure and example of human holiness. Lev. 11:44 emphasizes that the people of Israel were to "consecrate" themselves, and "be holy, for I am holy." Human holiness derives from, and is made possible through, God's holiness.

Cultic holiness came to expression in a variety of ways. The temple is to be "hallowed" (2 Ch. 36:14; cf. 1 K. 6:16; Ps. 5:7 [MT 8]), as well as the altar (Lev. 16:19) and the gifts (Ex. 28:38; Nu. 18:29; cf. Ex. 29:33; Lev. 2:3). Cultic time is to be hallowed in the year of Jubilee (Lev. 25:10).

God "hallowed" the seventh day (Gen 2:3; NEB "made it holy"; cf. Ex. 20:11; Ezk. 20:20). This comes as the climax of the creation account that opens the Bible. Just as the creation account is concerned with mankind, so the whole process of creation has its final goal in the institution of the seventh-day sabbath for all mankind. That the seventh day is the gift of God for mankind is seen in the fact that God made this day holy when He Himself "hallowed" (sanctified) it. In making the seventh day holy He separated it from all other days of creative activity through His rest and blessing. The holiness of the seventh day determines all ordered and fixed time, the origin of which is founded in creation. The regular workdays of the week find their goal in the seventh day as God's own property. The sabbath commandment enjoins mankind to "hallow" the sabbath (Ex. 20:11; Ezk. 20:20; Jer. 17:24, 27; cf. Neh. 13:22) by "keeping" it. Mankind's recognition of the holiness and separation of the sabbath, and his keeping it holy from the remaining days, is rooted in, and springs from, his acknowledgment of God as the Maker of heaven and earth who Himself made the seventh day holy, rested on it, and imbued it with blessing. *See* SABBATH.

II. In the NT.–The term *hagiázō,* infrequent in extrabiblical Greek, is employed a number of times in the NT but translated with the meaning "hallow" only in the Lord's Prayer: "Hallowed be thy name" (Mt. 6:9 par. Lk. 11:2). The logical subject of "hallowing" or treating as holy is God alone, not mankind. To the Semitic mind the name expressed and represented the person. Therefore, His name is the essence of His person, which is holy in itself and is revealed in its holiness (Ezk. 20:41; 38:16). The first petition of the Lord's Prayer echoes the third commandment (Ex. 20:7; Dt. 5:11) in a positive form. That is to say, the hallowing of God's name is achieved not merely by repeating a petition but also by human actions. To hallow the name of God requires that mankind speaks of the Supreme Being with words of reverence and that one manifests His name in every act of life. This hallowing of the name of God in the world can come about only as His name, His person, is hallowed first in the person that utters this petition. Historically the hallowing takes place first in the believer and then through the believer. But finally it takes place eschatologically in the Day of Judgment, because the petition, as the whole prayer, is oriented toward the eschaton.

See also HOLINESS, HOLY.

Bibliography.–A. Friedrichsen, *Teologisk Tidesskrift,* 8 (1917), 1-16; R. Astin, *Die Heiligkeit im Urchristentum* (1930), pp. 75-85; H. Ringgren, *Prophetical Conception of Holiness* (1948); R. Otto, *Idea of the Holy* (2nd ed. 1950); N. H. Snaith, *Distinctive Ideas of the OT* (1955), pp. 21-50; F. Horst, *RGG* (3rd ed. 1959), III, 148-151; W. H. Schmidt, *ZAW,* 74 (1962), 62-66; *TDNT,* I, *s.v.* ἅγιος κτλ.: ἅγιος (Procksch, Kuhn); *BhHW,* II, *s.v.* "Heilig" (Soggin); T. C. Vriezen, *Outline of OT Theology* (2nd ed. 1970), pp. 297-311.

G. F. HASEL

HALT [Heb. *'āmaḏ*–'stand'] AV TARRY (2 S. 15:17), STAND (2 K. 5:9; Nah. 2:8), STAND STILL (Neh. 12:39), REMAIN (Isa. 10:32); NEB also STAND (2 K. 5:9), STOP (Nah. 2:8), "pitch camp" (Isa. 10:32); [*bāṣaʿ*–'cut off'] (Joel 2:8); AV "wounded." In the RSV (and NEB) "halt" has the modern sense of "cease" or "stop." The AV uses "halt" in the obsolescent sense of "limp" for Heb. *ṣālaʿ* (Gen. 32:31; Mic. 4:6f.; Zeph. 3:19) and *pāsaḥ* (1 K. 18:21), "fall" for Heb. *ṣelaʿ* (Ps. 38:17 [MT 18]; Jer. 20:10), and "lame" for Gk. *chōlós* (Mt. 18:8 par.; Jn. 5:3).

HAM [Heb. *ḥām*]. Son of Noah, brother of Shem and Japheth, and thus grandson of Lamech (Gen. 5:28-32). Ham is said to be the youngest of Noah's sons (Gen. 9:24), though he is always mentioned second among the three (Gen. 5:32; 6:10; 7:13; 9:18; 10:1; 1 Ch. 1:4). One explanation for the apparent inconsistency of mentioning the youngest son before his elder brother (Japheth) is that "his youngest son" (Gen. 9:24) may be a reference to Canaan, Noah's grandson, rather than to Ham. Support for this is seen in that the curse of Noah fell on Canaan rather than upon Ham, and that in Hebrew "son" can also mean "grandson." The deed, however, is attributed to Ham rather than to Canaan. It could be that Noah's curse was prophetic; certainly the punishment of a son would punish equally his father. For the children to suffer for the sins of their parents is not unusual in the Bible, especially before the Exile (cf. Ezk. 18:1-24).

The meaning of the name "Ham" is not clear. It may be connected with the West Semitic deity Ḥammu (cf. J. Lewy, *HUCA,* 18 [1943/44], 473-76), or it may be akin to the Egyptian word *Kem,* which means "land of Egypt." Ham's descendants were Cush (Ethiopia), Egypt (AV, NEB, "Mizraim"), Put (Libya; AV "Phut"), and Canaan (Gen. 10:6). His territory was Egypt, and presumably the rest of Africa as well. Egypt was later called the "land of Ham" (Ps. 78:51; 105:23, 27; 106:22). The portion assigned to Canaan, Palestine, was for centuries under Egyptian control.

Noah's curse rested only upon Canaan, whose descendants included the residents of Palestine before the Israelite invasion; some of these became "hewers of wood and drawers of water" for the conquerors in apparent fulfillment of Noah's prophecy (Gen. 9:25; cf. Josh. 9:21-27).

The reference to "Ham" in 1 Ch. 4:40 is obscure; it is not clear whether the reference is to a people or to a place. In language similar to that of Jgs. 18:7-27, it is stated that some descendants of Simeon found attractive pastureland near Gedor, "for the former inhabitants there belonged to Ham." Unless the text is altered, as some have suggested, it is fair to assume that these peace-loving inhabitants were descendants of Ham who were expelled by the Simeonites. In any case, the author(s) of Genesis shows only a passing interest in the posterity of Ham and concentrates instead upon the descendants of Shem, the Semitic race which dominated the Middle East until the rise of Cyrus the Persian. Recent studies of African history reveal the existence in central Africa of a high level of civilization, probably nurtured by the posterity of Ham.

G. A. TURNER

HAM [Heb. *hām*] (Gen. 14:5). A city about 16 km. (10 mi.) E of Beth-shean on the King's Highway between Ashteroth-karnaim and Shaveh-kiriathaim. Chedorlaomer and his allies subdued the Zuzim there, and Thutmose III included a "Huma" in his list of conquered cities (*ANET,* p. 242), although M. Avi-Yonah (*Encyclopedia Judaica* [1971], VII, *s.v.*) doubted the identification of Ham with Huma.

Two problems are connected with Ham, one textual and the other archeological. The LXX, followed by the Vulg. and Pesh., reads "with them" (= Heb. *bāhem*) for MT *bᵉhām,* "in Ham," and 1QapGen 21:29 reads *bʿmn,* "in Ammon," probably under the influence of Dt. 2:20 (see J. Fitzmyer, *Genesis Apocryphon of Qumran Cave I* [rev. ed. 1971], pp. 164f.), but neither of these changes seems warranted. Excavations at Tell Hâm near the modern village of Hâm have uncovered three megalithic walls and some pottery but no remains from the patriarchal (Middle Bronze) age. G. A. L.

HAMAN hā'mən [Heb. *hāmān;* Gk. *Haman*]; AV also AMAN (Ad. Est. 10:7; 12:6; 13:3, 6, 12; 14:17; 16:10, 17). A Persian noble and vizier of the empire under Xerxes. He was the enemy of Mordecai, the cousin of Esther. Mordecai, being a Jew, was unable to prostrate himself before the great official and to render to him the adoration that was due to him in accordance with Persian custom. Haman's wrath was so inflamed that one man's life seemed too small a sacrifice, and he resolved that Mordecai's nation should perish with him. This was the cause of Haman's downfall and death. When ESTHER, wife of king Ahasuerus, revealed the plot, Haman was hanged on the very gallows that he had prepared for Mordecai. When the Jews were allowed to punish their enemies by way of retaliation, they also killed Haman's ten sons (Est. 9:6-10).

Haman's home was in an area adjacent to Media, described as "Agazi" in the Annals of Sargon. Thus the reference to Haman as an AGAGITE (Est. 3:1, 10; 8:3, 5; 9:24) is to his place of origin, not to any alleged relationship with Agag the Amalekite (cf. 1 S. 15:8f.). R. K. H.

HAMATH hā'math [Heb. *ḥ*^{a}*māṯ*–'citadel']; AV also HEMATH (1 Ch. 13:5; Am. 6:14), AMATHIS (1 Macc. 12:25). An important royal city of the Hittites, perched on a gigantic mound beside the Orontes 120 km. (75 mi.) S of Aleppo. The advantageous defensive position of the city makes its name especially apt. The modern town of some 65,000 is built in four quarters around the ancient citadel and is prosperous because it is located in a fruitful plain and serves as an important rail center.

A Danish archeological expedition under the leadership of H. Ingholt excavated at Hamath between 1932 and 1938, uncovering twelve occupational layers dating back to Neolithic times. Important Hittite hieroglyphic inscriptions came to light during the excavations.

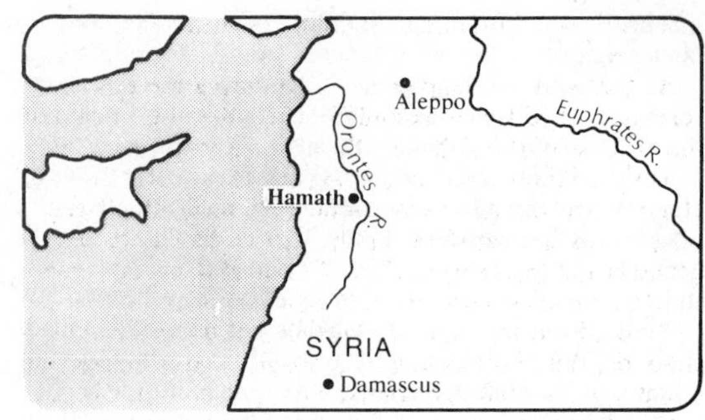

After the Hittite empire ended *ca.* 1200 B.C., numerous Hittite city-states sprang up in Syria. Hamath was one of the most powerful of these states and dominated the main trade route from Asia Minor to the south. Some idea of its power and wealth may be seen in the claim of Shalmaneser III of Assyria to have captured eighty-nine towns belonging to it. Although Assyrian rulers knew how to make a good story out of a military victory, this claim still indicates that Hamath was more than an isolated fort.

The Hamathites are mentioned in Gen. 10:18 among the sons of Canaan; but in historic times the population, as the personal names testify, seems to have been for the most part Semitic. The ideal boundary of Israel reached the territory, but not the city, of Hamath (Nu. 34:8; Josh. 13:5; Ezk. 47:13-21). David entered into friendly relations with Toi, its king (2 S. 8:9-12), and Solomon erected store-cities in the land of Hamath after an apparent show of force in the area (2 Ch. 8:4). Cuneiform inscriptions from the time of Ahab mention Hamath, and its king Irḫuleni was a party to the alliance of Syrian rulers that included Ben-hadad of Damascus and Ahab of Israel against Shalmaneser III of Assyria, who sought to extend his empire westward. At the Battle of Qarqar in 853 B.C. Irḫuleni contributed seven hundred chariots and ten thousand men. Although Shalmaneser claimed an overwhelming victory, he apparently greatly overstated his successes because Irḫuleni was active on more than one occasion in subsequent years defending his kingdom against Shal-

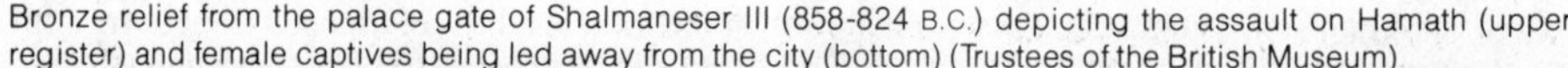
Bronze relief from the palace gate of Shalmaneser III (858-824 B.C.) depicting the assault on Hamath (upper register) and female captives being led away from the city (bottom) (Trustees of the British Museum)

maneser. But ultimately Hamath capitulated to Shalmaneser.

As the Assyrian empire declined during the 8th cent., Jeroboam II of Israel extended his borders northward at the expense of Hamath (*ca.* 780 B.C.; 2 K. 14:28; Am. 6:2). When Assyria revived under Tiglath-pileser III, Enilu of Hamath was forced to pay tribute (730 B.C.). But Tiglath-pileser was not satisfied; he divided its lands among his generals and transported 1223 of its inhabitants to Sura on the Tigris as hostages. Hamath rose again. In 720 Sargon II "rooted out the land of Hamath and dyed the skin of Ilu-bi'di [Yau-bi'di] its king, like wool," and colonized the country with 4300 Assyrians. Still not cowed, Hamath required the attention of Sennacherib, who claimed to have taken the kingdom *ca.* 700 B.C. (2 K. 18:34; 19:13; 1 Ch. 36:19; 37:13). In Isa. 11:11, Israelites are said to be in captivity at Hamath, and Hamathites were among the colonists settled in Samaria (2 K. 17:24) by Esarhaddon of Assyria in 675 B.C. Subsequently the kingdom fell under the power of Babylonia (Jer. 39:5).

The Hamathite country is mentioned in 1 Macc. 12:25 in connection with the movements of Demetrius and Jonathan. The Seleucid king Antiochus IV Epiphanes (175-164 B.C.) renamed it Epiphaneia after himself, and by this name it was known to the Greeks and Romans. Locally, however, the ancient name never disappeared, and since the Moslem conquest it has been known as Ḥama. Saladin's family ruled it for a century and a half, but after the death of the famous Arab historian Abulfeda, who was its prince from 1310 to 1331, it sank into decay.

In connection with the northern boundary of Israel, "the entrance of Hamath" is frequently mentioned (Nu. 13:21; 1 K. 8:65; etc.). It has been sought in the Orontes Valley, between Antioch and Seleucia, and also at Wâdī Nahr el-Barid, leading down from Homs to the Mediterranean N of Tripoli. But from the point of view of Palestine, it must mean some part of the great valley of Coelesyria (Beqaʿ). Probably instead of translating, we should read here a place name, "Lebo-Hamath." The presence of the ancient site of Lebo (modern Lebweh) 22 km. (14 mi.) NNE of Baalbek, at the headwaters of the Orontes and commanding the strategic point where the plain broadens out to the north and to the south, confirms this conjecture.

See Vol. I, Map X.

See H. Ingholt, *Rapport préliminaire sur sept campagnes de fouilles à Hama en Syrie, 1932-38* (1940).

H. F. VOS

HAMATH-ZOBAH hā'math-zō'bə [Heb. *ḥ^amāṯ ṣôḇâ*] (2 Ch. 8:3). Apart from the well-known Hamath on the Orontes, no site answering to this name is known. Zobah (Assyr. *Ṣubutu*) was the most powerful of the Aramean kingdoms of Syria in the late 11th cent. B.C., with its center of power in the region of modern Homs and apparently extending S to include Damascus and N to encompass Hamath (*WHAB*). Many would therefore simply identify Hamath-zobah with Hamath, and would see the double name as an effort on the part of the author to distinguish the site from Zobah in the Hauran (2 S. 23:36). The LXX B suggests a reading Beth-zobah ("house of Zobah") — omitting all reference to Hamath. If this reading is correct, 2 Ch. 8:3 may simply be saying that Solomon fought against the house or kingdom of Zobah and took territory from the kingdom, after which he built several fortified centers in the occupied land. In any case the reference is uncertain.

H. F. VOS

HAMMATH ham'əth [Heb. *ḥammaṯ*–'hot spring'].

1. [Gk. B *Mesēma*]; AV HEMATH. The father of the house of Recab (1 Ch. 2:55). The NEB reads: "Kenites who were connected by marriage with the ancestor of the Rechabites."

2. A fortified city included in the territory assigned to Naphtali after the conquest under Joshua (Josh. 19:35). The city is represented by modern Ḥammâm Ṭabarîyeh located about 3 km. (2 mi.) S of Tiberias on the western shore of the Sea of Galilee. Very probably this was the Naphtalite city assigned to the Levites (Gershonites) referred to as Hammoth-dor (Josh. 21:32) and Hammon (1 Ch. 6:76 [MT 61]).

At least since Josephus's day (the city is called Emmaus or Ammathus in *Ant.* xviii.2.3 [36]; *BJ* iv.1.3 [11]) the hot springs (about 60°C [140°F]) have been famous for treatment of the sick. Ancient fortifications and aqueduct remains are still visible on the slopes above the public baths.

See *EAEHL*, IV, *s.v.* "Tiberias, Hammath" (M. Dothan).

R. J. HUGHES, III

HAMMEDATHA ham-ə-dā'thə [Heb. *hamm^eḏāṯā'*] (Est. 3:1); AV also AMADATHUS (Ad. Est. 12:6). The father of Haman, generally called "the Agagite." The name may be of Persian origin, meaning "given by the moon."

HAMMELECH ham'ə-lek (AV Jer. 36:26; 38:6). The AV wrongly translates Heb. *hammeleḵ* ("the king") as a proper name.

HAMMER [Heb. *maqqeḇeṯ*] (Jgs. 4:21; 1 K. 6:7; Isa. 44:12; Jer. 10:4); [*paṭṭîš*] (Isa. 41:7; Jer. 23:29; 50:23); NEB also "gilder" (Isa. 41:7); [*kêlāp;* cf. Akk. *kalapāti*] (Ps. 74:6); NEB PICK; [*mappēṣ*] (Jer. 51:20); AV, NEB, BATTLE AXE. Pieces of shaped stone used for pounding or fashioning were among the earliest of human implements. Attempts at fitting handles seem to have been begun in the Early Bronze Age, and hammer heads with a hole bored for that purpose have been recovered from many sites. The *maqqeḇeṯ* was used for driving tent pegs into the ground and was the favored tool of the blacksmith and stonemason. The *paṭṭîš* was also used by the latter, whereas the *mappēṣ* of Jer. 51:20 was more correctly a weapon of war, as the AV and the NEB indicate. (*See* WEAPONS OF WAR.) The term *kêlāp* is a loanword which is probably better translated "axes."

R. K. H.

HAMMOLECETH ha-mol'ə-keth [Heb. *hammōleḵeṯ*–'the queen'] (1 Ch. 7:18); AV, NEB, HAMMOLEKETH. The daughter of Machir and sister of Gilead.

HAMMON ham'ən [Heb. *ḥammôn*–'hot spring'?].

1. A city included in the territory assigned to Asher after the conquest under Joshua (Josh. 19:28). Probably identified with modern Umm el-ʿAwāmîd, it is located on the Mediterranean coast about 16 km. (10 mi.) S of Tyre.

2. A city of Naphtali assigned to the Levites (Gershonites) (1 Ch. 6:76 [MT 61]), and probably identical with HAMMATH (Josh. 19:35) and HAMMOTH-DOR (Josh. 21:32).

R. J. HUGHES, III

HAMMOTH-DOR ham-oth-dôr' [Heb. *ḥammōṯ dō'r*–'hot springs of Dor']. A city in the territory of the tribe of Naphtali that together with the surrounding pastureland was given to the Gershonites of the tribe of Levi (Josh. 21:32). It is probably to be identified with the Hammath found in a list of the fortified cities of Naphtali (19:35) and with the Hammon in 1 Ch. 6:76 [MT 61], but not the Hammon in Josh. 19:28. The city was situated on the western shore of the Sea of Galilee just S of Tiberias at the location of modern el-Ḥammâm. The hot springs for which the city was named are still frequented by people seeking relief from various diseases. Josephus referred to the locality and its warm baths as the village of Emmaus (Gk. *Ammaous, Ant.* xviii.2.3 [36]; *BJ* iv.1.3 [11]).

D. H. MADVIG

HAMMUEL ham'û-əl [*ḥammû'ēl*]; AV, NEB, HAMUEL. A son of Mishma, a Simeonite, of the family of Shaul (1 Ch. 4:26).

HAMMURABI ham-ə-rä'bē. Sixth king of the 1st Babylonian Dynasty, Hammurabi is considered an outstanding statesman, military planner, and lawgiver. The main source of information concerning him comes from archeological finds that date to the 2nd quarter of the 2nd millennium B.C. These include about 150 tablets with Hammurabi's signature, the well-known law code found by the French expedition to Susa in the winter campaign of 1901/02, and a multitude of tablets from contemporary sites such as Mari and Alalakh.

I. Date
II. Name
III. Events of Reign
IV. Personal Traits
V. Code of Hammurabi
  A. Discovery and Description
  B. Editions of the Code
  C. Comparison with the OT

I. Date.–There has been much discussion concerning the date of Hammurabi. The earliest date assigned was 2123-2081 B.C. (S. A. Cook, *CAH*, I [1924], 154; originally supported by W. F. Albright, *Revue d'Assyriologie et d'archéologie orientale,* 18 [1921]). R. W. Rogers (*History of Babylonia and Assyria* [1915], pp. 492f.), utilizing a British Museum tablet of Nabonidus that claimed that Hammurabi preceded Burnaburiaš by seven hundred years, dated Hammurabi *ca.* 2075 B.C. From another British Museum tablet, which records the observations of the planet Venus during the twenty-one years of the reign of Ammi-ṣaduqa, the tenth king of the 1st Babylonian Dynasty, J. K. Fotheringham, in collaboration with S. H. Langdon and Carl Schoch, placed Hammurabi *ca.* 2067-2025 B.C. F. Thureau-Dangin reduced the date to 2003-1961. Subsequent discoveries at Mari revealed that the last years of Šamši-Adad I of Assyria were contemporary with the early years of Hammurabi, so that the above dates were much too early. Albright revised his date to 1870 B.C., and two years later, on the basis of new evidence from Mari, further reduced it to *ca.* 1800-1760.

One of the difficulties with using the material on the movements of the planet Venus is that it permits several dates for the end of the 1st Babylonian Dynasty. The most probable of these are 1651, 1595, 1587, and 1531. J. W. S. Sewell reduced the original calculation by 275 years, a full cycle, and put Hammurabi at 1792-1750 B.C. S. Smith, using a different approach, arrived at the same conclusion. This date has the support of M. B. Rowton (*JNES,* 17 [1958], 111), and is the consensus of most scholars. Albright reduced his own date to 1728-1686, and this date is supported by R. de Vaux and also by R. T. O'Callaghan (*Aram Naharaim* [1948]). P. van der Meer (*Chronology of Ancient Western Asia and Egypt* [1963]) and M. A. Beck (*Atlas of Mesopotamia* [1962]) have reduced the date by four years to 1724-1682. C. H. Gordon (*World of the OT* [1958]) and E. F. Weidner (*AfO,* 15 [1939/40], 1945-1951) agree on 1704-1662. For further information on dating, cf. R. K. Harrison, *Intro. to the OT* (1969), pp. 159-166.

II. Name.–The alphabetic writing of the name from Ugarit (*'mrpi*) would argue for a "p" instead of a "b," and "h" does not correctly represent the first consonant. Perhaps 'Ammurapi would be the best spelling.

Hammurabi was of West Semitic stock, an Amorite. His ascription of his victories to Dagan (Dagon) "his creator" and his title "King of the Amorites" indicate the pride he felt in his ethnic background. Later Babylonian scribes treated his name as foreign and translated it *kimtarapashtum,* "my family is great," taking *ḫammu* as the same as *ammi,* "people" and equivalent to *kimtu,* "family." Several variants of the name are found: Ammirabi, Ammu-rapi, Ḫammum-rabi and Hamu(m)-rabi. *Ammu* or *Ḫammu* is most likely a god, and the name should therefore be translated "Ammu is Great."

The first two decades of the 20th cent. saw an almost universal identification of the biblical AMRAPHEL with Hammurabi. From the same passage in Gen. 14, Arioch was thought to be Warad-Sin (Eri-Aku) of Larsa, Chedorlaomer to be Kudur-Lagamar of Elam, and Tidal to be one of the Hattic princes of Anatolia. As early as 1919, however, L. W. King (*History of Babylon,* p. 159) indicated that there were "too many difficulties in the way of accepting the suggested identification of Arioch with Warad-Sin." And 1QapGen 21:23 identifies this land as *Kptwk,* which is probably Cappadocia instead of Larsa. Tidal represents the cuneiform *Tudḫalias,* the name of at least five Hittite rulers. To identify Amraphel with Hammurabi is very precarious. The final *l* would be an error for *y,* and the initial *'aleph* a mistake for *'ayin,* which is highly suspect. The suggestions that Amraphel is a compressed form of Ammurapi-ilu, "Hammurabi is my god," or that the final *l* is the determinative *ilu,* "god," or that the *l* should be placed on the following word (thus *limlōk*) are unconvincing. It is best not to try to identify Amraphel with Hammurabi.

III. Events of Reign.–The predecessors of Hammurabi were occupied mainly with peaceful pursuits consisting of religious and defensive building and the digging of canals. The territory over which they exercised control was not extensive, probably within 80 km. (50 mi.) of the capital city, Babylon. Dogmatism must be avoided, however, since the materials for writing a history are scanty. Even for much of the period of Hammurabi himself evidence is scarce. Most of the letters written by him seem to be from the end of his reign, and little is known about his early years. His father Sinmuballit had ruled about twenty years, and since Hammurabi ruled for forty-three, it is presumed that he was a young man when he ascended to the throne. In his early years he seemed to have been content to follow his predecessors in strengthening his realm and seeking to gain for it the leadership of the south.

Social reform may have been initiated in his very first

year. The date-formula (*ANET,* pp. 269-271) for his second year indicates that he "established justice in the country." This act was not a novelty with Hammurabi, for it had a long-standing history going back to the kingdoms of Isin and Larsa, but with Hammurabi it became a regular practice. Each king, at his accession, issued a decree of "righteousness." The edict of Ammiṣaduqa has been preserved, and from this document it is clear that the main purpose of this action was to ease the burden of indebtedness — both to the state and to individuals — accumulated during the preceding reign, and to readjust the law to fit the necessities of an ever changing world.

In his seventh year Hammurabi conquered Isin and Uruk (Erech), two of the principal cities of Babylonia. The land of Yamutbal (Emutbal) fell to him in his eighth year. The ninth year was marked by one of his greatest nonmilitary achievements, the digging of the canal called *Hammurabi-hegal.* Years ten and eleven indicate military campaigns in which he crushed the army (or city) and inhabitants of Malgium (or Malgu, a kingdom situated on the banks of the river SE of Eshnunna), and conquered Rapiqum and Shalibi. The attack on Malgium may have been as a member of a coalition, with Šamši-Adad as the superior.

The eleventh year was the end of the first period of Hammurabi's military activity. Twenty years passed before he again mentioned a military campaign. During this period he bided his time and engaged in various building projects. In his twenty-fourth year he redug the *tilida*-canal for the benefit of the temple of Enlil, and he also dredged the bed of the Euphrates.

Hammurabi clearly saw his own limitations. He was content to wait for his opportunity and to play off one opponent against another. Much of the information for this activity is derived from the Mari tablets, which reveal the dealings of Hammurabi with Mari itself and with Rīm-Sin of Larsa in the early and middle periods of his reign. These letters indicate that the political and military situation in Babylonia and the surrounding countries was one of general weakness. This is perhaps expressed best in a letter written to Zimri-Lim by his emissary Itur-Asdu, who reported what he had conveyed to the local sheikhs along the Euphrates: "There is no king who is mighty by himself. Ten or fifteen kings follow Hammarubi, the man of Babylon, a like number Rim-Sin of Larsa, a like number Ibalpiel of Eshnunna, a like number Amutpiel of Qatana, and twenty follow Yarimlim of Yamkhad." (Cf. Gadd, *CAH,* II/1 [3rd ed. 1973], 181f.)

When Šamši-Adad died, Zimri-Lim came back from exile in Aleppo and regained his father's throne at Mari. Ibal-pīʾel of Eshnunna reasserted his independence, conquered Rapiqum, and defeated the army of Assyria. Now instead of one hostile power on his north Hammurabi had two states who were bitter rivals. He concluded an alliance with Zimri-Lim of Mari and with Rīm-Sin of Larsa. Evidence that Hammurabi was making preparations for expansion can be seen in the building of fortresses between his nineteenth and twenty-fifth years, and the prominent place this activity assumed in his date-formulas. But for a decade the whole of Mesopotamia experienced an uneasy peace. The land was split into two camps: Assyria, Malgium, Gutium, Elam, and Eshnunna were on one side; Babylon, Mari, and Larsa were on the other.

The thirtieth year of Hammurabi was decisive: it marked the beginning of his second period of military activity, which lasted almost a decade. He marched against the Assyrian coalition and defeated it soundly. In his date-formula he claimed to have "re-established the foundation of the empire of Sumer and Accad." The next year he promptly turned on his erstwhile confederate Rīm-Sin and destroyed the city of Larsa. In this campaign he seemed to have had the help of Mari and Eshnunna.

Hammurabi was now master of all Babylonia. In the north, however, the Assyrian coalition attempted to rise again; but it was defeated, and the lands along the Tigris as far as Assyria came under the control of Babylonia. Hammurabi was strong enough to turn again on his allies. Zimri-Lim was the target, and the city of Mari and the land of Malgium fell in his thirty-third year. That same year the famous *Hamurabi-nuhus-nisi* canal was dug. This canal provided water for Eridu, Ur, Larsa, Erech, Isin, and Nippur. No military action is recorded for the next year, but in the thirty-fifth year he destroyed Mari and Malgium because they had broken the terms of their peace treaties. Assyria and her allies were again defeated two years later. Eshnunna fell in the thirty-eighth year, when Hammurabi took advantage of a devastating flood that had hit the city and left its inhabitants helpless. Finally, Asshur and Nineveh were conquered the next year.

Hammurabi now reigned over an empire that stretched from the Persian Gulf along the Tigris, up to and including the Assyrian cities, and along the Euphrates to about the confluence of the Balîkh River. The Hittites probably prevented Hammurabi from extending his territory further west than Hit and Mari, and the Hurrians kept him from going further north and west than Nineveh. His last four years were devoted to lawgiving and matters of religion, but it is ominous that the last two of these years were named after defensive walls built on the Euphrates and at Sippar.

IV. Personal Traits.–Little is known about the personal life of Hammurabi, but this is common for ancient Near Eastern kings. From his code it can be inferred that he had a strong sense of justice, and his personal letters seem to bear this out. In a letter to Sinidinnam, Hammurabi mentioned a complaint which had come from an official by the name of Lalum against a certain judge named Ali-elatti. On the basis of evidence at court, Hammurabi decreed an investigation be made in the case, and if Lalum had been wronged, the matter was to be rectified and Ali-elatti was to be punished.

Such letters indicate that Hammurabi was a man who kept in close contact with events in his kingdom and took a personal interest in those who came to him with their complaints. A wide range of subjects received his attention and are mentioned in the letters: bribery, the claim of a grain merchant against a governor, regulation of food supplies, labor on public works, etc.

The letters from Mari describe the king through the eyes of the agents of Zimri-Lim. They portray him as a "busy and capable administrator immersed in affairs of war, diplomacy, and even society. He is ever prominent and in personal control — no ministers seem to be mentioned" (Gadd, *CAH,* II/1 [3rd ed. 1975], 189).

Hammurabi portrayed himself in the epilogue to his code as a shepherd and father to the black-headed people whom Enlil had given him and Marduk had committed to him. He claimed to have carried the people in his bosom, governing them in peace and sheltering them in wisdom. He was the protector of the weak and defender of the oppressed. He granted justice to orphans and widows. He was an efficient and perfect king, a king of justice whose words are choice and whose deeds have no equal.

See Vol. I, Map III.

V. Code of Hammurabi.–*A. Discovery and Description.*

During the winter campaign of 1901/02, the French expedition under M. J. de Morgan discovered at the acropolis of Susa a black diorite stone 2.25 m. (7.4 ft.) high and tapering from 1.9 m. (6.2 ft.) at its base to 1.65 m. (5.4 ft.) at the top. The stone was found in three pieces, but was easily assembled and now is in the Louvre in Paris. Fragments from other copies of its text were also found, indicating that stelae were erected in several places in the kingdom. Examination of the stele revealed that it was a codification by Hammurabi of the extant laws of his period. The stele had originally contained about 282 laws, arranged in forty-nine rows or registers of approximately four thousand lines and eight thousand words. Five registers on the front were erased by an Elamite king, presumably for the purpose of preparing the stone for a new inscription.

A bas-relief on the upper portion of the stele, measuring 0.65 m. (2.1 ft.) high and 0.6 m. (2 ft.) across, shows Hammurabi standing before the sun-god Šamaš with his right arm raised in a gesture of worship. The god, who is seated on a throne with his feet resting on conventionalized mountains, is presenting the king with a scepter and a ring. This scene probably represents the occasion when Hammurabi received the laws from the sun-god himself. The rest of the front of the stele is covered with a beautifully carved cuneiform writing in sixteen registers arranged horizontally, though each line in the register is read vertically. The reverse contains twenty-eight registers of text. This text is the longest Semitic inscription so far discovered, and the language, which is Akkadian, was already grammatically advanced and is now considered classical. The style of the Code was followed by later generations, and it seems to have made a greater contribution to the field of literature than to legislation. The stele was erected by the king toward the end of his long reign of forty-three years in the temple Esagila at Babylon, if the epilogue (lines 60-70) is interpreted correctly.

B. Editions of the Code. The first translation of the Code was published by V. Sheil in 1902 in the official report of the expedition, *Memoires de la délégation en Perse,* IV (1902), 11ff. Since then the text has been published many times and translations have appeared in many languages. The most comprehensive work is that of G. R. Driver and J. C. Miles, *The Babylonian Laws,* I (1952) and II (1955). Two other good English translations available are T. J. Meek's (includes prologue and epilogue) in *ANET,* pp. 163-180, and W. J. Martin's (laws only) in *DOTT,* pp. 29-37. The best source for the original text is A. Deimel, *Codex Hammurabi* (1930-1932); the cuneiform section now is in a third edition by E. Bergmann, *Codex Hammurabi: textus primogenius* (1953), and the transliteration and translation also in a third edition, *Codex Hammurabi: transcriptio et translatio latina* (1950), prepared by A. Pohl and R. Follet.

C. Comparison with the OT. The Code is a case-by-case formulation of customary law, covering civil, criminal, and administrative law, and reflects a well-developed commercial society. Subsequent discoveries of other law codes have made it clear that the Code of Hammurabi is neither the oldest nor the most original, but it is still the most detailed and most interesting. The wide variety of subjects covered, the types of crimes mentioned, and the penalties suggested tell us much about the society at that time.

The three social classes are specifically named: the *awīlu* (or *amīlu*), the *muškēnu,* and the *ardu* (or *wardum*). The last is the easiest to define: a slave, in the lowest rank of society. The *awīlu,* translated "free man," "patrician," or "seignior," is the highest in rank. *Muškēnu* seems to be

The top of the stele of Hammurabi showing the king (left) before the sun-god Šamaš, the god of justice. Below is part of Hammurabi's code. From Susa, *ca.* 1700 B.C. (Louvre)

a "commoner," a free person, but apparently subject to the corvée. Gadd suggests that the distinction between *awīlu* and *muškēnu* was one of social estimation only, not based strictly on ascertainable facts, and may have rested ultimately on wealth. The status of a person was important, for this affected the application of the law.

In the biblical legal system, a distinction is also made according to status or the ability to pay. Examples are found in the sin offering. A priest must offer a young bull (Lev. 4:3), a leader a male goat (4:23), and a member of the community a female goat (4:28) or a female lamb (4:32). Anyone not able to afford a lamb brought two doves or two young pigeons (5:7), or if that was beyond his means he brought a tenth of an ephah of fine flour (5:11). Purification of women after childbirth shows this same distinction: a year-old lamb and a pigeon or dove is required if the person is financially able (Lev. 12:6); otherwise two doves or two young pigeons are offered (12:8).

The first five paragraphs of the Code deal with standards or principles of legal process. A claim must be proved, and any accusation entailing the death penalty that is not proved means death for the accuser (§ 3). Dt. 19:16-21 states that the false accuser is to be punished with the same penalty he intended to bring on the accused.

Theft, burglary, robbery, and other such crimes are dealt with severely (§§ 6-15). Theft from private citizens requires multiple restitution, but theft from the government (temple or palace) is punishable by death (§ 6). The receiver of stolen goods is also put to death. Theft of an ox, sheep, ass, pig, or goat from the state requires a thirtyfold restitution, and similar theft from a private citizen a tenfold restitution. If the thief is too poor to make restitution, he is put to death (§ 8). Similar laws are found in Ex. 22:1-4,9. Anyone who steals an ox or a sheep and slaughters it or sells it, must pay back fivefold for the ox and fourfold for the sheep. If the thief has no means to make restitution, he must be sold to pay for the theft. If a stolen animal is found in his possession he must pay back double. Lev. 6:3-6 discusses property which is either entrusted to a person or is stolen or found. The guilty party must return the property, pay a 20 percent fine, and offer a ram as a guilt offering.

Kidnapping carries the death penalty (§ 14), as does abetting the escape of a slave (§ 15) or keeping the slave of another (§§ 16-19). Ex. 21:16 also requires the death penalty for kidnapping, but Dt. 23:15 (MT 16) prohibits a person from returning a fugitive slave to his master if he has come to him for refuge.

Laws concerning agriculture are extensive (§§ 42-58), and laws for horticulture are also emphasized (§§ 59-66), since the economic life of the Babylonians depended largely on the cultivation of grain and date palms. Babylonian laws suggest that much of the farmland was rented out to tenants, and many laws govern this procedure. In Israel this was not the case. Each man worked his own land. Only §§ 57 and 58, which discuss the damage done to a crop by sheep, have a parallel in the biblical text. Ex. 22:5 (MT 4) demands restitution from the man who lets his livestock stray and damage the crop in another man's field. Restitution must also be made if fire gets out of control and burns a field (22:6 [MT 5]). Unlike Mesopotamia, Israel was to allow the land to lie fallow every seventh year (Ex. 23:10f.). For the benefit of the poor the entire field was not to be harvested or gleaned (Lev. 19:9f.; Dt. 24:19-22). Anyone could enter a vineyard and eat all the grapes he wanted as long as he did not carry any away. Most of the orchards in Babylonia were date orchards; in Israel the laws concentrate on vineyards.

Several laws deal with deposits and debts (§§ 112-126). Failure to transport consigned goods carries a fivefold penalty (§ 112), stealing of goods on deposit requires double restitution (§ 113), while seizure of persons for a bogus debt carries a monetary payment (§ 114). According to Ex. 22:7-9 (MT 6-8), if valuables have been entrusted to a man by another and they are stolen, the thief is to pay back double. If the thief is not found, the owner of the house where the valuables were kept must be examined to determine his guilt or innocence.

Members of a family bound over for debt have to be released after three years (§ 117). The Babylonian law allows a man to subject his wife or children to slavery for three years. The Hebrew law (Ex. 21:2-11; Dt. 15:12-18) allows the man to enter slavery himself and serve six years. He may also sell his daughter, but a distinction is made between the treatment of a man and a woman. The woman is likely to become a wife, so she is not to be released at the end of six years. If her master is not pleased with her, she may be redeemed at any time.

The laws concerning the rights of a family are very extensive (§§ 127-195). Marriage requires a contract (§ 128) and the fidelity of the wife is presupposed, for the woman caught in adultery is to be drowned with the adulterer (§ 129) unless the husband wishes to save his wife, and then the king may reprieve the adulterer. A parallel is found in Lev. 20:10 and Dt. 22:22, except that the biblical law has no provision for clemency. Lev. 19:20-22 and Dt. 22:23-26 show some similarity to §§ 130 and 156, which speak of the rape of a married woman or one betrothed to the rapist's son. In the former the rapist is to die, and in the latter he pays a monetary penalty. The biblical text demands the death of both the man and woman in the former; in the latter both die only if the rape of the virgin takes place in the city, and only the man dies if the rape takes place in the country. In the case of a woman who is not pledged to be married (Dt. 22:28f.) a monetary payment must be made and the man must marry the woman. The law about a wife suspected of infidelity (§§ 131f.) is paralleled by Nu. 5:11-28. Both have trials by ordeal. The Code requires her to plunge into the sacred river, and the Mosaic law requires her to drink holy water that has been mixed with dust from the floor of the sanctuary. If nothing happens in either case, the wife is innocent. If she is guilty she drowns (§ 132) or swells up (Nu. 5:21f.).

Divorce is spelled out in detail in the Code (§§ 136-143), but only one law is found in the Bible (Dt. 24:1-4), and that gives the right of divorce to the man for almost any cause. The woman has no rights.

The Code gives specific penalties for incest. If a man has sexual relations with his daughter, he is expelled from the city (§ 154); with a daughter-in-law, he is bound and thrown into the water (§ 155); with a woman pledged to his son, he makes a monetary payment (§ 156); with his mother (after his father's death), both are burned (§ 157); with a wife of his father (after his father's death), he is expelled from his house (§ 158). Dt. 22:30 prohibits a man from marrying his father's wife, and Lev. 18:6-18; 20:11, 19-21 cover all other possible conditions with a penalty of being "cut off from the people."

The laws of inheritance in Babylonia are complicated and cover many situations. A son may receive a present of real estate from his father and also share equally with his brothers (§ 156). A young son who has not been given a wife may have money above his portion for a marriage settlement (§ 166). If a man has two wives, the children divide the dowries of their respective mothers and all share equally in the father's estate (§ 167). Other laws regulate disinheritance of children (§§ 168f.), the status of the children of slaves (§§ 170f.), the rights of the wife (§§ 171-74), the status of children of mixed marriages between persons of slave and nonslave classes (§§ 175f.), minor children of a widow (§ 177), and the rights of a priestess (§§ 178-182).

The biblical text (Dt. 21:15-17) is relatively simple. The firstborn son receives a "double portion." Favoritism must not be shown to the son of a favorite wife. Nu. 27:8-11 provides for daughters to inherit when there are no sons, and, if no daughters, for the nearest paternal relative. If a daughter inherits property she must marry within her tribe (Nu. 36:2-12). Children may be disinherited if the cause warrants (§§ 168f.), but the biblical text (Dt. 21:18-21) specifies death for a son who proves unworthy. Anyone who curses his father or mother is put to death (Ex. 21:17). In the Code (§ 195) the son who strikes his father has his hand cut off. Priestesses have special rights in matters of inheritance and support (§§ 185-194)

Damages are spelled out in detail, and there are many applications of the *lex talionis*: eye for eye (§ 196), bone for bone (§ 197), tooth for tooth (§ 200); but monetary payments are also frequent, generally for lesser offenses or when injuring one of a lower class. The status of the person responsible for the injury and the status of the injured person are taken into consideration. If one strikes the cheek of another and both are members of the *awīlu* class, the penalty is one mina of silver (sixty shekels) (§ 203); if both are from the *muškēnu* class, it is ten shekels (§ 204); but if a slave (*ardu*) strikes a member of the *awīlu,* he has his ear cut off (§ 205). Unintentional injury is covered by a fine (§§ 207f.). If an injury causes a miscarriage and death to a woman of high rank, the daughter of the one causing the injury is killed (§ 210), but the miscarriage and death of a lower-class woman carries only a monetary payment (§ 214). These laws are closely paralleled by Ex. 21:18-27. Wilful murder is punished by death. Accidental homicide is not punished (§ 206, he swears an oath that it was an accident; Ex. 21:13, he flees to the sanctuary). If a man injures another in a fight he pays for the physician (§ 206) or for the lost time and medical expense (Ex. 21:19). The two sources differ in reference to slaves. The biblical text deals with owners injuring or killing their own slaves (Ex. 21:20f., 26f.), while the Code deals with injury by others (§§ 199, 213f.). Both stress the principle of eye for eye and tooth for tooth (Ex. 21:23-25). The laws regulating Babylonian society are more complex because of the three distinct classes.

Several laws govern possible loss of animals from various causes, some of which are charged to the person who has hired them, while others, such as an act of God, are the responsibility of the owner. According to § 250, if an ox gores a person on the street and kills him, there is no penalty. If the ox has a habit of goring and he kills a man, the owner pays a monetary penalty (§§ 251f.). Ex. 21:28 requires the death of the ox if anyone is gored and killed. If the ox has a habit of goring and the owner has been warned, and the ox gores someone and kills him, the owner is put to death, or, if demanded, payment is made for redemption. If the ox gores a slave, a monetary payment is required (Ex. 21:32).

In the Code a surgeon is responsible for certain operations, and penalties are assessed to discourage abuses. Legally fixed fees are paid and are determined by the class of the patient (§§ 215-220). The work of the veterinary surgeon is also controlled by law (§§ 224f.). Various occupations are governed by laws, and hiring procedures are closely regulated. The last paragraphs concern slaves.

This brief examination of the Code reveals that offenses can be classified as being against the gods, against the state, or against the individual. These offenses cover nearly every situation in society, and the penalties, too, vary greatly. Thirty-two offenses call for the death penalty, and lesser punishment includes bodily mutilation such as branding, cutting off of the ear, hand, tongue, or breast, and destroying the eye. The motive behind the law seems to have been to uphold the authority of the state and to preserve the social organism. Whether the Code actually achieved this purpose is doubtful, for the numerous contemporary documents fail to give any evidence of its practical application. This may be because the Code appeared, in the form we now know it, shortly before the death of Hammurabi; there may not have been time for its implementation.

Much work has been done on a comparison of the Code of Hammurabi with the Mosaic legislation. There are many similarities since they are dealing with areas where there is universal agreement. In spite of resemblances there is no evidence of borrowing. The tone of the Hebrew law is most often more humane than that of the Babylonian.

Bibliography.–C. H. Gordon, *Hammurapi's Code: Quaint or Forward-Looking?* (1957); G. R. Driver and J. C. Miles, *The Babylonian Laws* (1952); H. W. F. Saggs, *The Greatness that was Babylon* (1962); D. J. Wiseman, *JSS,* 7 (1962), 161-172; C. J. Gadd, "Hammurabi and the End of His Dynasty," *CAH,* II/1 (3rd ed. 1973), 176-227; D. O. Edzard, "The Old Babylonian Period," in J. Bottero, *et al.,* eds., *The Near East: The Early Civilizations* (1967), pp. 177-231.

R. E. HAYDEN

HAMONAH hə-mō'nə [Heb. *hᵃmônâ*–'multitude'] (Ezk. 39:16). A city in the "Valley of Hamon-gog," where the forces of Gog will be destroyed. The NEB understands the word as a noun, "great horde," rather than a place name, but in order to do so the NEB emends the rest of the verse. Since there is no textual evidence for such an emendation, it is best to understand the verse as an explanatory gloss (cf. *GTTOT,* § 1439; W. Eichrodt, *Ezekiel* [Eng. tr., *OTL,* 1970], p. 528).

G. A. L.

HAMON-GOG hā'mən-gog' [Heb. *ḥᵃmôn gôg*–'the multitude of Gog']. A valley, possibly in Transjordan, where "Gog and all his multitude" are to be buried (Ezk. 39:11, 15).

HAMOR hā'môr [Heb. *ḥᵃmôr*–'ass'; Gk. *Emmōr*] (Gen. 33:19; 34; Josh. 24:32; Jgs. 9:28; Acts 7:16); AV, NEB, also EMMOR (Acts 7:16). Hamor was the father of Shechem from whom Jacob bought a piece of ground on his return from Paddan-aram for one hundred pieces of silver (Gen. 33:19), which became the burial place of Joseph when his body was removed from Egypt to Canaan (Josh. 24:32). "The men of Hamor" were inhabitants of Shechem and suffered a great loss under Abimelech, a prince over Israel (Jgs. 9:22-49).

Dinah, Jacob's daughter, was seduced by Shechem the son of Hamor. Afterward Shechem, with the cooperation of his father, requested her to be given to him in marriage. The sons of Jacob deceitfully agreed to intermarriage with the Shechemites on the condition that every male inhabitant of the city be circumcised, and when this was done, the sons of Jacob killed all the men in their weakened condition, thus taking vengeance upon Shechem and his father Hamor.

A clue to the name "Hamor" may be provided by the discovery that Middle Bronze Age Amorites at Mari frequently ratified treaties by the sacrifice of an ass. The custom survived among the seminomadic Canaanite stockbreeders of patriarchal and subsequent times, being particularly favored by the descendants of Shechem, the *bᵉnê-ḥᵃmôr,* or "sons of the ass."

B. H. DEMENT
R. K. H.

HAMRAN ham'ran [Heb. *ḥamrān*] (1 Ch. 1:41); AV, NEB, AMRAN. The first of four sons of Dishon, a clan chief. *See also* HEMDAN.

HAMSTRING [Heb. piel of *ʿiqqēr*]; AV HOUGH. To disable an animal by cutting the large tendon at the back of the knee on the hind legs.

It has been a common military act throughout mankind's history to disable an enemy's horses by hamstringing them. This rendered them useless for military action. It was often done when the force capturing the horses was too small or incapable of using them for themselves. Before his victory over Jabin of Hazor, God commanded Joshua to hamstring the horses that he would capture (Josh. 11:6, 9), since the Israelites were not yet trained in the use of the horses and chariots. David, who knew how to use chariots, captured too many horses and hamstrung those he could not use (2 S. 8:4 par. 1 Ch. 18:4). This prevented his enemies from recapturing the horses for their own use.

The hamstringing of oxen served no military function, and in Gen. 49:6f. is attributed to uncontrolled anger. Here the AV translates MT *ʿiqqᵉrû-šôr* as "they digged down a wall" on the basis of several versions (Vulg., Pesh., Targ., Aq., Symm.; cf. also Gen. 34:25); this translation, however, is based on the qal of *ʿqr,* "pull, root up" (cf. Eccl. 3:2), and follows the versions in reading *šûr,* "wall," for MT *šôr,* "ox."

H. W. LAY

HAMUEL ham'û-əl (AV, NEB, 1 Ch. 4:26). *See* HAMMUEL.

HAMUL hā'məl [Heb. *ḥāmûl*–'pitied,' 'spared']. A son of Perez, and head of one of the clans of Judah (Gen. 46:12; 1 Ch. 2:5; Nu. 26:21). His descendants were called "Hamulites."

HAMUTAL hə-mû'təl [Heb. *ḥ^a^mûṭal* (2 K. 23:31), *ḥ^a^mîṭal* (2 K. 24:18; Jer. 52:1)]. A daughter of Jeremiah of Libnah, and wife of King Josiah, and mother of Jehoahaz and Zedekiah. In the AV of 2 K. 24:18; Jer. 52:1, and in the LXX the name appears as "Hamital." Swete gives a number of variants, e.g., 2 K. 24:18: B, Gk. *Mitat*; A, *Amitath*; Jer. 52:1: B, *Hameitaal*; ℵ, A, *Hamitaal*; Q, *Hamital*.

HANAMEL han'ə-mel [Heb. *ḥ^a^nam'ēl*] (Jer. 32:7-9, 12); AV HANAMEEL. Jeremiah's cousin, son of Shallum, from whom the prophet, while in prison during the time when Jerusalem was besieged by the Chaldeans, bought a field with due formalities, in token that a time would come when houses and vineyards would once more be bought in the land (Jer. 32:6-15).

HANAN hā'nən [Heb. *ḥānān*–'gracious'].

1. A chief of the tribe of Benjamin (1 Ch. 8:23).

2. The youngest son of Azel, a descendant of Saul (1 Ch. 8:38; 9:44).

3. One of David's mighty men of valor (1 Ch. 11:43).

4. The head of a family of the temple servants who returned with Zerubbabel (Ezr. 2:46; Neh. 7:49; 1 Esd. 5:30, AV, NEB, ANAN).

5. An assistant of Ezra in expounding the law (Neh. 8:7; 1 Esd. 9:48, AV, NEB, ANANIAS). Possibly the same person is referred to in Neh. 10:10 (MT 11).

6. One of the four treasurers put in charge of the tithes by Nehemiah (Neh. 13:13).

7, 8. Two who "sealed the covenant" on the eve of the restoration (Neh. 10:22, 26 [MT 23, 27]).

9. A son of Igdaliah, "the man of God," whose sons had a chamber in the temple at Jerusalem (Jer. 35:4).

B. H. DEMENT

HANANEL han'ə-nel, **TOWER OF** [Heb. *migdal ḥ^a^nan'ēl*–'tower of God is gracious']; AV HANANEEL ha-nan'ē-el. A tower in the north wall of Jerusalem (Neh. 3:1; 12:39) named for an unknown person. It adjoined the Tower of the Hundred where the Mishneh Wall (Zeph. 1:10) crossed the ridge later called Bezetha, and may have been the west tower of the fortress (Neh. 2:8) that guarded the northern approach to the temple. Herod the Great later built the Antonia Tower here.

Alternately it is held to be the west tower of the Fish Gate. In Jer. 31:38 it is foretold that "the city shall be rebuilt for the Lord from the tower of Hananel to the Corner Gate" — possibly the whole north wall. In Zec. 14:10 it is said Jerusalem "shall remain aloft upon its sight . . . from the Tower of Hananel to the king's wine presses." These latter were probably at the south end of the city. Thus the entire N-S length of the city is described.

See M. Avi-Yonah, *IEJ*, 4 (1954), 241f.

D. J. WIEAND

HANANI hə-nā'nē [Heb. *ḥ^a^nānî*–'gracious']; AV and NEB Apoc. ANANIAS.

1. A musician and son of Heman, David's seer, and head of one of the courses of the temple service (1 Ch. 25:4, 25).

2. A seer, the father of Jehu. He was cast into prison for his courage in rebuking Asa for relying on Syria (1 K. 16:1, 7; 2 Ch. 19:2; 20:34).

3. A priest, of the sons of Immer, who had married a foreign wife (Ezr. 10:20; 1 Esd. 9:21).

4. A brother or kinsman of Nehemiah who carried news of the condition of the Jews in Palestine to Susa and became one of the governors of Jerusalem (Neh. 1:2; 7:2).

5. A priest and chief musician who took part in the dedication of the walls of Jerusalem (Neh. 12:36).

See also JOSHBEKASHAH. B. H. DEMENT

HANANIAH han-ə-nī'ə [Heb. *ḥ^a^nanyāhû, ḥ^a^nanyâ*; Gk. *Ananias*, "Yahweh has been gracious"]. This was a common name in Israel for many centuries.

1. A Benjaminite (1 Ch. 8:24).

2. A captain of Uzziah's army (2 Ch. 26:11).

3. Father of one of the princes under Jehoiakim (Jer. 36:12).

4. One of the sons of Heman and leader of the 16th division of David's musicians (1 Ch. 25:4, 23).

5. Grandfather of the officer of the guard who apprehended Jeremiah on a charge of desertion (Jer. 37:13).

6. A false prophet of Gibeon, son of Azzur, who opposed Jeremiah, predicting that the "yoke of Babylon" would be broken in two years, and that the king, the people, and the vessels of the temple would be brought back to Jerusalem. Jeremiah would have been glad if it should have been so; nevertheless it was not to be. The question arose, "Who is right, Jeremiah or Hananiah?" Jeremiah claimed that he was right because he was in accordance with all the great prophets of the past who had prophesied evil and whose words had come true. Therefore his words were more likely to be true. The prophet of good, however, had to wait to have his prophecy fulfilled before he could be accredited. Hananiah took off the yoke from Jeremiah and broke it in pieces, symbolic of the breaking of the power of Babylon. Jeremiah, seemingly beaten, retired and received a message from Yahweh that the bar of wood would become a bar of iron, and that Hananiah would die during the year because he had spoken rebellion against Yahweh (Jer. 28).

7. One of Daniel's companions in Babylon whose name was changed to Shadrach (Dnl. 1:7, 11, 19; Song Three 66; AV ANANIAS).

8. A son of Zerubbabel (1 Ch. 3:19, 21).

9. A Levite, one of the sons of Bebai, one of those who married foreign wives (Ezr. 10:28; 1 Esd. 9:29; AV, NEB, ANANIAS).

10. One of the perfumers (AV "apothecaries") who helped in rebuilding the wall under Nehemiah (Neh. 3:8).

11. One who helped to repair the wall above the Horse Gate (Neh. 3:30). This may be the same person as **10.**

12. A governor of the castle, i.e., the *bîrâ* or fortress, whom Nehemiah placed in charge of the whole city of Jerusalem, because "he was a more faithful and God-fearing man than many" (Neh. 7:2).

13. One of those who sealed the covenant under Nehemiah (Neh. 10:23 [MT 11]); a Levite.

14. A priest who was present at the dedication of the walls of Jerusalem (Neh. 12:12, 41).

15. One who returned with Ezra from Babylon to perform the functions of a priest in Jerusalem (1 Esd. 8:48; AV CHANNUNEUS; NEB CHANUNAEUS).

J. J. REEVE

HAND [Heb. usually *yāḏ,* also *kap*–'palm (of hand)'; Gk. *cheír*]. The hand is that part of the body which enables man to be a doer, a tool-making and tool-using being; thus it is associated with power or control (e.g., hands are called "keepers of the house" in Eccl. 12:3; in referring to parts of the body, Paul gives priority to the hand in 1 Cor. 12:15, 21).

The word "hand" appears in the RSV a total of 1782 times, five hundred of these in the literal sense. The basic notion is of the hand as a whole; thus to wear jewelry such as rings "on the hand" means on the fingers (Gen. 41:42; Jer. 22:24; Lk. 15:22), or bracelets "upon the hands" means on the wrists (Ezk. 23:42). Thumb (Heb. *bōhen*) is mentioned on only three occasions: the ordination of priests (Ex. 29:20; Lev. 8:24), the cleansing of lepers (Lev. 14:14-28), and the mutilation of an enemy (Jgs. 1:6f.). FINGER appears twenty-five times, twice with "right" (Lev. 14:16, 27), twice with "little" (1 K. 12:10 par. 2 Ch. 10:10). "Finger of God" (Ex. 8:19; 31:18; Lk. 11:20; cf. Dt. 9:10) is an expression used with the same force as "hand of God" (see below). PALM occurs only in Lev. 14:15, 26, and fist in the context of quarrels (Heb. *'egrōp,* "rake, hoe," Ex. 21:18; Isa. 58:4), as a gesture (Heb. *yaḏ,* Isa. 10:32; Zeph. 2:15), and as a symbol of power (*ḥōpen,* "hollow of hand," Prov. 30:4).

Benjaminites were distinguished as being ambidextrous (1 Ch. 12:2) or left-handed (Jgs. 3:15, 21; 20:16). References to "left and right" or "left or right hand" are numerous. As with Moslems and many oriental peoples today, the left hand may have been associated with uncleanness (since it was used in sanitation) and evil (Mt. 25:41), though there is little conclusive evidence for this (Jgs. 3:21; Prov. 3:16; Cant. 2:6; 8:3; Mk. 10:37, 40). The right hand, however, appears alone thirty-seven times, and with the left an additional thirty-nine times, suggesting preference for the right hand as the efficient agent (Ps. 118:16; Isa. 10:13). Thus, to be "on" or "seated at" the right hand is to be in the superlative and unique place of power, honor, and prestige, a notion which appears frequently in the OT (e.g., Ps. 110:1) and NT (e.g., Mt. 25:33f.), and also in the Apostles' Creed.

Frequently "hand" occurs in a variety of gestures (*see* GESTURES I). In Isa. 57:8, 10 it is a euphemism for the male sex organ (RSV "nakedness" and "strength," Heb. *yaḏ,* "hand"). In contexts of offering sacrifices, giving blessings, healing the sick, and ordination, hands were placed on animals or people (*see* HANDS, LAYING ON OF).

In the DSS (1QS) a penalty of ten days without food was laid on a member who, while in conversation, gesticulated with the left (unclean) hand. A penalty of thirty days without food was imposed upon a member for "bring[ing] out his hand from under his cloak," which may have meant to "expose himself that his private parts become visible" (7:12, 14, Gaster tr.). L. H. Silberman, however, interprets this to mean that in the community meetings the hands of a speaker had to be kept under his robe or in his pocket, and he cites a similar regulation in the court practice in Persia, possibly also in Babylonia. To cover the hands as an act of reverence in the presence of God is shown in the fresco paintings of the Dura-Europos Synagogue (*ca.* A.D. 250): "Abraham Receiving the Covenant Promise," where his arms are crossed and his hands are enveloped in his outer garment (Gk. *himátion*), and "Samuel Anointing David," where David's arms are crossed and his hands are wrapped in his outer garment (Kraeling).

A "sign [=mark] on the hand" (Ex. 13:9, 16; Dt. 6:8) for Israel meant the *t^epillîm,* or phylacteries (*see* PHYLACTERY). In pagan practice devotees honored gods by cutting or branding marks on the hand (Isa. 44:5; Rev. 20:4) and by kissing the hand in adoration (Job 31:27). A "handbreadth" is a rough linear measurement, the width of the hand at the base of the fingers, about 8 cm. (3 in., 1 K. 7:26; Ezk. 40:5; 43:13).

"Hand" is used figuratively in almost thirteen hundred passages in the RSV. The largest number of references is to the hand of God or of the Lord (186 times) in the sense of God's supreme and almighty power and authority. The phrase is modified frequently by adjectives, e.g., "right" (31 times), "mighty" (10 times), and "strong" (3 times). It signified the "mighty acts of God"; e.g., it is "by the finger of God that I [Jesus] cast out demons" (Lk. 11:20; cf. Mt. 12:28, "by the Spirit of God").

Other figurative uses of hand are "from, out of, into the hand of" (or "the hand of") denoting power and dominion (135 times), jurisdiction (180 times), or safekeeping or deliverance (42 times). Less frequent are "requiring something at your hand," or demanding an account for something for which one is responsible (sheep, Ezk. 24:10, and blood elsewhere); "take, hold life in one's hand," meaning to enter into a critical situation (e.g., 1 S. 19:5; 28:21); "under, by the hand of," or under the leadership of some person(s), with the connotation of prosperity or success (e.g., Ps. 77:20 [MT 21]); the "work of your hand," signifying the labor or the product of a skilled handcraftsman; "lay hands upon" or "lay the hand on the neck of," i.e., dominion. The expressions "with a high hand" (or defiantly, Nu. 15:30), "put forth thy hand" (or attack, Job 1:11f.; 2:5), "relax your hand" (or be slow or negligent, Josh. 10:6), and "strengthen the hand" (or comfort or encourage, 1 S. 23:16) are noteworthy.

From such a survey of the OT, it is clear that the Hebrews were especially conscious of the hand. Is this a trait common to all people? Expressions in the English language employing "hand" in both literal and figurative senses show a comparably wide variety, as in the phrase "under the hand and seal of" the owner. Perhaps the widespread use of "hand" in English reflects the influence which the English Bible has had on the vocabulary and idioms of English-speaking people.

Bibliography.–C. H. Kraeling, *The Synagogue: Excavations at Dura-Europos,* Final Report VIII, Pt. I (1957), 166f., Plate LXVI, 238f.; Plate LXXVIII, 261; T. H. Gaster, *Dead Sea Scriptures in English Translation* (1956), pp. 54, 99.

P. L. GARBER

HANDBAGS. *See* BAG.

HANDBREADTH [Heb. *ṭepaḥ, ṭōpaḥ*] (1 K. 7:26; 2 Ch. 4:5; Ps. 39:5 [MT 6]; Ex. 25:25; 37:12; Ezk. 40:5, 43; 43:13). A Hebrew linear measurement containing 4 fingers, or digits, and equal to about 8 cm. (3 in.). *See* WEIGHTS AND MEASURES.

HANDFUL. Four Hebrew words are used to indicate what may be held in the hand, either closed or open. (1) *Ḥōpen* in Ex. 9:8 is the fist or closed hand and signifies what can be taken in the two hands conjoined, a double handful. (2) *Kap,* "hollow of the hand," is an open handful, occurring literally in 1 K. 17:12 and figuratively in Eccl. 4:6. (3) *Šō'al,* "hollow hand," is the amount of dust Benhadad's soldiers can put into their hands in 1 K. 20:10 and the measured daily portion of barley in Ezk. 13:19. (4) *Qōmeṣ* is a measure of flour (Lev. 2:2; 5:12; 6:15 [MT 8]).

The RSV and the NEB correctly render Heb. *pissâ* "abundance" in Ps. 72:16 (AV "handful"). H. PORTER

HANDKERCHIEF [Gk. *soudárion*] (Acts 19:12). A loanword from the Lat. *sudarium,* found in the plural in

Acts 19:12 (*soudária*; cf. Lat. *sudor,* "perspiration"). Literally it means "a face-cloth used to wipe off perspiration" (Bauer, rev., p. 759). It may have been some sort of headdress. Elsewhere it is rendered "napkin" (Lk. 19:20; Jn. 20:7) or "cloth" (Jn. 11:44). *See also* NAPKIN.

HANDLE [Heb. *tāpaś* (Jer. 2:8; 46:9; 50:16; Ezk. 21:11; 27:29; Am. 2:15), *ʿāśâ* (Ezk. 23:3, 8), *ʾāḥaz* (2 Ch. 25:5), *yāḏ* (Isa. 45:9), *ʿēṣ* (Dt. 19:5), *kap* (Cant. 5:5); Gk. *psēlapháō* (Lk. 24:39), *háptō* (Col. 2:21), *orthotoméō* (2 Tim. 2:15)]; AV also HELVE (Dt. 19:5), BRUISE, TOUCH; NEB also CARRY, GRASP, PRESS, etc. The part of an object designed to be held by the hand, or the act of grasping the object.

In the OT the vb. *tāpaś* is used of scribes handling the law (Jer. 2:8), the armies of Ethiopia and Put handling their shields (Jer. 46:9), etc. In Jer. 50:16, the NEB translates *tāpaś* and its object by a single word which expresses both ideas: "reaper" rather than "one who handles a sickle" (RSV; cf. Ezk. 27:29; Am. 2:15). In Ezekiel, Heb. *ʿāśâ,* which usually means "make" (KoB, pp. 739f.), is translated "handle," and refers to an unchaste act performed upon Oholah and Oholibah in connection with their activity as harlots (23:3, 8, 21). The two women represent Samaria and Jerusalem and the passage is a critique of their unfaithfulness to God and a description of the punishment they received for it. In Ezk. 23:21, *lᵉmaʿan* ("for the sake of") is emended to *ʿāśâ* on the basis of the context.

Nouns translated "handle" in the RSV OT are Heb. *ʿēṣ* (lit. "wood," KoB, pp. 724f.), *kap* (usually "palm" of the hand, KoB, pp. 449f.), and *yāḏ* ("hand," KoB, pp. 362f.). In Isa. 45:9, *yāḏîm* is translated "handles" by the RSV, "hands" by the AV, and "you have no skill" by the NEB (see C. F. Whitley, *VT,* 11 [1961], 458f.; E. J. Young, *Book of Isaiah,* III [*NICOT,* 1972], 203f.).

In the NT Paul warned against a legalism which prohibited the handling of certain foods (Col. 2:21). After His resurrection, Jesus invited the disciples to handle Him in order to demonstrate the reality of His corporeal resurrection body (Lk. 24:39). The meaning of *orthotoméō* in 2 Tim. 2:15 is debated. It may mean "guide [the word of truth] along a straight path" (Bauer, rev., p. 580), "teach [the word] aright" (MM, p. 456), or "follow [the word]," i.e., obey it (*TDNT,* VIII, *s.v.* τέμνω κτλ.: ὀρθοτομέω [Köster]). The RSV rendering is to be preferred over the AV ("rightly dividing") and NEB ("be straightforward") translations.

P. L. BREMER

HANDMAID [Heb. *ʾāmâ*] (1 S. 25:24f., 28, 31, 41; Ps. 86:16; 116:16); NEB (HUMBLE) SERVANT, SLAVE-GIRL, "I," "me"; [*šipḥâ*] (1 S. 28:21f.; 2 S. 14:6f., 12, 15, 17, 19); NEB "I," "me"; [Gk. *doúlē*] (Lk. 1:38); NEB SERVANT; **HANDMAIDEN** [Gk. *doúlē*] (Lk. 1:48); NEB SERVANT. A term of humility or obeisance used by the speaker before a great man or God. The distinction between the two Hebrew words is not clear. It is thought that *sipḥâ* originally meant an unfree, untouched girl in the service of a woman, while *ʾāmâ* was an unfree woman, either a concubine or the wife of a slave. Heb. *ben-ʾāmâ* is also a term of humility, but is spoken by a man, "the son of thy handmaid" (Ps. 86:16; 116:16). The suggestion of M. Mansoor (*Thanksgiving Hymns* [1961], p. 31), followed by M. Dahood (comm. on Psalms, II [*AB,* 1968], p. 296), that the text be repointed to read "your true children" (Heb. *ben ʾᵃmitteḵā*), has little to commend it, especially in view of the parallelism and the absence of any other examples in the OT. Also, its occurrence in the Qumrân texts should probably be related to the Qumrân theology. The Gk. *doúlē* meant a "female slave," a common oriental expression of humility used when speaking to someone of higher rank; it is the word used by the LXX to translate both *šipḥâ* and *ʾāmâ* in all the above passages except 2 S. 14:17; Ps. 86:16; 116:16.

Bibliography.–F. C. Fensham, *VT,* 19 (1969), 312-321; A. Jepsen, *VT,* 8 (1958), 293-97; E. Neufeld, *Ancient Hebrew Marriage Laws* (1944), pp. 121-23.

A. L. PERLMAN

HANDPIKE [Heb. *maqqēl yāḏ*] (Ezk. 39:9); AV HANDSTAFF; NEB THROWING-STICK. A weapon perhaps like the staff used by travelers or shepherds (cf. Gen. 32:10 [MT 11]; Ex. 12:11; Nu. 22:27; 1 S. 17:40).

HANDS, LAYING ON OF [Heb. *sāmaḵ yaḏ ʿal–*'lean a hand upon' (Ex. 29:10, 15, 19; Lev. 1:4), *šîṯ yaḏ ʿal–*'place a hand upon' (Gen. 46:4), etc.; Gk. *títhēmi tás cheíras ep'* (Mk. 10:16), *epitíthēmi tás cheíras* (Mt. 19:15), *epíthesis tṓn cheirṓn* (1 Tim. 4:14), etc.]. The practice of laying hands upon the head of another person, usually a part of a religious rite, sometimes in order to impart a blessing. In Am. 5:19 the phrase "the laying of the hand upon" is used in a secular sense and is translated by the RSV as "[he] leaned with his hand against."

I. In the OT.–The laying on of hands was used in several distinct ways: in offering certain sacrifices, in consecrating or ordaining, in imparting blessings, and in passing judgment. The first two are connected with Heb. *sāmaḵ* and seem to connote a "leaning" of the hands. The third is expressed by Heb. *šîṯ* and connotes "placing" hands on the other.

A. In Offering. The person presenting a peace offering (Lev. 3:1f.) or a sin offering (Lev. 3:8, 13; 4:4; Nu. 8:12) was to lay his hands upon the animal so that he identified himself with the animal being offered. Most scholars believe that there was no transference of the guilt of sin. Rather, the value seemed to result from the offering of a pure and innocent life or of a being without blemish as an expiation for the guilt-laden life of the offerer. The only situation where the laying on of hands transferred the guilt of sin was that of the scapegoat (*see* AZAZEL). The high priest laid his hands upon the head of the animal, confessing the sins of the people. He then drove the goat, bearing the sins of the people, into the wilderness (Lev. 16:21).

B. In Ordaining. Beginning with the ordination of the Aaronic priesthood (Lev. 8:14, 22) and the consecration of the Levites (Nu. 8:12), the laying on of hands set apart a man for a special office. Moses laid his hands upon Joshua to symbolize his assumption of the leadership of the nation (27:23). Although Nu. 27:18 states that Joshua already had been given the Holy Spirit, the action does not seem to convey a special spiritual grace. The rite, however, was always accompanied with a special commission and the man commissioned was given special authority.

C. In Blessing. Jacob laid his hands on his grandsons' heads to bless them (Gen. 48:14). The laying on of hands was undoubtedly intended to convey some beneficial virtue.

In one instance God is said to lay (Heb. *šîṯ*) His hand upon David (Ps. 139:5) as a sign of blessing. We should not forget that the divine blessing underlies human blessing. There is no higher blessing, as Job acknowledged in his confrontation with God (Job 9:33).

D. In Passing Judgment. At the trial of a blasphemer each witness, to show his acceptance of the verdict of judgment, placed his hands upon the one to be executed (Lev. 24:14). In Ex. 7:4 the expression refers to an act of divine judgment by which God would visit the plagues upon Egypt. When a victim was spared death, as when God allowed the elders and leaders of Israel to see Him without executing the judgment of death (Ex. 24:11) or when Abraham was commanded not to sacrifice Isaac (Gen. 22:12), the sparing of judgment is described in terms of hands not being laid on the possible victim.

II. In the NT.–The same basic pattern is followed in the NT except that its sacrificial usage is dropped and the spiritual gifts are added. When Jesus blessed the children (Mt. 19:15 par. Mk. 10:16), He laid His hands upon them. Both Jesus (e.g., Mt. 9:18; Mk. 6:5) and His apostles (Acts 5:12; 28:8) healed by laying on their hands (cf. 9:12, 17). The miracles often occur, however, without the laying on of hands, so the miraculous power for the healings was surely a personal power and was not specifically connected to the action of the hands.

Special spiritual gifts seem to have been given through the laying on of hands. The Holy Spirit was given to the Samaritans (Acts 8:17-20) and to the disciples of John the Baptist (19:6) by the laying on of the apostles' hands. In each case it is possible that the laying on of the hands confirmed a questionable baptismal practice, for the gift of the Holy Spirit is more normally given at baptism. Timothy also received special spiritual gifts from the hands of the elders (1 Tim. 4:14) and from the hand of Paul (2 Tim. 1:6). Some consider these verses to be the basis for the modern practice of confirmation.

On two occasions the laying on of hands was part of the setting of persons aside for special tasks. The seven chosen to care for the widows were selected by the church (Acts 6:6), while Paul and Barnabas were set apart by the Holy Spirit (13:3). The laying on of hands was a part of the formal ceremony by which the church commissioned them and then sent them into their new service. Paul admonished Timothy that this act, probably connected with ordination, ought to take place only after the entire matter was properly considered (1 Tim. 5:22).

On He. 6:2 see the comms. for a discussion of the problematic context.

Bibliography.–J. Behm, *Die Handauflegung im Urchristentum nach Verwendung, Herkunft und Bedeutung* (1911); J. Coppens, *L'Imposition des mains et les rites connexes dans le NT et dans l'Eglise ancienne* (1925); D. Daube, "The Laying on of Hands," in *NT and Rabbinic Judaism* (1956), pp. 224ff.; *TDNT,* VIII, *s.v.* τίθημι κτλ. (Maurer).

D. W. WEAD

HANDSOME [Heb. *y^e^pēh-ṯō'ar* (Gen. 39:6), *ṭôḇ* (1 S. 9:2), *ṭôḇ rō'î* (1 S. 16:12), *ṭôḇ-tō'ar* ("very handsome," 1 K. 1:6), *ṭôḇ mar'eh* (Dnl. 1:4)]; AV GOODLY, GOODLY TO LOOK TO, WELL FAVOURED; NEB also BETTER (1 S. 9:2), STRIKING APPEARANCE, GOOD LOOKS. In 2 S. 23:21, the RSV, AV, and NEB follow the *Q 'îš mar'eh* (*K 'ašer mar'eh*); however, the JB, NAB, and NIV follow *BH*'s suggestion to emend *mar'eh* to *middâ,* "stature, size," on the basis of the par. 1 Ch. 11:23. This slight change vastly improves the sense of the text.

Joseph, Saul, David, Adonijah, the young Judean captives, and even the Egyptian slain by Benaiah are described as handsome. One interesting omission among the heroes so described is the name of Solomon, whose appearance may have been a serious disadvantage in his contest with Adonijah.

HANDSTAFF. *See* HANDPIKE.

HANDWRITING (Col. 2:14, AV). *See* BOND.

HANES hā'nēz [Heb. *ḥānēs,* meaning unknown, possibly Egyptian]. A place of uncertain identification mentioned in Isa. 30:4. The passage reads literally, "For his princes were [*hāyû*] in Zoan, and his messengers reach [*yaggî'û*] Hanes." The problem involved in translating perfects and imperfects in poetical passages is well known, but in this passage both verbs are in concessional clauses, and appear to be undefined general tense, as translated by the RSV, "For though his officials are at Zoan and his envoys reach Hanes. . . ." Hanes was formerly identified with Heracleopolis Magna, Coptic Ahnes, (modern) Arabic Ihnâsiyeh el-Medîna, on an island between the Nile and Baḥr Yûsûf opposite Beni Suef, about 30 km. (50 mi.) above (i.e., S of) Memphis. The objection has been raised (cf. *ISBE* [1929], II, *s.v.* [M. G. Kyle]) that Zoan is in the northeastern Delta, and that Hanes is therefore somewhere between that region and Israel. Tahpanhes has been suggested, but this requires an emendation of the MT to agree with the Targum. K. A. Kitchen (*NBD,* p. 504) offers two other suggestions. (1) W. Spiegelberg (*Aegyptische Randglossen zum AT* [1904], pp. 36-38) postulated a "Heracleopolis parva" in the eastern Delta, on the basis of Herodotus ii.137, 166. Kitchen equates the name "Anysis" with Egyp. **Ḥ(wt-nni-)nsw,* Akk. *Ḫininši.* (2) The second suggestion, proffered by Kitchen himself, is that the Hebrew is a transcription of Egyp. **ḥ(wt)-nsw,* "mansion of the king." In this case, "Zoan" is more closely defined by "the king's mansion." The problem is further complicated by the interpretation given to "his" — whether this pronoun refers to Pharaoh or to the (unmentioned) Israelite king who sent his official and envoys to make a league with Egypt (cf. 30:2). Straightforward grammar would require that the pronoun agree with the near antecedent, Pharaoh. In this case, the clause "and his envoys reach Hanes" does not necessarily require a location nearer Israel, although it must be admitted that the statement seems to lack significance if it is interpreted to mean that Pharaoh's messengers stretch from Zoan to Heracleopolis Magna. The suggestion that "Hanes" refers to the king's mansion in Zoan makes even less sense if "his" is taken to refer to Pharaoh, for why would Pharaoh's "messengers" (*mal'āḵāyw*) "reach" his palace? It therefore seems best to reject the suggested identifications, whether Heracleopolis Magna, or a smaller Heracleopolis otherwise unknown, or the king's mansion in Zoan, and to admit that Hanes is an unidentified location to which (probably) Egyptian envoys came to meet the Israelite envoys who were seeking to "make a league" (30:1).

W. S. L. S.

HANGING [Heb. *tālâ*; Gk. *kremánnumi*]. In the OT, where the word is used in connection with punishments, it refers to the hanging of the corpse in public after execution. Stoning was the usual form of capital punishment, but as an added warning (cf. Gen. 40:19; Josh. 8:29; 10:26; 2 S. 4:12) Deuteronomic law permitted the corpse to be hanged, so long as it was taken down and buried that same day (Dt. 21:22f.; cf. Josephus *Ant.* iv.8.6, 24 [202, 264f.]; Mish. *Sanhedrin* vi.4). However, there were times in Israelite history when this provision was not observed, as in the case of David, who handed over certain of the sons of Saul to the Gibeonites for execution (2 S. 21:5-9; hiphil of Heb. *yāqa'*, on which see S. R. Driver, *Notes on the Hebrew Text and the Topography of the Books of Samuel* [2nd ed. 1913], p. 351) and subsequent prolonged exposure. The Egyptians apparently did not remove a hanging corpse until it had been partially consumed by carrion birds (cf. Gen. 40:19), and perhaps the Philistines were following the same general practice in connection with the body of Saul (1 S. 31:10; 2 S. 21:12f.).

Scripture appears to contain only two clear examples of people who died by hanging, i.e., by strangulation, namely Ahithophel (2 S. 17:23 [Heb. *ḥānaq*]) and Judas Iscariot (Mt. 27:5, Gk. *apánchō*). Both of these were cases of suicide, not of execution. The method by which Pharaoh's baker was hanged (Gen. 40:18-22) is unknown. In Est. 2:23; 5:14; 6:4; 7:9f.; 8:7; 9:13f., 25, the verb *tālâ* ("hang up, suspend") is used of hanging. The "gallows" (Heb. *ʿēṣ*), however, most probably consisted of a stake on which the victim was impaled, since according to Herodotus this kind of punishment was practiced in Persia (iii.125, 159); *see* picture in CROSS. "Hanging on a tree" is applied to the crucifixion of Christ in Acts 5:30; 10:39 (cf. Lk. 23:39), and the "curse" associated with such a fate is quoted from Dt. 21:23 in Gal. 3:13. *See also* PUNISHMENTS.

R. K. H.

HANGINGS [Heb. *qᵉlāʿîm*] (Ex. 27:9-15; 35:17; 38:9-18; 39:40; Nu. 3:26; 4:26); [*bottîm*] (2 K. 23:7); NEB VESTMENTS. In Ex. 27:18 and Est. 1:6 the term "hangings" is supplied. The term represents curtains or drapes used to enclose or partition the tabernacle, its court, and the tent of the meeting. Those for the tabernacle (Ex. 27:9-15; 38:9-18; Nu. 3:26; 4:26) were made of "twined linen" of lengths corresponding to the sides of the enclosure. They were hung from silver hooks between supporter pillars. Another drape hung at the door of the tent of the meeting. The "hangings" were carried and cared for by Levites of the family of Gershon (Nu. 3:25; 4:26-28). The Heb. *bottîm* (2 K. 23:7; cf. Arab. *batt*, "woven garment"; J. Gray, *I & II Kings* [*OTL*, 2nd ed. 1970], p. 730) were probably woven garments used to clothe the Asherah.

See also CURTAIN; SCREEN; TABERNACLE; VEIL.

A. L. PERLMAN

HANIEL. *See* HANNIEL **2.**

HANNAH han'ə [Heb. *ḥannâ*–'grace, favor'; Gk. *Hanna*]. One of the two wives of Elkanah, an Ephraimite who lived at Ramathaim-zophim. Hannah visited Shiloh, where the tabernacle was located, yearly with her husband to offer sacrifices. She was greatly distressed because they had no children, so she prayed earnestly for a male child, whom she promised to dedicate to the Lord from his birth. The prayer was heard, and she called her son Samuel. When he was weaned he was carried to Shiloh to be trained by Eli the priest (1 S. 1:24-28). Hannah became the mother of five other children — three sons and two daughters (2:2). Her devotion in sending Samuel a little robe every year is one of the tenderest recorded instances of maternal love (2:19). She was a prophetess of extraordinary talent, as is evident from her song elicited by God's answer to her prayer (2:1-10). B. H. DEMENT

HANNATHON han'ə-thon [Heb. *ḥannāṯôn*–'gracious, favored']. A city on the northern boundary of the territory assigned to the tribe of Zebulun when Canaan was divided among the tribes of Israel after the Conquest (Josh. 19:14). It is mentioned in the Amarna Letters (Am. Tab. 8, 245). It was probably located about midway between Mt. Carmel and the Sea of Galilee, perhaps at modern Tell el-Bedeiwîyeh. R. J. HUGHES, III

HANNIEL han'ē-el [Heb. *ḥannîʾēl*–'God has been gracious'].

1. The son of Ephod and a prince of Manasseh who assisted in dividing Canaan among the tribes (Nu. 34:23).

2. A son of Ulla and a prince and hero of the tribe of Asher (1 Ch. 7:39; AV, NEB, HANIEL).

HANOCH hā'nok; **HANOCHITES** hā'nok-īts [Heb. *ḥᵃnôḵ*]; NEB ENOCH.

1. A grandson of Abraham by Keturah, and an ancestral head of a clan of Midian (Gen. 25:4; 1 Ch. 1:33; AV HENOCH.

2. The eldest son of Reuben (Gen. 46:9; Ex. 6:14; 1 Ch. 5:3). His descendants were known as "Hanochites" (Nu. 26:5, NEB "Enochites").

HANUN hā'nən [Heb. *ḥānûn*].

1. A son and successor of Nahash king of Ammon. Upon the death of Nahash, David sent Hanun sympathetic communications, which were misinterpreted and the messengers dishonored. Because of this indignity David waged a war against him, which caused the Ammonites to lose their independence (2 S. 10:1ff.; 1 Ch. 19:1ff.).

2. One of the six sons of Zalaph who assisted in repairing the east wall of Jerusalem (Neh. 3:30).

3. One of the inhabitants of Zanoah who repaired the Valley Gate in the wall of Jerusalem (Neh. 3:13), perhaps identical with **2.** B. H. DEMENT

HAP; HAPLESS; HAPLY. All three words are from the Old Norse *happ*, "luck, chance." "Hap" and "haply" are archaic terms used by the AV. "Hap" translates Heb. *miqreh*, "happening, occurrence," in Ruth 2:3. "If haply" translates Heb. *lûʾ*, "if only" (1 S. 14:30), Gk. *ei ára*, "if then" (Mk. 11:13), and *ei ára ge* (Acts 17:27). "Lest haply" translates Gk. *mḗpote*, "lest at any time" (Lk. 14:29; Acts 5:39), and *mḗ pōs*, "lest in any way" (2 Cor. 9:4).

"Hapless" is still used to denote "luckless" or "unfortunate," as in the RSV translations of Heb. *ḥēlᵉḵâ* (AV "poor"; NEB "poor wretch," "poor victim") in Ps. 10:8, 10, 14.

HAPAX LEGOMENON hä'pox lə-go'mə-non [Gk. *hápax legómenon*–'once read']. A word (or expression) that occurs only once in a certain writing or collection of writings (in biblical studies, usually either the Hebrew OT or Greek NT).

HAPHARAIM haf-ə-rā'əm [Heb. *ḥᵃpārayim*–'two pits']; AV HAPHRAIM haf-rā'əm. One of the sixteen cities, with their villages, assigned to the tribe of Issachar when Canaan was divided among the tribes of Israel after the Conquest under Joshua (Josh. 19:19). Sheshonq (Shishak) includes it in his list of conquered towns (cf. *ANET*, p. 242). Perhaps eṭ-Ṭaiyibeh, about 13 km. (8 mi.) NW of Beth-shean, represents it now. R. J. HUGHES, III

HAPPINESS [Heb. *ṭôḇâ*] (Lam. 3:17); AV, NEB, PROSPERITY. *See* PROSPER.

HAPPIZZEZ hap'ə-zez [Heb. *happiṣṣēṣ*]; AV, NEB, APHSES. A priest on whom fell the lot for the eighteenth of the twenty-four courses that David appointed for the temple service (1 Ch. 24:15).

HARA hā'rə [Heb. *hārāʾ*]. A place mentioned in 1 Ch. 5:26 as a location of Israelite exiles. Since this passage relates to the exiles of the Transjordan tribes and the time of Tiglath-pileser, whereas the seemingly parallel passages (2 K. 17:6; 18:11) refer to "the king of Assyria" and the fall of Samaria, the passage in Chronicles is problematic. Hara is not mentioned in either Kings passage, and the LXX of 1 Ch. 5:26 omits Hara. On the other hand, the LXX of 2 K. 17:6; 18:11 reads *horē mēdōn*, "the mountain of the Medes," where the MT reads *ʿārê māḏay*, "the cities of the Medes." The suggestion that *ʿārê*, "cities of," has been confused with *hārê*, "mountains of," possibly because the name Hara dropped out, is intriguing but involves a complicated series of textual problems.

Thus the location of Hara, if indeed there were such a place, is not known. W. S. L. S.

HARADAH hə-rā'də [Heb. *ḥ^a^rādâ*] (Nu. 33:24f.). A place where the Israelites stopped on their journey from Egypt. It is listed between Mt. Shepher and Makheloth, but its location is unknown.

HARAN hā'rən [Heb. *hārān*].

1. Son of Terah, younger brother of Abraham and Nahor, and father of Lot (Gen. 11:27). He had two daughters, Milcah and Iscah (v. 29).

2. A Gershonite of the family of Shimei (1 Ch. 23:9).

3. A Judahite, one of Caleb's sons by the concubine Ephah. He was the father of Gazez (1 Ch. 2:46).

HARAN hə-ran', hā'ran [Heb. *ḥārān*] (Gen. 11:31f.; 27:43; 28:10); NEB HARRAN; [Gk. *Charran*] (Acts 7:2, 4); AV CHARRAN, NEB HARRAN. A city in the northern loop of the Euphrates River, about 80 km. (50 mi.) E of Carchemish. Abraham's family moved to Haran after God had spoken to him in Ur of the Chaldees (Acts 7:2, 4).

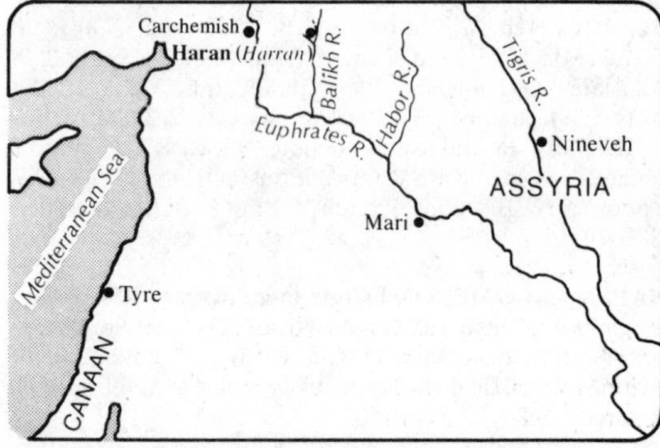

After Abraham's father Terah died in Haran (Gen. 11:31f.), Abraham, taking his possessions, wife, and nephew Lot, left Haran for Canaan (12:4f.). Jacob also went to Haran when he fled from Esau's anger, being sent by his mother Rebekah to her brother Laban (27:43; 28:10). Jacob arrived at a well, met men from Haran, and was introduced to Rachel, whom he eventually married after being tricked by Laban into first marrying her older sister Leah.

Haran (Harran) is included in the list of cities conquered by Sennacherib king of Assyria when he threatened Hezekiah (2 K. 19:12; Isa. 37:12). In his lament over Tyre, Ezekiel reflected the commercial interests of Haran when he referred to the clothing and carpets that Tyre had obtained from Haran (Ezk. 27:23).

A city by this name has been continuously occupied in this area since at least the 3rd millennium B.C. The Mari texts reflect life in the area during the early 2nd millennium B.C. very similar to that of the biblical patriarchs. Its continuous occupation may be due to its strategic position at the crossroads of trade routes going between the major commercial centers of that part of the world. This fits well with the biblical account of Abraham's prosperity, and the ease with which the patriarchs traveled and sent messengers to the area after settling in Canaan (cf. Gen. 24).

With Ur this city provided sites for famous temples of Sin, the moon-god. Assyrian rulers repeatedly added to the city, used it as a provincial capital, and embellished its temple. After Nineveh fell (612 B.C.), the final Assyrian government was located in Haran until defeated by the Babylonians in 609 B.C. The Babylonians restored the worship of Sin in both Ur and Haran. Nabonidus's mother (who died at age 104) was high priestess in the temple at Ur, and later his daughter was high priestess in the temple at Haran.

Crassus, a member of the first Roman triumvirate, was defeated, captured, and executed at Haran by the Parthians in 53 B.C. The city has been ruled by Zoroastrians, Nestorian Christians, Moslems, and Crusaders, and exists today as a town in southern Turkey.

See Vol. I, Map III.

See also C. F. Pfeiffer, ed., *The Biblical World: A Dictionary of Biblical Archaeology* (1966), *s.v.* (W. Hallo).

R. J. HUGHES, III

HARARITE hā'rə-rīt [Heb. *hah^a^rārî, hā'rārî*]. A gentilic (derived from an unknown place) applied to the fathers of some of David's mighty men.

1. Agee, father of Shammah (2 S. 23:11).

2. Shammah, son of Agee (2 S. 23:11, 33). The par. passage, 1 Ch. 11:34, has "Shagee" (AV, NEB, SHAGE) in place of "Shammah" and names him as the father of Jonathan.

3. Ahiam, son of Sharar the Hararite (2 S. 23:33). 1 Ch. 11:35 has "Sacher" (AV, NEB, SACAR) for Sharar.

HARBONA, HARBONAH här-bō'nə [Heb. *ḥar^e^bônā', ḥar^e^bônâ*]. One of the seven eunuchs who served Ahasuerus and who was commanded to bring Esther before the king (Est. 1:10). He suggested that Haman be hanged upon the same gallows that he had erected for Mordecai (7:9). The Persian equivalent of the name means "donkey driver."

HARD; HARDNESS [Heb. *gādôl*] (Ezk. 29:18); AV GREAT; NEB LONG; [*galmûd*] ("hard hunger," Job 30:23); AV FAMINE; NEB HUNGER; [*dābaq*] ("pursue hard," etc., Jgs. 20:45; 1 S. 14:22; Jer. 42:16); AV also CLOSE; NEB "hot pursuit," STILL; [*dāḥâ*] ("push hard," Ps. 118:13); AV SORE; [*ḥābā'*] (Job 38:30); AV HIDE; NEB COVER; [*ḥāzāq*] (1 S. 14:52; 2 S. 11:15; Job 37:18; Jer. 5:3; Ezk. 3:7-9); AV also HOTTEST, IMPUDENT, SORE, STRONG; NEB also BITTER, BRAZEN, FIERCEST, STUBBORN; [*ḥîdâ*] ("hard question," 1 K. 10:1; 2 Ch. 9:1); [*ḥāṭar*] ("row hard," Jonah 1:13); [*kābēd*] (Jgs. 20:34; 1 S. 31:3; 1 Ch. 10:3; Ezk. 3:5f.); AV also SORE; NEB also DIFFICULT, HEAVY; [*nāgaś*] ("hard pressed," 1 S. 13:6); AV DISTRESSED; [*'^a^bōdâ*] ("hard service," 1 K. 12:4; 2 Ch. 10:4; Isa. 14:3); AV also GRIEVOUS; NEB also CRUEL; [*'ōz*] (Eccl. 8:1); AV BOLDNESS; NEB GRIM LOOKS; [*'āmāl*] ("hard labor," Ps. 107:12); AV LABOUR; [*pālā'*] (Gen. 18:14; Dt. 30:11; Jer. 32:17, 27); AV also HIDDEN; NEB DIFFICULT, IMPOSSIBLE; [*pāṣar*] ("press hard," Gen. 19:9); AV SORE; NEB "crowded in"; [*ṣābā'*] ("hard service," Job 7:1); AV APPOINTED; [*ṣûq*] (Jgs. 14:17; 16:16; Job 41:24 [MT 16]; AV also FIRM, "press," SORE; NEB FIRM, "pester"; [*qāšâ*] (Gen. 35:16f.; Dt. 1:17; 15:18; Isa. 27:1); AV also SORE; NEB AMISS, CRUEL, DIFFICULT, PAINS, SEVERE PAINS; [*qāšeh*] (Ex. 1:14; 18:26; Dt. 26:6; Jgs. 4:24; 2 S. 3:39; 2 K. 2:10; Job 30:25; Ps. 60:3 [MT 5]); Isa. 19:4); AV also CRUEL, "prevailed against," TROUBLE; NEB also BITTER, CRUEL, DIFFICULT, MUCH, "pressed home"; [*rōb*] (Lam. 1:3); AV GREAT; NEB ENDLESS; [*rādap*] ("hard driven," Lam. 5:5); AV PERSECUTION; NEB OVERDRIVEN; [Gk. *báros*] (Mt. 23:4); AV GRIEVOUS; [*deinṓs*] (Lk. 11:53); AV VEHEMENTLY; NEB FIERCELY; [*dysbástaktos*] ("hard to bear," Lk. 11:46); AV GRIEVOUS; NEB INTOLERABLE; [*dysermḗneutos*] (He. 5:11); NEB DIFFICULT;

[*dýskolos*] (Mk. 10:24); [*dyskólōs*] (Mt. 19:23; Mk. 10:23; Lk. 18:24); [*dysnóētos*] ("hard to understand," 2 Pet. 3:16); NEB OBSCURE; [*thlíbō*] (Mt. 7:14); AV, NEB, NARROW; [*perissotérōs*] (1 Cor. 15:10); AV MORE ABUNDANTLY; NEB OUTDONE; [*polýs*] (Rom. 16:6, 12; Col. 4:13; He. 10:32); AV GREAT, MUCH; NEB also GREAT, SO LONG, TIRELESSLY; [*pṓrōsis*] (Mk. 3:5; Eph. 4:18); AV also BLINDNESS; NEB also OBSTINATE; [*sklērokardía*] ("hardness of heart," Mt. 19:8; Mk. 10:5); NEB CLOSED; [*sklērós*] (Mt. 25:24; Jn. 6:60); NEB also "more than we can stomach"; [*sklērótēs*] (Rom. 2:5); NEB RIGID; [*synéchō*] ("be hard pressed," Phil. 1:23); AV "in a strait"; NEB TORN.

(1) One of the main uses of the word "hard" in the OT is concerned with the idea of difficulty. The commandments given by Yahweh to Israel are not difficult to perform (Dt. 15:18; 30:11). Difficult judicial cases are to be resolved by Moses (Ex. 18:26; Dt. 1:17). The questions that the queen of Sheba poses to Solomon (1 K. 10:1; 2 Ch. 9:1) are called "hard," i.e., "difficult." Ezekiel is sent to the house of Israel because its language will not be difficult for him to understand (Ezk. 3:5f.). Elisha's request for a double share of Elijah's spirit is characterized as difficult of accomplishment (2 K. 2:10). Nothing is too difficult for Yahweh (Gen. 18:14; Jer. 32:17).

In the NT also the word "hard" is associated with the idea of difficulty. Some of the ideas of the Christian faith are difficult to understand (He. 5:11; 2 Pet. 3:16). Entry into the kingdom of God is difficult (Mt. 7:14; Mk. 10:24), especially for the rich (Mt. 19:23; Mk. 10:23; Lk. 18:24), as is Jesus' saying about the bread of life (Jn. 6:60; *see* HARD SAYING). The master in the parable of the talents is called a "hard man" (Mt. 25:24), difficult to satisfy. Paul has difficulty in deciding between life and death because of his devotion to Christ (Phil. 1:23).

(2) A second use is to characterize any activity that requires great exertion, effort, or persistence: the effort of Nebuchadrezzar's army against Tyre (Ezk. 29:18); the pursuit of the Benjaminites by the Israelites (Jgs. 20:45), of the Philistines by the Israelites (1 S. 14:22), of the Israelites by famine (Jer. 42:16); the rowing of the men in the boat with Jonah (Jonah 1:13); the persistence with which Delilah pursued Samson's secret (Jgs. 14:17; 16:16); Rachel's labor during the birth of Benjamin (Gen. 35:16f.). Severe fighting is often characterized as "hard" (Jgs. 4:24; 20:34; 1 S. 13:6; 14:52; 31:3; 2 S. 11:15; 1 Ch. 10:3). The psalmist says that he has been pushed so hard that he falls (Ps. 118:13); the men of Sodom pushed Lot hard (Gen. 19:9). In the NT this sense occurs particularly with respect to the efforts of Paul (1 Cor. 15:10) and his associates (Rom. 16:6, 12; Col. 4:13; He. 10:32).

(3) "Hard" occurs several times in the sense of "close" or "near to," as in "pursue hard" (Jgs. 20:45) and "follow hard" (Jer. 4:20; 42:16).

(4) Another use of "hard" concerns oppressive treatment or work; the treatment of the people of Israel by Solomon (1 K. 12:4; 2 Ch. 10:4) or by the king of Babylon (Isa. 14:3); the Israelites' life in Egypt (Ex. 1:14; Dt. 26:6) or in exile (Lam. 1:3; 5:5); the nature of life in general (Job 7:1; 30:25; Ps. 60:3; 107:12). The Egyptians are destined to become oppressed, says Isaiah (19:4, "hand of a hard master"). In the NT "hardness" is linked to oppressive burdens which the interpreters of the Jewish law lay upon the people (Mt. 23:4; Lk. 11:46).

(5) Yet another use characterizes those who are stubborn or pitiless as "hard" (2 S. 3:39; Jer. 5:3; Ezk. 3:7-9).

Qoheleth says that wisdom can change the hardness of a man's countenance to shining light (Eccl. 8:1). Isaiah says that Yahweh's sword is hard (Isa. 27:1). In Lk. 11:53 the Pharisees and scribes ask Jesus harsh and unfriendly questions. "Hardness of heart" is an affliction which hinders both belief (Mk. 3:5; Rom. 2:5; Eph. 4:18) and understanding (Mt. 19:8; Mk. 10:5).

The book of Job makes several uses of the term "hard." Job describes famine as "hard hunger" (30:3); Elihu describes the harsh, glaring sky as "hard" (37:18); and Yahweh describes frozen water as being "hard like stone" (38:30), as also is Leviathan's heart (41:24).

J. R. PRICE

HARD SAYING; HARD SENTENCES. In Dnl. 5:12 the AV renders "hard sentences" for Aram. *'ᵃḥîḏān* (RSV, NEB, "riddles"). The Hebrew equivalent, *ḥîḏâ,* denotes something obscure or enigmatic; cf. Nu. 12:8 ("dark speech"); Jgs. 14:12-19 ("riddle"); 1 K. 10:1 ("hard questions"); Ps. 49:4 ("riddle"). *See* DARK SAYINGS.

Greek *sklēros* (lit. "harsh" [Jn. 6:60; NEB "more than we can stomach"]; cf. Jude 15) conveys quite another meaning. Jesus' words about eating His flesh and drinking His blood were "hard" to His hearers because they could not accept His claims — not because His saying was enigmatic. As Calvin says, "To unbelievers . . . who obstinately oppose it, [Christ's teaching] will be a hammer breaking the rocks in pieces, as the prophet puts it in Jer. 23:29" (comm. on John, *in loc.*).

HARDEN; HARDENED [Heb. *ḥāzaq*] (Ex. 4:21; 7:3, 13, 22; 8:19; 9:12, 35; 10:20, 27; 11:10; 14:4, 8, 17; Josh. 11:20); NEB "make (be) obstinate," "make stubborn," "offer an obstinate resistance"; [*'āmaṣ*] (Dt. 15:7; 2 Ch. 36:13); NEB "be hard-hearted," "be stubborn"; [*kāḇēḏ*] (Ex. 7:14; 8:15, 32; 9:7, 34; 10:1; 1 S. 6:6); NEB "be (make) obdurate," "be stubborn"; [*qāšâ*] (Dt. 2:30; Job 9:4; Ps. 95:8; Prov. 28:14); NEB "make stubborn," "stubbornly resist," "grow stubborn"; [*qāšaḥ*] (Isa. 63:17); [*rāga'*] (Job 7:5); AV BROKEN; NEB omits; [Aram. *tᵉqēp*] (Dnl. 5:20); NEB "become stubborn"; [Gk. *pōróō*] (Mk. 6:52; 8:17; Jn. 12:40; Rom. 11:7; 2 Cor. 3:14); AV also BLINDED; NEB CLOSED, DULLED, "make blind," "make insensitive"; [*sklērýnō*] (Rom. 9:18; He. 3:8, 13, 15; 4:7); NEB "make (grow) stubborn"; **HARDENING** [Gk. *pṓrōsis*] (Rom. 11:25); AV, NEB, BLINDNESS.

"Harden" occurs most frequently in the phrase "to harden the heart." This hardening of people's hearts is attributed both to God and to people themselves, e.g., with reference to the hearts of Pharaoh and the Egyptians (Ex. 4–11). The verb *ḥāzaq* ("make strong") is used in both the qal and the piel, with the piel occurring where God hardens the heart and the qal where man is the subject. With the exception of Ex. 10:1, *kāḇēḏ* (in the piel and hiphil) is used where the hardening is attributed to man's own act, and means literally to "be heavy, dull, or insensitive." The verb *qāšâ* occurs only in the hiphil and is used both of hardening that is God's work and hardening that is man's work; this term is also used figuratively in the phrase "stiffen the neck" (*see* STIFF-NECKED). In the NT the verbs *pōróō* and *sklērýnō* are used only in the figurative sense of "harden the heart (or mind)."

The hardening of people's hearts by God is a way of punishment, but it is always a consequence of their own self-hardening. In Pharaoh's case we read that he "hardened his heart" against the appeal to free the Israelites. Hardening himself, he became more confirmed in his obstinacy, till he brought the final doom upon himself: sin is made to become its own punishment. In Hebrew religious thought everything was directly attributed to God, and the hardening *is* God's work, but it is always the consequence of human action out of harmony with God's will (cf. Rom. 1:18-32, esp. vv. 21, 24, 26, 28). W. L. WALKER

HARE [Heb. *'arneḇeṯ*] (Lev. 11:6; Dt. 14:7); cf. Akk. *annabu,* Ugar. *anhb,* Arab. *'arnab.* This animal is mentioned only in the lists of unclean animals in Leviticus and Deuteronomy, where it occurs along with the camel, the coney, and the swine. The camel, the hare, and the coney are unclean "because they chew the cud but do not part the hoof, the swine, because it parts the hoof but does not chew the cud." The hare and the coney are not ruminants, but might be supposed to be from their habit of almost continuously moving their jaws. Although *'arneḇeṯ* occurs only in the two passages cited, there is no doubt that it is the hare. The LXX has Gk. *dasýpous,* "rough-footed," which, while not the commonest Greek word for the hare (*lagṓs*), refers to the remarkable fact that in hares and rabbits the soles of the feet are densely covered with hair. The commonest Arabic word for "hare," *'arnab,* is from the same root as Heb. *'arneḇeṯ*.

Hares, which are rodents of the *Leporidae* family, are closely related to the rabbit (*Lepus cuniculus*), but have longer legs and ears, besides being much swifter than the rabbit. Hares are widely distributed in the northern hemisphere, whereas in Bible times there were no rabbits in Palestine. Tristram regarded the species *Lepus syriacus,* an animal closely resembling its English counterpart in size and coloring, as native to the northern regions of Palestine, although other species also occur elsewhere in the country. A. E. DAY

R. K. H.

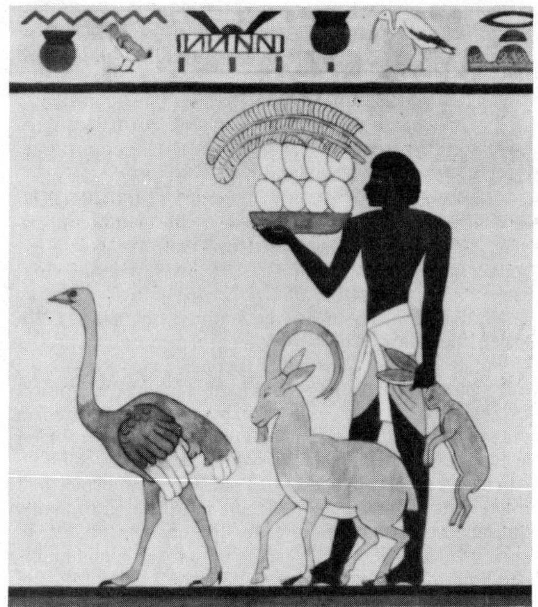

Desert creatures, including a hare, in a reconstruction of Egyptian wall paintings (Royal Ontario Museum, Toronto)

HAREM [Heb. *bêṯ hannāšîm*] (Est. 2); AV "house of the women," WOMEN'S HOUSE; NEB WOMEN'S QUARTERS. The young women chosen for Ahasuerus were taken into the women's quarters, under the care of a eunuch, to prepare for their night with the king. Having spent that night, they resided in a separate part of the harem in charge of another eunuch to await the king's command to return. Some might wait in vain. Esther was a favored one.

HAREPH hâr'əf [Heb. *ḥārēp*–'scornful']. A chief of Judah, one of the sons of Caleb and father of Beth-gader (1 Ch. 2:51).

HARETH hâr'əth [Heb. *ḥāreṯ,* in pause]. *See* HERETH.

HARHAIAH här-hā'yə [Heb. *ḥarh^{a}yâ*]. A goldsmith whose son Uzziel helped to repair the walls of Jerusalem under Zerubbabel (Neh. 3:8).

HARHAS här'has [Heb. *ḥarḥas*]. Grandfather of Shallum, husband of Huldah (2 K. 22:14). The name appears as Hasrah in the parallel passage 2 Ch. 34:22.

HAR-HERES. *See* HERES **1.**

HARHUR här'hûr [Heb. *ḥarḥûr*; Gk. *Hasour*]. One of the temple servants whose descendants came from Babylon with Zerubbabel (Ezr. 2:51; Neh. 7:53). 1 Esd. 5:31 has Asur and Pharakim in place of Harhur.

HARIM här'im [Heb. *ḥārim*]. A family name.

1. A nonpriestly family that returned from captivity with Zerubbabel (Ezr. 2:32; Neh. 7:35); mentioned among those who married foreign wives (Ezr. 10:31); also mentioned among those who renewed the covenant (Neh. 10:27 [MT 28]).

2. A priestly family returning with Zerubbabel (Ezr. 2:39; Neh. 7:42; 12:3, 15 [*see* REHUM]; 1 Esd. 5:25; AV CARME, NEB CHARME); members of this family covenanted to put away their foreign wives (Ezr. 10:21; Neh. 10:15 [MT 6]). A family of this name appears as the third of the priestly courses in the days of David and Solomon (1 Ch. 24:8).

3. In Neh. 3:11 is mentioned Malchijah, son of Harim, one of the wall-builders. Which family is here designated is uncertain. W. N. STEARNS

HARIPH hâr'if [Heb. *ḥārîp*]; NEB also HARIF. One of those who returned from exile under Zerubbabel and helped to seal the covenant under Nehemiah and Ezra (Neh. 7:24 [par. Ezr. 2:18 has "Jorah"]; 10:19 [MT 20]).

HARLOT; PLAY THE HARLOT [Heb. *zānâ, zōnâ* (Gen. 34:31; 38:15, 24; Ex. 34:15f.; etc.), *q^{e}ḏēšâ* (Gen. 38:21f.); Gk. *pórnē* (Mt. 21:31f.; Lk. 15:30; He. 11:31; Jas. 2:25; Rev. 17:1, 5, 15f.; 19:2)]; AV also WHORE, GO A WHORING, COMMIT FORNICATION, etc.; NEB COMMON WHORE, PROSTITUTE, TEMPLE-PROSTITUTE, etc.

A harlot is a woman who uses her sexual capacity either for gain or for pagan religious purposes. In contrast to the adulteress she is promiscuous and usually shows no regard for who her mate might be.

Prostitution is a very ancient practice. As early as Gen. 38 we read of it as an established custom. In the ancient world the harlot who worked for gain usually belonged to one of two classes of people. She might be a slave whose earnings as a harlot went to her masters. Baby girls were often deserted by their parents to die; these babies were frequently picked up and raised for the purpose of prostitution. On other occasions free women entered the profession. Prostitution was considered a profession, and licenses were often required from the state. Most of these women doubled as banquet musicians. If a prostitute was free she often became very rich. In ancient Greece Solon established houses of prostitution from which the state gained revenues.

The OT pictures the prostitute as having special clothing (Prov. 7:10), which probably included a veil that covered the face (Gen. 38:14f.). On occasions such women lived together in houses that might be called brothels (1 K. 3:16). They were available for hire at greatly varying prices. Prov. 6:26 says that a prostitute would make herself available for a loaf of bread, while the price Judah offered Tamar was a kid (Gen. 38:17). Joel illustrates the depth to which Israel's contempt for human life had fallen by saying that they would give a boy for a harlot's wages (Joel 3:3 [MT 4:3]). A harlot's earnings were not an acceptable offering to God (Dt. 23:18 [MT 19]).

The harlot is condemned in numerous places throughout the OT. A priest is excluded from marrying one, since he is allowed to marry only a virgin (Lev. 21:7-14). If at her marriage a young woman could not produce the tokens of her virginity, she could be stoned as a harlot (Dt. 22:21). The child of a harlot also was despised (Isa. 57:3; Hos. 2:4 [MT 6]). Because Jephthah was the son of a harlot, he was forced to withdraw from his clan and was not called to leadership until the situation was desperate (Jgs. 11:1-11).

Throughout the OT there are references to religious prostitution. Heb. *qᵉḏēšâ* comes from a root meaning "holy" (*qāḏôš*) and carries that connotation. It is the equivalent of the Gk. *hieródoulos* (lit. "temple slave"). While in the classical world these temple slaves were occasionally prostitutes, this often was not the case. Temple prostitution was a much more common practice in the Near East. The religions of this region commonly deified nature and its reproductive forces, and paid homage to these in licentious rites. The Code of Hammurabi allowed female prostitutes at any temple. The Gilgamesh Epic pictures such a woman in connection with the temple of Ishtar (cf. *ANET,* p. 75). Herodotus (i.199) says that the Babylonians compelled every native female to attend the temple of Venus once in her life and to prostitute herself in honor of the goddess. While this practice was not so widespread among the Greeks and Romans, Eryx and Corinth are known to have had vast numbers of temple prostitutes. Here they merely shared their gains with the temple with which they were connected.

When the Israelites entered the Promised Land religious prostitution was an immediate problem (Nu. 25:1). The extermination of the inhabitants of the land was commanded so that the Israelites would not fall into this practice (Ex. 34:11-16). Dt. 23:17 [MT 18] forbids cult prostitution for Israel and indicates that this was carried on by men as well as women. "Dog" in v. 18 (RSV mg. "sodomite") is usually interpreted to mean "male prostitute." In the period of the judges religious prostitution was one of the basic causes of the degradation of the people (Jgs. 2:17). They came to worship both the priestly ephod and certain Baals by means of sacred prostitution (8:27-35). Samson spent the night with a Philistine harlot (16:1). The captivity of the half-tribe of Manasseh resulted from their participation in the religious prostitution connected with the Canaanite gods (1 Ch. 5:25). The same can be said of the fall of both the northern and southern kingdoms, as the idolatrous practices they followed included such rites (Ezk. 16:16-58).

The degradation of the human being through religious prostitution becomes a figure for the spiritual infidelity that Israel and Judah show to God. The OT pictures Yahweh as the husband of Israel. For example, Israel and Judah are depicted as faithless sisters who play the harlot, being unfaithful to their beloved (see esp. Jer. 3:1-3 and Ezk. 23). The deep religious significance of such a figure is apparent when we see the close connection between idolatry and religious prostitution. To demonstrate the faithlessness of Israel, Yahweh commanded the prophet Hosea to take a wife who had been a harlot. Unable to break the habit of her former life, she became a living representation of Israel's faithlessness to Yahweh. Hosea filled the role of God, who was always willing to forgive. (*See* GOMER.)

In the NT we do not find the usual Greek word for harlot, *hetaíra.* Though this word is common in the LXX, Christian literature favors *pórnē.* Yet from the story of the Prodigal Son, who spent his inheritance on harlots (Lk. 15:30), and from the references to Rahab the harlot (He. 11:31; Jas. 2:25), we may be sure that the meaning is the same. Mt. 21:31f. shows that Jesus appealed to this class of people with His message. In this passage the harlot is pictured as a part of the lowest class of society, despised along with the tax collector. Although we cannot be sure that the woman taken in adultery (Jn. 8:1-10) belonged to this class, yet Jesus showed her forgiveness. In His statement of forgiveness, however, He commanded the woman to turn from her former ways.

Paul also joins in this condemnation of prostitution. In 1 Cor. 6:15-20 he shows that when the Christian goes to a harlot he actually becomes one flesh with such a sinful person. In a probable reference to the religious prostitution that was so rampant in Corinth, Paul says that one in whom the Holy Spirit dwells should not be joined to a prostitute. Such immorality is a sin against one's own body, which is the temple of God. The Christian should rather glorify God with his body.

In Rev. 17 an angel shows the judgment of the great harlot. In this vision a woman seated upon a great beast is called the mother of harlots. The final verse of the chapter suggests that the harlot is the city of Rome and her government which rules the world. Thus, the harlot here stands for that government which is opposed to God. She is condemned for being drunk with the blood of His saints. God is praised for destroying the one who corrupted the earth with her fornication and for avenging the blood of His saints (Rev. 19:2). In Rev. 18 the same judgment of the harlot is described in hymns. The first declares that Babylon the great (equivalent to the harlot) has fallen. The second hymn (vv. 4-8) calls for the people of God to come out from her lest they be charged with her sin. Finally, her fornication with the kings of the earth is portrayed in terms of the great wealth of the city. She is fallen, and within her is found the blood of the saints (Rev. 18:24).

Bibliography.–*EB, s.v.* (Cheyne); *ERE,* IV, *s.v.* "Hierodouloi" (G. Barton); *HDB, s.v.* (W. P. Peterson). D. W. WEAD

HARLOTRY. *See* CRIMES.

HAR-MAGEDON här-mə-ged'ən (Rev. 16:16, ASV). *See* ARMAGEDDON.

HARMON här'mən [Heb. *haharmônâ*] (Am. 4:3); AV PALACE; NEB DUNGHILL. The meaning of this hapax legomenon has been disputed from ancient times. The LXX translates it Gk. *tó óros tó Remman,* "the mountain of Remman." The Targum has Aram. *ṭûrê harmênî,* "the mountains of Armenia." The AV apparently reads Heb. *'armôn* and the NEB *hammaḏmēnâ* in its stead. Modern scholars have also suggested *ʿarummôṯ,* "naked," *ḥērem,* "devoted to destruction," and *hermônâ,* "to Hermon," the mountain N of Bashan.

HARMONY [Gk. *tó autó phroneín*] (Rom. 12:16; 15:5); AV SAME MIND, LIKE-MINDED; NEB EQUAL REGARD, AGREE; [*teleiótēs*] (Col. 3:14); AV "bond of perfection"; NEB "complete whole." Though there are several cognate forms in the NT, Paul is the only one to exhort the churches literally to "think the same thing." Only in the Roman passages does the RSV translate *tó autó phroneín* as "harmony," using "agree" in 2 Cor. 13:11 and Phil. 2:4, and "same mind" in Phil. 2:2.

"Harmony" is most closely related to Gk. *phrḗn* rather than Gk. *noús*. The Gk. *phrḗn* corresponds to the Heb. *nepeš*–'soul.' While not excluding intellectualization, *phrḗn* is broad enough in scope to include all the mental powers, though the emphasis here is on attitude. To "think the same thing" thus means to "have a similar disposition, outlook."

The idea of "living in harmony" occurs only in contexts addressed to the Church. In every case, Paul envisions full agreement as an aim, as his prayer for a congregation, not as something that has already happened. The goal of harmonious living, however, does not happen naturally among any people who desire unanimity. Harmony can be a guiding principle only in the Christian community, only "in accord with Christ Jesus" (Rom. 15:5). Harmony is not important simply as an experience in itself, but as the basis for worship. Paul challenges the Church to a healthy spirit of oneness, in order that "together you may with one voice glorify the God and Father of our Lord Jesus Christ" (Rom. 15:6).

The RSV uses the interesting phrase "perfect harmony" in Col. 3:14 for *teleiótēs* (lit. "completeness"). This passage specifies love as the golden key of harmony, its source and motivating power. It contrasts this liberating and healing harmony with the divisive self-centeredness of the non-Christian world (Col. 3:7f.; cf. Eph. 4:13). Gk. *teleiótēs* (cf. Gk. *teleióō*–'finish,' 'bring to an end') also suggests that harmony must be a supreme goal and purpose toward which the Christian community energetically aims.

See *TDNT*, VIII, *s.v.* τελέω κτλ. (Delling), esp. p. 79; IX, *s.v.* φρήν κτλ. (Bertram). C. G. CHRISTIANS

HARMONY OF THE GOSPELS. An arrangement of the material in the Gospels that takes their parallels into account. One type of harmony combines the Gospel material into a single continuous narrative. The earliest example is the *Diatessaron* of Tatian (*ca.* A.D. 175), which became the standard text of the Gospels in some churches until the 5th cent. (cf. *ODCC*, *s.v.* "Diatessaron," with bibliography). One example of the several English harmonies of this type is L. Boettner, *A Summary of the Gospels* (1933).

The much more common type of harmony, also known as a synopsis, developed from the work of Ammonius of Alexandria and Eusebius. It calls attention to the parallelisms, similarities, and differences among the Gospels without interweaving or conflating their materials, usually by printing the three "Synoptic" Gospels or all four Gospels in parallel columns. For this type of harmony *see* SYNOPSIS.

HARNEPHER här′nə-fər [Heb. *ḥarneper*]. A member of the tribe of Asher (1 Ch. 7:36).

HARNESS [Heb. *'āsar*–'bind'] (Jer. 46:4); [*rāṯam*–'bind fast'] (Mic. 1:13); AV BIND. The term "harness" is of Celtic origin, and in the AV refers to different types of armor (cf. 1 K. 22:24; 2 Ch. 9:24; 18:33; etc.). In the RSV it occurs only twice, with the meaning "saddle up," and with this sense it appears also in the NEB. R. K. H.

HAROD hä′rod [Heb. *ḥ^a^rōḏ*–'trembling'; *ḥ^a^rōḏî*–'Harodite'].

1. The location of the fountain beside which Gideon and his army were encamped (Jgs. 7:1). Smith (*HGHL*, pp. 397f.) shows how the terrain made Gideon's test of the army meaningful. There is no good reason to question the accuracy of the common view, which places this spring at ʿAin Jālûd, on the edge of the Valley of Jezreel, about 3 km. (2 mi.) E of Zerʿîn and just under the northern cliffs of Gilboa. A plentiful and beautiful spring of clear cold water rises in a rocky cave and flows out into a large pool, whence it drains off, in Nahr Jālûd, down the valley past Beisān to the Jordan. This spring may possibly be the fountain near which Saul encamped before the battle of Gilboa (1 S. 29:1).

2. The home of two of David's heroes, Shamma and Elika (thus the AV calls them Harodites). The LXX omits the second name. In 1 Ch. 11:27, the AV calls Shammoth "the Harorite"; the second is omitted. "Harorite" is a scribal error for "Harodite," ד being taken for ר. "Harodite" may be connected with the spring of Harod. R. P. DUGAN

HAROEH hə-rō′ə [Heb. *hārō'eh*–'the seer'] (1 Ch. 2:52); NEB REAIAH. A Judahite, son of Shobal. In 4:2 Shobal's son is Reaiah (Heb. *r^e'^āyâ*); probably *hārō'eh* in 2:52 should be emended to *r^e'^āyâ* (see the comms.).

HARORITE. *See* HAROD **2.**

HAROSHETH-HAGOIIM hə-rō′shəth hə-goy′əm [Heb. *ḥ^a^rōšeṯ haggôyim*] (Jgs. 4:2, 13, 16); AV HAROSHETH OF THE GENTILES; NEB HAROSHETH-OF-THE-GENTILES, HAROSHETH (Jgs. 4:16). The location (headquarters?) of Sisera, commander of the army of Jabin king of Canaan, prior to his battle with Barak. The term *ḥ^a^rōšeṯ* may be related to *ḥōreš*, "wooded height" (*pace* BDB, p. 361); *gôyim*, ostensibly the word for "nations," may be an entirely unrelated name (cf. Josh. 12:23, "king of Goiim in Galilee" [RSV, emending "Gilgal" to agree with the LXX]; Gen. 14:1, "Tidal king of Goiim"). If so, "Galilee of the Goiim" could be an earlier term that came to be understood later as "Galilee of the nations" (*see* GALILEE). Attempts to identify Harosheth-hagoiim with sites either in Galilee or in the Sharon plain are not convincing, but the general location near the scene of the battle by the Kishon is beyond question. Aharoni considers Harosheth-hagoiim "not a place name at all," preferring to regard it as the forest regions of Galilee (*LBHG*, p. 201). The name appears to be preserved in the Arabic village of *el-Ḥarithiyeh* (*GP*, II, 343f.), but excavations of nearby Tell ʿAmr (proposed by Albright, *JPOS*, 2 [1922], pp. 284ff.) indicate that it was not occupied until the 10th cent. B.C. Against Aharoni's suggestion, and the similar one of B. Maisler (Mazar) that the term applied to all of Galilee above the Valley of Esdraelon (*HUCA*, 24 [1952-53], 80f.), is the clear indication in Jgs. 4:2 that Sisera was located (lit. "was dwelling/sitting") at a specific place called Harosheth-hagoiim.

See *GTTOT*, § 548. W. S. L. S.

HARP [Heb. *nēḇel, neḇel, k^e^lî-neḇel, kinnôr*; Aram. *p^e^santērîn* < Gk. *psaltḗrion*; Gk. *kithára*]; AV also PSALTERY, VIOL; NEB also DULCIMER, LUTE, LYRE. *See* MUSIC.

HARPOON [Heb. *śukkâ*] (Job 41:7 [MT 40:31]); AV BARBED IRON. Both harpoons and fishing spears are of little use in catching Leviathan. Other methods of FISHING were by hook and line (Job 41:1 [MT 40:25]) and by net (Eccl. 9:12).

HARROW [Heb. *śāḏaḏ*] (Job 39:10; Isa. 28:24; Hos. 10:11); AV also "break (his) clods." The term generally means to break up and smooth the soil, but it is not known whether the process corresponds to what is involved in modern agriculture. The reasons for this uncertainty are: (1) the ancient Egyptians have left no records of the practice; (2) even before mechanization was introduced into Palestinian agriculture, it was not too common for harrowing to be performed, though on occasions the ground was leveled after plowing with the threshing-sledge or a log drawn by oxen. Cross-plowing was utilized for breaking up the lumpy soil (cf. the "clods" of Hos. 10:11, AV), particularly at the end of a long, dry summer. The verb *śāḏaḏ* could also refer to the plowing of border furrows, though this is doubtful. Equally uncertain is the view that "harrowing" refers to the dragging of branches over the soil to cover the seed, since the seed was normally sown before plowing. *See* AGRICULTURE III.A.1.

J. A. PATCH R. K. H.

HARROWS [Heb. *ḥārîṣ*] (AV 2 S. 12:31; 1 Ch. 20:3). *See* PICKS.

HARSHA här'shə [Heb. *ḥaršā'*]. Head of one of the families of the temple servants (Ezr. 2:52; Neh. 7:54); 1 Esd. 5:32, "Charea."

HART. *See* DEER.

HARUM här'əm [Heb. *ḥārûm*]. A Judahite (1 Ch. 4:8).

HARUMAPH hə-ro͞o'maf [Heb. *ḥ*ᵃ*rûmap*] (Neh. 3:10). Father of Jedaiah, who assisted in repairing the walls of Jerusalem under Nehemiah.

HARUPHITE hə-ro͞o'fīt [Heb. *K ḥ*ᵃ*rîpî, Q ḥ*ᵃ*rûpî*]. In 1 Ch. 12:5 (MT 6) Shephatiah, one of the companions of David, is called a Haruphite. If the *K* be the correct reading, it is connected with HARIPH or perhaps HAREPH.

HARUZ här'əz [Heb. *ḥārûṣ*]. Father of Meshullemeth, the mother of Amon king of Judah (2 K. 21:19).

HARVEST [Heb. *qāṣîr*]; NEB also CROP (Lev. 19:9; Isa. 17:11), VINTAGE (Isa. 18:5); [*m*ᵉ*lē'â*] (Ex. 22:29 [MT 28]); AV "ripe fruits"; [*p*ᵉ*rî*] (Dt. 26:2); AV FRUIT; NEB PRODUCE; [*'ōsep*] (Isa. 32:10); AV GATHERING; NEB PRODUCE; [*t*ᵉ*ḇû'â*] (Gen. 47:24; Jer. 2:3; 12:13); AV INCREASE, REVENUE; NEB also CROP; [Gk. *therismós*]; NEB also CROP; [*karpós*] (Rom. 1:13; Jas. 3:18); AV FRUIT; NEB also "(achieving) something"; [*génnēma*] (2 Cor. 9:10); AV FRUIT. For the Hebrew people — and indeed for any people engaged in agriculture — harvest was a most important season (Gen. 8:22; 45:6; *see* CALENDAR II.B.1 for a discussion of the Gezer Calendar, a tenth-century B.C. text that mentions three harvests). Events were reckoned from harvests (Gen. 30:14; Josh. 3:15; Jgs. 15:1; Ruth 1:22; 2:23; 1 S. 6:13; 2 S. 21:9; 23:13). Harvest time came to be the occasion for festivals and rejoicings on the part of all the people (Ex. 34:22; Isa. 9:3 [MT 2]). Harvest was more than a merely material and self-centered order, for from early times it was associated with requirements with respect to God and mankind. On the one hand the first fruits of the harvest must be offered to Yahweh (Ex. 22:29; Lev. 23:10); and on the other hand the harvester must leave a corner of his field without harvesting it, setting it aside for the poor person and the stranger (Lev. 19:9; 23:22; Dt. 24:19).

The three principal feasts of the Jews corresponded to the three harvest seasons (Ex. 23:16; 34:21f.): (1) the Feast of the Passover in April at the time of the barley harvest (cf. Ruth 1:22); (2) the Feast of Pentecost seven weeks later at the wheat harvest (Ex. 34:22); and (3) the Feast of Tabernacles at the end of the year (October) during the fruit harvest (Lev. 23:24). Olives were harvested from the middle of September to the middle of November by beating the trees with long sticks (Dt. 24:20; Isa. 17:6). Flax was harvested in March and April by cutting it off near the ground and then laying the stalks out to dry (Josh. 2:6).

There has been little change in the seasons since biblical days. Between the reaping of the barley in April and the wheat in June, most of the cereals are harvested. The grapes begin to ripen in August, but the gathering-in for making wine and molasses and the storing of the dried figs and raisins are at the end of September. Between the barley harvest and the wheat harvest only a few showers fall. They are welcomed because they increase the yield of wheat (cf. Am. 4:7). Samuel made use of the unusual occurrence of rain during the wheat harvest to strike fear into the hearts of the people (1 S. 12:17). From the wheat harvest until the fruit harvest no rain falls (2 S. 21:10; Jer. 5:24; cf. Prov. 26:1). The harvesters long for cool weather during the reaping season (cf. Prov. 25:13).

A sickle was used to cut the grain (Joel 3:13 [MT 4:13]; Dt. 16:9; Mk. 4:29), or it was pulled up by the roots. The latter method was practiced in both Palestine and Egypt. However, excavations have revealed evidence that the use of the sickle goes back to very early times. The grain stalks were usually cut about a foot beneath the head, and in some cases even higher (Job 24:24). The reaper grasped them in handfuls (Ruth 2:16), reaped them with his arm (Isa. 11:5), and laid them behind him. The binder then followed gathering them, as Ps. 129:7 says, into "his bosom." Then they were tied with straw into sheaves (Gen. 37:7) and set in heaps (Rev. 2:7).

A number of definite laws were instituted regarding the harvest. GLEANING was forbidden (Lev. 19:9; 23:22; Dt. 24:19). The children of Israel were enjoined to reap no harvest for which they had not labored (Lev. 25:5). The law that required the first fruits to be presented to Yahweh (Lev. 23:10) has continued through the centuries, and Christians in Syria who own vineyards bring their first bunches of grapes to the church.

The figurative use of harvest occurs frequently in Scripture. A destroyed harvest typified devastation or affliction (Job 5:5; Isa. 16:9; 17:11; Jer. 5:17; 50:16). The "time of harvest" frequently meant the day of destruction (Jer. 51:33; Hos. 6:11; Joel 3:13). "Joy in harvest" typified great joy (Isa. 9:3) and "harvest of the Nile" meant an abundant harvest (Isa. 23:3). "The harvest is past" meant that the appointed time was gone (Jer. 8:20). Yahweh chose the most promising time to cut off the wicked, namely, "when there is a cloud of dew in the heat of harvest" (Isa. 18:4f.). This occurrence of hot misty days just before the ripening of the grapes is still common and is welcomed because it hastens the harvest. In Proverbs the harvesting of the ant is mentioned as a lesson for the sluggard (6:8; 10:5; 20:4).

In the Gospels Jesus frequently refers to the harvest of souls (Mt. 9:37; 13:30; Mk. 4:29; Jn. 4:35). In explaining the parable of the tares Jesus spoke figuratively of the harvest as the end of the world (Mt. 13:39; cf. Rev. 14:15). Here the law of correspondence between sowing and reaping finds its perfect expression. The fruits of our actions will reach their full maturity only in the day when God Himself shall reap them. The task of separating the wheat from the tares is not entrusted to God's servants but to the divine harvesters (Mt. 13:30). So the time of harvest is in God's hands, but to mankind is committed the time of sowing, and the harvest is determined by what is sown. "For he who sows to his own flesh will from the flesh reap corruption; but he who sows to the Spirit will from the Spirit reap eternal life" (Gal. 6:8).

See also AGRICULTURE.

J. A. PATCH
L. HUNT

Various stages of the harvest: threshing and separating the grain from the straw (top); measuring the grain (center); carrying away the grain and picking flax (bottom, right to left). Mural from the tomb of Nakht at Thebes (15th cent. B.C.) (Service des musées, Cairo; picture Lehnert and Landrock)

HASADIAH has-ə-dī'ə [Heb. *ḥ^{a}sadyâ*–'Yahweh is kind']. A son of Zerubbabel (1 Ch. 3:20). In Bar. 1:1 the Greek is *Asadias*.

HASENUAH has-ə-nū'ə [Heb. *hass^{e}nu'â*]. The AV in 1 Ch. 9:7 for HASSENUAH.

HASHABIAH hash-ə-bī'ə [Heb. *ḥ^{a}šaḇyâ*].

1. Two Levites of the family of Merari (1 Ch. 6:45; 9:14).

2. A Levite who dwelt in Jerusalem at the time of Nehemiah (Neh. 11:15).

3. A son of Jeduthun (1 Ch. 25:3).

4. A Hebronite, chief of a clan of warriors who had charge of West Jordan in the interests of Yahweh and the king of Israel (1 Ch. 26:30).

5. A Levite who was a "ruler" (1 Ch. 27:17).

6. One of the Levite chiefs in the time of Josiah, who gave liberally toward the sacrifices (2 Ch. 35:9). In 1 Esd. 1:9, the AV has "Assabias," the NEB "Sabias."

7. A Levite whom Ezra induced to return from exile with him (Ezr. 8:19). The AV in 1 Esd. 8:48 has "Asebia," NEB "Asebias."

8. One of the twelve priests set apart by Ezra to take care of the gold, the silver, and the vessels of the temple on their return from exile (Ezr. 8:24). In 1 Esd. 8:54 the AV has "Assanias," the NEB "Asamias."

9. Ruler of half of the district of "Keilah," who helped to repair the walls under Nehemiah (Neh. 3:17), and also helped to seal the covenant (Neh. 10:11 [MT 12]; 12:24).

10. A Levite (Neh. 11:22).

11. A priest (Neh. 12:21). J. J. REEVE

HASHABNAH hə-shab'nə [Heb. *ḥ^ašaḇnâ*]. One who helped to seal the covenant under Nehemiah (Neh. 10:25 [MT 26]).

HASHABNEIAH hash-ab-nə-ī'ə [Heb. *ḥ^ašaḇn^eyâ*]; AV, NEB, HASHABNIAH.

1. Father of one of the builders of the wall (Neh. 3:10).

2. A Levite mentioned in connection with the prayer preceding the signing of the covenant (Neh. 9:5); possibly identical with HASHABIAH **7, 8, 9,** or **10.**

HASH-BADDANAH hash-bə-dā'nə [Heb. *ḥašbaddanâ*]; AV HASHBADANA. Probably a Levite. He was one of those who stood at Ezra's left hand when he read the law, and helped the people to understand the meaning (Neh. 8:4). 1 Esd. 9:44 has "Nabariah" (Gk. *Nabareías*; AV, NEB, NABARIAS).

HASHEM hā'shem [Heb. *hāšēm*] (1 Ch. 11:34). A Gizonite, one of David's thirty heroes. The AV and the RSV in the par. passage, 2 S. 23:32, have "sons of JASHEN."

HASHMONAH hash'mō-nə [Heb. *ḥašmōnâ*–'fatness'). A desert camp of the Israelites between Mithkah and Moseroth (Nu. 33:29f.). *See* WANDERINGS OF ISRAEL.

HASHUB hash'əb. *See* HASSHUB.

HASHUBAH hə-sho͞o'bə [Heb. *ḥ^ašuḇâ*–'consideration(?)']. One of the sons of Zerubbabel (1 Ch. 3:20).

HASHUM hā'shəm [Heb. *ḥāšum*].

1. In Ezr. 2:19; Neh. 7:22, "sons of Hashum" are mentioned among the returning exiles. In Ezr. 10:33 (also 1 Esd. 9:33; AV, NEB, ASOM), members of the same family are named among those who married foreign wives.

2. One of those who stood on Ezra's left at the reading of the law (Neh. 8:4; 1 Esd. 9:44, "Lothasubus"). The signer of the covenant (Neh. 10:18 [MT 19]) is possibly the same.

HASIDEANS has'ə-dē'ənz; **HASIDIM** has-ə-dēm' [Heb. *ḥ^asîḏîm*; Gk. *hasidaíoi*]; AV ASSIDEANS. The Hebrew term is a masculine plural of *ḥāsîḏ*; it frequently means "pious" in the OT and is usually translated "SAINTS" (cf. 2 Ch. 6:41; Ps. 30:4 [MT 5]; 31:23 [MT 24]; 37:28; 50:5; etc.). The Greek term, a transliteration of the Hebrew, is never used in canonical Scripture, though it is used in the Apocrypha (1 Macc. 2:42; 7:13; 2 Macc. 14:6). The Hasideans were pious Jews who staunchly defended the law against the encroachments of Hellenism.

Although they are not mentioned before the Maccabean struggle, it seems that the Hasideans were already in existence. Soon after the Maccabees revolted against Antiochus IV Epiphanes' demands that the Jews give up their ancestral worship of Yahweh, "there united with them a company of Hasideans, mighty warriors of Israel, every one who offered himself willingly for the law" (1 Macc. 2:42). After the death of Mattathias, the Hasideans recognized the leadership of Judas Maccabeus (son of Mattathias) and fought with him against the Hellenistic intrusion into the Jews' worship of God. The Maccabees fought and won many difficult battles against Antiochus Epiphanes' forces. In 163 B.C., however, the Syrian forces had laid siege to Jerusalem. Judas Maccabeus was in a desperate situation because of a food shortage due to a Sabbatical Year. Fortunately, because of internal problems due to Antiochus's death, the Syrians were anxious to make a peace treaty with Judas and guaranteed the Jews religious freedom (1 Macc. 6:28-63).

Having achieved religious freedom, Judas also wanted to gain political freedom. The Hasideans did not agree with Judas in this. In fact, in 161 B.C., when Alcimus was selected as high priest by the Syrians and came to Jerusalem with General Bacchides, the Hasideans sought to establish peace with Alcimus and Bacchides and thus split from Judas's ranks. Although the reason for this move is not given, it is probable that the Hasideans were satisfied that Alcimus was from the Aaronic line and that the Syrians had guaranteed them freedom of worship. Alcimus, however, who had promised no harm to the Hasideans, seized and slew sixty of them. Hence, they turned against him and returned to Judas (1 Macc. 7:10-18; Josephus *Ant.* xii.10.2 [393-97]). Alcimus asked the Syrians for more military help against Judas and the Hasideans, who were causing trouble and thus preventing tranquillity in the kingdom (2 Macc. 14:6).

After this, nothing is explicitly heard of them. It is thought by most scholars that they were the forerunners of the Pharisees and the Essenes.

Bibliography.–S. Tedesche and S. Zeitlin, *First Book of Maccabees* (1950); *Second Book of Maccabees* (1954); J. C. Dancy, *Comm. on I Maccabees* (1954); V. Tcherikover, *Hellenistic Civilization and the Jews* (Eng. tr. 1959); D. S. Russell, *The Jew from Alexander to Herod* (1967); F. F. Bruce, *New Testament History* (1969), pp. 69-73; J. R. Bartlett, *First and Second Books of the Maccabees* (1973); M. Hengel, *Judaism and Hellenism* (Eng. tr. 1974).

H. W. HOEHNER

HASIDIM has-ə-dēm'. *See* HASIDEANS; SAINTS.

HASMONEANS haz'mə-nē'ənz [Gk. *Asamomaios*; Heb. *ḥašmônay*]. In the broader sense the term Hasmonean refers to the whole "Maccabean" family (*see* MACCABEES). According to Josephus (*Ant.* xii.6.1 [265]), Mattathias, the first of the family to revolt against Antiochus IV's demands, was the great-grandson of Hashman. This name may have derived from the Heb. *ḥašmān*, perhaps meaning "fruitfulness," "wealthy." Hashman was a priest of the family of Joarib (cf. 1 Macc. 2:1; 1 Ch. 24:7). The narrower sense of the term Hasmonean has reference to the time of Israel's independence beginning with Simon, Mattathias's last surviving son, who in 142 B.C. gained independence from the Syrian control, and ending with Simon's great-grandson Hyrcanus II, who submitted to the Roman general Pompey in 63 B.C. Remnants of the Hasmoneans continued until A.D. 100.

I. Revolt of the Maccabees
II. Rule of the Hasmoneans
  A. Simon (143-135 B.C.)
  B. John Hyrcanus (135-104 B.C.)
  C. Aristobulus I (104-103 B.C.)
  D. Alexander Janneus (103-76 B.C.)
  E. Salome Alexandra (76-67 B.C.)
  F. Aristobulus II (67-63 B.C.)
III. Demise of the Hasmoneans
  A. Hyrcanus II (63-40 B.C.)
  B. Antigonus (40-37 B.C.)
  C. Mariamne and Her Sons (37-7 B.C.)

I. Revolt of the Maccabees.–The Hasmonean name does not occur in the books of Maccabees, but appears in Josephus several times (*Ant.* xi.4.8 [111]; xii.6.1 [265]; xiv.16.4 [490f.]; xv.11.4 [403]; xvl.7.1 [187]; xvii.7.3 [162]; xx.8.11 [190]; 10.3 [238]; 10.5 [247, 249]; *BJ* i.7 [19]; 1.3 [36]; *Vita* 1 [2, 4]) and once in the Mishnah (*Middoth* i.6). These references include the whole Maccabean family beginning with Mattathias. In 166 B.C. Mattathias, the aged priest in Modein, refused to obey the order of Antiochus IV's envoy to sacrifice to the heathen gods, and instead slew the envoy and a Jew who was about to comply. He then destroyed the altar and proclaimed, "Let every one who is zealous for the law and supports the covenant come out with me" (1 Macc. 2:15-27; *Ant.* xii.6.1-2 [265-272]; Dnl. 11:32-35). Mattathias and his five sons fled to the mountains. This marked the beginning of the Maccabean revolt. They waged war against the Jews who complied with Antiochus, tore down heathen altars, circumcised children who had been left uncircumcised, and exhorted all Jews to follow in their struggle. Mattathias died (166 B.C.) and left the crusade in the hands of his third son Judas, with whom a new era of fighting commenced (1 Macc. 2:42-70; *Ant.* xii.6.2-4 [273-286]).

Judas was very able and at Emmaus defeated the three generals sent by the Syrian regent Lysias and at Beth-zur defeated Lysias himself (1 Macc. 4:1-35; *Ant.* xii.7.4f. [305-315]). Judas had regained the entire country and this allowed him to restore the worship in the temple in Jerusalem. On Chislev 25 (14 December, 164 B.C.), exactly three years after its desecration, the temple with its altar was rededicated and the daily sacrifices were reinstituted (1 Macc. 4:36-59; 2 Macc. 10:1-8; *Ant.* xii.7.6f. [316-326]). This marked the commencement of the Jewish Feast of Dedication or Lights (Heb. *ḥ^{a}nûkkâ*).

Judas continued to fight Lysias. Finally in 163 B.C. Lysias had laid siege to Jerusalem. Because of adverse situations on both sides, Lysias and Judas made peace and guaranteed religious freedom for the Jews (1 Macc. 6:28-63). But Judas also wanted to have political freedom and continued in this struggle until his death at Eleasa in 160 B.C. (1 Macc. 7:14–9:22; *Ant.* xii.9.7–11.2 [384-434]). This brought disarray to Maccabean forces and the Hellenists were temporarily in control under the leadership of the Syrian general Bacchides.

Judas's brother Jonathan (fifth son of Mattathias) continued the guerilla warfare against Hellenism. In 157 B.C. Jonathan's defeat of Bacchides at Beth-basi (10 km. [6 mi.] S of Jerusalem) resulted in a peace treaty, and Bacchides returned to Antioch. This weakened the Hellenists and because of the internal struggles of Syria Jonathan gained strength for the next five years (1 Macc. 9:23-73; *Ant.* xiii.1.1-6 [1-34]). In 152 B.C. Syria had further internal struggles when Alexander Balas, who claimed to be the son of Antiochus IV, challenged the Seleucidian king Demetrius I. In 150 B.C. Alexander Balas won and made Jonathan a general, governor, and high priest of Judah (the king of Syria selected the high priest but none had been chosen since the death of Alcimus in May, 159 B.C.) and considered Jonathan one of his chief friends (1 Macc. 10:22-66; *Ant.* xiii.2.3f. [46-61]; 4.1f. [80-85]). This was a strange combination: Alexander Balas, professed son of Antiochus Epiphanes, was in league with a Maccabean! Alexander Balas's rule was challenged by Demetrius's son, Demetrius II Nicator, in 147 B.C. and Balas was

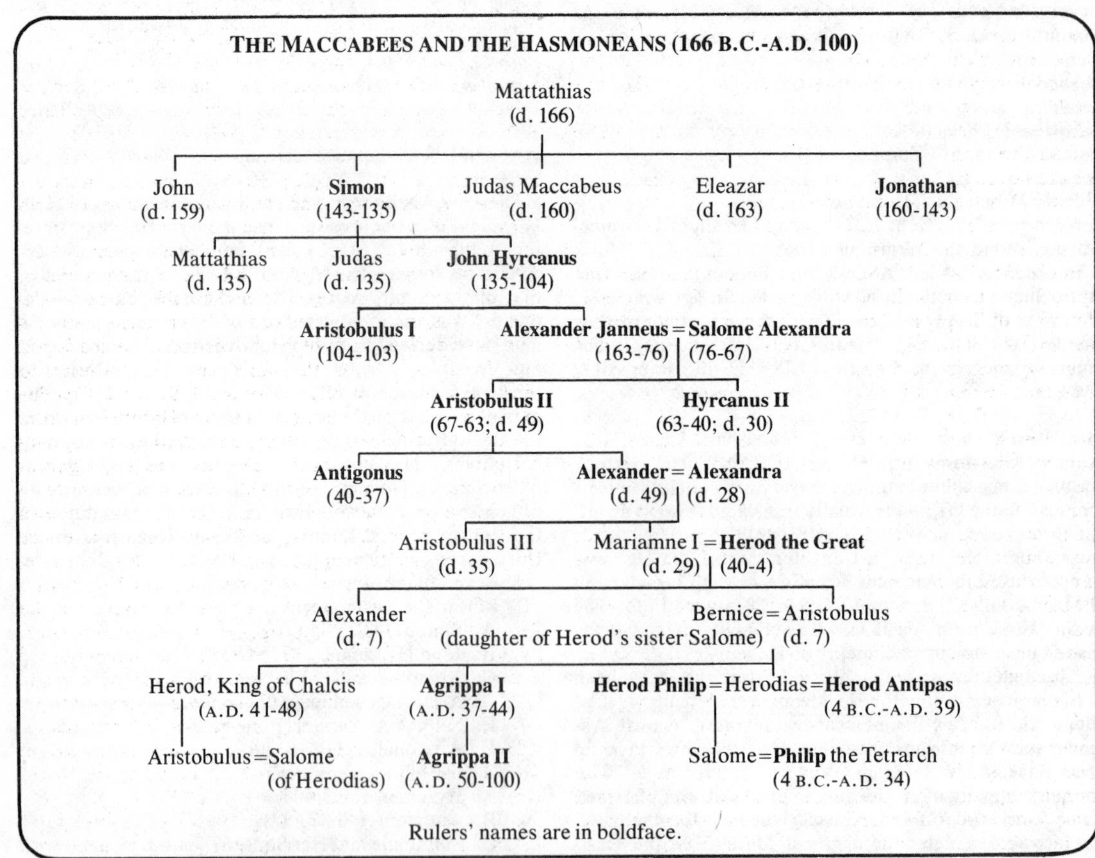

finally defeated in 145 B.C. Demetrius II confirmed Jonathan's high priesthood and gave Jonathan the three districts of southern Samaria that he had requested. In 143 B.C. Demetrius II's army rebelled, and Diodotus Tryphon (a general of Alexander Balas) claimed the Syrian throne for Alexander Balas's son, Antiochus VI. Jonathan took advantage of the situation and sided with Tryphon, who in turn made Jonathan head of the civil and religious affairs and his brother Simon head of the military. Tryphon, however, fearful of Jonathan's success, deceived him, arranged a meeting with him, and subsequently killed him (1 Macc. 10:67–13:30; *Ant.* xiii.4.3–6.6 [86-212]).

II. Rule of the Hasmoneans.–A new phase of the Maccabean rule had emerged. Although the term "Hasmonean" is sometimes applied to the whole of the Maccabean family, it is more strictly applied to the high-priestly house, from the time of Simon to 63 B.C. The reason for this is that the Maccabean dream had finally come true, namely, that the Israelites had become politically and religiously an independent nation.

Judas had already achieved religious freedom, and Jonathan had become both the religious leader, by being appointed high priest, and the political leader, by becoming the sole ruler over Judea and by ousting the Hellenistic elements. Simon attempted and achieved complete independence from the Seleucid rule. This independence endured until Rome's intervention in 63 B.C.

A. Simon (143-135 B.C). Simon, the second oldest son of Mattathias, succeeded his younger brother Jonathan. There was a great upheaval in Syria because Tryphon killed Antiochus VI and reigned in his stead as a rival to Demetrius II (1 Macc. 13:31f.; *Ant.* xiii.7.1 [218-222]; Diodorus xxxiii.28.1; Livy *Epit.* lv; Appian *Syr.* 68; Justinus xxxvi.1.7). Because of the dastardly act of Tryphon against Simon's brother, Simon naturally attached himself to Demetrius II on the condition of Judea's complete independence. Since Demetrius II no longer controlled the southern parts of the Syrian empire, he extended to Simon complete exemption from past and future taxation. The significance of this is that the gentile yoke over Israel had been removed for the first time since the Babylonian Captivity, and Judea's political independence meant that they could write their own documents and treaties. This was in 142 B.C. (1 Macc. 13:33-42; *Ant.* xiii.6.7 [213f.]).

In order to insure the security of the new independent state, Simon took two actions. First, because of the possible threat of Tryphon, Demetrius II's rival, Simon seized the fortress of Gazara (Gezer) between Jerusalem and Joppa, expelling the Gentiles and replacing them with Jews, and appointed his son John Hyrcanus as governor (1 Macc. 13:43-48, 53; 16:1, 21; *Ant.* xiii.6.7 [213-17]). Second, Simon shortly afterward captured the fortress of Acra in Jerusalem. Acra had never been in the hands of the Maccabeans but had been in the control of the hellenizers for more than forty years, serving as a reminder of the Syrian control. With the last vestige of Syrian control overthrown, the Acra was purified on the twenty-third day of the second month in 141 B.C. (3 June, 141 B.C.) (1 Macc. 13:49-52; *Ant.* xiii.6.7 [215-17]). Like his brothers Judas (1 Macc. 8:17) and Jonathan (1 Macc. 12:1), Simon made a peace treaty with Rome and Sparta, who guaranteed the freedom of worship.

In commemoration of Simon's achievement, in 140 B.C. (Sept. 13) the Jews conferred upon him the position of leader and high priest forever until a faithful prophet should arise (1 Macc. 14:25-40, esp. v. 41). The high priesthood formerly belonged to the house of Onias but this had come to an end in 174 B.C. The Syrian kings had selected the intervening high priests, namely, Menelaus, Alcimus, and Jonathan. But now the Jews appointed Simon and his descendants as successors of the high priesthood. This marked the beginning of the Hasmonean dynasty, in that Simon and his successors had both the priestly and political power vested in their persons, and thus had far greater power than the political power of Judas and Jonathan or the religious power of the family of Onias.

In 139 B.C. Demetrius II was captured by the Parthians. In Demetrius II's place his brother Antiochus VII Sidetes took up the struggle against Tryphon. He invited Simon's help in his struggle against Tryphon by confirming to him all the rights and privileges already granted to him with the additional right to strike his own coins. Simon, however, refused the invitation. When Tryphon finally fled and committed suicide, Antiochus VII turned his attention to Simon. He accused Simon of unlawful expansion and demanded the surrender of Joppa, Gazara, and the Acra in Jerusalem along with tribute he received from the captured cities outside of Judea. If Simon refused these demands, he could pay an indemnity of one thousand talents. Simon refused to comply because he insisted that all these territories were rightly a part of Judea. Antiochus VII sent his general, Cendebeus, but was defeated by Simon's two sons, Judas and John Hyrcanus (1 Macc. 15:1-14, 25–16:10; *Ant.* xiii.7.2f. [223-27]; *BJ* i.2.2 [50-53]). This brought peace to Judea.

Finally, in 135 B.C. Simon and his two sons, Mattathias and Judas, were slain at a banquet near Jericho by his son-in-law Ptolemy, who had been appointed governor over the plain of Jericho but had ambitions for greater power. Ptolemy sent men to kill Simon's second son, John Hyrcanus, at his residence in Gazara (where, also, he was the military governor). John, however, being warned of their coming, captured and killed them. John Hyrcanus went to Jerusalem and was well received (1 Macc. 16:11-23; *Ant.* xiii.7.4–8.1 [228-235]; *BJ* i.2.3f. [54-60]).

Simon's rule of eight years (*Ant.* xiii.7.4 [228]) had accomplished much for the Jews. He brought independence both politically and religiously. He had extended the boundaries of the nation, gained control over the land, and brought peace to the people whereby "each man sat under his vine and his fig tree, and there was none to make them afraid" (1 Macc. 14:4-15).

B. John Hyrcanus (135-104 B.C.). John Hyrcanus succeeded his father as high priest and ruler of the people. In the first year of his reign he had trouble because Antiochus VII, who had failed to take over Judea under Simon, asserted his claim of ruler over Judea, seized Joppa and Gazara, ravaged the land, and finally besieged Jerusalem for more than a year. With food supplies dwindling, Hyrcanus asked for a seven-day truce in order to celebrate the Feast of Tabernacles. Antiochus not only complied but also sent gifts to help them in their celebration. This action indicated Antiochus's willingness to negotiate a peace settlement. The result was that the Jews had to hand over their arms; pay heavy tribute for capture and possession of Joppa and other cities bordering on Judea; and give hostages, one of whom was Hyrcanus's brother. The walls of Jerusalem were destroyed, but the Syrians could not establish a garrison in Jerusalem (*Ant.* xiii.7.4–8.3 [228-248]; *BJ* i.2.5 [61]). The independence won by Jonathan and Simon was destroyed by a single blow, though only because Syria could concentrate its efforts. In 130 B.C., however, Antiochus VII became involved in a campaign against the Parthians that resulted in his death in 129 B.C. Demetrius II, released by the Parthians, again gained control of Syria (129-125 B.C.), but because of the troubles within Syria Demetrius II was unable to bother Hyrcanus. Hyrcanus renewed the alliance with

The Hasmonean palace, originally built by Hyrcanus I; part of M. Avi-Yonah's Jerusalem Temple Model (W. S. LaSor)

Rome whereby Rome confirmed his independence and warned Syria against any incursion into Hyrcanus's territory. Also, Hyrcanus's payment of indemnity for Joppa and other cities ceased. The long struggle between the Hasmoneans and the Seleucids came to an end (*Ant.* xiii.9.2 [259-266]). Hyrcanus took advantage of the situation and extended his borders to the east by conquering Medeba in Transjordan, to the north by capturing Shechem and Mt. Gerizim and by destroying the Samaritan temple at Mt. Gerizim (128 B.C.), and to the south by taking over the Idumean cities of Adora and Marisa, where he forced the Idumeans to be circumcised and to obey the Jewish law or emigrate (*Ant.* xiii.8.4–9.1 [249-258]; *BJ* i.2.6f. [62-66]). Later in 109 B.C. Hyrcanus and his sons conquered Samaria and thus were able to occupy the Esdraelon Valley all the way up to Mt. Carmel (*Ant.* xiii.10.2f. [275-283]; *BJ* i.2.7 [64-66]). Hyrcanus's independence was further demonstrated by the minting of coins bearing his own name, an unprecedented action for a Jewish king (110/109 B.C.).

With Hyrcanus's successes came a rift between him and the Pharisees. Although the origins of the Pharisees and the Sadducees are somewhat obscure, they were well established and influential by the time of Hyrcanus's reign. The Pharisees, who were descendants of the Hasideans, were somewhat indifferent to the political success of the Hasmoneans and felt that the high priesthood had become worldly by hellenization and secularization. Hence they questioned whether Hyrcanus should be the high priest. The Sadducees, however, a party of mostly wealthy priestly aristocracy, were antagonistic toward the Pharisees and sided with Hyrcanus. Consequently, Hyrcanus joined in with the Sadducees. This indicates both the thinking of the Sadducees and the decline of the office of the high priest (*Ant.* xiii.10.5f. [288-296]; T.B. *Berakhoth* 29a).

After thirty-one years of rule Hyrcanus died peacefully (104 B.C.), leaving five sons (*Ant.* xiii.10.7 [299f.]; *BJ* i.2.8 [67-69]).

C. Aristobulus I (104-103 B.C.). Hyrcanus desired that his wife would head the civil government while his oldest son Aristobulus I would be the high priest. Displeased with this, Aristobulus imprisoned all his brothers except Antigonus, who shared in ruling until Aristobulus became suspicious and had him killed. Aristobulus's rule lasted only a year, but he was able to conquer Galilee, whose inhabitants he compelled to be circumcised. Aristobulus died of a severe illness (*Ant.* xiii.11.1-3 [301-319]; *BJ* i.3.1-6 [70-84]).

D. Alexander Janneus (103-76 B.C.). On the death of Aristobulus, his wife Salome Alexandra released his three brothers, one of whom was Alexander Janneus, from prison. She appointed him as king and high priest and subsequently married him, though he was thirteen years her junior (*Ant.* xiii.12.1 [320-24]; *BJ* i.4.1 [85]). This marriage was against the law, for the high priest was to marry only a virgin (Lev. 21:13f.). Alexander Janneus endeavored to follow in the footsteps of his father and brother in territorial expansion. He captured the coastal Greek cities from Carmel to Gaza (except Ascalon), compelling the inhabitants to follow the Jewish law. He was successful in his conquests in Transjordan and the south, so that the size of his kingdom was equal to that of David and Solomon (*Ant.* xiii.12.2–13.4 [324-371]; *BJ* i.4.2 [86f.]).

There were, however, real conflicts within his domain. The Pharisees saw that the Hasmoneans were deviating more from their ideals, for Alexander Janneus was a drunkard who loved war and was allied with the Sadducees. Tension came to a head at a celebration of the Feast of Tabernacles when Alexander Janneus poured the water libation over his feet instead of on the altar as prescribed by the Pharisaic ritual. The people, enraged, shouted and pelted him with lemons. Alexander ordered his mercenary troop to attack, and six thousand Jews were massacred (*Ant.* xiii.13.5 [372-74]; *BJ* i.4.3 [88f.]; T.B. *Sukkah* 48b). This act brought great bitterness, and the people awaited an opportunity for revenge.

The time came in 94 B.C. when Alexander Janneus attacked Obedas king of the Arabs, but suffered a severe defeat and barely escaped with his life. Upon his return to Jerusalem the people turned against him; with the help of foreign mercenaries Alexander Janneus fought six years against his people, slaying no less than fifty thousand Jews. The Pharisees finally in 88 B.C. called upon the Seleucid Demetrius III Eukairos to help them. Wars bring strange allies, for the descendants of the Hasideans asked the descendants of Antiochus Epiphanes to aid them in their fight against the descendants of the Maccabees! Alexander Janneus was defeated at Shechem and fled to the mountains. Six thousand Jews, however, realizing that their national existence was threatened, sided with Alexander Janneus because they felt it the lesser of two evils to side with him in a free Jewish state than to be annexed to the Syrian empire. But when Alexander Janneus reestablished himself, he forced Demetrius to withdraw, and he ordered eight hundred Pharisees to be crucified and their wives and children to be killed before their eyes while he was feasting and carousing with his concubines. Because of these atrocities eight thousand Jews fled the country (*Ant.* xiii.13.5–14.2 [375-383]; *BJ* i.4.4-6 [90-98]).

After this there were upheavals in the Seleucid empire that affected Alexander Janneus. The Nabateans were becoming strong and opposed a Seleucid rule. Around 85 B.C. the Nabatean king Aretas invaded Judea, and Alexander Janneus retreated to Adida (32 km. [20 mi.] NW of Jerusalem), but Aretas withdrew after coming to terms with Janneus. From 83 to 80 B.C. he was successful in his campaign in the east, conquering Pella, Dium, Gerasa, Gaulana, Seleucia, and Gamala. The last three years of his life (79-76 B.C.) he contracted an illness due to his overdrinking, and when he died he was buried with great pomp (*Ant.* xiii.14.3–16.1 [384-406]; *BJ* i.4.7f. [99-106]).

E. Salome Alexandra (76-67 B.C.). On his deathbed, Alexander Janneus appointed his wife, Salome Alexandra, as his successor. Because the Law barred a woman from the priesthood, Salome selected her oldest son Hyrcanus II as the high priest. This did not please her younger son Aristobulus II, who was ambitious for power. Alexander Janneus also advised his wife to make peace with the Pharisees since they controlled the mass of the people. She followed his advice and this marked the revival of the Pharisaic influence. This change was not difficult since her brother, Simeon ben Shetah, was the leader of the

Pharisees. It soon became obvious that though she had the title, the Pharisees were really the power behind the throne. The Pharisees reintroduced Pharisaic legislation that had been abandoned by John Hyrcanus a few years earlier. Also, the Pharisees sought revenge for the slaughter of the eight hundred Pharisees, their wives, and their children during Alexander Janneus's reign, and thus put to death some of those who had advised Alexander Janneus in this atrocity. The Sadducees, who saw that as an attack on them, sent a delegation to Alexandra to protest this revenge. One of the delegates was her son Aristobulus II, who openly sided with the Sadducees against the Pharisees. With Alexandra's permission, the Sadducees were allowed to leave Jerusalem and to take control of several fortresses in various areas of the land. With Aristobulus II as their military leader, Hyrcanus II complained to Alexandra of Aristobulus's strength. When Alexandra became sick, Aristobulus II realized that he must win support if he, rather than Hyrcanus II, were to gain the throne. Aristobulus II left Jerusalem to enlist support of the surrounding cities, and within fifteen days he had the support of most of the country and control of twenty-two fortresses. Hyrcanus II and his advisers became alarmed and sought Alexandra's advice. She wanted Hyrcanus II to succeed her, but before anything could be done she died. Her reign was marked with peace both at home and abroad, except for the family turmoil (*Ant.* xiii.15.6–16.6 [399-432]); *BJ* i.5.1-4 [107-119]).

F. Aristobulus II (67-63 B.C.). With Alexandra's death Hyrcanus II assumed the positions of king and high priest. This, however, was short-lived, for Aristobulus II declared war on him. With many of Hyrcanus II's soldiers deserting him, Hyrcanus II fled to Jerusalem's citadel (later known as Fortress Antonia) and finally was forced to surrender. The two brothers agreed that Hyrcanus II was to relinquish his positions as king and high priest to Aristobulus II and to retire from public life and that Aristobulus II was to leave Hyrcanus II's revenue undisturbed. Hyrcanus II ruled for only three months.

Hyrcanus II was willing to accept this, but the Idumean Antipater II (the son of Antipater I, who had been appointed governor of Idumea by Alexander Janneus, and the father of Herod the Great) had other plans for him. Antipater realized that Hyrcanus II was a weak and idle man and that he could control him. Yet he himself could not be the high priest because he was an Idumean. Antipater convinced Hyrcanus II that Aristobulus unlawfully took the throne and that Hyrcanus II was the legitimate king. Furthermore, he convinced him that Hyrcanus II's life was in danger, and so he traveled by night from Jerusalem to Petra, the capital of Edom. Aretas was willing to help Hyrcanus II on the condition that he would give up the twelve cities of Moab taken by Alexander Janneus. Hyrcanus and Aretas having agreed, Aretas attacked Aristobulus II, who was defeated and retreated to the temple mount at the time of Passover in 65 B.C. Many people sided with Hyrcanus II (*Ant.* xiv.1.2–2.2 [4-28]; *BJ* i.6.1f. [120-26]; cf. also Justin Martyr *Dial.* lii; Eusebius *HE* i.6.2; 7.11; T.B. *Baba Bathra* 3b-4a; *Kiddushin* 70a).

Meanwhile the Roman army under Pompey was moving through Asia Minor after defeating Mithridates in 66 B.C. Pompey sent Scaurus to Syria, and upon his arrival at Damascus he heard of the dispute between the two brothers. When he had hardly arrived in Judea, both brothers sent emissaries asking for support. Aristobulus II offered four hundred talents, and Hyrcanus II followed suit, but Scaurus accepted Aristobulus II, for he felt he would be able to pay. He commanded Aretas to withdraw or else be declared an enemy of Rome. He pursued Aretas, inflicting a crushing defeat, and then returned to Damascus. Shortly after, Pompey arrived in Damascus, and three envoys approached him: one from Hyrcanus II who complained that Aristobulus II seized the power unlawfully; a second from Aristobulus II who claimed he was justified in his actions and that his brother was incompetent to rule; and a third from the Pharisaic element who asked for the abolition of the Hasmonean rule and the restoration of the high-priestly rule. Pompey wanted to delay his decision until after the Nabatean campaign.

Aristobulus II, displeased with this, quit fighting for Pompey against the Nabateans. Pompey dropped the Nabatean expedition and went after Aristobulus II. Aristobulus II lost heart and Pompey asked for the surrender of Jerusalem in exchange for Pompey's dropping his hostilities. Pompey's general Gabinius was sent to Jerusalem but was barred from the city. Pompey was outraged and attacked the city. Within the city Aristobulus II's followers wanted to defend themselves while Hyrcanus II's followers wanted Pompey as an ally and wanted to open the gates. Because the majority were with Hyrcanus II, the gates were opened, but Aristobulus II's men held out at the temple mount. After a three-month siege, Pompey entered the temple mount, and twelve thousand Jews were killed (autumn of 63 B.C.). Pompey entered the holy of holies, but he did not disturb it. In fact, on the following day he gave orders for cleansing it and for resuming the sacrifices there. Hyrcanus II was reinstated as high priest, and Aristobulus II, his two daughters and two sons, Alexander and Antigonus, were taken to Rome as prisoners of war. Alexander escaped. In the triumphal parade in 61 B.C. Aristobulus II was made to walk before Pompey's chariot.

This marked the end of the seventy-nine years (142-63 B.C.) of independence of the Jewish nation as well as the end of the Hasmonean house. Hyrcanus II, the high priest, was merely a vassal of the Roman empire (*Ant.* xiv.2.3–4.5 [29-79]; *BJ* i.6.3–7.7 [128-158]; Tacitus *Hist.* v.9; Appian *Mithridactic Wars* 106, 114; Florus i.40.30; Livy 102; Plutarch *Pompey* xxxix; cf. Dio Cassius xxxvii.15-17).

III. Demise of the Hasmoneans.–The loss of independence brought about the decline of the Hasmoneans. Their power was weakened and what power they had was gradually being transferred to the Herods (*see* HEROD).

A. Hyrcanus II (63-40 B.C.). Although Hyrcanus II was reappointed high priest, Antipater was the power behind the throne who was responsible for Hyrcanus II's position and honor. Antipater proved himself useful to the Romans in government. On the other hand, the Romans helped Antipater quell troubles caused by some of the Hasmoneans. Aristobulus II's family bitterly resented Rome's favoring Hyrcanus II over his brother Aristobulus II, and they made attempts to regain his status of high priest and political ruler. In 57 B.C., while Alexander (son of Aristobulus II), a Roman prisoner, was being taken to Rome, he escaped and succeeded in collecting an army of ten thousand heavily armed soldiers and one thousand four hundred horsemen, but he was finally defeated by Gabinius, the new Roman governor of Syria, and Mark Antony. In 56 B.C. Aristobulus II and his other son Antigonus escaped from their Roman imprisonment and caused a revolt in Judea, but a Roman detachment attacked his little band and they were driven across the Jordan. Although attempting to defend themselves in Machaerus, Aristobulus II and Antigonus had to yield after two days and they were again sent to Rome as prisoners. The Roman Senate decided to keep Aristobulus II in prison but released his two sons, Alexander and Antigonus, because of their mother's helpfulness toward Gabinius. They returned to Judea. In 55 B.C. Alexander revolted again and won many people to his side, but this was quickly brought to an end. Gabinius then went to Jerusalem and reorganized the government according to Antipater's wishes (*Ant.* xiv.5.1–6.1 [80-97]; *BJ* i.8.2-7 [160-178]; Dio Cassius xxxix.56; Plutarch *Antony* iii).

Antipater married a woman named Cypros, of an illustrious Arabian family, by whom he had four sons — Phasael, Herod, Joseph, Pheroras — and a daughter, Salome (*Ant.* xiv.7.3 [121]; *BJ* i.8.9 [181]).

When Julius Caesar became ruler of Rome in 49 B.C., Pompey and the party of the Roman Senate fled from Italy. This left Antipater and Hyrcanus II in the precarious situation of possibly being unable to handle revolts. In fact, Caesar released the imprisoned Aristobulus II and gave him two legions to fight the party of Pompey in Antioch and finally take control of Syria and Judea. But before he could leave Rome, Aristobulus II was poisoned by friends of Pompey. In addition, Aristobulus II's son, Alexander, who sided with Caesar, was beheaded at Antioch by order of Pompey. This means that only Antigonus, the other son of Aristobulus II, remained as a threat to Hyrcanus II and Antipater (*Ant.* xiv.7.4 [123-25]; *BJ* i.9.1f. [183-86]; Dio Cassius xli.18.1).

When Julius Caesar defeated Pompey in Egypt in 48 B.C., Hyrcanus and Antipater attached themselves to the victor. Caesar made Antipater a Roman citizen with exemption from taxes. He appointed him procurator of Judea and reconfirmed Hyrcanus II's high priesthood. He also gave Hyrcanus the title of Ethnarch of the Jews (*Ant.* xiv.8.1-5 [127-155]; 10.2 [191]; *BJ* i.9.3–10.4 [187-203]). Immediately after, Antipater went about the country to suppress disorder and appealed to the restless Judean population to be loyal to Hyrcanus II. In essence, however, Antipater was ruling, and it was he who appointed his son Phasael as the governor of Jerusalem and his second son Herod as governor of Galilee in 47 B.C. (*Ant.* xiv.9.1f. [156-58]; *BJ* i.10.4 [201-203]). Herod was successful in ridding Galilee of bandits.

In 47 B.C. or early 46 B.C., some Jews complained to Hyrcanus II that Herod was becoming too powerful and that he had violated the Jewish law and consequently should be tried before the Sanhedrin. So Hyrcanus II ordered Herod to a trial. Herod came to the trial, not appearing as an accused person, but as a king, decked in purple and attended by a bodyguard. Sextus Caesar, the new governor of Syria, ordered Hyrcanus II to acquit Herod or serious consequences would follow. Herod was released and fled to join Sextus Caesar at Damascus. Sextus appointed Herod as governor of Coelesyria because of his popularity and thus Herod became involved with the affairs of Rome in Syria. Herod began to march against Jerusalem in order to avenge himself for the insult Hyrcanus II had directed toward him, but was persuaded by his father and brother to abstain from violence (*Ant.* xiv.9.3-5 [163-184]; *BJ* i.10.6-9 [208-215]; cf. T.B. *Kiddushin* 43a).

After Cassius, Brutus, and their followers murdered Julius Caesar in 44 B.C., Cassius came to Syria. Needing to raise certain taxes required by Cassius, Antipater selected Herod, Phasael, and Malichus for the job. Herod was very successful in this, and Cassius appointed him governor of Coelesyria (as he had been under Sextus Caesar). Since the Herods were gaining strength, Malichus, whose life Antipater had previously saved, bribed the butler to poison Antipater. Herod killed Malichus (*Ant.* xiv.11.3-6 [277-293]; *BJ* i.11.2-8 [220-235]).

Herod was growing in power but was not always liked by the Jews because he was an Idumean. Although he was married to Doris, who was probably Idumean also, he became betrothed to Mariamne, who was the granddaughter of Hyrcanus II (her mother was Alexandra) and the daughter of Aristobulus II's son, Alexander, and thus a niece to Antigonus, the rival of Herod (*Ant.* xiv.12.1 [300]; *BJ* i.12.3 [241]). This strengthened Herod's position immensely, for he would marry into the royal house of the Hasmoneans and would become the natural regent when Hyrcanus II, who was growing old, passed away.

In 42 B.C. when Antony defeated Cassius, the Jewish leaders accused Herod and Phasael of usurping the power of the government while leaving Hyrcanus II with titular honors. Herod's defense nullified these charges (*Ant.* xiv.12.2-6 [301-323]; *BJ* i.12.4-6 [242-45]; Plutarch *Antony* xxiv; Dio Cassius xlviii.24; Appian *Civil Wars* v.4). Since Hyrcanus II was there, Antony asked him who would be the best qualified ruler, and Hyrcanus II chose Herod and Phasael. Antony appointed them as tetrarchs of Judea (*BJ* i.12.5 [243f.]; *Ant.* xiv.13.1 [324-26]).

B. Antigonus (40-37 B.C.). The next year (40 B.C.) the Parthians appeared in Syria. They joined Antigonus in the effort to remove Hyrcanus II. After several skirmishes, the Parthians asked for peace. Phasael and Hyrcanus II went to Galilee to meet the Parthian king while Herod remained in Jerusalem, suspicious of the proposal. The Parthians treacherously put Phasael and Hyrcanus II in chains, and Herod with his close relatives, Mariamne, and his troops moved to Masada and then to Petra (*Ant.* xiv.13.3-9 [335-364]; *BJ* i.13.2-9 [250-264]). Antigonus was made king (Dio Cassius xlviii.41; inferred in *Ant.* xiv.13.10 [368f.]; *BJ* 1.13.9 [268-270]; cf. also Dio Cassius xlviii.26). In order to prevent the possibility of Hyrcanus II's restoration to high priesthood, Antigonus mutilated him. Phasael died either of suicide or poisoning (*Ant.* xiv.13.10 [367-69]; *BJ* i.13.10f. [271-73]). Hyrcanus II was taken to Parthia (*Ant.* xv.2.1 [12]).

Herod went to Rome where Antony, Octavius Caesar, and the Senate designated him King of Judea (*Ant.* xiv.14.6 [381-85]; *BJ* i.14.4 [282-85]; cf. also Strabo *Geog.* xvi.2.46; Appian *Civil Wars* v.75; Tacitus *Hist.* v.9). In late 40 or early 39 B.C. Herod returned to Palestine, and with the help of Antony's legate Sossius, was able to recapture Galilee. In the spring of 37 B.C. he prepared for the siege of Jerusalem. While assigning his army several duties he left for Samaria to marry Mariamne to whom he had been betrothed for about five years. This was a contemptuous act against Antigonus, the uncle of Mariamne, for her being a Hasmonean strengthened Herod's right to the throne. After the wedding he returned to Jerusalem, which fell in the summer of 37 after a long and bitter struggle (*Ant.* xiv.15.8–16.2 [439-480]; *BJ* i.16.7–18.2 [320-352]; Tacitus *Hist.* v.9; Dio Cassius xlix.22). At Herod's request, the Romans beheaded Antigonus (*BJ* i.18.3 [357]; Plutarch *Antony* xxxvi; cf. also Dio Cassius xlix.22), which meant the end of the Hasmonean rule. Herod, therefore, ceased to be the nominee for king and became king *de facto*.

C. Mariamne and Her Sons (37-7 B.C.). One of the first moves Herod made as king was to appoint Ananel (Hananeel), who was of the Aaronic line, as high priest to replace Hyrcanus II who, although just returning from the Parthian exile, was disqualified because Antigonus had mutilated him (*Ant.* xv.2.1-4 [11-22]). Herod chose a priest who had no influence. Alexandra, who was Herod's mother-in-law as well as Hyrcanus II's daughter, was infuriated by his choice of a priest outside the Hasmonean line, especially because he overlooked her own sixteen-year-old son, Aristobulus III, the brother of Herod's wife Mariamne. Finally, Alexandra, with Cleopatra's pressure upon Antony, forced Herod to set aside Ananel (which was unlawful because a high priest was to hold the office for life) and make Aristobulus III high priest when he was only seventeen years old (late 36 or early 35 B.C.). Because of Aristobulus III's growing popularity, Herod managed to have him accidentally drowned in a swimming pool at Jericho right after the Feast of Tabernacles. Herod arranged for an elaborate funeral. Although the people never questioned the official versions, Alexandra believed that her son had been murdered. She reported this to Cleopatra, who persuaded Antony to summon Herod for an account of his actions. Realizing that his life was in danger, Herod put his wife Mariamne under surveillance and secretly instructed those in charge to kill Mariamne if he were killed so that she would not become someone else's lover. By eloquence and bribery, Herod persuaded Antony to free him of any charges. Upon his return in 34 B.C. Herod realized that Mariamne found out about his plan to kill her, but he also heard the charge that she had an affair with the one who was to watch her while he was away. She denied the charge, and after some debate they were reconciled. Herod surmised that some of the troubles were caused by her mother Alexandra, so he put her in chains and under guard (*Ant.* xv.2.5–3.9 [23-87]; *BJ* i.22.2-5 [437-444]).

Antony was defeated by Octavius in the Battle of Actium on 2 September, 31 B.C. Herod, in the spring of 30 B.C., went to Rhodes to meet Octavius and convince him that he was loyal. Before Herod left for Rhodes, he sentenced and executed Hyrcanus II, the only remaining rival claimant to the throne. Also, he had Mariamne and her mother Alexandra placed under observation and instructed two guards to execute them if he did not return from Rhodes. At their meeting in Rhodes in the spring of 30 B.C., Octavius was convinced of Herod's loyalty and confirmed his royal rank (*Ant.* xv.5.1–6.7 [108-201]; *BJ* i.19.3–20.3 [369-395]).

While Herod was at Rhodes, however, Mariamne found out from the two guards that she was to be killed in the event that he did not return. This caused an intense situation for Herod, and after a complicated series of events, he condemned and finally executed Mariamne at the end of 29 B.C. (*Ant.* xv.7.1-5 [202-236]). But Herod never accepted Mariamne's death. He fell ill, and because his recovery was doubtful, Alexandra tried to win over two fortified places in Jerusalem so that she could secure the throne. When Herod heard of this plot, he had her executed in 28 B.C. (*Ant.* xv.7.6-8 [237-252]). Finally, the governor of Idumea, Costobarus (husband of Herod's sister Salome), who had earlier conspired with Cleopatra against Herod, once again came under suspicion for alleged pro-Hasmonean sympathies. Herod killed Costobarus and his followers, the influential sons of Babas, who remained loyal to Antigonus. Herod now could console himself that all of the male relatives of Hyrcanus II (who could dispute the occupancy of the throne) were no longer living (*Ant.* xv.7.9f. [253-266]).

The only Hasmoneans who would claim the throne were Herod's own sons by Mariamne. She bore him five children. The two daughters were Salampsio and Cypros (*Ant.* xviii.5.4 [130-32]). The youngest son died during the course of his education in Rome (*BJ* i.22.2 [435]). The older sons were Alexander and Aristobulus (*Ant.* xvi.4.6 [133]; xvii.5.4 [134]). Herod made out a will in 22 B.C. that would make these two sons his successors. Both of these sons had no real fondness for their father, for he had killed their mother. When Herod heard and believed the rumors that these two sons planned to kill him to avenge their mother's death, he made out a new will in 13 B.C. declaring Antipater, son of his first wife Doris, the sole heir (*BJ* i.23.2 [451]). Antipater realized that Herod could again change his mind about the will, so he repeatedly wrote letters from Rome, kindling his father's anger against Alexander and Aristobulus and ingratiating himself. Finally, in Italy in 12 B.C., Herod brought Alexander and Aristobulus to trial before Augustus to prove that they were not worthy of the throne. The outcome of the trial, however, was reconciliation, and when they returned home Herod made out his third will, naming Antipater as his first successor and after him Alexander and Aristobulus (*Ant.* xvi.3.1–4.6 [66-135]; *BJ* i.23.1-5 [445-466]).

Scarcely had they arrived home when Antipater, being helped by Herod's sister Salome and Herod's brother Pheroras, began to slander the two sons of Mariamne. Alexander and Aristobulus became decidedly more hostile in their attitude. Herod became more morbid about the situation, and Antipater played on Herod's morbid fears. Although there was a reconciliation in 10 B.C., finally in 7 B.C. with Augustus's instruction his sons were tried at Berytus (Beirut) and found guilty. Herod had Alexander and Aristobulus executed by strangulation at Sebaste, where he had married their mother thirty years before (*Ant.* xvi.8.1–11.8 [229-404]; *BJ* i.24.7–27.6 [488-551]).

The remaining Hasmonean influence came after Herod's death. Aristobulus had married Bernice, the daughter of Herod's sister Salome, and they had three notable children (*BJ* i.28.1 [552f.]). First, there was Herod who was king of Chalcis from A.D. 41 to 48. Second, there was Herod Agrippa I who was king of the Jews from A.D. 37 to 44 (Acts 12), being succeeded by his son Herod Agrippa II, who was king of the Jews from A.D. 50 to 100 (Acts 25–26). Third, there was Herodias who married Herod Antipas, who ruled as tetrarch over Galilee and Perea from 4 B.C. to A.D. 39 (Mt. 14:3-12; Mk. 6:17-29; Lk. 3:1, 19f.; 13:31-33; 23:6-12). Herodias had a daughter, Salome, from a previous marriage, who married Herod Antipas's brother, Philip the tetrarch (Lk. 3:1).

See also HASIDEANS; HEROD.

Bibliography.–E. R. Bevan, *The House of Seleucus* (1902); *Jerusalem under the High-Priests* (1904), pp. 100-162; *CAH,* VIII (1930), 495-533; IX (1932), 397-417; E. Bickerman, *From Ezra to the Last of the Maccabees* (1947), pp. 136-182; S. Tedesche and S. Zeitlin, *First Book of Maccabees* (1950); J. C. Dancy, *Comm. on I Maccabees* (1954); V. Tcherikover, *Hellenistic Civilization and the Jews* (1959), pp. 235-265, 403f.; S. Zeitlin, *Rise and Fall of the Judaean State,* I (1962), 141-201, 317-411; D. S. Russell, *The Jews from Alexander to Herod* (1967), pp. 57-102; B. Reicke, *New Testament Era* (Eng. tr. 1968), pp. 63-107; Y. Aharoni and M. Avi-Yonah, *Macmillan Bible Atlas* (1968), pp. 129-139; J. R. Bartlett, *First and Second Books of the Maccabees* (*CBC,* 1973); E. Schürer, *HJP*², I, 189-242, 267-286.

H. W. HOEHNER

HASRAH haz'rə, has'rə [Heb. *ḥasrâ*].

1. Grandfather of Shallum, who was the husband of Huldah the prophetess (2 Ch. 34:22; in 2 K. 22:14, HARHAS).

2. In 1 Esd. 5:31 (AV AZARA, NEB ASARA), the head of a family returning to Jerusalem with Zerubbabel. His name is omitted in the par. passages (Ezr. 2:49; Neh. 7:51).

HASSENAAH has-ə-nā'ə [Heb. *hassᵉnā'â*]. In Neh. 3:3 the "sons of Hassenaah" are mentioned among the builders of the wall. Probably the same as SENAAH (Ezr. 2:35; Neh. 7:38) with the definite article, i.e., has-Senaah. The latter, from the connection, would appear to be a place-name. *See also* HASSENUAH.

HASSENUAH has-ə-nōō'ə [Heb. *hassᵉnu'â, hassᵉnû'â*]. A family name in the two lists of Benjaminite inhabitants of Jerusalem (1 Ch. 9:7, AV "Hasenuah"; Neh. 11:9, AV "Senuah"). The name is possibly the same as HASSENAAH, yet the occurrence of the singular ("son of

Hassenuah") does not accord so well with the idea of a place name.

HASSHUB hash'ub [Heb. *haššûḇ*–'considerate']; AV everywhere Hashub except 1 Ch. 9:14.

1. A builder of the wall (Neh. 3:11).
2. Another builder of the same name (Neh. 3:23).
3. One of the signers of the covenant (Neh. 10:23).
4. A Levite chief (Neh. 11:15; 1 Ch. 9:14).

HASSOPHERETH has-o-fē'reth [Heb. *hassōpereṯ*–'the scribe' (Ezr. 2:55); Gk. *Assaphiōth* (1 Esd. 5:33)]; AV SOPHERETH, AZAPHION; NEB Apoc. ASAPPHIOTH. Father of some of the "sons of Solomon's servants" who returned to Jerusalem with Zerubbabel.

HASTE; HASTEN; HASTY verbs: [Heb. piel of *māhar, ḥûš, bāhal, ḥāpaz, 'āmēṣ, 'ûṣ, nāḥaṣ* (1 S. 21:8 [MT 9]), *dāḥap* (Est. 3:15), *rûṣ* (Cant. 1:4), *bāraḥ* (Cant. 8:14), *nûs* (Jer. 46:5), *qāḏam* (Jonah 4:2), *rāpas* (Prov. 6:3), *'ûš* (Joel 3:11 [MT 4:11]), *šā'ap* (Eccl. 1:5), *pû(a)ḥ* (Hab. 2:3); Gk. *speúdō* (Acts 22:18)]; AV also "make speed" (2 S. 15:14), SPEEDILY (Ps. 69:17), "be swift" (Prov. 6:18), RUN (Cant. 1:4), etc.; NEB also QUICKLY (Gen. 19:22), "be overcome" (Gen. 43:30), "rose with all speed" (Josh. 8:14), PROMPTLY (Josh. 8:19), SUDDEN (Jgs. 20:37), URGENT (1 S. 21:8), etc.; substantives: [Heb. *ḥippāzôn, mahēr, meherâ* (Jgs. 9:54); Aram. *behîlû* (Ezr. 4:23); Gk. *spoudḗ* (Lk. 1:39), *tachéōs* (1 Tim. 5:22)]; AV also SUDDENLY (1 Tim. 5:22); NEB also HURRIEDLY (Jgs. 9:54), etc.

The Hebrew verb most often represented by the word-group "haste," "hasten," etc., is *māhar* (in the piel, "make haste, hasten"). Used independently, the verb *māhar* consistently has the meaning "hurry, hasten, act quickly" (cf. Gen. 18:7; 1 S. 9:12; Isa. 5:19; Nah. 2:5). Far more frequently, however, *māhar* is followed by a finite verb or infinitive (cf., e.g., Gen. 45:9, "make haste and go up"; 18:7, "who hastened to prepare it") so that it has an adverbial force (in the above examples, "go up quickly" and "prepare it quickly"). A slightly extended sense is apparent in the rare instances when the simple passive (niphal) stem of *māhar* is used; i.e., "be hurried" may connote "anxious" or "hasty." In Hab. 1:6 the Chaldeans, ever eager to annex more territory, are thus characterized as "hasty" or "impetuous." The cognate substantives *meherâ*, "haste" (Jgs. 9:54), and *mahēr*, "swift, quick" (Prov. 25:8), similarly have an adverbial force.

In Prov. 13:11 the translations for *mēheḇel* ("by vanity," AV) in the RSV ("hastily") and NEB ("quickly") follow the LXX and Vulgate and assume an emendation to *meherâ* or *meḇōhāl*, "by haste." The MT *mēheḇel*, if authentic, would perhaps refer to speculatively derived wealth (vis-à-vis that derived from honest effort). The emendations meaning "hastily gotten wealth" imply that which comes by questionable or fraudulent means (see W. McKane, pp. 458f.). In 1 S. 9:12 the NEB follows the LXX in assuming *hārō'eh*, "the seer," for MT *mahēr*, "make haste."

The synonymous verb *ḥûš* in the simple active (qal) stem basically means "be quick," as, e.g., in Ps. 119:60, "I hasten and do not delay," and in the familiar plea of the psalmist, "make haste to help me!" (Ps. 38:22 [MT 23]; etc.). The causative (hiphil) stem of *ḥûš* is used to express several nuances: (1) "act quickly, manifest haste" (Ps. 55:8 [MT 9]); (2) "cause to hurry" (Isa. 60:22); and (3) "be hasty, precipitous" (Isa. 28:16; NEB here assumes *mûš* for MT *ḥûš* and translates "waver"). In effect, *ḥûš* also frequently has an adverbial force.

There is a duality of meaning in both the Aramaic and Hebrew cognates of the root *bhl*: (1) "hurry," and (2) "be alarmed, terrified." Which meaning is the original is uncertain (see *TDOT*, II). In any event, the use of Heb. *bāhal* with the sense "hasten, hurry" (cf. 2 Ch. 35:21; Est. 6:14; 8:14; Prov. 20:21) is a development that occurred late in biblical Hebrew under the influence of the Aramaic cognate *behal* (cf. Dnl. 2:25; 3:24; 6:19 [MT 20]). The duality of meaning can be detected in Est. 6:14 and 8:14, in the sense that one who is alarmed acts in haste. The basic sense of "urgency" that underlies both meanings is apparent in the use of the Aramaic substantive *behîlû*, "haste," in Ezr. 4:23.

The English word group is used to translate a number of other Hebrew verbs for which this sense is an extension of its original meaning. Thus, *ḥāpaz*, "be alarmed, in trepidation," may also have the sense "be in a hurry." In contexts of retreat or escape the RSV renders it with "making haste" (e.g., 1 S. 23:26; cf. NEB "trying desperately"), and "haste" (2 S. 4:4; 2 K. 7:15). The cognate substantive *ḥippāzôn*, "haste" (lit. "trepidation"), is used in Ex. 12:11 to characterize the manner of the eating of the Passover meal (cf. also Isa. 52:12, where with the same language the prophet says that in the second Exodus the people will not leave in "haste").

The reflexive (hithpael) stem of *'āmēṣ*, "make oneself strong, alert," has the connotation of "making haste" or "acting with dispatch" in 1 K. 12:18 par. 2 Ch. 10:18 (AV "make speed"). J. Gray suggested that *hiṯ'ammēṣ* expresses "not so much the haste with which Rehoboam mounted his chariot as his rallying of his faculties to do so" (*I & II Kings* [*OTL*, rev. ed. 1970], p. 307).

The verb *'ûṣ*, "be narrow, pressed," is naturally extended to mean "make haste, be in a hurry, be anxious" (cf. Josh. 10:13; Prov. 19:2; 28:20). Similarly, *dāḥap*, "drive," in late Biblical Hebrew and Mishnaic Hebrew has the meaning "hasten." Est. 3:15 illustrates this: the king's runners "hasten" in the sense that they are "driven" under the compulsion of their task (cf. also 2 Ch. 26:20). That *rûṣ*, "run," should have the connotation "hasten, hurry" as, e.g., in Cant. 1:4 (AV, NEB, "run"), is natural and expected.

Bāraḥ, "flee," is in one instance in the OT (Cant. 8:14) translated "make haste" (NEB "come into the open"), since flight implies quick or hurried movement (cf. the similar treatment of *nûs*, "flee, escape," in Jer. 46:5). The synonymous verbs *šā'ap*, "gasp," and *pû(a)ḥ*, "pant," are each used once in the extended sense of "hasten." In Eccl. 1:5 the sun is figured as a "gasping" (i.e., "hurrying") racer, and in Hab. 2:3 the prophet describes his vision as one that "pants" (i.e., "hastens") to the end (AV "it shall speak"; NEB "in breathless haste").

For the hapax legomenon *'ûš* in Joel 3:11 (MT 4:11), the meaning "help, lend aid" is suggested by the Arabic cognate. The RSV translation, "hasten," assumes the emendation *ḥûš*. Another possibility, relevant to the context, is *'ûr*, "rouse (yourselves) up." The renderings of the AV ("assemble yourselves") and NEB ("rally") follow the LXX.

Another hapax legomenon, *nāḥaṣ*, which the RSV renders as "haste" in 1 S. 21:8 (NEB "urgent"), deserves mention. The meaning, "be urgent," is derived from the context and the LXX reading (*spoudḗ*, "haste, urgency").

An occurrence of *rāpas*, "tread, stomp, befoul by treading" (cf. Akk. *rapāsu*, "trample"), in the reflexive (hithpael) stem in Prov. 6:3 is translated "hasten" by the RSV. The precise meaning of the reflexive stem of *rāpas*, however, is uncertain. The AV rendering, "humble yourself," was based on the assumption that "stomping oneself down'' meant "humbling oneself" or "swallowing one's pride" (see McKane, pp. 322f.). But the context of going to importune (*rāhaḇ*, lit. "storm, act boisterously with") one's neighbor has been considered by some scholars to be a serious difficulty for the above interpretation. Thus it has been reasoned that "trampling oneself" could mean instead "wearying oneself" or "not flagging" in one's task (see G. R. Driver, *JTS*, 30 [1929], 374f.). This and the LXX reading, "do not slacken," are cited in support of the translation "hasten." The NEB follows another conjecture, "bestir yourselves."

The intensive (piel) stem of *qāḏam*, "go before, meet, be in front," is translated "make haste" in Jonah 4:2. The context is one of precipitate flight as Jonah "made haste to flee" (lit. "went beforehand to flee"; see N. H. Snaith, *Notes on the Hebrew Text of the Book of Jonah* [1945], p. 36).

The Greek verb *speúdō* has the intransitive sense "hurry, make haste" in Lk. 2:16; 19:5f.; Acts 20:16; 22:18. Like Heb. *māhar*, *speúdō* commonly has an adverbial force (e.g., in Acts 22:18 "make haste and get quickly out" means "leave as quickly as possible"). In 2 Pet. 3:12 *speúdō* has the transitive meaning "hasten, strive for" (the reference being the Parousia; cf. NEB "work to hasten").

The related substantive *spoudḗ*, "haste, speed," appears in the phrase *metà spoudḗs*, "with haste, in a hurry," in Mk. 6:25 and Lk. 1:39 (cf. also Ex. 12:11, LXX; Josephus *Ant.* vii.223). The extended sense of *spoudḗ*, "zeal, zealous concern," also appears in the NT in such passages as Rom. 12:11 ("zeal"); 2 Cor. 7:11 ("eagerness"); *see* EAGER; ZEAL. The Greek adverb *tachéōs*, "(too) quickly," is translated "hasty" in 1 Tim. 5:22 (AV "suddenly"; NEB "over-hasty").

Bibliography.–*TDOT*, II, *s.v.* "bāhal" (Otzen); *TDNT*, VII, *s.v.* σπουδάζω κτλ. (Harder); W. McKane, *Proverbs* (*OTL*, 1970).

D. G. BURKE

HASUPHA hə-so͞o'fə [Heb. *ḥ*ᵃ*sûpā'*, *ḥ*ᵃ*supā'*]. Head of a family of temple servants among the returning exiles (Ezr. 2:43; Neh. 7:46). Neh. 7:46 AV has "Hashupha," and in the par. passage 1 Esd. 5:29 the AV and the NEB have "Asipha."

HAT [Aram. *karb*ᵉ*lā'*] (Dnl. 3:21). Worn by Daniel's three friends when they were cast into the furnace. The term *karb*ᵉ*lā'*, a hapax legomenon, recalls the Akk. *karballatu* ("cap," "helmet"), and reflects accurately the Babylonian cultural milieu against which the book of Daniel was written (*see* DANIEL, BOOK OF). Little is known about the early headgear, and even the Beni-hasan tableau, an Egyptian relief from the early patriarchal period (*ca.* 1900 B.C.) that depicts a group of seminomads entering Egypt, shows only that the women held their hair in place by means of bands (*ANEP*, no. 3). The "ropes" worn on the head in connection with mourning in the monarchy period (1 K. 20:31) have been paralleled on Egyptian monuments by scenes depicting Syrians who wore cords tied around their heads. On the sculptures that illustrate Sennacherib's capture of Lachish in 701 B.C. the men wear circular caps that come to a shallow point, while many of the women wear long wimples (*ANEP*, no. 373). Attire of this kind, like the turbans of the high priest, tended to change but little throughout the period of biblical history.

R. K. H.

HATACH hā'tak. *See* HATHACH.

HATCHET [Heb. *kaššîl*] (Ps. 74:6); AV "axes." *See* AX.

Horseman with unusual hat surrenders to Assyrians. Relief from the palace of Tiglath-pileser III (745-727 B.C.) at Nimrûd (Trustees of the British Museum)

HATE; HATRED [Heb. *śānē'*, *śin'â* (Gen. 24:60; 26:27; etc.), *śāṭam* (Gen. 27:41; 49:23; 50:15; Job 16:9; Ps. 55:3 [MT 4]); Aram. *ś*ᵉ*nē'* (Dnl. 4:19); Gk. *miséō* (Mt. 5:43; Mk. 13:13; etc.), *stygētós* (Tit. 3:3)]; NEB also "enemies" (Gen. 24:60), "bore a grudge" (Gen. 27:41), "not loved" (Gen. 29:31), "odious" (Tit. 3:3), etc. To have intense emotions of animosity for another person or persons, or, as a noun, the animosity itself. The Hebrew and Greek terms manifest distinct variations in their semantic range, from the malicious hatred of a person who seeks the death of an enemy, a hate seated both in the feelings and the will, to the hate that is disregard, rejection, and dislike without deliberate determination to do harm. Other occurrences simply denote a lack of love.

I. In the OT
  A. Human Hatred
  B. Divine Hatred
II. In the DSS
III. In the NT
  A. Human Hatred
  B. Divine Hatred

I. In the OT.–The most frequently used Hebrew word for "hate" is *śānē'*, from the root *śn'*. In Hebrew poetical texts derivatives of this root often designate the "ENEMY" (e.g., NEB in Gen. 24:60 [Heb. *śōnē'*]; Nu. 10:35; Dt. 32:41; 33:11; etc. [*m*ᵉ*śanā'*]). This designation for an enemy can be compared to two other OT terms for enemy. Heb. *ṣar* (Gen. 14:20; Nu. 10:9; Dt. 32:41; etc.) is a derivative of the root *ṣrr* ("be hostile toward," "be in a state of conflict with"; Ex. 23:22; Nu. 10:9; Isa. 11:13; etc.). The cognate Akk. *ṣerru* means "enemy," "adversary" (*CAD*, XVI, 137f.). In Ugaritic, *ṣrt* means "enemy" and *ṣrr* means "hurt," "afflict" (Gordon, *UT*, p. 476).

The Hebrew word *śāṭam* occurs several times in the OT for "hate" (Gen. 27:41; 49:23; 50:15; Job 16:9; Ps. 55:3). Heb. *śāṭan*, with final *-n*, is identical in meaning and is attested in Akkadian, Arabic, Ethiopic, etc. (see KoB, pp. 918f.). The most widely used OT term for "enemy" is *'ōyēḇ* (Gen. 22:17; Ex. 15:6, 9; 23:4, 22, 27; etc.), which is attested in Akkadian as *ajābu* (*CAD,* A/I, 221-24; von Soden, pp. 23f.) and in Ugaritic as *ib* (cf. Donner, pp. 344ff.). The "enemy" whose name is derived from the root *śn'* is primarily a "hater" whose disposition of soul and mind has produced outright hostility and enmity. Other meanings of this Hebrew root are discussed below.

A. Human Hatred. In the Hebrew mentality "hate" is not necessarily always the direct antonym to the feeling of "love" in relations between human beings. When the patriarch Jacob is said to have "hated" his first wife Leah (Gen. 29:31), it does not mean so much the emotion of hate in the traditional sense as it expresses that she was "unloved" (NEB) or "disliked" (NAB), i.e., strong overtones are present in the context that show that he disregarded and rejected her in restricting his marital rights toward her and favoring Rachel. A significant semantic counterpart is found in the Code of Hammurabi where "a woman dislikes [*i-ze-er-ma,* "hates"] her husband and says, 'You have no marital rights (anymore) to me . . .'" (§ 142 as quoted in *CAD,* XXI, 97; cf. *ANET,* p. 172a). Here the "hating" (Akk. *zêru,* "dislike, hate, avoid," *CAD,* XXI, 97-99) involves a dislike that leads to the denying of sexual relations. Other nuances of the Akkadian verb *zêru* are "disregard" or "spurn" (Atra-ḫasis Epic iii.1.23; Gilgamesh Epic xi.26; cf. *ANET,* pp. 95, 105).

Ancient Israelite divorce law prohibited divorce for a man who "spurns" (NAB "dislikes," NEB "turns against") his wife and falsely accuses her of not having been a virgin when he married her (Dt. 22:13-21). It is likely that "hate" here means that the marriage partner sought to force a divorce by foregoing sexual relations as in Babylonian divorce law (Code of Hammurabi § 142; *ANET,* p. 172a). But no such "hate" provided sufficient legal grounds for divorce in Israelite family law. That this kind of "hate" was an adequate ground for divorce among Israel's neighbors is evident from Babylonian law (*ANET,* p. 172a) and Philistine custom (Jgs. 14:16; 15:2). The Hebrew laws of inheritance stipulated that the firstborn son of a "hated" (NEB "unloved," NAB "disliked") wife in a polygamous marriage was to be accorded the full right of a double share of the property, even if the "loved" wife had a son, provided that the latter was not the firstborn son of that home (Dt. 21:15-17). The personal disregard for one wife and corresponding preference of another by a polygamous husband was to have no legal bearing on the Israelite law that secured the inheritance of the firstborn (cf. Code of Hammurabi §§ 168-170; *ANET,* p. 173b). It is fairly certain that Israelite law was written in such a way as to discourage a situation of "hate" from arising in a polygamous home. It would certainly not bring legal advantage to the husband or to his "loved" wife or her offspring. The "hated" wife and her offspring were protected.

Different kinds of hate in relations between people are reflected in various passages of the OT. Isaac experienced the selfish hate of the Philistines when they drove him out of their territory because of the dispute over water rights (Gen. 26:27). This hate was characterized by a deliberate determination to do no physical harm (vv. 26-29). Esau "hated" (NEB, NAB, "bore a grudge against") Jacob (Gen. 27:41) because Jacob acquired the deathbed blessing from Isaac (cf. E. A. Speiser, *JBL,* 74 [1955], 252ff.). This hate sought revenge and forced Jacob to seek physical safety abroad (cf. Dt. 19:11). A despising hate led to Jephthah's rejection by his brothers and drove him from his house in Gilead, because he was the innocent victim of an illegitimate birth (Jgs. 11:1, 7). Absalom hated Amnon for the rape of his sister Tamar (2 S. 13:22). This hate not only led to a rejection of Tamar or a dislike of him; it was a deep-seated animosity that caused Absalom to have Amnon murdered (v. 28).

Hate, then, can be that innermost disposition of hostility and enmity that leads to premeditated killing. Hebrew criminal law required that in the case of homicide it should be ascertained whether or not the manslayer had "hated" the victim (Dt. 19:11; NEB "enemy of another"). Should such malicious hate be established by at least two or three witnesses, then the manslayer was to be judged a murderer worthy of death; but if no such hate could be established, then the killing was to be judged accidental (Dt. 4:42; 19:4, 6, 11; Josh. 20:5). In order to curb all such hurtful and destructive hate, the divine command prohibited it comprehensively and unequivocally, "You shall not hate your brother [neighbor] in your heart" and charged, "You shall love your neighbor as yourself" (Lev. 19:17f.; cf. Mt. 5:43ff.; Lk. 10:29-37). Here love and hate are contrasted; love is to take the place of malicious hate. In view of the Israelite laws prohibiting the "alien" or "sojourner" (Heb. *gēr,* Ex. 20:10; Dt. 5:14; 10:18f.; 14:29; 16:11, 14; 24:17-21; 26:12f.; 27:19; cf. Josh. 9), it is not possible to support the suggestion that originally the substitution of love for hate was to occur only toward members of the covenant community. The Israelite is indeed commanded to "love" the alien (Dt. 10:19).

A lack of love is equal to hate. Thus the father who withholds the punishment due to his son (Prov. 13:24) is failing to give love its due expression in the best interests of the person. There is no suggestion here of ill will, aversion, hostility, or rejection.

The psalmist speaks of the enemies as the ones who "hate" (Ps. 18:17; 21:8; 25:19; 34:21; 41:5, 7; 44:7) the worshiper of God "without cause" (35:19; 69:4) and "wrongfully" (38:19). Regardless of how the enemies are identified (G. W. Anderson, *BJRL,* 48 [1965], 18-29), there is no reason for doubting that they are real human beings and not demons or mythical powers of death. The enemies of the psalmist are also the enemies of God, for they "hate" God (Ps. 68:1; 81:15). Those who "hate" God plot crafty plans against God's people (83:2), and "hate" Zion (129:5), the city of God's choice and blessing. They also "hate" peace (120:6) and discipline (50:17). The psalmist's prayer for deliverance, preservation, and salvation from these hateful enemies (25:20f.; 86:17; 109:3, 5) makes it clear that these wicked ones may meet exactly the same fate that they intend "without cause" for the righteous (7:12-16; 9:16; 34:31; 35:7f., 19; 69:4; 141:10). The upright man "hates" evil (97:10), falsehood (119:163), and the false way (119:104, 128); he also hates the one who acts perversely (101:3), who is double-minded (119:113), and the whole assembly of evildoers (26:5).

The person who fears God hates not so much because these wicked ones threaten the well-being and existence of those whom they hate, but because they threaten the very foundation of all human order, which God has established at His creation in the beginning of time. The enemies and evildoers have placed themselves into a sphere apart from God and joined in a covenant with forces that have purposed the disruption and destruction of the divinely established order (cf. Ps. 22:13-17; 57:5; 73:6-9). The psalmist asks, therefore: "Do I not hate them that hate thee, O Lord? And do I not loathe them that rise up against thee?" (139:21). There is thus a hatred that is natural for the God-fearing one (Ex. 18:21; Ps. 97:10; 119:104, 128, 163; Prov. 8:13; 13:5; 28:16; Isa. 33:15). But this hatred is not a personal, malicious hatred which seeks the death of the enemy (cf. Prov. 24:17f.). Punishment of the enemies is to come from God and not from those whom the enemies hate. In the Song of Moses (Dt. 32) the hate of the enemies remains until the day of vengeance and requital (v. 35) when Yahweh will repay His foes and requite those who hate Him (v. 41). Because of their sin and rebellion, the just man hates those who hate his God; nevertheless, the righteous man maintains an attitude of nonretaliation. He refrains from usurping what is God's prerogative. He hates evil and loves good (Am. 5:15), while the wicked man hates good and loves evil (Mic. 3:2). The prophetic message shows that the act of decision between hate and love over against good and evil is not a matter based on the emotions of the human heart. To the contrary, it is a decisive choice of the will, for it is a choice for life or death.

As man is able to love God, so he is able to hate Him (Ex. 20:5; Dt. 5:9; 7:10; 32:41, 43; Ps. 68:1; 74:4, 23; 83:2). Man's hatred of God comes to expression in conscious opposition to God's revealed will, commandment, and law. Hatred against God is thus a sign of persistent rejection and constant obduracy (*TDNT,* IV, 687). God punishes the parental wrongdoing down to the third and fourth generation of those who hate Him (Ex. 20:5; Dt. 5:9). This does not mean that punishment comes for parental guilt alone (Ezk. 18:21f.), but only as the children participate in the sins of their parents by themselves walking in sinful ways. Certain natural results of a sinful course of life are certainly passed on to future generations. Hate in this instance means to live a life opposed to the divine will and the revealed principles of God.

B. Divine Hatred. Yahweh "hates" (NAB "detests") the worship of heathen gods (Dt. 12:31; Jer. 44:4) and the erection of *maṣṣēḇôṯ,* or sacred pillars associated with pagan cult practices (Dt. 16:22; 2 K. 23:14; cf. C. F. Graesser, *BA,* 35 [1972], 34-63). The reason for the "hate" of Yahweh against these standing stones seems to rest upon the desire to keep Israel free from foreign cults and influences, to separate them from the other nations, and to avoid the use of "images" (1 K. 14:23f.; 2 K. 17:8-11; Ex. 20:4; Lev. 26:1; Mic. 5:13). An Ugaritic text states that "Baal hates [*šn'a.b'l*]" certain cultic "banquets" which are unacceptable to the deity (II AB III.17:21; *ANET,* p. 132). The OT employs this same strong language (Heb. *śn'*) to condemn Canaanite forms of worship.

It must have been shocking and repulsive to the Israelite leaders and ordinary citizens to learn through the prophets of Yahweh that their God "hates" their worship (Isa. 1:14; 61:8; Hos. 9:15; Am. 5:21; Zec. 8:17; Mal. 2:13; cf. Jer. 12:8; 44:4). Israel's worship was thereby reduced to the level of idolatry, which God detests. The reason for God's hate of Israel's sacrifices, new moons, sabbaths, etc., lies in the deterioration of Israelite worship to an empty and meaningless ritual in which the worshiper engaged without inner devotion, wholehearted obedience, and complete justice in daily life. Thus God hates injustice (Isa. 61:8) and those who are evildoers (Ps. 5:6). Because of their wicked deeds, God will love His people no longer (Hos. 9:15f.). Such vices as self-assertiveness, lying, perjury, and acts disrupting society, which are based upon a deep-seated corruption of motives, are an abomination to Yahweh which He hates (Prov. 6:16-19). A list of vices hated by personified Wisdom begotten by Yahweh mentions pride, arrogance, evil conduct, and twisted speech (Prov. 8:13). God's hatred of sin is expressive of His utter abhorrence, disgusting repugnance, and vehement aversion. Thus God hates both sin and sinners, insofar as they persist in a way of life opposed to God's will and purpose, because this rebelliousness attracts the hatred due to sin. God desires the wholehearted repentance of the sinner, but if he refuses to repent and persists in turning away from the ways of God, He is obliged in justice and love to punish and destroy (Hos. 11:5-12).

II. In the DSS.–The sectarian literature of the Qumrân community provides a unique insight into an aspect of Judaism in late pre-Christian and early Christian times. The Qumrân covenanters considered themselves to be the only true REMNANT of Israel, the Chosen People, the "sons of Aaron" and "Israel" (1QS 5:21f.). All those outside their ranks were considered to be "sons of darkness" (1QM 1:1–2:14), who are under the sway of the spirit of darkness which issues from the Angel of Darkness. God "loathes and forever hates its [the spirit of darkness'] ways" (1QS 3:26–4:1). According to the Community Rule one should love one's neighbor (cf. Lev. 19:17f.), who was by their definition a member of the Qumrân community: "love all the sons of the light" (1QS 1:10). The "sons of light" or Qumrân covenanters in turn are to "hate all the sons of darkness, each according to his guilt in God's vengeance" (1QS 1:10), i.e., all those outside their community of faith, who were considered their enemies. This hate is unqualified as an "everlasting hatred in a spirit of secrecy for the men of perdition" (1QS 9:21). The "everlasting hatred" is thus practiced in a "spirit of secrecy" or concealment, in that it does not interfere in worldly affairs. This means that the "son of light" practices nonretaliation by refraining from repaying evil with evil. "I will pay to no man the reward of evil; I will pursue him with goodness" (1QS 10:17). To pursue the "son of darkness" with goodness is not the result of love but a special case of the application of the concealed "everlasting hatred." The member is "to love all that He has chosen and to hate all that He has rejected" (1QS 1:3f.). As the ones who once were members now "hate the neighbor [member of the community]" (CD 8:6), so the members themselves "will have no compassion on all who depart from the way" (1QS 10:20); i.e., love remains restricted to the faithful members of the community whereas the unfaithful ones are hated just as are the nonmembers. The Qumrân covenanters follow this unusual two-edged ethic because of their imminent eschatology, which taught that God would soon execute vengeance.

III. In the NT.–The Greek term *miséō* as used in the NT reflects a variety of semantic ranges, which must each be evaluated in its own context.

A. Human Hatred. In relations between human beings "hate" has been radically called into question by Jesus. In the Sermon on the Mount Jesus quoted a popular (SB, I, 253) maxim: "You shall love your neighbor and hate your enemy" (Mt. 5:43). Whereas the command to love one's neighbor is based upon Lev. 19:18, there is in the OT no positive teaching that one should hate one's enemy. To the contrary, it is possible to speak of the love of one's enemy (Ex. 23:4f.; Dt. 22:4). It can also be maintained that in Lev. 19:18 the demand of love for one's neighbor means also love of one's enemy (v. 17). It has, therefore, been said that Jesus was slanderous in referring to the hate of one's enemy when neither Judaism nor the OT explicitly taught such hate. The finds from Qumrân in 1947 have thrown totally new light on this issue. The Manual of Discipline demands that as part of an oath upon entering the Qumrân community the one seeking entrance must vow to "love all the sons of light, . . . and hate all the sons of darkness" (1QS 1:10). It has been shown above (II) that the "sons of darkness" are nonmembers or outsiders, who are the enemies of the Qumrân covenanters. This Qumrân concept of hate comes as close to the corresponding phrase in Mt. 5:43 as could be, and it provides a vivid background that demonstrates that there was actually such a demand in a segment of the Judaism of NT times. Jesus overturned this concept of hate toward one's enemy by commanding His disciples to live by a new principle: "love your enemies" (Mt. 5:44). This is much more than treating an enemy well, as is shown by the demand to pray for one's enemy (v. 44b). Jesus' charge to "do good to those who hate you" (Lk. 6:27) is a corollary of love and not an outgrowth of an "eternal hatred" (1QS 9:21) as in Qumrân. Jesus' ethic, by a total application of the absolute mandate of love in all situations of life, overcomes the irreconcilable tension of the two-edged ethic of love toward one's brother and hate toward one's enemy as practiced by the community and other segments of Judaism. Man is unable to live with the attitudes of both hate and love (Mt. 6:24; Lk. 16:13). One cancels the other.

Discipleship to Jesus involves a certain kind of hate. A prerequisite for becoming a follower of Jesus is the "hate" (Gk. *miseí,* NAB "turning his back on") of one's father, mother, brothers, sisters, wife, and children (Lk. 14:26). This is no malicious hate that seeks wrong; it is neither to lack love, nor to dislike, nor to disregard, but it is to put one's total commitment to someone higher and more important than even those to whom one has the closest ties in the human sphere. No personal interest is to take precedence over loyalty to the Master. To "hate" here means to "love less" as the Matthaean form of this saying shows: "He who loves father and mother more than me is not worthy of me" (10:37). In true discipleship relatives must take second place; first place must be given to Jesus and His kingdom (Mt. 6:19ff., 33). The Fourth Gospel contains another related saying of Jesus: "He who loves his life loses it, and he who hates his life in this world will keep it for eternal life" (Jn. 12:25; cf. Dodd, pp. 78-81). The basic antithesis is between loving and hating one's life. The follower of Jesus must not treasure his life "in this world" more than the life that will last into and throughout eternity. "Hate" here means a repudiation of a life apart from the Source of life. Man cannot live at the same time in the spheres of both the old and new life (cf. Tit. 3:3).

Of all the NT witnesses, the Johannine writings employ the word "hate" more often than any of the others. In Jn. 3:20 (cf. 1QS 4:24) the evildoer is said to "hate" the light. Evildoers are unbelievers who continue to practice wickedness; they can see the light of Jesus shining into their hearts, but through their evil deeds they demonstrate their hate and thus their rejection of the light of Jesus (1:4, 9; 8:12; 9:5; 12:35f.). Not only the Jews (Jn. 7:1) but also the world hates Jesus because of the evidence He brings that what it does is evil (v. 7). Since the world hates Jesus, it will also hate His followers (15:18f.), who are not of the world (17:14; cf. 1 Jn. 3:13) but do the works of Jesus. He who hates the follower of Jesus hates Jesus Himself. He who hates Jesus hates the Father also (Jn. 15:23). In 1 John hate belongs to the old aeon and not to the new one. These two aeons are contrasted by the typical Johannine dualism of darkness and light. Corresponding to this dualism is the antithesis of hate and love. He who hates belongs to the realm of darkness and has no part in the sphere of light. He who hates his brother, therefore, is still in the darkness of the old aeon (1 Jn. 2:9), walking in the darkness that has blinded his eyes (v. 11) from the light of the new aeon. The hate of the brother is not merely dislike, lesser love, or disregard; it is equal to murder (3:15). He who makes a profession to love God but hates his brother is a liar (4:20), for one cannot hate the one seen and love the One unseen.

In the Synoptic Gospels hate is a characteristic of the enemy and of the nonbeliever (cf. Tit. 3:3 [Gk. *stygētos*]). The first advent of Jesus Christ means deliverance from "all who hate us" (Lk. 1:71). This deliverance may not be immediate for each believer, for the follower of Jesus must expect to be hated by all for Jesus' name's sake (Mt. 10:22). As one of the eschatological woes, the hate of all nations will be directed against the followers of Jesus (Mt. 24:9; Mk. 13:13; Lk. 21:17). This hate will cause a falling away, a betraying, and a hating of one another (Mt. 24:10). Hate is therefore a sign of the eschaton at the second coming of Christ. The follower of Jesus will expect hate from the nonbeliever and should even rejoice in it (Lk. 6:22), because in experiencing it he is associated with the destiny of the Lord. The believer does not live by the *lex talionis,* but by love as the only rule for his life, also in relation to his enemies. The follower of Jesus does not live in a state of nonresistance, but of nonretaliation based on love. The Christian's task is to resist by doing good to those who hate him (Lk. 6:27; cf. Rom. 12:20; Klassen, pp. 345-350).

B. Divine Hatred. The NT is noted primarily for its presentation of the love of God. There are, however, some instances in which the idea of divine hate comes to expression. Basic to both OT and NT is the notion that the God of love is also the holy and jealous God who is obliged to destroy in the day of final judgment those who persist in rebellion against Him. The NT never speaks of hate in God. Still it knows the idea of God's hate. Paul quotes in Rom. 9:13 a saying from Mal. 1:2f.: "Jacob I loved, but Esau I hated." The prophetic saying maintains that God's choice of Jacob was an act of His grace and was not conditioned by the merit or failure of either of these twin brothers. God's freedom of choice is preserved. The "hatred" of Esau and the peoples descended from him does not involve ill will or the intention to harm and destroy on the part of God. The preference of Jacob is like that of the husband who "loves" one of his spouses and "hates" or "loves less" the other. God's "hatred" of Esau does not imply eternal damnation; it is expressive of God's freedom in working out the counsels of His own will. Paul's point in quoting this complex declaration is to illustrate that God still maintains His freedom of choice as to who shall be the recipient of His promises. The present "hate" of literal Israel and choice of spiritual Israel to accomplish God's purpose for the world is not guided by an arbitrary love or hate of God and it does not imply injustice on His part. It demonstrates God's righteousness in making salvation possible for all mankind, because "Israel" means the elect and not Jews by physical descent. By election God follows a unique plan of love and salvation for all mankind.

The hate of Jesus (and the Church) for the works of the Nicolaitans in Ephesus (Rev. 2:6) differentiates between the ones who work evil and their evil works. Only the evil works are hated. An extension of this differentiation leads to the well-known idea of hating the sin and loving the sinner. This idea is already embedded in the OT, where God hates sin but has no pleasure in the death of the sinner, and desires only that he be converted from his ways and live (Ezk. 18:23).

Hebrews 1:9 applies the sentence of Ps. 45:7, "thou hast loved righteousness and hated lawlessness," to the lordship of Jesus Christ. Hate is here again directed against sin but not the sinner. The purpose of this quotation is to support the supremacy of Jesus Christ.

Bibliography.–A. Carr, *Expos.* 6th ser., 12 (1905), 153-160; J. Denney, *Expos.T.,* 20 (1909), 41f.; *TDNT,* IV, *s.v.* μισέω (Michel); M. Smith, *HTR,* 45 (1952), 71-73; C. H. Dodd, *NTD,* 2 (1955), 75-86; E. F. Sutcliffe, *RQ,* 2 (1959-60), 345-355; *Dictionary of Biblical Theology* (Eng. tr. 1967), *s.v.* "Hate" (J. Brière); A. Dihle, *Die goldene Regel* (1962), pp. 114-16; K. Stendahl, *HTR,* 55 (1962), 343-355; W. Klassen, *NTS,* 9 (1962-63), 337-350; W. von Soden,

Akkadisches Handwörterbuch (1965); H. Donner, *ZAW*, 79 (1967), 344-46. G. F. HASEL

HATHACH hā'thak [Heb. *hᵃṯāḵ*; Gk. *Hachrathaios*]; AV HATACH. One of the eunuchs of Ahasuerus, appointed to attend on Esther (Est. 4:5f., 9f.), through whom she learned from Mordecai of Haman's plot.

HATHATH hā'thath [Heb. *ḥᵃṯaṯ*] (1 Ch. 4:13). Son of Othniel and grandson of Kenaz.

HATIPHA hə-tī'fə, hat'i-fə [Heb. *ḥᵃṭîpā'*–'taken, captive'(?)]. The ancestral head of a family of temple servants that returned from Babylon (Ezr. 2:54; Neh. 7:56; 1 Esd. 5:32 [AV Apoc. ATIPHA, NEB Apoc. ATEPHA]).

HATITA hə-tī'tə, hat'i-tə [Heb. *ḥᵃṭîṭā'*]. Head of a family among the "sons of the gatekeepers" who returned from exile (Ezr. 2:42; Neh. 7:45; 1 Esd. 5:28 [AV Apoc. TETA, NEB Apoc. ATETA]).

HATTIL hat'il [Heb. *ḥaṭṭîl*]. A company of servants of Solomon appearing in the postexilic literature (Ezr. 2:57; Neh. 7:59; 1 Esd. 5:34 [AV, NEB, Apoc. HAGIA]).

HATTUSH hat'ush [Heb. *ḥaṭṭûš*].

1. Son of Shemaiah, a descendant of the kings of Judah, in the 5th generation from Zerubbabel (1 Ch. 3:22). He returned with Zerubbabel and Ezra from Babylon to Jerusalem (Ezr. 8:2; Neh. 12:2). In 1 Esd. 8:29 Hattus (AV LETTUS; NEB ATTUS) is called the son of Shecaniah, as in Ezr. 8:2. It is possible that the Hattush of the house of David and the priest of the same name, mentioned in Neh. 10:4; 12:2, are identical. The latter was one of those who signed the covenant with Nehemiah (Neh. 10:4).

2. Son of Hashabneiah; he aided Nehemiah in repairing the walls of Jerusalem (Neh. 3:10).

HAUGHTY; HAUGHTINESS [Heb. *rûm*] (2 S. 22:28 par. Ps. 18:27 [MT 28]; Prov. 6:17; 21:4; Isa. 10:12; Jer. 48:29); AV also HIGH, PROUD; NEB also PROUD, VAINGLORY, INSOLENT; [*ga'ᵃwâ*] (Isa. 13:11); NEB ARROGANCE; [*gāḇâ*] (Ps. 101:5; 138:6; Prov. 16:18; 18:12; Isa. 2:11, 17; 3:16; 5:15; Ezk. 16:50; Zeph. 3:11); AV also HIGH, PROUD, LOFTY; NEB also PROUD, ARROGANCE, "hold themselves high," "flaunt your pride"; [*yāhîr*] (Prov. 21:24); [Gk. *hyperḗphanos*] (Rom. 1:30); AV PROUD; NEB ARROGANT; [*hypsēlós*] (Rom. 12:16); AV HIGH THINGS; [*hypsēlophronéō*] (1 Tim. 6:17); AV HIGHMINDED; NEB PROUD; [*megála*] (Rev. 13:5); AV GREAT THINGS; NEB BOMBAST; **HAUGHTILY** [Heb. *mārôm* (2 K. 19:22 par. Isa. 37:23), *rômâ* (Mic. 2:3)]; AV also "on high"; NEB also UPRIGHT; [*ga'ᵃwâ*] (Ps. 31:23 [MT 24]); AV PROUD; NEB ARROGANT.

The OT and NT terms all have the meaning of holding oneself high or exalted. The haughtiness of mankind is hated by the Lord (Prov. 6:17) and will be brought down in the day when the Lord is glorified (Isa. 2:17).

N. J. O.

HAUNT [Heb. *regel*–'foot'] (1 S. 23:22); NEB omits; [*nāweh*] (Isa. 34:13; 35:7); AV HABITATION; NEB ROUGH LAND; [*mā'ôn*] (Jer. 49:33; 51:37); AV DWELLING, DWELLING PLACE; [Gk. *phylakḗ*] (Rev. 18:2); AV HOLD, CAGE. A haunt is generally a place frequented with some regularity. David hid in the rocky strongholds in the Wilderness of Ziph (1 S. 23:14-24; 26:1-5) during his flight from Saul. Heb. *regel* refers, literally, to the place where David's "foot" was. Jackals (Isa. 34:13; 35:7; Jer. 49:33; 51:37) usually inhabit a desolate or ruined place — in these passages, places devastated as a result of God's judgment. Gk. *phylakḗ* usually refers to a place of detention for those awaiting sentence — thus, a "prison" (cf. He. 11:36; 1 Pet. 3:19; Rev. 20:7). In this sense, fallen Babylon (Rev. 18:2) would be equivalent to the abode of Satan, the fallen angels, and the spirits of unbelievers as they await the final sentence of divine judgment. It is also possible, however, that here *phylakḗ* designates the habitation from which these beings keep watch (cf. R. Mounce, comm. on Revelation [*NICNT*, 1977], p. 323; H. B. Swete, comm. on Revelation [repr. 1954], p. 227).

Bibliography.–W. J. Dalton, *Christ's Proclamation to the Spirits* (1964), pp. 158ff.; M. H. Scharlemann, *Concordia Theological Monthly*, 27 (1956), 81-94. J. T. DENNISON, JR.

HAURAN ho'ran, hôr'ən [Heb. *ḥawrān*–'black-land'? (see BDB, p. 301; KoB, p. 284); Gk. *Auranitis*; Gk. *Loraneitis* in Ezk. 47:18 appears to be a copyist's error]. A province in Transjordan N of the Yarmuk River and E of the Sea of Galilee. The term occurs in the Bible only in Ezk. 47:16, 18 and serves to mark the boundary of the ideal land of Israel at its northern and eastern extent.

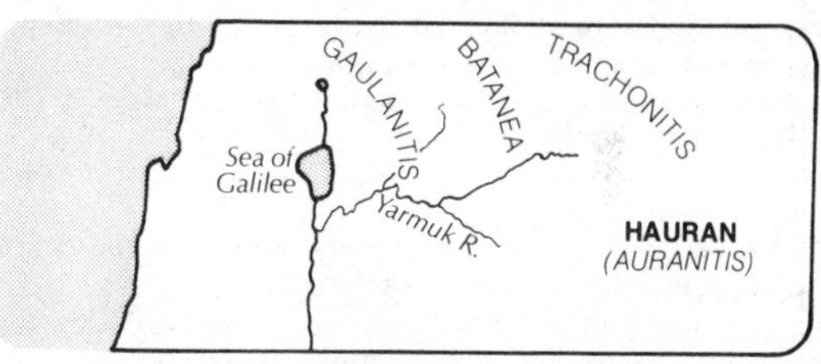

The name occurs in Egyptian texts of the 19th Dynasty as *Ḫu-ru-na*, and four centuries later in Assyrian texts. In his eighteenth year, Shalmaneser III (859-824 B.C.) crossed the Euphrates for the sixteenth time, moving against the Aramean city-states. He records, "I advanced as far as the mountains of Hauran" (*šadêᵉ* ᵐᵃᵗ*ḫa-ú-ra-ni*; see *ARAB*, I, § 672; *ANET*, p. 283). According to Y. Aharoni, Tiglath-pileser III (745-727 B.C.) reorganized sixteen districts of Aram-Damascus into four or five Assyrian provinces, one of which was Hauran (*LBHG*, p. 333). In an accompanying map, Aharoni shows the province of Hauran lying E of the provinces of Karnaim and Gilead, hence only the eastern portion of what is generally included in the term. (He does not provide specific documentation for these data. The reference to "sixteen districts of Aram" is found in *ARAB*, I, § 777; *ANET*, p. 283.) Ashurbanipal (669-631), in his ninth campaign, which was chiefly against Uate' king of Arabia, records a victory in a bloody battle "in the district of Haurina" (*ARAB*, II, § 818; *ANET*, p. 298).

Jews, Greeks, and Nabateans settled in Hauran in the 4th and succeeding centuries B.C., and there were continuing struggles for control. The Maccabeans conquered the region in the 2nd cent., and the Nabateans took it from Alexander Janneus in 90 B.C. It was then known as Auranitis, a province bounded on the north by Trachonitis and on the northwest by Gaulanitis (Josephus *Ant.* xvii.11.4 [319]; xviii.4.6 [106]). It was made part of the Decapolis by Pompey. About 23 B.C. Augustus gave it to Herod the Great, and upon his death it passed to Herod Philip (Lk. 3:1). Caligula gave it to Herod Agrippa I in A.D. 37, and subsequently it was ruled by Agrippa II until the Roman war. For a brief period (A.D. 85-106) it was ruled by the Nabateans, but it was finally passed to the Romans and was made part of the province of Syria (*BJ* i.20.4 [398-400]; ii.6.3 [94f.]; ii.17.4 [421]).

The extent of the identification of Hauran with BASHAN cannot be determined, but the names refer in part at least to the same territory, which is tableland at an elevation of between 490 and 700 m. (1600 and 2300 ft.), extremely fertile, with well-watered soil of volcanic origin. Except for the slopes of Jebel ed-Druze to the east, the region is almost without trees, and is important for the production of wheat.

Modern Hauran (Ḥaurân) is approximately equivalent in extent to the province of Auranitis, extending from Jebel el-ʿAswad in the north to the Yarmuk River in the south, and from el-Jōlân (Golan) on the west to Jebel ed-Druze on the east. It is thus the eastern portion of Hauran as the term is generally applied, and constitutes a region about 80 km. (50 mi.) long and 72 km. (45 mi.) wide. Ḥaurân is divided into three districts: (1) el-Lejâ in the northwest, a region filled with volcanic rocks; (2) en-Nuqra in the southwest, a region of decomposed lava; and (3) el-Jebel, the mountain range on the east, known as Jebel Ḥaurân and as Jebel ed-Druze. It received the latter name because the Druzes settled in this region after they were driven from the Lebanon in 1860. Jebel Ḥaurân is mentioned in the Mishnah as one of the heights where the fire signals were lighted to announce the beginning of the New Year (*Rosh ha-Shanah* ii.4).

Bibliography.–*GP*, I, 274f.; II, 8-11; *HGHL*, pp. 603-620; *GB*, pp. 219-226; W. F. Albright, *AJSL*, 53 (1936), 1-12.

W. S. L. S.

HAVEN [Heb. *ḥôp*; cf. Arab. *ḥaffat*–'border'] (Gen. 49:13); [*māḥôz*] (Ps. 107:30); NEB HARBOUR; [*bô'*] (Isa. 23:1); AV "entering in"; NEB "port of entry." *Ḥôp* means primarily "shore" (cf. RSV "shore" in 49:13a); the context, however, indicates a place where ships are harbored. Heb. *māḥôz* occurs only once in the OT and seems to refer to a "shipyard" (KoB, p. 512). The verb *bô'* means literally to "enter."

In biblical times Palestine possessed no good harbors. South of Mt. Carmel the coastline is almost straight. The Bay of Accho, called Ptolemais in NT times (Acts 21:7), offered the best natural harbor, but it lacked adequate shelter from the winds. Dor and Joppa were also used, but they provided even less protection in stormy weather. Phoenicia's shoreline is much rougher, and natural ports at places such as Tyre and Sidon encouraged the development of trade. *See* SHIPS.

See *WBA*, p. 18. N. J. O.

HAVILAH hav'ə-lə, hav'ē-lä [Heb. *ḥ^{a}wîlâ*–perhaps 'a stretch of sand' as diminutive of *ḥôl*–'sand'].

1. A son of Cush and a grandson of Ham (Gen. 10:7; 1 Ch. 1:9).

2. A son of Joktan and a grandson of Eber (Gen. 10:29; 1 Ch. 1:23).

HAVILAH hav'ə-lə, häv'ē-lä [Heb. *ḥ^{a}wîlâ*–perhaps 'a stretch of sand' as diminutive of *ḥôl*–'sand']. A land (or lands?) of uncertain location. Gen. 2:11f. associates it with the Pishon River and with the natural resources of gold, bdellium, and onyx stone. The Pishon has been variously identified with a lower branch of the Nile (Aharoni, p. 21), the Indus or Ganges rivers (cf. Skinner, pp. 64f.), the Wâdī el-Dhawasir in central Arabia (Glaser, pp. 319-326), and other rivers. Gold and fragrant gums are found in various places in the Arabian peninsula. No certainty of location is therefore achieved by these associations. Gen. 10:30 places it somewhere between Mesha (northern Arabia?) and the "hill country of the east," but neither of these can be identified with certainty. Gen. 10:7 places it near Seba (southwestern Arabia?), Sabtah (northwestern or southern Arabia?), Raamah (southwestern Arabia?), and Sabteca (?), but again no certainty of location can be attained. Gen. 25:18 makes it, with Shur (on the northeastern border of Egypt), a boundary of the Ishmaelites. This might suggest a location in eastern Arabia, but a southern location cannot be ruled out. 1 S. 15:7, in language akin to Gen. 25:18, traces Saul's routing of the Amalekites from "Havilah as far as Shur," thus locating it somewhere in the northeastern Sinai peninsula (however, in this passage an original Hachilah may have been corrupted to Havilah; cf. 1 S. 23:19; 26:1, 3). The ancient geographer Strabo mentions a people called Chaulotaioi who lived in northern Arabia (*Geog.* xvi.4.2) and who may in some way be connected. Another possible connection is the ancient city of Avalitis (Pliny *Ep.* vi.28), modern Zeila in Somalia.

None of this evidence is conclusive, and it may well be that more than one area was known as Havilah. It is also possible that a single Havilah encompassed a large geographical area.

Bibliography.–Y. Aharoni and M. Avi-Yonah, *Macmillan Bible Atlas* (rev. ed. 1977); E. Glaser, *Skizze der Geschichte Arabiens*, II (1890); J. A. Montgomery, *Arabia and the Bible* (1934); J. Skinner, comm. on Genesis (*ICC*, 2nd ed. 1930).

J. E. H.

HAVOC. In the RSV the word is used only once. The apostle Paul is described in Acts 9:21 as "the man who made havoc [Gk. *porthéō*] in Jerusalem." The Greek verb means "pillage" or "destroy" (cf. AV "destroy"; NEB "try to destroy").

HAVVOTH-JAIR hav'əth jā'ər [Heb. *ḥawwōṯ yā'îr*–'the tent-villages of Jair'; Gk. *Ayōth Iaïr*]; AV HAVOTH-JAIR, "towns of Jair" (1 Ch. 2:23). A number of villages in Bashan (hence AV Bashan-havoth-jair in Dt. 3:14) and/or Gilead (Nu. 32:40f.; Dt. 3:14; Jgs. 10:4; 1 Ch. 2:23; cf. "towns of Jair," Josh. 13:30; "villages of Jair," 1 K. 4:13). According to Dt. 3:14 Jair of the tribe of Manasseh took possession of "all the region of ARGOB," defined as "Bashan, as far as the border of the Geshurites and the Maacathites," and called the villages after his name, Havvoth-jair. This seems clear, but other passages complicate the problem. In Josh. 13:30 "all the towns of Jair" (lit. "all Havvoth-jair") were in Bashan, specifically "sixty cities." Jgs. 10:4, however, specifies "thirty cities, called Havvoth-jair" and locates them "in the land of Gilead." According to 1 K. 4:13 a certain Ben-geber "had the villages of [Heb. *ḥawwōṯ*] Jair the son of Manasseh, which are in Gilead, and he had the region of Argob, which is in Bashan, sixty great cities with walls and bronze bars." 1 Ch. 2:23 records that Jair had 33 cities in the land of Gilead, but Geshur and Aram "took from them Havvoth-jair, Kenath and its villages, sixty towns."

There are several problems. (1) Jair is a descendant of Manasseh in all references except 1 Ch. 2:23, which traces his descent from Judah through Tamar, Perez, and Hezron. Possibly traditions have become intertwined, and two persons named "Jair" are to be distinguished. However, Machir the son of Manasseh settled in Gilead (Nu. 32:40), and Jair was the son of Segub and grandson of Hezron and the daughter of Machir (1 Ch. 2:21f.). It is therefore possible to conclude that only one Jair is intended. (2) Were there 60, 30, or 33 villages? The assumption that there were 30 (or 33, with 30 serving as a round number) in Gilead and either another 30 (totaling 60) or an additional 60 in Bashan agrees with 1 K. 4:13. (3) The precise boundaries of Bashan cannot be determined (*see*

BASHAN), but the Yarmuk River is generally taken to be the boundary between Gilead (to the south) and Bashan (to the north). (4) The inclusion of "as it is to this day" indicates that part or all of the passage in Dt. 2:14 is a scribal gloss of a later date and cannot be used as an earlier and therefore more definitive description. (5) The relationship of Argob to Bashan is problematic. The above problems prevent a clear solution at present.

Bibliography.–*HGHL*, p. 355 and notes, p. 387 n. 3; *GP*, I, 274f., II, 8-11; *GTTOT*, §§ 21, 33, 302, 307, 309, 931, 1685.

W. S. LASOR

HAWK [Heb. *nēṣ*; Gk. *hiérax*] (Lev. 11:16; Dt. 14:15; Job 39:26). One of several small or medium-sized birds of prey of the genus *Accipiter*. In biblical times the largest Palestinian hawks were 60 cm. (2 ft.) long with flat heads, hooked beaks, strong talons, and extremely keen eyes. They nested on Mt. Carmel and on the Galilean hills in large trees and on mountain crags. Flocks of them were found near Beer-sheba and in the region of the Dead Sea. They constructed crude nests of twigs, and most of the food they found was carried off alive to their young. The lists of Lev. 11:13-19f. and Dt. 14:11-18 each included hawks of several species. The sparrow hawk (*Accipiter nisus*) may be referred to in Lev. 11:16; Dt. 14:15; Job 39:26, while in Lev. 11:14; Dt. 14:13; Job 28:7 (Heb. *'ayyâ*, "falcon, buzzard"; AV KITE, VULTURE; NEB also KITE) either the falcon (*Falco peregrinus*), the buzzard (*Buteo ferox*), or the harrier (*Circus aeruginosus*) could be indicated. Perhaps the kite (*Milvus migrans*) was referred to in Lev. 11:14 (possibly the "buzzard" of Dt. 14:13). The allusion in Job 39:26 appears to be to the soaring flight of these birds.

The species of bird designated by Heb. *qā'aṯ* in Isa. 34:11 is uncertain. The RSV translates "hawk," whereas the AV has "cormorant" and the NEB "horned owl."

See also FALCON; KITE. R. K. H.

HAY [Gk. *chórtos*] (1 Cor. 3:12). Used metaphorically by Paul to describe faulty "work" built on the foundation of Jesus Christ. *See* GRASS.

HAZAEL hā'zə-el [Heb. *ḥ^azā'ēl, ḥ^azā'ēl*, Akk. *Ḫaza'ilu*]. A highly placed court official under Ben-hadad (II?). Hazael was first mentioned in a statement by God to Elijah that the prophet was to anoint Hazael as king of Syria (1 K. 19:15). Subsequently Ben-hadad became ill and sent Hazael to Elisha for a prognosis (2 K. 8:7-9). While visiting the prophet in Damascus, Hazael was informed that he himself would succeed to the throne of Syria, a prospect that dismayed Elisha considerably even though he was the bearer of the tidings (2 K. 8:11-13). On his return Hazael suffocated his ailing master and succeeded immediately to the throne (*ca.* 843 B.C.). In the annals of Shalmaneser III king of Assyria (859-824 B.C.), the incident was recorded in the following terse statement: "Adad-'idri forsook the land; Hazael, the son of a nobody [i.e., one without royal parentage], seized the throne."

In an early demonstration of Syrian power, Hazael resisted the attack of a coalition formed by Jehoram of Israel and Ahaziah of Judah (*ca.* 842 B.C.). Ramoth-gilead, which had been recaptured by Jehoram, was besieged by Hazael, and in the ensuing battle Jehoram sustained severe wounds and returned to Jezreel (2 K. 8:28f.; 9:14f.). The annals of Shalmaneser III recorded that in his 18th year (*ca.* 841 B.C.) he fought a battle against Hazael at Damascus, in which the Syrian capital and its king survived, although the surrounding countryside and its villages were devastated. The annals claimed the defeat of the Syrian king, who was described as losing 1121 chariots, 6000 soldiers, and 470 horsemen, along with large quantities of supplies and a considerable amount of Syrian territory. Hazael survived yet another Assyrian attack on Damascus (*ca.* 837 B.C.), after which Shalmaneser abandoned any further attempts to curb the increasing strength of the city-states in Syria.

Hazael's name in cuneiform (2nd line: *ᵐḫa-za-'i-il*). Detail from the Black Obelisk of Shalmaneser III (Trustees of the British Museum)

Freed from the threat of Assyrian military intervention, Hazael was able to move against Israel and Judah at will. Jehu of Israel (841-813 B.C.) found himself in a state of almost continuous submission to Hazael, having to forfeit all of his lands E of the Jordan (2 K. 10:32f.; Am. 1:3) from the Arnon to Bashan in the north. Jehu's successor Jehoahaz (813-798 B.C.) fared little better than his predecessor. The Syrians swept through the country (2 K. 13:1-9), and the forces of Jehoahaz were reduced in numbers to such an extent that Israel was in complete servitude to Syria.

This eventuality was viewed in 2 K. 13:3 as an outpouring of divine anger upon an apostate nation, and would have resulted in the extermination of Israel had not God shown some compassion (2 K. 13:22f.). Not content with subjugating Israel, Hazael also turned his attention to the southern kingdom. Apparently he was eager to control the lucrative caravan trade routes which terminated in Philistia. Accordingly Hazael marched southward, reducing Gath (2 K. 12:17) and other Philistine cities. Having secured his flank he turned to attack Jerusalem, but was dissuaded from his objective by Joash of Judah (837-796 B.C.), who offered him large amounts of palace and temple treasure if he would spare the capital city (2 K. 12:17f.; 2 Ch. 24:23f.).

Hazael died *ca.* 798 B.C., shortly after the decease of Jehoahaz of Israel (2 K. 13:24), and it was only then that the northern kingdom was able to halt further Syrian aggression under Hazael's son Ben-hadad. Hazael did much to ensure that Damascus became a prosperous and attractive capital city, and for this enterprise he was commemorated in subsequent ages (Josephus *Ant.* ix.4.6 [93]). Archeological excavations at Arslan Tash, the site of a provincial capital known to the Assyrians as Ḫadâtu, revealed the presence of a small ivory inlay from a couch or bed. On the inlay was written ". . . belonging to our lord Hazael. . . ." The bed may have been taken as spoil to Assyria during a raid by the armies of Adadnirari III (805-782 B.C.).

See also BEN-HADAD.

Bibliography.–M. F. Unger, *Israel and the Aramaeans of Damascus* (1957; repr. 1980), pp. 75-82, 158-163; D. W. Thomas, ed., *DOTT*, pp. 46-52, 242-250; K. A. Kitchen, *The Bible in Its World* (1977), p. 111. R. K. H.

HAZAIAH hə-zā'yə [Heb. *ḥ^azāyâ*–'Yahweh sees']. Among

the inhabitants of Jerusalem mentioned in the list of Judahites in Neh. 11:5.

HAZAR-ADDAR hā'zər-ad'ər [Heb. *ḥ^aṣar-'addār*–'noble (or 'wide') village'; Gk. *épaulis Arad*]. A place named among the settlements of southern Judah, near the border with Edom (Nu. 34:4). The site of Khirbet el-Qudeirât, 11 km. (7 mi.) NW of Kadesh-barnea, fits the context very well (cf. Ezk. 47:17). Evidently it is the same place mentioned in Josh. 15:3 by the name HEZRON, although in this passage ADDAR follows as a separate locality.

A. H. LEWIS

HAZAR-ENAN hā'zər-ē'nən [Heb. *ḥ^aṣar 'ênān*–'village of the spring'; Gk. *aulḗ toú Ainan*; *Asernain*]; **HAZAR-ENON** [Heb. *ḥ^aṣar 'ênôn*]. A place at the easternmost point of the ideal northern boundary of the Promised Land, midway between Damascus and the land of Hamath (Nu. 34:9; Ezk. 47:17 [NEB also 16; RSV also 18]; 48:1). Simons (*GTTOT*, §§ 283f.) places it at modern Qaryatein, about 112 km. (70 mi.) NE of Damascus in the direction of Palmyra. From its name and position, Hazar-enan must have been an important desert oasis. A. H. LEWIS

HAZAR-GADDAH hā'zər-gad'ə [Heb. *ḥ^aṣar gaddâ*–'village of good fortune'; Gk. B *Seri*, A *Asergadda*]. One of the southern towns taken and inhabited by the tribe of Judah (Josh. 15:27). Some have suggested a locality near the western shore of the Dead Sea. "Cliff" or "riverbank" is an alternate connotation of *gaddâ* (Aram. *gûddā'*), which could indicate a site overlooking one of the wadis such as the towering Masada. A. H. LEWIS

HAZAR-HATTICON. *See* HAZER-HATTICON.

HAZARMAVETH hā-zər-mā'veth [Heb. *ḥ^aṣarmāweṯ*–'court of death'; Gk. *Asarmōth*]; NEB HAZARMOTH. A place founded by descendants of the Semite Joktan (Gen. 10:26; 1 Ch. 1:20). Its location along the southern coast of Arabia is still marked by the cognate name (Wâdī) Hadramaut, which is a region of the Aden Protectorate. Excavations in this area have produced evidence of an ancient and powerful civilization; its capital was at Sabteca.

Bibliography.–H. von Wissman and M. Höfner, *Beiträge zur historischen Geographie des vorislamischen Südarabien* (1952); *BASOR*, 129 (1953); W. L. Brown and A. F. L. Beeston, "Sculptures and Inscriptions from Shabwa," *Journal of the Royal Asiatic Society* (1954), 43-62. A. H. LEWIS

HAZARMOTH. *See* HAZARMAVETH.

HAZAR-SHUAL hā'zər-sho͞o'əl [Heb. *ḥ^aṣar šû'āl*–'village of the fox'; Gk. *Arsōla, Asersoual, Esērsoual, Esēreoulab*]. One of the localities of the Negeb assigned to the tribe of Simeon (Josh. 19:3; 1 Ch. 4:28). It occurs only three times in the OT and always in connection with Beer-sheba. It may be identified hypothetically with Khirbet el-Meshash, 24 km. (15 mi.) E of Beer-sheba (*GTTOT*, § 317). Postexilic Judah again occupied Hazarshual (Neh. 11:27). A. H. LEWIS

HAZAR-SUSAH hā'zər-sū'sə [Heb. *ḥ^aṣar sûsâ*–'horse corral'; Gk. B *Sarsousin*, A *Asersousim*] (Josh. 19:5); **HAZAR-SUSIM** sū'sim [Heb. *ḥ^aṣar sûsîm*; Gk. *hḗmisy Sōsim*] (1 Ch. 4:31). A place listed among the villages of Simeon in the central part of the Negeb (Josh. 19:5). The neighboring village of Beth-marcaboth, whose name means "house of chariots," strengthens the idea that these towns were either depots for horse traders or military stations. The plural form of the name in 1 Ch. 4:31 suggests that the name is to be understood generically, rather than as "station of the mare." The exact site has not been identified, though *WHAB* suggests Sbalat Abū Sûsein, about 32 km. (20 mi.) W of Beer-sheba.

A. H. LEWIS

HAZAZON-TAMAR haz'ə-zon-tā'mar [Heb. *ḥaṣ^eṣōn tāmār*–'Hazazon of the palm trees']; AV HAZEZON-TAMAR. A place described (Gen. 14:7) as the home of an Amorite (Canaanite) group that was conquered along with En-mishpat and the territory of the Amalekites by an Elamite coalition under Chedorlaomer. In 2 Ch. 20:2 it is identified with En-gedi, a freshwater spring situated at about the midpoint of the west coast of the Dead Sea, whose ancient name has survived to modern times. The Chronicler's identification may be only approximate, since the site of the village has yet to be uncovered. Quite possibly it was the same place as the Tamar Solomon fortified (1 K. 9:18) in southeast Judah, which was located by Ezekiel (Ezk. 47:19; 48:28) in the southeast corner of the land of Israel. Tamar may perhaps be the modern Kurnub, 32 km. (20 mi.) WSW of the southern end of the Dead Sea, or if Hazazon-tamar is identified with En-gedi, its name has been preserved in the nearby oasis of Wâdī el-Ḥaṣāṣa NW of 'Ain Jidi. R. K. H.

HAZEL. *See* ALMOND.

HAZELELPONI. *See* HAZZALELPONI.

HAZER-HATTICON hā'zər-hat'ə-kon [Heb. *ḥ^aṣēr hattîḵôn*–'the middle village'; Gk. *aulḗ toú Saunan*] (Ezk. 47:16); AV HAZAR-HATTICON; NEB HAZAR-ENAN. From its context the name appears to be another name for HAZAR-ENAN. A. H. LEWIS

HAZERIM hə-zir'im [Heb. *ḥ^aṣērîm*] (Dt. 2:23, AV); RSV VILLAGES; NEB HAMLETS. This term is found only in the AV's transliteration in Dt. 2:23. It should be translated as "villages" (unwalled settlements; cf. Lev. 25:31) as in the RSV here and in the RSV and AV in Josh. 19:8; Neh. 11:25; etc. The villages were located in southwest Palestine, near Gaza, and were inhabited by the Avvim.

HAZEROTH ha-zē'rōth, haz'ə-roth [Heb. *ḥ^aṣērôṯ*–'enclosures']. An Israelite camp during the wilderness wanderings, the third from Sinai (Nu. 33:17f.; 11:35; 12:16; Dt. 1:1). It was there that Miriam and Aaron spoke against Moses' marriage to the Cushite woman and against his position as the sole mediator between God and Israel (Nu. 12:1f.). Miriam's resultant leprosy caused a week's delay in their journey (12:15f.; cf. *GTTOT*, § 432). The probable location is 'Ain Ḥaḍrā ("spring of the enclosure"), about 48 km. (30 mi.) NE of Jebel Mûsā (Mt. Sinai?), on the way to Aqabah.

See *GP* (1938), II, 214, 344. D. M. WATSON

HAZEZON-TAMAR. *See* HAZAZON-TAMAR.

HAZIEL hā'zi-əl [Heb. *ḥ^azî'ēl*–'divine vision'] (1 Ch. 23:9). A Levite of the sons of Shimei, of David's time.

HAZO hā'zō [Heb. *ḥ^azô*] (Gen. 22:22). Fifth son of Nahor. Possibly the eponym of a Nahorite family or clan.

HAZOR hā'zôr, hot'sôr [Heb. *ḥāṣôr*; Gk. *Asōr*].

1. A major urban center of Galilee during the 2nd mil-

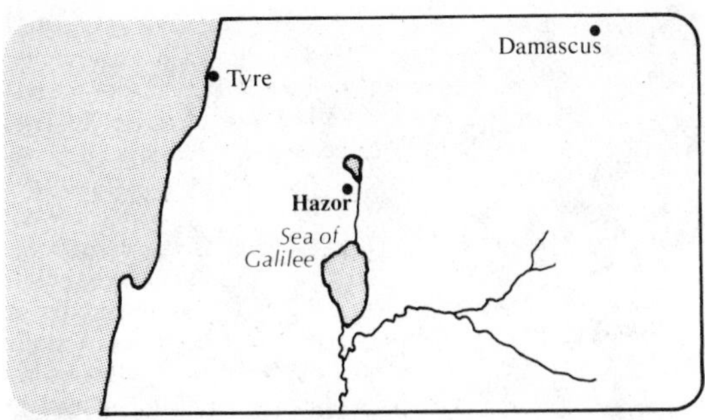

lennium B.C., perhaps the capital of the region; later an important city in the Israelite monarchy.

I. Name.–The Middle Bronze Age forms in nonbiblical sources, *ḥdw3i* (Egyptian Execration Texts) and uru*ḫa-ṣú-ra(-a)*ki (Akkadian from Mari), and from the Late Bronze Age, *ḥ-ḏ-r* (Thutmose III, *et al.*) and uru*ḫa-ṣú-ra/ri* (Am. Tab.), all point to an original **Ḥaṣōr(ā)*, evidently < **Ḥaḏār-*, meaning "settlement" (cf. BDB, p. 347). The shift of ā > ō suggests that the form is Canaanite in origin.

II. History.–The earliest historical allusion (12th Dynasty = M. B. II A, *ca.* 20th cent. B.C.) to Hazor is in the Egyptian Execration Texts' list of enemies to be cursed. The ruler of Hazor had the apparently non-Semitic name *Geṯ3i*; evidently he was not a vassal of Egypt, or he would not have been designated for the curse.

Hazor next appears in the archives of Mari, the famous Amorite center on the Euphrates. An ambassador to Hazor from Babylon, accompanied by an escort from Hazor, passed through Mari on his way back to Mesopotamia (*ARM,* VI, 78:5-17). Another group of ambassadors from several Babylonian cities traveled by way of Mari to the cities of north Syria and Hazor (*ARM,* VI, 23:19-24). An unpublished text records that the king of Hazor, Ibni-Adad, sent gifts to Ugarit and to Kaptara (Caphtor); Hazor also received a shipment of valuable metal from Mari (*ARM,* VI, 236). All of these passages agree with information from an ancient itinerary embedded in the text of a Babylonian "Dream Book." Hazor was the southernmost station on the route from Babylon to the West. It was evidently a major city in the Amorite milieu of that day (the Mari-Hammurabi age, M. B. II B, *ca.* 19th-18th cents. B.C.). That its ruler had an Akkadian name (Ibni-Adad) rather than an Amorite one (which would be Yabni-Addu) is remarkable, but this conforms with the find of an Išme-type name incised on a jar in the excavations at Hazor.

In the Late Bronze Age, Hazor again appears as one of the major cities of Galilee. It was conquered by Thutmose III (mid-15th cent. B.C.), but its appearance in a list from the reign of Amenhotep II (*ca.* 1430) suggests that it had some part in the rebellions against Egyptian rule under the 18th Dynasty. On the other hand, an emissary from Hazor (with an unusual spelling) appears in the Leningrad (St. Petersburg) Papyrus 1116A along with other representatives from some of the principal city-states in the Levant, especially Galilee.

During the 14th cent. B.C. Hazor continued to play an important role in the political foment of the so-called Amarna age. The ruler of Hazor is known to have sent two epistles to Pharaoh (Am.Tab. 227f.). In one he dares to call himself "king," but in the other he is more circumspect vis-à-vis the Egyptian overlord and gives himself the customary title "man" of Hazor. He is the only Canaanite ruler to adopt the royal title in correspondence with Egypt. He avers that he is faithfully preserving "Hazor together with its cities" for Pharaoh. Apparently an Egyptian military campaign was at hand and the monarch's arrival at Hazor was imminent. The local ruler, ʿAbdi-tirši, pleaded for Pharaoh's attention to the hostile activity against Hazor. But two other rulers in Canaan accused Hazor of disloyalty and sedition. Ayyāb (Job), apparently ruler of Ashtaroth in Bashan, accused Hazor's king of taking three towns from him (Am.Tab. 364:17-23); thus Hazor may have been expanding its influence eastward. Abimilki king of Tyre charged that "the king of Hazor has left his house [i.e., his proper sphere of influence] and aligned himself with the ʿApiru" (Am.Tab. 148:41-43). The outcome of these intrigues is unknown.

The disturbances that rocked the Levant during the transition from the 18th to the 19th Egyptian Dynasty probably permitted city-states such as Hazor a short breathing space of independence until Seti I succeeded in reimposing Egyptian suzerainty over the area; then Hazor appears again on that pharaoh's topographical list. Its geographical significance on the major route leading from Galilee to the Lebanese Beqaʿ is emphasized by the "Satirical Scribe" (*ANET,* p. 477b). A survey in Golan has shown that Bronze Age sites do not lie along the Roman road from Hazor to Damascus (across the "Bridge of Jacob's Daughters"); the more ancient highway must have followed the western side of the Huleh Valley to Abel-beth-maacah and Dan.

When the Israelites entered Galilee they experienced a confrontation with the royal house of Hazor on two fronts: in upper Galilee near the waters of MEROM (not Lake Huleh!) as depicted in Josh. 11, and in lower Galilee (Jgs. 4f.). Its fate was exceptionally hard in contrast to the other Canaanite centers in the area: ". . . none of the cities that stood on mounds did Israel burn, except Hazor only . . ." (Josh. 11:13). Hazor had formerly been the acknowledged leader in Galilee (Josh. 11:10), a position she had probably enjoyed sporadically from the Middle Bronze Age until the arrival of the Israelites. Either the same ruler of Hazor, Jabin, or a member of his dynasty, seems to have ruled southern Galilee (Harosheth-ha-goiim) through his viceroy Sisera. The Israelite victory under Deborah (Jgs. 4f.) marked the decline of Hazor's power in the region (Jgs. 4:23f.).

The city was allotted to the territory of Naphtali (Josh. 19:36), and its position in the list of Naphtali's towns (after Ramah) suggests that it was reckoned with upper Galilee in spite of its position in the valley below. During the united monarchy Hazor assumed a major role as one of Solomon's chief fortified cities (1 K. 9:15) along with Gezer and Megiddo (concerning the similar fortifications at all three sites, see below). Although it is not specifically mentioned, Hazor can scarcely have avoided destruction during the attack by Ben-hadad king of Aram in Galilee (1 K. 15:20; 2 Ch. 16:4).

Around 733 B.C. Tiglath-pileser III of Assyria invaded Galilee and brought Israelite independence there to an end. Hazor was one of the major towns captured at that time (2 K. 15:29). The city then fell into obscurity until the Hellenistic period, when Jonathan Maccabeus achieved a great victory over the Seleucid Demetrius (1 Macc. 11:67-74). The enemy retreated to the high ground around Kadesh (cf. Tob. 1:2).

III. Site.–Josephus (*Ant.* v.5.1 [199]) stated that Hazor was located "above Lake Semachonitis," the modern Lake Huleh (drained 1956); but he does not, as often supposed, equate the lake with the "waters of Merom" (Josh. 11:5). The first modern investigator to identify Hazor correctly with the mound of Tell el-Qedaḥ (also known as Tell el-Waqqâṣ) was J. L. Porter (*Handbook for Travellers in*

House at Hazor from the time of Amos showing earthquake damage (cf. Am. 1:1) (Institute of Archaeology, Hebrew University of Jerusalem)

These pillars at Hazor, at one time thought to be part of Solomon's stables, are now identified as part of a large storehouse (9th cent. B.C.) (W. S. LaSor)

Syria and Palestine [1875], pp. 415f.). His proposal was ignored or forgotten by other scholars until J. Garstang revived it (apparently unaware of Porter's priority) and conducted some excavations on the site (*Joshua-Judges* [1931], pp. 183-198, 381-83).

During the years 1955-58 four extensive seasons of excavation were carried out at Tell el-Qedaḥ under the direction of Y. Yadin. A further season was devoted to special problems during the fall of 1968. The abundance of finds has revealed much about the development of Hazor as an ancient urban center. *See* Plate 22.

Between Areas A and B, for example, later excavations have brought to light a shaft from the Israelite period that evidently was part of a water system similar to those at Megiddo and elsewhere. Area H reveals a temple whose plan has affinities with those of north Syria. Its later phases saw certain modifications in the ornamentation and utilization of the various rooms, including the addition of a "porch." Two pillars stood *within* the porch (note the striking parallel to 2 Ch. 3:17); the general arrangement is reminiscent of that later established for the Solomonic temple, with two major differences: the temple was already oriented N to S, and the innermost room contained the principal cult apparatus, altars, basins, etc. The niche in the northernmost wall would logically correspond to the holy of holies of the Israelite shrine; the image of the deity must have stood there, perhaps behind a veil.

Bibliography.–W. G. Dever, *BA*, 32 (1969), 71-78; J. Gray, *VT*, 16 (1966), 26ff.; K. M. Kenyon, *Bulletin of the Institute of Archaeology, University of London*, 4 (1964), 143-156; A. Malamat, *JBL*, 79 (1960), 12-19; "Northern Canaan and the Mari Texts," in J. A. Sanders, ed., *Near Eastern Archaeology in the Twentieth Century* (1970), pp. 164-177; Y. Yadin, *et al.*, *IEJ*, 6 (1956), 120-25; *Hazor I-II* (1958f.); *III-IV* (1964); Y. Yadin, *BA*, 19 (1956), 2-12; 20 (1957), 34-47; 21 (1958), 30-47; 22 (1959), 2-20; *IEJ*, 7 (1957), 118-123; 8 (1958), 1-14; 9 (1959), 74-88; *AOTS*, pp. 244-263; *Archaeological Discoveries in the Holy Land* (1967), pp. 57-66; *IEJ*, 19 (1969), 1-19; *BA*, 32 (1969), 49-71; "Symbols of Deities at Zinjirli, Carthage and Hazor," in Sanders, pp. 199-231; *Hazor* (1972); *Hazor: The Rediscovery of a Great Citadel of the Bible* (1975); *EAEHL*, III, *s.v.*

A. F. RAINEY

2. An unidentified town in southern Judah (Josh. 15:23). On the basis of the LXX B reading (*Asōrionaín*), some scholars (e.g., *WHAB*) would read it as Hazor-ithnan (cf. HAZOR-HADATTAH) and identify it with el-Jebarîyeh on the Wâdī Umm Ethnān, about 60 km. (37 mi.) SW of Beer-sheba.

3. Another town in southern Judah, identified with KERIOTH-HEZRON (Josh. 15:25).

4. A town inhabited by Benjaminites after the Exile (Neh. 11:33). It is now Khirbet Hazzûr, about 5 km. (3 mi.) NW of Jerusalem.

5. An unidentified place in Arabia conquered by Nebuchadnezzar (Jer. 49:28-33). It is uncertain whether the reference is to one town or several villages (cf. J. Bright, *Jeremiah* [*AB*, 1965], p. 336). G. A. L.

HAZOR-HADATTAH hā'zôr-hə-dat'ə [Aram. (?) *ḥāṣôr ḥ^a^ḏattâ*–'new Hazor'] (Josh. 15:25); AV HAZOR, HADATTAH. A city of Judah in the south, toward Edom (15:21). The presence of the Aram. adj. *ḥ^a^ḏaṯ* (cf. Heb. *ḥāḏāš*) is peculiar, since Aramaic influence is generally thought to be limited to the northeastern area of Palestine. Although Eusebius *Onom.* lists an *Asōr tēn kainēn*, it is located E of Ashkelon, and thus too far north to be Hazor-hadattah. It may be that residents of Hazor (which probably had some Aramean influence) resettled in the Negeb and named their town "New Hazor," using their native language, Aramaic. G. A. L.

HAZZELELPONI haz-ə-lel-pō'nē [Heb. *haṣṣ^e^lelpônî*]; AV HAZELELPONI. A feminine name in the list of the genealogy of Judah (1 Ch. 4:3).

HE hā [ה]. The fifth letter of the Hebrew alphabet, transliterated in this encyclopedia as *h*. It came also to be used for the numeral five and with the diaeresis for five thousand. *See* WRITING.

HEAD [Heb. *barzel*] (Dt. 19:5; 2 K. 6:5); [*gulgōleṯ*] (Ex. 38:26; Nu. 1:2, 18, 20, 22; 1 Ch. 10:10); AV also MAN, POLLS; NEB also SKULL; [*lehāḇâ*] (1 S. 17:7); [*lipnê*] ("at the head," Dt. 3:28; 10:11; 31:3; Jgs. 3:27; 9:39; 2 S. 10:16; 1 Ch. 19:16; Zec. 12:8); AV "before"; NEB also "across," "before," "led out"; [*m^e^ra'^a^šâ*] (Gen. 28:11, 18; 1 S. 19:13, 16; 26:7, 11f., 16; 1 K. 19:6; Jer. 13:18); AV also BOLSTER, PILLOW, PRINCIPALITY; NEB also "pillow for his head"; [*nûḏ*] ("wag the head," Ps. 64:8 [MT 9]; Jer. 48:27); AV "flee from," "skip for joy"; [*nāṣaḇ*] ("stand as head," 1 S. 19:20); AV APPOINTED; [*nāśî'*] (Nu. 3:24, 30, 35; 7:2; 25:14); AV CHIEF, PRINCE; NEB also CHIEF; [*pāqaḏ*] ("set as head," Jer. 13:21); AV CHIEF; [*ṣawwā'r*] (Cant. 7:5 [MT 6]); [*ṣemaḥ*] (Hos. 8:7); AV STALK; [*qāḏaḏ*] ("bow the head," Gen. 24:26, 48; 43:28; Ex. 4:31; 12:27; 34:8; Nu. 22:31; 1 Ch. 29:20; 2 Ch. 20:18; Neh. 8:6); NEB also "down," "low," etc.; [*qoḏqōḏ*] ("crown [or scab] of the head," Dt. 28:35; 33:16, 20; 2 S. 14:25; Job 2:7; Isa. 3:17; Jer. 2:16); AV also CROWN; NEB also BROW, SCALP; [*qāraḥaṯ*] ("bald head," Lev. 13:42f.); NEB FOREHEAD; [*rō'š*] (Gen. 3:15; 40:13, 16ff.; 47:31; 48:14, 17f.; 49:26; Ex. 6:14, 25; 12:9; etc.); AV also CAPTAIN, CHIEF, CHIEF MAN, CHIEFEST PLACE, FOREFRONT, LEAD, RULER, TOP, etc.; NEB also ABOVE, CHIEF, CHIEF CITY, CORNER, CROWNED, "in authority," LEADER, LORD, MASTER, etc.; [*śêḇâ*] (Lev. 19:32; 1 K. 2:6, 9; Prov. 16:31); NEB GREY HAIR; [*śar*] (1 Ch. 29:6; Ezr. 8:29); AV CHIEF; [Aram. *rē'š*] (Ezr. 5:10; Dnl. 2:28, 32, 38; 3:27; 4:5, 10, 13 [MT 2, 7, 10]; 7:1, 6, 9, 15, 20); AV also CHIEF; NEB also LEADER; [Gk. *akatakályptos*] ("head uncovered," 1 Cor. 11:13); AV UNCOVERED; NEB BARE-HEADED; [*ákron*] (He. 11:21); AV, NEB, TOP; [*kephalḗ*] (Mt. 5:36; 6:17; 8:20; 10:30; 14:8, 11; 21:42; 26:7; 27:29f., 37, 39; Mk. 6:24ff.; etc.); NEB also CORNERSTONE, HAIR, KEYSTONE, MAIN, etc.; [*kephalióō*] ("wound in the head," Mk. 12:4).

I. In the OT.–In the OT the primary meaning of "head" is its literal sense of the upper part of the body (Gen. 28:11, 18; 40:16f.; etc.).

A. Of People. In the OT gestures and expressions involving the head had great symbolic significance. Bowing the head was an indication of prayer (Ps. 35:13), worship (Gen. 24:26, 48; Ex. 4:31; 12:27; 34:8; Nu. 22:31; 1 Ch. 29:20; 2 Ch. 20:18; Neh. 8:6), or obeisance (Gen. 43:28). Obeisance might also be indicated by winding ropes about the head (1 K. 20:31f.). Blessings were conferred on the heads of men (Gen. 48:14, 17f.; 49:26; Prov. 10:6; 11:26). The installation of priests and kings involved crowning and anointing the head with oil (Ex. 29:6f.; Lev. 8:9, 12; 1 S. 10:1; 2 K. 9:3, 6); anointing also indicated the receipt of God's blessing (Ps. 23:5; 133:2), and good men would not be anointed with the oil of the wicked (Ps. 141:5).

What was done to the head could also indicate mourning, which usually involved putting dust or ashes on it (Lev. 10:6; Josh. 7:6; 1 S. 4:12; 2 S. 1:2; 13:19; etc.). Shame called for covering the head (Jer. 14:3f.). Mockery or derision was expressed by wagging the head (2 K. 19:21; Job 16:4; Ps. 22:7 [MT 8]; 64:8; 109:25; Isa. 37:22; Jer. 18:16; 48:27; Lam. 2:15). Feeding a hungry enemy heaps coals on his head (Prov. 25:22; Rom. 12:20), but joy rests on the heads of God's ransomed ones (Isa. 35:10; 51:11).

A man's responsibility for his deeds was indicated by the statement that they would return upon his head, whether murder (Josh. 2:19; 2 S. 1:16; 3:29; 1 K. 2:32ff.; Ezk. 33:4), other evil acts (1 S. 25:39; 1 K. 2:44; 8:32; 2 Ch. 6:23; Est. 9:23; Ezk. 9:10; 11:21; 16:43; 17:19; 22:31; Joel 3:4, 7 [MT 4:4, 7]; Ob. 15), taunts (Neh. 4:4), or mischief (Ps. 7:16 [MT 17]). To lift up one's head was to show pride (Jgs. 8:28; Job 10:15; Ps. 83:2 [MT 3]; 140:9 [MT 10]), but if Yahweh were the lifter, it was evidence of His favor (Ps. 3:3 [MT 4]; 27:6; 110:7; Jer. 52:31). The story of Joseph's encounter with Pharaoh's butler and baker contains an interesting juxtaposition of two meanings of "to lift the head," one indicating the restoration of someone to favor and the other indicating decapitation (Gen. 40:13, 19f.).

The head is also the center of the intellect and imagination (Dnl. 2:28; 4:5, 10, 13; 7:1, 15). "From head to foot" indicates the involvement of a man's entire body (Lev. 13:12; Dt. 28:35; Job 2:7; Isa. 1:5f.) or physical appearance (2 S. 14:25).

Finally, a "head" represents simply one person, as numbered for tax (Ex. 38:26) or census (Nu. 1:2, 18, 20, 22) purposes.

B. Of Animals. "Head" occurs also in the literal sense when it is used of animals: the serpent in Eden (Gen. 3:15); the Passover lamb (Ex. 12:9); bulls (Ex. 29:10; Lev. 1:4, 8; 3:2; 4:4, 11, 15; 8:14; Nu. 8:12), rams (Ex. 29:15, 17, 19; Lev. 8:18, 20, 22), sheep or goats (Lev. 1:12; 3:13; 4:24, 29; 16:21), lambs (Lev. 3:8; 4:33), calves (Lev. 9:13), and turtledoves or pigeons (Lev. 1:15; 5:8) used in regular or special sacrifices; mythical creatures, e.g., Leviathan (Job 41:7; Ps. 74:14), dragons (Ps. 74:13), and the creatures of the visions of Ezekiel (1:22, 25f.; 10:1) and Daniel (7:6, 20). Solomon's throne had a calf's head

Wooden headrest from Egypt (18th Dynasty, 16th-14th cents. B.C.) inscribed for the head gardener Daya (Royal Ontario Museum, Toronto)

on the back (1 K. 10:19). A famine caused the price of an ass's head to be drastically inflated (2 K. 6:25). Abner protested any implication of disloyalty to Saul by his denial of being a dog's head (2 S. 3:8).

C. Of Things. "Head" is also used of the top or upper end of a variety of other things: beds (Gen. 47:31; 1 S. 19:13, 16), idols (1 S. 5:4; Dnl. 2:32, 38), grain (Job 24:24; Hos. 8:7), gates (Ps. 24:7, 9), streets (Lam. 2:19; 4:1; Ezk. 16:25, 31; Nah. 3:10) and highways (Ezk. 21:19, 21), valleys (Isa. 28:1, 4), and the table at a feast (1 S. 9:22). It is the part of an axe (Dt. 19:5; 2 K. 6:5) or spear (1 S. 17:7) used for striking.

D. Position of Leadership. Another major meaning of "head" is the position of leadership, greatest authority, or honor (Dt. 1:15; 3:28; 10:11; 20:9; 28:13, 44; 31:3; Jgs. 3:27; 9:39; 10:18; 11:8f., 11; 2 S. 10:16; 1 Ch. 19:16; 2 Ch. 13:12; 20:27; Ps. 18:43 [MT 44]; Isa. 7:8f.; etc. Closely related to this meaning is the understanding of "head" as the one who holds this position of leadership, particularly among the families or tribes of Israel (e.g., Ex. 6:14, 25; 18:25; Nu. 1:4, 16; 2:24, 30, 35; 7:2; 10:4; 13:3; 17:3; 25:14f.; 30:1; 31:26; 32:28; 36:1; Dt. 1:13, 15; etc.).

II. In the NT.*–*A. Of Persons. In the NT the primary meaning of "head" is also the literal (Mt. 5:36; 6:17; 10:30; Mk. 12:4; Lk. 7:38, 46; 12:7; 21:18, 28; Jn. 13:9; 20:7, 12; Acts 21:24; 27:34; 1 Cor. 12:21). Jesus' head receives considerable attention: He has nowhere to lay it (Mt. 8:20; Lk. 9:58); it is anointed (Mt. 26:7; Mk. 14:3); it receives a crown of thorns (Mt. 27:29; Jn. 19:2) and blows (Mt. 27:30; Mk. 15:19), and the charge against Him is put over it (Mt. 27:37); He bows it in death (Jn. 19:30). Wagging the head is again a sign of mockery (Mt. 27:39; Mk. 15:29). In Mt. 14:8, 11 and Mk. 6:24ff. the decapitation of John the Baptist is graphically described.

Paul instructs the Corinthians that men should pray with heads uncovered, while women should cover theirs (1 Cor. 11:4f., 7, 10, 13). In Acts 18:6 ("Your blood be upon your head!") he reminds them of their responsibility for their own fate, while for the Romans (Rom. 12:20) he recalls the admonition of Prov. 25:21f.

B. Of Visionary Creatures. The book of Revelation contains references to the heads of a variety of visionary creatures: "One like a son of man" (1:14; 14:14), the twenty-four elders (4:4), sailors (18:19), an angel (10:1), a woman (12:1), one "called Faithful and True" (19:12), locusts (9:7), horses (9:17), lions (9:17), serpents (9:19), a dragon (12:3), and assorted beasts (13:1, 3; 17:3, 7, 9).

C. Of Things. In the NT "head" refers also to the top of a staff (He. 11:21) and to the most important stone in the foundation of a building, used metaphorically of Christ as the cornerstone of the Church (Mt. 21:42; Mk. 12:10; Lk. 20:17; Acts 4:11; 1 Pet. 2:7).

D. Position of Leadership. A head is also the one who holds a position of leadership and authority: Christ in the Church (1 Cor. 11:3; Eph. 1:22; 4:15; 5:23; Col. 1:18; 2:10, 19), a man in the family (1 Cor. 11:3; Eph. 5:23).

See GESTURE V. J. R. PRICE

HEADBAND. *See* GARMENTS.

HEADDRESS. *See* GARMENTS.

HEADSTONE (Ps. 118:22, AV). *See* CORNERSTONE.

HEADY. An obsolete term, meaning "wilful" or "rash," employed by the AV to translate Gk. *propetḗs* (lit. "falling forward, headlong") in 2 Tim. 3:4. The word is used figuratively here of those who are ready to rush into anything without thought (cf. RSV "reckless"; NEB "adventurers"). *See* RECKLESS.

HEAL [Heb. *rāpā'* almost exclusively] (Nu. 12:13); AV MAKE WHOLE (Job 5:18), CURE (Jer. 33:6); NEB CURE (2 K. 20:8), RECOVER (2 K. 8:29), DRESS (A WOUND, Jer. 6:14), TEND (THE SICK, Ezk. 34:4), etc.; also [*gāhâ*–'remove'] (Hos. 5:13), AV, NEB, CURE; [*ḥāyâ*] (Josh. 5:8); AV BE WHOLE; NEB RECOVER; [Gk. *therapeúo*–'serve'] (Mt. 8:7); AV CURE (Mt. 17:16); NEB most often CURE (Mt. 8:7), also SET FREE (Lk. 8:2); [*iáomai*]; AV MAKE WHOLE (Mt. 15:28); NEB most often CURE (Mt. 8:9), RECOVER (Mt. 8:13), RESTORE TO HEALTH (Mt. 15:28); BUT REGAIN ITS FORMER POWERS (*iathḗ dé mállon,* He. 12:13); [*hygiḗs génesthai*–'become healthy'] (Jn. 5:4, 6, 9); AV MAKE WHOLE; NEB RECOVER; [*hygiḗs poieín*–'make healthy'] (Jn. 5:11, 15); AV MAKE WHOLE; NEB CURE; [*sṓzō*– 'rescue'] (Acts 4:9); AV MAKE WHOLE; NEB CURE; [*diasṓzō*–'preserve'] (Lk. 7:3); NEB SAVE (LIFE); **CURE** [Heb. *'āsap*–'remove'] (2 K. 5:3); AV RECOVER; NEB RID; [*rāpā'*] (Hos. 5:13); AV HEAL; [Gk. *therapeúō*] (Lk. 9:1); AV HEAL; **MAKE WELL** [Gk. *sṓzō*] (Mt. 9:21); AV most often MAKE/BE WHOLE (Mt. 9:21), HEAL (Mk. 5:23), SAVE (Lk. 18:42); NEB most often CURE (Mt. 9:21); [*poieín hygiḗs*] (Jn. 7:23); AV MAKE WHOLE; NEB GIVE HEALTH; **HEALER** [Heb. *rōpē'*] (Ex. 15:26); [*ḥōḇēš*] (Isa. 3:7); NEB BE MASTER; **PHYSICIAN** [Heb. *rōpē'*] (Jer. 8:22); NEB STITCHING A PATCHWORK OF LIES (*rōpᵉ'ê 'ᵉlil,* Job 13:4); [Gk. *iatrós*]; NEB DOCTOR (Mt. 9:12); **HEALING** [Heb. *marpē, marpēh*]; AV HEALTH (Prov. 4:22), REMEDY (Prov. 6:15), CURE (Jer. 33:6); NEB HEALTH (Prov. 4:22), REMEDY (Prov. 6:15), HEAL (Prov. 12:18, etc.); [*tᵉ'ālâ*] (Jer. 46:11); AV CURE; NEB (NEW) SKIN (Jer. 30:13; 46:11); [*tᵉrûpâ*] (Ezk. 47:12); AV MEDICINE; NEB ENJOYMENT; [*yāgôn*] (Jer. 8:18, meaning uncertain), AV, NEB, SORROW; [*'ᵃrûḵâ*–'new skin (over a healing wound)'] (Isa. 58:8); AV HEALTH; [*rāpā'*] (Isa. 19:22); AV HEAL; [Gk. *therapeúō*]; NEB CURE (Mt. 4:23); [*therapeía*] (Lk. 9:11); [*íasis*] (Acts 4:22); [*íama*] (1 Cor. 12:9, 30); **CURE** [Gk. *íasis*] (Lk. 13:32); **MEDICINE** [Heb. *rᵉpu'â*] (Jer. 30:13; 46:11); NEB REMEDY; [*gēhâ*] (Prov. 17:22); NEB COUNTENANCE; **REMEDY** [Heb. *marpē'*] (2 Ch. 36:16); **HEALTH** [Heb. *'ᵃrûḵâ*]; NEB SKIN (Jer. 8:22); [*marpē'*] (Prov. 16:24); [*šālôm*] (Ps. 38:3 [MT 4]); AV REST; [*ḥālam*] (Isa. 38:16, "restore to health"); AV RECOVER; NEB RESTORE; [Gk. *holoklēría*–'wholeness'] (Acts 3:16); AV SOUNDNESS; NEB COMPLETELY WELL; [*hygiaínō*] (3 Jn. 2).

Health is a condition in which the components of the body-mind complex are free from disease and function together to promote the person's well-being. A person can be healthy even with minor pathological conditions, such as benign swellings or degenerated bodily tissues due to normal aging.

Healing is a process, often involving medical, surgical, or psychiatric treatment of a pathological condition, that culminates in the functional repair, and sometimes the actual regeneration, of a previously diseased or damaged part of the body or mind.

I. Health and Healing in the Ancient Near East.–In antiquity elevated or mountain areas, such as inland Anatolia or the Palestinian uplands, were considerably more healthy than swampy river bottoms, lowlands, or marshy districts, where mosquitoes and other disease carriers could breed. Egypt was notorious for its diseases (Dt. 28:60; cf. Ex. 15:26; Dt. 7:15), which were popularly attributed to demons or other unseen forces. Although the river regions of Mesopotamia did not seem to be so pestilential, the *Utukku* and *Ṭi'i* series of cuneiform texts suggest that the people did suffer from diseases such as malaria, smallpox, boils, water-borne infections (including amoebiasis, cholera, spirochetal jaundice, and typhoid fever), and environmental afflictions (including sandfly fever and the ophthalmic diseases hinted at in the Code of Hammurabi, §§ 215-220). More sinister diseases of demonic origin included the obscure "pestilence" in the Akkadian myth known as "Series Irra," as well as "plague," an affliction of uncertain nature.

In Egypt the priest-physicians began to establish their traditions in the late 4th millennium B.C., and early evidences of their medical practices are fiber splints for fractures (*ca.* 2800 B.C.) and the engraved representations of surgery (circumcision and perhaps amputation) on a tomb near Memphis (*ca.* 2500 B.C.). Some ancient papyri deal with medical treatment and surgery (Ebers papyrus), pharmacy and medicine (Hearst papyrus), and the treatment of surgical cases (Edwin Smith papyrus). This material probably dates from the very early 3rd millennium B.C. In what is sometimes regarded as a "pre-scientific" age, the ancient Egyptians discovered the correct (and only) way of reducing a dislocated lower jaw and established the four basic elements of a compound prescription (basis, adjuvans, corrigens, excipient) used to prepare many modern medicines. Although most of their therapeutic procedures were heavily overlaid with magic and superstition, the Edwin Smith papyrus, probably the earliest extant systematic record of surgical case histories, contains records of the examination, diagnosis, and treatment of conditions including hemiplegia, cranial traumata, fevers, and spinal and other dislocations.

The Babylonian priest-physicians generally used an etiological rather than an empirical approach to healing, although they too understood the principles involved in such matters as the treatment of fractures and certain eye problems, including cataract. Because disease was attributed to demonic activity, healing could occur only after the evil power had been exorcised and the patient given relief and peace of mind. Again, in a supposedly "pre-scientific" age, this procedure was in fact thoroughly rational, since it has been discovered in the late 20th cent. that healing of tissues is hindered if the patient is greatly worried or otherwise disturbed emotionally.

In the exorcism, the priest called upon Ea (Enki), the powerful water-deity, for help and often sprinkled the suf-

Votive relief (first half of the 4th cent. B.C.) from the sanctuary of Amphiaraus at Oropus, between Attica and Boeotia. At left, Amphiaraus, a divinized epic hero, heals Archinos, who successively sleeps in a bed (center) and dedicates a stele to the shrine (right) (National Archaeological Museum, Athens)

ferer with water to assure him that he was in direct contact with the omnipotent god. Sometimes the priest poured water upon the patient while reciting an incantation or "powerful word," a practice suggesting that the ailment would drain from his body into the ground along with the water. A ceremony of this sort, replete with spiritual power and psychological suggestion, could hardly fail to bring immediate relief to Mesopotamians afflicted with a form of emotogenic disease.

Apart from their reliance upon magic and sorcery, the Mesopotamians were at one with the Egyptians in their empirical use of a wide variety of therapeutic substances, especially herbs. The Sumerians were the first to discover the antipyretic and analgesic qualities of acetylsalicylic acid ("aspirin," the world's most widely used drug), which they made either by infusion or decoction from the bark and leaves of willow trees (one of the species of *Salicaceae*, perhaps *Salix babylonica*). They were also familiar with the healing properties of many shrubs and plants, and among other achievements they have been credited with the discovery of the cathartic qualities of castor oil (*Oleum ricini*). During the period of Hammurabi (*ca.* 1792-1750 B.C.), patients were charged according to their means, and penalties were prescribed for malpractice (*see also* DISEASE II.B, C, D).

Though superstition and magic were prominent in attempts at healing in the ancient Near East, no doubt certain therapeutic procedures were prompted by essentially rational considerations. There is very little evidence that serious attention was given, either in Egypt or in Mesopotamia, to regulating diets in order to promote and maintain good health. No doubt a person would avoid substances that, when ingested, produced an allergic reaction. But aside from personal choice or religious taboo all edible substances were potentially available as food; by contrast, the restrictive dietary traditions of the Hebrews were unique in the ancient Near East. Thus, methods to ensure health and healing in the ancient Near East were based upon etiological or empirical rather than preventive considerations, and, despite their rational aspects, they were ultimately based on superstition, magic, and fear of the gods.

II. Prophylactic Legislation for Israel.–One of the unique features of ancient Hebrew life was the manner in which life was regulated in terms of divine holiness. Although other nations observed religious traditions that penetrated their daily lives to varying degrees, the Hebrews were distinctive in being bound to the one true living God by a covenant relationship intended to make the Israelites a kingdom of priests and a holy nation (Ex. 19:6). The physical, emotional, and spiritual health of the nation was one important aspect of this relationship to the all-provident God of Sinai, and like other elements of promised prosperity could be obtained only by implicit obedience to God's will. Thus anyone who resorted to the medical practices of contemporary pagan societies demonstrated a lack of faith in God's ability to keep His covenant promise to be His people's healer (15:26). If obedience and trust resulted, among other things, in bodily health, anyone who became ill was by implication a sinner who was being punished visibly for his transgressions.

The Sinaitic and associated pentateuchal legislation, which represented God's will for His people's welfare, enshrined specific principles which, if observed, would contribute to good health. Their concept of preventive medicine and absolute repudiation of anything that resembled magic fundamentally differed from ancient medical or hygienic procedure.

A. Sabbath Observance. The practice of regarding specific days of each month as restricting the activities of certain classes of people apparently arose during the 3rd millennium B.C. in Mesopotamia. Later Babylonian tablets spoke of the fifteenth day of the month as the *šabattu* (*šapattu*), which designated the full moon in the Babylonian lunar calendar. Other days, such as the seventh, fourteenth, twenty-first, and twenty-eighth, were also regarded as ill omened or evil, and the texts placed restrictions upon certain forms of activity (*see* SABBATH). Whereas the Babylonians calculated their "sabbaths" from the beginning of each month, the Hebrew sabbath occurred every seventh day throughout the calendar year and had no relationship to lunar phases. It was based upon the concept of the divine rest from creative activity on the seventh day (Gen. 2:3); the covenant nation was required to keep it holy by worshiping God and ceasing all normal work (Ex. 20:8). Three obvious purposes were served by the enactment of sabbath observance. First, it constantly reminded the Israelites of their moral responsibility to venerate regularly and in community the deity to whom they owed their very being. Second, it legitimated the person's important biological need to abstain from normal work one day each week so that the body's cells might be renewed more readily. Third, because the law of sabbath rest applied also to domesticated animals (Ex. 23:12), it brought an extremely significant humanitarian influence to bear upon an area of God's creation that was otherwise subject to gross exploitation. Even the land on which the Israelites lived was required to remain fallow every seventh year after the harvest (Lev. 25:2-7), so that the mineral and nutrient reserve of the soil would not become impoverished unduly.

Some societies in more recent times have experimented with a different interval of time for the day of rest or have repudiated completely the need for a regular day of rest, much less divine worship. Medical science has shown, however, that the ideal rest period for the healthy operation of the human body and mind is that of one day in seven. Some persons appear to survive for a time without a regular "sabbath" interval, but it is doubtful that they are performing at anything approaching their maximum and they are certainly making themselves vulnerable to physical or mental breakdown. Thus the biblical concept of the sabbath has not merely positive and recuperative values for the individual but also serves to guard against disease.

B. Circumcision. Most Semitic peoples customarily removed the prepuce, or foreskin, of the male sexual organ. Some Levantines, however, such as the Philistines and the Greeks, did not observe the practice and in consequence were sometimes reviled by others as "the uncircumcised" (Jgs. 14:3; 15:18; 1 S. 14:6; Acts 15:1; Gal. 5:1-12; etc.). Those who had been circumcised, especially the Hebrews, felt morally superior. God had instituted the procedure for them as a covenantal sign (Gen. 17:10-14; cf. Ex. 12:48; Lev. 12:3), in which the small amount of blood shed sealed the relationship between God and man. Just as among other peoples CIRCUMCISION marked the initiation of a person into a tribe or manhood, among the Hebrews it indicated that the individual had become formally a member of the covenant community. The Torah permitted only this form of laceration because of its specifically religious associations.

The ancient Egyptians regarded circumcision as a special indication of culture that conferred certain hygienic benefits upon the nation. Others thought that circumcision prevented certain kinds of boils and venereal disease. Modern medical science has discovered that the *glans penis* secretes a certain amount of sebum from the *corona glandis,* which forms the prominent posterior border of the glans. This substance (*smegma*) is a carcinogen thought to cause much of the cervical cancer in women. In cases of phimosis, or narrowness of the aperture of the prepuce, an accumulation of smegma can produce irritation of and preoccupation with the glans. Cancer of the penis appears to be a rare complication of uncircumcision. Some advocate resection of the prepuce to reduce male sexual desire, but the evidence for this suggestion is of uncertain validity. While some decry the value of the procedure, it must not be forgotten that circumcision for the ancient Hebrews, as for their descendants, was not so much a medical procedure as a a distinctive religious symbol of the ideals of the covenant relationship. Physical hygiene may have resulted from circumcision, but it was always subsidiary to the spiritual meaning of the rite.

C. Sexual Relationships and Hygiene. Considerations of physical and spiritual health underlay the legislation in Israel dealing with sexual relationships. Among contemporary pagan nations, abhorrent sexual perversions continually threatened the stability of family and social life. These practices endangered the spirituality of the covenant people in Palestine because of their association with cultic idol worship. In consequence, an important body of legislation dealing with sexual activity from a spiritual, social, and biological standpoint was imposed on the Israelites. The Decalogue prohibited adultery and lust (Ex. 20:14, 17), and the bestiality found among the Hittites, Egyptians, and others was deemed a capital offense (22:19). Homosexuality, common to most Near Eastern religions, was condemned as an abomination (Lev. 18:22), for which the penalty in the Torah was death (20:13).

Since sexual activity was legislated to preserve the spiritual distinctiveness of the chosen people, it is unfortunate that Israel sometimes disregarded these sanctions of divine authority. Levitical law discouraged polyandrous, polygamous, and matriarchal relationships, even though such unions were well known in the Near East during the Bronze Age; the Hebrews instead were required to marry within the clan or tribe. Since even this type of endogamy could be fraught with danger, specific legislation prevented marriage within certain degrees of blood relationship. From the time of Moses onward a man was forbidden to marry his paternal half-sister, even though Abraham and Sarah had been thus related (Gen. 20:12). Lev. 18 set out representative prohibitions of six consanguineous relationships (vv. 7, 9-13) and eight instances of affinity, or connections through marriage (vv. 8, 14-18).

Degrees of affinity were regarded as being of blood or kinship, on the basis that husband and wife were "one flesh" (Gen. 2:24). As a result, regulations applied to maternal as well as paternal consanguinity. A careful reading of Leviticus seems to indicate that the regulations governed both marriage and casual sexual relations outside marriage. Many unions frequently found in Near Eastern nations were designated as incestuous by this legislation, which attempted to avoid rather than to prevent incest. Genetic studies have shown that the closer the blood relationship between husband and wife, the more probable is the incidence of detrimental or lethal genes. On the other hand, close inbreeding can purge recessive lethal and other damaging genes, a process that is accompanied by genetic deaths among the offspring. After many generations of such inbreeding the genetic deaths subside, since lethal genes have been largely eliminated from the stock. The covenant community could avoid all these genetic problems, with their accompanying personal and social hardships, and reflect divine holiness by following scrupulously the biblical regulations governing permissible degrees of relationships in marriage.

The prophylactic approach of the Levitical regulations is seen clearly in the matter of sexual hygiene. Sexual relations were considered ceremonially defiling, and the participants had to wash themselves and be treated as ceremonially "unclean" until the evening. Spontaneous seminal emission rendered the male unclean for the same period of time (Lev. 15:16-18). Menstruation made the woman unclean for seven days. Coition during this period defiled the male for seven days (vv. 15:19-24) because it involved contact with blood, which was prohibited to the Hebrews. (*See* CLEAN AND UNCLEAN II.B, IV.B.1.)

Near Eastern peoples may have had coition during menstruation as a contraceptive method, but it was specifically forbidden to the Hebrews (Lev. 20:18). In fact, Israelites apparently were not encouraged to practice contraception of any kind, since for them, as for other peoples, the chief aim of marriage seems to have been reproduction of the species. Coitus interruptus, practiced by Onan (Gen. 38:9), was thus judged to be a perversion of natural functions.

Physical and moral cleanness was fundamental to the life of the Hebrew community, and the associating of defilement with coitus helped to safeguard the nation against the gross promiscuity of surrounding peoples. It also introduced a sense of moral responsibility toward sexual behavior in general, so that those who indulged in coition were accountable at a level other than the purely physical.

Women were defiled by unusually lengthy menstruation, profuse bleeding, or intermittent hemorrhaging, such as might occur with uterine growths. Personal hygiene was again emphasized by regarding the woman as unclean till seven days after the discharge had ceased. Cleansing ceremonies followed the complete cessation of hemorrhagic discharge (Lev. 15:25-30) so that the highest possible standards of personal hygiene were assured. Although childbirth was a ceremonially defiling occasion because of the involvement of blood, the newborn child was always considered clean. Because of the postpartum secretion known as the *lochia*, the mother was unclean for two weeks if she bore a female child but only one week if she had a son; no explanation is given for the distinction (Lev. 12:2-5). The health of the offspring was protected by a nursing period of two or more years. Parents possibly did not cohabit between conception and the weaning of the child, a period that could exceed three years. During the incapacity of the legal wife, the husband could have recourse either to a concubine, if he could afford one, or a prostitute. But since prostitution usually impaired covenant spirituality, the less affluent married men in the community were clearly placed under some self-discipline, and even hardship, by Mosaic enactments. Nevertheless, the laws emphasizing the great significance of rest and personal hygiene after childbirth did protect the health of the mothers. Because the rules governing sexual activity carried the force of covenant law, sexual activity had a moral character that affected community health and was inextricably connected with the larger morality of the covenant deity.

D. Regulations Concerning Edible Food. Many diseases, both ancient and modern, have been shown to result from dietary deficiencies or imbalances that reduce the blood's ability to combat infection or repair damaged tissues. Some have argued from Gen. 1:29 that humans lived as vegetarians until the fall (cf. 3:18), and only after the Flood began to eat flesh (cf. 9:3). If humans had been designed as vegetarians, however, they would have one or more additional stomachs and a much larger intestinal system. Moreover, humans obtain more readily assimilable protein from meat than from commonly accepted substitutes and need iron and vitamins, especially of the B complex, not provided in a purely vegetarian diet.

Levitical legislation concerning foods, unique in the ancient Near East, embodied dietary principles that accord with modern scientific discoveries. Based on the distinction between "clean" and "unclean" which goes back at least to the Flood (Gen. 7:2), legislation protected individual and communal health and prevented infections or epidemic disease. Although the origin of the "clean" and "unclean" differentiation is unknown, there is no reason to associate it with primitive religions' totemism and taboos, which involved magical and superstitious concepts foreign to Hebrew covenantal life.

"Clean" animals parted the hoof and chewed the cud (Lev. 11:3-8; Dt. 14:4-8); all other mammals were "unclean." Although humans were not commanded to be vegetarian, all the mammals Scripture permitted them to eat had to be exclusively herbivores. Aquatic creatures with fins and scales were permitted for food, but all other species, including the edible crustaceans, were forbidden (Lev. 11:9-12). Hebrews could not eat rapacious, aquatic, and predatory birds (vv. 13-19) because they could acquire infection from them. All insects except the locust were "unclean."

Blood, the symbol of life, was strictly prohibited as food (Lev. 7:26), as was the flesh of "clean" animals that had not been slaughtered in such a manner as to drain the blood completely from the tissues. Animals that had died from natural causes (Dt. 14:21) or that had been mutilated by other animals and left to die also could not be eaten. Like the blood, the fat of an animal belonged to God and could not be consumed at any time (Lev. 7:22). The rationale underlying these prohibitions has become clear in modern times. Blood sustains bodily health when its components are properly balanced, but it can cause death when that balance is impaired. Thus to ingest whole blood except under the most carefully controlled clinical conditions is to run grave risk of infection from any noxious elements it contains. Similarly, the fat of certain animal species contains parasitic organisms that can produce illness and death in humans.

The "unclean" animals cataloged in Leviticus included the pig, an animal reared quite widely in the Near East. Modern studies indicate that the pig is the intermediate host for the parasitic tapeworm *Taenia solium,* which if ingested by humans can cause small nodules to form under the skin and in the eyes and muscular tissue. When these swellings occur in the brain, epileptiform convulsions can occur. Humans readily develop trichiniasis (*trichinosis*), a nematode (roundworm) infestation frequently accompanied by gastrointestinal problems and severe muscular pain, by eating poorly cooked pork and pork products. A small tapeworm, the *Echinococcus granulosus,* which people can acquire by drinking water polluted by pigs, causes cysts to form in the brain, heart, liver, and elsewhere in the body. Pigs which have eaten the flesh of dead or infected animals may transmit the protozoan causing toxoplasmosis, a disease damaging the tissues and central nervous system of humans and animals.

Carrion-eating birds and crabs, snails, and other shellfish also could transmit infection and so were forbidden as food.

Even the Hebrew diet of "clean" species of birds, animals, and fish could be unhealthy. For example, poorly cooked beef may contain a large tapeworm, *Taenia saginata,* and the *Echinococcus granulosus,* mentioned above. People ingest the parasitic worm *Diphyllobothrium latum* in caviar or improperly cooked fish. Tularemia, an affliction whose symptoms resemble those of both bubonic plague and undulant (Malta) fever, usually results from being bitten by insects, especially the fly *Chrysops discalis,* but also from handling carcasses of animals that died from the disease. The people of the primitive, semitropical Near East had to take scrupulous care to avoid the many sources of infections that often caused death. Thus the strictures of Leviticus are necessary and important guides to individual and communal health, directed at preventing rather than curing the diseases.

E. Sanitation and General Cleanliness. Usually seminomadic or nomadic communities are not concerned with sanitary practices, since they can move to a different environment if necessary. Desert nomads, unlike river-dwelling peoples, may have so little water that they must save it for their animals and for cooking. Where water happens to be in more ample supply, as at an oasis, the tradition of conservation still discourages the use of water for baths. Even today among Arab bedouin tribes, the women tend to use scents, ointment, and rose water instead of washing themselves, while the men often contrive to dispense with washing altogether.

Because of a lack of personal hygiene, communities of this sort are open to various infections from sources of human pollution, especially during the heat of Near Eastern summers. This is true for sedentary occupants unless they take strict measures to ensure sanitary conditions. In contrast to the Bronze Age cities of Sumer and other Mesopotamian centers, which had good sanitary facilities in middle- and upper-class houses and royal palaces, Jerusalem for much of its history had only rather rudimentary forms of sanitation. Garbage of all sorts accumulated in the streets although it could be dumped in the Valley of Hinnom, and as a result the city was a very unhealthy place in which to live during the hot summers. It is hardly surprising that food- and water-borne infections would take their toll, possibly with such frequency that they were accepted as an inevitable fact of life and thus were barely if ever alluded to in the biblical writings.

In addition to minimizing the threats to health by regulating "clean" and "unclean" foods, Levitical law protected the sources of food and water from pollution by by the carcasses of "unclean" species (Lev. 11:31-39). Observance of these rules would reduce the incidence of infectious fevers and diseases such as cholera, spirochetal jaundice, polioencephalitis, and bubonic plague. The legislation was the first of its kind to recognize that infection could be transmitted by both food and water.

The emphasis upon the burying of feces (Dt. 23:13) away from the camp in the wilderness period is a noteworthy attempt to control the spread of such insect-borne diseases as ophthalmia and poliomyelitis.

III. Healing in the OT.–Since God was His people's physician, health and other forms of prosperity could be expected as the result of implicit obedience to the divine commands. Only God could restore the sick to health. The penal view of disease was a natural consequence under such circumstances, but the book of Job disproves the idea of a necessary connection between sin and disease. What it does demonstrate, however, is that a positive response to suffering (as distinct from disease) results in emotional and spiritual maturity. Job's symptoms, which included fever (Job 30:30) and an occurrence of irritating, disfiguring sores on his entire body (2:7), were probably caused by allergies and thus could disappear rapidly when he began to submit himself to God in faith and obedience (cf. 40:4f.; 42:2-6). (*See also* DISEASE III.J.)

Healing also occurred from a deepening of spirituality in the case of King Hezekiah (2 K. 20:1-31), where tears evidently showed contrition as well as shock. He appeared to be in a poor state of health and was suffering from a carbuncle, a condition resembling a boil (*furuncle*) but considerably more extensive and dangerous in nature. The healing followed the pattern of some of Christ's miracles, where some material factor was involved in the restorative process (cf. Jn. 9:6f.). As far as Hezekiah was concerned, a fig poultice removed the suppuration and promoted cutaneous healing. A hippiatric prescription recovered from Ugarit testified to the value of figs in treating certain ailments affecting horses (C. H. Gordon, *Ugaritic Literature* (1949), pp. 128f.).

Another Judean ruler, Asa, was not healed of his ailment (*see* DISEASE III.J) because he trusted in the physicians rather than in God (2 Ch. 16:12f.). Physicians (Heb. *rōpᵉʾîm,* from a root meaning "repair, stitch together") probably cared for those wounded in wars and may have had some experience also with empirical herbal remedies. Contemporary Near Eastern medicine posed a real threat to Israel's faith because the Sinai covenant demanded that the nation trust in God alone for healing, not in human skills, magic, or superstitious practices. This tradition was being observed even when the prophets occasionally furnished advice about specific ailments or prognoses.

These functions were elements of the prophetic office, and in that respect the prophet was a surrogate for God Himself. Thus Nathan (2 S. 12:14), Elijah (2 K. 1:4), Ahijah (1 K. 14:4-16), and Elisha (2 K. 5:27; cf. 2 K. 8:10) predicted sickness and death. Prophetic intervention brought about the healing of Naaman (2 K. 5:3-14), the son of the Zarephath widow (1 K. 17:19-23), the son of the Shunammite (2 K. 4:18-37), a dead man who was cast into a grave containing Elisha's bones (2 K. 13:21), and Hezekiah (2 K. 20:1-7). Preexilic prophets neutralized the poisons in the impure waters of Jericho (2 K. 2:20f.) and pottage seasoned with lethal herbs (2 K. 4:41). In the early days of the covenant it is possible that fractured limbs were left unset (cf. Lev. 21:19), as happened periodically in Egypt, but by the exilic period they were apparently treated with some kind of pressure bandage (AV "roller," Ezk. 30:21). Presumably splints were used to keep the fractured bones properly aligned and supported. Wounds and suppurating sores were treated by a variety of folk remedies, including balsamic resin and oil (cf. Isa. 1:6). The resinous gums of Palestine and Arabia were mostly antiseptic and astringent in nature and could thus be used empirically for minor dressings.

Priests as well as prophets promoted health, but they were not so much healers as diagnosticians who supervised certain purification rituals to promote and ensure individual and communal health. Leviticus prescribed seven purificatory procedures controlled by the priests. These procedures were used for childbirth (Lev. 12), suspected and actual leprosy (ch. 13), venereal disease (15:2-15), emissions of semen (vv. 16-18), menstruation (vv. 19-30), and priestly contact with the dead (15:19-30; 22:4; cf. Nu. 5:2). The priest could administer a potion only in the so-called jealousy ordeal (Nu. 5:11-31), in which powerful suggestive mechanisms tested a woman's fidelity to her husband as she drank holy water containing dust from the tabernacle floor.

By the 2nd cent. B.C. the physician was more prominent than previously in Jewish life; this eventuality coincided with a marked increase of superstition and magic in Palestine. Although Ben Sira taught that medicines were the gift of God because they were natural products intended for the well-being of His children (Sir. 38:1-15), contemporary physicians employed magical charms, incantations, and spells to bolster the efficacy of the medicaments they administered.

IV. Jesus' Teaching on Health and Healing.–Diseases and infirmities that had plagued people for millennia were very much in evidence in Christ's time. Although His curing the afflicted was a rather minor part of His total ministry, it nevertheless perpetuated in the minds of His followers the biblical tradition that God was His people's physician. Jesus made no attempt to explain the rationale of disease any more that He expounded the larger problem of evil. The whole problem of evil was dealt with on the cross, where the Lord's Servant (Isa. 53:4) bore our griefs (Heb. *ḥᵒlî,* "disease") and carried our sorrows (Heb. *makʾōḇ,* "pain"). Christ's atonement not merely took away human sin (Jn. 1:29) but brought sickness and disease within His saving work as well. If this identification of the Servant with the crucified Lord is correct, it is entirely proper to see in the cross a basis for physical as well as spiritual healing.

Christ's ministry to individuals as body-spirit complexes needing proper integration is evident from both His teachings and miracles. The Sermon on the Mount (Mt. 5–7) and didactic material reveal His tremendous emphasis on human motivation and His recognition of powerful emotions like love, fear, hatred, lust, and anxiety as causes of mental and physical diseases. His first recorded address, given in the synagogue at Nazareth, expressed His concern for the sick, disabled, and oppressed (Lk. 4:18; cf. Isa. 61:1) — a very different attitude from that of many of His contemporaries, who found the sick and infirm exasperating and contemptible.

In a significant advance upon the OT penal concept of disease, Jesus regarded sickness as an evil influence that had disrupted the delicate holism of the human personality. His healing reunified body and mind so that the believer might have abundantly the life God willed for him (Jn. 10:10). The man who was born blind had not sinned any more than his parents (9:1-41) but was in that condition to show how God might be glorified through faith. When the man submitted in obedience and faith to the ministrations of the Great Physician, he received not merely physical sight but greater spiritual perception. Thus Christ showed that sickness was not the will of God for mankind, nor was it imposed on individuals either as a punishment or as a means of acquiring fortitude or patience. When, immediately after the Sermon on the Mount (Mt. 8:2-4; cf. Mk. 1:40; Lk. 5:12f.), a leper tentatively suggested that divine healing might not, after all, be his privilege, Christ abruptly dismissed the notion and healed him instantly with a touch of His hand.

Because Christ promulgated no doctrine about healing but instead responded spontaneously in loving concern to cases of sickness, the processes by which He restored people to health must be largely inferred. Jesus attributed certain types of pathology unhesitatingly to the influence of the devil (cf. Lk. 13:16), whose works He had come to destroy (1 Jn. 3:8). He therefore repudiated any suggestion that His own healings were performed under demonic influences (Mk. 3:23-27; Lk. 11:17-23). Christ was clearly aware of the nature-nurture relationship from which so much disease proceeds and was at pains to deal effectively with the sin that was an evident part of the situation. His conversation with the Samaritan woman (Jn. 4:7-29), who had come to the well for water, not for spiritual healing, bypassed a topic of general historical and theological argument (4:20) to concentrate on the way in which the woman's marital escapades had repeatedly broken God's laws. His analysis of her disreputable condition and His presentation of Himself to her as the Messiah (4:26) who would fulfill her deepest needs is a classic demonstration of spiritual counseling.

Christ's intuitive diagnostic powers, as evident in the Gospel narratives as His willingness to heal, probably attracted the deranged and desperate alike, who looked to

Christ as their only hope of healing. The healing of Mary Magdalene, an acutely psychoneurotic person (Lk. 8:2), the woman with a chronic hemorrhage (Mt. 9:20; Mk. 5:25; Lk. 8:43f.), lepers, and the blind depended upon their demonstration of faith in God's restorative power (cf. Mt. 9:29; Lk. 17:19), but the narrative form of the Gospels does not necessarily record this prerequisite (cf. Mt. 9:1-8; 12:9-13). Indeed, in some healings the matter of faith on the part of the sick seems to have been ignored completely in the spontaneity of Christ's response (Mk. 1:31, 34; Lk. 13:11-13; 14:4; 22:51) and may reveal that Christ's absolute healing abilities do not depend on any human response. He intended to heal the sin-damaged personality, knowing that once the imbalance was corrected and the turmoil of the subconscious mind calmed, the person would enjoy a new relationship with God characterized by health.

V. Healing in the NT.–Christ's occasional references to physicians, which do not seem particularly negative in tone, indicate that they were active in society (cf. Mt. 9:12; Lk. 4:23). As always, some afflictions defied the best efforts of the physicians, and in at least one instance (Mk. 5:25-34) Christ intervened to effect a cure. The author of the Third Gospel was described elsewhere as the "beloved physician" (Col. 4:14), indicating that, despite the magical accompaniments of contemporary medical therapy, some physicians were acclaimed for their work.

Votive foot with Greek dedication from Lucilla Pompeia to the Greek god of healing, Asclepius. It was found near the Sheep Pool in Jerusalem (Louvre)

The diseases that Jesus healed were the ordinary afflictions of the day, of which blindness (*see* DISEASE IV.C) was prominent. The Jerusalem beggar was congenitally blind (Jn. 9:1) though not mentally retarded; another person, who seems to have become blind gradually, perhaps through physical agents, had his sight restored by stages so as not to impair his new visual accommodation (Mk. 8:22-25). Bartimaeus when a child (Mk. 10:46-52) and two other beggars (Mt. 20:29-34) may have been blinded by ophthalmia.

The healing of cutaneous afflictions (*see* DISEASE IV.D) included the curing of ten lepers (Lk. 17:12-19), who, because of their isolation from society, appear to have been genuine victims of Hansen's disease. Luke's clinical observation (Lk. 5:12) of the disease indicates a stage in which the subcutaneous tissues and nerves of the patient had been grossly affected by leprosy. Probably other skin afflictions healed by Christ included acquired leucoderma, psoriasis, impetigo, and acne, although specific evidence is lacking.

Christ healed several paralytics, whose affliction apparently resulted from disease in the central nervous system. The centurion's servant (Mt. 8:5-13; Lk. 7:1f.) seems to have suffered from Landry's paralysis, which usually causes death within three weeks. The Capernaum paralytic (Mt. 9:2; Mk. 2:3; Lk. 5:18-25) was probably paraplegic, perhaps from a birth injury. The sick man of Bethzatha (Jn. 5:2) had a disease that produced progressive muscular atrophy, perhaps amyotrophic lateral sclerosis. The man with the atrophied hand (Mt. 12:9-13; Mk. 3:1-5; Lk. 6:6-10) probably had contracted anterior poliomyelitis as a child. (*See also* DISEASE IV.B.)

Christ healed a man with dropsy (Lk. 14:2), which is really a symptom of disease elsewhere in the body; a woman with a hemorrhage (Mt. 9:20-22 par. Mk. 5:25f.; Lk. 8:43-48), who may have had a uterine fibroid; a nobleman's son (Jn. 4:46-53), perhaps a victim of cerebro-spinal meningitis; and Peter's mother-in-law (Mt. 8:14f. par. Mk. 1:30f.; Lk. 4:38f.), who probably had malaria. A complete lack of evidence prevents identification of the fatal ailments of Jairus's daughter (Mk. 5:22-43 par. Lk. 8:41-56), Lazarus (Jn. 11:1-44), and the widow's son at Nain (Lk. 7:11; *see* DISEASE IV.G). Psychosomatic illness probably caused a woman's spinal deformity (Lk. 13:11), and Zechariah's functional aphonia (Lk. 1:11-22).

In the primitive Church the disciples performed healings in the manner of the Master (cf. Acts 2:43; 5:12; 8:7) and confronted exactly the same pathology. Thus Peter restored a Tabitha, who had died from unknown causes, in the classic manner (9:40f.); Paul healed Publius's father by the imposition of hands (28:8). The latter miracle attracted a crowd of sick people, just as the healing works of Christ had done. Paul's own blindness was clearly psychogenic in origin (9:3-9) and disappeared once his emotional and spiritual tensions were resolved (*see* DISEASE IV.F). Apostles healed the cripple at the temple gate (3:2-8) and one at Lystra (14:8-10). Their paralysis may have resulted from a birth injury or cerebral palsy.

Mental illness was prominent among pathologies in Christ's day, and numerous instances of healings took place in His ministry. Insanity was uniformly attributed to demons, and even Christ's power to heal was credited by some of His enemies to demonic sources (Mt. 12:24 par. Mk. 3:22; Lk. 11:15). The complaint of the disciples (Mk. 9:38; Lk. 9:49) and an incident in Paul's ministry (Acts 19:14) indicate that exorcisms were frequent in Christ's time. Demon possession (*see* DEMON, DEMONOLOGY) was distinguished from epilepsy, which is a chronic functional disorder of the nervous system, usually marked in its later stages by mental disturbance. Psychogenic forms of epilepsy should be distinguished from symptomatic and uncinate epilepsy in which there is demonstrable brain disease. Christ dramatically healed a boy whose severe epilepsy was attributed to a "dumb spirit," after the disciples had failed in the attempt (Mt. 17:14-18 par. Mk. 9:17-27; Lk. 9:37-42). Both epilepsy and demon possession were regarded as caused by demons (cf. Lk. 8:2), but probably some distinctive behavioral feature, perhaps suicidal or homicidal impulses (cf. Mk. 5:5; Acts 19:16), helped people differentiate the two conditions.

VI. Herbs and Medicaments.–Because health and healing came from God alone, Scripture contains no information on the preparation and administration of therapeutic substances like those in the extensive pharmacopeias of Egypt and Mesopotamia. Nevertheless, from early times certain substances were credited with therapeutic qualities, even though, as with the mandrake, the association was of a purely superstitious nature. Folk medicine was widespread in the ancient Near East, and without doubt the Hebrews employed some herbs and other substances empirically to restore and maintain health.

Incense and pomegranate rind were burned as fumigants and disinfectants in Bible times. Aromatic oils and scents were used for personal hygiene. Olive oil was employed widely to keep exposed parts of the skin supple, to relieve chafing, and to heal bruises and lacerations. Shepherds used it to treat sheep injured while grazing or traveling (Ps. 23:5).

A famous therapeutic substance in Palestine was the BALM OF GILEAD, exported to Egypt and Phoenicia (Gen. 37:25; Ezk. 27:17). It is actually difficult to identify botanically, and though commonly associated with the shrub *Balsamodendron opobalsamum* L., it has been thought also to be the gummy exudate of more than one shrub in Gilead. The balm was renowned for its soothing qualities and for its ability to promote tissue repair. A less elaborate unguent was the mixture of oil and wine that the Good Samaritan (Lk. 10:33f.) used to treat the battered traveler from Jerusalem in Jesus' story that undoubtedly drew upon real-life circumstances. The alcohol in the wine would act as an astringent and antiseptic; the oil would soothe and heal the tissues. Olive oil was boiled with sodium carbonate, or when more convenient, glasswort or saltwort plants, to make all-purpose soap.

Herbs traditionally renowned for promoting health found their way into the diet of the Hebrews. They included gastric stimulants and tonics such as dill, cummin, garlic, the caper berry, coriander, and fennel. In addition to the "bitter herbs" of the PASSOVER (Ex. 12:8), which probably were chicory, lettuce, watercress, dandelion, and endive, popular culinary herbs included anise, spelt, rosemary, thyme, mint, marjoram, and sage. Some shrubs, flowers, and gourds were poisonous (2 K. 4:39; Hos. 10:4) and no doubt took a toll of the uninitiated. The "deadly thing" of Mark 16:18 (mg.) was a drink into which some kind of poison, probably vegetable, had been put, but deliberate poisoning was not very common in Palestine during Christ's time.

Bibliography.–R. L. Moodie, *Antiquity of Disease* (1927); H. N. and A. L. Moldenke, *Plants of the Bible* (1952); A. R. Short, *Bible and Modern Medicine* (1953); F. Dunbar, *Emotions and Bodily Changes* (1954); R. K. Harrison, *Healing Herbs of the Bible* (1966); *Leviticus* (*Tyndale OT Comms.*, 1980); S. N. Kramer, *The Sumerians* (1963); J. R. Porter, *Leviticus* (*CBC*, 1976).

R. K. HARRISON

HEALING, GIFTS OF [Gk. *charísmata iamátōn*].

"Gifts of healing" are among the spiritual gifts enumerated in 1 Cor. 12:4-11, 28-30. The current revival of interest in the so-called charismata warrants a thorough study of gifts of healing.

I. Terminology.–Greek *chárisma* (pl. *charísmata*) means "grace," "favor," "a benefit conferred." It is used of divine gifts, especially of the supernatural kind enumerated in Rom. 12:6-8 and 1 Cor. 12:4-11, 28-30. Specific occurrences of Gk. *chárisma* and its derivatives are: Rom. 1:11; 5:15f.; 6:23; 11:29; 12:6; 1 Cor. 1:7; 7:7; 12:4, 9, 28-31; 2 Cor. 1:11; 1 Tim. 4:14; 2 Tim. 1:6; 1 Pet. 4:10. The charismata are not received *in abstracto* but always in the form of specific aptitudes for service to the entire Church. The charismata of 1 Cor. 12 are literally benefits or graces conferred upon certain individual members of the body of Christ for the use and benefit of the worshiping Church (v. 7). They are not the personal possession of the members who exercise them within the church community. They are, rather, manifestations of the Spirit through Christians who are serving the spiritual edification of the Church as a whole (vv. 8-11).

Greek *íama* (pl. *iámata*) means "healing" (1 Cor. 12:9, 30). In order to understand the gifts of healing it is helpful to consider healing in the Bible as a whole.

II. Healing in the OT.–The OT shows little concern with the biological causes of sickness. What predominates, rather, is the growing conviction that Yahweh gives and prevents sickness (Ps. 32:3f.; 38:3-11 [MT 4-12]; 103:3; etc.). Sickness and disease are often regarded as signs of God's wrath (Isa. 38:10-20 par. 2 K. 20:1-11), but the idea that *all* sickness is punishment for sin is rejected (e.g., Job's disease had another cause; cf. Job 2:4-8).

Deliverance from sickness by Yahweh is considered a mark of divine pleasure (Gen. 20:17; Ex. 15:26); conversely, Job's friends interpreted God's failure to deliver Job as a mark of divine displeasure. The chief means of such healing in the OT and in Judaism was prayer. Prayer for physical healing is very early linked with the temple cultus (Ps. 5:3, 7 [MT 4, 8]; 28:2; 38:6; 42:9 [MT 10]; 88:13 [MT 14]; etc.). Regular patterns of such prayers and thanksgiving for resultant healings appear in Ps. 6; 16:10; 30:2 [MT 3]; 32:3f.; 38; 41:4 [MT 5]; 51:7f. [MT 9f.]; etc.

The Jews of the Dispersion, however, developed a more scientific and secular attitude toward medical cures, largely due to the influence of the Greeks (see Sir. 38:1-15, esp. v. 4: "The Lord created medicines out of the earth, and a prudent man will have no disgust at them"). Conflicting attitudes about whether the diseases had natural causes and medical cures are evident in the NT period. It was into this state of affairs that Jesus came.

III. Healing in the NT.–The view that sickness is closely related to sin appears in Lk. 13:11-16, where it is called bondage to Satan; cf. also Mt. 12:22-28; Acts 12:23; Rev. 16:2. Furthermore, in Mk. 2:1-12 Jesus connects His authority over disease with His authority to forgive sins. Other instances where Jesus links sin and sickness are Mk. 5:34 and Lk. 7:9f. (where faith, the antithesis of sin [Rom. 14:23], brings healing); Jn. 5:14.

Jesus, however, rejected the belief of some OT writers that sickness is always divine punishment for sin. It is He, in fact, who removed the view of a causal relationship between sin and sickness; cf. Jn. 9:2f.: "And his disciples asked him, 'Rabbi, who sinned, this man or his parents, that he was born blind?' Jesus answered, 'It was not that this man sinned, or his parents, but that the works of God might be made manifest in him'"; also Jn. 11:4 and Lk. 13:2ff. Thus Jesus removed the idea of sickness as divine retribution for sin from its central place in the understanding of the earliest disciples.

Paul, following the lead of Jesus and applying His insight, maintained strictly and consistently that sickness, like all suffering, is due primarily to natural causes and not to divine retribution (see Rom. 8:28; 2 Cor. 4:17). While God can and does work *through* sickness for His own glory and purpose (Rom. 8:28; 2 Cor. 12:7ff.), He does not ordinarily place sickness upon one as a punishment for sin. Rather, disease and sickness are evils that contradict and hinder God's will and purpose for His creatures.

Those in the apostolic Church who followed the lead of Jesus and Paul regarded without disgust physicians and the development of medical science, while at the same time looking to God and praying for His deliverance from sickness and disease. For example, the good Samaritan uses natural means to cure illness (Lk. 10:34); Col. 4:14

calls Luke the beloved physician; and 1 Tim. 5:23 counsels the use of wine to counter stomach infirmities. At the same time that this understanding and appreciation of medical science grew, the Church developed its own more spiritual means of dealing with sickness and disease. The two approaches, however, were not thought to be mutually exclusive; they were, rather, complementary, because sickness was no longer viewed as God's punishment of sin.

IV. Gifts of Healing in the Apostolic Church.–There was an order of "healers" in the early ministry of the NT Church (1 Cor. 12:28) and "gifts of healing" were considered to be a grace conferred by the ascended Lord upon His body the Church (v. 9). This means that gifts of healing were part of the equipment of the witnesses to Christ's kingdom. Acts 3:6 and 14:8-10 demonstrate these gifts in action, as do other NT references (e.g., Jas. 5:13ff.). Col. 1:24 on the other hand shows Paul's "rejoicing in infirmities," and 1 Tim. 5:23 speaks of temporary sickness that might be cured by natural rather than by supernatural means.

From this we may conclude that throughout the apostolic age the power to heal sickness and disease was a spiritual gift conferred by the risen Lord upon certain members of His Church. But spiritual "gifts of healing" are in no way to be understood as contrary to the fullest development of medical knowledge and technique. The point is that God is concerned that people be whole, that is, sound in flesh, mind, and spirit. Yahweh is the God who heals and Jesus came to make human beings whole. The Church receives and transmits "gifts of healing" through its ministries.

V. Gifts of Healing in the Church Today.–The gifts of healing continued in use during the first two centuries after Christ, according to Justin Martyr (*Apol.* ii.6), Irenaeus (*Adv. haer.* ii.32, 34), Tertullian (*Apol.* xxii), and Origen (*Contra Celsum* 6.4). The operation of these gifts gradually diminished, due, no doubt, to the growth of ecclesiasticism and asceticism. The ritual of the Church became formalized and impersonal while the ascetic temper relegated physical healings to a relatively insignificant place. In fact, pain and sickness were sometimes considered to be the indispensable ministers of God to the soul.

Gifts of healing, however, have never been totally absent from the Church's life. Francis of Assisi, Luther, Wesley, the Waldenses, the early Moravians, the Quakers, and others have experienced these gifts intermittently throughout church history. Since the turn of the century, Pentecostals and others have laid heavy stress upon the revival of all the charismata conferred upon the Church, including gifts of healing. Charismatics and neo-Pentecostals from all branches of the Christian church have experienced and are emphasizing a renewal of these apostolic charismata.

Perhaps this revival of interest and emphasis upon the gifts of healing within the modern Church will help all Christians to reaffirm the reality and permanence of the *charísmata iamátōn* while relating them to the modern practice of medicine as a complementary ally in the quest for human wholeness.

Bibliography.–J. Héring, comm. on 1 Corinthians (*Comm. du NT,* 1949); *TDNT,* III, *s.v.* ἰάομαι (Oepke); Richardson, *RTWB, s.v.* "Heal."

R. E. COTTLE

HEAP. The noun "heap" is used in several different ways in the OT. Usually it refers to a heap of ruins or rubble. Several Hebrew words are used in this sense: *tel* (Dt. 13:16 [MT 17]; Josh. 8:28); *'ašpōṯ* (1 S. 2:8; Ps. 113:7; Lam. 4:5); *'î* (Isa. 17:1; Mic. 1:6; 3:12); *gal* (2 K. 19:25; Job 15:28; Isa. 25:2; 37:26; Jer. 9:11 [MT 10]; 26:18; 51:37; Hos. 12:11 [MT 12]; *'ᵃrēmâ* (Neh. 4:2 [MT 3:34]; possibly Jer. 50:26).

The Heb. *'ᵃrēmâ* usually refers to heaps of grain (Ruth 3:7; Cant. 7:2; Hag. 2:16; Neh. 13:15; possibly Jer. 50:26). In 2 Ch. 31:6-9 *'ᵃrēmâ* is used five times of heaps that probably include both fruit and grain.

The Heb. *gal* refers to heaps of stones (cairns) set up for some special purpose. Jacob and Laban set up stones to serve as a witness to the compact they made (Gen. 31:46-52). On three occasions a heap of stones was piled on top of a dead body (Josh. 7:26, Achan; Josh. 8:29, King of Ai; 2 S. 18:17, Absalom). Each of these cases involved an ignominious death, so that the heap of stones was a reminder of the shameful deeds of the person buried underneath.

The Heb. *nēḏ* is used four times in the special sense of a heap (or bank) of waters, in reference to the Red (Reed) Sea (Ex. 15:8; Ps. 78:13) and to the Jordan River (Josh. 3:13, 16). (In Isa. 17:11, therefore, where the MT makes unusual reference to a harvest heap, the RSV and NEB emend.)

Several passages refer to heaps of dead bodies. In Ex. 8:14 [MT 10] *ḥōmer* refers to heaps of frogs. With a play on the Hebrew words for "ass" and "heap" (both *ḥᵃmôr*), Jgs. 15:16 refers to heaps of Philistines who had been slain by Samson with the jawbone of an ass. The NEB, following an etymological conjecture, translates this passage "I have flayed them like asses." In Nah. 3:3 *kōḇeḏ* also refers to heaps of the slain. Heb. *ṣibbur* is used once — Jehu piles the heads of the slain members of the royal house in two heaps at the entrance of the city gate (2 K. 10:8). This was a common practice of the Assyrians after conquering a territory (M. Astour, *JAOS,* 91 [1971], 388).

Several Hebrew verbs are occasionally translated "heap." In Ex. 15:8 *'āram* is used in the niphal to refer to the waters of the Red (Reed) Sea forming a bank on each side, enabling the Israelites to pass through. The hiphil of *sāpâ* (which should probably be emended to *yāsap,* "add to" [KoB, p. 664]), is used once of heaping on punishment (Dt. 32:23). In Prov. 25:22 *ḥāṯâ,* usually used of snatching up fire or coals, is translated "heap" (coals on the enemy). The verb *ṣāḇar* refers on three occasions to the heaping up of riches (Job 27:16; Ps. 39:6 [MT 7]; Zec. 9:3). In Hab. 1:10 it refers to the heaping up of earth as part of a siege. The Heb. *rāḇâ,* meaning "multiply," is translated "heap" where it refers to the punishment of Jerusalem (Ezk. 24:10), and "heap up" where it refers to someone appropriating what is not his (Hab. 2:6). The Heb. *kānas,* translated "heap up" in Eccl. 2:26, refers to the amassing of wealth.

"Heap" is also used in the translation of some difficult passages. In Job 30:24 the MT has *bᵉ'î,* meaning "in a heap of ruins," and the RSV has made good sense of the passage using this translation. The NEB, however, emends *bᵉ'î* to *bᵉ'ānî* and translates it "beggar," while the AV translates it "grave."

In 1 S. 20:19 the RSV emends the MT *hā'eḇen hā'āzel,* "the stone Ezel," to agree with the LXX and reads "beside yonder stone heap" (cf. NEB "by the mound"). In v. 41 the RSV ("beside the stone heap") and NEB ("beside the mound") again follow the LXX, emending the MT *mē'ēṣel hanneḡeḇ,* "from beside the south."

In 1 K. 9:8 the MT has *'elyôn,* meaning "high" (AV). The RSV and NEB emend to *lᵉ'îyîn,* "(heap of) ruins," following the Old Syriac, Aquila, and the Old Latin.

In Hab. 3:15 *ḥōmer,* rendered by the AV "heap," is better understood as a verb; cf. the RSV, "surging," and the NEB, "boil."

In Isa. 3:6 reference is made to a "heap of ruins" (Heb. *makšēlâ*), probably referring to the future destruction of Jerusalem. The NEB emends this to "family" (*mišpāḥâ*), probably because of the context of v. 6, but without sufficient justification.

The RSV once translates Heb. *šûḇ*, "return," as "heaping (oppression upon oppression)" (Jer. 9:6 [MT 5]), based on a redivision of the consonants following the LXX (see J. Bright, *Jeremiah* [*AB*, 1965], p. 72). This is superior to the literal AV, "Thine habitation is in the midst of deceit."

In the NT "heap" translates three verbs. Prayer is not to consist of heaping up empty phrases (Gk. *battalogéō*, "utter meaningless words, babble," Matt. 6:7). Rom. 12:20 is a quotation of Prov. 25:21f., Gk. *sōreúō* translating Heb. *ḥāṯâ*, "heap" (coals on the enemy). In Rev. 18:5 Gk. *kolláō* means "unite" or "come in close contact with"; so Babylon's sins have "reached unto heaven" (AV) or are "heaped as high as heaven" (RSV).

J. C. MOYER

HEAR; HEARKEN; LISTEN; OBEY; etc. These words overlap in meaning, as is indicated not only by these various translations of the same Hebrew or Greek words, but also by frequent synonymous parallelism (e.g., Ps. 17:1; Isa. 28:23; 42:23; Jer. 23:18). The most frequent words are Heb. *šāma'* (Aram. *šᵉma'*), *qāšab* (hiphil), *'āzan* (hiphil), Gk. *akoúō* and *hypakoúō*. The semantic field ranges from the physical reception of a sound to the active response to what is heard: a response either of assent (to one of equal or lesser authority) or of obedience (to one of greater authority).

I. In the OT.–On the most basic level, to hear is to perceive a sound (always Heb./Aram. *šāma'*); thus one hears a whisper (Job 26:14), music (Am. 5:23; Dnl. 3:5, 15), the voice of a god (Dt. 4:33), and the sound of tools being used (1 K. 6:7). In silent prayer a voice is not heard (1 S. 1:13). The deaf cannot hear (Ps. 38:13 [MT 14]), nor can idols (Dt. 4:28; Dnl. 5:23). In Eden God could be heard walking (Gen. 3:8, 10; cf. 2 S. 5:24 for similar use of *qôl*, "sound"). Amos prophesied that God's words would cease to be heard (through the prophets, 8:11). The references to God hearing prayers (Gen. 17:20; 30:6; 2 S. 22:7; etc.; *see* ANTHROPOMORPHISM) and grumblings (Ex. 2:24; 6:5, 17; etc.) also may be regarded as passive, although a more active sense, implying some response, is apparent when God "hearkens" (Gen. 30:17, 22; Nu. 21:3; etc.) or "listens" (Jgs. 13:9; Ezr. 8:23; Ps. 66:19), or when He does not "hearken, give ear," e.g., Dt. 1:45.

This ambiguity between the passive and active senses may also be seen in the frequent introductory imperatives "give/incline (the) ear, hear, hearken, listen"; these may be viewed either as attention-getting devices, which indicate the urgency or importance of what follows, or as a call to the hearer to understand (so the RSV translates *šāma'* in Gen. 11:7; 42:23; Isa. 33:19; etc.) and respond to what is said. Thus in Gen. 4:23 Lamech perhaps desires a response of fear; Dt. 6:4f. certainly implies a response of faith (*see* SHEMA). In Job 34:16; 37:14 Elihu presents an argument to which he hopes Job will assent. A similar sense may be seen in people's responses to each other ("hearkened," Gen. 16:2; 34:24; 1 S. 12:1; etc.; "listened," Gen. 42:21f.; Ex. 6:9, 12; etc.).

Three special uses of this imperative should be noted. First, prayers often include such injunctions (2 K. 19:16; Ps. 5:1 [MT 2]; 17:6; etc.), and in several instances a response seems to be in view (71:2; 86:1; 102:2 [MT 3]; etc.). Second, in proclaiming judgment the prophets frequently admonish the rulers (Isa. 28:14; 39:5; Jer. 19:3; etc.) and the people (Isa. 66:5; Jer. 2:4; 10:1; etc.) to "hear the word of the Lord." (Even where this phrase is not in the text, e.g., Isa. 34:1; Am. 4:1; Mic. 3:9, it is frequently implicit.) Such denunciations may be viewed as calls to repentance. Third, a similar use occurs in conjunction with apostrophe in Dt. 32:1; Isa. 1:2; Mic. 6:1f.; cf. Ps. 50:1 (on the covenant background of these texts cf. M. G. Kline, *Structure of Biblical Authority* [1975], pp. 116, 141; P. C. Craigie, *Deuteronomy* [*NICOT*, 1976], pp. 139, 366, 376; J. Limburg, *JBL*, 88 [1969], 291-304).

In some texts this call for attention and understanding has obedience as a consequence. This is especially clear in instructions or commands, both human (Prov. 4:20; 5:1, 13; etc.) and divine (Jer. 34:14; 35:15; 44:5; etc.).

The common expression for "obey" is *šāma' bᵉqôl*, "hear the voice of." (The NEB frequently translates simply "obey," thus avoiding the unnecessary and somewhat awkward literalness of the RSV, AV, "obey the voice of.") Usually it is the voice of God that is to be obeyed. The vital importance of such obedience as the proper response to God is obvious from the many texts that call for obedience (Ex. 19:5; Dt. 13:4, 18; etc.) and denounce disobedience (Dt. 8:20; 9:23; 28:5; etc.; *see also* DISOBEDIENCE). (*Šāma'* alone may mean obey; cf. Nu. 27:20; Josh. 1:17; 1 K. 2:42; etc.) The classic text on obedience is 1 S. 15:22, which clearly demonstrates that the inward aspect of hearing and obeying is more important than the outward conformity to law (cf. Isa. 1:11-17; Hos. 6:6). The motivation for obedience is not only spiritual, however; there are more earthly, practical reasons (cf. Dt. 11:13-15; 28:1-13; Isa. 1:19; etc.).

In the realm of human relations, children are to obey their parents (cf. Dt. 21:18-21 and Prov. 30:17 for the dire consequences of disobedience), and subjects obey their rulers (2 S. 22:45; 1 Ch. 29:23).

II. In the NT.–NT uses are similar. One may hear a sound, such as a whisper (Mt. 10:27), a voice wailing (Mt. 2:13), a heavenly voice (Acts 9:4; 22:9), music (Lk. 15:25), or wind (Jn. 3:8). Jesus heals the deaf, so that they can hear (Mt. 11:5 par.). To hear "the word of God," i.e., the gospel, usually does not imply a response (Lk. 11:28; Acts 13:7, 44; 15:7; 19:10; Rom. 10:14; etc.). James especially points out the vital difference between hearing the word and responding to it in obedience (1:22-25).

The basic difference between hearing and understanding is pointed up in Mt. 13:19 par. and Acts 28:26, although the overlap in meaning is also apparent when people are directed to hear a parable (Mt. 13:18; 21:33), a word of judgment (Lk. 18:6), or a sermon (Acts 2:22); in these instances a response seems desired. "Listen" is often used in a way that could be interpreted either as an attention-getting device, or as a call to hear and understand and perhaps even respond in obedience or faith (Mt. 17:5 par.; Mk. 4:3; Acts 13:16; 15:13; Jas. 2:5). Jesus' repeated saying "He who has ears to hear, let him hear" (Mt. 11:15; 13:9, 43; etc.; *see also* EAR) entails understanding and perhaps also a response of faith.

Although the NT quotes no cries for God to hear prayers, it is said that He does hear them, and this hearing implies response (cf. Mt. 6:7; Lk. 1:13; Acts 10:31; Heb. 5:7 [all of which use *eisakoúō*]; Jn. 9:31; 11:41; 1 Jn. 5:14 [all of which use *akoúō*]; note that the RSV does not use "hearken" in the NT).

A similar use of *akoúō* may be seen in Mt. 18:15f., where human relations are in view, and in Lk. 16:29, 31, where Moses and the prophets are to be heard with a response of repentance. The phrase "He who has an ear, let him hear [*akoúō*] what the Spirit says" (Rev. 2:7, 11, 17; etc.) recalls the prophetic admonitions, which call for repentance and obedience (cf. Ezk. 3:27).

The close association of faith and obedience is manifested in several ways. Obedience is used as a synonym for conversion (Acts 5:32; 6:7; Rom. 1:5; 15:18; 16:26; 1 Pet. 1:22), and as a primary characteristic of believers (Rom. 6:17; 16:19; 2 Cor. 2:9; 7:15; Philem. 21; 1 Pet. 1:2); hence, believers are called "children of obedience" (1 Pet. 1:14). When they are misled and cease to "obey [*peíthōmai*] the truth" (Gal. 5:7), they require reproof and correction in order to avoid judgment (Rom. 2:8).

Believers then are to obey the leaders of state (Tit. 3:1; *see also* SUBJECT) and church (Heb. 13:17); children are to obey their parents (Eph. 6:1; Col. 3:20), wives their husbands (1 Pet. 3:6), and slaves their masters (Col. 3:22); and of course God and His word are to be obeyed (Jn. 3:36; Acts 5:29; Gal. 5:2; etc.).

Jesus' authority was dramatically demonstrated when nature (Mt. 8:27 par.) and demons (Mk. 1:27) obeyed him.

See also HEED; OBEDIENCE OF CHRIST; OBSERVE.

Bibliography.–*TDNT*, I, *s.v.* 'ακούω κτλ. (Kittel); VI, *s.v.* πείθω κτλ. (Bultmann). G. A. LEE

HEART [Heb. *lēḇ, lēḇāḇ, libbâ* (Dt. 20:8; Ps. 73:26; Ezk. 16:30; etc.), *nepeš*–'soul' (Ex. 23:9; etc.), *kᵉlāyôṯ*–'reins, kidneys' (Job 19:27; etc.) *mēʿîm*– 'bowels' (Job 30:27; etc.), *qereḇ*–'interior' (Jer. 9:8 [MT 7]; etc.), *beṭen*–'belly' (Job 15:35; 32:19; etc.), *raḥᵃmîm*–'compassion' (Gen. 43:30; 1 K. 3:26; etc.), *kāḇēḏ*–'liver' (Lam. 2:11; etc.), *ḥēleḇ*–'fat' (Ps. 17:10; etc.), *sāṯûm*–'enclosure' (qal pass. part., Ps. 51:6 [MT 8]), *moṯnayim*–'loins' (Ezk. 21:6 [MT 11]; etc.); Aram. *lᵉḇaḇ* (Dnl. 5:20, 22; etc.); Gk. *kardía* (Mk. 7:6 par. Mt. 15:8; Rom. 8:27; 2 Cor. 4:6; Eph. 1:18; etc.), *splánchnon*–'inward part' (2 Cor. 7:15; Philem. 7, 12, 20; 1 Jn. 3:17; etc.), *koilía*–'belly' (Jn. 7:38; etc.), *psychḗ*–'soul' (Eph. 6:6; Col. 3:23; cf. Acts 4:32)]; AV also SOUL (Prov. 19:18), MIND (Jer. 15:1), REINS (Job 19:27; Jer. 12:2), BOWELS (Job 30:27; Philem. 7, 12, 20), etc.; NEB also APPETITE (1 S. 2:33), DESIRES (Ps. 10:3), "single-minded" (Ezk. 25:15), MIND (Ps. 7:9), "inward parts" (Ps. 16:7), KIDNEYS (Lam. 3:13), BOWELS (Job 30:27; Cant. 5:4), etc.

In the OT the Hebrew substantives *lēḇ* and *lēḇāḇ* dominate the terms translated "heart" in the RSV (about 850 occurrences, in stark contrast to the eleven occurrences of Heb. *nepeš* for RSV "heart"). Similarly, Gk. *kardía* is predominant in the NT.

I. Physical Organ of the Body.–Ancient Hebrew anthropological thought, being prescientific, did not always clearly differentiate the internal organs of the body. Also, because the inner organs are concealed, Hebrew thought tended to attribute psychical as well as physical activities to them.

OT anthropology considered the heart more important than the other organs, probably because it can be located accurately by its beating (cf. Ps. 38:10 [MT 11]) in the chest cavity. Thus it is mentioned more often than *nepeš*, "soul," and *bāśār*, "flesh"; indeed, the heart can even be considered the place where the *nepeš* resides. Because of its important role as a life-sustaining organ (as well as the mystery of its concealed nature — a secret, inner place where thoughts can supposedly be "hidden" [Job 10:13; Ps. 36:1 (MT 2); 40:10 (MT 11); 51:6]), "heart" takes on a wide range of psychical meaning in the OT and can represent the human person in the totality of psychical and physical life.

In Ps. 84:2 (MT 3) *lēḇ* forms a hendiadys with *bāśār* ("my heart and my flesh") to express the total unity of the inner and outer person (NEB "my whole being"). The heart in OT thought performs the functions now generally associated with the brain. "Heart" in both the OT and NT only rarely (e.g., 1 S. 25:37; 2 K. 9:24; Ps. 38:10) represents the actual physical organ that sustains the human circulatory system. In most OT references the "heart" governs the intellectual, emotive, volitional, and physical dimensions of the inner person. Gk. *kardía* in the LXX has approximately the same range of nuances as Heb. *lēḇ* and *lēḇāḇ* in the OT (cf. Hatch).

The very limited NT (and LXX) use of *kardía* as bodily organ and center of human physical vitality (e.g., Acts 14:17; Jas. 5:5) directly contrasts with the use of the term in Josephus and Philo. Josephus used Gk. *diánoia*, "mind," or *psychḗ*, "soul," where the OT has "heart," and he reserved *kardía* for the central circulatory organ of humans and animals (cf. *Ant*. v.4.2 [193]; vii.10.2 [241]). Philo had learned from physicians (cf. *Legum allegoriae* ii.6) that the heart is that marvelous organ, located within the human *stḗthos*, "chest" (*Legum allegoriae* i.68), one of the seven inner parts of the body (*Legum allegoriae* i.12), which functions as the center of the bloodstream (*De specialibus legibus* i.216, 218). The much more prominent biblical use of heart in the metaphorical sense (as the center of the spiritual, intellectual, and emotive life) is not reflected in Philo, though he did wrestle with the Hellenistic anthropological problem of whether the *hēgemonikón*, "guiding reason," is located in the heart or brain. The classical Greek authors used *kardía* in its full range of meanings, from the physiological sense as central circulatory organ (e.g., Homer *Il*. x.94; xiii.442; Aristotle *De somno et vigilia* iii.456) and thus of the physical life in general, to the metaphorical sense as center of the inner life (e.g., Homer *Il*. xxi.547; Euripides *Akestis* 837; Sophocles *Antigone* 1105; cf. *TDNT*, III, 608-611).

II. Center of the Inner or Psychical Human Life.–*A. Emotions*. The heart may be glad (Ex. 4:14; Dt. 28:47; Jgs. 18:20 [NEB "pleased"]; Acts 2:26), merry, i.e., "drunk" (Jgs. 16:25; Ruth 3:7; 1 S. 25:36; Est. 1:10), thrilled (Cant. 5:4, Heb. *mēʿîm*), find delight (Prov. 29:17 [cf. H. Donner and W. Röllig, *Kanaanäische und aramäische Inschriften*, I (3rd ed. 1971), 26.A.I.13]) or pleasure (Eccl. 2:10), and be thankful (Col. 3:16).

Contrarily, the heart is also the locus of grief (Gen. 43:30; 1 S. 2:33 [Heb. *nepeš*; NEB "appetite"]; Lam. 2:11, 19 [Heb. *kāḇēḏ*]). It may even be "broken" in grief (Ezk. 21:6) or despair (Ps. 69:20; 34:18; 109:16; cf. Barn. 2:10), etc. Depression occurs when hearts are bowed down under hard labor (Ps. 107:12) and are heavy (Prov. 25:20) or dull (Lam. 3:65). The heart may throb in pain (Jer. 4:19; Isa. 65:14) or despondency (Ps. 38:10), know bitterness (Prov. 14:10), or be wrung within because of remorse (Lam. 1:20).

The angry person's heart becomes hot within (Ps. 39:3), carries him away (Job 15:12), and rages against the Lord (Prov. 19:3) when he has foolishly ruined himself. The avenger of blood is said in Dt. 19:6 to pursue the manslayer "in hot anger" (RSV; cf. AV "while his heart is hot"; NEB "in the heat of passion"). But the heart burning within may also signify excitement rather than anger (Lk. 24:32).

Empathy or compassion is expressed by the phrase "the heart goes out to" in Jgs. 5:9 and 2 S. 14:1 (cf. 15:13), or "cries out for" in Isa. 15:5. Israel, because of its sojourn in Egypt, knows the heart of a stranger (Ex. 23:9; NEB "how it feels to be") and thus should not oppress foreigners. Yahweh's compassion for His people is expressed in Isa. 63:15 as the "yearning" (Heb. *mēʿîm*) of His heart (AV "the sounding of thy bowels"; cf. Jer. 31:20; 2 Cor. 7:15).

The heart is particularly subject to fear (Dt. 28:67; Ps. 27:3). In fear the heart is said to melt (Dt. 1:28; 20:8) like water (Josh. 7:5) or like wax (Ps. 22:14 [MT 15]) as courage slips away (Josh. 2:11) or spirit departs (Josh. 5:1). Cf. also Gen. 42:28; 45:26; Lev. 26:36; Dt. 20:3; 28:65; 1 S. 4:13; 17:32; 28:5; Job 19:27; 37:1; Ps. 40:12; 61:2; 143:4; Isa. 7:2. (The RSV "losing heart" in 2 S. 22:46 par. Ps. 18:45 [MT 46] translates Heb. *yibbōlû* as a form of *nāḇēl*, "wither, droop" [cf. AV] rather than *yāḇal*, "carry away" [cf. NEB]. In the NT "lose heart" translates Gk. *enkakéō*, "tire, become weary" [Lk. 18:1; 2 Cor. 4:1, 16; Eph. 3:13] and *eklýō*, "slack, give out" [Gal. 6:9].)

The same human heart, so easily discouraged and fearful, is also the center of courage (2 Ch. 17:6; Ps. 27:14; Jer. 4:9), bravery (Ps. 76:5, RSV "stouthearted"; Am. 2:16, RSV "stout of heart"), and daring (2 S. 7:27, RSV "courage"; Jer. 30:21; cf. Dnl. 11:25). Thus the idiom from the language of love, "speak to the heart" (Heb. *dibbēr ʿal-lēḇ*), may mean encourage or move to decision, as in Gen. 34:3 (RSV "spoke tenderly"; cf. 50:21; Jgs. 19:3; etc.). The NT uses the Gk. *parakaléō* with *kardía* in the idiom "encourage the heart" (Eph. 6:22; Col. 2:2; 4:8; cf. 2 Th. 2:17), and imperative forms of *tharséō* and *euthyméō* to mean "take heart" (Mt. 9:2, 22; Mk. 6:50; 10:49; Acts 27:22, 25).

The heart may be weighed down with anxiety (Prov. 12:25) or worry (1 S. 9:20, RSV "set your mind on"). The heart suffers anguish (Ps. 55:4 [MT 5]; Jer. 4:19), sometimes as a burning fire (Jer. 20:9), so that one must cry out (Isa. 15:5). Yet it may also experience tranquillity (Prov. 14:30, Heb. *lēḇ*, RSV "mind") and freedom from anxiety (Isa. 60:5, lit. "enlargement of heart").

B. Volition and Purpose. The heart's role as the center of emotions is important, but its role as the center of will and purpose, intentionality and decision making, is even more significant.

Will and purpose originate in the heart (Dt. 8:2; 1 S. 2:35; 2 S. 7:3, 21; 1 K. 8:17; 1 Ch. 17:2; 28:2) and thus also intentionality (Jer. 23:20 [Heb. *mᵉzimmôṯ libbô*]; RSV "intents of the mind"), which is often a matter of "setting the heart" (1 Ch. 22:19; Ezr. 7:10). Resolve comes from the heart (Acts 11:23 [Gk. *prothései tḗs kardías*, NEB "resolute hearts"; RSV "steadfast purpose"]; Dnl. 1:8, lit. "put on the heart"; RSV "resolved") as does presumption (Est. 7:5; cf. AV "presume in his heart"). Paul indicates in 1 Cor. 4:5 that the Lord at His coming will "disclose the purposes of the heart" (Gk. *boulás tṓn kardiṓn;* cf. Jgs. 16:15; Ps. 55:21 [MT 22]; 139:23; etc.).

The heart's desire (2 S. 3:21; Ps. 10:3; 21:2; 37:4) often refers to determination, i.e., that on which one's heart is set (Dt. 24:15; Prov. 19:18; Eph. 6:5; Col. 3:22). Ezekiel speaks of idolatry in terms of the heart's desire: "takes his idols into his own heart" (Ezk. 14:3f., 7; NEB "sets his heart on idols"). It is idolatry also, though in a more subtle form, that Jesus has in mind when He says in Mt. 6:21 (par. Lk. 12:34), "For where your treasure is, there will your heart be also."

An idiomatic way of expressing wilful purpose or intent is that of "incline the heart" (Heb. hiphil of *nāṭâ* + *lēḇ;* Josh. 24:23; Jgs. 9:3; 1 K. 8:58; Ps. 117:36). The idiom "direct the heart" (Heb. hiphil of *kûn* + *lēḇ*) in 1 S. 7:3; Job 11:13; etc., is similar. As a causative form in Hebrew, either idiom may denote external influence in the human heart (e.g., that of God: 1 Ch. 29:18; cf. 2 Th. 3:5; of David: 2 S. 19:14 [MT 15]; and of Satan: Acts 5:3).

The inner impulse (Ps. 108:1 [MT 2]) for decision or choice comes from the heart (Ex. 35:21, 29; 2 K. 12:4 [MT 5]) and leads a person to be willing to contribute offerings (Ex. 25:2; 35:22; 2 Ch. 29:31) or work (Ex. 36:2) with a generous heart (Ex. 35:5; Acts 2:46; cf. Nu. 16:28; 1 S. 10:26; etc.). Reluctance or indecision can be seen in the expression "slow of heart to believe" (Lk. 24:25). Persistence in a decided course of action even against sound advice is stubbornness or obduracy of heart (Dt. 29:19 [MT 18]; Isa. 46:12), a heart that is, or is made, hard (Ex. 4:21; 7:3; Dt. 2:30; 15:7 [against the poor]; Prov. 28:14; Ezk. 2:4; Mk. 3:5; Rom. 2:5; Eph. 4:18; He. 3:8). When people agree, they have "one heart" (Heb. *lēḇ ʾeḥāḏ*, i.e., unanimity; 1 Ch. 12:38 [MT 39]; 2 Ch. 30:12; Jer. 32:39 [par. *dereḵ ʾeḥāḏ*, "one way"]; Ezk. 11:19). A person "after one's own heart" (1 S. 13:14; Jer. 3:15; Acts 13:22; cf. Jgs. 16:15) thinks or wills the same things one does. The idiom for discord or duplicity is having a "double heart" (Heb. *lēḇ wālēḇ;* 1 Ch. 12:33 [MT 34]; Ps. 12:2 [MT 3]).

C. Intellectual Activity, Perception, and Knowledge. Quite frequently Heb. *lēḇ*, *lēḇāḇ*, and Gk. *kardía*, etc., have the meaning "mind" (Dt. 5:29 [MT 26]; 28:28 [Heb. *timhôn lēḇāḇ*, "confusion of mind"]; 1 K. 3:9, 12; Job 17:4; Prov. 11:20; 12:8; Lk. 21:14; Rom. 1:21; etc.). Similar expressions using *lēḇ* or *lēḇāḇ* can be translated as a changing of mind (Ex. 14:5) or as receiving "another heart" (1 S. 10:9). In the NT "heart" and "mind" (Gk. *noús*) are closely related. Both designate the self as willing, intending, thinking, etc. In 2 Cor. 3:14f. the two terms are parallel in content (RSV uses "mind" for both), and in Phil. 4:7 they appear together in hendiadys. When so connected *noús* represents knowledge and *kardía* emotion and volition, so that together they signify the total person as a fully responsible self before God (see Bultmann, pp. 220ff.).

Expressions using "heart" signify various intellectual processes: "lay [something] to heart" means "consider carefully" (Dt. 4:39; 1 K. 8:47; Eccl. 7:2; 9:1) and "take seriously" (Ex. 7:23; Dt. 32:46; 1 S. 21:12 [MT 13]; cf. Dt. 11:18; Job 22:22; 2 S. 13:20; etc.). To "give the heart" (Prov. 23:26) means to pay attention, as does "set the mind" (Heb. *lēḇ*, Ezk. 40:4; NEB "mark well"; cf. Prov. 8:5 and Dt. 8:5, NEB "take to heart"; cf. also Ex. 9:21; 1 S. 25:25; Eccl. 1:13, 17; etc.). The heart also ponders (Ps. 4:4 [MT 5]; 77:6 [MT 7]; Lk. 2:19, 51), meditates (Ps. 19:14 [MT 15]; 49:3 [MT 4]), and is the locus of belief (Josh. 23:14; Rom. 10:9f.).

One's heart contains thoughts and ideas (1 Ch. 29:18; Lk. 2:35; 9:47) which may often be base (Dt. 15:9), evil (1 S. 17:28; Mt. 12:34; 15:18f.), or deceitful (Prov. 26:24; Jer. 12:2; 23:26). Similarly, one questions (Mk. 2:6, 8; Lk. 5:22; 24:38) and doubts (Mk. 11:23) in his heart. A frequent idiom for "think" is "say or speak in one's heart" (i.e., think to oneself; Gen. 24:45; Dt. 7:17; 8:17; 1 S. 1:13; 27:1; 1 K. 12:26; Rom. 10:6; Rev. 18:7; cf. Job 1:5, "cursed God in their hearts").

The heart does not simply store up ideas and impressions; it can devise plans to put these ideas quickly into action (Heb. *ḥāšaḇ*, "think, devise"; e.g., Ps. 33:11; 140:2 [MT 3]; cf. Jer. 9:8 [MT 7]; Acts 5:4). Creative thought, ascribed to the heart in Gen. 6:5 (Heb. *kol-yēṣer maḥšᵉḇōṯ libbô*, "every imagination of the thoughts of his heart"); 8:21, is particularly focused in the *yēṣer*, "invention, creation," which in the human is here said to tend toward some base purpose. In Lk. 1:51 the "imaginations of the heart" (Gk. *dianoía kardías*) are the fabric of false pride (cf. Ps. 45:1 [MT 2]; Jer. 14:14).

The heart as the seat of knowledge and understanding is closely associated with *ḥoḵmâ,* "wisdom," and *t^{e}ḇûnâ,* "understanding," in Prov. 2:2 and Ex. 31:6, and with *da'aṯ,* "knowledge," in Dt. 29:4 [MT 3]. The heart is also particularly associated with Solomon (1 K. 4:29 [MT 5:9]) to whom God gave "largeness of mind [Heb. *lēḇ*] like the sand on the seashore" (cf. 1 K. 3:12). The ancient Egyptians also perceived the heart as the seat of understanding (see *TDNT,* IX, 627).

The heart can recall things (Heb. hiphil of *šûḇ* + *'el-lēḇ*) e.g., Isa. 44:19, "consider"; Dt. 30:1, "call . . . to mind").

Something turned aside from the heart (Heb. *sûr* + *mill^{e}ḇāḇ*) is forgotten (Dt. 4:9; cf. Ps. 31:12 [MT 13]).

III. Center of the Ethical and Religious Life.–In the OT it is the heart that most closely approximates what we call conscience. The heart as conscience "smites" David (2 S. 24:5 [MT 6]). Similar is 1 Jn. 3:20f., "whenever our hearts condemn us" (cf. 1 S. 25:31; 2 K. 22:19; 2 Ch. 34:27). The heart functions as the seat of moral and ethical thought and thus is often described in terms of purity (e.g., Ps. 24:4; 73:1 [Heb. *bar lēḇāḇ,* "pure in heart"]; cf. "blameless" in 2 Ch. 15:17; Mt. 5:8).

Integrity (Heb. *tom-lēḇāḇ;* Gen. 20:5f.; 1 K. 9:4; Ps. 78:72; 101:2) and uprightness or straightforwardness (Heb. *yōšer,* lit. "on the level"; e.g., Dt. 9:5; 1 K. 3:6; 9:4; Ps. 119:7) come from the heart. A righteous life (Heb. *ṣ^{e}dāqâ*) results from responding to Yahweh "with all [one's] heart" (1 S. 7:3; 12:20, 24; Jer. 3:10; 24:7; cf. Dt. 4:29; 6:5; Mk. 12:30 par. Mt. 22:37; Lk. 10:27).

Faithfulness (Heb. *'^{e}meṯ* or *ne'^{e}mān;* 1 S. 12:24; 1 K. 2:14; Neh. 9:8), steadfastness or firmness (Heb. *nāḵôn;* Ps. 57:7 [MT 8]; 78:37; 112:7; cf. Akk. *libbu kēnu,* "steadfast heart"), and humility (Mt. 11:29, "I am gentle and lowly in heart"; cf. Dnl. 5:22; T. Reub. 6:10) are desirable qualities of the heart.

By nature, however, the human heart is not pure or faithful; it tends to be perverse (Heb. *'iqqēš;* Ps. 101:4; Prov. 11:20 [RSV "mind"]). The heart can function ethically only by the help of God (Ps. 73:26, "My flesh and my heart may fail, but God is the strength of my heart").

Thus God examines or tests (Heb. *bāḥan*; Gk. *dokimázō*) human hearts (1 Ch. 29:17; Ps. 7:9 [MT 10]; 17:3; Prov. 17:3; Jer. 11:20; 12:3; 17:10; 1 Th. 2:4; etc.).

God knows all the weaknesses of the human heart because He "searches" (Heb. *dāraš*; Gk. *eraunáō*) all hearts (1 Ch. 28:9; Rom. 8:27) and minds (Rev. 2:23). He knows that the heart's imagination or creativity (Heb. *yēṣer*) is often intent on evil (Heb. *ra'*) rather than on His own standard of uprightness, as in Gen. 6:5 and 8:21 (cf. 1 S. 17:28, where "the evil of your heart" parallels "presumption"). The idol-worshiping heart "turns away" (Heb. *pānâ*; Dt. 29:18 [MT 17]; 30:17; cf. 1 K. 11:2ff.; Acts 7:39) or "turns aside" (Heb. *sûr*; Dt. 11:16; 1 S. 12:20; etc.) from God. Perhaps the heart's greatest weakness is pride (2 Ch. 26:16; 32:25f.; Isa. 9:9 [MT 8]; Jer. 49:16; Ezk. 28:2; Hos. 13:6; Ob. 3; Lk. 1:51; 2 Cor. 5:12), which causes the heart to be haughty (Prov. 18:12) or lifted up (Dt. 8:14; 2 K. 14:10; Ps. 131:1; Dnl. 5:20). The heart may dull its moral sensitivity with a layer of fatness so that it fails to act uprightly (Ps. 119:70; Isa. 6:10; Acts 28:27; Jas. 5:5; cf. 1 Jn. 3:17). Indeed, it can even become petrified (Job 41:24 [MT 16]; Ezk. 11:19; 36:26; Zec. 7:12).

Only God can open (Acts 16:14) or illumine (2 Cor. 4:6) the heart to bring a person to faith. He can give the heart firmness and integrity and cause it to be true to Him (1 K. 8:61; 9:4; 15:3, 14; Heb. *šālēm;* RSV "wholly true"; NEB "perfect in loyalty," "faithful"). Ezekiel warned, "Get yourselves a new heart" (18:31; 36:26; cf. Ps. 51:10 [MT 12], "a clean heart" parallel to "a new and right spirit"; Acts 15:9, "cleansed"; and He. 10:22, "sprinkled clean from an evil conscience"). Jeremiah envisioned this new relationship between God and His people as a new covenant in which God's Torah would be inscribed on the hearts (Jer. 31:31-33). The heart deserves careful attention, for in it the "wellsprings of life" are found (Prov. 4:23).

See picture in DEATH.

IV. Synecdoche.–Since it includes so many dimensions of emotional, mental, and volitional activity, the term "heart" is often used in synecdoche — a figure of speech in which a part is used to represent the whole. The heart thus frequently stands for the whole person, e.g., "let not your heart be glad" in Prov. 24:17 (for "yourself"; cf. Lev. 26:41; Dt. 11:16; 1 K. 9:3 par. 2 Ch. 7:16; cf. 2 K. 5:26; cf. also *ANET,* p. 322).

V. Heart as "Remote Place."–The heart, as a concealed organ, connotes inaccessibility and thus is sometimes used in anthropomorphisms: the "heart of the sea" (Ex. 15:8; Prov. 23:34; 30:19; Ezk. 27:4, 25ff.; 28:2; 2 Esd. 13:3) means the unknown and unexplored "high seas" or the sea's awesome depths (Ps. 46:2 [MT 3]; Ezk. 28:8; Jonah 2:3 [MT 4]); the "heart of heaven" to which the mountain (Horeb) burned with fire (Dt. 4:11) refers to the inaccessible heights of the great mountain; the "heart of the earth" refers to the grave.

VI. Related Terms.–Greek *sklērokardía* denotes "hardness of heart" and is a LXX neologism created to translate Heb. *'orlāṯ lēḇāḇ* (Dt. 10:16; Jer. 4:4; Sir. 16:10). It occurs in the NT only in Mk. 10:5; 16:14 (cf. Mt. 19:8) and in various intertestamental and patristic writings (see *TDNT,* III, 614). The Gk. *kardiognṓstēs,* "the one who knows the heart," occurs only in the NT and later literature (see *TDNT,* III, 613). Gk. *eúsplanchnos,* "tenderhearted" (Eph. 4:32; 1 Pet. 3:8), describes kind and compassionate relationships. Its antonym, Gk. *ástorgos,* occurs only in Rom. 1:31 ("heartless") and 2 Tim. 3:3 ("inhuman"), in each instance in a catalog of vices. The phrase *ek psychḗs* is rendered "heartily" (i.e., "gladly" or "from the heart") in Col. 3:23 and "from the heart" in Eph. 6:6.

VII. Heart of God.–"Heart" is applied to God in much the same way as to humans. God seeks people "after his own heart" (1 S. 13:14, disobedient Saul's loss of the kingdom), for what is in His heart is His will. Thus the word comes to Eli in 1 S. 2:35, "I will raise up for myself a faithful priest, who shall do according to what is in my heart and in my mind" (Heb. *ka'^{a}šer bil^{e}ḇāḇî ûḇ^{e}napšî,* lit. "according to my will and desire"). The kindness of His heart (Lam. 3:33) and the profound way in which human evil has "grieved him to his heart" are readily apparent. In Hos. 11:8 God, in contemplating judgment, speaks of the "overthrow" (Heb. *hāpaḵ*) of His mind (RSV "my heart recoils within me"), the reversal of His own decision. As Wolff (p. 58) puts it, "God's heart, i.e., his free resolve of love, turns against his decision of anger. So Hosea promised that decision in the heart of God which has been sealed for all nations in Jesus Christ."

Bibliography.–G. C. Berkouwer, *Man: The Image of God* (Eng. tr. 1962), pp. 194-278; C. A. Briggs, "A Study of the Use of לֵב and לֵבָב in the OT," in *Semitic Studies in Memory of A. Kohut* (1897), pp. 94-105; R. Bultmann, *Theology of the NT,* I (Eng. tr. 1952), 220-27; R. Dentan, *Knowledge of God in Ancient Israel* (1968), pp. 37f.; W. Eichrodt, *Theology of the OT,* II (*OTL,* Eng. tr. 1967), 142-45; E. Hatch, *Essays in Biblical Greek* (repr. 1970), pp. 94-109; R. Jewett, *Paul's Anthropological Terms* (1971), pp. 305-333, 447f.; A. R. Johnson, *Vitality of the Individual in the Thought of Ancient Israel* (2nd ed. 1964), pp. 75-87; P. Joüon, *Bibl.,* 5 (1924), 49-53; L. Kuyper, *SJT,* 27 (1974), 459-474; F. H. Van Meyenfeldt, *Het Hart (leb, lebab) in Het Oude Testament* (1950); N. Schmidt,

EvTh, 24 (1964), 374-388; *THAT,* I, *s.v.* לֵב (F. Stolz); *TDNT,* III, *s.v.* καρδία (Baumgärtel, Behm); IX, *s.v.* ψυχή (Bertram, Dihle, Jacob, Lohse, Schweizer, Tröger); H. W. Wolff, *Anthropology of the OT* (Eng. tr. 1974), pp. 40-58, 63-77. D. G. BURKE

HEARTH [Heb. *môqᵉḏâ*] (Lev. 6:9 [MT 2]); AV BURNING; [*yāqûḏ*] (Isa. 30:14); NEB "glowing embers"; [*har'ēl*] ("altar hearth," Ezk. 43:15); AV ALTAR; [*'ᵃri'ēl*] ("altar hearth," Ezk. 43:16f.); AV ALTAR; [*mᵉḇaššᵉlôṯ*] (Ezk. 46:23); AV "boiling places"; NEB "fire-places."

In tents, the hearth was nothing more than a depression in the ground in which a fire burned, either for cooking or for providing warmth. Cakes were baked in the ashes on the hearth or on hot stones. The smoke escaped from the tent through the door, since there was no chimney. Such primitive facilities were also present in the poorer houses.

While the function of the hearth is thus clear, the Hebrew terms exhibit a variety of meanings. In Lev. 6:9, the "hearth" was the uppermost level of the altar of the burnt offering where the fire was kindled to consume the sacrifice (cf. RV mg., "on its firewood"). This may be what is implied by the terms in Ezk. 43:15f., namely, the area of a sanctuary in which a fire was maintained for the burning of offerings. In Isa. 30:14 the expression means simply "that which is kindled," referring to the bed of live coals, while the rare term in Ezk. 46:23 designates the kitchen hearths in Ezekiel's visionary temple (cf. v. 24).

R. K. H.

HEARTILY. The translation of Gk. *ek psychḗs,* lit. "out of the soul": "whatever your task, work heartily, as serving the Lord and not men" (Col. 3:23; NEB "put your whole heart into it"). "Heartily" also occurs in the AV of 2 Macc. 4:27, "Antiochus was heartily sorry" (Gk. *psychikṓs,* "from the soul").

HEAT [Heb. *ḥōm* (Gen. 8:22; 18:1; 1 S. 11:11; 2 S. 4:5; Job 24:19; Jer. 17:8), *ḥōreḇ* (Gen. 31:40; Job 30:30; Isa. 4:6; 25:4f.; Jer. 36:30), *ḥarḥur* (Dt. 28:22), *ḥᵒrî* (Dt. 29:24 [MT 23]), *rešep* (Dt. 32:24), *ḥammâ* (Ps. 19:6 [MT 7]), *ḥᵃrāḇôn* (Ps. 32:4), *ḥēmâ* (Isa. 42:25; Ezk. 3:14; Hos. 7:5), *zal'āpâ* (Lam. 5:10), *ḥārôn* (Nah. 1:6; Zeph. 3:8); *'awwaṯ nepeš* (Jer. 2:24); *zāraḇ* (Job 6:17); Gk. *kaúsōn* (Mt. 20:12; Lk. 12:55; Jas. 1:11), *thérmē* (Acts 28:3), *kaúma* (Rev. 7:16; 16:9)]; AV also DROUGHT, BURNING, HOT, FURY, FIERCE, etc.; NEB also HOT, ANGER, OUTBURST, BLAZING SUN, etc. The RSV understands Ps. 58:9a as a case of ellipsis and supplies "heat" before "thorns." In Isa. 18:4b the NEB, with the support of twelve Hebrew MSS, LXX, Vulgate, and Syriac, emends the MT to read *bᵉyôm (qāṣîr),* "at harvest time," instead of *bᵉḥōm,* "in the heat (of harvest)." The AV takes the consonants *ḥmt* in Hos. 7:5 as being from *ḥēmeṯ,* "waterskin," instead of *ḥēmâ,* and so reads "with bottles of wine" instead of "with the heat of wine" (RSV).

The various terms for "heat" represent different usages. The Heb. *ḥōreḇ* is used particularly of the dryness of the ground resulting from the heat of the sun, and is rendered "drought" three times by the AV. For *ḥarḥur,* on the other hand, KoB (p. 333) suggests "feverish heat," and for *rešep* (Dt. 32:24), "pestilence" (p. 911). In Palestine the most blasting heat is produced by the east wind, the sirocco. Some have understood Gk. *kaúsōn* to refer to these winds, especially in Mt. 20:12 and Jas. 1:11 (the LXX uses *kaúsōn* to refer to these winds, but generally accompanied by *ánemos* or *pneúma*); most commentators, however, think *kaúsōn* in the NT refers only to the heat of the sun. The term *thérmē,* which occurs only once in the NT, is used of the heat of a fire (Acts 28:3).

Many of the occurrences of "heat" show that it was an oppressive enemy. The heat of the day consumed a person (Gen. 31:40), the hot summer wore one out (Ps. 32:4). Noontime is referred to as "the heat of the day" (Gen. 18:1). People generally sought rest during the hot afternoon; however, an enemy could take advantage of this fact to commit treachery, such as the assassination of Ishbosheth while he was resting in his house (2 S. 4:5-8). The sun is the source of heat (Ps. 19:6: "there is nothing hid from its heat"). But too much sun and wind without rain create drought. Consequently, the versions fluctuate between translating *ḥōreḇ* as "heat" (Gen. 31:40 and Ps. 32:4, RSV) or "drought" (AV).

"Heat" is a word with numerous metaphorical uses, particularly in the areas of sickness (Dt. 28:22), anger (Isa. 42:25; Nah. 1:6), and sex (Jer. 2:24). During his intense suffering Job exclaimed, "My bones burn with heat" (Job 30:30). No doubt he was describing both the fever and the intense discomfort he felt in his body. Another sickness, that of becoming intoxicated, is described in Hos. 7:5 as "became sick with the heat of wine" (cf. Jer. 51:39). Heat is also one of the curses that the Lord brings on those who break the covenant. Since the word appears between physical diseases and natural plagues in Dt. 28:22, it is difficult to tell if it applies to the person (NEB) or to nature (RSV). Heat dries up vegetation and causes famine. The intensity of famine is called "the burning heat of famine" (RSV) or "the ravages of starvation" (NEB) in Lam. 5:10. Viewed as a curse, heat becomes part of the imagery of the catastrophic judgments against sinners described in Rev. 16:8f.: "the fourth angel poured his bowl on the sun, and . . . men were scorched by the fierce heat" (RSV).

Heat is connected with anger to stress the dynamic intensity of this emotion (Dt. 29:24; Zeph. 3:8; frequently *ḥēmâ* and *ḥārôn*), especially when God comes forth to judge the disobedient. Ezekiel's initial reaction to being coerced by the Holy Spirit was to respond in bitterness and in "the heat of [his] spirit" (Ezk. 3:14, RSV). Such a reaction indicates that he maintained his own inner emotional life in spite of the Spirit's directional force. After the initial encounter, it took seven days before the events gained their perspective and he could begin his prophetic task. The NEB understands the import of the passage differently; it renders "in the heat of my spirit" as "full of exaltation" (cf. *TDOT,* IV, 463f.). If this is correct, then Ezekiel became exhilarated rather than angry. Jeremiah, however, Ezekiel's contemporary, experienced intense anger in response to the Word of God (Jer. 15:17). This evidence may suggest that Ezekiel's experience was one of anger.

The RSV translates the word for "desire" as "heat" in reference to a wild ass in its time of mating (Jer. 2:24). The Hebrew, however, uses heat in reference to sex more frequently; e.g., "bred" in Gen. 30:38f., 41, "mating season" in Gen. 31:10, and "conceive" in Ps. 51:5 (MT 7).

In the time of judgment the wrath of God is intense against the disobedient, but the righteous experience God like "a shade by day from the heat" (Isa. 4:6). Then in the new age all the discomforts in this life will be gone. According to Rev. 7:16, those who have been cleansed by the blood of the Lamb "shall hunger no more, neither thirst any more; the sun shall not strike them, nor any scorching heat."

See also WRATH; FAMINE; FURY.

Bibliography.–G. Fohrer, *Das Buch Hiob* (1963); E. Dhorme, *The Book of Job* (Eng. tr. 1964). J. E. HARTLEY

HEATH. The AV translation of Heb. *'ar'ār* in Jer. 17:6

(RSV SHRUB; NEB JUNIPER) and of *ʿarôʿēr* in 48:6 (RSV "wild ass"; NEB "sand-grouse"). In the latter passage, the RSV emends the text, following the LXX and Aquila.

See also FLORA; TAMARISK.

HEATHEN. *See* GENTILES.

HEAVE OFFERING. *See* SACRIFICE.

HEAVEN [Heb. *šāmayim*–'heights,' *mārôm*–'height' (Job 25:2; Isa. 24:18, 21), *maʿaleh*–'ascent' (Isa. 7:11); Aram. *šemayim* (Dnl. 4:11 [MT 8]); Gk. *ouranós*–'that which is raised up']; AV also AIR (cf. Gen. 1:26), SKY, SKIES, ON HIGH, HEAVENS (Zec. 6:5; He. 8:1), HEAVENLY (1 Cor. 15:48), "places," "the high ones" (Isa. 24:21), HEIGHT; NEB also SKY, SKIES, HEAVENS, HEAVENLY, "realm on high," etc.; **HEAVENS** [Heb. *šāmayim, mārôm* (Ps. 78:69); Aram. *šemayim* (Jer. 10:11); Gk. *ouranoí* (cf. Mk. 13:25)]; AV also HEAVEN (cf. Gen. 1:1), HEAVENS OF HEAVEN (Ps. 68:33 [MT 34]), VERY HIGH, "palaces" (Ps. 78:69), "astrologers" (Isa. 47:13); NEB also HEAVEN (cf. Gen. 1:1; Ps. 68:33), HIGH PLACES, "astrologers" (Isa. 47:13). "Heaven" denotes the sky, outer space, the abode of God, angels, and other spiritual creatures, or may be used as a circumlocution for God, depending on the context.

I. OT.–In the OT, heaven is often metaphorically conceived as something fixed and material: it has windows (Gen. 7:11), pillars (Job 26:11), foundations (2 S. 22:8), and it can be torn (Isa. 63:19) like a curtain (cf. Mk. 1:10). In these senses, heaven is related to the "firmament" (Heb. *rāqî[a]ʿ*; cf. Gen. 1:8).

Heaven often refers to the space immediately enveloping the earth, i.e., the atmosphere, and a number of meteorological phenomena are mentioned: rain (Gen. 8:2), snow (Isa. 55:9-11), frost (Job 38:29), dew (Dt. 33:13, AV, RSV mg.), hail (Josh. 10:11), thunder (1 S. 2:10), wind (Zec. 6:5), and clouds (Ps. 147:8). Thus, heaven is the realm of various signs, both natural (Mt. 16:2f.) and supernatural (Ex. 10:21f.). In a combination of these two views, heaven is also the realm wherein the rainbow, God's sign of his covenant with Noah, is seen (Gen. 9:13-17).

Heaven can also denote outer space, where the lights (Gen. 1:14) and stars (Dt. 4:19) are located. The planets Venus and Saturn are referred to (Isa. 14:12; Am. 5:26), though they are not distinguished from the fixed stars. (*See* ASTRONOMY II.B, C.) Several constellations are mentioned (Job 9:9; 38:31). Though cultic worship was often associated with astrology among the peoples of the Near East, such practice was forbidden to the Hebrews (Ex. 20:4). The prophets condemned sacrificial offerings to the stars (Jer. 44:17-25), and astrological speculations were forbidden (Isa. 47:13). Such warnings reflect the conviction that the heavens, too, were part of the created order (Gen. 1:1; cf. Ps. 33:6) and therefore not to be worshiped in the place of the Creator. (*See also* ASTROLOGY IV.)

In many passages, "heaven" is the abode of God: "Look down from heaven and see, from thy holy and glorious habitation" (Isa. 63:15). Both God's habitation (Ps. 33:14) and His sanctuary (Ps. 102:19 [MT 20]; cf. Ps. 61:4 [MT 5]) are "in the heavens." God's throne is in heaven (Ps. 14:2; 103:19), and at times heaven is called the throne of God (Isa. 66:1; Mt. 5:34; He. 8:1). God's house is in heaven (Ps. 61:4; Jn. 14:2) and He dwells there (1 K. 8:12). Thus, God is often called "the God of heaven" (e.g., Gen. 24:3, 7; 2 Ch. 36:23; Ezr. 1:2; Neh. 1:4f.; Dnl. 2:37, 44). Yahweh, the God of heaven, is implored in prayer (Dt. 26:15) to "look down from thy holy habitation from heaven, and bless thy people Israel." Since God was thought to be above, people lifted their hands in oaths (Dt. 34:20) and in prayer (Ex. 9:29).

II. NT.–In postexilic Judaism the term heaven came to be used as a circumlocution for the divine name Yahweh or for the term "God." This phenomenon occurs only once in the OT (Dnl. 4:23 [MT 20]) but is frequent in the NT. In the parable of the Prodigal Son, the son returns and confesses to his father: "I have sinned against heaven," meaning that he had sinned against God (Lk. 15:21). Jesus referred to this common practice of using heaven as a substitute for God when He said, ". . . he who swears by heaven, swears by the throne of God and by him who sits upon it" (Mt. 23:22). Similarly Jesus asked the priests and elders whether John's baptism was "from heaven or from men" (Mt. 21:25), and John the Baptist is reported to have said, "No one can receive anything except what is given him from heaven" (Jn. 3:27). This phenomenon can also be seen in Jesus' preaching of the kingdom: Mark and Luke consistently use the phrase "the kingdom of God," but Matthew usually substitutes the phrase "the kingdom of heaven" (cf. Mk. 1:15 par. Mt. 3:17; Mk. 4:11 par. Mt. 13:11, etc.). (*See also* KINGDOM OF GOD V.A.)

Reference to heaven is made as a means of establishing the authority of someone or something. Thus "the heavens were opened" at Jesus' baptism (Mt. 3:16), indicating the authoritative nature of His mission. The heavenly voice (Mt. 3:17) was also indicative of divine authority. Similarly, Paul testified before King Agrippa, justifying his apostolic mission with reference to "the heavenly vision" (Acts 26:19).

Of great significance is the ambivalent portrayal of heaven given in the biblical materials. The popular conception of heaven revolves around clouds, harps, and angels, with humanity marching through the Pearly Gates to live a life of bliss. This conception is far removed from the biblical witness. Rather, the Bible depicts heaven under the wrath of God, the scene of cosmic warfare, and finally subject to dissolution prior to the creation of a new heaven. This ambivalence surrounding heaven is to be expected because of the fundamental antithetical structure of biblical eschatology, which is conceived in terms of this present evil age and the age to come (*see* ESCHATOLOGY; KINGDOM OF GOD). It must be stressed that in this framework this whole age experiences turbulence, disquiet, and flux; both heaven and earth experience the wrath of God, the powers of evil, personal incompleteness, and temporality. Only the age to come is "heaven" in any idyllic sense. In support of this view attention should be given to the following points.

(1) Heaven is populated by angels that are not absolutely good. Rom. 8:38 implicates heavenly angels in the execution of the wrath of God. This is also seen in Paul's warning that the saints will judge the angels (1 Cor. 6:3). This judgment is not restricted to the fallen angels (cf. Jude 6; 2 Pet. 2:4), but rather, in light of the absence of any qualifying epithet (Gk. *angélous*), the angels in view here must be considered "good" angels.

(2) The heavenly tribunal was accessible to the accuser, Satan (Job 1:6; cf. Zec. 3:1). In Lk. 10:17-20 we are told that the accuser had been refused hearing before the heavenly tribunal and had been cast down. This occurred initially during the temptation and the exorcistic activities of Jesus and His disciples. This event is symbolically depicted at Rev. 12:7-12, a description of a war in heaven. At vv. 8, 10, and 12 we are told that Satan was "cast out"

and that "no longer" was there any place for him in heaven. Hence, only since Christ's death and ascension to heaven has Satan's access to heaven been terminated.

(3) Some of the cosmic powers created by God (Col. 1:16) stand in need of redemption and reconciliation (v. 20), which was accomplished in the cross of Christ. Some of these heavenly powers will be destroyed, being beyond redemption (cf. 1 Cor. 15:24). These cosmic powers are evil, and Paul describes the Christian's warfare as against them (cf. Eph. 6:12). *See* HEAVENLY.

(4) Even in those heavenly precincts where God's presence is manifested there is disquiet and turmoil: the souls of the martyrs kept under the altar cry out and complain, saying, "O Sovereign Lord, . . . how long?" (Rev. 6:9f.). They are perplexed and even impatient at the postponement of judgment. Only Jesus' parousia and the subsequent completed judgment will bring these souls full blessedness. Though they are given white robes and told to rest "a little longer" (6:11), it is difficult to understand how the souls of the righteous could enjoy rest knowing that their fellow servants are being slaughtered. This "rest" is certainly not the rest of perfection, of completed blessedness.

(5) Paul tells us (2 Cor. 5:1-10) that the saints now in heaven are naked (Gk. *gymnoí*, v. 3), having not yet received their spiritual bodies (1 Cor. 15:44), which await the Parousia. Thus the intermediate state of the righteous prior to the eschatological consummation must not be one of complete felicity. Indeed, in 2 Cor. 5:1-5 Paul seems to shrink before the prospect of dying and going to heaven prior to the Parousia.

(6) Lastly, and perhaps most significantly, the Bible indicates that heaven will experience an eschatological catastrophe that will bring this age to a close. Heaven and earth were created together (Gen. 1:1), they will experience dissolution together (Isa. 51:6), and they will be redeemed together. In Mt. 24:29 Jesus said that "the powers of the heavens will be shaken," referring to the angelic or cosmic powers (Gk. *dynámeis*) that are "in the heavenly places" (Eph. 6:12): the heavens will perish (Ps. 102:26-28; Isa. 34:4), but they will be remade (cf. Isa. 65:17; 66:22).

It is in the NT that this final catastrophic judgment of heaven is clearly seen (cf. He. 1:10-12). He. 12:6, which refers to Hag. 2:6, says that the Lord will shake "not only the earth but also [Gk. *allá kaí*] the heaven," with this adversative construction stressing heaven's participation in the final cataclysm. Not only the visible, celestial heavens will be destroyed, but rather heaven in its entirety is subjected to the judgment of God. He. 1:10 and 2 Pet. 3:7, 10, 12 stress the plural "heavens" (*ouranoí*), which is explained not only with reference to the commonly used Heb. plural *šāmayim* but also by the Jewish belief in the plurality of the heavens (cf. 2 Cor. 12:2).

Whereas other religions often conceive of heaven, the beyond, as the place of complete felicity and look upon the celestial sphere as a place of pure light and untainted glory, the NT tradition never entertains such thinking. Rather, heaven was and is, even in the period after Christ, a place of conflict. God exercises wrath against the demonic attack that threatens to remove Him from his sovereign throne. It is this representation, the picture of a total age including the heavens of this age taken up in the catastrophe of evil, which finds normative expression in the NT. Thus the Christian does not seek ultimate release in this age or in the heaven of this age, for this age is impregnated with evil and hence subject to wrath. Rather, those who are "in Christ" here on earth and those who are "with Christ" in heaven anticipate that splendid day when Christ the Lord shall appear and by divine power end the demonic threat and inaugurate the coming age of glory. Then shall the saints of God fully rejoice and in transformed bodies eternally reign with the Father, Son, and Holy Spirit in the new heavens and new earth. *See also* HEAVENS, NEW.

Bibliography.–H. Bietenhard, *Die himmlische Welt im Urchristentum und Spätjudentum* (1951); K. Schilder, *Heaven: What Is It?* (Eng. tr. 1950); U. Simon, *Heaven in the Christian Tradition* (1958); W. M. Smith, *Biblical Doctrine of Heaven* (1968); C. R. Schoonhoven, *Wrath of Heaven* (1966); *TDNT*, V, *s.v.* οὐρανός κτλ. (Traub). C. R. SCHOONHOVEN

HEAVEN, HOST OF. *See* ASTROLOGY IV; HOST OF HEAVEN.

HEAVEN, ORDINANCES OF. In Job 38:33 the term refers to the constellations of certain stars (*see* ASTRONOMY IV.C) and signifies their laws. In Jer. 33:25 the term (Heb. *ḥuqqôṯ*, "regulations," KoB, p. 327) may mean the "natural laws" of the universe (cf. *IB*, V, 1052).

HEAVEN, WINDOWS OF. In a few OT passages "the windows [Heb. *ʾᵃrubbâ*, "openings," KoB, p. 82; "lattice," "window," "sluice," BDB, p. 70] of heaven" symbolize the way God, who is in heaven, interacts with His creatures on earth. These "windows" can be opened and closed (cf. Gen. 7:11; 8:2). In the Flood account (Gen. 7:11) they are the atmosphere from which heavy rains fell (cf. Isa. 24:18). In 2 K. 7:2, 19 "windows in heaven" symbolizes Yahweh's deliverance of Samaria (cf. Mal. 3:10). *See also* HEAVEN.

HEAVENLY [Heb. *bᵉnê ʾēlîm*–lit. 'sons of gods' (Ps. 29:1; 89:6 [MT 7]); Gk. *ouránios* (Mt. 5:48; 6:14, 26, 32; 15:13; 18:35; etc.), *ouranós* (Lk. 11:13; 2 Cor. 5:2), *epouránios* (Eph. 1:3, 20; 2:6; 3:10; 6:12; 2 Tim. 4:18; He. 3:1; 6:4; etc.)]; AV also "ye mighty" (Ps. 29:1), "sons of the mighty" (Ps. 89:6 [MT 7]), "from heaven" (2 Cor. 5:2), "high places" (Eph. 6:12), etc.; NEB also "gods" (Ps. 29:1), "court of heaven" (Ps. 89:6 [MT 7]), "of heaven" (Jn. 3:12), "realms of heaven" (Eph. 3:10), "in the heavens" (Eph. 6:12). Adjectival form of HEAVEN. "Heavenly" occurs only twice in the RSV OT, where "heavenly beings" translates Heb. *bᵉnê ʾēlîm* (lit. "sons of gods"). The "heavenly beings" are the gods of the pagan pantheons who must pay homage to Yahweh (cf. M. Dahood, *Psalms I* [*AB*, 1965], pp. 175f.; A. Weiser, *Psalms* [Eng. tr., *OTL*, 1962], p. 262).

In the NT, "heavenly" is used in a variety of contexts. In Jn. 3:12 it means that certain matters can be known by people with reference to their own abilities ("earthly") while other matters can be known only by revelation ("heavenly"). In 1 Cor. 15:40, 48f. the thought is eschatological and refers to the glorious resurrection bodies of believers that will correspond to the body of the resurrected Lord. In Ephesians the phrase "in the heavenlies" occurs at 1:3, 20; 2:6; 3:10 and 6:12 as a formulaic expression, so its meaning must therefore be consistent throughout the Epistle. From these passages the startling conclusion must be drawn that not only God, Christ, and believers who are "in him" dwell in the "heavenly places," but that evil cosmic powers also dwell there (cf. 3:10; 6:12). The phrase "in the heavenly places" in this Epistle is equivalent to "in the heavens" and so signifies a supernatural location. This idea of locale is seen in Phil. 2:10 and 2 Tim. 4:18. In Hebrews the thought appears to be of the superior value of the "heavenly things" as compared with the earthly things, not because of their heavenly location per se but because of their association with Christ, the High Priest (9:23f.).

Bibliography.–C. R. Schoonhoven, *Wrath of Heaven* (1966), pp. 60-62; *TDNT*, V, *s.v.* οὐρανός κτλ.: οὐράνιος, ἐπουράνιος (Traub).

C. R. SCHOONHOVEN

HEAVENS, NEW [Heb. *šāmayim ḥ^a^dāšîm* (Isa. 65:17; 66:22); Gk. *kainós ouranós* (2 Pet. 3:13; Rev. 21:1)]. "New heavens and a new earth" is a technical term referring to an important element of biblical eschatology. The phrase itself is found in only four passages. In Isaiah the new creation is promised in these words, "For behold, I create new heavens and a new earth; and the former things shall not be remembered or come into mind" (Isa. 65:17; cf. 66:22). In 2 Pet. 3:13 the new creation is identified as the focus of our hope: "But according to his promise we wait for new heavens and a new earth in which righteousness dwells." The apostle John saw the inauguration of the age to come in which the promise is fulfilled: "Then I saw a new heaven and a new earth; for the first heaven and the first earth had passed away" (Rev. 21:1).

The new heaven and new earth have through the centuries of biblical proclamation comprised the apogee of the eschatological hope of the pious Jew and the devout Christian, a hope for an age of complete blessedness in which the destruction of evil would be complete. The biblical hope, however, is separated from surrounding religious expectations by the conviction that man's emancipation could not occur apart from the redemption of the created order, for HEAVEN as well as earth was implicated in the revolt against God.

The character of the eschatological hope of a new heaven and new earth is variously described. He. 12:28 refers to it as a "kingdom which cannot be shaken." Although the present earth and heaven are impermanent, the new heaven and new earth will remain forever (cf. Isa. 66:22). 2 Pet. 3:13 describes the new creation as one in which "righteousness dwells." Indeed the stress in vv. 7, 10, and 12 is on the present lack of righteousness in the heaven of this age, which will be remedied only in the new heaven of the age to come.

The writer of Revelation draws a marked contrast between the new heaven and new earth and the present heaven and earth. The new heaven and new earth are distinguished by absolute purity (21:27) and freedom from the wrath and curse of God (22:3). Indeed, the author's purpose in these final two chapters of the Revelation is to tell the reader that the new heaven and new earth are in every way different from their predecessor. Also, it is important to observe that the "dualism" of heaven and earth is not retained after Rev. 21:1, for the new Jerusalem has come down out of heaven so that now is the time of consummation, "Behold, the dwelling of God is with men" (Rev. 21:2f.). The heavenly order is now subsumed in a terrestrial kingdom where all things are new. In this way God's redemption of a fallen cosmos is completed in the re-creation of the heavens and the earth wherein this age is taken up into the age to come and God dwells with men so that He may be all in all.

Bibliography.–C. R. Schoonhoven, *Wrath of Heaven* (1966), pp. 92-95; U. Simon, *Heaven in the Christian Tradition* (1958), pp. 50-512; *TDNT*, III, *s.v.* καινός (Behm).

C. R. SCHOONHOVEN

HEAVY; HEAVIER; HEAVILY [Heb. *gešem*] ("heavy rain," Ezr. 10:9, 13); AV GREAT; NEB RAINY SEASON; [*kāḇēḏ*] (Ex. 5:9; 9:18, 24; 14:25; 18:18; Nu. 11:14; Jgs. 1:35; 1 S. 4:18; 5:6, 11; 2 S. 14:26; 1 K. 12:10f., 14; etc.); AV also "chargeable," GRIEVOUS, MORE, REPLENISHED; NEB also BURDEN, MORE BURDENSOME, "deafened," DEEPLY, HARD, "increased pressure," "outweigh," etc.; [*ma^ʿa^māsâ*] (Zec. 12:3); AV BURDENSOME; [*sāḇal*] (Ps. 144:14); AV STRONG; NEB "fat and sleek"; [*siḇlôṯ*] ("heavy burden," Ex. 1:11); [*sāmaḵ*] ("lies heavy," Ps. 88:7 [MT 8]); AV LIE HARD; NEB "rises"; [*qāšâ*] (1 S. 5:7; 1 K. 12:4; 14:6; 2 Ch. 10:4); AV also GRIEVOUS, SORE; NEB also CRUEL; [*rāḇâ*] (Eccl. 6:1; 8:6); AV COMMON, GREAT; NEB also GREATLY; [*raʿ*] (Prov. 25:20); [Gk. *baréō*] (Mt. 26:43; Lk. 9:32); NEB also DEEP; [*baréōs*] (Mt. 13:15; Acts 28:27); AV DULL; NEB DULLED; [*katabarýnō*] (Mk. 14:40); [*mégas*] (Rev. 11:19); AV GREAT; NEB "storm"; [*talantiaíos*] (Rev. 16:21); AV WEIGHT; NEB WEIGHING; [*phortízō*] (Mt. 11:28); [*phortíon*] (Mt. 23:4).

The major meaning of "heavy" in the OT is "hard to bear, burdensome, harsh, oppressive." It has a variety of referents: (1) Yahweh's wrath (Ps. 88:7), or His hand laid in punishment on His people (1 S. 5:6f., 11; Job 23:2; Ps. 32:4), or His chains put on those who are in exile (Lam. 3:7); (2) the hand of the house of Joseph on the Amorites (Jgs. 1:35) and of Babylon on Israel (Isa. 47:6); (3) the work imposed on the Israelites by the Egyptians (Ex. 1:11; 5:9) and the work imposed by Solomon (1 K. 12:4; 2 Ch. 10:4), by Jeroboam (1 K. 12:10f., 14; 2 Ch. 10:10f., 14), and by Nehemiah's predecessors (Neh. 5:15, 18); (4) Moses' responsibilities (Ex. 18:18; Nu. 11:14); (5) Job's calamity (Job 6:3); (6) the psalmist's iniquities (Ps. 38:4), the earth's transgressions (Isa. 24:20), and mankind's troubles in life (Eccl. 6:1; 8:6); (7) Elihu's pressure on Job — which, he says, will not be oppressive (Job 33:7). In the NT Jesus says that He comes to relieve people of their oppressive burdens (Mt. 11:28), even those imposed by the law and its interpreters (23:4).

Another meaning is "of great physical weight" and refers to Eli (1 S. 4:18), Absalom's hair (2 S. 14:26), or, figuratively, to Jerusalem as an immovable stone (Zec. 12:3). This meaning is combined with the preceding to describe metaphorically the relationship between a large stone and a fool's provocation (Prov. 27:3).

Great amounts of hail (Ex. 9:18, 24; Rev. 11:19), rain (Ezr. 10:9, 13), and large hailstones (Rev. 16:21) are called "heavy," as are pregnant cattle (Ps. 144:14) and well-loaded ships (Ezk. 27:25). Mud-clogged chariot wheels drive "heavily" (Ex. 14:25).

Yet other meanings refer to emotional states: "depressed with trouble or sorrow" (1 K. 14:6) and "without vivacity or interest" (Prov. 25:20). "Heavy eyes" denotes sleepiness in Mt. 26:43; Mk. 14:40; Lk. 9:32.

The message that Isaiah received from Yahweh in his temple vision included the injunction to make the ears of the people "heavy" so that they would be unable to hear the word of salvation until the time which Yahweh should choose (Isa. 6:10). This verse is quoted twice in the NT (Mt. 13:15; Acts 28:27), each time indicating that the hour of salvation has arrived.

J. R. PRICE

HEBER hē'bər [Heb. *ḥeḇer*–'associate'; Gk. *Eber*]. Occurs several times in the OT as the name of an individual or of a clan.

1. A member of the tribe of Asher and son of Beriah (Gen. 46:17; Nu. 26:45; 1 Ch. 7:31f.).

2. A Kenite, whose wife Jael deceptively slew Sisera, captain of the army of the Canaanite king Jabin (Jgs. 4:17; 5:24). Heber had separated himself from the main body of the Kenites, which accounts for his tent being near Kedesh, the place of Sisera's disastrous battle (Jgs. 4:11).

3. Head of a clan of Judah, and son of Mered by his

Jewish, as distinguished from his Egyptian, wife. He was father, or founder, of Soco (1 Ch. 4:18).

4. A Benjaminite, or the clan or family of Elpaal of the tribe of Benjamin (1 Ch. 8:17).

5. Heber, of Our Lord's genealogy (Lk. 3:35, AV; the RSV and the NEB have "Eber"). E. B. POLLARD

HEBERITES hē'bər-īts [Heb. *haheḇrî*]. Descendants of Heber, a prominent clan of Asher (Nu. 26:45); *see* HEBER **1.** Some suppose them to be connected with the HABIRU.

HEBREW (PEOPLE) [Heb. *ʿiḇrî*; Gk. *Hebraios*].

An ethnic term originally designating the ancestral lineage of the Israelite nation down to the *bᵉnê Yiśrāʾēl,* "sons of Israel," who were sojourning in Egypt. As a gentilic noun for a proto-Israelite, *ʿiḇrî* was applied to the patriarch Abraham (Gen. 14:13), to the land of patriarchal pilgrimage (40:15), and to Joseph and his brothers (39:14; 43:32).

Most uses of *ʿiḇrî* occur in two biblical episodes: (1) the Israelite-Egyptian narratives in the Pentateuch (five times in the Joseph cycle [Gen. 39:14–43:32] and thirteen times in the Exodus story [Ex. 1:15–10:3]), and (2) the Israelite-Philistine narratives in Samuel (eight times in 1 S. 4:6–29:3).

These passages use *ʿiḇrî* in one of three ways. (1) A non-Israelite may identify an *ʿiḇrî* in contrast to himself or other non-*ʿiḇrî*. Thus it is used five times by Egyptians (Gen. 39:14, 17; 41:12; Ex. 1:16; 2:6; cf. 1:22[?]) and six times by Philistines (1 S. 4:6, 9; 13:3, 19; 14:11; 29:3). A legitimate contextual inference from these passages is that *ʿiḇrî* is an ethnic term used in contradistinction to "Egyptian" or "Philistine." Such an inference is reinforced by the antithesis *ʿiḇrî-miṣrî* of Gen. 43:32 and Ex. 1:19, in which the ethnic character of the term is vividly illustrated. The argument that proposes that the basis of differentiation in Gen. 39:14–Ex. 10:3 is master-servant, not Israelite-Egyptian (but see Gen. 40:15; 43:32!), cannot adequately account for the basic Israelite-Philistine parity in 1 Samuel. Furthermore, the alternation "the Lord God of *Yiśrāʾēl*" (Ex. 5:1) and "the Lord God of the *ʿiḇrîm*" (Ex. 5:3) clearly identifies the *ʿiḇrî* with the Israelite; it would be inconceivable that the author should consider Yahweh as God of any but Israelites.

(2) One may identify himself or another as *ʿiḇrî* in contrast to non-Israelites. Joseph used the appellation in this way (Gen. 40:15), as did a number of Israelites in the Exodus narratives (Ex. 1:19; 2:7; 3:18; 5:3; 7:16; 9:1, 13; 10:3; cf. Jonah 1:9).

(3) A writer or speaker of Scripture may wish to distinguish the *ʿiḇrî* ethnos from another (Gen. 43:32; Ex. 1:15; 2:11, 13; 1 S. 14:21; cf. Acts 6:1; 2 Cor. 11:22; Phil. 3:5). In the same way laws distinguish the *gôyim* (non-Israelite) slaves, whose servitude was lifelong (Lev. 25:44-46), from the *ʿiḇrî* slave, who suffered only temporary servitude (Ex. 21:2; Dt. 15:12; cf. Jer. 34:9, 14 [note the *ʿiḇrî-Yᵉhûḏî* alternation]).

These passages suggest that the normal usage of *ʿiḇrî* conveyed no derogatory nuance. Moreover, no passage provides explicit ground for extending the meaning of *ʿiḇrî* to include non-Israelites. On the plausible assumption that it is intended to mean "Eberite" (see below), *ʿiḇrî* ought logically to apply to non-Israelites as well (e.g., Gen. 10:21-31; 11:14-26; 1 Ch. 1:17-27). In fact, however, no passage uses *ʿiḇrî* to denote anyone but a descendant of Abraham-Isaac-Jacob, nor is *ʿiḇrî* attested in extrabiblical literature. Sometimes 1 S. 14:21 is cited in an attempt to adduce support for an *ʿiḇrî*-Israelite distinction. But in the preceding chapter (13:19f.), the author shows that the Philistines had been preventing the Israelites (*ʿiḇrîm*) from forging their own swords and spears: the Israelites were forced to journey to the Philistines for such services.

With the advent of the Exodus-Sinai events inaugurating the nationhood of Israel came a corresponding change in its official nomenclature to the honorific *bᵉnê Yiśrāʾēl,* to which religious and national pride came to be attached.

No etymological hypothesis advanced for *ʿiḇrî* has been totally convincing or garnered common consensus. It is suggested that *ʿiḇrî* derives from the root *ʿbr,* "cross over, go beyond." Accordingly, an *ʿiḇrî* was one who had crossed over a river (cf. Gen. 14:13 [LXX], *Abram tṓ perátē*), though it is unclear whether the river involved was the Jordan, the Euphrates, or the Balîkh. Building on the same root, others aver that an *ʿiḇrî* was one who had crossed over a boundary (i.e., a pejorative term signifying a boundary jumper, trespasser). Still less convincing are those theories that seek to identify *ʿiḇrî* with the Ḫapiru, suggesting that the *ʿiḇrî* were donkey drivers or state benefactors (*see* HABIRU). The term has been interpreted as referring to the patriarchal ancestor Eber, grandson of Shem (Gen. 10:21, 24f.); in this sense an *ʿiḇrî* was an Eberite (note the gentilic ending).

Bibliography.–H. Cazelles, "The Hebrews," in D. J. Wiseman, ed., *Peoples of OT Times* (1973), pp. 1-28; M. Greenberg, *The Hab/piru* (1955); M. Weippert, *Settlement of the Israelite Tribes in Palestine* (*SBT,* 2/21, 1971), pp. 84-102; F. F. Bruce, "Tell el-Amarna," in *AOTS,* pp. 6-14; J. Lewy, *HUCA,* 28 (1957), 1-14; R. de Vaux, *RB,* 72 (1965), 20; *RB,* 75 (1968), 301f.

B. J. BEITZEL

HEBREW LANGUAGE. The original language of most of the OT, used by the Hebrews from the 2nd millennium B.C. onward.

I. Semitic Languages
  A. Members of the Semitic Family
  B. Comparative Semitic Studies
II. History of the Hebrew Language
  A. Origin of the Hebrew Language
  B. Earliest References to Spoken Hebrew
  C. Earliest References to Written Hebrew
  D. Early Hebrew Inscriptions
III. Hebrew Literature
  A. Uniform Language
  B. Stylistic Differences
  C. Dialectal Differences
  D. Foreign Influences
  E. Extinction of Spoken Hebrew
IV. Chief Characteristics of Hebrew
  A. Phonology
  B. Use of Vowel Letters
  C. The Syllable
  D. Triconsonantal Roots
  E. Nouns and Adjectives
  F. Formation of Adjectives
  G. Verbal System
  H. Syntax
V. Conceptual Characteristics of the Semites
  A. Concrete and Abstract
  B. View of Nature
  C. Pictorial Imagination
  D. Poetry

The entire OT was written in Hebrew except for 268 verses that were written in Official or Imperial ARAMAIC (Dnl. 2:4–7:28; Ezr. 4:8–6:18; 7:12-26; Jer. 10:11). Both Hebrew and Aramaic belong to the Semitic family of languages.

I. Semitic Languages.–Relatively few words in the OT do not have their counterpart in some other Semitic language, though seldom with an exact correspondence of

HEBREW LANGUAGE

form or meaning. The Semitic family itself belongs to a still larger group of languages called Afroasiatic or Hamito-Semitic, which comprises Chadic, Berber, Egyptian, Cushitic, and Semitic. The languages spoken in the Middle East during the historical period dealt with in the Bible have been called Semitic, after Shem the son of Noah from whom the majority of peoples speaking these languages — Arabs, Hebrews, Arameans, and Assyrians (Gen. 10:21-31) — were descended. Yet not all of Shem's descendants spoke Semitic; cf., e.g., Elam (Elamite) and Lud (Lydian). Even non-Semitic peoples are found speaking a Semitic language, e.g., Canaan and Cush (Ethiopic) who were sons of Ham (Gen. 9:18; 10:6-20). Gen. 1:11 records a time when all the descendants of Shem, Ham, and Japheth spoke a common language. The biblical record and Jewish tradition imply that Hebrew was the original language of mankind, but this is not the view among Semitists today.

A. Members of the Semitic Family. About seventy distinct forms of Semitic have been classified to date, the latest being Eblaic (discovered in 1975). These languages and dialects were spoken in an area extending from the Caspian Sea to the Horn of Africa, and from the Mediterranean Sea to the Tigris valley. It is customary to fit them into one of the following three divisions:

(1) East Semitic. This is made up chiefly of Akkadian with its two main dialects, Babylonian and Assyrian. Written in cuneiform and attested from 2500 B.C. to 75 B.C., Akkadian was the lingua franca of the Middle East until it was superseded by Official Aramaic in the 8th cent. B.C.

(2) Northwest Semitic. The oldest attested member of this group is probably Eblaic. Written in cuneiform, it dates back to *ca.* 2350 B.C. Dated between 1900 and 1500 B.C. are the fragmentary Sinai inscriptions. West Semitic personal names appear in the Mari Letters *ca.* 1760 B.C. (*see* AMORITES). The Râs Shamrah tablets date from the 14th-12th cents. B.C. and are in alphabetic cuneiform script. The Canaanite glosses in the Amarna Letters date from the 14th cent. B.C. The earliest Aramaic records date from the 10th cent. B.C. Later developments are grouped into East and West Aramaic. To the former belong Syriac, Mandean, and the language of the Babylonian Talmud; to the latter, Samaritan, Nabatean, Jewish Palestinian Aramaic (found in the Palestinian Talmud and the Targums), Palmyrene, and Biblical (or Official) Aramaic. Other members of this group are Hebrew (Old Canaanite), Phoenician-Punic (10th cent. B.C. to 2nd cent. A.D.), Moabite (mid-9th cent. B.C.), and Ya'udi (8th cent. B.C.).

(3) South Semitic. This group is composed of (a) North Arabic and (b) South Arabian plus Ethiopic. To the former belong the preclassical North Arabic dialects (Thamūdic, Liḥyānite, and Ṣafāitic) and classical Arabic. To the latter belong Sabean, Minaean, Qatabanian, Ḥaḍramut, and Awsanian. The modern Semitic languages of Ethiopia are represented by Tigrina, Tigre, Amharic, Harari, and Gurage.

B. Comparative Semitic Studies. Early Hebrew customs, folklore, laws, architecture, and religious ideas show remarkably close affinities with those of surrounding Semitic peoples. It is not surprising, therefore, to find that this affinity extends to their respective languages also. Most modern commentators recognize and exploit this fact. The cognate languages are consulted to elucidate the meaning of rare Hebrew words and to clarify the nuances of various Hebrew words. Although there is a remarkable agreement morphologically (i.e., with regard to the forms of the words) among all the Semitic languages once the phonetic laws have been taken into account, this agreement cannot be taken for granted in the area of semantics (the meanings of the words). The table illustrates the close morphological affinity:

	Prefix form	Suffix form	Active Participle
***Ugaritic**	yaqbur	qabara	qābir
Hebrew	yiqbór	qābár	qōbḗr
Aramaic	yiqbúr	q^{e}bár	qābḗr
Syriac	neqbór	q^{e}bár	qāber
Ethiopic	yéqber	qabára	qā́ber
Arabic	yáqburu	qábara	qā́bir
Akkadian	íqbur	(qabir)	qābiru(m)
Eblaic	iqbur	qabara	?

*The vowel system is not fully indicated in Ugaritic, so the Proto-Semitic system has been supplied here.

Extreme caution, however, is needed in the area of comparative semantics, as J. Barr has demonstrated (*Semantics of Biblical Language* [1961]). Samples of roots taken from two such closely related languages as Syriac and Hebrew were found to have similar meanings in only 30 to 40 percent of the cases. Between Arabic and Hebrew the results were similar, but for Ethiopic there was only 17 percent agreement in meaning. If, however, a wider comparison is made between the names for objects, occupations, etc., there is about 65 percent agreement between Syriac and Hebrew (*Encyclopaedia Judaica* XIV, 1155a).

II. History of the Hebrew Language.–The Hebrew language of the OT is in a very stable state linguistically. The variations between the strata of the language are slight compared with the difference between modern and classical Arabic.

A. Origin of the Hebrew Language. According to Gen. 11:1f. the whole post-Flood civilization dwelt in one locality — the Plain of Shinar. Abraham's family (and ancestors?) dwelt at Ur. Presumably they were an integral part of this city-state socially and linguistically. Abraham's family may well have spoken a language akin to Old Akkadian or early Babylonian. Later, Abraham moved to Haran where the principal language was apparently Aramaic (cf. Gen. 31:47; Dt. 26:5). It may well be that bilingualism was common among the Semites (see E. Ullendorff, *BJRL,* 44 [1962], 455-465).

A common trend is to view the Hebrews who conquered Canaan under Joshua's leadership as primitive nomadic desert tribes speaking a tribal dialect of Old Aramaic, probably with close affinities to the speech of Canaan. After the Conquest these primitive tribes from across the Jordan appear to have been assimilated gradually into the culture and civilization of the conquered Canaanites and to have adopted their speech. On this view, then, we do not know the precise nature of the original language of the Hebrew invaders. For further discussion of the history of the Hebrews *see* ISRAEL, HISTORY OF THE PEOPLE OF.

B. Earliest References to Spoken Hebrew. The earliest biblical reference to spoken Hebrew occurs in Gen. 31:47 where Laban and Jacob refer to a heap of stones in their own native speech. Laban calls it *Jegarsahadutha,* which is Aramaic, while Jacob calls it *Galeed* and a nearby pillar *Mizpah,* two Hebrew words. This would place spoken Hebrew in the 18th cent. B.C., at the latest. One thousand years later we find Hebrew being called *y^{e}hûḏîṯ* or the "language of Judah" (2 K. 18:26). In Isa. 19:18 it is called "the language [Heb. *ś^{e}paṯ,* "lip"] of Canaan," possibly because this was how the Egyptians referred to it. The designation "Hebrew" for the language first occurs in Ben Sira's prologue (*ca.* 130 B.C.).

C. Earliest References to Written Hebrew. On numerous occasions Moses was commanded to write down what God had spoken (e.g., Ex. 17:14). This took place either in the 15th or the 13th cent. B.C., depending on the date of the Exodus (*see* EXODUS, DATE OF). In the period of the judges a young man could write down the names of the seventy-seven elders of Succoth without any apparent difficulty (Jgs. 8:14). The Book of Jashar may have been in existence in the early period of the monarchy (Josh. 10:13; 2 S. 1:18). Court records of the kings of Israel and Judah were kept from the earliest times. Records of prophecies were kept either by the prophet himself or by his disciples. We have no reason to cast doubt on the biblical references to Hebrew writing, although extant evidence only takes it back to the 11th cent. B.C.

D. Early Hebrew Inscriptions. The chief extrabiblical evidence for written Hebrew is as follows. (1) The ʿIzbet Ṣarṭah inscription was discovered in 1976. Dated to the 11th cent. B.C., it contains around eighty letters (M. Kochavi, *Tel Aviv,* 4 [1977], 1-13 [also pp. 14-27]). (2) The schoolboy's GEZER CALENDAR lists the agricultural significance of the successive months of the year. It is dated *ca.* 925 B.C. and is written in the Paleo-Hebrew script. (3) In 1976 about seventy Hebrew and Phoenician inscriptions were found at Kuntillet ʿAjrûd in Sinai, and dated between the 9th and 8th cents. B.C. (Z. Meshel, *Biblical Archaeology Review,* 5/2 [1979], 24-35). One text refers to God — under His covenant name *YHWH* — in conjunction with the goddess Ashtaroth, reminding one of the Elephantine papyri parallel. (4) The Siloam inscription dates from *ca.* 705 B.C. (5) The Samaria Ostraca date from the reign of Jeroboam II (*ca.* 770 B.C.), and consist mainly of receipts for taxes. (6) The Lachish Letters date from *ca.* 587 B.C., and consist largely of military communications from a Jewish outpost to its headquarters. These inscriptions indicate the way Hebrew was written and spelled in those periods. By the time the DEAD SEA SCROLLS were written (2nd cent. B.C.) the Paleo-Hebrew script had given way to the Aramaic "square script" (*see* INSCRIPTIONS; WRITING).

III. Hebrew Literature.–Israel may have had a vast literature before the close of the OT period, yet nothing of it has come down to us except the OT writings. The biblical books refer to other works and are themselves composite in character. The period between the Old and New Testaments saw an increase in works of an apocalyptic nature, but these and many other works were not so carefully preserved. The writings of the Qumrân sect survived because they were hidden in jars in the favorable climate of the Dead Sea valley.

A. Uniform Language. One of the most remarkable facts connected with the Hebrew of the OT is that, although its literature covers a period of over a thousand years, the language (grammar and vocabulary) of the oldest parts differs little from that of the latest. That is not to rule out dialectal differences, which we know did exist (see C below). Rather, just as the Koran — the first extensive work composed in Arabic that has survived — became the pattern for all future compositions, so the books of Moses became the pattern for all future Hebrew compositions because of their dominant influence on Hebrew life and culture. Note especially the influence of Deuteronomy on the language and outlook of the major prophets.

Many other reasons can be given for this uniformity and much will depend on one's view of the literary development and the date of composition of the OT. Some OT books (e.g., Genesis) incorporate a good deal of oral tradition, in which case the written form of the tradition may not be an exact reproduction of its first telling. For example, a "modern" place name may replace an earlier one which the readers or listeners would not have known, as in Gen. 14:14 where we read that Abram "went in pursuit as far as Dan." The oral tradition probably said "Leshem," as "Dan" did not exist in Abraham's time (cf. Josh. 19:47). Sometimes the old and the "modern" names are given (e.g., Gen. 23:2; 35:19). It also appears that later custodians of the written oral tradition felt it necessary to insert explanatory comments for the benefit of their readers or listeners; hence the information is supplied that "At that time the Canaanites were in the land" (Gen. 12:6; 13:7); or the observation that a custom or monument exists "unto this day" (see B. S. Childs, *JBL,* 82 [1963], 279-292). Some of these glosses in the Pentateuch are clearly post-Mosaic, e.g., Gen. 36:31; Ex. 6:26f.; 11:3; 16:35f. (cf. Josh. 5:11f.); and Dt. 34:5-12. It is safe, therefore, to assume that the purpose of these glosses was to keep these stories and traditions alive and relevant to each new generation; this may contribute to the apparent uniformity. The following factors, however, may have played a part also. (1) Behind much of Israel's early writings lies a strong oral tradition, which would itself have had an overall uniform character before it was committed to writing. (2) On the assumption that oral tradition underwent a continuous gradual development or updating over the centuries, this development would be "frozen" once it was written down. The written form would then set the pattern for any further writing of it or additions to it. (3) It is possible that the consonantal text is original but not its present Masoretic vocalization, which was added to the text sometime between the 6th and 9th cents. A.D., hence the apparent uniformity.

B. Stylistic Differences. When one considers the contributors — prophets, priests, kings, rich men, poor men, poets, philosophers, and historians — one is not surprised to find such a variety of styles. The style of Hosea is noticeably distinct from that of his contemporary Amos. The same author may reveal a number of styles depending on subject matter, genre, and time of writing, e.g., Isaiah and Daniel.

C. Dialectal Differences. Many attempts have been made to reconstruct the pre-Masoretic vocalization of the Hebrew writings without any major agreement among scholars. When the Masoretes vocalized the consonantal text Deborah's idiolect (the distinctive pronunciation, grammar, and vocabulary of an individual speaker) was made indistinguishable from Esther's, which can hardly have been the case from a diachronic point of view. That there were dialectal differences as early as the period of the judges is certain from Jgs. 12:6. In the Ephraimite dialect initial *š* became *ś,* whereas in the Gileadite dialect these two phonemes remained distinct. This meant that a man from Ephraim would say *sibboleth* when he tried to pronounce the word *shibboleth.* In both dialects the word meant "a stream in flood" (cf. Ps. 69:2 [MT 3], 15 [MT 16]; Isa. 27:12). It would appear that northern Israelites used *ʾty* for the 2nd fem. sing. pronoun, as against *ʾt* elsewhere (see BDB, p. 61b). The book of Job is also thought to be written in a dialect different from classical Hebrew (see comms.).

D. Foreign Influences. It is a recognized fact that the chronological stages of a nation's literature can be determined by the foreign elements imbedded in its vocabulary and structure. Thus, in Anglo-Saxon literature the numerous Latin ecclesiastical terms indicate that the English derived their religion from the Romans. Chaucer's *Canterbury Tales* show clearly that the Norman-French conquerors had imposed their civilization upon the Saxons and had dominated them in government, social customs, and nearly every sphere of life and thought. The Hebrews, too, came under the dominion of great empires — Babylonian (Abraham's time), Egyptian (400 years), Assyrian (*ca.* 853-612 B.C.), Neo-Babylonian (612-539 B.C.), Persian (539-331 B.C.), Greek (331-63 B.C.), and finally the Roman Empire. In one way or another these empires left their mark on Israel, especially on its language. According to

M. Ellenbogen, 50 percent of the loanwords in the OT came from the Akkadian, including words of Sumerian origin. Egyptian contributed 22 percent, Iranian (Persian) 18 percent, and the remaining 10 percent comprises words of Indian and Greek origin. According to Strong's concordance, Biblical Hebrew has a vocabulary of 8674 words, and of these, according to Ellenbogen, only 146, or less than 2 percent, are loanwords. This makes Biblical Hebrew a relatively pure language compared with English.

E. Extinction of Spoken Hebrew. The Babylonian Exile began the demise of Hebrew as the common language of the people. The educated classes were deported to Babylon or fled to Egypt. Those who remained quickly adopted the language of their conquerors or their foreign spouses. When Nehemiah arrived back in Jerusalem in 432 B.C. he found the people speaking hybrid languages (Neh. 13:24). Whatever may be the correct interpretation of Neh. 8:8, it proves that the people of that time had great difficulty understanding spoken Hebrew. It is very likely that Aramaic replaced Hebrew as the spoken language by the 3rd cent. B.C., but that Hebrew continued as the literary and sacred language. We have examples of literary Hebrew in the 2nd cent. B.C. in the works of Ben Sira (*ca.* 130 B.C.) and the Qumrân scribes. Hebrew was used on coins minted during the Maccabean period. It was used as late as A.D. 135 in Bar Cochba's letters and in fragments of Hebrew Christian prayers found at Dura-Europas (late 3rd cent. A.D.; cf. J. L. Teicher, *JQR,* 54 [1963], 99-109). Whether Hebrew was spoken as an everyday language in NT times is still debated (see J. A. Emerton, *JTS,* 24 [1973], 1-23).

IV. Chief Characteristics of Hebrew.–The Hebrew language, like Phoenician, Aramaic, and Arabic, but unlike English, is written from right to left. The language itself differs no less strikingly from English.

A. Phonology. Unlike English, which includes the vowels in its twenty-six-letter alphabet, the Hebrew alphabet consists of twenty-two consonantal sounds or phonemes. The first letter in the Hebrew alphabet is not *a* but the glottal stop *'ālep* (a breathing sound produced by the glottis). The nearest equivalent in English would be the "gap" in the Cockney pronunciation of "water." There are no equivalents for *'ayin, ḥēṯ,* or *qôp* in English. On the other hand, Hebrew has no equivalents for the English *j* (as in Jeremiah), or *ch* (as in Charles), or *x* (as in six).

The Masoretes distinguished fourteen different vowel sounds. These consist of long and short forms of the five English vowels, plus half-vowels of three of them, namely, ^{a}, $^{\breve{e}}$, and ^{o}, and finally an extremely brief indeterminate sound called *shewa* (^{e}). The diphthongs *ay* and *aw* were formed with the help of vowel letters.

B. Use of Vowel Letters. Until *ca.* 1000 B.C. only the consonants were written in Hebrew. The vowels were supplied by the reader from memory or from his knowledge of the language. Around 900 B.C. Hebrew scribes began to use the letters *hê, wāw,* and *yôḏ* in a semiconsonantal function. *Hê* was used to indicate final *ā* (sometimes final *ō*), *wāw* final *û,* and *yôḏ* final *ī*. Around 600 B.C. these three semiconsonants occur unambiguously as vowel letters in both medial and final positions. Thus these three consonants, while retaining their own consonantal value, served to indicate the type of vowel to be read until new methods were devised to indicate more accurately the quality and quantity of the vowels. The Masoretic system is the most elaborate of all and is used in the Hebrew Bible today.

C. The Syllable. In Hebrew no word or syllable may begin with a vowel such as the English *easy* and *age.* No syllable or word may begin with two or more consonants as happens in English, e.g., *blow.* In Hebrew this would have to be read as *b*^{e}*low,* e.g., the initial consonant *b* would have to take at least the brief shewa vowel (^{e}) after it in order to pronounce it properly and to break up the initial pair or cluster of consonants.

D. Triconsonantal Roots. Practically every word in the Hebrew language has at its heart a root consisting of three consonants (also characteristic of the other Semitic languages). Indeed, once a root has been learned it is not difficult to form verbs, nouns, etc., from it. Hebrew has around 1800 roots, of which only about thirty are quadriradicals (i.e., consisting of four consonants). In modern Hebrew quadriradicals comprise between 35 and 50 percent of all roots. With twenty-three consonants (including *ś* and *š*) Hebrew could theoretically form 12,167 three-letter roots (i.e., 23^3). It has substantially fewer than this because of certain phonetic difficulties or incompatibilities. For example, two identical consonants or two consonants with a similar point of articulation cannot appear as the first two consonants in any root (see J. H. Greenberg, *Word,* 6 [1950], 161-181; 18 [1962], 262-68).

E. Nouns and Adjectives. Following the Arab grammarians, medieval Jewish grammarians divided Hebrew grammar into three parts, namely, verbs, nouns, and particles. They made no distinction between nouns and adjectives. This is not surprising when we consider that both are formed in an identical manner, e.g., *sûs ṭôḇ,* "a good horse (*sûs*)" (masc. sing.); *sûsâ ṭôḇâ,* "a good mare" (fem. sing.); *sûsîm ṭôḇîm,* "good horses" (masc. pl.); and *sûsôṯ ṭôḇôṯ,* "good mares" (fem. pl.). To make these definite the article (*ha* + doubling of the first consonant where possible) is prefixed to both the noun and the following "adjective," thus: *hassûsîm haṭṭôḇîm,* "the good horses" (masc. pl.). There are four points to note here. (1) The masc. sing. form of the noun and adjective serve as the basis for the formation of the other genders and numbers (i.e., they are the unmarked forms). In Hebrew everything is either masculine or feminine; there is no neuter gender. (2) Both noun and adjective take the same gender and number endings: *-â* for fem. sing., *-îm* for masc. pl., and *-ôṯ* for fem. plural. (3) If the noun has the definite article, the adjective must also have it. (4) The adjective almost always follows the noun. There are, of course, exceptions to every general rule; the reader should consult a good Hebrew grammar for these.

For the sake of clarity we shall divide the broad category of nouns into the following three subdivisions: (1) substantive nouns, (2) pure and generic adjectives, and (3) epithet nouns.

(1) The substantive nouns are easily identifiable since they are usually an arbitrary name given to an object without reference to its quality or any other attribute, e.g., *ḥ*^{a}*môr,* "an ass," *sûs,* "a horse."

(2) Pure adjectives are those words which can be used to describe *both* animate and inanimate subjects or objects, e.g., *ṭôḇ,* "good," *lāḇān,* "white," *ḥāzāq,* "strong," *rāḥôq,* "distant, far," etc. Such adjectives are very rarely substantivized, though Hebrew can, like English, use the adjective to express the abstract, e.g., *haṭṭôḇ,* "the good." Generic adjectives, on the other hand, qualify only animate beings, and it is from this type of adjective that Hebrew forms its epithet nouns which require special notice.

(3) Biblical Hebrew almost exclusively uses epithet nouns rather than its adjectives, which are not nearly as numerous. Most of the generic adjectives are easily transformed into epithet nouns by simply using them on their own. For example, *k*^{e}*sîl* in *bēn k*^{e}*sîl,* "a foolish son" (Prov. 17:25), is an adjective, whereas in *'ênê k*^{e}*sîl,* "eyes of a fool" (Prov. 17:24), it is an epithet noun. Similarly, *ḥērēš* on its own would mean "a deaf man," and

it is not necessary to write or say *'îš ḥārēš* "a man, a deaf one." There is a semantic difference between the epithet noun and the adjective. "The man is foolish" (adjective) is not as strong or as harsh as "The man is a fool" (epithet noun). The adjective conveys the indefinite and the general, while the epithet noun conveys the specific; the adjective imputes an external quality while the epithet noun describes the nature of the man, or his permanent state. A wise man can make a mistake, but a fool does nothing else, hence the saying: "The tongue of the wise [*ḥ^{a}ḵāmîm*] dispenses knowledge, but the mouths of fools [*k^{e}sîlîm*] pour out folly" (Prov. 15:2).

F. Formation of Adjectives. Hebrew has a paucity of pure adjectives, i.e., a paucity of that category of words which express an indefinite external quality, but the language has made good this deficiency in a number of ways. This paucity is particularly noticeable in the Psalms where a total of forty-seven psalms have not a single pure adjective (i.e., where the adjective follows the noun it qualifies). The same is true of nine chapters in Job, five in Genesis, ten in Numbers, etc. Indeed, there is not a book in the Bible that can boast of an adjective in every chapter. On the other hand, there is hardly a chapter that does not have an epithet noun in it, or one or more of the following ways of forming adjectives.

(1) In the construct state, Hebrew brings two nouns together in apposition to create a compound idea, e.g., *'îš '^{e}lōhîm* means "a godly man" (lit. "a man of God"); likewise, *har qōḏeš* means "a holy mountain" (lit. "a mountain of holiness"). To make these compounds definite the article is prefixed only to the genitive or second noun, e.g., *'îš hā'^{e}lōhîm,* "the man of God." The construct state is used only where the language does not have a single word for the concept being expressed. In such cases the Hebrew speaker circumvented the problem in much the same way that anthropologists circumvent the problem of inventing new names to describe new species of men, i.e., first the genus is identified, *homo,* then a further defining or limiting word is added, such as *sapiens* or *erectus.* Hebrew did not have a single word for "silver sockets," so it mentioned the object first, *'aḏnê,* "sockets," and then limited the class of socket to the "silver" ones, as opposed to gold or bronze sockets, hence *'aḏnê kesep* or "sockets, silver" = "silver sockets."

(2) Adjectives are formed from the nominal qualities of the participle when these are placed in apposition with a noun, thus *'ēš 'ōḵeleṯ,* "a devouring fire" (Ex. 24:17).

(3) Relative nouns and adjectives are formed by suffixing *î* to the noun stem. The difference between them is that the relative noun is formed from a proper noun, e.g., from *miṣrayim,* "Egypt," is formed *miṣrî,* "Egyptian," and from *y^{e}hûḏâ,* "Judah," is formed *y^{e}hûḏî,* an inhabitant of Judah (the termination corresponds to the -ish in Irish, English, etc.); while the relative adjective is formed from a common noun, e.g., *'ēṯ,* "time," but *'îš 'ittî* means "a man, a fit (or 'ready, timely') one" (Lev. 16:21).

So fluid is the category of adjective in Hebrew that the same word may be used as a pure adjective, a common noun, or a proper name. For example, *b^{e}lîya'al,* "worthless," in *'îš rā' ûḇ^{e}lîya'al,* "the wicked and base fellows" (1 S. 30:22), is a pure adjective; in *'îš habb^{e}lîya'al,* "you worthless fellow" (2 S. 16:7), it is a common noun (note that it takes the definite article); and in *b^{e}nê-ḇ^{e}lîya'al,* "sons of Belial," it is a proper noun, which very rarely takes the definite article (see Gesenius, *et al.,* §§ 125f.).

A point often overlooked in Hebrew grammars is that Hebrew does have three word patterns which are purely adjectival; these are *qaṭlāl, q^{e}ṭalṭāl,* and *q^{e}ṭalṭōl.* While it is true that Hebrew does not have many pure adjectives, it is also clear that it has many other ways of expressing the adjectival idea.

G. Verbal System. Alongside its quota of participles, infinitives, and its various moods (imperative, jussive, and cohortative), Hebrew has seven indicative themes in two basic forms, perfect and imperfect. The perfect form is:

qal	*kāṯaḇ 'eṯ haddāḇār*	"he wrote the word" (base or ground form)
niphal	*niḵtaḇ haddāḇār*	"the word was written" (pass. of qal)
piel	*šibbēr 'eṯ hakkaḏ*	"he smashed the pitcher" (intensive)
pual	*šubbar hakkaḏ*	"the pitcher was smashed" (pass. of piel)
hiphil	*he'^{e}ḇîr 'eṯ hā'ām*	"he led the people across" (causative)
hophal	*ho'^{o}ḇar hā'ām*	"the people were led across" (pass. of hiphil)
hithpael	*hiṯqaddēš*	"he sanctified himself" (reciprocal)

The chief morphological difference between the perfect (or suffix form) and the imperfect (or prefix form) is that the former suffixes the pronominal subject to the verbal root, whereas the latter prefixes it. The main semantic difference between the two forms is still a matter of debate. It used to be thought that the suffix form indicated past time, and the prefix form the present and future times. This view was abandoned last century in favor of a complete (or perfect) and incomplete (or imperfect) opposition. This theory, while certainly an improvement on the former, is not without its difficulties. Another view regards these two verb forms as representing different ways of communicating events and ideas. We might illustrate this as follows. A family could hand down a visual account of its history to future generations in the form of (1) an album of "still" snapshots, or (2) "live" pictures by means of videotape or cine-camera film. Both would be equally valid, and, indeed, the biblical writers record the same event using the equivalent of both methods (cf. esp. the parallel passages in Kings-Chronicles, e.g., 1 K. 22:41 and 2 Ch. 20:31). The nearest parallel to the "still" and "live" forms of recording or retelling historical events in English would be the use of the past tense (= "still") and the historic present tense (= "live"), which is seldom used today. But the parallel should not be pressed as there are no "tenses" as such in Hebrew, which uses both forms in any time sphere.

A modification of the above view suggests that when the biblical writers used the suffix form (*qāṭal*) they were attributing or imputing actions or states to the subject of the verb, e.g., "In the beginning God created [*bārā'*] the heavens and the earth" (Gen. 1:1); whereas in using the prefix form (*yiqṭōl*) they intended to let the subject "speak for himself," as it were, and we see the original action once again being acted out, e.g., "And God said [*wayyō'mer,* or "proceeds to say"], 'Let there be [*y^{e}hî*] light,' and there was [*way^{e}hî*] light" (Gen. 1:3). The prefix form, then, on this view, has more the flavor of an "on-the-spot" reporting of an event; whereas the suffix form presents the listener with the facts themselves.

H. Syntax. Hebrew literature can be divided into three categories for the sake of discussing its syntax; these are (1) prose, (2) prophecy, and (3) poetry. The first two follow the same normal word order, namely, verbal predicate + noun subject + noun object + adverb or prepositional phrase, e.g., (prose) *wayyāḇē' yôsēp 'eṯ dibbāṯām rā'â 'el '^{a}ḇîhem,* "and Joseph brought an ill report of them to their father" (Gen. 37:2). Any deviation from the normal word order will be for emphasis (e.g., Gen. 3:13) or contrast (e.g., Gen. 13:12). Poetry, on the other hand, tends to be much more flexible in its clause structure.

An analysis of the way the RSV has translated the Hebrew verb forms is interesting.

	Indicative Mood			Other Moods
	Past	Present	Future	
wā + prefix	14,205	307	27	490
wᵉ + prefix	70	196	435	734
prefix	773	3,374	5,452	4,705
wᵉ + suffix	488	541	2,929	2,418
suffix	10,820	2,671	256	335

("Other moods" includes other translations, such as nouns or adjectives, and untranslated verbs.)

(1) Prose syntax shows a distinct preference for *wā* + prefix in initial position to describe or relate historical events, and the suffix form (without a prefixed *wāw*) in a noninitial position. Generally a narrative will commence with a suffix form in a noninitial position, and this will be followed by a series of prefix forms in initial position, e.g., *'îš hāyâ bᵉ'ereṣ 'ûṣ 'îyôḇ šᵉmô . . . wayyiwwālᵉḏû . . . wayhî. . .* , "There was a man in the land of Uz, whose name was Job . . . and there was born to him . . . and he had . . ." (Job 1:1-3). Normally when the series or chain of *wā* + prefix forms is interrupted so that the prefix form is detached from the initial conjunctive *wāw*, the following verb will be in the suffix form, e.g., *wayyiqrā' 'ᵉlōhîm lā'ôr yôm wᵉlaḥōšeḵ qārā' lāylâ*, "God called the light Day, and the darkness he called Night" (Gen. 1:5). Occasionally the prefix form is retained in a noninitial position if there is some special emphasis on the initial word, e.g., "And it [the little ewe lamb] grew up [*wattigdal*] . . . it used to eat [*ṯō'ḵal*] of his morsel, and drink [*ṯišteh*] from his cup, and lie [*ṯiškāḇ*] in his bosom, and it was like [*wattᵉhî*] a daughter to him" (2 S. 12:3).

(2) Prophecy shows a distinct preference for *wᵉ* + suffix in initial position to relate future events, and the prefix form (without a prefixed *wāw*) in a noninitial position. Prophecies seldom begin with a prefix form in noninitial position, followed by suffix forms in initial position, as one might expect on the analogy of prose syntax. Instead, the prophetic formula: "Thus said the Lord" is followed by *lāḵēn*, "Therefore" plus either a participial phrase, *hinnî nôṭeh yāḏî*, "Behold, I will stretch out my hand" (Ezk. 25:16), or a suffix form, *hinᵉnî nāṭîṯî*, "Behold, I have stretched out my hand" (Ezk. 25:7), or *wᵉ* + suffix, as in *wᵉnāṭîṯî yāḏî*, "I will stretch out my hand" (Ezk. 25:13).

Normally when a series or chain of *wᵉ* + suffix forms is interrupted so that the suffix form is detached from the initial conjunctive *wāw*, the following verb will be in the prefix form, e.g., *wᵉnāṯaṯi lāḵem lēḇ bāśār wᵉ'eṯ rûḥî bᵉqirbᵉḵem*, "and I will give you a heart of flesh. And I will put my spirit within you" (Ezk. 36:26f.).

A striking feature of Hebrew syntax, especially in prose, is the relative rarity of subordinating conjunctions marking adverbial clauses as such. Instead, one finds long sequences of clauses and even single verbs (cf. 2 Ch. 28:17 [MT 15]), connected only by a form of the conjunctive *wᵉ* ("and"). Because of this, it is obviously impossible to translate literally into acceptable English. For example, see the various translations of *wayyāqem* in Jgs. 2:16.

(3) The syntax of poetry is a little freer as regards word order and sentence structure. A comparison of the parallel passages in Ps. 18 and 2 S. 22 shows that the poet can dispense with the conjunctive *wā* before the narrative prefix form without in any way affecting the meaning, e.g., Ps. 18:6 [MT 7] = 2 S. 22:7; Ps. 18:13 [MT 12] = 2 S. 22:12.

Poetic language is also distinguished from prose, not only by a rhythm due to more strictly balanced (parallel) members and stress patterns, but also by peculiar words and meanings, inflexions and syntactical constructions that are used in addition to those usual in prose. Peculiar words in poetry, for which others are customary in prose, are *'ᵉnôš*, "man" = *'āḏām* in prose; *'ōraḥ*, "path" = *dereḵ*; *millâ*, "word" = *dāḇār*; *ḥāzâ*, "to see" = *rā'â*; *'āṯâ*, "to come" = *bô'*. It also has longer forms of prepositions of place: *'ᵃlê* = *'al*, *'ᵉlê* = *'el*, *'ᵃḏê* = *'aḏ*; the endings *-î*, *-ô* in the noun; the pronominal suffixes *-mô*, *-āmô*, *-ēmô* for *-m*, *-ām*, and *-ēm*, the plural (Aramaic) ending *-în* for *-îm*. With regard to syntax there is a more sparing use of the article, of the relative pronoun, and of the accusative particle *'eṯ*. The construct state is used even before prepositions, which have a wider governing power, and in general there is a forcible brevity of expression.

Because Hebrew does not have tenses as such (the table above shows that every verb form can be translated by any tense), only the context can supply this information. Thus *wᵉhāyû šᵉmōnâ qᵉrāšîm* is translated as "There were eight frames . . ." in Ex. 36:30; but in the parallel passage, the same clause is translated, "And there shall be eight frames . . ." (Ex. 26:25). Similarly, *yihyû* in Ex. 26:24 is future, but in Ex. 36:29 it is past; *wᵉlō' yizzaḥ* is future in Ex. 28:28, but past in Ex. 39:21; *wᵉṣippîṯâ* is future in Ex. 26:37, but *wᵉṣippâ* in 36:38 is past.

The beginner in Hebrew is often surprised to find the verb "to be" missing in most of the cases where it would be necessary in English. Where the AV supplied the verb "to be" it put it in italics as follows: "and darkness *was* upon the face of the deep" (Gen. 1:2, but cf. Gen. 15:17); "And Noah *was* six hundred years old" (Gen. 7:6, but cf. 2 S. 4:4); and "for she *was* a virgin" (2 S. 13:2, but cf. 1 Ch. 22:11).

V. Conceptual Characteristics of the Semites.–Almost every aspect of research into the ancient civilizations of the Near East throws some light on the literature, laws, and customs of the Hebrew people. This research makes the student of the Bible aware of the fact that the Hebrews were a Semitic people, thoroughly at home in their Semitic environment.

A. Concrete and Abstract. The thinking of the Hebrews, like that of other Semitic peoples, was done not in the abstract but in the concrete. Thus we find the material put for the immaterial, the expression for the thought, the instrument for the action, the action for the feeling. This mode of thought frequently gives rise to striking physical metaphors, e.g., the abstract "stubborn" is literally "hard of neck"; "impudent" = "hard of face"; "extensive" = "broad of hands"; "miserable" = "bitter of soul." The "eye" stands for "watchfulness" or "care" (cf. Ps. 33:18); the "long hand" for "far-reaching powers" (Isa. 59:1); "broken teeth" for "defeated malice" (Ps. 3:7 [MT 8]); the "sword" for "slaughter" (Ps. 78:62); "haughty eyes" for "superciliousness" (Prov. 6:17); "to say in one's heart" for "to think" (Ps. 10:6); and "to lift up the eyes" for "to see." A number of these and similar Hebraisms have come into the English language through the AV.

B. View of Nature. Hebrew poets hardly seem to draw any distinction between the animate and inanimate creation on occasions. All nature is animate (Ps. 104:29). The hills rejoice (Ps. 65:12 [MT 13]), the mountains skip (114:4), the trees clap their hands (Isa. 55:12). Such expressions were never intended to be taken literally but express the intensity and imaginative nature of the poets' feelings. All nature is one under man's dominion (Ps. 8:6 [MT 7]).

C. Pictorial Imagination. The highly imaginative nature of the Hebrew writer comes into play when he is recounting past events or telling stories. To his mind's eye all past events come alive and he recounts them as if they were unrolling before his very eyes. In English the historic present tense is used to achieve a similar effect, though Hebrew seems to have its own historic present in the form of the participle; thus, "So they went up [*wayyaʿalû*] to the city. As they were entering [*hēmmâ bāʾîm*] the city, they saw Samuel coming out [*šemûʾēl yōṣēʾ*] toward them on his way up to the high place" (1 S. 9:14). The writers prefer to let the characters in the stories speak for themselves, hence their frequent use of direct quotation. Moreover, the historian writes in much the same manner as the professional storyteller narrates, that is, he will often repeat himself (1 S. 5:1f.).

D. Poetry. Semitic poetry possesses no regular meter or rhyme. Its essential characteristic is rhythm — the rhythm of balancing thought against thought, and word against word. The Hebrew language is characterized by a vigorous terseness and power of condensation which cannot be preserved in English. On the special vocabulary and syntax of Hebrew poetry, see IV.H.3 above; *see also* POETRY, HEBREW.

Bibliography.–I: J. Barr, *Comparative Philology and the Text of the OT* (1968); *Enc.Brit.*, Macro, VIII, *s.v.* "Semitic Languages"; *Encyclopaedia Judaica,* XIV, *s.v.* "Semitic Languages" (C. Rabin); H. L. Ginsberg, "Northwest Semitic Languages," in B. Mazar, ed., *World History of the Jewish People: Patriarchs,* II (1970), 102-124; S. Moscati, *et al.*, eds., *Introduction to the Comparative Grammar of the Semitic Languages* (1969).

II: D. Diringer, *Revista degli studi orientali,* 32 (1957), 301-313; I. J. Gelb, *JCS,* 15 (1961), 27-47; C. H. Gordon, "Abraham of Ur," in D. W. Thomas, ed., *Hebrew and Semitic Studies* (1963), pp. 77-84; Z. Harris, *Development of the Canaanite Dialects* (1939); R. K. Harrison, *Intro. to the OT* (1969), pp. 201-210; C. F. Pfeiffer, *Patriarchal Age* (1965); E. Ullendorf, *Is Biblical Hebrew a Language? Studies in Semitic Languages and Civilizations* (1977).

III: M. Ellenbogen, *Foreign Words in the OT: Their Origin and Etymology* (1962); R. Polzin, *Late Biblical Hebrew: Toward an Historical Typology of Biblical Hebrew Prose* (1976); D. A. Robertson, *Linguistic Evidence in Dating Early Hebrew Poetry* (1972); R. D. Wilson, *Princeton Theological Review,* 25 (1927), 353-388; 26 (1928), 177-247; *Scientific Investigation of the OT* (rev. ed. 1959).

IV: F. I. Andersen, *Hebrew Verbless Clause in the Pentateuch* (1970); *The Sentence in Biblical Hebrew* (1974); H. Bauer and P. Leander, *Historische Grammatik der hebräischen Sprache des AT* (1965); W. Gesenius, E. Kautzsch, and A. E. Cowley, *Hebrew Grammar* (1910); P. Joüon, *Grammaire de l'hébreu biblique* (2nd ed. 1947); R. H. Kennett, *Short Account of the Hebrew Tenses* (1901); P. Kustár, *Aspekt im Hebräischen* (1972); T. O. Lambdin, *Introduction to Biblical Hebrew* (1971); W. S. LaSor, *Handbook of Biblical Hebrew* (1979); A. Sperber, *Historical Grammar of Biblical Hebrew* (1966); J. W. Watts, *Survey of Syntax in the Hebrew OT* (1951).

V: J. Barr, *Semantics of Biblical Language* (1961); T. Boman, *Hebrew Thought Compared with Greek* (Eng. tr. 1960); D. W. Hill, *Greek Words and Hebrew Meanings* (1967); A. R. Johnson, *Vitality of the Individual in the Thought of Ancient Israel* (1949); B. J. Le Frois, *American Ecclesiastical Review,* 134 (1956), 374-394; A. C. Partridge, *English Biblical Translation* (1973); H. W. Robinson, *Religious Ideas of the OT* (1913); W. H. Saulez, *Romance of the Hebrew Language* (1913); N. Snaith, *Distinctive Ideas of the OT* (1944); H. W. Wolff, *Anthropology of the OT* (Eng. tr. 1974).

L. MCFALL

HEBREWS, EPISTLE TO THE.

- I. Title
- II. Literary Form
  - A. Author's Culture and Style
  - B. Literary Category
  - C. Unity of the Letter
- III. Author
  - A. External Evidence
    1. Pauline Tradition
    2. Barnabas Tradition
    3. Tradition of Anonymity
  - B. Internal Evidence
  - C. Various Suggestions
- IV. Destination
- V. Readers
- VI. Purpose
- VII. Date
- VIII. Background
- IX. Analytical Outline

I. Title.–The oldest title for which we have any evidence contained the words "to Hebrews" (Gk. *prós Hebraious*). Even here the earliest attestation is not before the 3rd century. It is often supposed that this brief title may not have been original but was rather a scribal addition. If so, it may well have been no more than an inference from the contents of the book. The additional words "The Epistle of Paul the Apostle" found in the AV are a still later addition and reflect the tradition of the churches regarding the authorship of the book. Yet even if the briefer title is treated as editorial, it may not necessarily be assumed to be inaccurate. It is certainly vague, and this has raised suspicions in the minds of many regarding its authenticity.

Early tradition knows of no alternative title, however, and this may be taken to indicate that the consensus of opinion in the early period of the Church was that this letter was addressed to Hebrew people. There will be further discussion of the correctness of this assumption in V below, but it is evident that uncertainty regarding the title is a disadvantage when considering the historical setting. We are left to draw inferences from the book's

Chester Beatty papyrus (***p***[46]), 3rd cent. A.D., Rom. 16:23–Heb. 1:7. Note the heading *pros ebraious*, "to the Hebrews" (University of Michigan Library)

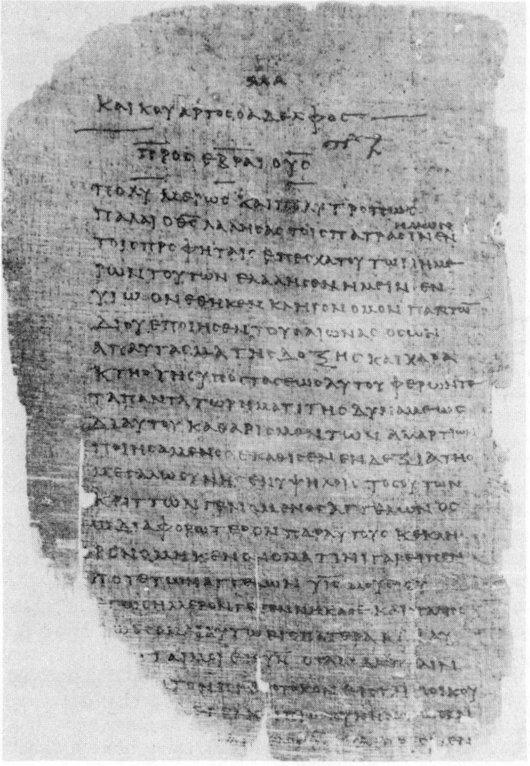

historical allusions, which at best are very vague and fragmentary. Nevertheless, there are some advantages for the exegete in this indeterminacy, for his interpretation of the contents is not greatly dependent upon conclusions regarding authorship, destination, and date, none of which is ascertainable with a great degree of certainty. Indeed, for the exegete the background of thought is of much greater importance. It may be said at once that criticism of the book may proceed with the primary intention of elucidating this background.

II. Literary Form.–A. Author's Culture and Style. The writer was evidently a man of culture who had a masterful command of the Greek language. He was well read in Hellenic literature (e.g., the Wisdom of Solomon) and showed some points of contact with Philo's system of thought, although it is by no means certain that he had read the works of that writer. This latter factor will be touched upon when dealing with the background, but for the present it is sufficient to note that the similarities in thought are indications of the author's level of culture. The writer's method of argument generally proceeds in accordance with the rules of Greek rhetoric. He does not digress the way Paul does in most of his letters. As Moffatt commented, "Where the literary skill of the author comes out is in the deft adjustments of the argumentative to the hortatory sections" (*Intro.*, pp. 424f.). He has been classified with Luke as the most "cultured" of the early Christian writers.

B. Literary Category. Since the book opens without an introductory greeting or address but concludes normally with personal references and salutations, the problem of its literary character becomes difficult to answer and gives rise to a variety of hypotheses.

Does the book fulfil the conditions of a true letter? Certain features support the view that it does. The concluding chapter provides evidence that the writer has had personal contact with the readers, details of which will be given below when discussing the readership. A reference to Timothy (13:23) implies that he was well known to writer and readers alike. Moreover, the body of the letter contains other indications that the writer is addressing a particular community.

There are no parallels, however, for a letter without an address, and the absence of one in Hebrews demands an explanation. Two different lines of approach have been taken in attempting to solve the problem. Either it is assumed that an address originally stood at the head of the work, or it is assumed that it is not a letter at all, in which case the concluding chapter or parts of it are regarded as not original. A variation of the former alternative is to suppose that the writer designed his work as a real letter but for some reason suppressed the introduction.

The idea that the introduction was lost in the course of the transmission of the book raises considerable difficulties, although it is not altogether impossible. In the absence of the slightest textual indication of any variation in the opening portion, it is questionable to build upon such a supposition. It would be necessary to supply an adequate reason why the introduction dropped off. If by accident, it must have been from the original itself, and this would be highly unlikely. If by intention, there must have been a strong motive. Harnack's suggestions that the suppression may have been occasioned by prudence in a time of persecution, or by its being unnecessary because the bearer could communicate to the recipients details of the letter's origin are quite unconvincing. It is much better to proceed from the known data and to attempt to explain Hebrews as it stands, without an introduction. It may well be that the author never intended the book to fit into the Greek category of a letter, in which case the lack of an introduction would lose some of its significance (cf. Roller's discussion of ancient Greek literary practice, *Das Formular der Paulinischen Briefe* [1933], pp. 213ff.).

The remaining suggestion, that it was never originally intended to be a letter but was really a homily, deserves careful consideration. There are some features that strongly support this contention. It possesses the oratorical character of a sermon. It contains hortatory asides, which might well suggest a preacher pausing in the course of his argument to address direct appeals to his audience (cf. 2:1; 3:1-12; 4:1, 14; 5:11; 6:9; 10:9; 13:7). Moreover, the carefully thought-out argument would fit in well with the idea of a preacher who before he begins has his conclusion clearly in mind. The digressions are carefully controlled and the drift of the main theme is never lost. This latter consideration does not necessarily point to a sermon but would be well explained by such a hypothesis.

But if the subject matter originally constituted a sermon, other problems arise. Was it actually delivered to one community and sent to another? Did the hearers of the original sermon request that it be written down and preserved? Or did the preacher prepare his message for a particular community only to be prevented from visiting them, with the result that he forwarded his address for their edification? In the event of any of these, the concluding greetings must have been added by the writer as a kind of covering letter; but there is a good measure of conjecture in all of these suggestions. It is probably better to assume that the subject matter had previously formed part of an address given by the writer and that he himself incorporated the main features of it, which were still in his mind, when dealing with the general problems of a particular community with which he was in direct personal touch. A. B. Bruce raised the objection to the sermon theory that Hebrews is too long and abstruse (p. 10). But what seems abstruse to modern minds might not have been so to early Christians, and the length is often exceeded by modern preachers. The sermon idea did not appeal to A. Nairne (*CGT,* p. lxxiii) either, who was impressed by the fact that the letter appears to have been called forth by some very urgent occasion.

A variation of the sermon idea is that of Deissmann, who regarded Hebrews as an example of Christian literary art. According to him, Hebrews belongs to the category of a written treatise, a kind of literary exercise (G. A. Deissmann, *Bible Studies* [2nd ed., Eng. tr. 1909], pp. 49f.; *The NT in the Light of Modern Research* [Eng. tr. 1929], p. 51). But the writer's purpose is too serious to be regarded in this light (cf. W. Manson, p. 5). The historical allusions, however vague, demand a more adequate explanation.

C. Unity of the Letter. Because of the problems raised by the letter as it stands, some scholars have proposed that parts of the concluding chapter do not belong to the original. The idea that 13:22-25 was a later addition, appended to give the original letter a Pauline flavor in order to make it more canonically acceptable, was first advanced by F. Overbeck in *Zur Geschichte des Kanons* (1880). He incorporated with this the suggestion that at first another name was attached, but was later dropped. But if 13:22-25 was appended for canonization purposes, would it not have been more effectual to have incorporated an introductory formula? This would hold even under the theory that 13:22-25 was genuinely Pauline although the rest was not.

A variation of this hypothesis is that of W. Wrede (pp. 2ff.), who advanced the view that the writer twice changed his mind in the course of writing Hebrews. His first intention was a homily, but after ch. 12 he decided on a letter and finally gave it a Pauline flavor in 13:22-25. A similar theory was suggested by C. C. Torrey (*JBL,* 30 [1911], 137-156), who extended the Pauline additions to include vv. 1-7, 16-19. But the evidence of change in style in ch. 13 is inadequate to warrant such a theory. C. Spicq (*ConNT,* 11 [1946], 226-236) argued that four of the main themes of chs. 1–12 are echoed in ch. 13; such thematic continuity strongly supports the unity of the whole book. There does not appear to be adequate evidence for suggesting that the whole or part of ch. 13 is not original, so this solution of the problem of the literary form must be excluded.

III. Author.–A. *External Evidence.* A survey of the early Christian approach to the book of Hebrews shows that no firm tradition existed regarding its authorship, at least in the earliest period. It is certain that Clement of Rome knew it, although he cites it without acknowledgment (cf. He. 11:7 and 1 Clem. 9:4; He. 1:3f. and 1 Clem. 36:1f.). In the passages cited from Hebrews in 1 Clement, the sequence of thought is so closely reproduced that there can be no doubt that Clement wrote with this work before him. This shows that Hebrews possessed authority in Rome at an early date. There are a few similarities of expression with the Shepherd of Hermas. The possible marks of its influence on the works of Polycarp and Justin Martyr are very uncertain, while Marcion did not include it in his canon — although this omission may have been for dogmatic reasons, since he would have found the theme of Hebrews unpalatable. Its omission from the Muratorian Canon is more significant, but this could possibly be accounted for by the fragmentary character of the canon. In any case, Paul's church Epistles are said to be seven in number, which would exclude Hebrews.

When the book emerges into the clear light of history toward the end of the 2nd cent., the tradition as to its authorship is divided into three different streams.

1. Pauline Tradition. The idea that Hebrews was the work of Paul first appeared in Alexandria. Clement tells how his teacher, apparently Pantaenus, explained why Paul did not in this letter, as in others, address his readers under his own name. He supposed that Paul refrained from putting his own name to a work addressed to Hebrew people out of reverence for the Lord, who Himself had been their Apostle. Clement accepted this explanation and in addition supposed that the original had been written in Hebrew and that Luke had translated it into Greek. This latter speculation was probably not based on any genuine tradition but was rather an inference drawn by Clement himself from the title, from the dissimilarity of the Greek from that of Paul's Epistles, and from the similarities observed between Hebrews and Acts.

Origen noted the differences in style between Hebrews and Paul's Epistles but was impressed by the Pauline character of the thoughts. His own suggestion was that some disciple had written down what he had heard from Paul. He knew of traditions that held Luke or Clement of Rome to be the author, but he himself was not prepared to venture upon any identification. He declared that "God alone knows." Origen's caution was not heeded by his successors in Alexandria, who assumed without question the Pauline authorship, an assumption which by the 4th cent. had spread throughout the Eastern churches.

2. Barnabas Tradition. The only other tradition that can claim ancient attestation is that of Barnabas, and even this seems to have been held in only a restricted area, for its sole authority is Tertullian, who, when introducing a quotation from He. 6:1, 4-6, writes: "There is also an Epistle to the Hebrews under the name of Barnabas . . . and the Epistle of Barnabas is more generally received among the churches than that apocryphal 'Shepherd' of adulterers" (*De pudicitia* 20). Tertullian is not expressing his mere personal opinion but quoting a tradition that had so far established itself as to appear in the MS title of the book; and he betrays no consciousness of the existence of any other tradition. Vernon Bartlet (*Expos.* 6th ser., 5 [1885], 423) considered that Tertullian was here magnifying Hebrews at Hermas's expense. In any case, he does not appear to regard it very highly, for the quotation referred to is the only one he makes from Hebrews, whereas he has copious citations from Paul's Epistles. Moffatt (*Intro.,* p. 437) thought that behind this view of authorship was some Roman tradition, but the evidence is too slight to be certain. Later, the African Church, whose opinion Tertullian appears to be representing, embraced the Alexandrian view, for at the councils of Hippo (393) and Carthage (419) Hebrews was included among the Epistles of Paul.

3. Tradition of Anonymity. No tradition of authorship appears elsewhere in the West until the 4th century. The earliest definite evidence in support of the Pauline authorship of this book is found in the works of Jerome and Augustine. Yet neither of these seems convinced of Pauline authorship, even though they cite it as Paul's. Since Hebrews was known as early as Clement in Rome, but without mention of author, it seems most probable that the book circulated in the West anonymously until through Jerome and Augustine the Eastern view was mediated to the West.

The theory of anonymity finds support in the fact that the earliest evidence for the Pauline tradition seems to have arisen in an attempt to explain the absence of Paul's name, i.e., the anonymity. But how did the strong Pauline tradition arise? It is highly probable that the superficial similarities of doctrinal presentation struck the early Alexandrians. To Origen the Pauline flavor of the thoughts was apparent. Since the work so clearly possessed apostolic authority, it is not difficult to see why the assumption arose that Paul was the author. There is no certain evidence that the Pauline ascription was added to make Hebrews acceptable from a canonical point of view. It is more probable that its canonicity was accepted before its apostolic authorship and not vice versa. In other words, its own spiritual authority and value made it impossible to exclude it from the canon, and the same cause led it to be classed with that other body of theological writings, the Pauline Epistles.

Until the time of the Reformers the Pauline tradition remained unchallenged. But Erasmus, Luther, and Calvin all questioned it. Luther suggested Apollos as author, but he seems to have been the first to do so. Later, Grotius returned to the theory of Lukan authorship, which had been current in Origen's time. Since Grotius many different views have been held and these will be considered next.

B. Internal Evidence. The failure of the external tradition to solve the problem of authorship throws the onus on the internal evidence, which is so sparse that the solution remains a matter of conjecture. The absence of the author's name is further complicated by the paucity of hints about his personality. But a few details may be inferred. He was probably a Hellenist, a Greek-speaking Jew. He was familiar with the OT Scriptures and with the religious ideas of the Jews. He claims the inheritance of their sacred history, traditions, and institutions (1:1) and dwells on these with an intimate knowledge and enthusiasm that would have been improbable, though not impossible, in a proselyte, and even more so in a Christian convert from heathenism. But he apparently knew the OT only in the

LXX, which he follows even where it deviates from the Hebrew. He writes Greek with a purity of style and vocabulary to which the writings of Luke alone in the NT can be compared. Like Philo, his mind is imbued with a combination of Hebrew and Greek thought. His general typological mode of thinking, his use of the allegorical method, as well as his use of many terms that are most familiar in Alexandrian thought, all reveal the Hellenistic mind. Yet his fundamental conceptions are in full accord with the teaching of Paul and of the Johannine writings.

The central position assigned to Christ, the high estimate of His person, the saving significance of His death, the general trend of the ethical teaching, the writer's opposition to asceticism, and his esteem for the rulers and teachers of the Church all bear out the inference that he belonged to a Christian circle dominated by Pauline ideas. Neither the author nor the readers appear to have been personal disciples of Jesus; rather, they had received the gospel from those who had heard the Lord (2:3). By the time of writing some of these may have been dead (13:7). The writer had probably lived among those whom he addressed and had probably been their teacher. He is anticipating visiting them again soon (13:18). Although the foregoing data are not inconsiderable, they are hardly conclusive enough to be attached to any specific person. Yet many attempts have been made.

C. Various Suggestions. Since much tradition points to Paul, he must be considered first. There are a number of reasons why scholars are almost unanimous in rejecting Pauline authorship. (1) Paul makes no claim to be the author. This contrasts strikingly with his practice as we know it from his acknowledged Epistles. If he had been the author, it is difficult, if not impossible, to suggest a reason why he would have omitted his name. Pantaenus's view that it was from reverence for the Lord, the true Apostle to the Hebrews, is quite unconvincing. Moreover, the author nowhere shows any consciousness of apostolic authority, which was of concern to Paul. (2) The style of Hebrews differs in many respects from that of Paul. As mentioned above, it is nearer to the classical Greek style, and it lacks digressions so frequent in Paul. Its theme is also more carefully worked out according to a definite pattern. All this does not automatically exclude Pauline authorship, since the different occasion and subject matter may have had some bearing on these matters. (3) The author does not show evidence of the same spiritual experience so characteristic of Paul. There is no allusion to the great crisis on the Damascus road. (4) The writer quotes the OT in a different way from Paul. Instead of "It is written" or "The scripture says," he has "God says," or "The Holy Spirit says," or "One somewhere says." The writer also keeps closer to the LXX. (5) The doctrinal emphases are also somewhat different, although not in conflict, with those of Paul. The dominant theme of Hebrews, the high-priesthood of Christ, finds no direct allusion in Paul's Epistles (although O. Moe, *TLZ,* 72 [1947], 335-38, finds a few hints of it). The author's view of the work of Christ also differs in emphasis, being less concerned with the redemptive aspect and more with the cleansing and purifying work. Unlike Paul, there is no reference to the tension between flesh and spirit. It must not, of course, be supposed that any author is obliged to reproduce all his doctrinal positions in every letter he writes, and to this extent care must be taken not to overstress the differences. (6) The historical situation seems much more conclusive in excluding Paul, for that apostle could hardly have written He. 2:3, where the author states that he had received instruction from those who had heard the Lord. Paul was constantly stressing that he was taught through supernatural revelation (cf. Gal. 1:12). The writer of Hebrews quite definitely seems to class himself with his readers among those who had received the tradition secondhand. In view of these considerations and the uncertainty of the external tradition, it is reasonable to conclude that Paul is not likely to have been the author.

Is there any more to be said for Barnabas? The African tradition that Tertullian mentions was probably a conjecture, but there are a few considerations that might support it. As a Levite, Barnabas would certainly have been acquainted with the temple ritual, but this consideration carries little weight, inasmuch as the author of Hebrews is more interested in the biblical cultus than in the current ritual. At the same time, a converted Levite would certainly have been deeply concerned about the issues raised in this book. It has been maintained that the author's knowledge of Jewish ritual is derived from Jewish tradition rather than from his acquaintance with the temple worship (cf. Moffatt, *Intro.,* p. 438). Whatever the source of his knowledge, there is nothing in the author's arguments that would make it impossible for Barnabas to have written it. The Hellenistic background might have made its mark upon him in Cyprus. On the other hand, it is difficult to suppose that Barnabas would have written He. 2:3, although the absence of any data regarding the way in which he became a Christian makes it impossible to be certain. The impression given by Acts is that Barnabas was closely linked with the Jerusalem church, although no indication is given of the length of his residence there.

Luke has found various supporters, who have mainly based their contentions on certain verbal similarities between Hebrews and Acts, particularly some affinities with Stephen's speech (cf. F. D. V. Narborough, p. 11; Manson, comm., p. 36, for details of the latter). The argument rests on the assumption that the speech of Stephen is Luke's own composition, but if Luke is reproducing the genuine ideas of Stephen himself the evidence would not necessarily point in the direction of the Lukan authorship of Hebrews. Moreover, it is evident that the predominantly Jewish background of Hebrews is not shared by the Lukan writings.

There is some slight tradition favoring Clement as author, but a careful comparison of 1 Clement with Hebrews does not lead to the conviction that they were both written by the same author. The parallels are well accounted for on the supposition that Clement was acquainted with Hebrews.

Silvanus (or Silas) has been proposed as author, and there are things to be said in his favor. He was known at Rome and at Jerusalem. He knew Timothy and had worked with him. He may have become acquainted with the temple cultus during his stay in Jerusalem. And if he were the virtual writer of 1 Peter as some scholars believe, it is clear that he was versed in the LXX (cf. G. Wohlenberg, *Neue Kirchliche Zeitschrift,* 24 [1913], 742-762; and Hewitt, pp. 26-32). This is a conjecture that can neither be confirmed nor rejected. There are inadequate data for determining whether Silvanus possessed the necessary background to write Hebrews.

There would seem to be more to be said for Apollos, for according to Acts 18 he was an Alexandrian and therefore could have been well versed in the type of thought current there. Acts mentions his great biblical knowledge and his oratorical gifts, both of which would support the claim of his authorship of Hebrews. Moreover, he also knew Timothy and had had close association with Paul. This theory, first suggested by Luther, is a plausible conjecture, although it is no more than a conjecture. If a name must be attached, that of Apollos would be as good as any.

The suggestion of Harnack that the author was Priscilla, aided by her husband, is based on a number of questionable suppositions. It was argued that Priscilla was the more important of the two because she is so often mentioned first in the NT, that she must have possessed high intelligence to instruct Apollos, that she uses the plural in 13:18 to include her husband, and that her name was omitted owing to prejudice against women teachers. But while these suppositions may be true, the evidence does not in fact require them. Apollos was in need more of spiritual than intellectual instruction; and there is nothing in Acts to show that Priscilla was equipped for the task of writing Hebrews.

This list has not exhausted all the proposals that have been made, but enough has been said to show that the only reasonable course is to maintain an open verdict. If we reject Pauline authorship, attaching the letter to any other person will not materially affect our understanding of the background.

IV. Destination.–Just as there is no certain knowledge of the author, so there are no certain indications of the destination. The three main suggestions are Jerusalem, Alexandria, and Rome. The first of these should probably be excluded in view of He. 2:3, the Hellenistic background of the book, the known poverty of the Jerusalem church (contrast 6:10; 10:34; 13:16), the use of the LXX, and 12:4, which suggests that no one in the church had as yet suffered martyrdom. These objections would not be so strong for Palestine generally, but a more predominantly Hellenistic area would better suit the background of Hebrews.

Concepts identified as "Alexandrian" do not support an origin in Alexandria itself, since Alexandrian thought was widely distributed throughout the Greek-speaking areas. Moreover, the Alexandrian church did not lay claim to it. On the contrary, we have seen that this church was the first to maintain Pauline authorship.

The arguments in favor of Rome are much more impressive. Hebrews was known there at an early date and was cited authoritatively by Clement. The reference in 13:24 to "those from Italy," whether it means Italians in Italy or away from home, points to some connection with Rome. If it indicates a greeting from Italians away from home, it would be most intelligible if these people were saluting those at home, i.e., at Rome. The words might also mean the alternative, but in that case they would indicate the location of the writer rather than the readers. On the whole, it seems easier to interpret the phrase as referring to a small group of Italians away from home rather than to Italian Christians generally. Timothy was known at Rome, while the allusions to the readers' generosity would agree with what is known of the Roman church. Furthermore, the Roman Christians had suffered spoliation of goods as had the recipients of Hebrews (He. 10:32).

Yet none of the above factors is conclusive; they can all be explained on the basis of many other destinations. Moreover, He. 2:3 is a problem if the destination were Rome, for the readers appear to have been taught by eyewitnesses; this could hardly have been the experience of the whole Roman church. There is much to be said for the view that the readers formed only a small group within a larger church, which could easily have happened at Rome.

Among other suggestions that have been made are Colossae, Ephesus, Galatia, Syria (Antioch), Corinth, Cyprus, and Berea (for details see Guthrie, p. 41). Since most of these are pure conjecture there is little point in discussing them, but the variety of hypotheses is evidence enough that no view can be anything more than tentative. Of more importance is the character of the readers.

V. Readers.–(1) They were a particular community. These Christians had received the word from eyewitnesses (2:3), had seen signs and wonders (2:4), knew the principles of Christian teaching (6:1), were fruitful in good works (6:10), and had ministered to those who had been ill-treated (10:32-34). All of these details are known to the writer. He speaks of "former days" (10:32) and of earlier persecutions (10:32; 12:4). He is aware of their present state of mind (5:1ff.; 6:9f.), which indicates that a specific community was in view.

(2) They were a community known to the writer. The preceding details might have been received from an informant, but it is clear from 13:19, 23 that the writer has himself visited them and hopes to return soon. He urges them to pray for him (13:18) and mentions Timothy's release as if it were a matter of mutual interest.

(3) They were a community that formed part of a larger community. When the writer tells them (5:12) that they ought by now to be teachers, it seems clear that he could hardly have had in mind the rank-and-file members of a church. He must have been thinking of a group of those who were capable of a teaching ministry, perhaps a small group of more intellectually inclined people. This must not be overstressed, however, since the most effective teachers in the Church have not always been the most intellectual. They were not in any case the leaders, for they are exhorted to remember these. The injunction not to forsake the assemblies (10:25) may well point to a small group of Christians who had segregated themselves from the main body of the church, as many another small group has subsequently done. It is possible that the recipients were a house community in Rome (or in some other city). But the next question that arises is whether they were Jews or Gentiles.

(4) Were they a community of Jewish Christians? Whatever value is attached to the title, the description "To the Hebrews" bears testimony to a strong belief that the readers were Hebrew Christians. The internal evidence would seem to support this belief. The dominance of the OT in the argument, the detailed interest in the Levitical cultus, the significant place given to the high-priesthood of Christ and to the New Covenant, the reference in 2:16 to Abraham's descendants, and the whole trend of the argument itself would be more relevant to Jewish Christians than to Gentiles. But if this is so, the community must have been made up of Jews of the Dispersion, since the original language was Greek and the LXX was used throughout.

(5) Were they a community of gentile Christians? The preceding arguments have not satisfied all scholars that the readers were Jewish. It has been maintained that Gentiles as well as Jews would be acquainted with the OT, since this was the Scripture of the early Church. Admittedly, the development of the argument in Hebrews would not be easy for Gentiles, but the same might be said for parts of the Epistle to the Romans, and Rome is generally assumed to have been a predominantly gentile church. The absence of reference to the temple is also brought forward as evidence of gentile rather than Jewish readers, but this is inconclusive, since the argument deals rather with biblical principles than the ritual procedure. According to E. F. Scott, the writer did not understand Judaism (*The Literature of the NT* [1932], p. 200), but even if this were true it would not necessarily indicate gentile readers. It has further been pointed out that the list of first principles in 6:1 would be inapplicable to Jews (cf. Vos, pp. 14-18). The apostasy mentioned in Hebrews could, according to von Soden (*Hand-Kommentar zum NT* [1899], pp. 12-16), mean apostasy to heathenism rather than to Judaism. But the argument of Hebrews would hardly answer such a threat.

(6) Or were they a mixed community? Since neither the evidence for Jewish nor for gentile readers is conclusive,

it might be better to assume that the writer had in mind neither group, but rather, Christians generally who needed encouragement (cf. Scott, *op. cit.*). But the peculiar nature of the theme would certainly seem to be more biased toward Jewish Christians. Further light may, however, be thrown on the problem by a consideration of the author's purpose.

VI. Purpose.–A discussion of the writer's aim is important for a correct interpretation of Hebrews. But again, many different opinions have been expressed. It is possible here to do no more than summarize them. Before doing so, we should note that the author has described his own work as "my word of exhortation" (Gk. *paráklēsis,* 13:22). If by this description he intended to refer to the whole preceding work, it is clear that Hebrews was designed not primarily as a theological treatise, but as a practical exhortation. When this is kept in mind, it will be seen that the hortatory passages are not interludes but are essential to the purpose.

Theories regarding the author's purpose will clearly be influenced by the decision about the nationality of the readers. Those assuming a Jewish Christian destination will be enumerated first.

(1) To warn against apostasy. The strong language of chs. 6 and 10 is obviously intended to warn against a serious situation, and the most generally accepted interpretation is that the readers were on the point of returning to Judaism. The glories of the cultus they had left might have appeared in striking contrast to the absence of such external glories in Christianity. The whole theme of Hebrews sets forth the superiority of Christianity over the old order and thus would be well designed to offset any temptation to return to Judaism. Although chs. 6 and 10 could be otherwise interpreted, it is reasonable to interpret them in the light of the argument as a whole, and this view of the threat of apostasy has much to recommend it in this respect.

Some have attempted to define this purpose more specifically. Nairne envisaged the author addressing a group of his intellectual friends who were finding it difficult to give up Judaism (*CGT,* p. lxxii). Bornhäuser, and more recently Spicq (pp. 226-231), favor the view that a group of converted priests was being addressed, and the argument of Hebrews would have strongly appealed to them. Such men might well have been exhorted to be teachers (5:12), but the difficulty is that no supporting evidence exists of a community composed exclusively of converted priests. Yet another possibility is that the readers were converts from Qumrân who had not been fully emancipated from the attractions of the sect. The priestly emphasis would thus be explained as would the interest in OT exegesis; but the absence of emphasis upon the ancient law in Hebrews would be a problem. Nevertheless, the conjecture is not impossible and should be kept in mind.

(2) To encourage the world mission. W. Manson agreed that the readers were Jewish Christians, but disputed that the danger was apostasy to Judaism. He maintained that the threat to these Christians was a failure to recognize that Christianity was universalistic in its appeal. The writer's aim was therefore to show that the universal truths of Christianity were far more important than the restricted Jewish cultus. In comparing Hebrews with Stephen's speech, Manson detected a similar approach to that cultus. The suggestion is a fascinating one, but the strong terms of warning in chs. 6 and 10 seem out of place in such a cause.

(3) To set out the absolute character of Christianity. If the readers were mainly Gentiles, it might be argued that the purpose of Hebrews was to show that Christianity is superior to all other religions. But the author's method of demonstrating this would then be somewhat baffling. Why in that case is there so much emphasis upon the cultus, unless, as Moffatt maintained (*Intro.* p. 445), the readers were affected by speculative Judaism? In any case, there is no reference to pagan rites or ablutions. Moreover, the elaborateness of the argument from biblical material could hardly have convinced a gentile Christian who was not already convinced of the absolute character of his new faith.

(4) To counteract a heresy. Some scholars have supposed that a form of Gnosticism of a Jewish type is being combated. Narborough (pp. 20-27) has suggested a general sect of Jewish Gnostics who were attempting to influence some of the Christians to apostatize to their views; T. W. Manson was more specific in supposing the author to have had the Colossian heresy in mind (*BJRL,* 32 [1949-50], 1-17). In the latter case, He. 1–4 would answer the idea of intermediaries (cf. Col. 2:18) and chs. 5–10 the ritual tendencies (cf. 2:14ff.). Manson's theory is tied to his acceptance of Apollos as author, and if this is granted it is not altogether impossible. The type of heresy at Colossae, however, may well have been widespread.

VII. Date.–Although it is difficult to fix any precise date, the general period may be deduced from certain data in Hebrews itself, even though these data are differently interpreted by different scholars. One point of disagreement concerns the fall of Jerusalem: did Hebrews appear before or after that event? It may be argued that if it appeared afterward the author would surely have quoted it as a significant historical indication that the old order was finished. On the other hand, if the author is not concerned with the Jerusalem temple ritual he may not have been so deeply impressed with the theological significance of its fall. Nevertheless, the reference to Timothy, the primitive ecclesiastical situation, and the fact that many of the readers appear to be first converts in the community would support an early dating. The passing reference to "former days" requires some interval of time to allow for the community to possess a history, but all these conditions would be satisfied by a date in the early 60's.

Many scholars, however, prefer a much later date, i.e., *ca.* A.D. 80 or soon after. Evidence for this view is the reference to an earlier persecution (He. 10:32f.), which is thought to be identical with Nero's outburst against the Church. The text suggests that this happened soon after their conversion, in which case the letter could not have been issued until some time after A.D. 64. Yet the major difficulty in this view is the statement that they had not yet resisted to the point of shedding their blood (12:4), which is difficult to imagine in view of the intensity of the Neronian persecutions.

Some have argued from the writer's supposed use of the Pauline Epistles, which would require a sufficient interval for these to have circulated and would push the date of Hebrews considerably later than the death of Paul. But literary affinities are uncertain supports on which to base calculations of date. Few scholars would date Hebrews after Clement's letter, even if they are impressed by this latter argument. Some suggest it was received only just before Clement wrote his; indeed, Goodspeed (*Intro. to the NT* [1937], pp. 258f.) suggested that Clement's letter was written in response to He. 5:12. But even if Goodspeed's theory is correct, this would tell us nothing about the date of Hebrews. The evidence as a whole seems to make the earlier date preferable.

VIII. Background.–It is important to analyze the constituent parts of an author's background, if possible, in order to be able to place his work correctly in the development of Christianity. In the case of Hebrews there were several influences at work. The author's acquaintance with the writings of Philo of Alexandria has been much emphasized. Indeed, at one time it was assumed that Hebrews could not be properly interpreted without reference to Philo. This movement was at its zenith at the turn of the century. The most important features in which Hebrews shows parallels with Philo are the tendency to allegory and especially the use of Melchizedek as a type, the widespread use of the LXX as authoritative, the similar method of quoting Scripture, and the assumption that the present order is but a copy of the real. It is this last consideration that has caused some to assume that the writer is interpreting Christianity in the light of current Hellenistic philosophical ideas. Hebrews contrasts the new and the old in a series of antitheses very similar to Philo's theory of ideas. Philo's fundamental approach to the OT is to treat it as allegory, which leaves him free to superimpose his own philosophical system upon it.

Hebrews, however, treats the OT essentially as history rather than allegory, although there may be a trace of allegorization in the Melchizedek story. The approach is in short more biblical. What similarities exist are on the surface, and it cannot be assumed that Philo's influence upon Hebrews is great. The author may have been, as Spicq claims (p. 198), a converted Philonist; but the evidence is not conclusive.

Another problem of continuing interest is the extent of the influence of Paul's thought on the author of Hebrews. As noted above, the similarities impressed the early Christians to such an extent that the assumption of common authorship remained unchallenged for centuries. There are certainly some strong grounds for maintaining that the writer was in close touch with Paul's teaching, whether from personal acquaintance or from knowledge of his letters. There is a similar doctrine of Christ, His part in creation, His humiliation, obedience, and self-offering. There are also similar conceptions of the new covenant and of Abraham as an example and a similar use of OT passages (both appeal to Ps. 8; Dt. 32:35; Hab. 2:4). Differences from Paul's approach have already been pointed out, but the evidence seems to show that the author had inherited much from Paul. Indeed, it seems safe to assume that he was a member of the Pauline circle.

An influence that earlier scholars tended to overlook, but which now has been brought to the fore, is that of the primitive tradition. No longer can it be maintained that Hebrews stands midway between Paul and John with no contacts with the primitive period. Such a view is the product of a unilateral conception of Christian development. It is nearer the truth to maintain that Paul, John, and Hebrews all represent parallel and complementary developments from the earliest period. The similarities with Stephen's speech noted above are evidence of the close affinities between Hebrews and the primitive period. Moreover, the writer appears to have had close acquaintance with early Jewish Christianity.

It is hardly necessary to emphasize the powerful influence of OT thought upon the author. Indeed, it may be said that Hebrews is a Christian assessment of the OT cultus. It is as if the author is attempting to answer the problem of the place of OT cultic thought in Christian theology. He finds that a good deal of the imagery points to Christ as its perfect fulfillment. Christianity is a "better way" than the old.

IX. Leading Themes.–A large portion of Hebrews is taken up with the theme of Christ's high-priesthood (4:14–10:18), and this may at once be said to be the dominating thought. Not only is it made clear that Christ has the necessary qualifications to be the perfect high priest, but His order of priesthood is contrasted with that of Aaron. Furthermore, the priesthood of Christ is shown to operate within a more perfect sanctuary than that of Aaron or his successors. The greatest feature of all in Christ's superiority was that as priest He offered Himself. This is the only perfect offering that has ever been made, and because of its perfection it requires no repetition. Within this main section there are various digressions such as strong exhortations to the readers (5:11–6:12).

The problem arises over the remaining portions. In 1:1–4:13 the writer deals with the superiority of Christ's person, and he does so against the background of the history of Israel at the time of the Exodus. The events of this period clearly exercised a molding influence upon his thought. Christ's superiority to angels was to offset the angelic agencies that had a part in establishing the Israelite nation. The loss of inheritance by the generation of wilderness wanderers is contrasted with the Christian's inheritance in the present day of grace (ch. 3). Great as Moses was in Jewish eyes, Christ is as much greater as a son is compared with a servant. Even the inheritance ultimately secured by Joshua was but a pale pattern of that secured in Christ (4:1-13). The whole of the first part of Hebrews is therefore designed to show that Christianity is a kind of spiritual reenactment of the most critical events in the development of Israel as a nation. In the emergence of a spiritual Israel, One greater than either Moses or Joshua took up the leadership and led His people into a more perfect "rest."

If the idea that Christians are on a spiritual pilgrimage toward a perfect inheritance is borne in mind, the relevance of the high-priest theme will become clearer. The Israelite wanderers needed an established order of worship with its official priestly representative and its sacrificial system. But the new Christian order, called by the writer the order of Melchizedek, is superior to this and substitutes spiritual for cultic worship on the basis of Christ's sacrifice.

The practical portion of Hebrews continues the same strain. The heroes of faith in ch. 11, apart from the brief concluding summary in vv. 32-38, are wholly from the period up to the wilderness wanderings. The great attention paid to Abraham reaches its climax in the statement that he never possessed his own inheritance, but pressed on toward a more enduring city prepared by God. Even when dealing with the theme of chastening, the writer comes back to the theme of the wilderness wanderings and, recalling the terrifying fire of Mt. Sinai, draws a contrast between this and the blessedness of Mt. Zion. In the concluding exhortations he remembers the imagery of the tabernacle and calls attention to the need to go forth outside the camp (13:13), while the magnificent concluding prayer appeals to the efficacy of the blood of the eternal covenant (13:20). There can be no doubt that the theme that holds the whole book together is that of the Christian Church as a new and better Israel, with Christ Himself fulfilling all the offices imperfectly performed by the great heroes of the past.

X. Analytical Outline

I. The Superiority of Christ and Christianity (1:1-10:18)
   A. To Old Revelation (1:1-3)
   B. To Angels (1:4–2:18)
   C. To Moses (3:1-19)
   D. To Joshua (4:1-13)
   E. The Priesthood of Christ (4:14–7:28)
   F. The Priestly Work of Christ (8:1–10:18)

II. Exhortations Based on Preceding Arguments (10:19–13:17)
   A. Use of the Superior Method (10:19-25)
   B. Danger of Apostasy (10:26-31)
   C. Memory of Past Days (10:32-39)

D. Examples of Historic Endurance (11:1-40)
E. The Example of Christ (12:1-11)
F. Avoidance of Moral Inconsistency (12:12-17)
G. Reminder of the Superiority of the New Covenant (12:18-29)
H. Practical Results (13:1-17)
III. Conclusion (13:18-25)

Bibliography.–I. Comms.: J. P. Alexander (1937); F. F. Bruce (*NICNT,* 1964); G. W. Buchanan (*AB,* 1972); M. Dods (*Expos.G.T.,* 1910); J. Héring (*Comm. du NT,* 1954); T. Hewitt (Tyndale, 1960); P. E. Hughes (1977); W. Manson (Baird Lectures, 1951); O. Michel (*KEK,* 1960); J. Moffatt (*ICC,* 1924); H. Montefiore (1964); A. Nairne (*CGT,* 1917); *Epistle of Priesthood* (2nd ed. 1915); F. D. V. Narborough (1930); E. F. Scott (1922); A. Snell (1959); C. Spicq (1952); H. Strathmann (*NTD,* 1956); G. Vos (1956); B. F. Westcott (3rd ed. 1903); E. C. Wickham (*WC,* 1910); H.Windisch (*HNT,* 1931).

II. Background: F. J. Badcock, *The Pauline Epistles and the Epistle to the Hebrews in their Historical Setting* (1937); D. Guthrie, *NT Intro.* (3rd ed. 1970), pp. 685-735; A. H. McNeile, C. S. C. Williams, *Intro. to the NT* (2nd ed. 1953); W. Michaelis, *Einl. in das NT* (3rd ed. 1961); J. Moffatt, *Intro. to the Literature of the NT* (2nd ed. 1912); A. Wickenhauser, *NT Intro.* (1958).

III. Destination and Authorship: H. H. B. Ayles, *Destination, Date and Authorship of the Epistle to the Hebrews* (1899); K. Bornhäuser, *Empfänger und Verfasser des Hebräerbriefes* (1932); V. Burch, *Epistle to the Hebrews, Its Sources and Message* (1936); A. Harnack, *ZNW,* 1 (1900) 16-41; E. Käsemann, *Das wandernde Gottesvolk, Eine Untersuchung zum Hebräerbrief* (1939); W. Leonard, *Authorship of the Epistle to the Hebrews* (1939); F. C. Synge, *Hebrews and the Scriptures* (1959); W. Wrede, *Das literarische Rätsel des Hebräerbriefes* (1906).

IV. Theology: A. B. Bruce, *Epistle to the Hebrews* (1899); W. P. Du Bose, *High Priesthood and Sacrifice* (1908); E. Ménégoz, *Théologie de l'Épître aux Hébreux* (1894); G. Milligan, *Theology of the Epistle to the Hebrews* (1899); R. H. Strachan, *Historic Jesus in the NT* (1931); R. V. G. Tasker, *The Gospel in the Epistle to the Hebrews* (1950).

D. GUTHRIE

HEBREWS, GOSPEL ACCORDING TO THE. *See* APOCRYPHAL GOSPELS IV.

HEBREWS, RELIGION OF THE. *See* ISRAEL, RELIGION OF.

HEBRON hē'brən [Heb. *ḥeḇrôn*–'league, association'].

1. The third son of Kohath, son of Levi (Ex. 6:18; Nu. 3:19, 27; 1 Ch. 6:2, 18; 23:12, 19).

2. A son of Mareshah and descendant of Caleb (1 Ch. 2:42f.). *See also* KORAH.

HEBRON hē'brən [Heb. *ḥeḇrôn*–'league' or 'confederacy'; Gk. *Chebrōn*]. A city known in ancient times as Kiriath-arba, located about 30 km. (19 mi.) SSW of Jerusalem on a sloping hill, er-Rumeideh. The hill is 1110 m. (3040 ft.) above sea level and overlooks a fertile valley to the west with an unusual supply of wells and springs. About 3 km. (2 mi.) to the north is Mamre, modern Râmet el-Khalîl. Modern Hebron since the time of the Crusades was rebuilt just E of this ancient site.

The Hebron district, especially the terebinth of Mamre, marks the residence of Abraham for numerous events recorded in Gen. 12–25. Here he purchased from the Hittites the cave of Machpelah, which became the burial place for the patriarchs Abraham, Isaac, and Jacob and the matriarchs Sarah, Rebekah, and Leah (Gen. 23:1-20; 49:31; 50:13).

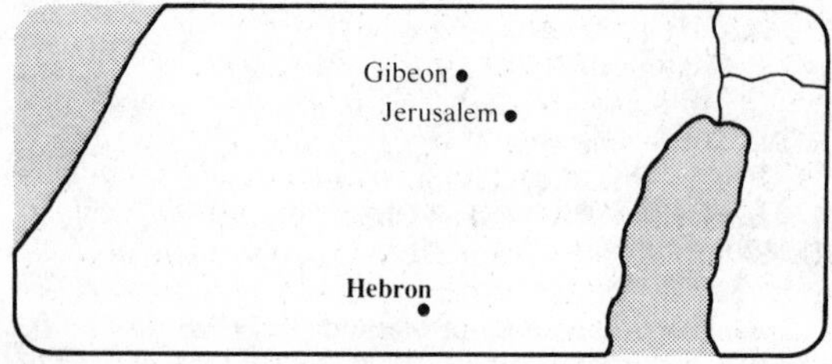

The ancient city of Hebron was built seven years before the Egyptian city of Tanis (Nu. 13:22 [MT 23]). If the building of Tanis (also called ZOAN) is correctly identified with the Hyksos rebuilding project, then the date for the beginning of Hebron is *ca.* 1700 B.C. This would account for the apparent explanatory references on the temple of Karnak in Upper Egypt to the "Field of Abram," perhaps the first outside source reference to Abraham's connection with Hebron (cf. *WBA,* p. 149).

When the Israelite spies explored the region of Hebron the Anakim occupied this area (Nu. 13:22, 28, 33). In the conquest of Canaan, Joshua killed Hokam the king of Hebron, who had joined the anti-Gibeonite coalition (Josh. 10:1-27). Caleb received Hebron and the surrounding territory for his family possession after defeating the Anakim (Josh. 14:12f.; 15:13f.; Jgs. 1:10, 20). Later it served as a Levitical city and a city of refuge (Josh. 20:7; 21:11). David was anointed king of Judah in Hebron (2 S. 2:4) and continued to use Hebron as his capital for seven and a half years. Absalom launched his unsuccessful rebellion at Hebron (2 S. 15:7ff.). Rehoboam fortified Hebron during his reign (2 Ch. 11:10). Many large storage jars from the 8th cent. onward stamped with the royal seal bear the name of Hebron, indicating that Hebron was a place where jars were produced in this era of the monarchy of Judah. These jars, with a capacity of 2 baths or 38 liters (10 gallons), were used for commerce and payment of taxes (cf. *WBA,* pp. 193f.).

Jar handle (8th cent. B.C.) with royal seal and "Hebron" (*ḥbrn*) inscribed in old Hebrew (Trustees of the British Museum)

Modern Hebron is a town that was within the boundaries of the Hashemite kingdom of Jordan (1949-1967; occupied by Israel in 1967). In A.D. 1167 it was the see of a Latin bishop but was captured by Saladin's forces in 1187. The traditional site of the cave of Machpelah is marked by a mosque in an enclosure measuring 60 by 34 m. (198 by 111 ft.), around which the modern city has been built. The mosque formerly was a Crusader church and stands on the site of the Justinian basilica of the 6th century. In the mosque, the cenotaphs, presumably over the site of the patriarchal and matriarchal tombs, are covered with elaborate gold and embroidered textiles in green and crimson. Regarded as a sacred spot by the Islamic world, the cave apparently has not been accessible since the time of the Crusades.

Crusaders regarded Hebron as the castle of Abraham. The Arabs designate Hebron or the oaks of Mamre as el-Khalîl, "the friend" (cf. Isa. 41:8; Jas. 2:23); in the LXX the words "my friend" are inserted after the word "Abraham" in Gen. 18:17. S. J. SCHULTZ

HEBRONITES hē'brən-īts [Heb. *ḥeḇrônî*]. A family of Levites, descendants of Hebron, third son of Kohath (Nu. 3:27; 26:58; etc.).

HEDGE [Heb. *meśûḵâ* (Isa. 5:5; Mic. 7:4, "thorn hedge"; cf. Prov. 15:19), *geḏērâ* (Jer. 49:3), vbs. *sāḵaḵ* (Job 3:23), *śûḵ* (Job 1:10; Hos. 2:6); Gk. *phragmós* (Mt. 21:33; Mk. 12:1; Lk. 14:23)]; NEB also FENCE (Isa. 5:5), BRIARS (Mic. 7:4), GASHES (Jer. 49:3), BLOCK (vb.) (Hos. 2:6), WALL (Mt. 21:33; Mk. 12:1), HEDGEROW (Lk. 14:23). Hedges were generally made of cut thorn branches or formed from thorny plants. A "fence" normally comprised a loose stone wall, such as surrounded fields and vineyards.

See also FENCE (Nah. 3:17); WALL; GEDERAH (1 Ch. 4:23). R. K. H.

HEDGEHOG [Heb. *qippōḏ*; Gk. *echínos*; cf. Arab. *qunfuḏ* (Isa. 14:23; Zeph. 2:14); AV BITTERN; NEB (RUFFED) BUSTARD. The RSV translates *qippôḏ* as "porcupine" in Isa. 34:11; here the animal is a member of the family *Hystricidae*, perhaps the European porcupine, *Hystrix cristata*. That *qippōḏ* is probably derived from a word meaning "roll up" has led to the traditional identification with the porcupine, of which three species have been reported in Palestine. Zephaniah obviously saw a ruined Nineveh as the home of hedgehogs or porcupines, and if a destroyed city was in fact being contemplated, it would be unnecessary to try to find some bird species to fit the idea of *qippōḏ*, as in the NEB.

See also PORCUPINE. R. K. H.

HEED [Heb. *šāmaʿ*]; AV also HEAR, HEARKEN, OBEY; NEB also HEAR, LISTEN, ACCEPT, PAY ATTENTION, OBSERVE; [qal and niphal of *šāmar*]; AV also HEARKEN, GIVE EAR, BEWARE, "be circumspect," OBSERVE, etc.; NEB also BE CAREFUL, ACCEPT, TAKE (GOOD) CARE, LISTEN, etc.; [hiphil of *qāšaḇ*]; AV also HEARKEN, REGARD, HEARD, ATTENDED; NEB also LISTEN, ATTEND, GIVE A READY EAR, etc.; [Gk. *blépō*]; NEB TAKE CARE, BEWARE, TAKE NOTE, "all you can expect" (Gal. 5:15), etc.; [*proséchō*]; AV also HAD REGARD, ATTENDED TO; NEB KEEP (A) WATCH, RESPONDED, GIVE THEIR MINDS TO, etc.; [*horáō*]; NEB BEWARE; [*akoúō*]; AV HEAR; NEB PAID NO HEED, LISTEN; [*parakaléō*] (2 Cor. 13:11); AV "be of good comfort"; NEB TAKE OUR APPEAL TO HEART; [*epéchō*] (1 Tim. 4:16); NEB MAKE THESE MATTERS YOUR BUSINESS; [*ameléō*] (He. 8:9); AV REGARDED (NOT); NEB ABANDONED; [*eulabéomai*] (He. 11:7); AV "moved with fear"; NEB TOOK GOOD HEED; [*hypakoúō*] (Rom. 10:16); AV OBEYED; NEB RESPONDED; **HEEDLESS** [Heb. *rēq*] (Prov. 13:10).

In the OT the RSV translates many Hebrew words as "(give) heed": *šāmaʿ*, "hear" (Dt. 21:18), qal and more frequently niphal of *šāmar*, "keep," "watch," "preserve" (Dt. 6:12; NEB "be careful," "take care" [8:11]), hiphil of *qāšaḇ*, "give attention to" (Ps. 66:19); occasionally *bîn*, "discern" (Dnl. 10:11), *ʿāṯar*, "pray," "supplicate" (2 S. 24:25), hiphil of *śāḵal* (Dnl. 9:13), hiphil of *ʾāzan* (Ps. 5:1 [MT 2]); only once *lāqaḥ*, "take" (Prov. 10:8), *nāṯan lēḇ*, "give heart" (Eccl. 7:21); *śîṯ lēḇ*, "set heart" (1 S. 4:20), *yāḏaʿ*, "know" (Job 35:15), *ʿānâ*, "answer" (Prov. 29:19), *zāʿaq*, "cry" (Ps. 142:6), *šûḇ*, "turn" (Prov. 1:23; NEB RESPOND).

In Dnl. 3:12; 6:13 the Jews do not pay heed to the Babylonian king. Here the verb is Aram. *śîm* with a basic meaning of "set, make," plus *ṭeʿēm*, "judgment." So the best translation would be "show proper respect to" (the king).

A few problem passages deserve special attention. "Take heed" is the RSV translation of Heb. *pillēś*, "weigh," "make level" (Prov. 4:26; 5:6; AV "ponder"; NEB "look out" [4:26], "watch" [5:6]). Though there can be no certainty, the context would lend support to the NEB and RSV translations. On three occasions the RSV takes the common word for "see" (Heb. *rāʾâ*) as "heed." In Jer. 2:31 the NEB confines to a footnote the whole sentence "You, O generation, see the word of the Lord." This is an unsound approach, even if it is a later marginal comment as some commentators have argued. In Prov. 13:10 the RSV "heedless" and the NEB "brainless fool" are based on reading Heb. *rēq* instead of *raq*. This change of vowels is probably correct. (Vowels were not originally written in Hebrew.)

In the NT nine different Greek words are translated "(give or take) heed." Of these *blépō*, "see" (cf. Gal. 5:15) and *proséchō*, "turn one's mind to" (e.g., Acts 8:10) occur frequently, *horáō*, "see," three times (Mt. 16:6 par. Mk. 8:15; Lk. 12:15), *akoúō*, "hear," twice (Jn. 10:8, 16), and the remaining five once. *Horáō* and *proséchō* occur together in Mt. 16:6 "take heed and beware" (NEB "beware . . . be on your guard"), and *horáō* and *blépō* in Mk. 8:15.

There are at least four uses of "heed": (1) things are to be "heeded," i.e., to be listened to and acted upon (the sound of the trumpet [Jer. 6:17], or wisdom [Prov. 1:23]), to be used (one's talents [Lk. 8:18]), to be aware of (pride [1 Cor. 10:12]), to be properly prepared for (leprosy [Dt. 24:8]), not to be touched (the mountain of the Lord [Ex. 19:12]), not to be taken (the land of Edom [Dt. 2:4]), not to be listened to (the curses of others against oneself [Ecc. 7:21]).

(2) People are "heeded," i.e., listened to (Ex. 18:24), obeyed (Dt. 21:18), responded to (1 S. 4:20), recognized in terms of their rights (Dt. 15:9).

(3) Man is to "heed" God's commandment (Ex. 15:26), His statutes (Dt. 4:1), His covenant (Jer. 11:3), His offerings (Nu. 28:2), and His prophets (Dt. 18:15) (which few do [Jer. 23:18]). Finally, we are to await the return of Christ (Mk. 13:33).

(4) God "heeds" the affliction of Hagar (Gen. 16:11), of Jacob (31:24), of Joseph in prison (39:23), of Job (Job 23:6), and countless others.

See also HEAR.

Bibliography.–*TDNT*, I, *s.v.* ἀκούω (Kittel); II, *s.v.* εὐλαβής, κτλ. (Bultmann); V, *s.v.* παρακαλέω (Schmitz). J. C. MOYER
R. W. V.

HEEL [Heb. *ʿāqēḇ*] (Gen. 3:15; 25:26; 49:17, 19; Job 18:9; Ps. 41:9 [MT 10]; Hos. 12:3 [MT 4]); AV also "at the last"; NEB also FETLOCK, "from the rear," paraphrases in Ps. 41:9; Hos. 12:3; [*regel*–'foot'] (Jgs. 4:10; 5:15; Job 18:11); AV FEET, "on foot"; NEB FEET, omits in Jgs. 4:10; 5:15; [Gk. *ptérnan*] (Jn. 13:18).

The heel or calx is the posterior rounded extremity of the foot, the heel bone itself being known anatomically as *os calcis*. Though occurring mostly in a literal sense in Scripture, the allusion in Gen. 3:15 is figurative, describing the partial victory of evil over humanity. The reference to the tribe of Dan is also of a figurative nature (Gen. 49:17), describing the stealthy tactics of the Danites in time of war. The use of "heel" in Jn. 13:18 (a quote from Ps. 41:9) may allude either to a cunning blow inflicted by a wrestler or to an action symbolizing rejection (cf. 1QH 5:24, which is a clear reference to Ps. 41:9 and which parallels "lift the heel" to *zll*, "mock, sneer").

R. K. H.

HEGAI hē'gī [Heb. *hēgay* (Est. 2:8, 15), *hēgē'* (2:3); Gk *Gaí*]; AV HEGE. A eunuch under the Persian king Ahasuerus. Hegai was placed in charge of the young women from whom Esther, Queen Vashti's successor, was chosen.

HEGEMONIDES heg-ə-mon'ə-dēz, hej-ə-mō-nī'dēz [Gk. *Hēgemonídēs* < *hēgemoneúō*–'be leader, rule'] (2 Macc. 13:24). A Syrian officer placed in command of the district extending from Ptolemais to Gerar. In this verse, the AV understands both *Hēgemonídēs* and *stratēgós* as adjectives referring to Maccabeus and translates "principal governor."

HEGLAM heg'ləm [Heb. *heglām*] (1 Ch. 8:7); AV "he removed them"; NEB "he it was who removed them." The AV and NEB take the Hebrew to be the hiphil of *gālâ*, "remove, take into exile." The RSV rendering interprets it as an alternate name for GERA, the son of Ehud and father of Uzza and Ahihud.

HEIFER hef'ûr [Heb. *pārâ*] (Nu. 19; *see* HEIFER, RED; Hos. 4:16); [*ʿeglâ* elsewhere in the OT]; [Gk. *dámalis*] (He. 9:13). For the "heifer of three years old" in the AV, RV mg. of Isa. 15:5; Jer. 48:34, *see* EGLATH-SHELISHIYAH. A young cow that has yet to produce a calf. The *ʿeglâ* figures specifically in religious rites only in the ceremony of Dt. 21:1-9 for the cleansing of the land, where an unexpiated murder had been committed. This was not a sacrificial rite — the priests are witnesses only, and the animal was slain by breaking the neck — but sacrificial purity was required for the heifer. In the sacrifices proper the heifer could be used for a peace offering (Lev. 3:1), but was forbidden for the burnt (Lev. 1:3) or sin (4:3, 14) offerings. Hence the sacrifice of 1 S. 16:2 was a peace offering. In Gen. 15:9 the ceremony of the ratification of the covenant by God makes use of a heifer and a she-goat, but the reason for the use of the females is altogether obscure. *See* HEIFER, RED.

Figuratively, the heifer appears as representing sleekness combined with helplessness in Jer. 46:20 (cf. the comparison of the soldiers to "fatted calves" in the next verse). In Jer. 50:11; Hos. 10:11, the heifer is pictured as engaged in threshing. This was particularly light work, coupled with unusually abundant food (Dt. 25:4), so that the threshing heifer served especially well for a picture of contentment. ("Wanton" in Jer. 50:11, however, is an unfortunate translation in the RV, RSV.) Hosea, in contrast, predicts that the "heifers" shall be set to the hard work of plowing and breaking the sods. In Jgs. 14:18, Samson uses "heifer" in his riddle to refer to his wife. This, however, was not meant to convey the impression of licentiousness that it sometimes gives the modern reader.

B. S. EASTON
R. K. H.

HEIFER, RED. In Nu. 19 a rite is described in which the ashes of a "red heifer" and of certain objects are mixed with running water to obtain the so-called "water for impurity" (Nu. 19:9, 13, 20f.; 31:23). This water was employed in the removal of the uncleanness of a person or thing that had been in contact with a dead body, and also in removing ritual defilement from booty taken in war.

I. Origin and Significance of the Rite.–The general origin of the rite is clear enough, as is the fact that this origin is related to the official sacrificial system of Israel. For the removal of impurity, ritual as well as physical, water, preferably running water (v. 17; cf. Lev. 14:5ff.; 15:13), is the natural means, and is employed universally. But where the impurity was unusually great, mere water was not felt to be adequate, and various substances were mixed with it in order to increase its efficacy. So (among other things) blood is used in Lev. 14:6f., and dust in Nu. 5:17 (*see* WATER OF BITTERNESS). The use, however, of ashes in Nu. 19:17 is unique in the OT, although parallels from elsewhere can be adduced — e.g., Ovid *Fasti* iv.639f., 725, 733; the last of these references, "The blood of a horse shall be a purification, and the ashes of calves," is remarkably close to the OT. The ashes were obtained by burning the heifer completely, "her skin, her flesh, and her blood, with her dung" (the contents of the entrails) (v. 5; cf. Ex. 29:14). Here only in the OT is blood burned for a ceremonial purpose, and here only is burning a *preliminary*; elsewhere it is either a chief act or serves to consume the remnants of a finished sacrifice — Lev. 4:12 and Nu. 19:3 are altogether different.

The heifer is a *female*. For the regular sin offering for the congregation, only the male was permitted (Lev. 4:14), but the female was used in the purificatory ceremony of Dt. 21:3 (a rite that has several points of similarity to that of Nu. 19). An individual sin offering by one of the common people, however, required a female (Lev. 4:28), but probably only in order to give greater prominence to the more solemn sacrifices for which the male was reserved. A female is required again in the cases enumerated in Lev. 5:1-6, most of which are ritual defilements needing purification; a female was required at the purification of a leper (in addition to two males, Lev. 14:10), and a female, with one male, was offered when a Nazirite terminated his vows (Nu. 6:14). Some connection between purification and the sacrifice of a female may be established by the list, for even in the case of the Nazirite the idea may be removal of the state of consecration. But the reason for such a connection is anything but obvious, and the various explanations that have been offered are hardly more than guesses. It was required also that the heifer be "red," i.e., reddish brown (Nu. 19:2). Likeness in color to blood is at first sight the most natural explanation, but likeness in color to ripe grain is almost equally plausible. It may be noted that certain Egyptian sacrifices also required red cattle as victims (Plutarch *De Iside* 31). The heifer is to be "without defect" ("faultless"), "in which there is no blemish," the ordinary requirement for sacrifices. (The Jewish exegetes misread this "perfectly red, in which there is no blemish," with extraordinary results; see below.) But an advance on sacrificial requirements is that she shall be one "upon which a yoke has never come." This requirement is found elsewhere only in Dt. 21:3 and in 1 S. 6:7. But in other religions this requirement was very common (cf. Homer *Il.* x.293; Vergil *Georgics* iv.550f.; Ovid *Fasti* iv.336).

II. Use of Cedar and Hyssop.–While the heifer was being burned, "cedar-wood, and hyssop, and scarlet" (i.e., scarlet wool or thread) were cast into the flames. The same combination of objects (although differently employed) is found at the cleansing of a leper (Lev. 14:4), but their meaning is entirely unknown. The explanations offered are almost countless. It is quite clear that hyssop was especially prized in purifications (Ps. 51:7 [MT 9]), but the use of hyssop as a sprinkler and the use of ashes of hyssop may be quite unrelated. Hyssop and cedar were supposed to have medicinal properties (*see* HYSSOP). Perhaps what was important was the use of aromatic woods. All that can be said definitely is that Lev. 14:4 and Nu. 19:6 show that the combination of objects was deemed to have a high purificatory value.

III. Application and Sacredness of the Ashes.–The ashes, when obtained, were used in removing the greatest of impurities. Consequently, they themselves were deemed to have an extraordinarily "consecrated" character, and they were not to be handled carelessly. Their consecration extended to the rite by which they were produced, so that every person engaged in it was rendered unclean (Nu. 19:7f., 10), an excellent example of how in early religious thought the ideas of "holiness" and "uncleanness" blend. It was necessary to perform the whole ceremony "outside the camp" (v. 3), and the ashes, when prepared, were also kept outside the camp (v. 9), probably in order to guard against contact that would defile anyone (as well as to keep them from being defiled). When used they were mixed with running water, and the mixture was sprinkled with hyssop on the person or object to be cleansed (vv. 17-19). The same water was used to purify booty (31:23), though whether it had any connection with the water of expiation (8:7) is doubtful. In addition to the similarities already pointed out between Nu. 19 and Dt. 21:1-9, the rites resemble each other also in the fact that, in both, laymen are the chief functionaries and that the priests have little to do (in Dt. 21:1-9 they are mere passive witnesses).

At the same time it should be noted that Eleazar the priest, and not a lay leader, was ordered to dip his finger in the animal's blood and sprinkle some of it at the front of the tent of meeting seven times (Nu. 19:4). The consequent ritual uncleanness of the priest and the requirement for cleansing (v. 7) place the rite in a category analogous to that of the sin offering of Lev. 4:6, 17. A ceremonial status of a priestly character was assigned even to the "clean" person whose responsibility it was to dispose of the ashes, for he, too, was considered unclean until the evening. The prescriptions of this ceremony are so much in accord with the ethos of the Levitical sacrificial system that it is difficult to believe that the rite had any connection whatever with contemporary non-Israelite bull-worship, as older liberal scholars used to urge. Indeed, the entire procedure is classified specifically as a "statute of the law which the Lord has commanded," and is totally different both in ethos and intent from the episode in the Ugaritic Baal myth in which the dead god somehow contrived to indulge in bestiality with a heifer in the underworld, thereby regaining his vitality (*UT*, 67:V:18-22; Eng. tr. in *ANET*, p. 139). Whereas the Baal myth was part of a fertility-cult tradition, the ceremony prescribed in Nu. 19 was intended to remove personal uncleanness or ritual defilement, and had no connection whatever with a pagan death-and-resurrection mythology.

See G. B. Gray, *Numbers* (*ICC*, 1903), pp. 241-256.

B. S. EASTON
R. K. H.

HEIGHT; HEIGHTS [Heb. *bāmâ*] (Nu. 21:28; 2 S. 22:34; Ps. 18:33 [MT 34]; Isa. 14:14; 58:14; Jer. 26:18; Ezk. 36:2; Am. 4:13; Mic. 3:12); AV HIGH PLACES; NEB also HIGH ABOVE, HIGH GROUND, HIGHLAND, MOUNTAINS, ROUGH HEATH; [*gaḇ*] (Ezk. 43:13); AV HIGHER PLACE; [*gāḇah*] (2 Ch. 33:14); [*gōḇah*] (1 S. 17:4; 2 Ch. 3:4; Ezk. 31:10; Am. 2:9); NEB also "grew," TALL; [*ḥᵃṣî*] ("half [its] height," Neh. 4:6); [*mārôm*] (Jgs. 5:18; 2 K. 19:23; Ps. 102:19 [MT 20]; 148:1; Isa. 22:16; 26:5; 33:16; etc.); AV also HIGH, HIGH PLACES, ON HIGH; NEB also HIGH, HIGHEST, HIGH TOWERS, HIGH UP, LOFTY, ON HIGH; [*qômâ*] (Gen. 6:15; Ex. 25:10, 23; 27:1, 18; 30:2; 37:1, 10, 25; 38:1; 1 S. 16:7; 1 K. 6:26; 7:2, 15f., 32; etc.); AV also HIGH, STATURE; NEB also HIGH, TALL, TALLEST; [*rō'š*] (Nu. 14:40, 44); AV TOP; [*rō'š-mᵉrōmîm*] (Prov. 8:2); AV "top of the high places"; NEB "top of the hill"; [*rûm*] (Prov. 25:3); [*rāmâ*] (1 S. 22:6); AV RAMAH; NEB HILL-TOP; [*śî'*] (Job 20:6); AV EXCELLENCY; NEB HIGH; [*šᵉpî*] ("bare height," Nu. 23:3; Isa. 41:18; 49:9; Jer. 3:2, 21; 4:11; 7:29; 12:12; 14:6); AV HIGH PLACES; NEB DUNES, SAND-DUNES, "forthwith," HIGH BARE PLACES; [*tāweḵ*] (Isa. 16:3); AV MIDST; NEB HIGH; [*tô'āpôṯ*] (Ps. 95:4); AV "strength"; NEB FOLDS; [Aram. *rûm*] (Ezr. 6:3; Dnl. 3:1; 4:10; NEB also HIGH; [Gk. *hýpsos*] (Eph. 3:18; Rev. 21:16); AV also DEPTH; [*hýpsōma*] (Rom. 8:39).

A "height" in the OT is primarily a geographical designation, referring to a high place above a level, a HILL, or mountain; it is used literally (e.g., Nu. 21:28; 23:3; 1 S. 22:6; 2 K. 19:23; Isa. 22:16; 37:24; Jer. 49:16; 51:53; Ezk. 36:2) and also figuratively, referring to Jerusalem itself and the site of the temple in Jerusalem (e.g., Jgs. 5:18; Isa. 26:5; Jer. 26:18; 31:12; Ezk. 17:23), to the location of those blessed by Yahweh (2 S. 22:34; Ps. 18:33; Isa. 33:16; 41:18; 49:9), to the seat of wisdom (Prov. 8:2). Jeremiah characterizes the "heights" as a particularly appropriate place to become aware of Yahweh's judgment (Jer. 3:2, 21; 4:11; 7:29; 12:12; 14:6).

"Height" is also a dimension of measure specifying extent or distance upward. It is used to refer to the stature of a man (1 S. 16:7; 17:4; Job 20:6; Am. 2:9) or of trees (Isa. 10:33; Ezk. 19:11; 31:3, 10, 14; Dnl. 4:10; Am. 2:9). It also refers to the measure of various constructed items: altars (Ex. 27:1; 30:2; 37:25; 38:1; Ezk. 43:13), walls (2 Ch. 33:14; Neh. 4:6; Ezk. 40:5), a vestibule (2 Ch. 3:4), Noah's ark (Gen. 6:15), the ark of the covenant (Ex. 25:10; 37:1), a table (Ex. 25:23; 37:10), a court (Ex. 27:18), a cherub (1 K. 6:26), the House of the Forest of Lebanon (1 K. 7:2), pillars (1 K. 7:15; 2 K. 25:17; Jer. 52:21), capitals (1 K. 7:16; 2 K. 25:17; Jer. 52:22), a wheel (1 K. 7:32), the house of God in Jerusalem (Ezr. 6:3), and an idol (Dnl. 3:1). Midday, when the sun reaches its highest point, is called the "height" of noon (Isa. 16:3). The height of the new Jerusalem will equal its length and its breadth (Rev. 21:16).

Height is listed with depth as being unable to separate the Christian from God's love (Rom. 8:39), for this love is all-encompassing (Eph. 3:18). J. R. PRICE

HEIR [Heb. *yôrēš* (Gen. 15:3f.; 21:10; 2 S. 14:7; Jer. 49:1), *ben-mešeq* (Gen. 15:2), *mānôn* (Prov. 29:21); Gk. *klēronómos* (Mt. 21:28; Mk. 12:7; Lk. 20:14; Rom. 4:14; 8:17; Gal. 3:29; 4:1, 7; Tit. 3:7; He. 1:2; 6:17; 11:7; Jas. 2:5), *synklēronómos*–'inheriting together with,' 'fellow heir' (Rom. 8:17; Eph. 3:6; He. 11:9; 1 Pet. 3:7)]; AV also STEWARD (Gen. 15:2), SON (Prov. 29:21); NEB also INHERITANCE (Gen. 21:10), SUCCESSION (2 S. 14:7), "ungrateful" (Prov. 29:21), "claim" (He. 11:7). Cognates of the Hebrew verb *yāraš*, "inherit," are Ugar. *yrṯ*, Old Aram. *yrt*, Syr. *yiret*, Moabite *yrš*, Late Bab. *yāritu*, "heir." An heir is a person who is legally entitled to inherit the parental or another's estate, which can be either material or spiritual.

I. In the OT
  A. Legal Aspects
    1. Sons
      a. Adopted Sons

b. Natural Sons
2. Daughters
3. Widows
B. Religious Aspects
II. In the NT
A. Christ as Heir
B. Christians as Heirs

I. In the OT.–This topic is closely related to the broader concept of INHERITANCE. The biblical concept of inheritance goes beyond the legal and religious aspects associated with the term "heir." Only the respective notions directly related to the concept "heir" are here treated.

A. Legal Aspects. The OT injunctions securing the right of possession by inheritance, namely, to inherit property or staple goods in any form and to gain their permanent title, are few. The reason for this seems to lie in a deeply religious view of property and inheritance. Property was usually not divided up among many heirs, and in accordance with the law of the Jubilee Year all alienated property was to return to the original owner (Lev. 25:8-34). Nevertheless, a number of OT texts address themselves to the question of who has the legal right to be heir.

1. Sons. The normal procedure according to the various OT injunctions is that sons were the heirs to the parental estate.

a. Adopted Sons. The earliest appearance of the term "heir" (Heb. *yôrēš*) is found in a narrative reflecting early patriarchal customs (Gen. 15:2-4). The noun here reflects the original meaning of the Hebrew verb *yāraš* from which it derives, namely, the legal notion associated with inheritance. The religious aspect seems to be a later development. Abraham's dialogue with God shows his concern that in spite of the promise (Gen. 12:1-4) he is still without physical offspring. Abraham has made arrangements for Eliezer of Damascus to be "the heir of my house" (Gen. 15:2). Since Abraham has no descendants his estate will pass to a chosen member of his household. The NUZI Texts throw much light on Hurrian family law, which was also normative for the patriarchs. These cuneiform texts are invaluable for explaining the legal aspects of this passage. Numerous Nuzi documents show the well-established custom for childless persons to adopt an heir, called *ewuru* (*CAD,* IV, 415) in distinction to the direct heir, *aplu* (*CAD,* A/II, 173-77), who was a physical descendant. The *ewuru,* or indirect heir, whom the law recognized when normal inheritors were lacking, owed his adoptive parents filial respect, maintained the estate, took care of the parents' physical needs, and performed the funeral rites at their death. In return, the adopted son became the legally recognized heir to the estate. If a natural son *(aplu)* was born after the adoption, the rights and obligations of both parties were clearly set forth. In such eventualities the natural son or direct heir *(aplu)* shall receive a "double portion" (*ANET,* p. 220). Abraham's slave Eliezer appears to have become his *ewuru* or adopted heir, whereas later, Isaac, the *aplu* or direct heir, was born.

b. Natural Sons. The legal rights of inheritance could be rather complicated in patriarchal society. Sarah followed the social custom of her society reflected in the Nuzi Texts, which specified that an upper-class wife who had borne her husband no sons would provide him with a slave girl. Thus Sarah gave the Egyptian maid Hagar to Abraham in order to "obtain children by her" (Gen. 16:2). After Hagar had borne Ishmael, Sarah was blessed with a son, Isaac. Resentful of Hagar and her son (cf. Gen. 16:4f.), Sarah tells Abraham: "Cast out this slave woman with her son; for the son of this slave woman shall not be heir with my son Isaac" (Gen. 21:10). But earlier Sarah had made the promise that the Egyptian maidservant Hagar's children should be recognized as her own (Gen. 16:2). According to the Nuzi Texts Ishmael had a right to inheritance, and Abraham was displeased at sending him away (Gen. 21:11). The Nuzi marriage contracts stipulate that the offspring of a slave woman must not be sent away (*ANET,* p. 200). Sarah's counsel to send away Ishmael does not appear to have been completely ruled out according to the presently known Nuzi contracts, because birthright was not so much a matter of physical birth as of parental decree. The clause that the wife should not drive out or send away the slave woman's offspring does not necessarily limit the right to do so, but may prevent a possible misuse. The Code of Hammurabi stipulates that if a female slave bears children to her owner and he acknowledges them as his own during his lifetime, then they "shall share equally in the goods of the paternal estate, with the first-born, the son of the first wife, receiving a preferential share" (§ 170; *ANET,* p. 173), but if they are not acknowledged, they receive no inheritance and are set free (§ 171; *ANET,* p. 173). The sons of the slave women Bilhah and Zilpah were given equal rank with those of Rachel and Leah (Gen. 49:1-28), having an equal share with them in the land of Canaan. The reason is that they had been adopted by Rachel or by Leah (Gen. 30:3-13), and named by them.

Only a few legal texts in the OT refer to the rights of the heir (Dt. 21:15-17; Nu. 27:1-11; 38:6-9). The basic rule is that only sons are considered heirs. Among the sons, the oldest or first-born had the privileged position and received a "double portion" (Dt. 21:17); by implication the other sons shared the remaining property equally. The provision that the oldest would receive a double share of his father's estate is also attested in the Code of Hammurabi (§§ 168-170; *ANET,* p. 173), the Middle Assyrian Law (*ANET,* p. 185), the Nuzi Texts (*ANET,* p. 220), and at Mari. The Lipit-Ishtar Code (*ca.* 1934-1924 B.C.), to the contrary, provides that all sons, whether of the first wife or the second wife, "shall divide equally the property of their father" (§ 24; *ANET,* p. 160). The "double portion" in Dt. 21:17 means that if a man had five sons the inheritance would be divided into six portions, the eldest son receiving two (cf. Gen. 48:22; 2 K. 2:9).

2. Daughters. In cases where there were no male heirs, daughters would inherit the estate (Nu. 27:1-11; 36:1-13), but with the proviso that they were to find husbands from a clan of their father's tribe, and so prevent the family estate from being passed to another tribe (Nu. 36:1-9). Under this law the daughters of Eleazar married their cousins (1 Ch. 23:22).

A notable exception is Job 42:13-15, where the three daughters of Job receive inheritance along with their seven brothers. This reflects an early and not a late custom as is sometimes assumed. In the Law Code of Lipit-Ishtar, a proviso gives legal right for equal shares of the estate among all children, including daughters (§§ 22, 24; *ANET,* p. 160).

3. Widows. Normally the wife of the deceased husband had no legal right to inherit the estate of her husband. If a man died without offspring, the estate passed to his male kinsmen on his father's side in the following order: his brothers, his father's brothers, the nearest family kinsman (Nu. 27:9-11). In contrast to this, the Babylonian Code of Hammurabi provides that the widow would receive her dowry and an equal share of the inheritance (§ 172; *ANET,* p. 173) and the gifts she received from her late husband (§§ 171f.). The laws at Nuzi also assure an inheritance to the widow, as do the Middle Assyrian Laws (*ANET,* pp. 182, 184) and the Neo-Babylonian Laws (*ANET,* p. 197). The contracts of the Elephantine papyri allow a childless widow to inherit from her husband (de Vaux, p. 54). The biblical evidence indicates that a childless widow could return to her father's house (Gen. 38:11; Lev. 22:13; Ruth 1:8) or could become a member of her husband's family by levirate marriage (Dt. 25:5-10). Thus, the widow was not entirely unprotected by law and custom. One of the reasons for levirate marriage was the concern to prevent the alienation of family property. To preserve both name and inheritance for the family and to provide for the widow, remarriage of the widow was required (cf. Mt. 22:24-26). If a widow had grown-up children, they would provide for her as the heirs; but if they were still young, she may have managed the estate left to them as a trustee. This seems to be the situation in 2 K. 8:3-6, where the Shunammite woman receives the estate of her late husband that had become the property of the king while she was in a foreign land.

B. Religious Aspects. It has been noted above that the earliest appearance of the noun "heir" is in connection with Yahweh's covenant with Abraham in Gen. 15, where the Lord ratified His promise even though Abraham was still without a physical heir. The promise that Abraham's own son shall be his heir (v. 4) climaxes in the covenant promise that Abraham's descendants shall be heirs of Canaan, the Promised Land (vv. 18-21). The heirs of Abraham will inherit both the promise and the land of inheritance (Gen. 26:3; 35:12; Ex. 6:8; etc.). In contrast to Israel's neighbors, the land of inheritance is not Yahweh's proper domain that He passes on to the heir Israel as an inheritance, for the whole earth belongs to Him (Ex. 19:5; Dt. 10:14). Yahweh is not the God of a local domain. Canaan, as the land of inheritance, is a gift of God (Dt. 4:1; 6:18; 8:1; 11:9). Yahweh "gives" the land to them to "possess" it (Gen. 15:7; Dt. 3:18; 5:28; 9:6; 12:1; 19:2, 14; 21:1; Josh. 1:11). If the Promised Land is Yahweh's gift, it is His inheritance for Israel, because He has given it to His people and has chosen to make His abode there (Ex. 15:17). The Israelites, as heirs to the promises of their patriarchal fathers, receive Canaan from their Lord, because the land is the Lord's (Lev. 25:23). Thus, the OT sees the descendants of Abraham as heirs of the promise and the land as the inheritance of Yahweh given to Israel for its inheritance.

II. In the NT.–The NT concept of "heir" is deeply rooted in the religious and theological aspects of the OT concept.

A. Christ as Heir. In a limited number of NT passages, Jesus is designated as "heir" (Gk. *klēronómos*). The root of this identification must be sought in the teaching of Jesus. In the Synoptic Gospels the term "heir" appears only in the parable of the wicked husbandmen (Mt. 21:38; Mk. 12:7; Lk. 20:14). It is widely recognized that this parable reflects the Isaianic Song of the Vineyard (Isa. 5:1-7), which stresses God's ownership of the vineyard. In the parable, the son (Jesus) of the owner (God) of the vineyard (Israel) "is the heir" (Mt. 21:38). The owner's son possesses (by birth) the legal rights of inheritance of his father's estate. "A firm link is established between sonship and inheritance such as we hardly ever find in the OT and later Judaism, and it runs through the whole of the NT" (*TDNT,* III, 781f.). The emphasis on the link between sonship and inheritance is absent from the version of this parable in Logion 65 of the gnostic Gospel of Thomas: "Those husbandmen, since they knew that he was the heir of the vineyard, they seized him (and) killed him" (H-S, I, 518). No mention is here made of sonship. The OT emphasizes, however, that sonship provided the right of inheritance. This is also the common view of both Greek and Roman law.

It should be noted that the husbandmen plotted to kill the son. They assumed that the father as holder of the title of inheritance was dead and thus they stupidly supposed that by murdering the son they would obtain the inheritance. The center of interest is the murder of the heir — the hearers were to recognize what the Jewish leaders (husbandmen) were plotting. In veiled manner Jesus spoke here of His death. Jesus made the point that the sonship that assures inheritance involves more than just birth. It is gained in its fulness only by doing the will of the Father (Jn. 5:30; 6:38-40; 7:17; Mt. 7:21; Mk. 3:35), which for Jesus meant death on the cross (Mt. 26:42; Lk. 22:42). Through death and resurrection Jesus Christ gained authority and thus inheritance (Mt. 28:18). The inheritance that Jesus gained is not the vineyard in its limited sense of literal Israel but "the kingdom of God" (Mk. 12:7; Mt. 21:43; 25:34; cf. 1 Cor. 6:9; 15:50; Jas. 2:5). By linking "son" and "heir" to "kingdom of God" Jesus breaks through the barriers of a limited and narrow conception of heirship and stresses also certain eschatological aspects of heirship.

The identity of Jesus with the "heir" rests on Jesus' own teaching and is found only in one other NT passage. The author of Hebrews shows his intensely christological emphasis in linking the "appointed heir of all things" to Him "through whom also he created the world" (He. 1:2). The Creator is here the one who is the divinely appointed heir.

B. Christians as Heirs. Since Christ is "heir" on the basis of His sonship, those who are followers of Jesus Christ are His brothers (He. 2:11, 17), and thus sons through Christ. "For in Christ you are all sons of God" (Gal. 3:26). The believer is a son of God not in his own right, but by being a follower of Christ. In Rom. 8:14-17 Paul applies the phrase "sons of God" to those who are led by the Spirit of God and who have thus received sonship. And if sons of God, "then [they are also] heirs, heirs of God and fellow heirs with Christ" (v. 17). Three ideas are brought together here by Paul: sonship, heirs, and fellow heirs. The sonship of the believer is not established by natural birth or physical descent; it comes through the redemption of Jesus Christ through which "we might receive adoption [*huiothesía*] as sons" (Gal. 4:5). God gives by His Spirit a "spirit of sonship" (Gk. *huiothesía,* Rom. 8:15, NAB "spirit of adoption"; NEB "a Spirit that makes us sons"), i.e., He has made "adoption" *(huiothesía)* possible through His Son, because "flesh and blood cannot inherit the kingdom of God" (1 Cor. 15:50). A unique NT emphasis is that sonship and adoption into sonship are possible only through the means God has established in Jesus Christ. Through the Son the believer becomes God's son, and "if a son then an heir" (Gal. 4:7; cf. 4:1). To be sons of God and thus "heirs according to the promise" (3:29) means to have been set free by God from the condition of slavery to the elemental spirits of the universe (4:3, 7).

The change from the condition of slavery to that of sonship which establishes heirship comes about by nothing less than a new creation that is to be found only "in Christ" (2 Cor. 5:17; 4:6; Gal. 6:15). Paul speaks of sonship that establishes inheritance as a gift of grace (Rom. 4:13-25) in terms of a present reality for the believer. On the other hand, he can also regard adoption into sonship with the heir's inheritance as a future experience of an eschatological nature (Rom. 8:23f.). This tension in Pauline theology reflects that adoption into divine sonship is a process: the first phase is the joining of the believers into the death of Christ at baptism (Gal. 3:23–4:7), and the final phase is experienced at the eschatological "redemption of our bodies" (Rom. 8:23). This is not unrelated to the believer's inheritance of the kingdom of God in the present and his expectation of experiencing the full manifestation of God's kingdom in power and glory in the future, when he will as Christ's fellow heir (Rom. 8:17; 1 Pet. 3:7) enter the Holy City (He. 11:10, 16), the new Jerusalem (Rev. 21:2). It is then that the heir will receive the reward (Col. 3:24).

The letter to the Hebrews moves from Christ as heir (1:2) to those who have become "heirs of the promise" (6:17). The context of the latter phrase indicates that God guaranteed the "heirs of the promise" by two unchangeable things that they shall receive the inheritance, namely, by His promise (v. 15; cf. Gen. 12:1-4; 15:1-5; etc.) and by His oath (v. 17; cf. Gen. 22:16-18). The author of this letter assures these heirs or Christians that they are the ones who are inheriting the promises through faith and patience (v. 12) and that they can therefore be fully assured of that for which they hope until the end (v. 11).

The proof that this hope of the heirs is not in vain rests not only in God's promise and oath but also in the fulfillment of God's promises to Noah, who "became an heir of the righteousness which comes by faith" (11:7). Furthermore, by faith (11:9) and patience (6:12) Abraham obtained his son (6:15) and was to obtain the Promised Land as his inheritance (Gk. *klēronomía,* 11:8f.). Isaac and Jacob were "fellow heirs" (Gk. *synklēronómoi*) with Abraham in the same promise (11:9). But these three heroes of faith "did not obtain what had been promised" (v. 13, NAB), viz., a heavenly country (v. 16) with a "city which has foundations, whose builder and maker is God" (v. 10). This is a clear indication that the inheritance that the "heirs of the promise" still await is the kingdom of God which will come at the Parousia. The letter to the Hebrews contributes to the NT concept of heirship in a twofold way: (a) the person who is an heir is a person of faith, patience, and hope; and (b) God guarantees the eschatological coming of the inheritance through divine promise and divine oath, which are pledges whereby the believer is to seize the hope that is placed before him. Although the believer is heir here and now, his inheritance in the form of the Promised Land is yet to come. It is also clear that the heirship established through the sonship of the believer anticipates in some way the inheritance he will obtain in "the world to come."

Bibliography.–E. Neufeld, *Ancient Hebrew Marriage Laws* (1944), pp. 259-265; *ILC*, I-II, 89-96; *TDNT*, III, *s.v.* κληρονόμος (W. Foerster); J. Dreyfus, *Revue des Sciences Philosophiques et Théologiques,* 42 (1958), 3-49; R. de Vaux, *Ancient Israel* (1961), pp. 53-55, 166; N. H. Snaith, *VT,* 16 (1966), 124-27; J. Weingreen, *VT,* 16 (1966), 518-522; H. Langhammer, *BZ,* 10 (1966), 273-280; J. D. Hester, *Paul's Concept of Inheritance* (1968); N. M. Sarna, *Understanding Genesis* (2nd ed. 1970); *THAT,* I, *s.v.* ירשׁ (Schmid).

G. F. HASEL

HELAH hē'lə [Heb. *ḥel'â*]. A wife of Ashur, father of Tekoa (1 Ch. 4:5,7).

HELAM hē'lam [Heb. *ḥêlām*; Gk. *Hailam*]. A city near the northern boundary of Gilead, near which David defeated the Aramean army under Hadadezer (2 S. 10:16f.). The LXX in Ezk. 47:16 located it between the territories of Damascus and Hamath. It may be identical with the ALEMA of 1 Macc. 5:26, 35 = ʿAlma, NE of Derʿā (Edrei) in Ḥaurân. The name appears as *Ḥlʾm* in the Egyptian Execration Texts (1850-1825 B.C.). B. E. HOVEY

HELBAH hel'bə [Heb. *ḥelbâ*–'fertile']. A town from which the tribe of Asher failed to drive out the Canaanites after settling in the land conquered under Joshua (Jgs. 1:31). It is identified with Maḫalib (Mehelab, AHLAB) of Sennacherib's prism inscription, and is located 6.4 km. (4 mi.) NE of Tyre near the Leontes River, as modern Khirbet el-Maḥâlib. R. J. HUGHES, III

HELBON hel'bon [Heb. *ḥelbôn*]. A region in the vicinity of Damascus famous for its high-quality wines. Ezekiel mentions the "wine of Helbon" among the chief articles of trade between the merchants of Tyre and Damascus (Ezk. 27:18). The site is to be identified with the productive valley of Halbûn, 29 km. (18 mi.) N of Damascus, where Moslem farmers continue to cultivate the terraced vineyards along the slopes of the Anti-Lebanon. From the Belino Cylinder we know that Nebuchadnezzar enjoyed wines from *mât helbûnim,* the land of Helbon. Persian kings also considered the wine of Helbon to be of great value (Strabo *Geog.* xv.3.22). A. H. LEWIS

HELCHIAH hel-kī'ə. *See* HILKIAH **7.**

HELDAI hel'dī [Heb. *ḥelday*].

1. A captain of the temple service, appointed for the twelfth month (1 Ch. 27:15). Same as Heled in the parallel list (1 Ch. 11:30), and is probably also to be identified with Heleb (NEB Heled), son of Baanah the Netophathite, one of David's heroic leaders (2 S. 23:29).

2. One of a company of Jews who brought gifts of gold and silver from Babylon to assist the exiles under Zerubbabel (Zec. 6:10, 14). In v. 14 the AV, following the MT, reads Helem (which the LXX translated by *hypoménō,* "wait for," apparently understanding Helem [Heb. *ḥēlem*] to be from *ḥîl* [as in Jgs. 3:25; Lam. 3:26]).

HELEB hē'ləb [Heb. *ḥēleḇ*] (2 S. 23:29); NEB HELEB. *See* HELDAI **1.**

HELECH hē'lək [Heb. *ḥêlēḵ*] (Ezk. 27:11); AV "thine army"; NEB CILICIA. The NEB is possibly correct. Assyrian records refer to Cilicia as Ḫilakku. The region was home to pirates and bandits from prehistoric times until the Roman empire. Such men would be willing mercenaries for Tyre. The AV takes it to be the common noun *ḥayil,* "army," with a pronominal suffix.

HELED hē'ləd [Heb. *ḥēleḏ*] (1 Ch. 11:30). *See* HELDAI **1.**

HELEK hē'lək [Heb. *ḥēleḵ*]. Son of Gilead the Manassite (Nu. 26:30; Josh. 17:2). Patronymic, "Helekites" (Nu. 26:30).

HELEM hē'ləm.

1. [Heb. *hēlem*; LXX B, Gk. *Balaam,* A, *huiós Elam*–'son of Elam'] (1 Ch. 7:35); NEB HOTHAM. A great grandson of Asher, called Hotham in v. 32.

2. [Heb. *ḥēlem*–'strength']. *See* HELDAI **2.**

HELEPH hē'ləf [Heb. *ḥēlep*; Gk. B *Moolam,* A *Meeleph*]. The first of nineteen cities, with their villages, listed in the territory assigned to the tribe of Naphtali when Canaan was divided among the tribes of Israel after the conquest under Joshua (Josh. 19:33). Its location is uncertain, although Khirbet ʿArbathah, NE of Mt. Tabor, has been suggested (cf. *GTTOT* §§ 333f.).

R. J. HUGHES, III

HELEZ hē'ləz [Heb. *ḥeleṣ*; Gk. *Sellēs, Chellēs*].

1. (2 S. 23:26; 1 Ch. 11:27; 27:10). One of David's mighty men; according to 1 Ch. 27:10, he belonged to the sons of Ephraim and was at the head of the seventh course in

David's organization of the kingdom. He is called a Paltite in 2 Samuel (but cf. LXX A "Peolonite"), but in 1 Chronicles he is called a Pelonite, which is probably correct since 1 Ch. 27:10 calls him an Ephraimite.

2. (LXX *Chellēs,* 1 Ch. 2:39). A man of Judah of the clan of the Jerahmeelites.

HELI hē'lī [Gk. *Hēlei* for Heb. *'ēlî*].

1. The father of Joseph the husband of Mary in Luke's genealogy of Jesus (Lk. 3:23).

2. AV form of ELI (2 Esd. 1:2).

HELIODORUS hē-li-ə-dō'rəs [Gk. *Hēliodōros*]. Treasurer of the Syrian king Seleucus IV Philopator (187-175 B.C.), the immediate predecessor of Antiochus Epiphanes who carried out to its utmost extremity the hellenizing policy begun by Seleucus and the "sons of Tobias." Greatly in need of money to pay the tribute due to the Romans as one of the results of the victory of Scipio over Antiochus the Great at Magnesia (190 B.C.), Seleucus learned from Apollonius, governor of Coelesyria (Palestine) and Phoenicia, of the wealth that was reported to be stored up in the temple at Jerusalem and commissioned Heliodorus (2 Macc. 3) to plunder the temple and to bring its contents to him. The temple seems to have served the purposes of a bank in which the private deposits of widows and orphans were kept for greater security, and 2 Macc. 3:15-21 narrates the panic at Jerusalem that took place when Heliodorus came with an armed guard to seize the contents of the temple. In spite of the protest of Onias the high priest, Heliodorus was proceeding to carry out his commission when "the Sovereign of all spirits and of all authority caused so great a manifestation" that he fell down, and deep darkness overcame him. While he was lying prostrate and speechless, and on the point of death, Onias interceded for him, as a result of which he was restored to health and glorified God for the great works that he had seen. The narrative given in 2 Macc. 3 is not mentioned by any other historian, though 4 Maccabees refers to the plundering of the temple, and assigns the deed to Apollonius.

Heliodorus is also mentioned by Appian (*Syr.* 45) and in an inscription found in the temple of Apollo on the Aegean island of Delos. J. HUTCHISON

HELIOPOLIS hē-li-op'ə-lis [Heb. *bêṯ šemeš*–'house of (the solar deity) Shemesh'; Gk. *hēlíou pólis*–'city of the sun'] (Jer. 43:13); AV, NEB, BETH-SHEMESH. The reference here is to the Egyptian city ON, also called the City of the Sun (Isa. 19:18) and Aven (Ezk. 30:17; *see* AVEN 3). Heliopolis was also the Greek name for the Lebanese city of BAALBEK.

HELKAI hel'kī [Heb. *ḥelqāy,* perhaps an abbreviation for Helkiah–'Yahweh is my portion.' Not in LXX B; LXX L *Chelkias*] (Neh. 12:15). The head of a priestly house in the days of Joiakim the high priest.

HELKATH hel'kath [Heb. *ḥelqaṯ*–'field, portion'] (Josh. 19:25; 21:31); also called **HUKOK** hōō'kək [Heb. *ḥûqōq*; Gk. *Hikak, Hakōk*] (1 Ch. 6:75 [MT 60]). The first city, with its villages, listed in the territory assigned to the tribe of Asher when Canaan was divided among the tribes of Israel after the conquest under Joshua (Josh. 19:25). It was a Levitical city assigned to the Gershonites (Josh. 21:31). Though the exact location is still disputed, it may be represented by the modern Tell el-Harbaj on the northeast slope of Mt. Carmel, about 8 km. (5 mi.) inland from the mouth of the Kishon River. The city may appear as *ḥrqt* in topographical lists of Pharaoh Thutmose III, *ca.* 1460 B.C. (cf. *NBD, s.v.*). R. J. HUGHES, III

HELKATH-HAZZURIM hel'kath haz'zōō-rim [Heb. *helqaṯ haṣṣurîm*–'field of flints' or 'field of sword edges'] (2 S. 2:16). The name of the area near the pool of Gibeon (v. 12) where twelve of Joab's men and twelve of Abner's men fought and killed each other. The meaning of the name is uncertain, as the variety of modern translations indicates: NEB "Field of Blades"; JB "Field of Sides," which requires only a slight change (*haṣṣurîm* to *haṣṣiddîm*) and which Driver prefers for its contextual appropriateness; NIV mg. "field of hostilities," which requires only a repointing of *haṣṣurîm* to *haṣṣārîm*. The LXX *Meris tōn epiboúlōn* offers yet another alternative, "field of the plotters [or 'liers in wait']," which also reflects only a slight change from MT *haṣṣurîm* to *haṣṣāḏîm* or *haṣṣōḏîm*. Curiously, although *BH* suggests all of these emendations, *BHS* has no notes at all on the verse.

See S. R. Driver, *Notes on the Hebrew Text and the Topography of the Books of Samuel* (2nd ed. 1913), pp. 242f. G. A. L.

HELL [Gk. *géenna*, *tartaróō*–'hold captive in Tartarus']. On Gk. *géenna, see* GEHENNA. In the NT Gk. *tartaróō* occurs only in 2 Pet. 2:4, where the angels who sinned were "cast . . . into hell" (cf. RSV mg. and NAB). The verb *tartaróō* is derived from the noun *Tartaros* (cf. LXX Job 40:20; 41:24 [Eng. 32]; Prov. 30:16), which in Greek mythology was the locale below Hades where the Titans were imprisoned (Homer *Il.* xiv.279; Josephus *CAp* ii.33 [240]). Homer also located it at the "undermost limits of earth and sea" (*Il.* viii.481). His description of it as murky (viii.13) apparently carried over to Sib. Or. 4:186 and perhaps to 2 Pet. 2:4, since Peter described Tartarus as having "pits of nether gloom."

See also DEATH. G. A. L.

HELL, HISTORY OF THE DOCTRINE OF.

I. Early Church.–The issues that have dominated the doctrinal discussion of hell — its nature, purpose, and duration — arose at once in the patristic age. Concerning its nature, many early fathers, including the apologist Justin (*Dial.* 45.4) and the Latin fathers Tertullian (*De res.* 5ff.) and Jerome (cf. *Ep.* 119), assumed a fiery hell. Origen, on the other hand, gave it a spiritualized sense, in which the emphasis fell on remorse and separation from God (*De prin.* ii.10.4). In the 4th cent. Basil of Caesarea (*De Spiritu sancto* 40) and Chrysostom (*Ad Theodorum lapsum* 1.9f.) offered vividly materialistic depictions, but Gregory of Nazianzus (*Oratio* 40[on baptism].36) and Gregory of Nyssa (*Oratio catechetica* 26) followed more in the steps of Origen. Augustine (*Ench.* 112f.) helped to shape Western thought by championing a combination of spiritual and natural (or sensory) penalties in keeping with his attempt to avoid the dualism that had tempted him in his Manichaean period.

For most of the fathers hell clearly served the purpose of retribution for demons and impenitent sinners. Origen (*In Ezech. Hom.* 1, 2), however, introduced the possibility of a remedial hell that might form a final stage of reclamation even for demons. This view found some support in eastern fathers such as Gregory of Nyssa (*Oratio catechetica* 26), who had plain inclinations toward universalism, but the official decision of the Church went against it at the 543 Council of Constantinople.

Hell could obviously be of limited duration if it served an educative or rehabilitatory goal. Where it was regarded

Devils taking away the damned: from left, a fashionable lady, a nun, and a miser. Right archivolt of the central south panel, Cathedral of Notre-Dame, Chartres (A.D. 1194-1260) (Rosenthal Art Slides)

as retributive it was also stated to be unending, although a few fathers thought that impenitent unbelievers were ultimately annihilated. A minor difference of opinion arose over the time of entry into hell. In the early period some writers, e.g., Justin Martyr (*Apol.* i.28), argued that hell commences only after the last judgment. The general opinion, however, was that hell began for the wicked immediately at death (cf. Jerome *In Joel* 2:1; Augustine *De praedestinatione sanctorum* 24).

II. Middle Ages and Reformation.–The medieval West contributed little that was essentially new to the doctrine of hell, but it added many interesting details. Aquinas (*Summa Theol.* III supp. qq. 69ff.) followed Augustine (*Civ. Dei* 20.22; 21.9) in postulating pains of sense as well as the supreme pain of spirit involved in deprivation of the vision of God. These torments of sense, being related to the resurrection body, were usually construed in very materialistic terms, the medieval imagination being spurred by Dante's *Inferno* and the common location of hell in the fiery depths of the earth. Degrees of retribution were discerned, but hell, as distinct from nearby purgatory, served only a retributive purpose and commenced immediately at death according to the important statement *Benedictus Deus* in 1336. Hell was eternal. Purgatory carried with it severe penalties, which could often be described no less vividly than those of hell itself, but they served a remedial purpose and were limited in duration.

The consignment of unbaptized infants to hell went hand in hand with an important differentiation. Infants were guilty only of original sin, not actual sin, and the penalty for this came to be understood as the more negative and spiritual one of loss of the beatific vision, sensory torments being related exclusively to actual sin (H. Denzinger, nos. 321, 410). Thus cartographers of the infernal regions divided hell into three separate compartments: the main area for the lost in general, a special "limbo" for unbaptized infants, and another "limbo" in which OT believers had been kept prior to Christ's "harrowing" of hell (from Middle English *harwen,* "harry, rob [hell of the souls of the righteous]") between His death and resurrection. To symbolize their special fate, those who died in infancy unbaptized were buried in an unconsecrated area that lay within the churchyard.

The Reformers accepted the retributive purpose of hell and its eternal duration but had reservations about its nature. Luther, for example, rejected the terrifying portrayals by artists ("I think nothing of the picture of the artists," *WA,* xviii, 225f.), refused to speculate about the condition of the lost (*WA, Tischreden* 4, no. 3962), and, while he regarded hell as a place (*WA,* xix, 225f.), argued that its worst torments are fear, terror, and despair (*WA,* xii, 591). He also contended strongly that God did not want hell (*WA,* lii, 726f.) and that in its own way it will be "full of God and the highest good" (*WA,* vi, 127). Calvin agreed with Luther that corporeal images are figurative representations of hell and found its real dreadfulness in alienation from God's presence and experience of the never-ending effects of His wrath (*Inst.* iii.25.12). All the Reformers also rejected the limbo of infants; they did not see any absolute necessity of baptism for salvation and replaced it by the milder necessity of precept. The doctrine of predestination, however, gave a somber touch to the Reformed development of the doctrine of hell, since it carried the implication that, as God had prepared heaven to give an eternal display of His grace in and to the elect, so He had prepared hell to give an eternal display of His justice in and to the reprobate.

III. Modern Period.–The more detailed discussion of hell in seventeenth-century dogmatics led to the reinstatement of the idea of physical as well as moral or spiritual penalties. Thus L. Riissen, who strongly opposed the idea of annihilation, argued for definite torments as well as the loss of the vision of God (*Francisci Turretini compendium theologiae didactico-elencticae* [Amsterdam, 1695], xviii, 20). He accepted degrees of punishment, but only in intensity, not in duration. J. H. Heidegger stated similarly that hell has a definite location (*Medulla theologiae christianae* [Zurich, 1696], xxvii, 52), and J. Cocceius believed that the pains of hell can be felt, though again to differing degrees (*Summa doctrinae de foedere et testamento Dei* [Amsterdam, 1648], xvi, 644). The Westminster Larger Catechism (q. 29) added "grievous torments in soul and body" to the chief penalty of "everlasting separation from the comfortable presence of God." Whether the fire of hell was itself material, however, was regarded as a debatable matter, e.g., by M. F. Wendelin (*Collatio doctrinae christianae* [Cassel, 1660], p. 510). (For a summary of these views, see Heppe, pp. 710-12.)

Eighteenth-century neology revived the universalistic thinking of Origen by virtually equating hell with purgatory. Impenitent and unbelieving sinners would be subjected to a process of education and purification, but this would not be eternal and would have final redemption as its goal. Schleiermacher (*Christian Faith,* § 163 Appendix) accepted this elimination of hell with his hope for a restoration of all human souls. During the 19th and early 20th cents. liberal Protestantism, while not wishing to minimize the importance or solemnity of personal decision, fairly consistently rejected the idea of eternal retribution, especially in a materialistic sense. Annihilationism also enjoyed a limited revival in some more orthodox circles that wished to maintain the idea of a definitive penalty but had difficulty with the concept of unending punishment; they thus equated hell with the extinction of being. Roman Catholicism and orthodox Protestantism, however, have generally continued to resist both the annihilationists with their dubious exegesis and the universalists with their dogmatic presupposition that God's love demands an ultimate restoration for all. They agree with patristic, medieval, and Reformation theologians that, according to biblical teaching, a final decision against God has an eternal and irreversible consequence. Since concepts of the nature of the resurrection body are less dogmatic now, attempts to portray hell in corporeal terms are usually more restrained. Nevertheless, the biblical unity of body and soul carries with it the undeniable implication that hell in some way affects the whole person

Bibliography.–H. Berkhof, *Christian Faith* (Eng. tr. 1979), pp. 525-533; Calvin *Inst.* iii.25; H. Denzinger, *Sources of Catholic Dogma* (Eng. tr. 1957); H. Heppe, *Reformed Dogmatics* (Eng. tr. 1950); J. N. D. Kelly, *Early Christian Doctrines* (1958), pp. 459-489; P. Schaff, *Creeds of Christendom,* III: *Evangelical Protestant Creeds* (4th rev. ed. 1919). G. W. BROMILEY

HELLENISM. A term that may be used in various senses: it has sometimes been applied to the whole of distinctively Greek culture, including that of the days before Alexander the Great (336-323 B.C.); it is more commonly employed, however, of the civilization that spread through much of the ancient world in the wake of Alexander's conquests. We shall here use it in this latter sense.

I. Introduction
II. Greek Language
III. Cosmopolitanism
IV. Greek Science
V. Literature
VI. Philosophy
VII. Religion

I. Introduction.–Alexander's conquests covered an immense area and brought him sovereignty over many nations. He proposed to solve the problems of ruling so heterogeneous a group of people and bringing coherence into his empire by eschewing a narrow nationalism and imposing a culture that would transcend national boundaries, in which all people could be at home. Basically, this meant that the Greek way of life would be extended to the non-Greeks, but in the process there ensued an amalgam of Greek and non-Greek ideas, so that the resulting Hellenism was far from being purely Greek. Nevertheless, Greek culture dominated the whole, and the result is not unjustly called Hellenism.

Sometimes Greek influence concerned more or less surface matters like the wearing of Greek dress, or athletic contests modeled after the Greek games. Sometimes it penetrated deeply into the realms of religion and philosophy. Hellenism was all-embracing. Alexander encouraged a thorough mixing of the conquerors and the conquered by intermarriage. He himself set the example and many of his officers and men likewise married women from the conquered peoples. Alexander died too soon to be able to accomplish his aim, but the policy of hellenization lived on after him.

We should not understand this as an unwelcome policy ruthlessly enforced from above. Doubtless it was this in some cases, and it was in this way that the Jews, for example, encountered it. Yet even they used the language and accepted some of the ideas, although many of them rejected the religion and the immorality. On the whole, people eagerly welcomed Hellenism. The Greeks had notable scholars, artists, and scientists, and many were impressed by the superiority of the Greek achievement. Thus people everywhere were ready to learn the language and adopt the culture of the conquering Greeks. It became fashionable to adopt the latest Greek fads.

The small city-state of earlier days seems to have been at the basis of the greatest Greek achievements. At their highest and best, Greek art and thought have never been surpassed in the minds of many. Names like Plato and Phidias conjure up thoughts of an excellence of which any civilization might well be proud. The little city-states of ancient Greece produced a notable group of outstanding men. Curiously, this did not persist when Greece became one nation and developed into a mighty empire. But although the city-state produced the men and the ideas, it was by means of the empire that the ideas were effectively spread abroad among the greatest number of people. Many factors were involved, but we shall concentrate only on the following.

II. Greek Language.–This was a potent force in the whole process. It became fnown in most places, with the result that it became a kind of lingua franca. It was a great convenience for the first Christian missionaries that when they went abroad with the gospel they did not have to learn another language. All over the known world people were brought into contact with one another by the medium of the Greek tongue; a further advantage was that with Greek they had access to the treasures of Greek literature.

III. Cosmopolitanism.–To a questioner who asked to what country he belonged, Socrates is said to have replied, "I am a citizen of the world"; and Diogenes gave his adherence to the same concept when he called himself *kosmopolítēs,* "world-citizen." In the days of the city-state, people had tended to confine themselves largely to local affairs; but with the stirring of the pulses brought about by Alexander's conquests and the consequent contact with new lands and peoples, people began to look down on narrow nationalism and to cultivate an outlook on life that deserved the name "cosmopolitan." This did not mean that on occasion there might not be a concentration on purely local issues, but it did mean that merely local concerns were never allowed to dominate.

This caused trouble for "provincials" like the Jews and later the Christians. When people of every nation other than the Jewish found it quite possible to subject local customs and ideas to cosmopolitan ones, it was a mystery to cultured people why the Jews could not. Specifically, the Jewish and Christian refusal to conform to custom by accepting a mild form of idolatry did not make sense to the Hellenists, who did not take the gods very seriously and could not see why these provincials did. When we read of Jews or Christians who came into conflict with those who embodied the Hellenistic spirit we should not understand this as a purely local clash. Nor, at least as far as the Hellenists were concerned, was it a purely religious issue. For them it represented a conflict between a small group with a provincial outlook and many others who had a worldwide outlook. The cosmopolitans never could understand the obstinacy with which the provincials clung to their narrow outlook.

IV. Greek Science.–The Greek spirit of free inquiry found outlet in many directions, and the scientific contributions of the age were impressive. In astronomy, the Ptolemaic geocentric picture of the universe is noteworthy. In the pre-Ptolemaic period many Greeks had quite different ideas, some thinking of the earth as a sphere moving around the sun. R. H. Pfeiffer draws attention to the work of Aristarchus of Samos, who gauged the sun's volume to be three hundred times that of the earth. He concluded from this and other considerations that the earth rotates on its axis and moves around the sun (*HNTT,* p. 112). With the acceptance of the Ptolemaic system, people came to think of the earth as central to the universe and of the sun, moon, and planets as moving around it. Another notable scientific feat was that of Eratosthenes of Cyrene, who calculated the circumference of the earth at 252,000 stadia. This has been worked out as 39,681 km. (24,662 mi.), not so very far from modern measurements. The mathematical studies of Euclid and the discoveries of Archimedes in the physical sciences are so well known they hardly need mentioning. It was a period when people were discovering a great variety of things about their environment.

V. Literature.–People were not interested only in scientific endeavor, for the humanities thrived as well and literature was popular. Poets like Callimachus of Cyrene and Theocritus of Syracuse flourished, and some poets wrote on more or less scientific themes. Menander wrote widely acclaimed comedies.

Special mention should be made of the historians. Hellenistic historians did not understand their task in quite the same way as does the modern scientific historian, being more concerned with the dramatic and the sensational. The abbreviator of Jason of Cyrene, who produced 2 Maccabees, tells us in well-known words: "We have aimed to please those who wish to read, to make it easy for those who are inclined to memorize, and to profit all readers" (2 Macc. 2:25). This was the kind of thing at which many historians aimed, and the results were varied. Some were too concerned with the pleasant and let the claims of literary form override respect for the facts; others were too didactic. But the best of them produced valuable histories, e.g., Polybius, who is normally regarded as first-rate. Josephus is another whose history is both well known and valuable. We owe a good deal to the historiographers of the Hellenistic period, even if we must be on our guard against attaching too much weight to the propagandizing and the striving for dramatic effect that characterizes some of them.

VI. Philosophy.–Philosophy was, of course, a prime interest of cultured Greeks. The great traditions of Plato and Aristotle were continued, although perhaps the best-known school was that of the Stoics. Many were attracted by its solutions of metaphysical problems and by its offer of peace of mind. Others were followers of Epicurus, though one should bear in mind that in modern times his teaching has often been misrepresented. He taught that pleasure is the aim of life, but he did not conceive of pleasure in merely sensual terms, since he held that it is virtue that enables one to enjoy true pleasure. Other schools also flourished and philosophical views varied greatly, including some that were highly skeptical. It is clear that the Greeks of this age took great delight in wrestling with profound problems and in examining critically the solutions others put forward.

They were not, however, concerned with only purely theoretical issues. Many of them were profoundly interested in ethics and made every effort to promote virtue. One reason why some philosophers were not interested in religion was that the religions they knew did little to promote morality. It is true that the philosophers found it difficult to achieve the ethical standards they advocated, but at least they were concerned with getting people to lead good lives.

They taught people not to be dominated by their passions. Detachment was a necessary characteristic of the wise person, and it enabled him to rise above the promptings of his own lower nature. Many saw mankind as nothing but the plaything of a blind fate. But the philosopher did not allow himself to yield to despair, aspiring, rather, to a freedom of spirit that would enable him to rise above the circumstances of life.

VII. Religion.–The Hellenistic world had many religions, though some of the variety was mitigated by the tendency to regard a god worshiped in one place under one name as identical with another god worshiped elsewhere under another name. Thus the Greek Zeus was identified with the Roman Jupiter. Hellenistic religion is of perennial interest to the Christian, for some maintain that certain features of Christianity are derived from the Hellenistic religious environment. Traditional Greek religion, centering on the gods of Olympus, had little influence at this time, for the development of Greek thought had deprived the earlier myths of their credibility. This does not mean that nobody took the Olympian deities seriously; some people undoubtedly did, although for most people there was no dynamic, no conviction in the official cultus.

It was otherwise with the mystery religions. Some, like the Eleusinian mysteries, were Greek and ancient. But more typically, they were comparatively recent arrivals from the East that flourished when transplanted to the West. Not a great deal is known about the details of these cults, for the devotees vowed to keep secret what went on and the vows must have been quite well kept. It is known, however, that the members were put through a horrifying initiation, which led to an experience of peace. The adherents were given the promise of immortality. These cults had an enthusiasm and a vitality that was lacking in the official Olympian religion. Thus they made a wide appeal and were a witness to the unsatisfied longings of the human heart.

The Eleusinian mysteries go back to great antiquity and, while not strictly Hellenistic, are typical of much Hellenistic religion. They center on the spring rites with the thought of the deity dying and rising again. The ritual was accompanied by the myth that told of Persephone, the daughter of Demeter, being carried off to the underworld by Hades, and of how eventually she was released for more than half of each year. Some of the other mysteries seem to have been of essentially the same type, such as those of Dionysus, Adonis, and Osiris, though each had its own variations. Thus the Dionysian rites were characterized by a wild ecstasy. Female devotees (the maenads) would be caught up in a supposedly divine frenzy in which they tore apart living animals and ate their bloody flesh.

Orphism was another religion with an air of wildness about it, though we should also notice that it had some interesting ideas about both heaven and hell. Probably the only other such religion we should notice is Mithraism. The worship of Mithras was of great antiquity in the East, but it did not become important in the Roman world until the 2nd cent. A.D. Mithras underwent many transformations during his long history, but at the time of his popularity in the West he appears to have been a sun god especially beloved by soldiers. It was the Roman legions who carried his worship everywhere. Associated with it was the *taurobolium,* a rite in which the initiate was placed in a pit covered with boards on which a bull was slain in such a manner that the blood flowed through and drenched the worshiper below. He believed that he thereby was filled with the strength and other qualities of the beast. Mithraism spread widely during the early centuries of our era and some scholars have seen it as a serious threat to Christianity. But it faded away before the reality and the vitality of the Christian faith.

Various Hellenistic religions contain parallels to Christian rites and teachings, which some of the Apostolic Fathers explained as parodies inspired by the devil. There is no reason for holding, as do some, that the Christians borrowed from the Hellenistic cults. While there is no reason why Christianity should not have taken over what was good from any source, the facts seem to show that Christianity was not inspired by the mysteries. It arose, rather, from the revelation made in the OT followed by the coming of the Son of God. Christianity brought people a real salvation, one accomplished by the Son of God Himself. The Hellenistic religions witness to the deep longings and needs of the human soul, but they cannot satisfy them. God in Christ does.

See also GREECE; RELIGIONS OF THE BIBLICAL WORLD: GRECO-ROMAN.

Bibliography.–E. Bevan, *Hellenism and Christianity* (1921); R. Bultmann, *Primitive Christianity in Its Contemporary Setting* (1956); J. Daniélou, *Gospel Message and Hellenistic Culture* (Eng. tr. 1973); F. C. Grant, *Roman Hellenism and the New Testament* (1962); E. Hatch, *Influence of Greek Ideas on Christianity* (1957); *HNTT,* pp. 93-165; M. Hengel, *Judaism and Hellenism* (Eng. tr. 1974); A. D. Nock, *Early Gentile Christianity and Its Hellenistic Background* (1964).

L. MORRIS

HELLENIST [Gk. *Hellēnistēs*]; AV GRECIANS; NEB "those of them who spoke Greek," "Greek-speaking Jews," "Gentiles." The word seems to derive not directly from *Hellēn,* but mediately through *hellēnízō,* by the addition of the termination *-tēs,* which denotes the doer of the action. Thus the word ought to point to one who practices or causes others to practice Greek ways (the causative force is often but not always present in such formations). There were many in the 1st cent. A.D. who tried to introduce Greek culture, so it is not difficult to see how the word might have come into use.

Unfortunately, however, we have no evidence that this conclusion from semantics accurately represents the historical facts. The situation is far from clear. The word "Hellenist" apparently was not used before its occurrence in Acts, where it is found three times (6:1; 9:29; 11:20; there is a textual problem in this last passage, where many MSS, and the RSV, read *Hellēnas,* "Greeks," instead of *Hellēnistas*; but most critics accept *Hellēnistas*). Since there are no previous examples we cannot appeal to a well-established sense. And when the word does begin to be used, its meaning seems indistinguishable from that of *Hellēn.* At a later time, then, the word meant "Greek," not "follower of Greek ways" or the like.

The big problem is the meaning of the term in Acts 6:1: "Now in these days when the disciples were increasing in number, the Hellenists murmured against the Hebrews because their widows were neglected in the daily distribution." Traditionally it has been held that the reference here is to Jews who were Greek-speaking, whereas "the Hebrews" were Jews who did not speak Greek. But in recent times it has often been pointed out that "Greek-speaking Jews" is a difficult way of taking "Hellenists," and one that is not elsewhere attested. It is also pointed out that "Hebrews" normally refers to Jews by race, not to people who spoke Hebrew. The inference is that "Hellenist" will have a corresponding meaning.

We should consider a number of possibilities.

(1) The traditional view may be supported in that up to this point Luke has said nothing about Gentiles being converted. The whole Church appears to be Jewish. If this is so, the natural way of distinguishing between "Hellenists" and "Hebrews" would be on the basis of Greek influence. The Hellenists would be those who spoke Greek and possibly had also imbibed something of the Greek outlook on life.

As evidence of this, when the difficulty arose, a committee of seven was set up, all of whom bear Greek names. One of them is called "a proselyte of Antioch" (Acts 6:5). Another, namely Stephen, had disputes in "the synagogue of the Freedmen" (Acts 6:9). This shows that they were Jews, and it seems natural to see in this synagogue one frequented by Greek-speaking Jews with both Stephen and his opponents belonging to the group.

(2) H. J. Cadbury argues powerfully for the view that "Hellenists" here must be taken to mean "Greeks." "Hebrews" is used outside this passage mostly in the sense "Jews" and we expect a corresponding meaning with "Hellenists." As we have already noted, when the word "Hellenist" appears in later writers it usually seems to mean much the same as "Greek." Cadbury meets the argument that Luke has thus far spoken only of Jews as members of the Christian movement by contending that he is not describing a straight line of development of Christianity from Jewish to Greek. Rather, Luke is showing that the acceptance of the gospel by Gentiles was a recurring phenomenon. Cadbury sees this as at least not contradicted by Acts 9:29 where the context does not demand conclusively any particular meaning. But to take the word in the sense "Gentiles" would give a suitable meaning, as it would show a prompt fulfillment of the prophecy that Paul would have a ministry to the Gentiles. In Acts 11:19f. Cadbury thinks the textual problem should be resolved in favor of *Hellēnistas* (*Hellēnas* has weaker attestation; transcriptional probability is also against it, for scribes would be more likely to alter the unusual word to the more usual one). He thinks the context shows that Jews cannot be meant, not even Greek-speaking Jews. The meaning "Gentiles" is demanded.

(3) Some have felt that the Hellenists were Jewish proselytes who had now become Christians. In favor of this is the fact that up to this point Acts has given no indication that Gentiles had joined the Christian Church; moreover, as already noted, at least one of the Seven was a proselyte. A division between proselytes and those who were

native-born Jews is held to be not unlikely. On the other hand, nowhere else do proselytes appear to be designated in this way.

(4) We know that there were groups in the early Church not unfairly called parties (e.g., in 1 Cor. 1). Some have thought that here we have evidence for the existence of a short-lived party, perhaps one which did not follow the Jewish way of life. This may be so, but the evidence cannot be said to be strong. "Hellenist" would be a natural correlative of "Judaist" or "Judaizer," but that seems as far as we can go. Of the same essential type is the view that the "Hellenists" were Christians of gentile origin in distinction from "Hebrews" who were Jews by race. Marcel Simon sees in them Jews who accepted Greek ways, or were thought to do so.

(5) F. F. Bruce favors the idea that the word is not used in any technical way but means simply "Greek-speakers" (*Acts of the Apostles* [2nd ed. 1952], p. 151). He thinks that the context will determine precisely what kind of Greek-speakers is in mind on each occasion. In Acts 6:1 it will probably mean Greek-speaking Jewish Christians, in Acts 9:29 Greek-speaking Jews in the synagogues, and in Acts 11:20 Gentiles. This might be supported by the fact that the verb *hellēnízō* normally seems to have been used in the sense "speak Greek" (cf. LSJ, *s.v.* Ἑλλην-). The natural meaning of the derived noun would accordingly be "Greek-speaker." Again, the word *Hellēnisti* refers to language and means "in Greek." It is formed independently of *Hellēnistēs*, but, as Cadbury points out, popular etymology might connect them.

From all this it is evident that the meaning of the term is far from clear. No one neat solution accounts for all the facts and excludes other views. On the whole it seems that the last-mentioned solution is most likely to be correct. The derivation of the word does make it look like "Greek-speaker." And this fits all the passages in Acts, especially when we bear in mind that rather diverse groups of people might well speak this language. It is a point in favor of this view that it does not demand that on every occasion the "Greek-speakers" be of the same national group. It is a weakness of the other views that they suit one context better than the rest.

See also GREEKS; HELLENISM.

Bibliography.–H. J. Cadbury, in *BC*, V, 59-74; M. Simon, *St. Stephen and the Hellenists in the Primitive Church* (1958); *TDNT*, II, *s.v.* Ἕλλην (Windisch).

L. MORRIS

HELM. *See* RUDDER.

HELMET. *See* WEAPONS OF WAR.

HELON hē'lon [Heb. *ḥēlōn*–'power'; LXX B *Chailōn*]. The father of Eliab, the prince of the tribe of Zebulun (Nu. 1:9; 2:7; 7:24, 29; 10:16).

HELP [Heb. nouns *yᵉšûʿâ* (Ps. 3:2 [MT 3]), *ʿēzer, ʿezrâ, ʿezrāṯ* (Ps. 60:11 [MT 12]; 108:12 [MT 13], *ṣᵉḏāqâ* ("righteous help," Ps. 71:24), *tᵉšûʿâ* (1 Ch. 19:12); Gk. nouns *boḗtheia* (He. 4:16), *epikouría* (Acts 26:22), *epichorēgía* (Phil. 1:19)]; [Heb. vbs. *ḥāzaq* (2 Ch. 29:34), *yāšaʿ* (2 S. 10:11), *nāśā'* (Est. 9:3), *ʿāzaḇ* (Ex. 23:5), *ʿāzar* (Gen. 49:25), *pāqaḏ* (Ps. 106:4), *qārā'* (Ps. 59:4 [MT 5]); Gk. vbs. *antéchō* (1 Th. 5:14), *antilambánomai* (Lk. 1:54), *boēthéō* (Mt. 15:25), *syllambánō* (Lk. 5:7), *symbállomai* (Acts 18:27), *synantilambánomai* (Lk. 10:40; Rom. 8:26), *synypourgéō* (2 Cor. 1:11)]; **HELPED** [Heb. *yāšaʿ* (Ex. 2:17); Gk. *syllambánō* (Acts 18:27)]; **HELPFUL** [Gk. *symphérō* (1 Cor. 6:12)]; **HELPING** [Heb. *sāʿaḏ*; Aram. *sᵉʿaḏ* (Ezr. 5:2), *yᵉšûʿâ* (Ps. 22:1 [MT 2])]; **HELPLESS** [Heb. *pûn* (Ps. 88:15 [MT 16]), *rāpâ* (Jer. 6:24); Gk. *asthenēs* (Rom. 5:6), *rhíptō* (Mt. 9:36)]; AV also SUCCOUR, VISIT WITH SALVATION, SAVE, SUPPORT, etc.; NEB also SUPPORT, AID, DELIVER, PROTECTOR, DEFENDER, FRIEND, etc.

Hebrew *ʿāzar* can be used with a human subject (2 S. 8:5), but often it is used of God who gives "help" to a person. God assisted the Israelites in battle and Samuel called the place Ebenezer — "Hitherto the Lord has helped us" (1 S. 7:12). Ps. 124:8 affirms, "Our help [*ʿēzer*] is in the name of the Lord." Many of the psalms praise God, for He is the God who "helps" His people in a time of need.

Gen. 2:18 uses *ʿēzer* to speak of woman's relation to man. Since man should not be alone, God makes a woman to be his "helper" (AV "help"; NEB "partner"; *see also* FIT). Since the same word is applied to God, it seems clear that the reader should not infer that woman is inferior to man simply because the Bible calls woman a "helper." The term serves to underscore her function rather than delimit her status.

Another important Hebrew verb is *yāšaʿ*. Here again a person can be designated as the one who gives assistance to another person, but often the term is used to describe God's gracious assistance to people (Ps. 20:6 [MT 7]; 21:1, 5 [MT 2, 6]).

"Help" becomes such a characteristic word for God's gracious assistance to His people that even Heb. *ṣᵉḏāqâ* (God's righteous activity that saves) can be translated as "help" (Ps. 88:12 [MT 13]; 71:24; AV "righteousness").

A number of Hebrew words convey the idea of "cry out for help" (*zāʿaq, ṣāʿaq*) and "help" occurs in the translation of such terms (Jgs. 4:3; 6:6).

In the NT the Canaanite woman and the father of the epileptic boy ask Jesus for "help" (Gk. *boēthéō*, Mt. 15:25; Mk. 9:22, 24); the man of Macedonia asks Paul to "help" (*boēthéō*, Acts 16:9). The NT urges Christians to "help" others (Acts 20:35; 1 Thess. 5:14). On two occasions Paul speaks of the "help" of the Spirit. Phil. 1:19 affirms that the Spirit will give him "help," "support" (Gk. *epichorēgía*) and enable him to be delivered from prison. Rom. 8:26 states that the Spirit comes to the assistance of the weak. Mary sings a song in which she praises God and one of the things that she singles out is that God has "helped" Israel (Lk. 1:54).

The Epistle to the Hebrews encourages the Christian to rely on Jesus, for Jesus is one who is able to "help" those who are being tempted (2:18); He is a high priest in whom the Christian can find "help" in time of need (4:16).

See also *TDNT*, II, *s.v.* βοηθέω κτλ. (Büchsel).

P. L. BREMER

HELPER [Heb. *ʿāzar*] (Gen. 2:18, 20; 1 Ch. 12:18; Job 9:13; Ps. 10:14; etc.); AV also HELP; NEB also PARTNER, PROTECTOR, DEFENDER, ALLY, PARTISAN, BODYGUARD, "those who aided"; [Gk. *prostátis*] (Rom. 16:2); AV SUCCOURER; NEB GOOD FRIEND; [*boēthós*] (He. 13:6); [*diakonéō*] (Acts 19:22); AV "them that ministered"; NEB ASSISTANTS; [*antílēmpsis*] (1 Cor. 12:28); AV HELPS; NEB "ability to help others."

The OT terms for "helper" are all based on the Hebrew verb *ʿāzar*, a very general term for "help" or "succor." The purpose for the creation of woman is included in this concept: she is a "helper," i.e., a partner who corresponds to a man, in contrast to any animal (Gen. 2:18, 20). The Lord is the ultimate Helper (Ps. 30:10 [MT 11]; 54:4 [MT 6]; cf. He. 13:6).

In the NT the Lord is the source of *antílēmpsis*, the ability to be a helper to others in the Church (1 Cor. 12:28); note that this is one of the "gifts of the Spirit," and not an office. The cognate verb means to help in a general sense, and is used in both the NT and the LXX (cf. *TDNT*,

I, *s.v.* αντιλαμβάνομαι κτλ. [Delling]). Those who have proved themselves able assistants are commended to others in this role (Rom. 16:2). The term used in Acts 19:22 of Paul's "helpers" Timothy and Erastus is a participle based on *diakonéō,* a verb denoting personal service done out of a motive of love (cf. Lk. 22:26f., where the RSV renders the part. *diakonōn* as "one who serves").

See *TDNT,* II, *s.v.* διακονέω (Beyer).

R. J. HUGHES, III

HELPS. 1. The AV translation of Gk. *antilēmpseis* in 1 Cor. 12:28 (RSV "helpers"; NEB "ability to help others"). *See* HELPER.

2. The AV translation of Gk. *boētheiai* in Acts 27:17 (RSV "measures"; NEB "tackle"). The more technical term in this case is probably *hypozṓmata. See* SHIPS III.

HELVE (Dt. 19:5, AV). *See* HANDLE.

HEM. In the RSV "hem" occurs as a verb only in Lk. 19:34, "your enemies will hem you in on every side" (Gk. *perikyklóō*; AV "compass thee round"). For the classic instance of the term in the AV of Mt. 9:20, *see* FRINGES; GARMENTS X.

HEMAM hē'mam [Heb. *hêmām*] (Gen. 36:22). The AV and NEB rendering of HEMAN. *See also* HOMAM.

HEMAN hē'mən [Heb. *hêmān*–'faithful'].

1. A musician and seer, Levite, son of Joel and grandson of the prophet Samuel; of the family of the Kohathites (1 Ch. 6:33), appointed by David as one of the leaders of the temple singing (1 Ch. 15:17; 2 Ch. 5:12). He had fourteen sons (and three daughters) who assisted their father in the chorus. Heman seems also to have been a man of spiritual power; he is called "the king's seer" (1 Ch. 25:5; 2 Ch. 35:15).

2. One of the noted wise men prior to, or about, the time of Solomon. He was one of the three "sons of Mahol," a guild of temple singers or dancers (1 K. 4:31 [MT 5:11]); also called a son of Zerah (1 Ch. 2:6).

Psalm 88 is inscribed to Heman the Ezrahite, who may have been the leader of a musical guild during the monarchy.

3. A Horite descendant of Esau (Gen. 36:22). He is called HOMAM in 1 Ch. 1:39.

HEMATH hē'məth (AV 1 Ch. 2:55; Am. 6:14). *See* HAMATH (Am. 6:14); HAMMATH **1.**

HEMDAN hem'dən [Heb. *ḥemdān*–'pleasant' (?)]. A descendant of Seir, the Horite (Gen. 36:26). In 1 Ch. 1:41 the name occurs as "Hamran" (AV, NEB, AMRAM).

HEMLOCK. *See* POISON; WEEDS **2**; WORMWOOD.

HEMORRHAGE [Gk. *pēgḗ toú haímatos*] (Mk. 5:29); AV "foundation of her blood"; [*haimorroéō*] (Mt. 9:20); AV "issue of blood"; **FLOW OF BLOOD** [*rhýsis toú haímatos*] (Lk. 8:43f.); AV "issue of blood." In the three parallel accounts of the story of the woman whose hemorrhage Jesus healed we find three different terms. Each of these is the equivalent of a corresponding phrase in the LXX. Mk. 5:29 has its parallel in Lev. 12:7, which deals with the normal secretions connected with childbirth; Mt. 9:20 has its parallel in Lev. 15:33, which deals with abnormal secretions unrelated to either childbirth or menstruation (gonorrhea?); and Lk. 8:43f. has its parallel in Lev. 15:19, which involves menstruation, and v. 25, which again involves neither childbirth nor menstruation and is abnormal. Most probably the woman healed by Jesus was troubled by a uterine fibroid that resulted in her hemorrhaging for twelve years.

The woman was burdened not only physically and financially (cf. Mk. 5:26) but religiously as well, because during those twelve years she was ceremonially unclean and made anyone unclean who associated with her (cf. Lev. 15:25). Perhaps this is why, in part at least, she was afraid (Mk. 5:33) for having touched Jesus.

R. H. STEIN

HEN hen [Heb. *ḥēn*–'favor']. In Zec. 6:14 the AV, following the MT, reads "And the crowns shall be to Helem . . . and to Hen the son of Zephaniah." But as this person is called Josiah in v. 10, the RSV and NEB (following the Syriac) read "Josiah." *See* JOSIAH **2.**

HEN. *See* CHICKEN.

HENA hen'ə, hē'nä [Heb. *hēnaʿ*; Gk. *Ana*]. One of the Syrian cities captured by Sennacherib and given as a warning of the coming fate of Jerusalem (2 K. 18:34; 19:13). Its location remains unknown, but evidently it was near the north Syrian provinces of Arpad and Hamath.

Cheyne (*EB, s.v.*) rejected a geographical connotation, "Hena and Ivvah," in favor of the translation "He has driven away and overturned" (so Tg.; cf. J. Gray, *I & II Kings* [*OTL,* 2nd ed. 1970], p. 677 n. g). This "witticism" (as he calls it) does not easily fit the context, but is preferable to Hommel's view that these are pagan deities (*Expos.T.,* 9 [1897/98], 330).

Isaiah quotes from this same message of the Assyrian king, thereby confirming the existence of the places mentioned, including Hena (Isa. 37:13).

A. H. LEWIS

HENADAD hen'ā-dad [Heb. *ḥēnāḏāḏ*–'favor of Hadad'; LXX *Hēnaad, Hēnadad, Hēnadab, Hēnalab* (Ezr. 3:9; Neh. 3:18, 24; 10:9). One of the heads of the Levites in the postexilic community.

HENNA [Heb. *kōper*; Gk. *kýpros*] (Cant. 1:14; 4:13); AV CAMPHIRE. The henna plant, *Lawsonia inermis* L., originally grown in northern India. The pulverized leaves had a cosmetic use, as attested by the orange-colored nails, palms, and fingertips of some Egyptian mummies. A reference to Hebrew disapproval of this custom is seen in Dt. 21:11f.

In Cant. 7:11 (MT 12) the NEB reads "henna-bushes" (so KoB), while the other English versions and the LXX translate "villages" (so BDB).

R. K. H.

HENOCH hē'nək [Heb. *ḥᵃnôḵ*].

1. AV in 1 Ch. 1:3 (RSV, NEB, ENOCH). *See* ENOCH **2.**

2. AV in 1 Ch. 1:33 (RSV HANOCH; NEB ENOCH). *See* HANOCH **1.**

HEPHER hē'fər; **HEPHERITES** hē'fer-īts [Heb. *ḥēper, ḥeprî*].

1. LXX *Hopher* (Nu. 26:32f.; 27:1; Josh. 17:2f.); the head of a family or clan of the tribe of Manasseh. The clan is called the Hepherites in Nu. 26:32.

2. LXX *Hēphal* (1 Ch. 4:6); a man of Judah.

3. LXX *Hopher* (1 Ch. 11:36); one of David's heroes. Note that the parallel text in 2 S. 23:34 differs substantially; one or both may be corrupt.

HEPHER hef'ər, hē'fər [Heb. *ḥēper*]. A Canaanite town, listed between Tappuach and Aphek, whose king Joshua defeated (Josh. 12:17). The "land of Hepher" is mentioned with Socoh (Shuweikeh, 3 km. [2 mi.] N of Tulkarm) and Arubboth (ʿArrābah, 19 km. [12 mi.] NE of Tulkarm) in one of Solomon's districts, under the direction of Ben-hesed. (Hepher may also be mentioned with Arubboth in one of the Samaria ostraca; cf. R. Dussaud, *Syria,* 6 [1925], 314-338.) Thus it is usually located in the northern area of the Plain of Sharon, although its precise location is uncertain. Some have suggested Hafireh, about 3 km. (2 mi.) E of Arubboth, or Tell Ibshar, about 13 km. (8 mi.) W of Tulkarm.

See J. Gray, *I & II Kings* (*OTL,* 2nd ed. 1970), p. 137.

HEPHZIBAH hef'zi-ba [Heb. *ḥepṣî-bāh*–'my delight is in her'].

1. LXX *Hopseiba, Hapseiba, Hophsiba*; the wife of Hezekiah and the mother of Manasseh (2 K. 21:1).

2. The new name of Zion (Isa. 62:4, AV, NEB, RSV mg.); LXX translates Gk. *thélēma emón,* "my delight" (cf. the RSV).

HERALD [Heb. *m^ebaśśēr*] (Isa. 40:9; 41:27); AV "(one) that bringeth good tidings"; NEB "(one) who brings good news" (Isa. 40:9); "defending counsel" (Isa. 41:27); [Aram. *kārôz*] (Dnl. 3:4); [Gk. *kḗryx*] (2 Pet. 2:5); AV, NEB, PREACHER.

Hebrew *bāśar* (root of *m^ebaśśēr*) is related to Ugar. *bšr* and Akk. *bussuru/passuru*. In the majority of cases in all three languages, the roots mean to "bring good news." Oppenheim argues that the Akkadian term carries the neutral sense "bring a message," regardless of content (cf. *TDOT*); however, the research of Fisher supports the positive, rather than the neutral, connotation of the term. The eschatological significance of the Isaianic passages finds inaugural fulfillment in the coming of the kingdom with the good news of Christ's advent (note the LXX translation of *bāśar,* i.e., *euangelízō*; cf. Mk. 1:14).

The Aram. *kārôz* was once thought to be derived from the Gk. *kērýssō*. However, Nuzi legal documents (*ca.* 1500 B.C.) contain the Hurrian *kirezzi,* meaning "proclamation." This proclamation was required for proper legal status and sheds light on the binding nature of the declaration in Dnl. 3:4-6.

The idea that Noah preached (cf. 1 Tim. 2:7) to his generation finds support in both Jewish (Josephus *Ant.* i.3.1) and early Christian (1 Clem. 7:6) tradition. However, if *dikaiosýnēs kḗryka* (2 Pet. 2:5) is not an objective genitive (as Dalton suggests), then the translation becomes "righteous herald," referring to Noah's personal character rather than the character of his preaching (cf. Gen. 6:9).

See GOOD NEWS.

Bibliography.–A. L. Oppenheim, *JNES,* 13 (1954), 141-48; *CAD,* II, *s.v.* "*bussuru*"; R. W. Fisher, "A Study of the Semitic Root BŚR . . ." (Diss., Columbia, 1966); A. Shaffer, *Orientalia,* 34 (1965), 32-34; W. J. Dalton, *Christ's Proclamation to the Spirits* (1964); *TDOT,* II, *s.v.* "bśr" (Schilling).

J. T. DENNISON, JR.

HERB; HERBAGE [Heb. *ʿēśeb* (Gen. 2:5; Dt. 32:2; Prov. 27:25; Isa. 42:15; Jer. 14:6), *ʾōrâ* (2 K. 4:39), *deše'* (Ps. 37:2), *yārāq* (Prov. 15:17); Gk. *láchanon* (Lk. 11:42)]; AV also GRASS (Dt. 32:2; Jer. 14:6); NEB also PLANT (Gen. 2:5), YOUNG PLANT (Dt. 32:2), VEGETABLES (Prov. 15:17), GREEN GROWTH (27:25), etc.

The RSV normally has "plants" or "grass" for Heb. *ʿēśeb* (cf. Akk. *išbabtu*) but translates "herb" in a few instances. Heb. *yārāq* (cf. Akk. *arqu*) indicates vegetables or greens (cf. RSV in Dt. 11:10; 1 K. 21:2; NEB in Prov. 15:17). Heb. *deše'* is usually "grass" in the RSV. Many biblical words for vegetation are of uncertain designation (cf. *MPB,* pp. 251-54).

AV references to herbs in Isa. 18:4; 26:19 have been altered in later versions. Mt. 13:32, RSV, has "shrubs."

See also BITTER HERBS (Ex. 12:8; Nu. 9:11); FLORA; GRASS.

R. K. H.

HERCULES hûr'kū-lēz [Gk. *Herakles*] (2 Macc. 4:19). The Greek god honored by games every five years in Tyre. The Greek name was used for the ancient Tyrian deity Melqart (cf. Josephus *Ant.* viii.5.3 [146]).

HERD. *See* CATTLE.

HERDSMAN [Heb. *rōʿeh*] (Gen. 13:7f.; 26:20; 1 S. 21:7); AV HERDMEN; NEB also SHEPHERDS; [*bôqēr*] (Am. 7:14); AV HERDMAN; [*šābeṭ*–'herdsman's staff'] (Lev. 27:32); AV "rod"; NEB "counting rod"; [Gk. *bóskontes*] (Mt. 8:33; Mk. 5:14; Lk. 8:34); AV "they that kept them," "they that fed the swine"; NEB "the men in charge of them." One who attended to the needs of any domesticated flocks of animals. He was responsible for their general well-being and was thus important in the kind of pastoral economy reflected in the OT. While the owner of flocks or herds might well have exercised a general oversight of the animals, the herdsman did the bulk of the work and was usually hired for that purpose. Heb. *nôqēḏ* occurs twice in the OT, once to describe Amos as a "shepherd" (Am. 1:1; AV "herdman"; NEB "sheep-farmer"), and once in reference to Mesha of Moab (2 K. 3:4) as a "sheep breeder" (AV "sheepmaster"). On the basis of Ugaritic and Akkadian evidence, Scandinavian scholars have thought that *nôqēḏ* was an official priestly or cultic title. While this might have been true of Mesha, it certainly was not of Amos, as he himself made clear.

R. K. H.

HERES hē'rēz, hē'res.

1. [Heb. *har-ḥeres*–'mountain of the sun'] (Jgs. 1:35); RSV HAR-HERES. A place from which the Danites failed to expel the Amorites. It is here associated with Aijalon and Shaalbim, which in Josh. 19:41 (Shaalabin) are associated with Ir-shemesh. Since *ḥeres* is a rare Hebrew word for "sun," the commoner word being *šemeš,* it is believed that Har-heres and Ir-shemesh are identical and refer to the well-known border fortress of BETH-SHEMESH, Heb. *har* ("mount") perhaps being a copyist's error for Heb. *ʿîr* ("city"). Other possibilities are Bain Harasheh, NE of Aijalon, and Bit Ninib of the Amarna Letters (Ninib being the fierce morning sun).

2. [Heb. *maʿ^alēh heḥāres,* "the ascent of Heres"] (Jgs. 8:13). A place where Gideon turned back from pursuing the Midianites. The AV reads "before the sun was up." The presence of the article before *ḥāres* is slightly against its being a proper name; however, *maʿ^alēh* elsewhere means the path ascending a hill, not the sun's path. If a place, Heres should lie E of the Jordan; but its site is unknown.

3. [Heb. *ʿîr haheres*] (Isa. 19:18). *See* CITY OF THE SUN.

F. WEDDLE

HERESH her'esh [Heb. *ḥereš*; LXX B, Gk. *Rharaiēl*; A, Gk. *Hares*]. A Levite among the returning exiles in 1 Ch. 9:15; he is not listed in the parallel Neh. 11:15f.

HERESY [Gk. *haíresis* < *haírein*–'take,' mid. 'select']. The term has three meanings in classical Greek: "seizure" (e.g., of a city); "choice" or "selection"; "resolve" or "effort directed to a goal." In Hellenism it acquired the related senses of "teaching" and "school." In the latter sense it came to be used of the philosophical schools, i.e., the groups that in a larger society follow the teachings of particular leaders in distinction from others.

I. Judaism.–In the LXX *haíresis* was still employed in the original sense of choice at Gen. 49:5. Philo, as one might expect, used the term for the philosophical schools of the Greek world. Josephus reapplied it, however, by speaking of the "heresy" of the Essenes and the three religious "heresies" of the Essenes, Sadducees, and Pharisees (*Ant.* xiii.5.9 [171]). So far, of course, the word had the neutral sense of a party with distinctive emphases and concerns. The rabbis of the time used the Hebrew equivalent in the same way. By A.D. 100, however, they began to reserve it for divergent movements and by A.D. 200 non-Jewish groups, especially Christians and Gnostics, were particularly in view.

II. NT.–For the most part *haíresis* has in the NT the same meaning as in Josephus. Acts 5:17 speaks of the school or party of the Sadducees and 15:5 of that of the Pharisees. Paul in 26:5 claimed to belong to "the strictest party of our religion," that of the Pharisees. Christianity itself was at first regarded as a sect or party in Judaism. Thus Paul in 24:5 is called "a ringleader of the sect of the Nazarenes," obviously in this instance a group that was viewed with disfavor. Paul himself seemed not to accept this designation in 24:14: "According to the Way, which they call a sect, I worship the God of our fathers." The term was also used unfavorably by the Jewish leaders in Rome: "For with regard to this sect we know that everywhere it is spoken against" (28:22).

Within the Church itself the term had from the very first a pejorative nuance. Paul in Gal. 5:20 put *haíresis* on his list of works of the flesh. It is unlikely that the word has a technical meaning here; "party spirit" (RSV) is probably what Paul had in mind. In 1 Cor. 11:19 the heresies seem to correspond to the "dissensions" of 1:10ff. and the "divisions" of 11:18 (both Gk. *schísmata*). They represent "factions" which are totally incompatible with the one being of the community; their only function is to bring the genuine members to recognition. The heresies of 2 Pet. 2:1 are more serious than ordinary divisions because they involve divergent teachings insidiously introduced by false teachers. The idea of incompatibility of opinion is thus added to that of faction and the term is well on the way to the technical sense it acquired in Christian history. In Tit. 3:9-11 the heretic, i.e., the person who "is factious," engaging in controversies and dissensions, is to be admonished twice and then, if stubborn, shunned by the community as perverted, sinful, and self-condemned.

III. Early Church.–The Christian writers of the first two centuries (e.g., Justin *Dial.* 82.3) could still use the term "heresies" for philosophical schools and Jewish parties. Nevertheless, they had an awareness that there is no place for parties in the Church, especially when those parties are not just schismatic but also hold divergent opinions under private and unauthorized leadership. Ignatius (Eph. 6:2) and Justin (*Dial.* 51.2) made this clear.

It is thus that the word finally undergoes the change of meaning that makes it a technical term in Christian history. The original sense may still be glimpsed, for heresy arises when a party develops around a particular leader (self-willed and possibly self-appointed) whose divergent opinion opposes some common teaching of the Church. The offense of heresy is threefold. (1) It represents an individualistic choice; (2) it diverges from basic teaching; (3) it repudiates the very being of the Church as not just an aggregate of parties but as the one body of the one Lord with one faith and one Spirit (cf. Eph. 4:4ff.).

IV. Christian Heresies.–As one might expect, over hundreds of years of Christian history divergent views have been held on almost all the Church's teachings. Only where these views have been actively promoted, however, have heresies arisen. To list all these would be tedious and unprofitable. Accounts of early heresies may be found in the *Panarion* of Epiphanius (4th cent.) and Book II of the *Fount of Divine Wisdom* of John of Damascus (8th cent.). All that will be attempted here is to indicate some of the more serious heresies in the successive historical periods.

A. Early Heresies. Apart from the Judaizing movement, Gnosticism posed the first heretical threat to Christianity. Incipient forms of Gnosticism appeared in the NT itself but the movement reached its peak in the 2nd century. Its general teachings included separation of the true God from the Creator, dualism of soul and body, denial of the bodily reality of Christ, and redemption of the soul alone, not the whole person. Marcionism, a distinct but related movement, opposed the NT God of grace to the OT God of retribution and rejected the OT canon.

Trinitarian and christological heresies entered the picture from the late 2nd century. In defense of the divine monarchy Adoptionists viewed Jesus as a man adopted to deity, Subordinationists arranged the divine persons in a descending hierarchy, and Modalists or Sabellianists treated Father, Son, and Holy Spirit as economic (revelational), not essential, modes of the one God, so that Patripassianists could say that the Father no less than the Son suffered on the cross.

In the 4th cent. Arianism insisted that Christ, while preexistent, was created. Semi-Arians resisted the consubstantiality of Father and Son. Macedonians, or, more accurately, Pneumatomachians, applied the same type of thinking to the Holy Spirit. In contrast, Apollinarianism, believing that the Logos replaced the rational soul in Jesus, truncated his full humanity. All these teachings were condemned at Constantinople in 381.

The Nestorians in the 5th cent. were accused of teaching two persons as well as two natures in Christ and consequently of denying the title *theotokos* (God-bearer) to the virgin. The Eutychians and Monophysites went to the opposite extreme and found only one nature as well as one person. Later the Monothelites tried a compromise and found only one will even though there might be two natures. The councils at Ephesus (431), Chalcedon (451), and Constantinople (681) excluded these deviations.

Dualism, revived in the 4th cent. by the Manichaeans, formed the first anthropological heresy. Speculations about the preexistence and transmigration of souls could be found in Origen. As originally presented, these hardly had the status of heresies, but they came under formal condemnation in the 6th century. Origen also suggested universalism and was followed at this point by Gregory of Nyssa, although again it was taught more as a possibility than a divergent doctrine. In the 5th cent. Pelagianism, while well-intentioned, took a heretical turn when it denied original sin and argued for freedom to live a righteous life and thereby to attain salvation without the divine forgiveness in Christ. After some vacillation, the Church rejected it at Ephesus in 431. The mediating movement known as Semi-Pelagianism, which tried to retain some initiative for mankind, failed to establish itself and was condemned a century later at the Council of Orange (529).

Differences on charismatic and disciplinary matters produced three important schismatic movements, Montanism, Novatianism, and Donatism, in the 2nd, 3rd, and 4th centuries. In relation to the main credal articles these were not heretical. Nevertheless, the Montanists were rejected for erroneous views on prophesying and ascetic practice, the Novatianists and Donatists for separatist concepts of the Church, and the Donatists for failure to accept the validity of acts of ministry performed by real or suspected apostates and those ordained by them. Divergent groups also arose on many minor issues. Thus the Aquarians were condemned for using only water at the Lord's Supper and the Cataphrygians for baptizing the dead.

B. Medieval Heresies. In the Western Church the centralizing of ecclesiastical power in the papacy brought all divergent groups under the risk not only of dogmatic condemnation but also of physical repression. Anathemas were exchanged between East and West over the question whether the Holy Spirit proceeds from the Father alone or also from the Son. By the 11th cent. a papal document proclaimed exclusion from salvation for anyone not in communion with the see of Rome. The same century saw the harsh treatment of Berengarius for his rejection of a bodily presence of Christ in the eucharistic elements. In the 13th cent. the Albigenses no doubt merited their condemnation as heretics because of their Manichaean tendencies, although this was no excuse for their brutal suppression. The Waldenses, in contrast, seem not to have denied traditional doctrines but simply to have resisted such later accretions as purgatory, invocations, and transubstantiation. Similarly the Wycliffites and Hussites in the 14th and 15th cents. were condemned only for their rejection of new dogmas and their opposition to papal authority and ecclesiastical abuses. Perhaps the only substantial charge against Wyclif is that like the Donatists he argued that bad priests cannot perform valid acts of ministry.

From the standpoint of the reforming "heretics" of the Middle Ages, the Western Church itself had adopted many heretical teachings which formed no part of basic Christian doctrine. Thus the concepts of papal primacy, purgatorial expiation, eucharistic sacrifice, and the treasury of merit might all be regarded as innovative heresies. Notwithstanding their lack of apostolic foundation or sanction, these ideas had been given the status of official dogmas. Certainly the older orthodoxy had been retained intact, but a new heterodoxy had now been added to it. Lacking ecclesiastical force, the reforming movements could not have these new doctrines officially declared heretical. Indeed, their own opposition received the heretical label. Nevertheless, the opposition arose because medieval developments brought the official Church itself under the charge of promoting new and serious heresies.

C. Reformation Heresies. The upheavals of the 16th cent. brought to the surface new or renewed teachings which came under general condemnation. The revolutionary millennialism of certain Anabaptists provides a clear example. So, too, does the odd christological view of Menno Simons that Christ did not take flesh from the Virgin. At more central points Servetus championed unitarianism, and the rationalistic Socinians departed from orthodoxy in relation to Christ's person and work.

From the Roman standpoint the Reformers were also guilty of teaching heresies. Individual Reformers were excommunicated and in some cases (e.g., Ridley and Cranmer in England) exterminated. The Council of Trent (1545-1563) anathematized their teachings, e.g., on Scripture, justification, and the eucharist, although in its positive statements it left some room for freedom of interpretation. Lutheranism, Zwinglianism, Calvinism, Anglicanism, and Anabaptism all took on the rank of new heresies according to the Tridentine understanding.

For their part the Reformers viewed the Tridentine formulations and the underlying medieval teachings as the real heresies, as may be seen in Calvin's *Antidote* or Jewel's *Apology.* Roman Catholicism, as distinct from the true catholicism which it had changed and distorted by addition, represented the real departure from the faith that had to be resisted and corrected. In particular it evaded the authority of Scripture, misunderstood justification, and promoted nonapostolic inventions in such questions as baptism, the eucharist, penance, purgatory, and papal primacy.

Differences between the Reformers, especially the Lutherans and Calvinists, led to a confused situation in which charges and countercharges of heresy were exchanged. Specific points at issue were the eucharistic presence, the related christological understanding of the communication of the attributes of the two natures of Christ, and the nature of election. All the main groups combined, however, to resist the spiritualism of Carlstadt and Franck, the antinomianism of Agricola, and the teaching of Osiander concerning justification by infused righteousness.

D. Modern Heresies. Within the post-Reformation churches various movements appeared which came to be stigmatized as heretical. Roman Catholicism moved against the strong Augustinianism of the Jansenists and the passivity of the Quietists in the 17th cent., against the suspected dangers of "Americanism" in the 19th cent., and against the liberal teachings of the Modernists (Loisy, Tyrrell) in the early 20th century. Those who would not assent to papal infallibility in 1870 were also ejected. In the Reformed churches Arminianism was condemned by the Synod of Dort in 1618-1619, although many Protestants would not regard Arminianism as heretical. Anglicanism in the 17th cent. opposed not only Puritanism but secondary groups like the Seekers, Levelers, and Quakers, although there was no formal dogmatic condemnation and coexistence with the Presbyterians, Congregationalists, and Baptists began by the end of the century. In twentieth-century Germany the so-called German Christians, who attempted a compromise with National Socialist (Nazi) doctrines, earned the unofficial theological anathemas of the Declaration of Barmen (1934).

When Roman Catholicism added three important dogmas, Protestants generally could only resist them as new and erroneous accretions. Two of these belonged to the sphere of Mariology: the Immaculate Conception of the Virgin (1854) and her bodily assumption (1950). The third was a declaration of papal infallibility in official pronouncements on faith and morals (1870).

On a broader front liberal Protestantism, of which Modernism was the Roman Catholic counterpart, has been considered by many the great heresy of the modern age. This comprised, and comprises, many individual heresies which it would be unprofitable to list in detail. Neither as a whole nor in detail has liberal Protestantism been generally defined as a heresy by the leading Protestant churches, although Barth explicitly treated it as such in his *Church Dogmatics*. Nevertheless, since many of its tenets revive ancient heresies, the movement as such, from the standpoint of biblical and apostolic orthodoxy, may plainly be viewed as heterodox.

Various sectarian forms or offshoots of Christianity have been considered modern heresies. Among these are Shakerism, Swedenborgianism, Mormonism, Christian Science, Jehovah's Witnesses, and perhaps the Unification Church. The Christianity of some of these groups is very tenuous. Nevertheless, to the extent that they have Christian sources or connections they come within the broader definition of heresy. Nor do they bear less likeness to authentic Christianity than the Gnostic sects of the early period or many liberal Protestant groups or schools that are contemporary with them.

See also FACTIONS. G. W. BROMILEY

HERETH, FOREST OF hē'rəth, hər'əth [Heb. *yaʿar ḥereṯ*–'forest of Hereth'; Gk. *pólis Sarich*–'city (of) Sarich']; AV, NEB, FOREST OF HARETH. The place where David went after the prophet Gad warned him to leave Mizpeh of Moab and return to Judah (1 S. 22:5). According to Grollenberg (*GAB*, p. 152) it is between Adullam and Giloh but the basis for this location is not given. Abel (*GP*, II, 343) locates it near Kharās (*ḫarās*), a hamlet about 11 km. (7 mi.) NW of Hebron near Khirbet Qila (Qᵉʿila); however, the equation of Heb. *ḥereṯ* with Arab. *ḫarās* is phonemically unlikely. The LXX reads "into the city Sarich," which is similar to Josephus's "into the city of Saris" (*Ant*. vi.12.4 [249]). The derivation of "Sarich" from "*Ḫarās*" requires a reversal of the consonants *ḫ*, *r*, and *s*, and since the equation of "*Ḫarās*" with Heb. *ḥereṯ* is doubtful, the identification of the forest of Hereth with the city of Sarich/Kharās is far from convincing. *See* ADULLAM. W. S. L. S.

HERETIC. The term is used by the AV and NEB in Tit. 3:10 for Gk. *hairetikós*. The RSV, with "factious," is probably closer to the intent of the passage. The Greek term refers to an agitator who creates divisions and parties. *See* FACTIONS; HERESY.

HERITAGE [Heb. *naḥᵃlâ* (Dt. 9:26, 29; 32:9; Josh. 18:7; etc.), *naḥᵃlāṯ* (Ps. 16:6), *nāḥal* (Ps. 119:111; Jer. 3:18), *yᵉruššâ* (Ps. 61:5 [MT 6]); Gk. *klēronoméō* (Rev. 21:7)]; AV also INHERITANCE, INHERIT (Rev. 21:5); NEB POSSESSION, PORTION, SHARE, INHERITANCE, PATRIMONY, etc. That which is passed down to descendants or succeeding generations, distinguished from "inheritance" in that "heritage" frequently refers to things other than property (e.g., traditions), while "inheritance" is used especially of property. The RSV makes no such distinction. *Naḥᵃlâ* denotes any sort of inherited possession; usually the reference is to land, a people, or material goods. In Ps. 136:21f. "heritage" is used of the land transferred by Yahweh from the Canaanites to Israel. Frequently Israel is spoken of as the heritage of the Lord (Dt. 9:26, 29; 32:9; 1 S. 10:1; etc.). *See* INHERIT.

HERMAS her'məs [Gk. *Hermas*]. One of the recipients of greetings in Rom. 16:14, otherwise unknown. Attempts to identify him with the author of the Shepherd of Hermas are unfounded.

HERMAS, THE SHEPHERD OF. *See* APOSTOLIC FATHERS IX.

HERMENEUTICS hûr-mə-nōō'tiks. *See* INTERPRETATION.

HERMES hûr'mēz [Gk. *Hermēs*].

1. A Greek god, son of Zeus and Maia, called "Mercury" by the Romans. In Greek mythology he functioned primarily as the attendant, herald, and interpreter of the gods. He was the god who conducted the souls of the dead to the underworld. Like his half brother Apollo, Hermes was celebrated as a skilled musician, being credited with the invention of the lyre and the pipes of Pan, and also as an athlete. He was popular as the patron of orators and the protector of travelers. Known as the god of gain — whether honest or dishonest — and renowned for his trickery, he was the patron of both merchants and thieves. His symbols were the caduceus, winged shoes, and purse. The caduceus was a golden rod he used as the shepherd-god who protected sheep and cattle. Though he played many roles in Greek mythology, in the cult he functioned primarily as a god of fertility, as is evidenced by the ithyphallic images erected to represent him. *See also* RELIGIONS OF THE BIBLICAL WORLD: GRECO-ROMAN.

Statue of Hermes found at Nineveh (State Antiquities Organization, Republic of Iraq)

In Acts 14:12 Paul is said to have been identified with Hermes because he was "the chief speaker." It was therefore to Hermes' character as the divine herald and god of oratory that the Lycaonians were referring. The people of Lystra were apparently familiar with the popular legends in which Zeus and Hermes had "come down . . . in the likeness of men" (v. 11) to their district; cf. the legend of Baucis and Philemon (Ovid *Metamorphoses* viii.611ff.). *See also* ZEUS.

2. The name of a Roman Christian, otherwise unknown, to whom Paul sent greetings (Rom. 16:14).

HERMOGENES hûr-moj'ə-nēz [Gk. *Hermogenēs*–'born of Hermes'] (2 Tim. 1:15). A Christian mentioned by Paul as having, along with Phygelus and "all who are in Asia," turned away from him. It is not clear when or where the defection of these Asiatic Christians from the apostle took place, whether it was at Rome at the time of Paul's second imprisonment there, and especially on the occasion of his being brought before the emperor's supreme court to be tried on a charge now involving the death penalty, or whether it was at some previous time in Ephesus.

If it was the latter, then Paul here wishes to inform or remind Timothy of how in Ephesus, where Timothy was the presiding minister of the church, these persons had turned away from him, i.e., had refused to submit to his authority and had rejected the Christian doctrine which he taught. Some expositors believe this to be the probable signification because the verb, Gk. *apestráphēsan,* "they turned away," is in the aorist tense, referring to a time long past.

On the other hand, there is no evidence that there ever was a time when "all who are in Asia" turned away from obedience to Paul. Whatever may have been the disloyalty and disobedience of individuals (and this certainly existed; see, e.g., Acts 20:29f.), the NT does not show that all who were in Asia — the Christian community as a whole in Ephesus, Miletus, Laodicea, Hierapolis, Colossae, and other places — repudiated his apostolic authority. If these words refer to all the Christians from the province of Asia who happened to be in Rome at the time of Paul's second imprisonment there, it can easily be understood that they should turn away from him at that testing time. It is impossible to say exactly what form their desertion of the apostle assumed. Their turning away would likely be caused by fear that they might be involved in the same imprisonment as had overtaken him, and probably also in the same death penalty.

It is altogether in favor of a reference to Rome that what is said about Phygelus and Hermogenes is immediately followed by a reference to the great kindness shown by Onesiphorus in diligently seeking out the apostle in Rome. On the whole, therefore, a reference to Asians who had accompanied Paul to Rome and then deserted him seems most probable. *See* PHYGELUS.

J. RUTHERFURD

HERMON hûr'mən, **MOUNT** [Heb. *har ḥermôn* < *ḥāram*–'devote']. The highest peak of the Anti-Lebanon Mountains, marking the southern end of that range. *See* Plate 21.

This majestic mountain has three peaks, the highest of which is 2813 m. (9232 ft.). The name appears in the plural form in Ps. 42:6 (MT 7), probably referring to these different peaks. (The word should not be rendered "Hermonites" as in the AV.)

The mountain is snow-covered most of the year, with patches of snow in protected gullies the year around. The sources of the Jordan River are to be found on its western slopes. Mt. Hermon marked the northern limits of Joshua's conquests (Josh. 11:17; 12:1).

The sacred character of the mountain is suggested not only by the etymology of the name, but also by the name Baal-Hermon (the mountain of the Baal of Hermon) used in Jgs. 3:3 and 1 Ch. 5:23. The mountain was also called Sirion by the Sidonians and Senir by the Amorites (Dt. 3:9; cf. Ps. 29:6; Ezk. 27:5; "Sion" in Dt. 4:48, AV, should also be read "Sirion," with the RSV and NEB, following the Syriac). The Arabs call the mountain Jebel esh-Sheikh or Jebel eth-Thalj, "mountain of the snow." Jebel esh-Sheikh is variously explained as the "gray-haired mountain," or the mountain of the elder or chief. Conder (in *HDB*) suggests that it is designated Jebel esh-Sheikh because the religious sheikh of the Druzes made Hermon his residence in the 10th century.

R. A. GWINN

HERMONITES hur'mən-īts [Heb. *ḥermônîm*]. AV in Ps. 42:6 (MT 7); RSV HERMON; NEB HERMONS. *See* HERMON, MOUNT.

HEROD hâr'əd [Gk. *Hērōdēs*]. The name of several members of a dynasty that was appointed to govern Jewish Palestine under Roman rule.

I. Herodian Dynasty
II. Herod the Great (47-4 B.C.)
  A. Governor of Galilee (47-37 B.C.)
  B. King of the Jews (37-4 B.C.)
    1. Consolidation (37-25 B.C.)
    2. Prosperity (25-14 B.C.)
    3. Domestic Troubles (14-4 B.C.)
III. Herod's Will Disputed
IV. Archelaus (4 B.C.-A.D. 6)
V. Antipas (4 B.C.-A.D. 39)
  A. Antipas's Realm
  B. Antipas's Reign
    1. Antipas and Archelaus
    2. Antipas and John the Baptist
    3. Antipas and Jesus
    4. Antipas and Exile
VI. Philip the Tetrarch (4 B.C.-A.D. 34)
VII. Agrippa I (A.D. 37-44)
VIII. Agrippa II (A.D. 50-100)

I. Herodian Dynasty.–The struggle between Hellenism and Judaism came to a climax during the Maccabean revolt against Antiochus Epiphanes when the Jews became more or less an independent nation beginning in 142 B.C. under the rule of Hasmoneans. During the reign of Alexander Janneus (103-76 B.C.) the Herodians began their influence in leadership. Herod the Great's grandfather Antipater (or Antipas) was appointed governor of Idumea by Alexander (Josephus *Ant.* xiv.1.3 [10]). On his deathbed Alexander appointed his wife, Salome Alexandra, to succeed him. Since she could not be high priest, she appointed Hyrcanus II as high priest. Upon her death in 67 B.C. Hyrcanus II assumed the position of king and high priest. His weak character enabled his brother Aristobulus II to force him to relinquish his position as king and high priest (*Ant.* xiv.1.2 [4-7]; xv.6.4 [180]; *BJ* i.5.4 [117-19]).

Antipater II, son of Antipater and father of Herod the Great, being an Idumean (*BJ* i.6.2 [123]; cf. also *Ant.* xiv.1.3 [9]; Justin Martyr *Dial.* lii.3; Eusebius *HE* i.6.2; 7.11; T.B. *Baba Bathra* 3b-4a; *Kiddushin* 70a), realized that though he could not become king and high priest he could nevertheless be the power behind the throne of a weak person like Hyrcanus II. He convinced Hyrcanus II that he had been deprived of his hereditary rights by his younger brother and persuaded him to flee to Aretas, king of Arabia, with a view to recovering his rightful place as king and high priest of Israel. He fled to Petra (*Ant.* xiv.1.3f. [8-18]). Aretas agreed to help Hyrcanus II provided he would give up twelve cities of Moab that were taken by Alexander Janneus. Having agreed, Aretas attacked and defeated Aristobulus, who retreated to the temple mount at the time of the Passover in 65 B.C.

Rome then came into the picture. Each brother (Hyrcanus II and Aristobulus II) asked Pompey, the Roman general, to side with him against the other. After some delay and signs of rebellion by Aristobulus II, Pompey joined with Hyrcanus (*Ant.* xiv.3.3 [46f.]). Pompey made war against Aristobulus II, besieged the Jerusalem temple for three months, and finally prevailed in the autumn of 63 B.C. This marked the end of Jewish independence and the Hasmonean house (142-63 B.C.). Pompey entered the holy of holies but did not plunder. In fact, on the following day he ordered its cleansing and the resumption of the sacrifices. He reinstated Hyrcanus as high priest (*Ant.* xiv.4.4 [69-73]; *BJ* i.6.5–7.6 [133-153]; Tacitus *Hist.* v. 9; Appian *Mithridatic Wars* 106, 114; Florus i.40.30; Livy *Epit.* cii; Plutarch *Pompey* xxxix; cf. Dio Cassius *Hist.* xxxvii.15-17). In the reorganization of the government in Palestine, Antipater initiated many of his own changes.

Antipater married Cypros, an illustrious Arabian woman, by whom he had four sons — Phasael, Herod, Joseph, Pheroras — and a daughter, Salome (*Ant.* xiv.7.3 [121]; *BJ* i.8.9 [181]).

After Julius Caesar defeated Pompey in Egypt (48 B.C.), Hyrcanus and Antipater attached themselves to Caesar's party. Because Antipater had risked his life for Caesar by fighting in Egypt in 48-47 B.C., Caesar made him a Roman citizen with exemption from taxes and appointed him procurator of Judea. Caesar also reconfirmed Hyrcanus's high-priesthood and gave him the title of Ethnarch of the Jews (*Ant.* xiv.8.1-5 [127-155]; 10.2 [191]; *BJ* i.9.3–10.4 [187-203]). Antipater was officially recognized as administrator of Judea and thus began to develop dynastic ambitions. He appointed his son Phasael as governor of Jerusalem and his second son Herod as governor of Galilee in 47 B.C. (*Ant.* xiv.9.1-2 [156-58]; *BJ* i.10.4 [201-203]). Although he encouraged the Jews to be loyal to Hyrcanus, Antipater was the real power behind the throne.

II. Herod the Great* (47-4 B.C.)–*A. Governor of Galilee (47-37 B.C.). Although Herod was only twenty-five when he became the governor of Galilee, he was admired by the Galilean Jews and the Roman officials in Syria for his efficient leadership in capturing and executing the brigand Ezekias and many of his followers (47/46 B.C.). Some persuaded Hyrcanus that Herod had violated Jewish law in executing Ezekias and his followers and consequently he should be tried before the Sanhedrin. Herod was brought to the trial, but Sextus Caesar, governor of Syria, ordered Hyrcanus to acquit Herod or suffer the consequences. Hyrcanus adjourned the trial and Herod fled to join Sextus Caesar in Damascus. Herod secured from Sextus Caesar the command of the city of Samaria and the district of Coelesyria and began to march against Jerusalem to avenge himself for the insult he received from Hyrcanus, but he was persuaded by his father and brother to refrain because this sort of rebellion would be looked upon with great disfavor by the Roman government (*Ant.* xiv.9.2-5 [158-184]; *BJ* i.10.5-9 [204-215]; cf. T.B. *Kiddushin* 43a).

Shortly thereafter Caecilius Bassus, a partisan of Pompey and foe of Julius Caesar, murdered Sextus Caesar and assumed the leadership of Syria (Dio Cassius xlvii.26.7–27.2; Livy *Epit.* cxiv; *Ant.* xiv.11.1 [268]; *BJ* i.10.10 [216]). The Caesarian commanders moved against Bassus and caused an indecisive war that lasted for about three years. After Cassius, Brutus, and their followers murdered Caesar on March 15, 44 B.C., Cassius arrived in Syria and by defeating Bassus assumed the leadership there.

Cassius was in desperate need of money. Herod was selected as one of those who would raise the funds. Because of his successful collection in Galilee, Cassius appointed him governor of Coelesyria (as he had been under Sextus) with the further promise of making him king after he and Brutus defeated Octavius and Antony. When Cassius left Syria to help Brutus, new disturbances arose in Judea but they were quelled by Herod (43 B.C.). Shortly thereafter Aristobulus's son Antigonus made an advance into Judea, but Herod, seeing the danger, drove him out (42 B.C.). Herod was received with acclamations by the people and with gratitude by Hyrcanus (*Ant.* xiv.11.3–12.1 [277-299]; *BJ* i.11.2–12.3 [220-240]).

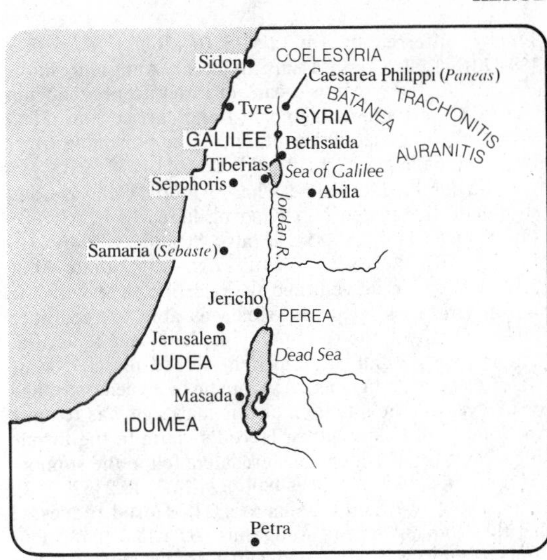

Herod's first wife Doris, who was probably an Idumean, had borne him a son named Antipater. Herod now became betrothed to Mariamne, whose mother was Hyrcanus II's daughter and whose father was Aristobulus II's other son, Alexander, and thus a niece to Antigonus, the rival of Herod (*Ant.* xiv.12.1 [300]; *BJ* i.12.3 [241]). This arrangement strengthened Herod's political base, for he was marrying into the royal house of the Hasmoneans and would become the natural regent when aging Hyrcanus passed away. Thus he gained acceptance in the Judean circles.

In 42 B.C. Antony defeated Cassius, and the Jewish leaders accused Herod and Phasael of usurping the power of the government while leaving Hyrcanus with titular honors. Herod's defense nullified these charges (*Ant.* xiv.12.2-6 [301-323]; *BJ* i.12.4-6 [242-45]; Plutarch *Antony* xxiv; Dio Cassius xlviii.24; Appian *The Civil Wars* v.30-38). In the autumn of 41 B.C. new accusations were made against Herod and Phasael, and a trial was held in Antioch with Antony present. Since Hyrcanus was at the trial, Antony asked him who he thought would be the best qualified ruler and Hyrcanus selected Herod and Phasael. Antony appointed them as tetrarchs of Judea (*BJ* i.12.5 [243f.]; *Ant.* xiv.13.1 [324-26]).

In the next year (40 B.C.) troubles arose for the two new tetrarchs. The Parthians arrived in Syria and joined Antigonus (whose father was Hyrcanus's deposed brother Aristobulus) in his struggle to remove Hyrcanus. Parthians had besieged Jerusalem and asked for peace. Herod was suspicious of the offer, but Phasael and Hyrcanus went to Galilee to meet the Parthian king, who betrayed them by putting them in chains. Hearing of the treachery, Herod with Mariamne, his close relatives, and his troops moved to Masada and then Petra (*Ant.* xiv.13.3-9 [335-364]; *BJ* i.13.2-9 [250-264]). Antigonus was made king (Dio Cassius xlviii.41; inferred in *Ant.* xiv.13.10 [368f.]; *BJ* i.13.9 [268-270]; cf. also Dio Cassius xlviii.26). Antigonus mutilated his uncle Hyrcanus's ears in order to prevent him from being restored as high priest and carried him off to Parthia. Phasael died either of suicide or poisoning (*Ant.* xiv.13.10 [365-69]; xv.2.1 [12]; *BJ* i.13.9-11 [270-73]).

Herod departed for Rome, where Antony, Octavius, and the Senate designated him King of Judea (*Ant.* xiv.14.6 [381-85]; *BJ* i.14.4 [282-85]; cf. also Strabo xvi.2.46; Appian *The Civil Wars* v.75; Tacitus *Hist.* v.9). In late 40 or early 39 B.C. Herod returned to Palestine, and with the help of Antony's legate Sossius was able to recapture Galilee. Finally in the spring of 37 he laid siege to Jerusalem. Before the fall of Jerusalem Herod married Mariamne, niece of Antigonus, to whom he had been betrothed for five years. The intention of this marriage was to spite Antigonus and to strengthen Herod's claim to the throne since she was a Hasmonean. Jerusalem fell in the summer of 37 (*Ant.* xiv.15.8–16.2 [439-480]; *BJ* i.16.7–18.2 [320-352]; Tacitus *Hist.* v.9; Dio Cassius xlix.22). Herod requested that the Romans behead Antigonus (*BJ* i.18.3 [357]; Plutarch *Antony* xxxvi; cf. also Dio Cassius xlix.22), thus ending the Hasmonean rule. Herod, therefore, became the king of the Jews.

B. King of the Jews (37-4 B.C.). Herod's reign can be divided into three periods: first, consolidation from 37 to 25 B.C.; second, prosperity from 25 to 14 B.C.; and finally, the period of domestic troubles from 14 to 4 B.C.

1. Consolidation (37-25 B.C.). First, it was necessary for Herod to gain loyalty from his subjects and to eliminate those hostile to his rule. He contended with four adversaries: the populace and the Pharisees, the aristocracy, the Hasmonean family, and Cleopatra of Egypt.

Since the Pharisees held sway over the majority of the people, there was a reluctance to have Herod rule because he was an Idumean, a half-Jew, and a friend of the Romans. Herod punished with severity those Pharisees and elements of the population that opposed him. On the other hand he rewarded with favors and honors those who showed signs of loyalty to him. Two Pharisees, Pollion and his pupil Samaias (Shammai?) rendered favorable service to Herod, for they felt the domination by a foreigner was a result of a divine judgment that the population should willingly bear (*Ant.* xv.1.1 [2f.]; *BJ* 1.18.4 [358]).

The second adversary was the aristocracy, who were supporters of Antigonus. Herod executed forty-five of the Sadducean aristocracy; many if not all of them were members of the Sanhedrin. He confiscated their property to pay the demands placed upon him by Antony (*Ant.* xv.1.2 [5f.]; cf. xiv.9.4 [175]; *BJ* i.18.4 [358]).

The third adversary was the Hasmonean family. Herod's mother-in-law Alexandra, the mother of Mariamne, was the cause of the trouble. One Hasmonean was Hyrcanus, the former high priest, who had a good relationship with Herod. Upon Hyrcanus's return from the Parthian captivity, however, he was not able to resume his office as high priest because of his physical mutilation. Therefore, since Herod was an Idumean and could not assume the rule of high priest, Herod selected Ananel (Hananeel) of the Babylonian Diaspora. He was an insignificant priest from the Zadokite family thought to be of the Aaronic line, and who had held the high priesthood before the Hasmoneans. Herod thought this to be a legitimate way of bypassing the Hasmonean priestly line (*Ant.* xv.2.1-4 [11-22]).

Herod's mother-in-law Alexandra felt insulted, for she wanted her sixteen-year-old son Aristobulus, Mariamne's brother, to be high priest since he was the only legitimate heir for that position from the Hasmonean line. Alexandra put pressure on Herod by appealing to her friend Cleopatra, who then convinced Antony of Herod's wrong conduct; consequently under Antony's urging Herod removed Ananel (an unlawful removal since the high priest's office was lifelong) and installed Aristobulus as high priest when he was only seventeen years of age, *ca.* late 36 or early 35 B.C. (*Ant.* xv.2.5–3.1 [23-41]).

Although this action brought some relief to the tension between Herod and Alexandra, it was short-lived, because Herod thought of the Hasmonean family as his enemies. This distrust was so overbearing that Alexandra and her son Aristobulus tried to escape to Egypt in two coffins but were caught in the act when the plan was betrayed to Herod. Although he overlooked the offense because of his fear of Cleopatra's reprisals, his suspicion of Alexandra only intensified (*Ant.* xv.3.2 [42-49]). At the following Feast of Tabernacles (35 B.C.) Aristobulus officiated as high priest and the populace showed great affection for him; his popularity caused Herod to view him as a dangerous rival who had to be removed. Immediately after the festivities, Alexandra invited Herod to be her guest in Jericho. Herod exhibited friendliness toward Aristobulus and on a hot day suggested that they go swimming to cool off. Some of Herod's servants and friends were swimming and playing in the water with Aristobulus. As if in sport Herod's friends held Aristobulus's head too long under water and he drowned. Herod simulated the most profound grief and provided a lavish funeral and a very fine tomb (*Ant.* xv.3.2-4 [42-61]; *BJ* i.22.2 [437]).

Although the populace accepted the official version of an accidental death, Alexandra knew the facts and devoted herself to revenge. She convinced Antony through Cleopatra of Herod's misdeeds and Antony summoned Herod to appear before him at Laodicea (on the coast of Syria). Realizing that he could be sentenced to death, Herod put his wife Mariamne under the surveillance of his uncle Joseph, who was also the husband of Herod's sister Salome, and ordered her death if Herod were sentenced to die. Herod convinced Antony by means of gifts and eloquence that he was not guilty. When he returned Salome accused her husband Joseph of having intercourse with Mariamne. Mariamne denied this and Herod believed her. She revealed, however, that Joseph had informed her of Herod's order to kill her if Antony sentenced him to death. In a fit of rage Herod was now convinced that Salome's charge of adultery was accurate, and without a trial Joseph was executed. Since he felt that many of these problems were caused by Alexandra, Herod put her in chains and under guard (*Ant.* xv.3.5-9 [62-87]; *BJ* i.22.4f. [441-44]).

The final adversary was Cleopatra. She was greedy, and wanted to eliminate Herod and Malchus of Arabia and possess their land. Antony would not permit this, but he did give her the whole of Phoenicia, the coast of Philistia S of the Eleutherus River (except the free cities of Tyre and Sidon), the district of Jericho, which was the most fertile land of Herod's territory, having palm trees and balsams, and a part of Arabia (*Ant.* xv.4.1f. [88-103]).

In 32 B.C. civil war broke out between Octavius and Antony. Herod wanted to help Antony but was prevented by Cleopatra, who wanted Herod to make war on the Arabian king because he was late in paying his tribute to Cleopatra. Ultimately she wanted Herod and the Arabian to weaken and exhaust each other so she could take over both of their territories. In 31 B.C., shortly after the war between these two vassal rulers had come to a standstill, there was a terrible earthquake in Palestine that killed thirty thousand people. The Arabs seized the opportunity to attack, but Herod was able to muster an army, completely rout the Arabs, and demand their surrender. Herod returned home a victor (*Ant.* xv.5.2-5 [121-160]; *BJ* i.19.2f. [369-385]).

Soon afterward, on September 2, 31 B.C., Octavius defeated Antony in the Battle of Actium. This was a blow to Herod, who now had to skillfully convince Octavius that he was the legitimate ruler of Palestine. Fortune was on his side. In Cyzicus there were gladiators of Antony who were training for the games that were to be a part of the victory celebration of Antony over Octavius. When they heard of Antony's defeat they attempted to go to Egypt to help him, but were prevented from passing through Syria by Didus, the governor of Syria, and Herod (*Ant.* xv.6.7 [195]; *BJ* i.20.2 [392]; Dio Cassius li.7).

With this demonstration of loyalty, Herod now could go to Octavius. Before he departed to meet him, however, he did two things. First, he accused Hyrcanus, the only remaining rival to the throne, of plotting with the king of the Nabateans and had him executed (*Ant.* xv.6.1-4 [161-182]; *BJ* i.20.1 [386]). Second, fearing that possibly his mother-in-law, Alexandra, might cause some problems, Herod put her and his wife Mariamne in Alexandreion under the surveillance of his steward Joseph (not his brother-in-law) and Soēmus, a trusted friend. He ordered their death if he were killed, and the preservation of the kingdom for his sons and his brother Pheroras (*Ant.* xv.6.5 [183-86]).

Herod met Octavius at Rhodes (spring, 30 B.C.) and handled the situation skillfully. Although he admitted his loyalty to Antony, he demonstrated that he actually did not fight Octavius during the civil war because of his skirmish with the Arabs. Octavius was convinced of his loyalty, and confirmed his royal rank. Leaving Asia Minor, Octavius went along the Phoenician coast to invade Egypt. With great pomp Herod met him in Ptolemais, giving him eight hundred talents, duly appreciated by Octavius (*Ant.* xv.6.6f. [188-201]; *BJ* i.20.1-3 [387-395]).

After Octavius defeated Antony in Egypt, Herod went to Egypt to congratulate him. Octavius returned Jericho (which had been taken by Cleopatra) to Herod, and added Gadara, Hippos, Samaria, Gaza, Anthedon, Joppa, and Strato's Tower (which later became Caesarea) (*Ant.* xv.7.3 [215-17]; *BJ* 1.20.3 [396]). Indeed, Herod had gained much. He accompanied Octavius as far as Antioch on their return from Egypt in late 30 B.C.

Although Herod was politically successful, his domestic affairs fell into disarray. While Herod was in Rhodes, Mariamne discovered from the guard Soēmus that she was to be killed in the event that he did not return. This caused great upheaval in Herod's life. With the encouragement of his sister Salome, and their mother Cypros, both of whom hated Mariamne, Herod finally executed Mariamne at the end of 29 B.C. (*Ant.* xv.7.1-5 [202-236]). Herod never fully accepted her death. He became ill, and because there was some doubt that he would recover, Alexandra attempted to seize control of two fortified places in Jerusalem in order to secure the throne. Hearing of this plot, Herod had her executed in 28 B.C. (*Ant.* xv.7.6-8 [237-252]). Finally, the governor of Idumea, Costobarus (husband of Herod's sister Salome), who earlier conspired with Cleopatra against Herod but was forgiven because of Salome's entreaty, once again came under suspicion for alleged pro-Hasmonean sympathies. Salome now wanted to get rid of her husband, and supplied information about his plans for a revolt. She charged that her husband was preserving the influential sons of Babas who remained loyal to Antigonus and always spoke ill of Herod. Herod was incensed and executed Costobarus and his followers (25 B.C.). All the male relatives of Hyrcanus had now been removed, and no living contenders for Herod's throne remained (*Ant.* xv.7.9f. [253-266]). This marks the end of the first period of Herod's rule.

2. Prosperity (25-14 B.C.). Although there were times of distress, this period of Herod's reign was marked with

M. Avi-Yonah's model of the Herodian temple in Jerusalem (W. S. LaSor)

splendor. Reference may be made first to the cultural developments. Although violating the Jewish law, Herod introduced the quinquennial games in honor of Caesar and constructed theaters, amphitheaters, and hippodromes (*Ant.* xv.8.1 [267-276]; xvii.10.3 [255]; *BJ* ii.3.1 [44]). He rebuilt many fortresses in the land and temples in gentile territories. Strato's Tower was restored and renamed Caesarea. In 24 B.C. he built for himself a royal palace in Jerusalem (*Ant.* xv.8.5–9.6 [292-341]). His greatest achievement in construction was the temple, which was begun in 20 B.C. and completed in A.D. 63, long after his death (*Ant.* xv.11.1-6 [380-425]). The rabbis stated, "He who has not seen the temple of Herod has never seen a beautiful building" (T.B. *Baba Bathra* 4a), and they saw its construction as an "atonement for having slain so many sages of Israel" (Midr. *Nu. Rabbah* 14:8). Herod acquainted himself with Greek culture by surrounding himself with men of Hellenistic education. Herod's tutor, Nicolas of Damascus, was the most noted of the Greek rhetoricians who advised him and was entrusted with complex diplomatic assignments. After Herod's death Nicolas was very much involved in the settlement of his will.

Second, there were domestic changes. Late in 24 B.C. Herod married Mariamne (who will be designated as Mariamne II), daughter of Simon, whom Herod appointed as high priest (23-6 B.C.). In 22 B.C. Herod sent his two sons by Mariamne I, Alexander and Aristobulus, to Rome for their education. They were received by Caesar personally and stayed at the home of one of Herod's close friends, Asinius Pollio. It seems that at this time Herod made the first of his six wills, wherein he was allowed by Caesar to give his kingdom to whichever son he wished (*Ant.* xv.10.1 [342f.]). Upon the completion of their education in 17 or 16 B.C., Herod went to Rome. Returning to Judea with Herod, Aristobulus married Bernice, the daughter of Herod's sister Salome, and Alexander married Glaphyra, the daughter of Archelaus king of Cappadocia (*Ant.* xvi.1f. [6-11]; *BJ* i.23.1 [445f.]).

Third, there were political advances. In 22 B.C. when Herod's two sons went to Rome, Augustus (Octavius's newly acquired title) awarded Herod the new territories of Trachonitis, Batanea, and Auranitis (*Ant.* xv.10.1f. [343-49]; *BJ* i.20.4 [398f.]). Two years later, Augustus came to Syria and gave to Herod the additional territory formerly belonging to Zenodorus that lay between Trachonitis and Galilee (containing Ulatha and Paneas), and the immediate area N and NE of the lake of Gennesaret. In addition, Augustus made the procurators of Syria responsible to Herod for all their actions (*Ant.* xv.10.3 [354-360]; *BJ* i.20.4 [400]; Dio Cassius liv.7.4-6; 9.3). Herod also obtained the tetrarchy of Perea for his brother Pheroras (*Ant.* xv.10.3 [362]; cf. *BJ* i.24.5 [483]). To show appreciation he erected a beautiful temple for Augustus in Zenodorus's territory near Paneion (later called Caesarea Philippi) (*Ant.* xv.10.3 [363]; *BJ* i.21.3 [404-406]). Herod made an internal political move when he remitted a third of the people's taxes. This tax cut was made under the pretext of crop failure, but actually it was to soothe the resentment of many people offended by his emphasis on Greco-Roman culture and religion, which was leading to the dissolution of their religion and customs. Fearing the possibility of revolts, Herod forbade the people to congregate. He also ordered them to take a loyalty oath. Two Pharisaic leaders, Pollion and Samaias, and their disciples refused to take the oath. Since both of these men were well known and had helped Herod earlier in his life, he thought it wise not to pursue the matter. Also, because of his high regard for the Essenes, they were exempted from the oath (*Ant.* xv.10.4 [365-372]). In 14 B.C. Herod again lowered the taxes by one-fourth (*Ant.* xvi.2.5 [64f.]).

In conclusion, the period from 25 B.C. to 14 B.C. was one of advancement. Herod had a good relationship with the Roman government, and although there was some resentment among the people, he had them under control. His domestic situation was reasonably calm although toward the end of this period there were rumblings of trouble to come.

3. Domestic Troubles (14-4 B.C.). The last ten years of Herod's life were marked by intrigue. He was getting old and there was much infighting among his sons. This problem was compounded since Herod had ten wives, each of whom wanted her son(s) to be his successor (*Ant.* xvii.1.3 [19-22]; *BJ* i.28.4 [562f.]). His first wife Doris bore him one son, Antipater. Herod repudiated her and Antipater when he married Mariamne I, the granddaughter of Hyrcanus, in 37 B.C. By her he had two daughters and three sons (*Ant.* xiv.12.1 [300]; *BJ* i.22.1f. [431-35]). Late in 24 B.C. Herod married his third wife, Mariamne II, by whom he had Herod (Philip). In late 24 or early 23 B.C. Herod married his fourth wife, Malthace, who was a Samaritan and by whom he had Archelaus and Antipas. He married his fifth wife, Cleopatra of Jerusalem, probably sometime during 22 B.C., and she bore him Philip. The other five wives played no significant role and only three of them, Pallas, Phaedra, and Elpis, are even mentioned by name (*Ant.* xvii.1.3 [19-22]; *BJ* i.28.4 [562f.]).

Herod's two favorite sons were those by Mariamne I, Alexander and Aristobulus. When they returned from their education in Rome in 17 or 16 B.C. new domestic troubles arose. Herod's sister Salome had an intense hatred toward these two sons of Mariamne I, even though her daughter Bernice was married to Aristobulus. Salome wanted her son to succeed to his uncle's throne. Being Hasmonean, Alexander and Aristobulus at times were arrogant. Consequently, Salome spoke ill of their mother whom Herod had killed. Salome and Pheroras (brother of Herod and Salome) warned Herod that these two sons were out to avenge their mother's murder by bringing charges against him before Caesar that would cause him to lose his throne (*Ant.* xvi.3.1f. [66-77]).

Disturbed, in 14 B.C. Herod recalled his oldest son Antipater (son of Doris) from exile to curb the reckless attitude of Alexander and Aristobulus. Consequently, in 13 B.C. Herod made his second will, wherein he made Antipater sole heir of his domain. Herod sent Antipater with Agrippa (a friend of Augustus) to be presented to the emperor and possibly to have the will ratified. Antipater realized that Herod could again change his mind, and from Rome he wrote to Herod slanderous letters against Alexander and Aristobulus. Herod became more infuriated toward these two sons and finally in 12 B.C. he brought them before Augustus in Aquileia (near Venice) to be tried. This case resulted not in execution but in reconciliation. Returning home with Alexander, Aristobulus, and Antipater, Herod made his third will naming all three sons as successors (*Ant.* xvi.3.3–4.6 [86-135]; *BJ* i.23.2-5 [451-466]).

Shortly after their return from Rome (*ca.* 11 or 10 B.C.) Antipater, with the aid of Herod's sister Salome and brother Pheroras, began once more to slander Alexander and Aristobulus, which again aroused Herod's suspicions. Antipater furnished proof from one of Alexander's friends that Alexander, with the help of Aristobulus, was planning to kill Herod and flee to Rome to lay claim on Herod's kingdom. Herod imprisoned Alexander, but Alexander's father-in-law Archelaus, king of Cappadocia, was concerned about the welfare of his own daughter, and was able to reconcile Herod and Alexander (*Ant.* xvi.7.2–8.6 [188-270]; *BJ* i.24.2–25.6 [467-512]). There was peace again in Herod's household.

Although his troubles subsided, Herod had some difficulties with external enemies and even with the emperor. About forty of Herod's subjects in Trachonitis had become rebellious and fled to a neighboring Arab territory under the ruler Syllaeus, who had overthrown the king Obodas. In consultation with Saturninus and Volumnius, governors of Syria, Herod entered the Arab territory to capture the brigands and killed twenty-five Arabs who had come in defense of the brigands. Syllaeus, however, went before Augustus in Rome to accuse Herod of devastating the Arab territory and killing 25,000 Arabs. Augustus believed Syllaeus and wrote to Herod that he was to be treated as a subject and no longer a "friend of Caesar," a most coveted title. Herod immediately sent an embassy to Rome to defend himself, and when this failed he sent a second under the leadership of Nicolas of Damascus (*Ant.* xvi.9.1-4 [271-299]).

Meanwhile, new domestic troubles arose. A certain Eurycles from Lacedemon, in behalf of Antipater, played Alexander and Aristobulus against Herod. Other troublemakers became involved and finally Herod became so suspicious that he imprisoned Alexander and Aristobulus and accused them of treasonable plots in a report to the emperor (*Ant.* xvi.10.1-5 [300-324]; *BJ* i.26.1–27.1 [513-535]; cf. also Pausanias ii.3.5; Strabo viii.5.1; Plutarch *Antony* 67).

In Rome Nicolas of Damascus had an audience with the emperor and explained to him the true situation concerning Herod and the Arabs. When the emperor fully understood the situation, he executed Syllaeus and reconciled himself to Herod. About that time messengers from Herod arrived in Rome seeking the emperor's advice regarding his sons. Augustus gave Herod full authority to deal with his sons as he wished, but advised him to have a trial outside of Herod's territory at Berytus (Beirut) with Roman officials attending it. In accordance with the emperor's advice there was a trial in Berytus and the court pronounced the death sentence upon Alexander and Aristobulus. Thus, at Sebaste (Samaria), where Herod married Mariamne thirty years before, her two sons were executed by strangulation, probably in 7 B.C. (*Ant.* xvi.10.6–11.8 [325-404]; *BJ* i.27.1-6 [536-551]). This wiped out the Hasmonean line with the exception of Herodias, Antipas's wife, and her brother Agrippa I, who began his rule in A.D. 37.

Herod now made his fourth will naming Antipater as the sole successor. Antipater was impatient, however, and had secret conferences with Herod's brother Pheroras, tetrarch of Perea. Salome, Herod's sister, knew of these conferences and reported to Herod their intention to kill him. Herod's relationship with Antipater became strained. Realizing this, Antipater arranged with his friends in Rome to have Augustus request Herod to send Antipater to him. Herod sent him to Rome with the new will that named Antipater as the sole ruler, and in the event that Antipater's death was before his own, he named Herod (Philip), son of Mariamne II, as his successor.

While Antipater was in Rome, Pheroras died. His death was the seal of Antipater's fate. Upon investigation, Herod found that Pheroras was killed by poison sent by Antipater, but that the poison had been intended for Herod himself. From the female slaves of Pheroras Herod learned of Antipater's meetings with Pheroras, his complaint about Herod's long life, and the uncertainties of his own prospects for the throne. Herod recalled Antipater from Rome under false pretenses. With no suspicion Antipater returned and Herod immediately imprisoned him in the king's palace. The next day he was tried before Varus, the governor of Syria, and was without defense. Herod put him in chains and sent a report to Augustus. Meanwhile, another plot of Antipater against Herod was unveiled. Becoming very ill and realizing that his death was near, Herod drew up his fifth will, wherein he omitted Antipater and his next two oldest sons, Archelaus and Philip, because Antipater had poisoned his mind against them. He selected his youngest son Antipas, son of the Samaritan Malthace, as his sole successor (*Ant.* xvii.2.4–6.1 [32-146]; *BJ* i.29.1–32.7 [567-646]).

In the winter of 5-4 B.C. (quite possibly) Jesus was born. Magi had come to Jerusalem inquiring about the birthplace of the newborn king of the Jews. Herod summoned the wise men to tell him of the exact location of the Christ child so that he could come also and worship Him. When the wise men found Jesus in Bethlehem they were warned in a dream to return home another way. The Lord appeared to Joseph in a dream instructing him to flee to Egypt because of Herod's desire to kill the child. After they fled to Egypt, Herod killed all the male children of Bethlehem who were two years old and younger (Mt. 2:1-16). *See also* STAR OF THE WISE MEN.

New troubles arose for the aging Herod. He was nearly seventy years old and his incurable diseases only grew worse. Because of his condition two rabbis, Judas son of Sepphoraeus, and Matthias son of Margalus, incited the people to tear down the offensive eagle from the temple gate, an action they thought would be pleasing to God. Although Herod was weak, he seized the offenders and ordered that they be burned alive.

When he realized that the warm spring baths at Callirrhoe were no longer helping his diseases, Herod returned to Jericho. He ordered the notable Jews from all parts of the nation to come to him, and when they arrived he locked them in the hippodrome. Realizing how the people disliked him, he ordered his sister Salome and her husband Alexas to slay all the leaders in the hippodrome at the moment of his death, in order to insure national mourning rather than a festival. While giving these instructions, he received a letter from Rome in which the emperor granted him permission to execute his son Antipater, and he did so immediately. Herod then made his final will in which he selected Archelaus, the older son of Malthace, as king, his brother Antipas as tetrarch of Galilee and Perea, and their half brother Philip as tetrarch of Gaulanitis, Trachonitis, Batanea, and Paneas.

Finally, only five days after Antipater's execution, Herod died at Jericho in the spring of 4 B.C. Rather than killing the leaders that were locked up in the hippodrome, Salome and Alexas released them. In a public assembly at the amphitheater in Jericho, Ptolemy, who had been entrusted with the king's seal, read Herod's last will in public and the crowd acclaimed Archelaus as their king. A royal funeral procession accompanied Herod's body from Jericho for about 1½ km. (1 mi.) in the direction of Herodium, where he was buried (*Ant.* xvii.6.1-8 [147-199]; *BJ* i.33.1-9 [647-673]).

Herod's reign was one of violence, lasting for thirty-four years if one reckons the beginning of his reign as 37 B.C. His rule, however, was not much different from that of other potentates of his day. In the eyes of the Romans

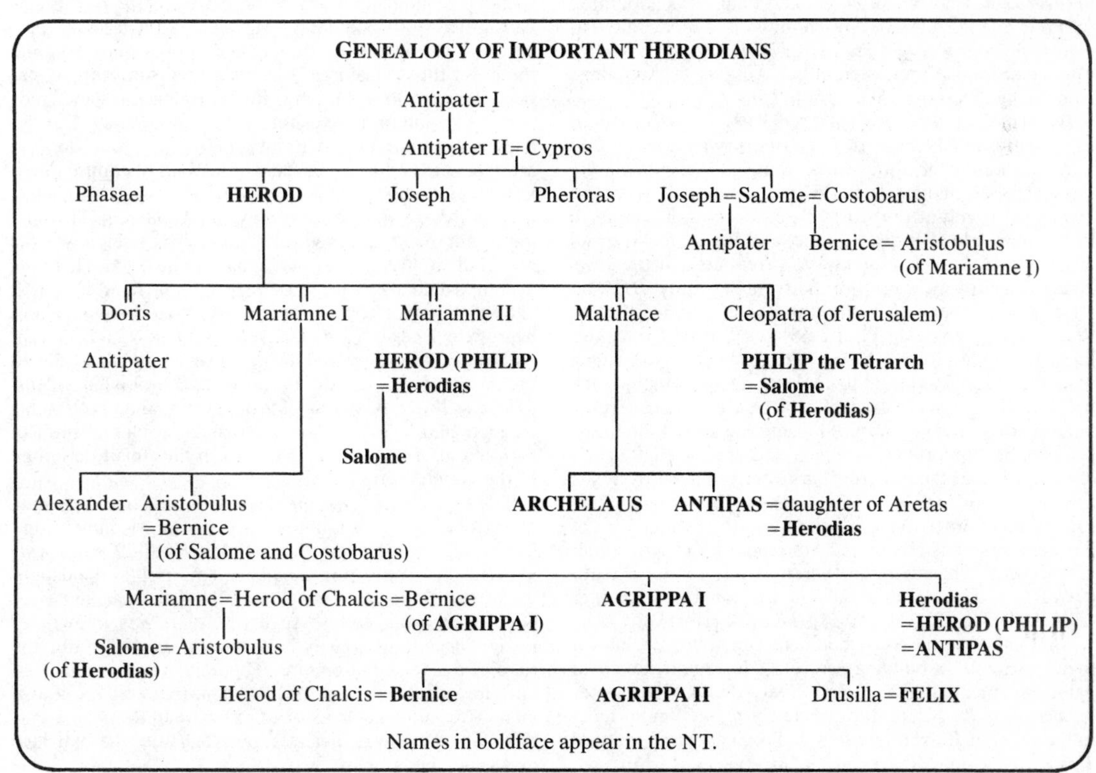

he ruled well; they realized that the Jews, because of their religious scruples, were not easy to satisfy. Since Herod was half Idumean, many Jews did not look upon him as a truly Jewish king.

III. Herod's Will Disputed.–During his life Herod made six wills, the last one only five days before his death. Archelaus took over the leadership, but did not accept the title of king nor allow himself to be crowned, for Herod's last will needed the emperor's ratification (*Ant.* xvii.8.4 [202f.]; *BJ* ii.1.1 [2f.]). The crowds, however, began making demands and Archelaus complied, thinking he would ingratiate himself with them. Some revolutionaries among the crowd sought to avenge the blood of those whom Herod killed for cutting down the eagle from the temple gate. Failing to pacify rioters who stirred up the crowd now attending the Passover, Archelaus sent in the army to suppress the crowd, and three thousand people were killed (*Ant.* xvii.8.4–9.3 [204-218]; *BJ* ii.1.2f. [4-13]).

Immediately after the Passover, Archelaus and Antipas left for Rome to contest Herod's last two wills, while Philip took care of the home front. Archelaus claimed that he should be king because that was the last will expressed by his father. Antipas contended for the validity of Herod's fifth will, which made Antipas king, because it had been ratified by the emperor and Herod was in good physical and mental health when he made it, in contrast to his health when he made his sixth will five days before his death. While the claimants were in Rome a revolt broke out in Jerusalem at the feast of Pentecost, and it took the Romans about two months to squelch it. As a result of the revolt a Jewish delegation was sent to Rome pleading autonomy for the nation and its unification with Syria. Philip also went to Rome. After considerable delay Augustus offered a compromise whereby he appointed Archelaus as ruler over Idumea, Judea, and Samaria. He gave him the title of ethnarch with the promise that he could become king if he provided good leadership. Antipas was made tetrarch over Galilee and Perea, and Philip was appointed tetrarch over Gaulanitis, Trachonitis, Batanea, and Paneas (*Ant.* xvii.9.5–11.4 [218-320]; *BJ* ii.2.1–6.3 [14-100]). This compromise prevented either Antipas or Archelaus from being given the coveted title *king*.

IV. Archelaus **(4 B.C.-A.D. 6).**–Archelaus, the son of Herod the Great and Malthace (a Samaritan), was born *ca.* 22 B.C. His killing of about three thousand people at the Passover before he left for Rome, combined with the prolonged revolt at the feast of Pentecost that spread to the countryside of Judea, Galilee, and Perea, made a bad beginning of Archelaus's rule. His treatment of the Jews and Samaritans was one of brutality and tyranny (*BJ* ii.7.3 [111]), as substantiated by Matthew (2:20-23), who states that when Joseph, Mary, and Jesus returned from their flight to Egypt, Joseph heard that Archelaus was ruling over Judea and was afraid to go there. Thus, being warned by God, they went to Nazareth of Galilee. Also, Archelaus removed the high priest Joazar, the son of Boethus, because he supported the rebels, and appointed Joazar's brother Eleazar whom Archelaus later replaced by Jesus son of See (*Ant.* xvii.13.1 [339-341]). He divorced his wife Mariamne in order to marry Glaphyra, the former wife of Alexander (son of Herod and Mariamne I and thus a half brother of Archelaus), and thereby transgressed the ancestral law, since she already had a son by Alexander (*Ant.* xvii.13.1, 4f. [341, 350-53]; *BJ* ii.7.4 [114-16]).

Although his rule was mediocre, he followed his father's example in building projects. He rebuilt the royal palace in splendid fashion, and diverted half of the water of the village of Neara into the newly planted palm trees in the plain of Jericho. He founded a village and honored himself by naming it Archelais (*Ant.* xvii.13.1 [340]).

Because of his oppressive rule he was finally deposed in A.D. 6. A delegation of Jews and Samaritans complained to Augustus about Archelaus's brutality and tyranny. For these two bitter enemies to join in their complaint against Archelaus indicated how bad the situation was. Also, Archelaus's brothers, Antipas and Philip, went to Rome and brought charges against him, probably because of his oversight of them while he was the ethnarch of the entire nation. As a result, Archelaus was banished to Vienna in Gaul (modern Vienne on the Rhone, S of Lyons) and Antipas and Philip retained their domains. Archelaus's territories were reduced to an imperial province under the rule of prefects (*Ant.* xvii.13.1-5 [342-355]; *BJ* ii.7.3–8.1 [111-18]; Strabo xvi.2.46; Dio Cassius lv.27.6).

V. Antipas **(4 B.C.-A.D. 39).**–Antipas, the son of Herod and Malthace (a Samaritan) and full brother to Archelaus, was born *ca.* 20 B.C.

A. Antipas's Realm. Of all the Herodians, he figures most prominently in the NT because he was the tetrarch over Galilee and Perea, the two territories in which John the Baptist and Christ had most of their ministries, and he reigned during their lives and activities.

Upon his return from Rome, Antipas had to restore order and rebuild that which had been destroyed from the revolt at the feast of Pentecost in 4 B.C. Following in the train of Alexander the Great and his father Herod the Great, Antipas founded cities. He rebuilt Sepphoris, the largest city in Galilee (*ca.* A.D. 8-10) and the capital of his territories until he built Tiberias. Joseph, Mary's husband, living in Nazareth only 6.4 km. (4 mi.) SSW of Sepphoris, may well have plied his trade as a carpenter (Mt. 13:55; Mk. 6:3) during its rebuilding. The second city to be rebuilt was Livias (or Julias) of Pereas in honor of Augustus's wife Livia. It was completed *ca.* A.D. 13 (*Ant.* xviii.2.1 [27]).

Although the Herodian family had built twelve cities, Tiberias was the first city in Jewish history to be founded within the municipal framework of a Greek *polis.* Antipas had difficulty in populating Tiberias because in the process of building the city they struck upon a cemetery, and the Jews thus considered the area unclean. Antipas enticed them to move there by offering free houses and lands and exemption from taxes for the first few years. The city, named in honor of the Emperor Tiberius, was finished around A.D. 25 and served as Antipas's capital (*Ant.* xviii.2.3 [36-38]).

B. Antipas's Reign. 1. Antipas and Archelaus. The only important event recorded early in Antipas's reign was the downfall of his brother Archelaus in A.D. 6. This was accomplished when he, his brother Philip, and a Jewish and Samaritan delegation went to Rome to complain about his rule to Tiberius (*Ant.* xvii.13.2 [342-44]; *BJ* ii.7.3 [111]). Although Antipas remained a tetrarch, he was able to obtain the dynastic title *Herod* (cf. *BJ* ii.9.1 [167]; *Ant.* xviii.2.1 [27]), which was of great significance both to his subjects and to the political and social circles of the Roman world. Tiberius may have given him this title in lieu of the coveted title *king*.

2. Antipas and John the Baptist. More than anything else Herod Antipas is known for his imprisonment and beheading of John the Baptist (Mk. 6:17-29 par.; *Ant.* xviii.5.2 [116-19]). Antipas had been married to the daughter of the Nabatean king Aretas IV. This marriage may have been arranged by Augustus, who was known for instigating intermarriages between various rulers for the sake of peace in the empire. This marriage provided not only for peace between the Jews and the Arabs, but also made Aretas available as a buffer between Rome and Parthia. Since this was arranged by Augustus, the marriage must have been before A.D. 14.

Coin of Antipas labeled (obverse) ΗΡΩΔΟΥ ΤΕΤΡΑΡΧΟΥ ("Herod, Tetrarch") and (reverse) ΤΙΒΕ ΡΙΑΣ ("Tiberias") (Trustees of the British Museum)

Antipas traveled to Rome *ca.* A.D. 29. On his way he visited his brother Herod (Philip), who apparently lived in one of the coastal cities of Palestine. Antipas fell in love with Herodias, his host's wife and his own niece. She saw the opportunity to become the wife of a tetrarch and agreed to marry Antipas upon his return from Rome, provided that he divorce his first wife (*Ant.* xviii.5.1 [109f.]). In some way Antipas's first wife discovered the plan and fled to her father. This divorce was an insult to Aretas, who later retaliated against Antipas.

When Antipas married Herodias, John the Baptist boldly criticized the marriage and was imprisoned by Antipas. The Mosaic law forbade the marriage of a brother's wife (Lev. 18:16; 20:21) except for levirate marriage (Dt. 25:5; Mk. 12:19). Since Antipas's brother had a daughter Salome, and more importantly, his brother was still living, levirate marriage did not apply.

Identifying Herodias's first husband is a problem. The Gospels state that he was Philip (Mt. 14:3; Mk. 6:17) but Josephus states that he was Herod, son of Herod the Great and Mariamne II, daughter of Simon the high priest (*Ant.* xviii.5.1 [109]). Since the Herodian family is confusing, it is thought by many that the Gospel writers had confused this Herod with Philip the tetrarch who later married Herodias's daughter Salome. However plausible this solution may seem at first, it is untenable for several reasons.

First, the Gospels would be guilty of three historical errors, namely, (1) that they confused this Herod with his half brother Philip, (2) that they made Philip the tetrarch (4 B.C.-A.D. 34) the husband of Herodias instead of the husband of her daughter Salome, and (3) that Salome would have been the daughter of Philip the tetrarch who, according to Josephus, had no children. These errors would seem to be incredible in light of the Evangelists' usual familiarity with historical matters. Also, when the early Christian community had people like Joanna, wife of Chuza, who was Antipas's financial minister (Lk. 8:3), and Manaen who was a close friend of Antipas (Acts 13:1), it seems that such a historical blunder is incredible.

Second, the Gospels speak of Herodias having a daughter previous to her marriage to Antipas (Mt. 14:6, 8-11; Mk. 6:22, 24-26, 28). This harmonizes exactly with Josephus's reference to her having a daughter named Salome from the former marriage (*Ant.* xviii.5.4 [136]). These details are more than coincidental, and thus it seems highly improbable that the Evangelists confused the Philips.

Third, some would argue that Herod the Great would not name two of his sons with the same name. It must be realized, however, that though both had the same father, they had different mothers. Furthermore, Herod the Great did have two sons named Antipas/Antipater and two sons named Herod.

Fourth, it is very probable that Herodias's first husband was called both Herod and Philip or Herod Philip. Although some argue that double names were not in use at that time, no one disputes that the Herod of Acts 12:1, 6, 11, 19-21 is the Agrippa of Josephus nor that Archelaus is Herod Archelaus.

Fifth, if the Gospel writers intended that Herodias's former husband was actually Philip the tetrarch, why did they not call him Philip the tetrarch as they had Herod Antipas within that same pericope (cf. Mt. 14:1, par. Mk. 6:14, 26, where Herod is first called tetrarch and then king)?

In light of the discussion above it seems most reasonable to conclude that the Philip in the Gospels and the Herod in Josephus are one and the same person; to do otherwise would seem to create inextricable confusion.

John's imprisonment was not enough for Herodias. At an appropriate time she arranged for a banquet, probably for Antipas's birthday, at Machaerus in Perea, in order to eliminate John the Baptist. There her daughter danced before dignitaries who served Antipas. Overwhelmed by her dance, Antipas promised with an oath to give her up to half of his kingdom. With the advice of her mother she asked for the head of John the Baptist on a platter. Although Antipas regretted his promise, he had to fulfil it because of his oath and because of the presence of his audience. John's death occurred *ca.* A.D. 31 or 32.

3. Antipas and Jesus. Antipas's relationship to Jesus is seen in three incidents. The first of these was when he heard of Jesus' ministry and, with a note of possible irony, concluded that this was John the Baptist resurrected (Mt. 14:1f.; Mk. 6:14-16; Lk. 9:7-9). Antipas thought he had eliminated a dangerous movement led by John, but now there seemed to be a more successful and remarkable people's preacher. Hence, he concluded it was John the Baptist all over again. Antipas desired to see Jesus, but was unable to do so because Jesus now withdrew from Antipas's territories. Furthermore, when Jesus did minister in his territories, Antipas did not want to have a confrontation that would cause resentment among his citizens as had occurred in his treatment of John the Baptist.

The second incident to be mentioned was Jesus' final journey to Jerusalem. While He was still in Antipas's territory of Galilee, some of the Pharisees told him that He ought to leave because Antipas wanted to kill Him (Lk. 13:31-33). Jesus told them to "Go tell that fox" that He would continue His ministry of casting out demons and healing the diseased for a short time, and when He accomplished His goal He would then go to Jerusalem to die. Apparently Antipas was fearful of Christ's popular movement, and although he threatened Him with death, it is highly improbable that he would have carried out his threat. He appeared fearful of an increase in resentment by the people who had not forgiven him for killing John the Baptist, whom they considered a prophet. Jesus intended to finish His ministry without interference. Although Antipas killed John the Baptist in his territory, he did not control the fate of Jesus.

The final incident was Jesus' trial by Antipas in A.D. 33 (Lk. 23:6-12). Since this incident is not in the other Gospels, some scholars think that this pericope is legendary. Luke, however, had an interest in the Herods, and since his addressee, Theophilus, was probably a Roman official, it is understandable that Luke would have included a pericope showing the relationship between the Herods and the prefects of Judea, especially since this pericope reports the reconciliation between Antipas and Pilate. On the other hand, since no progress in the trial of Christ is recorded in this pericope, it is understandable why the other Gospels omitted it. Some scholars argue that the source of this pericope is Acts 4:25f. (which quotes Ps.

2:1f.), but it seems that the opposite is true. Other scholars claim that the origin of this pericope was in the Gospel of Peter, but upon examination of this apocryphal work one will not find any real parallel to Luke's account of Antipas's trial of Jesus. In fact, the apocryphal account holds Antipas responsible for Jesus' death, whereas Luke does not mention his responsibility.

According to Luke, Pilate sent Jesus to Antipas, who was in Jerusalem for the Passover, when he heard that Jesus was from Antipas's territory, Galilee. Legally Pilate did not have to consult Antipas, but he wanted to extricate himself from an awkward situation. The Jews insisted on having Jesus killed; he felt that Jesus was innocent. Furthermore, Pilate needed to improve his relationship with Antipas because it had been strained by his killing some of Antipas's citizens (Lk. 13:1), and because Antipas had reported to Tiberius the trouble Pilate had caused the Jews when he brought votive shields into Jerusalem. As a result, Tiberius ordered Pilate to remove them immediately (Philo *Legatio ad Gaium* 299-304). Pilate had overstepped himself and needed to appease Antipas. On the other hand, Antipas did not want to give Pilate any reason to report him to the emperor, and so, after mocking Jesus, he sent Him back to Pilate without comment. As a result of this courtesy the two potentates became friends from that day forward (Lk. 23:12).

4. Antipas and Exile. In A.D. 36 Aretas attacked and defeated Antipas to avenge Antipas's treatment of Aretas's daughter when Antipas fell in love with Herodias. The Jews saw this defeat as a divine retribution upon Antipas for his killing of John the Baptist (*Ant.* xviii.5.1f. [109-119]). Tiberius ordered Vitellius, governor of Syria, to help Antipas, but before the governor attacked Aretas he went to Jerusalem with Antipas to celebrate the feast (probably Pentecost in A.D. 37). While in Jerusalem Vitellius learned of Tiberius's death (March 16, 37), and consequently called off his expedition against Aretas until he received orders from the new emperor Caligula.

Upon his accession, Caligula gave his friend Agrippa I, brother of Herodias, the land of Philip as well as the tetrarchy of Lysanius, with the title of king (*Ant.* xviii.6.10 [225-239]). Later (about August of 38), Agrippa went to see his acquisition in Palestine. When Agrippa I had received the coveted title of king, his sister Herodias became intensely jealous. She felt that her husband Antipas should have had the title for his faithful rule over the years. She prodded her husband into going to Rome to seek the same honor. Finally, in A.D. 39 Antipas and Herodias went to Rome, but meanwhile Agrippa sent one of his freedman to Rome to bring accusations against Antipas. This action resulted in Antipas's banishment to Lugdunum Convenarum, now Saint-Bertrand de Comminges in southern France, in the foothills of the Pyrenees. Caligula discovered that Herodias was the sister of Agrippa I and excused her from the exile; she chose to follow her husband. As a result, Agrippa I gained Antipas's territories (*Ant.* xviii.7.1f. [240-255]; *BJ* ii.9.6 [181-83]).

***VI. Philip the Tetrarch* (4 B.C.-A.D. 34).**–Philip was the son of Herod the Great and Cleopatra of Jerusalem, born *ca.* 22/21 B.C. In the settlement of Herod the Great's will, Augustus appointed him tetrarch over the northern part of Herod the Great's domain: Gaulanitis, Auranitis, Batanea, Trachonitis, Paneas, and Ituraea (*Ant.* xvii.8.1 [189]; 9.4 [319]; xviii.4.6 [106]; 5.4 [136]; *BJ* i.33.8 [668]; ii.6.3 [95]). The population of his territories was primarily Syrian and Greek (thus predominantly non-Jewish), and this is the reason he was the first and the only Herodian who minted coins with the emperor's image on them.

Philip the tetrarch rebuilt two cities (*Ant.* xviii.2.1 [28]; *BJ* ii.9.1 [168]). First, he rebuilt and enlarged Paneas, a city near the source of the Jordan. He renamed it Caesarea Philippi to honor the Roman emperor and to distinguish it from the Caesarea on the coast. It was here that Peter confessed Jesus' messiahship and received the revelation of the formation of the Church (Mt. 16:13-20 par. Mk. 8:27-30). Second, he rebuilt and enlarged the fishing village of Bethsaida (where the Jordan flows into the Sea of Galilee) to the status of a Greek *polis*. He renamed the city Julias in honor of Augustus' daughter Julia. It was here that Jesus healed the blind man (Mk. 8:22-26) and near this city He fed the five thousand and probably later the four thousand.

Coin of Philip the Tetrarch (4 B.C.-A.D. 34) showing head of Augustus (obverse) and the temple built by Herod to honor Augustus (reverse) (Trustees of the British Museum)

Philip lived a quiet and peaceable life. He was well liked by his subjects (*Ant.* xviii.4.6 [106-108]). He married Herodias's daughter Salome whose dance led to the execution of John the Baptist. They had no children (*Ant.* xviii.5.4 [137]).

When Philip died in A.D. 34, Tiberius annexed his territory to Syria. When Caligula became emperor in A.D. 37, he gave this territory to Agrippa I, brother of Herodias.

***VII. Agrippa I* (A.D. 37-44).**–Agrippa I, the son of Aristobulus (son of Herod the Great and Mariamne I) and Bernice (daughter of Herod's sister Salome and Costobarus), was born in 10 B.C. (*BJ* i.28.1 [552]; *Ant.* xix.8.2 [350]). He was the brother of Herodias.

Agrippa I was considered the black sheep of the Herodian family, for he accumulated many debts in his careless and extravagant life, especially after his mother's death. When his friend Drusus, son of the emperor Tiberius, was poisoned by Sejanus in A.D. 23, Agrippa lost the support and favor of the imperial family. Thus he was forced to retire quietly to Maltha, a fortress in Idumea, leaving many angry creditors behind him in Rome (*Ant.* xviii. 6.1f., 4 [143-47, 165]). Because of his bad situation, he contemplated suicide, but his wife Cypros pleaded with his sister Herodias for help. Sometime between A.D. 27 and 30 his uncle and brother-in-law, Antipas, provided him with a home and a small civil service position as an inspector of markets in Antipas's new capital Tiberias. Antipas and Agrippa I were not too favorably disposed toward one another, and their relationship was completely severed when at a feast (*ca.* A.D. 32/33) both had drunk too much wine and Antipas reproached Agrippa for his poverty and pointed out to the guests that the very food he was eating he owed to Antipas. Agrippa went to L. Pomponius Flaccus, legate of Syria, whom he had known intimately at Rome, but soon left for Rome after they quarrelled (*ca.* A.D. 35/36). He repaid old debts by incurring new ones (*Ant.* xviii.6.2f. [148-160]).

Upon returning to Rome he befriended Gaius Caligula. One day he made an unwise remark to Gaius, stating that he wished Tiberius would relinquish his office to Gaius, who was much more capable of ruling. This was reported to Tiberius by one of Agrippa's servants, and consequently Tiberius put Agrippa in prison, where he remained until Tiberius's death six months later (*Ant.* xviii.6.4-10 [161-236]; *BJ* ii.9.5 [178-180]; Dio Cassius lix.8.2).

When Caligula became emperor, he released Agrippa from prison and gave him a chain of gold equal in weight to the chain he had worn in prison. Furthermore, he conferred upon him the territory of Philip the tetrarch and the more northerly tetrarch of Lysanius and gave him the coveted title of king (*Ant.* xviii.6.10 [237]; *BJ* ii.9.6 [181]). The Senate also conferred upon him the honorary rank of praetor, a guardian of the state (Philo *In Flaccum* 40), and subsequently consular rank (Dio Cassius lx.8.2).

In late summer of A.D. 38 Agrippa went to Palestine to see his newly acquired domain. His presence in the land provoked Antipas's jealousy because he had obtained the title of king that Antipas had desired for many years. Agrippa's sister Herodias was even more incensed and she persuaded Antipas to ask the emperor for the title. Antipas departed for Rome in A.D. 39. When Agrippa heard of Antipas's mission he sent one of his freedmen, Fortunatus, to Rome to accuse Antipas of conspiracy against Rome. Agrippa's move was successful; it led to the downfall of Antipas and Agrippa's acquisition of Antipas's tetrarchy and property (*Ant.* xviii.7.1f. [240-256]; *BJ* ii.9.6 [181-83]).

When Caligula was murdered in A.D. 41, Agrippa happened to be in Rome and helped Claudius ascend to the throne (*Ant.* xix.4.1-6 [236-273]; *BJ* ii.11.1-4 [204-213]; Dio Cassius lx.8.2). As emperor, Claudius confirmed Agrippa in his rule and added Judea and Samaria to his domains. He now ruled over all the territory of his grandfather Herod the Great (*Ant.* xix.5.1 [274f.]; *BJ* ii.11.5 [214f.]).

In the NT Agrippa is remembered for his persecution of the early Church in order to gain the favor of the Jews (Acts 12:1-19). He killed James the son of Zebedee and imprisoned Peter, who was released by an angel. Agrippa ordered the execution of the prison guards. He was the most liked by the Jews of any of the Herods (*Ant.* xix.7.3 [328-331]; Mish. *Sotah* vii.8).

In A.D. 44 Agrippa died in Caesarea. There are two accounts of his death. Josephus states that on the second day of a festival in Caesarea, Agrippa appeared in a theater with a robe made of silver. The people, seeing his robe sparkling in the sunlight, cried out flatteries and declared him to be a god and begged for his mercy. While the king was basking in the adulation, he noticed an owl on a rope, an omen of his imminent death. Immediately, he had severe stomach pains and was carried to his house and died five days later (*Ant.* xix.8.2 [343-352]). On the other hand, Luke states that he was in Caesarea sitting on the judgment seat dressed in royal robes and was addressing the ambassadors from Tyre and Sidon with whom he had been displeased. While speaking, the people cried out that his voice was divine. Immediately an angel of the Lord struck him down because he did not give glory to God, and he was eaten by worms and died (Acts 12:20-23).

The principal parts of the two accounts are: (1) it occurred at Caesarea; (2) he was wearing a bright robe; (3) he was flattered by the crowd; and (4) a sudden death came upon him. The two accounts could be reconstructed as follows: Agrippa went to the festival in Caesarea as mentioned by Josephus, and on the second day (Acts 12:1 speaks of an appointed day), dressed in royal apparel he made the speech to the ambassadors of Tyre and Sidon and then died five days after he was struck down by an angel of the Lord. Thus, the two narratives can be harmonized.

His survivors were three daughters, Bernice, Mariamne, and Drusilla, and a son also named Agrippa who was seventeen years of age (*Ant.* xix.9.1 [354f.]; *BJ* ii.11.6 [218-220]). Because of Agrippa II's young age his father's territories were reduced to a Roman province.

***VIII. Agrippa II* (A.D. 50-100).**–Agrippa II, the son of Agrippa I and Cypros, daughter of Phasael (Herod the Great's brother's son) and Salampsio (Herod the Great's daughter) was born in A.D. 27 (*Ant.* xviii.5.4 [130-32]). Although Claudius wanted to make Agrippa II king over his father's territories, two freedmen persuaded him that a youth of seventeen years of age would not be able to rule such a large territory with so many diverse elements among the population. In A.D. 50, however, two years after the death of Agrippa II's uncle and brother-in-law Herod king of Chalcis, Claudius made Agrippa II king of Chalcis (*Ant.* xx.5.2 [104]; *BJ* ii.12.1 [223]). In 53 Claudius granted Agrippa II the tetrarchy of Philip — Abilene (or Abila), Trachonitis, and Arca (the tetrarchy of Varus) — in exchange for the territory of Chalcis (*Ant.* xx.7.1 [138]; *BJ* ii.12.8 [247]). Shortly after Nero became emperor in A.D. 54, he gave Agrippa the Galilean cities of Tiberias and Tarichea and their surrounding land as well as the Perean cities of Julias (or Betharamphtha) and Abila and their surrounding land (e.g., Julias had fourteen surrounding villages) (*Ant.* xx.8.4 [159]; *BJ* ii.13.2 [252]). In appreciation for the imperial favor, Agrippa enlarged his capital city Caesarea Philippi and renamed it Neronius (*Ant.* xx.9.4 [211]). Agrippa II now ruled Philip the tetrarch's territory with the added toparchies of Galilee and the three detached territories of Abilene, two middle toparchies of Perea, and Arca.

Agrippa II's private life was not exemplary. His sister Bernice came to live with him after their uncle, who was also her second husband, Herod king of Chalcis, died in A.D. 48. Because of the rumors of incest, she resolved to marry Polemo of Cilicia, but shortly after this she returned to her relationship with her brother. This incestuous relationship became the common chatter in Rome (*Ant.* xx.7.3 [145-47]; Juvenal *Satires* vi.156-160).

Like his father Agrippa I, and his uncle Herod king of Chalcis, Agrippa II had control of the vestments of the high priest and had the right to appoint the high priests (*Ant.* xv.11.4 [405-407]; xx.1.1-3 [9-16]; 5.2 [103]; 9.4 [213]). The Romans would consult him on religious matters and this may be why Festus asked him to hear Paul at Caesarea in A.D. 59. Agrippa was accompanied by his sister Bernice (Acts 25–26).

In May of 66 the revolution in Palestine began (*BJ* ii.14.4 [284]). Although Agrippa failed to quell the revolt, he sided with the Romans all through the war of 66-70. After Nero's suicide on June 9, 68, Vespasian sent his son Titus, with Agrippa accompanying him, to pay respects to the new emperor Galba. Before they reached Rome, however, they received the news of Galba's murder (Jan. 15, 69) and Titus returned to Palestine while Agrippa continued to Rome. After Vespasian was elected emperor (July 1, 69) by the Egyptian and Syrian legions, Agrippa returned to Palestine to take the oath of allegiance to the new emperor (Tacitus *Hist.* ii.81). Agrippa sided with Titus, who was in charge of the war in Palestine (Tacitus *Hist.* v.1), and after the capture of Jerusalem (Aug. 5, 70), Agrippa was probably present at the victory celebrations in Rome over the destruction of his people (*BJ* vii.1.2f. [5-40]).

Vespasian confirmed Agrippa in the possession of the kingdom he had previously governed and added new territories that are not recorded. In A.D. 75 he and his sister Bernice went to Rome where she resumed being Titus's mistress (as she had been during the war of 66-70). This became a public scandal (Tacitus *Hist.* ii.2). The Roman populace was against oriental queens because one of their choicest sons, Mark Antony, had been destroyed by the lust of the oriental queen Cleopatra. So Titus sent her away. When he became emperor in A.D. 79, Bernice returned again to Rome hoping to become the emperor's wife. But once again Titus sent her away (Dio Cassius lvi.18), and she returned to Palestine, fading out of the pale of history.

After this time, nothing is known of Agrippa except that he corresponded with Josephus about *The Jewish War*, praised him for his accuracy, and subsequently purchased a copy (*Vita* lxv [361-67]; *CAp* i.9 [47-52]). Some theorize that Agrippa II died in A.D. 93, but it seems more likely to have been *ca.* A.D. 100. Although the Talmud (T.B. *Sukkah* 27a) implies that Agrippa had two wives, Josephus gives no indication of his being married or having any children. His death marked the end of the Herodian family.

Bibliography.–M. Brann, *Monatsschrift für Geschichte und Wissenschaft des Judenthums,* 22 (1873), 241-256, 305-321, 345-360, 407-420, 459-474, 497-507; F. W. Farrar, *The Herods* (1898); W. Otto, *Herodes: Beiträge zur Geschichte des letzten judischen Königshauses* (1913); H. Willrich, *Das Haus des Herodes* (1929); J. S. Minkin, *Herod, King of the Jews* (1936); A. H. M. Jones, *The Herods of Judea* (1938); J. Blinzler, *Herodes Antipas und Jesus Christus* (1947); V. E. Harlow, *Destroyer of Jesus: The Story of Herod Antipas, Tetrarch of Galilee* (1954); S. Perowne, *Life and Times of Herod the Great* (1956); S. Perowne, *The Later Herods* (1958); F. O. Busch, *The Five Herods* (1958); G. Schofield, *Crime before Calvary: Herodias, Herod Antipas, and Pontius Pilate: A New Interpretation* (1960); F. F. Bruce, *Annual of Leeds University Oriental Society,* 5 (1963-65), 6-23; S. Sandmel, *Herod: Profile of a Tyrant* (1967); A. Schalit, *König Herodes: Der Mann und sein Werk* (1969); M. Grant, *Herod the Great* (1971); H. W. Hoehner, *Herod Antipas* (1972); E. Schürer, *HJP*² (1973), I, 287-357; M. Stern, "The Reign of Herod and the Herodian Dynasty," in S. Safrai and M. Stern, eds., *The Jewish People in the First Century* (1974), I, 216-307; R. T. France, *Nov.Test.,* 21 (1979), 98-120.

H. W. HOEHNER

HERODIANS hə-rō'de-ənz [Gk. *Hērōdianoi*]. The name of men of influence who were partisans of the Herodian house. They are mentioned specifically in three passages of the Gospels dealing with two incidents, one in Galilee and one in Jerusalem. Mark and Matthew associate the Herodians with the Pharisees in their opposition to Jesus (Mk. 3:6; Mt. 22:16= Mk. 12:13), but neither Luke nor John mentions them. Their origin may be traced to the time when Herod the Great sought to establish his right to rule in Palestine, because Josephus speaks of those both in Galilee and Judea who were of Herod's party (*Ant.* xiv.15.10 [450]; *BJ* i.16.6 [319]).

There has been much discussion of the origin of the name. Some think that the Latin suffix *-ianus* was appended to three adjectives employed as substantives in that period of Greek literature, meaning that they were domestic servants of Herod. Others hold that the suffix really represents the true Greek ending and would have the meaning of officers or agents of Herod. When one examines the Gospel narratives, however, it seems that the Herodians were neither domestic servants nor official agents of Herod, but rather adherents or partisans of Herod who were men of standing and influence. Their outlook was friendly to the Herodian rule, and consequently to the Roman rule upon which it rested.

Evidence from the Gospels seems to indicate that they were adherents of Herod Antipas. They preferred his rule to the direct rule of the Roman prefects. Although at the time of Herod the Great's death there were some Jews who wanted to put an end to the Herodian rule, later they found the rule of the prefects was less bearable than that of the Herodians. Consequently, Herod Antipas's rule was strengthened, and some Jews wanted a united nation under him. This may account for their being in Judea as well as in Galilee.

Were the Herodians an entirely separate group, or were they affiliated in some way to another party or sect? The problem comes to the fore when dealing with the meaning of the leaven of Herod in Mk. 8:15, and its replacement by the leaven of the Sadducees in Mt. 16:6. This becomes more acute if Mark's secondary reading, "the leaven of the Herodians" (p^{45} W, Θ, $f^{1, 13}$), is the correct one. The problem here is not the interpretation of the passage but whether there is any connection between the Herodians and the Sadducees. At first sight this connection seems incredible, because Herod the Great tried to discredit the Hasmonean house, and he never selected a priest from the Sadducees who was pro-Hasmonean. Rather, Herod the Great and Agrippa I selected most of the high priests from the house of Boethus (between Herod's death [4 B.C.] and Agrippa I's accession [A.D. 37] Judea was under Roman prefects and most of the high priests came from the house of Annas). It seems probable, therefore, that Boethusians who were pro-Herodian were really the Herodians, and the Sadducees were pro-Hasmonean. With Herod Antipas's marriage to Herodias (a Hasmonean on her mother's side), however, the political differences between the Boethusians (Herodians) and the Sadducees were less clear-cut. It may be possible that Antipas married Herodias to gain the support of the Sadducees. In fact, later rabbinic sources used the Boethusian name interchangeably with that of the Sadducees (Mish. *Menahoth* x.3). One might say that religiously and economically the Sadducees and the Herodians would have been very close if not identical. Although recently there has been an attempt to identify the Herodians with the Essenes, it seems impossible because the two groups are so different in character.

In conclusion, it seems best to identify the Herodians with the Boethusians who were religiously the same as the Sadducees, but were more pro-Herodian, while the Sadducees can be identified more with the Hasmoneans. As previously stated, these distinctions were less clear-cut with the marriage of Herod Antipas and Herodias. Furthermore, the Herodians and the Sadducees would have been on the same side of the political fence in opposition to the Pharisees; the former being pro-Roman while the Pharisees were anti-Hasmonean, anti-Herodian, and anti-Roman. Hence, it can be seen why the Herodians and the Pharisees, though political and religious enemies, would together oppose Jesus, because He was introducing a new kingdom that neither would have wanted. The Pharisees thought that Jesus misinterpreted the Mosaic law, and the Herodians felt that their mentor Herod Antipas should rule and have tribute money for the Roman coffers.

Bibliography.–W. Otto, Pauly-Wissowa, Suppl. II, 200-202; B. W. Bacon, *JBL,* 39 (1920), 102-112; E. Bickermann, *RB,* 47 (1938), 184-197; P. Joüon, *Revue des Sciences Religieuses,* 27 (1938), 585-88; H. H. Rowley, *JTS,* 41 (1940), 14-27; C. Daniel, *RQ,* 6 (1967), 31-55, 261-277; A. Negoiţă and C. Daniel, *Nov.Test.,* 9 (1967), 306-314; C. Daniel, *RQ,* 7 (1969), 45-79, esp. pp. 68-71; 7 (1970), 397-402; H. W. Hoehner, *Herod Antipas* (1972), pp. 331-342; W. J. Bennett, *Nov.Test.,* 17 (1975), 9-14; *DNTT,* III, 449-443.

H. W. HOEHNER

HERODIAS her-ō-dī'əs [Gk. *Hērōdias*]. The wife of Herod Antipas, who contrived the beheading of John the Baptist (Mt. 14:3-12; Mk. 6:17-29; Lk. 3:19f.). She was born *ca.*

8 B.C., the daughter of Aristobulus and Bernice. *See* chart in HEROD.

According to Josephus (*Ant.* xviii.5.1 [109]), Herodias's first husband was called "Herod," son of Herod the Great and Mariamne II, daughter of Simon the high priest. According to Mt. 14:3 and Mk. 6:17, however, he was called "Philip" (although a few Western MSS read "Herod" in Mt. 14:3, the best reading is clearly "Philip"; the name is not given in par. Lk. 3:19). Many scholars think that the Gospel writers confused him with Philip the tetrarch, who had married Herodias's daughter Salome. This is discussed in greater detail in HEROD V.

Herodias deserted her husband, Herod Philip, and married Herod Antipas in A.D. 27 after he divorced his first wife, a Nabatean princess (Josephus *Ant.* xviii.5.1 [110f.]). After John the Baptist publicly criticized her marriage to Antipas, Herodias contrived his execution. Later she shared Antipas's exile after Agrippa I arranged his downfall.

Bibliography.–K. Lake, *Expos.*, 8th series, 4 (1912), 462-477; W. Otto, Pauly-Wissowa, Suppl. II, 202-205; *Expos.T.*, 29 (1917), 122-26; G. Dalman, *PJ*, 14 (1918), 44-46; W. Lillie, *Expos.T.*, 65 (1954), 251; J. D. M. Derrett, *BZ*, N.F. 9 (1965), 49-59, 233-246; H. W. Hoehner, *Herod Antipas* (1972). H. W. HOEHNER

HERODION hə-rō'di-ən [Gk. *Hērōdiōn*] (Rom. 16:11). A Roman Christian to whom Paul sent greetings. The name seems to imply that he was a freedman of the Herods, or a member of the household of Aristobulus the grandson of Herod the Great (cf. v. 10). Paul calls him "my kinsman" (Gk. *syngenḗs*). In Rom. 9:3 this term is used with reference to the Jews with whom Paul shared his *génos*. Here however, Paul may be using the term in a different sense; for many of the persons referred to in ch. 16 are Jews, but he refers to only a few as *syngenḗs* (vv. 7, 11, 21). Thus, some have taken it to mean a close blood relative or close Christian companion.

HERODOTUS hə-rod'ə-təs. A fifth-century-B.C. Greek historian called "the father of history," who was initially a student of geography and ethnology. His historical research took him to Asia Minor, Mesopotamia, Phoenicia, and Egypt. Employing the accounts of eyewitnesses, plus his own accounts, archeological findings, traditions, and other written material, he attempted to probe the causes of important events; however, the limitations of his outlook place him at a distance from modern historiography. Among his notations about the people he called the "Syrians of Palestine" is a reference to their having originated in the area of the Red Sea. G. WYPER

HERON [Heb. *'ănāpâ*; Gk. *charadriós*; Lat. *Ardea cinerea*]; NEB CORMORANT. Herons are mentioned only in the abomination lists of Lev. 11:19 and Dt. 14:18. They are near relatives of the crane, stork, ibis, and bittern. The Hebrew term may have been a generic name for the seven or so varieties of *Ardeidae* still found in Palestine. Of these, the most common is *Ardea bubulcus*, the white ibis, which has Lake Huleh as its normal habitat. Closer to the Jordan, and also on the coast, are the common heron (*Ardea cinerae*) and the purple heron (*Ardea purpurea*). That several species existed in the 2nd millennium B.C. appears to be suggested by the association of the phrase "according to its kind" with the *'ănāpâ* in Lev. 11:19. The white herons are somewhat smaller than the purple variety, the latter being about 1 m. (3½ ft.) in length with a wingspread of approximately 1½ m. (5 ft.). The beak, neck, and legs constitute almost two-thirds of the length of the body, which is small, lean, and bony. Its general appearance of size results from its long, loose feathers. The heron eats fish and other aquatic animals, and was forbidden as food in the Mosaic legislation because of the possibility that it may have fed on unclean species. R. K. H.

HESED hē'səd, **SON OF** (1 K. 4:10, AV). *See* BEN-HESED.

HESHBON hesh'bon, hesh'bōn [Heb. *ḥešbôn*; LXX *Esebōn*]; AV also ESEBON (Jth. 5:15). A Transjordanian town mentioned thirty-eight times in the Bible. For geographical and linguistic reasons it is identified with Tell Ḥesbân, a mound rising 895 m. (2940 ft.) above sea level that guards the northern edge of the rolling Moabite plain where a southern tributary to the Wâdī Ḥesbân begins to cut down sharply toward the Jordan River about 24 km. (15 mi.) to the west. The tell is about 56 km. (35 mi.) E of Jerusalem, 19 km. (12 mi.) SW of Amman, 6 km. (4 mi.) NE of Mt. Nebo, and 180 m. (600 ft.) higher than ʿAin Ḥesbân, the perennial spring with which it is associated. Between 1968 and 1976 Andrews University sponsored five seasons of excavation there; in 1978 Baptist Bible College (Pennsylvania) continued the excavation of a Byzantine church.

- I. History
  - A. Biblical
  - B. Postbiblical
- II. Excavations
  - A. Iron Age Remains
  - B. Hellenistic and Roman Remains
  - C. Byzantine and Early Arab Remains
  - D. Ayyubid/Mameluke Remains

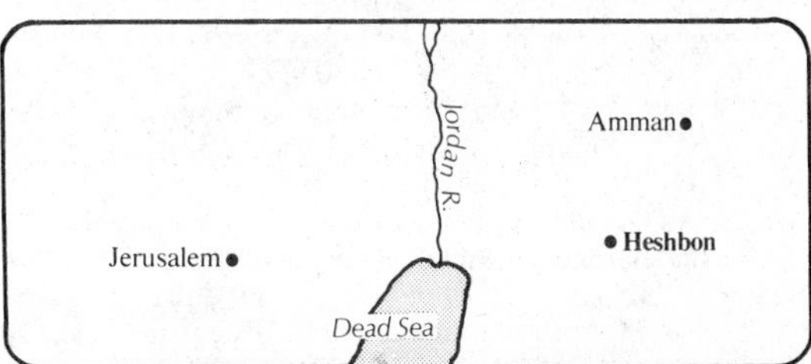

Tell Ḥesbân from the southeast (Heshbon Expedition, Andrews University; picture G. Unger)

I. History.–A. Biblical. The reference to Heshbon's earliest history is in Nu. 21:21-25 (cf. Dt. 2:16-37; Jth. 5:15), where it is referred to as the city of Sihon king of the Amorites, whose kingdom extended from the Jabbok in the north to the Arnon in the south, from the Jordan on the west to the Ammonites on the east (cf. Josh. 12:2; 13:10; Jgs. 11:22). Nu. 21:26-31 is an apparent attempt to justify

Israel's occupation, under Moses, of territory claimed at various times by Moab. This passage claims that at least the southern half of Sihon's kingdom, the geographical tableland known in the OT as the Mishor (Nu. 21:30; cf. Dt. 2:36), had indeed been Moabite, but that earlier Sihon had wrested it from Moabite control. As proof, the so-called Song of Heshbon (Nu. 21:27b-30), ostensibly an Amorite war taunt, was inserted in the narrative. The Israelite argument thus was that though Moabite territory was forbidden to them, the Mishor was an exception because it had been in Amorite hands during the Conquest. This claim was again made in Jgs. 11:12-28, where Jephthah denies the Ammonites ownership of the region between the Jabbok and Arnon on the basis that it was from the Amorites and not the Ammonites that it was originally taken by Israel.

The tribes of Reuben and Gad requested the territory that had been encompassed by Sihon's kingdom for their tribal allotment on the basis that it was good for their cattle (Nu. 32:1-5), but it was actually Reuben that built Heshbon and other nearby towns (Nu. 32:37), which were (according to the difficult and cryptic next verse) "changed as to name . . . and they called by [other?] names the names of the cities which they built." Josh. 13:15-23 confirms the allotment of Heshbon to Reuben, though vv. 24-28 indicate that it was contiguous to Gad's allotment. When Heshbon became a Levitical city it was considered a city of Gad (Josh. 21:34-40). If there is not outright confusion in the sources, apparently Reuben, like Simeon, soon lost its tribal identity and was absorbed, in this case, by Gad (cf. 1 Ch. 6:81 [MT 66]).

Though Heshbon is not mentioned by name in connection with the history of the united monarchy, 1 K. 4:19 puts "the land of Gilead, the country of Sihon king of the Amorites" in Solomon's twelfth district. Cant. 7:4 (MT 5) says, "Your eyes are like [with the versions] pools in Heshbon, by the gate [pl. in LXX and Vulg.] of Bath-rabbim."

The Mesha Stone (9th cent. B.C.) does not mention Heshbon, but since Medeba, Nebo, and Jahaz all came back into Moabite hands at that time, presumably Heshbon did as well. At least by the close of the 8th cent. and into the 7th cent., Heshbon appears to have been under firm Moabite control, for it figures in both extant recensions of a prophetic oracle against Moab (Isa. 15:4; 16:8f.; and Jer. 48:2, 34f.), in which its fields, fruit, and harvest are mentioned. By this time it may have been a steep tell, for fugitives stop in its shadow (Jer. 48:45). In Jer. 49:3, Heshbon appears again in the oracle against the Ammonites; perhaps it had changed hands again. Heshbon's final biblical mention is in Neh. 9:22, where it is included in a historical allusion to the Israelite Conquest.

B. Postbiblical. In the postbiblical literary sources, conveniently brought together by Vyhmeister, Heshbon is commonly called Esbus (though there are many variant spellings). Josephus says that in the 2nd cent. B.C. Tyre of the Tobiads was located "between Arabia and Judea, beyond Jordan, not far from the country of Heshbon" (*Essebōnitis, Ant.* xii.4.11 [233]). Further on he lists Heshbon among the cities (perhaps the capital) of the Moabitis, a district in dispute between the Ptolemies and the Nabateans (*Ant.* xiii.15.4 [397]). The Maccabean John Hyrcanus captured the cities of Medeba and Samaga in 129 B.C. (*Ant.* xiii.9.1 [255]). Even though Esbus is not specifically mentioned, it probably came into the hands of John Hyrcanus at this time because it is listed among the Jewish possessions in Moab during the reign of Alexander Janneus (103-76/75 B.C.), although not as a city captured by him (*Ant.* xiii.15.4 [397]).

Esbus is next mentioned in the late 1st cent. B.C. when Josephus includes *Esebōnitis* among several fortresses and fortified cities that Herod the Great built to strengthen his kingdom (*Ant.* xv.8.5 [294]); he populated it with veterans, probably to protect his border with the Nabateans. During the rule of Herod's son, Antipas (4 B.C.-A.D. 39), his territory of Perea was on the south "bounded by the land of Moab, on the east by Arabia, Heshbonitis, Philadelphia, and Gerasa" (*BJ* iii.3.3 [47]). Then at the beginning of the Jewish war (A.D. 66) the Jews sacked *Esebōnitis* (*BJ* ii.18.1 [458]). When the Roman province of Arabia Petrea was created in A.D. 106, Esbus was certainly a part of it; at least it appears there in Ptolemy's *Geog.* (v. 17), which reflects the political conditions of *ca.* A.D. 130-160. Ptolemy even gives its exact location, 68½ degrees longitude and 31 degrees latitude.

To summarize what is known about Esbus-Ḥesbân from later sources, the site should have been occupied in the following periods: 3rd cent., locally minted coins; 4th cent., Eusebius's *Onom.*'s site location; and all through this period, milestone evidence; Early Byzantine (4th-5th cent.), Christian council evidence; Late Byzantine (6th-7th cents.), continuing bishopric. Thereafter the evidence is skimpy until the Mameluke period (1260-1456), when once again the site enjoyed a resurgence of importance.

II. Excavations.–Six seasons of archeological excavation at Tell Ḥesbân have not uncovered any remains antedating *ca.* 1200 B.C. This poses a problem for the location of Sihon's Amorite capital, which may not have been found either because it is elsewhere on the site (unlikely) or because its (seminomadic) impermanent nature left no trace to be discovered (more likely). More extreme options are to consider the biblical account unhistorical or at least anachronistic (now favored by such OT scholars as Miller, Thompson, and Van Seters) or to seek the Amorite capital at another location, e.g., Jalul (a view favored by Horn). Most would at least identify Tell Ḥesbân with Greco-Roman Esbus, based on coin and milestone evidence coupled with such geographical specifications as required by Ptolemy and Eusebius. If one accepts Cross's reading of (Ammonite) Ostracon A.3 found at the site in 1978, it would support such an identification for Iron Age Heshbon as well. Altogether, the Andrews University expedition has reconstructed nineteen superimposed strata from the excavated remains, covering a period from *ca.* 1200 B.C. to A.D. 1500.

A. Iron Age Remains. The Iron Age remains (*ca.* 1200-500 B.C.) are very fragmentary due to periodic removals of earlier strata on top of the hill by later builders; nevertheless evidence for at least four strata remains. Stratum 19 (12th-11th cents.) probably represents a small unfortified village dependent on an agrarian-pastoral economy. In its earliest phase its most notable installation was a trench, 15 m. (50 ft.) long, 3.6 m. (12 ft.) deep, crudely carved out of bedrock on the tell's southern shelf. There is no real clue as to its purpose, though suggestions have included a moat for defense, storage, cultic activity, subterranean habitation, or a water channel (if not a narrow reservoir itself). In its later phase this installation was filled in with soil and into it were built both the cobbled floor of a room and a "filler" wall 2½ m. (8 ft.) wide. An egg-shaped cistern may also be associated with this phase, which produced so many loom weights that there may have been a cottage industry. Stratum 18 (10th cent.) left no *in situ* remains but its typologically later pottery was found in deep dump layers outside the contemporary settlement on the western slope; it may have been a continuation of the Stratum 19 village. Stratum 17 (9th-8th cents.) is also represented by sloping debris layers dumped to the west but it is better known for (perhaps) the initial construction, on the tell's

Reservoir at Heshbon. Note the header-and-stretcher construction (Iron II/Persian Period) and the plaster *in situ* on the right (Heshbon Expedition, Andrews University; picture A. Dick)

southern shelf, of an almost 2,000,000-l. (500,000-gal.) reservoir, 15 m. (50 ft.) to a side (its thrice-plastered eastern wall supplemented a bedrock cut by a header-stretcher retaining wall), and 6 m. (20 ft.) deep. Though several channels carved out of adjoining bedrock funneled rain water to the reservoir, its capacity appears to exceed the normal amount of winter rain that would fall on the catchment area; perhaps it was intended that extra water be transported up to the reservoir from below the mound. If so, this stratum may be what is left of Mesha's attempt to fortify his northern border with Israel. Could this be the pool referred to in Cant. 7:4?

Stratum 16 (7th-6th cents.) was the best preserved Iron Age stratum; its remains indicate a general prosperity and continued growth, probably clustered around a fort. A few scattered domestic units came to light on the western slope and the reservoir continued in use — perhaps a part of a way station or supply depot on the King's Highway. It was probably controlled by the Ammonites, to judge from the pottery and several ostraca found in the reservoir fill. (These ostraca have already been important in enlarging our knowledge of the Ammonite dialect and script.) Stratum 16 may have come to a violent end, considering the great quantity of ash in the debris scraped from the abandoned town into the reservoir by the (Maccabean?) rebuilders in the 2nd century.

B. Hellenistic and Roman Remains. After about a three-hundred-year abandonment of the site, Tell Ḥesbân was again occupied in the Late Hellenistic period. The remains from the Hellenistic and Roman periods (*ca.* 200 B.C.-A.D.

Heshbon Ostracon IV, containing a list of goods, e.g., grain, cattle, wine, "for the king" (*lmlk,* line 1). From the late 7th-early 6th cent. B.C. (Heshbon Expedition, Andrews University)

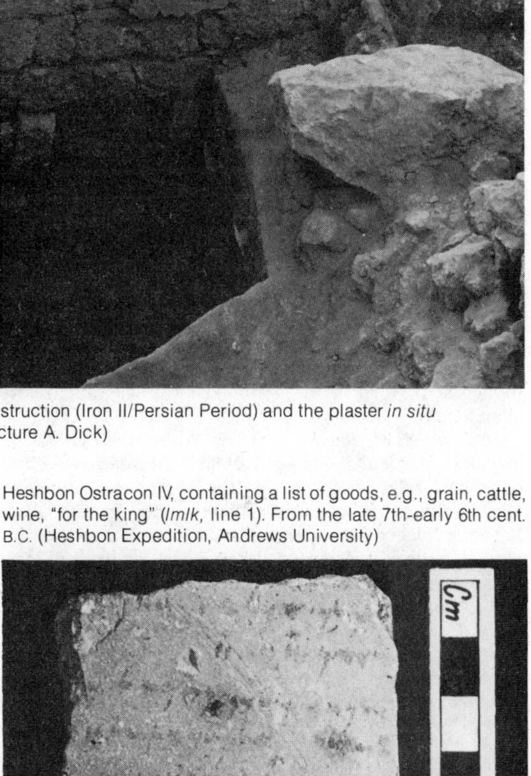

365) comprise at least five strata. Stratum 15 (*ca.* 200-63 B.C.) consisted primarily of a rectangular military fort at the site's summit, probably surrounded by the dwellings of dependents that were often associated with bell-shaped subterranean store silos. In Stratum 14 (*ca.* 63 B.C.-A.D. 130) Esbus came under the control of Herod the Great, probably as a border fort against the Nabateans. There is abundant evidence for extensive underground dwellings on the mound and characteristic Herodian-period family tombs in the cemetery (where two such tombs were found sealed by rolling stones). The town of Stratum 14 was destroyed by an earthquake, so Stratum 13 (A.D. 130-*ca.* 193) contained much new building. A new inn with an enclosed courtyard S of the fort testifies to the increased traffic past the road junction (*via nova* and Esbus-Livias) at which Roman Esbus was located. In Stratum 12 (*ca.* A.D. 193-284) the inn was partially rebuilt and well used. On the acropolis, earlier masonry was incorporated into what has been interpreted as a small temple — perhaps the one depicted on the Elagabalus coin minted for Esbus, a very fine example of which was found at the site in 1973. Access to the temple from the south was by a ramp. Stratum 11 (*ca.* A.D. 284-365) continued to demonstrate a modest level of prosperity. A porch was added to the temple and a double colonnade built eastward from it. The inn S of the acropolis platform was demolished, and a wide monumental stairway replaced the earlier earth ramp. The stratum came to an abrupt end with the severe earthquake of A.D. 365.

C. Byzantine and Early Arab Remains. Apart from the earthquake the transition from the Roman to the Byzantine periods was a gradual one. The Roman cemetery continued to be used. At least six strata encompass the Byzantine and Early Arab remains (A.D. 365-*ca.* 1000). Two basilica-type churches were built during this period, though at the end of the period the site was apparently abandoned.

D. Ayyubid/Mameluke Remains. Although it was a village of no particular significance during the earlier periods of Islamic rule, after a gap in the sedentary occupation Ḥesbân flourished again immediately after the Crusades. It even replaced ʿAmman as the capital of the Belqaʾ region of central Transjordan. Its remains comprise at least three strata (*ca.* 1200-1456) that were relatively well preserved compared to earlier remains. The tell was apparently deserted in the 15th cent., but the late 19th cent. marks the gradual return to limited occupation in the Ottoman and Modern periods.

Bibliography.–For detailed preliminary reports on each season at Tell Ḥesbân, see R. S. Boraas and S. H. Horn, *Andrews University Monographs,* 2 (1969); 6 (1973); 8 (1975); J. A. Sauer, 7 (1973); R. S. Boraas and L. T. Geraty, 9 (1976); 10 (1978); and the following issues of *Andrews University Seminary Studies*: W. Vyhmeister, 6 (1968), 158-171; A. Terian, 9 (1971), 147-160; 12 (1974), 35-46; E. N. Lugenbeal and J. A. Sauer, 10 (1972), 21-69; R. G. Bullard, 129-141. See also F. M. Cross, "An Unpublished Ammonite Ostracon from Hesban," in L. T. Geraty, ed., *Archaeology of Jordan and Other Studies Presented to S. H. Horn* (1981); *EAEHL,* II, *s.v.* (S. H. Horn); S. H. Horn, *BA,* 32 (1969), 26-41; R. S. Boraas and L. T. Geraty, *Archaeology,* 32 (1979), 10-20.

L. T. GERATY

HESHMON hesh'mon [Heb. *ḥešmôn*] (Josh. 15:27). An unidentified place on the border of Judah toward Edom, near Beth-pelet. This may have been the original home of the Hasmoneans (the name used by Josephus [e.g., *BJ* i.1.7(19)] and the rabbis [e.g., Mish. *Middoth* i.6] for the Maccabees).

HETH heth [ח]. The eighth letter of the Hebrew alphabet; transliterated in this encyclopedia as *ḥ* (guttural *h*). It came also to be used for the number eight and with the diaeresis for eight thousand. *See* WRITING.

HETH heth [Heb. *ḥēṯ*] (Gen. 10:15; 23:10 [AV]; 1 Ch. 1:13). In Gen. 23:10 the ancestor of the Hittites (Heb. *bᵉnê ḥēṯ*). In the Table of Nations (Gen. 10:15; cf. 1 Ch. 1:13) Heth is the second son of Canaan. The Hittites (AV "sons of Heth") who appear in Gen. 23; 25:10; 49:32 were probably early migrants or colonists from some part of the Hittite empire, which itself never actually extended so far south into Palestine. Perhaps an allusion to such a migration is reflected in the order of names in Gen. 10:15f., where Heth was placed between Sidon and the Jebusites.

See also HITTITES.

HETHLON heth'lon [Heb. *ḥeṯlôn*; Pesh. *ḥeṯrōn*]. A place mentioned on the ideal northern border of Israel (Ezk. 47:15; 48:1). Apparently its location would be between the Mediterranean coast and the "entrance of Hamath" in northern Palestine, or it may be identical to the "entrance of Hamath" (Nu. 34:8; Ezk. 47:15, LXX; 48:1). Perhaps the modern Heitela, NE of Tripoli, Syria, represents it. The exact location is unknown. R. J. HUGHES, III

HEW; HEWER; HEWN [Heb. *ḥāṣaḇ, ḥōṣēḇ*] (Dt. 6:11; 1 K. 5:15; 2 Ch. 26:10; Neh. 9:25; Isa. 5:2; 10:15; 22:16; 51:1; Jer. 2:13; Hos. 6:5); AV also DIG, MAKE; NEB also QUARRYMAN, DIG, LASH (Hos. 6:5); [*gāḏaʿ*] (Dt. 7:5; 12:3; 2 Ch. 14:3; 31:1; 34:4, 7; Isa. 10:33); AV also CUT DOWN; NEB also HACK DOWN; [*pāsal*] (Dt. 10:1, 3; 1 K. 5:18); NEB CUT, "shape the blocks"; [*tāzaz*] (Isa. 18:5); AV CUT DOWN; NEB STRIKE OFF; [*kāraṯ*] (Isa. 14:8; Jer. 6:6); AV also FELLER; NEB FELL, CUT DOWN; [*kārâ*] (Gen. 50:5; 2 Ch. 16:14); AV DIG, MAKE; NEB BUY; [*šāsap*] (1 S. 15:33); [*ḥāṭaḇ*] (Dt. 29:11; Josh. 9:21, 23, 27; 2 Ch. 2:10); NEB CHOP, WOODMAN; [*gāzîṯ*] (Ex. 20:25; 1 K. 6:36; 7:9, 11f.; Lam. 3:9; Ezk. 40:42; Am. 5:11); NEB also DRESSED, "blocks of"; [Aram. *gᵉḏaḏ*] (Dnl. 4:14, 23); [Gk. *latoméō*] (Mt. 27:60; Mk. 15:46); NEB CUT.

"Hew" is used to translate several Hebrew words having the meaning of "cutting." Heb. *ḥāṣaḇ* generally means to excavate a rock chamber, e.g., a cistern (Dt. 6:11; 2 Ch. 26:10) or a well (Jer. 2:13); *hḥṣbm,* "miners," occurs in the SILOAM inscription (lines 4, 6), describing those who tunneled through rock to supply Jerusalem with water. *Gāḏaʿ* expresses the idea of bringing down or "hacking" (NEB) the Asherah (Dt. 7:5; 2 Ch. 14:3). *Pāsal* means to cut into a shape, e.g., the tablets of the law (Dt. 10:1, 3), while *kāraṯ* means to cut down trees. The AV and RSV render *kārâ* by its meaning of cutting out or excavating; the NEB, on the other hand, renders the other meaning of "purchase." Though Heb. *ḥāṭaḇ* is translated "hew," it is probably closer in meaning to Arab. *ḥaṭaba,* meaning to "gather firewood"; it is usually found in construct with Heb. *ʿēṣîm,* "wood" or "trees." The Gibeonites were compelled to gather firewood as punishment for their subterfuge (Josh. 9:21, 23, 27). "Hewn" is generally Heb. *gāzîṯ* from the verb *gāzâ,* "cut off." It applies solely to hewn or dressed stone. The prohibition against the use of dressed stones on the altar is found in Ex. 20:25.

Aramaic *gᵉḏaḏ* appears only in Dnl. 4:14, 23, meaning to cut down a tree. "Hewn" appears twice in the NT for Gk. *latoméō,* meaning to hew out of rock.

A. L. PERLMAN

HEXATEUCH. This word, formed on the analogy of

"Pentateuch," "Heptateuch," etc., is used by modern writers to denote the first six books of the Bible (i.e., the Law and Joshua) collectively. The notion that the Hexateuch was a fundamental element of a consciously constructed history of Israel consisting of Genesis through 2 Kings was one of the offshoots of nineteenth-century literary-critical speculation. Indeed, for those scholars who held that the Pentateuch had been compiled on the basis of underlying "documents," which they designated by such symbols as J, E, D, P, H, and L, the existence of at least a Hexateuch seemed assured if only because they felt confidence in their ability to trace these alleged sources into Joshua, Judges, and even beyond. Unfortunately, it was not apparent to Wellhausen and his followers that the book of Joshua began an entirely new phase in Hebrew history, and had they appreciated this elementary fact they might have been less enthusiastic than they were about thinking in terms of a "Hexateuch."

More recent scholarship has necessitated a revision of this approach to pentateuchal criticism. Liberal writers, arguing from a seventh-century-B.C. date for Deuteronomy, have thought of the canonical compositions from Joshua through 2 Kings as a so-called "Deuteronomic history," which in part overlaps and conflicts with the idea of a history of Israel beginning at Genesis and ending with 2 Kings. Joshua, Judges, Samuel, and Kings had all undergone Deuteronomic editing, it was alleged. This presumably meant that a supposed Deuteronomic school of scribes, which Wellhausen and others had credited with the production of Deuteronomy in the 7th cent. B.C., had worked over the historical material in question and had compiled and edited a variety of literary sources until something approaching the canonical writings emerged. On the ground that the basic integrity of the Hexateuch has considerably less in its favor than that of the so-called Deuteronomic history, many liberals have arrived at the conclusion that the "Hexateuch" is at best an unreal postulate. Some have even conceded the folly of attempting to recover supposed J and E sources in Joshua, Judges, and beyond, and of identifying them with their alleged counterparts in the Pentateuch proper. For conservative scholars, the fact that the "sources" of nineteenth-century literary criticism are themselves entirely illusory, and that their existence at any time is totally undemonstrated, is in itself sufficient warrant for avoiding the concept of a "Hexateuch." When it is realized further that form criticism can be employed to refute decisively any possibility of the presence of such imaginary literary entities as "J" and "E" in Genesis, and, by implication, elsewhere in the Pentateuch (*see* GENESIS II), the fallacy of pursuing such nonexistent "documents" into the post-Mosaic historical writings becomes apparent immediately.

When the evidence for a second-millennium B.C. date and wilderness provenance for Deuteronomy is examined carefully (*see* DEUTERONOMY IV), it becomes obvious that any attempt to envisage Deuteronomy as a work composed just prior to 621 B.C., when a sacred law scroll was discovered in Jerusalem, lends active support to a fraudulent view of its authorship and date. This being the case, it is difficult to see precisely how a "Deuteronomic school" could ever have existed in the first place, and much more how such a "body" could have edited the post-Mosaic historical writings. If one turns from scholarly fantasies to the factual world of Hebrew tradition, it has to be admitted immediately that there has never been any work known to the ancient Hebrews as the "Hexateuch," since the Jewish canon made an entirely separate entity of the Pentateuch, and placed Joshua and the related historical writings in a different section. The Samaritans went even further, denying canonicity to any piece of writing except the books of the Pentateuch. Had there been a Hexateuch in existence when the Samaritans limited their scriptural canon to their Pentateuch, it would most certainly have been recognized at that time. At the hands of both liberal and conservative scholars, therefore, the concept of a Hexateuch appears to have met its fate.

See also PENTATEUCH; JOSHUA, BOOK OF III.

R. K. H.

HEZEKI hez'ə-kī. *See* HIZKI.

HEZEKIAH hez-ə-kī'ə [Heb. *ḥizqîyâ, ḥizqîyāhû*–'Yahweh strengthens'; Gk. *Hezekias*]; AV also EZEKIAS (Mt. 1:9f.). **1.** Son of Ahaz and king of Judah. His leadership marks a significant religious era in Judah's history, being a direct contrast to the idolatry and apostasy that prevailed under his father Ahaz and his son Manasseh. Sirach ranks Hezekiah with David and Josiah among the noteworthy pious rulers (Sir. 49:4). The scriptural accounts of his reign are given in 2 K. 18:1–20:21; 2 Ch. 29:1–32:33; Isa. 36–39. Cf. also Sir. 48:17-25.

Chronologically it seems reasonable to allot the twenty-nine-year reign of Hezekiah to the years 716-687 B.C. The references in 2 K. 17:1 and 18:9f. may represent an adjusted synchronism, according to E. R. Thiele (*MNHK*, pp. 139-148).

Throughout his reign Hezekiah encountered problems with the Assyrians, to whom Ahaz had committed the kingdom of Judah as a vassal. Although Hezekiah enjoyed periods of considerable freedom, the threat of Assyrian interference and occupation became acute on several occasions.

Hezekiah initiated a drastic reaction to the idolatry that prevailed under Ahaz. Being twenty-five years of age when he began to reign, he had observed the gradual disintegration and capitulation of the northern kingdom as the Assyrians advanced southward. Keenly did he realize that Israel had been taken into captivity because of its disobedience to God's laws. Placing his confidence in God, Hezekiah was concerned to renew the covenant his people had broken. Not only in Judah, but also extending north into Israel, he led an effective reform. Acknowledging the suzerainty of Sargon II (722-705), Hezekiah apparently encountered no serious impositions even when the Assyrian king conquered Ashdod in 711 B.C. Isaiah, walking barefoot and clad as a slave for a three-year period, dramatically warned his people that it was futile for them to look to Egypt for help even though Shabaka had successfully established the 25th Dynasty about this time.

The temple was immediately reopened. Hezekiah called in the Levites to repair and cleanse their place of worship. Things primarily used for idol worship were removed to the brook Kidron for destruction. Temple vessels that Ahaz had desecrated were sanctified. In sixteen days the temple was ready for worship.

Hezekiah and the officials of Jerusalem initiated the sacrifices in the temple. As had been the custom in Davidic times, musical groups accompanied by harps, lyres, and cymbals participated. The presentation of the burnt offerings was accompanied by liturgical singing. As the people worshiped, they sang praises to God using the words of David and Asaph.

Attempting to heal the breach that had separated Judah and Israel since Solomonic times, Hezekiah sent letters throughout the land inviting the people to come to Jerusalem for the Passover. Although some ignored Hezekiah's appeal, many responded, coming from Asher, Manasseh, Ephraim, and Issachar, as well as from Judah, to celebrate the festival. After consulting with the religious leaders, Hezekiah planned the celebration of the Passover one month later than prescribed so as to allow adequate time for preparation. In other respects the law of Moses was carefully observed; but the month's postponement was, most likely, a conciliatory measure to gain the participation of the northern tribes, who had been following the observance date instituted by Jeroboam I (1 K. 12:32). When some priests came without proper sanctification, Hezekiah prayed for their cleansing. A large congregation assembled in Jerusalem to participate in the reformation. Altars throughout the capital were removed to the Kidron Valley for destruction. Led by the priests and Levites, the people offered sacrifices, sang jubilantly, and rejoiced before the Lord. At no time since the dedication of the temple had Jerusalem seen such joyful celebration.

During this reformation Hezekiah destroyed the bronze serpent provided by Moses (Nu. 21:4-9), in order to terminate its use as an object of worship. Inspired by the king, the people went out to demolish pillars, Asherim, high places, and altars throughout the land. With the organization and employment of the priests and Levites, the tithe was reinstituted for their support. Feasts and seasons were again observed in accordance with the law.

Although Isaiah is not mentioned in the accounts of this great reformation, it is reasonable to assume that he cooperated fully in Hezekiah's attempt to restore worship according to the Mosaic law. The only reference to Isaiah's activity during the first half of Hezekiah's reign is the prophet's warning during the Ashdod rebellion in 711 B.C. This may have prevented an attack by the Assyrians on Jerusalem at this time.

Anticipating difficulties with Assyria, Hezekiah also developed an extensive defense program. Fortifications around Jerusalem were reinforced, the production of shields and weapons was increased, and combat forces were organized. To assure Jerusalem of an adequate water supply in time of siege, Hezekiah constructed a tunnel connecting the pool of SILOAM and the spring of GIHON. (This feat of engineering, whereby fresh water was channeled through 533 m. [1748 ft.] of solid rock, has attracted tourists in Jerusalem ever since its discovery in 1880, when Hezekiah's inscription was read in the tunnel.) The wall of Jerusalem was also extended to include this vital source of water, the pool of Siloam, in the city limits. Other springs of water in the surrounding area were cut off when it became apparent that the Assyrians were advancing on Jerusalem.

Having done all he could from the human standpoint, Hezekiah placed his trust in God. This attitude of confidence in God was boldly expressed by the king himself before the people assembled in the city square, with the words: "With him is an arm of flesh; but with us is the Lord our God to help us, and to fight our battles" (2 Ch. 32:8).

The biblical accounts of the Hezekiah-Sennacherib relations (2 K. 18–20; 2 Ch. 32; and Isa. 36–39) have been subjected to extensive interpretation in the light of new discoveries. Tirhakah (Isa. 37:9) was probably born *ca.* 709/708 B.C., which approximates to the period when Shabaka established himself on the Egyptian throne. Shabataka, who was associated with Shabaka in 699, became sole ruler *ca.* 697. Tirhakah became associated with Shabataka in 689 and became sole ruler in 684. Consequently, the account in which Tirhakah figures as a threat to the Assyrian king seems to refer to events after 689 B.C. (cf. K. A. Kitchen, *Ancient Orient and OT* [1966], pp. 82-84).

Sennacherib's accession to the Assyrian throne in 705 precipitated rebellions in Babylon. By 702 Merodach-baladan was forced to retreat from Babylon, leaving his throne to Bel-ibni, a native Chaldean. Subsequently, the Assyrian armies advanced westward in the Fertile Crescent, taking Sidon, Joppa, and Ekron, en route to Eltekeh, where they defeated the Egyptians. Hezekiah was forced to release Padi king of Ekron. In addition, the king of Judah paid a heavy tribute, stripping the temple of its silver and gold.

Apparently it was during this period of Assyrian pressure (*ca.* 701 B.C.) that Hezekiah became severely ill (Isa. 38:1-21; *see* BOIL). Although Isaiah warned the king to prepare for death, God intervened. The divine promise to

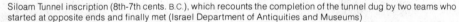

Siloam Tunnel inscription (8th-7th cents. B.C.), which recounts the completion of the tunnel dug by two teams who started at opposite ends and finally met (Israel Department of Antiquities and Museums)

Hezekiah was twofold — a fifteen-year extension of his life, and deliverance of Jerusalem from the Assyrian threat (Isa. 38:4-6).

In the meantime Sennacherib was besieging Lachish. Perhaps aware that Hezekiah had placed his confidence in God for deliverance, the Assyrian king sent his officers to the Fuller's Field highway near the Jerusalem wall to urge the people to surrender. Sennacherib even claimed that he was commissioned by God in demanding the capitulation of Jerusalem, citing an impressive list of conquests where other nations had trusted in their gods. Isaiah, who already in the days of Ahaz had predicted that the Assyrians would not wholly absorb the kingdom of Judah (Isa. 7:20; 8:8), now continued to reassure Hezekiah (Isa. 37:6f.).

Rumors of a Babylonian rebellion reached Sennacherib while he was besieging Libnah. Immediately the Assyrians departed, since Babylon was strategically more important than Egypt for Sennacherib. Even though he had conquered forty-six walled cities in the maritime plain, he makes no such claim for Jerusalem. In his records he boasts of taking some 200,000 Judean captives and reports that Hezekiah was shut up like a bird in a cage. Isaiah's prediction of Sennacherib's assassination was not fulfilled until twenty years later, but Hezekiah experienced immediate relief from the Assyrian threat.

Hezekiah's physical recovery and successful resistance to Assyria brought him the acclaim and recognition of surrounding nations, who bestowed upon him many gifts (2 Ch. 32:23). The powerful Babylonian leader Merodach-baladan, who was still stirring up rebellions, sent his congratulations to Hezekiah on his recovery — perhaps a recognition of the king's successful recovery from the economic hardships of Assyrian occupation (2 Ch. 32:27-29) as well as of his personal restoration to health. Hezekiah's triumph and his enthusiastic reception of the Babylonian embassy were tempered by the solemn warning by Isaiah that succeeding generations would be subjected to Babylonian captivity (Isa. 39:1-8). Nevertheless, this outstanding deliverance may have given the religious reformation a new impetus, while peace and prosperity continued under the reign of Hezekiah for another fifteen-year period. Apparently Manasseh, who became a "son of the law" at the age of twelve in 696/695, was officially made a co-regent with his father on the throne of David.

After numerous attempts to maintain control of the Babylonians, Sennacherib destroyed the city of Babylon in 689 B.C. Hearing of Tirhakah's advance, Sennacherib proceeded into Arabia toward Egypt, which may have been his real objective in his previous campaign in 701. Possibly hoping to ward off Judean interference, he dispatched letters addressed to Hezekiah personally with an ultimatum to surrender (Isa. 37:9-38). This time Hezekiah does not seem to be disturbed by this threat but confidently takes the letter to the temple and engages in prayer. Divine assurance of safety comes through a message sent by Isaiah to Hezekiah. The location of Sennacherib's army is not indicated in the scriptural account, which describes how 185,000 troops were slain through divine intervention. Immediately, the Assyrian king returned to Nineveh, so that Hezekiah's peaceful reign continued. When Hezekiah died he was buried in honor. S. J. SCHULTZ

2. An ancestor of Zephaniah (Zeph. 1:1; AV Hizkiah).

3. One of the returned exiles from Babylon (Ezr. 2:16; Neh. 7:21) who set his seal with Nehemiah on the covenant (Neh. 10:17 [MT 18]).

4. The AV rendering of HIZKIAH (1 Ch. 3:23).

HEZEKIAH, MEN OF. A body of men to whom is ascribed the compilation of a supplementary collection of Solomonic proverbs (Prov. 25:1). *See* PROVERBS, BOOK OF.

HEZEKIAH'S SICKNESS. *See* BOIL; DISEASE III.J.

HEZION hē'zi-ən [Heb. *ḥezyôn*; LXX B *Azein*, A *Azaēl*]. An ancestor of Ben-hadad I, king of Syria (1 K. 15:18).

HEZIR hē'zər [Heb. *ḥēzîr*; LXX B *Chēzein*, A *Iezir*].

1. A Levite in the time of David (1 Ch. 24:15).

2. [LXX *Hezeir*]. A chief of the people in the time of Nehemiah (Neh. 10:20 [MT 21]).

HEZRO hez'rō; **HEZRAI** hez'rī [Heb. *K ḥeṣrô, Q ḥeṣray*] (2 S. 23:35; 1 Ch. 11:37). A Carmelite, i.e., an inhabitant of Carmel, who was one of David's thirty mighty men. The ancient versions almost unanimously support the form "Hezrai," which is the reading of the AV and NEB in 2 S. 23:35.

HEZRON hez'ron [Heb. *ḥeṣrôn, ḥeṣrōn*; LXX *Asron*].

1. A son of Reuben (Gen. 46:9; Ex. 6:14), and head of the family of the Hezronites (Nu. 26:6).

2. A son of Perez and grandson of Judah (Gen. 46:12; Nu. 26:21; 1 Ch. 2:5, 9, 18, 21, 24f.; 4:1); a direct ancestor of David (Ruth 4:18f.). He appears also in the genealogy of Our Lord (Gk. *Esrōm*; Mt. 1:3; Lk. 3:33).

HEZRON hez'ron [Heb. *ḥeṣrôn*–'enclosure']. A town on the southern border of Judah between Kadesh-barnea and Addar (Josh. 15:3); the parallel passage Nu. 34:4 mentions HAZAR-ADDAR, which may be a combination of Hezron and Addar or a neighboring town. Conder suggested that the name has survived in Jebel Hadîreh, a mountain NW of Petra in the Tîh. It is to be distinguished from Keriath-hezron, which is also located in southern Judah.

HEZRONITES hez'rōn-īts [Heb. *haḥeṣrônî, haḥeṣrōnî*; LXX *ho Asrōnei*]. The name of the descendants of Hezron the son of Reuben (Nu. 26:6), and of the descendants of Hezron the son of Perez (26:21).

HIDDAI hid'ī [Heb. *hidday*; Gk. *Hatthai*]. One of David's thirty mighty men (2 S. 23:30), described as "of the brooks of Gaash." In the parallel list in 1 Ch. 11:32 the form of the name is Hurai (Heb. *hûray*).

HIDDEKEL hid'ə-kel [Heb. *ḥiddeqel*; Sum. Idiglat, Idigna; Akk. *Idiqlat*; Old Pers. *Tigrâ*; postbiblical Aram. *dîglaṯ*; cf. modern Turkish *Dicle*]. The AV rendering in Gen. 2:14 and Dnl. 10:4 for the TIGRIS River.

HIDE [Heb. *kāsâ* (Gen. 18:17; Ps. 32:5; Isa. 51:16), *kāḥaḏ* (Gen. 47:18; Josh. 7:19; 1 S. 3:17f.; etc.), *ṣāpan* (Ex. 2:2f.; Job 10:13; 14:13), *ʿālam* (Lev. 20:4; Job 6:16; 42:3; etc.), *sāṯar* (Ex. 3:6; Dt. 7:20; 31:17f.; etc.), *ḥāḇāʾ* (Gen. 3:8, 10; Josh. 2:16; etc.), *nûs* (Jgs. 6:11), *ṭāman* (Gen. 35:4; Ex. 2:12; Josh. 2:6; etc.), *maṭmôn* (Job 3:21), *taʿalumâ* (Job 28:11), *ḥāpaś* (Prov. 28:12), *kānap* (Isa. 30:20), *ḥaḇâ* (1 K. 22:25; 2 K. 7:12; Isa. 26:20), *mistār* ("hiding place," Ps. 10:8; Jer. 49:10; Lam. 3:10), *sēṯer* ("hiding place," Ps. 32:7; 119:114), *maḥaḇēʾ* (Isa. 32:2); Gk. *krýptō* (Mt. 5:14; 25:25; Lk. 18:34; Jn. 8:59; 12:36; Rev. 6:15f.), *kryptós* (Mk. 4:22), *apokryptō* (25:18), *apókryphos* (Lk. 8:17; Col. 2:3), *enkrýptō* (Mt. 13:33; Lk. 13:21), *lanthánō* (Mk. 7:24), *perikrýptō* (Lk. 1:24)]; AV also COVER, REMOVE; NEB also CONCEAL, SHELTER, WITHDRAW, BLIND, etc.; **HIDDEN** [Heb. *sāṯar* (Gen. 4:14; Ps. 19:12 [MT 13]; 38:9 [MT 10]; etc.), *ʿālam* (Lev. 4:13; 5:2-4; Nu. 5:13; etc.), *ṭāman* (Dt. 33:19; Josh. 7:21f.; Job 3:16; Ps. 31:4 [MT 5]), *kāḥaḏ* (2 S. 18:13; Ps. 69:5 [MT 6]; 139:15), *ḥāḇāʾ* (Isa. 42:22), *maṭmôn* (Prov. 2:4), *sôḏ* (Prov.

11:13), *nāṣar* (Isa. 48:6), *ṣāpan* (Josh. 2:4), *bāṣar* (Jer. 33:3); Gk. *krýptō* (Mt. 13:35, 44; 1 Tim. 5:25; Rev. 2:17), *kryptós* (Mt. 10:26; Lk. 12:2; 1 Cor. 4:5; 1 Pet. 3:4), *apokrýptō* (Mt. 11:25; Lk. 10:21; 1 Cor. 2:7; Eph. 3:9; Col. 1:26), *lanthánō* (Lk. 8:47), *aphanḗs* (He. 4:13)]; AV also SECRET, "lay privily," MIGHTY, etc.; NEB also BURIED, CONCEALED, SHIELDED, etc.

A large number of words are used in the English versions to render the concept of "hiddenness." A common usage of this idea in the Bible is that of "hiding" as the ordinary action of concealment for physical protection. In the OT, Moses' mother hid him at the river's brink to protect him from Pharaoh's command to kill all Hebrew boy babies (Ex. 2:2f.; cf. He. 11:23); Rahab the harlot hid two men prior to Israel's conquest of Jericho (Josh. 2:4f.); and David was urged by Jonathan to go into hiding when King Saul wished to kill him (1 S. 19:2; 23:19; 26:1). The command to hide came to Elijah from God (1 K. 17:3), and God provided for him. Yet this type of hiding was not always successful, as when Ahaziah was killed while hiding in Samaria (2 Ch. 22:9), and also in the case of evildoers who try to hide themselves from the eyes of God (Job 34:21f.). Occasionally in the OT the concept is used for that which is secret and concealed, e.g., sin (Job 31:33; Ps. 32:5; cf. 19:12) or love (Prov. 27:5; cf. 11:13).

Yet in the OT the usage of the idea of "hiddenness" goes far beyond physical actions and develops as an important theological concept. The wide variety of Hebrew synonyms for expressing the thought is an indication of the distinctive attitude of the Hebrew mind in its "deep sense of the hidden mystery of God" (Richardson, *Intro. to the Theology of the NT,* p. 58). "The mind of Israel was characterized by a profound sense of the hiddenness of things, in marked contrast to Greek thought with its sanguine capacity of reason to probe the inmost secrets of reality" (*RTWB,* p. 108). This is the presupposition of the doctrine of revelation, viz., that God is hidden from people's sight and therefore must reveal Himself if mankind is ever to know Him or His purposes.

In part, God's own "hiddenness" is due to His transcendence, His being "wholly other" than human. God is invisible to mankind and not observable like human beings or objects in the world (1 K. 8:12; Dt. 4:11). He and His wisdom are withdrawn from mankind and "hid from the eyes of all living" (Job 28:21). Yet nothing can be "hidden" from this God who controls all being; "everything that is hid he brings forth to light" (Job 28:11; cf. Ps. 139:15). "The OT takes God's omnipresence and omniscience more seriously than any other religion" (*TDNT,* III, 967).

But "hiddenness" is also a characteristic of God's dealings and presence in the world. This is due chiefly to the results of human sin. In the book of Isaiah the people are told: "Your iniquities have made a separation between you and your God and your sins have hid his face from you so that he does not hear" (Isa. 59:2; cf. Ezk. 39:23f.; Hos. 5:3). From a faithless generation God is said to "hide his face" (Dt. 31:16-18), leaving people in despair about His absence (Ps. 104:29; 143:7; 89:46 [MT 47]; etc.). Throughout the centuries "Israel had to bear the mystery of God's withdrawal and often spoke of the experience and trials which this entailed." Her experience taught her that "all true knowledge of God begins with a knowledge of his hiddenness" (von Rad, II, 374, 377; cf. Barth, pp. 179-204).

Though Yahweh may be hidden from His people, His people cannot hide from Him, for His eyes are "upon all their ways . . . nor is their iniquity concealed" from His eyes (Jer. 16:17). No one can find a place so secret that God cannot see him (Jer. 23:24; cf. Isa. 29:15); such was the experience of Adam and Eve when they tried to hide themselves among the trees of the garden (Gen. 3:8, 10; cf. 4:14). Death was the result for Achan, who broke the command not to steal during the battle of Jericho and was found out by Joshua after a word from Yahweh (Josh. 7:19-21). Ps. 139 gives a vivid portrayal of the vanity of trying to flee from God's omniscience.

The righteous person gives up this useless flight, no longer trying to conceal his iniquity (Ps. 32:5) but confessing every innermost sin (69:5) and disclosing all his perversity to God. This acknowledgment brings restored fellowship to him and enables him to receive the wonder of God's forgiveness (cf. Pss. 38, 51, 102, 130, 143, etc.).

Restored fellowship brings comfort to the righteous person, who finds now that his way is not hidden from the Lord (Isa. 40:27) and that he is given a share in the "hidden life" of Yahweh. God "covers" the righteous and hides them in the "shadow of his hand" (Isa. 49:2; 51:16); He is for them "a hiding place" (Ps. 27:5; 32:7; 119:114; etc.). According to Anderson, "the Hebrew *sēṯer* is the favourite term of the Psalmists. . . . The idea may have originated in the ancient belief and practice that the sanctuary offered a right of asylum" (II, 836).

Yet Yahweh is in continuing control of His revelation and may conceal it (Prov. 25:2), even from His prophets (2 K. 4:27). Increased incapacity to receive revelation may lead to increased concealment by Yahweh (Isa. 57:17) and "even the righteous knows the painful experience of God's concealing His face or His ear from him" (*TDNT,* III, 969; cf. Job 13:24; 34:29; Ps. 44:24 [MT 25]; etc.). This distress is almost unbearable (Ps. 69:17 [MT 18]) and the psalmist wonders how long the pain and sorrow of it all will last (13:1f. [MT 2f.]; *sāṯar* here can be rendered "turn your face" as *apostréphō* in the LXX, and "denotes divine displeasure or even punishment," as in Isa. 54:8; 59:2; etc.; see Anderson, I, 128). This experience of God is as a bear or lion waiting in ambush, ready to attack (Lam. 3:10). The believer's only hope is the remembrance of Yahweh's "steadfast love" and "faithfulness" (Lam. 3:22f.). The lamenter in Scripture "flees from the hidden God to the revealed God" in prayer (*TDNT,* III, 969).

As God's commandments (law) are like "hidden treasures" (Prov. 2:4) and His promises true (Ps. 119:140; cf. 2 S. 22:31), the "immediate task of the righteous is to hide this treasure in himself" (*TDNT,* III, 970; cf. Ps. 119:11, AV "Thy word have I hid [*ṣāpan*] in mine heart, that I might not sin against thee"). God's demand, however, is that what He says and does is not to be kept hidden but is to be proclaimed joyfully in the worshiping community (Ps. 40:10 [MT 11]; cf. 22:22 [MT 23]) and to the coming generations (78:4).

In the NT a similar pattern may be observed. The main words (Gk. *krýptō, kryptós,* and *apokrýptō*) agree with the oldest sense of the Hebrew terms, meaning to "cover" or "conceal." Jesus' simile of the kingdom of heaven being "like treasure hidden in a field, which a man found and covered up" (Mt. 13:44) is reminiscent of Yahweh's command to Jeremiah to hide a linen cloth by the Euphrates and then to dig it up again (Jer. 13:4-6), an action that became a sign of judgment on arrogant Judah. This concept of concealment is found throughout the Synoptic Gospels, where "everything divine is primarily and essentially hidden" and is "accessible only through God's revelation" (*TDNT,* III, 973, cf. 967f.). God has finally revealed Himself fully in the life and work of Jesus Christ, but the revealing of the salvation found in Him is "concealed" from the unreceptive, the proud, and the opinionated. Revelation is closed to human unreceptivity (Lk. 18:34; 19:42; cf. 9:45), for these things are "hidden from the wise and understanding" but are revealed to "babes" (Mt. 11:25; Lk. 10:21; cf. Mt. 13:35). Jesus impresses on His disciples that God's cause, having emerged from its original concealment, is now given over to them, and that now God will bring it out in the open (Mk. 4:22 par.). God's kingdom, like a buried treasure, is now found and brings great joy (Mt. 13:44); or like a tiny morsel of leaven mixed with a measure of meal, it will come forth from a most insignificant beginning (Jeremias, pp. 201, 149). Selfishness in hiding this message is condemned (Mt. 25:14-30 par.). The disciples' lives are to radiate its light, keeping the message as conspicuous as a city set on a hill (Mt. 5:14).

Though God's revelation to sinful mankind may be given and yet be "concealed," a person's secret acts or motives cannot be kept hidden from God. If one tries to cover his hypocrisy, one is engaged in a futile attempt to hide the truth (Mt. 10:26; Lk. 12:2), because "before God no creature is hidden" (He. 4:13; Gk. *aphanḗs*). "Nothing escapes the scrutiny of God's eyes and before him everything lies exposed and powerless" (Bruce, p. 83).

Yet for the person with an "inward beauty of character" (Beare, p. 155; cf. 1 Pet. 3:4), even his concealed good deeds will ultimately become known, for "they cannot remain hidden" (1 Tim. 5:25). At the final time of judgment, when the secret acts of people are brought to light, their motives will be the grounds for judgment, for at that time every person's work will be truly understood. This revelation of the counsels of the heart will be the basis for commendation from God (1 Cor. 4:5). Here "Paul's readers might learn with relief that the time of ultimate judgment is not necessarily a dreadful day of wrath. At last everyone will be fully understood, and God will disclose the basis for true praise" (W. F. Orr, *I Corinthians* [*AB*, 1976], p. 181).

This God who is hidden by nature has given His people a share in His "hidden life" (Rev. 2:17) by revealing His "secret and hidden wisdom" (1 Cor. 2:7) in the One "in whom are hid all the treasures of wisdom and knowledge," Jesus Christ (Col. 2:3). This wisdom is no secret, esoteric knowledge concealed from the "uninitiated" and claimed by false teachers. For the apostle, if there is a secret at all it is in Christ (see Moule, p. 86). This message of Christ, hidden for ages and generations, has now been made plain for all (Eph. 3:9), and for God's people to find new life through the "hiding" of their lives in His (Col. 3:3).

The NT uses this concept in the physical sense in its account of Jesus' detection in the crowd of the hemorrhaging woman (Lk. 8:47). Jesus could not escape the notice of the people when He was in Tyre and Sidon (Mk. 7:24), though in two instances He was able to hide from His enemies (Jn. 8:59; 12:36). The book of Revelation gives a vivid picture of people hiding in caves in the mountains, attempting to escape from the One seated on the throne and from the wrath of the Lamb (6:15f.).

Bibliography.–A. A. Anderson, *Psalms* (*New Century Bible*, 1972), I-II; K. Barth, *CD*, II/1; F. W. Beare, *First Epistle of Peter* (3rd rev. ed. 1970); F. F. Bruce, *Hebrews* (*NICNT*, 1964); J. Jeremias, *Parables of Jesus* (1963); C. F. D. Moule, *Colossians and Philemon* (1957); A. Richardson, *Intro. to the Theology of the NT* (1958); *RTWB*, *s.v.* (G. Hendry); *TDNT*, III, *s.v.* κρύπτω (Oepke); G. von Rad, *OT Theology*, II (1966).

D. K. MCKIM

HIEL hī'əl [Heb. *ḥî'ēl*; Gk. *Achiēl*]. A Bethelite who according to 1 K. 16:34 rebuilt Jericho in the time of Ahab (874-853 B.C.). This was done in defiance of the severe curse imposed by Joshua upon anyone who would dare to rebuild the city, which had been devoted to God. Such an act of rebuilding would cost the life of the person's firstborn as "payment" for the foundations, and his youngest son for the establishing of the gates (Josh. 6:26). The curse had its effect upon Hiel, who lost his eldest son Abiram and his youngest son Segub while the reconstruction was in progress. Precisely how they died is uncertain, but their demise was seen as the fulfillment of Joshua's curse. Human sacrifice was practiced at this period, and Garstang reported finding what he interpreted as foundation sacrifices of children at OT Jericho (Tell es-Sulṭân). In contemporary society, a period of acute crisis was sometimes thought to merit the sacrifice of a human being, as illustrated by the way in which the king of Edom offered up his eldest son to appease the national deity and gain success in battle (2 K. 3:27; cf. Mic. 6:7).

R. K. H.

HIERAPOLIS hī-ə-rap'ə-lis, hēr-ap'ō-lis [Gk. *Hierapolis*–'holy city'] (Col. 4:13; Sib. Or. 5:310; 12:280). A city of Asia Minor. The name originally may have been derived from Hiera, a mythical Amazon queen.

The city is situated nearly due E of Ephesus in the Anatolian hinterland, 10 km. (6 mi.) N of Laodicea and 19 km. (12 mi.) NW of Colossae, on a 150-m. (500-ft.) terrace overlooking the Lycus River. It was famed for its Plutonium or Charonion, a small hole opening deep into the earth and emitting deadly fumes, the vapors of which Strabo intimates poisoned even birds in flight (*Geog.* xiii.4.14). Likewise it is known for its gushing medicinal mineral pools, which flow at the rate of about 38,000 l. (10,000 gal.) per minute and deposit about 20 cubic m. (26 cubic yds.) of limestone sediment each day, so that the cliffs have been likened to an immense frozen cascade, whence also the nearby city's modern name Pamukkale, "cotton castle." *See* Plate 44. Hierapolis was thus positioned in a natural setting for the development of ancient religious traditions.

Colonizers from Macedonia and Pergamum established the Greek city in the early 2nd cent. B.C. when the Pergamenians wrested control of the area from the Seleucids. It then passed into Roman hands in 133 B.C. The city was subject to earthquakes (Tacitus *Ann.* xiv.27) and the gap in the presence of coins from the time of Nero to Trajan indicates that Hierapolis must have suffered a severe shock *ca.* A.D. 60.

The colonnaded main street of Hierapolis ran in a southeasterly direction; among the ruins (which fortunately have not suffered from local scavengers of building materials) can be found traces of Roman baths, arches, a gymnasium, a great "statuary" hall, both a Greek and a Roman theater (the latter being one of the best preserved in Asia Minor), and four possible churches, one of which seems to have been an octagonal building, probably from the 4th century.

The Phrygian god Sabazios was adopted at Hierapolis, symbolized by the snake, and worshiped under the name of Echidma. The Anatolian goddess Cybele under the name of Leto was likewise worshiped, together with her son Larbenos. Their sanctuaries were established very near the sacred Plutonium. During the Roman period other deities such as Asclepius and Isis were also introduced. A large Jewish community was established here, but it gradually disappeared with the growth of Christianity.

Christianity was probably brought to the city by Paul or one of his followers (W. M. Ramsay suggested Timothy rather than Paul, but this thesis depends on the meaning given to Col. 2:1). Some later traditions suppose that Philip the evangelist was the first Christian messenger to Hierapolis. At least it is fairly certain according to Polycrates of Ephesus that Philip spent his latter days in this vicinity, and two of his daughters were buried here (Eusebius *HE* iii.31.3). The existence of a church at Hierapolis in the 1st cent. is attested by Col. 4:13. Christianity apparently

General view of the Roman theater at Hierapolis (L. T. Geraty)

flourished in this city, and during the 4th cent. it seems to have been sufficiently strong to have had the Plutonium filled with stones, so that today it is no longer recognizable. In Byzantine times the city was the seat of a metropolitan bishop. Two of its most renowned residents were the Christian Papias and the philosopher Epictetus.

Bibliography.–C. Humann, *et al., Altertümer von Hierapolis (Jahrbuch des Kaiserlich Deutschen Archäologischen Instituts),* IV (1898); *CBP,* pp. 84ff.; S. E. Johnson, *BA,* 13 (1950), 12-17; *RRAM,* I, 47-49, 127f., etc.

G. L. BORCHERT

HIEREEL hī-er'e-əl (1 Esd. 9:21, AV). *See* JEHIEL **9.**

HIEREMOTH hī-er'ə-moth [Gk. *Ieremōth*] (1 Esd. 9:27, 30, AV). *See* JEREMOTH **6-8.**

HIERIELUS hī-er-i-ē'ləs (1 Esd. 9:27, AV). *See* JEHIEL **8.**

HIERMAS hī-ûr'məs [Gk. *Hiermas*] (1 Esd. 9:26, AV). *See* RAMIAH.

HIEROGLYPHICS hī-rō-glif'iks [< Gk. *hierós*–'sacred' + *glýphein*–'carve']. A system of writing using pictorial characters, especially the system of the priests of ancient Egypt. *See* ARCHEOLOGY OF EGYPT II.B; EGYPT V.C-E; WRITING.

HIERONYMUS hī-ə-ron'ə-məs [Gk. *Hierōnymos* (also Latin form of the name Jerome)] (2 Macc. 12:2). One of the regional governors in Palestine at the time of Antiochus V who would not permit the Jews to live in peace and security.

HIGGAION hi'gī-on, hi-gā'on [Heb. *higgāyôn*] (Ps. 9:16 [MT 17]). A musical notation of uncertain meaning. It is derived from the verb *hāgâ,* "mutter, speak, ponder," and occurs elsewhere with the meaning "meditation" (Ps. 19:14 [MT 15]) or "murmur" (Lam. 3:62, NEB). In Ps. 92:3 (MT 4) it occurs in a musical context, but the variety of translations indicates the uncertainty of its meaning (AV "solemn sound"; RSV, NIV "melody"; JB "rippling"; NEB "sounding chords"). In view of the general connotation of a quiet or low sound, JB's translation "muted music" in Ps. 9:16 seems preferable to Mowinckel's "musical flourish" (*Psalms in Israel's Worship* [Eng. tr. 1962], II, 211).

HIGH. Used by the AV in the obsolete sense of "haughty" in Ps. 101:5; Prov. 21:4; Isa. 10:12; etc.

HIGH DAY. Found in Gen. 29:7 as a rendering of the Heb. *yôm gāḏôl,* literally "great day" (NEB "the sun is still high"). The Hebrew means the day at its height, broad daylight, as contrasted with the time for getting the cattle to their sheds for the night (cf. Fr. *grand jour*). In Jn. 19:31, "high day" renders Gk. *megálē hēméra,* literally "great day" (NEB "day of great solemnity"), and refers to the Passover sabbath, a sabbath of special sanctity.

HIGH, MOST. *See* GOD, NAMES OF.

HIGH PLACE [Heb. *bāmâ*]. The Hebrews undoubtedly borrowed the word (as well as the installation itself) from the Canaanites, who in turn derived it from a common Semitic vocabulary where (in Akkadian and Ugaritic) it meant literally "back" or "ridge." It is now recognized that it could have the same literal meaning in Hebrew, though it also came to have the following extended meanings: "cultic platform," "sanctuary," "altar," "grave mound."

- I. Biblical Evidence
  - A. Poetic Usage
  - B. Prose Usage
  - C. Pre-Monarchial Period
  - D. United Monarchy
  - E. Northern Kingdom
  - F. Southern Kingdom
  - G. Deities Worshiped at High Places
  - H. Features of the Typical High Place
- II. Archeological Evidence
  - A. Surrounding Countries
  - B. Petra
  - C. Palestine
  - D. Models and Survivals

I. Biblical Evidence.–*A. Poetic Usage.* Among the nearly one hundred occurrences of *bāmâ* in the Hebrew OT, at least a dozen of them are best understood in the primitive, literal sense. Interestingly, each of these examples occurs in poetry. In the Lament of David (2 S. 1:19, 25), *bāmâ* refers to the ridge of Mt. Gilboa where Saul was slain. It is used in a similar way in an oracle of Micah against the temple, "Jerusalem shall become a ruin, and the temple mount a wooded 'ridge' [or 'height']" (3:12; this prediction was later remembered in the context of Jeremiah's Temple Sermon [26:18] and probably saved Jeremiah's life). In the taunt against the king of Babylon (Isa. 14:14), secondarily applied to Satan, the vocabulary used is identical to that found in Canaanite mythology, "I will climb on the *back* of the cloud; I will make myself like the Most High." This terminology is used also in descriptions of Yahweh in Job 9:8; Am. 4:13; and Mic. 1:3, where He is pictured as one "who treads on the *back* of Sea" or "Earth." "Sea" and "Earth" were mythological symbols in Canaan of the powers of chaos. It is possible that biblical poetry portrays Israel's God as having power over the Canaanite deities who were merely personifications of nature, but it is more likely that the authors were only making use of poetic imagery. That is certainly the case in the Song of Moses (Dt. 32:13), the Blessing of Moses (Dt. 33:29), and the blessing on sabbath observance (Isa. 58:14), where it is Israel whom Yahweh causes to ride on the back of its enemy. In the royal Psalm of thanksgiving (Ps. 18:33 [MT 34] par. 2 S. 22:34) and the Psalm of Habakkuk (Hab. 3:19), which is dependent on it, this corporate victory is individualized to celebrate personal victory. Here Yahweh is the one "who makes my feet like (the feet of) does, who makes me tread on the *back* (of Death)."

B. Prose Usage. In the majority of OT (mostly prose) occurrences, however, *bāmâ* has a meaning derived from the original "back" or "ridge." The term was first applied to the summits of either natural or artificial hills or mounds that were set aside for cultic purposes. As the cult at these open-air sites became more institutionalized, shrines were sometimes built and operated by cultic functionaries. The designation "high place" then came to refer not so much to the elevation of the site but rather to denote the entire installation wherever it was located.

C. Pre-Monarchial Period. The earliest chronological reference to such high places is found in the Amorite victory song of Heshbon (Nu. 21:28): "A fire went forth from Heshbon, a flame from the city of Sihon. It consumed the cities of Moab, engulfed the high places of Arnon." It was undoubtedly from a similar high place that Balak and Balaam surveyed the camp of Israel (Nu. 22:41; cf. Josh. 13:17) during their passage through Moab. Yahweh warned Moses of the high places in Cisjordan (Nu. 33:52; cf. Dt. 7:5), but near the time of the Exile these Moabite high places still existed (Isa. 15:2; 16:12; Jer. 48:35; cf. line 3 of the Moabite Stone: "I made this high place for Chemosh").

Apparently the Canaanite practices at the high places were proscribed for Israel rather than the use of such sites themselves. At least this is the inference derived from one of the sanctions at the end of the Holiness Code in which Yahweh says, "If you do not obey me, then I will destroy your high places, and knock down your incense altars, and throw your corpses on the memorial stelae of your idols, and my spirit will loathe you" (Lev. 26:30; cf. Ezk. 6:3-6). In any case, the high place seems to have survived as a legitimate site for sacrifice and worship in Israel until, ideally, the building of Solomon's temple (1 K. 3:2f.); in practice, however, it continued till the reforms of Hezekiah (2 K. 18) and Josiah (2 K. 23).

D. United Monarchy. Three Israelite high places are named in connection with permissible worship. Ramah (modern er-Râm) and Gibeath-elohim (Tell el-Fûl) both figure in the account of Saul's quest for Samuel in 1 S. 9–10. Both David and Solomon patronized the high place at Gibeon (modern el-Jîb, though the actual high place was very possibly the nearby Nabi Samwil or the traditional tomb of Samuel), where at the tent of meeting the priestly family of Zadok sacrificed on an altar and Solomon burned incense (1 Ch. 16:39; 21:29; 1 K. 3:2-4; 2 Ch. 1:3, 13). All three of these sites were in Benjamin just N of Jerusalem. Neither Ramah nor Nabi Samwil has been excavated, and though Tell el-Fûl was partially excavated by Albright and P. Lapp, only an Israelite fortress was found.

Solomon, however, supported not only the worship of Yahweh, but on the hill opposite Jerusalem he built high places to Chemosh of the Moabites, Molech (or Milcom) of the Ammonites, and Astarte of the Sidonians (1 K. 11:7f.; 2 K. 23:13). If not before, then certainly at this time, high places became associated with traditions and practices that tended to degrade Israelite religion.

E. Northern Kingdom. To prevent his subjects from worshiping at Jerusalem, where he would run the risk of losing their political allegiance as well, Jeroboam I encouraged the building of shrines, complete with illegitimate priests, at the local high places, and set up calves as pedestals for Yahweh at Dan and Bethel (1 K. 12:31f.; 13:33). This activity resulted in an oracle from an unnamed Judean prophet predicting the overthrow by Josiah of the shrines with their altars at the northern high places (1 K. 13:2, 32). Much later, Amos prophesied the desolation of these high places (Am. 7:9), and the Bethel high place was singled out by Hosea especially as deserving of condemnation (Hos. 10:8; cf. 4:13). In summary, 2 K. 17:9-12 attributes the fall of the northern kingdom and the Israelites' captivity in Assyria to this syncretism and idolatry. Even during the Exile, however, the high places had their devotees, because the Assyrians settled foreigners in the territory of the northern kingdom who repopulated the high places with priests to officiate in the shrines (2 K. 17:29-32).

F. Southern Kingdom. In the meantime, the kingdom of Judah was not free from the same syncretistic practices. In the reigns of most of the kings, high places were built and their cults patronized; those specifically mentioned include Rehoboam (1 K. 14:23; 2 Ch. 11:15), Asa (1 K. 15:14; 2 Ch. 15:17), Jehoshaphat (1 K. 22:43; 2 Ch. 20:33), Jehoram (2 Ch. 21:11), Jehoash (2 K. 12:3 [MT 4]), Amaziah (2 K. 14:4), Azariah or Uzziah (2 K. 15:4), Jotham (2 K. 15:35), and Ahaz (2 K. 16:4; 2 Ch. 28:4, 25). Though Asa (2 Ch. 14:3, 5 [MT 2, 4]) and Jehoshaphat (2 Ch. 17:6) apparently made some effort to stem the tide, the first real reform is attributed to Hezekiah, who destroyed the high places and their appurtenances throughout the land and attempted to centralize the cult in Jerusalem (2 K. 21:3; 2 Ch. 33:3, 19).

The reform was shortlived, however, because his son Manasseh rebuilt the high places, equipping them with the customary altars and Asherim (2 K. 21:3; 2 Ch. 33:3, 19). Jer. 7:31 (cf. 19:5) adds that they built the high place of Topheth in the valley of Ben-hinnom and sacrificed their children by fire. Obviously by this time the term "high place" had lost its connotation of height and connoted instead the standard cultic installation. After the captivity, conversion, and restoration of Manasseh, the people continued to sacrifice at the "high places," but only to Yahweh (2 Ch. 33:17). This reform, too, was a fleeting one.

It was left to Josiah to effect reforms that would really make an impact on the nation. He purged all the high places, from Samaria in the north to Beersheba in the south (including the Bethel high place, in fulfillment of prophecy [2 K. 23:16]), destroying their altars, incense stands, Asherim, pillars, and carved and molten images, and slaughtering their priests (2 K. 23; 2 Ch. 34:3-7). Again, as prophets looked back over the history of Israel, the high places were constantly adduced as primary reasons for Yahweh's displeasure with His chosen people (Ps. 78:58; Ezk. 16:16; 20:28f.; cf. Mic. 1:5; Jer. 17:3; Ezk. 36:2; 43:7-9).

G. Deities Worshiped at High Places. Though the worship of Yahweh appeared to predominate in many periods of Israel's history, syncretistic tendencies were usually present and were often fostered by what occurred at the high places. Among the other deities worshiped there was Baal (Jer. 19:5; 32:35), the fertility-god par excellence of the Canaanites. His proper name was Hadad, though he was popularly referred to as Baal, meaning "lord." Later he was identified with Greek Zeus Helios (the sun), who in turn was identified with the Roman Jupiter. Child sacrifice by fire, undoubtedly for votive offerings, was practiced in his cult.

Worship of Chemosh, Milcom or Molech, and Ashtoreth is mentioned in 1 K. 11:5-8; 2 K. 23:13. Ashtoreth was the main Semitic fertility-goddess worshiped throughout the ancient Near East, though in Mesopotamia, where she was also an astral deity, she was called Ishtar. Later she was identified with Greek Aphrodite and Roman Venus. Palestinian excavations often recover images of Ashtoreth that depict her as a nude woman with her sexual features accentuated; these artifacts are usually referred to as Astarte figurines or plaques (Astarte being the Greek transliteration of Ashtoreth), though it is now thought that many of these actually represented Asherah, the supreme Canaanite mother goddess, whose memory was obliterated in the Iron Age through the spread of the Mesopotamian Ishtar cult.

Chemosh was the name or (more probably) the title of the god of the Moabites, which in line 17 of the Moabite Stone is compounded with Athtar, the astral deity. Again, Molech or Milcom is probably not the name but the title of the national god of Ammon. From Jgs. 11:24 it is apparent that these two deities were actually one. Both, then, were local manifestations of the astral deity, the Venus star, Athtar. Finally, demons as well as deities were worshiped at certain high places (2 K. 23:8; cf. Lev. 17:7; 2 Ch. 11:15).

In general, one detects a strong interest in fertility and the reproductive powers of nature at the high places, and of course it was this that called forth strong denunciations from the prophets (Hos. 4:13f.; Isa. 57:3-10; Jer. 3:2; 1 K. 14:24).

H. Features of the Typical High Place. From such references as Lev. 26:30; Nu. 33:52; Dt. 12:2f.; 1 K. 14:23; and Ezk. 6:3-6, we may identify the essential features of a typical *bāmâ*, which was usually (though not always) situated on the wooded heights of a hill or mountain.

Standing stones (Heb. *maṣṣēḇôṯ*, sing. *maṣṣēḇâ*, usually translated "pillar") were commonly associated with high places. Etymologically, a *maṣṣēḇâ* could be any stone that is "set up"; its unnatural position would then serve the purpose of being some kind of a reminder. From the biblical point of view, the practice was both permitted (Gen. 28:18; 31:45-52; Ex. 24:4) and denounced (Dt. 16:22; 2 K. 23), depending, of course, on the purpose for setting up the stone. Though these stones have been variously interpreted as phallic symbols, sacred abodes of animistic spirits, and idols or representations of deity, a comprehensive study of standing stones by Graesser suggests that they normally perform one of four kinds of functions: (1) memorial, to mark the memory of a dead person or the position of his grave (Gen. 35:20; 2 S. 18:18); (2) legal, to mark a legal relationship between two or more individuals, such as boundary and treaty stones (Gen. 31:45-52; Ex. 24:4; Dt. 19:14; 27:17; Josh. 24:26f.); (3) commemorative, to commemorate an event and especially to call to mind its participants (1 S. 7:12; 15:12); (4) cultic, to mark the sacred area where the deity might be found or even the exact point where the deity is cultically immanent, i.e., where worship and sacrifice will reach the deity (Gen. 28:16-18; 35:14; 2 K. 3:2; 10:26f.). Naturally, the standing stones erected at the high places were most closely associated with this last function. As Graesser notes, "Cultic stones had a special tendency to assume transferred functions so that for many these stones 'enabled' or 'effected' the deity's presence" (p. 37). This is why certain biblical writers could consider standing stones to be idols (Lev. 26:1; Mic. 5:13 [MT 12]). At times, *maṣṣēḇôṯ* may even have been set up to serve as surrogates for worshipers themselves who wished to be continually represented before their deity at the high place.

Another object common to the high places was the *peger* (pl. *p*ᵉ*gārîm*), usually translated as "corpse." How such a meaning related to the *bāmâ* was enigmatic till the cognate *pgr* was found on two Ugaritic stone stelae recording a sacrifice to Dagon. Nieman suggests that the word refers to the stones themselves and that it appears with this meaning in such biblical passages as Ezk. 43:7, 9; Lev. 26:30. This suggestion permits the inclusion of "memorial stones" or "stelae" among the cult objects to be found at the high place.

Two kinds of altars are often mentioned in connection with the high place. The word *mizbē(a)ḥ* is the commonest designation for altar in the OT. Derived from the verb *zāḇaḥ*, "sacrifice," it does not specify the type of sacrifice made on it. *Ḥammānîm* (always in the plural) were also altars, but a type used exclusively for the burning of incense at the high place. Till recently this term was misunderstood and usually translated as "sun statues" (ASV) or "images" (AV). Known from excavations as small limestone altars with a "horn" or projection at each corner, their identification was finally assured by the appearance of the word itself on an altar from Palmyra. Thus the meaning "incense altar" well suits the meaning of the verb *ḥāmam*, "be hot, burn."

Another essential feature of the typical *bāmâ* was the *ʾᵃšērâ* (pl. *ʾᵃšērîm*), a term that has been translated by a variety of words, including "grove" and "sacred pole." Avoiding the problem altogether, the RSV just transliterates the term. Basically, *ʾᵃšērâ* refers either to the proper name for the Canaanite goddess of vegetation (the female counterpart of Baal) or the cult object which symbolized her. The latter was usually found at high places dedicated to Baal (Jgs. 3:7; 6:30; 1 K. 16:32f.; 2 K. 23:5f.). Unfortunately, the form of the cult object and its use at the high place are not described in the Bible, nor has any object been found in an excavation which can confidently be called an *ʾᵃšērâ*. Some of this information, however, can be inferred by a study of the biblical references to the object. Though it was not a tree it was upright and made of wood, or at least contained wood, and could be burned (Dt. 12:3; Jgs. 6:25f.; Isa. 27:9; etc.). W. L. Reed suggests that, as with the similar cult object made in the image of Dagon (1 S. 5:2-4), the *ʾᵃšērâ* was an image of the fertility-goddess Asherah.

Finally, various types of images are associated with the high place: (1) *pesel* (pl. *p*ᵉ*silîm*), derived from the verb *pāsal*, "hew," and usually translated "graven image"; (2) *massēḵâ* (pl. *massēḵôṯ*), derived from the verb *nāsaḵ*, "pour out," and usually translated "molten image"; (3) *ṣelem* (pl. *ṣ*ᵉ*lāmîm*), usually translated merely "image"; (4) *gillûlîm*, appearing only in the plural; though its derivation is uncertain, it is usually translated "idols"; (5) *maśkîṯ* (pl. *maśkîyôṯ*), perhaps from the root *śkh*, "to look out," and usually translated "carved stone."

II. Archeological Evidence.–Near Eastern archeology has provided evidence that may illustrate the biblical data. Unfortunately not too much of this evidence comes from Palestine in the biblical period — due probably to the nature of the high place itself. The summit of a mound, where the high place was frequently built, was often the first area of the mound to be denuded, either by natural or artificial causes. Since the typical simple installation was in the open air, perhaps it is expecting too much to find them today preserved "on every high hill and under every flourishing tree" (2 K. 17:10) as they were in the days of Israel's prophets.

An older generation of scholars found high places wherever they found standing stones, "cup marks," or cultic implements. No longer, however, are these phenomena considered sufficient evidence for a high place. It is now known that standing stones served as common structural elements in the buildings of the Iron Age (the archeological term for the Israelite period in Palestine). And when these stones were set up as markers, they may have served any of several functions, only some of which were cultic. It is now known, too, that "cup marks" which are common in Palestinian limestone bedrock are often a result of natural causes, but that even when they are made by humans they may serve some secular use, such as for mortars. Though cultic implements were obviously used for religious purposes, it is now clear they were appropriate almost anywhere, never being restricted solely to a high place. Thus older handbooks that use these phenomena to argue for the identification of high places must obviously be used with caution.

Having stated the case for the discovery of Israelite high places negatively, what remains to illustrate the biblical data? Apart from a few as yet unpublished examples such as Dan, one must leave either the biblical period (chronologically) or the Israelite territory (geographically) in order to find meaningful parallels from archeological discovery.

A. Surrounding Countries. Open-air temples — all possessing standing stones — that have been found in countries surrounding Israel have often been referred to as high places. The field of 140 stelae found at Asshur (modern Qalʿat-Sharqat in Iraq), one of the ancient capitals of Assyria, falls into this category. These two rows of stones — some crude, some squared, some as high as 3 m. (10 ft.), some inscribed with the names of kings who ruled from the 15th to the 7th cents. B.C. — were thoroughly excavated and published by W. Andrae when he worked for the Deutsche Orientgesellschaft between the turn of the century and the outbreak of World War I. Rather than being a high place in the biblical sense, however, these rows of stones may have served as a "walk-in calendar," since they were arranged in chronological order and the names inscribed on them were names from eponym lists which the Assyrians used to compute dates. To be compared to the standing stones of Asshur are the *maṣṣēḇôṯ* in the contemporary temple of Dagon at Ugarit (modern Râs Shamrah in Syria), though again, this phenomenon is probably not identical to the biblical high place.

Closer to Israel and closer to the Israelite high place was the Obelisk Temple of Byblos in Lebanon, excavated in the 1930's by Dunand. The installation dates to the 19th cent. B.C., and had more than forty standing stones of all sizes, grouped in an open court around a cella and procella which were built on a raised platform in the open air. Several of the *maṣṣēḇôṯ* even had offering tables positioned in front of them, so there is no doubt as to their cultic function. One of the stones contains a dedication to the Egyptian god Arsaphes, who may have been assimilated to Resheph, the well-known Canaanite god of the underworld.

South of Palestine at Serābîṭ el-Khâdim in the Sinai Peninsula, Sir Flinders Petrie in 1905 discovered a nineteenth-century-B.C. Egyptian temple in whose environs were many *maṣṣēḇôṯ*. This site, where several turquoise mines were worked by the Egyptians, is best known for its Proto-Sinaitic alphabet inscriptions from the 15th cent. B.C. In the same general vicinity along the ridges was a series of cairn cemeteries that Albright studied again in 1948. Albright was convinced that these phenomena provided the clue to the origin and development of the high place, which he saw to be funerary in character. His theory, however, has not found general acceptance.

At Timnah in the region of the Arabah where the Egyptians and Midianites exploited the copper deposits, B. Rothenberg discovered in the 1960's two installations that may have served as high places between the 14th and 12th cents. B.C. Each had curtain walls around an area that included a cella, *maṣṣēḇôṯ*, basins, and offering benches. One of them is built up against the sandstone formation known to tourists as Solomon's Pillars.

Across the valley and nearer the Dead Sea in Transjordan, surface exploration at such sites as Bâb edh-Dhrâʿ, Lejjun, and Ader has revealed various alignments of large standing stones out in the open air. Though there is no sure way of dating them, they are usually attributed to the 3rd millennium B.C. With no excavation and little evidence to go on, it is dangerous to speculate about the role they served. That some of these cultic installations from surrounding countries are parallel to the biblical high place at least in function is probable, but because of the distance in time and space, details cannot be pressed.

B. Petra. One of the best known and best preserved high places in the Middle East is Robinson's High Place (Zibb ʿAtuf) in the mountain fortress of Petra in Transjordan. Petra was in Edomite territory during biblical times, but by the end of the 4th cent. B.C. it had been taken over by the Nabateans, who carved their monuments out of the rose-red sandstone characteristic of the region. They also probably cut the famous high place out of the solid rock.

Despite the difference in time and place from the Israelite period, Albright stated that this class of high place "probably carries on the tradition of ancient Israelite high places more closely than any other extant installation" (*AP,* p. 163). It is approached by a flight of steps which, like the other features, is cut into the solid rock. The central court is about 14.3 m. (47 ft.) long and 6.7 m. (22 ft.) wide, and situated about midway of its length is a rock platform about 1.8 m. (5 ft.) long and half as wide. It has been suggested that this platform, 12.7 cm. (5 in.) high, was either the pedestal for the *ʾᵃšērâ,* or was the place where the sacrificial victim was killed (there is no positive evidence for human sacrifices). North of this is a bench, 8.2 m. (27 ft.) long, on which the sacrifice may have been prepared for the burnt offering, while S of the court was a water tank or laver (approximately 2.7 m. [9 ft.] square and 1.2 m. [4 ft.] deep) probably used for ablutions. Ascent to the rectangular (2.7 m. by 1.8 m. by 0.9 m. [9 ft. by 6 ft. by 3 ft.]) altar of burnt offering on the east was made by a flight of steps leading up to its top, which contains a shallow pan (perhaps to receive the fire). Slightly S of this first altar is another one with its own flight of steps, but this one is round. It probably served either for drink offerings or for the place of slaughter, because near its center are two concentric pans, the larger nearly 1.2 m. (4 ft.) in diameter, and the smaller ½ m. (1½ ft.) in diameter, and from this inner basin a conduit 1 m. (3 ft.) long leads to a tank where the liquid was caught. Near this installation, but farther to the south, are two 6-m. (20-ft.) obelisks which were exposed when the surrounding rock was hewn away, probably for buildings in the town below.

C. Palestine. Though most of them are not as spectacular as the one at Petra, several high places have been found in Cisjordan. They appear to be of at least four different types.

One type may be called a cairn high place. Such a heap, carefully constructed of rough stones, could serve either as an altar or as a commemorative installation. Albright and R. Amiran each excavated an example of the latter in 1924 and 1953 respectively, on a ridge near Malḥah, SW of

The Nabatean high place at Petra in Transjordan (E. K. Vogel; picture Department of Antiquities, Government of Palestine)

Jerusalem. The date of these two tumuli was fixed by pottery as near the end of the Judean monarchy (around the 7th cent. B.C.). Much earlier are the cultic cairns found at Megiddo by G. Loud and at Nahariyah by M. Dothan. The round altar platform of Megiddo (known as installation 401), also constructed of rough stones, is 7.6 m. (25 ft.) in diameter and 1.2 m. (4 ft.) high. It seems to date from the middle of the 3rd millennium B.C. when it was associated with three nearby sanctuaries. At a later time within the Middle Bronze Age (20th–16th cents. B.C.), some thirty to forty *maṣṣēḇôṯ* were erected over the high place, so that its cultic function continued for many centuries. The Nahariyah cairn, nearly 6 m. (20 ft.) in diameter, was found near a small shrine of the 18th cent. B.C. with which it was later associated. The shrine itself was probably dedicated to the Canaanite goddess Asherah.

A second type of high place is represented by the famous unwalled Gezer high place. It was first excavated and then covered over again by R. A. S. Macalister shortly after the turn of the century, but was reexcavated by the Hebrew Union College Expedition directed by W. G. Dever. The installation consists of a N-S line of ten monoliths or *maṣṣēḇôṯ*, the tallest of which is 3.3 m. (10 ft. 9 in.) and the shortest half that high. Just back of one of the pillars a square block was found with a rectangular hole 38 cm. (15 in.) deep cut in its upper side. Its function has been the subject of debate, with suggestions ranging from a laver or altar for blood sacrifice to a base for an Asherah. Around the bases of the stones, all of which were erected *ca.* 1600 B.C., were a low curb and a narrow paving of limestone chips. In the general vicinity Macalister found a number of infant jar burials, two interconnected caves in bedrock, and a cistern containing some human bones. Combining all these elements which modern scholars now know come from widely differing chronological periods, Macalister reconstructed an eclectic cultus which involved child sacrifice and oracular consultation in the two caves. Since there is no evidence for this fanciful interpretation, his theory must be abandoned. A. M. Furshpan-Walker, who reexcavated the installation for the Hebrew Union College Expedition, suggested that it functioned as a place of covenant making for groups around Gezer. Drawing on treaty and covenant-making parallels in Palestine and Syria, she thought that each of the stones might have been set up by a covenanting unit accompanied by a blood sacrifice on the block. This interpretation is, however, also far from certain.

A third type of high place is a smaller, walled installation of the kind made famous by Y. Yadin's excavation at Hazor. There he found among several shrines from the Late Bronze Age (15th-13th cents. B.C.) unroofed Shrine 6136 in Area C of the Lower City. It was built up against the slope of the earthen Hyksos rampart and contained ten small basalt *maṣṣēḇôṯ* in an apsidal niche at the back of the high place. The most interesting standing stone was inscribed with two forearms stretched upward toward a divine lunar symbol — a crescent and a disk. On one side of the row of stones was a basalt statuette of a seated male figure with an inverted crescent pendant on his chest. Benches for offerings lined the walls. A similar high place from the Israelite period may have been found at Beth-shemesh by D. Mackenzie. Unfortunately, since findings have not been completely published, the site is difficult to interpret.

A fourth type of high place in Palestine is Shrine E207 found at Samaria by the Joint Expedition in the 1930's. It is similar to the one at Petra in that it is formed by a trench, trapezoidal in layout and cut from solid rock. The trench itself is 6 m. (20 ft.) wide at the top, 4 m. (13 ft.) wide at the bottom, and about 3 m. (10 ft.) deep. The inner area, connected with the outer area by a rock bridge 2.4 m. (8 ft.) wide, is about 30 m. by 26 m. (100 ft. by 85 ft.). There was no sign of a building nor any other cultic artifacts, but the excavators presumed that it was a high place, dated ceramically to the 8th cent. B.C.

D. High Place Models and Survivals. Not only have some actual high places been found, but archeological discovery has provided us with several ancient models. The Louvre in Paris contains a bronze model from the 12th cent. B.C. of an Elamite high place found in Susa. Among the equipment of this *ṣît šamši* (as the model is known) are *maṣṣēḇôṯ*, lavers, altars, possible statues, and perhaps even an Asherah (*see* Vol. I, Plate 3). The Cyprus Museum in Nicosia displays two interesting clay models of ancient sacred enclosures from the northern coast of the island. From Tomb 22 at Vounous comes a model, late third millennium B.C., of a circular, open-air enclosure or *témenos* surrounded by a wall with a gate set in one side. Within the enclosure a ritual ceremony is taking place that focuses on three human figures who seem to be wearing bull masks and holding snakes. Figures of both people and bulls crowd the area. The seventh-century-B.C. sanctuary of Ayia Irini was excavated by the Swedes in 1929. Its enclosure contained a libation table and altar surrounded by two thousand terra-cotta votive figures representing bull figures, worshipers, war chariots, armed men, and centaurs — all of which now take up most of a room in the museum.

Besides these visual aids from ancient times, modern survivals of activities occurring at the high place may be helpful in understanding the biblical data. One such survival is the annual Samaritan Passover celebration, which takes place in a rectangular enclosure of rough stones on the summit of Mt. Gerizim. Another survival may be the cult of the hero shrines (Arab. *welis*) that dot the summits of mountains and hills throughout the Middle East. Here Arab peasants gather to mourn or rejoice, depending on the occasion.

Bibliography.–W. F. Albright, *ARI,* pp. 103-107; "The High Place in Ancient Palestine," *SVT,* 4 (1957), 242-258; R. Amiran, *IEJ,* 8 (1958), 205-227; W. Andrae, *Die Stelenreihen in Assur* (1913); R. L. Cleveland, *AASOR,* 34-35 (1960), 55-78; J. W. Crowfoot, K. M. Kenyon, and E. L. Sukenik, *Samaria-Sabaste I: The Buildings at Samaria* (1942), pp. 23f.; R. de Vaux, *Ancient Israel* (Eng. tr. 1961); M. Dothan, *IEJ,* 6 (1956), 14-25; *EAEHL,* s.v. "Dan, Tel" (A. Biran); "Gezer" (W. G. Dever); A. M. Furshpan, *BA,* 34 (Dec., 1971), 120-24; C. F. Graesser, Jr., *BA,* 35 (1972), 34-63; H. Ingholt, "Le Sens du mot ḥamman," in *Mélanges Syriens offerts à Monsieur René Dussaud,* II (1939), 795-802; S. Iwry, *JBL,* 76 (1957), 225-232; F. Jeremias, ΑΓΓΕΛΟΣ *Archiv für neutestamentliche Zeitgeschichte und Kulturkunde,* 4 (1932), 56-69; E. König, *Zentralkultstätte und Kultuszentralisierung im alten Israel* (*Beiträge zur Förderung christlicher Theologie,* 34/3, 1931); C. C. McCown, *JBL,* 69 (1950), 205-219; D. Nielsen, *JPOS,* 13 (1933), 192-96; D. Nieman, *JBL,* 67 (1948), 55-60; T. Oestreicher, *Reichstempel und Ortsheiligtümer in Israel* (*Beiträge zur Förderung christlicher Theologie,* 33/3, 1930); P. J. Parr, *RB,* 69 (1962), 64-79; W. L. Reed, *The Asherah in the OT* (1949); B. Rothenberg and A. Lupu, *ZDPV,* 82 (1966), 126f.; *TDOT, s.v.* "bāmāh" (K.-D. Schunk); E. Stockton, *Australian Journal of Biblical Archaeology,* 1 (1970), 58-81; R. Storr, *Die Frömmigkeit im Alten Israel* (1928), pp. 192f.; P. H. Vaughan, *Meaning of 'Bāmâ' in the OT* (1974); L.-H. Vincent, *RB,* 55 (1948), 245-278, 438-445; P. Volz, *Biblische Altertümer* (1914), pp. 14-23; A. von Gall, *Altisraelitische Kultstätten* (1898); G. Westphal, *Jahwes Wohnstätten* (1908); G. E. Wright, *BA,* 1 (May, 1938), 9f.; Y. Yadin, *Hazor* (1972).

L. T. GERATY

HIGH PRIEST. *See* PRIEST, HIGH.

HIGH THING. The AV uses this translation of Gk. *hypsēlós* ("high, lofty, elevated") in Rom. 12:16, and for *hýpsōma* ("height, loftiness, exaltation") in 2 Cor. 10:5. In both passages the reference is to pride, to things that are exalted in the eyes of the world.

HIGHEST HEAVEN. [Heb. *šᵉmê haššāmayim*] (1 K. 8:27; 2 Ch. 2:6; 6:18); AV HEAVEN OF HEAVENS; cf. the RSV in Dt. 10:14; Neh. 9:6. Although biblical cosmology shares features with the Semitic three-storied cosmology (e.g., pillars, Job 26:11; windows, Gen. 7:11; foundations, 2 S. 22:8), it is sometimes more akin to the modern viewpoint in its conception of the vastness of the universe; cf. Gen. 15:5; Ps. 147:4. In Akkadian mythology the highest heaven was the abode of the supreme god Anu. The Hebrew expression, however, may be nothing more than poetic imagery. *See* FIRMAMENT.

G. WYPER

HIGHMINDED. In modern usage "highminded" denotes elevation of principles and conduct, but in the AV it is used in the archaic sense of disdainful pride. In Rom. 11:20 and 1 Tim. 6:17 it translates Gk. *hypsēlophronéō* ("be proud, haughty"); in 2 Tim. 3:4 it renders *typhóomai* ("be puffed up with conceit"; cf. 1 Tim. 3:6; 6:4). "No one can be *highminded* without thinking better of himself, and worse of others, than he ought to think" (G. Crabb, *English Synonymes* [1916]).

HIGHWAY. *See* ROADS, HIGHWAYS; ROMAN EMPIRE AND CHRISTIANITY III.F; WAY.

HILEN hī'len [Heb. *ḥîlēn*] (1 Ch. 6:58 [MT 43]). A village in the hill country of Judah, assigned to the Levites. The form of the name in Josh. 15:51; 21:15 is HOLON.

HILKIAH hil-kī'ə [Heb. *ḥilqîyâ*–'Yahweh is my portion,' or 'Yahweh's portion']. The name of nine individuals in the OT, or eight, if the person mentioned in Neh. 12:7, 21 is the same who stood with Ezra at the reading of the Law (Neh. 8:4). The latter appears as Ezecias (AV) in 1 Esd. 9:43 (RSV Hezekiah; NEB Hezekias). Five of this name are clearly associated with the priesthood, and the others are presumably so, as the etymology suggests. Either interpretation of the name expresses the person's claim on Yahweh or the parents' recognition of Yahweh's claim on him.

1. The person mentioned above (Neh. 8:4, etc.).

2. A Levite of the descendants of Merari (1 Ch. 6:45).

3. Another Levite of Merari, son of Hosah (1 Ch. 26:11).

4. Father of the Gemariah whom Zedekiah of Judah sent to Nebuchadnezzar (Jer. 29:3).

5. The man in 2 K. 18:12ff. who is evidently more famous as the father of Eliakim, the majordomo of Hezekiah's palace (Isa. 22:20ff.; 36:3ff.).

6. A priest of Anathoth, father of Jeremiah (Jer. 1:1).

7. The son of Shallum (Bar. 1:7, AV Chelcias), and the best known of the name (1 Ch. 6:13). He was the great-grandfather of Ezra through his son Azariah (1 Esd. 8:1, AV Helchiah; NEB Chelkias; cf. 1 Ch. 9:11; Neh. 11:11). He discovered the lost book of the law during the repairing of the temple (2 K. 22:4, 8ff.), and became chief leader in the ensuing reformation in 621 B.C. (2 K. 23:4; 2 Ch. 34:9ff.; 35:8). He showed the recovered book to Shaphan the scribe, who in turn brought it to the notice of the king. At Josiah's request he led a deputation to Huldah the prophetess to "enquire of the Lord" concerning the new situation created by the discovery. The law scroll was originally thought to have been the canonical book of Deuteronomy, but further study shows that it was considerably smaller in size, and perhaps contained only a section of the covenant legislation, consisting possibly of the decalogue and some associated regulations. In the last analysis its content must remain uncertain. *See* DEUTERONOMY.

He may also be the father of Susanna (Sus. 2, 29, 63 [AV Chelcias]). According to tradition he was the brother of Jeremiah.

8. Ancestor of Jeremiah's servant Baruch (Bar. 1:1, AV Chelcias).

H. WALLACE

HILL; HILL COUNTRY; MOUNT; MOUNTAIN; etc.

I. Terms.–A. General. Several Hebrew words are used with some overlap in meaning, as suggested by the frequent synonymous parallelism (e.g., Dt. 33:15; Ps. 114:4, 6; Isa. 40:12; 54:10). But Heb. *giḇʿâ* (lit. "arch, swell") is generally a lower elevation than Heb. *har*; thus the RSV always translates *giḇʿâ* as "hill" (except where it is understood to be the town GIBEAH or part of another place name, e.g.,

Gibeath-haaraloth in Josh. 5:3 [cf. RSV mg., AV, "the hill of the foreskins"]). The AV is similar, except that four times "little hills" is used (Ps. 65:12 [MT 13]; 72:3; 114:4, 6). The NEB occasionally uses "hill-top" (2 K. 16:4; 2 Ch. 28:4; Jer. 3:23) and once "high summit" (Isa. 31:4).

Hebrew *har* is much more frequent and more ambiguous. In Jgs. 16:3 and 1 K. 16:24 the RSV translates it "hill," and in Cant. 4:1 "slopes" (cf. 6:5, where the RSV supplies "slopes" and the NEB "Mount"), but usually the RSV uses "hill country," "mount," or "mountain." In contrast, the AV uses "hill country" only in Josh. 13:6, and "hill" many times, though "mount" and "mountain" still predominate. In 1 K. 11:7 and Jer. 3:23 the NEB uses "height"; elsewhere the NEB usually agrees with the RSV, although it sometimes follows the AV (e.g., Josh. 15:9; 1 S. 25:20).

The RSV translates three other Hebrew words only rarely by "hill": *ʿōpel* (*see* OPHEL) in 2 K. 5:24 (AV "tower"; NEB "citadel"); Isa. 32:14 (AV "tower"; NEB "citadel"); Isa. 32:14 (AV "fort"; NEB "citadel"); Mic. 4:8 (AV "stronghold"); *qeren* (usually "horn") in Isa. 5:1 (NEB "hill-side"); and *maʿᵃleh* (from *ʿālâ,* "go up") in 1 S. 9:11.

Aramaic *ṭûr* (cf. Heb. *ṣûr* [*see* ROCK], Ugar. *ǵr*) is translated "mountain" in Dnl. 2:35, 45.

In the NT Gk. *bounós* ("hill") occurs only in Lk. 3:5 and 23:30 (both quotations from the LXX, although *bounós* usually translates Heb. *giḇʿâ* in the LXX). *Oreinē* ("hill country"; NEB "uplands") occurs in Lk. 1:39, 65, both times in reference to the Judean hill country (a reference that I. H. Marshall, comm. on Luke [*New International Greek Testament Comm.,* 1978], p. 80, calls "traditional practice"), although it occasionally translates Heb. *har* in the LXX. *Óros* is the predominant term, used for both "hill" and "mountain." Twice the RSV translates it "hillside" (Mk. 5:11, AV "mountain"; Lk. 8:32, AV "mountain," NEB "hill").

B. Parts. Various words are used for the top, sides, and bottom of the hill/mountain, often by analogy to the human body. Thus *rōʾš* (lit. "head") *hāhār* refers to the "top" (e.g., Gen. 8:5), "peak" (Cant. 4:8), or "summit" (e.g., 2 S. 15:32; Jer. 22:6; AV "head"; NEB "heights"); similarly *rōʾš giḇʿâ,* "top of the hill" (Ex. 17:9f.; Jgs. 16:3; 2 S. 2:25; 2 K. 1:9).

The sides or slopes of the hill/mountain are indicated by various Hebrew words. Thus in Gen. 48:22 Heb. *šᵉḵem* (lit. "shoulder") is "mountain slope"; Heb. *ʾᵃšēdâ* (either "leg, support," based on Akk. *išdu,* Ugar. *išd,* and post-biblical Aram. *ʾašdāṯaʾ*; or "watershed," based on post-biblical Aram. *ʾᵃšad* and Syr. *ʾᵉšaḏ*) is "slope" in Dt. 3:17; 4:49; Josh. 10:40; 12:3, 8; 13:20. *Kāṯēp̱* ("shoulder") is

The highlands of Gilead as seen from the castle of Ajlun (D. Baly)

The remains of the Byzantine castle Metzad Zohar, which guarded the road west from the south end of the Dead Sea. This road was considered one of the easiest routes in the Judean hill country (D. Baly)

used in Josh. 15:8, 10f.; 18:16; *ṣēlāʿ* (lit. "rib") *hāhār* is translated as "hillside" in 2 S. 16:13, and *ṣaḏ* (lit. "flank, side") *hāhār* as "side of the mountain" in 1 S. 23:26; 2 S. 13:34. *Yarkᵉṯayim* (lit. "two thighs") *hāhār* is "the remote parts of the hill country" of Ephraim in Jgs. 19:1, 18 (AV "on the side of mount Ephraim"; NEB "heart of the hill-country"), and "far recesses" in 2 K. 19:23 par. Isa. 37:24. *Taḥtîṯ* (lit. "lower") is the "foot" of the mountain in Ex. 19:17, as is *taḥaṯ* (lit. "under") in 24:4; 32:19; Dt. 4:11; Josh. 12:3. The "foundations" (Heb. *môsāḏ*) of the mountains are mentioned in Dt. 32:22 (MT 23; NEB "roots") and Ps. 18:7 (MT 8; cf. 2 S. 22:8, "foundations of heaven," which has been adduced, e.g., by L. I. J. Stadelmann, *Hebrew Conception of the World* [*Analecta Biblica*, 39, 1970], pp. 45f., 48, as evidence for the Hebrew belief that the mountains supported the heavens). Two words are translated "roots": Heb. *šōreš* (Job 28:9), apparently synonymous with the "foundations" mentioned in Ps. 18:7; and Heb. *qeṣeḇ* (lit. "extremity," Jonah 2:6 [MT 7]; AV "bottoms"; NEB "troughs"), perhaps a reference to the underworld, i.e., Sheol (cf. Stadelmann, p. 169).

The only similar Greek expression is *ophrýs*, for the "brow" of a hill in Lk. 4:29 (*see also* DESCENT).

II. Specific Topographical References.–The "hill country of" is often used with names of tribes, peoples, or towns to designate an area rather than one specific hill or peak: Gilead (Gen. 31:21), Seir (36:8), Israel (Josh. 11:16), Judah (11:21), Ephraim (17:15), Naphtali (20:7), Amalekites (Jgs. 12:15), Bethel (1 S. 13:2). "Mount" is usually more specific: Seir (Gen. 14:6), Sinai (Ex. 19:11), Horeb (33:6), Hor (Nu. 20:22), Shepher (33:23), Hermon (Dt. 3:8), Sirion (4:48), Gerizim (11:29), Ebal (11:29), Nebo (32:49), etc. (cf. "mountain[s]" of Ararat [Gen. 8:4], Gilboa [2 S. 1:21], Jerusalem [Isa. 66:20], etc.).

III. Characteristics and Use.–*A. Natural.* The elevated regions were sometimes quarried for stone (e.g., 1 K. 5:15; 2 Ch. 2:2, 18 [MT 1, 17]). The relatively high rainfall made such areas fertile, providing grass for grazing (Ps. 50:10; 104:14; 147:8; Ezk. 34:14), trees for timber (Josh. 17:18; 2 K. 19:23; Ezk. 17:23), and spices (Cant. 8:14). Wild animals lived there (Ps. 104:18), including birds (Isa. 18:6) and beasts (Cant. 4:8) of prey.

Hills and mountains had various other functions. They were the sites of ambush (Jgs. 9:25). Their peaks offered excellent vistas during times of war (Isa. 18:3) or peace (Dt. 3:27; 34:1). For auditory advantages elevated places were sometimes selected as speaking platforms (Jgs. 9:7; 2 Ch. 13:4; Isa. 40:9). Their inaccessibility made them refuges in wartime (Jgs. 6:2; 1 S. 13:6; 14:21f.; 23:14; Jer. 49:16; Ob. 3; Mt. 24:16), and hiding places for fugitives (Josh. 2:16, 22; 23:14; Ezk. 7:16). Hills also served as a natural boundary (Josh. 15:8-11).

Their ancient origin is frequently referred to, especially in passages about creation (Job. 15:7; Ps. 90:2; 104:5-8; Prov. 8:24-29; Ezk. 28:13f., 16).

B. Figurative. Hills and mountains are frequently personified. They rejoice (Ps. 98:8), leap (114:4, 6), sing (Isa. 44:23; 49:13; 55:12), and praise God (Ps. 89:12). At God's touch or presence they tremble and shake (Jgs. 5:5; Ps. 68:8 [MT 9]; Isa. 64:1; Nah. 1:5; Hab. 3:10) or melt (Ps. 97:5; Mic. 1:4). They are addressed by God (Ezk. 6:3) and called to witness a covenant lawsuit (Mic. 6:1f.; cf. J. Limburg, *JBL*, 88 [1969], 291-304).

Symbolically the mountains represent power (Jer. 51:25; Zec. 4:7), continuance or stability (Dt. 33:15; Ps. 30:7 [MT 8]; 125:1; Isa. 54:10; Hab. 3:6), and protection (Ps. 125:2). They are also symbolic of God's strength (Ps. 65:6 [MT 7]) and blessing (Dt. 33:15).

C. Religious. 1. Pagan. In much of the ancient Near East, the elevated regions were considered the dwellings of the gods (cf. Isa. 14:13f.), and thus centers of worship were established there (*see* HIGH PLACE). In OT times such Canaanite centers (often attended by Israelites) were located on hills (2 K. 17:9-12; Jer. 2:20; 17:2) and mountains (1 K. 11:7; 2 K. 23:13; Isa. 57:7; Ezk. 18:6, 11, 15; 22:9). (That there was no distinction between these terms is indicated by several texts where both are mentioned, e.g., Dt. 12:2f.; Isa. 65:7; Jer. 3:23; Ezk. 6:13; Hos. 4:13.) Balaam apparently favored the elevated regions (Nu. 22:41; 23:7, 9, 14, 28).

2. Israelite. Either through syncretism on the people's part or accommodation on God's part, the mountains and hills had special religious significance for the Hebrews (the extent of this significance and its impact on other nations may be seen in 1 K. 20:23, where the Syrians assume that Yahweh is a god of the hills). Divine appearances often occurred there (e.g., to Moses in Ex. 3:1–4:17; to Elijah in 1 K. 19:8-18), and God "came" from Teman, Paran, or Seir (Hab. 3:3; Dt. 33:2). Thus God spoke and made covenants from the mountaintop (Ex. 19–20). The people made sacrifices (Gen. 22:2-14; 31:54; Dt. 33:19; 1 K. 18:19-39) and worshiped God there (Josh. 8:30). Sanctuaries were established on various mountains, e.g., on Bethel (Gen. 12:8; 28:11-22; 35:1-15), on Ebal and Gerizim (Dt. 27:4-8; Josh. 8:30), on Shiloh (Josh. 18:1; Jgs. 18:31; 1 S. 1:3), and of course on Jerusalem/Zion. The ark was set on a hill at Bethel (Jgs. 20:18-28) and elsewhere before David brought it to Jerusalem (1 S. 7:1; 2 S. 6:3).

This close association of God and mountain is perhaps best seen in the frequent references to "the mountain of God/Yahweh," "the holy mountain," used of Horeb/Sinai (Ex. 3:1; 4:27; 18:5; 24:13; 1 K. 19:8) and Zion (Ps. 2:6; 3:4 [MT 5]; Isa. 27:13; 56:7; etc.). Zion is also called His city or abode (Ps. 48:1f. [MT 2f.]; 68:16 [MT 17]; 76:2 [MT 3]).

Prophecy is sometimes directly connected with a hill or mountain (1 S. 10:5f.; Ezk. 40:2; cf. He. 11:38). Elijah (1 K. 1:9) and Elisha (4:25) apparently lived in such areas.

References to mountains occur in eschatologies. Abundance of water will be found in the mountains during the last days (Isa. 30:25; Joel 3:18 [MT 4:18]; Zec. 14:8) and will bring tremendous fertility to the area (Ezk. 36:8; Joel 3:18; Am. 9:13). Judgment will also occur there, however. The terror and despair of unbelievers will drive them to seek a quick death in the mountains (Hos. 10:8). The battle with Gog will, at least in part, be fought in the mountains (Ezk. 38:8, 20; 39:2, 4). Yahweh Himself will fight from the Mt. of Olives (Zec. 14:3-5). In His wrath He will slaughter the nations so that the mountains will "flow with their blood" (Isa. 34:2-4). After His victory He will prepare a feast on Zion (Ezk. 38:17) and remove suffering and death from the people (Isa. 25:6-8). Then from the mountaintop Israel will proclaim its liberation (25:9; cf. 40:9-11; 52:7-10). The final reconciliation and ensuing worship of Yahweh will occur on Zion (2:1-4; 11:6-9; cf. Zec. 14:16). (In these eschatological references, Zion may be equivalent to the heavenly Jerusalem; see comms.)

3. NT. As in the OT, elevated regions are frequently mentioned. Sheep fed on the mountains (Mt. 18:12) and pigs on the hillside (Mk. 5:11). The Gerasene demoniac wandered in the mountains (Mk. 5:5). The Samaritans worshiped on Mt. Gerizim (Jn. 4:20).

Mountains played a significant role in Jesus' ministry. Not only did He mention them in striking illustrations, e.g., a city set on a hill cannot be hid (Mt. 5:14), and faith can move mountains (Mt. 17:20; 21:21 par.; cf. 1 Cor. 13:2); He also used them as a place to be alone (Jn. 6:15), to pray (Mt. 14:23 par.; Lk. 6:12), or to teach His disciples privately (Mt. 5:1; Mk. 3:13). He may have gone into the mountains to take advantage of the good acoustics for teaching large crowds or to force people to decide whether to follow Him (Mt. 15:29f.; Jn. 6:3-5; see *TDNT,* V, 485). The devil used a high mountain as a vista to tempt Jesus (Mt. 4:8; but cf. Lk. 4:5, where a visionary experience is implied). The Transfiguration occurred on a high mountain, perhaps Hermon (Mt. 17:1-8 par.). Finally, the Ascension apparently took place on the Mt. of Olives (Acts 1:3-12; cf. Lk. 24:50), although in Matthew Jesus' last recorded appearance is on a mountain in Galilee (Mt. 28:16).

Several references in Revelation indicate the role that the mountain plays in NT eschatology. In 6:14-16 a cataclysm removes the mountains and causes the people to hide among the rocks of the mountains, seeking either refuge or a quick death (cf. Lk. 23:30; both texts refer to Hos. 10:8). In 8:8 something like a fiery mountain is cast into the sea, destroying much of the sea. In 16:20 another cataclysm occurs, destroying the mountains. The seven mountains of 17:9 refer either to Rome or to world empires (see comms.). Like Ezekiel, the author is carried by the Spirit to a high mountain from which he views the new Jerusalem (21:10).

For fuller information on specific mountains, see separate articles.

See also HEIGHT.

Bibliography.–R. J. Clifford, *Cosmic Mountain in Canaan and the OT* (1972); *TDNT,* V, *s.v.* ὄρος (Foerster); *TDOT,* III, *s.v.* "har" (Talmon).

G. A. LEE

HILLEL hil'el [Heb. *hillēl*–'he greatly praised'; LXX Gk. *Ellēl*].

1. An inhabitant of Pirathon in the hill country of Ephraim, and father of Abdon, one of the judges of Israel (Jgs. 12:13, 15).

2. Hillel "the Elder" (Heb. *hazzāqēn*; *ca.* 60 B.C.-A.D. 20?). An eminent Jewish scholar and rabbinic leader in Jerusalem in the early Herodian period. Biographical details are scant, but it seems certain that Hillel was a native of Babylonia (T.B. *Pesahim* 66a; *Sukkah* 20a). He came to Jerusalem to study biblical exegesis, and Shemaiah and Abtalion, two of the early great "expositors" (Heb. *daršānîm,* T.B. *Pesahim* 70b), became his teachers. Hillel excelled in the elucidation of legal rules (Halakoth) from Scripture, and his zeal for Torah study, despite his poverty, became a model for later students (T.B. *Yoma* 35b). Other traditions state that Hillel, like Moses, lived one hundred twenty years (*Sifre* Dt. xxxiv.7 [357]) and that he was descended from David (T.B. *Ketuboth* 62b; "Rabbi" [*ca.* A.D. 135-220] was descended from Hillel), but these claims may be pious veneration rather than fact. It is still debated whether Hillel was the father or grandfather of Gamaliel I, the teacher of Paul (Acts 5:34; 22:3). The issue turns upon the questioned existence of a certain Simeon, mentioned only in T.B. *Shabbath* 15a in the rabbinic literature, who some scholars claimed was Hillel's son (R. T. Herford, "Pirke Aboth," in *APOT,* II, 694; recently reasserted by Guttmann, *Rabbinic Judaism,* p. 177; denied by E. Schürer, *HJP*², II, 367).

Hillel became leader (Heb. *nāśî,* "prince") of the rabbinic council after giving three arguments for the priority of the paschal sacrifice over the sabbath. The council had forgotten the Halakah on this issue and consulted Hillel, who finally silenced their arguments by appealing to previous tradition: "Thus have I heard from Shemaiah and Abtalion" (T.B. *Pesahim* 66a).

Hillel's exegesis was frequently opposed by Shammai (*ca.* 50 B.C.-A.D. 30), a Judean who, like Hillel, gathered a school of disciples about himself that continued after his death. Hillel generally favored a freer interpretation of the biblical text than Shammai, who usually adhered to the letter of the law. The difference between the two schools is illustrated by the issue of DIVORCE, which centered on the phrase "some indecency" (Heb. *ʿerwaṯ dāḇār,* lit. "nakedness of a thing") in Dt. 24:1. The school of Shammai restricted the meaning to illicit sexual conduct by focusing on *ʿerwaṯ* ("shamefulness," "nakedness"), but the Hillelites emphasized *dāḇār* ("thing," "matter") and construed the phrase to mean "*any* indecent thing," even as trivial as spoiling the husband's food (T.B. *Gittin* 90a). This controversy lies behind the question of the Pharisees in Mt. 19:3 (cf. Mk. 10:2), "Is it lawful to divorce one's wife *for any cause*?" The restriction of divorce to the one cause of UNCHASTITY in Mt. 5:32; 19:3 reflects the stricter interpretation of the school of Shammai (SB, I, 312-320).

On one occasion a non-Jew came to Shammai and asked to become a proselyte on the condition that Shammai teach him the whole law while the gentile stood on one foot. Shammai, apparently doubting his sincerity, chased him away with a measuring stick. Thereupon the man came before Hillel, who said, "What is hateful to you, do not do to your neighbor; that is the whole Torah, the rest is commentary" (T.B. *Shabbath* 31a). *See* GOLDEN RULE.

Another important decision rendered by Hillel was his issuance of the so-called *prozbul* (Heb. *peʳrôzbôl* or *peʳrôsbôl* from either Gk. *prós Boulē Bouleutōn,* "before the assembly of the counselors," or *prosbolḗ,* "delivery"; cf. *Jew. Enc.,* X, 219; *HJP*², II, 366f., etc.), a judicial edict that in effect canceled the OT ordinance that all debts should be remitted during the SABBATICAL YEAR (Dt. 15:1-11). Hillel's intent was to prevent transgression on the part of those who refused to give loans prior to the seventh year (cf. Dt. 15:9).

According to later tradition Hillel demonstrated seven hermeneutical rules (Heb. *middôṯ*) when he was called before the council (Tosefta *Sanhedrin* vii; *Aboth de Rabbi Nathan* xxxvii). The presence of several of these interpretative principles in the NT has led scholars to compare Hillel's use of Scripture with that of Jesus and Paul. Hillel's first rule, *qal wāḥômer* (lit. "light and heavy," i.e., what applies in a lesser case will certainly apply in a greater case), is exemplified in Mt. 7:11 (par. Lk. 11:13); Jn. 10:34-36; Rom. 5:15-21, which all have an "if . . . then how much more" argument (cf. R. Longenecker, *Biblical Exegesis in the Apostolic Period* [1975], pp. 32-38, 68, 117, etc.). Paul's use of other rules of Hillel led J. Jeremias to conclude that Paul was a Hillelite ("Paulus als Hillelit," in E. Ellis and M. Wilcox, eds., *Neotestamentica et Semitica* [1969], p. 89).

Glatzer argued ("Hillel the Elder in the Light of the Dead Sea Scrolls," in K. Stendahl, ed., *The Scrolls and the NT* [1957], p. 244) that Hillel's teaching may show an awareness of the Qumrân sect's break from Jerusalem Judaism. Hillel's purpose was thus one of reform within Judaism (contra H. L. Strack, *Intro. to the Talmud and Midrash* [Eng. tr. 1931; repr. 1969], p. 108) to counter the influence of that group.

Bibliography.–W. Bacher, *Tradition und Tradenten in den Schulen Palästinas und Babyloniens* (1914; repr. 1966), pp. 54-71; F. Delitzsch, *Jesus und Hillel* (3rd ed. 1879); *Encyclopaedia Judaica,* VIII, *s.v.*; N. Glatzer, *Hillel the Elder: The Emergence of Classical Judaism* (1956); J. Goldin, *JR,* 26 (1946), 263-277; A. Guttmann, *Rabbinic Judaism in the Making* (1970), pp. 59-104; *HUCA,* 23 (1950/51), 453-473; 28 (1957), 115-126; A. Kaminka, *JQR,* 30 (1939/40), 107-122; G. F. Moore, *Judaism in the First Centuries of the Christian Era,* I (1927; repr. 1971), 72-81.

R. J. W.

HIN hin [Heb. *hîn*]. A liquid measure containing 12 logs,

Basalt door pivot in its socket, from the Canaanite temple at Hazor (Institute of Archaeology, Hebrew University of Jerusalem)

Bronze pivot hinges from Egypt (Trustees of the British Museum)

equal to about 3 liters (6½ pints). *See* WEIGHTS AND MEASURES.

HIND. *See* DEER; GAZELLE.

HIND OF THE DAWN, THE. The translation of Heb. *'ayyeleṯ haššaḥar* in the title of Ps. 22, possibly the name of some well-known tune to which the psalm was intended to be sung, which may have had reference to the habits of deer in search of water and food, or to the flight of the hind from hunters in early dawn; or "dawn" may symbolize the deliverance from persecution and sorrow. *See* MUSIC III.B; PSALMS II; DAWN.

HINGE [Heb. *ṣîr*; Akk. *ṣirru*]. The Hebrew term in Prov. 26:14 refers to some device that enabled a door to turn on a pivot, and thus be opened or closed. Specimen hinges from ancient Near Eastern sites include metal bars having a piece at one end which projects downward at a right angle, so as to fit into a stone socket placed beneath the bottom corner of a wooden or stone door. In Mesopotamian temples these sockets were frequently inscribed with the name and titles of the reigning monarch who had constructed the temple. Presumably, the reference in Proverbs is to the slowness with which these usually massive doors moved on their hinges. R. K. H.

HINNOM hin'əm, **VALLEY OF** [Heb. *gê hinnōm*] (Josh. 15:8; 18:16); [*gê ḇen-hinnōm,* "valley of the son of Hinnom"] (Josh. 15:8; 18:16; 2 Ch. 28:3; 33:6; Jer. 7:31f.; 19:2, 6; 32:35; *Q* in 2 K. 23:10, read by the NEB); NEB "Valley of Ben-hinnom"; [*gê ḇ^enê-hinnōm,* "valley of the sons (AV "children") of Hinnom"] (*K* in 2 K. 23:10, read by the AV and the RSV); [*haggay'*, "the valley" (referring to Hinnom)] (2 Ch. 26:9; Neh. 2:13, 15; 3:13; Jer. 31:40; perhaps also Jer. 2:23). A deep narrow valley immediately S of Jerusalem, marking the boundary between Judah and Benjamin (Josh. 15:8; 18:16) — especially the E-W section of the Wâdī er-Rabâbi, though the name is commonly extended to include the N-S section just W of the present city walls. The forms *ben-* and *b^enê-hinnōm* suggest that Hinnom is a personal name.

I. Biblical References and History.–The Harsith Gate, or Gate of the Earthenware Pots (Jer. 19:2), and the Valley Gate (Neh. 2:13; 3:13) opened into the Valley of Hinnom. Here Ahaz (2 Ch. 28:3) made idols, burned incense, and offered his sons to the Baals; likewise Manasseh (2 Ch. 33:6) "burned his sons as an offering" here. Josiah stopped the offering of children to Molech by defiling Topheth, the eastern end of Hinnom near its confluence with the Kidron (2 K. 23:10). Because of the pagan rites practiced there, Jeremiah prophesied that the name would be changed to the "Valley of Slaughter" in the Day of Vengeance (7:31f.; 19:5f.). In view of its notoriety Jeremiah could refer to it simply as "the valley" (2:23). Lightfoot and others thought that it was used as the refuse dump of the city where dead animals and garbage were burned and smoke from the burning rose continually. Thus Hinnom became an appropriate symbol of woe and judgment (Jer. 7:31; 19:6; cf. Isa. 66:24).

The theological significance of the Valley of Hinnom (GEHENNA) heightens in the intertestamental Jewish literature, where, for example, the evil inherit Gehenna (Mish. *Pirke Aboth* i.5; v. 19f.) and the "furnace of Gehenna" is set over against the "paradise of delight" (2 Esd. 7:36, RSV mg.). In the NT Gehenna is the "hell of fire" (Mt. 5:22) associated with the last judgment.

II. Location.–The Valley of Hinnom has been identified by different scholars as each of the three great valleys of Jerusalem. Some early Christian, Moslem, and Jewish writers identified Hinnom with the Kidron. It is more likely, however, that the identification of the Kidron (because of its nearness to the temple) as the scene of the last judgment — the "valley of Jehoshaphat" of Joel 3:2 [MT 4:2] — probably led to its designation as Gehenna, the scene of the punishment of the wicked, after the ancient geographical position of the Valley of Hinnom had long been lost. The following arguments weigh heavily against the Kidron theory: (1) the Kidron Valley is always called a *naḥal* ("wadi") and not a *gay'* ("gorge"); (2) the Valley

Gate did not lie to the east of the city; (3) En-rogel, which lay E of the beginning of the Valley of Hinnom (Josh. 15:8; 18:16), cannot be the ancient Gihon (2 Ch. 33:14), but is rather to be identified with Bîr Ayyûb; (4) if Hinnom is identified with Kidron, Jerusalem would be in Judah, whereas Josh. 18:28 indicates that Jerusalem is in Benjamin.

The theory that the Valley of Hinnom was located originally in what was later known as the Tyropoeon Valley (the valley that separates the eastern hill, Ophel, from the western hill) does not flatly contradict the boundary description in Josh. 15:8; 18:6. But this theory requires the acceptance of two unlikely assumptions: (1) that the name Hinnom moved from the central valley to the southern one; (2) that the name of the plain of Rephaim moved from N of the city to SW of Jerusalem. Furthermore, Neh. 11:30 requires that Hinnom be an E-W valley. If the Tyropoeon was incorporated within the city walls before the time of Manasseh, it could hardly have been the place of sacrifice of children (2 K. 23:10), for this must have occurred outside the city limits.

The clearest geographical data (Josh. 15:8; cf. 18:16) state that the boundary of Judah and Benjamin passed from En-rogel "by the valley of the son of Hinnom" to "the northern end of the Valley of Rephaim. . . ." If the modern Bîr Ayyûb is En-rogel, as is probable, then the Wâdī er-Rabâbi is the Valley of Hinnom. The name may have extended to the wide-open land formed by the junction of the three valleys (some locate Topheth here), but there is no need to extend the name beyond the gorge. The Wâdī er-Rabâbi commences in a shallow, open valley W of the modern Jaffa Gate; near the gate it turns S for less than a kilometer (half mile) and then gradually curves to the east where it becomes a gorge (Heb. *gay'*) descending rapidly to its junction with the Kidron. *See* JERUSALEM II.B.

Well-founded tradition locates Akeldama on the south side of the Valley of Hinnom. Here Jewish and Christian tombs of Roman and Byzantine times may be seen.

Bibliography.–G. A. Smith, *Jerusalem*, I (1907), 170-180; J. Simons, *Jerusalem in the OT* (1952), pp. 10-12, 52 n.2.

D. J. WIEAND

HIP [Heb. *nāšeh*] (Gen. 32:32 [MT 33]); AV "which shrank"; NEB NERVE; [*ṣaḏ*–'side'] (Isa. 66:12); AV SIDES; NEB ARMS; [*šôq*] (Jgs. 15:8); [*šēṯ*–'buttock'] (2 S. 10:4); AV, NEB, BUTTOCKS; [*mipśā'â*] (1 Ch. 19:4); AV BUTTOCKS.

The Hebrew terms relate in a general way to the trunk, waist, or lower abdominal area of the body, although in Gen. 32:32 it is the muscular structure of the thigh which is designated. In Jgs. 15:8, the violent slaughter resulted in bodies being hacked into pieces and limbs piled upon each other (lit. "leg upon thigh") in heaps. The humiliation of David's servants (1 S. 10:4; 1 Ch. 19:4) involved among other things the exposing of their pudenda, following ancient Near Eastern custom. In Isa. 66:12, the child is being held by his mother's arms along one side of her body, with his main weight resting upon her hip. R. K. H.

HIRAH hī'rə [Heb. *ḥîrâ*] (Gen. 38:1, 12, 20-23). A native of Adullam and a "friend" of Judah. In v. 12 (cf. v. 20) both the LXX and the Vulgate designate Hirah "his shepherd" (Heb. *rō'ēhû*) instead of "his friend" (*rē'ēhû*).

HIRAM hī'rəm; **HURAM** hu'rəm (2 Chronicles) [Heb. *ḥîrām, ḥûrām, ḥîrôm,* probably an abbrev. of *'aḥîrām*–(my) brother is exalted'; Gk. *Chiram, Cheiram*].

1. Hiram I king of Tyre, who lived on friendly terms with both David and Solomon. Tyre, rebuilt by Sidonian Phoenicians in the 12th cent. B.C., was capital of a state that by this time controlled the whole southern Phoenician littoral from the Bay of Acre northward. Under Hiram I Tyre enjoyed considerable expansion and prosperity; and before the end of the 10th cent. B.C. colonies existed in Cyprus, Sicily, and Sardinia, where copper mines were exploited.

David, whom Hiram loved (1 K. 5:1) and whose Lord he acknowledged (2 Ch. 2:11f.), entered into a friendly alliance with Hiram (2 S. 5:11). The terms of the alliance included the sending of Tyrian workmen, who excelled in architecture, and also materials to build a palace for David at Jerusalem. Solomon also entered into a treaty, which had considerable advantages for both sides and was probably the most important of Solomon's alliances. Palestine became the "granary of Phoenicia," for Hiram received large quantities of wheat, barley, oil, and wine annually for both his household and his workers (1 K. 5:11; 2 Ch. 2:10). In return Solomon received cedar, fir, and algum trees, which came in rafts by sea to Joppa (land carriage would have been too slow and costly) for building the temple. No doubt this was not just a commercial agreement, for Phoenicia would welcome an alliance with a strong military power that would protect its eastern trade routes but not embark on any scheme of conquest.

At the end of twenty years Solomon gave Hiram twenty cities of Galilee. This has been interpreted as a measure of desperation on the part of Solomon. By this time Solomon's financial position must have been embarrassingly acute and the royal coffers severely overstrained. The cities were either sold outright or advanced as collateral against a cash loan and later redeemed. Hiram was not at all pleased with the cities and contemptuously called them "CABUL" (1 K. 9:10-14). Hiram apparently returned these cities, for later Solomon rebuilt them and settled his own people in them (2 Ch. 8:2).

Hiram and Solomon maintained merchant vessels on the Mediterranean and shared mutually in a profitable trade with foreign ports (1 K. 10:22). Hiram's sailors, men of considerable experience, taught Solomon's men seamanship. They used the route from Ezion-geber on the Gulf of Aqabah to Ophir, where large stores of gold, as well as almug wood, precious stones, ivory, apes, and baboons (RSV mg.) were brought to the royal palace every three years (1 K. 9:26-28; 10:22-25; 2 Ch. 8:17f.).

Josephus (*CAp* i.17f. [106-127]), on the authority of Menander of Ephesus and Dius the Phoenician, recounts that Hiram was the son of Abibaal and died at the age of fifty-three after a reign of thirty-four years. This, however, may be a different king, for the biblical account requires a longer reign. Josephus also tells us on the same authority that Hiram and Solomon sent riddles to one another, but that Hiram could not solve those sent to him by Solomon, whereupon he paid to Solomon a large sum of money which had first been agreed upon. Eusebius recounts that Hiram gave his daughter in marriage to Solomon (from Tatian; *Praep. ev.* x.11) and this compares well with 1 K. 11:1.

2. *See* HURAM **1.** J. A. BALCHIN

HIRCANUS hûr-kā'nəs (AV Apoc.). *See* HYRCANUS.

HIRE [(vb.) Heb. *śāḵar, sāḵar* (Ezr. 4:5), *tānâ* (Hos. 8:9f.); Gk. *misthóomai* (Mt. 20:1, 7)]; AV also REWARD (Prov. 26:10); NEB also "sell themselves" (1 S. 2:5), BRIBE (Neh. 6:12f.; Ezr. 4:5), BARGAIN (Hos. 8:9f.); [(subst.) Heb. *śāḵîr, śāḵār, 'eṯnān* (Dt. 23:18 [MT 19]; Isa. 23:17f.; Ezk. 16:31, 34, 41; Hos. 9:1; Mic. 1:7), *'eṯnâ* (Hos. 2:12 [MT 14]), *śeḵer* (Isa. 19:10), *m^{e}ḥîr* (Mic. 3:11); Gk. *místhios* (Sir. 7:20; Lk. 15:17, 19), *misthōtós* (Mk. 1:20)]; AV also REWARD (Ezk. 16:34; Hos. 2:12; 9:1), "sluices" (Isa. 19:10), HIRELING (Sir. 7:20); NEB also MERCENARIES (Jer. 46:21), WAGES (Dt. 24:15), REWARD (Gen. 30:18), FEE (Dt. 23:18), PROFITS (Isa. 23:18), TRADE (Isa. 23:17).

As a verb, "hire" in all but three instances represents the Hebrew verb *śāḵar* (sibilant confusion has yielded *sāḵar* in Ezr. 4:5; in later Aramaic *ś* became *s*). The meaning is to employ a person to perform a service for compensation. The cognate noun, *śāḵār,* represents the compensation or wage paid to the hired person for his service (cf. Dt. 24:15). An apparently synonymous term, *śeḵer* (also a derivative of *śāḵar*), occurs only once in the OT (Isa. 19:10) in the phrase *ʿōśê śeḵer,* "those who work for hire." Sibilant confusion again led to the AV translation "make sluices." The NEB has freely rendered the phrase as "artisans." Since the context of Isa. 19:10 is a brief catalog of skilled crafts, it is possible that a designation of "brewers" (*ʿōśê šēḵār*) has been obscured by the MT pointing; cf. LXX *zýthos,* "beer," and Syr. *šaḵrāʾ,* "strong drink."

The most common Hebrew substantive is the remaining cognate, *śāḵîr,* most often translated as "hired servant" by the RSV and "hired man" or "hired labourer" by the NEB (*see also* HIRELING). Dt. 24:14f. clearly delineates the meaning — the *śāḵîr* is the "wage-earner" or "day-laborer" who is paid the *śāḵār* in compensation for his labor. Though this paid laborer is usually human, *śāḵîr* may also be applied to a hired beast of burden (Ex. 22:15 [MT 14]) or even a figurative razor (Isa. 7:20).

The Hebrew substantive *'eṯnān* (and once the synonymous *'eṯnâ,* Hos. 2:12) constitutes a "wage" class all by itself, for in all its occurrences it denotes the "hire" or "fee" of the prostitute (cf., e.g., Dt. 23:18). The term is commonly employed in figurative depiction of Israel's unfaithfulness to Yahweh (cf. Ezk. 16:31, 34, 41; Hos. 2:12; 9:1); *see* HARLOT. *Meḥîr,* usually meaning simply "price" or "payment" (e.g., Isa. 55:1), has a particularly opprobrious connotation in Mic. 3:11, where the prophet laments the unethical practice of paying priests for decisions.

The NT terms are all derivatives of *misthós,* "wages, payment due a laborer for work accomplished" (cf. 1 Tim. 5:18; *see* WAGES). *Misthóomai* appears twice in the NT (Mt. 20:1, 7), both times in the strictly secular sense, "to hire for payment" (as, e.g., a laborer in a vineyard). *Místhios* also appears only twice (Lk. 15:17, 19), in each case as a noun denoting the simple, classical sense of the term "hired worker," or "day laborer." Similarly, *misthōtós* appears three times, always as a noun, and also in the above sense of "day laborer" (Mk. 1:20) or "hireling" (Jn. 10:12f.).

The precise nature of the work or service performed by the "hired" varied widely. Day laborers were hired for agricultural tasks (Lk. 15:17, 19), horticultural work (Mt. 20:1, 7), general labor (Dt. 24:14f.; 1 S. 2:5), and even crew service on a fishing trawler (Mk. 1:20). The hiring of skilled craftsmen is mentioned in Isa. 46:6 (a goldsmith) and 2 Ch. 24:12 (masons and carpenters), and of mercenary soldiers or military allies in Jgs. 9:4; 2 S. 10:6; 2 K. 7:6; 1 Ch. 19:6f.; 2 Ch. 25:6; Jer. 46:21; and Hos. 8:9f. Apparently, the practice of hiring oneself out in mercenary service was frequently viewed by impoverished and debt-ridden commoners as a more desirable alternative than bankruptcy and voluntary slavery. The hiring of a diviner (Dt. 23:4; Neh. 13:2), a prophet (Neh. 6:12f.), a priest (Mic. 3:11; Jgs. 18:4), advisors (Ezr. 4:5), a work animal (Ex. 22:15 [MT 14]), and a prostitute (Dt. 23:18; etc.) further exemplify the variety of services that may be rendered for hire. A caution against the hiring of a fool or drunkard is offered in Prov. 26:10.

While the OT gives no direct information about the amount of the wage earned by such hired workers, the NT in one instance (Mt. 20:1-15) expressly states that certain vineyard laborers were hired at the rate of a denarius a day. In addition to the common daily arrangement, hire could also be contracted by the year (cf. Lev. 25:50, 53).

The lot of the hired laborer was understandably no enviable one, and Israelite law thus included some safeguards of his rights (e.g., Lev. 19:13 and Dt. 24:14f. stipulate that the hired worker must be paid for his work each evening; cf. Mt. 20:8f.). While the hired laborer's livelihood was apparently harsh and precarious, he was at least not a slave. The use in Israel of both native and foreign-born freemen as hired laborers or craftsmen who render services in exchange for livelihood must not be confused on the one hand with the institution of slavery (*see* SLAVE), nor on the other with the custom of native Israelites selling or indenturing themselves to another out of economic necessity (cf. Dt. 15:12-18; see de Vaux, pp. 82f.).

The term *śāḵār* occurs once in the Qumrân literature. The Damascus Document contains a regulation (CD 14:12) that the earnings of at least two days out of each month be appropriated by the administration for public welfare.

While there were in Israel large-scale commercial concerns (e.g., the various textile and metallurgical industries) that certainly employed substantial numbers of laborers, direct references in the Bible to such guilds of workers are scarce (cf. 1 Ch. 4:21; 2 Ch. 2:7 [MT 6]; Neh. 3:31; *WBA*, p. 188; Mendelsohn, pp. 17-21).

Bibliography.–I. Mendelsohn, *BASOR,* 80 (1940), 17-21; *TDNT,* IV, *s.v.* μισθός (Preisker, Würthwein); R. de Vaux, *Ancient Israel* (Eng. tr. 1961), I, 76, 82f.

D. G. BURKE

HIRELING [Heb. *śāḵîr*] (Job 7:1f.; 14:6; Isa. 16:14; 21:16; Mal. 3:5); NEB HIRED LABOURER, SERVANT (Job 7:2); [Gk. *misthōtós*] (Jn. 10:12f.).

The Hebrew substantive *śāḵîr,* "hireling" or "hired man," is derived from the verb *śāḵar,* "to hire for payment," and thus denotes the "wage earner" or "day laborer" who is paid the "hire" (*śāḵār*) in compensation for his (usually temporary) manual or skilled labor. The Gk. *misthōtós* appears twice in the NT (Jn. 10:12f.) as a noun with the particular sense (in the context) of "hired shepherd," even though, like Heb. *śāḵîr,* the term itself has reference only to the hiring of service or labor in general and not to any specific craft or occupation (cf. *místhios,* "a man whom you will pay" [AV "hireling"] in Tob. 5:11 [LXX 12]). Elsewhere in the NT *misthōtós* occurs only in Mk. 1:20, where it denotes the hired crew of a fishing trawler.

The transience of the hireling's work is underscored in Jn. 10:12f., where Jesus contrasts the hireling shepherd or "paid keeper" with the good shepherd. In stark contrast to the permanent shepherd, such a temporary employee is depicted as being markedly less conscientious about the responsibilities of his job. While labor was commonly contracted on a per diem basis (cf. Lev. 19:13; Dt. 24:15), per annum hiring was also practiced (cf. Isa. 16:14; 21:16).

Mal. 3:5 is illustrative of the frequent prophetic protest against the cheating of the hireling out of his rightful earnings. That such employer malfeasance was common may be inferred from both the prophets' condemnations and the legal sanctions that protected the hireling's wage rights (cf. Lev. 19:13; Dt. 24:14f.; Job 7:2). Elsewhere, sympathy is expressed for the anxiety-ridden harshness of the day laborer's more or less hand-to-mouth existence on a subsistence wage (cf. Job 7:1f.; 14:6; Sir. 7:20).

For further details and bibliography, *see* HIRE.

D. G. BURKE

HIS. Used often in the AV with reference to a neuter or inanimate thing, or to a lower animal (Gen. 1:11, "after *his* kind"; Lev. 1:16, "pluck away his crop"; Acts 12:10, "of *his* own accord"; 1 Cor. 15:38, "*his* own body"; etc.). The RSV substitutes "its."

HISS [Heb. *šāraq*] (1 K. 9:8; 2 Ch. 29:8; Job 27:23; Jer. 18:16; 19:8; 25:9, 18; 29:18; 49:17; 50:13; 51:37; Lam. 2:15f.; Ezk. 27:36; Mic. 6:16; Zeph. 2:15); NEB also JEER, GASP (1 K. 9:8), WHISTLES (Job 27:23), "a thing (or object) of derision" (2 Ch. 29:8; Jer. 25:9, 18; 29:18; 51:37). The Hebrew root means "to whistle," and the RSV has used "hiss" to indicate contemptuous or derisive whistling. The note of bitter invective is clearly present in Lam. 2:15f. and Zeph. 2:15. However, some of the above passages (e.g., 1 K. 9:8; 2 Ch. 29:8) may be interpreted in a less pejorative sense; e.g., one may express astonishment by whistling through the teeth. J. T. DENNISON, JR.

HISTORY [Heb. *tôlēdôṯ*] (Gen. 37:2); AV GENERATIONS; NEB STORY OF THE DESCENDENTS; [*diḇrê*–'words'] (2 Ch. 9:29); AV BOOK. The former reference is to a family history or genealogy, of a type frequent in the book of Genesis, which points back to the beginnings of the family or other social unit in question. The latter concerns the royal annals kept by Nathan; cf. RSV 1 Ch. 29:29. G. WYPER

HITHERTO. In modern English usage the term means "up to this time." The RSV uses it in this sense for Heb. *tᵉmôl* (Ex. 5:14), *ʿaḏ kōh* (Josh. 17:14), *ʿaḏ hēnnâ* (1 S. 7:12; 1 Ch. 9:18; 12:29), and for Gk. *héōs árti* (Jn. 16:24; 1 Cor. 8:7).

The AV sometimes uses "hitherto" in the obsolete sense of "thus far," e.g., for Heb. *ʿaḏ hᵃlôm* (2 S. 7:18; 1 Ch. 17:16), *ʿaḏ pōh* (Job 38:11).

HITTITES hi'tīts [Heb. *bᵉnê ḥēṯ, ḥittîm*; Gk. *Chettaioi*]. A designation given in the OT (1) to a great nation which gave its name to the whole Syrian region, "from the wilderness and this Lebanon as far as the great river, the river Euphrates, all the land of the Hittites to the Great Sea [Mediterranean] towards the going down of the sun" (Josh. 1:4; cf. Jgs. 1:26), and (2) to one of the ethnic groups resident in Canaan from patriarchal times until after the Israelite settlement (Gen. 15:20; Dt. 7:1; Jgs. 3:5), whose eponymous ancestor was Heth, a son of Canaan (Gen. 10:15; 1 Ch. 1:13).

I. Anatolian Hittites
II. Neo-Hittite City-States
III. Hittites of Palestine

I. Anatolian Hittites.–The Hittites first make their appearance in history as Indo-European immigrants from the northeast who settled in east-central Asia Minor in the Early Bronze Age III B (*ca.* 2000 B.C.). They had been preceded two or three centuries earlier by another Indo-European group, the Luwian-speaking Arzawans, who settled farther west, around Beycesultan. The area in which the Hittites settled was occupied before their arrival by an indigenous Anatolian people called the Ḫatti, with whom the immigrants amalgamated and whose name they assumed. As in other parts of the Near East in the 2nd millennium B.C., we can recognize a dominant Indo-European caste united in one national entity with a subordinate non-Indo-European infrastructure.

In the records of the Assyrian trading colony at Kültepe (Kaneš) Hittite proper names appear *ca.* 1800 B.C. The Hittite archives from Boghazköy (Hattusas), later capital of the Hittite empire, preserve a half-legendary account of an early king named Pitḫanas, ruler of Kussaras (an

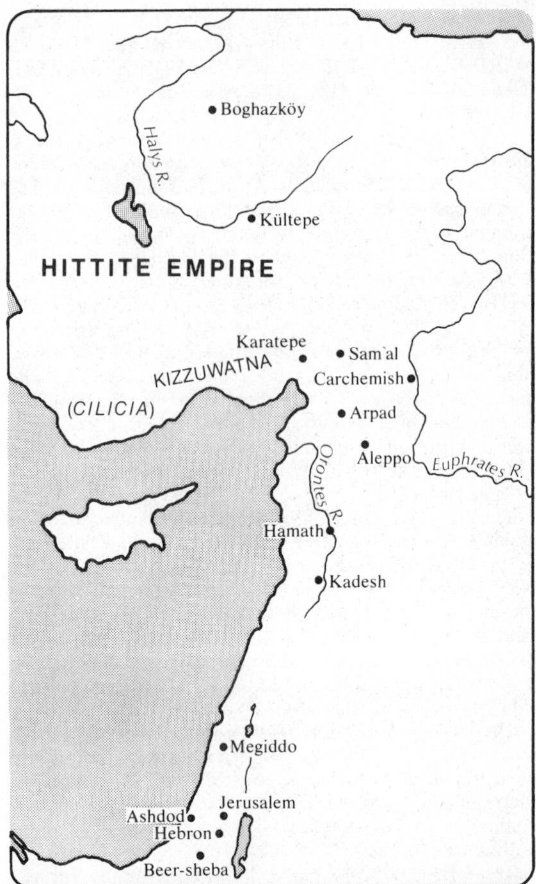

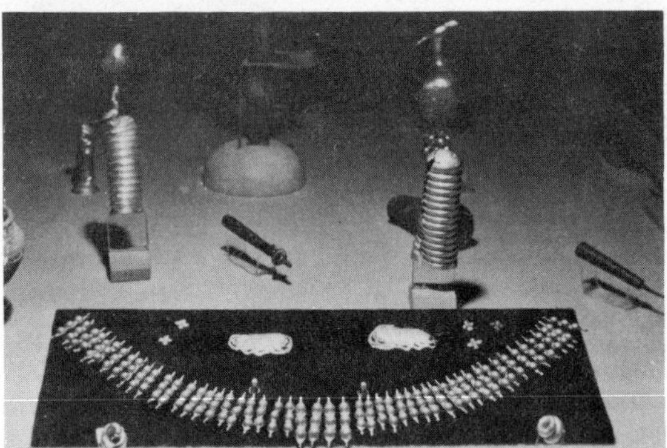

Proto-Hittite gold objects (23rd cent. B.C.) from Alaça Hüyük in present-day Turkey (Hittite Museum, Ankara; picture W. S. LaSor)

unidentified city), who conquered the city of Nesas (provisionally, but not certainly, identified with Kaneš), which his son Anittas adopted as his capital. From the name of this city the Hittites' Indo-European language is referred to in their own records as "Nesian" (*nasili, nesumnili*). (The language of the indigenous Ḫatti is referred to as *hattili*, conveniently translated "Hattic.")

Anittas was the first of the Hittite rulers to adopt the title of "Great King" — an index of his imperial ambition. His son Tudḫaliyas I (*ca.* 1720 B.C.) has been tentatively identified with "Tidal king of Goiim," one of the allies of Chedorlaomer in Gen. 14:1. A later king, Labarnas, extended his rule over a number of Hittite city-states

The site of Hattusas (Boghazköy), the capital of the Hittite kingdom (16th-13th cents. B.C.) (B. K. Condit)

in Anatolia that had previously been independent; his name is used by later Hittite kings as a title meaning "emperor" (cf. the development of the personal name Caesar in Roman imperial history). His son Ḫattusilis I extended his dominion into north Syria (*ca.* 1600 B.C.). He was succeeded by Mursilis I, who moved his capital to Hattusas, in the area enclosed by the curve of the river Halys (modern Kızıl Irmak). Here the seat of the empire remained for nearly four centuries, and it was the unearthing of the state archives on this site in 1906 and the following years that brought to light the lost history of early Hittite civilization. Mursilis I captured Aleppo and toward the end of his reign (*ca.* 1560 B.C.) raided Babylon — an event that precipitated the downfall of the 1st Babylonian Dynasty.

Early in the 15th cent. B.C. the Hittite constitution and laws were codified by King Telepinus. The Hittite king was not an absolute monarch; his authority was limited (in the earlier period at least) by a council or assembly called the *pankus*. Succession to the throne required ratification by this body. The king was a military, civil, and religious leader; the succession normally passed to his son or son-in-law. The role of the queen (*tawanannas*) was chiefly religious; she retained her authority for life, and not until the death of the queen mother did the king's wife acquire the title. The social status of women in general was better secured in Hittite law than among many of the neighboring peoples. In religious matters the Hittites appear to have taken over the practice of their predecessors, the Ḫatti. The Hittite laws were more humane than those of Babylonia and Assyria. They exhibit points of resemblance with the earliest OT law codes, but more in details than in basic principles. For example, while the OT laws, like several other ancient Near Eastern law codes, apply the law of retaliation (*lex talionis*), the Hittite code is characterized by the distinctively Indo-European principle of compensation (*Wergeld*). No degrading mutilations are imposed as penalties in the Hittite code, and conquered enemies are treated with clemency. Diplomacy is preferred, when possible, to military force; royal intermarriage is a recurring instrument of Hittite relations with foreign powers, and the sanctity of treaties is carefully respected.

Hittite wall at Boghazköy. Note how the massive stones are fitted together (F. E. V. LaSor)

In the reign of the next king, Tudḫaliyas II, the Hittites first came into close contact with Egypt, when Thutmose III, after his great victory at Megiddo (*ca.* 1468 B.C.), advanced to Carchemish on the Euphrates and Kadesh on the Orontes, thus approaching the southern frontier of the Hittite sphere of influence. Tudḫaliyas judged it wise to send to Thutmose an embassy with gifts.

Šuppiluliuma I (*ca.* 1380-1350 B.C.) consolidated his power in Asia Minor and established his supremacy over the Hurrian kingdom of Mitanni in upper Mesopotamia and over the city-states of Syria as far S as the Lebanon Range. It was during his reign that iron was first smelted on a significant scale in the Near East, in the province of Kizzuwatna (Cilicia). The manifest might of Šuppiluliuma moved some Syrian city-states, hitherto vassals of Egypt, to transfer their allegiance to him. Nevertheless he endeavored to maintain friendly relations with Egypt: he congratulated Akhenaten on his accession (*ca.* 1377 B.C.), and some twenty years later Akhenaten's daughter, the widow of Tutankhamen, sent a delegation to Šuppiluliuma to discuss the possibility of her marrying one of his sons. The failure of this plan, and the assassination of a Hittite prince who had been sent to Egypt to explore the situation, led to a state of intermittent war between the two imperial powers that culminated in the indecisive battle of Kadesh on the Orontes in the fifth year of Ramses II (*ca.* 1297 B.C.). This war was brought to an end seventeen years later with a nonaggression pact between Ramses and the Hittite king Ḫattusilis III, recognizing the common frontier of the two empires on the Orontes. This agreement was confirmed a few years later by a marriage between Ramses and one of the daughters of Ḫattusilis.

The following decades witnessed a continual weakening of the Hittite power: with the capture and destruction of Hattusas by invaders from the west (*ca.* 1200 B.C.) the Hittite empire came to an end.

II. Neo-Hittite City-States.–After the fall of the empire the Hittite home territory on the Anatolian side of the Taurus Range was encroached upon by the Phrygians; one Hittite state in that area was known to the Assyrians as Tabal (cf. Tubal in Gen. 10:2; Ezk. 27:13; 38:2; etc.). Seven city-states on the Syrian side of the range that had belonged to the Hittite sphere of influence continued for several centuries to bear the Hittite name, and their rulers were known as "the kings of the Hittites." Prominent among these neo-Hittite states were Carchemish, Sam'al (modern Zenjirli), Aleppo, Arpad, and Hamath on the Orontes. King Toi of Hamath entered into treaty relations with David (2 S. 8:9-12), whose kingdom stretched as far N as "Kadesh in the land of the Hittites" (2 S. 24:6, RSV, emended on the basis of the LXX from the meaningless MT Heb. *taḥtîm ḥoḏšî*). His son Solomon traded and intermarried with these "kings of the Hittites" (1 K. 10:28f.; 11:1). A century later the reputation of their military strength was sufficient to strike panic into an army of Damascus (2 K. 7:6). In the 8th cent. B.C., however, these city-states were reduced by the Assyrians: Hamath and Arpad fell to them in 720 B.C. and Carchemish three years later (as the Assyrians repeatedly boast in their attempts to intimidate Judah and other weak states; cf. 2 K. 18:34; 19:13; Isa. 10:9; etc.).

The Hittite inscriptions in north Syria are written in hieroglyphs, whereas the records of the Anatolian Hittites (and of some of their neighbors) are in cuneiform script on clay tablets. The two forms of Hittite are distinguished materially as well as in respect of script: "hieroglyphic Hittite" has affinities with Luwian, the Indo-European language of Arzawa (which was first identified in modern times in Am.Tab. 31f.). The credit for identifying the Indo-

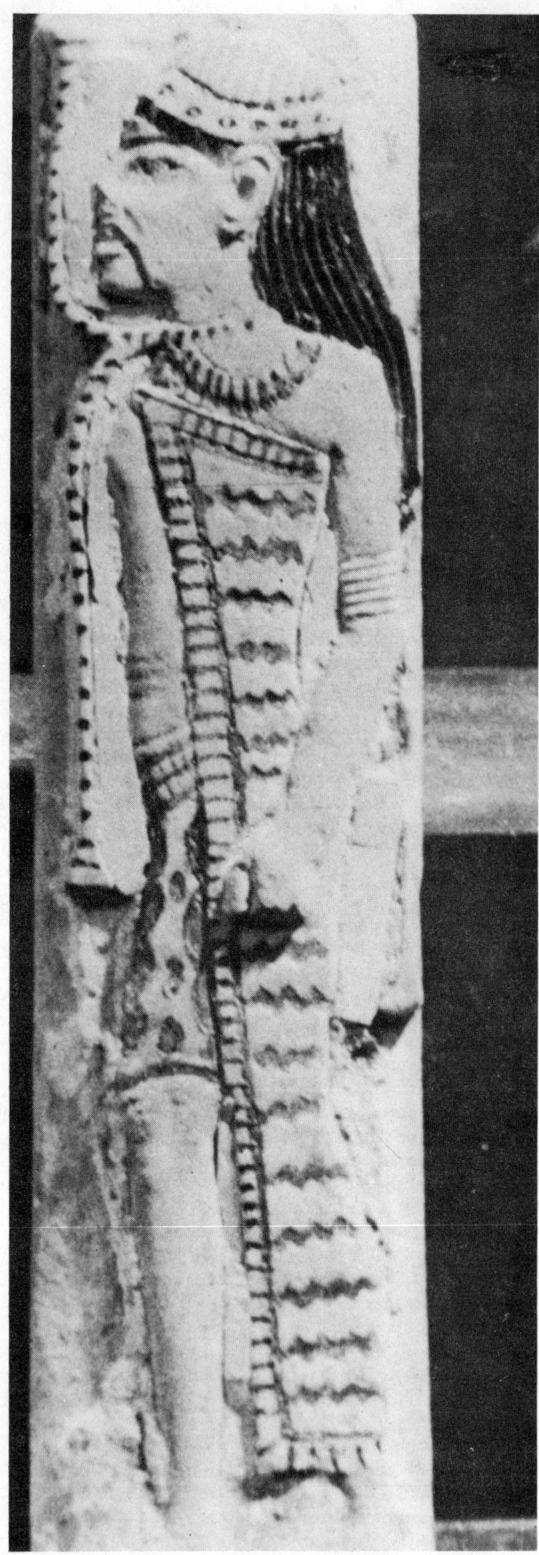

Faience tile (12th cent. B.C.) of a Hittite captured by the Egyptians. He wears a short kilt under a bright mantle baring the left shoulder, a decorated cap, and a beaded collar (Service des musées, Cairo)

Copy of a stamp seal with the portrait and name of a Hittite prince (Tarkondemos) in Hittite cuneiform and hieroglyphs (Ashmolean Museum, Oxford; picture W. S. LaSor)

European character of "cuneiform Hittite" belongs to the Czech scholar B. Hrozný (1917). Less progress has been made with the decipherment of "hieroglyphic Hittite," even after the study of the eighth-century-B.C. bilingual inscriptions in Phoenician and "hieroglyphic Hittite" discovered at Karatepe in Cilicia in 1946 and 1947.

From these city-states the whole Syrian territory in which they were situated is called "the land of the Ḫatti" in Assyrian records of this period; even the inhabitants of Ashdod are described by Sargon II as "the faithless Ḫatti" (711 B.C.). The term persists in the usage of the Neo-Babylonian empire: Nebuchadrezzar in his chronicles (*ca.* 600 B.C.) regularly speaks of Palestine as "the land of the Ḫatti" — so long a shadow did the long-extinct empire of Šuppiluliuma cast, far beyond its southern frontier.

III. Hittites of Palestine.–This Assyrian and Babylonian usage has nothing to do with the earlier OT listing of the Hittites as one of the seven nations in Canaan overthrown by the Israelites under Joshua (Dt. 7:1; etc.). The identity of these Hittites presents an unsolved problem. They appear as inhabitants of the central hill country (Nu. 13:29). In Gen. 23:3-20 they are the native population of the Hebron district, "the people of the land," among whom Abraham lives as "a stranger and a sojourner," and from whom he buys the field containing the cave of Machpelah as a family burying place. His grandson Esau annoys his parents, Isaac and Rebekah, by marrying two Hittite wives with Semitic names, "daughters of the land" — apparently in the Beer-sheba district (Gen. 26:34f.; 27:46). It is scarcely satisfactory to treat "Hittites" in these contexts as simply the designation for the native population employed in that particular strand of the tradition, when we consider other references to Hittites in Canaan in conjunction with, but in distinction from, other ethnic groups. Jerusalem, according to Ezk. 16:3, 45, had a mixed Hittite and Amorite foundation. This statement has been held to be confirmed by the Hittite etymology of the name of Araunah the Jebusite (2 S. 24:16-24), if it is rightly related to Hitt. *arawanis,* "freeman," "noble." (H. Hoffner relates it to Hurrian *ewri-ne,* "the lord.") In any case, Uriah the Hittite, one of David's mighty men, was evidently a Jerusalemite (2 S. 11:3-24; 23:39). Uriah's name, however, is not Indo-European: conceivably it may be connected with Hurrian *ewri* ("lord"), but is much more probably Semitic, as are all the names of other Hittites specifically mentioned in the OT, from Ephron son of Zohar in Gen. 23:8 to Ahimelech, one of David's outlaw companions (1 S. 26:6).

E. Forrer tried to link the presence of Hittites in Palestine with the reference in an inscription of the Hittite king Mursilis II (*ca.* 1330 B.C.) to certain of his rebel subjects whom the Egyptians allowed to settle in part of their territory — which then included the southern region of Palestine. But this doubtful interpretation of a Hittite document could have no bearing on the Hittites mentioned in the patriarchal narratives. Much more attractive is Sir Leonard Woolley's suggestion that the Hittites of Canaan in patriarchal times were survivors of a wave of Khirbet Kerak people who left the southern Caucasus toward the end of the 4th millennium B.C. and settled in the ʿAmuq plain, E of the Gulf of Alexandretta — the original producers of Khirbet Kerak pottery being the ancestors both of the Anatolian Hittites and of the Palestinian Hittites. The one difficulty about this suggestion is its failure to explain how the Palestinian wave acquired the name "Hittites." The Anatolian Hittites took over this name from the indigenous Ḫatti whom they found already occupying their new habitat after their entry into Anatolia, long after the time when (on Woolley's hypothesis) they had parted company with the wave of Khirbet Kerak people who continued south and ultimately reached Hebron and Beer-sheba. Whence then could the latter have come independently to be called Hittites? It would be mere speculation to envisage a group of Hittites leaving the main body after the settlement in Anatolia and migrating to the south of Palestine. It has been argued that the terms of Abraham's transaction with Ephron, as set out in Gen. 23:16-20, agree remarkably with Hittite mercantile procedure: "permeated with intricate subtleties of Hittite laws and customs, correctly corresponding to the time of Abraham" (M. R. Lehmann). But it is questionable if the Hittite laws and customs referred to can be attested so early as the time of Abraham; besides, the Hebrew terms are not so technical as to demand a distinctively Hittite provenance; they accord with general Near Eastern usage of the period, and exhibit no features that would be inconsistent with the practice of Semitic peasants in that area in the patriarchal age.

A further suggestion is that the Palestinian Hittites (of the patriarchal period at least) are the people whom we otherwise know as HURRIANS. No problem is presented by the presence of Hurrians in Palestine at this time: it was their presence that made the Egyptians refer regularly to Palestine as "the land of the Hurrians" (*ḫ'rw*). But this identification would raise fresh problems regarding the relation between the Palestinian Hittites and the HORITES or HIVITES. It is possible, after all, that the Palestinian Hittites were accidentally homonymous with the Hittites of Anatolia and the city-states of north Syria, to whom they bore no historical relation.

Bibliography.–E. Akurgal, *Art of the Hittites* (1962); F. F. Bruce, *Hittites and the OT* (1947); R. A. Crossland, *CAH,* I, ch. 27; E. Forrer, *PEQ,* 68 (1936), 190-203; 69 (1937), 100-115; J. Garstang, O. R. Gurney, *Geography of the Hittite Empire* (1959); O. R. Gurney, *The Hittites* (2nd ed. 1961); *CAH,* II, ch. 6; H. Hoffner, *Laws of the Hittites* (1964); "The Hittites and Hurrians," in D. J. Wiseman, ed., *Peoples of OT Times* (1973), pp. 197-228; G. L. Huxley, *Achaeans and Hittites* (1960); K. A. Kitchen, *Ancient Orient and OT* (1966); M. R. Lehmann, *BASOR,* 129 (1953), 15-18; S. Lloyd, *Early Anatolia* (1956); *Early Highland Peoples of Anatolia* (1967); E. Neufeld, *The Hittite Laws* (1951); H. Petschow, *JCS,* 19 (1965), 103-120; G. M. Tucker, *JBL,* 85 (1966), 77-84; M. Vieyra, *Hittite Art* (1955); C. L. Woolley, *A Forgotten Kingdom* (1953).

F. F. BRUCE

HIVITES hi'vīts [Heb. *ḥiwwî*; Gk. *Heuaioi*]. A name that occurs twenty-five times as a designation of one of the nations the Israelites found in Palestine W of the Jordan; the Samaritan text and the LXX have it also in Gen. 15:21 and Nu. 13:29.

Apart from the traditional enumerations of gentile nations in Palestine we find Hivites mentioned in Gibeon (Josh. 9:7, where the LXX has Horite, and 11:19, where they are absent from the LXX), in Shechem (Gen. 34:2, LXX "Horite"), and in the north (Josh. 11:3, "under Hermon in the land of Mizpah"; Jgs. 3:3 "on Mount Lebanon, from Mount Baal Hermon as far as Lebo-Hamath"; cf. also 2 S. 24:7).

Inasmuch as Zibeon, who is called a Hivite in Gen. 36:2, is mentioned as a Horite in Gen. 36:20, and the name Horites never occurs together with the name Hivites in the traditional enumerations, scholars assume that the Hivites and the Horites were the same nation; cf. also the LXX variants quoted above. Perhaps both names go back to the same self-designation of the Horites or Hurrians, *ḥurwî*, which might develop both into *ḥōrî*, "Horite," and into *ḥuwwî*, which by means of a popular etymology (cf. *ḥawwâ*, "tent village") might become *ḥiwwî*, "Hivite."

The name disappeared soon; it does not occur later than David's time (2 S. 24:7), though some scholars (cf. the RSV and NEB) read it in Isa. 17:9, following the Greek text.

A. VAN SELMS

HIZKI hiz'kē [Heb. *ḥizkî*; Gk. *Azaki*]; AV, NEB HEZEKI. A son of Elpaal, a descendant of Benjamin (1 Ch. 8:17).

HIZKIAH hiz-kī'ə [Heb. *ḥizqîyâ*–'strength of Yahweh'; Gk. *Ezekia*].

1. A son of Neariah, of the royal family of Judah (1 Ch. 3:23; AV HEZEKIAH).

2. AV form of HEZEKIAH in Zeph. 1:1.

HOAR, HOARY. *See* COLOR V.D; HAIR.

HOARFROST hōr'frost [Heb. *k^epôr*] (Ex. 16:14; Job 38:29; Ps. 147:16; Sir. 43:19); NEB also FROST (Job 38:29; Sir. 43:19). A synonym for FROST. In Ex. 16:14 the MANNA on the ground is as "fine as hoarfrost." All the other passages mention hoarfrost as another example of God's creative and sovereign involvement in nature.

HOBAB hō'bab [Heb. *ḥōbāb*–'beloved'; LXX *Obab*]. This name occurs only twice (Nu. 10:29; Jgs. 4:11). It is not certain whether it denotes the father-in-law (RSV) or the brother-in-law (cf. Jgs. 4:11, NEB) of Moses. The direct statement of Nu. 10:29 is that Hobab was "the son of Reuel" (AV "Raguel"). This is probably the correct view and finds support in Ex. 18:27, which tells us that sometime before the departure of the Israelites from Sinai, Jethro had departed and returned to his own land. The statement of Jgs. 4:11 is ambiguous, and therefore does not help us out of the difficulty, but is rather itself to be interpreted in the light of the earlier statement in Nu. 10:29.

Moslem traditions favor the view that Hobab was only another name for Jethro. But this has little weight against the statements of Scripture. However, whether father-in-law or brother-in-law to Moses, the service he rendered to the leader of the hosts of Israel was most valuable and beautiful. Hobab was an experienced sheikh of the desert whose counsel and companionship Moses desired in the unfamiliar regions through which he was to journey. His knowledge of the wilderness and of its possible dangers would enable him to be to the Israelites "as eyes."

The facts recorded of this man are too meager to enable us to answer all the questions that arise concerning him. A difficulty that remains unsolved is that in Jgs. 1:16 (cf. LXX A, Lucian, Origen) and 4:11 he is described as a Kenite, while in Ex. 3:1 and 18:1, the father-in-law of Moses is spoken of as "the priest of Midian."

J. L. COTTON

HOBAH hō'bə [Heb. *ḥôḇâ*]. A place N (AV "on the left hand") of Damascus, to which Abraham pursued the defeated army of Chedorlaomer (Gen. 14:15). It may be identical with the modern Ḥoba, about 96 km. (60 mi.) NW of Damascus. Some scholars have associated the place with the territory of Ube mentioned in the Amarna Tablets (e.g., 53:63), whose capital prior to the 16th cent. B.C. may have been located in the region of Tell el-Salihiye, about 16 km. (10 mi.) E of Damascus. Excavations at the site indicate traces of occupation from the Neolithic Age onward, but whether it is the Hobah of the Abrahamic period is uncertain.

HOBAIAH. *See* HABAIAH.

HOD hod [Heb. *hôḏ*–'majesty, splendor'; LXX A *Hōd*, B *Ōa*] (1 Ch. 7:37). One of the sons of Zophah, a descendant of Asher.

HODAIAH hō-dā'yə. *See* HODAVIAH **4.**

HODAVIAH hōd-ə-vī'ə [Heb. *hôḏawyâ, hôḏawyāhû*; LXX A, Gk. *Hōdouia*].

1. One of the heads of the half-tribe of Manasseh on the east side of the Jordan (1 Ch. 5:24).

2. A Benjaminite, the son of Hassenuah (1 Ch. 9:7).

3. A Levite, who seems to have been the head of an important family in that tribe (Ezr. 2:40). In Neh. 7:43 the name is Hodevah (Heb. *K hôḏ^ewâ, Q hôḏ^eyâ*–'splendor of Yahweh'; NEB Hodvah; cf. Ezr. 3:9).

4. A son of Elioenai, and a descendant of David (1 Ch. 3:24; Heb. *K hôḏaywāhû, Q hôḏawyāhû*; AV, NEB, Hodaiah).

HODESH hō'desh [Heb. *ḥōḏeš*–'new moon']. One of the wives of Shaharaim, a Benjaminite (1 Ch. 8:9).

HODEVAH hō-dē'və, hō'də-və. *See* HODAVIAH **3.**

HODIAH hō-dī'ə [Heb. *hôḏîyâ*–'splendor of Yahweh']; AV HODIJAH in all occurrences except 1 Ch. 4:19.

1. A brother-in-law of Naham (1 Ch. 4:19), and possibly for that reason reckoned a member of the tribe of Judah. The AV and NEB translation "his wife" is probably wrong (but cf. KD *in loc.*).

2. One of the Levites who explained to the people the law as read by Ezra (Neh. 8:7; 1 Esd. 9:48 [AV Auteas]) and led their prayers (Neh. 9:5). He is doubtless one of the two Levites of this name who sealed the covenant of Nehemiah (Neh. 10:10, 13 [MT 11, 14]).

3. One of the chiefs of the people who sealed the covenant of Nehemiah (Neh. 10:18 [MT 19]).

J. G. MCALLISTER

HOE [Heb. *ma'dēr*] (Isa. 7:25); AV MATTOCK; [*'āḏar*] (Isa. 5:6; 7:25); AV DIG; NEB also WORK. An implement used to loosen the earth and to weed. *See* MATTOCK.

HOGLAH hog'lä [Heb. *ḥoglâ*–'partridge']. The third of five daughters of Zelophehad of the tribe of Manasseh (Nu. 26:33). Zelophehad had no male heirs, and it was made a statute that the inheritance in such cases should pass to the daughters as joint heirs, on condition, however, of marriage within the tribe (Nu. 27:1-11; 36:1-12; Josh. 17:3f.). The name also occurs in the Samaria ostraca (no. 47).

HOHAM hō'ham [Heb. *hôhām*] (Josh. 10:3). An Amorite king of Hebron and one of the five kings of the Amorites who joined together for war on Gibeon because of its peace treaty with Joshua. The five were defeated in the decisive battle of Beth-horon and shut up in a cave at Makkedah in which they had taken refuge; after the battle, they were slain, hanged, and cast into the cave (Josh. 10:1-27).

HOISE. An archaic form of "hoist," used by the AV in Acts 27:40 to translate Gk. *epaírō,* "lift up."

HOLD [Heb. *'āḥaz, ḥāzaq, tāmaḵ* (Prov. 31:19), *tāpaś* (Jer. 49:16); Gk. *échō* (and compounds of it), *kratéō, epilambánomai, háptō*]; AV also CATCH, RETAIN, KEEP, etc.; NEB also GRASP, SEIZE, CLUTCH, CLING, ADHERE, etc.

Hebrew *'āḥaz* can refer to physical acts of holding or seizing, e.g., Jacob seizes Esau's heel (Gen. 25:26). It can, in addition, have a more figurative sense; Job says that affliction has "taken hold" of him (Job 30:16). The word is also used anthropomorphically to describe God's protection of His people (Ps. 73:23; 139:10). Similarly, Heb. *ḥāzaq* can be used to speak of a literal act of holding (Gen. 21:18), but it also is used with the preposition *be* to describe a person's "adherence" or "obedience" to various things — other gods (1 K. 9:9), God's covenant (Isa. 56:4), instruction (Prov. 4:13).

The NT uses Gk. *kratéō* in a literal sense (Mt. 12:11) but also in a more figurative sense. The Jews "hold" to traditions of their fathers (Mk. 7:8), and the Christian community must "hold" to certain teachings (2 Thess. 2:15; He. 4:14; Rev. 2:13, 25). The Epistle to the Hebrews exhorts its readers to "hold fast" (*katéchō*) to their confession (3:6, 14; 10:23). In 1 Tim. 6:12, 19 Christians are urged to "take hold of" the life that has been offered to them (*epilambánomai*).

In addition, the word "hold" can convey the sense of "hold back" or "prevent from going away" (Lk. 4:42, AV), "hold counsel" (Mk. 3:6), "hold down," or "suppress" (Rom. 1:18, AV), "hold in honor" (Acts 5:34), "hold one's peace," or "be silent" (2 S. 13:20), "hold out" (Est. 4:11), "hold up" (2 S. 2:22, AV), "consider," or "reckon" (Rom. 3:28), "contain" (2 Ch. 4:5), "place" (Ps. 66:9, AV), "prefer" (Mt. 6:24, AV).

One interesting usage is found in Jn. 20:17 where Jesus forbids Mary to "hold" Him since He has not yet ascended to His Father (AV "touch"; NEB "cling"). The imperative is in the present tense and thus lends support to the suggestion that the verse means "Do not cling to me." Jesus' work on earth has been completed, and He must now ascend to the Father.

Bibliography.–Bauer, rev., pp. 295, 422f., 448f.; BDB, pp. 28, 304f., 1069, 1074; *TDNT,* II, *s.v.* ἔχω κτλ. (Hanse); III, *s.v.* κρατέω (Michaelis).

P. L. BREMER

HOLD (ONE'S) PEACE AT. An archaic expression meaning "say nothing to," used by the AV to translate Heb. *ḥāraš* in Nu. 30:4, 7, 14; Est. 4:14; etc., and Gk. *sigáō* (e.g., Lk. 20:26), *siōpáō* (e.g., Mt. 20:31), and *phimóō* (Mk. 1:25; Lk. 16:13).

HOLDERS [Heb. *bāttîm,* pl. of *bayiṯ*] (Ex. 25:27; 26:29; 30:4; 36:4; 37:14, 27; 38:6); AV PLACES; NEB RINGS. The term refers to attachments upon some items of furniture in the tabernacle through which the poles used in transporting the articles would pass. Similar arrangements on the boards or frames of the structure provided a means of stabilizing the walls.

HOLIDAY [Heb. *yôm ṭôḇ*] (Est. 8:17; 9:19, 22; cf. 1 S. 25:8); AV GOOD DAY. The Feast of Purim, celebrating Israel's deliverance from its Persian enemies, was the only really secular Jewish festival and was given over to merriment. In postbiblical times a "good day" was any holy or feast day.

HOLINESS; HOLY. A fundamental element in the distinctive nature of God as revealed in Scripture and a basic response to His grace on the part of the people of God as they become molded into His likeness.

- I. Terminology
- II. In the OT
  - A. Holiness of God
  - B. Holiness of Israel
  - C. Holiness of the Cultus
- III. In the NT
  - A. Holiness of the Godhead
    - 1. Father
    - 2. Son
    - 3. Spirit
  - B. Holiness of God's People
    - 1. Their Calling
    - 2. Their Conduct
    - 3. Problems

I. Terminology.–Heb. *qōḏeš* (Ex. 15:11), used as adj. (Ex. 3:5); the adj. *qāḏôš* (Lev. 20:7); Gk. *hágios* (2 Pet. 1:18), NEB also "sacred"; *hagiázō,* "make holy," "consecrate" (1 Cor. 7:14); NEB also "belongs to God"; *hagiasmós,* "sanctification," "holiness" (Rom. 6:19); NEB also "a holy life"; *hagiótēs* (Heb. 12:10); *hagiōsýnē* (2 Cor. 7:1); NEB also "consecration"; adj. *hierós* (2 Tim. 3:15, AV); *hósios* (Acts 2:27); NEB also "loyal servant."

II. In the OT.–*A. Holiness of God.* It is no exaggeration to state that this element overshadows all others in the character of the deity so far as the OT revelation is concerned (Ps. 99:3, 5, 9). The lesser emphasis in the NT is readily accounted for on the assumption that the massive presentation under the old covenant is accepted as an underlying presupposition.

Judging from the usage of the root *qḏš,* the basic idea conveyed by the holiness of God is His separateness, i.e., His uniqueness, His distinction as the Wholly Other, the One who cannot be confused with the gods devised by men (Ex. 15:11), the One who stands apart from and above the creation. Secondarily the holiness of God denotes His moral perfection, His absolute freedom from blemish of any kind (Ps. 89:35 [MT 36]). This aspect is strikingly set forth in the account of Isaiah's call to the prophetic office, in that the reiterated angelic pronouncement of the divine holiness brought to him the overpowering awareness of his own sinfulness (Isa. 6:5). Even though the seraphim are not characterized by sin, their demeanor proclaims that a gulf is fixed between them as creatures and God the Creator and Lord of all. The verbal communication by the seraphim was coupled with the vision of God's glory, the luminous token of His presence. Glory and holiness are closely related concepts. The threefold proclamation of the holy nature of God (the trisagion) is significant for its uniqueness. No other attribute is so treated. Farnell notes that "wherever theistic belief has prevailed, holiness has belonged to the essence of the idea" (p. 186).

God's holiness is reflected in His demand for an exclusive worship rather than one that is shared with various deities of man's creation. This demand is clearly reflected in the first two commandments of the Decalogue. This demand is not a characteristic of the deities of other religions in ancient times.

The possible danger that the holiness of God should be taken as an indication of remoteness and aloofness is overcome by the close alliance between His holiness and His righteousness (Isa. 5:16). He asserts the right to monitor the conduct of His own people. Through the prophet God points out the incompatibility between Israel's conduct and His character. For example, "A man and his father go in to the same maiden, so that my holy name is profaned" (Am. 2:7). Because His holiness is flaunted, His wrath comes into action. When His people are holy in name but not in fact, He cannot in righteousness refrain from expressing His displeasure in terms of judgment (Hos. 13:4-14; Am. 4:2; Ezk. 2:17-22). Likewise, the arrogant cruelty of other nations offends His righteousness and calls for punishment (Ezk. 38:17-23). At times a prophet could become disconcerted that a holy God would permit an alien nation to overwhelm His own people, who by comparison were more righteous (Hab. 1:12f.). The very fact that both in the OT and in the NT the people of God, His chosen and beloved ones, are not exempt from chastening is a sure token that His holy and righteous character is never compromised.

B. Holiness of Israel. Clearly holiness is not something native to this people, but a quality derived only from God. As with God, so with His people, holiness has a twofold aspect. The first consists in a privileged position. This nation is chosen, in distinction from all the peoples of earth, to be the special possession of the Almighty (Dt. 7:6). The choice was not dictated by Israel's prominence, seeing that it was the fewest in number of all peoples, but was due to His love (Dt. 7:7f.). Thus, the nation's holiness is to be traced primarily to its position in God's purpose. But that very position makes it natural and inevitable that Israel will be summoned to honor His will by being obedient to His commandments and faithful to His covenant (Ex. 19:5f.). This is acquired holiness (Lev. 11:44f.; Dt. 28:9).

A serious threat to Israel's commitment to keep the law of God presented itself when the tribes took possession of Canaan and found themselves surrounded by neighboring peoples who worshiped other gods. Despite advance warnings by Moses about the peril of intermarriage with these peoples, a course of action that held the threat of apostasy to an alien worship (Dt. 7:2-4), Israel succumbed to this danger. The most notable example is the imposition of Baal worship on the northern kingdom by Ahab's marriage to Jezebel. Both the northern and the southern kingdoms suffered captivity because of their unfaithfulness to the Lord God of their fathers. Even then the lesson was not fully learned, for in the days following the return from Exile many took alien wives: "The holy race has mixed itself with the peoples of the lands" (Ezr. 9:2). This comment was motivated not by racism but by concern for the purity of the community's worship and life under God.

The concept of holiness permeated the life of Israel. Even the land occupied by the people was considered holy (Zec. 2:12), since it was the land of the Holy One of Israel and belonged to the nation as His gift. The capital city Jerusalem is designated as the city of God, the holy habitation of the Most High (Ps. 46:4 [MT 5]). What the holy of holies meant in relation to the rest of the sanctuary, Jerusalem the holy city meant in relation to the rest of the land. When the nation became involved in military action against neighboring peoples, the conflict was regarded as a holy war and those who participated as warriors understood that such a conflict laid on them the responsibility to refrain from intercourse with women (2 Sam. 11:11; cf. 1 Sam. 21:4f.). For the nation as a whole one day in the week, the sabbath, was to be kept holy to the Lord as a special day of rest on which a holy convocation was held (Lev. 23:3). The appointed festivals of the Lord, held at specified times during the year, were proclaimed as holy convocations (Lev. 23). One who took upon himself the vow of the Nazirite, whether for life or for a limited period, was regarded as holy, as separated to the Lord. He was to abstain from wine and strong drink, to let his hair grow long, and to avoid going near a dead body, even that of a loved one. These aspects of separation constituted his special holiness (Nu. 6). The claims of holiness reached deeply into the daily life of the people. An example is the law of the tithe: Of the products of the soil and of the flock and of the herd the people were required to set aside a tenth for the Lord (Lev. 27:30, 32). Those who lived at a distance from Jerusalem were permitted to convert these items into money which was to be regarded as holy, and as such was to be conveyed to the Lord's treasury (Lev. 27:30-33).

C. Holiness of the Cultus. Since any place where God is pleased to reveal Himself can rightfully be proclaimed holy (Ex. 3:5), it is natural that everything connected with His worship should be so designated. The tabernacle erected in the wilderness according to divine specifications was placed in the center of the camp as a constant reminder of the presence of a holy God in the midst of His people.

The division of this structure into two portions, the holy place and the most holy, was calculated to emphasize the awesomeness of the privilege of drawing near to the living God. In the former area the priests, duly consecrated for their ministrations, carried on their labors, but only the high priest was permitted access to the most holy place where God's presence was uniquely experienced once a year on the Day of Atonement.

In a special way the ark of the covenant symbolized and epitomized the divine presence. Its later history in the land of promise is revealing. The loss of it to the Philistines in battle was interpreted to mean that the glory of Israel had departed (1 S. 4:22). Its sojourn among an alien people brought to them affliction and terror, disclosing the fact that the Holy One of Israel would not permit Himself to be treated as a prize of war. Even on the soil of Israel the attempt to carry the ark by unconsecrated hands brought retribution (2 S. 6:6f.). Levites should have been assigned to bear it.

Not only were the Levites holy in order to be able to assist the priests (2 Ch. 35:3), but the priests themselves, who presented the offerings of the people to the Lord, were holy (Lev. 21:6), and above all the high priest as the head of a holy order. His garments (Ex. 28:2) and his crown were labeled holy (Ex. 39:30). He was consecrated to his office with holy anointing oil that was also used for his sons, for the tent of meeting, and for the utensils needed in worship (Ex. 30:22-33).

All these features were retained when the temple supplanted the tabernacle. It was likewise pronounced holy (Ps. 65:4 [MT 5]), being the place where holy offerings were presented and where God met with His people. Though the earthly sanctuary, constructed and used for His worship, was considered holy, heaven was recognized as the true sanctuary, God's proper and holy abode (1 K. 8:30; 2 Ch. 30:27). This recognition made more meaningful the divine condescension, "I dwell in the high and holy place and also with him who is of a contrite and humble spirit" (Isa. 57:15).

No doubt the element of beauty prominent in the vestments of the priests and the utensils used in the priestly service was intended to portray the beauty of holiness in the moral and spiritual sphere. The danger resident in cultic observance was that the worshiper would be content with going through the motions, making the prescribed sacrifices but failing to realize adequately the presence and holiness of God in a personal way. We read of priests and Levites being sent among the people of Judah to teach them (2 Ch. 18:7-9). While their instruction undoubtedly gave prominence to the ethical aspects of the law, it is probable that attention was paid also to the significance of the temple ritual, so that when worshipers presented their gifts and sacrifices they would realize the importance of dedicating themselves afresh to the Lord.

Holiness in the ceremonial sense is contrasted with various conditions. One is uncleanness due to eating food designated as unclean, coming into contact with a dead body, etc. (Dt. 23:14). Another area is the common (Lev. 10:10; Ezk. 44:23), that which is not consecrated or that which is ordinary, such as common bread in distinction from the sacred loaves in the holy place (1 S. 21:4). A third classification, this one having more than ceremonial aspects, involves what is so abhorrent to the divine holiness that a curse is placed upon it and it becomes marked for destruction. The term *ḥērem* is used to indicate it. An example is the city of Jericho and its inhabitants, utterly destroyed by God's command (Josh. 6:17-19).

III. In the NT.–Understandably the NT carries over much OT data, though the frame of reference may be altered. For example, we read of God as holy (1 Pet. 1:15), of holy angels (Lk. 9:26), holy prophets (Acts 3:21), the firstborn as being holy (Lk. 2:23), a holy priesthood (1 Pet. 2:5), a holy nation (1 Pet. 2:9), the Holy City (Mt. 4:5), the Holy Scriptures (Rom. 1:2), etc. The most striking difference is the virtual eclipse of the purely ceremonial aspect of holiness and a flooding of the sacred page with allusions to holiness as conformity to the nature of God.

A. Holiness of the Godhead. 1. Father. In His great prayer the Son of God addressed His Father as holy (Jn. 17:11) and in giving instruction to the disciples on prayer directed them to recognize the heavenly Father as worthy of being acclaimed and honored as unique, without a rival — "Hallowed be thy name" (Mt. 6:9). The seer of Patmos reports the angels' praise of God through the trisagion (Rev. 4:8), as well as the appeal of martyrs for their vindication by Him (Rev. 6:10) and the adoration of the saints who had defied the beast (Rev. 15:4).

2. Son. The angelic prediction that Mary would have a son included the observation that He would be called holy (Lk. 1:35). This was accented during His ministry by the admission of demons (Mk. 1:24), after His resurrection by the Church at prayer (Acts 4:27, 30), by the apostolic unfolding of the fulfillment of prophecy in His person (Acts 2:27; 13:35), and by epistolary writers (e.g., He. 7:26).

3. Spirit. Though by no means lacking mention in the OT, He is seldom designated there as the Holy Spirit ("the Spirit of the Lord" is the most common title). In the Synoptic Gospels He is represented as resting on Jesus for the accomplishing of His mighty works (Lk. 4:14, 18). When certain scribes attributed the exorcisms of Jesus (obviously a beneficent ministry) to the power of Satan (a malevolent source), Jesus pronounced this an unforgiveable sin, namely, blasphemy against the *Holy* Spirit (Mk. 3:22-30).

In the book of Acts the Holy Spirit assumes leadership of the Church by illuminating, empowering, and directing the servants of Christ (1:8; 2:4; 5:32; 13:2; 16:6f.), and by keeping the Church pure (5:1-11).

A shift is discernible in the letters to churches by Paul and others, for here the emphasis falls on the Spirit's work in the gathering of the saints and in individual lives. He is there to promote holiness (1 Thess. 4:7f.; 1 Cor. 6:19).

B. Holiness of God's People. 1. Their Calling. In view of the general parallelism between Israel and the Church, it is not unexpected that the NT children of God should be considered holy by virtue of their position. This is fundamental to any consideration of their condition. It may strike one who examines 1 Corinthians as contradictory that Paul should address his readers as saints or holy ones (1 Cor. 1:2; cf. 3:17), whereas much of what he says about them in the body of the letter seems to contradict this characterization. The apparent contradiction is ameliorated by translations that suggest a future frame of reference for holiness by inserting *to be* between "called" and "saints," as though the holiness is only a future, hoped-for reality. Such translations miss the point, for Paul is asserting that these people are holy by virtue of their call. It is a matter of position in relation to God rather than a condition. In keeping with this, the preceding statement about these believers, that they are sanctified in Christ, can only bring confusion if it is taken as a description of their state, since this is not confirmed by the contents of the letter. Clearly, they are being described here as set apart to God in Christ.

Once more, in the same letter, the apostle uses the term "sanctified" in a way that removes it from any possible human activity. He states that the Corinthian believers were washed, sanctified, and justified (1 Cor. 6:11). This was done, he states, in the name of the Lord Jesus and by the Spirit of God. Clearly this does not mean that the Corinthians were made holy in character. The term "sanctified," placed as it is before "justified," can only mean a positional holiness, something that was granted concurrently with justification but given prior mention because of the context.

It is helpful in this connection to consider Paul's description of himself (1 Cor. 1:1). He is not saying that people call him an apostle, but rather that he *is* an apostle by virtue of being summoned by God to this responsibility. The position of his readers as saints is parallel to his position as apostle, i.e., both relationships depend on the divine call. Issues concerning character or conduct *at this point* are irrelevant. That is not to assert or imply that they are unimportant in the overall consideration of holiness. But it is the habit of NT writers to base their appeal for holiness of life upon their readers' call, their choice by a holy God. Peter's approach is typical: "As he who called you is holy, be holy yourselves in all your conduct" (1 Pet. 1:15). That call is intimately connected with God's choice, His electing (1:2).

2. Their Conduct. Clearly the divine choice has in view also an actual life change, the molding of character, what may be described as progressive sanctification. So it behooves us to examine the second aspect of holiness, namely, an actual improvement in one's manner of life. Though the believer must involve himself in this process, his involvement is not something meritorious, as though it could become a contributing factor to his acceptance by a holy God. Salvation is already his as a gift of God's grace. But by virtue of being born into the family of God he should desire to reproduce the family likeness. This is the will of God. The starting-point for the development of a holy character is the realization that the mercies received from God call for an adequate response. Paul identifies this as the presentation of one's body as a living sacrifice, holy and acceptable to God (Rom. 12:1). He does not mean the body as a physical entity distinct from the inner life, but rather as the normal vehicle for implementing the desires and purposes of the one who has become a new creation in Christ. This dedication of the person will have to face the temptation to be conformed to this age, a temptation that can be met by the renewal of the mind (the thoughtful recollection and appreciation of the divine mercies) so as to experience an ever increasing transformation (v. 2) that is doubtless to be thought of as a growing conformity to the likeness of Christ (2 Cor. 3:18). In the latter passage it is made clear that the Holy Spirit is the agent of this transformation, but not the pattern, for that is Christ Himself, the holy Son of God. The apostle stresses this in writing to the Galatians, who were floundering in their misapprehension of the sufficiency of the Savior: "My little children, with whom I am again in travail until Christ be formed in you!" (Gal. 4:19). What was needed was the appropriation of the Lord in all the fulness of His power.

The Greeks were notorious for their laxity in sexual relations. Consequently Paul had to cope with the issue, especially among the Thessalonians and Corinthians. He makes several observations, based on the premise that it is God's will that they be holy (1 Thess. 4:3). God's call had in view for them a holy life (v. 7). Sexual deviation is an affront to the Holy Spirit who has been given to them (v. 8). The body is not meant for immorality but for the Lord (1 Cor. 6:13). The believer's body is a temple of the Holy Spirit (v. 19). Believers should not associate with a so-called brother who is guilty of immorality (5:11). Persistence in an unholy course should bring expulsion (5:13). The Church must be protected, for it is holy, the temple of God, as is the believer's body (3:17).

Not infrequently Christians are reminded to greet one another with a holy kiss (e.g., Rom. 16:16), holy because free from any erotic association. It was a token of mutual love in the Lord. This practice served as a reminder of the fact that the love of God shed abroad in human hearts is a holy love.

Growth in holiness is not possible apart from the means of grace. Scripture is an inspired record, given by God for the profit of His people, a holy, powerful instrument calculated to promote a life of godliness. Prayer should be linked with the Word as its natural and expected response, for whereas by Scripture God speaks to us, in prayer we respond to Him. The Holy Spirit who is indispensable for the interpretation of the Word (1 Cor. 2:12f.) is equally necessary for a satisfactory experience in prayer (Rom. 8:26f.). These two factors, the Word and prayer, both of them under the tutelage of the Spirit and working together, should produce the needed response of obedience to God that in turn results in holiness. Contrary to a rather widespread opinion, extreme asceticism does not promote holiness, for while it may remove outward temptation it does not deliver from inward desire.

3. Problems. One problem is antinomianism, a point of view overly intrigued by the truth that Christ is the end of the law for righteousness to everyone who believes (Rom. 10:4). What results is more interest in freedom to live as one chooses than to cultivate a holy life. Paul rebukes such a tendency with the observation that the believer, as God sees it, has died with Christ to sin. He has no further obligation to serve it. It is incongruous, therefore, to think that one should continue to live in sin (Rom. 6:1-11). Antinomianism can easily be refuted, and few would openly endorse it; nevertheless it remains a snare to believers who are content to come to terms with sin in their own lives and remain unwilling to seek a way of deliverance.

The opposite tendency is perfectionism, the position that it is possible for a believer to make such diligent use of the means of grace and to be so fully committed to the will of God that sin is effectually banished. It should be granted that the desire to attain such a state is praiseworthy. Consequently perfectionism can be set aside only for the best of reasons. Foremost is the serious doubt that Scripture endorses such a view. When we find that Paul, who is appealed to for support of the perfectionist position because of his teaching (e.g., 2 Cor. 7:1), actually denies perfection in his own case (Phil. 3:12) and assigns the realization of it to the age to come (1 Cor. 13:10), we begin to sense that the whole subject needs careful scrutiny and clarification. The word "perfect" must of course be given its full weight when used of God (Mt. 5:48). He is our ultimate standard of holiness and we should not desire a lesser one. But the word itself in its general manward use means fully grown or mature, and that is its meaning in the teaching on sanctification (Phil. 3:15; Col. 4:12). In Eph. 4:13 Paul presents as the goal of Christian ministry "a perfect man." He is not thinking in individual terms, but collectively ("we all"), so he does not have in mind the hope that a few individuals may arrive at sinless perfection. Rather, his desire is that his readers, all of them, may be no longer babes. So the perfection in view is spiritual maturity.

Furthermore, the picture of the Christian life presented in Scripture is one of incessant antagonism and conflict between the flesh and the Spirit (Gal. 5:17). There is no reason to think that this situation relates only to some believers or that it will be altered during one's earthly pilgrimage. The victory of which Paul writes in Romans is not the complete banishment of sin but the breaking of its dominion in the life of the Christian (6:12-14). One need be no longer a slave to its mastery. He can have deliverance by counting on the fact that he has died with Christ to sin and by presenting himself and his renewed powers of body and spirit to God for His holy use.

Finally, Scripture leads us to expect perfection for the whole person in the future, when Christ comes again (1 Thess. 5:23). After we have come to Christ for salvation, our minds are still limited. Only when we see Him face to face will we know as we have been known (1 Cor. 13:12). Our bodies are still subject to incursions of illness and to decrepitude, heralding the prospect of death. Why, in view of the unity of the whole person, should it be thought possible for the redeemed human spirit alone to anticipate the perfection that is reserved for the future? Maturity should be our goal for the present life. Perfection belongs to the day of Christ, when we will be fully transformed into His likeness. Meanwhile, only One has been able to ask without fear, "Which of you convicts me of sin?" (Jn. 8:46). Even though one may feel that he has not sinned for a considerable period, it is hazardous to make feelings the criterion. Furthermore, holiness is not simply the absence of sin but being filled with the Spirit and reflecting the love of Christ. Can anyone say in good faith that he has done this consistently?

In summary, holiness has a threefold aspect. All believers are positionally holy by virtue of their calling as saints. They are then summoned to such conduct as befits their new position in Christ. They are to seek by God's help to grow and mature with the life of Christ as their pattern for appropriation. Without this holiness, which confirms the salvation experience, no one will see the Lord (He. 12:14). The final phase of holiness will be reached when Christ completes the process of salvation by His return, when all His own will be like Him, seeing Him as He is, the perfect and glorious Son of God (1 Jn. 3:2).

See also ASCETICISM; SANCTIFICATION; GLORY.

Bibliography.–S. Charnock, *Existence and Attributes of God* (1958), pp. 440-532; J. H. Elliott, *The Elect and the Holy, Supplements to Nov.Test.*, 12 (1966); L. R. Farnell, *Attributes of God*

(1925); A. Köberle, *Quest for Holiness* (1936); S. Neill, *Christian Holiness* (1960); R. Otto, *The Idea of the Holy* (Eng. tr., rev. ed. 1929); *ILC,* III-IV (1959); G. von Rad, *OT Theology,* I (Eng. tr. 1962), 203-212, 272-79; J. C. Ryle, *Holiness* (1952); N. H. Snaith, *Distinctive Ideas of the OT* (1944), pp. 21-50; *TDNT,* I, *s.v.* ἅγιος κτλ. (Kuhn, Procksch); T. C. Vriezen, *Outline of OT Theology* (1970), pp. 297-311; B. B. Warfield, *Perfectionism* (1958).

E. F. HARRISON

HOLLOW. The RSV uses "hollow" to translate four Hebrew words:

(1) Heb. *kap* regularly means the palm of the hand but is also applied to other concave objects, including the hollow of the thigh (Gen. 32:25, 32; usually assumed to mean the socket of the thigh-joint) and the hollow of a sling (1 S. 25:29; AV "middle"; AV mg. "bought"; NEB omits).

(2) The "hollow" of the hand in Isa. 40:12 (NEB "palm") is Heb. *šōʿal.*

(3) Heb. *maḵtēš* is literally "mortar" (Prov. 27:22, and postbiblical Hebrew); it is applied to a hollow rock formation in Jgs. 15:19.

(4) The two great bronze pillars which flanked the entrance to Solomon's temple are called "hollow structures" (Heb. *nāḇûḇ*) in Jer. 52:21; a parallel passage occurs in the LXX of 1 K. 7:15, but is omitted by the MT (RSV and NEB follow the LXX, while the AV omits with the MT).

Ex. 27:8; 38:7 describe the wilderness altar as "a hollow structure of planks" (*neḇûḇ luḥōṯ*) overlaid with bronze. Its apparent unsuitability as an altar on which fires are to burn continually leads many scholars to regard it as an artificial retrojection of Solomon's altar, made portable by the priestly author to suit the needs of the wandering Israelites.

See M. Noth, *Exodus* (Eng. tr., *OTL,* 1962), pp. 215f.

D. J. HALPERIN

HOLM TREE [Heb. *tirzâ*; Vulg. *ilex*] (Isa. 44:14); AV CYPRESS; NEB ILEX. Omitted by the LXX, this term has been much disputed. The Douay, RV, and RSV have "holm tree"; but the true holm or holly (*Ilex aquifolium* L.) does not grow in the locality specified in Isaiah. It is perhaps the massive oriental plane tree, *Platanus orientalis* L., widely distributed throughout Lebanon and Palestine, or the slender *Cupressus sempervirens* L.

See also OAK (Sus. 58). R. K. H.

HOLOFERNES hol-ə-fûr′nēz [Gk. *Olophernēs*]; NEB HOLOPHERNES. According to the book of Judith, chief captain of Nebuchadrezzar, king of the Assyrians (Jth. 2:4), who was commissioned to make war upon the west country and to receive from the inhabitants the usual tokens of complete submission, earth and water. The object of the expedition of Holofernes, who thus became the typical persecutor of the Jews, was to compel people everywhere to worship Nebuchadrezzar. He was slain by Judith, the heroine of the book of that name, during the siege of Bethulia. There is no notice of Holofernes except in the book of Judith. The termination of the word would seem to indicate a Persian origin for the name.

HOLON hō′lən [Heb. *ḥōlōn, ḥōlôn*].

1. One of the towns in the hill country of Judah (Josh. 15:51) assigned to the Levites (21:15). In 1 Ch. 6:58 (MT 43) it is called HILEN. It is usually identified with Khirbet ʿAlîn, about 16 km. (10 mi.) NW of Hebron, although this location would place it in the region of Beth-zur (Josh. 15:58) rather than Debir.

2. Probably once an important town in the "tableland" of Moab (Jer. 48:21); the site is unknown.

HOLY. *See* HOLINESS.

HOLYDAY. This word occurs twice in the AV (Ps. 42:4 [MT 5]; Col. 2:16). In the latter case it renders Gk. *heortḗ,* the ordinary term for a religious festival (RSV, NEB "festival"). In the former instance "keeping holyday" renders Heb. *ḥôgēg.* The verb *ḥāgag* means "make a pilgrimage" or "keep a religious festival." The psalmist (who was perhaps an exiled priest) remembers with poignant regret how he used to lead religious processions on festival occasions. T. LEWIS

HOLY GHOST. *See* HOLY SPIRIT.

HOLY GHOST (SPIRIT), SIN AGAINST THE. *See* BLASPHEME; HOLY SPIRIT II.B.

HOLY OF HOLIES [Gk. *hágia hagíōn*] (He. 9:3). *See* MOST HOLY PLACE.

HOLY ONE. *See* GOD, NAMES OF II.E.2.

HOLY PLACE [Heb. *haqqōḏeš*] (Ex. 26:33; Lev. 16:2; 1 K. 8:8; 2 Ch. 5:11; Ezk. 41:21; etc.); AV also SANCTUARY; NEB also SANCTUARY, INNER COURT; [*māqôm qāḏôš*] (Ex. 29:31; Lev. 6:16 [MT 9]; etc.); NEB also SACRED PLACE; [*meqôm qāḏôš*] (Eccl. 8:10); AV "place of the holy"; [*meqôm qoḏšô*] (Ezr. 9:8); [*meqôm haqqōḏeš*] (Lev. 14:13); NEB SACRED PRECINCTS; [*hammiqdāš*] (Ezk. 45:4); AV, NEB, SANCTUARY; [*hāʾārôn*] (2 Ch. 5:9); AV ARK; [*môʿēḏ*] (Ps. 74:4); AV CONGREGATIONS; [Gk. *tópos hagíos,* and variants thereof] (Mt. 24:15; Acts 6:13; 21:28); NEB also SANCTUARY; [*hágia, tá hágia*] (He. 9:2, 12, 25); AV, NEB, also SANCTUARY. The outer compartment of biblical sanctuaries; also the outer court of the tabernacle (Lev. 6:16 [MT 9], 26 [MT 19]; 10:13), the "most holy place" of the temple (Ezk. 41:21, 23; He. 9:12, 25), the temple itself (Ezr. 9:8; Ps. 24:3; 74:4; Acts 21:28), the inside of the temple in general (2 Ch. 29:5), the temple grounds (Ezk. 45:4).

Each of the biblical sanctuaries had two main compartments, as originally exemplified in the tabernacle. Here the inner and outer rooms were separated by a tapestried curtain supported on four pillars (Ex. 26:33). The dimensions of the holy place in the tabernacle are usually calculated at twenty cubits length and ten cubits breadth and height (approx. 9 by 4.5 by 4.5 m. [30 by 15 by 15 ft.]). It was in this chamber that the priests performed many of their routine duties, tending the golden lampstand, the table of showbread, and the golden altar of incense. He. 9:1-5 implies that these all had symbolic value.

In Solomon's temple the measurements of the length and breadth of the holy place were probably double those of its tabernacle prototype. 1 K. 6:2 is normally understood to mean that the height was thirty cubits (approx. 14 m. [45 ft.]). There were now ten golden lampstands, five on either side (1 K. 7:49), and, according to 2 Ch. 4:8, there were also ten tables of showbread. This outer chamber had light from clerestory windows which appear to have had splayed jambs (cf. 1 K. 6:4). It was separated from the most holy place by a wall in which were set doors made of olivewood; these were carved and overlaid with gold (1 K. 6:31f.).

The length and breadth of the holy place in the Herodian temple were the same as in Solomon's building, but larger figures for the height are given by Josephus (*BJ* v.5.5) and in Mish. *Middoth* iv.6. The same passage in Josephus indicates that the Herodian temple had the standard items of furniture associated with the holy place (cf. 1 Macc. 1:21f. for the second temple in the time of Antiochus IV). Only the golden lampstand and the table of showbread are shown on the Arch of Titus, which commemorates the capture of Jerusalem in A.D. 70.

R. P. GORDON

HOLY SEPULCHRE. A term referring to the place in Jerusalem where Jesus was entombed. Nowhere in the NT is it referred to as "holy." It is simply called a *mnēmeíon,* the Greek term for "sepulchre" or "tomb." Certain information is given about this tomb. It was the private burial plot of Joseph of Arimathea (Mt. 27:57-60). No one had previously been buried in this tomb (Lk. 23:53). It was located in a garden near where He was crucified (Jn. 19:41). It was near but outside the city (v. 20).

It was not until the 4th cent. that a site was singled out for veneration as the tomb of Christ and declared "holy." Eusebius (*Vita Constantini* iii.25-40) states that Constantine the Great directed Bishop Macarius to locate the place of the crucifixion and burial. It seems he was led to the site through a vision of the Queen Mother Helena. Constantine then demolished the Temple of Aphrodite that stood on the spot and erected the Church of the Anastasis. It was replaced by later churches, and the present massive building known as the Church of the Holy Sepulchre dates to the Crusader period. It has undergone numerous renovations and remodelings through the years. *See* Plate 40.

Though the traditional identification of this site dates to the 4th cent., it is not without problems. One of the major questions that has never been satisfactorily answered is whether the place was outside the city walls in the Roman period. In sharp contrast to this massive ancient church, located in the heart of a city whose history is blighted with bigotry, greed, and selfishness, is another site which has been accepted by many as the Holy Sepulchre. It is known as the "Garden Tomb" and is located a short distance N of the Damascus Gate. Though it cannot be established as the tomb of Christ with any more certainty than the site of the Church of the Holy Sepulchre, it is a more meaningful place for many Christians because of its quiet surroundings so completely reminiscent of the biblical narrative.

See JERUSALEM III.H.14, 15.

Bibliography.–C. Coüasnon, *Church of the Holy Sepulchre in Jerusalem* (1974); W. S. McBirnie, *The Search for the Authentic Tomb of Jesus* (1975); A. Parrot, *Golgotha and the Church of the Holy Sepulchre* (1955).

J. F. PREWITT

HOLY SPIRIT [Heb. *rû(a)ḥ qāḏôš* (Ps. 51:11 [MT 13]; Isa. 63:10f.); Gk. *pneúma hágion*].

- I. The OT Doctrine of the Spirit
  - A. The Concept of the Spirit in the OT
  - B. The Spirit and God's People
    - 1. The Spirit and Prophecy
    - 2. The Spirit and Israel's Leadership
  - C. The Spirit and God
  - D. The Spirit and Man
  - E. The Spirit and Creation
  - F. The Spirit and the Age to Come
  - G. Intertestamental Developments
- II. The NT Doctrine of the Spirit
  - A. Introduction
  - B. The Holy Spirit in Luke-Acts
    - 1. Jesus and the Spirit
    - 2. Jesus, the Spirit, and Pentecost
    - 3. The Spirit and the Church in Acts
  - C. The Holy Spirit in the Pauline Epistles
    - 1. The Spirit in Eschatological Perspective
    - 2. The Spirit and Jesus
    - 3. The Spirit and the Body of Christ
    - 4. The Spirit and the Charismata
    - 5. The Spirit and the Christian Life
    - 6. The Spirit, the Law, and the Flesh
    - 7. The Spirit and God
  - D. The Holy Spirit in the Johannine Writings
  - E. The Holy Spirit in Other NT Writings
- III. Summary: The Development and Significance of the Biblical Doctrine of the Holy Spirit

I. The OT Doctrine of the Spirit.–*A. The Concept of Spirit in the OT.* Hebrew *rû(a)ḥ,* "breath," "wind," and "spirit," comes from a root meaning "breathe out violently," almost "snort." The noun connotes unusual force or energy as seen in the mysterious breath of life in man (Job 9:18; 12:10; Ps. 104:29; etc.), in the mighty and terrifying power of wind (Ps. 107:25; 148:8), in a dominating aspect of a person's disposition (Ex. 6:9; Nu. 5:14; 14:24; cf. Gen. 26:35), or most commonly in the ecstatic states of prophetic consciousness experienced as invasion by an external power (1 S. 10:6; 2 Ch. 24:20; Hos. 9:7).

From these fundamental experiences of spirit as intensity, mystery, and power are derived uses that pertain more directly to the Spirit as related to the covenant God of Abraham, Isaac, and Jacob. Breath in man is seen in association with the breath of God (Job 32:8). Combining the imagery of breath and wind, the breath of God is viewed as an overwhelming force (Isa. 30:28) or as a creative power (Ps. 104:30; cf. Gen. 1:2). In keeping with the primitive imagery of *rû(a)ḥ* the Spirit in relation to God is conceived more as an agency than as an agent, commonly using a quasi-liquid form as an analog of the Spirit (cf. Isa. 32:15; 44:3; Joel 2:28 [MT 3:1]).

B. The Spirit and God's People. The OT doctrine of the Spirit, rooted in religious phenomenology, is developed overwhelmingly within a theocratic context of the living God who acts, rather than in a context of metaphysics and science as later in the Greek concept of spirit as *pneúma.* Virtually all OT references to the Spirit, whether early or late, are related to the religious life of Israel as God's covenant people. Therefore, the preponderance of references pertain to the prophetic calling, state, and experience or to the charismatic powers given to Israel's leadership — prophets, priests, and kings.

1. The Spirit and Prophecy. The Spirit in the OT is above all the "Spirit of prophecy," for the most frequent manifestation of the Spirit of God is in relation to prophecy. Repeatedly, "the Spirit of Yahweh" (or "of 'Elohim" or simply "the Spirit") "came upon" someone to prophesy (Balaam, Nu. 24:2; Saul, 1 S. 10:10; Jahaziel, 2 Ch. 20:14) or, more vividly and violently, "clothed itself" with the one receiving prophetic power (cf. Amasai, 1 Ch. 12:18 [MT 19]; Zechariah, 2 Ch. 24:20). Indeed, Hosea equates the phrase "man of the Spirit" (Heb. *'îš hārû(a)ḥ*) with the term "prophet" (Heb. *nāḇî'*; Hos. 9:7); both were peculiarly characterized by the powerful activity of the Spirit of God.

Micah's classic statement makes clear that his mission as a prophet is related to God's powerful presence by His Spirit. He proclaims, "But as for me, I am filled with power, with the Spirit of the Lord, and with justice and might, to declare to Jacob his transgression and to Israel his sin" (Mic. 3:8). Ezekiel warns against false prophets who speak from their own spirits, having seen nothing from the Spirit of the Lord (Ezk. 13:3). The same role of the Spirit is seen in Zedekiah's scornful reply to Micaiah (1 K. 22:24), in Zechariah's interpretations of Israel's prophetic history (Zec. 7:12), and in the Levites' prayer (Neh. 9:20, 30). Significantly, many of Israel's great leaders, not generally considered prophets, are recognized as prophetic (e.g., Jacob, Joseph, Moses, Daniel). In fact it is understood that the whole people of God ought to be prophetic and indeed will be in the future (Nu. 11:29; Joel 2:28; cf. Ps. 105:15).

The manifestations of the Spirit in Israel's earliest prophecy were ecstatic in that unusual states of consciousness were generally involved. This is most clearly seen in the early bands or schools of prophets in which, evidently, prayer, music, and ritual dance were part of the prophetic context. The story of Saul's messengers who, "when they saw the company of the prophets prophesying, and Samuel standing as head over them," also began to prophesy because the "Spirit of God came upon them" (1 S. 19:20) is a classic example of ecstatic prophecy among the prophetic bands caused by the sudden action of the Spirit. The story of Saul's call to kingship (1 S. 10:1-13) specifically mentions musical instruments (and implied ritual dance) as well as the ecstatic experience of prophecy; "the spirit of the Lord will come mightily upon you, and you shall prophesy" (v. 6). The accounts of Moses and the seventy elders (Nu. 11:25), Eldad and Medad (Nu. 11:26), Balaam (Nu. 24:2), and Zechariah (2 Ch. 24:20) also indicate the sudden powerful action of the Spirit, with prophecy a sign of its presence or impartation, whether momentary or permanent.

Though of a somewhat different character, the later prophets indicate no absolute disjunction from the earlier prophets in terms of the role of the Spirit or the ecstatic nature of the prophetic experience. The emphasis, however, does shift from the Spirit as the *cause* of prophetic ecstasy to the Word as the *content* of that experience. Also, beyond prayer and fasting, there is no hint of the use of special means such as music and ritual dance as a context for prophecy. Ezekiel and Zechariah are the clearest examples of the continuity in psychologically unusual prophetic states. Nevertheless, the role of the Spirit in prophecy is often clearly stated (Isa. 48:16; Ezk. 11:5; Mic. 3:8). The prophets view the Spirit as the cause of earlier prophecy (Zec. 7:12) and as the source of the future prophetic ministry of the Messiah (Isa. 61:1) or among the whole people of God (Joel 2:28 [MT 3:1]).

This last point is of special significance for the development of the relation of the Spirit to prophecy in the OT. What begins as a sporadic and uncommon experience of prophecy limited to certain key leaders comes to a focus in a messianic figure, uniquely characterized as the man of the Spirit (Isa. 11:2; 42:1; 61:1), and finally is to be universalized and naturalized among the whole people of God in the age to come (Joel 2:28).

2. The Spirit and Israel's Leadership. A second dominant theme in the relation of the Spirit to the people of God is the charismatic endowment of Israel's leadership. The episode of Moses and the seventy elders was primarily intended to legitimate the authority of an administrative institution in Israel. A permanent endowment of the Spirit as found in Moses was evinced by a single experience of ecstatic prophesying and was required for true administrative authority. Through Moses' hands, Joshua also participates in the Spirit to serve as Israel's leader (Nu. 27:18-20; Dt. 34:9).

The same endowment for leadership can be seen in the experiences of the judges, including Gideon, Jephthah, Samson, and others (Jgs. 6:34; 11:29; 14:6). It is especially evident in Saul (1 S. 10:1-13) and David (1 S. 16:13f.) as the first kings of Israel. Even after the Exile Zerubbabel was to lead by the power of the Spirit (Zec. 4:6). Again it is important to note that this charismatic line of leadership culminates in a messianic figure especially equipped by the Spirit (Isa. 11:2; 42:1; 61:1) and followed by an age in which all are endowed with the Spirit and attended by His power (Isa. 44:3-5; Ezk. 39:29; Joel 2:28).

C. The Spirit and God. Because of the emphasis on Spirit in terms of religious experience and unusual power, the OT has little concern for the Spirit as personal or for His inner relationship to God. Isaiah stresses that "spirit" is essentially of God rather than of mankind or of anything in the created order, specifically setting a sharp disjunction between God and mankind, "spirit" and "flesh" (Isa. 31:3). Thus the Spirit, uniquely of God, is made virtually synonymous with God's power (Zec. 4:6; Mic. 3:8) or His presence (Ps. 139:7). The model underlying the OT conception of the relation of God and the Spirit is one of agent and agency, pictured anthropomorphically as God and the breath of His mouth (Isa. 30:28).

In the parallelism between God's presence and His Spirit there is, however, a place for a hypostatizing of the Spirit. The Spirit as God's presence and power active in the life and leadership of Israel is depicted as being grieved (Isa. 63:10), as giving rest (v. 14), as one who could not be directed by people (40:13), as being patient (Mic. 2:7), and as an instructor to God's people in the wilderness (Neh. 9:20). This lays the foundation for the further understanding of the Spirit as personal in the history and experience of the early Church.

D. The Spirit and Man. Apart from the chief religious experiences of the Spirit in prophecy and leadership, very little is said about the Spirit in relation to mankind in general. The most significant conception in the OT period was that He is the source of human life. The creation account in Gen. 2:7 presents man's self-consciousness as a living person (*nepeš*) as the result of a distinct action of God, who breathes into man the "breath of life" (Heb. *nišmaṯ ḥayyîm*). Man, as the image of God, is given a distinction not given to the rest of the sentient creation.

This notion of the Spirit of God as the ongoing source of man's life is found also in Gen. 6:3, which contrasts man as flesh with the continuation of God's *rû(a)ḥ* within him, and in the book of Job, which equates man's breath with the *rû(a)ḥ* of God within man's nostrils (Job 27:3; 33:4; 34:14). The function of God's spirit in man extends also to his creative and intellectual activities. Bezalel's skills as an artisan of the tabernacle are directly ascribed to his being "filled with the Spirit of God — with ability and intelligence, with knowledge and all craftsmanship" (Ex. 31:3; 35:31). The same connection of the Spirit of God ("the breath of the Almighty") to man's intellectual functioning is generalized in Job 32:8: "But it is the spirit in a man, the breath of the Almighty that makes him understand." These notions of the relation of God's Spirit to people are summed up in the phrase that characterizes God as "the God of the spirits of all flesh" (Nu. 16:22; 27:16).

A more general use of the Hebrew term *rû(a)ḥ* in relation to man focuses less on God as the source and more on the effects of *rû(a)ḥ* on man, construed in terms of his own psychical functioning. Of the 378 OT occurrences of *rû(a)ḥ*, perhaps one quarter (especially in Psalms and Proverbs) involve a conception bordering on the functions of *nepeš*. By Ezekiel's time *rû(a)ḥ* in relation to man was assimilated to *nepeš*, though generally with higher associations and with more profound intensity and significance.

E. The Spirit and Creation. The role of the Spirit in creation is not extensive. It is, however, in keeping with the primary experiential orientation to the Spirit as the mighty power of the living God, immanent and active among His people. Ps. 33:6 presents the basic biblical order and emphasis in creation as a coordination of God's creative Word (Heb. *dāḇār*) and His mighty *rû(a)ḥ*, which proceeds as breath from His mouth. This same coordination of *rû(a)ḥ* and *dāḇār* is majestically portrayed in the first account of creation (Gen. 1:1–2:4). Here the creative word is prominent, but all is prefaced by a reference to the "brooding" Spirit as the "wind of God" moving over the primal state of creation prior to its progressive ordering through the Word (unless *rû(a)ḥ 'ĕlōhîm* means simply "mighty wind"). Other references to the Spirit's role in creation are sparse and do not add any significant points (see Job 26:13). The Spirit of God is viewed in relation not only to the action of creation but also to the preservation of the life of man and beast (Ps. 104:27-30).

F. The Spirit and the Age to Come. The development of the OT doctrine of the Spirit within its theocratic context reaches its culmination in the eschatological hope of the age to come. In this final age of God's glory (Isa. 11:9; Hab. 2:14) and the glory of His people the Spirit really comes into His own, because that age is uniquely characterized as the age of the Spirit. This can be seen in a threefold way — first, in the figure of the coming messianic deliverer, perceived as prophetic (Dt. 18:15), as a kingly, charismatic leader (Isa. 11:1-10), and finally as a glorious supernatural person of divine qualities (Dnl. 7:13f.). Isaiah particularly characterizes this "one who comes" as a man of the Spirit (Isa. 11:2; 42:1; 61:1). Second, the age to come is inaugurated by the outpouring of the Spirit (Isa. 32:15; 44:3; Ezk. 39:29; Joel 2:28 [MT 3:1]). According to these passages there is to be an effusion of the Spirit in that age so that the people of God will experience the activity of the Spirit universally, permanently, and powerfully through inner, moral, and spiritual renewal. The Spirit's activity is to be so extensive that even the earth will be renewed as a fulfillment of the Spirit's role in the original creation. Third, this age of the Spirit is to be marked by a deeper, inward spirituality as summed up in Isaiah's and Jeremiah's expectation of a new covenant (Isa. 59:20f.; Jer. 31:31-34; 32:37-40). Although the Spirit's role in the new covenant is not delineated in these passages, His new and deepened inwardness is emphasized. However, Ezekiel's conception of this new covenant reality specifically mentions the role of the Spirit. God says, "I will put my spirit within you and cause you to walk in my statutes" (Ezk. 36:27). Here the role in the heart of the law (Jer. 31:33) and the fear of God (Jer. 32:40) are portrayed in terms of a new spirit and a new heart through the abiding inner presence of God's Spirit, guaranteeing an obedience never attainable prior to the future age.

Thus, a development can be perceived in the OT concept of the Spirit as the Spirit of the living God. That development is from sporadic, selective, and external activity of the Spirit, to His total pervasiveness both within God's people and within the created order. This eschatological hope, which within the OT remains only a hope, forms the only adequate basis for understanding the NT message of the kingdom of God established through Jesus Christ and inaugurated by the Spirit at Pentecost.

G. Intertestamental Developments. The intertestamental literature in the Apocrypha and Pseudepigrapha and the writings of Qumrân, Josephus, and Philo reveal no really significant changes beyond the OT conception. Generally, the Spirit is regarded as the prophetic Spirit that worked in the golden age of Israel's history but is now quiescent (Sir. 48:12, 24; 1 Macc. 9:27). In the wisdom literature the role of the Spirit is intellectualized as the Spirit of wisdom (Wisd. 7:22–8:1). Philo, a Jewish expositor of Platonic Mosaism, sees the Spirit in more philosophic terms or in terms of ecstatic or mystical inspiration. The pseudepigraphic writings, emerging within a context of heavy political oppression coupled with the lack of any authentic religious voice, do pick up and amplify the OT eschatological hopes of a coming age in which a man of the Spirit would appear and an effusion of the Spirit would take place (Ps. Sol. 17:37 [var. 42]; 18:7 [var. 8]; T. Levi 18:7; T. Jud. 24:2).

II. The NT Doctrine of the Holy Spirit. *–A. Introduction.* The NT teaching on the Spirit is incredibly rich and complex in comparison with OT materials. Yet there is a definite sense of continuity in one major aspect — the Spirit is above all still the experience of God powerfully present and active in the midst of His people. And this experience, as in the OT, is totally conditioned by the theocratic context of relation to the living God of Israel's patriarchs and by the eschatological framework of the two ages. This context is, however, at the same time both more focused and more universalized. It is more focused in that the NT experience is inextricably bound up with the historical Jesus. It is more universalized in that this experience is "naturalized" into the individual and corporate life of all of the people of God, who are now uniquely the people of the Spirit participating in the reality of the age of the Spirit.

It is important to note at the outset that the whole NT teaching regarding the Spirit is radically conditioned by the experience of the Spirit, Pentecostal and post-Pentecostal, so that even the pre-Pentecostal references to the Spirit are understood within the later experience and understanding of the Church. Further, it is necessary to remember always that the NT teaching arises from varied circumstances and over an extended period. This gives rise in the NT to a series of doctrinal strands regarding the Spirit that indicate both development and an underlying complementary unity. The thrust of NT teaching on the Spirit can best be reviewed by a survey of the various basic strands as they are presented, but especially as they reflect the development of the doctrine in terms of Jesus and the Church within the broadest framework of the two-age eschatological structure. Three fundamental strands of teaching on the Holy Spirit are to be discerned in the NT: (1) Lukan; (2) Pauline; (3) Johannine. Matthew and Mark can be assimilated to the more extensive frame of Luke-Acts, and the remaining NT writings provide materials requiring only brief comment. The order of treatment favors the coherency of the overall meaning of the NT doctrine of the Spirit rather than chronology.

B. The Holy Spirit in Luke-Acts. To Luke must go the title "Historian of the Holy Spirit," even as Paul and John must share the title "Theologian of the Holy Spirit." This is not to say that Luke is not theological in his treatment of the Church's experience of the Holy Spirit. Rather it is because he uses the vehicle of history preeminently to provide an external framework large enough to contain the full significance of the experience of the Holy Spirit, even as Paul and John plumb the depths of His meaning and content in a more detailed and personal fashion. Luke focuses on the movement of salvation-history, on the leadership of the Holy Spirit in the missionary task of the Church, and on the manifestation of the Holy Spirit in the external frame of history. In this way he provides the context within which may be contained the Pauline and Johannine analysis of the "inwardness" of the experience of the Spirit. Luke, Paul, and John all share the same basic frame of salvation-history, though in rather complementary ways and with definite variation of emphasis. Thus, within this external frame which Luke develops most obviously, the three fundamental NT strands on the Holy Spirit may be seen to cohere in presenting the full NT understanding of the Spirit.

Luke clearly sees himself as historian in the classical sense, as he announces in his introduction to the work (Lk. 1:1-4). But though his stated purpose is "to write an orderly account" of the "things which have been accomplished" among the community of believers, both internal observation and comparison with the other Gospels reveal that Luke's selection of materials uniquely reflects a concern for the activity of the Holy Spirit. The second part of his work leaves no doubt whatsoever as to this emphasis, which is particularly evident in Luke's conception of the Spirit as the Spirit of prophecy (as in the OT), as the agency of the progression of salvation-history, and as the agency and power of the Church's missionary movement.

Luke is especially convinced that the Spirit is the source of prophetic experience in strict continuity with the OT tradition. Accounts of the prophesying of Elizabeth (Lk. 1:41-45), Mary (1:46-55), Zechariah (1:67-79), Simeon (2:25-27), Anna (2:36-38), and John the Baptizer (3:15ff.), in which they are usually described as "filled with the Holy Spirit" (a phrase that must also be interpreted in the light of Acts 2:4; 4:8, 31; 6:3, 5; 7:55; 9:17; 13:9), clearly indicate Luke's interest in this aspect of the Spirit's activity. Luke sees this experience of the renewal of prophetic Spirit in the OT tradition as inaugurating a transition from the *status quo* of this age and anticipating the advent of something new. For Luke divine intervention in John's conception and that of Jesus by the Holy Spirit is the beginning of a transition in salvation-history, a transition especially marked by an accompanying renewal of the OT Spirit of prophecy.

This transition is continued at Jesus' baptism by John at the Jordan. Jesus, conceived by the Holy Spirit, is thus uniquely endued with the Spirit as a permanent reality, enabling Him to take the office of Messiah (anointed by the Spirit) and to carry out His ministry in the Spirit's power as one who is uniquely the man of the Spirit (Lk. 3:22; 4:1, 18-21). The transition is completed through the events of His "exodus" in death, resurrection, and ascension, after which He is portrayed as receiving the "promise of the Father" (Acts 1:4; 2:33). As the man of the Spirit now become the exalted Lord of the Spirit, He "pours" out the Holy Spirit, thus inaugurating the age to come, the age of the Spirit promised in the eschatological hope of the OT prophets, particularly Joel (Acts 2:16-21). Luke sees the OT structure of the two ages as fulfilled, in part yet also in actuality, through the history of Jesus the Messiah and its continuation in the history of the community of the Spirit.

It is within this revolutionary understanding of the history of Jesus as effecting the transition of the OT eschatological hope into a present (although partial) realization of the age to come, a history characterized at each critical point by the unique activity of the Holy Spirit, that Luke presents his narrative. Luke is able, then, to center on the Church, as the community of the Spirit of the age to come, in its missionary task of "preaching the kingdom of God and teaching about the Lord Jesus Christ" (Acts 28:31). Luke actually wrote within the context of the Church's missionary expansion; his concern is clearly along these lines, as Acts 1:8, which outlines the rest of the work, indicates. Therefore Luke, in strict conformity with the OT conception of the Spirit of prophecy, speaks primarily in terms of a dynamic power guiding (Acts 8:29; 10:19; 13:2, 4; 15:28; 16:6f.) and enabling the community of believers in His continuation of "all that Jesus began to do and teach" (1:1).

The very fact that Luke wrote two "treatises" indicates both a continuity and a parallelism between the ministry of Jesus and that of the Church. This is quite evident in the Gospel's beginning with Jesus' self-definition as one uniquely anointed with the Spirit to proclaim and to heal (Lk. 4:18f.), recalling Isa. 61:1f., and the second book's beginning with a unique, epochal empowering of the Spirit mediated from Jesus as the new exalted Lord of the Spirit, fulfilling Joel's prophecy (Joel 2:28-32 [MT 3:1-5]). Because of Luke's missionary concern, conceptualized as the Church's continuing Jesus' activity, and the fact that Luke essentially does not advance beyond the OT conception of the Spirit of prophecy, Luke-Acts emphasizes not the Spirit as the eschatological reality that totally conditions the believer (as found in Paul), but the manifestation of the Spirit as ecstatic and powerful, i.e., signs and wonders.

1. Jesus and the Spirit. In his Gospel Luke traces, basically from the same materials underlying all of the Synoptics, the relationship of Jesus and the Holy Spirit. His narrative gives the fullest account of the promise of Jesus' conception by the Holy Spirit (evidently learned from Mary herself; cf. Lk. 2:19, 51). The conception is described as a "coming upon" or an "overshadowing." The OT flavor is very strong in the parallelism between the Holy Spirit and the "power of the Most High" (1:35). The significance given to this fact of divine action in Jesus' conception is that Jesus' relation to the Spirit is not simply that of another pneumatic figure in the OT prophetic tradition (contrast with John who, though "filled with the Holy Spirit even from his mother's womb" [1:15], is not conceived by the Holy Spirit). Jesus is, rather, from the very beginning uniquely a man of the Spirit, even by origin, so that He is holy, the special Son of God (1:35).

The next event that indicates the relation of Jesus and the Spirit is His baptism by John at the Jordan (3:21f.). John the Baptizer, already introduced by Luke as a prophetic figure in the mold of Elijah (1:17), is presented as one whose ministry is preparatory to Jesus. John's message is freighted with intense eschatological expectation of the immediate appearance of a messianic deliverer and the violent inbreaking of the age to come, accompanied by a special baptism of judgment in wind and fire through the Holy Spirit (Mk. 1:7f.; Mt. 3:11f.; Lk. 3:15-17). Essentially a preparatory and not initiatory ministry, John's activity in the renewed OT Spirit of prophecy in itself was not a new beginning or eschatological but was a sign of a new beginning soon to take place through another, described by John as one who baptizes with the Holy Spirit (the reality) rather than with mere water (as John himself did). His call to the people was preparation for the ushering in of the new age and a pointing to the one who was actually to initiate that event. John's baptism was thus a preparation for the true baptism in the Holy Spirit.

The actual experience of Jesus' baptism is beautifully and delicately described by Luke. He carefully separates Jesus from the repentant crowd in His baptism (3:21), and as He is praying (a point of significance for the later Christians, cf. Lk. 11:13; Acts 4:31) the Spirit descends upon Him, symbolized by a dove, and a word of special divine approbation is given to Him. All the Evangelists attest to this special endowment with the Holy Spirit at the beginning of Jesus' public ministry. The Fourth Gospel notes explicitly and forcefully what is only implicit in the Synoptic Gospels, that the Spirit not only comes upon Jesus but remains there, thereby establishing Him as one who is characterized as "baptizer with the Holy Spirit" (Jn. 1:32f.).

The alternate reading in Codex Bezae messianically interprets Ps. 2:7. It is correct in its insight that this event constitutes Jesus' own entry into the reality of the age to come in terms of its *powers,* though not in terms of the *life* of that age. He already possessed the latter by virtue of His unique conception by the Holy Spirit. This special endowment of the Spirit is necessary if Jesus is to fulfil His role as initiator of the age to come. Through this experience Jesus is depicted as *the* man of the Spirit who, in the context presented by Luke, is also then the head of the renewed race of Adam (cf. Lk. 3:23-38, where Jesus is traced back to Adam, "the son of God").

Entrance into the coming eschatological reality was initially restricted to Jesus Himself, though He did give His disciples temporary authority over disease and demons (Lk. 9:1-6; 10:1-20). It was only as Jesus went through His representative messianic baptism (Lk. 12:50; Mk. 10:38) — His death, resurrection, and consequent exaltation as the Lord of the Spirit (Acts 2:33) — that the life and the power of the new age could be made available to the Church, the renewed people of the promised age. Only after the total transposition of the humanity of Jesus the Messiah into the form of the future age could the reality of the life and power of that age be poured out upon all flesh.

The implied motif of Jesus as the head of a renewed race of Adam is continued in Jesus' wilderness temptation, where He is led (Mark implies "compulsion" [RSV "drove him out"; Gk. *ekbállei*], Mk. 1:12) by the Holy Spirit. Luke describes Jesus as "full of the Holy Spirit," the result of the Spirit's descent. The newly endowed Jesus first experiences intense spiritual discipline and struggle in the desert (Lk. 4:1-13), in which Jesus, the Spirit-filled man, overcomes the devil's temptation, succeeding where Adam failed.

Significantly, Jesus, after the descent of the Holy Spirit upon Him, acts only in the Spirit's power rather than in His own power as the Son of God. Only after Jesus is anointed by the Spirit does He begin His messianic ministry. Thereafter, though references to the Holy Spirit are not frequent, Jesus' power and authority quite clearly result from the continuing presence of the Holy Spirit with Him as the man of the Spirit. Jesus' whole ministry is construed as being under the guidance and power of the Spirit. Luke emphasizes this by noting that, at the beginning of Jesus' public ministry, after His victory over temptation, He "returned in the power of the Spirit into Galilee" (Lk. 4:14).

Later references also indicate that Jesus always acted by the Holy Spirit's power rather than His own. In 5:17 "the power of the Lord was with him to heal," suggests OT idiom for "the Spirit of the Lord." In 11:20, a verse of key significance in interpreting Jesus' person and ministry in relation to the OT eschatological hope, Jesus makes it clear that His exorcisms (and by implication all of His deeds of power) were performed by the power of "the finger of God," or as in the parallel Mt. 12:28, by the Holy Spirit.

In this connection, the "blasphemy against the Holy Spirit" is specially relevant, particularly in the Markan account (Mk. 3:19-30; cf. Mt. 12:24-32; Lk. 12:8-12; cf. Mk. 13:11). The point specifically at issue is the source of Jesus' ministry of power in healing, especially exorcisms. Jesus' enemies attributed His power to Beelzebul. Jesus counters first by pointing out the absurdity of such a tactic on the part of Satan and second by referring to the sin against the Holy Spirit. It is clear that in this context this sin is one of wilful spiritual self-blindness in attributing to Satan the work of the Holy Spirit in Jesus' ministry (cf. Mark's comment "for they had said, 'He has an unclean spirit' " [3:30]).

It is important to note for historical reasons that this sin is very specific and therefore cannot be generalized to some unknown sin that is arbitrarily categorized as an "eternal" or "unforgiveable" sin. Untold amounts of useless and neurotic agony have been wrought in the experience of some who dreaded that they had committed this sin unknowingly.

Luke's presentation here indicates an extension of this sin in a direction particularly relevant to the early Church. In the context of Jesus' warnings against apostasy in persecution, he mentions the sin against the Holy Spirit, along with the promise that the Holy Spirit will provide the proper words to speak (cf. the experience of Stephen the first martyr; Acts 6:8–7:60). In the early Church apostasy was a serious issue and the question of the reinstatement of the lapsed was much debated. This saying of Jesus follows a serious warning about such apostasy. He then goes on to say that those who oppose the followers of Jesus are guilty of a sin more awful than apostasy, a sin not of timidity but of outright hostility to the Holy Spirit's activity in the midst of God's people. In post-Pentecostal perspective this saying of Jesus indicates that the sin against the Holy Spirit as active in the Spirit-filled community is of the same order as blasphemy against the Spirit as the source of Jesus' ministry, healing, and power. This conforms very much with Luke's main theme of the continuity of mission between Jesus and the Church in the same Spirit and dynamic.

Even more important than these indirect indications of the role of the Spirit in Jesus' ministry is His own inaugural address given in Nazareth, "where he had been brought up" (Lk. 4:16-22). In a dramatic setting Jesus opened the prophetic scroll to Isaiah and read the charter of His own ministry: "The Spirit of the Lord God is upon me, because the Lord has anointed me to bring good tidings to the afflicted; he has sent me to bind up the brokenhearted, to proclaim liberty to the captives, and the opening of the prison to those who are bound; to proclaim the year of the Lord's favor" (Isa. 61:1f.).

In this striking way Jesus takes to Himself the role of Isaiah's Servant of the Lord, thereby characterizing His own ministry as initiated, empowered, and justified only on the basis of His anointing with the Spirit of the Lord. He is *the* prophet, with plenary endowment of the Spirit for ministry. Isa. 61:1f. might well be taken as Luke's own introduction of the basic theme of Luke-Acts, the Spirit-empowered mission of Jesus begun in His own history and continued in the missionary expansion of the Church through the same initiative and power. Matthew, in his own unique way, reinforces this picture of Jesus as the Spirit-endued Servant of the Lord by quoting another passage in Isaiah: "Behold, my servant whom I have chosen, my beloved with whom my soul is well pleased. I will put my Spirit upon him, and he shall proclaim justice to the Gentiles . . ." (Mt. 12:18-21; Isa. 42:1-4). In view of Jesus' self-definition as the Spirit-endowed Servant of the Lord and the many indirect references to His ministry as empowered by the Spirit, it is clear that even where there is no explicit mention of the Holy Spirit the assumption is that all is done through His power.

The eschatological significance of Jesus' ministry in the power of the Spirit is epochal in nature. Jesus was not functioning simply as the latest in the long line of prophetic figures as a "man of the Spirit" (cf. Hos. 9:7). Rather Jesus is clearly perceived as *the* man of the Spirit, who both initiates and rules the coming age of glory and who *also* experiences and demonstrates this new age as the age of the Spirit. This becomes strikingly evident in the *logion* of Jesus in which He replied to the scribes and

Pharisees who attributed His power to Beelzebul. He said: "But if it is by the finger of God that I cast out demons, then the kingdom of God has come upon you" (Lk. 11:20; "by the Spirit of God," Mt. 12:28). By this saying Jesus provides the key to His self-interpretation. The power and authority He exercised were to Him evidence that the long-awaited kingdom of God was already present in some sense. Jesus experienced the reality of the age to come through the power of the age to come, the eschatological Spirit. This power to heal and to exorcise, which came so easily for Jesus, was but the smallest sample of the tremendous power of the kingdom of God — the mere "finger of God," a power that was clearly an expression of the activity of God's Spirit.

Luke has clearly interpreted Jesus, in the light of Jesus' self-definition, as *the* man of the Spirit, who brings about the age of the Spirit in which the Church also participates. Jesus' conception by the Holy Spirit and the attendant renewal of the Spirit of prophecy mark him from the very beginning as uniquely related to the Spirit. John the Baptizer's saying characterizing Jesus as the "one who baptizes with the Spirit" points to His eschatological mission. Jesus' experience, in His baptism, affirming His unique status as the Son of God, coupled with a plenary and permanent endowment of the Holy Spirit as the source of His direction and power, marks His own entry into the power of the age to come. His inaugural address recalling Isaiah's Servant of the Lord indicates His intense awareness of special anointment by the Spirit for an eschatological ministry of healing and proclamation. That for which John made preparation Jesus already experienced as present — at least in part.

2. Jesus, the Spirit, and Pentecost. For Luke, the final step in developing the eschatological meaning of Jesus' person and ministry in relation to the Spirit awaits the post-resurrection events of Ascension and Pentecost. Luke's first "treatise," the Gospel, ends with Jesus' ascension and His command for the disciples to wait before commencing the task of witnessing. Jesus Himself is to send the "promise of the Father" upon them through which they will be clothed, in OT metaphor, with the divine power of the Holy Spirit promised through the prophets in association with the coming glorious eschatological age.

Acts, Luke's second treatise, begins by retracing the Ascension in more detail in preparation for the narrative's real beginning. At this point Luke sets the stage masterfully, emphasizing the Gospel's focus on the ministry that Jesus had *begun* prior to the ascension. Then, in immediate anticipation of what was to follow, reference is made to John the Baptizer's depiction of Jesus' ministry as baptizing with the Holy Spirit, a characterization that Jesus Himself adopts. The fulfillment of that promise is imminent, laying the foundation both for Luke's concern with the mission of the Church and for the manifested power of the Spirit in that mission (Acts 1:8). All of this is set within an eschatological frame that sweeps aside inadequate conceptions of the kingdom of God as merely political (1:6), making room for the eschatological event about to take place, yet without bringing the final (but temporarily undetermined) apocalyptic coming of the kingdom of God.

Following this preparation Luke proceeds, after a transitional section (1:12-26), to describe briefly but vividly the epochal event of Pentecost. The disciples, gathered together in eschatological excitement anticipating the promised Holy Spirit and evidently observing the Jewish feast of Pentecost, suddenly experienced a powerful inrush of spiritual reality, described by Luke as being "filled with the Holy Spirit," and they overflowed with tremendous joy in a prophetic ecstasy of praise in other tongues (languages that were recognized by others). This was attended by other manifestations comparable to the rushing of a powerful wind (reminiscent of a common meaning of *rû(a)ḥ* and *pneúma*) and to the appearance of a divine fire resting upon each person present, symbolic of a participation in the new and wonderful spiritual reality. The noise and excitement of the event provided the opportunity for a Spirit-filled, prophetic explanation of the event's significance by Peter, along with the eleven. *See* Plate 38.

Eschatologically, this experience is the beginning of the age of the Spirit in its universal and naturalized form, fulfilling the OT promise, specifically as mentioned by Joel (Joel 2:28-32 [MT 3:1-5]). Not a matter of another prophetic band, it was the coming of the long-awaited promise of the Spirit "poured out upon all flesh" with attendant evidence of the Spirit's presence in terms of charismatic manifestations — visions, dreams, and prophecy — manifestations once restricted to a few but now universalized.

This fulfillment is possible only through the agency of the risen and exalted Jesus (Acts 2:32f.). The Pentecost event confirms both that Jesus is Lord and Messiah (v. 36) and that this eschatological experience is a result of His activity as the Lord of the Spirit, for it is the exalted Jesus who pours forth "this which you see and hear" (v. 33).

This is clearly the culmination of the Lukan development of the relation of Jesus to the Spirit of the age to come. He has now effected a new stage in the progress of salvation-history in which the endowment of the Spirit that He experienced at Jordan is made available to His people through the messianic baptism of death and the subsequent resurrection and ascension. What once He alone experienced as the Man of the Spirit, now as exalted Lord He provides to all of His disciples.

That the early Christians experienced the Spirit only as derived from the ascended Lord and not as their own, independent spiritual experience ties the experience of the early Church to the history of Jesus. It does not allow for a generalized "mysticism" of religious experience. Pentecost is clearly the beginning of a new era and marks the entrance of the disciples into the power of that age. The availability of this gift of the Spirit is expressed in terms of repentance — faith, baptism in water, and reception of the Holy Spirit — an opportunity extended to all who receive God's sovereign call (Acts 2:38f.). With this salvation-history has transited by means of the activity of the Holy Spirit and through the person of Jesus from the age of anticipation to the age to come, present and powerfully manifested but not fully realized (1:11).

Luke's method of historical narrative does not discuss directly the significance and mode of reception of this promised "baptism in the Holy Spirit" by Jesus as exalted Lord of the Spirit. No rigid pattern is to be found in Acts concerning the order and conditions of the baptism in the Holy Spirit. The composite picture for individual entrance into the community of the Spirit encompasses several events — hearing, repentance, baptism in water, laying on of hands, reception of the Spirit with charismatic manifestations (2:38; 8:12-19; 10:44-48; 18:8; 19:5f.) — the total initiation of the person, both conversion and empowering.

Theologically the phrase "baptism in the Spirit" is perceived as a unitary event with a twofold purpose and a twofold anthropological reaction. The giving of the Spirit by Jesus aims to communicate the new life of the age to come with the resurrected Lord as archetypal (Paul uses the concept "first fruits" [Gk. *aparchḗ*], which John implies in his account of the pre-Pentecostal giving of the Spirit; Jn. 20:22). It aims also at the communication of new power experienced as the person's total immersion into the reality of the Spirit with an attendant empowering for ministry, exactly parallel to Jesus' baptism at Jordan. Two experiences result. The communication of the life of the age to come is connected with the experience of conversion. The communication of new power is associated with the introduction to charismatic manifestation. The former is universally experienced by its very nature as dynamic life activity. The second, though potentially universal, is both conceptually and experientially separable from the first (cf. the Samaritans, Acts 8:14-17; and the Ephesian "disciples," 19:2-6) and must be actively received (cf. 2:38). A case can also be made for limiting the phrase "baptized in the Holy Spirit" to the introduction to the charismatic manifestation of the Spirit; thus the phrase "to receive the Holy Spirit" (Acts 2:38; 8:15, 17, 19; 10:47; 19:2; cf. Rom. 8:15; 1 Cor. 2:12; 2 Cor. 11:4; Gal. 3:2, 14) becomes a technical term indicating an active appropriation of this experience.

Though these two realities are separable in principle they were not generally separated in the experience of the early Church. The NT shows no concern for seeking any second, post-conversion experience. All Christians are viewed as having experienced the total complex of events. Indeed, the narrative of the Samaritan mission seems to imply that until that time all converts had experienced the total complex; the lack of the expected charismatic reception of the Spirit was recognized, so further action was taken by the apostles in the form of laying on of hands (Acts 8:9-19). This "pan-Pentecostal assumption" is one way to understand the overall experience of the Holy Spirit underlying the NT writings.

3. The Spirit and the Church in Acts. The rest of the narrative in Acts carefully reviews the experience of the early Church in its Spirit-directed and Spirit-empowered mission from Jerusalem "to the end of the earth" (1:8). This experience of the Spirit can be seen in the quality of the early Church's life as community, in relation to certain persons as especially filled with the Spirit, and in the very precise leading of the Holy Spirit in directing the mission.

The quality of life in the early Church is clearly connected to the promise of the Spirit. The beautiful picture of the initial community of believers (Acts 2:42-47), which depicts apostolic teaching, fellowship, breaking of bread, prayers, signs, wonders, holding "all things in common," and praise to God, indicates that all are implicitly connected with the first outpouring of the Spirit. The experience of Ananias and Sapphira (5:1) illustrates this point, for their sin is described as tempting the "Spirit of the Lord" (v. 9). Luke encapsulates the Church's situation as being "built up; and walking in the fear of the Lord and in the comfort of the Holy Spirit" (9:31). After the mission of Paul and Barnabas at Antioch in Pisidia the new converts were "filled with joy and with the Holy Spirit" (13:52).

While all believers are depicted as endowed with the Spirit, certain figures emerge as especially Spirit-endued. Peter speaks as one filled with the Holy Spirit not only at Pentecost but also before the high priestly commission (4:8). The Hellenists chosen to serve the widows are described as "full of the Spirit," particularly Stephen (6:3-6). Philip, also one of the seven, in the later evangelistic mission to the Samaritans performed signs, healings, and exorcisms by the Spirit (8:4-8). Barnabas is characterized as "a good man, full of the Holy Spirit and of faith" (11:24). Some persons such as Agabus were recognized by the community of the Spirit as prophets, much in the manner of the OT tradition (Acts 11:27f.; 21:10f.). Paul was clearly filled with the Spirit at his conversion through Ananias (9:17). He exercised a ministry of extraordinary power in signs and wonders (13:9-11; 14:8-11; 15:12; 19:11f.) and was unusually fruitful in bringing many into the community of the Holy Spirit (cf. Rom. 15:17-19).

The specific leading of the mission of the early Church by the Holy Spirit is quite pronounced. Philip, in the midst of his successful mission to the Samaritans, is led by the Spirit to the Ethiopian ruler (Acts 8:26, 29) and subsequently is "snatched away" by the Spirit, much after the fashion of Elijah or Ezekiel, to continue his mission (8:39). The variant reading in Codex Alexandrinus, "the Holy Spirit fell upon the eunuch and the angel of the Lord caught up Philip," shows both the strong expectation of the early Church that conversion should be attended by an identifiable spiritual experience and the dramatic leading of the Spirit. Similar influence of the Spirit upon missionary efforts is reflected in the experiences of Peter among the Gentiles (10:19f.; cf. 11:12), Barnabas and Saul (13:1-4), and Paul and Timothy (16:6f.; cf. 21:11). Even the appointment of elders in Paul's mission was related to the leading of the Holy Spirit (20:28). At the conclusion of the Jerusalem Council on the relation of gentile converts to the Mosaic customs the leaders expressed their conclusions in a letter delimiting conditions that "seemed good to the Holy Spirit" and to the Jerusalem leaders (15:28).

It is obvious that Luke and the Synoptists did not progress materially beyond the OT concept of the Spirit as the Spirit of prophecy. Yet, because of the new experience of the Spirit after Pentecost, it became more natural to speak of the Spirit in personal terms. Luke's description of the Holy Spirit as speaking (Acts 10:19f.; 11:12; 13:2; 21:11; cf. 15:28), being "tempted" (5:9), and forbidding Paul to preach (16:6f.) reveals a clear awareness of a personal dimension of the Spirit analogous to that of Jesus. Indeed, the Spirit is once described by Luke as the "Spirit of Jesus" (v. 7). Supplemented by the Matthaean liturgical form (Mt. 28:19), which links the Holy Spirit with the Father and the Son, this indicates that the personhood of the Spirit is recognized in the Luke-Acts-Synoptic strand of NT teaching. The full complement of NT teaching from Paul and John lays a very solid foundation for the theological formulation of the personhood and deity of the Spirit in trinitarian orthodoxy.

C. The Holy Spirit in the Pauline Epistles. The circumstances and literary form of the Pauline writings are compatible to express all aspects of the Spirit linked together in a basically coherent theological understanding. Paul combines Luke-Acts' external manifestation orientation and the Fourth Gospel's inward individualist approach in the two-age eschatological framework. These two interpretations he associates with the historical, resurrected Jesus through the corporate structure of the Church viewed as the body of Christ animated by the one Holy Spirit. His teaching encompasses both the life and the power of the age to come — the former in terms of inner renewal experienced in conflict with the "law" and the "flesh," the latter both as the Church's missionary dynamic and also as the source of its corporate unbuilding through the various manifestations of the Spirit. In short, the Pauline conception of the Spirit is one of totality. The Spirit is viewed as that which radically and totally determines the life and existence of the Christian, indeed, as that which defines the sphere of Christian existence. Participation in the reality of eschatological salvation is "in the Spirit." To be Christian is to be "in the Spirit" (Rom. 8:9). The wealth and complexity of the Pauline materials prohibit anything more than a look at their major points.

1. The Spirit in Eschatological Perspective. The eschatological framework in which the future age has already come in principle (if not in full manifestation) in the presence of the eschatological Spirit, first in Jesus Christ and then through Him as exalted Lord of the Spirit in the community of the Spirit viewed as a colony of that age (Phil. 3:20), is clearly accepted in the Pauline writings (Rom. 12:2; 1 Cor. 1:20; 2:6,8; 2 Cor. 4:4; Eph. 1:21; 2:7). This becomes especially clear in his reference to the Spirit as the "first fruits" (Gk. *aparchḗ*) in anticipation of the incomparable "glory that is to be revealed," the "glorious liberty of the children of God," and the "redemption of our bodies" (Rom. 8:18-25). Here the Spirit is looked upon as the initial stage of and in strict identity and continuity with the age to come — already experienced. Paul expresses the same concept through different images, referring to the Christian experience of the Spirit as a "guarantee" (Gk. *arrabṓn*) (2 Cor. 1:22; 5:5; Eph. 1:14) or under the figure of "sealing" (2 Cor. 1:22; Eph. 1:13).

This eschatological perspective provides the measure of the true nature of the Christian experience of the Spirit, whether it be in terms of a new life, "fruit of the Spirit" (Gal. 5:22) or the image of Jesus Christ (Rom. 8:29), or in terms of a new power, in the manifestations of the Spirit ("gifts"; "ministries"; "offices"; 1 Cor. 12:4-11, 28; Eph. 4:11). Obviously, both the new life and the new power are essential to the very nature of the Church and to the Christian life. There can be no mere passing manifestations of the Spirit designed only for the establishment of apostolic authority. Rather, all manifestations of the Spirit are signs and scintilla of glory exhibiting the true nature of the Church as possessing the "first fruits" of the coming glory.

2. The Spirit and Jesus. The Pauline conception of the relation of the Spirit to the historic and risen Jesus is not a simple one. Writing from a powerful experience of the Spirit and with pastoral rather than philosophical concern, he speaks of the Spirit both as the mode of the presence of the exalted Lord within the individual Christian and as distinct from yet intimately related to Jesus (Rom. 15:30; 1 Cor. 6:11; 12:4; 2 Cor. 13:14). The point of greatest significance in the Pauline awareness of the relation of Jesus and the Spirit is the existence of a reciprocity between the two. There is no experience of Jesus apart from the Spirit even as there is no recognition of any "spirit" that is not related to the Jesus of history now exalted. In Paul's complaint to the Corinthians this becomes evident: "For if some one comes and preaches another Jesus than the one we preached, or if you receive a different spirit from the one you received, or if you accept a different gospel from the one you accepted, you submit to it readily enough" (2 Cor. 11:4).

Paul does not recognize any spirit that is not related to Jesus, no matter what the phenomenon presented. Ecstasy is not enough (1 Cor. 12:3), nor is prophetic utterance (2 Thess. 2:2). Rather, the Spirit for Paul is preeminently the "Spirit of Jesus Christ" (Phil. 1:19). The Spirit, which produces true confession of Jesus in the Spirit-filled worshiper (1 Cor. 12:3), is the "Spirit of life in Christ Jesus" (Rom. 8:2).

Paul recognizes that the transposition of Jesus' humanity into the glorified form of the age to come through resurrection and ascension means that He can be experienced only as "spirit" — not in the natural, material mode. Paul expresses this in his development of the "last Adam" interpretation of the risen Lord (1 Cor. 15:45); this does not mean He became the Spirit, but that He is now in the mode of spirit and is experienced only as such (cf. v. 50). Similarly, Paul's admittedly difficult statement that "the Lord is the Spirit" (2 Cor. 3:17f.) certainly cannot mean "God [Yahweh] is Spirit" (in Johannine style, Jn. 4:24), nor can it mean any confusion of Jesus ("the Lord") with the Holy Spirit. Rather it means that Jesus is experienced as spirit in contrast to the letter, which kills (2 Cor. 3:6). Here Jesus, experienced as spirit, changes the Christian into the likeness of Jesus (v. 18), showing again that the Spirit Paul recognizes is tied to and conditioned by the Jesus of history (cf. also Rom. 8:15-17).

3. The Spirit and the Body of Christ. Paul exhibits special concern for the functional aspects of the community of the Spirit. He applies primarily the image of the Church as the body of Christ animated and unified by the Holy Spirit (Rom. 12:4-8; 1 Cor. 12:17-31; Eph. 1:22f.; 4:11-16; Col. 1:18, 24), though he also uses other images (e.g., "God's temple," 1 Cor. 3:16f.; "household of God" and the metaphor of a building, Eph. 2:19-22; "great house," 2 Tim. 2:20f.; "pillar and bulwark of the truth," 1 Tim. 3:15). Through these images he depicts the unity of the Church (Eph. 4:3), the character of its worship as "in spirit" (Phil. 3:3), and its power through the manifestations of the Spirit.

As in the Luke-Acts materials, Paul applies the familiar motif of the Spirit as the source of signs and wonders in missionary activity. Paul so summarizes his own ministry. "For I will not venture to speak of anything except what Christ has wrought through me to win obedience from the Gentiles, by word and deed, by the power of signs and wonders, by the power of the Holy Spirit . . ." (Rom. 15:18f.), and more succinctly, "my speech and my message were . . . in demonstration of the Spirit and power . . ." (1 Cor. 2:4; see also 1 Thess. 1:5).

Paul does provide, however, a new insight into the relation of the Spirit and the Church not found in the Lukan materials. He sees the power and manifestations of the Spirit in the charismata not only in relation to mission but also and especially in relation to the very nature and functioning of the Church as it builds itself up and matures corporately into "the stature of the fulness of Christ" (Eph. 4:13). Twice Paul speaks of the charismata of the Spirit when he discusses the Church as the body of Christ and the Spirit's activity within the Church (Rom. 12:3-8; 1 Cor. 12:4-30). Once in the same context he speaks of the "gifts" (Gk. *dōreá*; Eph. 4:7-16). Gifts, offices, and ministries in the Church are all perceived as manifestations of the Spirit (cf. especially 1 Cor. 12:7, 11; 14:12).

All of these are permanent to the Church both because they reflect its eschatological nature and because of their very purpose in nurturing it into a mature state. There is no real exegetical foundation for any view that dismisses any gift, office, or ministry as merely temporary, as existing simply for the establishment of apostolic authority, or as associated with a phase of immaturity in the Church. (Nevertheless, the office of apostle, though it may continue in one sense, certainly is not continued in terms of the establishing of normative teaching and practice for the Church; Eph. 2:20). This is reinforced by the theological view of the Spirit's various manifestations as eschatological.

4. The Spirit and the Charismata. In view of twentieth-century movements of the Spirit in the Church it is necessary here to mention specifically the more spectacular and psychologically unusual manifestations of the Spirit as cataloged in 1 Cor. 12:3-10, particularly prophecy and "tongues." The precise nature and manner of the functioning of these charismata are not stated specifically, so it is difficult exegetically to go beyond mere inferences. Present-day experiences identified with these gifts may provide much clarification. In any case it seems clear that though the manifestations of these charismata may have involved unusual ("Spirit-filled") states of consciousness they were generally not fully ecstatic. This is implied in the Pauline commands to exercise control over the expression of tongues or of prophecy. It is also stated as an explicit principle that "the spirits of prophets are subject to prophets" (1 Cor. 14:32).

In Pauline use prophecy is not the same as preaching or teaching but is an especially appropriate and powerful spontaneous utterance in the speaker's own language given to those present in worship for purposes of upbuilding, encouragement, and consolation (1 Cor. 14:3). Prophecy sometimes concerned the future and could be quite specific (1 Cor. 14:24f.; 2 Thess. 2:2; cf. Acts 11:27; 21:11). Such utterances were not to be uncritically received but were to be evaluated in relation to the criterion of the historical Jesus (1 Cor. 12:3) and by the Church as a whole (1 Cor. 14:29; 1 Thess. 5:19-21). Evidently gifts of discernment functioned here along with objective criteria related to apostolic teaching (1 Cor. 12:3; 2 Thess. 2:2). Prophecy was highly valued by Paul because of its value for the Church (1 Cor. 14:4). Therefore he urged all to seek with great intensity this manifestation of the Spirit even above the others, which they were also to seek (1 Cor. 14:1, 39).

Some question exists about the manifestations of tongues in Acts and that of which Paul speaks in the Corinthian situation. In Acts tongue-speaking clearly results from an unusual initiatory experience of the Spirit (Acts 2:4; 10:44-46; 19:6; cf. 8:18). The purpose was neither preaching the gospel nor upbuilding the Church as a worshiping community, but more a sign of receiving the Spirit. At least on Pentecost, the speaking was in known human languages (Acts 2:7-11). In the Corinthian circumstances internal evidence indicates that it was more self-initiated than a result of a sudden experience of the Spirit (1 Cor. 14:15, 27f.), and that its purpose was either as an individualized form of prayer (14:2, 4, 28), or, with the parallel gift of interpretation (which also could be sought; v. 13), as an equivalent to prophecy (v. 5), or as a sign to unbelievers who might be present (v. 22). Corporate or individual singing in tongues may have been practiced and encouraged by Paul (v. 15; Eph. 5:19; cf. Col. 3:16, "spiritual songs"). Paul seems to imply that all might speak in tongues (1 Cor. 14:5) but that only some exercised this gift and that of interpretation in the context of the worshiping community (1 Cor. 12:30). Further, in contrast to the picture presented in Acts, Corinthian tongues seem generally not to be known human languages (cf. "tongues of men and of angels"; 1 Cor. 13:1; "no one understands him, but he utters mysteries in the Spirit"; 14:2), though they are clearly languages of some sort because they bear a meaning that may be interpreted. There is no evidence whatsoever that Paul or any of the apostles used tongues as a means of preaching the gospel in their missionary efforts. The cessation and renewal of tongues and other of the more unusual charismata in the Church are historical rather than exegetical or theological matters.

5. The Spirit and the Christian Life. Most Pauline references to the Spirit relate to the individual Christian's inner experience and behavior as one totally determined by being "in the Spirit." They encompass the initial giving and receiving of the Spirit, the relation between the individual and the Church, and the ethical significance of being "in the Spirit," a concept uniquely and highly developed in Paul's writings.

As for the OT prophets, so for Paul the Holy Spirit was a gift from God, not something constitutive to man as man. Repeatedly Paul refers to this fact: "Now we have received not the spirit of the world, but the Spirit which is from God" (1 Cor. 2:12); "Your body is a temple of the Holy Spirit within you, which you have from God" (1 Cor. 6:19); "he [God] has . . . given us his Spirit in our hearts" (2 Cor. 1:22; see also 5:5; 11:4); "God has sent the Spirit of his Son into our hearts" (Gal. 4:6); "God, who gives his Holy Spirit to you" (1 Thess. 4:8). Paul correlates the fact of being given the Spirit by God with the actual reception of the Spirit in the individual Christian's experience. The very origin of the Christian life (as in Jn. 3:5) Paul attributes to the Spirit, which he describes as "renewal in the Holy Spirit" (Tit. 3:5). He epitomizes this point in his ethical injunction to the Galatians, "If [=since] we live by the Spirit, let us also walk by the Spirit" (Gal. 5:25). The Christian "lives by the Spirit" and the Spirit "dwells" in the Christian; the whole Christian life is premised upon this fact.

Paul deals with the reception of the Spirit most clearly in his Galatian Epistle. In refuting the error of the Judaizers and their legalism Paul states that Christ redeemed from the law "that we might receive [Gk. *lábōmen*] the promise of the Spirit through faith" (Gal. 3:14). Reception of the Spirit was not something merited or earned but a gift received by faith. In keeping with Acts and the Pauline pan-Pentecostal premise, however, this reception was not simply an acceptance of a divine fact but a definite experience to which Paul could appeal in his discussions with the Galatians. He asks them, "Did you receive the Spirit by works of the law, or by hearing with faith?" — a question that Paul knows can be answered not simply as a doctrinal affirmation but as an experience. The type of reception to which Paul refers is clearly the sort found in the Lukan descriptions in Acts. The whole dramatic episode of conversion-initiation with its suddenness and depth (repentance-faith), its active response in water baptism, and the crowning experience of the charismata, the outward, discernible manifestions of the Spirit, provides an unequivocal experience of reception of the Holy Spirit to which appeal could be made. Paul's further question, "Does he [Jesus] who supplies the Spirit to you and works miracles among you do so by works of the law, or by hearing with faith?" (Gal. 3:5), indicates this type of reception in no uncertain terms. Paul sees this same experience as universal to the Corinthians as they entered into the body of Christ, the sphere of the Holy Spirit who animates that body (1 Cor. 12:13). For Paul baptism by the exalted Jesus into the sphere of the Spirit is the basis both of diversity of manifestation of the Spirit and of a fundamental unity (1 Cor. 12:11).

Life in the Spirit is experienced in manifold ways. The Spirit is the source of divine love (Rom. 5:5), joy (1 Thess. 1:6; Rom. 14:17), and hope (Rom. 15:13), indeed of a whole constellation of moral and spiritual virtues, the "fruit of the Spirit" (Gal. 5:22f.). He leads the Christian (Rom. 8:14; Gal. 5:18), strengthens both his physical nature (Rom. 8:11) and his "inner man" (Eph. 3:16), produces a deep sense of sonship reflective of Jesus' own awareness (Rom. 8:15-17; Gal. 4:6; cf. Mk. 14:36), aids in prayer (Rom. 8:26, 27; Eph. 2:18; 6:18), enables him to "understand the gifts bestowed on us by God" (1 Cor. 2:12), teaches him (v. 13), is the source of any charismata he manifests (vv. 7, 11; 2 Tim. 1:6f.), provides the experience of true liberty in relation to the law (2 Cor. 3:17), inspires true worship both corporately and individually (Phil. 3:3; Eph. 5:18f.), and is generally the dynamic behind sanctification (2 Thess. 2:13).

This development of an all-encompassing activity of the Spirit in the life of the Christian, which combines enthusiastic, ethical, and eschatological elements into a unified whole, is the high point in the biblical doctrine of the Spirit in relation to the individual. Paul provides a balance between inner spiritual and moral renewal, "the fruit of the Spirit," and the proper functioning of the external manifestations of the Spirit, "the gifts of the Spirit," a balance found elsewhere only in the Johannine materials, yet without the corresponding balance of external, eschatological, and corporate elements.

6. The Spirit, the Law, and the Flesh. Two points of special significance in Paul's treatment of life in the Spirit are the contrast between law and Spirit and the struggle between flesh and Spirit. Paul does not fall into a false "perfectionism" in his awareness of the powerful present experience of the eschatological Spirit. Rather, he fully recognizes the element of struggle and conflict in the Christian life as well as its victory in anticipation of the final revelation of the "glorious liberty of the children of God" (Rom. 8:18-25).

One of the primary threats to true life in the Spirit was a threat from Paul's own background as a Pharisaic Jew, the threat of legalism. Law, as misunderstood in the Pharisaic tradition, reduces everything to the level of man's self-righteousness (Phil. 3:9) with its attendant tendency to self-adulation (Gal. 6:13-15) and bondage (Rom. 7:6; 8:15), and it leads ultimately to spiritual death (2 Cor. 3:6). The only law Paul acknowledges is the "law of the Spirit of life in Christ Jesus," which sets free "from the law of sin and death" (Rom. 8:2). This new law fulfils the requirements of the old (Rom. 13:10) without leading back to the error of self-justification (Gal. 2:15-21). So radical a disjunction did Paul see between the "letter of the law" and the Spirit who brings life and freedom (2 Cor. 3:6, 17) that to be under law is to be severed from Christ, outside the sphere of God's grace, and therefore not in the hope of righteousness through the Spirit (Gal. 5:3-5). Paul speaks of this disjunction in terms of death to the law and resurrection to a totally different sphere with a totally new relationship and life (Rom. 7:1-6). "Spirit" for Paul is no indefinite thing in comparison with the law but is quite vivid and precise so that one can not only enter into the life of the age to come as a result of the Spirit's activity but can also "walk in the Spirit," or conduct his total daily life "by the Spirit" (Gal. 5:18, 25).

Intimately connected with the contrast between the way of law and the way of the Spirit is the conflict between flesh and Spirit (spirit). The way of law is one expression of "the flesh" (Gal. 3:3). Paul uses the word "flesh" (Gk. *sárx*) in a variety of ways in his Epistles. Some uses are traditional and ethically neutral (see Rom. 3:20; 4:1; Gal. 1:16; etc.), but the most significant application of this term relates to the struggle and conflict between flesh and spirit (Rom. 8:1-9; Gal. 5:16-24). The primary significance of Paul's ethical use of the term "flesh" is man's functioning apart from the Holy Spirit. Paul makes this eminently clear by characterizing flesh as implacably hostile to God and spiritual things (Rom. 8:5-8), declaring that those occupied by the Spirit of God are "not in the flesh" but "in the Spirit" (v. 9). To be "in the flesh," then, is obviously not a matter of having bodily existence but of being in an inner state of separation from God, unresponsive to the activity of the Spirit and spiritually dead (Eph. 2:1). Such a state follows its own inner impulse leading to final corruption, even as walking in the Spirit (Paul uses the figure of "sowing") leads to the fulness of life (Gal. 6:8). This independence from God and from the influence of the Spirit is in constant conflict with the new principle (or "law of the Spirit of life in Christ Jesus"; Rom. 8:2). It accounts for spiritual conflict even in those who now enjoy the "first fruits" or "guarantee," through the Holy Spirit's indwelling, of the total redemption of the age to come (Rom. 7:13-25; Gal. 5:16-24). On the basis of the Spirit's indwelling, Paul exhorts and commands that Christians "live by the Spirit" (Gal. 5:25), i.e., as true "pneumatic Christians" (Gk. *pneumatikoí*), and not as "babes in Christ" or "men of the flesh" (Gk. *sárkinoi*; 1 Cor. 3:1-4). In experience it is through the Spirit that the flesh (="deeds of the body") is "put to death" (Rom. 8:13). Indeed, Christians are to be "aglow with the Spirit" (Rom. 12:11). This conflict between the flesh and the Spirit precludes any simplistic perfectionism or any passive acceptance of "the flesh" and leads into an ever increasing renewal in the image of God (Eph. 4:22f.; Col. 3:9f.) and in the image of the eschatological man of the Spirit, Jesus, now experienced as "spirit" (Rom. 8:29; 1 Cor. 15:45-49).

7. The Spirit and God. Paul's terminology for the Spirit indicates a continuity with the OT prophetic tradition in perceiving the Holy Spirit primarily as the dynamic presence and power of God. His teaching also reflects the post-Pentecostal experience of the Church, which understands the Spirit as emanating from Jesus Christ and as conditioned by the person and character of the historical Jesus. Thus both the deity and the personhood of the Spirit are implied.

Paul most frequently speaks of the "Holy Spirit" or "Spirit of God" rather than simply using the term "Spirit." In this he is true to his OT background. He conceives the Spirit as intimately connected with God, so much so that there is a special community of knowledge and will between God and the Spirit (Rom. 8:27; 1 Cor. 2:10f.). Yet even his mode of expression indicates the distinction between God as such and the Spirit. This is especially clear in the many references to God giving or sending His Spirit.

References to the relation between the Spirit and Jesus are rare but very significant, as demonstrated above ("Spirit of Christ," Rom. 8:9; "Spirit of his Son," Gal. 4:6; "Spirit of Jesus Christ," Phil. 1:19). Paul's teaching links the OT Spirit, which was conceived primarily in terms of God's presence and power, with Jesus, so that in turn Jesus' presence and power are mediated to the Christian through the Spirit. This close identification of Jesus and the Spirit provides further insight into the personhood of the Spirit. Paul speaks of grieving (Eph. 4:30) or quenching (1 Thess. 5:19) the Spirit, which also imply the personhood of the Spirit.

The Pauline association of the Spirit with "God" and with "the Lord Jesus Christ" in the apostolic benediction (2 Cor. 13:14), much as in the baptismal liturgical form in Mt. 28:19, attests the full coordination of the Spirit with God and the exalted Lord. This same harmony is found in 1 Cor. 12:4-6, which speaks of "same Spirit," "same Lord," "same God" in a direct parallel, and again in Tit. 3:4-6, which speaks of "God our Savior" pouring out the "Holy Spirit" through "Jesus Christ our Savior."

D. The Holy Spirit in the Johannine Writings. The Johannine interpretation of the Spirit in the Fourth Gospel, perhaps best understood in relation to growing institutionalism in the Church and an accompanying tendency toward a type of sacramentalism, emphasizes neither the external manifestations of the Spirit (as in Luke-Acts) nor the inner experience of the individual Christian sharing in the charismatic community of the Spirit (as in Paul). Rather, it emphasizes the immediacy of the relation of the individual disciple to Jesus through the Spirit. For John the Spirit is essentially *alter Christus*, "another counselor [Paraclete]" (Jn. 14:16) who comes from the glorified Jesus and takes His place.

John's Gospel is a marvelous example of the deep, penetrating, spiritual and theological grasp of the meaning of the person and history of Jesus that became possible after the Pentecostal effusion of the Spirit. In a sense, John himself is the example *par excellence* of the fulfillment of Jesus' own words regarding the Spirit's ministry, that "the Holy Spirit . . . will teach you all things, and bring to your remembrance all that I have said to you" (14:26) and "the Spirit of truth . . . will guide you into all truth; for he will not speak on his own authority, but whatever he hears he will speak" (16:13). John's presentation of Jesus has a unique style, a self-contained form and purpose, a careful reanalysis of the history of Jesus, and a clear relevance to his contemporary relation to the Church and the missionary task. Thus John clearly expresses the balance between the present and dynamic activity of the Spirit in the Church ("teaching" and "guiding") and the historical and normative significance of Jesus by which all genuine activity of the Spirit is determined ("all that I have said," "not on his own authority"). This balance requires that the background, situation, and purpose of John be especially kept in mind in attempts to grasp particular points in his presentation.

John presents the Spirit as especially related to the Jesus of history, perhaps more so even than Paul, but with a special awareness of Jesus' personal presence in the individual Christian's life and experience through the indwelling of the Spirit. This becomes clear at several points in John's presentation. He introduces Jesus as peculiarly endowed with the Spirit. The Spirit not only descended upon Jesus at Jordan (as the Synoptists note), but also remains upon Him (1:32). Thus Jesus is characterized as the one "who baptizes with the Holy Spirit" (Gk. *ho baptízōn en pneúmati hagíǭ*; v. 33). In his Gospel John never presents Jesus as fulfilling this role, but he does speak repeatedly of Jesus as the source of the Spirit for the individual Christian.

In 3:34 Jesus is again represented as uniquely endowed with the Spirit from the Father ("not by measure") for His ministry of proclamation of God's "words." The usual studied ambiguity of John's style allows Jesus also to be the one who gives the Spirit without measure. In Jesus' dialogue with the Samaritan woman, in symbolic reference to the Spirit through the image of "living water," He says He is the source of that water to all who ask Him (4:10) and that it becomes a wellspring of eternal life to the one receiving it (v. 14). The same thought is implied when Jesus, in the synagogue at Capernaum, presents His midrash on the text "He gave them bread from heaven to eat" (6:31). He says that "he who believes in me shall never thirst" (6:35).

John interprets Jesus' offer of "rivers of living water" to all who will believe in Him (7:38) as a reference to the giving of the Spirit by the glorified Jesus. From the perspective of the movement of salvation-history it is very important that the Spirit was not available (literally "the Spirit was not yet") to believers in the special way that Jesus alone can provide until He was "glorified" (i.e., until His death, resurrection, and ascension). This corresponds to the Lukan representation of Jesus as Lord of the Spirit only after His ascension (Acts 2:33). The same point is made in the Paraclete sayings: "It is to your advantage that I go away, for if I do not go away [i.e., ascend], the counselor [Paraclete] will not come to you; but if I go, I will send him to you" (16:7).

John ends his Gospel treatment of the relation of Jesus and the Spirit with a description of the risen Jesus acting as author of the life of the new age in clear parallelism to the account of man's original creation in Gen. 2:7 (Jn. 20:22). The LXX of Gen. 2:7 uses the same word as in Jn. 20:22 (Gk. *enephýsēsin*); significantly, the same root is used in Ezk. 37:9 (*emphýsēson*) with reference to the life-giving power of God's *rû(a)ḥ*. John clearly intends that Jesus be seen as the source both of the original creation as the divine Logos (1:1-3, 10) and of the new creation with its new life through the Spirit (cf. Jn. 3:5-8). John's emphasis on being born "from above" (Gk. *ánōthen*) in contrast to being born "of the flesh" or "of the earth" (3:31) is analogous to Paul's contrast of the "first Adam" or "man of dust" with the "last Adam" or "man of heaven" (1 Cor. 15:45).

The precise relation of this action of Jesus to the Pentecostal effusion recorded by Luke in Acts has been argued since the time of Theodore of Mopsuestia (A.D. 350-423). In terms of John's intention and the self-contained unity of the whole Gospel some have seen this as John's theological rendition of the historical Pentecost event, especially in view of references to Jesus' ascending (Jn. 20:17) and the immediate context for mission that precedes this action (v. 21) and follows it (v. 23). Internal evidence in John's work, however, indicates that he does not simply transpose theology into history, and the references to the earlier giving of the Spirit do not seem well fulfilled by the simple, symbolic action of breathing. Therefore it seems best to interpret this action as the initial impartation of the life of the new age, of resurrection life, the eternal life that is John's chief concern in writing his Gospel (v. 31). If this is correct, then Jesus' action, which takes place after the Resurrection but before the Ascension, bears the same relation to His effusion of the Spirit at Pentecost as quickening does to endowing (cf. the comms. on John by F. Godet [2 vols., repr. 1978] and B. F. Westcott [repr. 1954]).

A deep theological principle is involved in this distinction between the new life of the age to come, which derives from the Resurrection, and the new power of that age, which derives from Jesus' exaltation to the right hand of the Father. It thereby becomes clear that *in principle* the reality of the Christian experience of the Holy Spirit is separable into two aspects, new life and new power. It must be noted, however, that what the disciples experienced as two distinct events separated in time was the result of their unique position in relation to the transition of the stages of salvation-history. In the early Church, as has already been pointed out, there was no such separation in time (though the new life and new power were yet separable in principle; cf. Acts 8:14-17). The normative experience in the early Church was the experience both of new life as conversion and of new power as charismatic manifestation in one dramatic episode of initiation into the community of the Spirit.

In the unique Johannine material on the Holy Spirit as the Paraclete the close personal identification of the Spirit with Jesus becomes especially evident. Only in the Fourth Gospel is the Holy Spirit designated as the Paraclete (RSV "Counselor"; Gk. *paráklētos*). The word itself, which means literally "one called alongside," has multiple meanings, depending on interpretation of the Greek etymology. Literally, the noun indicates "defense attorney." If the verb *parakaleín* is taken as the background, then the word means "an intercessor" (RSV "advocate"; 1 Jn. 2:1) or "a comforter" or "consoler." If the noun *paráklēsis* is taken, the idea of "exhorter" or "encourager" prevails. All of these have some validity in expressing the complex ministry of the Holy Spirit. To allow the full range of possibilities of meaning it may be best simply to transliterate and speak only of the "Paraclete," allowing John's own rich usage to fill in the meaning of the term.

The Paraclete is above all an *alter Christus*, both a substitute for ("another Paraclete," Gk. *állon paráklēton*; 14:16) and a continuation (14:18) of the presence and ministry of Jesus. This substitution/continuation is only possible after the Ascension (16:7) in keeping with the Synoptic understanding. A comparison of Jesus' ministry with the future ministry of the Paraclete reveals a striking similarity, already implied by the reference to the Paraclete as "another Paraclete" (14:16). This means that Jesus is a Paraclete too. Both come from the Father (13:3; 14:26); both are sent (5:36f.; 15:26); both are related to the truth (Jesus is the Truth, 14:6 and the Paraclete is the "Spirit of truth," 15:26); both somehow remain in the disciple (compare 14:17 with vv. 20, 23); both are rejected by the world (14:17; 15:18); both testify against the world (7:7; 16:8). Moreover, there is a parallelism between the relation of Jesus to the Father and that of the Paraclete and Jesus, so that what Jesus is to the Father the Paraclete is to Jesus (cf. 5:19, 30; 14:13; 15:26; 16:13f.). This emphasis on the continuing relation of the believer with the glorified Lord clearly solves the problems related to a growing institutionalism and sacramentalism in the Church as well as those arising from the unexpected delay in the return of Jesus. In a significant sense later generations of believers are no more distant from Jesus' personal presence than the first (17:20) because Jesus is present through the Paraclete, having already returned functionally in the Spirit's coming.

The ministry of the Spirit/Paraclete in the life of the individual Christian is very rich. He is the source of his life (3:5-8). He is the "dimension" in which genuine worship takes place — a worship "in spirit," i.e., in charismatic, Spirit-inspired worship (4:24). He makes His home within the believer (14:17), teaching all the necessary things and guiding into all the truth — but only in relation to Jesus Himself as source, subject, and norm (14:26; 16:13-15). His presence with and in the believer is the prerequisite for the mission of the disciples (20:21-23), and through them the Paraclete will be a witness to Jesus (15:26f.) and will serve as a prosecuting attorney against the world for its sin and unbelief (16:7-11). The believer's ministry in charismatic power is also clearly related to the activity of the Spirit when Jesus promises that the one who believes in Him "will also do the works that I do; and greater works than these will he do, because I go to the Father" (14:12; cf. 16:7: "It is to your advantage that I go away").

In the first Epistle the Spirit's rich ministry is specifically related to the contemporary situation. The Spirit is the anointing given to each Christian and teaches truth (1 Jn. 2:20, 26f.). He is the "spirit of truth" in opposition to the "spirit of error" (4:6) and provides the relevant discernment of any "spirit" or spiritual experience (4:1-3). Indeed, He is the witness along with the history of Jesus, "water and blood," to Jesus' incarnation and deity (4:2; 5:7-9, 20). The giving of the Spirit to the believer is the evidence that assures the believer that God abides in him and he in God (3:24; 4:13). The individualism of all this should be noted, for very little explicitly points to the Pauline emphasis on the Church as the body of Christ charismatically ordered and endued. Also significant, in the Paraclete teachings the full personhood of the Spirit is clearly and strongly presented both in the grammar (masculine pronoun with neuter noun; Jn. 14:26; 15:26; 16:13) and in the close identification of the Spirit and Jesus as a kind of tandem.

The materials in the Apocalypse do not add a great deal. There is an interesting triadic coordination of the Spirit (as the sevenfold spirit of fulness) with God and Jesus Christ (Rev. 1:4). The Spirit is clearly presented here as the OT Spirit of prophecy (22:6), who speaks prophetically to the seven churches (2:7, 11, 17; etc.) and who is the ecstatic source of the visions recorded in the book (1:10; 4:2; 17:3; 21:10). The Spirit, in conjunction with the Church as the bride of Christ, invites all to enter into the life of the glorious age to come (22:17).

E. The Holy Spirit in Other NT Writings. The remaining NT documents add little to the understanding of the Holy Spirit beyond the three basic strands of NT teaching already surveyed. The Epistles of James, 2 and 3 John, and Philemon do not mention the Spirit at all. In Hebrews the Spirit is related mostly to the Scripture (He. 3:7; 9:8; 10:15). In 2:4 reference is made to charismatic manifestations of the Spirit in establishing the apostolic mission. In 6:4f. it is noted that Christian initiation, described in the comprehensive sense of enlightenment (Gk. *phōtisthéntas*), involves above all contact with and participation in the Holy Spirit and experience of the word (*rhḗma*) of God and the manifestations of the Spirit perceived as the "powers of the age to come." In view of 4:12, which speaks of the word of God (*lógos toú theoú*) in terms of the Spirit's almost personal presence (cf. the Pauline equation of the "word of God" [*rhḗma theoú*] with the "sword of the Spirit" [Eph. 6:17]), it appears that even the phrase "word of God" in He. 6:5 might be construed as a manifestation of the Spirit (perhaps of prophecy); thus all of the elements in Christian initiation are related to the Spirit or His activity. The death of Christ is portrayed as a high-priestly sacrifice offered through the "eternal Spirit" effecting purification of the conscience and thereby allowing true service to God (9:14). The Spirit is called the "Spirit of grace" in 10:29, a phrase which admirably describes both the Spirit and His overall ministry.

In 1 Pet. 1:10f. the Spirit in OT prophecy is specifically identified with the "Spirit of Christ," and 2 Pet. 1:21 strongly affirms that all true OT prophecy was initiated by the Holy Spirit rather than by the prophet. Christians are said to be "sanctified by the Spirit" (1 Pet. 1:2), and the good news is proclaimed "through the Holy Spirit sent from heaven" (1:12), a clear reference to the events of Pentecost. The Spirit is described as the "spirit of glory and of God" in 1 Pet. 4:14, an apt phrase for the eschatological Spirit. Indeed, the phrase sums up the diverse biblical portrayal of the essence of the Holy Spirit's total ministry as it moves from creation to new creation, from "this age" to the "age to come," the age of the Spirit, the age of doxophany. Jude speaks only of those "devoid of the Spirit" in contrast to those "who pray in the Holy Spirit" (Jude 19f.).

III. Summary: The Development and Significance of the Biblical Doctrine of the Holy Spirit.–The biblical doctrine of the Holy Spirit is the doctrine of God immanent and active in the experience of His people, a doctrine that begins and ends with experience. The primitive imagery underlying the biblical notion of spirit (Heb. *rû(a)ḥ*) is that of violent power encountered in human experiences within the dimensions of depth, mystery, and power. These experiences can be clearly perceived from the basic root meanings and uses of *rû(a)ḥ* — "hard breathing," "wind," and "dominating impulse or disposition of an individual."

This phenomenology of religious experience, first encountered in OT religion, is overwhelmingly construed by the biblical writers not in terms of philosophy or science, but in terms of the God who acts, the covenant God of Abraham, Isaac, and Jacob in the OT. Thus, in the OT, the points at which references to the Spirit emerge in the material are all theocratically oriented. The preponderance of the references to the Spirit in the OT pertain to the prophets' calling or state, to charismatic powers given to the leadership of Israel, or to the presence of God experienced as tremendous power and energy (*mysterium tremendum*).

A developmental process, however, may be perceived in the other OT references to the Spirit. The most significant development was in the eschatological framework of OT religion. The great prophets of Israel increasingly refer to the Spirit in terms of a coming glorious kingdom initiated by the Spirit (Isa. 32:15), ruled by a Davidic king especially endued by the Spirit (Isa. 11:1-10; 42:1; 61:1), and characterized by a general effusion of the Spirit upon the people through both inner renewal (Ezk. 36:26f.) and charismatic endowment (Joel 2:28 [MT 3:1]).

In the intertestamental period the only significant development of the doctrine of the Spirit was its increased intellectualization as seen in the wisdom writers and in Philo's Platonic interpretations of OT materials. The trauma of the Exile and return, the cessation of recognized prophetic activity, the state of constant servility to gentile powers, plus increased contact with Greek religious and philosophical speculations did produce a more explicitly apocalyptic understanding of the coming glorious kingdom. In particular the concept of history as divided into "this age" and "the age to come" is significant because of its adoption by Jesus and the early Church in explicating the OT eschatological materials.

Therefore, the OT demonstrates a development from the primary religious phenomenology of the Spirit through a theocratic understanding of that Spirit active in Israel's religious and political life to a state of expectation of a final glorious age and kingdom in which the presence, power, and activity of the Spirit are characteristic.

In the NT both fulfillment and expectation are represented. After centuries of prophetic silence in Israel, in quick succession came John the Baptizer with an arousing message ("Repent, for the kingdom of heaven is at hand"; Mt. 3:2), and Jesus of Nazareth proclaiming "the time is fulfilled, and the kingdom of God is at hand; repent, and believe in the gospel" (Mk. 1:15). Both came with a sense of urgency and immediacy. The apocalyptic inbreaking of the age to come was imminent. John saw his own message and baptism as preparatory to the "one who was coming," characterized as uniquely the man of the Spirit, who baptizes in the Spirit (Mk. 1:7f.; Lk. 3:16f.; Mt. 3:11f.; Jn. 1:26f., 33). Jesus perceived Himself as one anointed with this Spirit (Lk. 4:18f.; Isa. 61:1f.), already exercising by this same Spirit the powers of the age to come (Mt. 12:28; Lk. 11:20). Therefore, in a sense the age to come was already present in the ministry of Jesus. It was confined to Him alone until the events of the Passion, Resurrection, and Ascension were completed, when He became the Lord of the Spirit who received the "promise of the Father" (Acts 1:4) and who then baptized His waiting disciples in the Spirit on the day of Pentecost. Thus His ministry as the anointed man of the Spirit (the Messiah) was vindicated and the age of the Spirit was inaugurated more fully through the creation of the community of the Spirit (the Church) in fulfillment of Joel's prophecy (Acts 2:16, 33-36).

The early Church viewed itself as a "colony" of the age to come, experiencing the mighty workings of the Spirit both in terms of charismatic powers in the OT tradition of the Holy Spirit's theocratic activity and in terms of inner renewal, in fulfillment of the new covenant expectations of Jeremiah and Ezekiel. This can be seen in Paul's use of the comprehensive phrases "in Christ" (Rom. 8:1; 2 Cor. 5:17) and the equivalent "in the Spirit" (Rom. 8:9; cf. Gal. 5:25), as well as the specific notions of "the fruit of the Spirit" (Gal. 5:22f.) and "the gifts of the Spirit" (1 Cor. 12:4-11). The writer to the Hebrews encapsulated this, describing Christians as those who have "tasted the goodness of the word of God and the powers of the age to come" (He. 6:5).

The experience of the early Church was radically determined by its experience of the Spirit of the age to come, encountered only as the Spirit of Messiah, of Jesus. It cannot be understood apart from this experience. This is clearly seen in all strands of NT writings, including Luke-Acts, which stresses the external and charismatic experiences of the Spirit, Paul, who weaves together into a complex pattern both external manifestations and inner renewal, and the Johannine tradition, which highlights Jesus as the source of the Spirit (Jn. 7:37-39) and the full, present experience of the life of the age to come through the Spirit (Jn. 3:5).

Despite the emphases on the present realization of the future age of the Spirit, the community of the Spirit still anticipated the consummation of the OT promises of that age in terms of the parousia of Jesus. The Spirit was experienced now in reality, but only as a "pledge" (Gk. *arrabṓn*; RSV "guarantee"; Eph. 1:14) or as the "first fruits" (*aparchḗ*; Rom. 8:23) of the final manifestation of the glory of that age.

Only when understood in terms of the fundamental biblical framework of eschatology does the full meaning of the biblical teaching of the Holy Spirit attain final perspective and significance. In the biblical materials the "final cause" — the ultimate category of interpretation, the point of reference that provides the most universal scope — for the unfolding drama of creation and history is doxophany, the full manifestation of the glory of God. The doxology of Paul expresses it succinctly: "For from him and through him and to him are all things. To him be glory for ever. Amen" (Rom. 11:36). The song of the twenty-four elders before the throne of God is eloquent: "Worthy art thou, our Lord and God, to receive glory and honor and power, for thou didst create all things, and by thy will they existed and were created" (Rev. 4:11). All of this fulfils God's OT promises concerning the future age as that of His coming glory (Nu. 14:21; Isa. 11:9; 60:19; Hab. 2:14). In the NT this is adapted in terms of the light of glory from "God and . . . the Lamb" (Rev. 21:23; 22:5).

From this ultimate eschatological perspective the Holy Spirit is the "Spirit of Glory" (1 Pet. 4:14) — the eschatological glory of doxophany! To miss this point is to reduce the Spirit and the experience of the Spirit (whether charismatic or inner renewal) to a man-centered level. The role of the Spirit must not be seen simply in terms of creation or the redemptive process, but in terms of the glory of God. All the activity of the Spirit leads to doxophany in the created order and full doxology from all creation: "And I heard every creature in heaven and on earth and under the earth and in the sea, and all therein, saying, 'To him who sits upon the throne and to the Lamb be blessing and honor and glory and might for ever and ever!'" (Rev. 5:13).

Bibliography.–C. K. Barrett, *The Holy Spirit and the Gospel Tradition* (1947); H. Berkhof, *Doctrine of the Holy Spirit* (1964); R. E. Brown, *Gospel According to John II* (*AB*, 1970), 1135-1144; F. D. Bruner, *Theology of the Holy Spirit* (1970); R. Bultmann, *Theology of the NT*, I (Eng. tr. 1951), 153-164; C. H. Dodd, *Interpretation of the Fourth Gospel* (1970), pp. 213-227; J. D. G. Dunn, *Baptism in the Holy Spirit* (1970); *Jesus and the Spirit* (1975); M. Green, *I Believe in the Holy Spirit* (1975); J. H. E. Hull, *Holy Spirit in the Acts of the Apostles* (1967); A. Kuyper, *Work of the Holy Spirit* (1900); J. Lindblom, *Prophecy in Ancient Israel* (1962); J. Owen, *Pneumatologia* (repr. 1971); M. Ramsey, *Holy Spirit* (1977); H. W. Robinson, *Christian Experience of the Holy Spirit* (1928); N. H. Snaith, *Distinctive Ideas of the OT* (1964), pp. 143-158; G. Smeaton, *Doctrine of the Holy Spirit* (1958); H. B. Swete, *Holy Spirit in the NT* (1910); *TDNT*, VI, *s.v.* πνεῦμα, πνευματικός (Kleinknecht, Baumgärtel, Bieder, Sjöberg, Schweizer); J. R. Williams, *Era of the Spirit* (1971).

D. A. TAPPEINER

History of the Doctrine

I. Credal and Baptismal Witness.–As in the case of the Father and the Son, the baptismal formula and the creeds constitute basic evidence for the thinking of the Church on the being and role of the Holy Spirit. The church order known as the *Didache* confirms the practice of baptism in the name of the Father, Son, and Holy Spirit, probably in connection with the threefold immersion or pouring that is also prescribed. Second-century creeds express faith in the Father, the Son, and the Holy Spirit the Paraclete, with whom is associated the Church and also forgiveness or resurrection. In the Hippolytan rite of baptism (*ca.* 200) the credal interrogatory puts as the third question, "Dost thou believe in the Holy Spirit, in the holy church, and in the resurrection of the flesh?" and when the answer, "I believe," is given, the candidate is dipped the third and final time. The anointing which follows is also given in the name of the Father Almighty, and Jesus Christ, and the Holy Spirit.

II. The Spirit and Baptism.–One often hears the complaint that the Church has neglected the doctrine of the Holy Spirit. A glance at early baptismal thinking and practice will quickly show how untrue this is. From the very outset the Spirit plays an important role in relation to the baptismal remission and regeneration. In Hermas the white robe symbolizes the Spirit (Sim. 8:2:2f.). In Barnabas the Holy Spirit comes to indwell the believer and effects a new creation. Justin views Christian baptism as a baptism with the Spirit imparting enlightenment, forgiveness, and regeneration (*Apol.* 61). Irenaeus finds in the Spirit who is given at baptism a pledge of eternal life. Clement of Alexandria links regeneration with the Spirit, who is also the stamp or impress made on the believer at baptism. Origen speaks of baptism in Christ, in water, and in the Holy Spirit (*De prin.* ii.10.7).

Most of the early writers plainly associate baptism itself with the Spirit, who does the true baptismal work. In the West, however, a tendency develops to relate baptism to forgiveness and then to link the Spirit more narrowly with the included but ensuing anointing and laying on of hands. Tertullian holds this view in his work *De baptismo*. He describes the new birth as a work of the Spirit and then says that the Spirit is not received in the water. Rather, one invokes the Spirit by the laying on of hands (8). Developing this understanding, some third-century authors could even argue that the gift of the Spirit does not come with baptism at all, baptism with the Spirit being differentiated from water baptism and related exclusively to anointing and the laying on of hands. Cyprian in Carthage resisted this conclusion. He argued that those baptized in an emergency, without the laying on of hands, still receive the Spirit. He was not insensitive, however, to the fact that in Acts 8 the imparting of the Spirit comes, not with Philip's baptism, but with the apostles' laying on of hands.

The 4th and 5th cents. display no little confusion in this area. On the one side the relating of baptism to the work and gift of the Spirit finds strong support, as in Athanasius, Hilary, Cyril of Jerusalem (*Catechetical Lectures*), and Augustine. On the other side the descent of the Spirit is strongly associated with anointing, sometimes even in the same writers, e.g., Hilary and Cyril (cf. especially his *Mystagogical Lectures,* although their authenticity is in serious question). In explanation of this view appeal is made to the texts in Acts and also to the descent of the Spirit on Jesus after His baptism.

How could the apparent contradiction be reconciled? In a sense it did not have to be, for baptism, anointing, and the laying on of hands all formed parts of the same rite. Since, however, external separation might take place, and with the rapid increase of infant baptisms did so in the West, some solution had to be offered. Two related lines of thinking may be noted in this regard. The first is that with the anointing or laying on of hands the Spirit confers a strengthening, fortifying, or perfecting of those who have remission and regeneration in baptism. Hence the laying on of hands came to be known as confirmation. The second is that this strengthening is with the sevenfold gift of the Holy Spirit. Hence the Spirit could be associated with baptism in respect of the new birth and still connected with the anointing or the laying on of hands in respect of His fortifying gift or gifts.

III. The Spirit and Scripture.–If the Holy Spirit figured prominently in the baptismal thinking and practice of the first centuries, he claimed no less attention in the important sphere of the inspiration of Scripture. Here again the testimony goes back to the first period and is uniform throughout. Such diverse writers as Origen, Basil, and Jerome can all describe the Bible as written by the Holy Spirit. Inspiration is seen as applying equally to every book and to Scripture as a whole. All its writers were moved by the same Spirit and everything they wrote, including such details as lists of names, must be regarded as inspired, reliable, and profitable. As Jerome says, every word, syllable, accent, and point is "packed with meaning" (*On Eph.* 2).

In the earliest period, when the NT canon was still in process of formation, the importance of the inspiration of the OT was appreciated, as one sees from Justin Martyr. Both in small points and in its totality the OT is a prophecy of Jesus Christ. Only in the light of its fulfillment in the gospel can one understand its true meaning. The unity of the OT and NT, rejected by Marcion, is obviously based on their inspiration by the same Spirit. As He who inspired the OT the Spirit is often called "the prophetic Spirit." When Christ comes, the Spirit, who is the Spirit of Christ, imparts His gift to the Church instead of Israel. In this instance the gift is supremely that of understanding the prophetic writings (*Dial.* 82.7ff.). Irenaeus speaks similarly. Through the Spirit the prophets prophesied and at the end of the age he was poured out in a new way, renewing man to God. The emphasis on the Spirit's role in the composition of the OT finds an echo in the Nicene affirmation: Who spake by the prophets.

How did the Spirit work in the writing of Scripture? An early writer like the apologist Athenagoras suggested that the prophets spoke and wrote in an ecstatic state and that the Spirit played on them like a flute player (*Legatio* 7,9). This view, which was parallel to that of Philo, found support in Tertullian (*Adv. Marc.* iv.22) and is still heard in Chrysostom when he compares the apostolic authors to instruments on whom the Spirit played (*Hom. 1 in Jn.*). If it was ever a majority view, however, it came into discredit through Montanus and his associate prophetesses, who issued strange babblings, spoke as though they were the direct mouthpiece of God, and fell into a trance as they spoke. The Montanists, of course, are said to have laid claim to new revelations by the Spirit (Hippolytus *Ref.* vii.12), but the very mode of their prophesying scandalized the churches. Since Montanus himself used the figure of a lyre — "man is as a lyre and I fly over it like a plectrum" (Epiphanius *Haer.* 48) — it is not unnatural that the movement should promote a rethinking of the relation of the Spirit to the inspired prophetic and apostolic authors.

The third-century fathers and their successors still found a special ministry of the Holy Spirit in the composition of Scripture but they now defined inspiration in such a way as normally to give the authors an active and conscious role. Hippolytus, e.g., defined inspiration primarily as a clarifying of the mind, Origen as an apprehending of truth, Augustine as a stimulation and control that would rule out mistakes. In all this the authors would ordinarily engage in their own thinking, exercise freedom of will, rely on their memories and research, and display their individualities in style and expression. Augustine and Theodore even distinguished types or levels of inspiration, although not, of course, to the point of a differentiation between inspired and uninspired portions of Scripture.

As the Holy Spirit inspired Scripture, so He brought the illumination without which it could not be properly understood. The fathers differed in their procedures of interpretation. The Alexandrians, for example, favored allegorizing, whereas the Antiochenes stood for a more natural exegesis. All agreed, however, that a Christian understanding of the OT, and of its unity with the NT, involves the typological or christological exposition which rests on a total perception of the theme of Scripture that only the Holy Spirit can give. This is why illumination figures so persistently in the baptismal descriptions of the Spirit's work.

IV. The Spirit and the Trinity.–*A. The Early Period.* If the idea of a doctrinal neglect of the Spirit has merit, it can be only in the trinitarian sphere, where the dominant theme tends to be that of the relation of God and Christ. Even here, however, the Holy Spirit has a place in the discussions from the very first. Thus 1 Clement speaks of one Spirit as well as one God and one Christ (46:6). Ignatius of Antioch uses a fanciful image in which the Father builds up Christians as stones in His temple, Christ's cross is the derrick, and the Holy Spirit is the rope. Hermas tends to confuse the Son and the Spirit (Sim. 9:1), but if anything he is happier with the deity of the preexistent Spirit than with that of Christ, who seems to be adopted because the Spirit dwells in Him. Justin, too, shows some confusion, although in his case the focus is on God and the Logos. To be sure, Justin refers frequently to the holy prophetic Spirit, and he has a third person in view, but he seems to have difficulty in distinguishing between the Spirit and the Logos. Athenagoras could speak of the Spirit as a divine effluence and Theophilus identified Him with Wisdom (as distinct from Word). The prophetic ministry of the Spirit, however, was the main thing to capture the interest of the Apologists. Irenaeus, like Theophilus, equated Spirit and Wisdom as he equated Son and Word. Word and Wisdom were with God before the world was, and both were used by God in creation and self-revelation.

B. The Third Century. Thinking about the Spirit shared in the advances and problems of general trinitarian thinking during the period from the Apologists to Nicea. Concern for the divine unity led modalists to see in the Spirit, as in the Father and the Son, only a temporal mode of the one God for the purpose of His external works. A similar concern lay behind the adoptionist view that the man Jesus was deified when the Spirit, or Christ, came upon Him, the Spirit, of course, having no distinctive being in God. Meeting the two forms of monarchianism, Tertullian and Hippolytus contended for the otherness of the Spirit (and the Son) even within the oneness of the deity. As Tertullian saw it, the Spirit as the vicar of the Son proceeds from the Father through the Son (*Adv. Prax.* 4). The term *persona* commended itself as a suitable one to express the element of individuality within the one essential being. Origen had much the same in mind when he used the Gk. *hypóstasis*. As *hypóstasis* the Spirit derives from the Father through the mediation of the Son. Origen, of course, could used extremely subordinationist terms, as when he said that the power of the Father is greater than that of the Son, and that of the Son greater than that of the Spirit (*De prin.* i.3). Against this, however, should be set his concept of essential consubstantiality (iv.1.1).

C. The Nicene Theology. Arianism so focused attention on the status of the Son that little attention was paid at first to the Spirit. The creed of Nicea (A.D. 325) simply repeated the affirmation: I believe in the Holy Spirit. Nevertheless, Arians saw that if the Son is not truly God, neither is the Spirit. Indeed, Eunomius could regard the Spirit as the supreme creation of the Son. By the middle of the 4th cent., then, the deity of the Spirit emerged as an issue of its own. Cyril of Jerusalem described the Spirit as eternal, subsistent, and present with the Father (*Catecheses* xvii.5). Athanasius insisted that the Spirit comes from the Father, not from nothingness, is consubstantial with the Father and the Son (*Ad Serap.*1), and works with the Father in creation, inspiration, and incarnation (3). Semi-Arians, however, resisted this view, and a group named the Pneumatomachians (later the Macedonians) contended for a likeness, not a oneness, of substance, and gave to the Spirit the position of neither God nor creature. The Cappadocians finally corrected this aberration. Basil in his work *On the Holy Spirit* (375) ranked the Spirit with the Father and the Son, although not specifically calling him God. Gregory of Nyssa argued for a oneness of nature shared by the divine persons (*Oratio catechetica* 3). Gregory of Nazianzus plainly accepted the consubstantiality and deity of the Spirit (*Oratio* 31). As regards the relation of the Spirit to the Father and the Son, Gregory of Nyssa spoke of procession from the Father and reception from the Son, from whom He is not to be separated. This underlies the common formula: "From the Father through the Son." Meanwhile, Hilary, Ambrose, and Augustine completed the doctrine of the trinity in the West. Augustine strongly supported the equality of the divine persons. The whole trinity acts externally, although with specific "appropriations." The true distinction is in the inner relations. The Spirit is the bond of union and is thus the Spirit of the Father and also of the Son. How His procession differs from the Son's generation, Augustine cannot explain, but it is procession from the Father and the Son, although the Father is still the source of deity, since it is He who begets the Son from whom the Spirit also proceeds.

D. The Filioque. Augustine's phrase "from the Father and the Son [*filioque*]" was later to prove a source of friction between the eastern and western churches. These shared the Nicene Creed, which in its 381 version described the Spirit as simply "proceeding from the Father," with whom, as with the Son, He is worshiped and glorified together. In 447, however, a council at Toledo in Spain espoused the phrase "and from the Son [*filioque*]" and a further council at Toledo recited it in the creed in 589. In spite of its popularity in the West, Rome at first refused to accept the addition, but by 867 Constantinople excommunicated Rome for including the new clause. A main reason for the rift would seem to have been the ecclesiastical one of a credal alteration without consultation, but quickly theological arguments for and against the filioque were developed. Since the Reformation churches sided with Rome on the issue, the disagreement between East and West has continued to the present day, although Anglicans have shown some readiness to return to the original statement. The divergence can hardly be regarded as a crucial one, however, and a formula like "proceeding from the Father through the Son" would seem to provide an acceptable basis of theological reconciliation. Ruffled ecclesiastical feelings might be harder to settle, even after a thousand years and more.

V. The Spirit and the Word.–*A. Inner Witness of the Spirit.* The fathers, as we have seen, can only in ignorance be accused of ignoring the Holy Spirit. The same applies to the Reformers. Indeed, Calvin could be appropriately described as the theologian, not of election, but of the Holy Spirit, or of the Spirit and the Word. In this regard he is representative of many others. The Reformation doctrine of the inner testimony of the Holy Spirit points clearly in this direction. For the Reformers Scripture as God's Word has ultimate authority in the Church. But how can we be sure that it is God's Word? Because the Church says so? Because it has features (indicia or criteria) which prove it to be so? At most these can be only secondary grounds and can never give the certainty required. Does Scripture, then, bear witness to itself? It does, but not in isolation. To the self-witness of the Word is added the inner testimony of the Spirit who alone can provide us with the necessary assurance as to the divine nature and authority of the written Word.

B. Illumination. Nor does the Holy Spirit merely give assurance that Scripture is God's Word. In so doing, He speaks God's Word through Scripture in such a way that it is understood. The Spirit who inspired the authors also illumines the readers and hearers. Biblical hermeneutics involves many activities ranging from textual or lexical study to prayer. For a proper understanding, however, the expository work of the Spirit is needed too. This work of the Spirit is not mystical, of course, for it relates strictly to the Word, which is also its own interpreter. Yet the Word must be read in the Spirit if its real sense is to be apprehended, its saving truth appropriated, and its authority put into effect.

C. Effectual Calling. In and with the Word, the Spirit issues the divine call which not only gives enlightenment but at the same time brings sinners to repentance and faith. Hence the Christian life cannot even begin without the Spirit's work. Differences arise in relation to the human activity at this point. Yet all the main Reformation groups, Arminians as well as Dortians, recognize that without this prior ministry of the Spirit the possibility of human activity does not exist. In its own way the calling of the Spirit through the Word is no less vital to salvation than the reconciling work of Christ in His death and resurrection.

D. Renewal. As the Holy Spirit bears witness to the Word, brings its meaning to light, and through it issues the call that leads to personal faith, so through the Word the Spirit does the work of regeneration and renewal that includes mortification and sanctification as well as the beginning of the new life in Christ. As Calvin says, we are washed in Christ's blood by the Spirit and through the same indwelling Spirit we are mortified and sanctified. If the Christian life cannot begin, it cannot continue either without the ongoing ministry of the Spirit and the Word.

E. Faith. A special role is played in the Christian life by faith. Yet faith, by which alone we are justified before God, is the principal work of the Spirit, by whom Christ unites us to Himself. The Spirit is, in Calvin's phrase, the "inner teacher" by whom the promise of salvation penetrates the mind. Faith depends on the Word, yet on account of human blindness and obstinacy the Word cannot engender faith without the Spirit's enlightening of the mind and strengthening of the heart. Nor does the Spirit merely initiate faith; he also increases it. To come to faith in Christ, and to grow in Him, we have to be lifted above our own understanding. This can take place only as the Spirit does not let the Word flit about in the brain but pours it into the mind and confirms it in the heart, Himself serving as a seal and guarantee of the divine promises.

F. The Sacraments. In the strengthening of faith the Spirit works not only through the written and spoken Word but also through the visible Word of the sacraments. What the sacraments promise, the Spirit reveals and fulfils. By the Word and sacraments the Spirit ministers in us so that they do not merely strike our ears or eyes but enter into our hearts. Without the Spirit, baptism and the eucharist can do nothing. They can serve, but the Spirit alone has the power to act. It is because this power can be put forth in infants too that baptism may be extended to them. Similarly it is by the Spirit that Christ grants fellowship with His body, and one may thus speak of feeding on Him at the eucharist. Christ Himself is truly present at His table; He is present in the mode of the Holy Spirit.

G. Charisms. In Reformation theology the Holy Spirit gives graces (or charisms) to the Church, but only some of those listed in Romans and 1 Corinthians, namely, government and almsgiving, are thought to be permanent. In apostolic days the Spirit visibly gave additional wonderful gifts through the laying on of hands, but these served the special purpose of magnifying the new preaching and they have now ceased. The Spirit Himself remains. He still endows the Church. Yet He does His present work by less spectacular means. As they saw it, the historical fact of the cessation of the gifts — even when the laying on of hands continued — demonstrates their temporary nature.

H. Sin Against the Spirit. The sin against the Spirit is to be seen in the light of His preeminent role in bringing people to understanding and faith. When unbelievers attack God's truth in ignorance they sin against the Father and the Son, and this may be forgiven them. But when they continue this attack even though they know that what they reject is indeed God's Word, they sin against the Spirit, resisting the illumination which is His work, and for this there neither is nor can be any forgiveness. When knowledge, not ignorance, is joined with unbelief, forgiveness has no place.

I. General Grace. While the Holy Spirit brings salvation only by the Word and sacraments, He also does a work of general grace by which the human race is preserved from destruction and receives many real if not eternal blessings. For believers and unbelievers alike achievements are thus possible in the arts and the sciences. The Spirit is the Spirit of all truth, and knowledge of everything good in life is given us through Him. Special or individual graces may indeed be given to certain people within the common grace; hence their outstanding contributions in the various spheres of human life. Nevertheless, in spite of the common grace or individual graces, even those who most excel can have no knowledge of God apart from the saving grace of the Spirit that frees the ears to hear and the heart to understand. From the time of the Reformation the concept of general or common grace has had a fixed place in the doctrine of the Holy Spirit, especially among Dutch theologians. It is not to be confused, however, with the grace of salvation that is the Spirit's proper work.

***VI. The Spirit and Immanence.**–A. Unitarianism.* The various unitarian views of God that arose in the 17th cent. all tended to depersonalize the Spirit. Instead of seeing the Spirit as the third person of the trinity, Himself God, they identified Him directly with God — God is Spirit — or depicted Him as the power of God at work in the world. Indeed pantheism, equating God and the world soul, could even find in the Spirit the self-consciousness of the universe. Along these lines Hegelian Idealism is basically pantheistic. The Spirit for Hegel, whether as finite Spirit or eternal Spirit, has nothing to do with the Holy Spirit of Scripture. Nor indeed does the marching and smilingly triumphant Spirit of Schleiermacher's *Speeches on Religion*.

B. The Spirit and the Church. In his *Christian Faith,* of course, Schleiermacher attempted a more biblical approach. Here again, however, he swallowed up the Spirit of historical teaching, this time in the collective consciousness of the Church, which gave rise to Scripture in the form of the apostolic writings but whose work continued, and still continues, in all the activities of the Church. In line with his consistent reconstruction of theology as Christian anthropology, Schleiermacher saw in the Spirit simply a term for the common life and spirit of the believing community.

C. The Spirit and Immediacy. The concept of the Spirit became an even more tenuous one in Harnack's *What is Christianity?* Harnack related the Spirit very closely to religious experience. Receiving and acting by the Spirit denote immediacy of religious feeling without external constraints. Obedience to Christ and freedom in the Spirit characterize the primitive Church. Unusual phenomena may mark this at first, but the indispensable workings of the Spirit are holiness and love. From another angle the Church is by its very nature a community of the Spirit.

D. The Cosmic Spirit. Liberal Catholicism, represented by Charles Gore, followed the middle course of merging the general and special workings of the Spirit in a cosmic view. In his essay on "The Holy Spirit and Inspiration" in *Lux Mundi* Gore found in Christian experience the freest work of the Spirit. The Spirit works in all nature, but especially in rational creatures. Through his ministry He consecrates the natural but only gradually by a reuniting of spirit and flesh. Gore, of course, identified the Spirit as the third person of the trinity even if he could also use impersonal terms like "the Divine Energy." He seemed to postulate no ultimate distinction between the cosmic and the redemptive work. Even in illumination he recognized Holy Scripture only as the most conspicuous of the Spirit's works. Nevertheless, the Spirit was not for him a world soul, nor did he expect the fulfillment of the Spirit's ministry except by His special activity in Christ and His people.

VII. The Spirit and a Second Work.–A. Sanctification. The relation of the Spirit to sanctification took a new turn with the emphasis on Christian perfection deriving from the teaching of John Wesley. Theologians had consistently linked the Spirit to sanctification both in its first beginning and also in its progress. Wesley accepted this link, but he discerned a new possibility of entire sanctification resulting from the outpouring of the Holy Spirit at Pentecost. He also believed that ordinarily this perfection can be secured in an instantaneous experience which even in his day could be referred to as "the second blessing." Wesley himself did not specifically identify this experience with the Holy Spirit, but he undoubtedly implied this by associating it with Pentecost. Hence many of the holiness movements which have followed Wesley in different ways have seen in instantaneous sanctification a blessing of the Spirit that might be called the filling of the Spirit, the baptism of the Spirit, or the second work of the Spirit.

B. Confirmation. Paralleling in some sense the holiness movements, certain Anglo-Catholic writers, especially Mason, Dix, and Thornton, revived the patristic concept of a post-baptismal giving of the Holy Spirit. In this development confirmation took on a new importance as the "sacrament" of the Spirit's outpouring. What this second work entailed, they did not state with any precision. The older idea of strengthening or perfecting was still a common one. Equipment for Christian service offered an alternative. This could quickly merge into charismatic endowment in pentecostal Anglicanism and Roman Catholicism. Thornton found a typological basis for the second work of the Spirit in the sequence of Israel's deliverance. It was saved from Egypt at the crossing of the Red Sea (baptism) but had then to cross the Jordan to enter the Promised Land (confirmation).

C. Charismatic Endowment. Modern pentecostal movements share with the holiness and confirmation schools the general concept of a work of the Holy Spirit subsequent to regeneration. Their distinctive contribution is to relate this work to the imparting of spiritual gifts, more especially the gift of tongues, and to find in it, as an ongoing pentecostal experience, the true baptism of the Holy Spirit. Naturally the sanctifying ministry of the Spirit is not neglected, but the emphasis tends to fall on the charismatic distribution. The pentecostal groups reject the idea that the extraordinary gifts were imparted only for the apostolic period and that the modern Church can have nothing comparable to the experience of the Spirit that once came with the laying on of hands. They believe that across the centuries, though not always with appropriate strength or recognition, all the charisms have in fact been present in the Church, as Roman Catholics are, of course, more swift to acknowledge than many Protestants who too easily presume their absence. Their teaching undoubtedly needs to be set in the total context of the person and ministry of the Holy Spirit. When this is done, and the obvious overemphases are corrected, it can perhaps recapture for the Church a special feature of the Spirit's work, namely, the equipping of all Christians, in different ways, for the fulfillment of their priesthood in the common ministry of evangelism and edification.

Bibliography.–K. Barth, *CD,* I/1 and I/2; H. Bettenson, *Early Christian Fathers* (1956); *Later Christian Fathers* (1974); F. D. Bruner, *Theology of the Holy Spirit* (1970); Calvin *Inst.* i.7f.; ii.2; iii.1-3; iv.14-17; L. Dewar, *The Holy Spirit and Modern Thought* (1959); G. Dix, *Theology of Confirmation in Relation to Baptism* (1946); A. Harnack, *History of Dogma* (1961); H. Heppe, *Reformed Dogmatics* (Eng. tr. 1950); J. N. D. Kelly, *Early Christian Doctrines* (1960); G. W. H. Lampe, *The Seal of the Spirit* (1967); A. J. Mason, *Relation of Confirmation to Baptism* (1893); R. Riggs, *The Spirit Himself* (1949); P. Schaff, *Creeds of Christendom,* III: *Evangelical Protestant Creeds* (4th rev. ed. 1919); H. B. Swete, *The Holy Spirit in the Ancient Church* (1912); *John Wesley,* Library of Protestant Thought, ed. A. C. Outler (1964); J. R. Williams, *The Pentecostal Reality* (1972).

G. W. BROMILEY

HOMAGE [Aram. *s^egiḏ*] (Dnl. 2:46); AV, NEB, WORSHIPPED; [Gk. *proskynéō*] (Mk. 15:19); AV WORSHIPPED; NEB MOCK HOMAGE. The Aramaic (and its Hebrew cognate *sāgaḏ*) mean "do homage by prostration." These terms, by referring to the physical act of prostration, describe not only worship of God, or gods, but also the obeisance shown to human dignitaries. *See* picture in JEHU. Thus while the RSV has "worship" for *s^egiḏ* ten times in Dnl. 3, it appropriately has "homage" in Dnl. 2:46. It is not necessary to suggest that Nebuchadrezzar acted improperly in "worshiping" Daniel or that Daniel erred in accepting that "worship."

In Mk. 15:19, the pagan soldiers bow in "mock homage" (NEB) to the convicted Jesus. While *proskynéō* usually means "worship" in the NT (*see* WORSHIP), it is doubtful that this is meant here, unless the soldiers were parodying Caesar worship or some oriental idea of king worship.

H. VAN BROEKHOVEN, JR.

HOMAM hō'mam [Heb. *ḥômām*–'destruction']. A Horite descendant of Esau (1 Ch. 1:39). The name appears in Gen. 36:22 as Heman.

HOME substantives: [Heb. *bayiṯ*]; AV also HOUSE, FAMILIES (Ps. 68:6 [MT 7]); NEB also HOUSE, "in the family" (Lev. 18:9), STALL (1 S. 6:7,10), PALACE (2 S. 13:7), HOMEWARD (Job 38:20), TENTS (Ps. 68:12 [MT 13]), etc.; [*'ōhel*]; AV, NEB, also TENT; [*māqôm*]; AV also PLACE; NEB also COUNTRY (2 S. 15:19); [*mānô(a)ḥ*] (Ruth 3:1); AV REST; NEB "happily settled"; [*reḇeṣ*] (Prov. 24:15); AV "resting place"; NEB FARM; [*mizzᵉḇul*] (Ps. 49:14 [MT 15]); AV DWELLING; NEB HONOR; [Gk. *oíkos*]; AV also HOUSE; NEB also HOUSE, INDOORS (Mt. 17:25), "private houses" (Acts 5:42); [*oikía*] (Mt. 8:6); [*ídios*]; AV also "own," "all" (Lk. 18:28); NEB also "own realm" (Jn. 1:11a), BELONGINGS (Lk. 18:28); [*monḗ*] (Jn. 14:23); AV ABODE; NEB DWELLING; verbs: [Heb. *šûḇ*]; AV also RETURN, BRING Zec. 10:10); NEB also "is brought" (2 S. 17:3), "went back," etc.; [*bô'*]; AV also "come," "come again" (Ps. 126:6), BRING; NEB also RESTORE, "come back" (Ps. 126:6); [*šālaḥ*] (1 S. 13:2); AV, NEB, SENT; [*sûr*] (1 Ch. 13:13); AV "brought home"; NEB "take with him"; [*sāḇaḇ*] (1 Ch. 16:43); AV, NEB, RETURN; [*lûn*] (Job 39:28); AV ABIDE; NEB LODGE; [*'āsap*] (Dt. 22:2); AV BRING; NEB TAKE; [Gk. *endēméō*] (2 Cor. 5:6, 8f.); AV also "be present"; NEB also "go to live," "here"; [*analýō*] (Lk. 12:36); AV, NEB, RETURN; [*hypostréphō*] (Lk. 23:48); AV RETURN; NEB "went home"; [*apérchomai*] (Lk. 24:12); AV DEPART.

I. In the OT.–A. Substantives. 1. Bayiṯ. Although the Hebrew noun *bayiṯ*, "house, domicile, home," is one of the most common words in the OT, and the proto-Semitic **bayt* is widely diffused among the cognate Semitic languages (Akk. *bītu;* Ugar. and Phoen. *bt;* Aram. *byt;* Eth. *bēt;* Arab. *bayt*), there is no obvious verb from which the noun may be derived. An etymology has been sought by some scholars in the Aramaic root *bwt*, "go in, spend the night," but this is dubious. Even if such a connection were granted it is more likely that the verb is a denominative from the noun (see BDB, p. 108).

While "house" is by far the most common RSV translation for *bayiṯ* (*see* HOUSE), "home" is used more than fifty times. *Bayiṯ* in the OT reveals an extremely wide and varied range of meaning, and its manifold connotations cannot be captured merely by "house" or "home." It may refer to a "shelter" or "stable" for animals (1 S. 6:7, 10; cf. NEB "stall"). It sometimes refers to a tent (usually *'ōhel*), i.e., a temporary or nomadic dwelling (Gen. 27:15; 33:17; *see* TENT, and *TDOT*, I, *s.v.* "'ōhel" [Koch]). But essentially and most frequently it has reference to an edifice, something that has been built (Heb. *bānâ;* cf. Gen. 33:17; Dt. 20:5; 22:8; 28:30). If proto-Semitic **bayt* had any earlier meaning among the Semites in the prehistoric period of cave habitation, the OT has no trace of such a meaning. Indeed, the OT regularly uses *mᵉ'ārâ* (Gen. 19:30) for "cave" (*see* CAVE, and *TDOT*, II, *s.v.* "bayith" [Hoffner], 108).

Bayiṯ, then, represents many kinds of buildings that are made of various materials — stone, lumber, and plaster (Lev. 14:45; 1 K. 5:8, 15, 18 [MT 22, 29, 32]; 7:11f.; Hab. 2:11), or hewn stone (1 K. 5:17; 6:7; 7:9f.; Ps. 118:22; Am. 5:11). Most frequently *bayiṯ* denotes a building used as a dwelling or home by a family (Dt. 6:7; 19:1; etc.). In the biblical period such homes were erected within the protective walls of fortified cities, usually according to no discernible plan and in a heavily impacted, small area. City planning was apparently not practiced in any systematic way until Hellenistic times.

Such family living quarters were generally of two stories, with a door opening onto a street. They were usually attached to adjacent homes and/or the city wall itself (cf. Josh. 2:15-21; 2 Cor. 11:33). Interior room was provided for cooking on a centrally located hearth, for sleeping, and for quartering the domestic animals. Smoke escaped either through windows or open courtyards. The lower walls were usually of undressed stone and, as a result, often thick. Where stone was in short supply, sun-dried mud brick was employed for walls, but in these cases it was still important that at least the foundation be sturdily constructed of stone (especially because of the cumulative erosive effect of rain runoff and flooding at the ground level, and as a safeguard against earthquake).

Archeological excavations have revealed that these stone walls were not usually mortared, but were plastered on the interior surface. The floors of such homes were of clay (the use of flagstones in the floors and courtyards of homes was a feature of only the more luxurious dwellings). Ceilings consisted of a plaster surface over wooden beams. The rooftop was constructed of a thick layer of clay over reed matting, all supported by the wooden beams. This rooftop area usually received heavy use in warm weather (cf. 2 S. 11:2). To combat cracking of the clay, the roof surface had to be rolled periodically. In the springtime a short-lived growth of grass on the rooftop was commonplace (cf. Ps. 129:6; 2 K. 19:26; Isa. 37:27). The

Wooden model (12th Dynasty, 20th-19th cents. B.C.) of an Egyptian farm-steward's house. The lower floor was the kitchen and storage area and the upper floor the bedroom (Trustees of the British Museum)

roof was usually made accessible either by an external stairway or a ladder.

With the exception of the more luxurious homes, rooms in these dwellings were tiny, with ceilings about 2 m. (6 ft.) in height. The doors were of wood, set into sockets in the stone sill and wooden or stone lintel; the doorjambs were also of wood.

Independently or in combination, *bayiṯ* may also designate particular kinds of buildings or homes. *Bēṯ hammeleḵ* (lit. "house of the king") is thus the royal "PALACE" in 1 K. 9:1; but so is *habbayiṯ* (lit. "the house") in 1 K. 4:6. *Bēṯ hā'ĕlōhîm* (lit. "house of God") is the "temple" in Dnl. 1:2 ("shrine" in Jgs. 17:5), but so is *habbayiṯ* in 1 K. 6:12. *Bēṯ YHWH* is the "temple of the Lord" in Ex. 23:19; etc. This same combination has recently appeared in the Arad ostraca (see Y. Aharoni, *BA*, 31 [1968], 16f., and cf. the similar combination, *bēṯ dāḡôn,* "temple of Dagon," in 1 S. 5:2).

In Jer. 37:15 both *bēṯ hā'ēsûr* (lit. "house of binding") and *bēṯ hakkele'* (lit. "house of confinement") mean simply "prison." Also notable among numerous other such combinations is *bēṯ hannāšîm* (lit. "house of the women"), which means simply "the harem."

The great flexibility of the term may be seen through its less common and more remote extensions of meaning — e.g., the netherworld (Job 17:13), the grave (Ps. 49:11 [MT 12]; Eccl. 12:5), the human body (Job 4:19; Eccl. 12:3), a spider's web (Job 8:14), a bird's nest (Ps. 84:3 [MT 4]; 104:17), a badger's den (Prov. 30:26), and property (1 K. 13:8).

Apart from the literal sense of "dwelling, home" the most common connotation of *bayiṯ* is that of "household, family." This natural extension of the essential meaning occurs almost six hundred times in the OT, referring to an immediate FAMILY or HOUSEHOLD (i.e., the occupants of a *bayiṯ*; cf. Gen 7:1), a family of descendants or clan (Ruth 4:12), a tribe (Ex. 2:1), a family or guild of craftsmen (1 Ch. 4:21), a dynasty (2 S. 9:1; 1 K. 12:16; 2 K. 8:18; etc.; in 2 S. 7:11 *'āśâ bayiṯ* means "found a dynasty"), or even a political entity or nation (e.g., *bēṯ yiśrā'ēl* in 1 S. 7:2f.). The combination "house of the Torah" (*byt htwrh*) in CD 20:11-13 appears to have the sense of "community" and to be related to the NT conception of the community as the "house of God" (cf. He. 3:1-6; see *TDNT,* V, *s.v.* οἶκος, οἰκία [Michel], 121).

In the great majority of cases where the RSV translates *bayiṯ* by "home" the meaning is a residence or personal dwelling (cf., e.g., Gen. 39:16; Jgs. 18:26; Lam. 5:2). In a few instances the meaning is really closer to "family." In the incest legislation of Lev. 18:9 a "female born at home" (*môleḏeṯ bayiṯ*) is contrasted with a "female born outside" (*môleḏeṯ ḥûṣ*). This simply means a girl born "in the family" vis-à-vis one born "outside the family" (cf. also Ps. 68:6; 113:9).

The idiomatic use of the directional *h* with *bayiṯ,* yielding the sense "to the home" or "homeward," lies behind the RSV translation in several instances. In 2 S. 13:7 it is used of sending a message "homeward"; in 1 K. 13:7 of bringing a visitor to one's home; and in Ex. 9:19 and 1 S. 6:7, 10 of bringing animals back home.

2. 'Ōhel. The Hebrew noun *'ōhel,* "tent," is translated "home" fifteen times in the RSV. While its literal and original meaning is the impermanent, nomadic tent dwelling, *'ōhel* was still used in settled times in a much more general sense as "home, dwelling, habitation." In 2 K. 13:5, e.g., the people of Israel are said to dwell during the second reign of the Jehu dynasty (*ca.* 800 B.C.) in their *'ŏhālîm* (lit. "tents"; RSV "homes"). Such usage is anachronous, but it represents reapplication of the old vocable to the new realities of urban or sedentary life. In all of these examples the term simply means "residence," and the literal sense, "tent," is of no particular import. In six instances (1 S. 4:10; 2 S. 18:17; 19:8; 2 K. 8:21; 14:12; 2 Ch. 25:22) the immediate context is a variation of the idiomatic expression "each person fled to his home/tent" (cf. 2 S. 20:1, RSV; see *TDOT,* I, *s.v.* "'ōhel" [Koch]).

3. Māqôm. Eleven times in the OT the RSV renders *māqôm* (lit. "place, standing-place") as "home." In most instances its use is comparable to that of the above terms: it refers to a person's "place of residence" or "home." But in Gen. 30:25 and 2 S. 15:19 it has the wider, geographical sense of "homeland" (*see* PLACE).

4. Mānô(a)ḥ *and* Meꞏnûḥâ. Both the cognate synonyms *mānô(a)ḥ* (Ruth 3:1) and *meꞏnûḥâ* (1:9) have the literal and original sense of "resting place." By logical extension they are each used once in Ruth with the sense of "home," i.e., that place where one can rest securely (*see* REST). The original sense of these terms is illustrated in Gen. 8:9, where Noah's dove could find no *mānô(a)ḥ,* and Nu. 10:33, where *meꞏnûḥâ* denotes a campsite on the wilderness journey from Sinai.

5. Reḇeṣ *and* Mizzeꞏḇul. The use of *reḇeṣ* (lit. "a place of lying down, crouching place") to mean "home" is borrowed from the animal world (e.g., Isa. 65:10, the place where the flocks lie down to rest) and is applied to human beings only in Prov. 24:15. The RSV has rendered the very uncertain *mizzeꞏḇul* in Ps. 49:14 as "home" (cf. *zeꞏḇul,* "habitation," in Isa. 63:15) but this is at best a guess (cf. NEB "honor," from *zeꞏḇûl,* "elevation"). A. Weiser (p. 385) states that "the restoration of the seriously corrupt text is hopeless," and attempts no translation for the end of the verse.

B. Verbal Expressions. The RSV also uses "home" in English verbal expressions translating a number of Hebrew verbs: *šûḇ,* "return home" (Jgs. 7:3); *šûḇ* (hiphil), "bring home" (Jgs. 11:9); *bô',* "come home" (Ps. 126:6); *bô'* (hiphil), "bring home" (1 Ch. 13:12); *šālaḥ* (piel), "send home" (1 S. 13:2); *sûr* (hiphil), "take home" (1 Ch. 13:13); *sāḇaḇ,* "go home" (1 Ch. 16:43); *lûn* (hithpael), "make a home" (lit. "lodge oneself," Job 39:28); and *'āsap,* "bring home" (lit. "gather up," Dt. 22:2).

II. In the NT.–A. Substantives. 1. Oíkos. The Greek noun *oíkos,* "house, dwelling, home," is regularly used in the LXX to render Heb. *bayiṯ* and thus reflects in the NT a similar range of meaning as that possessed by its normal OT equivalent. Like *bayiṯ, oíkos* most often represents a building in which a family dwells. But it may refer to a palace (Mt. 11:8) or temple (21:13), or even a city or populace (23:38); also to the human body (Lk. 11:24 and Mt. 12:44, where the sick person is said to be the "house" of the evil spirit or demon), to the property of a house (Acts 7:10), and by extension to the household or family (Lk. 10:5) or clan (Lk. 1:27).

In the LXX *oíkos toú theoú* (lit. "house of God") is the regular translation for the Heb. *bēṯ (hā)'ĕlōhîm.* In NT usage it has reference to no other sacred building than the earthly temple of Israel (cf. also Josephus *BJ* iv.4.4 [281]). A few times in the NT, however, the Christian community itself is designated as the *oíkos toú theoú,* the "household of God" (1 Tim. 3:15; 1 Pet. 4:17; He. 3:6; cf. Eph. 2:19; and see *TDNT,* V, 125-28). In the apocryphal book of Baruch (3:24) the phrase "house of God" means the cosmos or created universe (cf. Philo *De aeternitate mundi* 112; *De cherubim* 52). But Philo was also able to conceive of the pure human soul as an *oíkos toú theoú* (see *TDNT,* V, 123).

The RSV translates "home" for twenty NT occurrences of *oíkos*. In each of these the term specifically has reference to a personal residence or dwelling (except perhaps for Lk. 9:61, where it may have the sense "family"; cf. 10:5). Also in each of these instances *oíkos* is always in the idiom *eis (toń) oíkon* plus a verb of motion (e.g., in Mt. 9:6, "go home"; in Mk. 8:26, "send home") or *en oíkō/kat' oíkon,* "at home" (e.g., Mk. 2:1; Acts 5:42).

2. Oikía. The Greek language originally distinguished between *oíkos* and *oikía,* the former representing the whole of a deceased person's possessions and the latter simply his residence. But in the NT the two have by and large fallen together (see *TDNT,* V, 131-34), and *oikía,* though less frequent in occurrence, displays much the same variety of meaning as does *oíkos*. In three of its NT occurrences the RSV translates "home." Occurring in the same idioms as does *oíkos,* it also refers in each case to a personal residence.

3. Ídia. The Greek adjective *ídios,* "one's own," has reference to what properly belongs to an individual (private property), vis-à-vis what is public property or another's. Used as a substantive it may refer to persons such as "relatives" or "fellow citizens" (cf. Jn. 1:11b; Sir. 11:34); or it may refer to one's own "home" (*tá ídia*) as in Jn. 1:11a; 16:32; 19:27; Acts 21:6. It may also mean simply "home" in Lk. 18:28, but it seems here to connote more precisely "property, possessions" (cf. NEB "belongings").

4. Monḗ. The noun *monḗ,* "staying, tarrying" (derived from *ménō,* "stay, wait, abide"), in one NT instance has the connotation "home" (Jn. 14:23; cf. also v. 2, "room").

B. Verbal Expressions. As in a number of OT passages, the RSV incorporates "home" into its translation of several verbs: *endēméō,* "be at home" (2 Cor. 5:6, 8f., employed figuratively); *apérchomai,* "go, depart (for home)" in Lk. 24:12; Jn. 20:10; *hypostréphō,* "turn back, turn around, return (home)," in Lk. 23:48; and *analýō,* "depart, return (home)," in Lk. 12:36.

See also BUILD; FAMILY; HABITATION; HOUSE; HOUSEHOLD.

Bibliography.–Y. Aharoni, *BA,* 31 (1968), 2-32; *TDNT,* V, *s.v.* οἶκος, οἰκία (Michel); *TDOT,* I, *s.v.* "'ōhel" (Koch); II, *s.v.* "bayith" (Hoffner); A. Weiser, *Psalms* (Eng. tr., *OTL,* 1962).

D. G. BURKE

HOMEBORN [Heb. *'ezrāḥ*]. A native-born Hebrew, as contrasted with a foreigner of different blood (Josh. 8:33, AV "he that was born among them"; NEB "native"). The same Hebrew word is found in Lev. 16:29; 18:26; and elsewhere, but is translated differently. "Homeborn servant" in Jer. 2:14 translates Heb. *y^elîḏ bayiṯ* (NEB "born in slavery"), which indicates a free-born person in contrast to a slave.

HOMER hō'mər [Heb. *ḥōmer*] (Lev. 27:16; Nu. 11:32; Isa. 5:10; Ezk. 45:11, 13f.; etc.). A dry measure equal to the cor, containing about 394 liters, or approximately 11 bushels. It was equal to ten ephahs. *See* WEIGHTS AND MEASURES.

HOMICIDE. The only occurrence of this term in the RSV is in Dt. 17:8, where Heb. *dām* ("blood") is employed in the absence of a specific Hebrew term for "murder." The narrative is endeavoring to distinguish between homicide proper, an act of physical violence against a person that culminates in his death, and an unpremeditated killing in which the death of the victim is accidental. Murder is definitely forbidden in the sixth commandment (Ex. 20:13; 21:12; cf. Gen. 9:5f.; Lev. 24:17, 21; Nu. 35:16-21; Dt. 19:11-13). It was always to be punished by death, as a crime against the image of God; the penalty of death, however, was not inflicted when the killing was unintentional or unpremeditated (Ex. 21:13; Nu. 35:22-25; Josh. 20:3-5). Refuge cities were founded to which the manslayer could escape from the "avenger of blood." There he had to abide until after the death of the officiating high priest. If he left the city before that event, the AVENGER who killed him was free from punishment (Ex. 21:13; Nu. 35:10-15, 25-28, 32; Dt. 19:1-13; Josh. 20:2-6; *see* REFUGE, CITIES OF).

Killing a thief who broke in during the night was not accounted murder (Ex. 22:2), although one who killed a thief in the daytime incurred bloodguilt (Ex. 22:3). If a man failed to build a parapet for his roof, and anyone fell over and was killed, bloodguiltiness also came upon that man's house (Dt. 22:8). Unintentional killing of a pregnant woman in a fray was punished according to the *lex talionis,* i.e., the husband of the woman killed could kill the wife of the man who committed the offence without being punished (Ex. 21:22f.). This was not usually carried out, but it gave the judge a standard by which to fine the offender. Where a body was found, but the murderer was unknown, the elders of the city nearest to the place where it was found were ordered by a prescribed ceremony to declare that they were not guilty of neglecting their duties, and were therefore innocent of the man's blood (Dt. 21:1-9). Two witnesses were necessary for a conviction of murder (Nu. 35:30). If a slave died under chastisement, the master was to be punished according to the principle that "whosoever strikes a man so that he dies shall be put to death" (Ex. 21:12; cf. v. 20).

See KILL; MURDER.

P. LEVERTOFF

HOMOEOTELEUTON. *See* TEXT AND MSS OF THE NT II.A.1.

HOMOSEXUALITY. *See* SEX; CRIMES.

HONEST [Heb. *kēn*] (Gen. 42:11, 19, 31, 33f.); AV TRUE; [*yāšār*] (1 S. 29:6); AV, NEB, UPRIGHT; [*yōšer*] (Job 6:25); AV RIGHT; NEB UPRIGHT; [*ṣeḏeq*] (Prov. 12:17); AV RIGHTEOUSNESS; [Gk. *agathós*] (Eph. 4:28; Tit. 2:1); AV GOOD; NEB HONESTLY, HONORABLE; [*kálos*] (Lk. 8:15); **HONESTLY** [Heb. *be'^emûnâ*] (2 K. 12:15 [MT 16]; 22:7; Isa. 59:4); AV FAITHFULLY, TRUTH; NEB TRUST; **HONESTY** [Heb. *ṣ^eḏāqâ*] (Gen. 30:33); AV RIGHTEOUSNESS.

The majority of Hebrew words translated by "honest" and "honestly" are derived from roots denoting firmness, straightness, steadfastness, and supportiveness (*kwn, yšr, 'mn*). Thus "honest" has to do with adhering to a particular standard, often with legalistic nuances (cf. Isa. 59:4). The two occurrences of Heb. *ṣeḏeq* and *ṣ^eḏāqâ* also indicate a correctness, an evaluative judgment based on legal practice, though the precise legal traditions are difficult to determine (esp. for Gen. 30:33).

The Gk. *kálos kaí agathós* was a well-known combination in Greek literature (cf. *TDNT,* pp. 538-540) and came to mean the ideal of life, with ethical and spiritual connotations. In Lk. 8:15 it probably connotes "morally good" (cf. Bauer, rev., p. 400). The "honest work" in Eph. 4:28 and Tit. 3:1 probably has a similar ethical or religious connotation (cf. *TDNT,* II, 649; Bauer, rev. p. 3).

See also GOOD.

Bibliography.–*TDOT,* I, *s.v.* "'āman" VII (Jepsen); *TDNT,* III, *s.v.* κάλος (Grundmann).

D. F. MORGAN

HONEY [Heb. *d^eḇaš*; Gk. *méli*]. The honey referred to in the OT was in most cases wild honey (Dt. 32:13; Jgs. 14:8f.; 1 S. 14:25f., 29, 43), although the offering of honey with the first fruits would seem to indicate that the bees were also domesticated (2 Ch. 31:5). The bees constructed their honeycomb and deposited their honey in holes in the ground (1 S. 14:25), under rocks, or in crevices between the rocks (Dt. 32:13; Ps. 81:16 [MT 17]).

In OT times, as at present, honey was rare enough to be considered a luxury (Gen. 43:11; 1 K. 14:3). Honey was used in baking sweets (Ex. 16:31). It was forbidden to be offered with the meal offering (Lev. 2:11), perhaps because it was fermentable, but was presented with the fruit offering (2 Ch. 31:5). Honey was offered to David's army (2 S. 17:29). It was sometimes stored in the fields (Jer. 41:8). It was also exchanged as merchandise (Ezk. 27:17). In NT times wild honey was an article of food among the lowly (Mt. 3:4; Mk. 1:6).

The OT uses "honey" in several figurative expressions. "A land flowing with milk and honey" suggested a land filled with abundance of good things (Ex. 3:8, 17; Lev. 20:24; Nu. 13:27; Dt. 6:3; Josh. 5:6; Jer. 11:5; Ezk. 20:6, 15). "A land of olive trees and honey" had the same meaning (Dt. 8:8; 2 K. 18:32), and similarly "streams flowing with honey and curds" (Job 20:17). Honey was a standard of sweetness (Cant. 4:11; Ezk. 3:3; Rev. 10:9f.). It typified sumptuous fare (Cant. 5:1; Isa. 7:15, 22; Ezk. 16:13, 19). The ordinances of Yahweh are "sweeter than honey and the drippings of the honeycomb" (Ps. 19:10 [MT 11]; 119:103); *see* picture of *Leipzig Mahẓor* in EDUCATION. "You ate . . . honey" (Ezk. 16:13) expresses Yahweh's goodness to Jerusalem.

J. A. PATCH

HONOR [primarily Heb. *kāḇēḏ* (e.g., Ex. 20:12) and the derivative noun *kāḇôḏ* (e.g., Nu. 24:11), also *hôḏ* (1 Ch. 16:27), *yeqār* (Est. 1:20), *yāqār* (Ps. 45:9 [MT 10]), *tāmîm* (Jgs. 9:16), *šēm* (Ezk. 39:13), *tip̄'ārâ* (Dt. 26:19), *neḏîḇâ* (Job 30:15), *geḏûllâ* (Est. 10:2), *ʿaḏ-lim'ōḏ* (2 Ch. 16:14), *nāśā'* (Isa. 9:15 [MT 14]), *zāḇal* (Gen. 30:20), *hāḏar* (Lev. 19:32); Aram. *haḏar* (Dnl. 4:34 [MT 31]), *reḇâ* (Dnl. 2:48); Gk. *timḗ* (Jn. 4:44), *timáō* (Mt. 15:4), *tímios* (Acts 5:34), *éntimos* (Phil. 2:29), *átimos* (Mt. 13:57), *dóxa* (2 Cor. 6:8), *doxáxō* (Rom. 1:21), *éndoxos* (1 Cor. 4:10), *megalýnō* (Acts 5:13), *prōtoklisía* (e.g., Mt. 23:6)]; AV MAGNIFY, GLORIFY, MAKE GREAT, etc.; NEB SHOW FAVOR, "have great reputation," GLORIFY, etc.; **HONORABLE** [Heb. *kāḇēḏ* (Nu. 22:15; 1 Ch. 4:9; Isa. 3:5; 58:13), *šô(a)ʿ* (Isa. 32:5); Gk. *kalós* (2 Cor. 8:21; Jas. 2:7), *átimos* (1 Cor. 12:23), *semnós* (Phil. 4:8)]; AV also BOUNTIFUL, HONEST, TRUE, WORTHY; NEB OF HIGHER RANK, MEN OF SUBSTANCE, PRINCE; **HONORABLY** [Gk. *kalṓs* (He. 13:18)]; AV HONESTLY; NEB "what is right."

The following difficult or unusual readings should be noted. On Heb. *yizbelēnî* (Gen. 30:20), see E. A. Speiser, *Genesis* (*AB*, 1964), p. 231; the AV "dwell with" reflects the older understanding derived from *zeḇûl*, "dwelling"; cf. *CHAL*, p. 86. The RSV and NEB "in his honor" (Heb. *ʿaḏ-lim'ôḏ*) in 2 Ch. 21:19 is an interpolation (omitted by the AV) on the basis of 2 Ch. 16:14. In Job 30:15 the NEB "resolution" is based on the LXX *elpís*, while the AV "soul" reflects Vulg. *desiderium* (cf. Syr. *neṯîḇâ*, "path [of life]"). Ps. 45:9 has several problems (see the comms.); *beyiqqerôṯeḵā* in v. 9 is often emended to *liqrā'ṯeḵā*, "to meet you" (cf. *BHS*; KoB, p. 399). Isa. 5:13 uses *kāḇôḏ* as a substantive, hence the RSV and AV "honored men" and the NEB "nobles." The Gk. *prōtoklisía* (Mt. 23:6 par. Mk. 12:39 par. Lk. 20:46; Lk. 14:7f.) means "place of honor" (so RSV, NEB); as A. Plummer (comm. on Matthew [1953], p. 315 n. 1) points out, the AV "uppermost rooms" is misleading now, although in Elizabethan English it corresponded fairly closely to the meaning of *prōtoklisía*. In Rom. 14:6 the RSV three times translates *kyríǭ* as "in honor of the Lord" (dative of advantage; cf. BDF § 188); the AV "to the Lord" is woodenly literal, but the NEB "has the Lord in mind" effectively communicates the meaning.

The Hebrew root *kbd* and its derivatives, more often translated "glorify, glory," denote weight or heaviness (cf. Assyr. *kabâdu* and Ugar. *kbd* [sometimes used in reference to money]). The root *yqr* has a similar denotation (cf. Assyr. *akâru* and Ugar. *yqr*) as well as *hdr*, "to adorn" (cf. Ugar. *hdrt*). The most frequent roots used in the NT stress the action of honoring (Gk. *timáō, megalýnō, doxázō*).

Honor usually results in people being elevated in the eyes of the community. This anthropocentric use of honor in the Bible has often been observed, and is easily understandable in view of the characteristics usually associated with final achievement of honor, namely, rank (Nu. 22:15), reputation (1 S. 9:6; Acts 5:34), status (1 Tim. 5:3), wealth (1 K. 3:13; Prov. 3:16; Dnl. 2:6), and character (Isa. 3:5). All of these are worthy of honor. What is sometimes blurred, however, is the issue of whether these characteristics are prerequisites for being an honorable person or the results of being such a person. It is probably safe to assume that the causal relationship will sometimes change its sequence (e.g., honor leading to wealth, or wealth leading to honor), but in the majority of cases most of these characteristics will be present. To the extent that honor is attributed to God and therefore interpreted as a sign of His favor, the prophets and other critics of Israelite society had real objections to the simple equation of honor with wealth and fame. There were real criteria for achieving honor (see below) and they were usually behavioral characteristics rather than economic achievements.

Sometimes the references focus upon honor as an object, on that which is given to a person, and therefore on those aspects and actions of man that are deserving of such honor. In Proverbs, e.g., wisdom, graciousness (Heb. *ḥēn*), humility (*ʿanāwâ*), a lack of contentiousness, righteousness (*ṣeḏāqâ*), kindness (*ḥeseḏ*), lowliness of spirit (*šepal-rû(a)ḥ*), and fear of the Lord — all these are characteristics of the honorable person. Honor here is seen as the result of doing the right things (cf. Rom 2:7-11). It is clear that honor is often found in contexts presenting a retributive theology, equating honor and good works with right action.

Sometimes the *action* of giving honor is stressed, emphasizing not only the merits of the receiver (Dnl. 2:48), but the merits of the giver as well. The best example of this use of honor is the well-known imperative to honor parents (Ex. 20:12; Mt. 15:4; Eph. 6:2), focusing on both the implicit attributes of the parents and the efficaciousness of the action for the children.

Though a study of honor in its many biblical occurrences will necessarily concentrate upon the human being, it must be remembered that a biblical anthropology begins and ends with theological assumptions. The honor that a person earns or is given by others is ultimately dependent upon God (2 Ch. 26:18; Ps. 62:7 [MT 8]; 84:11; Rom. 2:7-11). Moreover, God Himself is clothed with honor (Ps. 104:1), and His saving works, the necessary constituent for Israel's existence, are worthy of honor (Ps. 111:3). Thus, behind all the biblical references to honor can be found the assumption that without God as the giver of honor all is inconsequential (Rom. 2:6ff.). And the necessary prerequisite for such an understanding of honor is that ultimately God alone is not only the source and giver, but the most appropriate recipient of honor, as reflected in Rev. 4:11: "Splendor and honor and kingly power are yours by right, O Lord our God, for you created everything that is, and by your will they were created and have their being" (*Authorized Services* [1973], Protestant Episcopal Church of the USA).

Bibliography.–*TDNT,* II, *s.v.* δοκέω κτλ. (von Rad, Kittel); VIII, *s.v.* τιμή κτλ. (J. Schneider); *TDOT,* III, *s.v.* "hādhār" (Warmuth); "hôdh" (Warmuth).

D. F. MORGAN

HOOD [Heb. *ṣānîp*] (Isa. 3:23, AV). *See* TURBAN.

HOOF. *See* CLEAN AND UNCLEAN, II.A.; CLOVEN.

HOOK [Heb. *wāw*] (Ex. 26:32, 37; 27:10f.; 36:36, 38; 38:10-12, 17, 19, 28); [*qeres*] (Ex. 35:11; 39:33); AV TACHE; NEB FASTENER; [*ḥakkâ*–'fishhook'] (Job 41:1 [MT 40:25]; Isa. 19:8; Hab. 1:15); RSV, NEB, also FISHHOOK; AV also ANGLE; [*ḥāḥ*] (2 K. 19:28 par. Isa. 37:29; Ezk. 19:4, 9; 29:4; 38:4); AV also CHAIN; NEB also RING; [*ḥô(a)ḥ*] (2 Ch. 33:11; Job 41:2 [MT 40:26]); AV THORN; NEB also "spiked weapon"; [*ṣēn* (pl. *ṣinnôṯ*), "hook(s)," and *sîrôṯ dûgâ,* "fishhooks"] (Am. 4:2); NEB "shields and . . . fish-baskets"; [*mazmērâ,* "pruning hook"] (Isa. 2:4; 18:5; Joel 3:10 [MT 4:10]; Mic. 4:3); NEB also KNIVES, PRUNING KNIVES; [Gk. *ánkistron*] (Mt. 17:27); NEB LINE.

The book of Exodus conceives the tabernacle court as enclosed by a portable wall; posts were set up at regular intervals with curtains attached by "hooks" or pegs (Ex. 27:10; 38:10). Similar constructions (the "screen" and the "veil") are described in Ex. 26:32, 37; 36:35-38. The Hebrew word for these objects, *wāw,* is also the name of the sixth letter of the Hebrew alphabet; it is not clear whether the letter was so named because it looked like a "hook," or vice versa.

The "hooks" of Ex. 35:11; 39:33 (*qeres*) were used to join together the two great sets of curtains for the tabernacle (Ex. 36:10-13), and also those for the tent (36:14-18).

The Israelites, like the Egyptians and Assyrians, fished with hook and line (*ḥakkâ*); fishing rods, however, are not mentioned in the Bible. The monster crocodile (?) Leviathan cannot be caught with a *ḥakkâ* (Job 41:1; but cf. Herodotus ii.70). Jewish law knows the *ḥakkâ* as simple fishing equipment (T.P. *Moed Katan* ii.5; Tosefta *Baba Kamma* viii.17); it was apparently the hook used by Peter in Mt. 17:27 (Gk. *ánkistron,* used by the LXX to translate *ḥakkâ*).

The *ḥaḥ* or *ḥō(a)ḥ* was used for the capture of crocodiles (Ezk. 29:4; Job 41:2), wild beasts (Ezk. 19:4, 9), and human beings (2 Ch. 33:11; cf. 2 K. 19:28 par. Isa. 37:29; Ezk. 38:4). It was inserted in the victim's nose (2 K. 19:28) or jaw (Job 41:2; Ezk. 29:4; 38:4). It is sometimes thought of as a pointed stick or harpoon, but the passages referring to human beings suggest Assyrian illustrations of captives held by a ring in the lip attached to a cord (see *ANEP,* nos. 447, 524). Something similar may be intended in the obscure passage Am. 4:2, where the women of Samaria are led away with "hooks" (*ṣinnôṯ*) and "fishhooks" (*sîrôṯ dûgâ*). The RSV's "hooks" in Job 40:24 is based on the emendation *ṣinnîm* for *ʿênāw* (AV, NEB, "eyes"; AV mg. "sight"; see the comms.).

The "pruning hook" (*mazmērâ*) consisted of a sickle-shaped metal blade, its inner edge sharpened, attached to a wooden handle. It could be converted into a spear (possibly "scimitar") and vice versa (Joel 3:10; Isa. 2:4; Mic. 4:3). Isa. 18:5 describes its use.

"Hooks" (Ezk. 40:43) is a guess, from the context, at the meaning of Heb. *šᵉpattayim* (AV mg. "endiron"; NEB "ledges").

Bibliography.–G. Dalman, *Arbeit und Sitte in Palästina,* VI (1939), 359f.; E. Dhorme, comm. on Job (Eng. tr. 1967), pp. 624-26; S. Schwantes, *ZAW,* 79 (1967), 82f.; H. Tur-Sinai (Torczyner), *JQR,* 41 (1950), 171-75; S. Yeivin, *Leshonenu,* 27 (1962-63), 1-9.

D. J. HALPERIN

The hoopoe bird (Trustees of the British Museum)

HOOPOE ho͞o'pō, -po͞o [Heb. *dûkîpaṯ*; Gk. *épops*; Lat. *Upupa epops*] (Lev. 11:19; Dt. 14:18); AV LAPWING. One of the peculiar and famous birds of Palestine, having a curved bill and beautiful plumage. It is about the size of a thrush. Its back is a rich cinnamon color, its head golden buff with a crest of feathers of gold, banded with white and tipped with black, that gradually lengthen as they cover the head until, when folded, they lie in lines of black and white, and, when erect, each feather shows its exquisite marking. Its wings and tail are black banded with white and buff. It nests in holes and hollow trees. All ornithologists agree that it is a nasty, filthy bird in its feeding and breeding habits. The nest, never cleaned by the elders, soon becomes soiled and evil smelling. The bird is mentioned only in the lists of abominations (Lev. 11:19; Dt. 14:18), perhaps because it has bad habits, and undoubtedly because it was one of the sacred birds of Egypt.

G. STRATTON-PORTER

HOPE [Heb. *bāṭaḥ*–'trust,' *yāḥal*–'wait for,' *qāwâ*–'expect,' *tiqwâ*–'expectation'; Gk. *elpízō, elpís,* "hope," also "expect" (2 Cor. 8:5)]. A concept involving trustful anticipation, particularly with reference to the fulfillment of the promises of God.

I. General Considerations
II. OT
III. Intertestamental Period
  A. Normative Piety
  B. Apocalypticism
  C. Rabbinic Judaism
  D. Qumrân
IV. NT
  A. Gospels and Acts
  B. Epistles
    1. In Relation to Believers
    2. In Relation to the Creation
    3. Coordinates of Hope
    4. Symbols of Hope
  C. Book of Revelation
V. The "Larger" Hope

I. General Considerations.–Hope is one of the finest responses of which the human spirit is capable. It has kept people alive and buoyant when the conditions of life were almost unbearable. Men of letters have saluted it with language that has become axiomatic, such as "hope springs eternal in the human heart" and "where there is life there is hope." Scripture speaks similarly: "Anyone who is among the living has hope" (Eccl. 9:4, NIV).

Hope is also a mark of human limitation. Granted that

it owes much to the promises of God, yet those promises are especially welcome because of our lack of knowledge of the future and our inability to effect radical change. Hope is a testimony to man's humility in the face of his finiteness. It amounts to a protest against any assumption that the present contains the ideal situation for mankind.

We may assume that hope has no place in the being of God. True, Paul can refer to Him as the God of hope (Rom. 15:13), but probably only in the sense that He is the one who inspires hope in His people, unless we are to suppose that Paul is suggesting that God Himself lives in an aura of anticipation, pondering His plans for the future.

It is hardly adequate to define hope as expectation, for someone could expect judgment and on that account be utterly without hope. Expectation must be yoked with confidence and desire in order to qualify as hope. Frequently in our culture the familiar "I hope so" is really only an admission of a thinly veiled pessimism.

Hope sometimes appears in Scripture as a subjective entity, something that one possesses and exercises. Especially is this true of the OT, but in the NT this usage is less frequent, being overshadowed by the objective reality that draws the human response like a magnet. Paul can speak of Christ Jesus as the believer's hope (1 Tim. 1:1) and of the hope laid up in heaven for the child of God (Col. 1:5). The hope generated in one's heart (1 Pet. 3:15) is the echo of this heavenly reality. To exert hope would be futile apart from the person and pledges of the Almighty.

II. OT.–The Exodus from Egypt followed by the Sinaitic covenant, the preservation of the nation in the wilderness, and the successful occupation of Canaan, provided a firm basis for Israel's confidence in God's continuing provision and aid. By virtue of their largely agricultural economy, the people were dependent on God's faithfulness in respect to weather patterns. In time, competition from Baal worship seriously imperilled the nation's fidelity and also its Godward expectation. Yet even in the darkest days of apostasy hope was not extinguished among the godly. On the basis of God's covenant mercy, the remnant continued to look to Him for intervention, including deliverance from Israel's enemies (Jer. 14:8f.). Later, when the returnees from Babylonian captivity evidenced their repentance by putting away their foreign wives, they took fresh hope on the ground of God's forgiveness (Ezr. 10:2). Those who did not return from captivity were consoled by being addressed as prisoners of hope (Zec. 9:12).

A corollary of placing one's hope in God is refusing to put one's ultimate reliance on man, whether neighbor or friend (Mic. 7:5), princes (Ps. 118:9), or resources such as wealth (Ps. 52:7 [MT 9]) or horses (Ps. 33:17).

Hope is sometimes expressed by other terms, especially "wait" and "look." For the Hebrew, waiting on the Lord was not primarily a matter of spending time but was rather an attitude of trust and expectation. It could bring the reward of exchanging one's own weakness for divine strength (Isa. 40:31). God is represented as one who works for those who wait for Him (Isa. 64:4).

Hope is often present without specific mention of it. Abraham's attitude of faith in God's promise of a son stimulated within him a confidence that defied all human calculation (Rom. 4:18). When David and his men returned to Ziklag and found their homes burned and their wives carried off by marauders, all of them lamented, but David strengthened himself in the Lord his God (1 S. 30:6). He was exercising hope.

Hope may sometimes suffer partial eclipse or alternate with depression. The psalmist admits to being in low spirits, but this very condition prods him to hope in God (Ps. 42:11 [MT 12]). Unable to understand the affliction that has deprived him of possessions, family, and health, Job laments, "My days are swifter than a weaver's shuttle, and come to their end without hope" (Job 7:6). Yet resurgent hope enables him to triumph over these moments of near despair. "For I know that my Redeemer lives . . . I shall see God" (Job 19:25).

In the writings of the OT hope relates largely to one's earthly existence. Hezekiah, in the grip of serious illness, longs for restored health and pleads with God, "For Sheol cannot thank thee; those who go down to the pit cannot hope for thy faithfulness" (Isa. 38:18). Revelation was incomplete; Christ had not come, and the definite hope of eternal life, based on His resurrection, was lacking (2 Tim. 1:10).

One must turn to the OT prophets for the principal development of the concept of hope on a national and even universal scale. This element of hope is not predicated on the improvement of the character of the covenant people. The prophets lament the unfaithfulness, the disobedience of the nation, echoing the disappointment and pain of Yahweh. But they also voice His determination not to inflict such a sweeping judgment as to destroy the nation He has chosen. "How can I give you up, O Ephraim! How can I hand you over, O Israel! . . . I will not execute my fierce anger . . . for I am God and not man" (Hos. 11:8f.; cf. 2:15 [MT 17]). This mingling of judgment and promise in the prophets provides the stamp of authenticity for their utterances, since only God could make valid by His own decision and action the pattern of judgment followed by restoration. The crowning feature of the prophetic message of hope was the promise of a messianic king (Isa. 11:1, etc.).

III. Intertestamental Period.*–A. Normative Piety.* This era reflected the expectations of OT days in that hope was fixed on God rather than on mankind or favorable circumstances. "The spirit of those who fear the Lord will live, for their hope is in him who saves them. He who fears the Lord will not be timid, nor play the coward, for he is his hope" (Sir. 34:13f.). Hope for the life to come included resurrection at times (e.g., 2 Macc. 7:14), but where Greek influence was strong the prevailing expectation was immortality of the soul (e.g., 1 En. 103:4).

B. Apocalypticism. The intertestamental literature testifies to a growing preoccupation with apocalyptic, a feature readily understandable in the light of the political situation. Israel was under continuous domination by foreign powers, a condition relieved only during the era of independence under the Maccabees. Divine intervention from without was perceived as the only hope of the nation. It would occur through the inbreaking of the Messiah, who is given additional titles in 1 Enoch such as the Righteous and Elect One (53:6) and the Son of Man (69:27).

C. Rabbinic Judaism. With few exceptions the rabbis found their solace in the study and application of the Mosaic law rather than in the adoption of forcible measures designed to effect political freedom. Theoretically this spiritual concern should have stimulated hope in God and in His promises, but paradoxically this was not the result. The reason was the growth of legalism. No one could be confident of having observed fully the ramifications of the law that were extended into every area of human life and activity. The more conscientious one sought to be the more his assurance of salvation tended to become clouded (*TDNT,* I, 527-29).

D. Qumrân. This group was eschatologically oriented, living in the belief that its lot was cast in the end of the days. It anticipated a final conflict between the forces of righteousness and the forces of wickedness, involving both men and angels. The faithful could anticipate eternal salvation in the presence of God.

IV. NT.–A. Gospels and Acts. Regarding the Gospel

corpus, if one were to judge from terminology alone, there would be little to discuss, because the noun does not occur at all and the verb appears in only a few instances. Other terms are used, however, e.g., *prosdéchomai* (Lk. 2:38; 7:19f.; 23:51) and *prosdokáō* (Mt. 11:3).

Certainly when one appraises the atmosphere and the spirit generated by the coming of a new age, there was eager anticipation. The impact of the Baptist's preaching was felt throughout the land as he proclaimed the imminent arrival of the kingdom of God. Moreover, his proclamation of one greater than himself who would shortly appear was electrifying.

Jesus proclaimed His own mission basically in terms of the kingdom. It had come in His own person and was due to experience both growth and opposition, resulting in a glorious consummation. To His disciples He intimated that before the setting in of the age to come an era of gospel proclamation based on His forthcoming death and resurrection would intervene. The Master had much to say also about His return and the necessity that His followers be found serving and waiting, looking for the coming of their Lord (Mt. 24–25).

Since the disciples did not understand this perspective due to their preoccupation with a temporal kingdom, their hopes were dashed by the death of Jesus (Lk. 24:21); but His resurrection revived and intensified those hopes. This glorious event became the focus of gospel preaching as recorded in the early chapters of Acts. It meant that the rejection of Jesus as Israel's Messiah was a human blunder (Acts 4:10-12), and the chief value of the event was to awaken saving faith in the risen Lord. At Pentecost thousands became convinced by the Spirit-empowered preaching of Peter that Jesus had indeed fulfilled the prophecies of the OT regarding the Messiah. In the latter half of Acts, Paul's witness to his countrymen centered in Jesus the risen Lord as the hope of Israel (Acts 23:6; 26:6-8; 28:20).

B. Epistles. 1. In Relation to Believers. Here, as in Acts, the resurrection of the Lord Jesus provides the catalyst not only for the present enjoyment of Christian experience but also for the expectation of heavenly inheritance (1 Pet. 1:3). Peter was able to call it a living hope, due to its constant and unfading character. This prospect is confirmed by the dwelling of the living Christ in the hearts of believers, where He abides as the hope of glory (Col. 1:27). He provides introduction to the Father and access to the throne of grace for the saints (Rom. 5:2; He. 7:19), stimulating hope of eternal fellowship in the divine presence. This ultimate reality comes to God's people through the corridor of death (2 Cor. 5:8), but those who remain alive until the coming of the Lord will be spared the ordeal of death and will be translated to His heavenly kingdom (1 Thess. 4:15-17), exchanging the present body for one that resembles Christ's (Phil. 3:21). Small wonder that believers are encouraged to think of the return of the Lord as their blessed hope (Tit. 2:13)! It is a purifying hope as well, since it weans the people of God from the tempting allurements of a godless world (1 Jn. 3:3). Christian hope involves also the anticipation of seeing and enjoying once again the loved ones who have died in the faith (1 Thess. 4:17) as well as meeting the saints of all the bygone ages. This is part of the gain that death brings (Phil. 1:21). Another aspect of the hope is the prospect of receiving a reward for faithful service rendered to the Lord. Paul looked forward to this (2 Tim. 4:8) and encouraged his converts to make whatever sacrifice was necessary in order to enable them to receive their imperishable crown (1 Cor. 9:24-27).

Salvation relates to the future no less than to the past and the present (Rom. 13:11). To those already justified by faith Paul can speak of waiting for the hope of righteousness (Gal. 5:5; cf. Rom. 8:10f.). This final phase of salvation involves the redemption of the body (Rom. 8:23) but also complete deliverance from the sinful nature that has plagued them during their earthly pilgrimage. Only on this basis can it be said that we shall be like Christ (1 Jn. 3:2; cf. Rom. 8:29). Yet it should be noted that the Christian's hope of experiencing the glory of God (Rom. 5:2) rests on his justification (Rom. 5:1) rather than on his sanctification (even though the development of Christian character adds an element of expectancy), since what God does in His own rests on what He has done for them. All believers are called to one hope (Eph. 1:18; 4:4); this is understandable in light of the fact that salvation, including its final, eschatological aspect, is a matter of grace rather than human attainment (1 Pet. 1:13). This gives a strength and constancy to the hope of believers that it could not have if it were conditioned on some element of human achievement.

In passing, it should be noted that hope respecting the future was not a characteristic of the pagan world. The word itself was seldom used. Often enough, when it was employed, it denoted something illusory. Burial inscriptions reveal no confidence regarding an afterlife. The best one could do was to face death without fear or regret. "I am of good courage, I who was not, and became, and now am not. I do not grieve" (*Inscriptiones Graece Siciliae et Italiae,* No. 1879, line 11). This inscription no doubt expresses the Stoic outlook. Paul assessed the situation accurately when he referred to such people as having no hope and without God in the world (Eph. 2:12; cf. 1 Thess. 4:13).

Christian hope, whether related to the return of Christ or to the heavenly inheritance, should not be regarded as a form of escapism. It relates to the fulfillment of the divine promise and is confirmed by the witness of the Spirit (Rom. 15:13).

The central feature of Christian worship is the Lord's Supper. As believers gratefully remember the Savior's sacrificial death on their behalf, it is their privilege to look forward to the marriage supper of the Lamb (1 Cor. 11:26).

The heavenly hope is reflected in the depiction of believers as already possessing a heavenly citizenship (Phil. 3:20), with the result that they are sojourners in this world (1 Pet. 2:11) awaiting their summons to a better land. A similar outlook characterized the OT saints whose faith gave them assurance of things hoped for (He. 11:1, 13). Christ's followers are in the world but not of it (Jn. 17:14). This does not imply isolation from unsaved society, making witness impossible, but only a determination not to be conformed to its ideals and manner of life. Believers belong to the (coming) day, so they are challenged to live a life of sobriety and alertness, ready for participation in eschatological salvation (1 Thess. 5:4-11; Rom. 13:11-14). They are expected as well to be sufficiently informed about the implications of their faith to be able to explain their hope to those who inquire about it (1 Pet. 3:15).

One may legitimately raise the question as to whether the passing of time without the return of the Savior led to the diminishing of expectation on the part of the Church. It is natural to suppose that this was the case, at least to a degree. Apparently the writer of the Epistle to the Hebrews detected such a tendency among his prospective readers and tried to counteract it. Whatever may be conjectured about the rank and file of believers, clearly the apostles and leaders of the Church continued to emphasize the promised return and to urge alertness and expectancy. Toward the end of his life, roughly a generation after Jesus' death and resurrection, Paul could affirm that the Christian community eagerly awaited a Savior from heaven (Phil. 3:20). Peter treats the promised revelation of Jesus Christ as imminent (1 Pet. 1:13; 4:13; 5:4). John writes as though the coming could well be within his lifetime (1 Jn. 3:2f.). James pleads for patience in view of the apparent delay in the Lord's return, but holds fast to its factuality (5:7; cf. He. 9:28; 10:23-25, 37).

When the Gospels were published, a generation or more after the conclusion of our Lord's ministry, the Church received in these writings a reminder that the Master Himself promised to return, urging upon His followers the necessity of alertness and fidelity in view of that coming event (Mt. 24:42-44; 25:1-13; Jn. 21:22).

So hope was nourished despite the passing of the years. The Church apparently did not at this stage yield to complacency and begin to look on itself as a permanent institution with an indefinite tenure in the world.

2. In Relation to the Creation. In the notable passage Rom. 8:18-22 Paul draws a comparison between nature and man. As a consequence of the fall, man's environment was made subject to futility, being unable to realize the potential given to it originally by the Creator. Personifying the creation, the apostle pictures it as hoping and groaning, an experience similar to that of the believer as he awaits the coming transformation. Creation waits with eager longing for the revealing of the sons of God in their glorification, for that event will bring release from creation's present limitation (Rom. 8:19). Paul's teaching has affinity to that of Our Lord when He spoke of the regeneration or renewal of the world (Mt. 19:28).

3. Coordinates of Hope. The most noteworthy of these are faith and love (1 Thess. 1:3; 1 Cor. 13:13). In the former passage hope is put last because of its future reference. In the latter passage hope occupies the medial position and love is placed last for the reason that a final statement is to be made about love. The superiority of love is not due to its eternal character, since all three abide, but because it believes all things and hopes all things, and even more because it belongs to the essential nature of God. Since the chapter has love for its theme, no compulsion rested on the apostle to refer to faith and hope. Their close affinity to love made it natural for him to do so.

The absence of hope from Paul's list of the fruit of the Spirit (Gal. 5:22f.) is not strange, since the enumeration is representative rather than complete ("such" is used rather than "these"). Furthermore, "patience" implies hope.

In another setting the apostle asserts that hope does not disappoint for the reason that God's love has been poured into our hearts through the Holy Spirit (Rom. 5:5). This constant ministration of love assures us that the hope of experiencing it in glory is no illusion.

Hope and love are mutually and intimately involved in the expectation of the Lord's return. Paul looks forward to receiving the crown of righteousness that the Lord will award to him and to all who have loved His appearing (2 Tim. 4:8).

The connection between hope and faith is especially close. Hope depends on faith and is its forward-looking aspect. This is made clear by the definition of faith in He. 11:1 and by numerous examples from the lives of OT figures (vv. 10-23). With reference to Christ we read, "Through him you have confidence in God, who raised him from the dead and gave him glory, so that your faith and hope are in God" (1 Pet. 1:21).

Hope's linkage with steadfastness (or endurance) in 1 Thess. 1:3 is significant (cf. 2 Thess. 1:3f.). Endurance takes account of the length of the journey to be made and the obstacles along the way, but it gains its inspiration and strength from the vitality of hope.

Joy is an accompaniment of hope (Rom. 5:2). In the same letter Paul prays, "May the God of hope fill you with all joy and peace in believing, so that by the power of the Holy Spirit you may abound in hope" (15:13). This amounts to saying that hope is not only the inspiration for joy and peace but also the end result. It is both cause and consequence.

4. Symbols of Hope. First, it is described as an anchor of the soul (He. 6:19). Using the pattern of the tabernacle for the structuring of his thought, the writer pictures Christ as having passed through the inner veil by His ascension so that He is now in the presence of God. Whereas in human experience the anchor rope reaches down into the watery depths to where the anchor holds fast at the bottom, giving security to the ship from stormy winds, Christ has entered the unseen realm by proceeding to heaven. There He constitutes our hope, both sure and steadfast. This is explained in terms of His high-priestly ministry.

Excavations of the catacombs in the area around ancient Rome have disclosed that along with other symbols of the Christian faith such as the fish and the shepherd, the anchor was widely used. It expressed confidence that despite all the adverse winds of ill fortune and persecution, the believer would be preserved for the heavenly kingdom and would meet the Savior face to face.

A second symbol of hope is the helmet (1 Thess. 5:8; Eph. 6:17). In both passages Paul links it with (eschatological) salvation. In Ephesians the setting is one of conflict with the powers of darkness in the spiritual realm. However strong the foe, the Christian need not fear, since the hope of completed salvation provides a sure defense against all attacks of the evil one.

C. Book of Revelation. Superficially the absence of the word hope from this book may seem strange and disappointing, for it is so replete with victory and glory. But one should take into account that the writer is "seeing" the eschatological glory in the unveiling of Christ's victory over evil powers both human and superhuman. He is caught up in the assurance of prophetic fulfillment. He is standing for the time being amid the realities of the golden age, so there is no need for an expression of hope. This does not mean that the concept of hope is excluded, for it appears under the guise of endurance (e.g., 13:10; 14:12).

V. The "Larger" Hope.–This caption is sometimes given to the view that ultimately all mankind will be saved, not only those who have not heard the gospel but also those who have rejected it. Advocates of this position could argue that God withholds any plain indication of His purpose to do this lest people be content to rest in confidence that their eternal welfare is secure and therefore plan to enjoy the best of both worlds, self-satisfaction here and eternal life with God hereafter. But it is hazardous to posit any such reticence on the part of God in view of the clear teaching of Scripture that some "shall suffer the punishment of eternal destruction and exclusion from the presence of the Lord" (2 Thess. 1:9). If this sounds harsh, one should reflect on the fact that God's Son, the embodiment as well as the messenger of the love of God, addressed Himself to the theme of judgment without any vagueness or equivocation (e.g., Mt. 25:46). One could argue that "eternal" means age-long, something short of endless duration, and on this basis suppose that after punishment had run its course God would welcome the offenders by pardoning their transgressions. But this line of reasoning would cast doubt on the duration of eternal life for the saved, since the word "eternal" is the same in both situations. Furthermore, we know that God does not force His salvation on anyone. We have no evidence that punishment endured by sinners prepares them to accept God's forgiveness in case it should be offered. The linking of gnashing of teeth with weeping may well suggest continuing anger and rebellion as well as pain (Mt. 13:42, 50).

Appeal to Christ's preaching to the spirits in prison

(1 Pet. 3:19) is also dubious, because those who are indicated as the objects of the preaching, namely, those who were disobedient in Noah's time, can hardly be thought of as human, since the word "spirits" when used without further description (contrast He. 12:23) is not used of human beings in the NT but rather of evil spirits (e.g., Lk. 9:39). So 1 Pet. 3:19 should probably be linked to Gen. 6:2 (cf. 2 Pet. 2:4; Jude 6). Furthermore, the word rendered "preached" does not strictly mean that Christ preached the gospel (good news) to the spirits in prison, since it literally means "to proclaim." It could indicate an announcement of His triumph over all the hosts of darkness (cf. 1 Pet. 3:22; Col. 2:15).

Some would ground the hope of universal salvation on Paul's statement, "Then as one man's [Adam's] trespass led to condemnation for all men, so one man's [Jesus Christ's] act of righteousness leads to acquittal and life for all men" (Rom. 5:18). One needs to take into account the full sweep of Paul's teaching on sin and righteousness. All men do in fact share the consequences of Adam's disobedience, namely, sin and death, but a person comes to share in the benefits of Christ's saving work only on the basis of faith in Him. This limitation of the second statement about "all men" (v. 18) to the believing portion of mankind is not arbitrary exegesis. A parallel exists in the apostle's teaching on resurrection. "For as in Adam all die, so also in Christ shall all be made alive" (1 Cor. 15:22). The following sentence limits those who will be made alive to those "who belong to Christ." Nothing is said in the chapter about the resurrection of the unsaved. Nothing is said elsewhere in the NT to the effect that the resurrection of the unsaved will lead to eternal life (Jn. 5:28f.).

The consensus of Scripture is that life on earth is the theater wherein one's eternal destiny is determined (2 Cor. 6:2; He. 9:27). It is not kindness to raise false hopes by holding before people the possibility that despite their refusal to put their faith in Christ during this life they can count on God's love to set aside the verdict against them, enabling them ultimately to share in salvation. To glorify such an opinion by putting on it the label of hope is unfortunate and misleading. *See also* PAROUSIA; GLORY; ESCHATOLOGY.

Bibliography.–A. Barr, *SJT,* 3 (1950), 68-77; *TDNT,* II, *s.v.* ἐλπίς κτλ. (Bultmann, Rengstorf); G. B. Caird, *et al., The Christian Hope* (1970); J. E. Fison, *Christian Hope* (1954); P. S. Minear, *Christian Hope and the Second Coming* (1954); J. Moltmann, *Theology of Hope* (1967); C. F. D. Moule, *Meaning of Hope* (1953); H. Schlier, *Relevance of the NT* (1968), pp. 142-155; S. Travis, *The Jesus Hope* (1974); W. Zimmerli, *Man and his Hope in the OT* (Eng. tr., *SBT,* 2/20, 1968).

E. F. HARRISON

HOPHNI hof'nī, hof'nē, and **PHINEHAS** fin'ē-əs [Heb. *ḥopnî* < Egyp. *ḥfn(r),* "tadpole"; Heb. *pinḥās* (1 S. 1:3), *pînᵉḥās* < Egyp. *p' nḥsy,* "the Negro/Nubian"]. Sons of Eli, priests of the sanctuary at Shiloh. Their character was wicked enough to merit the designation "worthless men" (AV "sons of Belial," 1 S. 2:12). Their evil practices are described in vv. 12-17. Twice Eli was warned concerning them, once by an unknown prophet (vv. 27-36) and again by the lips of the young Samuel (3:11-18). The curse fell at the battle of Aphek (4:1-18) at which the brothers were slain and the ark was taken; these events caused Eli's death. Phinehas was father of the posthumous ICHABOD, whose name marks the calamity. A remoter sequel to the prophetic warnings is seen in the deposition of Eli's descendant Abiathar from the priestly office (1 K. 2:26f., 35).

H. WALLACE

HOPHRA hof'rə [Heb. *ḥoprаʿ*; Gk. *Houaphrē*; Egyp. *Ḥaʿaʿibrēʿ; Waḥibrēʿ*]. The Apries of the Greeks (e.g., Herodotus ii.169), the fourth king of the 26th Dynasty, who ruled 589-570 B.C. Heb. *Ḥopraʿ* is derived from Egyp. *(Wa)ḥibrēʿ*, the king's personal name.

In 589 B.C., Zedekiah of Judah broke his solemn oath of loyalty to Babylon and sent for troops to Egypt (Ezk. 17:11-21), heedless of what had befallen Jehoiachin in 597 B.C. Nebuchadrezzar II of Babylon promptly laid siege to Jerusalem, and Hophra in turn invaded Palestine in support of Zedekiah (Jer. 37:5; cf. 47:1?), possibly with his fleet (cf. Herodotus ii.161). The Babylonian army then left Jerusalem to fight Hophra, but Hophra appears to have retired, leaving the Jews in the lurch as prophesied by Jeremiah (cf. Jer. 37:5-11). At this time (*ca.* 588 B.C.) Ezekiel (29:1-16) added his voice in condemnation of Egypt.

Hophra appears only once more in the OT, and this time by name; at some time after the final fall of Jerusalem (587/586 B.C.), Jeremiah prophesied that God would "give Pharaoh Hophra king of Egypt into the hand of his enemies and into the hand of those who seek his life" (44:30). This was fulfilled in 570 B.C., after Hophra had sent an army to help the Libyans against the Greek colony of Cyrene. The Egyptian force was overwhelmingly defeated, and the Egyptians accused Hophra of having sent their countrymen to their deaths and of unduly favoring the Greeks. Revolt broke out, and Amasis became its leader, defeating and capturing Hophra. Hophra was then probably put to death; at any rate, soon afterward he was buried as befitted a pharaoh by Amasis his successor.

Several monuments of Hophra are known (e.g., a palace-fort at Memphis; see W. M. F. Petrie, *Palace of Apries* [*Memphis II*] [1909]), but they add very little to our knowledge of his foreign adventures.

Bibliography.–A. H. Gardiner, *Egypt of the Pharaohs* (1961), pp. 360f., 383; É. Drioton and J. Vandier, *L'Égypte* (Coll. Clio) (4th ed. 1962), pp. 596f., 619, 679.

K. A. KITCHEN

HOPPER. *See* LOCUST.

HOR hôr [Heb. *hōr hāhār*–'Hor the mountain'].

1. An elevation on the border of Edom where Aaron died and was buried (Nu. 20:22; Dt. 32:50; etc.). The name always appears with the definite article, suggesting that it was a prominent mountain ridge. It is sometimes alleged that two traditions conflict regarding the place where Aaron died and was buried, Dt. 10:6 stating that these events occurred at Moserah. There is, however, neither conflict nor a double tradition, for the name Moserah (Moseroth), meaning "chastisement(s)," was applied to the event, not the location, of Aaron's death. As punishment for the Meribah incident (Nu. 20:24; Dt. 32:51) he died in Edom on Mt. Hor, while the people were encamped below. To mark the occasion, the incident and the campsite were called Moseroth (Nu. 33:30f.).

Josephus (*Ant.* iv.4.7) identified Mt. Hor with one of the heights in the vicinity of Petra, localized traditionally in Jebel Nebī Harun, the "mountain of Aaron," a lofty, twin-crested sandstone peak some 1460 m. (4800 ft.) high. It lies to the west of Edom, and is by far the most rugged of the Edomite mountains. Its summit holds a tomb allegedly belonging to Aaron, the upper part of which is a Moslem mosque. The tomb itself, however, is probably a reconstructed Christian church from the time of Justinian (A.D. 527-565). Any tradition that places Mt. Hor in the middle of Edomite territory and not on the border (Nu. 20:22) is open to serious objections. Since the Edomites were able to deny the Israelites access to their territory, and could implement their decision with a powerful border force (Nu. 20:17-21), Israel could not have reached Jebel Nebī Harun without crossing Edom, which was clearly impossible. Furthermore, such a location is too far from Kadesh, and the mountain itself would be too lofty and inaccessible for the Hebrews to witness the ceremony by which high office was transferred from father to son (Nu. 20:22-29).

Jebel Madurah, a site about 24 km. (15 mi.) NE of Kadesh, has been suggested as a more likely location for Mt. Hor. This height stood at the extreme northwest boundary of Edom, though strictly outside Edomite territory. Topographically it is more suitable, since Israel began the detour around Edom at Mt. Hor (Nu. 21:4), and the entire area was more accessible for witnessing the ceremony involving transfer of religious office. Insufficient evidence, however, makes the identification of Mt. Hor uncertain.

2. A mountain peak (Nu. 34:7f.) marking the northern limit of Israel. Both Mt. Hermon and Jebel Akkar, a spur of Lebanon, have been suggested. R. K. H.

HORAM hō'ram, hôr'əm [Heb. *hōrām*–'height']. A king of Gezer who tried to help Lachish, which Joshua was besieging (Josh. 10:32), but was himself defeated by Joshua (v. 33).

HOREB hō'reb, hôr'əb. *See* SINAI.

HOREM hō'rem, hôr'əm [Heb. *ḥorēm*–'consecrated']. One of the fenced cities in the territory of Naphtali (Josh. 19:38), named with Yiron, Migdal-el, Beth-anath, and Beth-shemesh. Thus it was probably in northern Galilee, though its precise location remains unknown.

HORESH hō'resh, hôr'əsh [Heb. *hōreš*–'wood, forest'] (1 S. 23:15-19); AV WOOD. The name evidently referred to a location in the Wilderness of Ziph (although it is doubtful that this land was ever wooded) where David was hiding from Saul. It was in this area that David and Jonathan entered into a solemn agreement. Khirbet Khoreisa, a ruined site some 3.2 km. (2 mi.) from Tell Zîf (9.6 km. [6 mi.] SE of Hebron) has been associated with David's exploits at this time, although this association is speculative. Note that the LXX *tḗ Kainē* presupposes Heb. *ḥ*^{a}*ḏāšâ* or *ḥāḏāš,* "new," which could be confused with *hōreš*.

HOR-HAGGIDGAD hôr hə-gid'gad [Heb. *ḥōr haggidgāḏ*]. A place of encampment in the wilderness journeyings, listed between Bene-jaakan and Jotbatah (Nu. 33:32f.). In a parallel account in Dt. 10:6f., the campsite is called GUDGODAH, and is listed between Moserah and Jotbatah. In the account in Numbers, Moserah appears as Moseroth (plural form of the same word), and Bene-jaakan is placed between Moseroth and Hor-haggidgad. The LXX in both passages reads *Gadgad*. The attempted identification of either form of the name with *Wâdī Ghadhaghedh* or *Khadhâḥed* (cf. *GP,* II, 216) is phonemically improbable. W. S. L. S.

HORI hôr'ī [Heb. *ḥôrî, ḥōrî*–'cave-dweller'].

1. A Horite descendant of Esau (Gen. 36:22; 1 Ch. 1:39).

2. A Simeonite, father of Shaphat one of the twelve spies (Nu. 13:5).

HORITES hō'rīts [*ḥōrî,* pl. *ḥōrîm*; LXX *Chorraioi*]. The original inhabitants of Edom (Gen. 36:20-30) before the area was occupied by the Edomites, the descendants of Esau, who displaced them (Dt. 2:12, 22). They are also included among the peoples defeated by Chedorlaomer (Gen. 14:6). Their ancestor is given as Seir, the Horite (Gen. 36:20).

The identification of the biblical Horites with the extrabiblical HURRIANS is one that has frequently been made and has much at first glance to commend it. The Hebrew name *ḥōrî* is the equivalent of cuneiform *Ḫurru* (Ugar. *ḫry*), and the Hurrians are known to have been present in Palestine prior to the entry of the Israelites. A closer examination of the evidence, however, shows that the identification is fraught with difficulties. Hurrians first appear in the ancient Near East *ca.* 2300 B.C., entering northwestern Mesopotamia from the general region of the Armenian mountains around Lake Van. Prior to 2000 B.C. they are limited to the northern part of the east Tigris region, but in succeeding centuries their penetration continues with ever increasing speed and numbers into Mesopotamia. By 1500 B.C. they had inundated northwestern Mesopotamia and northern Syria and created the empire of Mitanni, whose brief hegemony controlled states from the Mediterranean to E of the Tigris River. Although their political control was short-lived, Hurrian immigration continued into southern Syria, reaching Palestine itself in the 15th cent. B.C., as sporadic references to Palestine as "Ḫurru-land" in texts of the pharaohs of the 18th Dynasty reveal. The more frequent use of this name in texts of the 19th Dynasty and the presence of a number of Mitanno-Hurrian names in the Amarna Tablets show that they reached Palestine in significant numbers by the 14th cent. B.C. The extent and depth of this penetration into Palestine remains difficult to assess, however, due to the paucity of the evidence. It is probable, nonetheless, that their presence and influence in Palestine were minimal, consisting mainly of a military aristocracy imposed at the upper levels on some of the city-states. The Hurrian substratum which appeared by this period everywhere N of the Beqaʿ in central Syria left no trace in the contemporary texts from Palestine. From documentation we know that the cities that were ruled by Mitanno-Hurrian overlords, or had such elements in their population, were all in Cisjordan and primarily in the north and the coastal region: Jerusalem, Shechem, Taanach, Megiddo, Acco, Achshaph, and in the south Ashkelon and possibly Hebron.

This evidence for the minimal presence of Hurrians in Palestine, and only in northern and coastal Cisjordan, presents difficult problems for identifying them with the biblical Horites. The Horites are confined to Edom in southern Transjordan and the names given in Gen. 36 are all Semitic. Further, the Bible locates Hivites in the areas where the extrabiblical evidence documents the presence of Hurrians: HIVITES dwell at Shechem (Gen. 34:2), Gibeon (Josh. 9:7; 11:19), the mountains of Lebanon (Jgs. 3:3), and the valley below Hermon (Josh. 11:3, 8). The matter is further complicated by textual problems: in Gen. 36:2 the Hebrew text identifies Zibeon, son of Seir the Horite (Gen. 36:20, 29), as a Hivite, and some LXX texts read Horites for Hivites in Gen. 34:2 and Josh. 9:7.

The resolution of this conflicting evidence is not appar-

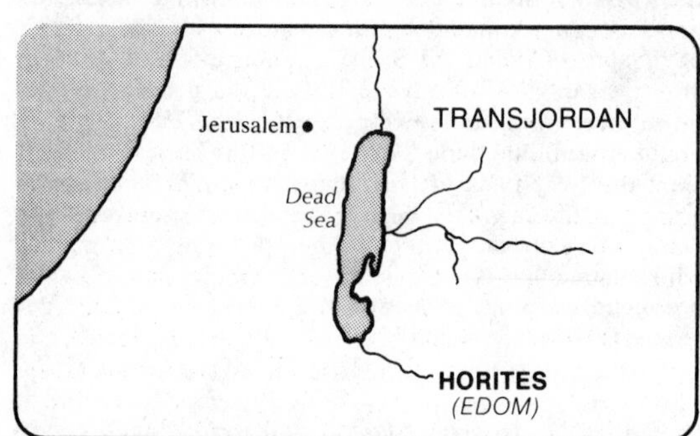

ent, although several different hypotheses have been advanced. Some scholars suggest that the two very similar names "Hivites" and "Horites" have been exchanged and simply reverse them. But such a desperate expedient is hardly satisfactory. Others, accepting the LXX reading of Horites for Hivites in Gen. 34:2 and Josh. 9:7 as correct, regard the two as synonyms, or hypothesize two homophonous names of different origin, the Semitic "Horites" of Edom and the non-Semitic "Horites" (i.e., "Hurrians") of north-central Cisjordan. The biblical writers, attempting to make a distinction, replaced the "Horites" (i.e., Hurrians) of Cisjordan with "Hivites," a name of local origin. Although preferable to the first hypothesis, this view is weakened by its reliance on textual variants that are most probably mistaken readings. Thus, the Bible uses the names Hivites and Horites in a consistent manner to designate two peoples, and, apart from Gen. 34:2 and Josh. 9:7, the LXX agrees with the MT in the more than twenty other places where the two names occur. Further, several versions support the MT (Aquila and Symmachus in Gen. 34:2; the Old Latin, the Syriac, the Ethiopic translations, and several MSS of the LXX in Josh. 9:7). It is also important to note that the Shechemites in Gen. 34 have Semitic names and are identified as Canaanites in v. 30; and the Gibeonites are identified as Amorites in 2 S. 21:2.

One more recent hypothesis views "Hivite" as a spelling variant or confusion for "Horite." The evidence for this view is that "Hivites," an ethnic term unknown elsewhere, occurs in twenty of the twenty-two lists of conquered peoples, while "Horites" (Hurrians), known to have been present in Cisjordan, never occurs in the lists, and that the names Hivite and Horite are close in biblical Hebrew (*ḥwy* and *ḥry*). This last point, however, is weak, since the *w* and *r* were never easily confused in Hebrew.

The most recent (and most likely) hypothesis to date treats the question as a special case of the general problem of the use made by the Israelites of the nomenclature they met in Palestine when they occupied it. For Cisjordan they adopted the Egyptian administrative term for that region, "Canaan," and they applied the term "Amorite" to northern and central Transjordan (as well as using it as a general term for all of Palestine, as they also used "Canaan"). Since the received nomenclature had no term for southern Transjordan (prior to the arrival of the Edomites), the Israelites used the term "Horite," i.e., *Ḫurru,* another general and imprecise term in Egyptian usage for the whole region.

See Vol. I, Map V.

Bibliography.–W. F. Albright, "The Horites in Palestine," in L. Leary, ed., *From the Pyramids to Paul* (1935), pp. 9-26; J. C. L. Gibson, *JNES,* 20 (1961), 217-238, esp. pp. 228f.; *IDB,* II, *s.v.* (E. A. Speiser); R. North, *Bibl.,* 54 (1973), 43-62; R. de Vaux, *RB,* 74 (1967), 481-503.

F. W. BUSH

HORMAH hōr'mə [Heb. *ḥormâ*–'devotion,' 'destruction']. A city first mentioned in connection with the defeat of the Israelites by the Amalekites and the Canaanites after the Israelites decided that they had made a mistake in not accepting the report of Joshua and Caleb that favored entering the land. Attempting to reverse their decision, the Israelites persisted against the will of Moses in going "up to the place which the Lord has promised," but were defeated (Nu. 14:40-45; Dt. 1:44). Later during the wilderness experience, Israel, at war with the king of Arad, took the place and utterly destroyed it and thus named it Hormah (Nu. 21:3). It was apparently rebuilt and is listed as one of the places conquered by Joshua (Josh. 12:14). Hormah was in the territory assigned to Judah (15:30); but it was reassigned to Simeon (19:4). Jgs. 1:17 relates that Judah and Simeon together once more subdued the Canaanites and destroyed Hormah. To Hormah David sent a share of the spoil taken from the Amalekites who had raided Ziklag (1 S. 30:30). It was reckoned as one of the cities of Simeon until the days of David (1 Ch. 4:30). Its location has been variously conjectured. W. F. Albright (*BASOR,* 15 [Oct. 1924], 6f.) suggested Tell esh-Sheriʿah, about 19 km. (12 mi.) NW of Beer-sheba; B. Mazar (*JNES,* 24 [1965], 297-303) identified it with Tell el-Milḥ, about 13 km. (8 mi.) SW of Tell ʿArâd; and most recently, Y. Aharoni (*EAEHL,* I, 88f.) has argued for Tell Meshash, about 6 km. (3.7 mi.) W of Tell el-Milḥ.

Bibliography.–*EAEHL,* III, *s.v.* "Masos, Tel" (A. Kempinski); *LBHG.*

J. F. PREWITT

HORN [Heb. and Aram. *qeren*]; AV also CORNET; NEB also "mountain fastness" (2 S. 22:3 par. Ps. 18:2 [MT 3]), HEAD (e.g., Ps. 89:17 [MT 18]), TRUMPET, etc.; [Heb. *qāran*–'have horns'] (Ps. 69:31 [MT 32]); [*šôpār*] (Josh. 6:4, 6, 8, 13; 2 S. 6:15); AV, NEB, also TRUMPET; [*tôʿăpôṯ*] (Nu. 23:22; 24:8); AV STRENGTH; NEB CURVING HORNS; [Gk. *kéras*] (Lk. 1:69; Rev. 5:6; 9:13; 12:3; 13:1, 11; 17:3, 7, 12, 16); NEB also "victorious power." *Qeren* is the general term for "horn," whether on the animal, as a musical instrument or noisemaker, as a container for liquids, as part of the whole offering and incense altars, or as a symbol of power associated with men.

Portrayal of gods with horns was common throughout the ancient Near East. The horns may have symbolized the power of the deity of the holy place, but it is not known if Yahweh was depicted with horns. *See also* ALTAR; HORNS OF THE ALTAR.

"Horn" is used figuratively to suggest aggressive power, e.g., in robbing one of power ("Moab's horn is cut off," Jer. 48:25; Ps. 75:10 [MT 11]) or bestowing power ("exalt the horn," Ps. 92:10 [MT 11]). Likewise "horn" symbolizes the power of kingship (Dnl. 7:7f., 11f., etc. where the succession of horns means the succession of kings; Ps. 132:17). The power can be abused ("thrust at the weak with your horns," Ex. 34:21), or called to use for the people (2 Ch. 18:10; 1 K. 22:11), or used to destroy (Zec. 1:19, 21). The horn is also used to represent two aspects of the divine: salvation (Ps. 18:2; 2 S. 22:3) and power (Hab. 3:4).

The horns used for musical instruments and noise makers (1 Ch. 15:28; Ps. 98:6) are traditionally ram's horns (T.B. *Rosh ha-Shanah* 26a). Cow's horns were forbidden for ritual (military or religious) purposes. *See also* MUSIC.

Bibliography.–R. de Vaux, *Ancient Israel* (Eng. tr. 1961), II, 414; H. Obbink, *JBL,* 68 (1949), 43-49.

A. L. PERLMAN

HORNET [Heb. *ṣirʿâ*; Arab. *ḍarʿa*]; NEB PANIC. Hornets, like wasps (which are smaller in size), belong to the family *Vespidae* of the order *Hymenoptera.* In Palestine, the commonest hornet species is the *Vespa orientalis,* a large yellow or reddish-brown insect which will sting anyone who molests it. As is frequently the case in the western world, hornets live in clusters in roundish, multicelled nests made from a type of cellulose which the hornets produce by chewing the bark of trees. Hornets are mentioned only in Ex. 23:28; Dt. 7:20; and Josh. 24:12, all of which refer to God's miraculous intervention on His people's behalf in dispossessing the indigenous inhabitants of the Promised Land. In these passages the hornet seems to be used in a dramatic metaphorical sense to show how God's onslaught would render the Canaanites immobile, just as the hornet's sting paralyzed its victim. An analogous usage occurs in Isa. 7:18, where the fly and the bee symbolize the military might of Egypt and Assyria.

R. K. H.

HORNS OF THE ALTAR [Heb. *qarnōṯ* (or *qarnôṯ*) *hammizbē(a)ḥ*]. Projections at each of the four corners of the altar of burnt offering (Ex. 27:2; 38:2; Ezk. 43:15) and of the altar of incense (Ex. 30:2f.; 37:25f.). In both cases they were to be of one piece with the altar. Blood was smeared on the horns of the altar of burnt offering at the consecration of Aaron and his sons (Ex. 29:12), in the sin offering for a ruler (Heb. *nāśî'*) or for one of the people (Lev. 4:25, 30, 34), and on the Day of Atonement (Lev. 16:18). The horns of the altar of incense were smeared with blood in the case of sin offerings for the high priest and the congregation of Israel (Lev. 4:7, 18). Fugitives seeking asylum could cling to the horns, thus putting themselves under the divine protection (cf. 1 K. 1:50-53; 2:28; an addition in the LXX [2:29] reads, "I fled to the Lord"), though not in the case of wilful murder (1 K. 2:31-34; cf. Ex. 21:14); the horns appear to epitomize the holiness of the altar. The cutting off of the horns in Am. 3:14 signifies the removal of Israel's last refuge from God's judgment. *See also* ALTAR.

The most significant suggestions concerning the nature of the horns are: (1) that they represent the horns of beasts actually offered in sacrifice (W. R. Smith, *Religion of the Semites* [3rd ed. 1927], p. 436 n.); (2) that they are stylized representations of Heb. *maṣṣēḇôṯ*, or pillars representing deity in Canaanite religion (H. Gressmann, *Die Ausgraben in Palästina und das AT* [1908], p. 28; J. R. Porter, *Leviticus* [1976], p. 38; against this view, see H. T. Obbink, *JBL*, 56 [1937], 43-49); (3) that the animal to be sacrificed was tied to them with cords; the only support for this view is found in Ps. 118:27, which is textually uncertain; it is also unclear why such binding would be necessary, and why the incense altar was also horned, unless Aharoni is correct (see below); (4) that they are the extremities which stress the holiness of the altar, being smeared with blood in the same way as the extremities of priests' bodies were (R. de Vaux, *Ancient Israel* [Eng. tr. 1961], II, 414); yet this does not explain the existence of the "horns" as such; (5) that the altar itself was symbolic of the deity who was often portrayed with horns (Obbink, *op. cit.*); in this case, Israel would have shared the form of the altar with her neighbors, but not its religious implications.

Altars with horns (i.e., vertical corner projections) have been discovered at such sites as Gezer (H. Gressmann, *Altorientalische Bilder* [1927], fig. 444), and Megiddo (H. G. May, *Material Remains of the Megiddo Cult* [1935], pp. 6-8 and illustration, pp. 12f. and plate xii; *AP*, plate 19), and more recently at Beer-sheba (Y. Aharoni, *BA*, 37 [1974], 2-6; Y. Yadin, *BASOR*, 222 [Apr. 1976], 11-17) and Dan (A. Biran, *BA*, 37, 106f.). These are of different sizes and dates; some are incense altars. Aharoni regards the latter as imitations of the altars of burnt offering. An Ugaritic sacrificial text perhaps speaks of "the horns of the table" (*qrnt ṯlḥn*, C. Virolleaud, *Ugaritica*, V [1968], 592f.), but the text is read differently by J. C. de Moor (*Ugarit-Forschungen*, 2 [1970], 323). According to Josephus, the altar of Herod's temple had "horn-like corner projections" (*BJ* v.5.6 [225]). For later representations of horned altars, see the references in S. A. Cook, *The Religion of Ancient Palestine in the Light of Archaeology* (1930), pp. 29-31, 160, 177 n.; see also O. Keel, *Symbolism of the Biblical World* (Eng. tr. 1978), p. 146.

E. BALL

Limestone horned altars from Megiddo (Oriental Institute, University of Chicago)

HORNS, RAMS'. *See* MUSIC.

HORONAIM hôr-ə-nā'əm [Heb. *ḥôrōnayim*–'two hollows']. A place in the south of Moab, close to Zoar, lying at the foot of a plateau (2 S. 13:34). It is mentioned on the Moabite Stone (line 32) as a city to which one descends. Isa. 15:5 speaks of "the way to Horonaim," and Jer. 48:5 of the "descent" or "going down" of Horonaim. Mesha says he was bidden by Chemosh to "go down" and fight against *Ḥwrnn* (Moabite Stone, lines 31f.). Probably, therefore, it lay on one of the roads leading down from the Moabite plateau to the Arabah. It is mentioned by Josephus as having been taken by Alexander Janneus (*Ant.* xiii.15.4 [395-97]). Hyrcanus promised to restore it, along with eleven other cities his father had taken from the Arabians, to Aretas (*Ant.* xiv.1.4 [14-18]). There is no indication that in early times it was ever possessed by Israel. It is probably to be identified with el-ʿAraq.

D. B. PECOTA

HORONITE hor'o-nīt [Heb. *ḥōrōnî*]. An appellation given to Sanballat, one of those who opposed Nehemiah (Neh. 2:10, 19; 13:28). It probably denotes that he was an inhabitant of BETH-HORON.

HORROR [Heb. *šammâ* (Dt. 28:37; Jer. 18:16; 19:18; 25:9; 42:18; Ezk. 23:33; etc.), *mᵉšammâ* (Ezk. 5:15), *zᵉwāʿâ* (Dt. 28:25; 2 Ch. 29:8; Jer. 15:4; 24:9 [*Q zaʿᵃwâ*]; 29:18; 34:17), *pallāṣûṯ* (Ps. 55:5 [MT 6]; Isa. 24:4; Ezk. 7:18), *tôʿēḇâ* (Ps. 88:8 [MT 9]), *mᵉḥittâ* (Jer. 48:39), *tipleṣeṯ* (Jer. 49:16), *śaʿar* (Job 18:20)]; AV also ASTONISHMENT, DISMAYING, DESOLATION, etc.; NEB also REPUGNANT, LOATHSOME, RUIN, SHUDDER, etc.; **HORRIBLE** [Heb. *šaʿᵃrûr* (Jer. 5:30; 23:14), *šaʿᵃrûrî* (Jer. 18:13; Hos. 6:10)]; NEB also OUTRAGE (Jer. 5:30); **HORRIBLY** [Heb. *śaʿar*] (Ezk. 27:35); AV SORE AFRAID; **HORRIFY; HORRIFIED** [Heb. *šāmēm* (Jer. 18:16; 19:8; 49:17; Ezk. 20:26)]; AV also ASTONISHED, MAKE DESOLATE; NEB also LAY WASTE.

A people or territory punished by God may become a "horror" in that observers are horror-struck by the enormity of its devastation. This sense is frequent in the book of Jeremiah.

The Heb. *pallāṣûṯ* and *tipleṣeṯ* are derived from *pālaṣ*, "shudder," and hence denote a shaking of the body due to fear or amazement. Similar is Heb. *zᵉwāʿâ*, "a trembling," "object of trembling," from *zûʿ*, "tremble, quake" (cf. Hab. 2:7; Eccl. 12:3; Est. 5:9). Heb. *śaʿar* means a bristling of one's hair (Heb. *śēʿār*) in horror. Heb. *tôʿēḇâ*, "abomination," comes from the verb *tāʿaḇ*, "be abhorred." The nouns *šammâ* and *mᵉšammâ*, from *šāmēm*, "shudder," "be deserted," or niphal, "be made to shudder," "be desolate," can designate the ruin and lifelessness of a devastated territory, as well as the analogous bodily manifestations of horror. The context is the criterion for the meaning, and it is sometimes ambiguous (e.g.,

Box from the tomb of Tutankhamen (1361-1352 B.C.). The pharaoh in his chariot leads an attack against Asiatics (Service des musées, Cairo)

Jer. 25:9; 51:37, 43; Ezk. 23:33; 2 K. 22:19; Mic. 6:16; etc.).

The RSV's "horror" in Ps. 31:11 (MT 12) is based on an emendation of the difficult Heb. *m^{e}'ōḏ* (usually "very"; cf. AV "especially"), presumably to *māgôr*, "terror" (cf. Jer. 20:3, 10), or *mōrā'*, "fear." The NEB's "burden" requires only a revocalization to **mā'ōḏ*, but this word is otherwise unattested (cf. G. R. Driver, *JTS*, 32 [1931], 256; KD *in loc.*).

See N. Lohfink, *VT*, 12 (1962), 267-69.

HORSE [Heb. *sûs*; Ugar. *ssw*; Akk. *sisû*; Egyp. *ssmt*] (Ex. 15:1; etc.); [Heb. *'abbîr*; Egyp. *ibr*]; RSV "steeds" (Jgs. 5:22), "stallions" (Jer. 8:16); AV "mighty ones," "strong ones," "bulls" (Jer. 50:11); NEB "chargers"; [Heb. *reḵeš*]; RSV "steeds" (Mic. 1:13), "swift horses" (Est. 8:14), "swift steeds"; AV "swift beasts"; [Gk. *híppos*] (Jas. 3:3; Rev. 9:9; 14:20; 18:13; 19:18). The most common is Heb. *sûs*, often occurring in parallelism with *'abbîr*. Heb. *rakkāḇ* usually refers to the rider or charioteer (e.g., 1 K. 22:34) and not to the animal being ridden. The RSV translates Heb. *pārāš* as "horsemen" (2 S. 8:4), or "war horses" (Ezk. 27:14; Joel 2:4); the AV has "horsemen"; the NEB "cavalry." *Rōḵēḇ hassûs* (2 K. 9:18) and *'al-hassûs* (Est. 6:9) are translated "horseback" by the AV and RSV and "horseman," "mounted" by the NEB.

Canticles 1:9 has textual difficulties; the RSV translates *sûsâ* as "mare," and the AV and NEB as "horses." Also difficult is Est. 8:10, where the RSV renders *rammāḵâ* as "royal stud," the AV "young dromedaries," and the NEB "royal stables."

In two instances the meaning of city names has retained etymological associations with horses: Hazarsusah (Heb. *ḥ^{a}ṣar sûsâ*, "village of a mare," Josh. 19:5), and Hazarsusim (Heb. *ḥ^{a}ṣar sûsîm*, "village of horses," 1 Ch. 4:31).

I. Horses in the Ancient Near East.–The original home of the horse appears to have been the steppes of Central Asia. References to horses are found in Cappadocian and Mitanni records at the beginning of the 2nd millennium B.C. in northern Mesopotamia. The Kassites in Babylonia also used the horse. The first reference to the horse in the eastern Mediterranean region occurred during the Hyksos rule in Egypt (18th-16th cent. B.C.). It is assumed that the horse was introduced to Egypt at that time. The Amarna Letters (14th cent. B.C.) mention horses in Palestine, although it seems clear that Israel did not rely upon the horse in warfare until the time of Solomon (see II.A below). Horses were trained to carry horsemen or pull chariots and represented a great advance over the foot soldiers. The Egyptians bred horses especially for war and sold them to other countries unable to raise enough horses for their armies (1 K. 10:29). Because of its military use the horse was associated primarily with the ruler and the state army (cf. Eccl. 10:7). Eventually cavalry systems developed as the use of horses in battle became regularized.

II. Biblical Uses of Horses.–Certainly the primary contextual connotations for horses in the Bible are dependent upon their use in war. Nevertheless, a few instances suggest a less glamorous domestic role. In addition, in a variety of contexts the horse is used to convey a broader figurative or symbolical meaning.

A. Military Use. Many passages refer to the characteristics of the horse in battle. He is swift (Jer. 12:5) and surefooted (Isa. 63:13); he is determined, and oblivious to others when charging in battle (Jer. 8:6). Horses are, nevertheless, capable of being panicked by Yahweh (Zec. 12:4). The most magnificent description of the war-horse occurs in Job 39:19-25, where the might, leaping ability, terrible snorting, fearlessness, ability to carry many weapons, fierceness, and desire for battle are all mentioned. It is clear from these references that the horse was a valuable and fearsome resource for the armies of the Near East. Horses were, as noted above, usually described as the property of the king (Est. 6:8f.; 1 K. 4:26, 28 [MT 5:6, 8]; 10:25; etc.).

The majority of references to horses in the Bible are concerned with them as the specific property of one nation or another. In the Mosaic period the horses of the Egyptians are mentioned frequently as illustrative of the might of Egypt and the greater power of God (Ex. 15:1, 21; Dt. 11:4; etc.). In the periods of the occupation and of the judges it was the enemies of Israel, the Canaanite city-states, that possessed horses (Josh. 11:4; Jgs. 5:22). For a variety of practical and theological reasons (Dt. 20:1; Josh. 11:6, 9) the tribes did not employ horses in their battles at this time.

With the increasing threat posed by the Philistines and the necessity for a unified effort against such enemies, it became clear that the army needed horses in order to fight successfully. David did not rely heavily upon horses (2 S. 8:4), but the way of the future was seen in the actions of Absalom and Adonijah, both of whom attempted to seize royal power with the aid of horses and horsemen (2 S. 15:1; 1 K. 1:5). The regular use of horses as an integral part of the army began on a large scale with Solomon. He was dependent upon Egypt for his horses (1 K. 10:28), with which he developed a sizable and powerful army.

The history of the divided kingdoms is interspersed with descriptions of the horses of Israel (1 K. 18:5; Isa. 2:7; Am. 4:10; etc.), Judah (Isa. 30:16; 31:1; Jer. 17:25; etc.), Syria (2 K. 5:9; 6:14), Egypt (Isa. 31:3), the "north" (Jer. 4:13; 6:23), Babylon (Jer. 50:37), and others. Sometimes reference is made to the horses of Yahweh (2 K. 2:11; 6:17; Hab. 3:8, 15). In each case the horse is seen as a determinant and symbol of military strength and its use is primarily for war.

The identification of the horse with royal authority explains the necessity for an entrance to the palace designated for horses (2 K. 11:16; 2 Ch. 23:15; Neh. 3:28; Jer. 31:40). The horse statues in the temple, connected with worship of the sun in Josiah's time, should also be noted (*see* HORSES OF THE SUN).

B. Nonmilitary Uses. Little attention is given to the nonmilitary uses of the horse, since these were clearly not its main use. In Gen. 47:17 and Ex. 9:3, however, horses are found in lists of possessions and appear to be referred to as ordinary livestock. In Isa. 28:28 (reading uncertain) reference may be made to the pulling of a cart by a horse. In Isa. 66:20 horses are one of many means of transport for the exiles. The horse is sometimes described as an animal which needs discipline in the form of a whip (Prov. 26:3): it is without understanding and "must be curbed by bit and bridle" (Ps. 32:9; cf. Jas. 3:3). Although these references cannot demonstrate the widespread use of the horse outside a military context, they offer some evidence to justify a nonmilitary use of the horse and a concern with characteristics not particularly pertinent to warfare. *See* picture of horse and chariot in HUNTING.

One of King Ashurbanipal's horses. Notice the fine trappings. Detail of an alabaster relief of a lion hunt from Nineveh (*ca.* 650 B.C.) (Staatliche Museen, Berlin)

C. Figurative and Symbolic Uses. Biblical literature affords many instances in which the horse is intended to represent more than just an animal carrying a rider. The best example of this is the famous Song of the Sea, which begins "Sing to the Lord, for he has triumphed gloriously; the horse and his rider he has thrown into the sea" (Ex. 15:20). Clearly the "horse and his rider" are meant to symbolize the entire Egyptian army on one level, and perhaps a more cosmological force on another level (cf. 15:1-18).

As the influence and military power of the state increased, so also did the importance of the horse as an integral part of the army. The horse, indeed, became a symbol of the strength of the nation. It is not surprising that those opposed to the growing ideology of state self-sufficiency would attack the horse as one example, a symbol, of the state's power. Thus the war-horse is described as a vain hope (Ps. 33:17), and the Lord's delight is not in the strength of a horse (Ps. 147:10). Akin to this judgment are the pronouncements of the prophets, who deny the horse's ability to save its rider's life (Am. 2:15) or provide military deliverance (Hos. 1:7).

Finally, the use of horse in apocalyptic contexts — both OT and NT — must be mentioned. The imagery accompanying the use of horse is vivid. In Joel, horses are used to describe locusts (2:4; cf. Rev. 9:7); the horses in Zechariah (1:8; 6:2, 3, 6) are patrolling the earth, signalling the beginning of the messianic age. A similar and parallel image appears in Revelation (6:2, 4, 5, 8; cf. 19:11, 19, 21, etc.; cf. R. H. Mounce, *Revelation* [*NICNT,* 1977], pp. 152-57, 342-350).

The horse, then, was an important part of the military life of Israel. It became a symbol of the power of the state, attacked by the prophets. Later it was used by other visionaries to help describe the final victory of God.

Bibliography.–V. Møller-Christensen and K. Jørgensen, *Encyclopedia of Bible Creatures* (1965); M. Noth, *The OT World* (Eng. tr. 1966); R. Pinney, *Animals in the Bible* (1964).

D. F. MORGAN

HORSE, BLACK [Gk. *híppos mélas*] (Rev. 6:5). Symbolizes famine (cf. Zec. 6:2, 6). *See* REVELATION, BOOK OF.

HORSE GATE. *See* JERUSALEM.

HORSE, RED [Gk. *híppos pyrrós*] (Rev. 6:4). Symbolizes war, bloodshed (cf. Zec. 1:8; 6:2). *See* REVELATION, BOOK OF.

HORSE, WHITE [Gk. *híppos leukós*] (Rev. 6:2; 19:11, 14). Symbolizes victory, conquest (cf. Zec. 1:8; 6:3, 6). *See* REVELATION, BOOK OF.

HORSELEACH (Prov. 30:15, AV). *See* LEECH.

HORSEMAN. *See* ARMY.

HORSES OF THE SUN (2 K. 23:11). In connection with the sun-worship practiced by idolatrous kings in the temple at Jerusalem (2 K. 23:5; cf. Ezk. 8:16), horses dedicated to the sun, with chariots, had been placed at the entrance of the sacred edifice. Josiah removed these in his great reformation, and burned the chariots. In Babylonian mythology Šamaš, the sun-deity, had his own charioteer, while a sculpture of Helios, the Greek sun-god, found in the Parthenon, showed him riding in a chariot pulled by horses.

HOSAH hō'sə [Heb. *ḥōsâ*]. One of the sons of Merari. He, his sons, and his brothers became responsible for the posting of guards at the west gate of Shallecheth (1 Ch. 26:10-19). He had previously been one of the gatekeepers in the tent of the ark when David brought the ark to Jerusalem (1 Ch. 16:37f.).

See also GATEKEEPER.

HOSAH hō'sə [Heb. *ḥōsâ*; Gk. B *Iasi(e)ph*]. A city on the border of Asher, in the neighborhood of Tyre (Josh. 19:29). The LXX B reading may suggest identification with Kefr Yasîf, NE of Acre. It is possible that Hosah represents the Assyrian Usu. Some scholars think that Usu was the Assyrian name for Palaetyrus. If "the fenced city of Tyre" were that on the island, while the city on the mainland lay at Râs el-ʿAin, 30 stadia to the south (Strabo *Geog.* xvi.2.24), this identification is not improbable.

B. E. HOVEY

HOSANNA hō-zan'nə [Gk. *hōsanná*]. "Hosanna" occurs six times in the NT, all in the story of Jesus' triumphal entry into Jerusalem. Twice this word is used absolutely (Mk. 11:9; Jn. 12:13), twice followed by the phrase "to the Son of David" (Mt. 21:9, 15), and twice followed by the words, "in the highest" (Mt. 21:9; Mk. 11:10). It was shouted at Jesus by the crowds of pilgrims in the street who acclaimed His arrival in the Holy City (Mt. 21:9), and later by the children who met Him in the temple (Mt. 21:15).

The origin and meaning of *hōsanná* are not certain. Some scholars suggest that it is derived from Gk. *hōs* (=*eis*, "into"), *aná* ("up"), an expression equal to *tḗn doxologían anapémpein,* "to send up the word of praise" (the doxology). Others consider the possibility that its origin lies in the Aramaic word *ʿûšᵉnāʾ* ("power"), and that it really means "praise." Most scholars, however, see it as a transliteration of Heb. *hôšîʿâ(-n)nāʾ*, an emphatic expression which appears in Ps. 118:25 as a cry to the Lord for salvation — "Save, we pray!" (RSV "save us, we beseech thee") or "Save now!" (LXX *ṓ kýrie, sṓson dḗ*). This last derivation is favored by Mark's use of a definite quotation from Ps. 118:26 following the crowd's "hosanna" (used absolutely): "Blessed is he who comes in the name of the Lord!" (11:9). Hence, C. C. Torrey (*Our Translated Gospels* (1936), p. 22) translates rather than transliterates *hōsanná* as "God save him!" (Mk. 11:9), and "God in heaven save him!" (11:10).

Although *hōsanná* originally may have been a cry for help addressed to God (or to a king for mercy; cf. 2 S. 14:4; 2 K. 6:26), it is quite likely that through liturgical usage (the Hallel Psalms, 113–118, were chanted both at the Feast of Tabernacles and at Passover, and the branches carried and waved then were known as "hosannahs") the original significance was lost, so that by NT times *hōsanná* may have become simply an expression of intense joy or a shout of welcome (cf. what happened through religious usage to the meaning of "hallelujah"). The phrase "to the Son of David," attached immediately to *hōsanná* (Mt. 21:9, 15), seems to confirm this understanding. Luke's translation of *hōsanná* by *dóxa* (19:38) does the same. The Greek-speaking church, no longer certain of the meaning of *hōsanná,* interpreted it to include the ideas of "light, and glory, and praise, with supplications to the Lord" (cf. Clement of Alexandria *Paed.* i.5).

"Hosanna" was associated with Jewish eschatological hopes in postbiblical times, and Judaism thought of the "one who comes in the name of the Lord" (Ps. 118:26) as the Messiah (T.B. *Pesahim* 119a; Midr. *Ps.* to Ps. 118:22; cf. SB, I, 849f.). Possibly this interpretation was very old, older than the rabbinic writings cited above. Thus it may also have been that of the crowd which hailed the coming of Jesus.

Mark seems to understand their hosannas in this way, for immediately upon quoting the substance of Ps. 118:25f. — "Hosanna! Blessed is he who comes in the name of the Lord!" (11:9) — he offers a commentary on the Psalm by including these additional words of the crowd: "Blessed is the kingdom of our father David that is coming! Hosanna in the highest!" (11:10). Matthew's "Hosanna to the Son of David" (21:9), which now precedes the quotation from Ps. 118:25f., strengthens this interpretation. Clearly praise is here being ascribed to Jesus, who, as the son of David, has fulfilled the promise to Israel (*TDNT,* IX, *s.v.* ὡσαννά 2 [Lohse]). Further, John's reference to the King of Israel — "Blessed is he who comes in the name of the Lord . . . even the King of Israel!" (12:13) — emphasizes this idea even more.

Thus the use of the familiar "hosanna" shouted to Jesus by pilgrims and children seems to indicate that for them every Jewish messianic expectation had now been fulfilled in Jesus. And the positioning of this story here in the outline of the life of Jesus, along with its modifications of the basic narrative, implies that the Evangelists also understood this ejaculation of praise and salvation in the same way.

Bibliography.–*TDNT,* IX, *s.v.* ὡσαννά (Lohse); F. C. Burkitt, *JTS,* 17 (1916), 139-149; J. S. Kennard, *JBL,* 67 (1948), 171-76; J. J. Petuchowski, *VT,* 5 (1955), 226-271; E. Werner, *JBL,* 65 (1946), 97-122.

G. F. HAWTHORNE

HOSEA hō-zā'ə [Heb. *hôšē(a)ʿ*]. A prophet of the 8th cent. B.C. whose oracles have been preserved in the book which bears his name.

- I. The Prophet
  - A. Name and Ministry
  - B. Historical and Religious Context
  - C. Marriage
- II. The Book
  - A. Form and Content
  - B. Message
  - C. Hosea and OT Traditions
  - D. Text and Redaction
  - E. Canonical Context

I. The Prophet.–*A. Name and Ministry.* The name Hosea, which occurs elsewhere in the OT (Nu. 13:8, 16, Joshua; 2 K. 15:30, the last ruler of the northern kingdom; etc.), is derived from the Hebrew root *yšʿ* ("help," "save"), and is probably to be understood simply as a 3rd masc. sing. pf. hiphil formation: "he [Yahweh] has helped, delivered" (cf. the name *hôšaʿyâ* [Jer. 42:1; 43:2; Neh. 12:32], a partially contracted form). Very little is known of Hosea's background, except the name of his father Beeri. While it is not explicitly stated, his ministry was certainly in, and chiefly to, the northern kingdom, and most probably Hosea was also (unlike his near contemporary Amos) a native of Israel, as is suggested by his intimate acquaintance with it. Note his mention and knowledge of the northern locations of Gilead (6:8; 12:11 [MT 12]), Tabor (5:1), Shechem (6:9), Gilgal (4:15; 9:15; 12:11), and Bethel ("Beth-aven," 4:15; 5:8; 10:5). Attempts to connect Hosea closely with the cult (cf. Brueggemann) lack conviction.

The only direct evidence for dating Hosea's ministry comes from the heading in 1:1 (in its present form a later editorial addition), which accurately matches the contents of the book — though it does not mention the last kings of Israel under whom Hosea was active. Jeroboam II of Israel died in 747/6 B.C., so the prophet must have begun his work before this; in 1:4 the house of Jehu, which came to an end with Jeroboam's short-lived son Zechariah, is still in power. If, as is suggested by the internal evidence of the book, Hosea's ministry continued till just a few years before the fall of Samaria in 722 B.C., this period would cover the Judean reigns mentioned in whole or in part. Hosea was thus the prophet of the final years of the northern kingdom, and his book represents, in skillful and impassioned language, the troubles of these years.

B. Historical and Religious Context. Israel's prosperity during the long reign of Jeroboam II (*ca.* 786-746 B.C.) is reflected in passages that probably come from the earliest period of Hosea's ministry (e.g., 2:2-15 [MT 4-17]). But the corruption and religious decay of Israel's last years, already apparent in the book of Amos, are also clearly reflected. After a reign of six months, Jeroboam's son Zechariah was murdered by Shallum, who after one month was in turn assassinated by Menahem (2 K. 15:8-15). Assyria, whose concentration on its own internal problems had been at least one factor that enabled the expansion of Israel under Jeroboam II, was resurgent under Tiglath-pileser III (745-727 B.C.), who was bent on expansion in the west; Menahem was forced to pay him heavy tribute (2 K. 15:19). Menahem was succeeded by his son Pekahiah who was slain by his officer Pekah (2 K. 15:25). The northern monarchy was in the throes of a bloody dissolution, as is apparent also in Hosea's portrayal of it (7:7; 8:4). Along with political anarchy went social chaos and a collapse of the moral fabric of society (4:2; 6:8f.; 7:1) which was condoned and shared by the ruling classes (7:3-7).

When Pekah and Rezin of Syria formed a coalition against Assyria and tried to force Jotham of Judah and his successor Ahaz to join them (2 K. 15:37; 16:5-9; Isa. 7), Ahaz' appeal to Tiglath-pileser precipitated Assyrian intervention to crush the rebels (733-732 B.C.). The events of the Syro-Ephraimite crisis of 735-732 B.C. are probably reflected in the details of Hos. 5:8–6:6 (cf. *KS,* II [1953], 163-187; for a different view see E. M. Good, *JBL,* 85 [1966], 273-286). In 733 B.C. the Assyrians overran Israelite territory, deporting large numbers of the population and carving up the occupied land into three provinces. Another bloody coup followed when Pekah was murdered by Hoshea (2 K. 15:30), who paid tribute to Assyria for a time during the reign of Shalmaneser V (727-722 B.C.) (2 K. 17:3). The political vacillation in this period between obedience to Assyria and rebellion with Egyptian support is reflected in Hos. 5:13; 7:11; 8:9f.; 12:1 (MT 2). When Hoshea withheld tribute from Shalmaneser and sought Egyptian aid (cf. 9:3 and 11:5), Israel was overrun by the Assyrians again, Hoshea was arrested, and Samaria besieged. The city fell in 722/1 B.C., and the northern kingdom came to an end. No prophecy of Hosea appears to come from so late a period as this (13:16 [MT 14:1] still looks to the fall of Samaria), though 13:10 may allude to the capture of Hoshea in 724 B.C. His work therefore takes us down to about the time of the siege, though it is conceivable that some of the hopeful prophecies come from a later period, after 722 B.C. (see below).

Along with the corrupt political situation, a central target of Hosea's invective is the prevalence of Baal worship, or a baalized form of Yahweh worship, in Israel. In the Ugaritic texts from Râs Shamrah, Baal (Hadad) is the great storm-god, the giver of rain and fertility, who, in one group of myths, dies at the hands of the god Mot, then comes back to life — just as the fertilizing autumn rains follow the drought and death of the summer. Thus these Canaanite deities were essentially mythological personifications of the forces of nature (see A. S. Kapelrud, *The Ras Shamra Discoveries and the OT* [1965], and N. C. Habel, *Yahweh Versus Baal* [1964]). Hosea shows clearly the increasing dominance in Israel of the Canaanite fertility cult associated with Baal and the sexual rites which belonged with it (as a means of insuring the fertility of the land), including sacred prostitution and bacchanalian orgies (4:11-13), and witnesses to the multiplication of altars and sacrifices in his day (8:11, 13; 9:4; 10:1). The Israelites tended increasingly to identify Yahweh with Baal, and to attribute Yahweh's good gifts of land and fertility to Baal (2:5-13). Probably the tendency was fostered by the apparently innocuous application of the epithet *baʿal* to Yahweh in the generic sense "master," "lord" (cf. 2:16 [MT 18]; note the occurrence of the name Bealiah, "Yahweh is baal," in 1 Ch. 12:5 [MT 6]). While it should not be supposed that the thought of Yahweh as controller of nature did not early play a part in the historically oriented faith of Israel, it is quite clear that Israel was increasingly attracted to the native Canaanite fertility deities after the settlement. The conflict had been fought and won for Yahwism at one level with Elijah (1 K. 18), and in the rebellion of Jehu with its prophetic support (2 K. 9–10), but the paganized cults did not die out. Hosea is concerned, probably, with this battle between the Mosaic faith and Baal worship at the level of both the local sanctuaries — hence his use of the Hebrew plural *beʿālîm* (2:13, 17 [MT 15, 19]; 11:2), suggesting a variety of local Baal cults — and the official bull cult introduced into the northern kingdom by Jeroboam I, which — whatever its original intention — must certainly have fostered syncretism (1 K. 12:26-33; Hos. 8:5f.; 10:5f.). Furthermore, the priests had failed in their duty of instructing the people; they were themselves greedy and corrupt (4:4-9; 5:1; 6:9). The situation, as Hosea saw it, was a total departure from faithfulness to Yahweh.

C. Marriage. Particular problems attach to the interpretation of the personal events of Hosea's life, recorded in chs. 1–3, which have a direct bearing on his message. Chapter 1 gives a third-person account of how Hosea, at Yahweh's command, married Gomer bath-Diblaim and had three children by her, to whom he gave symbolic names. Chapter 3, on the other hand, is couched in the first person, and tells how Hosea was instructed by God to go after an adulterous woman, whom he bought from her lover or from slavery, and brought to his own home, where she was to live for a time under disciplinary restriction; again this action symbolically expressed a divine message. It is clear that Hosea's prophetic word is here integrally linked with details of his personal life, and interpreters have long sought to clarify these details, though without attaining any consensus. (For a fuller discussion of older interpretations, see Harper, 208-210; S. Bitter, *Die Ehe des Propheten Hosea* [1975]; for a survey of more recent discussion, see Rowley.)

In trying to reach a decision on these matters, it should be stressed that (1) questions of historical reconstruction are here intimately related to questions concerning the literary composition of chs. 1–3; (2) there is a danger of arguing in a circle, i.e., building up a picture of the marriage relationship by analogy with Yahweh's relationship to Israel, and then using the former to interpret the latter (in particular, the issue arises as to how far we may use the prophetic oracles of ch. 2 as a key to the interpretation of chs. 1 and 3); and (3) these chapters are in no sense intended to give us material for a psychological study of the prophet. As with other apparently biographical passages in the prophetic books, Hosea does not want to tell us about himself, except insofar as it expresses his function as the messenger of Yahweh. It is necessary to beware, therefore, of the temptation to construct a romantic novel from chs. 1–3 and to use this as the interpretative key to the book. We have to start from the prophet's message and not from a reconstruction of his experience. This does not mean, of course, that the two are unrelated, but we must begin from what is clearly known, and what the prophet himself wishes to convey. It is customary to say that Hosea saw in his broken marriage and his enduring love for his wife (that is, taking chs. 1 and 3 as chronologically consecutive) a paradigm of Israel's apostasy from Yahweh, and of Yahweh's continuing love for Israel. But, while Hosea does indeed picture the relationship between God and His people as a marriage bond, this does not necessarily mean that a reconstruction of Hosea's married life would provide us with an overarching interpretative key for the prophecy.

Three questions call for clarification here. (1) Do chs. 1 and 3 give a record of actual events, or is this portrayal simply an oral or literary device? (It is better to avoid the term "symbolic," since the events in either case do have symbolic meaning.) The view that the account is allegorical is found, e.g., in Jerome, in medieval Jewish interpreters like Kimchi and Ibn Ezra, and more recently in Calvin, Hengstenberg, Keil, and Gressmann. E. J. Young argues that "the entire message was revealed to the prophet, and the prophet related this revelation to the people" (*Intro. to the OT* [1964], p. 253). This view was propounded largely because of the moral difficulty involved in supposing that God commanded Hosea to marry a prostitute. (A variant of this view takes ch. 1 to be historical, and ch. 3 as allegorical, but such an opinion seems unfounded.) A *prima facie* reading suggests that real events are in view in both cases, and some of the details do not seem to lend themselves easily to allegorizing (e.g., the name Gomer). Furthermore, serious exegetical evidence is lacking for the allegorical or visionary interpretation, which in any case does not have the desired effect of saving the morality of the divine command, but merely pushes the problem one stage further back. Everything favors, then, a literal interpretation of chs. 1 and 3, a view now generally accepted and found already in Irenaeus, Theodore of Mopsuestia, and Augustine. To the objection that God could not have commanded Hosea to do such a terrible thing as marry a prostitute, it may be replied that Israel's adultery with Baal was also a terrible thing.

(2) What, then, was Gomer's state at the time of the marriage? Some suggest that Gomer was not originally immoral, but only became so later (Hosea's growing suspicions perhaps being seen in the names given to the second and third children). While the views that Gomer was not an actual adulteress, but was only inclined toward adultery (Eichrodt, Soggin), or was so named simply as a member of the adulterous people of Israel, are unlikely (Rowley), many have argued that 1:2 is a proleptic view of Gomer's unfaithfulness, and that Hosea was commanded to marry a woman who only later turned out to be false to him (e.g., W. R. Smith, G. A. Smith, H. W. Robinson, Rowley, Ellison). This is not impossible, but the most natural reading of 1:2 is that Hosea actually was told to marry a woman known as a prostitute. It cannot be objected against this view that Gomer must originally have been pure, to parallel Israel's former relationship with Yahweh, since this is not the point of the marriage — which is concerned with the present situation existing between God and His people (1:2). An opinion commonly favored is that Gomer was in fact a ritual prostitute who took part in the Canaanite fertility cult (Mays, Fohrer, Wolff). Rowley's counterargument that Hosea would have had only condemnation for such an institution is no doubt true; but again it may be suggested that the whole point lies in the repulsiveness of the act, just as Israel's harlotry was repulsive to Yahweh.

(3) What is the relationship between chs. 1 and 3? Here a variety of interpretations have been proposed: (a) ch. 3 is in some sense parallel to ch. 1, but dwelling on different aspects of the marriage experience (Ackroyd, Clements, McKeating). In this case, "again" (*'ôḏ*) in 3:1 may be an editorial addition, or it may be taken with "Yahweh said" (resumptive of 1:2a) rather than with "go." The interpretation of the chapters as being in some way parallel does justice to the different forms of chs. 1 and 3, but at the same time this need not be decisive against a consecutive view; (b) chs. 1 and 3 concern different women, a second marriage being understood in ch. 3 (Keil, Fohrer, Rudolph); (c) both chapters concern the same woman and ch. 3 is a chronological sequel to ch. 1 (W. R. Smith, G. A. Smith, H. W. Robinson, Rowley, von Rad, Wolff). In this view, Gomer left Hosea some time after the birth of Lo-ammi, but in his undying love he bought her back from (probably) slavery.

Historically, the choice lies between regarding chs. 1 and 3 as chronologically sequential, and filling in the intervening events, or as in some sense parallel and describing the same marriage experience from different points of view. Perhaps a little more may be said for the former alternative (though the different options have their own problems), but it must be stressed again that the messages conveyed by the two chapters do not depend primarily on their chronological relationship. Chapter 1 is essentially concerned, not with the relationship between Hosea and Gomer as such, but with the symbolic names of the children (Rudolph) as signs of the judgment on Israel (cf. Isa. 7–8), while ch. 3 is concerned with God's continued love for His people and with the chastening punishment and hope of renewal which follows it. While it may be true that the second and third children were not Hosea's own (in fact, the message in the name of the first child is no less severe; and Jezreel is explicitly attributed to him) this is not said in the text, and as such is not part of the message of ch. 1. Much in the whole description (perhaps intentionally) relates only indirectly to the prophet's own experience. Views of Hosea's message that depend largely on a biographical reconstruction of his life as hinted at in chs. 1–3 should be eschewed (e.g., the opinion that Hosea heard his call from God in the very experience of his broken marriage, and that just as he continued to love his erring wife, so God continued to love His faithless people, particularly since 1:2 read in its most natural sense puts Hosea's call prior to his marriage). The "traditional" view is not necessarily wrong historically, but the text itself should not be interpreted in the light of this particular reconstruction. In addition, while the idea of Israel's adultery certainly occurs frequently, the text of chs. 4–14 does not directly indicate that the theme of God's continuing love for faithless Israel was based on Hosea's marriage experience; the marriage image is not the only one used by Hosea to express the relationship between Yahweh and His people (e.g., in ch. 11, where the theme of wrath wrestling with mercy is strongest, the father-son image is used). If we take 1:2 seriously, the significance of the marriage for the prophetic message is essentially that of prophetic symbolism (cf. Isa. 20; Ezk. 5). And, while Hosea appears to have been the first to express the relationship between Yahweh and Israel in terms of a marriage, it is not necessarily the case that he first drew the parallel from his own experience, since the husband-wife motif is already found in Canaanite religion (von Rad). Here 1:2 must be given full weight again, for this places Hosea's knowledge of the analogy prior to his own marriage. Possibly Hosea here, as elsewhere, was drawing on imagery used by those he was opposing, to give his message all the more force. At the same time, it is surely true that his own experience did deepen his understanding of Israel's faithless breach with Yahweh, even if it was not the source of that understanding.

II. The Book.–A. Form and Content. Most interpreters divide the prophecy into two unequal sections: chs. 1–3, which expound Hosea's message as conveyed through his family experiences, and chs. 4–14, a more loosely connected series of oracles conveying God's word to Israel. (There is no satisfactory reason to suppose, however, that chs. 1–3 ever circulated as an independent collection of prophetic material; cf. J. Lindblom, *Prophecy in Ancient Israel* [1962], p. 242.)

The prophecies of ch. 2 function quite clearly as a link between chs. 1 and 3. On the one hand, the mention of the children in ch. 2 is to be understood in the light of Hosea's children in ch. 1; ch. 2 clearly links the faithlessness of the wife with the birth of the children. Rudolph suggests that 1:2b should be regarded as a gloss, but in fact it forms the necessary background to the interpretation of the children's names, with their message of judgment on Israel. Judgment is coming because of Israel's faithlessness to Yahweh, symbolized in the marriage. On the other hand, ch. 2 also has close links with ch. 3 (Wolff, p. 59), so that chs. 1–3 belong together as a unit. Whether they were put in their present order by Hosea himself, or by later editors of the Hosea tradition, is uncertain. (An alternative suggestion is that if chs. 1 and 3 are parallel, then "perhaps the book should be divided into i+ii and iii+iv-xiv, the duplicate narratives each introducing a collection of sayings" [G. W. Anderson, *A Critical Intro. to the OT* (1959), p. 143]; but this is less likely.) In any case, it should be noted that chs. 1–3 are roughly parallel to each other in that prophecies of hope and restoration follow upon oracles of divine judgment. Many scholars argue that the hopeful prophecies are not from Hosea himself, but from later editors who arranged the material in its present form (see II.D below).

In chs. 4–14 we have a variety of oracles, from different periods of Hosea's ministry, whose exact delimitation is often difficult. The prophet's own deep sorrow about Israel's sin and the coming judgment is clearly evident in his language; but, at the same time, the words are not his own, but God's, whose messenger Hosea is (note the frequent use of the first-person divine-speech form). Hosea's threats of judgment are supported by invectives explaining why judgment is coming (for detailed studies of the speech forms used, see Wolff, pp. xxiii-xxv; Buss). Within these chapters, it is usually supposed, the units of material are grouped mainly according to similarity of subject matter (e.g., 4:1-11 and 12-19) and use of catchwords (e.g., "devour" in 8:7f., linking vv. 1-7 and 8-10), though questions of arrangement and structure here, as in other prophetic books, need fuller treatment. The prophecy has some movement, however, in that a roughly chronological arrangement is observable, and in that 9:10–14:9 (MT 10) look back more to Israel's past history and have a greater stress on the element of promise than 4:1–9:9.

We may outline the contents of the book thus:

Superscription (1:1)

I. Hosea's Marriage (Chs. 1–3)
   A. Hosea's Marriage to Gomer and the Birth of the Three Children (1:2–2:1 [MT 1:2–2:3])
      Words of Hope (1:7, 10–2:1 [MT 2:1-3])
   B. Yahweh's Legal Dispute with His Faithless Wife Israel (2:2-23 [MT 2:4-25])
      Words of Hope (2:16-23 [MT 18-25])
   C. Divine Command to Hosea to Bring Home a Woman (Perhaps Gomer) and Hosea's Disciplining of Her (3:1-5)
      Words of Hope (3:5)

II. Oracles Concerning Israel (Chs. 4–14)
   A. Israel's Sin and the Culpability of the Priests (4:1-10)
   B. Israel's Licentiousness and Idolatry; Participation in the Canaanite Fertility Cult (4:11-19)
   C. Israel's Defilement — Priests, King, and People (5:1-7)
   D. Threats Against Israel and Judah; Need for True Repentance (5:8–6:6)
   E. Israel's Breach with Yahweh; Bloodshed and Idolatry (6:7-11a)
   F. Israel's Wickedness (6:11b–7:7)
   G. Israel's Turning from God to the Nations and to Baal (7:8-16)
   H. False Worship and False Kings (8:1-14)
   I. Israel's Immoral and Idolatrous Worship (9:1-9)
   J. Israel's Apostasy at Baal-peor (9:10-14)
   K. Israel's Wickedness, Beginning at Gilgal (9:15-17)
   L. Growing Prosperity and Growing Sin: Fall of Calf and King (10:1-8)
   M. Israel's Wickedness, Beginning at Gibeah (10:9-15)
   N. Yahweh's Fatherly Love and His Sinful Son (11:1-11)
   O. Yahweh's Case Against Israel, Beginning with Jacob (11:12–12:14 [MT 12:1-15])
   P. Israel's Death-Bringing Departure from Yahweh, Past and Present (13:1-11)
   Q. Final Announcement of Coming Punishment (13:12-16 [MT 13:12–14:1])
   R. Plea for Israel to Return in Penitence to Yahweh; Promise of His Grace (14:1-8 [MT 14:2-9])
   S. Epilogue: "True Wisdom" (14:9 [MT 14:10])

B. Message. The great presupposition behind Hosea's message is the intimate relationship existing between Yahweh and His people Israel. Yahweh is Israel's God, who had entered into a covenant relationship with Israel (6:7; 8:1). This is pictured through a variety of images alongside that of the husband and wife (e.g., father and son [11:1-4], physician and patient [7:1; 11:3]). Hosea stresses God's tender care and compassion for His people, from the time that in grace He had brought them out from Egyptian bondage (11:1; 12:9 [MT 10]; 13:4), led them in the wilderness (9:10; 13:5), brought them into His good land, and gave them His good gifts (2:8 [MT 10]). He is the exalted Lord, the Holy One (11:9), who is not remote, but in a love relationship with Israel. This is clear throughout the prophecy. Hosea can vividly picture Yahweh's heart in turmoil, wavering between judgment and mercy (11:1-9). God's gracious acts of salvation are not just of antiquarian interest, but are relevant to Israel's present plight. Hosea can look back and see the present in the light of the past: "Wherever Israel's beginnings are examined, her present immediately appears" (Wolff, p. xxvii).

It is because of the relationship between Yahweh and Israel that Hosea and his God grieve deeply over Israel's sin. That sin is essentially a revolt against love, a breach of personal relationship — this is what breaking the covenant means for Hosea. Hence sin can be pictured as adultery or harlotry (1:2; 2:2, 4 [MT 4, 6]; 4:10-12; 5:3f.; 6:10; 9:1), manifested in social wickedness, but all the more in Israel's adultery with Baal, both individually (4:14) and corporately. Even this goes back to early days (9:10). It means making Yahweh into Baal (2:16 [MT 18]) and attributing Yahweh's gifts to him (2:5f. [MT 7f.]). Multiplying sacrifices and altars will prove useless (10:1f., 8), since the religion behind them is fundamentally corrupt. Thus the intended channels of grace have become channels of sin. The official northern bull cult is condemned (8:5f.; 10:5f.). Essentially the Baals are idols (4:17; 8:4; 11:2; 13:2) which God cannot tolerate (cf. Ex. 20:3-5).

In society Hosea singles out Israel's kings and priests for special condemnation (5:1). The kings are illegitimate because Yahweh did not choose them (8:4); at best they are "gifts" of His anger (13:10f.). They rejoice in Israel's wickedness and share it (7:1-7), they are proud and lack trust in Yahweh (7:7, 16) — the product of merely human machinations, taking no account of God's will and ways. Israel vacillates between Assyria and Egypt, neither of which can provide the necessary aid (5:13; 7:11; 8:9f.). The priests, too, are corrupt (4:4-9; 6:9), and because of them Israel lacks "knowledge of God" (4:1, 6; 5:4). While such knowledge undoubtedly has an intellectual element (note the parallel between lack of knowledge and forgetfulness of the divine Torah in 4:6; cf. 8:12), it is far more than this, embracing the whole personality. To know God means to be in an intimate relationship of cognition, love, and obedience (6:6; cf. 8:13; 12:6 [MT 7]; Jer. 22:16); it is Israel's highest good, which is now conspicuously lacking, even though it is claimed to be in evidence (8:2). (A covenantal basis for "know" in this sense has been suggested by H. B. Huffmon, *BASOR*, 181 [Feb. 1966], 131-37.) Linked with this is Hosea's frequent use of the term *ḥeseḏ* (RSV "steadfast love"), which, while difficult to translate, means for Hosea essentially warm and loving devotion to the relationship here created by the covenant (4:1; 6:4, 6; 10:12; 12:6 [MT 7]). In Israel, God's steadfast love contrasts to His people's lack of it. The ideal relationship (2:19f. [MT 21f.]) simply does not exist at present. Because of all this, and in the light of the way in which, though Yahweh desires to save His people, they will have none of it (7:1, 10, 13f.), judgment is coming.

Hosea stresses this judgment as vehemently as Amos ever did. More than Amos, however, he stresses that it is the judgment of love. This message of judgment is expressed clearly in the symbolic names given to the prophet's children (1:4-8): Jezreel, signifying that God would end the bloody kingship of Jehu's family; Lo-ruḥamah, "not pitied"; and Lo-ammi, "not my people," signifying a dissolution of the present covenant relationship (cf. Ex. 19:3-6). Like an adulterous wife, Israel would be punished. Prosperity and revelry would end (2:2-13 [MT 4-15]). Similarly, ch. 3 conveys a message of judgment, as is made clear by v. 4. At the same time, this is a disciplinary punishment inflicted by love (cf. v. 1), but terrible nonetheless. The prophecies that follow indicate the nature of the judgment as well as the reasons for it. It is pictured as a return to Egypt or exile in Assyria (8:13; 9:3, 6; 11:5); it means being cast out among the nations (8:8; 9:17). It involves the coming of the Assyrian enemy (8:3; 10:6), bringing war and barrenness, desolation and terrible atrocities (5:9; 9:11-16; 10:14; 11:6; 13:16 [MT 14:1]). In all this, Yahweh is the personal mover; He is bringing the end on Israel (1:4), the judgment of holy love.

Yet because it is the judgment of love, this is not the end of the story. The question of hope for the future in Hosea's prophecies has been widely discussed, and few would now accept the view that Hosea has no hope at all (Harper). Yet beyond this, scholars still disagree considerably. The whole problem of the redaction of the book arises here. To summarize in advance suggestions offered below (II.D), it is clear that Hosea does look beyond the coming judgment to restoration, salvation, and a renewal of the broken relationship (cf. 2:14-23 [MT 16-25]). Because God is holy love, mercy does not detract from judgment, but goes through and looks beyond it. Hosea proclaims a God whose free grace, not the sin of His people, has the last word.

C. Hosea and OT Traditions. Hosea's message, as indicated above, is firmly rooted in Israelite tradition, though he is never simply a mouthpiece for tradition but shows how past and present (and future) belong together as an indissoluble whole. For one thing, Hosea realizes that he stands in a tradition of Israelite prophecy (6:5; 9:7; 12:10 [MT 11]), which goes back to Moses (12:13 [MT 14]). Wolff argues that he belonged to a northern levitical-prophetic movement which stood firmly in the old Exodus traditions of Mosaic Yahwism, in opposition to the current Canaanization of Israel's faith. While this is possible, it does not seem necessary to tie Hosea down specifically to such a group, since we can assume "that all such circles as had a serious interest in the Israelite religion would also be acquainted with its traditions" (R. Rendtorff, *Journal for Theology and the Church,* 4 [1967], 19). Certainly Hosea does take up and use the old traditions of the Exodus and wilderness wandering (cf. R. E. Clements, *Prophecy and Covenant* [1965], pp. 45-49), and of the covenant between Yahweh and Israel (for a different view cf. J. Vollmer, *Geschichtliche Rückblicke und Motive in der Prophetie des Amos, Hosea, und Jesaja* [1971]). It has been argued that the idea of the relationship specifically as a *covenant* (though not the idea of a relationship in itself) is a view later than the eighth-century prophets, and that 8:1 must be seen as a later addition (L. Perlitt, *Bundestheologie im AT* [1969], pp. 146-49), but this view appears unnecessary. Hosea refers, further, to a number of other ancient traditions (e.g., Jacob in 12:2-6 [MT 3-7]), standing firmly within the stream of Israel's history. His links with Deuteronomy are particularly striking. For example, both see love as the link between God and Israel (3:1; 11:1, 4; 14:4 [MT 5]; Dt. 6:5; 7:8); both regard Moses as a prophet (12:13 [MT 14]; Dt. 18:15); both stress the dangers of satisfaction with God's gifts which leads to forgetting the Giver (13:5f.; Dt. 8:11-20). Such links are to be accounted for, not by supposing that Deuteronomy was written in dependence on Hosea (the older critical view), but by seeing Hosea as drawing on the particular streams of Israelite tradition represented in Deuteronomy. This does not prove an early date for Deuteronomy as such, but it does indicate that many traditions within that book are certainly very ancient.

Hosea's view of Israelite kingship shows his stance toward a newer aspect of tradition. The prophet was uniformly critical of the northern monarchy of his day, which was illegitimate because it was not chosen by God (8:4). Whether, as frequently supposed, Hosea was critical of kingship as such is more debatable (9:9, 15 are probably not to be regarded as alluding to the beginning of the monarchy under Saul). It is at least doubtful whether we should sharply distinguish between a "charismatic" view of kingship in the north, continuing the tradition of leadership of the judges period, and the southern "dynastic" view associated with the house of David. The OT distinguishes, rather, between kings who are chosen by God and those who are not, and Hosea seems to be in line with this view. Did he then regard the Davidic kingship of Judah as the only legitimate rule for "all Israel"? This will depend on the view taken of such verses as 1:11 [MT 2:2] and 3:5, but it is not impossible that this view does go back to Hosea himself. (On this topic, see the balanced and cautious discussion by A. Gelston, *Oudtestamentische Studiën,* 19 [1974], 71-85.)

D. Text and Redaction. The Hebrew text of Hosea appears badly preserved in places (more so in chs. 4–14 than in chs. 1–3), and in any case presents numerous translation difficulties (cf. the RSV mg.). The LXX is of some use in restoring corrupt passages, though in no sense superior as a whole to the MT. Some of the problems are caused by simple scribal errors; others may be caused by the difficulty that those who transmitted the prophecy after the fall of Samaria had with the language, which bears marks of a northern dialect of Hebrew influenced by Aramaic (cf., e.g., G. R. Driver, *JTS*, 36 [1935], 294ff.; A. Szabó, *VT*, 25 [1975], 522-24). Most probably the prophet himself had a share in writing down his oracles after their oral delivery (note the first-person narrative in 3:1-3), contrary to the views of Scandinavian scholars like Nyberg and Engnell that the prophetic oracles originally underwent a long period of oral transmission, being handed down in the circles of the followers of the various prophets, and constantly remolded according to contemporary needs. These scholars have overstressed the importance of oral, as opposed to written, transmission in the ancient Near East (cf. K. A. Kitchen, *Ancient Orient and OT* [1966], pp. 135-37). Furthermore, that certain prophets actually did have their oracles committed to writing appears to be attested to by the books themselves (cf. Isa. 8:16; Jer. 36; Hab. 2:2). Hosea himself most probably began the process of committing his own words to writing, so that they might live for the future as a witness to the truth of Yahweh's word (cf. Isa. 30:8). At a later time it was seen that the word had been fulfilled in the judgment which had come upon Israel in 722 B.C. (and on Judah in 587). So far as we can judge, then, Hosea's prophecies existed in written form not long after their oral proclamation, and were probably brought south to Judah after the fall of Samaria. (Whether Hosea himself came with them is impossible to say.)

In discussing possible editorial work in the book, we need not rule out in advance the possibility that editorial additions have been made, while we may wish to doubt whether these have been as extensive as often supposed. In Hosea's case, the chief question concerns the prophecies of hope beyond judgment which the book contains. Central to this issue is the status of the references to Judah (as opposed to the northern kingdom of Israel). A number of references which suggest that Judah will be punished alongside Israel are integral to the prophecy (5:10, 12, 13, 14; 6:4), and others may well be, though this is less clearly the case (e.g., 5:5c; 6:11a); in any event the latter merely highlight a theme found elsewhere in the book. Along with these, other verses indicate a much more positive attitude toward Judah (cf. 1:7; 11:12 [MT 12:1]). Critical scholars have tended to regard all or some of these references as secondary, along with others in the book (e.g., Fohrer sees the following as later additions: 1:10–2:1 [2:1-3]; 2:4f., 6f., 10, 12 [MT 6f., 8f., 12, 14]; 4:15; 5:5; 7:13b-14; 11:11f.). This goes too far. It is at least possible that some of the hopeful references to Judah were spoken by Hosea himself — perhaps in the period after the fall of Samaria (e.g., the hopeful reinterpretation of the names of the children in 1:10–2:1 [MT 2:1-3]). These do not give a detailed program of restoration, but they do affirm that God's grace must finally triumph. Such an attitude is already Hosea's own (cf. 11:8f.), and the reinterpretation can take place "not because judgment is escaped, but because the activity of God towards man is two-sided" (Ackroyd, p. 604).

At the same time, it seems clear that the book of Hosea has been subject to some editing at a later time, to draw out more clearly themes already implicit in the prophet's own preaching, and (with a basis in the convictions that God's word to Israel is also His word to Judah [since His people are in reality one] and that God's royal promises were given to the house of David [cf. 2 S. 7]) to apply the words of Hosea to Judah's situation. Hos. 1:1 is certainly redactional in its present form. It is important to stress that such editing was not a haphazard or arbitrary procedure, but was based on a theological understanding of the nature of Israel and its kingship deeply rooted in the OT, so that Hosea's book as we have it is oriented not simply toward the historical northern kingdom but toward the people of God as a whole. By this means it was affirmed that the prophetic word had continuing validity as God's word; Hosea's message was not simply preserved, but proclaimed afresh. A good case can be made for the view that other preexilic prophetic books have been subject to such editing. This is probably best attributed to the Deuteronomic school, active in the late preexilic and the exilic periods (contrast I. Willi-Plein, *Vorformen der Schriftexegese innerhalb des AT* [1971], pp. 115ff.). This group also (most probably) edited or compiled the historical books from Joshua to 2 Kings, showing how, in the light of the law of Deuteronomy, God's judgment on His people had been just, and yet pointing beyond present judgment to future hope (such a view does not, in itself, necessarily imply a late date for Deuteronomy). Thus the messages of the "writing" prophets and of the history of Israel stood alongside each other as witnesses to the rationale behind the events of 722 and 587/6 B.C., but also as witnesses to a hope of salvation. In this, and not least with Hosea, the Deuteronomists have not artificially tried to make the prophet say what he did not say, but have simply drawn out the real implications of what he did say. Their most important task was to let the prophet's own words speak, words which had already seen fulfillment in their threats of judgment. Now they proclaim the grace of God, who could not relinquish His hold on His people (cf. Dt. 4:29-31; 30:1-6).

E. Canonical Context. It is important to note that it is the book of Hosea in its final form which stands as canonical Scripture. Though Hosea himself was a northern prophet with a primary mission to the northern kingdom, in its present form the book is distinctly oriented toward Judah and the concept of "all Israel," and toward the Davidic kingship as exercising legitimate sovereignty over "all Israel" (1:11 [MT 2:1]; 3:5) in accordance with God's promises made to the house of David. A further stage of "redimensioning" is seen in the NT, where Hosea is quoted or distinctly alluded to in several important passages; it has been claimed that the whole book "was influential in early Christian thought" insofar as it stresses "the theme of judgement on a sinful people as the inevitable and indispensable, but also the certain, prelude to redemption, renewal, or resurrection" (C. H. Dodd, *According to the Scriptures* [1952], pp. 75-78).

Jesus Himself quoted Hos. 6:6 against His Pharisaic opponents (Mt. 9:13; 12:7), and in both cases the context is christologically oriented, i.e., it is not merely an inculcation of an ethical principle, but is integrally connected with Jesus' own work and claims. In Mt. 2:15, the Evangelist quotes Hos. 11:1 as fulfilled in Jesus' return from Egypt, or perhaps rather in His preservation from harm in Egypt, just as long before God had preserved and delivered His son Israel from Egypt (cf. R. H. Gundry, *Use of the OT in St. Matthew's Gospel* [1967], pp. 93f.). The messianic son, here viewed as the embodiment of the true people of God, recapitulates the experience of Israel. In a similar way, the idea of a resurrection of Israel "on the third day" (Hos. 6:2) lies behind the theme of Jesus' resurrection "in accordance with the scriptures" (1 Cor. 15:4; cf. B. Lindars, *NT Apologetic* [1961], pp. 60-66; H. K. McArthur, *NTS*, 18 [1971/72], 81-86). Indeed, the suggestion has been made that Hos. 11:1 may have been used as a pointer to the saving death and resurrection of Jesus (in His deliverance by God from the land of death), so that Matthew sees the last events of His earthly life as already prefigured in the events of His birth (Dodd, p. 103; Lindars, p. 217; D. Hill, *Matthew* [*New Century Bible*, 1972], p. 85). It is evident that we have in these references a further reinterpretation of Hosea's oracles within the setting of the total Christian canon: Jesus the Messiah embodies and represents the people of God. In His death and resurrection, He is the true Israel.

Furthermore, both Paul (Rom. 9:25f.), and Peter (1 Pet. 2:10) use the reversed "no people" prophecies of Hos. 1:10 and 2:23 (MT 2:1 and 25), applying them to the gentile mission (cf. J. H. Elliott, *The Elect and the Holy* [1966], pp. 44-48; F. F. Bruce, *NT Development of OT Themes* [1968], pp. 62-67) and no longer to the old Israel (though C. K. Barrett, *Romans* [1957], p. 191, suggests that there may be a secondary reference to Israel's temporary failure and subsequent return). Here again we see an extension of Hosea's prophecy within its overall canonical context, and it is not fanciful to link this with the applications of Hosea to Jesus as the embodiment of God's people. Thus Hosea directs us to Christ. With his insistence that divine grace does not remove divine judgment but goes through and beyond it to a future filled with hope, the book as Christian Scripture points to the gospel of the cross and says, "God loves like that!"

***Bibliography.**–Historical Setting: BHI* (2nd ed. 1972), pp. 254-274; N. K. Gottwald, *All the Kingdoms of the Earth* (1964), pp. 119-146; H. Donner, "The Separate States of Israel and Judah," in J. H. Hayes and J. M. Miller, eds., *Israelite and Judaean History* (*OTL*, 1977), pp. 421-434.

Survey of Recent Literature: J. F. Craghan, *Biblical Theology Bulletin*, 1 (1971), 81-100, 145-170.

Comms.: J. Calvin (repr. 1950); C. F. Keil (Eng. tr. 1871); G. A. Smith (*Expos.B.*, 1896); W. R. Harper (*ICC*, 1905); A. Weiser (*ATD*, 1949); J. Mauchline (*IB*, 1956); G. A. F. Knight (*Torch Comm.*, 1960); P. R. Ackroyd (*Peake's Comm.*, 1962); T. H. Robinson (*HAT*, 1964); W. Rudolph (*KAT*, 1966); J. M. Ward (1966); J. L. Mays (*OTL*, 1969); H. McKeating (*CBC*, 1971); H. W. Wolff (Eng. tr., *Hermeneia*, 1974); F. I. Andersen and D. N. Freedman (*AB*, 1980).

Intros. to the OT: O. Eissfeldt (Eng. tr. 1965); R. K. Harrison (1970); G. Fohrer (Eng. tr. 1970); J. A. Soggin (Eng. tr. 1976); B. S. Childs (1979).

Studies: W. R. Smith, *The Prophets of Israel* (2nd ed., repr. 1912), pp. 144-190; H. S. Nyberg, *Studien zum Hoseabuch* (1935); H. W. Robinson, *Two Hebrew Prophets* (1948), pp. 11-61; A. C. Welch, *Kings and Prophets of Israel* (1952), pp. 130-184; N. H. Snaith, *Mercy and Sacrifice* (1953); G. Östborn, *Yahweh and Baal* (1956); W. Eichrodt, *Interp.*, 15 (1961), 259-273; H. H. Rowley, "The Marriage of Hosea," in *Men of God* (1963), pp. 66-97; G. von Rad, *OT Theology*, II (Eng. tr. 1965), 138-146; E. M. Good, "The Composition of Hosea," *Svensk Exegetisk Årsbok*, 31 (1966), 21-63; W. Brueggemann, *Tradition for Crisis* (1968); M. J. Buss, *The Prophetic Word of Hosea* (1969); J. M. Ward, *Interp.*, 23 (1969), 387-407; H. L. Ellison, *Prophets of Israel* (1969), pp. 95-157; R. E. Clements, *Review and Expositor*, 72 (1975), 405-423; D. Kinet, *Baal und Jahwe: ein Beitrage zur Theologie des Hoseabuches* (1977); J. Schreiner, *BZ*, 21 (1977), 163-183.

E. BALL

HOSEN hō'zən [Aram. *paṭṭîš*] (Dnl. 3:21, AV); RSV TUNIC; NEB SHIRTS. An archaic term for "hose," "leggings." The precise meaning of the Aramaic word is unknown. *See* GARMENTS III.

HOSHAIAH hō-shā'yə [Heb. *hôša'yâ*–'Yah(weh) has saved'].

1. Father of Azariah (LXX Jer. 42:1; AV, following MT, has "Jezaniah"), who with other leaders antagonized the policy and counsel of Jeremiah after the fall of Jerusalem (Jer. 42:1–43:7).

2. A man, probably of Judah, who led half of the princes of Judah in procession at the dedication of the wall of Jerusalem (Neh. 12:32).

HOSHAMA hosh'ə-mə, hō-shā'mə [Heb. *hôšāmā'*, abbr. from *y^ehôšāmā'*–'Yahweh has heard']. One of the descendants of Jeconiah, the captive king of Judah (1 Ch. 3:18).

HOSHEA hō-shē'ə [Heb. *hôšē(a)'*–'little Joshua' or 'may Yahweh save']; AV OSHEA (Nu. 13:8, 16).

1. The early name of Joshua son of Nun, before Moses changed it (Nu. 13:8, 16). According to Dt. 32:44, the original form persisted for some time.

2. The son of Azaziah. An officer in David's army, he was set over the tribe of Ephraim (1 Ch. 27:20).

3. An eighth-century B.C. Israelite prophet, the son of Beeri, whose writings and oracles form part of the material known as the Minor Prophets (Hosea).

4. A signatory to the covenant in the time of Ezra and Nehemiah (Neh. 10:23 [MT 24]).

5. Son of Elah. He was Israel's nineteenth and final king, who reigned for nine years (*ca.* 732-722 B.C.), and was known in Assyrian records as *A-ú-si-'*. Hoshea succeeded to the throne of Israel at the end of a long period of social turmoil, political intrigue, and spiritual corruption. All this was reflected in the way Hoshea gained the throne — conspiring against and murdering his predecessor Pekah (*ca.* 740-732 B.C.).

Hoshea's action may have been prompted by Pekah's utter failure to contain the westward advance of Assyria under Tiglath-pileser III (*ca.* 745-727 B.C.), who had incorporated almost all of Israel into the Assyrian empire. Tiglath-pileser was apparently determined to annex the rest of Israel, and when Hoshea became king in Samaria the Assyrian monarch promptly put him under heavy tribute (2 K. 17:3). At the same time Tiglath-pileser boasted in his annals that he had put Hoshea on the throne over the Israelites (*ARAB*, I, § 816; *ANET*, pp. 283f.). Hoshea evidently did nothing to reverse the moral and spiritual corruption of the northern kingdom, although the compiler of Kings regarded him as somewhat less offensive than his precursors (2 K. 17:2). Apart from this brief evaluation, very little is known about the reign of Hoshea. He seems to have been an ardent patriot, however, and when Tiglath-pileser III died in 727 B.C. Hoshea probably thought that the time was opportune for him to revolt against Assyria by withholding the tribute.

Unquestionably his small realm could not afford the many talents of silver that the Assyrians demanded, but by refusing to pay the price of peace Hoshea placed his tiny kingdom in jeopardy. While Shalmaneser V was still in the process of succeeding his father Tiglath-pileser III, Hoshea made political overtures to Egypt by sending ambassadors to the pharaoh requesting assistance (2 K. 17:4). This ruler, named So (*sw'*), was probably Osorkon IV of Tanis (Zoan) (K. Kitchen, *The Bible in Its World* [1977], p. 113; but cf. Goedicke). He offered no help to Hoshea, however, and in 724 B.C. Shalmaneser launched an attack upon Israel.

Hoshea submitted to the Assyrians and paid tribute, but Shalmaneser suspected his professed loyalties and imprisoned him. After this there is no further information about the life or activities of Hoshea. Samaria withstood the enemy attacks for three years before falling in 722 B.C. About that time Shalmaneser V died and was succeeded by Sargon II (*ca.* 722-705 B.C.), who described in his annals how he captured the city (*ARAB*, II, § 55; *ANET*, pp. 284f.).

There is some doubt as to whether the city actually fell to Sargon, since, despite Sargon's repeated claims to have overthrown Samaria, the Assyrian ruler alluded to in 2 K. 17:6; 18:9f. appears to be Shalmaneser V. The fall of Samaria marked the end of the northern kingdom, since most members of the various tribes were taken as captives to Assyria. The prophet Hosea condemned the Israelites for their perfidy in attempting to deal with Egypt while still bargaining with Assyria (Hos. 7:11; 12:1 [MT 2]).

Bibliography.–W. F. Albright, *BASOR,* 130 (Apr. 1953), 4-11; 141 (Feb. 1956), 23-27; *WBA,* pp. 160-63; H. Tadmor, *JCS,* 12 (1958), 33-39; H. Goedicke, *BASOR,* 171 (Oct. 1963), 64-66; *MNHK,* pp. 141-47; *LBHG,* pp. 329-333. R. K. H.

HOSPITABLE; HOSPITALITY. *See* ENTERTAIN.

HOST. *See* ENTERTAIN.

HOST OF HEAVEN [Heb. *ṣ*[e]*ḇā' haššāmayim*]. The expression is employed in the OT to denote (1) the stars, frequently as objects of idolatry (Dt. 4:19; 17:3; 2 K. 17:16; 21:3, 5; 23:4f.; Jer. 8:2; 19:13; Zeph. 1:5), but also as witnesses, in their number, order, and splendor, to the majesty and providential rule and care of Yahweh (Isa. 34:4; 40:26, "calling them all by name"; 45:12; Jer. 33:22); and (2) the angels (1 K. 22:19; 2 Ch. 18:18).

(1) Star worship seems to have been an enticement to Israel from the first (Dt. 4:19; 17:3; Am. 5:26; cf. Acts 7:42f.), but attained special prominence in the days of the later kings of Judah. The name of Manasseh is particularly connected with it. This king built altars for "all the host of heaven" in the courts of the temple (2 K. 21:3, 5). Josiah destroyed these altars, and cleansed the temple from the idolatry by deposing the priests and burning the vessels associated with it (2 K. 23:4f., 12).

(2) In the other meaning of the expression, the angels are regarded as forming Yahweh's army, and He Himself is the leader of them — "the Lord of hosts" (Isa. 31:4; etc.) — though this designation has a much wider reference. *See also* ANGEL; LORD OF HOSTS. J. ORR

HOSTAGE. *See* WAR.

HOSTILE; HOSTILITY [Heb. *raʿ*] (Dt. 15:9); AV EVIL; NEB "look askance"; [Gk. *échthra*] (Rom. 8:7; Eph. 2:14, 16); AV, NEB, ENMITY; [*echthrós*] (Col. 1:21); AV, NEB, ENEMIES; [*antilogía*] (He. 12:3); AV CONTRADICTION; NEB OPPOSITION. The most frequently used Greek word describing the disposition or nature of the enemy is *échthra,* which appears in the NT six times. With the AV and NEB, the RSV translates *échthra* as "enmity" in Lk. 23:12; Gal. 5:20; Jas. 4:4, but in the other three instances it has "hostile/hostility." Perhaps the distinction between the two English words is that "hostility" more clearly reflects the active sense of *échthra.* Explicitly in Rom. 8:7, but also in Eph. 2:14, 16, man, more than merely being at odds with God, is the hostile party (*see also* HOSTILITY, DIVIDING WALL OF). So it is in Col. 1:21, where the RSV departs from the usual "enemy" for *echthrós* (cf. AV and NEB). "Enemy" is ambiguous, meaning either "hated (by God)" or "hostile (to God)." The RSV seems correct with "hostile." "It is the mind of man, not the mind of God, which must undergo change, that a reunion may be effected" (Lightfoot, comm. on Colossians [1879], *in loc.*).

Although the sense of active "opposition" (NEB) in *antilogía* was formerly disputed, so that the AV reads the more literal sense of "contradiction," the meaning "hostility" (RSV) or "rebellion" (cf. Jude 11) has been adequately attested (cf. MM). H. VAN BROEKHOVEN, JR.

HOSTILITY, DIVIDING WALL OF [Gk. *tó mesótoichon toú phragmoú*] (Eph. 2:14); AV, ASV, MIDDLE WALL OF PARTITION; NEB DIVIDING WALL BETWEEN THEM. The Greek expression *tó mesótoichon toú phragmoú* joins two words for wall. Gk. *mesótoichon,* which occurs only here in the NT, refers to a partition within a house. The other word for wall, Gk. *phragmós,* refers to a fence for protection and is so used in Mk. 12:1; Lk. 14:23. If the phrase is not merely a pleonasm, the joining of these words achieves the sense of a wall erected for both separation and protection.

Many have identified this wall with the stone wall of the Jerusalem temple, 1.5 m. (5 ft.) high, beyond which no Gentile was permitted to go. Inscribed on the pillars of the wall were warnings to Gentiles that trespassing was a capital offense. The destruction of this wall would be a particularly vivid metaphor for the new unity and equality between Jew and Gentile in the Christian Church.

Others have suggested that Gk. *tó mesótoichon toú phragmoú* be identified as the thick curtains that separated the holiest section of the temple from the rest. Only the high priest entered this holiest section and only on the Day of Atonement, when he performed the expiation for Israel's sins (cf. Mk. 15:38 par.; He. 10:19f.).

H. Schlier (pp. 125-133) suggested that the wall is a cosmic boundary that is broken through. He presupposed a mythological background for the passage, specifically Jewish Gnosticism, which gave to the principalities and powers a mediating position between God and mankind and made the law their instrument.

M. Barth took the wall to refer to "the fence around the law" created by the rabbis. This "fence," with its scribal interpretation, applications, and additions, protected God's law from being broken and effectively separated Jew from Gentile. Barth's interpretation takes "has broken down the dividing wall" as a synonymous parallel with "abolishing the law of commandments and ordinances." Barth also appealed to Gal. 2:18f., where Paul spoke of just such laws and statutes as having been torn down.

Each of these suggestions is plausible, but the "holy temple" image, which culminates the theological argument of Eph. 2:11-21, seems to favor the first suggestion. There is sustained contrast between the temple of Jerusalem and the new "holy temple" as well as between the restrictions on "access" (v. 18, Gk. *prosagōgḗ*; the verb *proságō* has cultic associations) in the old temple and the unrestricted "access in one Spirit" in the new temple. Just as the temple and cultic access are "spiritualized" (see Wenschkewitz), so are the holiness of the temple, the distinction between clean and unclean, and "the law of commandments and ordinances." Jesus Christ has created a "holiness" unrelated to race or nation. Thus Gentiles are no longer just "strangers and sojourners" vis-à-vis the temple but "built into it [the "holy temple in the Lord"] for a dwelling place of God in the Spirit" (v. 22). In view of this sustained contrast, the "dividing wall of hostility" seems to refer to the wall of the old temple separating Jews and Gentiles and restricting gentile access.

Bibliography.–M. Barth, *Ephesians 1–3* (*AB,* 1974), pp. 283-87; H. Schlier, *Der Brief an die Epheser* (*KEK,* 1958), pp. 125-133; H. Wenschkewitz, *Die Spiritualisierung der Kultusbegriffe, Tempel, Priester und Opfer im NT* (1932). A. D. VERHEY

HOSTS, LORD OF. *See* GOD, NAMES OF; LORD OF HOSTS.

HOTHAM hō'thəm, **HOTHAN** hō'thən [Heb. *ḥôṯām*–'seal'].

1. An Asherite, son of Heber, family of Beriah (1 Ch. 7:32).

2. An Aroerite, father of two of the mighty men of David (1 Ch. 11:44). The AV, following the LXX *Chōthan*, has, incorrectly, "Hothan."

HOTHIR hō'thər [Heb. *hôṯîr*–'abundance']. Mentioned in 1 Ch. 25:4, 28 among the sons of Heman, and one of those set apart by David for the musical service of the house of God (cf. v. 6). *See also* JOSHBEKASHAH.

HOUGH. *See* HAMSTRING.

HOUR [Heb. *môʿēḏ* (1 S. 9:24; Jer. 46:17); Gk. *hṓra* (Mt. 10:19; Rev. 3:3; etc.)]; AV also TIME (1 S. 9:24; Jer. 46:17; Mk. 6:35; Lk. 1:10; Jn. 16:2, 4, 25; Rom. 13:11; 1 Jn. 2:18; Rev. 14:15), INSTANT (Lk. 2:38); NEB also MOMENT, TIME, THEN, INSTANTLY (Acts 22:13), etc. Only the NEB uses "hour" to help translate the Greek terms *kairós* (Lk. 12:56; 2 Cor. 6:2; 11:25; 2 Tim. 4:6; Rev. 1:3; 22:10), *peirasmós* (Lk. 22:40), *krísis* (Jn. 12:31), and *árti* (Rev. 12:10). The term indicates either a point in time or a period of time, whether inexact or specified, and whether quantitatively measured or qualitatively assessed.

A point in time of no exact length is designated by Aram. *šāʿâ* in Dnl. 3:6, 15, etc. (which the AV often translates as "the same hour"; RSV "immediately"; NEB "suddenly," "at that very moment," "forthwith") and by Heb. *môʿēḏ* (< *yāʿaḏ*, "appoint"), "the time appointed" (Jer. 46:17, AV). Since in Greek the shortest length of time was expressed by *hṓra*, that word frequently meant "in a second," "without a moment's delay," "instantly," etc., as the NEB acknowledges more frequently than the AV or RSV (LXX Dnl. 3:6, 15; 4:19 [MT 16]; Mt. 9:22; 15:28; 17:18; Lk. 2:38; 24:33; Acts 16:18; 22:13; Gal. 2:5; Rev. 17:12; 18:10, 17, 19; see Bauer, rev., p. 896; MM, p. 702). "At that very moment" in Mt. 8:13b refers to the time of 8:13a.

The kind of time, its nature or quality, is often more important than its quantity or length. For instance, in the Fourth Gospel "hour" refers to the appointed time for either Jesus' sufferings in the Passion week or His glorification in the resurrection (Jn. 2:4; 7:30; 8:20; 12:23; 17:1). "Hour" is here a critical moment, marked for its meaning rather than its length. Whatever its duration, the "hour" of Jesus' betrayal (Mk. 14:41; cf. Lk. 22:53) or of His parousia (Mt. 25:13) or of His final judgment (Jn. 5:28f.) is different, in each case, from any other hour.

Frequently a temporal period is meant. Indefinite periods of time are indicated by: "as it was already late" (Mk. 11:11; cf. 6:35), "to the present hour" (1 Cor. 4:11), "hour by hour" (1 Cor. 15:30, NEB). Preexilic OT literature did not divide the day into hours, but after the Exile time was measured by sundials from sunrise to sunset. Since these were inaccurate chronometers that varied from one solstice to another, "hour" designated simply one twelfth of either day or night (Mt. 20:1-12; Jn. 11:9). Accordingly, "the third hour" was approximately 9:00 A.M. (Mk. 15:25), "the sixth hour" about noon (Mk. 15:33), "the ninth hour" about 3:00 P.M. (Mk. 15:33f.). There were three hours of prayer (Ps. 55:17 [MT 18]; Dnl. 6:10 [MT 11]), which could be designated more exactly by this sundial measurement: at morning sacrifice about 9:00 A.M. (Acts 2:15), at thanksgiving for the day's largest meal about noon (Mt. 15:36; Acts 27:35), and at afternoon sacrifice about 3:00 P.M. (Acts 3:1; 10:30). The most reliable MSS read *hēméra*, "day" (RSV, NEB), rather than *hṓra*, "hour" (AV), in Mt. 24:42.

Whatever the length of a period of time, the nature of that period is often most important. The silence of "half an hour" (Rev. 8:1) that followed the breaking of the seventh seal was a period of ecstatic suspense during which, unexpectedly, nothing happens — except almost unendurably tense expectation of judgment. The whole Christian era is "the last hour" (1 Jn. 2:18), a time known by the "many antichrists" that come during its duration. "The eleventh hour" (Mt. 20:6, 9), because of its context in a parable of the kingdom, accents the crisis of decision before impending judgment. "The hour to reap" (Rev. 14:15) is likewise quantitatively indefinite but qualitatively decisive.

See also DAWN; DAY; DAY AND NIGHT; DIAL OF AHAZ; NIGHT; TIME; WATCH.

Bibliography.–J. Barr, *Biblical Words For Time* (2nd ed., *SBT*, 1/33, 1969); O. Cullmann, *Christ and Time* (Eng. tr., rev. ed. 1964); C. Sandegren, *EQ*, 24 (1952), 241ff.

J. G. GIBBS

HOUR(S) OF PRAYER [Gk. *hṓra tḗs proseuchḗs*]. The phrase "hour of prayer" occurs only in Acts 3:1: Peter and John went up to the temple "at the hour of prayer, the ninth hour" (but see also Lk. 1:10; Acts 10:3, 9[?], 30). This narrative reflects the Jewish custom in NT times of regular hours of prayer three times a day.

The Jewish tradition of thrice-daily hours of prayer is already expressed in the OT (cf. Ps. 55:17 [MT 18]; Dnl. 6:10 [MT 11]; though 1 Ch. 23:30 reflects a twice-daily pattern). The exact times of the three hours, however, and the religious or cultic reasons for them are not easy to determine. The reference to morning, noon, and evening in Ps. 55:17 led some to regard the 3rd, 6th, and 9th hours of the day as the hours of prayer. But the more common and perhaps more important Jewish tradition was to regard the three hours of prayer as morning (3rd hour), afternoon (9th hour), and evening (12th hour). The morning and afternoon (sometimes translated "evening") sacrifices (Ex. 29:38-42; 2 K. 16:15) became the occasions for the morning (Ps. 5:3 [MT 4]) and afternoon (Ps. 141:2; Ezr. 9:5) hours of prayer. Another hour of prayer at sunset was then added.

Although the NT does not directly advocate regular hours of prayer (whether twice or thrice daily), the postapostolic Church soon came to call the 3rd, 6th, and 9th hours of the day the "apostolic hours" of prayer (based on the apostolic precedents in Acts 3:1; 10:3, 9, 30). These hours of prayer were connected generally with the trinity and specifically with two stages of Christ's passion (the 6th and 9th hours) and the descent of the Spirit at Pentecost (the 3rd hour). At first these were times for purely private devotions by all Christians, but later the stated hours of prayer became so extended and so regulated that they could be kept only by the religious orders under vows. Support for the monastic regulations was also found in the OT. The Benedictine Rule (xvi) calls for seven daytime hours of prayer and the night office. Warrant for this is found in Ps. 119:164, "Seven times a day I praise thee . . ." and Ps. 119:62, "At midnight I rise to praise thee. . . ."

That the NT does not specifically stipulate set hours of prayer suggests that the Christian has the freedom to regulate this for himself. Some will find regular hours of prayer a very helpful practice (e.g., grace before and after meals, Mt. 15:36; Acts 27:35; and prayer coupled with Bible reading, 1 Tim. 4:5); others may not find it helpful. In either case, each Christian will attempt to respond positively to the apostolic exhortation: "Pray constantly" (1 Thess. 5:17).

Bibliography.–For the Jewish tradition, SB, II, 696-702; for the

Christian tradition, *ERE,* XII, *s.v.* "Worship (Christian)" (J. V. Bartlet).
A. J. BANDSTRA

HOUSE [Heb. and Aram. *bayiṯ;* Gk. *oíkos, oikía*]. Hebrew *bayiṯ,* "house," occurs over 1750 times in the OT and embraces all dwellings, from the simplest (even a tent, Gen. 27:15) up to the king's palace (1 K. 7:1) or God's temple (1 K. 6:1). The term stems, presumably, from a root meaning "to get a night's shelter" (KoB, p. 122a; but cf. *TDOT,* II, 108).

- I. Cave Dwellings
- II. Surface Houses
  - A. Materials
  - B. Plans
- III. Details of Construction
  - A. Foundation
  - B. Floor
  - C. Doorway
  - D. Windows
  - E. Roof
- IV. Interiors
  - A. Walls
  - B. Fixtures
- V. Elaborated Structures
- VI. Extended Meanings

I. Cave Dwellings.–The earliest permanent habitations of the prehistoric inhabitants of Palestine were the natural caves that abound throughout the country. The OT refers frequently to reversions to the use of cave dwellings, particularly as refuges in distress (1 S. 22:1; Ezk. 33:27). Thus Lot dwelt with his two daughters in a cave (Gen. 19:30), and Elijah stayed in a cave when hiding from Jezebel (1 K. 19:9). As the people increased and grouped themselves into communities, these abodes were supplemented by systems of artificial caves. Such systems of burrowings, though of low headroom, might develop extensively into a series of adjoining compartments having several entrances. The latter were usually cut through the roof, with descent made by a few steps or simply a drop to the floor. During the rainy season caves were faulty dwellings, for when protection was most needed they might be flooded through the surface openings that formed their entrances.

II. Surface Houses.–*A. Materials.* The natural successor to the cave was a cavelike hut. For designed structures, the materials used were determined by local availability. Houses in most areas of the ancient Near East were therefore constructed of mud-dried bricks (Gen. 11:3; cf. Job 4:19). Thus some of the earliest known Palestinian houses, dating from 6800 B.C. in the silt-laden Jordan Valley at Jericho, were constructed of flattened cigar-shaped bricks, indented with thumb marks for more effective bonding (K. M. Kenyon, *Digging Up Jericho* [1957], pp. 54f.). Across the river from Jericho at Teleilât el-Ghassûl have appeared well-constructed houses of sun-dried brick roofed with wood, dating from Middle Chalcolithic (3500 B.C.). For most of Palestine, however, stone is the predominant material. Just as loose stones, and later quarried stones, could be carried out of Palestine's caves and used to erect extended fortifications, so these, together with the limitless field stones, constituted the natural materials for houses made in the hill country. Even for mud-brick buildings, foundations of unhewn stones were necessary to keep the bricks above the water that might collect (sometimes suddenly, Mt. 7:24-27); for protection against weathering, the walls were covered with a clay plaster or sometimes with a casing of stone slabs, as at Tell el-Ḥesī (F. J. Bliss, *Mound of Many Cities* [2nd ed. 1898]). Yet stone houses, in turn, seem frequently to have used mud brick for their upper story.

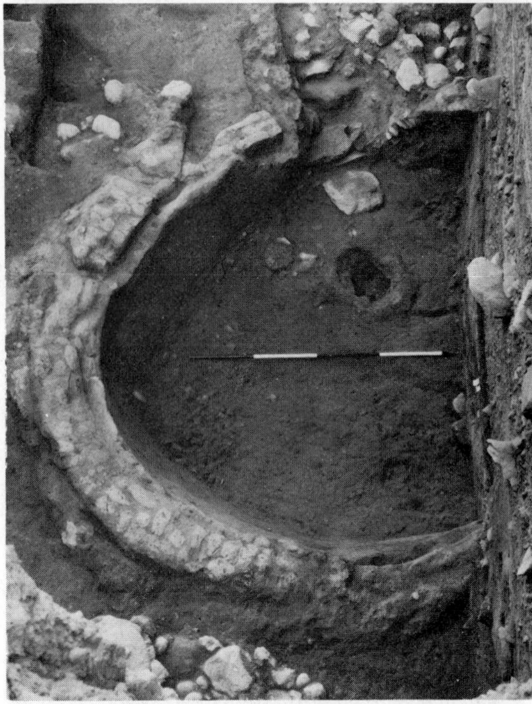

Excavated remains of a beehive-shaped house at Jericho. From the Pre-pottery Neolithic A Period, *ca.* 7000 B.C. (Jericho Excavation Fund, University of London; picture K. M. Kenyon)

A house from the Pre-pottery Neolithic B level at Jericho. Note the significant change to large, rectangular rooms (Jericho Excavation Fund, University of London; picture K. M. Kenyon)

B. Plans. Except in such rare periods of national security as the mid-8th cent. B.C., permanent houses were erected only within the fortified "cities that stood on mounds" (Josh. 11:13). Even those who worked on distant farms would make the long walk back to be within the walls at night (cf. Ps. 121:8, "Yahweh shall preserve thy going out and thy coming in"). Areas for dwellings were accordingly very crowded. The first houses of Jericho, built of oval "hogbacked" bricks which preceded even the indented mud bricks described above, were roughly circular, with floors sunk below the ground level and walls that inclined inward, forming a beehive shape. The upper part seems to have been of branches plastered with mud, the whole being suggestive of people only recently removed from cave dwellings, or from the circular tents or brushwood shelters of nomads (Kenyon, pp. 70-72). Plans of several apartments, allowing one to enter from what may be called a living room, followed as a matter of course; and these huddled together constituted the homes of the people. The more valuable animals would be stabled in a forecourt; the total enclosure provided storage for the entire property of a family. There is little sign of progress until the period of Hellenistic influence; and even then the improvement was slight, so far as the homes of the common people were concerned. Builders, of course, varied the plans to suit the requirements of cramped sites, and modifications were common. When members of a family married, extra accommodations or compartmentalizations would be necessary. In consequence, plans often became so jumbled that it is impossible to identify the respective limits of adjoining houses.

***III. Details of Construction.**–A. Foundation.* The combined threat of Palestine's all-too-frequent earthquakes and winter cloudbursts necessitated the laying of secure foundations, composed of rocks, and anchored to a cornerstone (Heb. *pinnâ,* Isa. 28:16; Jer. 51:26; Gk. *líthos akrogōniaíos,* 1 Pet. 2:6). In the construction of rude boulder walls, a large projecting boulder was built into the lower angle course. It tied together the return angles and was one of the few bondstones used in the building. This most necessary support claimed chief importance and as such frequently assumed a figurative meaning (Isa. 28:16; 1 Pet. 2:6; *see* CORNERSTONE). The importance given to the laying of a sure foundation is further emphasized by the dedication rites in common practice, evidence of which has been found on various sites in Palestine. The discovery of human remains placed diagonally below the foundations of the returning angle of the house gives proof of the practice of dedication rites both before and after the Conquest. Hiel sacrificed his firstborn to the foundations of Jericho and his youngest son to its gates (1 K. 16:34). But this was in a great cause compared with a similar sacrifice to a private dwelling. The latter manifests a respect scarcely borne out by the miserable nature of the houses so dedicated. At the same time, it gives proof of the frequent collapse of structures that the winter rains made inevitable and at which superstition trembled. The fear of impending disaster to the man who failed to make his sacrifice is recorded in Dt. 20:5: "What man is there that has built a new house, and has not dedicated it? Let him go and return to his house, lest he die in the battle."

B. Floor. When houses were built on rocky outcrops, the floor (Heb. *qarqa'*) could be roughly leveled on the rock surface; but it is more common to find floors of beaten clay, layer upon layer. Indeed, burnished plaster for both floors and walls characterized even the earliest houses of prehistoric Jericho. Flagstones were more sparingly used, primarily in courtyards and in the houses of the great. Wood was too precious to be employed extensively for flooring, although Solomon used it for his temple floor (1 K. 6:15). By Iron I and II (Israelite) times, with the invention of waterproof lime plaster, almost every house had its own cistern, sunk in the floor and supplied in winter by relatively pure rainwater from the roof (*AP,* pp. 113, 210). Channels for this purpose have been found, made of stones set in clay, sometimes leading through a silt pit into the cistern.

C. Doorway. The doorway (Heb. *peṯaḥ,* "opening") was a simple square entrance in the wall with a stone or wood lintel (Heb. *mašqôp*) and side posts (Heb. *meẓûzâ* [Ex. 12:7, 22] or *'ayil* [1 K. 6:31]). A stone sill, or threshold (*sap* [1 K. 14:17] or *miptān* [1 S. 5:4f.]), raised above the floor, was necessary to prevent flooding. Along with the cornerstone, this threshold was especially sacred, and in many instances foundation sacrifices have been found buried under the threshold. In later times, when the Hebrews had freed themselves from this unholy Canaanite practice, the rite remained with the substitution of a lamp enclosed between two bowls as a symbol of life. The doorposts were set into the stone at top and bottom, though when no wood was used the stone jambs of the opening simply constituted the doorposts. In either event, they were conspicuous as the points between which all those belonging to the house had continually to pass; hence the Mosaic injunction to inscribe God's commandments "on the doorposts of your house" (Dt. 6:9; 11:20). Judaism later took this command literally by attaching a small case at the doorway in which was placed a parchment containing the exhortation. The earliest wooden door (Heb. *deleṯ;* Gk. *thýra*) seems not to have been a permanent part of the house at all but to have consisted simply of a boarded cover, fixed vertically by a movable bar that slipped into sockets in the stone jambs. Later, true swinging doors were produced by the addition of the hinge (Heb. *ṣîr*), actually a pole attached vertically to one of the side edges of the door, projecting both above and below the door itself, and introduced permanently into sockets carved into the lintel and threshold. A more advanced form of construction was necessary to this type of door than in the previous instance, and skill was required to brace it, hold it together, and prevent sagging. In Israelite times a primitive "lock," or bolt (Heb. *man'ûl* [Neh. 3:3; Cant. 5:5]), and key (Heb. *maptē[a]ḥ* [Jgs. 3:25; Isa. 22:22]; Gk. *kleís* [Mt. 16:19]) made its appearance. (*See also* LOCKS AND KEYS.)

D. Windows. The window (Heb. *ḥallôn* [Josh. 2:15], *'arubbâ* [Eccl. 12:2]; Gk. *thyrís* [Acts 20:9; 2 Cor. 11:33]) was often simply an opening in the wall, though furnished with some method of closing which, it may be conjectured, was somewhat the same as the primitive door previously mentioned. The window of the ark (*ḥallôn,* Gen. 8:6), the windows in Gen. 26:8; Josh. 2:15, and the window from which Jezebel looked (2 K. 9:30) were presumably of the casement class. Ahaziah fell through a lattice (*śeḇāḵâ,* 2 K. 1:2) in the same palace, and the same word is used for the "networks" (1 K. 7:41) "covering the two bowls of the capitals." In Cant. 2:9 the beloved is "gazing in the windows [*ḥallōnôṯ*], looking through the lattice [*ḥarakkîm*]." It would appear, therefore, that some variety of treatment existed, and that the simple window opening with casement and the opening filled in with a lattice or grill were distinct. The door was a house's primary source of light. Windows were small, both for protection and for keeping the house cool. The lattice was open, without glass filling, a product that became available only in NT times, and only for the most wealthy. Heaven is spoken of figuratively as having "windows" (*'arubbâ*) for rain (Gen. 7:11; 8:2; 2 K. 7:2, etc.).

E. Roof. Contrary to the vaulted housetops seen in Palestine today, the roof (Heb. *gāg;* Gk. *stégē, dṓma*) of the biblical period was flat and usually not much over 1.8 m. (6 ft.) above the floor. Cf. "The beams of our house are cedar, our rafters are pine" (Cant. 1:17). To get over the difficulty of the larger spans, a common practice was to introduce a main beam (*qôrâ*) carried on the walls and strengthened by one or more intermediate posts let into stone sockets laid on the floor. Smaller timbers as joists ("rafters," *rāhîṭ*) were spaced out and covered in turn with brushwood; the final covering, being of mud mixed with chopped straw, was beaten and rolled. A tiny stone roller is found on every modern native roof, and is used to roll the mud into greater solidity every year on the advent of the first rains. Similar rollers have been found among the ancient remains throughout the country. Grass might grow temporarily on such roofs (Ps. 129:6; Isa. 37:27). "They let him down through the tiles [Gk. *kéramos*] with his couch into the midst before Jesus" (Lk. 5:19) refers to the breaking through of a roof similar to this. The roof ("housetop," Heb. *gāg;* Gk. *dōma*) was an important part of every house and was subjected to many uses. It was used for worship (2 K. 23:12; Jer. 19:13; 32:29; Zeph. 1:5; Acts 10:9). Absalom spread his tent on the "top of the house" (2 S. 16:22). In the Feast of Tabernacles temporary booths (*sukkôṯ*) were erected on the housetops. The Mosaic law required a parapet or railing for protection (Dt. 22:8). The people, as is their habit today, gathered together on the roof on high days and holidays (Jgs. 16:27). The wild wranglings which can be heard in any modern native village, resulting in vile accusations and exposure of family secrets hurled from the housetops of the conflicting parties, illustrate the passage, "And what you have whispered in private rooms shall be proclaimed upon the housetops" (Lk. 12:3).

IV. Interiors.–A. Walls. Life in a Palestinian village consisted primarily of outdoor activities; houses seem, therefore, to have functioned more for storage than for dwelling. Except for the rich, austerity was the rule. As previously noted, walls were plastered (Lev. 14:43, 48), and small fragments of painted plaster (Jer. 22:14) discovered from time to time show that some attempt at mural decoration was made, usually in the form of crudely painted line ornament. An exception exists in the polychrome fresco paintings recovered from Chalcolithic (3500 B.C.) Ghassul. As Albright has remarked, art here reached a higher level of achievement in Palestine than it did for thousands of years thereafter (*AP,* pp. 67f.). House walls were recessed here and there into various forms of cupboards at different levels. The smaller cuttings were probably for lamps, and in the larger and deeper recesses bedmats may have been kept and garments stored.

B. Fixtures. The OT references to the "hearth" (Heb. *'āḥ* [Jer. 36:22f.], *kîyôr* [Zec. 12:6], lit. "brazier") have been supplemented by archeological indications of fire pits in ordinary homes. It is unlikely that chimneys were provided (AV "chimney," Hos. 13:3, renders Heb. *'ᵃrubbâ,* RSV "window"): the smoke from the wood or charcoal fuel was allowed to find its way through the door and windows and cracks in the rough stone workmanship. Most cooking was done in the outdoor court when possible; but during the cold season the people had to huddle around and warm their hands at tiny interior fires (cf. Jer. 36:22). The use of cow or camel dung for cooking fires appears to have continued from the earliest time to the present day (Ezk. 4:15). A clay baking oven (Heb. *tannûr* [Gen. 15:17; Ex. 8:3]), approximately 0.6 m. (2 ft.) in diameter and 0.3 m. (1 ft.) in height, was located in the court. Household equipment was, for the poor, limited to bedding and kitchen utensils, storage bins of stone or pottery, water jars, clay cooking pots and serving bowls, and a stone mortar for grinding grain. Better homes could afford the furniture mentioned in the room of Elisha: a bed, table, seat, and lamp (2 K. 4:10), but not much more.

V. Elaborated Structures.–From Palestine's Early Bronze Age (3000-2000 B.C.) have appeared private houses of substantial construction, e.g., the thick-walled homes found in Early Bronze Ai. Thus Lot's house in Sodom provided a refuge against mob violence (Gen. 19:1-11). The Late Bronze (1575-1200) patrician establishments of the Canaanites were succeeded by relatively poor Israelite houses in Iron I. But in Iron II, accompanying the rise of wealth and commerce under Solomon, came a corresponding improvement in house building, though primarily in areas occupied by the rich. The northern capital of Tirzah, e.g., demonstrates a marked shift from homes of approximately uniform quality and arrangement in the 10th cent., to mansions on the one hand and hovels with thin walls and small rooms on the other in the 8th (R. de Vaux, *Ancient Israel* [Eng. tr. 1961], I, 72f.). Both Scripture and archeology attest to the spacious dwellings and ivory-inlay furniture of the nobles of Samaria (Am. 3:15; 6:4).

Most families, however, by this time located their living quarters in upstairs rooms (Heb. *'ᵃlîyâ* [2. K. 4:10]; Gk. *hyperṓon* [Acts 9:37], "upper chambers"; cf. *AP,* p. 210). Ahaziah was fatally injured by falling from the window of his palace, and a somewhat similar fate befell his mother, Jezebel (2 K. 1:2; 9:33). The escape of the spies from the house on the wall at Jericho (Josh. 2:15) and that of Paul from Damascus (2 Cor. 11:33) give substantial evidence of window openings at a considerable height. Elijah carried the son of the widow of Zarephath "up into the chamber." The Last Supper was held in an upper chamber (Mk. 14:15). Some sort of stairs (Heb. *ma'ᵃlâ*) on the outsides of the houses (cf. Mk. 13:15) must have existed; and the paucity of the remains of stone steps suggests that they were wooden, probably in the form of ladders in poorer homes.

Palaces (Heb. *'armôn, bîrâ* [1 K. 16:18; Ezr. 6:2; etc.]) were part of every city and were more elaborate in plan, raised in all probability to some considerable height. The Canaanite castle discovered by Macalister at Gezer shows a building of enormously thick walls and small rooms. Reisner has unearthed Ahab's palace at Samaria, revealing a plan of considerable area. Solomon's palace is detailed in 1 K. 7 (*see* TEMPLE). In this class may also be included the megalithic fortified residences with the beehive guard towers of an earlier date, described by Dr. Mackenzie (*PEF,* I).

Luxurious structures come into particular prominence with the Persian period; witness for example the residence of the provincial official in Lachish, which covered an area 36 m. by 52 m. (120 ft. by 170 ft.), and was equipped with bathrooms, and even underground pipes. In Greco-Roman times came the first truly planned cities. Their Herodian palaces and other structures, however, belong more to classical than to Palestinian architecture.

VI. Extended Meanings.–"House" often carries the expanded sense of "household," and this term is frequently substituted in the RSV for AV "house" (e.g., Ex. 12:4; 2 K. 7:11; 15:5; Isa. 36:3; 1 Tim. 5:14); in certain cases for phrases with "house" RSV has "at home" (Acts 5:42). *See* HOME; HOUSE OF GOD; HOUSEHOLD.

Bibliography.*–*AP; A. C. Bouquet, *Every Day Life in NT Times* (1954), ch. 3; W. A. Corswant, *Dictionary of Life in Bible Times* (Eng. tr. 1960), I.A.8, *s.v.* "Dwellings"; E. W. Heaton, *Every Day Life in OT Times* (1956), pp. 71-77; *TDOT,* II, *s.v.* "bayith" (Hoffner).

A. C. DICKIE
J. B. PAYNE

HOUSE, FATHER'S. *See* FATHER'S HOUSE.

HOUSE, GARDEN. *See* BETH-HAGGAN.

HOUSE OF GOD [Heb. *bêṯ (hā)'ᵉlōhîm;* Gk. *oíkos theoú*]. In Judges, 1 and 2 Chronicles, Ezra, Nehemiah, Psalms, etc., *bêṯ (hā)'ᵉlōhîm* designates the sanctuary of the tabernacle (Josh. 9:23; Jgs. 18:31), the temple (1 Ch. 6:48 [MT 33]; 9:11, 26f.; 2 Ch. 3:3; Ps. 42:4 [MT 5]; etc.), and the second temple (Ezr. 2:68; 3:9; Neh. 6:10; etc.; cf. Mt. 12:4 par.). The designation "house of the Lord" is used synonymously. On Gen. 28:17, 22, *see* BETHEL.

In the NT *oíkos theoú* is used spiritually of the church

or community of believers (1 Tim. 3:15; He. 10:21; 1 Pet. 4:17; cf. 1 Cor. 3:9, 16f.; 1 Pet. 2:5).

HOUSEHOLD [Heb. *bayiṯ*; Gk. *oikía, oíkos*]. A term that signifies the members of a family and others living together as a social unit, often under the same roof. It is used interchangeably with "house" and "family," and the translations vary considerably in their use of these terms, the AV frequently retaining the translation "house."

Households could include husbands, wives, concubines, children, close relatives, slaves, and even strangers. For example, Noah's household (Gen. 7:1; AV "house") consisted not only of himself and his wife, but also of his three sons and their wives. Gen. 14:14 says that 318 trained men who had been born into Abraham's household tried to rescue Lot. Later Abraham was commanded to put the sign of the covenant on all the male members of his household: "every male throughout your generations, whether born in your house, or bought with your money from a foreigner who is not your offspring" (Gen. 17:12; cf. 17:27). The *bayiṯ* (house or household) of Jacob (Gen. 46:27) included all his offspring — his unmarried daughters, his sons, their wives, and his sons' sons and daughters — seventy in all (46:1-27).

Yet a *bayiṯ* (household, family, or house) must not be thought of as being too large. It is not to be identified with a clan (*mišpāḥâ*), which is a subdivision of a tribe; rather, it is a subdivision of the clan (Josh. 7:14).

The Scriptures are much more corporate minded than we are today, and the OT use of "household" reflects that difference. God does not deal with each believer in a merely atomistic fashion. Once Abraham believed, then his whole household was considered to be in the covenant and the males were required to receive the covenant sign, circumcision. God gave a charge of holiness not only to Abraham, but also to his whole household (Gen. 18:19). He commanded various religious ceremonies to be observed by the household as a unit: the Passover (Ex. 12:3f.; 2 Ch. 35:6), the sin offering on the Day of Atonement (Lev. 16:17), the sacrifice of the firstborn of the flocks (Dt. 15:20), tithing (Dt. 14:26; 12:7), and eating of the Levitical tithe (Nu. 18:31). God punished not only Korah, Dathan, and Abiram, but also their households (Nu. 16:32; Dt. 11:6). Conversely, when God blessed Obed-edom for taking care of the ark, He also blessed "all his household" (2 S. 6:11).

On the human level, Jacob treated his whole household as a religious unit, commanding them to put away their foreign gods and to accompany him to Bethel, where he would set up an altar (Gen. 35:2f.). When Jacob was in danger of famine, Joseph invited him and his household to Egypt (Gen. 45:11). When Joshua saved Rahab for her act of faithfulness, he also saved her father's household and all who belonged to her (Josh. 2:18; 6:23-25). When he punished Achan for his sin, he also punished his household — "his sons and daughters, and his oxen and asses and sheep, and his tent, and all that he had" (Josh. 7:24).

The NT is likewise corporate minded. When Jesus healed the son of a royal official, not only did the official believe, but also all his household (Jn. 4:53). And when Jesus saved Zacchaeus, salvation came to his household also (Lk. 19:9). So closely are the members of a household related that Jesus observed that if its master is called Beelzebul, how much more its members (Mt. 10:25). In Acts we read that households were saved and baptized along with their heads: the household of Cornelius (10:2; 11:14), Lydia (16:15), the Philippian jailer (16:31-34), and Crispus (18:8). Paul tells of baptizing the household of Stephanus (1 Cor. 1:16; 16:15). He prayed that God would show mercy to the household of Onesiphorus (2 Tim. 1:16), and he sent his greetings to them (2 Tim. 4:19). The Christians in Caesar's household, i.e., the people in and about the emperor's palace, sent their greetings to the church in Philippi (Phil. 4:22; Rom. 16). *See also* CAESAR'S HOUSEHOLD.

In harmony with this pattern, the Bible figuratively calls the entire Church the household of God (Eph. 2:19; 1 Tim. 3:15; 1 Pet. 4:17) and the household of faith (Gal. 6:10).

See FAMILY. E. H. PALMER

HOUSEHOLD, CAESAR'S. *See* CAESAR'S HOUSEHOLD.

HOUSEHOLDER [Gk. *oikodespótēs*] (Mt. 13:27, 52; 20:1, 11; 21:33; 24:43; Mk. 14:14; Lk. 12:39; 13:25; 14:21; 22:11); AV also "goodman of the house," "master of the house"; NEB also "master (of the house)," LANDOWNER, EMPLOYER. The word denotes the master or owner of a "household," i.e., of servants. The Greek term emphasizes the authority of the master.

HOUSETOP. *See* HOUSE III.E.

HOWLING CREATURES [Heb. *'ō(a)ḥ,* only in the pl. *'ōḥîm*] (Isa. 13:21); AV DOLEFUL CREATURES; NEB PORCUPINES. The animal referred to by this word is not known, although the eagle-owl and the hyena are possible identifications (*CHAL,* p. 9). The context describes the animal inhabitants of the destroyed and abandoned city of Babylon. It is inhabited by scavenger birds, wild beasts, and "satyrs" (*see* DEMON I) instead of people. The hyena is likely because of its habit of digging up graves in order to eat the bones. Its howling cry adds to the eerie desolation of the landscape. For similar prophetic oracles describing a destroyed city or country, see Isa. 34:13f. (Edom) and Jer. 50:39f. (Babylon).

"Hyenas" in v. 22 translates a different word, Heb. *'îyîm* (AV "wild beasts"; NEB "jackals").

See also HYENA. H. W. LAY

HOZAI hō'zī [Heb. *ḥôzay,* or as it stands at the close of the verse in question, 2 Ch. 33:19, *ḥôzāy;* LXX *tṓn horṓntōn;* Vulg. "Hozai"; AV, RSV, NEB, "the seers"; AV mg. HOSAI; RSV mg. HOZAI. LXX not improbably reads (Heb.) *haḥōzîm* as in v. 18, an easy error, since there we find *w^e^diḇrê haḥōzîm,* "the words of the seers," and here *diḇrê ḥôzāy,* "the words of Hozai." Kittel, following Budde, conjectures as the original reading *ḥôzāyw,* "his (Manasseh's) seers"]. A historiographer of Manasseh king of Judah. Thought by many of the Jews, incorrectly, to be the prophet Isaiah, who, as we learn from 2 Ch. 26:22, was historiographer of a preceding king, Uzziah. This "History of Hozai" has not come down to us. The prayer of Manasseh, mentioned in 33:12f., 18f., and included in this history, suggested the apocryphal book, "The Prayer of Manasseh," written, probably, in the 1st cent. B.C. J. G. MCALLISTER

HUBS [Heb. *ḥiššurîm*] (1 K. 7:33); AV SPOKES. The term appears in a description of the ten bronze stands constructed for Solomon by Hiram from Tyre. KoB (p. 342) supports the RSV rendering. If, as it seems, the NEB rearranges the parts of the wheel in a progression outward from the axle, that version would also agree.

G. WYPER

HUKKOK huk'ok [Heb. *ḥûqōq*] (Josh. 19:34). A town on the border of Naphtali named with Aznoth-tabor. It is usually identified with the village of Yâqûq, which is about 5 km. (3 mi.) W of Chinnereth (cf. *GTTOT,* §§ 334, 337).

HUKOK ho͞o'kok. *See* HELKATH.

HUL hul [Heb. *ḥûl*]. The name of one of the "sons" of Aram" in the list of nations descended from Noah, but a people of uncertain identity and location (Gen. 10:23; 1 Ch. 1:17).

HULDAH hul'də [Heb. *ḥuldâ*–'weasel'; Gk. *Holda*]. A prophetess who lived in Jerusalem during the reign of Josiah. She was the wife of Shallum, keeper of the wardrobe, and resided in the "Mishneh" or second part or quarter of Jerusalem (location unknown; *see* JERUSALEM III.D.5.d). The standing and reputation of Huldah in the city are attested by the fact that she was consulted when the Book of the Law was discovered. The king, high priest, counselors, etc., appealed to her rather than to Jeremiah, and her word was accepted by all as the word of Yahweh (2 K. 22:14-20; 2 Ch. 34:22-29). Her prophecy relating to God's judgment on the nation began to be fulfilled with the death of Josiah at Megiddo in 609 B.C. While it was unusual for a woman to act in such a prophetic capacity, there is no doubt that her utterances were genuine in nature, as were the words of Anna when Christ was presented in the temple. J. J. REEVE

R. K. H.

HUMAN [Heb. *'āḏām, 'îš* (Isa. 52:14; cf. 53:2, NEB), *nepeš* (Ezk. 22:25); Gk. *ánthrōpos, anthrṓpinos, sárx, sárkinos*]; AV also "of man," "souls" (Ezk. 22:25), "flesh," etc.; NEB also "in a man" (Lev. 5:3), "men" (Ezk. 22:25), "living thing," "man-made" (Col. 2:8), etc.; **HUMANKIND** [Gk. *anthrṓpinos*] (Jas. 3:7); AV, NEB, MANKIND; **HUMANLY (SPEAKING)** [Gk. *katá ánthrōpon*] (1 Cor. 15:32); AV "of men"; NEB "as the saying is."

I. OT.–The Heb. *'āḏām* can denote an individual, "someone," or "man" in the generic sense, "mankind" (cf. Lev. 13:2; Gen. 6:2). Heb. *'āḏām* also functions as the proper name for Adam (Gen. 4:1), who was formed from the earth, *'ᵃḏāmâ* (2:7). The precise derivation of the word is debated (cf. *TDOT,* I, *s.v.* "'ādhām" [Maass]).

"Human" designates what is peculiar to mankind in distinction from other creatures (e.g., "cow," Ezk. 4:15; "cherub," 10:8), or what is characteristic of mankind (e.g., "semblance," Isa. 52:14; "hands," Ezk. 1:8). In Job 34:20; Dnl. 2:34, 45; 8:25, the RSV supplies "human" to emphasize the distinction between divine and human action.

II. NT.–A. *Common Uses.* As in the OT, "human" is used to distinguish mankind both from other creatures (Jas. 3:7; 2 Pet. 2:16; Rev. 9:7; 18:13) and from God (Acts 17:25; Rom. 3:5; 6:19; 1 Cor. 2:13; 9:8; Gal. 3:15; Phil. 2:8). In 2 Cor. 3:3 the *kardíai sárkinai* (lit. "hearts of flesh") are the new tablets on which Christ has written, in contrast to the old tablets of stone (cf. Ex. 24:12). The phrase "human being" occurs several times (Mt. 24:22; Mk. 13:20; Rom. 2:9; 3:20; 1 Cor. 1:29; Jas. 3:8), and there are frequent references to human practices or institutions (1 Cor. 4:3; Col. 2:8, 22; 1 Pet. 2:13; 4:2; Rev. 13:18).

B. Katá Sárka *in 2 Cor. 5:16.* Paul's usage here has sparked widespread and continuing discussion (cf., e.g., Allo, Fraser, Windisch). One's understanding of "human" or "worldly" (*katá sárka*) in 2 Cor. 5:16 depends on solutions to the following problems.

1. The Nature of the Phrase. Fraser has argued persuasively that since Paul's use of *katá sárka* to modify a noun has in all other cases placed the phrase immediately after the noun, the phrase in 5:16a and b, preceding *Christón* in 16b and separated by a verb from *oudéna* in 16a, must be used adverbially to modify *oídamen* in 16a and *egnṓkamen* in 16b.

2. The Nature of Paul's Knowledge of the Historical Jesus. The issue in 5:16 is not Christology but epistemology. Thus 5:16 tells us nothing about Paul's attitude toward the Jesus of history, and certainly it does not contrast the Jesus of history and Paul's Christ of faith (so Barrett contra Bultmann, *Primitive Christianity,* p. 197).

3. The Temporal Terms apó toú nýn *and* allá nýn. If 5:16 and 17, each introduced by *hṓste,* are taken as parallel (so Allo, Barrett, Fraser, Martyn), the contrast in 5:16 is between *katá sárka,* the "old" way of knowing before one becomes a Christian, and *en Christō̂,* the "new" way of knowing "in Christ." Since the person in Christ remains human (e.g., 2 Cor. 3:18; 4:6; Col. 1:28), the phrase *katá sárka* cannot mean that Christian knowledge is antihuman; the NEB "worldly standards" communicates the idea more effectively.

4. The Context. Far from being a gnostic gloss that denies the crucified Jesus (i.e., *katá sárka Christón*), as Schmithals argues, 5:16 is Paul's own statement of the contrast between the knowing that is empowered by Christ and the knowing that is empowered by *sárx* (for the contrast here between weakness and power, cf. Schütz, pp. 240f.). The contrast is not between exalted and crucified Christ. Rather, the contrast, evident also in Gal. 4:21-31, is the apocalyptic one between old and new aeons (Jewett, pp. 453ff.), or between old and new environments, old and new orders and powers.

Accordingly, *sárx* is not used by Paul to express dualism between man's body and mind or soul; rather it refers to "the whole man wrongly directed" (Barrett, p. 72; cf. Rom. 8:4f.; 1 Cor. 3:3, jealousy and strife as behavior originating in *sárx,* synonymous with *katá ánthrōpon,* RSV "behaving like ordinary men"; 2 Cor. 1:17, plans being made *katá sárka*; 2 Cor. 11:18, boasting that is *katá sárka* in contrast to speaking *katá kýrion*; Col. 2:11, "the body of the flesh"; Col. 2:18, "the mind of the flesh").

C. Other Uses of Katá Sárka. Knowledge "according to the flesh" is perverted by its self-serving character. "What Paul projects is man's habit (which affects Christians as well as Jews) of making a Messiah in his own image" (Barrett, p. 171). Thus *katá sárka* thinking is not guided by the Holy Spirit (Rom. 8:5), not controlled by the love of Christ (2 Cor. 5:14; cf. Mk. 10:35-45), whether one is considering other people (2 Cor. 5:16a) or Christ (16b). In the theological sense this is subhuman thought, less than that for which humanity was created, and contrary to thinking that is captivated by Christ (cf. 1 Cor. 9:19-23; 2 Cor. 1:12f.; 5:11; 10:5b; Gal. 1:10). Truly human thought is eschatologically determined, destined by the *kainḗ ktísis* (2 Cor. 5:17; cf. Schütz, 177f.).

Readers of the Greek NT will observe that Paul sometimes uses *katá sárka* nonpejoratively to designate kinship (RSV "according to the flesh" in Rom. 1:3; 4:1; 9:3, 5; 1 Cor. 10:18). Elsewhere (Rom. 8:3-5, 12f.; 1 Cor. 1:26; 2 Cor. 1:17; 5:16; 10:2f.; 11:18; Gal. 4:23, 29; 5:17; Eph. 6:5) the phrase carries the negative meaning found in 2 Cor. 5:16.

See also MAN.

Bibliography.–E. B. Allo, *La Seconde Épître aux Corinthiens* (1956), pp. 179ff.; C. K. Barrett, comm. on 2 Corinthians (*HNTC,* 1973), pp. 170ff.; R. Bultmann, *Primitive Christianity* (Eng. tr. 1956); *Theology of the NT,* I (Eng. tr. 1951), 232-246; E. Burton, comm. on Galatians (*ICC,* 1921), pp. 37f., 177f.; J. W. Fraser, *NTS,* 17 (1971), 293-313; R. Jewett, *Paul's Anthropological Terms* (1971), pp. 453ff.; W. Schmithals, *Gnosticism in Corinth* (Eng. tr.

1971), pp. 155-166, 302-315; J. H. Schütz, *Paul and the Anatomy of Apostolic Authority* (*Society for NT Studies Monograph Series*, 1975), pp. 175ff., 240ff.; *TDNT*, I, *s.v.* ἄνθρωπος, ἀνθρώπινος (J. Jeremias); VII, *s.v.* σάρξ κτλ. (Schweizer); H. Windisch, *Der zweite Korintherbrief* (*KEK*, 1924), pp. 186ff. J. G. GIBBS

HUMAN SACRIFICE. *See* SACRIFICE, HUMAN.

HUMBLE [(verb) Heb. *ʿānâ* (Gen. 34:2; Ex. 10:3; Dt. 8:2f., 16; Ezr. 8:21; Job 30:11; Ps. 55:19 [MT 20]; 89:22 [MT 23]; Isa. 58:3, 5; Ezk. 22:10; Dnl. 10:12), *kānaʿ* (Lev. 26:41; 1 K. 21:29; 2 K. 22:19; 2 Ch. 7:14; 12:6f., 12; 30:11; 32:26; 33:12, 19, 23; 34:27; 36:12), *šāpēl* (Isa. 5:15), *šāḥah* (Isa. 2:9, 11, 17), *bāḵâ* (Ps. 69:10 [MT 11]), *dāḵāʾ* (Jer. 44:10), *qālâ* (Prov. 12:9); Aram. *šᵉpēl* (Dnl. 5:22); Gk. *tapeinóō* (Job 22:23, LXX; Mt. 18:4; 23:12; Lk. 14:11; 18:14; 2 Cor. 12:21; Phil. 2:8; Jas. 4:10; 1 Pet. 5:6)]; AV also ANSWER, AFFLICT, "bowed down," "wept and chastened" (Ps. 69:10), "lightly esteemed" (Prov. 12:9), etc.; NEB also DISHONOURED; MORTIFY (Ezr. 8:21; etc.), MORTIFICATION (Isa. 58:5), BRING LOW, SPOKEN, SUBMIT, DEFER, SHOW REMORSE, HUMILIATE, etc.; [(noun or adjective) Heb. *ʿānî* (2 S. 22:28 par. Ps. 18:27 [MT 28]; Prov. 3:34; Isa. 66:2; Zeph. 3:12; Zec. 9:9), *ʿānāw* (Ps. 25:9; 149:4; Zeph. 2:3), *ṣānû(a)ʿ* (Prov. 11:2), *šāpāl* (Isa. 57:15; Ezk. 17:14), *tᵉḥinnâ* (Jer. 37:20; 38:26); Gk. *tapeinós* (2 Cor. 10:1; Jas. 4:6; 1 Pet. 5:5), *praús* (Mt. 21:5), *tapeinóphrōn* (1 Pet. 3:8)]; AV also AFFLICTED, LOWLY, POOR, MEEK, SUPPLICATION; NEB also MEEK, DOWN-TRODDEN, AFFLICTED, PETITION, FEEBLE, GENTLENESS, etc.; **WALK HUMBLY** [Heb. *ṣānaʿ*] (Mic. 6:8); NEB WALK WISELY; **HUMBLEST** [Heb. *ṣāʿîr*] (1 S. 9:21); AV LEAST; NEB LEAST IMPORTANT; **HUMILITY** [Heb. *ʿᵃnāwâ*] (Prov. 15:33; 18:12; 22:4; Zeph. 2:3); AV also MEEKNESS; NEB also "a humble heart"; [Gk. *tapeinophrosýnē*] (Acts 20:19; Phil. 2:3; 1 Pet. 5:5); AV also "lowliness of mind"; NEB also HUMBLY. "Humble" has a range of meanings that extends from vile acts to Christian virtue.

I. OT.–A. As a Verb. 1. Sexual Intercourse. Heb. *ʿānâ* is used in Gen. 34:2 of Shechem's rape of Dinah. Ezekiel condemns the men of Jerusalem who "humble" (*ʿānâ*) women "unclean in their impurity" (22:10). The verb is thus a euphemism for sexual intercourse (cf. Dt. 21:14; 22:24, 29) and is frequently equivalent to rape (Jgs. 19:24; 20:5; 2 S. 13:12, 14, 22, 32; Lam. 5:11). The broader meaning which renders the word usable in such contexts is "make submissive."

2. God's Sovereignty and Its Recognition. The term *ʿānâ* is related to the presence and use of power and coercion, of sovereignty and authority. It makes no distinction between *de jure* and *de facto* power, between legitimate and illegitimate authority; thus the verb has two main referents: "make submissive" and "afflict." Similarly, the cognate noun and adjective may denote either "the submissive" or "the afflicted."

Both meanings are present in Dt. 8. The first verse exhorts the people of God to keep His commandments, to be submissive to His will. The ground for that exhortation is the memory of the wilderness wanderings and how God humbled His people there (vv. 2f.). He afflicted them surely, but as discipline (v. 5). He "humbled" them, but to do them "good in the end" (v. 6). God's authority and power are legitimate as well as actual. Then follows the significant contrast by which the virtue of being humble suddenly bursts into view: "Beware lest you say in your heart, '*My* power and the might of *my* hand have gotten me this wealth'" (v. 17, italics added). The attitude of pride is not fitting for a people whose life and prosperity are due to the kindness and power of Yahweh.

That passage is paradigmatic for the Hebrew people's interpretation of their own history: when they exalted themselves God humbled them, and when they humbled themselves God exalted them. Undergirding such an interpretation of history is the conviction of the sovereignty of God: that His power and authority may not be ignored and cannot be escaped. From such an interpretation of history issues the appeal that people submit to Yahweh. Such is one of the themes of the historical books (which prefer Heb. *kānaʿ* to *ʿānâ*). The king who humbles himself before God, who submits to God, is exalted (Ahab, 1 K. 21:29; Josiah, 2 K. 22:19; 2 Ch. 34:27; Rehoboam and princes, 2 Ch. 12:6f., 12; Hezekiah, 2 Ch. 32:26; Manasseh, 2 Ch. 33:12, 19, 23; cf. Daniel, Dnl. 10:12). The king who does not humble himself, who does not submit, is afflicted (Amon, 2 Ch. 33:23; Zedekiah, 2 Ch. 36:12; even the Babylonian kings, Nebuchadnezzar and Belshazzar, Dnl. 5:22 [Aram. *šᵉpēl*], and the Egyptian pharaoh, Ex. 10:3 [Heb. *ʿānâ*]). Not only the king, however, but the whole people must submit to Yahweh (2 Ch. 7:14; cf. Jer. 44:10, Heb. *dāḵāʾ*). And the conviction of God's authority and power that undergirds such appeals explains the connection of "humbling" oneself with loyalty to God and performance of His commands (Lev. 26:41; 2 Ch. 7:14; 30:11; Jer. 44:10).

The conviction that God is sovereign also provided the background for the psalmists' appeals for deliverance. In Ps. 55 the people of God plead for deliverance from "the oppression of the wicked" (v. 2 [MT 3]). They voice their confidence that God will "humble" their enemies, and they give expression to the ground of their confidence, viz., that God is sovereign ("is enthroned from of old") and that their enemies have not acknowledged that sovereignty ("they keep no law and do not fear God," v. 19). Their confidence, then, is that God will humble the exalted, will make submissive the unsubmissive. God's authority and power may not be ignored and cannot be escaped. Ps. 89:22 speaks to this latter point straightforwardly: the wicked shall not humble God.

The situation is not really different with Heb. *šāpēl* and *šāḥah* in Isa. 2:9, 11, 17 and 5:15. These words do approach "humiliate," but they do not — at least in these contexts — surrender the connection with the sovereignty of God. Indeed, these threats that the proud will be humiliated occur in the context of Isaiah's vision of the Lord's universal reign: "For the Lord of hosts has a day against all that is proud and lofty, against all that is lifted up and high" (2:12). Moreover, Isaiah's vision itself constitutes an appeal to Judah and Jerusalem to submit to the Lord's authority; "O house of Jacob, come, let us walk in the light of the Lord" (2:5).

It is clearly a presupposition of the foregoing discussion that the sovereignty of God is both *de facto* and *de jure*. That presupposition, however, seems to have been questioned in Job. Eliphaz tells Job to humble himself before

God, to submit to God's sovereignty (22:23, LXX *tapeinóō*; MT *bānâ*). The implicit judgment in this is rejected by Job, who complains that God has "humbled" or afflicted him (30:11). The presence and use of power are clearly part of the question of Job. That God is sovereign is undenied, but the questions with which Job struggles are his own righteousness and the righteousness of God's exercise of power. He will let go of neither, but is it possible to hold to both? Job finally realizes that not even a genuinely righteous man can make any claims against Yahweh (chs. 40–42).

3. Fasting. *ʿĀnâ* sometimes means "fast" (cf. Lev. 16:29, 31; 23:27, 32; Nu. 29:7; Ps. 35:13; Isa. 58:3, 5; Ezr. 8:21; Dnl. 10:12; the RSV sometimes translates "afflict." Cf. also Ps. 69:10, where *bāḵâ* is rendered "humbled," probably on account of the following word *baṣṣôm* ["in fasting"] although it might also be a selection of the textual variant, a form of *dāḵâ*). The use of this word, however, discloses that the intention of the fast is not simply asceticism but submission to God's judgment. Ezr. 8:21 reports that the people fasted in order to humble themselves before God and to seek His will. Indeed, Isaiah issues a prophetic denunciation of the external observance when it is torn loose from its intention of submission to God and His judgment (58:3ff.). The fast God demands is submission to His will, "to loose the bonds of wickedness," "to share your bread with the hungry" (vv. 6f.). In Mic. 6:8 the contrast is with sacrifice rather than with fasting, but it is equally clear that the demand of God is not outward religious observances. The demand of God is rather to do justice, to love kindness, and to walk humbly (*ṣānaʿ*) with God.

B. As a Noun or Adjective. 1. "Afflicted" and/or "Submissive." The noun and adjective forms, Heb. *ʿānāw* and *ʿānî*, are also capable of meaning either "afflicted" or "submissive." The suggestion of S. R. Driver in *HDB* that *ʿānāw* refers to "the submissive" and *ʿānî* to "the afflicted" seems less likely than that these were virtual synonyms, each with both connotations. Driver's suggestion has some plausibility when, e.g., Zephaniah instructs "the humble" [*ʿānāw*] of the land, who do his commands," to seek righteousness and humility (2:3) and then promises to preserve a remnant "humble [*ʿānî*] and lowly" (3:12). But the plausibility vanishes when this remnant is contrasted with the unsubmissive "proudly exultant ones" who "have rebelled against me" (3:11), and when it is described as a people who "seek refuge" in God and do His will (v. 13). It seems here that *ʿānî* at least includes the idea of submission. Isa. 66:2 also counts against a clear distinction, for it uses *ʿānî* in a phrase that clearly refers to a man who is submissive to the authority of God, a man who "is humble and contrite in spirit and trembles at my word." Such a man stands in obvious contrast to those who fasted without submitting themselves to God's reign and purposes (Isa. 58:3ff.). These — in their religious pride — thought themselves to have earned God's blessing. The humble man is he who acknowledges that he has no claim on God but that God has a total claim on him. If religious observances, whose meaning is the acknowledgment of that claim of God, can tempt a man away from that acknowledgment, it is understandable that power and riches too can tempt a man to pride. And thus the connection of affliction with humility, of the poor and the powerless man with the humble man, can also be seen. Because of that connection it is very often difficult to discern whether "the humble" refers to "the afflicted," to "the submissive," or to both.

To the humble (*ʿānāw*) is promised victory in war (Ps. 149:4). David praises God for giving the victory to the humble (*ʿānî*) while He afflicts the haughty (Ps. 18:27 par. 2 S. 22:28, David's song of victory over Saul).

2. Wisdom. Of the conviction that God exalts the humble and humbles the exalted, Proverbs makes a general prudential rule, a piece of wisdom: "Toward the scorners he is scornful, but to the humble [*ʿānî*] he shows favor [*ḥēn*]" (3:34). Similarly, 11:2 teaches that the effect of arrogance is disgrace, "but with the humble [*ṣānûaʿ*] is wisdom [*ḥoḵmâ*]." *Ṣānûaʿ* is a hapax legomenon derived from *ṣānaʿ* (cf. Mic. 6:8); but given the antithesis and the wisdom context, it is probably to be understood as "not thinking of oneself more highly than one ought to think." Such a characteristic is not likely to bring the kind of disgrace which arrogance effects. (The wisdom of Prov. 12:9 is even more difficult to understand. The AV "lightly esteemed" [*qālâ* in contrast to *kāḇēḏ*], however, is probably a better rendering than RSV "humble.")

The same general rule is expressed elsewhere in Proverbs in terms of "humility" (Heb. *ʿᵃnāwâ*). As the fear of the Lord is the way to wisdom, so humility is the way to honor (15:33). As the result of pride is destruction, so honor is the result of humility (18:12). And 22:4 expresses forthrightly that "the reward for humility and the fear of the Lord is riches and honor and life."

These proverbs all point to the fact that the sovereignty of God cannot be ignored without consequence. A danger, however, is that subtlety of pride can use even humility as a claim upon God. The best remedy for this is the instruction of Zeph. 2:3 to the humble that they should seek humility (*ʿᵃnāwâ*) and righteousness. Similarly, in Ps. 25:9 the humble are taught what is right. Their humility makes no claims upon God but listens to His claims upon them.

3. Šāpāl *and* Tᵉḥinnâ. The Heb. *šāpāl*, a cognate of the verb *šāpēl*, approaches the meaning "humiliated," and maintains the connection with the sovereignty of God. Indeed, this connection is a presupposition of the comfort Isaiah offers the afflicted people: God dwells in the high and holy place *and* with the humble (Isa. 57:15; cf. Ezk. 17:14).

The "humble plea," Heb. *tᵉḥinnâ*, of Jer. 37:20; 38:26 is derived from the verb *ḥānan* and is thus related to *ḥēn* ("favor"). *Tᵉḥinnâ* usually refers to supplication for God's favor. Here it refers to Jeremiah's supplication to Zedekiah. In either case it is a recognition of the presence of authority and power and represents a plea rather than a claim. The request is based on the generosity and favor, the *ḥēn*, of the one who is asked rather than on the rights or merits of the one who is asking.

In summary, the OT calls people to submit themselves to the God who is sovereign and demands righteousness, who humbles the proud and blesses the humble.

II. NT.–A. The Transformation of Vocabulary. As is well known, the Greek moralists used the term *tapeinós* disparagingly. It was used in the sense of "groveling" and "mean-spirited" (*DNTT*, II, 259f.). Epictetus placed this quality at the very head of those he found censurable (*Discourses* iii.2.14). But because the Christian gospel and the Christian community did not lose touch with their Jewish heritage, they were able to change the status of this word in the Greek vocabulary. This transformation is represented within the NT itself. Paul iterates the charge of his Corinthian opponents: "I who am humble when face to face with you, but bold to you when I am away" (2 Cor. 10:1; cf. 10:10). "Humble" is meant disparagingly here. But Paul's response first appeals to the "meekness and gentleness of Christ" and finally vindicates humility and convicts his opponents: "For it is not the man who com-

HUMBLE

mends himself that is accepted, but the man whom the Lord commends" (2 Cor. 10:18; cf. 12:21).

Tapeinophrosýnē occurs in a bad sense in Col. 2:18, 23. "Self-abasement" (RSV) and severity with oneself is not to be demanded. That is part of the old aeon. But the Greek term soon recurs in a list of virtues with which the Christian is to clothe himself; the person who dies and was raised with Jesus Christ is to put on "lowliness" (RSV, *tapeinophrosýnē*, Col. 3:12; cf. Eph. 4:2). It is part of the new aeon. The possibility of a wrong kind of humility clearly exists and is condemned by the Christian community. The "humility" of the old aeon is to be distinguished from the humility of the new aeon in that it is really a device of pride; it lets go of the head, Christ, and destroys the unity of the new community (Col. 2:18f.). The self-abasement whose end is some claim upon God or some favorable comparison with the neighbor is condemned. That kind of humility is at bottom religious pride. The Christian virtue makes no claim on God but submits to the reign of God; it makes no claim over against the brother but serves, forgives, and loves the brother and thus serves the harmony and peace of the new community.

B. The Transformation of Values. The Magnificat of Mary stands at the beginning of the NT story and indicates both the continuation of the OT heritage and a radical revision of values. Mary praises the God who puts down the mighty and exalts the humble (Gk. *hýpsōsen tapeinoús*, RSV "exalted those of low degree," Lk. 1:52). In Mary's understanding, God's blessing upon her is a part of the decisive episode of God's activity of humbling the proud and exalting the humble.

The same theme is present in the preaching of Jesus Himself. Mt. 23:12 and Lk. 14:11; 18:14 all attribute to Jesus the saying, "For everyone who exalts himself will be humbled, and he who humbles himself will be exalted." Moreover, the same thought is expressed in Mt. 20:16; Mk. 10:31; Lk. 13:30, "Some are last who will be first, and some are first who will be last"; also in Mk. 9:35 and Mt. 20:27, "If any one would be first, he must be last of all and servant of all," and in Mt. 18:4, "Whoever humbles himself like this child, he is greatest in the kingdom of heaven." The profusion of this teaching — occurring in each of the Synoptic Gospels and at least nine times in the Synoptics altogether — is an indication both that the teaching is from Jesus Himself and also that it was very important in the early Church (cf. Minear, pp. 83-97).

In Mt. 23:12 the saying occurs in the context of Jesus' denunciation of the scribes and Pharisees. They taught humility (cf. SB, I, 191ff.), but they did not practice it. Here Christ prophetically announces the kingdom, with its promise to the humble, its judgment on pride — even moral and spiritual pride — and its radical demand to submit to the rule of God.

In Luke the saying appears twice in the central section (9:51–19:10): once as the conclusion to the parable about the places of honor at a marriage feast (14:11) and once as the conclusion to the parable about the Pharisee and the publican (18:14). The publican made no claim on God; he humbly made his plea for God's mercy; and "this man went down to his home justified rather than the other" (18:14). We do the parable no injustice if we take its lesson to be the doctrine of justification by grace through faith; but injustice is done to the parable — and that doctrine — if we take it to be teaching merely a theological abstraction or a purely individualistic and introspective reality. The lesson of justification by grace through faith speaks to a social reality. The Pharisee's lack of humility before God entails arrogance toward others. The publican's humility establishes solidarity and unity with all people.

Such a social reality is a matter of direct instruction in Lk. 14:11 and Mt. 18:4. Arrogance in social relations does not belong in the eschatological community. The people who know their salvation to be of grace do not act presumptuously toward their neighbors. The reign of God constitutes a realm in which all previous ideas of prestige, privilege, and protocol are transformed. To submit to God's kingship is to participate in a new social reality. "Who is the greatest in the kingdom of heaven?" (Mt. 18:1). The one who submits to the rule of God.

Jesus could not be accused of the error of the Pharisees; He practiced humility as well as taught it. His life is an even more eloquent testimony to the meaning of humility than His teachings. He was submissive to the purposes and will of God, and although He was master and lord of His disciples, yet He lived among them as one who served (Lk. 22:27; Jn. 13:13). The prophecy of Zechariah, fulfilled in Christ, gives eloquent expression to this theme: "Lo, your king comes to you . . . humble and riding on an ass" (9:9).

Paul, referring to the life of Jesus, appealed to the members of the Christian community to give up their pride of place, to seek unity, equality, and service, "in humility [to] count others better than yourself" (Phil. 2:3). He instructed them to "have this mind among yourselves, which you have in Christ Jesus," who made no claim on God but humbled Himself, submitting to the purposes and will of God (vv. 5-8). Therefore God exalted Him (v. 9), for God exalts the humble. Jesus' life, death, and resurrection are thus the decisive episode in God's historical activity of exalting the humble.

James and 1 Peter refer directly to the OT heritage (Jas. 4:6 and 1 Pet. 5:5 quote Prov. 3:34). Both preserve the connection of humility with the sovereignty of God and obedient submission to His will. On the basis of the proverb James issues the call to "submit yourself therefore to God" (Jas. 4:6); or as he puts it later, "Humble [*tapeinóō*] yourselves before the Lord and he will exalt you" (v. 10). Similarly Peter concludes, "Humble [*tapeinóō*] yourselves therefore under the mighty hand of God, that in due time he may exalt you" (1 Pet. 5:6). What James joins simply by the coordinating conjunction "and" (*kaí*, probably parataxis), Peter joins by the subordinating "(in order) that" (*hína*). While Peter's expression can be taken as result rather than purpose, there is nevertheless in his advice the same subtle danger we noted in the proverb itself: that humility be sought with a view to the consequent exaltation, that self-abasement be made a means to self-exaltation.

Both James and Peter are alert to the social consequences of submission to the reign of God. Peter introduces his quotation of the proverb to back his appeal that all members of the community clothe themselves with humility (*tapeinophrosýnē*) toward one another (1 Pet. 5:5; cf. *tapeinophrōn*, "humble-minded," in 3:8). Members of the Christian community ought to have a readiness to serve and to forgive.

James 2 recalls Jesus' parable of places of honor at the wedding banquet. Submission to the reign of God places one in an eschatological community in which there can be no partiality, for the pride of position and protocol is part of the old aeon. This conviction is already present in Jas. 1:9f. The RSV translates *tapeinós* as "lowly" and *tapeínōsis* as "humiliation"; nevertheless, the meaning is clear: God exalts the humble and humbles the exalted.

In conclusion, then, the heritage is important, but its fulfillment in Jesus Christ and the radical transformation of values God wrought in Him are decisive. From different angles of vision, different authors, genres, and bases, the NT speaks with one voice the conviction that the God who reigns is also the God who raises the humble, and that His reign establishes a new social reality. With one voice the NT calls people to accept that reign and its social consequences.

Bibliography.–*HDB,* IV, *s.v.* "Poor" (S. R. Driver); P. Minear, *Commands of Christ* (1972); *TDNT,* VIII, *s.v.* ταπεινός κτλ. (W. Grundmann). A. D. VERHEY

HUMILIATION OF CHRIST. *See* KENOSIS; PERSON OF CHRIST I.

HUMOR IN THE BIBLE.

I. The Source and Appropriateness of Biblical Humor
II. The Nature of Humor
  A. The Role of the Incongruous
  B. "Laughter" and "Joy"
III. Types of Biblical Humor
  A. Human Personality
  B. Situation
  C. Wit
IV. Conclusion

I. The Source and Appropriateness of Biblical Humor.–Our God is the God of laughter, merriment, and joy, as well as the God of righteousness, judgment, and love. When He created mankind in His own image, God imparted that mysterious capability called "a sense of humor." Those of His servants who recorded the words of the Bible by the inspiration of the Holy Spirit were in no degree diminished in their rich human personalities. Hence, it is not surprising that the Bible, despite its austerity, high seriousness, and urgency, should display many humorous events, personalities, and instances of wit. Indeed, it undoubtedly contains more humor than we realize, for it is both an ancient and a largely oriental book, and a sense of fun is often dependent on cultural and linguistic features peculiar to certain times and regions. A notoriously poor traveler from one language to another is wit, or verbal humor, arising from such things as paronomasia, alliteration, onomatopoeia, double meanings, clever rhythms, and the like.

II. The Nature of Humor.–Questions about what humor is and why it should stimulate that strange paroxysm called laughter have bewildered people through the ages. They need not detain us here. Two general characteristics of humor, however, are germane to our purpose, and must be mentioned.

A. The Role of the Incongruous. First, as to the nature of humor, its taproot seems to lie close to a recognition of the incongruous, the sense of difference from what normally is to be expected. It is, e.g., normal for people to speak intelligibly; so, when the unfortunate laborers on the Tower of Babel lapse involuntarily into gibberish (Gen. 11:7), and when (we may imagine) their shouts for more bricks produce only angry bewilderment from their fellows, we laugh at the incongruity. The original author underlines the fun with a pun: "Therefore its name was called Babel [*bāḇel*], because there the Lord confused [*bālal*] the languages of all the earth" (Gen. 11:9).

To be amused by the incongruous, it is important to realize, requires that one have a sense of the congruous. Confusion is funny only to the unconfused. Laughter is the judgment of order upon disorder. As George Meredith points out in his *Idea of Comedy and the Uses of the Comic Spirit* (1877), only an orderly society can recognize the incongruity of folly and laugh it off the stage. Even evil, if considered apart from the horror of its consequences, is laughably absurd, as Milton's unfallen angels discover when they view the arrogant posturings of Satan and his fellow rebels, and rejoice in their sprawling defeat at the hands of the Son (*Paradise Lost,* Book vi). There is much similarly exultant laughter in the Bible.

B. "Laughter" and "Joy." The second general point to be made about humor, as we treat the term in this writing, is that it is distinguishable from simple joy, though the outward manifestations of the two may be similar. "A glad heart makes a cheerful countenance" (Prov. 15:13). The Bible has much to say about the joy, the sheer happiness, of the redeemed; but these passages are not to be touched on here.

III. Types of Biblical Humor.–Humor arises most commonly from three sources: (1) individual personality; (2) events and situations; (3) wit (essentially wordplay, as defined above). In most instances, at least two of these categories operate at the same time.

A. Human Personality. We start with humor arising from personality, for the word "humor" itself starts with it. At least from the time of Hippocrates (*ca.* 400 B.C.), the term has related to the imagined four chief "humors" (or fluids — Latin *umor*) of the body which were anciently believed to determine the distinctive personality of every individual. To medieval interpreters Jonah, e.g., was a "choleric" man, owing to an excess of yellow bile. An excess of black bile bred melancholy, as in Jeremiah. An excess of phlegm produced phlegmatic Lot. And an excess of blood produced the warlike Joab. Needless to say, neither the Bible nor we view matters in this naive way; but from of old laughter has been caused by the quirks, foibles, and excesses of human personality.

Very early in the biblical story we find a deplorable but wryly amusing human trait: the tendency to blame someone else — anyone else — for one's own follies. "Rightly viewed," Adam in effect tells the Lord after Adam's sin, "it's not really my fault at all. The woman (whom, I must remind you, you gave me) made me do it." "Don't look at me," responds Eve, "the serpent tempted me to eat the fruit" (cf. Gen. 3:12f.). More endearing is the amusement we both share with, and aim at, Sarah, that lively, strong-willed woman, when the Lord promises her and Abraham a son in their old age (Gen. 18:10). Sarah, listening at the tent door, cannot refrain from laughing to herself (at the incongruous, incidentally), and is abashed when the Lord asks Abraham: " 'Why did Sarah laugh . . . ?' But Sarah denied, saying, 'I did not laugh'; for she was afraid. He said, 'No, but you did laugh' " (Gen. 18:13-15). Our kindly amusement at Sarah's discomfiture blends into a lovely culmination; for Sarah, after the birth of the promised son, says: "God has brought me laughter, and everyone who hears about this will laugh with me" (Gen. 21:6, NIV). So they name their son Isaac (Heb. *yiṣḥāq,* "laughter" or "he laughs"), from whose line comes the Savior, bringing joy and laughter not only to Sarah, but to all the company of the redeemed.

Jacob is one of the most fascinatingly complex personalities of the Bible, keeping us in a whirlwind of varying emotions, ranging from admiration for his persistence and energy to amusement triggered by his irrepressible trickery. To read of Jacob's long battle of wits with Laban over wives and sheep (Gen. 29–31), including Jacob's employment of primitive eugenics in the latter case, is to enjoy the kind of laughter accessible at once to the most primitive and the most sophisticated cultures. The narrative is capped with a delightful instance of litotes: "And Jacob noticed that Laban's attitude toward him was not what it had been" (Gen. 31:2, NIV). Even Jacob's wrestling match with the Lord (32:24-28) bears a kind of glowing corona of amusement around the luminous spiritual center, for the arrogant Jacob (whose name signifies "supplanter" or "heel-grabber"), now walking with a limp, is renamed "Israel," to be variously translated "God persists" or "rules," but permissibly to be colloquially rendered "God won the match!"

From the scores of delectably quirky personalities of the OT, our last illustration is Jonah. This taciturn, irascible character delights from beginning to end. His story starts abruptly, when God commands Jonah to go to Nineveh and pronounce judgment upon it (Jonah 1:1f.). Jonah's response is equally abrupt. Without a word (so far as the record shows), Jonah departs at top speed — in the opposite direction, not stopping until he comes to the port of Joppa where he takes ship for Tarshish (1:3)! When the great sea storm arises and lots have been cast, fixing Jonah as the cause, his advice to the sailors is typically dour and artless: "Take me up and throw me into the sea" (v. 12). His face, as he was swung by reluctant hands (for the sailors had tried to save him by reaching shore) arching him into the tumultuous waves, was no doubt expressionless. Rescued from the great fish God had provided, Jonah finally, and with the dark misgiving that in the end God would graciously withhold His hand from Nineveh, goes to the great city and pronounces its doom forty days hence. But his forebodings are realized. God, seeing Nineveh's repentance, spares the city; whereupon Jonah cries, in effect: "I knew it! Didn't I say so when I was back home — that you are a gracious God, merciful and slow to anger? I knew you'd never go through with it. That's why I headed for Tarshish. I want to die!" (cf. 4:2f.). And so he sits grumpily down and waits to see what will happen, making a booth to protect himself from the sun, aided by God's providential provision of a fast-growing vine — which promptly dies, to Jonah's intense anger. "Do you do well to be angry for the plant?" the Lord asks him. "I do," Jonah replies, "angry enough to die" (4:9). Whereupon the Lord teaches His gentle lesson (4:10f.), and one hopes, without great confidence, that Jonah's heart was touched. (An added fillip of pleasure may have been available to the ancient reader, for one etymology of the name "Nineveh" relates it to Akk. *nūnu,* "fish," and it was ideographically indicated by the drawing of a fish within a line denoting city walls. If Jonah would not go to the city-enclosed fish, he would himself become a fish-enclosed Jonah!)

The NT is not so richly sown with various kinds of humor as the OT, but it has its share. The personality of Peter, e.g., draws our admiration and laughter in full measure — Peter feeling it incumbent upon him to make a speech and take charge of the arrangements at the Transfiguration (Mt. 17:4); Peter drawing his sword, ready to take on the entire temple guard (Jn. 18:10); Peter undertaking to correct the Lord Himself, and to set Him on the right path (Mt. 16:22); Peter, told that the risen Lord stands on the shore in the dawn, leaping overboard to get to Him (Jn. 21:7). Often in error, but never in doubt; and when right, gloriously right!

B. Situation. Turning to our second category of humor — that arising from situations — we confront another embarrassment of riches; but we cannot do better than to turn first to the life and adventures of Samson, as recorded in Jgs. 14–16. Every age delights in the adventures, usually extravagant and sometimes farcical, of the prankster, the trickster, whose cleverness and physical strength reduce the enemy to laughable impotence. As usual, incongruous juxtapositions lie at the root of the fun — Samson burning the grain fields of the Philistines by tying torches to the tails of foxes; Samson carrying off the gates of the enemy's city, gates which were both the symbol and the reality of its security; Samson slaying a thousand men with the "fresh jawbone of an ass" (Jgs. 15:15); Samson paying his gambling debts by slaying thirty men of Ashkelon, turning the tables on those who had tricked the secret of his riddle from him by "plowing with his heifer" (Jgs. 14:18). Even his last great "labor" (to use a term legitimately reminding us of Hercules, another hero sometimes given to brutal fun), though it ended his life, was a great national victory, bringing exultant laughter to his countrymen and "calm of mind, all passion spent" (Milton, *Samson Agonistes,* line 1758). In quite a different vein is Balaam's controversy with his clear-seeing ass (Nu. 22:21-30). Three times the poor little donkey tries to avoid the fearful spectacle of the angel of the Lord, once dashing into a field, and being struck for her pains (v. 23); once, "in a narrow path between the vineyards, with a wall on either side" (vv. 24f.), bumping Balaam's foot against the wall, and being beaten again; and lastly, in another narrow path "where there was no way to turn either to the right or to the left" (vv. 26f.), just lying down, in pathetic distress — and of course being beaten again. We are ready to enjoy Balaam's ultimate discomfiture. Tacking again, we find that the life of the great David provides frequent occasion for the pleasure we always enjoy with the "comeuppance" of the boastful and the powerful. One such situation is David's victory over Goliath (1 S. 17:1-54), and another his conflict with Nabal, whose name means "fool" (1 S. 25:1-38). The final scene of the Nabal episode is particularly skillful in mingling incongruous contrasts for humorous effect: the gentle and beautiful Abigail; the noble David; and the gross Nabal, who, after a drunken night, wakes up sober (with a hangover) just in time to die of fright. Humorous for the same reason (the discomfiture of the haughty) are: the defeat of the Midianites by a handful of men under Gideon (Jgs. 7:19-23); the ironic jeers of Elijah at the priests of Baal (1 K. 18:27); and the terror of the wicked Haman, begging for his life from Queen Esther, whom he had tried to destroy ("falling on the couch where Esther was," Est. 7:8), and being hanged on the very gallows he had built for Mordecai (vv. 9f.). A brilliant instance of such exulting laughter (admittedly cruel, but very human) occurs in the victory song of Deborah and Barak, after the defeat of Sisera (Jgs. 5:1-31). Sisera's mother peers out of the window, wondering why her son's victorious chariot is delayed: "She gives answer to herself, 'Are they not finding and dividing the spoil? — A maiden or two for every man. . . ?' " (Jgs. 5:29f.). The word *raḥam* here euphemistically translated "maiden" is, in context, sexually crude, and intensely ironic, since the reader knows that Sisera lies dead of a tent peg driven clean through his head and into the ground, *by a woman,* Jael, wife of Heber the Kenite (Jgs. 4:21).

In the NT, Peter is again the central figure in two situations in which wickedness is frustrated to amusing effect, both of them involving supernatural rescues from prison. In the first, he and John, having been imprisoned in Jerusalem to prevent them from preaching, are summoned before "the council and all the senate of Israel" (Acts 5:21) sitting in solemn authority. Everyone is there — except the prisoners, who, according to the officers, seem to have disappeared. But not entirely: they are back in the temple preaching again (vv. 22-25)! In the second episode, Peter, having been led from Herod's prison by an angel, knocks for admission at the door of the house of Mary, mother of John Mark, causing such dismay to the maid Rhoda, who recognizes his voice but cannot believe he is real, that she leaves him pounding on the still unopened door while she runs to report to her mistress (Acts 12:6-16).

C. Wit. Instances of humor arising from our third category are the most numerous in the Bible, and the least translatable. From scores of examples we can mention only a few. A striking example of onomatopoeia (a word which imitates the sound of its referent) occurs in Isa. 28:10, where is culminated the condemnation of the "proud crown of the drunkards of Ephraim," and the "priest and the prophet reeling with strong drink," staggering and incoherent (vv. 1, 3, 7). With them, writes Isaiah, it is "precept upon precept, precept upon precept, line upon line, line upon line, here a little, there a little." This sounds innocent enough in English; but the Hebrew words translated "precept" and "line" repeat themselves in witless rhyme: *"ṣaw lāṣāw ṣaw lāṣāw qaw lāqāw qaw lāqāw zᵉʿêr šām zᵉʿêr šām."* A notable instance of paronomasia occurs in Am. 8:1f., wherein the prophet is shown a "basket of summer fruit" (*qāyiṣ*), and the Lord declares that the "end" (*qēṣ*) is come upon His people Israel. Similar is Jer. 1:11: " 'Jeremiah, what do you see?' And I said, 'I see a rod of almond [*šāqēḏ*].' Then the Lord said to me, 'You have seen well, for I am watching [*šōqēḏ*] over my word to perform it.' " A grim double meaning is used by Joseph in Gen. 40:13, 19 when he interprets the dreams of Pharaoh's chief butler ("Pharaoh will lift up your head, and restore you to your office") and chief baker ("Pharaoh will lift up your head — from you!"). The similarity in sound between certain common and frequently used words (such as "sun" and "son" in English) generates the same pun a number of times in the Bible, as in the case of the Hebrew for "see" and "fear"; e.g., "Ashkelon shall see [*tēreʾ*] it, and be afraid [*tîrāʾ*]" (Zec. 9:5).

In the NT, verbal humor is to be found in several of the utterances of Jesus, including hyperbole (the "speck" and the "log" of Mt. 7:3; the "straining out a gnat and swallowing a camel" of 23:24; and the passing of a camel through the eye of a needle of 19:24). Parallelism is used to good effect as he entangles the Pharisees and the Sadducees in their own wiles (22:15-46), and paronomasia in his naming of Peter (16:18). In the writings of Paul, instances of humor are infrequent, though he effectively employs irony, notably in his defense of himself in 2 Cor. 10:1f. and 11:1, 16-21; and perhaps against Ananias in Acts 23:2-5.

IV. Conclusion.–After examining a preponderance of rather satiric, often bitter, examples of humor, it may be appropriate to conclude with instances of gentle laughter in the NT. One thinks, e.g., of earnest little Zacchaeus, suffering not only from being "small of stature" (Lk. 19:3) but from the scorn of his neighbors, since he was not only a tax collector but the chief of that hated trade in Jericho and its environs. One can see him running ahead of the crowd, not welcome within it, for "he sought to see who Jesus was" (v. 4). Climbing the sycamore, he sits in imagined unobtrusive security, until Jesus Himself calls to him before the whole company: "Zacchaeus, make haste and come down; for I must stay at your house today" (v. 5). Oblivious now to the hostile upward stares of the crowd, Zacchaeus suits action to the command, scrambling down and rushing home to meet Jesus "joyfully" at the door, tumbling over himself to declare his integrity as a Jew, whatever his despised occupation may be. "Behold, Lord, the half of my goods I give to the poor; and if I have defrauded anyone of anything, I restore it fourfold" (v. 8). Jesus' gracious words in response (vv. 9f.) complete Zacchaeus's joy, and our own participation in it.

Two other episodes touch on that lovely thread woven into the NT, namely, Jesus' response to the women who came to Him. In one, He meets the Samaritan woman at the well, answers her blunt and perceptive questions, and approves her cautious statement that she has no husband at the moment, but adds that she has had five husbands, and the man she is now living with is not her husband (Jn. 4:16-18). After further conversation, the woman, with amusing exuberance and a disposition for exaggeration that comments on the breadth of her amatory and connubial history, runs back to the city and cries out to the people: "Come, see a man who told me all that I ever did!" (v. 29). The second episode concerns a Greek woman, Syrophoenician by birth, who begs Jesus to cast the demon out of her daughter (Mk. 7:25f.). Jesus tells her that His mission is only to the lost sheep of the house of Israel. "Let the children first be fed," He says, "for it is not right to take the children's bread and throw it to the dogs" (v. 27). Her reply reveals a smiling whimsy even in the midst of her distress for her daughter: "Yes, Lord; yet even the dogs ["little puppy dogs" — Gk. *kynárion*] under the table eat the children's crumbs." And He said to her, "For this saying you may go your way; the demon has left your daughter" (v. 29).

God's incomparable Book is addressed to a fallen world, where, truly, "even in laughter the heart is sad" (Prov. 14:13a); but the urgent proclamation of salvation is lightened by smiling, and Our Lord Himself has promised: "Blessed are you that weep now, for you shall laugh" (Lk. 6:21b).

Bibliography.–A. Bentzen, *Intro. to the OT* (1954); M. Eastman, *Enjoyment of Laughter* (1936); E. M. Good, *Irony in the OT* (1965); S. Leacock, *Humour: Its Theory and Technique* (1935); A. Repplier, *In Pursuit of Laughter* (1936); D. E. Trueblood, *The Humor of Christ* (1964).

C. D. LINTON

HUMPS [Heb. *dabbešeṯ*] (Isa. 30:6); AV BUNCHES. This is the only RSV reference to a camel's hump. While its meaning is clear from the context, its etymology has long been disputed. Some (e.g., Gesenius, *Hebrew-Chaldee Lexicon,* S. Tragelles, trans. and ed. [repr. 1976], p. 189) suggest that it orginally meant "bee hive" (cf. *dᵉḇaš,* "honey"), and developed the meaning "(camel's) hump" because of the similar shape. Others (e.g., KoB, p. 203) relate it to Akk. *gupšu,* "mass, lump," and Ugar. *gbṯt,* which refers to an animal's hump (cf. H. Cohen, *Biblical Hapax Legomena in the Light of Akkadian and Ugaritic* [1978], p. 132 n. 64).

G. A. L.

HUMTAH hoom'tə [Heb. *ḥumṭâ*]. An unidentified place mentioned between Aphekah and Hebron in the hill country of Judah (Josh. 15:54).

HUNCHBACK [Heb. *gibbēn*]; AV CROOKBACKT; NEB "mis-shapen brows." One of the disqualifications for the priesthood listed in Lev. 21:20. The affliction was probably Pott's disease, an angular curvature of the spine resulting from tubercular caries of the vertebrae. Its presence has been demonstrated in mummies, and it was also portrayed unmistakably in models of humans and on bas-reliefs in Egypt. The NEB rendering is based on postbiblical Heb. (and Aram.) *gᵉḇîn(āʾ),* "eyebrow," but the traditional rendering has the support of all the versions.

R. K. H.

HUNDRED [Heb. *mēʾâ*; Gk. *hekatón*]. *See* NUMBER II.

HUNDRED, TOWER OF THE [Heb. *migdal hammēʾâ*– 'tower of the hundred'; Gk. *pýrgos tṓn hekatón*] (Neh. 3:1; 12:39); AV TOWER OF MEAH. A tower of the wall of Jerusalem, possibly the eastern tower of a fortress that lay between the Sheep Gate and the Fish Gate, at the northernmost part of the walls restored by Nehemiah, approximately where Herod the Great later built Antonia. Alternately, it may have been the eastern tower of the

Sheep Gate, or an independent tower on the north wall.

The number may refer to 100 cubits in height, or to a hundred steps, or to a garrison of a hundred, or to the headquarters of a centurion in charge of a hundred men, or less likely to the distance from the Sheep Gate to the Tower of Hananel.

See JERUSALEM III.F.2.x. D. J. WIEAND

HUNGER, HUNGRY verbs: [Heb. *rā'ēḇ*]; AV "suffer to famish" (Prov. 10:3); NEB STARVE (Prov. 19:15; Isa. 65:13; Jer. 42:14), "afraid" (Isa. 8:21); [*ḥāḏal*] (1 S. 2:5); AV "have ceased"; NEB "grow strong"; [Gk. *peináō*]; AV "an hungred" (Mt. 4:2; 12:1, 3; 25:35, 37, 42, 44; Mk. 2:25; Lk. 6:3); NEB FAMISHED (Mt. 4:2 par. Lk. 4:2), "go hungry" (Lk. 6:21, 25; 1 Cor. 4:11); substantives: [Heb. *rā'āḇ*]; AV FAMISHED (Isa. 5:13); NEB FAMINE (Ezk. 34:29), "starve," "starving to death" (Ex. 16:3; Isa. 5:13); [*rā'ēḇ*]; AV, RSV, HUNGER-BITTEN (Job 18:12); NEB STARVING (2 K. 7:12; Isa. 29:8), HUNGRILY (Job 5:5), "fear" (Isa. 8:21), "paralyzed with fear" (Job 18:12); [*kāpān*] (Job 30:3); AV FAMINE; [*nepeš*]; AV "soul(s)" (Isa. 29:8; Ezk. 7:19; Hos. 9:4); NEB "himself" (Isa. 29:8); [*yešaḥ*] (Mic. 6:14); AV "(thy) casting down"; NEB "(your) food shall lie heavy"; [Gk. *limós*] (Lk. 15:17; 2 Cor. 11:27); NEB STARVING (Lk. 15:17); [*nēsteía*] (2 Cor. 6:5); AV FASTINGS; NEB STARVING; [*nēstis*] (Mt. 15:32 par. Mk. 8:3); AV FASTING; NEB UNFED; [*próspeinos*] (Acts 10:10).

In the OT "hunger" is most frequently expressed by the root *r'b* (vb., *rā'ēḇ*; noun, *rā'āḇ*; adj., *rā'ēḇ*). The verb *rā'ēḇ* denotes "be hungry, suffer hunger." With the exception of Isa. 44:12, where the ironsmith is said to weaken from not eating, *rā'ēḇ* refers to the deprivation or lack of the normal fruits of work (cf., e.g., Ex. 16:3; Jer. 38:9; Ezk. 34:29), rather than the recurrent appetite for food. In Prov. 6:30 it represents the desperate lack that spurs a man to thievery. Thus it often may refer to FAMINE, whether as the result of fire (Isa. 9:20), as a national phenomenon (Gen. 41:55), or as the result of war (Dt. 28:48; 32:24; Jer. 42:14).

Famine was a common phenomenon in OT times, largely because a successful harvest in Palestine was dependent on an adequate winter rainfall. Timing was the crucial factor — a late winter rain brought crop failure and the hunger of famine. The OT references to famines lasting over a period of years probably reflect periods of deficient rainfall. A total lack of rainfall in any given year is unusual in Palestine and highly improbable over a span of several years (see Dalman, pp. 195-99).

The threat of the painful hunger of famine, and thus the need to ensure the earth's fertility and yield of nourishment, underlies the powerful attraction that the Canaanite fertility gods had for Israel, in particular the Baal cult. Indeed, throughout the religions of antiquity, the desire to ensure the constant fertility and productivity of the earth was of paramount importance in worship (particularly in the early stages), and crop failure and famine were universally interpreted as signs of divine anger. Thus from early times in Palestine, and throughout the ancient Near East, it was incumbent upon the king as one of his primary socio-political responsibilities to ensure for all subjects at the least a subsistence level of nourishment to avoid hunger. Ps. 72 exemplifies this royal obligation to provide justice for the disadvantaged, to be an exemplar of compassion for those of the society who suffer deprivation of any sort, and an active vindicator of their cause. The negative counterpart of this appears in the Ugaritic epic *Krt,* usually but inaccurately called "Keret" (*UT* 127:45-50; cf. *ANET,* p. 149; *TDNT,* VI, 13).

It was thus a matter of individual ethics also, especially incumbent upon the prosperous, to share food with the hungry (Job 22:7; Isa. 32:6), a more significant form of devotion to God than fasting (Isa. 58:7, 10; cf. Ps. 50:12). This obligation extended even to the enemy who was hungry (Prov. 25:21; cf. Rom. 12:20). The pattern for such compassion is set by Yahweh Himself, who "fills the hungry with good things" (Ps. 107:9), "gives food to the hungry" (Ps. 146:7), and "does not let the righteous go hungry" (Prov. 10:3). The stark contrast between the "hungry" and the "full" does not go unnoticed (Isa. 65:13; 1 S. 2:5; Prov. 27:7). It avails nothing for people to be full, mighty, prosperous, etc., for Yahweh at will can exalt the hungry, the poor, and the needy into their place.

The OT manifests several theological perspectives on hunger. It is proclaimed as a future judgment in the prophetic demand for repentance (cf. Isa. 5:13; 8:21, where "hunger" is said to accompany the enemy's conquest), and as one of the signs of abandonment by God because of stubborn disobedience (Isa. 8:21; 65:13; cf. Dt. 28:48). Another perspective is that hunger is a saving abasement. The hunger on the wilderness wandering is understood in Dt. 8:3 as having a significance beyond the physical need for bread; it was a historical means of testing and training. In contrast, Isa. 49:10 offers an eschatological perspective on the people's current abasement by declaring that on the return through the desert "they shall not hunger or thirst" (cf. Ezk. 34:29). Hunger as saving abasement is also a feature of the promises of salvation to the hungry "poor," a theme often parallel to judgment against the "full." In 1 S. 2:5; Ps. 107:36-43; 146:7, e.g., the satisfying of the hungry already in history is considered a saving revelation of the One who abases only to exalt.

Three other Hebrew substantives appear five times as "hunger" in the RSV. In Job 30:3 *kāpān* is an Aramaic loanword meaning "hunger, famine, acute lack of food." Elsewhere in the OT it appears only in Job 5:22. The common noun *nepeš,* "soul, being, person, breath, appetite, etc." (lit. "that which breathes") occasionally is used in the OT to designate appetite in general, and hunger (or thirst) in particular (Isa. 29:8; Ezk. 7:19; Hos. 9:4). The meaning of the hapax legomenon *yešaḥ* in Mic. 6:14 has usually been conjectured from context to mean "emptiness (of hunger)." In 1 S. 2:5 the Hebrew verb *ḥāḏal,* while literally meaning simply "ceased," is translated by the RSV in context as "ceased to hunger."

In the RSV NT the translation "hunger" or "hungry" occurs twenty-nine times. In twenty-three of these it represents the Greek verb *peináō,* "be hungry, hunger." As in the classical literature, this verb has an extended meaning beyond its literal sense — "to desire (something) strongly (as necessary to life)" (cf. Mt. 5:6; Jn. 6:35). In addition are four substantives. Gk. *limós* is twice rendered "hunger" (2 Cor. 11:27; Lk. 15:17; cf. also Isa. 5:13 LXX and Josephus *BJ* iii.7.13 [189]). This term primarily means "famine," referring to an acute lack of food (in the LXX *limós* is regularly the equivalent of Hebrew *rā'āḇ*). As used in the NT it usually denotes circumstances of deprivation or lack (i.e., famine), rather than desire. Only in the above two passages is it used to connote appetite. In only one instance does the RSV translate *nēsteía,* "fasting, abstention from food," as "hunger." This term is usually used with regard to fasting as a religious rite or act of private piety, but in 2 Cor. 6:5 it refers to "hunger" in the sense of forced or necessitated abstention from food. The cognate *nēstis* (lit. "not eating") is translated "hungry" twice in the NT (Mt. 15:32 par. Mk. 8:3; cf. AV "fasting," NEB "unfed"). *Próspeinos,* related to the verb *peináō,* is a NT hapax legomenon translated "hungry" in Acts 10:10.

In Mt. 5:6 par. Lk. 6:21 Jesus calls the hungry blessed. In so doing he refers not to any social or religious group, but simply to those persons who (externally and internally) are lacking in the things essential to life as God meant it to be. They are believers who seek Jesus' help because of their own helplessness. The hungry are thus an object lesson of utter dependence on God.

The conception of "hungering after righteousness" is a feature of Matthew's Gospel. In Mt. 25:34-40 Jesus mentions the surprising reward given to those who are merciful to the hungry (thirsty, imprisoned, etc.). The rationale is that such mercy is actually given to Jesus Himself in the person of the less fortunate (i.e., all who are in need of mercy). Jesus deliberately identified Himself with the humiliation of hunger (Mt. 4:1-4) and in the course of everyday life was merciful to the hungry (Mt. 12:1-7), and thus He was able to invest the old command for mercy with the authority of a "new commandment." In Mt. 4:1-4 Jesus' temptation was the result of hunger, but He upheld the faith which Israel learned in the desert (Dt. 8:3). In Mt. 12:1, 3 Jesus refers to the scriptural record regarding David's eating of consecrated bread when he was desperately hungry. Jesus' point is not that the hungry have a right to help themselves, but that discipleship carries with it freedom — everything is at the disposal of the person who offers himself to God. Since it is Jesus who provides what is really essential to life, mundane bread is put in proper perspective and the hunger for life's essentials finds its true satisfaction in Him.

In Lk. 1:53 the OT promise is reflected in the Magnificat's praise of the God who in His mercy fills the hungry with good things (cf. Ps. 107:9) and sends the rich away empty. Luke also stresses the contrast between that hunger which brings salvation and that which signifies damnation: "Blessed are you that hunger now, for you shall be satisfied" (6:21), and "Woe to you that are full now, for you shall hunger" (v. 25; cf. the parable of the rich man and Lazarus, 16:19-31).

For Paul, his own hunger (and thirst) was an indication that he still awaited the consummation of salvation, even though it had already begun in Christ; it was an authenticating sign (among many others) to him that he was a "minister" of Christ (2 Cor. 11:27). In 1 Cor. 4:11 (and its context) Paul applied the beatitude of the blessed hungry to his own time, understanding life to be by faith rather than sight. In Phil. 4:12, however, hunger and fulness are simply understood as two vicissitudes of life. But in the light of Jesus' crucifixion and resurrection Paul accepted both as related aspects of the way of life he followed.

In 1 Cor. 11:21 Paul described the attitude of one part of the Corinthian community as a misconception of the meaning of redemption that allowed some to remain hungry at the fellowship meal while others became drunk. Paul concluded that hunger was better appeased at home, and he demanded, not equality of concern for all, but that everything (and especially the communal meal) should be under the rule of love, the kind of love that accepts as a new commandment even the obligation to feed a hungry enemy (Rom. 12:20).

The content of the beatitude is presented in yet a different manner in Jn. 6:35 as a self-witness by Jesus — "I am the bread of life; he who comes to me shall not hunger. . . ." What was originally promised for the age of salvation (cf. Isa. 49:10) is to be the experience of the believer in Jesus — the satisfying of hunger and thirst is here presented as feeding on the bread of life. John modified the OT language — this hunger is not an acute state of hunger, but rather the regularly recurring need for nourishment. This is a craving that cannot be satisfied by mundane bread (not even by manna, cf. Jn. 6:31-58). It is only commitment to Jesus that will really satisfy the appetite for "bread" in that it directs the craving to its true goal. Being free from hunger means that the insistent desire encompassed in the need for "bread" is both removed and satisfied.

Revelation 7:16 reflects more concretely the Hebraic concept (cf. Isa. 49:10) than do the more hellenized expressions in the Gospel of John. The promise of the Beatitude and the offer of the bread of life is experienced now in the earthly tribulation only in the context of that harsh dissonance to which Paul testified. In the new world it will be experienced in physical totality.

See also FAMINE; FAST.

Bibliography.–G. Dalman, *Arbeit und Sitte in Palästina*, I/1 (1928), 195-99; *TDNT*, VI, *s.v.* πεινάω (Goppelt).

D. G. BURKE

HUNTING [Heb. *ṣayiḏ*]. One should distinguish hunting for protection (of self, flocks, or crops), hunting for sport, and hunting for sustenance.

Hunting wild animals for self-protection was important in ancient days when the scarcity of human population left most of the land to nature. Many nations tell in their sagas of ancient heroes who delivered their peoples from the attacks of lions, bears, or wild swine. Gen. 10:8f. describes Nimrod as such a hero; his name is related to Babylonian and Assyrian king names composed with the name of the Sumerian-Babylonian god of war and the hunt, Ninurta. In historical times, even in the early centuries of the Christian era, lions, bears, and panthers were a real threat, and shepherds had to protect their flocks against them (1 S. 17:34-36). When the inhabitants of a certain region were exiled, wild animals could take possession again of the desolated country (e.g., Jer. 10:22; 2 K. 17:25). The Madeba Map shows a lion in the jungle at the shores of the Jordan River. Samson encountered a lion in the neighborhood of Timnah (Jgs. 14:5f.), a region where one would not expect one, as it was well cultivated and rather densely populated. Near Bethel, on the fringe of the desert descending to the Jordan Valley, bears sometimes appeared (2 K. 2:24), and a lion slew the disobedient man of God on his way from Bethel to Judah (1 K. 13:24). Wolves and jackals have always been a danger for the flocks.

The Assyrian and Egyptian kings were great hunters of lions and wild oxen, as we know from their boasting in inscriptions and reliefs. With them we can observe the transition from hunting for self-protection to hunting for sport; the later Assyrian kings kept lions in cages from which they were let free when the king wanted to indulge in his favorite sport (cf. Ezk. 19:9). A trace of this custom is to be found in Dnl. 6:7-24 (MT 8-25), which mentions the lions' den, a pit where lions were kept and fed until the king (in this case Darius the Mede) wanted to hunt. *See* pictures in ASHURBANIPAL; CALAH; DARIUS. The only example of hunting for sport in the OT is Benaiah's slaying of a lion in a pit (2 S. 23:20).

Hunting for sustenance did not play an important role in the economic life of Israel. From Sinuhe's description of his life in Palestine-Syria it appears that in the first centuries of the 2nd millennium B.C. gazelles and deer were plentiful, and a few centuries later men like Ishmael and Esau made hunting their trade (Gen. 21:20; 25:27ff.); but no professional hunters are mentioned after Israel's settlement in Canaan (Jer. 16:16 is figurative speech). Nevertheless, the "harts, gazelles, and roebucks" mentioned in the list of Solomon's daily provision (1 K. 4:23 [MT 5:3]) point to the existence of at least a group of hunters connected with the royal household. The name Pochereth-hazzebaim ("catcher of gazelles") as a family

Relief from Nineveh (*ca.* 650 B.C.) showing men trapping deer in a net (Trustees of the British Museum)

belonging to "the children of Solomon's servants" (Ezr. 2:57; Neh. 7:59) might be quoted as a corroboration of this assumption. In general, however, hunting was done only occasionally and by people who in their daily life were shepherds or farmers. Lev. 17:13 prescribes that the hunter should pour out the blood of his victims and cover it with dust; unlike the Canaanites, the Hebrews did not think game fit for sacrifice.

Partridges and other birds were hunted on the mountains (cf. 1 S. 26:20; Prov. 12:27) simply by following them till they were tired and could be caught or stunned by throwing a stone. Tired birds of passage like quails could sometimes be caught in large numbers (Ex. 16:13; Nu. 11:31f.). All kinds of weapons and means were used: arrows, lances, swords, slings, clubs (cf. Job 41:26-29 [MT 18-21]). Larger animals were often caught in a pit (Isa. 24:17f.; Jer. 48:43f.; Ezk. 19:4, 8; Ps. 7:15 [MT 16]; etc.). In order to manage the trapped beast a net was often spread over it after it had fallen into the pit (e.g., Ezk. 19:8). In other cases a net was spread over some place where animals were likely to pass by (Isa. 51:20; Ps. 140:5 [MT 6]). Snares were used in the same way.

Different kinds of nets and snares were also used for catching birds. Job 18:8-10 mentions six different names of devices used for catching game or birds. Heb. *rešeṯ* is a net both for large animals and smaller mammals or birds; it was stretched out on the ground and drawn together by the hunter when he observed that the feet of the animal were entangled in it. According to Hölscher (comm. on Job [*HAT,* rev. ed. 1952]), Heb. *śᵉḇāḵâ* ("grate") is the light cover of branches laid over the pit; most scholars think it is a kind of net, as indicated by the related word in Arabic. Heb. *paḥ* denotes a bird trap; some scholars describe it as a pair of wooden frames (cf. Ps. 124:7) each spanned with a net. They were laid flat on the ground, and if a bird touched one of them they automatically sprang up (Am. 3:5) and clapped together. It was thus a rather intricate instrument, as it depended on the working of one or more springs. In connection with the *paḥ* the verb *yāqaš (nāqaš, qôš)* is used in Ps. 124:7; 141:9; a *môqēš* might be the part on which the bait was placed, and a *yāqûš* or *yāqôš* was a man who made use of a *paḥ* (Hos. 9:8; Ps. 91:3) with a *môqēš,* probably a semiprofessional bird catcher, whose bag could be sold in the market (Mt. 10:29; Lk. 12:6). When caught, the birds might have been placed in a cage woven from branches or reeds like a basket (Jer. 5:26f.). Job 5:5; 18:9 have also the word *ṣammîm* (AV "robber"), perhaps a very fine mesh (cf. *ṣammâ,* "veil"). A *ḥeḇel* is a snare; the word itself means simply "rope"; it was laid on

Assyrian archers hunt birds and other game in a wooded area. Relief from the palace of Sargon II (721-705 B.C.) at Khorsabad (Trustees of the British Museum)

Neo-Hittite orthostat of archers hunting from a chariot. From Malatia in Anatolia, 9th cent. B.C. (Louvre)

the ground and was therefore not a specific instrument of the bird catcher. Finally, Heb. *malkōḏeṯ* is a general word for an instrument to catch mammals (Jgs. 15:4) or birds (Jer. 5:26). *See* FOWLER.

Josephus (*Ant.* iv.8.9 [206]) supposes that dogs were used in hunting; Egyptian and Assyrian monuments confirm this, but in the Bible neither hunting with hounds nor hunting with hawks or falcons is mentioned. The Greek text of Sir. 11:30 speaks of a "decoy partridge in a cage," but the Hebrew text has simply "a bird caught in a cage." Hunting on horseback or from chariots, frequently pictured in Assyrian and Egyptian works of art, is neither mentioned nor pictured in Israel.

The abundant use of imagery taken from hunting, in both the OT and NT, is remarkable in view of the comparative rarity of literal references and the small importance of hunting from an economic standpoint. Probably many of the OT similes borrowed from hunting belonged to the accepted literary language of Canaan as fixed in the centuries preceding the Israelite Conquest.

From the OT, the imagery was taken over in the NT. Mt. 22:15 uses the Greek vb. *pagideúō,* which occurs in Jewish Hellenistic literature only; it is derived from Gk. *pagís,* the word the LXX uses for rendering Heb. *paḥ*. In the NT *pagís* occurs in Lk. 21:34; Rom. 11:9; 1 Tim. 3:7; 6:9; 2 Tim. 2:26. Heb. *môqēš* is rendered *thḗra* ("trap," but generally "hunt") in Rom. 11:9; but the general rendering of *môqēš* in the LXX is *skandálēthron,* a word which does not occur in the NT, but which is closely allied to the frequent biblical word *skándalon,* "cause of stumbling." In some instances an allusion to the hunter's trap (or snare) is still recognizable. In 1 Cor. 7:35 *bróchos,* "noose" (Heb. *ḥeḇel*), is used. Two words for "hunt, catch," *agreúō* and *thēreúō,* occur in Mk. 12:13 and Lk. 11:54 respectively. The general idea of the imagery is the sudden action of the trap resulting in loss of freedom and power.

See A. G. Barrois, *Manuel d'archéologie biblique* (1939), I, 343-47.

A. VAN SELMS

HUPHAM hū'fəm, hōō'fəm [Heb. *ḥûpām*–'coast inhabitant']. One of Benjamin's sons and head of the "Huphamite" family (Nu. 26:39). *See* HUPPIM.

HUPPAH hup'ə [Heb. *ḥuppâ*–'protection']. The priest in charge of the thirteenth course as prescribed under David (1 Ch. 24:13).

HUPPIM hup'im [Heb. *ḥuppîm*–'coast people']. Probably a variant form of HUPHAM. From the only mention made of him (Gen. 46:21; 1 Ch. 7:12, 15), his direct descent is difficult to establish.

HUR hûr [Heb. *ḥûr*].

1. A prominent official in Israel. With Aaron he held up Moses' hands during the battle against the Amalekites (Ex. 17:10, 12) and assisted Aaron as judicial head of the people during Moses' stay on the mount (Ex. 24:14).

2. Grandfather of Bezalel, the head artificer in the construction of the tabernacle (Ex. 31:2; 35:20; 38:22; 2 Ch. 1:5). He is here assigned to the tribe of Judah, and in 1 Chronicles is connected with the same by descent through Caleb (2:19f., 50; 4:1, 4). Josephus (*Ant.* iii.2.4; 6.1 [54, 105]) makes him identical with **1** and the husband of Miriam.

3. One of the five kings of Midian slain along with Balaam when Israel avenged the "matter of Peor" upon this people (Nu. 31:8; cf. vv. 1f., 16). In Josh. 13:21 these kings are spoken of as "leaders of Midian" and "princes of Sihon" king of the Amorites.

4. According to 1 K. 4:8 (AV), the father of one of Solomon's twelve officers who provided food for the king's household, and whose district was the hill country of Ephraim. Here the RSV and NEB have "Ben-hur," taking the Heb. *ben,* "son of," as part of the proper name; and the same is true in reference to the names of four others of these officers (cf. vv. 9-11, 13).

5. Father of Rephaiah, who was one of the builders of the wall under Nehemiah, and ruler of half the district of Jerusalem (Neh. 3:9).

B. R. DOWNER

HURAI hūr'ī, hûr'î [Heb. *ḥûray*]. One of David's thirty mighty men mentioned in 1 Ch. 11:32 as "of the brooks of Gaash," i.e., from Mt. Gaash. In the par. 2 S. 23:30 he appears as Hiddai.

HURAM hūr'əm, hōō'rəm; **HIRAM** hī'rəm [Heb. *ḥûrām, ḥîrām*; Gk. *Chiram, Hōim, Hiwim, Houram*].

1. A skillful worker in all kinds of metals and furnishings whom Hiram king of Tyre lent to Solomon for work on the temple (1 K. 7:13f.; 2 Ch. 2:13). His father was a Tyrian brassworker and his mother an Israelite of the tribe of Naphtali (1 K. 7:14), "a woman of the daughters of Dan" (2 Ch. 2:14), for Dan lay in the territory of Naphtali. It may be that he was chosen because of his half-Hebrew blood, which would make him more acceptable in Jerusalem.

He is also called Huram-abi (2 Ch. 2:13; 4:16); the addition "-abi" here probably means "master," a title of respect and distinction (so NEB, "master Huram").

2. Huram son of Bela (1 Ch. 8:5) and grandson of Benjamin.

3. *See* HIRAM **1.**

J. A. BALCHIN

HURAM-ABI hūr'əm-ā-bī, hōōr'əm-ə-bē [Heb. *ḥûrām 'āḇî* –'Huram my father'; Gk. *ho Chiram ho patḗr mou*]; AV "Huram my father" (2 Ch. 2:13), "Huram his father" (4:16); NEB "master Huram." *See* HURAM **1.**

HURI hūr'ī, hōōr'ē [Heb. *ḥûrî*]. One of the immediate descendants of Gad and father of Abihail; a chief man of his family (1 Ch. 5:14).

HURRIANS hûr'ē-ənz. A people who entered Mesopotamia toward the end of the 3rd millennium B.C. By the middle of the 2nd millennium they had created the powerful empire of Mitanni in northwestern Mesopotamia. They played an important role in the spread of Sumero-Akkadian culture westward to Syria, Anatolia, and possibly Palestine.

I. Origin and Language.–The Hurrians were a non-Semitic people who entered Mesopotamia from the Armenian mountain mass to the northeast, the area in which the Urartians, a related people known from the 1st millennium, were located. The Hurrians spoke a language related to Urartian that has some distant relationship to the modern northeastern Caucasian family of languages.

II. History and Geographical Distribution.–Before *ca.* 2000 B.C., the Hurrians were located in the region E of the Tigris and N of the Upper Zab, although a few Hurrian names appear in texts from Babylonia. One major and important exception to this limit of early Hurrian influence was the kingdom of Urkish in the hilly region of Upper Mesopotamia, the region which remained the center of Hurrian penetration of Mesopotamia throughout their history. An interesting text from this site has demonstrated that in this early period the Hurrians had borrowed the cuneiform syllabary, while other finds document a high level of cultural attainment.

During the centuries following 2000 B.C., after the fall of Ur III, Hurrians moved in ever increasing numbers into Upper Mesopotamia from the northeast, although our documentation of this migration is sporadic and incomplete. In the south at Mari the Hurrian pressure was minimal, although Hurrian religious texts occur in the Mari archives. In the north the Hurrian numbers were much larger; e.g., about one-third of the population of Chagar Bazar was Hurrian. The Hurrian presence gradually grew and moved southward. Thus, the Hurrians formed more than a third of the population of Alalakh (*ca.* 1700), and it is likely that Hurrian was the language of the scribes, if not of the court. By the 15th cent., however, the vast majority of Alalakh's population was Hurrian, and its society was thoroughly Hurrianized. Hurrian influence further south at Ugarit (15th cent.) was significant, although West Semites predominated. Southern Syria and Palestine, however, show no trace of Hurrians throughout the first half of the 2nd millennium.

The Hittite archives from Anatolia document the same expansion. In the early years of the rise of the Hittite Old Kingdom, the Hurrians were virtually an unknown people in the east. Toward the end of the dynasty in the 16th cent., however, the Hittites struggled for their very existence against Hurrian states in north Syria. Because of this limited Hurrian penetration into Syria before the 16th cent., it is most unlikely that they, and the Indo-Aryans associated with them in the later kingdom of Mitanni, could have been part of the peoples called Hyksos who gained control of Egypt *ca.* 1750.

The next evidence available from the central area of Hurrian penetration, northwestern Mesopotamia, is from *ca.* 1500, when the Hurrians created the Mitannian empire, which controlled territory from Alalakh on the Mediterranean to Nuzi E of the Tigris. Of the development of this state we know almost nothing, except for the names of several of its early kings. These names are Indo-Aryan, rather than Hurrian, and it appears that the formation of Mitanni is linked with their arrival, the first significant appearance of Indo-Aryans in the ancient Near East. In actuality the Indo-Aryans formed a small ruling aristocracy at the head of the Mitannian state and of a number of others that fell under Hurrian influence after 1500 B.C. Their contribution to the Mitannian civilization has often been pictured as major, but the evidence clearly suggests that this view is greatly exaggerated. They were never more than a political veneer; the language and dominant culture of Mitanni was Hurrian. It is quite improper to speak of a Hurro-Indo-Aryan "symbiosis," as has sometimes been done.

The state of Mitanni soon fell before the rising might of Šuppiluliuma and the Hittite New Kingdom. Nonetheless, the wave of Hurrian immigration that created Mitanni spread Hurrian influence further and more deeply through the Near East. Hurrians formed the vast majority of the population of Nuzi in the 15th cent., and they deeply influenced the Hittite New Kingdom, the dynasty of which seems to have been of Hurrian extraction. They were now present in southwestern Syria at Qatna and Tunip, where the official language was Hurrian.

Their penetration into Palestine is indicated by the appearance of a few Hurrian and a larger number of Indo-Aryan names in the Amarna Tablets (14th cent. B.C.). A close examination of the evidence, however, suggests that they represented only a ruling class, a military aristocracy imposed in feudal style on the city-state system. Certainly Palestine shows no trace of the Hurrian substratum that appears in the 14th cent. throughout the area N of the Beqaʿ in central Syria. This Hurro-Indo-Aryan presence explains why the Egyptians in the 19th Dynasty increasingly called Syria-Palestine "Ḫurru-land."

When the Israelites entered Palestine in the Conquest, it is reasonable to suppose that they would have encountered the descendants of the Hurro-Indo-Aryans whom we find there in the texts of the 14th cent. B.C. On the vexed question of biblical evidence for this, *see* HORITES.

After it fell to the Hittites, the state of Mitanni continued for a time in a much abbreviated form as a tributary state of the Hittite empire, only to fall in the course of the 13th cent. to the rising power of Assyria. After this period, Hurrian names became increasingly infrequent, eventually disappearing altogether during the early centuries of the 1st millennium. In this last period Hurrian names are associated exclusively with the mountain region between northwestern Mesopotamia and Lake Van, the region from which they originally came. With the sparseness of the evidence one can only assume that, given the end of Hurrian political rule, the apparent cessation of Hurrian immigration from the northeast, and the radical transformation in the ethnic and political status of the whole area brought about by the incursions of new peoples (particularly the sea-peoples in the 12th cent. B.C.), the Hurrian population was slowly assimilated through intermarriage and cultural amalgamation.

III. Cultural Influence.–As mentioned above, the Hurrians came into contact with the Sumero-Akkadian civilization of Mesopotamia early in their penetration into the Near East. Here the cultural relationship was markedly one-sided: the Hurrians, far less culturally sophisticated than their Mesopotamian contemporaries, were deeply influenced by that society and borrowed from it in the areas of religion, law, literature, art, economics, and language.

In their movement to the west, however, the situation was reversed. Here the Hurrians played an important role in the transmission of Sumero-Akkadian culture, imprinted with their own indigenous contribution, to Anatolia and Syria. The dynasty of Šuppiluliuma in the Hittite New Kingdom period was Hurrian by race, each king bearing a Hurrian personal name as well as a Hittite throne name. The Hurrians made a major contribution to the religious sphere, with many Hurrian deities included in the Hittite pantheon and frequent passages in the Hurrian language appearing in Hittite religious texts. Hurrian contributions can also be documented in the area of writing, literature, law, and art; and the Hittite language teems with Hurrian loanwords. At Ugarit in Syria a large number of Hurrian religious texts have been found, together with one Akkado-Hurrian bilingual text and a quadrilingual vocabulary, one column of which was Hurrian.

The Hurrian cultural impact on Palestine, once assumed by some scholars to have been extensive, can now be seen to have been minimal. The detailed comparisons made between the so-called Hurrian socio-juridical customs from Nuzi and certain features of the patriarchal texts in Gen. 12–50 have now been largely discredited and the relation between the Hurrians and the "Horites" of the OT is highly problematical (*see* HORITES).

Other Hurrian contributions to the ancient world can be documented. It has often been alleged that the Mitanno-Hurrians introduced the horse and chariot to the ancient world. Although there is good evidence that the horse and chariot were known previously, there is little doubt that the Mitannians developed them into very effective weapons of war and that they particularly pioneered in the breeding of horses.

It also seems highly probable that they introduced the composite bow and the defense for it, a type of armor with metal scales used on men and horses, the Hurrian name of which appears in Egyptian, Akkadian, Hittite, Ugaritic, and Hebrew. These weapons created a new warrior class, termed *Maryannu,* and became decisive in battle from the 15th cent. B.C. on.

Bibliography.–Origin, Geographical Distribution, and History: CAH, II (3rd ed. 1970), chs. 1 (J. R. Kupper), 6 (O. R. Gurney), 10 (M. S. Drower), 20 (W. F. Albright); I. J. Gelb, *Hurrians and Subarians* (1944); *JCS,* 15 (1961), 27-47; R. T. O'Callaghan, *Aram Naharaim* (1948); R. de Vaux, *Early History of Israel* (Eng. tr. 1978), pp. 64-66, 83-89; *RB,* 74 (1967), 481-503.

People and Culture: E. A. Speiser, "The Hurrian Participation in the Civilization of Mesopotamia, Syria, and Palestine," in *Oriental and Biblical Studies* (1967), pp. 244-269; H. G. Güterbock, *Journal of World History,* 2 (1954), 383-394.

Hurrians and the OT: W. F. Albright, "The Horites in Palestine," in L. Leary, ed., *From the Pyramids to Paul* (1935), pp. 9-26; E. A. Speiser, *Genesis* (*AB,* 1964), pp. 282f.; R. de Vaux, *RB,* 74 (1967), 481-503; T. L. Thompson, *Historicity of the Patriarchal Narratives* (1974), pp. 196-297; M. E. J. Selman, *Tyndale Bulletin,* 27 (1976), 114-136.

F. W. BUSH

HURRICANE [Heb. *sûpâ*] (Ps. 83:15 [MT 16]); AV STORM; NEB STORM-WIND. Elsewhere the RSV has STORM or WHIRLWIND. The commencement of the rainy season in October or November frequently brought severe thunderstorms. Hurricanes, however, were unusual. When they did come, usually along the coast, they appeared like a huge wall, were terrifyingly destructive, and ceased abruptly.

G. WYPER

HURT. The term (noun and vb.) represents a large number of Hebrew words, of which the chief are *raʿ* (vb. *rāʿaʿ,* "evil" (Gen. 26:29; 1 S. 24:9; etc.), and *šeḇer* or *šeḇer* (from *šāḇar*), a "fracture" or "breaking" (Jer. 10:19; cf. Ex. 22:10, 14). In the NT a principal verb is *adikéō,* "do injustice" (Lk. 10:19; Rev. 2:11; 9:10). Such references illustrate adequately the meaning of the term as alluding to general harm, bruising, breaking, and the like, whether literal or figurative.

HUSBAND. *See* FAMILY; MARRIAGE; RELATIONSHIPS, FAMILY.

HUSBANDMAN hus'bənd-mən. The Hebrew *'ikkar,* translated by the AV as "husbandman," is rendered by the RSV "plowman" (Isa. 61:5), "farmer" (2 Ch. 26:10), or "tiller of the soil" (Joel 1:11); the phrases *'îš hā'ᵃḏāmâ* (Gen. 9:20) and *'îš ʿōḇēḏ 'ᵃḏāmâ* (Zec. 13:5) are rendered "tiller of the soil." The Gk. *geōrgós* is translated as "farmer" (e.g., 2 Tim. 2:6), "vinedresser" (Jn. 15:1), and "tenant" (Mk. 12:7), and the Gk. *oikodespótēs* as "householder."

In the OT the term "husbandman" refers to someone connected with the soil. In the NT it can mean the owner of a vineyard (Gk. *oikodespótēs* [Mt. 21:33]), or the tenant (Gk. *geōrgós* [Mk. 12:7]). In some cases Gk. *oikodespótēs* is connected with the soil (Mt. 21:33; Mk. 12:1; and Lk. 20:9 have "a man who planted"), in other cases with the house; it is properly rendered "householder" (cf. Mt. 24:43; Lk. 12:39), its more original meaning. The Bible does not use the term "animal husbandry," though the idea is present in the OT (cf. Gen. 30:31-43).

Usually the term "husbandman" is applied to people, but at least twice to God, who is the vinedresser (Gk. *geōrgós* [Jn. 15:1]) or the householder (Gk. *oikodespótēs* [Mt. 20:1]). In 1 Cor. 3:9 the church is said to be the "field" (Gk. *geṓrgion*) of God.

See *TDNT,* II, *s.v.* οἰκοδεσπότης (Rengstorf).

D. W. WEAD
R. W. V.

HUSBAND'S BROTHER [Heb. *yāḇām*–'brother-in-law'; Gk. *epigambreúō;* Late Lat. *levir*]. He was required (Dt. 25:5-10; Mt. 22:24) "to perform the duty of a husband's brother" (*yibbᵉmâ*); that is, if his brother, living with him on the paternal estate, died without male issue, he should take the widow to wife, and "perpetuate his brother's name," the firstborn of the new marriage inheriting the deceased brother's estate. Refusal of the duty was possible, but entailed public ceremonial disgrace and lasting reproach. This provision for a specific case modified the general law which forbade the marriage of a sister-in-law (Lev. 18:16, 18). It was a patriarchal custom (Gen. 38, Judah and Tamar), and is alluded to in Ruth 1:11-13. A related custom is found in Ruth 4:1, Boaz playing, however, the part, not of *levir* ("brother-in-law"), but of *gō'ēl* ("redeemer"). It was at least theoretically in force in Our Lord's time (Mt. 22:23-28, the question of the Sadducees concerning the resurrection). For the origin and object of this custom *see* MARRIAGE II; RELATIONSHIPS, FAMILY.

P. W. CRANNELL

HUSHAH ho͞osh'ə [Heb. *ḥûšâ*]. In 1 Ch. 4:4, the home of one of David's heroes (2 S. 23:27; cf. 1 Ch. 27:11). It was probably located in the Judean uplands, and has been identified by some scholars with Husan, a site SW of Bethlehem.

HUSHAI ho͞osh'ī [Heb. *ḥûšay*; Gk. *Chousei,* Josephus *Chousi*]. An Archite, native of Archi, SW of Bethel on the northern border of Benjamin and southern border of Joseph (Josh. 16:2). Hushai was one of David's most faithful and wise counselors. When David was fleeing from Jerusalem and Absalom, Hushai met him, having his coat rent and earth on his head. The king persuaded him to return to Jerusalem, feign submission to Absalom, and try to defeat the counsel of Ahithophel (2 S. 15:32f.). Whatever Absalom decided on, Hushai was to send word to David through two young men, sons of the priests Zadok and Abiathar (15:34-36). Hushai obeyed, and succeeded in persuading Absalom to adopt his counsel rather than that of Ahithophel (2 S. 16:16–17:14). He sent word to David of the nature of Ahithophel's counsel, and the king made good his escape that night across the Jordan. The result was the suicide of Ahithophel and the ultimate defeat and death of Absalom.

J. J. REEVE

HUSHAM ho͞osh'əm [Heb. *ḥušām,* Gen. 36:34; *ḥûšām,* 1 Ch. 1:45f.]. According to the former reference, Husham was one of the kings of Edom, and according to the latter he was "of the land of the Temanites" and (1 Ch. 1:35f.) descended from Esau.

HUSHATHITE ho͞osh'ə-thīt [Heb. *ḥûšāṯî,* "a dweller in

Hushah"]. The patronymic given in two forms, but probably of the same man, Sibbecai (AV, NEB, also SIBBECHAI), one of David's thirty mighty men (2 S. 21:18; 1 Ch. 11:29; 20:4; 27:11), or Mebunnai as named in the par. passage (2 S. 23:27).

HUSHIM hōōsh'im [Heb. *ḥûšîm, ḥušîm, ḥušim*].

1. Family name of the children of Dan (Gen. 46:23), but cf. the form "Shuham," by interchange of consonants, in Nu. 26:42.

2. The sons of Aher, of the lineage of Benjamin (1 Ch. 7:12).

3. One of the wives of Shaharaim, of the family of Benjamin (1 Ch. 8:8, 11; NEB MAHASHAM).

HUSKS (Lk. 15:16, AV). *See* PODS.

HUT [Heb. *m^e^lûnâ*] (Isa. 24:20); AV COTTAGE; NEB WATCHMEN'S SHELTER. The term *m^e^lûnâ* refers to a temporary structure from which watchmen could guard the fields during the night (translated "lodge" in Isa. 1:8).

HUZ huz (Gen. 22:21, AV). *See* UZ.

HUZZAB huz'əb (Nah. 2:7, AV). *See* MISTRESS.

HYDASPES hī-das'pēz [Gk. *Hydaspēs*]. A river mentioned in Jth. 1:6 in connection with the Euphrates and Tigris, but otherwise unknown. It is possible there may be a confusion with the Hydaspes of India. Some have conjectured an identification with the Choaspes (modern Kerkha, also called Ulai; cf. Jth. 1:6 [Syr.]; Dnl. 8:2 [Heb. *'ûlay*]), which flows from the Zagros mountains to the delta at the Persian Gulf where the Tigris and Euphrates meet.

HYENA [Heb. *'îyîm*; Gk. *hýaina*; cf. Arab. *ḍabuʿ*] (Isa. 13:22; 34:14; Sir. 13:18); AV "wild beasts of the islands"; NEB JACKALS.

The Palestinian hyena is the striped hyena (*Hyaena striata*) which ranges from India to North Africa. The striped, the spotted, and the brown hyenas constitute a distinct family of the order of Carnivora, having certain peculiarities of dentition and having four toes on each foot, instead of four behind and five in front, as in most of the order. The hyena is a nocturnal animal, rarely seen though fairly abundant, powerful but cowardly, a feeder on carrion and addicted to grave-robbing. The last habit in particular has won it the abhorrence of the natives of the countries which it inhabits. In the passage cited in Sirach, it is to be noted that it is to the hyena that the rich man is compared. The jaws and teeth of the hyena are exceedingly strong and fitted for crushing bones which have resisted the efforts of dogs and jackals. Its dens are in desolate places and are littered with fragments of skeletons.

The name ZEBOIM (Neh. 11:34) means "hyenas," and the "hyena valley" of 1 S. 13:17f. is most probably the Wâdī Abū Dabāʿ, a tributary of the Wâdī Qelt.

The name of Zibeon the Hivite (Gen. 36:2; etc.) is more doubtfully connected with "hyena."

See HOWLING CREATURES. A. E. DAY

HYKSOS hik'sos. A people associated with OT history, although not mentioned by name in the Bible. The Egyptian priest Manetho, cited by the Jewish historian Josephus (*CAp* i.14 [75-82]), speaks of them as "Shepherd Kings" but the term "Hyksos" is derived from the Egyp. *ḥq3w ḫ3swt,* "rulers of foreign countries." Manetho (3rd cent. B.C.) compiled a history of Egypt and ascribed Dynasties 15-16 to them. Josephus attributed to the Hyksos a rule in Egypt of some five hundred years, but recent chronologies assign them about 100-150 years, e.g., *ca.* 1700-1550 B.C. *See* EGYPT VIII.F.

In attempting to correlate secular history with the biblical data, some scholars have tried to equate the expulsion of the Hyksos from Egypt with the Israelite Exodus, but the chronology rules out this identification, and other factors as well make this hypothesis untenable. Others have associated the Hyksos rule with the Israelite sojourn in Egypt, seeing in Joseph's meteoric rise to the vizierate some favoritism based on common Semitic background. In support of this synchronism is the apparent singling out of Potiphar as "an Egyptian," in apparent contrast to others in Egypt (Gen. 39:1f.), and the mention of chariots (41:43), which were a Hyksos introduction into Egypt. On the other hand, a reference to Egyptian discrimination against foreigners (43:32) shows that persons in Egyptian officialdom were generally Egyptians.

There are chronological difficulties in placing Joseph in the Hyksos period, for the biblical figures indicate that Joseph lived some time before the current dates of the 15th and 16th Dynasties. But the Israelites must have been in Egypt throughout the Hyksos domination, although many matters of chronology hinge on the date of the Exodus. There can be little doubt that the reference to "a new king over Egypt, who did not know Joseph" (Ex. 1:8) refers to the appearance of a native Egyptian dynasty that followed the expulsion of the Hyksos.

The origin of the Hyksos is uncertain; they came from somewhere in Asia and bore Semitic names for the most part. Arriving in Egypt during the time of political weakness and confusion known as the Second Intermediate Period, they were in Egypt some years before their rise to power; their usurpation of rule was the result of gradual infiltration rather than of concentrated military activity. Their capital was located at Avaris (biblical Zoan, modern Ṣân el-Ḥagar; *see* ZOAN), in the northeast Delta. Their influence was widespread in the Mediterranean world and their monuments have been found as far abroad as Baghdad and Crete. Among their most famous kings were Khayan and Apophis.

The Kamose stele shows that late in their period of supremacy the Hyksos were allied with the Nubians against an Egyptian line of princes centered in Thebes (17th Dynasty). Theban rulers, Sekenenre and Kamose, initiated military action against the Hyksos and it is probable that the wounds which caused Sekenenre's death were incurred in such a battle. According to the autobiographical inscription of Ahmose son of Ebana, the Theban Ahmose (founder of the 18th Dynasty) successfully besieged Avaris and pursued the fleeing Hyksos to Sharuhen (Tell el-Fârʿah) in southern Palestine.

In typical Egyptian fashion, later Egyptian records mention the Hyksos rarely. Hatshepsut claims to have restored temples which the Hyksos had desecrated, and Thutmose III seemed to regard his military campaigns in Palestine-Syria as punitive expeditions against the Hyksos.

By the time the Hyksos attained political rule in Egypt they were largely Egyptianized, but they are credited with the introduction of numerous elements into Egyptian culture. Among these were military innovations that were adopted by the Egyptians: the horse and chariot, the composite bow, new types of dagger and sword, and a different kind of battle-ax. Other contributions may be the shaduf (a water-lifting device), an improved loom, and a lyre. The Hyksos made wide use of scarabs and developed

Blue faience tile (18th Dynasty, 16th-14th cents. B.C.) with a drawing of a typical Hyksos chariot. The Hyksos introduced horses and chariots into Egypt (Metropolitan Museum of Art, gift of J. Pierpont Morgan, 1917)

a scarab style that is a useful chronological criterion for archeologists.

Bibliography.–P. Labib, *Die Herrschaft der Hyksos in Ägypten und ihr Sturz* (1936); T. Säve-Söderbergh, *JEA*, 37 (1951), 53-71; J. Van Seters, *The Hyksos* (1966); H. E. Winlock, *Rise and Fall of the Middle Kingdom in Thebes* (1947), esp. pp. 150-170.

C. E. DEVRIES

HYMENAEUS hī-men'ē-əs [Gk. *Hymenaios,* from Hymen, the god of marriage in classical mythology] (1 Tim. 1:20; 2 Tim. 2:17). A heretical teacher at Ephesus and opponent of the apostle Paul, associated in the former reference with Alexander, and in the latter with Philetus.

In 1 Tim. 1:19f. Hymenaeus is included with certain persons who had made shipwreck of their faith by "rejecting conscience." For this he and Alexander were to be "delivered" to Satan, "that they might learn not to blaspheme." Here, as in 1 Cor. 5:5, the purpose of the separation from the fellowship of the Church was remedial. By their being given over to the powers of evil it was hoped that repentance and a change of conduct would ensue. Since Satan functions as the destroyer of the body and life, many have thought that the infliction of bodily suffering or disease was involved.

Paul does not describe the blasphemy, but in 2 Tim. 2:16f. he admonishes Timothy to avoid "godless chatter" which leads people into ungodliness and "eats its way like gangrene." Hymenaeus and Philetus are examples of this activity in their teaching that the resurrection had already taken place with the implicit denial of the resurrection of the body. It appears probable that Paul was dealing with some form of Gnosticism, which, due to its idea of the necessarily evil nature of all material substance, taught that the resurrection was to be understood in only a spiritual sense and was realized in the present blessings of the Church — thus removing any place for eschatology.

See also ALEXANDER **4.** W. W. BUEHLER

HYMNS IN THE NT. ***I. Encouragements for This Study.***– The Church that meets us in the pages of the NT is a worshiping community of believing men and women. This is clear from the descriptions in the Acts (1:14; 2:42, 46; 4:31; 5:12, 42; 13:1-3; 20:7-12) and from the statements of Paul in his letters (notably 1 Cor. 10–14). It is therefore only to be expected that these chapters and references will contain some allusion to a specific part of the Christian cultus, namely, the worship of God in religious song.

The data lie mostly beneath the surface of the text, however, and have to be explored by the biblical discipline of form criticism as applied to the NT Epistles. But there are, in addition to some explicit references to Christian hymns (in 1 Cor. 14:26; Col. 3:16; Eph. 5:19), some encouragements of an inferential character, to which attention should be drawn. We may list these with a brief comment appended.

First, the origin of the Church in the womb of the Jewish faith made it inevitable that the first followers of the risen Lord Jesus, themselves Jews by birth and tradition, who formed the nucleus of the Jerusalem community, would wish to express their religious devotion in a way to which they were accustomed, and this would include the use of religious song. It is this background which leads to the suggestion that the Lukan canticles (Lk. 1–2; see below) had their first use as canonical Scripture in the context of the worship of the Jewish Christianity which cherished and preserved these messianic psalms.

Then, as the message spread to confront the world of Hellenism, gentile converts entered the Church from a religious world which sang hymns to the deities of Greco-Roman religion. There are some superficial correspondences between the literary form and language used in both pagan and Christian hymnody (see the definitive work of E. Norden, *Agnostos Theos* [2nd ed. 1923]), but on the more serious levels of theological content and human aspiration (noted by Karl Keyssner in another authoritative study, *Gottesvorstellung und Lebensauffassung im griechischen Hymnus* [1932], esp. pp. 166ff.) there are fundamental differences. These differences center in the way in which Christian compositions appeal to God whose nature is known in Jesus Christ as a loving and faithful Father (the nearest we come to this conviction is Cleanthes' Hymn to Zeus, but that trails off in a sad identification of the father of the gods and men with impersonal Fate) and the clear declaration that the God and Father of Jesus Christ is the God who acts in history. Much of the NT hymnology stands in the OT tradition of confessional statements (e.g., Dt. 26:5ff.; Ps. 105) which celebrate the mighty acts of God in salvation-history. Pagan prayer as expressed in personal hymns is largely self-centered and does not break out of the circle of egocentricity (see for a good example the suppliant's appeal to Serapis in Aristides' Hymn to Serapis, which manages to contain some lofty thoughts but without the involvement of personal religion: so G. Delling, *Worship in the NT* [Eng. tr. 1962], p. 114; A. J. Festugière, *Personal Religion Among the Greeks* [1960 ed.], p. 99). NT examples of hymnic prayer are quite different as they focus on objective realities which are at the same time intimately related to the believer's experience in the Christian community — the coming of God's kingdom, the progress of the gospel in the world, and the upbuilding of the Church.

In sum, Christian hymns in the NT Church stand in relation to both Jewish antecedents and pagan examples of Greco-Roman religion as the fulfillment stands to the longing which precedes it. That which explains the transition is the gospel of God's grace in Jesus Christ. This good news of man's salvation brought to Christians an awareness of living in days of eschatological fulfillment; and it was only to be expected that Christian lips should be opened in praise of the mighty deeds of God and in tribute to His goodness. Much closer to the ethos of the apostolic hymns are the confessions of the community at Qumrân (e.g., in 1QS 10:9 and in the Hymn scroll, 1QH 11:3f.). These fine expressions offer examples of personal faith and a desire to give glory to God for His saving acts. But even these tributes lack the note that is characteristic of the NT hymns. Though parts of the NT data are simply creation hymns (Rev. 15:3f.), the most distinctive feature is seen in those hymnic confessions of faith which praise the redeeming power of God in the gospel and share in the element which is taken from the OT and given a richer connotation in the incarnation and redemption of Israel's Messiah. As R. Deichgräber (in his *Gotteshymnus and Christushymnus in der frühen Christenheit* [1967], p. 201) puts it, "The praise of the community is the response to God's saving act," thus making Christian hymns reflexive and expressive of gratitude to God for all that He has done for the world's reconciliation. Encouragements like this give added depth to our study, for Christian hymns expose the nerve ends of the gospel itself.

II. Presence of Hymns in the NT.–The detection of hymnic forms in the literature of the NT is a product of comparatively recent scholarly work, and includes the results of an analysis of the literary features which are present in the documents. For some further discussion of these features *see* POETRY IN THE NT.

The line that divides poetry from hymnody is finely drawn, and indeed the terms overlap. What distinguishes the latter as such is the subject matter that is expressed in poetic form. Invariably the hymn is focused on God or Christ and praises some aspect of the divine nature or activity.

It is just as difficult and delicate a task to separate out a species of Christian hymn from an early confession of faith, but the chief test (offered by R. Bultmann in his essay in *ConNT*, 11 [1947], 9) is simply one of length. The creed in early times was short and was used as a baptismal confession of faith (e.g., Rom. 10:9). As the credal statement became lengthened in definition of the person and work of Christ and the character of God — both enlargements even in NT times arose as a result of pressure exerted by false teaching and polemics — so the hymnic forms were drawn into use. Adaptations of Jewish hymns (seen in Lk. 1–2 and Rev. 15) were insufficient to ward off the strange teachings which threatened the apostolic gospel; and the distinctive Christian hymn was born out of a need to assert (1) the centrality of Christ in God's saving plan and His unique relationship to God; (2) the true meaning of the Christian life as one of moral excellence; and (3) the freedom of the believer from all forms of bad religion and superstition which would hold him prey to fears and doubts. We can sum up the chief enemy as a gnosticizing teaching which quickly challenged the apostolic message and imposed its presence in the churches of the Pauline mission. The tenets are seen in a denial of the lordship of Christ as the sole intermediary between God and the world (Colossians), the insidious relaxing of the moral fiber which leads Christians to be indifferent to bodily lusts and sins (Ephesians), and the uncertainty that underlies the meaning of life since the star-gods still hold sway and need to be placated. It is not accidental that the main examples of NT hymns address the various situations in which the presence of Gnostic ideas is suspected and form the polemic counterthrust to heretical teaching in the areas of both doctrine and morals. For an elaboration of this thesis see J. T. Sanders, *NT Christological Hymns* (1970).

III. Classification of the Hymns.–In the light of the above discussions, we may attempt to classify the material which is germane.

(1) The Nativity Canticles (Lk. 1:46-55 — the Magnificat; vv. 68-79 — the Benedictus; 2:14 — the Gloria in Excelsis; vv. 29-32 — the Nunc Dimittis) all share common features in their OT coloring and reminder of God's covenant faithfulness. They show that Jesus came as the climax of the OT's hope and longing, and that the God of the Jews is the same as the true God whom Christians know and worship. Contrast Marcion's denial of this and the Gnostic idea of Israel's God as inferior to the high God.

(2) Hymns in the Apocalypse stress the same truth, taken from the synagogues of Hellenistic Judaism (Rev. 4:11; 11:17f.; 14:7; 15:3f.). Into the same category we should place the fragments of Rom. 11:33-35; 1 Tim. 1:17; 6:15f.

(3) Distinctively Christian compositions may in turn be subdivided as follows.

(a) Sacramental. Here parts of Ephesians (2:19-22) and the Pastoral Epistles (Tit. 3:4-7) have been placed; Eph. 5:14, the clearest illustration of a NT hymn, also falls in this grouping. It divides naturally into three lines on grounds of style and finds its obvious *Sitz im Leben* in a baptismal setting. The convert is summoned to moral endeavor, and promised divine aid to live a life worthy of his profession. In the context of the letter it challenges the view of an indifferent moral attitude — a wrong-headed notion which was plaguing the Asia Minor churches (so Eph. 4:17ff.; 5:3ff.; see R. P. Martin, *Expos.T.*, 79 [1968], 296ff.).

(b) Meditative. Eph. 1:3-14 is a good example of a Christian rhapsody on the themes of trinitarian faith and redemption. Possibly a Jewish pattern drawn from the synagogue in which God is blessed (hence the term Berakah) lies in the background, but if so it has been dramatically christianized by impressive Christian concepts of election, salvation, and adoption.

(c) Confessional. The nature of the Christian life comes to vivid expression when believers are called upon to attest their faith in time of trial. Passages of the Pastorals (e.g., 2 Tim. 2:11-13) read like hymns of the martyrs' confession, and illustrate the strenuous quality of Christian living which was expected in the early Church in its incipient conflict with the persecuting state.

(d) Christological. Here we touch the heart of the matter, for as we have seen, the NT teaching on the person of Christ is virtually contained in its hymns. Outstanding specimens are: Jn. 1:1-18; Phil. 2:6-11; Col. 1:15-20; 1 Tim. 3:16; He. 1:1f. All these passages have been the subject of in-depth studies in recent times and collectively are discussed in detail by Sanders and by Deichgräber. Let it suffice to extract a modicum of common teaching. The Christians' Lord is depicted in a cosmological role in the double sense of that adjective. First, His preexistence and pre-temporal activity in creation are made the frontispiece of the hymns, and from the divine order in which He eternally is He "comes down" as the incarnate one in an epiphany. Second, at the conclusion of His earthly life He takes His place in God's presence by receiving the universal homage and acclamation of the cosmic spirit-powers, which confess His lordship and so are forced to abandon their title to control over human destiny. His saving work is seen as that of bringing together the two orders of existence (the celestial and the terrestrial), and His reconciliation is described in a cosmic setting. The hymns are essentially soteriological in their purpose, and set forth the person of Christ in relation to His work as reconciler and world ruler. But inasmuch as He accomplishes what God alone can do — the pacification of the hostile powers of the universe and the enthronement of a true lordship, in particular — and has received from the Father's hands the right to rule human life and to be the judge of history, it was but a short step for the early Christians to set Him on a level with God in their cultic worship. Hymnology and Christology thus merge in praise of the one Lord, soon to be hailed after the close of the NT canon as worthy of hymns "as to God" (Pliny's report of Bithynian Christians' worship, A.D. 112). And it was this close drawing together of the Father and the Son which laid the foundation for the trinitarian creeds and raised a bulwark against classical Gnosticism, the incipient presence of which in NT times impelled, we may believe, the creation of these inspired hymns.

See also MUSIC.

Bibliography.–On the form of hymns, G. Schille, *Frühchristliche Hymnen* (1965); on the history of hymns, J. Kroll, *Die christliche Hymnodik bis zu Klement von Alexandreia* (1921); and for a general survey, R. P. Martin, *VE,* 2 (1963), 6-33.

Studies on the individual hymns include: H. J. Gabathuler, *Jesus Christus, Haupt der Kirche — Haupt der Welt* (on Col. 1:15-20) (1965); R. P. Martin, *Carmen Christi* (on Phil. 2:5-11) (1967); M. E. Boismard, *St. John's Prologue* (Eng. tr. 1957); and R. H. Gundry, "Form, Meaning and Background of the Hymn Quoted in I Tim. 3:16," in W. W. Gasque and R. P. Martin, eds., *Apostolic History and the Gospel* (1970), pp. 203-222.

On the Christology of the hymns see D. M. Stanley, *Studies in Salvation History,* ed. C. L. Salm (1964). R. P. MARTIN

HYPOCRISY [Gk. *hypókrisis*] (Mt. 23:28; Mk. 12:15; Lk. 12:1); NEB also "crafty" (Mk. 12:15); **HYPOCRITE** [Gk. *hypokritḗs*] (Mt. 6:2, 5, 16; 7:5; 15:7; etc.); NEB also HYPOCRISY.

I. OT Use.–In the OT the AV translates Heb. *ḥōnep̱* as "hypocrisy" (Isa. 32:6) and *ḥānēp̱* as "hypocrite" or "hypocritical" (Job 8:13; 13:16; 15:34; 17:8; 20:5; 27:8; 34:30; 36:13; Ps. 35:16; Prov. 11:9; Isa. 9:17 [MT 16]; 10:6; 33:14). The verb *ḥānēp̱,* however, means "be polluted, profane, godless." Thus, the Eng. "hypocrisy" and related words do not correctly represent the Hebrew terms. In the LXX the Gk. *hypokritḗs* was used to translate *ḥānēp̱* and is therefore to be understood as meaning "a godless man" rather then one who pretends to be what he is not. This usage of *hypokritḗs* to refer to evil in general is found in much of the Jewish dispersion literature (*TDNT,* VIII, 563-66). It may be that NT usage is occasionally influenced by this meaning.

II. NT Use.–For the most part, however, the NT meanings of *hypókrisis* and *hypokritḗs* reflect the classical and Hellenistic use of the words to refer to "acting" and "actor." In Greek literature the *hypokritḗs* was a person who played a part on the stage. He usually wore a mask, and in speech and action imitated the character whom he represented in the stage production. There was no necessary connotation of evil or deception involved in the early use of the terms. Context always made it clear whether the action was to be viewed as evil or not. In the NT the terms are invariably evil in sense, and it was this use that gave our English transliterations of the terms ("hypocrisy," "hypocrite") the persistent meaning of "pretending to be what one is not," especially in the areas of religion and morality.

A. In the Synoptic Gospels. The majority of the NT occurrences of the words are found in the Synoptic Gospels (*hypókrisis* three times; *hypokritḗs* eighteen times). In the Sermon on the Mount Christ described as hypocrites those whose giving, praying, and fasting are paraded in public (Mt. 6:2, 5, 16). These are people who with ulterior motives openly play the part of righteous persons. One who criticizes another for that of which he himself is guilty is also a hypocrite (Mt. 7:5; Lk. 6:42). The Pharisees belonged in this category because they performed the external actions of religion without an inner devotion to God (Mt. 15:7f.; Mk. 7:6f.). They are also accused of pretense in Lk. 12:1, where Christ speaks of hypocrisy as "the leaven of the Pharisees." Here He seemed to refer to the pervasive character of hypocrisy. On another occasion Christ spoke of the people in general as hypocrites because they could interpret and predict the weather but pretended not to understand the meaning of the times (Lk. 12:56). Lk. 13:15 was addressed to religious leaders who covered their hatred for Christ with the cloak of meticulous concern for the sabbath. They were exposed by Christ's reminder that they even took care of their animals on the sabbath day. Again the religious leaders were designated as hypocrites when they posed as sincere men asking if it was right to pay Roman taxes (Mt. 22:18; Mk. 12:15). Seven times in Mt. 23 (vv. 13-15, 23, 25, 27, 29) Jesus pronounced woe on the scribes and Pharisees because they were hypocrites. Their hypocrisy is most explicitly set forth in vv. 23, 25, 27, and 29. In v. 28 hypocrisy is listed as one of the sins they attempted to hide. In Mt. 24:51 hypocrites are apparently classed among the worst of sinners.

B. In the Pauline Epistles. Paul employs *hypókrisis* only twice, and *hypokritḗs* not at all. Peter's act of withdrawing from table fellowship with gentile Christians when Jews from Jerusalem came to Antioch is called hypocrisy (RSV "insincerity," Gal. 2:13). In 1 Tim. 4:2 false teachers are said to be characterized by hypocrisy (RSV "pretensions") because they pose as teaching the truth.

C. In the Petrine Epistles. Peter's only use of either of the terms is found in his inclusion of *hypókrisis* (RSV "insincerity") in a list of sins to be avoided (1 Pet. 2:1).

See *TDNT,* VIII, *s.v.* ὑποκρίνομαι (U. Wilckens); *DNTT,* II, 468-470. D. W. BURDICK

HYRCANUS hûr-kā'nəs [Gk. *Hyrkanos*]; AV HIRCANUS. "Son of Tobias, a man of very high standing," who had a large sum of money deposited in the temple of Jerusalem when Heliodorus was sent to confiscate it in 187 B.C. (2 Macc. 3:11ff.). Opinions differ about whether to identify this Hyrcanus with Tobias's grandson, whose birth and history are related at considerable length by Josephus (*Ant.* xii.4.6-11 [186-236]), or with another Hyrcanus mentioned in *Ant.* xiii.8.4 (249-253). *See* HASMONEANS; MACCABEES.

HYSSOP [Heb. *'ēzôḇ*; Gk. *hýssōpos*] (Ex. 12:22; Lev. 14:4, 6, 49ff.; Ps. 51:7 [MT 9]; etc.); NEB also MARJORAM. A plant, the identity of which has been a subject of prolonged and inconclusive discussion. It is not the labiate that Linnaeus named *Hyssopus officinalis,* since that species is indigenous only to southern Europe. Probably "hyssop" refers to several plants, as does Arab. *zaʿtār,* a name given to a group of plants like marjoram and thyme. The hairy stems of marjoram would serve excellently as an aspergillum when bunched together. In addition, these species are widely distributed, growing even in desert areas. On this basis, OT references to hyssop may well be to *Origanum syriacum* L., and the Egyptian marjoram *O. maru* var. *aegyptiacum* (L.) Dinsm., both of which favor terrace walls and rock crevices (cf. 1 K. 4:33).

Attempts to identify hyssop with the *Capparis spinosa* or caper (Arab. *'aṣaf*) are fanciful philologically as well as botanically. The caper bears flat leaves on stiff prickly stems, and would furnish neither a satisfactory aspergillum nor a "sponge" (Jn. 19:29; cf. Mt. 27:48; Mk. 15:36). For the latter purpose the *Origanum* would also be entirely unsuitable. Some authorities maintain that the hyssop, sponge, and vinegar were lifted up to the dying Jesus on a stalk of Indian millet (*Sorghum vulgare* var. *durra*), while others have argued that Gk. *hyssṓpō* is a corruption of *hýssō,* "javelin," and that the passage should read, "they put a sponge full of vinegar upon a javelin" (cf. NEB). R. K. H.

I AM; I WILL BE. *See* God, Names of.

IACIMUS. *See* Alcimus.

IBEX ī'beks [Heb. *dîšōn*] (Dt. 14:5); AV PYGARG; NEB WHITE-RUMPED DEER. A kind of antelope or mountain goat (BDB, p. 190). Heb. *dîšōn* is derived from *dûš,* "to tread, thresh" (cf. Hos. 10:11; cf. also Assyr. *daššu,* "mountain goat"). The ibex must be similar to the other "clean" animals with which it is listed in Dt. 14:5. The LXX *pýgargos* (from *pygḗ,* "rump," and *argós,* "white") also occurs in Herodotus iv.192 as the name of an antelope. It has been used as a specific name of *Cervus pygargus,* the Tartarian roe, and *Bubalis pygargus,* a small South African antelope. Both the AV and NEB derive their translations from the LXX: the NEB by paraphrase and the AV by transliteration. A. E. Day

IBHAR ib'här [Heb. *yiḇḥār*–'He (God) chooses'; Gk. *Ebear, Baar, Iebaar*]. One of David's sons, born at Jerusalem; he was the son of a wife, not of a concubine (2 S. 5:15; 1 Ch. 3:6), but is otherwise unknown. His name in all three lists follows Solomon's.

IBIS ī'bəs [Heb. *yanšûp*; Gk. *eíbis*] (Lev. 11:17); AV GREAT OWL; NEB SCREECH-OWL. This is the only instance where the ibis is mentioned in the RSV, which here follows the LXX and Vulgate. In Dt. 14:16 and Isa. 34:11 the RSV retains the "owl" of the AV and RV, so the rendering *yanšûp* as "ibis" in Lev. 11:17 seems unjustified. Instead, the eagle-owl (*Bubo ascalaphus*) or the long-eared owl (*Asio otus*) would seem to be indicated. The ibis (*Threskiornis aethiopica*) was familiar in antiquity as the sacred bird of the Egyptian deity Thoth.

IBLEAM ib'lə-am, ib'lē-əm [Heb. *yiḇlᵉʿām*; Gk. *Ieblaam*]. A fortified city with its villages, apparently located in or near the territory of Issachar, but included in the northern part of the territory assigned to the half-tribe of Manasseh that settled W of the Jordan, when Canaan was divided among the tribes of Israel after the conquest under Joshua (Josh. 17:11). It may be the Levitical city Bileam of 1 Ch. 6:70 (MT 55) and also the Belmain of Jth. 4:4. Ibleam occurs as Ybrʿm in Egyptian lists. The site is represented by Khirbet Belʿameh, about 16 km. (10 mi.) SE of Megiddo.

Manasseh failed to drive the Canaanites from Ibleam but forced them into the tribe's service (Jgs. 1:27f.). When Jehu was destroying the family of Ahab, he mortally wounded Ahaziah king of Judah as he fled in his chariot "at the ascent of Gur, which is by Ibleam" (2 K. 9:27). According to the Lucian text, Zechariah king of Israel was killed there by Shallum (2 K. 15:10).

R. J. Hughes, III

IBNEIAH ib-nē'yə [Heb. *yiḇnᵉyâ*–'Yahweh builds up']. A Benjaminite, son of Jeroham (1 Ch. 9:8).

Winged ibex, silver with partial gilding, originally used as a handle on a vessel. Susa, 4th cent. B.C. (Louvre)

IBNIJAH ib-nī'jə [Heb. *yiḇnîyâ*–'may Yahweh enlarge']; NEB IBNIAH. A Benjaminite, father of Reuel (1 Ch. 9:8).

IBRI ib'rē [Heb. *ʿiḇrî*–'a Hebrew']. A Merarite Levite, son of Jaaziah (1 Ch. 24:27).

IBSAM ib'sam [Heb. *yiḇśām*–'fragrant']; AV, NEB, JIBSAM. Descendant of Issachar, family of Tolah (1 Ch. 7:2).

IBZAN ib'zan [Heb. *'iḇṣān*]. The tenth judge of Israel. His city is given as Bethlehem (whether of Judah or Zebulun is not stated). He judged Israel seven years, and when he died he was buried in his native land. The only personal details given about him in the biblical narrative are that he had thirty sons and a like number of daughters. He sent all of his sons "outside" for wives and brought husbands from "outside" for all his daughters. The exact meaning of Heb. *haḥûṣ,* "outside," is a matter of speculation, but the great social importance of the man and possibly alliances among tribes are suggested in the brief narrative (Jgs. 12:8–10). Jewish tradition identifies Ibzan with Boaz of Bethlehem in Judah (T.B. *Baba Bathra* 91a).

E. D. ISAACS

ICE [Heb. *qeraḥ*]. Ice is almost unknown in Palestine and Syria except on the highest mountains. At moderate heights of less than 1200 m. (4000 ft.) some ice may form during the night in winter, but the warm rays of the sun melt it the next day. A great quantity of snow collects in caves in the mountains during the winter and is thus preserved for use in the summer months. The OT uses the word in three descriptions of God's power: "From whose womb did the ice come forth, and . . . the hoarfrost" (Job 38:29); "By the breath of God ice is given" (37:10); "He casts forth his ice like morsels" (Ps. 147:17).

Figuratively, untrue friends are compared to streams "which are dark with ice" (Job 6:16). A. H. JOY

ICHABOD ik'ə-bod, ī'kə-bod [Heb. *'î-ḵāḇôḏ*–'inglorious'; LXX B *ouaí barchabṓth,* A *ouaí chabṓth, Atimos*]. Son of Phinehas, Eli's son, slain at the battle of Aphek when the ark was taken. Ichabod was born after his father's death. His mother named him on her deathbed to indicate that the "glory [had] departed from Israel" (1 S. 4:19-22). He was thus important as a symbol, though little is recorded of him as an individual. His nephew Ahijah was one of those who waited with Saul and the six hundred at Gibeah just before Jonathan's brave attack upon the Philistines (1 S. 14:2f.). H. WALLACE

ICONIUM ī-kō'nē-əm [Gk. *Ikonion* (Acts 13:51; 14:1, 19, 21; 16:2; 2 Tim. 3:11), *Eikonion* (Acts 14:21 B D)]. A city of south-central Asia Minor in which Paul proclaimed the gospel on his first missionary journey (Acts 14:1-6) and which he apparently revisited on the second and third missionary journeys.

I. Topography and History.–In what remains the definitive essay (in *Cities of St. Paul*), Sir William Ramsay likened Iconium to Damascus. The physical setting is similar: Iconium is close to the mountains on a high, fertile plateau that is well watered by large streams. Again, Iconium is not suited to military defense, and it thus became a prosperous city of peace and commerce as well as a center of agriculture. Furthermore, Iconium was on a major trade route (between Ephesus and Syria) and was an important crossroads of the Roman empire, with no less than five roads radiating from it. Another point is that the origins of Iconium are lost in antiquity. Two legends, one Phrygian and the other Greek, exist as explanations of the beginning

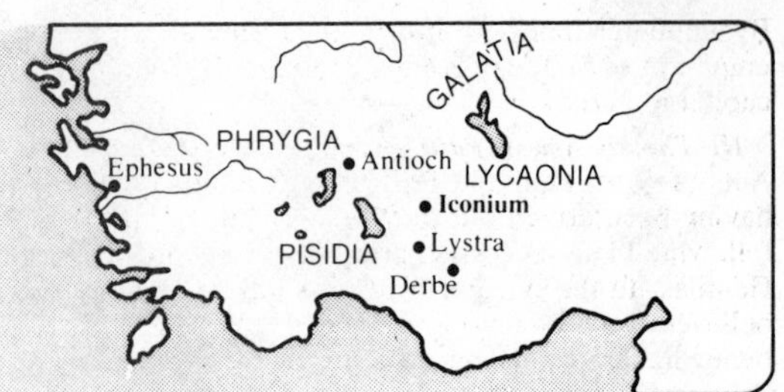

of Iconium, each playing in a different way on Gk. *eikṓn* ("image") as the source of the name Iconium. Between the 11th and 14th cents., Iconium (Konya) was similar to Damascus in that it became the capital of the Seljuk empire of Roum and the possessor of so many beautiful buildings that the Turks spread the epigram: "See all the world; but see Konya." Modern Konya remains known for its plum and apricot orchards.

Iconium lies close to the border between Phrygia and Lycaonia, and thus it has been associated with both regions. So far as topography is concerned, Iconium is naturally suited to be the capital of the region of Lycaonia. Yet the city was regarded in earliest times as Phrygian; its inhabitants were of Phrygian (not Lycaonian) descent, although in later times the educated classes took pride above all in their Hellenism. Archeological evidence verifies the persistence of the Phrygian language. The religion of the area was the native Phrygian Cybele worship, which, however, took on Greek dress in the Hellenistic period. In this period Iconium was governed successively by the Seleucids, Galatians, and the kings of Pontus. This period was followed by the Roman conquest under Mithradates VI. Mark Antony gave Iconium to Polemon of Cilicia and shortly thereafter it came under the rule of Amyntas of Galatia. Iconium was commonly regarded as a city of Lycaonia from 100 B.C. to A.D. 100, despite the existence of references (both before and after this period) to the city as Phrygian. When Amyntas died in 25 B.C., the city was given back to the Romans and belonged to the Roman province of Galatia until the end of the 3rd century.

Ramsay regarded Acts 14:6 as a "striking instance of local accuracy" when it says that Paul and Barnabas fled from Iconium to Lystra and Derbe, "cities of Lycaonia." This phrase implies that Iconium was a city of Phrygia and agrees with Xenophon (4th cent. B.C.) that Iconium was "the last city of Phrygia" on Cyrus' eastward march (*Anabasis* i.2.19). From the perspective of the author of Acts, Iconium probably belonged with the Phrygia of 16:6 and 18:23.

After becoming a part of the Roman empire, the city retained its Hellenistic character: only in reference to Iconium, of all the cities of Asia Minor, does Acts mention "Hellenes" (Acts 14:1; 16:1, 3). Nearby Lystra and Antioch were utilized as military outposts and were more subject to Romanization. Nevertheless, Iconium was honored by Rome for loyalty, receiving from Claudius the imperial name Claudiconium (*ca.* A.D. 41) and achieving the favored status of a Roman colony from Hadrian (*ca.* A.D. 135). The later history of Iconium includes an ecclesiastical council held there in 235; numerous inscriptions point to a thriving Christian population in the early centuries. Iconium became a secondary city in the new province of Pisidia (with its capital Antioch) created by Diocletian in 295. Less than a century later (372) Iconium was made the capital of the province of Lycaonia. Iconium fell to the Moslems in 708 and was part of the

Byzantine empire until it was made capital of the Seljuk empire in 1097. Today Konya continues to be a provincial capital in Turkey.

II. The Mission of Paul.–According to the narrative of Acts (14:1-6), Paul and Barnabas came to Iconium after having been driven out of Pisidian Antioch by the Jews, following their success in preaching the word among the Gentiles. In the synagogue at Iconium "a great company believed, both of Jews and Greeks [*Hellēnōn*]." The unbelieving Jews poisoned the minds of the Gentiles, but Paul and Barnabas were able "for a long time [*hikanón chrónon*]" to continue their preaching and to perform "signs and wonders." The populace were divided in their response; the opposition stirred up by the unbelieving Jews culminated in a plot by Jews and Gentiles "with their rulers" to assault and stone the apostles. The reference to the rulers may suggest some formal authorization of the Jewish penalty of death by stoning. The whole context, however, suggests the precipitant action of a mob, with no concern for legality. When Paul and Barnabas heard of the plan they escaped to the Lycaonian cities of Lystra and Derbe. Undaunted by Paul's escape, Jews of Iconium (and Antioch) turned the people of Lystra against him and accomplished their purpose of stoning Paul (to death, as they supposed). In an autobiographical reminiscence at the end of his life (2 Tim. 3:11), Paul mentions his persecution at Iconium (as at Antioch and Lystra) to Timothy, who was from Lystra, but known and well spoken of by the brethren in Iconium (Acts 16:2).

After preaching at Derbe, Paul and Barnabas returned to Iconium (as to the other cities) to strengthen new disciples and to appoint elders for the church (14:21-23). Although Iconium is not mentioned by name, Paul very probably visited the city on his second (16:6) and third (18:23) missionary journeys. According to the so-called South Galatian theory, Iconium (with Antioch, Lystra, and Derbe) was one of the churches addressed by Paul's Epistle to the Galatians (*see* GALATIANS, EPISTLE TO THE). This church may also have been among those addressed by 1 Peter (1:1).

III. Thecla.–The apocryphal Acts of Paul and Thecla, a book dating from the late 2nd cent. but well known in the early Church, tells the story of Thecla, a young woman of Iconium who overheard Paul's preaching from her window. Thecla became a convert, renounced marriage, and engaged in preaching following Paul's example. She suffered many trials and eventually became the most famous virgin martyr and the source of a growing legend — especially among the Christians at Iconium, where much evidence of her influence has been discovered. Ramsay reconstructed a putative first-century version of the story, but the extent to which the romance rests upon a historical kernel (if at all) cannot be established. A conical hill near Konya bears the name of St. Thecla to this day.

Bibliography.–F. F. Bruce, *Acts of the Apostles* (2nd ed. 1952); W. M. Ramsay, *Cities of St. Paul* (1907); *CRE*; *SPT*.

D. A. HAGNER

IDALAH id'ə-lä, īd'ə-lə [Heb. *yiḏ*ʾ*ᵃlâ*] (Josh. 19:15). One of the towns allotted to Zebulun. It is named immediately before Bethlehem, and thus it is generally identified with Khirbet el-Ḥawârah (cf. Ḥuryēh in T.P. *Megillah* i.1), about 10 km. (6 mi.) NW of Nazareth, just S of BETHLEHEM **2.**

IDBASH id'bash [Heb. *yiḏbāš*–'honey-sweet'(?)]. A man of Judah, one of the sons of the father of Etam (1 Ch. 4:3; LXX "sons of Etam").

IDDO id'ō.

1. [Heb. *ʾiddô*] (Ezr. 8:17). The "leading man at the place Casiphia," who provided Ezra with Levites and temple servants; the head of the Levitical body or school, said to be one of the temple servants, but perhaps an "and" has slipped out, and it should read: "his brethren *and* the temple servants." In 1 Esd. 8:45f., the AV has "Saddeus" and "Daddeus," while the NEB has "Doldaeus."

2. [*yiddô*] (1 Ch. 27:21). Son of Zechariah, and captain of the half-tribe of Manasseh in Gilead, under David.

3. [*yiddô*] (Ezr. 10:43). One of those who had taken foreign wives. Another reading is "Jaddai" (AV "Jadau"). In 1 Esd. 9:35 the AV has "Edes," the NEB "Edaes."

4. [*ʿiddô*] (1 K. 4:14). Father of Abinadab, Solomon's commissary in Mahanaim in Gilead.

5. [*yiddô*] (1 Ch. 6:21). A Gershomite Levite, son of Joah, called Adaiah in v. 41; ancestor of Asaph.

6. [*K yeʿdî, Q yeʿdô,* also *ʿiddô* (2 Ch. 12:15; 13:22)]. A seer and prophet who provided one of the Chronicler's sources for the reigns of Solomon (2 Ch. 9:29), Rehoboam (12:15), and Abijah (13:22). He may have been the prophet who denounced Jeroboam (1 K. 13), whom Josephus and Jerome call Jadon or Jaddo. Jerome makes Iddo and Oded the same.

7. [*ʿiddô*] (Zec. 1:1). Grandfather (father, according to Ezra) of the prophet Zechariah. See also Zec. 1:7; Ezr. 5:1; 6:14 (*ʿiddôʾ*). In 1 Esd. 6:1 the AV and NEB have "Addo."

8. [*ʿiddôʾ*] (Neh. 12:4, 16). A priest who went up with Zerubbabel (v. 4); one of the priestly clans which went up (v. 16); perhaps same as **7.**

P. W. CRANNELL

IDLE [Heb. *rāpâ*] (Ex. 5:8, 17); NEB LAZY; [*rᵉmîyâ*] (Prov. 19:15); NEB IDLERS; [*pāraṭ*] ("sing idle songs," Am. 6:5); AV CHANT; NEB "pluck the strings"; [Gk. *argós*] (Mt. 20:3, 6); NEB also "nothing to do"; [*lēros*] (Lk. 24:11); NEB NONSENSE; [*átaktos*] (1 Thess. 5:14); AV UNRULY; NEB CARELESS; [*ataktéō*] (2 Thess. 3:7); AV DISORDERLY; NEB IDLERS; [*argéō*] (2 Pet. 2:3); AV LINGER; **IDLENESS** [Heb. *ʿaṣlûṯ*] (Prov. 31:27); [Gk. *atáktōs*] (2 Thess. 3:6, 11); AV DISORDERLY; **IDLER** [Gk. *argós*] (1 Tim. 5:13); (SPEAKING) **IDLY** [Heb. *dabbēr dāḇār*] (Isa. 58:13); AV "speaking thine own words"; NEB "attending to your own affairs."

To be idle is to neglect one's own responsibilities so that one becomes dependent on the generosity of others for the necessities of life. Hebrew Wisdom said that idleness led to poverty and want (Prov. 19:15; Eccl. 10:18; Tob. 4:13). A mark of a good wife is that she will "not eat the bread of idleness" (Prov. 31:27); i.e., she will not sit by while others work and then enjoy the fruits of their labor.

The NT description of "idlers" is found primarily in Paul's letters to the Thessalonians. The verb *ataktéō* was used originally of "soldiers marching out of order or quitting the ranks, hence 'to be neglectful of duty, to be lawless, to lead a disorderly life'" (Thayer, p. 83). Hence when Paul exhorts his readers to "admonish the *atáktous*" (1 Thess. 5:14), it may be inferred that he is referring to those who have committed some moral wrong or deviated from a prescribed rule (so Chrysostom; AV "unruly"). A contemporary papyrus from Egypt (Oxy. P. II, 275, 24), however, shows the word to mean "a loafer," or "not being at one's post"; thus the reference is to absenteeism from work, hence being "idle" or "lazy." Such laziness seems to have been a long-standing problem in Thessalonica, where in the general excitement surrounding the anticipation of an imminent Parousia some Christians had quit working and had begun to live off the generosity of their fellow Christians. This refusal to work directly violated the tradition Paul had passed on (2 Thess. 3:6) and his own example (v. 7). These "idlers" were severely rebuked not only because they failed to work but also because they interfered with the work of others of the community (2 Thess. 4:11), being "mere busybodies," instead of attending to their own affairs (1 Thess. 4:11).

The problem of "busybodies" in connection with idleness is also found in 1 Tim. 5:13. In this case, widows who were not engaged in doing good deeds tended to "gad about from house to house" and became "not only idlers but gossips and busybodies, saying what they should not." It is well known that a definite office of widow emerged in the early Church (1 Tim. 5:3, 9; Ign. *Smyrn.* 13:1; Polyc. *Phil.* 4:3), and it seems that these women especially were expected to perform good works (1 Tim. 5:10). House-to-house visitations were evidently a part of these duties, and the very real danger was that these "pastoral calls" would degenerate into opportunities for prying into neighbors' affairs.

The men in the marketplace in Jesus' parable of the laborers and the vineyard (Mt. 20:3, 6) were "standing idle." These men were not "lazy" but rather unemployed and looking for work (v. 7). The "idle" (*lḗros*—occurring only here in the NT) tale of the women returning from the empty tomb on Easter morning seemed to the disciples to be "pure nonsense," so they did not initially believe that Christ had risen from the dead (Lk. 24:11).

Bibliography.–MM, p. 89; M. Dibelius, *Pastoral Epistles* (Eng. tr. 1972), p. 75; J. E. Frame, *Thessalonians* (*ICC*, 1912), p. 197.

D. K. McKim

IDOL [Heb. *semel* (2 Ch. 33:7, 15), *pesel* (Isa. 40:19; 44:17; Jer. 10:14; etc.), *'āwen* (Isa. 66:3), *'āṣāḇ* (1 Ch. 10:9; 2 Ch. 24:18; Hos. 10:6; Ps. 106:36; 115:4; Isa. 10:11; etc.), *'ĕlîl* (Lev. 19:4; 26:1; 1 Ch. 16:26; Ps. 96:5; 97:7; Isa. 2:8; etc.), *gillûlîm* (Lev. 26:30; 1 K. 15:12; Ezk. 6:4-6, 9, 13; etc.), *heḇel* (Dt. 32:21; 1 K. 16:13; 2 K. 17:15; etc.), *šiqqûṣ* (2 Ch. 15:8; Jer. 16:18), *ṣîr* (Isa. 45:16), *'êmâ* (Jer. 50:38); Gk. *eídōlon* (Acts 7:41; 15:20; Rom. 2:22; Rev. 9:20; etc.), *eidōlóthytos* (Acts 15:29; 21:25; 1 Cor. 8:1, 4; 10:19; Rev. 2:14, 20; etc.), *eidōlolatría* ("worship of idols," 1 Cor. 10:14; cf. 1 Pet. 4:3), *kateídōlos* (Acts 17:16)]; AV also GRAVEN IMAGE (Isa. 40:19; Hab. 2:18; etc.), A GOD (Isa. 44:17), "vanities" (Dt. 32:21; 1 K. 16:13; etc.), "detestable things" (Jer. 16:18), etc.; NEB also IMAGE (2 Ch. 33:7; Isa. 40:19; etc.), FALSE GOD (1 Cor. 8:4), WORTHLESS IDOLS (1 K. 16:13, 26; etc.), "heathen consecration" (1 Cor. 8:7), etc.; **IMAGE** [Heb. *ṣelem* (Gen. 1:26f.; 5:3; 9:6), *teraphîm* (1 S. 19:13, 16), *'ĕlîl* (Isa. 10:11), *mipleṣeṯ* (1 K. 15:13; 2 Ch. 15:16), *taḇnîṯ* (Ps. 106:20), *'āṣāḇ* (Jer. 44:19), *neseḵ* (Jer. 10:14; 51:17); Aram. *ṣelēm* (Dnl. 2:31f.; etc.); Gk. *eikṓn* (Rom. 8:29; 1 Cor. 11:7; 15:49; Col. 1:15; Rev. 14:9, 11; etc.)]; AV also IDOL (1 K. 15:13; 2 Ch. 15:16), "similitude" (Ps. 106:20); NEB also HOUSEHOLD GODS (1 S. 19:13, 16), "obscene object" (1 K. 15:13; 2 Ch. 15:16), LIKENESS (Rom. 8:29; 1 Cor. 15:49), etc.; **GRAVEN IMAGE** [Heb. *pesel*] (Ex. 20:4; Lev. 26:1; Dt. 4:16, 23, 25; Jgs. 18:18; 2 K. 21:7; etc.); NEB also FIGURE (Dt. 4:16), CARVED FIGURE (Dt. 4:23, 25; 5:8; etc.), IDOL (Jgs. 18:30f.; Isa. 44:15), etc.; **MOLTEN IMAGE** [Heb. *messēḵâ* (Dt. 9:12; 27:15; Jgs. 18:17f.; Ps. 106:19; etc.), *neseḵ* (Isa. 41:29; Dnl. 11:8)]; NEB also IMAGE OF METAL (Dt. 9:12), EFFIGIES (Isa. 41:29); etc. A material object representing a deity to which religious worship is directed. "Idol" is a transliteration of the Gk. *eídōlon,* "image." The prohibition of idol worship and manufacture occurred early in Israel's history and remained an important concern, often occupying a central place in the prophetic literature. These prohibitions were continued in the primitive Church, and after the conversion of large numbers of Gentiles, the APOSTOLIC COUNCIL issued a written admonition to the gentile churches prohibiting any association with idols and idolatry (Acts 15:20-29).

I. Vocabulary.–The Heb. *semel* denotes a figure of anything (Dt. 4:16) as well as the image of a particular deity (BDB, p. 702). Heb. *pesel* is derived from *pāsal,* "hew," "cut," hence, something carved or cut from wood or stone (BDB, pp. 820f.). The *terāpîm* (Gen. 31:19, 34f.; 2 K. 23:24) were probably small statues of household gods (*see* TERAPHIM). Heb. *massēḵâ* designates a molten image (KoB, pp. 541f.).

Canaanite graven image of silver (*ca.* 1600 B.C.) from Nahariyah on the northwestern coast of Israel (Israel Department of Antiquities and Museums)

In addition to terms for objects of worship, the Hebrew OT contains derogatory epithets that denote idols, expressing the contempt of the Hebrews for foreign deities. Thus, Heb. *'ĕlîlîm,* the plural of *'ĕlîl,* "nothing," "vain," means "nonentities" (KoB, pp. 53f.). Heb. *'āṣāḇ* is derived from the verb *'āṣaḇ,* "form," "fashion," hence, something made by hand, but a double meaning is intended because of the similarity to Heb. *'āṣaḇ,* "hurt," "grieve." Heb. *mipleṣeṯ,* "object of trembling," is derived from *pālaṣ,* "shudder." Heb. *'āwen* can mean "sorrow," "trouble" (e.g., Gen. 35:18; Nu. 23:21), but also is a term for "idol" (Isa. 66:3). The verb *hāḇal,* "be vain, empty," is a cognate of *heḇel,* "vanity." Thus the AV translates "vanities" and the NEB "worthless idols." The plural noun *gillûlîm,* found most frequently in the books of Kings and in Ezekiel, is possibly derived from *gālal,* "roll." Hence, idols are "those rolled about"; they must be carried and have no life of their own. Another derivation is possible from *gēl,* "dung" (KoB, pp. 181, 183f.). Heb. *'ēmîm,* literally "objects of fright," is a cognate of *'êmâ,* "fright," "horror." The verb *šāqaṣ,* "be unclean, detestable," gives the noun *šeqeṣ,* "detestable thing," thus "loathsome idols" in the NEB (2 Ch. 15:8) and "detestable things" in the AV (Jer. 16:18).

Frequently two words are combined to form a compound expression denoting an idol. Thus Heb. *'ēṣ pislām* literally means "wooden idols" and is so translated in the NEB (Isa. 45:20). Heb. *haḇlê nēḵār,* "foreign vanities," is rendered "strange vanities" in the AV, "foreign gods" in the NEB, and "idols" in the RSV (Jer. 8:19). Similar translations are followed for Heb. *haḇlê šāwᵉ',* "worthless vanities"; the NEB renders "useless idols," the AV has "lying vanities," and the RSV translates simply "idols." The expression *sēmel haqqin'â,* "image of jealousy" (Ezk. 8:3, 5), is obscure. W. Eichrodt interprets the expression to mean "image of passionate love," since Heb. *qin'â* can mean the ardor of love as well as jealousy (KoB, pp. 842f.). Thus, Eichrodt understands the image to be that of the deity ASHERAH, a goddess of love. This suggestion accords with 2 K. 21:7, which states that King Manasseh set up an image of Asherah in the temple. The image was destroyed by Josiah (2 K. 23:6), but may have been restored later (W. Eichrodt, *Ezekiel* [Eng. tr., *OTL,* 1970], p. 122).

The NT terms for "idol" include Gk. *eídōlon,* used most frequently, and several of its cognates. Gk. *eidōlóthyton* specifically refers to meat sacrificed to idols. In 1 Cor. 10:14, the NEB renders Gk. *eidōlolotría,* "idolatry," literally; the RSV reads "worship of idols." Gk. *kateídōlos* appears only in Acts 17:16 and means "full of idols." The phrase *homoiṓmati eikónos* in Rom. 1:23 literally means "likeness, image" (Bauer, rev., pp. 221, 421, 567).

II. Form.–The familiarity of the Hebrews with the forms of foreign deities is due not only to the geography of Palestine in OT times, but also to the pagan background from which the Israelite nation emerged. Israel was in close political, social, and economic contact with Syria, Phoenicia, Philistia, and Canaan, and thus was widely exposed to foreign gods. Also, Israel was situated on the main route between Egypt and the rest of the Near East, so that the Hittites, Assyrians, Babylonians, and Egyptians had frequent contact with Israel. The Mesopotamian background of the patriarchs is well known, and coupled with Israel's sojourn in Egypt, it exposed the early Israelites to a variety of idolatries.

Jeroboam I had golden bulls built for his sanctuaries of Bethel and Dan (1 K. 12:28-30), an event reminiscent of the golden calf of Aaron (Ex. 32:1-6). The bulls were probably wooden statues covered with gold plate. Although Jeroboam was not advocating a departure from Yahweh the God of Israel, the images of the bull had idolatrous connotations (R. de Vaux, *Ancient Israel* [Eng. tr. 1961], II, 333-35). The Egyptian gods Apis and Hathor were both represented by a bull (*ANEP,* nos. 570, 573), as was 'El, the head of the Canaanite pantheon. Ahab built a temple to BAAL, the Canaanite storm god. A stone stele found at Ugarit depicts Baal as a mighty warrior, wielding a club and a lightning bolt (*ANEP,* no. 490). Ahab's temple undoubtedly made use of similar images. The worship of the goddess Asherah was widespread in Syria, Canaan, and throughout Israel in different periods. The exact form and construction of the Asherim are uncertain; whether they were phallic pillars or stele inscribed with an image is not known. Several stone pillars (Heb. *maṣṣēḇâ,* "pillar") manufactured for the worship of Egyptian deities were unearthed at Timnah in 1969 (*see* PILLAR). Other findings there included the remains of a sanctuary dedicated to the goddess Hathor, incense altars, and smelting equipment (*EAEHL,* IV, 1186-1197). The Israeli archeologist Y. Aharoni directed the excavation of a solar shrine at Lachish in 1966 and 1968 (cf. Ezk. 8:16). The date of the shrine has been fixed in the Hellenistic period, but there is evidence that the solar shrine was preceded by other kinds of cults at the same site; a stone pillar, the remains of a buried olive tree, possibly an Asherah, and various cult vessels and incense burners have been recovered (*EAEHL,* III, 747-49).

Bronze statuette, covered with gold leaf, of a god, possibly Baal. From Megiddo, *ca.* 1200 B.C. (Oriental Institute, University of Chicago)

Besides the upright pillars, engraved stelae, and gold- and silver-covered idols, much smaller objects served as representations of deity. A small seal from Bethel depicts the goddess Astarte (*see* ASHTORETH), along with an unnamed deity. Small bronze figurines of the Egyptian deities Horus and Osiris have been recovered at Ashkelon (*EAEHL*, I, 122, 124). Findings at Beth-shean include a small stele of the goddess Anat, consort and sister of Baal, and temple cult objects covered with birds and serpents (cf. Ezk. 8:10). Earlier strata contain objects of Egyptian origin, including a stele erected to the honor of Mekal (*ANEP*, no. 487), the god of Beth-shean (*EAEHL*, I, 213-17). Nude figurines of female goddesses, some with exaggerated features, are common among artifacts from various Palestinian sites (*ANEP*, nos. 464-473).

Cylindrical pottery cult object from Beth-shean (11th cent. B.C.). Four serpents writhe up its sides, and birds perch on handles and in triangular openings (University Museum, University of Pennsylvania)

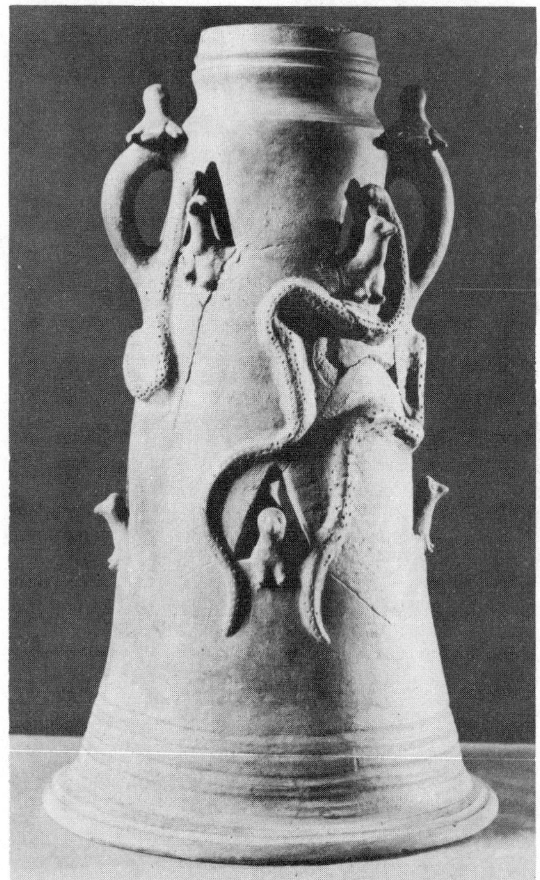

Though idols and images as objects of worship were prohibited, a few images were permitted in Israel. The "bronze serpent" erected by Moses was not intended to be an object of worship, but a device for healing (Nu. 21:8; cf. Jn. 3:14). Later Jewish tradition, found in the Palestinian Targum to the Pentateuch and Wisd. 16:7, made it clear that the healing was from God, not the brazen serpent (see M. McNamara, *Targum and Testament* [1972], pp. 147f.). Hezekiah destroyed the bronze serpent because the people had been burning incense to it (2 K. 18:4). The ARK OF THE COVENANT was constructed with figures of CHERUBIM facing each other over the mercy seat (Ex. 26:18-20). Apparently their purpose was to symbolize the glory of God. The EPHOD, an outer garment worn during certain religious ceremonies, often aroused superstitious reverence among those who viewed it (Jgs. 8:27; 17:5), though it could be used to determine God's will in certain situations (1 S. 23:9-12; 30:7f.).

Idols occupied an important place in the life of Gentiles in the NT world. During his second missionary journey, Paul visited Athens, which was "full of idols" (Acts 17:16). The Athenians had even erected an altar with an inscription "to an unknown god." A similar altar with the inscription "unknown god" has been discovered at Pergamum (*LAP*, rev. ed., plate 126). Demetrius and other silversmiths rioted in protest against Paul when he preached at Ephesus; profits from their manufacture of silver shrines of Artemis had been reduced (Acts 19:23-39). Artemis was a fertility goddess and patron deity of the city. Statues of her depict a woman whose chest is covered with multiple oval shapes, either breasts or eggs, apparently symbols of fertility. Excavations at Ephesus have identified shops of silversmiths (C. H. Pfeiffer, ed., *The Biblical World* [1966], p. 230).

Jewish monotheism and antipathy to idols were affirmed in the primitive Church (1 Cor. 8:4). Paul taught that pagan sacrifices were an offering "to demons" (1 Cor. 10:20; cf. Dt. 32:17). John likewise urged Christians to "keep yourselves from idols" (1 Jn. 5:20).

See also GODS; IDOLATRY; RELIGIONS OF THE BIBLICAL WORLD.

Bibliography.–G. A. Barrois, *Manuel d'archéologie biblique*, II (1939-1953), 389-398; M. Burrows, *What Mean These Stones?* (1941); J. B. Pritchard, *Palestinian Figurines in Relation to Certain Goddesses Known Through Literature* (1943); W. F. Albright, *Yahweh and the Gods of Canaan* (repr. 1979); F. M. Cross, *Canaanite Myth and Hebrew Epic* (1973); *TDOT*, I, *s.v.* "'ᵉlōhîm" (Ringgren).

P. L. GARBER R. J. W.

IDOLATRY [Heb. *tᵉrāpîm* (1 S. 15:23), *gillûlîm* (Ezk. 23:49), *zᵉnûṯ* (Ezk. 43:9); Gk. *eidōlolatría* (Gal. 5:20; Col. 3:5; 1 Pet. 4:3); AV also IDOLS (Ezk. 23:49), "whoredom" (Ezk. 43:9); NEB also "wanton disloyalty" (Ezk. 43:9), WORSHIP OF IDOLS (1 Pet. 4:3). The TERAPHIM were apparently "household idols" (Gen. 31:19, 34f.), although no text states that they were worshiped. In 1 S. 15:23 Heb. *tᵉrāpîm* may be used as a general word for idols (P. K. McCarter, *I Samuel* [*AB*, 1980], p. 268). Heb. *gillûlîm* is perhaps another general word for idols (cf. 2 K. 23:24, where both *gillûlîm* and *tᵉrāpîm* occur), although its etymology is uncertain; it may be related to Heb. *gēl*, "dung," and may have been coined by Ezekiel (cf. *TDOT*, III, 2). Heb. *zᵉnûṯ* is derived from *zānâ*, "have illicit intercourse"; its sexual connotations suggest the involvement of cultic prostitutes, who were a regular feature of Canaanite pagan worship.

I. Ancient Near East.–Deities of the non-Hebrew religions of the ancient Near East were commonly associated with animal forms. It is generally held today that this theriomorphic representation of deity was either a concrete expression of the attributes of the god (e.g., in *UT* 49:IV:34, 'El, the chief god of the Canaanite pantheon, is called *ṯr* [Heb. *šôr*], "bull," which connotes his power), or a localization of the spiritual presence of the deity, similar to the presence of Yahweh over the cherubim. Yet a stele from Râs Shamrah depicts 'El as a human figure (*ANEP*, no. 493), and the portrayal of the deities in the Ugaritic epic material makes it highly unlikely that they were thought to have an essential animal form. W. F. Albright observes that in the Canaanite, Aramean, and Hittite cultures, a god was almost always depicted standing on the back of an animal. He also observes, "The storm-god of Mesopotamia is actually represented on seal-cylinders of the second millennium B.C. as a schematic bolt of lightning set upright on the back of a bull, and this iconographic device may go back to Sumerian seals showing the bull who was the central figure in the ritual of consecration of a sacred drum with the winged shrine of music (so labelled!) on his back" (*FSAC*, p. 300).

This conception of the nature of idolatry seems to be consonant with the cult of the golden calf, which manifested itself early in Israelite history at Sinai (Ex. 32:1-6), and which resurfaced in the state cultus of the northern kingdom of Israel (1 K. 12:25-30). The worship of the golden calf was evidently a syncretistic form of Yahwism and not an outright rejection of Yahweh. This is clear from the attribution of the deliverance from Egypt to the image of the bull (Ex. 32:4), and from the fact that the worship associated with the image was directed to Yahweh (vv. 5f.). Evidently the image of the golden calf was understood as a visual representation of the spiritual presence of Yahweh. The plural verbs associated with the word "god" (*'ĕlōhîm*) need not indicate a plurality of gods (only one image was constructed); they may have been used by the writer to emphasize that the golden calf was not the true god. The word *'ĕlōhîm* ("God, gods") is plural, but when used of God it is always construed with singular verbs. (For a viewpoint opposing this concept of the golden calf see Bailey.)

This concretization of the presence and attributes of deity could easily have degenerated in the popular religion to the point where the image was regarded as the deity itself. It is likely that this occurred in many ancient cultures. The use of the image of a bull was inherently dangerous in the Israelite cultus because of the close associations of that symbol with the pagan fertility cults.

See RELIGIONS OF THE BIBLICAL WORLD: ASSYRIA AND BABYLONIA, CANAANITE, EGYPT.

II. Relation to Israel.–*A. Patriarchal Period.* The nature of the patriarchal religion has been the subject of much scholarly research. One of the most influential contributions to this field of study is that of Albrecht Alt. In his essay "The God of the Fathers" (in *Essays in OT History and Religion* [Eng. tr. 1966], pp. 1-100), Alt contends that much of the material in the patriarchal narratives is secondary and only the most archaic strands are trustworthy. On this supposition Alt concludes that the individual patriarchs worshiped distinct numina which were identified with Yahweh by later writers. Thus Yahwistic monotheism developed long after the patriarchal times.

This view, as well as others of a similar nature, regards the patriarchal traditions as an idealistic representation of what was in reality a somewhat primitive religion, vestiges of which are observable in the narratives. It is asserted by some that the patriarchal religion involved the worship of deities other than Yahweh. Some scholars appeal to Josh. 24:2 to support this assertion. This verse states nothing more, however, than that Terah, Abraham's father, worshiped other deities. Abraham may have been involved with these deities before his call, but there is no reason to assume that he was an idolator after his call by Yahweh. It is difficult to understand why this verse would follow the prohibition against worship of other gods in Josh. 23:16 if that were its implication.

Rachel's theft of the household gods (*tᵉrāpîm*) in Gen. 31:19, 25-35, has been illuminated by archeological finds at the site of ancient NUZI. While Rachel may still have had an affinity for the religion of her youth, it is more probable that the household gods had a legal or monetary value for her, rather than simply a religious one. The Nuzi material indicates that one who possessed the household gods stood to inherit the family estate; e.g., one tablet indicates, "Should Nashwi beget a son, [the latter] shall divide equally with Wullu but [only] Nashwi's son shall take Nashwi's gods . . ." (C. Gordon, pp. 24ff.). If Laban had natural sons during Jacob's sojourn with him, the *tᵉrāpîm* would have been rightfully theirs. Rachel wished the advantage for Jacob her husband.

The pillar (*maṣṣēḇâ*) erected by Jacob (Gen. 28:18, 22; 35:14) need not be regarded as a concrete representation of Yahweh, although such pillars were certainly common to the Canaanite religion (Ex. 23:24; 34:13; Dt. 7:5; 12:3). The term *maṣṣēḇâ* is used in the OT of a memorial (2 S. 18:18), a grave marker (Gen. 35:20), representations of the Israelite tribes (Ex. 24:4), and the visible sign of an agreement (Gen. 31:45, 51f.).

The most common function of the *maṣṣēḇâ* was that of memorializing individuals or solemn events. The pillar set up by Jacob seems to be best understood as a memorial of the extraordinary encounter that Jacob had with God at Bethel. The erection of the pillar would not only distinguish the area where the divine encounter occurred, but also serve as a token of the vow Jacob made to the Lord at that place (Gen. 31:13).

The command Jacob gave to his household to give up their foreign gods (Gen. 35:2-4) does not indicate that idolatry was an essential part of patriarchal religion. Rather, it demonstrates that Jacob recognized the inconsistency of idolatry with his Yahwistic faith.

There seems to be no compelling reason for believing that the use of representational forms of deity was an essential part of pre-Mosaic religion among the Hebrews. Still less is there reason for positing a primitive animism in ancient Hebrew religion because of the theophany that occurred to Abraham at the oaks of Mamre (Gen. 18:1). The reference to the oaks may be understood as a topographical reference similar to other such references in the Pentateuch (Gen. 13:10; Ex. 15:27). Any essential connection between the theophanic appearance and the oak trees is purely conjectural.

B. Mosaic Era. The Mosaic covenant expressly forbids the practice of idolatry in its opening statements (Ex. 20:3-5 par. Dt. 5:7-9). Not only does the Decalogue prohibit the Israelites from having any gods that would rival Yahweh (Ex. 20:3; Dt. 5:7), but it forbids the fashioning of images as objects of worship. The words "you shall not bow down to them or serve them" (Ex. 20:5; Dt. 5:9) make it clear that the command does not preclude the pursuit of art, nor the use of certain representations in worship, such as the cherubim on the ark of the covenant, but that one is not to worship an image or venerate it by bowing before it. Thus the Israelites were to make no symbolic representations of Yahweh in any form (Dt. 4:15-18). This commandment made Israel's faith unique among the nations of the ancient world.

This prohibition of idol worship may not have encouraged advancement in the visual arts, but it served to make the concept of God intensely spiritual. Efforts to concretize the spiritual nature of God were made in the realm of bold literary anthropomorphism. It may be that this verbalizing of the divine attributes caused Israelite religion to find its greatest expression in word rather than in artistic depiction.

The first major defection to idolatry on the part of the Israelites took place in the Mosaic era in the worship of the golden calf (Ex. 32:1-6). The representation of deity in the form of a bull calf may have had its origin in the worship of the Egyptian god Apis, who was so depicted. As mentioned above the bull was also a representation of

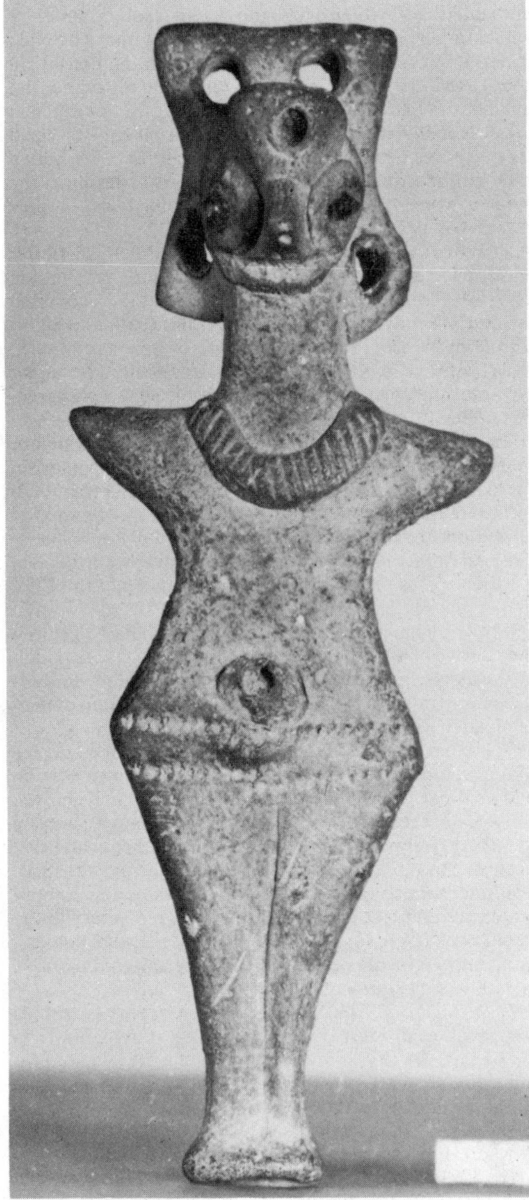

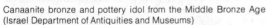

Canaanite bronze and pottery idol from the Middle Bronze Age (Israel Department of Antiquities and Museums)

Statue of Baal (Service des musées, Cairo; picture W. S. LaSor)

the Canaanite god 'El. The institution of the bull cult in Israelite history was the first expression of a religious syncretism that was never entirely suppressed.

C. Historical Books. Several passages in the historical books indicate that images continued to be made in Israel long after Moses' time (Jgs. 3:19; 8:27; 17:3-6; 2 K. 21:7). These instances do not mean that idolatry had a legitimacy in early Yahwism. The period of the judges was one of blatant lawlessness, and much that cannot be considered normative for Israelite faith and practice occurred then. Solomon's lapse into idolatry (1 K. 11:4-8) was clearly denounced (vv. 9-13). The syncretistic religion of Manasseh cited in 2 K. 21:7 is depicted by the historian as contrary to the spirit of Israelite faith (vv. 6-9). Even the bronze serpent that Moses fashioned in the wilderness (Nu. 21:9) became an object of worship (2 K. 18:4). In his reform Josiah removed both the high place at Topheth (2 K. 23:10) and the "horses . . . dedicated to the sun" that had been installed in the temple (v. 11).

These accounts testify that the desire for a visual representation of deity had not been completely expunged from the hearts of many generations of Israelites. The tendency toward syncretism that manifested itself during Moses' absence at Sinai (Ex. 32:1) continued to steal back into the Israelite cultus, creating a tension that ultimately led to a rending of the social fabric of Israel.

The tension between idolatry and the essential spirit of Israelite religion is reflected in the early prophetic protest of Samuel: "For rebellion is as the sin of divination, and stubbornness is as iniquity and idolatry" (1 S. 15:23). In this statement Samuel places disobedience to God and idolatry in the same category. In the final analysis idolatry was rebellion, for it constituted a violation of God's commands.

The syncretistic expressions of religion that run like a thread through the early history of Israel were ultimately given legitimacy by Jeroboam I, king of the northern kingdom of Israel. The division of the nation into the northern and southern kingdoms posed a serious theological crisis for the northern kingdom. The geopolitical rift brought to the fore the question of access to the cultic center at Jerusalem. Jeroboam understood that if he was to bring stability to his fledgling kingdom, he could allow nothing that would foster the loyalties to the Davidic dynasty that were so deeply ingrained in the minds of the people (1 K. 12:26f.). The temple had been built by Solomon the son of David, and Jerusalem was rich with Davidic traditions. Clearly, a new form of religious expression distinct from any association with David would have to be instituted. This was done in a revival of the cult of the golden calf (1 K. 12:28).

Once again the historian expresses displeasure with the use of concrete forms of deity, for he says, "And this thing became a sin, for the people went to the one at Bethel and to the other as far as Dan" (1 K. 12:30). The displeasure seems to be because the law of the central sanctuary had been broken. The placement of sanctuaries in different locations was dangerous because it could lead to the fractionalizing of the concept of Yahweh in the minds of the people, similar to the geographical localizations of the Canaanite god Baal.

The reference to *t^erāpîm* in 1 S. 19:13 ("image") seems best understood according to the suggestion of W. F. Albright as "old rags." He points out that no images "of comparable size have ever been found in Palestinian excavations" (*ARI,* pp. 110f., 206f. n. 63).

D. Classical Prophets. The 8th cent. B.C. witnessed a resurgence of Israel and Judah. Economic prosperity, unparalleled in their history except for the golden age of David and Solomon, fostered a growing class of wealthy, influential people whose loyalty to the covenant stipulations of Yahweh was at best questionable. The erosion of the strong core of covenant obligation marked the 8th cent. and led to the dissolution of the nation. One of the most obvious violations of the covenant standards was the popular religion of the day, a strange syncretism of Yahwism and the symbols and mind-set of pagan idolatry.

The situation in the northern kingdom seems to have been particularly dismal. Rites associated with the fertility cults of Canaan were practiced at a number of shrines in Israel (Hos. 4:11-19; Mic. 1:7) and may even have been widespread.

The internal sickness affected the southern kingdom of Judah as well, although probably to a lesser degree. Isaiah presents a picture of Judahite syncretism that is remarkably similar to that of Israel (2:8; 57:4-10).

The prophets engaged in a bitter polemic against idolatry. They observed the incongruity of worshiping that which one fashions with one's own hands (Isa. 2:8; 44:12-20; Hab. 2:18), and pointed out that idols are impotent and therefore a delusion to those who worship them (Isa. 42:17; 44:9; 45:20; Jer. 10:14f.; 51:17f.). Idols provoke Yahweh to anger (Jer. 8:19) and they are a form of spiritual fornication (Mic. 1:7). The practice of idolatry will lead to Israel's downfall (Isa. 2:8f.). The prophetic condemnation of idolatry had a more positive side, however. God will abolish the images that vie with Him for supremacy (Isa. 2:18; 10:10f.; 31:6f.).

Isaiah's denunciation of idols is the most theologically based of all the prophets. He finds the source of the inclination for the worship of idols in spiritual blindness (44:18) and self-delusion (44:20). Idolatry is thus the external manifestation of a spiritually impoverished mind.

Isaiah points to the impossibility of likening anything on earth to God (40:18-20) and thus roots his polemic against idolatry in the spiritual nature of the deity. At the heart of Isaiah's theological polemic is the fact that God cannot be likened to anything that is finite or temporal (cf. Dt. 4:15). Because God is pure spirit, any attempt to represent Him in symbolic form is a distortion of His person and hence a falsification of truth.

Isaiah also points his hearers to the attributes of Yahweh and then contrasts Yahweh and His glorious attributes with the brooding idol of stone or wood, incapable of thought, speech, or action. He speaks of the Lord's ability to declare future events, and denounces the idol as "empty wind" (41:26, 29; 44:7). The idol cannot stand before the inexorable progress of God's will in history (41:5-7; cf. vv. 8-16). The Lord is the creator of the worlds, controlling the destinies of nations (40:21-23); an idol cannot compare with Him (40:25).

The later prophets also denounced idolatry. Jeremiah foresaw judgment on those who defiled the temple (7:30) and built high places (to Baal) where child sacrifice was practiced (7:31; 19:5). Ezekiel also was faced with idolatrous practices in the temple (8:3-18), where apparently the sun and the Babylonian god Tammuz (Dumuzi) were being worshiped (vv. 14, 16).

Bibliography.–*ERE,* VII (1915), *s.v.* "Images and Idols, Hebrew and Canaanite" (A. Lods); C. Gordon, *BA,* 3 (1940), 1-12 (repr. in D. N. Freedman and E. F. Campbell, eds., *Biblical Archaeologist Reader,* 2 [1964], 21-33); *ARI* (5th ed. 1968); H. H. Rowley, *Faith of Israel* (1956); *FSAC*; Y. Kaufmann, *Religion of Israel* (Eng. tr. 1961); W. F. Albright, *Yahweh and the Gods of Canaan* (1965); L. R. Bailey, *HUCA,* 42 (1971), 97-115; F. M. Cross, *Canaanite Myth and Hebrew Epic* (1973); *TDOT,* III, *s.v.* "gillûlîm" (Preuss).

T. E. MCCOMISKEY

III. Intertestamental Period.–What finally established the Jewish people in immovable opposition to idolatry is told in the Apocrypha (1 Macc. 2:1-48) and in Josephus (*Ant.* xii.5.4 [248-256]). The issue between Antiochus Epiphanes and the Jewish people in the time of the early Maccabees was idolatry. Antiochus demanded that as a pledge of political allegiance to his sovereignty, Jews make a sacrifice at an altar dedicated to the Olympian Zeus, perhaps before his statue (2 Macc. 6:2). Refusal resulted in execution. The HASMONEANS, Mattathias and his sons, and their followers, the HASIDEANS, defied the king's decree. They raised a guerilla army and fought a three-year civil war. With much heroism, they succeeded in obtaining from the state freedom to follow their own religious practices. Never again were Jews to take idolatry seriously. Rather, idol worship became for them a matter of semi-humorous satire and ridicule (cf. Bel and the Dragon).

IV. NT.–Idolatry was prevalent in the NT world. Idols were venerated in temples dedicated to the traditional gentile gods, in popular magic and superstition, as well as in the mystery religions and in emperor worship (Mk. 12:16 par.; Rev. 13:14f.). The subject is scarcely mentioned in the Gospels but receives attention in Paul's letters due to the circumstances of his mission (cf. Luke's comment that Athens was a "city full of idols," Acts 17:16; AV "wholly given to idolatry").

Reflecting his Jewish background, Paul stated plainly, "We [Christians] know that an idol has no real existence" (1 Cor. 8:4). Idolatry is "earthly" (Col. 3:5; Phil. 3:19). The idolaters are "immoral men," with whom Christians are not to associate (1 Cor. 5:10f.), who will not inherit the kingdom of God (1 Cor. 6:10; Gal. 5:21; Eph. 5:5). Cf. "Little children, keep yourselves from idols," 1 Jn. 5:21; "abstain from the pollution of idols," Acts 15:20. Rev. 21:8 states that idolaters are doomed to be destroyed by fire; the new Jerusalem has no place for idolaters who love and practice falsehood (Rev. 22:15).

In Rom. 1:18-32, Paul taught that sexual laxness and social disorder among Gentiles were ultimately traceable

Relief of a god, probably Zeus-Hadad, with thunderbolt and a young bull on each side, from Khirbet et-Tannur SE of the Dead Sea. The relief shows Hellenistic-Parthian influences (E. K. Vogel; picture American Schools of Oriental Research)

to their idolatry, which he described as exchanging "the glory of the immortal God for images." The wrath of God is against all such ungodliness and wickedness (v. 18). God's decree is that idolaters deserve to die (v. 32). At Ephesus Paul was accused of successfully persuading a considerable company of people "that gods made with hands are no gods" (Acts 19:26).

In their dealings with gentile converts from Greco-Roman religious backgrounds, the early Christian evangelists encountered a new problem related to idolatry — eating food, especially meat, that had been offered to idols (Acts 15:29; 1 Cor. 8; Rev. 2:14, 20). Although to the enlightened Christian such food had not been contaminated by idolatrous rites, his eating it could possibly cause a weak brother to fall. To preserve the solidarity of the Christian community, the well-informed Christian was to choose voluntarily to avoid customary social engagements where eating food offered to idols was involved (1 Cor. 8:1-13; 10:14-30).

Idolatry in the NT is also used figuratively. This was an interiorizing extension of the commandment against idolatry (Ex. 20:3). Especially in Paul's letters, idolatry is used of a person's commitment to any value other than to Jesus Christ as Lord. In Rom. 1:18-32, it is evident that the ultimate idolatry for Paul is putting love of self before honoring and serving God (cf. "You cannot serve God and mammon," Mk. 6:24). For Paul, "the works of the flesh" — sexual immorality, impurity, licentiousness, sorcery, enmity, strife, jealousy, anger, selfishness, dissension, party spirit, and envy — were all, like idolatry, products of putting self before God (Gal. 5:19-21). In Col. 3:5 is a similar list of "what is earthly in you" — sexual immorality, impurity, passion, evil desire — to which is added "covetousness," which, Paul says, "is idolatry." What is suggested again is that at the root of sinful actions is the idolizing of self, the pursuit, regardless of all else, of that which seems to offer self-gratification. The opposite of idolatry is self-giving, as in agape love (1 Cor. 13).

Bibliography.–R. M. Grant, *Early Christianity and Society* (1977), ch. 7; *LAP* (1959), pp. 459-501; M. C. Tenney, *NT Times* (1965), ch. 5; M. F. Unger, *Archaeology and the NT* (1962), chs. 12–13.

P. L. GARBER

IDUEL id'yo͞o-əl [Gk. *Idouēlos*] (1 Esd. 8:43); NEB IDUELUS. *See* ARIEL **1**.

IDUMEA id-ū-mē'ə [Gk. *Idoumaia, Idoumea*–'(land) of the Edomites']. The Greek name for EDOM as found in the LXX and sometimes used interchangeably with Edom in the AV. The name was eventually attached to the region S of Judea occupied by Edomites (Idumeans) who moved there after the fall of Jerusalem in 586 B.C. and who were later joined by compatriots pressed out of their homeland by Nabatean Arabs. Diodorus, writing of fourth-century-B.C. events, once called Idumea a satrapy and once an eparchy, possibly a corruption of hyparchy, the official designation of a district in Ptolemaic times (xix.95.2; 98.1). For a short period during the Maccabean wars the Seleucids controlled parts of the region under Gorgias, "the governor [*stratēgós*] of Idumea" (2 Macc. 12:32).

In general the region extended as far N as Beth-zur, 24 km. (15 mi.) S of Jerusalem, and reached Beer-sheba to the south. Neither the territories E of the Dead Sea nor those surrounding the coastal cities to the west were part of Idumea. In describing the region, Josephus speaks broadly of Upper Idumea, "extending in length to Jerusalem and in breadth reaching down to the lake of Sodom"; and Lower Idumea "bordering on Egypt and Arabia" (*Ant.* v.1.22 [81f.]). It would be more accurate, however, to speak of East Idumea, with its capital at Adoraim in the Hellenistic period and En-gedi in the Herodian period; and West Idumea, with its capital at Marisa in the Hellenistic period (transferred from Lachish) and Betogabris in the Herodian period (*P. Zenon,* Cairo 59006; Josephus *BJ* i.2.6 [63]; i.8.4 [166]; iii.3.5 [55]; iv.8.1 [447]).

Judas Maccabeus in 164 B.C. fortified Beth-zur against the encroaching Idumeans and ravaged their territory (1 Macc. 4:61; 5:3, 65). In 125 B.C. another Maccabean, John Hyrcanus I, subjugated the Idumeans, forced them to accept Judaism, and annexed their territory to the Hasmonean state (Josephus *Ant.* xiii.9.1; 15.4 [257f., 396]). Still another Maccabean, Alexander Janneus, in *ca.* 80 B.C. appointed an Idumean chief, Antipater the Elder, as governor (*stratēgós*) of the region (*Ant.* xiv.1.3 [10]). With the coming of the Romans in 63 B.C., Idumea was detached from Judea and was entrusted to local rule (*BJ* i.7.7 [155-57]; *Ant.* xiv.4.4 [74-76]). Through careful handling of opportunities during the feuds between Hyrcanus II and Aristobulus II and by benefiting from Roman endeavors in the East, Antipater the Younger in 47 B.C. became "procurator [*epítropos*] of Judea" and thus paved the way to the throne for his son Herod the Great (*Ant.* xiv.*passim*, esp. 8.1, 5 [127, 143]). In 37 B.C. Idumea was reannexed as part of Herod's kingdom (xv.7.9f. [254-59]). After Herod's death, Idumea, with Judea and Samaria, was part of Archelaus' ethnarchy (*BJ* ii.6.3 [96]; *Ant.* xvii.11.4 [319]) and after him shared the fate of Judea, of which it had become an integral part.

In the NT Idumea is mentioned only once, in a description of the wide area from which people came to hear Jesus (Mk. 3:8).

A. TERIAN

IEZER ī-ē'zûr, **IEZERITES** ī-ē'zûr-īts [Heb. *'î'ezer*] (Nu. 26:30); AV, NEB, JEEZER, JEEZERITES. Contracted from ABIEZER **1** (Josh. 17:2; etc.).

IGAL ī'gal [Heb. *yig'āl*–'he [God] redeems'; LXX Gk. *Igal, Gaal, Iōēl*].

1. One of the twelve spies sent by Moses from the wilderness of Paran; son of Joseph, tribe of Issachar (Nu. 13:7).

2. One of David's thirty mighty men, son of Nathan of Zobah (2 S. 23:36). In 1 Ch. 11:38 he is "Joel [Heb. *yô'ēl*] the brother of Nathan."

3. Son of Shemaiah of the royal house of David, descendant of Zerubbabel (1 Ch. 3:22, AV, NEB, IGEAL).

IGDALIAH ig-də-lī'ə [Heb. *yigdalyāhû*–'Yahweh is great']. Ancestor of certain persons who had a "chamber" in the temple in Jeremiah's time (Jer. 35:4).

IGEAL ī'gē-əl, ī'jē-əl. *See* IGAL **3.**

IGNATIUS. *See* APOSTOLIC FATHERS.

IGNORANCE [Heb. *p^eṯî* (Ezk. 45:20); Gk. *ágnoia* (Acts 3:17; 17:30; Eph. 4:18; 1 Pet. 1:14), *agnōsía* (1 Pet. 2:15)]; AV also SIMPLE; NEB also FOOLISH (Ezk. 45:20); **IGNORANT** [Heb. *lō' yāḏa'* (Ps. 73:22); Gk. *agnoéō* (Rom. 10:3; 2 Cor. 1:8; 2:11; 1 Thess. 4:13; 1 Tim. 1:13; He. 5:2; 2 Pet. 2:12), *amathḗs* (2 Pet. 3:16)]; AV also UNDERSTAND NOT (2 Pet. 2:12), UNLEARNED (2 Pet. 3:16); NEB also IGNORE (Rom. 10:3), "should like you to know" (2 Cor. 1:8), "know too well" (2 Cor. 2:11), DO NOT UNDERSTAND (2 Pet. 2:12), etc.

In the RSV the terms "ignorance" and "ignorant" occur only twice in the OT; however, the general concept that these terms imply is found throughout the OT and is often translated in the RSV as "error" or "sin."

Asaph confesses his guilt by admitting he was "stupid and ignorant," without perception or understanding of God in his heart (Ps. 73:21f.). Ignorance as sin is set within a ritual context in Ezk. 45:20, where the priest is to bring before God the sins of those who "sinned through error and ignorance." This practice had its roots in the Levitical legislative passages which describe sins committed "inadvertently" or "unwittingly" (Lev. 4:2; 22:14; 5:18; cf. Nu. 15:24ff.; 35:11, 15; Josh. 20:3, 9; He. 5:20) that could be forgiven on the great Day of Atonement (Nu. 15:28; Lev. 16:16-34). These are set in contrast to sins committed "with a high hand" (*b^eyāḏ rāmâ*), i.e., deliberately or "presumptuously" (Nu. 15:30; cf. Ps. 19:13; Dt. 17:12), for which there is no cultic atonement (Nu. 15:30; cf. Mish. *Yoma* v. 6-9; viii.9; SB, I, 636-38). Thus, it is clear that in the OT a sin committed in ignorance is not excusable, but incurs guilt and must be atoned for.

In the NT the chief words used to describe "ignorance" are *agnoéō* ("not know") and *ágnoia*. They were used originally in the Greek for "not knowing" something specific, and then for a general ignorance in the sense of not being "civilized" (see *TDNT,* I, 116). Thus it became parallel to or was linked with "lack of education" (*apaideusía*), and for the Stoics this was the basis of wickedness. This Stoic thought had a partial influence on the LXX. In some of the later apocryphal books, "ignorance" describes the state of the heathen who "err in their knowledge of God" (Wisd. 14:22). Along with this is the LXX's expansion of the Hebrew root *šgg,* which basically means "erring" or "going astray," to describe as *ágnoia* inadvertent or unintentional sin (Lev. 22:14; 5:18; cf. 2 Ch. 28:13; Josephus *Ant.* vi.5.6 [92]; xi.5.1 [130]). Here the sin is "ignorance" of the Law. Judaism, with its heavy emphasis on the Law, could make use of such a designation and among the rabbis knowledge of the Torah came to be seen as the basis of piety (see *TDNT,* I, 117f.).

This understanding of "ignorance" reflects the OT view of knowledge. In the OT knowledge is not intellectual alone, but is connected with experience (Heb. *yāḏa',* "learn to know") and means "insight into the will of God in command and blessing. It is primarily acknowledgment, and obedient or grateful submission to what is known" (*TDNT,* I, 704). *See* KNOW.

While ignorance as lack of intellectual knowledge is found in the NT in the Pauline formula "I would not have you to be ignorant" (AV 1 Thess. 4:13; cf. 2 Cor. 1:8), and though the term is used in other cases to denote the absence of awareness or understanding (2 Cor. 2:11; 2 Pet. 2:12), "ignorance" is used predominantly in a religious sense. Paul contrasts his life as a Pharisee "in which I had acted ignorantly in unbelief" (e.g., his blaspheming, persecuting, and insulting of Jesus Christ) with his conversion, when he received mercy (1 Tim. 1:13). Pagans are seen as ones who do not know God (1 Thess. 4:5), and thus also the former lives of believers are seen as "times of ignorance" (Acts 17:30; Eph. 4:18; 1 Pet. 1:14; cf. Justin *Apol.* i.12.11). "To know God" is to be converted (1 Clem. 59:3; 2 Clem. 17:1), and to speak of living "ignorantly in unbelief" is to speak of "the dark night of unknowing that preceded Jesus Christ" (Berkouwer, p. 291). This is true to the OT sense in which "knowledge means election and ignorance rejection" (*TDNT,* I, 116).

Ignorance is rejection in that it is disobedience. Paul speaks of the unenlightened zeal of the Jews who "being ignorant of the righteousness that comes from God, and seeking to establish their own, . . . did not submit to God's righteousness" (Rom. 10:3). Berkouwer notes that for this ignorance "there is no hint of self-excuse, for through this very ignorance they came to seek their own righteousness" (p. 292). "Ignorance" led to the crucifixion of Christ (Acts 3:17). According to Haenchen, the guilt of the Jews lies precisely in their ignorance (*ágnoia*): "if men had not hardened their hearts against God, they would have recognized Jesus. Only so does it become plain that in the Cross our guilt is revealed" (p. 207). Thus "ignorance did not eliminate their guilt, but it did describe the *situation* in which they committed their sin" (Berkouwer, p. 292). This is reflected in Jesus' prayer for those who "know not what they do" (Lk. 23:34). As the great High Priest, this same Christ can also "deal gently with the ignorant and the wayward" (He. 5:2; cf. Bruce, p. 91). In Christian thought, then, the only "knowledge" which can remove *ágnoia* is that which comes not from "human reflection or enquiry, but from the proclamation which demands faith" (*TDNT,* I, 116). Now, because of what has happened in Jesus Christ, God has "overlooked" the "times of ignorance" (Acts 17:30) and "commands all men everywhere to repent" (1 Pet. 1:14). Ignorance and error are now sin against the One who has made Himself known in Jesus Christ.

Agnōsía, used to describe the "ignorance of foolish men" (1 Pet. 2:15), has the same force as *ágnoia* in the sense that it refers not primarily to an intellectual ignorance but to "a lack of religious experience or *lack of spiritual discernment*" (Bauer, rev., p. 12; cf. 1 Cor. 15:34; Job 35:16; and Wisd. 13, where it describes the state of the gentile world). In 2 Pet. 3:16 the heretics who are "uninstructed and unwilling to learn the traditional teaching" (Kelly, p. 373) are called *amathḗs* ("ignorant").

Bibliography.–G. C. Berkouwer, *Sin* (1971); F. F. Bruce, *Hebrews* (*NICNT,* 1964); M. Dibelius, *Pastoral Epistles* (Eng. tr. 1972), p. 27; E. Haenchen, *Acts of the Apostles* (Eng. tr. 1971); J. N. D. Kelly, *Epistles of Peter and Jude* (1969); *TDNT,* I, *s.v.* ἀγνοέω (Bultmann); I, *s.v.* γινώσκω (Bultmann).

D. K. MCKIM

IIM ī'im [Heb. *'iyîm* (Josh. 15:29)]; NEB IYIM. (The NEB rendering is preferable, since it better reflects the Hebrew.) An unidentified town in the extreme south of the territory of Judah, toward the border of Edom.

IJE-ABARIM. *See* IYE-ABARIM.

IJON ī'jon [Heb. *'iyôn*; Gk. *Ain, Nain, Aian, Iō, Aiōn*]; NEB IYYON. A store-city in the northern frontier hill area of Naphtali. It was captured from Baasha king of Israel by Ben-hadad king of Syria, in response to a request by Asa king of Judah (1 K. 15:20; 2 Ch. 16:4). In the days of Pekah king of Israel, Tiglath-pileser of Assyria captured the city along with others and deported the people to Assyria (2 K. 15:29).

Ijon is probably represented by Tell ed-Dibbîn at the north end of Merj-ʿAyûn ("meadow of springs"), a fertile oval plain about 9.5 km. (6 mi.) long, 3 km. (2 mi.) wide, located about 29 km. (18 mi.) N of Lake Huleh, about 39 km. (24 mi.) ENE of Tyre, between the Leontes and Jordan rivers.

The NEB reads IYYON also at 2 S. 24:6 (*see* DAN-JAAN).

R. J. HUGHES, III

IKKESH ik'esh [Heb. *ʿiqqēš*–'crooked']. A man of Tekoa and father of Ira, one of David's thirty mighty men (2 S. 23:26; 1 Ch. 11:28; 27:9).

ILAI ī'lə-ī, ī'lī [Heb. *ʿîlay*]. An Ahohite, one of David's thirty mighty men (1 Ch. 11:29), called Zalmon in 2 S. 23:28.

ILEX ī'leks [Heb. *tirzâ*] (Isa. 44:14, NEB). *See* HOLM TREE.

ILIADUN i-lī'ə-dun, il'ē-ə-dun [Gk. *Iliadoun*] (1 Esd. 5:58 [LXX 56]); AV ELIADUN. An ancestor of some of the Levites who oversaw the rebuilding of the temple. Possibly corresponding to Henadad in Ezr. 3:9.

ILL REPORT; ILL REPUTE [Heb. *dibbâ rāʿâ* (Gen. 37:2), *dibbâ* (Prov. 25:10); Gk. *dysphēmías* (2 Cor. 6:8)]; AV also EVIL REPORT (Gen. 37:2), INFAMY (Prov. 25:10); NEB also BAD REPORT, BLAME; **TREAT ILL; GO ILL; BE ILL; DO ILL** [from the Hebrew root *rʿʿ*, qal–'be evil, bad' (Ps. 106:32), hiphil–'do evil, hurt, injure' (Gen. 43:6; Zeph. 1:12)]; AV also "dealt . . . ill," "do evil," "shall be ill"; NEB also "treated so badly," "suffered," "goes ill," "do nothing good or bad"; **ILL** [Heb. *'āwen*] (Prov. 12:21); AV EVIL; NEB MISCHIEF; **ILL-BEHAVED** [Heb. *raʿ maʿalālîm*–'evil of practices'] (1 S. 25:3); AV "evil in his doings"; NEB MEAN; **ILL-CLAD** [Gk. *gymnitéuō* (1 Cor. 4:11), *gymnoí* (Jas. 2:15)]; AV NAKED; NEB IN RAGS; **ILL-NATURED** [Heb. *ben-beliyaʿal* (1 S. 25:17), *'îš habbeliyaʿal* (1 S. 25:25)]; AV also "son of Belial" (1 S. 25:17), "man of Belial" (1 S. 25:25); NEB "good for nothing"; **ILL-TREAT** [piel of Heb. *ʿānâ*–'afflict' (Gen. 31:50); Gk. *kakóō* (Acts 7:6, 34; He. 11:37; 13:3), *synkakouchéomai*–'suffer with others' (He. 11:25)]; AV also AFFLICT (Gen. 31:50; Acts 7:34), "tormented" (He. 11:37), "suffer adversity" (He. 13:3), "entreat . . . evil" (Acts 7:6), "suffer affliction" (He. 11:25); NEB also "oppression" (Acts 7:6, 34), "misery" (He. 11:37), "mal-treated" (He. 13:3), "hardship" (He. 11:25). A group of expressions denoting a reputation as an evildoer, suffering due to persecution or one's sins, or rude behavior and speech.

Joseph's ill report of his brothers was probably a true report of their evil doings rather than slander (BDB, p. 179). The ill repute of Paul and his companions was undeserved (2 Cor. 6:8). A talebearer, however, brings ill repute upon himself (Prov. 25:10).

"Ill" denoting unfortunate or adverse circumstances is found in several OT passages. Israel felt he had been purposely ill-treated when his sons revealed to Joseph that they had another brother, Benjamin (Gen. 43:6). Circumstances "went ill" with Moses due to the sins of the Israelites (Ps. 106:32). Problems will plague the wicked person (Isa. 3:11), but "no ill will befall the righteous" (Prov. 12:21). God promised that He would punish those who claimed He had ceased to act: "The Lord will not do good nor will he do ill" (Zeph. 1:12).

In the NT, ill-treatment is synonymous with persecution, but all references except one (He. 13:3) are to the sufferings of Israel and its leaders during the OT period, rather than Jewish or Roman persecution of the Church. Stephen recounted the four hundred years of affliction suffered by the Israelites in Egypt (Acts 7:6, 34). The writer to the Hebrews used Moses as an example of one who was willing to suffer with others (11:25) and also referred to an anonymous group of OT martyrs who underwent terrible sufferings (11:37). Paul and his companions were ill-clad and homeless as they traveled from place to place (1 Cor. 4:11). James also mentioned the ill-clad members of a church who were discriminated against by their more affluent brethren (2:15).

Three disparaging terms are applied to Nabal, the "fool" (Heb. *nāḇāl*) in 1 S. 25:3-38. In v. 3, "ill-behaved" (Heb. *raʿ maʿalālîm*) literally means "evil [in his] doings." Nabal is termed ill-natured in v. 17, but the Heb. *ben-beliyaʿal* is literally translated "son of Belial" (AV). Verse 25 has a slight variation: the Hebrew is *'îš habbeliyaʿal*, "man of Belial" (cf. 1 S. 1:16; Dt. 13:14 [MT 13]; Prov. 16:27). The precise meaning of *beliyaʿal* is debated, but the word does seem related to Hebrew conceptions of the underworld, chaos, and spiritual evil (*TDOT*, II, *s.v.* "beliyyaʿal" [Otzen]). *See* BELIAL.

R. J. W.

ILLNESS. *See* DISEASE.

ILLUMINATION. *See* ENLIGHTENED.

ILLUSTRIOUS, THE [Gk. *thaumastós*]; AV THE ADMIRABLE; NEB THE FAMOUS. A title of rank and merit attached to the name of Bartacus, the father of Apame (1 Esd. 4:29). Instead of "the illustrious" we should possibly read "colonel" (cf. Josephus *Ant.* xi.3.5 [54]; *EB, s.v.*). *See* BARTACUS; APAME.

ILLYRICUM i-lir'i-kəm [Gk. *Illyrikon*] (Rom. 15:19). A Roman province in the northwest part of the Balkan peninsula, along the east coast of the Adriatic Sea, NW of Macedonia. The province corresponds approximately to modern Yugoslavia, although its borders varied, at times including part of what is now Albania.

At the end of his letter to the church in Rome, Paul describes the vast extent of his missionary labors in the following terms: "so that from Jerusalem and as far round as Illyricum I have fully preached the gospel" (Rom. 15:19). Whether Paul intended to include Illyricum as part of the area in which he had evangelized or to say simply "as far west as the border of Illyricum" is not clear. The words "as far as" (Gk. *méchri*) can be interpreted either way. If Jerusalem were the eastern limit of Paul's preaching, it might be clear that he intended to say that he went through Macedonia to the border of Illyricum as the western limit; but we know that Paul preached further east in Damascus (Acts 9:19f.). In describing the Egnatian Way, Strabo (vii.7.4) indicated that in going from the coast of the Adriatic to Macedonia it passed through a portion of Illyria. Perhaps Paul worked his way west along this road and actually entered a part of Illyricum. On the other hand, Illyricum, like the term "Galatia," could designate the Roman province or the entire area inhabited by Illyrians. It is possible, though not likely, that Paul meant to indicate that he had preached to Illyrians in western Macedonia. The statement in Acts 20:1f., "when he had gone through these parts," indicates considerable activity in Macedonia at the end of Paul's third missionary journey, but does not specify the precise area he covered. In some sense Paul must have considered that he had gone as far east as possible, since he explained to the Christians in Rome that he was now ready to come to them (on his way to Spain) because he had no other place

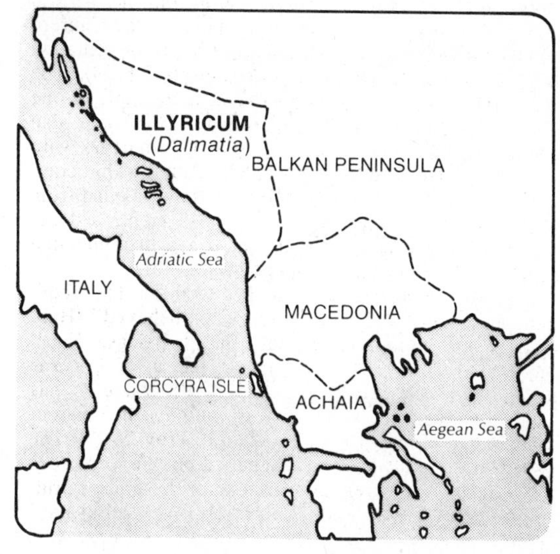

to work (Rom. 15:23f.). In 2 Tim. 4:10 Paul states that he had sent Titus to DALMATIA. Dalmatia was one of two major divisions of Illyricum. It was known as "Illyria Superior" and the other, Pannonia, as "Illyria Inferior."

Illyricum had many favorable harbors along the coast as well as on the nearby islands. The land was described by Strabo (vii.317) as sunny and fertile along the coast, but cold and mountainous in the inland area. The Illyrians, an Indo-European people, settled in the area *ca.* 1000 B.C.

The first known contact with Greece was in the 8th cent. B.C. when Chersikrates of Corinth settled on the island of Corcyra. In the centuries following, the Greeks established colonies in Illyricum and a significant amount of trade developed. After a long period of conflict with Macedonia the Illyrians were defeated by Philip II in 359/8 B.C. Before they were constituted as a Roman province the Illyrians were divided into many separate tribes. In the south a rather strong kingdom developed whose raids on the Greek colonies and piracy on Greek and Roman shipping provoked the wars with Rome in 229/8 and 219 B.C. This southern area was finally subjugated by Rome in 168 B.C. Then uprisings broke out in the north (Dalmatia), resulting in the burning of the capital, Delminium, in 156 B.C. The province was made subject to Caesar in 46 B.C., and then in 27 B.C. when the provinces were divided between Augustus and the senate Illyricum was assigned to the latter. Renewed disturbances led, however, to its transference to the emperor in 11 B.C. The severity of Roman taxes caused a new outbreak among the Pannonians and Dalmatians in A.D. 6. After three years of vicious fighting the uprising was crushed and Pannonia and Moesia were organized as separate provinces. The Romanizing of this area proceeded rapidly and thoroughly due to the numerous cities, army camps, and good roads.

D. H. MADVIG

IMAGE. *See* IDOL.

IMAGE OF GOD [Lat. *imago Dei*]:

I. Man as Made in the Image of God
 A. Image and Likeness
 B. Meaning of the Image
 C. The Image and the Fall
 D. The Image and the Christian
II. Christ the Image of God
 A. Eternal Son
 B. Prototype of Man
 C. The God-Man
 D. The Servant Form
 E. Prototype of the New Man

I. Man as Made in the Image of God.–Genesis 1:26 (cf. 5:3) says that God resolved to make man in His own image (Heb. *ṣelem*) and likeness (*d^e mûṯ*), and in Gen. 1:27 we read that He did create man in His own image. The word "image" is used alone in 1:27 and also in 9:6, while "likeness" occurs alone in 5:1. It is only here that the terminology occurs in the OT, though the thought is present in Ps. 8:5-8 (MT 6-9); and cf. Sir. 17:3; Wisd. 2:23 in the Apocrypha. The relevant NT passages are 1 Cor. 11:7; Col. 3:10; Jas. 3:9.

A. Image and Likeness. The exact significance of the terms is the subject of considerable discussion. A first question is whether any distinction is to be seen between image and likeness. When such distinction has been attempted, it has usually been along the lines of theological interpretation. Thus Irenaeus and Tertullian refer the image to man's bodily nature and the likeness to his spiritual. The Alexandrians think in terms of mental and moral perfections as compared with divine perfections. In the Middle Ages this interpretation led to a distinction between the natural gifts of rationality and freedom on the one side and the supernatural endowments of grace on the other; this distinction gave rise to an explanation of the fall in terms of a loss of grace and an impairment of rationality and freedom. Yet the basic premise is open to serious question, for elsewhere in Scripture the terms appear to be used more or less interchangeably; and it seems more likely that Gen. 1:26 is simply an example of synonymous parallelism, or of what Driver has called a duplication of synonyms.

B. Meaning of the Image. The problem of meaning and interpretation remains. A first point to be noted is that man is said to be made in the image of God, not to be the image of God. This wording seems to indicate that the image here is fundamentally the original or example rather than the copy, and that man is the copy. But too much stress should not be laid on this distinction, for usage is not always clear and strict at this point, and 1 Cor. 11:7 also has to be taken into account. Certainly, metaphysical speculation along the lines of patterns and shadows is to be avoided. On the other hand, even when it is said that man is the image of God it is realized that God is the true original and that "image" is here given the sense of "copy." This statement has three important implications: (1) that man is not to create God in his own image, (2) that he is to learn his true nature from God and not vice versa, and (3) that Christ, who is the express image of God, is the true original of man, so that even apart from the fall and restoration man would still have borne the image of Christ.

In what respect, however, is man a copy or reflection of God? Physical resemblance is ruled out, for God is not represented as having a human form, or any other material form, except in theophany or incarnation. The most that might be said along these lines is that the incarnate Christ is the prototype of man; but physical form is not as such essential to deity, and it hardly seems possible to make much sense of Gen. 1:26f. in terms of a physical interpretation.

A second possibility of a very different kind is to see in man's dominion over nature a reflection of the lordship of God. This possibility has the merit of construing the divine resolve of 1:26 with a divinely imposed task in 1:28, in terms of the immediate context. No doubt man as God's vicegerent does, as it were, stand in the place of God (as Moses later did for Aaron, Ex. 4:16), so that a representation is thereby given of God. While there is an element of truth here, it is surely too narrow to be the whole truth. For man also has the endowment with which to exercise lordship, e.g., rationality, volition, and moral responsibility; and this, too, has called for notice as the true reference of the *imago*. That similar qualities are also revealed with reference to God is a strong argument in favor of this widely accepted interpretation, and perhaps the only argument against it is that it does not actually belong to the context of Gen. 1 but has to be imported in the light of other considerations.

Finally, the image has been interpreted in terms of relationship. Karl Barth (*CD,* III/1f.) makes a strong plea for this interesting view. His main argument is that in Gen. 1:27 "male and female created he them" is not an odd and detached bit of information but stands in strict relation to "in the image of God created he him." This does not mean, of course, that there is sexual distinction in God. It does mean, however, that within God there is a relationship in unity (the plural *'ĕlōhîm,* later more fully revealed as the trinity), which finds reflection in the indestructible relationship in unity of man as essentially man-and-woman. In other words, intrapersonal relationship is the essential mark of man as it is also of God. To be created in the divine image is to be created in this relationship.

Two or three objections may be made to this interpretation. First, it is not wholly certain that 1:27b does stand in this stricter parallelism to 1:27a. Second, the doctrine of the trinity has to be read back into the plural of 1:26, though the plural itself is undoubtedly in the text. Third, the beasts, too, are created male and female; and therefore the endowment of rationality, volition, and ethical sense is still necessary for human intrapersonal relationship in the image of the divine. Barth has to assume this traditional aspect of the *imago* even though he may be right in giving the interpretation a slightly different emphasis or focus.

C. The Image and the Fall. How far does man still bear the image in his fallen state? This problem has constantly exercised theology, and the paucity of biblical data and the paradoxical nature of fallen man make it difficult to give any very sure or convincing answer. In fact, many different solutions have been proposed, and the differences in the interpretation of the image itself naturally affect these. Where a distinction is seen between image and likeness, it is often argued that the one is weakened and the other effaced. Where emphasis is thrown on the ordinary endowment of man, it is agreed that the formal aspects remain but that an element of distortion arises at the material level. Thus man is still rational, but his rationality no longer imparts true knowledge of God. The same holds true in respect of relationship. Nothing man does can alter the fact that he stands in relation to the fellow man, specifically in the form of woman; but the actual outworking of the relationship is in no sense a reflection of the true relationship within the Godhead.

A similar distinction arises in respect of man's dominion over the cosmos. Man is still the lord of creation and in this formal sense he represents God, the ultimate Lord. But now man is to a very large degree a selfish tyrant who rules over nature for his own ends, and in this sense he is the very opposite of God. It will be noted that all these answers to the question realize that fallen man is basically paradoxical. He cannot cease to be man. Hence he cannot cease to be made in the image of God. But the actual content of his life is at odds with its underlying reality. God is reflected only in the structure, not in the material content of his being. The *imago* is not now partial or blurred; it is on the one hand intact from the standpoint of basic structure and on the other unrecognizable from the standpoint of outworking or content.

This continuity and discontinuity seem to lie behind the presentation in the NT. Thus true relationship between man and woman is established on the basis of the *imago Dei* in 1 Cor. 11:7. Incidentally it is worth noting that in this passage only man is said to be created directly in the divine image (woman indirectly), though Paul does not say that woman is created in the image of man. Perhaps the true point of the introduction of the image here is that the relation between man and woman should reflect the relation between Father and Son within the Godhead. Insofar as this relationship is demanded by the very structure of human life, the image is inescapably present. Insofar as it is perverted in practice, the intertrinitarian relationship is no longer perceived. The true course is to remodel the practice on the divine original, so that this will be reflected not only in structure but in practice, too.

The paradoxical nature of fallen man may also be seen in Jas. 3:9. Here the fact remains that man is made after the likeness of God. Hence it is self-contradictory to bless God (the original) and curse man (the likeness) at the same time. That man is sinful does not remove the element of contradiction, for, even though he is sinful, he is still made in the divine image and it is thus fundamentally natural for him to bless God. On the other hand, that he can be guilty of contradiction is evidence that the content of the *imago* is lost, for contradiction exists only because (1) men do not in fact reflect the divine nature in their character and conduct, and (2) their thinking and utterance are at odds with their creation in the divine image.

D. The Image and the Christian. Yet the NT also advances a further consideration, namely, that in and by God's saving work in Christ the content of the image is brought back into harmony with the structure. Thus in Col. 3:10 the believer is said to be renewed unto knowledge after the image of Him who created him (cf. Eph. 4:24, "after God"). But this is now equivalent to being conformed to the image of God's Son (Rom. 8:29). As we now bear the image of Adam (cf. Gen. 5:3), the earthly man, so we shall bear the image of Christ, the heavenly man (1 Cor. 15:49). Beholding as in a glass the glory of the Lord, we are changed into the same image from glory to glory (2 Cor. 3:18). The NT, then, is not content merely to state the doctrine of the *imago* in terms of the fall. In keeping with its true character as the message of salvation, the NT adds a soteriological and eschatological element. The message of salvation is the message of salvation in Christ. Hence the soteriological and eschatological dimension is the christological. The *imago Dei* is redefined in terms of Christ as Himself the true image.

II. Christ the Image of God.–In three NT passages Christ is called the image of God. The first is 2 Cor. 4:4, which refers to "the light of the gospel of the glory of Christ, who is the image of God." Then in Col. 1:15 it is said that Christ is "the image of the invisible God, the firstborn of every creature." Finally, He. 1:3 speaks of the Son as "the very image of his substance." Two different words are used in these passages. In 2 Corinthians and Colossians we find the familiar Gk. *eikṓn,* the LXX rendering of Heb. *ṣelem* (Vulg. *imago*). In Hebrews the term is Gk. *charaktḗr,* which derives from *charássō,* "engrave," and which bears the sense of engraved stamp, image, or impression (Lat. *figura*).

A. Eternal Son. The *imago Dei* as applied to Christ is capable of many different interpretations, though we need not be forced to choose among them. So long as proper balance is kept, the reality of Christ should be big and rich enough to embrace many different aspects. In this field perhaps the main danger is to seize on one factor and to press it to the exclusion of others. Certainly, a place must be found for Christ's being in His essential deity the exact image of the Father in the sense that He is Himself equally God. He is not just a copy, an impression from the original fount. He is Himself also the original. He does not merely give a representation of God. As Paul says, in Him dwells all the fulness of the Godhead bodily (Col. 1:19; 2:9). If there is real distinction between the Father and the Son, as the term "image" suggests, Christ is the *imago substantialis,* whereas man is the *imago accidentalis*. The term *imago* is here designed to express what is implied in the word *lógos* in Jn. 1:1 and the phrase "in the form of God" in Phil. 2:6.

B. Prototype of Man. In His preexistent life as the Son, Christ is also the prototype of man, even in respect of the first creation. Colossians makes this clear by equating the "image of God" with the "firstborn of every creature." Similarly Jn. 1:4, 9 indicates that man is in some sense the mirror of the Logos. While there is a danger of speculation in this field, whether in terms of a necessary incarnation or in the direction of an ultimate universalism, the christological aspect of creation is so plainly established in Scripture that it is not to be evaded. According to God's eternal counsel the Son has always been the prototype and goal of humanity, so that even if man had never sinned — a mere hypothesis — he would still have come to the fulfillment of his destiny in relation to Christ. This does not mean, of course, that Adam is created in the divine image only by anticipatory promise. It means that at his creation Adam is already fashioned according to the prototype, i.e., Christ. In Himself Christ already sums up all that humanity is to be. In this respect Christ is not, of course, to be abstracted from the Father and the Holy Spirit. To be made in the image of Christ is to be made in the image of God, for Christ is God, not alone, but in the eternal triunity of Father, Son, and Holy Spirit.

C. The God-Man. In His incarnate life as true God and true Man, Christ is again the image of God. He is a perfect representation of God to man. The word "image" is not actually used of Christ in this connection but the thought is present throughout the NT. Thus it is said of the incarnate Word: "We beheld his glory, the glory as of the only begotten of the Father, full of grace and truth" (Jn. 1:14). Paul tells believers that they are changed into the same image as they behold "as in a glass the glory of the Lord" (2 Cor. 3:18). Jesus Himself says plainly: "He that hath seen me hath seen the Father" (Jn. 14:9). What ought to be true of every man, namely, that he is a representation of God, is supremely true of the man Jesus, whose whole life, character, and work bear the stamp of the divine approval (Mt. 3:17; Mk. 9:7; Acts 2:22) and who is finally declared to be the Son of God with power by His resurrection from the dead (Rom. 1:4).

D. The Servant Form. Yet, as in the case of the fallen Adam, so in that of the incarnate Jesus, though in a very different way, there is a paradoxical element. For in fulfillment of the work of salvation Christ, who is the image of God, was sent in the likeness of sinful flesh and condemned sin in the flesh (Rom. 8:3): "taking the form of a servant, being born in the likeness of men" (Phil. 2:7). "Therefore, he had to be made like His brethren in every respect" (He. 2:17). The paradoxical element in this is twofold. First, it is paradoxical that the original should be made in the likeness of the likeness, though it will also be seen that just because Adam was made in the divine image, and Christ was thus the prototype, the incarnation does not in fact involve any self-alienation on the part of the divine Son. Second, and more profoundly, it is paradoxical that as Adam bears the image of God and yet lives a sinful life, so Christ bears the image of man and yet lives a sinless life (He. 4:15).

It is to be noted, however, that there is here no inherent paradox as in the case of Adam, for only what is sinful can be really paradoxical. For even fallen Adam still bears the divine image, and the sinless Christ is simply bringing the content back into line with the structure. In other words, Christ is true man whereas fallen Adam is perverted man. It is also to be noted that Christ bears the likeness of sinful flesh only that He may do the work of salvation. He becomes man in order to die for man. He takes the likeness of the sinner, not to be a sinner, but to live the life the sinner ought to live, to offer Himself the righteous offering for the sinner's sin, and to effect the restoration of the sinner to the likeness of God. It is part of the substitutionary ministry of Christ that He, the express image of God, should be made in the likeness of men that man may be wholly and truly refashioned in the likeness of God.

A final point is that His bearing the likeness of sinful flesh prevents the *direct* recognition that would impede the sifting of the heart and true repentance and faith by the Holy Spirit. At the end of the age, when He comes again in His glorified humanity (cf. Rev. 1:13-16), Christ will be manifested directly as the express image of God. In the days of His earthly life, however, He bore the servant form, which is no less truly the image of God, which is related directly to His work for the restoration of the image, but which conceals His glory from the impenitent and unbelieving who resist the illumination of the Holy Spirit (cf. Mt. 16:13-17).

E. Prototype of the New Man. As the God-Man, Christ is the prototype of the new, redeemed humanity. The Christian is the person who in repentance and faith, by the Holy Spirit, is identified with the Christ who died and rose again for him. He is dead, and the life he now lives is that of Christ in him (Gal. 2:20). He is a new creature (or creation); the old things have passed and new things have come (2 Cor. 5:17). This redemption has an ethical implication. He is born again in Christ, and hence the whole movement of his life is to be one of being made conformable to Christ. Every thought is to be brought captive to Christ's obedience (2 Cor. 10:5). The mind of Christ is to be his mind (Phil. 2:5). As the mind is renewed, so conduct should be transformed. The old man is to be put off with his wicked works, the new man put on, which after God is created in righteousness and true holiness (Eph. 4:22ff.; Col. 3:9ff.). The process of the Christian life is that of the fashioning of the image of Christ in His people. But there is also an eschatological implication. As Paul says in 1 Cor. 15:49, at the last day we shall finally bear the image of the heavenly. The Lord Jesus "will change our lowly body to be like his glorious body" (Phil. 3:21). "We shall be like him, for we shall see him as he is" (1 Jn. 3:2). The original purpose of God, that man be created in His own image and after His likeness, will thus be brought to perfect and glorious fulfillment in the new creation, when the redeemed people of God bear the image of their Lord and Head, who bore the image of sinful man for them, and who is Himself the express image of God.

See ADAM; ANTHROPOLOGY; CHRIST.

Bibliography.–BDTh, *s.v.* "image," "man"; *TDNT,* I, *s.v.* εἰκών (Kittel, von Rad, Kleinknecht); G. Berkouwer, *Man: The Image of God* (Eng. tr. 1962); E. Brunner, *Man in Revolt* (Eng. tr. 1947); J. Machen, *Christian View of Man* (1937).

G. W. BROMILEY

IMAGERY, CHAMBERS OF (Ezk. 8:12, AV). *See* PICTURES, ROOM OF.

IMAGES. *See* IDOL.

IMAGINE [Heb. *ḥāšab̠*] (Ps. 41:7 [MT 8]); AV DEVISE; NEB "love to make"; [Gk. *meletáō*] (Acts 4:25); NEB LAY PLOTS; [*dokéō*] (1 Cor. 8:2); AV THINK; NEB FANCY; [*nomízō*] (1 Tim. 6:5); AV SUPPOSE; NEB THINK; **IMAGINATION** [Heb. *yēṣer*] (Gen. 6:5; 8:21); NEB INCLINATION; [Gk. *diánoia*] (Lk. 1:51); NEB MIND; [Gk. *enthýmēsis*] (Acts 17:29); AV DEVICE; NEB DESIGN.

The Hebrew verb *ḥāšab̠* means "plot" or "devise," as does Gk. *meletáō. Dokéō* and *nomízō*, on the other hand, mean to "think, believe, consider." Heb. *yēṣer* may denote the "plan" or "purpose" which a person proposes to enact. It is not the organ of reasoning but the product of that organ. The "plan" may be evil (so Gen. 6:5; 8:21; Dt. 31:21) or acceptable to God (so 1 Ch. 28:9; 29:18; Isa. 26:3). The AV sometimes uses "imagination" in the obsolete sense of "stubbornness" to render Heb. *šᵉrirût* (Dt. 29:19 [MT 18]; Jer. 3:17; 7:24; etc.).

The usual meaning of Gk. *diánoia* is either "mind," i.e., the organ of thinking (cf. Bauer, rev., p. 187) or "thoughts," i.e., the ideas, conceptions, or chains of reasoning which thinking produces (cf. Col. 1:21; 2 Pet. 3:1). *Enthýmēsis* represents an idea that arises in the mind and is given mental consideration (cf. Mt. 9:4; 12:25; He. 4:12).

J. A. HEWETT

IMALKUE ī-mal-kū'ē [Gk. *Imalkouē*]; AV SIMALCUE; NEB IMALCUE. An Arabian prince to whom Alexander Balas entrusted the upbringing of his young son Antiochus. Trypho, who had formerly been on the side of Alexander, persuaded Imalkue to set up the young Antiochus (Antiochus VI) against Demetrius, who had incurred the enmity of his men of war (1 Macc. 11:39f.). Antiochus confirmed Jonathan in the highpriesthood and appointed him to be one of the king's friends (v. 57). In Josephus (*Ant.* xiii.5.1 [131]) the name is given as Malchus.

J. HUTCHISON

IMITATE [Gk. *miméomai*] (2 Thess. 3:7, 9; He. 13:7; 3 Jn. 11); AV FOLLOW; NEB also COPY-, FOLLOW THE EXAMPLE OF; **BE(COME) IMITATORS** [Gk. *mimētaí gínesthai*] (1 Cor. 4:16; 11:1; Eph. 5:1; 1 Thess. 1:6; 2:14; He. 6:12; 1 Pet. 3:13 var.); AV BE(COME) FOLLOWERS; NEB also IMITATE, FOLLOW THE EXAMPLE OF, "try to be like" (Eph. 5:1), "fare like" (1 Thess. 2:14); **JOIN IN IMITATING** [Gk. *symmimētaí gínesthe*] (Phil. 3:17); AV BE FOLLOWERS TOGETHER; NEB "agree together to follow my example."

The noun *(sym)mimētḗs* is always in the NT joined with the verb *gínomai*, "be," "become," usages equivalent to those of the simple verb *miméomai*. The word-group may thus be treated as a unit. These words, absent from Homer, are common in most later Greek literature in the sense "imitate," "follow a pattern (*týpos*)," as distinct from the literal *akolouthéō*, "follow." *Týpos* as "pattern," "example," recurs in several of these passages (Phil. 3:17; 1 Thess. 1:7; 2 Thess. 3:9). Timothy was to be a *týpos* to the believers (1 Tim. 4:12). Most of the occurrences are in the present imperative, or an equivalent, as exhortations to a habitual standard of conduct.

There are, however, difficulties. The basic meaning is not quite appropriate in all cases, and we may question in what sense believers are to be "imitators" of God (Eph. 5:1) or Paul an "example" to them. Michaelis distinguished three nuances in Paul. (1) Simple comparison is intended in 1 Thess. 2:14, where the Christians in Thessalonica are imitators of the churches in Judea only in that they have suffered alike at the hands of their fellows. They may imitate the conduct of their model, but scarcely their fate (cf. the NEB rendering). (2) The idea of imitation is dominant in passages in which Paul presented himself as the *týpos* (2 Thess. 3:7, 9; Phil. 3:17). (3) In other passages Michaelis found the connotation of obedience prominent: he regarded this as exclusively the sense of 1 Cor. 4:16, where the relationship pictured is that of a son to his father. In this case Paul was again the object, but in Eph. 5:1 the readers were called to be imitators of their Father God in terms of forgiveness (4:32). 1 Cor. 11:1 notes a double relationship: "be imitators of me as I am of Christ." The believer is to follow in obedience the pattern that his model represents.

He. 13:7 is probably to be linked with the thought of 6:12, urging the readers to "imitate" their first leaders, who are now dead (cf. 11:4ff.; 12:1f.), a view supported by the immediate context. It is possible, however, that the living are in mind here, since *hēgoúmenoi* ("leaders") in 13:17, 24 clearly refers to the living (cf. Bauer, rev., p. 237; G. E. Ladd, *Theology of the NT* [1974], pp. 586f.).

The whole word-group is absent from the canonical books of the LXX, though the concept was applied by Philo to mankind's relationship to God (e.g., *De opificio mundi* xxvi.79), perhaps under the influence of philosophical concepts of the correspondence of the heavenly and earthly realms. The NT thought is different. Paul did not hold himself up as an ideal of mature perfection (cf. 1 Cor. 9:27; Phil. 3:12): the believer is to follow him in spirit and purpose rather than in performance. Christ Himself was the supreme example; He ran in advance the course His disciples are called to follow (cf. He. 12:1f.). The Christian life involves a measure of identification with the sufferings of Christ. That is very different from the notion of justifying oneself by seeking to emulate His works.

Bibliography.–Bauer, rev., pp. 521f.; MM, p. 412; *TDNT*, IV, *s.v.* μιμέομαι κτλ. (Michaelis); *DNTT*, II, 490-92.

C. J. HEMER

IMLAH im'lə [Heb. *yimlâ*–'fulness'(?)]; AV, NEB, IMLA (2 Ch. 18:7f.). Father of the prophet Micaiah (1 K. 22:8f.; 2 Ch. 18:7f.).

IMMACULATE CONCEPTION. *See* MARY **6.**

IMMANUEL i-man'ū-el [Heb. *ʿimmānû ʾēl*–'with us (is) God']. A symbolic name or title given at birth to one or more male infants in the OT (Isa. 7:14; 8:8; see also 8:10) and NT (**EMMANUEL** [Gk. *Emmanouēl*], Mt. 1:23). The phrase is two words in all three Isaiah references in the MT; in 1QIsa[a] from Qumrân, however, it is combined into one word in all three places. The LXX transliterates as *Emmanouēl* in Isa. 7:14 but translates as *meth' hēmṓn ho theós* in 8:8 and *meth' hēmṓn kýrios ho theós* in 8:10. The NT quotation of Isa. 7:14 in Mt. 1:23 adds the LXX Isa. 8:8 translation: (*hó estin methermēneuómenon*) *meth' hēmṓn ho theós*. Names similar to Immanuel have been found on an early Hebrew seal (*ʿImmadiyahu*, "with me [is] the Lord") and in an Elephantine papyrus from the 5th cent. B.C. (*ʿImmanuyah*, "with us [is] the Lord").

I. Historical Background
II. Exegetical Issues
III. Identification of Immanuel and His Mother
IV. Relationship to NT
V. God with His People

I. Historical Background.–Isaiah 7:1–12:6, a section often called "The Book of Immanuel," begins by stating that Rezin king of Aram and Pekah king of Israel marched out against Ahaz king of Judah with the intention of capturing

Jerusalem and replacing Ahaz with a certain "son of Tabeel" (perhaps an Aramean; cf. Ezr. 4:7). In 735/4 B.C. they slaughtered large numbers of people in Judah and took captive even larger numbers (2 Ch. 28:5-8). The ferocity of the attack may have been prompted by the posited refusal of Ahaz to join Rezin and Pekah in a western alliance against Tiglath-pileser III of Assyria. In any event Ahaz appealed to the Assyrian king for help, sending him tribute and becoming his vassal in the bargain (2 K. 16:7f.; 2 Ch. 28:16-21). The Assyrians were only too willing to oblige; they destroyed Damascus the capital of Aram (2 K. 16:9) in 732 and Samaria the capital of Israel in 722. It was probably shortly before the Aramean-Israelite invasion of Judah in 735/4 that Isaiah uttered his famous Immanuel oracle to Ahaz (Isa. 7:10-17).

II. Exegetical Issues.–Although "The Book of Immanuel" abounds with interpretative difficulties, we shall focus our attention on Isa. 7:14. The heart of the verse, *hinnēh hāʿalmâ hārâ wᵉyōleḏeṯ bēn* ("Behold, the virgin shall conceive and bear a son"), reflects an ancient annunciation formula, found elsewhere not only in the OT itself in the form *hinnāḵ hārâ wᵉyōlaḏt bēn* (Gen. 16:11; Jgs. 13:5, 7) but also earlier in Ugaritic: *hl ǵlmt tld b*[*n*] (*UT* 77:7). The use of so solemn a phrase underscores the significance of the child to be born. "The virgin" in Isa. 7:14 can also be read "a virgin" (i.e., indefinitely) or "virgins" (i.e., generically), but a specific mother seems intended in the context.

It is not self-evident that Heb. *ʿalmâ* means "virgin" since most of the ancient Semitic languages had no word for *virgo intacta,* a concept that could be expressed only by means of circumlocution. Contrary to common opinion, *bᵉṯûlâ* does not always or even necessarily mean "virgin"—nor does Gk. *parthénos* (the LXX rendering of *ʿalmâ* in Isa. 7:14, quoted in Mt. 1:23; cf. Acts 21:9, NIV). The most that can be said of *ʿalmâ* is that in all of its OT occurrences it seems to be used of an unmarried woman, a "damsel"—which, in situations such as the one before us, carries with it a strong presumption in favor of virginity. The verbal adjective *hārâ* in our text could be either present or future, but to render it as future seems safest in the context.

Proceeding to the next clause in Isa. 7:14, we observe that the Masoretes vocalized *wqrʾt* as an archaic third person feminine singular perfect form with *wāw* conversive (*wᵉqārāʾṯ*; "and she will call"). They were following the tradition represented by LXX Sinaiticus and the Targum. Although LXX A B, Aquila, Symmachus, Theodotion, and Old Latin read "you [sing.] will call," it is perhaps best to stay with the MT in the light of Gen. 16:11, where the same vocalization is found (without variants). The Syriac and Vulgate have a passive form in Isa. 7:14, probably reflecting the reading *wqrʾ* in 1QIsa[a] (to be vocalized as a pual passive; see especially Isa. 62:2, and note *kalésousin,* "they will call" his name = his name "will be called," in Mt. 1:23).

III. Identification of Immanuel and His Mother.–This is the most vexing question of all. Three basic approaches have been suggested: the nonfulfillment view, which asserts that the *ʿalmâ* and Immanuel were people living in Ahaz' time only; the one-fulfillment view, which understands Isa. 7:14 as only a prediction of the virgin birth of Christ; and the double-fulfillment view, which sees a near fulfillment in the days of Ahaz and a remote fulfillment in the NT period. The first theory is unsatisfactory because of its refusal to take Mt. 1:23 seriously, and the second is unsatisfactory because it fails to do justice to the context of which Isa. 7:14 is an integral part. Only the third, which provides contemporary fulfillment as a sign to Ahaz and fulfillment centuries later as a sign to the "house of David" as a whole, is worthy of our consideration here.

Numerous suggestions have been made concerning the contemporary identification of Immanuel, the two most popular being a son of Ahaz or a son of Isaiah. The former, however, flounders in a sea of difficulties both theological and chronological. Arguments favoring the latter proposal are much stronger. We begin by noting that many have observed the similarity of form between Isa. 7:10-17 and 8:1-4. So similar are they that Immanuel and Maher-shalal-hash-baz may be two names for the same child, the former given by his mother, the latter by his father. Just as Shear-jashub (7:3), the name of Isaiah's other son, has a double significance ("a remnant will return" and "only a remnant will return"), so also Immanuel ("God is with us") and Maher-shalal-hash-baz ("the plunder hastens, the prey speeds") represent salvation and judgment respectively. Alternate names are common in both the OT (cf. Isa. 62:4; Jer. 20:3; and esp. Ruth 1:20) and the NT. The interplay between promise and threat in Isa. 7–8 corresponds to the alternation between Immanuel and Maher-shalal-hash-baz in the same section. Isa. 7:15f. and 8:4 complement each other and refer to the same period of time (approximately two years; in 732 B.C. Assyria destroyed Damascus and replaced Pekah with the puppet king Hoshea, thereby setting Samaria on its irreversible path to ruin). The term "sign," referring to Immanuel in Isa. 7:14, is echoed in the summary statement of 8:18 where Isaiah refers to himself and his children as signs and portents in Israel. All the contextual evidence indicates that Immanuel is to be regarded as one of Isaiah's sons.

Though some have claimed that Isaiah would not use *ʿalmâ* in 7:14 to refer to his own wife, this is not a valid objection. Here is a plausible reconstruction: His first wife, the mother of Shear-jashub (7:3), had died. He predicts that the girl who is to become his second wife — a virgin at the time of the prediction — will become pregnant and give birth to a son (7:14), whom she will name "Immanuel." The wedding ceremony is alluded to in 8:1f. Isaiah takes his new bride and in due course she bears the predicted son (8:3f.), whom Isaiah names Maher-shalal-hash-baz. It is not surprising or unprecedented that she is called both a "virgin" and a "prophetess" (8:3); cf. the description of Miriam in Ex. 2:8; 15:20.

IV. Relationship to NT.–Understanding the *ʿalmâ* of Isa. 7:14 as Isaiah's second wife, and Immanuel as their son, does not exhaust the meaning of that text. Isaiah and his children are viewed typologically in He. 2:13, which quotes Isa. 8:18 and applies it in a bold figure to Christ as the father of His adopted children. And the Immanuel of Isa. 7:14 cannot be separated, ultimately, from the child/son whose story is embedded in 9:1-7 (MT 8:23–9:6) or the Branch/Root described in 11:1-10. Both of these passages are integral to "The Book of Immanuel" and are quoted in part in Mt. 4:15f. (cf. Isa. 9:1f.) and Mt. 2:23 (cf. Isa. 11:1, where Heb. *nēṣer,* "branch," corresponds to Greek *Nazōraios,* "Nazarene," in Matthew). Matthew quotes yet a third time from "The Book of Immanuel" when he applies Isa. 7:14 to the virginal conception of Jesus Christ in Mt. 1:23. The "Mighty God" of Isa. 9:6 (MT 7) is the "God with us" of Matthew's Gospel. The relationship of the "virgin" in Isa. 7:14 and the Virgin Mary in Mt. 1:23 is that of type and antitype. Matthew's "God with us," reflecting as it almost surely does deity incarnate, lifts the Immanuel of Isa. 7:14 to an infinitely higher plane.

V. God with His People.–In a sense, "God with us"

is the story of Scripture in summary. The key covenant statement of relationship, "I will be their God, and they will be my people," is sometimes called the "Immanuel theme" in covenant theology. From the fellowship with God that mankind enjoyed in Eden to "the grace of the Lord Jesus . . . with all" God's people in Rev. 22:21, the concept of God's search for His children and His dwelling with them (cf. Jn. 1:14) is prominent throughout the Bible. As "God with us" was the sign (*'ôṯ*) to Ahaz and his people in Isa. 7:14, so also "I will be with you" (rather than "you will serve me on this mountain"; cf. the MT accentuation) was the sign (*'ôṯ*) to God's people at the beginning of their pilgrimage as a nation (Ex. 3:12). God's relationship "with us" distinguishes us "from all other people that are upon the face of the earth" (Ex. 33:16). It is "with us" that God enters into covenant (Dt. 5:2f.); it is "with us" that God speaks (AV Hos. 12:4 [MT 5]); it is "with us" that God walks as He gives help and guidance and protection (Jgs. 6:12-18; 1 K. 8:57; 2 Ch. 13:12; 32:7f.).

Bibliography.–In addition to the standard comms. on Isaiah, the reader should note the following: G. L. Archer, *Wycliffe Bible Comm.* (1962), pp. 617-19; R. G. Bratcher, *Bible Translator,* 9/3 (July, 1958), 97-126; G. Brunet, *Essai sur l'Isaïe de l'histoire: Étude de quelques textes notamment dans Isa. VII, VIII & XXII* (1975), pp. 3-120; *HDB,* II, *s.v.* (A. B. Davidson); C. H. Gordon, *JBR,* 21 (1953), 106; N. K. Gottwald, *VT,* 8 (1958), 36-47; R. Gundry, *Use of the OT in St. Matthew's Gospel* (*Nov.Test.Supp.,* 18, 1967), pp. 226f.; E. E. Hindson, *Grace Journal,* 10/3 (Fall, 1969), 3-15; C. D. Isbell, *Biblical Archaeology Review,* 3 (1977), 18f., 52; E. G. Kraeling, *JBL,* 50 (1931), 277-297; W. S. LaSor, *Isaiah 7:14—'Young Woman' or 'Virgin'?* (n.d.); C. Lattey, *CBQ,* 8 (1946), 369-376; W. McKane, *VT,* 17 (1967), 208-219; S. Mowinckel, *He That Cometh* (1956), pp. 110-19; M. Noth, *IP,* pp. 33, 160; *TDNT,* V, *s.v.* παρθένος (Delling); R. D. Wilson, *Princeton Theological Review,* 24 (1926), 308-316; H. M. Wolf, *JBL,* 91 (1972), 449-456; *NBD, s.v.* (E. J. Young).

R. F. YOUNGBLOOD

IMMER im'ər [Heb. *'immēr*–'lamb'; LXX Gk. *Emmērouth* (1 Esd. 5:24, A), *Amar* (1 Esd. 5:36; *Alar,* A; *Aalar*), *Emmēr* (1 Esd. 9:21)]; AV also AALAR (1 Esd. 5:36), EMMER (9:21), MERUTH (5:24); NEB also ALAR (5:36), EMMER (9:21), EMMERUTH (5:24).

1. A priest of David's time (1 Ch. 24:14), whose descendants are mentioned in Ezr. 2:37; 10:20; Neh. 3:29; 7:40; 11:13 (cf. 1 Esd. 5:24; 9:21).

2. A priest in Jeremiah's time (Jer. 20:1).

3. A place in Babylonia from which Jewish exiles returned (Ezr. 2:59; Neh. 7:61; 1 Esd. 5:36).

IMMORAL [Gk. *pórnos* (1 Cor. 5:9f.; 6:9; Eph. 5:5; 1 Tim. 1:10; He. 12:16; 13:4), *porneúō* (1 Cor. 6:18)]; AV also FORNICATION (1 Cor. 6:18), WHOREMONGER (Eph. 5:5; He. 13:4); NEB also FORNICATOR (1 Cor. 6:9; etc.), LOOSE LIVERS (1 Cor. 5:9), "pagans who lead loose lives" (1 Cor. 5:10); **IMMORALITY** [Gk. *porneía* (1 Cor. 5:1; 6:13, 18; 7:2; 2 Cor. 12:21; Gal. 5:19; Eph. 5:3; Col. 3:5; 1 Thess. 4:3; Rev. 2:21; 9:21), *pórnos* (1 Cor. 5:11), *porneúō* (1 Cor. 10:8; Rev. 2:14, 20)]; AV FORNICATION (1 Cor. 5:1; 6:13; etc.); NEB also SEXUAL IMMORALITY (1 Cor. 5:1), LOOSE LIFE (1 Cor. 5:11), LUST (1 Cor. 6:13); **IMMORALLY** [Gk. *ekporneúō* (Jude 7)]; AV, NEB, FORNICATION. The RSV uses these three words (only in the NT) to denote sexual behavior that is not in accord with OT regulations and the teaching of the apostles and other leaders in the primitive Church.

The word *porneúō* is derived from Gk. *pórnēmi,* "sell, prostitute oneself." Several cognates are derived from *porneúō.* A *pórnē* is a female prostitute. A man who fornicates with prostitutes is a *pórnos,* but the word is also used of male prostitutes. *Porneía* means fornication, harlotry, and other illicit sexual activities in general, including those of a homosexual nature. In the LXX, *porneúō* and its cognates almost always translate Heb. *zānâ,* "have intercourse with another," "be unfaithful," "play the harlot" (*DNTT,* I, 497; *TDNT,* VI, 581f., 584).

The Pauline Epistles are highly illustrative of the use of the word group *pórnē,* with the bulk of occurrences found in 1 Corinthians. Although "any kind of illegitimate sexual intercourse" is an adequate definition of the terms (*DNTT,* I, 500), the various contexts in which these terms occur show their application to specific situations. According to 1 Cor. 5:1, *porneía* refers to the incestuous relationship between a man and "his father's wife" (*gynaíka toú patrós*). Paul's phrase is similar to that of Lev. 18:8 (LXX), "you shall not uncover the nakedness of your father's wife" (*gynaikós patrós sou*). This command forbids sexual relations with one's stepmother, as distinguished from one's mother (v. 7). Whether the man's father had died or divorced his wife is not clear (see comms.), but the present relationship is forbidden (cf. Lev. 20:11; Mish. *Sanhedrin* vii.4). In 5:9-11 Paul addressed a more widespread problem among the Corinthians: sexual intercourse with prostitutes (cf. 6:12-20). Paul emphasized the seriousness of *porneía.* The person who commits *porneía* with a prostitute "sins against his own body" (v. 18), i.e., defiles his body, which is the temple of the Holy Spirit (cf. 1 Thess. 4:4-8).

In ch. 7 Paul responded to various questions raised by the Corinthians concerning marriage. He advocated marriage as a preventative measure against *porneía* and rejected any idea of sexual asceticism within marriage (vv. 1-7). Paul combined the example of the death of the Israelites who "yoked themselves" to Baal-peor (Nu. 25) with a warning to avoid idol worship in 10:8-22. It is possible that the immorality in the Corinthian church included prostitution, which involved participation in temple meals. The warning in v. 8 is followed by teaching concerning food offered to idols (vv. 14-30). Paul's comment in v. 20, "they offer to demons and not to God," indicates the influence of Lev. 17:7 and Dt. 32:17. If Paul already referred to Lev. 18:8 in 1 Cor. 5:1, he might have alluded to Lev. 17:7 in 10:20. Lev. 17:7 combines the ideas of immorality and participation in pagan sacrifice: "So they shall no more slay their sacrifices for satyrs [AV "devils," NEB "demons"] after whom they play the harlot" (LXX *ekporneúō*).

It is clear that Paul regarded immorality in all its forms as a serious breach of God's will. The offender in 1 Cor. 5:1 is to be cut off from all fellowship with other believers. This was initiated in an announcement at the next assembly of the congregation. Such a separation had the effect of handing the offender over to Satan, with the possibility of death (5:5). Immorality is not only a sin against oneself (1 Cor. 6:18), but also against God, for He has given His Holy Spirit to dwell in the believer, whose body is thus called "the temple of the Holy Spirit" (1 Cor. 3:16f.; 1 Thess. 4:3-8). Whoever persists in such behavior will bring severe judgment upon himself, possibly death (1 Cor. 3:17; 5:5; cf. 10:29f.; 1 Thess. 4:6). Those who pursue an immoral life-style will not enter the kingdom of God (Eph. 5:3).

"Immoral" occurs twice in Hebrews. Esau is termed "immoral" in 12:16. Some commentators construe v. 16a to mean "let no one among you be immoral or, like Esau, irreligious" (Bruce, pp. 366f.). Postbiblical tradition, however, portrays Esau as a licentious character who was interested only in satisfying his physical needs. The Palestinian Targum to Gen. 25:29 explains Esau's exhaustion as the result of his having committed five transgressions on that day, including adultery with a betrothed maiden (cf. Jub. 25:1; Philo *Legum allegoriae* iii.2). Such traditions were probably familiar to the Epistle's Jewish audience (Hughes, p. 540). Immorality (*pórnos*), meaning nonmarital sexual intercourse, is distinguished from adultery (*moichós*), or extramarital sexual intercourse, in 13:4. The writer was countering both promiscuity and an antimarriage asceticism (Hughes, p. 365).

The author of Revelation refers to immorality four times. In 2:14, 20f. the churches of Pergamum and Thyatira are rebuked because they committed immorality and ate food sacrificed to idols. As in 1 Cor. 10:8-22, fornication was apparently part of the pagan festivities (Mounce, p. 98). The meaning of *porneía* in 9:21 is more general. It occurs with murder, sorcery, and theft, and together they form a catalog of vices (Lohmeyer, p. 83).

"Immorally" (*ekpornéuō*) occurs in Jude 7, which refers to the sexual excesses of Sodom and Gomorrah as an example of God's judgment on licentious behavior.

See also FORNICATION; MARRIAGE; UNCHASTITY.

Bibliography.–*DNTT*, I, 497-501; MM, p. 529; *TDNT*, VI, *s.v.* πόρνη κτλ. (Hauck, Schulz); comms. on 1 Corinthians by H. Conzelmann (*Hermeneia*, 1975); C. K. Barrett (*HNTC*, 1968); H. Lietzmann (*HNT*, 1949); comms. on Hebrews by F. F. Bruce (*NICNT*, 1964); P. Hughes (1977); comms. on Revelation by E. Lohmeyer (*HNT*, 1953); G. E. Ladd (1972); R. Mounce (*NICNT*, 1977); B. Malina, *Nov.Test.*, 14 (1972), 10-17; J. Jensen, *Nov.Test.*, 20 (1978), 161-184.

R. J. WYATT

IMMORTAL i-môr'təl; **IMMORTALITY** im-ôr-tal'ə-tē [Heb. *'al-māweṯ*] (Prov. 12:28); [Gk. *athanasía*] (1 Cor. 15:53f.; 1 Tim. 6:16); [Gk. *aphtharsía*] (Rom. 2:7; 2 Tim. 1:10); [Gk. *áphthartos*] (Rom. 1:23; 1 Tim. 1:17); AV also UNCORRUPTIBLE (Rom. 1:23). The noun *athanasía*, "deathlessness," denotes the immunity from death enjoyed by God (1 Tim. 6:16) and by resurrected believers (1 Cor. 15:53f.). The noun *aphtharsía*, "incorruptibility," "imperishability," signifies the immunity from decay that characterizes the divine state (Eph. 6:24) and the resurrection state (1 Cor. 15:42, 50, 53f.). It was "brought to light" by Christ as indicated in the gospel (2 Tim. 1:10) and is the divine gift granted to the righteous (Rom. 2:7). Finally, the adjective *áphthartos*, "imperishable," describes the quality of the divine nature (Rom. 1:23; 1 Tim. 1:17; 1 Pet. 1:23), the gentle and quiet disposition of the Christian woman (1 Pet. 3:4), the Christian's reward (1 Cor. 9:25) or inheritance (1 Pet. 1:4), and the future state of resurrected believers (1 Cor. 15:52).

Several points are noteworthy: (1) All uses of the nouns are Pauline. (2) All three terms are associated with Paul's description of the spiritual body (seven instances, all in 1 Cor. 15), but never with the "soul." Immortality and resurrection are inseparable ideas (see IV.A below). (3) Although the three terms are formed with "alpha privative," a negative prefix comparable to the English *in-* or *un-*, each takes on positive overtones relating to "(eternal) life." For example, just as God is "never-dying" (Rom. 1:23; 1 Tim. 1:17; 6:16) because he is "ever-living" (Jer. 10:10; Jn. 5:26), so believers are destined to become free from decay and death because they will participate fully and immediately in the eternal divine life (2 Pet. 1:4). Moreover, the ideas of immortality and life are closely related in Rom. 2:7; 2 Tim. 1:10, so that inheriting immortality (1 Cor. 15:50) is equivalent to reaping eternal life (Gal. 6:8). (4) Immortality may therefore be defined as the immunity from decay and death that results from sharing the divine life in the resurrected state.

I. Immortality in the Pre-Christian Era.–*A. Greek World.* An essential ingredient of Orphic religion was belief in the essential divinity of the soul and in embodiment as the soul's exile from its true heavenly home. Hence the celebrated Orphic pun *sṓma sḗma*, "the body is the tomb (of the soul)." This belief in the eternal survival of the soul gained intellectual respectability in the writings of Plato. According to Plato, in its rational or divine function the soul is preexistent and apparently eternal and has relations with both the phenomenal world and the unchanging ideal world. He adduces five arguments for the immortality of the rational soul: the argument from opposites (*Phaedo* 70c-72e) and the complementary argument from reminiscence (*Phaedo* 72e-77d); the argument from affinity (or from the simplicity of the soul) (*Phaedo* 78b-84b); the argument from "forms" (*Phaedo* 102a-107b) which he regarded as the most conclusive proof; the argument from destructibility (*Respublica* 608d-611a); the argument from motion (*Phaedrus* 245c-246a). Aristotle reserves divinity, eternality, and immortality for "active intellect" (*De an.* 415a; *De generatione animalium* 738b), the highest phase of soul. Since the faculty of memory belongs to the passive and perishable part of the intellect (*De an.* 408b), the discarnate active intellect will lack continuity with earlier bodily existence. All that survives the death of the individual is the impersonal reason or divine *noús* (intellect).

B. OT. The OT has no distinct term for immortality, although the coinage "not-death" (*'al-māweṯ*) occurs once (Prov. 12:28): "In the way of righteousness is [eternal] life; the treading of her path is not-death [= immortality]." The RSV, however, follows the LXX (*eis thánaton*) in reading *'el-māweṯ* ("to death") in the second line: "the way of error leads to death." Adducing an instance of the synonymous parallelism of "[eternal] life" and "immortality" in an Ugaritic poem (2 Aqht vi. 27-29), M. Dahood claims to have found ten instances in the Psalms (e.g., 16:11; 133:3) and four in Proverbs (e.g., 12:28; 15:24) where the Heb. *ḥayyîm* ("life") signifies "life eternal" (*Psalms*, III [*AB*, 1970], xlvi-xlvii).

The common OT phrase "for ever(more)" sometimes denotes eternality and immortality, as when it refers to Yahweh's existence and character (Ps. 9:7 [MT 8]; 111:3), but generally it points to unlimited duration, "as long as life lasts" (e.g., Ex. 21:6, of slavery in perpetuity). Note also the customary royal greeting, "O king, live for ever!" (Dnl. 2:4). Even "living for ever" in Gen. 3:22 denotes merely a permanent continuation of man's earthly, corporeal existence, not direct participation in the eternal, divine life brought about by a somatic transformation. Only in Dnl. 12:2 is immortality related to resurrection: some of those who sleep in the dust of the earth "shall awake . . . to everlasting life," the positive corollary of immortality. As to man's original state, we may say that he was created neither immortal (Gen. 3:22-24) nor mortal (Gen. 2:17) but with the potentiality to become either, depending on his obedience or disobedience to God. If not created *with* immortality, he was certainly created *for* immortality.

C. Intertestamental Judaism. During the period 200 B.C. to A.D. 100 the concept of immortality gained a new prominence in Jewish texts. Some emphasize or refer exclusively to immortality (Palestinian Judaism: Jubilees [e.g., 23:31]; Testament of Moses [e.g., 10:8-10]; Testament of Abraham [e.g., Recension A, 1, 7]; Diaspora Judaism: 4 Maccabees [e.g., 16:13; 18:23]; Wisdom [e.g., 2:23; 3:1-4]; Philo [e.g., *De opificio mundi* 135]). Other texts juxtapose the ideas of resurrection and immortality without attempting to interrelate them (Palestinian Judaism: 1 En. 91–104 [e.g., 92:3f.; 103:3f.]; XII P. [e.g., T. Jud. 25:1, 4; T. Ash. 6:5f.]; Diaspora Judaism: Testament of Job [e.g., 4:9; 52:2-9]). But some texts do interrelate the two ideas, often through recourse to the notion of an intermediate state occurring between a person's gaining of immortality at death and his resurrection at the last day (Palestinian Judaism: 1 En. 1–36 [e.g., 22:1-12]; 37–71 [e.g., 51:1f.; 58:3f.]; 2 Esd. 3–14 [e.g., 7:88-101]; 2 Baruch [e.g., 30:2-4; 51:9]; Diaspora Judaism: 2 Maccabees [e.g., 7:9-11, 14]; Josephus [e.g., *BJ* iii.8.5 (372-78)]).

II. Immortality of God in the NT.–1 Tim. 6:16 asserts the uniqueness of God's immortality. He is "the blessed and only Sovereign . . . who alone has immortality." This means not simply that decay and death have no place in His existence but that He is the sole and eternal source of life and holiness. Significantly, the same Greek sentence that includes the phrase "who alone has immortality" affirms that He perpetually "gives life to all things" (1 Tim. 6:13) and "dwells in unapproachable light" (1 Tim. 6:16). On the principle that behind each explicit negative definition of God's character (such as immortality) there lies some implicit positive assertion, immortality may be said to imply that creative energy (Ps. 36:9 [MT 10]; Jn. 5:26; 6:57) and purity (Ex. 15:11; Isa. 6:3; He. 12:29) are constantly present in God as well as that death and sin are permanently absent.

III. Immortality of Man in the NT.–*A. As a Divine Gift to the Righteous.* If only God is inherently immortal, man may gain immortality only as a gracious gift of the divine will (cf. Rom. 2:7; 6:23). Man's immortality is not essential or intrinsic but derived or extrinsic. The acquisition of immortality is a privilege reserved for the righteous rather than the prerogative of all mankind. This is clear from Rom. 2:7f., where eternal life is promised to "those who by patience in well-doing seek for glory and honor and immortality" but wrath and fury to "those who . . . do not obey the truth but obey wickedness"; and from 1 Cor. 15, where investiture with imperishability and immortality (vv. 53f.) is pledged to "those who have fallen asleep in Christ" (v. 18). There is a resurrection that leads to eternal life, the positive aspect of immortality, and a resurrection that leads to judgment (Jn. 5:29). Sharing the divine nature is a future experience reserved for those who belong to Christ (1 Cor. 15:23, 49, 53f.; 2 Pet. 1:4). Potentially immortal by nature, man actually becomes immortal through grace. Immortality is conditional in the sense that there is no eternal life except in Christ. But this does not imply, of course, that existence beyond death is conditional. Because, in its NT sense, immortality has positive content, being more than mere survival beyond death, its opposite is not nonexistence but the "second death" (Rev. 20:6, 14; 21:8), "the punishment of eternal destruction and exclusion from the presence of the Lord" (2 Thess. 1:9).

B. As a Future Acquisition. It was suggested above (I.B) that man was not created unable to die (*non posse mori*) but able not to die (*posse non mori*). If, then, man was not created immortal and since the fall has been subject to death, when is this gift of immortality received? Although immortality was "brought to light" and made available by the death and resurrection of Jesus (2 Tim. 1:10) and is gained *potentially* at the time of regeneration when a person comes to be in Christ (1 Cor. 15:22; 2 Cor. 5:17; 1 Pet. 1:23), it is not until the believer experiences a resurrection transformation that immortality becomes an *actual* possession. For those who die this may occur at the moment of death (if indeed that marks the receipt of the spiritual body) or at the Parousia; for the living it occurs at the Parousia. But more in accord with the NT use of the terms "immortal" and "immortality" than this "potential-actual" distinction, is the conclusion that the NT simply portrays immortality as a divine gift gained through somatic resurrection at or after the death of the believer (Lk. 20:35f; Jn. 11:25f.; 1 Cor. 15:51-54; 2 Cor. 5:1-4). Whereas resurrection occurs in two stages, a spiritual resurrection at baptism (Rom. 6:4; Col. 2:12) and a somatic resurrection in the future (1 Cor. 15:23, 49, 52), immortality lies totally in the future, since as long as the believer is alive he remains subject to physical death.

C. Immortality and Eternal Life. Both expressions describe conditional divine gifts (Acts 11:18; 13:48; Rom. 2:7; 6:23; Gal. 6:8; 1 Cor. 15:52-54) that are inseparably related to the resurrection transformation (compare Rom. 6:22f. with 8:11, 23, for eternal life; 1 Cor. 15:35-57, for immortality). Both depict the final state of blessedness or the heavenly mode of existence. But they are not identical concepts: (1) Formally, one is a positive expression, referring to life; the other negative, relating to death. Each implies the other, however, for to have eternal life is to be ultimately free from death (Jn. 5:24) and to be immortal is to live forever (Jn. 6:51, 58). (2) In the Fourth Gospel, eternal life is both a present reality (Jn. 3:36; 5:24; 17:3) and a future blessing (Jn. 4:14, 36; 5:29; 6:27), whereas for Paul both eternal life (Rom. 2:7; 5:21; 6:22f.; Gal. 6:8) and immortality are future acquisitions. This distinction may perhaps best be explained by observing that in John eternal life (or life) signifies (negatively) an immunity from spiritual death (Jn. 5:24) but not from physical death (Jn. 11:25), while immortality (and eternal life) in Paul involves immunity from both spiritual and physical death. (3) Eternal life is the positive aspect of immortality (viz., participation in the divine life), and immortality is the future aspect of eternal life.

IV. Immortality and Resurrection.–It is sometimes thought that the idea of immortality may be safely jettisoned without losing an essential ingredient of Christian doctrine. There is a distinction between a Platonic belief in the immortality of the soul alone and biblical teaching regarding the resurrection of the dead. The NT data, however, point to the complementarity of the ideas of resurrection and immortality.

A. As Inseparable Ideas. First, a resurrection transformation is the only means of gaining immortality (Lk. 20:35f.; Acts 13:34f.; Rom. 6:9; 1 Cor. 15:42, 52-54). Although those alive at the Parousia will not be "raised from the dead," they will experience a transformation into the image of Christ comparable to the change effected in the dead (1 Cor. 15:49-54). Second, immortality is the inevitable outcome of a resurrection transformation (Lk. 20:36; Jn. 11:25f.; Rom. 6:9; 1 Cor. 15:53f.; Rev. 1:18; 20:6). From a Christian perspective, the two ideas stand or fall together. To deny resurrection is to deny immortality, since the embodiment guaranteed by resurrection is (from a Jewish or Christian outlook) necessary for meaningful existence. To deny immortality is to deny resurrection, since the divine life pledged by immortality is necessary to sustain transformed persons.

B. As Complementary Ideas. First, NT teaching about resurrection insures that immortality is regarded as personal rather than racial, ideal, or pantheistic; as corporate rather than individualistic; and as somatic rather than merely spiritual. Resurrection involves dead persons who are raised in spiritual bodies to enjoy the corporate life of the redeemed. Second, NT teaching about immortality guarantees that resurrection is seen as a continuing state rather than simply as a single event. It is a permanent rather than a temporary condition, a transformed state sustained by divine life and power. Immortality involves entrance upon a state of freedom from decay and death that is permanent because it has the constant invigoration of God's endless power.

V. Platonic and Biblical Immortality.–The biblical doctrine of immortality differs from the Platonic doctrine in several important ways. First, in the NT immortality is not an inherent characteristic of the rational part of the human soul but a natural attribute of God alone (1 Tim. 6:16). Second, the NT depicts immortality as a future acquisition gained by the righteous through a resurrection transformation effected by God, not as a natural property of every rational soul. Third, whereas Platonic anthropology is dichotomistic so that only release from corporeality achieved at death enables the soul to reenter its true abode in the world of Forms, NT anthropology is basically monistic so that the destiny of the Christian is somatic immortality, with the spiritual body being the organ of resurrection life. Fourth, according to the NT, possession of immortality depends on one's relationship to the second Adam, not the first Adam. It is death or a propensity to death, not immortality, that man inherits from Adam (Rom. 5:12; 1 Cor. 15:22). Deathlessness and imperishability result from union with Christ (1 Cor. 15:22f., 42, 52-54). Fifth, for Plato assurance of immortality was grounded in belief in the soul's divinity, but for Paul it was based on the fact that God gives all believers His Spirit as a pledge of a resurrection transformation that will result in immortality (2 Cor. 5:4f.). Sixth, although both Plato and NT writers understand immortality as involving "becoming like God," for the Christian this means conformity to the image of Christ (Rom. 8:29; Col. 3:10), rather than "a never-ending union with true Reality" (Rohde, *Psyche,* p. 475).

See also RESURRECTION.

Bibliography.–*I. Greek Concepts:* J. Burnet, *Proceedings of the British Academy,* 7 (1915), 236-260; C. H. Moore, *Ancient Beliefs in the Immortality of the Soul* (1931); M. P. Nilsson, *Eranos,* 39 (1941), 1-16; R. L. Patterson, *Plato on Immortality* (1965); A. S. Pringle-Pattison, *The Idea of Immortality* (1922); E. Rohde, *Psyche: The Cult of Souls and Belief in Immortality among the Greeks* (8th ed. 1925).

II. Jewish Concepts: H. C. C. Cavallin, *Life After Death* (1974), I; R. B. Laurin, *JSS,* 3 (1958), 344-355; J. Lindblom, *Das ewige Leben* (1914); R. Martin-Achard, *From Death to Life* (1960); G. W. E. Nickelsburg, Jr., *Resurrection, Immortality and Eternal Life in Intertestamental Judaism* (1972); A. T. Nikolainen, *Der Auferstehungsglauben in der Bibel und ihrer Umwelt* (1944-1946); F. Nötscher, *Altorientalischer und alttestamentlicher Auferstehungsglauben* (1926); E. Sellin, *Neue Kirchliche Zeitschrift,* 30 (1919), 232-289; J. van der Ploeg, *Bibliotheca Orientalis,* 18 (1961), 118-124; P. Volz, *Die Eschatologie der jüdischen Gemeinde im neutestamentlichen Zeitalter* (1934).

III. Christian Concepts: P. Badham, *Christian Beliefs about Life after Death* (1976); J. Baillie, *And the Life Everlasting* (1936); C. K. Barrett, *London Quarterly and Holborn Review,* 190 (1965), 91-102; P. Benoit and R. Murphy, eds., *Immortality and Resurrection* (1970); R. H. Charles, *Eschatology: The Doctrine of a Future Life in Israel, Judaism and Christianity* (repr. 1963); O. Cullmann, *Immortality of the Soul or Resurrection of the Dead?* (1958); C. S. Duthie, ed., *Resurrection and Immortality* (1979); G. Greshake and G. Lohfink, *Naherwartung, Auferstehung, Unsterblichkeit* (1975); M. J. Harris, *Themelios,* 1 (1976), 50-55; *Raised Immortal: Resurrection and Immortality in the NT* (1981); J. H. Hick, *Death and Eternal Life* (1976); P. Hoffmann, *Die Toten in Christus* (2nd ed. 1969); S. D. F. Salmond, *The Christian Doctrine of Immortality* (1895); K. Stendahl, ed., *Immortality and Resurrection* (1965); A. E. Taylor, *The Christian Hope of Immortality* (1938).

M. J. HARRIS

IMMUTABILITY, IMMUTABLE (He. 6:17f., AV). *See* UNCHANGEABLE.

IMNA im'nə [Heb. *yimnā'*]. A descendant of Asher (1 Ch. 7:35).

IMNAH im'nə [Heb. *yimnâ*].

1. Eldest son of Asher (Gen. 46:17 [AV JIMNAH]; Nu. 26:44 [AV JIMNA; NEB IMNA]; 1 Ch. 7:30).

2. A Levite of Hezekiah's time (2 Ch. 31:14).

IMNITES im'nīts [Heb. *yimnî*] (Nu. 26:44); AV JIMNITES. Descendants of Imnah (*see* IMNAH **1**).

IMPART [Gk. *dídōmi* (Eph. 4:29), *metadídōmi* (Rom. 1:11), *laléō* (1 Cor. 2:6f., 13)]; AV also MINISTER (Eph. 4:29), SPEAK (1 Cor. 2:6f., 13); NEB also BRING A BLESSING (Eph. 4:29), SPEAK (1 Cor. 2:6f., 13). The term can mean either "give a share of" (Eph. 4:29; Rom. 1:11) or "communicate," "disclose" (1 Cor. 2:6f., 13).

IMPEDIMENT [Gk. *mogilálos*] (Mk. 7:32). The Gk. *mogilálos* is composed of *mógis,* "with difficulty," and *lálos,* "speech," i.e., one who speaks with difficulty. In the LXX the word is used as a translation of Heb. *'illēm,* "dumb" (Isa. 35:6).

IMPERISHABLE. *See* IMMORTAL.

IMPIOUS. *See* PIETY.

IMPLANTED WORD [Gk. *émphyton lógon*] (Jas. 1:21); AV ENGRAFTED WORD; NEB MESSAGE PLANTED IN. *Émphytos,* appearing only here in the NT, may mean "inborn," "innate," or "natural" (cf. MM; e.g., Wisd. 12:10). In Jas. 1:21, however, the "Word" is to be "received"; thus *émphytos* here may mean "implanted (from without)" (cf. 1 Cor. 3:6). The word is "sown," not "engrafted" (cf. Mt. 13:18-23 par. Mk. 4:13-20).

H. VAN BROEKHOVEN, JR.

IMPLEAD [Gk. *enkaléō*] (Acts 19:38, AV). Archaic term for "bring charges" (RSV).

IMPLEMENTS [Heb. *k^elî*] (1 S. 8:12; Zec. 11:15); AV INSTRUMENTS; NEB WEAPONS, "equip yourself." The Heb. *k^elî* is a general term for various items. In 1 S. 8:12, it refers to weaponry, and in Zec. 11:15 to a shepherd's equipment.

See also INSTRUMENT.

IMPORT [Heb. *môṣā'*] (1 K. 10:28f.; 2 Ch. 1:16f.; 9:28). *See* COMMERCE I.A.

IMPORTUNITY [Gk. *anaídeia*]; NEB VERY SHAMELESSNESS. Occurring only in Lk. 11:8, this Greek word implies an element of impudent insistence to the point of shamelessness that the English "importunity" does not fully express. This weakens the parable's argument, which is that if by shameless insistence a favor may be won, even from one unwilling and ungracious, still more surely will God answer the earnest prayer of His people. God's willingness to give exceeds our ability to ask. The parable teaches by way of contrast, not by parallel.

D. F. ESTES

IMPOSITION OF HANDS. *See* HANDS, LAYING ON OF.

IMPOSSIBLE [Heb. *bāṣar* (Gen. 11:6), *pālā'*–'be too hard' (2 S. 13:2); Gk. *adynatéō* (Mt. 17:20; Lk. 1:37), *adýnatos* (Mt. 19:26; Mk. 10:27; Lk. 18:27; He. 6:4, 18; 10:4; 11:6)]; AV also NOT POSSIBLE, HARD, "be restrained"; NEB also "beyond their reach," "can never fail," NOT POSSIBLY. The verb *adynatéō* and adjective *adýnatos* are both cognates of *dýnamai,* "be powerful," "be able," and hence they mean "powerless" (adj.) and "be powerless" (vb.). In several of these passages it is affirmed that "nothing is impossible with God," but, of course, this means nothing that is consistent with the divine nature, e.g., it is not possible for God to lie (cf. He. 6:18). So, when it is said that nothing is impossible to faith, the same limitation applies, as well as that of the mind or will of God for the believer (cf. 1 Jn. 5:14).

W. L. WALKER

IMPOSTOR [Gk. *plános*] (Mt. 27:63; 2 Cor. 6:8); AV DECEIVER; [*góēs*] (2 Tim. 3:13); AV SEDUCER; NEB CHARLATAN. *Plános* appears in the NT only four times as a substantive. The RSV has "deceiver" in 2 Jn. 7, but "impostor" in Mt. 27:63 and 2 Cor. 6:8. The Jews regarded Christ's resurrection as the second deception and thought of Christ Himself as the first fraud (Mt. 27:63f.); already they may have feared a fraudulent messiah (cf. *TDNT,* VI, *s.v.* πλανάω κτλ. [Braun]). The apostles were regarded as "impostors" although they were in fact *alētheís* — "true" in the sense of "genuine" and not merely "truthful" (2 Cor. 6:8). The focus here is upon the person's character rather than activity.

In 2 Tim. 3:13 "charlatan" (NEB) perhaps captures the nuance of Gk. *góētes* better than "impostor" (RSV). The *góēs* was a cheap, even a false and slick magician, a quack, who was regarded by the educated as despicable or ludicrous. The apostle, interested in correct doctrine, painted a rather humorous picture of these hustlers (3:6-13), whom he described as not only "deceiving but themselves deceived."

H. VAN BROEKHOVEN, JR.

IMPOTENT. Used by the AV for Gk. *adýnatos,* "powerless" ("could not use," Acts 14:8), *asthenḗs,* "without strength" ("cripple," Acts 4:9), and *asthenéō,* "be without strength" ("invalid," Jn. 5:3; "sick man," v. 7). The English term is used to characterize those who are paralyzed or crippled. In this sense the word is used by Shakespeare (*Love's Labour's Lost* V, 2, line 864; *Hamlet* I, 2, line 29). The impotent folk referred to in the Letter of Jeremiah (6:28) were those weak and feeble from age and want; cf. "impotent and snail-paced beggary" (*Richard III,* IV, 3, line 53).

A. MACALISTER

IMPRISONMENT. *See* PUNISHMENT IV; PRISON.

IMPURITY. *See* CLEAN AND UNCLEAN.

IMPUTATION im-pū-tā'shən.

I. Meaning and Use of the Term
II. The Threefold Use of the Term in Theology
III. The Scriptural Basis of These Doctrines
   A. Imputation of Adam's Sin to His Posterity
   B. Imputation of the Sins of His People to Christ
   C. Imputation of the Righteousness of Christ to His People

I. Meaning and Use of the Term.–The word "imputation," according to the scriptural usage, denotes an attributing of something to a person, or a charging of one with anything, or a setting of something to one's account. This takes place sometimes in a judicial manner, so that the thing imputed becomes a ground of reward or punishment. Impute is used three times in the RSV. In 1 S. 22:15, it translates Heb. *'al-yāśēm* (lit. "do not put"; NEB "not accuse"). In Ps. 32:2 and Lev. 17:4, "impute" translates Heb. *ḥāšaḇ,* "think," "account," "reckon" (BDB, pp. 362f.). Lev. 17:4 teaches that bloodguilt was imputed to a man who killed a sacrificial animal without bringing it to the tent of meeting for sacrifice. Ps. 32:2 called the man blessed to whom the Lord did not impute sin. The RSV uses "reckon" for Gk. *logízomai* when Paul quotes Ps. 32:2 in Rom. 4:8 (*see* RECKON). The RSV does not use "impute" for any word in the NT. The AV uses "impute" for both *ḥāšaḇ* (Lev. 17:4; Ps. 32:2) and *logízomai* (Rom. 4:6, 8; etc.) (cf. "count" in Gen. 15:6; Rom. 4:3; etc.). The NEB has "count" (Gen. 15:6; Rom. 4:3f., 6; etc.), "held guilty" (Lev. 17:4), and "account" (Ps. 32:2).

These synonyms of the verb "impute" bring out the idea of reckoning or charging to one's account. It makes no difference, so far as the meaning of imputation is concerned, who it is that imputes, whether man (1 S. 22:15) or God (Ps. 32:2); it makes no difference what is imputed, whether a good deed for reward (Ps. 106:30f.) or a bad deed for punishment (Lev. 17:4); and it makes no difference whether that which is imputed is something which is personally one's own prior to the imputation, as in the case above cited, where his own good deed was imputed to Phinehas (Ps. 106:30f.), or something which is not personally one's own prior to the imputation, as where Paul asks that a debt not personally his own be charged to him (Philem. 18). In all these cases the act of imputation is simply the charging of one with something. It denotes just what we mean by our ordinary use of the term. It does not change the inward state or character of the person to whom something is imputed. When, for example, we say that we impute bad motives to anyone, we do not mean that we make such a one bad; and just so in the Scripture the phrase "to impute iniquity" does not mean to make one personally bad, but simply to lay iniquity to his charge. Hence when God is said "to impute sin" to anyone, the meaning is that God accounts such a one to be a sinner, and consequently guilty and liable to punishment. Similarly, the non-imputation of sin means simply not to lay it to one's charge as a ground of punishment (Ps. 32:2). In the same manner, when God is said "to impute righteousness" to a person, the meaning is that He judicially accounts such a one to be righteous and entitled to all the rewards of a righteous person (Rom. 4:6, 11).

II. The Threefold Use of the Term in Theology.–Three acts of imputation are given special prominence in the Scripture, and are implicated in the scriptural doctrines of original sin, atonement, and justification, though not usually expressed by the words *ḥāšaḇ* and *logízomai.* Because, however, of its "forensic" or "judicial" meaning, and possibly through its use in the Vulg. to translate *logízomai* in Rom. 4:8, the term "imputation" has been used in theology in a threefold sense to denote the judicial acts of God by which the guilt of Adam's sin is imputed to his posterity; by which the sins of Christ's people are imputed to Him; and by which the righteousness of Christ is imputed to His people. The act of imputation is precisely the same in each case. It is not meant that Adam's sin was personally the sin of his descendants, but that it was set to their account, so that they share its guilt and penalty. It is not meant that Christ shares personally in people's sins, but that the guilt of His people's sin was set to His account, so that He bore its penalty. It is not meant that Christ's people are made personally holy or inwardly righteous by the imputation of His righteousness to them, but that His righteousness is set to their account, so that they are entitled to all the rewards of that perfect righteousness.

These doctrines have had a place in the theology of the Christian Church from the earliest Christian cents., though the doctrine of the imputation of the righteousness of Christ was first fully and clearly stated at the time of and following the Reformation. The first two of these doctrines have been the possession of the entire Christian Church, while the third one of them is affirmed by both the Reformed and Lutheran branches of Protestantism.

III. The Scriptural Basis of These Doctrines.–These three doctrines have a basis in the Scripture, and underlie the Scripture doctrines of original sin, atonement, and justification.

A. Imputation of Adam's Sin to His Posterity. The doctrine of the imputation of Adam's sin to his posterity is implied in the account of the fall in Gen. 2 and 3, taken in connection with the subsequent history of the human race as recorded in Genesis and in the rest of the OT. Many ancient and modern interpreters regard this narrative as an allegorical, mythical, or symbolical representation in historical form, either of a psychological fact, i.e., of something which takes place in every individual, or of certain general truths concerning sin. By some exegetes, following Kant, it has been held to depict an advance of the race in culture or ethical knowledge (but see Clemen); by others it has been regarded as a symbolical representation of certain truths concerning sin (Oehler, Schultz); by others it has been regarded as historical (KD, I, 28-32). This latter view is the one which accords with the narrative itself. It is evidently intended as historical by its author, and is so regarded by the NT writers. It is, moreover, introduced to explain, not an advance of the race, but the entrance of sin into the world, and the connection of certain penal evils with sin. It does this by showing how these evils came upon Adam as a punishment for his disobedience, and the subsequent history shows that his posterity were subjected to the same evils. It is true that the threat of punishment to Adam in case of disobedience was made to him alone, and that the penalties threatened are said to have come only upon him and Eve (Gen. 3:16-19). Nevertheless, it is clear from the account of the subsequent history of the race that it actually shared in the punishments inflicted upon Adam, and that this was in consequence of his sin. This implies that in Gen. 2:16f. are contained the terms of a covenant in which Adam acted as the representative of the race. If, therefore, the race shares in the penalty of Adam's sin, it must also share in his guilt or the judicial obligation to suffer punishment. And this is precisely what the theology of the entire Christian Church has meant by saying that the guilt of Adam's sin was imputed to his posterity. This is in accordance with God's method of dealing with people in other recorded instances (Gen. 19:15; Ex. 20:5; Dt. 1:37; 3:26); and the assertion of the principle of personal responsibility by Ezekiel and Jeremiah against an abuse of the principle of representative responsibility implies a recognition of the latter (Ezk. 18:2, 4; 33:12; Jer. 31:29).

The universality of sin and death is not brought into connection with the fall of Adam by the other OT writers. This is done, however, by Paul. In 1 Cor. 15:21f., Paul says that the death of all people has its cause in the man Adam in the same way in which the resurrection from the dead has its cause in the man Christ. The death of all people, accordingly, is not brought about by their personal sins, but has come upon all through the disobedience of Adam. Upon what ground this takes place, Paul states in the passage Rom. 5:12-21. He introduces the subject of Adam's relation to the race to illustrate his doctrine of the justification of sinners on the ground of a righteousness which is not personally their own. In order to do this he takes the truth, well known to his readers, that all people are under condemnation on account of Adam's sin. The comparison is between Adam and Christ, and the specific point of the comparison is imputed sin and imputed righteousness. Hence in v. 12 Paul does not mean simply to affirm that as Adam sinned and consequently died, so people sin and die. Nor can he mean to say that just as God established a precedent in Adam's case that death should follow sin, so He acts upon this precedent in the case of all people because all people sin, the real ground of the reign of death being the fact that all people sin, and the formal ground being this precedent (B. Weiss); nor that the real ground is this precedent and the subordinate ground the fact that all people sin (Hünefeld). Neither can Paul intend to say that all people are subject to death because they derive a corrupt nature from Adam (Fritzsche); nor that people are condemned to die because all have sinned (Pfleiderer). Paul's purpose is to illustrate his doctrine of the way in which people are delivered from sin and death by the way in which they are brought into condemnation. The main thought of the passage is that, just as people are condemned on account of the imputation to them of the guilt of Adam's sin, so they are justified on account of the imputation to them of the righteousness of Christ. Paul says that it was by one man that sin and death entered into the world, and it was by one man that death passed to all, because all were implicated in the guilt of that one man's sin (v. 12). In proof of this the apostle cites the fact that death as a punishment was reigning during a period in which the only possible judicial ground of this fact must have been the imputation of the guilt of that one man's sin (vv. 13f.). Hence there is a precise parallel between Adam and Christ. Just as people are condemned on account of Adam's disobedience, so they are justified on account of the obedience of Christ (vv. 18f.). The thought of the passage is imputed sin and imputed righteousness as the ground of condemnation and of justification respectively.

B. Imputation of the Sins of His People to Christ. That our sins are imputed to Christ is not expressly stated in the Scripture, but is implied in those passages which affirm that Christ "bore our sins," and that our iniquities were "laid upon him" by the Lord. To bear iniquity or sin, though it may sometimes mean to bear it away or remove it, is an expression often applied in Scripture to persons charged with guilt and subjected to the punishment of their own sin (Lev. 5:17; 7:18; 19:8; 22:9). That the Heb. verb *nāśā'* has this meaning is also indicated by its being interchanged with the verb *sāḇal*, which means "to bear as a burden" and is used to denote the bearing of the punishment of sin (Isa. 53:11). In the OT sacrificial system, which according to the NT is typical of the sacrifice of Christ, the imposition of hands on the head of the victim signified the substitution of it for the offender and the transfer of his guilt to it. This idea is brought out clearly in the case of the two goats on the great Day of Atonement (Lev. 16). When, therefore, the Servant of the Lord in Isa. 53 is said "to bear iniquity" (v. 11), or that "the chastisement of our peace was upon him" (v. 5, AV), or that "the Lord has laid [lit. "caused to fall"] on him the iniquity of us all" (v. 6), the idea expressed is that Christ bore the punishment of our sin vicariously, its guilt having been imputed to Him. The thought of the prophecy is, as Delitzsch says, that of vicarious punishment, which implies the idea of the imputation of the guilt of our sins to Christ.

The same idea underlies these expressions when they occur in the NT. When Peter wishes to hold up Christ as an example of patience in suffering, he takes up the thought of Isaiah, and adduces the fact that Christ "himself bore our sins in his body upon the tree" (1 Pet. 2:24). The context indicates that Peter had the prophecy of Isa. 53 in mind, so that his meaning is, not that Christ carried our sins even up to the cross, but that in His death on the cross Christ bore the punishment of our sin, its guilt having been imputed to Him. The same thought is expressed by the writer of Hebrews, where the contrast between the first and second advents of Christ is made to hinge upon the fact that in the first He came to be sacrificed as a sinbearer, burdened with the guilt of the sin of others, whereas in His second coming He will appear without this burden of imputed or vicarious guilt (He. 9:28). Paul also gives expression to the same thought when he says that God made Christ "to be sin" (2 Cor. 5:21), and that He became "a curse for us" (Gal. 3:13). In the former passage the idea of substitution, although not expressed by the preposition *hypér* which indicates that Christ's work was for our benefit, is nevertheless clearly implied in the thought that Christ, whose sinlessness is emphasized in the verse, is made sin, and that we sinners become righteous in Him. Paul means that Christ was made to bear the penalty of our sin and that its guilt was imputed to Him in precisely the same way in which we sinners become the righteousness of God in Him, i.e., by the imputation of His righteousness to us. The same thought is expressed in Gal. 3:13, where the statement that Christ was made a curse for us means that He was made to endure the curse or penalty of the broken law. In all these passages the underlying thought is that the guilt of our sin was imputed to Christ.

C. Imputation of the Righteousness of Christ to His People. The righteousness upon the ground of which God justifies the ungodly is, according to Paul, witnessed to in the OT (Rom. 3:21). In order to obtain the blessedness which comes from a right relation to God, the pardon or nonimputation of sin is necessary, and this takes place through the "covering" of sin (Ps. 32:1f.). The nature of this covering by the vicarious bearing of the penalty of sin is made clear in Isa. 53. It is, moreover, the teaching of the OT that the righteousness which God demands is not to be found among people (Ps. 130:3; 143:2; Isa. 64:6). Accordingly, the prophets speak of a righteousness which is not from human works, but which is said to be in the Lord or to come from Him to His people (Isa. 32:16f.; 45:23f.; 54:17; 58:8; 61:3; Jer. 51:10; Hos. 10:12). This idea finds its clearest expression in connection with the work of the Messiah in Jer. 33:16, where Jerusalem is called "the Lord is our righteousness" because of the coming of the messianic king, and in Jer. 23:6 where the same name is given to the Messiah to express His significance for Israel. Although the idea of the imputation of righteousness is not explicitly asserted in these passages, the idea is not merely that the righteousness spoken of is recognized by the Lord (Cremer), but that it comes from Him, so that the Lord, through the work of the Messiah, is the source of His people's righteousness.

This idea is taken up by Paul, who makes explicit the way in which this righteousness comes to sinners, and who puts the idea of imputed righteousness at the basis of his doctrine of justification. By the righteousness of Christ Paul means Christ's legal status, or the merit acquired by all that He did in satisfying the demands of God's law, including what has been called His active and passive obedience. Notwithstanding the fact that some of the modern expositors of Paul's doctrine have denied that he teaches the imputation of Christ's obedience, this doctrine has a basis in the apostle's teaching. Justification leads to life and final glorification (Rom. 5:18; 8:30); and Paul always conceives the obtaining of life as dependent on the fulfillment of the law. If, therefore, Christ secures life for us, it can only be in accordance with this principle. Accordingly, the apostle emphasizes the element of obedience in the death of Christ, and places this act of obedience at the basis of the sinner's justification (Rom. 5:18). He also represents the obedience of the cross as the culminating point of a life of obedience on Christ's part (Phil. 2:8). Moreover, Paul affirms that our redemption from all the demands of the law is secured by the fact that Christ was born under law (Gal. 4:4). This cannot be restricted to the fact that Christ was under the curse of the law, for He was born under law and the result of this is that we are free from all of its demands. This doctrine is also implied in the apostle's teaching that justification is absolutely gracious, taken in connection with the fact that it leads to a complete salvation.

The importance in Paul's thought of the doctrine of the imputation of the righteousness of Christ to the believer can be seen from the fact that the question how righteousness was to be obtained occupied a central place in his religious consciousness, both before and after his conversion. The apostle's conversion by the appearance of the risen Christ determined his conception of the true way of obtaining righteousness, since the resurrection of Christ meant for Paul the condemnation of his entire past search for righteousness by works of the law.

That the imputation of the righteousness of Christ to the believer does lie at the basis of Paul's doctrine of justification can be further seen from the fact that justification is absolutely free and unmerited so far as the sinner is concerned (Rom. 3:24; 5:15; Gal. 5:4; Tit. 3:7); its object being one who is ungodly (Rom. 4:5); so that it is not by works (Rom. 3:20, 28; Gal. 2:16; 3:11; 5:4; Phil. 3:9); and yet that it is not a mere pardon of sin, but is a strictly "forensic" or judicial judgment, freeing the sinner from all the claims of the law, and granting him the right to eternal life. This last truth is plain because God's retributive righteousness lies at the basis of Paul's doctrine of justification (Rom. 2); is manifested in it (Rom. 3:25f.); because Christ's expiatory work is its ground (Rom. 3:25); and because our redemption from the curse of the law rests upon Christ's having borne it for us, and our redemption from all the demands of the law depends upon their fulfillment by Christ (Gal. 3:13; 4:4). Hence the gracious character of justification, according to Paul, does not consist in its being merely a gracious pardon without any judicial basis (Ritschl); or in God's acceptance of a subjective righteousness produced by Him in the sinner (Tobac); or in the acceptance of faith instead of a perfect righteousness (Cremer). The gracious character of justification consists for Paul in the fact that the righteousness on the ground of which God justifies the ungodly is a righteousness which is graciously provided by God, and which Paul contrasts with his own righteousness which comes from works of the law (Phil. 3:9). The sinner, therefore, is pardoned and accepted as a righteous person, not on account of anything in himself, but only on account of what Christ has done for him, which means that the merits of Christ's suffering and obedience are imputed to the sinner as the ground of his justification.

This truth is explicitly affirmed by Paul, who speaks of God's imputing righteousness without works, and of righteousness being imputed (Rom. 4:6, 11). The idea of the imputation of righteousness here is made clear by the context. The one who is declared righteous is said to be "ungodly" (4:5). Hence he is righteous only by God's imputation of righteousness to him. This is also clear from the contrast between imputation according to grace and according to debt (4:4). He who seeks righteousness by works would be justified as a reward for his works, in antithesis to which, imputation according to grace would be the charging one with a righteousness which he does not possess. Accordingly, at the basis of justification there is a reckoning to the sinner of an objective righteousness. This same idea is also implied and asserted by Paul in the parallel which he draws between Adam and Christ (Rom. 5:18f.). The apostle says that just as people are condemned on account of a sin not their own, so they are justified on account of a righteousness which is not their own. The idea of imputed sin and imputed righteousness, as was said, is the precise point of the parallelism between condemnation in Adam and justification in Christ. This is also the idea which underlies the apostle's contrast of the Old and New Covenants (2 Cor. 3:9). The New Covenant is described as a "dispensation of righteousness," and contrasted with the Old Covenant, which is described as a "dispensation of condemnation." If, therefore, this last expression does not denote a subjective condition of people under the old dispensation, but their relation to God as objects of His condemnation, righteousness must denote the opposite of this relation to the law, and must depend on God's judicial acquittal. The same truth is expressed by Paul more concretely by saying that Christ has been "made unto us righteousness from God" (1 Cor. 1:30). Here the concrete mode of expression is chosen because Paul speaks also of Christ being our sanctification and redemption, so that an expression had to be chosen which would cover all of these ideas. One of the clearest statements concerning this objective righteousness is Phil. 3:9. The apostle here affirms that the righteousness which the believer in Christ obtains is directly opposite to his own righteousness. This latter comes from works of the law, whereas the former comes from God and through faith in Christ. It is, therefore, objective to mankind, comes to him from God, is connected with the work of Christ, and is mediated by faith in Christ.

The idea clearly stated in this last passage of a righteousness which is objective to the sinner and which comes to him from God, i.e., the idea of a new legal standing given to the believer by God, explains the meaning, in most cases, of the Pauline phrase "righteousness of God." This phrase is used by Paul nine times: Rom. 1:17; 3:5, 21-26; 10:3 (twice); 2 Cor. 5:21. It denotes the divine attribute of righteousness in Rom. 3:5, 25f. The customary exegesis was to regard the other instances as denoting the righteousness of a sinner that comes to him from God, in accordance with Phil. 3:9. Häring, following Kölbing in general, interpreted all these instances as denoting God's justifying action. But this interpretation is most strained in 2 Cor. 5:21, where we are said to "become the righteousness of God," and in Rom. 10:3-6, where the righteousness of God is identified with the righteousness which comes from faith, this latter being contrasted with a person's own inward righteousness. That a righteousness of man which he receives from God is here referred to, is confirmed by the fact that the reason given for the error of the Jews in seeking a righteousness from law works is the fact that the work of Christ has made an end of this method of obtaining righteousness (Rom. 10:4). This righteousness, therefore, is one of which man is the possessor. The phrase, however, cannot mean a righteousness which is valid in God's sight (Luther), although this thought is elsewhere expressed by Paul (Rom. 3:20; Gal. 3:11). It means a righteousness which comes from God and of which He is the author. This is not, however, by making man inwardly righteous, since all the above passages show the purely objective character of this righteousness. It is the righteousness of Phil. 3:9; the righteousness which God imputes to the believer in Christ. Thus we "become the righteousness of God" in precisely the same sense in which God made Christ to be sin (2 Cor. 5:21). Since Christ was made sin by having the guilt of our sin imputed to Him so that He bore its penalty, Paul must mean that we "become the righteousness of God" in this same objective sense through the imputation to us of the righteousness of Christ. In the same way, in Rom. 10:3, the contrast between God's righteousness and the Jew's righteousness by works of the law shows that in each case righteousness denotes a legal status which comes from God by imputation. It is this same imputed righteousness which makes the gospel the power of God unto salvation (Rom. 1:17), which has been revealed by the law and the prophets, which is received by faith in Christ by whose expiatory death God's retributive righteousness has been made manifest (Rom. 3:21f., 25f.), and which is represented by Peter as the object of Christian faith (2 Pet. 1:1).

In two passages Paul affirms that Abraham believed God and "it was reckoned to him for righteousness" (Rom. 4:3; Gal. 3:6). The old Arminian theologians, and some modern exegetes (H. Cremer) assert that Paul means that Abraham's faith was accepted by God instead of a perfect righteousness as the meritorious ground of his justification. This, however, cannot be the apostle's meaning. It is diametrically opposed to the context where Paul introduces the case of Abraham for the very purpose of proving that he was justified without any merit on his part; it is opposed to Paul's idea of the nature of faith which involves the renunciation of all claim to merit, and is a simple resting on Christ from whom all its saving efficacy is derived; and this interpretation is also opposed to Paul's doctrine of the absolutely gracious character of justification. The apostle in these passages wishes to illustrate from the case of Abraham the gracious character of justification, and quotes the untechnical language of Gen. 15:6. His meaning is simply that Abraham was justified as a believer in God, and not as one who sought righteousness by works. *See* SIN; ATONE; JUSTIFICATION; RECKON.

Bibliography.–Biblical: T. Häring, Δικαιοσύνη θεοῦ *bei Paulus* (1896); Kölbing, *Theologische Studien und Kritiken* (1895), pp. 7-51; G. E. Ladd, *Theology of the NT* (1974), pp. 449f.; L. Morris, *Apostolic Preaching of the Cross* (3rd ed. 1965); G. F. Oehler, *Theology of the OT* (Eng. tr. 1883), pp. 158-164; H. Schultz, *OT Theology* (Eng. tr. 1892), II, 292-320; B. Weiss, *Biblical Theology of the NT,* I (Eng. tr. 1882), 437-447.

Theological: Original Sin: H. Bavinck, *Our Reasonable Faith* (Eng. tr., repr. 1978), pp. 224-230, 240-46; G. C. Berkouwer, *Sin* (Eng. tr. 1971), pp. 436-465; Calvin *Inst.* ii.1.5-9; C. C. Clemen, *Die christliche Lehre von der Sünde,* I (1897), 151-179; Hünefeld, *Rom 5 12-21* (1895); J. Murray, *Imputation of Adam's Sin* (1959); H. Ridderbos, *Paul: An Outline of His Theology* (Eng. tr. 1975), pp. 174-78.

Atonement: T. J. Crawford, *Doctrine of Holy Scripture Respecting the Atonement* (2nd ed. 1874), pp. 33-45, 188-190.

Justification: H. Bavinck, *Our Reasonable Faith,* pp. 455-461; H. Cremer, *Paulinische Rechtfertigungslehre im Zusammenhange ihrer geschichtlichen Voraussetzungen* (2nd printing 1900), pp. 329-349; M. Luther, *Lectures on Romans* (*LCC,* XV, 1961); O. Pfleiderer, *Zeitschrift für wissenschaftliche Theologie* (1872), 161-200; A. B. Ritschl, *Christian Doctrine of Justification and Reconciliation* (Eng. tr., 3rd ed. 1966), pp. 86-93; Tobac, *Le Problème de la justification dans saint Paul* (1908), pp. 206-225.

C. W. HODGE

IMRAH im'ra [Heb. *yimrâ*]. A descendant of Asher (1 Ch. 7:36).

IMRI im'rī [Heb. *'imrî*].

1. A Judahite (1 Ch. 9:4).

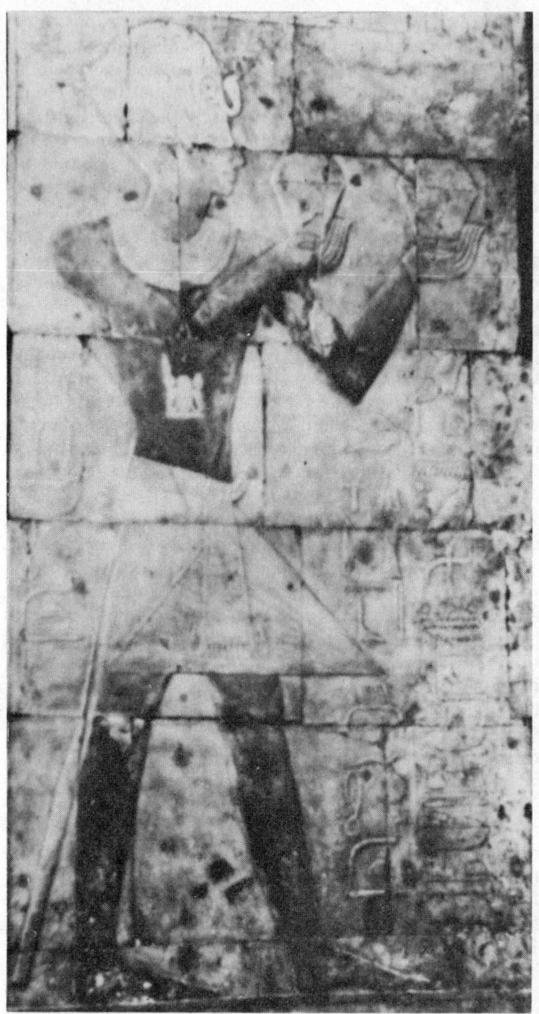

Thutmose III offering incense to Amon. Relief from the temple of Hatshepsut at Deir el-Baḥri (early 15th cent. B.C.) (Royal Ontario Museum, Toronto; picture A. C. Myers)

2. Father of Zaccur who helped to rebuild the walls of Jerusalem under Nehemiah (Neh. 3:2).

IN THE LORD [Gk. *en Kyriō*]. A favorite Pauline expression, denoting intimate union and fellowship of the Christian with the Lord Jesus Christ that supplies the basis of all Christian relations and conduct, and the distinctive element that gives the Christian life its specific character. Cf. the synonymous Pauline phrases "in Christ," "in Christ Jesus," and the Johannine expressions "being in Christ," "abiding in Christ." "In the Lord" denotes: (1) the motive, quality, or character of a Christian duty or virtue, as based on union with Christ, e.g., "Free to be married to whom she wishes, only in the Lord" (1 Cor. 7:39), i.e., provided the marriage is consistent with the Christian life (cf. 1 Cor. 15:58; Phil. 3:1; 4:1f., 4, 10; Eph. 6:1, 10; Col. 3:18; etc.); (2) the ground of Christian unity, fellowship, and brotherly salutation, e.g., Rom. 16:2, 8, 22; 1 Cor. 16:19; Col. 4:7; (3) by implication "Christian" (noun or adj.), "as Christians," or "as a Christian," e.g., "Greet those in the Lord who belong to the family of Narcissus" (Rom. 16:13); 1 Cor. 9:1f.; Eph. 6:21 ("faithful minister in the Lord" = faithful Christian minister); Col. 4:17 (see Bauer, rev., pp. 259f.). D. M. EDWARDS

INCARNATION. *See* PERSON OF CHRIST.

INCENSE [Heb. *qᵉṭōreṯ, qᵉṭôrâ* (Dt. 33:10), *qiṭṭēr* (Jer. 44:21), *muqṭār* (Mal. 1:11)]; AV also PERFUME (Ex. 30:35), SACRIFICE (2 Ch. 2:6); NEB also SACRIFICE, FRAGRANT SACRIFICE, SMOKE OF SACRIFICE, REEK OF SACRIFICE, OFFERINGS, SMOKE OFFERINGS, etc.; [*lᵉḇônâ*] (1 Ch. 9:29; Jer. 41:5); AV also FRANKINCENSE (1 Ch. 9:29); NEB also FRANKINCENSE (Jer. 41:5); [Aram. *nîḥô(a)ḥ*] (Dnl. 2:46); AV SWEET ODOURS; NEB SOOTHING OFFERINGS; [Gk. *thymíama, thymiáō*]; AV ODOURS (Rev. 5:8); [*thymiatḗrion*] ALTAR OF INCENSE (He. 9:4); AV CENSER. Aromatic resins or spices, usually compounded; known to the Bible as an element of cultic worship — and of the secular "good life" as well (Ps. 45:8 [MT 9]; Prov. 7:17; 27:9; Cant. 3:6; cf. Mish. *Berakoth* vi.6).

I. In the Ancient Near East
II. In the Priestly Code
III. In the First Temple
IV. In the Second Temple

Limestone incense burners (3rd-1st cents. B.C.) with South Arabic inscriptions (University Museum, University of Pennsylvania)

I. In the Ancient Near East.–Egyptian use of incense can be traced back to the 5th Dynasty (2494-2345 B.C.). The Egyptians imported some aromatics from Nubia; others — myrrh, and the still more popular frankincense — came from south Arabia and north Somaliland.

With the establishment of overland trading routes toward the end of the 2nd millennium, south Arabia became the incense land par excellence. The Queen of Sheba brought "spices" (*beśāmîm*) to Solomon (1 K. 10:2, 10); Isa. 60:6 and Jer. 6:20 speak of the frankincense of Sheba; Abraham's Arabian concubine is appropriately named Keturah, "incense" (*qeṭûrâ*) in Gen. 25:1-6. Cuneiform sources suggest that the Mesopotamians normally burned aromatic woods (cypress, cedar) rather than incense; yet Herodotus (i.183) claims that "the Chaldeans offer something like two and a half tons of frankincense every year at the festival of Bel." The earliest Greek allusion to incense (frankincense, *libanōtós*) dates from the 6th cent. (Xenophanes 1.7).

The south Arabian states grew rich on the enormous popularity of frankincense and myrrh in the Greco-Roman world (cf. Rev. 18:13). Transportation costs increased the price; G. Van Beek has calculated that in the 1st cent. A.D. frankincense cost the equivalent of $87.50 to $175.00 (1964 values) per pound, depending on its quality. Mt. 2:11 considers frankincense and myrrh, like gold, gifts fit for an infant king.

II. In the Priestly Code.–Most of the biblical passages dealing with incense occur in the priestly stratum (P) of the Pentateuch, which regards it as an important element of the Mosaic cult. Its recipe, in which frankincense is the chief ingredient, is revealed by God Himself (Ex. 30:34-36; cf. 37:29; 1 Ch. 9:30); no secular use may be made of it (vv. 37f.). Conversely, no other compound may be burned upon the incense altar (Ex. 30:9; see below). Incense may be offered only by a descendant of Aaron (Nu. 16:35, 40; cf. 2 Ch. 26:16-21), and only the proper fire may be used for it (presumably, fire from the altar of whole offering; Lev. 10:1f.; cf. 16:12; Nu. 16:46); violation of these restrictions brings the most drastic punishment (Nu. 16:35; cf. 2 Ch. 26:19).

P specifies two fixed incense offerings: (1) the *tāmîḏ* ("perpetual") incense, burned every morning and evening upon the altar of incense (Ex. 30:7f.); (2) the censer offering, performed by the high priest in the holy of holies once every year, on the Day of Atonement (Lev. 16:2, 12f.). We may mention also the burning of frankincense (Heb. *leḇônâ*) with vegetable offerings (Lev. 2:1f., 15f.; 6:15 [MT 8]; 24:7; expressly omitted in Lev. 5:11; Nu. 5:15). Elsewhere, incense is offered *ad hoc*: to test the legitimacy of priestly claimants (Nu. 16:5-7, 16-18); to halt a plague (vv. 46-48); even — if this may be gathered from Lev. 10:1f. — as a spontaneous expression of joy and devotion.

One might suppose that the purpose of the incense was to offer the deity the aromas enjoyed by His worshipers — or, perhaps, to mitigate the stench of the burning sacrifices. But neither assumption finds support in P. Incense is never mentioned in connection with animal sacrifices; P's recurring phrase, "a soothing odor for the Lord" (*rê(a)ḥ nîḥô(a)ḥ leYHWH*), is normally applied to the smoke of animal sacrifice, never to incense. Two passages (Lev. 16:13; cf. v. 2; Nu. 16:46-48) suggest that the cloud of incense smoke serves to protect people from the dangers inherent in contact with the holy.

Exodus 30:1-10 prescribes a gold-plated incense ALTAR to be set up in the tabernacle for the burning of the *tāmîḏ* incense (cf. Lev. 4:7, 18; it is called "the golden altar" in Ex. 40:5, 26). Literary critics argue that the passages referring to the incense altar belong to a secondary stratum of P — note the silence of Ex. 26:35; Lev. 16:11-20. (This *literary* question is not the same as the *historical* question of the existence of such an altar; see below.) In the main stratum, incense is offered in censers (*maḥtâ*, Lev. 16:12; cf. *miqṭereṯ*, Ezk. 8:11), assumed to be in the possession of priests (Lev. 10:1) and laymen (Nu. 16:6, 17, 38); they may have been shaped like coal shovels or even cups. The "dishes for incense" (Ex. 25:29, etc.; Heb. *kap*, lit. "palm"; AV "spoons"; NEB "saucers") seem to have been containers for incense, rather than instruments for burning it (Nu. 7:14, 20, etc.; *see* INCENSE, DISH FOR).

III. In the First Temple.–As the view became widespread that P was the latest of the pentateuchal documents, hardly to be dated before the early second temple period, the history of incense in the Israelite cult underwent a radical revision. From the silence of such passages as Am. 4:4f.; 5:21f.; Isa. 1:11-13; Mic. 6:6f., J. Wellhausen argued that incense was unknown in Israel before the late 7th cent. B.C., when it began to figure in the polemics of Jeremiah (6:20; cf. 41:5) as "a rare and far-fetched offering." Not until after the Exile did it acquire the importance attributed to it by P.

Wellhausen did not deny that nouns and verbs from the root *qṭr* occur frequently in preexilic literature; but he held that they refer to the burning of animal or vegetable offerings, not incense. The first meaning is in fact clear in 1 S. 2:15f.; 1 K. 12:33; 13:1f.; 2 K. 16:13, 15; Ps. 66:15; the second in Am. 4:5; Jer. 33:18; 44:19 (cf. 7:18). We do not find an unambiguous use of *qṭr* for incense before Ezekiel (8:11; 16:18; 23:41; but cf. Prov. 27:9; Cant. 3:6; and the name Keturah). In such important passages as Dt. 33:10; 1 S. 2:28; Isa. 1:13, *qeṭōreṯ*/*qeṭôrâ* may thus be translated, according to predilection, either "incense" or "smoke of sacrifice." (Wellhausen's "argument from silence" is surely somewhat circular: it requires the assumption that *qeṭōreṯ* in Isa. 1:13 refers to animal or vegetable offerings, an assumption which in turn rests on the premise that incense was not a part of the contemporary cult.)

Wellhausen's hypothesis is not without influence today (it evidently underlies the NEB's renderings of *qṭr* — "incense" in the Pentateuch [except Dt. 33:10], Chronicles [sometimes], Ps. 141:2; Isa. 40–66; Ezekiel; but "sacrifice," "offering," etc. in Dt. 33:10; Samuel-Kings, Chronicles [sometimes], Isa. 1–39, Jeremiah, Hosea, Habakkuk, and Malachi), but it is generally out of favor. Most scholars accept the late dating of P (Y. Kaufmann is a notable exception), but do not believe that P's *material* must therefore be late. Indeed, it is hardly likely that incense was a novelty in Jeremiah's time: early Israelite trade with south Arabia is indicated by the story of Solomon and the Queen of Sheba, and confirmed by a south Arabian clay stamp discovered in the ruins of Bethel.

Archeologists have unearthed a number of small, stone altars in Palestine, generally dating from the 8th to the 6th century. The top is square, flat (or with a shallow depression), and often has a "horn" at each corner (cf. Ex. 30:2). *See* pictures in ALTAR; HORNS OF THE ALTAR. On the basis of Nabatean parallels, many scholars identify these altars with the mysterious *ḥammānîm*, which are mentioned disapprovingly in several biblical passages (Lev. 26:30; Ezk. 6:4; etc.; RSV, NEB, "incense altars"; AV "images," "idols"). It is generally agreed that they were used for burning incense. This does not quite prove that incense was part of any official Israelite cult; the objects may have been used for secular incense burning or as part of a pagan (or at least unauthorized) cult — as the biblical condemnation of *ḥammānîm* may indicate. But these discoveries have led scholars to question the view

Side panel of an incense altar from Khirbet et-Tannur SE of the Dead Sea. Winged Tyche holds a palm branch and wreath (E. K. Vogel; picture American Schools of Oriental Research)

that the priestly incense altar is a baseless fabrication, and that the allusions to a gold-plated altar (presumably for incense) standing inside Solomon's temple (1 K. 6:20f.; 7:48; cf. 2 Ch. 26:16, 19) are interpolations based on P. Isa. 6:6 seems to assume an altar *inside* the temple, therefore *not* the altar of whole offering (and cf. the "smoke," v. 4). W. F. Albright has conjectured that Jachin and Boaz, the pillars flanking the entrance to the temple, were gigantic incense burners patterned after Canaanite models.

A letter written by the Jews of Elephantine (408 B.C.) speaks of frankincense (Aram. *l^eḇônṯâ*) as an element of the temple cult, alongside whole offerings and vegetable offerings; this may reflect preexilic Israelite practice (cf. Jer. 41:5).

IV. In the Second Temple.–Use of incense in the second temple is attested by postexilic writings (Neh. 13:5, 9; 1 Ch. 9:29f.; cf. Isa. 66:3), the Apocrypha (1 Macc. 4:49f.; 2 Macc. 10:3; Song Three 15), and the NT (Lk. 1:8-11). The Mishnah gives vivid and circumstantial descriptions of the *tāmîḏ* incense offering (*Tamid* ii.5; v.2–vi.3), and that of the Day of Atonement (*Yoma* v.1; vii.4). These accounts presumably reflect second temple practice; yet the anachronistic reference to the ark in *Yoma* v.1 (cf. T.B. *Yoma* 52b) suggests that some details may derive from biblical exegesis rather than historical recollection (compare Mish. *Menahoth* xi.5 to Josephus *Ant.* iii.10.7 [255-57]).

Even if Ex. 30:7f. intends that only the high priest may offer the *tāmîḏ* incense, no such provision was in force in NT times. The Mishnah provides that he may perform the ritual whenever he desires but is required to do so only on the Day of Atonement and the seven days preceding it (*Yoma* i.2; iii.4f.; vii.4; cf. Josephus *Ant.* xiii.10.3 [282]). Normally, the office was assigned by lot (Lk. 1:9; *Tamid* v.2; *Yoma* ii.4); it was highly desirable (later rabbis explained that it brought prosperity) and could not be performed more than once by any one priest (T.B. *Yoma* 26a). Stories in Josephus (*Ant.* xiii.10.3 [282]) and the NT (Lk. 1:8-23) suggest that the solitary officiant might be favored with a divine revelation. Both Josephus and Luke (1:10, 21f.) have a crowd of people waiting "outside" for the priest. The Mishnah confirms that the priest must be alone (*Tamid* vi.3; *Kelim* i.9; cf. Lev. 16:17); when the ritual is completed, his fellow priests enter the temple to worship, then emerge and bless the people (*Tamid* vii.1f.).

The censer offering of the Day of Atonement was the focus of a controversy between the Pharisees and the Sadducees: the former held that the high priest must enter the holy of holies before he puts the incense on the coals, the latter the reverse (T.B. *Yoma* 53a). Terrifying stories were told of a high priest who flouted the Pharisaic norm: he was found dead in the temple (according to one version), his face to the ground, the imprint of a calf's foot (Ezk. 1:7) between his shoulders (T.B. *Yoma* 19b; cf. T.P. *Yoma* i.5; *Sukkah* iv.6). The root of the controversy remains obscure; J. Z. Lauterbach suggests that the Sadducees, against the Pharisees, believed that the deity made Himself visible in the holy of holies on the Day of Atonement (Lev. 16:2).

Exodus 30:34 specifies four ingredients for the incense; Josephus (*BJ* v.5.5 [218]) speaks of "thirteen spices from sea and land"; T.B. *Kerithoth* 6a lists eleven major and five minor components, all indispensable (6b). One ingredient, the "smoke-raiser," is said to have been the secret of the Abtinas family, who thereby had a monopoly on incense (*Yoma* iii.11; T.B. *Yoma* 38a; T.P. *Yoma* iii.9; *Shekalim* v.1). The incense was compounded in the temple area, but it was so pungent that (the Mishnah claims) "people could smell it in Jericho. R. Eliezer b. Daglai said, 'When they compounded the incense my father's goats on Mt. Machwar [on the other side of the Jordan] used to sneeze'" (*Tamid* iii.8).

See also FRANKINCENSE; MYRRH.

Bibliography.–*Ancient World:* G. Van Beek, "Frankincense and Myrrh," in E. Campbell and D. N. Freedman, eds., *Biblical Archaeologist Reader,* II (1964), 99-126.

Priestly Code: M. Haran, *VT,* 10 (1960), 113-129.

First Temple: W. F. Albright, *ARI,* pp. 144-48; R. de Vaux, *Ancient Israel* (Eng. tr. 1961), pp. 286, 411, 423, 430-32; *IDB,* II, *s.v.* "Incense Altar" (K. Galling); N. Glueck, "Incense Altars," in H. Frank and W. Reed, eds., *Translating and Understanding the OT* (1970), pp. 325-339; M. Löhr, *Das Räucheropfer im AT* (1927); J. Wellhausen, *Prolegomena to the History of Ancient Israel* (Eng. tr. 1957), pp. 64-67.

Second Temple: J. Z. Lauterbach, *Rabbinic Essays* (1951), pp. 51-83.

D. J. HALPERIN

INCENSE ALTAR. *See* INCENSE; ALTAR I.A.2; III.B.

INCENSE, DISH FOR [Heb. *kap*–'palm (of the hand)']. A golden dish or shallow bowl which held incense in the Israelite tabernacle and temple. Heb. *kap* usually denotes the "hand," or more specifically the "palm." Therefore when this word is used for a vessel of the sanctuary, it suggests a dish (RSV Ex. 25:29; 37:16; etc.) somewhat like a cupped hand and so moderately shallow, or possibly a "spoon" (AV Ex. 25:29; etc.). The use of the word in certain verses (e.g., Ex. 25:29; Nu. 7:14) seems to imply that it was a dish-like container, or perhaps an incense burner, rather than a utensil for pouring. The tabernacle ritual used twelve of these dishes, each weighing ten shekels (Nu. 7:84-86). Solomon had a duplicate set of vessels made for the temple; Nebuchadrezzar later carried this set to Babylon (2 K. 25:14; Jer. 52:18f.).

Suggestive parallels from archeology include the following:

(1) An ornately decorated incense dish in the form of a lion's mouth, having the lower jaw extended as a bowl, was found at Tell Beit Mirsim and is dated about the 8th cent. B.C. It was carved from steatite and had a hollow handle through which air could be gently blown (through a wooden extension) to aid the burning of the incense. Similar objects were found at Megiddo and in northern Syria, some of them having a human hand carved in relief on the bottom, apparently indicating that they were hand held. The problem with interpreting these objects as incense burners is that they do not show convincing evidence of burning. They may have been simply reservoirs of incense, receiving their supply through the hollow tube. One additional example from Megiddo was made of ivory and so could hardly have been for burning incense.

(2) A small zoomorphic libation bowl found at Beth-shemesh had an animal head mounted on the rim, and the long neck of another animal extended into the bowl as a handle. Likewise, at Tell Qasile a cultic bowl in the shape of a bird, dating to the last period of Philistine occupation (11th-10th cents.), was found.

Many other simple bowls with and without handles from various sites and periods may be similar to the biblical *kap*.

Bibliography.–W. F. Albright, *AASOR*, 21–22 (1943), 1-229, esp. 70-73; *BASOR*, 47 (Oct. 1932), 3-17, esp. 15-17; *EAEHL*, I, 249; III, 832; IV, 974; H. G. May, *Material Remains of the Megiddo Cult* (1955), pp. 18f., plate XVII; G. E. Wright, *BA*, 4 (1941), 17-31, esp. 30.

L. WILLIS

INCENTIVE [Gk. *paramýthion agápēs*] (Phil. 2:1); AV COMFORT OF LOVE; NEB LOVING CONSOLATION. *Paramýthion* appears only in Phil. 2:1, although its cognates appear five times elsewhere in the NT (fem. noun, 1 Cor. 14:3; vb., Jn. 11:19, 31; 1 Thess. 2:11; 5:14). The neuter noun suggests the content of "friendly address" and may mean either "consolation" (for what *has* happened; cf. the cognate, Jn. 11:19, 31) or "persuasion" (to what *may* happen; see 1 Thess. 2:11; 5:14).

The translations of Phil. 2:1 reflect these two possibilities. Here Paul based his exhortation to like-mindedness upon four conditional statements. If this verse looks to a future condition, it is appropriate that *paramýthion* be read "incentive" rather than "comfort." Further, the genitive *agápēs* seems to be subjective (rather than qualifying as in the NEB) so that we may understand that love ought to provide incentive to unity, as in the JB: "If love can persuade at all."

H. VAN BROEKHOVEN, JR.

INCEST. *See* CRIME.

INCONTINENCY. Used by the AV in 1 Cor. 7:5 for Gk. *akrasía* (RSV "lack of self-control") and in 2 Tim. 3:3 for *akratḗs* (RSV "profligate"). In both references the meaning is a lack of self-control which leads to licentiousness and dissipation.

INCORRUPTION; INCORRUPTIBLE. Used by the AV for Gk. *aphtharsía* (1 Cor. 15:42, 50, 53f.) and *áphthartos* (1 Cor. 9:25; 15:52; 1 Pet. 1:4, 23) in reference to the believer's inheritance and resurrection body. Both words are translated as "imperishable" in the RSV.

See IMMORTAL; IMMORTALITY.

INCREASE [Heb. *rāḇâ* (Gen. 7:17f.; 30:30; Ex. 1:7; Lev. 25:16; Ezk. 23:19; Dnl. 12:4; etc.), *yᵉḇûlâ* (Lev. 26:4; Nu. 32:22; Ps. 85:2 [MT 3]; etc.), *yāsap* (Nu. 32:14; Ps. 115:14; Prov. 1:5; 9:9; Eccl. 1:18; etc.), *tarbîṯ* (Lev. 25:36; Ezk. 18:8, 13, 17; 22:12), *šeger* (Dt. 7:13; 28:4, 18, 51), *nûḇ* (Ps. 62:10 [MT 11]; Ezk. 36:30), *pāraṣ* (1 Ch. 4:38; Job 1:10), *tᵉḇû'â* (Job 31:12), *śāgâ* (Ps. 73:12), *marbîṯ* (1 S. 2:33); Gk. *pleonázō* (Rom. 5:20; 2 Cor. 4:15; 1 Thess. 3:12; etc.), *auxáno* (Jn. 3:30; Acts 6:7; 2 Cor. 9:10; etc.), *prostíthēmi* (Lk. 17:5), *prokóptō* (Lk. 2:52), *endynamóō* (Acts 9:22), *perisseúō* (Acts 16:5), *epathroizō* (Lk. 11:29), *plēthýnō* (Acts 6:1)]; AV also STRENGTHENEDST (Ps. 138:3), MULTITUDE (Eccl. 5:7), MULTIPLIED (Ezk. 23:19; Nah. 3:16; Acts 6:1), ABOUND (Rom. 5:20; Phil. 4:17; 2 Thess. 1:3), REDOUND (2 Cor. 4:15), "gathered thick" (Lk. 11:29); NEB also SWELLED (Gen. 7:17), PROLIFIC (Ex. 1:7), ADDED (Ezr. 10:10; Job 1:10), ENLARGED (Isa. 26:15), PRODUCE (Lev. 26:4, 20), ADVANCED (Lk. 2:52), MULTIPLY (Rom. 5:20), GROW GREATER (Jn. 3:30), "wealth breeds wealth" (Ps. 62:10), "more and more" (Hos. 10:1), "the more . . . the more" (Eccl. 1:18), etc. To grow in number, amount, or stature. The idea of increase is used with physical objects, abstract ideas, and the stature of persons.

The most common use involves physical objects. The increase of water lifted up Noah's ark (Gen. 7:17f.). The Israelites increased in number prior to the pharaoh "who did not know Joseph" (Ex. 1:7f.). Receiving an increase in monetary interest on loans to fellow Israelites was forbidden (Lev. 25:36; Ezk. 18:8, 13, 17; *see* INTEREST). Heb. *yᵉḇûlâ* and *šeger* denote an increase in crops and cattle, respectively (Lev. 26:4; Ezk. 34:7; Dt. 7:13; 28:4, 18, 51). God will increase the population of Israel in the time of restoration (Ezk. 36:37). Absalom attracted increasing numbers of men to his revolt against David (2 S. 15:12).

Material prosperity was often seen to have a spiritual dimension. Thus, the favor of God was necessary for material prosperity: "may the Lord give you increase" (Ps. 115:14), although the wicked sometimes increased their riches with little or no effort (Ps. 73:12). God could destroy material blessings on account of iniquity (Job 31:12). Hosea saw a direct relationship between the physical well-being of Israel and their subsequent decline into apostasy: "The more they increased, the more they sinned against me" (4:7), "The more his fruit increased, the more altars he built" (10:1; cf. Dt. 32:15).

Learning can be increased by the study of proverbs (Prov. 1:5). Knowledge shall increase in "the time of the end" (Dnl. 12:4). The rule of the messianic king will increase to worldwide proportions and endure forever (Isa. 9:7 [MT 6]). The disciples asked Jesus to increase their faith (Lk. 17:5). The sins of men are "increased," i.e., made to look more despicable, by the introduction of the Mosaic law (Rom. 5:20). Those Jews who married foreign wives in Israel after the captivity "increased the guilt of Israel" (Ezr. 10:10).

As a youth, Jesus "increased in wisdom and in stature" (Lk. 2:52). John the Baptist foresaw the rising popularity of Jesus and the eclipse of his own ministry and exclaimed, "He must increase but I must decrease" (Jn. 3:30). R. J. W.

INDESTRUCTIBLE LIFE [Gk. *zōḗs akatalýtou*] (He. 7:16); AV ENDLESS LIFE; NEB "a life that cannot be destroyed." This expression appears only here in the RSV. The author of Hebrews argues that the priesthood of Jesus is superior to that of Aaron, for Jesus is "a priest forever after the order of Melchizedek" (7:17 = Ps. 110:4). Since Melchizedek was not subject to an end of life (7:3), neither was Jesus. R. J. W.

INDIA [Heb. *hōddû*; Gk. *hē Indikḗ*]. The name occurs in canonical Scripture only in Est. 1:1; 8:9, of the country which marked the eastern boundary of the territory of Ahasuerus. The Hebrew word comes from the name of the Indus, *Hondu,* and denotes, not the peninsula of Hindustan, but the country drained by that great river. This is the meaning also in 1 Esd. 3:2; Ad. Est. 13:1; 16:1. The drivers of the elephants (1 Macc. 6:37) were doubtless natives of this land. The name in 1 Macc. 8:8 is certainly an error. India never formed part of the dominions of Antiochus the Great. It may possibly be a clerical error for "Ionia," as Media is possibly a mistake for Mysia. If the Israelites in early times had no direct relations with India, many characteristic Indian products seem to have found their way into Palestinian markets by way of the Arabian and Syrian trade routes, or by means of the Red Sea fleets (1 K. 10:11, 15; Ezk. 27:15-36; etc.). Among these may be noted "ivory tusks and ebony," "cassia, and calamus," almug (sandalwood), apes, and peacocks. W. EWING

INDIAN DRIVER (1 Macc. 6:37). *See* ELEPHANT; INDIA.

INDICTMENT [Heb. *sēper*] (Job 31:35); AV BOOK; [*rîḇ*] (Jer. 25:31; Hos. 12:2 [MT 3]); AV CONTROVERSY; NEB CHARGE. The term *sēper* refers to a written charge brought against someone. *Rîḇ* refers to a legal case brought by Yahweh against the nations which had offended Him.

INDIGNANT; INDIGNATION [Heb. *zā'am* (Ps. 7:11 [MT 12]; Isa. 66:14; Zec. 1:12), *za'am* (Ps. 38:3 [MT 4]; 69:24 [MT 25]; Isa. 10:25; etc.), hithpael of *'āṣaḇ* (Gen. 34:7), *qāṣar napšô* (Jgs. 10:16; cf. 16:16), *ka'as* (Ps. 85:4 [MT 5]), *zal'āpâ* (Ps. 119:53), *qeṣer gāḏôl* (Jer. 32:37), *qin'â* (Ezk. 23:25), *'eḇrâ* (Hab. 3:8); Gk. *aganaktéō* (Mt. 20:24; 21:15; 26:8; Mk. 10:14, 41; 14:4; etc.), *aganáktēsis* (2 Cor. 7:11), *pyróō* (2 Cor. 11:29)]; AV also ANGRY, ANGER (Ps. 7:11; 38:3), WRATH (Ps. 78:49; Hab. 3:8), JEALOUSY (Ezk. 23:25), GRIEVED (Gen. 34:7; Jgs. 10:16), DISPLEASED (Mt. 21:15; Mk. 10:14; 10:41), BURN (2 Cor. 11:29); NEB also WRATH (Ps. 78:49; 102:10, etc.), ANGER (Isa. 10:25; Mic. 7:9; etc.), JEALOUS WRATH (Ezk. 23:25), FURY (Jer. 10:10), DISPLEASURE (Ps. 85:4), GUSTS OF ANGER (Ps. 119:53), ANGRILY (Mk. 14:4), BLAZE WITH INDIGNATION (2 Cor. 11:29). Emotion of extreme displeasure expressed by God toward people (e.g., Ps. 7:11; Lam. 2:6; Ezk. 21:31; etc.), people toward each other (e.g., Gen. 34:7; Ps. 119:53; Mk. 10:41; etc.), the religious leaders of Judaism toward Jesus (Mt. 21:15; Lk. 13:14), and Jesus toward the disciples (Mk. 10:14). Heb. *za'am* as used in Dnl. 8:19; 11:36 does not refer to an emotion but designates the reprehensible acts of the ruler who is to arise in the last days in Israel (Dnl. 8:11-14, 18-26, etc.).

The Heb. *za'am* is predominant in the OT in depicting God's indignation, which is provoked on account of unrighteousness and iniquity, whether it be that of Israel (Lam. 2:6), the psalmist (Ps. 38:3), or the gentile nations (Jer. 10:10). This word is always reserved for the indignation of God, with the exception of Dnl. 11:30. There the ruler of the last days becomes "enraged" (RSV) against the covenant. *Za'am* is found in the Qumrân scrolls in both the Manual of Discipline (1QS) and the War Scroll (1QM). The word means to curse or to damn: the expression of indignation is depicted. Whoever casts his lot with Belial will be damned (*w^e zā'ûm*) to the gloom of eternal fire (1QS 2:7) and Belial himself is "cursed in the dominion of his guilt" (1QM 13:4; cf. 13:1, 5).

Hebrew *zal'āpâ,* "hot indignation" (Ps. 119:53), is a metaphoric usage. The literal use is found in Ps. 11:6 of a burning wind and in Lam. 5:10 of the fever of famished persons. Heb. *qin'â* can also mean jealousy or ardor (cf. Cant. 8:6), hence the NEB translation "jealous wrath" in Ezk. 23:25. In Jgs. 10:16, God's indignation is aroused, not by Israel's iniquities, but by Israel's bondage to the Ammonites. The Heb. *wattiqṣar napšô* literally means "his [God's] soul was shortened." All versions have a more idiomatic translation: "he became indignant" (RSV), "he could endure no longer" (NEB), "his soul was grieved" (AV). The AV translates the Heb. *'im-yišmōr lāneṣaḥ* of Jer. 3:5 literally: "Will he keep it to the end?" The RSV supplies "indignant" on the basis of the immediate context (cf. 3:12): "Will he be indignant to the end?" The NEB paraphrases similarly: "Will he rage eternally?"

The use of *aganaktéō* in the NT remains on the human level of provocations among the disciples (Mt. 20:24; Mk. 10:41), Jesus and the religious leaders of the Jews (Lk. 13:14), and the Corinthians (2 Cor. 7:11). *Pyróō,* always occurring in the passive in the NT and literally meaning to burn up (cf. 2 Pet. 3:12), is used by Paul metaphorically of anger in 2 Cor. 11:29. He also uses the word of sexual desire (1 Cor. 7:9). R. J. W.

INDIGNITIES. *See* PUNISHMENTS IV.

INDITE [Heb. *rāḥaš*]. An archaism of the AV in Ps. 45:1 (MT 2), "My heart is inditing a good matter." Here *rāḥaš* means "be stirred up" (*CHAL,* p. 338), "keep moving, stir" (BDB, p. 935). Thus the excited psalmist pours out praise for the king. The RSV renders, "My heart overflows with a goodly theme," and the NEB, "My heart is stirred up by a noble theme."

INERRANCY. *See* INFALLIBILITY.

INFALLIBILITY. Belief in an infallible, authoritative, reliable Scripture has always been a part of the faith of the Church. Faith, by biblical definition, requires a sure Word of God. The very reality of faith as a sure knowledge and hearty confidence depends upon a Scripture whose truth is certain and unfailing.

While such concepts as infallibility, inerrancy, and reliability have commonly been predicated of the Scriptures, they are theological rather than biblical terms. Because they arose within the Church's theological reflection upon its Scriptures, their validity cannot be deduced from biblical usage. Their validity and justification, therefore, depend on their serviceability in expressing the Bible's own thought about itself. For only what the Bible thinks about itself belongs to the truth of the Bible and to that faith which must be surely believed. Everything else lacks those qualities of infallibility, inerrancy, authority, and trustworthiness that adhere alone in the nature of the Church's sacred writings. The very uniqueness of Holy

Scripture determines that such predications as can properly be attributed to Scripture also have their own unique meaning.

While the term "inerrancy" does not appear in any of the creeds of the Church, the term "infallibility" appears frequently. Those who speak of inerrancy usually mean freedom from any kind of error — scientific, historical, chronological, etc. As used within the Church's credal formulas, infallibility expresses the thought of *unfailing certainty,* and does so especially on two matters. First, it expresses the faith that the Scriptures are unfailingly and certainly true as regards all those matters of doctrine and life that are necessary for mankind's salvation. Second, the gracious saving actions of God that are recorded and interpreted in the Scriptures are confessed to be such actions as will certainly bring the believing sinner to salvation.

This usage of "infallibility" reflects the most distinctive religious motif of Reformation faith. Against the claims the Roman Church made for itself and its tradition, the Reformers confessed that the Scriptures alone are normative and wholly trustworthy since they alone infallibly present all matters of doctrine and life necessary for salvation. Alongside this *sola Scriptura,* the *sola gratia, sola fide* of Reformation thought expressed the Reformation faith in the efficacious and triumphant power of divine grace that alone — and unfailingly — brings sinners to a full and final salvation.

Thus the Canons of Dort employ the term "infallible" in their discussion of God's gift of faith to the elect and declare that God through the gift of faith will "bring them infallibly to salvation" (Second Head, art. 8). The Canons also speak of "the infallible fruits of election" (First Head, art. 12). Describing God's renewal of the sinner, the Canons declare "that all in whose heart God works in this marvelous manner are certainly, infallibly, and effectively regenerated, and do actually believe" (Third and Fourth Heads, art. 12), and the Canons use the term in their rejection of those who deny that believers "infallibly continue in faith" (Fifth Head, Rejection of Errors, para. 9).

This usage of "infallibility" to express certainty concerning the efficacy of God's gracious actions was not, however, peculiar to the Reformers. Thomas Aquinas, discussing the grace of regeneration, declared that although God does not coerce men, they to whom God gives such grace will "infallibly attain" to regeneration (*Summa Theol.* ii/1.112.3).

The term "infallibility" is also frequently applied in Reformation and post-Reformation thought to the Bible. The Belgic Confession speaks of the Bible as "this infallible rule" (art. 7); the Westminster Confession declares that Scripture is the "infallible rule of interpretation of Scripture" (chs. 1, 7); the Confession of the Free-Will Baptists asserts that the Scriptures "are a sufficient and infallible guide in religious faith and practice" (ch. 1); and the Confession of the Evangelical Free Church of Geneva claims that the Scriptures "are the only and infallible Rule of Faith" (art. 1).

Thus the term infallibility was widely used in credal statements to express the deep religious motif that God in His gracious redemptive action and the Bible in its truth are unerringly reliable and certain, a sure foundation for the certain knowledge and hearty confidence of faith.

Does the Bible think of itself in such a way as gives warrant to the predications of infallibility and reliability? Unless this question can be answered affirmatively, these terms lose their validity and serviceability, no matter how desirable it might seem for the Bible to possess such qualities. The task of the Church is not to enhance the Scriptures, even for what might seem the best of reasons. Its task is to listen to the Scriptures and in its theological reflections upon what it hears to echo and confess about Scripture only what Scripture says about itself.

Moreover, if the nature of Scripture by its own claim gives sanction to these theological predications, great care must be taken to ensure that the definitions given these concepts be themselves derived from the Scriptures, and not from common usage or from dictionary definition. The meaning, e.g., of that perspicuity which the Reformers, contra the Roman Church, attributed to the Bible was itself derived from the Bible. Clearly, any definition of perspicuity derived from common usage or a dictionary would never include that biblical understanding of itself reflected in Paul's statement that "now we see through a mirror darkly." If indeed the Bible is infallible in all matters of doctrine and life, it is also its own infallible and unique guide as to the truth of its own nature. We may neither add to nor subtract from the words of the Bible; by the same token we may not add to or subtract from the Bible's teaching about its nature. If it is a basic principle of theology and hermeneutics that the Scriptures must themselves define such biblical concepts as election, grace, faith, justification, and righteousness, it is no less essential that such concepts as we adopt and predicate of the Bible derive their unique definition from the unique character of the Bible. A more expansive procedure would be to bring strange fires to the altar.

That the Scriptures regard themselves as a sure, unfailing, certain, and trustworthy Word of God cannot be doubted. While specific proof texts are of limited number, the Scriptures in their entirety present themselves as the true and, therefore, reliable Word of God. It is true, and it should be recognized, that the Scriptures, for reasons that derive from their very nature as the Word of God, do not indulge in an apologetic effort to demonstrate their reality and truth as God's Word by reference to something other than themselves. The Scriptures no more attempt to prove the existence of God apart from His Word than they attempt to prove the authority, infallibility, and reliability of His Word apart from His Word. For this very reason, the Word of God in the Scriptures presents itself throughout as possessing these qualities without any special, introductory, self-conscious demonstration that it is what it asserts itself to be, namely, the Word of God. It merely speaks in terms of what it is: the Word of God. The Bible has no introductory or prefatory word by which it would commend its peculiar quality to its reader or special texts to prove what the rest of the Bible asserts. When the Scriptures do explicitly and self-consciously urge their certainty, infallibility, authority, and reliability, they do so only to induce acceptance and belief by doubtful and unbelieving sinners. Thus the Word of prophecy is said to be a sure word (2 Pet. 1:19); a word worthy of all acceptance (1 Tim. 1:15, etc.); a word that, unlike all flesh which is grass, abides forever; a word that should induce people to turn from their evil ways to God because it is an efficacious word of the God whose ways and thoughts are not like those of people (Isa. 55:6-9); a word of God that men should not doubt, because it is the word of Him who has built for them a city, because He is not ashamed to be called their God (He. 11:16). Similarly, Jesus urged the infallibility of the Scriptures upon the disputatious Sadducees when He said, "You are wrong, because you know neither the scriptures nor the power of God" (Mt. 22:29).

But for the rest, the Scriptures present the Word of God as being authoritative, infallible, and true just because it is what it is, the Word of God, quite independent of human acknowledgment. God is faithful to His Word, even though Israel is unfaithful; indeed the latter cannot undo the former, and God's Word is true even though every person is a liar (Rom. 3:3f.). The OT prophet has no higher credential than "Thus saith the Lord." Jesus has need of no higher appeal than "I am the way, and the truth, and the life" (Jn. 14:6). For the Word of God uttered in the Scriptures is the Word by which the world was created, which wrought life from the dead (Rom. 4:17), which caused light to shine out of darkness in creation and to shine in the face of Jesus Christ in redemption (2 Cor. 4:6), the word which both in creation and redemption "calls into existence the things that do not exist" (Rom. 4:17).

This is the nature of the Word of God as it appears in Scripture. It is a Word that carries its authority, truth, and infallibility in its own reality and precisely for this reason can neither itself appeal to something other than itself, namely, to that which it has created and redemptively recreated, nor allow what it has created and recreated (the believer, the Church) to step outside the context of its faith to seek proof of the authority and truth of that in which it believes and to which it owes its own reality.

The limited purpose and the specific scope within which the Bible claims to be infallible, authoritative, a wholly trustworthy object of faith, are clearly indicated by the Scriptures. They declare "that the testimony of the Lord is sure, making wise the simple" (Ps. 19:7 [MT 8]). This wisdom imparted by the Scriptures is that which instructs people for salvation (2 Tim. 3:15), which in its beginnings is the fear of the Lord (Prov. 9:10), and in its fulfillment is the Christ whom God has made to be that wisdom which is for us (1 Cor. 1:30), i.e., which is salvific. Paul tells the church at Rome that the Scriptures were written "for our instruction, that by steadfastness and by the encouragement of the Scriptures we might have hope" (Rom. 15:4). He tells Timothy that "these sacred writings" are indeed "able to instruct you for salvation through faith in Jesus Christ" (2 Tim. 3:15), and are "profitable for teaching, for reproof, for correction and for training in righteousness" (2 Tim. 3:16). Here the specific nature and the limited purpose of the Holy Scriptures are clearly indicated. Jesus says plainly concerning the Scriptures that "these are they which witness of me" (Jn. 5:39); and concerning the writings of Moses, "he wrote of me" (Jn. 5:46). Jesus adds that if the Jews whom He was addressing believed what Moses wrote, they would believe in Him (Jn. 5:47).

The Scriptures clearly indicate that their specific limited purpose, within which their claims of infallibility, authority, and trustworthiness coincide, is to utter that sure Word of God that alone contains all that mankind needs to know about doctrine and life in order to be saved. If the Scriptures were something other and less than this they could not be the sufficient and sure ground for that faith to which they summon people, and which they portray as a sure knowledge and hearty confidence.

The Holy Scriptures meet the test of every claim which they make for themselves. They are infallible, authoritative, and trustworthy in terms of their own stated nature, purpose, and demands. This has always been confessed by the Church. Some claim that the Scriptures are either fallible or infallible, reliable or unreliable, according to the demands of extraneous, extrabiblical norms derived from rationalism, natural science, or modern historiography, that leave no room for the unique truth of Scripture that is above all that mankind knows, and on account of which Scripture employs symbol, image, parable, poetry, and its own peculiar kind of historical writing. But these people import human notions into the Word of God. Nor is the importation any less real when done by those whose intentions are on the side of the sacred Scriptures but who nonetheless surrender to speculative rationalism and modern science the right to dictate the nature of biblical infallibility, authority, and trustworthiness, and who thus forfeit the true certainty and supreme authority of Scripture in their very attempt to establish it.

The great need of the Church today is not to try to prove an infallibility extraneously defined. It is to learn from the Bible, as a real norm, what the Bible has to say about its own infallibility. It is to take this infallibility seriously from the very outset, so that Scripture is indeed the infallible basis of a faith that is not an uncertain grasping at straws of human verification, but a sure and unquestioned knowledge.

Scripture as God's own word attests to its own truthfulness within our hearts through the function of the Holy Spirit, for as Paul says, the ministry of the Word is itself a "ministration of the Spirit" (2 Cor. 3:8). *See* HOLY SPIRIT: HISTORY OF THE DOCTRINE V.A. J. DAANE

INFANCY, GOSPEL OF THE. *See* APOCRYPHAL GOSPELS II.

INFANT BAPTISM. *See* BAPTISM.

INFANTICIDE. *See* CRIME.

INFIDEL. The AV uses this word twice to translate Gk. *ápistos,* "unbelieving": "What part hath he that believeth with an infidel?" (2 Cor. 6:15); "If any provide not for his own, [he] . . . is worse than an infidel" (1 Tim. 5:8). In both passages the RSV has "unbeliever" in harmony with numerous other instances of *ápistos* in the NT. The word nowhere corresponds to the modern conception of an infidel as one who denies the existence of God or repudiates the Christian faith, but always signifies one who has not become a believer in Christ. It was formerly so used in English, and some of the older versions have it in other passages besides these two.

W. O. CARVER

INFINITE in'fə-nət. The word "infinite" does not occur in the RSV. The AV uses it only three times: Ps. 147:5, "his understanding is infinite" (Heb. *'ên mispār,* lit. "no number"; RSV "beyond measure"; NEB "beyond all telling"); Job 22:5, "[are not] thine iniquities infinite?" (Heb. *'ên-kēṣ,* lit. "no end"; RSV "no end to"; NEB "passes all bounds"); Nah. 3:9, the strength of Ethiopia and Egypt is "infinite" (Heb. *'ên qēṣeh,* lit. "no end"; RSV "without limit"; NEB "boundless"). The RV retains "infinite" in Nah. 3:9 and Ps. 147:5. Both the AV and the RV apply "infinite" to God in Ps. 147:5.

The Hebrew OT and the LXX do not contain the word "infinite," but Scripture does employ the concept. Concerning God, we read that His years have "no end" (Ps. 102:27 [MT 28]), that we cannot find out "the limit [Heb. *taḵlîṯ*–'completeness,' 'end'] of the Almighty" (Job 11:7), and that there is no end to His promises (Ps. 77:8 [MT 9]). In sharp distinction, man has an end (Ps. 90:9; Job 32:22), even his boasting (2 Cor. 10:13, 15).

The Bible teaches that people by virtue of their creation in the *imago Dei* have within their minds the idea of infinity. Without this ability, the human mind could have no idea of God. Indeed, it is the inclusion of the idea of infinity that makes it difficult for the human mind to conceive of a finite space-time universe beyond which is nothing. Because the human mind can exhaustively comprehend neither finitude nor infinity, it tends to define each in reference to the other.

As stated above, the Bible at times conveys the idea of infinity by "no end" and "no number," for "end" and "number" are expressions of limitation. Infinity is defined as that which is not finite.

Such thought and expression is unavoidable; indeed, it has biblical precedence. Yet care should be observed so as not to confuse infinity with quantity. God's infinity is a matter of quality, not quantity.

God's infinity, which applies to all His perfections, means that God's perfect omniscience conveys, not merely that God knows all that can be known, but that nothing can exist beyond the reach of His knowing. Similarly God's omnipotence is not an infinite quantity of power but that potentiality of God to accomplish without limit everything that is possible for power to accomplish. A quantity cannot be infinite, for it is subject to limits and boundaries, to measurement and enumeration. All God's perfections have the quality of infinitude and, therefore, none of His perfections is subject to any form of measurement or limitation.

The infinity of God must be "defined" and understood, as best we can, in terms of God Himself, and not in terms of those created realities that are not God. God's infinity is not comprised or constituted by the finitude of the created universe. Being circumscribed by His own internal qualities, God's infinity is not limited by any aspect of the finite creation — neither by mankind's logical, conceptual thought as rationalism is prone to forget, nor by mankind's free will as Arminian theology tends to ignore. The finite cannot contain or delimit the infinite.

God can become human without in any sense qualifying His own infinitude. In the shorthand of theology, God became man in Jesus Christ without in any sense ceasing to be God. In the mystery of the Incarnation, God can in Jesus Christ enter into finite time and space and thus subject Himself to the finitude of His own creation. He is born at a specific place and time (Lk. 2:4-7) and at no point in time or space ceases to be the infinite Lord of time and space and of all things in them. Hence, God in Christ at the moments of His greatest weakness can assert His infinite lordship. When about to be seized by Judas and the mob, He speaks and His enemies fall backward upon the ground (Jn. 18:6), and on the cross, in the moment of death, Christ Himself commends His spirit into the hands of His Father (Lk. 23:46).

Only God is infinite; infinity is a divine quality. It must therefore not be defined with reference to finitude, which is a quantity, as though infinity were an infinite amount of finitude. In biblical thought the question is not whether the infinite can tolerate or allow, or have room for the finite, for one can no more comprehend creation than that other truth which one can know but not comprehend — the infinity of God. Nor is it a question, in biblical thought, whether the infinite can become finite, for God can, acording to Scripture, become man, exist in time and space, as He does in Christ, precisely because God is the infinite who creates the finite and therefore is not subject to it, but can in it remain infinite. The life of Christ on earth reflects that enduring insistence of the Church that God can become man and be numbered among them, without ceasing to be God. That is the revelation of infinity.

See also ETERNAL; ETERNITY; IMAGE OF GOD.

J. DAANE

INFIRMITY. *See* DISEASE.

INFLAME [Heb. *dālaq*–'kindle' (hiphil, Isa. 5:11); *hāmam*–'be hot' (Jer. 51:39)]; AV "in their heat," NEB "to end in fever." Both terms are used figuratively, although the precise sense is disputed in each text because of enigmatic contexts. The former may speak of the desire or passion often accompanying drunkenness, or of the consuming effects of such drunkenness. The latter might refer to anger (cf. v. 38) or to appetite (see comms.).

INFLAMMATION [Heb. *dalleqeṯ*; Gk. *rhígos*]; NEB AGUE. Occurs only in Dt. 28:22 and was considered by Jewish writers as "burning fever," by the LXX as a form of ague. Both this and typhoid fever are now, and probably were, among the commonest of the diseases of Palestine. *See* DISEASE III.H. In Lev. 13:28 AV has "inflammation" as the rendering of Heb. *ṣārebeṯ,* where the LXX has Gk. *charaktḗr,* and for which the proper English equivalent is "scar," as in the RSV and NEB.

INFLUENCES (Job 38:31, AV). *See* CHAIN.

INGATHERING, FEAST OF. *See* BOOTHS, FEAST OF.

INHABIT [Heb. *yāšaḇ, šāḵan*; Gk. *katoikéō*]; AV also DWELL, REMAIN (Jer. 17:25), SETTLE (hiphil of *yāšaḇ,* Ezk. 36:11); NEB also LIVE, DWELL, MAKE POPULOUS (hiphil of *yāšaḇ,* Ezk. 36:11), LIE; **INHABITANT** [Heb. part. *yōšēḇ, šāḵēn*; Aram. construct part. of *dûr* (*Q* Dnl. 4:35 [MT 32]); Gk. part. *katoikṓn*]; NEB also NATIVE, CITIZEN, TOWNSMAN, PEOPLE.

The Hebrew term most frequently rendered "inhabit" by the RSV is *yāšaḇ,* which elsewhere in the OT has the meanings "sit" (e.g., Gen. 18:1) and "remain" (e.g., Gen. 24:55). Six times the term *šāḵan* is rendered "inhabit" (Job 26:5; Prov. 2:21; Isa. 33:24; 57:15; Jer. 46:26; Hos. 10:5), while elsewhere it may mean "remain" (Jgs. 5:17; Prov. 7:11). Both uses of "inhabitants" in Dnl. 4:35 render Aram. *dāy^{e}rê* (< *dûr*). In the NT the Gk. *katoikṓn,* which frequently renders *yāšaḇ* and *šāḵan* in the LXX, is rendered "inhabitant" three times (Acts 1:19; 4:16; 13:12). There appears to be no appreciable semantic difference among these terms in the passages where they are rendered "inhabit(ant)." *See* DWELL; HABITATION.

J. E. H.

INHERIT [Heb. *nāḥal*] (Ex. 32:13; Nu. 26:55; Jer. 12:14; etc.); NEB also POSSESS, PATRIMONY, POSSESSION, etc.; [*yāraš*] (Lev. 20:24; Dt. 16:20; Isa. 65:9; etc.); AV also POSSESS; NEB POSSESSION, OCCUPY, HEIR, POSSESS; [*'^{a}ḥuzzâ*] (Lev. 27:28); AV POSSESSION; NEB ANCESTRAL; [*naḥ^{a}lâ*] (Prov. 19:14); AV INHERITANCE; NEB "come down"; [Gk. *klēronoméō*] (Mt. 5:5; Mk. 10:17; 1 Cor. 6:9; etc.); AV also BE HEIR; NEB also GAIN, WIN, CLAIM, etc.; [*klēronómos*] (Rom. 4:13); AV BE HEIR; NEB INHERITANCE; [*patroparádotos*] (1 Pet. 1:18); AV RECEIVED; NEB BOUGHT; **INHERITANCE** [Heb. *naḥ^{a}lâ*] (Gen. 31:14; Nu. 16:14; Josh. 11:23; etc.); AV also HERITAGE; NEB also PATRIMONY, POSSESSION, PROPERTY, DOMAIN, etc.; [*nāḥal*] (Ex. 34:9; 1 Ch. 28:8; Prov. 13:22; etc.); AV, NEB, also POSSESSION; [*'^{a}ḥuzzâ*] (Lev. 27:16, 22, 24); AV also POSSESSION; NEB LAND, PATRIMONY; [*gôrāl*] (Nu. 26:56); AV LOT; NEB LAND; [*y^{e}ruššâ*] (Jgs. 21:17); NEB HEIRS; [*yāraš*] (Ezr. 9:12); NEB POSSESSION; [Gk. *klēronomía*] (Mt. 21:38; Acts 20:32; Col. 3:24; etc.); NEB also PROPERTY, HERITAGE, SHARE; [*kataklēronoméō*] (Acts 13:19); AV LOT; NEB HERITAGE; [*klḗros*] (Col. 1:12); NEB HERITAGE; **INHERITOR** [Heb. *yāraš*] (Isa. 65:9); NEB HEIR.

The concept of "inheritance" played an important role for the Israelites. The chief terms used are the verb *nāḥal* and the noun *naḥ*ª*lâ*. In their widest application these terms refer not only to an estate received by a child from his parents but also the the land received by the children of Israel as a gift from Yahweh.

This latter theological use of "inheritance" has its beginnings in the promise God made to Abraham when he entered the land of Canaan. In Gen. 12:7 God said, "To your descendants I will give this land." This promise was passed down through Abraham's descendants and reaffirmed to Moses: "I will bring you into the land which I swore to give to Abraham, to Isaac, and to Jacob; I will give it to you for a possession. I am the Lord" (Ex. 6:8; cf. 3:7f.; 32:13; *TDNT,* III, 770). In Deuteronomy Moses repeatedly reminds the people of the promise of the land as made to Abraham, always with the recognition that the land is Yahweh's and that He is giving it to His people (Dt. 4:21,38; 12:9; 15:4; 19:10; etc.; see *TDNT,* III, 769-776).

With the entrance of Israel into Canaan after Moses' death, a new focus comes into view. As the nation holds the entire land as an inheritance, so it is now distributed among the people for an inheritance (see Nu. 32:18f.; 34:14-18; 36:2-12; etc.). Here again, as throughout the OT, a clear distinction is made between real and personal property, the fundamental idea regarding the former being that the land is Yahweh's, and the people hold it as an "inheritance" only through His favor — not by right; therefore the Israelites are still called "strangers and sojourners" in the land, and the portion allotted to them could not be sold into perpetuity (Lev. 25:23-28). The terms *nāḥal* and *naḥ*ª*lâ* are used most frequently in this sense, to denote the possession of a portion of the land by a tribe or family.

Joshua was the one chosen by Yahweh to lead the people into the land (Josh. 1:1f.), and when with God's help the land had been successfully taken, Joshua was commanded to apportion the land (13:7). This was done by casting lots to determine the specific piece of land to be owned by each family head (18:6; cf. Nu. 26:53-56; 33:54).

Israel's social legislation was designed to protect a family's inheritance. In case, through necessity of circumstances, a homestead was sold, the title could pass only temporarily; for in the year of Jubilee every homestead had to return again to the original owner or heir (Lev. 25:25-34). Priests were to receive no inheritance (Ezk. 44:28). Real estate given to the priesthood had to be appraised and could be redeemed by the payment of the appraised valuation, thus preventing the transfer of real property even in this case (Lev. 27:14-25). A father's possessions were all to be passed on to his sons (Prov. 13:22; Lev. 25:46), who had preeminent rights (though Job's three daughters shared the inheritance with their brothers [42:15]). The right to inheritance was not affected by the status of the mother, and "a slave who acts wisely will rule over a son who acts shamefully" (Prov. 17:2). A father's firstborn son received a "double portion of all that he has," twice as much as was given to the other sons (Dt. 21:15-17). If there were no sons but only daughters, the inheritance went to them. If there were neither sons nor daughters, a man's possessions would go to his brothers, and if he had no brothers, they would go to his father's brothers; if his father had no brothers the possessions would go to his next of kin (Nu. 27:1-11). In order to keep the inheritance from going to another tribe, daughters were prohibited from marrying outside the tribe of their father (Nu. 36:6-9).

Naboth's vineyard (1 K. 21:1, 3) was a part of his family's inheritance; thus, he was right in refusing to sell the property. Ahab's illegal seizure of the vineyard was severely condemned by Elijah and brought grievous punishment upon the family of Ahab (vv. 20-24). The prophet Micah later warns that the Lord will devise evil against those who "covet fields, and seize them; and houses, and take them away; they oppress . . . a man and his inheritance" (2:2).

The psalmist found comfort in the thought that God remembers His covenant promise for inheritance (105:11). The land is called the inheritance of God in Ps. 79:1, but in 69:36 (MT 37) it is the inheritance of Israel over which God had set David as shepherd (78:71).

The prophet Jeremiah speaks of Israel as "the tribe of his [Yahweh's] inheritance" (10:16). He cries that the people have polluted the land with idols and "have filled my [Yahweh's] inheritance with their abominations" (16:18), so Yahweh has forsaken His house and given up His heritage to its enemies (12:7-10). In Ezekiel, however, comes the promise that after the Exile the land will be resettled and inhabited as an "inheritance" forever (36:12). As in the days of Joshua, the land will again be divided and each will receive his inheritance by lot (Ezk. 47:13f.; 48:29; etc.), a prince being allowed neither to take inheritance away from the people nor to give away any of his own (46:16-18).

In the NT inheritance as the ordinary transmission of property from father to son is found in the parables of Jesus (Mt. 21:38; Mk. 12:1-8; Lk. 15:11-13; cf. Lk. 12:13; 20:14). In these instances sonship is firmly linked with inheritance, reflecting the common Greek and Oriental view. But the NT also uses the verb *klēronoméō* and noun *klēronomía* in a theological sense as an eschatological concept. In such cases these terms refer to the kingdom of God (see Lk. 10:25; 18:18) as the inheritance now to be claimed by the heirs, the sons of God (Mt. 19:29; 25:34; Mk. 10:17; 1 Cor. 6:9ff.). This sonship is based "not . . . on physical descent . . . but on the divine call and appointment" (*TDNT,* III, 782; see 1 Cor. 15:50). Christ as Son is heir, and His people set in sonship are *synklēronómoi* ("fellow heirs," Rom. 8:17). While the "inheritance" of the kingdom (Gal. 5:21; Eph. 5:5) is eschatological (Eph. 1:14,18; Col. 3:24) and imperishable (1 Pet. 1:4), the promise to the meek of inheriting the *earth* (Mt. 5:5) gives it also a distinctly this-worldly element.

This metaphor of inheritance used by Christ (here from Ps. 37:11; cf. 1 En. 5:7; Ps. Sol. 14:5), "speaks of the meek and their ultimate prosperity in this life and triumph over the wicked" (McNeile, p. 51). Similar is 1QM 11:7-18: the *kittîyîm* are defeated by the Messiah and become His inheritance. He vindicates the poor. This idea has its roots in the promise to Abraham and his descendants (cf. Acts 13:19). Paul faces the question of who now are the true descendants (Gk. *spérma*) of Abraham, in light of the Judaizer concept that the sons of Abraham were the physical descendants who kept the law. Paul declares that the promise of inheritance to Abraham and his descendants "did not come through the law but through the righteousness of faith" (Rom. 4:13; Gal. 3:18; cf. 4:30). This promise was fulfilled with the coming of Christ as Messiah; to His sons now go the promised blessings (Col. 1:12; *klḗros,* meaning "lot" or "portion," is used in the LXX for Heb. *gôrāl, yāraš,* and *naḥ*ª*lâ* in the apportioning of the land of Canaan; see *TDNT,* III, 759; cf. Acts 20:32).

In He. 12:17 the ordinary, father-to-son type of inheritance is mentioned in reference to Esau, who "desired to inherit the blessing" but was rejected. Generally, though, in the book of Hebrews "inheritance" is linked with the content of the OT promise to Abraham (9:15), who went out "not knowing where he was to go" (11:8); and it is that same "faith and patience" which Christians now are exhorted to have, that they may "imitate" those who "through faith and patience inherit the promises" (6:12).

Bibliography.–G. Dalman, *Words of Jesus* (1902), pp. 125-27; W. D. Davies, *The Gospel and the Land* (1974); A. H. McNeile, *Gospel According to St. Matthew* (1915); A. Richardson, *Intro. to the Theology of the NT* (1959); B. F. Westcott, *Epistle to the Hebrews* (1889), p. 167; *RTWB*, *s.v.* "Inherit" (Cranfield); *TDNT*, III, *s.v.* κλῆρος (Herrmann); MM, pp. 346-48.

F. E. HIRSCH
D. K. MCKIM

INIQUITY [Heb. *ʿāwôn*]; AV also PUNISHMENT (Gen. 4:13), MISCHIEF (2 K. 7:9), etc.; NEB also PUNISHMENT, RESPONSIBILITY, GUILT, PENALTY OF GUILT, etc.; [*ʾāwen*]; AV also WICKEDNESS (Job 11:11); NEB also MISCHIEF, TROUBLE, WRONG (Ps. 119:133), etc.; [*ʿāwâ*]; NEB DOES WRONG (2 S. 7:14), HAVE ERRED (Ps. 106:6), DEEP IN THEIR SIN (Jer. 9:5 [MT 4]); [*ʿāwel*, fem. *ʿawlâ*]; NEB also WRONG, EVIL (Job 15:16), EVIL WAYS (Ezk. 18:26, twice), LOATHSOME (Ps. 53:1), INJUSTICE (Ezk. 18:8), FRAUD (Hab. 2:12), MISCHIEF (Hos. 10:13); [Gk. *anomía*]; AV also UNRIGHTEOUSNESS (2 Cor. 6:14); NEB LAWLESS DEEDS (Rom. 4:7), CRIME (Mt. 23:28), LAWLESSNESS (Rom. 6:19), WICKEDNESS (2 Cor. 6:14, Tit. 2:14); [*adikía*]: NEB WICKED DEEDS (He. 8:12), WICKED WAYS (Lk. 13:27), SIN (Acts 8:23), WICKEDNESS (2 Tim. 2:19); [*adíkēma*]; NEB CRIMES (Rev. 18:5). A variety of connotations is conveyed by these words.

In the OT, the term *ʿāwôn* occurs more frequently (over 200 times) than any other Hebrew word translated "iniquity." It conveys three ideas: (1) the iniquitous act itself; (2) the guilt accompanying the act; (3) the punishment for the act. These ideas are so closely related that they are not always clearly distinguishable, hence the differences in translation. In Job 7:21 the RSV has "Why dost thou not pardon my transgression and take away my iniquity?" (NEB "guilt"); in Isa. 53:11 the RSV has "he shall bear their iniquities" (NEB "penalty of their guilt"). A frequently occurring expression is *nāśāʾ ʿāwôn*. The AV and RSV translate as "bear iniquity" while the NEB usually has "accept responsibility." It may have moral or theological implications as in Lev. 5:17 where it refers to sins of omission. Or it may refer to the breaking of ritual laws as in Lev. 17:16 where the washing of clothes and body are necessary after being mauled by wild animals or eating an animal which died a natural death.

Several times the OT refers to God as "visiting the iniquity (*ʿāwôn*) of the fathers upon the children and the children's children to the third and fourth generation" (Ex. 34:7; cf. 20:5; etc.). It is extremely difficult for the modern western mind to accept the fact that God would punish children for the iniquity of their ancestors. The solution is to be found in differing conceptions of the basic unit in society. In the modern West the emphasis is on the individual and individual accountability, while in ancient Israel the emphasis was on the group or the community. This concept of "corporate solidarity" was reflected in an unbroken genealogical relationship of families (witness all the genealogies in the OT), and in the idea that God punished children for the deeds of their ancestors or blessed them for the righteousness of their ancestors (Gen. 17:6-8). (Cf. R. Shedd, *Man in Community* [1964], pp. 3-41.)

The Heb. *ʿāwôn* occurs in several passages that are difficult to interpret. In 1 S. 3:13, punishment is predicted for Eli's house "for the iniquity which he knew, because his sons were blaspheming God" (RSV) or "because he knew of his sons' blasphemies against God" (NEB). The NEB translation has omitted "for the iniquity" (or "in guilt") although the resulting translation achieves the sense of the passage very well. In Ps. 36:2 (MT 3) the RSV reads "that his iniquity cannot be found out and hated," while the NEB considers the Hebrew unintelligible and translates "when he is found out he does not mend his ways." In Ps. 106:43 the NEB deletes the last phrase "and were brought low through their iniquity" without justification. In Ezk. 18:17 the RSV follows the Greek in reading "(withholds his hand from) iniquity" where the Hebrew reads "the poor." The NEB translates "he shuns injustice."

The verb *ʿāwâ* is translated "commit iniquity" on three occasions (2 S. 7:14; Ps. 106:6; Jer. 9:5). It also has the idea of "do wrong" as reflected in the NEB translations.

The nouns *ʿāwel* (masc.) and *ʿawlâ* (fem.) convey the idea of "injustice" or "unrighteousness." The masculine form is used frequently in Ezekiel; it often occurs with the verb *ʿāśâ* to mean "commit iniquity" (RSV) or "do wrong" (NEB), e.g., Ezk. 33:13. In Ezk. 18:8 *ʿāwel* occurs in an extensive list of things which do not characterize the righteous person. Similarly God is not characterized by *ʿāwel* but by *ʾᵉmûnâ*, "faithfulness." Job 36:33 is variously translated because of the difficulties. The MT has *ʿôleh*, literally "one who rises," AV "vapor," RSV "iniquity," NEB "in his anger he calls up the tempest, and thunder is the herald of its coming" (cf. M. Pope, *Job* [*AB*, 3rd ed. 1973], pp. 276f.).

Another term, *ʾāwen*, is translated "iniquity" most of the time by the AV, only some of the time by the RSV, and almost never by the NEB. It means "trouble, sorrow, wickedness" as is reflected in the NEB translations. The usage of the term is concentrated in Job, Psalms, Proverbs, and Isaiah, never appearing in legal portions of the OT and rarely in narrative texts (1 S. 15:23). The expression *pōʿᵃlê ʾāwen* (RSV, AV "workers of iniquity," NEB "wrongdoers, evildoers") is frequent. It refers to evildoers in both the political (Isa. 31:2) and moral spheres (Job 31:3). In 1 S. 15:23 the NEB emends the first half to read "Defiance of him is sinful as witchcraft, yielding to men as evil as idolatry." Although the precise meaning is debated, the RSV translation is preferable: "For rebellion is as the sin of divination, and stubbornness is as iniquity and idolatry." Another difficult passage is the first part of Hos. 12:11 where NEB takes *ʾāwen* to refer to idolatry (RSV and AV "iniquity"). It is more likely in the light of Hos. 6:8 that bloody transgressions characterize Gilead, and therefore "iniquity" is the correct translation. (See H. W. Wolff, *Hosea* [Eng. tr., *Hermeneia*, 1974], p. 215.) In Ps. 141:4 the NEB unnecessarily emends to "the evildoers appal me." The RSV translation makes very good sense, however: "in company with men who work iniquity."

In the NT, three Greek terms are translated "iniquity." The first, *anomía*, means "lawlessness," either as a frame of mind (Mt. 23:28) or the lawless deeds themselves (Rom. 4:7). It is also most frequently used in the LXX to translate *ʿāwôn*. The second term, *adikía*, means "unrighteousness" (Lk. 13:27) or misdeeds (He. 8:12). The third term, *adíkēma*, refers to the crimes of Babylon in Rev. 18:5 where it is parallel to *hamartía*, "sin."

See also SIN.

Bibliography.–*TDOT*, I, *s.v.* "ʾāwen" (Bernhardt); *TDNT*, I, *s.v.* ἄδικος κτλ. (Schrenk); IV, *s.v.* νόμος (Kleinknecht, Gutbrod).

J. C. MOYER

INJURIOUS. *See* INSULT.

INJURY. *See* CRIME.

INK [Heb. *dᵉyô*, from a root meaning "slowly flowing" (see BDB, p. 188); Gk. *mélan*–'black']. Any fluid substance used with pen or brush to form written characters. In this sense ink is mentioned once in the OT (Jer. 36:18) and three times in the NT (2 Cor. 3:3; 2 Jn. 12; 3 Jn. 13), and it is implied in all references to writing on papyrus or leather. Hebrew ink was a fluid made from lampblack or soot mixed with gum arabic or gum acacia to form a nonmetallic writing mixture. It could be washed off (cf. Ex. 32:33; Nu. 5:23). A red metallic ink was made by replacing the soot or lampblack with a red ocher or iron oxide. The Dead Sea Scrolls show that both types of ink were in use in Palestine in the pre-Christian period. Egyptian scribes wrote with moistened pens dipped on pellets of dried ink; this practice may also have been followed in Palestine as early as the preexilic period. The Samarian ostraca and the Lachish Letters provide specimens of writing in ink from the times of Ahab (873-853 B.C.) and Zedekiah (597-587 B.C.), respectively. When the scriptorium at Qumrân was excavated (*see* DEAD SEA SCROLLS), inkwells were recovered containing dried flakes of the ink in which some of the scrolls had actually been written.

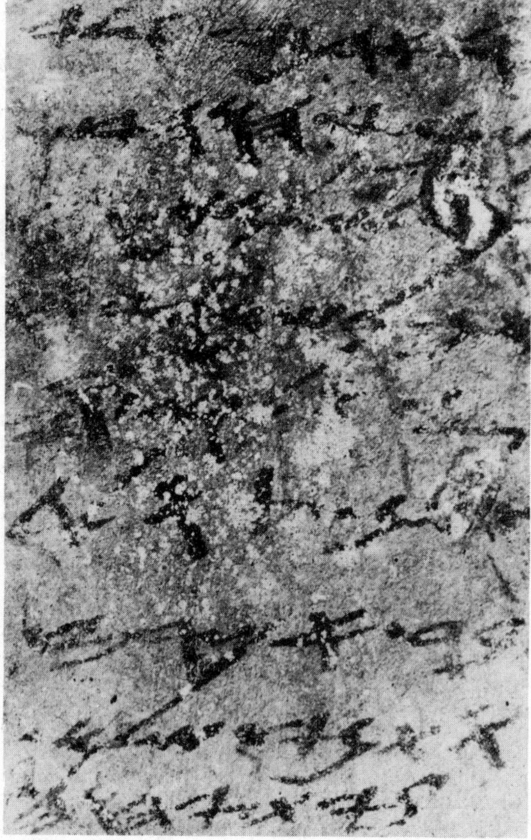

Arad Ostracon III, written in Paleo-Hebrew script, with Hebrew tetragrammaton in second and last lines (Israel Department of Antiquities and Museums)

Terra-cotta and bronze inkwells from the scriptorium at Qumrân (Israel Department of Antiquities and Museums)

INK-HORN. *See* WRITING CASE.

INLAY [Heb. *qaršēḵ ʿāšû-šēn*] ("made your deck . . . inlaid with ivory," Ezk. 27:6); AV "have made thy benches of ivory"; NEB "made your deck strong." The RSV has seen the verse as referring to ivory inlays, which have been used decoratively in the Near East from Sumerian times. *See also* IVORY.

INMOST SELF (Rom. 7:22). *See* INNER MAN.

INN; LODGE; LODGING PLACE [Heb. *mālôn*–'night resting place,' *m^e lûnâ* < *lûn*–'pass the night'; Gk. *katályma, pandocheíon, xenía*].

Among the Semitic people of ancient times, as among Arabs today, hospitality to strangers was a recognized duty. The ordinary traveler would be cared for in private homes (houses or tents). The Heb. *mālôn* might be applied to any spot where caravans (Gen. 42:27; 43:21), individuals (Ex. 4:24; Jer. 9:2), or even armies (Josh. 4:3, 8; 2 K. 19:23; Isa. 10:29) encamped for the night (cf. NEB). The slightly altered form *m^e lûnâ* is used of a night watchman's lodge in a garden (Isa. 1:8; in 24:20 RSV has "hut," AV "cottage"). The word *mālôn* in itself does not imply the presence of any building, and in the case of caravans and travelers was doubtless originally, as very often at the present day, only a convenient level bit of ground near a spring, where baggage might be unloaded and animals watered and tethered, and where people could sleep on the bare ground.

In NT times the case was quite different, due to the influence of Greek and Roman culture and the wide travel that went with it. The Gk. *katályma* comes from the verb *katalýō,* which literally means "unloose" or "unyoke." Hence the noun suggests a stopping place for travelers, where the horses are unharnessed or unsaddled, and baggage is unpacked.

Generally speaking, inns had a bad reputation. In Mish. *Yebamoth* xvi.7, the word of an innkeeper was doubted, and Mish. *Abodah Zarah* ii.1 places them lowest on the scale of degradation. The NT specifically mentions Rahab as "the harlot" (He. 11:31; Jas. 2:25). The Tg. designates her an "innkeeper," and Rashi translates *zōnâ* as "a seller of kinds of food." Kimchi, however, accepts both meanings. This ill repute of public inns, together with the Semitic spirit of hospitality, led the Jews and the early Christians to recommend the keeping of open house for the benefit of strangers. In the Jewish Morning Prayers, even to this day, such action is linked with great promises, and the NT repeatedly commends hospitality (He. 13:2; 1 Pet. 4:9; 3 Jn. 5); both the Talmud (T.B. *Shabbath* 127a) and the NT (He. 13:2) cite the same passage (Gen. 18:3) in recommending it.

The Gk. *katályma* is used in Mk. 14:14 and Lk. 22:11 for the "guest chamber" in a private home where Jesus and His disciples ate the Last Supper. This circumstance raises the question of the term's significance in its only other occurrence in the NT (Lk. 2:7). Was the "inn" at Bethlehem, where Joseph and Mary sought a night's lodging, an upper guest room in a private home or some kind of public place for travelers? The question cannot be answered with certainty. It is thought by some that it may have been a guest chamber provided by the community. We know that visitors to the annual feasts in Jerusalem were entertained in the guest rooms of private homes (*Aboth de Rabbi Nathan* 34). It may be that Joseph and Mary hoped to be received into the home of some relative in Bethlehem, but found the guest chamber already taken, and so had to sleep in the stable. Dalman thinks the "inn" may have been a guest room in a private home (cf. NEB "house") — but without adequate privacy for the birth of a baby — or a more public place of hospitality provided by the villagers (*SSW*, pp. 41-44).

A different word is used for "inn" in Lk. 10:34. Here it is Gk. *pandocheíon*, which rather clearly means a public khan or caravanserai. It was a place where a wounded traveler could be taken care of for the night. Not only rooms, but food for man and beast were evidently provided. It would seem that there was a set charge for these, or at least a payment was expected. The present Good Samaritan Inn, located about halfway between Jerusalem and Jericho (just off the new Jericho Road), marks the traditional site of the inn of Jesus' parable. The place is now used for a police post. At the back of the building, with its high arched door, is a spacious courtyard surrounded by a wall. In the center of the courtyard is a well. Parts of the back wall are made of immense stones which may well go back to Roman times. It is probable that Khan Hathrur, as it is called, is on the same site as the inn of Jesus' day. By a strange coincidence, the Mishnah (*Yebamoth* xvi.7) states that some Levites going along the Jericho Road left a sick companion at an inn in the care of an innkeeper — very possibly the same place.

Greek *xenía* occurs in Acts 28:23 as the word for Paul's quarters in Rome, when he was under house arrest. For AV "into his lodging" and RSV "at his lodging," the NEB has "as his guests." The same word occurs in Philem. 22, where the AV has "lodging," the RSV "guest room," and the NEB "room," and in Sir. 29:27. Usage of the word outside the NT points more in the direction of "hospitality" than of a place of lodging.

Bibliography.–Bauer, rev., p. 547; BDB, pp. 533f.; MM, p. 433.

R. EARLE

INNER MAN; INNER NATURE; INMOST SELF [Gk. *ho ésō ánthrōpos*]. An expression used by Paul (Rom. 7:22; 2 Cor. 4:16; Eph. 3:16) for the true self in contrast with the "outward self" (*ho éxō ánthrōpos*, 2 Cor. 4:16) that is visible to others, and the outward "members" that are subject to the law of sin (Rom. 7:23). It corresponds to the "hidden person of the heart" (*ho kryptós tḗs kardías ánthrōpos*) spoken of by Peter as that part of a person that is visible only to God (1 Pet. 3:4). Thus the "inner man" is practically synonymous with the "heart" (cf. 1 S. 16:7c, "man looks on the outward appearance, but the Lord looks on the heart"). The domain of the Spirit's transforming power is the heart (Eph. 3:16); however, the strengthening of the inner self should issue into a transformation of the outward behavior as well (4:1-3). Paul confesses that his outward nature (or his "members") is still at war with his inward nature, which delights in the law of God (Rom. 7:22f.); but he is confident that one day the outward nature will also be redeemed (cf. 8:19-23).

See also NEW NATURE I.

N. J. O.

INNER NATURE. *See* INNER MAN.

INNER ROOM.

1. [Heb. *qubbâ*, a hapax legomenon (unless *qᵒḇāṯāh* in this verse is the same word incorrectly vocalized in the MT)] (Nu. 25:8). Views of the meaning of this term have varied since ancient times. No doubt influenced by early rabbinic exegesis, Aq., Symm., and Vulg. render this term "brothel" (respectively Gk. *tégos*, *porneíon*; Lat. *lupanar*), i.e., a tent used for immoral relations with the Midianite woman (S. C. Reif, *JBL*, 90 [1971], 202). The LXX has "oven" (Gk. *káminos*); perhaps this, like postbiblical Heb. *kûr* that it frequently translates, is a euphemism for "womb," and thus by extension "place of [Zimri's] immoral activities" (Reif, p. 202). Reif also notes the possibility that *káminon* is corrupt for an original *kamáran*, "vault, arched structure." The Pesh. has *qelāyṯā'*, "alcove," i.e., a recessed room in Zimri's tent.

The medieval Jewish grammarians Rashi, Ibn Ezra, and Ibn Jannach related Heb. *qubbâ* to Arab. *qubbatun*, "tent," and Ibn Ezra interpreted the present reference as a "tent-brothel" for Zimri and his brothers (Reif, p. 203).

Modern commentators have added to the possibilities. J. Morgenstern, also comparing the Arabic term, suggests "marriage-tent," i.e., a prototype of the tent used by the modern bedouin in which marriage is consummated (*HUCA*, 17 [1942/43], 260f.). F. M. Cross relates the term to the tabernacle, or at least to the sacred enclosure (*Biblical Archaeologist Reader*, 1 [1975], 218f.). Perhaps most attractive is Reif's suggestion that this was a tent shrine in which the Midianite woman practiced divination or was consulted regarding the origin and reason for the plague (pp. 204f.).

2. [Heb. *pānîm*] (1 K. 6:29); AV WITHIN; NEB INNER CHAMBER; [*pᵉnîmâ*] (1 K. 6:30; Ezk. 41:3); AV INWARD; [*pᵉnîmî*] (Ezk. 41:15); [*habbayiṯ happᵉnîmî*] (Ezk. 41:17a); AV INNER HOUSE; NEB INNER CHAMBER (41:17b); AV WITHIN; NEB INSIDE. Some of these are difficult to identify (Ezk. 41:15, 17; perhaps 1 K. 6:29f.), but in most the referent is probably the *dᵉḇîr*, the "most holy place" of the TEMPLE.

3. [Heb. *'îr*] (2 K. 10:25). The RSV rendering is based on A. Klostermann's old and quite popular emendation of *'îr* to *dᵉḇîr*, "most holy place" (*Die Bücher Samuelis und der Könige* [*Kurzgefasste Kommentäre*, 1887], *ad loc.*). More recent interpretations include "citadel" (F. Frick, *The City in Ancient Israel* [1977], p. 33), "temple quarter" (L. Fisher, *JSS*, 8 [1963], 37, cites parallels in Nuzi texts), "altar" (N. H. Snaith, *IB*, III, 242), and "inmost shrine" (J. Gray, *I & II Kings* [*OTL*, 2nd ed. 1970], p. 562, compares Ugar. *ǵr*).

4. [Gk. *tameíon*] (Mt. 24:26); AV SECRET CHAMBERS. The word can mean "innermost, hidden, (or) secret room" (of a house) or "storeroom" (Bauer, rev., p. 803). In this passage "in the inner rooms" probably means "in a residence somewhere" (cf. Lk. 17:23).

J. E. H.

INNOCENT; INNOCENCE [Heb. *nāqî*, *nāqî'*, *nāqâ*, *niqqāyôn*]; AV INNOCENCY; [*ṣaddîq*]; AV RIGHTEOUS; NEB also "those in the right" (Isa. 5:23); FAIR JUDGES (2 K. 10:9); [*ṣāḏaq*]; AV also BE RIGHTEOUS, JUSTIFY (Job 9:20); NEB RIGHT; [Gk. *akéraios*]; AV HARMLESS; NEB ABOVE REPROACH (Phil. 2:15); [*díkaios*]; AV RIGHTEOUS; [*athṓos*]; NEB CLEAN (Mt. 27:24); [*katharós*]; AV also CLEAN (Acts 18:6), PURE (Acts 20:26); NEB PURE (Acts 18:6), "no man's fate can be laid at my door" (Acts 20:26). The condition of being free from sin and guilt.

In the OT, two Hebrew roots are translated innocence — *nqh* and *ṣdq*. The Hebrew verb *nāqâ* means "be clean" or "innocent" in the sense of "free from guilt," e.g., Jer. 2:35, where the people claim they are innocent despite the fact that they have killed the poor unjustly. The psalmist requests God to keep him from presumptuous sins so he will be innocent (Ps. 19:13 [MT 14]). It also means to "count as innocent" or "acquit," e.g., Job 9:28 and 10:14.

The noun *niqqāyôn* from the same root is used rarely. Twice it is used of washing the hands in innocence (Ps. 26:6; 73:13) and once of Abimelech's protest to God that he took Sarah in all innocence (Gen. 20:5). More common is the adjective *nāqî*. It means "clean, exempt, free from guilt" and therefore is often translated "innocent." The majority of occurrences are coupled with *dām*, "blood," and translated by the RSV as "innocent blood." Occasionally the NEB translates this expression "innocent man," e.g., Jonah 1:14, "do not charge us with the death of an innocent man." The expression clearly refers to blood that has been shed unjustly and cruelly. Jeremiah uses it several times to characterize the social sins of Judah (e.g., Jer. 7:6). The other occurrences refer to innocent people, either in a negative or positive context. The interpretation of Job 22:30 is difficult; both the RSV and NEB understand the sense to be God delivering the innocent (person). However, the Hebrew has "not innocent," which is probably correct in light of the second half of the verse (M. Pope, *Job* [*AB*, 3rd ed. 1973], pp. 168f.).

The verb *ṣāḏaq* means to "be just" or "righteous." On a few occasions the RSV translates it "be innocent" where the meaning is to "be in the right" or "have a just cause" (Job 9:15, 20; 34:5). The adjective *ṣaddîq* means "just, righteous." It can mean "just in one's cause" or "right" in a legal sense. Dt. 25:1 is a good example of this legal aspect, where the innocent are acquitted and the guilty are condemned.

In the NT, the RSV renders four different adjectives as "innocent." The first term *akéraios* means "pure" in the sense of unmixed and is used figuratively in Mt. 10:16 where the twelve disciples are to be as innocent as doves. It occurs elsewhere in Phil. 2:15 where the command is to be blameless (*ámemptos*) and innocent, and in Rom. 16:19 (RSV "guileless"). A second term, *athǭos*, means "innocent" or "to be innocent of something." Judas recognizes his sin in betraying the innocent Jesus (Mt. 27:4), and Pilate washes his hands to be innocent of Jesus' blood (Mt. 27:24). Both of these terms tend to emphasize the negative, while the next two terms stress the positive. The first of these is *díkaios*, which translates *ṣaddîq* in the LXX and means "just, righteous, upright." On two occasions the RSV translates it as "innocent" — once of innocent martyrs of the OT (Mt. 23:35) and once when the centurion observes the innocence of Jesus after His death (Lk. 23:47). Finally, *katharós* — "clean" or "pure" — can convey both a ceremonial sense and a moral or religious sense of freedom from sin or guilt. The latter meaning is in view in Acts 18:6 and 20:26 where Paul's conscience is pure because he has carried out his obligation to preach the gospel. *See* JUSTIFICATION.

Bibliography.–BDB, pp. 667, 841f.; *TDNT,* I, *s.v.* ἀκέραιος (Kittel); II, *s.v.* δίκαιος (Schrenk); III, *s.v.* καθαρός (R. Meyer, Hauck).

J. C. MOYER

INNOCENTS, MASSACRE OF THE. The conventional, ecclesiastical name given to the slaughter by HEROD I of male children two years old and under in Bethlehem and its environs at the time of the birth of Jesus (Mt. 2:16).

I. Meaning and History of the Term
II. Analysis of Narrative with Special Reference to Motive
  A. Focus of Narrative — Residence at Nazareth
  B. Corollaries from Above Facts
  C. Marks of Historicity

I. Meaning and History of the Term.–The accepted title for this event may be traced through Augustine to Cyprian. Irenaeus (d. A.D. 202) called these children "martyrs," and interprets the tragedy as a gracious and tender "sending before" into His kingdom by the Lord Himself. Cyprian (d. A.D. 258) said: "That it might be manifest that they who are slain for Christ's sake are innocent, innocent infancy was put to death for his name's sake" (*Epistula* 55.6). Augustine (b. A.D. 354), following Cyprian, speaks of the children, formally, as "the Innocents" (Comm. on Ps. 43:5).

The ecclesiastical treatment of the incident is remarkable because of the exaggerations about the extent of the massacre and the number of victims. At an early date the Greek church canonized 14,000, and afterward, by a curious misinterpretation of Rev. 14:1, 3, the number was increased to 144,000.

According to H. H. Milman the liturgy of the Church of England retains a reminiscence of this ancient error in the use of Rev. 14 on Holy Innocents' Day (*History of Latin Christianity,* I, 107 n. e). This exaggeration, of which there is no hint in the NT, is worthy of note because the most serious general argument against the historicity of the narrative is drawn from the silence of Josephus. As in all probability there could not have been more than twenty children involved (cf. F. W. Farrar, *Life of Christ,* I, 45 n.), the incident could not have seemed very significant among the series of horrors perpetrated or planned by Herod in the last months of his life (cf. Farrar, *The Herods,* pp. 144f.).

II. Analysis of Narrative with Special Reference to Motive.–In estimating the value of such a narrative from the viewpoint of historicity, the first and most important step is to determine the motive. Why was the story told? This question is not easy to answer, but in the present instance a very simple and effective test is at hand.

A. Focus of Narrative — Residence at Nazareth. In Matthew's infancy section (chs. 1–2) five quotations from the OT are set into the narrative of events. These five quotations represent the outstanding points of interest. The quotations are placed (1) at the announcement of the Virgin Birth (1:23); (2) at the birth at Bethlehem (2:6); (3) at the visit to Egypt (2:15); (4) at the murder of the children (2:18); (5) at the Nazareth residence (2:23). It is significant that no quotation is attached to the visit of the Magi. This omission is the more noteworthy because Nu. 24:7; Ps. 72:15; Isa. 60:6, and numerous references to the ingathering of the Gentiles have such appropriate passages to link the birth with the visit of the strangers from the Far East. This peculiar omission, on the part of a writer so deeply interested in prophecy and its fulfillment, can be explained only on the ground that the visit of the Magi did not, in the writer's view, occupy a point of special interest. Their visit is told, not for its own sake, but because of its connection with the murder of the children and the journey to Egypt. The murder of the children is of interest because it discloses the character of Herod and the perils surrounding the newborn Messiah. It also explains the visit to Egypt and the subsequent residence at Nazareth. The latter is evidently the objective point, because it is given a place by itself and marked by a quotation. Moreover, the one evidence of overstrain in the narrative is in the ambiguous and obscure statement by which the OT is brought into relationship with the Nazareth residence. The center of interest in the entire section which is concerned with Herod and the Magi is the Nazareth residence. The story is told for the express purpose of explaining why the heir of David, who was born at Bethlehem, lived at Nazareth.

This brings the narrative of Matthew into striking relationship with Luke. The latter's concern is to show how it was that the Messiah who lived at Nazareth was born at Bethlehem. We have here an undesigned unity that binds together these two narratives, which are seemingly so divergent. That Matthew says nothing about a previous residence at Nazareth and that Luke says nothing about a forced return there may be explained, in accordance with the balance of probabilities, on the ground either that each evangelist was ignorant of the fact omitted by himself, or that in his condensed and rapid statement he did not see fit to mention it. In any case the harmony immeasurably outweighs the discrepancy.

B. Corollaries from Above Facts. The fact that the focus of the entire narrative lies in the residence of Jesus at Nazareth effectually disposes of a number of current hypotheses as to its origin.

(1) The idea that it is merely legend told for literary embellishment. The dovetailing of what would be the main item into the rest of the narrative and its subordination to secondary features cannot be explained on this hypothesis. The absence of adornment by available passages from the OT alone is conclusive on this point (W. C. Allen, comm. on Matthew [*ICC*, 1907], pp. 14f.).

(2) The idea that the story is told for the purpose of illustrating the scope of the Messiah's influence beyond Israel. Here again the subordinate position assigned to the story of the Magi, together with the absence of OT material, is conclusive. Moreover, the story of the Magi is abruptly dropped with the statement of their return home. Interest in them disappears as soon as their brief connection with the movement of the history through Herod ceases. Also, the intensely Hebraic character of Matthew's infancy section as a whole is incidental evidence pointing in the same direction.

(3) The idea that the story is told to emphasize the miraculous element in connection with the birth of Christ. The facts contradict this. In addition to the primary consideration (the Magi's subordinate position in the narrative), there are others of great value. That the Magi were providentially guided to the feet of the Messiah is evidently the firm conviction of the narrator.

The striking feature of the story is that with this belief in mind the narrator keeps so strictly within the limits of the natural order. In vv. 9, 12 only is there apparent exception. Of these the statement in v. 9 is the only one peculiar to this part of the narrative. Two things are to be remembered concerning it. It is clear that the verse cannot be interpreted apart from a clear understanding of the whole astronomical occurrence of which it forms a part. It is also evident that v. 9 must not be interpreted apart from the context. From the viewpoint of a wonder-tale the writer makes a fatal blunder at the most critical point of his story. The popular notion that the Magi were miraculously led to the Messiah finds no support in the text. The Magi did not come to Bethlehem, but to Jerusalem, asking: "Where is he that is born King of the Jews?" Verse 9 comes after this statement and after the conclave called by Herod in which Bethlehem was specified. In view of all this it seems clear that the Magi were led, not miraculously, but in accordance with the genius of their own system, and that the providential element lay in the striking coincidence of their visit and the birth of Jesus. The interest of the writer was not in heightening the miraculous element; otherwise, he would have sharpened its outlines and expurgated all ambiguity about the nature of the occurrence.

C. Marks of Historicity. 1. The centering of the narrative upon the residence at Nazareth not only brings Luke's Gospel in support of the center, but groups the story around a point of known interest to the first generation of believers. It is interesting to note that the residence in Egypt has independent backing of a sort. There are in existence two stories, one traced by Origen through Jews of his own day to earlier times, and the other in the Talmud, which connect Jesus with Egypt and attempt to account for His miracles by reference to Egyptian magic (F. F. Bruce, *Jesus and Christian Origins Outside the NT* [1974], pp. 54-65).

2. Another mark of historicity is the telling of the story of the Magi so objectively and with such personal detachment. Both Jews and early Christians had strong views about astrology and magic in general, but the author of this Gospel tells the story without emphasis and without comment and from the viewpoint of the Magi. His interest is purely historical and matter-of-fact.

3. The portrait of Herod the Great supports historicity. So far as Herod is concerned, the incident is usually discussed with reference to the savagery involved. Many affirm that we have here a hostile and unfair portrait. This contention could hardly be sustained even if the question turned entirely upon the point of savagery. But there is far more than savagery in the incident. First there is this undeniable element of inherent probability in the story. Practically all of Herod's murders, including those of his beloved wife and his sons, were perpetrated under the sway of one emotion and in obedience to a single motive. They were in practically every instance for the purpose of consolidating or perpetuating his power. He nearly destroyed his own immediate family in the half-mad jealousy that on occasion drove him to the very limits of ferocity, simply because they were accused of plotting against him. The accusations were largely false, but the suspicion doomed those accused. The murder of the Innocents was another crime of the same sort. The old king was obsessed by the fear of a claimant to his petty throne; the messianic hope of the Jews was a perpetual secret torment, and the murder of the children, in the attempt to reach the child whose advent threatened him, was so original in method and so characteristic in purpose as to give verisimilitude to the whole narrative. Also, Herod's prompt discovery of the visit of the Magi and their questions is in harmony with what we know of the old ruler's watchfulness and his elaborate system of espionage. Third, the subtlety with which Herod deals with the whole situation is characteristic of him. How striking and vivid, with all its rugged simplicity, is the story of the king's pretended interest in the quest of the strangers, the solemn conclave of Jewish leaders with himself in the role of earnest inquirer, his urgent request for information that he may worship also, followed by his swift anger (note that *ethymṓthē*, "be enraged" [v. 16], is not used elsewhere in the NT) at being deceived, and the blind but terrible stroke of his questing vengeance.

All this was so true of Herod, of the atmosphere that always surrounded him, and of the historic situation, that we are forced to conclude, either that we have veracious history more or less directly received from one who was an observer of the events described, or the work of an incomparably clever romancer.

See also WISE MEN.

Bibliography.–R. E. Brown, *The Birth of the Messiah* (1977), pp. 104-119, 202-230; D. Hill, comm. on Matthew (*New Century Bible*, 1972), pp. 84-86.

L. M. SWEET

INORDINATE. A term derived from Lat. *in*, "not," and *ordinatus*, "set in order," hence "immoderate," "excessive." In the two AV occurrences the original has no corresponding adjective, but the word is inserted by the translators as being implied by the noun. The term does not occur at all in the RSV. For "inordinate love" (Heb. *ʿagāḇâ*, Ezk. 23:11) the RSV has "doting"; for "inordinate affection" (Gk. *páthos*, Col. 3:5), the RSV gives "passion." In classical Greek *páthos* denotes any affection or emotion of the mind, whether good or bad. In the NT, however, it occurs only in a negative sense.

D. M. EDWARDS

INQUIRE [Heb. *dāraš* (1 K. 22:5; Am. 5:14; etc.), *šā'al* (1 S. 10:22; etc.), *bāqar* (Lev. 27:33; 2 K. 16:15), *bā'â* (Isa. 21:12), *bāqaš* (Est. 2:23; Ps. 27:4; Dnl. 1:20); Gk. *pynthánomai* (Jn. 4:54; etc.), *zētéō* (Acts 9:11), *ereunaō, exereunaō* (1 Pet. 1:10f.)]; **INQUIRY** [Heb. *biqqōreṯ* (Lev. 19:20), *pāqaḏ* (Job 31:14); Aram. *b^eqar* (Ezr. 7:14); Gk. *dierōtáō* (Acts 10:17)]; AV also ASK, ENQUIRE, SEARCH, MAKE INQUISITION, etc.; NEB also SEEK GUIDANCE or COUNSEL, MAKE CAREFUL or DILIGENT EXAMINATION, CONSULT, FIND OUT, INVESTIGATE. Of the Hebrew words, *šā'al, bāqar,* and *bā'â* have the direct sense of "inquire" or "ask," while *dāraš, bāqaš,* and *pāqaḏ* mean "seek" or "search" and so "inquire" and "investigate" (cf. Est. 2:23). There is not, however, much distinction between the words, and they may be found together in a single verse in synonymous parallelism (Zeph. 1:6), sometimes to intensify the sense (Dt. 13:14: "You shall inquire and make search and ask diligently"; cf. NEB "careful examination").

While the OT speaks of normal human inquiry — whether informal (e.g., Gen. 43:27, into the health of Joseph's family; 2 S. 11:3, into the identity of Bathsheba) or formal investigation (e.g., Dt. 13:14; Est. 2:23; on Ps. 9:12 [MT 13], *see* AVENGE) — it is largely concerned with approach to God, especially for specific purposes. For example, when the Israelites had disputes with their neighbors, they came to Moses to "inquire of the Lord" for judgment (Ex. 18:15); the tribe of Dan "inquired of the Lord" whether they should move north (Jgs. 18:5); Hazael went to Elijah to inquire of God whether he would recover from his illness (2 K. 8:8); Jehoshaphat desired to inquire of the Lord before going into battle with Ahab against Syria (1 K. 22:5-8; cf. 2 Ch. 18:4-7) and with Jehoram against Moab and its allies (2 K. 3:11). In fact the question of doing battle is the most frequent inquiry made of God, especially in the historical books and particularly by David (e.g., Jgs. 20:18, 23, 27; 1 S. 14:37; 23:2, 4; 2 S. 2:1; 5:19, 23; cf. 1 Ch. 14:10-14).

Israelites made this inquiry in specific ways. Generally, in the earlier history of Israel, "inquiry" was made through the priest (e.g., Nu. 27:21; cf. Jgs. 18:5; 1 S. 22:9-15; 2 K. 22:13, 18) by the use of the URIM AND THUMMIM. Although the method is not certain, from 1 S. 14:36-42 especially it would seem that the Urim and Thummim involved casting lots.

According to 1 S. 9:9 the priestly inquiry was replaced by inquiry through the prophets in the early days of the monarchy (cf. 1 K. 14:5; 22:5, 7f.; 2 K. 3:11; 8:8; 2 Ch. 11:2-4; Jer. 21:2; 37:7; Ezk. 14:3, 7, 10; 20:1-3). With the apparent exception of David, most inquiry of God was made through the priest or the prophet. David's seemingly direct inquiry of God (cf. 1 S. 23:2, 4; 2 S. 2:1; 5:19, 23) may be instructive. Perhaps such inquiry was made possible when Abiathar — the son of Ahimelech, the priest through whom David had earlier inquired of the Lord (1 S. 22:9f.) — brought to David the ephod. Presumably, the ephod contained the Urim and Thummim, and thus enabled David to inquire of the Lord for himself.

"Inquiry of the Lord" was not always rewarded with a response. In contrast with the specific direction which David received, Saul's inquiry of the Lord met with no response on at least two occasions (1 S. 14:37; 28:6), due to sin (cf. 1 S. 14:41f.). That sin prevents the Lord from responding is the message of the prophets, especially of Ezekiel, through whom the Lord refuses "to be inquired of at all" by idolaters and sinners (Ezk. 14:1-5; 20:1-3). Apparently, God speaks only to those who have a proper attitude of heart.

Nowhere do these elements come together more clearly than in 1 S. 28:6. There Saul inquires of the Lord concerning a battle with the Philistines but receives no response, whether by dreams, or by Urim (through the priest?), or by prophets. In desperation, Saul resorts to the witch of Endor in direct violation of the Mosaic law (cf. Ex. 22:18; Lev. 19:26; 20:27; Dt. 18:10-14). This sin, following the transgressions that had already stilled the voice of God, was the last straw: the next day Saul and all his successors were killed in battle.

Israel was constantly tempted to inquire of other gods (2 K. 1:2-16), or of idols (Hos. 4:12), as well as of false priests (Jgs. 18:5) and false prophets (1 K. 22:5-23).

In the NT the sense is predictable. While *pynthánomai* always means "ask" (cf. *erōtáō* and its compounds), *eraunáō* or *ereunáō* means "search." *Zētéō* means "strive for," "follow after" (Mt. 6:33; Rom. 10:3; etc.) rather than "ask," and implies an act of the will (cf. *DNTT,* III, 531f.). Most of these NT uses are found in narrative sections in normal human dialogue. *Ereunáō (exereunáō)* suggests the idea of research, study, or investigation. Sometimes it is God who searches the hearts of men (cf. Rom. 8:27; 1 Cor. 2:10; Rev. 2:23) and sometimes it is people who search or inquire into Scripture, specifically for evidence of the Messiah (cf. 1 Pet. 1:10f.; Jn. 5:39; 7:52). The OT sense of "inquiry of the Lord" is not apparent in the NT.

H. VAN BROEKHOVEN, JR.

INSCRIPTION [Heb. *miḵtāḇ*] (Ex. 39:30); AV WRITING; NEB ENGRAVING; [*pittû(a)ḥ*] (Zec. 3:9); AV GRAVING; NEB "meaning"; [Gk. *epigraphḗ*] (Mt. 22:20; Mk. 12:16; 15:26; Lk. 20:24; 23:38); AV SUPERSCRIPTION; [*epigráphō*] (Acts 17:23); **INSCRIBE** [Heb. *ḥāqaq*] (Job 19:23; Isa. 30:8); NEB also ENGRAVE; [*rāšam*] Dnl. 10:21); AV NOTED; NEB WRITTEN; [Aram. *r^ešam*] (Dnl. 5:24f.); AV WRITING; [Gk. *gráphomai*] (Rev. 19:12, 16); AV, NEB, WRITTEN; [*epigráphō*] (Rev. 21:12); AV WRITTEN. In Zec. 14:20 the RSV and NEB supply "inscribed," while the AV translates literally, "shall be upon."

The Heb. *kāṯaḇ,* of which *miḵtāḇ* is a cognate, means simply "write," while *pittû(a)ḥ* refers more specifically to an engraving. The context, however, indicates that the inscription in Ex. 39:30 was also engraved (cf. 28:36). The inscription "Holy to the Lord" signified that the priest was set apart for special service to Yahweh. Zechariah prophesied that in the last days, after the annihilation of all the forces of evil, this same phrase would be inscribed on the bells of the horses (Zec. 14:20).

One way of preserving testimony for succeeding generations was to inscribe it in a book. Isaiah was told to write his oracles in a book "that it may be for the time to come as a witness for ever" (30:8). Job desired to have his words written down so that he might be vindicated by posterity (19:23). On Dnl. 10:21, *see* BOOK OF TRUTH.

In the NT the term *epigraphḗ* is used by each of the Synoptics for the legend on a coin designating the person in whose honor or by whose authority the coin was issued (Mt. 22:20; Mk. 12:16; Lk. 20:24). It is also used for the charge against Jesus that was fixed to the cross in accordance with Roman custom (Mk. 15:26; Lk. 23:38; cf. Mt. 27:37; Jn. 19:19).

Archeology has not uncovered an altar with the inscription "To an Unknown God" in Athens, but such altars have been found in other cities, and ancient writers reported seeing them in Athens (cf. Pausanias i.1.4; Philostratus *Life of Apollonius* vi.3.5).

See also ARCHEOLOGY; INSCRIPTIONS; WRITING.

N. J. O.

INSCRIPTIONS. Documents written or engraved on hard surfaces and intended for public display as lasting records. They may be distinguished on the one hand from writings on perishable materials, such as PAPYRUS, and on the other from those intended for private use, including LETTERS and seals; to the latter category also belong many graffiti and most OSTRACA (*see also* SEALS AND SCARABS).

I. Form and Content
- A. Writing Systems and Materials
  1. Egyptian Hieroglyphic
  2. Cuneiform
  3. The Alphabet
- B. Purposes of Inscriptions
  1. Commemorations of Military Victories
  2. Commemorations of Other Public Events
  3. Proclamations and Decrees
  4. Treaties
  5. Law Codes
  6. Epitaphs
  7. Religious Texts

II. Ancient Israel: Inscriptional Evidence
- A. Pre-Israelite Syria and Palestine
- B. Conquest and Settlement
- C. Early Monarchy
- D. Age of Assyrian Invasions
- E. Exile
- F. Persian Age

III. The Early Church: Inscriptional Evidence
- A. Jerusalem
- B. Scythopolis
- C. Caesarea
- D. Delphi

I. Form and Content.–Several kinds of information were communicated by inscription in the ancient world, and the variety of uses to which public documents were put seems to have transcended cultural boundaries; but the materials and techniques involved in the production of inscriptions in the earliest centers of civilization differed.

A. Writing Systems and Materials. The great majority of inscriptions that bear upon biblical history are in Egyptian hieroglyphic, cuneiform, or the alphabet, the three great writing systems which arose in Egypt, Mesopotamia, and Syria-Palestine respectively. In the cases of both cuneiform and alphabetic writing special developments carried the systems beyond the boundaries of their lands of origin.

1. Egyptian Hieroglyphic. Public documents in Egypt were usually written in the complex pictographic script known as hieroglyphic, less often in its cursive derivatives, hieratic and demotic. The discovery in 1799 of the ROSETTA STONE, a trilingual inscription of 196 B.C. honoring Ptolemy V Epiphanes in equivalent texts of hieroglyphic, demotic, and Greek, led eventually to the decipherment of the hieroglyphic writing system as well as the ancient Egyptian language, itself almost unknown previously. An enormous number of hieroglyphic texts are now known and understood, many with direct or indirect relevance to biblical studies. *See also* ARCHEOLOGY OF EGYPT II.A; IV.D.

2. Cuneiform. CUNEIFORM was a type of wedge-shaped writing developed in Mesopotamia for use on clay tablets, but for the execution of public documents the system was transferred to stone. The language of most cuneiform inscriptions of direct relevance to biblical studies is Akkadian, the Semitic language of Mesopotamia, in its dialectal subdivisions, Assyrian and Babylonian. A large number of Assyrian and Babylonian inscriptions from the 2nd and 1st millennia B.C. shed important light on biblical history. Among the several peoples who adapted Mesopotamian cuneiform to their own needs were the early inhabitants of Syria, Asia Minor (the Hurrians, the Hittites), and Persia, and it was the simplified system of Old Persian that provided modern scholars with clues for the decipherment of cuneiform. The key inscription in this regard was the accession memorial of DARIUS the Great (522-486 B.C.) at BEHISTUN (modern Bisitun, Iran) with its trilingual (Old Persian, Babylonian, and Elamite) text. *See also* ARCHEOLOGY OF MESOPOTAMIA II; BABYLONIA V.C.

3. The Alphabet. The alphabet probably was invented sometime in the first half of the 2nd millennium B.C. The oldest known writing that is indisputably alphabetic in character is that of the so-called Proto-Sinaitic inscriptions, rock-cut graffiti from an ancient turquoise-mining community at Serābîṭ el-Khâdim in the Sinai Peninsula. These texts, still incompletely understood, seem to be votive in character, engraved to accompany offerings made by Asiatic slaves in the Egyptian mines of the region; Egyptian monuments from the same period also survive (cf. *ANET,* pp. 29-30). Linear alphabetic inscriptions do not become plentiful, however, until after the beginning of the Iron Age (*ca.* 1200 B.C.), when documents in the various local branches of the parent Canaanite script — viz., Phoenician, Hebrew, Aramaic, Ammonite, Moabite, and Edomite — begin to appear. Most of the inscriptions that survive from this period are incised in stone, but there is reason to believe that at least among the Israelites and their Transjordanian neighbors public documents were written frequently with ink on surfaces prepared with plaster (cf. Dt. 27:2f., 8), as discoveries from Tell Deir ʿallā in southern Transjordan and Kuntillet ʿAjrūd in the wilderness of northern Sinai suggest (see II.E, F below). Such materials may have seemed sufficiently durable to those who employed them, but plaster inscriptions are permanent only under exceptional conditions of climate and archeological context. This is probably a chief reason that the corpus of public documents that survive from the period of the Israelite monarchy is quite small.

The economy and utility of alphabetic writing prompted a rapid extension of its use beyond the boundaries of Syria and Palestine during the 1st millennium B.C. The Aramaic script and language were adopted for official use in the chancellery affairs of the Assyrian empire, a role they maintained during the later period of Persian ascendancy. The transmission of the alphabet from Phoenicia to Greece led to its further expansion and refinement. Inscriptions of relevance to NT studies are predominantly in the Greek and Roman alphabets, less often in the indigenous systems of the Levant, such as Aramaic and Paleo-Hebrew, an archaizing Jewish script that survived in limited use after the general spread of Aramaic in the Persian Age to be revived briefly in the Hasmonean and Herodian periods.

B. Purposes of Inscriptions. Committing information to an inscription was believed to accomplish two things. First, it placed the information officially before the public. A decree or edict went into effect formally upon its publication as an inscription; it became generally obligatory or effective. Second, information so published could be thought of as permanently enshrined; it would endure, carrying its message to future generations. Public monuments were believed to accord a kind of permanency to the glory of particular human achievements, and this belief must have been an important part of the motivation for making inscriptions, underlying most of the purposes to which they were put, as listed below.

1. Commemorations of Military Victories. Success at war was routinely memorialized in stone, and victory stelae are uniquely valuable to modern scholars because of their relative abundance and the specific historical information they supply. As detailed below, much of our knowledge of the peoples and places of second-millennium Palestine comes from the monuments made by Egyptian pharaohs to commemorate their conquests in Asia. Similarly, the biblical picture of the history of the Israelite and Judean monarchies and their neighbors in Iron Age Syria-Palestine is considerably filled out by information culled from the annalistic accounts of the triumphs of the Assyrian kings that appear on the monuments they left behind in the west or erected at home.

2. Commemorations of Other Public Events. Other achievements were also recorded for posterity in inscriptions. To this category belong especially those documents which celebrate the completion of buildings or other public works, many examples of which are cited below.

3. Proclamations and Decrees. As noted above, royal edicts were often published as inscriptions in order to place them formally in public view and, therefore, to make them generally binding or effective. So it is, for example, that copies of the decrees of Xerxes mentioned in Est. 3:12f. and 8:9-12 are said to have been promulgated to the people (Est. 3:14; 8:13) so that they would "be ready" for the execution of the king's instructions.

4. Treaties. Treaties between nations were often recorded in inscriptions and publicly displayed. Such documents shed invaluable light on the political relationships of involved parties and frequently on the general history of a particular period as well. Treaties have survived in gratifying numbers from some of the politically most complex ages in Syria-Palestinian antiquity, such as the period of independence and realignment in eighth-century Syria that preceded the arrival of Tiglath-pileser III (see III.E below).

5. Law Codes. The existence of a common legal tradition spread throughout ancient western Asia is demonstrated by a number of surviving collections of law, especially from Middle Bronze Age Mesopotamia. Such legal "codes," as they are somewhat improperly called, were preserved in inscriptions for the purpose of honoring the kings responsible for promulgating them. Anonymous collections of law, on the other hand, sometimes survive on clay tablets, but they tend not to have been incorporated into public inscriptions. All of these materials are useful to students of the legal parts of the OT.

6. Epitaphs. Tomb inscriptions identifying and sometimes eulogizing the dead survive from all parts of the ancient Near East. Such texts frequently contain deterrents to grave robbers in the form of grievous curses invoked upon anyone who disturbs the rest of the deceased or, alternatively, assurances of the absence of valuable grave goods.

7. Religious Texts. On occasion written monuments were set up for specifically religious purposes. Sacred texts of special importance might be publicly displayed (cf. Dt. 27:2f.; Josh. 8:30-32). Hymns and prayers were sometimes included in inscriptions. Amulets or plaques bearing apotropaic incantations were worn or attached to doorposts as insurance against demons.

II. Ancient Israel: Inscriptional Evidence.–In the following synopsis the principal inscriptions from Egypt, Mesopotamia, and Syria-Palestine that bear directly or indirectly on the study of the OT are listed by historical periods.

A. Pre-Israelite Syria and Palestine. The illumination of the history and civilization of Syria-Palestine by articulate records begins long before the arrival of the Israelites in Canaan. Biblical scholars study the earlier periods as background to the later history and as the arena of the patriarchal sojourns described in Genesis.

1. Early Bronze Age (*ca.* 3100-2200 B.C.). Much of our knowledge of the political history of Bronze Age Syria-Palestine comes from the information provided in the military records of Mesopotamian and Egyptian kings, whose interest in the area was already active in the 3rd millennium B.C. The kings of Akkad erected monuments describing their campaigns in the west; and although the stelae themselves have not survivied, copies of the texts on clay tablets (*ANET,* pp. 267f.) refer to victories over major Syrian cities, including Mari and Ebla, by the first and fourth dynasts, Sargon (2371-2316) and Naram-Sin (2291-2255), who are said to have marched as far as "the Cedar Mountain" (the Amanus) and "the Upper Sea" (the Mediterranean).

Egyptian activity to the south in Palestine during this period is illustrated by the cenotaph inscription of Uni, military commander in Asia under Pepi I (2332-2283), found at Abydos (*ANET,* pp. 227f.). Uni speaks of his successes against the "Sand-Dwellers," as he contemptuously calls the Asiatics, in five separate campaigns.

2. Middle Bronze Age (*ca.* 2200-1550). Another cenotaph inscription from Abydos, that of a nobleman called Djaa (*ANET,* p. 230), provides information about an Asiatic campaign undertaken during the Middle Kingdom by Sen-Usert III (1878-1843), who is said to have won a great victory over "the wretched Retenu," as the peoples of Syria and Palestine are collectively described, including in particular "a foreign country of which the name was Sekmem," probably Shechem.

Shechem is also among the enemies of Egypt listed in the Execration Texts from the time of Sen-Usert and later (*ANET,* pp. 328f.). These are ceramic bowls and figurines inscribed with the names of enemies and ritually smashed. In addition to Shechem, later Israelite cities such as Hazor, Beth-shemesh, and Jerusalem are also mentioned, as well as Iy-ʿanaq, a name which has been compared to that of the biblical "sons of Anak" (*ʿᵃnāq*), aboriginal inhabitants of the Hebron area (Josh. 15:14; Jgs. 1:20), and Shutu, possibly equivalent to Moab (cf. Nu. 24:17), one of whose princes was named Ayyabum, that is, Job (Heb. *ʾîyōḇ*).

The Middle Bronze Age is the time from which the great Mesopotamian collections of law derive (cf. I.B.5 above). These include not only the famous Code of Hammurabi (1792-1750), the sixth and greatest king of the 1st Dynasty of Babylon (*ANET,* pp. 163-180; *see also* HAMMURABI, CODE OF), but also the earlier Sumerian law codes of Ur-Nammu (2112-2095), founder of the 3rd Dynasty of Ur (*ANET,* pp. 523-25), and Lipit-Ishtar (1934-1924), a ruler of the 1st Dynasty of Isin (*ANET,* pp. 159-161); in neither of the latter two cases does the original stele survive, but the texts can be largely restored from later copies. In all three collections the laws themselves are introduced by a prologue, in which the king responsible for them identifies himself and speaks of a divine commission he has received to promote justice and equity in his land.

The great cuneiform archives from Alalakh and especially Mari provide extensive information about the history of Syria and western Mesopotamia in the Middle Bronze Age as well as about the economic, legal, and social customs of the region, but public monuments from these sites are relatively rare. An important exception is a brick inscription from Mari in which King Yaḫdun-

Lim (*ca.* 1800) dedicates a temple to Šamaš, the sun-god, with whose help he claims to have campaigned westward as far as the Mediterranean, quelled an uprising of nomadic kings, and erected the Šamaš temple within a single year (*ANET,* pp. 556f.).

3. Late Bronze Age (*ca.* 1550-1200). Another exception is a statue of Idrimi, a king of Alalakh early in the Late Bronze Age, inscribed with a first-person account of his early life as a political refugee from Syria living in Canaan among the *ḫapiru* and his subsequent return to Syria, where he became king of the district of Mukiš, the capital of which was Alalakh (*ANET,* pp. 557f.). The story, which is reminiscent in many ways of the biblical account of David's rise to power (1 S. 16–2 S. 5), is valuable for its high literary quality as well as the light it throws on the civilization of contemporary Canaan and north Syria.

Statue of King Idrimi (*ca.* 1450 B.C.) of Alalakh in northern Syria. The cuneiform text is inscribed across the front of his garment (Trustees of the British Museum)

The reassertion of Egyptian power in Palestine and Syria after the 2nd Intermediate Period, the Hyksos interlude, is well documented by the inscriptions of the kings of the 18th Dynasty. Greatest of these was Thutmose III (1483-1450), who conducted seventeen Asiatic campaigns in his first twenty years of independent rule and recorded most of them on the walls of the temple of Amon-Re at Karnak (*ANET,* pp. 234-241). These Annals of Karnak provide considerable information about the situation en-

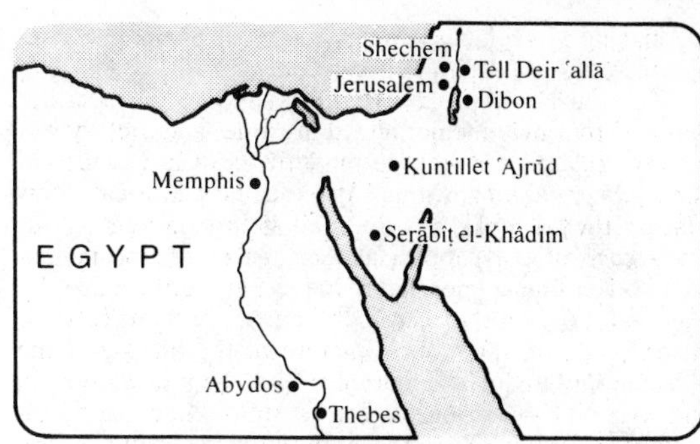

countered in Asia during the campaigns, of which the most important were probably the first, when Thutmose won a dramatic victory at Megiddo over a coalition that had been organized at Kadesh on the Orontes, and the eighth, when he marched as far as the Euphrates, breaking the power of the Hurrian state of Mitanni, which had become Egypt's chief rival for control of Syria. Another inscription from the same temple contains a roster of enemy states in "Upper Retjenu" (i.e., the mountains of Syria-Palestine) and "the mysterious lands of the marshes of Asia," from which Thutmose took prisoners (*ANET,* pp. 242f.); this text represents an invaluable topographical resource and is important not only in its own right but also because it established a precedent followed by subsequent kings, who expanded the roster. Thutmose's successors, Amenhotep II (1450-1425) and Thutmose IV (1425-1417), also made incursions into the land of "Retjenu," Syria-Palestine, and recorded them in inscriptions at Memphis, Karnak, and elsewhere (for Amenhotep's, see *ANET,* pp. 245-48); but these were little more than punitive raids — hardly campaigns — and Egypt's Asiatic empire, especially in its northern reaches, was eroding.

The public documents of the Amarna period show little interest in Egypt's territories in Asia and, therefore, provide scant information about contemporary Syria-Palestine, especially in contrast to the riches of the cuneiform archive of the famous AMARNA TABLETS. On the other hand, the religious pronouncements in the inscriptions of Amenhotep IV, Akhenaten (1379-1362), are of great interest to biblical scholars and students of religion in general for the light they cast on the heretical "Aten monotheism" of the period. Of particular interest is the "long hymn" to the Aten from the tomb of an official of the Amarna court named Ay (*ANET,* pp. 369-371), which has been compared in its general spirit and in some particulars to Ps. 104.

The reassertion of Egyptian power in Asia after the Amarna interlude is illustrated by the inscriptions of the great warrior-kings of the 19th Dynasty, Seti I (1318-1304), Ramses II (1304-1237), and Merneptah (1236-1223). Seti's inscriptions at Karnak (*ANET,* pp. 254f.) describe his campaigns in the Sinai and Palestine and as far north as Kadesh on the Orontes, where he confronted the power of the new Hittite Empire. He won a major victory over insurgents from Hamath at BETH-SHEAN (Tell el-Ḥuṣn) and recorded the event in two basalt stelae (*ANET,* pp. 253-55); Beth-shean was a city in "Upper Retjenu" that had been captured by Thutmose III after his victory at Megiddo (cf. *ANET,* p. 242) and where Ramses II subsequently campaigned, leaving behind his own stele (*ANET,* p. 255). Ramses, rebuilder of the old Hyksos capital Avaris as "the House of Ramses" (cf. Ex. 1:11) and generally regarded as the pharaoh of the Exodus, campaigned extensively in Asia during his long reign and left

Victory stelae of Seti I (left) and Ramses II (right) from Beth-shean (University Museum, University of Pennsylvania)

monuments to his accomplishments at several sites in Syria and Palestine as well as at home at Karnak and other Egyptian cities. The texts of these inscriptions (*ANET,* pp. 255-58) document the resolution of the conflict with the Hittites and, after initial difficulties, the establishment of Egyptian control of Palestine and the Phoenician coast as far north as Byblos.

B. Conquest and Settlement. A *terminus ante quem* for the arrival of Israel in Canaan is established by the so-called Israel Stele of Ramses II's son and successor Merneptah (1236-1223). The text (*ANET,* pp. 376-78) contains a series of victory hymns listing conquered enemies, including "Israel," of whom it is said that he "is laid waste, his seed is no more." The stele designates settled peoples with the hieroglyphic determinative for foreign countries, but Israel is marked only as a people, a detail that has been taken to mean that the Israelites, though they had arrived in Canaan by the time of Merneptah, were not yet settled there. *See also* ARCHEOLOGY OF EGYPT IV.D.

The arrival of the Israelites was roughly contemporaneous with the arrival of a number of other peoples, among them the Arameans and the "Peoples of the Sea," including in particular the Philistines, who would rival Israel for control of Palestine. The problems the sea-peoples created for Syria-Palestine as well as Egypt are illustrated by Egyptian inscriptions of the period. Merneptah lists several of the sea-peoples among the conquered enemies of the Israel Stele (see above), but he gave them only a temporary check. The inundation came in the time of Ramses III (1198-1166), the ablest king of the 20th Dynasty, who left an inscription in his temple at Medinet Habu (Thebes) recounting his partly successful war against the Philistines and other sea-peoples.

The earliest unambiguous references to Arameans in Syria are in the inscriptions of the Assyrian conqueror Tiglath-pileser I (1115-1077) (*ANET*, pp. 274f.), who found it necessary to cross the Euphrates twenty-eight times during his reign to keep the Arameans under control.

No Israelite inscriptions from the time of the Conquest and the period of the judges have survived. Even in the absence of extant monuments (such as the one described in Josh. 8:30-35), however, we are assured that there was literacy in the premonarchial period by the discovery of a number of ostraca, seals, inscribed arrowheads, etc., as well as a scribal practice tablet from ʿIzbet Ṣarṭah, near biblical Aphek, dating to the early 12th cent. B.C. (see M. Kochavi, *Tel Aviv*, 4 [1977], 1-13).

C. Early Monarchy. The time of Israel's united monarchy is not represented by surviving public monuments, though at least two such inscriptions are mentioned in the Bible. We are told in 1 S. 15:12 that Saul erected a monument to himself at the village of Carmel (modern Kermel, S of Hebron) after his victory over the Amalekites, and David, when his march of conquest reached the Euphrates, is said to have set up a monument there (1 Ch. 18:13; cf. 2 S. 8:3), just as the Egyptian kings Thutmose I and Thutmose III (see II.A, B above) had done before him.

From contemporary Phoenicia comes a series of sepulchral inscriptions from the tombs of five tenth-century kings of Byblos. The earliest of these is incised on the rim of the sarcophagus of Ahiram of Byblos, who died early in the 10th cent. (*ANET*, p. 661). Another, that of Abibaal, was incised on a seated statue of the founder of the 22nd

Sarcophagus of King Ahiram of Byblos (Gebal). This side shows him seated on a throne and attendants approaching him. The inscription is on the edge of the lid (Direction générale des antiquités, Republic of Lebanon)

(Bubastite) Dynasty of Egypt, Sheshonq I (*ca*. 947-927), and may be dated *ca*. 940 B.C. (cf. McCarter, *Antiquity*, pp. 31-34).

Sheshonq, biblical SHISHAK, campaigned in Palestine and commemorated his successes in an inscription on the Bubastite Portal at Karnak (cf. B. Mazar, "The Campaign of Pharaoh Shishak to Palestine," in *SVT*, 4 [1957], 57-66); the campaign is also described in 1 K. 14:25-28, though the widespread devastation Sheshonq inflicted on both Israel and Judah, as indicated in the Karnak inscription and supported by archeological data, is not hinted at in the biblical account. A fragment of a stele of Sheshonq has been found at Megiddo.

In the 9th cent. B.C., Phoenician westward expansion into the Mediterranean basin reached its zenith. Earlier Phoenician visits to Mediterranean ports are attested by a fragment of an eleventh-century stele from Pula, ancient Nora, in Sardinia (see F. M. Cross, *CBQ*, 36 [1974], 490-93) and an inscribed bronze bowl of the 10th cent. from Tekke, near Knossos, Crete (see M. Sznycer, *Kadmos*, 18 [1979], 89-93). From Cyprus comes the so-called Honeyman inscription, a weathered gravestone of the early part of the 9th cent., and a painted ceramic bowl from the temple of Astarte at Kition dated archeologically to *ca*. 800 B.C. The famous Nora Stone from ninth-century Sardinia has long

been supposed to contain a dedication to the god Pummay, but Cross (*BASOR*, 208 [Dec. 1972], 13-19) interprets it as a military inscription referring to King Pummayyaton (Pygmalion) of Tyre. Other Phoenician maritime inscriptions include (1) fragments of a bronze bowl from Cyprus dedicated by a provincial governor in the service of Hiram II of Tyre to a god called Baal ("lord of") Lebanon and roughly datable to the middle of the 8th cent., (2) the inscribed base of a small statue of a goddess, evidently the Hurrian Ishtar (F. M. Cross, *HTR*, 64 [1971], 189-195), found near Seville in southwestern Spain and deriving from the middle or second half of the 8th cent., and (3) a votive stele from Malta of the late 8th century. See further McCarter, *Antiquity*, pp. 39-50; M. G. Guzzo Amadasi, *Le iscrizioni fenici e puniche delle colonie in occidente* (1967).

D. Age of Assyrian Invasions. In the 9th cent., with the beginning of Assyrian expansion, the annals of the Neo-Assyrian kings become an important resource for the history of Palestine and Syria. Ashurnasirpal II (884-860), a contemporary of Omri of Israel, campaigned in northern Syria and the Lebanon and recorded his exploits in the temple of the war-god Ninurta in Calah (Nimrûd) (*ANET*, pp. 275f.). But of more interest to biblical scholars are the several inscriptions of Shalmaneser III (859-825), whose ambitions in the west were challenged by a large coalition of Syria-Palestinian states led by Irḫuleni of Hamath, Hadadezer (Ben-hadad II) of Damascus, and Ahab of Israel, Hadadezer's erstwhile enemy (1 K. 20; cf. BEN-HADAD **2**). In Shalmaneser's Monolith Inscriptions from Kurkh (*ANET*, pp. 277-79 *passim*), Ahab is said to have contributed two thousand chariots and ten thousand foot-soldiers to the coalition for an indecisive battle at Qarqar on the Orontes in 853. In 841 he achieved a decisive victory over Damascus, whose king was now Hazael (1 K. 19:15f.; 2 K. 8:13-15), and its allies, as recorded on the famous Black Obelisk found at Nimrûd (*ANET*, pp. 278-281 *passim*). Among the tributaries of that year this obelisk lists Tyre, Sidon, Byblos, and Israel, whose king, "Yaw [Jehoram or Jehu], son of Omri," is depicted in a relief on the obelisk kneeling before the Assyrian monarch.

After the accession of Jehu the Transjordanian state of Moab, which during the Omri dynasty had been under Israelite sway, was able to assert its independence. Mesha king of Moab is said in 2 K. 3:4 to have paid Ahab an annual tribute of 100,000 lambs and the wool of 100,000 sheep. After gaining his independence Mesha erected a stele at Dibon (modern Dhībân) commemorating his victories and praising Chemosh the god of Moab (*ANET*, pp. 320f.; *see* MOABITE STONE). A second Transjordanian inscription of the same period is the Amman citadel inscription, a fragment of a limestone slab on which a mid-ninth-century Ammonite king inscribed the dedication of a temple or other sacred precinct to the god Milcom.

To this same period belongs the inscription of Kilamuwa, king of the northern Syrian state of Ya'udi or Sam'al (modern Zenjirli), near which Shalmaneser III had fought his first battle. The text, which is in the local dialect and the Aramaic script, recounts Kilamuwa's achievements (*ANET*, pp. 654f.).

The Aramean kings of the time of Shalmaneser III left their own inscriptions. A stele found near Aleppo bears a votive inscription to the Tyrian god Melqart from a certain Ben-hadad (*ANET*, p. 655; cf. BEN-HADAD **1**); it has long been assumed that this is an inscription of Ben-hadad II, i.e., Hadadezer, of Damascus (see above), but another proposal argues that the king's name is given as Ben-hadad, *son of Ezer*, and that he should be considered Ben-hadad III, perhaps Hadadezer's son and co-regent at the end of his reign (see F. M. Cross, *BASOR*, 205 [Feb. 1972], 36-42; cf. W. H. Shea, *Maarav*, I/2 [1979], 159-176). Fragments of ivory inlay, parts of a bed (cf. Am. 6:4) found at Arslan Tash, were inscribed by the craftsmen "to our lord, Hazael," evidently the Damascene king. His succession by Ben-hadad III (or, if the proposal cited above is correct, IV) (2 K. 13:24) is illustrated by another Aramaic inscription, a stele from Apish (modern Āfis 45 km. [28 mi.] SW of Aleppo), erected by a certain Zakkur (formerly known as Zakir) king of Hamath in honor of the god Ilu-wer. Zakkur speaks of the same kind of hostilities and successes against Damascus that Jehoash of Israel was experiencing at this time (cf. 2 K. 13:14-25); *see also* BEN-HADAD **3**.

A stele found in 1967 at Tell er-Rimah in northern Mesopotamia identifies Jehoash (Joash) of Israel as a tributary of Adadnirari III (811-784). Shalmaneser's successor, Šamši-Adad V (824-812), had not been strong enough to maintain a firm hand on his father's western dominions, but Adadnirari reasserted Assyrian control at least temporarily, campaigning to the Mediterranean in 805-802. His slab inscriptions from Nimrûd (*ANET*, pp. 281f.) describe his victories at that time. The Rimah stele probably commemorates a later campaign to northern Syria that he is known to have made in 796.

The oldest known public documents in the Hebrew language come from Kuntillet ʿAjrūd, a remote outpost in the northern Sinai which flourished in the late 9th or early 8th cent. B.C. In addition to a number of inscribed pithoi and other objects the site has yielded ink-on-plaster inscriptions with religious themes *in situ* on the walls of the single building. When published this material will provide scholars with unique evidence of the religious situation in Israel and Judah during the divided monarchy (see provisionally Z. Meshel, *Biblical Archaeology Review*, 5/2 [1979], 24-34).

From later in the 8th cent. comes the crude inscription of a man named Uriah on the entrance to a rock-cut tomb in the Judean hills at modern Khirbet el-Qom. The text invokes the help of Yahweh.

The several states of eighth-century Syria are represented by a number of extant inscriptions. The Aramaic Sfire treaties record the pact made by Mati'el (Mati'-ilu) king of Arpad with a Mesopotamian suzerain (*ANET*, pp. 659-661) sometime before the fall of Arpad to Tiglath-pileser III in 740 B.C.; they are an invaluable source of information about covenant forms in the Iron Age. Three inscriptions from Ya'udi or Sam'al (Zenjirli) in the strange Ya'udic dialect shed further light on northern Syria in this period. The oldest, dating to the middle of the 8th cent., is that of King Panammu I; the others, dating *ca*. 730 B.C., belonged to Panammu II and his son Barrakib (*ANET*, p. 655), both of whom were vassals of Tiglath-pileser. A group of long Phoenician-Hittite bilinguals, engraved on a leonine gate, its orthostats, and a statue of a god, comes from Karatepe in southern Turkey. They are the inscriptions of a King Azitawadda of Que, the little state that controlled the area, and are to be dated *ca*. 725. Like Arpad and Sam'al, Que was a tributary of Tiglath-pileser III (744-727).

Tiglath-pileser's own inscriptions (*ANET*, pp. 282-84) describe his consolidation of Assyrian power in Mesopotamia, his rigorous reorganization of the empire, and his two great western campaigns. In the records of his first campaign (743-738), on which he reasserted Assyrian control of northern Syria, he lists among his tributaries Menahem of Israel (cf. 2 K. 15:19). In an inscription of an unknown year he claims credit for the replacement of Pekah of Israel by Hoshea (cf. 2 K. 15:29-30). His second campaign (734-732) was directed principally against an insurgent coalition led by Rezin of Damascus, a city that fell in 732; the relevant biblical material, involving Ahaz of Judah — Tiglath-pileser's records give us a longer form of his name, viz., Jehoahaz (*ia-ú-ḫa-zi*) — is found in 2 K. 16 (cf. Isa. 7).

Both the Assyrian chronicles and the biblical account (2 K. 17:3) assign the fall of Samaria to Shalmaneser V (726-722), of whose own inscriptions almost nothing survives. Shalmaneser's successor, Sargon II (721-705), claimed credit for the achievement, which is described in detail in his own inscriptions from Nimrûd, Khorsabad (ancient Dūr-Šarrukin, "Sargon City," his new capital), and elsewhere (*ANET,* pp. 284-87). Among the spoil from Samaria was a votive plaque expertly incised with a Hebrew inscription including an invocation of divine retribution on anyone who defaced it; fragments of this text were recovered at Nimrûd in 1961.

The siege of Jerusalem in 701 by Sargon's successor Sennacherib (704-681) is described in great detail in the Taylor and Oriental Institute Prisms of Sennacherib's annals (*ANET,* pp. 287f.). His destruction of Lachish at the same time is graphically illustrated by reliefs from his palace at Nineveh and their accompanying epigraph. The corresponding biblical material is found in 2 K. 18:13–19:37=Isa. 36–37; 2 Ch. 32:1-23. The completion of the underground water system HEZEKIAH devised for the siege (cf. 2 Ch. 32:2-4) was commemorated by the engraving of an inscription on the wall at the outer entrance to the tunnel (*ANET,* p. 321); it describes the excavation of the

Two funerary stelae with Aramaic texts from Nerab in northern Syria (7th cent. B.C.), both by priests of Shahr the moon-god. The stele of Agbar (left) mentions Shahr and the Babylonian deities Nikkal and Nusku, and the stele of Sin-zera-ibni mentions Šamaš as well (Louvre)

shaft by two teams of workers, who cut their way through the rock from both directions until they met in the middle (*see also* SILOAM).

From approximately this same period comes the Royal Steward inscription from the necropolis at Silwan, Jerusalem. Inscribed above the entrance to a large tomb, it identifies the deceased as "[ ]yahu, who is over the house"; the title has been compared to that of Shebna, Hezekiah's majordomo (Isa. 22:15). *See* picture in ARCHEOLOGY OF PALESTINE AND SYRIA.

Sennacherib's successor, Esarhaddon (680-669), in two baked clay prisms designated A and B, described his one significant western campaign (*ANET,* pp. 290f.), which was directed principally against an insurgent king of Sidon; mention is made of tribute received from Manasseh of Israel, a loyal Assyrian vassal (cf. 2 K. 21; 2 Ch. 33), Baal of Tyre, and others. There is no Assyrian reference to Manasseh's visit to Babylon (2 Ch. 33:10f.). The treaty Esarhaddon made with Baal of Tyre (*ANET,* pp. 533f.) survives as an important illustration of the treaty forms of this period and, because of the divine names listed in the curses that conclude the text, is a valuable witness to the Tyrian pantheon. Esarhaddon's successor, Ashurbanipal (668-633), also includes among the accounts of his western campaigns (*ANET,* pp. 294-97) reference to tribute received from both Manasseh and Baal in "Cylinder C," a text made up of fragments of a number of prisms. *See* picture in ESARHADDON.

An alphabetic inscription of *ca.* 700 B.C. from Tell Deir ʿallā in southern Transjordan is of special interest to biblical scholars as containing the earliest extrabiblical reference to a named pentateuchal figure. The ink-on-plaster text, originally attached to a wall or stele in a sanctuary, relates a story involving Balaam son of Beor in phrases strikingly reminiscent of the material in Nu. 22–24. The language of the inscription displays affinities with both Old Aramaic and South Canaanite (Hebrew and Moabite). See J. Hoftijzer and G. van der Kooij, *Aramaic Texts from Deir ʿAllā* (1976).

From Nerab, modern Nayrab near Aleppo, come two basic basalt gravestones inscribed with the seventh-century Aramaic epitaphs of two priests of Shahr, the Aramaic form of the name of the Assyrian moon-god Sin. For the second, that of a certain Agbar, see *ANET,* p. 661.

E. Exile. The siege and conquest of Jerusalem by Nebuchadrezzar II of Babylon (604-562), though included in the Babylonian chronicles (*ANET,* pp. 536f.), are not described in surviving public inscriptions. Hebrew inscriptions, found in 1961 and paleographically datable to the early 6th cent. B.C., have been interpreted as providing moving evidence of the plight of the refugees in Judah (cf. F. M. Cross in J. A. Sanders, ed., *Near Eastern Archaeology in the 20th Cent.* [1970], pp. 299-306). They are crude graffiti incised on the walls of a cave at Khirbet Beit Lei in the Judean hills near Lachish. The difficult texts seem to invoke Yahweh's help in phrases reminiscent of many of the prayers in the book of Psalms.

To the 6th cent. belong two Aramaic incantations on limestone plaques found at Arslan Tash in northern Mesopotamia. Both seem to be apotropaic devices to be hung on doorposts to ward off demons. For the first, see *ANET,* p. 658.

F. Persian Age. The fall of Babylon to CYRUS (557-529) is described in the Cyrus Cylinder, a clay barrel bearing a cuneiform text composed by a Babylonian devotee of the god Marduk. The inscription describes the liberation of Babylon by Cyrus as an achievement inspired and abetted by Marduk; its general spirit has been compared to that of Isa. 40–55, where Cyrus's victories and the liberation of the Jews are said to have been made possible by the involvement of Yahweh, the god of Israel.

Evidence that the Arabian tribes who were pressing into southern Palestine in the postexilic period were also in the eastern Egyptian Delta comes from Tell Maskhuta near Ismailia, where a number of silver bowls inscribed with fifth-century Aramaic legends have been discovered. One (*ANET,* p. 657) is identified as having belonged to a son of Geshem the Arab, Nehemiah's nemesis (Neh. 2:19; 6:1f.,6), called "king of Kedar" in the inscription.

To the Persian Age also belong the Sidonian inscriptions of the Eshmunʿazar dynasty (cf. Peckham, pp. 78-86). We have inscribed sarcophagi of Tabnit, son of Eshmunʿazar I (*ca.* 470-465), who describes himself as "priest of [the goddess] Aštart" as well as "king of Sidon," and Eshmunʿazar II (*ca.* 465-451), especially valuable for its description of the Sidonian temple district (*ANET,* p. 662), and the building inscriptions of Bodʿaštart (*ca.* 451-?) from the temple of the god Eshmun. *See* picture in BURIAL.

II. The Early Church: Inscriptional Evidence.—Inscriptions from Palestine, Syria, and the Mediterranean basin in the Roman period illuminate the NT background in a general way. Several items of specific relevance are listed below.

A. Jerusalem. Among the best-known inscriptions from Herodian Jerusalem is the so-called Balustrade Inscription, a Greek text with two extant copies, forbidding foreigners to enter the temple precinct, "the balustrade and enclosure," on penalty of death. This brings to mind the charge against Paul that he had defiled the temple by bringing in Trophimus the Ephesian (Acts 21:28f.).

Greek inscription from the Jerusalem temple (*ca.* A.D. 30) forbidding Gentiles to enter the temple court (Israel Department of Antiquities and Museums)

Several interesting tomb inscriptions have been recovered from Herodian Jerusalem. An ossuary inscription from Givʿat ha-Mivtar, e.g., identifies the deceased as "Simon, builder of the temple." Another tomb from the same cemetery bears a long Aramaic inscription, notable for its use of the archaizing Paleo-Hebrew script (see I.A.3 above); the unusual text begins by identifying not the deceased but the man who buried him, a certain Abba.

An inscription of the emperor Vespasian and his son Titus, discovered in 1970, is a reminder of the destruction of Jerusalem in A.D. 70.

A Greek building inscription from the Ophel identifies the builder of a synagogue as a certain Theodotus, apparently a freed Roman captive. This brings to mind the "synagogue of the Freedmen [Libertini]" mentioned in Acts 6:9.

See also ARCHEOLOGY OF PALESTINE AND SYRIA II.L.

B. Scythopolis. Another important synagogue text, in

this case a Hebrew inscription on a mosaic floor, comes from Tell el-Ḥuṣn (OT Beth-shean, NT Scythopolis). The text reviews the Halakic agricultural regulations incumbent upon Jews living in border districts like Scythopolis.

C. Caesarea. Among important discoveries from Caesarea Maritima is a stone inscription from the period when the city was the administrative capital of Palestine; it mentions Pontius Pilate.

D. Delphi. A fragment of an inscription from Delphi publishing the text of a letter from the emperor Claudius makes reference to Gallio, the proconsul of Achaia mentioned in Acts 18:12-17. The reference is important for the chronology of Paul's journeys. *See* CHRONOLOGY OF THE NT II.F.

See also WRITING.

Bibliography.–*General: ANET; ARAB; DOTT.*

Specific Studies: W. F. Albright, *Proto-Sinaitic Inscriptions and Their Decipherment* (1969); H. Donner and W. Röllig, *Kanaanäische und Aramäische Inschriften* (3 vols., 2nd ed. 1966-1969); J. A. Fitzmyer, *Aramaic Inscriptions of Sefîre* (1967); J. C. L. Gibson, *Textbook of Syrian Semitic Inscriptions* (3 vols., 1971-); P. K. McCarter, *Antiquity of the Greek Alphabet and the Early Phoenician Scripts* (1975); J. B. Peckham, *Development of the Late Phoenician Scripts* (1968); *CCK.* For bibliography on Northwest Semitic inscriptions before 1970, see Donner and Röllig; for more recent studies, see J. Teixidor, "Bulletin d'épigraphie sémitique," published annually in *Syria.* P. K. MCCARTER

INSECTS [Heb. *šereṣ hāʿôp̱*] (Lev. 11:20f., 23; Dt. 14:19); AV FOWLS THAT CREEP, CREEPING THING THAT FLIETH, FLYING CREEPING THINGS; NEB TEEMING WINGED CREATURES. The prescription in Dt. 14:19 prohibited for food "all winged insects" as unclean, but the more detailed regulations of Lev. 11:20f. made a distinction between winged insects going on all fours, i.e., that move like quadrupeds, and those having "legs above their feet." This latter presumably referred to bending rear legs which were larger and higher than the corresponding forelegs. Such insects were regarded as suitable for food, and included species of locust, of which the order *Orthoptera* is divided into more than forty.

The different species of Lev. 11 cannot be identified by means of the Hebrew words given, so that the nature of the "bald locust" (NEB "long-headed locust"), the cricket (NEB "green locust"), and the grasshopper (NEB "desert locust") must remain indeterminate. Terms such as cricket or grasshopper may merely denote the locust at various stages of its development and may not allude to separate insects.

See also LOCUST, and the articles under the names of the various insects. R. K. H.

INSIGHT [Heb. *haśkēl*–'prudence, sense' (Job 34:35), *bînâ* < *bîn*–'have discernment' (cf. *bên,* "between") (Prov. 1:2; 9:10, etc.), *m^{e}ḇînîm*–'they who give (or possess?) understanding' (Ezr. 8:16); Gk. *phrónēsis* (Eph. 1:9), *sýnesis* (Eph. 3:4)]; AV UNDERSTANDING, PRUDENCE (Eph. 1:9), KNOWLEDGE (Eph. 3:4); NEB also DISCERNMENT, DISCRETION, UNDERSTANDING.

The hiphil part. *m^{e}ḇînîm,* which the RSV renders "men of insight" in Ezr. 8:16 (cf. the similar use of the hiphil part. in Neh. 8:3; 10:29), could alternatively mean "they who cause (the people) to have insight," i.e., "teachers" (cf. 1 Ch. 10:22; 25:8; Neh. 8:7, 9; *TDOT,* II, 103). The noun *bînâ,* a favorite word of wisdom authors, occurs several times in Proverbs, often denoting the discernment and understanding that results from heeding wisdom teaching (2:3 [cf. vv. 1f.]; 4:1, 5, 7; 7:4 [cf. vv. 1-3]). In 3:5, however, it refers to one's natural perception, which is inadequate without Yahweh's guidance. In 8:14 personified Wisdom (Heb. *ḥoḵmâ*) says that she is, or perhaps has (cf. W. McKane, *Proverbs* [*OTL,* 1970], pp. 347f.), insight, and in 9:6 insight is contrasted with simpleness (LXX; Pesh.; MT "simple ones"; cf. also v. 4).

Greek *phrónēsis,* collocated with *sophía,* "wisdom," in Eph. 1:9, probably differs little in meaning from the latter, and like the latter denotes "knowledge of how to do something — i.e., the right handling of the right thing at the right moment" (M. Barth, *Ephesians 1–3* [*AB,* 1974], pp. 84f.). Thus the phrase "in all wisdom and insight" probably indicates the source of God's decision to lavish His grace upon us (vv. 7-8a). Greek *sýnesis* in 3:4 means "understanding, grasp."

See also UNDERSTANDING; WISDOM. J. E. H.

INSOLENCE; INSOLENT [Heb. *zāḏôn, zēḏ, zîḏ*] (Prov. 13:10; Ps. 54:3 [MT 5]; 86:14; 119:21; Jer. 43:2; Neh. 9:10); AV PRIDE, PROUD, PROUDLY; NEB PRESUMPTION, PROUD, EFFRONTERY, ARROGANTLY; [*ʿeḇrâ*] (Isa. 16:6; Jer. 48:30); AV WRATH; NEB ARROGANCE; [*ḥerpâ*] (Job 16:10; Dnl. 11:18); AV REPROACHFULLY; NEB CHALLENGE, "with knives"; [*zaʿam*] (Hos. 7:16); AV RAGE; NEB "lies"; [*ʿāṯāq*] (Ps. 31:18 [MT 19]; 75:5 [MT 6]); AV STIFF, "grievous things"; NEB ARROGANTLY, WITH CONTEMPT; [*rāhaḇ*] (Isa. 3:5); AV BEHAVE PROUDLY; NEB BREAK OUT; [*maḏhēḇâ*] ("insolent fury," Isa. 14:4); AV "golden city"; NEB FRENZY; [*ʿāzaz*] (Isa. 33:19); AV FIERCE; NEB BARBAROUS; [hiphil of *gāḏal*] (Ps. 55:12 [MT 13]); AV MAGNIFY HIMSELF; NEB "treat with scorn"; [Gk. *hybristḗs*] (Rom. 1:30); AV DESPITEFUL.

The AV rendering of Isa. 14:4 assumes a Hebrew derivation from the Aram. *d^{e}haḇ,* "gold." 1QIsa^a, however, would appear to indicate that *maḏhēḇâ* has been a misreading of *marhēḇâ,* "turmoil." A similar confusion may account for the two readings of Ps. 54:3; the AV used MSS reading *zār,* "stranger," while the RSV and NEB used others, including the Targum, which read *zēḏ,* "insolent." The term *ḥerpâ,* "reproach," is based on the verb *ḥārap,* "be sharp," or "say sharp things against." This may account for the NEB rendering "with knives." G. WYPER

INSPECTORS (Ezr. 5:6; 6:6, NEB). *See* APHARSACHITES.

INSPIRATION. A term used in the discussion of the nature of the canon of Scripture that concerns the influence of the Spirit of God upon the biblical writers to produce a divinely authoritative Scripture. If God is viewed as the author of Scripture, a natural corollary of a doctrine of inspiration is the concept of the INFALLIBILITY of Scripture.

I. Meaning of Terms
II. Relevant Passages
III. Christ and Scripture
IV. Scripture in the Primitive Church
V. Human and Divine Aspects

I. Meaning of Terms.–The use of "inspire" in a technical, theological sense is derived from the usage of the word *inspiro* in the Vulg. (Gen. 2:7; Wisd. 15:11; Sir. 4:12; 2 Tim. 3:16; 2 Pet. 1:21), and the noun *inspiratio* (2 S. 22:16; Job 32:8; Ps. 18:15; Acts 17:25). In the RSV, "inspired" occurs in three passages relevant to the discussion. In Mt. 22:43, Jesus speaks of David writing Psalm 110 "inspired by the Spirit" (*en pneúmati*). The parallel passage in Mk. 12:36 has "inspired by the Holy Spirit" (*en tǭ pneúmati tǭ hagíǭ*). Luke (20:42) makes the reference more specific by substituting "in the Book of Psalms" (*en biblǭ psalmōn*). The AV translates Mt. 22:43 literally, "in Spirit," and for Mk. 12:36 has the

INSPIRATION

archaic "by the Holy Ghost." The NEB has "by inspiration" for Mt. 22:43 and "inspired by the Holy Spirit" in Mk. 12:36.

II. Relevant Passages.–The most important verse, however, is 2 Tim. 3:16: "All scripture is inspired by God" (*pāsa graphḗ theópneustos*). The AV translates, "All Scripture is given by inspiration of God." The NEB, less correctly, has "every inspired Scripture." The important Greek word in this passage, however, is not correctly translated "inspired by God." This phrase is the rendering of the Latin *divinitus inspirata,* restored from the Wyclif ("Al Scripture of God ynspyrid is. . . .") and Rhemish ("All Scripture inspired of God is. . . .") versions of the Vulg. The Greek word does not even mean, as AV translated it, "given by inspiration of God," although that rendering (inherited from Tyndale: "All Scripture given by inspiration of God is. . . ." and its successors; cf. Geneva: "The whole Scripture is given by inspiration of God and is. . . .") is a somewhat clumsy, perhaps, but not misleading, paraphrase of the Greek term in the theological language of the day. The Greek term has, however, nothing to say of *in*spiring or of *in*spiration: it speaks only of "aspiring" or "aspiration." What it says of Scripture is, not that it is "breathed into by God" or is the product of the divine "inbreathing" into its human authors, but that it is breathed out by God, "God-breathed," the product of the creative breath of God. In a word, what is declared by this fundamental passage is simply that the Scriptures are a divine product, without any indication of how God has operated in producing them. No term could have been chosen, however, which would have more emphatically asserted the divine production of Scripture than that which is here employed. The "breath of God" is in Scripture just the symbol of His almighty power, the bearer of His creative word. "By the word of the Lord" we read in the significant parallel of Ps. 33:6, "were the heavens made, and all their host by the breath of his mouth." And it is particularly where the operations of God are energetic that this term (whether *rû(a)ḥ* or n^{e}*šāmâ*) is employed to designate them — God's breath is the irresistible outflow of His power. When Paul declares, then, that "every scripture" or "all scripture" is the product of the divine breath, "is God-breathed," he asserts that Scripture is the product of a specifically divine operation.

(1) 2 Tim. 3:16: In the passage in which Paul makes this energetic assertion of the divine origin of Scripture he is engaged in explaining the greatness of the advantages which Timothy had enjoyed for learning the saving truth of God. He had had good teachers; and from his very infancy he had been, by his knowledge of the Scriptures, made wise unto salvation through faith in Jesus Christ. The expression, "sacred writings," used here (v. 15), is a technical one, not found elsewhere in the NT, it is true, but it occurs in Philo and Josephus designating that body of authoritative books which constituted the Jewish "law." It appears here anarthrously because it is set in contrast with the oral teaching which Timothy had enjoyed, as something still better. To enhance further the great advantage of the possession of these sacred Scriptures the apostle adds now a sentence throwing their nature strongly up to view. They are of divine origin and therefore of the highest value for all holy purposes (3:16bf.).

There is room for some difference of opinion as to the exact construction of this declaration. Shall we render "Every scripture" or "All scripture"? Shall we render "Every [or all] scripture is God-breathed and [therefore] profitable," or "Every [or all] scripture, being God-breathed, is as well profitable"? No doubt both questions are interesting, but for the main matter now engaging our attention they are both indifferent. Whether Paul, looking back at the sacred Scriptures he had just mentioned, makes the assertion he is about to add, of them distributively, of all their parts, or collectively, of their entire mass, is not important: to say that every part of these sacred Scriptures is God-breathed and to say that the whole of these sacred Scriptures is God-breathed, is, for the main matter, all one. Nor is the difference great between saying that they are in all their parts, or in their whole extent, God-breathed and therefore profitable, and saying that they are in all their parts, or in their whole extent, because God-breathed as well profitable. In both cases these sacred Scriptures are declared to owe their value to their divine origin; and in both cases this their divine origin is asserted of their entirety. On the whole, the preferable construction would seem to be, "Every scripture, seeing that it is God-breathed, is as well profitable." In that case, what the apostle asserts is that the canon of Scripture in every passage — for it is just "passage of scripture" which "scripture" in this distributive use of it signifies — is the product of the creative breath of God, and, because of this divine origination, is of supreme value for all holy purposes.

The apostle does not stop here to tell us either what particular books enter into the collection which he calls sacred Scriptures, or by what precise operations God has produced them. It was the value of the Scriptures, and the source of that value in their divine origin, which he asserts leaving to other occasions any further facts concerning them. The apostle does not tell us here everything for which the Scriptures are made valuable by their divine origination. He reminds Timothy of the value which these Scriptures, by virtue of their divine origin, have for the "man of God." Their spiritual power, as God-breathed, is all that he had occasion here to refer to. Whatever other qualities may accrue to them from their divine origin, he leaves to other occasions to speak of.

(2) 2 Pet. 1:19-21: What Paul tells us about the divine origin of the Scriptures is enforced and extended by 2 Pet. 1:19-21. Peter is assuring his readers that what had been made known to them of "the power and coming of our Lord Jesus Christ" did not rest on "cunningly devised fables." He offers them the testimony of eyewitnesses of Christ's glory. Then he intimates that they have better testimony than even that of eyewitnesses. "We have," says he, "the prophetic word" (AV, unhappily, "the word of prophecy"); and this, he says, is "more sure," and therefore should certainly be heeded. He refers, of course, to the Scriptures. Of what other "prophetic word" could he, over against the testimony of the eyewitnesses of Christ's Majestic Glory (v. 17), say that "we have" it, that is, it is in our hands? And he proceeds at once to speak of it plainly as "scriptural prophecy." You do well, he says, to pay heed to the prophetic word, because we know this first, that "every prophecy of scripture. . . ." It is questionable, however, whether by this phrase he means the whole of Scripture, designated according to its character, as prophetic, that is, of divine origin; or only that portion of Scripture which we discriminate as particularly prophetic, the immediate revelations contained in Scripture. The former is the more likely view, inasmuch as the entirety of Scripture is elsewhere conceived and spoken of as prophetic. In that case, what Peter has to say of this "every prophecy of scripture" — the exact equivalent, it will be observed, in this case of Paul's "every scripture" (2 Tim. 3:16) — applies to the whole of Scripture in all its parts. What he says of it is that it does not come

"by the impulse of man"; that is, it is not the result of human investigation into the nature of things, the product of its writers' own thinking. This is as much as to say it is of divine gift. Accordingly, he proceeds at once to make this plain in a supporting clause which contains both the negative and the positive declaration: "because no prophecy ever came by the impulse of man, but men moved by the Holy Spirit spoke from God." In this singularly precise and pregnant statement there are several things which should be carefully observed. First, there is the emphatic denial that prophecy owes its origin to human initiative. Then, there is the equally emphatic assertion that its source lies in God: it was spoken by men, indeed, but the men who spoke it "spoke from God." And a remarkable clause is here inserted, and thrown forward in the sentence that stress may fall on it, which tells us how it could be that men, in speaking, should speak not from themselves, but from God: it was as they were "moved by the Holy Spirit" that they spoke. Speaking thus under the determining influence of the Holy Spirit, the things they spoke were not from themselves, but from God.

Here is as direct an assertion of the divine origin of Scripture as that of 2 Tim. 3:16. But there is more here than a simple assertion of the divine origin of Scripture. We are advanced somewhat in our understanding of how God has produced the Scriptures. It was through the instrumentality of men who spoke from Him. More specifically, it was through an operation of the Holy Spirit on these men which is described as "moving" them. The term here used is a very specific one. It is not to be confounded with guiding, or directing, or controlling, or even leading in the full sense of that word. It goes beyond such terms, in assigning the effect produced specifically to the active agent. What is "moved" is taken up by the "mover" and conveyed by the "mover's" power, not its own, to the "mover's" goal, not its own. The men who spoke from God are here declared, therefore, to have been moved by the Holy Spirit and brought by His power to the goal of His choosing. The things which they spoke under this operation of the Spirit were therefore His things, not theirs. And that is why "the prophetic word" is so sure. Though spoken through the instrumentality of men, it is, by virtue of the fact that these men spoke as "moved by the Holy Spirit," an immediately divine word. The stress is laid here, not on the spiritual value of Scripture (though that, too, is seen in the background), but on the divine trustworthiness of Scripture. Because that is the way every prophecy of Scripture came it affords a more sure basis of confidence than even the testimony of human eyewitnesses. Of course, if we do not understand by "the prophetic word" here the entirety of Scripture described, according to its character, as revelation, but only that element in Scripture which we call specifically prophecy, then it is directly only of that element in Scripture that these great declarations are made. In any event, however, they are made of the prophetic element in Scripture as written, which was the only form in which the readers of this Epistle possessed it, and which is the thing specifically intimated in the phrase "every prophecy *of scripture*." These great declarations are made, therefore, at least of large tracts of Scripture; and if the entirety of Scripture is intended by the phrase "the prophetic word," they are made of the whole of Scripture.

(3) Jn. 10:34-36: How far the supreme trustworthiness of Scripture, thus asserted, extends may be conveyed to us by a passage in one of Our Lord's discourses recorded by John (Jn.10:34-36). The Jews, offended by Jesus' "making himself God," were ready to stone Him, when He defended Himself thus: "Is it not written in your law, 'I said, you are gods'? If he called them gods, to whom the word of God came (and scripture cannot be broken), do you say of him whom the Father consecrated and sent unto the world, 'You are blaspheming,' because I said, 'I am the Son of God'?" It may be thought that this defense is inadequate. It certainly is incomplete: Jesus made Himself God (Jn. 10:31) in a far higher sense than that in which "You are gods" was said of those "to whom the word of God came": He had just declared in unmistakable terms, "I and the Father are one." But it was quite sufficient for the immediate end in view — to repel the technical charge of blasphemy based on His making Himself God: it is not blasphemy to call someone God in any sense in which he may fitly receive that designation; and certainly if it is not blasphemy to call such men as those spoken of in the passage of Scripture adduced gods, because of their official functions, it cannot be blasphemy to call Him God whom the Father consecrated and sent into the world. The point for us to note, however, is merely that Jesus' defense takes the form of an appeal to Scripture; and it is important to observe how He makes this appeal. In the first place, He adduces the Scriptures as law: "Is it not written in your law. . . ?" The passage of Scripture which He adduces is not written in that portion of Scripture which was more specifically called "the Law," i.e., the Pentateuch; nor in any portion of Scripture of formally legal contents. It is written in the book of Psalms and in a particular psalm which is as far as possible from presenting the external characteristics of legal enactment (Ps. 82:6). When Jesus adduces this passage, then, as written in the "law" of the Jews, He does it, not because it stands in this psalm, but because it is a part of Scripture at large. In other words, He here ascribes legal authority to the entirety of Scripture, in accordance with a conception common enough among the Jews (cf. Jn. 12:34), and finding expression in the NT occasionally, both on the lips of Jesus Himself, and in the writings of the apostles. Thus, on a later occasion (Jn. 15:25), Jesus declares that it is written in the "law" of the Jews, "They hated me without a cause," a clause found in Ps. 35:19. And Paul assigns passages both from the Psalms and from Isaiah to "the law" (1 Cor. 14:21; Rom. 3:19), and can write such a sentence as this (Gal. 4:21f.): "Tell me, you who desire to be under law, do you not hear the law? For it is written. . . ," quoting from the narrative of Genesis.

We have seen that the entirety of Scripture was conceived as "prophecy"; we now see that the entirety of Scripture was also conceived as "law": these three terms, the law, prophecy, Scripture, were indeed, materially, strict synonyms. Our present passage demonstrates this by using the terms "law" and "scripture" in contiguous verses. And what is thus implied in the manner in which Scripture is adduced, is immediately afterward spoken out in the most explicit language, because it forms an essential element in Our Lord's defense. It might have been enough to say simply, "Is it not written in your law?" But Our Lord, determined to drive His appeal to Scripture home, sharpens the point to the utmost by adding with the highest emphasis: "and scripture cannot be broken." This is the reason why it is worthwhile to appeal to what is "written in the law," because "scripture cannot be broken." The word "broken" here is the common one for breaking the law, or the sabbath, or the like (Jn. 5:18; 7:23; Mt. 5:19), and the meaning of the declaration is that it is impossible for the Scripture to be annulled, its authority to be withstood, or denied. The movement of thought is to the effect that, because it is impossible for the Scripture — the term is perfectly general and witnesses to the unitary character of Scripture (it is all, for the purpose in hand, of a piece) — to be withstood, therefore this particular Scripture which is cited must be taken as of irrefragable authority. What we have here is, therefore, the strongest possible assertion of the indefectible authority of Scripture; precisely what is true of Scripture is that it "cannot be broken." Now, what is the particular thing in Scripture, for the confirmation of which the indefectible authority of Scripture is thus invoked? It is one of its most casual clauses — more than that, the very form of its expression in one of its most casual clauses. This means, of course, that in the Savior's view the indefectible authority of Scripture attaches to the very form of expression of its most casual clauses. It belongs to Scripture through and through, down to its most minute particulars, that is of indefectible authority.

III. Christ and Scripture.–It is sometimes suggested, it is true, that Our Lord's argument in Jn. 10:34-36 is an *argumentum ad hominem,* and that His words, therefore, express not His own view of the authority of Scripture, but that of His Jewish opponents. It will scarcely be denied that there is a vein of satire running through Our Lord's defense: that the Jews so readily allowed that corrupt judges might properly be called "gods," but could not endure that He whom the Father had consecrated and sent into the world should call Himself Son of God, was a somewhat striking fact to set in such a high light. But the argument from Scripture is not *ad hominem* but *e concessu;* Scripture was common ground with Jesus and His opponents. If proof were needed for so obvious a fact, it would be supplied by the circumstance that this is not an isolated but a representative passage. The conception of Scripture thrown up into such clear view here supplies the ground of all Jesus' appeals to Scripture, and of all the appeals of the NT writers as well. Everywhere, to Him and to them alike, an appeal to Scripture is an appeal to an indefectible authority whose determination is final; both He and they make their appeal indifferently to every part of Scripture, to every element in Scripture, to its most incidental clauses as well as to its most fundamental principles, and to the very form of its expression. This attitude toward Scripture as an authoritative document is, indeed, already intimated by their constant designation of it by the name of Scripture, and by their customary citation of it with the simple formula "It is written." What is written in this document admits so little of questioning that its authoritativeness required no asserting, but might safely be taken for granted. Both modes of expression belong to the constantly illustrated habits of Our Lord's speech. The first words He is recorded as uttering after His manifestation to Israel were an appeal to the unquestionable authority of Scripture; to Satan's temptations He opposed no other weapon than the final "It is written" (Mt. 4:4, 7, 10; Lk. 4:4, 8)! And among the last words which He spoke to His disciples before He was received up was a rebuke to them for not understanding that all things "written . . . in the law of Moses and the prophets and psalms" concerning Him — that is in the entire "Scriptures" — "must be" (very emphatic) "fulfilled" (Lk. 24:44f.). "Thus it is written," says He (v. 46), as rendering all doubt absurd. For, as He had explained earlier upon the same day (v. 25), it argues only that one is "foolish" and "slow of heart" if he does not "believe" (if his faith does not rest securely on, as on a firm foundation) "all" (without limit of subject matter here) "that the prophets" (explained in v. 27 as equivalent to "all the scriptures") "have spoken."

The necessity of the fulfillment of all that is written in Scripture, strongly asserted in these last instructions to His disciples, is frequently referred to by Our Lord. He repeatedly explains that occurrences have come to pass "that the scripture might be fulfilled" (Mk. 14:49; Jn. 13:18; 17:12; cf. 12:14; Mk. 9:12f.). On the basis of scriptural declarations, therefore, He announces with confidence that given events will certainly occur: "You all will fall away because of me this night; for it is written. . . ." (Mt. 26:31; Mk. 14:27; cf. Lk. 20:17). Although holding at His command ample means of escape, He bows before oncoming calamities, for, He asks, how otherwise "should the scriptures be fulfilled, that it must be so?" (Mt. 26:54). It is not merely the two disciples with whom He talked on the way to Emmaus (Lk. 24:25) whom He rebukes for not trusting themselves to the teaching of Scripture. "You search the scriptures," he says to the Jews, in the classical passage (Jn. 5:39f.), "because you think that in them you have eternal life; and it is they which bear witness to me; yet you refuse to come to me, that you may have life!" These words surely were spoken more in sorrow than in scorn: there is no blame implied either for searching the Scriptures or for thinking that eternal life is to be found in Scripture. What the Jews are blamed for is reading with a veil lying upon their hearts which He could take away (2 Cor. 3:15f.). "You search the scriptures" — that is right — and "even you" (emphatic) "think that in them you have eternal life" — that is right, too. But "it is these very Scriptures" (very emphatic) "which are bearing witness" (continuous process) "of me; and" (here is the irony) "you refuse to come to me that you may have life!" — that you may, that is, reach the very end you have so properly in view in searching the Scriptures. Their failure is due, not to the Scriptures but to themselves, who read the Scriptures to such little purpose.

Quite similarly Our Lord often finds occasion to express wonder at the little effect to which Scripture had been read, not because it had been looked into too curiously, but because it had not been looked into earnestly enough, with sufficiently simple and robust trust in its every declaration. "Have you not read this scripture?" He demands, as he adduces Ps. 118 to show that the rejection of the Messiah was already intimated in Scripture (Mk. 12:10; Mt. 21:42 varies the expression to the equivalent: "Have you never read in the scriptures?"). And when the indignant Jews came to Him complaining of the Hosannas with which the children in the temple were acclaiming Him, and demanding, "Do you hear what these are saying?" He met them (Mt. 21:16) with, "Yes; have you never read, 'Out of the mouths of babes and sucklings thou hast brought perfect praise'?" The underlying thought of these passages is spoken out when He intimates that the source of all error in divine things is just ignorance of the Scriptures: "You are wrong," He declares to His questioners, on an important occasion, "you neither know the scriptures nor the power of God" (Mt. 22:29); or, as it is put, perhaps more forcibly, in interrogative form, "Is not this why you are wrong, that you know neither the scriptures nor the power of God?" (Mk. 12:24). Clearly, he who rightly knows the Scriptures does not err.

The confidence with which Jesus rested on Scripture, in its every declaration, is further illustrated in a passage like Mt. 19:4f. Certain Pharisees had come to Him with a question on divorce and He met them thus: "Have you not read that he who made them from the beginning made them male and female, and said, 'For this reason a man shall leave his father and mother and be joined to his wife, and the two shall become one'? . . . What therefore God has joined together, let no man put asunder." The point to be noted is the explicit reference of Gen. 2:24 to God as its author: "*He who made them* . . . said"; "what therefore *God* has joined together." Yet this passage does not give us a saying of God recorded in Scripture, but just the word of Scripture itself, and can be treated as a declaration of God only on the hypothesis that all Scripture is a declaration of God. The passage in Mk. 10:5ff. just as truly, though not as explicitly, assigns the passage to God as its author, citing it as authoritative law and speaking of its enactment as an act of God. It is interesting to observe that Paul, having occasion to quote the same passage, also explicitly quotes it as a divine word: "For two, saith he [Gk. *phēsín*], shall be one flesh" (1 Cor. 6:16, AV) — the "he" here, in accordance with a usage to be noted later, meaning "God."

Thus it is clear that Jesus' occasional adduction of Scripture as an authoritative document rests on an ascription of it to God as its author. His testimony is that whatever stands written in Scripture is a word of God. Nor can we evacuate this testimony of its force on the plea that it represents Jesus only in the days of His flesh, when He may be supposed to have reflected merely the opinions of His day and generation. The view of Scripture He announces was, no doubt, the view of His day and generation as well as His own view. But there is no reason to doubt that it was held by Him, not because it was the current view, but because, in His divine-human knowledge, He knew it to be true; for, even in His humiliation, He is the faithful and true witness. And in any event we should bear in mind that this was the view of the resurrected as well as of the humiliated Christ. It was after He had suffered and had risen again in the power of His divine life that He pronounced those foolish and slow of heart who do not believe all that stands written in all the Scriptures (Lk. 24:25); and that He laid down the simple "Thus it is written" as the sufficient ground of confident belief (Lk. 24:46). Nor can we explain away Jesus' testimony to the divine trustworthiness of Scripture by interpreting it as not His own, but that of His followers, placed on His lips in their reports of His words. Not only is it too constant, minute, intimate and in part incidental, and therefore, as it were hidden to admit of this interpretation; but it so pervades all our channels of information concerning Jesus' teaching as to make it certain that it comes actually from Him. It belongs not only to the Jesus of our evangelical records but as well to the Jesus of the earlier sources which underlie our evangelical records, as anyone may assure himself by observing the instances in which Jesus adduces the Scriptures as divinely authoritative that are recorded in more than one of the Gospels (e.g., "It is written," Mt. 4:4, 7, 10 par. Lk. 4:4, 8, 10; Mt. 11:10 par. Lk. 7:27; Mt. 21:13 par. Lk. 19:46; Mk. 11:17; Mt. 26:31 par. Mk. 14:21; "the scripture" or "the scriptures," Mt. 19:4 par. Mk. 10:9; Mt. 21:42 par. Mk. 12:10; Lk. 20:17; Mt. 22:29 par. Mk. 12:24; Lk. 20:37; Mt. 26:56; Mk. 14:49; Lk. 24:44). These passages alone would suffice to make clear to us the testimony of Jesus to Scripture as in all its parts and declarations divinely authoritative.

IV. Scripture in the Primitive Church.–The attempt to attribute the testimony of Jesus to His followers has in its favor only the undeniable fact that the testimony of the writers of the NT is to precisely the same effect as His. They, too, cursorily speak of Scripture by that pregnant name and adduce it with the simple "It is written," with the implication that whatever stands written in it is divinely authoritative. As Jesus' official life begins with this "It is written" (Mt. 4:4), so the evangelical proclamation begins with an "As it is written" (Mk. 1:2); and as Jesus sought the justification of His work in a solemn "Thus it is written, that the Christ should suffer, and on the third day rise from the dead" (Lk. 24:46), so the apostles solemnly justified the gospel which they preached, detail after detail, by appeal to the Scriptures, "That Christ died for our sins in accordance with the scriptures" and "That he was raised on the third day in accordance with the scriptures" (1 Cor. 15:3f.; cf. Acts 8:35; 17:3; 26:22; and also Rom. 1:17; 3:4, 10; 4:17; 11:26; 14:11; 1 Cor. 1:19; 2:9; 3:19; 15:45; Gal. 3:10, 13; 4:22, 27). Wherever they carried the gospel it was as a gospel resting on Scripture that they proclaimed it (Acts 17:2; 18:24, 28), and they encouraged themselves to test its truth by the Scriptures (Acts 17:11). The holiness of life that they inculcated, they based on scriptural requirement (1 Pet. 1:16), and they commended the royal law of love which they taught by scriptural sanction (Jas. 2:8). Every detail of duty was supported by them by an appeal to Scripture (Acts 23:5; Rom. 12:19). The circumstances of their lives and the events occasionally occurring about them are referred to Scripture for their significance (Rom. 2:26; 8:36; 9:33; 11:8; 15:9, 21; 2 Cor. 4:13). As Our Lord declared that whatever was written in Scripture must be fulfilled (Mt. 26:54; Lk. 22:37; 24:44), so His followers explained one of the most startling facts which had occurred in their experience by pointing out that "the scripture had to be fulfilled, which the Holy Spirit spoke beforehand by the mouth of David" (Acts 1:16).

Here the ground of this constant appeal to Scripture, so that it is enough that a thing "stands in scripture" (1 Pet. 2:6) for it to be of indefectible authority, is plainly enough declared: Scripture must be fulfilled, for what is contained in it is the declaration of the Holy Spirit through the human author. What Scripture says, God says; and accordingly we read such remarkable declarations as these: "For the scripture says to Pharaoh, 'I have raised you up for the very purpose . . .'" (Rom. 9:17); "And the scripture, forseeing that God would justify the Gentiles by faith, preached the gospel beforehand to Abraham, saying, 'In you shall all the nations be blessed'" (Gal. 3:8). These are not instances of simple personification of Scripture, which is itself a sufficiently remarkable usage (Mk. 15:28; Jn. 7:38, 42; 19:37; Rom. 4:3; 10:11; 11:2; Gal. 4:30; 1 Tim. 5:18; Jas. 2:23; 4:5f.), vocal with the conviction expressed by James (4:5) that Scripture cannot speak in vain. They indicate a certain confusion in contemporary speech between "Scripture" and "God," the outgrowth of a deep-seated conviction that the word of Scripture is the word of God. It was not "Scripture" that spoke to Pharaoh, or gave the great promise to Abraham, but God. But "Scripture" and "God" lay so close together in the minds of the writers of the NT that they could naturally speak of "Scripture" doing what Scripture records God as doing. It was, however, even more natural to them to speak casually of God saying what the Scriptures say; and accordingly we meet with forms of speech such as these: "Therefore, as the Holy Spirit says, 'Today when you hear His voice'" (He. 3:7, quoting Ps. 95:7); ". . . who by the mouth of our father David, thy servant, didst say by the Holy Spirit, 'Why did the Gentiles rage . . . ?'" (Acts 4:25 quoting Ps. 2:1); "that He raised him from the dead . . . he spoke in this way, 'I will give you . . .' Therefore he says also in another psalm. . . ." (Acts 13:34f., quoting Isa. 55:3 and Ps. 16:10), and the like. The words put into God's mouth in each case are not words of God recorded in the Scriptures, but just Scripture words in themselves. When we take the two classes of passages together, in the one of which the Scriptures are spoken of as God, while in the other God is spoken of as if He were the Scriptures, we may perceive how close the identification of the two was in the minds of the writers of the NT.

This identification is strikingly observable in certain catenae of quotations, in which there are brought together a number of passages of Scripture closely connected with one another. The first chapter of the Epistle to the Hebrews supplies an example. We may begin with v. 5: "For to what angel did God ever say, 'Thou art my Son, today I have begotten thee'?" — the citation being from Ps. 2:7 and very appropriate in the mouth of God — "or again, 'I will be to him a father, and he shall be to me a son'?" — from 2 S. 7:14, again a declaration of God's own — "And again, when he brings the first-born into the world, he says, 'Let all God's angels worship him'" — from Dt. 32:43 (LXX) or Ps. 97:7, in neither of which is God the speaker — "Of the angels he says, 'Who makes his angels winds, and his servants flames of fire'" — from Ps. 104:4, where again God is not the speaker but is spoken of in the third person — "But of the Son he says, 'Thy throne, O God...'" — from Ps. 45:6f. [MT 7f.] where again God is not the speaker, but is addressed — "Thou, Lord...," — from Ps. 102:25-27 [MT 26-28], where again God is not the speaker but is addressed — "But to what angel has he ever said, 'Sit at my right hand...'?" — from Ps. 110:1, in which God is the speaker. Here not only passages in which God is the speaker but also passages in which God is not the speaker (but is addressed or spoken of) are indiscriminately assigned to God, because they all have in common that they are words of Scripture, and as words of Scripture are words of God. Similarly in Rom. 15:9-12 we have a series of citations the first of which is introduced by "As it is written," and the next two by "again it is said," and "again," and the last by "and further Isaiah says," the first being from Ps. 18:49 [MT 50]; the second from Dt. 32:43; the third from Ps. 117:1; and the last from Isa. 11:10. Only the last (the only one here assigned to the human author) is a word of God in the text of the OT.

This view of the Scriptures as a compact mass of words of God occasioned the formation of a designation for them by which this their character was explicitly expressed. This designation is "the sacred oracles," "the oracles of God." It occurs with extraordinary frequency in Philo, who very commonly refers to Scripture as "the sacred oracles" and cites its several passages as each an "oracle." Sharing, as they do, Philo's conception of the Scriptures as, in all their parts, a word of God, the NT writers naturally also speak of them under this designation. The classical passage is Rom. 3:1f. (cf. He. 5:12; Acts 7:38). Here Paul begins an enumeration of the advantages which belonged to the chosen people above other nations. Declaring these advantages to have been great and numerous, he places first among them all their possession of the Scriptures: "Then what advantage has the Jew? Or what is the value of circumcision? Much in every way. To begin with, the Jews are entrusted with the oracles of God." That by "the oracles of God" here are meant just the Holy Scriptures in their entirety, conceived as a direct divine revelation, and not any portions of them, or elements in them more especially thought of as revelatory, is perfectly clear from the wide contemporary use of this designation in this sense by Philo, and is put beyond question by the presence in the NT of habits of speech which rest on and grow out of the conception of Scripture embodied in this term. From the point of view of this designation, Scripture is thought of as the living voice of God speaking in all its parts directly to the reader. Accordingly, it is cited by some such formula as "it is said," and this mode of citing Scripture duly occurs as an alternative to "it is written" (Lk. 4:12, replacing "it is written" in Matthew; He. 3:15; cf. Rom. 4:18). It is due also to this point of view that Scripture is cited, not as what God or the Holy Spirit "said," but what He "says," the present tense emphasizing the living voice of God speaking in Scriptures to the individual soul (He. 3:7; Acts 13:35; He. 1:7-10; Rom. 15:10). And especially there is due to it the peculiar usage by which Scripture is cited by the simple "says," without expressed subject, the subject being too well understood, when Scripture is adduced, to require stating; for who could be the speaker of the words of Scripture but God only (Rom. 15:10; 1 Cor. 6:16; 2 Cor. 6:2; Gal. 3:16; Eph. 4:8; 5:14)? The analogies of this pregnant subjectless "says" are very widespread. It was with it that the ancient Pythagoreans and Platonists and the medieval Aristotelians adduced each their master's teaching; it was with it that, in certain circles, the judgments of Hadrian's great jurist Salvius Julianus were cited; African stylists were even accustomed to refer by it to Sallust, their great model.

There is a tendency, cropping out occasionally, in the OT, to omit the name of God as superfluous, when He, as the great logical subject always in mind, would be easily understood (cf. Job 20:23; 21:17; Ps. 114:2; Lam. 4:22). So, too, when the NT writers quoted Scripture there was no need to say whose word it was: that lay beyond question in every mind. This usage, accordingly, is a specially striking intimation of the vivid sense which the NT writers had of the divine origin of the Scriptures, and means that in citing them they were acutely conscious that they were citing immediate words of God. How completely the Scriptures were to them just the word of God may be illustrated by a passage like Gal. 3:16: "It does not say, 'And to offsprings,' referring to many; but, referring to one, 'And to your offspring,' which is Christ." We have seen Our Lord hanging an argument on the very words of Scripture (Jn. 10:34); elsewhere His reasoning depends on the particular tense (Mt. 22:32) or word (Mt. 22:43) used in Scripture. Here Paul's argument rests similarly on a grammatical form. No doubt it is the grammatical form of the word which God is recorded as having spoken to Abraham that is in question. But Paul knows what grammatical form God employed in speaking to Abraham only as the Scriptures have transmitted it to him; and, as we have seen, in citing the words of God and the words of Scripture he was not accustomed to make any distinction between them. It is probably the Scriptural word as a Scriptural word, therefore, which he has here in mind: though, of course, it is possible that what he here witnesses to is rather the detailed trustworthiness of the Scriptural record than its direct divinity — if we can separate two things which apparently were not separated in Paul's mind. This much we can at least say without straining, that the designation of Scripture as "scripture" and its citation by the formula "It is written" attest primarily its indefectible authority; the designation of it as "oracles" and the adduction of it by the formula "It says" attest primarily its immediate divinity. Its authority rests on its divinity and its divinity expresses itself in its trustworthiness; and the NT writers in all their use of it treat it as what they declare it to be — a God-breathed document, which, because God-breathed, is through and through trustworthy in all its assertions, authoritative in all its declarations, and down to its last particular, the very word of God, His "oracles."

V. Human and Divine Aspects.–That the Scriptures are throughout a divine book, created by the divine energy and speaking in every part with divine authority directly to the heart of the readers, is the fundamental fact concerning them which is witnessed by Christ and the sacred writers to whom we owe the NT. But the strength and constancy with which they bear witness to this primary fact do not prevent their recognizing by the side of it that the Scriptures have come into being by human agency. It would be inexact to say that they recognize a human element in Scripture: they do not parcel Scripture out, assigning portions of it, or elements in it, respectively to God and man. In their view the whole of Scripture in all its parts and in all its elements, down to the least minutiae, in form of expression as well as in substance of teaching, is from God; but the whole of it has been given by God through the instrumentality of men. There is, therefore, in their view, not, indeed, a human element or ingredient in Scripture, and much less human divisions or sections of Scripture, but a human side or aspect to Scripture; and they do not fail to give full recognition to this human side or aspect. In one of the primary passages which has already been before us, their conception is given, if somewhat broad and very succinct, yet clear expression. No "prophecy," Peter tells us (2 Pet. 1:21), "ever came by human impulse but men moved by the Holy Spirit spoke from God." Here the whole initiative is assigned to God, and such complete control of the human agents that the product is truly God's work. The men who speak in this "prophecy of scripture" speak not of themselves or out of themselves, but from "God": they speak only as they are "moved by the Holy Spirit." But it is they, after all, who speak. Scripture is the product of man, but only of man speaking from God and under such control of the Holy Spirit as that in their speaking they are "moved" by Him. The conception obviously is that the Scriptures have been given by human instrumentality; and this conception finds repeated incidental expression throughout the NT.

It is this conception, for example, which is expressed when Our Lord, quoting Ps. 110, declares of its words that "David himself, inspired by the Holy Spirit, declared" (Mk. 12:36). There is a certain emphasis here on the words being David's own words, which is due to the requirements of the argument Our Lord was conducting, but which nonetheless sincerely represents Our Lord's conception of their origin. They are David's own words which we find in Ps. 110, therefore; but they are David's own words, spoken not of his own motion merely, but "in the Holy Spirit," that is to say — we could not better paraphrase it — "as moved by the Holy Spirit." In other words, they are "God-breathed" words and therefore authoritative in a sense above what any words of David, not spoken in the Holy Spirit, could possibly be. Generalizing the matter, we may say that the words of Scripture are conceived by Our Lord and the NT writers as the words of their human authors when speaking "in the Holy Spirit," that is to say, by His initiative and under His controlling direction. The conception finds even more precise expression, perhaps, in such a statement as we find — it is Peter who is speaking and it is again a Psalm which is cited — in Acts 1:16, "the Holy Spirit spoke beforehand by the mouth of David." Here the Holy Spirit is adduced, of course, as the real author of what is said (and hence Peter's certainty that what is said will be fulfilled); but David's mouth is expressly designated as the instrument (it is the instrumental preposition that is used) by means of which the Holy Spirit speaks the Scripture in question. He does not speak except through David's mouth. Accordingly, in Acts 4:24f., the "Lord, who didst make the heaven and the earth," acting by His Holy Spirit, is declared to have spoken another Psalm "by the mouth of our father David," His "servant"; and in Mt. 13:35 still another Psalm is adduced as "spoken by the prophet" (cf. Mt. 2:5). In the very act of energetically asserting the divine origin of Scripture the human instrumentality through which it is given is constantly recognized. The NT writers have, therefore, no difficulty in assigning Scripture to its human authors, or in discovering in Scripture traits due to its human authorship. They freely quote it by such simple formulas as these: "Moses says" (Rom. 10:19); "Moses said" (Mt. 22:24; Mk. 7:10; Acts 3:22); "Moses writes" (Rom. 10:5); "Moses wrote" (Mk. 12:19; Lk. 20:28); "Isaiah . . . to say" (Rom. 10:20); "Isaiah said" (Jn. 12:39); "Isaiah cries" (Rom. 9:27); "as Isaiah predicted" (Rom. 9:29); "said Isaiah the prophet" (Jn. 1:23); "did Isaiah prophesy" (Mk. 7:6; Mt. 15:7); "David says" (Lk. 20:42; Acts 2:25; Rom. 11:9); "David said" (Mk. 12:36). It is to be noted that when thus Scripture is adduced by the names of its human authors, it is a matter of complete indifference whether the words adduced are comments of these authors or direct words of God recorded by them. As the plainest words of the human authors are assigned to God as their real author, so the most express words of God, repeated by the scriptural writers, are cited by the names of these human writers (Mt. 15:7; Mk. 7:6; Rom. 10:5, 19f.; cf. Mk. 7:10 from the Decalogue). "Moses says" or "David says" is evidently thus only a way of saying that "Scripture says," which is the same as to say that "God says."

Such modes of citing Scripture, accordingly, carry us little beyond merely connecting the name, or perhaps we may say the individuality, of the several writers with the portions of Scripture given through each. How it was given through them is left meanwhile, if not without suggestion, yet without specific explanation. We seem safe only in inferring this much: that the gift of Scripture through its human authors took place by a process much more intimate than can be expressed by the term "dictation," and that it took place in a process in which the control of the Holy Spirit was too complete and pervasive to permit the human qualities of the secondary authors in any way to condition the purity of the product as the word of God. The Scriptures, in other words, are conceived by the writers of the NT as through and through God's book, in every part expressive of His mind, given through people after a fashion which does no violence to their human nature and constitutes the book also mankind's book as well as God's, in every part expressive of the mind of its human authors.

If we attempt to get behind this broad statement and to obtain a more detailed conception of the activities by which God has given the Scriptures, we are thrown back upon somewhat general representations, supported by the analogy of the modes of God's working in other spheres of His operation. It is very desirable that we should free ourselves at the outset from influences arising from the common employment of the term "inspiration" to designate this process. This term is not a biblical term and its etymological implications are not perfectly accordant with the biblical conception of the modes of the divine operation in giving the Scriptures. The biblical writers do not conceive of the Scriptures as a human product breathed into by the divine Spirit, and thus heightened in its qualities or endowed with new qualities, but as a divine product produced through human instrumentality. They do not conceive of these people, by whose instrumentality Scripture is produced, as working upon their own initiative, though energized by God to greater effort and higher achievement, but as moved by the divine initiative and borne by the irresistible power of the Spirit of God along ways of His choosing to ends of His appointment. The difference between the two conceptions may not appear great when the mind is fixed exclusively upon the nature of the resulting product. But they are differing conceptions, and look at the production of Scripture from distinct points of view — the human and the divine; and the involved mental attitudes toward the origin of Scripture are very diverse. The term "inspiration" is too firmly fixed, in both theological and popular usage, as the technical designation of the action of God in giving the Scriptures, to be replaced; and we may be thankful that its native implications lie as close as they do to the biblical conceptions. Meanwhile, however, it may be justly insisted that it shall receive its definition from the representations of Scripture, and not be permitted to impose upon our thought ideas of the origin of Scripture derived from an analysis of its own implications, etymological or historical. The scriptural conception of the relation of the divine Spirit to the human authors in the production of Scripture is better expressed by the figure of being "moved" than by the figure of "inbreathing"; and when our biblical writers speak of the action of the Spirit of God in this relation as a breathing, they represent it as a "breathing out" of the Scriptures by the Spirit, and not a "breathing into" the Scriptures by Him.

So soon, however, as we seriously endeavor to form for ourselves a clear conception of the precise nature of the divine action in this "breathing out" of the Scriptures — this "moving" of the writers of the Scriptures to their appointed goal of the production of a book of divine trustworthiness and indefectible authority — we become acutely aware of a more deeply lying and much wider problem, apart from which this one of inspiration, technically so called, cannot be profitably considered. This is the general problem of the origin of the Scriptures and the part of God in all that complex of processes by the interaction of which these books, which we call the sacred Scriptures, with all their peculiarities, and all their qualities of whatever sort, have been brought into being. For, of course, these books were not produced suddenly, by some miraculous act — handed down complete out of heaven, as the phrase goes; but, like all other products of time, are the ultimate result of many processes through long periods. There is to be considered, for instance, the preparation of the material which forms the subject matter of these books: in a sacred history, say, for example, to be narrated; or in a religious experience which may serve as a norm for record; or in a logical elaboration of the contents of revelation which may be placed at the service of God's people; or in the progressive revelation of divine truth itself, supplying their culminating contents. And there is the preparation of the men to write these books to be considered, a preparation physical, intellectual, spiritual, which must have attended them throughout their whole lives, and, indeed, must have had its beginning in their remote ancestors, and the effect of which was to bring the right men to the right places at the right times, with the right endowments, impulses, acquirements, to write just the books which were designed for them. When "inspiration," technically so called, is superinduced on lines of preparation like these, it takes on quite a different aspect from that which it bears when it is thought of as an isolated action of the divine Spirit operating out of all relation to historical processes. Representations are sometimes made as if, when God wished to produce sacred books which would incorporate His will — a series of letters like those of Paul, for example — He was reduced to the necessity of going down to earth and painfully scrutinizing the men He found there, seeking anxiously for the one who, on the whole, promised best for His purpose; and then violently forcing the material He wished expressed through him, against his natural bent, and with as little loss from his recalcitrant characteristics as possible. Of course, nothing of the sort took place. If God wished to give His people a series of letters like Paul's, He prepared a Paul to write them, and the Paul He brought to the task was a Paul who spontaneously would write just such letters.

If we bear this in mind, we shall know what estimate to place upon the common representation to the effect that the human characteristics of the writers must, and in point of fact do, condition and qualify the writings produced by them, the implication being that, therefore, we cannot get from man a pure word of God. As light that passes through the colored glass of a cathedral window, we are told, is light from heaven, but is stained by the tints of the glass through which it passes; so any word of God that is passed through the mind and soul of a man must come out discolored by the personality through which it is given, and just to that degree ceases to be the pure word of God. But what if this personality has itself been formed by God into precisely the personality it is, for the express purpose of communicating to the word given through it just the coloring which it gives it? What if the colors of the stained glass window have been designed by the architect for the express purpose of giving to the light that floods the cathedral precisely the tone and quality it receives from them? What if the word of God that comes to His people is framed by God into the word of God it is, precisely by means of the qualities of the men formed by Him for the purpose, through which it is given? When we think of God giving by His Spirit a body of authoritative Scriptures to His people, we must remember that He is the God of providence and of grace as well as of revelation and inspiration, and that He holds all the lines of preparation as fully under His direction as He does the specific operation which we call technically, in the narrow sense, by the name of "inspiration."

The production of the Scriptures is, in point of fact, a long process, in the course of which numerous and very varied divine activities are involved, providential, gracious, miraculous, all of which must be taken into account in any attempt to explain the relation of God to the production of Scripture. When they are all taken into account we can no longer wonder that the resultant Scriptures are constantly spoken of as the pure word of God. We wonder, rather, that an additional operation of God — what we call specifically "inspiration," in its technical sense — was thought necessary. Consider, for example, how a piece of sacred history — say the book of Chronicles, or the great historical work, Gospel and Acts, of Luke — is brought to the writing. There is first of all the preparation of the history which will be the theme: God leads the sequence of occurrences through the development He has designed for them that they may convey their lessons to His people: a "teleological" or "aetiological" character is inherent in the very course of events. Then He prepares a man, by birth, training, experience, gifts of grace, and, if need be, of revelation, capable of appreciating this historical development and eager to search it out, deeply interested in its lessons and bent upon making them clear and effective to others. When by His providence, God sets this man to work on the writing of this history, will there not be spontaneously written by him the history which it was divinely intended should be written? Or consider how a psalmist would be prepared to put into verse a piece of normative religious experience: how he would be born with just the right quality of religious sensibility, of parents through whom he should receive just the right hereditary inclination, and from whom he should get precisely the right religious example and training, in circumstances of life in which his religious tendencies should be developed precisely on right lines; how he would be brought through just the right experiences to quicken in him the precise emotions he would be called upon to express, and finally would be placed in precisely the exigencies which would call out their expression. Or consider the providential preparation of a writer of a didactic epistle — by means of which he should be given the intellectual breadth and acuteness, and be trained in habits of reasoning, and placed in the situations which would call out precisely the argumentative presentation of Christian truth that was required of him. When we give due place in our thoughts to the universality of the providential government of God, to the minuteness and completeness of its sway, and to its invariable efficacy, we may be inclined to ask what is needed beyond this mere providential government to secure the production of sacred books which should be in every detail absolutely accordant with the divine will.

The answer is that nothing is needed beyond mere providence to secure such books — provided only that it does not lie in the divine purpose that these books should possess qualities which rise above the powers of men to produce, even under the most complete divine guidance. For providence is guidance; and guidance can bring one only so far as his own power can carry him. If heights are to be scaled above man's native power to achieve, then something more than guidance, however effective, is necessary. This is the reason for the superinduction, at the end of the long process of the production of Scripture, of the additional divine operation which we call technically "inspiration." By it, the Spirit of God, flowing confluently in with the providentially and graciously determined work of men, spontaneously producing under the divine directions the writings appointed to them, gives the product a divine quality unattainable by human powers alone. Thus these books become not merely the word of godly men, but the immediate word of God Himself, speaking directly as such to the minds and hearts of every reader. The value of "inspiration" emerges, thus, as twofold. It gives to the books written under its "moving" a quality which is truly superhuman; a trustworthiness, an authority, a searchingness, a profundity, a profitableness which is altogether divine. And it speaks this divine word immediately to each reader's heart and conscience; so that he does not require to make his way to God, painfully, perhaps even uncertainly, through the words of His servants, the human instruments in writing the Scriptures, but can listen directly to the divine voice itself speaking immediately in the scriptural word to him.

That the writers of the NT themselves conceive the Scriptures to have been produced thus by divine operations extending through the increasing ages and involving a multitude of varied activities, can be made clear by simply attending to the occasional references they make to this or that step in the process. It lies, for example, on the face of their expositions, that they looked upon the biblical history as teleological. Not only do they tell us that "whatever was written in former days was written for our instruction, that by steadfastness and by the encouragement of the scriptures we might have hope" (Rom. 15:4; cf. Rom. 4:23f.); they speak also of the course of the historical events themselves as guided for our benefit: "Now these things happened to them as a warning" — in a typical fashion, in such a way that, as they occurred, a typical character, or predictive reference impressed itself upon them; that is to say, briefly, the history occurred as it did in order to bear a message to us — "but they were written down for our instruction, upon whom the end of the ages has come" (1 Cor. 10:11; cf. v. 6). Accordingly, it has become a commonplace of biblical exposition that "the history of redemption itself is a typically progressive one" (Küper), and is "in a manner impregnated with the prophetic element," so as to form a "part of a great plan which stretches from the fall of man to the first consummation of all things in glory; and, in so far as it reveals the mind of God toward man, carries a respect to the future not less than to the present" (P. Fairbairn).

It lies equally on the face of the NT allusions to the subject that its writers understood that the preparation of men to become vehicles of God's message to mankind was not recent, but had its beginnings in the very origin of their being. The call by which Paul, for example, was made an apostle of Jesus Christ was sudden and apparently without antecedents; but it is precisely this Paul who reckons this call as only one step in a long process, the beginnings of which antedated his own existence: "But when he who had set me apart before I was born, and had called me through his grace, was pleased to reveal his Son to me" (Gal. 1:15f.; cf. Jer. 1:5; Isa. 49:1, 5). The recognition by the writers of the NT of the experiences of God's grace, which had been vouchsafed to them as an integral element in their fitting to be the bearers of His gospel to others, finds such pervasive expression that the only difficulty is to select from the mass the most illustrative passages. Such a statement as Paul gives in the opening verses of 2 Corinthians is thoroughly typical. There he represents that he has been afflicted and comforted to the end that he might "be able to comfort those who are in any affliction, through the comfort with which" he had himself been "comforted by God." For, he explains, "If we are afflicted, it is for your comfort and salvation; and if we are comforted, it is for your comfort, which you experience when you patiently endure the same sufferings that we suffer" (2 Cor. 1:4–6). It is beyond question, therefore, that the NT writers, when they declare the Scriptures to be the product of the divine breath, and explain this as meaning that the writers of these Scriptures wrote them only as moved by the Holy Spirit in such a fashion that they spoke, not out of themselves, but "from God," are thinking of this operation of the Spirit only as the final act of God in the production of the Scriptures, superinduced upon a long series of processes, providential, gracious, miraculous, by which the matter of Scripture had been prepared for writing, and the men for writing it, and the writing of it had been actually brought to pass. It is this final act in the production of Scripture which is technically called "inspiration"; and inspiration is thus brought before us as, in the minds of the writers of the NT, that particular operation of God in the production of Scripture which takes effect at the very point of the writing of Scripture — understanding the term "writing" here as inclusive of all the processes of the actual composition of Scripture, the investigation of documents, the collection of facts, the formation of conclusions, the adaptation of exhortations as means to ends and the like — with the effect of giving to the resultant Scripture a specifically supernatural character, and constituting it a divine, as well as human, book. Obviously the mode of operation of this divine activity moving to this result is conceived, in full accord with the analogy of the divine operations in other spheres of its activity, in providence and in grace alike, as confluent with the human activities operative in the case; as in a word, of the nature of what has come to be known as "immanent action."

It will not escape observation that thus "inspiration" is made a mode of "revelation." We are often exhorted, to be sure, to distinguish sharply between "inspiration" and "revelation"; and the exhortation is just when "revelation" is taken in one of its narrower senses, of, say, an external manifestation of God, or of an immediate communication from God in words. But "inspiration" does not differ from "revelation" in these narrowed senses as genus from genus, but as a species of one genus differs from another. That operation of God which we call "inspiration," the operation of the Spirit of God by which He "moves" men in the process of composing Scripture, so that they write not of themselves, but "from God," is one of the modes in which God makes known to us His being, His will, His operations, His purposes. It is as distinctly a mode of revelation as any mode of revelation can be, and therefore it performs the same office which all revelation performs. In the words of Paul, it makes people wise, and makes them wise unto salvation. All "special" or "supernatural" revelation (which is redemptive in its very idea, and occupies a place as a substantial element in God's redemptive processes) has precisely this for its end; and Scripture, as a mode of the redemptive revelation of God, finds its fundamental purpose just in this: if the "inspiration" by which Scripture is produced renders it trustworthy and authoritative, it renders it trustworthy and authoritative only that it may the better serve to make us wise unto salvation. Scripture is conceived, from the point of view of the writers of the NT, not merely as the record of revelations, but as itself a part of the redemptive revelation of God; not merely as the record of the redemptive acts by which God is saving the world, but as itself one of these redemptive acts, having its own part to play in the great work of establishing and building up the kingdom of God. What gives it a place among the redemptive acts of God is its divine origination, taken in its widest sense, as inclusive of all the divine operations, providential, gracious, and expressly supernatural, by which it has been made just what it is — a body of writings able to make wise unto salvation, and profitable for making the child of God perfect. What gives it its place among the modes of revelation is, however, specifically the culminating one of these divine operations, which we call "inspiration"; that is to say, the action of the Spirit of God in so "moving" its human authors in their work of producing Scripture, that in these Scriptures they speak, not out of themselves, but "from God." It is this act by virtue of which the Scriptures may properly be called "God-breathed."

It has been customary among a certain school of writers to speak of the Scriptures, because thus "inspired," as a divine-human book, and to appeal to the analogy of Our Lord's divine-human personality to explain their peculiar qualities as such. The expression calls attention to an important fact, and the analogy is true to a degree. There are human and divine sides to Scripture, and, as we examine it, we may perceive in it, alternately, traits which suggest first the one, then the other factor in its origin. But the analogy with Our Lord's divine-human personality may easily be pressed beyond reason. There is no hypostatic union between the divine and the human in Scripture; we cannot parallel the "inscripturation" of the Holy Spirit and the incarnation of the Son of God. The Scriptures are merely the product of human forces working under the initiation and prevalent direction of the divine; the person of Our Lord unites in itself divine and human natures, each of which retains its distinctness while operating only in relation to the other. Between such diverse things there can exist only a remote analogy; and, in point of fact, the analogy in the present instance amounts to no more than that in both cases divine and human factors are involved, though very differently. In the one they unite to constitute a divine-human person; in the other they cooperate to perform a divine-human work. Even so distant an analogy may enable us, however, to recognize that as in the case of Our Lord's person, the human nature remains truly human and can never fall into sin or error because it can never act out of relation with the divine nature into conjunction with which it has been brought; so in the case of the production of Scripture by the joint action of human and divine factors, the human factors have acted as human factors and have left their mark on the product as such, and yet cannot have fallen into that error which we say it is human to fall into, because they have not acted apart from the divine factors, by themselves, but only under their unerring guidance.

The NT testimony is to the divine origin and qualities of "Scripture"; and "Scripture" to the writers of the NT was fundamentally, of course, the OT. In the primary passage, in which we are told that "every" or "all Scripture" is "God-breathed," the direct reference is to the "sacred writings" which Timothy had known since his infancy, and these were, of course, just the sacred books of the Jews (2 Tim. 3:16). What is explicit here is implicit in all the allusions to inspired Scriptures in the NT. Accordingly, it is frequently said that our entire testimony to the inspiration of Scripture concerns the OT alone. In many ways, however, this is overstated. Our present concern is not with the extent of "Scripture" but with the nature of "Scripture"; and we cannot present here the considerations which justify extending to the NT the inspiration which the NT writers attribute to the OT. It will not be out of place, however, to point out simply that the NT writers obviously themselves made this extension. They do not for an instant imagine themselves, as ministers of a new covenant, less in possession of the Spirit of God than the ministers of the old covenant: they freely recognize, indeed, that they have no sufficiency of themselves, but they know that God has made them sufficient (2 Cor. 3:5f.). They perform their work of proclaiming the gospel, therefore, in full confidence that they speak "by the Holy Spirit" (1 Pet. 1:12), to whom they attribute both the matter and form of their teaching (1 Cor. 2:13). They, therefore, speak with the utmost assurance of their teaching (Gal. 1:7f.); and they issue commands with the completest authority (1 Thess. 4:2, 14; 2 Thess. 3:6, 12), making it, indeed, the test of whether one has the Spirit that he should recognize what they demand as commandments of God (1 Cor. 14:37). It would be strange, indeed, if these high claims were made for their oral teaching and commandments exclusively. In point of fact, they are made explicitly also for their written injunctions. It was "the things" which Paul was "writing," the recognition of which as commands of the Lord he makes the test of a Spirit-led person (1 Cor. 14:37). It is his obedience to "what we say in this letter" that makes the condition of Christian communion (2 Thess. 3:14). There seems involved in such an attitude toward their own teaching, oral and written, a claim on the part of the NT writers to something very much like the "inspiration" which they attribute to the writers of the OT.

And all doubt is dispelled when we observe the NT writers placing the writings of one another in the same category of "Scripture" with the books of the OT. The same Paul who, in 2 Tim. 3:16, declared that "every [or "all"] scripture is God-breathed" had already written in 1 Tim. 5:18, "for the scripture says, 'You shall not muzzle an ox when it is treading out the grain,' and 'The laborer deserves his wages.'" The first clause here is derived from Deuteronomy and the second from the Gospel of Luke, though both are cited as together constituting, or better, forming part of the "scripture" which Paul adduces as so authoritative as by its mere citation to end all strife. Who shall say that, in the declaration of the later epistle that "all" or "every" Scripture is God-breathed, Paul did not have Luke and, along with Luke, whatever other new books he classed with the old under the name of Scripture, in the back of his mind, along with those old books which Timothy had had in his hands from infancy? And the same Peter who declared that every "prophecy of scripture" was the product of men who spoke "from God," being "moved" by the Holy Spirit (2 Pet. 1:21), in this same epistle (3:16), places Paul's epistles in the category of Scripture along with whatever other books deserve that name. For Paul, says he, wrote these epistles, not out of his own wisdom, but "according to the wisdom given him," and though there are some things in them difficult to understand, yet it is only "the ignorant and unstable" who wrest these difficult passages — as what else could be expected of men who wrest "the other scriptures" (obviously the OT is meant) — "to their own destruction"? Is it possible to say that Peter could not have had these Epistles of Paul also lurking somewhere in the back of his mind, along with "the other scriptures," when he told his readers that every "prophecy of scripture" owes its origin to the prevailing operation of the Holy Spirit? What must be understood in estimating the testimony of the NT writers to the inspiration of Scripture is that "Scripture" stood in their minds as the title of a unitary body of books, throughout the gift of God through His Spirit to His people; but that this body of writings was at the same time understood to be a growing aggregate, so that what is said of it applies to the new books which were being added to it as the Spirit gave them, as fully as to the old books which had been previously received. It is a mere matter of detail to determine precisely what new books were thus included by them in the category "Scripture." They tell us some of them themselves. Those who received them from their hands tell us of others. And when we put the two bodies of testimony together we find that they constitute just our NT. It is no distortion of the witness of the writers of the NT to the inspiration of the Scripture, therefore, to look upon it as covering the entire body of "Scriptures," the new books which they were themselves adding to this aggregate, as well as the old books which they had received as Scripture from the fathers. Whatever can lay claim to the appellation of "Scripture," as employed in its eminent sense by those writers, can by the same just right lay claim to the "inspiration" which they ascribe to this "Scripture."

Bibliography.–C. Hodge, *Systematic Theology* (1871), I, 151-186; H. B. Smith, *Inspiration of Holy Scripture* (2nd ed. 1891); A. Kuyper, *Encyclopedia of Sacred Theology* (Eng. tr. 1898), pp. 341-563; J. Orr, *Revelation and Inspiration* (1910).

B. B. WARFIELD

INSPIRATION, HISTORY OF THE DOCTRINE OF.

I. Early Church
II. Patristic Period
III. Medieval Church
IV. Reformation
V. Post-Reformation Period
VI. Eighteenth-Century Rationalism
VII. Conclusion

The starting point of the Church's doctrine of inspiration is obviously to be found in the self-witness of the Bible itself. As far as the OT is concerned, both the Law and the prophetic writings purport to come from God; and in specific cases the NT links the giving of messages through human speakers or writers with the activity of the Holy Spirit. Inspiration thus arises naturally and necessarily from the divine source and authority. Nor does it refer only to an ecstatic upsurge of the human spirit; the reference is plainly to the inworking of the Holy Spirit. In the NT it is made clear that divine authority extends to the whole of the OT; for example, Our Lord shows His disciples "in all the scriptures the things concerning himself" (Lk. 24:27). Again, the activity of the Holy Spirit is given a general reference. We read that the psalmist speaks in the Spirit in Ps. 110 (Mt. 22:43). And finally, the two primary verses in 2 Tim. 3:16 and 2 Pet. 1:21 tell us that "all scripture is given by inspiration of God," and that "holy men of God spake as they were moved by the Holy Ghost" (AV).

It is to be noted that the linking of the biblical writings with the Holy Spirit means that they are brought into direct relationship with the work of the Spirit, namely, to bear witness to Jesus Christ. This is true of the OT with its prophetic testimony, for we read that Jesus Himself said of these writings: "They are they which testify of me" (Jn. 5:39). But it is also true of the NT, and gives the backward-looking apostolic testimony an assured place alongside the prophetic. For in Jn. 14:26 we are told that the Holy Spirit would bring all things to the remembrance of the apostles; in Acts (e.g., 2:4; 4:8; *et passim*) we find that the Holy Spirit is their coworker, and in 2 Pet. 3:16 there is a classification of the Epistles of Paul with the Scriptures which certifies the divine authority of this written testimony.

A derivative point specifically developed in 2 Cor. 3 (cf. 1 Cor. 1 and 2) is that the Holy Spirit who gave the Scriptures is the living Lord, whose voice must be heard in and through Scripture if its message is to be understood and received. This continuing work of the Spirit does not seem to be described by the Bible as the proper work of inspiration. But it is an unavoidable implication. If the message is really from the Holy Spirit, it cannot be received merely by the natural understanding. Without the Holy Spirit it can be read only on the level of the human letter. What is given by the Spirit must be read in the Spirit. To the objective inspiration of Scripture there corresponds the subjective illumination of the understanding, which safeguards the doctrine against the constant threat of an "Apollinarian" interpretation and the consequent notion of *ex opere operato* (automatic operation).

I. Early Church.–It is as well to mention this derivative point at once because one of the alien influences to which the early Church was also exposed tended to press it in the direction of this distorted interpretation. This was the Jewish or Judaistic understanding to which there is an oblique allusion in Jn. 5:39f., and to which Paul is specifically referring in 2 Cor. 3. To be sure, the Jews stood for a high doctrine of inspiration, particularly in relation to the Law. To the extent that their teaching helped to safeguard the Church against the equation of the Bible with "inspired" religious literature we may describe it as salutary. For after all, it had its roots in the Bible itself. But it carried with it a threefold danger. In the first place, it tended to abstract the divine nature and authority of the Bible from the human authors and situations, i.e., from the whole movement of God's saving work in and through the history of Israel and the persons concerned. Second, it clearly abstracted the Bible from the object of its witness when it failed or refused to see in Jesus Christ the object of its witness, thus being left with a mere textbook of doctrine, ethics, and ceremonies. Third, in rejecting Jesus Christ it refused the witness of the Holy Spirit, so that in its reading the OT was deprived of its living power. The result of this threefold abstraction is the contradiction that the human element in the Bible is almost completely subsumed into the divine on the one side, whereas in practice the divine and authoritative text falls victim to only too human exegesis and schematization on the other.

The Judaistic was not, of course, the only danger threatening the infant Church. Gentile Christians especially were perhaps even more vulnerable to pagan notions. For the heathen religions also had their inspiration, whether in the ecstatic utterances and movements of devotees, the pronouncements of the oracles, the writings of the Sybillines, or literature generally. A writer like Philo had already succumbed to the temptation to bring together the prophetic inspiration of the OT and these pagan phenomena. After all, had not the early prophets given evidence of this type of ecstatic possession? The statement of Plato: "And for this reason God takes away the mind of these men and uses them as his ministers, just as he does soothsayers and godly seers, in order that we who hear them may know . . . that it is God Himself who speaks and addresses us through them" (*Ion* 533), thus finds a clear parallel in Philo's interpretation of the OT: "For a prophet has no utterances of his own, but all his utterances come from elsewhere, the echoes of another's voice . . . he is the vocal instrument of God smitten and played by His invisible hand" (*Quis rerum divinarum heres* 259). In some sense, this is no less a high view than that of Judaism, and it has the advantage of emphasizing the living movement. But apart from its pagan associations, it has the same twofold and apparently contradictory disadvantage of destroying the human element on the one side, yet in so doing, of reducing inspiration to a familiar and psychologically explicable human phenomenon on the other.

II. Patristic Period.–When we turn to the patristic period we are struck at once by the way in which all writers accepted the inspiration and authority of Holy Scripture as self-evident. The actual writings of the OT and NT are seen to derive from the Holy Spirit and therefore carry the divine message. Nor is this merely a general inspiration; it extends to the detailed phraseology of the Bible in accordance with the saying of Christ in Mt. 5:18. Thus Clement of Alexandria tells us that not one jot nor tittle can pass because all has been spoken by the mouth of the Lord (*Protrepticus* ix.82.1); and Gregory Nazianzus writes that even the smallest lines in Scripture are due to the minute care of the Holy Spirit, so that we must pay careful attention to every slightest shade of meaning (*Oratio* 2.105). In order to emphasize the perfection and authority of the Scriptures, Irenaeus can say that its words are actually spoken by God Himself through His Word and Spirit (*Adv. haer.* ii.28.2). What the authors say is really said by God Himself, and must be received and studied not merely or primarily as the word of man but as the Word of God. This emphasis on the divine inspiration of the Bible is obviously reflected again in the many statements in the fathers which refer to the supreme authority of the Bible in the Church, as in the dictum of Augustine quoted in Cranmer's *Confutation of Unwritten Verities:* "For I do not account Cyprian's writings as canonical, but weigh them by the canonical scriptures; and that in them which agreeth with canonical I allow to his praise; but that that agreeth not, by his favour I refuse" (Parker Society ed., II, p. 33).

There can be little doubt that a sound and scriptural doctrine of inspiration was for the most part maintained and developed in the patristic period. The primary fact of inspiration was never in doubt. There was no temptation to restrict its range to favored passages of the Bible. It was not abstracted from the true theme of the Bible in Jesus Christ, the temptation in most writers being to find rather fanciful and extravagant allusions to Christ and His work in the most unlikely ways and places (cf. especially the Epistle of Barnabas). And no attempt was made to work out a systematic understanding of inspiration along lines which might replace its true miracle and mystery by a false.

At the same time there are elements in the patristic teaching which show that the pressure of Judaistic and pagan doctrine was not without its effect. This is reflected in the typical attempt by the Apologists to commend the Bible by comparing it with the Sibyllines (cf. Theophilus of Antioch, *Ad Autolycum* ii.9), and more seriously perhaps by the doubtful suggestions of Athenagoras that the Holy Spirit uses the prophets as a flautist uses his flute (*Supplicatio* 7, 9); or of Hippolytus that He plays on them as on a zither or harp (*Demonstratio de Christo et antichristo* 2). Fortunately, perhaps, the excesses of Montanism served as a decisive check to thinking in terms of pagan ecstacism. But the impulse to depreciate the human element found no less serious expression in another form. Augustine, for example, approached the thought of a dictation of the Holy Scriptures when he stated that the Christ used the Evangelists "as if they were his own hands" (*Harmony of the Gospels* i.35), although in the context this does not mean more than that the members of Christ's body act on behalf of Christ Himself as the head. This was pressed almost unbearably (though with an element of truth) by Gregory the Great when he said of Job: "He Himself wrote them, who dictated the things that should be written. He did Himself write them, who both was present in the saint's work, and by the mouth of the writer," the identity of the author being of no consequence (*Magna moralia praef.* i.2). This tendency was the more dangerous because the reaction against Montanism entailed a concentration upon the given letter at the expense of the free movement of the Holy Spirit, not in divorce from the letter as in Montanism, but in His disposal of it.

We must not exaggerate these weaknesses in relation to the real strength of the patristic doctrine and its avoidance of cruder errors especially in relation to pagan ecstaticism. Indeed, even the human element is not altogether lost in the divine, for Augustine can find a place for this side by side with his doctrine of dictation (*Harmony of the Gospels* ii.12); and it was realized that the unpolished style of some of the authors could not be attributed to the Spirit except by way of condescension. Indeed, some writers like Origen and Theodore of Mopsuestia were prepared to go further and speak of various levels of inspiration, although fortunately this opposite extreme did not find general acceptance in the early Church. On the other hand, it has to be conceded that there were dangerous tendencies in this primitive period. The phrase "dictation" can be understood, and was probably intended, in a true sense; but it opens the way to a mechanical view which makes it difficult to appreciate the original setting of the messages, and at the same time eliminates the present work of the Holy Spirit in the illumination of the reader. In addition, there is involved a possible relativization of the Bible which in the long run jeopardizes rather than secures its true authority, placing it side by side with other historically demonstrable phenomena such as extrabiblical tradition, the Church, and at a later date the Papacy.

III. Medieval Church.–The incipient dangers in the patristic doctrine come to fruition in the medieval Church, which presents us with the paradox of a high doctrine of inspiration accompanied by a muzzling of its authority and in the later stages a virtual elimination of its living power. In point of fact the Scholastic period is particularly sterile in the matter of inspiration, being far more interested in defining the status of the Bible in relation to that of other authorities in the Church. Abelard, as might be expected, makes a plea for a more human understanding, and expresses doubt as to the inerrancy of Scripture from a historical standpoint. Aquinas has a full and careful discussion of the relation of the human authors and readers to the Holy Spirit as the true author, and with his usual acuteness he finds a real place for the ordinary element (cf. *Summa Theol.* ii.2.171ff.). But the whole discussion relates to a Bible Judaistically understood as a textbook of divine truth, divinely given and therefore to be approached with respect, but accessible to human study like any other textbook (i.e., in virtual abstraction from the Holy Spirit as its necessary interpreter), and accompanied by other and hardly less important authorities. In these circumstances it is not surprising that over large tracts of medieval life the Bible could not do its vivifying and reforming work, although its inspiration was so fully accepted. It is not surprising that the human element excluded from the understanding of the Bible should rise up the more strongly in other spheres and successfully challenge and subjugate the divinely dictated Scriptures. It is not surprising that the Bible should become a mere source book for dogmatic disputation, ossified in an alien tongue, instead of the living Word of Jesus Christ to the churches. This is not to say that the medieval doctrine was wrong in basic substance. It is not to say that a less high doctrine of inspiration is demanded. It is not to say that the Bible should be understood in terms of religious philosophy or poetry. But it is a warning that even a materially impeccable doctrine may be held and taught and applied in such a way that the true insights of the Bible are suppressed, and the result is a distortion which achieves the very opposite of what is intended, and is almost worse than naked error.

IV. Reformation.–This was the kind of situation which the Reformers had to remedy in their understanding of the Bible, and it is against this background that we must try to understand their doctrine of inspiration. In the first place, we can hardly fail to note that this doctrine does not play any decisive part in their theology. Their concern is primarily with other matters. Yet this does not mean that it is unimportant, let alone that it is absent. It simply means that they can almost afford to take it for granted. The high inspiration of the Bible; the fact that God Himself is the true author of Scripture; the divine origin of even the detailed wording — these are matters which are not disputed. Luther makes it plain that the whole of the Bible must be accepted as the inspired Word of God (cf. *WA* liv,158,28). Zwingli appeals consistently to the divinely inspired record of the OT and NT in assertion and defense of pure Christian doctrine. Calvin is perhaps the clearest and firmest on this point. He describes the Scriptures as the "only record in which God has been pleased to consign his truth to perpetual remembrance," and says that we cannot have an established faith in doctrine "until we have a perfect conviction that God is its author," i.e., through Scripture (*Inst.* i.7.2, 4). In his sermon on 2 Tim. 3:16, he constantly refers to God as the author of the Bible, and in his commentary on this passage he can even speak in terms of "dictation" (*Corpus Reformatorum,* LIV, 283f.). Among the Anglicans, Whitaker has a similar passage in answer to the Romanist contention that the Bible is only mediately the voice of God: "We confess that God hath not spoken of himself, but by others. Yet this does not diminish the authority of scripture. For God inspired the prophets with what they said, and made use of their mouths, tongues, and hands: the scripture, therefore, is even immediately the voice of God. The prophets and apostles were only the organs of God" (Parker Society ed., p. 296). In view of the controversy regarding Reformation teaching, and the suggestion in some quarters that the Reformers more or less abandoned the traditional doctrine of inspiration, it is as well to emphasize this primary element in their thinking. Nowhere, perhaps, is it more authoritatively summed up than in Barth's *Church Dogmatics:* "The Reformers took over unquestioningly and unreservedly the statement on the inspiration, and indeed the verbal inspiration, of the Bible, as it is explicitly and implicitly contained in those Pauline passages which we have taken as our basis, even including the formula that God is the author of the Bible, and occasionally making use of the idea of a dictation through the biblical writers" (I/2, 520).

Yet even a cursory examination of the Reformation literature makes it plain that in three important respects the Reformers moved back from the traditional teaching and its Judaistic basis to a more genuinely scriptural understanding. In the first place, they had a clear realization that Christ is the true theme of the Bible. The Bible is not a mere source book of Christian teaching to be handled with legalistic rationalism (i.e., for attainment of self-righteousness and self-wisdom) by scholars, ecclesiastics, and canonists. It is the book to lead us to Christ, not merely to a mystical Christ, but to Christ prepared and prophesied in the OT, and incarnate, crucified, risen, and ascended in the NT. Luther makes this point with greatest clarity: "But Holy Scripture refuses to know or put before us anything but Christ. And whoso therefore goes to Scripture or is led by Scripture to Christ, it is well with him and he is on the right path" (*WA* xvi,113,22). But Zwingli has it, too: in the Bible "Christ stands before you with open arms, inviting you and saying, 'Come unto me . . .'" (*LCC,*XXIV, 84). And although Calvin does not make it quite so explicitly, it is the theme of his whole understanding of the biblical story as developed in the main part of the *Institutes* (ii.6f.; and cf. his comm. on Jn. 5:39, "We ought to read the Scriptures with the express design of finding Christ in them").

Second, and in consequence, there is a better appreciation of the human aspects of the Bible, not in isolation from the divine work but in conjunction with it. The Bible tells us the story of God's dealings in salvation and judgment. It treats of a people, of the men of this people, and of the One to whom they led and in whom they found fulfillment. The authors have their own place in the development or outworking or recounting of this story. God uses them in their own place and time, and according to their own capacity and endowment. The fact that the Bible is fully inspired does not mean that we have to look for a hidden or allegorical sense, but that the divine message is given in and through the human. It is for this reason that the Reformers dismiss the complicated exegesis of the Middle Ages and insist upon straightforward exposition (cf. Whitaker, pp. 405f.), relating the various passages primarily to their human setting. But they are also aware that in this respect the Bible conforms to a christological pattern. As the Word became flesh, and was very man no less than very God, so the written Word is no less fully a human word than a divine. To allow the human word to be minimized or even swallowed up in the divine is not to do true honor to the Bible, but to miss its true miracle and message.

Third, the Reformers all have a vivid sense that, although the meaning of the Bible is for the most part clear and simple in itself, its message cannot be received merely by human reading or scholarship or historical research. There is needed in the reader the work of the same Spirit who gave the writings. This is one of the most widely and firmly attested of all the points made by the Reformers, for it was of crucial importance in their attack on the medieval doctrine and their whole resistance to the traditional view of authority. Luther puts it in this way: "The Bible cannot be mastered by study or talent; you must rely solely on the influx of the Spirit" (*Briefwechsel*, ed. Enders and Kawerau, I, 141). Zwingli bases his appeal to the nuns of Oetenbach upon it: "Even if you hear the gospel of Jesus Christ from an apostle, you cannot act upon it unless the heavenly Father teach and draw you by the Spirit" (*op. cit.*, p. 79, and cf. the whole context, pp. 75-95). Calvin gives us the forceful statement: "For as God alone can properly bear witness to his own words, so these words will not obtain full credit in the hearts of men, until they are sealed by the inward testimony of the Spirit. The same Spirit, therefore, who spoke by the mouth of the prophets, must penetrate our hearts, in order to convince us that they faithfully delivered the message with which they were divinely entrusted" (*Inst.* i.7.4, and see esp. comms. on 1 Cor. 20ff.; 2 Cor. 3:6). The same emphasis is to be found in Whitaker: "We say that the Holy Spirit is the supreme interpreter of scripture, because we must be illuminated by the Holy Spirit to be certainly persuaded of the true sense of scripture," and again: "For no saving truth can be known without the Holy Ghost" (p. 415).

Two subsidiary points are to be noted in passing. The first is that, since Christian understanding rests upon the work of the Spirit, the Bible cannot be treated as a Euclid of Christian faith and conduct to be learned, schematized, and applied by the ordinary ways of reason and scholarship. On the basis of a sound doctrine of inspiration, biblical theology is always a venture of prayer, humility, and obedience in the Spirit; and nowhere is this better illustrated than in the works of the Reformers themselves. But second, since the Holy Spirit Himself attests the word He has given, there can be a relative unconcern regarding its human qualifications. It does not have to be proved that the Bible is the oldest of books, or the best literature, or of superior majesty, though some of these points may well be made by way of confirmation. Again, it need not be *demonstrated with absolute finality* that all the predictions of the OT are fulfilled to the letter, although Christians taught by the Spirit will rejoice as the Reformers did if this is the case. Finally, the credibility of Scripture does not stand or fall with the *ability to prove* that all the events recorded took place exactly as reported, although for all their freedom in face of apparent contradictions the Reformers have obviously not the slightest doubt that this is the case. As Calvin judiciously points out, these proofs are "not so strong as to produce and rivet a full conviction in our minds," but when the necessary foundation of a higher assurance is laid "they become most appropriate helps" (*Inst.* i.8.1).

V. Post-Reformation Period.–The post-Reformation period presents us with a multiplicity of material on the theme of inspiration which makes it impossible to do more than pick out the leading tendencies. As in Reformation doctrine, it was commonly accepted that God is the true author, not merely of the doctrine of Scripture but of the writings themselves (J. Gerhard, *Loci communes theologici*, II, 17; J. Cocceius, *Summa theologiae*, IV [Amsterdam, 1665], 39). Inspiration applies to the whole Scripture, and not merely to particular parts (Hollaz, *ETA*, p. 90). It does not rule out a concomitant action on the part of the human authors (*ibid.*, p. 91; *Leiden Synopsis*, III, 7). Yet it is more than a mere guidance of the authors in their human action, and is not equivalent to ordinary artistic "inspiration" (J. Quenstedt, *Theologia didactico-polemica*, I, 69). It extends to the very words in which the statements are clothed (*ibid.*, I, 72; Cocceius, IV, 41), and includes passages which deal with historical and scientific as well as doctrinal and ethical matters (Hollaz, p. 89). It is supported both by the witness of Scripture itself and by the inner witness of the Holy Spirit through the word (Quenstedt, I, 87).

In all these matters it is evident that the Lutheran and Reformed dogmaticians of the 17th cent. are in line with the main teaching of the Reformers themselves. But certain features call for notice which pose the question whether their full and careful codification of doctrine has not involved certain shifts of emphasis, slight in themselves but serious in their historical consequences. In the first place, there is a tendency to return to the patristic overwhelming of the human author by the divine. This must not be exaggerated, for most theologians agree that the authors write intelligently and voluntarily, and are certainly not to be regarded as mere machines (H. Heidegger, *ST*, II, 36; Scherzer, *Systema theologiae*, p. 8). But there is a distinct development of the theory of dictation, not merely in the use of the rather ambiguous *dicto* (Calov, *Systema*, I, 555), but also in the employment of such phrases as "assistants and amanuenses" (Gerhard, II, 26ff.; Bucan, *Institutiones theologicae* . . . [Geneva, 1609], 1.4.2), and even in the revival by Heidegger of the dubious image of the flautist (H. Heidegger, *Corpus theologiae*, II [Zurich, 1700], 34). Second, there is a tendency to press to an unnecessary extreme the intrinsically true doctrine of verbal inspiration, as in the insistence that even the Hebrew vowel points must be regarded as inspired (Gerhard, 265). Third, there is a tendency to give a false importance to the doctrine of inerrancy, as if the inspiration of Scripture were finally suspended upon the ability to prove it correct in every detail. To be sure, inspiration is itself the basis of inerrancy, and there is no obligation to prove the latter (Quenstedt, I, 77). But in face of attacks upon the inerrancy of the Bible, whether by those who do not regard it as essential to inspiration or by those who deny both, it is only too easy to reverse the true relationship and to come to think of inerrancy as the basis of inspiration (Calov, I, 552). Fourth, and in consequence, there is a tendency to subordinate the inner witness of the Holy Spirit, still forcefully maintained, to the external and internal criteria of the authenticity and authority of the Bible. If final assurance comes only with the Holy Spirit, the criteria are of great importance in engendering intellectual conviction and even giving spiritual certainty (Hollaz, p. 121), so that even a careful and sympathetic student like Preus is forced to see in the Lutherans "a certain concession to rationalism" at this point (R. Preus, *The Inspiration of Scripture*, p. 114). Finally, and underlying the whole conception, there is a tendency to subject genuinely scriptural material to alien Aristotelian or Cartesian principles and modes of presentation which result in a measure of distortion from the standpoint of true biblical and Reformation doctrine, which give an ambiguity still reflected in scholarly assessments of the period, and which, contrary to the intentions of the dogmaticians, expose the doctrine of inspiration to the violent reactions of the period of the Enlightenment and theological liberalism.

Whether the post-Reformation orthodox could have contended for the truth of inspiration along other lines is a point worth considering before we rush on to the sweeping and exaggerated condemnations which mark some dogmatic scholars. After all, they were faced by very real difficulties: the demand of the Romanists that they should produce as evident an authority as that of the Church and papacy (Preus, pp. 93ff.); the attacks of Socinians upon the historical reliability of Scripture (pp. 81f.); and the revived Montanism of the sectaries with their appeal to inward illuminations of the Spirit apart from the letter of the Bible (p. 46). It is also to be recalled that in the matters referred

INSPIRATION, HISTORY OF THE DOCTRINE OF

to we are dealing for the most part only with tendencies within a general loyalty, or intention of loyalty, to the Reformation position. Yet the fact can hardly be disputed that a new and nonbiblical rationalism of presupposition, method, and approach threatens the Protestant doctrine with these dogmaticians (pp. 210f.), that they clearly repeat in some degree the same kind of Judaizing movement as that of the early and medieval Church, and that in so doing they incur a measure of both positive and negative responsibility for the disasters which follow.

*VI. **Eighteenth-Century Rationalism.***–By the inversion characteristic of theological history, the application of inspiration to the minutiae of the biblical text led to a concentration of interest on the actual documents and history. Hence the 18th cent. saw a rapid and intensive development (e.g., by Michaelis and Semler) of the linguistic and textual studies which had commenced with the Renaissance (cf. K. Aner, *Die Theologie der Lessingzeit,* pp. 202ff.). Much of this work had no direct bearing upon the doctrine of inspiration. But the case was different when literary and historical questions were raised, for rationalistic attacks upon the reliability and even the authenticity of the records implied a rejection of its inspiration. The calumnies of Voltaire and the Encyclopedists were too outrageous to be seriously effective; but the *Wolffenbüttel Fragmente* constituted a direct challenge with their discussion of the resurrection narratives, and theologians who had already committed themselves to rationalist presuppositions found it difficult to avoid some kind of compromise solution. After all, it was argued, "historical truths cannot be demonstrated," as Lessing maintained (*Werke,* ed. Gosche, VI, 241). To try to defend inspiration in terms of inerrancy is thus to commit it to inevitable relativization. Surely the better course is to intellectualize the concept. Irrespective of its historical reliability, the Bible contains general truths which are inspired, not in a special or supernatural sense, but insofar as they conform to the teaching of pure reason. This was the new version of inspiration in theological circles (Aner, p. 296), and the tragedy was that orthodox apologists like Schumann, Riss, and Goeze, attempting to meet the attackers on their own ground, accepted the basic presuppositions instead of challenging the real enemy in the name of a genuinely biblical and Reformation understanding.

In its own way, rationalism was no less an evasion of the historical element than pure supernaturalism. But many forces were making for a study of the Bible, not merely as an ancient text, nor as a repository of abstract divine or human truth, but as divine truth in the form of a human product. This was the contention of Herder, first expressed in his Riga *Sermon on the Bible,* and then worked out in the *Theological Letters* and *The Spirit of Hebrew Poetry.* As Herder saw it, the human element in the Bible must be taken quite seriously. The Bible is a work of literature, written at a particular time, by a particular people, in particular situations, and conditioned by race, language, thought-forms, and historical and geographical milieu (*Werke,* ed. Müller, II, X, 257). Its inspiration is not to be denied, but it is not to be absolutized. It is that of great religious thinkers and poets through whom God is speaking as He speaks elsewhere through nature, philosophy, and the arts (*ibid.,* p. 271). It is simply a heightened form of true conviction, of religious enthusiasm in the purer and deeper sense (XVIII, 53f.). As such, it commends itself to the sincere and seeking reader, not by its outward singularity but by the direct message which it carries to the soul (p. 275). Herder can thus unite a conception of the inward testimony of the Spirit with his basic reduction of inspiration to the aesthetic level. The gain in this understanding is that it does take the human element in the Bible with a sympathetic seriousness hardly attained before in the whole history of the doctrine. But this gain does not offset the failure to see that on its own terms the biblical literature and history cannot be classified as merely one manifestation of the divine Spirit among others, nor its inspiration regarded as one particular species in a common genus. And it is no real compensation that a place is found for the direct speech of the Bible to the heart; for although this contains an element of truth it is a highly emotionalized and subjectivized version of the authentic witness of the Holy Spirit, and no less exposed than the biblical history to empirical criticism and interpretation in the form of psychological analysis.

With this program of historical biblical study, Herder initiated the intensive research of the modern period and its more-or-less sustained polemic against the inerrancy and therefore the special inspiration of the Bible. But theologically his subjectivization of inspiration was no less important, for it combined with Empiricism, Pietism and Kantian Idealism to produce the thoroughgoing subjectivization of Christianity by Schleiermacher, which has dominated the whole movement of liberal Protestantism. As Schleiermacher sees it, all religions are relative formulations or descriptions of the basic religious feeling of dependence (*Reden,* p. 21). Of these Christianity is the best because in it this feeling finds perfect expression (p. 212). The doctrines of Christianity are all true and important as the more detailed expressions of emotional states (pp. 84ff.), the Holy Spirit being the common spirit of the Church (*Der Christliche Glaube,* II, 372ff.), the Scriptures the first of a series of attempts to express the Christian faith, and inspiration the working of the common spirit of believers no less evident in any great doctrinal or devotional work than in the apostolic literature. The almost complete supernaturalizing of the 17th cent. is thus completely reversed and avenged by a no less thorough absorption of the divine element into the human; and the stage is set for the long tragedy of an anthropocentric understanding with all its vanities and vulnerabilities, with its illusory hopes and eventual disillusionment and despair.

*VII. **Conclusion.***–Why is it that, for all the tenacity displayed and scholarship deployed, orthodoxy has proved so feeble and ineffective in claiming the Bible and its inspiration for itself in face of this upsurge of the human spirit? The answer to this question is undoubtedly to be found in the approximation of orthodoxy itself to an abstract, schematized, and basically Judaistic understanding of inspiration instead of a genuinely biblical and Reformed. The attack on the historical reliability of the Bible was damaging just because orthodoxy no longer had full confidence in the witness of the Spirit but had to find for it rationalistic support by a reversal of the relationship between inspiration and inerrancy, suspending the former on the latter. The neological compromise was tempting and misleading just because orthodoxy was already finding in the Bible a mere textbook of dogmatic truth rather than a concrete and living attestation of Jesus Christ. The historical program was convincing and dangerous just because orthodoxy found so little place for the human and historical element, and could not contend for the genuinely historical understanding of the Bible in terms of itself to which biblical scholarship is finding its way after so much debate and confusion. The subjectivization of the Bible and its inspiration was so powerful just because orthodoxy was guilty of all these unfortunate tendencies, suppressing man in his proper place yet exalting him in his rationality, losing sight of Jesus Christ as the true theme and center of the Bible, and showing so little genuine appreciation for the illumination of the Holy Spirit and His work.

In this as in so many matters, the way forward is the way back, namely, to the Reformers, and through them to the Bible and its self-witness, by which all our views of inspiration must be tested, corrected, strengthened, and empowered. This certainly does not mean that the doctrine of inspiration must be weakened, or a compromise arranged. It means that it must be genuinely asserted, not only in face of error, but also in face of distortions or dilutions of the truth. The prophetic and apostolic word is the word of divine wisdom by which all the rationalism of man is summoned to repentance and renewal. The historical record of the Bible is the account of the divine dealings with man which alone give meaning and direction to all other history. The theme of the Bible is the incarnate Word in whom alone we find truth, freedom, and salvation, and to whom the written Word conforms in divine and human structure. The inspiration of Scripture is genuinely the work of the sovereign Spirit, whose operation cannot finally be subjected to human analysis, repudiation, or control, but who remains the internal Master of that which He Himself has given, guaranteeing its authenticity, and declaring its message with quickening and compelling power.

See also INFALLIBILITY.

Bibliography.–*BDTh*; K. Barth, *CD*, I/1-2; H. Berkhof, *Christian Faith* (1979); G. C. Berkower, *Holy Scripture* (1975); H. Heppe, *Reformed Dogmatics* (Eng. tr. 1950); A. Kuyper, *Principles of Sacred Theology* (Eng. tr. 1954); J. Orr, *Revelation and Inspiration* (1910); *TDNT*, VI, *s.v.* πνεῦμα κτλ.: θεόπνευστος (Schweizer); B. B. Warfield, *Inspiration and Authority of the Bible* (1927).

Note: The above article is reprinted from C. F. H. Henry, *Revelation and the Bible* (1958) by kind permission of the editor and publisher (Baker Book House). G. W. BROMILEY

INSTANT; INSTANTLY [Heb. *peṯaʿ* (Hab. 2:7; Nu. 6:9), *piṯʾōm, piṯʾōm* (Prov. 3:25; Nu. 12:4), *lᵉpeṯaʿ piṯʾōm*–'in an instant, suddenly' (Isa. 29:5), *piṯʾōm lᵉpeṯaʿ*–'suddenly, in an instant' (Isa. 30:13); Gk. *apó tēs hōras ekeínēs* (lit. 'from that hour,' Mt. 9:22; 15:28; 17:18), *euthéōs* (Acts 22:29)]; AV also SUDDENLY, STRAIGHTWAY (Acts 22:29); NEB also SUDDENLY, HASTILY (Acts 22:29). As used in the RSV, the phrase "in an instant" and the adverb "instantly" have the usual sense of "immediately," of an event occurring in an infinitesimal space of time (Isa. 29:5; 30:13; Mt. 9:22; 15:28; 17:18; Acts 22:29). The AV uses these terms in this sense, but it also uses the phrases "to be instant" (Lk. 23:23; 2 Tim. 4:2) and "to continue instant" (Rom. 12:12) in the sense of "persevere," "be urgent, pressing," and "instantly" in the sense of "earnestly, intently" (Lk. 7:4; Acts 26:7).

INSTINCT [Gk. *physikós*] (2 Pet. 2:12); AV NATURAL; NEB "in the course of nature"; [Gk. *physikṓs*] (Jude 10); AV NATURALLY. In these parallel passages 2 Peter and Jude are both concerned to contend against antinomianism. Jude succinctly describes the people under attack as "ungodly persons who pervert the grace of our God into licentiousness" (v. 4). Both 2 Peter and Jude compare such people to Gk. *tá áloga zṓa*, "irrational animals." It is in that comparison that 2 Peter and Jude use "instinct," and it is in terms of that comparison that "instinct" is to be understood: as the appetitive drives unbridled by reason. This definition is confirmed by the fact that in writings of antiquity Gk. *physikṓs* was often paralleled by Gk. *chōrís lógou* ("apart from reason") as in Diogenes Laertius X.137. That it need not always be contrasted to rationality, however, is clear from Rom. 1:26, where Gk. *physikós* is properly rendered "natural" by the RSV because it stands in contrast to Gk. *parà phýsin*, "unnatural." 2 Peter and Jude accuse their opponents of living like irrational animals, according to instinct, i.e., according to the dictates of their appetites and drives rather than their reason. Such a way of life leads men to the same end as the brutes: to death. "The instinct of nature alone rules in brute animals; but reason ought to govern men and to bridle their appetites" (Calvin, comm. on Jude).

A. D. VERHEY

INSTRUCT [Heb. *yārâ* (1 S. 12:23; 2 K. 12:2 [MT 3]; Ps. 25:8, 12), *zāhar* (2 Ch. 19:10), *śāḵal* (Neh. 9:20; Ps. 32:8; Prov. 21:11), *ṣāwâ* (Gen. 32:4 [MT 5], 17 [MT 18], 19 [MT 20]; Ruth 2:15; 2 S. 11:19; Jer. 38:27), *bîn* (2 Ch. 26:5), *yāsar* (Job 4:3; Isa. 28:26; Ps. 105:22), *yāḏaʿ* (Isa. 40:13; Jer. 31:19)]; AV also TEACH, WARN (2 Ch. 19:10), "bind" (Ps. 105:22), COMMAND, CHARGE, "have understanding" (2 Ch. 26:5); NEB also TEACH, WARN, ADVISE, etc.; [Gk. *noutheteō* (Rom. 15:14), *symbibázō* (1 Cor. 2:16), *katēchéō* (Acts 18:25; Rom. 2:18; 1 Cor. 14:19), *sophízō* (2 Tim. 3:15), *paideúō* (Acts 7:22), *chrēmatízō* (He. 8:5), *diatássō* (Mt. 11:1)]; AV also ADMONISH, TEACH, "make wise" (2 Tim. 3:15), LEARN, COMMAND; NEB also ADVISE, TRAINED, "make wise," "give instructions," "benefit" (1 Cor. 14:19); **INSTRUCTION** [Heb. *yārâ* (Ex. 24:12), *tôrâ* (Dt. 17:11; Job 22:22; Isa. 30:9; Mal. 2:6-9), *mûsār* (Job 36:10; Prov. 1:2ff.; 4:1, 13; 8:10, 33; etc.), *leqaḥ* (Isa. 29:24)]; AV also TEACH, LAW, DISCIPLINE, DOCTRINE; NEB also CORRECTION, LESSON, etc.; [Gk. *didaskalía* (Rom. 15:4), *nouthesía* (1 Cor. 10:11; Eph. 6:4), *parakaléō* (Tit. 1:9), *didachḗ* (He. 6:2), *diastéllomai* (Acts 15:24), *diatássō* (Acts 23:31), *parangéllō* (1 Cor. 11:17), *entolḗ* (Col. 4:10), *parangelía* (1 Thess. 4:2), *taúta* (1 Tim. 3:14; 4:6)]; AV also LEARNING, ADMONITION, DOCTRINE, etc.; NEB also ORDERS, INJUNCTIONS, etc.; **INSTRUCTOR** [piel part. of Heb. *lāmaḏ*] (Prov. 5:13); AV "them that instruct"; NEB MASTERS.

I. OT.–A basic OT meaning of Eng. "instruction" has to do with education in the broader sense. The Heb. *yāsar* and its derivative *mûsār* have this denotation. (In Ps. 105:22 the RSV and NEB emend MT *ʾāsar,* "bind," to read *yāsar,* following the LXX, Vulgate, and Syriac versions.)

For the people of Israel God's law served as an "educative force." The law regulated life for the Hebrew and was passed on from generation to generation by the fathers, whose responsibility it was to guard the tradition (Ex. 12:26; Dt. 6:7, 20). Thus education is very "intrapersonal," and *yāsar/mûsār* includes the whole process of "rearing" or "moral correction," "but can also take on a more intellectual sense and stand for 'culture' in the sense of possession of wisdom, knowledge, and discernment" (*TDNT,* V, 604). Both for the individual Israelite and for his nation, "chastisement" and "discipline" were an important part of "instruction" by the fathers and by God (Prov. 13:24; 29:15; Jer. 2:19; Hos. 10:10).

This theme is common in the wisdom literature, which goes beyond the parent-child relationship to point to the marks of the "wise person." The beginning of knowledge is the "fear of the Lord," while "fools despise wisdom and instruction" (Prov. 1:7; 15:33). The goal of "instruction" (1:2) is that people might learn "righteousness, justice, and equity" (1:3). "Instruction" makes a wise person "still wiser" (9:9; cf. 19:20; 4:1; 8:33). It is better than silver and gold (8:10). "He who heeds instruction is on the path to life" (10:17; 4:13), while "poverty and disgrace" come to him who ignores it (13:18), since by doing so he really "despises himself" (15:32). It is the parents' responsibility to instruct their children, but the education one receives from one's father comes from undergoing discipline voluntarily (1:8; 13:1; 19:27; 23:12); only a fool rejects his father's "instruction" (15:5). Children are urged to buy "wisdom, instruction, and understanding" (23:23), while the lazy man who has neglected his property is depicted as a warning example to others (24:32). Thus the picture is of a God who corrects and chastises His children, but who does so as a Father.

God is often seen as the "corrector" or "chastiser" and hence the "educator" of His people. Yahweh has persistently sought to teach His people, but they have stubbornly refused to accept any discipline or instruction (Jer. 17:23; 32:33; 35:13). Jeremiah declares that the "instruction of idols is but wood" compared to the greatness and power of the Lord (10:8). Isaiah maintains parabolically (28:26) that as God teaches the farmer what to do, his actions varying from plowing to sowing, so also God's educating or guiding (*CHAL*, p. 137) of His people does not always follow the same pattern.

The verb *yārâ,* meaning "teach," expresses the purpose of the law and commandments given to Moses on Sinai (Ex. 24:12). It is also used by Samuel, who tells the people that he will "instruct [them] in the good and the right way" (1 S. 12:23; cf. 2 K. 12:2). The psalmist confesses that Yahweh will instruct sinners (25:8) and those who fear Him (25:12) in the way they should go (cf. 32:8).

Derived from *yārâ* is the term *tôrâ,* which can mean "direction" and can in ordinary usage refer to parents teaching their children or to Job's comforters putting forth their theological views. In most places, however, *tôrâ* is used for cultic or ritual practices and for the instruction of the prophets and priests regarding the will of Yahweh (Mal. 2:6f.). In Isaiah's day the rebellious people of Israel would not hear the *tôrâ* of the Lord, which warned them of the folly of trusting in Egypt (Isa. 30:9). Job 22:22 uses the term in the sense of "Divine guidance inwardly received" (Dodd, p. 32). This is one of the few places where the LXX (*ezēgoría*–"utterance") deviates from the strict legal use of *tôrâ* as "law" (cf. Dt. 17:11).

The educative aspect of both divine and human "instruction" is further seen in the use of the hiphil of *bîn* in 2 Ch. 26:5, where Zechariah is said to have instructed the young King Uzziah in "the way of the Lord," while a piel form of the verb *lāmaḏ* describes the instructors of Prov. 5:13 (cf. *ḥāḵam* in Ps. 105:22). *Sāḵal* is used in the sense of instruction in Neh. 9:20 and Prov. 21:11, while God is the One who will give instruction *(leqaḥ)* to those who murmur in Isa. 29:24. Yet there is no one wise enough to give advice to Him or tell God's Spirit that He should have acted differently (*yāḏa'*, Isa. 40:13; cf. Jer. 31:19).

"Instructing" in the sense of "warning" is found with the use of *zāhar* (2 Ch. 19:10), while examples of its use in the sense of "command" or "give an order" are found with *ṣāwâ* (e.g., Jer. 38:27).

In the LXX, the Heb. *yāsar/mûsār* was most often translated by the Gk. *paideúō*. The oldest use of the Greek term (Aeschylus in the 5th cent. B.C.) stressed the "nourishing" and "chastising" elements of bringing up a child, but by the time of Plato and Isocrates (4th cent. B.C.) the term was no longer limited to the teaching done by fathers and pedagogues. By this time "instruction" had come to mean "culture, the formation of the human soul" (Jaeger, III, 314). The stress was laid on philosophy as the main element of education, and the ideal became "the philosophical man, the Hellenistic cosmopolitan" (*TDNT,* V, 598). The effect of this on the LXX translation was that the Hebrew root meanings of "correction" and "chastisement" were in many cases subsumed under the Greek notion of "culture." In the wisdom literature, e.g., the use of *paideía patrós* ("father's instruction," Prov. 1:8; 4:1, 13; 15:5; 19:20, 27; etc.), which is praised as "wisdom," shows that "the interest of the Greek translators was not in discipline or chastisement, but in intellectual instruction" (*TDNT,* V, 609). This same tendency is found in the Psalms and some of the prophetic writings. The LXX sees the content of the prophetic revelation as being concerned with God's education of His people. "Fundamentally, however, the concept of education presupposes in the OT the belief in election. Education by God is a gift of grace allotted only to God's people" (*TDNT,* V, 611).

II. NT.–In the NT, Acts 7:22 describes Moses as having been "instructed [*paideúō*] in all the wisdom of the Egyptians." Moses' instruction included the elements of a foreign pagan culture and secular learning. Josephus speaks of his superior "understanding" (*Ant.* ii.9.6) as does Philo, who credits him with proficiency in all branches of education (*Vita Mosis* i.20ff.; cf. Sir. 45:3; Bruce, p. 168).

Other NT expressions of "instruction" include *didaskalía,* which Paul uses in Rom. 15:4 to designate the "teaching" which comes from Scripture (in this case Ps. 69:9 [MT 10]). Related to this is the term *didachḗ,* of prime importance in early Christianity, which is used in an exceptional NT sense in He. 6:2, where it refers to an already established doctrine rather than the usual "teaching." In close relationship with these terms is *katēchéō* (lit. to "sound from above"). This term, from which we derive "catechism" and "catechumen," is used for the act of "instructing" someone, particularly in religious matters. Paul uses it usually in reference to instruction in Christian doctrine, but in Rom. 2:18 he speaks of the Jews as *katēchoúmenos* in the law. In the congregation Paul says he would prefer to speak five words understandably to instruct others in the faith than ten thousand words in tongues (1 Cor. 14:19). Thus is seen the high importance he attaches to the preaching and teaching offices. The specifically Christian content of the teaching that was passed on, originally as oral information, is summed up in the description of Apollos as one who had been "instructed in the way of the Lord" and who spoke and taught [*didáskō*] accurately the things concerning Jesus" (Acts 18:25). Beyer notes that already *katēchéō* seems to denote "elementary instruction in the Christian faith" while *didáskō* refers to "the teaching constantly given to believers" (*TDNT,* III, 639 n. 8).

Less formal and more in line with Hebrew thought is the term *noutheteō* (from *noús*), the usual LXX rendering of Heb. *bîn,* with the sense of imparting understanding or having a corrective influence on someone, hence to "teach." The teaching referred to here, however, concerns not so much the intellect as the will, the mind set, or the attitude. It involves an attempt to discipline the will and disposition through teaching and exhortation (see *TDNT,* IV, 1019). The corresponding noun *nouthesía* ("admonition") is used in Eph. 6:4, where fathers are urged to bring up their children "in the discipline and instruction of the Lord," meaning that nurture which is designed to educate and correct without arousing bitterness or resentment in the child. Paul uses this same term in 1 Cor. 10:11, where he reminds his readers that the judgments of God recorded in the OT serve as warning examples, and in Rom. 15:14, where he acknowledges that the Roman Christians are able to exercise a ministry of pastoral admonition toward each other so that his own instruction need only be by way of reminder.

Another traditional Jewish usage is seen in 2 Tim. 3:15 where Timothy is told that the sacred writings are "able to instruct [*sophízō*–'make wise'] you for salvation." Here the OT concept that knowledge of the law can make people wise is transferred to a setting in the primitive Church without change. This wisdom brings salvation through "faith in Jesus Christ." The use of *symbibázō* ("bring together") in 1 Cor. 2:16 is based on the LXX rendering of Isa. 40:13 (cf. Justin *Dial. with Trypho* 50.5); Paul asks, "Who has known the mind of the Lord so as to instruct him?" His point is that only those who have the mind of Christ are able to understand and instruct others concerning the gifts of the Spirit. One of the responsibilities of a bishop, Paul tells Titus (1:9), is to "give instruction [*parakaléō*–'exhort'] in sound doctrine."

"Instruction" in the sense of a revelation of God given to mankind is expressed by *chrēmatízō* in He. 8:5, where Moses was "advised" or "warned solemnly" by God to follow the specified pattern for the tabernacle. Giving precise commands or injunctions is the meaning of both *entolḗ* in Col. 4:10 and *diatássō* in Mt. 11:1 and Acts 23:31. *Parangelía* has a related meaning stemming from military usage for "passing on an announcement" (among the ranks). It is used in 1 Thess. 4:2 to express apostolic "orders," in this case ethical precepts which have their basis in the authority of the Lord Jesus Himself.

See also EDUCATION.

Bibliography.–G. W. Buchanan, *To the Hebrews* (*AB*, 1972), p. 136; F. F. Bruce, *Acts of the Apostles* (2nd ed. 1952); D. Daube, *NT and Rabbinic Judaism* (1956), pp. 106ff.; C. H. Dodd, *The Bible and the Greeks* (2nd ed. 1954); *NT Essays* (1952), pp. 106-119; W. Jaeger, *Paideia*, I (2nd ed. 1945), II (1943), III (1944); E. G. Selwyn, *First Epistle of St. Peter* (1946), pp. 18ff.; *TDNT*, IV, *s.v.* νοέω (Behm); V, *s.v.* παιδεύω (Bertram); VII, *s.v.* σοφία (Wilckens), στέλλω (Rengstorf), συμβιβάζω (Delling).

D. K. MCKIM

INSTRUMENT. In Gen. 4:22 the participle of Heb. *ḥāraš* denotes a craftsman (*CHAL*, p. 118). *K^{e}lî* is used in the OT for many kinds of implements (e.g., NEB "anything made of iron," Nu. 35:16). The RSV translates it "instruments" when it refers to the musical instruments used in cultic practice (e.g., 1 Ch. 15:16; 16:42; 2 Ch. 5:13; Neh. 12:36). The AV often uses "instruments" when denoting other items connected with the sanctuary and weapons of war. Some of the "instruments of music" (1 S. 18:6) specifically mentioned are the *šālîš* (NEB "tambourine"), *mēn* (RSV "stringed instrument," Ps. 45:8 [MT 9]), and *n^{e}gînâ* (RSV "stringed instrument," Isa. 38:20). The verb *nāgan* means "play a stringed instrument" (Ezk. 33:32). *See also* MUSIC.

In the NT, the Gk. *skeúos* of Acts 9:15 (AV "vessel") is something especially chosen (a "chosen instrument") *by* God for His use; the *hópla* of Rom. 6:13 are the members of the human body which are yielded *to* God. Both terms are used in the sense of an implement (Rom. 6:13, NEB), something that is usable. The RSV also translates *tá ápsycha phōnḗn didónta* (1 Cor. 14:7) as "lifeless instruments."

See also UTENSILS. D. J. KELLY

INSTRUMENTS OF MUSIC. *See* MUSIC.

INSULT [Heb. *ḥārap, ḥerpâ*] (1 S. 25:39; Ps. 69:9, 20 [MT 10, 21]; Prov. 14:31; 17:5; Lam. 3:30); AV REPROACH; NEB REPROACH, ABUSE, SNEER AT; [*ṣāḥaq*] (Gen. 39:14, 17); AV MOCK; NEB "make a mockery of"; [*qālôn*] (Prov. 12:16); AV SHAME; NEB "slighted" [*k^{e}limmâ*] (Job 20:3); AV "putteth (me) to shame"; NEB "is a reproach"; [Gk. *hýbris, hybrízō*] (2 Cor. 12:10; 1 Tim. 1:13); AV INJURIES, INJURIOUS; NEB CONTEMPT, OUTRAGE; [*eípon raká*] (Mt. 5:22); AV "say . . . Raca," NEB "sneer at." In Ps. 89:50 (MT 51), the RSV emends the MT *kol-rabbîm,* "all of many," to either *kol-ribê,* "all the disputes of" (cf. NEB), or *k^{e}limmaṯ,* "disgrace of," in order to complete the parallelism. The AV supplies "reproach" from the first part of the verse; this solution seems at least as satisfactory as the above emendations (but cf. KD *in loc.*).

I. Insulting God.–The wisdom of Prov. 14:31 and 17:5 declares that to oppress or mock the poor is to insult the Maker of mankind. This correlation of respect for the poor and respect for the Creator is pervasive in the Wisdom literature of the OT and elsewhere in the Scriptures (cf. Job 31:13-15; Jas. 3:9). The reason for the correlation is that God created both rich and poor (Prov. 22:2). Every person, whether rich or poor, bears the image of God. To mock a poor person, therefore, is to mock God, and to be kind to a poor person is to honor God. If Jesus was the first to join Dt. 6:5 (the love of God) to Lev. 19:18 (the love of mankind) as a summary of the law (Mt. 22:37-40), He was following the Hebrew tradition of correlating relations to God with relations to people. 1 Tim. 1:13 speaks on the same order, where Paul's former persecution of the Church is described as blaspheming, persecuting, and insulting Jesus Christ: to treat people without respect and care is to insult God. Indeed, although Gk. *hýbris* and its derivatives are used infrequently in the NT, the term seems particularly apt to express the arrogance in human relations that is a result of insolence before God (*TDNT,* VIII, 306).

II. Insulting People.–The correlation of relations to God with relations to people must be kept in mind when insults against people are considered. Because of that correlation, the insult invites Yahweh's displeasure against the insulter. This is the case in 1 S. 25:39, e.g., where David blesses Yahweh for having avenged the insult he received from Nabal. Nabal had responded to the polite solicitation of David's men with an insolent refusal. David was intending to avenge himself, but Abigail, Nabal's wife (and later David's), successfully appealed to him not to take vengeance with his own hands. When that decision was made, "the Lord smote Nabal, and he died" (1 S. 25:38).

Numerous passages in the Psalms call upon Yahweh to act against the psalmists' insulters. In Ps. 69 the psalmist says, "the insults of those who insult thee fall upon me" (v. 9). Here the correlation is between insults to God and insults to the people of God. It is on the basis of this correlation that, after eloquent expression of the insults that have been given him (v. 20), the psalmist appeals to God to pour out His indignation upon those who have insulted him (vv. 22-28).

This correlation, however, does not warrant vengeance by the insulted person. This is clear in David's case against Nabal. Indeed, Lam. 3:30 tells us that it is good for a young man to "give his cheek to the smiter, and be filled with insults" (cf. Mt. 5:39). The principle of reciprocity is clear here (cf. Lam. 3:61-66), but it is balanced by the recognition that we also have sinned (v. 42), by appeals for modesty and educability (v. 40), and especially by the assurance of the compassion of God (vv. 31-33). Similarly, one is a fool who reacts passionately to insult (Prov. 12:16); a wise person stays calm when insulted. Passionate retaliation for insult is always wrong. This advice concerning reaction to insult is both followed and developed by Paul, who endured insults "for the sake of Christ" (2 Cor. 12:10).

Jesus' explication of the true meaning of the law in Mt. 5:21ff. moves from the prohibition of murder to the prohibition of insult. Both the murderer and the person calling another "Raca" count the object of their act, a person made in the image of God, as of little worth. That the correlation of relationships to people with the relationship to God is operative here too is clear from the subsequent saying about leaving the altar to make peace with an offended brother. Gk. *raká* is a transcription of the Aram. *rêqā'*. This Aramaic insult, in turn, is related to Heb. *rêq,* an adjective meaning "empty," to which the vocative ending is added (*TDNT,* VI, 974). It very likely meant "empty-headed one" and thus something like our "blockhead." Like "blockhead," *raká* was thought a harmless insult even though it expressed disparagement and sometimes contempt. By putting such an insult on the same level as murder, Jesus clearly demands that insults, even "harmless" insults, be avoided.

Two instances of "insult" remain in which the correlation motif is not involved. In Job 20:3 Zophar accuses Job of having insulted him. Job had argued that even his friends (including Zophar) failed to understand and support him. Joseph is accused by Potiphar's wife of insult in Gen. 39:14, 17 when she charges him with having made an illicit sexual advance. Heb. *ṣāḥaq,* which only here is translated "insulted," means to "laugh at," "make sport of," "toy with."

Bibliography.–*TDNT,* VI, *s.v.* ῥακά (J. Jeremias); VIII, *s.v.* ὕβρις (G. Bertram). A. D. VERHEY

INSURRECTION. Used by the RSV only in the NT for Gk. *stásis* in Mk. 15:7 and Lk. 23:19, 25. In both passages *stásis* is used in the sense of a rebellion against civil authority. The revolt in which Barabbas participated was only one of many that took place in Judea during that period, being preceded by the revolts of a certain Theudas (cf. Josephus *Ant.* xx.5.1) and Judas the Galilean (cf. Josephus *BJ* ii.7.1; Acts 6:36f.; 21:38).

INTEGRITY [Heb. *tōm*] (Gen. 20:5f.; 1 K. 9:4; Job 4:6; Ps. 25:21; 101:2; Prov. 2:7; 10:9); AV also PERFECT, UPRIGHTLY, UPRIGHTNESS; NEB also BLAMELESS LIFE, CLEAR CONSCIENCE, PURITY; [*tummâ*] (Job. 2:3, 9; 27:5; 31:6; Ps. 7:8 [MT 9]; 26:1, 11; 41:12 [MT 13]; Prov. 11:3; 19:1; 20:7; 28:6); AV also UPRIGHTNESS; NEB also "without reproach," "claim to innocence," INNOCENT, HONESTY, etc.; [*tāmîm*] (Prov. 2:21; 28:18); AV PERFECT, UPRIGHTLY; NEB BLAMELESS, HONEST; [Gk. *aphthoría*] (Tit. 2:7); AV UNCORRUPTNESS. In Prov. 14:32 the RSV and NEB follow the LXX in amending the MT to read *ḇᵉṯummô,* "in his integrity (honesty)," to develop the antithesis of the verse between the fate of the wicked and the righteous, whereas the AV follows the MT in reading *ḇᵉmôṯô,* "in his death."

The basic meaning of "integrity" in the OT is "soundness of character and adherence to moral principle," i.e., uprightness and honesty, whether referring to Abraham (Gen. 20:5f.), David (1 K. 9:4), Job (Job 2:3, 9; 4:6; 27:5; 31:6), or the psalmist (Ps. 7:8; 25:21; 26:1, 11; 41:12; 101:2). A common expression is "to walk in integrity," indicating an habitual manner of life. In Proverbs integrity is seen as an essential characteristic of the upright life: Yahweh will protect those who walk in it (2:7); their security is assured (2:21; 10:9; 20:7; 28:18); it is a trustworthy guide for living (11:3), and better than wealth (19:1; 28:6).

Titus 2:7 specifies integrity as an indispensable ingredient in Christian teaching. The meaning is essentially the same as that in the OT. J. R. PRICE

INTELLIGENCE [Heb. *ḥoḵmâ*] (Ex. 31:3; 35:31; 36:1); AV WISDOM; NEB "skilful"; [Gk. *synetós*] (Acts 13:7); AV PRUDENT. The Hebrew term designates various facets of ability, whether technical skill (Ex. 36:1), shrewdness of different kinds (2 S. 20:22; 1 K. 2:6), spiritual insight (Ps. 90:12), or a personified concept of wisdom (Prov. 8:1ff.). Ancient Near Eastern cognates (Akk. *ḫakamu*; Ugar. *ḥkmt*) denote perception or understanding.

The AV translates Heb. *bîn* ("discern, understand") in Dnl. 11:e0 (RSV "take heed"; NEB "take note") as "(he shall) have intelligence." In 2 Macc. 3:9 the AV translates Gk. *gegonótos* as "intelligence" (RSV "disclosure"; NEB "allegations"), in the sense of information.

See also WISDOM. R. K. H.

INTEND [Heb. *'āmar*] (2 Ch. 28:10; Jer. 18:10); AV PURPOSE, SAY; NEB PROPOSE, "have in mind"; [*ḥāšaḇ*] (Neh. 6:2, 6; Jer. 18:8; 26:3; 36:3); AV THINK, PURPOSE, etc.; NEB PLOTTING, PURPOSE, PLANNING, etc.; [*dāmâ*] (Isa. 10:7); AV MEAN; NEB THINK; [*pāneh*] (2 Ch. 32:2); AV PURPOSE; NEB DETERMINE; [*hālaḵ*] (Jer. 41:17); AV "to go"; [Gk. *méllō*] (Jn. 7:35; Acts 20:7, 13; 25:4; 2 Pet. 1:12); AV also WILL, READY; [*boúlomai*] (Acts 5:28; 12:4); NEB "meaning to," "trying to"; [*protíthēmi*] (Rom. 1:13); AV PURPOSE; NEB PLAN; **INTENT** [Heb. *rā'â*–'evil (intent)'] (Ex. 32:12); AV MISCHIEF; NEB MEANT; [*bišᵉgāgâ*] ("without intent," Nu. 35:11, 15; Josh. 20:3, 9); AV UNAWARES; NEB BY ACCIDENT, INADVERTENTLY; [*lēḇ*] (1 Ch. 12:38 [MT 39]); AV "one heart"; NEB THOUGHT; [*zāmam*] (Prov. 21:27); AV MIND; NEB "at heart"; [*mᵉzimmâ*] (Jer. 23:20; 30:24); AV also THOUGHTS; NEB DESIGNS, DESIRES; [Gk. *epínoia*] (Acts 8:22); AV THOUGHT; NEB IMAGINING; **INTENTIONS** [Gk. *énnoia*] (He. 4:12); AV INTENTS; NEB PURPOSES; **INTENTLY** [Gk. *diablépō*] (Mk. 8:25) AV LOOK UP; NEB LOOK HARD; [*atenízō*] (Acts 13:9; 14:9; 23:1); AV "set his eyes," STEADFASTLY, EARNESTLY; NEB "fix his eyes." In 2 Ch. 11:22 the AV, RSV, and NEB insert Heb. *ḥāšaḇ,* "plan" or "intend," following the LXX and Vulgate. In Gen. 31:20; 1 Cor. 16:5; and 2 Cor. 8:20 the RSV supplies "intend" where there is no single word it translates.

The inner thoughts, plans, and purposes of the will are expressed by the concept of "intention." The most significant OT designations occur in Jeremiah and refer to the purposes of God. God tells Jeremiah that if a nation turns from its evil, "I will repent of the evil I intended to do to it" (18:8). But if it does not listen to His voice, "I will repent of the good which I intended to do to it" (18:10). Jeremiah was to stand in the court of the Lord's house and pronounce God's words with the hope that the cities of Judah might listen, "that I may repent of the evil which I intend to do to them because of their evil doings" (26:3; cf. 36:3). Nonetheless, "the anger of the Lord will not turn back until he has executed and accomplished the intents of his mind" (23:20; cf. 30:24).

Another important OT usage is the provision in Hebrew law for those who kill someone "without intent." Those who accidentally kill another can find asylum in any one of six cities designated for that purpose (Nu. 35:11, 15; Josh. 20:3, 9).

In the NT several words are used to denote human planning or proposing (Acts 20:7; Rom. 1:13). *Boúlomai* usually means the "decision of the will after previous deliberations," stressing the meditative aspects of the plan (Acts 12:4), though it may also mean "wishing" or "desiring" (Acts 5:28; Bauer, rev., p. 146).

All the secret "intentions of the heart" (*énnoia*) are unerringly discerned by the Word of God, which is "living and active, sharper than any two-edged sword, piercing to the division of soul and spirit, of joint and marrow" (He. 4:12; cf. *TDNT,* IV, 971). God is the One who knows what is in the heart ("For he is a searcher of designs and intentions," 1 Clem. 21:9; cf. v. 3); as 2 Bar. 83:3 says, the Most High will "carefully scrutinize the deep thoughts" *(cogitationes),* and prayer must be directed to Him that the "evil or hostile schemes" therein might be forgiven (Acts 8:22).

It is not certain in the story of the healing of the blind man whether *diablépō* means "he looked fixedly" — as "staring" — or he "saw clearly" (Mk. 8:25). *Atenízō,* a medical term denoting a certain "fixed" look (Bruce, p. 71) and frequently found in miracle stories, is used to describe Paul's gaze on the crippled man whom he healed (Acts 14:9) and also his "looking steadily" without anxiety at his judges in Jerusalem (Acts 23:1). According to Haenchen, the use of this term in Acts 13:9 to describe Paul's intense look at Elymas the magician "does not mean that Paul possessed the withering glance that Jewish legend attributed to the rabbis" (p. 400). This was the belief in the power of the rabbi's eye for good or evil, and according to one rabbi "ninety-nine die of the evil eye" for every one who dies a natural death (see SB, II, 713f.).

Bibliography.–F. F. Bruce, *Acts of the Apostles* (2nd ed. 1952); E. Haenchen, *Acts of the Apostles* (Eng. tr. 1971); F. Jackson and K. Lake, *Beginnings of Christianity,* IV, 33, 146; *TDNT,* IV, *s.v.* νοέω (Behm).

D. K. MCKIM

INTERCESSION [Heb. vb. *pāgaʿ*–'assail with petitions' (Isa. 53:12); Gk. *énteuxis,* vbs. *entynchánō, hyperentynchánō*]. A pleading with one party on behalf of another, usually with a view to obtaining help for that other. In the Bible, intercession normally is in the form of prayer on behalf of another.

I. In the OT
   A. Official Intercession
   B. As a Personal Burden
   C. Arising out of Natural Affection
   D. In the Psalms
   E. Its Effect
II. In the NT

I. In the OT.–Throughout the Bible, prayer is a deeply important aspect of the activity of the people of God. Those who live by prayer express in their prayers concern not only for their own needs but also for those with whom they are bound up by natural affection, and for other members of the community.

A. Official Intercession. Intercession sometimes appears as primarily an official duty, though often it arises also from deep personal concern. Some examples in the OT are: (1) king interceding for people: David (2 S. 24:17; 1 Ch. 21:17; 1 Ch. 29:10-19); Asa (2 Ch. 14:11); Solomon (1 Ch. 6:14-42); Jehoshaphat (2 Ch. 20:5-12); Hezekiah (2 Ch. 30:18; Isa. 37:15-20); (2) prophet for people: Elijah (1 K. 18:36f.); Samuel (1 S. 7:5f.); Amos (7:1-6); Joel (2:17); Malachi (1:9); Ezekiel (9:8; 11:13); Jeremiah (10:23ff.; 14:7-9; 42:4); Isaiah (63:7–64:12); cf. Lam. 5:1-22; (3) prophet for king: Samuel (1 S. 9:6–10:8); (4) priest for king and nation: Hilkiah (2 Ch. 34:20-28); Ezra (9:5-15); cf. Joel 2:17; Mal. 1:9.

B. As a Personal Burden. Intercession often arises as the distinct burden of the individual who has been called to serve God among His people. It becomes the inevitable accompaniment of his work for God, especially in the midst of crisis and failure. Intercession becomes more prominent as the servant of God increasingly identifies himself with the guilt of the people to whose service he has been called.

Moses is the supreme illustration of such intercession in the OT. His prayers are always vivid and passionate utterances, especially his intercession for Israel after the episode of the golden calf (Ex. 32:11-14, 31f.; 34:9; cf. Dt. 9:18-21, 25-29). Equally illustrative are a series of prayers recorded in Numbers (11:2; 11:11-15; 12:13; 14:13-19; 21:7; 27:5; 27:15-17). For other prayers of Moses, cf. Ex. 15:25; 17:4; 17:8-13; Nu. 10:35; Dt. 10:10; 33.

Other prayers of intercession arising from the burden of special concern are found in Josh. 7:6-15; Jgs. 6:13; 2 S. 24:17; 1 K. 18:36f.; Neh. 1:5-11; Ezr. 9:5-15; Isa. 63:14–64:12; Jer. 14:19-22; Ezk. 9:8; 11:13; cf. also Joel 2:17; Isa. 53:6, 12.

C. Arising out of Natural Affection. Frequently natural affection and kinship play a large part in intercession, e.g., in Abraham's prayers for Ishmael and Lot (Gen. 17:18; 18:23-33), in those of David for his children and house (2 S. 12:16; 1 Ch. 17:16-27; 1 Ch. 29:10-19), of Manoah for Samson (Jgs. 13:8-20), and of Job for his children (Job 1:5).

Intercession may be inspired also by gratitude and friendship: cf. 1 K. 17:20; 2 K. 4:33; 6:17; Dnl. 2:18.

D. In the Psalms. A lack of intercession is sometimes noted in the Psalms. But many of the prayers for the common salvation of Israel, while they appear simply as petitionary prayers, undoubtedly contain a large element of intercession. The individual identifies himself with the community, and intercessions take the form of public prayers of the people of God for the common welfare; cf. Pss. 74, 79, 122. Occasionally the element of intercession is more clearly expressed: cf. Ps. 20; 25:22; 28:9; 35:13; 51:18 (MT 20). Ps. 67 is a prayer of intercession for all nations.

E. Its Effect. The incident of Israel prevailing over Amalek as long as Moses lifted up his hands (Ex. 17:8-16) could be taken (allegorically perhaps) as a sign to Israel that God answers intercession. Cf. also Gen. 20:17; Ex. 9:27f.; Nu. 12:11-13; Job 42:8. But intercession is not always so successful (cf. Gen. 18:17–19:23; Ex. 32:30-35; Am. 7:2-9).

II. In the NT.–In the Gospels, the works of Jesus are constantly inspiring ordinary people to come to Him on behalf of others. Parents plead with Him in desperation for sick children (Mk. 5:22-43; Mt. 15:22-28; Jn. 4:47-53; Mk. 9:21-29). Mothers bring Him their infants (Mk. 10:13). Friend pleads on behalf of friend (Lk. 7:3-10; Mk. 2:3-12). A man pleads for his servant (Mt. 8:6-13). The mother of James and John displays her ambitions for her sons (Mt. 20:20f.).

Jesus commands intercession (Mt. 5:44; 9:38). He also encourages intercession by promising an answer to prayers made "in my name" (Jn. 14:3; 15:16; 16:23-26), especially if two or three persons agree in making the request (Mt. 18:18-20). To pray "in Jesus' name" seems to mean to pray emboldened and inspired by the word that He has spoken (Jn. 15:7), by the grace He has shown, and out of the difficulties and problems of the situation into which His service has led (cf. Mk. 11:22-24). The petitions of the Lord's prayer involve a large element of prayer for others. It is significant that the importunate praying described in the parable of the man at midnight (Lk. 11:5-13) involves intercession on behalf of another.

In the rest of the NT, the ordinary member of the community is able to pray confidently to God. The Church is understood as a royal priesthood (cf. 1 Pet. 2:9) which is required to make intercession for all mankind (cf. 1 Tim. 2:1) and engage spontaneously in prayer for others in a way that is different from OT practice.

The prayers of the Church are part of the wide vision and scope of the book of Acts. Signs are given of the effectiveness of intercession. Men are healed through it (Acts 3:16; 9:40; 28:8). Peter is delivered from prison by it

(Acts 12:8, 12). It forms the basis of the missionary enterprise of the Church (Acts 13:1-3 implies intercession and Acts 14:27 is a report of missionary success to a praying Church). The intercession of the Church is behind the advance of the word of God (cf., e.g., Acts 1:14; 2:2; 4:31; 16:25).

In the Epistles intercession is less a dramatic experience than an act of faith that Jesus is indeed Lord and has promised to hear and answer. Intercession is made in concrete and particular terms: "I appeal to you, brethren, by our Lord Jesus Christ, and by the love of the Spirit, to strive together with me in your prayers to God on my behalf; that I may be delivered . . ." (Rom. 15:30). Paul mentions his own intercession for the churches with whom he communicates (Rom. 1:9; 2 Cor. 13:7; Eph. 1:16-23; 3:14-21; Phil. 1:3-11; Col. 1:3, 9; 1 Thess. 1:2; 5:23); cf. also his personal prayers for individuals in 2 Tim. 1:3; Philem. 4. He mentions intercession "for all saints" as a necessary aspect of the healthy Christian life (Eph. 6:18). He seeks the prayers of others (Rom. 15:30; Col. 4:3; 1 Thess. 5:25), and expresses confidence in their efficacy (Phil. 1:19). The same confidence is expressed in other Epistles with reference to prayers for the sick (Jas. 5:14-18), and "for those whose sin is not mortal" (1 Jn. 5:16f.). The writer of Hebrews expects that the intercession of the Church can hasten the working of God's providence (He. 13:18f.).

In the life of NT Christians a free and confident outburst of intercessory prayer is a result of certain basic convictions. Their intercession arises out of confidence in the supreme sovereignty and love of God. J. M. Campbell points out (*Nature of the Atonement* [1873], p. 238) that "it is the tendency to deal with God as a fate, and with the accomplishment of the high designs of His grace for man simply as the coming to pass of predetermined events, that is the real source of our difficulty with respect to prayer." In the NT there is no trace of this fatalistic outlook. God is the living God, as loving as He is sovereign; and prayer is an expression of confidence in His goodness. This goodness inspired the prayer of Jesus Himself, and it inspires constant and confident praying in those who come to God through Him. In facing God they are facing a loving heart who desires to be asked, and they are responding to the promises and challenges of His Word that they should "ask" (Lk. 11:9).

The intercession of the NT Church arose from its sense of the service it owed the world. The Church was conscious of being elected to share the prophetic ministry of Christ toward the world — to speak the word of witness to Him as Lord and Christ, crucified and risen from the dead. It was equally conscious of being called to share the priestly ministry of Christ on behalf of the world that as yet did not know Him and could not pray for itself. Though Christ's intercessory bearing of the burdens of all people had been unique and redemptive, the Church could nevertheless in its own way, according to His example, take upon its heart a loving burden of intercession that He would now make effective, according to His promises, in the fulfillment of His redemptive purposes. For the early Christians, the love of God for all men, "shed abroad in their hearts" by the Spirit (Rom. 5:5), enabled them to participate in the effective bearing of others' burdens (cf. Rom. 10:1; 9:1-3).

The intercession of the NT Church arose, further, out of the belief that God had called the Church to fulfil before Him not only a priestly ministry on behalf of others, but also a kingly ministry (Rev. 1:6). It is precisely in the sphere of prayer and intercession that God gives a person real freedom in His presence to influence the course His providence is going to take, and perhaps, can take. In its ministry of intercession the Church is given a share in the universal Lordship of God. "The will of God," says Karl Barth, "is not to preserve and accompany and rule the world . . . in such a way that He is not affected and moved by it, that He does not allow Himself to converse with it. . . . God is not the prisoner of His own resolve and will and action. . . . His sovereignty is so great that it embraces the possibility . . . and the actuality that the creature can actually be present and cooperate in His overruling" (*CD*, III/3, 285; cf. p. 287).

The intercession of the Church in the NT is linked with Christ's heavenly intercession, in the understanding that the inspiration of the Holy Spirit enables the Church to imitate within its own earthly life the intercession of its High Priest. The love, prayers, and faith that give rise to intercession are the work of the Holy Spirit. "Likewise the Spirit helps us in our weakness; for we do not know how to pray as we ought: but the Spirit himself intercedes for us with sighs too deep for words" (Rom. 8:26; cf. 8:14-16). The Church prays "in the Spirit" (Eph. 6:8; Jude 20). In such intercessory prayer the Church is not engaging in a fresh work of redemption, but is furthering the effects in this present age of the redemption that Christ has provided.

See also INTERCESSION OF CHRIST, Bibliography.

R. S. WALLACE

INTERCESSION OF CHRIST.

I. During His Earthly Life.–Intercession for others was a basic element in Our Lord's earthly life of prayer, as is implied, e.g., in His groaning as He approached the grave of Lazarus (Jn. 11:33), and His sighing as He looked up to heaven in curing the deaf man (Mk. 7:34). His assurance to Peter that He had constantly prayed for him (Lk. 22:32) reminds us of the night of prayer He spent before choosing His disciples (Lk. 6:12f.), and of the great high-priestly prayer in Jn. 17, in which the apostles themselves, and all who will believe through their word, are His special concern. This prayer, in which Christ's intercession for His disciples rises to its supreme height of expression, reveals a basic element in His relationship with His disciples all through His life. Jn. 17 is also the revelation, in an earthly form, of the mediating prayer relationship between God and His people that Christ will eternally assume in the life to come.

The intercession Jesus made during His earthly life for sinners, on whose behalf He was suffering and offering His perfect obedience, must be regarded as an important element in His achievement of the atonement. The Suffering Servant of God "made intercession for the transgressors" whose sins He bears (Isa. 53:12). His resurrection and exaltation, as an answer to the prayers of One who perfectly trusted His Father, are the pledge also of God's answer to those intercessions. Such intercession is involved in Jesus' fulfillment of the office of His high-priesthood, and it is when we preserve the real intercessory character of His fulfillment of this role that we can avoid conceptions of His atoning work that show Him merely as acting a part in some divine drama.

II. His Heavenly Intercession.–In the NT, when the state and activity of the exalted Christ are pictured, He is shown not simply to be fulfilling eternally the role of King, seated and reigning on the heavenly throne, but also as fulfilling eternally the role of high priest. "He holds his priesthood permanently because he continues for ever" (He. 7:24). He has entered into heaven itself "now to appear in the presence of God on our behalf" (He. 9:24). Rom. 8:34 explicitly states that making intercession for

His people is one aspect of His heavenly activity as high priest. In 1 Jn. 2:1 He is described as an advocate (Gk. *paráklētos*) with the Father. Since in the midst of the fulfillment of this heavenly office He still retains a feeling for our infirmities (He. 4:15), this heavenly intercession on our behalf is pointed to as a source of encouragement and comfort.

The heavenly intercession of Christ has been variously interpreted within the Church. (1) On the one hand His intercession has been spoken of as if it were the means by which He carries on eternally the mystery of propitiation before the throne of God. On this view, the resurrection, ascension, and intercession of Christ are all integral parts of Christ's one sacrifice, and His intercession implies a continuation and consummation of what He did on the cross — a perpetual pleading of His sacrifice at the heavenly altar. (2) On the other hand writers like Westcott insist that "the modern conception of Christ pleading in Heaven His passion, and offering His blood on behalf of men" has no foundation in Scripture. He pleads simply by His presence on the Father's throne. The first view does not seem to allow for Christ's "sitting down" at the right hand of God after a completed work (He. 10:12). The second view seems to forget the sympathy of the exalted Lord for the present condition of His people.

The Church has discussed at various times whether the heavenly intercession of Christ is to be understood simply as a symbol of the eternal self-identification of Christ with the cause and needs of His people, or whether it must also be understood as actual prayer "vocal and real." Lutheran theology has tended to think of it as the literal offering of petition. Reformed theology has tended to think of the continual self-offering of Christ at the hand of the Father as a pledge and guarantee of His people's salvation.

In thinking of the relationship of His intercession to His sacrifice, Our Lord's own word in Jn. 17:4 must be remembered: "I glorified thee on the earth, having accomplished the work which thou gavest me to do" (cf. He. 7:27; 10:12-14). The intercession must rest on the complete sacrifice, and can be thought of only as proclaiming the completed atonement, or as actualizing and giving effect to whatever is already included within this completed atonement.

In the face of Arian suggestions that Christ's intercession signified His inferiority to the Father, the church fathers asserted that the intercession was a proof "not of inferiority but of love" (Chrysostom). In His intercession, Christ is not to be thought of as casting Himself at the Father's feet in abjection, but as presenting His people in Himself.

The ascension of Christ in no way separates Him from His people. In He. 7:24f. we are reminded that His intercession is an aspect of His unchangeable priesthood on behalf of those who came unto God by Him. "As Messiah, Christ cannot be thought of as existing without His people, neither can the heavenly high priest without His church. When He enters the heavenly realm, He enters not alone. He comes in fellowship with those who belong to the New Covenant established in His blood, and the fellowship expresses itself in intercession for them" (Aulen, p. 152).

III. The Intercession of Christ and the Prayer of the Church.–The intercession of Christ for the Church and for the world should be the source and inspiration of the Church's prayer for itself and for the world. To live by prayer means to live by grace, by asking and receiving from a gracious Father. When Christ was on earth He not only taught that people should live this way, but also sought to draw them into the fellowship of His own prayer life. The Church that understands this and is caught up into the grace of God "will not allow the Lord to be alone in prayer, but will be at his side with its own asking, however impotent its petitions enclosed in his asking" (*CD*, III/3, p. 277). Since Christ prays for the Church and for all mankind, the Church, in union with Him, will learn to pray truly for itself and for all mankind. This intercession will not be an amplification of completion of Christ's intercession, but an echoing of it and a witness to it. All human intercession is thus the fruit of Christ's intercession, and must indeed itself be basically the pleading of Christ's sacrifice. In Rev. 5 it is after the Lamb, who has been slain, ascends to the throne that the praises and prayers of the Church become heard there; and the ascent of the Lamb to the throne is followed by the vision (Rev. 8:3-5) of the prayers of the saints ascending before God and becoming an effective factor in fulfilling His purposes.

Bibliography.–G. Aulén, *Eucharist and Sacrifice* (Eng. tr. 1958), pp. 149ff.; J. M. Campbell, *Nature of the Atonement* (1873), pp. 231ff.; H. Heppe, *Reformed Dogmatics* (Eng. tr. 1950), pp. 458, 479f.; G. E. Ladd, *Theology of the NT* (1974), pp. 578-584.

R. S. WALLACE

INTERDICT [Aram. *'ĕsār*] (Dnl. 6:7-9, 12f., 15 [MT 8-10, 13f., 16]); AV DECREE; NEB ORDINANCE. A written prohibition, in this instance the banning of prayer to any god or man for thirty days, except to King Darius.

INTEREST [Heb. *nešeḵ* (Ex. 22:25 [MT 24]; Lev. 25:36f.; Dt. 23:19 [MT 20]; Ps. 15:5; Prov. 28:8; Ezk. 18:8, 13, 17; 22:12), *nāšaḵ*–'bite' (Dt. 23:20 [MT 21]), *maššā'* (Neh. 5:7, 10); Gk. *tókos* (Mt. 25:27 par. Lk. 19:23)]; AV USURY; NEB also USURY (Ps. 15:5), "holding as pledges" (Neh. 5:7), "taking . . . as pledges" (Neh. 5:10); **INCREASE** [Heb. *tarbîṯ*] (Lev. 25:36; Ezk. 18:8, 13, 17; 22:12), NEB "adding on repayment" (Lev. 25:36); **PROFIT** [Heb. *marbîṯ*] (Lev. 25:37); AV INCREASE; NEB "add interest." A sum paid to a creditor in money or goods at a fixed percentage rate for the use of borrowed money or goods. Although Heb. *nešeḵ* and *marbîṯ* or *tarbîṯ* have sometimes been equated in meaning (T.B. *Baba Metzia* 60b) because they occur together in some passages, *nešeḵ* probably denotes interest on money, and *marbîṯ* and *tarbîṯ* denote interest on grain or other produce. Akkadian documents make a similar distinction (Loewenstamm, p. 79).

Collection of interest from fellow Israelites was forbidden (Ex. 22:25; Dt. 23:19; Ezk. 18:18; etc.). Foreigners, however, were subject to interest on borrowed money and goods (Dt. 23:20; cf. 15:6). Specific interest rates in Israel are unknown. They may have been 20 percent on silver and 33⅓ percent on produce, the standard rate found in the law codes of Eshnunna and Hammurabi (Maloney, pp. 3, 7), but some rates exceeded this amount (de Vaux, p. 171). Although some of the codes had safeguards against manipulation of interest in favor of the creditor (see Maloney, pp. 5-11), other repeated abuses may have led to the ban on interest-taking among Israelites.

The prohibitions against receiving interest reflect the seriousness of this particular transgression. Lev. 25:36-38 closes with the solemn assertion, "I am the Lord your God who brought you forth out of the land of Egypt." Dt. 23:19 adds a promise to the prohibition, "that the Lord your God may bless you in all that you undertake." Ezekiel's condemnation is severe: taking interest is grouped with adultery, robbery, and idolatry (18:10-13). The one who lends at interest will, in the end, give his ill-gotten gain to the poor (Prov. 28:8).

Nehemiah 5:1-13 provides an example of the violation of these prohibitions and its result — poverty for the lower classes. As a result of famine (v. 3), some families had been forced to mortgage (Heb. *ʿāraḇ,* "pledge") their land and vineyards to buy grain. Others could not afford to pay their taxes and were selling their sons and daughters into slavery (cf. Lev. 25:39; Dt. 15:12-14), having already lost their fields and vineyards to creditors who were fellow Jews. After Nehemiah confronted the rulers with their illegal practices, lands were returned and payment of interest was immediately suspended.

The RSV has only two occurrences of "interest" in the NT, both in Q's parable of the talents (Mt. 25:27 par. Lk. 19:23). The Gk. *tókos* is a cognate of *tíktō,* "bear," "give birth." Hence *tókos* is a metaphoric usage for interest or usury because it "breeds" or multiplies money (MM, p. 637).

See also DEBT; PLEDGE.

Bibliography.–S. E. Loewenstamm, *JBL,* 88 (1969), 78-80; R. P. Maloney, *CBQ,* 36 (1974), 1-20; R. de Vaux, *Ancient Israel* (Eng. tr. 1961), I, 170-73. R. J. W.

INTERLACING [Heb. *śāraḵ*] (Jer. 2:23); AV TRAVERSING; NEB TWISTING AND TURNING. The figure is that of a young camel, possibly in heat, running about aimlessly; it represents the life of one who has forsaken the direction of God.

INTERMARRIAGE [Heb. hithpael of *ḥāṯan*–'become each other's son-in-law'] ("intermarry," Ezr. 9:14); AV JOIN IN AFFINITY; NEB JOIN IN MARRIAGE. Intermarriage of the returned exiles with the surrounding pagans would lead Israel back into the idolatry and abomination for which God's judgment had fallen upon them in the form of the captivity. This explains the severity of Ezra's stricture. G. WYPER

INTERMEDIARY [Gk. *mesítēs*] (Gal. 3:19f.); AV MEDIATOR. The role which Moses fulfilled by receiving the law on Sinai and delivering it to Israel. Well-attested in classical and Hellenistic Greek, the noun *mesítēs* is derived from the adj. *mésos,* "middle." Thus *mesítēs* means one who functions as a mediator between two parties or bodies in conflict. The corresponding verb *mesiteúō* means "function as a mediator" (*DNTT,* pp. 372f.; Bauer, rev., p. 506). In the papyri *mesítēs* often denotes an arbiter in legal transactions (MM, p. 399). The RSV translates *mesítēs* as "mediator" where it refers to Christ (1 Tim. 2:5; He. 9:15; 12:24).

In Gal. 3:19f. the giving of the law involves angels — an early Jewish tradition reflected also in Acts 7:35, 52 and He. 2:2 (cf. Dt. 33:2; Job 1:29; T. Dan 6:1). Burton (*Galatians* [*ICC,* 1920], p. 189) refers to Josephus *Ant.* xv.5.3 (136) as another example of this tradition, but in that passage Gk. *ángeloi* is better understood as "messengers," i.e., the OT prophets rather than angels.

Paul uses this tradition to argue for the superiority of the promise over the law. The law did not come to mankind directly as did the promise: both Moses and the angels had a part in its transmission to Israel. R. J. W.

INTERMEDIATE STATE. *See* ESCHATOLOGY VII.

INTERPRET; INTERPRETATION [Heb. *pāṯar* (Gen. 40:8), *piṯrôn* (Gen. 40:12), *pēšer* (Eccl. 8:1), *šeḇer* (Jgs. 7:15), *mēlîṣ* (Gen. 42:23); Aram. *pᵉšar* (Dnl. 2:4; 5:12); Gk. *diermēneúō* (1 Cor. 12:30), *diakrínō* (Mt. 16:3), *dokimázō* (Lk. 12:56), *synkrínō* (1 Cor. 2:13), *hermēneía* (1 Cor. 12:10), *epílysis* (2 Pet. 1:20), *diermēneutḗs* (1 Cor. 14:28)]; AV also "discern" (Mt. 16:3; Lk. 12:56); NEB also "meaning" (Eccl. 8:1). In the biblical world, the act or process of explaining dreams (e.g., Gen. 40:12), languages (e.g., 1 Cor. 12:10), circumstances (Lk. 12:56; Mt. 16:3), and biblical texts (e.g., 2 Pet. 1:20). In the modern sense, interpretation is the concern of hermeneutics, the discipline or the methodology of expounding all kinds of texts, including the Bible, poetry, and other literature. The word "interpret" has come into English from the Latin *interpres,* "go-between, agent, interpreter," and its deponent verb *interpretari,* "expound, explain, interpret."

I. OT–A. Hebrew. In the Hebrew portion of the OT the RSV uses "interpret" and "interpretation" almost without exception to translate the Hebrew verb *pāṯar* and its cognate noun *piṯrôn.* Use of these terms is confined to the Joseph narrative in Gen. 40–41, where the meaning has to do exclusively with the interpreting of dreams. In these chapters Joseph demonstrates his gift for the interpretation of dreams, first to the royal butler and baker, and then, dramatically, to the pharaoh himself. In each instance he is very careful to attribute to *Yahweh* the interpretations that he is able to expound (Gen. 40:8; 41:16; cf. 41:39). Heb. *pāṯar* is generally understood to be cognate with Aram. *pᵉšar,* "dissolve," and thus figuratively, "solve, interpret." In two instances (Gen. 40:5; 41:11) the RSV translates *piṯrôn* as "meaning" in the formulaic expression "a dream with its own meaning."

In Eccl. 8:1, within a context of seeking and finding wisdom, Heb. *pēšer,* "interpretation," makes its lone OT appearance, perhaps as a loanword from Aram. *pᵉšar,* "solution, interpretation" (see KoB, p. 785). This Aramaic term appears quite frequently in the Aramaic portion of Daniel.

The Heb. noun *šeḇer,* which ordinarily conveys the literal sense of "shattering, fracture," or the like (e.g., of pottery, Isa. 30:14; of a wall, Isa. 30:13; of a bone, Lev. 24:20), in one instance in the OT (Jgs. 7:15) is used figuratively. Again, in this instance the application is that of interpreting dreams. Heb. *šeḇer* is used to refer to the interpretation of a dream in the sense that an interpretation is figuratively a "shattering" or "breaking up" of the overwhelming whole of a dream into its constituent pieces and thus into clarity of meaning.

In the Joseph narrative Heb. *mēlîṣ* occurs with the meaning "interpreter." While the verbal root *lîṣ* appears to have the sense of "scorn, deride," the hiphil participle *mēlîṣ* nevertheless clearly means "interpreter" in Gen. 42:23 (Joseph's brothers assume that he cannot understand them because "there was an interpreter [*mēlîṣ*] between them"). The LXX here translates *mēlîṣ* with *hermēneutḗs,* "interpreter" (cf. Phoen. *mlṣ,* "interpreter"; see H. Donner and W. Röllig, *Kanaanäische und Aramäische Inschriften* [1968], II, 40). In the other three OT occurrences of *mēlîṣ* the RSV translates "mediator" (Job 33:23; Isa. 43:27) and "envoy" (2 Ch. 32:31). The rare cognate noun *mᵉlîṣâ,* "figure, enigma" (Prov. 1:6; Aquila and Theodotion have *hermēneía,* "interpretation"), may actually refer to the speech of a *mēlîṣ* (i.e., the artistically crafted and fluent articulation that enables an interpreter or envoy to bridge language barriers; see W. McKane, *Proverbs* [*OTL,* 1970], pp. 266f.), but it occurs only twice in the OT and in each case is understood more by context (cf. Sir. 47:17 where *mᵉlîṣâ* = *hermēneía*).

B. Aramaic. The Aramaic noun *pᵉšar,* "interpretation," occurs 31 times, exclusively in the Aramaic portion of Daniel. The cognate verb *pᵉšar* also appears twice in Daniel with the meaning "interpret." The noun appears repetitively in relation to the interpretation of a dream (*ḥēlem;* 2:4-7, etc.), usually in the formula *ḥelmāʾ ûpišrēh,* "the dream and its interpretation"). Both noun and verb are used in reference to a cryptic writing (*kᵉṯaḇ;* 5:7f., 15f., etc.), and the noun is used once (7:16) in Daniel's reference to "the visions of my head" (*ḥezwê rēʾšî*). The LXX uses the nouns *synkrísis, krísis,* and *kríma* to render *p^e^šar* as "interpretation." Daniel, as Joseph before him, attributes all interpretative ability to God, the revealer of mysteries (2:18ff., 28ff., 45ff.). It is assumed here, as in the Joseph story, that dreams remain an impenetrable mystery to humans even though they may have been given by God Himself. But it is for this reason that interpretation of dreams can come only as God's gift.

II. Qumrân.–The Habakkuk Comm. from Qumrân best illustrates the use of the term *pšr* as applied to scriptural texts in that community. In a thoroughgoing attempt to apply the prophet's words to contemporary history, the Qumrân interpreter of Habakkuk relentlessly quotes verse by verse, and in each instance applies the exposition with the formula *pšrw ʿl,* "its (hidden) interpretation is thus. . . ." This example is illustrative of the origin of the literary form of the pesher. It incorporates not only interpretation, but also application and commentary, and endeavors to elucidate hidden meanings in the words of the prophet, the import of which are known only in the inner circle of the chosen (cf. 1QpHab 2:5, 8, 12; 3:4, 7, etc.).

III. Classical and Hellenistic Greek.–The Gk. verb *hermēneúō* usually has the meaning "explain, interpret" in the classical authors, but it can also simply mean "speak plainly" or "be spokesman for" (see J. M. Robinson, "Hermeneutic Since Barth," pp. 2f.). Thus *hermēneía,* "interpretation," may also simply be "plain speaking" (e.g., Plato *Respublica* vii.7 [524]). A related meaning in the classical sources, not found in the biblical examples, is "articulate, express thoughts in words." A third sense is that of "translate," the meaning *hermēneúō* most frequently has in the LXX (e.g., Est. 10:3). Ezra 4:7 refers to an official letter "written in Aramaic and translated" (RSV; Gk. *hērmēneukénai* = Heb. *m^e^ṭurgām*). In the second ending of Job (42:18, LXX only) *hermēneúō* has the sense "described as" in a phrase referring to a translation: "described in the Aramaic book as. . . ." In the prologue to Sirach both *hermēneía* and *methermēneúō,* "translate," are used in the translator's apologetic for the shortcomings of the translation from Hebrew into Greek.

The Gk. *hermēneía* is also used in the LXX in the first sense listed above, e.g., in Sir. 47:17, where "interpretations" are itemized among songs, proverbs, and parables as one category among the many marvels that made Solomon the wonder of the world in his day ("illuminations" are suggested as the sense of *hermēneía* in this passage by J. M. Robinson ["Hermeneutic Since Barth," p. 2]; cf. Prov. 1:6 [Aquila and Theodotion]). The function of the official interpreter in the Joseph narrative (Gen. 42:23) would also have been to translate foreign languages into the familiar Egyptian (cf. also *Letter of Aristeas* 3). Gk. *diermēneúō,* "explain, interpret, translate," appears in 2 Macc. 1:36, where it refers to translation of a foreign term, yet is best rendered into English simply as "means" (cf. Acts 9:36 where *diermēneúō* is used in exactly the same way to translate the word Tabitha or show what it means).

Josephus uses *methermēneúō* in his assertion that he was "translating" his *Antiquities* from the holy Scriptures (*ek tṓn hierṓn grammátōn, CAp* i.10 [54]; cf. also *Ant.* xii.2.2 [20] for the sense "translate," but also *Ant.* ii.5.3 [72] for *hermēneutḗs* as an interpreter of dreams). Philo of Alexandria usually used these terms in the second general sense, that of putting thought into words (e.g., *De vita contemplativa* 28-31). It is not entirely clear in his portrayal of Aaron's role as Moses' "spokesman" (*De migratione Abrahami* 81) whether this role is one of conveying the thoughts of Moses or of interpreting his words. Josephus also uses the closely related term *hermēneús* (not used in biblical texts) to describe Moses' role as the "interpreter" or "spokesman" for God (*Ant.* iii.5.3 [87]).

The use of *hermēneutḗs* by Papias, an early Christian bishop in Asia Minor, to describe the role played by Mark the Evangelist in relation to the apostle Peter (Eusebius *HE* iii.39.15: *Márkos hermēneutḗs Pétrou genómenos*) has most often been understood to mean "translator." It may, however, mean simply "spokesman" — the middleman who conveys the apostle's thought (*TDNT,* II, *s.v.* ἑρμηνεύω [Behm], p. 663 n.3) — or perhaps "private secretary" (see R. P. Martin, *Mark: Evangelist and Theologian* [1972], p. 52). The main concern of Papias was, after all, to authenticate the Gospel of Mark, suspect in some circles, by tracing its authority directly to Peter himself.

IV. NT.–The Gk. *diermēneúō* has the meaning "interpret, expound" in Lk. 24:27, where along the Emmaus road the risen Jesus expounds the OT as it relates to Himself: "beginning with the law and the prophets, he interpreted to them in all the scriptures the things concerning himself" (cf. the parallel "opened" [*diḗnoigen*] the Scriptures in Lk. 24:32). The messianic interpretation of the OT, cherished and developed in the early NT Church, is here founded by Jesus Himself. This interpretation understands the OT in terms of promise and fulfillment, a pattern of divine preparation and deeds that reach their climax in the life, death, and resurrection of the Christ (cf., e.g., the handling of the Suffering Servant of Isa. 53 in Acts 8:32f. and Lk. 22:37; cf. also Mk. 14:27; *et al.*).

In several passages in 1 Corinthians (12:10, 30; 14:5, 13, 26-28) the related Gk. terms *diermēneúō, hermēneía,* and *diermēneutḗs* all have to do with the interpretation of tongues or glossolalia (e.g., *hermēneía glṓssōn* in 1 Cor. 12:10). This sort of interpretation is clearly not to be understood in the sense of "translation." The phenomenon of *glossolalia* is not speech that can be "translated" into a familiar language, but the ecstatic (or "angelic," 1 Cor. 13:1) utterance of praise directed to God (see *TDNT,* I, *s.v.* γλῶσσα κτλ. [Behm]). The gift of "interpretation" under consideration in these verses of 1 Cor. 12 and 14 is that of rendering intelligible the pre-conceptual spiritual ecstasy of the tongues-speaker. Paul's orientation in these verses is not toward the dramatic phenomena of the Spirit as ends in themselves, but toward the holistic upbuilding of the community (1 Cor. 14:5, 26-28). So *hermēneía* properly functions for the edification of the whole community of faith as it serves to explain or interpret the Spirit-filled experience of the ecstatic person who is addressing God (1 Cor. 14:2, 26-28). Paul indicates in these verses that it is possible for the gift of *hermēneía* to be given to the person already possessing the gift of tongues (1 Cor. 14:13), but also that the one who interprets is usually a different person (1 Cor. 12:10; 14:5, 27f.). Because the gift of tongues is essentially an inner experience between the individual ecstatic person and God (1 Cor. 14:2ff., 16-19, 23, 26ff.), Paul argues on the principle of the upbuilding the whole that if the *chárisma* of interpretation is not also present in someone, then speaking in tongues should not occur in the worshiping assembly (1 Cor. 14:27f.). Paul's concern in this portion of this Corinthian letter is that the dramatic, ecstatic gift of tongues not become exaggerated in importance beyond that of other more ordinary gifts that the one and same Spirit has distributed among the varied members of the body of Christ. Because his orientation is toward the community of believers as the goal of the Spirit's working rather than the phenomenon itself, Paul can reverse the Corinthians' priorities and place tongues near the end of his catalog of gifts (e.g., in 1 Cor. 12:4-10), so that ordinary deeds of loving service may be seen as equally the gifts of the same Spirit. Since there was at

Corinth a tendency to rank spiritual gifts according to the degree of intensity of the ecstatic element and the degree of unintelligibility of the experience (unintelligibility in Corinth being considered preeminently an indicator of authentic connection to the Spirit), Paul underscores the role of intelligibility in worship as essential to the upbuilding of the whole (see H. Conzelmann, *1 Corinthians* [*KEK*, 1969; Eng. tr., *Hermeneia*, 1975], pp. 209, 232ff.).

The Gk. *synkrínein* is translated "interpreting" in 1 Cor. 2:13 ("interpreting spiritual truths to those who possess the Spirit"), although its two other meanings, "combining" and "comparing," are possible. The Gk. *epílysis*, "explanation, interpretation" (lit. "a releasing"), occurs only once in the NT, in 2 Pet. 1:20, "no prophecy of scripture is a matter of one's own interpretation." This term occurs frequently in the similitudes of Hermas with reference to the interpretation of a parable. Its literal sense has to do with releasing what is bound or hidden. Gk. *diakrínō*, "judge, distinguish," is translated "interpret" twice in Mt. 16:3, "you know how to interpret the appearance of the sky, but you cannot interpret the signs of the times." The parallel account in Luke (12:56) uses Gk. *dokimázō*, "examine, test out."

The Gk. verbs *hermēneúō* (Jn. 1:38, 42; 9:7; He. 7:2), *diermēneúō* (Acts 9:36), and *methermēneúō* (Mt. 1:23; Mk. 5:41; 15:22, 34; Jn. 1:41; Acts 4:36) may also have the sense "translate" in the NT. This usage appears typically in parenthetical explanations (e.g., Jn. 1:42 where it is explained parenthetically that Cephas "means" Peter). In all the above instances the RSV translates "[which] means" (AV usually has "[which] being interpreted").

*V. **Hermeneutics**.*–The Gk. verb *hermēneúō* has given the name to that aspect of theological study known as hermeneutics. In brief, hermeneutics has traditionally been understood to be the working out of rules and methodologies for interpreting scriptural texts. Already in the time of Aristotle rules were derived for the interpretation of literary texts; a number of these are still in effect. Biblical critical scholarship has made increasingly clear in recent years the difficulty involved in applying general hermeneutical rules or principles uniformly to all types of biblical literature. Methodology must differ according to the peculiarities of the varied kinds of literary material under study. Universal principles are thus few in number: interpretation must first come to grips with the language used, the historical context, the literary genre, the identity of the author and his addressees, the aim of the author, and the process of the work toward canonical shape.

Hermeneutics traditionally has been understood as part of a triangular relationship with exegesis and interpretation, although the distinctions once made are no longer always so clearly drawn. Exegesis was that part of the process of the study of biblical texts that had to do with determining the meaning of the text for its author and addressees. Interpretation had to do with determining the text's meaning for the present age, and hermeneutics then referred to the rules and methodology applied in the movement from exegesis to interpretation. This distinction among three interrelated disciplines neither was nor is always easily made. There is a degree of overlap and synonymity that can be detected already in the ancient use of the Gk. terms *hermēneía* and *exḗgēsis*. This also carried over into their Latin counterparts, *interpretatio* and *expositio*, and it persists in English.

See INTERPRETATION, HISTORY OF.

Bibliography.–R. E. Palmer, *Hermeneutics* (1969), esp. pp. 12-32; J. M. Robinson, "Hermeneutic Since Barth," in J. M. Robinson and J. Cobb, eds., *New Frontiers in Theology*, II (1964), 1-77; *TDNT*, II, *s.v.* ἑρμηνεύω κτλ. (Behm); *DNTT*, I, 579-584; H. W. Wolff, "The Hermeneutics of the OT," in C. Westermann, ed., *Essays on OT Hermeneutics* (1963), pp. 160-199.

D. G. BURKE

INTERPRETATION, HISTORY OF.

*I. **Definition**.*–Interpretation is an activity in which a reader or hearer seeks to gain the shareable verbal meanings that an author or speaker has sought to transmit by linguistic signs. Not every meaning in an author's mind can be conveyed by language. Matters concerning his unique individuality that draw on a complex of private experiences in his past cannot be shared. Certain experiences, such as the taste of apricots, also cannot be represented by words. Likewise, the visual images that often accompany the matters we wish to transmit cannot be represented verbally. But over and above these limits much is shareable. As E. D. Hirsch has put it, "An author's verbal meaning is limited by linguistic possibilities but is determined by his actualizing and specifying some of those possibilities. Correspondingly, the verbal meaning that an interpreter construes is determined by *his* act of will, limited by those same possibilities" (*Validity*, p. 47).

*II. **Validity in Interpretation**.*–The chance that an interpreter will succeed in grasping an author's verbal meaning is greatly enhanced by the limitations of possible meanings that have been imposed upon words by cultural norms and conventions. A linguistic symbol can represent an identical meaning for two persons because the range of what it can mean has been limited by convention. Of course words often have several meanings, as any dictionary makes evident. But the association a word has with other words in its context does much to indicate the unambiguous meaning which the author intended it to have at a certain place in his writing. Nevertheless, the interpreter always has to guess at the meaning of a communication he wants to grasp. He tries out several possible meanings which certain crucial words or phrases can have until coherency with all such crucial terms and the text as a whole is reached. Virtually absolute certainty that one person has understood another can be achieved when the two are in direct conversation with each other, for then it is possible to ask questions to see if the meanings guessed at were correct. But in construing a text whose author cannot be consulted, a claim to validity in interpretation can never have more than a high probability.

Yet the more willingly an interpreter submits his proposed construction of a text to the scrutiny of others who have also worked hard to understand it, the higher will be the probability of achieving a consensus regarding the meaning its author wanted to transmit. The greatest difficulty to be overcome in the interpretation of texts is the famous "hermeneutical circle." (One's mind is so delighted with all the "evidence" and "coherency" its construction draws from the text that anger is easily generated against different constructions of that text, which also claim coherency and cite much "evidence" in their support.) But the interpreter who is aware of the alluring power of the hermeneutical circle and who desires truth more than the ego satisfaction of hanging onto his pet ways of construing a text will want to consider seriously the objections another interpreter brings against his way of gaining a supposedly coherent view of a text.

To be sure, if all facets of a text were equally capable of being made into "evidence" to support several different ways of construing a text, then the hermeneutical circle could never be broken, and interpreters would waste their time discussing which view was correct. But as Hirsch points out, ". . . not all traits are genre-dependent . . . and not everything in verbal understanding is variable. Understanding is difficult, but not impossible, and the hermeneutical circle is less mysterious and paradoxical than many in the German hermeneutical tradition have made it out to be" (p. 77). So discussion with a fellow interpreter about how a text should be construed is indispensable precisely because another mind is able to bring one to see some of those relatively few invariable traits in a text which will fit only one interpretation of it. Therefore validity in interpretation is possible as a matter of high probability, albeit not absolute certainty, and this makes the interpretation of texts to be as worthy a pursuit of knowledge as that of many other fields where only high probability rather than absolute certainty is attained.

III. Literary-Historical Method.–Two particular barriers arise in construing texts coming from another culture and time such as those in the Bible. The first consists of the language conventions the authors have used. Translations of the Bible are indispensable for imparting a great many of its meanings to vast numbers of people, but in each generation a certain number of serious interpreters are needed who will expend the time and energy necessary for grasping the linguistic world of the Bible's various books. "Verbal meaning," says Hirsch, "can be construed only on the basis of its own presuppositions, which are not given from some other realm, but must be learned and guessed at — a process that is obviously intrinsic to a particular social and linguistic system" (p. 134).

Hirsch's reference to "a particular social . . . system" indicates the second barrier to be overcome in interpreting texts outside our culture: one must seek to think in terms of the culture of biblical times. Much help in learning of this culture comes from the allusions biblical writers make to their customs and outlook. For example, in OT times instituting a covenant was spoken of as "cutting a covenant" (Jer. 34:18 [Heb. *habbᵉrîṯ ʾᵃšer kārᵉṯû*, "the covenant which they cut"]), and this explains why God, when entering into a covenant with Abraham, moved between the divided carcasses of animals (Gen. 15:10, 17). Though one depends on the associations that surround a word in its immediate context in order to determine its unambiguous meaning, one may go to any source that promises knowledge of the culture alluded to in a biblical passage. In Mt. 3:9, e.g., John the Baptist says, "Do not presume to say to yourselves, 'We have Abraham as our father,' for I tell you, God is able from these stones to raise up children to Abraham." Justin Martyr shows that Jews in his day regarded physical descent from Abraham as a guarantee of their salvation: "[The Jews] beguile themselves . . . supposing that the everlasting kingdom will be assuredly given to those of the dispersion who are of Abraham after the flesh . . ." (*Dial.* 140). Whereas in the literary aspect of interpretation one works from the immediate context, in the historical aspect any source which casts light on the world in which an author was writing is greatly valued because it helps the interpreter to escape from his own culture and make progress toward thinking in the alien terms of the text's culture.

Thus one thesis of this article is that even though the Bible is the verbally inspired Word of God, it is nevertheless to be interpreted like any other book, i.e., by recourse to the literary-historical method. As the ensuing survey of the history of biblical interpretation will show, however, many schools of interpretation from the early centuries down to the present argue that because the Bible was written under the inspiration of the Holy Spirit, it should be interpreted by means of a special hermeneutic.

A second thesis of this article is that the task of interpretation is not completed simply when an interpreter regards it as highly probable that he has understood what the author intended to communicate. The interpreter must still determine to what extent the author has succeeded in giving a true picture of his subject matter. If the only reason for grasping what another mind is trying to communicate is to be entertained, there would be no need to ask whether the message the author sought to impart truly represents some aspect of the world. M. Adler and C. Van Doren affirm that "the reader must do more than make judgments of agreement or disagreement. He must give reasons for them. . . . Otherwise he is treating a matter of knowledge as if it were an opinion" (*How to Read a Book* [rev. ed. 1972], p. 150). So asking how one may know that the Bible is true after he has grasped the intended meaning of its authors is certainly not an act of irreverence. On the contrary, not to give reasons for agreeing with the Bible's teachings but just to accept them by a leap of faith would be blasphemous, for it would be implying that the teachings of the biblical writings were no more worth bothering with than mere opinions. We honor God, therefore, as we, like the Bereans, examine the Scriptures "to see if these things [are] so" (Acts 17:11).

IV. History of Biblical Interpretation.–*A. Origen.* Origen (d. 254) expounded the first theory of biblical interpretation. He not only wrote voluminously, interpreting many biblical books, but also worked out a complete hermeneutical theory (*De prin.* iv). According to this theory, the Bible must be interpreted in a very special way because of its inspiration. For Origen, inspiration did not mean that the biblical books' own sequence of words and historical events set forth, by themselves, a true message from God. Rather, it meant that behind the words and details of the text was a deeper meaning, which was the unblemished Word of God. Thus in interpreting the triumphal entry into Jerusalem, Origen asserted that Jesus would have acted unworthily as the Son of God if he had had need of an ass and a colt, that He would have been stupid if He had been pleased by the placing of garments on the animals, and that the strewing of branches in His way could only hinder His progress (*Comm. on John* x.17f.). The account, therefore, is to be allegorized: Jesus as the Word of God enters into the soul. The ass is the literal sense of the OT, the colt is the literal sense of the NT, and these become a vehicle for the Word of God as it is loosed by the two disciples, whom Origen makes representatives of the two phases of the deeper meaning, namely, the moral and the spiritual sense (x.18). Origen's allegorical method derives directly from Philo of Alexandria, who used the Greek method of allegorizing myths to fit philosophy in order to make the OT accord with Platonism (R. P. C. Hanson, *Allegory and Event* [1959], p. 249). Likewise, Platonism is the presupposition dominating all of Origen's thinking (*ibid*., p. 361).

B. Antiochean School. The Antiochean School arose in opposition to Origen, and it included such men as Theodore of Mopsuestia (d. 429), the greatest exegete of the early Church, and Chrysostom (d. 407), the greatest preacher of the early Church. Instead of approaching the Bible with Hellenistic preconceptions, these men interpreted the Bible from the vantage point of its own Semitic thought. Theodore stressed the necessity of studying a passage's phraseology, separate clauses, and sequence of thought until the whole is seen as a sum of its parts. He was adamant in his rejection of Origen's allegorical interpretation and insisted that the biblical books be understood in their historical setting. He saw that when these books were interpreted literally and historically, they set forth a unified record of God's redemptive work in time (cf. the prologue to his comm. on Amos). Hence he acknowledged the validity of prophetical and typological passages in the OT, whose complete meaning did not become clear until the NT. This objective approach to the Bible is reflected in Chrysostom's sermons and comms., which even today make a valuable contribution to exegesis.

C. Middle Ages. The Antiochean School, however, had no lasting effect on the subsequent history of interpretation. Its influence vanished when it was included under the anathema on Nestorius at the Council of Ephesus in 431. Some form of Origen's allegorism, in which the Bible was expounded in at least two senses and sometimes as many as seven, prevailed for the next thousand years. The fourfold sense was most common: the literal-historical; the allegorical, to which faith gives assent; the moral, which governs conduct; and the anagogical, which tells something of the goal at which the faithful will arrive. As long as the Bible was thought to have more than one sense, it could easily be regarded as an "authority" alongside of, but not over, church tradition.

In the years between Origen and the Reformation, however, there were a few influences toward giving priority to the literal sense. Aquinas made the other meanings of Scripture dependent upon the literal meaning and thus elevated it above them. He said, ". . . all the senses [of Scripture] are founded on one — the literal — from which alone can any argument be drawn, and not from those intended in allegory . . ." (*Summa Theol.* i.1.10).

The prominent Jewish exegete Rashi (Rabbi Shelomo ben Isaac, d. 1105) and his followers influenced the teachers of the school of St. Victor in Paris to seek the meaning in OT books that their writers had in mind when they wrote. In the 14th cent. Nicholas of Lyra, the first author of a printed commentary, gives evidence of dependence on the leading teachers of the school of St. Victor. He in turn seems to have had some influence on Martin Luther, whose enemies composed the jingle, "If Nicholas had not played on his lyre, Luther would not have danced" (Farrar, p. 277).

D. Reformation. The impulse for the Reformation came as the Bible was given more freedom to speak for itself. Luther remarked, "When I was a monk, I was an expert at allegorizing Scripture, but now my best skill is only to give the literal, simple sense of Scripture, from which comes power, life, comfort, and instruction" (*Tischreden*, 5285, Oct. 1540). Whereas Romanism had considered the Bible to be so abstruse that it could be properly interpreted only by the clergy, who with the help of allegory kept the Scriptures submissive to church tradition, the Reformation advanced the principle of the Bible's perspicuity. This did not deny its inexhaustible profundity, but rather asserted that the Bible was understandable to all insofar as it was interpreted historically and grammatically. Thus the Reformers stressed both the study of the Bible in the original languages and the translation of it into the language of the people.

Unfortunately, however, Luther did not grant the literary-historical method exclusive rights in the interpretation of Scripture. He once quoted Paul's warning in 1 Cor. 3:10ff. that others should be careful to build upon the foundation of Jesus Christ, and commented, "All this is spoken of the ministry, so that he who would treat Scripture and explain it well may be sure so to treat it as to teach nothing but what agrees with the doctrine of faith, which alone stands firm and is founded on Christ" (*WA*, XXIV, 549). Luther never explained why his understanding of justification by faith alone was the "doctrine of faith" by which all the Bible should be interpreted. Some parts of Scripture fared badly as Luther applied his rule to them. In his disputation thesis, *De fide*, September 11, 1535, he affirmed that "Scripture is to be understood not contrary to, but in accordance with Christ. . . . If adversaries urge Scripture against Christ, we will urge Christ against Scripture. . . . If it is to be a question of whether Christ or the Law is to be dismissed, we say, Law is to be dismissed, not Christ." Some of the NT books urged Christ more than others, according to Luther. In the last paragraph of his *Preface to the NT* (1522) Luther said, "In a word St. John's Gospel [not the Synoptics!] and his first epistle, St. Paul's epistles, especially Romans, Galatians, and Ephesians, and St. Peter's first epistle are the books that show you Christ and teach all that is necessary and salvatory for you to know, even if you were never to see or hear any other book or doctrine. Therefore St. James' epistle is really an epistle of straw, compared to these others, for it has nothing of the nature of the Gospel about it" (quoted by E. Reuss, *History of the Canon* [2nd ed. 1884], p. 329).

Like Luther, Calvin also urged a literary-historical interpretation of the Bible. In the preface to his commentary on Romans Calvin said, "It is the first business of an interpreter to let the author say what he does, instead of attributing to him what we think he ought to say." But Calvin also set certain books of the NT above others. In the preface to his commentary on John's Gospel he said, "The doctrine which points out to us the power and fruit of Christ's coming appears far more clearly in [John] than in [Matthew, Mark, and Luke]. . . . For this reason I am accustomed to say that this Gospel is the key to open the door to the understanding of the others." Calvin was troubled by the parable of the sheep and the goats (Mt. 25:31-46). Here Christ taught that the blessed will inherit the Kingdom of God and eternal life because they have done such things for "Jesus' brethren" as feeding them when they were hungry. To keep this passage from teaching salvation by works, Calvin felt he must go to Eph. 1:5f., which teaches that people become children of God through His grace, and to Eph. 1:18 and Gal. 4:7, which teach that God's children receive the inheritance by grace. Calvin concluded, "Even in these very passages [e.g., Mt. 25:31-46] where the Holy Spirit promises everlasting glory as a reward for works, [yet] by expressly terming it an 'inheritance' he is showing that it comes to us from another source [than works]" (*Inst.* iii.18.2). In allowing passages so remote from Mt. 25 as Eph. 1 and Gal. 4 to control the author's meaning, Calvin was certainly not letting "the author say what he does, instead of attributing to him what we think he ought to say."

But the problem of gospel and law, or faith and works, which analogy-of-faith hermeneutics is called on most often to solve, evaporates as one probes more deeply into biblical theology. As Luther and Calvin perceived, a good starting-point for solving this problem is an understanding of what Paul meant by a "work of faith" (1 Thess. 1:3; 2 Thess. 1:11) and the "law of faith" (Rom. 3:27; cf. 9:31f.). Works done from the motivation of faith preclude the possibility of boasting and instead give all glory to God. These works are so vital to a saving faith that those lacking them are not saved. To be saved people must render the obedience of faith (Rom. 1:5) — less than perfectly! — to the law of faith (Rom. 3:27; 9:31f.). (See D. P. Fuller, *Gospel and Law: Contrast or Continuum?* [1980], p. 110 *et passim.*)

E. 16th and 17th Centuries. Reacting against the Reformation, Roman Catholicism became more adamant about the primacy of church tradition. At the fourth session of the Council of Trent (Apr. 8, 1546), it decreed, "No one shall presume to interpret the said sacred Scripture contrary to that sense which the holy mother Church hath held and doth hold." In seeking to establish their hermeneutic as over against that of Rome, the Reformers adopted as their motto, "The Bible is its own interpreter." This motto was good as long as it meant that no competing voice should interfere with the Bible's message. But in reaction against the Council of Trent, M. Flacius in his *Clavis scripturae sacrae* (1567) implied that the catechisms and creeds of the Reformation were the controlling norm for interpretation (W. G. Kümmel, p. 30). Following this trend, Protestant interpretation in the 17th cent. concerned itself not so much with literary-historical interpretation as with the support of its creeds through deductions gained from disconnected proof texts.

F. Bengel. As a revolt against Protestantism's polemicism and dry scholasticism in the post-Reformation era, a movement called Pietism arose; its greatest biblical expositor was J. A. Bengel. In his early years he was troubled by the textual variations in the few Greek MSS of the NT that were available to him. He wanted to follow Chrysostom's example of basing all exposition on the text alone, and so, to the collection of sermons by a famous preacher that he was publishing (1725), he attached a preface in which he outlined the strategy for his life work: first, to determine as nearly as possible from all available MSS the NT author's original wording, and then to write a commentary based on this text. He appealed to others to send him NT MSS. The readings selected for his Greek NT published nine years later were based on the division of MSS into "families" and on the principle that ever since has been employed in textual criticism: "The more difficult reading is to be preferred." But this strict scientific effort was for a practical purpose, as the rule laid down in the preface of his NT shows: *Te totum applica ad textum, rem totam applica ad te* ("Apply yourself fully to the text, and then apply all its subject matter to yourself").

As planned, his NT comm. *Gnomon* appeared eight years later (1742). The hermeneutical ideal toward which Bengel strove in this monumental work of exegesis is summed up in the preface to his comm. on Revelation (1740), where he says, "I desire to transmit to others nothing of myself, but simply what is found in the Scriptures. . . . An interpreter is to be compared with a fountain builder. He may not pour any water into the spring, but may work only to cause the fountain to run freely, sufficiently, and without impurity." His *Ordo temporum* (1741) indicates that as Bengel allowed the individual words, assured by textual criticism, to have their say, he came to see that the Bible is an organic unity centered on a redemption unfolding in history.

G. Rise of Historicism. Bengel's textual and historical efforts are both a reflection of and a contribution toward the rise of historicism, which was to have a decisive influence on subsequent biblical interpretation. Men like Theodore of Mopsuestia, Chrysostom, and the Reformers to some extent had sought to interpret the Bible historically, but as man's understanding of what constitutes a precise historical science increased, the Bible was subjected to a more rigorous historical investigation than ever before.

1. Beginnings. a. Textual Criticism. When the new study of ancient texts begun during the Renaissance was applied to the Bible, it became evident that the biblical text had been affected by the same historical forces that affect other documents. Thus J. Buxtorf's (d. 1664) insistence that the very vowel points of the MT were inspired had to give way before the labors of L. Capellus (d. 1658), J. Morinus (d. 1659), and R. Simon (d. 1712), who demonstrated the variations between the LXX and the MT. Likewise, Protestantism's virtual canonization of the Greek "Textus Receptus" in 1633 had finally to yield before the more thoroughgoing labors of such men as Bengel and J. A. Wettstein (d. 1754). Since it was discovered that historical procedure could bring about a more accurate knowledge of the original biblical texts, it was only natural to seek also for a more precise understanding of biblical content through historical investigation.

b. Secular Philosophy. Repulsed by the deadness and intolerance of organized religion, Hugo Grotius (d. 1645), René Descartes (d. 1650), Baruch Spinoza (d. 1677), and John Locke (d. 1704) shucked away what they considered the theological "husk" of the Bible and sought, by means of a historical investigation, to find the simple "kernel" of biblical truth. An investigation of secular parallels to the Bible, a historical testing of all traditional views of the authorship and purpose of the biblical books, and a reconsideration of their claim to canonicity were elements in the programs upon which these men embarked. Though the results of their investigations were controlled by their philosophical presuppositions, their methods became the foundation upon which future historical investigations were carried out with greater profit.

2. Turretini's Ground Rules. At the dawn of the rise of historicism, J. A. Turretini, a Reformed theologian from Geneva, set forth in *De Sacrae Scripturae interpretandae methodo* (1728) the basic hermeneutic that should control the literary, and especially the historical, interpretation of the Bible (Kümmel, pp. 58-60). This hermeneutic can be summarized in four propositions. (1) Since the God who gave revelation in the Bible also endowed people with the rational faculty necessary for receiving communication, the Bible's communication is to be grasped in the same way as other communications. (2) Since the Bible presumes the validity of the law of contradiction, which states that a thing cannot be both true and not true at the same time, no biblical interpretation can be accepted as true that clashes with what is already known to be true. Otherwise we could not live in relation to the world about us (for if yes could be no, how could we be sure of any fact?) or think coherently about God and His revelation. (3) Since it is a historical book, the Bible must be understood from the vantage point of its own writers as they lived in their own times and places, rather than from any modern vantage point. (4) Since the Bible is to speak for itself like any other book, the mind, subject to the law of contradiction, must come to the Bible as a *tabula rasa,* emptied of all cherished concepts derived from our modern view of life. Such ideals are more easily stated than carried out in practice. Thus the history of biblical interpretation had to go through several phases before any influential interpreter came close to realizing them. Even the first full proposal for producing a biblical theology left the door open for the popular philosophy of the time to exercise a prevailing influence.

3. Concept of Biblical Theology. It was J. P. Gabler, in his inaugural speech as professor of theology at the University of Altdorf in 1787, who first outlined the theory of how a biblical theology was to be differentiated from dogmatic theology (Kümmel, pp. 98-104). He declared that the individual biblical authors and writings must be understood in terms of their own historical settings, and that in comparing these writings with each other, their differences must be forthrightly acknowledged. But then he transgressed Turretini's third rule, for instead of allowing biblical writers to explain these differences in their own way as God's different administrations in a progressive history of redemption, he insisted that the only kernels of truth that could finally be extracted from the Bible were the timeless truths that did not reflect historical conditioning. Then he transgressed the fourth rule by explaining miracles in a mythological, rationalistic way.

4. Hegelian Historicism. Hegel's concept of history as an evolutionary, dialectical process inspired the attempt to trace this process in biblical history. Beginning in 1833, F. C. Baur outlined apostolic history as being controlled at first by the Jewish party dominated by Peter. Against this arose the gentile antithesis under Paul's leadership. Then came the conciliatory, synthetic movement reflected by Acts and the supposedly non-Pauline Epistles, Ephesians and Colossians. J. Wellhausen attempted to show the same dialectic for the OT in his *Geschichte Israels* (1878). Proceeding on the basis of what he felt were documents (JE, D, and P) which could be discerned as underlying the Pentateuch, he declared that first (*ca.* 800 B.C.) there was the preprophetic religion (JE), in which God was regarded as a local tribal deity countenancing revenge on enemies and ritual sacrifice. In antithesis to this arose (*ca.* 623 B.C.) the prophetic religion (D), whose God exemplifies love and which considers a high ethical life to be more important than sacrifice. The synthesis came (*ca.* 500 B.C.) in the priestly religion (P), with its codification of laws and ritual.

Subsequent investigations, however, showed that these reconstructions of biblical history were neater than the facts warranted. Even the Jerusalem church had its Hellenistic side, and Paul's churches had their Jewish members. As for the Graf-Wellhausen theory of the development of the Pentateuch, R. K. Harrison has chronicled the serious objections against this theory that were raised by people scrutinizing the Pentateuch through various avenues of historical research (*Intro. to the OT* [1969], pp. 27-61). J. Dahse (1910), e.g., showed that the supposedly more primitive parts of the Pentateuch actually reflected a far more advanced degree of maturity than Wellhausen and his followers were willing to concede. But all this historical research, stimulated by Hegel's philosophy of history, enabled scholarship to come to a clearer understanding of biblical history.

5. Liberalism and the "Historical" Jesus. Through K. Lachmann (d. 1851) and C. H. Weisse (d. 1866), the argument gained ground that Matthew and Luke were composed on the basis of Mark and a hypothetical document called Q, whose existence in Matthew and Luke could be perceived. Consequently, H. J. Holtzmann in *Die synoptischen Evangelien* (1863) sought, by working from these two sources, to set forth a more accurate picture of Jesus "as He actually was." The resulting picture, however, was controlled by the presuppositions of liberalism, whose ideology stemmed from Kant, Hegel, and Schleiermacher. In accordance with liberalism's tenets of God's universal fatherhood and ethical idealism, the resulting "historical" Jesus did not announce the kingdom of God as an impending, apocalyptic intervention into history, but merely as that ethical reign of God which should exist in human hearts. Only after Albert Schweitzer (*QHJ*) pointed out liberalism's unwillingness to do justice to Jesus' eschatological views did the would-be champions of the historical method take account of this most basic aspect of Jesus' teaching.

6. History of Religions. This more recently developed historical approach poses the question of the significance of certain similarities that exist between some biblical vocabulary and thought forms and those found in the ancient Semitic religions, Jewish apocalypticism, and the Hellenistic mystery religions. When carried to an extreme, this method has sought to explain the Bible simply by reference to these religions, e.g., R. Reitzenstein's attempt (*Die hellenistischen Mysterienreligionen* [1910]) to represent Paul as a proponent of a Hellenistic mystery cult. But such an extreme application of this method fails to explain why, if the biblical religion is a duplication of other religions, it was able to prevail against them. As E. von Dobschütz put it in his *Probleme des Apostolischen Zeitalters* (1904), "If Christianity from the beginning had been nothing more than such a syncretistic religious structure of an ecstatic, magical, ascetic sort, it would not have been worth outliving those sects of the Ophites, etc. And in accordance with the brazen laws of history, it would have had to perish instead of finally emerging as victor . . . in the gigantic struggle with all the powers of the ancient world. There must have been something in Christianity which was different from that religiosity, a power that raised it above all those formations. This distinctive element is the Gospel and the impression it conveyed of the person of Jesus Christ" (quoted by Kümmel, p. 314).

7. Form Criticism. This approach investigates the function and history of certain biblical literary forms as they were used in the life of the religious community prior to their becoming fixed in their present scriptural sequence. The method was applied to the OT by H. Gunkel (though from a confessed naturalistic premise) in his *Genesis* (1901) and *Ausgewählte Psalmen* (1904), and to the Gospels by K. L. Schmidt in his *RGJ* (1919). Schmidt argued that before the Gospels were written and while their events were still being transmitted orally, the stress naturally fell on those aspects of gospel tradition that were useful for edification and evangelism. These aspects became fixed while such incidental matters as chronological and geographical settings (except in the case of the Passion narratives) became a thing of indifference. Consequently, when the Gospels were written the various pericopes concerning Jesus' ministry could be put into settings and sequences that suited the Gospel writers' particular purpose. Thus form criticism points out that each of the Gospels is an interpretation of the life of Jesus, and the expositor therefore does well to make his first task that of seeing each Gospel as an independent literary unity before trying to work out harmonies among them.

Form criticism is carried to an extreme, however, when

it is argued that the interpretational element in the Gospels so discredits their historicity that "we can now know almost nothing concerning the life and personality of Jesus" (R. Bultmann, *Jesus and the Word* [repr. Eng. tr. 1958], p. 8). All historical reports reflect the interpretation their writers ascribe to the events recorded, but no one concludes from this that Julius Caesar does not tell us actual history about Gaul *ca.* 50 B.C., or that Josephus does not give us actual history about the fortunes of the Jews in the Roman empire of the 1st century. Likewise, each of the Gospel writers arranges and edits his knowledge about Jesus' ministry, suffering, death, and resurrection, in order to set forth his particular interpretation of these matters. But the respective interpretations complement each other, and the historically valid basis for their interpretations is vouchsafed by (1) a general agreement regarding the fundamental historic framework of Jesus' life, (2) the express effort to be historically accurate (Lk. 1:1-4; 3:1-3), and (3) the greater ease in explaining the apostles' faith and understanding of Jesus from Jesus as He actually was than from their own imagination.

H. Revolt Against Historicism. During historicism's rise there were many biblical scholars, e.g., F. Delitzsch, G. F. Oehler, T. Zahn, J. B. Lightfoot, and B. F. Westcott, who, avoiding its extremes and biases, welcomed its development and were themselves among the greatest contributors to our present exegetical and historical knowledge of the Bible. Others, however, have felt that at best, historical exegesis could have only a limited value, because it tended to remove the Bible from the solid ground of revelation and inspiration to the flux and uncertainty that accompany history. In the preface to his commentary on Romans (Eng. tr., 2nd ed. 1933), K. Barth related how burdensome it had been for him as a pastor to climb the pulpit Sunday after Sunday with a desire to give his people the word of God, but unable to do so because from his university training he had learned to have such an awe before the verdicts of history that a reverent understanding of the Bible had become impossible (p. 9). Revolting from this, Barth attempted an interpretation of Romans controlled by Paul's concern (*Sache*) in writing it, namely, God's revelation in Jesus Christ, which at the time, however, Barth understood in terms of Kierkegaard's concept of the infinite qualitative difference between time and eternity (p. 10). In such an interpretation, historical and philological considerations could have their place, but if exegesis concerned itself only with these, it would be "preliminary" (p. 7). As a result, this commentary was more of a theological treatise than an exegesis, and Adolf Jülicher charged in a review that by this "theological" interpretation Barth, rather than explaining Paul, had succeeded only in putting himself and his own ideas in front of Paul (*Die Christliche Welt* [1920], p. 468). Nevertheless, Barth's approach has found such sympathetic response that some have claimed that, whereas the 19th cent. is known as the century of historical interpretation, the 20th cent. will be known as the century of theological interpretation.

1. Demythologizing the Bible. R. Bultmann joined with Barth and argued (*Zwischen den Zeiten,* 3 [1925], 334-357) for the inadequacy of the historical method because: first, it inevitably assumed a view of history and human possibilities that limited in advance what a historical document could say, and second, it encouraged the interpreter to be so detached in striving for objectivity that he was immune to any claim history might make upon him. To remedy the problem, Bultmann borrowed from the philosophy of existentialism by insisting that the interpreter must consider a historical document not as a specific instance of a general category that he already understands, but rather as a special and concrete instance in itself that cannot be subsumed under any generalization. He must be ready to have an encounter with the new possibilities of human existence that it may set forth. Since the NT was written by those for whom the possibility of faith in Jesus Christ had become a reality, it can be understood properly only by an interpreter who has such faith. The interpreter is made ready for this decisive event of faith by coming to the NT with a readiness to believe made possible by the Church's witness. Hence, according to Bultmann, decision is the requisite for understanding. The literary-historical method has no final control. While it can clarify NT faith, faith in turn supplements what can be learned by historical exegesis.

In Bultmann's subsequent expositions of this hermeneutic, he frankly admitted his indebtedness to the existentialism of M. Heidegger (in H. W. Bartsch, ed., *Kerygma and Myth* [rev. Eng. tr. 1961], p. 25). Consequently, he saw NT faith as pointing toward an "authentic existence" in which a person, freed from all regrets for the past, fears of the future, fixed systems of thought, and dependence on things of the world, takes full responsibility for his actions and lives fully in the moment. The NT, in its proclamation of the death and resurrection of Christ, asserts that God works graciously to bring people out from the old into this new and authentic existence.

Since NT proclamation is accompanied by concepts and ways of thinking that pertain to inauthentic existence, however, these must be "demythologized" so that the NT's central purpose of bringing about authentic existence may be enhanced. Thus one must acknowledge the invalidity of such NT features as (1) the evidences cited to support Christ's resurrection (*ibid.,* pp. 39f.), for all "proofs" militate against authentic faith; (2) the assertion that regeneration means receiving a new nature (p. 21), for this encourages one to depend on a "thing"; and (3) the thought of a future coming of Christ (p. 20), for this hinders an openness for the future. The NT concept of grounding all God's redemptive work in the historical, once-for-all event of Christ's death and resurrection must not, according to Bultmann, be understood as a datable event of the past but as one in which God acts in the decisive present in church proclamation (p. 209). Modern man's scientific world view is one argument Bultmann used for this demythologizing, but his main argument for it was existentialism (pp. 210f.). Bultmann would demythologize even if he were living in the Stone Age. Hence it is apparent that his presuppositions controlled his interpretation of history as fully as was the case with nineteenth-century liberalism. Not the witness of the apostles, which was for him intermixed with concepts leading to inauthentic living, but the "faith" purified by existentialism had the final say.

A small modification in the Bultmannian hermeneutic appeared in the writings of two of Bultmann's pupils, G. Ebeling and E. Fuchs. These men continued to demythologize the NT so that it would aid authentic living, but unlike Bultmann they stressed (in accordance with the supposed philosophy of the later Heidegger) that language, rather than being an obstacle that must be demythologized before it can convey the truth, is really the means for bringing people to authenticity, for language itself confronts people with authenticity. Hence while the NT language must be demythologized with Ebeling and Fuchs just as much as with Bultmann, the emphasis is upon the positive benefit of language rather than on the need to purge out the mythological elements.

2. Barth's Revised Hermeneutic. In the years directly

after the publication of *Römerbrief,* when Barth and Bultmann considered themselves as allies in a new cause, Barth revised his hermeneutic to such an extent that he came to oppose Bultmann. In the preface to his *Kirchliche Dogmatik* I, 1 (Eng. tr. *CD*), he expressly renounced the existentialist presuppositions that controlled his thinking for his *Christliche Dogmatik* (1927) because he felt they dethroned God by making Him conformable to our prior knowledge of existence. Over against any generalization, only Christ, the concrete and specific revelation of God, is to be the source for understanding the Bible.

The full expression of Barth's hermeneutic appears in *CD,* I/2, pp. 457-472 and 722-740. Decision is a requisite for understanding; biblical interpretation can be carried out properly only by one who has come to know God in Christ through church proclamation. Such a one, instead of sinfully evading the biblical message by endless historical and literary consideration of its details, grasps the center of the biblical message and thus has the proper perspective for letting literary and historical data make pertinent contributions.

Barth's novel ways of interpreting Scripture become understandable from this hermeneutic. Regarding his exposition of election, Barth declared that his "hermeneutical decision" not to depart one step from the Word of God, which calls us and exhausts our knowledge of God, must control the entire interpretational process (*CD,* II/2, p. 152). Christ is this Word of God, who not only elects but who Himself is God's elect, and who, by having become reprobate for us, shows us that now only God's blessings are to be enjoyed. But as the Church concerns itself simply with proclaiming this gospel, it must not wonder whether there will be a final universalism or whether some will not believe, for such questions are themselves a turning aside from the concrete Word of God to abstractions (pp. 417f.).

Barth's hermeneutic also controls his doctrine of Scripture. Since God is known only in Christ, the Bible is not an inscripturation of propositional revelation but rather is God's word as witness to Christ (I/2, p. 463). The OT witnesses to Christ by looking forward to His coming, the NT by recollecting His coming (pp. 70-121). Christ did not fully reveal God during His earthly ministry but only during His resurrection appearances, when He manifested God's pure presence in the triumph of life over death (p. 114). Yet even the Resurrection accounts cannot mediate this high moment of revelation; in describing it, human language can only stammer and grope for words (p. 115).

3. The New Hermeneutic. Despite their differences, Bultmann and Barth both proposed a theory of interpretation that regarded *die Sache* ("the subject matter") about which a text spoke as the basis for understanding its statements. Barth's method of interpretation in the 20th cent. was very similar to that of Luther and Calvin, who in their application of the rule of faith forced the Bible to be interpreted by a subjectively chosen subject matter. Nevertheless, J. M. Robinson has attached to Barth's method of interpretation the name "New Hermeneutic."

Robinson climaxed his essay "Hermeneutic Since Barth" by referring to the hermeneutic advocated by Heidelberg philosophy professor Hans-Georg Gadamer in his *Truth and Method* (Eng. tr., 2nd ed. [1975]). Like Barth, Gadamer regards "the subject matter" (*die Sache*) as the key for understanding what another human mind has sought to express. He says, e.g., ". . . The hermeneutical problem is not one of the correct mastery of language, but of the proper understanding of that which takes place [*der rechten Verständigung über die Sache*] through the medium of language" (Eng. tr., pp. 346f.). For Gadamer, "that which takes place [*die Sache*]" is the force which grips an interpreter when the horizon of the text (the author's intended meaning modified by subsequent history) fuses with the horizon of the interpreter — a horizon that is shaped by his individuality as it carries on a friendly conversation with the text under consideration.

Gadamer has written a very penetrating advocacy for subject-matter exegesis. We can see his influence both in some Protestant exegesis and in Roman Catholic exegesis since Vatican II.

a. Gadamer's Influence on Protestantism. Perhaps the most articulate spokesman in Protestant hermeneutics in the later 20th cent. is P. Stuhlmacher. According to Stuhlmacher, "Gadamer's hermeneutic which is based on a sympathetic grappling [*Einverständnis*] with the great history of the humanities set forth in a written tradition, and on reflecting on this tradition in which the interpreter is aware that both he and the text are a product of ongoing history [*Wirkungsgeschichte*] — this hermeneutic has such a great significance for theology because it spurs us on to view in a new light aspects of the church's consideration of its texts which have been virtually ignored. Gadamer's hermeneutic also holds us back from following only a critically-oriented, scientific understanding of the text which keeps us from a dialogue with the peculiar biblical language and its historical setting" (p. 200). As Stuhlmacher sees it, Gadamer has helped keep the Protestant theologian from being so committed to the historical method that the Church's own confessions can play no role in the development of a biblical theology.

Stuhlmacher is also convinced that Gadamer has made evident the great defect in Bultmann's hermeneutic. He cites in support the criticism that the French hermeneutical theorist P. Ricoeur has made of Bultmann's hermeneutical approach in Ricoeur's foreword to the French edition (1973) of Bultmann's *Jesus and the Word* (1926) and Bultmann's essay *Jesus Christ and Mythology* (1941). Stuhlmacher quotes with approval (p. 201) Ricoeur's critique: "A theory of interpretation which at the outset runs straight to the moment of decision is running too fast. It leaps over the moment of meaning, which is the objective stage. . . . There is no exegesis without a 'bearer [*teneur*] of meaning', which belongs to the text and not to the author of the text" ("Preface to Bultmann," *Conflict of Interpretations* [Eng. tr. 1974], p. 397). In putting meaning in the text rather than in the intention of the author who wrote it, Ricoeur's hermeneutic is very much like that of Gadamer. As Stuhlmacher states, "Ricoeur has given utterance to the classical statement that a true understanding of the text completes itself not behind [in authorial intention], but before the texts, and indeed in a dialogue which goes on with the tradition regarding matters of truth that are vital to life" (p. 208).

So Stuhlmacher believes that the hermeneutic of Gadamer and Ricoeur provides the way in which biblical studies can be free from the "agony" caused by the historical method in that it denies the very essence of biblical theology by insisting that all happenings in the world have only immanent, non-supernatural causes. As an example of this "agony" Stuhlmacher says, "It is more than bewildering to hear from one and the same Bible critic the view represented that Jesus from Nazareth [and] his messianic work and word are the peculiar content and basis of Christian faith, and at the same time see him affirm that according to norms of the historical critical method nothing reliable about this Jesus can be learned. . . . Here indeed one detects a sigh of agony" (p. 210).

Two steps must be taken, according to Stuhlmacher, to be relieved of this "agony." First, biblical exegesis must reflect on the limited ability of the critical method to handle the basic Bible documents. In 1898 E. Troeltsch laid down the supposed ground rules of the historical critical method ("Über die historische und dogmatische Methode in der Theologie," *Gesammelte Schriften* [4 vols., 1919-1925], II, 729-753). One rule is that a historical report is doubtful until a verdict regarding its authenticity is rendered by the historical method and its use of "control." This "control" is that events cannot have occurred without analogous causes already existent in the world. But Stuhlmacher objects that such a rule is unsuited for biblical interpretation, because the central message of the Bible is how God has entered history and reconciled humanity to Himself in Christ — a matter which the principle of analogy cannot handle (p. 23).

To the question of how anyone, then, is to know the truth of this biblical message, Stuhlmacher answers that "biblical exegesis must establish an obligation backwards to church dogmatics. . . . Only then will biblical exegesis become aware of her subjectivity and understand herself as a part of the hermeneutical circle which draws the historical critical point of view into the context of a faith responsibility established by the church [*kirchliche Glaubensverantwortung*]. This hermeneutical circle also gives to exegesis a steadying support [*Hilfestellung*], and relieves the exegete of the task of having to establish, by the historical method, what is the normative body of Christian teaching [*massgebliche Glaubenswahrheit*]" (p. 210).

According to Stuhlmacher, if the exegete understood Gadamer's (and Ricoeur's) insight that no one is a neutral observer who stands, as it were, on the bank of the flowing river of history, but is himself borne along by that flow, then he would acknowledge that the Church's tradition regarding the meaning of the various biblical texts inescapably affects his work with those texts. Stuhlmacher insists that only this understanding of the exegete's historicity allows him to have "an open dialogue with the truth. . . . This dialogue is not only open because the interpreter is free to examine the textual tradition [of the Bible] for himself, but also because, according to Protestantism, the great confessional traditions of the church are the residue of the church's past interpretation of scripture, whose validity must, from time to time, be verified and, if necessary, be made more precise by reworking the primal witness of the Bible" (p. 221).

b. Gadamer's Influence on Roman Catholicism. We saw how the Council of Trent (1545-1563) forbade anyone from interpreting Scripture contrary to church tradition. But the power of the historico-critical method that prevailed for Protestant biblical interpretation in the 19th cent. made it necessary for the encyclical letter, *Providentissimus Deus* (1893), to affirm that expositors, while continuing to uphold the teachings of the Fathers, are nevertheless permitted "in those passages of Holy Scripture which have not as yet received a certain and definite interpretation, such labors [of the private student possessed of exegetical skill] [as] may, in the benignant providence of God, prepare for and bring to maturity the judgment of the Church" (*Rome and the Study of Scripture* [7th ed. 1964], § 109). Fifty years later in the *Divino Afflante Spiritu* (1943) the Catholic exegetes were told that their greatest task was that "of discovering and expounding the genuine meaning of the Sacred Books. . . . Aided by context and by comparison with similar passages, let them therefore by means of their knowledge of languages search out with all diligence the literal meaning of the words . . . so that the mind of the author may be made abundantly clear" (*ibid.*, § 550).

Church tradition, nevertheless, must continue to play a decisive role in Roman Catholicism, but just how it would fit in with the diligent search for "the mind of the [biblical] author" remains ambiguous in Vatican II's dogmatic constitution *De Revelatione* (Nov. 28, 1965). According to 2:9, "Sacred Tradition and sacred Scripture . . . are bound closely together and communicate one with the other. For both of them, flowing out from the same divine wellspring, come together in some fashion to form one thing. . . . Thus . . . the Church does not draw her certainty about all revealed truths from the holy Scriptures alone. . . . Both Scripture and Tradition must be accepted and honored with equal feelings of devotion and reverence."

R. Brown ("Hermeneutics") tries to describe clearly how biblical exegesis will always mesh with church tradition. He declares that Roman Catholicism wants the interpreter of Scripture to go beyond the author's intended meaning of a text to the deeper meaning (*Sensus Plenior*) which has been "sponsored by writings to which Christians give authority, e.g., the NT, the Fathers, [and] Church Pronouncements" (§ 59). He argues that the NT on a number of occasions gives a deeper meaning to the OT. For example, Mt. 1:23 interprets Isa. 7:14 to apply to the Virgin Birth of Christ when the immediate context of the Isaianic passage speaks only of a child that is soon to be born. Likewise, "Even after the end of the biblical era and the close of the public revelation . . . God guides the Church and Christians in the understanding of revelation" (§ 58). "The surest guide to [the fuller interpretation] is an authoritative interpretation of the words of Scripture in a more-than-literal way — authoritative in the sense that it comes from one of the guides to revelation, e.g., the NT, the Church Fathers, Church Pronouncements, etc. . . . If there are real meanings of Scripture that . . . are of importance to the divine plan for man's salvation, the most likely matrix for their emergence to clarity and acceptance is the context of Church life" (§ 63).

For Brown the probability of *Sensus Plenior* arises from the fact that the Bible is a divinely inspired book. "Since it is God who reveals and who inspires, God can tell man through revelation what he intended in inspiring earlier passages of Scripture" (§ 58). For biblical scholars who do not hold Catholicism's view of biblical inspiration, Brown suggests that "perhaps the solution is to take the emphasis off the mechanics of the divine and human intentions and to concentrate rather on the close relationship between the idea of [*Sensus Plenior*] and the modern interest in the hermeneutical value of language" (§ 68). Earlier Brown had invoked Gadamer and the "new hermeneutic" as favoring the idea of *Sensus Plenior*: "H. G. Gadamer has written on hermeneutic from a philosophical viewpoint, and he insists that one *always* understands the text differently from the way in which the author himself understood it. . . . The new hermeneutic is a modern tendency in favor of a more-than-literal exegesis" (§ 50).

4. Structuralism. Mention should also be made of "structural exegesis," or "structuralism," as another contemporary instance of the revolt against historicism. Instead of placing texts so fully under the control of the historical method, structuralism emphasizes the reading of biblical books as literature. This means that rather than trying to catch on to what the author wanted to say to the original readers, one simply regards the text as it stands as the "author," and oneself as the intended reader. Structuralism is advocated by a group of biblical scholars from diverse traditions, and, quite possibly, even more by teachers in secular schools who have no specifically religious or theological interest in the Bible. Following the lead of the linguist Ferdinand de Saussure and the anthropologist Claude Lévi-Strauss, who claim to have observed similar structures among the most diverse cultures at the deep levels of both language and behavior, these literary structuralists believe they can find recurrent patterns in the many different literary units of the Bible. Although no consensus has emerged about any book's structure and forthcoming meaning, the practitioners of structuralism argue that in diverse narratives, for instance, one nevertheless finds such recurrent themes as subject, object, ordainer, recipient, opponent, and helper. So R. Spivey observes that "at the heart of structuralism is the assumption that the 'uninvited guest' for all cultural phenomena is the human brain" (*Interp.*, 28 [1974], 133). But if this means that all human activity (both speaking and doing) is, at root, a repetition of the structure by which the brain operates, then all study of the humanities would soon become monotonous. Perhaps this is why in the editorial at the beginning of that 1974 issue of *Interp.* the remark is made that "there is at present nothing like a unanimous and hearty welcome for the uninvited guest, even among the scholarly initiates" (p. 131).

I. Cullmann's Revelational History. In contrast to the new hermeneutic, which scoffs at seeking an "objective" interpretation of the text, a minority of reputable biblical scholars, in accordance with classical hermeneutics, insist on discovering the consciously intended meaning which the author or redactor of a text wanted to share with his readers. K. Stendahl affirmed that the textual and historical material of the Bible "itself gives us means to check whether our interpretation is correct or not. . . . Our only concern is to find out what these words meant when uttered or written by the prophet, the priest, the evangelist, or the apostle — and regardless of their meaning in later stages of religious history, our own included. Such a program is by and large a new feature in biblical studies, a mature fruit of the historical method. . . . This descriptive task can be carried out by the believer and agnostic alike. The believer has the advantage of automatic empathy with the believers in the text — but his faith constantly threatens to have him modernize the material, if he does not exercise the canons of descriptive scholarship rigorously" (*IDB*, I, 422).

B. Childs objected that Stendahl, by sharply dividing the task of biblical theology first into the "descriptive task" — indicated by the quotation above — after which homiletical applications could be made for the world of today, had "struck a blow at the very heart of the [biblical theology] movement, as it was originally conceived" (p. 79). Like Stuhlmacher, Childs wants a biblical theology that will revitalize the Church by letting faith and church confessions temper the results of the historical method, which, he feels, can never support the central affirmations of the Bible because they bear no analogy to ordinary history. Childs also complained that Stendahl's insistence that we carry out first the "descriptive" task and only then the "hermeneutical" task of applying the results of biblical theology in some real-life, present-day situation was "not widely held by American Biblical theologians" (p. 26).

Stendahl cites O. Cullmann as one who insists on first engaging oneself in the descriptive task before proceeding to the all-important work of applying the results of descriptive interpretation to the needs of the particular life situations faced by various individuals and groups. In his early years Cullmann became disenchanted with liberalism and then with dialectical theology because he saw how both tried to make the facts of Scripture fit a modern philosophical point of view. Then he espoused the methodology of form criticism as the best way to rediscover the faith of the early Church. "As I prepared my lectures," he relates, "I sought to hold every modern or personally cherished idea regarding the nature of Christianity at a distance. Through this purely *scientific* approach, I came gradually to a deeper theological understanding of those concepts in the NT, which at the outset had been foreign to my ways of thinking" ("Autobiographische Skizze," in *Vorträge und Aufsätze, 1925–1962* [1966], p. 685).

The results of this interpretational procedure can be seen clearly in his *Christ and Time* (Eng. tr., 3rd ed. 1962), *Christology of the NT* (Eng. tr. 1960), and *Salvation in History* (Eng. tr. 1967). Cullmann affirms that the "legitimate limits . . . by which we seek to make the NT relevant to modern thought . . . are overstepped when, for example, in the story of the Fall [Gen. 3], as one finds it used in the NT, the sin of man is seen psychologically as the timeless condition of all men rather than the original rebellion against God. To interpret the story in this way is to fail to understand sin in the light of the 'second Adam' who comes *after* the first. Here too the sequence of events must be allowed to stand" ("The Connection of Primal Events and End Events with the NT Redemptive History," in B. Anderson, ed., *The OT and Christian Faith* [1969], p. 123). Cullmann insists that faith is "a decision to align my existence with that concrete [redemptive] history revealed to me, with that sequence of events" (*Salvation in History,* p. 69). In his view, a substantial part of "the central portion of salvation history [is] open to historical investigation. . ." (*ibid.*, p. 139). The rest of redemptive history, especially what lies back in the early chapters of Genesis (and of course forward, in the redemptive events yet to transpire), is not open to historical investigation. Yet "both are prophecy [i.e., revealed truth]; but the stories of the beginning and the end are only prophecy, while the middle section [of redemptive history], which is open in part to historical testing, is prophecy of a kind that refers to facts that can be historically established, and [the middle section] makes these facts [also] an object of faith" (*Christ and Time,* p. 97).

Unlike R. Brown (see IV.H.3.b above), Cullmann affirms that while the NT does place events of the OT in a new light, it does not do this by negating or giving an entirely new meaning to the OT events. Cullmann says, to be sure, that as the kerygma is taken up from the OT and goes into the NT it "passes through new interpretations more radical than all those undertaken within the sphere of the OT . . ." (*Salvation in History,* p. 113). But earlier he had declared that this radical transformation of meaning "never happens in such a way that an earlier account is disputed. Rather, aspects formerly unnoticed are by virtue of the new revelation now placed in the foreground, creating a correspondingly wider horizon" (*ibid.*, p. 88). So the revelation connected with the earlier events in redemptive history retains its integrity, although certain aspects of them (e.g., that Abraham received circumcision *after* he believed God in Gen. 15:6) are, in the larger perspective provided by later revelation, given an importance and significance which they did not originally have. Like pieces of a jigsaw puzzle, elements of earlier redemptive history continue to make their individual contributions, but as the later pieces of redemptive history are fitted in, the significance of those earlier pieces undergoes a radical change. In that all parts of the Bible therefore retain their integrity even though later revelation changes their significance, Cullmann is able to affirm that "a dogmatics . . . of salvation history . . . ought to be written some day" (*ibid.*, p. 292).

Unlike Stuhlmacher, Cullmann does not want church confessions to play a decisive role, along with the historical method, in finally ascertaining the meaning of a text. "When I approach the text as an exegete," Cullmann says, "I may not consider it to be certain that my Church's faith in Christ is in its essence really that of the writers of the NT.... In the same way, my personal self-understanding [contra Bultmann], and my personal experience of faith must not only be seen as exegetical aids, but also as possible sources of error" (*ibid.*, pp. 68f.). Pertinent philological and historical data alone are determinative for arriving at the meaning that the author or redactor intended to impart in the text he was composing.

V. Adequacy of the Literary-Historical Method for Biblical Interpretation.–We argue that the method of interpretation advocated by K. Stendahl and O. Cullmann, which echoes that of Theodore, Turretini, and Bengel, is the proper one for interpreting the Bible. The foregoing history of biblical interpretation teaches us that only as biblical spokesmen are allowed to speak for themselves about the meaning of events occurring in history does the consequent message of the Bible concern a revelation from God. This message became so much a part of the stuff of history that, corresponding to God's revelation in Christ, the message the apostles and prophets proclaimed was, to use their words, "that which we have heard, which we have seen with our eyes, which we have looked upon and touched with our hands" (1 Jn. 1:1).

A. The Bible and the Historical Method. We have seen how Stuhlmacher (and others) argue that the nature of the historical method is unsuited for handling the message of the Bible, whose essence is that God has, in events of redemptive history and most especially in the Incarnation, produced happenings within time and space whose cause lies outside the immanental world. This view would be valid if Bultmann's description of historiography were correct. He said, "The historical method includes the presupposition that history is a unity in the sense of a closed continuum of effects in which individual events are connected by the succession of cause and effect.... This closedness means that the continuum of historical happenings cannot be rent by the interference of supernatural, transcendent powers and that therefore there is no 'miracle' in this sense of the word" ("Is Exegesis Without Presuppositions Possible?" in *Existence and Faith* [Eng. tr. 1960], pp. 291f.). J. M. Robinson has gone a step farther and argued that the possibility of miracles must be excluded from positivistic historiography not because of certain dogmatic presuppositions but because of the demands of the historical method itself (*Kerygma und historischer Jesus* [2nd ed. 1966], pp. 24f. n.).

Just what are these demands which are supposed to make it necessary to exclude the possibility of the supernatural in pursuing the historical method? In the book entitled *The Historian's Craft* (Eng. tr. 1954), written by the late French historian Marc Bloch, we find a typical example of how the historical method works. From this illustration it can be seen how the admission of the possibility of miracles might seem to make it impossible to gain any historical knowledge. Bloch cites the example of a certain Marbot, an officer in Napoleon's army, who in his memoirs relates how on the night of May 7, 1809, he crossed the raging torrents of the Danube in order to free some French prisoners from the Austrians. But a petition for promotion drawn up by Marbot himself on June 30, 1809, contains no mention of this daring exploit during the preceding month. There is no conceivable reason why Marbot would have kept silent about such a feat especially when applying for an advancement in rank. On the basis that everything is happening according to regularity, the historian easily concludes that Marbot was lying when he recorded this exploit in his memoirs. Though a braggart, he would not fabricate a tale about some deed of bravery when his superiors would all know that no such heroic deed had taken place less than two months earlier. But later, when writing for an audience most of whom would not question his story, Marbot's desire to depict himself in the most praiseworthy light would perfectly explain this lie.

Robinson's argument is that if the historian had to acknowledge that miracles, or irregularities, can happen in the immanental, then it would be impossible to conclude that Marbot was lying. If the world can be so irregular that Marbot the braggart becomes modest in not recounting his exploit at the very time when it would be to his advantage to recount it and his superiors would expect it of him, then it becomes impossible to check the veracity of his or any other reported occurrence.

Going back to Bultmann's statement of how the historical method operates, we observe that he makes two separate affirmations. First, he insists that "individual events are connected by the succession of cause and effect." Second, he insists that this succession of cause and effect is closed. "This closedness," Bultmann declared, "means that the continuum of historical happenings cannot be rent by the interference of supernatural transcendent powers." But we should observe how completely separate the two parts of this presupposition of the historical method are. The affirmation that every effect has a cause does not have to limit the source of that cause to what is immanental. The possibility that an event could have a supernatural cause without destroying the integrity of the historical method could be accomplished by never postulating the supernatural until all attempts to find immanental explanations have been exhausted.

The report of Paul's conversion provides an illustration of how the historical method retains its integrity while affirming that the explanation for Paul's radical change of behavior arises neither from his own inclinations nor from the circumstances of his life as an up-and-coming leader in Pharisaism. There is virtually universal consensus that Paul wrote Galatians. In 1:13f. of that Epistle he described the kind of person he was before his conversion. The all-important historical control for verifying his description is provided by the introductory words, "You have heard. . . ." Since it was generally known what kind of person Paul was before his conversion, the Judaizers at Galatia, who were attempting to turn the Galatian believers away from Paul's teachings, could not deny that Paul had once zealously insisted on circumcision and conformity to the Jewish dietary regulations in order to claim the blessings God had promised to Abraham's seed. We know that Paul could not have affirmed that he was once such a person if that were not general knowledge, for the Judaizers then could easily have discounted that Paul ever had undergone the radical change that made him the person he now was. Thus, relying upon a view of history in which individual *reports* of happenings can be verified by assuming that all effects in history result from appropriate causes, but denying the possibility that supernatural causes ever happen to affect the *reportage* of events, we are able to admit the possibility of supernatural events without destroying the possibility of all historical knowledge.

For example, there is universal consensus that Paul spearheaded the gentile mission and announced to Gentiles far and near that the great blessings which God had promised to Abraham and his seed (e.g., "I will be your God") could be enjoyed by all those who would simply repent and believe by banking their hope upon such promises. In order to be saved they did not have to submit to circumcision or dietary restrictions. In carrying out the Gentile mission Paul himself repudiated the strong Jewish disinclination to dine with Gentiles (cf. Acts 10:12-14, 28), and so he must often have eaten so-called unclean foods himself.

The historical method wants to discover adequate causes to explain the effect of how Paul, a promising young Pharisee, renounced his adherence to Jewish distinctives. This adherence had given him the confidence that God approved of him (Phil. 3:4-6). Only factors which would have caused Paul to flee from a gentile dining table can be found in his motives and circumstances before his conversion. But since there must be an appropriate cause or set of causes to explain Paul's spearheading the Gentile mission — or else all possibility for gaining historical knowledge vanishes — we honor the explanation Paul himself gave for the change, namely, that the risen Jesus, whose followers he had been relentlessly persecuting, appeared to Paul as one possessing the power of the supreme deity and commissioned him henceforth to be His apostle, His spokesman on earth. (See D. P. Fuller, *Easter Faith and History* [1965], pp. 224-29.)

Paul's conviction that he is Jesus' apostle is expressed often enough in connection with his assurance that Jesus had commanded him to head up the Gentile mission (Rom. 1:5-7; 15:15ff.; Gal. 1:15-17; Eph. 3:2ff.; 1 Thess. 2:13-16) to make it difficult to think of his carrying on that mission apart from this conviction. So, starting with the controllable historical phenomenon of Paul's radical change of behavior, we can argue to his being the spokesman for Jesus Christ. Since he occupied such a position, it is not surprising to find him claiming that he and other apostles uttered words given them by the Holy Spirit (1 Cor. 2:13). Working outward from Paul it would be possible to show (if we had sufficient space) that the "we" of 1 Cor. 2:6-13 indicates that Paul regarded another apostle like Peter and a close associate of apostles like Apollos likewise as spokesmen for Jesus Christ. Thus in the centuries following the close of the apostolic age (*ca*. A.D. 100) when many were claiming to speak and write as Jesus' spokesmen, the churches instinctively fell back upon the writings of the apostles and their close associates as the authority to keep them from following false teachers. Working outward from the controllable history of Paul and the gentile mission, it is possible therefore to establish the validity of the twenty-seven books of the NT canon. Then, because Paul and the other apostles regarded the OT as inspired (cf. 2 Tim. 3:16f.), and because two Jewish sources definitively state the composition of the OT canon (2 Esd. 14:19-48 [117 B.C.]; Josephus *CAp* i.8 [39-46] [A.D. 90]) and omit the apocryphal and pseudepigraphical books, we accept the thirty-nine books of the OT as the extent of the rest of the Scriptures.

This use of the historical method — a use that insists that every effect in history must have a sufficient cause but does (unlike Troeltsch and Bultmann) allow transcendent causes when immanental causes are insufficient — does not go contrary to the peculiar nature of Scripture, as Stuhlmacher would have us believe. This method should be used not only to find the intended meanings of the authors and redactors of the sixty-six books of the canon, but also to gain knowledge of the truth and extent of the canon. Surely if redemptive history is inextricably interwoven with ordinary history, and if Jesus Christ, the culmination of revelation, became a part of history by becoming flesh (Jn. 1:14; 1 Jn. 4:2), then it is the historical method that should be used to interpret and validate the sixty-six books of the canon. Docetism becomes a threat in the hermeneutics of those who regard knowledge of divine things as something gained in ways other than through the literary-historical method. An attempt to understand a part of revelatory truth as being known in a manner that bypasses history and the way historical happenings and utterances are known, necessarily implies that that part of revelation was not history but was somehow transmitted immediately to the believer.

B. The Holy Spirit and Biblical Interpretation. Although the literary-historical method is adequate for determining and verifying the intentional meanings of authors and redactors, people in their totally depraved condition have no inclination to welcome the message of the Bible. Scripture gives God all the credit for the benefits and blessings that people enjoy and for the redemptive acts that finally mark an end to sin and death and bring in the reign of God in a condition completely free from all evil and infirmity. Inclined as people are to boasting in themselves and seeking the praise of others, they rebel against this message. A person's inability to "receive" (Gk. *déchomai*) spiritual things in 1 Cor. 2:14 means his unwillingness to welcome them (Bauer, rev., p. 177).

An unregenerate person can be cognizant of the spiritual things taught in Scripture, but since he accounts them to be foolishness, he does not "know" them in the sense of accepting them as true. If, however, his being a minister or Bible teacher in a Christian school prohibits him from denying the essential truthfulness of the Bible, he will, in defiance of the literary-historical method, appear to uphold the truth of Scripture by a process of distortion. Consequently he does not expound "the whole counsel of God" (Acts 20:27). A. H. Francke, one of the founders of the pietistic revival in Germany in the 18th cent., affirmed that "to the extent that you are crucified to the world you will be able to grasp what the holy Scriptures are saying" (E. Peschke, *TLZ*, 89 [1964], 103).

Regenerated people, too, must realize how the power of sin can gain the ascendancy in their lives, so that they will distort the intended meaning of some important statement in Scripture or even omit it altogether. In addition, therefore, to being skilled exegetes, they must spend time seeking fellowship with God. Only by fulfilling these two requirements will they succeed in declaring "the whole counsel of God."

C. Unity of the Bible. If our argument above (see V.A) regarding the canonicity and divine inspiration of the sixty-six books constituting the Bible is valid, a necessary corollary is that the Bible sets forth a coherent message. We have seen how, according to Cullmann, later revelatory spokesmen, in addition to providing new material, reemphasize facets of earlier revelation as part of the whole counsel of God. It is significant that Paul, as one of the last revelatory spokesmen, regards as worthy of hell anyone who teaches a message contrary to what has already been given (Gal. 1:8f.). As one of the revelatory spokesmen, Paul considered the teaching which he gave as being so in concert with the message of the earlier spokesmen that he used quotations from these earlier sources of revelation to affirm his point (Rom. 3:9) that all the peoples of earth are under sin (Rom. 3:10-18). Later revelatory spokesmen also regarded their interpretation of contemporary revelatory events to reflect so accurately God's moving of redemptive history toward its final climax that they could regard an event whose occurrence and meaning they reported to be a partial or typological fulfillment of prophecy uttered by an earlier revelatory spokesman (e.g., Acts 2:16-21; cf. Joel 2:28-32 [MT 3:1-5]). In establishing the unity of the Bible, each literary unit of the Bible must be allowed to contribute its teaching equally with every other literary unit.

Thus by letting only the literary-historical method operate in the handling of Scripture, we come to a knowledge of divine revelation in the same way we come to knowledge about everything else in our experience, namely, by a process of trying out various possibilities until coherency is attained. E. D. Hirsch calls this method the "hypothetico-deductive process" (p. 264), and those familiar with M. Polanyi's *Personal Knowledge* (1958) will see how similar the pathway to knowledge indicated in this article has been to his.

Bibliography.–Since the field of interpretation (hermeneutics) covers many diverse aspects, the following bibliography cites several important works on a number of hermeneutical subjects.

Bibliographies: N. Heinrichs, *Bibliographie der Hermeneutik* (1968), 430 pages of aspects of secular and theological hermeneutics from Schleiermacher to 1968; I. H. Marshall, ed., *NT Interpretation* (1977), helpful bibliographies on pp. 368f. for each of the eighteen essayists; P. Stuhlmacher, *Vom Verstehen des NTs* (1979), bibliography for history of interpretation on pp. 248-255.

Theory of Interpretation: D. E. Fuchs, *Hermeneutik* (2nd ed. 1958); H. G. Gadamer, *Truth and Method* (Eng. tr. 1975), the basic philosophy behind the "new hermeneutic"; E. D. Hirsch, Jr., *Aims of Interpretation* (1976), and *Validity in Interpretation* (1967), best thinking for classical hermeneutics instead of the "new hermeneutic"; D. Ihde, *Hermeneutic Phenomenology* (1971), the American interpreter of P. Ricoeur; R. E. Palmer, *Interpretation* (1969), the American spokesman for the "new hermeneutic" in secular usage; P. Ricoeur, *Conflict of Interpretation* (1974), a hermeneutical theorist for secular and biblical hermeneutics.

Histories of Biblical Hermeneutics: F. W. Farrar, *History of Interpretation* (1885; repr. 1961), excellent work up until the Reformation; R. M. Grant, *Short History of the Interpretation of the Bible* (rev. ed. 1965); W. G. Kümmel, *The NT: The History of the Investigation of Its Problems* (Eng. tr. 1972); J. M. Robinson, "Hermeneutic Since Barth," in J. Robinson and J. Cobb, eds., *The New Hermeneutic* (1964), pp. 1-77, the best orientation to the "new hermeneutic"; B. Smalley, *Study of the Bible in the Middle Ages* (1952); P. Stuhlmacher, *Vom Verstehen des NTs* (1979), a consistently fine history of interpretation from the early Church down to 1979.

Hermeneutical Books on the Bible: L. Berkhof, *Principles of Biblical Interpretation* (1952); K. Froer, *Biblische Hermeneutik* (1961); B. Ramm, *Protestant Biblical Interpretation* (rev. ed. 1956); M. S. Terry, *Biblical Hermeneutics* (2nd ed. 1890; repr. 1952).

Special Areas of Hermeneutics: The OT: C. Westermann, ed., *Essays in OT Hermeneutics* (Eng. tr. 1963); NT and OT: F. F. Bruce, *NT Development of OT Themes* (1968); D. P. Fuller, *Gospel and Law: Contrast or Continuum?* (1980); R. V. G. Tasker, *OT in the NT* (1957).

Biblical Theology: B. Childs, *Biblical Theology in Crisis* (1970); O. Cullmann, *Salvation in History* (Eng. tr. 1967); D. P. Fuller, "Biblical Theology and the Analogy of Faith," in R. Guelich, ed., *Unity and Diversity in the NT* (1978), pp. 195-213; *IDB*, I, *s.v.* "Biblical Theology, Contemporary" (K. Stendahl).

The Historical Method: G. W. Bromiley, *Biblical Criticism* (1948); D. P. Fuller, *Easter Faith and History* (1965); *Theologische Zeitschrift* 24 (1968), 93-101; E. Krentz, *The Historical-Critical Method* (1975); G. Maier, *The End of the Historical Method* (Eng. tr. 1977).

Structuralism: J. Barr, *BJRL*, 56 (1973/74), 10-33; *Interp.*, 27 (1974), entire issue devoted to structuralism; G. E. Bryce, "Structural Analysis of Didactic Texts," in G. A. Tuttle, ed., *Biblical and Near Eastern Studies* (1978), pp. 107-121; D. Patte, *What Is Structural Exegesis?* (1975).

Miscellaneous: D. P. Fuller, *Journal of the American Scientific Association*, 24 (1972), 47-51; "Holy Spirit's Role in Biblical Interpretation," in W. W. Gasque and W. S. LaSor, eds., *Scripture, Tradition, and Interpretation* (1978), pp. 189-198.

Roman Catholic Hermeneutics: R. S. Brown, "Hermeneutics," *Jerome Biblical Comm.* (1968), pp. 605-623; *Sensus Plenior in Sacred Scripture*, (1955); "Dogmatic Constitution on Divine Revelation," in A. Flannery, ed., *Documents of Vatican II*, (1965) pp. 750-765; *Rome and the Study of Scripture* (7th ed. 1964). Consists of texts of papal enactments concerning Scripture from 1893 (*Providentissimus Deus*) to just before Vatican II.

D. P. FULLER

INTERPRETATION OF TONGUES. *See* TONGUES, INTERPRETATION OF.

INTERPRETER [Heb. *mēlîṣ*]. In Gen. 42:23 the term denotes one who translates languages for another; but it can also be used in the sense of a mediator (Job 33:23) or ambassador (Isa. 43:27).

INTERTESTAMENTAL PERIOD.

I. Definition
II. World History
III. Jewish History
IV. MSS Discoveries
V. Theological Concepts

I. Definition.–The intertestamental period denotes here the history of postexilic Judaism from the time of the completion of the book of Malachi to the destruction of the temple of Jerusalem (A.D. 70). The period is characterized by the struggle of the Jews in Palestine to attain political and religious autonomy from a series of dominant foreign powers, by the emergence of different movements within Judaism (*see* DISPERSION; ESSENES; SADDUCEES; ZEALOT), by the process of hellenization carried on by the Macedonians and Romans, and finally by the emergence of Christianity.

Intertestamental Judaism was characterized, not by a continuing stream of OT prophecy, but by the interpretation of prophecy and revelation already given — the correct exposition and application of the OT to all areas of life. The Jews were aware of the cessation of prophecy. Josephus postulated the reign of Artaxerxes I — the Ahasuerus of the book of Esther (465-424 B.C.) — as the time when prophecy ceased (*CAp* i.8 [41]). This date concurs with the Mishnah (*Aboth* i.1), which names the men of the Great Synagogue — the scribes of Ezra's time — as the successors of the prophets (cf. 1 Macc. 4:46; 9:27; 14:41).

The OT canon probably closed before 400 B.C., though some scholars reject this position, postulating later dates for Joel, Jonah, and other OT books. In particular, Daniel is often considered a pseudepigraphon written after 167 B.C. But the appearance of fragments of the book of Daniel at Qumrân that are related paleographically to 1QIsa[a] argues for a date earlier than the Maccabean period (*see* ARAMAIC III; CANON OF THE OT; DANIEL, BOOK OF VI). By A.D. 70 the formation of the NT canon was well underway and Judaism and Christianity had parted company.

II. World History.–Persia and Greece were the dominant powers at the beginning of this period. Cyrus had founded the Persian dynasty (559-530 B.C.) and was succeeded in turn by Cambyses (530-522), Darius I (522-486), Xerxes I (486-465), and Artaxerxes I (465-424). Cambyses conquered Egypt in 525, but later attempts to extend rule over the Greek world failed when the Persians were defeated at Marathon (490), Salamis (480), and Plataea. Artaxerxes I was assassinated in 424 and Darius II ascended the throne.

A situation developed in which Persia attempted to play off the Greek city-states, especially Athens and Sparta, against each other. Infighting and intrigue, however, were also characteristic of Persian politics. Darius II sent his son Cyrus II to Sardis with instructions to give increased help to Sparta. While on this mission, however, Cyrus began collecting Greek mercenaries to further his own plans. In 403 Artaxerxes II, brother of Cyrus, ascended the throne. Cyrus soon attacked his brother's forces at Cunaxa and was defeated (401). The retreat of Cyrus's Greek mercenaries is described in Xenophon's *Anabasis;* most of them eventually joined the Spartans.

Egypt threw off Persian control and began its 30th Dynasty (380). The forces of Artaxerxes II, with the help of Greek mercenaries, attempted to reassert Persian rule in 373, but with mixed success. Artaxerxes III led a second attack in 343 that was victorious, terminating the rule of the pharaohs. The Persian Empire, however, was in a state of disintegration, with continual rebellions in the various satrapies. Artaxerxes III attempted to reorganize the Persian government when he came to the throne (358).

The rise of Macedonia was on the horizon. Philip II of Macedon (359-336), father of Alexander, first conquered the Greek cities of Pydna, Methone, and Amphipolis. He then incorporated into his alliance Thrace, Chalcidice, and Thessaly. The economy of this alliance, supplemented by mines at Pangaeum, enabled him to support a large standing army, which became the army of his son Alexander.

While attending the wedding feast of his daughter, Philip was murdered (336), and Alexander, age twenty, was elected as his father's successor. He crushed a revolt by Thebes (335) and began his assault against the Persians, defeating them first at the battle of Granicus (334). He met Darius III in battle at the river Issus (333) and defeated him, capturing his family. Alexander then moved to the south, conquering Tyre after a long siege (333/2) and arriving in Egypt in 332. He began the process of hellenization in the Near East by founding ALEXANDRIA, his largest colony. After leaving Egypt, Alexander defeated a vast army led by Darius, and thus became master of the Persian Empire. He penetrated as far east as India and then returned to Babylon, where he developed a fever and died (323).

Alexander's empire was divided among his generals, the *Diadochoi* ("successors"): Ptolemy (Egypt); Seleucus (Babylon and Syria); Antipater and his son Cassander (Macedonia and Greece); Antigonus (Phrygia and parts of Asia Minor), Lysimachus (Thrace and Pergamum); Eumanes (Pontus). A power struggle developed among them as they attempted to develop their own dynasties.

Palestine assumed the role of a buffer state between the domains of Ptolemy and Antigonus as it had centuries earlier between Egypt and Assyria. First Palestine was under Ptolemaic rule (320-198), but a Seleucid victory at Panion (200) began the period of Seleucid rule which lasted until the end of the Maccabean revolt when the Seleucid king Demetrius II granted Jewish independence and freedom from tribute (142). Antiochus IV tried unsuccessfully to reimpose tribute but his death in 128 brought a final end to the Seleucid dynasty.

The Jews enjoyed relative independence until 64, when Pompey annexed Syria as a province of Rome. Pompey proceeded to Jerusalem in 63 and the Jews came under Roman rule, losing their political independence until modern times. Pompey was killed in a civil clash with Julius Caesar (48), and shortly thereafter Caesar was assassinated (44). Octavian succeeded Caesar and defeated the rival forces of Mark Antony and Cleopatra at Actium (31). Tiberius succeeded Augustus (Octavian), and Caligula, Claudius, and Nero were emperors in turn. Nero, reigning from A.D. 54 to 68, initiated the persecution of Christians by the Roman state. Vespasian (69-79) succeeded Nero, and under his direction Titus conquered Jerusalem (70) and crushed Jewish resistance at Masada, ending the First Jewish Revolt. The final attempt by the Jews to throw off Roman rule was the Bar Cochba revolt during the reign of Hadrian (117-138), also unsuccessful (see H. E. L. Mellersh, *Chronology of the Ancient World* [1976], pp. 96-326).

The process of hellenization initiated by Alexander and continued later by the Romans was of central importance in this period. Its basis was the Greek practice of colonization, already current in classical times. In the Hellenistic period, soldiers were needed in distant areas under Greek control. Land was given to soldiers in return for military service, and this obligation passed to the occupant of the property in succeeding generations. By this method, a Greek population was attracted to cities of strategic or economic importance. Alexandria was Alexander's first and greatest colony, a trading and administrative center. Other cities developed by colonization included EPHESUS, founded by Ionian colonists in the classical period; CORINTH, refounded by the Romans as a colony in 44 B.C. after its destruction in 146; and PHILIPPI, subject to colonization by Alexander's father Philip in 356 and later by Antony and Augustus.

Such colonization brought with it the Greek language, Greek standards of weights and measures, coinage, and the gymnasium (Gk. *gymnásion*), which was a public facility for sports that also provided instruction in philosophy, literature, and music (see Hengel, I, 6-88; *Oxford Classical Dictionary, s.v.* "Colonization, Hellenistic" [A. T. Griffith], "Education" [F. A. G. Beck]).

III. Jewish History.–The rebuilding of the temple, completed in 516 B.C., was followed in the next century by the reforms of Ezra and Nehemiah. It is generally agreed that Nehemiah restored the walls of Jerusalem (444), stayed for twelve years, and then returned from Susa after a brief absence (*ca.* 430; Neh. 13:6f.). Ezra came to Jerusalem in 457, the seventh year of Artaxerxes I (Ezr. 7:1, 8), and collaborated with Nehemiah in 444 (Neh. 8:1). (For another view *see* EZRA; JERUSALEM III.F.1.) During this period, Malachi condemned the sins of an unrepentant nation and a corrupt priesthood, though a small remnant continued to follow in the footsteps of Ezra and Nehemiah (Mal. 3:16f.).

In Palestine during this obscure period the Jews and Samaritans became religiously and ethnically separated, a fact reflected in the Gospel narrative and still quaintly perpetuated by the contemporary Samaritan high priest at Nâblus. Earlier, Aramaic began to replace Hebrew as the vernacular. This development is discernible even within the canon, notably in the book of Daniel. From Alexander the Great onward, Judaism became increasingly threatened by the cultural forces of a highly intellectual Hellenism, both in Palestine and the Diaspora. Jewish resistance to such hellenization often explains the vast bulk of intertestamental literature, much of it valuable and fine, none of it canonical. The discerning reader perceives that divine guidance kept the right books within the compass of Scripture. Eventually, and gradually, Judaism manifested itself in the "Three Pillars of Judaism": the tripartite OT canon of Law, Prophets, and Writings; the synagogue, with its new, liturgical, and entirely nonsacrificial worship; and Rabbinism, which culminated in the Talmud and Midrash.

The Jerusalem temple and priesthood were corrupt in Malachi's day, but when Antiochus IV Epiphanes came to the Syrian throne in 175 B.C. their apostasy and deliberate policy of hellenization were even more notorious. The new monarch (nicknamed Epimanes, "the madman"), in a policy of forced hellenization, overestimated the extent to which he could insult the seemingly decadent Jewish religion; and in view of its official representatives, one cannot entirely blame him. From the still faithful remnant was sparked off the celebrated Maccabean revolt, led in turn by Mattathias, Judas Maccabeus, Jonathan, and Simon (168-135 B.C.) (*see* MACCABEES). Daniel's "abomination of desolation" was proximately and typically fulfilled in the erection by Antiochus Epiphanes (168) of an altar to the Olympian Zeus in the very temple of God, an action that fired the immediate revolt of Mattathias.

By their revolt, God's chosen people slowly regained a

precious if transitory freedom. This liberation culminated under Simon in 142 B.C., when they gained exemption from the taxes, virtually from the overlordship, of the Seleucids (1 Macc. 13:41f.). In gratitude to the deliverer, but in violation of the scriptural requirements of direct hereditary succession, the high priesthood, now Hasmonean, became invested and ratified in the person of Simon in 140. This break with tradition, however, was never wholly acceptable to the pious and orthodox, and it was a cause of later frictions. Simon's life ended tragically; he was murdered in 134 by his son-in-law, an ambitious hellenizer. But his son John Hyrcanus, another intended victim, escaped and became his successor (*see* HASIDEANS; HASMONEANS).

During the long dominion of John Hyrcanus (134-104), who was virtually king as well as high priest, the Pharisaic and Sadducean parties became clearly differentiated, with their respective legal and priestly emphases. John abruptly transferred his allegiance from the first to the second. We have seen already that his high priesthood was not entirely satisfactory to the orthodox; neither was his kingship, so far as monarchy could be acceptable at all in a theocratic and covenant community, for he was not of the house and lineage of David. The quarrel with the Pharisees probably flared up on these grounds. There followed the brief reign of Aristobulus I, and the lengthy one of Alexander Janneus (102-76). Alexander, able and successful in many political respects, entirely alienated the Pharisees by his obvious personal unfitness for the high priesthood. Pelted with citrons by the common people for a technical and ritual mistake, he retaliated with defiance and massacre (Josephus *Ant.* xiii.13.5 [372-76]). At the close of his life, he counseled his queen and successor Alexandra Salome to make peace with the Pharisees. This she did, according them increased powers in the Sanhedrin, which they retained right into NT days (*Ant.* xiii.16.1 [405]). Her son Aristobulus usurped the place and power of his older brother Hyrcanus and reigned till 63 B.C. Then Pompey intervened, and Palestine, shorn of its recent conquests, was integrated into the Roman province of Syria.

The first phase of Roman domination in Palestine extended from 63 till 37, and then as later the Jews were uneasy under the yoke. Pompey entered the holy of holies in 63, though he seems merely to have looked around, and Crassus, proconsul of Syria, plundered the temple treasury in 54 (*Ant.* xiv.4.4 [72]; 7.1 [105-109]). During most of this period Hyrcanus II, a pitifully ineffective puppet, held nominal rule, civil and ecclesiastical. Freed from his younger brother, yet now subject to the Roman governor, he tended to delegate such real power as he possessed to the Idumean Antipater, whose Edomite origins gave the deepest offense to Jewish sentiment. The incumbency of Hyrcanus ended pathetically after more than twenty years, when his intending successor Antigonus confined him in bonds and then bit deeply into his ears, thereby rendering him ritually unfit for office (Josephus *BJ* i.13.9 [270]). Antigonus himself did not last very long, and with him the Hasmonean line came to its end. HEROD, a son of Antipater and therefore also of Edomite blood, secured the backing of Rome in 40 B.C., and was able three years later to consolidate his kingship over a torn and troubled Palestine. During his rivalry with Antigonus he had used and equipped the fortress of Masada W of the Dead Sea.

Herod, rightly or wrongly styled "the Great," was capable, loyal to Rome, and reasonably successful in his control of Palestine. But his political leanings, his Idumean blood, and his ten wives did not commend him to Jewish subjects. He rebuilt in lavish manner the Jerusalem temple, but the heathen sanctuaries that were also indebted to his munificence suggest religious views mixed or skeptical. Filson (p. 22) sums him up by remarking trenchantly, "He preserved order almost everywhere except in his polygamous palace." Since Herod features prominently in the Matthaean Infancy narratives, his death in 4 B.C. gives a date before which Jesus must have been born. The domains granted to his sons, the various Roman procuratorships in Palestine, in short, the general affairs of relevant history down to about the mid-60's A.D., are well known and need not be recapitulated here.

About A.D. 66, warned by such predictions as Mk. 13:14, the Christians in Jerusalem fled to Pella. This was the beginning — perhaps effectively the end — of the split between Church and synagogue. The prolonged siege of Jerusalem by Titus followed, culminating in A.D. 70 in the butchery of Jews in the Holy City, and in the total ruin of the cherished temple, even as Christ had predicted (Mk. 13:2).

The conquest of Titus was virtually final, but there were pockets of resistance. Nine hundred sixty Jewish men, women, and children gathered on the summit of the old Herodian fortress of Masada; on the east side was a sheer drop of about 400 m. (1300 ft.) to the Dead Sea. From here they defied, almost successfully, the embattled might of Rome. Flavius Silva and his men nearly retired in frustration and defeat. But wind, fire, and catapult stones at last smashed the Jewish defenses; and the conquering legions proudly mounted the high platform, only to find that the defenders had committed suicide. Yigael Yadin, with others, uncovered the skeletons of these people in the 1960's; he aptly calls them an "undying symbol of desperate courage" (*EAEHL,* III, 806, 810f.).

Outside of Jerusalem, Judaism assumed slightly different forms. The Qumrân community, associated by some scholars with the Essenes, carried on its own kind of scriptural exegesis and religious practice with the belief that they were a righteous remnant living in the last days. Large numbers of Jews made up the Dispersion (Gk. *diasporá*), i.e., those who were scattered throughout the countries outside Palestine. Such a group lived on the island of Elephantine in the Nile, close to modern Aswân. Their recovered documents, the famous Aramaic papyri edited by Cowley, reflect their affairs for the quarter century ending in 399 B.C. Thereafter, they disappear from recorded history. Other important Jewish communities existed in Alexandria, Rome, Antioch, and numerous cities in Asia Minor (see Safrai and Stern, I, 117-215; Smallwood, pp. 120-143, 201-255).

IV. MSS Discoveries.–Discoveries of MSS fragments at various locations in Palestine have made a great contribution to the study of this period. The scrolls found at Qumrân consist of Scripture texts and commentaries; Hebrew and Aramaic portions or transcripts of apocryphal, targumic, and pseudepigraphical literature, some of it previously known only in Greek; sectarian documents that had long disappeared; etc. This recovered Essene library is filling many gaps in intertestamental history and Christian antecedents and forms an immensely valuable area of biblical study (*see* DEAD SEA SCROLLS).

Other Judean caves have yielded fragmentary MSS, letters, and coins. Remains of Greek, Hebrew, and Aramaic MSS from the Cave of Horror (Naḥal Heber) include a fragmentary Greek translation of the Minor Prophets closer to the MT than the LXX. The caves at Naḥal Ṣe'elim yielded a small parchment containing Ex. 13:1-16 in a form almost identical to the MT. More impressive are the discoveries from the Cave of Letters: small fragments of Pss. 15–16, Nu. 20:7f., and letters written by Simon Bar Cochba to his cohorts. The cave at Wâdī Murabba'ât con-

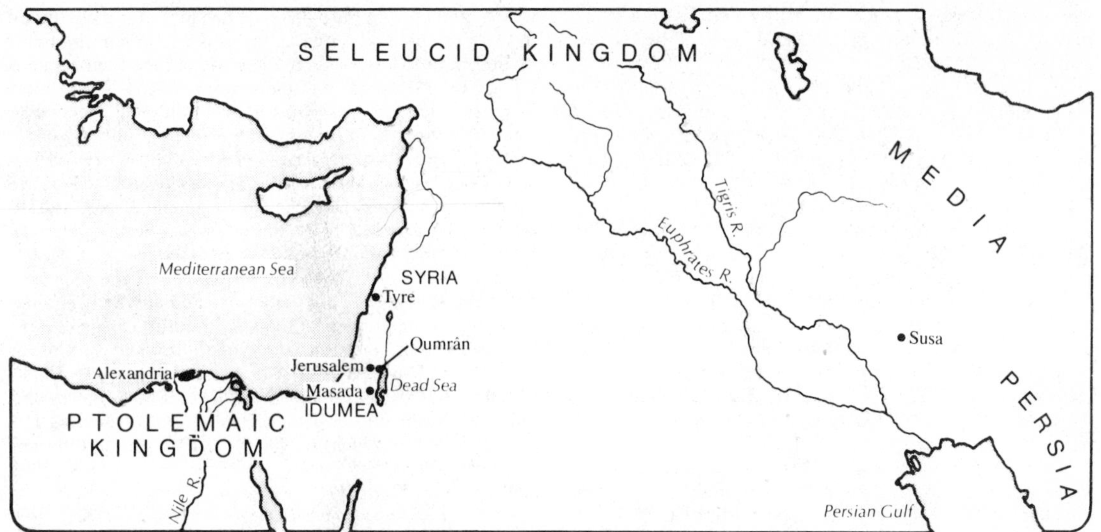

tained a scroll of the Minor Prophets, other biblical books, and papyri in Greek, Latin, and Arabic. The excavations carried on at Masada (1963-65) under the direction of Y. Yadin discovered fragments of biblical scrolls including Genesis, Leviticus, Deuteronomy, and Ezekiel. Nonbiblical fragments included a small portion of the book of Jubilees in Hebrew and large fragments of chs. 39–44 of the Hebrew original of Sirach. A Hebrew text of Sirach was found in the Cairo Genizah in 1910, and some scholars hotly disputed its genuineness, stigmatizing it as a late translation from the Greek; but this MS from Masada has proved them wrong. Some argue that this book would have been included in the canon had its original been known at the right time (see *EAEHL,* III, 665-694, 812-14).

V. Theological Concepts.–Intertestamental Judaism in Palestine particularly included quiet orthodoxy, fierce Zealot nationalism, subconscious assimilation, and decadent hellenization. OT theology advanced in certain respects, with important NT consequences, partly by internal development, partly by naturalization of Zoroastrian and other elements. Diaspora Jews, devout if less strictly orthodox, attempted allegorically and otherwise to blend Greek philosophy with Hebraic tradition — the extreme example is the Alexandrian Philo. Usually the amalgam was recognizably Jewish. In 1909 Schürer exhaustively examined the Palestinian (*HJP,* II/3, 1-155) and the Hellenistic (II/3, 156-381) literature. To the Apocrypha, Pseudepigrapha, Josephus, and Diaspora literature must now be added the Dead Sea Scrolls. (These topics are discussed elsewhere in this encyclopedia under their separate titles. On rabbinic Judaism, oral and secondary at this state, supremely important later, *see* COMMENTARIES, HEBREW; TALMUD; TARGUM.)

Loyalty to external Judaism reached its pinnacle in the Masada martyrs (see III above); in the butchered thousand who would not break the sabbath by resisting attack (1 Macc. 2:29-38; cf. 2 Macc. 6:11); and in those who endured torture and death, rather than break the law by eating pork (1 Macc. 2:61f.; 2 Macc. 6:18-31; 7:1-42). The same spirit sent the Qumrân covenanters to the stricter life of the desert. Aristobulus (104-103 B.C.) exercised on Galileans and neighboring Ituraeans a policy of forcible Judaizing by circumcision, though this was somewhat rare (cf. Mt. 4:15). At the opposite extreme were skeptical hellenizers such as those sporting youths under Antiochus Epiphanes, naked runners so apostate from Judaism as to submit to surgical uncircumcision — Gk. *akrobystía* means foreskin, hence by metonymy the artificial restoration thereof (1 Macc. 1:15; Asm.Mos. 8).

Intertestamental Jewish literature, historically and theologically important, often differs in content from the books that Protestantism considers inspired. Protestantism excludes all of it from the canon, and thus rejects prayers for the dead (2 Macc. 12:43-45) and a doctrine of salvation by works (2 Esd. 7:77; Tob. 4:9-11; etc.), concepts found in the Roman Catholic Church, which regards these books as canonical. That humanistic commonplace of rabbinic Judaism, the good and evil impulse in man, is found in germ. The *cor malignum* of 2 Esd. 3:20 (NEB "wicked heart") foreshadows the evil impulse (cf. vv. 48, 92; Gen. 8:21); for the so-called good impulse, cf. Sir. 1:14.

Noncanonical apocalyptic, child of OT prophecy, emphasizes national and individual judgment, eternal rewards and punishments, usually postulating imminent eschatological climax. These apocryphal apocalypses — symbolic, dualistic, esoteric, usually pseudonymous, and "history in the guise of prediction" — claimed that they had been written by Moses, Enoch, or some ancient worthy, and hidden since that author's time for this very emergency — a claim intolerable within the inspired canon and to modern believers yet widely accepted at that time. Such writers of such works, feeling deep spiritual affinity with their prototypes, possessed a unitary Hebraic time sense, with a weakened apprehension of chronological separation. They believed themselves to be God's chosen instruments to build up the people in dark days. Within Judaism, apocalyptic lost its place to Rabbinism after A.D. 70, yet profoundly influenced Christian theology, where it reached its high-water mark in the book of Revelation. For apocalyptists and time, see Thorleif Boman, *Hebrew Thought Compared with Greek* (Eng. tr. 1960); D. S. Russell, *Apocalyptic,* pp. 205-223.

Intertestamental Jewry sought to approach the transcendent God through intermediaries; thus angelology became elaborated. In the Ezra Apocalypse (2 Esd. 3–10) the prophet is instructed by the archangel Uriel (cf. canonical Zechariah), and also by Tobit and Enoch. Evil, rebellious angels, including Satan under his various designations, also came to prominence. In certain sources (cf. 1 Enoch; Jubilees) the fallen angels who united themselves to human females are designated "watchers." They, not God, are the source of evil, which has an extent much wider than this terrestrial globe. In other sources evil is explained by Adam's original transgression, or by the evil impulse in mankind.

A conception resembling the doctrine of original sin, consistently bypassed by later rabbinic Judaism, is found in 2 Esd. 4:30-32; 7:11, 48, 118; these passages should be compared with key phrases in 1 Cor. 15. Individual responsibility is also stressed, in the spirit of Ezk. 18 (2 Esd. 7:102-106; cf. vv. 112-15). Into this doctrine the idea of the treasury of merits inconsistently intrudes (7:77). Comparable with Mt. 7:13f. is the stern doctrine of majority damnation; some apocryphal devices to justify the ways of God to man are not appealing (7:49-61; 8:1-3, 40f.). The writer also stresses (8:55-60) that most people have abused their free will, spurned God's law, and brought condemnation upon themselves. Original sin is implied clearly in Sir. 8:5; 25:24; cf. also Wisd. 10:1. The possibility of avoiding direct transgression, or sin with a high hand, is stressed in Tob. 4:5.

Vitally important are the interconnected concepts of Word and Wisdom. The creative Word goes back by implication to the repeated "and God said" of Gen. 1, but assumes firmer contours in the constantly recurring paraphrastic *Memra* of the Targums — cf. sample passages translated in TARGUM. The Greek form *lógos* began probably with the pagan Heraclitus (*ca.* 500 B.C.), passed through the hands of the Stoics several centuries later, reappeared in theological form in Philo of Alexandria (d. A.D. 40), then found its highest expression in Jn. 1:1-14. In classical Greek philosophy, logos meant roughly the rational principle undergirding the universe and its lifestream; for Philo, who intermingled metaphysics with revealed religion, the concept, still impersonal, came to mean the rational thought of God, the impress of His creative power on the scheme of things. John ascribes all this and infinitely more to the incarnate Son. The analogous concept of Wisdom, created by God and personified, begins canonically with Prov. 8:22-31, becoming more sharply etched in Sir. 1:1-10; Wisd. 7:22-26. The latter passage makes Wisdom "a pure effluence from the glory of the Almighty... the flawless mirror of the active power of God and the image of his goodness" (NEB). The creative Word is found in Wisd. 9:1f., the decreeing Word in 18:15.

There are three levels of Jewish future expectation — a revived, extended "Golden Age" Davidic kingdom in Palestine; a catastrophic, destructive climax to this world (cf. 2 Pet. 3:5-11), with an eternal age supervening; and the two combined, the first reappearing as some kind of millennium. The popular first view falls below ESCHATOLOGY proper, but explains some reactions to the ministry of Jesus (cf. Jn. 6:15; Acts 1:6). Bultmann describes apocalyptic eschatology as "a pessimistic-dualistic view of the Satanic corruption of the total world-complex" — but this tabloid statement must not be too blindly generalized.

Outstanding in Christian interest is the eschatology of 2 Esdras. The age to come is first delineated as succeeding this one without pause or interval (6:7-10). Messiah is to appear, inaugurating a reduced "millennium" of four hundred years, after which he, and all living beings, will die. Then after seven days of the silence of death will come a general resurrection, followed by divine judgment (7:28-36). The bliss of paradise is briefly described (8:52-54). These passages should be compared with Dnl. 12; Rev. 20–21; etc. Chapter 6 must mean that there is no interval between the present age and Messiah's glorious earthly reign — otherwise it would contradict ch. 7. A thousand-year millennium is found in the Slavonic Enoch, one of indefinite length in 2 Baruch. Angelology, the precosmic angelic fall, final judgment, the destruction of the world, and eternal bliss and woe are more fully portrayed in the Ethiopic and Slavonic versions of Enoch; the latter incorporates the celestial architecture of the seven heavens (cf. 2 Cor. 12:2-4). The Assumption of Moses (*ca.* 4 B.C.) has probable Qumrânic links. Its lost ending is, according to some scholars, quoted in Jude 9.

Apocalyptic writers frequently recognized two Messiahs, one associated with the priestly tribe of Levi, the other with the royal Davidic tribe of Judah. This is carried over (with variations) into the Dead Sea Scrolls (cf. 1QS 9:11) and into Talmud and Midrash (see R. A. Stewart, *Rabbinic Theology* [1961], pp. 46-53). Under the new covenant the Messiah is, of course, one and unique. There is, however, a dual strain in the OT, the Suffering Servant, who reflects the passion, atonement, and substitution of Christ's first advent (Isa. 42:1-4; 49:4-9; 50:4-9; 52:13–53:12) and the Son of man, who will come with power and judgment at the end of the age (Dnl. 7:13f.), reflecting His second advent (cf. Isa. 63:1-6; Rev. 19:11-16; and innumerable parallels).

See Vol. I, Maps XII-XVI.

See also ALEXANDER THE GREAT; JOSEPHUS, FLAVIUS; PHILO JUDAEUS.

Bibliography.–F. F. Bruce, *Israel and the Nations* (2nd ed. 1969), pp. 112-240; *NT History* (1969); J. H. Charlesworth, *Pseudepigrapha and Modern Research* (1976); W. H. Davies and E. A. McDowell, *Source Book of Interbiblical History* (1948); S. Dubnov, *History of the Jews,* I (Eng. tr. 1967), 447-904; F. V. Filson, *NT History* (1965); W. Förster, *From the Exile to Christ* (Eng. tr., 2nd ed. 1967); *Palestinian Judaism in NT Times* (Eng. tr. 1964); R. Furneaux, *Roman Siege of Jerusalem* (1973); F. C. Grant, *Roman Hellenism and the NT* (1962); M. Grant, *Jews in the Roman World* (1973); M. Hengel, *Judaism and Hellenism* (2 vols., Eng. tr. 1975); *HJP*[2]; *HNNT; IB,* VII, 75-113; J. Jeremias, *Jerusalem in the Time of Jesus* (Eng. tr., 3rd ed. 1969); W. S. McCullough, *History and Literature of the Palestinian Jews from Cyrus to Herod* (1975); A. D. Nock, *Conversion* (1933, repr. 1961); *ORHI,* II; D. S. Russell, *Between the Testaments* (1960); *Method and Message of Jewish Apocalyptic* (1964); *The Jews from Alexander to Herod* (1967); S. Safrai and M. Stern, eds., *The Jewish People in the First Century,* section one of *Compendia Rerum Judaicarum ad Novum Testamentum* (1974); E. M. Smallwood, *The Jews under Roman Rule,* vol. I of J. Neusner, ed., *Studies in Judaism and Late Antiquity* (1976); W. W. Tarn, *Hellenistic Civilization* (3rd ed. 1952); Y. Yadin, *Masada* (Eng. tr. 1966); *IEJ,* 7 (1957), 1-65 and plates; 15 (1965), 1-120 and plates; S. Zeitlin, *Rise and Fall of the Judean State* (2 vols., 2nd ed. 1967).

R. A. STEWART
R. J. W.

INTREAT. Archaic term used in the AV for ENTREAT.

INVESTIGATE; INVESTIGATION [Heb. piel of *bāqaš* (Est. 2:23), *ḥēqer* (Job 34:24); Gk. *zētéō* (Acts 25:20)]; AV INQUISITION (Est. 2:23), "without number" (Job 34:24), "such a manner of questions" (Acts 25:20); NEB also INQUIRY (Job 34:24), "discussions" (Acts 25:20). *See* INQUIRE.

INVISIBLE [Gk. *aóratos*–'unseen' (Rom. 1:20; Col. 1:15f.; 1 Tim. 1:17; He. 11:27)]. This term is used as an attribute of God in every biblical occurrence except Col. 1:16, where it refers to ranks of unseen angels and other spiritual powers. That no one had seen God at Sinai is stated in the OT (Ex. 34:20; Dt. 4:12), and, in spite of God's special self-disclosure to Moses (Ex. 33:18-23; Nu. 14:14), it became axiomatic in Judaism that no one had seen or could see God in this present age (SB, II, 362f.; cf. Mt. 5:8). The influence of this concept is reflected in the Johannine writings, with their emphasis that "no one has seen God" (Jn. 1:18; 5:37; 6:46; 14:9; 1 Jn. 4:12), and in the Pauline tradition as well (Rom. 1:20; Col. 1:15f.; 1 Tim. 1:17; 3:16). The use of *aóratos* in the context of a doxology (1 Tim.

1:17) and in an adjectival clause with the pronoun "who" ("who is invisible"; He. 11:27) shows that "invisible" was one of the ascriptions to God used in early Christian liturgy (*see* GOD, ASCRIPTIONS TO). R. J. W.

INVITE [Heb. *qārā'* (Nu. 25:2; Josh. 24:9; 1 K. 1:9; etc.); Gk. *kaléō* (Lk. 7:39; 14:8; 1 Cor. 10:27; etc.), *hoi keklēménoi* (Mt. 22:4; Lk. 14:7; etc.), *parakaléō* (Acts 8:31; 28:14), *antikaléō* (Lk. 14:12), *phonéō* (Lk. 14:12; cf. Mt. 20:32)]; AV also CALL (Isa. 13:3; Lam. 2:22; Lk. 14:12; etc.), BID (Mt. 22:9; Lk. 14:12, 17; etc.), DESIRED (Acts 8:31; 28:14); NEB also SUMMON (Lam. 2:22), ASK (Lk. 14:12f.), THOSE WHO WERE INVITED (Lk. 14:24), GUESTS (Lk. 14:17; Jn. 2:2), COMPANY (1 S. 9:13, 22). The Heb. *qārā'* can mean call or summon, hence invite, especially in cultic contexts (e.g., 1 S. 9:13, 22). The Gk. *kaléō* with the passive participle *keklēménoi* corresponds to the Hebrew usage: "call," "invited guests." The compound form *antikaléō,* occurring in the NT only in Lk. 14:12, means "be invited again," and *parakaléō* literally means "call to one's side," hence summon or invite (Acts 8:31; 28:14; cf. Mt. 20:28).

Israel is cautioned in Ex. 34:15 against accepting invitations (LXX *kaléō*) to the sacrificial worship of other nations in which the sacrifices are eaten by the participants. Paul may be alluding to this passage, among others (cf. Dt. 32:17), as he admonishes the Corinthians concerning participation in the meals and worship of unbelievers (1 Cor. 10:20-29). Sometimes an invitation is quoted (e.g., Gen. 18:3-5; 19:2; Jgs. 19:9; Lk. 24:29; Acts 16:15) or a visit is announced (e.g., Lk. 19:5). Often servants were used to convey the invitation (Mt. 22:3f., 8). Ancient invitations written on papyri have been studied by C.-H. Kim (*JBL,* 94 [1975], 391-402).

See also ENTERTAIN. R. J. W.

INWARD MAN (AV Rom. 7:22; 2 Cor. 4:16). *See* INNER MAN.

INWARD PART. An expression in the OT, occurring only in Ps. 139:13 (Heb. *kilyâ;* AV REINS) and Mic. 6:14 (Heb. *qereḇ;* AV MIDST; NEB STOMACH). The former term occurred only in the plural, and denoted either the kidneys as such (cf. Ex. 29:13, 22) or the interior of the abdomen in general, in which the most secret part of man was held to be located (Ps. 7:10; Jer. 11:20; etc.). *Qereḇ* (Akk. *qirbu*) also referred in a broad sense to the contents of the abdominal cavity, and was regarded symbolically as the seat of laughter (Gen. 18:12) or thought (Jer. 4:14). It was clearly an area of emotional sensitivity and reaction (cf. AV "bowels of mercies," Col. 3:12), whose receptive functions were the gift of the Creator. R. K. H.

IOB yōb [Heb. *yôḇ*]; AV JOB. Third son of Issachar (Gen. 46:13). In parallel passages (Nu. 26:24; 1 Ch. 7:1) the name is Jashub (Heb. *yāšûḇ*), which the versions in Genesis also support as the correct form.

IOTA ī-ōt'ə [Gk. *iōta*] (Mt. 5:18); AV JOT; NEB LETTER. The English transliteration of the Gk. *iōta* (ι), the ninth (originally the tenth) letter of the Greek alphabet. *Iōta* is the nearest equivalent of the Heb. *yōḏ* (י), the tenth letter of the Hebrew alphabet. The DOT also mentioned here (Gk. *keraía,* "horn") is the smallest projection of any part of a letter, or an accent or breathing mark of a text (cf. Lk. 16:17). The sense, therefore, of Mt. 5:18 is "not the smallest letter or even the smallest part of a letter will be abolished in the law or the prophets until all things are accomplished." The statement is based on the practice, well known at the time, of the copying of Hebrew and Aramaic texts by scribes.

See Bauer, rev., pp. 386, 428. B. S. EASTON R. J. W.

IPHDEIAH if-dē'yə [Heb. *yipdᵉyâ*–'Yah(weh) redeems']; AV, NEB, IPHEDEIAH. A descendant of Benjamin (1 Ch. 8:25).

IPHTAH if'tə [Heb. *yiptaḥ*]; AV JIPHTAH. An unidentified town in the Shephelah of Judah, named with Libnah, Ether, and Ashan (Josh. 15:43). It may be modern Tarqūmīya, about 10 km. (6 mi.) NW of Hebron.

IPHTAHEL if'tə-el [Heb. *yiptaḥ-'ēl*–'God shall open' or 'may God open']; AV JIPHTHAH-EL; NEB JIPHTAH-EL. A valley in Galilee, described as the western boundary of the tribal allotment of Zebulun (Josh. 19:14) and as the place where the allotment of Asher touches Zebulun (v. 27). F.-M. Abel (*GP,* I, 398) rejects the identification with Wâdī el-Qurein as too far north and Wâdī 'Abellin as unimportant. He finds the reasons on which Dalman selected Wâdī el-Melek unconvincing and opts for *Sahl el-Baṭṭôf,* "which moreover is traversed by the upper course of Wâdī el-Malik." Sahl el-Baṭṭôf (Biq'ath Beth Neṭôphah) is a broad valley running NE-SW, 11 km. (7 mi.) N of Nazareth, but the meeting point of Asher and Zebulun would probably be located NW of Nazareth. The modern 1:100,000 map of the State of Israel marks *Ḥ. Yiptaḥ'ēl* 1 km. (0.6 mi.) SW of where Biq'ath Beth Neṭôphah and the highway northwest from Nazareth intersect (coordinates 171.240). *See* ASHER. W. S. L. S.

IR ir [Heb. *'îr*]. A descendant of Benjamin (1 Ch. 7:12), called Iri in v. 7.

IRA ī'rə [Heb. *'îrā'*; Gk. *Eiras*].

1. A person referred to in 2 S. 20:26 as a priest (AV "a chief ruler") of David. The RSV translation is the only possible one; but, according to the text, Ira was "a Jairite," and thus of the tribe of Manasseh (Nu. 32:41) and not eligible to the priesthood. On the basis of the Peshitta some would correct "Jairite" of 2 S. 20:26 into "Jattirite," referring to Jattir, a priestly city within the territory of Judah (Josh. 21:14). Others point to 2 S. 8:18, "David's sons were priests," as an indication that in David's time some non-Levites were permitted to serve — in some sense — as priests.

2. An Ithrite, or (with a different pointing of the text) a Jattirite, one of David's thirty mighty men (2 S. 23:38 par. 1 Ch. 11:40); possibly identical with **1.**

3. Another of David's thirty mighty men, son of Ikkesh of Tekoa (2 S. 23:26; 1 Ch. 11:28) and a captain of the temple guard (1 Ch. 27:9). F. K. FARR

IRAD ī'rad [Heb. *'îrāḏ*]. Grandson of Cain and son of Enoch (Gen. 4:18).

IRAM ī'ram [Heb. *'îrām*]. A "clan chief" of Edom (Gen. 36:43 par. 1 Ch. 1:54).

IR-HA-HERES. *See* CITY OF THE SUN.

IRI ī'rī [Heb. *'îrî*]. *See* IR; URIAS.

IRIJAH i-rī'jə [Heb. *yir'îyāyh*–'Yahweh sees']. A captain at the gate of Benjamin in Jerusalem, who arrested Jeremiah the prophet on suspicion of intending to desert to the Chaldeans (Jer. 37:13f.).

IR-MELACH (Josh. 15:62, NEB). *See* SALT, CITY OF.

IRNAHASH ir-nā′hash [Heb. *ʿîr nāḥāš*–'city of (the) serpent(-god)'; Gk. *póleōs naas*–'city of Na(h)as'] (1 Ch. 4:12). A person or a city. The passage in 1 Chronicles is a genealogy of the descendants of Judah, and Tehinnah is named as the father of Irnahash. This statement, taken alone, could mean that Tehinnah founded the city of Nahash, but the preceding context deals only with fathers and their offspring. The LXX, however, whether from an ancient tradition or from misunderstanding of the Hebrew (i.e., taking *ʿîr nāḥāš* literally), translates "city of Naas" and thus raises the problem of identifying such a city.

The reading in 1 Ch. 4:14, "Joab [was] the father of Ge-harashim ["valley of craftsmen"], so called because they were craftsmen," lends support to the interpretation that Irnahash, like Ge-harashim, is not a personal name. Heb. *nāḥāš* is cognate with *n^eḥōšeṯ,* "copper" (Dt. 8:9, etc.), and with *n^eḥuštān,* "bronze serpent" (2 K. 18:4), although BDB derives them from separate roots (with no supporting evidence); hence it is possible to translate Irnahash as "copper city" or Cypropolis. Aharoni (*LBHG,* p. 224) describes it as an Edomite city, in the northeastern part of the Arabah (p. 33). Until it is determined whether Irnahash is a person or a place, attempts to locate a place are academic. W. S. LASOR

IRON [Heb. *barzel*; Aram. *parzel* (Dnl. 2:33ff.; 4:15 [MT 12], 23 [MT 20]; 5:4, 23; 7:7, 19); Akk. *parzillu*; Ugar. *brḏl*; Phoen. *brzl*; Hitt. *barzillu*; all loanwords deriving from Sum. BAR.GAL; Gk. *sídēros,* adj. *sidḗreos*].

- I. Beginning of Ironworking
  - A. Egypt
  - B. Mesopotamia
  - C. Anatolia
  - D. Syria-Palestine
- II. Iron in the Pentateuch
  - A. Tubal-cain
  - B. Og's Iron Bed
  - C. Palestine's Iron Ore
- III. Iron as a Symbol

I. Beginning of Ironworking.*–A. Egypt*. Modern archeology has brought to light iron objects in the form of tools, implements, weapons, and jewelry from as far back as predynastic and early dynastic Egypt. Jewelry in the form of iron beads from the predynastic period came from Gerzah. Iron tools and an iron plate were found embedded in the masonry of the pyramid of Cheops and the pyramid temple of Mendure (Mycerinos), both of the 4th Dynasty (*ca.* 2500 B.C.). A lump of iron from Abydos dated to the 6th Dynasty (*ca.* 2200 B.C.) differs from the meteoric iron used by primitive man. The low nickel content has led A. Lucas to conclude that it is made of nonmeteoric iron and R. Forbes suggests that it may have been manufactured as a by-product of the process of refining gold. Other iron objects come from the 11th (*ca.* 2000 B.C.) and the 18th dynasties (*ca.* 1500 B.C.). The meteoric origin of early iron in Egypt is directly implied by its Egyptian name, "metal of heaven," but iron was originally also produced as a by-product of gold. Literary evidence for the early use of iron comes from various Egyptian texts and the Amarna Letters (14th cent. B.C.).

B. Mesopotamia. In Mesopotamia chance survivals of iron objects have been found primarily from the ruins of Ur, Tell Chagar Bazar, Tell Asmar, and Mari from the first half of the 3rd millennium B.C. An iron dagger of Ur from the 3rd millennium B.C. is made of meteoric iron. The Sumerian ideogram for iron and the later derivative cuneiform signs point again to the celestial (meteoric) origin of iron. However, an iron dagger blade from Tell Asmar in Iraq (*ca.* 2800 B.C.) is shown to be of man-smelted iron (Maryon, p. 173). Thus there is evidence that

Dagger with iron blade, gold and glass handle, rock-crystal knob, and gold sheath, from the tomb of Tutankhamen (Egyptian Museum, Cairo; picture Lehnert and Landrock)

iron in small quantities was produced from terrestrial ores. There is also a considerable amount of literary evidence for iron in early times in documents many of which are from the time of Hammurabi (18th cent. B.C.).

C. Anatolia. The earliest evidence is an iron sword from Alaca Hüyük, near Ankara, from *ca.* 2400-2100 B.C. The reason for the scarcity of iron objects, even from the time of the Hittites (*ca.* 1400-1200 B.C.), may be explained by the oxidation of iron in wet climates. It is quite certain that the art of iron smelting was discovered by the Hittites of Anatolia at *ca.* 1400 B.C. Thus iron was in the ancient Near East both a newcomer and a metal known of old. There is literary evidence from the time of the Hittite king Hattusilis III (1289-1265 B.C.) which indicates that the Hittite territory was the source of iron for Assyria in the 13th cent. B.C. (Gurney, p. 83). It seems that the Hittites maintained a monopoly on iron until their final destruction *ca.* 1200 B.C. Then Hittite ironsmiths settled here and there in the ancient Near East, taking with them their trade secrets.

D. Syria-Palestine. An iron inset in a gold ring from Byblos comes from as early as *ca.* 1825 B.C. At Ugarit an iron battle-axe was discovered from the 15th-14th cent. B.C., but in the 14th cent. B.C. iron in Ugarit was apparently more expensive than silver (*Syria,* 30 [1953], 194). It is generally believed that the Philistines introduced iron into Syria-Palestine, but if the Philistines came from Crete rather than from the north (Anatolia), this hypothesis is difficult to maintain (see Winnett).

The OT literary evidence contributes significantly to a more complete understanding of the availability and use of iron in Syria-Palestine. On one occasion Israelite soldiers under the leadership of Moses returned from combat against the combined Midianite forces and brought with them rich spoils among which was iron (Nu. 31:22). The iron and other metal objects captured at the destruction of Jericho were dedicated to Yahweh (Josh. 6:24). On another occasion the Israelites were allowed to divide among themselves the iron and other spoils taken from their Canaanite enemies (Josh. 22:8). The possession of "iron chariots" (*see* IRONSMITH) by the Canaanites proved to be a major obstacle in Joshua's conquest of Beth-shean, the Valley of Jezreel, and the coastal plain (Josh. 17:16, 18; Jgs. 1:19). During the time of the judges Israel was sorely oppressed by the "iron chariots" of the Canaanite king Jabin of Hazor (Jgs. 4:2f.). The early references to iron from the time of the Conquest clearly indicate that the Canaanites were in possession of iron before the invasion of the sea-peoples (Philistines) *ca.* 1200 B.C. Later passages show indisputably, however, that the Philistines were able to establish and enjoy a local monopoly on the production and sale of iron which gave them an unusual advantage that they knew how to exploit (1 S. 17). The Philistines prevented Israel from the manufacture of iron weapons and tools in order to protect their own monopoly on iron and made Israel dependent on Philistine ironsmiths for all services (1 S. 13:19-22). Iron was still not plentiful in Israel at that time.

The first material evidence for iron in Palestine in well-authenticated associations consists of an iron dagger, an iron knife, and iron jewelry from Late Bronze tombs (late 12th or early 11th cent. B.C.) of Tell el-Fâr'ah (Sharuhen). Also from twelfth- and eleventh-century-B.C. tombs (nos. 58, 84, 85) at Gezer came various iron implements. At Megiddo the Canaanite city of stratum VI yielded an iron dagger and an iron knife from about 1150 B.C. At Beth-shemesh iron objects in the form of weapons, jewelry, ornaments, and tools date from the late 11th cent. B.C. (stratum III). The excavations at Gerar yielded a number of iron objects (dagger, lance-head, knife) from the 11th cent. B.C. An iron plough-tip was found at Saul's Gibeah (11th cent. B.C.). Iron was introduced at Tell el-Ḥesī and at Lachish before the 10th cent. B.C.

An authentic ancient iron mine on the soil of Palestine is the one at Mugharet el-Wardeh not far from Tulûl edh-Dhahab, the ancient Penuel. The reference to the bed of iron of Og, king of Bashan (Dt. 3:11), points to the working of this mine, or some other in that part of Transjordan, as early as the time of Moses, or earlier. Tell Deir 'allā (Succoth?) has revealed an advanced metallurgical industry for smelting and casting of iron and copper both prior to and after the time of Solomon (cf. 1 K. 7:45; 2 Ch. 4:17). The presence of iron slag at the mining and smelting camps along the Wâdī el-'Arabah is evidence that iron ore was mined and smelted there during the Iron Age. In Cisjordan an iron foundry was excavated at Tell el-Qasîleh. Iron ores were also found near Mt. Carmel, Mt. Hermon, southwest Midian, and the Lebanon Mountains.

This extrabiblical evidence coincides with the biblical records which indicate that a change took place with the establishment of the Hebrew monarchy. Iron became plentiful in Israel during the reign of David. The Chronicler reports that David laid up "great stores of iron" (1 Ch. 22:3) which were later employed for the construction of the temple (1 Ch. 29:7). There is evidence that in the Davidic period the iron-tipped plow was employed on a large scale (Wright, p. 95), which led to increased productivity of the soil and permitted the Israelite population to increase significantly. In David's day almost every farmer was able to own iron axes, mattocks, plowpoints, pruning hooks, and sickles (2 S. 12:31 = 1 Ch. 20:3). The recovery of the iron axe-head from the Jordan by Elisha (2 K. 6:5) adds evidence for the use of iron implements in the 9th cent. B.C. The expression "iron from the north" in Jer. 15:12 may suggest that the Hebrews got their iron from the Phoenicians in the north, who probably brought it from Anatolia (Ezk. 27:12, 19).

Iron hoe (left) and plowshare, 10th cent. B.C., found at Tell Jemmeh, 10 km. (6 mi.) S of Gaza (Israel Department of Antiquities and Museums)

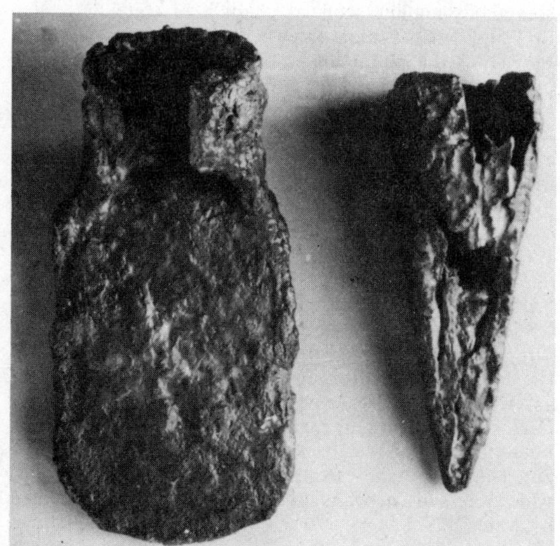

II. Iron in the Pentateuch.–Scholars have often taken exception to the mention of iron in certain parts of the Pentateuch (cf. Gen. 4:22; Dt. 3:11; 8:9). The finds of iron objects in the ancient Near East from prehistoric and historic times provide conclusive archeological evidence that iron was known and used long before the time of Moses, and that statements in the Pentateuch about the early use of iron are in harmony with known facts.

A. Tubal-cain. According to ancient Hebrew tradition Tubal-cain is associated with the beginning of ironworking in that he produced various implements of bronze and iron (Gen. 4:22). This is no anachronism. The author of this passage traces in summary fashion the origin of bronze-working and ironworking to the ancestor of all metallurgical experts. The "hammering" (*lṭš*) of iron does not imply the complex art of mining, smelting, casting, and forging of iron as developed later. Archeology has shown that early iron was hammered.

B. Og's Iron Bed. In Dt. 3:11 Og king of Bashan is said to have had a "bedstead of iron" (NEB "sarcophagus of basalt"). The iron for this "bedstead" (*'ereś*) may have come from the rich iron ores and smelting area of Mugharet el-Wardeh. The entire bed may not have been of solid iron. It probably had iron fittings or trimmings like the "beds of ivory" (Am. 6:4) which were inlaid with ivory, or the bronze bed from Tell el-Fâr'ah which was a bed with bronze fittings. Sometimes the word "iron" in this passage has been translated as "basalt," and correspondingly the word for "bed" as "sarcophagus." These suggestions lack contemporary literary support, as does the suggestion that the bed refers to a dolmen (*see* DOLMENS).

C. Palestine's Iron Ore. Palestine is described as a land "whose stones are iron-ore and from whose hills you will dig copper" (Dt. 8:9, NEB). The discussion above (I.A) has shown that Palestine is a country of iron ore. The fact that both iron and copper were mined and smelted within the confines of Solomon's realm was a literal fulfillment of this passage.

III. Iron as a Symbol.–In many instances iron is a colorful biblical symbol. The strength of iron is contrasted with that of straw in Job 41:27 (MT 19). The strength of life is like bolts of iron and bronze (Dt. 33:25). The stump and roots of a tree are as strong as iron and bronze fetters (Dnl. 4:15, 23). The iron sky and the bronze earth are symbols for drought and infertility (Lev. 26:19; Dt. 28:23). Bronze and iron as compared with gold and silver refer to Israel's corruption (Jer. 6:28; cf. Ezk. 22:18). The smelting of iron in the furnace is a symbol of testing, cleansing, and suffering (Dt. 4:20; 1 K. 8:51; Jer. 11:4; Ezk. 22:18). The "pillar of iron" (Jer. 1:18) is a symbol of strength; the "iron sinew" is a symbol of stubbornness (Isa. 48:4); the "iron rods" are a figure of speech for strength (Job 40:18); the "rod of iron" of rulership is symbolic of harshness (Ps. 2:9; Rev. 2:27; 12:5; 19:15). The sharpening process of iron with iron symbolizes the sharpening of one man's wits with that of another so that his capacity of perception becomes as keen as a razor blade (Prov. 27:17).

The comparative valuation of metals plays an important role in the symbolism of the four world empires of Dnl. 2: gold = Babylon, silver = Medo-Persia, bronze = Greece, and iron = Rome. Iron is the least valued metal in this scale (cf. Hesiod's five ages in *Works and Days* 106-201). Though inferior in value as compared with the other metals, iron is superior in strength. The powerful iron teeth of the fourth beast in Dnl. 7:7, which symbolize the same power that is portrayed by the iron legs of Dnl. 2:40, speak of the superior strength and intense power of destruction of this beast as it devours and subdues other nations. From these examples it is apparent that iron is a symbol of unsubdued power, unusual force, and firm persistence while it is at the same time inferior in value to gold, silver, and bronze on the symbolic scale.

Bibliography.–A. C. Richardson, *American Journal of Archaeology,* 38 (1934), 555-583; V. G. Childe, *New Light on the Most Ancient East* (1935); G. A. Wainwright, *Antiquity,* 10 (1936), 5-24; W. Witter, *Forschungen und Fortschritte,* 17 (1941), 223-25; A. Lucas, *Ancient Egyptian Materials and Industries* (3rd ed. 1948); W. F. Albright, *BASOR,* 120 (1950), 22-25; *AP*; O. Johannsen, *Geschichte des Eisens* (3rd ed. 1953); R. North, *Orientalia,* 24 (1955), 78-88; H. Maryon, *American Journal of Archaeology,* 65 (1961), 173-184; *IDB,* II, *s.v.* "Iron" (F. V. Winnett); *RAC,* VI, *s.v.* "Erz" (Hill, Mundle); *WBA*; R. J. Forbes, *Studies in Ancient Technology,* IX (1964), 175-290; O. R. Gurney, *Hittites* (rev. ed. 1966).

G. F. HASEL

IRON. *See* YIRON.

IRONS. *See* CHAINS; PRISON V.

IRONSMITH [Heb. *ḥāraš barzel*] (Isa. 44:12); AV SMITH; NEB BLACKSMITH. A metalworker who works with iron. The first "forger" (*lōṭēš*) of bronze and iron is said to have been Tubal-cain (Gen. 4:22). Iron objects were used in early times (*see* IRON; cf. Nu. 35:16; Dt. 3:11; Josh. 6:19, 24). The Canaanite "chariots of iron" (Josh. 17:16; Jgs. 1:19; 4:3, 13) probably were not made completely of iron. They were war vehicles on which some fittings or trimmings were of iron. This is illustrated by the reference of Thutmose III to Canaanite "chariots of gold," which he mentions in another place as having gold decorations.

From the time of David onward iron objects made by ironsmiths became more plentiful (cf. 1 S. 17:7; 13:19-22), consisting of harrows and axes (1 Ch. 20:3; cf. Dt. 19:5), nails and tools for builders (1 K. 6:7; 1 Ch. 22:3; cf. Job 19:24), bars, chains, sheets to cover city gates (Ps. 105:18; 107:10, 16; 149:8; Isa. 45:2; Acts 12:10), and idols (Dnl. 5:4).

See also METALLURGY.

Bibliography.–*AP,* pp. 110, 127; *BhHW,* I, *s.v.* "Eisen" (Forbes); Pauly-Wissowa, VI, 2142-49.

G. F. HASEL

IRPEEL ir′pi-əl [Heb. *yirpᵉʾēl*–'God heals'] (Josh. 18:27). An unidentified city allotted to the tribe of Benjamin. It may have been located in the hill country NW of Jerusalem. Rafat, N of Gibeon and 10.5 km. (6.5 mi.) NW of Jerusalem, has been suggested as the site.

IRRIGATION. The artificial supplying of water to crops or gardens where rainfall is insufficient or irregular. A pivotal invention in the history of civilization, it is attested in eastern Iraq (Choga Mami) *ca.* 5500 B.C. and inferred at Jericho *ca.* 7000 B.C. The earliest flowering of civilization, in the Tigris-Euphrates basin before 3000 B.C., is defined by a group of developments associated with irrigation: social specialization, laws, a working judiciary, art (from a leisure class). Without it urban life in the great centers of Mesopotamia and Egypt would have been impossible.

In the past irrigation was uncommon in Palestine because (1) unlike Egypt (Dt. 11:10) and Mesopotamia, Palestine had enough rain for agriculture (minimum 25 cm. [10 in.] per year) — "The rain," the Talmud says, "is the husband of the soil" (*Taanith* 6b); (2) much of the country is mountainous, unsuited for large-scale farming and for canal networks; (3) cisterns conserve, and springs (Dt. 8:7) and wells augment the rainfall; (4) there is no large river system from which a continuing water supply might be drawn (the Jordan lies below sea level at every point, posing formidable technical problems).

At the same time, peculiarities of the Palestinian climate make irrigation desirable: rainfall is badly distributed, coming (except for rare showers) entirely during the rainy season of October to April; and the desert borders directly on cropland and grazing land, especially in the Jordan Valley and the Negeb, where archeology provides some evidence for irrigation.

At Jericho monumental walls dating *ca.* 7000 B.C. enclosed a settlement of two to three thousand people. Food for so many could have been grown in the Jordan Valley only by irrigation, with canals carrying water from Jericho's flowing springs.

In the Buqeicah (the Valley of Achor, Hos. 2:15; Isa. 65:10), about 19 km. (12 mi.) E of Jerusalem near Qumrân, farmers of the 8th or 7th cent. B.C. built terraces to hold the soil and dams to catch and distribute water coming down from the mountains of southern Judea. Irrigation here made possible three settlements (perhaps the Middin, Secacah, and Nibshan of Josh. 15:61f.) composing an eastern zone of defense. At Khirbet Abu Ṭabaq the system included a massive wall 250 m. long across the wadi and a series of seven terraces, which are still effective in holding moisture for several weeks after the rains.

In the Bible specific references to irrigation are infrequent (as the practice itself is in Palestine), and do not show a specialized vocabulary. "Irrigate" is a nuance of Heb. *hiškâ,* "to water" (BDB, p. 1052), and is used of a vineyard (Isa. 27:3), a grove (Eccl. 2:6), and an Egyptian vegetable garden (Dt. 11:10). The last refers to opening and closing irrigation runnels with the gardener's foot. Nu. 24:6 may refer to the *šaduf* or sweep, a water-lift still (sometimes) used today. In Prov. 17:14 the releasing (*pāṭar*) of water from an irrigation sluice is a simile for the beginning of a quarrel. The "wheel" (*galgal*) of Eccl. 12:6 is an axle-and-rope device to draw water from a well.

The Heb. *peleg,* "channel, stream" (cognate with Akk. *palgum,* the commonest word for Mesopotamian canals), sometimes implies artificial conduct of water (Ps. 46:4 [MT 5], "canals" bring water from the "river"; Isa. 32:2). In Ps. 1:3 the plural implies irrigation and suggests an ornamental garden where the tree's prosperity is guaranteed by a gardener's oversight (cf. Jer. 17:8). In Prov. 21:1 the Lord's direction of the king is symbolized by the ease with which a gardener may direct the flow of water in irrigation runnels. The piel of the denominative verb *pālag* means "split, divide," thus "cleave a channel" (Job 38:25).

A "pool" (*bᵉrēḵâ*) is mentioned at Gibeon (2 S. 2:13), Hebron (2 S. 4:12), and Jerusalem (Neh. 3:16, Heb. *habbᵉrēḵâ hāʿᵃśûyâ,* "the pool, the one made," hence "artificial"; cf. Eccl. 2:6), serving as a collecting basin for domestic use and probably for gardens and light agriculture. Ornamental gardens required special sources of water (Is. 1:30; 58:11), and the Jordan Valley is once described as "well watered everywhere like the garden of the Lord" (Gen. 13:10). Egyptian canals and Nile branches are frequently mentioned (Heb. *yᵉʾôrîm*: Ex. 7:19; 8:5; 2 K. 19:24 par. Isa. 37:25; Isa. 7:18; 19:6; Ezk. 29:3f.; and Nah. 3:8, which refers to Thebes as "sitting on the canals, surrounded by water").

Reconstruction of the impression of a cylinder seal from Mesopotamia (*ca.* 2300 B.C.). It shows a *šaduf* or water lift. The man holds the rope and basket, which he has raised from the water by the lever and counterweight; the upright pole is a date palm.

Modern Egyptians still employ the ancient *šaduf* for irrigation (Lehnert and Landrock)

Watercourses were used metaphorically for spiritual prosperity (Isa. 58:11), the blessings of the king's rule (Isa. 32:2), wisdom herself (Sir. 24:30), and God's favor (Nu. 24:6f.; Isa. 30:25), although it is not always certain that artificial channels are meant. Babylonian dependence on irrigation underlies Jeremiah's apostrophe, "You who dwell on many waters, rich in treasures" (51:13). The reference is to the network of canals, and the Talmud explains that Babylon was rich because she could "harvest without rain" (*Taanith* 10a). A Babylonian allusion is probable in the name of Peleg ("canal"), who is associated with the beginning of irrigation, for "in his days the earth was canalized" (*nipl^e gâ,* Gen. 10:25). Several verbs of the OT flood story reflect the technical language of Babylonian irrigation (*kālā',* "hold back," and *sāḵar,* "stop up," Gen. 8:2; *pāṯaḥ,* "open," Gen. 7:11).

A large irrigation system has social drawbacks as well as benefits. It requires slave labor, is baroque in its complexity, and breeds perpetual conflict among users (the word "rival" derives from Roman law where it denotes a person who shares the water of a *rivus,* "watercourse"). Since the physical life of the state depended on irrigation, an autocratic agro-managerial bureaucracy developed, with religious personnel frequently given official roles. One might argue that in Palestine the rise of the prophetic criticism of king and state was facilitated by the absence there of the totalitarian and despotic control that irrigation cultures seem to require.

Bibliography.–*General:* K. Wittfogel, *Oriental Despotism* (1957); M. S. Drower, "Water-Supply, Irrigation, and Agriculture," in O. Singer, *et al.*, eds., *A History of Technology,* I (1965), 520-27; R. J. Forbes, *Studies in Ancient Technology,* II (1965), 1-79; J. Laessøe, *JCS,* 7 (1953), 5-26; B. Brentjes, *Altorientalische Forschungen,* 1 (1974), 43-54.

Sites: J. Oates, *Iraq,* 31 (1969), 115-123; *EAEHL,* I, *s.v.* "El-Buqeiʿa" (F. M. Cross); II, *s.v.* "Jericho" (K. Kenyon, E. Netzer, G. Foerster, G. Bacchi), esp. pp. 553f.; L. E. Stager, *RB,* 81 (1974), 94-96.

S. D. WALTERS

IR-SHEMESH ir-she'məsh [Heb. *ʿîr-šemeš*–'city of the sun'] (Josh. 19:41). A city originally allocated to Dan but later designated as a city of Judah (2 K. 14:11). *See* BETH-SHEMESH.

IRU ī'ro͞o [Heb. *ʿîrû*] (1 Ch. 4:15). The oldest son of Caleb. The word should probably be read Ir, the final vowel being the conjunction "and" belonging to the following word (cf. the LXX).

ISAAC ī'zək [Heb. *yiṣḥāq, yiśḥāq*–either 'laughing,' 'he laughs,' or 'he laughed'; Gk. *Isaak*]. An OT patriarch, son of Abraham and father of Jacob and Esau.

I. Significance of the Name.–Whether *yiṣḥāq* is to be taken as an imperfect or as a past tense, it is necessary to consider the subject of the verb. The most common solution is to supply *'ēl,* "God," as the subject. It might then be understood as indicating divine benevolence, or else the fearful laughter of God's scorn for His enemies (Ps. 2:4). A strong objection to this analysis is that the name is never so written in the text preserved; cf. Albright (*FSAC,* p. 245), who translates Heb. *yiṣḥāq-'ēl* "May 'El smile favorably upon me in my distress." The narratives concerning the promise and the birth of Isaac suggest that some person may be the subject: his father (Gen. 17:17); his mother (Gen. 18:12-15; separation from the specific subject might result in the name taking the simple masculine form *yiṣḥāq* and not the feminine *tiṣḥaq*); or "everyone who hears" (Gen. 21:6). Other occurrences of the root in the Isaac stories cannot be connected with his naming since they followed that event (Gen. 21:9; 26:8). The name may well be understood as indefinite, "one laughs," or, since Abraham named his son, it may refer back to his own incredulous laughter, "he laughed."

II. Family.–The two events of Isaac's life that Genesis treats in detail emphasize his significance as the heir of the covenant first made with his father and as the one whose son was to become the nation Israel.

A. Birth and Position. The birth of Isaac was peculiar in several respects: the age of his parents, the purity of his lineage, the special divine promises. In the birth of Isaac (when his mother was ninety and his father one hundred years old [Gen. 17:17]) may be seen the faithfulness of Yahweh, who had promised an heir twenty-five years before (Gen. 12:1-4). His mother was not only Abraham's wife but also his half sister, so Isaac was a member of the family of Terah on both sides. As son of Sarah, Isaac had legal precedence over Ishmael; but Hagar's son could be excluded from inheriting along with Isaac only by the explicit command to expel him from the family (Gen. 21:11-14; *see* ABRAHAM II).

B. Relation to the Religious Birthright. The removal of Ishmael and of Abraham's other sons (Gen. 25:1-6) avoided a division of Abraham's material wealth at his death and ensured that Isaac alone would inherit the blessings associated with the Promised Land. It also avoided the possibility of disagreement and difficulties arising from subjection to Isaac. Some sense of the importance of the spiritual inheritance is evident in Isaac's relationship to

Interior capital of San Pedro de la Nave, near Zamora, Spain, late 7th cent. A.D. God stops Abraham from sacrificing Isaac and provides a ram as a substitute offering (Rosenthal Art Slides)

his sons. Although he favored the elder, he could not withdraw the blessing he had bestowed upon the younger son, but rather recognized that this was in accordance with the divine plan and confirmed it (Gen. 28:3f.).

III. Biography.–Prior to his marriage, Isaac's life is a part of the story of Abraham; after his marriage it merges into that of his children, emphasizing his role as an intermediary.

As he was the first child of God's promise, Isaac was the first to receive the sign of circumcision at the prescribed age of eight days; and his survival to the end of weaning (perhaps at the age of two) was marked by a great feast. These indications of the important position he held underline the enormous sacrifice later demanded of Abraham. Isaac was probably fully grown at the time and evidently familiar with the act of sacrifice (Gen. 22:7). The divine interposition to save the one who was thus devoted to God constituted him afresh the heir of the promise, confirmed by its renewal on that occasion.

The account of the central event of Isaac's life is prefaced by the genealogies of Abraham's brother in Haran (Gen. 22:20-24) and the death of Sarah, an event that caused Abraham, an old man, to think of his duty to obtain a wife for his son (Gen. 24:3, 67). The wife could be found only among the cousins at Haran if the purity of descent was to be maintained and the family distinguished from surrounding clans. Eliezer was sent there and found Rebekah, whose hand he sought in the approved way (*see* MARRIAGE III.B). The match was accomplished under divine guidance. The first meeting of Isaac and Rebekah is described at the close of Gen. 24 with the tender interest natural to blood descendants.

If the phrase "these are the generations of" is taken as marking the end of a section of Genesis, the history of Isaac finishes at Gen. 25:19 (see P. J. Wiseman, *New Discoveries in Babylonia about Genesis* [1936], pp. 54f.). The next paragraphs describe the birth of the twin sons Esau and Jacob, and continue into their stories. Like Abraham, Isaac learned of the faithfulness of God in this matter, for it was not until twenty years after his marriage that his sons were born.

Life in Palestine followed an unchanging pattern for several generations, so that similarity of the events in the life of one person with events in the life of another need not be explained as duplication of tradition. When there was famine in the land the natural reaction of inhabitants of the south was to look to Egypt for food. Abraham and Joseph's brothers went there for corn, and Isaac intended to do so (Gen. 26:2). At this time of distress the covenant promises were reiterated and confirmed to Isaac. Although he was prevented from going to Egypt, he copied his father in telling the men of Gerar that Rebekah was his sister. Although ancient customs (*see* MARRIAGE II.B.2) may make this move understandable and Heb. *ʾāḥôṯ* may have had a wider connotation than "sister," Isaac clearly intended to deceive. His status, wealth, and the size of his household served to protect him from attack by the local peoples, especially in disputes over watering rights (Gen. 26).

The favoritism Isaac showed for Esau and Rebekah showed for Jacob culminated in the deceit by which the younger son received the elder's share and led to his flight to the relatives at Haran. Esau also left his father and settled in Transjordan. About twenty years later Jacob returned with his family and soon thereafter Isaac died. Just as his sons Isaac and Ishmael together buried Abraham, so also Esau and Jacob together laid their father in the family tomb at Hebron (Gen. 35:27-29).

IV. Biblical References.–Although Isaac is often mentioned in the formula "Abraham, Isaac, and Jacob [or Israel]" (so 23 times in the OT, 7 times in the NT), he is otherwise far less prominent than either his father or his son. Jacob calls Yahweh the "Fear" of Isaac (Gen. 31:42), perhaps simply referring to the God whom Isaac reverenced; possibly it is a name of deeper, unexplained significance. Isaac is called the "gift" of God to Abraham, just as Esau and Jacob are called God's "gifts" to Isaac (Josh. 24:3f.; cf. Koran 6:84). Amos uses Isaac in poetic parallel with Israel (Am. 7:9, 16, but the LXX reads Jacob in v. 16).

In the NT are noted Isaac's importance as the first to be circumcised on the eighth day (Acts 7:8), his position as first of the elect seed (Rom. 9:7), and his begetting two sons so dissimilar in their relation to the promise as were Esau and Jacob (Rom. 9:13). That Isaac was heir to the promise, a child of old age, and the father of an innumerable progeny are emphasized in He. 11:9-12, where the deeper significance of the sacrifice in Moriah is also discovered (He. 11:17-19; cf. Jas. 2:21); in the same context is noted the faith in God implicit in Isaac's blessing of his sons. Paul uses Isaac and his mother as allegorical representations of Christians, who are justified by faith in the promise of God and who are freeborn heirs of all its spiritual inheritance (Gal. 4:21-31).

V. Views Other Than Historical.–Philo, the chief allegorizer of the scriptural narratives among ancient authors, has little to say of Isaac, whom he calls "the self-instructed nature." More recent critics have taken the view that together with Edom he is a personification of an ethnic group (J. Wellhausen, *Prolegomenon to the History of Israel* [repr. 1959], p. 316) or that Isaac was a deity at Beer-sheba, with the suggestion also that the name of a god might be applied to the intended victim of sacrifice (cf. E. Meyer, *Israeliten und ihre Nachbarstämme* [1906], p. 255). H. Gunkel (*Schriften des AT* [1910], p. 41) allows that the patriarchs were actual persons, but have survived only as names around which cycles of folk stories have crystallized. The position of M. Noth is somewhat similar; he sees Isaac and Abraham as names that were associated with the religion of the southern tribes in Palestine and around which various traditions collected (*NHI,* pp. 122f.). Increasing knowledge of the history of the early centuries of the 2nd millennium B.C. has resulted in the recognition of factual material in the narratives by many historians. J. Bright concludes that, when account is taken of the oral transmission through which they are assumed to have passed, "although the essential historicity of the traditions cannot be impeached, detailed reconstructions are impossible" (*BHI,* p. 68).

A. R. MILLARD

ISAIAH ī-zā'ə.

I. Name
II. Personal History
III. Call
IV. Literary Genius and Style
V. Traditions Concerning His Martyrdom
VI. Historical Background
VII. Analysis and Contents
VIII. The Critical Problem
  A. History of Criticism
  B. Arguments for Divided Authorship
  C. Arguments Against Divided Authorship
  D. The Prophecy as an Anthology
  E. Evidence from Qumrân
  F. Composition and Date of Isaiah
  G. Servant Oracles
  H. Cyrus

Of all the prophets of Israel, Isaiah stands out as incomparably the greatest. Writing with majestic grandeur, this gifted eighth-century B.C. author exalts the grace of God in salvation. For this, if for no other reason, he has well been called "the evangelical prophet."

I. Name.–The Heb. *y^e^šaʿyāhû* was the form current in the 8th cent. B.C., the shorter variant *y^e^šaʿyâ* becoming more popular subsequently, and occurring in the fifth-century-B.C. Elephantine papyri. Greek and Latin equivalents were *Hsaias* and *Isaiae* respectively. Thus the AV uses "Esay" in 2 Esd. 2:18; Sir. 48:22, and "Esaias" in the NT (Mt. 3:3; 4:14; etc.). The name means "Yahweh is salvation," and is thus similar to names such as Joshua, Elisha, and Jesus.

II. Personal History.–Little is known about the man himself. He is said to have been the son of Amoz (not the contemporary prophet Amos), and he exercised his ministry in and around Jerusalem. Inasmuch as he had ready access to kings (cf. 7:3), it has been thought that he was of royal descent. By tradition he was the cousin of King Uzziah (791/90-740/39 B.C.). Whether this was actually the case or not, it must be remembered that it was the custom in ancient times for prophets to move freely in court circles and to associate with monarchs, sometimes on a friendly basis (cf. 1 K. 19:15f.) and sometimes not (cf. 2 Ch. 18:4-27). In the same way some prophets exhibited a decided interest in temple worship and its implications for national destiny, and thus it would not have been unusual for Isaiah to have had the kind of contact with the Jerusalem temple implied in the vision that resulted in his call, or the personal friendship with a priest that 8:2 seems to indicate.

As appears from 8:3 he was married, and designated his wife "the prophetess," perhaps because she also prophesied. He had two sons, who each bore a symbolic name. One of these, Shear-jashub ("a remnant shall return"), held out the promise that a faithful minority would survive the collapse of national life (7:3), while the other, Maher-shalal-hash-baz ("hasten booty, speed spoil"), symbolized Assyria's mad desire for conquest (8:3). Like Elijah before him, Isaiah normally would have been clad in a garment of sackcloth, and would have worn sandals. This customary prophetic garb was discarded for three years, however, when in obedience to God's command and as a means of reinforcing his statements about the pointlessness of Judah's reliance on Egypt against Assyria, Isaiah walked about Jerusalem wearing only a loincloth (Isa. 20:2-6). No doubt his behavior must have appeared somewhat bizarre in the eyes of his fellow Judeans, and may have led some of them to describe him in terms of the "mad fellow" epithet used in 2 K. 9:11 of the young prophet sent to anoint Jehu. Precisely how long Isaiah functioned as prophet, evangelist, and adviser to the royal court is unknown. His last appearance that can be dated with reasonable certainty was at the time of Sennacherib's campaign in 701 B.C. If there was factual evidence to show that Sennacherib had launched a second attack against Jerusalem, this date could be lowered to *ca.* 688 B.C. There is no a priori reason why Isaiah should not have survived into Manasseh's reign, since the absence of that king's name from the superscription of the prophecy (1:1) need only mean that Isaiah played a modest public role at the end of his life. The date of his death, however, must remain entirely conjectural.

III. Call.–From the superscription it is legitimate to conclude that Isaiah's ministry must have involved at least a portion of the reign of Uzziah, perhaps during the time of his leprosy when Jotham acted as co-regent and subsequently as king (2 K. 15:5), since he received visions at that time. Such an indication that Isaiah was already active as a prophet challenges the popular view that he received his call in connection with the events mentioned in ch. 6. Instead, it would seem to indicate that Isaiah experienced on that occasion a reconsecration or rededication to his prophetic task, which was in effect to warn his contemporaries of impending disaster and divine judgment (6:9-13), and at the same time to promise that redemption would be the lot of a repentant remnant (6:13). (Or ch. 6 may describe a calling to speak to the people, whereas formerly he had spoken to the king.) Isaiah in his vision found himself in the temple, where he received the symbolical assurance of the forgiveness of his sins and a commission to preach to his own people for the Lord. His remarkable readiness to serve in this capacity appeared in his eager response to the commission, which proved to be one whose discharge resulted in the hardening of the will of the nation to which he had been sent. The entire ministry of Isaiah was one of faithful fulfillment of his responsibilities as a prophet of God. His horizons, both political and spiritual, were virtually unbounded, and he was in every sense of the term the universal prophet of Israel.

IV. Literary Genius and Style.–For versatility of expression and brilliance of imagery Isaiah had no superior, not even a rival. His style marks the climax of Hebrew literary art. Epigrams and metaphors, particularly of flood, storm, and sound (1:13; 5:18, 22; 8:8; 10:22; 28:17, 20; 30:28, 30), interrogation and dialogue (6:8; 10:8f.), antithesis and alliteration (1:18; 3:24; 17:10, 12), hyperbole and parable (2:7; 5:1-7; 28:23-29), even paronomasia, or play upon words (5:7; 7:9), characterize Isaiah's book as the great masterpiece of Hebrew literature. He is also famous for his richness of vocabulary and synonyms. For example, Ezekiel uses 1535 words; Jeremiah, 1653; the psalmists 2170; while Isaiah uses 2186. Isaiah was also an orator: Jerome likened him to Demosthenes; and a poet: he frequently elaborates his messages in rhythmic or poetic style (12:1-6; 25:1-5; 26:1-12; 38:10-20; 42:1-4; 49:1-9; 50:4-9; 52:13–53:12; 60–62; 66:5-24); and in several instances slips into elegiac rhythm, e.g., in 37:22-29 there is a fine taunting poem on Sennacherib, and in 14:4-23 another on the king of Babylon.

V. Traditions Concerning His Martyrdom.–Nothing definite or historical is known concerning the prophet's end. Toward the close of the 2nd cent. A.D., however, there was a tradition to the effect that he suffered martyrdom in the heathen reaction that occurred under King Manasseh, because of certain speeches concerning God and the Holy City that his contemporaries alleged were contrary to the law. Indeed the Mishnah explicitly states that Manasseh slew him. Justin Martyr also (A.D. 150), in his controversial dialogue with the Jew Trypho, reproaches the Jews with this accusation, "whom ye sawed asunder with a wooden saw"; this tradition is further confirmed by a Jewish apocalypse of the 2nd cent. A.D., Ascension of Isaiah, and mentioned by Epiphanius in the 4th century. It is barely possible that there is an allusion to his martyrdom in He. 11:37, which reads, "They were stoned, they were sawn in two," but this is by no means certain. In any case Isaiah probably survived the great catastrophe of the siege of Jerusalem by Sennacherib in 701 B.C., and possibly also the death of Hezekiah in 699 B.C., for in 2 Ch. 32:32 it is stated that Isaiah wrote a biography of King Hezekiah. If so, his prophetic activity extended over a period of more than forty years, ending presumably in the early part of Manasseh's reign (687/6-642/1 B.C.), and certainly during the period of his co-regency (696/5-687/6 B.C.).

VI. Historical Background.–According to the title of his book (1:1f.), Isaiah prophesied during the reigns of Uzziah, Jotham, Ahaz, and Hezekiah, kings of Judah. He dates his inaugural vision (6:1) in the year of Uzziah's death, which was approximately 740 B.C. This marks, therefore, the beginning of his prophetic ministry. And we know that he was still active as late as the siege of Jerusalem by Sennacherib in 701 B.C. Hence the minimum period of his activity as a prophet was from 740 to 701 B.C. As a young man Isaiah witnessed the rapid development of Judah into a strong commercial and military state; for under Uzziah Judah attained a degree of prosperity and strength not enjoyed since the days of Solomon. Walls, towers, fortifications, a large standing army, a port for commerce on the Red Sea, increased inland trade, tribute from the Ammonites, success in war with the Philistines and the Arabians — all these became Judah's during Uzziah's long and prosperous reign of approximately fifty-two years, this period of time including his co-regency from 791/90 B.C. with his father Amaziah (796-767 B.C.). But along with power and wealth came also avarice, oppression, religious formality, and corruption. The temple revenues indeed were greatly increased, but religion and life were too frequently dissociated; the nation's progress was altogether material. During the reign of Jotham (740/39-732/1 B.C.), who for several years was probably associated with his father as co-regent, a new power began to appear over the eastern horizon. The Assyrians, with whom Ahab had come in contact at the Battle of Qarqar in 853 B.C., and to whom Jehu had paid tribute in 841 B.C., began to manifest anew their characteristic lust of conquest. Tiglath-pileser III (called "Pul" in 2 K. 15:19), who reigned over Assyria from 745 to 727 B.C., turned his attention westward, and *ca.* 740 B.C. reduced Arpad, Calno, Carchemish, Hamath, and Damascus, causing them to pay tribute. His presence in the West led Pekah king of Israel and Rezin king of Damascus to form an alliance in order to resist further encroachment on the part of Assyria. When Ahaz refused to join their confederacy they resolved to dethrone him and set in his stead the son of Tabeel upon the throne of David (2 K. 16:5; Isa. 7:6). The struggle that ensued is commonly known as the Syro-Ephraimitic war (734 B.C.) — one of the great events in Isaiah's period. Ahaz in panic sent to Tiglath-pileser for help (2 K. 16:7), who of course responded with alacrity. The result was that the great Assyrian warrior sacked Gaza, carried all of Galilee and Gilead into captivity (734), and finally took Damascus (732 B.C.). Ahaz was forced to pay dearly for his protection and Judah was brought very low (2 K. 15:29; 16:7-9; 2 Ch. 28:19; Isa. 7:1). The religious as well as the political effect of Ahaz' policy was decidedly baneful. To please Tiglath-pileser, Ahaz went to Damascus to join in the celebration of his victories, and while there saw a Syrian altar, a pattern of which he sent to Jerusalem and had a copy set up in the temple in place of the brazen altar of Solomon. Thus Ahaz, with all the influence of a king, sponsored idolatry in Jerusalem, even causing his sons to pass through the fire (2 K. 16:10-16; 2 Ch. 28:3).

Hezekiah succeeded Ahaz, beginning to rule at the age of twenty-five as co-regent (729 B.C.) and reigning until his death in 687/6 B.C. Isaiah was at least fifteen years his senior. The young king inherited from his father a heavy burden. The splendor of the reigns of Uzziah and Jotham was rapidly fading before the ever menacing and avaricious Assyrians. Hezekiah began his reign with many reforms. "He removed the high places, and broke the pillars, and cut down the Asherah" (2 K. 18:4, 22). He even invited the surviving remnant of Israel to join in celebrating the Passover (2 Ch. 30:1). But Israel's end was drawing near. Hoshea, the vacillating puppet-king of Israel (732/1-723/2 B.C.), encouraged by Egypt, refused to continue to pay Assyria his annual tribute (2 K. 17:4); whereupon Shalmaneser IV, who had succeeded Tiglath-pileser, promptly appeared before the gates of Samaria in 724 B.C., and for nearly three years besieged the city (2 K. 17:5). Finally, the city was captured by Sargon II (or by Shalmaneser, but claimed by Sargon), who succeeded Shalmaneser IV in 722 B.C., 27,292 of Israel's choicest people (according to Sargon's own description) were deported to Assyria, and colonists were brought from Babylon and other adjacent districts and placed in the cities of Samaria (2 K. 17:6, 24). Thus the kingdom of Israel passed into oblivion, and Judah was left exposed to the direct ravages, political and religious, of her Assyro-Babylonian neighbors. In fact Judah itself barely escaped destruction by promising heavy tribute. This was the second great political crisis during Isaiah's ministry.

Other crises were soon to follow. One was the desperate illness of King Hezekiah, who faced certain death *ca.* 714 B.C., though the chronology presents some difficulties. Being childless, he was seriously concerned for the future of the Davidic dynasty. He resorted to prayer, however, and God graciously extended his life fifteen years (2 K. 20; Isa. 38). His illness occurred during the period of Babylon's independence under Merodach-baladan, the ever ambitious, irresistible, and uncompromising enemy of Assyria, who for twelve years (722-710 B.C.) maintained independent supremacy over Babylon. Taking advantage of Hezekiah's wonderful cure, Merodach seized the opportunity, sending an embassy to Jerusalem to congratulate him on his recovery (712 B.C.), and at the same time probably sought to form an alliance with Judah to resist Assyrian supremacy (2 K. 20:12-15; Isa. 39). Nothing, however, came of the alliance, for the following year Sargon's army reappeared in Philistia in order to discipline Ashdod for conspiracy with the king of Egypt (711 B.C.).

The greatest crisis was yet to come. Its story is as follows: Judah and her neighbors groaned more and more under the heavy exactions of Assyria. Accordingly, when Sargon was assassinated and Sennacherib came to the throne in 705 B.C., rebellion broke out on all sides. Merodach-baladan, who had been expelled by Sargon in 709 B.C., again took Babylon and held it for at least six months in 703 B.C. Hezekiah, who was encouraged by Egypt and all Philistia, except Padi of Ekron, the puppet-king of Sargon, refused to continue to pay Assyria tribute (2 K. 18:7). Meanwhile a strong pro-Egypt party had sprung up in Jerusalem. In view of all these circumstances, Sennacherib in 701 B.C. marched westward with a vast army, sweeping everything before him. Tyre was invested though not taken; on the other hand, Joppa, Eltekeh, Ekron, Ashkelon, Ammon, Moab, and Edom all promptly yielded to his demands. Hezekiah was panic stricken and hastened to bring rich tribute, stripping even the temple and the palace of their treasures to do so (2 K. 18:13-16). But Sennacherib was not satisfied. He overran Judah, capturing, as he tells us in his inscription, forty-six walled towns and smaller villages without number, carrying 200,150 of Judah's population into captivity to Assyria, and demanding as tribute eight hundred talents of silver and thirty talents of gold (a talent equaled about 30 kilograms, or 65 pounds); he took also, he claims, Hezekiah's daughters and palace women, seized his male and female singers, and carried away enormous spoil.

But the end was not yet. Sennacherib himself, with the bulk of the army, halted in Philistia to reduce Lachish; thence he sent a strong detachment under his commander-in-chief, the Rabshakeh, to besiege Jerusalem (2 K. 18:17–19:8; Isa. 36:2–37:8). He describes this blockade in his own inscription: "I shut up Hezekiah in Jerusalem like a bird in a cage." The Rabshakeh, however, failed to capture the city and returned to Sennacherib, who meanwhile had completely conquered Lachish, and was now warring against Libnah. A second expedition against Jerusalem was planned, but hearing that Tirhakah (at that time the commander-in-chief of Egypt's forces and only afterward "king of Ethiopia") was approaching, Sennacherib was forced to content himself with sending messengers with a letter to Hezekiah, demanding immediate surrender of the city (2 K. 19:9ff.; Isa. 37:9ff.). Hezekiah, however, through Isaiah's influence held out; and in due time, though Sennacherib disposed of Tirhakah's army without difficulty, his immense host in some mysterious way — by plague or otherwise — was suddenly smitten, and the great Assyrian conqueror was forced to return to Nineveh, possibly because Merodach-baladan had again appeared in Babylonia. Sennacherib never again returned to Palestine, so far as we know, during the subsequent twenty years of his reign, though he did make an independent expedition into north Arabia (691-689 B.C.). This invasion of Judah by Sennacherib in 701 B.C. was the great political event in Isaiah's ministry. Had it not been for the prophet's statesmanship, Jerusalem might have capitulated. Isaiah had at this time been preaching forty years. How much longer he labored is not known.

VII. Analysis and Contents.–There are six general divisions of the book: (1) chs. 1–12, prophecies concerning Judah and Jerusalem, closing with promises of restoration and a psalm of thanksgiving; (2) chs. 13–23, oracles of judgment and salvation, for the most part concerning those foreign nations whose fortunes affected Judah and Jerusalem; (3) chs. 24–27, the Lord's world-judgment in the redemption of Israel; (4) chs. 28–35, a cycle of prophetic warnings against alliance with Egypt, closing with a prophecy concerning Edom and a promise of Israel's ransom; (5) chs. 36–39, history, prophecy, and song intermingled, serving both as an appendix to chs. 1–35 and as an introduction to chs. 40–66; (6) chs. 40–66, prophecies of comfort and salvation, and also of the future glory awaiting Israel.

By examining in detail these several divisions we can trace better the prophet's thought. Thus, chs. 1–12 reveal Judah's social sins (chs. 1–6) and its political entanglements (chs. 7–12); ch. 1 is an introduction, in which the prophet strikes the chief notes of his entire book: thoughtlessness (vv. 2-9), formalism in worship (vv. 10-17), pardon (vv. 18-23), and judgment (vv. 24-31). Chapters 2–4 contain three distinct pictures of Zion: (a) its exaltation (2:2-4), (b) its present idolatry (2:5–4:1), and (c) its eventual purification (4:2-6). Chapter 5 contains an arraignment of Judah and Jerusalem, composed of three parts: (a) a parable of the Lord's vineyard (vv. 1-7); (b) a series of six woes pronounced against insatiable greed (vv. 8-10), dissipation (vv. 11-17), daring defiance against the Lord (vv. 18f.), confusion of moral distinctions (v. 20), political self-conceit (v. 21), and misdirected heroism (vv. 22f.); and (c) an announcement of imminent judgment. The Assyrian is on the way and there will be no escape (vv. 24-30). Chapter 6 recounts the prophet's inaugural vision and commission. It is really an apologetic, standing as it does after the prophet's denunciations of his contemporaries. When they tacitly object to his message of threatening and disaster, he is able to reply that, having pronounced "woe" upon himself in the year that King Uzziah died, he had the authority to pronounce woe upon them (6:5). Plainly Isaiah tells them that Judah's sins are hopeless. They are becoming spiritually insensible. They have eyes but they cannot see. Only judgment can avail: "the righteous judgment of a forgotten God" awaits them. A "holy seed," however, still existed in Israel's stock (6:13).

In chs. 7–12, Isaiah appears in the role of a practical statesman. He warns Ahaz against political entanglements with Assyria. The section 7:1–9:7 (MT 6) is a prophecy of Immanuel, history and prediction being intermingled. It describes the Syro-Ephraimitic uprising *ca.* 734 B.C. when Pekah of Israel and Rezin of Damascus, in attempting to defend themselves against the Assyrians, demanded that Ahaz of Jerusalem should become their ally. But Ahaz preferred the friendship of Assyria, and refused to enter into alliance with them. In order to defend himself, he applied to Assyria for assistance, sending ambassadors with many precious treasures, both royal and sacred, to bribe Tiglath-pileser. It was at this juncture that Isaiah, at the Lord's bidding, expostulated with Ahaz concerning the fatal step he was about to take, and as a practical statesman warned Ahaz, "the king of No-Faith," that the only path of safety lay in loyalty to the Lord and avoidance of foreign alliances; that "God is with us" for salvation; and that no "conspiracy" could possibly be successful unless God too was against them. When, however, the prophet's message of promise and salvation found no welcome, he committed it to his disciples, bound up and sealed for future use, assuring his hearers that to them a child was born and a son was given, in whose day the empire of David would be established upon a basis of justice and righteousness. The messianic scion was the ground of the prophet's hope. This hope, though unprecedented, he thus early in his ministry committed, written and sealed, to his inner circle of "disciples." *See* IMMANUEL.

The section 9:8 (MT 7)–10:4 contains an announcement to Israel of accumulated wrath and impending ruin, with a refrain (9:12, 17, 21 [MT 11, 16, 20]; 10:4). Here, in an artistic poem composed of four strophes, the prophet describes the great calamities that the Lord has sent down upon Israel but that have gone unheeded: foreign invasion (9:8-12), defeat in battle (9:13-17), anarchy (9:18-21), and impending captivity (10:1-4). Yet the Lord's judgments have been ignored: "For all this his anger is not turned away, and his hand is stretched out still." Divine discipline has failed; only judgment remains.

In 10:5-34, Assyria is declared to be an instrument of the Lord, the rod of the Lord's anger. Chapters 11–12 predict Israel's return from exile, including a vision of the Messiah's reign of ideal peace. For Isaiah's vision of the nation's future reached far beyond mere exile. To him the downfall of Assyria was the signal for the commencement of a new era in Israel's history. Assyria has no future, its downfall is fatal; Judah has a future, its calamities are only disciplinary. An ideal Prince will be raised up in whose advent all nature will rejoice, even dumb animals

(11:1-10). A second great exodus will take place, for the Lord will set His hand again "a second time" to recover the remnant of His people "from the four corners of the earth" (11:11f.). In that day, "Ephraim shall not be jealous of Judah, and Judah shall not harass Ephraim" (11:13). On the contrary, the reunited nation, redeemed and occupying their rightful territory (11:14-16), shall sing a hymn of thanksgiving, proclaiming the salvation of the Lord to all the earth (ch. 12).

Chapters 13–23 contain oracles of judgment and salvation, for the most part concerning those foreign nations whose fortunes affected Judah and Jerusalem. They are grouped together by the editor, as similar foreign oracles are in Jer. 46–51 and Ezk. 25–32. Isaiah's horizon was worldwide. First among the foreign prophecies stands the oracle concerning Babylon (13:1–14:23), in which he predicts the utter destruction of the city (13:2-22), and sings a dirge or taunt-song over its fallen king (14:4-23). The king alluded to is almost beyond doubt an Assyrian (not a Babylonian) monarch of the 8th cent.; the brief prophecy immediately following in 14:24-27 concerning Assyria tacitly confirms this interpretation. Another brief oracle concerning Babylon (21:1-10) describes the city's fall as imminent. Both oracles stand or fall together as genuine prophecies of Isaiah. Both seem to have been written in Jerusalem (13:2; 21:9, 10). It cannot be said that either is unrelated in thought and language to Isaiah's age (14:13; 21:2); each foretells the doom to fall on Babylon (13:19; 21:9) at the hands of the Medes (13:17; 21:2); and each describes the Israelites as already in exile — but not necessarily *all* Israel.

The section 14:24-27 tells of the certain destruction of the Assyrian.

The passage 14:28-32 is an oracle concerning Philistia.

Chapters 15–16 are ancient oracles against Moab, whose dirgelike meter resembles that of chs. 13–14. These oracles consist of two separate prophecies belonging to two different periods in Isaiah's ministry (16:13f.). The three points of particular interest in the oracles are: (1) the prophet's tender sympathy for Moab in her affliction (15:5; 16:11). As Delitzsch says, "There is no prophecy in the book of Isaiah in which the heart of the prophet is so painfully affected by what his mind sees, and his mouth is obliged to prophesy." (2) Moab's pathetic appeal for shelter from her foes; particularly the ground on which she urges it, namely, the messianic hope that the Davidic dynasty shall always stand and be able to repulse its foes (16:5). The prophecy is an echo of 9:5-7. (3) The promise that a remnant of Moab, though small, shall be saved (16:14). The prophet predicts that Moab, wearied of prayer to CHEMOSH in the high places, will seek the living God (v. 12).

The passage 17:1-11 is an oracle concerning Damascus and Israel, in which Isaiah predicts the fate of the two allies — Syria and Ephraim — in the Syro-Ephraimitic war of 734 B.C., with a promise that only a scanty remnant will survive (17:6). In 17:12-14, the prophet boldly announces the complete annihilation of Judah's unnamed foes — the Assyrians.

Chapter 18 describes ETHIOPIA as in great excitement, sending ambassadors here and there — possibly all the way to Jerusalem — ostensibly seeking aid in making preparations for war. Assyria had already taken Damascus (732 B.C.) and Samaria (722 B.C.), and consequently Egypt and Ethiopia were in fear of invasion. Isaiah bids the ambassadors to return home and quietly watch the Lord thwart Assyria's confident attempt to subjugate Judah; and he adds that when the Ethiopians have seen God's hand in the coming deliverance of Judah and Jerusalem (701 B.C.), they will bring a present to the Lord to His abode in Mt. Zion.

Chapter 19, which is an oracle concerning Egypt, contains both a threat (vv. 1-17) and a promise (vv. 18-25), and is one of Isaiah's most remarkable foreign messages. Egypt is smitten and thereby led to abandon its idols for the worship of the Lord (vv. 19-22). Still more remarkable, it is prophesied that in that day Egypt and Assyria will join with Judah in a triple alliance of common worship to the Lord and of blessing to others (vv. 23-25). Isaiah's missionary outlook here is remarkable.

Chapter 20 describes Sargon's march against Egypt and Ethiopia, containing a brief symbolic prediction of Assyria's victory over Egypt and Ethiopia. By donning a captive's garb for three years, Isaiah attempts to teach the citizens of Jerusalem that the siege of Ashdod was but a means to an end in Sargon's plan of campaign, and that it was sheer folly for the Egyptian party in Jerusalem, who were ever urging reliance upon Egypt, to look in that direction for help. In 21:11f. is a brief oracle concerning Seir or Edom, "the only gentle utterance in the OT upon Israel's hereditary foe." Edom is in great anxiety. The prophet's answer is disappointing, though its tone is sympathetic. In 21:13-17 is a brief oracle concerning Arabia. It contains a sympathetic appeal to the Temanites to give bread and water to the caravans of Dedan, who have been driven by war from their usual route of travel.

Chapter 22 concerns the foreign temper within the theocracy. It is composed of two parts: (1) an oracle "of the valley of vision," i.e., Jerusalem (vv. 1-14); and (2) a tirade against Shebna, the steward of the palace. Isaiah pauses, as it were, in his series of warnings to foreign nations to rebuke the foreign temper of the frivolous inhabitants of Jerusalem, and in particular Shebna, a high official in the government. The reckless and God-ignoring citizens of the capital are pictured as indulging themselves in hilarious eating and drinking, when the enemy is at that very moment standing before the gates of the city. Shebna, on the other hand, seems to have been an ostentatious foreigner, perhaps a Syrian by birth, quite possibly one of the Egyptian party, whose policy was antagonistic to that of Isaiah and the king. Isaiah's prediction of Shebna's fall was evidently fulfilled (36:3; 37:2).

Chapter 23 concerns Tyre. In this oracle Isaiah predicts that Tyre shall be laid waste (v. 1), its commercial glory humbled (v. 9), its colonies made independent (v. 10), and Tyre itself forgotten for "seventy years" (v. 15); but "after the end of seventy years," its trade will revive, its business prosperity will return, and it will dedicate its gains in merchandise as holy to the Lord (v. 18).

The third great section of the book of Isaiah embraces chs. 24–27, which tell of the Lord's world-judgment, issuing in the redemption of Israel. These prophecies are closely related to chs. 13–23. They express the same tender emotion as that already observed in 15:5; 16:11, and sum up as in one grand finale the prophet's oracles to Israel's neighbors. For religious importance they stand second to none in the book of Isaiah, teaching the necessity of divine discipline and the glorious redemption awaiting the faithful in Israel. They are a spiritual commentary on the great Assyrian crisis of the 8th cent.; they are messages of salvation intended not for declamation but for meditation, and were probably addressed more particularly to the prophet's inner circle of "disciples" (8:16). These chapters partake of the nature of apocalypse. Strictly speaking, however, they are prophecy, not apocalypse. No one ascends into heaven or talks with an angel, as in Dnl. 7 and Rev. 4. They are apocalypse only in the sense that certain things are predicted as sure to come to pass. Isaiah was fond of this kind of prophecy. He frequently lifts his reader out of the sphere of mere history to paint pictures of the distant future (2:2-4; 4:2-6; 11:6-16; 30:27-33).

In ch. 24 the prophet announces a general judgment of the earth (i.e., the land of Judah), and of "the city" (collective for Judah's towns), after which will dawn a better day (vv. 1-15). The prophet fancies he hears songs of deliverance, but alas! they are premature; more judgment must follow. In ch. 25 the prophet transports himself to the period after the Assyrian catastrophe and, identifying himself with the redeemed, puts into their mouths songs of praise and thanksgiving for their deliverance. Verses 6-8 describe the Lord's bountiful banquet on Mt. Zion to all nations, who, in keeping with 2:2-4, come up to Jerusalem to celebrate "a feast of fat things," rich and marrowy. While the people are present at the banquet, the Lord graciously removes their spiritual blindness so that they behold Him as the true dispenser of life and grace. He also abolishes war (cf. 2:4), and its sad accompaniment, "tears," so that "the earth" (i.e., the land of Judah) is no longer the battlefield of the nations, but the blessed abode of the redeemed, living in peace and happiness. The prophet's aim is not political but religious.

In 26:1-19 Judah sings a song over Jerusalem, the impregnable city of God. The prophet, taking again his stand with the redeemed remnant of the nation, vividly portrays their thankful trust in the Lord, who has been to them a veritable "everlasting rock" (26:4). With hope he joyfully exclaims, Let the Lord's dead ones live! Let Israel's dead bodies arise! The Lord will bring life from the dead! (v. 19). This is the first clear statement of the resurrection in the OT. But it is national and restricted to Israel (cf. v. 14), and is merely Isaiah's method of expressing a hope of the return of Israel's faithful ones from captivity (cf. Hos. 6:2; Ezk. 37:1-14; Dnl. 12:2).

In 26:20–27:13 the prophet shows that Israel's chastisements are temporary. He begins by exhorting his own people, his disciples, to continue a little longer in the solitude of prayer, till God's wrath has shattered the world-powers (26:20–27:1). He next predicts that the true vineyard of the Lord will henceforth be safely guarded against the briers and thorns of foreign invasion (27:2-6). And then, after showing that the Lord's chastisements of Israel were light compared with His judgments upon other nations (27:7-11), he promises that if Israel will only repent, the Lord will spare no pains to gather "one by one" the remnant of His people from Assyria and Egypt (cf. 11:11); and together they shall once more worship the Lord in the holy mountain at Jerusalem (27:12f.).

The prophet's fundamental standpoint in chs. 24–27 is the same as that of 2:2-4 and chs. 13–23. Yet the prophet not infrequently throws himself forward into the remote future, oscillating between his own times and those of Israel's restoration. It is especially noteworthy how he sustains himself in a long and continued transportation of himself to the period of Israel's redemption. He even studies to identify himself with the new Israel that will emerge out of the present chaos of political events. His visions of Israel's redemption carry him in ecstasy far away into the remote future, to a time when the nation's sufferings are all over; so that when he writes down what he saw in vision he describes it as a discipline that is past. For example, in 25:1-8 the prophet, transported to the end of time, celebrates in song what he saw, and describes how the fall of the world-empire is followed by the conversion of the heathen. In 26:8f. he looks back into the past from the standpoint of the redeemed in the last days, and tells how Israel longingly waited for the manifestation of God's righteousness which has now taken place, while in 27:7-9 he places himself in the midst of the nation's sufferings, in full view of its glorious future, and portrays how the Lord's dealings with Israel have not been the punishment of wrath, but the discipline of love. This kind of apocalypse, or prophecy, was indeed to be expected from the very beginning of the group of prophecies, which are introduced with the word "Behold!" Such a manner of introduction is peculiar to Isaiah, and of itself leads us to expect a message that is unique.

The practical religious value of these prophecies to Isaiah's own age would be very great. In a period of war and repeated foreign invasion, when but few people were left in the land (24:6, 13; 26:18), and Judah's cities were laid waste and desolate (24:10,12; 25:2; 26:5; 27:10), and music and gladness were wanting (24:8), when the nation still clung to its idols (27:9), and the Assyrians' work of destruction was still incomplete, other calamities were sure to follow (24:16). It would certainly be comforting to know that forgiveness was still possible (27:9), that the Lord was still the keeper of His vineyard (27:3f.), that His judgments were to last but for a little moment (26:20), that though His people should be scattered, He would soon carefully gather them "one by one" (27:12f.), that in company with other nations they would feast together on Mt. Zion as the Lord's guests (25:6-10), and that Jerusalem should henceforth become the center of life and religion to all nations (24:23; 25:6; 27:13). Such faith in the Lord, such exhortations and such songs and confessions of the redeemed, seen in vision, would be a source of rich spiritual comfort to the few suffering saints in Judah and Jerusalem, and a guiding star to the faithful disciples of the prophet's most inner circle.

Chapters 28–35 contain a cycle of prophetic warnings against alliance with Egypt, closing with a prophecy concerning Edom and a promise of Israel's ransom. As in 5:8-23, the prophet indulges in a series of six woes.

(1) Woe to drunken, scoffing politicians (ch. 28). This is one of the great chapters of Isaiah's book. In the opening section (vv. 1-6) the prophet points in warning to the proud drunkards of Ephraim whose crown (Samaria) is rapidly fading. He next turns to the scoffing politicians of Jerusalem, rebuking especially the bibulous priests who stumble in judgment, and the staggering prophets who err in vision (vv. 7-22). He closes with a most instructive parable from agriculture, teaching that God's judgments are not arbitrary; that as the husbandman does not plow and harrow his fields the whole year round, so God will not punish His people forever; and as the husbandman does not thresh all kinds of grain with equal severity, no more will God discipline His people beyond their deserts (vv. 23-29).

(2) Woe to formalists in religion (29:1-14). Isaiah's second woe is pronounced upon Ariel, the altar-hearth of God, i.e., Jerusalem, the sacrificial center of Israel's worship of the Lord in Zion. But now Zion's worship has become wholly conventional, formal, and therefore insincere; it is learned by rote (v. 13; cf. 1:10-15; Mic. 6:6-8). Therefore, says Isaiah, the Lord is forced to do an extraordinary work among them, in order to bring them back to a true knowledge of Himself (v. 14).

(3) Woe to those who hide their plans from God (29:15-24). What their plans are, which they are devising in secret, the prophet does not yet disclose; but he doubtless alludes to their intrigues with the Egyptians and their purpose to break faith with the Assyrians, to whom they were bound by treaty to pay annual tribute. Isaiah bravely remonstrates with them for supposing that any policy will succeed that excludes the counsel and wisdom of the Holy One. They are but clay; He is the potter. At this point, though somewhat abruptly, Isaiah turns his face toward the messianic future. In a very little while, he says, Lebanon, which is now overrun by Assyria's army, shall become a fruitful field, and the blind and deaf and spiritually weak shall rejoice in the Holy One of Israel.

(4) Woe to the pro-Egyptian party (ch. 30). Isaiah's

fourth woe is directed against the rebellious politicians who stubbornly, and now openly, advocate making a league with Egypt. They have at length succeeded apparently in winning over the king to their side, and an embassy is already on its way to Egypt, bearing across the desert of the Exodus rich treasures with which to purchase the friendship of their former oppressors. Isaiah now condemns what he can no longer prevent. Egypt is a Rahab "who sits still," i.e., a mythological sea monster, menacing in appearance but slow to act. When the crisis comes, Egypt will do nothing, causing Israel only shame and confusion.

(5) Woe to those who trust in horses and chariots (chs. 31–32). Isaiah's fifth woe is a still more vehement denunciation of those who trust in Egypt's horses and chariots, and disregard the Holy One of Israel. Those who do so forget that the Egyptians are but men and their horses flesh, and that mere flesh cannot avail in a conflict with spirit. Eventually the Lord means to deliver Jerusalem, if the children of Israel will but turn from their idolatries to Him; and in that day Assyria will be vanquished. A new era will dawn upon Judah. Society will be regenerated. The renovation will begin at the top. Conscience also will be sharpened, and moral distinctions will no longer be confused (32:1-8). As Delitzsch puts it, "The aristocracy of birth and wealth will be replaced by an aristocracy of character." The careless and indifferent women, too, in that day will no longer menace the social welfare of the state (32:9-14); with the outpouring of the Lord's spirit an ideal commonwealth will emerge, in which social righteousness, peace, plenty, and security will abound (32:15-20).

(6) Woe to the Assyrian destroyer (ch. 33). Isaiah's last woe is directed against the treacherous spoiler himself, who has already laid waste the cities of Judah, and is now beginning to lay siege to Jerusalem (701 B.C.). The prophet prays, and while he prays, behold! the mighty hosts of the Assyrians are routed and the long-besieged but now triumphant inhabitants of Jerusalem rush out like locusts upon the spoil that the vanishing adversary has been forced to leave behind. The destroyer's plan to reduce Jerusalem has come to naught. The whole earth beholds the spectacle of Assyria's defeat and is filled with awe and amazement at the mighty work of the Lord. Only the righteous may henceforth dwell in Jerusalem. Their eyes shall behold the Messiah-king in his beauty, reigning no longer like Hezekiah over a limited and restricted territory, but over a land unbounded, whose inhabitants enjoy the Lord's peace and protection, and are free from all sin, and therefore from all sickness (vv. 17-24). With this beautiful picture of the messianic future, the prophet's woes find an appropriate conclusion. Isaiah never pronounced a woe without adding a corresponding promise.

In chs. 34–35, the prophet utters a fierce cry for justice against "all the nations," but against Edom in particular. His tone is that of judgment. Edom is guilty of high crimes against Zion (34:8f.); therefore it is doomed to destruction. On the other hand, the scattered ones of Israel shall return from exile and "obtain joy and gladness, and sorrow and sighing shall flee away" (ch. 35).

Chapters 36–39 have history, prophecy, and song intermingled. These chapters serve both as an appendix to chs. 1–35 and as an introduction to chs. 40–66. In them three important historical events are narrated, in which Isaiah was a prominent factor: (1) the double attempt of Sennacherib to obtain possession of Jerusalem (chs. 36–37); (2) Hezekiah's sickness and recovery (ch. 38); (3) the coming of the embassy from Merodach-baladan (ch. 39). With certain important omissions and insertions these chapters are duplicated almost verbatim in 2 K. 18:13–20:19. They are introduced with the chronological note, "In the fourteenth year of King Hezekiah." Various attempts have been made to solve the mystery of this date. If the author is alluding to the siege of 701 B.C., difficulty arises, because that event occurred not in Hezekiah's "fourteenth" but in his twenty-sixth year, according to the biblical chronology of his life; or, if with some we date Hezekiah's accession to the throne of Judah as 729 B.C., then the siege of 701 B.C. occurred, as is evident, in Hezekiah's twenty-eighth year. It is barely possible of course that "the fourteenth year of King Hezekiah" was the fourteenth of the "fifteen years" which were *added* to his life, but more probably it alludes to the fourteenth year of his reign. On the whole it is better to take the phrase as a general chronological caption for the entire section, with special reference to ch. 38, the story of Hezekiah's sickness, which actually fell in his fourteenth year (714 B.C.), and which, coupled with Sargon's expected presence at Ashdod, was *the* great personal crisis of the king's life. *See also* CHRONOLOGY OF THE OT V.B.

Sennacherib made two attempts in 701 B.C. to reduce Jerusalem: one from Lachish, with an army headed by the Rabshakeh (36:2–37:8), and another from Libnah with a threat conveyed by messengers (37:9-13). The brief section contained in 2 K. 18:14-16 is omitted from between vv. 1 and 2 of Isa. 36, because it was not the prophet's aim at this time to recount the nation's humiliation. Isaiah's last "word" concerning Assyria (37:21-35) is one of the prophet's grandest predictions. It is composed of three parts: (1) a taunt-song, in elegiac rhythm, on the inevitable humiliation of Sennacherib (vv. 22-29); (2) a short poem in different rhythm, directed to Hezekiah, in order to encourage his faith (vv. 30-32); (3) a definite prediction, in less elevated style, of the sure deliverance of Jerusalem (vv. 33-35). Isaiah's prediction was literally fulfilled.

The section 38:9-20 contains Hezekiah's Song of Thanksgiving, in which he celebrates his recovery from some mortal sickness. It is a beautiful, plaintive "writing," omitted altogether by the author of the book of Kings (cf. 2 K. 20). Hezekiah was sick in 714 B.C. Two years later Merodach-baladan, the veteran archenemy of Assyria, having heard of his wonderful recovery, sent letters and a present to congratulate him. Doubtless, also, political motives prompted the recalcitrant Babylonian. But be that as it may, Hezekiah was greatly flattered by the visit of Merodach-baladan's envoys, and, in a moment of weakness, showed them all his royal treasures. This was an inexcusable blunder, as the sight of his many precious possessions would naturally excite Babylonian cupidity to possess Jerusalem. Isaiah not only solemnly condemned the king's conduct, but he announced with more than ordinary insight that the days were coming when all the accumulated resources of Jerusalem would be carried away to Babylon (39:3-6; cf. Mic. 4:10). This final prediction of judgment is the most marvelous of all Isaiah's minatory utterances, because he distinctly asserts that not the Assyrians, who were then at the height of their power, but the Babylonians would be the instruments of the divine vengeance in consummating the destruction of Jerusalem. There seems to be no real reason to doubt the genuineness of this prediction. In it, indeed, we have a prophetic basis for chs. 40–66, which follow.

Coming now to chs. 40–66, we have prophecies of comfort, salvation, and of the future glory awaiting Israel. These chapters naturally fall into three sections: (1) chs. 40–48, announcing deliverance from captivity through Cyrus; (2) chs. 49–57, describing the sufferings of the "Servant" of the Lord, this section ending like the former with the refrain, "There is no peace, says my God, for the wicked" (57:21; cf. 48:22); (3) chs. 58–66, announcing the final abolition of all national distinctions and the future glory of the people of God. Chapter 60 is the characteristic chapter of this section, as ch. 53 is of the second, and ch. 40 of the first.

In greater detail, the first section (chs. 40–48) demonstrates the deity of the Lord through His unique power to predict. The basis of the comfort that the prophet announces is Israel's incomparable God (ch. 40). Israel's all-powerful Lord is incomparable. In the prologue (40:1-11) he hears the four voices: (1) of grace (vv. 1f.); (2) of prophecy (vv. 3-5); (3) of faith (vv. 6-8), and (4) of evangelism (vv. 9-11). Then, after exalting the unique character of Israel's all-but-forgotten God (vv. 12-26), he exhorts the people not to suppose that the Lord is ignorant of, or indifferent to, Israel's misery. Israel must wait for salvation. They are clamoring for deliverance prematurely. Only wait, he repeats; for with such a God, Israel has no reason to despair (vv. 27-31).

In ch. 41 he declares that the supreme proof of the Lord's sole deity is His power to predict. He inquires, "Who stirred up one from the east?" Though the hero is left unnamed, Cyrus is doubtless in the prophet's mind (cf. 44:28; 45:1). He is not, however, already appearing upon the horizon of history as some fancy, but rather *predicted* as sure to come. The verb tenses that express completed action are perfects of certainty, and are used in precisely the same manner as those in 3:8; 5:13; 21:9. The answer to the inquiry is, "I, the Lord, the first, and with the last; I am He" (41:4). Israel is the Lord's servant. The dialogue continues; but it is no longer between the Lord and the nations, as in vv. 1-7, but between the Lord and the idols (vv. 21-29). Addressing the dumb idols, the Lord is represented as saying, Predict something, if you are real deities. As for myself, I am going to raise up a hero from the north who will subdue all who oppose him. And I announce my purpose now in advance "from the beginning," "beforetime," before there is the slightest ground for thinking that such a hero exists or ever will exist (v. 26), in order that the future may verify my prediction, and prove my sole deity. I, the Lord, alone know the future. In vv. 25-29, the prophet even projects himself into the future and speaks from the standpoint of the fulfillment of his prediction. This, as we saw above, was a characteristic of Isaiah in chs. 24-27.

In 42:1–43:13 the prophet announces also a spiritual agent of redemption, namely, the Lord's "Servant." Not only a temporal agent (Cyrus) shall be raised up to mediate Israel's redemption, which is the first step in the process of the universal salvation contemplated, but a spiritual factor. The Lord's "Servant" shall be employed in bringing the good tidings of salvation to the exiles and to the Gentiles also. In 42:1-9 the prophet describes this ideal figure and the work he will execute. The glorious future evokes a brief hymn of thanksgiving for the redemption that the prophet beholds in prospect (42:10-17). Israel has long been blind and deaf to the Lord's instructions (42:18f.), but now the Lord is determined to redeem them even at the cost of the most opulent nations of the world, that they may publish His law to all peoples (42:18–43:13).

In 43:14–44:23 forgiveness is made the pledge of deliverance. The Lord's determination to redeem Israel is all of grace. Salvation is a gift. The Lord has blotted out their transgressions for His own sake (43:25). "This passage," Dillmann observes, "marks the highest point of grace in the OT." Gods of wood and stone are nonentities. Those who manufacture idols are blind and dull of heart, and are "feeding on ashes." The section 44:9-20 is a most remorseless exposure of the folly of idolatry.

In 44:24–45:25 the prophet at length names the hero of Israel's salvation and describes his mission. He is Cyrus. He shall build Jerusalem and lay the foundations of the temple (44:28); he shall also subdue nations and let the exiles go free (45:1, 13). He speaks of Cyrus in the most extraordinary, almost extravagant terms. He is the Lord's "shepherd" (44:28); he is also the Lord's "anointed," i.e., Messiah (45:1), "the man of my counsel" (46:11), whom the Lord has called by name, and surnamed without his ever knowing Him (45:3f.); the one "whom the Lord loves" (48:14), whose right hand the Lord grasps (45:1), and who will perform all the Lord's purposes (44:28); though but "a bird of prey from the east" (46:11). The vividness with which the prophet speaks of Cyrus leads some to suppose that the latter is already upon the horizon. This, however, is a mistake. Scarcely would a contemporary have spoken in such terms of the real Cyrus of 538 B.C. The prophet regards him (i.e., the Cyrus of his own prediction, not the Cyrus of history) as the fulfillment of predictions spoken long before. That is to say, in one and the same context, Cyrus is both predicted and treated as a proof that prediction is being fulfilled (44:24-28; 45:21). Such a phenomenon in prophecy can best be explained by supposing that the prophet projected himself into the future from an earlier age. Most extraordinary of all, in 45:14-17 the prophet soars in imagination until he sees, as a result of Cyrus' victories, the conquered nations renouncing their idols, and attracted to the Lord as the Savior of all mankind (45:22). On any theory of origin, the predictive element in these prophecies is written large.

Chapters 46–47 describe further the distinctive work of Cyrus, though Cyrus himself is but once referred to. Particular emphasis is laid on the complete collapse of the Babylonian religion, the prophet being apparently more concerned with the humiliation of Babylon's idols than with the fall of the city itself. Of course the destruction of the city would imply the defeat of its gods, as also the emancipation of Israel. But here again all is in the future; in fact, the Lord's incomparable superiority and unique deity are proven by His power to predict "the end from the beginning" and bring His prediction to pass (46:10f.).

Chapter 47 is a dirge over the downfall of the imperial city, strongly resembling the taunt-song over the king of Babylon in 14:4-21.

Chapter 48 is a hortatory summary and recapitulation of the argument contained in chs. 40–47, the prophet again emphasizing the following points: (1) the Lord's unique power to predict; (2) that salvation is of grace; (3) that Cyrus' advent will be the crowning proof of the Lord's abiding presence among His people; (4) that God's chastisements were only disciplinary; and (5) that even now there is hope, if they will but accept the Lord's proffered salvation. Alas! that there is no peace or salvation for the godless (48:20-22). Thus ends the first division of Isaiah's remarkable vision of Israel's deliverance from captivity through Cyrus.

The second section (chs. 49–57) deals with the spiritual agent of salvation, the Lord's Suffering Servant. With ch. 49 the prophet leaves off attempting further to prove the sole deity of the Lord by means of prediction, and drops entirely his description of Cyrus' victories and the overthrow of Babylon, in order to set forth in greater detail the character and mission of the suffering Servant of the Lord. In chs. 40–48 he had alluded several times to this unique and somewhat enigmatical personage, speaking of him both collectively and as an individual (41:8-10; 42:1-9, 18-22; 43:10; 44:1-5, 21-28; 45:4; 48:20-22); but now he defines with greater precision both his prophetic and priestly functions, his equipment for his task, his sufferings and humiliation, and also his final exaltation. Altogether in these prophecies he mentions the Servant some twenty times. But there are four distinctive servant passages in which the prophet seems to rise above the collective masses of all Israel to at least a personification of the pious within Israel or, better, to a unique person embodying within himself all that is best in the Israel within Israel. They are the following: (1) 42:1-9, a poem descriptive of the Servant's gentle manner and worldwide mission; (2) 49:1-13, describing the Servant's mission and spiritual success; (3) 50:4-11, the Servant's soliloquy concerning His perfection through suffering; and (4) 52:13–53:12, the Servant's vicarious suffering and ultimate exaltation. In this last of the four servant passages we reach the climax of the prophet's inspired symphony, the acme of Israel's messianic hope. The profoundest thoughts in the OT revelation are to be found in this section. It is a vindication of the Servant, so clear and so true, and wrought out with such pathos and potency, that it holds first place among messianic predictions. Polycarp called it "the golden passional of the OT." According to the NT (cf. Acts 8:32f.) it has been realized in Jesus Christ.

Chapters 58–66 describe the future glory of the people of God. Having described in chs. 40–48 the temporal agent of Israel's salvation, Cyrus, and in chs. 49–57 the spiritual agent of their salvation, the Servant of the Lord, the prophet proceeds in this last section to define the conditions on which salvation may be enjoyed. He begins, as before, with a double imperative, "Cry aloud, spare not" (cf. 40:1; 49:1).

In ch. 58 he discusses true fasting and faithful sabbath observance.

In ch. 59 he beseeches Israel to forsake their sins. It is their sins, he urges, that have hidden the Lord's face and retarded the nation's salvation. In vv. 9-12 the prophet identifies himself with the people and leads them in their devotions. The Lord is grieved over Israel's forlorn condition, and, seeing their helplessness, He arms himself like a warrior to interfere judicially (vv. 15-19). Israel shall be redeemed. With them as the nucleus of a new nation, the Lord will enter anew into covenant relation, and put His spirit upon them, which will abide with them henceforth and forever (vv. 20f.).

Chapters 60–61 describe the future blessedness of Zion. The long-looked-for "light" (cf. 59:9) begins to dawn: "Arise, shine; for your light has come, and the glory of the Lord has risen upon you" (60:1). The prophet pauses at this point to paint a picture of the redeemed community. As in 2:3f. the Gentiles are seen flocking to Zion, which becomes the mistress of the nations. Foreigners build its walls, and its gates are kept open continually without fear of siege. The Gentiles acknowledge that Zion is the spiritual center of the world. Even Israel's oppressors regard it as "the city of the Lord," as "majestic for ever," in which the Lord sits as its everlasting light (60:10-22).

In ch. 61, which Drummond has called "the program of Christianity," the Servant of the Lord is again introduced, though anonymously, as the herald of salvation (vv. 1-3). The gospel monologue of the Servant is followed by a promise of the restoration and blessedness of Jerusalem (vv. 4-11). Thus the prophecy moves steadily forward toward its goal in Jesus Christ (cf. Lk. 4:18-21).

In 62:1–63:6 Zion's salvation is described as drawing near. The nations will be spectators of the great event. A new name that will better symbolize its true character shall be given to Zion, Heb. *ḥepṣî-ḇāh,* "My delight is in her"; for Jerusalem shall no more be called desolate. On the other hand, Zion's enemies will all be vanquished. In a brief poem of peculiar dramatic beauty (63:1-6), the prophet portrays the Lord's vengeance, as a victorious warrior, upon all those who retard Israel's deliverance. Edom in particular was Israel's insatiate foe. Hence the prophet represents the Lord's judgment of the nations as taking place on Edom's unhallowed soil. The Lord, whose mighty arm has wrought salvation, returns as victor, having slain all of Israel's foes.

In 63:7–64:12, the Lord's "servants" resort to prayer. They appeal to the Lord as the Begetter and Father of the nations (63:16; 64:8). With this thought of the Fatherhood of God imbedded in his language, Isaiah had opened his very first oracle to Judah and Jerusalem (cf. 1:2). As the prayer proceeds, the language becomes increasingly tumultuous. The people are thrown into despair because the Lord seems to have abandoned them altogether (63:19). They recognize that the condition of Jerusalem is desperate. "Our holy and beautiful house, where our fathers praised thee, has been burned by fire, and all our pleasant places have become ruins" (64:11). Such language, however, is the language of fervent prayer and must not be taken with rigid literalness, as 63:18 and 3:8 plainly show.

Finally, in chs. 65–66, the Lord answers His people's supplications, distinguishing sharply between His own servants and Israel's apostates. Only His chosen seed shall be delivered (65:9). Those who have obdurately provoked the Lord by sacrificing in gardens (65:3; 66:17), offering libations to Fortune and Destiny (65:11), sitting among the graves to obtain oracles from the dead, and, like the Egyptians, eating swine's flesh and broth of abominable things that were supposed to possess magical properties, lodging in vaults or crypts in which heathen mysteries were celebrated (65:4), and at the same time fancying that by celebrating such heathen mysteries they are holier than others and thereby disqualified to discharge the ordinary duties of life (65:5) — such the Lord designs to punish, measuring their work into their bosom and destroying them utterly with the sword (65:7, 12). On the other hand, the servants of the Lord shall inherit His holy mountains. They shall rejoice and sing for joy of heart, and bless themselves in the God of amen, i.e., in the God of truth (65:9, 14, 16). The Lord will create new heavens and a new earth, people will live and grow old like the patriarchs; they will possess houses and vineyards and enjoy them; for an era of idyllic peace will be ushered in with the coming of the messianic age, in which even the natures of wild animals will be changed and the most rapacious of wild animals will live together in harmony (65:17-25). Religion will become spiritual and decentralized, mystic cults will disappear, and incredulous scoffers will be silenced. Zion's population will be marvelously multiplied, and the people will be comforted and rejoice (66:1-14). Furthermore, all nations will flock to Zion to behold the Lord's glory, and from one new moon to another, and from one sabbath to another, all flesh will come up to worship in Jerusalem (66:15-23).

It is evident that the book of Isaiah closes, practically as it begins, with a polemic against false worship, and the alternate reward of the righteous and punishment of the wicked. The only essential difference between the prophet's earlier and later oracles is this: Isaiah, in his riper years, on the basis of nearly half a century's experience as a preacher, paints a much brighter eschatological picture than was possible in his early ministry. His picture of the messianic age not only transcends those of his contemporaries in the 8th cent. B.C., but he penetrates regions beyond the spiritual horizon of any and all OT seers. Such language as that contained in 66:1f., in particular, anticipates the great principle enunciated by Jesus in Jn. 4:24, namely, that "God is spirit, and those who worship him must worship in spirit and truth."

VIII. The Critical Problem.–A. History of Criticism. The Isaianic authorship of the entire prophecy was never questioned either in the OT period or that of early Christendom. The frequency with which the NT referred to Isaiah, who was cited more than all the other OT prophets combined, confirmed the view in the minds of early Christians that the composition was an integer, consciously composed by a single person. The NT references are as follows: Mt. 3:3; 8:17; 12:17-21; 13:14f.; 15:7-9; Mk. 1:2f.; 7:6f.; Lk. 3:4-6; 4:17-19; Jn. 1:23; 12:38-41; Acts 8:28-33; 28:25-29; Rom. 9:27-29; 10:16, 20f. If these quotations are examined, it will be seen that they refer to all parts of the prophecy, with citations from the first thirty-nine chapters being about the same in number as those from the last twenty-seven chapters. Many of these do not refer to the book as such, but rather attribute the utterance quoted to the man Isaiah himself. Hence we meet such phrases as "Isaiah the prophet," "the prophet Isaiah," "Isaiah prophesied," "Isaiah said again," "Isaiah said . . . saw . . . spoke," "Isaiah cries," "Isaiah says," "As Isaiah said before," "Isaiah becomes bold and says," "Well spoke the Holy Ghost through Isaiah the prophet." Thus it appears that the NT attributes various sections of the prophecy to the man Isaiah himself.

The unity of Isaiah was maintained in Christendom without question until the late 18th cent., though this degree of unanimity was not as evident in certain Jewish circles. It may have been that the talmudic tradition (T.B. *Baba Bathra* 15a) furnished some freedom for speculation in this respect, affirming that "Hezekiah and his company wrote Isaiah, Proverbs, the Song of Songs and Ecclesiastes," even though the verb "wrote" was being employed technically in the sense of "edited" or "compiled." The allusion to the "company" of Hezekiah was evidently to his eighth-century B.C. contemporaries who were responsible, under his direction, for the compilation and arranging of certain literary products (cf. Prov. 25:1). Be this as it may, the Talmud clearly set the writings of Isaiah against an eighth-century B.C. Palestinian milieu and credited Hezekiah's "company" with their arrangement in extant form. Some medieval Jewish commentators, however, began to question this tradition; e.g., Ibn Ezra (A.D. 1092-1167) denied that Isaiah was the author of the last twenty-seven chapters. In the following century a Spanish Jew, Moses Ibn Gekatilla, also wrote a commentary on Isaiah in which he denied that chs. 40–66 were the work of the eighth-century prophet, and attributed them instead to the postexilic period. These tendencies exerted no influence upon contemporary Christian opinion, however, and it was not until the 18th cent. that the impact of European rationalistic thought began to be felt on the prophecy of Isaiah.

Modern literary criticism of the book can be said to have begun with Döderlein's *Esaias* (1775), in which the author suggested, without any compelling evidence, that the book comprised two distinct works. In the German edition (1779-81) of the commentary on Isaiah by R. Lowth, J. B. Koppe advanced the view that ch. 50 might have come from an exilic writer, perhaps Ezekiel, but again nothing was adduced in the nature of historical evidence. Almost immediately this trend attracted the attention of German scholars, and in his OT introduction Eichhorn adopted the position held by the medieval Jewish commentators, regarding chs. 40–66 as the work of some person other than Isaiah ben Amoz. With the commentary by Gesenius (1821) there emerged the view that, while chs. 40–66 were non-Isaianic in character, they were still an essential literary unity. This opinion was supported by scholars such as Knobel, G. A. Smith, König, and Torrey, though not all critics who reviewed the problem were convinced that these chapters were the work of a single author, an unknown exilic prophet who by this time had become known for convenience as Second or Deutero-Isaiah. Thus Stade, in his *Geschichte des Volkes Israel* (1888), stoutly refuted the possibility that the last five chapters of the prophecy in their extant form could have been written by Isaiah at all. Budde enlarged this number in 1891 to include at least chs. 56–59, but Duhm and Marti found that even this suggestion was inadequate. Instead, in 1892, they advanced the opinion that chs. 40–55 had been composed by a Second Isaiah in Babylon somewhat before the liberating decree of Cyrus in 538 B.C., while a third or Trito-Isaiah was credited with having written chs. 56–66, probably in Palestine and subsequent to 538 B.C.

The opinions of Duhm and Marti found quick acceptance and were soon adopted as the official literary-critical view of the composition of Isaiah. Not all liberal scholars were attracted to it, however, because some of them, caught up in the fervor of source-fragmentation, were already challenging the postulated unity of chs. 40–55. In this the way had been opened up by Rückert, who as early as 1831 had used the pronouncement "there is no peace, says the Lord, to the wicked" (48:22), which occurred in similar form in 57:21, to divide chs. 40–55 into two subsections consisting of chs. 40–48 and 49–55. Kuenen in 1889 maintained that the bulk of chs. 50–55 had come from a period later than 536 B.C., and that Second Isaiah could conceivably have had a hand in composing the material. Kosters, however, denied any section of chs. 40–55 to a Second Isaiah, and this view was adopted by Cheyne in the *Polychrome Bible* (1898). The pervasive influence of Duhm was seen in the writings of Skinner, especially his *Cambridge Bible* commentary on Isaiah (1896–98), and he, along with A. B. Davidson and G. A. Smith, was responsible for promoting German literary-critical views relating to the composition of Isaiah among English-speaking peoples.

When the form-critical procedures of Gunkel began to be applied to Isaiah, some scholars regarded chs. 40–55 as an anthology of poetic material composed by Second Isaiah and arranged without regard to particular order. Those who supported such a position included Gressmann, Mowinckel, Eissfeldt, and Volz. The speculations of Duhm regarding the possibility of a Trito or Third Isaiah who had supposedly been the author of chs. 56–66 also found advocates in Europe, among whom were Kosters, Littmann, Box, Elliger, and Sellin. Other liberal critics wondered if chs. 56–66 could in fact be assigned with confidence to a single author, and the results of their speculations, which attributed various sections of these chapters to the work of anonymous individual writers, tended to increase still further the fragmentation of the prophecy and carry the process to all sorts of subjective extremes. Writers who pursued this line of approach included Cheyne, Budde, Buttenwieser, Marti, Levy, and Lods.

As part of the general literary criticism of Isaiah, some sections of the prophecy that became known as the servant passages (42:1-4, or perhaps 1-9; 49:1-6, or perhaps 1-9; 50:4-9, or perhaps 4-11; 52:13–53:12) fell under scholarly scrutiny, and provoked wide divergences of opinion in consequence. For the first three hundred years of its existence, the Church commonly identified the Servant of Isaiah with the righteous, whether on an individual or collective basis, while at the same time interpreting ch. 53 as a messianic prophecy. Subsequently the messianic interpretation became the standard way of regarding the

Servant of the Lord, but when European scholars began to reject Isaianic authorship of the prophecy, the Davidic messiah was gradually abandoned in favor of seeing the Servant in terms of the whole nation of Israel. In the 18th cent. this was begun by Semler (1771), Koppe (1779), and Eichhorn (1794), and continued in the following century with some variations by Vatke (1835), Ewald (1840), Davidson (1863), Cheyne (1870), and Driver (1888) among others, most of whom thought of an ideal and spiritual Israel rather than an actual historical people.

While these attempts at interpretation were taking place, the significance of which will be considered subsequently, scholars were attempting to relate the composition of the servant passages to the work of one or more of the "Isaiahs" allegedly involved in the writing of chs. 40–66. Fullkrug, Ley, and Blank thought that the poems were composed by Second Isaiah during the Exile as part of the section of the prophecy attributed to him, while Condamin, Sellin, Levy, and others maintained that, while Second Isaiah was the author, the material was late rather than early, and was incorporated into the prophecy in the postexilic period. Some European scholars, including Fischer, Rudolph, and Hempel, thought that the servant passages had been written by Second Isaiah after the bulk of his work had been completed, and as a result had been interpolated into the Hebrew text. Wellhausen offered a variant form of this hypothesis in suggesting that the poems had been composed by an earlier unknown author and had been taken over by Second Isaiah, who incorporated them later into his own work. Yet another view, supported by Duhm, Kittel, Kennett, and others, suggested that the oracles were the work of an anonymous composer who wrote at a later time than Second Isaiah and whose compositions were added subsequently to the prophecy by an equally unknown editor. In all of these speculations the appeal to ignorance was a marked feature, and none of the scholars involved apparently thought it either desirable or necessary to attempt to adduce objective data by which their conclusions could be tested, preferring instead to follow the highly subjective a priori procedures employed by the Graf-Wellhausen school.

These attempts to fragment the prophecy of Isaiah were more than essays in literary criticism. They were in fact a microcosm of the age, and one expression of the evolutionary *Zeitgeist* that could be found both in the humanities and in the descriptive sciences in the 19th century. The philosophical speculations of Hegel had encouraged the European savants to think in terms of a social and intellectual environment in which progress and development were assured. Consequently it was confidently imagined that the ratiocinative processes of the nineteenth-century European intelligentsia could, by their essential superiority, challenge definitively the cogitations and the literature of earlier ages, expose the fallacies and frailties of non-European thought as never before, strip away firmly the mythological accretions which were thought to have accumulated over the millennia, and reveal for the first time the true nature and content of the material under consideration. The confidence which the nineteenth-century literary critics had in their ability to unravel the mysteries of the authorship and date of OT books seemed boundless; even when they were based on only the flimsiest evidence, or as often happened on no evidence at all, the pronouncements of liberal scholars were made with a breathtaking degree of assurance and finality. Consequently it is not surprising to read in the literature of the day that the division of Isaiah among several authors represented "one of the most assured results of modern literary criticism."

Needless to say, the approaches and conclusions espoused by the Graf-Wellhausen school were not by any means shared by more conservative scholars, and the emotional fervor engendered by the fragmenting of Isaiah provoked an equally vigorous reaction among those who viewed the prophecy as a literary unity. While there were undoubted diatribes and denunciations on both sides, there were also discussions of an extremely high academic order, and in some respects the erudition of late nineteenth-century OT scholarship reached its apogee in the controversy about the literary and historical criticism of Isaiah. One of the earliest, and perhaps the most outstanding conservative study of Isaiah, and one which anticipated many later objections to the literary unity of the book, was made in 1846 by J. A. Alexander. He began by attacking the basic weaknesses in the a priori approach of contemporary liberal scholarship (*see* PENTATEUCH; CRITICISM), and went on to uphold the Isaianic authorship of chs. 40–66. In this connection he stated that it would be unparalleled in all literary history for a brilliant and erudite author such as Isaiah to have produced a series of prophecies of such vital importance for the Babylonian exiles, and then to have disappeared both from the local scene and from human memory without leaving any trace of his own personality upon them. He also asked how it was possible for this anonymous material to have been attached to the writings of Isaiah ben Amoz when, according to liberal critics, they had little or nothing in common. In addition he pointed out how comparatively few references to Babylon and the Exile occurred in chs. 40–66, a matter that C. C. Torrey was to take up with perception and insight many years later.

In a commentary on Isaiah begun in 1845 by Drechsler and completed in 1857 by Delitzsch and Hahn, the literary unity of chs. 40–66 and their Isaianic authorship were again maintained. Delitzsch held that chs. 36–39 formed a link between the Assyrian and Babylonian periods, and suggested that chs. 1–39 served as a preparation for chs. 40–66. From the same period came a brilliant commentary on Isaiah by Rudolph Stier, in which the literary integrity of the prophecy was emphasized. Five years later, in 1855, a Jewish-Italian commentary on Isaiah was published by Luzzatto. In this book the author advanced the view that the last twenty-seven chapters had been written by Isaiah ben Amoz, and that they differed from some other sections of the book in comprising prophecies concerning the future.

In 1866 the first edition of Franz Delitzsch's commentary on Isaiah appeared, and at once was recognized as an outstanding combination of philological expertise and spiritual insight. By the time the fourth edition was translated into English (1889) and furnished with an introduction by S. R. Driver, it became apparent that Delitzsch had accommodated his views throughout the work to those of most contemporary liberal scholars. He never capitulated completely, however, to the current critical speculations regarding the authorship of Isaiah, for he chose to think of chs. 40–66 as "testamentary discourses of the one Isaiah, and the entire prophetic collection as the progressive development of his incomparable charism" (*Biblical Comm. on the Prophecies of Isaiah* [1880], II, pp. 125f.). Elsewhere he thought that the author of chs. 40–66 was "in any case a prophet of the Isaianic type, but of an Isaianic type peculiarly developed," and of the material itself as being attributable ultimately to Isaiah, if, in fact, he was not the immediate author (pp. 129, 133).

Despite unremitting opposition from conservative scholars, the divisive theories of Duhm held the field in liberal circles, and conveyed the general impression that the literary-critical problems of Isaiah were settled to all intents and purposes. Impressive though this show of critical unanimity appeared, it was not destined to survive more than the first four decades of the 20th century. Unmistakable fissures in the facade began to appear by about 1940, and became evident in 1944 when Sidney Smith delivered a series of lectures on what he deemed to be the historical material illustrative of chs. 40–55. Instead of employing the type-analytical (*Gattungsforschung*) techniques of Gunkel and Gressmann, Smith related the historical events of the period between 547 and 538 B.C. to the section of Isaiah that he was studying. Having achieved this objective, he then set out the material in the original structure of speeches composed by the prophet that had then been circulated, according to Smith, in the form of approximately twenty-two pamphlets. These included all of the servant passages, the last of which (52:13–53:12) Smith connected with the death of Isaiah himself.

A barrage of criticism greeted the publication of the book, and there can be no question but that some of the strictures were richly deserved. Smith's treatment of the servant passages, the fourth one in particular, was very unsatisfactory, and much of the historical material that he had adduced to support his thesis was extremely tenuous. His treatment of the problem was outstanding, however, in the way in which he proposed serious historical links between the period of 547-538 B.C. and the material in chs. 40–55 of Isaiah. It is difficult to resist the conclusion that the criticisms of his position were aroused in no small measure by a fear of what the future might hold for the entire scheme of liberal criticism of Isaiah.

In 1962, Mauchline published a commentary on chs. 1–39 of the prophecy, and a notable feature of the work was the conservative position adopted toward sections that had been regarded previously as interpolations by later editors. The results of his study enabled him to see Isaiah as the substantial author of chs. 13–27, and in this conclusion he diverged considerably from many liberal scholars, who had commonly assigned certain sections of that material to a postexilic period. There were certain contradictions in his method, however, and they seemed to be of a kind that would beset anyone writing from a general liberal background. Thus he saw no inconsistency, as other critics had done, between the references to Babylon in ch. 39 and Isaianic authorship of that section; at the same time he utilized the mention of the Medes and Babylon in Isa. 13:17-19 as a reason for adhering to an exilic date for the passage. Had he allowed room for a genuinely predictive element in the narrative, however, the apparent problem would have been resolved immediately.

The literary-critical position was reemphasized by the publication of J. L. McKenzie's commentary on Second Isaiah (*AB*, 1968). He studiously ignored any position other than his own, and seemed blissfully unaware of the effect that certain evidence from Qumrân (see below) has had upon the literary-critical problem of Isaiah. Meanwhile, conservative scholars were continuing to argue for the integrity and Isaianic authorship of the prophecy, and their writings included works by Allis (1950), Young (1965-74), and Buksbazen (1971-74).

B. Arguments for Divided Authorship. From the preceding survey it will have become apparent that, as long as only internal evidence is considered, the polarization of views concerning the authorship and date of the prophecy is much the same now as it was a century ago. Before any attempt is made to resolve this situation, it would seem desirable to subject the arguments for a divided authorship of the prophecy to careful examination so as to test their validity. According to S. R. Driver (*Intro. to the Literature of the OT* [9th ed. 1913], pp. 236ff.), these fell into three broad categories. First, chs. 40–66 seemed to point to a period of composition toward the close of the Babylonian Exile rather than to a time in the 8th cent. B.C. According to this view the Exile was presupposed, not predicted, and those addressed were thought to be already exiled and awaiting a return to Palestine. In consonance with their general disavowal of a predictive element in prophecy, liberal literary critics held that it was impossible for Isaiah to have sustained so lengthy a futuristic standpoint and to have addressed persons who were more than a century in the future.

The second argument for separating chs. 40–66 and assigning them to some author other than Isaiah ben Amoz rested upon stylistic considerations. Accordingly it was argued that new imagery and phraseology occurred to replace (to some degree at least) the ideas and terminology of chs. 1–39, with phenomena such as the duplication of words occurring more prominently in chs. 40–66. The literary style of this latter section was held to be marked by a personification of cities and nature alike, a dramatic depicting of the fortunes of individuals and nations, and an impassioned lyricism that made the section one of outstanding literary quality. By contrast, the style of Isaiah ben Amoz in chs. 1–39 was described as terse and compact, and the thought and ideas as moving in a measured, unexceptional manner.

The third criterion for the division of the prophecy involved the theological concepts of chs. 40–66. Thus it was alleged that, whereas earlier chapters spoke of God's majesty, later ones described His uniqueness and eternity. In the first part of the prophecy it was maintained that the remnant constituted the faithful left behind in Jerusalem, whereas in later chapters the remnant consisted of the exiled Judeans about to be brought back to Palestine. A third supposition was that the messianic king of chs. 1–39 was replaced by the servant concept of chs. 40–66.

C. Arguments Against Divided Authorship. Conservative scholars met the first of these objections by recognizing that the difference in the time-perspective between the first and second supposed divisions of the prophecy was of an ideal rather than a real nature. Taking their cue from remarks such as those made by Driver (*Intro.*, p. 237) to the effect that there were instances where Isaiah ben Amoz projected himself into the future and then described certain events yet to take place as though they had already occurred (cf. 5:13-17; 9:1-7; 23:1, 14), they asked why it would not have been possible for a prophet as great as the author of chs. 40–66 to have maintained exactly the same kind of ideal standpoint for some prolonged period also. In addition it was pointed out that the Exile was not an event that was still very much in the future for Isaiah, but a process that had for long been initiated by God's people, and whose culmination was in fact a commonplace of prophetic observation and prediction.

Issue was also taken with the way in which critical scholars either minimized or else rejected completely the predictive element in prophecy, and in particular their allegation that it would be unprecedented for the name of Cyrus to have been mentioned more than a century and a half before his birth. Conservative writers then cited the prophetic utterance that foretold the name of Josiah more than three hundred years before he was born (1 K. 13:1f.), the mention of Bethlehem by Micah, Isaiah's contemporary, as the birthplace of the Messiah (Mic. 5:2; Mt. 2:6) some six hundred years before the event, and the subjugation of Tyre by the Babylonians as predicted both by Ezekiel (26:2-21) and Zechariah (9:1-4). The first of these prophecies proved particularly embarrassing to liberal scholars, since there was absolutely no possibility whatever of the Hebrew text being corrupt at that point, and in the end they quietly gave up the task of attempting to meet this devastating criticism of their position, other than insisting that there could be no predictive element in prophecy.

Equally difficult for liberal scholarship was the task of furnishing convincing evidence for the theory that chs. 40–66 were written in Babylonia. Duhm and others followed the general tradition of the Graf-Wellhausen school by formulating speculative accounts of the way in which this eventuality could have happened, but no amount of critical ingenuity could furnish any actual proof. C. C. Torrey, one of the more extreme critics of his day, was so skeptical of this kind of approach that he asserted flatly that the few references to Babylon and Cyrus in chs. 40–66 were bungling editorial insertions, and that the bulk of the material could be assigned without question to a Palestinian milieu. Some liberal scholars made a determined attempt to see a Babylonian background in the description of religion, buildings, and local scenery, but when pressed they were forced to concede that nothing of a cultural, geographical, or topographical nature suggested any locale other than Palestine as the place of origin of the prophecy. That no place other than Judah or Jerusalem was mentioned in chs. 40–66 as the actual home of the Judeans supported this Palestinian provenance. From the foregoing discussion it would therefore appear that the Babylonian Exile was in fact being predicted rather than being presupposed in chs. 40–66, and that those addressed were still living in Palestine and had not yet been transported as captives to Babylonia.

Arguments from literary style have always been rather tenuous and highly subjective in nature, though this fact was unfortunately not recognized by the members of the Graf-Wellhausen school. Curiously enough, the adherents of this approach to OT study saw no inconsistency whatever in investigating material ascribed to some biblical author, and then denying to his literary activity certain parts of that corpus simply because the literary form and vocabulary of each chapter did not happen to correspond in minute detail. Conservative scholars were not slow to point out the anomalies involved, and this, along with the much wider knowledge of ancient Near Eastern languages that scholars now possess, has resulted in far less reliance being placed upon this form of argument than was the case previously. It is now conceded openly that arguments based on style can prove to be extremely precarious in nature, and not infrequently to be resting upon a complete misunderstanding of the literary situation, as the following example will show. Liberal scholars have commonly argued that, because a Mesopotamian literary idiom occurs in Isa. 45:7, an exilic date and a Babylonian provenance must obviously be indicated for the chapter in question, and by implication, for chs. 40–55 at the least. The idiom referred to is known to modern scholars as *merismus,* in which antonyms used in pairs are employed to designate the totality of a given situation. This particular form originated with the Sumerians, and is one of the oldest literary idioms known. At an early period its usage diffused northward into the subsequent Babylonian culture, and westward into the language and thought of Egypt. On prima facie grounds, the incidence of *merismus* in Isa. 45:7 could equally well imply an Egyptian or a Mesopotamian origin for the material. Yet because purely speculative considerations demanded for liberal scholars a Babylonian provenance, the possibility that the chapter could have come (at least on the grounds of this particular piece of linguistic evidence) from Egypt was never even considered, let alone dismissed. If the incidence of *merismus* were to be in fact the deciding criterion, however, the very first chapter of the prophecy would have to be attributed to someone other than Isaiah ben Amoz, and to a period other than the 8th cent. B.C., since the second verse contains an obvious *merismus* ("heavens . . . earth"). Yet not even the most radical literary critic has been presumptuous enough to make this suggestion. Obviously Isaiah's use of *merismus,* which of course is not restricted to the two verses mentioned above, cannot possibly determine the date of any section of any composition, prophetic or otherwise. Certain *merismus* expressions do have another extremely important function in the prophecy of Isaiah, the significance of which will be examined subsequently.

Even with the information that was then at their disposal, nineteenth-century scholars were clearly wrong in suggesting the kind of wide stylistic divergences that they did, because a close study of the prophecy shows that chs. 1–39 and 40–66 have close verbal agreement in specific instances. For example, emphatic reduplication occurs in 2:7, 8; 6:3; 8:9; 24:16, 23; 40:1; 43:11, 25; 48:15; 51:12; 57:19; and 62:10. The agonies of a woman in labor are mentioned in 13:8; 21:3; 26:17, 18; 42:14; 54:1; 66:7, while the position occupied by Zion in the prophet's thoughts can be seen in 2:3; 4:4; 18:7; 24:23; 28:16; 29:8; 30:19; 31:9; 33:5, 20; 34:8; 46:13; 49:14; 51:3, 16; 52:1; 59:20; 60:14; 62:1, 11; 66:8. It is rather interesting from a stylistic standpoint that the expression "the mouth of the Lord has spoken" should occur in 1:20; 40:5; 58:14, and be found nowhere else in the OT, and that the phrase translated "running with water" (30:25) and "flowing streams" (44:4) should not be found anywhere else in the Hebrew scriptures. The terseness of literary style allegedly confined to chs. 1–39 occurs also in chs. 40–66, with ch. 53 being a case in point. Chs. 40–66 contain both verbal agreements with 1–39 and similarities in thought or figure, as the following chart indicates.

Verbal Agreements

40:5; 58:14	1:20	56:8	11:12
43:13	14:27	61:2; 63:4	34:8
45:11; 60:21	19:25; 29:23	65:25	11:9
51:11	35:10		

Similarities in Thought or Figure

40:3f.; 49:11	35:8-10	54:7f.	26:20
41:17f.; 43:19	35:6f.	55:12	14:8; 32:15; 35:1f.
42:1; 61:1	11:2	56:7	2:2
42:7	9:2 (MT 1)	56:8	11:12
42:13	31:4	56:12	22:13
42:18-20; 43:8	6:9	59:3	1:15
43:13	14:27	59:11	38:14
43:24	1:14	60:13	35:2
43:26	1:14-19	60:18	26:1
45:9; 64:8 (MT 7)	29:16	60:21	11:1
45:15	8:17	61:8	1:11, 13
47:3	3:17; 20:4	62:10	11:12
47:10	29:15; 30:1	63:17	6:10
49:2	11:4	65:3; 66:17	1:29
49:26	9:20 (MT 19)	65:19	35:10
51:4	2:3	65:25	11:6
51:9	27:1	66:16	27:1
53:2	11:1, 10		

An examination of the foregoing shows that so far from diverging midway through the extant prophecy, the literary style of the book exhibits an amazing consistency. It also makes clear that Isaiah's literary style differed significantly from that of every other OT prophet, and in particular shows that it diverged widely from that employed by Ezekiel and the postexilic prophets.

The same considerations hold good for the theological

differences alleged for chs. 1–39 and 40–66. In this connection notice should be taken of a characteristic name for God, "the Holy One of Israel." It occurs twenty-six times in the prophecy, and only six times elsewhere in the OT, one of which is in a parallel passage in Kings (2 K. 19:22; cf. Ps. 71:22; 78:41; 89:18 [MT 19]; Jer. 50:29; 51:5). This unique description unifies the various sections in which it appears, and stamps them with the personal imprimatur of the one who saw the vision of the most high God seated on His throne, and heard the angelic choir singing His praise and glory (6:3). Against the unproven assertion that the two supposed divisions of the prophecy exhibit substantial theological differences, the presence of this concept of God as the Holy One of Israel is a strong argument for the theological unity of the work, distributed as it is twelve times in chs. 1–39 (1:4; 5:19, 24; 10:20; 12:6; 17:7; 29:19; 30:11f., 15; 31:1; 37:23) and thirteen times in chs. 40–66 (41:14, 16, 20; 43:3, 14; 45:11; 47:4; 48:17; 49:7; 54:5; 55:5; 60:9, 14). Such an even and consistent distribution would have been impossible had the prophecy as a whole arisen from such diverse historical circumstances as the liberal critics claimed. Another concept which occurs with some frequency in the prophecy is that of a highway (11:16; 35:8; 40:3; 43:19; 49:11; 57:14; 62:10). References to the temple and its worship also presuppose a uniform preexilic Palestinian milieu throughout. Thus 1:11-15 reflects a situation when all was flourishing in the land, whereas the attack of Sennacherib has brought about different conditions in 43:23f. In 66:1-3, 6, 20, not only is the existence of the temple and its ritual presupposed, but the prophet is active in condemning those very features that were to occupy Jeremiah's thoughts so much in the following century.

One of the most important unifying theological concepts has to do with the strictures of Isaiah concerning idolatry. Such references, especially as they occur in chs. 40–66, present a uniform picture of preexilic veneration of Canaanite deities and indulgence in the sensual rituals now illustrated by archeological discoveries at Ugarit (Râs Shamrah). Critical scholars have failed to observe that, apart from the description of Babylonian idolatry in 47:13, all other references to such practices in chs. 40–66 are specifically to the preexilic Canaanite variety mentioned in 1:13, 29; 2:8; 8:19, and elsewhere. Such allusions in later chapters of the extant prophecy include 40:19; 41:7, 29; 42:17; 44:9, 25; 45:16; 46:6f.; 48:5; 57:5f.; 66:3, 17. Of the preceding, it is impossible to interpret 44:9, 25 and 57:5 in any terms other than those of the familiar preexilic Canaanite idolatry. If this material had in fact come from the Exile and had been written by an unknown prophet, it is most strange that the author was so actively concerned with something that was meaningless to his compatriots in Babylonia, and which in fact, both socially and religiously, was a completely dead issue. But since the ancient Hebrew prophets were not given to answering questions that their hearers were not asking, it can only be concluded that those who interpret the material of chs. 40–66 in terms of an exilic or postexilic standpoint are construing incorrectly such evidence as they purport to possess. There can be no doubt that, in reality, the social and religious background of the content of chs. 40–66 is that of the preexilic period, as Kissane showed so competently (E. J. Kissane, *Book of Isaiah* [1943], II, xlvi ff.). If nineteenth-century literary critics had made an honest attempt to relate chs. 40–66 to Hebrew history, it would have become clear to them immediately that certain portions of that section could not be relegated to any point within the exilic period. Thus in 40:9 the stronghold of Zion and the cities of Judah are still in existence, a situation vastly different from the known conditions at the time of the Exile. Again, in 62:6 the walls of Jerusalem were mentioned explicitly in a context of well-being and prosperity, and it is impossible to interpret this state of affairs either in terms of the Exile or the early postexilic period. By contrast, against an obvious background of eighth-century-B.C. life in the southern kingdom, Isaiah regards the Exile as an already accomplished fact, as in 1:7-9; 5:13; and 14:1-4. Theology, religion, and history thus combine to emphasize the unity of background and provenance of the extant work.

The later chapters of the prophecy of Isaiah have a far greater degree of consonance with the statements of the eighth-century B.C. prophets about current religious and moral conditions than most liberal critics have been prepared to concede. Such reflections can be seen in 44:23f.; 45:8; 50:1; 55:12f.; 56:1; 57:1; 59:3; 61:8; 63:3-5. Especially striking are the similarities between the doctrines of Isa. 40–66 and the teachings of Micah. The following resemblances should be noted: Isa. 41:15f. and Mic. 4:13; Isa. 47:2f. and Mic. 1:11; Isa. 48:2 and Mic. 3:11; Isa. 49:23 and Mic. 7:17; Isa. 52:12 and Mic. 2:13; Isa. 58:1 and Mic. 3:8. Quite obviously the same confident expectation of the future under God's providence, the same overall conception of the ancient Near Eastern nations, and the joyous hope that a remnant would return from exile to perpetuate the ancestral faith, were characteristic of both prophets.

Conservative scholars generally answered the arguments relating to supposed differences in theological standpoint and perspective by demonstrating that the concepts elaborated in later sections of the prophecy were broader and more extended in scope than their counterparts in chs. 1–39. Thus the messiah, who had been described in earlier parts of the prophecy in terms of a king who would be of Davidic stock, was subsequently thought of as the Servant of the Lord. But even here the mention of David in 55:3 makes it evident that the earlier concept of a royal Davidic descendant had not by any means been abandoned in favor of the servant ideal. As will be shown subsequently, the extant prophecy exhibits a remarkable parallelism of both structure and thought so that specific theological emphases occur in a context that makes it extremely difficult to argue against the integrity of the work and an eighth-century-B.C. Palestinian provenance. There is no evidence for the assertion that in chs. 1–39 the remnant comprised the faithful left behind in Jerusalem, but in chs. 40–66 it was understood as the exiled group of Judeans preparing to return to Palestine. As observed above, it is impossible to show that any locale other than Judean soil was the place from which chs. 40–66 emerged. The topography, the references to Canaanite idolatry, and the significance of the temple and the house of David all point to a distinctively Palestinian background and refute any suggestion of a Babylonian provenance.

One other strong argument against a divided authorship should be noted in passing, and this has to do with the predictive element in the prophecy. Prediction was of the essence of prophetic activity (cf. Dt. 18:22), and Isaiah was particularly gifted in this direction. Without any warning he repeatedly leaped from despair to hope, from threat to promise, and from the actual to the ideal. While he spoke of his own age, of course, he also addressed himself to the days that would follow, as shown by the fact that his verb tenses are typically futures and prophetic perfects. The following historical situations in the prophecy are worthy of note. Before the Syro-Ephraimitic war (734 B.C.), he predicted that within sixty-five years Ephraim should be broken to pieces (7:8); and that before the child

Maher-shalal-hashbaz should have knowledge to cry, "My father," or "My mother," the riches of Damascus and the spoil of Samaria should be carried away (8:4; cf. 7:16). These are, however, but two of numerous predictions, as shown above, among his earlier prophecies (cf. 1:27f.; 2:2-4; 6:13; 10:20-23; 11:6-16; 17:14). Shortly before the downfall of Samaria in 722 B.C. Isaiah predicted that Tyre should be forgotten seventy years, and that after the end of seventy years its merchandise should be dedicated to the Lord (23:15, 18). In like manner, prior to the siege of Ashdod in 711 B.C., he proclaimed that within three years Moab should be brought into contempt (16:14), and that within a year all the glory of Kedar should fail (21:16). And not long prior to the siege of Jerusalem by Sennacherib in 701 B.C. he predicted that in an instant, suddenly, a multitude of Jerusalem's foes should be as dust (29:5); that yet a very little while and Lebanon should be turned into a fruitful field (29:17); and that Assyria should be dismayed and fall by the sword, but not of men (30:17, 31; 31:8). And more, that for days beyond a year, the careless women of Jerusalem should be troubled (32:10, 16-20); and that the righteous in Zion should see Jerusalem a quiet habitation, and return and come with singing (33:17ff.; 35:4, 10); but that Sennacherib, on the contrary, should hear tidings and return without shooting an arrow into the city (37:7, 26-29, 33-35).

In like manner, *after* the siege of Jerusalem by Sennacherib in 701 B.C. was over, the prophet seems to have continued to predict; and, in order to demonstrate to the suffering and unbelieving remnant about him the deity of the Lord and the folly of idolatry, pointed to the predictions which he had already made in the earlier years of his ministry, and to the fact that they had been fulfilled. These references include 41:21-23, 26; 42:9, 23; 43:9, 12; 44:7f., 27f.; 45:3f., 11, 13; 46:10f.; 48:3, 5; 48:6-8, 14-16. There can be no doubt that these predictions are as consistent throughout the extant prophecy as they are explicit and emphatic.

D. The Prophecy as an Anthology. As W. F. Albright pointed out (*FSAC*, p. 275), scholars are becoming increasingly aware that most OT prophecies are really anthologies of oracular and sermonic material, since their contents are seldom in chronological order. The Hebrew prophets did not set out to elaborate a system of theology in their teachings, but instead spoke the divine word as they received it in spiritual fellowship with God. They addressed themselves to the needs of their age, and were infinitely more concerned about speaking to the contemporary situation than in correlating specific utterances to a given phase or epoch of history, in the manner that a chronicler might have done. Thus it is not surprising, even in fairly short prophecies, to encounter chronologically different sections in juxtaposition. It would seem that, in most instances, the aim of the written prophecy was to afford permanence for the spoken word in that and subsequent generations, mindful of the fact that, in the ancient Near East, anything of importance was committed to writing either when it happened or shortly afterward.

By definition, an anthology of written work can, and most frequently does, emerge from an extended period of the author's literary activity, and thus can be expected not only to reflect specific differences of literary style, but an equal diversity of social, historical, or religious circumstances, many of which would have prompted the composition of various items of the collection in the first instance. Again, an anthology normally comprises selections from the author's works, where a single individual is involved, and not his entire production of literature. While some of the Minor Prophets may have written or spoken little else beyond what is attributed to them in extant works, major writers such as Jeremiah or Isaiah probably produced far more than has actually survived. Certainly it is correct to regard Isaiah as an anthology in the sense described above because of the evidence furnished by the superscription of 1:1. This verse comprises a heading for the prophecy and speaks specifically of the revelatory material received by Isaiah in visions in the reigns of Uzziah, Jotham, Ahaz, and Hezekiah. The nature of the prophecy as an anthology is further indicated by the presence of superscriptions in 2:1 and 13:1; these may well have pointed to the presence of earlier collections of prophetic pronouncements.

Although Isaiah may be regarded properly as an anthology, it must not be imagined that the book is a rather arbitrary selection of discourses compiled haphazardly. That the work received its extant form from the specific application of a special type of literary structure familiar to the ancient Near Eastern peoples will be made evident below. For the moment it should be noted that the extant composition manifests a certain degree of chronological order as it stands. In chs. 1–39, the utterances in chs. 2–5 seem to have emerged from the earliest stages of Isaiah's ministry, while 7:1–9:7 probably came from a period about 734 B.C., during the Syro-Ephraimite conflict. While some doubt remains, it may well be that chs. 18–20 were the product of the period between 715 and 711 B.C. The historical material of chs. 36–39, which varies only slightly from 2 K. 18:13–20:19, has been held to be later than Isaiah since it mentioned Sennacherib's death (681 B.C.). This would be later than Isaiah unless he survived to the early years of Manasseh (687/6-642/1 B.C.), as Jewish tradition has long maintained. It may be that this historical material was arranged by the disciples of Isaiah after his death. It is exceedingly difficult, however, to maintain as liberal scholars have done that chs. 36–39, in which Isaiah himself played such an important part, were in fact extraneous and specifically non-Isaianic in origin. There seem to be good grounds for thinking that this material comprised an Isaiah source upon which the compiler of Kings drew. The existence of a separate Isaianic source dealing with the life of Hezekiah appears to be indicated by 2 Ch. 32:32, which suggests that the excerpt from the Book of the Kings of Israel and Judah might have been taken from the vision of Isaiah. Furthermore, that the song of Hezekiah (Isa. 39:9-20) occurred in the prophecy but not in the section in Kings indicates that the editor of the latter apparently thought the material unsuitable for his purposes. That the preservation of strict chronological sequences was not the overriding concern of the author is plain from Isa. 9:8-21, which may well comprise the earliest pronouncements of Isaiah. Again, the utterances concerning Damascus (17:1-14) may be dated somewhat before 735 B.C., a period that is probably very close to the events narrated in ch. 7.

Evidence of some sort of chronological arrangement appears in chs. 40–55, which predict the return from Exile and the time of restoration of national life. These include sections dealing with the work of Cyrus (41–45), predictions concerning the downfall of Babylon (46–47), and utterances describing the glories of the new Jerusalem (49–54). Nor should one ignore the suggestion that the compiler(s) arranged the material of chs. 56–66 in a way that presented in alternate form prophecies whose standpoints were preexilic (56:1–57:12; 59:1–60:22; 62:1–63:19; 65:1-25) and exilic (58:1-14; 61:1-11; 64:1-12; 66:1-14), with 57:14-21 and 66:15-24 perhaps comprising fragments of such oracles.

Another suggestion regarding the manner in which the

The great Isaiah Scroll from Qumrân (1QIsa[a]) open to 2:21–3:22 (Israel Museum)

Isaianic anthology was compiled relates to the arrangement of material according to subject matter. Some scholars have seen the opening chapters (1–35) as a series of oracles emerging from Isaiah's contemporary situation, followed by a section of historical material (36–39). The next group of utterances (40–55) presupposed the Exile in Babylon, as some earlier references had done, while the remainder of the extant prophecy (56–66) comprised a diverse group of oracles that picked up themes already prominent in earlier chapters. The presence of three superscriptions in the prophecy (1:1; 2:1; 13:1) was seen as perhaps representing three separate written compilations by Isaiah, upon which the editor(s) drew subsequently. Although an approach of this sort partially explains the parallelism between different portions of the book, it does so from a purely occidental standpoint, and therefore does not offer a satisfactory explanation of the mechanics involved in the compilation of the prophecy. Quite clearly, then, the questions associated with the way in which the anthology reached its present form are much more involved than has been imagined by anyone, whether liberal or conservative, who has been approaching this piece of oriental literature on the basis of occidental theoretical presuppositions.

E. Evidence from Qumrân. A new approach to the problem of the authorship and compilation of Isaiah became possible as the result of the recovery from Qumrân of the celebrated Dead Sea Scrolls. From Cave 1 came a complete copy of the book of Isaiah, known to scholars as 1QIsa[a]. Surprisingly well preserved, it comprised fifty-four columns of clearly written Hebrew script inscribed on seventeen sheets of leather that had been stitched end to end. When unrolled it measured about 7.3 m. (24 ft.) in length, and was approximately 30 cm. (1 ft.) in width. The text averaged twenty-nine lines to each column, and instead of being set out in chapter-and-verse form, as in the more modern style, it was divided up into clearly marked sections and paragraphs. Although the scroll had obviously been used a great deal in antiquity, the manuscript had only ten lacunae and about one dozen small holes, a circumstance that made restoration of the text a comparatively easy matter. Copyists' errors were evident in the text, as were the corrections of such mistakes, and the work of several different hands is apparent in a few instances in the manuscript. Aside from differences in orthography and the use of certain consonants as vowel letters, the text of Isaiah in 1QIsa[a] was identical with that in the much later editions of the MT.

When the scholarly world learned of the existence of an ancient Isaiah scroll among the Qumrân writings, many hoped that at long last it would be possible to say something of a positive nature about the number of Isaiahs who were responsible for the extant prophecy. A photographic edition of the scroll showed that no gap occurred between the end of ch. 39 and the beginning of ch. 40, as is the case in some modern translations of the prophecy. Since ch. 40 began on the bottom line of a column, it would have been very easy for a copyist to have followed a division in the Hebrew text if such had actually existed in the manuscript from which he was working. But it was noticed that a break in the text occurred at the end of ch. 33, where a space of three lines occurred before the commencement of ch. 34. If at that stage of investigation the scholars attributed any significance to this phenomenon, it was merely to suggest that the change of authorship occurred some six chapters earlier than the literary ana lysts had supposed. Indeed, at least one nineteenth-century scholar, W. Robertson Smith (*Prophets of Israel* [1895], p. 355) had actually raised that possibility, but had been ignored by those who were acclaiming an "unknown prophet of the exile" as the author of at least some of the material from ch. 40 onward.

Paul Kahle (*Die Hebraïschen Handschriften aus der Höhle* [1951], pp. 72f.) was the first to comment on the incidence of a gap in the text after ch. 33; he claimed that it substantiated C. C. Torrey's notion that chs. 34 and 35, along with chs. 40–66, belonged to the activities of a Deutero-Isaiah. Unfortunately this observation afforded no explanation whatever of the reason why chs. 36–39 came to form part of the work of this Second Isaiah. The matter remained unresolved until W. H. Brownlee published a treatise (*Meaning of the Qumrân Scrolls for the Bible* [1964]) that for the first time attempted to visualize the composition of the book from the standpoint of an ancient Near Eastern, rather than an occidental, author. Brownlee noted that in antiquity it was not unusual for books to be produced in two parts (cf. H. St. John Thackeray, *Septuagint and Jewish Worship* [1923], pp. 130ff.), perhaps for convenience in handling bulky writings. Furthermore, there are good reasons for believing that literary works of high quality were often planned with a natural division in the middle of the composition. Josephus obviously attributed this sort of activity to certain of the Hebrew literary prophets in observing that Ezekiel, Daniel, and Isaiah had left their writings behind in "books" (*Ant.* x.5.1; x.2.2; x.11.7). The plural form would thus describe quite properly a work produced in two halves, or in bifid form, to use a more modern term. In the extant Isaiah, such a structure would encompass two sections of thirty-three chapters each, and thus it is now possible, as Brownlee has shown, to regard the break in the text of 1QIsa[a] that occurs at the end of ch. 33 as indicating that the ancient practice of bisecting an important literary work was being followed. For Brownlee, the extant prophecy comprised the outcome of effort by an Isaianic school, whose major achievement was the publication in two volumes of the utterances of the master.

Brownlee analyzed the structure and contents of the prophecy to show the way in which chs. 1–33 were parallel to chs. 34–66. The results can be set out in tabular form as follows:

Subject	1–33	34–66
Ruin and Restoration	1–5	34–35
Biographical Material	6–8	36–40
Agents of Divine Blessing and Judgment	9–12	41–45
Oracles Against Foreign Powers	13–23	46–48
Universal Redemption and the Deliverance of Israel	24–27	49–55
Ethical Sermons	28–31	56–59
Restoration of the Nation	32–33	60–66

This arrangement for Brownlee was not so much an analysis of the literary units from which the book was derived as a way of viewing the complete composition from the standpoint of the original editors, whose primary interest was in literary balance and parallelism, not in literary origins.

Such an analysis constitutes the best attempt on the part of liberal scholarship to come to grips with the book's real problems, which involve method rather than history or theology. Literary criticism in the past has been far too subjective and speculative in nature, and has failed to face the implications of objective data. The grave methodological weakness of past literary criticism was that it examined oriental literature from an occidental point of view, an error that was compounded by the application of an overriding a priori approach. Modern literary research will have to reexamine the problems upon which the nineteenth-century scholars pronounced with such authority and finality, using all of the pertinent data and applying a scientific, a posteriori method of investigation in order to interpret correctly the significance of the material under consideration. In the case of Isaiah, the evidence relating to the structure of the prophecy as furnished by 1QIsa[a] indicates clearly that the extant canonical work was one of the most elaborate and artistically constructed anthologies ever to have emerged from the ancient Near East. Brownlee is correct in stating that it was written as a two-volume work, and on closer examination it can be actually seen to have been linked in series in the typical Mesopotamian scribal fashion by means of the ancient Sumerian literary figure known as *merismus*. This device, already described above, involved the use of antonymic pairs to denote totality, and in the case of Isaiah such pairs were used to comprise markers at the beginning of volumes one and two. They occur in 1:2 ("O heavens . . . O earth"), introducing the first section of the scroll, and again in 34:1 ("O nations . . . O peoples . . . the earth . . . the world"), which introduces the second section of the two-part composition.

With this kind of notation there can be no possible doubt that the balance of sections and themes as outlined by Brownlee was deliberate rather than accidental. The prophecy obviously was assembled in bifid form so that each half could circulate independently if necessary, and owing to the size of the composition there can be little question but that this would have actually taken place. It is equally clear that this arrangement was carefully planned, claimed a high degree of literary and functional artistry, and was constructed in full accord with certain accepted compilatory techniques familiar to the scribes of antiquity. All of this the large Qumrân Isaiah scroll has now made evident. Whatever may have been the history of independent circulation of the two units forming the extant Isaiah, the prophecy had evidently been known as a unity long before the copyists of the Qumrân settlement commenced their labors.

F. Composition and Date of Isaiah. On the basis of the foregoing information it is possible to make a new and responsible approach to the problems involving the compilation and date of the prophecy. Taking the latter first, the cumulative evidence from Qumrân demands a much closer look at the tradition of eighth-century-B.C. authorship for Isaiah. The Qumrân fellowship is now known to have originated as a schismatic group during or perhaps a little prior to the Maccabean period. All of its scriptural manuscripts were copies, and not originals; thus it is obvious that none of them could have originated in the Maccabean period, since an adequate amount of time would not have elapsed between the original autograph and the general acceptance of the composition as canonical scripture. One criterion for canonical status of material in the second and third divisions of the Hebrew canon was a comparison with the ethos of the Mosaic Law. Because of the need for manuscripts to circulate among both the religious authorities and the devout, a certain interval of time between the compilation of potentially canonical material and its final recognition as such was obviously inevitable, even if that same material, or something approximating it, had already been proclaimed orally.

If Burrows and others were correct in dating 1QIsa[a] *ca.* 100 B.C. (cf. M. Burrows, *Dead Sea Scrolls* [1955], p. 118), it is clear that the extant prophecy was in its final form at least by the beginning of the 2nd cent. B.C. That it evidently came from a considerably earlier period was made plain by Burrows: "The book of Isaiah certainly comes from a time several centuries before the earliest date to which this manuscript can be assigned on any grounds" (Burrows, p. 109). How early, then, was the original bifid Isaiah set? Here again the Qumrân manuscripts throw important light on the situation. From Cave 4 a fragmentary copy of the Psalter (4QPsa[a]) dated to the 2nd cent. B.C. showed incontrovertibly that the collection of canonical Psalms had already been fixed by the time of the Maccabees (F. M. Cross, *Ancient Library of Qumran and Modern Biblical Studies* [1961], p. 165). This evidence alone has persuaded scholars to abandon the once popular concept of "Maccabean psalms" and instead to date the latest canonical psalms, not in the Greek period (331-65 B.C.), but in the even earlier Persian period (539-331 B.C.). The evidence from this fragmentary copy of the Psalter thus indicates that no part of the canonical OT was put in written form later than 330 B.C., and in the case of Isaiah it would seem to advance the date of composition to the middle of the Persian period at the latest.

This factual evidence immediately challenges the critical theories concerning the authorship of the prophecy. For one thing, it repudiates unequivocally the view of Volz (*Jesaja* [1932], II, 200) that chs. 65–66 were written after 331 B.C. For another, it demonstrates the fallacy of the view of Kennett and others that the concept of the Suffering Servant arose as the result of the persecution of pious Jews under Antiochus IV Epiphanes (R. H. Kennett, *Composition of the Book of Isaiah* [1909], p. 85; *OT Essays* [1928], p. 146). In the same way, Duhm's theory (*Das Buch Jesaia* [1892], pp. 9f.) that chs. 24–27 belonged to the time of John Hyrcanus is shown to be untenable, as is any suggestion of a Third Isaiah or additional Isaiahs, credited from time to time with having had a hand in writing parts of chs. 50–66 (cf. J. L. McKenzie, *Second Isaiah* [*AB*, 1968], pp. lxvii-lxxi). Suppositions of this kind are entirely a product of critical speculation, without factual basis, as the evidence from Qumrân now makes clear.

Although the theory of a Trito-Isaiah can now be dismissed without further consideration, that which involved the so-called Second Isaiah must be refuted on somewhat different grounds. Almost all liberal scholars regarded the assumption of the existence of a Second Isaiah as constituting "one of the most assured results of modern literary criticism." But liberal scholars have never demonstrated the existence of this unknown prophet of the exile, and it would appear from a perusal of writings in this area that no demonstration seems to be thought necessary by proponents of the Second Isaiah theory, since to mention the unknown prophet is to preclude automatically any further need to prove his alleged existence. Liberal orthodoxy in this matter has permeated even the otherwise admirable researches of Brownlee, as noted above, where he supposed that the exilic prophet had arisen from the group of Isaiah's disciples credited with having produced the Isaianic anthology.

This concept of an alleged exilic Second Isaiah is by far the weakest point in Brownlee's argument, and obviously vitiates some of his conclusions. As in other instances, it was not examined critically by the author because it was a fundamentally important element of orthodox theory, inadequate though it may be. Taken at face value, the assertion that a Second Isaiah was active during the exilic period has important implications for history as well as literature and spirituality. It could be held to indicate that up to 150 years after the death of the master, members of an Isaianic school were busily perpetuating the traditions of the prophet in what can only be described as a theological vacuum. A vacuum indeed, because the work of Isaiah had long given place to the lengthy and immensely significant ministry of Jeremiah and its theology of calamity, and this in turn had been followed by the tribulations of captivity in Babylonia and the ministry of Ezekiel as prophet, priest, and pastor to the exiled Jewish community. In addition there was the work of Daniel as a Jewish statesman in a heathen court, setting for the Neo-Babylonian regime a model of Hebrew piety and gaining such stature by his spiritual deportment and wisdom as to succeed ultimately to membership in a triad that governed the kingdom. Yet the work of the supposed school shows no recognition whatever of the work or thought of Jeremiah, the witness and teachings of Ezekiel, whose activities marked a decisive turning point in Hebrew religious life, or the life and example of Daniel, the gifted Hebrew seer and saint.

Despite the fact that chs. 40–66 afford no basis for thinking that they were composed in Babylonia, those who have postulated the existence of the so-called school have placed this group of Isaianic supporters in Babylonia itself, where, if sheer historical circumstances have any meaning at all for the situation, they could not have failed to come into contact with other Judean exiles and their outstanding leaders. Nor could they possibly have avoided reflecting (to some extent at least) the teachings and traditions of Jeremiah and Ezekiel as fostered by the deported Judeans. Furthermore, the assertions concerning the existence of Deutero-Isaiah would have the credulous reader believe that the Palestinian Isaianic tradition received a new lease of quite independent life in Babylonia during the time of the Exile as the result of the work of this unknown prophet, who added to the already existing compositions of the deceased master in language that for beauty of expression and literary elegance has seldom been surpassed; but that this work bore almost no relationship to the crucial theological issues of the day as expressed particularly in the writings of Ezekiel. Had this unknown prophet actually had any existence other than in the fervid imaginations of nineteenth-century European scholars, and had he in fact been teaching and writing during the Exile, he would hardly have reflected a preexilic Palestinian background such as occurs in chs. 40–55, but would instead have been in accord with Ezekiel and Daniel in depicting contemporary Mesopotamian environmental, social, moral, and religious conditions. A careful reading of chs. 40–55 reveals only the most general allusions to the coming Exile, and nothing whatever pertaining to the details of life as it was ultimately experienced by the deported Judeans at *Tīl Abūbi*, probably located near Nippur.

Perhaps the most important repudiation of the fallacy entertained by postulating the existence of a so-called Second Isaiah is to be seen in the ignorance that he exhibited in the matter of the theological continuity between Jeremiah and Ezekiel with respect to the new covenant. Jeremiah (31:31-34) had predicted a time when the older corporate concept of covenantal relationship would be replaced by an individual one. Ezekiel went further (18:1-24) and emphasized that the individual in his dealings with God would have to bear personal responsibility for his own wrongdoings. By contrast, the postulated unknown prophet of the Exile knew nothing of the new covenant and its spiritual implications. On two occasions where the concept of covenant was introduced (Isa. 42:6; 49:8), it was related to the work of the Servant as a "covenant of the people," while Isa. 54:10 referred to it in a general manner as "my peaceful covenant" and embraced ideas of divine compassion. So formidable is this particular objection to the liberal supposition of a Second Isaiah that it has almost invariably tended to be evaded, and to date no liberal scholar has even begun to resolve the problem posed by the relationship of the historical ministry and writings of Ezekiel to that of the wholly hypothetical Deutero-Isaiah. This failure is hardly surprising in the light of a passage such as Ezk. 2:5, which suggests that there was no other prophet living in the community who was issuing the same warnings as Ezekiel. Again, in Ezk. 22:30, God was represented as telling the prophet that He had looked for a man to fill the breach, but that He had found no one. This situation would not have existed had the celebrated unknown prophet of the Exile been living and ministering in the Judean community of exiles at the time of Ezekiel, and by his utterances and example bringing his dejected hearers out of despair to new heights of creative spirituality, as is popularly supposed to have happened by those who for so long have been advocating the existence of a Second Isaiah. Surely under such conditions a man of his outstanding gifts would have been ideally suited for whatever ministry God had for him to perform on behalf of the dispirited exiles.

The evidence furnished by the book of Ezekiel, however, knows nothing of an unknown prophet of the Exile. Any ministering that was undertaken to the exiled community was the sole responsibility of Ezekiel, since Daniel was functioning at an entirely different level in Babylonian affairs; also there is no doubt that Ezekiel was a genuine historical figure, as opposed to the imaginary Deutero-Isaiah. It would be without parallel in Hebrew history for one of the greatest, if not the greatest of the Hebrew prophets, to lavish on his contemporaries, at a time when they were experiencing one of the most serious spiritual crises of their history, some of the most exalted language and lofty spirituality in the whole of divine revelation, and having done all this to pass so completely from Hebrew tradition that not even his name managed to survive. It is even more incredible to suppose that his incomparable literary work could ever have become a mere appendix to that of a much inferior and less renowned Palestinian prophet, however much the latter might have commended himself to the former, and that for two millennia his writings should have been uniformly regarded by Jewish tradition as comprising the work of this inferior prophet. Liberal scholarship has yet to establish the degree of probability by which sections of literature emerging from a later period should have become intermingled with the writings of Isaiah ben Amoz by an inexperienced or incompetent editor in such a way that it has become virtually impossible for anyone to extract the work of the eighth-century B.C. prophet and arrange it in something like chronological order. Were any further objection needed, it can only be regarded as totally incredible that the Jews, with their almost superstitious veneration of sacred Scripture, could ever have permitted it to be mutilated in such a manner.

If this supposedly unknown individual is to be regarded as anything other than an imaginative creation of nineteenth-century critical scholarship, it will be mandatory for his place in the history of Hebrew thought and religious institutions to be established firmly. As noted above, however, he was evidently totally unknown to both Ezekiel and Daniel, despite the outstanding talents and abilities credited to him. In the postexilic period, neither his name nor his teachings seem to have exerted the slightest influence over Haggai and Zechariah on the one hand, or over Ezra and Nehemiah on the other. By contrast, however, it is known that the thought of Ezekiel exercised a profound effect upon both temple and synagogue worship in the postexilic theocracy. In the same way it was the wholehearted application of the law of Moses, not the teachings of an unknown prophet of the Exile, that furnished Judaism with its characteristic stamp of legalism. The preoccupations of Deutero-Isaiah with the kind of idolatry typical of preexilic Canaan would have been as out of place in Babylonia, where the conditions for indulgence in Canaanite religious rites simply did not exist, as they would have been in the postexilic theocracy, if only because the Exile had made Canaanite Baal worship a completely dead issue.

That the Jews of the exilic or postexilic periods never had a tradition of a Second Isaiah or a Third Isaiah makes the supposition of his (or their) existence not merely hypothetical but extremely suspect. On purely objective grounds no evidence supports the contention of liberal scholars that there was more than one author of the extant prophecy. As with the Pentateuch, the liberal studies of the book of Isaiah are littered with undemonstrated assumptions, tendentious arguments, and unwarranted conclusions for which there is no factual evidence, and this despite the confidence with which they were promulgated. It is because such research was so far removed from accredited scientific method that it will need to be undertaken afresh, this time against a background of a posteriori scientific method and the full use of all objective data, before credible conclusions can be reached.

On the basis of the foregoing survey of hypotheses concerning the authorship of Isaiah, the present writer can only reject in all honesty any hypothesis adduced in favor of establishing the existence of a Second or Third Isaiah on the ground that such a hypothesis has been shown to be totally lacking in anything that the modern scientific approach would recognize as evidence. It seems difficult to avoid the further conclusion that Second and Third Isaiahs constitute some of the most successful myths ever foisted upon a gullible scholarly world by nineteenth-century liberal thinkers. In view of the data presented by 1QIsa[a], it appears that the prophecy was the work of the one attributive author, Isaiah ben Amoz, with some possibility of assistance from his disciples. It seems to have been compiled as an anthology of this Isaiah's writings, and may well have been circulated in bifid form from the very beginning of its literary history. Its sophisticated and artistic structure would make it highly probable that the master prophet himself played a large part in shaping the final form of the work. In that event it appears likely that the prophecy was closely approaching its extant state within fifty years after the death of the prophet, and thus may be assigned with reasonable confidence to a date *ca.* 630 B.C.

G. Servant Oracles. Few subjects have evoked more discussion in OT theology than the problems raised by the passages relating to the work of the Servant of the Lord. As already noted, the servant passages have generally been held to comprise, as a minimum, 42:1-4; 49:1-6; 50:4-9 or 50:1-11; and 52:13–53:12. For the first three centuries of its existence the Church identified the Servant with the righteous, sometimes on an individual basis but at other times on a collective basis. This was then replaced by a general messianic interpretation, which lasted until the 19th century. For liberal scholars such as Semler, Koppe, and Eichhorn, the messiah was no longer to be regarded as a scion of the house of David, but rather as a picture of the entire nation of Israel. Under Vatke and Ewald this view was basic to the expectation that the spiritual Israel would somehow be the means of restoring the moribund physical Israel. Though others such as Cheyne, A. B. Davidson, and S. R. Driver took up this view with enthusiasm, they failed to show how an ideal Israel could suffer and die vicariously or representatively in order to redeem the actual nation. A variation of this theory envisaged the Servant as the faithful minority within the larger corpus of unrepentant Israel. This involved one portion of the nation dying to atone for and redeem the rest of the people, but the theory simply did not match the known historical facts when it was transferred to the exilic situation as depicted in Ezekiel and Daniel. Other equally unsuccessful attempts to identify the Servant related him in some way to the prophetic order, or to some specific individual such as Hezekiah, Isaiah, or Jeremiah. Delitzsch (p. 236) suggested that at its lowest level the servant concept was rooted in the entire nation of Israel. In a more developed form it was concerned with a spiritual rather than with a physical Israel, and at the highest level it represented the personage of the Redeemer-Messiah.

The view that the Servant was in fact Second Isaiah was advanced by S. Mowinckel (*Der Knecht Jahwäs* [1921]) as a reaction against the collective interpretation favored by many liberal scholars. He held that in material contiguous to the oracles, the Servant was the actual nation, whereas in the oracles themselves the missionary vocation of the Servant indicated his individuality. This theory ran into trouble in connection with the fourth oracle (52:13–53:12), to say nothing of all the problems associated with the assumption that there actually was such a person as the unknown prophet of the Exile, as noted above. Mowinckel subsequently modified his position (cf. *He That Cometh* [1956], pp. 228f.) by stating that the Servant had been killed before the completion of the oracles, which had been assembled by the disciples of Deutero-Isaiah (*ZAW*, 49 [1931], 87ff., 242ff.).

Another Scandinavian scholar, Nyberg, thought of the Servant as a supra-individual personage belonging alike to the past, present, and future (*Svensk Exegetisk Årsbok,* 7 [1942], pp. 5ff.). Not merely did this concept thus enshrine the best of all possible worlds, but it also drew upon religious and mythological elements from other beliefs. This latter element reflected to some extent the mythological view of the Servant espoused by Gressmann and Gunkel (cf. H. Gressmann, *Der Ursprung der israelitisch-jüdischen Eschatologie* [1905]; H. Gunkel, *RGG* [1912], III, cols. 1540ff.), a theory which encountered lasting difficulties because of its inability to demonstrate a positive link between the nature myths and the biblical sources.

The problems that scholars had to confront are immediately evident upon reading the oracles themselves. The personage of the Servant and the scope of his work make possible the simultaneous recognition of individual, collective, actual, and ideal elements. If a purely collective interpretation is advanced, it immediately faces the fact that the Servant of Isaiah is very different in character from Israel as depicted in the OT. Since the description of the Servant was most probably never intended to be the portrait of any specific individual, attempted identifications with known historical figures such as Uzziah, Jeremiah, or Cyrus can only be regarded as highly speculative at the best. The same conclusion must be leveled against the kind of messianic interpretation that saw the Servant in the role of some preexilic king who was thought to have undergone certain ritual punishments as part of an annual "enthronement liturgy." Redemption and atonement ceremonies were matters for the priests, not the preexilic kings, and in any event there is absolutely no factual evidence produced to date that could be cited in support of an annual enthronement ceremony in Israel such as was represented by the Babylonian *akîtu* rituals.

Certain scholars have felt that those who were satisfied with the classical liberal delineation of the servant oracles took a rather restricted view of the available textual material. Thus Brownlee (pp. 193ff.) suggested that additional servant songs can be found in Isa. 51:4-6, or perhaps 1-8; 61:1ff., and 62:10-12. Similarly, Harrison (*Intro. to the OT* [1969], p. 797) has pointed out that, probably because of liberal preoccupations with theories of divided authorship, a prose oracle in the earlier chapters has been overlooked completely. Occurring in 22:20-25, it described the function of the divine servant, whose name was given as Eliakim, son of Hilkiah. He would have authority over Jerusalem and the house of Judah, but ultimately he would be removed from office and his powers would disappear. This oracle is of some interest historically because archeologists have found both at Tell Beit Mirsim and Beth-shemesh three stamped jar handles of the 6th cent. B.C. inscribed, "belonging to Eliakim, attendant of Yaukin [Jehoiachin]" (cf. 2 K. 18:18, 26, 37 par. Isa. 36:3, 11, 22; cf. also 37:2).

Of the various identifications proposed for the Servant, the one that seems to suit all the data most adequately is the traditional messianic approach. In its overall construction the picture of the divine Servant is sufficiently fluid to admit of differences between the Servant and Christ the Messiah. It needs to be remembered that the Servant is not the only messianic figure in Isaiah, but this impression has been conveyed by an entirely unwarranted and arbitrary dissection of the prophecy into portions alleged by the literary critics to have come from widely separated historical periods. It is extremely difficult to believe that Isaiah was not aware, at least in part, of the historical and spiritual significance of the servant oracles, even though his eighth-century-B.C. contemporaries may have been so immersed in pagan ways as to have remained completely indifferent to any meaning, eschatological or otherwise, that the material may have had. Certainly there were those in the time of Christ who were unable to interpret such passages in terms of His status as Messiah. C. R. North is undoubtedly correct in stating that, regardless of the original of the Servant, Christ alone furnished its fulfillment (*IDB*, IV, 294).

H. Cyrus. The appearance of this renowned Persian ruler's name in Isa. 44:28 and 45:1 has supplied many liberal scholars with what they regarded as valid reason for attributing chs. 40–55 to the exilic period and a specific Babylonian background. The problems posed by the incidence of the name of Cyrus (539-530 B.C.) have been met by conservative scholars in three principal ways. The first has been to reject the liberal view of an exilic date for the material as being based on a disregard for a genuinely predictive element in OT prophecy, and to assert that, in any event, Cyrus was represented by Isaiah as the subject of prediction. This latter element of the argument, which obviously would preclude anything later than an early exilic date, was even accepted by some liberal scholars, e.g., G. A. Smith (*HDB*, II, 493). The second approach to the problem, adopted by some modern conservative scholars such as Allis (*Unity of Isaiah* [1950], pp. 51ff.) and Young (*Intro. to the OT* [2nd ed. 1960], pp. 237f.), has been to see the references as comprising prophetic previsions of the work of Cyrus that occurred 150 years later. Allis accepted somewhat uncritically the view of Josephus (*Ant.* xi.1.1) that Cyrus, having read of his destiny in Isaiah, made serious attempts to fulfil all that had been written about him. Young and Allis, however, insisted upon the predictive element in OT prophecy, and thus saw Cyrus as the subject of foretelling by Isaiah.

A third way of viewing the references to Cyrus has been to see them as explanatory glosses, inserted by a post-exilic copyist who may well have felt that Cyrus was discharging the functions of the Servant about whom Isaiah had spoken. The references in 44:28 and 45:1 are actually the only places in the prophecy where Cyrus was mentioned by name, and if the word *l*ᵉ*ḵôreš* ("of Cyrus") is removed from the Hebrew text, it not only makes for greater smoothness in the verses involved, but focuses attention upon Jerusalem and gives promise of future restoration and glory, in consonance with other sections of chs. 40–66. C. C. Torrey (*Second Isaiah: A New Interpretation* [1928], pp. vii-viii) was one of the first scholars to recognize the possibility that the references to Cyrus were later glosses by maintaining that if the few direct and indirect allusions to him could be eliminated, almost all of chs. 40–66 could be relegated to a Palestinian origin. The suggestion that *l*ᵉ*ḵôreš* has been miscopied from *ḥōreš*, "workman," is improbable, if only as a totally inadequate description of the "anointed one" of 45:1.

Bibliography.–*Commentaries:* Among the early church fathers, Eusebius, Basil the Great, Chrysostom, Theodoret, Procopius of Gaza, Ephraim Syrus, and Jerome wrote comments on parts or the whole of the prophecy. Among the Jewish expositors Ibn Ezra, David Kimchi, Abarbanel, and the Tanchum Jerushalmi should be noted. Of the Reformers see comms. by both Luther and Calvin. The work of Campegius Vitringa (1732) is particularly valuable. Among the later commentaries on the entire prophecy may be mentioned E. F. Rosenmüller's *Scholia* (1826); Wilhelm Gesenius' *Jesaja* (1821); J. A. Alexander (1865); Moritz Drechsler (1845), completed by Hahn and Delitzsch; S. D. Luzzatto (1855); Franz Delitzsch (repr. 1949); G. A. Smith (1888-90); Bernhard Duhm (1892); A. Dillmann (rev. ed. 1898); G. H. Box (1908); J. Ridderbos (1922); F. Feldmann (1925-26); J. Fischer (1939); E. J. Kissane (1941-43); A. Bentzen (1944); A. Penna (1958); I. W. Slotki (*Soncino*, 1959); E. J. Young (1961); V. Buksbazen (1971-74).

Commentaries on Chs. 1–39: G. B. Gray (*ICC*, 1912); O. Procksch (*KAT*, 1930); R. B. Y. Scott (*IB*, 1956); J. Mauchline (1962); A. S. Herbert (1973); O. Kaiser (*OTL*, 1973).

Commentaries on Chs. 40–55 or 40–66: R. Levy (1925); C. C. Torrey (1928); P. Volz (1932); J. Muilenburg (*IB*, 1956); C. R. North (1964); J. L. McKenzie (*AB*, 1968); C. Westermann (*OTL*, 1969).

Standard Introductions (some obsolete): S. R. Driver (9th ed. 1913); R. H. Pfeiffer (1941); W. O. E. Oesterley and T. H. Robinson (3rd ed. 1958); A. Weiser (5th ed. 1963); A. Bentzen (1952); O. Eissfeldt (Eng. tr. 1965); E. J. Young (2nd ed. 1960); G. L. Archer (1964); R. K. Harrison (1969); B. S. Childs (1979).

Special Studies: H. Gunkel, *Ein Vorläufer Jesu* (1921); S. Mowinckel, *Der Knecht Jahwäs* (1921); J. Fischer, *Wer ist Ebed?* (1922); L. Köhler, *Deuterojesaja (Jesaja xl-lv) stilkritisch untersucht* (*BZAW*, 37, 1923); J. Begrich, *Der Psalm des Hiskia* (1926); A. Boutflower, *Book of Isaiah in the Light of Assyrian Monuments* (1930); K. Elliger, *Deuterojesaja in seinem Verhältnis zu Tritojesaja* (*Beiträge zur Wissenschaft vom AT*, 4, 1933); L. Glahn and L. Köhler, *Der Prophet der Heimkehr* (1934); J. Lindblom, *Die Jesaja-Apokalypse* (1938); W. A. Wordsworth, *En Roeh* (1939); S. Smith, *Isaiah Chapters xl-xv: Literary Criticism and History* (1944); O. T. Allis, *Unity of Isaiah* (1951); E. S. Mulder, *Die Teologie van die Jesaja-Apokalipse* (1954); E. J. Young, *Studies in Isaiah* (1954); S. H. Blank, *Prophetic Faith in Isaiah* (1958); S. P. Schilling, *Isaiah Speaks* (1958); E. J. Young, *Who Wrote Isaiah?* (1958); B. S. Childs, *Isaiah and the Assyrian Crisis* (*SBT*, 2/3, 1967); J. W. Whedbee, *Isaiah and Wisdom* (1971); R. N. Whybray, *The Heavenly Counsellor in Isaiah 40:13-14* (1971); W. S. LaSor, *Israel* (1976), pp. 11-29; A. A. MacRae, *The Gospel of Isaiah* (1977).

G. L. ROBINSON
R. K. HARRISON

ISAIAH, ASCENSION OF. *See* APOCRYPHAL APOCALYPSES II.A.

ISCAH iz'kə, is'kə [Heb. *yiskâ*]. Daughter of Haran and sister of Milcah the wife of Nahor (Gen. 11:29). Tradition identifies her with Sarai, Abram's wife, but without sufficient reason.

ISCARIOT. *See* JUDAS ISCARIOT.

ISDAEL iz'dā-əl [Gk. *Isdaēl*]. *See* GIDDEL.

ISH [Heb. *'îš*]. In the following Hebrew proper names, a prefix meaning "man of," or, collectively, "men of"; Ish-bosheth, Ishhod, etc. *See also* JUDAS ISCARIOT.

ISHBAAL ish'bā-əl. *See* ISH-BOSHETH.

ISHBAH ish'bə [Heb. *yišbaḥ*]. A member of the tribe of Judah, father of Eshtemoa (1 Ch. 4:17).

ISHBAK ish'bak [Heb. *yišbāq*]. A name in the list of sons of Abraham by Keturah (Gen. 25:2; 1 Ch. 1:32). Cf. the personal name Shobek in Neh. 10:24 (MT 25).

ISHBI-BENOB ish-bī-bē'nob [Heb. *yišbî ḇ*ᵉ*nōḇ*]. A descendant of the giants of Gath who sought to take advantage of David's weariness and kill him (2 S. 21:15-22). However, Ishbi-benob was killed by Abishai, and David's life was saved. There is some problem with the text, and the name can be pointed to read "they dwelt in Nob." Hence v. 15 could have ended with a note about where the exhausted David stayed. Perhaps Nob is a miscopying for "Gob," as in v. 19, but this is uncertain. If the above emendation is adopted, the name of the giant (NEB "Benob") would disappear.

ISH-BOSHETH ish-bō'sheth [Heb. *'îš-bōšeṯ*–'man of shame'; Gk. *Iebosthe*]. Called *'ešbaʿal*–'man of Baal' (1 Ch. 8:33). The original form of the name seems to have been Ishbaal, but because of the reluctance of the post-seventh-century-B.C. Hebrews to use the name Baal, the form Ish-bosheth was substituted. The reflection of "shame" was as much on the name itself as on the licentious rites of Baal worship.

Ish-bosheth was one of the sons of Saul (1 Ch. 8:33; 9:39) who, when his father and brothers were slain in the battle of Gilboa (1 S. 31:1-6), was proclaimed king over Israel by Abner, the captain of Saul's host, at Mahanaim (2 S. 2:8-10). Ish-bosheth was forty years old at this time and reigned over Israel two years (2 S. 2:10). Judah, however, proclaimed David its king. The consequence was war (2 S. 2:12ff.). The house of David prevailed against the house of Saul (2 S. 3:1), but the war did not come to a close until Abner, angry on account of the rebuke he suffered from Ish-bosheth for unlawful intimacy with Saul's concubine Rizpah, joined David (2 S. 3:6ff.). David's condition, that Michal his wife be returned to him before peace could be made, was fulfilled by Ish-bosheth (2 S. 3:14-16); but it was not until after Abner's death that Ish-bosheth seems to have given up hopes of retaining his power (2 S. 4:1). The shameful murder of Ish-bosheth by his own captains is recorded in 2 S. 4:5-7. David punished the murderers, who had expected reward, and buried Ish-bosheth in the grave of Abner at Hebron (2 S. 4:12).

A. L. BRESLICH

ISHHOD ish'hod [Heb. *'îšᵉhôḏ*–'vitality']. A man of the tribe of Manasseh (1 Ch. 7:18; AV ISHOD).

ISHI ish'ī, ish'ē [Heb. *yišʿî*–'salutary'].

1. A Jerahmeelite (1 Ch. 2:31); the genealogy may denote his membership by blood, or only by adoption, in the tribe of Judah.

2. A Judahite (1 Ch. 4:20).

3. A Simeonite, whose sons led five hundred of their tribe against the Amalekites in Mt. Seir (1 Ch. 4:42).

4. One of the chiefs of Manasseh E of the Jordan (1 Ch. 5:24).

ISHI ish'ī, ish'ē [Heb. *'îšî*–'my husband']. The name symbolic of Yahweh's relation to Israel which Hosea (2:16) declares shall be used when Heb. *Baali,* "my lord," has become hateful on account of its associations with the worship of the Baals.

ISHIAH i-shī'yə. *See* ISSHIAH.

ISHIJAH i-shī'jə. *See* ISSHIJAH.

ISHMA ish'mə [Heb. *yišmā'*–'may God listen']. A brother of Jezreel and Idbash (1 Ch. 4:3).

ISHMAEL ish'mā-əl [Heb. *yišmāʿē'l*–'may God hear,' 'God hears,' 'God will hear'; Gk. *Ismaēl*].

1. The son of Abraham by Hagar, Sarah's Egyptian servant; thus Isaac's older half brother (Gen. 25:12).

The circumstances connected with his birth, once thought bizarre, have been clarified by Middle Bronze Age discoveries in Mesopotamia. In ancient Sumer and such Babylonian cultures as Mari and Nuzi, the primary purpose of marriage was procreation rather than companionship. Marriage was by contract, which often obliged a wife who subsequently proved to be infertile to supply her husband with a concubine through whom he could obtain an heir. One clause of such a marriage tablet states, "If Gilimninu (the bride) will not bear children, Gilimninu shall procure a woman of N/Lullu-land (the source of choice slaves) as a wife for Shennima (the bridegroom)." The wife's position in the household was safeguarded by making it clear that the concubine was inferior to her in status. At Nuzi, it was illegal to expel either the concubine or her offspring, since survival was impossible outside a family community. In the light of this situation, the provision in the ancient Sumerian law code of Lipit-Ishtar (*ca.* 1850 B.C.) that the freedom received by the dispossessed slave was adequate recompense for the act of expulsion is a masterpiece of ancient casuistry.

In view of these discoveries it is clear that the childless Sarah was obliged to give her Egyptian slave to Abraham in order to provide an heir (Gen. 16:2). The pregnant Hagar behaved indiscreetly by looking "with contempt on her mistress" (16:4), so infuriating the already very frustrated Sarah that she abused Hagar, whereupon Hagar fled to a wilderness oasis on the way to Shur. A divine messenger instructed her to return and submit to her mistress's demands. In return, Hagar's descendants through Ishmael would be without number (16:10) and Ishmael himself would be a "wild ass of a man" (16:12). Although this description seems to connote a revolutionary and a fugitive, it was actually highly complimentary, since in the Middle Bronze Age the wild ass of the steppes was the preferred animal of the chase, and anyone who could catch and kill one was a hunter of obvious prowess.

The child was born when Abraham was eighty-six years old (17:24f.) and at the age of thirteen Ishmael was circumcised in accordance with the divine command received by Abraham: "Every male among you shall be circumcised" (17:10). The adolescent Ishmael thus became party to the covenant which God had established with his father. The fact that Abraham, Ishmael, and all the males of Abraham's household were circumcised on the same day indicates the importance of the rite.

Abraham might then have entertained the hope that from Ishmael would come the innumerable offspring promised (Gen. 13:16; 17:7f.; 18:18), but this was changed abruptly when Sarah herself conceived and bore a son (21:1-7). The infant Isaac was nursed for two years, in accordance with contemporary practices, and then weaned at a ceremonial banquet, a custom still followed in certain parts of the Near East. In the midst of the festivities Sarah's fury was aroused by the sight of Ishmael playing. (The RSV adds "with her son Isaac" [21:9], following the LXX and the Vulgate, but omitted by the MT. The NEB reads "laughing at him" [cf. AV "mocking"], which seems to be the sense of the participle of Heb. *ṣāhaq* [cf. Paul's interpretation in Gal. 4:29].) Sarah demanded the banishment of Hagar and Ishmael from Abraham's dwellings, whether or not local law was broken. The adolescent Ishmael, without visible means of support, had nothing more than some bread and a skin containing water. With these spent, the prospect of death was imminent, and the narrative describes with great pathos the last tender acts of a grieving mother toward her languishing son (21:15f.). When all seemed lost, God intervened again in her life (21:17-20), renewing His earlier promise concerning Ishmael and giving them water. Ishmael grew up in the wilderness of Paran and became an archer. He was subsequently married by his mother to an Egyptian wife (21:21).

Following Abraham's death, his exiled son Ishmael returned to assist in the task of burial (25:9). The names of Ishmael's twelve sons are listed in 25:13-16, and 25:17 has a brief report of his death at the age of 137 years. According to Gen. 28:9 he also had a daughter named Mahalath, whom Esau married; in Gen. 36:3 her name was given as Basemath. Ishmael is regarded as the progenitor of the Arabs, who trace their ancestry back to Abraham, as do the Jews through Isaac. The character of Ishmael as represented in the Genesis narratives is amply illustrated by his descendants, the bedouin Arabs.

The person and the history of Ishmael, the son of Abraham, "born according to the flesh," is of special interest to the student of the NT because Paul uses him, in the Epistle to the Galatians, as a type of those Jews who cling to the paternal religion in such a manner as to be unable to discern the transient character of the OT institutions, and especially those of the Mosaic law. By doing so they could not be made to see the true meaning of the law, and instead of embracing the grace of God as the only means of fulfilling the law, they most bitterly fought the central doctrine of Christianity and even persecuted its advocates. Like Ishmael, they were born of Hagar, the handmaid or slave woman; like him, they were Abraham's sons only "according to the flesh," and their ultimate fate is foreshadowed in the casting out of Hagar and her son. They could not expect to maintain the connection with the true Israel, and even in case they should acclaim Christ their Messiah they were not to be the leaders of the Church or the expounders of its teaching (Gal. 4:21-28).

2. The son of Nethaniah (Jer. 40:8–41:18; cf. 2 K. 25:23-25). It is a dreary story of jealousy and treachery that Jeremiah has recorded in chs. 40–41 of his book. After the destruction of Jerusalem and the deportation of the better class of Jewish citizens, it was necessary to provide for a government in the depopulated country. Public order had to be restored and maintained; the crops of the fields were endangered and had to be taken care of. It was thus only common political prudence that dictated to the king of Babylon the setting up of a governor for the remnant of Judah. He chose Gedaliah the son of Ahikam for the difficult position. The new officer selected for his place of residence the city of Mizpah, where he was soon joined by Jeremiah. All the captains of the Jewish country forces came to Mizpah with their men and put themselves under Gedaliah's orders (Jer. 40:13). Ishmael the son of Nethaniah, the son of Elishama "of the royal family" (2 K. 25:25) was among their number — all of which must have been rather gratifying to the new governor. But he was destined to be cruelly disappointed. A traitor was among the captains that had gathered around him. Yet the governor might have prevented subversion. Johanan the son of Kareah and other loyal captains warned him of the treachery of Ishmael, telling him he was induced by Baalis the Ammonite king to assassinate the governor. But the governor's faith in Ishmael was not to be shaken; he even looked upon Johanan's report as false and calumnious (Jer. 40:16).

About two months after the destruction of Jerusalem, Ishmael was ready to strike the mortal blow. With ten men he came to Mizpah, and there, at a banquet given in his honor, he killed Gedaliah and all the Jews and Chaldeans that were with him. He succeeded in keeping the matter secret, for, two days after the horrible deed, he persuaded a party of eighty pious Jews to enter the city and killed all but ten of them, throwing their bodies into a pit. These men were coming from the ruins of the temple with the offerings which they had intended to leave at Jerusalem. Now they had found out, to their great distraction, that the city was laid waste and the temple destroyed. So they passed by Mizpah, their beards shaven, their clothes rent, and with cuts about their persons (Jer. 41:5). We may, indeed, ask indignantly, Why this new atrocity? The answer may be found in the fact that Ishmael did not kill all of the men. He spared ten of them because they promised him some hidden treasures. This shows his motive. He was a desperate man and just then carrying out a desperate undertaking. He killed those peaceful citizens because of their money, which he needed to realize his plans. They were those of a traitor to his country, inasmuch as he intended to deport the inhabitants of Mizpah to the land of his high confederate, the king of the Ammonites. Among the captives were Jeremiah and the daughters of the Jewish king. But his efforts came to nothing. When Johanan and the other captains were told of Ishmael's unheard-of actions, they immediately pursued the desperate adventurer and overtook him by "the great pool which is in Gibeon." Unfortunately, they failed to capture Ishmael, for he managed to escape with eight men to the Ammonites. *See* GEDALIAH.

3. A descendant of Benjamin and the son of Azel (1 Ch. 8:38; cf. 9:44).

4. The father of Zebadiah who was "the governor of the house of Judah, in all the king's [Jehoshaphat, 2 Ch. 19:8] matters" (2 Ch. 19:11).

5. The son of Jehohanan, and a "commander of hundreds," who lived at the time of Jehoiada and Joash (2 Ch. 23:1).

6. One of the sons of Pashhur the priest. He was one of those men who had married foreign women and were compelled to "put away their wives" (Ezr. 10:22; cf. 1 Esd. 9:22). W. BAUR R. K. H.

ISHMAELITES ish'mā-el-īts, ish'mē-el-īts [Heb. *yišmᵉʿēʾlî*]. The descendants of Ishmael, the son of Abraham and Hagar, whom Abraham sent away from him after the birth of Isaac (Gen. 21:14-21). The sons of Ishmael are given in Gen. 25:13f.; they were twelve in number and gave rise to as many tribes, but the term Ishmaelite has a broader signification, as appears from Gen. 37:28, 36, where it is identified with Midianite. From Gen. 16:12 it may be inferred that it was applied to the bedouin of the desert region E of the Jordan generally, for the character there assigned to Ishmael, "his hand against every man, and every man's hand against him," fits the habits of bedouin in all ages. Such was the character of the Midianites as described in Jgs. 7, who are again identified with the Ishmaelites (8:24). These references show that the Ishmaelites were not confined to the descendants of the son of Abraham and Hagar, but refer to the desert tribes in general, like "the children of the East" (Jgs. 7:12).

H. PORTER

ISHMAIAH ish-mā'ya [Heb. *yišmaʿyâ*–'Yahweh hears'].

1. A man of Gibeon, chief of David's thirty great warriors, who came to him at Ziklag (1 Ch. 12:4; AV "Ismaiah").

2. Chief of the armed contingent of the tribe of Zebulun, which served David in the monthly order of the tribes (1 Ch. 27:19).

ISHMEELITES ish'mē-el-īts [Heb. *yišmʿēʾlî*]. AV variant of ISHMAELITES (Gen. 37:25, 27f., 39:1; 1 Ch. 2:17).

ISHMERAI ish'mə-rī [Heb. *yišmᵉray,* from *šāmar*– 'hedge about,' i.e., 'guard,' and therefore 'guard,' 'protector'] (1 Ch. 8:18). A descendant of Benjamin, son of Epaal, resident of Jerusalem, one of the "heads of fathers' houses, according to their generations, chief men" (1 Ch. 8:28).

ISHOD. *See* ISHHOD.

ISHPAH ish'pə [Heb. *yišpâ*]; AV, NEB, ISPAH. A man of the tribe of Benjamin, of the house of Beriah (1 Ch. 8:16).

ISHPAN ish'pan [Heb. *yišpān*]. Descendant of Benjamin, son of Shashak; he lived at Jerusalem (1 Ch. 8:22, 29).

ISHTAR. *See* RELIGIONS OF THE BIBLICAL WORLD: ASSYRIA AND BABYLONIA.

ISH-TOB (2 S. 10:6, 8, AV). *See* TOB.

ISHUAH. *See* ISHVAH.

ISHUAI. *See* ISHVI.

ISHVAH ish'və [Heb. *yišwâ*]; AV ISHUAH, ISUAH. Second son of Asher (Gen. 46:17; 1 Ch. 7:30). As only the families of his brothers Ishvi, etc., are mentioned in Nu. 26:44, the supposition is that he left no descendants.

ISHVI ish'vī [Heb. *yišwî*].

1. The third son of Asher (Gen. 46:17; 1 Ch. 7:30), and founder of the family of Ishvites (Nu. 26:44); AV "Isui," "Jesui," and "Ishui."

2. One of the sons of Saul (1 S. 14:49); AV "Ishui."

ISIS. *See* RELIGIONS OF THE BIBLICAL WORLD: EGYPT.

ISLAND [Gk. *nēsíon* (Acts 27:16); *nēsos* (Acts 13:6; 27:26; 28:1, 7, 9, 11; Rev. 1:9; 6:14; 16:20)]; **ISLES; ISLANDS** [Heb. *'îyîm*] (Ps. 72:60; Isa. 40:15; 42:15; Ezk. 28:16); NEB also "coast-lands," "islands of the sea" (Ezk. 28:16); **ISLES OF THE GENTILES** [Heb. *'îyê haggôyim*] (Gen. 10:5, AV); RSV "coastland peoples"; NEB "peoples of the coasts and islands." Depending upon the context, either the islands of the Aegean and eastern Mediterranean, or the coastal area of the same region, particularly Egypt, Philistia, and Phoenicia. The NT refers to the islands of CAUDA, CYPRUS, MALTA, and PATMOS.

The NEB translation of *'îyîm* as "desert wastes" in Isa. 42:15 is a conjecture based on the context, but without any textual support. The AV expression "isles of the Gentiles" (Gen. 10:5) refers to the region and the inhabitants of the eastern Mediterranean coastal areas. Thus the RSV translates "coastal peoples." The NEB uses both meanings of *'îyîm*: "the peoples of the coasts and islands." *See* TABLE OF NATIONS.

See also COAST. R. J. W.

ISMACHIAH iz-mə-kī'ə [Heb. *yiśmakyāhû*–'Yahweh sustains']. A temple official who assisted Coniah and Shimei, appointed by King Hezekiah and Azariah the high priest (2 Ch. 31:13).

ISMAEL. AV Apoc. for ISHMAEL **1** (Jth. 2:23) and **6** (Esd. 9:22).

ISMAERUS (1 Esd. 9:34, NEB). *See* AMRAM.

ISMAIAH. *See* ISHMAIAH **1.**

ISPAH. *See* ISHPAH.

ISRAEL iz'rē-əl [Heb. *yisrā'ēl*; Gk. *Israēl*]. The name given to Jacob and later adopted by his descendants as their political-religious title.

I. Etymology.–Gen. 32:28 (MT 29) implies a connection between "Israel" and the verb *śārâ*, "strive." This popular explanation has several problems, however, some of which seem insurmountable. First, as Albright (p. 159) and others have pointed out, in personal names the divine element is (as a rule) always the subject. Thus the name apparently cannot refer to Jacob's striving with God. Second, that *śārâ* means "strive" is uncertain, since it occurs only here and in Hos. 12:3f. (MT 4f.), which apparently used the Genesis text as an illustration. Third, the Masoretic vocalization of the name is not what one would expect (cf. Albright, pp. 161-65).

In view of these problems, scholars have offered a number of alternative explanations of the name's origin (see Albright, Danell, and Sachsse for summaries and evaluations of the various proposals). Three of the more popular explanations are: S. R. Driver's proposal that Heb. *śārâ* is related to Arab. *šariya*, "persevere, persist"; the ancient derivation from *śrr*, "rule" (cf. Symm., Aq., Onk.), espoused by Noth among others; and the more radical view that the root is *yšr*/*'šr*, "reliable, successful, happy," held by Sachsse and somewhat modified by Naor and Danell. Driver's suggestion seems to fit the biblical context best, though it is not without problems. One of the main problems with the second proposal is that it is difficult to understand why or how the proper origin and meaning of the name came to be forgotten, since *śrr* continued in use throughout the biblical period. The third option is more radical in that it supposes a shift from *š* to *ś*, and in Naor's modification (followed by Danell) a shift from ' to *y* as well. This last conjecture also posits that the name originally meant "Asher is god ['El]," and thus identifies 'El with a Canaanite deity Asher, perhaps the male counterpart of Asherah. Aside from the incredibility that the people of Yahweh got their national name from a lesser Canaanite deity, this theory confuses two distinct roots, *yšr*, "upright, just," and *'ṯr*, "happy." It also does not account for the Ugaritic personal name *yšril*, which many (e.g., C. Gordon, *UT*, p. 415, and KoB [3rd ed. 1974], p. 422) think is equivalent to Israel, and which therefore rules out a deity Asher here on two counts: the spelling with *y* (not ') and with *š* (not *ṯ*, which is required by Ugar. *aṯrt*).

II. The People of Israel.–As a designation for the entire people of Israel, the name derives from the idea of Jacob/Israel as the ancestor of the nation, since he was the father of twelve sons from whom the twelve tribes descended (thus the more common designation for the whole nation is "children/people/men of Israel," *b^e^nê yiśrā'ēl*; cf. the similar expressions that denote various peoples supposedly descended from other ancient figures, e.g., "sons of Ammon," Dt. 2:19; "sons of Edom," Ps. 137:7; Gen. 25:30; 36:1, 8). Although some passages differ as to whether the twelve tribes were the twelve sons of Jacob (Gen. 49; note that vv. 16, 28 call them "tribes," not individuals) or whether Ephraim and Manasseh were substituted for Joseph (and Simeon?) (Dt. 33; cf. 3:13f.; Jgs. 5:4), it is quite possible that the original twelve sons of Jacob founded these clans or tribes, which in the course of time were altered somewhat. Many scholars who reject the historicity of the text conjecture that the patriarchs were legendary figures, perhaps representing tribes and associated with cult centers (e.g., Abraham with Hebron, Isaac with Beer-sheba, and Jacob with Bethel, Peniel, or Shechem; some would even see another patriarch named "Israel" who was associated with Shechem; cf. H. Seebass, *Der Erzvater Israel* [*BZAW*, 98, 1966]). Thus the twelve-tribe system is relegated to a later era, and is said to have originated in Palestine.

Aside from Gen. 34:7, which is commonly regarded as an anachronism or later gloss (see comms.), the first use of "Israel" as a nation is in Gen. 49:7 (note that it is parallel to "Jacob," as also in v. 2, where the two names are used personally). That this "Blessing [Testament] of Jacob" is one of the oldest pieces of Hebrew literature is well known, and since the name "Israel" occurs in other very early Hebrew poetry (Nu. 23:7, 10, 23; Dt. 33:10; etc.), it seems that the name must have been known and used for the nation/people at least in the time of the judges. The well-known occurrence of "Israel" in the Merneptah stele (*ca.* 1225 B.C.) obviously establishes the people of Israel in

The name Israel on a detail of the Merneptah stele (*ca.* 1220 B.C.) (Service des musées, Cairo)

Palestine and shows that they were known by that name in the 13th century. (Though some see here instead a reference to Jezreel, rather than Israel, the reading *ya-si-r-'i-ra* seems clearly to indicate Israel; see W. F. Albright, *Vocalization of the Egyptian Syllabic Orthography* [1934], p. 34.)

As a designation for all Israelites, "Israel" was used throughout the biblical period, though it developed more specialized uses as well.

III. The Northern Kingdom.–When the kingdom split, the northern ten tribes kept the name Israel (1 K. 11:37; 12:1-3, 16, 19f.; etc.), as they had earlier used it (e.g., 2 S. 2:9; 3:10, 17-21; 20:1f.), and the southern kingdom became Judah, an appropriate name since that tribe was the dominant one in the south (cf. 2 S. 2:10f.; 3:10; 20:2; 1 K. 12:17, 20).

IV. Other Uses.–Even after the kingdom split, the southern kingdom was occasionally called Israel (Isa. 5:7; 8:18; Jer. 10:1), especially after the fall of the northern kingdom. This is no doubt a reflex of the general use of Israel to refer to the people of God. In postexilic times Israel was again used to designate the whole people (e.g., Ezr. 2:2), though its use as a national name was obviously secondary to its function indicating the people of God, since the nation was no longer autonomous. This religious or cultic use is apparent throughout the Psalms and is strikingly lacking in the wisdom literature (the only references there being political, not religious), which is perhaps to be expected in view of the special interests of that genre in contrast to the more cultic literature (which, however, was very often tied up with a nation's politics in the ancient Near East).

V. Intertestamental Period.–The Apocrypha and the Pseudepigrapha use "Israel" in ways similar to the OT, though naturally the predominant use is for the people of God and/or those of Jewish descent (Sir. 17:17; 24:8; Jth. 4:1, 8; 1 Macc. 1:11, 20; Jub. 1:29; T. Reub. 6:8; Ps. Sol. 2:24; etc.). At Qumrân the name Israel was adopted by the covenanters to indicate that they were the people of God (see F. F. Bruce, *Second Thoughts on the Dead Sea Scrolls* [2nd ed. 1961], p. 147; M. Burrows, *Dead Sea Scrolls* [1955], pp. 231, 263). The name also had other significances, however. Especially in connection with the two messiahs (of Aaron and Israel), Israel seems to refer to the laity, whereas Aaron refers to the clergy (cf. Burrows, p. 265; G. Vermes, *Dead Sea Scrolls in English* [1965], p. 17; cf. also K. G. Kuhn, "The Two Messiahs of Aaron and Israel," in K. Stendahl, ed., *The Scrolls and the NT* [1957], pp. 54-64 [repr. with some revisions of *NTS*, 1 (1954/55), 168-180]).

VI. NT.–The NT continues the usages found in the OT and intertestamental periods. Usually the name is used of the nation, i.e., those of Jewish descent (e.g., Mt. 10:6; Jn. 3:10; Acts 2:22; Phil. 3:5). Paul uses the term Israel predominantly for the historic people of the covenant, but also for the whole nation as represented in the last times. His thought seems to emphasize the spiritual nature of Israel, although some theological issues arise in his use of Israel and lead to various interpretations. Reformed thinkers identify Israel with the Church, i.e., the community of true believers, whereas dispensationalists argue that the terms "Israel" and "church" are always distinct. Bauer (rev. ed., p. 381) lists three different uses: the patriarch Jacob (Rom. 9:6; Phil. 3:5; etc.), the nation of Israel, and the "figurative" sense of Christians as "the true nation of Israel in contrast to . . . *Israel in the physical sense*" (1 Cor. 10:18; cf. *TDNT*, III, 383-88).

The incarnate Christ, being God's Anointed, is thoroughly representative in His person of the chosen people of God. On Calvary, Jesus the Jew partook of the sufferings of Israel, but transcended any purely local or national concepts of vicarious representation by atoning for the sins of the whole world. The realization by the primitive church that Jesus was indeed the Messiah that had been long promised to the nation was a factor underlying the urge to evangelize Palestinian Jews (cf. Mt. 15:24), and under the guidance of the Spirit to take the message throughout the Levant. The comparative lack of success that Paul experienced in persuading the Jews to acknowledge Christ as Messiah did not shake his pride in being a member of the people of Israel (2 Cor. 11:22), but at the same time he saw Israel as an obstinate nation after a fashion that was in complete harmony with the thought of the Hebrew prophets. This stubborn attitude, however, also worked for the benefit of the Gentiles, whose evangelization enabled them to share in the blessings of the covenant people (Gen. 12:3). Paul refused to entertain the idea that God had cast off His people (Rom. 11:1), and instead envisaged a time at the end of the age when all Israel would be saved (Rom. 11:26). He was able to do this with some assurance by regarding himself and other Jewish converts as the first fruits of such an act of salvation.

Bibliography.–W. F. Albright, *JBL*, 46 (1927), 151-185; G. A. Danell, *Studies in the Name of Israel in the OT* (1946); M. Naor, *ZAW*, 49 (1931), 317-321; M. Noth, *IP*, pp. 207-209; E. Sachsse, *ZAW*, 34 (1914), 1-15; *TDNT*, III, *s.v.* Ἰσραήλ κτλ. (v. Rad, Kuhn, Gutbrod).

G. A. LEE

ISRAEL, HISTORY OF THE PEOPLE OF.

***I. Introduction.**–A. Name.* The Israelites are named for their patronymic ancestor Jacob (Israel), whose story is recorded in Gen. 25–49. Although Abraham is accounted the father of the nation, the Israelite tribes traced their lineage from Abraham through Isaac to Jacob. The promises to Abraham were conveyed through Isaac (not Ishmael his half-brother) and Jacob (not Esau his twin). With Jacob, however, the line separates into twelve parts — the twelve sons or tribes of Jacob — each of which has a part in subsequent Israelite history. The blessings of Jacob (Gen. 49) indicate specific callings. Judah was to be the governing tribe (49:10; David was of the tribe of Judah), but all are reckoned as heirs to the covenant promises. In this sense Israelite history is the history of the *bᵉnê yiśrāʾēl,* the sons of Israel (*see also* TRIBE).

B. Sources. 1. The OT. The OT provides two accounts of Israelite history. One begins with the Pentateuch and continues through Joshua, Judges, Samuel, and Kings. It traces history from creation to the Exile of Judah (587 B.C.). A second, in part parallel, includes Chronicles, Ezra, and Nehemiah. This also traces its genealogies back to Adam, but it stresses the history of the Davidic family in the southern kingdom and the temple rites. Its history extends beyond the Exile to the return following the decree of Cyrus and to the reforms of Nehemiah (445 B.C.).

2. Archeology. Within the past century archeological discoveries in Palestine and neighboring lands have illuminated Israelite history. Key Palestinian towns, including Hazor, Megiddo, Jericho, Lachish, and Samaria, have been excavated. Fortifications have been traced, buildings unearthed, and written materials collected and edited. The discovery of the MOABITE STONE has given a contemporary account of the conflict between Moab and Israel during the period of the divided kingdom. The Lachish Letters provide a view of life in the provinces during the time of Nebuchadrezzar's invasion of Judah. The DEAD SEA SCROLLS have given us source material for the study of sectarian Jewish life in the last two centuries before the Christian era. Discoveries in Egypt, Babylonia, and Assyria have helped us to understand Israelite history in the light of its contemporary Near Eastern setting. Discoveries from Nuzi and Mari have thrown much light on life during the patriarchal age. The Amarna Letters illustrate life in Canaan during the 15th and 14th cents. B.C.; and the epics discovered at Ugarit describe Canaanite religion at the same period. Annals of Assyrian and Babylonian kings illustrate the problems faced by Israel and Judah during the time of the divided kingdom. Sennacherib actually describes his siege of Jerusalem. We learn from the Cyrus Cylinder the goals of the Persian empire and the circumstances that permitted the Jews to return from exile. The Elephantine papyri show something of the life of a Jewish colony in Egypt during the period of Persian rule, and the letters of the Murašu family at Nippur show how Jews prospered in Babylon during postexilic times (*see also* ARCHEOLOGY; ARCHEOLOGY OF MESOPOTAMIA; ARCHEOLOGY OF PALESTINE AND SYRIA).

3. Ancient Historians. The sources of Israelite history after Nehemiah are scanty. The apocryphal 1 Maccabees gives a reliable account of the conflict with Hellenism in the days of Antiochus Epiphanes and the rule of Judas and his successors of the Hasmonean period (174-135 B.C.). The Jewish historian Flavius Josephus (*ca.* A.D. 37-100) wrote a history of the Jewish wars *(BJ)* in which he surveyed the history of his people from the time of the MACCABEES to the suppression of the Jews following the fall of Jerusalem to Rome (A.D. 70). Since he was an eyewitness to the Jewish wars his work is a valuable historical document. A second work, *Antiquities of the Jews,* traced the history of Israel from creation to the outbreak of the revolt against Rome (A.D. 66). It is based largely on the LXX, but also contains legendary material and quotations from other sources available to Josephus, including the Egyptian historian Manetho, Philo of Alexandria, Dius the Phoenician, Menander of Ephesus, and Nicolas of Damascus. These quotations, more than the work of Josephus himself, make his work a valuable source for the history of the Jews during the centuries immediately preceding the fall of Jerusalem (A.D. 70).

***II. Pre-Mosaic Israel.**–A. Homeland.* According to the biblical records, Israelite history began with the call of Abraham while he was resident in Ur of the Chaldees, usually identified with the mound el-Muqaiyar in lower Mesopotamia. The Israelites of patriarchal times had close relations with the city of Haran on the Habor River in upper Mesopotamia and with the surrounding area known as Paddan-aram ("the fields of Aram") or Aram-naharaim ("Aram of the two rivers," AV "Mesopotamia"). It is to this district that Abraham's servant went to find a bride for Isaac (Gen. 24). Years later, Jacob fled there to escape the wrath of his brother Esau and to get a wife for himself. Since upper Mesopotamia is uniformly presented in Scripture as the ancestral homeland of the Israelites, a northern Ur has been posited as the possible site of Abraham's birthplace instead of the now famous el-Muqaiyar. Cyrus Gordon suggests that the biblical Ur of the Chaldees was a commercial colony founded in the far north by the 3rd Dynasty of Ur (*ca.* 2000 B.C.) and named after the capital city (p. 132).

Both Isaac and Jacob made their home in Canaan, although Jacob subsequently went to Egypt. During a time of famine Jacob's sons sought food in Egypt, and found that their brother Joseph, who had been sold into slavery, was vizier of the country. Joseph encouraged his father and brothers to migrate to Egypt, where they remained until the time of Moses. The eastern Delta region, known as Goshen, became the temporary home of the Israelites. In the Exodus, Israel left Egypt and, after a generation in the wilderness, entered Canaan from the east.

B. Genealogy. The Israelites formed a part of two larger ethnic groups: Semites and Hebrews. The Semites of the Table of Nations (Gen. 10:21ff.) comprise Assyrians, Arameans, and a number of Arabian tribes, as well as the ancestors of the Israelites. A descendant of Shem was named Eber (11:14), a name that gives us our word "Hebrew." Abraham was a descendant of Eber, making the term "Hebrew" more inclusive than the later "Israelite." Groups known as Ḫabiru (Ḫapiru) or ʿApiru are described in the literature of Mari, Nuzi, Ugarit, and Amarna, which regarded them as beyond the pale of the organized urban communities of the 2nd millennium B.C. The term is not equivalent to Israelite, but the Israelites were probably included in that category by the inhabitants of the city-states of Canaan before the conquest of that land by Joshua and its subsequent Israelite settlement (*see* MARI IV; HABIRU).

C. Patriarchal Origins. The family is the earliest unit in biblical history. Abraham with his family and retainers comprised a sizable company — so large that he could organize an army of men to rescue his nephew from a powerful coalition of foreign invaders (Gen. 14). There is no reason to doubt that servants and others who voluntarily associated themselves with the patriarchal family were regarded as Israelites, regardless of their own genealogy. The later Israelites contained numerous racial strains — Amorite, Hurrian, Hittite, and Aramean.

According to Gen. 11:31, Terah the father of Abraham migrated from the territory of Ur to the region of Haran in northwestern Mesopotamia. Although exact dates for the patriarchal period are debatable, a date *ca.* 2000 B.C. for Abraham is acceptable (*see* ABRAHAM III). Following the migration from Ur, Terah and his family settled in Haran, which, like Ur, was a center for the worship of the moon-god. Terah was content to remain in Haran; but Abraham, mindful of the call of God, moved on to the land of Canaan.

The region around Haran continued to be recognized as the ancestral home of the family of Abraham. Haran, or Harran as it is spelled in the cuneiform literature (cf. LXX *Charran*), was an important trading center. Its name is similar, although not identical in the original, to Haran, a brother of Abraham. The city of Haran is mentioned in contemporary letters and documents as an important trading center during the 19th and 18th cents. B.C. Other towns in the neighborhood of Haran, mentioned in the Mari Letters, which date from the patriarchal age, include Nahor (also the name of a brother of Abraham), Til-Turakhi (Terah), and Sarugi (Serug). When Abraham sent his servant to find a bride for Isaac, it was to the city of Nahor that the servant went (Gen. 24:10).

The Mari Letters illustrate the freedom of movement that characterized the Amorite world in the late 18th century. The king of Assyria, from his capital at Asshur on the Tigris, negotiated with the king of Qatna in central Syria for the marriage of his son with the latter's daughter. Assyrian merchants had established trading communities in Cappadocia, where they maintained trading relations with the homeland. The records of this commerce are preserved in the Cappadocian Tablets. The movement of the patriarchs is thus seen as part of a manner of life in which mobility formed an important element.

The term "Amorite" or "westerner" was originally used of all the peoples who spoke dialects that grammarians call Northwest Semitic. This included the people whom we know as the Arameans and the Hebrews. In later use, however, the name was applied to groups of inhabitants of Palestine with which the Israelites came into conflict. All of northern Palestine is called "the land of the Amorites" in Egyptian records dating *ca.* 1300 B.C.

The Mari Letters mention names that form interesting parallels to those of the Bible. The name Abram has a close parallel in *Abam-ram* and Jacob in *Jacob-el.* An Amorite tribe of Benjamites is frequently mentioned, although it has no relation to the biblical tribe of the same name. The Ḫabiru were a troublesome group at Mari. They are also met in many parts of Mesopotamia, Anatolia, Canaan, and Egypt, where they appear as raiders, mercenary soldiers, captives, government employees, rebels, and slaves. The term seems to be one of social or legal status, rather than nationality. It was used of the unsettled, nomadic peoples who harassed the civilized communities around the Arabian Desert. The name Ḫabiru may have been applied to the biblical Hebrews, or Israelites, in that sense. Abraham is specifically termed *hāʿiḇrî* (Gen. 14:13). (*See also* TELL MARDIKH.)

III. Moses and the Exodus.–A. Israel in Egypt. The Israelites voluntarily entered Egypt under Joseph, but later unfriendly pharaohs reduced them to slaves. According to Gen. 15:13 their entire sojourn was 400 years in duration, or according to Ex. 12:40, 430 years. The LXX of Ex. 12:40 interprets the 430 years as the time of sojourn both in Canaan and in Egypt — a period of 215 years in Canaan and 215 in Egypt. This reckoning is followed also by the Samaritan Pentateuch, Josephus (*Ant.* ii.15.2 [318]), and the NT (Gal. 3:17).

B. The Exodus. Suffering in Egypt, the Israelites cried to God for deliverance, which came in the person of Moses. After a series of plagues that came upon the land of Egypt, Moses led the people across the Sea of Reeds (N of the Red Sea) into the Sinai Peninsula.

According to 1 K. 6:1 Solomon dedicated the Jerusalem temple in the 480th year after the Exodus from Egypt. The first year of Solomon's reign is known to have been *ca.* 970 B.C. By adding the two figures together we would have a date of *ca.* 1450 B.C. for the Exodus. This would fall during the reign of Thutmose III (1490-1435 B.C.), who is known to have employed Asiatic captives in his extensive building projects. On the basis of this chronology, Ahmose (or Amosis), who expelled the Hyksos and founded the New Kingdom (*ca.* 1570 B.C.), may have been the "new king over Egypt who did not know Joseph" (Ex. 1:8) and Hatshepsut may have been the pharaoh's daughter of Ex. 2:5-10. If the Exodus took place *ca.* 1440, the Israelites would have attacked Jericho forty years later, *ca.* 1400 B.C.

Other evidence, however, points to a later date for the Exodus. The building operations of Thutmose III were, as far as we know, in Upper Egypt, and the Israelites labored in the Delta, where they "built for Pharaoh store-cities, Pithom and Raamses" (Ex. 1:11). Raamses appears definitely to have been Per-Ramses, the "House of Ramses (II)," which has been identified with the Delta city of Tanis-Avaris-Qantir. Those who hold to a 1440 date for the Exodus suggest that the use of the name "Raamses" is an example of scribal emendation whereby an older name is replaced in the text by a contemporary name for the same place. Those who hold the so-called late date for the Exodus suggest that Ramses II (1290-1224 B.C.) was the pharaoh of the Exodus, which may have taken place *ca.* 1280 B.C. Ramses II had his court at Tanis, a location that agrees with the biblical statement that the Israelites

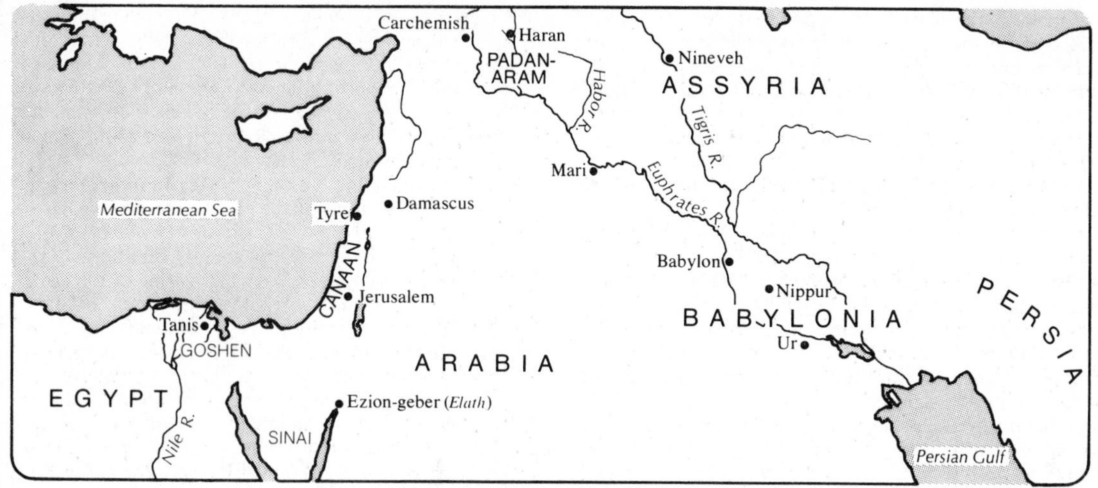

lived nearby "in the land of Egypt, in the field of Zoan" (i.e., Tanis) (cf. Ps. 78:12,43).

The first actual mention of Israel in any Egyptian document is in the Israel stele of Merneptah (1224-1216 B.C.). Pharaoh Merneptah professes to have gained a decisive victory over "the people of Israel." We thus have a *terminus ad quem* for the Exodus — Israel was definitely in Palestine by *ca.* 1220 B.C.

The chief argument against the 1280 B.C. date for the Exodus is the 480 years of 1 K. 6:1. This figure may represent twelve generations, conventionally figured at forty years each, and it need not represent an exact number. Actual generations may be less than forty years apart, leaving us no fixed chronology. With our present state of knowledge it is best not to be dogmatic, but to leave the exact date an open question.

See EXODUS, DATE OF THE.

C. Wilderness Wandering. The most important event of the forty years of wandering near Kadesh was the giving of the law at Mt. Sinai. There the Decalogue was received by Moses and the tabernacle was constructed according to instructions received by revelation. Within the tabernacle was a chamber known as the holy of holies (or most holy place), which served as the throne room of Israel's God. The sacred ark of the covenant was located there and the glory cloud hovered over the ark between two cherubim. The two tablets of the Decalogue were placed within the ark.

Having resisted Moses' leadership, faithless Israel refused to enter Canaan and a whole generation perished in the wilderness. It was only after the death of Moses that Joshua led Israel into Canaan.

IV. Conquest of Canaan.*–*A. Entrance into Canaan. Victories in Transjordan formed a prelude to victories in the Promised Land itself. Sihon and Og, powerful kings ruling the area of Ammon and Bashan, had been defeated by the Israelites before Joshua led his people into western Palestine.

After crossing the Jordan, Joshua established his camp at Gilgal. Here twelve symbolic stones taken from the Jordan were erected as a monument to God's faithfulness (Josh. 4:1-9, 20). The encampment at Gilgal formed a period of transition for the Israelites, who recognized Joshua as the successor to Moses. The miraculous manna ceased, and Israel began to eat from the produce of the land of Canaan. The rite of circumcision, which appears to have been neglected during the wilderness period, was reestablished, and the Passover was celebrated.

B. Joshua's Campaigns. Joshua's military strategy was designed to divide the Canaanite forces. Victories at Jericho and Ai in central Palestine would divide the land and provide a wedge from which the Israelites might gain effective control. Jericho was the walled and fortified city that was the key to the Canaanite defense of central Palestine. Joshua laid siege to the city, which fell into Israelite hands following an earthquake that destroyed its walls. The city was burned and only Rahab, who had received Israelite spies into her house, was spared.

The book of Joshua states that the conquest of a place named Ai (lit. "the ruin") took place shortly after the conquest of Jericho (Josh. 7:2–8:28). A mound known as et-Tell (lit. "the mound," a synonym for Ai) was excavated in 1933-1934 by Mme. Judith Marquet-Kraus. The remains indicate that the city located at et-Tell flourished 3300-2400 B.C. It was destroyed, however, *ca.* 2400 B.C., and never again became a city of any consequence. It was occupied by a few Israelites during the period 1200-1000 B.C. The absence of an account of the conquest of Bethel, only 2½ km. (1½ mi.) from Ai, has caused some scholars to conclude that the account of the battle of Ai refers actually to a battle at Bethel. L. H. Vincent has suggested that Ai may have served as a military outpost for Bethel. It may have seemed wise for the Canaanites to meet the Israelite threat at Ai to prevent the disaster of a battle at Bethel itself. It is, of course, possible that the identification of et-Tell with Ai is incorrect and that subsequent discoveries will provide a solution to the problem.

Now fearful of the Israelites, the inhabitants of Canaan prepared to defend themselves, although the Gibeonites determined to make an alliance with Israel as a means of self-preservation. Feigning themselves travelers from a distant country, they tricked Joshua into making an alliance, which he honored even after the deceit was detected. Unwilling to see their land absorbed by the armies of Joshua, Adoni-zedek of Jerusalem and the kings of Hebron, Jarmuth, Lachish, and Eglon marched against Gibeon. Joshua staged a night march, rushed up the pass, and at daybreak came upon the kings from southern Canaan in their encampment near Gibeon. The armies of the southern coalition were forced to flee down the western slope of the hill, past Beth-horon. Many of the fleeing Canaanites were killed in a hailstorm. The rest continued their flight down the Valley of Aijalon as far as Makkedah, where the five kings were trapped and slain.

Jabin, the king of the city-state of Hazor in northern Canaan, led another resistance movement. The threat was so great that Jabin had no difficulty enlisting the help of the other city-states and ethnic groups of northern Canaan. The Hazor confederacy grouped its forces in the vicinity of the waters of Merom. (Older maps identify the waters of Merom with Lake Huleh, N of the Sea of Galilee; subsequent studies indicate a location SW of Hazor.) Joshua took the offensive and launched a surprise attack. The armies of the Hazor confederacy fled, with Joshua pursuing them as far as the city of Sidon on the Phoenician coast. Although pockets of resistance were to continue throughout Canaan, large-scale organized resistance ended with the defeat of the Hazor confederacy. Hazor itself was completely destroyed. The smaller cities "that stood on their mounds" (Josh. 11:13) were not burned. These could be readily defended by Joshua and could be used by the Israelites who were about to settle throughout the land of Canaan.

Joshua's victories were decisive, yet much of Canaan was still in enemy hands at the time of his death. The Philistines occupied the land along the Mediterranean from the Brook of Egypt (Wâdī el-ʿArîsh) to Joppa. They remained a foe of Israel until David's reign, and did not finally disappear as a potential threat until Judas Maccabeus inflicted a crushing defeat on them (Josephus *Ant.* xii.8.6 [353]). The Phoenician cities of Tyre, Sidon, and Gebal (Byblos) did not fall before the armies of Joshua and never were a part of Israelite territory. David and Solomon found it profitable to make commercial treaties with the Phoenicians. Hiram of Tyre provided valuable building materials and architects for Solomon's building projects.

C. Division of the Land. Although the land was not wholly occupied by Israelites during Joshua's lifetime, it was divided among the tribes both as a recognition of victory and as an encouragement to the tribes to go in and possess the territory assigned to them. Judah was assigned the territory of southern Canaan, E and SE of the Dead Sea. A part of this land was later assigned to Simeon (Josh. 19:1-9) because "the part of the children of Judah was too much for them."

The important central part of Canaan was assigned to the Joseph tribes, Ephraim and Manasseh. This was a rich and fertile region; but Canaanite fortresses at Beth-shean, Ibleam, Dor, Taanach, and Megiddo proved a barrier to the occupation of the area. When complaints were received about the inadequacy of their territory, Joshua assured Ephraim and Manasseh that they would conquer the Canaanites "though they have chariots of iron, and though they are strong" (Josh. 17:11-18). Between Judah and the "Joseph tribes" territory was assigned to Benjamin (Josh. 18:11-28) and Dan (19:40-48). Jerusalem was located at the border between Judah and Benjamin. The tribe of Dan had difficulty maintaining itself in the coastal area and later migrated to the far north (Jgs. 1:34f.). It is with respect to northern Dan that the borders of Israel are said to be "from Dan to Beer-sheba." Asher, Zebulun, Issachar, and Naphtali received their inheritance in the northern part of the country (Josh. 19:10-39). Reuben, Gad, and the half-tribe of Manasseh had already taken their territory on the east of the Jordan (Nu. 32:1-42; Josh. 13:8-33).

The Levites, whose concern was public worship, were not given tribal inheritance. They were assigned forty-eight cities with the pasture land or "suburbs" of each. These cities were scattered among the tribes. They included the six "cities of refuge," which were set apart as an asylum for those who had committed unintentional homicide. The fugitive had to convince the elders of the city that he had had no murderous intent. He then stood trial before the entire congregation. If declared innocent he remained within the city of refuge until the death of the high priest, after which he could return home without fear of the "avenger of blood."

V. Period of the Judges.—A period of spiritual decline that was characterized by the licentious worship of Baal and the Asherim (Jgs. 2:11-13) and combined with weakness and defeat on the field of battle followed the death of Joshua. A succession of oppressions is recorded in the book of Judges, during each of which Israel cried to God for deliverance. When Israel turned to God in repentance, He raised up a judge, or deliverer, who served as leader of the tribes until his death.

A. Political Life of the Period. The Israelite tribes formed a loose confederation during the period of the judges. The tribes settled in their respective territories and had to defend themselves against marauding tribes from a distance and against the local Canaanites who had not been dispossessed. During the 12th cent. B.C. a migration of Philistines from Crete and the Aegean region settled along the coastal regions of southern Palestine and became the greatest threat to Israelite independence. The Philistine threat continued through the period of the judges and was resolved only during the reign of King David. The presence of Philistines along the coastal regions of southern Canaan made it impossible for the tribe of Dan to secure adequate territory for its population. Thus a large portion of the tribe migrated to the extreme north of the country, where they took the city of Laish (Leshem) and renamed it Dan (Jgs. 18).

The lack of a strong central government was keenly felt during the period of the judges. In southern Canaan Judah and Simeon fought their own battles (Jgs. 1:3), as did the tribes in the territory E of the Jordan known as Gilead (11:5-11). The northern tribes of Zebulun and Naphtali united to repulse Canaanite attacks upon their territory (4:6). Men from Naphtali, Asher, and Manasseh supported Gideon in his attack on the Midianites (7:23). The Ephraimites were unhappy with Gideon's attitude toward them (8:1) and they threatened to avenge a fancied slight that they attributed to Jephthah (12:1). Jephthah met their challenge by marshaling his Gileadite forces and defeating Ephraim in battle (12:4-6).

Civil war broke out when a Levite's concubine died as the result of mistreatment by Benjaminites of Gibeah (Jgs. 19:22-26). The Benjaminites would not deliver the murderers into the hands of the other Israelites for punishment, with the result that the other tribes were arrayed against Benjamin. After several unsuccessful attempts to take Gibeah by frontal attack, the other Israelites captured the city by a ruse (Jgs. 20:18-48). So great was the slaughter that the tribe was almost annihilated, and wives had to be provided from the other tribes for the surviving Benjaminites (Jgs. 21). The author of the book of Judges characterizes the period as one in which "every man did that which was right in his own eyes" (Jgs. 21:25). Although theoretically the tribes were a theocracy, it was practically a time of anarchy.

B. The Judges. Israel's first oppression came from Cushan-rishathaim, a king of Aram-naharaim (Mesopotamia), and lasted eight years (Jgs. 3:8). This may be a king from Mitanni who attacked Israel during his campaigns against Egypt. Since the Hebrew word "Edom" is similar to "Aram," and since all Israel's oppressors were neighbors of Israel, some scholars identify Cushan-rishathaim as an Edomite ruler. Othniel, a Kenizite, delivered Judah from Cushan. After a time of peace, Eglon of Moab oppressed Israel until he was killed by a Benjaminite named Ehud (3:12ff.). Then the Canaanites of northern Palestine formed an alliance under Jabin of Hazor and afflicted Israel for twenty years. Deborah, a prophetess, encouraged Barak to marshal the forces of Israel to fight the Canaanites in the Valley of Esdraelon. In the plain of the Kishon River Barak defeated the forces of the Canaanite general Sisera, whose chariots had to be abandoned when the Kishon overflowed its banks. Sisera himself was killed by Jael, the wife of Heber the Kenite (Jgs. 4–5). In the same region bands of Midianites oppressed the Israelite tribes until Gideon marshaled his small but loyal band to drive out the oppressor (Jgs. 6–8). Abimelech, a son of Gideon, established a kingdom at Shechem and attempted to rule Israel (Jgs. 9). His brother Jotham expressed contempt for the concept of monarchy (9:7-20), and Abimelech's kingdom was soon ended.

The minor judges Tola of Issachar and Jair of Gilead (Jgs. 10:1ff.) judged Israel for twenty-three and twenty-two years, respectively. Details of their work are not recorded. When Ammonites crossed the Jordan from the east and attacked Israel, the Israelites sent for Jephthah, an illegitimate youth who had been an outcast from society before being recalled to lead the armies against Ammon (Jgs. 11). After the victory over the Ammonites, Jephthah had to settle a civil war brought about by the jealousy of the Ephraimites (Jgs. 12), who had not taken part in the expedition against Ammon.

The most detailed account of the book of Judges concerns Samson, a Nazirite of the tribe of Dan who lived during the time when the Philistines were making serious inroads against Israel. Samson's exploits show that friendly relations were possible between Philistines and Israelites on a personal basis even when the peoples were national enemies.

C. Chronology of the Judges. The chronological data given in the record of the judges (Jgs. 3:8–16:31) add up to a total of 410 years for the periods of oppression and the rule of the judges themselves. This figure is too large to harmonize even with the 480 years of 1 K. 6:1, and archeological considerations argue for a much shorter period. Jewish tradition eliminates the years of oppression, incorporating them into the periods of the individual judges (cf. *Seder Olam Rabbah*). Many biblical scholars note the prevalence of forty-year periods (or fractions or multiples thereof) and suggest that some of the figures are part of an epic frame of reference and should not be taken literally. It is also highly probable that some of the oppressions and judgeships were contemporary in Jgs. 10:7, and it is likely that this was true of others. For this reason it is not possible to establish an absolute chronology for the period of the judges (*see also* JUDGES, BOOK OF).

VI. United Kingdom.–A. International Scene. The books of Samuel record the beginning of Israel's golden age, the one period of history during which Israel was a world power. Palestine usually served as a buffer state between Egypt and the empires of the Tigris-Euphrates Valley, Assyria and Babylonia. The world situation of the 11th and 10th cents. B.C., however, produced a power vacuum. The empire period of Egyptian history had come to an inglorious end. Following the death of Ramses III (1144 B.C.) Egypt was ruled by a succession of weak pharaohs. Aggressive foreign policies were resumed by Shesonq I (biblical Shishak), who came to the Egyptian throne (935 B.C.) while Solomon was reigning in Jerusalem.

In the east Tiglath-pileser I (1115-1077 B.C.) laid the groundwork for the Assyrian empire, which became the scourge of Syria and Palestine. The Assyrian nation remained quiescent, however, from the death of Tiglath-pileser until the accession of Ashurnasirpal II (885 B.C.), about forty years after Solomon's death. It is precisely during the period between Tiglath-pileser and Ashurnasirpal that Israel experienced its golden age under Saul, David, and Solomon.

Although not confronted with armies from the Euphrates or the Nile, Israel faced formidable foes nearer home. During the time of the judges there were battles with the Arameans, Moabites, Canaanites, Midianities, Ammonites, and Philistines. Difficulties with most of these tribes were sporadic, but the Philistines continued as an active threat. The uncircumcised Philistines were a non-Semitic people who had come to Canaan (to which they later gave the name of "Palestine") from Caphtor, an ancient name for Crete (Jer. 47:4; Am. 9:7). Although some Philistines settled in patriarchal Canaan (Gen. 26:1, 14, 18), a large influx occurred following an unsuccessful Cretan attempt to invade Egypt during the 12th cent. B.C. The Philistines settled in the southwestern part of the land. A clash was inevitable. One result of the struggle was the establishment of the Israelite monarchy.

B. Samuel. Samuel was a transitional figure. He was the last of the judges (1 S. 7:15), a priest (1 S. 2:18; 7:9), and a prophet (2 Ch. 35:18). Under his leadership Israel passed from a group of more or less independent tribes with common traditions and a common loyalty to the Lord, to a limited monarchy under Saul and, subsequently, David.

Dedicated from birth to God's service, Samuel was trained by Eli the priest at the house of God in Shiloh (1 S. 2:11, 18-21; 3:1-10). The ark of the covenant was kept in this structure, which seems to have been more permanent than the tabernacle used during the period of wilderness wandering. Samuel in his youth acted as the mouthpiece of God in condemning the immoral practices (1 S. 2:22) and greed (2:12-17) that marred the usefulness of Eli's sons in the service of the Shiloh shrine. Eli himself appears as a moral but weak individual, unwilling or unable to cope with the situation. God, through Samuel, declared that the family of Eli would not continue in the sacred office (3:11-18).

The Philistine victory at Aphek marks the low point of Israelite power at this period. It also serves as a commentary on the spiritual condition of the days before the establishment of the monarchy. Experiencing the bitterness of defeat, Israel determined to bring the sacred ark to the field of battle as a kind of fetish (1 S. 4:3). The momentary sense of relief at the sight of the ark changed to sorrow when the Philistines fought victoriously, captured the ark, and slew Hophni and Phinehas, the sons of Eli (4:11). At the tidings of the loss of the ark and the death of his sons, the aged Eli died.

God would not allow the Israelites to make a fetish of the ark, but neither would he allow the Philistines to prosper through its presence in their camp. It became a source of embarrassment in the Dagon temple (5:2-5). When "tumors" afflicted the men of Ashdod (5:6-12), they determined to rid themselves of the ark, which had brought evil instead of good. Thus they put it on a new cart with unyoked oxen and sent it to Beth-shemesh, along with golden jewels (6:1-16). The men of Beth-shemesh "gazed" at the ark, perhaps opening it and examining its contents. As a result of this irreverence, they too were smitten (6:19). Thereupon the men of Beth-shemesh sent to Kiriath-jearim, in the hill country of Judah, asking that the men of Kiriath-jearim come and take the ark (6:21). The Philistines had evidently destroyed the sanctuary at Shiloh (cf. Jer. 7:12). The ark was placed in the house of Abinadab at Kiriath-jearim (7:1), where it remained until the time of David (2 S. 6:3f.).

With the ark in Israel once more, the nation experienced a time of spiritual revival which began in "yearning after the Lord" (1 Sam. 7:2). The Philistine oppression quickened a sense of spiritual need in Israel. Samuel urged the necessity of putting away the Baalim and the Ashtaroth (7:3), the Canaanite deities that had such a grip on Israel during much of its preexilic history. At Mizpah (7:5-9), Samuel called together the people of Israel, and in repentance they acknowledged their sin (7:6). The Philistines, learning of the Mizpah convocation, attacked (7:7-17), but God enabled the Israelites to achieve a great victory. Here they set up a monument, which they called Ebenezer, "stone of help," with the testimony: "Hitherto hath the Lord helped us" (7:12).

During the wise judgeship of Samuel, Israel had no cause for complaint. With his advancing years, however, fear of the future became a paramount concern. Samuel's sons were not following the godly paths of their father. The Philistines constituted a continuing threat. Israel desired to have a king to lead them in battle as was the custom among other peoples (8:1-9).

C. Saul. Samuel was disheartened when the people requested a king. It seemed to be a rejection of the theocracy, and of Samuel himself. Assured that it was God's will to anoint a king over Israel, Samuel sought the one who should reign as the first king.

Benjamin, Saul's tribe, was very small. The choice of a Benjaminite as Israel's first king was a conciliatory gesture to Ephraim to the north and Judah to the south. Tribal rivalries were thus held in abeyance while Israel passed from a loose federation of tribes to a centralized monarchy. Saul was anointed as king by Samuel, but it was his prowess on the field of battle that brought him the enthusiastic support of his people. Israel had requested a king who could lead his people in battle, and Saul was not a disappointment in that respect.

The Ammonites, living E of Moab and Gilead, were a roving, predatory people. Under their king Nahash they invaded the Israelite territory E of the Jordan and besieged Jabesh-gilead. When Saul learned of the threat to Jabesh-gilead, he summoned the Israelite warriors to Bezek, S of the mountains of Gilboa, and put the Ammonites to flight. This decisive victory gave Saul prestige as a king who had proved himself successful on the field of battle (11:1-11).

Since the time of the judges, the Philistines had occupied strategic Israelite cities. Geba of Benjamin, 9.6 km. (6 mi.) N of Jerusalem, and Bethel, 19 km. (12 mi.) N of Jerusalem on the Shechem road, were among the important cities in Philistine hands. Saul sought to lead Israel against the Philistines. His son Jonathan struck the first blow by attacking them at Geba, and soon followed it with a second victory at Michmash, across the valley from Geba. The Israelites then pursued the Philistines to their own borders. The Philistines, however, continued to hold fortresses in Israel throughout the reign of Saul, and there were constant wars between the two peoples.

The Aramean state of Zobah, N of Damascus, had frontiers extending as far as the Euphrates. The chariotry of Zobah proved a serious obstacle to Israelite military power (1 Ch. 19:6). Saul's campaign there was very likely defensive, protecting his borders against Aramean raids.

The marauding nomads who attacked the Israelites during their migration from Goshen (Dt. 25:17-19) had been defeated by Joshua at Rephidim (Ex. 17:8-16). They continued to be Israel's inveterate foes. Saul defeated them in battle but incurred the wrath of Samuel when he spared Agag, the Amalekite ruler, and refrained from killing the cattle. Although Saul expressed a desire to sacrifice the best of the cattle to the Lord, Samuel insisted that obedience was better than sacrifice. The beginning of the rift between Samuel and Saul may be traced to the Amalekite war.

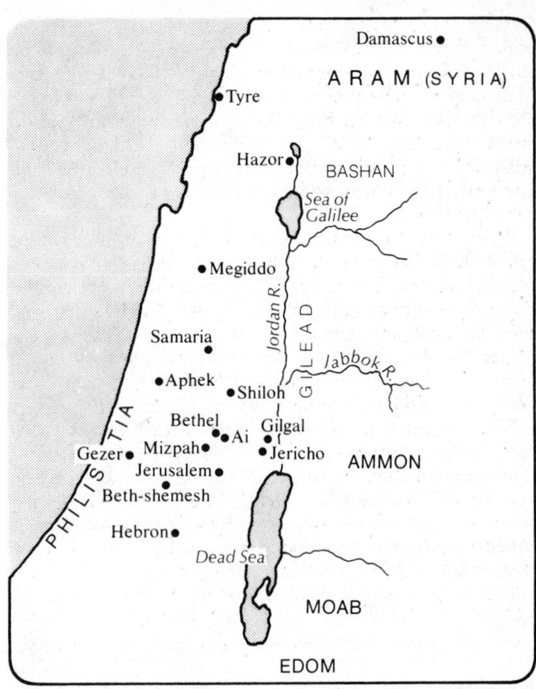

There were doubtless many conflicts between Israelites and Philistines during the reign of Saul. The second war was notable in that David, who had been anointed privately by Samuel, appeared on the field of battle for the first time. In the Valley of Elah, David met and slew the Philistine hero, Goliath of Gath. The Israelite victory that followed made David a national hero. Saul, however, was enraged, and determined to rid himself of a rival.

The last years of Saul's life were filled with tragedy. Literally insane with jealousy over David, Saul was in no position to lead his people. The Philistines were a growing threat, and they prepared for a complete victory over Israel. They assembled at Aphek in Benjamin, and marched northward to the Israelite encampment on the plain of Esdraelon at the foot of Mt. Gilboa. Saul, fearing for his life, left the Israelite camp by night and sought out a "woman having a familiar spirit" at Endor, S of Mt. Tabor. During this clandestine interview, the deceased Samuel warned Saul that he would die on the morrow. The next day a battle was fought between Israel and the Philistines at Mt. Gilboa. Saul and three of his sons, including Jonathan, were killed. Saul's body was fastened to the wall of the Canaanite fortress city of Beth-shean, overlooking the Esdraelon Valley. It was retrieved, however, by the warriors of Jabesh-gilead, who remembered Saul's deliverance of their city when it had been attacked by the Ammonites. The Philistine victory at Gilboa was one of the darkest episodes of OT history.

D. David. After the death of Saul, David left his place of refuge, the Philistine city of Ziklag, and went to Hebron where he was proclaimed king over Judah. In the meantime Saul's son Ish-bosheth ruled over the northern tribes, although Abner, who had been Saul's general, exercised the real power. The forces of Joab, David's general, and Abner, commander of Ish-bosheth's army, met at Gibeon. The ensuing battle resulted in victory for the partisans of David. In the retreat, however, Joab's brother Asahel was slain by Abner. After a stormy career, during which Abner changed allegiance to David, Ish-bosheth was murdered by two of his own henchmen, who took his head to

David at Hebron, expecting a reward. David hanged the criminals and gave the head of Ish-bosheth an honorable burial at Hebron. Jealous of his position, David's general Joab slew his potential rival Abner, ostensibly to avenge the death of Asahel. King David mourned Abner as "a prince and a great man" (2 S. 3:38). With the death of Ish-bosheth, opposition to the kingship of David over the northern tribes was removed. He was subsequently anointed king over all Israel.

When David became heir to the kingdom of Saul he ruled the hill country of Ephraim and Judah; Philistines and Canaanites still occupied strategic cities on the coastal plain, the Shephelah, and the Esdraelon Valley. The Jebusites, a Canaanite tribe (Gen. 10:16; cf. 1 Ch. 1:14), occupied the ancient city of Jerusalem, which they called Jebus. In the Amarna Tablets (*ca.* 1400 B.C.) the city was called Urusalim, meaning "city of peace" or "city of Salim," an ancient Canaanite deity. Although the Jebusites felt their fortress city high in the Judean mountains to be impregnable, Joab, David's general, risked his life to conquer it for the king. Jebus bordered Judah and Benjamin, but had not been incorporated into the territory of either tribe during the period of Jebusite occupation. After capture by Joab, Jerusalem became "the city of David."

The Philistines became apprehensive at the growing power of David and entered the Judean mountain region with their armies. In the Valley of Rephaim, running about 5 km. (3 mi.) SW of Jerusalem toward Bethlehem, David utterly routed his Philistine foes (2 S. 5:20). Following up his victory in the Judean highlands, David pursued the Philistines to the Shephelah and the maritime plain. He took the stronghold of Gath (1 Ch. 18:1) and so completely subjugated the Philistine confederacy that they could not trouble Israel again until after the division of the kingdom.

Although not permitted to build the temple, David made the initial plan for it. He centralized worship in Jerusalem by bringing the ark from Kiriath-jearim, on the western border of Benjamin, to the new capital (1 Ch. 13:3-14). The ark was installed in Jerusalem, where it remained until the Exile (587 B.C.).

The reign of David marks — politically speaking — Israel's golden age. A power vacuum in both Egypt and Mesopotamia made it possible for the tribes that had entered Canaan under Joshua a few centuries earlier to become a mighty nation. The lands conquered by David included Moab (2 S. 8:2), Zobah (vv. 3-5), Damascus (vv. 5f.), Edom (vv. 13f.), and Ammon (2 S. 10–11). The Ammonite war was the longest in David's career. Aided by fighting men from Zobah, Maacah (Aram-maacah), Beth-rehob, and Tob, the Ammonites were able to offer stiff resistance to David. The first battle was fought near Medeba, an old Moabite town about 26 km. (16 mi.) SE of where the Jordan enters the Dead Sea. The Arameans were routed and the Ammonites took refuge within a fortress. Joab met the army of Hadadezer of Zobah, led by his chief Shobach, at an unidentified place named Helam (10:16) in the east Jordan country. After peace was concluded with the Arameans, David turned his attention to the extended siege of Rabbah, or Rabbath-ammon, modern ʿAmmân. While back in Jerusalem, David ordered the death of Uriah the Hittite, in order to cover his sin with Bathsheba, Uriah's wife, and marry her (1 S. 11:15-17). When victory was assured, David went to Rabbah and put the crown of Milcom, the god of Ammon, on his own head, thus taking to himself the title "king of the Ammonites" (1 S. 12:30).

With the successful conclusion of the Ammonite war, David was king of an area extending from the Red Sea to the Euphrates. He was at the pinnacle of success, but already the seeds of future trouble were evident. From the death of Saul to the siege of Rabbah, David was successful in all his major undertakings, but during his declining years he experienced a series of personal and national tragedies.

Absalom, David's son, killed his half brother, David's oldest son Amnon, who had defiled and mistreated Tamar, Absalom's full sister. Fearing the anger of David, Absalom fled to the small Aramean state of Geshur, E of the Sea of Galilee, the home of his maternal grandparents. Through a stratagem of "the wise woman of Tekoa," David was reconciled to Absalom and the youth returned home (1 S. 14). Difficulties continued, however, when Absalom took advantage of a sacrificial ceremony at Hebron to have himself declared king of Israel. David with his foreign mercenaries, Cherethites (probably Cretans) and Pelethites (from southern Philistia), fled from Jerusalem and made his way to the east Jordan territory (2 S. 8:18). He and his retinue reached Mahanaim, N of the Jabbok, before Absalom and his army crossed the Jabbok (2 S. 17:24). In the Forest of Ephraim nearby, the battle took place and Absalom was killed.

Soon after Absalom's rebellion, a Benjaminite, Sheba, led a revolt against David (1 S. 20:1f.). Since Saul had been a Benjaminite, this may be interpreted as an effort to bring the throne back to the tribe of Benjamin. Joab pursued Sheba and his followers to Abel-beth-maachah, in northern Palestine W of Dan. There Sheba was decapitated by a "wise woman" in order to save her city from destruction by Joab's army (1 S. 20:19-22).

Toward the end of his reign, David took a census, and a severe pestilence fell upon the people (2 S. 24). David also purchased the stone threshing floor from Araunah, or Ornan, which was used as the base for an altar dedicated by David to the Lord (24:16-25). This became the site of Solomon's temple, and is thought to be the rugged natural scarp preserved under the mosque known as the Dome of the Rock in the old city of Jerusalem.

David's last days were comparatively uneventful. When his son Adonijah attempted to secure his own succession to the throne, David heeded the warning of Bathsheba and Nathan, and had Solomon anointed at the Spring Gihon outside the east wall of Jerusalem.

E. Solomon. Solomon fell heir to an empire formed largely through the leadership of David. Early in his reign Solomon reorganized the government of his kingdom, dividing it into twelve provinces or administrative districts (1 K. 4:7-19). Judah is not mentioned among the provinces. It may have been ruled directly from Jerusalem. Solomon is said to have ruled from the Euphrates to the border of Egypt (1 K. 4:21). The Aramean states as well as the people of Edom and Moab regularly presented their tribute to Solomon at Jerusalem. As a commercial outpost he built "Tadmor in the wilderness" (2 Ch. 8:3f.), about 225 km. (140 mi.) NE of Damascus. In Roman times Tadmor was known as Palmyra.

By a trade alliance with Hiram, king of the Phoenician seaport Tyre, Solomon was able to promote Israel's commercial interests. He personally developed Ezion-geber, on the Gulf of Aqabah, as a port through which Israelite trade with Arabia and Africa could pass (1 K. 9:26-28). Hiram of Tyre also helped Solomon by providing building materials and skilled labor for the palace and temple that he built in Jerusalem. Solomon was able to supply farm products to the Tyrians as a partial payment for their assistance. Ten thousand men are said to have been employed to cut down the cedars and transport them to the sea. Stone for Solomon's building operations was quarried in the mountain country adjacent to Jerusalem.

The financial difficulties of Solomon are noted in the account of his ceding a tract of land in Galilee containing twenty towns as partial payment for his debt (1 K. 9:11-24). One of these towns was Cabul, a border city in the tribe of Asher. The territory was evidently not desirable, for Hiram expressed dissatisfaction over the payment. Solomon's control of Zobah, Damascus, Ammon, Moab, and Edom gave him a monopoly of the caravan routes between Arabia and the north. Horses from Cilicia (1 K. 10:28f.) and chariots from Egypt were handled at a fixed price by Solomon's merchants.

The building of chariot cities was an important defensive measure of Solomon. The great Canaanite stronghold of Hazor in upper Galilee had important chariot installations. (Similar installations at Megiddo, previously thought to be Solomonic, have been dated to the time of Omri; cf. *EAEHL,* III, 853f.) Other chariot cities included Accho (Acre), N of Mt. Carmel; Achshaph, 8 km. (5 mi.) SE of Accho; and Tell el-Ḥesī (perhaps Eglon), W of Lachish. There were also Solomonic chariot installations at the towns at the border of Cilicia, from which horses were imported. The city of Gezer W of Jerusalem was given by the Egyptian pharaoh to his daughter on the occasion of her marriage to Solomon (1 K. 9:16). Important chariot installations were subsequently placed there.

Copper mining and smelting was developed in the Jordan Valley in the region between Succoth, near the Jabbok, and Zarethan, 19 km. (12 mi.) NE of Adamah. The whole region between Succoth and Zarethan provided suitable clay for the molds in which the copper was cast. Metal objects produced here later adorned and equipped the temple in Jerusalem. (The ruins at Ezion-geber that were first identified as a copper smelting industry have now been identified as a storehouse and granary. *See* TELL EL-KHELEIFEH.)

International alliances were made not only with Egypt and Tyre but also with other states. Solomon's harem of a thousand wives and concubines represented many alliances sealed by marriage (1 K. 11:1-3). The visit of the queen of Sheba (probably from Saba in southwestern Arabia) probably was concerned at least partially with commercial matters. Important caravan roads led from Saba northward along the western borders of Arabia (Job 6:19; Isa. 60:6; Jer. 6:20; Ezk. 27:22f.). Solomon carried on trade with Ophir, from which he imported "almug wood" and precious stone. Ophir was probably located in southwestern Arabia in the area now called Yemen. From distant lands ships brought gold, silver, ivory, apes, and peacocks (or baboons, RSV mg.) to Solomonic Israel (1 K. 10:22). Egypt and Kue, a part of Cilicia, provided horses for Solomon's extensive chariot installations (10:28, RSV).

The latter years of Solomon marked the beginning of Israel's economic and political decline. A change in dynasties in Egypt brought to the throne a pharoah unfriendly to Solomon. Hadad, an Edomite who had been in Egypt, returned to his native country to spark a rebellion against Solomon (1 K. 11:14-22). Rezon, an Aramean chief, seized Damascus and severed its ties with Israel. The loss of these territories resulted in a serious decline of revenue to the government of Solomon.

Further troubles came, however, from within Israel. Jeroboam, Solomon's high official who had the responsibility for the labor conscriptions in the "tribe of Joseph" (i.e., Ephraim and Manasseh), became the leader of a revolt against the king. Although forced to flee to Egypt, he remained in readiness to return when called upon by his countrymen.

VII. Divided Kingdom.–A. Disruption. After the death of Solomon, Rehoboam his son refused to come to grips with the economic chaos of the nation. Jeroboam, a former officer of Solomon, returned from exile in Egypt to lead a revolt that resulted in the establishment of an independent northern kingdom. This included the larger portion of Palestine proper, an area of about 24,300 sq. km. (9400 sq. mi.) as over against 8800 (3400) for the rival kingdom of Judah. The boundary between Israel and Judah ran S of Jericho, Bethel, and Joppa. The line was variable, however, being moved northward or southward depending on the relative strength of the two nations. The capital of Israel was first at the historic city of Shechem, then at Tirzah. Omri, the founder of the third dynasty, chose Samaria as the site of his permanent capital and it remained there until the kingdom was destroyed by the Assyrians. Religious sanctuaries were maintained at Dan in northern Israel and at Bethel near the southern border.

The kingdom of Judah included the tribe of that name, a portion of Benjamin, and Simeon, which had been incorporated earlier into Judah. The Shephelah and the coastal plain were nominally a part of Judah, but actually they seem to have been controlled by the Philistines. Kings of the Davidic line reigned over Judah until the fall of Jerusalem to Nebuchadrezzar king of Babylon (587 B.C.).

Solomon had retained control over Moab (1 K. 11:1, 7), but the land E of the Dead Sea subsequently gained its independence from the northern kingdom. On the Moabite Stone, discovered at Dibon in Jordan in 1868, Mesha king of Moab recorded that his land had been subdued by Omri of Israel, and held by Omri's son Ahab until Mesha freed his country during the latter part of Ahab's reign. Israel's counterattack failed (2 K. 3:21-27). According to Assyrian records Moab paid tribute to Tiglath-pileser III after his invasion of the West (733-732 B.C.), and subsequently to Sennacherib (701 B.C.). Moab disappeared as a political power when Nebuchadrezzar subjugated the country (605-562 B.C.).

South of the Dead Sea was the kingdom of Edom, which had been conquered by David and remained tributary during the reign of Solomon. It held about the same relationship to Judah that Moab held to Israel. During the reign of Jehoram son of Jehoshaphat (*ca.* 849-842 B.C.) the Edomites gained their independence (2 K. 8:20-22). Like its neighbors, Edom fell to Nebuchadrezzar.

B. Period of Warfare. The three kingdoms that developed from Solomon's kingdom in western Palestine — Syria, Israel, and Judah — strove for supremacy. They waged intermittent warfare from the reign of Jeroboam to that of Jehu in the northern kingdom, and from Rehoboam to Joash in Judah. During the early part of this period wars between Israel and Judah were continual. With the rise to power of the Syrian state of Damascus, Israel and Judah tended to draw closer together.

Shortly after the division of the kingdom, Jeroboam of Israel called upon Sheshonq of Egypt (biblical Shishak) to invade Judah. Thus Judah was confronted with a war on two fronts, Israel to the north and Egypt to the south. Sheshonq despoiled the temple and palace of treasures accumulated by David and Solomon (2 Ch. 12:2-12). It is noteworthy that Sheshonq did not limit his Palestinian campaign to Judean cities, for the Egyptian inscriptions at Karnak depicting his successful Palestinian campaign show captives from the northern kingdom as well as from Judah.

During the reign of Asa, Judah was invaded by a large force of chariotry under Zerah, an Ethiopian or Cushite. This Zerah, who may be one of the Osorkons of the 22nd Dynasty of Egyptian history, was defeated at the Judean city of Mareshah on the old road from Gaza to Hebron (2 Ch. 14:8-15).

Under Ahab and his Phoenician wife Jezebel, the worship of the Tyrian Baal became a serious challenge to the faith of Israel (1 K. 16:28–19:21), but the ministry of the prophet Elijah helped stem the tide of Baalism. Meanwhile, Ahab was faced with danger from Syria. After an initial defeat by Israel, Ben-hadad's Syrian forces concluded that Israel's God was "a god of the hills" (20:23), and that victory for Syria would be achieved if Israel could be brought down from its mountain strongholds. This proved to be wishful thinking, however. At Aphek, a town about 6.5 km. (4 mi.) E of the Sea of Galilee on the highway between Damascus and Esdraelon, Ben-hadad was decisively defeated. Cities earlier taken from Israel by the Syrians were restored and the northern kingdom was given commercial privileges in Damascus (1 K. 20:26-34).

In 853 B.C., Ahab was numbered among the allies of Ben-hadad against the Assyrian ruler, Shalmaneser III, at Qarqar on the Orontes River. The major threat from Assyria made it necessary for the smaller states of Syria-Palestine to reconcile their differences. Assyrian records tell us that Ahab placed in the field of battle two thousand chariots and ten thousand foot soldiers (probably an exaggeration). Although Shalmaneser III claimed a great victory, it was not a decisive one. When the Assyrian armies returned home, conditions returned to normal in Syria and Palestine — war again broke out between Ben-hadad and Ahab. In a battle to regain Ramoth-gilead, E of the Jordan, Ahab was struck with an arrow. He bled to death and was buried in the Israelite capital, Samaria.

Contemporary with the reigns of Omri, Ahab, and Jehoram in Israel, Jehoshaphat reigned as Judah's fourth king. Early in his reign, Jehoshaphat sought to cement relations with Israel by marrying his son, the crown prince Jehoram, to Athaliah the daughter of Ahab and Jezebel. This act, while politically expedient, gave Baal worship a foothold in the southern kingdom comparable to its hold upon the north. Jehoshaphat was allied with Ahab against the Syrians at the battle of Ramoth-gilead, near the Syrian border (2 Ch. 18:18). During his reign a strong confederacy of Edomites, Moabites, and Ammonites invaded Judah. Due to a misunderstanding, however, the invading peoples began fighting among themselves and Jehoshaphat won the day without drawing a sword.

During the reign of Joram (Jehoram) of Judah, Edom revolted. Joram encamped at Zair, about 8 km. (5 mi.) NE of Hebron, before successfully attacking the Edomites. Judah was unable to retain supremacy over Edom, however.

C. Period of Aramean Dominance. The dynasty of Omri in Israel was brought to a violent end by Jehu, who was as zealous for the worship of Israel's God as Ahab and Jezebel had been for Baal worship. A countermovement took place in the south, when Athaliah the daughter of Ahab and Jezebel seized the throne of Judah and attempted to force Baalism on her people. While both Israel and Judah were going through these periods of trial, Hazael succeeded Ben-hadad II as king of Syria (2 K. 8:7-15). Hazael was so powerful that during a period of Assyrian weakness he was able to dominate both Israel and Judah. He seized Israel's land E of the Jordan (10:32f.; cf. Am. 1:3) and spared Jerusalem only after plundering the city and temple (2 K. 12:17f.). During this period the usurpation of Athaliah was ended through the activity of the high priest Jehoiada, who had rescued the infant Joash of the Davidic line from the murderous plans of Athaliah. Joash was instrumental, in cooperation with Jehoiada, in a program of renovation and repair of the temple (2 K. 12:1-16). During the latter part of his reign, however, he lapsed into idolatry. It was during Joash's reign that Hazael conquered the Judean city of Gath and plundered Jerusalem itself.

D. Period of Prosperity. With the death of Hazael, Syrian power waned. Jeroboam (II) son of Joash (Jehoash) was a powerful and able king of Israel. Lost territory was regained and nearly all of Syria was reconquered; Samaria was now the capital of a nation that approached in size the empire over which Solomon had ruled. The period of Joash of Israel and his son Jeroboam II has been called Israel's "Indian summer," a brief time of prosperity before its fall.

This prosperous period in Israel is paralleled in Judah during the reigns of Amaziah and Uzziah (otherwise rendered Azariah). After a victorious campaign against Edom in which he took Sela, the capital, Amaziah of Judah fought Jehoash of Israel at Beth-shemesh. Amaziah's Judean army was defeated and Israel proceeded to attack Jerusalem itself. For the only time in history, an army from the northern kingdom entered Jerusalem as victor, plundered its treasures, and made Judah virtually subject to Israel.

The reign of Uzziah of Judah was more successful. He raised a large, well-equipped army and provided for the defense of Jerusalem (2 Ch. 26:11-15). Successful military campaigns were carried on against the Philistines, and Ammon was made tributary to Judah (2 Ch. 26:6-8). Ezion-geber (Elath) was recovered for the southern kingdom (2 K. 14:22).

The prosperity during the reigns of Jeroboam II of Israel and Uzziah of Judah was not matched with spiritual progress. The prophets of the day, particularly Hosea and Amos in the north and Isaiah in the south, underscored the externalism and hypocrisy that characterized much of religious life. Sacrifices were brought to the altars and sacred seasons of the year were punctiliously observed. At the same time oppression, bloodshed, and greed were commonplace. The prophets declared the imminent judgment of God upon a nation that had forgotten its Maker and Protector.

E. Fall of Samaria. Israel's prosperity under Jeroboam II was short-lived. Assyrian power was on the increase, and the entire Syria-Palestine area was considered suitable prey. In the reign of Menahem, Israel became tributary to Assyria. Northern Israel, including Naphtali, was carried into captivity by Tiglath-pileser (733 B.C.). His son Shalmaneser V besieged Samaria, which fell to Shalmaneser's successor, Sargon II (722 B.C.). Israel had placed confidence in Egypt for assistance against Assyria, but the days of Egyptian might were past.

The Assyrian policy of transportation had an important effect upon subsequent history. Captive peoples were transported to various new areas in an attempt to break up any possible national resistance. Israelites were taken to Halah and Gozan on the banks of the river Habor in northern Mesopotamia. Similarly, peoples from Babylonia, Syria, Elam, and elsewhere were settled in Samaria (2 K. 17:24). The subsequent intermarriage of these peoples with the Israelites who were left in the land produced the people known as Samaritans (v. 29). It was precisely this policy of transportation that made impossible the return of the people of the northern kingdom in a way comparable to the return of the Judeans after the decree of Cyrus.

F. Judah Alone. Judah continued for almost a century and a half after the fall of Samaria. During much of this period, however, it was tributary to Assyria. Ahaz and most of his successors maintained their throne by the payment of tribute. An influential party in the Judean court was active in seeking an alliance with Egypt as an alternative to this payment of Assyrian tribute.

During the reign of Hezekiah (715-687 B.C.), the Assyrian king Sennacherib, a son of Sargon II, invaded western Palestine and occupied the principal Philistine, Phoenician, and Judean cities. Hezekiah paid tribute to Sennacherib (2 K. 18:13-16), but refused to surrender the besieged city of Jerusalem (19:9-34). Assyrian annals tell how Sennacherib shut up Hezekiah "like a bird in a cage." The siege of Jerusalem was lifted, however, when the Assyrian armies were smitten by the "angel of the Lord" (19:35). Secular history suggests that bubonic plague broke out in the Assyrian camp (Josephus *Ant.* x.1.5 [21]).

Following the godly reign of Hezekiah two idolatrous kings, Manasseh and Amon, ruled over Judah. Manasseh had a policy of religious syncretism, adopting the worship of Baal and Astarte, and encouraging the worship of the sun and "all the host of heaven" (2 K. 21:1-18 par. 2 Ch. 33:1-20). The worship of Molech in the Hinnom Valley included the rite of passing living children through the fire. Tradition suggests that the prophet Isaiah was "sawn asunder" during the reign of Manasseh (He. 11:37; cf. the pseudepigraphic Martyrdom of Isaiah, *APOT,* II, 155-162).

The last spiritual revival of preexilic Israel occurred during the reign of Josiah, who succeeded to the throne after courtiers murdered his father Amon because they resented his idolatrous policy. The discovery of the "book of the law of the Lord" during Josiah's program of temple renovation was the chief element in this revival. Religion was centralized in the Jerusalem temple to the exclusion of the notorious "high places." Josiah died at the fortress of Megiddo in an attempt to prevent Pharaoh Neco of Egypt from joining forces with the Assyrians, who were now fighting for their national existence against the Neo-Babylonian empire. In this act, Josiah was doubtless honoring commitments to Babylon.

G. Fall of Jerusalem. The rise of the Neo-Babylonian (Chaldean) empire was one of the important factors during the last days of Judah's history. Nabopolassar the Chaldean revolted against his Assyrian lords and established one of the great empires of antiquity. The city of Babylon was reconstructed during his reign. With Cyaxeres the Mede and the Scythian king, he captured the Assyrian capital of Nineveh (612 B.C.). In concert with his son Nebuchadrezzar II, Nabopolassar took part in the Battle of Carchemish (605 B.C.) in which the Egyptian Pharaoh Neco received a crushing defeat. Syria and Palestine, earlier considered parts of the Assyrian empire, were now theoretically subject to Babylon.

Judah's pro-Egyptian king Jehoiakim, the second son of Josiah, was permitted to reign until he rebelled against Babylon (2 K. 24:1-6). Jehoiakim was succeeded by his eighteen-year-old son Jehoiachin, who reigned only three months before being taken into captivity with ten thousand other men of Judah (24:11-16). After looting the temple treasury, Nebuchadrezzar appointed Jehoiachin's twenty-one-year-old uncle Mattaniah king under the name of Zedekiah. In spite of the counsel of Jeremiah, Zedekiah favored the pro-Egyptian party and rebelled against Nebuchadrezzar, precipitating the eighteen-month siege of Jerusalem. This ended with the destruction of the city and its temple and the deportation of the citizens to Babylon (587 B.C.).

VIII. Babylonian Exile.–The Jews who were deported from Jerusalem were permitted to settle in their own communities in Babylon. The prophet Ezekiel prophesied to such a community located at Tel-abib on the river Chebar (Ezk. 1:1) near Nippur. Although unwilling exiles in a foreign land, the Israelites did not find life in Babylon intolerable. Jeremiah urged the exiles taken at the time of Jehoiachin's captivity (597 B.C.) to build houses, marry, and live normal lives (Jer. 29:5-7).

A. Changes in Israelite Life. During the years of exile, Israel became a religious community unrelated to any political entity or cultic center. This caused changes in its thinking and in its political institutions that have continued to the present. Although some Jews would later return to Jerusalem, the majority continued to live at a distance from the Holy Land. Their ties were cultural and religious, but not political.

The term "Israel" is frequently used to describe the earlier period of Hebrew life, when the tribes dwelt in proximity to one another and religious life could conveniently center in one sanctuary. As a political unit Israel was a power to be reckoned with in the days of David and Solomon, and even after the division of the kingdom it maintained a semblance of autonomy until the Exile. On the other hand, postexilic Judah, except for the Maccabean interlude, was dependent upon the great powers among whom it lived: Persia, Macedonia, the Ptolemies of Egypt, the Syrian Seleucids, and the Romans. The people lived not only in Palestine, but also in Egypt, Persia, Babylon, Syria, Asia Minor, Greece, and Rome. These Jews might visit Jerusalem on the occasion of the religious festivals (cf. Acts 2:8-11), but they had found their livelihood in a wider world and made some adaptations to a wider culture.

1. Place of Scripture. Exilic and postexilic Judaism was the heir to the Law and the prophetic writings of preexilic Israel. The Exile itself had underscored the need for faithfulness to Israel's God. Idolatry had been the besetting sin of the preexilic period, and those who had suffered the loss of home and temple could be expected to turn in horror from the sins that had brought on the Exile. The rejection of idolatry had, as its positive side, a deepening appreciation of Israel's historic monotheistic faith as enunciated in the body of sacred writings known as the Torah, or Law. The Torah — our Pentateuch — includes much more than rules for conduct. Exodus, Leviticus, and Deuteronomy contain codified law, but much of the Torah instructs by example. Biographies of godly people — Abraham, Joseph, Noah, Moses, and a host of others — provide instruction. The evil deeds of people so realistically described provide instruction also. Bad examples as well as good examples are necessary if we are to understand life in its totality. The evil must be shunned and the good followed; both are illustrated and described in the Torah of Israel.

Not only the Law, but preexilic prophetic writings were studied by faithful Jews in Babylon. Daniel tells us that it was his study of the prophecies of Jeremiah that caused him to humble himself before God in anticipation of the day when the Exile would come to an end (Dnl. 9:1-19). In contemplating the time when a new temple would be built in Jerusalem, the priests and their descendants concerned themselves with the minutiae of the Levitical laws. Those whose hearts were still in Zion occupied themselves with the Scriptures. There they learned both the reason for the Exile and the manner of life proper to the people of God in the land of their captivity and, at a later time, in a restored Zion.

2. Synagogue. The synagogue, the characteristic institution of postexilic Judaism, had its roots in the religious needs of those who could not attend the temple worship to which they were accustomed. Orthodox Judaism reckoned but one sanctuary, that which had first been built by Solomon in Jerusalem. The temple was the successor to the older tabernacle, a movable structure that had been built during the period of the wilderness wandering before Joshua led Israel into Canaan. The sacred ark, the most important element in the tabernacle, had later been located at Shiloh where "the temple of Yahweh" (1 S. 1:9) was located in the days of Samuel. Shiloh was destroyed during the battles between the Israelites and Philistines, and the ark had no permanent abode until David brought it to Jerusalem (2 S. 6:1-19). From that time to the present,

Jerusalem was considered the religious center of Jewish life and the only appropriate place for the holy temple.

No temple was built in the Jewish settlements of Babylon. The exiles needed to have occasions of fellowship in prayer and Bible study to augment their personal devotional times. Out of this very real need the institution known as the synagogue gradually developed. The synagogue became the community center for Jewish life.

3. Aramaic Language. During the Exile the linguistic habits of the Jews changed. In the days of Hezekiah, the common language of the Jews was Hebrew, although ARAMAIC was understood as a language of diplomacy (cf. 2 K. 18:26). Hebrew was never totally displaced, but the Aramaic language became the common tongue during the exilic period, and it was the spoken language of most of the Jews who returned to Palestine. Jews who spoke only Aramaic would not be able to understand the Hebrew Scriptures without an interpreter. The custom arose in the synagogue service of first reading the Hebrew Bible and then giving an explanation in the vernacular Aramaic. This oral explanation in time became a discourse, interpreting and applying the biblical message. Generations later these explanations or "Targums" were themselves written down, but in their early history they were simple explanations of the biblical text, ranging from word-by-word translations to quite free paraphrases. More liberties were permitted with the prophetic literature than with the Torah, which was accorded the highest degree of inspiration in Jewish thought.

4. Worship. The reading of Scripture was probably preceded by a prayer. In later Jewish practice the reading from the Torah was preceded by the recitation of the Shema (Dt. 6:4-9; 11:13-21; Nu. 15:37-41), which gets its name from the Hebrew for "hear," the first word of Dt. 6:4-9 ("Hear, O Israel!").

The institution of the sabbath, poorly observed in the preexilic communities, became the hallmark of Judaism during the exilic period. From sundown on Friday to sundown on Saturday the Jew refrained from all work. The sabbath became a day of rest and worship. In addition to the sacred festivals of the Levitical calendar, the Jews of the Exile observed fasts in memory of the national calamities attending the fall of Jerusalem (Zec. 7:3, 5; 8:19). Later the Feast of Purim was observed to commemorate the victory of the Jews over their foes in Persian times (Est. 9:27-32).

Corporate worship did not take the place of personal devotion for the godly Jew. Daniel made it a practice to pray three times daily with his face turned toward Jerusalem (Dnl. 6:11 [MT 10]). Confession of sin and prayers for divine compassion were certainly stimulated by the Exile. Those who had presumed upon God's goodness during preexilic times now saw their predicament in the light of God's holiness. The author of Lamentations cried out, "Restore us to thyself, O Lord, that we may be restored! Renew our days as of old!" (Lam. 5:21).

5. Relations with Non-Jews. It is impossible to generalize on the attitude of Babylonian Jews to their idolatrous neighbors. Some had little contact with non-Jews, but we know of many Jews who rose to important positions in the political and business world of the time. Daniel in the courts of Babylon and Persia, Nehemiah the cupbearer to Artaxerxes Longimanus, and Esther the queen serve as notable examples of Jews who were in no sense isolated. We also know that some Jews made a name and fortune for themselves in the world of commerce. The business archives of the Murašu family of Nippur provide an early example of Jews who became successful in business.

One result of this new chapter in Jewish life was the Jews' impact on their non-Jewish associates. Prior to the Exile, conversion was largely a matter of living in the land of Israel and assimilating Israelite culture. Ruth the Moabitess determined to serve Naomi's God when she returned with her to Bethlehem, whereas Orpah, Ruth's sister-in-law, returned to Moab and served the gods of Moab (Ruth 1:14-16). During and after the Exile, however, Judaism became a missionary religion. The Jews looked with scorn on the idolatry that once had been so great a temptation to their fathers. They saw idolatry as something evil not only for themselves as Jews, but for all people. A significant and growing number of converts or "God-fearers" looked upon Judaism as the true religion and turned their backs on paganism. The early Church found a ready audience that had been providentially prepared by postexilic Judaism for the preaching of the Christian gospel.

B. Judah During the Exile. With the destruction of Jerusalem, Judah ceased to exist as a sovereign state. Zedekiah died shortly after being taken to Babylon. Jehoiachin, although looked upon as the legitimate king, had no reasonable hope of returning to his land.

1. Rule of Gedaliah. The Babylonians established a military government for Judah with headquarters at Mizpah, about 13 km. (8 mi.) N of Jerusalem. Gedaliah, a Judean, was named governor. He was the son of Ahikam, who had protected Jeremiah from the wrath of Jehoiakim and his nobles (Jer. 26:24). Gedaliah was considered pro-Babylonian and thus suitable for an appointment that would be sympathetic to Babylonian rule. After Jerusalem fell to Nebuchadrezzar, the Babylonian military officers asked Gedaliah to look after the safety of Jeremiah (39:11-14).

Gedaliah formed a center around which the Judeans who had not been taken into exile might gather. Those who had fled to Edom, Moab, and Ammon trickled back. Gedaliah advocated loyalty to Nebuchadrezzar: "Dwell in the land, and serve the king of Babylon, and it shall be well with you" (Jer. 40:9). Evidently a degree of prosperity ensued, for "they gathered wine and summer fruits in great abundance" (40:12).

In the ruins of Tell en-Naṣbeh (Mizpah?) a seal was found bearing the identifying inscription "To Jaazaniah, servant of the king." Jaazaniah was one of the officials associated with Gedaliah (2 K. 25:23; Jer. 40:8). A seal impression found among the ruins of Lachish (thus antedating its destruction) bears the inscription, "Gedaliah who is over the house." Thus G. Ernest Wright (*WBA*, p. 181) suggests that Gedaliah had served as one of the last prime ministers of Judah, because the words "who is over the house" refer to the office of prime minister. Not only was Gedaliah's father a high official in his own right (Jer. 26:24), but his grandfather Shaphan had served Josiah as scribe, or secretary of state (2 K. 22:3, 8-12).

The rule of Gedaliah at Mizpah came to a violent end. Ishmael, a man of royal blood who sought the throne for himself (Jer. 41:1; 2 K. 25:25), had fled to Ammon during the siege of Jerusalem. He found a ready ally in Baalis king of Ammon. Learning that Gedaliah was governor of the remnant of the Judeans at Mizpah, Ishmael went there with a band of ten men and treacherously killed Gedaliah. Gedaliah had been warned about the plot, but he refused to believe the evil report concerning Ishmael (Jer. 40:16).

In addition to Gedaliah, Ishmael killed eighty men who had come to worship at the shrine at Mizpah (Jer. 41:4-7), and took captive the others who had settled at Mizpah, intending to take them to Ammon (41:10). At Gibeon, Ishmael was challenged by the forces of the loyal Judean, Johanan the son of Kareah. Although Ishmael escaped, his captives were freed and subsequently, contrary to the counsel of Jeremiah, fled southward to Egypt.

2. Silent Years. The history of Judah between the destruction of Jerusalem (587 B.C.) and the return of the first group of exiles following the decree of Cyrus (536 B.C.) is largely a blank. The province of Judah that Gedaliah had ruled was probably abolished, and its territory incorporated into the neighboring province of Samaria. Although the land was not repopulated, as the northern kingdom had been following its fall to Assyria in 722 B.C., the Samaritans doubtless occupied much of the territory that had been vacated. Other groups — Ammonites, Arabians, and Edomites, in particular — must also have profited from the exile of the Judeans. In the years after 536 B.C. these peoples became adversaries of the group of Jews that returned from exile, and by political intrigue and limited warfare they sought to hinder the rebuilding activities.

The Babylonians, like the Assyrians before them, made it a matter of policy to burn and raze captured cities. Treasures would be pillaged and city walls reduced to rubble. Archeologists note that no town in Judah was continuously occupied throughout the exilic period. There was a complete break in the history of Judah. This is not true, however, of the cities N of the Judean border. Bethel and the Samaritan cities were not destroyed. Similarly the towns of the Negeb, S of Judah, were undisturbed. Among the towns of Judea that were destroyed and never rebuilt were Beth-shemesh and what is now known as Tell Beit Mirsim (Debir?). Excavators have found that there were periods when sites were not used prior to the 6th cent. B.C., but it was only after the Babylonian conquest of Judah that large numbers of sites permanently ceased to be occupied.

Unlike the Assyrians, who repopulated the northern kingdom after its fall in 722 B.C. (2 K. 17:24), the Babylonians did not make it a policy to repopulate areas from which captives had been taken. Instead the land was gradually occupied by neighboring tribes: Edomites and Arabians pressed in from the south, and Ammonites and other tribes from E of the Jordan crossed the river to occupy such territory as they could claim. Before the return of exiles from Babylonia, Judah was dominated by alien peoples along with descendants of the former Jewish population who had not been deported. The area occupied by the Jews who returned following the decree of Cyrus was little more than Jerusalem and its suburbs.

The Jews who were in Palestine during the period of the Exile had much in common with their Samaritan neighbors to the north. Both groups worshiped the same God, Yahweh, and both accepted the Torah as Holy Writ. The syncretism that marked the earliest Samaritans (2 K. 17:33) seems to have disappeared in later Samaritan history. Their distinctive faith was in the sanctity of Mt. Gerizim as the temple site (Jn. 4:20). This, however, was not implemented until a sanctuary was built on Mt. Gerizim in postexilic times.

Judging by the problems faced by reformers of a later day, e.g., Ezra and Nehemiah, the Jews and Samaritans of Palestine must have had friendly relations. Intermarriage must have been common, for it became the great problem of the later reformers (cf. Ezr. 10:18-44; Neh. 13:23-28). Sanballat the governor of Samaria gave his daughter to a grandson of the high priest Eliashib in the days of Nehemiah (Neh. 13:28). But the Jews who returned from exile insisted on strict separation from the Samaritans and other non-Jewish peoples of Palestine.

For fifty years after the destruction of Jerusalem, Judah was left to its own devices. While exiles in Babylon dreamed of returning to their Palestinian homes, the inhabitants of Judah, Jews and non-Jews, had adjusted to a new mode of life. It is understandable that Samaritans should resent the return of exiles from Babylon and that some Jews would desire to keep ties of friendship with them.

C. The Last Kings of Babylon. Nebuchadrezzar reigned over Babylon for more than forty years. He did not, however, prepare successors who would be ready to rise to the needs of a succeeding generation. In the first year of the reign of his son Amēl-Marduk (Evil-merodach of Scripture), Jehoiachin king of Judah was released from prison in Babylon and given a position of honor among the vassal kings. After a reign of only two years Evil-merodach was assassinated by his brother-in-law Neriglissar, who usurped the throne. After a nine-month reign, Neriglissar's son Labāši-Marduk was in turn assassinated by Nabonidus, who had no ability as a king. Nabonidus was more interested in religion and the study of antiquities than in the details of government. He was consequently unpopular with the priests, who wished to restrict his interest to the established religion, and with the populace, who cared little for his unorthodox ways. Belshazzar the son of Nabonidus served as prince regent in the place of his father and is best known as the "king" under whom Babylon fell to the Persians.

IX. Return from Exile and Restoration. *–A. Career of Cyrus.* The Persian empire came into being as the result of the efforts of Cyrus, who first appeared in history in 559 B.C. when he inherited the small kingdom of Anshan. This territory was tributary to the Median empire, one of the eastern rivals of Babylon. After revolting against his Median overlord, Cyrus sought to build a world empire. He marched his armies into Asia Minor and subdued Croessus of Lydia. Then he turned toward Babylon, where the weak rule of Nabonidus and his son Belshazzar was resented by both priests and populace. In October, 539 B.C., Gobryas the governor of Elam (whom some identify with the DARIUS of Dnl. 6) conquered the city of Babylon in the name of Cyrus. When Cyrus became lord of Babylonia, the dependencies of Babylon also came under his control. He adopted a benevolent policy toward the former Babylonian provinces, expecting thereby to secure their cooperation for his own policies. Phoenicia pledged its loyalty and its fleet, which was the match of any in the Mediterranean.

Cyrus' avowed policy of restoration of captive deities and captive peoples had special application to the Jews, whose religious ideals were respected by Cyrus and his successors. Cyrus restored the gods of other nations and authorized the return of the vessels used in the worship of the God of Israel (cf. Dnl. 5).

Many Jews were happy in Babylon, and had no desire to leave. They were permitted to remain, and many prospered in business and government during the Persian period. Daniel, who had earned a place of respect in the courts of Babylon and Persia, was among those who remained. Nehemiah and Esther subsequently rose to positions of influence in the Persian court.

B. First Return. The temple utensils were taken from Esagila, the temple of Babylon, and entrusted to a Jewish prince who had been appointed governor of Judah, Sheshbazzar (perhaps Šamaš-apal-uṣur). About fifty thousand Jews availed themselves of the opportunity to return to their homeland with the blessing and help of Cyrus. Aside from the assertion that he "laid the foundation of the house of God which is in Jerusalem" in 537 B.C., we read no more of the activity of Sheshbazzar (Ezr. 5:16).

The leadership of the band of returned exiles passed to Zerubbabel (Zer-babili, "seed of Babylon") and Jeshua (or Joshua) the priest. Consonant with the edict of Cyrus, they built the altar of burnt offerings and began the offering of daily morning and evening sacrifices on the site of their former temple (Ezr. 3:3). In the second year of the return, the foundations of the temple were laid amid scenes of great rejoicing (3:12), although nothing more was accomplished in the work of rebuilding the temple during the lifetime of Cyrus (4:5). The joyful enthusiasm of the early days of the return gave way to the gloomy frustration that resulted from the activities of "the adversaries of Judah and Benjamin" (Ezr. 4:1) who attempted to hinder the Jews from making effective use of their homeland. These peoples had profited from the expulsion of the Jews in the days of Nebuchadrezzar, and they resented their return to Palestine.

Due to pressures from Judah's foes, the work of rebuilding the temple came to a halt. The last days of Cyrus and the reign of Cambyses were times of disillusionment and adjustment for the returned exiles. Harassed by unfriendly neighbors, they found they had all they could do to provide for the necessities of life. The people were agreed on one thing: "The time is not come, the time that the Lord's house should be built" (Hag. 1:2).

This spirit of defeat was not shared by Haggai and Zechariah, who began to prophesy to Judah during the second year of Darius. They were aware of the problems the Jews faced, but they urged the people to trust God and take heart (Hag. 2:4f.). The work of rebuilding began in earnest. Perhaps at the instigation of "the adversaries of Judah and Benjamin," the Persian governor "beyond the river," Tattenai (perhaps "Thithinaia" in Persian), made a visit to investigate the activities of the Jews. Tattenai asked who had authorized the building of the temple and the Jews told him of the decree of Cyrus (Ezr. 5:3), suggesting that a search be made in the royal archives. The decree was found in the royal archives at Ecbatana. Darius determined to honor it and issued an order to that effect (Ezr. 6:7). He further decreed that an endowment be given the Jews from the royal treasury to expedite the work (6:8). Darius honored the decree and encouraged the Jews in their labors. In the sixth year of Darius (516 B.C.) the temple was completed. Special dedicatory sacrifices were offered, and the priests and Levites were assigned their respective tasks (6:15-18).

Over fifty years pass in silence between the dedication of the second temple (515 B.C.) and the arrival of Ezra in Palestine in the seventh year of Artaxerxes (457 B.C.). Although successful in building the temple, the Palestinian Jews were certainly not prosperous during this period. Their city had no walls and it was open to attack from their numerous enemies. The people had become dispirited. Earlier resolves to live in separation from their neighbors had been quietly forgotten, and mixed marriage was common.

C. Return under Ezra. In Babylon and other parts of the Persian empire numerous Jews still looked with fond associations upon Jerusalem as the center of their religious life and their spiritual hopes. One of these was Ezra, a pious Levite who devoted his life to the study of the law. As a lover of Zion, Ezra appealed to Artaxerxes for help in making it possible for a fresh company of exiles to return to Palestine. The king complied (Ezr. 7:11-26) and authorized Ezra to assemble such Jews as would volunteer to join him, and to take offerings for the temple. Sacrificial animals were to be purchased, and the rest of the money used as he saw fit. Ezra was also authorized to appoint magistrates and judges and to enforce the law of God and of the Persian king. Thus Ezra was not merely a pious pilgrim but a representative of the Persian empire. Provincial rulers were ordered to provide Ezra and his company with food and money for their journey.

In all, about eighteen hundred men and their families responded to Ezra's appeal. Forty Levites and 220 temple servants joined the party after a special appeal was made. After praying for divine protection they journeyed almost 1600 km. (1000 mi.) to Jerusalem, a trip that took about three and a half months. The temple treasures were returned to the temple in Jerusalem and special sacrifices were made on the altar in the temple court.

Ezra's mission in Jerusalem is conveyed in his title, "scribe of the law of the God of heaven" (Ezr. 7:12), which had the significance of "Minister of State for Jewish Affairs." The Persians were tolerant of the many religions in their empire, but they did wish them to be regularized under responsible authority. Armed with his official rescript, Ezra was responsible for Jewish affairs in the province of Abar-nahara ("beyond the river"), i.e., Syria and Palestine (7:25).

One of the first practical problems Ezra faced was that of mixed marriages. The reformer took an uncompromising attitude and insisted that such marriages be dissolved (Ezr. 9–10). While insuring the purity of Jewish faith against heathen dilution, this action most certainly stirred up the non-Jewish population of the province to renewed hostility against the Jews.

Ezra brought with him from Babylon the "book of the law of Moses" (Neh. 8:1), which he publicly read from a wooden pulpit. Along with the reading there was an explanation, probably in Aramaic, which had become the popular language of the Jews during the exilic period (8:7f.). When the people learned that it was time for the Feast of Tabernacles, which through ignorance they had not observed, they built booths for themselves and observed the ancient feast. Each day during the week of the observance they listened to the reading of God's law.

D. Nehemiah. A Persian Jew named Nehemiah had risen to the post of cupbearer to Artaxerxes Longimanus (465-424 B.C.). This was a position of honor, for it involved an intimate relationship with the king. When his brother Hanani and others from Judah came to visit Nehemiah at the Persian court, they told him of the difficulties of the Jews in Palestine (Neh. 1:1-3). Jerusalem had no walls to protect it from its many enemies. Although it was reckoned as the Holy City because the temple of the Lord had been built there, few people dared live among its ruins.

The report grieved Nehemiah, who sought an opportunity to tell the king. Artaxerxes readily granted him a leave of absence to visit Jerusalem and do the work that was on his heart. The length of the leave was agreed upon (Neh. 2:6), and Artaxerxes issued a royal rescript authorizing the building of the city walls. Letters were sent to the governors of the provinces W of the Euphrates and to Asaph, the keeper of the royal forest, directing that Nehemiah be provided with the materials he would need for the gates of the citadel, for the wall of the city, and for the temple itself (2:7f.). Nehemiah was appointed governor of Judah (5:14), thus making it a province separate from Samaria. This was to be one factor in the rivalry that developed between Nehemiah and Sanballat governor of Samaria.

The generosity of Artaxerxes was not without political implications and possible benefit to Persia. Egypt had been perennially restive, and Persia wanted its Palestinian provinces that bordered Egypt to be in loyal hands. The Jews, moreover, had smarted under Samaritan officialdom and were generally demoralized.

After making necessary preparations, Nehemiah and a group of companions made the long journey from Susa to Jerusalem. His first concern was for building the walls of the city. In the company of a few associates he inspected the ruins by night (Neh. 2:12-15). His heart was heavy, for he looked upon the ruined walls as a reproach both to Judah and to Judah's God (2:17). After inspecting the ruins, Nehemiah sought out the leaders of the Jerusalem community (2:16f.) and explained his mission. They caught something of Nehemiah's enthusiasm and determined to build the walls (2:18).

The opposition found its peak in three non-Jews: Tobiah, an Ammonite slave; Sanballat, the governor of Samaria; and Geshem, probably the chief of a tribe in northwestern Arabia. These men mocked the Jews for their efforts and insinuated that this rebuilding was an act of rebellion against Persia (2:19f.).

Nehemiah pressed on with his plans. The people responded to his appeal for help, and soon labor battalions were assigned to the various sections into which the wall had been divided. Workers came from outside villages — Jericho, Gibeon, Mizpah, Beth-haccerem, Beth-zur, Keilah, and Tekoa. Priests, Levites, goldsmiths, and merchants all labored together (Neh. 3). In less than two months (6:15) the wall was completed. Josephus tells us that it was further strengthened with battlements and gates over an additional two years and four months (cf. *Ant.* xi.5.8 [179]).

Nehemiah appointed his brother Hanani and a man named Hananiah, the governor of the castle, to assume responsibility for the welfare of Jerusalem. He charged them to keep the city gates closed until the sun was well up in the heavens, and to keep a guard posted (Neh. 7:2f.). The inhabitants of Jerusalem were few, for houses were still in ruins. It was necessary to encourage people to settle within the city, for life was more pleasant in other parts of Judah. Those who volunteered to live in Jerusalem were esteemed patriots, and a forced draft brought one-tenth of the country people into the Holy City (11:1).

The completion of the walls was an occasion of celebration and spiritual dedication. After ceremonies of purification (12:30), Ezra and Nehemiah each led a procession around the walls in opposite directions. They met near the temple area, where they gave expression to their joy and offered appropriate sacrifices (12:31-43).

When the wall was completed and adequate provision was made for the observance of the sacrifices and holy days prescribed in the Mosaic law (12:27-30), Nehemiah was free to end his leave of absence and return to the Persian court (13:6). The problems in Judah were not over, however. Within a short time — perhaps one to three years — he was granted a second leave of absence to return to Jerusalem.

During Nehemiah's stay at the Persian court, the situation in Jerusalem deteriorated. Although freed from the threat of enemies from without, the Jews themselves grew careless and internal dissension and infidelity brought on a new crisis. The wine presses were in operation on the sabbath day, and Tyrian merchants brought their fish and other merchandise into Jerusalem contrary to the sabbath law (Neh. 13:15f.). The perennial problem of intermarriage came to the fore again (13:23). Nehemiah made a second journey to Jerusalem in order to call his people back to the sacred law and their spiritual responsibilities.

For about a century after Nehemiah's time the Persian empire exercised control over Judea. The period was relatively uneventful, for the Jews were permitted to observe their religious institutions without molestation. Judea was ruled by high priests who were responsible to the Persian government, a fact that insured the Jews a large measure of autonomy but degraded the priesthood into a political office. Jealousy, intrigue, and even murder are reported in the contests for the office of high priest. Johanan son of Joiada (Neh. 12:22) is reported to have slain his brother Joshua in the temple itself.

Johanan was succeeded as high priest by his son Jaddua, whose brother Manasseh, according to Josephus (*Ant.* xi.7.2 [302f.]), married the daughter of Sanballat governor of Samaria, and established a sanctuary on Mt. Gerizim that was to vie with the Jerusalem temple as the true place of worship (cf. Jn. 4:20). Although this temple was destroyed during the reign of John Hyrcanus (134-104 B.C.), Mt. Gerizim continued to be regarded as the Samaritan holy mount, as it is today. The Sanballat in the histories of Josephus cannot have been the man of the same name mentioned by Nehemiah (Neh. 4:1 [MT 3:33]), but the establishment of a rival temple about this time is known to have taken place.

Persia and Egypt were engaged in constant struggles during this period; and Judea, situated between the two powers, could not escape involvement. During the reign of Artaxerxes III (Ochus) many Jews were implicated in a revolt against Persia, and they were deported to Babylonia and the shores of the Caspian.

During the 5th cent. B.C. a Jewish colony was located on Elephantine, an island at the First Cataract of the Nile River near modern Aswân. Contrary to the Mosaic law, these colonists built a temple for themselves and worshiped other divine beings (e.g., Eshem-bethel, Herem-bethel, Anath-bethel) along with Yahweh. These names may have been identified with Yahweh, but their very existence shows tendencies toward syncretism. The Elephantine Jews had dealings with the Samaritans as well as with the Judeans, and were not a part of the mainstream of Israel's religious life.

X. The Jews under Alexander and His Successors.–A. Alexander. The defeat of Persian armies in Asia Minor (333 B.C.) brought Alexander the Great into Syria and Palestine. After stubborn resistance, Tyre was taken and Alexander marched south toward Egypt. Legend states that he was met by Jaddua the high priest, who told him of Daniel's prophecies that the Greek army would be victorious (Dnl. 8). The story is not taken seriously by historians, but it is true that Alexander dealt kindly with the Jews. He permitted them to observe their laws, granted exemption from tribute during sabbatical years, and, when he built Alexandria in Egypt (331 B.C.), he encouraged the Jews to settle there and gave them privileges comparable to those of his Greek subjects.

B. The Ptolemies. Following the death of Alexander (323 B.C.), Judea was first subject to Antigonus, one of his generals; but it ultimately fell to another general, Ptolemy I, surnamed Soter or "Deliverer," who seized Jerusalem on a sabbath day in 320 B.C. Ptolemy followed Alexander's liberal attitude toward the Jews. Many of them settled in Alexandria, which continued as an important center of Jewish thinking for many centuries. Under Ptolemy II (Philadelphus) the Jews of Alexandria translated their Torah (the Pentateuch) into Greek. This translation was known later as the Septuagint, from the legend that seventy (more correctly seventy-two — six from each of the twelve tribes) translators were supernaturally inspired to produce an infallible translation (cf. the Letter of Aristeas, *APOT,* II, 83-122).

The Jews in Palestine enjoyed a period of prosperity in the days of Simon the Just, the ruling high priest whose character is described in the apocryphal book of Sirach (50:1-21). He is reputed to have repaired the walls and fortified the city of Jerusalem and to have built a spacious reservoir to provide water for the city. Tradition links his name with the completion of the OT canon. In his time the books of Ezra, Haggai, Zechariah, Nehemiah, Esther, and Malachi are said to have been canonized.

C. The Seleucids. After about a century during which the Jews were subject to the Ptolemies, Antiochus III (the Great) wrested Syria and Palestine from Egyptian control (198 B.C.). The Syrian rulers are known as Seleucids because their kingdom, built on the ruins of Alexander's empire, was founded by Seleucus (Nicator). Most of the earlier rulers bore the names of Seleucus or Antiochus. The seat of government was in Antioch on the Orontes River. During the early years of Syrian rule the Seleucids allowed the high priest to continue to govern the Jews according to their law. Strife broke out, however, between the Hellenistic party and the orthodox Jews. Antiochus IV (Epiphanes) allied himself with the hellenizing group, and appointed to the priesthood a man who had changed his name from Joshua to Jason and who encouraged the worship of the Tyrian Hercules. Jason was displaced in two years, however, by another Hellenist, a rebel named Menahem (Gk. Menelaus). When the partisans of Jason contended with those of Menelaus, Antiochus marched on Jerusalem, plundered the temple, and killed many of the Jews (170 B.C.). Civil and religious liberties were suspended, the daily sacrifices were prohibited, and an altar to Jupiter was erected on the old altar of burnt offering. Copies of the Scriptures were burned and the Jews were forced to eat swine's flesh, contrary to their law. A sow was offered on the altar of burnt offering in contempt for the Jewish religious conscience (Josephus *BJ* i.1.2 [34f.]; *Ant.* xii.5.4 [253]).

D. Maccabean Revolt. The oppressed Jews were not long in finding a champion. When the emissaries of Antiochus arrived at the small town of Modin, about 25 km. (15 mi.) W of Jerusalem, they expected the aged priest Mattathias to set a good example for his people by offering a pagan sacrifice. He not only refused, but he also killed an apostate Jew at the heathen altar as well as the Syrian officer who was presiding at the ceremony. Mattathias fled to the Judean highlands and with his sons waged guerrilla warfare on the Syrians. Although the aged priest did not live to see his people freed from the Syrian yoke, he commissioned his sons to complete the task. Judas, surnamed Maccabeus, took the leadership at the death of his father. By 164 B.C. Judas had gained possession of Jerusalem. He purified the temple and reconstituted the daily offerings. Soon after the victories of Judas, Antiochus died in Persia. Struggles continued between the Maccabees and the Seleucid rulers for about twenty years. Following the death of Judas, his brother Jonathan, who was already high priest, became leader. When Jonathan was murdered (143 B.C.) the last of the sons of Mattathias, Simon, became ruler. He was able to gain full independence from Syria, but he too was murdered (135 B.C.), by a son-in-law, Ptolemy. The surviving son of Simon, John Hyrcanus, succeeded his father and thereby established a dynasty. Hyrcanus determined to build Judea into a powerful, independent state. He conquered Samaria and destroyed the schismatic temple on Mt. Gerizim. The borders of Judea were also extended in the directions of Syria, Phoenicia, Arabia, and Idumea. During the reign of Hyrcanus the pro-Hellenistic Sadducean party gained control and the orthodox principles of the older Maccabees tended to be neglected.

E. The Hasmoneans. Aristobulus I, the son of Hyrcanus, was the first of the Maccabean rulers to take the title "king of the Jews." After a short reign he was succeeded by the tyrannical Alexander Janneus, who in turn left the kingdom to his mother Alexandra. Alexandra's reign was relatively quiet. The Pharisees assumed control, but they persecuted the Sadducees as they themselves had been persecuted in the days of Janneus. Alexandra's older son Hyrcanus II served as high priest. At Alexandra's death a younger son Aristobulus (II) dispossessed his brother. The governor of Idumea, Antipater (see XI.A below), espoused the cause of Hyrcanus, and civil war threatened until Pompey appeared with his Roman legions to settle matters and further the aims of Rome. Aristobulus sought to defend Jerusalem from Pompey, but the Romans took the city and entered the temple. Pompey left the temple treasures untouched, however.

XI. The Jews under the Romans.–With the defeat of Aristobulus, Judea was made a part of the Roman province of Syria. Hyrcanus was rewarded for his loyalty to Pompey by being named ethnarch of Judea and high priest of the Jews. He paid an annual tribute to Rome.

A. Antipater. An Idumean named Antipater gained considerable power in Judean affairs during the reign of Hyrcanus II. He was loyal to the Romans and used his office to seek positions of influence for his two sons Phasael and Herod. Antipater was loyal to Cassius after the death of Julius Caesar, but he espoused the cause of Anthony when he defeated Brutus and Cassius at Philippi. Herod, a son of Antipater, was named procurator of Judea with the promise that he would later be named king.

B. Herod. The Parthians, eastern foes of Rome, attacked and subdued Jerusalem in 41 B.C., installing Antigonus, a son of Aristobulus II, as king and high priest. Herod fled to Rome, where Anthony made him king of the Jews and sent a Roman army to Palestine to drive out the Parthians and back up Herod's right to the throne. From 37 to 4 B.C. Herod ruled as king. He did much to enhance the prestige of Judea. An immense building plan included the rebuilding of the temple on a magnificent scale. His Idumean background and his personal cruelties, however, made him highly unpopular with the Jews.

C. Herod's Successors. After the death of Herod (4 B.C.) the kingdom was divided among his three sons: Archelaus was tetrarch of Judea, Samaria, and Idumea; Herod Antipas was tetrarch of Galilee and Perea (4 B.C.–A.D. 39), and Philip was tetrarch of Gaulanitis, Trachonitis, Batanea, Auranitis, and Panias (4 B.C.–A.D. 34). In A.D. 6 Archelaus was deposed by the Romans and Judea became a part of the province of Syria under a resident Roman proconsul with headquarters at Caesarea; the best-known proconsul was Pontius Pilate (A.D. 26-36). The proconsuls were opportunists whose policies impoverished the people.

Pontius Pilate, the Roman proconsul at the time of Jesus' crucifixion, was deposed in A.D. 36 following an attack he made upon the Samaritans. Agrippa, a grandson of Herod the Great, became ruler of Judea and most of the territory earlier ruled by his grandfather. At his death the Romans appointed a series of rulers who were generally unprincipled. One of these was Felix, procurator of Judea A.D. 52-60, whose injustices and cruelties caused the outbreak of the Jewish war, according to Josephus (*Ant.* xx.8.5-8 [160-181]).

D. The Zealots. The Zealots, who opposed paying taxes to Rome and attempted to follow the older Maccabees in seeking political independence, gained many adherents. In A.D. 65 a group of Jews captured the Roman fortress at Masada overlooking the Dead Sea, and killed the Roman garrison there. Revolts sparked by the Zealots broke out in many cities of Judea and Galilee. After a series of Roman defeats, Nero sent Vespasian to command the forces of Syria and lead the battle against the Jews. Between A.D. 67 and 70 a series of battles was fought. Vespasian was made emperor and returned to Rome, but Titus marched against Jerusalem and in A.D. 70 destroyed the city after a long siege. The temple was burned to the ground, the walls of the city were leveled, and more than a million lives were lost. Jerusalem became a heap of ruins in the charge of the tenth Roman legion.

Although the Jews made another attempt at independence under Bar Cochba (A.D. 132-135), Rome maintained its hold on Palestine and the Jewish dispersion continued. In the years after the destruction of Jerusalem many Jews lived in Palestine, but it was not until 1948 that an independent Jewish state was again established, using the ancient name of Israel.

See also INTERTESTAMENTAL PERIOD.

Bibliography.–Archeology: *AOTS*; *AP*; *ARI*; *EAEHL*; K. Kenyon, *Bible and Recent Archaeology* (1978); K. Kitchen, *Bible in Its World* (1977); K. Schoville, *Biblical Archaeology in Focus* (1978); *WBA*.

Geography: GAB; *GB*; *GTTOT*; *HGHL*; *LBHG*; *WHAB*.

Relevant Texts and Pictures: ANEP; *ANET*; W. Beyerlin, ed., *Near Eastern Religious Texts Relating to the OT* (Eng. tr. 1978); *DOTT*; B. Mazar, *et al.*, *Views of the Bible World* (1959-1961).

Histories of Israel: BHI; R. de Vaux, *Early History of Israel* (Eng. tr. 1978); J. H. Hayes and J. M. Miller, eds., *Israelite and Judaean History* (1977); S. Herrmann, *History of Israel in OT Times* (1975); *HJP*[2]; R. Kittel, *History of the Hebrews* (Eng. tr. 1895); A. Lods, *Israel from Its Beginnings to the Middle of the 8th Cent.* (Eng. tr. 1932); *NHI*; *ORHI*; J. Wellhausen, *Prolegomena to the History of Ancient Israel* (Eng. tr. 1957).

Historical and Cultural Background: R. de Vaux, *Ancient Israel* (Eng. tr. 1961); C. H. Gordon, *World of the OT* (1958); N. Gottwald, *Tribes of Yahweh* (1979); R. K. Harrison, *OT Times* (1970); S. Moscati, *Ancient Semitic Civilizations* (1957); *Face of the Ancient Orient* (1960); A. T. Olmstead, *History of Palestine and Syria to the Persian Conquest* (1931).

C. F. PFEIFFER

ISRAEL, KINGDOM OF. The nation founded by the northern ten Hebrew tribes when the Solomonic empire collapsed. It existed from 930 to 722 B.C. on territory extending from Bethel and Jericho northward to Mt. Hermon (except for Phoenicia on the coast).

I. First Half-Century
- A. Origin of the Divided Kingdom
- B. Struggles of the Fledgling State

II. Zenith under the House of Omri
- A. Stabilization and Progress
- B. Elijah and the Religious Crisis
- C. End of the Omri Dynasty

III. Fortunes under the House of Jehu
- A. Period of Aramean Supremacy
- B. Resurgence under Jehoash and Jeroboam II
- C. Prophetic Diagnosis of Terminal Illness

IV. Catastrophic End
- A. Rise of Assyria
- B. Political Instability and Turmoil
- C. Syro-Ephraimite War
- D. Fall of Samaria and Its Aftermath

I. First Half-Century.–*A. Origin of the Divided Kingdom.* The collapse of the united kingdom is a sad tale quickly told. Though the northern and southern tribes had united under David and Solomon, the arrogant refusal of Rehoboam, Solomon's son, to relieve them of his father's harsh policies of taxation and forced labor resurrected long-buried divisions between north and south (2 S. 2:4; 5:1-5; 20:1f.). The elders of the northern tribes crowned Jeroboam, a former appointee of Solomon, as king over the new nation "Israel." For further details, *see* ISRAEL, HISTORY OF THE PEOPLE OF; JUDAH, KINGDOM OF.

B. Struggles of the Fledgling State. Rehoboam's desire for a buffer zone between the new nation Israel and his own capital, Jerusalem, spawned two generations of warfare in Benjaminite territory over their common border (1 K. 14:30; 15:16; 2 Ch. 13:3-20). Only the devastating invasion by the Egyptian Shishak (Sheshonq I; 1 K. 14:25f.) interrupted the warfare. Such warfare certainly disrupted the economic life of the state and brought hardship on many.

Jeroboam (930-909) is remembered for two things. First, he established his capital successively at Shechem, Penuel (1 K. 12:25), and Tirzah (1 K. 14:17) — an oddity reflecting

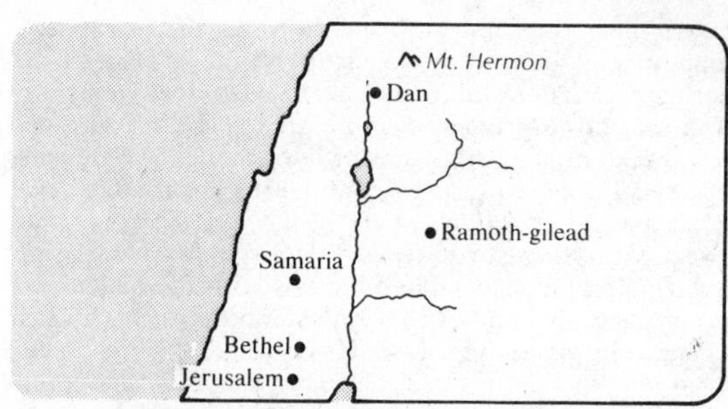

either an official policy of rotating capitals or his attempts to elude Shishak. Second, he provided two royal shrines at the ends of his realm (Dan in the north, Bethel in the south) to discourage pilgrimages to Jerusalem that might tempt his people to shift their loyalty to Rehoboam (1 K. 12:26-33). Unfortunately, he fitted those shrines with golden bulls, perhaps as pedestals over which the invisible Yahweh was presumably enthroned. This act not only earned the condemnation of Ahijah of Shiloh, the prophet who had designated him to be king (1 K. 11:29-39; 13–14), but was long thereafter remembered as "the sin of Jeroboam," the classic act of apostasy from which Israel never recovered.

In tune with the instability of this period, the reign of Jeroboam's son Nadab (909-908) was abruptly ended by the conspiracy of Baasha amid warfare with Philistia (1 K. 15:25-27; cf. Ahijah's prophecy, 1 K. 15:29f.). Of Baasha's long reign (908-886) little is known except his retreat from a fortress at Ramah, which Ben-hadad I of Syria attacked at the behest of Asa of Judah (1 K. 15:16-21). That retreat probably signaled the end of the border dispute.

II. Zenith under the House of Omri.–*A. Stabilization and Progress.* Baasha did not bequeath political stability to Israel. His son Elah (886-885) was assassinated, after a two-year rule, by Zimri, a chariotry officer (1 K. 16:8-10). Seven days later, however, Zimri perished in a palace fire which he himself had set while under attack by Omri, commander of the army, whom the army had just crowned king (1 K. 16:15-19). The ensuing four-year civil war between factions supporting Omri and Tibni finally ended with the death of Tibni and Omri's accession to the throne (1 K. 16:21f.). Thus, Israel received its first dynasty and a thirty-year period of stability that lifted it to the zenith of its power.

Omri (885-874) and Ahab (874-853) were remarkably able rulers. Through royal marriages they established friendships with neighboring Phoenicia and Judah (1 K. 16:31; 2 K. 8:26; 2 Ch. 21:6; 22:2). Their subjection of Moab enabled them to reacquire territory in Transjordan once part of the Davidic empire and to settle Israelites there (2 K. 3:4; cf. the testimony of Moab's King Mesha, *ANET*, pp. 320f.). By dominating city-states in Transjordan (notably Aphek and Ramoth-gilead; cf. 1 K. 20:26, 30; 22:3-36), they successfully kept the powerful Arameans at bay — often in military league with Judah (1 K. 22:2-36; 2 K. 3:4-27). They even participated in a coalition that fought the Assyrian monarch Shalmaneser III (859-825) to a draw at the Battle of Qarqar (853; *ANET*, pp. 278f.).

Prosperity accompanied that military might. The Omrides not only maintained a royal residence at Jezreel (1 K. 21) but also constructed a new one called "Samaria," the dynasty's one lasting legacy (1 K. 16:24; 22:39). Excavations there have unearthed fortifications and luxurious ivory inlays that illustrate the wealth of the dynasty (cf. Am. 3:15). On the other hand, the lot of the common folk worsened. A lengthy drought hurt many (1 K. 17), and the poor were at the mercy of the rich (2 K. 4:1).

B. Elijah and the Religious Crisis. The period's political stability and material prosperity could not hide its severe religious crisis. Ahab's Phoenician wife Jezebel established the worship of the Tyrian god Baal Melqart. Prophets of Baal enjoyed royal status (1 K. 18:19), altars of Yahweh were torn down (19:10, 14), and prophets who protested were either killed or driven underground (18:4). As he was only a nominal Yahwist, Ahab had a temple for Baal built at Samaria (16:32f.). While many stood for Yahweh (18:3-13; 19:18; 22:8-28), the majority seemed undecided (18:21). Elijah, the awesome "troubler of Israel" (v. 17), stood against this tide of apostasy. He called for Israel to choose between Baal and Yahweh (v. 21), condemned Ahab for his complicity in the apostasy and predicted Ahab's downfall (21:17-24), and made plans to rid Israel of the Omrides altogether (19:15-21).

C. End of the Omri Dynasty. Elijah's prediction soon was fulfilled. Ahab died in battle against Aram (1 K. 22), his son Ahaziah (853-852) died a few months after a fall (2 K. 1:2-17), and another son, Jehoram (Joram) (852-841), suffered the loss of Transjordan under Mesha's rebellion (2 K. 1:1; 3:4f.; cf. Moabite Stone, *ANET,* pp. 320f.) and battled Damascus (2 K. 6–7; 8:28; 9:14). Although he removed a highly offensive pillar of Baal from Samaria (2 K. 3:2) and enjoyed the support of Elisha and the prophets in his war efforts (2 K. 3:11-19; 6:11f.), Jehoram fell victim to Yahweh's intervention and probably to popular resentment as well.

While Jehoram nursed battle wounds in Jezreel (2 K. 9:15), Elisha dispatched a prophet to Ramoth-gilead to anoint as king a military officer named Jehu — much to the delight of the army's officers (2 K. 9:1-13). Jehu immediately carried out his mandate by hastening toward Jezreel, killing Jehoram on its outskirts, and later wounding his visitor, King Ahaziah of Judah, who fled to Megiddo and died (2 K. 9:27f.). Jehu had Jezebel thrown to her death from the palace window (2 K. 9:30-37) and, by an exchange of diplomatic correspondence, persuaded leaders in Samaria to execute Ahab's seventy sons (2 K. 10:1-7). He then went to Samaria himself, exterminated the remains of Ahab's retinue (2 K. 10:17) as well as the land's Baal worshipers, and converted the temple there into a latrine (2 K. 10:18-27). The house of Omri was gone forever.

III. Fortunes under the House of Jehu.*–*A. Period of Aramean Supremacy. Though Jehu (841-814) gave Israel its longest dynasty, the first half-century of that house was an unhappy one. His actions against the house of Ahab and the Baal worshipers cost him the friendship of Phoenicia and Judah. At the same time, Hazael, one of Israel's most dreaded foes (2 K. 8:11f.; Am. 1:3-5; cf. Isa. 9:11f. [MT 10f.]), led a resurgent Damascus to deprive Jehu of all territory in Transjordan (2 K. 10:32f.; cf. Am. 1:3) and to reduce the army of his son Jehoahaz (814-798) to a nominal force (2 K. 13:7). Moab also attacked a weakened Israel (2 K. 13:20). While Jehoahaz enjoyed some military successes (2 K. 13:4f.), only Yahweh's compassion enabled the helpless state to survive during Hazael's oppressive campaigns (2 K. 13:22f.).

B. Resurgence under Jehoash and Jeroboam II. The four western campaigns of the ambitious Assyrian ruler Adadnirari III at the dawn of the 8th cent. crippled Damascus and gave Israel new political freedom. Jehoash (798-782) recaptured from Ben-hadad II, Hazael's son, all the cities that his father Jehoahaz had lost to the Arameans in Transjordan (2 K. 13:25). When King Amaziah of Judah, intoxicated with his recent victory over Edom, demanded war, Jehoash reluctantly obliged. He prevailed, even damaging Jerusalem itself (2 K. 14:7-14; 2 Ch. 25:5-24).

This resurgence crested during the reign of Jeroboam II (793-753). He extended Israel's borders to their location during Solomon's day (2 K. 14:25; cf. 1 K. 8:65), possibly even subduing Damascus, Hamath (2 K. 14:28?), and Moab (Am. 6:14?). His control of the lucrative trade routes crossing Israel blessed the state — particularly the upper classes — with a prosperity unknown since Solomon's empire. It was an era so great that only Yahweh Himself could be credited with responsibility for it (2 K. 14:26f.).

C. Prophetic Diagnosis of Terminal Illness. Unfortunately, behind the glitter of the "golden age" lay cancerous social and religious decay. The prophets Amos and Hosea listed the symptoms: shocking oppression of the poor by the rich (Am. 2:6f.; 5:10-12; 8:4-6), unbridled self-indulgence (4:1-3; 6:1-7), a presumptuous sense of security in Israel's election (3:1f.; 9:7) and in busy cultic activity (5:21-24), and adulterous pursuit of Baal's fertility cult (Hos. 4:7-19; 6:8-10; 8:5f.).

Such symptoms demanded a terminal prognosis. They pronounced the nation's doom (Am. 5:2; 7:7-9; Hos. 7:13; 9:11-17); Yahweh would divorce His adulterous people and abandon them to destruction (Hos. 2:2-13 [MT 4-15]). Contrary to popular expectations, the "day of Yahweh" would bring them disaster, not victory (Am. 5:18-20).

IV. Catastrophic End.*–*A. Rise of Assyria. The reign of Tiglath-pileser III in Assyria (745-727) launched all of Syro-Palestine toward its destiny. Whereas his predecessors had contented themselves with merely taking tribute from there, he sought permanent conquest of the area and its rich timber, mineral deposits, access to Egypt, and lucrative Mediterranean commerce. His climactic conquest and incorporation of Hamath into the Assyrian provincial system (738) served notice that henceforth history in the West would be guided by the "Great King" of Assyria.

B. Political Instability and Turmoil. The death of Jeroboam II (753) plunged Israel into chaos. Within ten years, Israel had five kings, three of whom seized the throne by violence. Jeroboam's son Zechariah was murdered by the usurper Shallum ben Jabesh after a six-month rule (2 K. 15:10) — thus fulfilling the earlier promise to Jehu's house (2 K. 15:12; cf. 2 K. 10:30; Hos. 1:4f.). He in turn fell a month later to Menahem ben Gadi in a brutal civil war (2 K. 15:14-16). To prop up his shaky regime, Menahem paid tribute to Tiglath-pileser III (Pul) by taxing his wealthy citizens (2 K. 15:19f.).

Menahem's lengthy reign (752-742) proved to be only the calm before the storm. His son Pekahiah was assassinated after only two years by one of his officers, Pekah ben Remaliah (740-732), in a coup that may have had Aramean and Philistine backing (Isa. 9:8-12 [MT 7-11]). On the problem of the length of Pekah's reign, *see* CHRONOLOGY OF THE OT V.

C. Syro-Ephraimite War. The vassals of Assyria soon became restive. In 734 Rezin of Damascus and Pekah of Israel formed a coalition to resist Assyria along with Edom and Philistia (2 Ch. 28:17f.). Judah, well aware of Assyria's expedition into Philistia earlier that year, refused to join. When Rezin and Pekah attacked Jerusalem to enthrone the son of Tabeel, an Aramean sympathetic to their cause (Isa. 7:6), Ahaz rejected Isaiah's advice (Isa. 7) and sent a sizable present to Tiglath-pileser himself with an appeal for military intervention (2 K. 15:37; 16:5-8). The Great King gladly obliged (2 K. 16:9), thereby forcing the coalition to suspend its attack and face the Assyrians. The next year (733) the Assyrians overran Transjordan and Galilee, destroyed many cities (cf. the archeological evidence from Megiddo and Hazor), parceled the territory

ISRAEL, RELIGION OF

into three new Assyrian provinces, deported the ruling classes, and imported their own officials (2 K. 15:29). In 732 Tiglath-pileser took Damascus, executed Rezin, and made it an Assyrian province. A large part of Syro-Palestine was now under his control.

With its territory virtually reduced to the mountains of Ephraim and the city of Samaria, Israel escaped total destruction when Hoshea ben Elah (731-722), possibly a member of a pro-Assyrian faction, murdered Pekah (2 K. 15:30) and submitted to Assyria (cf. *ANET,* p. 284).

D. Fall of Samaria and Its Aftermath. For some unknown reason, the accession of Shalmaneser V (726-722) in Assyria tempted Hoshea to shatter a five-year peace with rebellion. He foolishly solicited aid from one So, King of Egypt — aid which never came — and withheld tribute from Assyria (2 K. 17:4). These proved to be suicidal steps, probably taken, however, to prevent a coup by an anti-Assyrian party in Samaria.

Shalmaneser responded quickly. In 724 he took Hoshea prisoner and occupied everything but the capital city. Two years later (722) he overcame its resistance; 27,290 captives were later taken to Mesopotamia and Media (cf. Sargon's account, *ANET,* pp. 284f.; 2 K. 17:3-6), where they vanished from history. The two-hundred-year-old state of Israel had come to an end.

The territory was organized as the Assyrian province of Samerina (cf. the NT term "Samaria") under the administration of peoples imported by Shalmaneser's successor, Sargon II (721-705), the ancestors of the NT Samaritans (2 K. 17:24f.). The immigrants added Yahweh to their list of gods and established local religious customs (2 K. 17:29-33). To end a plague of lions, Sargon returned a deported priest to Bethel to instruct the new residents in the "law of the god of the land" (2 K. 17:25-28). Over the next four decades, more foreign colonists immigrated and mixed with the population of Samaria (Ezr. 4:2, 10).

Bibliography.–BHI; NHI; MNHK; H. Donner, "The Separate States of Israel and Judah," in J. H. Hayes and J. M. Miller, eds., *Israelite and Judaean History* (*OTL,* 1977), pp. 381ff.

R. L. HUBBARD, JR.

ISRAEL, RELIGION OF. This article describes the development of the faith and religious practices held within that circle of the patriarchal seed from which the normative OT canon emerged. Thus no attempt is made here to present the pagan religious convictions occasionally embraced by the mass of the patriarchal stock except to the extent that they influenced the religious persuasions of so-called spiritual Israel. Archeological evidence and, to a much lesser extent, form-critical studies have essentially verified the biblical witness to the progressive development of this religion, and therefore the Bible's own outline of the development of this religion is followed here.

- I. Patriarchal Religion
  - A. Identity of Their God
  - B. Names of God and His Character
  - C. Cult of the Patriarchs
- II. Mosaic Religion
  - A. Sources
  - B. God's Name, Yahweh
    - 1. Form
    - 2. Meaning
    - 3. Origin
  - C. God
  - D. Covenant
  - E. Cultus
- III. From Moses to Monarchy
  - A. Gift of the Land
  - B. Holy War
  - C. Gifts and Charisma
  - D. Angels and the Angel of Yahweh
- IV. From Monarchy to Exile
  - A. Israel's Attitude Toward the Monarchy
  - B. Davidic Covenant and Son of God
  - C. Davidic Covenant and Earlier Covenants
  - D. King and Cult
  - E. King and Wisdom
  - F. Prophetic Movement
- V. Exilic and Postexilic Periods
  - A. Institutions for Preserving Israelite Religion
    - 1. Cultus
    - 2. Law
    - 3. Canon
  - B. Eschatology
    - 1. New Covenant
    - 2. Messiah
    - 3. Apocalyptic
  - C. Rise of Personal Religion

It will become obvious through this study that Israel wore the garments and behaved in the manner of its age, but it always remained distinctive in its religious convictions.

I. Patriarchal Religion.*–A. Identity of Their God.* Many OT scholars agree that the stories about the patriarchs cannot be used just as they stand in order to present the religion of Israel's fathers. According to their consensus, the text of Genesis contains at least three earlier narratives — J, E, P (to be discussed below) — each of which was separated from the time of the patriarchs by many centuries, during which time the stories contained in them were transmitted orally, more or less uncontrolled by written sources, and were reformulated time and again in order to meet the changing needs of the people transmitting these stories. In the opinion of these scholars E (Ex. 3:13-15) and P (Ex. 6:2f.), although claiming an identity between the God of the patriarchs and Yahweh, who for the first time revealed himself to Moses, in fact betray a vast cleavage between the god of the fathers and Yahweh. J, by contrast, simply assumed the use of Yahweh in pre-Mosaic times (cf. esp. Gen. 4:26) and reshaped his material in this light.

Older critics, e.g., J. Wellhausen and W. Robertson Smith, attempted to reconstruct the patriarchal religion by assuming that this religion existed in an early and primitive form. Imposing upon Genesis a model that assumed the progressive evolution in mankind's religious ideas, they sifted the sources for primitive religious features such as animism, fetishism, and totemism and credited these features to the patriarchs. Moreover, they tried to validate their reconstruction by appealing to customs and ideas of the pre-Islamic Arabs.

This idealistic reconstruction, however, was demolished by the hard historical fact established from archeological sources that the religious ideas of the ancient Near East at the time of the patriarchs were much more sophisticated than was assumed by these critics.

Instead of imposing an arbitrary idealistic model on the text, modern critics use the form-critical tools forged by H. Gunkel ("Fundamental") at the turn of the century. Using these tools A. Alt began the modern discussion of patriarchal religion by noting two groups of epithets for the gods of the patriarchs. One set, characterized by an *ʾēl* element followed by a substantival form, included *ʾēl ʿôlām* (Gen. 21:33), *ʾēl ʿelyôn* (Gen. 14:18-22), *ʾēl rᵒʾî* (Gen. 16:13), etc. Alt understood the *ʾēl* element as an appellative, "god," and the second as a proper name; thus he rendered them as "the god ʿŌlām," "the god ʿElyōn," etc., and he thought of them as local deities tied to Palestinian shrines encountered by that element of Israel that entered the land.

In Alt's second group of epithets, the god is identified by the name of a patriarch; thus, "the Fear of Isaac" (Gen. 31:42, 53), "the Mighty One of Jacob" (Gen. 49:24), "the God of Abraham" (Gen. 31:42), etc. He thought that these gods were originally separate deities, but that in the development of Israel's traditions they were assimilated into a single family god by artificially linking the patriarchs together into a common genealogy. This was done at the same time they were associated with Yahweh. According to Alt these tutelary deities were nameless and were not attached to a local shrine but to clans with whom they entered into a covenantal relationship. These deities assumed the responsibility to guide the clan's destiny, lead them in battle, and establish justice for them. Such, he contended, was the true nature of the patriarchal religion.

Later critical research has modified his concept about the clan deities and has radically altered his view about the meaning and nature of the god(s) with the *'ēl* element. J. Lewy demonstrated from parallels in the Old Assyrian Cappadocian texts of the early 2nd millennium B.C. that the Amorites called on their ancestral god as "the god of your [our, etc.] father," and that this god had the personal name Ilabrat, just as the patriarchs called 'El Shaddai the "god of your father" (*RHR,* 110 [1934], 29-65; cf. Gen. 49:25). Cappadocian texts published later included the god Amurru, who also was called "the god of my father." F. M. Cross (pp. 9-11) collected additional evidence corroborating Lewy's modification of Alt's view and modified it further by noting that "the Amorite gods of the Father are neither anonymous gods nor minor genii," but are commonly the high gods in the cult at Ugarit, namely, 'El, Haddad, and Dagan. Moreover, most modern critics, e.g., O. Eissfeldt (*JSS,* 1 [1956], 34), U. Oldenburg (*Conflict Between El and Ba'al in Canaanite Religion* [1969]), and Cross (pp. 46-60), regard the first element as the proper name of the high god in the Ugaritic pantheon, 'El, whose cult flourished no later than 1400 B.C., and the second element as an attributive modifier; thus, "'El, the Everlasting One," "'El, the Most High," etc. In favor of taking *'ēl* as a proper name, it is argued, are the facts that this is its most common usage in the oldest strata of the Semitic languages, that this must be its meaning in Gen. 33:20 and 35:7, and that Alt's suggestion would attribute to an 'Elyon the function of creator, a function ascribed to 'El in the Ugaritic mythologies.

If one accedes to this plausible suggestion that *'ēl* is a proper name, then a strong case can be made for merging or identifying Canaanite 'El with the 'El of the patriarchs. First, 'El was probably the dominant figure in this pantheon at the time of the patriarchs, and significantly his role among the gods reflects a patriarchal society. Second, to judge from the proto-Sinaitic inscriptions (cf. W. F. Albright, *Proto-Sinaitic Inscriptions and Their Decipherment* [1966]), his cult was widespread in south Canaan, even as the epithets with *'ēl* in Genesis are associated with southern sanctuaries (cf. 14:18; 16:13f.; 17:1; 21:33; etc.). Third, 'El shares the same attributes as those ascribed to *'ēl* in Genesis: both are called "the ancient/eternal one" and "creator of all creatures." Fourth, Canaanite 'El's characteristic mode of manifestation appears to be through visions, spoken messages, and dreams (cf. 15:1, 12; 17:1; etc.). Fifth, according to Cross (p. 44), it is extraordinary that "*'Ēl* is rarely if ever used in the Bible as the proper name of a non-Israelite, Canaanite deity in the full consciousness of a distinction between 'Ēl and Yahweh, god of Israel."

But there are even stronger reasons against merging or equating Canaanite 'El with the God of the Fathers. First, one should note not only the similarities between Canaanite 'El and the God of the Fathers, but also the striking differences between them. In *UT* 51:iv:27-30, e.g., we are told of 'El's reception of 'Asherah: "As soon as 'El spied her he unfastened his scabbard and laughed; he put his feet on his footstool and wiggled his toes" (translation by Cross, p. 37). He thereupon offered her food, drink, and his conjugal bed. In another text his lackeys made him so drunk he passed out, and in yet another he took his sisters to wife and emasculated his father. There is no evidence that the patriarchs worshiped such a god. To argue that earlier crude features have been purged from the texts begs the issue. Second, the Bible ingenuously admits that Israel's forefathers worshiped pagan gods on the other side of the Euphrates and in Egypt (Josh. 24:14), that Israel emerged out of the nations of the earth (Gen. 10), and that Jerusalem originated as a pagan cult center (Ezk. 16:3). Why, then, should we discredit its claim that the patriarchs worshiped the one true God? Third, *'ēl* is both a proper name and a generic appellative in the earliest strata of the Semitic languages; thus there is no good reason to deny that the patriarchs understood *'ēl* as designating the one true God — it must have been understood in this way in the canonical text. In Gen. 31:13 the identification of *'ēl* with the true God is safeguarded by the addition of the article: "I am *the* God of Bethel." The construction in Gen. 33:20 finds parallels in Nu. 16:22 and Josh. 22:22. Fourth, the temple of El-berith in Jgs. 9:46 is named after Canaanite 'El in contrast to Yahweh. Thus the Bible consciously distinguishes Canaanite 'El from Israel's God. Fifth, it seems highly tenuous to base an equation on similar attributes when these attributes are consistent with Israel's faith. Sixth, there is no warrant for replacing the presentation of the patriarchal religion in Genesis, a book whose historicity has been validated many times by archeology, with a reconstruction of that religion deduced from archeology and comparative religion.

The similarities among the clan god of the Amorites, Canaanite 'El, and the God of the fathers show two things: the antiquity of the stories in Genesis and the revelation of God in forms common to the age. J. van Seters (*Abraham in History and Tradition* [1975]) challenged the antiquity of the patriarchal stories, but his work serves to criticize scholarly interpretation of the biblical text and not the antiquity of the stories themselves.

B. Names of God and His Character. These epithets reveal to us in part what the patriarchs believed about God: He is "God Most High, Maker of heaven and earth" (Gen. 14:18f.), "God of seeing" (16:13), "the Everlasting God" (21:33), and above all "God Almighty" (*'ēl šadday,* Gen. 17:1; Ex. 6:3; etc.), which is now understood to mean "the Ruling God" on the basis of the Deir 'allā texts (so P. K. McCarter, *"ēl šadday,"* a paper read at the Nov. 1979 meeting of the Society of Biblical Literature in New York). This transcendent God is the "God of Abraham" (24:27; cf. 31:42, 53), "God, the God of Israel" (33:20), the God of the Fathers (31:5, 29, 42; 46:3; 50:17). He is "the Fear of Isaac" (31:42), "the Mighty One of Jacob . . . the Shepherd, the Rock of Israel" (49:24). (In many of these texts He is called Yahweh, which we shall discuss below.) He became their God by calling them and entering into covenant with them with promises to bless them (12:2), to make them fertile (17:5), to give them the land of Canaan (12:7, etc.), and to protect them (15:1).

C. Cult of the Patriarchs. As a sign that this God had so favored them, the patriarchs circumcised themselves (Gen. 17:9-14), a fertility rite performed on marriageable males in the ancient Near East and transposed in the pa-

ISRAEL, RELIGION OF

triarchal rites to the eighth day after birth as an initiatory rite into the blessed stock.

They filled other cultic practices borrowed from their pagan neighbors with their new faith. In ancient Canaan the pagans performed fertility rites under green trees that served as symbols of fertility. The patriarchs also worshiped under green trees where their God, who abhorred Canaanite practices (15:16), appeared to them with His covenant promises to bless them (12:1) and make them fertile (17:5; cf. 12:6f.; 18:1). Abraham planted a tamarisk tree at Beer-sheba and called on God (Gen. 21:33). Thus God appeared to them at sites where they might expect to see Him, but the texts do not suggest that they adopted the Canaanite practices. They also built altars and offered sacrifices at these sites; the forms of these practices probably resembled those in the neighboring religions, but their meaning was filled with the patriarchs' unique faith. God credited this faith to them as righteousness (15:6) and rewarded it with innumerable offspring.

It is sometimes said that stones also played a vital part in Jacob's religious practices. But the stones mentioned in Gen. 31:45-49 are clearly commemorative and functioned in the same way as in modern Israel. In 28:18-22 and 35:14, however, the stone is called a *maṣṣēḇâ* and anointed with oil. A *maṣṣēḇâ* in the Canaanite religion was a stone smeared with blood or fat, moistened with drink offerings, and kissed by the worshiper as an idol. Jacob, however, set up his *maṣṣēḇâ* not as an idol but as a consecrated memorial of the mercy shown him.

Finally, we note that whereas the patriarchs adopted and adapted Canaanite practices such as circumcision and worship under trees, their God made it clear to them by His substitution of a ram for Isaac that He repudiated child sacrifice (Gen. 22:1-18), an aspect of the Canaanite 'El cult (cf. Albright, *Yahweh,* pp. 234-244).

II. Religion of Moses.*–*A. Sources. One's understanding of the development of Israelite religion is related to one's view of the date and historical credibility of these sources. Source critics accept most of the classic division of the Pentateuch into a Yahwistic tradition (J), an Elohistic tradition (E), a Deuteronomistic tradition (D), and a Priestly tradition (P), but they disagree on how the material within these sources was transmitted, on how they were edited, and on how much actual history they contain.

Wellhausen began his study with the persuasion that the Pentateuch consisted of these four sources and with W. M. L. de Wette's conclusion that D, the law that figured in Josiah's reform (2 K. 22–23), was in fact a pious forgery composed at that time (*ca.* 625 B.C.). Whereas earlier scholars had tended to regard P as the oldest and most fundamental source, he immediately leaped upon the suggestion of E. Reuss and H. Graf that P was the latest source. According to Wellhausen, P set forth the ceremonial law with the underlying assumption that Israel was a priestly theocracy, a situation that prevailed either at the time of the second temple (*ca.* 500 B.C. onward) and not during the monarchy, or at the nation's primitive beginnings presented in the more reliable historical evidence of the books of Judges and Samuel. Thus the idea that Moses founded the theocracy on "ethical monotheism" was a postexilic creation. In Wellhausen's view the prophets, in order to explain Israel's fall into gentile hands, interpreted Israel's history by elevating Yahweh from a national god unequal to the crisis posed by the imperial powers of Assyria, Babylon, and Persia to a universal God over all the nations who directed history by rewarding the righteous and by punishing the wicked. Moreover, in his scheme the earliest hexateuchal source had not been composed before the middle of the 9th cent., and it reflected the historical situation at the time of its composition.

H. Gunkel (*Schöpfung*) radically altered Wellhausen's entrenched views by two new insights: (1) an awareness of the continuity between the religion of the OT and the religions of Mesopotamia and Egypt, and (2) his introduction of the methods of form criticism to the analysis of the four documentary sources. Instead of regarding these literary strands as original compositions, he saw them as a relatively late phase in the history of the oral traditions embedded in them. According to Gunkel these earlier, oral sources had original "settings in life" (*Sitze im Leben*) and these settings gave them fixed forms (*Gattungen*). In order to obtain a picture of Israel's religious life centuries earlier than the literary strands, the scholar must trace the history of these independent, originally oral units (*Gattungsgeschichte*). Modern scholarship almost universally adopts this practice, but as the following survey will show, it has yielded no consensus on the identification of these units or on their historical credibility.

On the setting of the Decalogue, H. Gressman (*Mose und seine Zeit* [1913]) argued that it originated in the worship which Israel's ancestors had brought with them from the desert because it bore no evidence of the influence of Canaan. Gunkel's student S. Mowinckel (*Le Décalogue* [1927]) ascribed the Decalogue to the cultic setting of a great autumnal celebration in the first temple that he entitled "the festival of Yahweh's enthronement." This proposed setting of the cult for the transmission of pentateuchal materials substantially modified Gunkel's picture, which emphasized the popular folk settings. A. Alt contended that the distinctively Israelite apodictic law (best exemplified in Ex. 20:2-17) was transmitted in the cult, and the case law represented in the book of the covenant (Ex. 20:22–23:19) may have circulated at the city gate. But G. E. Mendenhall (*BA,* 17 [1954], 26-46) argued that the Decalogue was formulated according to the pattern of Hittite suzerainty treaties that were couched in a style resembling Alt's apodictic laws.

Regarding the confessions of Yahweh's mighty acts, G. von Rad ("The Form-Critical Problem of the Hexateuch," in *Problem of the Hexateuch and Other Essays* [1965], pp. 1-78) found short historical credos in the Hexateuch (esp. Dt. 6:20-24; 26:5b-9; Josh. 24:2b-13) whereby early Israel, possibly at the Feast of Weeks in Gilgal, affirmed its faith in Yahweh's saving acts. Since these confessions do not mention the giving of the law at Sinai, von Rad argued that this later element of the tradition had been woven into it by J. Some argued that the Sinai story was just as primary as the Exodus tradition, but they thought it was handed down at the covenant renewal ceremonies at the fall festival. By contrast M. Noth (*History of Pentateuchal Traditions* [Eng. tr. 1972]) detected five great themes — the promise to the patriarchs, the Exodus from Egypt, the wanderings in the wilderness, the revelation at Sinai, and the entry into the land — which, he contended, were originally isolated traditions later creatively linked together to construct one unified history of Israel. But F. M. Cross (pp. 83-90) disagreed with both von Rad and Noth in their separation of Israel's confession of the *Magnalia Dei* from the stipulations of the law. Following Mendenhall, Cross argued that the discovery of the covenant forms from the ancient Near East shows that the recital of the suzerain's mighty acts was followed by covenant stipulations; thus these elements belong together. He suggested, therefore, that the confessions of Yahweh's mighty acts belonged to the first movement of a covenant renewal festival and the recitation of the law was the consequent act in the ritual drama. Cross's reconstruction, more plausible than that of von Rad or Noth, underscores the inability of form critics to identify authoritatively original, primitive units.

The same sort of confusion prevails with respect to the identity and date of the literary sources. For example, Y. Kaufmann (pp. 175-200) demonstrated the preexilic date for many of the cultic prescriptions contained in P, and on this account dated P to the preexilic era before D. Noth (*op. cit.*) thought P was primarily a historical narrative into which various collections of priestly instructional material were incorporated in progressive stages. B. A. Levine (*IDB Supp.*, pp. 683-87) preferred to see a chronological overlapping of code and narrative with a mutual influence of one on the other. According to I. Engnell ("Pentateuch," in *Rigid Scrutiny* [Eng. tr. 1969], pp. 50-67), no literary narrative source "P" ever existed. For him P was the "circle" that last handled the complex of traditions called the Tetrateuch. R. Rendtorff (*Das überlieferungsgeschichtliche Problem des Pentateuch* [*BZAW*, 147, 1977]) sought to undermine a basic tenet of source criticism by denying P's existence as a complete and continuous strand in the Pentateuch. Cross (pp. 295-325) argued that P was never an independent code but a systemizing expansion of the JE epic tradition completed in the 6th cent. B.C. B. Childs (*Intro. to the OT as Scripture* [1979], p. 132) supposed that a hiatus remains between the older sources including P and the final editing of the Pentateuch.

In sum, form-critical research has left us with the conclusion that much of the material in the Pentateuch is ancient but with no agreement about the development of the pentateuchal sources that present Israel's faith and with little prospect of adjudicating between rival theories.

Form critics also cannot speak authoritatively on the amount of real history preserved in the allegedly earlier oral traditions. I. Engnell (*op. cit.*) presented the strange picture that Israel's cultus grew out of a progressive historicizing of mythological elements found in the liturgies and hymns employed at the cultus during the monarchy. M. Noth (*NHI* [2nd. ed. 1960], pp. 42-50) held that there is historical memory in the traditions, but he thought that the national entity we call Israel first took shape on Palestinian soil. W. F. Albright (*FSAC*, pp. 64-81) and most American scholars view these traditions as historically valuable.

Apart from a few exceptions, however, there is general agreement that Moses founded the Israelite religion. Most scholars accept N. Söderblom's dictum that if Moses did not exist, then some other figure must be invented to explain the existence of the nation and its religion (*Das Werden des Gottesglaubens* [1916], p. 310). The new consensus is highly significant, for against the older criticism it corroborates the biblical picture that Moses founded Israel's unique religion and that the prophets were reformers, not innovators (Jer. 2:5-8; Mal. 3:6).

Good evidence supports the persuasion that the Pentateuch is historically accurate and that the religion it credits to Moses is not anachronistic. Ringgren argued: "A nation is unlikely to invent a period of slavery in its past" (*Israelite Religion*, p. 29). Furthermore, it has long been noted that several Egyptian personal names are found in the genealogies, especially in the tribe of Levi: Phinehas, Pashhur, Moses (from an Egyptian root meaning "to bear" or "to beget"), etc. Then, too, the Israelite covenant form has a remarkable similarity to that of the Hittite treaties (mid 2nd millennium B.C.), consisting of a preamble, historical prologue, stipulations, a provision that the document be deposited in a temple and regularly read in public, a calling of witnesses, and formulas of curses and blessing (cf. M. G. Kline, *Treaty of the Great King* [1963]). Moreover, stipulations in the book of the covenant have striking analogies in earlier Mesopotamian law codes, and E. Gerstenberger (*JBL*, 84 [1965], p. 44) has convincingly shown that these casuistic laws "are expressions of a former agreement." The Mosaic legislation calling for a portable tent-shrine finds analogies among the pre-Islamic Arabs, in a bas relief from the period of Ramses II (*ca.* 1285 B.C.), in earlier prefabricated structures in Egypt that resemble the one called for by Moses, in analogous religious structures known from the earliest times in Egypt's history, and in a Ugaritic text calling for King Krt to practice certain rituals in a tent despite the fact that his was an age of roofed houses (C. H. Gordon, *Ugaritic Literature* [1949], pp. 5f.). Finally, religions with a highly organized priesthood and sacrificial system existed in Mesopotamia, Egypt, and Canaan at the time of Moses.

We conclude then that one need not be skeptical regarding the biblical claim that when Israel entered into the land of Canaan its religion had already assumed its basic beliefs. Cundall (comm. on Judges [*Tyndale OT Comms.*, 1968], p. 37) noted: "It was a near-miracle that this religion survived the searching test of the crucial centuries in Canaan. It would have been more than a miracle had such a religion developed after the settlement, with all the forces making for disintegration and deterioration pressing in upon it."

B. God's Name, Yahweh. 1. Form. God's personal name occurs in the Pentateuch in three forms: usually in a long form *YHWH* (Ex. 6:3), rarely in the short independent form *Yāh* (Ex. 15:2) and in personal names as the element *Yô* or *Y^ehô* (presumably from **Yā*, **Yaw*, or **Yhw* (Ex. 6:20; 17:9; etc.). The full form is probably a nominal formation with a prefixed *yodh* from the root *hwh* ("to be"; cf. L. Koehler, "Vom hebräischen Lexikon," in *Oudtestamentische Studiën*, 8 [1950], 153-55). It is most instructive to note that *Yô-* (< **Yā* or **Yaw*) occurs in the name of Moses' mother, Jochebed ("*Yaw* is glorious"), and we have no reason to doubt the antiquity of the name.

In extrabiblical, preexilic literature only the forms *YHWH* and *Yw* occur. *YHWH* is found in the Moabite Stone (*ca.* 850 B.C.), on a seal from the 8th cent. B.C., in the Arad Letters (late 7th cent. B.C.), and in the Lachish Letters (587 B.C.). The element *-yw* (= *yaw*) occurs in seals and in the Samaria ostraca. The form *Yhw* occurs in postexilic Aramaic texts (*THAT*, I, *s.v.* יהוה [E. Jenni]).

From postexilic times Jews substituted in their reading of the Bible the title *'^adōnāy* ("lord") for the tetragrammaton *YHWH*, and the Masoretes reflected this practice by imposing the vowels of this word into the tetragrammaton, eventually resulting in the hybrid reading *J^ehōvāh*. Because the Jews ceased to pronounce the name, its original vocalization is uncertain, but on the basis of philological considerations and some Greek transcriptions of the name in the Church Fathers it is generally agreed that it should be pronounced "Yahweh."

2. Meaning. Numerous conjectures have been made about the meaning of "Yahweh." We shall limit ourselves here to a consideration of those meanings proposed on the basis of Ex. 3:14f., where its authoritative meaning for the religion of Israel is given in the sentence *'ehyeh '^ašer 'ehyeh* ("I am the one who I am"). The variations between *'ehyeh* and *yahweh* need not trouble us because divine titles in the Near East can be derived from the first person (here *'ehyeh*) and the third person (here *yahweh*), and the alternation between *hwh* and *hyh* can be expected in Biblical Hebrew. In any case, the text makes clear that *'ehyeh* and *yahweh* are acceptable alternate forms of the divine name by paralleling "*'ehyeh* has sent me" (v. 14) with "*yahweh* ... has sent me" (v. 15).

Unfortunately, the sentence is grammatically enigmatic.

Some suggest that it is deliberately evasive. "We are left with the impression that this god does not want to surrender his name to men. The widespread conception that whoever knows a person's name has power over that person makes this evasion intelligible" (Ringgren, *Israelite Religion,* p. 33). Against this interpretation weighs the fact that all other divine names carry significance, and, as we shall see, such a response is unlikely in this context. The LXX rendered the sentence, "I am the Being," and many have understood it to be an ontological statement about God's eternal or pure being. But such an interpretation is too abstract a concept for Hebraic thought and ill suits the context. Others think it expresses God's independence and sovereignty. "He is from-within-determined not moved by outside influences" (Vos, pp. 118f.). This suggestion fits the grammar but not the context.

The suggestion that most readily meets the contextual requirement is that of W. Robertson Smith, G. von Rad, B. Childs, etc., who argue that it means, "I am present, the one truly present." Yahweh stated His name in this full-sentence form in response to Moses' second of four objections against his accepting the divine call to lead Israel out of Egypt. His first objection, framed in the form of a question, was: "Who am I" (3:11), to which God responded, *"ʾehyeh ʿimmāḵ* ("I will be with you," v. 12). His second objection, also phrased in the form of a question begging for reassurance, was: "What is [your] name?" (v. 13). The most likely response of those meanings proposed is: "I am present, count on me!" (For the other two questions and responses see 4:1-9, 10-16.) Vriezen (p. 181) further noted: "More important than the correctness of the etymology is the fact that in the faith of Israel . . . the name Yahweh had this meaning."

3. Origin. The name Yahweh may be attested outside of the Bible at or before the time of Moses in Egyptian place names (14th-13th cents. B.C.; cf. R. Giveon, *VT,* 14 [1964], 239-255, esp. p. 244) and in the Ebla texts (*ca.* 2300 B.C.; Kitchen, p. 47), but the evidence is flimsy. Other suggested occurrences in Akkadian proper names and in the Ugaritic texts have not been able to withstand close linguistic scrutiny. A popular theory is that Yahweh was a god of the Kenites, a tribe in the district of Sinai to which Moses' father-in-law belonged, and this fact, it is suggested, explains Yahweh's association with that mountain. But this theory ignores the Yahweh element in the name of Moses' mother, and has no textual or artifactual support. Cross (p. 72) thinks that Yahweh is a south Canaanite cultic name of the Canaanite 'El and that the god Yahweh later split off from 'El. But this speculation is based on the faulty assumption that the patriarchs worshiped Canaanite 'El (see I.A. above), and fails to take Yahweh's holiness seriously.

According to Genesis people began to call on the name of Yahweh both before and during the time of the patriarchs (Gen. 4:25; 12:8; etc.). But how can we reconcile this claim with the account in Ex. 6:3 that the name Yahweh was not known to the patriarchs? It is highly unlikely that the author of the unified Pentateuch thought he was contradicting himself. These epic narratives can be reconciled by correctly understanding the crucial terms "name" and "know" in Ex. 6:3. It is generally recognized that among the Semites a name was not so much a label as a revelation of a person's character, nature, and role. J. A. Motyer (*Revelation of the Divine Name* [1959], pp. 11f.) helpfully paraphrased Ex. 6:3: "in the character expressed by my name Yahweh I did not make myself known to them." Furthermore, unlike Greek and Western thought, in Hebrew "to know" does not connote cognitive knowledge as much as effective, existential knowledge. For example, when a man married the Hebrew expression says that he "knew" his wife. Though the patriarchs worshiped God as 'El Shaddai, the Ruling God, they had not yet "known" him. God had committed Himself to them with promises to protect them, to guide them, to give them the land, etc., but still they in fact remained guests in alien lands, depending on the goodwill and hospitality of the indigenous populations wherever they migrated (cf. Gen. 26). Eventually they lost favor with the host nation, Egypt, and were reduced from guests to slaves. Now after four hundred years of slavery and facing a hopeless future with the pharaonic edict that their male babies be put to death to control their numbers, they were turning to pagan gods (cf. Josh. 24:14; Ezk. 23:8, 19, 21; Lev. 17:7) and were calling God's being and presence into question (Ex. 3:12). Under Moses, however, they would experience in a way heretofore unknown to them the dynamic presence of God. Now for the first time in their history they would shatter a mighty nation and its gods and in so doing they would "know" the "I am."

C. God. For practical reasons the discussion regarding Israel's convictions about God at the time of Moses is limited to those stated in the first four commandments of the Decalogue.

Because the first commandment tacitly assumed the existence of other gods, most scholars contend that at the time of Moses, Israel had not yet arrived in its religious development to a doctrine of monotheism but only to a belief in henotheism, the worship of one god that admits the existence of other gods. This formulation distorts the picture. The first commandment offers religious instruction and not theological statement. In the OT there is an ambivalence about the existence of pagan gods: *de facto* they were served with practices that debased mankind (cf. Dt. 32:12, 16; Jgs. 11:24; 1 S. 26:19), but *de jure* they were not gods (Dt. 32:21, 39; Isa. 41:24). In religious commandment Israel was forbidden to serve them (Dt. 6:40), but in religious statement their reality was denied (Dt. 32:17). The same tension exists in Paul's letter to the Corinthians (1 Cor. 8:1-13).

The word for God, *'ĕlōhîm,* from a root meaning either "be first, foremost" or "be powerful, strong," is morphologically a plural form, and this feature has suggested to some that the word preserves an earlier Israelite polytheism, and to others that it expresses the conviction that the one God exists as a plurality. It seems more likely, however, that since its modifiers are normally singular in form and since the word is used for Yahweh, we are dealing with a form that often elsewhere in the Hebrew language expresses intensification or majesty.

This belief in one God profoundly influenced Israelite thought and radically distinguished Israel from its neighbors. J. Bright commented: "Here is the sharpest break with paganism imaginable. The ancient paganisms were all polytheistic, with dozens of gods arranged in complex pantheons. These gods were for the most part personifications of the forces of nature or other cosmic functions; they were in and of nature and, like nature, without any particular moral character. Their will could be manipulated in the ritual (which re-enacted the myth) so that they would bestow on the worshiper the desired tangible benefits. In such religions no moral interpretation of events, nor indeed any consistent interpretation, was possible, for no one god ruled history" (*Kingdom of God* [1953], pp. 25f.).

In addition, Israel's religion proscribed idolatry (Ex. 20:4). This universal prohibition against images expressed the conviction that God is a spiritual being (cf. Dt. 4:12f.), dissimilar in kind to any and every material form. In contrast to the hundreds of unearthed pagan fertility figurines that crudely emphasize the sexual organs, no image of Yahweh has ever been found.

Another characteristic feature of Israel is its belief that God is jealous, an attribute connected with His uniqueness. The sublime, incomparable, and only God will not tolerate any other god or human to usurp the glory that rightfully belongs to Him alone (Ex. 34:14; Isa. 42:8; 48:11). He is a consuming fire against the intransigent rebel that, despising his elect privilege to serve the only God, gives his life instead in the service of gods and images made in the likeness of fallen creation.

On the other hand, God exercises an unfailing love (Heb. *ḥeseḏ*) for those loyal to him (Ex. 20:6). This word *ḥeseḏ* denotes both God's loyalty to His covenant commitment to Israel and His sentiment of love informing that loyalty (cf. also K. Sakenfeld, *Meaning of* Hesed *in the Hebrew Bible* [1978], p. 233). Israel's history confirmed the truthfulness of this revealed quality in God, and consequently it was singled out for celebration in Israel's hymns (1 Ch. 16:41).

God's ability to punish those that reject Him and reward those that choose Him for a thousand generations clearly implies that He is the eternal, living, and sovereign Lord over history.

God forbids Israel to appropriate His name to anything false (Ex. 20:7), a proscription that gives a firm basis for Israel's demand for truthfulness in all areas of life, especially at court. Moreover, in contrast to pagan practices, no place is allowed for the magical manipulation of His name.

Finally, by observing the sabbath (Ex. 20:8-11) Israel bore testimony to its faith that Yahweh is the Creator of all things, a truth that implies He is the universal God. Paradoxically Yahweh stands apart from His creation and above it, and at the same time He was immanently present on a mountain in the Sinai, expressing His righteous will for Israel.

D. Covenant. Foundational to Israel's religion is its commitment made at Sinai (Ex. 19–24) to enter into covenant with Yahweh, who had centuries earlier committed Himself with promises to bless the obedient patriarchs. Now, prompted by gratitude for Yahweh's gracious deliverance of them from grievous Egyptian servitude, the clans of Israel ratified the covenant drawn up by Yahweh, their Great King, and gave promise of becoming Yahweh's prized possession, a kingdom of priests among the nations, and a mirror of His holiness on earth (Ex. 19:4-6). Thus Israel's relationship to Yahweh was based on His election of them and His grace and love for them. Consequently the covenant relation is less legal than familial; its demands are less legal justice than unfailing loyalty (*ḥeseḏ*). The covenant served both Yahweh's interests (Dt. 10:1-13; etc.) and Israel's interests (Dt. 4:40; etc.) by guiding them toward the fullest enjoyment of life (R. Clements, *God's Chosen People* [1968], p. 58).

Deuteronomy, a covenant renewal document (Dt. 5:2; 29:1 [MT 28:69]), expanded the Decalogue and gave a complete expression of God's will for the people. For this reason it is called "the Law" not only in the book itself, but also in the prophets and the Psalms (cf. B. Lindars, "Torah in Deuteronomy," in P. Ackroyd and B. Lindars, eds., *Words and Meanings* [1968], pp. 128-132). Its basic stipulation, like that of the parallel Hittite treaties, is that Israel love the Great King with all its heart (Dt. 6:5; cf. K. Baltzer, *Covenant Formulary* [Eng. tr. 1971]). From this "circumcised heart" (Dt. 10:16) was to issue obedience to the other commands that had in view life in the land from which the Canaanites were dispossessed (Dt. 12:1).

The covenant called for Yahweh's blessings and curses in response to Israel's obedience and disobedience, respectively (Dt. 28). According to this religion, history is the arena for the interplay between Yahweh and Israel. In this arena it will be demonstrated that ethics, not magic or chance, determines Israel's future. Moreover, the rewarding of righteousness and the punishment of evil is not due to some ineluctible force in the order of creation but is brought about through divine intervention in history. On this stage Israel will prove that its heart is naturally uncircumcised (30:6; 31:29), and Yahweh will prove that He is both righteous and faithful (30:1–32:43). Of utmost importance for understanding the Israelite religion is the conviction that in spite of Israel's sins God's promises to the patriarchs remain unchanged and in force. The point is made dramatically at Horeb. At precisely that moment when the Israelites reneged on their promise to serve Yahweh alone by making a golden bull around which they gathered in a pagan religious orgy, Yahweh revealed that He is merciful, gracious, longsuffering, and abounding in love and faithfulness (Ex. 34:6). To be sure, the guilty are punished, but the promise stands firm. For this reason Israel constantly and robustly affirmed the future, even though it included harsh judgment for infidelity.

E. Cultus. Israel's beliefs found their visible and audible expression in regulated holy sites, objects, seasons, actions, personnel, and diet. The *sacred site* at first was a nomad's tent, the tent of meeting, and wherever Yahweh moved His tent, that site became sanctified by His presence (Ex. 40:34f.).

Sacred objects included: Moses' rod, an appanage that signaled Yahweh's presence with Israel, especially in battle (Ex. 4:2-5; 7:8; 14:16); the ark, the seat where Yahweh sat enthroned between the cherubim and from which He ruled Israel (Nu. 10:35); the tent of meeting where Yahweh met with Israel's officially appointed representatives and mediated His will to Israel (Ex. 33:7); and the sacred lot that served to mediate His will to the priests (Dt. 33:8).

The *three pilgrimage festivals,* when all the men of Israel gathered at the central sanctuary, included: (1) the Passover, in March-April, the time of barley harvest and the end of the rainy season; in sacred ritual Israel dramatically reenacted its exodus out of Egypt, and offered the first fruits of the barley harvest; (2) Pentecost, in May-June, fifty days after Passover, at which time Israel presented to Yahweh the new grain of the wheat harvest as an expression of gratitude for the gift of the land; and (3) the Feast of Tabernacles, in September-October, at the time the olive oil and wine were pressed and just before the rainy season. This feast had three aspects: on the first day Israel blew trumpets, on the tenth day the Israelites purified themselves in a day of atonement, and from the fifteenth to the twenty-first of the month the Israelites lived in booths to remind themselves that Yahweh had them live in booths when He brought them out of Egypt (Ex. 23:14-19; Nu. 28:1–29:40; Dt. 16:1-10).

Sacred actions included the offering of many kinds of sacrifices that served many different purposes: to bring a gift expressing dependence upon Yahweh (Lev. 1–2), to express appreciation mostly for answered prayer (Lev. 3), to make a covenant (Ex. 24:1-8); to effect ritual cleansing (Lev. 14; Nu. 19), to provide a substitute for the first-born child (Ex. 34:19f.); to appease God's wrath against sin (Lev. 4, 16), and to compensate for the damage done to the sanctuary (Lev. 5). Like many aspects of the cultus it appears likely that these sacrifices were adopted from the religions around Israel and adapted to its beliefs. Thus, e.g., the sacrificial meal included a full diet of meat, bread, cereal, wine, and salt, and is even called "the food of

God" in Lev. 21:6, but in contrast to the pagan religions, where the gods had to be fed or the demons placated, there is no suggestion that Yahweh actually ate the food to sustain His life or that they had an apotropaic intent. Other sacred acts included the sacerdotal blessing (Nu. 6:22-27), prayer (Ex. 32:32, etc.), an initiatory consecration by circumcision (Ex. 4:26; Josh. 5:8), and purity rites, mostly rituals to effect ceremonial cleansing in connection with sexual emissions, leprosy, and death (Lev. 12–15, Nu. 19).

Sacred personnel included priests from the house of Aaron (Ex. 29; Lev. 9–10), his ministers from the tribe of Levi, called priests in Deuteronomy (Nu. 3:9; Dt. 18:1-6), and the Nazirite who, regardless of his clan, separated himself to Yahweh by abstaining from strong drink, from having his hair cut, and from coming into contact with the deceased (Nu. 6:1-21). See Eichrodt, I, 98-177.

Israel's *sacred diet* (Lev. 11:1-47; Dt. 14:3-21) consisted of agricultural and dairy produce and of animals "pure" with respect to their forms and habits (in contrast to animals "unclean" in either of these areas). By this practical measure the Law inculcated in Israel the mind to be a pure and holy people to Yahweh (cf. G. Wenham, *Book of Leviticus* [*NICOT,* 1979], p. 169).

III. From Moses to Monarchy.–*A. Gift of the Land.* M. Noth has pointed out that three factors are typically prerequisite for a nation's existence: a common people, a common constitution, and a common homeland. Yahweh's promises to the patriarchs, that their offspring would be His nation to bring universal salvation (Gen. 12:1-3; 22:16f.) focused on these three themes: the gift of an innumerable progeny (Gen. 15:5; 22:17; 26:4; 28:14), the gift of Himself as their God and their descendants' God forever (17:7; 28:15), and the gift of the land extending from the river of Egypt to the Great River, Euphrates (12:7; 13:15-17; 15:7-21; 28:15). He began to give the land to Israel under the leadership of Joshua and fulfilled the promise in the time of David. He delayed in giving the land until the time of Joshua that the iniquity of the Amorite might become full (Gen. 15:16) and to prove His faithfulness to keep promises made centuries earlier.

The land is also important in the Israelite religion because of its sacramental value. Throughout the Mosaic covenant, Israel's possession and retention of the good land was made contingent upon obedience to the Mosaic covenant (Dt. 4:25; etc.). The conquest of the land was made contingent upon obedience (Dt. 28:7, 36). Moreover, the rainfall and consequent harvest depended on Israel's adherence to Yahweh. Indeed, God chose this land precisely to discipline the people. In contrast to Egypt and Mesopotamia where a person could irrigate his land "with his feet" (Dt. 11:10), Canaan depended on rain from heaven. Thus Israel could be made to turn back to God by drought (Dt. 11:10-15). This persuasion that possession of the land depended on obedience to the divine will also sharply differentiated Israelite thought from pagan mythical notions of an inherent bond, or even blood kinship, among the people, the land, and its god.

This theology posed a tension, however. According to the patriarchal covenants Yahweh had promised to give Israel the land, but according to the conditions of the Mosaic covenant it was apparent that God still owned the land. The tension is made explicit in Lev. 26:23 where Israel's possession of the land is likened to that of a tenant farmer. The tension can be relieved somewhat, however, by thinking of the land as a usufruct. Israel had a right to all the enjoyment and advantages of the land as long as it fulfilled Yahweh's intention to sanctify it. Furthermore, since Yahweh had given the land as an everlasting possession (Gen. 17:8), Israel could be confident that one day all Israel would have a circumcised heart in order that God's faithfulness and righteous purpose might be brought into harmony (Dt. 30:1-10).

B. Holy War. Israel's wars were religious wars, as is attested alike by the historical narratives and the ancient poetry preserved in them (Gen. 49:22-26; Ex. 15:1-18; Dt. 33; Jgs. 5). Von Rad (*Der heilige Kriege im alten Israel* [1958]) showed that Israel destroyed the Canaanites and occupied their land by strict adherence to the religious rules of what he labeled "holy war." This kind of war dictated that Yahweh begin the battle and consummate it, and thus the true glory was His (Josh. 3:10; 4:23; etc.). Israel, on its part, need only trust and obey (1:6-8). Throughout the book of Joshua one can note a pattern of divine command followed by the obedience of His faithful nations (1:1f., 10f.; 8:1f., 3-9; 11:6f., 9). In two incidents the Israelites failed to look to Yahweh and in both instances they went down in defeat (Josh. 7:2-5; 9:14, 18). This kind of war also called on occasion for *ḥērem,* an institution by which persons (and their possessions) hostile to the deity were given over to the deity, often by totally destroying them. This "ban" served to bring God's righteous judgment on flagrant and incorrigible sin, to protect Israel from defaulting on its commitment to Yahweh by intermarriage with the Canaanites (Dt. 7:2f.), to keep Israel from engaging in war for personal gain (Josh. 6:14; 7:1-26), and to encourage the enemy's wholehearted submission (Josh 6:24f.). When the elect nation later in its history embraced the Canaanite religion, "the ban" was pronounced against it (Isa. 43:28). In short, it had a moral purpose (cf. O. T. Allis, *Five Books of Moses* [1964], pp. 156f.).

C. Gifts and Charisma. Yahweh, Israel's king (Dt. 33:5), gave gifts to elect individuals both indirectly and directly by the conferral of His Spirit on them in order to perform various tasks in the theocracy. Thus for the building of His sanctuary Yahweh gave "wisdom," i.e., all sorts of skills in designing and craftsmanship, to people who distinguished themselves from the masses by their obvious capability (Ex. 28:3; 35:35–36:1). Then too, for the local administration of the clans he gave "wisdom," i.e., the right temperament and mind for judging Israel (cf. Ex. 18:13-27; Nu. 11:30; Dt. 1:9f.). Israel attributed these gifts to Yahweh (cf. Job 12:13-25; Ezk. 7:26; Prov. 2:6) and as a result it could be said "judgment belongs to Yahweh" (Dt. 1:17).

In the case of Moses, however, this leadership ability was attributed to a direct conferral of the divine Spirit upon him. So great and so powerful was this Spirit that when only a portion of it was taken from him and distributed to seventy elders they all prophesied (Nu. 11:24-30).

Yahweh's rule by means of placing His Spirit upon elect individuals was a prominent feature of the time of the judges. During this disturbed period when the legacy inherited from Joshua broke down due to Israel's repeated sin, Yahweh raised up individuals gifted with military prowess (the judges) whenever Israel repented and cried out to Him for relief from the oppressor. At those times Israel's Great Judge and Warrior (Ex. 15:3) settled the dispute not by arbitrating but by empowering people for battle (Jgs. 11:27).

D. Angels and the Angel of Yahweh. Although the OT writers inveigh against consorting with the spirits of nature or of the dead, throughout the history of the Israelite religion we encounter spiritual beings created by Yahweh to serve in His heavenly court and to accomplish His will on earth (cf. Gen. 28:12; Dnl. 10:11). These beings are called "sons of God," "angels," "hosts of heaven/of the heights," "council of the holy ones." Some, e.g., the cherubim and seraphim, worship Him, but others, e.g., "evil spirits" and Satan, do not share God's character or design. But occasionally all must appear in Yahweh's heavenly court to wait upon Him (Job 1:6; 1 K. 22). None compares to God (Ps. 89:6), and the psalmist calls upon them to praise Him (Ps. 29:1). In the ancient Near East the stars were considered among the highest gods, but in the OT they are God's servants. As King over all these heavenly beings Yahweh is called Yahweh of hosts, a title we encounter for the first time during the period of the judges when His tent was at Shiloh (1 S. 1:3).

The angel of Yahweh, however, is not one of these creatures. Rather, he appears to be a manifestation of Yahweh Himself in Israel's epic narratives (Gen. 16:9-13; 22:9-14; Jgs. 6:11-27). This hypostatic manifestation of God bore witness in yet another way to the Israelites that God was with them.

IV. From Monarchy to Exile.–Israel's kings, who reigned from *ca.* 1000 B.C. to 587 B.C., are religious figures like their pagan counterparts. In Mesopotamia, e.g., it was believed that kingship was lowered from heaven, and each king sought divine legitimation for his claim to the throne. These kings interpreted the will of the gods, took responsibility for building the temple, and were the subject of many of the prayers offered at these sanctuaries. In Egypt, the king was held to be the son of god, an incarnation of Horus and Seth. In Israel similar features were found, as we shall see, but they were transformed and pressed into the service of the incomparable Yahweh.

A. Israel's Attitude Toward the Monarchy. The OT reflects an ambivalence toward the monarchy. Samuel, Israel's last judge, both condemned Israel for demanding the institution and promoted it. The classic critical solution to this tension is to suppose that there are two contradictory sources in the books of Samuel: an earlier source promonarchial in sentiment (1 S. 9:1–10:16; 11:1-15) and a later antimonarchial source (8:1-22; 10:17-27; 12:1-25). In spite of the protests by some scholars (H. Wildberger, *Theologische Zeitschrift*, 13 [1957], 442-469) that this formulation is overly simplistic, it still remains the standard starting point in most critical discussions about Israel's attitude toward the monarchy. It seems unlikely, however, that a good writer, like the one we meet in this book, illogically incorporated two contradictory viewpoints. Rather, it appears that he consciously confronts his reader with the theological tension between God's good and sovereign will and human sin. On the one hand, Yahweh brings Israel to the acme of its history in the OT by installing David as king. By this act He fulfilled the patriarchal vision (Gen. 49:10), provided the answer to Hannah's hope (1 S. 2:10), and consummated the promises to the fathers regarding the land (Gen. 15:18-21; 2 S. 8). On the other hand, he punished them with kings who abused their office because they demanded a king out of a spirit of unbelief. A similar tension can be observed in Yahweh's use of the proud Assyrian to discipline Israel and His later breaking of that insolent rod (Isa. 10:1-19), and in His offering of His Servant for the sins of His people and His punishment of those that killed Him (cf. Lk. 22:22).

B. Davidic Covenant and Son of God. R. A. Carlson (*David, the Chosen King* [1964]) argued persuasively that the author of the books of Samuel arranged his material so as to present "David under the Blessing" (2 S. 2–8) and then "David under the Curse" (9–24), with the Bathsheba incident constituting the turning point between these two poles. The blessings on David climaxed with the Davidic covenant, wherein Yahweh promised among other things to make David's son the son of God forever (2 S. 7:14f.; 1 Ch. 17:13-15; Ps. 2:7; 89:19-37). The OT makes it clear that (in contrast to Egypt) this promise must not be understood in a mythical sense. Solomon, whose lineage is well known, is explicitly designated by David as God's son (1 Ch. 22:8-10; 28:6). The reference to "today" in Ps. 2:7 precludes a mythical sense, and the verb "beget" used there is used elsewhere figuratively (Dt. 32:18; Isa. 1:2 (LXX); Jer. 2:27). For these and other reasons, scholars speak of Israel's king as being adopted by Yahweh (cf. G. Cooke, *ZAW*, 43 [1961], 202-205). In any case, in the unfolding drama of Israel's religion the earlier naming of the nation of Israel as Yahweh's first-born (Ex. 4:22) and son (4:23) is now applied to the king. Thus the king becomes the nation's representative head. From now on all that concerned the son of God also concerned the people "in him"; nothing that happened to him was a purely private affair. Israel's fortunes now rested on "the anointed."

This promise constituted the basis for the messianic expectation in Israel. Israel's hymns celebrating the king gave clear expression that it understood this promise to include both the everlasting duration of David's house (Ps. 72:5-7) and the universal extension of that rule over all the earth (Ps. 2:8; 72:8-14). In the course of Israel's history it became clear that none of the kings associated with the first temple had shoulders broad enough to fill this magnificent purple robe, and with the certainty of the Exile looming ominously on the horizon the prophets projected this yearning for an ideal king to a future king who would emerge from the line of David after Israel's return from the strange land (Isa. 7:10-17; 9:2-7; Mic. 4:14–5:3; Hos. 3:5; Am. 9:1-12; etc.).

C. Davidic Covenant and Earlier Covenants. The Davidic covenant provided yet another step in the fulfillment of the promises made to the fathers and did not in any way replace the Mosaic covenant made between Israel and Yahweh (cf. R. Clements, *Abraham and David* [*SBT*, 2/5, 1967]). As the people's representative the king was responsible to the law and for it (cf. 1 S. 10:25; 1 K. 2:2; 11:11; 2 K. 21:8; 23:25). He had to copy it under priestly tutelage upon his inauguration and to read it daily (Dt. 17:18f.). His success or failure was understood to be contingent upon his loyalty or dissaffection to the Author of the covenant (1 S. 12:25; 1 K. 2:2). Though he sat on God's throne (1 Ch. 17:14, 24; 29:23), nevertheless he was a man under the "law" of the priests, and, as we shall see, under the "word" of the prophet. The law's demand that he not multiply wealth, military resources, or political alliances (Dt. 17:16f.) aimed at inculcating in him a spirit of dependence upon Yahweh.

But failure on the part of the Davidic scion to keep the law could not negate Yahweh's promise to the house of David. Again, to be sure, sin had to be judged, but God's promise to the house of David stood firm forever. The writer of the book of Samuel drove this conviction home by recording David's sin with Bathsheba, a debacle in which he broke the law almost immediately after Nathan's oracle communicating the divine and eternal promises to him. David passed immediately from "under blessing" to "under curse," but the messianic promise remained unchanged and in force (cf. B. Childs, *Intro. to the OT as Scripture* [1979], p. 276).

D. King and Cult. Ideally the king's roles included his behaving as "the Servant of Yahweh," as "the Shepherd of Israel," and as the patron of the cult. Like other oriental monarchs he demonstrated his fidelity to the deity by selecting the site for the temple, building it, making arrangements for the worship in it, and offering gifts (1 Ch. 15–16, 22–29). In contrast to Saul, David would allow himself no sleep until he had found a resting place for God

(Ps. 132:5; 2 S. 6). With David's choice of Jerusalem as that resting place for the ark and with Solomon's building of the temple there, Mt. Zion became God's final throne on earth and His central sanctuary forever (Ps. 87). Sanctuaries similar to Solomon's temple have been excavated in northern Syria, particularly at Tell Taʿyinat, both corroborating the Bible and showing in yet another way that Israel's faith developed in forms common to the times (*WBA*, pp. 137f.).

H. Gunkel (*Einleitung*) demonstrated that Israel's hymnic forms closely paralleled those of Egypt and Mesopotamia. Parallel Sumerian hymns contain musical notations as unintelligible to Sumerologists as the musical notations in the Psalms are unintelligible to Hebraists (cf. S. N. Kramer, *The Sumerians* [1963], p. 207). Mowinckel (*Psalms*) demonstrated from internal evidence in the psalms that they were sung in the cultus connected with the first temple, and Dahood (*Psalms I-III* [*AB*, 1965-1970]) backed up this conclusion with linguistic evidence from the Ugaritic texts, though he marred his work by overextending the argument. John Eaton (*Kingship in the Psalms* [1976]) argued convincingly that the Scandinavian scholars are right in their contention that the bulk of prayers had the king as their subject. Gunkel (*Einleitung*, p. 161) had already noticed that the prayers for the king in Mesopotamia are "extraordinarily numerous." These studies have driven from the field the older critical view that the spiritual content of the psalms is so advanced that they must have been composed during the time of Israel's second temple.

But Mowinckel went too far in his contention that approximately forty-four of the psalms were sung as a libretto accompaniment to a ritual drama in which Yahweh was enthroned annually at the great fall festival. According to him (*Psalms*, p. 118), through this cultic event "the bond made with the deity in the harvest festival causes the rain to return so that the curse of drought and death is overcome, dormant nature revives and life awakens for the benefit of mankind." Other scholars belonging to the myth-and-ritual school went even further, and against Mowinckel's protestations, they argued that the psalms accompanied a ceremony in which Israel's king, representing Yahweh, went through a ceremony wherein he died and was raised again and whereby the recreative forces of life were released (cf. A. R. Johnson, *Sacral Kingship in Ancient Israel* [2nd. ed. 1967]; S. H. Hooke, ed., *Myth and Ritual* [1933]). Now admittedly such rites led by the king were carried out both in Mesopotamia at a new year's (*akītu*) festival in order to reenact and mythically recreate Marduk's victory over Tiâmat, the goddess of chaos, and in Egypt at a Sed festival and at a new year and harvest festival for the god Min. (For a thorough treatment of the relationship between the king and the cult in the ancient Near East, see H. Frankfort, *Kingship and the Gods* [1948, 1978]; I. Engnell, *Studies in Divine Kingship in the Ancient Near East* [2nd. ed. 1967].) Moreover, it appears highly likely that in the Israelite Feast of Tabernacles the king figured prominently and psalms were sung and composed for it. But it is incorrect to take the next step and conjecture that Israel filled this ritual with mythical convictions borrowed from its pagan neighbors. The superscriptions in fourteen of the psalms bear witness that these psalms originated out of David's historical experiences, and there is no compelling reason for brushing these notices aside. Furthermore, Mowinckel's argument is based on the persuasion that the phrase *ʾᵃḏōnāy mālaḵ* must be translated "Yahweh has become king," but many scholars (e.g., N. Ridderbos, *VT*, 4 [1954], 87-89; D. Michel, *VT*, 6 [1956], 40-68) have argued persuasively on philological and literary evidence that the traditional rendering "Yahweh reigns" is to be preferred.

Then too, it is possible that David and the other poets who gave us the psalms belonged to that circle within Israel that gave us the canon, and it is unthinkable that this school of thought would have replaced the conviction that obedience to Yahweh's will constituted the only basis for future blessings with cultic activity procuring benefits for mankind. To be sure, Zechariah (14:16f.) speaks of an age in which rain will fall on the nations in accordance with whether they have gone up to Jerusalem at the Feast of Tabernacles to worship Yahweh as their King. But we must not think of "worship" here as a mythical act recreating the bond between Yahweh and the forces of life latent in the creation. Rather, it means that they will have submitted their lives to the King, and the test of their submission is whether they observe the Feast demanded in the law. The psalms repeatedly call for fidelity to Yahweh and His law (Ps. 1:2; 2:3; 4:5; etc.) and the very psalms to which Mowinckel appeals affirm that Israel's future and the earth's future depend on Yahweh conforming to His righteous statutes and character (Ps. 93:5; 96:10; 97:10f.; 98:9; 99:6-9). The psalms themselves do not lead the reader to the mythical interpretations of these Scandinavian and English scholars, and it is exegetically unsound to impose pagan notions on the text.

Worship on Mt. Zion did not originate in pagan myth but in Yahweh's work in moving history towards its destiny. At the Exodus, Moses foresaw the day when Yahweh would rule from His mountain sanctuary (Ex. 15:17). Centuries later David fulfilled the vision.

E. King and Wisdom. Scholarship confirms the biblical claim that Solomon (Prov. 1:1; 10:1; 1 K. 4:29f.) and other kings (Prov. 25:1; 31:1) coined and collected sayings consistent with the notion of ethical monotheism. G. Pettinato (*BA*, 39 [1976], 45) alerted the world that he had uncovered thousands of tablets in the royal archives at Tell Mardikh (Ebla) from 2350 B.C., and that some of these tablets contained collections of proverbs. E. I. Gordon (*Sumerian Proverbs* [1969]) published two collections of Sumerian proverbs pieced together from the hundreds of clay tablets dug up at Nippur, Susa, and Ur and dated them to the Old Babylonian period (*ca.* 1700 B.C.). Instructional literature in Egypt dates back to the Old Kingdom period and onward (cf. L. Perdue, *Wisdom and Cult* [1977], pp. 28-61), and C. Kayatz (*Studien zu Proverbien 1–9* [1966]) carefully documented the remarkable parallelism in syntactical constructions between these texts and Prov. 1–9. In short, wisdom literature existed around the Fertile Crescent not only before Solomon but even before the Hebrews appeared in history! Moreover, this kind of literature appears to have had its original setting in the home of the courtier (cf. H. Frankfort, *Ancient Egyptian Religion* [1961]; W. G. Lambert, *Babylonian Wisdom Literature* [1960]). In sum, Moses gave the law; the king gave wisdom.

F. Prophetic Movement. Israel's prophets also had their counterparts in the surrounding pagan nations and religions. Thus, e.g., Kitchen states (p. 54) that at Ebla the *nabiʾutum* (cf. Heb. *nāḇîʾ*, "prophet") occurs as a class of "prophet" alongside the better known *maḫḫu*. The knowledge of the function of such people, however, must await publication of the Ebla tablets. In both Babylon and Assyria the king sought prophetic sanction to validate his claim to kingship. In a Mari Letter (*ca.* 1750 B.C.) we are told of a certain *maḫḫu*, "seer," who threatened the king of Mari that if he did not satisfy the demands of the gods Hadad and Dagan, his kingship would be withdrawn. In Moab King Balak hired the prophet Balaam to pronounce a curse on Israel (Nu. 24), and centuries later Moab's King Mesha (*ca.* 850 B.C.) commemorated his victory over Israel by erecting a stele on which he boasted that his god Chemosh had encouraged him in his campaign.

The Aramean king Zakir of Hamath (8th cent. B.C.) speaks of a *ḥāzîn,* "seer," who delivered an oracle promising him victory (cf. *ANET,* pp. 655f.).

But in spite of these obvious similarities with Yahweh's prophets, who likewise appointed kings (1 K. 12:29), assisted them in battle (2 K. 6:8–8:6), and deposed them when they fell into disfavor (1 K. 16:1-4), Yahweh's prophets were imbued with the conviction that their message came directly from God. They contrasted their own experience in receiving Yahweh's words with that of prophets who served dumb idols (Isa. 41:22-26; 43:4; Jer. 30:5; Hab. 2:10) and with false prophets of Yahweh who spoke out of "their own hearts" (Jer. 14:14; 23:16, 25). So real was their experience in hearing God's word that they confounded the words from Yahweh's mouth with the human voice, if we may universalize Samuel's experience (1 S. 3:8).

In the early period of the monarchy they "prophesied" with such extraordinary manifestations caused by the overwhelming and irresistible influence of Yahweh's Spirit falling upon them, that they could not continue their normal functions (Nu. 24:4; 1 S. 10:6-10). Yet Elijah scoffed at the frenzied practices of his pagan peers and at their impotency in prayer (1 K. 18:27f.). It is also instructive to note that a king who shared the faith of the true prophet of Yahweh could distinguish him from false ones who prophesied in Yahweh's name (1 K. 22:7).

But above all they distinguished themselves from pagan prophets by their legacy of prophecies that are remarkable for their specificity and continuity over centuries. No movement in the history of religions can be compared with prophecy in Israel (Isa. 41:21-29).

Yahweh's true prophets were bound together by their common experience with Yahweh and by their common conviction about Yahweh's sovereign will for Israel as proclaimed by Moses, the prophet par excellence. Both the Former Prophets (i.e., the authors of Joshua to Kings) and the Latter Prophets (Isaiah to Malachi) interpreted the nation's fortunes and predicted its future on the basis of the threats and promises contained in the Mosaic covenant. Thus, e.g., the writer of Kings framed each of Israel's kings within a very strict literary form (cf. 1 K. 14:21f., 29-31) and evaluated his heart and his reign in terms of the first stipulation of the law, i.e., Israel was to have but one central sanctuary, which, as it turned out, was Jerusalem. As impracticable as it might appear to human judgment, the prophets of both the north and the south called for a political division of Yahweh's kingdom between the northern tribes and the southern tribes and at the same time attempted to preserve the religious unity of the kingdoms by insisting that all the people continue to worship at Jerusalem. None of the kings of the north had the faith to accept this arrangement, and hence all of them failed the test of loyalty to Yahweh's covenant. According to our prophet-historian the doom of the northern kingdom was sealed when Jeroboam I set up his rival cult centers at Bethel and Dan. Likewise, our writer found guilty those sons of David who tolerated or set up cultic centers to other gods around about Jerusalem, and this travesty against the law brought about the collapse of the southern kingdom.

It is sometimes argued that this historian distorted Israel's history in order to support his fabricated interpretation of history, but it may be noted that, although like all historians he carefully edited his material, he did not oversimplify historical reality. It is this prophet-historian who tells us, e.g., of the prosperity of the "evil" Jeroboam II and of the untimely death of "good" king Josiah (cf. 1 K. 14:24-27; 2 K. 23:26-29). Jacques Ellul (*The Politics of God and the Politics of Man* [Eng. tr. 1972], p. 91) said: "Historians who think the history told in the Bible is pious and distorted ought to ask themselves why it is that these biblical historians who supposedly want to prove something always tell us about the disasters under good kings and victories under idolatrous kings" (cf. 1 K. 19, 21).

The author of Kings not only interpreted Israel's past history on the basis of the Mosaic covenant's demand for cultic purity, but also hinted at a future messianic expectation based on his belief in the immutability of God's promise to David that his line would never be extinguished. Thus he concluded his work with the hope that a son of David still lived and that even though he was in captivity his throne was set above the thrones of all the other captive kings (2 K. 25:27-30). This conviction about Yahweh's judgment upon sin along with a sure confidence that God's promises were irrevocable informed all the prophets.

Yahweh's prophets not only interpreted and predicted history in the light of the covenants binding Israel and Yahweh together; they also directed its progress through their dynamic words. The book of Kings might better be labeled the book of prophets, for in truth they planted nations and uprooted them with their powerful oracles. Von Rad (*Studies in Deuteronomy* [1953], pp. 78ff.), taking note of a series of prophecy-fulfillment patterns in the books of Kings (e.g., 2 S. 7:13 par. 1 K. 8:20; 1 K. 11:29 par. 12:15; 13:2 par. 2 K. 23:16-18; etc.), concluded that the prophetic word should be conceived of as "a history creating force" that is unleashed in the world and accomplishes its purpose (cf. also Jer. 1:9f.; Isa. 55:10f.).

Yahweh favored Israel with prophets throughout its history, though at times His words were scarce (1 S. 3:1). Even the patriarchs were called prophets (Ps. 105:15) because the word of God came to them in dreams, visions, and spoken messages and proceeded from them. Moses, however, stands singularly above all the prophets because only he saw God face to face, and unlike his successors spoke plainly and not in riddles. Moreover, all subsequent prophecy must be tested by whether it conformed with Moses' revelation. The word of God came to those who succeeded him without respect to class or sex. Thus it came to men of royal degree (Zephaniah), priests (Ezekiel), common men (Amos), and women (Miriam, Deborah, Huldah).

Prophets assumed a most important place in Israel's religion with the coming of the monarchy. They were never a mere appendage to it, but, as noted above, elected Israel's kings and stood over them. In the earlier period (Samuel to Elisha) they were usually friendly toward Israel's kings, displaying a fostering and protective attitude toward them, and when the kings sinned they called them back to repentance. Later on, however (Amos to Jeremiah), they arraigned the kings before the law, and finding them guilty of having broken the covenant, they sentenced them to judgment at the hands of the great imperial powers of Assyria, Babylonia, and Persia and predicted the birth of a new nation out of the ashes.

The prophets' teaching nowhere opposes any of the priestly Torah of the Mosaic law. Their minimizing of its cultic provisions did not constitute a rejection of it but a subordination of it to the more important moral and social concerns found in their heritage (Hos. 4:6; 5:1f.; Mic. 3:11; 6:8). They did not reject the priesthood or the sacrificial system, but they did rebuke dereliction in the priesthood and the substitution of ritual for heartfelt commitment to Yahweh.

V. Exilic and Postexilic Periods.–The fall of Jerusalem in 587 B.C. had a decisive effect upon the development of the Israelite religion. Israel's unique religious identity was now constantly threatened by the changing attitudes toward Israel on the part of their capricious oriental overlords and by the unchanging fickleness of the human heart. Nebuchadrezzar deported them, Cyrus restored them, and Xerxes first ordered their annihilation and then armed them to slay their adversaries. Rival states in their homeland offered first to help them rebuild the temple, and then, when refused, opposed them. Some of the people returned to the homeland and others did not, and of those that did return many sought their own comforts and intermarried with the foreigners now living in the land. Israel's survival through these changing fortunes, which the people likened to wandering in desert wastes, sitting in dungeons, and becoming seasick on stormy seas, caused the Israelites to give thanks to Yahweh who protected and preserved them (Ps. 107). At the same time Israel's spiritual leaders sought to preserve their precious and unique spiritual trust by recreating ancient religious institutions, by pointing the people beyond the present to their glorious future, and by calling upon them individually to make a decision in the present to serve Yahweh.

A. Institutions for Preserving the Israelite Religion. 1. Cultus. Encouraged by the preaching of Isaiah (Isa. 40–55) and taking advantage of Cyrus' edict to return from Babylon and to rebuild the temple, many Israelites returned to Jerusalem in 539 B.C. and recreated the Mosaic cultus, but without the ark. At the first Feast of Tabernacles they rebuilt the altar on its original site and offered the sacrifices prescribed in the law. In the second year they laid the foundations for the second temple with the accompaniment of the liturgy instituted by David, but they soon became discouraged by opposition from without and abandoned the work to pursue personal gain (Ezr. 3; Haggai). In 520 B.C., however, under the provocative preaching of Haggai and Zechariah they resumed the work and finished it in 516 B.C. (Ezr. 4). But the nation continued to be plagued by weary priests perfunctorily performing their duties and by people who did not share the prophetic zeal.

2. Law. For the apostates from Yahweh, Judah's state god had shown himself impotent before the imperial might of Babylon, and consequently, facing the threat of deportation, they clung to all conceivable deities and cults (Jer. 7:18; 44:17-25; Ezk. 8:7-16). For true Israel, however, it was apparent that the privileged nation had fallen because of its failure to keep the covenant and to heed the prophetic warnings of judgment (2 K. 17:7-23). History confirmed them in the conviction that the nation's hope for a blessed future lay in knowing the law and in keeping it. Moreover, its laws originally intended to keep Israel separate from the Canaanites were needed as much now as at the beginning. At *ca.* 450 B.C. Ezra and Nehemiah (Neh. 8–9), along with Malachi (cf. Mal. 4:4), founded the Second Jewish Commonwealth squarely on the law and terminated the mixed marriages. The language and ideas of Deuteronomy clearly influenced the literature of the period (cf. Neh. 1:5 and Dt. 7:9, 21; Neh. 1:8 and 20:1-4; Neh. 1:10 and Dt. 9:29; etc.).

3. Canon. Sometime after these reforms and before 132 B.C., the spiritual leaders of Israel gave the canon its final shape. This written document, taught and studied both at the temple and in local synagogues, uniquely conserved Israel's heritage and preserved them as a spiritual community (cf. Sir. 39:1-4, 7f.).

B. Eschatology. 1. New Covenant. The first Hebrew nation failed because it depended on people to keep God's law. History had confirmed the Israelite belief that mankind was at heart rebellious against God and lawless. Accordingly, amid the nation's wreckage, Israel's prophets became convinced that one day Yahweh would make a new covenant with all the patriarchal stock (Jer. 31:31-34; Ezk. 36:25-27; etc.). This new covenant would contain the same stipulations as the earlier one, but in addition to providing for Israel's cleansing, it would depend on God's promise to put His law into Israel's heart to be an everlasting covenant of peace. Isaiah foresaw, moreover, that the Servant of Yahweh, by taking away the sins of His people through death, would mediate this covenant (Isa. 42:6; 49:6).

2. Messiah. The preexilic expectation of an ideal son of David who would restore the fortunes of David's house was picked up by the postexilic prophets associated with the rebuilding of the second temple (Hag. 2:21-23; Zec. 6:9-14). But this son did not emerge during the time that the OT canon achieved its final form. Accordingly, those who gave us the canon must have interpreted the ancient promises regarding Israel's glorious future under the Messiah as referring to one yet to come. Thus, e.g., the psalms sung at the first temple to celebrate the coronation of the king (Pss. 2, 110, etc.), his marriage (Ps. 45), his victories over the enemy (Pss. 18, 30, etc.), were reinterpreted as references to the coming Christ.

3. Apocalyptic. It is impossible to make a sharp distinction between prophecy and apocalyptic because apocalyptic literature builds upon the prophetic vision that one day the ideal son of David will come with righteousness, victory, and dominion over the nation. In the apocalyptic literature, however, the dynamic tension between God's plan and mankind's responsibility is severed and only the divine side of history is presented. Here we encounter angels and spiritual forces shaping history from without, and we are given the divine plan and timetable behind history. The plan is revealed to the favored person in a vision, and the revelation is presented in the form of fantastic and arresting images that often require an angel to interpret them. Thus, e.g., Daniel, who putatively served in Nebuchadrezzar's court, received a vision in which the four imperial empires that subjugated Israel between the Captivity and the advent of Jesus Christ are represented by a lion (Babylon), a bear raised on one side with three ribs in its mouth (Medo-Persia with its conquests of Babylon, Lydia, and Egypt), a leopard with four heads (Greece and its subsequent fourfold division) and a dreadful beast with iron teeth (Rome). He then saw the Ancient of Days (God) sitting in His heavenly court and a son of man (Messiah) presented to Him to whom He bequeathed the eternal, universal kingdom.

C. Rise of Personal Religion. When the nation existed as a political entity under a king, the individual member of the state tended to think of himself as a leaf upon a tree. But when the tree was cut down, the historical reality dictated that he think of himself more individualistically. Without the hermetical seal of the political entity, and exposed constantly to foreign influences, the individual was forced to choose his own identity. The exilic prophets Ezekiel (18:2-30) and Jeremiah (31:29f.) began this emphasis with their doctrine that each individual was responsible for his own sin. The substitution of the local synagogue for the central temple reinforced the new emphasis. The Chronicler not only sought to show the links of the postexilic community with its past through genealogies and Israel's glorious royal heritage by not dwelling on the kings' sins, but he also elected, in contrast to the writer of Kings, to include in his history the personal choices of Rehoboam when he confronted Shishak (2 Ch. 12:1-12), of Asa when he faced Zerah the Ethiopian (14:9f.), and of Manasseh who repented when held captive in Assyria (33:10-13). All of these men found God's salvation when they humbled themselves and sought the Lord.

For the intertestamental and NT periods, *see* RELIGIONS OF THE BIBLICAL WORLD: JUDAISM.

Bibliography.–W. F. Albright, *ARI; Yahweh and the Gods of Canaan* (repr. 1979); A. Alt, "Origins of Israelite Law," in *Essays on OT History and Religion* (Eng. tr. 1966), pp. 79-132; F. M. Cross, *Canaanite Myth and Hebrew Epic* (1973); W. Eichrodt, *Theology of the OT* (2 vols., Eng. tr., *OTL*, 1961-1967); G. Fohrer, *History of Israelite Religion* (Eng. tr. 1972); H. Gunkel, *Einleitung in die Psalmen* (1933); "Fundamental Problems of the OT," in *What Remains of the OT* (Eng. tr. 1928), pp. 57-68; *Schöpfung und Chaos in Urzeit und Endzeit* (1895); Y. Kaufmann, *Religion of Israel from Its Beginnings to the Babylonian Exile* (trans. and abridged by M. Greenberg, 1960); K. Kitchen, *Bible in Its World* (1977); S. Mowinckel, *Psalms in Israel's Worship* (2 vols., Eng. tr. 1962); H. Ringgren, *Israelite Religion* (Eng. tr. 1966); *Religions of the Ancient Near East* (Eng. tr. 1973); W. R. Smith, *Religion of the Semites* (repr. 1956); R. de Vaux, *Ancient Israel* (2 vols., Eng. tr. 1961); G. von Rad, *OT Theology* (2 vols., Eng. tr. 1962-1965); G. Vos, *Biblical Theology* (1948); T. C. Vriezen, *Outline of OT Theology* (Eng. tr., 2nd ed. 1970); J. Wellhausen, *Prolegomena to the History of Israel* (Eng. tr., repr. 1957); G. E. Wright, *God Who Acts* (*SBT*, 8, 1952); *OT Against Its Environment* (*SBT*, 2, 1950).

B. K. WALTKE

ISRAEL STELE. *See* MERNEPTAH.

ISSACHAR [Heb. *Q yiśśāḵār*].

1. The ninth son of Jacob, the fifth born to him by Leah (Gen. 30:17f.); also the tribe named for him. His birth is, in this passage, connected with the strange story of Reuben and his mandrakes; and the name given him is apparently conceived as derived from Heb. *'îš śāḵār,* "a hired workman." There is a play upon the name in this sense in Gen. 49:15. Wellhausen (*Text der Bücher Samuelis* [1871], p. 95) thinks that the second element of the name may denote a deity; Sokar, an Egyptian god, has been suggested. The name in that case would mean "worshiper of Sokar."

Practically nothing is preserved of the personal history of this patriarch beyond his share in the common actions of the sons of Jacob. Four sons were born to him before Jacob's family removed to Egypt (Gen. 46:13). In that land he died and was buried.

At Sinai the tribe of Issachar numbered 54,400 men of war over twenty years of age (Nu. 1:29). At the end of the wanderings the numbers had grown to 64,300 (Nu. 26:25). In the days of David, the Chronicler puts the figure at 87,000 (1 Ch. 7:5). The place of Issachar in the desert march was with the standard of the tribe of Judah (along with Zebulun) on the east side of the tabernacle (Nu. 2:5), this group forming the wing of the host (10:14f.). The captain of the tribe was Nethanel the son of Zuar (Nu. 1:8, etc.). Later this place was held by Igal the son of Joseph, the tribal representative among the spies (Nu. 13:7). The prince chosen from Issachar to assist in the division of the land was Paltiel son of Azzan (34:26). The position of Issachar at the ceremony near Shechem was on Mt. Gerizim, "to bless the people" (Dt. 27:12).

According to Yeivin this tribe belonged to the second wave of settlement, which took place in the middle of the 14th cent. B.C., and which included the majority of the sons of Leah: Reuben, Judah, and Simeon (Jgs. 1:3ff.). Yeivin bases his theory on the completed reading of an Egyptian stele from the time of Sethis I (1310 B.C.) found in Beth-shean, which gives an account of a military campaign into the territory of Issachar. According to Yeivin the campaign was against the family of Tola, which belonged to the tribe of Issachar. It seems that the sons of Issachar and the sons of Zebulun were more closely connected with each other than with other tribes. Possibly they had a common sanctuary on Mt. Tabor (Dt. 33:18f.). With the strengthening of the Egyptians and the Canaanites, soon after their settlement they became subjected to them. This is reflected in the Blessing of Jacob: "He saw a resting-place that it was good, and the land that it was pleasant; and he bowed his shoulder to bear, and became a servant under task-work" (Gen. 49:15).

When the Egyptian rule weakened and the third wave of settlement took place, the southern area of the territory of Issachar was captured by families of the tribe of Manasseh. Issachar took part in the battle with Sisera (Jgs. 5:15). To Israel Issachar gave one judge, Tola (Jgs. 10:1), and two kings, Baasha and his son (1 K. 15:27, etc.). The genealogical lists of this tribe are concentrated in Gen. 46:13; 1 Ch. 7:1-5.

Of the two hundred "heads" of the men of Issachar who came to David at Hebron it is said that they were "men that had understanding of the times, to know what Israel ought to do" (1 Ch. 12:32). According to the Targum, this meant that they knew how to ascertain the periods of the sun and moon, the intercalation of months, and the dates of solemn feasts, and could interpret the signs of the times. A company from Issachar came to the celebration of the Passover when it was restored by Hezekiah (2 Ch. 30:18). Issachar has a portion assigned to him in Ezekiel's ideal division of the land (48:25); he appears also in the list in Rev. 7:7.

Into the description of the tribe's territory mentioned in the book of Joshua (19:17-22), as in those of the territories of the other northern tribes, two lists have been worked. One is the description of the borders, the other a list of the cities. In the process of combining the two lists they may have been shortened. According to Yeivin the beginning of v. 18 and two parts of v. 12 belong to the list of the boundaries; they deal with the northern and western boundaries. It is possible to reconstruct the northern border in its entirety by comparing it with that of the tribe of Naphtali. Thus it ran from Mt. Tabor NE to the upper Brook of Jabneel, and from there eastward to the Jordan near Lakum. The eastern border followed without doubt the course of the Jordan River. The southern border cannot be reconstructed because the description of the territory of Manasseh's northern border is not mentioned in detail. It can be assumed, however, that the southern border of the territory of Issachar passed between the mountains of Gilboa and the central hills of Ephraim. Thus the territory included the mountains of Gilboa, the northeastern part of the plain of Dothan, and the eastern part of the plain of Esdraelon. The western border ran in a more or less straight line S-N; from Ibleam it passed by the city of Jezreel to Mt. Tabor.

The cities of the plain fell into the hands of the Israelites only in a comparatively late period, and the strip of independent Canaanite cities separated the southern from the northern part of the territory. Because of the lack of contact the southern area was held by families belonging to the tribe of Manasseh. Fifteen towns are mentioned in the list of towns; they are subdivided in a manner not yet clear, as most of them have not been satisfactorily identified.

See Vol. I, Map VI.

Bibliography.–K. Budde, *ZAW*, 7 (1887), 132; R. Kittel, *Geschichte des Volkes Israels* (7th ed. 1925-1932), I, 12ff.; A. Alt, *PJ*, 20 (1924), 34ff.; W. F. Albright, *JPOS*, 5 (1925), 35; *ZAW*, 44 (1926), 225; 45 (1927), 64ff.; A. A. Saarisalo, *Boundary Between Issachar and Naphtali* (1927); M. Noth, *Das Buch Josua* (1938), pp. 86f.; *NHI*; W. F. Albright, *BASOR*, 125 (1952), 24ff.; Y. Aharoni, *IEJ* 3 (1953), 153ff.; W. F. Albright, *JAOS*, 74 (1954), 222f.; S. Yeivin, *Mélanges A. Robert* (1957), pp. 100ff.

2. A Korahite doorkeeper, the seventh son of Obededom (1 Ch. 26:5).

A. A. SAARISALO

ISSHIAH ish-shī'ə [Heb. *yiššîyāhû*]; AV also ISHIAH (1 Ch. 7:3), JESIAH (12:6; 23:20).

1. Mentioned among David's heroes, a great grandson of Tola (1 Ch. 7:3).

2. Mentioned among the men who came to David at Ziklag (1 Ch. 12:6).

3. A member of the priesthood of the house of Rehabiah (1 Ch. 24:21).

4. Another Levitical priest of the house of Uzziel (1 Ch. 23:20; 24:25).

ISSHIJAH ish-shī'jə [Heb. *yiššîyâ*]; AV ISHIJAH. A man of the household of Harim, named among those who, at Ezra's command, were induced to put away their "foreign wives" (Ezr. 10:31). Also called ASAIAS in 1 Esd. 9:32 (AV ASEAS, NEB ASAEAS).

ISSUE. Occurs with a variety of meanings:

(1) [Heb. *śîm, śûm* (Ezr. 5:17; 6:3), *nāṯan* (Est. 3:14f.; etc.), *yāṣā'* (Ezk. 47:1); Aram. *n^egaḏ* (Dnl. 7:10); Gk. *ekporeúomai* (Rev. 1:16; 4:5; 9:17f.; 19:15, 21), *ek* (1 Tim. 1:5; Rev. 16:13)]; AV also MAKE, GIVE, GO, PROCEED, etc.; NEB also "stream out," SPRING, "come out," etc. As a verb "issue" can mean "publish" a decree (Ezr. 5:17; 6:3; Est. 3:14f.; 4:8; 8:13f.; 9:14); it can also refer to the emission of water (Ezk. 47:1), fire and smoke (Dnl. 7:10; Rev. 9:17), lightning (Rev. 4:5), a sword (Rev. 1:16; 19:15, 21), spirits (Rev. 16:13), or love (1 Tim. 1:5) from a source.

(2) [Heb. *rē'šîṯ* (Dt. 21:17; Ps. 78:51; 105:36), *ṣ^epi'ôṯ* (Isa. 22:24), *zîrmâ* (Ezk. 23:20), *'aḥ^arîṯ* (Dnl. 12:8)]; AV also BEGINNING, CHIEF, END; NEB FIRST-BORN, SEED, etc. As a noun "issue" generally occurs in the sense of "offspring" or "semen" (Ezk. 23:20). In Dnl. 12:8, however, it means "final outcome" or "end."

(3) The AV frequently uses "issue" for a bodily DISCHARGE or HEMORRHAGE (e.g., Lev. 15:2ff.; Nu. 5:2; Mt. 9:20; Mk. 5:25; Lk. 8:43). N. J. O.

ISTALCURUS is-täl'ko͞or-əs [Gk. *Istalkouros*]. A name in 1 Esd. 8:40 corresponding to ZACCUR in Ezr. 8:14. LXX B has Istakalkos.

ISUAH. *See* ISHVAH.

ISUI. *See* ISHVI.

ITALA VERSION. *See* VERSIONS.

ITALIAN COHORT (AV ITALIAN BAND). *See* ARMY, ROMAN II.B; COHORT.

ITALY [Gk. *Italia*]. The name Italy appears four times in the NT: Acts 18:2; 27:1, 6; He. 13:24. The adjectival form is found in the appellation "Italian band" (*kalouménēs Italikēs,* Acts 10:1). Originally the name Italy was restricted to the extreme southern part of the Italian peninsula, the area now called Calabria. As early as Polybius, Italy was sometimes considered an appellation for all the country between the Tyrrhenian and Adriatic seas, and stretching from the Alps in the north all the way S to Sicily. The Italians (Lat. *Itali*), after whom the country is named, derive their name from a legendary ruler Italus (Dionysius i.12.35; Vergil *Aen.* i.533).

Like a fishback the Apennines run down the middle of Italy from modern Lombardy (once part of Cisalpine Gaul) to Sicily. The only navigable river is the Tiber, which slants across the upper middle section of the peninsula and flows through Rome.

Very little information is available about life from antiquity. The oldest inhabitants were the Ligurians and Iberians, closely related to the aborigines of Spain and Gaul. In the Late Bronze Age some Indo-European clans came with more advanced weapons and drove the early settlers, who were lake dwellers, into the background. They divided into three groups — the Latins, Samnites, and Umbrians — as they penetrated the peninsula. The Illyrian clans of the Apulian valleys and the Venetian plains gave them resistance. The Celts (Gauls) were the last invaders, and began to drive out the Etruscans on the west coast of central Italy (M. I. Rostovtzeff, *Rome* [Eng. tr. 1960], pp. 8f.).

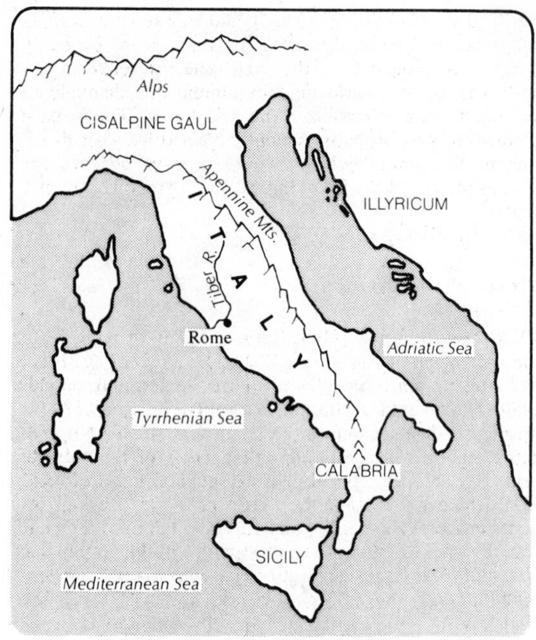

Archeological excavations have uncovered the most valid source of historical information about the culture and characteristics of the people. Pottery, art, and jewelry tell us that Greece influenced the culture through commerce and military training. No serious construction of the economic history from the 7th to the 4th cents. B.C. has been developed.

From a tendency toward democracy in the 4th cent. B.C., Rome through the threat of wars realized a need for a centralized government, and gave the senate governmental authority. From the Knights (class of businessmen), who were rivals to the senate, Octavian arose to be recognized as supreme ruler over Italy and Rome. The office was given the title of emperor, and later Octavian's name was changed to Augustus; he was in power when Paul was taken to Rome (Acts 27:1).

See also ROME. E. S. MAST

ITCH [Heb. *neṯeq* (Lev. 13:30-37); Gk. *thraúsma*; Heb. *gārāḇ,* Gk. *lichḗn* (Lev. 22:22; AV "scurvy"; NEB "scab"); Heb. *ḥāres,* Gk. *psṓra* (Dt. 28:27)]. In Lev. 13:30-37, *neṯeq* was part of a diseased condition affecting the scalp (AV "dry scall"; NEB "scurf"). Its presence indicated that the skin disease was malignant, and if after a fourteen-day period of isolation the ailment had spread, the sufferer was pronounced unclean. The "itch" seems to have been that of a fungus infestation such as ringworm (*favus*), a vegetable parasitic disease of the skin. *Alopecia areata,* a disease resulting in circumscribed bald patches, may also be indicated. In Lev. 22:22 the Hebrew refers to a skin disease affecting animals and marked by eczema and inflammation of the affected area. Most probably mange was indicated by the text. The reference in Dt. 28:27 was to some parasitic skin ailment that disqualified persons from membership in the priesthood. The disease in question was probably scabies, caused by a small organism, *Sarcoptes scabiei*, which burrows beneath the skin, especially that of the fingers, and is readily communicated.

See also DISEASE III.I. R. K. H.

ITHAI ith'ī. *See* ITTAI **2.**

ITHAMAR ith'ə-mär [Heb. *'îṯāmār*–'oasis of palms'(?)]. The fourth son of Aaron (Ex. 6:23; 28:1; 1 Ch. 6:3), Eleazar being the third, Nadab and Abihu the first and second. While Nadab and Abihu were prematurely cut off for offering strange fire before the Lord (Lev. 10:1f.; Nu. 3:4; 26:61), and Eleazar was appointed chief of the tribe of Levi (Ex. 6:23, 25) and ultimately succeeded Aaron (Ex. 28:1), Ithamar was made the treasurer of the offerings for the tabernacle (Ex. 38:21), and superintendent of the Gershonites and Merarites in the service of the tabernacle (Nu. 4:28, 33). A descendant of Ithamar, Daniel, is mentioned among the exiles who returned from Babylon (Ezr. 8:2). T. WHITELAW

ITHIEL ith'i-el [Heb. *'îṯî'ēl*–'God is with me'(?)].

1. A son of Jeshaiah of the tribe of Benjamin, mentioned among the inhabitants of Jerusalem in Nehemiah's day (Neh. 11:7).

2. The name is perhaps also found in the oracle of Agur (Prov. 30:1). *See* ITHIEL AND UCAL.

ITHIEL AND UCAL i'thē-əl, ōō'kal [Heb. *'îṯî'ēl wᵉ'uḵāl*] (Prov. 30:1). The names of two persons to whom Agur addressed his words. The text is obscure, however; such an introduction seems strange — nowhere else in Proverbs is the audience named. Although T. Mauch (*IDB, s.v.* "Ucal") points to "Surely you know" in v. 4 as evidence for retaining the proper names, several factors weaken the force of this observation. First, the LXX and Vulg. did not render the Hebrew words as proper names; rather, they translated them. Second, the verb is in the sing. in v. 4, and one might expect the pl. if the two persons of v. 1 are being addressed. Third, addresses like that of v. 4 need not have any specific previous referent; cf., e.g., 22:20f., 27; 26:12; 29:20. Thus several modern versions and many commentators prefer to repoint and redivide the Hebrew words to make sense of the consonantal text. For example, the prep. *lᵉ*, "to," is combined with *'îṯî*, and the phrase is revocalized *lā'îṯî* ("I am weary") *'ēl* ("O God") *wā'ēḵel* ("and worn out") (cf. NEB; NIV mg.; KD *in loc.*). As D. Kidner (*Proverbs* [*Tyndale OT Comms.*, 1964], p. 178) notes, this rendering introduces the theme of vv. 2-4 well. Less likely is the NAB's rendering, "I am not God, I am not God, that I should prevail" (cf. *BH*), though this at least fits the context better than M. Dahood's "I, El, prevail" or "I am strong, O El" (*Proverbs and Northwest Semitic Philology* [1963], p. 57). Although the comms. by C. H. Toy (*ICC*, 1899, pp. 519f., 526) and W. McKane (*OTL*, 1970, pp. 643-47) discuss the problem in some detail, they offer no satisfactory solution, and no consensus has yet been reached. G. A. L.

ITHLAH ith'lə [Heb. *yiṯlâ*]; AV JETHLAH. An unidentified town in the territory of Dan, named with Aijalon and Elon (Josh. 19:42).

ITHMAH ith'mä [Heb. *yiṯmâ*]. A citizen of the country of the Moabites, David's deadly enemies, yet mentioned as one of the king's thirty mighty men (1 Ch. 11:46).

ITHNAN ith'nan [Heb. *yiṯnān*]. A town in southern Judah mentioned along with Hazor and Ziph (Josh. 15:23), apparently the Ethnan of Jerome (*Onom.* 118.13). It has not been identified.

ITHRA ith'rə [Heb. *yiṯrā'*]. The father of Amasa, commanding general in the rebel army of Absalom. It seems that his wife was Abigail, a sister or half sister of King David (1 Ch. 2:17). She is called the sister of Zeruiah, Joab's mother (2 S. 17:25). In this passage Ithra is called an Israelite, but "Jether the Ishmaelite" in 1 Ch. 2:17. *See* JETHER.

ITHRAN ith'ran [Heb. *yiṯrān*].

1. A descendant of Seir the Horite, son of Dishon (Gen. 36:26; 1 Ch. 1:41).

2. One of the sons of Zophah of the tribe of Asher (1 Ch. 7:37).

ITHREAM ith'rē-əm [Heb. *yiṯrᵉ'ām*]. The sixth son born to David at Hebron. His mother's name was Eglah (2 S. 3:5; 1 Ch. 3:3).

ITHRITE ith'rīt [Heb. *yiṯrî*]. A family in Israel whose home was Kiriath-jearim (1 Ch. 2:53). Among the heroes of David, two are mentioned who belonged to this family, Ira and Gareb (2 S. 23:38; 1 Ch. 11:40).

ITTAH-KAZIN it-ə-kā'zin. *See* ETH-KAZIN.

ITTAI it'ī [Heb. *'ittay, 'îṯay*].

1. A Gittite or native of Gath, one of David's chief captains and most faithful friends during the rebellion of Absalom (2 S. 15:11-22; 18:2, 4, 12). The narrative reveals David's chivalrous and unselfish spirit in time of trouble, as well as the most self-sacrificing loyalty on the part of Ittai. He seems to have left his native city recently and joined David's army through personal attachment to the king. David rapidly promoted him. Hearing of Absalom's rebellion and approach to Jerusalem, he fled with David. The latter remonstrated and urged him to go back and join Absalom, as he was a foreigner and in exile. His interests were in the capital and with the king; there was no reason why he should be a fugitive and perhaps suffer the loss of everything; it was better for him, with his band of men, to put himself and them at the service of Absalom, the new king. Ittai, with a double oath, absolutely refused to go back, but would stand by David until the last. Remonstrance being useless, the monarch ordered him across the river, doubtless glad that he had such a valiant warrior and faithful friend by his side. On mustering his hosts to meet Absalom, David made Ittai a chief captain with the intrepid Joab and Abishai. He doubtless did his part in the battle, and as nothing more is said of him it is possible that he fell in the fight.

2. A Benjaminite, one of David's thirty mighty men (2 S. 23:29; called Ithai in 1 Ch. 11:31). J. J. REEVE

ITURAEA i-tūr-ē'ə, it-oor-ē'ə [Gk. *Itouraioi, Ityraioi, Itouraia* (*xōra*)–'(land) of the Ituraeans']. A region along the Lebanon and Anti-Lebanon Ranges deriving its name from the Jetureans, an Arab tribe descended from Ishmael through JETUR (Gen. 25:15; 1 Ch. 1:31), who had formerly lived in Transjordan but had moved NE of Galilee either when overthrown by the Israelite tribes in Transjordan:

Reuben, Gad, and Manasseh (1 Ch. 5:18f.; Eupolemus attributes the conquest to David, Eusebius *Praep. ev.* ix.30) or, more likely, for better pastures if not because of the Nabateans. The Ituraeans were formidable archers according to Vergil (*Georgics* ii.448) and Lucan (*De bello civili* viii.514), notorious robbers according to Strabo (*Geog.* xvi.2.18, 20), and "of all tribes the most barbarous" according to Cicero (*Philippicae* ii.112; cf. 19; v.18).

By the end of the 2nd cent. B.C., the Ituraeans had apparently spread southward to upper Galilee. When the Hasmonean Judas Aristobulus (or rather his brother Antigonus at his command) set out to complete the conquest and Judaization of Galilee in 104 B.C., "he fought against the Ituraeans, annexed a large part of their land to Judea, and forced the inhabitants, if they wished to remain in their country, to submit to circumcision and live according to the laws of the Jews" (Josephus *Ant.* xiii.11.3 [318]), just as his father, John Hyrcanus, had earlier forced the Idumeans in the south (*Ant.* xiii.9.1; 15.4 [257f., 396]).

The subsequent, still fragmentary history of the remaining part(s) of the region may be summed up as follows. At the height of the Syrian civil wars culminating with the fall of the Seleucid kingdom and the coming of the Romans, the son of a certain Mennaeus, Ptolemy (*ca.* 85-40 B.C.), controlled among vast territories in the Lebanon "the mountainous country of the Ituraeans" with its capital at Chalcis, from where he terrorized Damascus (Strabo *Geog.* xvi.2.10; Josephus *BJ* i.4.8; 5.3; 9.2 [103, 115, 185f.]; *Ant.* xiii.15.2; 16.3 [392, 418]; xiv.7.4 [126]). He continued to rule the region after submitting to Pompey in 64 B.C. and paying an indemnity of 1000 talents (*Ant.* xiv.3.1f. [34-39]). His son Lysanias (40-36 B.C.), called king of the Ituraeans by Dio Cassius (*Hist.* xlix.32.5; cf. *Ant.* xiv.13.3 [330]), was killed at the instigation of Antony, who gave the domain with other territories to Cleopatra (*Ant.* xv.4.1 [91f.]; Plutarch *Antony* xxxvi.2). Following her death in 30 B.C., a certain Zenodorus (23-20 B.C.) leased the former domain of Lysanias and controlled harshly a number of principalities between Trachonitis and Galilee, leading Augustus to add certain of these principalities to the kingdom of Herod the Great; and upon the death of Zenodorus, the rest of his principalities were added (*BJ* i.20.4 [398-400]; ii.6.3 [95]; *Ant.* xv.10.1-3 [344f., 349-352, 359f.]). Herod in turn bequeathed the region to his son Philip (*Ant.* xvii.11.4 [319]), whose tetrarchy later became the initial kingdom of Herod Agrippa I, given to him by Gaius Caligula in A.D. 38 (*BJ* ii.9.6 [181]; *Ant.* xviii.6.10 [237]).

Another part of the region, the tetrarchy of ABILENE, which received its name from the city of Abila and was ruled for a time by another LYSANIAS (Lk. 3:1; cf. *CIG*, 4521, 4523), was added to the kingdom of Agrippa I in A.D. 41 by Claudius (*Ant.* xviii.6.10 [237]; xix.5.1 [275]; Dio Cassius *Hist.* lix.8.2), who also gave the central Ituraean city of Chalcis and its surroundings to a brother (later son-in-law) of Agrippa I, known as Herod of Chalcis (*BJ* ii.11.5 [217]). The kingdom of Chalcis passed in A.D. 50 to Herod Agrippa II (*BJ* ii.12.1 [223]; *Ant.* xx.5.2 [104]). In A.D. 53 Claudius deprived the young Agrippa of Chalcis and granted him instead the former tetrarchy of Philip and Lysanias' former tetrarchy of Abilene, along with Batanea and Trachonitis (*Ant.* xx.7.1 [138]). Upon the death of Agrippa II in A.D. 93, his kingdom was once more incorporated into the vast province of Syria, just as the Ituraean tetrarchy of Arca, which Gaius Caligula had granted to a certain Sohaemus in A.D. 38 (Dio Cassius *Hist.* lix.12.2), was incorporated earlier (Tacitus *Ann.* xii.23).

The dividing of the region by the Romans into various tetrarchies and principalities, and their occasional annexation to neighboring provinces, add to the difficulty of defining its boundaries.

A. TERIAN

IVAH ī'və. *See* IVVAH.

IVORY [Heb. *šēn*] (1 K. 10:18; 22:39; 2 Ch. 9:17; Ps. 45:8 [MT 9]; Cant. 5:14; 7:4 [MT 5]; Ezk. 27:6, 15; Am. 3:15; 6:4); NEB also "strong" (Ezk. 27:6); [*šenhabbîm*] (1 K. 10:22; 2 Ch. 9:21); [Gk. *elephántinos*] (Rev. 18:12). The Hebrew term *šēn* is a specialized use of the common noun for tooth. This is an appropriate designation for ivory, which is a kind of dentin constituting the tusks of some large mammals, most familiarly elephants, as the Greek term reflects. The biblical references to ivory are part of a large body of textual and archeological evidence illustrating the extent of highly skilled ivory carving in the ancient Near East during the first two millennia B.C.

Drawing of ivory plaque from Megiddo with Hittite figures (Oriental Institute, University of Chicago)

The single NT reference (Rev. 18:12) places ivory among special woods in the cargo for the symbolic Babylon; it occupies the same place in Assyrian and Babylonian royal tribute lists and building inscriptions. The hardness and grain of ivory required carving techniques similar to those of woodworking, and the two materials were used together, the ivory applied as inlay to wooden articles or attached to wooden foundations. The Canaanites, Phoenicians, and their neighbors in northern Syria were particularly adept in these skills, perhaps because they had access to local timber and to raw ivory from native elephant herds in the upper Euphrates region (until Assyrians hunted them to extinction about the 7th cent. B.C.) as well as from African and Indian sources through maritime trade. This concentration of materials, expertise, and sea commerce explains why most of the excavated second-millennium sites where Syro-Phoenician ivories have been found are in a narrow band along the eastern Mediterranean coast. Only under the Assyrians did the products of the Levantine ivory industry reach the interior in significant quantities.

The parallel passages in 1 K. 10:22 and 2 Ch. 9:21 use *šenhabbîm* to designate the raw ivory tusks imported by Hiram of Tyre and Solomon in their overseas commercial ventures (cf. 1 K. 9:26-28, joint voyages from Ezion-geber to Ophir through the Red Sea). The Hebrew term has been explained as a contraction derived either from *šēn*

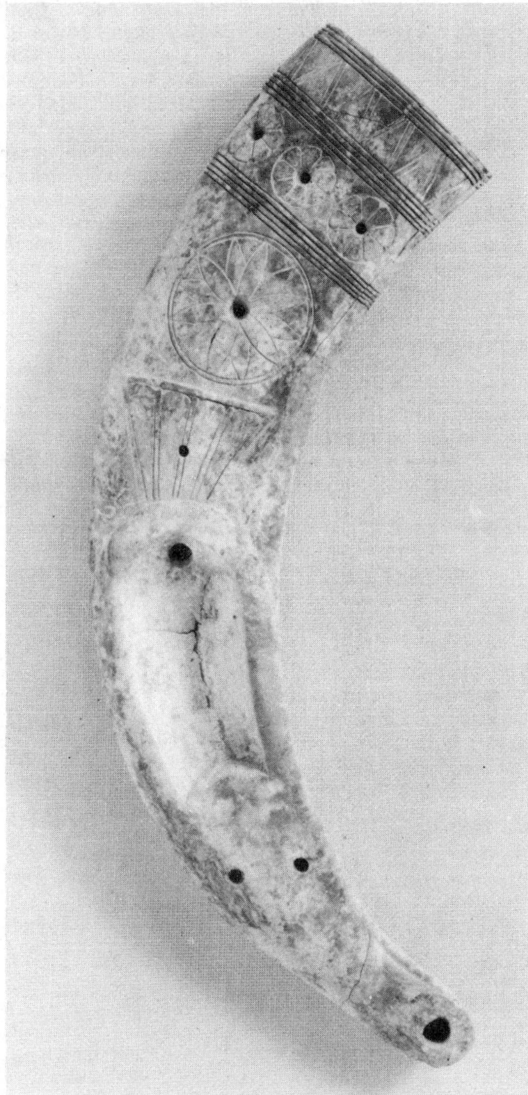

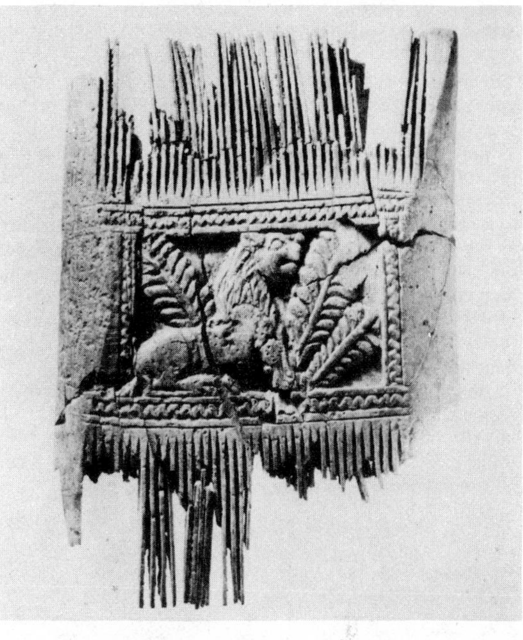

Ivory objects from Megiddo (Late Bronze II). Clockwise from left: incised tusk, double comb ornamented with a lion among trees, carved ivory bird heads, and griffin (Oriental Institute, University of Chicago)

IVORY

habbîm, "elephants' tooth" (*habbîm* understood as an otherwise unattested Hebrew form for elephants; cf. the LXX here [1 K. 10:22; 2 Ch. 9:21], *odóntes elephantínoi,* "elephants' teeth"), or from *šēn (wᵉ)hoḇnîm,* "ivory and ebony" (cf. Ezk. 27:15, *qarnôṯ šēn wᵉhoḇnîm,* "horns of ivory and ebony").

More than half of the OT references to ivory use *šēn,* the common noun without an article, suggesting a general reference to ivory. The lamentation over Tyre in Ezk. 27 twice mentions that Phoenician port's ivory interests, first as the inlaid decking of the metaphorical ship (v. 6), second as a payment from its coastal markets (v. 15). Solomon not only imported ivory but had a magnificent throne of it, overlaid with gold (1 K. 10:18-20; 2 Ch. 9:17-19). Although the text does not specify that Phoenician craftsmen were employed for making the throne (as they were for the temple, 1 K. 5), the design suggests that they were responsible for it. Ivory lions in the round, which could have stood at the armrests or steps of a throne, have been found at Samaria and Nimrûd, and the calf motif is familiar among Syro-Phoenician carvings of the period.

Ivory plaques detached from their original frames and even recognizable pieces of furniture have been excavated from other royal collections, including the footboard of a bed and a round table from Ugarit, a bedframe from Arslan Tash, screens from Nimrûd, and footstools from Zenjirli. A stone relief at Nineveh shows Ashurbanipal reclining on an elaborately carved couch, his queen seated nearby on a chair with footstool, as they share a ceremonial garden feast and review a parade of prisoners (cf. Ps. 149:5-9). Amos alludes to the furnishings of such a royal banquet in the oracle of woe "to those who lie upon beds of ivory, and stretch themselves upon their couches, and eat lambs from the flock . . ." (6:4). The Psalms refer to royal suites, furnished in ivory and paneled with carved plaques inlaid in cedar, as ivory palaces (45:8).

Smaller objects — cosmetic boxes, game boards, and figures in the round — were also carved from ivory. The lover in Cant. 5:14 is compared to a statue with a torso of ivory inset with lapis lazuli (NEB) or sapphires (RSV, AV). Fragments of several male ivory figures decorated with blue paste inlay and gilt were recovered from Nimrûd.

Ivory plaque, 7.5 cm. (2.9 in.) square, from the palace of Shalmaneser III at Nimrûd, 9th cent. B.C.: trellis work with floral designs (Royal Ontario Museum, Toronto)

Ivory female head used as a furniture or spoon ornament. From Megiddo, Late Bronze II (Oriental Institute, University of Chicago)

Some of the ivories buried in Mesopotamian sites may have come originally from the Hebrew courts: Menahem of Samaria is listed among the western tributaries who provided elephants' hides and ivory to Tiglath-pileser III, while Sennacherib boasts of having exacted "ivory beds, house chairs of ivory, elephants' hides, ivory (elephants' teeth)" from Hezekiah of Jerusalem (*ARAB,* II, § 284).

The remaining OT references to ivory use the definite article with the noun, *haššēn,* and all describe buildings. In the formulaic report of the close of Ahab's reign, "the ivory house which he built" receives special notice (1 K. 22:39). The fragmentary remains of its carvings have been excavated at Samaria, and they show the Syro-Phoenician style one might expect in the palace of the son-in-law of a a Sidonian king (1 K. 16:31). Similarly, the building inscriptions of Tiglath-pileser III, Sargon, Sennacherib, and Esarhaddon conventionally designate their royal houses by their materials: e.g., "Palaces of ivory, maple, boxwood, mulberry, cedar, cypress, juniper, pine and pistachio-wood, I erected herein for my royal dwelling" (Sargon, *ARAB,* II, § 102). The features of a queenly maiden are compared to recognizable landmarks (Cant. 7:4): the ivory tower, pools of Heshbon, the tower of Lebanon. In Amos' prophecy that "the houses of ivory shall perish" (3:15), the royal house in its literal and figurative senses is clearly the target. The historical counterpart to this literary practice of using the destruction of ivory to symbolize the monarch's downfall may have been the deliberate gathering and burning of royal ivory furnishings from the sacked palace, as reported by excavators of Megiddo, Alalakh, Ugarit, and Nimrûd.

In their participation in the international ivory trade, the Hebrew monarchs evidently favored the popular Phoenician motifs, which were religious at least in their origins. Stylized sacred trees, guardian sphinxes (cherubim), adapted Egyptian deities, cow and calf, the woman at the window, stags drinking, lions in the round — these characteristic designs brought the iconography of the Canaanite and Phoenician cultures into Israelite temple and palace.

Bibliography.–R. D. Barnett, *PEQ,* 71 (1939), 4-19; *Catalogue of the Nimrud Ivories* (1957); J. W. and G. M. Crowfoot, *Early Ivories from Samaria* (1938); C. Decamps de Mertzenfeld, *Inventaire commenté des ivoires phéniciens et apparentés découverts dans le Proche-Orient* (1954); G. Loud, *Megiddo Ivories* (1939); M. E. L. Mallowan, *Nimrud and Its Remains* (1966); I. J. Winter, *Iraq,* 38 (1976), 1-22.

E. B. JOHNSTON

IVORY TOWER [Heb. *migdal haššēn*]. In Cant. 7:4 (MT 5) the neck of Shulammite is compared in whiteness and stateliness to a (or the) tower of ivory. The definite article may suggest that the comparison is with some actual tower in or near Jerusalem, but probably the language is simply figurative (cf. M. Pope, *Song of Songs* [*AB,* 1977], pp. 624f.).

IVVAH iv'ə [Heb. *ʿiwwâ*; Gk. *Aba*]; AV IVAH; also **AVVA** av'ə [Heb. *ʿawwāʾ*; Gk. *Aia*] (2 K. 17:24); AV AVA. A city-state in Syria captured by the Assyrians in the 8th cent. (2 K. 18:34; 19:13) along with Hamath, Arpad, Sepharvaim, and Hena. Of these, only Arpad and Hamath have been identified. Ivvah could be related to the modern site of ʿImm (older form Emma) between Aleppo and Antioch (cf. Isa. 37:13).

Ivvites were among the displaced persons who were brought into Palestine by the Assyrians after the deportation of the northern tribes of Israel (2 K. 17:24). Later they became infamous for making the pagan idols of "Nibhas and Tartak" (2 K. 17:31). Arguments against the historicity of the state of Ivvah (*see* HENA) are weakened by these concrete facts of captured city and king, deported people, and national gods. A. H. LEWIS

IVY [Gk. *kissós*]. The only mention of the word in all the sacred writings is in 2 Macc. 6:7 in connection with the oppression of the Jews by Antiochus Epiphanes. The plant referred to was the *Hedera helix*, which was sacred to Bacchus (Dionysus), the Greek god of wine and of the culture of the vine (cf. Euripides, *Bacchae, passim*). It was of ivy or of pine that the "perishable wreath" of the famous Isthmian games was made (1 Cor. 9:25)
J. HUTCHISON

IYE-ABARIM ī-yə-ab'-ə-rim [Heb. *ʿîyê hāʿᵃḇārîm*–'mounds of the Abarim']; AV IJE-ABARIM. A place occupied by the Israelites in their wanderings, located somewhere between Oboth and the Wâdī Zered (Nu. 21:11f.) on the border of Moab (Nu. 33:44). A site on the southeastern edge of Moab seems to be indicated, but no certain identification has yet been made. In Nu. 33:45 it is called IYIM.

IYIM ī'yim [Heb. *ʿîyîm*–'heaps, mounds' (Josh. 33:45)]; AV IIM. A short form of IYE-ABARIM.

IYYAR ē'yär [Heb. *'îyār*; Gk. *Iar*]. The second month of the Jewish year, corresponding to May. It is not mentioned in the Bible. *See* CALENDAR.

IYYON. *See* IJON.

IZEHAR iz'ə-här (Nu. 3:19, AV). *See* IZHAR.

IZHAR iz'här [Heb. *yiṣhār*].

1. The father of Korah (Nu. 16:1), descended from a Kohathite Levite of this name, whose descendants formed a family in the tribe of Levi (Ex. 6:18, 21; Nu. 3:19, 27; 1 Ch. 6:18, 38). AV also IZEHAR (Nu. 3:19).

2. A descendant of Judah whose mother's name was Helah (1 Ch. 4:7; AV, NEB JEZOAR).

IZHARITES iz'hə-rīts [Heb. *yiṣhārî*]. The descendants of Izhar son of Kohath and grandson of Levi (Nu. 3:19, 27; 1 Ch. 26:23).

IZLIAH iz-lī'ə [Heb. *yizlîʿâ*]; AV, NEB JEZLIAH. A son of Elpaal, of the tribe of Benjamin (1 Ch. 8:18).

IZRAHIAH iz-rə-hī'ə [Heb. *yizraḥyâ*–'Yahweh appears,' or 'Yahweh shines']. A descendant of Issachar, grandson of Tola, only son of Uzzi (1 Ch. 7:3); same as Jezrahiah (Neh. 12:42, RSV, AV), leader of the temple singers.

IZRAHITE iz'rə-hīt [Heb. *yizrāḥ*–'rising, shining']. Shamhuth the captain of the fifth monthly course (1 Ch. 27:8) is called an "Izrahite." The name may be derived from the town or family of Izrah, but more likely is a corruption of the word "Zerahite," descendant of Zerah of Judah.

IZRI iz'rī [Heb. *yiṣrî*]. A man of the "sons of Jeduthun," leader of the fourth band of musicians, who served in the sanctuary (1 Ch. 25:11). He may be the Zeri mentioned in v. 3.

IZZIAH iz-ī'ə [Heb. *yizzîyâ*–'Yahweh purifies']; AV JEZIAH, EDDIAS. One of the faithful Jews who put away their foreign wives. He belonged to the family of Parosh (Ezr. 10:25; 1 Esd. 9:26; NEB JEDDIAS).

J. *See* CRITICISM II.D.

JAAKAN jā'ə-kən [Heb. *ya'ᵃqān*] (1 Ch. 1:42); AV JAKAN. The third son of Ezer, a Horite. The text is uncertain, however, and seems to lack the necessary conjunction *wᵉ*, "and." Thus *BH* and *BHS* suggest reading *wᵉya'ᵃqān* or *wa'ᵃqān* (so NEB, "and Akan") on the basis of some MS evidence and the parallel Gen. 36:27. *Wᵉya'ᵃqān* seems preferable in both texts, since this form also occurs in Nu. 33:31f. (Bene-jaakan) and Dt. 10:6 (Beeroth Bene-jaakan). That Gen. 36:27 is not without problems is clear from the LXX, which has *kaí Iōukam kaí Oukan*, perhaps the result of a conflation of variants or a marginal gloss that has crept into the text. G. A. L.

JAAKOBAH jā-ə-kō'bə [Heb. *ya'ᵃqōḇâ*–for meaning *see* JACOB **1**]. A Simeonite prince (1 Ch. 4:36).

JAALA jā'ə-lə [Heb. *ya'ᵃlā'*] (Neh. 7:58); **JAALAH** [Heb. *ya'ᵃlâ* (Ezr. 2:56); Gk. *Ieēli* (1 Esd. 5:33)]; AV also JEELI. The name of a family of returned exiles.

JAALAM jā'ə-ləm. *See* JALAM.

JAANAI jā'ə-nī. *See* JANAI.

JAAR jā'ər [Heb. *ya'ar*–'forest' or 'wood']. Only once taken as a proper name: "We found it in the fields of Jaar" (Ps. 132:6). It may be a shortened form of the name KIRIATH-JEARIM, where the ark had rested twenty years.

JAARE-OREGIM jā'ə-rə-ôr'ə-jim [Heb. *ya'ᵃrê 'ōrᵉgîm*]. In 2 S. 21:19, given as the name of a Bethlehemite, father of the ELHANAN who is said to have slain Goliath the Gittite (cf. 1 S. 17). The name is an evident scribal error in which the term *'ōrᵉgîm*, "weavers," was copied accidentally from the end of the verse. The name Jaare should be modified to correspond with the textual variant of 1 Ch. 20:5, Jair. *See* JAIR **4**.

JAARESHIAH jar-ə-shī'ə [Heb. *ya'ᵃrešyâ*]; AV JARESIAH. In 1 Ch. 8:27 a Benjaminite, son of Jeroham.

JAASAU jā'ə-sô. *See* JAASU.

JAASIEL jā'ā-zə-əl [Heb. *ya'ᵃśî'ēl*–'God makes'(?)]; AV JASIEL. In 1 Ch. 11:47, a Mezobaite, one of David's mighty men, probably the same as "the son of Abner" in 1 Ch. 27:21, a Benjaminite tribal prince of David.

JAASU jā'ə-sōō [Heb. *K ya'ᵃśû*; *Q ya'ᵃśāy*]; AV JAASAU. In Ezr. 10:37, one of those who had married foreign wives. The LXX translates the consonantal text as a verb, *kaí epoíēsan*, "and they did."

JAAZANIAH jā-az'ə-nī'ə [Heb. *ya'ᵃzanyāhû* (2 K. 25:23; Ezk. 8:11); *ya'ᵃzanyâ*–'Yahweh hears' (Jer. 35:3; Ezk. 11:1)].

1. In 2 K. 25:23, "son of the Maacathite," and one of the Judean "captains of the forces" who joined Gedaliah, the Babylonian governor appointed by Nebuchadrezzar over Judah, at Mizpah. He is the Jezaniah of Jer. 40:8; 42:1. Though not mentioned by name, he was presumably one of those captains who joined Johanan in his attack on Ishmael after the latter had slain Gedaliah (Jer. 41:11-18). He is also the Azariah of Jer. 43:2, a name also found in LXX B in 42:1. Jer. 43:5 relates how Johanan and his allies, Jaazaniah (= Azariah) among them, left Judah with the remnant and took up their abode in Egypt.

2. In Jer. 35:3, son of Jeremiah (not the prophet), and a chief of the Rechabite clansmen. Jeremiah used their loyalty to their ancestral tradition as an example as he preached to his own people.

3. In Ezk. 8:11, son of Shaphan, and one of the seventy men of the elders of Israel whom Ezekiel saw in a vision of Jerusalem offering incense to idols.

4. In Ezk. 11:1, son of Azzur, and one of the twenty-five men whom Ezekiel saw in his vision of Jerusalem, at the eastern door of the Lord's house, and against whose iniquity he was commanded to prophesy (11:1-13).

Excavations at Lachish have uncovered several letters dating from the 6th cent. B.C., one of which contained the name "Jaazaniah, son of Tob-Shillem." Obviously the name was fairly common in Palestine in the preexilic period. D. F. ROBERTS R. K. H.

JAAZER jā'ə-zər. *See* JAZER.

JAAZIAH jā-ə-zī'ə [Heb. *ya'ᵃziyāhû*–'Yahweh strengthens']. In 1 Ch. 24:26f., a Levite, "son" of Merari. But the MT is corrupt. LXX B reads Gk. *Ozeia*, which some take to suggest Uzziah (cf. 27:25). (See E. L. Curtis, comm. on the books of Chronicles [*ICC*, 1910], pp. 274f.)

JAAZIEL jā-ə-zī'əl [Heb. *ya'ᵃzi'ēl*–'God strengthens']. In 1 Ch. 15:18, a Levite, one of the musicians appointed to play upon instruments at the bringing up of the ark by David. Jaaziel should probably replace "Jeiel" in 1 Ch. 16:5, which seems to have been a transcriptional error.

JABAL jā'bəl [Heb. *yāḇāl*]. In Gen. 4:20, a son of Lamech by Adah. He was the earliest nomadic shepherd mentioned in the OT.

JABBOK jab'ək [Heb. *yabbōq*]. One of the main streams of Transjordan. Now known as the Wâdī Zerqā, from the blueness of its water, it rises near ʿAmmân, the biblical Rabbath-ammon, and flows north and then northwest; finally about due E of Shechem it turns west in an ever deepening gorge until it enters the Jordan Valley and flows into the Jordan just N of Adam. If we ignore its meanderings, the length of the Jabbok is about 100 km. (60 mi.).

In Nu. 21:24 it is given as the boundary of Sihon's kingdom; i.e., the upper course separated it from that of the Ammonites and the lower from the area claimed by Og king of Bashan. Under Israel the lower course ceased to form a boundary, except as part of the border between Gad and half Manasseh, though only in the hill country. On its course lay the important settlements of Succoth, Zarethan, Penuel, and Mahanaim.

Only in the story of Jacob does the Jabbok play any part (Gen. 32:22), but it is in the background of other events. Gideon's pursuit of the Midianites (Jgs. 7–8) must have passed that way, and somewhere near it Absalom met defeat and death (2 S. 18). Jephthah's defeat of Ephraim (Jgs. 12) was probably also in its vicinity.

H. L. ELLISON

River Jabbok in Transjordan (W. S. LaSor)

JABESH jā'besh [Heb. *yāḇēš*]. The father of Israel's King Shallum (2 K. 15:10, 13f.). Noth (*IP*, p. 244) suggests that this may be a place name, i.e., Shallum of Jabesh, an interpretation that the grammar allows (cf. Isa. 7:6, where "son of Tabeel" means a person from the land of Tabeel). Gray (*I & II Kings* [*OTL*, 2nd ed. 1970], pp. 620-23) modifies this idea by suggesting that Yasib be read for Jabesh (basically a simple transposition of the last two consonants in Hebrew). According to Gray, Yasib was located near Tappuah, which Menahem brutally destroyed (v. 16); Gray sees Menahem's only possible motivation for this unprecedented brutality as a retaliation against Shallum's hometown. Evidence for a town in this vicinity comes from the Samaria Ostraca (cf. J. Gibson, *Textbook of Syrian Semitic Inscriptions,* I [1971; repr. 1973], 12); Aharoni (*LBHG,* p. 325 n. 101) concludes that this town is to be identified with Yasuf near Tappuah, and may be intended in Josh. 17:7 (LXX *Iassib*; MT *yōšᵉḇê*, "inhabitants of"), where a place name does improve the sense (cf. the NEB and JB).

G. A. L.

JABESH jā'besh [Heb. *yāḇēš*]. A short form of JABESH-GILEAD.

JABESH-GILEAD jā'besh-gil'i-əd [Heb. *yāḇêš gilʿāḏ*–'dry place of Gilead']; also Jabesh. A city belonging to the half-tribe of Manasseh in the highlands E of the Jordan about 16 km. (10 mi.) SE of Beth-shan. It is situated beside the Wâdī Yâbis (Jabesh), which flows into the Jordan about 30 km. (20 mi.) S of the Sea of Galilee. Several OT passages refer to Jabesh-gilead.

The city was destroyed for its refusal to appear at the Mizpah assembly called by Israel to deal with Benjamin (Jgs. 21:8). Four hundred maidens were spared — to be given to Benjaminites for wives (Jgs. 21:14), lest Benjamin become extinct.

When Nahash king of Ammon threatened to put out the right eye of the men of Jabesh-gilead, Saul came to their rescue (1 S. 11:1-11). His act of mercy was not forgotten. When Saul was defeated on the slopes of Mt. Gilboa by the Philistines, and he and his sons were slain, the men of Jabesh-gilead trekked about 30 km. (20 mi.) by night to recover the decapitated bodies of Saul and his sons from the walls of Beth-shean (1 S. 31:12). They cremated the bodies and buried them with honor in Jabesh-gilead, where they remained until David ordered them exhumed and reinterred in the tomb of Saul's father Kish, at Zela in Benjaminite territory (2 S. 21:1-14; 1 Ch. 10:11f.).

When David learned of the courage of the men of Jabesh-gilead he commended them and promised them compensation (2 S. 2:5-7).

F. E. YOUNG

JABEZ jā'bez [Heb. *yaʿbēṣ*] (1 Ch. 4:9f.). The head of a family of Judah, noted for his honorable character. The popular explanation of his name is that his mother bore him in pain (Heb. *ʿōṣeḇ*); this play on words is continued in Jabez' prayer that God would keep him from pain (Heb. *ʿāṣaḇ*; cf. the NEB). J. Myers (*I Chronicles* [*AB,* 1965], p. 28) points out that this pericope, which rather abruptly appears in a somewhat continuous genealogy (but cf. vv. 14, 27), "may have been intended as a comment on ii 55 where Jabez is a place name."

JABEZ jā'bez [Heb. *yaʿbēṣ*] (1 Ch. 2:55). An unidentified town probably in the territory of Judah near Bethlehem, occupied by scribes.

JABIN jā'bin [Heb. *yāḇîn*–'one who is intelligent,' 'discerning'(?)]. The word may have been a hereditary royal title among the northern Canaanites (cf. the familiar usage of Heb. *parʿôh meleḵ-miṣrayim*).

1. The king of Hazor, the leading city in northern Palestine, who led an alliance against Joshua. He was defeated at the waters of Merom, his city was taken, and he was slain (Josh. 11:1-12).

2. The king of Canaan, who reigned (or had reigned) in Hazor. It is not clear whether he dwelt in Hazor or Harosheth, the home of Sisera the captain of his host at the time of the story narrated in Judges. He oppressed Israel in the days preceding the victory of Deborah and Barak. To the Israelites he must have been but a shadowy figure as compared with his powerful captain Sisera, for the song makes no mention of him and there is nothing to indicate that he even took part in the battle that freed Israel (Jgs. 4:2, 7, 17, 23f.; Ps. 83:9f. [MT 10f.]).

E. D. ISAACS

JABNEEL jab'nə-əl [Heb. *yaḇnᵉʾēl*–'God causes to build'; Gk. *Iabnēl*].

1. Also **JABNEH** jab'nə [Heb. *yaḇneh*–'he causes to

build'; Gk. *Iabnē*]; Josephus, Apoc., **JAMNIA** jam'ni-ə [Gk. *Iamneia*]; AV Apoc., NEB Apoc., also JEMNAAN (Jth. 2:28). A town on the northern border of Judah, about 6 km. (4 mi.) from the Mediterranean Sea on the Nahr Rubin. It had a port a short distance S of the river's mouth. In early times it was a Philistine city, but King Uzziah captured it for Judah and demolished its wall in his war against the Philistines (2 Ch. 26:6).

During the Hellenistic period its name was changed to Jamnia. It served as a Syrian stronghold against the Maccabees and was occupied by the Seleucid generals Georgias (1 Macc. 4:15; 5:58), Apollonius (10:69), and Cendebeus (15:40). Judas Maccabeus burned its harbor and fleet (2 Macc. 12:9); in his battles he found "consecrated tokens of the idols of Jamnia" under the clothing of the dead (2 Macc. 12:40). It was Simon, however, who finally conquered the town in 142 B.C. (Josephus *Ant.* xiii.6.7 [215]). Later Jamnia was under the jurisdiction of Alexander Janneus (*Ant.* xiii.15.4 [395]).

In 62 B.C. Pompey joined Jamnia to the province of Syria (*Ant.* xiv.4.4 [75]), after which Gabinius ordered the city to be rebuilt (*BJ* i.8.4 [166]). Caesar Augustus restored Jamnia to Herod, who presented it to his sister Salome with 5000 drachmas of silver (*Ant.* xvii.8.1 [189]); she bequeathed it to Julia the wife of Augustus (*Ant.* xviii.2.2 [31]; *BJ* ii.9.1 [167]).

Before the fall of Jerusalem, according to talmudic tradition, Vespasian gave Rabban Johanan ben Zakkai permission to found a *Yeshiva* (academy) at Jamnia. (The title "Rabban" ["our master"] was reserved for the rabbinic patriarch or head of the academy [Baron].) After Titus sacked Jerusalem (A.D. 70), the Sanhedrin was transferred to Jamnia (*BJ* ii.16.1f.), where it remained until the Bar Cochba revolt in A.D. 132. It became the hub of Jewish spiritual and intellectual life, leading to significant internal reforms. Under Johanan's leadership an assembly of Jewish scholars met there in A.D. 90 to make consequential decisions relating to the canon of the OT (*see* CANON OF THE OT II.D.3).

The Crusaders conquered the city, giving it the name Ibelin. It remained a commercial center of some importance during the Middle Ages.

The site is represented by the modern city of Yebnā, belonging to the state of Israel; in 1948 it was colonized by Jewish immigrants. Its population is about 2500.

2. A town of Naphtali (Josh. 19:33). The site is likely modern Yemmā, about 6 km. (4 mi.) SW of the Sea of Galilee.

Bibliography.–S. W. Baron, *Social and Religious History of the Jews* (8 vols., 2nd ed. 1952); M. I. Dimont, *Jews, God, and History* (1962); S. Landman and B. Efron, *Story Without End* (1949).

K. G. JUNG

JABNEH (2 Ch. 26:6). *See* JABNEEL **1.**

JACAN jā'kən [Heb. *ya'kān*] (1 Ch. 5:13); AV JACHAN. A chief of a family from Gad.

JACHIN jā'kən [Heb. *yāḵîn*–'he will establish'].

1. The fourth son of Simeon (Gen. 46:10; Ex. 6:15; Nu. 26:12). In 1 Ch. 4:24 his name is given as "Jarib" (cf. AV mg.). "Jachinites," the patronymic of the family, occurs in Nu. 26:12

2. Head of the twenty-first course of priests at the time of David (1 Ch. 24:17). It is used as a family name in 1 Ch. 9:10 and Neh. 11:10, where some of the course are included in the list of those who, having returned from Babylon, willingly accepted the decision of the lot, and abandoned their rural retreats to become citizens and guardians of Jerusalem (Neh. 11:1f.). J. CRICHTON

JACHIN jā'kən **AND BOAZ** bō'az [Heb. *yāḵîn*–'he will establish'; *bō'az*–'in it is strength' (1 K. 7:15-22; 2 Ch. 3:15-17)]. These were the names of the two bronze pillars that stood before the temple of Solomon. The precise purpose of the pillars is uncertain, since there is no explicit biblical statement about their function. They were probably not used to support the building. They may have been the metal equivalents of the sacred wooden poles among the cultic equipment of Canaanite shrines. Albright suggested that they functioned as cressets or giant incense stands, after the fashion of those depicted on some Roman coins. Such pillars were often inscribed, and since 2 K. 11:14; 23:3 mention the king standing by the pillars, a dynastic use similar to the inscribed pillar of the Sumerian ruler Gudea at Lagash may be reflected.

A difficulty arises concerning the height of the pillars. The writers in Kings and Jeremiah affirm that the pillars before the porch were each 18 cubits (8.2 m., 27 ft.) high (1 K. 7:15; Jer. 52:21), while the Chronicler states that they were 35 cubits (16 m., 52.5 ft.) (2 Ch. 3:15). Various methods have been suggested to reconcile this discrepancy, but it is more probable that there is a corruption in the Chronicler's number.

On the construction of the pillars and their capitals, *see* TEMPLE. At the final capture of Jerusalem they were destroyed, and the metal of which they were composed was sent to Babylon (2 K. 25:13). The two pillars are represented in Ezekiel's ideal temple (Ezk. 40:49).

Similar columns have been excavated in front of temples at Tyre, Khorsabad, and elsewhere. At Khorsabad, a cylindrical bronze pillar nearly 9 m. (30 ft.) in length was unearthed, very close to the dimensions of the Jachin and Boaz pillars. At Hazor, two basalt pillars were recovered from each side of a temple entrance, but these were integrated into the total structure.

Bibliography.–R. B. Y. Scott, *JBL*, 58 (1939), 143ff.; *ARI*, pp. 138ff.; H. G. May, *BASOR*, 88 (Dec. 1942), 19ff. R. K. H.

JACINTH jā'sinth. *See* STONES, PRECIOUS.

JACKAL [Heb. *tannîm* (cf. Arab. *tînân*–'wolf,' *tinnîn*–'sea monster')]; AV DRAGONS; NEB also WOLF, SEA SERPENT; [*tannîn*] (Lam. 4:3); AV "sea monsters"; NEB "whales"; [*šû'āl*] (Ps. 63:10 [MT 11]; Lam. 5:18); AV FOX. In Mal. 1:3 the NEB follows the LXX *dómata* ("dwellings"), and the RSV follows the MT. A member of the carnivorous *Canidae* family.

The jackal (from Pers. *shaghal*), *Canis aureus*, is found throughout the Mediterranean except in western Europe. It ranges southward to Abyssinia, and eastward, in southern Asia, to India. It is smaller than a large dog, has a moderately bushy tail, and is reddish brown with dark shadings above. It is cowardly and nocturnal. Like the fox, it is destructive to poultry, grapes, and vegetables, but is less fastidious and readily devours the remains of others' feasts. Jackals generally go about in small companies. Their peculiar howl may frequently be heard in the evening and at any time during the night. It begins with a high-pitched, long-drawn-out cry, which is repeated two or three times, each time in a higher key than before. Finally there are several short, loud, yelping barks. When one raises the cry others often join in. Jackals are not infrequently confused with foxes. They breed freely with dogs. In Ps. 63:10; Lam. 5:18, the reference appears to be to the fox, whether the northern Palestinian *Vulpus flavescens* or the *Vulpus niloticus* found in southern Palestine.

See also WOLF; ZOOLOGY. R. K. H.

JACKAL'S WELL [Heb. *'ên hattannîn;* LXX Gk. *pēgḗ tṓn sykṓn*–'fountain of the figs']; AV DRAGON WELL.

Wooden funerary chest from the tomb of Tutankhamen with the Egyptian god Anubis as a jackal (Service des musées, Cairo)

A well or spring in the valley of Hinnom between the Valley Gate and the Dung Gate (Neh. 2:13). No such source exists in the Wâdī er-Rabâbi (*see* HINNOM, VALLEY OF) today, though it is very probable that a well sunk to the rock in the lower parts of this valley might strike a certain amount of water trickling down the valley bottom. It probably received its name from the jackals which frequented the locality, much as the pariah dogs did in later times. *See* JERUSALEM III.F.2.b.

JACOB jā'kəb [Heb. *yaʿ"qōḇ*–(see below); Gk. *Iakōb*].

1. An OT patriarch, son of Isaac and father of the twelve eponymous ancestors of the tribes of Israel.

- I. Significance of the Name
- II. Life of Jacob
  - A. Early Life in Canaan
  - B. To Paddan-aram
  - C. Return to Canaan
  - D. To Egypt
- III. Jacob's Religion
  - A. Background
  - B. Jacob's Growth; First Crisis
  - C. Second Crisis
  - D. Third Crisis
  - E. Fourth Crisis
  - F. Fifth Crisis and Triumph
  - G. Israel: Man and Nation
- IV. References Outside Genesis
  - A. OT
  - B. NT
- V. Modern Interpretations of Jacob
  - A. Documentary Theories
  - B. Views of Alt and Noth
  - C. View of Albright
  - D. Summary

The history of Jacob's life has been preserved in Gen. 25–50. There are many opinions about the form and compilation of these stories (see V below), but for the purposes of this study they will be considered as authentic records of historical events. A century of archeological exploration, combined with the study of documents from the period in which the patriarchs must have lived, has shown that Genesis reflects accurately the social conditions of the time. This information enables parts of the biography of Jacob to be better understood. Evidence quoted as contemporary with Jacob is taken from material of the 18th and 17th cents. B.C.

I. Significance of the Name.–Two other names from the same root are found in the OT, Akkub and Jaakobah. It has long been known that a similar name was also in use in ancient Babylonia. Further discoveries of many more contemporary documents indicate that it is one of a large group of names borne by the West Semites who gained control of Mesopotamia at the beginning of the 2nd millennium B.C. "Jacob-el" (*yaʿ"qub-il*) occurs not only in Babylonia (e.g., Kish and Khafadje) but also on the mid-Euphrates at ʿAna and in the north at Chagar-Bazar. Several other names with the same root are recorded from Mari and other sites. Egyptian sources provide contemporary examples of Asiatic slaves with Semitic names, including some formed from *ʿāqaḇ*. An inscription of Thutmose III (*ca.* 1450 B.C.) mentions a place in Palestine named *yaʿ"qub-el*. One of the major rulers of the Hyksos period was named *yaʿ"qub-her*. At a later period such names are found in the Palmyrene inscriptions.

The root *ʿqb*, meaning "heel," is found in Arabic and Assyrian as well as in Hebrew. From this basic noun was derived a simple verb "follow closely," with various nuances. In Jer. 9:4 it has the connotation of "overtaking" (cf. 17:9; Ps. 49:6 [MT 7]). Yet it may equally have a more favorable significance, "follow closely" and then "guard, protect," as in Sabean (cf. Job 37:4, "restrain").

There can be little doubt that the name *yaʿ"qub-il* had the sense of "protection," perhaps as a prayer uttered at the birth of the child, "May God protect (him)" (so *FSAC*, p. 245). "Jacob" would be an abbreviated form of the name. According to G. R. Driver (*Problems of the Hebrew Verbal System* [1936]), however, *yaʿ"quḇ* can be interpreted as a past tense as well as an imperfect (future). "God has protected" is a plausible translation of the name, one especially suitable if the birth had been difficult (cf. Gen. 25:22). In Jacob's case the circumstances of his birth were likely to give rise to an allusive wordplay upon a current name, for he "grasped the heel" of his brother (25:26).

II. Life of Jacob.–"A wandering Aramean was my father" (Dt. 26:5). This is an apt description of Jacob's history, which may be considered in four sections according to his place of residence.

A. Early Life in Canaan. The conception of Isaac's sons is remarkable in that it did not occur until twenty years after his marriage to Rebekah. As Abraham had been required to exercise faith in the promise of an heir, so was Isaac. The peculiar nature of his birth may have given Jacob his name, but even earlier he was designated as the chosen son through whom the promise given to Abraham should pass. Although born in Canaan, he was racially distinct, being the grandson of a man from Ur of the Chaldees, a Semite among the descendants of Ham.

The relationship of Esau and Jacob, twin brothers and full-born sons of Isaac, could not be eased by such a separation as divided Isaac and Ishmael. Later teachings (e.g., Mal. 1:2f.) show that it was by the sovereign will of God that one was chosen over the other. The supremacy of God over human customs was exemplified by the choice of Jacob, the younger son. The contrast between the two brothers may be seen as the contrast between the agriculturalist and the nomad-hunter who lives "from hand to mouth." These were the characteristics of the later nations of Israel and Edom. Esau's thoughtlessness lost him his birthright (the privilege of the firstborn son to inherit a double share of the paternal estate), thus allowing

Jacob the material superiority. His equally heedless marriage to local women of Hittite stock (Gen. 26:34) rendered him unsuitable to become the father of the chosen people. Nevertheless, Isaac intended to bestow the blessing of the firstborn upon Esau. The oracle given to Rebekah before the birth of her sons (25:23) probably encouraged her to counter Isaac's will and to gain the blessing for her favorite son by a fraud. The blessing that was given to Jacob conveyed the status of head of the family, apparently apart from the status of heir. Esau had disposed of this many years before, an action comparable to the sale of a birthright recorded at Nuzi. The blessing, once pronounced, was irrevocable; and so Jacob was sent to the safety of Rebekah's home until Esau should forgive him.

B. To Paddan-aram. Jacob was well over forty years old when he left home, for Esau had already married at the age of forty (Gen. 26:34; 27:46). The journey from Beer-sheba may be reckoned, however, as the commencement of his life as an individual. He had received the paternal blessing, and doubtless knew of the God who had made great promises to his father and to his grandfather; yet it was not until he slept at Luz that he realized that he was required to participate in the fulfillment of these promises. He was following the road to the north along the central hills when night fell, and he lay down with a convenient stone as his pillow. The text does not indicate that he had arrived at a recognized shrine, although Abraham had built an altar in that region (12:8) and archeological evidence suggests that it was an ancient holy place (*see* BETHEL **1**). In the dream God revealed Himself to Jacob and renewed the promise to him by His name Yahweh, the name in which the promise had first been given. The traveler was given reassurance for his journey and of his eventual return. The erection of a stone pillar, in this case only a small boulder, was a common practice for the commemoration of some notable event. For Jacob this place was henceforth sanctified as "the gate of heaven" where God first communicated with him. It was for him Beth-el, "the dwelling of God."

Jacob moved northward to the "fields of Aram" (*see* PADDAN-ARAM). The relatives of Bethuel were evidently prosperous citizens of Haran who cultivated the land surrounding the town in the valley of the Jullab and pastured their flocks on the hills. Jacob was welcomed into his mother's family. An agreement was made that he should give seven years of service and then take as his wife his cousin Rachel, whom he had first met at the well outside the town. A partially comparable transaction is known from NUZI, where a man entered into servitude for seven years in return for a wife; but there the marriage probably took place at the beginning of the time. When the day of Jacob's marriage arrived, Rachel's father Laban substituted his elder daughter Leah, on the plea of a local custom that the elder was always wed first. Perhaps the narrator knew of another reason: Leah had "weak eyes" (Gen. 29:17), i.e., she was not beautiful, so it might have been more difficult to find a suitable husband for her (cf. E. Speiser, comm. on Genesis [*AB*, 1964], p. 225). After the week of celebration had passed, Rachel also was given to Jacob. He had to promise another seven years of service in return. Jacob remained in Laban's employ for six years after he had worked out his contract in order to earn sufficient capital for the support of his family.

Leah bore his first four sons (Reuben, Simeon, Levi, and Judah). Rachel, jealous of her sister since she herself was barren and eager to remove that reproach, gave her maid Bilhah to her husband. By this means, which was an accepted practice at the time (cf. Abraham and Hagar), any child born would be counted as Rachel's (note 30:3). The two sons borne by Bilhah were named by Rachel, as if they were her own, Dan and Naphtali. Leah then did likewise with her maid Zilpah, who bore two sons, named by her mistress Gad and Asher. At this juncture Reuben, Leah's firstborn and now about twelve years old, found mandrakes, which he brought to his mother. Rachel purchased this herb from her sister for its supposed aphrodisiac qualities. As a result of the bargain, Leah bore two more sons to Jacob, Issachar and Zebulun, and at some time a daughter Dinah. Then at last Rachel gave birth to her first son Joseph.

Now Jacob pressed for permission to return to Canaan. Laban could not afford to lose so good a herdsman and offered him any wage he cared to name. Yet even when Jacob had suggested his reward, Laban tried to avoid payment. The evasion was overcome by Jacob's experience with the flocks. He succeeded in breeding fine sheep of the type he had asked from Laban, while his father-in-law was left with inferior stock. This prosperity aroused the jealousy of Laban's own sons and of Laban himself. Rachel and Leah supported their husband when he related to them the divine command to return to his father's home. They claimed that their father had not given them any dowry but had spent it instead, treating them as foreigners.

C. Return to Canaan. Jacob departed while Laban and his sons were away shearing sheep in the hills. Thereby he gained a two-day head start, and it was not until he reached the highlands of Gilead that Laban overtook him. The seven days indicated as the time taken by Laban's party to cover about 650 km. (400 mi) from Haran to Gilead are within the capabilities of good riding camels (*see* CAMEL). Jacob, with his family and his flocks, took a little longer. Laban complained that he had had no opportunity to bid farewell to his daughters with the accustomed feasting. More important, he wanted to find the "gods" that had been stolen (31:30, 32). These "gods" (Heb. *t^e^rāpîm*, 31:19, 34) were almost certainly small metal or terra-cotta figures of deities such as are commonly found in the ruins of ancient towns. Possession of these images was vested in the head of the family, according to evidence from Nuzi. Certain texts specify that they are to pass to the son of the owner upon the latter's decease, rather than to an adopted son, even if he has been made principal heir. Rachel's theft can now be seen as an attempt to obtain for her husband the status of head of the household. Laban's anxiety arose partly from this consideration and partly from the loss of the magical protection they were thought to afford. This value may well have been in Rachel's mind, too, as she took them with her at the outset of a long journey. Divine command prevented Laban from using force against Jacob, and his daughter's ingenuity deprived him of his gods.

No fault could be found in Jacob's conduct in Haran either. In his own defense (31:36-42) he mentioned that he had not eaten any of Laban's rams and had himself replaced those animals seized by wild beasts. Records from Nuzi describe the prosecution of shepherds who had made their own use of their masters' flocks. The Babylonian laws of Hammurabi (*ca.* 1750 B.C.) impose a fine of ten times the value of the animal taken on a shepherd convicted of such an offense. By the same laws, however, the loss of an animal killed by a marauding lion is to be borne not by the herdsman but by the owner (§§ 265-67).

Laban could do little but suggest a pact of friendship with his son-in-law. He proposed as terms of the treaty that Jacob should neither ill-treat his wives nor marry any other women, a clause often found in marriage records of this time. Moreover, the site of the covenant was to be a boundary which neither party should cross with evil intent. Ancient treaties frequently stipulate that rulers of states should not permit raids from their territory into the neighboring country and that they should be responsible for the punishment of any of their subjects who did so raid. Such treaties were solemnized by the naming of various important deities as witnesses and the deposit of a copy in a temple (*see* COVENANT [OT] II). The covenant of Jacob and Laban was ratified solely by the invocation of the God of Abraham and of their common ancestor Terah. If either Jacob or Laban broke the terms of the agreement, the curse of God would fall upon him. The cairn and the pillar were visible expressions of the treaty, reminding them of it if ever they passed that way again. Stone slabs, simple boulders, rough-hewn monoliths, and carefully carved stelae have been discovered throughout the ancient Near East. Some are isolated on a hillside; some are grouped in a shrine or temple; all originally commemorated a notable event or person. When a treaty was to be recorded, a picture was carved, on some occasions, representing the contracting parties sharing a meal to indicate their unanimity and good faith, as Jacob and his kin ate together in Gilead (31:54).

The parting from Laban marked another stage in Jacob's development. He was now head of his own household. He also climbed to a higher plane of spiritual experience. An encounter with angels at Mahanaim impressed upon him the might of the God who protected him, encouraging him for the journey southward to meet Esau. His brother's seemingly hostile advance prompted a call for clear evidence of God's guarding. Shrewdly, he sent a handsome gift to his brother and strategically divided his retinue into two parts; so large had his following become that each would be able to defend itself, or to escape if the other was captured. When all had crossed the stream of the Jabbok, Jacob was hindered by a stranger. The two struggled without one gaining advantage on the other, until the adversary dislocated Jacob's hip. The disabled man still refused to release his antagonist, but, clinging to him, demanded his blessing. This could not be given until the stranger knew Jacob's name. By telling it, Jacob acknowledged his defeat. His opponent, himself incognito, could command him as an individual. He emphasized his superiority by renaming the patriarch. No longer was he the man whose name had an unfavorable connotation.

A ford in the Jabbok River near the traditional scene of Jacob's wrestling with the angel (W. S. LaSor)

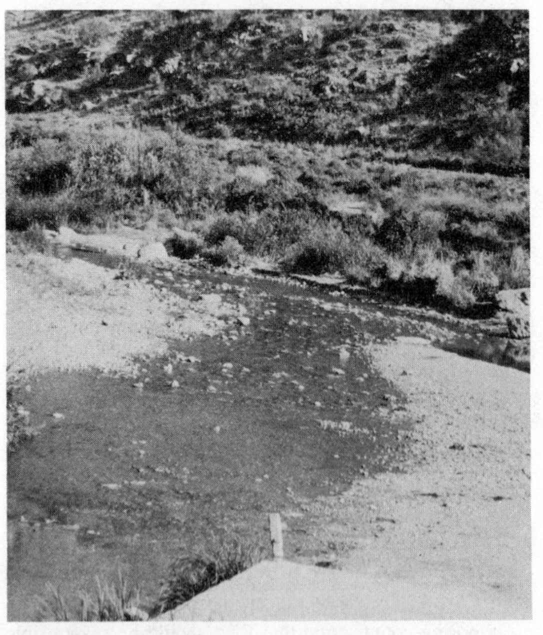

He became Israel, the one on whose behalf "God strove" or "God strives" and with whom "God strove." The withholding of the adversary's name, perhaps, caused Jacob to realize whom he had met. So Jacob called the place Peniel (Heb. *p*[e]*nî'ēl,* "face of God"), "For I have seen God face to face, and yet my life is preserved" (32:30 [MT 31]).

Jacob's fear of meeting his brother proved groundless. Esau was content to forget the wrongs of the past and to share his life with his brother. The juncture of their two households would bring them greater security and standing among the alien peoples around them. As two men of so contrary natures were unlikely to live together long in harmony, Jacob chose the better course in turning westward, leaving the road to Edom.

Succoth was the first halting place before the Jordan was crossed. The length of his stay there is not indicated. It may be that the cattle were breeding and it was necessary to stop and provide shelter (the "booths") for them.

Now Jacob entered the Promised Land. It was a natural course for him to follow the valley of the Wâdī Fâr'ah, which joins the Jordan almost opposite Succoth, and so penetrate into the hill country. In Canaan the patriarch was landless, a wanderer, the type of person called Ḫabiru, or 'Apiru, in ancient texts (*see* HABIRU). He traveled until he reached a place of good pasture where he might settle for a time. The town of Shechem was well established in the center of the area, and it was from the rulers of this place that Jacob purchased a plot of land on which he pitched his tent and built an altar. Inevitably the family chosen by God was brought into contact with the local population, of which the ruling class at least were apparently of non-Semitic, Hurrian stock (*see* HURRIANS). The son of the city's ruler was attracted to Jacob's daughter and took her by force. Although the prince, Shechem, afterward made an honorable proposal of marriage, this act alone could not restore amity between the clans. Jacob's sons demanded that the Shechemites be circumcised before intermarriage could be permitted. The narrator comments that the brothers "replied deceitfully" (34:13); therefore it may be supposed that they understood that more than a physical sign was required to distinguish the inheritors of the promise from their neighbors. The leading citizens of Shechem all followed their lord in submitting to circumcision, motivated, no doubt, by the possibility of absorbing the "Hebrews" and adding their property to their own. While recovering from this surgery, they were incapable of defending themselves against Simeon and Levi, who killed them to avenge their sister. This treacherous deed, however effective in overcoming the evil that caused it and in preventing the adulteration of the tribe, was roundly condemned by Jacob (34:30; 49:5-7; cf. 34:31).

For safety's sake, Jacob had to leave the domain of Shechem. He was instructed by God to return to Bethel and to sacrifice there. All danger of evil influence from Canaanites, Arameans, or other pagan peoples was left behind at Shechem. The journey was accomplished in peace; Bethel itself was outside the jurisdiction of Shechem. The promise given to Jacob fleeing to Paddan-aram was confirmed to Israel returning to the land of the promise. As he had done previously, Jacob set up a memorial stone, making a libation and anointing it with oil.

A brief note records the death of Rebekah's nurse at Bethel. Evidently she was going with Jacob in the hope of meeting his mother at Hebron. A greater sorrow befell Jacob at Ephrath, for there Rachel died while giving birth to her second son. To call him "son of my pain" (Benoni), as she did, would have stigmatized the child all his life. Jacob changed his name to the honorable "son of the right hand" (Benjamin).

Illustration of Jacob blessing his sons in the *Vienna Genesis* Codex (6th cent. A.D.). The text is Gen. 49:31-33a (LXX) (Bild-Archiv des Österreichischen Nationalbibliothek, Vienna)

At last the caravan reached Hebron. This was the family "home," for it contained the cave Abraham had purchased to serve as his sepulchre. Together, Jacob and Esau buried their father. Esau returned to his Edomite hills, while Jacob took his place as head of the family in Canaan. In Gen. 37–50 the writer narrates events in the lives of various members of Jacob's family, the children of Israel. Their father's biography can still be traced through theirs, however, for they were still dependent on him.

In Hebron Jacob lived as he had in Haran, sowing crops each year and pasturing his flocks wherever there was good grazing, even as far away as Dothan. His sons grew up, married, and begot children of their own. The favorite son was, naturally enough, Rachel's firstborn, Joseph. His sale into Egypt (*see* JOSEPH II.A) was the consequence of the treatment his father lavished on him. After Joseph's disappearance from home, his brother Benjamin became his father's dearly loved son.

Famine had driven Abraham to Egypt, and Isaac had intended to make the same journey. Similarly, Jacob sent to the Egyptian granaries for corn when he was in want and presently left Canaan with all his immediate family to settle in Goshen. Every major change of Jacob's life had been marked with God's approval. On this occasion Jacob sought reassurance when he reached Beer-sheba, the place near the border of Canaan where both Abraham and Isaac had met with God (21:33; 26:23-25). The promise given to Jacob reiterated the promises of Bethel, that he would be the ancestor of a great nation which would return and possess the land, even as he himself had returned from Paddan-aram.

D. To Egypt. The caravan passed from Gerar along the main route to Egypt until it came to Goshen, the fertile area E of the Nile Delta. Here Joseph had arranged for his father's family to settle. As Israel arrived in Egypt they

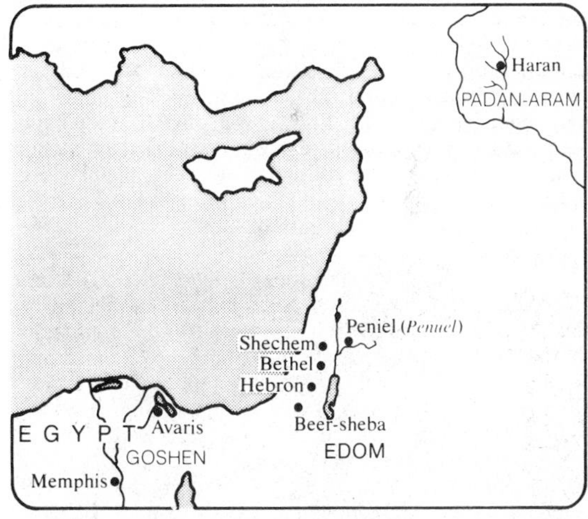

must have appeared like the figures painted in a noble's tomb at Beni-hasan *ca.* 1800 B.C. (see *ANEP,* no. 3), their curly black hair and beards and their long, colored tunics contrasting with the shaven heads and linen kilts of the Egyptians. Visitors and settlers from Palestine were no novelty. A list of slaves in an Egyptian household of *ca.* 1740 B.C. included a number of Asiatics bearing Semitic names. Among them are some formed from the same verbal roots as the names of the family of Israel (e.g., *škr,* cf. Issachar; *'šr,* cf. Asher; cf. W. F. Albright, *JAOS,* 74 [1954], 222-233). At the close of the 18th cent. B.C. the native rulers in Lower Egypt had been ousted by the Hyksos invaders from Palestine and Syria. These people dominated the whole country until their expulsion *ca.* 1567

B.C. Evidence suggests that Jacob entered Egypt during the earlier phase of Hyksos rule, roughly *ca.* 1700 B.C.; but this cannot be established with certainty. At that time the royal residence was either at Avaris (Tanis) or at Memphis, within easy reach of Goshen, as Gen. 46–47 suggests. Jacob was introduced to the court, where the pharaoh, with true Egyptian courtesy, inquired about his age.

In the pastures of Goshen, Jacob's sons were able to live as they had in Canaan, with the extra security afforded by Joseph's high position at the court. They inhabited an area separate from Egypt proper, in close contact with the land from which they had come.

As Jacob felt death approaching, he made arrangements for the inheritance of his property. Reuben, Jacob's eldest son by Leah, had disqualified himself, as far as his birthright was concerned, by his sin (35:22). Rachel's son stood far higher in his father's eyes than any of the sons of Leah, and so it was to Joseph that the extra portion was assigned (48:22). In addition Joseph's two eldest sons, Ephraim and Manasseh, were adopted by their grandfather as his own sons. This action may find a later parallel in a document from Ugarit recording the adoption by a man of his grandson as his heir, but in that instance he was the sole heir. Numbers of ancient wills have survived in written form, but there is evidence that oral dispositions were equally valid in law if duly witnessed. The complete control of the testator over his bequests and his ability to show favor or disfavor are clearly shown in the testament of a Hittite king, Ḫattusilis I (*ca.* 1650 B.C.). Several of the king's sons had rebelled against him, so a nephew was adopted as successor. He, too, made plots against the king, who eventually designated his grandson(?) Mursilis as his "son" while he, the king, lay dying.

The poetic form of the Blessing of Jacob doubtless enabled each of its hearers to remember the pertinent passage easily. The subsequent history of the several tribes is lucidly, and by divine inspiration, contained within the few lines of each section. There are no good grounds for doubting its authenticity, although the language may have been "modernized" by a later editor (as was done on occasion in Egypt). Through Jacob's blessing the promise and covenant of God were no longer borne by one man in each generation. With the death of Jacob commences the history of the nation of Israel.

Jacob's final injunction concerned his burial. His sons accordingly made their way back to Hebron and there placed his embalmed body in the cave Abraham had purchased as an earnest of his inheritance. All the pomp Egypt could muster was provided for the vizier's father. The size and lamentations of this cortege so impressed the Canaanites that they named a place after it. So the "wandering Aramean" rested in his homeland.

III. Jacob's Religion.–Any attempt to study the beliefs of individuals apart from their life story is apt to become unbalanced. The stages on the road of Jacob's experience of God have already been noted. As the religion of Israel and thus the roots of Christianity claim to derive from the patriarchs, it is necessary to attempt to understand Jacob's spiritual life.

A. Background. The religious thought of the common people of western Asia at the time of Jacob can be discovered only from chance references in letters and other documents, and from material remains. Each city had its patron god associated with various minor attendant deities. Citizens could go to the major shrine or to smaller chapels to offer sacrifice or to join in the festivals connected with the particular cult. To what extent private persons could participate in the services of these temples is unknown. The life of the king depended largely upon the commands and wishes of the different gods as interpreted by their priests, who did not hesitate to threaten disaster if their desires were not met. Most of the individual's devotion was paid to his "private" gods. It is likely that these were represented by small images kept in the house and passed from father to son (cf. II.C). Many cuneiform texts, notably but by no means exclusively the records of Assyrian merchants in Anatolia *ca.* 1900 B.C., refer to the god of such a man or the god of his father. This is not evidence of monotheism — the same letter may contain a greeting, "May Ashur [the chief god] and your god bless you" — but of a choice and devotion to a single member of the pantheon. While the evidence is incomplete, it appears that the individual venerated lesser gods in his personal devotion while honoring as a citizen the local chief deity and naming his children after him.

Abraham left the multitudinous gods of Ur for the worship of the God who revealed Himself by the name of Yahweh. He was no minor god or even a leader among others; He alone was God. The simple term God (Heb. *'ēl*) or the emphatic plural form (Heb. *'ᵉlōhîm*) sufficed to identify Him. Perhaps it was because the Canaanites placed a god 'El at the head of their pantheon that this title seldom appears alone. In the story of Jacob the names 'El Shaddai (43:14) and 'El Bethel (31:13; 35:7) occur together with Yahweh. They do not point to an underlying polytheism or a syncretism of local deities or clan totems. Each name has its own significance in the place it occupies.

B. Jacob's Growth; First Crisis. Jacob's religion can be viewed as consistent with the beliefs and practices of his fathers. No doubt he received some instruction from Isaac in the faith of the family, the history of Abraham, of the covenant, and of the promise. He first encountered God at Bethel, at the moment of greatest need in his life, fleeing from home to distant and unknown relatives. He received a vision of majesty, glorious and terrifying. Jacob saw the God of Abraham, the God of Isaac, Yahweh Himself. God repeated to him the promise given to Abraham in Ur. His immediate reaction was to think that he had rested in a notable holy place (28:17). In the morning, however, he consecrated it by erecting and anointing the stone pillow. The name given expresses the significance of this place for Jacob. Above all else it was "the house of God." It is not to be deduced that Jacob believed God to be confined to the stone or to reside therein, although such ideas are not unknown in the ancient world. Jacob returned to the place, but he also sacrificed and worshiped elsewhere. He vowed to take Yahweh as his God, if he should journey in safety and eventually return home. Moreover, he would devote a tenth of his income to God (cf. Abraham, Gen. 14:20).

C. Second Crisis. After twenty years in Paddan-aram came the command to return to Canaan. There could be no doubt of its authenticity, for it came in the name of the God of Bethel. The following events shed light on the beliefs of Jacob's wives and their father. Already in the naming of their children Leah and Rachel had shown that they acknowledged Yahweh as God (Gen. 29:31, 33, 35; 30:24). Upon the announcement of the vision and of the order to leave home, they recognized it as God's guidance (31:16). Their life and education among the pagans of Haran, however, had imbued them and their father with pagan superstitions. The family was thought to be protected by the presence of images of gods, the teraphim. Rachel's theft of these laid the household in Haran open to the mischief of demons of disease and workers of black magic. Laban's eagerness to regain possession of the figurines implied confidence in their power and apprehension at the disasters their loss might entail. The servants in Jacob's train also brought images of their own. These were buried at Shechem before the visit to Bethel, together with earrings, no doubt decorated with heathen symbols (35:2-5). Yet Laban was not an apostate from the family religion. He attributed Jacob's successes as a herdsman to the blessing of Yahweh (30:27), and he knew who it was that warned him not to harm Jacob (31:24, 29). Most significant is the oath he swore at Mizpah, invoking God as witness, the God of Abraham (Jacob's grandfather), the God of Nahor (his own grandfather), and the God of their father Terah (31:50-53). The identity of the God of each generation in both branches of the family is proclaimed here. In this way the covenant was guaranteed by the witness of the Power proved constant by the ancestors of either party. Jacob added an oath by the "Fear" of Isaac. This epithet (31:42, 53) seemed to have been part of the personal relationship between God and Isaac. A different translation, "Kinsman," has been proposed (*FSAC*, p. 248; but *see* Fear II.C). A single reference might admit of Jacob's using a similar private epithet for God, "the Mighty One of Jacob" (49:24).

D. Third Crisis. The third crisis was the encounter at Peniel. Before Jacob met Esau he had seen the strength of his "Mighty One" in the angelic host at Mahanaim. Fear of his brother brought him to pray humbly for the protection of his father's God. The plan he conceived for palliating Esau's anger and for safeguarding his property was not allowed to supplant trust in God. The wrestling at the ford showed Jacob how weak he was before his God. It taught him the value of the continued prayer of one who is helpless. The awe that was aroused by the revelation at Bethel recurred as Jacob named the place, awe that a mortal should survive a meeting with God "face to face."

E. Fourth Crisis. When Jacob setled at Shechem he built an altar to 'El, with whom the local inhabitants might possibly identify their chief god. To emphasize the distinction Jacob called the name 'El, God of Israel. There is no record of his erecting an altar and making a sacrifice — a natural sequel — before this time, apart from the sacrifice that solemnized his treaty with Laban (31:54). Here at Shechem he had become an independent man, head of his own family. The problem of Esau had been circumvented and Isaac was a very old man at Mamre. As the leader of the chosen race Jacob could offer sacrifices to God. He constructed another altar at Bethel when he went there the second time (35:1, 7) with all his household to worship. The promise given as he left Canaan a solitary fugitive was renewed now to Israel, father of eleven sons, head of his own family. All the experiences of the past had their culmination at this moment. The new name, plus the promise of nationhood and of the land, were confirmed by the God in whom Jacob had been taught to trust. Remembrance of this occasion was insured by the erection of another pillar and reiteration of the name Bethel, not in solitude but before many witnesses, notably his sons, who would remember its meaning.

F. Fifth Crisis and Triumph. The altar at Beer-sheba marked the final crisis. Here the patriarch worshiped for the last time in the land promised to him. This was the great test of his faith in God. As a counter to it he had the joyful anticipation of reunion with his favorite son. The piety of the elderly Hebrew is seen in his interview with the pharaoh. In the blessings of his sons is shown the mature expression of the patriarch's trust in God, a confidence resulting from trying experiences. The immediate concern was the continuance of his name and that of his father (48:16), but he looked farther ahead to his children's return to Canaan and to the part of each son's family in the life of the clan. When viewed from the NT perspective, the blessing of Judah assumes greater import in its mention of the coming ruler. As the writer to the Hebrew church says, "By faith Jacob . . . blessed" (He. 11:21). What Jacob expected after his death is not revealed. He spoke of himself as "going down to Sheol" (37:35; 42:38), but this was no gloomy prospect after he had met Joseph and his two sons (48:11). The concluding phrase of the blessing of Dan (49:18, "I await thy salvation, O Lord!") may hint at a deeper belief; it certainly implies great faith in God. Throughout his life his faith had grown, strengthened by the visions at Bethel. This was the faith he passed on to his sons, the outcome of his experience of the God who did not change, "before whom . . . Abraham . . . walked, . . . who has led me all my life long" (48:15). No wonder that a later Israelite could sing, "Happy is the man whose help is the God of Jacob!" (Ps. 146:5).

G. Israel: Man and Nation. The narratives of Genesis paint a vivid picture of Jacob's character. His failings are recounted as much as his triumphs; he has a personality of his own, distinct from his relatives, distinct from any other ancient hero. Parallels may be found in folklore, legend, or history to one incident in his life or another, but they should all be recognized as common experience rather than cultural borrowings. The story of the patriarch's progress is a consistent whole. The many incidental details and dissimilarities discredit theories that the stories are retrojections of events in the history of Israel the people.

That some similarities exist is obvious. Indeed, the ancient prophets realized this. Hosea applied to Israel the story of Jacob, for it was their story too (Hos. 12:2-4, 12 [MT 3-5, 13]). Less precise resemblance occurs between Jacob's story and the teachings of Isaiah, Jeremiah, and Habakkuk concerning the faithful among the Israelites and the stages through which Jacob passed. Further exploration for "types" in Jacob's sojourn in Haran or his "exile" in Egypt exceed the limits of reasonable exegesis. Malachi stressed the most important typical relation, the possession of the covenant, the distinction of the choice of God (Mal. 1:2). Later Jacob became an illustration and a type of the Church (Rom. 9:10-13).

IV. References Outside Genesis.—"Jacob" and "Israel" are the two names most frequently met with in the OT. In most cases these denote the children of Israel, particularly in the parallelism of poetic compositions. To this day the name of the patriarch is thus perpetuated. There remain, however, biblical passages that refer to Jacob himself.

A. In the OT. A considerable group of verses associate him with Abraham and Isaac in naming God as the God of the fathers, underlining the continuity and the identity of the God of the past with the God of the present (e.g., Ex. 3:13-15). The collection of a small number of passages about the patriarch himself permits the reconstruction of a fairly complete epitome of his life. His birth as the younger twin, clutching his brother's heel, is recounted by Hosea (12:3 [MT 4]). God's choice of Jacob over Esau is mentioned in Malachi (1:2f.), together with the inheritance of the covenant and all that it contained (Ps. 105:10f.). Hosea tells specifically of the flight to Aram and the servitude by which Jacob gained his wife (12:12 [MT 13]). He is mentioned as the father of the twelve tribes (1 S. 12:8; 1 K. 18:31). His escape from Laban is probably referred to in Dt. 26:5, where a "Syrian ready to perish" (AV, RV) may be better translated "a fugitive Syrian" (RSV "a wandering Aramean"; NEB "a homeless Aramaean"; see A. R. Millard, *JNES*, 39 [1980], 153-55). The hand of God protected the small clan as it moved from place to place among hostile neighbors (Ps. 105:12-15), for the only land Jacob owned was the plot he had purchased near Shechem (Josh. 24:32). Hosea again summarizes the encounter at Peniel and the communion with God at Bethel (12:4 [MT 5]). The sale of Joseph as a slave to Egypt was God's preparation for the future need of Jacob and his family when famine struck Canaan. So he was enabled to travel to Egypt and prosper there (Dt. 26:5; Josh. 24:4; Ps. 105:16-24). He died there, bequeathing the land at Shechem to Joseph's sons (Josh. 24:32), who are counted as two of the tribes as if they had been Jacob's own sons (Josh. 16–17). Here is evidence for the antiquity of the Jacob story and its diffusion, and it is noteworthy that all is consistent with the Genesis presentation. If the latter had been lost, it would still have been possible to write a biography of the father of the children of Israel.

B. In the NT. Four NT passages recall events in the life of Jacob. The conversation of Jesus (a descendant of the patriarch, Mt. 1:2; Lk. 3:33f.) and the woman at the well of Sychar includes a declaration by the woman that Jacob provided the well (Jn. 4:12), besides the author's note that this was the ground given by Jacob to Joseph (5:6). Samaritan pride can be felt in the woman's words "our father Jacob." Stephen mentions the famine and Jacob's journey to Egypt in the course of his defense before the Sanhedrin (Acts 7:8-16). When the patriarch and his sons died in Egypt they were carried to Shechem and buried in the tomb Abraham bought from the sons of Hamor (vv. 15f.). This is one of the curious discrepancies in Stephen's speech — the result, it is conjectured, of his endeavor to include all he could of Jewish history in his argument. For the apostle Paul, Jacob is an outstanding example of the sovereign choice of God, of the predestination of the elect (Rom. 9:10-13). The writer of Hebrews takes Jacob as one of his examples of active faith, a faith that acknowledges the present protection and worship of God and that can look forward fearlessly into the future (He. 11:9, 20-22).

V. Modern Interpretations of Jacob.–Evolutionary theories, and the critical spirit engendered by them, were largely responsible for the analyses and reinterpretations of Genesis published in considerable number at the end of the last century. (See *ISBE, s.v.* "Genesis" [W. Möller].)

A. Documentary Theories. The most widely taught reconstructions of patriarchal history stemmed directly from the analysis of the Hexateuch into four main documents coming from different sources and dates and compiled in the 5th cent. B.C. This hypothesis was supported by noting variations of style and by observing religious development. Its parallel was the approach to Israelite religion that sought to trace the advance from animism or demonism to henotheism and then to the monotheism found in the later prophets. The effect of such views upon the stories of Jacob may be seen, e.g., in *ORHI,* I, ch. 4. The Jacob stories describe for the most part events "affecting whole clans and not merely isolated persons" (p. 58). So Jacob's relations with Esau depict Israel's political contacts with Edom, and the treaty of Jacob and Laban reflect a border agreement between neighboring tribes. Other stories are attached to local shrines, notably Bethel, where there were two, one perhaps from the northern tribes and one from the southern. The incident at Peniel is considered a myth, to be compared with other stories of a hero fighting a god, used to explain a food taboo. It is not denied, however, that Jacob was a historical person and the account of the vision at Bethel a personal story.

B. Views of Alt and Noth. The documentary theories have undergone many revisions and alterations at the hands of various scholars over the past forty years. The work of two German scholars, A. Alt and M. Noth, has commanded considerable attention. This view followed the documentary analysis, but at the same time made use of the form-critical approach, examining the types of narrative, and also made use of archeological discoveries. The study of the Pentateuch and its sources has led to the view that there was no nation of Israel before the settlement in Canaan. Consequently events described as happening before that time are to be connected with the individual tribes, whose traditions have been mixed together. Alt ("God of the Fathers," in *Essays on OT History and Religion* [Eng. tr. 1967]) drew a comparison between worship of "the gods of the fathers" in Hellenistic and Roman Transjordan and the Israelite conception of the God of Abraham, Isaac, and Jacob. He reached the conclusion that such persons must have existed to give rise to such a creed. This study and one on the connection of Shechem with Bethel are utilized by M. Noth in *NHI,* section 10, and in his more detailed *Überlieferungsgeschichte des Pentateuch* (1948).

The theories of Alt and Noth were well summarized by J. Bright in *Early Israel in Recent History Writing* (1960). Jacob is considered the original and most important patriarch, associated with a shrine at a tree near Shechem in the territory of Ephraim. His vision of the ladder was located there until the transference of the shrine of the ark to Bethel during the time of the judges caused the scene of the dream to be changed also. A separate group of traditions, placed in Gilead, relates the association of Jacob and Esau. The stories reflect encounters of Ephraimite settlers (Jacob) with native woodsmen (Esau). The Jacob-Laban affair constitutes a third group, in "saga" style, and later than the others. This, too, is of Transjordanian origin, yet linked with the central Palestine group by the Ephraimitic settlers. The strong influence of the central shrine at Shechem led to the recognition of Jacob as the ancestor of all the tribes when they formed their confederacy. The patriarchs of the other tribes were then incorporated into Jacob's family tree. Little more can be said than that Jacob was a wandering shepherd on the desert fringe, for almost all the narratives now linked with his name are the speculations of later Israelites about the origins of their customs and beliefs or the accretions of local etiological tales.

C. View of Albright. The third school of thought was dominated by the American scholar W. F. Albright. While adhering to the documentary analysis, he placed far greater reliance on the correctness of the traditions preserved in the Pentateuch. These were handed on, mainly in oral form, from the time of the patriarchs. Some anachronisms have been added in the process, notably the mention of camels. Albright's more constructive approach is due to his insistence upon the primacy of archeology. His views can best be illustrated by quoting from *FSAC,* p. 241:

> So many corroborations of details have been discovered in recent years that most competent scholars have given up the old critical theory according to which the stories of the Patriarchs are mostly retrojections from the time of the Dual Monarchy (9th-8th centuries B.C.). Conflicting versions of a given episode in the J and E documents warn us against depending too slavishly on the present form of the tradition. On the other hand they are altogether too close in form and content to be of distinct origin, especially when we remember that much closer parallelism between them has presumably been eliminated by the redactor, who saw no purpose in unnecessary repetition. The most reasonable view is that of R. Kittel, that they reflect different recensions of an old national epic, based on poems which came down . . . from the Patriarchal Age. . . . A unitary background for J and E is also suggested by their remarkably homo-

geneous characterizations of the Patriarchs. The figures of Abraham, Isaac, Jacob, and Joseph appear before us as real personalities, each one of whom shows traits and qualities which would suit his character but would not harmonize with the characters of the others. This is particularly true of Jacob and Joseph.

This approach was taken up by Albright's pupils. Among the most widely known is J. Bright. In his study of the patriarchs (*BHI,* ch. 2) he suggested that they were "chieftains of sizeable clans" reaching Palestine "in various waves over a period of time" from Mesopotamia. (For a good summary of this position, see *BANE,* chs. 1–2.)

In reaction to Albright's attitude, attacks have been made on this use of archeological and textual evidence from the ancient Near East. In some cases these attacks are justified, for too much weight has been put upon isolated discoveries or events; in other cases, however, attempts to discount the witness of antiquity clearly result from predetermined views. Most who are critical in this way adhere firmly to the documentary theory that empties the stories of their apparent historical meaning. The major works in this vein are J. Van Seters, *Abraham in History and Tradition* (1975), and T. L. Thompson, *Historicity of the Patriarchal Narratives* (*BZAW,* 133, 1974), while W. McKane, *Studies in the Patriarchal Narratives* (1979), reasserts the primacy of literary study. It is impossible, however, to treat the patriarchal narratives justly without setting them in their ancient context, and that context is found best in the world of the early 2nd millennium. Arguments for this positive view are found in K. A. Kitchen, *Bible in Its World* (1977), ch. 4; D. J. Wiseman and A. R. Millard, eds., *Patriarchal Narratives and Their Study* (1980); M. J. Selman, *Tyndale Bulletin,* 27 (1976), 114-136.

D. Summary. Archeological discoveries and the studies of the Albright school acted as a stimulus to conservative scholarship. Despite the many attractive ideas to be found in these studies — and their conclusions must frequently command assent — the basic attitude of doubting whatever cannot be supported by extrabiblical evidence is unacceptable. Acquiescence in the documentary theory carries with it this hypercritical approach, easily leading to groundless assumptions. The emphasis on the role of oral tradition (a contribution of some Scandinavian scholars; see E. Nielsen, *Oral Tradition* [*SBT,* 1/11, 1954]) allows as much freedom for the introduction of anachronisms of material detail and of thought as the old documentary analysis. So long as there are envisaged "editors" or "redactors" who collected old stories and wrote them down, rewrote, and expanded them as they thought fit, little confidence can be placed in the resultant work as a true representation of events long before their age. No doubt the stories were told orally; yet it is unlikely that no written record existed at the same time and from an early date. Comparison with the place of oral tradition in later Islam is misleading. The study of Babylonian or Egyptian practice of the 2nd and 1st millennia B.C. is far more profitable. In those societies the "classics" were written in ancient days, copied out, and then memorized by boys at school even when Jacob was a youth. Cuneiform texts were often signed by the copyist and checked against the exemplar by another scribe. Respect for the written word in all civilizations of the ancient Near East and the careful preservation of documents are arguments against the primacy of oral tradition. Occasional examples of scribal fraud exist, but early writers were not in the habit of "composing" history or of altering it, however biased they may have been. Editors worked over the old books. Many Egyptian and Babylonian manuscripts attest this, a natural action in any culture of which the language developed. Their work was not necessarily to modernize the story or its thought; they were only editors.

Thus it is likely that the life history of Jacob was written at an early date, perhaps during his own last days in Egypt. It was written for our learning, and we have no conclusive reason for disbelief in any part. A. R. MILLARD

2. The father of Joseph the husband of Mary (Mt. 1:15f.).

3. Patronymic denoting the Israelites (Isa. 10:21; 14:1; Jer. 10:16).

JACOB'S WELL [Gk. *pēgḗ toú Iakōb*]. In John we read that Jesus "came to a city of Samaria, called Sychar, near the field which Jacob gave to his son Joseph. Jacob's well was there" (4:5f.). When Jacob came to SHECHEM on his return from Paddan-aram, he camped "before" the city, presumably to the east of it, and bought the land on which he had pitched his tent (Gen. 33:18f.). This may well be the "mountain slope" (Heb. *šeḵem*) spoken of in Gen. 48:22, although there the text states, "I took it from . . . the Amorites with my sword and my bow." Where the pass of Shechem opens to the east, on the south, close to the base of Gerizim, is the well known as Bîr Yaʿqûb, "the well of Jacob." The main road from Beer-sheba, Hebron, Bethlehem, and Jerusalem divides S of the well, one arm leading westward to Nâblus, about 3.4 km. (1.5 mi.) distant, the other more directly to the north toward Jenîn and east to the Jordan Valley. The well is about 76 m. (250 ft.) from Tell Balâṭah, ancient Shechem.

Although the OT does not refer to it, Jewish, Samaritan, Moslem, and Christian traditions associate this well with the patriarch Jacob. It is mentioned *ca.* A.D. 333 by the Bordeaux pilgrim. Since water apparently filters through its soft limestone sides as well as through a superimposed thick bed of soil, it may be considered, as Jn. 4 suggests, both a *pēgḗ,* "spring," and in the main a *phréar,* "rain pit" or CISTERN. The water is said to last until the end of May and to return with the fall rains.

Major Anderson, who in 1866 descended into it, described it as having "a narrow opening, just wide enough to allow the body of a man to pass through with arms uplifted, and this narrow neck, which is about 4 ft. long, opens into the well itself, which is cylindrically shaped, and about 7 ft., 6 in. in diameter. The mouth and upper part of the well are built of masonry, and the well appears to have been sunk through a mixture of alluvial soil and limestone fragments, till a compact bed of mountain limestone was reached, having horizontal strata which could be easily worked; and the interior of the well presents the appearance of having been lined throughout with rough masonry." The depth to the accumulated debris has been measured at 23 m. (75 ft.). In 1935 the total depth was measured at 41 m. (135 ft.).

From the narratives of the pilgrims, we learn that at different times churches were built over the well. The first was probably a cruciform church of the 4th century. The Crusader Church was destroyed after the Moslem victory of 1187. Now the Greek Orthodox own the walled enclosure and an unfinished church. Stairs to the crypt lead to the well, the top of which is now above the floor. The text of p^{66} suggests that in ancient times the top of the well was at ground level and that Jesus sat on the ground or *at* the well rather than *on* it.

A stone found in 1881 may have been an old cover of the well. It measured 1.1 m. (3.8 ft.) by 0.7 m. (2.6 ft.) by 0.4 m. (1.5 ft.). The aperture in the center measured 0.3 m. (13 in.) in diameter. In its sides were grooves worn by the ropes used in drawing up the water.

Bibliography–R. E. Anderson, *Recovery of Jerusalem* (n.d.), p. 465; C. W. Barclay, *PEQ,* 1881, pp. 212ff.; G. E. Wright, *Shechem* (1965), pp. 215f.

W. EWING
D. J. WIEAND

JACUBUS jə-kū'bəs [LXX *Iakoubos*, B *Iarsouboos*]. *See* AKKUB **4.**

JADA jā'də [Heb. *yāḏā'*–'the caring one']. Son of Onam and grandson of Jerahmeel by his wife Atarah (1 Ch. 2:26, 28, 32).

JADAU jā'dä, jā'dou [Heb. *K yiddô*; *Q yadday*]. *See* IDDO **3.**

JADDAI jad'ī, jad'ə-ī. *See* IDDO **3.**

JADDUA jad'o͞o-ə [Heb. *yaddû(a)'*–'known'].

1. One of the "chiefs of the people" who with Nehemiah sealed the covenant, thus signifying their voluntary acceptance of the law and their solemn promise to submit to its yoke (Neh. 10:21 [MT 22]).

2. Son of Jonathan or Johanan, and great-grandson of Eliashib, the high priest in Nehemiah's time (Neh. 12:11, 22). He is the last of the high priests mentioned in the OT and held office during the reign of Darius the Persian, i.e., Darius III Codomannus, the last king of Persia (336-332 B.C.), who was overthrown by Alexander the Great (*see* DARIUS **3**). It is doubtless to him that Josephus refers in his romantic account of Alexander's entrance into Jerusalem (*Ant.* xi.8.4f. [326-339]). J. CRICHTON

JADDUS jad'əs [Gk. LXX B *Iaddous*, A *Ioddous*]; AV ADDUS. Jaddus was removed from the office of the priesthood because he could not prove his right to it after the return to Jerusalem under Zerubbabel (1 Esd. 5:38). He is called Barzillai in the OT (Ezr. 2:61; Neh. 7:63), because he married Agia, the daughter of Zorzelleus (OT Barzillai the Gileadite), and adopted his father-in-law's name. *See* BARZILLAI **2.**

JADINUS jə-dī'nəs [Gk. *Iadinos*] (1 Esd. 9:48, NEB). *See* JAMIN **3.**

JADON jā'don [Heb. *yāḏôn*]. One who helped to rebuild the wall of Jerusalem in company with the men of Gibeon and of Mizpah (Neh. 3:7). He is called the "Meronothite," and another Meronothite is referred to in 1 Ch. 27:30, but there is no mention of a place Meronoth. Perhaps the reference was to a site about 5 km. (3 mi.) NW of Gibeon, now known as Beit-Unia, but this is uncertain.

JAEL jā'əl [Heb. *yā'ēl*–'a wild or mountain goat,' as in Ps. 104:18]. The wife of Heber the Kenite and the slayer of SISERA (Jgs. 4:17-22; 5:2-31). Jael obtained fame by a single act. For years Jabin king of the Canaanites had oppressed Israel with iron chariots led by his general Sisera. Deborah, the prophetess of Israel, was seized with a passion for freedom and roused the Israelites to do battle against Sisera. They defeated him at "Taanach by the waters of Megiddo," but Sisera fled for his life. When he came to the "oaks of the wanderers," where the tribe of Heber lived, he was invited to turn aside into the tent of Jael (4:17f.). The subsequent events are depicted in two accounts: one in prose (4:19-22), and the other in poetry (in Deborah's song of victory, 5:24-27).

The tribe of Heber was probably neutral in the struggle; but they were descendants of Jethro and had the confidence of the Israelites. Even though they no doubt suffered at the hands of the Canaanites, they made a peace pact with Jabin. Because of this, as well as the current law of hospitality, Sisera entered the tent of Jael with confidence. Whether Jael met Sisera and invited him to enter the tent and rest (4:18), or he requested the sanctuary of her home, is not clear.

She gave him buttermilk ("butter in a lordly dish") to drink and a blanket for covering, and heeded his request that she stand guard at the door of the tent to foil any pursuers. When sleep came to the tired general, she took a tent-pin and a hammer in her hands, went quietly to him, and drove the pin through his temples, so that he died (cf. 4:21). With blood dripping from her hands, she went forth to meet Barak the Israelite general, to collect the reward. There is no evidence that Sisera insulted or mistreated her. Jael's motive may have been a mixed one. She could have been in sympathy with Israel and with the religion of Israel. But perhaps she was merely prudent. Sisera was in flight, Barak in pursuit. Since Sisera would be killed anyway, why should she not kill him and cement a friendship with the conqueror?

Deborah (5:24) immortalized Jael's deed, because anyone who would kill her country's enemy was a friend of Israel. The method of his death mattered little to her, for all things were fair in war; therefore Jael was blessed among women by all who loved Israel.

See also DEBORAH **2.** D. W. DEERE

JAGUR jā'gər [Heb. *yāḡûr*]. An unidentified town on the Edomite frontier of Judah in the south (Josh. 15:21), perhaps Tell Gur, 16 km. (10 mi.) E of Beer-sheba.

JAH jä, alternate spelling of **YAH** yä. An abbreviated form of the name Yahweh (*see* GOD, NAMES OF II.C). It occurs, e.g., in the Hebrew text of Ex. 15:2, in personal names like Adonijah ("Yah is my master"), and in the liturgical expression "hallelujah" ("praise Yah").

JAHATH jā'hath [Heb. *yaḥaṯ*, perhaps a shortened form of *yaḥteh*, *yaḥ^{a}ṯeh*–'he [God] will snatch up'].

1. Son of Reaiah, son of Shobal, a descendant of Judah and father of Ahumai and Lahad, the families of the Zorathites (1 Ch. 4:2).

A frequent name for a descendant of Levi:

2. Son of Libni, son of Gershom, the oldest son of Levi (1 Ch. 6:20 [MT 5]; in v. 43 [MT 28] "son of Libni" is omitted).

3. Son of Shimei, son of Gershom (1 Ch. 23:10f.).

4. One of the "sons" of Shelomoth, a descendant of Izhar, son of Kohath, the second son of Levi (1 Ch. 24:22).

5. A descendant of Merari, the third son of Levi, and an overseer in the repairing of the temple during the reign of Josiah (2 Ch. 34:12). J. CRICHTON

JAHAZ jā'haz [Heb. *yahaṣ* (Isa. 15:4; Jer. 48:34); *yāh^{e}ṣâ* or *yah^{e}ṣâ* (Nu. 21:23; Dt. 2:32; Josh. 13:18; 21:36; Jgs. 11:20; 1 Ch. 6:78 (MT 63)]; AV also JAHAZAH (Jer. 48:21; RSV JAHZAH), JAHAZA. This is the place where in a great battle Israel overwhelmed Sihon king of the Amorites and then took possession of all his territory (Nu. 21:23f.). It is named along with Beth-baal-meon and Kedemoth (Josh. 13:17f.), with Kedemoth (21:37) pointing to a location in the southeast of the Amorite territory. It was given to Reuben by Moses and was one of the cities in the portion of that tribe assigned to the Merarite Levites. Mesha (Moabite Stone, lines 18-21) states that the king of Israel lived in Jahaz when at war with him. Mesha drove him out, and the city passed into the hands of Moab. It is referred to as a city of Moab in Isa. 15:4; Jer. 48:21, 34. Khirbet et-Teim, 0.5 km. (1 mi.) SW of Medeba, Umm el-Walid, 11 km. (7 mi.) SE of Medeba, and Jālûl, 5.6 km. (3.5 mi.) E of Medeba, have all been suggested as possible locations. A. C. M.
R. K. H.

JAHAZIAH jā-ha-zī'ə (Ezr. 10:15, AV). *See* JAHZEIAH.

JAHAZIEL jə-hā'zē-əl [Heb. *yaḥ^{a}zî'ēl*–'God sees'; LXX *Oziēl*].

1. In 1 Ch. 12:4 (MT 5), one of David's recruits at Ziklag, a Benjaminite or maybe a Judean.

2. In 1 Ch. 16:6, one of two priests appointed by David to sound trumpets before the ark on its journey to Jerusalem.

3. In 1 Ch. 23:19; 24:23, a Levite, "son" of Hebron, a Kohathite.

4. In 2 Ch. 20:14, an Asaphite, son of Zechariah. He encouraged King Jehoshaphat of Judah and his subjects to fight against the Moabite and Ammonite invaders.

5. In Ezr. 8:5, an ancestor of one of the families of the Restoration. Read probably "of the sons of Zattu, Sheconiah the son of Jahaziel," following 1 Esd. 8:32 (AV, NEB, Jezelus). D. F. ROBERTS

JAHDAI jä'dī [Heb. *yāhdāy*–'may God guide']. A descendant of Judah mentioned in 1 Ch. 2:47.

JAHDIEL jä'dē-əl [Heb. *yaḥdî'ēl*]. In 1 Ch. 5:24, head of a Manassite family.

JAHDO jä'dō [Heb. *yaḥdô*–'may God rejoice']. The head of a Manassite tribe mentioned in 1 Ch. 5:14.

JAHLEEL jä'lē-əl [Heb. *yaḥl^e'ēl*–'wait for God' or possibly 'may God show Himself friendly']. The third son of Zebulun and ancestor of the Jahleelites (Nu. 26:26).

JAHLEELITES jä'lē-əl-īts [Heb. *hayyaḥl^e'ēlî*; collective]. In Nu. 26:26, the descendants of the clan of Jahleel.

JAHMAI jä'mī [Heb. *yaḥmay*; perhaps the same as Heb. *yaḥm^{e}yâ*–'may Yahweh protect']. In 1 Ch. 7:2, head of a clan of Issachar.

JAHWEH yä'wā, alternate spelling of **YAHWEH** yä'wā. *See* GOD, NAMES OF II.C.

JAHZAH jä'zə. *See* JAHAZ.

JAHZEEL jä'zē-əl [Heb. *yaḥṣ^e'ēl*–'God divides, apportions' (Gen. 46:24; Nu. 26:48; 23 MSS in 1 Ch. 7:13)] and **JAHZIEL** [Heb. *yaḥ^{a}ṣî'ēl* (1 Ch. 7:13)]. A descendant of Naphtali and ancestor of a clan.

JAHZEELITES jä'zē-əl-īts [Heb. *hayyaḥṣ^e'ēlî*; collective]. In Nu. 26:48, descendants of the clan of Jahzeel.

JAHZEIAH jä-zē'yə [Heb. *yaḥz^{e}yâ*–'Yahweh sees']; AV JAHAZIAH. In Ezr. 10:15, son of Tikvah and a contemporary of Ezra. Along with Jonathan he opposed Ezra's action in prosecuting those who had married foreign women (but cf. 1 Esd. 9:14; AV Ezechias; NEB Hezekias).

JAHZERAH jä'zə-rə [Heb. *yaḥzērâ*]. In 1 Ch. 9:12, an ancestor of Maasai and apparently the same as Ahzai of Neh. 11:13 (AV Ahasai).

JAHZIEL jä'zē-əl. *See* JAHZEEL.

JAILER. *See* PRISON.

JAIR jā'ər [Heb. *yā'îr*–'may he shine'; (**4**) *Q yā'îr*–'may he arouse,' *K yā'ûr*].

1. Son, i.e., descendant, of Manasseh (Nu. 32:41; Dt. 3:14; Josh. 13:30; 1 K. 4:13; 1 Ch. 2:22). According to 1 Ch. 2:21f. he was the son of Segub, son of Hezron, a descendant of Judah, who married the daughter of Machir, son of Manasseh. He was thus descended both from Judah and Manasseh. At the time of the Conquest he distinguished himself by taking the tent-villages HAVVOTH-JAIR.

2. One of the judges. He is said to have had thirty sons, who rode on thirty ass colts, and who had as many cities, known as Havvoth-jair (Jgs. 10:3f.). He was probably a descendant of the person mentioned above (**1**).

3. The father of Mordecai (Est. 2:5; Ad. Est. 11:2 [AV Jairus]).

4. The father of Elhanan, the giantslayer (1 Ch. 20:5). In the parallel passage (2 S. 21:19) his name is given as Jaare-oregim, but the text should be corrected to Jair, "oregim" (Heb. *'ôr^{e}gîm*) having crept in from the line below through a copyist's error.

See also ELHANAN. J. CRICHTON

JAIRITE jā'ə-rīt [Heb. *yā'irî*–'of Jair']. In 2 S. 20:26, Ira the Jairite is "David's priest." He was a descendant of Jair who was a Manassite (Nu. 32:41, etc.) and whose territory was in Gilead. LXX, Lucian, and Syr. suggest Heb. *yattirî,* "Jattirite," a native of Jattir mentioned in 1 S. 30:27 as one of the towns friendly to David when he was in Ziklag. It is not improbable that a native of Jattir would be given such a post by David. *See* IRA **1** (cf. 2 S. 23:38).

JAIRUS jā'ə-rəs, jī'rəs [Gk. *Iaïros*].

1. (Ad. Est. 11:2, AV). *See* JAIR **3**; REAIAH.

2. A ruler in a synagogue near Capernaum whose only daughter, about twelve years of age, was raised from the dead by Jesus (Mt. 9:18-26 par. Mk. 5:22-43; Lk. 8:41-56).

The accounts of the miracle are substantially the same, but vary in detail. According to Mark and Luke the arrival of Jairus in Capernaum fell immediately after the return of Jesus from Gadara; but according to Matthew the sequence of events was that Jesus had returned to Capernaum, had called Matthew, had joined the feast of the publicans, and had just finished His discourse on fasting when Jairus came to Him. Matthew and Mark both testify to the great faith of Jairus, who begged Jesus merely to lay His hand upon the girl so that she would live. According to Matthew she was already dead when Jairus came to Capernaum; according to the others she was at the point of death; but all agree on her death before the arrival of Jesus and His followers at her home. Matthew implies that Jesus alone was present at the actual raising; Mark and Luke state that Peter, James, John, and the parents were also there. All three Synoptists record Jesus' healing along the way of the woman with the hemorrhage.

C. M. KERR

JAKAN jā'kən. *See* JAAKAN.

JAKEH jā'kə [Heb. *yāqeh*–'discerning']. The father of AGUR, the author of the sayings recorded in Prov. 30. No other information is available about either Agur or Jakeh. The Hebrew text is rather uncertain at this point, and consequently has been interpreted in various ways. One attempt to give Jakeh a pedigree suggests emending Heb. *hammaśśā'*, "the prophecy," to *hammaśśā'î,* "the Massite"; Massa is the land of an Ishmaelite tribe (cf. Gen. 25:14; 1 Ch. 1:30; Prov. 31:1). J. CRICHTON

JAKIM jā'kim [Heb. *yāqîm*–'may (God) establish'; cf. ELIAKIM].

1. A Benjaminite, a son of Shimei (1 Ch. 8:19).

2. A priest, the head of the twelfth of the twenty-four courses into which the priests were divided (1 Ch. 24:12).

JALAM jā'ləm [Heb. *ya'lām*]; AV JAALAM. In Gen.

36:5, 14, 18; 1 Ch. 1:35, a son of Esau, mentioned as the second son by Oholibamah; probably an Edomite clan.

JALON jā'lən [Heb. *yālôn*]. In 1 Ch. 4:17, a son of Ezra, a Judahite.

JAMB [Heb. *'ayil*] (Ezk. 40–41); AV POST; NEB PILASTER. The "jambs" of the temple gates in Ezekiel's vision were an ornamental feature at the opening of the vestibule into the court. *See also* HOUSE III.C.

JAMBRES jam'brēz. *See* JANNES AND JAMBRES.

JAMBRI jam'brī [Gk. *hoi huioí Iambri*; 1 Macc. 9:36f.]. The sons of Jambri are said to have come from Medeba, a city of the Moabites and subsequently a possession of the Amorites, and to have carried off John, the brother of Jonathan, who succeeded Judas Maccabeus as leader of the Jews. The Israelites took possession of the place and assigned it to the tribe of Reuben. No mention is made elsewhere of the Jambri. In Josephus (*Ant.* xiii.1.2 [11]) they are called "sons of Amaraius."

JAMES. The name of two or more persons who were active in the early Church. James is the English equivalent of Gk. *Iakōbos,* which in turn is derived from Heb. *ya'ᵃqōḇ* (Jacob).

The forty-one instances of this name in the NT seem to refer to two or three persons. Nineteen clearly refer to James the brother of John and son of Zebedee. Four more refer to a son of Alphaeus. Three others refer to a son of a Mary, two to a half brother (or cousin?) of Jesus, and eight to an unspecified James, a pillar of the Jerusalem Church. Finally, two refer to the father of Jude (Lk. 6:16; Acts 1:13). Most scholars narrow down these references to two or three persons.

1. James the son of Zebedee. This was one of the first disciples who were called in Galilee (Mt. 4:21 par. Mk. 1:19). He is mentioned before his brother John in every instance but one (Lk. 9:28), possibly because he was older (or because he was the preeminent member of the family). Customarily John has been given the larger place because of his extensive writings, but these all came after the death of James, the first martyr of the apostolic circle. The two men were named BOANERGES by Christ (Mk. 3:17), which is Aramaic for "sons of thunder" and which may refer to their impetuosity or their power in their later ministry. With their mother they sought a privileged position for themselves from Jesus, but were told that they should drink of the cup of His suffering and serve as He came to serve (Mt. 20:20-23; Mk. 10:35-38). Their mother's name seems to have been SALOME (Mt. 27:56; cf. Mk. 15:40). It is not certain whether the sister of Jesus' mother in Jn. 19:25 is this Salome or Mary the wife of Clopas. From the wording of the related passages it seems more likely that the sister of Jesus' mother was Mary, the mother of James the younger and Joses (or Justus). One objection to this view is the oddity of having two Marys in the same family. But some Egyptian parallels suggest that this was common practice and the two children were distinguished by some epithet — the other Mary, e.g., or James the younger. If this conclusion is adopted, then Salome was the mother of Zebedee's children, but was not the sister of Jesus' mother.

James, John, and their father were partners with Peter and Andrew in the fishing trade (Lk. 5:10; Mt. 4:18-21). Fishing in Galilee was an important business and some have thought that through such business connections John was able to gain entrance to the high priest's house (Jn. 18:15). James, however, is not mentioned as entering with his brother.

Neither James nor John is specifically mentioned as a disciple of John the Baptist, as Peter and Andrew are (Jn. 1:35-40). But the unnamed disciple here was likely John. James apparently was not there, though with John he heeded Jesus' call in Galilee to leave the nets and become fishers of men (Mt. 4:21f. par. Mk. 1:19f.; Lk. 5:3-11).

James was one of the early disciples (Mk. 1:29) and was also, with Peter and John, one of the inner circle of three. Only these were taken into the house at the raising of Jairus' daughter (Mk. 5:37; Lk. 8:51). They were also witnesses of the Transfiguration (Mt. 17:1 par. Mk. 9:2; Lk. 9:28) and of the agony in Gethsemane (Mt. 26:37; Mk. 14:33). These three with Andrew asked Jesus privately the questions about eschatology that elicited the Olivet discourse (Mk. 13:3).

James and John not only took it upon themselves to request the highest place in the Kingdom, but also asked that fire be brought down on Jesus' opposition. He rebuked them for their ignorance of His true mission (Lk. 9:52-56).

In the lists of the apostles James always occupies a place of prominence (Mt. 10:2; Mk. 3:17; Lk. 6:14; and Acts 1:13). It was possibly this prominence, together with James' forthrightness, that led Herod Agrippa I to kill "James the brother of John with the sword" (Acts 12:2). And so one of the two brothers became the first apostolic martyr; the other brother, John, became, according to tradition, the only apostle to escape martyrdom — living on till nearly the close of the century.

2. James the son of Alphaeus. In the four lists of the apostles (Mt. 10:3; Mk. 3:18; Lk. 6:15; Acts 1:13), a James is always mentioned as the son of Alphaeus. It seems probable that James the son of Alphaeus is the one called the son of Mary or "the other Mary" (see **1** above). Mk. 15:40 clearly speaks of a Mary the mother of James the younger (AV "the less") and of Joses (*see* JOSES **2**). This Mary seems clearly to be the wife of CLEOPHAS (or CLOPAS) according to Jn. 19:25, and therefore the equation is often given of Cleophas with ALPHAEUS. A Cleopas was one who met Jesus on the road to Emmaus. Again, if this Mary is indeed the sister of Mary the mother of Jesus, as argued above, then James the apostle was the cousin of Jesus.

Whether James the apostle was the brother of Jude the apostle or his father depends on the interpretation of the genitive (Gk. *Ioudas Iakōbou*) in Lk. 6:16 and Acts 1:13. Modern versions tend to take the view that Jude was the son of James (RSV, NEB, JB), but it is a bit strange to have father and son apostles and possibly the grandfather (Lk. 24:18) a disciple as well. Nothing of special import is said of this James in the Gospels. He is always identified by his father or mother. It must be noted that Mary the mother of James the younger is never said to have had a son Jude. Quite possibly this Jude the apostle was indeed the grandson of Mary and Alphaeus (*see* JUDAS **7**).

3. The alleged half brother of Christ. This James is mentioned twice by name in the Gospels (Mt. 13:55 par. Mk. 6:3). The brothers of Jesus are named by the people of Nazareth as "James and Joseph [or Joses or Justus] and Simon and Judas." Another reference to Jesus' brothers is in Jn. 7:3-5, where they are said not to believe. The brothers of the Lord are also mentioned in 1 Cor. 9:5. Gal. 1:19 speaks of James the Lord's brother.

The usual Protestant view has been that there was a third James, the half brother of Christ. The usual Roman Catholic view has been that the so-called half brother of Christ was really by a Semitic idiom the cousin of Christ and was identical with the son of Alphaeus. (Cf. *New Catholic Encyclopedia,* II, *s.v.* "Brothers of Jesus" [G. H. Guyot].)

Whether this James was a cousin of Christ and one of the twelve, or the half brother of Christ and later counted as an apostle, has been much discussed. Further questions are whether the Epistle of James was written by this man if he were not of the twelve, and whether the Epistle of Jude written by "Jude the brother of James" was likewise by one of the twelve, or by one of the Lord's half brothers, or by the apostle Jude, brother of a totally different James? The various possible combinations of these views are obviously numerous.

It should be admitted that the word "brother" is in Semitic expression broad enough to include "cousin." Nonetheless, the disbelief of Jesus' "brothers" in Jn. 7:5 is emphasized. Actually, the circle of "cousins" would be rather broad. The incident of Lk. 2:44 shows a closely knit clan grouping where a twelve-year-old boy might feel quite at home with several cousins. Conceivably, some cousins did not believe in Jesus and others did. Jn. 7:5, however, is probably the strongest point against the cousin theory.

It is nevertheless strange that James the son of Alphaeus and of Mary is regularly referred to with this qualification in the Gospels, but after the death of James the son of Zebedee, the Epistles and Acts regularly refer simply to "James" without qualification, as if there were only one (Acts 12:17; 15:13; 21:18; 1 Cor. 15:7; Gal. 2:9, 12; Jas. 1:1). An apparent exception is Gal. 1:19, but it should be remembered that James the Son of Zebedee was still alive on that first visit of Paul to Jerusalem. This peculiar fact could support the cousin theory and argue that the James, Joses, Jude, and Simon of Mk. 6:3 were really children of the other Mary and Alphaeus. This strange silence with regard to another James may be explained, however, by the eminence of the Lord's brother over the son of Alphaeus. Luke does not always distinguish his characters. There are several Simons! Yet it is a point against the third James theory.

The reference of Gal. 1:19 to James, the Lord's brother, is of special interest, for some would hold that he is here designated an apostle. Does the verse include James among the other apostles besides Peter? Not necessarily; yet in a very similar situation in 1 Cor. 1:14 Paul gives an exception for Crispus and Gaius, who were of the number spoken of there. By the same token, James would be one of the apostles, or at least had an eminence calling for similar recognition.

The other references to this unspecified James certainly give him a considerable eminence: after his deliverance Peter says, "Tell this to James and to the brethren" (Acts 12:17). At the Apostolic Council in Jerusalem James gave the deciding argument concerning the relation between Jews and Gentiles (*see* APOSTOLIC COUNCIL IV, V). It does not say, however, that James presided in any capacity of "bishop of the Jerusalem Church" (Jerome *De vir. ill.* 2). James did appear to be the leader among the elders referred to in Acts 21:18, however, though the decisions are given in the name of the whole company of elders. In the list of resurrection appearances in 1 Cor. 15, James is mentioned apart from the twelve as singled out for special honor. Then (v. 7), it says, "[Christ] appeared to all the apostles" as if James were indeed not among the Twelve, but counted as one of the apostles, who by this time officially included Matthias and Paul, in addition to the original twelve. In Gal. 2:9, James, Cephas, and John are spoken of as "pillars" in Jerusalem. Later the emissaries who came from Jerusalem to Antioch are referred to as "from James" (Gal. 2:12). These facts would seem to imply a sufficient eminence to account for the lack of extra designation for a third James. There is here, however, more than a hint that this James was classified as apostolic, doubtless by virtue of his relation to Christ and the special resurrection appearance to him.

In view of all these facts, it is probably most reasonable to hold that there were indeed three men named James and that James the younger, like most of the other Twelve, achieved no position occasioning special mention. What is left then is the surprising but not impossible situation that Jesus had half brothers, James, Joseph (or Joses or Justus), Simon, and Judas, and that his mother Mary had a sister Mary, the wife of Alphaeus, with James the younger and Justus (or Joses) as sons. Still, the two-James theory is a possibility.

This James, the half brother of the Lord, is mentioned prominently in Christian tradition and even by the Jewish historian Josephus. Josephus says that the high priest Ananus had James stoned to death, but that the people revolted against him as a result (*Ant.* xx.9.1 [200f.]). Eusebius (*HE* ii.23.3-18) quotes Hegesippus to the effect that James was noted for his piety and constant prayers in the temple. He was called "camel-knees" and was respected by Christians and Jews alike, especially as he was (like Jesus) of David's line. Eventually the Jews cast him down from a pinnacle (or corner) of the temple and, as he still lived, they stoned him to death. The major points of this tradition agree with the NT picture.

The question of the authorship of the Epistles of James and Jude is not easily answered. Jude calls himself the brother of James, but again, we cannot be sure of which James he spoke. Tertullian says this Epistle was written by the apostle Jude. We cannot tell whether this means (1) that the Judas who wrote the Epistle was one of the Twelve and brother of James the younger (assuming that Jude was the brother and not the son of James the younger), or (2) that this Judas, one of the Twelve, was a son of James and had a brother also by that name, or (3) that this Judas was another half brother of the Lord and like his full brother James was recognized as an apostle. The possibilities are numerous and, of course, other men by the name of James or Jude may be thought of, but it would seem that one of the above possibilities is the more likely. (*See also* JAMES, EPISTLE OF IV; JUDE, EPISTLE OF II.)

See also BROTHERS OF THE LORD. R. L. HARRIS

JAMES, EPISTLE OF.

- I. Contents
  - A. Outline
  - B. Main Theological Themes
    1. Temptation (Trials)
    2. Law
    3. Faith, and Faith *v.* Works
    4. Wisdom
    5. Eschatology
- II. Literary Character
  - A. Diatribe Theory
  - B. Parenesis Theory
  - C. Homily Theory
    1. Dialogue
    2. Method of Address
    3. Variability of Subject Matter
  - D. Other Sources for the Literary Forms
- III. Language
  - A. Vocabulary
  - B. Style
    1. Evidences of Good Greek Style
    2. Semitic Influences

JAMES, EPISTLE OF

C. Aramaic-Original Theory

IV. Authorship

A. Evidences for the Traditional Authorship

B. Objections to the Traditional Authorship

1. Good Greek of the Epistle
2. Late Acceptance of the Epistle

C. Other Theories of Authorship

1. Pseudonymous
2. Another James
3. Jewish-Original Theory

V. Readers and Their Circumstances

VI. Date

VII. Place

***I. Contents**.–A. Outline*.

1. Salutation (1:1)
2. Trials (1:2-8)
3. Poverty and Wealth (1:9-11)
4. Trial and Temptation (1:12-18)
5. Reception of the Word (1:19-25)
6. True Religion (1:26f.)
7. Social Distinctions and the Royal Law (2:1-13)
8. Faith and Works (2:14-26)
9. The Tongue (3:1-12)
10. The Two Wisdoms (3:13-18)
11. The World and God (4:1-10)
12. Judging (4:11f.)
13. Sinful Self-confidence (4:13-17)
14. Judgment of the Unscrupulous Rich (5:1-6)
15. Patience Until Christ's Return (5:7-11)
16. Oaths (5:12)
17. Prayer (5:13-18)
18. Reclaiming the Sinning Brother (5:19f.)

B. Main Theological Themes. The Epistle of James is the least dogmatic book of the NT. Scarcely a trace of the great theological themes that dominate the Pauline Epistles and the rest of the NT books is to be found. James, e.g., makes no mention of the Incarnation. The name of Christ appears only twice (1:1; 2:1). There is no mention, directly or by implication, of His sufferings, death, or resurrection.

A second feature of the Epistle is the great emphasis on the practical aspects of Christianity. Herder admirably summarized this emphasis:

> What a noble man speaks in this Epistle! Deep unbroken patience in suffering! Greatness in poverty! Joy in sorrow! Simplicity, sincerity, firm direct confidence in prayer! . . . How he wants action! Action! not words, not dead faith! (Quoted in F. W. Farrar, *Early Days of Christianity* [1883], II, 324.)

A third feature of the content of the Epistle is its evident Judaistic flavor. Ropes well remarked that the "religious attitudes of rabbinical Judaism would in most respects sum up the fundamental ideas of the Epistle of James" (p. 31). The distinctive Christian features of course remain; James has baptized these rabbinical ideas into Christ. The outstanding theological themes of the Epistle are:

1. Temptation (Trials). The typically Jewish teachings, namely, (1) joy in trial and (2) the use of trial for the building and perfecting of character, are both found in the Epistle (1:2-4). More significant is the teaching in 1:13-15 concerning the origin of temptation. Here the author reflects contemporary Jewish theology. The rabbinical solution to the problem of the origin of sin was the doctrine of the *yēṣer hārāʿ*, the evil tendency in man, whose function it was to lure him to sin. Jas. 1:13-15 looks very much like a refutation of the Jewish idea that since God created everything, including the evil tendency in people, people are not responsible for their sin. Not so, according to James, for "each person is tempted when he is lured and enticed by his own desire. Then desire when it has conceived gives birth to sin; and sin when it is full-grown brings forth death" (1:14f.).

2. Law. The transitional nature of the Epistle is clearly seen in the treatment of the concept of law. The entire Epistle is concerned with ethics (*didachē*), not proclamation (*kērygma*). Thus Christianity is presented with great emphasis on its ethical teachings as a perfect law, a law of freedom and a royal or kingly law. James seems to be reassuring his Jewish Christian readers that for them there is still the law (the priceless possession of every Jew), though by "law" he does not mean the same thing as a non-Christian might understand by that term. He has baptized this concept into Christ.

The law is a perfect law (1:25, not a strange expression from a Palestinian Jew; cf. Ps. 19:7 [MT 8]). James seems to be deliberately ascribing to *didachē* the attributes of the law. For James, the Christian, it is perfect because it was perfected by Jesus Christ.

It is also "a law of freedom" (1:25), a seemingly contradictory phrase since law implies commandments and they in turn imply restrictions. Dibelius suggested that the concept of law as freedom is Stoic and came into Judaism through Philo (pp. 111f.). James, however, does not seem to be describing the *results* of law, ethically speaking, on the individual. It is a law of freedom, i.e., a law that applies to those who have the status of freedom, not from law but from sin and self, through the "word of truth." Thus "law of freedom" is a Palestinian Jew's way of describing the Christian standard of conduct found in the *didachē*.

This tendency to describe *didachē* as law is found in 2:8-13, a paragraph that arises out of a rebuke for the partiality James's readers were showing toward the rich. This partiality was condoned by an appeal to the law of love to one's neighbor. So James writes, "If you really fulfil the royal law . . . you do well." (The intimation is that they are not fulfilling it.) The "royal law" is connected with the statement in v. 5 where James reminds his readers that God has chosen the poor in the world to be rich in faith and heirs of the Kingdom He has promised to those that love Him. The "royal law," then, is for those who are of God's kingdom; it is the rule of faith for those who have volitionally subjected themselves to the rule of God. This identification of law with the ethical side of Christianity runs through the entire Epistle (cf. 2:8-13; 4:11f.).

3. Faith, and Faith v. Works. Faith, for James, is the basic element of piety (1:3; cf. 2:5), the belief in God — not merely in the existence of God, but in His character as being good and benevolent in His relations with people (1:6, 13). Faith includes belief in the power of God, in His ability to perform miraculous acts; and it is closely associated with prayer (5:15f.; cf. 1:6). These passages illustrate James's dynamic concept of faith and together clearly show his contact with Judaism. James, of course, goes beyond the bounds of Judaism by speaking of faith directed toward the Lord Jesus Christ (2:1).

Similarities exist between the concept of faith in James and that in the teachings of Jesus. For Jesus, too, faith meant access to the divine power and was often associated with healing. Such statements as: "All things are possible to him who believes" (Mk. 9:23); "Therefore I tell you, whatever you ask in prayer, believe that you received it, and it will be yours" (11:24); and "Daughter, your faith has made you well; go in peace" (5:34) reveal a dynamic concept of faith strikingly similar to that of James.

The best-known passage in which faith is mentioned is

2:14-26, and here faith and works are contrasted. A study of this passage reveals that the author is not attempting to refute Paul. The two stand basically in agreement. For both James and Paul faith finds its object in the Lord Jesus Christ, and both are agreed that the first thing to do with faith is to live by it. The "faith" of which James speaks in 2:14-26 is really not faith at all, in the true Hebraic sense of confidence and trust in God that elicits appropriate action. It is not recognized as true faith by James (cf. "if one *says* he has faith") and would not be considered such by Paul.

James's use of the word "works" differs significantly from Paul's. For James, "works" are works of faith, the ethical outworking of true piety and include especially the "work of love" (2:8). (Paul would probably call these the fruit of the Spirit.) When Paul speaks of works, he has in mind primarily the works of the law, i.e., works righteousness. And it is against these that he directs his strongest polemic in Galatians and Romans. (*See* PAULINE THEOLOGY VI.B, C.)

It is best then to understand 2:14-26 as a refutation, not of Paul, but of a misunderstanding of Paul's doctrine of justification by faith.

4. Wisdom. James's treatment of wisdom also reveals the basic Jewish tone of the Epistle. Wisdom is primarily practical, not philosophical. It is not to be identified with reasoning power or the ability to apprehend intellectual problems. It has nothing to do with the questions why or how. It is to be sought by earnest prayer, and it is a gift from God (1:5). Both of these ideas find their roots in the wisdom literature (cf. Wisd. 7:7; Prov. 2:6; Sir. 1:1).

Another more extensive passage (3:13-18) on wisdom has given rise to some difficult problems. Schammberger, Schoeps, and Preisker see in this passage, with its contrast between the wisdom from above and the earthly, devilish wisdom, a refutation of the Gnostics. This may well be, since an incipient type of GNOSTICISM was present among both Jews and Christians long before the full flowering of this heresy in the 2nd century. Such anti-Gnostic sentiments, however, are not a reliable guide for dating the Epistle, particularly for insisting on a late date.

5. Eschatology. Three distinct eschatological themes are found in the Epistle.

a. Kingdom of God. Mention of the kingdom of God grows out of the discussion of partiality (2:1-7). No partiality is to be shown to the rich, for "has not God chosen those who are poor in the world to be rich in faith and heirs of the kingdom which he has promised to those who love him?" This echoes Christ's teaching in Lk. 6:20: "Blessed are you poor, for yours is the kingdom of God." The Kingdom is the reign of God partially realized in this life, but fully realized in the future (cf. Jas. 2:5, "promised"). It is almost synonymous with salvation or eternal life.

b. Judgment. This is the dominant eschatological theme of the Epistle. In 2:12 Christians are admonished to "so speak and so act as those who are to be judged under the law of liberty" and they are reminded that "judgment is without mercy to one who has shown no mercy" (v. 13). Judgment, in other words, will be administered on the basis of works. In 3:1 the author addresses teachers and reminds them that privilege is another basis for judgment.

The judgment of the non-Christian rich is also emphasized in the Epistle. Thus 1:10f. depicts judgment on the wicked rich, whose destruction is likened to the swift withering of the grass due to the burning heat of the sun. In the midst of his pursuits the rich person will fade away. The theme of judgment reappears in 5:1-6. Here the author reaches prophetic heights. The wealthy landowners have indulged themselves and defrauded the poor farm laborers. They have even condemned and killed the righteous. All this has made them ripe for certain judgment (5:5, "you have fattened your hearts in a day of slaughter").

The final passage on judgment (5:9) is addressed to James's Christian readers who have become somewhat frustrated and impatient with the difficult situation in which they find themselves. His word of exhortation is: "Do not grumble, brethren, against one another, that you may not be judged; behold, the Judge is standing at the doors." Judgment is to be based on character, and the imminency of the judgment is paralleled by the imminency of the Parousia, because the same Person is involved in both.

c. Parousia. The hope of the Parousia is presented as the great stimulus for the kind of Christian living advocated in the Epistle. Every kind of suffering and trial must be endured because the Parousia is at hand (5:8). This expectancy of the Parousia is powerful and immediate, and reminds one of the eschatological tenor of the Thessalonian letters.

See ESCHATOLOGY IV, VIII, X.

II. Literary Character.–The importance of the literary character for understanding the Epistle is seen in the fact that some of the best commentators deal with this question first and in considerable detail (e.g., Ropes and Dibelius). To understand the literary form of the Epistle is to solve one of its most baffling problems and to come into possession of a valuable key toward the solution of other problems.

James purports to be an epistle. The opening statement, "James, a servant of God and of the Lord Jesus Christ, To the twelve tribes in the Dispersion: Greeting," is a typical epistolary address. Hundreds of papyrus letters have been uncovered from the sands of Egypt that bear similar opening addresses. But the apparent or purported literary character of the Epistle does not explain the literary forms that underlie it. These are discovered by a careful study of the Epistle itself, and by a comparison with the commonly employed literary forms of the period.

A. Diatribe Theory. From a study of its literary forms J. H. Ropes concluded that the Epistle reveals many of the characteristics of the diatribe — the short moral or ethical address developed initially by the Stoics and Cynics.

Certain stylistic features of the Epistle are similar to the peculiar style of the diatribe: dialogue (2:20); brief questions and answers (5:13f.); rhetorical questions (2:14); harsh speech (2:20; 4:4); the introduction of an opposing speaker with "but someone will say" (2:18); etc. The choice of illustrations, especially in 3:2-12, is significant. This passage with its *ho trochós tḗs genéseōs* reveals some connection, either directly or indirectly, with Hellenistic thought and culture. The author certainly is familiar with Hellenistic literary forms, as is evidenced by the diatribelike character of 2:1-13; 2:14-26; 4:1-10; but his basic circle of ideas is Semitic, not Hellenistic, and Jewish, not Greek. W. L. Knox suggested that the "lively dialogue form had penetrated into the Greek-speaking synagogues of Jerusalem and even into the general usage of the synagogue sermon" (*JTS*, 46 [1945], 10).

B. Parenesis Theory. This theory, rejected by Ropes, was extensively developed by Dibelius. The chief literary characteristics of the parenetic tract are to be found in the Epistle of James. Dibelius lists four in particular: (1) a manifest eclecticism; (2) a lack of real coherence (artificial coherence is attained by means of catchwords, e.g., *leípomai . . . leípetai,* 1:4f.); (3) the repetition of the same theme in different places; (4) the lack of a definite situation to which the exhortations are addressed.

There is much in Dibelius' view of the literary character

of the Epistle of James that commends itself. The presence, e.g., of traditional exhortative material, especially in 4:1-10, is evident. On the other hand, the strong personality of the author is clearly seen through most of the Epistle. Again, the Epistle is not without some coherence of thought. Indeed, some commentators have argued with great force for the complete coherence of the Epistle. Furthermore, the Epistle has some indications of being addressed to a definite situation (e.g., 2:1-7; 2:14-26; 3:1-12; 5:1-6).

C. Homily Theory. The theory that identifies the Epistle with a sermon (especially a synagogue sermon), or perhaps excerpts from a number of sermons, accounts best for all the facts. Martin Luther first hinted at this theory in one of his pronouncements on the Epistle. Attempting to explain its origin, he said, "I imagine it was some good pious man or other who took up a few statements from the disciples or the apostles and so threw them on paper, or perhaps it was composed by another from his sermons" (*WA*, lxiii, 157). J. S. Stevenson expresses a similar idea (*Expos.T.*, 24 [1912-1913], 44).

An examination of the literary character of the Haggadah as preserved in the homiletical and expositional midrashim reveals striking similarities to the literary forms found in the Epistle of James. Of special significance are:

1. Dialogue. The author of the Epistle of James is especially adept at using dialogue (see II.A above) along with the introduction of an alleged or real objector, as in 2:18, using the formula *all' ereí tis*. The Jewish homilists had at least four formulae with which they introduced an alleged or real objection or objector. The one most similar to James's *all' ereí tis* is *'m 'mr lk 'dm*, "but if someone tells you [so reply to him]." This formula is found in the Haggadah of the Tannaim as early as the 2nd cent. (A. Marmorstein, *HUCA*, 6 [1929], 192).

2. Method of Address. Another striking similarity between the Epistle of James and the Jewish homilies is the method of addressing the audience. Fifteen times James addresses his hearers as "brethren." This method of address is common in the OT (Jgs. 19:23; 1 S. 30:23; 1 Ch. 28:2) and is often used in the NT (Rom. 7:4; 1 Cor. 1:10; 1 Thess. 1:4; 1 Jn. 3:13). The Gk. *adelphoí* as an address occurs most frequently in the speeches in Acts, e.g., 1:16; 2:29; 3:17; 6:3; 7:2; 13:15, 26, 38; etc. Its occurrence in Acts 13:15 is especially important because there it is used by Paul in the synagogue sermon preached at Antioch in Pisidia. Ropes suggested that this method of address may have "belonged to the homiletical style of the synagogue and was brought thence into the Christian hortatory language" (p. 132). Marmorstein cited impressive evidence that "brethren" or "our brethren" was a principal method of address used by the Jewish preachers of the first three centuries A.D. (*London Quarterly Review* [Oct. 1916], p. 238).

3. Variability of Subject Matter. The Epistle of James in a very short space deals with a large number of seemingly isolated subjects. If the Epistle is in reality a collection of sermonic materials used by James in the synagogue, then the variability of subject matter can be explained by assuming that the material is collected from a number of sermons on different subjects. (It does not follow, however, that the collection was arbitrarily made without a thought given to the needs of the readers.)

The variety of the material in the Epistle is paralleled by that found in the Jewish synagogue sermons. One would have to list all the themes of Jewish theology in order to include the multiplicity of subjects dealt with in the synagogue sermons (cf. L. Zunz, *Die Gottesdienstliche Vorträge der Juden historisch entwickelt* [2nd ed. 1892], pp. 329-360).

Of special interest is the closing section of the synagogue sermons, since they usually conclude with an eschatological passage — a prophecy of the glorious future of Israel. A typical example is found in a homily from the *Pesikta de Rab Kahana* (p. 213 in Wünsche's translation). The Epistle of James likewise contains a strong eschatological passage, and it appears in the final chapter.

These and other similarities (e.g., use of alliteration) between the literary characteristics of the Epistle and the homiletical and expositional midrashim at least open up the possibility that the Epistle consists of excerpts from numbers of synagogue sermons which have been brought together (not without a definite purpose in mind) and given an epistolary address.

It is highly probable that a Jewish-Christian teacher of Pharisaic background and training would be familiar with the literary style and form of the synagogue sermon. By the 1st cent. A.D. the homily was a regular part of the synagogue service in both Palestine and the Diaspora. The book of Acts records how the freedom that was afforded anyone of competence to deliver the sermon in the synagogue was used by the apostle Paul as a means of evangelism. This freedom existed in the synagogues of Jerusalem as well as those of the Diaspora. It seems unlikely that, with such a splendid opportunity as the synagogues afforded James in Jerusalem to reach his own people, he would have overlooked or neglected this opportunity for evangelism and teaching any more than would the apostle Paul.

D. Other Sources for the Literary Forms. Although the basic orientation of the Epistle is probably to be found in the Jewish synagogue sermon, this does not exclude the use of other materials that were in common use in the Christian community. The most important of these is catechesis. The research of Selwyn and Carrington has shown that common catechetical material underlies many of the NT Epistles. The Epistle of James contains some of this material, and this has to some degree affected its literary form. The high frequency of the use of the imperative (see III.B below) may be due to the presence of catechetical material in the Epistle.

Another source is the *verba Christi*. No other NT book so echoes Christ's words as does the Epistle of James. The early catechetical forms undoubtedly drew from collections of the *verba Christi*, and James seems to have had contact with this tradition while it was still in a plastic form. The author's aphoristic style may be attributable in part to this influence.

III. Language.–The Greek of the Epistle ranks with the best to be found in the NT. This is not, however, to say that the author was a classicist. There are only three periodic sentences in the Epistle (2:2-4; 2:15f.; 4:13-15), and only two of these exceed four lines. The use of Greek particles is very sparse; and although participles are numerous, there is not a single instance of a genitive absolute. No optative occurs and there is no accusative with an infinitive. Nevertheless, the author is obviously at home in the Greek language, a fact revealed by the vocabulary and style of the Epistle.

A. Vocabulary. There are 570 different words in the Epistle. Of these about seventy (this figure varies according to decisions made on variant readings) do not occur elsewhere in the NT. All but twenty-five of the seventy occur in the Greek OT. Only six words in the Epistle (*brýō, enálios, eupeithḗs, euphḗmeros, thrēskos, katḗpheia*) are found neither in the NT nor in the LXX.

The author uses words and phrases in good literary

koine style, e.g., *deleázomai* (1:14), *apokyéō* (1:15, 18), *epitḗdeia toú sṓmatos* (2:16), *katḗpheia* (4:9). He seems to be fond of compounds, e.g., *adiákritos, chrysodaktýlios, prosōpolēmpsía*, etc., and picturesque words, e.g., *ololýzō, deleázomai, dípsychos*. He employs technical terms, e.g., *pēdálion, psychikós*, and phrases, e.g., *trochós tḗs genéseōs* and *émphytos lógos*, without using them in their strict technical sense.

Deissmann stated that "the Epistle of James will be best understood in the open air beside the piled sheaves of a harvest field" (Deiss.*LAE*, p. 232). Its vocabulary reflects the local color of the countryside. Numerous words are drawn from agriculture (*amáō, ámpelos, bréchō, brýō, geōrgós, elaía, maraínō, ópsimos, próimos, sḗpō, sýkon, sykḗ*). Words used in fishing are also employed, e.g., *alykón, anemízō, enálios, exélkō*, and *rhipízō*.

An outstanding feature of the Epistle is the use of rare words. There are about twelve words that have their first known occurrence (assuming the precedence of the Epistle of James to Hermas, Clement, and the Pauline Epistles) in James.

B. Style. The author exhibits a remarkable active literary susceptibility to, and feeling for, a good Greek style. He may be favorably compared to the writer of Hebrews.

1. Evidences of Good Greek Style. The following examples may be cited:

a. Paronomasia (Assonance). This literary device of linking together clauses or sentences by the repetition of the leading word or a cognate permeates the entire Epistle (cf. 1:1f., 3f., 5f., 13f., etc.).

b. Alliteration. This is obviously deliberate (cf. 1:1f., 21; 3:8).

c. Rhyme (Homoeoteleuta). (Cf. 1:6, 14; 2:12; 4:8.)

d. Frequent Use of the Imperative. There are fifty-nine of these (thirty-one in the present tense, twenty-eight in the aorist). A terseness and forcefulness is given to the Epistle by the presence of such a large number of imperatives.

2. Semitic Influences. Despite the good Greek of the Epistle, Semitic influences are evident. It is somewhat precarious to offer a list of Hebraisms or Semitisms, since so many of these constructions have been shown to be a part of a large number of "international vulgarisms," and since experts differ among themselves as to what is or is not a Semitism in the NT. Despite these difficulties there are several indications of possible Semitisms in the Epistle: the use of the attributive genitive for the adjective (1:23, 25; 2:1, 4; 3:6, 13; 5:15); periphrastic tenses (1:17; 3:15); use of the dative for the Hebrew infinitive absolute (5:17, *proseuchḗ proseúxato*); pleonasms (1:7f., 12, 19, 23; 2:22); parallelism (1:15, 17, 22; 3:11f.).

C. Aramaic-Original Theory. This theory arose from (1) the recognition of Hebraic turns of expression in the Epistle, and (2) the refusal to concede such good Greek to James, the Lord's brother. Toward the close of the 19th cent. Bishop Wordsworth (*Studia Biblica*) proposed this theory on an entirely different basis from previous attempts. His study of the Epistle of James in the Latin Codex Corbeiensis convinced him that a text different from our present Greek text of the Epistle underlay it. He explained the differences between the readings in Corbeiensis and in our Greek text by postulating two independent Greek versions of the supposed Aramaic original of the Epistle, the one corresponding to our present Greek text, and the other underlying the Latin Codex Corbeiensis.

Mayor has shown that the variations in Codex Corbeiensis can be explained by the usual principles of textual criticism, without necessitating the theory of an Aramaic original. Fatal to the theory of an Aramaic original is the literary style of the Greek text. It is difficult, if not impossible, to account for James's alliterations, homoeoteleuta, plays on words, etc., on the basis of an Aramaic original.

F. C. Burkitt (*Christian Beginnings* [1924], pp. 25-71) attempted to revive the Aramaic-original theory. His view is that the original of the Epistle was in Aramaic and was translated by a member of the gentile Greek-speaking church of Aelia. The arguments fatal to Wordsworth's theory are likewise fatal to Burkitt's. It can be affirmed with great confidence that Greek was the original language of the Epistle.

IV. Authorship.–According to the superscription, the Epistle was written by "James, a servant of God and of the Lord Jesus Christ." The traditional view has identified this James with the brother of the Lord and the head of the Jerusalem church (Acts 12:17; 15:13; 21:28; 1 Cor. 15:7; Gal. 2:9, 12).

A. Evidences for the Traditional Authorship. There are three main evidences. First, the language of the Epistle is similar to that of the circular letter of Acts 15 and to James's speech. The most important of these similarities are: the use of Gk. *chaírein* in the salutation (Jas. 1:1; Acts 15:23); the close parallel between the phrase *tó kalón ónoma tó epiklēthén eph' hymás* (Jas. 2:7) and *eph' hoús epikéklētai tó ónoma mou ep' autoús* (Acts 15:17); the close relationship between *akoúsate, adelphoí mou* (Jas. 2:5) and *ándres adelphoí, akoúsaté mou* (Acts 15:13). Other verbal coincidences and similarities are *agapētós* (Jas. 1:16, 19; 2:5; Acts 15:25); *tēreín* (Jas. 1:27) and *diatēreín* (Acts 15:29); *episképtesthai* (Jas. 1:27; Acts 15:14); *epistréphein* (Jas. 5:19f.; Acts 15:19).

Although caution should be exercised in ascribing too much significance to these parallels, they remain an important factor in determining authorship.

Second, the historical reports concerning the life and character of the Lord's brother are consistent with the contents of the Epistle. The NT reveals that the brothers of the Lord were not believers before His resurrection (Jn. 7:5). A special postresurrection appearance of Our Lord was made to James (1 Cor. 15:7). This no doubt was the means of his conversion, and subsequently he and his brothers are numbered with the believers (Acts 1:14). James immediately took his place in the Christian community at Jerusalem. Here he associated himself with Peter, John, and other apostles. How he became head of the Jerusalem church is not told, but it is likely that it was prior to the famine of *ca*. A.D. 43, for when Paul named the three "pillars," James is mentioned first (Gal. 2:9). His relations with Paul show that no basic antagonism existed between the two men. Indeed, on at least two occasions James defended Paul's mission among the Gentiles (Acts 15:13-18; Gal. 2). After Paul's return to Jerusalem at the close of his third missionary journey, the NT tells nothing more of James. The popular portrait of James as a strong advocate of the law, an ascetic, and a martyr is derived largely from an account of his death by Hegesippus (see Eusebius *HE* ii.23; but cf. Jerome *De vir. ill.* 2). This account is obviously legendary and unreliable (cf. Lightfoot's evaluation in his comm. on Galatians [1900], pp. 366f.). The NT record and additional information from Josephus (*Ant.* xx.9.1 [200]) are our only reliable sources, and nothing is revealed in either about the character of James the Lord's brother that is inconsistent with what is written in the Epistle.

Third, the Epistle shows the author's knowledge of and dependence upon the Jewish tradition. Several examples will be found in the section on contents (see I.B above). One further example is cited here, namely, the author's use of the tradition concerning Elijah in 5:17f. In this passage, prayer for the return of rain is specifically mentioned, while the OT has no reference to prayer at all. Later Jewish tradition, however, does mention Elijah's prayer in connection with the cessation of rain (cf. Sir. 48:3); and apparently it is this tradition that James is following.

The same is true relative to the duration of the drought. The OT is not explicit. It simply states that the rain came in the third year (1 K. 18:1). This would mean that the drought lasted less than three years. The rabbinic tradition of the drought's precise length is not uniform (cf. SB, III, 760f.), but it is clear from the researches of Kittel (*Die Probleme des palästinischen Spätjudentums* [1926], p. 43; and *ZNW,* 41 [1948], 81) that three-and-a-half in the rabbinic tradition was used as a round number (one-half of seven — very much like our half dozen). Thus James here is again dependent on the Jewish tradition, a tradition one would expect James the Lord's brother to know.

B. Objections to the Traditional Authorship. 1. Good Greek of the Epistle. No objection to the traditional authorship has as much force as this one. How was it possible for one reared at Nazareth in a pious peasant Jewish home to possess a command of the Greek language such as is revealed in the Epistle? The answer to this question may be found first in that the Greek of the Epistle, although good, has evidences of Semitic influences (see III above); and second in that such a knowledge of Greek was required by James's position as head of the Jerusalem church. A large segment of the church in Jerusalem was made up of Hellenists who had lived in the lands of the Dispersion and to whom Greek was the native tongue. James certainly would have associations with these people, and the prestige of the Jerusalem church would demand that its leader be able to speak with them in a manner appropriate to his position. We do not know what linguistic aptitudes the Lord's brother possessed, but it is not too much to assume, in view of the widespread diffusion of Greek in Jewish Palestine (cf. S. Lieberman, *Greek in Jewish Palestine* [1942]) and the need for James to possess a mastery of the language, that the Greek of the Epistle was penned by him.

2. Late Acceptance of the Epistle. Origen (3rd cent.) is the first to cite it as Scripture and to name the author as James, even though passages in noncanonical authors before Origen seem to reveal acquaintance with the Epistle. (For a listing and discussion of these cf. M. Meinertz, *Der Jakobusbrief und sein Verfasser in Schrift und Überlieferung* [1905].) What prevented its earlier recognition if written by James, the head of the Jerusalem Church? The nontheological character of the Epistle, the Jewish nature of its contents, the supposed refutation of the Pauline doctrine of justification by faith, and particularly its lack of claim to apostolic authorship — all may have proved to be hindrances to its universal acceptance in the Church.

C. Other Theories of Authorship. 1. Pseudonymous. The chief problem with this view is that the author is not likely to have used the name James without further identification.

2. Another James. James son of Zebedee is an unlikely candidate, since there is no evidence that he attained a position of leadership in the Church that would warrant a letter addressed to the Church generally. Another objection is his early death (A.D. 44). An unknown James has been suggested by some. This appears to be too easy a solution to a difficult problem.

3. Jewish-Original Theory. F. Spitta and L. Massebieau arrived at the conclusion independently that the Epistle is a Jewish document Christianized by the interpolation of the words *Iēsoú Christoú* in 1:1 and *hēmōn Iēsoú Christoú* in 2:1.This hypothesis has failed to gain the general support of scholars because it overlooks the basic Christian element in the Epistle. It has, however, helped to emphasize that the writer of the Epistle was intimately acquainted with the OT Scriptures and the wisdom literature of the Jews of the Dispersion.

A. Meyer developed a unique theory built on Spitta and Massebieau. He viewed the Epistle as a Jewish document of a special type: an allegorical treatise that utilizes the more-or-less stereotyped allegorical interpretations of the names of Scripture for the purpose of edification. *Jakobus* is Jacob, and he writes a letter to the twelve tribes in the Dispersion through their eponymous founders. The names of the characters in the story of Jacob are played upon throughout the Epistle. Simeon, e.g., is derived from the Hebrew word "to hear." James 1:19-24, then, with its recurrent references to "hearing" and "hearers," is a play on the name Simeon. In like fashion Dan is associated with "judgment," Asher with "riches," etc. The Christian editor, according to Meyer, did his work *ca.* A.D. 80-90, and the Jewish *Grundschrift* dates back to the time of Philo. Although Meyer's theory has been adopted to a degree by Windisch and Easton, it is too ingenious and subtle to warrant general acceptance.

V. Readers and Their Circumstances.–The only direct hint in the Epistle that might help discover who the readers are is found in the superscription, "To the twelve tribes in the Dispersion." This is generally taken to mean the Jews living outside of Palestine, and then, on the basis of the contents of the Epistle, to Christian Jews, at least primarily. The basic objection to this position is that the phrase "the twelve tribes" is a term that traditionally meant the entirety of the Jewish nation (cf. Sir. 44:23; Asm. M. 2:4f.; Bar. 1:2; 62:5; 63:3; 64:3; Acts 26:7) which, no matter how widely it may have been scattered in the Diaspora, could not be considered to have had its entire existence outside of Palestine. Furthermore, if James were writing to the part of the Jewish nation that had taken up its abode in the Diaspora, he could easily have made it clear by such a phrase as "to those out of (*ek*) the twelve tribes that are in the diaspora."

It therefore seems best to take "to the twelve tribes" in a symbolic sense. The phrase would then refer to the Christian Church, conceived of as the new Israel, which inherits the spiritual privileges of the people of God.

Now if "to the twelve tribes" is taken figuratively to mean the Christian Church, it seems best to give a figurative meaning to "in the Dispersion" also. Thus, taken as a whole, the superscription would mean "to the Christian Church, the new Israel, which in reality has its home in heaven but which for the present is resident in a hostile and alien world." This is as far as the superscription can take us in determining the readers of the Epistle. Further indications can be derived from the Epistle itself.

An examination of the contents reveals nevertheless that the Epistle was written primarily for Jews. Some of the most obvious evidences for this are: (1) the tendency of the readers to blame God for their sin — a tendency that sprang from the Jewish doctrine of the evil *yēṣer* (1:13-15); (2) the use of *tḗs dóxēs* in 2:1, a reference to the Shekinah, which would be unintelligible to non-Jewish readers; (3) the evident pride in a monotheistic faith (2:19); (4) the use of the feminine *moichalídes,* "ye adulteresses" (4:4 [RSV "unfaithful creatures"]) in a passage addressed to both men and women, recalling the OT figure of the Lord as the faithful husband and Israel as His unfaithful wife, which also would hardly be intelligible to gentile readers (cf. Cadoux, pp. 10-18, for a formidable list of indications of Jewish readers).

The Jews addressed are primarily Christians (cf. 2:1), but one passage (5:1-6) seems clearly to be addressed to non-Christians. This passage may represent a prophetic attempt to reach non-Christians who were frequenting Christian assemblies (cf. 1 Cor. 14:23f.) just as non-Jews (the God-fearers of Acts 13:26) were often in attendance at Jewish synagogues.

In the shorter disconnected passages of the Epistle it is impossible to discover anything about the readers' circumstances. Most of these exhortations are general and relate to social and spiritual conditions to be found among any group of Christians in any age. This does not apply, however, to the more extended passages in the Epistle that treat social conditions (2:1-12; 5:1-11). In these the author's knowledge of the situation is more evident. James is addressing poor Christians who are employed as farm laborers for wealthy landowners. A few rich may be included among his Christian readers (cf. 4:13-17), but James is primarily concerned with the poor. His statements denouncing the rich (especially 5:1-6) are among the strongest in the NT.

VI. Date.–A wide range of opinion exists on the date of the Epistle. The various dates suggested fall into three groups: (1) pre-Christian (Spitta, Massebieau, Meyer); (2) during the lifetime of the Lord's brother (A.D. mid-40's to 62); (3) late date (*ca.* A.D. 70-150). Admittedly the dating of the Epistle is difficult. Since there is no mention of historical events or personages that might help to fix a date, dogmatic assertions are not possible. Internal evidence, however, favors an early date.

(1) The social conditions revealed in the Epistle suggest a date before the destruction of Jerusalem. The Hasmonean nobility was superseded by a new aristocracy, which oppressed the poor as did its predecessors. The new aristocracy, however, disappeared during the war of A.D. 66-70. G. F. Moore pointed out that subsequent to the Jewish War and the wars under Trajan and Hadrian, the old social cleavage between rich and poor had noticeably diminished (*Judaism in the First Centuries of the Christian Era,* II [1932], 157). The new social cleavage was between those who were instructed in their religion and those who were not. In the Epistle of James the social cleavage was still between the pious poor and the wicked rich.

(2) The concept of faith in the Epistle suggests an early date. Faith, which is associated with prayer, healing, and the miraculous intervention of God, strongly resembles the concept in the Synoptic Gospels. "If James is a late work, it provides us with an example of faith connected with bodily healing (5:15) which is quite without parallel in the Pastorals and any other late book of the NT" (C. Powell, *Expos.T.,* 13 [1901-1902], 314). Indeed, the general similarity of tone and teaching that the Epistle displays with the Synoptic tradition is strong evidence for an early date.

(3) The eschatology of the Epistle points to an early date. The Parousia expectation rates in intensity with that found in the Thessalonian Epistles. There is no indication of a delayed Parousia as we find in some of the late books of the NT, and there are no apocalyptic visions or similar developments as found in later Christian apocalyptic literature. James's readers are living in the active and powerful expectation of an imminent Parousia. Nothing in the Christian literature of the 2nd cent. matches the simple and powerful eschatological teaching of the Epistle of James.

(4) The organization of the churches of the Epistle also points to an early date. The elders alone seem to be regarded as possessing pastoral authority. The office of bishop is not mentioned as it almost certainly would have been in the 2nd century. The only other church officers referred to in the Epistle are the teachers (ch. 3), who seem to be loosely organized.

(5) The debate concerning the Gentiles is wholly absent. This, of course, can be explained by assuming a late date, i.e., at a time when the argument had cooled off and had largely been forgotten. But it also can be explained by assuming an early date, before the contention had become bitter. If James wrote *ca.* A.D. 44, the problem would already have arisen (cf. the discussion in Gal. 2:1-20, which arose primarily out of Paul's preaching to Gentiles at Antioch, Acts 11:26), but would not as yet have assumed great importance. The mission to the Gentiles brought it into clear focus.

(6) The superscription is addressed to the entire Church (see V above), but the contents reveal that the hearers are primarily Jews. The only time in the history of the Christian Church that one could address the entire Church and be speaking primarily to Jews was before the mission to the Gentiles *ca.* A.D. 47.

(7) A crucial passage for dating the Epistle is the well-known one on faith and works (2:14-26). These verses are inexplicable without presupposing a knowledge of certain Pauline formulae; yet it is hard to believe that the author of 2:14-26 is refuting Paul. This would involve an almost inconceivable miscomprehension of the Pauline doctrine of justification by faith. The passage is best explained as having been occasioned by a misunderstanding of Paul, not by the author, but by the readers. Such a misunderstanding would have been more likely at the very outset of Paul's public preaching than later on. The book of Acts records his first extended public preaching as taking place at Antioch (11:26). This yearlong ministry preceded the famine visit to Jerusalem of *ca.* A.D. 46 (cf. Acts 11:27-29; Gal. 2:1-10) and the Herodian persecution of A.D. 44. How long it was before the misunderstanding and misapplication of Paul's doctrine of justification by faith came to the attention of James is not known. Since Jews, including Christian Jews, from all over the Mediterranean world were constantly moving in and out of Jerusalem, it probably was not long. A date *ca.* A.D. 44, during or immediately following the Herodian persecution, would best fit all the known factors.

(8) The most serious objection to the early date is that the churches addressed show signs of apathy, which seems to indicate that they are past the early stages of their life. But is this a valid argument against an early date? Time is not the only factor involved in apathy; the people themselves, their background and circumstances, are also important considerations. In periods of general intense enthusiasm and zeal there are always some who are not carried along on the wave of excitement. And even if it is insisted that time is needed for a state of apathy to set in, about ten years had elapsed in which this could have taken place.

VII. Place.–Although a number of opposing suggestions have been made from time to time, there can be little doubt that the Epistle was written in Palestine. The author draws pictures that are Near Eastern generally and Palestinian particularly (cf. "the early and the late rain" [5:7]; the spring of brackish water [3:11]; the fig, olive, and vine [3:12]; and the "scorching heat" [1:11]).

Bibliography.–Comms. by J. Adamson (*NICNT,* 1976); A. Carr (*CGT,* 1895); M. Dibelius (*KEK,* rev. ed. 1964; Eng. tr., *Hermeneia,* 1976); B. S. Easton, (*IB,* 1957); F. Hauck (1926); R. J. Knowling (*WC,* 1910); J. Marty (1935); J. B. Mayor (3rd ed. 1913); J. Moffatt (*MNTC,* 1928); B. Reicke (*AB,* 1964), J. H. Ropes (*ICC,* 1916); R. V. G. Tasker (*Tyndale,* 1956); H. Windisch and H. Preisker (*HNT,* 3rd ed. 1951).

A. T. Cadoux, *Thought of St. James* (1944); A. Meyer, *Das Rätsel des Jacobusbriefes* (1930); H. Schammberger, *Die Einheitlichkeit des Jacobusbriefes im antignostischen Kampf* (1936); H. Schoeps, *Theologie und Geschichte des Judenchristentums* (1949). W. W. WESSEL

JAMES, PROTEVANGELIUM prə-tē-van-jel'-i-əm, prō'tə-van-jel'i-əm **OF.** *See* APOCRYPHAL GOSPELS II.B.

JAMIN jā'min [Heb. *yāmîn*].

1. A "son" (clan) of Simeon (Gen. 46:10; Ex. 6:15; Nu. 26:12; 1 Ch. 4:24).

2. A Judahite, son of Ram and grandson of Jerahmeel (1 Ch. 2:27).

3. A Levite, one of those who "helped the people to understand" the Torah when Ezra enforced it (Neh. 8:7; 1 Esd. 9:48; AV Adinus; NEB Jadinus).

JAMINITES jā'min-īts [Heb. *hayyāmînî*]. Descendants of Jamin (Nu. 26:12). *See* JAMIN **1.**

JAMLECH jam'lek [Heb. *yamlēḵ*–'may he (God) cause to reign']. A prince or chief of the tribe of Simeon (1 Ch. 4:34). If v. 41 refers to the preceding list, he lived at the time of Hezekiah.

JAMNIA jam'ni-ə. *See* JABNEEL **1.**

JAMNITES jam'nīts [Gk. *Iamnitais*] (2 Macc. 12:9, AV). The inhabitants of Jamnia, the ancient Jabneel, a town on the northern border of Judah near the sea. Its port and navy were burned by Judas Maccabeus.

JANAI jā'nī [Heb. *yaʿnay*–'may he answer']. A chief of a family descended from Gad (1 Ch. 5:12; AV Jaanai).

JANGLING. An obsolete term used in 1 Tim. 1:6, AV, for Gk. *mataiología* (RSV "vain discussion"). Cf. *mataiológoi,* "empty talkers," in Tit. 1:10.

JANIM jā'nim [Heb. *yānîm*]; AV JANUM. A place in the Hebron uplands named with Eshan and Beth-tappuah (Josh. 15:53), possibly Beni Naʿim, about 6 km. (4 mi.) E of Hebron.

JANNAI jan'ī [Gk. *Iannai*]; AV JANNA. An ancestor of Jesus in Luke's genealogy, the fifth before Joseph the husband of Mary (Lk. 3:24).

JANNES AND JAMBRES jan'əz, jam'brēz [Gk. *Iannēs kaí Iambrēs*]. Two Egyptian magicians or soothsayer priests who withstood Moses before Pharaoh. The names occur in the Bible only in 2 Tim. 3:8, although the incident referred to is undoubtedly that described in Ex. 7:11, 22, in which Pharaoh "called for the wise men and the sorcerers, and they also, the magicians of Egypt, did the same [as Moses and Aaron] with their secret arts." In both Jewish and Greek traditions the names Jannes and Jambres are given to two of these magicians.

I. Function.–The word "magicians" (Heb. *ḥarṭummîm*) occurs also in Gen. 41:8, 24 (grouped in v. 8 with *ḥᵃḵāmîm,* "wise men"); Ex. 8:7, 18f. (MT 3, 14f.); and Dnl. 1:20 and 2:2 (grouped with *'aššāpîm,* "conjurers" or "enchanters," and *mᵉḵaššᵉpîm,* "sorcerers"). The root idea, although obscure in Hebrew, is probably to be connected with some aspect of occult knowledge, or scripts used in magical practices. The alternate translation, "soothsayer priest," probably best expresses the sense of the word in the Egyptian context.

II. Orthography.–The names Jannes and Jambres occur in a variety of Greek and Aramaic forms. Jannes, which is possibly a Grecized form of the Aram. *Yôḥānā'*, is reflected as *ynys* or *ywnys* (Tg. Ps. Jon.), *ywnws* (Yalkut Shimeoni), *ywḥn'* (T.B. *Menahoth*), *yḥnh* (CD 5:17-19), and *ywḥny* (Midr. *Ex. Rabba*). Jambres, the original of which is in doubt, occurs as *ymrys* or *ymbrys* (Tg. Ps. Jon.), *ywmbrys* (Midr. *Tanhuma*), *mmr'* (T.B. *Menahoth,* Midr. *Ex. Rabba*), *Mambrēs* (Origen on Mt. 27:9), and the Latin *Mambre* (*Decretum* of Gelasium).

III. Rabbinic References.–Although the names do not occur in the OT, Philo, or Josephus, they are common in late Jewish rabbinical traditions. Tg. Ps. Jon. on Ex. 1:15 and 7:11 names both as the chief magicians who opposed Moses and Aaron. The tractate T.B. *Menahoth* 85a quotes Jannes' and Jambres' mocking Moses' and Aaron's attempt to do magic in Egypt, the home of such arts. Tg. Ps. Jon. on Nu. 22:22 considers the magicians servants of Balaam, while *Yalkut Shimeoni* on Ex. 2:15 makes them the sons of that soothsayer. In the Jerusalem Targum to Nu. 22:22 they escape with Balaam to Ethiopia, eventually fleeing that country to Egypt, where they become the chief of Pharaoh's magicians. *Yalkut Shimeoni* on Ex. 14:25 also attributes to Jannes and Jambres an attempt to destroy Israel during its passage through the Red Sea by restricting the power of the angelic beings who were holding back the waters. Another Jewish tradition (Midr. *Tanhuma*) has them accompanying Israel's Exodus as part of the "mixed multitude" and makes them responsible for the instigation of the golden calf incident. Without doubt some of these confused legends, possibly collected in a now-lost book, were known and reflected in 2 Tim. 3:8.

IV. Non-Jewish References.–Jannes and Jambres, one or both, are mentioned by Pliny (*Nat. hist.* xxx.2.11; 1st cent. A.D.), Apuleius (*Apology* 90; 2nd cent. A.D.), and the Pythagorean philosopher Numenius (2nd cent. A.D. cited in Eusebius *Praep.ev.* ix.8), who refers to them as Egyptian *hierogrammateís,* "sacred scribes." In early Christian circles Origen (*Contra Celsum* iv.51) speaks of a history concerning Moses, Jannes, and Jambres, and elsewhere (on Mt. 27:9) cites the tradition of a "secret book which was written by Iamnes and Mambres." The sixth-century *Decretum Gelasianum* not only alludes to an apocryphal *Book of Jannes and Jambres (Mambre),* but reinforces the legend that they eventually became penitents and joined the community of Israel. These traditions, like those of the Jews, are confused and no evidence of such a book remains.

Bibliography.–The most important primary sources are given in *HJP,* III, 402-405; SB, III (1926), 661f. See also J. Charlesworth, ed., *Pseudepigrapha and Modern Research* (1976), pp. 133f.; M. Dibelius and H. Conzelmann, *Pastoral Epistles* (Eng. tr., *Hermeneia,* 1972), pp. 116f.; L. Grabbe, *JBL,* 98 (1979), 393-401; *TDNT,* III, *s.v.* 'Ιαννης, 'Ιαμβρης (Odeberg); also pp. 990f.

C. E. ARMERDING

JANNES AND JAMBRES, BOOK OF. *See* JANNES AND JAMBRES.

JANNEUS jə-nē'əs [Gk. *Iannaios*]. The Hasmonean king and high priest of Judea (*ca.* 103-76 B.C.), also named Alexander, under whose imperialistic policies that kingdom enjoyed its greatest expansion. Although during his lifetime he ruthlessly crushed the bitter opposition of the Pharisees to his rule, after his death his wife and successor, Salome Alexandra, at Janneus's request, was friendly toward that sect and introduced Pharisaic rule.

See HASMONEANS; PHARISEES.

JANOAH jə-nō'ə [Heb. *yānô(a)ḥ* (with *hê* directive *yānôḥâ*)–'resting-place'] (Josh. 16:6f.); AV JANOHAH.

1. A town on the northern boundary of the tribal territory of Ephraim, between Taanath-shiloh and Ataroth. It has been identified with Khirbet Yānûn, 11 km. (7 mi.) SE of Shechem (*LBHG,* p. 236; *GTTOT,* p. 166) — but no explanation is offered for the identification. The form *yānôḥâ* in v. 6 is clearly with *hê* directive, but it cannot be in v. 7 (*miyyānôḥâ,* "from Janoah"), although the accent is penultimate.

2. A town in upper Galilee captured by Tiglath-pileser in 733/32 B.C. (2 K. 15:29). If the order of names is significant, Janoah was located between Abel-beth-maacah and Kedesh. Simons (*GTTOT,* § 932) rejects the suggestion of Janûḫ E of Tyre, which would mean "an impossible break in the line of cities enumerated," and identifies Janoah instead with Tell en-Nâʿimeh, 8 km. (5 mi.) NE of Kedesh. Tiglath-pileser's account mentions the conquest of Abel<ma>akka on the borderland of Bit-Ḫumri (Beth-Omri = Israel) (D. J. Wiseman, *Iraq,* 18 [1956], 117ff.; cf. *ANET,* pp. 283f.).
W. S. L. S.

JANUM jā'nəm. *See* JANIM.

JAPHETH jā'fəth [Heb. *yepeṯ, yāpeṯ*; Gk. *Iapheth*] (Gen. 9:27). This name is the hiphil jussive of Heb. *pāṯâ,* "to open," and means "may God enlarge." Japheth had seven immediate descendants (Gen. 10:2; 1 Ch. 1:5-7), represented by the nations designated GOMER (perhaps the ancient Cimmerians who conquered Urartu before the 8th cent. B.C.), MAGOG (Asia Minor?), Madai (the MEDES), JAVAN (the Ionians and their descendants), TUBAL (most probably the Tabal in Cappadocia mentioned in ninth- and eighth-century-B.C. Assyrian sources), MESHECH (the Mushki, who came to the ancient Near East from the Russian steppes), and TIRAS (identification uncertain, but perhaps the Tursha, mentioned in the 13th cent. B.C. by Merneptah as a warlike northern people). The sons of Gomer were Ashkenaz (represented by the Scythians), Riphath (identified with a region in Anatolia), and Togarmah (probably the area surrounding the Anatolian city known in eighth-century-B.C. Assyrian sources as Til-Garimmu). The sons of Javan (Elishah, Tarshish, Kittim, and Dodanim) were the western division of the family that passed through Ionia and settled in the islands and coastlands of the Aegean (cf. Gen. 10:5). Elishah has been identified with Alashia in Cyprus, while Dodanim, which may be a corruption of Rodanim, can be identified with Rhodes.

In Gen. 9:27, as in other passages, Japheth is third in the enumeration of Noah's sons, but he is really regarded as the second son, Ham being the youngest. In the genealogical table (Gen. 10), however, the descendants of Japheth are given first, and those of Shem last, in order to set forth Semitic affinities at greater length. This ordering seems to indicate that the Jews knew the fair races and moreover were well disposed toward them, for Japheth was (ultimately) to dwell in the tents of Shem and therefore to take part in Shem's spiritual privileges.

Some connection between the Hebrew Japheth and the Greek giant-hero, Iapetos, father of Prometheus, who was regarded by the Greeks as the father of the human race, may exist, but is far from easy to establish. The original Hebrew record is much too early to permit any form of borrowing from Greek mythological sources, even if such were thought desirable. Yet the closeness of linguistic form between Heb. *yepeṯ/yāpeṯ* and Gk. *Iapetos* might indicate that the early Greeks borrowed the name from Near Eastern traditions regarding the existence of ancient peoples, since they adopted other elements of culture from Near Eastern sources.

See also HAM; SHEM; TABLE OF NATIONS.
T. G. PINCHES
R. K. H.

JAPHETH jā'fəth [Gk. *Iapheth*]. A region mentioned only in Jth. 2:25, where its southern borders are described as "fronting toward Arabia." We should not think of this area as being too far south, however, for Holofernes had just seized Cilicia (in southeastern Asia Minor) and had not yet attacked Damascus (v. 27).

JAPHIA jə-fī'ə [Heb. *yāpî(a)ʿ*; Gk. *Iephtha*].

1. King of Lachish, one of the five "kings of the Amorites" who formed an alliance in an expedition against Gibeon on account of its treaty with the Israelites (Josh. 10:3-5). After their rout by Joshua in the battle of Beth-horon (v. 10; *see* BETH-HORON, BATTLE OF), they fled and hid themselves in the cave at Makkedah (v. 16). As Joshua passed, he was informed of this, but, unwilling to delay his pursuit of the fugitives, he ordered great stones to be rolled into the mouth of the cave, leaving a guard in charge (vv. 17f.). On the completion of his victory, Joshua returned to Makkedah, commanded the Israelites to bring forth the imprisoned kings, and summoned the chiefs of his army to plant their feet upon their necks. Then he put them to death; and after he had hung their bodies on five trees, he ordered the Israelites in the evening to take them down and cast them into the cave (vv. 22-27).

2. [Gk. LXX *Iephies, Iaphie*]. One of the sons of David who were born to him at Jerusalem (2 S. 5:15; 1 Ch. 3:7; 14:6).
J. CRICHTON

JAPHIA jə-fī'ə [Heb. *yāpî(a)ʿ*]. A town on the southern boundary of Zebulun named with Chisloth-tabor and Daberath (Josh. 19:12). It is represented by the modern Yâfā, about 2½ km. (1½ mi.) SW of Nazareth, near the foot of the hills. It was one of the places fortified by Josephus (*Vita* 45 [230]; 52 [270]; *BJ* ii.20.6 [573]).

See *EAEHL,* II, *s.v.* (D. Barag).

JAPHLET jaf'lit [Heb. *yaplēṭ*]. In 1 Ch. 7:32f., a son of Heber, an Asherite.

JAPHLETITE jaf'lə-tīt, jaf-lē'tīt [Heb. *yaplēṭî*] (Josh. 16:3); AV JAPHLETI. A clan said to border on the territory of Joseph.

JAPHO jā'fō (Josh. 19:46, AV). *See* JOPPA.

JAR. Most of the vessels in antiquity were made of fired clay, and the jars mentioned in the Bible are no exception. Only rarely was stone, metal, glass, or alabaster used.

I. In the OT.–There are several Hebrew terms that refer to jars of different sizes, shapes, and uses. Not all of these terms can be connected with archeological finds. Heb. *nēḇel* refers to a large storage jar (Jer. 13:12; AV "bottle"; NEB "wine-jars") about 0.6 m. (2 ft.) high that held about 29 l. (5½ gals.). Only about half as large as the *nēḇel* was the *kaḏ,* which served as a water jar (Gen. 24:14-46; NEB "water-jug," "[water-] jar") or a storage jar for flour (1 K. 17:12). The mouth was big enough to allow removal of a handful of flour but small enough to be covered with a large potsherd, stone, small bowl, or lid. Thus the *kaḏ* was smaller than a "barrel" (AV, 17:14, 16; 18:33 [MT 34]). Heb. *ṣappaḥaṯ* apparently denotes two different vessels. One was a water canteen or pilgrim flask made for travelers or soldiers. The mouth of the canteen allowed for quick and easy drinking and could be easily stoppered for traveling. This is probably the meaning of 1 S. 26:11f., 16 (NEB "water-jar"); here David takes the *ṣappaḥaṯ* from Saul, who is chasing him (cf. 1 K. 19:6; NEB "pitcher"). On the other hand, the *ṣappaḥaṯ* in 1 K. 17:12 (RSV "cruse") was most likely an oil juglet (*see* CRUSE). These juglets ranged from 7.5 to 15 cm. (3-6 in.) in height. The *baqbuq*

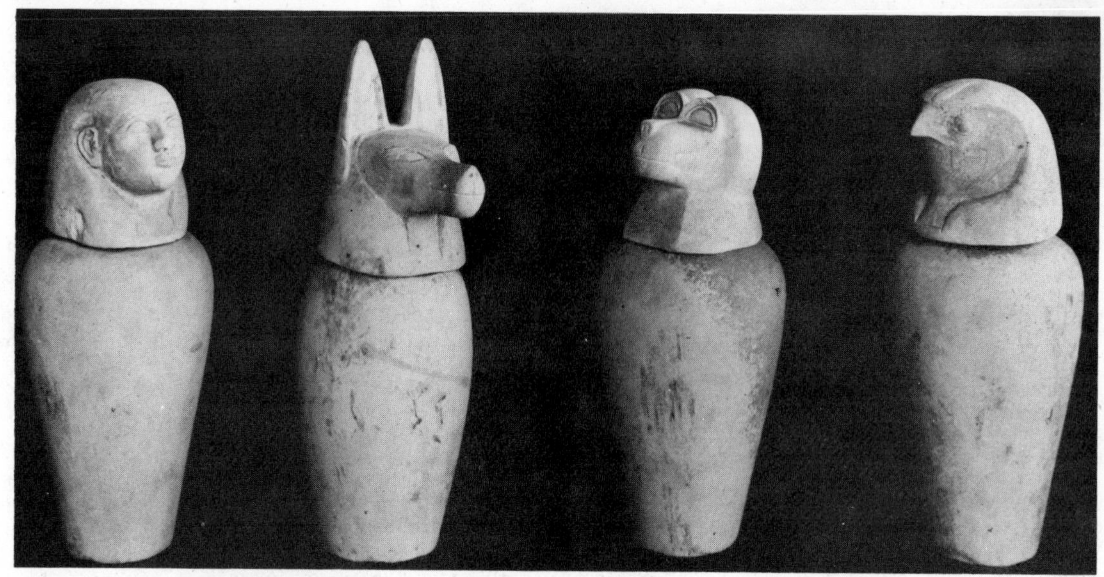

Set of limestone canopic jars (7th-6th cents. B.C.) from Medinet Habu, used to hold the viscera of the mummy with whom they were buried (Royal Ontario Museum, Toronto)

Polychrome glazed pottery jar (*ca.* 800 B.C.) showing a kneeling bull, from Zawiyeh, about 240 km. (150 mi.) E of Nineveh (Royal Ontario Museum, Toronto)

was an expensive decanter with a narrow neck that aerated the water as it was poured for drinking. This produced a gurgling sound that may have led to the name *baqbuq*. The vessel was also used for honey and water (1 K. 14:3; NEB "flask"). Two terms occur only once each in the OT. The first, *'āsûḵ*, refers to a jar used to store oil (2 K. 4:2; NEB "flask"). This jar had a special spout with a small hole, making it easy to fill all kinds of jars, especially small oil juglets. The other term, *ṣinṣeneṯ*, indicates a container for manna (Ex. 16:33); the size and shape are uncertain.

In Jgs. 7:8 the term *ṣēḏâ* means "provisions," but the RSV and NEB read *kaddê* and translate "jars." The support of the versions for "provisions," however, makes it improbable that "jars" is correct (R. G. Boling, *Judges* [*AB*, 1975], p. 146).

II. In the NT.–The Gk. term *hydría*, a cognate of *hýdōr*, "water," denotes a water jar. In Jn. 2:6f. the term refers to large stone jars holding 75 or 115 l. (20 or 30 gals.) each. In Jn. 4:28, however, the jar is probably smaller since it was most likely carried. The term *kerámion* is qualified as a jar of water (*hýdōr*) (Mk. 14:13 par. Lk. 22:10). The term *alábastros* refers to a small alabaster juglet (Mt. 26:7 par. Mk. 14:3; NEB "small bottle"). Alabaster was reserved for expensive perfumes (*see* ALABASTER).

See also FLASK; POTTER, POTTERY.

Bibliography.–R. Amiran, *Ancient Pottery of the Holy Land* (1970); J. L. Kelso, *Ceramic Vocabulary of the OT* (*BASOR Supp. Studies*, 5–6, 1948).

J. C. MOYER

JARAH jā'rə [Heb. *yaʿrâ*–'honeycomb'(?); Gk. *Iada* (= Heb. *yaʿdâ*)]. A descendant of King Saul (1 Ch. 9:42). Some Hebrew MSS have *yaʿdâ*, and it should probably be accepted as the correct reading, for *yaʿdâ* is linguistically the same as *yᵉhôʿaddâ* (Jehoaddah, 1 Ch. 8:36; Gk. *Iada*).

JAREB jā'rəb, jär'əb [Heb. *yārēḇ*–'let him contend'; Gk. *Iareim*]. The name given to an Assyrian king who received tribute from Israel (AV Hos. 5:13; 10:6).

A. H. Sayce (*Higher Criticism and the Monuments* [1895], pp. 416f.) thinks it was the original name of Sargon II, the usurper who succeeded Shalmaneser V after his death in 723/722 B.C., and who took the name of "one of the most

Alabaster lid of a canopic jar in the shape of a queen's head, from the Valley of the Kings near Thebes, *ca.* 1350 B.C. (Egyptian Museum, Cairo)

illustrious of Babylonian monarchs." But it seems likely that Hosea's prophecies were delivered earlier than 722. A more probable suggestion is that Jareb is simply a scornful nickname for a king who would prove a scourge rather than an ally, e.g., "king Combat" (Farrar), "king Fightingcock" (Guthe), "king Contentious" (American-Jewish version), or "king Pick-Quarrel" (G. A. Smith). Another suggestion is "the great king," reading Heb. *mlky rb* instead of *mlk yrb* (W. M. Müller, *ZAW,* 17 [1897], 334; cf. Moffatt, RSV, NEB), or "high king," reading *mlk rm* (following LXX). Cheyne would amend to read "king of Arabia." (For other suggestions see W. R. Harper in *ICC.*)

The historical reference may be to the attempt by Menahem of Israel to win over Tiglath-pileser in 738 B.C. (2 K. 15:19). Wellhausen, however, inserted the name "Judah" in Hos. 5:13 to complete the parallelism; and if this is accepted the reference would probably be to the bribe offered to Tiglath-pileser by Ahaz of Judah in 734 B.C. (2 K. 16:7f.). On the other hand, the reference may simply be to the general tendency of Israel and Judah to seek foreign aid instead of relying on Yahweh.

J. G. G. NORMAN

JARED jā'rəd, jär'əd [Heb. *yereḏ*–'descent'; pausal form *yāreḏ* (Gen. 5:15; 1 Ch. 1:2); Gk. *Iared*]; AV JERED (1 Ch. 1:2). In Gen. 5:15-20; 1 Ch. 1:2; Lk. 3:37, son of Mahalaleel and father of Enoch.

JARESIAH jär-ə-sī'ə (1 Ch. 8:27, AV). *See* JAARESHIAH.

JARHA jär'hə [Heb. *yarḥā'*]. An Egyptian slave of Sheshan, about Eli's time, who married his master's daughter and became the founder of a house of the Jerahmeelites (1 Ch. 2:34f.).

JARIB jā'rib, jär'ib [Heb. *yārîḇ*–'he contends,' or 'takes [our] part,' or 'conducts [our] case'].

1. In 1 Ch. 4:24, a son (clan) of Simeon, the same as Jachin of Gen. 46:10; Ex. 6:15; Nu. 26:12.

2. In Ezr. 8:16, one of the "chief men" for whom Ezra sent, and dispatched by him to Casiphia to fetch ministers for God's house (1 Esd. 8:44; AV Joribas; NEB Joribus).

3. In Ezr. 10:18, a priest who had married a foreign wife (1 Esd. 9:19; AV, NEB, Joribus).

JARIMOTH jär'ə-moth (Ezr. 10:27, AV; 1 Esd. 9:28, AV, NEB). *See* JEREMOTH **7.**

JARMUTH jär'muth [Heb. *yarmûṯ*].

1. A city of the Canaanites in the Shephelah of Judah (Josh. 15:35) whose king Piram joined the league of the five kings in an attempt to stop Joshua's invasion (Josh. 10:3-5). They were defeated at Gibeon and executed at Makkedah (Josh. 10:3-5, 22-27; 12:11). After the Exile, Jarmuth was occupied by remnant Jews (Neh. 11:29). The site of this once important place is Khirbet Yarmûk, about 13 km. (8 mi.) NNE of Eleutheropolis (Beit Jibrîn).

2. [Heb. *yarmûṯ*; LXX B *Remmath,* A *Iermōth* (Josh. 21:29); in the duplicate list (1 Ch. 6:73 [MT 58]) Heb. *rā'môṯ*; Gk. *Ramōth* (6:65); in Josh. 19:21 Heb. *remeṯ* occurs in the list of the cities of Issachar; Gk. B *Remmas,* A *Ramath*]. A town of Issachar, probably to be identified with REMETH of Josh. 19:21 and RAMOTH of 1 Ch. 6:73.

See *EAEHL,* II, *s.v.* "Jarmuth, Tel" (A. Ben-Tor).

K. G. JUNG

JAROAH jə-rō'ə [Heb. *yārô(a)ḥ*]. A Gadite chief (1 Ch. 5:14).

JASAEL jā'sə-əl (1 Esd. 9:30, AV). *See* SHEAL.

JASHAR jā'shər, **BOOK OF** [Heb. *sēp̄er hayyāšār*]; AV BOOK OF JASHER, mg. THE BOOK OF THE UPRIGHT. The title of an ancient collection of Hebrew literary material, referred to as though it were a familiar source. Two quotations were made from it in the OT: (1) Josh. 10:12-14, in which the sun and moon were commanded to stand still; (2) 2 S. 1:18-27, the "song of the bow" or lament of David over Saul and Jonathan. Some scholars have suggested a third extract in 1 K. 8:12, "Then Solomon said, 'The Lord has set the sun in the heavens, but has said that he would dwell in thick darkness.'" The LXX quotes Yahweh's words (LXX v. 53) as "written in the book of the song" (Gk. *en biblíǭ tḗs ōdḗs*), and scholars have suggested that the words "the song" (Heb. *haššîr*) might easily be a corruption of Heb. *hayyāšār.* A similar confusion ("song" for "righteous") may explain the fact that the Syriac Peshitta of Joshua has for a title "the book of praises or hymns."

The book seems to have been a collection of poetry which probably included epics and religious songs. In 2 S. 1:18 the RSV "it" and the NEB "this dirge" unfortunately replace the MT "the bow," the title of the lament composed by David on the occasion of Saul's death and taken from the body of the poem. The AV mg. reading, "the ode of the bow," while nearer to the sense of the MT, still failed to see the use of "bow" as the title. The use of a word in the body of a poem as the title of the composition is a familiar Arabic poetic convention, as illustrated by the suras of the Koran. The term "Jashar," which is the Hebrew adjective "upright," has led some scholars to suppose that the collection either honored individual heroes or reflected the character of Israel as the upright nation in the ancient Near East.

The provenance of the work has been the topic of considerable discussion. The comparatively poor state of preservation of the OT quotations indicates the antiquity of the material itself. There can be no doubt about the authenticity of the extracts from the work. Their linguistic affinities suggest that the book originated in the late Amarna period; additions were made at least until the time of Solomon. It seems to have had some affinity with the Book of the Wars of the Lord (Nu. 21:14), and both compositions may have commenced at approximately the same time. Some scholars have conjectured that the Book of Jashar contained such poems as the Song of Deborah (Jgs. 5) and the Song of Miriam (Ex. 15:21), but this cannot be proved.

See J. A. Montgomery, comm. on Kings (*ICC*, 1951), pp. 189ff. J. ORR R. K. H.

JASHEN jā'shən [Heb. *yāšēn*]. Seemingly the father of some of David's thirty mighty men (2 S. 23:32f.). The MT reads "Eliahba of Shaalbon, the sons of Jashen, Jonathan, Shammah the Hararite. . . ." 1 Ch. 11:33f. has "Eliahba of Shaalbon, the sons of Hashem the Gizonite, Jonathan the son of Shagee the Hararite. . . ." It is clear that "sons of" is a dittography of the last three consonants of the previous word. The LXX Lucian in 2 Samuel and 1 Chronicles has Gk. *ho Gouni,* "the Gunite," for "the Gizonite," perhaps correctly (cf. Gen. 46:24; Nu. 26:48 for "Guni," "Gunite"). 2 S. 23:32 may be corrected thus: "Eliahba of Shaalbon, Jashen the Gunite, Jonathan the son of Shammah the Hararite." Jashen thus becomes one of the thirty, the same as Hashem of 1 Ch. 11:34. D. F. ROBERTS

JASHER jā'shər, **BOOK OF** (AV Josh. 10:14; 2 S. 1:18). *See* JASHAR, BOOK OF.

JASHOBEAM jə-shō'bē-əm [Heb. *yāšoḇʿām*]. Jashobeam is mentioned in three passages (1 Ch. 11:11; 12:6 [MT 7]; 27:2f.), but opinions vary about the number of persons referred to. In 1 Ch. 11:11 he is called "a Hachmonite" (reference unknown) and "chief of the three" ("three," the best reading, RSV, NEB; AV, "captains"), mighty men of David. He is said to have slain three hundred (eight hundred in 2 S. 23:8) at one time, i.e., one after another. In the parallel passage (2 S. 23:8) he is called, "Josheb-basshebeth, a Tah-chemonite." This verse, however, is probably corrupt, and the text should be corrected in accordance with 1 Chronicles to "Ishbaal, the Hachmonite." In 1 Ch. 27:2f. Jashobeam is said to have been "the son of Zabdiel," of the family of Perez, and the commander-in-chief of the division of David's army which did duty the first month. The army consisted of twelve divisions of 24,000 each, each division serving a month in turn. In 1 Ch. 12:6 (MT 7) Jashobeam is mentioned among those who joined David at Ziklag in the time of Saul, and is described as a Korahite, probably one belonging to a family of Judah (cf. 2:43). J. CRICHTON

JASHUB jā'shəb [Heb. *yāšûḇ, yāšîḇ* in 1 Chronicles, but *Q yāšûḇ*–'may he return'].

1. In Nu. 26:24; 1 Ch. 7:1, a son of Issachar. Gen. 46:13 has incorrectly Iob (cf. LXX *Iasoub*).

2. In Ezr. 10:29; 1 Esd. 9:30 (AV, NEB, Jasubus), one of those who had married foreign wives.

3. In Isa. 7:3, part of the name SHEAR-JASHUB.

JASHUBI-LEHEM jə-sho͞o'bī-lē'hem [Heb. *yāšuḇî-leḥem*]. A name in 1 Ch. 4:22 read as such by AV, but changed in the RSV to "and returned to Lehem," based upon a slight difference in the pointing of the first word. The NEB, following some commentators, inserted *bêṯ* between the two words and rendered the phrase "came back to Bethlehem."

JASHUBITES jā'shə-bīts [Heb. *hayyāšuḇî*; collective]. In Nu. 26:24, descendants of JASHUB.

JASIEL jā'zə-əl (1 Ch. 11:47, AV, NEB). *See* JAASIEL.

JASON jā'sən [Gk. *Iasōn*]. A common name among the Hellenistic Jews, who used it for Jesus or Joshua, probably connecting it with the Greek vb. *iásthai* ("heal").

1. Son of Eleazar, sent (161 B.C.) by Judas Maccabeus with other deputies to Rome "to establish friendship and alliance" (1 Macc. 8:17; Josephus *Ant.* xii.10.6 [417]), and perhaps to be identified with **2.**

2. The father of Antipater who went as ambassador of Jonathan to Rome in 144 B.C. (1 Macc. 12:16; 14:22; Josephus *Ant.* xiii.5.8 [169]).

3. Jason of Cyrene, a Jewish historian, who is known only from what is told of him in 2 Macc. 2:19-23. 2 Maccabees is in fact simply an abridgment in one book of the five books written by Jason on the Jewish wars of liberation. He must have written after 162 B.C., as his books include the wars under Antiochus Eupator.

4. Jason the high priest, second son of Simon II and brother of Onias III. The change of name from Jesus (Josephus *Ant.* xii.5 [237-264]) was part of the hellenizing policy favored by ANTIOCHUS IV EPIPHANES from whom he purchased the high-priesthood by a large bribe, thus excluding his elder brother from the office (2 Macc. 4:7-26). He did everything in his power to introduce Greek customs and Greek life among the Jews. He established a gymnasium in Jerusalem, so that even the priests neglected the altars and the sacrifices, and hastened to be partakers of the "unlawful proceedings" in the palaestra. The writer of 2 Maccabees calls him "ungodly" and "vile." He even sent deputies from Jerusalem to Tyre to take part in the worship of Hercules; but what he sent for sacrifices, the deputies expended on the "construction of triremes." After three years of this hellenizing work he was replaced in 172 B.C. by MENELAUS, who gave a large bribe for the high priest's office. Jason took refuge with the Ammonites; on hearing that Antiochus was dead he tried with some success to drive out Menelaus, but ultimately failed (2 Macc. 5:5-10). He took refuge with the Ammonites again, and then with Aretas, the Arabian, and finally with the Lacedaemonians, where he hoped for protection "because of their kinship," but there "he met a miserable end." J. HUTCHISON

5. The host of the apostle Paul during his stay in Thessalonica (Acts 17:5-9). During the uproar organized by the Jews, who were jealous of the success of Paul and Silas, Jason and several other "brethren" were severely attacked by the mob. When the mob failed to find Paul and Silas, they dragged Jason and "some of the brethren" before the politarchs, accusing Jason of treason in receiving into his house those who said "there is another king, Jesus." The magistrates, being disturbed at this charge, took security from them and let them go.

The immediate departure of Paul and Silas seems to show that security was given so that the strangers would leave the city and remain absent (*see* PLEDGE).

6. Jason was one of the companions of Paul who united with him in sending greetings to the Roman Christians (Rom. 16:21). He is probably the same person as **5.** Paul called him a kinsman, which means a Jew (cf. Rom. 9:3; 16:11, 21). S. F. HUNTER

JASPER. *See* STONES, PRECIOUS.

JASUBUS jə-so͞o'bəs (1 Esd. 9:30, AV, NEB). *See* JASHUB **2.**

JATAL jā'təl (1 Esd. 5:28, AV). *See* ATER.

JATHAN jā'thən [Gk. *Iathan*; LXX A *Nathan*]; NEB NATHAN. For "Jonathas" (AV), which is the Latin form for the Heb. "Jonathan." Jonathan was brother of Ananias and "son of the great Shemaiah" (Tob. 5:13 [LXX 14]).

JATHNIEL jath'ni-əl [Heb. *yaṯnî'ēl*]. Fourth son of Meshelemiah, a Korahite (1 Ch. 26:2), who was one of the gatekeepers of the sanctuary.

JATTIR jat'ər [Heb. *yattîr*]. A Levitical town (Josh. 21:14; 1 Ch. 6:57 [MT 42]) in the hill country of Judah midway between Hebron and Beer-sheba, mentioned with Shamir and Socoh (Josh. 15:48). After his victory over the Amalekites David sent a present from the booty to the inhabitants of Jattir (1 S. 30:27). The site is now known as Khirbet ʿAttîr, about 21 km. (13 mi.) SW of Hebron.

D. J. WIEAND

JAUDI jə-o͞o'dē, jou'dē [Heb. *yehûḏâ*] (2 K. 14:28, NEB); AV, RSV, JUDAH. The phrase in the MT, *lîhûḏâ beyiśrā'ēl*, literally "to Judah in Israel," poses a twofold problem, namely, the meaning of the prepositions, and the variance from known history. The Syriac version, sensing the difficulties, omits "to Judah" and reads instead *leyiśrā'ēl*, "to Israel." Both the AV and RSV emend the text to read that Jeroboam recovered "for Israel" what had belonged "to Judah." Keil sees *lîhûḏâ* as a periphrastic form of the genitive, "of Judah," so that the meaning of the clause is "whatever in the two kingdoms of Damascus and Hamath had formerly belonged to Judah in the times of David and Solomon" (cf. RSV). As the text stands, a cooperative dominance of Judah and Israel over Damascus and Hamath may be indicated, in which case, Gray thinks, it is strange that Chronicles would be silent about such a resurgence of Judah's power (*I & II Kings* [*OTL*, 2nd ed. 1970], pp. 616f.). The NEB emendation, "Jaudi," refers to a small city-state in north Syria that, in alliance with Hamath, rebelled against Tiglath-pileser III in 738 B.C. (*see* YA'UDI).

G. WYPER

JAVAN jā'vən [Heb. *yāwān*; Gk. *Iōvan, Iaōn, Hellas, hoi Hellēnes*]. A son of Japheth son of Noah (Gen. 10:2; 1 Ch. 1:5), and father of Elishah, Tarshish, Kittim, and Rodanim (Rhodes or Dodanim, Gen. 10:4; 1 Ch. 1:7). The name is listed among the Ionian islands, probably referring to Javan's "descendants" Cyprus (Isa. 66:19; Ezk. 27:13; cf. the pl. in Joel 3:6 [MT 4:6]); and the Hebrew refers to the Greeks or Macedonians in Dnl. 8:21; 10:20; and 11:2. The term appears in the MT of Ezk. 27:19, followed by the AV; but the LXX reads "and wine" (end of v. 18), which is adopted by the RSV and NEB (*see* DAN AND JAVAN). The Javanites are viewed as enemies of Judah, particularly because of their involvements in slave trading (Joel 3:6; Ezk. 27:13); and in Zec. 9:13 their judgment is announced ("Greece"; NEB omits).

The term is known in other ancient literature. The *Yevana* or Ionians were aligned with the Hittites against Ramses II. In the Amarna Letters *yivana* seems to equal Tyre, while in the Persian records from the time of Darius *yauna* equals the Ionians of Asia Minor. *See also* GREECE.

See J. Skinner, comm. on Genesis (*ICC*, 2nd ed. 1930), pp. 196-98.

G. L. BORCHERT

JAVELIN. *See* WEAPONS OF WAR.

JAW [Heb. *leḥî, malqô(a)ḥ*]. The term *leḥî* designated one of the two osseous structures from which the teeth grow and which constitute the framework of the mouth. The dual form *malqôḥayim* denoted both upper and lower maxillae (Ps. 22:15 [MT 16]). In Job 41:2 (MT 40:26) God asked Job if he were able to pierce the jaws of Leviathan (Heb. "the crocodile") with a fishhook, implying that he could not. The expression "to place on the jaws of the people" (Isa. 30:28) was used figuratively to describe the ultimate check of the Assyrian military power at Jerusalem. The taming of an adversary was alluded to metaphorically in Ezk. 29:4 (of Pharaoh) and 38:4 (of Gog). God's gentleness with regard to human trials and difficulties was the subject of the reference in Hos. 11:4. In Jgs. 15:15-17, Samson used the fresh (NEB "all raw") jawbone of an ass as a weapon against his Philistine opponents; the place name Ramath-lehi, "the hill of the jawbone," commemorated this event.

R. K. H.

JAZER jā'zər [Heb. *ya'zēr, ya'ᵃzēr*]; AV also JAAZER. The RSV follows the LXX in reading Jazer (Gk. *Iazēr*) in Nu. 21:24 (AV "strong" [Heb. *ʿaz*]; NEB "difficult"). A fortified Amorite city N of Heshbon, not far from ʿAmmân in the land of Moab. Eusebius (*Onom.*) and Jerome speak of an Azer or Iazer about 16 km. (10 mi.) W of ʿAmmân. It may be Khirbet Jazzir, near es-Salt. The Amorites, Israelites, Moabites, and Ammonites all contested for possession of it.

After the defeat of Sihon king of the Amorites, Moses sent spies to scout Jazer and subsequently captured the town (Nu. 21:32). The region surrounding Jazer was so well suited for cattle grazing that the tribes of Reuben and Gad requested it (Nu. 32:1-5). Gad received it and the men of Gad fortified it. Later it was assigned to the Merarite levitical family (Josh. 21:39; 1 Ch. 6:81 [MT 66]). It lay in a district that was noted for its luxuriant grapevines and fruit trees (Isa. 16:8f.; Jer. 48:32).

During the reign of David, troops from Hebron (1 Ch. 26:31) were stationed in Jazer to protect the area against an attack from the Ammonites. After the death of Ahab (853 B.C.) Mesha king of Moab conquered the whole area, and Jazer is referred to in Isaiah and Jeremiah as a Moabite city. Later the Ammonites took it, and finally it was retaken for Israel in the Maccabean era by Judas Maccabeus (1 Macc. 5:8).

F. E. YOUNG

JAZIZ jā'ziz [Heb. *yāzîz*]. The Hagrite who was over David's flocks (1 Ch. 27:30 [MT 31]).

JEALOUS [Heb. *qannā'* (Ex. 20:5; 34:14; Dt. 4:24; 5:9; 6:15), *qannô'* (Josh. 24:19; Nah. 1:2)]; **JEALOUS WRATH** [Heb. *qin'â*] (Ps. 79:5; Ezk. 36:6; Zeph. 1:18; 3:8); AV JEALOUSY; NEB JEALOUSY, ANGER; **BE JEALOUS** [Heb. piel of *qānā'* (Gen. 37:11; Nu. 11:29; 1 K. 19:10, 14; etc.); Gk. *zēlóō* (Acts 7:9; 17:5; 1 Cor. 13:4)]; AV also ENVY, ZEALOUS (Nu. 25:11, 13); NEB also SUSPECT (Nu. 5:14, 30), ZEAL, etc.; **MAKE JEALOUS** [Gk. *parazēlóō*] (Rom. 10:19; 11:11, 14); AV PROVOKE TO JEALOUSY; NEB also STIR ENVY; **JEALOUSY** [Heb. *qin'â* (Nu. 25:11; Job 5:2; Prov. 6:34; 27:4; Ezk. 8:3, 5; etc.); Gk. *zēlos* (Acts 5:17; 13:45; Rom. 13:13; 1 Cor. 3:3; 2 Cor. 11:2; 12:20; Gal. 5:20; Jas. 3:14, 16)]; AV also ZEAL (Ezk. 5:13), ENVY, ENVYING; NEB also RESENTMENT (Dt. 29:20), etc.; **JEALOUSLY** [Gk. *prós phthónon*] (Jas. 4:5); AV UNTO ENVYING; NEB TOWARDS EVIL DESIRES. Jealousy is the intense emotion aroused by the infringement of one's right (or presumed right) to exclusive possession or loyalty.

I. Terminology
 A. In the OT
 B. In the NT

II. Varieties of Usage
   A. In the OT
      1. God's Jealousy
      2. Human Jealousy
   B. In the NT
      1. Pauline Literature
      2. Acts
      3. James

I. Terminology.–The Eng. "jealousy" derives from Gk. *zḗlos,* the same root from which Eng. "zeal" derives. The Hebrew and Greek vocabularies do not distinguish, as modern English does, between these two intense emotions. In the English versions, only the context determines whether Heb. *qin'â* and Gk. *zḗlos* are to be translated as "zeal" or "jealousy." *See also* ZEAL.

A. In the OT. All the Hebrew terms translated by "jealous" or "jealousy" come from the root *qn',* which ranges in meaning from "be zealous for" to "be envious of." Frequently the Hebrew terms refer to a righteous or godly jealousy (e.g., the intensive nominal forms *qannā'* and *qannô'* are used only in reference to God's jealousy); both the noun *qin'â* and the verb *qānā',* however, are also used of sinful human jealousy.

B. In the NT. The NT derived its vocabulary for "jealousy" from the LXX, which generally translated Heb. *qn'* by Gk. *zēlóō* and cognates. Thus *zḗlos,* like *qin'â,* etc., can refer to a "divine jealousy" (2 Cor. 11:2). More often, however, it refers to a sinful emotion that is linked with other sins such as *éris* (quarreling), *thýmos* (hostility), and *phthónos* (envy) (cf. 2 Cor. 12:20; Gal. 5:20f.).

In Jas. 4:5 the RSV renders Gk. *prós phthónon* as "jealousy." The text is problematic, because elsewhere *phthónos* always designates the negative emotion of envy — never the divine jealousy sometimes designated by *zḗlos.* The NEB attempts to resolve this problem by taking *tó pneúma* ("spirit") as the subject — rather than the object — of the verb, and rendering *phthónos* with its usual negative sense.

II. Varieties of Usage.–In the OT. 1. God's Jealousy. Repeatedly in the OT, Yahweh is described as a "jealous God" (e.g., "I the Lord your God am a jealous God," Ex. 20:5; cf. Dt. 4:24; 5:9; 6:15; Josh. 24:19; etc.). In addition, there are numerous references to Yahweh's jealous wrath (e.g., Ps. 79:5) and to His being provoked to jealousy (e.g., Ps. 78:58). Several things about this prominent OT theme deserve notice.

(1) It is important to recognize that the description of Yahweh as jealous is an anthropomorphism, i.e., it is the attribution to God of a human emotion. It should therefore not be assumed that Yahweh's jealousy is identical with the human emotion of jealousy. The analogy between divine and human jealousy lies in the demand for exclusive possession or devotion.

(2) The term is used in the context of the covenantal relationship between Yahweh and Israel (*see* COVENANT [OT]). As Israel's sovereign, Yahweh had a right to demand His people's exclusive loyalty. This was the first and most basic stipulation of the covenant (cf. the first commandment: "You shall have no other gods before me," Ex. 20:3). Nonetheless, the OT records Israel's perpetual lapses into idolatry, and it was this unfaithfulness that provoked Yahweh's jealous wrath (cf. Nu. 25:3, 11; Dt. 29:18-20; 32:16, 21; 1 K. 14:22f.; Zeph. 1:18; 3:8; cf. also Ezk. 8:3, 5, where the idol in Ezekiel's vision is called "the image of jealousy" because it provoked Yahweh to jealousy). Frequently the metaphor of a marriage was used to describe the relationship between Yahweh and His people, with Yahweh depicted as the jealous husband and Israel as the adulterous wife (cf. Ezk. 36:41f.). There is another side, however, to Yahweh's *qin'â,* namely, His jealousy *for* His covenant people, which is expressed in pity and zeal for Israel's renewal and results in judgment upon Israel's enemies and the restoration of Jerusalem (e.g., Ezk. 36:5-7; 38:18f.; 39:25; Joel 2:18f.; Zec. 1:14-17; 8:2f.).

(3) Yahweh's claim to the exclusive allegiance of His people arises out of His unique nature as the only true God, the sovereign Lord of all creation. No other gods can rival Him; thus Yahweh alone is deserving of His creatures' exclusive and wholehearted devotion (cf. Pss. 95–97, etc.; Dt. 6:4f.). Yahweh's jealousy is an expression of His holiness (cf. Josh. 24:19; Ezk. 39:25). His very name is Jealous (Ex. 34:14).

2. Human Jealousy. In the OT human jealousy may be either a positive or a sinful emotion, depending upon whether it represents a selfless concern for another's due, or a selfish demand for exclusive possession of something to which one has no exclusive right.

Jealousy as a positive emotion is illustrated by the priest Phinehas, described by Yahweh as "jealous with my jealousy" (Nu. 25:11-13). Similarly, Elijah, after his confrontation with the priests of Baal on Mt. Carmel, described himself as having been "very jealous for the Lord" (1 K. 19:10, 14). A selfless — though misguided — jealousy is also displayed by Joshua in his devotion to Moses (Nu. 11:29). This type of jealousy is practically synonymous with zeal. (*See also* ZEALOTS.)

The husband's exclusive right to his wife's sexual faithfulness was recognized by Mosaic law. Thus, a wife who was suspected of adultery was required to undergo an ordeal in which she drank "water of bitterness" (i.e., holy water mixed with dust from the floor of the tabernacle) while holding the "cereal offering of jealousy" (Nu. 5:11-31). If she was guilty, "the water that brings the curse shall enter into her and cause bitter pain, and her body shall swell, and her thigh shall fall away, and the woman shall become an execration among her people" (v. 27). If, however, she was innocent, she would not become sick and she would be free to conceive children (v. 28).

The OT contains many examples of sinful jealousy. In only a few instances does the term "jealousy" appear. The sons of Jacob were jealous of their brother Joseph because of his dreams (Gen. 37:11; also vv. 19f.; cf. Acts 7:9). Dathan and Abiram rebelled against Moses because they were jealous of his position of leadership (Ps. 106:16-18; cf. Nu. 16:1-40). Bitter jealousy divided the northern kingdom (Ephraim) from the southern kingdom (Judah); but Isaiah prophesied of a time when this jealousy would be broken down and the two kingdoms reunited (Isa. 11:13). Wisdom literature warned of the destructiveness of jealousy, both for the one possessed by the emotion (e.g., Job 5:2) and for the one who provoked it (e.g., Prov. 6:34; 27:4; Cant. 8:6).

B. In the NT. The use of jealousy in the NT, as in the OT, denotes both a godly and a sinful emotion.

1. Pauline Literature. Most occurrences of *zēlóō* and cognates in the NT are found in Paul's letters. In Rom. 10:19; 11:11, 14, jealousy is mentioned as Paul describes God's inclusion of the Gentiles in His redemptive plan. The jealousy of Israel at the sight of gentile redemption has the intended purpose of leading some Jews to faith in the gospel (11:14). Thus, God is seen to be using human jealousy for a divine purpose — the expansion of redemption to worldwide proportions. In the catechetical section of Rom. 13:8-14, jealousy is listed with other vices to be avoided. Jealousy is likewise termed a "work of the flesh" in Gal. 5:20. The sinful manifestation of "jealousy and strife" among the Corinthians was a result of their divisive attitude (1 Cor. 3:3; cf. 1:12). In condemning the participation of the Corinthians in meals sacrificed to idols, Paul asks the rhetorical question, "Shall we provoke the Lord to jealousy?" (10:22), a question based on the many statements of God's divine jealousy for His people in the OT (cf. Dt. 32:16f.). Love, the paragon of Christian virtues, "is not jealous" (1 Cor. 13:4). Paul feared finding jealousy and other sinful attitudes when he returned to Corinth (2 Cor. 12:20), and he described his concern for the Corinthians (11:2) as a "divine jealousy" (*theoú zḗlǭ*).

2. Acts. In several instances in Acts, the jealousy of the Jewish religious leaders was aroused when early Christian preaching threatened to make converts of numerous Jewish laymen and proselytes (5:12-16; 17:1-15). In 7:9, Stephen recounted the jealousy of Joseph's brothers.

3. James. James uses *zḗlos* twice: in 3:14f. "bitter jealousy" (*zḗlon pikrón*) is termed an "earthly wisdom," and in 3:16, the presence of "jealousy and selfish ambition" is said to lead to "disorder and every vile practice." As was noted above, the phrase *prós phthónon* in 4:5 is one of several ambiguities in this verse, which may be best rendered by the NEB, "the spirit which God implanted in man turns towards envious desires" (see comms. by J. Adamson [*NICNT,* 1976], pp. 170-73; C. L. Mitton, *Epistle of James* [1966], pp. 153-56; M. Dibelius [Eng. tr., *Hermeneia,* 1976], pp. 220-24).

Bibliography.–DNTT, I, 558; III, 1166-1170; S. S. Laws, *NTS,* 20 (1973/4), 210ff.; *New Catholic Encyclopedia,* VII, *s.v.* "Jealousy of God" (M. A. Freund); G. F. Oehler, *Theology of the OT,* I (Eng. tr. 1892), 165-68; A. C. Welch, *Prophet and Priest in Old Israel* (1953), pp. 61f.

N. J. OPPERWALL R. J. W.

JEALOUSY, IMAGE OF. *See* IDOL.

JEARIM jē'ə-rim, **MOUNT** [Heb. *har yᵉʿārîm*–'mountain of forests'; LXX *pólin Iarim*–'city of Jarim']. A mountain or hill on the northern border of the area given to Judah after the Conquest (Josh. 15:10). It is identified in this passage with the city of Chesalon (Heb. *kᵉsālôn,* "loins"[?], "back"[?]), modern Kesla, 16 km. (10 mi.) W of Jerusalem. It is mentioned here with Mt. Ephron (v. 9) and Mt. Seir (v. 10), all of which were probably hilltops in the forested regions between Jerusalem and Beth-shemesh (*LBHG,* p. 235).

J. E. H.

JEATHERAI jē-ath'ə-rī [Heb. *yᵉʾāṯray*]; AV JEATERAI. A descendant of Gershom son of Levi (1 Ch. 6:21), and probably an ancestor of Asaph. In 1 Ch. 6:41 (MT 26) the form ETHNI appears to be a scribal variation.

JEBERECHIAH jə-ber'ə-kī-ə [Heb. *yᵉḇerekyāhû*–'Yahweh blesses']. The father of the Zechariah whom Isaiah (8:2) took as a witness for his prophecy against Syria and Ephraim (*ca.* 734 B.C.).

JEBUS jē'bəs; **JEBUSITE** jeb'yə-sīt [Heb. *yᵉḇûs; hayᵉḇûsî*]; AV JEBUSI (Josh. 18:16, 28). The name "Jebusite" described an ethnic group living in the uplands of Canaan (Nu. 13:29; Josh. 11:3) near Jerusalem (Josh. 15:8; 18:16). A comparatively small clan, they claimed descent from the third son of Canaan (Gen. 10:16), and lived among the Amorites, Canaanites, and Girgashites (Gen. 15:21), though always separate from them. Their principal city was known as Jebus (Jgs. 19:10f.; 1 Ch. 11:4f.), which led to their becoming known as Jebusites (Gen. 15:21; Ex. 3:8). In exilic and postexilic writers the term Jebusite was used of the former inhabitants of the city (Zec. 9:7). In Josh. 18:28; Jgs. 19:10 a scribal gloss explained that Jebus meant "Jerusalem," while a similar gloss in 1 Ch. 11:4 gave its converse. Apparently these attempts at explanation are comparatively late and show that the name Jebus, by which Jerusalem was known, designated the pre-Israelite occupation of the region. *See* JERUSALEM I.C.

Archeological excavations in the general area of Mt. Zion have shown that its earliest occupational levels date from the 3rd millennium B.C., representing a significant advance on the Neolithic flint scrapers and crude pottery found to the south and west of the site of later Jerusalem. In the nineteenth-century-B.C. Egyptian Execration Texts from Luxor, the fortified settlement was known as *Urushalim* ("foundation [shrine] of [the deity] Shalim"); in the fourteenth-century-B.C. Amarna Letters as *Urusalim*; and in later Assyrian texts as *Urusilimmu* — all of which relate the site to the deity worshiped there. The Jebusites seem to have moved into the area early in the Middle Bronze Age (*ca.* 1950-1550 B.C.), perhaps as part of a migration of Hurrians (HORITES). Once in control they enlarged the defenses of the city and constructed underground tunnels to divert the waters of the spring of Gihon and bring them within their city walls.

The first mention of a king of Jebus is in Josh. 10:1, during the Hebrew Settlement period. Earlier scholars frequently identified the Salem of which Melchizedek was king (Gen. 14:18) with Jerusalem, following Josephus (*Ant.* i.10.2 [180f.]). Since the Genesis narrative speaks of the king of Sodom going out to meet Abraham in the Jordan Valley, however, a location for Salem better than Jerusalem would seem to be somewhere in the area known in NT times as Perea, a well-watered district where John the Baptist was active (Jn. 3:23), and where the name "Salim" was preserved many centuries later. Nevertheless, the Amarna Tablets indicate that in the 15th cent. B.C. a man named Abdu-Ḫeba ruled *Urusalimmu,* and like the later Jebusite king Araunah (2 S. 24:24) or Ornan (1 Ch. 21:15) was of non-Semitic origin.

When the soldiers of Judah raided Jebus (Jgs. 1:8) they set it on fire, but apparently the devastation did not prevent the Jebusites from reoccupying the site. Although assigned to Benjamin at the division of Canaan, the Jebusite stronghold was independent of any form of Hebrew rule during the judges period, as illustrated by the incident of the Levite of Mt. Ephraim (Jgs. 19:10-12). David was the first Hebrew to mount a successful campaign against Jebus (2 S. 5:6-8; 1 Ch. 11:4f.), but precisely how it was accomplished is not made clear by the narratives. Earlier scholars thought that he had gained access to the fortress by means of the underground water conduits, but W. F. Albright (in H. C. Alleman and E. E. Flack, eds., *OT Comm.* [1954], p. 149) showed that Heb. *ṣinnôr* (2 Sam. 5:8; AV "gutter"; RSV "water shaft") was a Canaanite word for a "hook" (NEB "grappling-iron"), implying that David's men went over the walls by means of grappling hooks (but *see* JERUSALEM III.C.1.a). The surviving Jebusites yielded to David, who later purchased part of the land from ARAUNAH to house the ark of the covenant (2 S. 24:24 par.). From that time the Jebusites were absorbed by the Judeans.

Excavations at the site of the limestone promontory known as Ophel have uncovered very old fortifications consisting of massive walls, bastions, and gates, which were evidently Jebusite in origin. An underground tunnel made by the Jebusites to bring water from the spring of Gihon in the Kidron Valley SE of Ophel was also discovered, as was the deep cistern some 12 m. (40 ft.) below ground level into which the tunnel emptied. Another aqueduct designed to divert the spring of Gihon emptied into the "old pool" (Isa. 22:11) just outside the city walls (cf. F. Kenyon, *The Bible and Archaeology* [1940], p. 176). From the Ophel region archeologists have uncovered several links with the Davidic period, including the corner of a Jebusite or Davidic wall and the probable location of the royal necropolis at the south end of Ophel.

Bibliography.–*GP*, I (1933), 320f.; J. Simons, *Jerusalem in the OT* (1952), pp. 60f., 246f.; D. R. Ap-Thomas, "Jerusalem," in *AOTS*, pp. 276-295. R. K. H.

JECAMIAH jek-ə-mī'ə (1 Ch. 3:18, AV). *See* JEKAMIAH **2.**

JECHOLIAH jek-ə-lī'ə (2 K. 15:2, AV). *See* JECOLIAH.

JECHONIAH jek-ə-nī'ə. *See* JEHOIACHIN.

JECHONIAS jek-ə-nī'əs. The AV spelling of JEHOIACHIN in Mt. 1:11f., and the NEB spelling of JECONIAH (**2**).

JECOLIAH jek-ə-lī'ə [Heb. *yᵉkolyāhû* (2 K. 15:2); *Q yᵉkolyâ, K yᵉkîlyâ* (2 Ch. 26:3)]; AV also JECHOLIAH. The mother of King Uzziah (Azariah) of Judah.

JECONIAH jek-ə-nī'ə [Gk. *Iechonias*]; AV NT JECHONIAS, AV also JECONIAS (1 Esd. 1:9), JOACHAZ (1 Esd. 1:34); NEB also JECHONIAS (1 Esd. 1:9), JOACHAZ (1 Esd. 1:34).

1. The alternative designation of JEHOIACHIN king of Judah.

2. In 1 Esd. 1:9, a Levite in the time of Josiah, equivalent to Conaniah in 2 Ch. 35:9.

3. In 1 Esd. 1:34, an alternate designation of Jehoahaz king of Judah. *See* JEHOAHAZ **3.**

JECONIAS jek-ə-nī'əs (1 Esd. 1:9, AV). *See* JECONIAH **2.**

JEDAIAH jə-dā'yə, jə-dī'ə [Heb. *yᵉdaʿyâ*–'Yahweh knows'; (**6, 7**) *yᵉdāyâ*–'Yahweh has favored'].

1. A priest in Jerusalem (1 Ch. 9:10; 24:7).

2. Ezr. 2:36; Neh. 7:39, where "sons of Jedaiah" are mentioned (1 Esd. 5:24; AV, NEB, Jeddu).

3. Jedaiah is among "the priests and the Levites" who returned with Zerubbabel (Neh. 11:10; 12:6, 19).

4. Another priest of the same name (Neh. 12:7, 21).

5. One of the exiles whom Zechariah was commanded to send with silver and gold to Jerusalem (Zec. 6:10, 14).

6. Father of a Simeonite prince (1 Ch. 4:37).

7. One of the repairers of the wall of Jerusalem (Neh. 3:10). D. F. ROBERTS

JEDDIAS jed-dī'əs (1 Esd. 9:26, NEB). *See* IZZIAH.

JEDDU jed'o͞o (1 Esd. 5:24, AV, NEB). *See* JEDAIAH **2.**

JEDEUS jə-dē'əs (1 Esd. 9:30, AV). *See* ADAIAH **6.**

JEDIAEL jə-dī'əl [Heb. *yᵉdîʿaʾēl*–'known by God'].

1. A son of Benjamin or probably of Zebulun (1 Ch. 7:6, 10f.).

2. One of David's mighty men (1 Ch. 11:45), probably the same as the Manassite who deserted to David at Ziklag (1 Ch. 12:20 [MT 21]).

3. A Korahite doorkeeper during David's reign (1 Ch. 26:2).

JEDIDAH jə-dī'də [Heb. *yᵉdîdâ*–'beloved']. Mother of King Josiah of Judah, daughter of Adaiah of Bozkath (2 K. 22:1).

JEDIDIAH jed-ə-dī'ə [Heb. *yᵉdîdyâ*–'the beloved of Yahweh']. The name conferred by God through Nathan upon Solomon at his birth (2 S. 12:25).

JEDUTHUN jə-do͞o'thən [Heb. *yᵉdûṯûn, yᵉduṯûn, yᵉdîṯûn*–'praise'(?); Gk. *Ideithoun*].

1. A Merari Levite of the Davidic period who with Asaph and Heman was responsible for the music in temple worship (1 Ch. 25:1; 2 Ch. 5:12). In 1 Ch. 25:1, 3; 2 Ch. 35:15; 1 Esd. 1:15 (assuming Eddinus [LXX *Eddinous*] = Jeduthun), his music was linked with prophecy, not an uncommon link in Israel (cf. 1 S. 10:5f.; 2 K. 3:15). In 1 Ch. 6:44 (MT 29); 15:17, 19, Asaph and Heman were mentioned with Ethan, perhaps Jeduthun's family name before he was appointed to his temple duties (cf. 1 Ch. 16:41). Jeduthun occurs in the titles of Pss. 39, 62, and 77, indicating either that he directed their composition or that "Jeduthun" was the name of a melody to which they were sung. Jeduthun's descendants carried on his ministry in the times of Hezekiah (2 Ch. 29:14), Josiah (2 Ch. 35:15), and Nehemiah (Neh. 11:17).

See also ASAPH **2.**

2. A Korahite, father of Obed-edom (1 Ch. 16:38; cf. 26:1, 4). G. A. L.

JEELI jə-ē'lī (1 Esd. 5:33, AV, NEB). *See* JAALA, JAALAH.

JEELUS jə-ē'ləs (1 Esd. 8:92, AV). *See* JEHIEL **8.**

JEEZER jə-ē'zər (Nu. 26:30, AV). *See* ABIEZER **1.**

JEEZERITES jə-ē'zər-īts (Nu. 26:30, AV). *See* ABIEZER **1.**

JEGAR-SAHADUTHA jē'gər-sā'ə-do͞o'thə [Aram. *yᵉgar śāhᵃdûṯā'*; LXX Gk. *bounós tḗs martyrías*–'(the) mound of witness']. The name given by the Aramean Laban to the heap of stones called by Jacob GALEED and set up to commemorate their agreement (Gen. 31:47). The cairn was located in northern Transjordan, but the Hebrew name Galeed was the one ultimately given to the site.

JEHALLELEL jə-hal'ə-lel [Heb. *yᵉhallelʾēl*–'may God shine forth']; AV JEHALELEEL.

1. A Judahite (1 Ch. 4:16).

2. A Levite, a descendant of Merari (2 Ch. 29:12).

JEHDEIAH jə-dē'yə, jə-dī'yə [Heb. *yeḥdᵉyāhû*–'may Yahweh rejoice'].

1. A Levite, head of the family of Shubael (1 Ch. 24:20).

2. An officer of David "over the she-asses" (1 Ch. 27:30).

JEHEZKEL jə-hez'kel [Heb. *yᵉḥezqēʾl*–'God strengthens']; AV JEHEZEKEL. A priest of the twentieth priestly order in David's time (1 Ch. 24:16).

JEHIAH jə-hī'ə [Heb. *yᵉḥîyâ*–'may Yahweh live']. Keeper of the ark with Obed-edom (1 Ch. 15:24).

JEHIEL jə-hī'əl [Heb. *yᵉḥîʾēl*–'may God give life'].

1. A Levite, one of the musicians appointed to play upon instruments at the bringing up of the ark by David (1 Ch. 15:18, 20; 16:5).

2. A Gershonite, head of a Levitical house (1 Ch. 23:8; 29:8), who supervised the treasury of the temple in the early monarchy. He was the father of a priestly family known as Jehieli (1 Ch. 26:21f.).

3. Son of a Hachmonite; he attended the king's sons, i.e., as the tutor of David's boys (1 Ch. 27:32).

4. A son of King Jehoshaphat (2 Ch. 21:2).

5. A Hemanite Levite who took part in cleansing the temple in Hezekiah's reign (AV, NEB 2 Ch. 29:14; *K yᵉḥûʾēl*; RSV Jehuel) and later became a temple overseer (2 Ch. 31:13).

6. One of the three "rulers" of the temple during Josiah's reign (2 Ch. 35:8; 1 Esd. 1:8 [Gk. *Esyelus*; NEB, RSV mg., Esyelus; AV Syelus]).

7. Father of Obadiah, a returned exile (Ezr. 8:9; cf. 1 Esd. 8:35 [AV, NEB, Jezelus]).

8. Father of Shecaniah (Ezr. 10:2; cf. 1 Esd. 8:92; NEB Jeel) who assisted Ezra in promoting marriage reforms in postexilic Judea. He was probably the Jehiel of Ezr. 10:26 (cf. NEB 1 Esd. 9:27; AV Hierielus) who divorced his foreign-born wife.

9. A priest who obeyed Ezra's injunction about divorcing foreign-born wives (Ezr. 10:21; cf. 1 Esd. 9:21 [AV Hiereel]).

JEHIELI jə-hī'ə-lī [Heb. *yᵉḥî'ēlî*] (1 Ch. 26:21f.). The gentilic of Jehiel. *See* JEHIEL **2.**

JEHIZKIAH jə-hiz-kī'ə [Heb. *yᵉḥizqîyāhû*–'may Yahweh strengthen']. One of the Ephraimite chiefs (2 Ch. 28:12) who with Obed is said to have opposed the enslavement of the Judahites taken captive by Pekah in his war against Ahaz (*ca.* 724 B.C.).

JEHOADDAH jə-hō'ə-də [Heb. *yᵉhô'addâ*]; AV JEHOADAH. A descendant of King Saul (1 Ch. 8:36), known as JARAH in 1 Ch. 9:42, where the LXX reads Gk. *Iada*.

JEHOADDAN jə-hō'ə-dən [Heb. *yᵉhô'addān*–'Yahweh is delight'(?)]. The mother of King Amaziah (2 Ch. 25:1), known in the *kethibh* of 2 K. 14:2 as Jehoaddin, and so rendered by the RSV, NEB.

JEHOADDIN jə-hō'ə-dən (2 K. 14:2). *See* JEHOADDAN.

JEHOAHAZ jə-hō'ə-haz [Heb. *yᵉhô'āḥāz*–'Yahweh will hold fast,' lit. 'Yahweh has taken hold'].

1. King of Judah (2 Ch. 21:17). *See* AHAZIAH **2.**

2. The son of Jehu and the eleventh king of Israel (814-800 B.C.). He reigned for fourteen years but ruled for seventeen, sharing with his father the governing of the kingdom when the latter was incapacitated by extreme old age (cf. 2 K. 13:1, 10).

The political situation had evidently deteriorated since Jehu's death. Israelite territories E of the Jordan were even then under constant attack from Hazael's forces, who inflicted blow after blow on them (2 K. 10:32f.). During Ahaziah's reign, Hazael or his son captured several cities (13:25) and destroyed Israel's military power, which was now reduced to the size of a police force, so much so that although Ahab was able to send two thousand chariots into battle, Ahaziah had no more than ten chariots altogether (2 K. 13:7). It is highly probable that the temporary relief from Syrian attacks during this reign (13:4f.) came in the wake of a crushing defeat inflicted on the Arameans by Adadnirari III (810-783) in the course of his campaigns (*ANET,* pp. 281f.).

Jehoahaz patronized the fertility cult, which was introduced by Jeroboam, for political reasons. But he was not on that account entirely lacking in true religion. When hard pressed he turned to God for help, and help came; Assyria, the Lord's "rod of anger" (Isa. 10:5), was on this occasion the deliverer of His sinful and wayward people: "Then Jehoahaz besought the Lord, and . . . the Lord gave Israel a savior" (2 K. 13:4f.). M. S. SEALE

3. King of Judah, son of King Josiah, enthroned immediately after his father's sudden death in 609 B.C. (2 K. 23:30-34; 2 Ch. 36:1-4). He is named SHALLUM in 1 Ch. 3:15; Jer. 22:11 and Jeconiah in 1 Esd. 1:34. He was the choice of the people in spite of his being younger than Jehoiakim. His enthronement, however, did not meet the approval of Pharaoh Neco of Egypt, whom Josiah attempted to stop at Megiddo.

Pharaoh Neco marched his forces N to Carchemish, where he temporarily halted the westward advance of the Babylonians in the Fertile Crescent. After three months Neco removed Jehoahaz from his throne in Jerusalem, took him captive to Riblah, which was the occupational headquarters for the Egyptians, and ultimately transferred him to Egypt. Neco exacted a heavy tribute from Judah and enthroned Jehoiakim in Jerusalem.

Jeremiah offered his people no hope for Jehoahaz. According to the prophet's word, Jehoahaz did not return but died in Egypt (Jer. 22:10-12). S. J. SCHULTZ

JEHOASH jə-hō'-ash. *See* JOASH **1, 2.**

JEHOHANAN jə-hō-hā'nən [Heb. *yᵉhôḥānān*–'Yahweh is (or has been) gracious'].

1. A Korahite doorkeeper in David's reign, son of Meshelemiah (1 Ch. 26:3). The LXX Lucian has Jehonathan.

2. One of the five captains over King Jehoshaphat's army (2 Ch. 17:15), probably the father of Ishmael, son of Jehohanan (2 Ch. 23:1).

3. Ezr. 10:6 (AV Johanan), the same as Johanan (Neh. 12:22f.) and Jonathan (Neh. 12:11), son of Eliashib (Ezr. 10:6; but "grandson" in Neh. 12:11). He was high priest in Ezra's time (cf. 1 Esd. 9:1; AV, NEB, Joanan).

4. One of those who had married foreign wives (Ezr. 10:28; 1 Esd. 9:29, AV Johannes, NEB Joannes).

5. Son of Tobiah the Ammonite, Nehemiah's opponent (Neh. 6:18; AV Johanan).

6. Head of the priestly family of Amariah (Neh. 12:13).

7. A priest present at the dedication of the walls of Jerusalem (Neh. 12:42). D. F. ROBERTS

JEHOIACHIN jə-hoi'ə-kin [Heb. *yᵉhôyāḵîn*–'Yahweh will uphold']; also **JECONIAH** jek-ō-nī'ə [Heb. *yᵉḵonyâ, yᵉḵonyāhû*]; **CONIAH** kō-ni'ə [Heb. *konyāhû*] (Jer. 22:24, 28; 37:1); NT **JECHONIAH** jə-kō-nī'ə [Gk. *Iechonias*] (Mt. 1:11f.); AV NT JECHONIAS; NEB NT JECONIAH; Apoc. [Gk. *Iōakim*] (1 Esd. 1:43 [LXX 41]; AV JOACIM; NEB JOAKIM. The son of Jehoiakim, and his successor to the Davidic throne in 598 B.C. (2 K. 24:8-17; 2 Ch. 36:9f.; 1 Esd. 1:43 [the LXX reading here is an obvious scribal error]). He ruled only three months in Jerusalem.

Apparently Jehoiakim precipitated Babylonian aggression, so Jehoiachin was suddenly faced with the invading Babylonians after his father's death. (*See* BABYLONIA IV.J.) Realizing the futility of resisting so strong a power, the young king surrendered. Consequently, the Babylonians stripped the temple and the royal treasures. Jehoiachin and his queen mother were taken prisoners. Accompanying them into captivity were palace officials, executives, artisans, and the leading citizens of Jerusalem. Not least among them was Ezekiel (but *see* EZEKIEL III). Whereas previously (605) the Babylonians had merely taken hostages, this was a massive exile from the kingdom of Judah.

Jeremiah (22:24-28) not only indicated that Jehoiachin would be taken into captivity, but also predicted that he would not have his throne reestablished. In Babylon, Jehoiachin received favorable treatment. In all likelihood, he is the Yaukin, "king of the land of Yahud," who is listed in cuneiform tablets with persons from Egypt, Philistia, Phoenicia, Asia Minor, Elam, Media, Persia, and Judah. The reference to his five sons immediately after his name in these tablets, unearthed near the Ishtar

Gate in Babylon and dating between 595 and 570 B.C., may indicate that Jehoiachin was living with his family in Babylon and received rations such as barley and oil (cf. 1 Ch. 3:17f.).

Jehoiachin apparently was regarded as the legitimate claimant to the throne of Judah by the Babylonians as well as by the Jewish exiles. Ezekiel dates events by the years of captivity beginning in 597 when Jehoiachin was taken captive. Since Jehoiachin received such favorable treatment in 592 B.C., the date of one of these cuneiform tablets from Babylon, it seems quite probable that subsequent Judeo-Babylonian relationships resulted in the imprisonment of Jehoiachin. In 562, after Nebuchadrezzar's death, when Jehoiachin was restored to more preferential treatment, the city of Jerusalem had long since been reduced to ruins.

S. J. SCHULTZ

JEHOIADA jə-hoi'ə-də [Heb. *yᵉhôyāḏā'*–'Yahweh knows'; Gk. *Iōdae*].

1. Father of Benaiah, captain of David's bodyguard (2 S. 8:18; 20:23; 23:20-22; 1 K. 1:8; etc.). Jehoiada was "the son of a valiant man of Kabzeel" (AV, 2 S. 23:20); the RSV and NEB omit with the LXX and Ewald the second (Heb.) *ben* as an accidental repetition, the reference then being understood as to "Benaiah, a valiant man" (see S. R. Driver, *Notes on the Hebrew Text and Topography of the Books of Samuel* [rev. ed. 1913]; H. P. Smith, comm. on Samuel [*ICC*, 1899]). In 1 Ch. 27:5 Jehoiada is called a priest (AV, NEB, "chief priest"), which may find support in 1 Ch. 12:27, where among those who supported David in Hebron was "the prince Jehoiada, of the house of Aaron." The reference in 1 Ch. 27:5, however, may be to Benaiah (as LXX, Vulg., Josephus *Ant.* vii.5.4 [110]), though some, e.g., H. L. Ellison, discount this. In 1 Ch. 27:34 there is named among David's counselors "Jehoiada the son of Benaiah." Some commentators, and two MSS, would reverse the names; E. L. Curtis, however (comm. on Chronicles [*ICC*, 1910]), retains the MT. *See* BENAIAH **1.**

2. A priest during the reigns of Ahaziah, Queen Athaliah, and Joash of Judah (2 K. 11:4–12:16 [MT 17] par. 2 Ch. 23:1–24:14; 2 Ch. 22:11; 24:14-25). In 2 K. 12:10 (MT 11) he is called "high priest," the first to receive the title; but as the priest lived in the temple, it is meaningless to say that he "came up," so most commentators omit the words "and the chief priest" as being a later addition.

I. Revolt Against Athaliah.–He was the leader of the revolt against the queen mother ATHALIAH, who had assumed full authority in Judah after the death of her son Ahaziah. Jehoiada's wife Jehosheba, sister of Ahaziah, had protected her brother's youngest son Joash when Athaliah had slain all the others. Jehoiada planned the revolt carefully and with the aid of the royal guard proclaimed Joash king and slew Athaliah (2 K. 11:4-20; 2 Ch. 23:1-21).

There are several textual problems in these accounts. (1) Stade (*ZAW*, 5 [1885], 280ff.) suggested that there were two main sources in 2 K. 11:4-20, namely, the original narrative (vv. 4-12, 18b-20) and an interpolation (vv. 13-18a). This has been widely accepted, and the historicity of the interpolation doubted. J. A. Montgomery (*ICC*), however, prefers to see here an amalgamation of contemporary accounts, holding that "the alleged interpolation... tells true history" that gives information otherwise unknown, e.g., the reference to the temple of Baal and the priest Mattan. (2) According to some v. 6 is difficult and ought to be omitted because of confusion concerning the numbers of the companies involved in the operation (e.g., Wellhausen, Skinner). Montgomery says that the omission of the whole verse with its exact local details is arbitrary, the point being that all the troops were kept on duty for the intended coup.

(3) The account in 2 Ch. 23:1-21 follows that of 2 Kings in the main, with the important modification that the leading part in the revolt was played by the Levites, and that only they were permitted in the temple. Whether the Chronicler was reading back into the past customs contemporary to him, or whether he deliberately altered his sources "in the interests of the ecclesiastical order to which he belonged" (W. A. L. Elmslie, *CBSC* on 2 Chronicles), is a matter of conjecture. H. L. Ellison suggested that the writer of Kings omitted to mention the Levitical guard because he "considered them ornamental rather than useful." (On all these and other critical questions see comms.)

II. Restoration of the Temple.–Joash determined to repair the temple, but when the money came in so slowly that nothing was done, he called in Jehoiada and rebuked him for his lethargy. A chest was then prepared as a collection box for the offerings ("the first collection box in history," Montgomery), and the work was speedily accomplished (2 K. 11:21–12:16 [MT 17]; 2 Ch. 24:1-14). The Chronicler seems to have followed a different tradition in some details, notably when he recorded that the surplus money was used to supply vessels for the sanctuary, whereas Kings seems expressly to deny this. A. Van Hoonacker (*Le Sacerdoce lévitique dans la loi et dans l'histoire des Hébreux* [1899], pp. 101-114) defends the account in Chronicles.

III. Death and Significance.–Jehoiada died at a good age and was held in such high esteem that he was buried among the kings. It appears that he was the predominating force for good in the kingdom, and after his death the piety and character of Joash noticeably declined (2 Ch. 24:15-18; cf. 2 K. 12:2).

3. (Neh. 3:6, AV). *See* JOIADA **1.**

4. The priest referred to in Jer. 29:26 is taken by some, e.g., Giesebrecht, to be the priest of Athaliah's time (see **2** above). H. Freedman saw a reference to 2 K. 11:18. Others, e.g., Duhm, simply said that nothing is known of him.

J. G. G. NORMAN

JEHOIAKIM jə-hoi'ə-kim [Heb. *yᵉhôyāqîm*–'Yahweh will establish']; originally **ELIAKIM** ē-lī'ə-kim [Heb. *'elyāqîm*–'God will establish']; AV Apoc. JOACIM [Gk. *Iōakim*] (1 Esd. 1:37-39; Bar. 1:3); NEB also JOAKIM (1 Esd. 1:37-39).

1. The son of Josiah, and king of Judah enthroned by Pharaoh Neco of Egypt in 609 B.C. to replace Jehoahaz his brother, whom the people had chosen to succeed Josiah (2 K. 23:34; 2 Ch. 36:4). Judah paid a heavy tribute to Egypt, to whom Jehoiakim remained subservient until 605 B.C. when the crucial Battle of Carchemish caused Neco to retreat to the borders of Egypt. From 605 until the end of his reign in 598 B.C., Jehoiakim encountered problems with the Babylonians.

Jehoiakim was not in sympathy with the reforms promoted by his father Josiah. His attitude and antagonism toward the prophets is significantly reflected in the book of Jeremiah. Undoubtedly, Judah reverted to idolatry during his reign.

During the early years of Jehoiakim's reign, Jeremiah boldly declared in the temple court that the temple would be reduced to ruins. The mob reacted violently (Jer. 26). Probably Jeremiah had proclaimed this message previously during the reign of Josiah without any serious difficulties (cf. Jer. 7). When the princes from the palace came, the prophets and priests demanded the execution of Jeremiah; but apparently Ahikam was effective in defending him. About this time, however, Jehoiakim was responsible for the arrest and execution of a prophet named Uriah, who proclaimed the same judgment announced by Jeremiah.

The fourth year of Jehoiakim's reign (605) was crucial in many respects. During this year Jeremiah's scroll was read in the presence of Jehoiakim, who defiantly cut it up and threw the pieces into the fire (Jer. 36). It was during this year that Jeremiah boldly declared that Nebuchadrezzar would subdue Judah and many surrounding nations (Jer. 25). In his denunciation (22:13-19) the prophet reflects some of the selfish policies Jehoiakim followed in his administration, causing oppression and injustice. Unlike Josiah, who provided pious leadership, Jehoiakim showed no signs of repentance or favorable response to the divine warnings.

In 605 Jehoiakim was confronted with a Babylonian invasion. In the decisive battle at Carchemish in early summer the Egyptians were routed by the Babylonians. By August, Nebuchadrezzar had advanced far enough into southern Palestine to claim treasures and hostages in Jerusalem — Daniel and his friends being the most noteworthy among the Judean captives (Dnl. 1:1). Although Jehoiakim retained his throne, the return of the Babylonians into Syria in 604 and to Ashkelon in 603, and their clash with Neco on the borders of Egypt in 601, frustrated any attempts to terminate Babylonian vassalage. Since this Egyptian encounter was indecisive, with both armies retreating after heavy losses, Jehoiakim may have taken this opportunity to withhold tribute (Wiseman, *CCK*, pp. 26-28). Although Nebuchadrezzar did not send his conquering army to Jerusalem for several years, he incited raids on Judah by marauding Chaldean bands supported by Moabites, Ammonites, and Syrians. In the course of this warfare Jehoiakim's reign was abruptly terminated by death, leaving a precarious anti-Babylonian policy to his young son Jehoiachin. (*See also* BABYLONIA IV. J.)

The way in which Jehoiakim met death is not reported in Kings or Chronicles. The burning of Jeremiah's scroll precipitated divine judgment upon Jehoiakim — his body would be exposed to the heat by day and the frost by night, indicating that he would not have a royal burial (Jer. 36:27-32). On another occasion Jeremiah predicted that Jehoiakim would have the burial of an ass — his body would be cast out beyond the gates of Jerusalem (22:18-19). Since neither of the historical accounts reports the circumstances of Jehoiakim's death, nor mentions even his burial, the conclusion that this defiant king was killed in battle seems warranted. In wartime it was impossible to provide an honorable burial.

2. (Bar. 1:7; AV JOACHIM). A priest (Gk. *hiereús*) to whom the Babylonian exiles sent a collection of money.

S. J. SCHULTZ

JEHONADAB jə-hō'nə-dab = **JONADAB** jō'nə-dab [Heb. *yᵉhônāḏāḇ, yônāḏāḇ*–'Yahweh is noble, liberal,' or 'Yahweh has impelled'].

1. Son of Shimeah, the brother of King David (2 S. 13:3, 5, 32, 35; RSV, NEB Jonadab), who helped Amnon seduce his sister. This scheme was probably intended to assist Amnon in claiming the throne, according to the principles of matriarchal succession which are reflected elsewhere in the narratives of the early monarchy (cf. 1 S. 25:43; 2 S. 3:3). Two years later when Absalom murdered Amnon, and David heard that all the king's sons were assassinated, Jehonadab assured him that only Amnon was killed; and his reassuring tone was justified (v. 35); possibly he knew of Absalom's intentions. The LXX Lucian has "Jonathan" in 13:3ff.; and in 2 S. 21:21 par. 1 Ch. 20:7, there is mentioned a son of Shimei (= Shammah, 1 S. 16:9), whose name is Jonathan.

2. Jehonadab in 2 K. 10:15, 23 and in the MT of Jer. 35:8, 14, 16, 18 = Jonadab in the MT of Jer. 35:6, 10, 19 and in the RSV of vv. 8, 14, 16, 18. "Son" of Rechab, of the Kenite clan (1 Ch. 2:55). Jehonadab is described in 2 K. 10 as an ally of Jehu in the abolition of Baal worship in Samaria. Jehu met him after slaying the son of Ahab (10:15). In Jer. 35 (where the RSV has Jonadab throughout), he is called the "father" of the Rechabites, who derived from him their ordinances for their nomadic life and abstention from wine.

See RECHAB. D. F. ROBERTS

JEHONATHAN jə-hon'ə-thən [Heb. *yᵉhônāṯān*–'Yahweh has given'].

1. A Levite who took part in teaching the Torah in the cities of Judah under Jehoshaphat (2 Ch. 17:8).

2. Head of the priestly family of Shemaiah (Neh. 12:18).

3. AV and MT in 1 Ch. 27:25; *see* JONATHAN.

JEHORAM jə-hôr'əm, contracted form: **JORAM** jôr'əm [Heb. *yᵉhôrām, yôrām*–'Yahweh is exalted'].

1. The son of Ahab and Jezebel, and the ninth king of Israel (852-841 B.C.). He succeeded his brother Ahaziah, who had died prematurely as a result of a fall; and he reigned twelve years (2 K. 3:1–9:26).

I. His Religious Character.–The sacred historian clears him of the idolatrous excesses of his royal parents. He put away Baal's image which his father had made, although he did not destroy it; that was left for Jehu to do (2 K. 10:26f.). He had, however, a poor idea of the God of Israel, thinking of Him as a malevolent deity. Thus when the allied armies marching against Moab were suffering from a serious lack of water, he thought that it was God who was thus deliberately delivering them into the hands of the Moabites (2 K. 3:13). Again, when the country was suffering from famine, at a time when the capital was besieged by the Arameans, he thought that these evils, too, had come from God, in whom one trusted in vain and from whom no good could be expected (2 K. 6:33).

II. Moabite War.–Mesha king of Moab was paying a yearly tribute to Ahab of 100,000 lambs and the wool of 100,000 rams; finally he revolted (2 K. 3:4). The biblical account agrees with what is recorded on the Moabite Stone, that the revolt took place after many years of oppression by Omri and his sons, or rather his son and grandson. In the war with Moab that followed, Jehoram was aided by the king of Judah as well as by the vicegerent of Edom, Judah's vassal. The allied armies miraculously escaped perishing from thirst on their long march into Moab around the southern end of the Dead Sea. After making some gains they besieged Kir-hareseth. In desperation, King Mesha offered up his eldest son as a holocaust on the city wall in sight of the besiegers, who were so affected that they gave up the siege and withdrew.

III. Conflict with the Arameans.–The Arameans, who were no less hostile, sent out raiding parties (2 K. 5:2), laid ambushes (6:8), and once, as already noted, besieged the capital (6:24). The most serious clash seems to have taken place at Ramoth-gilead E of the Jordan. This was no new battlefield, since Ahab had fought here and lost his life. Jehoram, wounded in battle, went down to Jezreel to recuperate.

IV. Jehoram's Death.–Jehu was the instrument of Jehoram's death. Jehu, who was secretly anointed by a young prophet sent to him by Elisha, was charged with avenging the blood of the prophets and the blood of the Yahweh worshipers killed by Jezebel. Acclaimed king by his fellow officers, Jehu made a dash for Jezreel; and when Jehoram went out to meet him he was shot down by an arrow from Jehu's bow. Jezebel, the queen mother, was ignominiously killed; and all the members of Ahab's house were exterminated, together with the entire pro-Baal party. M. S. SEALE

2. [Gk. *Iōram* (Mt. 1:8)]. King of Judah, and son of Jehoshaphat (2 K. 8:16-24; 2 Ch. 21). He began to rule *ca.* 849 B.C. and reigned eight years. It is not easy to reconcile the synchronism of 2 K. 1:17 with that of 8:16, but it may be that Jehoram of Judah was co-regent with his father Jehoshaphat for some years before he became sole ruler in 849 B.C. The commencement of his sole reign must then be referred to in 8:16. But *see* JEHORAM **1.**

I. His Marriage.–In the beginning of the reigns of Ahab and Jehoshaphat, an attempt was made to end the old feud between Israel and Judah. At the suggestion of Ahab, the two kingdoms for the first time joined forces against the common foe from the north, the Syrians. To seal the alliance, Athaliah daughter of Ahab was married to Jehoram son of Jehoshaphat. Thus Jehoram was brother-in-law to Jehoram son of Ahab. No doubt this was considered as a master stroke of conciliatory policy by the interested parties. It proved disastrous for Judah, however. Beyond a doubt, the unholy zeal of Jezebel included the baalizing of Judah as well as of Israel. This marriage was a step in that direction.

II. His Idolatry.–"A man shall leave his father and mother, and shall cleave unto his wife." Jehoram did so. "He walked in the ways of the kings of Israel, as did the house of Ahab" (2 K. 8:18). According to 2 Ch. 21:11, 13 Jehoram not only accepted the religion of Athaliah, but he became a persecutor, compelling the inhabitants of Jerusalem to become apostates.

Because of his gross idolatry and his wickedness, he is said (2 Ch. 21:12ff.) to have received a denunciatory letter from the prophet Elijah, which, however, had no effect on him. This leads to a chronological difficulty. Was Elijah still alive? The inference from 2 K. 3:11 is that he was not. A possible explanation is that the strictures applied to Ahab by Elijah were now reapplied by somebody to Jehoram almost word for word, so that the document could be called Elijah's. The simplest solution, however, is to read "Elisha" instead of "Elijah." On the other hand, it is just possible that Elijah was still alive.

A person's religion cannot be divorced from his character. Baal worship had in it the elements of tyranny and civic unrighteousness. In keeping with his religion and in true oriental fashion Jehoram began his reign by murdering his brothers and other princes of the land, to whom Jehoshaphat had given valuable gifts and responsible positions.

III. Edomite Revolt.–The only event of his reign recorded in Kings is the revolt of Edom. Edom was subdued by David, and it had remained subject to the united kingdom and then to Judah until the revolt under Jehoram. The text is somewhat obscure, but both accounts indicate that the expedition of Jehoram against Edom ended in failure. It appears that the army of Jehoram was surrounded, and that it managed to fight its way out, inflicting heavy casualties on the Edomites. But it was the Edomites who won the battle.

IV. Raid into Judah.–Perhaps the revolt of Libnah (2 K. 8:22) should be taken in connection with the invasion of the Philistines and of the Arabians, mentioned in 2 Ch. 21. Libnah was located on the southwestern border of Judah. Since it was a border city, it is possible that the compiler of Kings considered it as belonging to Philistia. In the account in Chronicles, Jehoram is represented as having lost all his possessions and his family, except for Jehoahaz his youngest son, when the town was sacked and the palace plundered by the invading force of Philistines and Arabians. The account appears to be based on reliable sources.

V. His Death.–In his last days, he was afflicted with a disease in the bowels (*see* DISEASE III.J). His death was unregretted, and his burial without honor (cf. 2 K. 8:24; 2 Ch. 21:20). Ahaziah, also called Jehoahaz, his youngest and only surviving son, succeeded him. Athaliah (who must have escaped capture by the raiders) retained her influence, now occupying the powerful position of queen mother. S. K. MOSIMAN

D. F. PAYNE

JEHOSHABEATH jə-hō-shab'ē-əth [Heb. *y^e^hôšaḇ'aṯ*]. In 2 Ch. 22:11, the same as JEHOSHEBA of 2 K. 11:2.

JEHOSHAPHAT jə-hosh'ə-fat [Heb. *y^e^hôšāpāṭ*–'Yahweh has judged'].

1. King of Judah. See separate article below.

2. Son of Ahilud. He was recorder under David (2 S. 8:16; 20:24; 1 Ch. 18:15) and Solomon (1 K. 4:3).

3. Son of Paruah, and Solomon's overseer in Issachar to provide victuals for the royal household for one month of the year (1 K. 4:17).

4. Son of Nimshi, and father of Jehu, king of northern Israel (2 K. 9:2, 14). His name is omitted in 9:20 and 1 K. 19:16, where Jehu is called "son of Nimshi."

D. F. ROBERTS

JEHOSHAPHAT jə-hosh'ə-fat [Heb. *y^e^hôšāpāṭ*–'Yahweh has judged'; Gk. *Iōsaphat* (Mt. 1:8)]. The fourth king of Judah, and son of Asa. His mother was Azubah the daughter of Shilhi. He was thirty-five years of age at his accession, and reigned twenty-five years, *ca.* 873-849 B.C. The history of his reign is contained in 1 K. 22:41-50 and in 2 Ch. 17:1–21:1. The narrative in 1 K. 22:1-35a and in 2 K. 3:4ff. belongs to the history of the northern kingdom. The absence from Kings of the details contained in 2 Chronicles affords no presumption against their truth. Neither do high numbers, embellished statements, and the coloring of the writer's own age destroy the historical perspective.

I. His Religious Policy.–The reign of Jehoshaphat appears to have been one of unusual religious activity. It was characterized, however, not so much by striking religious measures as it was by the religious spirit that pervaded every act of the king, who sought the favor of Yahweh in every detail of his life (2 Ch. 17:3f.). He evidently felt that a nation's character is determined by its religion. Accordingly, he made it his duty to purify the national worship. The "sodomites," the male cult prostitutes of Canaanite worship, were banished from the land (1 K. 22:46). The Asherim were taken out of Judah (2 Ch. 17:6; 19:3), and "the people from Beer-sheba to the hill country of Ephraim were brought back unto the Lord, the God of their fathers" (19:4). Because of his zeal for Yahweh, Jehoshaphat was rewarded with power and "riches and honor in abundance" (17:5).

II. Domestic Programs.–Believing that religion and morals, the foundation and bulwarks of civilization, suffer from ignorance, Jehoshaphat introduced a system of public instruction for the whole land (2 Ch. 17:7ff.). He appointed a commission, composed of princes, Levites, and priests, to go from city to city to instruct the people. Their instruction was to be based on the one true foundation of sound morals and healthy religious life, "the book of the law of the Lord" (17:7-9).

Next in importance to his system of public instruction was his provision for the better administration of justice. He appointed judges to preside over courts of common pleas, which he established in all the fortified cities of Judah. In addition to these local courts, two courts of appeal, an ecclesiastical and a civil court, were established at Jerusalem to be presided over by priests, Levites, and leading nobles as judges. At the head of the ecclesiastical court of appeal was the high priest; a layman, "the ruler of the house of Judah," headed the civil court of appeal (2 Ch. 19:4-11). The insistence that a judge was to be in character like Yahweh, with whom there is "no iniquity . . . nor respect of persons, nor taking of bribes" (19:7), is worthy of note.

III. His Military Defenses.–According to 2 Ch. 17:2, Jehoshaphat began his reign with defensive measures against Israel. Furthermore, he built castles and store-cities in the land of Judah, "and he had many works," probably military supplies, "in the cities of Judah" (17:13). He appears to have had a large standing army, including cavalry (1 K. 22:4; 2 Ch. 17:14ff.). However, the numbers in Chronicles seem to be impossibly high.

IV. His Foreign Policy.–Godliness and security at home were followed by respect and peace abroad. That the Philistines and the Arabians brought tribute (2 Ch. 17:11) and that Edom had no king (1 K. 22:47), but a deputy instead who was probably appointed by Jehoshaphat, indicate that he held the suzerainty over the nations and tribes bordering on Judah to the south and west. Holding the suzerainty over the weaker nations, and being allied with the stronger, Jehoshaphat for the greater part of his reign secured the peace that fostered the internal development of the kingdom (1 Ch. 17:10).

In contrast to the former kings of Judah, Jehoshaphat saw greater benefit in an alliance with Israel than in civil war. Accordingly, the old feud between the two kingdoms (1 K. 14:30; 15:6) was dropped, and Jehoshaphat made peace with Israel (22:44). The political union was cemented by the marriage of his son Jehoram to Athaliah daughter of Ahab. Shortly after the marriage, Jehoshaphat joined Ahab in a campaign against Syria (2 Ch. 18:1-3). It is clear from the narrative that he had a subordinate position in this campaign (1 K. 22:4, 30), and many historians have deduced from this that Judah must have become a dependency of Israel. It was only natural that Israel should take the lead, however, since it was not only the larger nation but also the claimant to Ramoth-gilead, which lay in Gadite territory. It is not easy to prove that Judah was Israel's vassal, in view of Jehoshaphat's own military prowess and resources (2 Ch. 17:2; 20:27-30); moreover, the marriage between Athaliah and Jehoram probably implies that their fathers ranked as equals.

It is evident that the union and cooperation of Israel and Judah gave them the necessary strength to defy Syria and to subjugate other neighboring states. But the introduction of an Israelite princess to the court of Judah was ultimately disastrous. Her propagation of the Tyrian Baal cult in Judah outweighed any political and material advantages gained through the alliance, and in the succeeding reigns it led indirectly to the almost total extinction of the royal family of Judah (11:1ff.).

In spite of the denunciation of the prophet Jehu for his expedition with Ahab, thus "help[ing] the wicked" (2 Ch. 19:2), Jehoshaphat entered into a similar alliance with Jehoram of Israel (2 K. 3:4ff.). On the invitation of Jehoram to join him in an expedition against Moab, Jehoshaphat was ready with the same set speech of acceptance as in the case of Ahab (2 K. 3:7; cf. 1 K. 22:4). For the details of the expedition *see* JEHORAM 1.II.

V. Victory over the Moabites and Ammonites.–The Chronicler has given us a very remarkable account of a victory gained by Jehoshaphat over the Moabites and Ammonites. No doubt he made use of a current historical midrash. Many find the historical basis of the midrash in the events recorded in 2 K. 3:4ff. The localities are different, however, and there a defeat is recorded, while in this case we have a victory. The story in outline bears the stamp of authenticity. 1 K. 22:45 seems to suggest wars of Jehoshaphat that are not mentioned in Kings. The tribes mentioned in the account are represented as trying to make a permanent settlement in Judah (2 Ch. 20:11). In their advance through the south of Judah, they were doubtless harassed by the shepherd population of the country. Jehoshaphat, according to his custom, sought the help of Yahweh. The invading forces fell to quarreling among themselves (2 Ch. 20:23), and destroyed one another. The spoil was great because the invaders had brought with them all their goods, expecting to remain in the land.

VI. Destruction of Jehoshaphat's Fleet.–The destruction of Jehoshaphat's fleet is recorded in 1 K. 22:48f. and in 2 Ch. 20:35-37. The two accounts are quite different, however. According to Kings, Jehoshaphat built ships of Tarshish to sail to Ophir for gold, but the vessels were wrecked at Ezion-geber. Thereupon Ahaziah of Israel offered to assist him with seamen, but Jehoshaphat refused to enter into the alliance. According to Chronicles, the alliance had been formed, and together they built ships at Ezion-geber, which were destroyed because Jehoshaphat had made an alliance with the wicked king of Israel. The two accounts may well be describing two separate events, of which the Chronicles episode was the earlier. The text of the passage in Kings is somewhat corrupt, and, taking the LXX into consideration, some scholars conclude that there was only one ship, and that it was built by the "deputy" of v. 47. If this is so, then without doubt Chronicles must be describing a different event — an event that must have damaged the economy of Judah considerably.

VII. His Death.–Jehoshaphat died at the age of sixty. Josephus says (*Ant.* ix.3.2 [44]) that he was buried in a magnificent manner, for he had imitated the actions of David. The kingdom was left to his son Jehoram. E. R. Thiele (*MNHK*) contends on chronological grounds that Jehoshaphat figured in two co-regencies, at the start of his reign with his father Asa, and with his son Jehoram at the end of it (*see also* CHRONOLOGY OF THE OT V.B). If so, the Bible gives no specific indication of it.

S. K. MOSIMAN
D. F. PAYNE

JEHOSHAPHAT jə-hosh'ə-fat, **VALLEY OF** [Heb. *ʿēmeq yᵉhôšāpāṭ*–the second element means "Yahweh shall judge"; Gk. *koiláda Yosaphat*]; NEB VALLEY OF THE LORD'S JUDGEMENT. The scene of the judgment of the nations (Joel 3:2, 12 [MT 4:2, 12]). No location is given in Scripture for this final assize of the nations that were hostile to God's people, but it is clear both from the contexts of 3:2, 12 and from the term used twice in 3:14, "the valley of decision" (cf. Zeph. 3:8), that the name is to be interpreted as the scene of judgment, and not taken from the king of the same name. Ezk. 39:11 and Rev. 16:16 seem to locate it in the plain of Esdraelon (Armageddon).

By a curious process Jews, Christians, and Moslems have come to associate the last judgment with a portion of the Kidron Valley E of Jerusalem including the slopes on either side. As a result, a great number of tombs can be seen there, Moslem for the large part on the western side and Jewish on the eastern. Eusebius in the *Onomasticon*

Traditional Valley of Jehoshaphat E of Jerusalem (W. S. LaSor)

(ed. Klostermann, p. 70) located the valley of Jehoshaphat in the Valley of Hinnom, possibly because of the judgments that were associated with that place in connection with the idolatrous kings of Judah (cf. Jer. 7:31f.; 19:5f., where it is called "the valley of Slaughter"). Since the time of the Pilgrim of Bordeaux (A.D. 333), however, the Kidron has become increasingly the site popularly accepted. (For a sketch of the development, cf. *HDB*, II [1899], 562.) According to Jewish tradition, that portion of the Kidron that lies between the temple mount and the Mt. of Olives is the valley of Jehoshaphat, hence the large number of Jewish burial sites there. Some rabbis taught that it was necessary to be buried in the Holy Land in order to have a share in the resurrection, and the tradition developed that the bodies of those buried elsewhere would roll underground "like bottles" until they reached Palestine (T.P. *Ketuboth* xii.3, quoted in C. G. Montefiore and H. Loewe, eds., *Rabbinic Anthology* [repr. 1974], p. 600). In Moslem tradition, the angel Israfel on the day of resurrection will stand on es-Sakhra (the rock under the Dome of the Rock) to blow his trumpet. The multitude of the faithful then will follow Muhammad across *al-Sirât*, a bridge as narrow as a finely honed scimitar. One end of this bridge begins at Jerusalem and is marked by a column set horizontally in the wall of Ḥaram esh-Sherîf (*see* JERUSALEM II.B), and it crosses the gulf of Jahannum (obviously drawn from "Gehenna," but whether from a Christian or a Jewish source is not clear). Christians look for the return of Jesus to take place on the Mt. of Olives, based in part on Acts 1:9, 11, and in part on Ezk. 14:1 and Zec. 14:4. The Christian tradition, that the triumphal entry was made through the Golden Gate and that the return would be by that same gate, and a Moslem tradition that attempts to thwart any such occurrence, have given rise to the inclusion of the Golden Gate in the Moslem concept of the last day. Christian monks and nuns in the Middle Ages lived in caves in the Kidron and later a monastery, St. Mary of Josaphat, was built there. The Lion Gate ("St. Stephen's Gate") was formerly known as the Gate of the Valley of Josaphat. It was probably from the association of this area with the name "valley of Jehoshaphat" that a prominent tomb near "Absalom's Pillar" came to be called "the tomb of Jehoshaphat."

Bibliography.–J. Simons, *Jerusalem in the OT* (1952), pp. 10, 372; L.-H. Vincent and F.-M. Abel, *Jérusalem nouvelle*, IV (1926), 813-16, 849-852; *HDB*, II (1899), 561f. (C. Warren); E. Hoade, *Guide to the Holy Land* (7th ed. 1973), pp. 289-291.

W. S. LASOR

JEHOSHEBA jə-hosh'ə-bə, jē-hə-shē'bə [Heb. *yᵉhôšeḇaʿ*–'Yahweh is opulence']. Called "Jehoshabeath" in 2 Ch. 22:11; daughter of Jehoram king of Judah, possibly by a wife other than Athaliah (2 K. 11:2). According to 2 Ch. 22:11, she was the wife of Jehoiada, the priest. She hid Jehoash, the young son of King Ahaziah, and so saved his life from Queen Athaliah.

JEHOSHUA jə-hōsh'o͞o-ə [Heb. *yᵉhôšu(a)ʿ*] (AV Nu. 13:16; 1 Ch. 7:27). *See* JOSHUA **5.**

JEHOVAH jə-hō'və. *See* GOD, NAMES OF II.C.

JEHOVAH-JIREH jə-hō'və-jī'rə [Heb. *YHWH yirʾeh*–'Yahweh will find']. The AV and NEB transliteration of Abraham's name for the place where Yahweh provided him a lamb as a substitute sacrifice for Isaac (Gen. 22:14). Abraham's choice of name was no doubt based on his response to Isaac's question (v. 7) regarding the whereabouts of the lamb needed for a sacrifice: "God will find [*yirʾeh*; cf. 1 S. 16:1] for Himself the lamb" (v. 8). The meaning of the related popular saying in v. 14b is not immediately discernible because the narrator, communicating with an audience familiar with the saying, did not feel compelled to provide any further explanation for later audiences (see comms.).

Jehovah-jireh has been traditionally identified with the site of Solomon's temple, but later scholars have suggested the sanctuary of the oak of Moreh at Shechem (cf. O. Procksch, comm. on Genesis [*KZAT*, 3rd ed. 1924], *in loc.*). Neither identification is certain. J. E. H.

JEHOVAH-NISSI jə-hō'və-ni'sī [Heb. *YHWH nissî*–'Yahweh is my banner']. The AV and NEB transliteration of Moses' name for the altar that he erected to commemorate the Israelites' defeat of the Amalekites at Rephidim (Ex. 17:15). The BANNER was frequently used to rally an army for battle (cf. Ps. 60:4 [MT 6]); thus the altar would witness to all who saw it that Yahweh was responsible for the Israelites' victory over the Amalekites. For discussion of the problems involved in interpreting the related saying in v. 16, see B. S. Childs, comm. on Exodus (*OTL*, 1974), pp. 311f., 315.

JEHOVAH, SERVANT OF. *See* SERVANT OF THE LORD.

JEHOVAH-SHALOM jə-hō'və-shä-lōm [Heb. *YHWH šālôm*–'Yahweh is peace'] (Jgs. 6:24); RSV "The Lord is peace." The AV transliteration of the name that Gideon gave to the altar he built at Ophra, in allusion to the word spoken to him by the Lord, "Peace be to you" (Jgs. 6:23).

JEHOZABAD jə-hō'zə-bad [Heb. *yᵉhôzāḇāḏ*–'Yahweh has bestowed'].

1. A servant of King Jehoash of Judah. According to 2 K. 12:21 (MT 22), he was a son of Shomer, but 2 Ch. 24:26 makes him "son of Shimrith the Moabitess."

2. A Korahite doorkeeper, son of Obed-edom (1 Ch. 26:4).

3. A Benjaminite, one of King Jehoshaphat's warriors (2 Ch. 17:18).

JEHOZADAK jə-hō'zə-dak [Heb. *yᵉhôṣāḏāq*] (1 Ch. 6:1f. [MT 5:40f.]; Hag. 1:1, 12, 14; 2:2, 4; Zec. 6:11); **JOZADAK** jō'zə-dak [Heb. *yôṣāḏāq*] (Ezr. 3:2, 8; 5:2; 10:18; Neh. 12:26); AV also JOSEDECH (Hag. 1:1, 12, 14; 2:2, 4; Zec. 6:11), JOSEDEC (1 Esd. 5:5, 48, 56; 6:2; 9:19); NEB also JOSEDEK (1 Esd. 5:5, 48, 56; 6:2; 9:19). The father of Joshua the priest and a priest himself at the time of the captivity under Nebuchadrezzar (1 Ch. 6:14f.; Hag. 1:1; etc.).

JEHU jē'ho͞o [Heb. *yēhûʾ*–'he is Yahweh'; 1 K. 19:16f.; 2 K. 9–10; Gk. *Eiou*].

1. Son of Jehoshaphat and descendant of Nimshi, hence commonly called "the son of Nimshi"; tenth king of Israel and founder of its fourteenth dynasty. He reigned for twenty-eight years, *ca.* 842-814 B.C.

I. Officer of Ahab.–A soldier of fortune, Jehu appears first as an officer in the bodyguard of Ahab. He saw the judicial murder of Naboth and Naboth's sons (2 K. 9:26). He was there when Ahab drove from Samaria to inspect his new possession, Naboth's vineyard, in Jezreel and witnessed the dramatic encounter between the king and the prophet Elijah (cf. 1 K. 21:16-24). Years after, Jehu reminded Bidkar his aide (lit. "third [officer]") of the doom they had heard pronounced there upon Ahab and his house (2 K. 9:25f.). In fulfillment of this doom Jehu ordered the body of the slain Jehoram to be thrown into the enclosure that had once been Naboth's. Ahab's temporary repentance averted the punishment from himself for a few years (1 K. 21:27-29), but the blow fell at the battle of Ramoth-gilead, and Jehu remembered the prophet's words as he beheld the dogs licking Ahab's blood "by the pool of Samaria" (22:38).

II. Jehoram at Ramoth-gilead and Jezreel.–Ahab's elder son, Ahaziah, after a short reign died from the effects of an accident (2 K. 1). He was succeeded by his brother Jehoram, who toward the close of his twelve-year reign (2 K. 3:1) decided to recover Ramoth-gilead, where his father had been fatally stricken, from Hazael of Syria. He succeeded (2 K. 9:14) but in the attack was severely wounded and was taken to Jezreel to recover (v. 15). The city meanwhile was left under the supervision of Jehu and his fellow commanders. At Jezreel his ally Ahaziah of Judah visited him (8:28f.; 9:16).

III. The Anointing of Jehu.–Elisha the prophet, the successor of Elijah, took the decisive step that precipitated the predicted vengeance on the house of Ahab. Hazael and Jehu had already been named to Elijah as the persons who were to execute the divine judgment, the one as king of Syria, the other as king of Israel (1 K. 19:15-17). Elisha, doubtless aware of this commission, quickly dispatched to Ramoth-gilead a messenger, who took Jehu aside, anointed him king of Israel in Yahweh's name, and charged him to strike down the house of Ahab to avenge the righteous blood shed by Ahab and Jezebel. The messenger, as instructed, then fled (2 K. 9:1-10).

IV. The Revolution and Death of Jehoram.–Events now moved rapidly. Jehu's companions, learning that Jehu had been anointed king, at once improvised a throne by throwing their garments on the top of some steps, blew the trumpet, and proclaimed "Jehu is king." Not a moment was lost. No one was permitted to leave the city to carry news, and Jehu himself, with characteristic impetuosity, set out in his chariot with Bidkar as charioteer and a small body of horsemen to Jezreel (2 K. 9:25). As they came within sight of the city, a watchman reported their advance, and messengers were sent to inquire about their errand. These were ordered to fall into the rear. This conduct awakened suspicion, and Jehoram and Ahaziah — who was still with his invalided kinsman — proceeded in person to meet Jehu. At the ill-omened field of Naboth, their anxious query "Is it peace?" was answered by a storm of denunciation from Jehu, and when Jehoram turned to flee, an arrow from Jehu's powerful bow pierced him through the heart, and he sank dead in his chariot. Ahaziah likewise was pursued and wounded "at the ascent of Gur, which is by Ibleam." He died at Megiddo and was buried in Jerusalem in the sepulchre of the kings (9:11-28). A somewhat variant account of Ahaziah's death is given in 2 Ch. 22:9. It is possible that Jehu came to Megiddo or its neighborhood and killed him there.

V. Death of Jezebel.–The slaughter of Jehoram was quickly followed by that of the main instigator of all the crimes for which the house of Ahab suffered — the queen mother Jezebel. Returning from the pursuit of Ahaziah, Jehu arrived at Jezreel. Jezebel, now an aged woman, but still defiant, had painted and attired herself and, looking from her window, met him as he drove into the palace court with the insulting question, "Is it peace, you Zimri, murderer of your master?" (cf. 1 K. 16:9-12). Jehu's answer was an appeal for aid from those inside. Two or three eunuchs of the palace gave signs of their concurrence and at Jehu's bidding threw Jezebel down into the courtyard, where, lying in her blood, she was trampled by the chariot horses. A little later, when her remains were sought for burial, she was found to have been almost completely devoured by dogs — a lurid commentary on Elijah's earlier threat which was now remembered (2 K. 9:30-37). Jehu was a fearless executor of judgment, but the pitiless zeal, needless cruelty, and deceit with which he accomplished his mission withdraw one's sympathy from him, as it did that of a later prophet (Hos. 1:4).

VI. Slaughter of Ahab's Descendants.–The next deeds of Jehu even more clearly reveal his thoroughness of purpose, promptness of action, ruthlessness, and lack of principle. Samaria was the capital of the kingdom and headquarters of the Baal worship introduced by Jezebel, though it is recorded of Jehoram that he had removed, at least temporarily, an obelisk of Baal that his father had set up (2 K. 3:2; cf. 10:26). The city was still held for the house of Ahab, and seventy of Ahab's "sons" — to be taken here in the sense of male descendants — resided in it (10:1, 6). Jehu here adopted a bold and astute policy. He sent letters to Samaria challenging those in authority to set up one of their master's sons as king and fight for the city and the kingdom. The leaders knew well that they could make no effective resistance to Jehu and at once humbly offered their submission. Jehu, in a second message, challenged them to prove their sincerity by delivering to him the heads of the seventy princes in baskets. Their compliance irrevocably committed them to Jehu's cause (v. 9). The ghastly relics were piled up in two heaps at the gate of Jezreel — a horrible object lesson to any still inclined to hesitate in their allegiance. Friends and partisans of the royal house shared the fate of its members (v. 11).

VII. Slaughter of Ahaziah's Brethren.–Apart from the faultiness in the agent's motive, the deeds recounted up to this point fell within the letter of Jehu's commission. As much cannot be said of the bloody deeds that follow. Jehu had killed Ahaziah, king of Judah. Now, on his way to Samaria, he met forty-two persons described as "kinsmen of Ahaziah" — evidently blood relations of various degrees, as Ahaziah's own brothers had been earlier killed by the Arabians (2 Ch. 21:17; 22:1) — and, on learning their identity and their purpose to visit their kinsmen at Jezreel, gave orders that they be killed on the spot and their bodies disgracefully thrown into the pit (or "cistern") of the shearing house where he had encountered them. It was a cruel excess for which there was no justification (2 K. 10:12-14).

VIII. Massacre of the Worshipers of Baal.–Still less can the deceit and violence be condoned by which, when he reached Samaria, Jehu displayed his "zeal for Yahweh" (2 K. 10:16) by exterminating the worshipers of Baal. Jehu had secured the support of a notable man — Jehonadab the son of Rechab (vv. 15f.; cf. Jer. 35:6-19) — and his entrance into Samaria was marked by further slaying of all adherents of Ahab. Then, doubtless to the amazement of many, Jehu proclaimed himself an enthusiastic follower of Baal. A great festival was organized, to which all proph-

Panel of the Black Obelisk from Nimrûd showing Jehu (or his emissary) bowing before Shalmaneser III (859-824 B.C.). This is the only contemporary representation of an Israelite king (Trustees of the British Museum)

ets, worshipers, and priests of Baal were invited from every part of Israel. Jehu himself took the leading part in the sacrifice (2 K. 10:25). Vestments were distributed to distinguish the true worshipers of Baal from others. Then, when all were safely gathered into "the house of Baal," the gates were closed, and Jehu sent in eighty soldiers to massacre the whole deluded company. The temple of Baal was destroyed. Thus Jehu indeed "wiped out Baal from Israel" (v. 28), but at a terrible cost of falsehood and treacherous dealing (vv. 18-28).

IX. Wars with Hazael.–The history of Jehu in the Bible is mainly the history of his revolution. His reign itself is summed up in a few verses, which mostly tell of the attacks made by Hazael king of Syria on the Transjordanian territories of Israel (10:32f.). These districts were overrun and remained lost to Israel till the reign of Jehu's great-grandson, Jeroboam II (14:28).

X. Latter Years.–There are some indications that in his latter years, which were clouded with misfortune, Jehu involved his son Jehoahaz in the government (cf. 2 K. 13:1, 10 where Jehoahaz comes to the throne in the 23rd and dies in the 37th year of Jehoash of Judah — fourteen years — yet has a total reign of seventeen years). Jehu is not mentioned in Chronicles, except incidentally in connection with the death of Ahaziah (2 Ch. 22:9), and as the grandfather of Jehoash (25:17).

XI. Character.–The character of Jehu is apparent from the deeds recorded of him. His energy, determination, promptness, and zeal equipped him for the work he had to do. It was rough work and was executed with relentless thoroughness. Gentler measures probably would have failed to eradicate Baal worship from Israel. His impetuosity was demonstrated in his furious driving (2 K. 9:20). He was bold, daring, unprincipled, masterful, and astute in his policy. But one seeks in vain in his character for any touch of magnanimity or of the finer qualities of the ruler. His "zeal for Yahweh" was too much a cloak for merely worldly ambition. The bloodshed in which his rule was founded early provoked a reaction, and his closing years were dark with trouble. He is especially condemned for tolerating the worship of the golden calves (2 K. 10:29-31). Nevertheless the throne was secured to his dynasty for four generations (10:30; cf. 15:12). W. S. CALDECOTT

XII. Assyrian Records.–Further information about Jehu's reign comes from two inscriptions of Shalmaneser III of Assyria (859-824 B.C.). The first is a fragment of an annal recording the eighteenth year of Shalmaneser's reign (841/40), describing his campaign westward. After an exaggerated account of his victories he says, "At that time I received the tribute of the people of Tyre, Sidon, and of Jehu, son of Omri" (Akk. *Ia-u-a mar Ḫu-um-ri-i*; *ANET*, p. 280). In the well-known Black Obelisk of Shalmaneser, set up by him in the main square of Nimrûd, this act of submission is depicted. The superscription below the relevant panel reads: "The tribute of Jehu, son of Omri. Silver, gold, a golden bowl, a golden vase, golden cups, golden buckets, tin, a staff for the royal hand[?], *puruchati*-fruits" (*DOTT*, p. 48). *See* ASSYRIA III.E.2. J. E. H.

2. The son of Hanani, who prophesied the downfall of Baasha's line (1 K. 16:1, 7, 12). This may be the same person who rebuked Jehoshaphat of Judah for allying with Ahab of Israel against the Syrians at Ramoth-gilead (2 Ch. 19:2f.). The "chronicles of Jehu the son of Hanani, which are recorded in the Book of the Kings of Israel" (2 Ch. 20:34) may have been written by this prophet.

3. One of David's heroes, a Benjaminite from Anathoth (1 Ch. 12:3).

4. Son of Obed of the family of Jerahmeel (1 Ch. 2:38).

5. Son of Joshibiah, of the tribe of Simeon (1 Ch. 4:35). R. K. H.

JEHUBBAH jə-hub'ə [Heb. *yᵉḥubbâ*]. A descendant of Asher mentioned in 1 Ch. 7:34, where *Q* (followed by LXX B) is *wᵉḥubbâ*, "and Hubbah," but *K* is *yaḥbâ*.

JEHUCAL jə-hōō'kəl [Heb. *yᵉhûḵal*–prob. 'Yahweh is powerful']. A courtier sent by King Zedekiah to Jeremiah to ask the prophet to pray for the king and the people (Jer. 37:3). Most versions except LXX have "Jucal" (Heb. *yûḵal*), as in 38:1.

JEHUD jē'hud [Heb. *yᵉhûḏ*]. A town in the lot of Dan named between Baalath and Bene-berak (Josh. 19:45). The only possible identification seems to be with el-Yehudīeh, which lies about 13 km. (8 mi.) E of Joppa, although *WHAB* (p. 14) prefers to follow LXX B *Azōr* and read "Jazar" (modern Yazur), a town about 6 km. (4 mi.) SE of Joppa.

JEHUDI jə-hōō'dī [Heb. *yᵉhûḏî*–'a Jew']. An officer of King Jehoiakim (Jer. 36:14, 21, 23). He was sent by the princes to summon Baruch to read the roll containing Jeremiah's prophecies to them; he afterward read them to the king, who destroyed the roll. His name, along with that of his great-grandfather Cushi (i.e., "Ethiopian"), is noteworthy, indicating foreign origin of the family and the possible naturalization of Jehudi.

JEHUDIJAH jə-hōō-dī'jə [Heb. *hayᵉhuḏîyâ*] (1 Ch. 4:18, AV). The proper name of the wife of Eshtemoa in the AV. The word literally means "the Jewish (one)" and is translated "his Jewish wife" in the RSV and NEB.

JEHUEL jə-hōō'əl [Heb. *K yᵉhû'ēl*; *Q yᵉḥî'ēl*; AV, NEB, JEHIEL (2 Ch. 29:14)]. A Levite; *see* JEHIEL **5.**

JEHUSH jē'hush (1 Ch. 8:39, AV). *See* JEUSH **3.**

JEIEL jə-ī'əl [Heb. *yᵉʿî'ēl*–'God has kept'(?)].

1. A Reubenite (1 Ch. 5:7).

2. In 1 Ch. 8:29, added in the RSV from 9:35, where *K* is "Jeuel," an ancestor of King Saul; AV Jehiel.

3. One of David's mighty men, son of Hotham the Aroerite (1 Ch. 11:44; *K* Heb. *yeʿû'ēl*; AV Jehiel).

4. A Levite, keeper of the ark with Obed-edom (1 Ch. 15:18, 21; 16:5; 2 Ch. 20:14), called "Jehiah" in 1 Ch. 15:24.

5. A Levite (1 Ch. 16:5), the JAAZIEL of 1 Ch. 15:18.

6. A scribe under King Uzziah (2 Ch. 26:11).

7. A chief of the Levites, present at King Josiah's great Passover feast (2 Ch. 35:9).

8. One of those who had married foreign wives (Ezr. 10:43), the same as Joel in 1 Esd. 9:35 (AV Juel).

JEKABZEEL jə-kab'zē-əl [Heb. *yᵉqaḇṣᵉ'ēl*–'God gathers'] (Neh. 11:25). *See* KABZEEL.

JEKAMEAM jek-ə-mē'əm [Heb. *yᵉqamʿām*– prob. 'may kinsman establish']. Head of a Levitical house (1 Ch. 23:19; 24:23).

JEKAMIAH jek-ə-mī'ə [Heb. *yᵉqamyâ*–'may Yahweh establish'].

1. A Judahite, son of Shallum (1 Ch. 2:41).

2. A son of King Jeconiah (Jehoiachin) in 1 Ch. 3:18; AV Jecamiah.

JEKUTHIEL jə-kōō'thi-əl [Heb. *yᵉqûṯî'ēl*–'may God sustain'(?)]. A Judahite who was descended from Mered (1 Ch. 4:18).

JEMIMAH jə-mī'mə [Heb. *yᵉmîmâ*–perhaps a diminutive meaning 'little dove']. The first daughter of Job (42:14) born after his restoration from affliction.

JEMNAAN jem'nə-än [Gk. *Iemnaan*] (Jth. 2:28, AV, NEB); RSV JAMNIA. A coastal city in Palestine terrorized by the Holofernes. *See* JABNEEL **2.**

JEMUEL jə-mōō'əl, jem'yōō-əl [Heb. *yᵉmû'ēl*]. A son of Simeon (Gen. 46:10; Ex. 6:15), the same as Nemuel in Nu. 26:12; 1 Ch. 4:24.

The Pesh. has "Jemuel" in the four passages, but Gray (*Studies in Hebrew Proper Names*, p. 307 n. 6) thinks it more likely that "Jemuel" is a correction in Genesis than that "Nemuel" is a correction in Numbers.

JEOPARD jep'ərd. The verbal form of an English word that referred originally to a game in which the chances were even (from Old French *jeu parti*), now used to designate any great risk. In the RSV it occurs once only, in Jgs. 5:18 for a Hebrew idiom, "despise the soul," i.e., they placed a small value upon their lives (Vulg. "offered their souls to death").

JEPHTHAH jef'thə [Heb. *yiptāḥ*–'opened', or 'opener,' prob. signifying "Yahweh will open"; Gk. *Iephthae*]; AV NT JEPHTHAE (He. 11:32). The designation also appears as a place name, Iphtah (Josh. 15:43). Jephthah was the ninth judge of Israel, who gave charismatic leadership for six years (Jgs. 11:1–12:7). He was the son of a harlot and a man named Gilead and appears to have been the only illegitimate child in the household. The name "Gilead" was in use among the Canaanites of the late Amarna Age, as indicated by its occurrence in Ugaritic texts from *ca.* 1300 B.C. Because of his origin he was denied a share in the family inheritance by the legitimate offspring of Gilead (Jgs. 11:2) and subsequently became leader of a band of robbers in the area known as Tob. This place was located NE of Ramoth-gilead and has been identified with eṭ-Ṭaibiyeh, a site about 24 km. (15 mi.) ENE of Ramoth-gilead. The marauding band under Jephthah's leadership would survive by making periodic raids on merchant caravans and settled communities in the Tob district.

These exploits must have become known to the Israelites in the north, for it was to Jephthah that the elders or leaders (Heb. *śārîm*) of Gilead turned when the Ammonites declared war on the Hebrews during a time of religious apostasy in Israel. In bargaining with the elders, Jephthah agreed to fight the Ammonites provided that he became the official leader of all the Gileadite clans once victory had been assured. A lengthy section (Jgs. 11:12-28) described Jephthah's preliminary negotiations with the Ammonites, in which the Hebrew leader rejected the claim that both Ammon and Moab had been deprived of some ancestral holdings when the Israelites left Egypt under Moses.

This passage recounted accurately the events described in Nu. 20–22 and pointed out that a victory had been won over the Amorites, resulting in the occupation of their land and not Moabite or Ammonite territory. It is incorrect to regard this section as an interpolation of much later date, based upon alleged pentateuchal sources, as some literary critics have done, if only because the practice of issuing charges and countercharges before battle was joined was a feature of the Mediterranean Heroic Age (12th and 11th cents. B.C.) and later periods (cf. 1 S. 17:41-47; 2 K. 14:8-10; etc.). Nor is there any real confusion of Ammonite and Moabite history in the mention of Chemosh, the national god of Moab, as though he were an Ammonite deity, because at that period Ammon and Moab worshiped each other's gods. When the text is read carefully within the context of Heroic Age traditions, the account appears as a contemporary description of Hebrew attempts to ward off a marauding Transjordanian people who were posing a threat to the security of the chosen people in the pre-monarchy period.

Jephthah endeavored to secure victory by promising God that he would sacrifice whoever came out of his house first to greet him on his return home. Human sacrifices of this and other kinds were not unknown then, either in Israel (cf. 2 K. 16:3; 17:17; Jer. 7:31; etc.) or in Greek tradition, as with the account by Aeschylus of the sacrifice of Iphigenia daughter of Agamemnon (Aeschylus *Agamemnon* 228-247). When Jephthah defeated the Ammonites (Jgs. 11:32f.), he was shocked on his return to be greeted by his only daughter. Because of his vow he had no option but to offer her in sacrifice, perhaps feeling that God would intervene at the last moment, as He had done with Abraham (Gen. 22:11f.). The death of the young woman initiated the tradition of a four-day annual pilgrimage of lamentation by Israelite females (Jgs. 11:39f.), perhaps as a protest against human sacrifice. The view, formerly espoused by liberal scholarship, that the procession was part of a pagan mourning ceremony for the dead vegetation-gods Tammuz or Baal cannot be upheld any longer, since the time of year when the Hebrew ritual was conducted is unknown and thus cannot be associated with pagan Canaanite ceremonies of cultic mourning.

Shortly after his victory over the Ammonites, Jephthah was accused by the Ephraimites of neglecting them when calling for assistance against Ammon. He defended himself by saying that he had in fact appealed to the Ephraimites, but also pointed out that he and his followers had their own feud with the Ammonites (Jgs. 12:2). Scholars are probably correct in suggesting that there was long-standing hostility between Ephraim and Gilead, since some people from the latter group had been derided at one point as "fugitives of Ephraim" (Jgs. 12:4). Jephthah's answer to the Ephraimites was apparently unsatisfactory, and war broke out between the two groups. The Gileadite guards at the Jordan fords adopted an unusual pronunciation test to detect fleeing Ephraimites that resulted in 42,000 of them being killed (Jgs. 12:6).

Although Jephthah never claimed the title of "judge," he was one of the most illustrious leaders of that period of Hebrew history. A man of energy and conviction who was used by the Spirit of God, he fought valiantly against the pagan Ammonites. He was faithful in his vow to God, even though it cost him dearly, and in the NT was included in the category of great people of faith (He. 11:32).

Bibliography.–R. G. Boling, *Judges* (*AB*, 1975); *IP*, pp. 28f., 179, 200; C. A. Simpson, *Composition of the Book of Judges* (1957).

R. K. HARRISON

JEPHUNNEH jə-fun'ə [Heb. *y^epunneh*].

1. Father of Caleb (Nu. 13:6; 14:6, 30; etc.). According to Nu. 13:6 he was of the tribe of Judah; according to 32:12 and Josh. 14:6 a Kenizzite; the Kenizzites were incorporated in Judah (cf. 1 Ch. 4:15).

2. A son of Jether, an Asherite (1 Ch. 7:38).

JERAH jē'rə, jer'ə [Heb. *yeraḥ*–'moon']. A descendant of Joktan (Gen. 10:26; 1 Ch. 1:20). The others named include Hazarmaveth (Hadramaut), Sheba, and Ophir, all of whom are considered eponymous founders of places in South Arabia (and possibly in the case of Ophir, eastern Africa, e.g., Somaliland). A place named Jerah has not been identified; the preponderance of words for "moon" and their compounds in South Arabic further complicates the situation. W. S. L. S.

JERAHMEEL jə-rä'mē-əl [Heb. *y^eraḥm^e'ēl*–'may God have compassion'].

1. In 1 Ch. 2:9, 25-27, 33, 42, he is described as the son of Hezron, the son of Perez, the son of Judah by Tamar his daughter-in-law (Gen. 38). 1 S. 27:10 mentions the Negeb of the Jerahmeelites. This tribe was first alluded to in the early days of David (cf. 1 S. 30:29), and in postexilic writings was regarded as a clan of the tribe of Judah. Historians have assumed that the Jerahmeelites, like the Calebites (cf. 1 Ch. 2:9, 18), felt the pressure of Edomite expansion after the Exile and moved from their cities to the areas around Jerusalem (cf. *ORHI*, I, 101, 135).

2. A Merarite Levite, son of Kish (1 Ch. 24:29).

3. A contemporary of Jeremiah (cf. Jer. 36:26) who served as an official under King Jehoiakim (609-598 B.C.). The king of whom he was a "son" could hardly have been Jehoiakim, who would only have been about thirty at the time (cf. Jer. 36:9), but perhaps the term "son" merely meant "descendant," implying royal birth. The AV took the MT "the king" as a proper name, Hammelech.

R. K. H.

JERECHUS jer'ə-kəs (1 Esd. 5:22, AV, NEB). *See* JERICHO.

JERED jer'əd [Heb. *yereḏ*]. A Judahite, father of Gedor (1 Ch. 4:18). *See also* JARED.

JEREMAI jer'ə-mī [Heb. *y^erēmay*]. One of those who had married foreign wives in the time of Ezra (Ezr. 10:33); AV, NEB, JEREMIAS (1 Esd. 9:34).

JEREMIAH jer-ə-mī'ə [Heb. *yirm^eyāhû, yirm^eyâ;* Gk. *Ieremias;* Latin *Jeremias*]. A name of uncertain meaning, suggestions being "Yahweh founds," "Yahweh exults," "Yahweh loosens," or "Yahweh throws." The OT mentions nine different people by this name:

1. The prophet, son of Hilkiah (*see* JEREMIAH, BOOK OF).

2, 3, 4. A Benjaminite and two Gadites who, with other warriors, joined David at Ziklag (1 Ch. 12:4, 10, 13 [MT 5, 11, 14]).

5. Head of a Manassite family (1 Ch. 5:24).

6. Father of King Josiah's wife Hamutal, hence grandfather of King Jehoahaz (2 K. 23:31) and King Zedekiah (2 K. 24:18; Jer. 52:1).

7. Father of Jaazaniah, the head of the Rechabites in the time of Jeremiah the prophet (Jer. 35:3).

8. A priest who, with Zerubbabel, went up to Jerusalem from exile and became head of a priestly family (Neh. 12:1, 12).

9. A priest who, with Nehemiah, set his seal to the covenant (Neh. 10:2 [MT 3]) and took part in the dedication of the wall of Jerusalem (Neh. 12:34).

S. K. SODERLUND

JEREMIAH, BOOK OF. The book which goes by the name of one of Israel's greatest prophets, who was active in the last years of the kingdom of Judah (*ca.* 645-575 B.C.); Jeremiah stands second among the Major Prophets, following Isaiah and preceding Ezekiel (except in one rabbinic tradition, preserved in T.B. *Baba Bathra* 14b, where it stands first, followed by Ezekiel and Isaiah).

I. Historical Background
II. Jeremiah's Message and Character
III. The Book
  A. Structure
  B. Sources
  C. Texts

I. Historical Background.–Our sources for reconstructing the life and times of Jeremiah the prophet are principally (1) the book of Jeremiah; (2) the historical narratives in 2 K. 21–25 and 2 Ch. 33–36; (3) the books of other prophets active around his time (Zephaniah, Nahum, Habakkuk, Ezekiel); and (4) archeological discoveries of extrabiblical records (e.g., D. J. Wiseman, *CCK; ANET,* pp. 321f.; *DOTT,* pp. 212-17; and W. F. Albright, *JBL,* 51 [1932], 77-106).

According to Jer. 1:1f. (henceforth references are always to the book of Jeremiah unless stated otherwise), Jeremiah was born in the village of Anathoth, which was located at or near the present-day village of ʿAnâtâ, some 5 km. (3 mi.) N of Jerusalem. His father was Hilkiah the priest, possibly a descendant of the priest Abiathar banished to that village by Solomon (1 K. 2:26), but probably not the high priest of that name who discovered "the book of the law" in Josiah's reign (2 K. 22:8). While still a youth, in the thirteenth year of the reign of King Josiah, 627/6 B.C., Jeremiah was called to be a prophet. Some scholars discount this chronology and reinterpret 1:1-3, claiming that Jeremiah did not begin his ministry till considerably later (cf. J. P. Hyatt, *IB,* V [1956], 779f.; for a reply, cf. T. W. Overholt, *CBQ,* 33 [1971], 165-184).

According to the traditional date, the time of his call coincided approximately with the death of the last great Assyrian ruler, Ashurbanipal, an event which signaled the disintegration of the Assyrian empire under whose yoke Judah had served for nearly a century. Against the waning power and influence of the Assyrians, Judah asserted its independence under Josiah, and for a time the prospects for a secure national future appeared promising. But the next generation was destined to experience the most catastrophic reversal of fortune in the nation's history, leading to ultimate destruction and captivity in 586 B.C. at the hands of the Neo-Babylonians, who by that time had emerged as the undisputed rulers of the ancient Near East. Into these turbulent and tragic times Jeremiah was called to be God's spokesman. Since his career spanned the reigns of the last five kings of Judah and the first years of the Captivity, the principal events of his life and times may be summarized under the following chronological headings.

A. Under Josiah (639-609 B.C.). King Josiah was a pious man who, in marked contrast to his immediate predecessors Manasseh and Amon, early in his reign "began to seek the God of David his father" and institute religious reforms (2 Ch. 34:3). This reforming spirit was greatly accelerated in the eighteenth year of his reign (622/1 B.C.) upon the discovery in the temple precincts of the Book of the Law which, when read to Josiah, brought a sudden realization of the seriousness of the nation's backsliding, motivating king and people to make a new covenant with Yahweh, their God (2 K. 22:3–23:23; 2 Ch. 34:8–35:19). There can be little doubt that this national repentance warmed the heart of the young prophet, and for a time at least he may have actively supported the reformation by speaking on behalf of its ideals (cf. the "Covenant Sermon" [11:1-8], which may be derived from this period).

It seems certain, however, that with the passing of years, Jeremiah became increasingly disillusioned with the superficiality of the reformation and his preaching became more critical (cf. the "Sabbath Sermon" [17:19-27], which possibly reflects this stage). In fact, from the earliest days of his ministry Jeremiah had been convinced of the ultimate fate of his people and had not hesitated to describe it (cf. the bulk of the judgment oracles of chs. 2–6). This kind of preaching made him the object of much hostility, especially in his native town of Anathoth where his brethren or close relatives planned a conspiracy against him (11:21; 12:6). Nevertheless, the condition of Jeremiah under Josiah was probably the happiest of his career. When the popular king was tragically killed at Megiddo in vain pursuit of the Egyptians who were hurrying to the aid of the beleaguered Assyrians, Jeremiah uttered a sad lament on his untimely death (2 Ch. 35:25).

B. Under Jehoahaz (609 B.C.) *and Jehoiakim* (609-598 B.C.). With the death of Josiah, his son Jehoahaz (called Shallum in the book of Jeremiah) was immediately proclaimed king, but after a short rule of three months he was summarily deposed by Pharaoh Neco (then master of Palestine) and deported to Egypt. The first leader of Judah to die in exile, Jehoahaz received the announcement of his judgment from Jeremiah (22:10-12). In his place, Neco put another of Josiah's sons, Jehoiakim, on the throne of Judah. This was an unhappy choice, both for the nation and for Jeremiah. Jehoiakim was not inclined to follow the godly example of his father Josiah, but reverted to idolatry, self-indulgence, and rebellion. Surrounded by a circle of ambitious nobles and self-appointed prophets, Jehoiakim and his party lived under the illusion that their future was guaranteed by the presence of the Solomonic temple in their midst and by eternal divine favor to David's royal lineage. Their corrupt behavior and false sense of security elicited the most vigorous protests from Jeremiah (cf. 22:13-19 and the "Temple Sermon," 7:1-15; 26:1-6), an outspokenness which nearly cost the prophet his life (26:7-24).

In the critical fourth year of Jehoiakim's reign, 605 B.C., the armies of Babylon under the leadership of Nebuchadrezzar defeated the forces of Pharaoh Neco at Carchemish, and thus gained control of the upper Euphrates and Syro-Palestine (46:2). Jeremiah clearly foresaw the course of events from there: Nebuchadrezzar would advance into Palestine, take Judah captive, and send the people into exile for seventy years (25:1-14). It was in that year, too, that Jeremiah was commissioned to write his oracles on a scroll which was later burned by the king. In reply, Jeremiah uttered a prophetic judgment concerning Jehoiakim's ignominious death and proceeded to dictate a second scroll (ch. 36). For three years Jehoiakim served Nebuchadrezzar as his vassal but then rebelled (2 K. 24:1), possibly due to a temporary Babylonian setback at the hands of the Egyptians in 601 B.C. When Nebuchadrezzar had reequipped his army, retaliation by the Babylonians was a foregone conclusion, and in 598 B.C. they marched on Palestine, capturing Jerusalem in March of the following year, 597 B.C. Jehoiakim had died three months before the fall of the city, perhaps assassinated by pro-Babylonian parties in Jerusalem or slain in battle. In his stead, his son Jehoiachin (in the book of Jeremiah called Jeconiah or simply Coniah) was made king.

C. Under Jehoiachin (597 B.C.) *and Zedekiah* (597-586 B.C.). When the armies of Babylon entered Jerusalem they carried off the temple treasures and took Jehoiachin captive together with a large number of his nobles and the best part of the people (2 K. 24:10-16; Jer. 24:1), as Jeremiah had predicted (22:24-30). As local ruler in Jerusalem the conquerors installed the exiled king's uncle, Zedekiah. But this signified no improvement in the quality of the city's leadership. Although he seems not to have been personally hostile to Jeremiah, Zedekiah was completely under the sway of his pro-Egyptian advisers, who continually plotted evil against Jeremiah and urged rebellion against Babylon (e.g., 28:1-4). Jeremiah insisted that the only sane course was submission to Babylon, but for this counsel he was branded unpatriotic and apprehended as a traitor. At one point he would have died in a murky cistern but for the intervention of a benevolent foreigner, Ebed-melech (38:1-13). In the end, Jeremiah's worst predictions were fulfilled when, in response to another rebellion in Judah, the Babylonians again marched on Palestine and after a long siege — temporarily lifted by the approach of the Egyptians (37:5) — breached the walls of Jerusalem and set the city to the torch, this time being content with nothing less than total destruction. Zedekiah himself was taken in flight, blinded, and transported to Babylon. The year was 586 B.C. (for the date 587 cf. *BHI* [2nd ed. 1972], p. 329, and literature cited there), and it terminated for many generations the nationhood of Judah.

D. After the Fall of Jerusalem (586-*ca.* 575 B.C.). At the time of the capture of the city, Jeremiah was under arrest in the court of the guard, but because of his pro-Babylonian pronouncements he was given preferential treatment by the invaders (39:11-14). Presented with the choice of either going to Babylon under royal protection or staying in Judah, Jeremiah decided to cast his lot with the poor remnant that was left in the land. But his troubles were by no means over. When conspirators murdered the Babylonian-appointed governor Gedaliah, the Jews became alarmed; fearing retaliation by their overlords, they fled to Egypt, unheedful of Jeremiah's warnings and protestations (42:7-22). They even forced the aged prophet to go with them, but they could not silence him; at Tahpanhes, where they settled, Jeremiah continued to the end of his days to prophesy against his people and other nations, including Egypt (43:8–44:30). The circumstances of his death are unknown. The church fathers report that he was stoned by Jews in Tahpanhes, but according to a rabbinic tradition (*Seder Olam Rabbah* 26) he was eventually taken to Babylon with Baruch and died there; however, neither story is well founded.

II. Jeremiah's Message and Character.–The account of Jeremiah's call in ch. 1 serves as a convenient introduction to the main elements of his message. In this passage, Jeremiah relates how he was commissioned "to pluck up and to break down, to destroy and to overthrow, to build and to plant" (v. 10). At the outset, therefore, we learn that his preaching was to be both destructive and constructive, reproving as well as edifying. The call pericope, moreover, recounts the international scope of Jeremiah's message: he was appointed "a prophet to the nations" (v. 5), these nations being in the first instance Israel and Judah, but also "all the kingdoms of the world" (25:26).

In the continuation of the narrative Jeremiah is presented with two ominous visions. The first is that of an almond rod (Heb. *šāqēḏ*), which is a reminder that God is watching (Heb. *šōqēḏ*) over His word to perform it, i.e., He will keep His promise of judgment (1:11f.). The second vision, that of the boiling pot facing away from the north, serves notice that the agents of the divine judgment will be a people from the north, unspecified here (1:13-16), but later (25:8-14) identified with the Babylonians (for the view that in his early ministry Jeremiah identified the foe from the north with the Scythian raiders see the comment and bibliography in R. K. Harrison, *Intro. to the OT* [1969], pp. 803f.). Next the causes of the impending judgment are specified, these being chiefly apostasy and idolatry (1:16). Taken together these two sins constitute a fundamental breach of the covenant between the chosen people and their God.

This theme of the broken covenant was destined to become one of Jeremiah's major preoccupations in his subsequent ministry. In the covenant enacted between God and His people at Mt. Sinai, the Israelites promised to render total loyalty and obedience to Yahweh their God in return for His everlasting care and protection. According to the book of Deuteronomy, this covenant was renewed on the plains of Moab prior to entry into Canaan, and it was the Deuteronomic version of the covenant (for the view that the book itself is a covenant-renewal document, cf. P. C. Craigie, *Book of Deuteronomy* [*NICOT,* 1976], pp. 36-45) which most profoundly influenced Jeremiah — not surprisingly, if it was this book, or some portion of it, that was rediscovered at the time of Josiah's reformation.

Modern archeological discoveries and scholarly discussions have illuminated the significance that the covenant motif had for Jeremiah and his contemporaries. In 1954, G. E. Mendenhall pointed out the resemblance in structure between Hittite suzerainty treaties of the late 2nd millennium and the biblical Sinaitic covenant (*BA*, 17 [1954], 26-46 and 50-76), the implication being that Israel conceived of itself as a vassal nation to Yahweh, the Great King. Since Jeremiah more than any other prophet employs the vocabulary of the covenant, the relevance of these comparisons for an understanding of his message is immediately obvious. Although scholarly discussion has probably gone too far in making the treaty model the determining principle in the interpretation of the prophetic message (cf. R. E. Clements, *Prophecy and Tradition* [1975], pp. 14-23), it seems fairly established that in his use of the covenant theme the prophet was deliberately referring to a concept familiar to many of his hearers.

Of particular significance in this connection is Jeremiah's appeal to the curses that would attend the nation's rebellion against Yahweh. Like the suzerainty treaties, the book of Deuteronomy provided for a set of curses to be invoked upon the violation of the covenant (Dt. 28:15-68), and it may be that Jeremiah had these in mind when he announced Yahweh's message, "Cursed be the man who does not heed the words of this covenant" (Jer. 11:3). Jeremiah's stern indictment against Judah was that by idolatry and apostasy the people had violated their agreement with Yahweh to the point that judgment was inevitable. Under various images, e.g., the unfaithful wife, the ox that breaks its yoke, the vine that bears strange fruit, the stain that will not wash — some of which he learned from previous prophets, notably Hosea and Isaiah — Jeremiah reinforced his message of the broken relationship between Yahweh and His people as well as the catastrophic consequences of their faithlessness.

But Jeremiah had a difficult — nay, impossible — time convincing his countrymen of the seriousness of their action. Essentially the problem was one of different views of the covenant, for the religious hierarchy of Jerusalem had a covenant theology too, but of a different sort. Whereas Jeremiah insisted that Yahweh's protection was conditional upon the faithful performance of the terms of the covenant, the popular theology sponsored by the temple priests and prophets taught that Yahweh was irrevocably committed to the preservation of Jerusalem, the temple, and the Davidic line. This theology could accommodate the prospects of intermittent divine discipline, but never of total destruction.

Such diametrically opposed views of Israel's election were inevitably on a collision course, and the issue came to a head in Jeremiah's famous "Temple Sermon" (7:1-15; 26:1-6). In this address, Jeremiah unconditionally rejected the official theology of trust in an inviolable temple. The temple of Jerusalem was no more sacrosanct, he declared, than the sanctuary at Shiloh which God had destroyed. This kind of language raised passions to a feverish pitch, and Jeremiah barely escaped being lynched on the spot. In response to Jeremiah's charges the promoters of the official religion could point to a flourishing temple cult, in their opinion surely evidence of true worship. But to Jeremiah this cult was utterly reprehensible (cf. 6:20f.). Not that he seems to have condemned the system as such, but Jeremiah could not stomach the hypocrisy that attended it. For even while the people were bringing their oblations and professing their innocence their hands were full of blood with oppression of the guiltless poor (2:34f.). For Jeremiah, ceremonial worship had no validity apart from the attitude of the heart. The external observances of an apostate people were the final insult that would culminate in the outpouring of divine wrath.

In spite of Jeremiah's gloomy predictions, he also was able to see beyond the immediate tragedy of his people to a brighter future. Occasionally, even in the earliest chapters, the gloom of a procession of judgment oracles is punctured by a message of promise and restoration (cf. 3:15-18), but the fullest expression of this aspect of Jeremiah's message is found in the consolation oracles and narratives of chs. 31–34. According to the core of this section (31:31-34, quoted twice by the author of Hebrews [He. 8:8-12; 10:16f.], and alluded to by Paul [2 Cor. 3:3]), the old covenant which was being abrogated would be replaced by a new covenant. Whereas the old had been written on tables of stone, the new would be engraved on hearts of flesh.

Included in Jeremiah's vision of a new future for Judah and Israel was also a restored line of David, embodied in the person of the Messiah (33:14-26). It is remarkable that even as Jeremiah's worst predictions were being fulfilled and the Babylonian army surrounding Jerusalem was preparing for the coup de grace, Jeremiah set out for Anathoth to invest in a piece of real estate in his native village — a powerful symbolic action demonstrating his faith in a restored future. Such action was consistent with Jeremiah's message of judgment, because in the final analysis his faith was grounded in a view of God as the supreme Lord of history whose purpose for the good of His people could not finally be frustrated.

Thanks to the preservation of several autobiographical poems (principally 11:18-20; 15:10-18; 17:9-18; 18:18-23; 20:7-18) and many narrative passages by a sympathetic observer, we are unusually well informed about the person and character of Jeremiah. The biographical narratives provide the dramatic background for his life, while the personal poems (sometimes rather inappropriately called the "Confessions") reveal the prophet's inner struggles. In the biographical narratives we are presented with the picture of a man of action and fortitude who, in spite of tremendous opposition and physical persecution, fearlessly proclaimed God's word and boldly denounced the evils of his day, especially corruption in high places and religious idolatry among the populace. The picture thus drawn is a true one, for only a man of great personal courage could persist in the proclamation of an unpopular message in defiance of the politico-religious establishment of his day. But this is only half the story; the other half is told in the autobiographical meditations.

In these moving compositions we meet a very human prophet, indeed, one plagued by a sense of inadequacy, given to moods of depression, doubt, and despair. At the root of Jeremiah's problem was the tension between his naturally tender disposition and the hard message of judgment he was called to proclaim. Deeply involved emotionally in his message and the fate of his people, his sensitive soul recoiled at the thought of the impending destruction of Jerusalem and the inevitable suffering of the people he loved. Their rejection of his message he took as a personal affront, while their scorn and plots of physical violence frequently demoralized his spirit. This led him to a love/hate relationship with his countrymen: sometimes he wanted to intercede and weep for them; other times he was tempted to abandon them altogether and condemn his personal enemies to Sheol.

Besides being at odds with himself and with his brethren, Jeremiah carried on an agonizing quarrel with God. Pleading immaturity and inability, Jeremiah felt called to the prophetic office against his will and complained of having been overpowered by One stronger than himself. For a time he had rejoiced when God spoke to him, but later he felt betrayed. The prophecies spoken in God's name did not immediately materialize and Jeremiah became the laughingstock of his peers. Instead of the vindication of divine justice on wrongdoers, the wicked seemed to prosper and Jeremiah's opponents flourished — apparently protected by God Himself! Thus humiliated, Jeremiah wanted to quit, but could not; he cursed the day of his birth, but had to go on living. In the light of these spiritual and emotional crises it is remarkable that he did not collapse under the pressure. But his weaknesses also revealed his strengths; for underneath his frustration and disquieting meditations, Jeremiah was a man of extraordinary faith, confidence, and above all prayer. This is highlighted dramatically when, in one of his depressed moments, he was nevertheless able to say, "Heal me, O Lord, and I shall be healed; save me, and I shall be saved; *for thou art my praise*" (17:14; italics mine). Such demonstration of personal faith has been an inspiration for generations of believers.

A challenge to the traditional way of understanding the character of Jeremiah has come in the form-critical study by H. G. Reventlow, *Liturgie und prophetisches Ich bei Jeremia* (1963). According to this work, Jeremiah was the holder of a cultic office who submerged his individuality in his role as public spokesman. The first-person mode of speech was simply a convention for giving expression to communal feelings, hence it may not be used to sketch the personality of the prophet. Reventlow's theory, however, has not met with widespread acceptance (for critiques cf. J. Bright, "Jeremiah's Complaints: Liturgy or Expression of Personal Distress?" in J. I. Durham and J. R. Porter, eds., *Proclamation and Presence* [1970], pp. 189-214, and J. M. Berridge, *Prophet, People, and the Word of Yahweh* [1970]).

III. The Book.–A. *Structure*. A person approaching the book of Jeremiah for the first time is likely to be disconcerted. If he comes with modern notions regarding coherent structure, logical development, and chronological sequence, he is sure to be disappointed. But then Jeremiah is not a modern book and must not be judged by those standards. In fact, it is not a book at all, according to the usual sense of the word. A more apt comparison might be the anthology, but the great variety of material included (oracles, sermons, autobiographical poems, and historical narratives) makes it doubtful that even this category is wholly adequate. Probably no modern term exists which adequately describes the nature of this ancient document, and we are thrown back to the Bible itself for the only valid frame of reference.

In this context — specifically, the prophetic corpus of the OT — the book finds its natural setting as a record of the words and deeds of the prophet Jeremiah, similar to some other prophetic books. But even so, the problem of structure will not go away; of all the prophetic books, this is the most complex. Particularly acute is the problem of chronology, examples of which abound, e.g., episodes dated during the reign of Jehoiakim (609-598 B.C.) are found dispersed in chs. 25, 26, 36, and 45, while passages from the time of Zedekiah (597-586 B.C.) occur in chs. 21, 24, 27 (MT 27:1 "Jehoiakim" is probably a scribal error), 32, and 39. Additional problems such as the apparently random juxtaposition of oracles of judgment with those of blessing, and prose sermons with autobiographical poems, have led some scholars to adopt a counsel of despair and abandon the MT altogether in their expositions of the book (cf. the comms. of Leslie and Bright). Other scholars, however, claim to have discovered structural principles underlying the present arrangement and have accordingly proposed various outlines by which to survey the contents of the book. The fact that these outlines are as numerous and as varied as the commentators who have proposed them ought to say something about the difficulty — perhaps impossibility — of the task. Nevertheless, the situation is not altogether desperate. Within limits, it is possible to identify certain blocks of material in the book, some of which, at least, are determined by chronological considerations.

For the purpose of this article it will be most convenient to begin at the end of the book. Ch. 52 is obviously a unit by itself, forming what can best be described as a historical appendix to the book. It is, in fact, a near duplicate passage of 2 K. 24:18–25:30, the latter part of which carries the history of the period down to the thirty-seventh year of Jehoiachin's captivity and his ultimate restoration at the hands of Evil-merodach, king of Babylon. In chs. 46–51 is found another clearly defined unit: the "Oracles Against the Nations" (for similar collections in the prophetic books, cf. Isa. 13–23; Ezk. 25–32; Am. 1–2:4). Preceding this section comes a long, almost unbroken narrative (chs. 37–45) dealing with events immediately prior to and following the fall of Jerusalem. This section preserves chronological continuity throughout, except for ch. 45, which is a private message from Jeremiah to Baruch in Jehoiakim's fourth year.

Working back from ch. 36, division markers become more diffuse, notwithstanding that traditionally the most popular approach has been to see a pivotal dividing point in the book at ch. 25. The main reason for this is the finale-like sentence found in 25:13, "I will bring upon that land all the words which I have uttered against it, everything written in this book," at which point the LXX (see III.C below) inserts the section of the "Oracles Against the Nations." Although the witness of the LXX gives a certain plausibility to this scheme, and although it conveniently divides the book into two nearly equal halves, other considerations make ch. 25 a less convincing division point. There appears to be no obvious difference between the material contained in the chapters immediately preceding ch. 25 and those immediately following it. They all relate miscellaneous incidents from the life of Jeremiah during the reigns of Jehoiakim and Zedekiah (an exception being the "book of consolation," chs. 30–31). Since these miscellaneous incidents from the life of Jeremiah commence with ch. 21, it seems better to take chs. 21–36 as a loose historical section by itself.

We are thus left with chs. 1–20 as the remaining unit. This section appears to contain a collection of Jeremiah's oracles, sermons, and personal meditations from the first half of the prophet's ministry, i.e., from the time of his call to the early part of Jehoiakim's reign, perhaps the critical fourth year of his reign, 605 B.C. With one exception (3:1), this section is characterized by an absence of the type of chronological formula so common in later chapters, e.g., "the word which came to Jeremiah from the Lord, when King Zedekiah sent to him Pashhur . . ." (21:1). The one exception, 3:1, is the only dated oracle from the time of Josiah. New support for the isolation of chs. 1–20 as a self-contained unit comes from the studies on rhetorical structure by J. Lundbom, pp. 28-30, and W. L. Holladay, *Architecture of Jeremiah 1–20* (1976).

On the basis of the preceding discussion, we may propose the following basic outline for the book of Jeremiah:

I. Prophecies and Poems of Jeremiah (627/6–605 B.C.), chs. 1–20
II. Historical Narratives from the Time of Jehoiakim and Zedekiah (605-587 B.C.), chs. 21–36
III. Events Immediately Prior to and Following the Fall of Jerusalem (587-*ca.* 570 B.C.), chs. 37–45
IV. Oracles Against the Nations, chs. 46–51
V. Historical Appendix, ch. 52

B. Sources. In ch. 36 we are given a unique insight into the circumstances that brought part of this book into being. The chapter relates how, in the crucial fourth year of King Jehoiakim's reign, Jeremiah dictated to his secretary Baruch all the words that God had spoken to him since the beginning of his ministry twenty-three years earlier (cf. 25:1-3). When in the fifth year of Jehoiakim's reign the king in utter contempt of Jeremiah's message burned the scroll column by column as it was being read to him, Jeremiah resolutely dictated a second scroll, to which "many similar words were added" (36:32). This suggestive narrative has not failed to attract the attention of scholars, for it would be most instructive to know what material was contained in Baruch's scroll (*Urrolle*) and whether it is possible to isolate its contents within the present Jeremianic corpus.

If the contents of the scroll are retrievable at all, they must be found within certain limits imposed by the narrative itself. One such limit is the divine command that the oracles deal with messages spoken "against Israel and Judah and all the nations" (v. 2). Another limit is the chronological one of Jehoiakim's fourth year for the first scroll and his fifth year for the second scroll. A third consideration is the fact that it must not be longer than what could be read publicly three times in one day. These limits have led scholars to focus their search for the *Urrolle* on the first half of the book, usually within chs. 1–25. The reference in 25:13 to "everything written in this book" may suggest the original scroll, but the appearance in chs. 21 and 24 of episodes from the time of Zedekiah eliminates the totality of chs. 1–25 as constituting the *Urrolle.* On the basis of rhetorical structures in chs. 1–10, J. Lundbom has proposed those chapters as designating the limits of the *Urrolle* (pp. 28-30). Most commentators, however, think a smaller unit, e.g., chs. 1–6, or a collection of smaller units within chs. 1–25 serves as a more likely size for a scroll that was read three times in one day. Probably we shall never be able to reconstruct the contents of Jeremiah's scroll, and it must be admitted that the search for the

Urrolle can become something like chasing a will-o'-the-wisp. But this is not to doubt that the formation of the book of Jeremiah had its beginnings in the events related in ch. 36, particularly in Baruch's secretarial activity.

To the same Baruch, however, has been attributed much more than just a secretarial role in the formation of this book. The question arises whether he may not also have been Jeremiah's "biographer." A basic observation with regard to the book is that it uses both the first person and the third person. The characteristic formula introducing the former is: "The word of the Lord came to me, saying . . ." (2:1), found mostly in the first half of the book, while the typical heading introducing the latter is: "The word that came to Jeremiah from the Lord" (7:1). Some third-person narratives are without any such formula altogether and simply relate episodes from the prophet's life and times, e.g., "Now when the Chaldean army had withdrawn from Jerusalem at the approach of Pharaoh's army, Jeremiah set out from Jerusalem . . ." (37:11-21). Such passages were obviously not written by Jeremiah himself but by someone else. The suggestion lies near at hand that this person was Baruch the son of Neriah, Jeremiah's friend and secretary.

While this "Baruch hypothesis" is not amenable to proof, it is the most reasonable proposition in the light of the limited information at our disposal (but cf. G. Wanke, *Untersuchungen zur sogenannten Baruchschrift* [*BZAW*, 122, 1971]). Whether he wrote a separate book which was later combined with Jeremiah's oracles or whether he simply expanded on Jeremiah's collection is, of course, impossible to say. Probably he should not be thought of as a "biographer" in the modern understanding of the term, though some have found it convenient to speak of the third-person material as Baruch's "memoirs." But whether from Baruch or somebody else, there appears to be no convincing reason for doubting that this material preserves authentic highlights from the life of Jeremiah.

Thus far, the book of Jeremiah is composed of a minimum of two sources. Many scholars, however, discern at least a third source for much of its material. Delineation of this third source proceeds from a further basic observation concerning the nature of the book, namely, that there exist side by side in the prophecy both poetry and prose, the prose in turn being of two types, narrative and sermonic. The rediscovery of poetry in the Hebrew Bible is a relatively modern, yet well-established, phenomenon. The pioneering work was done by R. Lowth in the 18th cent., and the first Hebrew Bible to print poetry as poetry was Kittel's edition of 1906. Although perfect unanimity does not exist among scholars on what distinguishes poetry from prose (cf., e.g., 3:14, which is printed as poetry in the RSV and as prose in Bright's comm., while the reverse is true of 3:24f.; see also W. L. Holladay, *JBL*, 85 [1966], 401-435), the distinction is nevertheless secure in the great majority of passages. The poetry is concentrated in 1–20, the prose in the historical narratives of the following chapters.

The first scholar to make the poetry/prose dichotomy a determining principle in his analysis of the book was B. Duhm, who, following certain critical fashions of his time, believed that Jeremiah wrote only in verse, and only in verse of a certain meter (the dirge or qinah). On this basis Duhm assigned 280 verses to Jeremiah; the rest he apportioned between Baruch (220 verses) and later redactors (580 verses). He made the distinction between the Baruch source and the later redactors on the basis of differences in style between the narrative and sermonic prose. This three-source theory, which slowly crystallized in the 19th cent., was given classic and fresh expression by S. Mowinckel in his book *Zur Komposition des Buches Jeremia* (1914). Avoiding Duhm's extreme views on prophetic meter, Mowinckel outlined the three sources as follows: Source A consists of poetry and represents Jeremiah's words; Source B consists of historical narratives, perhaps from a contemporary observer; Source C consists of prose sermons in the first person scattered throughout the book, e.g., 7:1–8:3; 11:1-5, 9-14; 18:1-12; 21:1-10, originating from the exilic or postexilic era (Mowinckel excluded from his consideration the "Oracles Against the Nations"; he also proposed a small D Source of minimal significance). In this form, Mowinckel's study has had a profound effect on the source analysis of the book of Jeremiah; with relatively few modifications his study has formed the basis for the comms. of Volz, Rudolph, and Hyatt.

As a description of the main types of material found in the book of Jeremiah, Mowinckel's contribution is very helpful; problems attach themselves to the interpretation and significance of the results. The center of this controversy has undoubtedly been Mowinckel's C Source, the prose sermons. Impressed by the stylistic similarities of these sermons and discourses to many passages and stereotyped expressions in the book of Deuteronomy, both Duhm and Mowinckel regarded these passages as composed (or edited) in the Exile under Deuteronomic influence with correspondingly negative historical worth for the time of Jeremiah. Many have followed this approach, though with various modifications (cf. E. Nicholson, *Preaching to the Exiles* [1970], and W. Thiel, *Die deuteronomistische Redaktion von Jeremia 1–25* [1973]). However, counter arguments defending the essential authenticity of the prose sermons have not been wanting. Of these, the most persuasive viewpoint has consistently been that of the existence of a contemporary rhetorical style employed by Jeremiah. In various ways this argument has been advanced by W. O. E. Oesterley and T. H. Robinson (*Intro. to the Books of the OT* [1934], pp. 298f.), J. Bright (*JBL*, 70 [1951], 15-35), W. L. Holladay (*JBL*, 79 [1960], 351-367; *JBL*, 81 [1962], 44-54), and H. Weippert (*Die Prosareden des Jeremiabuches* [1973]). In the attacks on the authenticity of the prose sermons and discourses, two arguments appear particularly vulnerable, namely, (1) the suggestion that poetry and prose are such radically different functions of the human mind that the same person could not regularly have employed both, and (2) the contention that certain things could not have been said by Jeremiah because they do not fit his message (e.g., the "Sabbath Sermon," 17:19-27). The first is plainly an overstatement, while the second is too arbitrary and subjective a judgment to carry the weight put upon it. It is methodologically objectionable to set up criteria for the limits of preexilic and exilic theology and then proceed to divide the contents of a book like Jeremiah accordingly.

A radical challenge to the literary analysis of the prose tradition has come from a different quarter altogether, namely, the traditio-historical school associated with certain Scandinavian scholars, notably I. Engnell. Emphasizing the role of oral tradition in the transmission and shaping of the prophetic material, this school rejects as totally inadequate the almost exclusive preoccupation with literary sources that has tended to characterize the study of Jeremiah (as well as other books of the OT). Instead of literary sources, these scholars prefer to think of the coalescence of large blocks of "tradition complexes," e.g., 1–24; 25; 46–51; 26–35; 36–45 (for a demonstration of the method at work, cf. E. Nielsen, *Oral Tradition* [*SBT*, 1/11, 1954], pp. 64-79). While much of this hypothesis is untenable (general critiques may be found in G. W. Anderson, *HTR*, 43 [1950], 239-256; C. R. North, in H. H. Rowley, ed., *OTMS*, pp. 76-81), the point is well taken that an exclusive interest in literary sources at the expense of oral factors does not do justice to the complexities of the origins of this book.

C. Texts. The text of Jeremiah has been preserved in two different forms: the Hebrew Masoretic Text (MT) and the Greek Septuagint Text (LXX). The principal differences between these texts are length (the LXX has about 2700 fewer words and thus is seven-eighths the length of the MT) and arrangement (the LXX has the section of the "Oracles Against the Nations" [MT chs. 46–51] in the middle of the book following 25:13). The relationship between these two texts has intrigued scholars ever since Origen in the 3rd cent. A.D. first found evidence for "much transposition and variation in the prophecies" of this book (*Ad Africanus* 4). Although most of the quantitative differences between the two texts concern such minor things as shorter forms of the divine name (the LXX frequently omits "of Hosts" in the phrase "Lord of Hosts"), the omission of prophetic formulas like "says the Lord," and the second occurrence of some duplicate passages (cf. the omission in the LXX of 8:10b-12, which in the MT parallels 6:13-15), some larger sections are also missing in the LXX, most notably the messianic passage (33:14-26). Transpositions occur not only in the "Oracles Against the Nations" but also in a few other places (e.g., 10:9 in the LXX comes in the middle of 10:5, while 23:7f. in the LXX comes at the end of the chapter). In addition, there are the usual qualitative differences between the two texts where one text gives a different reading from the other (e.g., in 36:2 the MT reads "Israel" where the LXX [43:2] reads "Jerusalem").

In the history of the problem, four different theories, broadly speaking, have been proposed to account for the divergencies of the two texts: (1) The "editorial" theory. This theory holds that the two texts are derived from different editions of the book produced either by Jeremiah himself (J. G. Eichhorn, *Einl. in das AT,* IV [1824], 170-220) or by Jeremiah and Baruch respectively (A. van Selms, *VT,* 26 [1976], 99-112). (2) The "abbreviation" theory. According to this view, the MT is the best witness to the text of Jeremiah, the LXX being an abbreviated account with many accidental and deliberate omissions blamed on the translator (e.g., M. G. L. Spohn, *Ieremias vates e versione Iudaeorum Alexandrinorum* [1824], pp. 1-21, and the comms. by K. H. Graf [1862], C. F. Keil [1880], and C. von Orelli [1905]). (3) The "expansion" theory. On this view the LXX is the best witness to the text of Jeremiah, the Hebrew having suffered greatly from expansion and interpolation in the course of transmission (e.g., F. C. Movers, *De utriusque recensionis vaticinorum Ieremiae* [1837]; A. Scholz, *Der masorethische Text und die LXX-Uebersetzung des Buches Jeremias* [1875]; G. C. Workman, *The Text of Jeremiah* [1889]; A. W. Streane, *The Double Text of Jeremiah* [1896]; J. G. Janzen). (4) The "mediating" theory. This theory holds that it is impossible to generalize on the relative merits of the two texts; instead, each reading has to be evaluated on its own merits, resulting sometimes in a preference for the Hebrew, sometimes for the Greek (e.g., the comms. of F. Hitzig [1866], B. Duhm [1901], F. Giesebrecht [1907], P. Volz [1922], W. Rudolph [3rd ed. 1968], J. Bright [1965]).

At mid-century, the mediating position seemed firmly entrenched as the consensus view, particularly as expressed in the comms. of Rudolph and Bright. As a result of the Qumrân discoveries, however, some of which contain fragments from the text of Jeremiah, the whole problem of the Hebrew-Greek relationship has been reopened. Fragments from three different MSS of Jeremiah — 4QJer[a], 4QJer[b], and 4QJer[c]— have been identified among these finds. For a preliminary transcription of most of the extant fragments of 4QJer[a] and 4QJer[b], see Janzen (pp. 173-184). Whereas the texts of 4QJer[a] and 4QJer[c] follow that of the MT quite closely, 4QJer[b] is more independent of the MT and shows instead several correspondences with the LXX.

A portion that has been singled out for special notice is one containing ends of lines from 9:22–10:18. In his book *Ancient Library of Qumran* (1958; repr. 1980), F. M. Cross showed that in matters of omission and dislocation of verses, this fragment corresponds to the order of verses found in the LXX. Here is positive proof, therefore, that, at least for this passage, a text similar to that of the LXX already existed in Hebrew, and it was presumably from one such MS that the LXX was translated. Taking the Qumrân discoveries as his cue, Janzen has restudied other internal phenomena of the book of Jeremiah where the Greek differs quantitatively from the Hebrew (e.g., double readings, parallel and related contexts, and stereotyped formulas) and has argued convincingly that the LXX was translated from a Hebrew text already shorter than the MT.

For Cross and Janzen these findings fit into a larger scheme that seeks to explain the development of the Hebrew text of the entire OT in the pre-Masoretic period. As elaborated by Cross, the theory of "local texts" postulates the development of distinct varieties of texts in three centers of Jewish learning in the era of the Second Temple: Babylon, Palestine, and Egypt. In this scheme, the Babylonian text represents a pure tradition, the Palestinian text is characterized by heavy expansion and editing, while the Egyptian text is an early off-shoot from the Palestinian branch, hence less conflated than the latter. Applied to the book of Jeremiah, the MT represents the Palestinian tradition while the Hebrew archetype behind the LXX corresponds to the Egyptian text, there being no third or Babylonian text for the book of Jeremiah. Both implicitly and explicitly this hypothesis favors the LXX tradition as representing the more original form of the book of Jeremiah (cf. Janzen, pp. 127-135; Cross, "The Evolution of a Theory of Local Texts," in F. M. Cross and S. Talmon, eds., *Qumran and the History of the Biblical Text,* [1975], pp. 308f.).

It is by no means certain, however, that we can settle the Hebrew/Greek priority issue on the basis of this theory (for a general critique see the remarks by S. Talmon in *Cambridge History of the Bible,* I [1970], 193-99, and in *Qumran and the History of the Biblical Text* [1975], pp. 321-400). Certainly it would be misleading to suggest that the mere existence at one time of a shorter Hebrew text weighs the scales in favor of the LXX as the better text. Moreover, Janzen's study was limited to one aspect of the Hebrew/Greek relationship, namely, the Greek "omissions" (or "zero variants" as he calls them). Further work needs to be done on the qualitative or content variants. As for 4QJer[b], all that this MS can do is corroborate the actual existence of an LXX-type text; it cannot decide between the two texts. It must be remembered, furthermore, that the extant portions of 4QJer[b] are extremely fragmentary and even where the MS has been preserved it is by no means consistent in its agreement with the LXX. Sometimes it follows the MT; sometimes it goes its own way.

In connection with the critical portion from 10:1-16, R. Davidson has shown that in this passage the MT has superior literary merit and hence a better claim to originality than the LXX (*Transactions of the Glasgow University Oriental Society,* 25 [1973-74], 41ff.). Other studies suggest that in certain LXX omissions it is possible to discern patterns that go back to the translators rather than to Hebrew copies (e.g., Z. Zevit on the translation of *'eḇeḏ,* "servant," in the LXX of Jeremiah, *JBL*, 88 [1969], 74-77; and *Bulletin of the International Organization for Septuagint and Cognate Studies*, 8 [1975], 17f.). At the same time, if and where it can be shown that the LXX has a better reading or order than the MT, the wise Bible student rejoices in the preservation of a text that more accurately reflects the wording and/or position of the original documents.

Bibliography.–*Comms*.: J. Bright (*AB*, 1965); A. Condamin (*EtB*, 1920); H. Cunliffe-Jones (*Torch*, 1960); S. R. Driver, *Book of the Prophet Jeremiah* (1906); B. Duhm (*Kürzer Hand-Kommentar zum AT*, 1901); H. L. Ellison, a continuous series in *EQ*, 31-40 (1959-1969); R. K. Harrison (*Tyndale OT Comms.*, 1973); KD; E. A. Leslie, *Jeremiah* (1954); E. W. Nicholson (*CBC*, 2 vols., 1973, 1975); A. S. Peake (*Century Bible*, 2 vols., 1910, 1911); W. Rudolph (*HAT*, 3rd ed. 1968); J. A. Thompson (*NICOT*, 1980); P. Volz (*KZAT*, 1922); A. Weiser (*ATD*, 2 vols., 1955).

Monographs: J. Bright, *Covenant and Promise* (1977), pp. 140-170; W. L. Holladay, *Jeremiah: Spokesman out of Time* (1974); J. P. Hyatt, *Jeremiah: Prophet of Courage and Hope* (1958); J. G. Janzen, *Studies in the Text of Jeremiah* (1973); J. Lundbom, *Jeremiah: A Study in Ancient Hebrew Rhetoric* (1975); J. W. Miller, *Das Verhältnis Jeremias und Hesekiels sprachlich und theologisch untersucht* (1955); S. Mowinckel, *Prophecy and Tradition* (1946); T. W. Overholt, *Threat of Falsehood* (*SBT*, 16, 1970); C. Rietzschel, *Das Problem der Urrolle* (1966); J. Skinner, *Prophecy and Religion* (1922); E. Tov, *The Septuagint Translation of Jeremiah and Baruch: A Discussion of an Early Revision of the LXX of Jer. 29–52 and Baruch 1:1–3:8* (1976); A. C. Welch, *Jeremiah: His Time and His Work* (1951).

Articles and Essays: H. Bardtke, *ZAW*, 53 (1935), 209-239; and *ZAW*, 54 (1936), 240-262; J. Bright, *Interp.*, 9 (1955), 259-278; R. Davidson, *VT*, 14 (1964), 407-416; T. R. Hobbs, *CBQ*, 34 (1972), 257-275; W. L. Holladay, *VT*, 25 (1975), 394-412; J. P. Hyatt, *ZAW*, 78 (1966), 204-214; H. G. May, *JBL*, 61 (1942), 139-155; J. Muilenburg, "Baruch the Scribe," in J. I. Durham and J. R. Porter, eds., *Proclamation and Presence: OT Essays in Honour of G. Henton Davies* (1970), pp. 215-238; T. H. Robinson, *ZAW*, 42 (1924), 209-221; H. H. Rowley, "The Prophet Jeremiah and the Book of Deuteronomy," in H. H. Rowley, ed., *Studies in OT Prophecy Presented to T. H. Robinson* (1950), pp. 157-174; *Men of God* (1963), pp. 133-168; R. P. Vaggione, *JBL*, 92 (1973), 523-530.

S. K. SODERLUND

JEREMIAH, LAMENTATIONS OF. *See* LAMENTATIONS, BOOK OF.

JEREMIAH, LETTER OF [Gk. *Epistolē Ieremiou*; AV EPISTLE OF JEREMY]. A letter of the Apocrypha purporting to be written by Jeremiah the prophet to the exiles of Judea who were being deported to Babylon. It warns the captives of the dangers of idolatry and apostasy.

I. Name.–In LXX MSS B and A the title is simply "An Epistle of Jeremiah." These MSS also have a superscription introducing the letter: "Copy of a letter which Jeremiah sent to the captives about to be led to Babylon by [Pesh. adds "Nebuchadnezzar"] the king of the Babylonians, to make known to them what had been commanded him by God." What follows is a satirical exposure of the folly of idolatry and not a letter. The idea of introducing this as a letter from Jeremiah was probably suggested by Jer. 29.

II. Canonicity and Position.–The early Greek Fathers were on the whole favorably disposed toward this tract, recognizing it as part of the canon. It is therefore included in the lists of canonical writings of Origen, Epiphanius, Cyril of Jerusalem, and Athanasius, and it was recognized as authoritative by the Council of Laodicea (300 A.D.).

In most Greek MSS of the LXX (B A Codex Marchalianus, Syrohexapla), it follows Lamentations as an independent piece, closing the supposed writings of Jeremiah. In the best-known printed editions of the LXX (Tischendorf, Swete, etc.), the order is Jeremiah, Baruch, Lamentations, Letter of Jeremiah. But in Latin MSS, including those of the Vulgate, it is appended to Baruch, of which it forms ch. 6, though it really has nothing to do with that book. This last is the arrangement in the Apocrypha of the AV, RSV, and NEB.

III. Contents.–In the so-called letter, the author shows the absurdity and wickedness of heathen worship. The Jews, for their sins, will be removed to Babylon, where they will remain seven generations. In that land, they will be tempted to worship the gods of the people. The writer's aim is ostensibly to warn them beforehand by showing how helpless and useless the idols worshiped are, and how immoral as well as silly the rites of the Babylonian religion are. For similar polemics against idolatry, see Isa. 44:9-20 (which in its earnestness closely resembles the Letter of Jeremiah); Jer. 10:3-9; Ps. 115:4-8; 135:15-18; Wisd. 13:10-19; 15:13-17.

IV. Original Language.–From traces of translation in the Greek text some scholars have argued for a Hebrew original. This is by no means impossible, since as the Qumrân materials show, letters were written in Hebrew at the beginning of the Christian era. R. H. Pfeiffer and C. C. Torrey proposed an Aramaic original on the ground that the instructions mentioned in 2 Macc. 2:1f. actually alluded to this letter, but this must be regarded at best as conjectural. Since Hellenistic Greek contained certain Semitisms, it is difficult if not actually impossible to determine the original language from a study of the text.

V. Authorship, Date, and Aim.–The letter has every appearance of being a typical Hellenistic-Jewish attack upon contemporary idolatry. Its author was almost certainly a resident in Alexandria toward the close of the last century B.C. The Greek of the book, with references to Egyptian religion (v. 19, where the Feast of Lights at Saia [Herodotus ii.62] is referred to), and the allusion to the Letter of Jeremiah in 2 Macc. 2:2 make this conclusion very probable. The author had in mind the dangers to his countrymen's religion presented by the fascinating forms of idolatry existing at Alexandria. Certainly Jeremiah is not the author, for the book was written in Greek and never formed part of the Hebrew canon. Besides, the treatment is far below the level of the genuine writings of that prophet.

VI. Text and Versions.–This letter occurs in the principal Greek MSS of the LXX uncials (B A Q Γ contain vv. 7b-24a, etc.) and cursives (except 70, 96, 229). The Syriac Peshitta follows the Greek in a free rendering, but the Syrohexapla follows the text of B closely, often at the expense of Syriac idioms. The Latin Vulgate is translated directly from the Greek. A different Latin version with a freer rendering than the Vulgate was published by Sabatier in his *Bib. Sacr. Lat. Versiones Antiquas*, II, 734ff. There are also an Arabic version, which follows LXX A, and Coptic (ed. Quatremère, 1810) and Ethiopic (ed. Dillmann, 1894) versions.

T. W. DAVIES
R. K. H.

JEREMIAS jer-ə-mī'əs [Gk. *Ieremias*].

1. Named among the sons of Baani as one of those who had married foreign wives (1 Esd. 9:34). In Ezr. 10:33 Jeremai is listed among the sons of Hashum. In 1 Esdras the name should come in 9:33 before Manasses.

2. *See* JEREMIAH.

JEREMIEL jer-ə-mī'əl [Lat. *Hieremihel*, prob. for Heb. *y^eraḥm^e'ēl*–'may God have compassion']. AV mg., RSV, NEB in 2 Esd. 4:36 for AV Uriel. He is here called the "archangel" who answers the questions raised by the souls of the righteous dead. He is probably identical with the Ramiel of 2 Bar. 55:3 or Remiel of 1 En. 20:8.

JEREMOTH jer'ə-mōth [Heb. *y^e^rēmôṯ, y^e^rîmôṯ* (1 Ch. 27:19)–'swollen']; AV also JERIMOTH (1 Ch. 7:8; 27:19); NEB also JERIMOTH (1 Ch. 27:19).

1, 2. Benjaminites (1 Ch. 7:8; 8:14). *See* JEHORAM **2.**

3. A son of Mushi (1 Ch. 23:23), the same as Jerimoth in 1 Ch. 24:30.

4. The head of a Levitical house (1 Ch. 25:22), the same as JERIMOTH **4.**

5. A Naphtalite, one of David's tribal princes (1 Ch. 27:19; AV, NEB, Jerimoth).

6. A Jew married to a foreign wife in the time of Ezra (Ezr. 10:26; 1 Esd. 9:27, AV Hieremoth).

7. Another Jew married to a foreign woman in Ezra's day (Ezr. 10:27; 1 Esd. 9:28, AV, NEB, Jarimoth).

8. Another Jew married to a non-Jewish wife in Ezra's period (Ezr. 10:29, *K; Q,* AV, Ramoth; 1 Esd. 9:30, AV Hieremoth).

JEREMY, EPISTLE OF. *See* JEREMIAH, LETTER OF.

JERIAH jə-rī'ə [Heb. *y^e^rîyāhû*–'may Yahweh see']. In 1 Ch. 23:19; 24:23 the same as Jerijah (Heb. *y^e^rîyâ*) in 26:31 (NEB Jeriah), head of a Levitical house; called chief of the Hebronites in 24:23 (cf. v. 30).

JERIBAI jer'ə-bī [Heb. *y^e^rîḇay*]. One of David's mighty men (1 Ch. 11:46) whose name is among those not found in the list in 2 S. 23:24-39.

JERICHO jer'ə-kō [Heb. *y^e^rēḥô, y^e^rîḥô, y^e^riḥô, y^e^rîḥōh*; Gk. (LXX) *Ierichō,* (NT) *Hierichō*]; AV, NEB, also JERECHUS (1 Esd. 5:22). A city just N of the Dead Sea, mentioned sixty times (54 OT; 6 NT) in the Bible.

- I. Biblical References
  - A. Geographical and Topographical
  - B. The Ancient City and Its King
  - C. Substantive Accounts of Historical and Traditional Events
- II. Archeology of Jericho of the Bronze and Iron Ages
- III. Hasmonean and Herodian Jericho

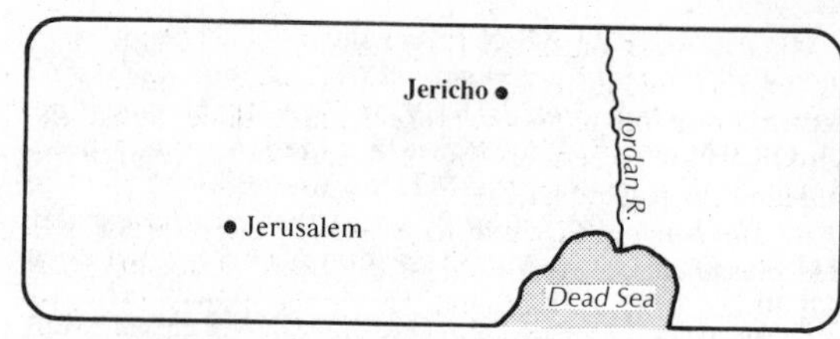

I. Biblical References.–A. Geographical and Topographical. Jericho was situated in the southern portion of the Jordan Valley about 16 km. (10 mi.) NW of the mouth of the Dead Sea, at one of the largest freshwater springs in all of Palestine, ʿAin es-Sulṭân, and near the E-W roadway that connected Transjordan with the hill country of Palestine. Thus the city has been prominent from its earliest occupation.

The first mention of Jericho in the Bible uses the city as a reference point to describe the location of the Israelite tribes moving toward the Promised Land. The characteristic phrase found in many verses is "in the plains of Moab by the Jordan at [opposite] Jericho" (Nu. 22:1; 26:3, 63; 31:12; 33:48, 50; 34:15; 35:1; 36:13; Dt. 32:49; Josh. 13:32). A second general designation refers to the area "in the plains of Jericho," the place where the Israelite army under Joshua encamped after crossing the Jordan (Josh. 4:13; 5:10). Twice the oasis fed by the great spring of ʿAin es-Sulṭân is indicated by the phrase "Jericho the city of palm trees" (Dt. 34:3; 2 Ch. 28:15).

The city of Jericho was also used as a boundary marker for the tribal allotments (Josh. 16:1f., 7; 1 Ch. 6:78) while the city itself was allotted to the tribe of Benjamin (Josh. 18:12, 21). Some scholars have seen a relationship of the name Jericho to the clan name *Yariḫû,* one of the subtribes of the *Banū-yamīna* mentioned in the Mari correspondence (*ca.* 1750 B.C.). Despite the similarity in names, the evidence for a relation between this northern Mesopotamian tribe and the biblical Benjaminites is not conclusive. Further, the city and its boundaries are referred to in locating the cities of refuge (Josh. 20:8).

View westward toward modern Jericho from Tell es-Sulṭân (ancient Jericho) (W. S. LaSor)

Finally, most of the NT references (Mt. 20:29; Mk. 10:46; Lk. 10:30; 18:35; 19:1) show Jericho as a first-century city on a major route from Galilee down the Jordan Valley to Jericho and then up (WSW) through the Judean hills to Jerusalem.

B. The Ancient City and Its King. All the references in this classification are found in the book of Joshua (6:2; 8:2; 10:28, 30; 12:9; 18:21) and refer to the Canaanite period of occupation (*ca.* 1350 B.C.). The names of the kings are never given. "Jericho with its king" (Josh. 6:2) appears most often in lists naming those cities conquered by Joshua and his troops when claiming the land of Canaan as the Promised Land.

C. Substantive Accounts of Historical and Traditional Events. In addition to its mention as a geographical point of reference in the Mosaic period, Jericho is included in the Canaanite land that Moses is permitted to see from Mt. Nebo, E of the Jordan (Dt. 32:49; 34:1, 3).

The story of Joshua's conquest of Jericho reports many items of significance for Israel's history and subsequent Jewish and Christian theology. From the narrative of the spies at Rahab's house one learns that Jericho was a walled city with houses, gates, and windows, and that some houses were built into the walls of the city (Josh. 2:1). The account of the stoppage of the Jordan's water at Adamah reports the crossing "opposite Jericho" (Josh. 3:16). Earth slides and the shutting off of the water of the serpentine Jordan have been reported periodically (1267, 1907, 1927). At the east border of Jericho after the crossing twelve stones were erected to serve as a memorial of the event and as a teaching aid for later generations (Josh. 4:19-24). In an event reminiscent of Moses' call, Joshua had a vision before Jericho of the "commander of the Lord's army." Joshua was told, "Put off your shoes from your feet; for the place where you stand is holy" (Josh. 5:13). The familiar story of Jericho's fall is reported in Josh. 6, including a curse uttered against anyone who would rebuild the city (Josh. 6:26). The final reference in Joshua lists Jericho among those cities which fought against Israel (Josh. 24:11).

The Davidic period yields only one reference to Jericho (2 S. 10:5 par. 1 Ch. 19:5). David's delegates to the Ammonites were shamed by having their beards cut off. David sent word for them to remain at Jericho until the beards were grown again. Nothing is learned of the city's size or influence, but presumably, though occupation continued at the site after Joshua's conquest, no walled city existed until Jericho was rebuilt in the period of the divided kingdom.

During the days of Ahab and Jezebel, when Baalism was a threat to Israel's religious life, one named Hiel of Bethel undertook the rebuilding of Jericho. The narrator reports that laying the foundation cost him his first-born son Abiram, and laying the gates cost him his youngest son Segub, in fulfillment of Joshua's curse (1 K. 16:34; cf. Josh. 6:26). It is unclear whether child sacrifice as practiced in Baalism is intended in this report. Later, the Qumrân community interpreted the violent death of Simon Maccabeus at the hand of Ptolemy in 134 B.C. as a fulfillment of Josh. 6:26. The reference is found in a Cave IV fragment of a work called the Psalms of Joshua, which bears witness to the Hellenistic-Hasmonean rebuilding of Jericho (at Tulûl Abū el-ʿAlâyiq) by "a cursed man, a man of Belial" and his two sons.

Elijah's translation occurred at the Jordan near Jericho. He was accompanied by Elisha, who succeeded the great prophet. The account includes a reference to fifty "sons of the prophets" believed to be from a "school of the prophets" in existence at Jericho at this time (2 K. 2:4f., 15, 18). Also reported at Jericho is the freshening of the spring by Elisha (2 K. 2:19-22). During Ahaz's reign in Israel a group of captives were spared, clothed, and cared for at Jericho (2 Ch. 28:15).

The final references to Jericho in the period of the divided kingdom tell of the Chaldean army pursuing King Zedekiah. He was overtaken in the plains of Jericho and was forced to watch the slaughter of his sons; then he was blinded by his captors and carried off to Babylon (2 K. 25:2-7; Jer. 39:1-7 par. 52:4-11).

On return from the Exile under Zerubbabel, Jericho's inhabitants, listed as "sons of Jericho, three hundred and forty-five," had a role in rebuilding the walls of Jerusalem (Ezr. 2:34 par. Neh. 3:2; 7:36).

The NT references to Jericho include an event outside the city on the road to Jerusalem in which two blind men were healed (Mt. 20:29; cf. Mk. 10:46, the healing of Bartimaeus; cf. also Lk. 18:35). In two of Luke's narratives Jericho is prominent. The parable of the Good Samaritan (Lk. 10:30) refers to the Jerusalem-Jericho road, and the story of Zacchaeus (19:1) has its setting in Jericho. The last NT reference to the city recalls the active faith of God's people that was illustrated by the collapse of Jericho's walls and by Rahab's salvation (He. 11:30).

R. A. COUGHENOUR

*II. **Archeology of Jericho of the Bronze and Iron Ages.***–The identification of remains that could be associated with the account in Josh. 6 has for long been the objective of archeologists. If precise evidence could be obtained of a destruction that could definitely be ascribed to the Israelites, it would be of great help in determining the date of the entry of the Israelites into Canaan.

J. Garstang, in his excavations of 1930-1936, believed that he had found the evidence of the collapse of the town walls by earthquake (the most probable explanation of the episode) at a date of *ca.* 1400 B.C. More precise evidence concerning pottery (the main basis for dating evidence in Palestine) accumulated after Garstang's excavations and suggested the need for further examination, which was carried out between 1952 and 1958.

Garstang traced a succession of four town walls encircling the mound of Tell es-Sulṭân. The wall that he considered (in fact erroneously) to be the latest was heavily burned and showed evidence of collapse, probably from earthquake. Excavation methods in Palestine at that time were not sufficiently precise for the rather complex process of dating a town wall by the levels belonging to it. Garstang, considering this wall to be the latest, associated it with the latest buildings he found. He correctly ascribed these and some tombs to the Late Bronze Age (*ca.* 1550-1200 B.C.), but was misled by incorrect dating of comparable pottery from Beth-shean into suggesting that the terminal date was *ca.* 1400 B.C.

The 1952-1958 excavations at Jericho showed that the history of the Bronze Age town walls of Jericho is extremely complex. Those of the Early Bronze Age (covering most of the 3rd millennium) were of mud brick and were very frequently repaired; in one area investigated as many as seventeen builds and rebuilds could be identified. It was one of the latest of these E.B. walls that was ascribed by Garstang to the L.B. All these E.B. walls were in fact buried by the great earth bank belonging to the Middle Bronze Age. The upper part of this bank has for the most part been destroyed by erosion, and only in one place do the foundations of the wall on its summit survive. Erosion during centuries of abandonment has in fact removed almost all the remains of the M.B. town, and therefore to a still greater extent those of the overlying L.B. town.

Enough, however, did exist to prove that there had been a L.B. town, built on top of the eroded ruins of the M.B. town after a century and a half of abandonment. Since the remains of the L.B. town survive over such a limited area, and no part of the town wall survives, nothing can be said of its plan. The pottery evidence, including that from the tombs discovered by Garstang, suggests that it was destroyed in the last quarter of the 14th century. Excavation has thus recovered enough evidence to prove that a L.B. town had existed at Jericho and was abandoned after a destruction. This destruction could have been the work of one of the groups of infiltrating Israelites and thus could be reflected in the account of the book of Joshua, though the date is rather earlier than that which most scholars would prefer.

The excavations showed clearly that a long period of abandonment followed this destruction. The site was not reoccupied until Iron Age II. Most of the material found belongs to the 7th cent. B.C. There is some material — including one tomb (Kenyon, *Jericho,* II, 482ff.) — that may be associated with the rebuilding of the town by Hiel the Bethelite (1 K. 16:34) early in the 9th cent. B.C. The final abandonment of the site of Tell es-Sulṭân came in the 6th cent. B.C., probably as a result of the Babylonian destruction of the kingdom of Judah in 587 B.C.

Although excavations have produced such meager remains of the OT period at Jericho, they have made a considerable contribution to OT studies by the light they have thrown on the Canaanite Palestine which the Israelites penetrated and its culture which they absorbed. New groups entering Palestine *ca.* 1900 B.C. introduced the urban culture that developed on the Phoenician coast (K. Kenyon, *Amorites and Canaanites* [1966]). This culture of fairly small-scale city-states lasted till 1200 B.C. and later, with no significant break. The great wealth of evidence recovered by excavations at Jericho concerning M.B. life is therefore very relevant to the identification of the material culture that the Israelites found and absorbed to a considerable extent when they entered Palestine.

As already stated, most of the M.B. town had disappeared in successive phases of erosion. In one area, however, a group of houses survives. They show cobbled streets, with draining beneath, ascending from the spring to the east up the slope of the mound, which was by that date steep. Relatively small houses — certainly two-storied, and probably with single-roomed shops at street level (Kenyon, *Digging Up Jericho* [1957], p. 229) — opened onto the streets. The last of a long succession of M.B. buildings in the area were violently destroyed by fire in the first half of the 16th cent. B.C. The ruins provided good evidence of the domestic equipment of the period.

Reconstruction of a room at Jericho (*ca.* 1650 B.C.) (Royal Ontario Museum, Toronto; picture A. C. Myers)

Still greater evidence came from the tombs (of which details are given in Kenyon, *Jericho,* I and II). The dead of Jericho were provided with purely material equipment for the afterlife. The absence of any evidence for the provision of spiritual needs is in very striking contrast with contemporary Egypt. The dead person was buried with what was obviously the normal furnishings of his home. He had a basket containing toilet requisites, combs, small boxes, perfume or oil containers, and in one case a wig. The standard article of furniture was a table, usually about 1 m. (3 ft.) long, the largest example being 1.5 m. (5 ft.) long and about 35 cm. (14 in.) wide, standing on legs about 40 cm. (16 in.) high, of which there were invariably two at one end and one at the other as an aid to stability on an uneven floor. This must have been the sole article of furniture in most households, and the inhabitants must have slept and sat on rush mats, on which many of the bodies were laid. In one case the principal burial lay on a narrow bed with a wooden frame while the rest of his family lay on the floor of the tomb chamber. Wood-framed stools were also provided; and in all cases where stools were found, there were indications of the special importance of the person buried, e.g., that he was placed on a brick platform. There was usually a generous provision of food, with parts or whole carcasses of sheep or goats, and jars containing liquid. The skin left in these jars as the liquid evaporated was often intact, but analysis has not shown what the liquid was. In the mouth of these jars were suspended dipper flasks to ladle it out. Dishes of pottery and wood and drinking vessels were provided.

Fragments of the clothing of the dead persons survived and were sufficient to show that the material was usually flax or some form of leaf bast. The surviving fragments were inadequate to indicate the shape of the garments; it could, however, be deduced from the position of the bronze toggle pins which must have held them in position that some individuals had a loose garment which was draped over one shoulder and under the other and secured there by a toggle pin, while others wore a kiltlike garment secured at the waist. The general burial practice was certainly that of successive burials in what were presumably family tombs. As space was required for a later burial, a place was cleared in the front of the tomb by unceremoniously pushing back the bones and associated offerings of earlier burials to the walls of the tomb chamber. This process inevitably damaged the earlier burials and their offerings. From the archeological point of view it is fortunate that just before the final destruction of M.B. Jericho there had been a number of burials of many members of (presumably) the same family that were not thereafter disturbed, and the evidence from these tombs is the main basis for the conclusions described here.

The town of Jericho destroyed in the early 16th cent. B.C. and the accompanying tombs provide evidence for the culture of Palestine in the period of the biblical patriarchs. The patriarchs were not town dwellers, but this was the culture with which they would have been in contact. More importantly, it was the culture found and absorbed by the infiltrating Israelite tribes of the 14th and 13th cents. B.C.

At the time when Jericho impinged on the Joshua story and the preceding period of the patriarchs it was already a very old town. The major contribution of the excavations of the site to the history of the development of civilization has been to show that Palestine was one of the centers of the change from a wandering, food-collecting way of life to a settled way of life based on agriculture and the domestication of animals — one from which villages, towns, and cities could emerge.

Trench I at Jericho at the Pre-pottery Neolithic B level (Jericho Excavation Fund, University of London; picture K. M. Kenyon)

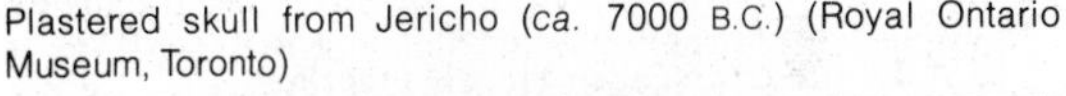

Plastered skull from Jericho (*ca.* 7000 B.C.) (Royal Ontario Museum, Toronto)

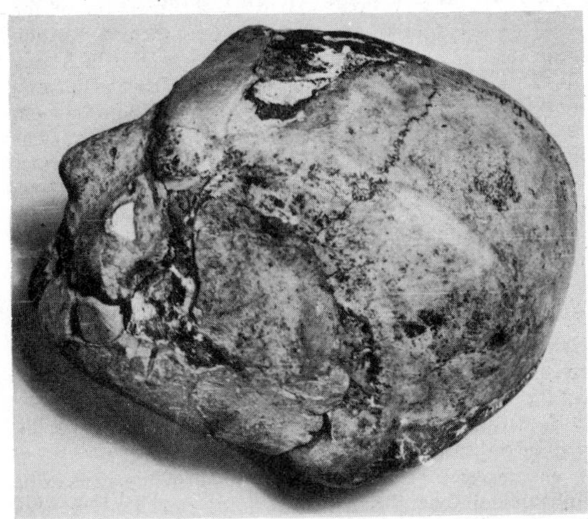

Early Jericho shows the full range. The first stage is the arrival of the hunters of the final food-collecting stage (the Mesolithic), who built a structure that can be interpreted as a shrine associated with the life-giving properties of the spring of ʿAin es-Sulṭân, *ca.* 9000 B.C. The descendants of these hunters gradually settled down at Jericho, and by *ca.* 8000 B.C. they were building permanent houses, successors to the slight structures of which the intervening strata provide evidence. The climax of this development was the construction of an imposing town wall, enclosing an area of about 4 ha. (10 acres), associated with at least one massive stone tower. By 8000 B.C., therefore, the inhabitants of Jericho had achieved a coherence and organization very far removed from that of the Mesolithic nomads who had appeared on the site a thousand years before.

Excavations at Jericho showing Neolithic tower (lower left), *ca.* 7000 B.C. (Israel Government Tourist Office)

The first Neolithic culture of Jericho was indigenous, derived from the flourishing Mesolithic culture of Palestine. It provides the only sequence so far traced for this crucial stage in the development of civilization. The second culture was not indigenous. It superseded the original one *ca.* 7000 B.C., and probably provides evidence of the arrival of a new group from some area to the north where a parallel development had taken place. Town life was again highly organized. After *ca.* 6000 B.C. there was a recession, and a town reappears at Jericho only in the E.B. period of the 3rd millennium B.C. Between that town and the one ascribed to the period of the patriarchs there was a break, which may be ascribed to the arrival of the nomadic Amorites *ca.* 2300 B.C. K. M. KENYON

III. Hasmonean and Herodian Jericho.–The modern site of Tulûl Abū el-ʿAlâyiq is the ruin of ancient Hasmonean and Herodian Jericho (formerly designated as NT Jericho [Kelso] and Herodian Jericho [Pritchard]). It was built in the days of the late Maccabean (Hasmonean) period, possibly as early as 134 B.C., by Simon Maccabeus. The city lies on the two banks of the Wâdī Qelt about 1½ km. (1 mi.) W of the modern city of Jericho and about 27 km. (17 mi.) ENE of Jerusalem.

The Hasmoneans rediscovered the great agricultural and economic potential of Jericho with its mild winter climate, abundance of water, and availability of land in the valley. Harnessing the water sources by means of aqueducts from ʿAin es-Sulṭân, ʿAin Dûq, ʿAin Nuʿeima, the three springs of Wâdī Qelt, and the spring of ʿAuja NW of the valley, the Hasmoneans and especially Herod turned Jericho into a garden city and royal estate which from 134 B.C. to A.D. 70 covered hundreds of acres and was inhabited by tens of thousands of Jews. After A.D. 70 the Roman procurators paid less attention to the site, which declined rapidly to a very small settlement.

Excavations at the site by James L. Kelso (1950), James B. Pritchard (1951), and more recently Ehud Netzer and his colleagues (1973-1979) uncovered a number of remarkable features of Jericho. A large (1.2-ha. [3-acre]) winter palace complex of the Hasmonean kings built possibly by Alexander Janneus (103-76 B.C.) consisted of a central building, a huge swimming pool (32 by 18 by 4 m. [105 by 59 by 13 ft.]), a large reception hall facing east and giving a breathtaking view of the Wâdī Qelt and the Jericho valley, and paved promenades around the pool (more than 2000 sq. m. [½ acre]), bathing and ritual bath installations, a storage hall with several rooms, and aqueducts. Most of the coins found in the palace area belong to the period of Alexander Janneus, but a cache of twenty rare Mattathias Antigonus coins was found west of the swimming pool. In Jericho Herod overcame Mattathias, the last of the Hasmonean kings, and became, according to Josephus, the ruler of the valley in 37 B.C. Shortly thereafter Anthony gave the fertile oasis to Cleopatra queen of Egypt, but Herod, recognizing the economic worth of the area, rented it back and continued to develop the valley (*BJ* i.18.5 [362]; see Netzer, pp. 1, 6, 9).

Herod's expansion of the complex was even more magnificent. Choosing a 300-m. (1000-ft.) straight portion of the wadi, Herod built a well-planned coordinated architectural complex straddling the Wâdī Qelt. Herod's winter palace included four wings with such features as courtyards surrounded by columns, an ornate Roman bath, small rooms, and two halls. One of the halls is 29 m. by 19 m. wide (95 by 62 ft.) with three rows of columns surrounding it. The wide opening to the west faced the Wâdī Qelt. The hall was paved with imported marble and local colored stones. Its center had a mosaic panel. A large sunken garden and an exotic formal garden elaborately constructed in mirror image and symmetry with niches were included. The buildings were crafted in *opus reticulatum,* a peculiar use of small, uniform, rectangular stones set in mortar. This feature is Roman in origin from the time of Augustus and dates most likely to a period between 18 B.C. and A.D. 6. Herod's successor Archelaus rebuilt some of the buildings (Josephus *Ant.* xvii.13.1 [340]), though excavation has not yet revealed the extent of the rebuilding.

The most recent discoveries at Jericho are inscriptions from a first-century A.D. Jewish monumental tomb revealing three generations of a family. The tomb shows great wealth, having been plastered, decorated with a brightly colored fresco depicting a vine with leaves, trellis, ripe grapes, and birds perched on the branches (Hachlili, p.31).

A total of thirty-two inscriptions, many of them in both Greek and Aramaic, reveal much about the occupants of the tomb. The most important inscription reads, "Theodotos, freedman of Queen Agrippina." "This is the first time that a non-literary source mentions a Judean Jew who was most likely taken slave as a result of the political turmoil in Judea at this time and who was manumitted by a Roman Empress" (Hachlili, p. 62). This Queen Agrippina, empress of Rome A.D. 50-54, should be identified with Agrippina the younger (A.D. 15-59) who in A.D. 49 married the emperor Claudius, her uncle (Tacitus *Ann.* xii.1-8). She was co-regent with her son Nero (Tacitus *Ann.* xii.64; xiii.21f.). She was in close contact with the Jewish King Agrippa II interceding on behalf of Jews during the Samaritan-Jewish riots of A.D. 52 (Josephus *Ant.* xx.6.3 [134f.]).

These recent findings with anthropological, inscriptional, archeological, and historical data demonstrate a large, wealthy, sophisticated city during NT times. Thus, when Jesus visited Jericho and was invited to the home of the tax collector Zacchaeus, he entered a remarkably rich setting (Lk. 19:2-10).

Jericho was captured by Vespasian's troops *ca.* A.D. 68 and the city declined but was not destroyed. A brief revival of its glory came at the time of Bar Cochba's rebellion against Rome in A.D. 132-135. Later a Byzantine Jericho was built about 1½ km. (1 mi.) E of Herodian Jericho. The present city of Jericho is built on the Byzantine site.

Bibliography.–*EAEHL,* II, *s.v.* (K. Kenyon, *et al.*); R. Hachlili, *BASOR,* 235 (Summer 1979), 31-65; J. L. Kelso, *BA,* 14 (1951), 34-43; J. L. Kelso and D. C. Baramki, *Excavations at NT Jericho and Khirbet en-Nitla* (*AASOR,* 29-30, 1955); K. Kenyon, *Excavations at Jericho* (2 vols., 1960-1965); L. Mowry, *BA,* 15 (1952), 26-42; E. Netzer, *BASOR,* 228 (Dec. 1977), 1-13; E. Netzer and E. Meyers, *BASOR,* 228 (Dec. 1977), 15-27; J. B. Pritchard, *BASOR,* 123 (Oct. 1951), 8-17.

R. A. COUGHENOUR

JERIEL jer'i-əl [Heb. *y^erî'ēl*–'may Yahweh observe']. A chief of Issachar (1 Ch. 7:2).

JERIJAH jə-rī'jə [Heb. *y^erîyâ*–'may Yahweh notice']. In 1 Ch. 26:31 the chief of the Hebronites in the days of David. *See* JERIAH.

JERIMOTH jer'i-moth [Heb. *y^erîmôṯ*–'swollen'].

1. A Benjaminite (1 Ch. 7:7).

2. A Benjaminite who joined David at Ziklag, or perhaps a Judean (1 Ch. 12:5 [MT 6]).

3. In 1 Ch. 24:30 the same as JEREMOTH **3.**

4. A Levite musician in David's time (1 Ch. 25:4), the same as JEREMOTH **4.**

5. Son of David and father of Mahalath, Rehoboam's wife (2 Ch. 11:18). He is not mentioned (2 S. 3:2-5; 5:14-16; 1 Ch. 3:1-9; 14:4-7) among the sons of David's wives.

6. A Levite overseer in Hezekiah's time (2 Ch. 31:13).

D. F. ROBERTS

JERIOTH jer'i-oth, jer'i-ōth [Heb. *y^erî'ôṯ*–'(tent-)curtains']. The MT presents certain problems in 1 Ch. 2:18, reflected by the English versions in making Jerioth appear to be the second wife of Caleb son of Hezron. It is possible to regard Azubah as the former wife of a man named Jerioth, but it is more probable that Jerioth was an alternative name for Azubah. In the latter case the "and" of the RSV should be rendered "even." The NEB reads "had Jerioth by Azubah his wife."

JEROBOAM jer-ə-bō'əm [Heb. *yārob'ām*–'(may God) increase the nation'; Gk. *Hieroboam*]. The name of two kings of the northern kingdom.

1. Jeroboam I, the first king of Israel (931-910 B.C.) and son of Nebat.

I. Sources.–The writer of the book of Kings derives his information from the history of Solomon (1 K. 11:41), the history of the kings of Judah, and the history of the kings of Israel; the Chronicler refers to certain prophetic writings and genealogies (2 Ch. 9:29; 12:15; 13:22), none of which is extant. The last work is called midrash, but it would be presumptuous to assume that it was a work of imaginative homiletics; the word "midrash" did not have this meaning in those early days, and the midrashic works we have are postbiblical and rabbinical.

There is no real ground for supposing that the writer of Kings displays any animus toward Jeroboam or is in any way prejudiced in favor of some of the kings belonging to David's house. If the writer tells the story of Jeroboam's apostasy and failure he does not fail to mention his valor and vigor, or the nobility of his son who died young, although these qualities are not detailed (1 K. 14:13). The text of the story of Jeroboam in the MT is to be preferred to that of the LXX, which even a cursory reading will show to be a clumsy attempt to straighten things out in the Hebrew text, which in places is admittedly difficult.

II. Jeroboam's Revolt.–While engaged on one of Solomon's vast building projects, Jeroboam displayed such ability that he was put in control of the porterage allotted to Joseph or the Israelitish clans (1 K. 11:27f.), and was sub-overseer under Adoniram, or Adoram (4:6; 11:28). Jeroboam revolted, or "lifted up his hand against the king." The juxtaposition of the corvée and the revolt warrants the supposition that Jeroboam's people revolted because of the forced labor exacted from them, not because of intrigue or their leader's personal ambition as has been suggested (J. Montgomery, *ICC* on Kings); Jeroboam's prophetic backing would otherwise be hard to explain.

The story of Jeroboam's encounter with the prophet Ahijah is told in 1 K. 11:29. The prophet tells him that, provoked by Judah's idolatrous practices, God was going to split the kingdom and give him ten of its twelve parts. The prophet corroborated the oral message by tearing his upper garment into twelve pieces and giving Jeroboam ten of them. But Jeroboam's plot, if it was ever a full-blown plot and not merely the airing of a grievance, was discovered by the authorities; Jeroboam fled to Egypt to find asylum with the famous Shishak (Sheshonq).

III. Secession of the Ten Tribes.–The protest against the corvée gathered force at Solomon's death and embraced all the northern tribes; Jeroboam, who had returned from Egypt, became his people's spokesman (1 K. 12:2; see J. Gray, *I & II Kings* [*OTL*, 2nd ed. 1970], p. 301; cf. N. Sarna, *JBL*, 78 [1959], 313). When Rehoboam came to Shechem to be confirmed as king over all Israel, the protesting tribesmen said that they were willing to serve him on condition that he reduce the forced labor and taxation, which were so burdensome and galling. But Rehoboam allowed himself to be influenced by his young courtiers and spoke roughly to them; so the cry went up:

"What portion have we in David?
We have no inheritance in the son of Jesse:
To your tents, O Israel:
Look now to your own house, David." (1 K. 12:16)

Events followed in rapid succession. Adoniram, whom Rehoboam sent as chief of the corvée, presumably to force people to submit, was stoned by "all Israel," i.e., the representatives of all the tribes, an act that sealed the secession for good. Rehoboam mounted his chariot in haste and fled to Jerusalem. Once safely among his people, he summoned his Judean and Benjaminite troops and prepared to fight for his lost provinces. But the king's intention to fight was opposed immediately by the prophet Shemaiah (1 K. 12:21-24).

IV. Jeroboam Becomes King of Israel.–Jeroboam, who first aired the grievance against the forced labor, and who led the aggrieved Ephraimites when Rehoboam sought election, was then called to the throne. He first fortified Shechem, which became the capital of the kingdom. He later built up Penuel E of the Jordan, no doubt as a war measure. Later still, Tirzah seems to have become the capital, since it housed the palace (1 K. 14:17; cf. *WHAB*, p. 50b). But if prophetic interference prevented the war over the secession, intermittent fighting took place later between the two parts of the now irreparably divided kingdom, and in one battle Jeroboam fared badly (1 K. 14:30; 2 Ch. 13:2-20). When Shishak (*ca.* 935-914) attacked Palestine, Israel suffered as well as Judah, as is shown by the inscriptions in the temple of Karnak, though Judah must have suffered more than Ephraim (1 K. 14:25).

V. His Apostasy.–Prophetic support notwithstanding, Jeroboam failed miserably because he became involved in Baal worship (cf. Hos. 13:1). Anxious to keep his throne, Jeroboam adopted a disastrous religious policy. He feared that the periodic pilgrimages to the temple at Jerusalem would make his people transfer their allegiance to the heirs of David and Solomon and destroy the dynastic hopes he had entertained as a result of the prophetic oracle (1 K. 11:38). He therefore set up two official shrines for the pilgrimage, one at Bethel and the other at Dan, which were situated south and north at the ends of the realm. Bethel was associated in the public mind with the patriarchs, and with Jacob in particular, who recognized the place as "the house of God and . . . the gate of heaven" (Gen. 28:17). Dan may have been associated with some local cult.

The charges leveled against Jeroboam are many. He set up high places. He enrolled into the priesthood people who did not belong to Levitical families. He altered the religious calendar. He set up two golden calves, or young bulls, symbols of fertility, which were part and parcel of Canaanite Baal worship (1 K. 12:28-32). This was not only wrong in itself but it also opened the way for the abominations associated with Canaanite Baal worship.

(*See also* DISEASE III.C.)

VI. End of the Dynasty.–The same Ahijah, the prophet from Shiloh, who brought Jeroboam the promise of a "sure house" or a stable dynasty (1 K. 11:38), brought him on a second occasion a message of doom: "Therefore behold, I will bring evil upon the house of Jeroboam and will cut off from Jeroboam every male . . . because of the sins of Jeroboam which he sinned and which he made Israel to sin" (1 K. 14:10, 16). Jeroboam died in the twenty-second year of his reign and was succeeded by his son Nadab, who was cut down by a usurper after a short reign of two years, when the whole royal family was massacred.

2. Jeroboam II, the tenth king of Israel, a son of King Jehoash and a great-grandson of Jehu (2 K. 14:23-29).

I. His Wars.–His long reign of forty-one years was truly an Indian summer. It began not long after the nation's deliverance from the atrocious oppression of the Arameans, when the Israelites were "like the dust of threshing" (2 K. 13:7). Helped by Aramean internecine wars, as well as Assyria's temporary incapacity, Jeroboam was able to regain lost territory, or territories, and was rightly called the savior of his people (14:27). "He restored the border of Israel from the entrance of Hamath," i.e., from the pass between Lebanon and Anti-Lebanon in the valley of the Beqaʿ, "to the Sea of the Arabah," at the southern end of the Dead Sea (14:25).

Some have flatly denied the biblical statement of 14:28 that Jeroboam took Damascus and Hamath (see Montgomery, *ICC* on Kings, p. 444), but this is to deny what the Bible does not assert. The meaning of the passage is clear only when the Semitic word order is understood correctly. The passage says that Jeroboam did two things: he fought against Damascus and Hamath, and also recovered territory. What he recovered or restored, the verse does not name; it does say, however, that the beneficiary was not his own northern kingdom but Judah. The place recovered was Elath. The verse may be read: "Now the rest of the acts of Jeroboam . . . how he warred against Damascus and Hamath, and restored (what he restored) to Judah by the hand of Israel, are they not written in the book of the Chronicles of the kings of Israel?" (cf. Montgomery's criticism, *ICC* on Kings, p. 444).

The same passage relates that Jonah, who prophesied against Nineveh and threatened it with quick destruction, also prophesied during Jeroboam's reign, and that Israel like Nineveh was reprieved, at least for a time, because of God's mercy and long-suffering.

II. Spiritual Decay and Prophetic Condemnation.–Amos, one of the prophets who lived during Jeroboam's reign (Am. 1:1), has left us a picture, or rather a series of pictures, of the moral and spiritual decay that was fast leading the nation to destruction. The people bragged about their military victories (6:13) and suffered from a false sense of security (6:1). They were inordinately proud of their great houses of dressed stone decorated with inlaid ivory work and of their pleasant vineyards with their trailing grape vines and luscious fruit; but they were not concerned that it all came from exactions from the depressed poor and needy (5:11).

They were shamelessly immoral (Am. 2:7). They ate and drank and sang; they perfumed themselves and listened to music lying about on fine couches; but the woes of the common folk and their grinding poverty did not concern them at all (6:4-6). They celebrated their religious festivals with many blood offerings and with an elaborate choral worship, but there was flagrant injustice everywhere, and a judge could be bribed with a piece of silver or the gift of a pair of shoes (2:6).

> "I hate, I despise your feasts. . . .
> Take away from me the noise of your songs;
> to the melody of your harps I will not listen.
> But let justice roll down like waters,
> and righteousness like an everflowing stream."
> (Am. 5:21-24)

Amos' powerful pleading did not change the nation; he was insulted for his pains, and when he prophesied the speedy end of the dynasty he was accused of plotting against Jeroboam and was asked to leave the country (Am. 7:12). M. S. SEALE

JEROHAM jə-rō'həm [Heb. *yᵉrōḥām*–'may he be tender'(?)].

1. An Ephraimite, the father of Elkanah and grandfather of Samuel (1 S. 1:1; 1 Ch. 6:27, 34 [MT 12, 19]). Jerahmeel is the name in LXX B in 1 Samuel and in LXX L and MSS in 1 Chronicles.

2. A Benjaminite (1 Ch. 8:27), apparently the same as JEREMOTH (cf. v. 14), and probably the same as the Jeroham of 1 Ch. 9:8.

3. Ancestor of a priest in Jerusalem (1 Ch. 9:12, the same as Neh. 11:12).

4. A man of Gedor, father of two of David's Benjaminite recruits at Ziklag, though Gedor might be a town in southern Judah (1 Ch. 12:7 [MT 8]).

5. Father of Azarel, David's tribal chief over Dan (1 Ch. 27:22).

6. Father of Azariah, one of the captains who supported Jehoiada in overthrowing Queen Athaliah (2 Ch. 23:1). D. F. ROBERTS

JERUBBAAL jer'ə-bāl, jə-rub'bā-əl [Heb. *yᵉrubbaʿal*–'let Baal contend'(?)]. The name given to Gideon by his father Joash and the people in recognition of his destruction of the altar of Baal at Ophrah (Jgs. 6:32). For this name the form "Jerubbesheth" (2 S. 11:21) was substituted after the analogy of "Ishbosheth" and "Mephibosheth," in which *bōšeṯ*, the Hebrew word for "shame," displaced the word *baʿal*, no doubt because the name resembled one given in honor of Baal. *See* GIDEON.

JERUBBESHETH jer-ub-bē'sheth, jə-rub'ə-sheth [Heb. *yᵉrubbāšeṯ*–'let shame contend']. It is found once (2 S. 11:21) for JERUBBAAL.

The Hebrew word *bōšeṯ*, "shameful thing," was substituted by later editors of the text for *baʿal*, "lord," in the text of Jer. 3:24; Hos. 9:10; in 2 S. 2:8, etc., we find Ishbosheth, the same as Eshbaal (Ishbaal) in 1 Ch. 8:33; 9:39. The reason for this was reluctance to pronounce the word *baʿal*, which had by their time been associated with Canaanite forms of worship. In 2 S. 11:21, LXX Lucian has "Jeroboal," which LXX B has corrupted to "Jeroboam." Cf. MERIBBAAL; MEPHIBOSHETH. For a NT case cf. Rom. 11:4 and see Sanday and Headlam, comm. on Romans (*ICC*, 1902), *in loc*. *See* JERUBBAAL. D. F. ROBERTS

JERUEL jə-rōō'əl, jer'ōō-əl [Heb. *yᵉrûʾēl*–'founded by El']. Jahaziel prophesied that King Jehoshaphat should meet the hordes of Moabites and Ammonites, after they had come up by the "ascent of Ziz," "at the end of the valley [i.e., *wâdī*], before the wilderness of Jeruel" (2 Ch. 20:16). The particular part of the wilderness intended seems to have been between En-gedi and Tekoa.

JERUSALEM jə-rōō'sə-ləm [Heb. *yᵉrûšālayim, yᵉrûšālēm*–'city of wholeness'; Gk. *Ierosalēm, Hierosolyma*]. The principal city of ancient Israel, location of the temple, capital of the kingdom of Judah, chief city of nascent Judaism, the city where Jesus Christ was tried and crucified, the place visited (according to tradition) by the prophet Muhammad on his way to heaven, and hence the holiest city of Jews and Christians and (after Mecca and Medina) the third holiest city of the Moslems.

D. Divided Kingdom
1. Ninth Century
2. Eighth Century
a. Amaziah of Judah
b. Amaziah of Judah and Joash of Israel
c. Uzziah of Judah
d. Jotham and Ahaz of Judah
e. Hezekiah of Judah
f. Siloam Tunnel
g. Hezekiah's Walls
h. Sennacherib's Siege
3. Eighth-Century Prophets
4. Seventh Century
5. Before the Exile: A Synthesis
a. Southwest Hill
b. Population Explosion
c. Walls
d. Mishneh
e. Mortar
f. Tower of Hananel
g. Corner Gate
h. Ephraim Gate
i. Hill Gareb and Goah
j. Upper Pool, the Highway, Fuller's Field
k. Valley Gate
l. Topheth
m. Potsherd Gate
n. Uzziah's Towers
o. Horse Gate and Benjamin Gate
p. Court of the Guard, Gate of the Foundation, Gate of the House
q. Fish Gate
r. Ophel
s. Millo
t. Waters of Shiloah, Lower Pool, King's Garden
u. Gate Between the Walls
v. Manasseh's Wall
E. Destruction of Jerusalem (586 B.C.)
F. From the Return until Herod
1. Persian Period
2. Nehemiah's Jerusalem
a. Valley Gate
b. Jackal's Well
c. Dung (Ashpot) Gate
d. Fountain Gate
e. En-rogel
f. King's Garden
g. King's Pool
h. Pool of Shelah
i. Stairs That Go Down from the City
j. Sepulchres of David
k. House of David
l. House of the Mighty Men
m. Water Gate on the East
n. Ascent to the Armory at the Angle
o. House of Eliashib
p. House of Azariah
q. Projecting Tower
r. House of the King
s. Gate of the Guard
t. Ophel
u. Horse Gate
v. Muster Gate
w. Sheep Gate
x. Tower of the Hundred
y. Tower of Hananel
z. Fish Gate
a'. Old Gate (Mishneh Gate)
b'. Gate of Ephraim
c'. Broad Wall
d'. Tower of the Furnaces
e'. Corner Gate
3. Religious Situation
4. Hellenistic and Hasmonean Periods
G. Herodian Jerusalem
1. General Observations
2. Josephus's Account
H. Jerusalem in the Time of Christ and the Apostles
1. First Years
2. Early Ministry
3. Approach to Jerusalem
4. Passion Ministry
5. Palace of Caiaphas
6. Upper Room
7. Gethsemane
8. Peter's Denial
9. Before the Sanhedrin
10. Before Pilate: The Praetorium
11. Akeldama
12. Location of Herod Antipas
13. Stations of the Cross
14. Golgotha (Calvary)
15. Gordon's Calvary and Garden Tomb
16. "Galilee"
17. Place of Appearance to the Eleven
18. Place of the Ascension
19. Upper Room of Disciples
20. Pentecost
21. Gate Beautiful
22. Solomon's Portico
23. Synagogue of the Freedmen
24. St. Stephen's Gate
25. House of Mary the Mother of Mark
26. Paul's Arrest in the Temple
27. Paul in the Barracks
28. Paul Before the Sanhedrin
29. James the Bishop of Jerusalem
30. Population of Jerusalem
I. Destruction of Jerusalem (A.D. 70)
J. Destruction of Jerusalem (A.D. 135)
K. Subsequent History of Jerusalem
1. Byzantine Period (A.D. 324-638)
2. Moslem Period (A.D. 638-1099)
3. Crusader Period (A.D. 1099-1187)
4. Mameluke Period (A.D. 1250-1517)
5. Ottoman-Turk Period (A.D. 1517-1917)
6. British Mandate (A.D. 1917-1948)
7. State of Israel (A.D. 1948–)
IV. Jerusalem in Eschatology
A. Location of the Throne of God's Great King
B. Center of a Cosmic Struggle
C. Perfect and Eternal Dwelling Place of God

I. Names.*–*A. Jerusalem. The name "Jerusalem" has traditionally been interpreted to mean "city of peace," from the component parts (as found, e.g., in the Amarna Tablets) *uru,* "city," and *salim,* "peace." This etymology has been challenged and even rejected by some (e.g., M. Burrows, *IDB,* II, 843). The accuracy of the etymology depends on whether the original name was Hebrew or another language.

The earliest appearance of the name is in the Egyptian Execration Texts of the 12th Dynasty, where the city is named *Aushamem* and its ruler is called Setj-ʿanu. The name appears in the Amarna Letters (14th cent. B.C.) as ^{al}*u-ru-sa-lim* and ^{al}*u-ru-sa-lim*^{ki} (Am.Tab. 287:25, 46; *ANET,* p. 488); ^{al} is a determinative for a city and ^{ki} a postpositive determinative for a place. Early discussions of the Ebla discoveries reported that the name occurred in an Ebla tablet as *urusalima* (*Los Angeles Times,* June 7, 1976). Later reports gave the name as *Salim* (G. Pettinato, *BA*, 39 [1976], p. 46). Pettinato's *Catalogo dei testi cuneiformi di Tell Mardikh-Ebla* (1979) lists neither form, however; *sal-lim*^{ki} and *uə-ru*$_{x}^{ki}$ do appear in tablet 6522 r.IV, but there is no indication in the catalog of their geographical location or their relationship to one another. In Sennacherib's account of his siege of Jerusalem (Taylor Prism) the name occurs as ^{al}*ur-sa-li-im-mu* (or *-ma*). It may be worth noting that the determinative ^{al} is the Sumerian sign uru, meaning "city." It is possible that the original name was something like *^{uru}*sa-lim,* which came to be read as *urusalim,* to which a new determinative was added pleonastically (but see B below).

The suggestion that the name is a Hebrew derivative must also be considered. Burrows traced the first part of the word to the Hebrew root *yrh,* which regularly means "throw, shoot," and in a derived sense "teach." But Burrows appealed to Job 38:6, where the root occurs in the context of laying a cornerstone, and analyzed "Jerusalem" as meaning "foundation of Shalem." He found the same root in the names Jeruel, Jeriel, and Jeriah, which are theophoric names and therefore would be close parallels to "Jerushalem." Further support for this etymology is found in the name Salem (see B below). But the appearance of the name in fourteenth-century texts, or possibly even in eighteenth-century texts, raises the question of how far back Hebrew etymologies can be traced. The names Jeruel, Jeriel, and Jeriah are quite late (only in Chronicles), and therefore are hardly valid for the study of a word that occurs many centuries earlier. The name of the city could, of course, be "proto-Hebrew" or "early Canaanite." If so, the shift of initial *w* to *y* probably had not yet occurred, and the root *yrh* would have been **wry*. This could account for the form *uru* (from **wuru*), found in the Amarna Tablets.

The biblical form *y^{e}rûšālayim,* as vocalized in the perpetual *Q* of the MT, was formerly taken as a dual form and explained as referring to the two parts of the early city, Lower and Upper Jerusalem. It is now generally recognized that the early form of the name was *y^{e}rûšālēm,* as found in the Aramaic of Daniel and Ezra. This form has the support of the Akkadian forms and the Greek of the LXX. The so-called dual ending of the Masoretic vocalization is probably a back-formation, similar to that of *šāmayim* < **šāmēm,* "heaven." The ending *-ê(n),* however, is an oblique dual form in Akkadian, and thus this explanation must not be too carelessly rejected.

The two Greek forms of the name, *Hierosolyma* and *Ieroysalēm,* are somewhat interchangeable (note that both forms occur in Acts 1:4, 8). The LXX, Josephus, Luke, and Paul seem to prefer the second form, but textual variants make such conclusions uncertain. Two Latin forms, *Hierosolym* and *Ierusalem,* are found, generally corresponding to the Greek forms, but again, textual variants complicate the problem.

B. Salem. The city is called "Salem" (Heb. *šālēm,* Gk. *salēm*) in Gen. 14:18 and Ps. 76:2 (MT 3); in the LXX (75:3) the latter is translated *eirḗnē* (cf. also He. 7:1f.). Salem has been taken as an abbreviation of *y^{e}rûšālēm,* but this view has now generally been abandoned. In fact, in spite of the parallelism with "Zion" in Ps. 76:2 (MT 3), the identification of Salem with Jerusalem has been questioned, and other locations have been suggested, such as the Salim of Jn. 3:23 in the Jordan Valley S of Beth-shean, or the Shalem of the ancient versions (Gen. 33:18) not far from Shechem.

Whether "Salem" is to be associated with the deity "Shalem" is a question that needs further study. It is well known that *ś* and *š* have developed from phonetic shifts, and that this was recognized in biblical times in the Shibboleth-Sibboleth password (Jgs. 12:6). But the alternation of *ś/š* is not a haphazard phenomenon that can be called on at will by philologists and commentators to make the equations they would establish (cf. W. S. LaSor, "Semitic Phonemes," Ph.D. diss., Dropsie, 1949; *JQR*, 48 [1957], 161-173). The god *šlm* is found in Ugaritic literature, where the births of Shaḥar and Shalem are mentioned (*UT* 52:53). Shaḥar and Shalem have been described as the morning and evening stars (Heb. *šaḥar* is "dawn" [Ps. 22, title (MT 1)]), and Shalem has been identified as Venus (cf. *IDB*, IV, 304) and as Saturn (*IDB Supp.*, p. 821). The names Solomon and Shulamit have been interpreted as coming from the worship of Shalem. But the initial identification of Salem with Shalem has not been confirmed. The *š* in Ugar. *šlm* and Heb. *šlm* is regularly also *š* in Akkadian (*šalâmu*). This same *š* occurs in the word Salem (Heb. *šālēm*) in Gen. 14:18. But in the Akkadian form *urusalim(mu),* it is *s* and not *š*. Complicating the identification further is the fact that proper nouns were often borrowed after a phonetic shift had occurred and therefore do not reflect that shift. (The Akkadian syllabogram *sa* is also read as *ša*$_{10}$, but this is rare and does not occur with this value in the periods of the Amarna texts or the Assyrian royal inscriptions.)

C. Jebus. In Jgs. 19:10, in what could be a scribal gloss, Jerusalem is identified with Jebus. (The same identification occurs in explanatory phrases in Josh. 18:28; 1 Ch. 11:4.) The Jebusites were one of the tribes or groups included in the larger term "Canaanites," and are regularly listed with other such tribes or groups (cf. Gen. 10:15-18 and many other passages where the various "-ites" are named [e.g., Josh. 3:10]). See III.B below.

D. City of David. With the conquest of Jebus, the name City of David came to be used for Jerusalem (2 S. 5:9; cf. Lk. 2:4, 9). The City of David was but a part of Jerusalem, although the term could be used in synecdoche for Jerusalem (see III.C.2.a below).

E. Zion. "The stronghold of Zion" occurs in connection with the capture of Jebus (2 S. 5:7), and the name Zion became a synonym for the City of David and for the city of Jerusalem. The name does not occur often in historical passages, but it is quite common in poetical and figurative language, and therefore is used with reference to the heavenly Jerusalem (cf. Isa. 60:14; He. 12:22; Rev. 14:1). The term is also applied to the temple and to the people. No satisfactory etymology or explanation of the name has been given. The expression "stronghold of Zion" does not necessarily imply that a portion of Zion was the stronghold; it is more likely that the terms are used in apposition and that Zion itself was the stronghold (see III.C.1.b below).

F. Moriah. In 2 Ch. 3:1 we read that Solomon began to build the house of the Lord "in Jerusalem on Mount Moriah." Josephus identified this with "the very place that Abraham brought his son Isaac, to sacrifice him as a burnt-offering" (*Ant.* vii.13.4 [333]), a belief found also in Jub. 18:13 and in Moslem tradition. The term Moriah occurs in the Bible only in Gen. 22:2, where Abraham is instructed to go to "the land of Moriah" and offer Isaac on "one of the mountains," and in 2 Ch. 3:1; hence there is little biblical basis for the traditions that have grown up about this term. It might be worth noting that the LXX of 2 Ch. 3:1 reads *toú Amoria* (or *Amoreia*), a form found in 2 Esd. 9:1 for "Amorite," suggesting that a variant reading of the Hebrew word is possible.

G. The City. "The city" and several modifications of

the term frequently stand for Jerusalem: "the city," Jer. 32:24; Ezk. 7:23; "the city of God," Ps. 46:4 (MT 5); 87:3; "the city of our God," Ps. 48:1, 8 (MT 2, 9); "the city of the Lord [Yahweh]," Ps. 101:8; Isa. 60:14; "the city of the Lord [Yahweh] of hosts," Ps. 48:8 (MT 9); "the city of righteousness," Isa. 1:26; "the holy city," Isa. 48:2; 52:1; Neh. 11:1, 18; cf. "your holy city," Dnl. 9:24; "the faithful city," Zec. 8:3; "the city of Judah," 2 Ch. 25:28; Babylonian Chronicle (*CCK*, pp. 33, 73). There are also derogatory modifications of the term, such as "the oppressing city," Zeph. 3:1, and "the bloody city," Ezk. 22:2; 24:6, 9.

H. Ariel. "Ariel," *'ᵃrî'ēl,* occurs five times in Isa. 29. The meaning of the term is disputed; some scholars take it to mean "lion of God" (*'ᵃrî,* "lion"), and others "hearth of God," i.e., His home (cf. Ezk. 43:15f., *'ᵃrî'ēl,* "altar-hearth"). R. Youngblood's suggestion that "Ariel" means "city of God" deserves careful consideration ("Ariel, 'City of God,'" in A. I. Katsch and L. Nemoy, eds., *Essays on the Occasion of the Seventieth Anniversary of Dropsie University, 1909-1979* [1980], pp. 457-462).

I. Yahweh Is There. "Yahweh Is There," *YHWH šāmmâ* (Ezk. 48:35), is the name given to the eschatological city (cf. Rev. 21:22; see IV below).

J. New Jerusalem. "New Jerusalem," Gk. *Ierousalēm kainḗn* (Rev. 21:2), is the name given to the city that John saw in his vision of the new heaven and the new earth. It is also called "the above Jerusalem," *hē áno Ierousalēm* (Gal. 4:26) — contrasted with "the now Jerusalem," *tę̄ nýn Ierousalēm* (v. 25) — and "the heavenly Jerusalem," *Ierousalḗm epouraníǭ* (He. 12:22), where it is also called "Mount Zion" and "the city of the living God."

K. Aelia Capitolina. "AELIA CAPITOLINA" is the name given to the city built by the Romans after Jerusalem was destroyed in A.D. 135. See III.J below.

L. El-Quds. El-Quds (pronounced locally *el-ʿuds*) is the common Arabic term today, meaning "the holy (city)." A more classical term with the same meaning is *el-Muqaddes.*

II. Physical Features.–A. *Location.* Jerusalem is situated on the central mountain ridge of Palestine, almost exactly opposite the north tip of the Dead Sea, 58 km. (36 mi.) E of the Mediterranean and 26 km. (16 mi.) W of the Dead Sea (direct measurements). On the Palestine Survey grid the location is 1723.1316 (Dome of the Rock), or 31°46′45″ N Lat. and 35°13′25″ E Long. (dome of the Holy Sepulchre). The city's altitude is between 640 and 770 m. (2100 and 2526 ft.) above sea level. Just N of the city Mt. Scopus (Râs el-Mešârif) rises to about 820 m. (2690 ft.), and just S of the city Jebel Mukabbir (Hill of Evil Counsel) rises to 895 m. (2936 ft.). East of Jerusalem, across the Kidron Valley, the Mt. of Olives reaches an elevation of 818 m. (2684 ft.). West of Jerusalem are heights of 848 m. (2782 ft.) and 842 m. (2762 ft.). In other words, Jerusalem, "to which the tribes go up" (Ps. 122:4), is not the highest point; on the contrary, from whatever direction the city is approached it cannot be seen until one of the surrounding heights is reached. In antiquity it lay just E of the infrequently traveled N-S route and just S of an E-W route of no great importance.

B. Topography. Understanding the defenses of Jerusalem as well as its growth and development requires a thorough knowledge of its peculiar situation. Unfortunately, more than twenty sieges (cf. J. Simons, p. 27) have altered the topography of the city considerably since it was first occupied by King David. This description attempts to picture the situation as it was from 2000 B.C. to the beginning of the Christian era.

The basic area of the city resembles a square with no definite top line. The eastern side is marked by the ravine of the Kidron (Heb. *naḥal qiḏrôn* [2 S. 15:23]; Gk. *kedrōn* [Jn. 18:1]), "the ravine [*cheímarros*] to the east of the city" (1 Macc. 12:37). In the region NE of Jerusalem, beyond the junction of Wâdī ej-Jōz, the Kidron cuts its way from an elevation of about 720 m. (2360 ft.) to about 610 m. (2000 ft.) in a distance of about 1600 m. (1 mi.). The present Kidron (known today as Wâdī Sitti Maryam, farther south as Wâdī Ṭanṭur Farʿûn, then Wâdī Silwān) is 12 m. (39 ft.) higher and 27 m. (89 ft.) farther east than it was in Jebusite times, according to soundings.

The western and southern sides of the square are formed by the Valley of Hinnom, *gê hinnōm* (Josh. 15:8), more often *gê ben hinnōm,* "Valley of the son of Hinnom" or "sons of Hinnom" (also in Josh. 15:8), from which is derived Gk. *géenna,* "Gehenna" (Mt. 23:33). The Valley of Hinnom descends from the northwest, where it is known as Wâdī el-Mês, turns toward the south, where it is known as Wâdī er-Rabâbeh, at an altitude of 750 m. (2362 ft.) above sea level, bends rather sharply toward the east at an altitude of 710 m. (2329 ft.), and then joins the Kidron ravine at the southeastern corner of the city, where they become Wâdī en-Nâr. The rectangular area between the valleys is therefore decidedly marked by these deep ravines on the east and south, and shallower ones on the west. It thus becomes apparent that any attacks on the city would be normally from the north, and any growth of the city had to be toward the north and northwest.

This basic area of the city was further cut by two interior valleys, one running approximately N-S, the other E-W. The former is by far the more significant. Since it is unnamed in Scripture, it has come to be known simply as the Central Valley. Beginning approximately midway between the Hinnom and the Kidron N of what is today known as the Damascus Gate, the Central Valley, to which

Cross section showing the Central Valley between the northwest hill (left) and the northeast hill, the Ḥaram esh-Sherîf (right). On the far right is the Kidron Valley.

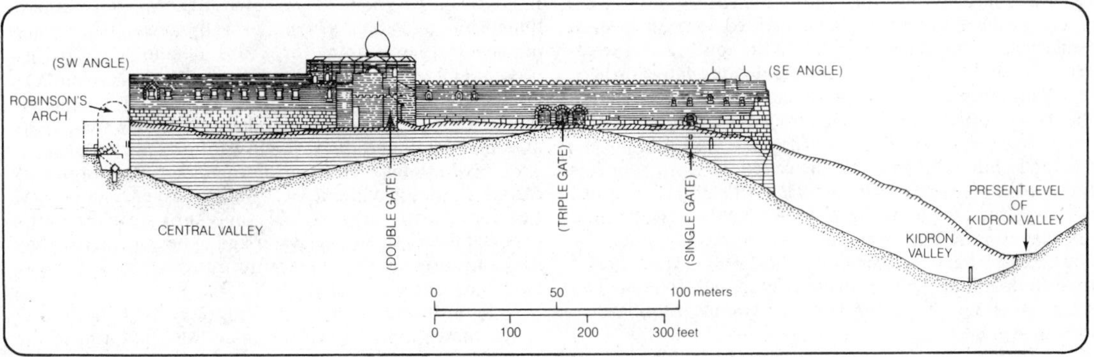

Aerial view of Jerusalem from the south. In the center is the Ḥaram esh-Sherîf (the temple mount). To its left, running through the center of the city, is the Tyropoeon (Central) Valley. To the right of the Ḥaram is the Kidron Valley, which joins the Hinnom Valley just SW of the Ḥaram (Matson Photo Service)

Josephus gave the name "valley of the cheesemakers" (*tṓn tyropoiṓn,* whence Tyropoeon, cf. *BJ* v.4.1 [140]), but more commonly known today as simply *el-Wâd,* cuts a deep gash until it joins the Kidron just before its confluence with the Hinnom. The Central Valley has become filled with rubble as the result of many destructions of the city, so that the present valley bottom (at the southwest corner of the temple mount) is 35 m. (115 ft.) higher than and 30 m. (98 ft.) W of its location prior to the Herodian period.

The east-west valley, which Simons (p. 21) called the "Cross-Valley" (also called the "Transverse Valley"), is a branch of the Tyropoeon Valley, coming from the west about where the Hinnom turns to the south (the modern Citadel and Tower of David), and joining the Central Valley about where the Plaza of the Western Wall is located today (near Wilson's Arch). A similar depression along the same line flows westward to join the Hinnom, so that these two depressions appear to form a division of the basic area into northern and southern quarters.

The basic city, then, can be divided into an eastern (smaller) part, tapering to a point in the south, and a western part, and each of these can be divided into northern and southern parts. Josephus called the southwest hill the "first," on which was the "upper city," which he mistakenly believed to be David's City (*BJ* v.4.1 [137]). His "second" hill or "lower city" he called the Acra, which is David's City (see III.C.1 below; *BJ* v.4.1 [138]). The "third hill" was the temple mount (*BJ* v.4.1 [139]). Josephus did not mention the northwest hill — a point that should be considered when discussing his "third wall." He did refer to a "fourth hill," which he associated with Bezetha (*BJ* v.4.2 [149-151]), the region N of the Ḥaram esh-Sherîf in the modern city.

The northeast hill (the temple mount, Ḥaram esh-Sherîf) rises to an altitude of 744 m. (2441 ft.). Originally it sloped off rather sharply to east and west, but the sides were built up in the Herodian period. It would seem that at one time a depression separated the northeast from the southeast hills, and Josephus indicated that the southeast hill was formerly higher (cf. *Ant.* xiii.6.7 [217]; *BJ* v.4.1 [139]). The southeast hill, often called Ophel, was somewhat broader in the Jebusite period than it is today; destruction of the walls and erosion have cut away the eastern slope. The southwest hill (the Upper City, the southern portion of which is today called Mt. Zion) rose to 768 m. (2519 ft.). The northwestern portion rises gradually from the Central Valley, reaching an elevation of 770 m. (2526 ft.) at the northwestern corner of the present walls. The Old City, within the present walls, occupies the northwest, Bezetha, the Ḥaram, and the northern part of the southwest hills.

From the Hinnom on the west to the Kidron on the east, the basic city is about 750 m. (2460 ft.) across its southern dimension, and about 875 m. (2871 ft.) across its northern dimension, while from "St. Anne's Valley" (N of the present Golden Gate) to the junction of the Kidron and the Hinnom the distance is about 1000 m. (3200 ft.). As already noted, however, the northern boundary was indefinite and continued to move outward as the city grew.

C. Hydrography. A major determining factor in the location of cities in antiquity was the available water supply. For Jerusalem there was only one spring. To meet the needs of the growing city, water had to be collected during the rainy season or brought in by aqueducts and stored in pools and underground cisterns.

1. Spring Gihon. The one spring was the Gihon (1 K. 1:33), known today as ʿAin Umm ed-Darāj ("spring of the

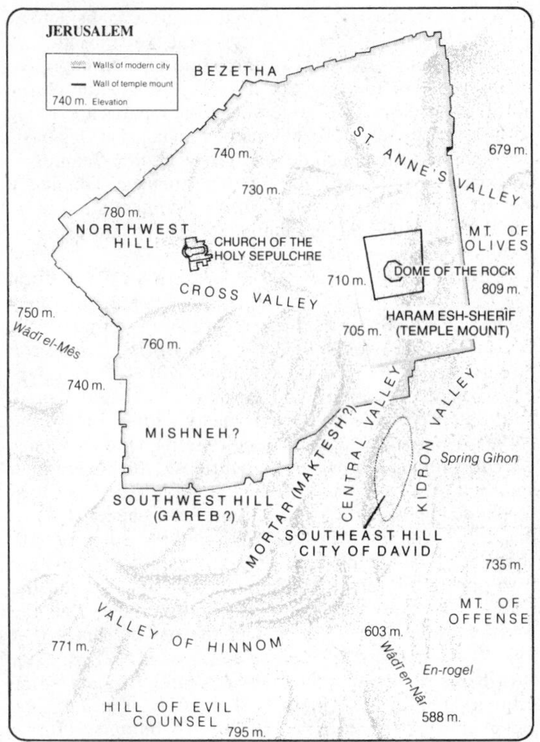

mother of the steps"), ʿAin Sittī Maryam ("spring of our Lady Mary"), and the Virgin's Fountain. It is located in the Kidron Valley about 250 m. (820 ft.) S of the present south wall of the Ḥaram, approximately at the northeastern end of the ancient City of David. "Gihon" very likely comes from the root *gyḥ,* "gush," with the elative ending *-ôn,* hence "the great gusher," so named from the fact that it gushes for a period of about forty minutes, at intervals of six to eight hours, depending on the season. Its flow is about 1200 cu. m. (42,400 cu. ft. = 317,000 U. S. gals.), less in the dry season. As a result, some provision had to be made to conserve or use the water as it became available. To that end aqueducts were built, and the water from them was used for watering gardens or collected in a pool (see III.C.2.g; D.2.f below). Because of the peculiar gushing property of the Gihon it was formerly incorrectly identified as the pool of Bethesda (cf. Jn. 5:2). The pool of Bethesda has been excavated near the Church of St. Anne.

2. En-rogel. Because of its name (*ʿên* = "spring"), EN-ROGEL (Josh. 15:7) was formerly thought to be a second source of water for Jerusalem. It is generally identified with Bîr Ayyûb ("Job's well" — a *bîr* is not a spring), on the right bank of Wâdī en-Nâr, about 210 m. (690 ft.) beyond the confluence of the Kidron and the Hinnom. The source of the water is at the bottom of a shaft 30 m. (100 ft.) deep. According to one report, this source had been lost and was rediscovered by the Crusaders in A.D. 1184, when they cleared the tunnel. It is possible that the original En-rogel was covered as the result of an earthquake (cf. Josephus *Ant.* ix.10.4 [225], who took *Erōgē* to mean En-rogel). Whether or not the present well is the location of the ancient "spring," En-rogel was certainly in this vicinity (Josh. 15:7f.). Modern studies in the area suggest that the water that supplies Gihon is carried by the hard limestone strata to feed En-rogel also.

3. Jackal's Well. Also known as the Dragon's Well (*ʿên hattannîn,* Neh. 2:13), the Jackal's Well has not been identified, but the suggestion of G. A. Smith (I, ch. 4) that it may have been formed by an earthquake around the time of Nehemiah and later dried up offers one possibility. The location is in the Valley of Hinnom between the Valley Gate and the Dung Gate, i.e., S of the southwest hill. There is no indication that this was a significant source of water in any other period of the city's history (see III.F.2.b below).

D. Geology. The watershed of the region is principally the product of the Cretaceous period. To the west it is Turonian, to the east Senonian, but the immediate vicinity of Jerusalem is a Cenomanian outcropping, the result, according to Baly (*GB* [2nd ed. 1974], p. 36), of erosion caused by the rains from the west. This Cenomanian limestone is of major importance for the history and development of the city. It is found in regular strata, of which three may be mentioned.

The superior mizzi (Arab. *mizzi ḥelû,* "sweet mizzi"), found in a stratum 21 m. (70 ft.) or more thick, is hard, reddish grey, fine-grained with bands of flint, and capable of taking a polish. It is well adapted for stairs, cornices, and the framing of doors and windows. The Sakhra or Stone under the Dome of the Rock is an outcropping of *mizzi ḥelû.*

Royal mizzi (*mizzi melekeh*) is found in a stratum often 11 m. (35 ft.) thick, and is characterized by its softness while in the ground, and its gradual hardening when it is exposed to the air. It is therefore easy to cut and shape. A large number of caverns, cisterns, tombs, and several aqueducts are cut into this rock. The "royal caverns" (Josephus *BJ* v.4.2 [147]), popularly called Solomon's Quarries, are cut in the royal mizzi stratum.

Jewish mizzi (*mizzi yahûdi*) is hard and highly valued as a building material, but it is difficult to work. Red mizzi (*mizzi ʾaḥmâr*), a variety of *mizzi yahûdi* (which is yellowish grey, sometimes described as flame color), is found in red, pink, and shades of brown, takes a polish, and is known locally as "marble." This stratum forms a deep layer under the entire city and surfaces only in the Kidron Valley. Water from the rains percolate into the ground and are held by this stratum, which drains them toward the Kidron. The water of the Spring Gihon is probably a result of the *mizzi yahûdi* stratum (*GP,* I, 181-84).

E. Climate. Jerusalem has the same general climate as the rest of Palestine, namely, that dominated by the Etesian winds, resulting in a two-season year, the rainy season ("winter") and the dry season ("summer"). However, since Jerusalem is situated at an altitude of about 750 m. (2460 ft.), almost astride the central mountain range, its weather is somewhat different from either that of the western slopes or that of the Jordan Valley (Ghor).

The wind is prevailingly from the west: from the northwest in the rainy season and from the southwest in the dry season. The temperature therefore is generally moderate, 8°-14°C (46°-56°F) in January, 18°-28°C (64°-82°F) in June and September, 19°-29°C (66°-84°F) in July, and 20°-30°C (68°-86°F) in August. Summer days are warm, but a cool breeze usually springs up in the late afternoon, and the evenings are cool. When the wind shifts to the southeast (the khamsîn or sirocco), the air becomes sultry, and the temperature may climb to 36°C (98°F) and has been known to reach 40°C (104°F). This usually occurs in May and September-October. The day in Jerusalem at its longest is 14 hours 10 minutes, and at its shortest, 9 hours 50 minutes.

Precipitation at Jerusalem averages 63 cm. (25 in.) annually, with an average of fifty-seven days of rain, including six days of steady rain. The rainy season is divided into three parts: (1) the "early rain" (*yôreh,* Dt. 11:14; Jer. 5:25), which, in a good year, begins around Sukkoth (Tabernacles, 15 Tishri), approximately the beginning of October; (2) the "rain in its season" (*māṭār beʿittô,* Ex. 9:33; 1 K. 8:33), usually coming in Kislev (late November or early December) and continuing into Nisan; and (3) the "latter rain" (*malqôš,* Hos. 6:3; Jer. 5:24), which normally comes in Nisan (late March or April) and may extend to about fifteen days before Shabûʿôt (Pentecost, i.e., around the middle of May). There is an average of 5 cm. (2 in.) or more in January-March, 2 cm. (¾ in.) or less in April-May and September-October, and none in June-August. In January the temperature may drop below freezing, possibly bringing snow (snow falls about once in five years). This is similar to the climate of the southern California coastal region, e.g., Los Angeles.

F. Sources of Information. The Bible is a major source of information for the biblical period, even though it contains no systematic presentation of the data, with the sole exception of Nehemiah's observations. Details in Sirach and in the two books of Maccabees must be added to the material in the Hebrew Bible, and additional details can be added from the Greek Bible (both Testaments).

Josephus must be considered a primary source, in spite of constant denigration of his historical reliability, for he lived in Jerusalem in the 1st cent. A.D., and when he speaks as an eyewitness (particularly in *BJ*) his witness should not be too quickly dismissed. Other details may be picked up from the Mishnah (completed *ca.* A.D. 200) and the Jerusalem and Babylonian Talmuds (to *ca.* A.D. 500), from visitors such as the Pilgrim of Bordeaux (early 4th cent. A.D.), Eusebius (*ca.* 260-340), Chrysostom (A.D. 354-407), and from the Madeba mosaic map (6th cent. A.D.). All such data must be carefully checked whenever possible, because measurements, locations, local names, etc., are often inaccurate or suspect.

For a survey of modern exploration and excavation, cf. Simons, pp. 27-34; B. Mazar, pp. 11-39; Yadin, pp. 131, 133, 135, 137; *see also* ARCHEOLOGY OF PALESTINE AND SYRIA.

III. History of Jerusalem.–A. Before 2000 B.C. At the present, scholars are entirely dependent on archeological discoveries for the earlier history of Jerusalem. If reports on the Ebla tablets from Tell Mardikh are confirmed by the publication of the pertinent texts, this may be somewhat altered.

In 1877 Germer-Durand found hand axes in the plain of el-Buqeiʿa, SW of the city. In 1933 an entire settlement dated to the Acheulo-Levalloisian culture was found. It therefore appears that there was a Paleolithic settlement in the Jerusalem area (I. Anati, *Palestine Before the Hebrews* [1963], p. 69; Anati preferred to call the artifacts Early Bifacial; cf. M. Stekelis, *JPOS,* 21 [1947], 80-87). Mesolithic sites have also been found in the region around Jerusalem (Anati, p. 146).

The earliest settlement in Jerusalem, by general consensus, was on the southeast hill, which had steep slopes on both sides (the Kidron and the Central valleys) for defense, and the necessary spring (Gihon) for water supply. Objects found in rock-cut tombs included pottery that K. Kenyon classified as Proto-Urban, more commonly called late Chalcolithic. The development of the city may be connected with the advent of newcomers, probably Semites, *ca.* 3300 B.C., but just who the previous inhabitants were is still not clear (cf. *CAH,* I/2 [3rd ed. 1971], 233f.; R. de Vaux, *Early History of Israel* [Eng. tr. 1978], p. 52, simply called them "Canaanites"). The suggestion has been made that they were HORITES (Hivites) or Hittites, but these terms are rather loosely used. Attempts to equate the Horites with the HURRIANS and the Hittites of Genesis with the Hittites of Anatolia are unsatisfactory, and the rendering of the terms in the versions further complicates the problem. In the Table of Nations (Gen. 10:15-18), Heth (usually taken as the progenitor of the Hittites by biblical interpreters) and the Hivites are, along with the Jebusites, descendants of Canaan. On this basis we would have to conclude that they were non-Semites — but the Canaanites spoke a Semitic language! Obviously no one is yet in a position to make definitive statements about either the earlier inhabitants or the more recent invaders.

B. Between 2000 and 1000 B.C. There was a cultural break between what J. H. Iliffe has called the Intermediate Early Bronze-Middle Bronze (the former M.B. IA) and Middle Bronze I (formerly M.B. IIB), which can be dated *ca.* 1850 B.C. (cf. *CAH,* II/1 [1973], 77-116). Egyptian Execration Texts found in 1926, of about the same date (late 12th or early 13th Dynasty), may contain the earliest references to Jerusalem. The names of enemies were inscribed on bowls or on figurines, which were then smashed. According to popular superstition, the smashing would accomplish the destruction of the enemy. One of these has the following inscription: "the ruler of Aushamem, Iyqa-ʿammu, and all the retainers(?) who are with him; the ruler of Aushamem, Setj-ʿanu, and all the retainers who are with him. . . ." On another, "all the Asiatics" are mentioned, and in the list of names that follows, "Aushamem" is given again (cf. *ANET,* p. 329). "Aushamem" is generally taken to mean Jerusalem, some scholars reading the hieroglyphic *3w.w* as *uru.* Since Egyptian has no sign for *l* (*m* sometimes, but more often *n* or *r,* being used for *l*), *s3.m.m* could be read as *šāmēm* (=*sālēm*). But the reading is problematic. The names Iyqa-ʿammu and Setj-ʿanu appear to be a mixture of non-Semitic and Semitic elements. B. Mazar read these names as "Yqrʿm" and "Shasʿan" and classified them as "West Semitic" (*Mountain,* p. 45).

Although the date of Abraham is far from settled, the account in Gen. 14:18-20 is relevant here. Kings invaded the cities of the plain (vv. 1-12) and captured Lot, who was rescued by Abram (Abraham). The mysterious Melchizedek king of Salem blessed Abram, and Abram gave him "a tenth of everything" (vv. 17-20). In He. 7:2 "king of Salem" is interpreted to mean "king of peace." (It does no violence to the doctrine of inspiration to allow a popular etymology to become a vehicle of divine revelation, and even the king's name [*Malkî ṣeḏeq,* "my king is Sadqu"] is given the meaning "king of righteousness.") It was previously noted that "Salem" has been considered a synonym of Jerusalem (see I.B above), but this is far from certain. The location of Salem is given in Gen. 14:17f. as near "the Valley of Shaveh (that is, the King's Valley)," and in 2 S. 18:18 the King's Valley is near Jerusalem. But it is well known that over a period of time place names are transferred from one location to another (e.g., Mt. Olympus, which was originally in Asia Minor, was transferred to northern Greece).

In Gen. 22:2, Yahweh tells Abraham to take Isaac to "the land of Moriah" and sacrifice him "upon one of the mountains." In 2 Ch. 3:1 the location of Solomon's temple is given as "in Jerusalem on Mount Moriah" (see I.F above).

We move toward firm historical ground with the references to Jerusalem in the Amarna Tablets (14th cent. B.C.). Abdu-Ḫeba of Jerusalem wrote a number of letters (six of which are included in the published material) to the pharaoh of Egypt requesting aid against his enemies, who were being supplied by Gazri (Gezer), Ašqaluna (Ashkelon), and Lakisi (Lachish). Abdu-Ḫeba refers to his city as

Plate 23. Mycenaean gold death mask (University Museum, University of Pennsylvania; picture Rosenthal Art Slides)

Plate 24. Perseus slays the Gorgon-headed Medusa with Athena's help. Red-figured, black-glazed Attic vase (*ca.* 450-440 B.C.) attributed to Polygnotos (Metropolitan Museum of Art)

Plate 25. Relief of two sphinxes from Achaemenian Susa (5th-4th cents. B.C.) (Louvre; picture Rosenthal Art Slides)

Plate 26. Reconstruction of the throne room of the pharaoh Merneptah (*ca.* 1227-1217 B.C.) (University Museum, University of Pennsylvania; picture W. S. LaSor)

Plate 28. Lens-shaped flask, 10.1 cm. (3.94 in.) tall, from the 18th Egyptian Dynasty (1400-1360 B.C.) (Corning Museum of Glass)

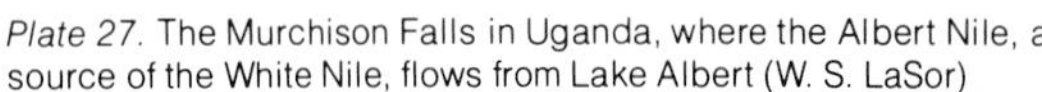

Plate 27. The Murchison Falls in Uganda, where the Albert Nile, a source of the White Nile, flows from Lake Albert (W. S. LaSor)

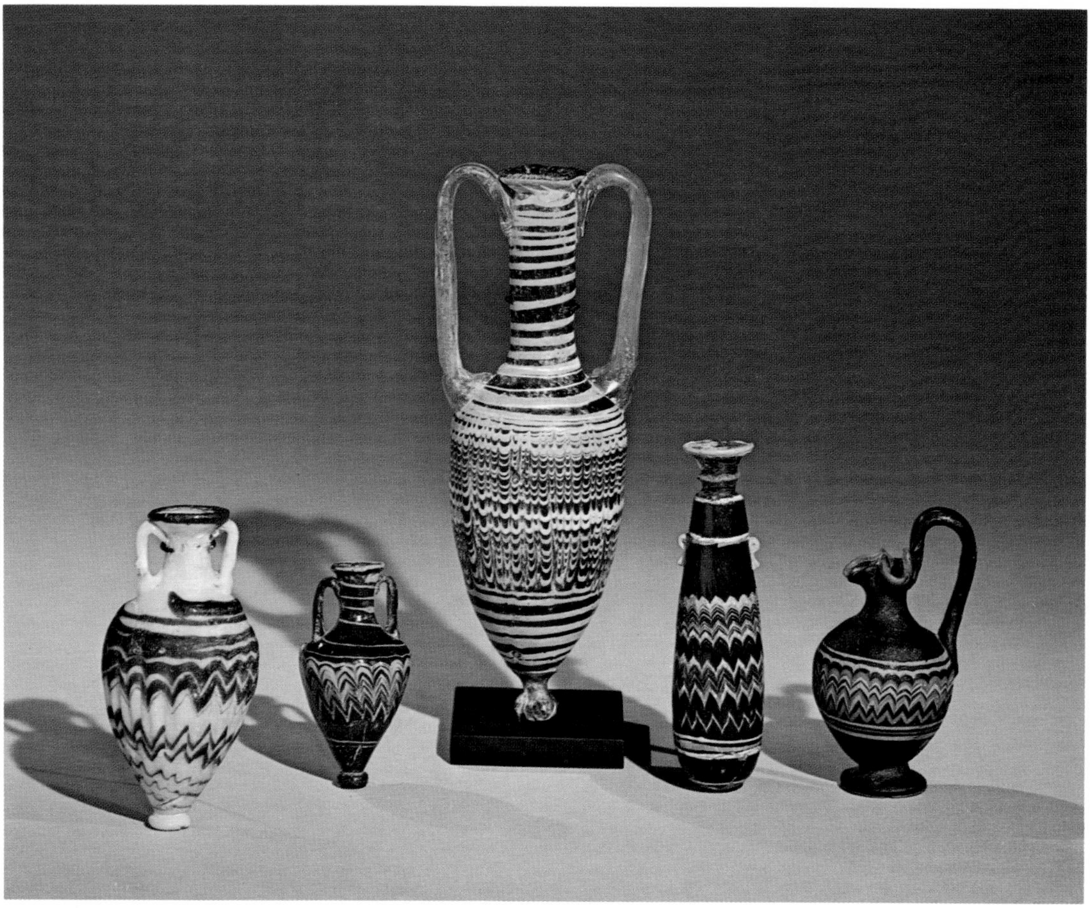

Plate 29. Core-formed vessels from the eastern Mediterranean area (5th-1st cents. B.C.) (Corning Museum of Glass)

Plate 30. Blown-glass Roman tableware from a tomb (1st cent. A.D.) (Corning Museum of Glass)

Plate 31. Nativity relief, carved by an unknown artist *ca.* A.D. 1500, from the Netherlands (Bode Museum, Staatliche Museen, Berlin)

Plate 32. Giotto di Bondone, The Marriage at Cana. Fresco (*ca.* A.D. 1305) in the Arena Chapel, Padua, Italy (Museo Civico, Padua)

Plate 33. Giotto di Bondone, Christ's Washing of the Feet. Fresco (*ca.* A.D. 1305) in the Arena Chapel, Padua, Italy (Museo Civico, Padua)

Plate 34. The Flagellation of Christ. Silk and metal thread on canvas. Italy, mid-14th cent. A.D.

Plate 35. Mosaic of Jerusalem (4th cent. A.D.) in the Church of St. Pudentiana, Rome. Behind the enthroned Christ is Calvary and a jeweled cross (G. Nalbandian)

Plate 36. Georges Roualt, *Ecce Homo* ("Behold the man" — the humiliated Christ), *ca.* A.D. 1939 (Staatsgalerie, Stuttgart; picture Rosenthal Art Slides)

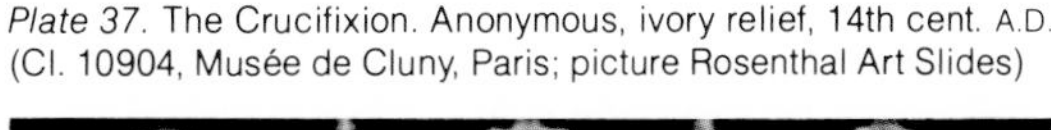

Plate 37. The Crucifixion. Anonymous, ivory relief, 14th cent. A.D. (Cl. 10904, Musée de Cluny, Paris; picture Rosenthal Art Slides)

Plate 38. Pentecost. Panel from the Amiens Altarpiece (A.D. 1480) by the Master of Amiens (Art Institute, Chicago)

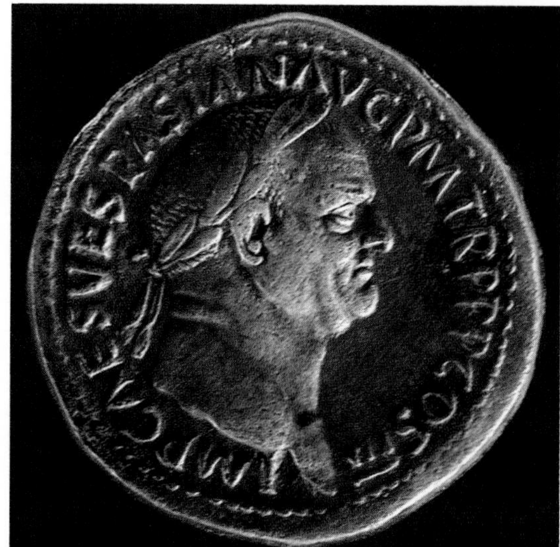

Plate 39. Coin of Vespasian wearing a victory wreath. He was emperor when his son Titus captured Jerusalem in A.D. 70 (G. Nalbandian)

Plate 40. Entrance to the Church of the Holy Sepulchre, Jerusalem, built on the traditional site of Golgotha (W. S. LaSor)

Plate 41. Silver shekels struck in Jerusalem in "Year 3" (left) and "Year 5" of the Jewish revolt, *ca.* A.D. 68 and 70, respectively (G. Nalbandian)

Plate 42. Olive trees in the traditional garden of Gethsemane (W. S. LaSor)

Plate 43. View from the southwest of part of the Jerusalem Temple Model. Visible above the wall surrounding the temple mount are the temple (upper left) and the royal stoa (upper right). The Central (Tyropoeon) Valley runs below the Western (Wailing) Wall (upper left) and next to the hippodrome (right center) (W. S. LaSor)

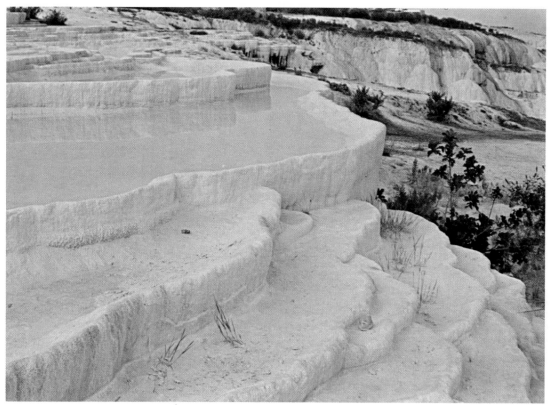

Plate 44. Calcareous basins with ribbed rims from the mineral deposits at Pamukkale, near Hierapolis in Anatolia (L. T. Geraty)

Plate 45. The upper Euphrates River at Kale, between Malatya and Elazis in Anatolia (D. Baly)

Plate 46. Ağri Dağ in eastern Turkey, the highest peak of the Ararat range and the traditional landing place of Noah's ark (W. S. LaSor)

mat ^{al}*u-ru-sa-lim,* "the land of (city) Jerusalem" (Am.Tab. 287:25). The name Jerusalem occurs also in lines 46, 61, and 63 of the same tablet, written *mat* ^{al}*u-ru-sa-lim*^{ki}, *mat u-ru-sa-lim*^{ki}, and *matât* (pl. "lands") ^{al}*u-ru-sa-lim*^{ki}. The variants are of little consequence. The name is found also in Am.Tab. 289:14, 29 and in 290:15 where it occurs as *âl mat u-ru-sa-lim*^{ki}, "a city of the land of Jerusalem." (See I.A above.)

The name Abdu-Ḫeba is written with a logogram meaning "servant," and syllabograms for *ḫe* and *ba*. The logogram is often given the value ARAD, based on the Akkadian value; the Sumerian value, according to bilingual lists, may have been arda, erum, erad, or arad (*CAD,* I/2, 243; R. Labat, *Manuel d'épigraphie akkadienne* [1948], reads ÈR, ÈRI, ERUM). The rendering "Abdu-Ḫeba" presupposes that the Canaanite or West Semitic value was used at Jerusalem; many scholars have taken up the practice of leaving the question open by writing the name as ARAD-Ḫeba, as W. F. Albright suggested (cf. *JBL,* 45 [1924], 384; he read the name as ARAD-Gepa, thus inserting a second a priori while removing the first). The second sign can be read either *ḫi* or *ḫe,* and the third can be read *ba* or *pá*. The rendering Ḫeba (Ḫepa, Khepa) assumes (quite reasonably) that the name is theophoric, the deity being the Hurrian goddess Ḫebat. As a matter of fact, the whole name could be read as (Hittite) Puti-ḫeba, "servant of Ḫebat." Several scholars have pointed out that the expression "land of the city of" (reading *al* as "city" and not as a determinative) is a Hittite expression.

Abdu-Ḫeba (or Puti-Ḫeba) was king of the city-state of Jerusalem, although he does not call himself by that title. In some other Amarna Letters the authors slip (perhaps deliberately) and call themselves "king." Thus the ruler of Hazor opens his letter with the words "thus says the king of Hazor" (*šar* ^{al}*ḫa-zu-ri*^{ki}, Am.Tab. 227:3). The official title of these kings, who reigned under Egyptian protection, was *awêlu,* "freeman" or *ḫaziânu,* "inspector, overseer." Abdu-Ḫeba in one letter says, "I am not an inspector; I am only a petty-officer [^{awel}*ú-e-ú*] to the king my lord" (Am.Tab. 288:9f.). The term *ú-e-ú* is perhaps an Egyptian term (cf. Egyp. *wʿw,* "soldier"). He recognizes that the king of Egypt has given him the throne of Jerusalem when he says, "I said, 'Not my father and not my mother established me in this place'" (Am.Tab. 286:9-11), but it appears that he had indeed inherited the throne when he goes on to say, "The strong hand of the king has caused me to enter unto the house of my father," i.e., the palace (Am.Tab. 286:12f.).

From a study of the Amarna Letters the following picture emerges. Egypt had long maintained hegemony over Palestine, with administrative centers at Gaza and Joppa. There were petty kings over the several city-states, all under Egyptian control. But Egypt had declined in strength, the Hittites and the Mitanni were having their own problems, and a group called the Ḫa-BI-ri was causing trouble (BI can be read either *bi* or *pí*; to avoid prejudging the value, *Ḫa-BI-ri* will be used). The petty kings were slandering one another. Abdu-Ḫeba complains to Pharaoh that Lab'aya and his sons gave [aid] to the Ḫa-BI-ri (Am.Tab. 289:24). Milkili of Gazri (Gezer) and Lab'aya of Šikmi (Shechem) are often accused (cf. Am.Tab. 287:29-31), but so is Šuwardata of Ki-el-te (cf. Heb. *qeʿîlâ,* near Hebron) (Am.Tab. 290:6f.). On the other hand, Šuwardata writes to Pharaoh, "Verily Abdu-Ḫeba is another Labaya and he takes our cities" (Am.Tab. 280:33-35). Ašqaluna (Ashkelon) and Lakisi (Lachish), along with Gezer, have given food, oil, etc., to the Ḫa-BI-ri (Am.Tab. 287:14f.). Abdu-Ḫeba is asking for "archers," probably a general term for infantry, much as "cavalry" is still used for tank corps.

Because some works still equate the Habiru (Hapiru, ʿApiru) with the Hebrews and the conquest of Canaan (*see* HABIRU), it is necessary to note several facts in connection with the history of Jerusalem. The ideogram SA.GAZ — the pronunciation of which is unknown, but which in the Amarna Letters is equated with the ḫa-BI-ri — has a long history in cuneiform records. In Sumerian-Akkadian bilingual lexical lists, specifically ḪA.ra = *ḫubullu* II.330 (cf. *CAD,* VI, 13), SA.GAZ is translated as *ḫab-ba-tum,* "robber." The term SA.GAZ is found ten or eleven centuries before the Amarna Letters. The equation of SA.GAZ with *ʿapiru* is based on parallel cuneiform alphabetic and syllabic lists of towns found at Ugarit, where URU *ḫal-bi* LU.SA.GAZ ("city Aleppo of the SA.GAZ," probably meaning the SA.GAZ quarter of Aleppo) is parallel with *ḫlb ʿprm* ("Aleppo of the ʿApiru"; cf. C. Virolleaud, *Syria,* 21 [1940], 143; Nougayrol in J. Bottéro, ed., *Le Problème des Ḫabiru* [1954], p. 178). This equation proves, according to some scholars, that Akkadian *ḫ* is found in Northwest Semitic as ʿ— but this is not true. I have shown, with many illustrations, that the *ayin* and the *ghayin* phonemes occur in Akkadian as *aleph,* frequently influencing a vocalic shift of *a* to *e* in the words in which they occur. The exception, which could hold true here, is in foreign words which were borrowed after the phonetic shift had taken place ("Semitic Phonemes," Ph.D. diss., Dropsie, 1949). The suggestion that *ʿapiru* is derived from the root for dust and means something like "dusty ones" (cf. W. F. Albright, *Yahweh and the Gods of Canaan* [1969], pp. 73-78) presents another difficulty that seems to have gone unrecognized. The word occurs in Akkadian as *epêru* and derived forms (all spelled with *aleph,* not *ḫ*; the *e*-vowel indicates an original *ḥ,* ʿ, or *ǵ,*), and therefore it is not to be equated with Akk. *ḫa-BI-ru* (cf. *CAD,* IV, 184ff.). The same is true of the attempt to equate *ḫa-BI-ru* with *epêru,* "provide food" (*CAD,* IV, 190, 238). Albright's suggestion that *ʿapiru* shifted to *ʿabiru* (cf. *Yahweh and the Gods of Canaan,* p. 86 n. 84) will not stand up under scientific investigation of the phonetic shift of Semitic phonemes. The whole problem of the relationship of SA.GAZ-*ḫa-BI-ru-ʿapiru*-Hebrews still needs refining, but there seems to be little justification for trying to make the ḫa BI-ru of the Amarna Letters the Hebrews of the conquest of Canaan.

At a date not definitely determined the Israelites invaded Canaan under the leadership of Joshua. Adonizedek king of Jerusalem led a federation of five Amorite kings against the Gibeonites (Josh. 10:1, 3-5). The Gibeonites, who by a ruse had involved Joshua in a mutual-assistance pact (9:3-15), called on him for aid against the Amorites. Joshua defeated the Amorites in the valley of Aijalon, and the five kings were slain (10:26). Some scholars have thought that the account of the battle with Adonibezek (cf. Jgs. 1:4-7) is another version of the one recorded in Joshua. F.-M. Abel (*GP,* II, 24) and J. Simons (*GTTOT,* § 511), however, located Bezek much farther north. Jgs. 1:7f. locates the death of Adoni-bezek at Jerusalem and continues with an account of the capture and burning of Jerusalem. The Jebusites (the inhabitants of Jerusalem), however, were not driven out (Josh. 16:63).

In the tribal allotments, the portion given to Judah included En-rogel and the Valley of the son of Hinnom as boundary marks, but the mention of "the southern shoulder of the Jebusite" (Josh. 15:8) suggests that Judah's border did not include the southeast hill. Later, when the conquests are summarized, it is specifically stated that Judah could not drive out the Jebusites (15:63). The portion of the tribe of Benjamin seems to have followed the same boundaries as that of Judah, which suggests that the portion of the region that did not belong to Judah, namely, that E of the boundary line, was the lot of Benjamin (18:16). The cities of Benjamin included Jebus/Jerusalem (v. 28).

Obviously these accounts present a few problems, which scholars have attempted to solve by various means. According to one view, the Israelite tribes invaded Canaan twice, earlier when the Joseph tribes entered the land (probably from the north) and later under Joshua, or earlier under Joshua and later under Moses (cf. W. F. Albright, *BASOR*, 74 [Apr. 1939], 11-23). According to yet another view, only some of the Israelites went into Egypt, perhaps in the Amarna age, and returned under Moses (cf. H. H. Rowley, *From Joseph to Joshua* [1950], pp. 109-163). The variations are almost innumerable. The problem of the apportionment among the tribes and the possession of Jerusalem is a part of a larger problem: was the Benjamin allotment earlier than the Judah allotment? Was Jerusalem captured? What was the name of the king of Jerusalem — Adoni-zedek or Adoni-bezek? A solution that satisfies everyone and handles all the problems may never be found in this age. But two facts stand out: the Jebusites were an enclave in Israel (cf. Josh. 15:53; Jgs. 3:5), and Jebus was not taken until David took it (2 S. 5:6-9).

It is possible, as Simons observed (p. 245), that the geography of Jerusalem yields a clue to the answer. The southeast hill, standing on steep slopes above the Kidron and Central valleys, was fortified in the early 2nd millennium, shafts and tunnels were drilled to maintain the supply of water from the Gihon spring, and the first aqueduct was probably built at that time (cf. K. Kenyon, *Jerusalem*, ch. II). As we shall see, this was "the stronghold of Zion" (2 S. 5:6), which David captured only with great difficulty. Was this the impregnable fortress that the Jebusites were able to hold, even though the surrounding parts of Jerusalem, particularly the southwest hill, fell to the Israelites?

C. Israelite Monarchy. 1. David. In the eighth year of his reign, David moved against the Jebusites. They were confident that their city was impregnable (2 S. 5:6), but David was apparently aware of a chink in their armor, the *ṣinnôr*. (The expression "to attack the lame and the blind" [v. 8] must be taken as a bit of sarcasm, turning the Jebusites' own taunt back on them; obviously David was interested not in attacking the lame and blind but rather the defenders of the city.)

a. Ṣinnôr. The meaning of *ṣinnôr* in 2 S. 5:8 is uncertain. The LXX translators apparently did not understand the word, for they translated it by *en paraxiphídi*, "with a dagger, dirk," which makes little sense. W. F. Albright suggested "hooks," i.e., using a device to scale the walls (*JPOS*, 2 [1922], 286-290). In Ps. 42:7 (MT 8), what appears to be the plural of the same word is translated "cataracts" (RSV), "waterspouts," or "sluices." In Josephus's account, the Davidic forces capture the Lower City first, and then David offers rewards to those who can take the citadel by climbing up from the valley beneath (*Ant.* vii.3.1 [63]). English versions translate *ṣinnôr* as "water shaft" (RSV, NIV), "water tunnel" (NASB), "grappling-iron" (NEB), "gutters of the roofs" (Knox), etc.

But as Simons pointed out (pp. 171f.; cf. S. R. Driver, *Notes on the Hebrew Text and the Topography of the Books of Samuel* [2nd ed. 1913], p. 259), the basic problem is not the meaning of *ṣinnôr*, but the force of *nāgaʿ b-*. With this preposition, the verb usually means "reach, touch, arrive at" (cf. BDB, p. 619). The *ṣinnôr*, then, is not a weapon or an instrument, but a goal. Mazar may give us the clue, although it appears that he missed the force of the verb. He pointed out that climbing up the shaft, which had been dug inside the walls for the purpose of reaching Spring Gihon, would have been impossible and unnecessary. The shaft led to a tunnel, and the tunnel brought the water from the spring (*Mountain*, pp. 43, 168f.; for a modern study of "Warren's Shaft," discovered 1867-1870, see K. Kenyon, *Jerusalem*, pp. 19-22). Now, if a person or a small force could get through the tunnel and reach the "shaft" (*ṣinnôr*), the water supply would be cut off and the city would have to surrender. Mazar's solution, however, is somewhat different. He translated and interpreted the passage as "'and he struck (and damaged)' the horizontal conduit which led the water of the spring below to the mouth of the spring shaft" (*Mountain*, p. 168). In the account in 1 Ch. 11:4-6, where the *ṣinnôr* is not mentioned, Joab is the first to achieve the goal and is made commander-in-chief.

b. Zion. Having taken the city, David dwelt in the "stronghold of Zion" (*mᵉṣuḏaṯ ṣîyôn*, 1 Ch. 11:5; simply "the stronghold" in 2 S. 5:8), and called it "the city of David." The etymology of *ṣîyôn*, "Zion," is uncertain. If the word is Semitic, its meaning may be related to Arab. *ṣahî*, "ascend to the top," *ṣuhhay*, "tower, or the top of a mountain." But it has been suggested that the word is Hurrian, related to *šeya*, "river, brook," and that "the stronghold of the river" would then refer to the location at Spring Gihon. Neither suggestion is convincing, and "the stronghold of Zion" may be an appositional genitive meaning "the stronghold Zion," if "Zion" is taken as the Jebusite name of the place. Whatever the etymology of the word, "Zion" came to be synonymous with "City of David," and developed into a term for the people of God and for the idealized city to be established in an age to come (see IV below).

c. Millo. "David built the city round about from the Millo inward" (2 S. 5:9). The exact meaning is not clear, and the word translated "inward" (*wāḇaytâ*), although being used in this sense, literally means "toward the house." The expression (lit. tr.) "round about, from the Millo and inward" gives the impression of building from the outside toward the inner part, suggesting that the Millo was something on the outer part. The root of the word *millô'* conveys the meaning "be full," in the piel "fill," and the word may mean "that which fills." K. Kenyon understood the word to mean "tower," so named because it was solid, i.e., constructed of stone and filled with earth (*HDB* [rev. one-vol. ed. 1963], p. 473; cf. Jgs. 9:6, located near Shechem). Mazar thought that the Millo may have been "the terraces on the eastern slope of the southeastern spur, forming supporting walls for the structures above" (in *Jerusalem Revealed*, p. 6). It is not stated that David "built" the Millo; rather, both 2 S. 5:9 and 1 Ch. 11:8 give the site as a landmark. It is clearly stated, however, that Solomon built the Millo (1 K. 9:15, 24; 11:27; 2 K. 12:20 [MT 21]); hence we could take the reference in David's time as proleptic, a use of the name by which it was later known. 1 K. 11:27, "Solomon built the Millo, and closed up the breach of the city of David his father," seems to imply that David had left a breach (in the wall? — hardly likely!) and that the Millo filled this breach.

A suggestion made in various forms by several scholars, particularly by L.-H. Vincent (*Jérusalem antique*, pp. 172ff.), is that the Millo was a fill in the low area between the southeast hill (David's citadel) and what later became the south wall of the temple mount. The view has gained very little support — but it would be the kind of project that could be "built" by David, further "built" (or filled) by Solomon, and still further strengthened by Hezekiah (cf. 2 Ch. 32:5).

Two or three points should be emphasized. (1) The word *millô'* is regularly translated in LXX by *ákra*, "citadel." While this equivalence is inconclusive because of the length of time between the use of the word in the Hebrew Scriptures and the translation into Greek, it may preserve an ancient understanding of the word. (2) The word *millô'* occurs only in the earlier writings (and Chronicles, but presumably the Chronicler was using an earlier account) and is replaced in later writings by the word *'ōpel* (Ophel), which also is translated "citadel" (see III.F.2.t below). (3) The term, used frequently and without further explanation, must have been thoroughly familiar at the time of writing and thus cannot be much later than the monarchy. See III.C.2.e; III.D.5.s below.

d. Cult Center. David not only made Jebus his capital, but he also proceeded to make it the cultic center of the nation. First he moved the ark to Jerusalem (2 S. 6:15), locating it in a tent. Then he set about collecting the materials to build a temple (lit. "house"). Just when this idea first came to him is not clear, and the account in 2 S. 7 does not give many details. The passage in 1 Ch. 22 is much more detailed, but scholars often question its reliability and suggest that the Chronicler was influenced by a desire to make David rather than Solomon the originator of the plans. Josephus went still farther than Chronicles by giving elaborate details of the amounts of materials collected by David (*Ant.* vii.14.1 [335]).

The selection of the temple site seems to have come late in David's reign, following his census of the nation (2 S. 24). The prophet Gad instructed David to build an altar to Yahweh on the threshing floor of Araunah the Jebusite (24:16; in 1 Ch. 21:15 the name is given as Ornan). We may assume that he purchased the threshing floor of Araunah (Ornan) some time prior to his decision to build a temple, since it was to be the place of an altar (2 S. 24:18). Araunah is called "the king" (*'ᵃrawnâ hammélek̲*) in the MT of 2 S. 24:23; the *kethibh* of 24:16 is *hā'ᵃwarnâ hayᵉb̲usî,* "the Jebusite *'ᵃwarnâ.*" B. Mazar suggested that this is a Hurrian title, *ewrine,* "lord," found in Hittite as a title and in Ugaritic as a personal name (in *Jerusalem Revealed,* p. 4). If the text and these suggestions are accepted, Araunah, or whatever his personal name may have been, was the last king of the Jebusites, the "lord" of the city.

The location of the threshing floor of Araunah is reasonably identified with the site of Solomon's temple, N of David's City (Josephus's "third hill"), where the Dome of the Rock now stands. According to tradition, the Rock (Arab. *eṣ-Ṣakhra*) over which the Dome stands is the surface of the threshing floor and the location of the altar in front of Solomon's temple.

e. Capital. David also had other building projects in Jerusalem. His own house is known as "the house of cedars" (2 S. 5:11), built by Tyrian workmen, carpenters, and masons using cedars sent by Hiram king of Tyre (*ca.* 979-945 B.C.). "The house of the mighty men" (Neh. 3:16) is probably the name of a building of David's time (cf. 2 S. 10:7; 15:17; 17:8; 23:8-39; 1 K. 1:10, 38). "The tower of David" (Cant. 4:4) is also attributed to David. Of the walls and gates no clear picture emerges due to the almost complete destruction of the structures on the southeast hill. The king's house was probably in the lower part of the city, with stairs that went down to the lower gate (the Fountain Gate?; cf. Neh. 3:15). David was buried in the city (Neh. 3:16; cf. B. Mazar, *Mountain,* p. 316). The lower aqueduct and the lower pool (see III.C.2.g below), as well as the king's garden (see III.D.5.t below), were almost certainly there in David's day.

2. Solomon. Toward the end of David's reign, his son Adonijah staged a coup and had himself crowned king at "the Serpent's Stone," near En-rogel (1 K. 1:5-10). Nathan the prophet heard of it and took steps to have Solomon crowned the legitimate heir, although Adonijah was certainly senior. David had Solomon anointed as king near

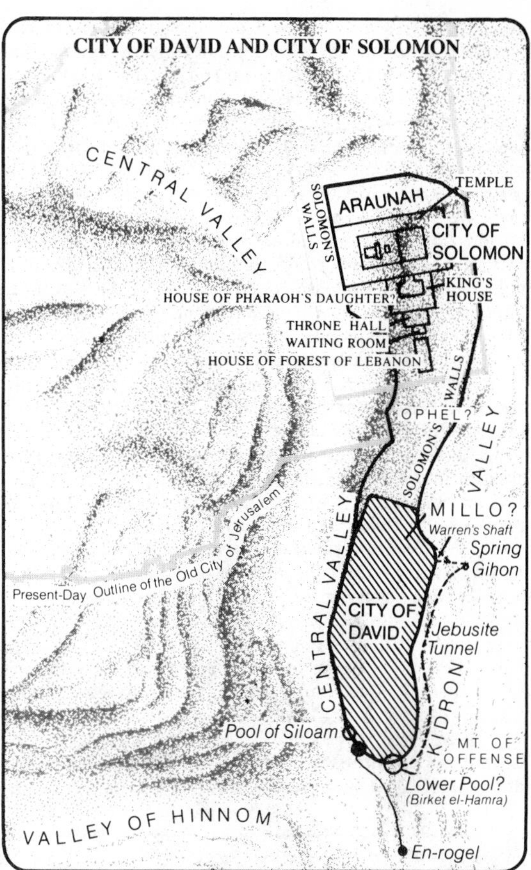

Spring Gihon, not far from En-rogel, and those who had joined Adonijah could hear the noise of the ceremony at Gihon (cf. vv. 40f.). The coup collapsed and Solomon became David's successor.

a. "City of David" and "Jerusalem." At the time of Solomon's marriage alliance with Pharaoh's daughter, there was a distinction between "the city of David" and "Jerusalem"(cf. 1 K. 3:1). A similar distinction between "Zion" and "Jerusalem" is reflected in a number of poetic passages in the Prophets and Psalms. There can be no doubt that the city was expanding. The only questions are in which direction and how far. David was doubtless building toward the future temple site. Some have thought that the "breach" mentioned in 1 K. 11:27 was in the north wall and that the Millo was a fill N of that area. But the text does not say that the "breach" was in the wall (*'eṯ-pereṣ 'îr dāwîḏ,* "the breach [or "bursting-out"] of the city of David"), and a king of David's military experience would hardly leave a breach in the most vulnerable wall. In any event, Solomon "closed" it, possibly the result of building the Millo (note the absence of a conjunction: "he built the Millo; he closed the breach"). Had the city also expanded to the southwest hill? (See III.C.2.f; III.D.2.g below.)

b. House of Yahweh. In the fourth year of his reign Solomon began construction of the house of the Lord (1 K. 6:1). Details of the arrangements with Hiram are given (1 K. 5:1-18 [MT 15-32]; 7:13f.; 2 Ch. 2:1, 3-16 [MT 1:18; 2:2-15]; for details, *see* SOLOMON'S TEMPLE). There can be little doubt that the location was approximately where the Dome of the Rock is today, although archeological excavation around and under a sacred building like the Dome of the Rock is impossible. The temple hill was considerably narrower, the Central Valley farther east, and the Kidron farther west than they are today (see II.C above). "Solomon's stables" are Herodian and Umayyad construction (see III.G below), built to support the expanded platform of the second temple. A tradition that the stone for the temple was quarried in the area near the modern Damascus Gate, known as Solomon's Quarries, Royal Quarries, Royal Caves, King Solomon's Mines, and the cave of Zedekiah, is without archeological support, but the tradition is not unreasonable (cf. 1 K. 6:7).

c. House of the Forest of Lebanon. This building was so named because of the use of cedar beams made from trees imported from Lebanon. The port at which these huge tree trunks were landed is the modern Tell el-Qasîleh, N of Tel Aviv, by the Yarkon River. The site was excavated by B. Maisler (Mazar). Cedar was used for pillars, beams, roofing, ceilings, and paneling (1 K. 6:15, 18; 7:2-5). It is a reasonable assumption that this house was part of the royal palace ("his entire house," 7:1-5). The most probable location of the royal house was S of the temple area.

d. Hall of Pillars. The term should perhaps be emended to "Audience Hall," reading *hʿwmdym* instead of *hʿmwdym* (1 K. 7:6). It was part of the royal palace, as was "the Hall of the Throne," or "the Hall of Judgment" (v. 7). The king's private quarters were "in the outer court back of the wall" (v. 8), and Pharaoh's daughter had a similar house. Some idea of the size and splendor of the royal palace complex may be seen in the fact that it took seven years to build the Lord's house, and thirteen to build Solomon's (1 K. 6:38–7:1).

e. Temple-Palace Complex. The accounts in Kings and Chronicles are probably not always in chronological order, and rearrangements are somewhat arbitrary. It is possible, e.g., to take the "twenty years" of 1 K. 9:10 (2 Ch. 8:1) as applying to regnal years rather than to the time of the building program, and to assume that there was some overlap of the building of the temple and the building of the palace. It is even possible that the dedication of the temple took place before the palace complex was completed — in fact, this would almost seem to be the necessary course of events. From the data in the books of Kings a tightly interwoven chronology of the kings of Judah may be constructed (cf. *NBC* [rev. ed. 1970], p. 323), which almost certainly establishes 931 B.C. as the date of the accession of Rehoboam. If the figure of forty years for Solomon's reign is accepted, then his accession, or possibly his co-regency with David, took place in 971 or 970, and the beginning of the building of the temple in 968 or 967. The dedication of the temple, then, could have taken place *ca.* 960, and the completion of the building program in Jerusalem *ca.* 951. This would have allowed the remaining twenty years for Solomon to establish his royal navy at Ezion-geber and to build Hazor, Megiddo, Gezer, and many other places (1 K. 9:15, 17-19, 22).

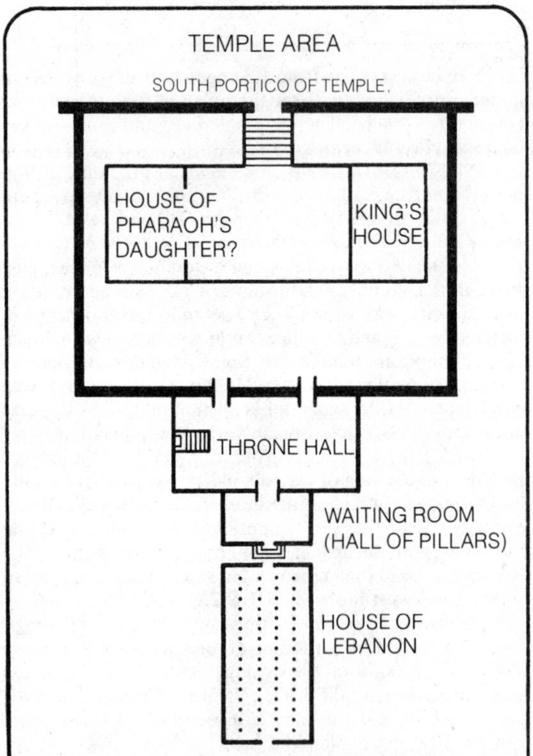

According to Josephus (*Ant.* viii.3.1 [61f.]), the beginning of the construction of the temple was in the eleventh year of Hiram of Tyre. Using the dates 979-945 for Hiram's reign, the eleventh year would be 969 B.C. — reasonably close to the figure 968/7 given above. Josephus also dated this event 592 years after the Exodus, differing from both the MT (480 years) and the LXX (440 years) of 1 K. 6:1. *See* CHRONOLOGY OF THE OT; EXODUS, DATE OF THE.

The temple was surrounded by an inner court (1 K. 6:36; 7:12), also called the "upper court" (Jer. 36:10), and characterized as "the court of the priests" (2 Ch. 4:9). A gateway faced north (Ezk. 8:3), and no doubt others faced east, south, and possibly west. No size is given for the inner court, and the speculations that it was twice the size of the temple or that its dimensions can be figured on the basis of Ezekiel's temple are without solid basis.

The outer court (1 K. 7:9, 12), was called "the great court" (2 Ch. 4:9). Since the inner court is termed "the upper court" (Jer. 36:10), the outer court was by implication on a lower level than the temple and the inner court. Again, no size is given, and calculations cannot be based on the size of the modern Ḥaram, for the original area was increased by Herodian constructions. According to Josephus (*BJ* i.21.1 [401]), Herod doubled the size of the courts of Zerubbabel's temple. If these courts were approximately equal to those of Solomon's temple — a view admittedly not established but not completely unreasonable — we might work back from these data. But precisely what does Josephus's statement ("he enlarged the surrounding area to double its former extent") mean? Did Herod double each dimension (giving it four times the area), or did he double the area? If he doubled the area, did he do it by multiplying each dimension by 1.4, or did he double its width?

Likewise, the relationship of the location of the palace complex to the temple is not clear. Ezekiel indicated that the king's house was separated from the Lord's house by only a wall, and the two houses were connected by an entrance (Ezk. 43:7f.), but this could be effected by placing the entire palace complex immediately S of the outer court. A number of scholars have looked upon the temple as the king's chapel. There was an "outer entrance for the king" (2 K. 16:18), possibly the same as "the king's gate on the east side" (1 Ch. 9:18). We know that Solomon, as also his father David, performed priestly functions on occasion (1 K. 8:62f.; 9:25) — unless we are to understand that this means that the king ordered the priest to perform the actual sacrificial ritual. Nor would it be surprising to

TEMPLE AREA
SOUTH PORTICO OF TEMPLE
HOUSE OF PHARAOH'S DAUGHTER?
KING'S HOUSE
THRONE HALL
WAITING ROOM (HALL OF PILLARS)
HOUSE OF LEBANON

Based on the reconstruction by L. H. Vincent, in Vincent and A.-M. Steve, *Jerusalem de l'AT,* II, 428, fig. 134

find that later kings, under the strong influence of surrounding religious practices, arrogated to themselves the use of the temple as a royal chapel. But the OT nowhere indicates that this was part of the religion of Israel as given by Moses or as maintained by the prophets.

Solomon also built the Millo (see III.C.1.c above). If the sequence in 1 K. 9:24 is significant, the building of the Millo took place after Solomon had moved Pharaoh's daughter to her house in the palace complex. The Millo might have been a landfill on the west, or more likely the east, of the saddle between the city and the palace, or it may have been fill behind retaining walls on the Kidron side of the area between the city and the palace.

f. Walls. Solomon also built the walls of the city (1 K. 3:1). It is reasonable to assume that the walls of David's City were maintained, and that they were extended toward the north to enclose the palace-temple complex. But how far to the north did these walls run? Did they encompass any part of the Central Valley and southwest hill? Excavations on the Ḥaram are impossible, but it seems reasonable to assume that the temple was the northern limit. Excavations in the Tyropoeon Valley (the Central Valley) indicate that the northern part was uninhabited until the time of the Maccabees. That Israelites lived on the southwest hill is a most reasonable assumption, for this area was inhabited before the Conquest; there is no evidence, however, that Davidic or Solomonic walls enclosed any part of the area. An argument frequently made against including the southwest hill in Solomon's Jerusalem is that it would make the city much too large in comparison with other cities of the period. This line of reasoning is questionable. Solomon had a large kingdom, very well organized administratively. This required a large number of retainers. At Ebla, e.g., according to G. Pettinato's reading of a text, there were fourteen governors under the king, each with between three hundred and eight hundred functionaries, and in addition there were 4700 palace functionaries, each with a support group of twenty persons (cf. G. Pettinato, *Ebla, Un impero inciso nell'argilla* [1979], p. 135). Some indication of the size of Solomon's royal house and its retinue is given in the provisions listed in 1 K. 4:8-19, 22-28 (MT 5:2-8). Moreover, the size of Jerusalem, including the southwest hill, is approximately 64 ha. (160 acres), compared with 72 ha. (182 acres) for Hazor (which Solomon built), and 56 ha. (140 acres) for Ebla (which was built *ca.* 1500 years earlier). It is not unreasonable to assume that Solomon's capital was as large as his fortress in Galilee — but such an assumption admittedly lacks archeological support.

g. Water Supply. The water supply in Solomon's day was no doubt similar to that of David's time. The single source known to us was Spring Gihon. The tunnel and shaft, discovered by Warren and fully excavated and studied in 1961-1967, are earlier than Hezekiah's tunnel. Since the shaft was definitely shown to be *inside* the Jebusite and Davidic walls (cf. R. Amiran, "The Water Supply of Israelite Jerusalem," in *Jerusalem Revealed,* pp. 75f.), it is reasonable to assume that it served the city of those periods. Two aqueducts were discovered, the first of undetermined age but clearly earlier than the second, and the second lower than and therefore earlier than Hezekiah's tunnel. These carried water from the spring, the first perhaps to the "king's garden" supposedly at the junction of the Kidron and Central valleys (but without substantiating evidence), and the second to the lower pool, known as Birket el-Ḥamra, now a garden but formerly SE of the pool of Siloam. The aqueduct was constructed partly underground, and partly in the open, with openings or sluices in its walls, apparently for the purpose of watering gardens

Possible location of the King's Garden (foreground) at the junction of the Kidron and Hinnom valleys (W. S. LaSor)

along the slope of the city outside its east wall. It is believed that 2 Ch. 32:2-4 refers to this system, particularly in the words "he planned . . . to stop the water of the springs that were outside the city. . . ." Isaiah may also refer to this system when speaking of "the waters of Shiloah which flow gently" (Isa. 8:6) and "the channel between the walls for the water of the old pool" (22:11). Warren's Shaft is made up of three parts: (1) a tunnel from within the walls, probably starting at a complex of public buildings on the east side of the city (see III.F.2.m below), hewn in the rock, 39 m. (128 ft.) long, descending 12.7 m. (41.7 ft.); (2) a vertical shaft 11 m. (36 ft.) deep; and (3) a horizontal channel 20 m. (66 ft.) long, bringing the water from Gihon to the foot of the shaft (possibly the *ṣinnôr;* see III.C.1.a above; cf. R. Amiran, in *Jerusalem Revealed,* p. 76).

According to tradition, Solomon constructed "Solomon's Pools" 4 km. (2.5 mi.) SW of Bethlehem (cf. Eccl. 2:4-6, esp. "I made myself pools from which to water the forest of growing trees"). The present pools and the aqueduct leading from them to Jerusalem are of later construction (see III.G below). The reference in Ecclesiastes, if indeed it is Solomonic in origin, probably refers to the king's gardens at the confluence of the Kidron and Central (or Hinnom) valleys, watered by Spring Gihon and the aqueduct mentioned above.

Solomon built a high place for Chemosh and for Molech "on the mountain east of Jerusalem" — probably on Baṭn el-Hawa (the Mt. of Offense), just S of the Mt. of Olives, and he built religious places "for all his foreign wives" (1 K. 11:7f.).

D. Divided Kingdom. For most of this period (*ca.* 931-586 B.C.) no detailed accounts of the building and expansion of the city are available. Yet it is known from many explicit and implicit statements that the city was considerably larger at the end of the period. We can only record the details and, for the most part, leave their interrelationships to speculation.

The prophet Jeremiah gave a description of the future rebuilding of the city. Since the passage is bracketed by dated passages, the first in 597 B.C. (Jer. 28:1) and the second between April and October, 587 B.C. (32:1), and since it appears to be the end of a message to the elders of the exiles in Babylon (29:1, 27), it cannot be dated before the early 6th century. It obviously deals with the future rebuilding of the city, but since Jeremiah included place names, some of which are undeniably historic, the assumption is reasonable that he was using terms that would have been meaningful to his readers. The passage reads: "Behold, the days are coming . . . when the city shall be rebuilt from the tower of Hananel to the Corner Gate . . . straight to the hill Gareb, and shall then turn to Goah, the whole valley of the dead bodies and the ashes, and all the fields as far as the brook Kidron, to the corner of the Horse Gate toward the east . . ." (31:38-40).

There can be little question that this forms a circuit of the city, counterclockwise, starting in the northeastern part of the city. The "Corner Gate" has been identified by many as in the vicinity of the present Jaffa Gate. "The whole valley of the dead bodies and the ashes" is almost certainly the Hinnom Valley, and there is no question about the Kidron. "The corner of the Horse Gate toward the east" must be somewhere near the starting point in the northeastern part of the city.

Here we shall not impose this plan on Jerusalem, but use it merely to check details given in other passages. If this description is indeed based on the Jerusalem of Jeremiah's day, it indicates that Jerusalem occupied some or all of the southwest hill as well as the City of David and the temple hill. Other evidence of this is suggested in Mic. 3:12:

Zion shall be plowed as a field;
Jerusalem shall become a heap of ruins,
and the mountain of the house a wooded height.

Admittedly this is poetry. "Zion," "Jerusalem," and "the mountain of the house" are synonymous terms — but are they identical, or are they parts of the whole? The question deserves further study than can be made here. It seems very probable, however, that they are supplementary terms. One should note that the Israelites under Joshua captured Jerusalem, but they did not take Jebus (Zion) (see III.B above).

When the northern tribes separated from Rehoboam's kingdom, Jeroboam of Israel (931-910 B.C.) took steps to keep his subjects from going to Jerusalem to worship (1 K. 12:27-29). This account certainly must be accepted as historical; therefore centralized religion at Jerusalem was already established in the monarchy and was not a product of the "Deuteronomic" reforms of the 7th century. There would have been no reason to include these statements about Jeroboam if the events had not occurred. And if it is assumed that the Deuteronomist was responsible for the final writing of Kings, this way of making his point would be sophisticated beyond credibility. There is something basically wrong with critical theories that require on the one hand such sophistication, while presuming on the other hand that the final editors overlooked obvious contradictions.

In the fifth year of Rehoboam (*ca.* 927 B.C.) Shishak (Sheshonq) of Egypt invaded Judah and Jerusalem and took away the treasures of the temple (1 K. 14:25). During the reign of Asa (910-870 B.C.), in the face of aggression by Israel, the southern king took the remaining temple treasures and sent them to Ben-hadad of Damascus to cause him to break his alliance with the north (15:18). These and similar events in subsequent reigns indicate a constant flow of wealth into the temple at Jerusalem — which certainly requires Jerusalem to have been the cult center of the nation.

1. Ninth Century. Little is recorded about Jerusalem during the 9th century. A full record exists of the kings of Judah who ruled from Jerusalem, but the religious problems mostly stemmed from Israel. The abominable sins of the southern kings are recorded, but it is certain that the invasion of Baal worship in Israel was the more serious problem. Ahab of Israel (874-853 B.C.) and his Phoenician queen Jezebel were Elijah's chief enemies (and Yahweh's). Their daughter Athaliah was married to Jehoram of Judah (853-841; cf. 2 K. 8:18), and after the death of their son Ahaziah, who reigned briefly (841), Athaliah seized the throne and attempted to replace Yahweh worship with Baal worship. Her sons plundered the temple for the Baals (2 Ch. 24:7), and she attempted to exterminate the Davidic line (2 K. 11:1). Joash, however, was hidden by his aunt, and when Athaliah was assassinated after a seven-year reign (841-835), Joash, age seven, became king (835-796).

The account of the coup against Athaliah gives a few details of the temple-palace complex. One-third of the guards were at the gate Sur (1 K. 11:6) or Sud ("foundation," 2 Ch. 23:15), and another third at the gate behind the guards (2 K. 11:6), called "gatekeepers" (2 Ch. 23:15; see III.D.5.p below). Apparently the king's house was directly connected to the temple, with, it would seem, outer and inner guardposts. Athaliah fled to the temple, but the priest objected to an assassination in the house of the Lord (2 K. 11:15), and she was taken "through the horses' entrance to the king's house," where she was slain (2 K. 11:16, called "the horse gate" in 2 Ch. 23:15).

Joash made repairs on the temple (2 K. 12:4-16 [MT 5-17]), completing them in his twenty-third year (*ca.* 813 B.C.). Thereafter, Hazael of Syria (843-796 B.C.) attacked Gath and then planned to move against Jerusalem (v. 17 [MT 18]). Joash plundered the temple to buy his way out of this predicament, but he was later slain in a palace coup (vv. 18, 20 [MT 19, 21]). According to the account in Chronicles, the Syrians actually attacked Jerusalem, wounding Joash during the battle (2 Ch. 24:23-25). The detail that he was slain "in the house of Millo, on the way that goes down to Silla" (2 K. 12:20 [MT 21]) adds little if anything to our knowledge of the city. "Beth Millo" may have been a city quarter in Jerusalem.

2. Eighth Century. a. Amaziah of Judah (796-767 B.C.). Amaziah "mustered" the men of Judah twenty years old and older, numbering 200,000 fit for war (2 Ch. 25:5). He also hired 100,000 mighty men from Israel (v. 6). Such numbers seem to be highly inflated, from what is known about the size of armies at that time. Yet the figures found in the OT are remarkably consistent, and some reevaluation of the evidence — biblical as well as archeological — is in order.

b. Amaziah of Judah and Joash of Israel. Amaziah and Joash (798-782 B.C.) engaged in battle at Beth-shemesh (2 Ch. 25:21), and Joash was victorious. He took Amaziah back to Jerusalem, "broke down the wall of Jerusalem for four hundred cubits, from the Ephraim Gate to the Corner Gate" (24:23), and plundered the temple and the palace. He then returned to Samaria. (For discussion of these gates, see III.D.5.g, h below.)

c. Uzziah of Judah. Uzziah (Azariah, co-regent 790-782, king 782-740) built towers "at the Corner Gate, and at the Valley Gate, and at the Angle" (2 Ch. 26:9). Uzziah undertook several other building operations throughout the land. The "many cisterns" he hewed out (v. 10) probably included some in Jerusalem. Also, the "engines" for shooting arrows and hurling great stones were placed "on the towers and the corners" in Jerusalem (v. 15). The rise of the Assyrian empire under Tiglath-pileser III (747-727 B.C.) was quite likely the cause of Uzziah's extensive fortification. Uzziah's attempt to usurp the priestly prerogative of burning incense in the sanctuary resulted in leprosy, "because the Lord had smitten him" (v. 20). This may have led to a co-regency with Jotham (co-regent 751-740; king 740-732), and probably was the reason that Uzziah was not buried in the sepulchre of David (26:23). A stone found in 1931 on the grounds of the Russian Church at the foot of the Mt. of Olives has an Aramaic inscription reading, "To this place were brought the bones of Uzziah king of Judah; do not open" (cf. B. Mazar, *Mountain,* figure on p. 188). The carved stone is dated to Maccabean times and is the result, it is believed, of a transhumation.

d. Jotham and Ahaz of Judah. Jotham built "the upper

gate of the house of the Lord, and did much building on the wall of Ophel" (2 Ch. 27:3; cf. 2 K. 15:35). He also built cities in the hill country of Judah and erected forts and towers on wooded hills (cf. 2 Ch. 27:4). The test of the fortifications came sooner than expected, for in the days of Ahaz (735-716 B.C.) the Syro-Ephraimite coalition, under Rezin of Damascus and Pekah of Israel, attacked Jerusalem, but the attack failed (2 K. 16:5). According to the account in Chronicles, Rezin took many captives to Damascus, and Pekah slew 120,000 men of valor in Judah in one day (2 Ch. 28:5f.) and took 200,000 of the inhabitants captive — but at a word from a prophet of Yahweh, he returned the captives (2 Ch. 28:8-15).

e. Hezekiah of Judah (co-regent 728-716, king 716-687 B.C.). Hezekiah was one of Judah's greatest kings, and his reign covered one of the critical periods in Judah's history. It was also the time of one of the greatest prophets, if not *the* greatest — Isaiah. From Isaiah comes much of the local color of the city. There was a very wealthy class, the result of foreign trade arrangements (Isa. 2:6) that brought in silver and gold and endless treasures, so that the land was filled with horses and chariots (2:7), not to mention idols (2:8). Their formal religion was meaningless (1:11-15). They lived in large and beautiful houses (5:9), and at their feasts there was music and drinking (5:12). Their women were haughty, walking with outstretched necks, glancing wantonly as they walked with mincing steps and tinkling feet (3:16). Men's and women's finery included anklets, headbands, crescents, pendants, bracelets, scarves, headdresses, armlets, sashes, perfume boxes, amulets, signet rings, and nose rings. They were dressed in mantles, festal robes, cloaks, garments of gauze, and garments of linen, and wore turbans and veils (3:18-23). All of this was seen as evil, because there was no true faith in Yahweh; it would all be stripped away.

Hezekiah began his reign in 716 B.C., after a co-regency of twelve years. His first act was to undertake extensive religious reforms. It took sixteen days to clean the accumulation of material from the temple, and the debris was thrown into the Kidron Valley (2 Ch. 29:3-19). Then he sanctified the place with the prescribed offerings (vv. 20-36). He next made preparations to hold the Passover — apparently it had not been observed for many years — and he invited Israelites of the northern tribes, including the Transjordanian tribes, to come to Jerusalem for the celebration. This was, it seems, after the fall of the northern kingdom (722 B.C.). Most scorned the invitation (30:1-10); some, however, did come. The temple was not ready in time for the fixed date (14 Nisan; cf. 30:2-4, 15), so the Passover was held in the second month (Iyar). "Since the time of Solomon . . . there had been nothing like this in Jerusalem" (30:26).

Hezekiah, sensing growing danger from Assyria, was concerned about his water system. Spring Gihon was indeed vulnerable. It was located outside the east wall, and could easily be cut by an enemy. Hezekiah "planned with his officers and his mighty men to stop the water of the springs that were outside the city . . . and they stopped all the springs and the brook that flowed through the land . . ." (Ch. 32:2-4). One interpretation is that the "brook" (Heb. *nāḥāl*) here refers to the aqueduct, and the "springs" are the openings through which the gardens were watered — a reasonable view, but an unusual use of the words. Hezekiah further "closed the upper outlet of the waters of Gihon and directed them down to the west side of the city of David" (32:30). This is interpreted to mean that he cut the tunnel that brought the waters of the Gihon inside the walls.

f. Siloam Tunnel. According to 2 K. 20:20 Hezekiah "made the pool and the conduit and brought water into the city," and Isaiah says, "You made a reservoir between the two walls for the water of the old pool" (Isa. 22:10). Sir. 48:17 reads, "Hezekiah fortified his city, and brought water into the midst of it; he tunneled the sheer rock with iron and built pools for water." The Siloam tunnel was known to early explorers, but it was only in 1880 that the inscription was found at the point where the workmen joined the two bores. The tunnel is quite tortuous, including a large S-bend. At one time it was suggested that this bend was made in order to avoid tombs, possibly the royal sepulchres, but this is now known to be false. The suggestion made by H. Sulley (*PEQ* [1929], p. 124), that the tunnel follows the course of a natural underground stream running from Spring Gihon to the southern end of the southeast hill, was revived by R. Amiran (in *Jerusalem Revealed,* p. 77). Such a route would have provided ventilation from a natural flow of air and would account for the assurance that the project could be carried out successfully by digging from each end. Amiran also suggested that this water course, with its "upper Gihon" source and "lower Gihon" exit, would explain the phrase "the brook that ran through the midst of the land" (2 Ch. 32:4). The tunnel is 533 m. (1749 ft.) long, although the straight-line distance is only 320 m. (1050 ft.). According to the wall inscription, its length was 1200 cubits. *See* HEZEKIAH; SILOAM.

g. Hezekiah's Walls. If the southwest hill had not been previously enclosed, it was certainly walled by Hezekiah. B. Mazar, following Avigad, identified Hezekiah's wall with Josephus's First Wall: "It encircled the present-day Mount Zion [i.e., the southwest hill] and was linked with the segment of the great wall discovered by Professor Avigad in the present Jewish Quarter of the Old City. The same wall also encompassed the new quarter called the *Mishneh* (Second) Quarter, on the Western hill in the latter days of the Judean Kingdom" (*Mountain,* p. 176). He associated with this wall the statement in 2 Ch. 32:5. The wall discovered by Avigad is 7 m. (23 ft.) thick, built of large, unhewn stones, and the portion that remains is of two to seven courses, extending for 40 m. (131 ft.; cf. N.

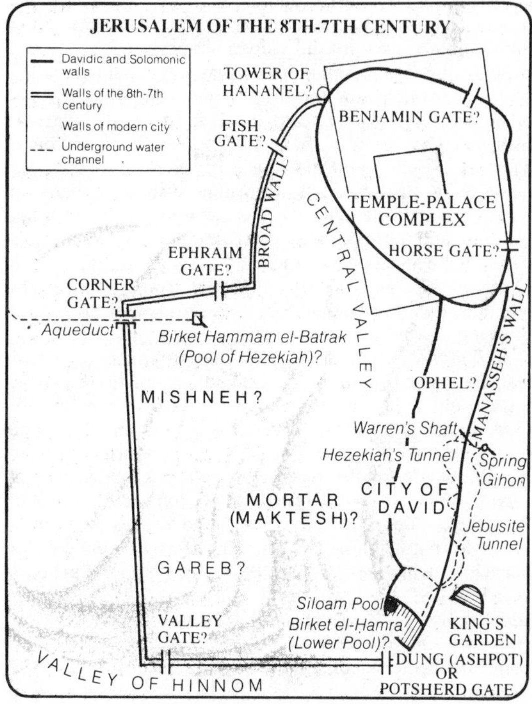

Avigad, "Excavations in the Jewish Quarter of the Old City, 1969-1971," in *Jerusalem Revealed,* pp. 41-51).

h. Sennacherib's Siege. Sennacherib king of Assyria (705-681) began his reign peaceably enough, but in a short time he had problems with Babylon, and while he was attending to those, the western regions began to withhold the payment of tribute. So in his "third campaign" (701) he moved into Hatti-land (i.e., Syria and Palestine). His story is recorded in the Taylor Prism, ii.37–iii.49 (*DOTT,* pp. 66f.; *ARAB,* II, §§ 239f.; cf. *ANET,* pp. 287f., which is from another text, not the Taylor Prism). Hezekiah was one of those who had rebelled (2 K. 18:7), and in a campaign against the Philistines Hezekiah had seized Padi, the pro-Assyrian governor of Ekron (cf. 18:8; *ARAB,* II, § 240). When Sennacherib invaded Judah, Hezekiah hastened to offer restitution, and was forced to strip the temple and the palace to pay the tribute (18:14-16). According to Sennacherib's record, Padi was also handed over at that time (*ARAB,* II, § 240). The tribute paid was thirty talents of gold and three hundred talents of silver (2 K. 18:14; Sennacherib records thirty talents of gold and eight hundred talents of silver; a talent was three thousand shekels, 34.27 kg. or 1209 Troy oz.).

Sennacherib thereupon sent the Tartan (second-in-command) and two other officials with an armed contingent to demand surrender of the land (2 K. 18:17-25; Isa. 36:1-10). The scene took place "by the conduit of the upper pool" (see III.D.5.j below). When Hezekiah's officers reported the Assyrian message, Hezekiah sent to Isaiah, who told the king not to fear, for Yahweh would defend the city (2 K. 19:1-34; Isa. 37:33-35). Sennacherib tells in glowing terms how he had shut Hezekiah in Jerusalem "like a bird in a cage" (*ARAB,* II, § 240), but he does not claim to have captured Jerusalem. The biblical account, on the other hand, tells of the destruction of the Assyrian army (2 K. 19:35f.; Isa. 37:36f.), of which no Assyrian record exists. A. L. Oppenheim (*IDB,* IV, 271) made the point that if there had been such a large destruction of Assyrian forces, there would have been widespread rebellion of the vassal states. He recognized that the incident is curiously reported in Herodotus (ii.174) — which appears to be strong evidence that an event like the one recorded in the biblical account did indeed happen.

Sennacherib's prism indicates that Hezekiah had called on Egypt for help, and this may be implied in 2 K. 19:9, for when the Assyrian king heard that Tirhakah was advancing, he sent a message of warning to Hezekiah. The mention of TIRHAKAH (Taharqa, 690-664 B.C.) creates a problem, for he was not pharaoh in 701; according to some scholars he was not even old enough to lead a campaign at that time. This fact and the apparently close linking of Sennacherib's catastrophe at Jerusalem and his assassination in Nineveh (2 K. 19:36f.; Isa. 37:37f.) have led some scholars to advance the theory that SENNACHERIB made a second invasion *ca.* 687 B.C.

3. Eighth-Century Prophets. The prophecy of Amos was delivered to the northern kingdom, but there can be little doubt that it was intended for all of the people of God. Judah is addressed (Am. 6:1). Amos is concerned for Jacob, "for he is so little" (7:4). The word is spoken to "the whole family which I brought out of the land of Egypt" (3:1). Amos has his closing vision with Yahweh in the temple, "beside the altar" (9:1), and he sees the "booth of David that is falling" (9:11). (The Heb. *hannôpelet̠* is a participle, which may mean "that which is in the process of falling"; cf. W. S. LaSor, *Handbook of Biblical Hebrew* [1979], § 32.3711; W. Gesenius, E. Kautzsch, and A. Cowley, *Hebrew Grammar* [2nd ed. 1910], § 116d.)

In Micah the sin of Judah is Jerusalem (Mic. 1:5); the wound has reached Jerusalem (1:9). But the days are coming when the exaltation of "the mountain of the house of Yahweh" (the temple mount) shall be the occasion of the Torah going to all the world (4:1f.; cf. Isa. 2:2f.).

Hosea, the northern prophet, in contrast to Amos who was a Judean sent to preach to the north, does not direct his message to Jerusalem. Since the message was preserved and ultimately canonized by Judeans, its relevance to all the people of God must have been recognized before the original scrolls were lost.

The prophecy of Isaiah furnishes a number of details for the reigns of Ahaz and Hezekiah. The Syro-Ephraimite siege of Jerusalem is the background of Isa. 7 (cf. vv. 7-9). To deliver this message Isaiah took his son Shear-jashub ("a remnant shall return") to meet Ahaz "at the end of the conduit of the upper pool on the highway to the Fuller's Field" (v. 3). The same location is mentioned in 2 K. 18:17 (see III.D.2.h above). Several explanations have been given. Two cisterns were located on the northwest side of the city — Birket Mamilla, at some distance beyond the Jaffa Gate, and Birket Hammam el-Batrak, also known as the Pool of Hezekiah (Amygdalon in Josephus *BJ* v.11.4 [568]), inside the walls, NE of the Jaffa Gate. An aqueduct leads from the first to the second. G. Dalman claimed that Birket Mamilla came from the 8th cent. B.C. (*Jerusalem,* p. 203; cited by Simons, p. 49 n. 1), but scholars have not been convinced. The location would be the most likely for the Rabshakeh of Sennacherib and his army to confront the officials of Hezekiah's kingdom. A second location is on the northern side of the city, where the remains of a conduit from the north have been found. According to Josephus (*BJ* v.4.2 [147]) a "so-called Fuller's Tomb" was near the northeast corner of the wall. Josephus's knowledge of the days of the first temple, however, is at many points erroneous or questionable. The location preferred by most scholars is in the Kidron Valley; however improbable a place it may seem for a highway, it would be a likely place for Ahaz to meet with Isaiah, particularly in the king's garden (not mentioned in the account).

Disregarding Isaiah's word, Ahaz turned to Tiglath-pileser for aid against Israel and Syria, i.e., he became a vassal of Assyria (2 K. 16:7f.). The Assyrian was quick to seize this opportunity, conquering Damascus and taking a large part of Israel. Ahaz was summoned to Damascus to meet with Tiglath-pileser, and while there "he sacrificed to the gods of Damascus" (2 Ch. 28:23). He also had plans made for a copy of an altar that he saw at Damascus, and replaced Solomon's bronze altar with the copy of the Damascene altar (2 K. 16:10-16). Ahaz also removed the twelve bronze oxen that supported the large sea, and set it on a pediment of stone (v. 17). He made other alterations in the temple-palace complex (v. 18), and erected altars on every corner (2 Ch. 28:24). It was in connection with these events that Isaiah, realizing that there was no hope for reform, wrote chs. 8–10, foretelling the Assyrian attack (cf. Isa. 10:5-12).

4. Seventh Century. Hezekiah (see III.D.2.e-h above) was succeeded by his son, Manasseh, who probably served as co-regent 696-687 B.C. because of Hezekiah's illness and the prediction of his death, and as king 687-642 B.C. The Bible records that Manasseh returned to the idolatries of Ahaz, added soothsaying, auguries, and sorcery, and even offered his sons as burnt offerings in the Valley of Hinnom (2 Ch. 33:3-7, 11). It is possible that Manasseh built Topheth as a high place for such immolations (cf. 2 K. 23:10), and scholars have suggested that the Ashpot Gate (also translated "Dung Gate") of Neh. 2:13; etc. was so named because it was the gate used by worshipers taking sacrifices to Topheth (see III.D.5.l; III.F.2.c below).

According to Chronicles, Manasseh was taken to Babylon as a prisoner, and when he humbled himself before God he was returned to Jerusalem (2 Ch. 33:10-13). Babylonian documents record no such captivity; nor is there any indication in Kings of his subsequent acts of repentance (cf. 2 K. 21:16f. with 2 Ch. 33:14-19). Instead, the acts of Manasseh are presented as the last trying of God's patience, resulting in His decision to destroy Jerusalem as He had destroyed Samaria (2 K. 21:10-15).

According to the Chronicles account, Manasseh built an outer wall to the City of David, "west of Gihon, in the valley [= Kidron], to the entrance by the Fish Gate, and carried it round Ophel, and raised it to a very great height" (2 Ch. 33:14). This may be the wall discovered by K. Kenyon, W of the ancient wall (Jebusite or Davidic). B. Mazar connected this narrowing of Ophel with the westward expansion into the Tyropoeon Valley and the western hill (*Mountain*, p. 57).

Josiah (639-609 B.C.) became king at the age of eight upon the assassination of his father Amon. He undertook to purge Jerusalem of the pagan places of worship when he was about twenty (2 Ch. 34:3f.). In the course of repairing the temple, the "book of the law" was discovered (2 K. 22:8; 2 Ch. 34:14). According to a widely held view, this was part or all of the book of Deuteronomy, and by one version of this view, it was a "pious fraud," a recently composed work that was "discovered" to give it credibility (cf. *NBC* [rev. ed. 1970], p. 320). The accepted date of the discovery is 621 B.C., and it led to reforms that, regrettably, had no great depth (cf. 2 K. 23:4-20). Josiah was slain at Megiddo, trying to prevent Pharaoh Neco from going to the aid of Assyria (2 K. 23:29f.). In Josiah's day we find the first reference to the Mishneh ("second" [quarter]), part of the western development of Jerusalem (2 K. 22:14; 2 Ch. 34:22). (See III.D.5.d below.)

In considering Jerusalem of the 7th cent. we must not overlook the evidence of the prophets who lived there at that time, i.e., Jeremiah and Zephaniah. Zephaniah's contributions are few: he mentions the Fish Gate and the Mishneh (Zeph. 1:10), and the Maktesh ("Mortar," v. 11).

Since Jeremiah foretold that "the city shall be rebuilt upon its tell, and the palace shall stand where it used to be" (Jer. 20:18), it seems reasonable to infer that the terms he used to describe this restoration are the names of places in existence in his day (see III.D above). Jeremiah mentions the high place of Topheth in the Valley of the son of Hinnom, which shall be called the valley of Slaughter (7:32), and locates the Potsherd Gate there (19:2, 6). Jeremiah also mentions the Benjamin Gate (37:13; 38:7), more closely defined as the "upper Benjamin Gate of the house of the Lord" (20:2) where he was put in stocks. Burrows, however, conjectured that the "upper Benjamin Gate" implies a lower Benjamin Gate, the latter a gate of the city and the former a gate of the temple (*IDB*, II, 853). Twice Jeremiah refers to "the gate between the two walls" (39:4; 52:7; cf. 2 K. 25:4); it led "to the Arabah" (39:4) and was the way that Zedekiah fled, probably via Wâdī en-Nâr toward the Jordan Ghor. This gate was "by the king's garden" (52:7), located in the Kidron Valley near the confluence with the Hinnom, doubtless watered by the overflow from Spring Gihon.

On one occasion Jeremiah was commanded to "stand in the gate of the Lord's house" and proclaim his message to those who entered to worship (Jer. 7:2). The temple itself was not available to the ordinary worshiper; hence this gate was one of the entrances to the court. There was also a "New Gate of the house of the Lord" (26:10), which was in the upper court (36:10). There was a Benjamin Gate (20:2) and a "third entrance of the temple of the Lord" (38:14). Since this was the place of a clandestine meeting between Jeremiah and the king, it was probably on the palace side of the temple, possibly "the outer entrance for the king" (2 K. 16:18). Jeremiah also mentions a court of the guard, bakers' street (37:21), the king's garden, and the gate between the two walls (39:4; 52:7; see III.D.5.u below). Some inhabitants of Jerusalem were poor (5:4) and some great (5:5); some rode in chariots or on horses (17:25); they gathered wood or kneaded dough (7:18). The city received silver from Tarshish and gold from Uphaz (10:9).

Some idea of the kaleidoscopic character of the day can be seen in the fact that Jeremiah lived under seven kings of Judah and his ministry extended through the reign of five kings (627-586 B.C., 1:2f.). He witnessed the revival under Josiah and three invasions of the city. Egypt and Assyria fell during his lifetime and Babylonia became dominant. Josiah was killed trying to halt Neco and the Egyptian forces at Megiddo (2 K. 23:29f.). Jehoahaz (Shallum) was deposed by Neco after a reign of three months (v. 33). Jehoiakim (Eliakim) was put on the throne by Neco (v. 34); he was opposed to Jeremiah, and was cruel and oppressive. During his reign (608-597 B.C.), Babylon, which had overcome the Assyrians at Nineveh in 612 B.C., defeated the Egyptians at Carchemish and conquered all of Hatti (605 B.C.; cf. 24:1; *CCK*, pp. 66f.). Jehoiakim, who had been a vassal of Egypt (23:35), transferred his loyalty to Nebuchadrezzar of Babylon for three years, and then rebelled (24:1). He was to be taken to Babylon, but he died and was succeeded by Jehoiachin (Coniah; 2 Ch. 36:6, 9). Jehoiachin was removed by Nebuchadrezzar and taken to Babylon, and Zedekiah was made a puppet king of Judah (597-586 B.C.).

5. Before the Exile: A Synthesis. This survey permits an attempted synthesis, although with the recognition that many points are still unclear and are subjects of scholarly disagreement. There are three basic guides for this synthesis: (1) the topography, which is reasonably certain; (2) the outline in Jeremiah (see III.D above); and (3) the outline based on Nehemiah's three descriptions (see III.F.2 below).

a. Southwest Hill. The most severely debated region is the southwest hill. Two questions need to be answered. When was the southwest hill incorporated into the walled city? Certainly it was not within David's walled city, although it may have been the "Jerusalem" taken by the Israelites when Jebus was left as a Jebusite enclave (see III.B above). Did Solomon extend the walls to include part or all the southwest hill? Simons, and others whom he cited, believed that he did (p. 242). K. Kenyon rejected the idea, stating succinctly, "The western ridge, or at least its southern end, was not incorporated into the city until the first century A.D." (*Jerusalem*, p. 70).

The second question grows out of the first: how much of the southwest hill, if any, was walled? Kenyon pointed out that the rebuilding of Jerusalem's walls in Nehemiah's time was completed in fifty-two days (Neh. 6:15). The only way that a 4000-meter (2½-mile) wall (which Simons and others postulated) could have been completed in such a short time would have been if the earlier walls had survived "to a very substantial extent" (*Jerusalem*, p. 110). This is not a strong objection, for after breaching the walls, an enemy did not spend time tearing them down. There would have been some destruction in the course of time, due to natural causes, goats running on walls, men robbing the stones for other building, etc., but most of the material (field stone for the walls, some ashlar at the gates) and the foundations would have been in place. Newer excavations, however, place the wall much earlier than

Kenyon's estimate. (Cf. H. Geva, *IEJ,* 29 [1979], 84-91: ". . . this longstanding controversy is now an anachronism; the westward expansion of the city prior to the second century B.C.E. has been proven, in recent excavations on the southwestern hill, by the discovery of pottery deposits and building remains dating from the eighth-seventh centuries B.C.E." [p. 84].) Caution must be exercised in accepting this view, for there is the concomitant problem of population.

b. Population Explosion. M. Broshi said, "Jerusalem at about 700 B.C. had mushroomed, historically speaking, overnight" (*IEJ,* 24 [1974], 23). He estimated that it had grown from the 44 dunams (4.4 ha. or 11 acres) of David's city, to 130-180 dunams (13-18 ha. or 32.5-45 acres) in the 8th cent., to 500-600 dunams (50-60 ha. or 125-150 acres) in the 7th century. Using an accepted figure of 40-50 inhabitants per dunam, Broshi arrived at an estimated population of 24,000 (*IEJ,* p. 24 n. 20; cf. *Biblical Archaeology Review,* 4/2 [1978], 10-15). The figures from Ebla (Tell Mardikh) work out to 446 persons per dunam (250,000 in 56 ha.), and comparable density would have given Jerusalem of the 7th cent. a population about the same as that of Ebla. Incidentally, Broshi's seventh-century size of Jerusalem is very close to the area of present-day Jerusalem within the walls (i.e., the Old City) — 77 ha. or 192.5 acres.

Two methods of estimating population are common, each with serious weaknesses. One is to work from density, as Broshi has done. But the disparity between his 40 to 50 per dunam and Ebla's density ten times as great raises questions about the validity of the "accepted" figure. The figures from Ebla are not simply a round number (250,000), but a detailed breakdown of various officials and retainers adding up to 249,716. The consistently "large" figures in biblical and other ancient records suggest that density-population estimates are in need of restudy. The second method is to work on a straight-line basis. If the population of a given city-state was only one thousand in 800 B.C., it could not have been 75,000 in 400 B.C. — the same holds true for whatever figures and dates are used. This reasoning can easily be shown to be false. The population of Israel, e.g., tripled between 1948 and 1962. Extrapolating from these figures we would get a population of only around 3200 seventy years earlier — which we know to be completely wrong. Or working from the world's population, which is supposed to have doubled in the past fifty years, we would be back to Adam and Eve in less than 1600 years! Population explodes, holds steady for a time, is decimated by war or pestilence, undergoes both immigration and emigration, and does many other unpredictable things. Figures from ancient records, incredible as they seem, are often no more erroneous than scholarly estimates.

c. Walls. Hezekiah's wall enclosed the southwest hill (a conclusion from evidence presented in 5.a above), forming a "second" city.

d. Mishneh. This "second" city was probably the Mishneh ("second quarter," 2 K. 22:14), first mentioned in Josiah's day (many scholars take it to be a northern addition to the southwest hill).

e. Mortar. Zephaniah 1:11 mentions the Mortar (*maḵtēš*) with the Fish Gate, the Mishneh, and the hills. The Mortar would be named from its shape, and the most likely location would be in the Central Valley, either in the vicinity of the cross valley, or perhaps the lower slopes of the southwest hill descending to the Central Valley (identified as "the Lower City" in Avi-Yonah's model of Jerusalem).

f. Tower of Hananel. The north wall extended from the tower of Hananel to the Corner Gate (Jer. 31:38-40). Hananel, according to scholarly consensus, was at the northwest corner of the temple area (cf. Neh. 3:1; 12:39; Zec. 14:10). Perhaps it is erroneous to locate this where the Antonia was later built, for the temple area may not have extended that far north in the 7th cent. or the 5th century. A topographical location for the north wall would be along the cross valley, from the citadel on the west to Wilson's Arch on the east. It must be borne in mind that St. Anne's Valley, prior to the Herodian enlargement of the temple platform, cut off a sizable portion of the northeast end of the temple mount.

g. Corner Gate. This gate must now be located in the vicinity of the citadel near the Jaffa Gate. Scholars formerly held that the west wall (if it did exist at that time) was considerably farther east, but Avigad's discoveries indicated that the wall was toward the west (N. Avigad, *IEJ,* 22 [1972], 194), on the summit of the hill.

h. Ephraim Gate. This gate must be located in the north wall, if for no other reason than that Ephraim was to the north. Joash broke down the wall for 400 cubits from the Ephraim Gate to the Corner Gate (2 Ch. 24:23); hence the Ephraim Gate was about 200 m. (650 ft.) E of the Corner Gate. The distance from the Corner Gate to the temple mount is about 600 m. (1950 ft.). The Middle Gate (Jer. 39:3) is possibly the Gate of Ephraim, as is Josephus's Gennath Gate (Garden Gate; *BJ* v.4.2 [146]).

i. Hill Gareb and Goah. The hill Gareb is possibly the top of the southwest hill, at which point the wall turned toward Goah (Jer. 31:39), neither place being positively identified. The "whole valley of the dead bodies" indicates that Jeremiah is moving toward the Hinnom.

j. Upper Pool, the Highway, Fuller's Field. The "upper pool" may be in the area of the west wall (see III.D.3 above). The "pool of Hezekiah" (Birket Hammam el-Batrak) at least preserves a tradition that Hezekiah built a pool on that side of the city, and since the population explosion had moved to the southwest hill by Hezekiah's day, some provision for water was of vital necessity. The northwest side of the city would be an appropriate place for the highway, but there is no indication of where "Fuller's Field" (Isa. 7:3) was located. Josephus's reference to a "so-called 'Fuller's tomb'" near the northeast corner of the wall (*BJ* v.4.2 [147]) is apparently of no help. Scholars are inclined to locate the Fuller's Field near En-rogel in Wâdī en-Nâr.

k. Valley Gate. This gate has often been identified with the ruins discovered by Crowfoot on the west side of David's City, opposite the Water Gate. But the name in Hebrew is *šaʿar haggay'*, "gate of the valley." The Kidron is always called *naḥal,* and the Central Valley (Tyropoeon) is not mentioned in either the OT or the NT. Of the valleys around Jerusalem, only the Hinnom is called *gay'*. Hence some scholars locate the Valley Gate in a wall above the Hinnom, generally in the south wall. M. Burrows put it, cautiously, at the southwest corner, where the Hinnom turns toward the east (*IDB,* II, 850), which would be, in this reconstruction, on the hill Gareb, or between Gareb and Goah (see III.F.2.a below).

l. Topheth. Jeremiah 7:32 locates this place in the Valley of the son of Hinnom; it will be called the valley of Slaughter, doubtless the valley of dead bodies (31:40; cf. 7:33). It is possible that Manasseh built Topheth (cf. 2 K. 23:10; see III.D.4 above). See III.F.2.c below.

m. Potsherd Gate (Jer. 19:2, *Q*). Also located in the Valley of Hinnom, the Potsherd Gate (*šaʿar haḥarsîṯ, Q* 19:2) has been identified with the Dung Gate (Neh. 2:13; see III.F.2.c below). The suggestion that this is where broken pottery was thrown away (BDB, p. 360) is not necessarily valid; broken pottery was often left where it was broken, as any archeologist knows. Simons suggested that the Potsherd Gate was where pottery was sold (p. 230). Possibly Jeremiah used the term to conform to his action and message.

n. Uzziah's Towers. This survey, following Jeremiah's outline, brings us to the Kidron (Jer. 31:40), and we have completed a circuit of the southwest hill. A few details remain to be fitted into this reconstruction. Uzziah built towers "at the Corner Gate, and at the Valley Gate, and at the Angle" (2 Ch. 26:9). The first two would be at the northwest and southwest corners of the wall, in this synthesis. But where (and what) is "the Angle"?

The "Angle" (Heb. *hammiqṣō[a]ʿ*, possibly "place of cutting off, corner where one wall intersects another") is mentioned by Nehemiah four times (Neh. 3:19f., 24f.) as though it were a well-known place in the city. Once he speaks of the "ascent to the armory at the Angle" (v. 19; see III.F.2.n below). For the present it will be identified as a tower in a location not previously protected, possibly where the north wall of the southwest hill joined the west wall of Solomon's palace-temple complex.

An attempt to synthesize the information about the temple mount (the "mountain of the house," Jer. 26:18) has fewer difficulties textually but receives very little archeological help. The eastern, western and southern limits of the mount are topographically determined. The north is not established, but since Josephus spoke of Bezetha as a "recently built quarter" (*BJ* v.4.2 [151]), one can assume that there had been little expansion N of the temple mount before his time.

o. Horse Gate and Benjamin Gate. The tower of Hananel (see III.D.5.f above) was at the northwest corner of the temple mount. The Horse Gate (Jer. 31:40; see III.F.2.u below) was the end of the circuit sketched by Jeremiah, but this gate had to be nearer the palace; hence the southeast corner of the temple area would be its extreme northern limit. The Benjamin Gate (37:13; 38:7) is a better candidate for the northeast gate, since the road to Benjamin lies in that direction. Moreover, Jeremiah speaks of the "upper Benjamin Gate of the house of the Lord" (20:2), where he was put in stocks; hence this was a temple gate. Burrow's conjecture, however, that "upper" (*ʿelyôn*) implies a "lower Benjamin Gate," probably in the city (*IDB*, II, 853), does not necessarily follow (ʾEl ʿElyon does not imply the existence of a lower god).

p. Court of the Guard, Gate of the Foundation, Gate of the House. The location of the "court of the guard"(Jer. 37:21) is not specified. There were also a "gate behind the guards" (lit. "the gatekeepers of the threshold," 2 Ch. 23:4) and a gate of the foundation (v. 5 par. 2 K. 11:6, if *swr* is emended to *swd* in the latter reference), both connected with the palace. "The horse gate of the king's house" (2 Ch. 23:15) was also at the palace. There was an "upper gate of the house of the Lord" built by Jotham (2 Ch. 27:3; see III.D.2.d above) and a "new gate of the house of the Lord" (Jer. 26:10), which was in the upper court (36:10). Since gates are the weakest part of a city's defense, it is probable that some duplication occurs in the names, and some gates may be located in the wall that Manasseh built. It would be reasonable to assume that if a "lower" Benjamin Gate existed it would be in Manasseh's wall, below the "upper" Benjamin Gate.

q. Fish Gate (2 Ch. 33:14; Zeph. 1:10). This gate is generally located in the north wall — an unlikely place to sell or deliver fish, if the north wall only extended the width of the temple! Because it is located between Gihon and Ophel in the description of Manasseh's wall, one hesitates to locate it in the north wall, but the most logical place would be between the Ephraim Gate and the temple mount, probably in the Central Valley area of the north wall of the Mishneh. See III.F.2.z below.

r. Ophel. On the southeast hill (David's City) are several landmarks. The Ophel (2 Ch. 27:3; see III.F.2.t below) can almost certainly be located between David's City and the temple mount, approximately at the southeast corner of the modern Ḥaram. This "swelling" (the meaning of *ʿōpel*) was protected by a wall, on which Jotham "did much building." In the time of Nehemiah, the Nethinim (temple servants) lived on Ophel (Neh. 3:26).

s. Millo. This is still very much of a problem. It seems likely that it was a fill in the depression between the City of David and the palace, preferably on the west side, although the preponderance of scholarly opinion has taken it to be the walls and back-filling on the east side of the city on the Kidron slopes.

t. Waters of Shiloah, Lower Pool, King's Garden. Spring Gihon (see II.C.1 above) is positively located, even to the present. The second aqueduct ("the waters of Shiloah") conducted the water of Gihon to the lower pool (Birket el-Ḥamra or the pool of Siloam, not necessarily the same) and watered the king's garden (see III.F.2.f). Hezekiah's tunnel offers no problem; it is still in existence (see III.D.2.f above).

u. Gate Between the Walls. This gate was at the lower end of Zion, "by the king's garden" (Jer. 52:7), and since it was the way "to the Arabah," Zedekiah fled by that route (39:4; 2 K. 5:24), probably going by Wâdī en-Nâr toward the Jordan Ghor.

v. Manasseh's Wall. This wall presents a problem, chiefly because of the order of landmarks. Clearly it was on the east side of the Lower City and "west of Gihon" (2 Ch. 33:14) and thus inside the ancient Jebusite or Davidic wall and the opening of Warren's Shaft. This may be the wall discovered by K. Kenyon, who reported that the original wall on Ophel was about 50 m. (160 ft.) further east and 25 m. (83 ft.) lower on the slope, dating from *ca.* 1800 B.C. to the 8th century. B. Mazar connected this narrowing of the Lower City with the westward expansion into the Tyropoeon Valley and the west hill (*Mountain*, p. 57).

Very few details of the water system are available other than those listed above. Every house and public building had its cistern to collect rain water (plastered cisterns were an invention of the Late Bronze Age; G. A. Barrois, *Manuel d'archéologie biblique*, I [1939], p. 226), and the large cisterns under the temple, some of which have been explored, indicate that Solomon and his successors made such provision. There must have been open pools also but we do not have sufficient data to describe them.

E. Destruction of Jerusalem (586 B.C.). The publication of the Babylonian Chronicle should resolve the question of the dates of the capture and the destruction of Jerusalem. A fourfold record is available, calculated according to the years of Nebuchadrezzar's reign, of the Exile, of Zedekiah's reign, and of the captivity of Jehoiachin; these are found in 2 Kings, Jeremiah, Ezekiel, and the Babylonian Chronicle. Part of the past confusion about the date resulted from a misunderstanding of how months were named. According to 2 K. 25:2f. the siege of Jerusalem lasted from the tenth day of the tenth month of the ninth year of Zedekiah's reign to the ninth day of the fourth month of the eleventh year. As we reckon months, this is about 1½ years. But it is beyond argument that, whether the year began in Nisan or Tishri, Nisan was always considered the first month. Thus in Jer. 36, the reading and burning of the scroll took place in the ninth month (v. 9), which was in the winter (v. 22). At that time Judah was on a Tishri year; hence the first month of the calendar (by our reckoning) would have been Tishri, and the ninth month would have been in May/June. "Month 9," however, is always Kislev (Dec./Jan.). This is similar to the use of ancient names for our ninth to twelfth months, which are literally months 7 (sept-), 8 (oct-), 9 (nov-), and

10 (dec-). The siege of Jerusalem lasted from Jan., 588, to July, 586, and the city was burned in Aug., 586 (dates are calculated from R. A. Parker and W. H. Dubberstein, *Babylonian Chronology 626 B.C.–A.D. 75* [1956], pp. 27f.; cf. *DOTT,* pp. 80f.; see detailed chronology below).

Nebuchadrezzar (Nebuchadnezzar) ascended to the throne of Babylon on the death of his father Nabopolassar, which was 8 Abu of Nabopolassar's twenty-first regnal year (Aug. 15/16, 605 B.C.). Nebuchadrezzar did not return to Babylon until 1 Elul (Sept. 6/7, i.e., the day that began at sundown on the 6th) of that year. Nebuchadrezzar calls this his "accession" year (British Museum 21946, line 12; *CCK,* pp. 68f.). His "first year" began in Nisanu 604, when he had taken the hand of Bel (line 14), and the Chronicle records events of years 1-11 (*CCK,* pp. 68-75).

It is possible to make the following reconstruction.

608	Sept. 10 =	1 Tishri, Jehoiakim's first regnal year, 2 K. 23:34; 2 Ch. 36:5; Jer. 45:1
605	Apr. 12 =	1 Nisan, Nabopolassar's twenty-first regnal year (Parker and Dubberstein, p. 27)
	May-June	Nebuchadrezzar defeated Egyptians at Carchemish (Jer. 46:2; *CCK,* p. 67)
	Aug.	Nebuchadrezzar reached Egypt; Aug. 16, Nabopolassar died; Nebuchadrezzar hurried home (*CCK,* p. 69)
	Sept. 6	Nebuchadrezzar ascended throne, accession year (British Museum 21946, line 12; *CCK,* p. 69)
	Oct. 7 =	1 Tishri, Jehoiakim began fourth regnal year (2 K. 24:7; *Ant.* x.6.1 [86]) Cf. Berossus's account in Josephus *CAp* i.19 (132-39); *Ant.* x.11.1 (219-223)
604	Apr. 2 =	1 Nisan, Nebuchadrezzar's first regnal year (British Museum 21946, line 14; *CCK,* p. 69) Jeremiah's prophecy, Jer. 25:1; cf. 25:3 with 1:2
	June-Nov.	Nebuchadrezzar against Hatti-land (Dnl. 1:1?) (British Museum 21946, line 16), defeated Ashkelon (cf. Jer. 47:1?)
	Sept. 26 =	1 Tishri, Jehoiakim's fifth regnal year; he served Nebuchadrezzar three years (2 K. 24:1)
603	Mar. 22 =	1 Nisan, Nebuchadrezzar's second regnal year; he assembled a large army; possibly a revolt at home
	Oct. 15 =	1 Tishri, Jehoiakim's sixth regnal year
	Dec.	Jeremiah's scroll read and burned (Jer. 36:9)
601	Mar. 30 =	1 Nisan, Nebuchadrezzar's fourth regnal year; marched against Egypt (British Museum 21946, rev. 5-7); the battle a standoff, both sides weakened
	Sept. 22 =	1 Tishri, Jehoiakim's eighth regnal year; revolt against Babylonia (*Ant.* x.6.1 [87]; 2 K. 24:1)
600	Mar. 19 =	1 Nisan, Nebuchadrezzar rebuilt his army (British Museum 21946, rev. 8)
599	Oct. 1 =	1 Tishri; Jehoiakim's tenth regnal year
	Nov.	Nebuchadrezzar marched on Hatti-land
598	Feb./Mar.	Nebuchadrezzar returned to Babylon
	Mar. 27 =	1 Nisan; Nebuchadrezzar's seventh regnal year (cf. Jer. 52:28)
	Oct. 20 =	1 Tishri; Jehoiakim's eleventh regnal year
	Dec.	Nebuchadrezzar went to Hatti-land
	Dec. 6	Jehoiakim died (2 Ch. 36:9; *Ant.* x.6.1 [88]; Jer. 37:7); Jehoiachin became king
597	Mar. 16 =	2 Adar; Jerusalem captured, Jehoiachin taken to Babylon (2 K. 24:12; 2 Ch. 36:10; Ezk. 40:1); accession year of Zedekiah
	Apr. 13 =	1 Nisan; Nebuchadrezzar's eighth regnal year
593	Jan.	Nebuchadrezzar went to Hatti-land
	Apr. 30 =	1 Nisan; Nebuchadrezzar's twelfth regnal year
	July 31 =	5 Tammuz (Ezk. 1:1)
	Aug./ Sept. =	Ab; Hananiah's false prophecy? (Jer. 28:1-4)
592	Sept. 17 =	5 Elul; Ezekiel's temple vision (Ezk. 8:1)
591	Aug. 14 =	10 Ab; Ezekiel's address to the elders (Ezk. 20:1)
589	Oct. 10 =	1 Tishri; Zedekiah's ninth regnal year
588	Jan. 15 =	10 Tebet; siege of Jerusalem began (2 K. 25:1; Jer. 39:1; 52:4; Ezk. 24:1f., "this very day")
587	Jan.	Zedekiah rebelled against Babylon (Jer. 52:4)
	Jan. 7 =	10 Kislev; Ezekiel's prophecy against Egypt (Ezk. 29:1); siege lifted briefly (Jer. 37:5); Jeremiah attempted to go to Benjamin (37:12); Jeremiah put in prison (32:1)
	June 21 =	1 Sivan; Ezekiel's message to Egypt (Ezk. 31:1)
	Oct. 18 =	1 Tishri; Zedekiah's eleventh regnal year
586	Apr. 13 =	1 Nisan; Nebuchadrezzar's nineteenth regnal year
	July 18 =	9 Tammuz; famine in the city; breach in the walls; the king and his men fled, were captured (2 K. 25:3f.; Jer. 39:2; 52:6)
	Aug. 12 =	7 Ab (2 K. 25:8) or 15 Aug. = 10 Ab (Jer. 52:12); Jerusalem destroyed and burned (52:13f.); people taken captive (52:28-30); Gedaliah made governor over Judah, located at Mizpeh (2 K. 25:22-26; Jer. 40:5f.)
585	Mar. 3 =	5 Tebet; news reached Ezekiel of fall of Jerusalem (Ezk. 33:21)
	Sept. =	Tishri (or 586?); Gedaliah slain (Jer. 41:2)
562	Oct.7 =	26 Elul; Awel-Marduk (Evil-Merodach) succeeded Nebuchadrezzar
561	Apr. 2 =	25 Adar; Evil-Merodach's accession year; Jehoiachin released from prison in thirty-seventh year of captivity (Jer. 52:31; *DOTT,* p. 86)

F. From the Return until Herod. For the period from the destruction of Jerusalem to the return from Exile we have no information of any kind. Those left in the ruined city were the unfit and the misfits, under foreign rulers. The period of the second temple in reality includes Herod's reconstructed temple, which was never known as a "third temple." Practically, however, one must consider Herodian Jerusalem separately because of the great changes that were made in the city, especially in the temple and its platform.

1. Persian Period. The Jews were permitted to return to Jerusalem in the first year of the reign of Cyrus (2 Ch. 36:22f.; Ezr. 1:1f.). Although Cyrus had been king of the Medes since 559 B.C., he dated his reign from the conquest of Babylon. His accession year began *ca.* Oct. 12, 539, and his first regnal year was dated from 1 Nisan = Mar. 24, 538 B.C. (cf. W. H. Dubberstein, *AJSL,* 55 [1938], 417). The rebuilding of the temple commenced in Iyyar (Apr./ May), 537 (Ezr. 3:8), was halted by the objections of adversaries, and was resumed only in the second year of Darius (520 B.C.; Ezr. 4:24; Hag. 1:1f.). Work was completed on 3 Adar (= Mar. 10), 516 B.C. (Ezr. 6:15). Passover was observed on 14 Nisan (= May 1) of that year (Ezr. 6:19). Next to nothing is known about the details but it is reasonably certain that the second temple was located on the site of Solomon's temple, since some were present who had seen the former temple (Hag. 2:3), and no protest was raised against the location of Zerubbabel's temple.

Jerusalem in the Persian period was in the satrapy of Beyond-the-River (*ʿaḇar nahªrāʾ*, Transeuphrates), which included Syria and Palestine. According to Herodotus there were twenty satrapies ("protectors of the kingdom"), of which Beyond-the-River was the fifth, extending from the border of Cilicia to the border of Egypt (iii.88, 91). The governor of a satrapy was very powerful, and he had a staff of subordinates. One can assume that Tattenai was the satrap of Beyond-the-River (Ezr. 5:3, etc.), that Sanballat was his lieutenant governor in Samaria (Neh. 2:10, etc.; cf. *DOTT*, pp. 260-64; A. Cowley, *Aramaic Papyri of the Fifth Century B.C.* [1923], pp. 108-119), that Tobiah the Ammonite (Neh. 2:10) was a similar official in part or all of Transjordan, and that Geshem the Arab (2:19) was an important person over the province of Arabia, which according to Herodotus included Edom and southern Judah and was exempt from the taxes levied on Beyond-the-River.

Nehemiah was cupbearer in the court of Artaxerxes, undoubtedly Artaxerxes I Longimanus (464-425 B.C.). Because of his concern for Jerusalem, Nehemiah asked permission to visit the city and was appointed "governor" of Judah (Neh. 5:14; cf. 2:1, 9). The sequence of dates in 1:1 and 2:1 is not necessarily an error; if Nehemiah was using a Tishri year for Artaxerxes, Kislev (month 9, but the second month in the Tishri calendar) would precede Nisan (month 1, but the seventh month in the Tishri calendar).

The date of Ezra's journey to Jerusalem is a problem, due in part to uncertainty about which Artaxerxes is meant and in part to details in Ezra and Nehemiah that do not harmonize well. If Artaxerxes is the first (Longimanus, 464-425 B.C.), the seventh year (Ezr. 7:7) would be 458 B.C. But if it was Artaxerxes II Mnemon (404-359 B.C.), Ezra's journey would have been in 398 B.C. In the latter case, Ezra and Nehemiah could not have been contemporary, for according to Elephantine Papyrus 30, Bigvai (Bagohi) was governor of Jerusalem at that time. On the other hand, if Ezra reached Jerusalem in 458 B.C., a number of details do not fit: walls were already built, but Nehemiah found them in ruins; Nehemiah did not mention the previous work of Ezra; Nehemiah found people abusing the law, although Ezra had corrected them; etc. As a result, some scholars suggest emending the text of Ezr. 7:7 to read "in the thirty-seventh year," making his arrival in Jerusalem in 428 B.C., sixteen years after Nehemiah's first visit (*BHI* [rev. ed. 1972], pp. 392-403). This is not the place to try to solve the problem, but any solution that fails to take into consideration all of the biblical data is less than satisfactory as an exegetical work (J. S. Wright, *The Date of Ezra's Coming to Jerusalem* [1958]; H. H. Rowley, "The Chronological Order of Ezra and Nehemiah," in *The Servant of the Lord and Other Essays* [1952], 129-159).

The numbers of exiles and returnees are also significant — but no satisfactory data exist. The figures in 2 K. 24:14-16 (ten thousand either including or in addition to the eight thousand in the following verses) and Jer. 52:28-30 (4600) are far too small, in the light of the biblical picture. Likewise the number of 42,360 who returned with Sheshbazzar, plus the servants and the singers (7537, a total of around fifty thousand), while reasonable, does not seem to fit in with Nehemiah's method of selecting ten percent to live in Jerusalem (Neh. 11:1) — unless we are willing to settle for an extremely small Jerusalem — and again is not consistent with the biblical data. W. F. Albright suggested that the population of Judah was more than 250,000 in the 8th cent., possibly half that figure after the first deportation in 597 B.C., and around twenty thousand after the first exiles had returned (*Biblical Period from Abraham to Ezra* [rev. ed. 1963], pp. 87, 105f., 110f.). It is extremely difficult to believe that the very small number of twenty thousand Jews in all Judah could have survived the years that followed.

The Babylonians had damaged the city extensively, particularly the palace-temple complex. K. Kenyon's excavations revealed terrible destruction of the east side of David's City, due in part to the steepness of the slope, which had been retained by walls with back-filling. Once these walls had been broken, houses, fill, and upper walls had tumbled down the side of the Kidron ravine, making archeological excavation extremely difficult and somewhat hazardous. Nehemiah recognized the need for sound walls if the city was to be safe.

The book of Nehemiah describes the city walls three times: first, in a record of Nehemiah's night inspection (Neh. 2:11-16), which began at the Valley Gate and ended at the Kidron because he could not go further; then, in an account of the work gangs on the wall (ch. 3); and finally, in an account of the processional around the walls for the dedication (12:31-43). The walls were finished in fifty-two days (6:15) — a point used by the minimalists to support the view that Jerusalem at that time was confined to the east hill. The question is now moot. But even apart from the evidence of archeology, the biblical text contains the record of other work besides that of the fifty-two days. Those who had returned with Zerubbabel in 538 B.C. had obviously made some effort to rebuild the walls and thus caused the complaint to the Persian ruler (Ezr. 4:12). Moreover, the rebuilding under Nehemiah was principally on the east hill, specifically on the eastern side of that hill, as the text indicates, because that is where the palace complex and official buildings were located. An enemy had little reason to do more than destroy the gates and towers on the rest of the city walls — and it was on these that Nehemiah's workers labored. The stones, as excavations have shown, were not dressed; hence there was no involved masonry except around the gates. The walls were finished to half their height (Neh. 4:6) and were not notably strong walls at that, for Sanballat made sarcastic remarks about the material and the structure (vv. 2f.). One other point should be noted: Josephus reported that the rebuilding of the wall took two years and four months (*Ant.* xi.5.8 [179]) — a figure which he must have found in some record.

2. Nehemiah's Jerusalem. Because of their importance for reconstructing both the city of the preexilic period and that of the subsequent period, Nehemiah's descriptions will be examined in detail.

In Nehemiah's night inspection (Neh. 2:3f.) he mentions the Valley Gate, the Jackal's Well (or Dragon's Well), the Dung Gate, the Fountain Gate, and the King's Pool (discussed below).

In ch. 12 Nehemiah describes the procession to the temple for the dedication. The two groups apparently started from the southwestern part of Jerusalem, where Nehemiah himself had started his tour of the walls. Group A moved counterclockwise and Group B clockwise. Their goal was the same; hence one may suppose that their respective routes would take about the same amount of time, even though the B itinerary lists more landmarks. It will be assumed, merely so that we can visualize the situation, that the groups started somewhere in the vicinity of the modern Zion Gate, in the southwest corner of the walled city. We shall trace the first group and then continue with the second group in reverse order, hence completing a circuit of the city in a counterclockwise direction. The places mentioned in this sequence are: the Dung Gate (12:31), the Fountain Gate (v. 37), the Stairs of the City of

David, the Water Gate on the east (v. 37), the Gate of the Guard (v. 39), the Sheep Gate, the Tower of the Hundred (v. 39), the Tower of Hananel, the Fish Gate, the Old Gate, the Gate of Ephraim (v. 39), the Broad Wall, the Tower of the Furnaces (v. 38). These will be discussed in order, and other locations or places will be inserted where they seem most appropriate.

a. Valley Gate (*šaʿar haggay'*, Neh. 2:13, 15; 3:13; 2 Ch. 26:9). This gate has often been located in the west wall of David's City, i.e., leading to the Central Valley. As seen above (III.D.2.k), only the Hinnom was known as the *gay'* (*haggay'*, Jer. 2:23); thus some scholars have identified the Hinnom of David's day with the Central Valley (e.g., L.-H. Vincent, *Jérusalem antique*, pp. 124ff.), but this is an argument of desperation totally at variance with all other biblical data. The Valley Gate was located 1000 cubits W of the Dung Gate (a reasonable inference from Neh. 3:13). Three different cubits were known to the Jews: the small cubit of 465 mm. (1.5 ft.), the cubit of Moses, 525 mm. (1.7 ft.), and the large cubit of 560 mm. (1.8 ft.) (A. Ben-David, *IEJ*, 20 [1970], 235). One will not be far wrong if he figures roughly that 2 cu. = 1 m.; thus the two gates were about 500 m. (1640 ft.) apart. This would locate the Valley Gate approximately on a line with the west wall as proposed by N. Avigad, based on the excavations of 1971 (see map, *IEJ*, 22 [1972], 195), or roughly S of the Zion Gate in the modern wall.

b. Jackal's Well (Dragon's Well, *ʿên hattannîn*, Neh. 2:13). This well is usually identified as En-rogel (see II.C.2, 3 above), but this does not fit the general direction of the journey, for the spring was between the Valley Gate and the Dung Gate. No spring is known in the Hinnom, but this does not preclude the possibility that at one time there was a source of water (cf. II.C.3 above). It should also be noted that *ʿên hattannîn* could be translated "dragon's eye"; hence it might refer to a local landmark other than a spring.

c. Dung (Ashpot) Gate (Neh. 2:13; 3:14; 12:31; cf. *šaʿar hāšᵉpôṯ*, 3:13, "gate of the ash heap, refuse pile, dung hill"). This gate would obviously be on the side of the city where it would be least offensive. This certainly was in the Valley of Hinnom at some distance from the king's garden. It is probably to be identified with Jeremiah's Potsherd Gate (see III.D.5.m above). The suggestion has been made that the word *'ašpōṯ* or **šāp̱ôṯ* is etymologically related to "Topheth," based on a hypothetical root **ṯpy*, which became *tp'* in Aramaic and *špy* in Hebrew (cf. BDB, p. 1046). This would require Topheth to be an Aramaic loanword — a possibility, since Ahaz had imported pagan elements from Damascus.

d. Fountain Gate (Gate of the Spring; Neh. 2:14; 3:15; 12:37). This gate is probably the one at the lower end of David's City (see III.D.5.u above) that led to En-rogel, for it was near "the stairs that go down from the City of David" (3:15; 12:37), and it is distinguished from the Water Gate on the east.

e. En-rogel. See II.C.2 above.

f. King's Garden (Neh. 3:15). This was probably a fertile area watered by the overflow of the Gihon, but whether it was in the valley at the confluence of the Kidron and the Hinnom, or along the lower slopes of the City of David, where the second aqueduct had openings providing for the watering of the adjacent land, cannot be positively determined. See III.D.5.t above.

g. King's Pool (Neh. 2:14). This is possibly the pool made by Hezekiah (2 K. 20:20; Isa. 22:11), perhaps the Pool of Shelah of the king's garden (Neh. 3:15).

h. Pool of Shelah (Neh. 3:15). As previously noted, there were two older aqueducts in the Kidron Valley, antedating Hezekiah's tunnel. To the later of these Isaiah may have been referring when he spoke of "the waters of Shiloah" (Isa. 8:6), which may have led to the Pool of Shelah, since the words are derived from the same root.

i. Stairs That Go Down from the City (Neh. 3:15; 12:37). These were located in the lower part of David's City, near the Fountain Gate (see III.F.2.d above).

j. Sepulchres of David (Neh. 3:16). These were doubtless in the Lower City, but their exact location may never be known, due to the extensive quarries of the Roman period (cf. S. Yeivin, *JNES*, 7 [1948], 40-43). According to the biblical accounts, fifteen kings of the Davidic line were buried in the City of David: David, Solomon, Rehoboam, Abijah, Asa, Jehoshaphat, Joram, Ahaziah, Joash, Amaziah, Azariah (Uzziah), Jotham, Ahaz, Hezekiah, and Josiah. David's tomb was known in the time of John Hyrcanus (Josephus *Ant.* vii.15.3 [393]) and Herod (*Ant.* xvi.7.1 [179-187]), and even into the early Christian era (Acts 2:29). The location of the "tomb of David" on the southwest hill (modern "Zion") is without biblical or archeological foundation; it dates no earlier than the 9th cent. A.D. (Mazar, *Mountain*, p. 185). The argument that the southwest hill was not inhabited in Israelite times because burial places were found there is based on a later stricture of Judaism; it was obviously not in force in the preexilic period.

k. House of David (Neh. 12:37). This was probably not standing in Nehemiah's day, but its location may have been traditionally marked. It was not in the palace complex, for that was built by Solomon (see III.C.2.e above), but in the Lower City, near the stairs also mentioned in the procession (12:37).

l. House of the Mighty Men (Neh. 3:16). This was near David's palace; again, it may have been a historical site by Nehemiah's time.

m. Water Gate on the East (*šaʿar hammayim mizrāḥ*, Neh. 12:37, or *lammizrāḥ*, 3:26). This is possibly to be distinguished from another water gate (west), but if so we have no direct reference to it. There was a Water Gate (lit. "gate of the waters," Neh. 8:1, 3, 16) that had a plaza or town square before it, as did the Gate of Ephraim (3:16). Above Spring Gihon, where the Water Gate on the east is generally located, there would have been little room for a town square due to the topography, but no other location suggests itself. The Water Gate on the east appears to be the same as the East Gate (3:28).

n. Ascent to the Armory at the Angle (Neh. 3:19). This is very difficult to locate because the words "ascent," "armory," and "angle" may not be correctly translated. The word *ʿᵃlōṯ* can be read as an infinitive construct meaning "the going up" or "ascending of," but it is usually emended to *ʿᵃlîyâ*, "upward, northward" (cf. 3:31f.) or to *maʿᵃlôṯ*, "stairs" (cf. 3:15). The word *nešeq* means "equipment, weapons"; "armory" is a translational facilitation here (cf. BDB, p. 676). It can be made to mean "armory" by emending the text to read *bêṯ nešeq*. But the versions are against this reading. The root *nšq* also gives rise to the word for "kiss," and an Arabic cognate means "fasten together." The LXX reads "the tower of the ascent where it meets the corner." The word *miqṣô(a)ʿ*, translated "angle, place of corner-structure, corner-buttress" (BDB, p. 893), occurs ten times (Ex. 26:24; 36:29; 2 Ch. 26:9; Neh. 3:19f., 24f.; Ezk. 41:22; 46:21f.). The root seems to mean "cut off, break off, end abruptly." Avi-Yonah said that both *pinnâ* and *miqṣô(a)ʿ* mean "angle," the former the outer angle and the latter the inner angle (*IEJ*, p. 243 n. 4). But one place in Jerusalem was known specifically as the *miqṣô(a)ʿ*. Since every corner of a wall has both an outer and an inner angle, it is unreasonable to suppose that only one of these would be called without further qualification "the inner angle." Moreover, both words are used in the phrase "to the Angle and to the corner" (Neh. 3:24f. [MT 23f.]).

Furthermore, neither the LXX nor the Vulgate so understood it. The "ascent" could hardly meet an inner corner of an angle (LXX), and the Vulgate has an entirely different idea in *contra ascensum firmissimi anguli* ("opposite the ascent of the strongest angle"). In the Exodus passages some kind of a join or joint is meant. In the Ezekiel passages, the meaning is simply "corners." In 2 Ch. 26:9, the Angle is one of the three places where Uzziah built towers (see III.D.2.6 above). Perhaps the *miqṣô(a)ʿ* was a particular location where the wall was strengthened or buttressed (hence the Vulg. *firmissimi*) at a corner and joined by another wall. The context of Neh. 3:19 seems to locate the Angle on the temple mount near the houses of the high priest and other prominent persons (cf. 3:20-25), possibly on the west side where the wall that extended from the Gate of the Corner to the temple mount joined the wall of the temple court.

o. House of Eliashib (Neh. 3:20). This seems to have been a large building, befitting the high priest, for work on the wall at that area was divided into two parts (3:20f.). It was located near the priests' house (interpreting 3:22).

p. House of Azariah (Neh. 3:23). Since many persons were named Azariah, the meaning of "the house of Azariah" (3:23) is obscure. From the location of his house one should assume that he was an important person, possibly a priest, perhaps one of those who joined in attaching their seals to the covenant (10:10), as well as the priest (?) who marched with the princes and with Ezra in the procession (12:33).

q. Projecting Tower (*hammigdāl hayyôṣēʾ*, Neh. 3:25-27). This is also difficult to locate — or even to define. Heb. *yôṣēʾ* means "the (one) coming/going out"; but what, exactly, is a "tower that comes out"? The RSV translates "projecting tower," which is accurate but not satisfyingly descriptive. Did the tower project outward from the line of the wall, or inward, or in both directions? In v. 25 the tower projects "from the upper house of the king," meaning the palace built on Solomon's palace location, rather than on David's, which was in the Lower City. But was the tower built on the palace and was the palace built against the outer wall? In v. 26 the Nethinim ("temple servants" who lived on Ophel) "repaired to a point opposite [*ʿaḏ neḡeḏ*] Water Gate on the east and the projecting tower." Certainly the Water Gate on the east was on the east wall; was the projecting tower there also? Was it the tower that Uzziah built at the *miqṣô(a)ʿ* (2 Ch. 26:9)? Was it the tower of David (Cant. 4:4)? Warren thought that he found the remains of a tower where the Ophel wall assumes the direction of the modern Ḥaram wall (cf. Simons, p. 119), but the remains of that tower do not come from Nehemiah's day (cf. K. Kenyon, *Jerusalem,* pp. 114f.). Kenyon pointed out that the excavations of 1961 show that Nehemiah did not (probably could not) follow the line of the earlier wall on the eastern slope of Ophel, because of the tumble of stones, but rather constructed a wall higher up on the ridge, reducing the width of the city at that point (*HDB* [rev. one-vol. ed. 1963], p. 474).

r. House of the King (Neh. 3:25). This was almost certainly located in the general area of Solomon's palace, near the court of the guard (see III.D.5.p above); it had a projecting tower (see III.F.2.q above).

s. Gate of the Guard (*šaʿar hammaṭṭārâ,* Neh. 12:39). This gate, probably close to the court of the guard near the king's house, was perhaps in Manasseh's second wall, further down on the slope and slightly E of the temple mount (cf. Simons, p. 342). The word *maṭṭārâ,* from the root *nṭr,* "to watch," sometimes means "prison" as well as "warden," and thus this has been referred to as the Prison Gate; but it is unclear why a prison would be located near the temple, and why the procession, planning to hold a dedication service, would station itself by the prison. It is a peculiar feature of this word that it can be developed either from the qal or the piel, and if the latter, it would mean "watchman" (cf. Heb. *ṣôpēh*; Gk. *skópos*). Could there be a connection between this gate and the nearby hill that came to be known as *har haṣṣôpēh,* Mt. Scopus? There was, of course, a prison or "court of the guard" located in the palace complex (Jer. 32:2), well away from the outer wall, as prisons should be.

t. Ophel (Neh. 3:27). This name is often given to the entire City of David, but no scriptural basis exists for this practice. Josephus referred to Ophel as "a certain place" (*chōrou tinós, BJ* v.4.2 [145]). The Ophel was between the northern end of David's City and the southern end of the temple mount, with its own portion of wall. The Nethinim (temple servants) lived on Ophel (3:26).

u. Horse Gate (*šaʿar hassûsîm,* Neh. 3:28; Jer. 31:40; see III.D.5.o above). This gate was located N of the Water Gate, the projecting tower, and the wall of Ophel, if the details in Neh. 3:28 are intended to be sequential. It therefore was probably a gate in the outer wall at the southeast end of the temple complex (but see Simons, pp. 338f.).

v. Muster Gate (*šaʿar hammipqāḏ,* "gate of the muster/appointment," Neh. 3:31). This gate was probably, from the name, the place for mustering the guard and was located near the northeastern corner of the city wall (cf. Neh. 3:31f.). Most likely it was in the eastern wall just S of the "upper chamber of the corner," since the Sheep Gate was in the northern wall. Simons stated that the Horse Gate and the Muster Gate (which he called "Inspection Gate") were the only two gates in the eastern side of Manasseh's outer (second) wall (p. 342).

w. Sheep Gate (*šaʿar haṣṣōʾn,* Neh. 3:1, 32; 12:39; Jn. 5:2). This gate was on the northern or northeastern side of the city. Because of its location it can hardly be the gate by which the inhabitants of the city led their flocks out to pasture. More likely it was the gate used for bringing sheep for sacrificial offerings to the temple. Since merchants were located in that region (Neh. 3:32), one could assume that animals were sold here for the sacrifices. The Sheep Gate of Jn. 5:2 would have been located in the Herodian wall, which was somewhat farther north.

x. Tower of the Hundred (Tower of Meʾah, Neh. 3:1; 12:39). This tower was also on the northern wall, if indeed it was a separate tower. It is possible to read the phrase as an appositive defining Hananel (note the wording of 3:1) and to take "hundred" as either a measurement or as the number of persons connected with an event no longer understood (cf. the Israeli Kiryat Shemoneh, "the village of Eight").

y. Tower of Hananel (Neh. 3:1; 12:39; Jer. 31:37-39; Zec. 14:10). This tower was a landmark serving as the northern extremity of the city (Zec. 14:10) and as the eastern extremity (Jer. 31:38). It is generally located at the northwestern corner of the Ḥaram, being replaced by the Hasmonean Baris and the Herodian Antonia, but one must keep in mind that the northern end of the temple area in earlier times was probably not as far north as the Ḥaram extends today. One must also bear in mind that the depression known as "St. Anne's Valley" was deeper and provided a natural location for a city wall.

z. Fish Gate (2 Ch. 33:14; Neh. 3:3; 12:39; Zeph. 1:10). This gate was located in the northern wall, perhaps where it crossed the Central Valley (see III.D.5.g above). It would be the location of the fish markets, or at least the gate by which catches were brought from Galilee and from the Mediterranean. If the Mishneh was near Ephraim Gate (see III.D.5.h), then the juxtaposition of "Fish Gate," "Mishneh," and "the Mortar" in Zeph. 1:10 becomes more meaningful. If the Mishneh was the "second" quarter of the city, on the southwest hill, and the Maktesh (Mortar) was a new addition northward along the Central Valley, this would fit the details well — but at present this is no more than a hypothesis, not agreeing with the more generally accepted view that the Mishneh was a northern addition to the settlement on the southwest hill.

a'. *Old Gate* (*haššaʿar hayy^{e}šānâ*; this cannot be translated "old gate," for *šaʿar* is masc. and *y^{e}šānâ* is fem.; hence "Gate of the Old [Wall]" or, with a minor emendation, "Gate of the Mishneh," Neh. 3:6; 12:39). If formerly a wall extended westward from the Central Valley to the ridge above the Hinnom (now generally accepted), to which a later wall was added that embraced the more northerly part of the Central Valley (the two probabilities on Avigad's map), this may have been a gate opening between these two parts of the city.

b'. *Gate of Ephraim* (2 K. 14:13; 2 Ch. 25:23; Neh. 8:16; 12:39). This gate was 400 cubits (about 200 m., 656 ft.) from the Corner Gate (2 Ch. 25:23; see III.D.5.g above). It has been identified with the "Old Gate," but the presence of the preposition (*w^{e}ʿal*) in Neh. 12:39 makes it impossible to read "even the Old Gate." The two were in the same vicinity; it is possible that the addition of the "Mishneh wall" necessitated the opening of a new Ephraim Gate in order to give access to the road north to Ephraim or Samaria.

c'. *Broad Wall* (*haḥômâ hār^{e}ḥāḇâ,* Neh. 3:8; 12:38). This may be the wall of which part was discovered in the excavations of 1969-1971 (N. Avigad, *IEJ*, 20, 1-8, 129-140; 22, 193-200). The suggestion that it be translated "wall of the plaza/city square," while enticing, is impossible without emending the text. (The LXX can be translated either way, but at least it supports the MT.) Avigad described a broad wall, 6.4 to 7.2 m. (21 to 24 ft.) wide.

d'. *Tower of the Furnaces* (Tower of the Ovens, Neh. 3:11; 12:38). This was in the northwestern part of the city, probably near the Corner Gate (see III.D.5.g above; 2 K. 14:13; 2 Ch. 26:9; Jer. 31:28; cf. 2 Ch. 25:3 and Zec. 14:10, both with slight emendations), and was possibly one of the towers built by Uzziah (2 Ch. 26:9; see III.D.2.c above).

e'. *Corner Gate* (2 K. 14:13). This gate was located at the northwestern corner of the city of that period, 400 cubits from the Ephraim Gate (see III.D.5.h above). The Tower of the Ovens (Furnaces) may have been built on or by the Corner Gate.

This completes a circuit of the city of Nehemiah, using the material in Nehemiah and the sequence found in Neh. 2:11-15; 3:1-32; and 12:31-43. It is clear that the city of Nehemiah's day could in no way have been limited to the eastern hills (the temple mount and David's City), as has been widely held. While it is true that no archeological discoveries from the Persian period have been found on the southwest hill — at several sites, Hellenistic or Hasmonean remains are immediately above Israelite, allowing no place for a Persian interval — the following facts still cannot be ignored. (1) Nehemiah describes the city as an eyewitness, and the Persian-period date of his work cannot be challenged. (2) In his description he uses names and locations that we now know were in existence in the preexilic period, and which, as has long been recognized, continued in use into the Hellenistic and Roman periods, some of these locations being on or related to the southwest hill. (3) The walls of Nehemiah's Jerusalem, as de-

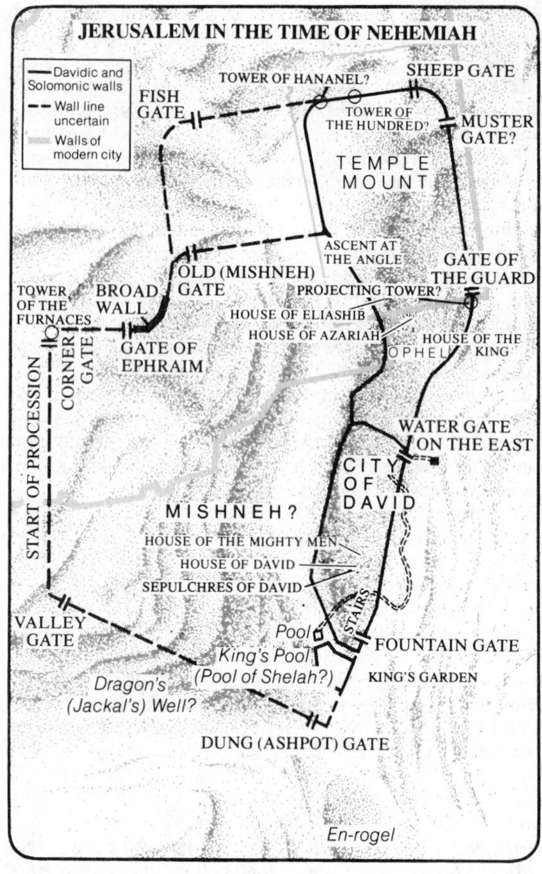

scribed in this synthesis, are quite similar to Josephus's First Wall (see III.G below).

3. Religious Situation. Since Jerusalem (Yahweh's holy city) and the temple (Yahweh's house) had been destroyed and the people decimated by wars (from *ca.* 742 to 586 B.C.) and finally exiled, since some had lived in Babylonia for a generation and others for three or four generations, and since those who had returned were thrown in with those who had remained in the land, many of them non-Israelites, one can readily see that the religion of Yahweh's Torah needed something to keep it from vanishing completely. Ezra and Nehemiah were given that task.

Building the walls to protect the city and the temple was only incidental. The time would come when another Prophet would point out, as Jeremiah had done, that God does not need temples and sacred cities. But meanwhile, the preservation of God's law, both in the lives of the people and in the form of Scripture for future generations, was of primary importance.

Ezra gathered the people in the city square before the Water Gate (Neh. 8:1, 3) and read the law. Since it was the time for the Festival of Booths (15-22 Tishri), the people built their "tabernacles" in the city square. Ezra read the law daily from early morning until midday (vv. 3, 18). He is also given credit for the formation of the Great Synagogue, becoming the "father" of Judaism (G. F. Moore, *Judaism,* I [1927], 29-47). The men of the Great Synagogue collected the Scriptures (T.B. *Baba Bathra* 15a), and Ezra copied them in the "Assyrian" (square) letters (T.B. *Sanhedrin* 21b-22a). According to some scholars, Ezra wrote the "P" document, 1 and 2 Chronicles, Ezra-Nehemiah, and Malachi, or various combinations. However these statements are interpreted, they lead to the conclusion that Ezra was an essential link between the religion of Israel and the religion of Judaic and Christian origins.

Ezra is sometimes seen as a legalist. He and Nehemiah put great stress on rigid sabbatarianism and were strongly opposed to mixed marriages. But it is a fact of sociology, as Nehemiah recognized (Neh. 13:23f.), that children grow up to speak the language of their mother; in other words, the more influential of the parents in the early training of the child is the mother. If Jewish men had been permitted freely to marry gentile women, within two or three generations the religion of the Jews probably would have disappeared entirely. Legalism had to be given its proper balance, and Jesus and Paul did so; but for the intervening period, a strong dedication to the law was necessary, if revealed religion were to survive.

4. Hellenistic and Hasmonean Periods. Information about Jerusalem from *ca.* 400 to 200 B.C. is almost nonexistent. There was, according to Josephus, some persecution by the Persians, although as a general rule they left the Jews alone. Josephus quoted Hecateus of Abdera, who said that "many ten-thousands" of Jews were taken to Babylon (*CAp* i.22 [194]; Thackeray said in a note [*LCL*, I, 241 n. b] that Hecateus was in error and confused the Persians with the Babylonians — yet some historical background for the Esther story exists). Alexander conquered the Persian empire in stages (334-326 B.C.) and the age of hellenization had come. The story of Alexander's visit to Jerusalem (Josephus *Ant.* xi.8.5 [329-339]) is branded by scholars as fictitious.

The Jew-Samaritan schism had its roots at an earlier time, but the break came toward the middle of the 4th cent. B.C., when the Samaritans built a temple on Mt. Gerizim. It was destroyed by John Hyrcanus in 128 B.C. (Josephus *Ant.* xiii.11.1 [254-58]; *BJ* i.2.6 [62f.]; cf. H. H. Rowley, *BJRL*, 38 [1955], 166-198, with full bibliography).

Alexander left no heir and his empire dissolved in struggles among the Diadochoi, the principal ones for our purpose being the Lagides (Ptolemies) of Egypt and the Seleucids of Syria (Josephus *Ant.* xii.1.1 [1f.]). The Ptolemies controlled Palestine until 198 B.C., when the Seleucids took over. Ptolemy I Soter (satrap 323-305, king 305-283 B.C.), son of Lagos, entered Jerusalem on a Sabbath and took many Jews from Judah to Egypt (*Ant.* xii.1.1 [4-7]), among them a number of soldiers (Josephus drew material from the Letter of Aristeas 12f.). The date is not known but one suggestion is 312 B.C., following the battle of Gaza (R. Marcus, note to *Ant.* xii.i.1 [5] in *LCL*, VIII, 5 n. d). Ptolemy II Philadelphus (283-245 B.C.) released "some hundred and twenty thousand natives of Jerusalem who were slaves in Egypt" (*Ant.* xii.2.1 [11]) as partial payment for the privilege of copying the Hebrew Scriptures for the library at Alexandria (*Ant.* xii.2.1-3 [11-33]). Josephus, using the Letter of Aristeas, told in detail the story of the version known as the Septuagint (*Ant.* xii.2.4f., 7, 11 [39, 49, 57, 85-93], and particularly the translating, in xii.2.13 [101-109]).

Of particular interest is the material quoted by Josephus from Hecateus of Abdera "who rose to fame under King Alexander, and was afterward associated with Ptolemy, son of Lagos" (*CAp* i.22 [183]). There were many cities and forts in Judah, but only one fortified city, Jerusalem, which had a circumference of 50 stades (9250 m., 5¾ mi.; in *BJ* v.4.3 (158) Josephus gave the circumference of the city in the 1st cent. A.D. as 33 furlongs, about two-thirds the size given by Hecateus) and a population of 120,000 inhabitants (*CAp* i.22 [198]). Near the center of the city a stone wall enclosed an area which is clearly the temple. The wall was 5 plethra long (149 m., 490 ft.) and 100 cubits broad (about 50 m., 164 ft.) with a pair of gates (i.22 [198]). Inside the wall was an altar of unhewn stones, 20 by 20 cubits and 10 cubits high (about 10 x 10 x 5 m., 32 x 32 x 16 ft.), and a great edifice with a golden altar and lampstand, but not a single statue or votive offering (199). The chief priest was Hezekiah (178), a statement often disputed, but apparently substantiated by Seller's discovery of a coin at Beth-zur that contained the names of Jehohanan and Hezekiah in Hebrew (O. R. Sellers, *Citadel of Beth Zur* [1933], pp. 73ff.). Jehohanan was Honnai (Onias I), the high priest, and Hezekiah (Ezechias) was his chief priest. Hecateus remarked on the high status of the priesthood, which consisted of fifteen hundred men, and the august position of the high priest. In the Birah (cf. Neh. 2:8) there was a garrison of five hundred soldiers.

Even allowing for some exaggeration in the various numbers quoted, a reasonable portrayal of Jerusalem is given, one not greatly different from that which has been established by the excavations of the 1970's in the Old City.

Onias I was high priest from 320 to 290 B.C. His son, Simon I, is often identified as Simon (Simeon) the Just (Josephus *Ant.* xii.2.5 [131ff.]), but the panegyric of Simon in Sir. 50:1-24 and the confusion of later events and persons in Josephus's accounts have led scholars to suggest that Simon II was the Just. Repairs to the temple, strengthening of the fortifications of temple and city, and other details would fit the time after Jerusalem had been ravaged by Antiochus III (*ca.* 198 B.C.; *Ant.* xii.4.10 [224]). A well-known saying attributed to Simon is "On three things the world rests, on Torah, on worship, and on works of charity" (*Pirqe Aboth* i.2). He is considered the last leader of the Great Synagogue. After Simon the high priesthood deteriorated through secularization (cf. G. F. Moore, *Judaism,* III (1930), 8f.).

The highly complex and confused accounts of the struggles between the houses of Onias and Tobias, of the pro-Egyptian and pro-Syrian parties, and of intrigues to gain positions lie beyond this article. The process of hellenization had been at work in Judaism for some time. Hecateus (306-283 B.C.) refers to it (*ORHI*, II [1932], 217 n. 1; scholars are inclined to doubt statements by Hecateus relating to the time before Alexander), and history gives evidence of its effects (cf. 1 Macc. 1:43). Alongside the struggle in Judah was the constant struggle between the Seleucids and Ptolemies. This ended in 198 B.C. when the Seleucid Antiochus III took over all of Coelesyria (Syria and Palestine) with a victory at Paneas (later Caesarea Philippi). The hellenizers among the Jews were thus given more authority. Antiochus IV Epiphanes (175-164 B.C.) succeeded his elder brother Seleucus Philopator and at once set in motion his plan to hellenize ("civilize" was his term) his entire realm. Greek altars were set up at many places and the worship of Greek gods was required. He made Jason (who had hellenized his name from Joshua/Jesus) high priest on Jason's promise that he would vigorously pursue the program of hellenization. When a false report reached Jerusalem that Antiochus had been killed in battle with Egypt, Jason, who had been replaced by Menelaus, staged a revolt. Antiochus retaliated savagely, leaving his general Apollonius to occupy Jerusalem. The city walls were razed to the ground. A new fortress, the Akra, was erected on the citadel of David. A gymnasium was built and Greek names were to be used. No kind of separatism was to be tolerated; all were to be fused into one people with one religion. An image of Jupiter was set up on the altar (the "desolating sacrilege," Mt. 24:15 par. Mk. 13:14), and the courts of the temple were filled with Greek soldiers, hierodules, and the performance of licentious pagan rites. The sacred Scriptures were defiled or destroyed.

Resistance to hellenization came under the leadership of the MACCABEES or HASMONEANS. It began in 167 B.C. when Mattathias, a priest of the house of Hashmon in the town of Modin (Modein), near Lydda (modern Lud), was ordered to perform a pagan sacrifice at a pagan altar. He refused, and when another would have done so, he slew the apostate and the Syrian soldier, destroyed the altar, and called for an uprising (1 Macc. 2:1-28; Josephus *Ant.* xii.6.2 [268-278]). Mattathias had five sons: Simon, the second oldest, whom Mattathias designated as "father" because of his excellent understanding; Judas the "Maccabee" (spelled with either *k*, meaning "extinguisher," or *q*, meaning "hammer"), whom the father designated as commander of the army; John, the oldest; Jonathan, the youngest; and Eleazar. The revolt started slowly, but with the addition of the Hasidim and others who opposed hellenization the Hasmoneans finally gained a peace treaty. Judas took over Jerusalem, cleansed the temple, and on 25 Kislev (Dec. 13) 164 B.C. the temple was rededicated. The eight-day celebration is known as Hanukkah ("dedication," hence *tá enkaínia*, Jn. 10:22), also as "Lights" (*phōta* in Josephus) and "the feast of the Asmoneans."

Jonathan was appointed high priest, and after him Simon became high priest and ethnarch (141-135 B.C.). Fortifications were built and the Second Commonwealth was established. John Hyrcanus (135-105) suffered a siege of Jerusalem, when the walls were broken down, but then his fortunes changed and his reign became perhaps the high point of the Commonwealth.

Among those who resisted hellenization, the Hasidim were perhaps the "right wing," and from them probably developed the Pharisees, who were more centrist (possibly the Hasidim moved to the right and the Pharisees broke away). Another "sect" was the Sadducees, who were more sympathetic with hellenization. We first hear of the Pharisees and Sadducees in the days of Jonathan (*Ant.* xiii.5.9 [171]). When John Hyrcanus shifted his support from the Pharisees to the Sadducees, bitterness between the parties developed and continued into NT times. Somewhere in the same period the Essenes emerged, possibly as a group more to the right than the Pharisees, and perhaps from the Essenes the Qumrânians developed (cf. W. S. LaSor, "A Preliminary Reconstruction of Judaism in the Time of the Second Temple in the Light of the Published Qumran Materials," Th.D. diss., University of Southern California, 1956; *Amazing Dead Sea Scrolls* [rev. ed. 1962], pp. 222-239).

Later Hasmoneans seemed to forget the original struggle against hellenization. Judas Aristobulus I (104 B.C.) extended his kingdom northward, forcing Galilean Gentiles to become proselytes, while encouraging hellenization. He may have called himself Philhellene ("friend of the Greek"). Alexander Janneus (104-78 B.C.) extended the kingdom to its greatest limits. Possibly the inclusion of so many Gentiles contributed greatly to the spread of Hellenism among the Jews. Alexandra (78-69 B.C.) went to excesses in trying to make peace with the Pharisees. Aristobulus II (69-63 B.C.) gained the throne in victory over his older brother Hyrcanus, and when Antipater (father of the Herod to be known as "the Great") sought to undermine Aristobulus and put Hyrcanus on the throne, both sides appealed to the Roman commander Pompey, who had taken Damascus. In a swift move to put down a threatened revolt Pompey attacked Jerusalem, battered down the walls of the temple enclosure, and with some soldiers entered not only the temple but even the holy of holies. He permitted the Jews to continue their worship, however, and for a while under the Romans the Jewish people enjoyed better times.

Scholars have generally agreed that it was in this period, beginning *ca.* 200 B.C., that Jerusalem was greatly enlarged and many buildings were constructed on the southwest hill. Although the excavations of the 1970's require considerable revision of theories, it is true that there was much building just before the Herodian period. Some Herodian walls rest on Hasmonean foundations. The Citadel was fortified. Wilson's Arch, which supported a causeway between the southwest hill and the temple mount, was built in the Hellenistic period and reconstructed in the Herodian period. Likewise the eastern supporting wall of the temple mount is partly of pre-Herodian construction. The Hasmonean palace was built on the eastern slope of the southwest hill with a view over the temple mount. According to B. Mazar, it, too, was linked with the temple mount by a causeway (*Mountain*, p. 204). The capital of a column in the Ionic order was discovered in excavations of the Old City, indicating that hellenization had influenced even the architecture. Simon the Just is credited with the building of a great city pool to augment the water supply (cf. Sir. 50:1-3), identified as the Pool of Bethesda (cf. Jn. 5:2-4).

G. Herodian Jerusalem. For the complex story of the Herodian family, *see* HEROD. In this article only his building activities in Jerusalem are relevant.

1. General Observations. It is exceedingly difficult for the visitor to Jerusalem today to visualize what it was like just before and during the Herodian period (or at the time of Jesus). First, the walls of the Old City are not where they were then; at least the south wall is much farther north, and the north wall likewise is probably partly or entirely much farther north. As a result, the Old City has shifted anywhere from 300 to 600 m. (1000 to 2000 ft.) N of the site of the Herodian city. Especially the portion S of the present wall, which slopes down to the Hinnom, is unlike the Herodian city, for this is where many of the houses, as well as some of the important buildings (e.g., the palace of the high priest and the Hippodrome) were

The southeastern corner of the Ḥaram esh-Sherîf showing the vertical junction of the Herodian wall and Nehemiah's wall (right). The smaller bricks in the upper portion of the wall are later additions (D. Baly)

located. In the second place, the Ḥaram does not give a true picture of the temple area. It is larger, occupying the enlarged temple platform built by Herod, and much more open than it was when Herod began his building. Third, the Central Valley (which Josephus called Tyropoeon, "Cheesemakers'") has almost disappeared, having been gradually filled with debris. Its location is still identified as *el-Wâd,* the street with the shops, running through the city from the Damascus Gate to the Dung Gate. But even this has been interrupted by buildings and later by the worship area (plaza) in front of the western wall. Fourth, the modern level is considerably higher than it was in the 1st century. At the southwest corner of the Ḥaram, for example, the modern ground level is about 20 m. (66 ft.) above the level of the Roman street, and the original bed of the Central Valley (about where the wall of the Old City abuts the south wall of the Ḥaram), was about 30 m. (100 ft.) lower. As a result, no clear picture emerges of the Upper City on the west and the deep ravine that separated it from the Lower City (David's City) on the east. Moreover, the leveling of the temple platform to coincide with its highest point has raised it markedly above the Ophel S of it. Fifth, the filling of St. Anne's Valley (done to complete the rectangular shape of the temple platform), the alteration of the topography around the Antonia, the cutting of a fosse, and the quarrying of stone have all changed the northeast end of the Old City. The best way to get a clear idea of what the Herodian city was like is to visit Avi-Yonah's scale model of Jerusalem on the grounds of the Holy Land Hotel in a western suburb of Jerusalem.

2. Josephus's Account. Josephus gave a detailed account of the three walls of Jerusalem and the towers (*BJ* v.4.1-4 [136-183]) and of the temple (v.5.1-8 [184-247]). Simons discussed these structures extensively (pp. 35-59). His basic conclusions are sound and many of them, formerly rejected by some scholars, have been confirmed by the excavations of the 1970's.

Josephus's First Wall started at the tower Hippicus and extended to the Xystus, joined the Council Chamber, and terminated at the western portico of the temple (*BJ* v.4.2 [144]). Hippicus was located at the Citadel, near the present Jaffa Gate; hence this northern wall ran west-east. The Xystus was a gymnasium, apparently in the open with polished flagstones (= Gk. *xystós*) (cf. *BJ* ii.16.3 [344]), close to the Hasmonean palace (*Ant.* xx.8.11 [189-190]), near the bridge that crossed the Central Valley. The remains of the bridge are known as Wilson's Arch (*BJ* vi.3.2 [199]; vi.6.2 [325]; vi.8.1 [377]). It would not be far from the modern Plaza of the Western Wall. The Council Chamber has been identified as the place where the Sanhedrin usually met, called in the Mishnah (*Middoth* v.4) *Lishkath ha-Gazith* ("Chamber of Hewn Stone," but possibly "Chamber of the Xystos," since *xystós* in the LXX translates *gāzîṯ* [1 Ch. 22:2; Am. 5:11]). The first northern wall approximately paralleled the cross valley (see II.B above).

The balance of the first wall is more difficult to trace. It began "at the same point" (generally taken to mean the Hippicus), "in the other direction, westward," past "Bethso," to the gate of the Essenes. It turned south above the "fountain of Siloam," east again toward "Solomon's pool," past Ophel, and finally joined the eastern portico of the temple (*BJ* v.4.2 [545]). Yadin (apparently alone) takes the first part literally, on the basis of his translation of the Temple Scroll from Qumrân, and locates Bethso (*bêṯ ṣô(a)ʿ*, the latrines) NW of the city (Y. Yadin, "The Gate of the Essenes and the Temple Scroll," in *Jerusalem Revealed,* pp. 90f.; cf. Josephus *BJ* ii.8.9 [147-49]). But this raises two objections. First, the northwestern side of the city, with wind generally from the west and particularly with the palace located there, is no place for latrines. Second, to extend the wall west — with no way to join it to the rest of the wall as described — makes little sense. The wall is generally described as enclosing the western and southern sides of the southwest hill (the Upper City), although the locations of Bethso and the Gate of the Essenes are not identified. The directions in the following portion of Josephus seem to be confused ("then [the wall] turned southward above the fountain of Siloam; thence it again inclined to the east toward Solomon's pool, and after passing a spot which they call Ophlas, finally joined the eastern portico of the temple") — but Josephus was certainly describing a wall that passed the southern part of David's City and then ran north along the Kidron Valley.

The tower Hippicus, named for a friend of Herod, is described in detail (*BJ* v.4.3 [163-65]). It was one of three towers built close together on the crest of a hill at the northwestern side of the Upper City (v.4.3 [161]; v.4.4 [173]), the others being Phasael, named for his brother (166), and Mariamne, named for his wife (170). Within the area was a cistern with provision for collecting rainwater from the roofs (164). Hippicus was 25 by 25 cubits, 30 cubits high; Phasael was 40 by 40 cubits, 90 cubits high, and Mariamne was 20 by 20 cubits, 55 cubits high, according to Josephus (the cubit = about ½ m. or 1½ ft.). Since the foundations of one of these, now identified as Phasael, are at the base of the Tower of David on the citadel, and since the general location and topography fit Josephus's numerous statements, there can be no doubt that the citadel is where these three towers were built (cf. R. Amiran and A. Eitan, "Excavations in the Jerusalem Citadel," in *Jerusalem Revealed,* pp. 52-54).

Josephus's second wall started from a gate in the first wall called Gennath, and enclosed the northern district of the town, going as far as Antonia (*BJ* v.4.2 [146]). Gennath may be the Ephraim Gate (see III.D.5.h above). Theories about the wall vary from taking it to be a rather small enclosure of the northern part of the Central Valley adjacent to the temple mount, to understanding it as part or all of the present north wall of the Old City.

Beginning at Hippicus the third wall went north to the tower Psephinus, which is described as "where the circuit of the wall bends back from the north to the west" (v.3.5 [133]), and N of Hippicus (v.4.2 [147]). Then it descended "opposite [*antikrý*] the tombs of Helen" (147), i.e., Helen of Adiabene. This site is now identified as "the Tombs of the Kings," located on the edge of Wâdī el-Jôz beyond St. George's Cathedral on Nablus Road, and provides a strong argument for those who have accepted the Sukenik-Mayer wall as the third wall (cf., e.g., E. L. Sukenik and L. A. Mayer, *Third Wall*; Simons, pp. 470-481; S. Ben-Arieh and E. Netzer, *IEJ,* 24 [1974], 97-107; M. Avi-Yonah, *IEJ,* 18 [1968], 98-125). The wall proceeded past the royal caverns, identified with the caves or quarries E of the Damascus Gate; this seems to be a strong point against the Sukenik-Mayer wall. The third wall then bent round a corner tower across from the so-called Fuller's tomb (location not identified) and joined the ancient rampart ending at the Kidron; this description could fit the present north wall from the quarries to the northeastern corner (*BJ* v.4.2 [147]).

In spite of a number of problems, it seems clear that the city of Josephus's time extended at least from the present north wall to the junction of the Kidron and Hinnom valleys, and from the citadel (Jaffa Gate) to the east wall of Ḥaram esh-Sherîf (the temple platform). It seems best to understand Josephus's first wall as the approximate location of the wall in the 7th cent. (B.C.), his second wall as that which enclosed the Mishneh, and the third as roughly

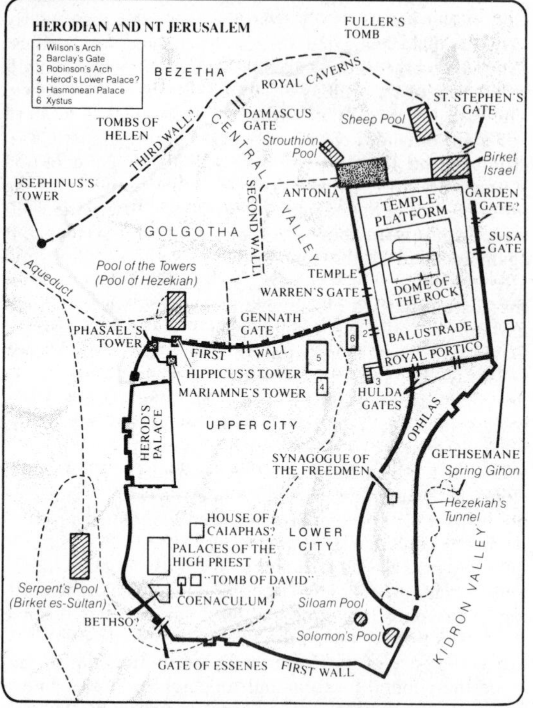

equivalent to the north wall of the present Old City — yet this view must remain tentative.

Herod built a palace "adjoining and on the inner side" of the three towers (*BJ* v.4.4 [176]), i.e., on the inner side of the region now known as the citadel. Josephus described it in some detail (176-183). He referred to the Upper City as the "upper market [*agorá*]," leading to the inference that there was a market or bazaar there. On the basis of Mishnaic references, J. Jeremias located such markets in both parts of the city: "The Upper and Lower Cities thus contained the two principal market streets" (p. 19). The house of Caiaphas is now identified with excavated remains on the southwest hill (modern Mt. Zion), just outside the Zion Gate of the Old City, but the identification is not certain. Some scholars are still inclined to locate it in one of the Hasmonean palaces near the Xystus.

The theater was built on the eastern slope of the southwest hill, opposite the southern end of the temple platform. The hippodrome, if indeed one existed in that period, was located in the Central Valley S of the temple platform.

Herod's greatest project was his rebuilding of the temple and enlarging of the temple platform. The size and shape of the previous platform are not known and probably will never be known while the present Ḥaram stands. The east hill (Josephus's "third hill") was arched, sloping down on the east to the Kidron, on the west to the Central Valley (Josephus's Tyropoeon Valley), and on the northeast to St. Anne's Valley, which ran diagonally (NW-SE), joining the Kidron somewhere around the Golden Gate of the present wall. Between the third hill and the City of David there was apparently a shallow depression or valley. Herod filled the area on the northeast (St. Anne's Valley) and on the southwest (the Tyropoeon) and raised the level of the temple platform to that of its highest point, "the Rock" under the Dome of the Rock. This enlarged platform was about twice the area of the preceding, and the filled areas were supported by retaining walls built of huge "Herodian" blocks of limestone.

The southern width was 900 *pódes,* the western length 1550 *pódes,* the northern width 1000 *pódes,* and the eastern length 1500 *pódes,* with the Herodian *poús* ("foot") equal to 0.31 m. (1.017 ft.). These figures were obtained by calculating the *poús* from a known measurement and applying the result to the entire platform; since the figures are all integers in multiples of 50 or 100, it is reasonable to assume that this is the original plan (cf. R. Grafmann, *IEJ,* 20 [1970], 60-66). Converting these figures to more familiar forms yields the following: 279 m., 480.5 m., 310 m., and 465 m. The Herodian foot is approximately equal to the Greek foot of the period as well as the later Byzantine foot of 30.8 cm. found beneath an inscription near Bethlehem (cf. F.-M. Abel, *RB,* 35 [1926], 284-88) and two-thirds of the small cubit of 46.5 cm. (18.3 in.).

Excavations carried out along the south wall and the southern part of the west wall have uncovered the Herodian masonry to bedrock. Robinson's Arch, which before the excavations stood only a few feet above ground level, springs from the eighteenth course above the foundation, and the street level in the 1st cent. was at the seventh course of stones. Under the street was a huge drain. The first seven courses had large protruding bosses, but above ground the bosses were finely combed, and only a little higher than the drafted margins.

It we assume that the Dome of the Rock stands over the original site of the altar (which obviously cannot be proved), the temple was located W of that point, facing east and surrounded by courts or enclosures. "Temple" in the NT translates two Greek words. The *hierón* was the entire sacred area, and the *naós* was the temple itself. Priests, Israelite men, Israelite women, and Gentiles approached the *naós* in their respective courts (the Court of the Gentiles being outermost), but only the high priest could enter it. Thus, e.g., when Matthew says that Jesus "entered the temple of God and drove out all who sold and bought in the temple" (21:12), it means that He entered the *hierón,* the sacred area, but not the *naós,* the temple itself. The Mishnah distinguishes between "the Temple Mount" and "the Temple Court" (Mish. *Middoth* i.1-4; ii.1-6). For further description, *see* TEMPLE.

At the northwest corner of the temple area, where the Hasmoneans had built the Baris, Herod rebuilt it and named it Antonia (cf. Josephus *BJ* i.3.3 [75]; i.5.4 [118]). Formerly it was portrayed as having four huge towers and extending over an area that included the northwest part of the Ḥaram and the convent of Notre Dame de Sion on the opposite side of the Via Dolorosa. The excavations of P. Benoit have severely restricted this to a portion adjoining the Ḥaram, probably having four small corner towers and a larger central tower (cf. P. Benoit, *HTR,* 64 [1971], 135-167; "The Archaeological Reconstruction of the Antonia Fortress," in *Jerusalem Revealed,* pp. 87-89). Mazar's excavations on the south wall have uncovered the Hulda Gates: a double gate toward the west and a triple gate toward the east. These led to tunnels under the southern basilica that opened in the Court of the Gentiles.

Herod also enlarged the water supply of Jerusalem. Since it is inconceivable that the city could have existed with only one spring, considerable development must have occurred at earlier times. At any rate, Herod and the Romans developed systems of aqueducts, built pools and cisterns, and made other improvements. These include the sheep pools in Bezetha, the area N of the temple mount, Strouthion Pool near Antonia, Birket Israel at the northeast end of the Ḥaram, the Pool of the Towers (called Amygdalon by Josephus, possibly corrupted from Heb. *hammiḏgālîm*), which was fed by an aqueduct from the Mamilla pool to the northwest, the Serpent's Pool (Birket

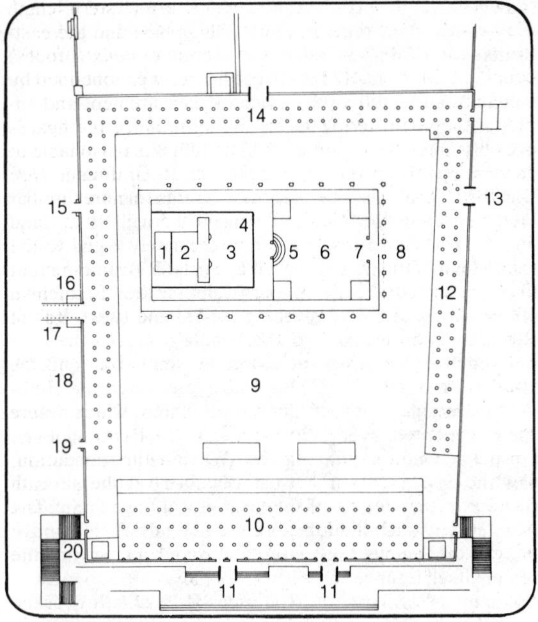

1 Holy of Holies
2 Sanctuary
3 Court of the Priests
4 Court of Israel (men)
5 Nicanor Gate
6 Court of the Women
7 Gate Beautiful
8 Balustrade with Greek and Latin inscription forbidding Gentiles to enter the sanctuary under penalty of death
9 Court of the Gentiles
10 Royal Basilica
11 Hulda Gates
12 Solomon's Porticoes
13 Susa Gate
14 Tadi Gate
15 Warren's Gate
16 Chamber of Hewn Stone
17 Wilson's Arch
18 Wailing Wall
19 Barclay's Gate
20 Robinson's Arch

es-Sultan), also fed by aqueduct from Mamilla, and repair of Solomon's Pools and the aqueduct from S of Bethlehem to the temple area. The aqueduct to the temple area, which fed a number of underground cisterns, was repaired by Pilate.

The 1969 study of the aqueducts presented by A. Mazar ("The Aqueducts of Jerusalem," in *Jerusalem Revealed,* pp. 79-84) gives some idea of the extent of the system. Three areas are of concern here: Wâdī ʿArrub, 20 km. (12 mi.) SSW of Jerusalem; the Pools of Solomon, 4 km. (2.5 mi.) SW of Bethlehem and 12 km. (7.5 mi.) SSW of Jerusalem; and Jerusalem. For the waters to flow by gravity to the temple mount, all sources had to lie above that altitude — a fact known to the rabbis and incorporated into the Babylonian Talmud: "The spring of Etam is higher than the floor of the court [of the temple] 23 cubits" (*Yoma* 31a) — and the aquifer had to maintain a continuous descent. The temple mount is 735 m. (2411 ft.) above sea level. The springs in Wâdī ʿArrub (ʿAin ʿArrub, ʿAin el-Dible, ʿAin Kuweiziba) are at 810 m. (2657 ft.). ʿAin Wâdī Biyar lies at 870 m. (2854 ft.). Solomon's Pools (three at slightly different levels) are around 780 m. (2559 ft.). The ʿArrub aqueduct carries water from ʿAin Kuweiziba, ʿAin el-Dible, and ʿAin ʿArrub to the middle of Solomon's Pools, a direct distance of 8 km. (5 mi.), by a very tortuous route measuring 40 km. (25 mi.). The Biyar aqueduct is much straighter, carrying the waters of springs in Wâdī Biyar to Solomon's Pools, a distance of 4.7 km. (2.9 mi.). From ʿAin ed-Daraj this is one long tunnel, built by digging tens of shafts and connecting their bottoms, similar to the construction of the Persian *qanât,* an engineering method that the Romans put to good use. These shafts were dug into the soft limestone and, according to A. Flexer, the geologist who examined the tunnel, the principle combined an aquifer and an aquiclud, so that all of the ground waters along the route were gathered. The method is so effective that when the British undertook the Mandate (1918), they provided water for Jerusalem by refurbishing Solomon's Pools and clearing and repairing the Biyar aqueduct. The system is still in use. From Solomon's Pools to Jerusalem there were two aqueducts, the lower aqueduct leading to the temple mount, 21 km. (13 mi.) long, and the upper aqueduct, which generally follows the Bethlehem-Jerusalem road leading to Hezekiah's pools. The lower aqueduct tunneled beneath Bethlehem (400 m., 1312 ft.) and beneath Jebel Mukabbir (370 m., 1214 ft.) and entered the temple mount over Wilson's Arch. Some of the construction of this elaborate system can be dated to Herodian times or earlier, and some was accomplished under the Mamelukes.

Herod the Great died in 4 B.C., at most two years after the birth of Jesus (cf. Mt. 2:16). He was followed by Archelaus (4 B.C.-A.D. 6), and then Jerusalem was placed under a Roman procurator. The succeeding Herodians, with the exception of Agrippa I (A.D. 41-44), were not

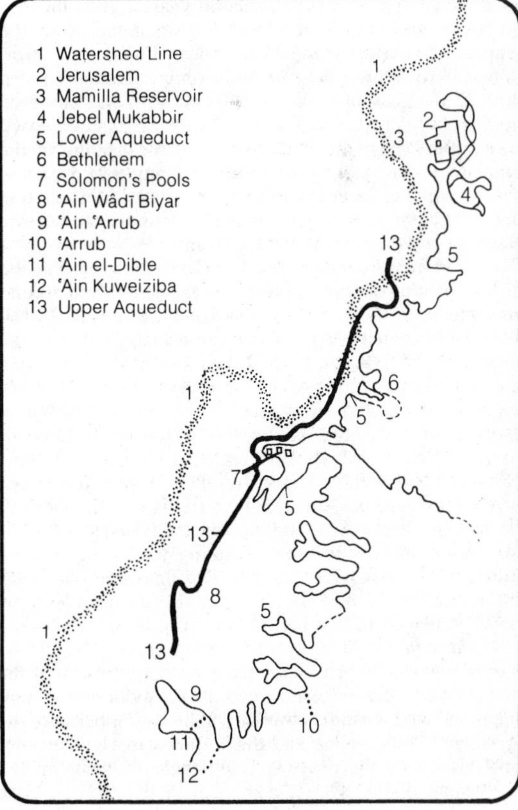

rulers of Judea, but rather ethnarchs of various outlying regions. Agrippa II ruled over Chalcis, portions of Galilee and Perea, and a part of Judea. With his death *ca.* A.D. 100, the Herodian period ended.

H. Jerusalem in the Time of Christ and the Apostles. The NT data can be fitted into what is known of Herodian Jerusalem.

1. First Years. The life of Jesus as presented in the Gospels had little contact with Jerusalem. The baby Jesus was presented in the temple (Lk. 2:22-40), but He spent the subsequent years in Egypt and Nazareth. At the age of twelve, possibly for a bar-mitzvah ceremony (if, indeed, this custom was already observed at that date), He was again in the temple (vv. 41-50), and possibly made annual visits, of which we have no record, to the city. Until He was about thirty no other data exist except that He grew up in Nazareth and was known there as "the carpenter's son" and "the carpenter."

2. Early Ministry. After Jesus was baptized by John the Baptizer, He was tempted by Satan; one of these temptations took place in the Holy City "on the pinnacle of the temple" (Mt. 4:5; Lk. 4:9). It was generally held that this was the southeast corner of the temple platform overlooking the Kidron, but it is now believed to have been the southwest corner, because of the discovery of an inscribed stone marking the place of the blowing of the shofar. The Synoptics give no other information about Jesus in Jerusalem until the end of His earthly ministry. The Fourth Gospel, however, records an "early Judean" ministry, located in the temple (2:13-25; possibly 3:1-21). Later Jesus performed a miracle at the pool of Bethesda (Bethzatha) by the Sheep Gate (5:1-18). This site is now occupied by the Church of Saint Anne. The discourse that followed (5:19-47) may have taken place in the temple (i.e., the *hierón;* see III.A above). On the occasion of the Feast of Tabernacles, possibly in the second year of His ministry, He again went to Jerusalem (7:1-15) and taught in the temple. The Gospel account continues without any indication of a break through 10:40, and a time reference is given in 10:22, the Feast of Dedication. Tabernacles was observed in Tishri (Sept./Oct.) and Dedication in Kislev (Nov./Dec.). Between these two indicators, the healing of the blind man took place at the pool of Siloam (9:7). Hence it seems that John intended to show that Jesus continued in the Jerusalem area for two months or more, to set the stage, as it were, for His final appearance.

3. Approach to Jerusalem. The Gospels agree that the closing portion of Jesus' ministry took place in and around Jerusalem. In the long Lukan account (Lk. 9:56–18:14), Jesus is presented as approaching Jerusalem. This was the intention (9:51), but just when He reached the city is not clear. Was the parable of the Good Samaritan (10:25-37), e.g., told in the Jerusalem area? The visit to the home of Martha and Mary (10:38-42) certainly was, but what of the following teachings? The reference to the tower of Siloam (13:4) and the warning about Herod (v. 31) may have been uttered in the Jerusalem area, but v. 22 is set elsewhere. It is clear that Luke was working toward Jerusalem (v. 33), but he certainly was not attempting to give a detailed itinerary (cf. also 17:11; 18:31). The final approach was from Jericho (Lk. 18:35; 19:1, 11), and the raising of Lazarus must be placed in this period (Jn. 11:6, 18; cf. 11:46-53).

4. Passion Ministry. The triumphal entry (Mt. 21:1-11 par.; Jn. 12:12-19) proceeded from Bethany (just E of the Mt. of Olives) to Jerusalem. According to modern tradition, the procession wound its way down the mount between the Armenian Gethsemane and the Franciscan Gethsemane, but this cannot be proved. From there, it went up the west bank of the Kidron and through the Golden Gate (now walled up). Scholars, however, are inclined to trace the journey along the north wall, which would join the old Roman road from Jerusalem to Jericho. If so, the procession would have moved north from Bethany to pick up the Roman road, and then descended the Mt. of Olives just S of Mt. Scopus, entering the city by a gate in the north wall, possibly the gate called Tadi Gate. But this view is not convincing. The southern end of the temple enclosure was the larger, the portion by the royal portico where the merchants and the money changers were located. It is more reasonable to suppose that the procession wound round the temple mount, possibly by the Kidron but more likely by way of the Tyropoeon Valley, gathering a crowd all the way, and finally reaching the Huldah Gates. In the Synoptics the cleansing of the temple occurred the next day. Each night was spent at Bethany (cf. Mk. 11:12, 19; Lk. 21:37).

The Dominus Flevit Chapel traditionally marks where Jesus lamented over Jerusalem (Lk. 19:41-44), but the Gospel account is quite vague: "When he drew near and saw the city" (v. 41). Likewise it is not possible to locate the site of the cursing of the fig tree — in fact, one must wonder why such identifications are sought. Jesus taught daily in the temple (the *hierón,* the sacred area around the temple itself). Since the early Christians chose to meet in Solomon's Portico (Acts 3:11; see III.H.22 below), possibly they had an emotional bond to the place; was it there that Jesus taught and disputed with the Pharisees and Sadducees?

Jesus discoursed on the destruction of Jerusalem and the end of the age while He and His disciples were sitting on the Mt. of Olives opposite the temple (Mk. 13:3). It is not necessary to demand absolute conformity with the words "There will not be left here one stone upon another" (Mt. 24:2). The utter frustration of explorers and archeologists who have tried to reconstruct the temple from the ruins is sufficient testimony to the essential truth of the prophecy. Was Jesus talking of the destruction in A.D. 70, or of the end of the present age, or of the end of the Satan-dominated world? Just as the prophets did of old, He telescoped near and distant fulfillment into a single prophecy. For further discussion, see the commentaries.

5. Palace of Caiaphas (Mt. 26:3). Traditionally this has been located on the southwest hill, outside Zion Gate. Modern archeologists have found remains that could be the palace (cf. M. Broshi, "Excavations in the House of Caiaphas, Mount Zion," in *Jerusalem Revealed,* pp. 57-60), but the identification remains conjectural. The palace of Ananias (cf. Acts 23:2) is generally located near the Hasmonean palace on the eastern part of the southwest hill (*BJ* ii.17.6 [426]).

6. Upper Room (Mk. 14:15 par.). The traditional location is at the Coenaculum (Cenacle) near the tomb of David on Mt. Zion, S of the house of Caiaphas. All of these terms are questionable. Mt. Zion, as previously shown, was on the southeast hill (see III.C.1.b above). David's tomb, likewise, was in the City of David (see III.F.2.j above). Both identifications presently given are from the Middle Ages. The building in which the upper room is located is, architecturally, from Crusader times, with later reconstructions. From the Gospel narrative, however, we can locate the Last Supper on the west of the Kidron (cf. Mk. 14:13, 26), and, since security was a problem (Judas having already agreed to deliver Jesus to the authorities), a remote spot on the southwest hill would not be incredible. To locate it so close to the palace of Caiaphas, however, may raise a question of credibility.

7. Gethsemane (Mt. 26:36 par.). Gethsemane was located across the Kidron on the Mt. of Olives (Lk. 22:39;

Jn. 18:1). Tradition has identified three sites: the grotto of Gethsemane E of the Basilica of the Assumption, the Franciscan Garden of Gethsemane somewhat to the south, and the Russian Garden near the church of St. Mary Magdalen, somewhat higher on the mount SE of the garden. The grotto best preserves original features, but this does nothing to prove or disprove the location. The old, gnarled olive trees in the Franciscan Garden are presented to the tourist as the trees that were there when Jesus prayed, "Let this cup pass from me" (Mt. 26:39 par.), but since the Romans cut down every tree for hundreds of meters in the siege of Jerusalem, it is highly unlikely that these survived. A modified theory claims that newer trees were grafted on the ancient roots — but even this is hard to accept. *See* Plate 42.

8. Peter's Denial (Mt. 26:69-75 par.; Jn. 18:25-27). Jesus was taken by the guard from Gethsemane to Caiaphas the high priest (Mt. 26:57; Jn. 18:13 says "to Annas," the father-in-law of Caiaphas), "where the scribes and the elders had gathered" (Mt. 26:57). Was this an official meeting of the Sanhedrin in the Chamber of Hewn Stone (see III.G above)? The reference to the courtyard (Mt. 26:58 par.; Jn. 18:15) seems to indicate that it was the house of the high priest (see III.H.5 above). According to the Mishnah a trial of such nature could not be held at night, but the Sanhedrin ceased to exist after A.D. 70, and the laws of the Mishnah, whenever they do not reflect earlier laws, do not bind the earlier Sanhedrin. G. F. Moore's comment is worth noting: "The inquiry whether the trial of Jesus was 'legal,' i.e. whether it conformed to the rules in the Mishnah, is futile because it assumes that those rules represent the judicial procedure of the old Sanhedrin" (*Judaism,* II [1927], 187 n. 5). It is better to consider this a preliminary hearing to prepare the grounds for a trial, and not a trial. The denial of Peter, which occurred in connection with the event, is traditionally located at the Church of St. Peter in Gallicantu, on the southeastern slopes of the southwest hill. Leading down from the church to the valley is an old flight of stone steps, which some authorities consider Roman and suggest as the route by which Jesus and the disciples journeyed from the upper room to Gethsemane.

9. Before the Sanhedrin. The following morning (which was but a few hours later) "all the chief priests and the elders of the people took counsel against Jesus to put him to death" (Mt. 27:1). The language suggests that this group was the Sanhedrin. According to J. Jeremias, the Sanhedrin was an aristocratic senate, a "small close circle composed of the heads of Jerusalem families" (pp. 223, 225), and every description of them points to the conclusion that they were more concerned about their status and power than about their spiritual leadership. Their meeting place was the Chamber of Hewn Stone (see III.G above), which according to Mish. *Middoth* (v.4) was on the south side of the temple, but according to Josephus (*BJ* v.4.2 [144]) it was near the Xystus, which could still adjoin the southwest retaining wall of the temple. In vi.6.3 [354] it is said to be between the Akra and the Ophel, which according to some studies would place it on the southeast hill S of the temple platform, but according to others in the Tyropoeon or on the slope of the southwest hill.

10. Before Pilate: The Praetorium. (Mt. 27:2 par.; "the praetorium," Jn. 18:28). According to tradition, the governor (procurator), whose official residence was in Caesarea-by-the-Sea, made his headquarters in the Antonia when in Jerusalem. This view has been challenged by some scholars, partly because the trips from the hearing before the chief priests to the hearing before Pilate would require too much travel through crowded city streets and therefore provide opportunity for rioting. A number of scholars, therefore, incline to the view that when in Jerusalem the Roman procurator made his official residence in the Herodian palace (cf. P. Benoit, "The Archaeological Reconstruction of the Antonia Fortress," in *Jerusalem Revealed,* p. 87; cf. Philo *De legatione ad Gaium* 38). This change also involves the location of the "Pavement" (Gk. *lithóstrōtos* [Gabbatha], where Pilate pronounced judgment on Jesus [Jn. 19:13]; part under the convent of the Dames de Sion), the Ecce Homo Arch, and the Via Dolorosa, for the journey to Calvary would have been on the northwest side of the city.

The theory of P. Benoit raises a few questions. The biblical account, whether one uses the Synoptic or the Johannine record, involves a crowd. No biblical basis exists for supposing that either the high priests or the Romans were avoiding the people. The release of Barabbas was a token gesture to the crowd (Mt. 27:15). Pilate's scourging of Jesus was a weakling's way of trying to satisfy the crowd's thirst for blood, and then an attempt to evade personal responsibility (Jn. 19:1-16). At Passover the entire city was crowded, but the one place in the city where crowds would have been most susceptible to psychological manipulation was in the shadow of the temple — which is precisely where Antonia was located. This observation does not, of course, constitute proof. It is simply a factor that must be taken into consideration. P. Benoit stated, "Josephus and Philo both testify that the Roman governors stayed there [Herod's palace] while in Jerusalem, and the Gospel's description would suit this site better than any other" (in *Jerusalem Revealed,* p. 87). The statements of Josephus and Philo will not bear that much weight, and the support that the Gospel accounts give to the Herodian palace location are questionable. It must be admitted, however, that the arch inside the convent of the Dames de Sion is to be attributed to Hadrian in the 2nd cent. (A.D.), and the pavement in the same area is also most likely of the same period.

11. Akeldama (Mt. 27:3-10; Acts 1:18f.). Traditionally "Akeldama" or "the Field of Blood" is located in the southern part of the Hinnom Valley, on the southern slopes, where the Crusaders built a Church of St. Mary in 1143, which the Greeks rebuilt in 1874 and named for St. Onophrius. One tradition locates the conversation between the representatives of Sennacherib and Eliakim (2 K. 18:17f.; see III.D.3 above) on this spot (cf. E. Hoade, *Guide to the Holy Land* [7th ed. 1973], p. 303). (J. Jeremias, pp. 138-140, took the account of Judas as spurious, but brought out the point that by returning the money to the temple Judas was complying with a provision for revoking a sale that appears in Mish. *Arakhin* ix.4.)

12. Location of Herod Antipas (Lk. 23:6-12). In an effort to dodge responsibility, Pilate sent Jesus to Herod. At that time there was no Jewish king over Judea. Herod Antipas was tetrarch of Galilee (Lk. 3:1; Josephus *BJ* ii.6.3 [94f.]; *Ant.* xii.11.4 [188]) and was in Jerusalem only for Passover (Lk. 23:7). He should have had no jurisdiction in the case — but Pilate was obviously desperate. The concern here is the location of Herod in Jerusalem. If the high priest was occupying the Hasmonean palace (not proved), Herod would not have been there. If Pilate was occupying the Herodian palace (also not proved), Herod Antipas would not have been there, for Pilate "sent him [Jesus] over to Herod" (23:7). On one map there is a "Lower Palace" of Herod next to the Hasmonean palace, as well as "Herod's Upper Palace" near the citadel (*Student Map Manual* [1979], 14-2), but there appears to be no confirmation of this. Since Herod was accompanied by soldiers (v. 11), the location must have been one of the palaces, but identification of the site is at present not possible.

13. Stations of the Cross (Mk. 15:21; etc.). The pilgrim to Jerusalem is shown fourteen Stations of the Cross, traditional locations of places where Jesus stopped or was stationed as He moved from the judgment to Calvary (cf. Hoade, *Guide,* pp. 195-212). At present, there is no objective support for any of these locations. Some of them are quite attractive and can produce an emotional or spiritual effect.

14. Golgotha (Calvary) (Mt. 27:33 par.; Jn. 19:17). For many decades the discussion of the location of Calvary has been heated and often bitter. Emotionalism has too often replaced scholarly objectivity. According to a Roman Catholic theologian, the identification of the Church of the Holy Sepulchre with the place of the crucifixion is not *de fide,* i.e., it is not required as an item of faith. But Catholic scholars have sometimes given the appearance of defending the faith when defending the site. Protestants, on the other hand, have often opposed this site simply because it is supported by Catholics.

The argument of primary consideration involved the location of the wall, for Calvary was outside the city (He. 13:12; cf. Mt. 28:11; Jn. 19:20), and if the site of the Church of the Holy Sepulchre was then inside the wall, that church cannot mark the authentic site. K. Kenyon's excavations demonstrated, on the basis of a quarry (which, in her view, must have been outside the city), that the church's site was outside the city (*Jerusalem,* pp. 153f.; this supersedes her article in *HDB* [rev. one-vol. ed. 1963], p. 475, where she came to a different conclusion). The history of the site must be considered. When Hadrian sought to wipe out every trace of Jerusalem and establish a new city, Aelia Capitolina (see III.H.32 below), he built a temple of Venus on the place where Christians marked the sepulchre (Eusebius *Vita Constantini* 3.26). When Constantine declared Jerusalem a Christian city (A.D. 325), the temple was destroyed and a basilica was erected on the site (A.D. 335, Eusebius *op.cit.* 3.26-32). The Bordeaux Pilgrim (A.D. 333) also described the church (quoted in *LAP* [2nd ed. 1959], p. 528). Excavations in and around the church confirm the location of Constantine's building (cf. B. Mazar, *Mountain,* pp. 245f.; C. Coüasnon, *The Church of the Holy Sepulchre in Jerusalem* [1974]).

15. Gordon's Calvary and Garden Tomb. A hill near the modern bus terminal close to Damascus Gate was identified as "the place of the skull" (Mt. 27:33 par.) by O. Thenius in 1842. His sole reason, it seems, was that the hill looked like a skull. When General C. Gordon, later of Khartoum fame, visited Jerusalem in 1883-1884, he declared this to be Calvary. His reasons are curious, indeed (originally published in *PEQ* [1885], reprinted in J. Wilkinson, *Jerusalem as Jesus Knew It* [1978], pp. 198-200; for an interesting discussion, see J. Simons, pp. 287-290). Near Gordon's Calvary is a garden with a tomb which had been discovered earlier, but which came to be known as "Gordon's Tomb," later "the Garden Tomb." The tomb may be from the 2nd cent. or later; it certainly has no ancient tradition. Nevertheless, it has become a touchstone of faith to many sincere Protestants. (Cf. L.-H. Vincent, *RB,* 34 [1925], 401f.; E. T. Richmond, *Sites of the Crucifixion and the Resurrection* [1934].)

16. "Galilee." After the Resurrection, an angel told the women who visited the tomb, "He is going before you to Galilee" (Mt. 28:7 par.). Since the Gospel record has no place for a visit to Galilee at that time, some have sought a site of this name near Jerusalem. According to one view, visitors to Jerusalem on the occasion of the feasts, having traveled together, often made their temporary residence together. Those from Galilee, it is suggested, stayed on the Mt. of Olives, near Bethany, and this was called "Galilee." No historical support for the suggestion has been offered. Jeremias simply said, "We may presume that the quarters for Galilean pilgrims were to the east of the city" (p. 62). Hoade located the site at Viri Galilee, the residence of the Greek Orthodox Patriarch (*Guide,* p. 306).

17. Place of Appearance to the Eleven (Jn. 20:19-25). Tradition locates the appearance to the Eleven in the upper room, but this does not have scriptural support, although some claim to find such in Acts 1:13.

18. Place of the Ascension (cf. Lk. 24:50f.; Acts 1:9-12). Tradition locates the Ascension at the Chapel of the Ascension on the top of the Mt. of Olives. The building is Crusader with a cupola added by Moslems, and inside is a stone slab imprinted with the reputed footprints of Jesus. Luke, however, records that "he led them out as far as Bethany" (24:50), and Acts indicates that it was a sabbath day's journey (2000 cubits, approximately 1 km. or 2/3 mi.) away.

19. Upper Room of Disciples (Acts 1:13). The room where the disciples stayed after the Ascension is called "the upper room," but whether it is the same as the room where the Last Supper was held is not specified. In addition to the Eleven there were "the women and Mary the mother of Jesus, and . . . his brothers" (1:14). If the next verse is to be considered part of the same account, "about a hundred and twenty" were present (1:15).

20. Pentecost (Acts 2:1). No location is given. The disciples were "in one place" (2:1), and after the glossolalial phenomenon Peter addressed the crowd that had assembled. Speculation sometimes locates the event in the temple court, possibly at Solomon's Portico. Where the baptism of the three thousand (2:41) took place is entirely a matter of speculation.

21. Gate Beautiful (Acts 3:2). The followers of Jesus attended the temple together daily (2:46). A miracle took place at "that gate of the temple which is called Beautiful" (3:2), the ornate gate on the east of the Court of the Women, separating it from the Court of the Gentiles; in effect, it was the main entrance for those wishing to approach the temple.

22. Solomon's Portico (Acts 3:11; 5:12; Jn. 10:23). The four sides of the temple platform (the *hierón* or "mountain of the house") were surrounded by colonnaded stoas, of which the eastern was known as "Solomon's" and the southern as "Royal" (*Ant.* xv.11.5 [411]; xx.9.7 [220f.]). Josephus apparently believed that the east portico remained from Solomon's temple, but this is contradicted not only by the structure itself but also by Josephus's own testimony concerning the Herodian expansion of the temple platform. It would seem, from the several Scripture references, that Jesus and later His disciples made the east portico their place of worship and teaching (cf. Acts 5:12f.).

23. Synagogue of the Freedmen (Acts 6:9). According to one tradition there were 480 synagogues in Jerusalem when it was destroyed in A.D. 70 (T.P. *Megillah* 73d). The "freedmen" were Jews whom Pompey had taken captive to Rome and later freed. Those who returned to Jerusalem established a synagogue. Weill discovered the ruins of a synagogue at the southern end of the southeast hill (Ophel); among the remains was a stone inscribed by Theodotus, who had restored the synagogue. It was built or rebuilt *ca.* A.D. 65, possibly on the location of the Synagogue of the Freedmen, as indicated on some maps. The connection lacks solid proof (cf. Simons, pp. 75f.). *See* FREEDMEN, SYNAGOGUE OF THE.

24. St. Stephen's Gate (cf. Acts 7:58–8:1). The gate in the east wall, known as St. Stephen's Gate, St. Mary's Gate, and Lions' Gate, is shown to tourists as the place where Stephen was stoned to death. The identification as St. Stephen's Gate is late, however, for when the Basilica of St. Stephen was erected on the north side of the city, the Nablus Gate, now known as the Damascus Gate, was the traditional site (cf. Simons, p. 14 n. 4).

25. House of Mary the Mother of Mark (Acts 12:12). Since this was the location of "many" who were gathered for prayer, some have identified it with the location of the "upper room" (see III.H.6 above). The site is unknown but is shown on some maps on the southwest hill not far from the Hasmonean palace. "Herod the king" of 12:1 was Herod Agrippa I, who was given the title of "king" by Caligula and ruled A.D. 41-44. Passover (14 Nisan) in A.D. 44 was May 1. Peter had probably been imprisoned in Antonia. For a fuller account see W. S. LaSor, *Church Alive! An Exposition of Acts* (1972), pp. 174-183.

26. Paul's Arrest in the Temple (Acts 21:17-36). Paul and Luke, returning from the third mission, were lodged in the house of Mnason of Cyprus (v. 16), location unknown. Paul's meeting with James and all the elders likewise was at an unspecified location. It is unlikely that at that date the Christians were still meeting in Solomon's Portico. Paul was to sponsor some men who had taken a vow, and for this he went into the temple (v. 26) — meaning, of course, the *hierón,* the enclosure, clearly beyond the balustrade with the signs forbidding Gentiles to go any closer to the temple, since he was accused of taking "Greeks" into the temple (vv. 28f.). The mob dragged Paul out of the temple, and the tribune of the cohort was informed of the ensuing riot. The charge that Paul had taken Gentiles into the "Court of Israel" was a capital offense; hence Paul was arrested and taken to Antonia. Two of the notices that were attached to the barricade surrounding the Court of Israel have been found, one in 1871, the second in 1935, both in Greek, reading: "No foreigner may enter within the barricade which surrounds the temple and enclosure. Anyone who is caught doing so will have himself to blame for his ensuing death" (cf. F. F. Bruce, *Book of the Acts* [*NICNT,* 1956], p. 434). *See* picture in INSCRIPTIONS.

27. Paul in the Barracks (Acts 21:37–22:29). The Roman soldiers were stationed in Antonia overlooking the temple enclosure. Antonia was separated from the temple mount by a ditch or fosse; likewise it was cut off from the "fourth hill," Bezetha, by a deep fosse dug for that purpose (*BJ* v.4.2 [149]). There were at least two "centuries" of soldiers since there were at least two centurions (21:32). An outside staircase apparently was open to public view, for from it Paul addressed the people (v. 39). If P. Benoit is correct in his reconstruction of Antonia (cf. "The Archaeological Reconstruction of the Antonia Fortress," in *Jerusalem Revealed,* p. 89), one can no longer visualize it in the form of the well-known models of Vincent, Avi-Yonah, *et al.*

28. Paul Before the Sanhedrin (Acts 23:1-10). According to T.B. *Abodah Zarah* 8b, *Shabbath* 15a, *Sanhedrin* 41a, and *Middoth,* the Sanhedrin had been exiled from the Chamber of Hewn Stone (see III.G, H.9 above), to a bazaar forty years before the destruction of Jerusalem (Jeremias, p. 210 n. 201). There is confusion concerning the location of the Chamber of Hewn Stone, some interpreting the Mishnah to mean that the council chamber was within the temple enclosure (e.g., on the south side of the Court of Israel), while others, attempting a harmonization with Josephus, have placed it adjacent to but outside the temple area. B. Mazar, however, located the bazaar in the *Ḥanuyot* in the temple enclosure, most likely in the Royal Portico (*Mountain,* p. 112). The high priest at that time (*ca.* A.D. 57) was Ananias ben Nebedaius (cf. Jeremias, p. 378; Josephus *Ant.* xx.9.2 [205]). Gamaliel (22:3), under whom Paul studied, was the Rabban Gamliel I, who was prominent in the first generation of the Tanna'im (cf. C. G. Montefiore and H. Loewe, *A Rabbinic Anthology* [repr. 1974], pp. 695f.), probably *ca.* A.D. 30-60.

29. James the Bishop of Jerusalem (Acts 15:13; Gal. 2:9; cf. Jas. 1:1; Jude 1). The leadership of James in the Jerusalem church is indicated by his position in the Jerusalem Conference (Acts 15) and by his priority over Peter and John (Gal. 2:9). He came to be known as "James the Just," and his death in A.D. 62 by stoning is recorded in Josephus (*Ant.* xx.9.1 [200]). Both Josephus and Paul (Gal. 1:19) refer to him as "James the brother of Jesus" (cf. Mt. 13:55; *see* BROTHERS OF THE LORD). Ananus, the high priest responsible for James's death, was deposed after a tenure of only three months (*Ant.* xx.9.1 [203]). According to Hegesippus (quoted in Eusebius, *HE* ii.23.11-18), James was thrown from the pinnacle of the temple, stoned, and clubbed to death with a fuller's club.

30. Population of Jerusalem. Estimates of the population of Jerusalem in the 1st cent. A.D. vary. The extreme figure, taken from Talmudic sources, is about twelve million (cf. Jeremias, p. 78). Josephus gave three million (*BJ* ii.14.3 [280]) or 2,700,000 (vi.9.3 [425]). These figures are based on the number of sacrificial animals at the time of Passover, averaging ten persons per animal. Josephus also gave the figures of those taken prisoner (97,000) and those killed (1,100,000) during the siege (vi.9.3 [420]). Jeremias, working from the available area in the temple for those offering sacrifices, arrived at a figure of 180,000, of which about 55,000 were inhabitants of Jerusalem and 125,000 were pilgrims (pp. 79-83). Or again, working from the area of the city and a density of 160 persons per acre, he arrived at a figure of 55,000 to 95,000 for the population of Jerusalem, and believed that even the lower figure may be too high (p. 83 n. 24). In an additional note dated 1966 Jeremias arrived at a figure of "about 20,000 inside the city walls at the time of Jesus, and 5,000 to 10,000 outside" (p. 84). T. W. Manson, *The Servant-Messiah* (1953), p. 11, estimated 30,000 to 35,000. (See III.D.5.b above.)

I. Destruction of Jerusalem (A.D. 70). After A.D. 6 Jerusalem was under Roman procurators, with the exception of the years 41-44 under Herod Agrippa I. Judea was apparently the least desirable post in government service, and the province's procurators were among the worst Roman officials. The Jews were increasingly restive under Roman control and the procurators were increasingly violent, cruel, and dishonest. Open rebellion broke out in A.D. 66. Two years earlier Gessius Florus, the procurator, had sent his troops on a mad rampage in Jerusalem, and the extreme Zealot faction of the Jews had reacted violently. The war began when the Zealots seized Masada and then, under Menahem, marched on Jerusalem. Simultaneously Jews in the gubernatorial city of Caesarea were massacred, and news of this atrocity spread throughout the country. New coins were marked Year 1 through Year 5 of the revolt (A.D. 66-70; *see* Plate 41). The emperor Nero dispatched Vespasian to Judea to put down the revolution; in 68 Vespasian had isolated Jerusalem and was ready to begin a siege. The empire, however, was in turmoil, with unrest in the east and revolt in the west. Nero committed suicide. Vespasian, who was acclaimed emperor in 69, left for Rome to secure his throne and gave his son Titus responsibility for ending the Jewish war.

Titus had four legions. The Tenth had moved from Jericho to the Mt. of Olives, destroying the Qumrân community on its way. The Twelfth had come from Caesarea and was encamped W of the city, along with the Fifth and Fifteenth that had come from the north. In the spring of 70 the offensive was launched. The Jewish forces were under Simon bar-Giora and Yohanan of Gush-Halab (John of Gischala). The Romans breached the third wall on the west and then the second wall, but their attempt to take Antonia failed. Titus thereupon decided on a siege, and a circumvallation was thrown up, according to Josephus almost 8 km. (5 mi.) long, built in three days (*BJ* v.12.1f. [491-511]). According to some scholars, the "third wall" of Sukenik and Mayer was part of this circumvallation (but see S. Ben-Arieh, "The 'Third Wall' of Jerusalem," in *Jerusalem Revealed,* pp. 60-62). The horrors of the six-month siege are graphically told by Josephus (*BJ* v.12.3 [512-18]). Antonia was taken, and the Jews barricaded themselves in the temple. On 9 Ab (Aug. 5, A.D. 70) the temple was burned and the Roman soldiers carried out a campaign of slaughter along the entire east ridge. The Jews made their last stand in Herod's palace but the end was inevitable. Titus ordered the entire city razed to the ground except for the three large towers at the northwest corner. Many Jews were executed, others were carried off as slaves, the Tenth Legion was quartered in Jerusalem, and Titus held a triumphal procession in Rome in which he displayed the golden candelabra from the temple. The Arch of Titus in Rome was built to commemorate the triumph and on one of its panels is carved in high relief the scene of his soldiers carrying the candlestand.

J. Destruction of Jerusalem (A.D. 135). The Christians had fled from Jerusalem in 66, basing their action, it is said, on the Lord's words in Mt. 24:15f. They located at Pella and returned to Jerusalem later. A Jewish center of learning was established at Yavneh (Jamnia) under the leadership of Rabban Johanan ben Zakkai. The next sixty years were rather uneventful. But when the emperor Hadrian visited the province in A.D. 130 and sensed the feeling of revolt still strong in the hearts of the Jews, he decided to crush it once for all. The rigid demands he imposed touched off the War of Freedom led by Ben-Koziba (Bar Cochba) in 132. Once again Jewish coinage was minted, with years 1, 2, and 3 of the Liberation appearing on the coins. The Roman troops, led by Julius Severus, triumphed in 135. This time Hadrian made good his plan to wipe out Jewish resistance in Jerusalem by destroying the city completely, pulling down every wall and plowing the entire area. Then he built a new city named Aelia Capitolina, with a main north-south street from the location of the Damascus Gate southward, a main east-west street about where David Street is today, and a forum at the intersection of the two. Streets were laid out on a grid, not following contours as previously. Walls were built, approximately where they are located today. A temple of Jupiter was built on the site of the temple and a temple of Venus on the site of Golgotha. The city had the usual Roman structures such as a theater, a hippodrome, public baths, and an aqueduct. No Jews were allowed in the city, or even within sight of it — a condition that prevailed until the 4th cent., and even then they were allowed to visit the city only on 9 Ab to bewail the destruction of the temple. Jesus' prophecy had become stark reality: Jerusalem was trodden down by the Gentiles (Lk. 21:22-24).

K. Subsequent History of Jerusalem. 1. Byzantine Period (A.D. 324-638). Constantine made Christianity the religion of the empire. His mother Queen Helena visited Jerusalem, located many sites, and erected buildings, including the Anastasia (later the Church of the Holy Sepulchre). The Madeba Map of Jerusalem was made toward the end of the 6th century. A brief Persian conquest lasted from 614 to 629.

2. Moslem Period (A.D. 638-1099). Caliph Omar entered Jerusalem in 638. The Dome of the Rock ("Mosque of Omar") was built by Caliph Abd el-Malik, 687-705, using Byzantine architects and craftsmen. The walls of the city had been rebuilt, following the earlier line along the Hinnom in the south. In 975 Caliph el-Aziz rebuilt the walls, reverting to the lines of Aelia Capitolina, approximately where they are today.

3. Crusader Period (A.D. 1099-1187). When Caliph Hakim ordered the destruction of Christian shrines in 1010, particularly when the Church of the Holy Sepulchre was destroyed, a major incentive for the Crusades was provided. This curious kind of Christianity left a mark on the religious world that has never been completely erased. Jews in the Holy Land suffered more from Crusaders than they had in 450 years of Moslem rule. Christian Arabs were slaughtered by Christian Crusaders as "infidels." The Latin (Christian) Kingdom of Jerusalem came to an end with the conquest by Salaḥ ed-Dîn (Saladin) in 1187. The unbelievable number of crusader fortresses, walls, and towers that spread across the Middle East is mute evidence of the power and wealth that was poured into this effort to wrest the Holy Land from the "infidels."

4. Mameluke Period (A.D. 1250-1517). Jerusalem was in Christian hands for brief periods (1229-1239 and 1243-1244). In 1244 Jerusalem was sacked by Khwarizmian Tatars, and in 1247 the city fell to Egypt under the Ayyubids. But in 1249, Aybak, a *mamluk* ("owned," i.e., a former slave), began a rule that was to last for nearly three centuries. The Mamelukes were peoples brought from Russia, the Caucasus, and central Asia by the caliphs of Baghdad to serve as soldier-slaves. They had gained great power, and Jerusalem came under that power. They rebuilt the walls, built *madrasa*s (school-mosque compounds), and beautified the Dome of the Rock, the Ḥaram esh-Sherîf, and the city. Christians and Jews were tolerated, but taxation was excessive.

5. Ottoman-Turk Period (A.D. 1517-1917). In 1517 Selim I took Jerusalem. Suleiman I (the Magnificent) ruled from Constantinople (1520-1566) and established a well-organized empire. He erected the present walls of Jerusalem. The Damascus Gate was the pride of his structures in Jerusalem. He built or repaired aqueducts, pools, and fountains. Christians and Jews were given full freedom but had to pay a high head tax imposed on all non-Moslems, in return for which they were exempt from military service.

6. British Mandate (A.D. 1917-1948). When the Turks became allies of Germany in World War I, the British, under Allenby, occupied Palestine and it became a British Mandate. Constant strife between Jews and Arabs, aggravated by the influx of Jews driven from Europe by persecution and finally by the Nazi efforts at a "final solution" (the Holocaust), caused Britain to terminate the Mandate. On November 29, 1947, the United Nations established two separate states, one Jewish and the other Arab. When the Mandate ended on May 14, 1948, the State of Israel was proclaimed and Arab opposition broke out in a war in which Lebanon, Syria, Iraq, Transjordan, Egypt, and Saudi Arabia were allied against Israel. Armistice agreements were signed in the early months of 1949, leaving Jerusalem divided between the Jews and the Arabs, with the newly formed Hashemite Kingdom of Jordan controlling the Old City and Israel controlling the western part of the city outside the walls.

7. State of Israel (A.D. 1948–). The State of Israel was proclaimed on May 14, 1948, and on Dec. 13, 1949, Jerusalem was declared its capital — a claim not recognized by a number of nations. On June 5, 1967, Jordan shelled the new city and the Six Day War began. When it ended, all of Jerusalem was in Israeli control. The area in front of the Western Wall (the Wailing Wall) was cleared and excavated to create a worship area. The old Jewish Quarter in the Old City was cleared of rubble and reconstruction

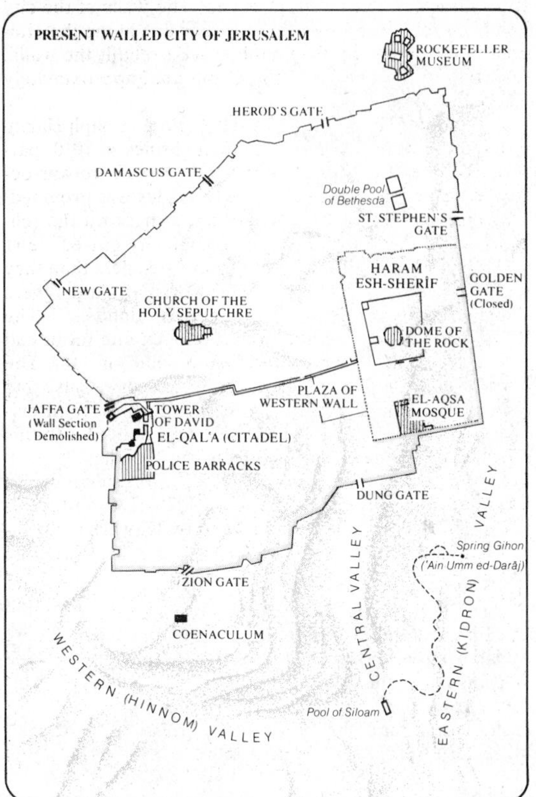

began. Archeological excavations were conducted in and around the Old City. The Dome of the Rock and the Ḥaram are open to all, including Arabs of all Arab states, but pilgrims from Arab nations are rarely present, due to political and emotional forces. Christian antiquities, particularly the Church of the Holy Sepulchre, are undergoing extensive repair and beautification.

IV. Jerusalem in Eschatology.–ESCHATOLOGY is a complex subject, beset with many difficulties of interpretation that are best considered elsewhere. Here the concern is simply to note certain truths in the main outline, without attempting to fit them into a system or to use them to preview history.

A. Location of the Throne of God's Great King. From the time that it was taken by David for his throne, Jerusalem has been both a reality and an ideal. As a reality, it can be sinful, apostate, abominable, subject to God's wrath, besieged by enemies, and finally destroyed. "I will send a fire upon Judah, and it shall devour the strongholds of Jerusalem," says the Lord (Am. 2:5). "Zion shall be plowed as a field; Jerusalem shall become a heap of ruins, and the mountain of the house a wooded height" (Mic. 4:1; cf. Isa. 2:2). "And when your people say, 'Why has the Lord our God done all these things to us?' you shall say to them, 'As you have forsaken me and served foreign gods in your land, so you shall serve strangers in a land that is not yours'" (Jer. 5:19). "They will fall by the edge of the sword, and be led captive among all nations; and Jerusalem will be trodden down by the Gentiles, until the times of the Gentiles are fulfilled" (Lk. 21:24).

Nevertheless, Jerusalem remains the hope of the world. "I have set my king on Zion, my holy hill," says the Lord (Ps. 2:6). "Great is the Lord and greatly to be praised in the city of our God! His holy mountain, beautiful in elevation, is the joy of all the earth, Mount Zion, in the far north, the city of the great King" (48:1f.). "Come, let us go up to the mountain of the Lord, to the house of the God of Jacob; that he may teach us his ways and that we may walk in his paths. For out of Zion shall go forth the law, and the word of the Lord from Jerusalem" (Isa. 2:3; cf. Mic. 4:1-3). Jerusalem is to be the seat of government of the wonderful counselor, the prince of peace, of whom alone it could be said, "Of the increase of his government and of peace there will be no end, upon the throne of David, and over his kingdom, to establish it, and to uphold it with justice and with righteousness from this time forth and for evermore" (Isa. 9:7). "Rejoice greatly, O daughter of Zion! Shout aloud, O daughter of Jerusalem! Lo, your king comes to you; triumphant and victorious is he" (Zec. 9:9). *See* Plate 35.

No matter how evil the king, no matter how sinful the people, the word of the Lord to His prophets was never a word of despair, never a message that He had given up His original plan. Through His chosen people He will work out His redemptive plan. Through His chosen king He will rule the nations in righteousness and peace.

B. Center of a Cosmic Struggle. Jerusalem is not simply the capital of a kingdom that must fight against other kingdoms of the world for survival. It is the city of God, and there is a cosmic, satanic opposition against God and against His redemptive purpose. A clear doctrine about the satanic is rarely expressed although greatly needed in the present age. Paul said it well: "For we are not contending against flesh and blood, but against the principalities, against the powers, against the world rulers of this present darkness, against the spiritual hosts of wickedness in the heavenly places" (Eph. 6:12). Ezekiel foretold the days when the Lord will restore His people to their own land (Ezk. 36:28), when by His spirit He will make His dead people live again (37:11), take them from the nations and bring them to the mountains of Israel, and place one king, His servant David, over them (vv. 21f., 24).

But these restorations will not ultimately solve the problem, for opposition to God's plan and His people remains. Ezekiel portrays the opposition as Gog of the land of Magog (Ezk. 38:1) who will go against these regathered people on the mountains of Israel (v. 8). Ezekiel makes clear that this will be no ordinary war, for this time God will not call upon Egyptians or Assyrians or Babylonians to do His work. He Himself will destroy Gog and his satanic forces (vv. 21-23). "I will set my glory among the nations; and all the nations shall see my judgment which I have executed, and my hand which I have laid on them," says the Lord (39:21). The author of the book of Revelation uses the same figure. After portraying war in heaven (Rev. 12:7) and the defeat of the deceiver of the whole world (v. 9), the revelator sees a struggle on earth (v. 13), but on Mt. Zion stands the Lamb with myriads of His own (14:1). Even after the song of triumph (19:1-10), however, there is still a satanic opponent to be destroyed. Satan is loosed from prison and enlists by deception the forces of Gog and Magog (20:7f.). "But fire came down from heaven and consumed them" (v. 9), and the devil and Death and Hades were thrown into the lake of fire (vv. 10, 14).

C. Perfect and Eternal Dwelling Place of God. In Ezekiel's temple vision, which he carefully dated, 10 Nisan of the fourteenth year after Jerusalem was captured (= Apr. 28, 575 B.C.), the prophet saw the new temple (cf. Ezk. 40:1-4). Much of the imagery is difficult to understand, but the message is clear: "The name of the city henceforth shall be, The Lord is there" (48:35).

The book of Revelation closes with a vision of the new Jerusalem, set in the new heaven and the new earth, "coming down out of heaven from God" (Rev. 21:2). The writer heard a great voice from the throne saying, "Behold, the dwelling of God is with men" (v. 3). Death, sorrow, and pain are no more, as the prophets of old foretold, "for the former things have passed away" (v. 4). The holy city hanging down from heaven like a splendid satellite has the glory of God, which is radiant like a rare jasper, clear as crystal (vv. 10f.). It has walls and gates; the gates bear the names of the twelve tribes of Israel and the foundations bear the names of the twelve apostles, for there is no longer any division of the people of God (vv. 22, 24). The gates shall never be shut (21:25; 22:5), either to keep out the enemy — for the last enemy has been destroyed and nothing unclean shall enter it, nor anyone who practices abomination or falsehood (21:23-27) — or to keep in the citizens, for the Ruler is not of this world. John saw no temple in the new Jerusalem, "for its temple is the Lord God the Almighty and the Lamb" (21:22). The temple made with hands was only a symbol of God's presence and could not, as Solomon recognized from the beginning, contain the eternal God (1 K. 8:27). What need is there for a symbol when God Himself dwells in the city? There is no need of the light of the sun or the moon, for the glory of the One who created the luminaries is the light and in that light shall the nations walk. The river of the water of life flows from the throne of God, and the tree of life grows on its banks, "and the leaves of the tree were for the healing of the nations" (22:1f.).

Bibliography.–F.-M. Abel, *Géographie de la Palestine,* I (1933), 181-84; W. F. Albright, *CAH,* II/2 (3rd ed. 1975), 98-116; R. Amiran and A. Eitan, *IEJ,* 20 (1970), 9-17; N. Avigad, *Archaeological Discoveries in the Jewish Quarter of Jerusalem — Second Temple Period* (1976); *IEJ,* 20 (1970), 1-8, 129-140; 22 (1972), 193-200; M. Avi-Yonah, *IEJ,* 4 (1954), 239-248; *Madeba Mosaic Map* (1954); M. Ben-Dov, *Christian News from Israel,* 26 (1978), 138-142; *Biblisches Reallexikon, s.v.* (K. Galling); F. J. Bliss and A. C. Dickie, *Excavations at Jerusalem, 1894-1897* (1898); M. Broshi, *IEJ,* 24 (1974), 20-26; *BA,* 40 (1977), 11-17; C. R. Conder, *City of Jerusalem* (1909); J. W. Crowfoot and G. M. FitzGerald, *Excavations in the Tyropoeon Valley, Jerusalem, 1927* (1929); G. Dalman, *Jerusalem und sein Gelände* (1930); *Sacred Sites and Ways: Studies in the Topography of the Gospels* (1935); *EAEHL,* II, *s.v.* (N. Avigad, *et al.*); J. Germer-Durand, *Topographie de l'ancienne Jérusalem des origines à Titus* (1912); R. Grafman, *IEJ,* 20 (1970), 60-66; E. Hamrick, *BA,* 40 (1977), 18-23; E. Hoade, *Guide to the Holy Land* (7th ed. 1973); O. Holtzmann, *Middoth: Text, Übersetzung, und Erklärung* (1913); J. Jeremias, *Jerusalem in the Time of Jesus* (Eng. tr. 1969); *Jerusalem Revealed* — see Y. Yadin; C. Johns, *Quarterly of the Department of Antiquities of Palestine,* 14 (1950), 121-190; K. M. Kenyon, *Jerusalem: Excavating 3000 Years of History* (1967); *Digging Up Jerusalem* (1974); *PEQ,* 94 (1962), 72ff.; 95 (1963), 7ff.; 96 (1964), 5ff.; 97 (1965), 18-20; T. Kollek and M. Pearlman, *Jerusalem, Sacred City of Mankind: A History of Forty Centuries* (2nd ed. 1974); R. A. S. Macalister and J. G. Duncan, *Excavations on the Hill of Ophel, Jerusalem, 1923-1925* (1926); W. S. McBirnie, *The Search for the Tomb of Jesus* (1975); R. M. Mackowski, *Jerusalem: City of Jesus* (1980); A. Mazar, *IEJ,* 26 (1976), 1-8; B. Mazar, *Mountain of the Lord* (1975); C. Schick, *PEQ* (1892), 120-24; N. Shaheen, *PEQ,* 109 (1977), 107-112; J. Simons, *Jerusalem in the OT* (1952); G. A. Smith, *Jerusalem* (2 vols., 1907-1908); E. L. Sukenik and L. A. Mayer, *Third Wall of Jerusalem* (1930); P. Thomsen, *Palästina-Literatur* (5 vols., 1894-1934); Y. Tsafrir, *RB,* 82 (1975), 501-522; A. D. Tushingham, *PEQ,* 100 (1968), 109-111; L.-H. Vincent, *Underground Jerusalem: Discoveries on the Hill of Ophel, 1909-1911* (Eng. tr. 1911); *Jérusalem antique* (1912), I; L.-H. Vincent and F.-M. Abel, *Jérusalem nouvelle* (3 vols., 1914-1926); L.-H. Vincent and A. Steve, *Jérusalem de l'Ancien Testament* (3 vols., 1956); C. Warren, *Underground Jerusalem* (1876); C. Warren and C. R. Conder, *Survey of Western Palestine: Jerusalem* (1884); R. Weill, *La Cité de David* (2 vols., 1920, 1947); Y. Yadin, ed., *Jerusalem Revealed: Archaeology in the Holy City, 1967-1974* (1976).

W. S. LASOR

JERUSALEM COUNCIL. *See* APOSTOLIC COUNCIL.

JERUSALEM, NEW. *See* JERUSALEM IV.C.

JERUSHA jə-ro͞o'shə [Heb. *yᵉrûšā'*–'possession']. In 2 K. 15:33, the same as Jerushah (Heb. *yᵉrûšâ,* same meaning) of 2 Ch. 27:1, the mother of King Jotham of Judah. Zadok was her father's name; he may be the priest of 1 Ch. 6:12 (MT 5:38).

JESHAIAH jə-shā'yə, jə-shī'ə [Heb. *yᵉšaʿyāhû* **(2, 3)**, *yᵉšaʿyâ* **(1, 4-6)**–'deliverance of Yahweh']; NEB ISAIAH.

1. Son of Hananiah, and grandson of Zerubbabel, according to 1 Ch. 3:21; AV Jesaiah.

2. A son of Jeduthun, and like him a temple musician; head of the family of that name (1 Ch. 25:3, 15).

3. A Levite, ancestor of Shelemoth, one of David's treasurers (1 Ch. 26:25).

4. A descendant of Elam; he went with Ezra from Babylon to Jerusalem (Ezr. 8:7, AV), the same as Josias (1 Esd. 8:33, AV; NEB Jessias).

5. A descendant of Merari and a contemporary of Ezra (Ezr. 8:19; 1 Esd. 8:48; AV Osias; NEB Jessias).

6. A Benjaminite (Neh. 11:7); AV Jesaiah; NEB Hosaeas.

D. F. ROBERTS

JESHANAH jesh'ə-nə, jə-shä'nə [Heb. *yᵉšānā*–'old (city)'? (2 Ch. 13:19); *šēn* (1 S. 7:12)]. A city named with Bethel and Ephron (variant Ephrain) among the places taken by Abijah from Jeroboam (2 Ch. 13:19). Most authorities agree that this name should be read for *šēn* in 1 S. 7:12, as evidence from the versions (LXX *tḗs palaías* < **hayᵉšānā*; Pesh. *yāšān*) and the geographical relation to Mizpah suggest. It is probably identical with the Isana of Josephus (*Ant.* xiv.15.12 [458]), where Antigonus's general Pappus had his headquarters. It is also probably to be identified with modern Burj el-Isaneh, about 5 km. (3 mi.) N of Jifneh (W. F. Albright, *BASOR,* 9 [Feb. 1923], 7). J. E. H.

JESHARELAH jesh-ə-rē'lə [Heb. *yᵉśar'ēlâ*]; NEB ASARELAH. One of the group of Levitical musicians appointed to serve in temple worship in the time of David (1 Ch. 25:14). A variant form of the same name (Asharelah; AV, NEB, Asarelah) appears in 1 Ch. 25:2.

JESHEBEAB jə-sheb'ē-ab [Heb. *yešeḇ'āḇ*–meaning uncertain]. A Levite of the fourteenth course (1 Ch. 24:13). LXX A reads "Ishbaal" while LXX B omits it. If *baʿal* was an original element of the name, the change of form in the MT and the omission from LXX B are understandable.

JESHER jē'shûr [Heb. *yēšer* or *yešer*–'uprightness'(?)]. A son of Caleb (1 Ch. 2:18).

JESHIMON jə-shē'mən, jə-shī'mən [Heb. *hayyᵉšîmôn*–'the desert'].

1. In the AV of Nu. 21:20; 23:28, and the NEB of 23:28, the desert N of the Dead Sea and E of the Jordan River. Pisgah overlooked this area, a bare and sterile land, saturated with salt and very little vegetation. In the RSV, and the NEB of 21:20, the word is translated "the desert."

2. The barren eastern part of the Judean mountains stretching toward the Dead Sea. The Hill of Hachilah was on the edge of this desert (1 S. 23:19; 26:1, 3), and the Arabah was to its south (1 S. 23:24). This desolate region of waterless land and soft chalky hills with numerous caves has been throughout history a refuge for fugitives, outlaws, and those who withdrew from society. David was forced to hide himself in this area to escape the wrath of Saul and took refuge at the oasis of En-gedi. Centuries later, the people of Qumrân built their community at Wâdī

Precipitous valley cut by a wadi in the rugged area known as Jeshimon, W of the Dead Sea (D. Baly)

Qumrân and the oasis of ʿAin Feshkha. The followers of Bar Cochba found refuge in the Jeshimon and later the Christian monastics of Mar Saba retired to this area.

The word is often used as a common noun in referring to the desert of Sinai (Dt. 32:10; Ps. 78:40; 106:14; Isa. 43:19; etc.). J. F. PREWITT

JESHISHAI jə-shish'ī [Heb. *yᵉšîšay*]. A Gadite chief (1 Ch. 5:14).

JESHOHAIAH jesh-ə-hī'ə [Heb. *yᵉšôḥāyâ*]. A prince in Simeon (1 Ch. 4:36).

JESHUA, JESHUAH jesh'o͞o-ə, je-sho͞o'ə [Heb. *yēšûa(a)ʿ*–'Yahweh is deliverance'; *see* JOSHUA].

1. Head of the ninth course of priests, and possibly of "the house of Jeshua" (1 Ch. 24:11, AV Jeshuah; Ezr. 2:36; Neh. 7:39; 1 Esd. 5:24).

2. A Levite of Hezekiah's time (2 Ch. 31:15).

3. The son of Jozadak who returned as high priest to Jerusalem after the Exile and supervised, with Zerubbabel the civil leader, the rebuilding of the temple and the restoration of worship (Ezr. 3:2, 8f.; 4:3; 5:2; Hag. 1:1, 12, 14; 2:2, 4; Sir. 49:11f. [his name appears as Joshua in Haggai and Zechariah]). He was a contemporary of the prophets Haggai and Zechariah, and the latter makes him the subject of two of his apocalyptic visions (3:1-10; 6:9-14). Some of his sons were among those who married "foreign women" after the return from captivity (Ezr. 10:18).

4. A man of Pahath-moab, some of whose descendants returned from Babylon to Jerusalem with Zerubbabel (Ezr. 2:6; Neh. 7:11), the same as Jesus in 1 Esd. 5:8.

5. Head of a Levitical house that had oversight of the workmen in the temple (Ezr. 2:40; 3:9; Neh. 7:43). He is mentioned again in Neh. 8:7 as taking part in explaining the Torah to the people, in 9:4f. (cf. 12:8) as leading in the worship, and in 10:9 (MT 10) as sealing the covenant; this Jeshua is called son of Azaniah (Neh. 10:9). To these references should be added probably Neh. 12:24 (NEB "Jeshua, Binnui, Kadmiel"). Perhaps Jozabad (Ezr. 8:33) is a "son" of this same Jeshua; cf. Ezr. 8:33 par. 1 Esd. 8:63, where the AV has Jesu. He is the same as Jessue (AV; NEB Jesue) in 1 Esd. 5:26.

6. Father of Ezer, a repairer of the wall (Neh. 3:19).

7. JOSHUA, son of Nun (Neh. 8:17, NEB).

D. F. ROBERTS J. E. H.

JESHUA jesh'o͞o-ə, je-sho͞o'ə [Heb. *yēšûa(a)ʿ*]. A place occupied by the children of Judah after their return from captivity (Neh. 11:26), evidently, from the places named with it, in the extreme S of Judah. It may correspond to the Shema of Josh. 15:26, and possibly to the Sheba of 19:2. The site may be Khirbet Saʿwī, a ruin upon a prominent hill, Tell es-Saʿwī, 19 km. (12 mi.) ENE of Beer-sheba. The hill is surrounded by a wall of large blocks of stone.

JESHURUN jə-sho͞o'rən, jesh'ə-rən [Heb. *yᵉšurûn*–'upright one'; Dt. 32:15; 33:5, 26; Isa. 44:2]. The LXX translates it "the beloved one" (Gk. *ēgapēménos,* the pf. pass. part. of *agapáō*), and in Isa. 44:2 adds "Israel"; Vulg. has Lat. *dilectus* in Dt. 32:15, elsewhere *rectissimus*; Aq., Symm., Theod. have "upright." Most modern scholars regard it as a hypocorism from the name Israel (Heb. *yiśrāʾēl*), of which the first three consonants are almost the same. In Nu. 23:10 the term "the righteous" (*yᵉšārîm*) is supposed to contain a similar reference. The name occurs only in poetry. The poems in Deuteronomy in which it occurs belong properly to the 2nd millennium B.C. In 32:15 Jeshurun, the chosen of God, became apostate and was promised divine retribution for abandoning the covenant ideals (vv. 23-25). The latter are reflected in 33:5, 26, where at Sinai the Israelite tribes had acknowledged in a pledge of obedience the lordship of the covenant (cf. Ex. 24:3). Divine election is indicated in Isa. 44:2, where the LXX renders the name "beloved Israel." In the NT the term "beloved" was used both of Christ (Mt. 3:17; Mk. 1:11; Eph. 1:6, etc.) and of the primitive church (Col. 3:12; 1 Thess. 1:4; Jude 1; etc.), again implying divine election to spiritual mission in the world. D. F. ROBERTS

JESIAH jə-sī'ə (1 Ch. 23:20, AV). *See* ISSHIAH **2, 4.**

JESIMIEL jə-sim'i-əl [Heb. *yᵉśîmiʾēl*–'God establishes']. A prince of Simeon (1 Ch. 4:36).

JESSE jes'ē [Heb. *yišay*; Gk. *Iessai*]. Grandson of Boaz, son of Obed, and father of King David. A member of the tribe of Judah, he owned land S of Jerusalem. Later his principal significance was as David's father; the phrase "son of Jesse," applied to David by his opponents (cf. 1 S. 20:27ff.; 22:7-9; 25:10; 1 K. 12:16) carried ridicule and scorn, as though Jesse were of no account in Hebrew society.

In 1 S. 16:1-13 Jesse is described as "the Bethlehemite" to whom Samuel was sent in his search for a successor to King Saul, who already was becoming mentally deranged. Jesse does not seem to have been wealthy, for he was apparently unable to have all his sons present at one time, thus leaving unattended his herds and flocks. On the occasion of Samuel's visit, David, the youngest son, was responsible for tending the flocks; when finally he was summoned into Samuel's presence he was anointed as Saul's successor.

When Saul's mental condition deteriorated further, Jesse's youngest son was recommended as a skillful harpist whose playing would help to soothe the deranged king; 1 S. 16:18 describes David as embodying the qualities of the ideal Hebrew aristocrat. Although Jesse sent with David a gift for King Saul — a donkey load of bread, a skin of wine, and a kid (v. 20) — and permitted David to reside at the court, Saul's and others' references to Jesse from this period seem to have been mostly contemptuous (20:27ff.). Jesse's three oldest sons served under Saul against the Philistines; when Jesse sent David with supplies for them the boy became involved with the giant Goliath (17:12ff.).

When David was harassed by Saul he took his parents

to Moab for safety (1 S. 22:3f.); Jesse was an aged man at the time (cf. 1 S. 17:12). At his death Jesse had fathered eight sons — Eliab, Abinadab, Shimea (Shammah), Nethanel, Raddai, Ozem, Elihu, and David — and two daughters, Zeruiah and Abigail. In contrast with his contemporaries' reproach, the prophets honored Jesse as the "stump" from which the Messiah would come (Isa. 11:1; AV "stem"). For Paul (Rom. 15:12) the "root [NEB "Scion"] of Jesse" was a synonym for the Messiah. R. K. H.

JESTING. Used once in the RSV for the piel of *ṣāḥaq* (Gen. 19:14). Here it refers merely to playful joking. "Jesting" also occurs once in the AV for Gk. *eutrapelía* (Eph. 5:4; RSV "levity"). Aristotle uses the original in his *Ethics* iv.14 as an equivalent of "quick-witted," from its root meaning "something easily turned," adding that, since the majority of people love excessive jesting, the word is apt to be degraded. This is the case in Eph. 5:4, where it clearly has a flavor of the coarse or licentious.

JESUI jes'o͞o-ī (Nu. 26:44, AV). *See* ISHVI.

JESUITES jes'o͞o-īts (Nu. 26:44, AV). *See* ISHVI.

JESUS jē'zəs [Gk. *Iēsous* < Heb. *y^ehôšu(a)ʿ*].

1. Joshua, the son of Nun (AV Acts 7:45; He. 4:8; cf. 1 Macc. 2:55; 2 Esd. 7:37).

2 and **3.** High priest and Levite. *See* JESHUA **2** and **5.**

4. Son of Sirach. *See* SIRACH I.

5. An ancestor of Jesus Christ (Lk. 3:29, AV Jose).

6. Jesus Christ. See the next two articles.

7. Jesus "called Justus" (Col. 4:11). *See* JESUS JUSTUS.

JESUS CHRIST [Gk. *Iēsous* < Heb. *yēšû(a)ʿ*–'savior'; Gk. *ho Christos*–'the anointed'].

I. Did Jesus Ever Live?
  A. Roman Witness
  B. Jewish Witness
II. Gospel History in the Light of Recent Study
III. Birth of Jesus
IV. An Outline of the Public Ministry of Jesus
V. Theological Significance of Jesus' Life

I. Did Jesus Ever Live?–The natural tendency may be to assume quite confidently that of course Jesus lived, for we have the witness of the Gospels and the continuing existence and influence of the Church that bears His name in the world. Nonetheless, now and again doubts have been cast upon the historical life of Jesus. This skepticism has taken various forms.

Over the last two hundred years or so, some skeptics have sought to explain the NT witness to Jesus and the rise of Christianity in terms of the Christ-myth theory. This view states that the story of Jesus is a piece of mythology, possessing no more substantial claims to historical fact than the old Greek or Norse stories of gods and heroes, and its basis is sought in the parallels, actual or legendary, to the Gospel records concerning Jesus. Sometimes these parallels are supposed to be comparable to the broad outline of the Gospel story; sometimes they refer to small details and isolated incidents. Thus, for instance, the account of His birth (it is claimed) may be paralleled from the traditions attached to the Buddha, Krishna, and Mithras. His miracles are set in comparison with those of Hellenistic "divine men," like the famous Apollonius of Tyana — an argument against the originality of Christianity that goes back to the first centuries of the Church, when the early skeptic Lucian tried to show that Jesus was but a pale reflection of Apollonius (see V. Taylor, *Formation of the Gospel Tradition* [2nd ed. 1935], pp. 127f.). His death and resurrection suggest to some minds a variant of the myth of the dying-and-rising god, so popular in the world of ancient pagan religion and represented in the cults of Attis, Adonis, Osiris, and Mithras.

Since these alleged analogies seem farfetched — and there is hardly a reputable scholar today who supports the legitimacy of these so-called parallels (G. A. Wells, *The Jesus of the Early Christians* [1971], being a solitary exception; see review in *Christian Graduate*, 25 [1972], 19) — recourse is made to some other possibilities. The most sensational of these is the reconstructed figure of the Teacher of Righteousness of the Qumrân community of the Dead Sea Scrolls. But the figure of the Teacher is altogether too shadowy and bloodless to have been the inspiration of the later followers. His ethical teachings as codified in the beliefs of the sect are scarcely up to the level of the Gospel records (*see* DEAD SEA SCROLLS II.I). That he was hung upon a tree — if indeed he died this way, at the hands of the Lion of Wrath — says nothing about the meaning of that death, while the supposition that he was raised in triumph is based on a dubious reading of the text (see G. Graystone, *The Scrolls and the Originality of Christ* [1958], pp. 73ff.).

These examples of the Christ-myth idea appeal to those who imagine that the origins of Christianity are obscure. They overlook the fact to which Acts 26:26 pays tribute, as Paul makes the public evidence of Christian origins the ground for the skeptic's acceptance: "These things were not done in a corner." And Peter adds his witness: "We have not followed cunningly devised fables" (2 Pet. 1:16). Those who doubt the historical validity of the Gospel records approach the documents with preconceived ideas, as a short list of some of the wilder specimens of speculation will show. Full details are given in F. C. Conybeare, *The Historical Christ* (1914) and Bruce, *Jesus and Christian Origins*.

Bertrand Russell leaves open the question of whether there was such a figure as Jesus of Nazareth as the Gospels portray Him. This negative attitude is shared by P. Graham, *The Jesus Hoax* (1974). But the question presses. Is it an open question about which reasonable doubt may be entertained? What is the verdict of history outside the Christian literature? Have we any independent testimony, uninfluenced by Christians, on which the unbiased historian may draw with certitude? A little independent evidence does exist. But a mass of data is unimportant here. Rather, the vital matter is evidence that is trustworthy and illuminating. It is the quality that counts.

Considering the contempt in which Roman society held the Jews and also the obscurity of Judea in the empire, it is not surprising that voluminous testimony to Our Lord's person is lacking. Yet some detail is given, and this must be accorded an important place.

A. Roman Witness. (1) Of Thallus the Samaritan, Julius Africanus writes, "Thallus, in the third book of his history, calls this darkness an eclipse of the sun, but in my opinion he is wrong." The allusion in question is to the preternatural darkness that accompanied the crucifixion of Jesus (Mk. 15:33 par.). A significant comment on this testimony is given by M. Goguel in his *Life of Jesus* (Eng. tr. 1933), p. 93: "This shows that this detail [of the darkness] was known in Rome, in the middle of the first century, in a circle near to the Imperial House. A small detail like this could not have been preserved and transmitted save within the setting of a narrative of the Passion." And thus a fragmentary allusion becomes sufficient to dispel the idea that Christ's story grew like a legend over the decades and centuries. Within twenty years or so of the actual event in the Gospels a secular writer is aware that a phenomenal happening was reported in connection with the event of the Cross.

(2) Suetonius' famous words (*Claudius* 25) are an indirect witness: "Claudius expelled the Jews from Rome because of their continual quarrelling at the instigation of *Chrestus*." The last word is doubtful of interpretation, but it is likely that the name intended is *Christus* and that Jewish-Christian controversies are in mind. Compare Acts 18:2 for this edict of the emperor Claudius, which is a further piece of evidence of the historical setting of the Christian gospel.

(3) In his description of the fire of Rome in A.D. 64 in the reign of Nero Caesar, the historian Tacitus (*Ann.* xv.44) adds this note: "Christ from whom they [the Christians whom Nero accused of arson] took their name had been put to death as a punishment during the reign of Tiberius at the hands of one of our procurators, Pontius Pilate, and a most mischievous superstition thus checked for the moment, again broke out not only in Judaea, the first source of the evil, but even in Rome, where all things hideous and shameful from every part of the world find their centre and become popular." This testimony speaks for itself and by linking the names of Pilate and Tiberius (as in Lk. 3:1) firmly anchors Christianity in the historical stream.

(4) The Roman official Pliny was governor of the province Bithynia-Pontus in Asia Minor in A.D. 111-112. In one extant piece of his correspondence with the emperor Trajan (*Ep.* x.96) he relates some information about the church's worship and witness in that area. In particular, he describes how the Christian believers were in the habit of meeting "before dawn on a set day and singing alternate verses to Christ as to a God." This evidence sheds light on early Christian worship. We note simply the plain allusion to the practice of the cultic adoration of Christ (see further R. P. Martin, *Carmen Christi* [1967], pp. 1-9).

B. Jewish Witness. The fall of Jerusalem in A.D. 70 destroyed most of the Jewish writings that bear upon our theme; and after that date, with a bitter cleavage between Church and synagogue now established, the revived Judaism apparently kept a deliberate silence concerning the practices of Christians, now regarded as apostates. Occasional innuendoes are made, however. An example is the twelfth of the "Eighteen Benedictions," a set of synagogue prayers, petitions: "To slanderers let there be no hope, and let all workers of wickedness perish in a moment." For the first term in this extra prayer the authentic reading seems to be not "slanderers" — a general term for the synagogues' opponents — but the *Minim*, i.e., the heretics. If so, this would be a reference to the Jewish believers in the Messiah. The prayer may have been an effective means of detecting in the synagogue service such believers, who would not use the prayer lest they call down condemnation on their own heads.

From the mass of rabbinic allusions to Jesus in the Talmud J. Klausner (*Jesus of Nazareth* [1926], p. 46) compiles the following summary: "There are reliable statements to the effect that his name was Yeshua (Yeshu) of Nazareth; that he 'practiced sorcery' (i.e., performed miracles) and beguiled and led Israel astray; that he mocked at the words of the wise; that he expounded Scripture in the same manner as the Pharisees; that he had five disciples; that he said that he was not come to take aught away from the Law or to add to it; that he was hanged (crucified) as a false teacher and beguiler on the eve of the Passover which happened on a Sabbath; and that his disciples healed the sick in his name."

Much more interesting and controversial is this description by the Jewish historian Josephus (*Ant.* xviii.3.3 [63f.]): "Now about this time arises Jesus, a wise man, if indeed he should be called a man. For he was a doer of marvellous deeds, a teacher of men who receive the truth with pleasure; and he won over to himself many Jews and many also of the Greek(s). He was the Christ. And when, on the indictment of the principal men among us, Pilate had sentenced him to the cross, those who had loved [or perhaps 'been content with'] him at the first did not cease; for he appeared to them on the third day alive again, the divine prophets having (fore)told these and ten thousand other wonderful things concerning him. And even now the tribe [or 'race'] of Christians, named after him, is not extinct." *See* JOSEPHUS, FLAVIUS.

It is true that this account in Josephus has been suspected as a Christian interpolation, although "it is difficult to imagine what sort of Christian could have deemed it worth his while to interpolate this cool, objective, patronizing, and faintly contemptuous paragraph into the text of Josephus" (T. W. Manson, *Studies in the Gospels and Epistles* [1962], pp. 18f.). Yet some textual doubts remain, and it is far from certain that Josephus penned a full confession of Jesus' messiahship. Nevertheless, we may grant that this *testimonium* is at least a witness that Jesus existed, was a wonder-worker who gathered followers, and paid the price for His novelties by death on a cross.

In fact, the common residuum of factual witness from the sources of Roman writers, rabbinic authorities, and Josephus, agrees in this simple, unvarnished summary. All our evidence adds up to the description, "a crucified false teacher." However inadequate this summary may be from a Christian standpoint, it at least focuses on the basic element in the gospel story, is not contradictory of it, and affirms the historical reality of Jesus as a first-century figure in Palestine.

II. Gospel History in the Light of Recent Study.–The modern study of the Gospels makes three widely shared assumptions.

(1) Source criticism, since the time of B. H. Streeter (*The Four Gospels* [1924]), has evaluated the chief literary sources of the Synoptic Gospels as "Mark, a hypothetical sayings-source labeled Q, special material in Matthew and special material in Luke." Recently doubt has been cast on the existence of Q as a written document (*see* Q article), and thus even more uncertainty is shown about complicated theories involving imponderables like Q, e.g., the proto-Luke hypothesis. The priority of Mark, although assailed, commands a wide acceptance, and recent challenges to the preliterary history of the Gospels as classically stated by Streeter have produced no substantial dislocation of the critical position.

(2) Form criticism, an attempt to probe beneath the surface of the canonical Gospels to discover the literary forms of the narratives and sayings of the individual sections that make up the records, is now an established tool in biblical research. The burning question is how far its (often) negative judgments on the historical worth of the material may be taken.

(3) Current debate on the "new quest of the historical Jesus" has highlighted the importance of historiography, and the consensus is that the Evangelists were not biographers or historians like von Ranke who describe "what exactly happened" in a disinterested and impartial way. They were not biographers, but evangelists, telling of the incursion of the divine into human life in the person of Jesus of Nazareth. By relating His life to His work, and that work to God's saving purposes in the hope of Israel, they were showing the achievement of the world's salvation. At heart, then, the Gospels are theological documents; they incorporate history, but it is interpreted his-

tory, which sets forth the fulfillment of God's redeeming motive and activity in Jesus, the Messiah and Lord.

Because these modern presuppositions lie at the center of the contemporary discussion of the life of Jesus, a survey of historical background is required. The place to begin is the work and influence of the European Life of Jesus School in the middle of the 19th century.

The aim of the Life of Jesus movement was clearly defined: it was to press back from the credal Christ to the Jesus of history. Albert Schweitzer, whose monumental book *The Quest of the Historical Jesus* chronicled the chief contributions of the *Leben-Jesu-Forschung,* expresses it thus: "They were eager to picture Him as truly and purely human, to strip from Him the robes of splendour with which he had been apparelled, and clothe him once more with the coarse garments in which He had walked in Galilee" (*Quest,* p. 4). This quotation shows that there were many motives that inspired the members of the Life of Jesus School. They had a genuine devotion to the humanity of Jesus, which they felt was obscured and overlaid by the Church's credal forms and by metaphysical doctrine. The Byzantine Christ in His transcendent majesty seemed remote and inhuman, and they were concerned lest this tendency to separate Jesus the man from the Christ of glory should result in Docetism. But they were equally alive to the danger of a revived Monarchianism which would exclude Jesus from the Godhead in the interest of stressing the unity of God. Precisely this peril appeared in the Harnackian theology, for which the quintessence of Christianity lies in the dictum: "The Gospel, as Jesus proclaimed it, has to do with the Father only and not with the Son" (*What is Christianity?* [Eng. tr. rev. ed. 1950], pp. 68f.).

Other motives may be detected. Strauss and the Mythical School had sought to show that Jesus was a legendary figure whose historicity was a debatable issue. The various "Lives of Jesus" asserted that He was, on the contrary, to be placed within the historical frame of the first-century world. Yet this insistence upon the historical Jesus invited the philosophical criticism that (as Lessing put it in his *Theological Writings,* III, 12) "accidental historical truths can never become proofs for the necessary truths of reason." Thus the historians of the life of Jesus were driven into the arms of "historicism," which admits of no unique cases.

Furthermore, biblical criticism in the mid-19th cent. was hospitable to the writings of these lives. Since the work of H. J. Holtzmann (*Die synoptischen Evangelien* [1863]) a high evaluation had been placed on Mark's Gospel as the first of the canonical Gospels; and it was assumed that this Gospel describes a purely human Jesus for whom no claims to divinity are made. There is no doubt, as Albert Schweitzer noted (*Quest,* pp. 204ff.), that Holtzmann's statement of the Markan hypothesis, i.e., that Mark's Gospel is the foundation document underlying the other Synoptics and contains a clear, factual, unembellished record of the life and public career of Jesus, had a tremendous influence in the second half of the 19th century. Holtzmann's vindication of Mark's priority and historicity held the field until the turn of the century, when powerful forces already at work assailed and destroyed it, at least for German scholarship.

Already in the 19th cent. the ground was being prepared for an assault on the Holtzmann doctrine, and more specifically on the generally accepted notion that a portrait of Jesus as He lived in Galilee and Jerusalem could be sketched by a careful and sympathetic drawing together of the Gospel data. Martin Kähler's *The So-called Historical Jesus and the Historic, Biblical Christ* (1892; Eng. tr. 1964) is a heated polemic against the historicism of his day that had produced the vagaries of the Life of Jesus portraits. Kähler objected that inevitably such an attempt at portraiture obscured the transcendental qualities of the biblical Christ. The living Christ is essentially the Christ of apostolic proclamation, accessible to us today in a spiritual encounter and not to be ferreted out of historical documents by psychological inquiry.

Many reasons (carefully noted by Carl E. Braaten in the introduction to his translation of Kähler's book) may be supplied for Kähler's about-face and antagonism to the historiographical methods and theological presuppositions of his day. Of central importance, however, was his conviction that the Gospels do not provide biographical data, giving us a window of access into the inner life of Jesus. They are "passion narratives with extended introductions" (to use Kähler's now celebrated phrase), containing the content of early Christian preaching and intended to awaken faith in Christ as Redeemer. The Gospels are, by design, theological documents, written from "faith to faith" (another now well-known sentence, which derives from Johannes Weiss), and serving an exclusively religious interest. The Christ they portray is the Christ of faith, the proclaimed Lord, whose encounter with His people is not at the mercy of historical investigation and systematic doubt. Only by insisting on the exact nature of our access to the "historic, biblical Christ" can we be delivered from the clutches of historical relativism (for which nothing in the past is absolutely certain) and be given an "invulnerable area" (Ger. *sturmfreies Gebiet*), unassailed and unassailable by historical inquiry. Kähler's discussion seriously questioned the current doctrine that Mark records plain, uninterpreted history which is capable of treatment by the methods of historical science and reveals to the impartial investigator Jesus as He was and is.

Influences at work in the early part of the 20th cent. developed the historical radicalism of Kähler.

(1) Wilhelm Wrede's book on the messianic secret in the Gospels (which first appeared in 1901) concluded that Mark's Gospel is not a record of unvarnished history, portraying Jesus as He really was, but a dogmatic treatise in which the doctrine of the messianic secret was imposed upon the materials by the Evangelist (*see* Mark, Gospel According to IV).

(2) K. L. Schmidt considered the "framework of the story of Jesus," to translate the title of his work, *Der Rahmen der Geschichte Jesu*; and by a form-critical analysis of the sections of the Gospel material he came to a startling verdict: "As a whole there is no life of Jesus in the sense of a developing biography, no chronological sketch of Jesus' history, but only pericopes [isolated paragraphs], which are put into a framework" (p. 317).

(3) The doctrine of *Sitz im Leben* (i.e., the principle that each section of the Gospel narrative may be suggestively placed in its historical context on the basis of its literary form and theological content) was taken by the early practitioners of the form-critical method a step beyond a purely literary exercise. From an analysis of the "types" or "forms" (Ger. *Gattungen*) of the literary materials of the Gospels into such categories as "miracle stories," "conflict stories," and biographical "tales," the form critics (or at least some of them) moved on to appraise the historical worth of the data. Thus, the historical value of the Synoptic incidents that appear as straightforward events of factual, episodic history is evaporated into whatever worth such hypothetical idealized reconstructions had for the post-Easter Church. The *Sitz im Leben Jesu* was transformed into the *Sitz im Leben der alten*

Kirche by a stroke of the form critics' pen, and Gospel history was subsumed under the ominous category of the theology of the community (*Gemeindetheologie*).

The name of Rudolf Bultmann occurs in this discussion as the author of the study *Jesus* (1926; Eng. tr. *Jesus and the Word,* 1934), based on his form-critical work *History of the Synoptic Tradition* (Eng. tr. 1963). These works may be taken as indicative of the effect of a radical form-critical approach to the Gospels' historical data. Emerging from Bultmann's literary analysis is the conclusion that the Jesus of the Gospels is the Christ of the apostolic experience. No historical foundation may legitimately be sought in the Synoptics — a judgment based on a twofold premise.

(1) Form-critically, it is impossible, Bultmann avers, to recapture Jesus as He moved in Galilee and Jerusalem and to know precisely what took place A.D. 30-33. The Gospels do not give us scientific biography, show any interest in Jesus' personality, nor offer a psychological study. There is no fascination with His charm, no window into His inner life. In Schweitzer's phrase, there is no estimate of the "inner and outward course of development in the life of Jesus." The Gospels accentuate not Jesus' personality, but His work, and that work is seen through the eyes of the later Church.

(2) From a theological point of view, the question "Can we know the Jesus of history as a figure of the past?" is answered in the negative. Even if it were possible to learn of the Jesus of history, it is illegitimate so to inquire, for faith can never be at the mercy of historical criticism and suspend its activity while the historians debate the issue, "Did it happen?" The person in whom the Christian faith confides is the risen Christ, living in the Church and present supremely in the ministry of preaching the kerygma. The Gospels perform the necessary function, not of directing faith to a past figure of whom certain historical values may be predicated, but of certifying that Jesus of Nazareth once embodied the Word of God in His existence in time. About this "Christ-event," i.e., the appearance of Jesus as an eschatological prophet of God who announced the imminent reign of God, nothing of *theological* significance is required to be known except that He once lived, taught, and died. The mere *Thatness* (That — Ger. *Dass* — He once existed) is sufficient; the character of Jesus (How — Ger. *Wie* — He acted) and the content of His message (What — Ger. *Was* — He said, in words that ruffled the air in Palestine long ago) are both beyond recovery and unnecessary to faith. The real importance of the Gospel testimony lies in its endorsement of Jesus' bare facticity, about which, to be sure, certain features may be predicated (stated clearly in Bultmann's *Jesus* in 1926 and repeated in 1960 in his essay translated in C. E. Braaten and R. A. Harrisville, eds., *The Historical Jesus and the Kerygmatic Christ* [1964], pp. 22ff.). Both the early and later Bultmann make much of a distinction (traceable also in E. Brunner, *The Mediator* [Eng. tr. 1934], pp. 265ff., 318ff., 345ff.) between Jesus' person (including His existence and certain features that belong to His activity and mission as healer and prophetic teacher, announcing the impending in-breaking of the divine rule) and His personality (i.e., the traits of His character and our knowledge of the inner working of His mind).

Bultmann is willing to affirm cautiously the facticity of Jesus' person, although he goes on immediately to deny to it any real theological value (pp. 24f.), because the Gospels are, by definition, not concerned with "objective historicity." Yet he stoutly denies any hint that Jesus' personality may be seen in the Gospels. Thus he is led to say that we have no sure knowledge of His understanding of His death. Mk. 10:45 is a "prophecy after the event," read back into the lifetime of Jesus. It is conceivable, he says, that He died in utter bewilderment and abject despair, a frustrated and rejected prophet of God.

Accepting, therefore, J. M. Robinson's revised estimate of Bultmann's skepticism concerning the historical Jesus, we may use his words to summarize the situation that led to the "New Quest" debate: "Bultmann's form-critical analyses corroborated the view that a Life of Jesus research after the style of the nineteenth century is impossible, and his existential interpretation undermined the thesis that such a Life of Jesus research was legitimate" (*Kerygma und historischer Jesus* [2nd ed. 1967], pp. 16f.). "Therefore it is not surprising that the critical restudy of his [Bultmann's] position by his pupils should begin here" (*A New Quest of the Historical Jesus* [1959], p. 12).

The central issues of the debate — how may we know the person of Jesus Christ, the preached Word of God, and what is His relation to history — may be read in some detail in the present writer's essay contributed to *Jesus of Nazareth: Savior and Lord,* ed. C. F. H. Henry (1966). That contribution may be supplemented by a summary of the writer's conclusions:

(1) In any sound approach to the Gospels — and we are dependent upon the canonical Gospels for our historical knowledge of Jesus — the first question is what these books purport to be. R. H. Lightfoot (in his books *Locality and Doctrine in the Gospels* [1938] and *History and Interpretation in the Gospels* [1935]) pinpointed this issue of methodology. In considering what sorts of questions we ought to ask of the Gospels, we must realize that the Gospels do not offer us biography in the modern sense of that term by tracing the Lord's career from His antecedents, the formative influences upon His character, and a day-to-day chronicle of His doings. Nor do they profess to supply objective history by telling a story in an impartial and disinterested way. And they are certainly not mythological accounts of a legendary figure, the cult-hero of a first-century religion.

The Gospels are theological documents, setting forth the interpreted history of the person in whom God visited and redeemed His people (Lk. 1:68). In the phrase "interpreted history," both aspects are to be given equal prominence. "History" is of vital importance because the Gospels record what actually took place in time and space. They are a standing denial of the Docetism that early afflicted the Church, i.e., the notion that Jesus was an appearance only and did not assume a true human nature (explicitly countered in the Johannine literature). Hans Conzelmann has sought to find an explanation of the source and origin of the canonical Gospels in the early appearance of a docetizing tendency, which denied a veritable incarnation; and it is still debated whether his attempt to detect Gnostic influences in centers of early Christianity (such as Corinth, as in W. Schmithals, *Gnosticism in Corinth* [Eng. tr. 1971], and R. M. Grant, *Historical Intro. to the NT* [1963], which call attention to 1 Cor. 12:3 as evidence of an attempt to separate the heavenly aeon Christ from the earthly Jesus, who is anathematized) can be sustained. But the Gospels do deny any docetic Christology in advance.

"Interpreted" or, perhaps better, "kerygmatic" draws attention to the purpose for which the Gospels were composed, stated in Jn. 20:31. The Gospels report history not for its own sake, but as the vehicle of God's redeeming grace in His Son. They declare that in this segment of history certain disclosure situations were created which reveal to faith that Jesus was God's messianic agent and is now the Church's exalted Lord.

(2) The axiom stated succinctly by T. W. Manson (*The*

Servant-Messiah, p. 67) — "a single story or saying may contain the whole Gospel in miniature" — fits the above proposition. Each Gospel pericope may be approached with the anticipation that it will disclose something of God's activity in Jesus. In Him God laid Himself bare to the eye of faith, and to examine the Gospel stories in this way and in the attitude of expectant faith means to anticipate discovering there what God is like. Having disclosed Himself once in Jesus, He has given a once-for-all revelation (represented in Gk. *eph' hápax*) that is accessible to the modern reader. This distinction, made by E. Käsemann in his celebrated address on the problem of the historical Jesus (Eng. tr. "The Problem of the Historical Jesus," in *Essays on NT Themes* [*SBT,* 41, 1964], pp. 15-47), between what happened once (upon a time — Ger. *einmal*) and what took place once and for all (*ein für alle Mal*) is one of the most fruitful suggestions to come out of the current New Quest controversy (pp. 30f.). In the life and death of Jesus certain patterns of life were displayed once upon a time. This anchors the Gospel in a historical stream. From this pattern (and one of the chief features is the tension "humiliation/exaltation," on which J. M. Robinson has written in W. Klassen and G. F. Snyder, eds., *Current Issues in NT Interpretation* [1962], pp. 91-110) once enacted in a human life, we can learn what is the eternal nature of God.

(3) The historian's task then is severely limited. By "indirect" research — of which E. Stauffer's *Jesus and His Story* is the best example — the historian can place Jesus in His setting of first-century Palestinian Judaism with its religious and cultural milieu. He can show that the historical evidence implies strongly that God is present and active in the man Jesus. But nothing except faith can grasp the implication "Jesus is Lord" and confess that God's presence is here mightily at work. History as a science operates with the category of "once" — "so it occurred." Faith alone perceives a transcendental significance in the historical event, giving it *Einmaligkeit* value, i.e., its uniqueness as revelation.

(4) In answer to the urgent summons "How then is Jesus known today?" the Christian historian with the Gospels before him will reply: "Not simply by inspection of these records." Then a knowledge of Jesus as the Christ and Lord of all would depend upon (a) human cleverness and (b) scholarly aptitude in handling ancient texts. The disclosure is made through the apostolic testimony in the Gospels within the context of the Church's life, faith, worship, and service, i.e., the revelation works only in the atmosphere of faith. The media of revelation include the *consensus fidelium* ("agreement of the faithful") of the past, making us debtors to all Christians who have led us in the way of Christ by their example, prayer, writing, and influence. Other media are the ministry of the preaching office by which the words of Christ are read, expounded, and applied to the concrete situations of modern life; the Gospel sacraments, instituted by dominical authority and pledges of the presence of the living Christ according to His express word; and the road of life, where we meet Him in the face of our neighbor and in situations of human need (Mt. 25:31-46). Thus the cup of water offered in His name becomes sacramental of His presence and grace, and the knowledge of Jesus Christ is mediated in the context of doing His will (Jn. 7:17) and serving one another as He did (Lk. 22:27).

III. Birth of Jesus.–The event of the Messiah's entry into the world is variously anticipated in the OT and in Judaism (see D. Edwards, *Virgin Birth in History and Faith* [1943]; R. E. Brown, *The Birth of the Messiah* [1977]) and described in full detail in the Infancy narratives (Mt. 1–2; Lk. 1–2), whose chief apologetic value lies in their opposition to Docetism (cf. 2 Jn. 7, and O. Cullmann's illuminating comments in *Christ and Time* [Eng. tr. 1951], pp. 125-130).

The scriptural data of the VIRGIN BIRTH are these. (1) Mary was betrothed to Joseph, a descendant of David, and was a virgin at that time (Mt. 1:18ff.). (2) The conception of the baby was due to the action of the Holy Spirit (Lk. 1:35). (3) An angelic messenger instructed the parents to name Him Jesus, a name with intense significance (Mt. 1:21). (4) Jesus was born in Bethlehem in the reign of Herod I, who died in 4 B.C. A suggestive discussion of the chronological problems connected with the Birth stories and the massacre of the innocents in Mt. 2:16-23 is given by H. E. W. Turner, in D. E. Nineham, *et al.,* eds., *History and Chronology in the NT* (1965), pp. 60ff. His conclusions are (1) that the massacre of the children by Herod, although otherwise unattested, is in keeping with the known character of Herod, especially if he was at that time under pressure from Rome; and the same circumstance may well account for a census under Sentius Saturninus, governor of Syria 9-6 B.C., which Tertullian (*Adv. Marc.* iv.9) speaks of as a "fact" (*constat*); and (2) that the star in Mt. 2 may be a conjunction of Jupiter and Saturn, visible in Palestine *ca.* 7 B.C. according to Kepler's computation. *See* STAR OF THE WISE MEN.

Turner has also treated the theological difficulties of the Birth narratives (*Expos.T.,* 68 [Oct. 1956]). The issues concern (1) the supposed parallels of Jesus' birth with stories of the births of Greek "holy men," such as Apollonius of Tyana (the strong Semitic coloring of the Lukan chapters is a cogent argument against the view that the Christian Gospels are indebted to a pagan source for this material; see J. G. Machen, *The Virgin Birth* [1930], pp. 317-379), and (2) the alleged silence of the rest of the NT about this doctrine. Admittedly the NT shows a marked reserve and does not blazon this teaching on every subsequent page. The evidence points to the conclusion that the Virgin Birth did not belong to the public kerygmatic message of the Church. But this same token suggests that the reserve was intentional because the facts came into circulation among believers through the mother herself (so J. K. S. Reid, in *RTWB,* pp. 275-77); or else, as Jeremias' conclusions (*Eucharistic Words,* pp. 72ff.) have shown, the Virgin Birth belonged to the so-called *disciplina arcani* or esoteric teaching of the Church, intended for those within the fellowship of the Christian fold and not for public debate.

The values of the Birth stories are manifold. Historically they show that early Christology developed the belief that the divinely given heir of the house of David was qualified for true messiahship as the "stem of Jesse's rod." They also emphasize the atmosphere of the supernatural and the miraculous in which the gospel, no less than the Lord Himself, was cradled; and they find no incompatibility between this assertion of His miraculous birth and His true incarnation. Jn. 1:14 is the classic statement of this.

Hints of the universality of the Christian gospel are seen in the visit of the Magi, who are identified by W. K. L. Clarke (*Divine Humanity* [1936], pp. 41-51) as Babylonian magicians and representatives of astral religion, bowing down in submission before the infant King.

Above all, Lk. 2:11 stands as a Christmas text which is complementary to the important passage in Ps. Sol. 17:36, "and their king shall be the Lord's Christ." The militant warrior-prince is hailed in language closely parallel with the Lukan verse, but the picture of the Savior is quite distinctive in the Christian writing. Jesus' messiahship is to be declared and acknowledged by His lowliness and obedience unto death, not by armed might. The cradle at Bethlehem is thus an epitome of His entire ministry.

IV. An Outline of the Public Ministry of Jesus (Based Chiefly on Mark).–The record in Mark's Gospel falls into some fairly obvious sections. After a brief introduction (1:1-13; for this division see R. H. Lightfoot, *Gospel Message of St. Mark* [1950], ch. 2), the first phase of the public career of Jesus — the call of the Twelve and the growing popularity of the Galilean ministry — is described in 1:14–7:31. Then 7:31–10:52 includes a period of withdrawal from Galilee and a more intensive training of the Twelve once they have confessed Jesus as Messiah (8:27ff.). The final period (11:1–15:47) carries the story to its climax in the last journey to Jerusalem, the final appeal to the nation, and the preparation for the betrayal, the arrest, the trial, and the crucifixion of the Messiah, to be followed by the denouement, which reveals that the last word is not one of tragedy and loss, but of victory and vindication (16:1-8a, at which point the authentic text of Mark ends).

A. Introduction. The appearance of John the Baptist marks the historical setting of Jesus' public ministry. It is possible that the exordium of the entire Gospel in this paragraph (1:1-8) should read: "The beginning of the Good News of Jesus . . . was John the Baptist's preaching of a baptism of repentance." This view, adopted by some Greek church fathers and in modern times by C. H. Turner (in C. Gore, *et al.*, eds., *A New Comm. on Holy Scripture* [1928], *in loc.*), would find confirmation in Acts 1:22; 10:37; and 13:24f., all of which see John's baptizing ministry as preceding the public appearance of Him in whom the gospel was actualized. Verses 1-8 focus attention upon John's distinctive practice, for of the many features of this messianic herald's work (see T. W. Manson, *Servant-Messiah* [1953], pp. 36-49) none is more important than his baptizing his fellow Jews in preparation for the coming of God's rule; and in that record of his baptisms no single baptism is more significant than his receiving and baptizing his cousin, Jesus of Nazareth (1:9-11). Cf. Mt. 3:13-17; Lk. 3:21-23; Jn. 1:24-34. This event provided a fixed starting-point for the public ministry.

At His baptism Jesus received an anointing of the Holy Spirit (cf. Acts 10:38) and a summons to His messianic service. The pattern of that service is clearly shown in the Father's announcement, "Thou art my Son, the Beloved; with thee I am greatly pleased" (1:11). This verse, in combining two OT passages (Ps. 2:7 and Isa. 42:1), strikingly links together a coronation formula for the messianic Son and a portrayal of the suffering Servant of God. There is also a possible underlying motif in the wording that recalls Gen. 22, where Isaac is depicted as Abraham's beloved child. This chapter received a targumic interpretation in the light of Isa. 53 (so G. Vermes, *Scripture and Tradition in Judaism* [1961], pp. 202ff.), so the various backgrounds may very well merge together. Thus the messianic Servant-Son begins a ministry of service and obedience that will culminate in His atonement for His people's sins (cf. O. Cullmann, *Christology of the NT,* pp. 66f.).

Jesus' baptism and temptation are inextricably joined (1:12f.). In the Jordan the call came marking the commencement of His public work. What that call meant and involved was made clear in His weeks of solitude in the wilderness. Mark simply notes the fact; the other Synoptics give a dramatic and revealing account in which the lines of temptation are clearly drawn, and the significance for Jesus and His future ministry carefully spelled out. William Manson (*Gospel of Luke* [1930], p. 36) rightly observes: "In the background of the experience there undoubtedly lie the Messianic ideas of Jesus' race and

The second temptation of Christ (Mt. 4:5-7). Relief, Cathedral of St. Lazarus, Autun, France, 12th cent. A.D.

time." To Him "these traditional Messianic ideas of his people [to be a political deliverer or an apocalyptic savior] appear not as divine inspirations but as Satanic perversions of the truth." The importance of this background cannot be overrated. Jesus, the temptations tell us, will not use any of the possible methods by which success can be achieved or accept any contemporary role open to Him. To use the apt description of H. E. W. Turner (*Jesus, Master and Lord,* pp. 98ff.), He will not be an economic Messiah, ministering solely to the bodily and social needs of people, nor a sign-giving Messiah, compelling belief by a theatrical display of supernatural ability, nor a political leader, ambitious to captivate the kingdoms of the world by Caesar's methods.

Instead, He began His ministry with the clear intention of being God's Servant in God's way. His first announcement (1:14f.) of the in-breaking of God's rule into human life picks up an earlier promise (in Psalms of Solomon 17:21: "Behold, O Lord, and raise up for them their king at the decisive hour [Gk. *kairós,* as in Mk. 1:15] which Thou didst choose"), but His subsequent activity will show how He was to purify and disinfect the current notion of the kingdom from all misconceptions and political associations and give it a content in terms of service and suffering unto death (Mk. 10:45).

B. Ministry in Galilee. Jesus' activity, following the initial declaration of 1:14f., began with a call to the masses in Galilee, accompanied by a call to individuals (1:16-20). This latter call is important because it shows that Jesus purposed from the beginning to create a new society. He was not simply teaching people in a vague, amorphous group; He intended to collect disciples (as the fine study by R. N. Flew, *Jesus and His Church* [2nd ed. 1943], shows convincingly) who should later be His messengers (3:14; for the concept of "discipleship" cf. E. Schweizer, *Lordship and Discipleship* [Eng. tr. 1960]). These disciples were learners of a practical craft, and in the company of their Master they were to catch His spirit.

A sabbath day's teaching in the synagogue (1:21-34) makes an impression not only on the human bystanders but also on the spirit world, now stirred to violent resistance. A summary paragraph (1:32-34) speaks of His healing ministry, directed to both physically sick and mentally disordered people. Both afflictions were thought to be caused by demonic influence; He must first "expel the demon."

Jesus' fame was spreading (1:28), and He sought retirement and renewal, responding to an insistent request to meet the crowds with a quiet determination not to get too caught up in a growing popular movement (1:35-39).

At some unspecified place (1:40) He was confronted by a leper, who doubted more His willingness than His ability to help (cf. 9:14-27). Jesus was moved with anger (so v. 41 in a good MS tradition, and to be preferred as the more difficult reading), for reasons at which we can only guess; and He cleansed the leprous man, bidding him comply with the law (which had proved powerless to aid him in his extremity) and cautioning him to keep a secrecy that would conceal the identity of the healer. D. E. Nineham (comm., *in loc.*) comments on the point of the story in Mark: the account and its sequel are placed here because they depict Jesus as fully obedient to the law of ritual cleansing (based on Lev. 14), as an earlier verse had shown His respect for the sabbath (1:32). Jesus' loyalty is illustrative of what follows because it shows that Jesus is no ruthless iconoclastic reformer, but breaks with rabbinic Judaism only when it comes into fundamental collision with the will of God expressed in His ministry.

In the healing of the paralytic (2:1-12) that controversy with official Judaism becomes apparent. The question of the debate in this story turns on v. 9: "Which is easier?" The declaration of healing and that of forgiveness are easy to say — and equally difficult to accomplish. Jesus then criticized His adversaries who raised objection to His ministry: "You have nothing to say to either his moral or physical condition: I have both the solving word and the effective help!" But the really criminal offense in the eyes of the rabbis was that Jesus pronounced forgiveness Himself, thus usurping a prerogative belonging exclusively to God (see Jn. 5:18 in the context of Jn. 5:1-16).

The call to Levi the tax official (2:13-17) is inserted into a group of stories that show the developing controversy between Jesus and His opponents. These narratives, first isolated and examined by M. Albertz in *Die synoptischen Streitgespräche* (1921) and more recently discussed by A. J. Hultgren, *Jesus and His Adversaries* (1979), indicate the nature of the disagreement between Jesus and scribal orthodoxy and orthopraxis in His day. The way the conflict would be resolved is not in doubt (3:6). They would destroy Him, for He had made claims that shocked His rabbinic audience:

(1) He claimed to forgive sins, and drew out the murmured comment, Why does this man talk like this? Who can forgive sins except God Himself?

(2) He chose to consort with tax-collectors and other bad company, treated by the Pharisees as beyond the pale of true religion, as "people of the land" (Heb. *ʿam hāʾāreṣ*) for whom no hope of salvation is possible (Lk. 15:1; Jn. 7:49). Further, He even called one of them to be His disciple. The position of *publicanus* in Roman-occupied Palestine was particularly obnoxious to the loyal Jews, smacking of compromise with the hated invaders and affording an opportunity for extortion and fraud.

(3) That His disciples did not fast occasioned serious questioning (2:18-22). The immediate background here is the Jewish picture of the messianic "good time coming," which is likened to a wedding feast. Jesus, in refusing to fast and to commit His followers to this practice, was tacitly announcing that the messianic age had begun. The feast is now to be enjoyed and everyone is to be happy. But He is under no illusion that everyone shares that joy, and darkly hints that an ominous future will await Him and His followers (2:20) because God's kingdom in Him and official Judaism are scarcely compatible, and must affect each other either by way of Jesus' revitalizing Judaism or (more probably) by a distinct break and a new beginning. "New wine calls for fresh wineskins" (v. 22).

(4) Jesus' sabbath violations offended the Jews, who treated His disciples' practice of plucking the ears of corn as falling within the category of "reaping and threshing," one of the thirty-nine schedules of work forbidden on the holy day. Jesus countered this objection with the assertion that the claims of the ministry override the sabbath rules, and even the venerable sabbath day (believed by the rabbis to antedate creation) is to give place to the Son of man, i.e., Him and His followers, in the work of the kingdom (see T. W. Manson, *ConNT,* 11 [1947], 138-146, on this meaning of Son of man). Later He was to turn this claim to priority into a prayer: "Give us today bread for the coming day" (of service in the interests of the kingdom).

(5) A further case of sabbath breaking — healing the man with the withered hand (3:1-6) — brings this series of conflict stories to a close; yet the notice of v. 6 points unmistakably to the way in which the future will be shaped.

A generalizing summary (3:7-12) epitomizes the first phase of the ministry. The Lord's immense popularity is attested, calling forth reactions of gratitude and more importantly hope that here may be the new leader of God's people, the heaven-sent Messiah. Yet official Judaism was shocked by His unconventional ways and annoyed by the carefree attitude He showed to the law whenever the claims of the ministry cut across the law's authority. As He fulfilled the messianic program enunciated in Lk. 4:16-39, the Jewish leaders grew alarmed and suspicious at His mounting success and influence.

The appointment of the Twelve (3:13-19) served a double purpose. They were to learn the secrets of the kingdom by personal acquaintance as learner-apprentices (for the underlying Aramaic of "disciple" in direct contrast to the rabbinic idea, see T. W. Manson, *Teaching of Jesus,* pp. 237-243); and they were then to become missionary-apostles to the world. In both ways they form the nucleus of the Church.

The reader is thereafter introduced to Jesus' immediate family ("And He came home," 3:20) and relatives (this is the sense of the Greek in 3:21). This section reminds us that Jesus encountered misunderstanding and opposition from those who were His own kinsfolk and friends as well as from those who took up an attitude of official animosity (cf. E. Trocmé, *Formation of the Gospel According to Mark* [1975]). Judaism failed to perceive that His power was a sign of His divine credentials. His wonders they attributed to an alliance with Satan. The family, on the other hand, credited Him with madness because of the strange behavior He showed and His obstinacy vis-à-vis the authorities. Both charges are frankly rebutted as blasphemy against the Spirit, a deliberate ridiculing of what is God-given; the rebuttals are invested with solemn warnings.

Up to this point the public ministry had been conducted either in the network of Galilean synagogues or in private conversation. With the mounting hostility of the synagogue leaders He turned to open-air preaching (4:1) and to a new type of teaching: instruction by parables. Parables are vivid observations (said T. W. Manson) of nature and human nature. They speak of commonplace things, events, and situations. Having gained our interest and sympathy, they bid us take a further step: to consider the best in life as a hint of, or a stepping-stone toward, what God is like.

Thus they set out a standard by which we can measure what we ought to be. "The parables show us what kind of God we must believe in and what kind of persons we must be" (T. W. Manson). Jesus taught by parables to make clear the nature and genius of God's kingdom in direct contrast to misconceptions and perversions of the nature of God current in popular and official teaching. This designation of the parabolic method is one of the chief contributions of J. Jeremias (*Parables of Jesus* [Eng. tr. 1955], p. 19), who describes them as Jesus' "weapons of warfare." By these powerful words Satan's realm is invaded and his "house robbed" (3:27).

The sower and the seeds speak of the effectiveness of Jesus' own teaching and form a parable about parables. In the explanation appended to the simple tale (4:14-20) we learn that despite wastage, failure due to human unresponsiveness, and Satanic countermeasures, there is a crop that crowns the preacher's task (likened to the farmer's work) with success, and gives him encouragement to go on. Jesus' own ministry is illumined by this piece of self-revelation, and its application in this parable to early Christian preaching in Mark's day is obvious.

Further parabolic warnings and encouragements indicate more about the kingdom's nature and outward growth. This may be summed up simply: speed and tardiness of growth are human standards not always applicable to farming. The farmer is known for his patience (Jas. 5:7), and is not overanxious concerning the seed he buries in the ground. Preachers may similarly leave the issue with God whose word they sow. God will take care of His own kingdom and fervid nationalist calls to arms are misplaced.

In the mustard seed simile (4:30-32) the accent falls on the inclusiveness of the rule of God, embracing the Gentiles, who are pictured as "birds of the air" (as in Ezk. 17:23; 31:6; Dnl. 4:9, 11, 18, and in rabbinic usage; cf. the evidence in J. Jeremias, *Jesus' Promise*, pp. 68f.).

Three examples of Jesus' acts of power follow in 4:35–5:43. First, the storm on the lake (4:35-41) recalls parallel OT passages which teach that ability to control the sea and subdue tempests is a characteristic sign of divine power (Ps. 89:8f.; 93:3f.; 106:8f.; Isa. 51:9f.). The nearest parallel is Ps. 107:23-30. In the background of these OT texts lies the imagery of the monster "chaos" (Akk. *Tiâmat*, Ugar. *thm*, Heb. *t*[e]*hôm*) subdued by the powerful god in Near Eastern thought (for this background cf. G. von Rad, *OT Theology*, I [Eng. tr. 1962], 150-52, 360f.). Of more significant interest to Mark's first readers would be the OT picture of sleep in the midst of upheaval as a token of perfect trust in the sustaining and protective power of God, exemplified in such cases as Ps. 4:8 (MT 9); Prov. 3:23f.; Job 11:18f.; Lev. 26:6. And when Yahweh seemed to be "asleep," i.e., inactive, in the face of His people's danger, He would be invoked to "awake" (Ps. 44:23f. [MT 24f.]; 35:23; 59:4 [MT 5]; Isa. 51:9). To the Church in Mark's day, threatened by persecution and fearful of the outcome, the reassuring and commanding word of its unseen Lord, "Peace! Be still," would come home with special relevance.

The second act of divine power — the cure of the Gerasene madman — is notable for its wealth of personal detail involving a reported conversation between Jesus and the demoniac (5:6-10, 18-20). (For a tradition-historical study of the story see R. Pesch, *Ecumenical Review*, 23 [1971], 349-376.) The incident is set in gentile territory, although the exact location is hard to determine. The "Gerasenes" were Gentiles who lived in the ten-town federation on the east of the Sea of Galilee (see v. 20), and there is some plausibility in the suggestion of Hoskyns and Davey (*Riddle of the NT* [1931], pp. 92-94) that this incident directly follows the preceding one to parallel the activity of God in Ps. 65. God stills the roaring of the sea and the tumult of the peoples (Ps. 65:7 [MT 8]). The Lord's power over disease and death (5:21-43) is shown in the third narrative; in fact, two stories are here merged into a unit of Gospel tradition. The raising of Jairus' daughter is obviously the chief event, and the finale receives an extra dramatic effect by the intercalation of the other account of the woman with the hemorrhage (vv. 25-34), which interrupted Jesus' movement to the scene of need and hopelessness. Early Christian confidence in the face of man's last enemy (1 Cor. 15:26) is well illustrated by the report of Jesus' explanation, "The child has not died, she is only asleep" (cf. *RTWB*, pp. 60f., for a discussion of NT passages that use this verb, "to sleep," of death). The skeptical reaction that greeted this sentence ("They only laughed Him to scorn") may portray pagan derision at the claim of eternal life made by Mark's church (see A. Richardson, *Miracle-Stories of the Gospels* [1956], p. 74).

After these impressive accounts of the Lord's wonder-working power and the human response of faith and devotion, the next pericope by way of stark contrast picks up the unsympathetic attitude of His family in ch. 3. Not surprisingly in such a hostile atmosphere of rejection and disbelief at Nazareth, Mark appends the realistic comment (compare Matthew and Luke, who modify this statement): "He could not perform any miracle there, except that He put His hands on a few sick people and healed them. And He was astonished at their unbelief." This is a quiet reminder that the Markan Jesus was not a Hellenistic thaumaturge, a *theíos anḗr* ("divine man"), bestowing his favors to build up his reputation, but worked in a congenial atmosphere where hope, expectancy, faith, and spiritual sensitivity were present, at least in germ. The plain declaration of His inability to perform miracles as though they were akin to conjuring tricks may be a sign of Mark's antidocetic strain, as well as a sad commentary on the rejection of the apostolic message by the Messiah's own people in the later decades.

Nor is it fortuitous that the success of the Twelve, whose mission is placed in the next section (6:7-13), also points in the direction of the subsequent mission to the Gentiles in the apostolic Church, as R. H. Lightfoot notes (*History and Interpretation*, p. 113).

Such a "sending forth" (v. 7 has the important Greek verb *apostéllō*) completes the purpose hinted at in ch. 3. "Their task is an extension of the Ministry of Jesus" (T. W. Manson, *Church's Ministry* [1948]), coupling a call to repentance with a ministry of healing. From all indications (e.g., in Lk. 10:1-20) this mission met with some success, and as an indirect proof of such a response from the people, Herod's reaction of alarm is noted (7:14-16). The

The traditional Mt. of Precipitation, from which the enraged people of Nazareth would have cast Jesus down (Lk. 4:29f.) (W. S. LaSor)

interesting comparison of Jesus with John *redivivus* (returned to life) leads on to the narrating of John's death, also reported in Josephus (*Ant.* xviii.5.2f. [116-19]).

The popularity of Jesus, assisted by the measure of success granted to the apostles' mission, provoked a crisis. The climax is reached at the conclusion of the following two pericopes (6:30-56). Various motives seem to have entered into Mark's placing of these stories side by side. Both accounts illustrate the disciples' dullness (vv. 51f.) in the face of the manifest evidence of Jesus' power, first, to provide a messianic banquet (on which see A. Schweitzer, *Mystery of the Kingdom of God* [Eng. tr. 1950], pp. 103ff.), and second, to assert His control of natural forces (as earlier at 4:35-41). But the historical context of v. 44 has been perceptively noted by T. W. Manson (*Servant-Messiah,* p. 71), namely, that Jesus was confronted here with an ugly situation which dangerously foreboded a messianic uprising (cf. H. Montefiore, *NTS,* 8 [1961/62], 135-141). The crowd comprised five thousand *men* (Gk. *ándres,* which may be significant; Mt. 14:21 adds "not counting women and children," perhaps to stress that these were strong men, colloquially "he-men"), and they are described as "sheep without a shepherd." It is true that Mt. 14:13f. tends to moralize this incident by observing the compassion of Jesus shown to a hapless crowd. But Mark's use of the sheep-shepherd metaphor points in a different direction. They are likened to a leaderless mob, an army without a general (1 K. 22:17) — a danger to all if they were stirred to a violent anti-Roman demonstration. Jn. 6:15 states this possibility expressly. So Jesus faced the real problem, not simply of feeding the crowd, but of quieting it and persuading it to go home in peace. Shortly after this incident, on which the Fourth Gospel's commentary is most revealing (Jn. 6:66-71), Jesus retired from Galilee; and it is possible that the dangerous enthusiasm of His professed followers urged Him to this course of action (7:24-30). F. C. Burkitt's suggestion that the northern journey was virtually a flight from the long arm of the police of Herod Antipas is also compatible with this reconstruction. H. E. W. Turner (*Jesus, Master and Lord,* p. 110) adds a further note with the reminder that He withdrew partly to prepare His disciples more thoroughly for the true understanding of His messianic vocation. Recent events had shown how little they had imbibed this teaching and how greatly they needed fresh insight into the meaning of His ministry, if they were to be His "apostles" (6:30, i.e., His accredited representatives or *šᵉlûḥîm,* the rabbinic term underlying Gk. *apóstoloi*).

Opposition to His ministry was felt not simply from Herod and the Romans. Jewish leaders were mounting an attack, and the discussion of ritual washings (7:1-23) focuses attention upon the gravamen of the charge the scribes brought against Him: He was disregarding "the tradition of the elders" (7:5, 8f.) because of His sovereign freedom and tacit assumption (Mark's account does not draw out its implications) that He, as Messiah, brought in the new age in which the authority of the Torah is rendered invalid. On the surface, the conflict gathered round the scribal interpretation of the Mosaic law, particularly in the matter of solemn vows, which, if taken deliberately as distinct from rash vows undertaken in error, were treated as irrevocable, and had the effect of making property "offered to God" (Heb. *qorbān*) sacrosanct, even though the plainest human obligations were neglected. Jesus recalled the discussion of the legitimacy of such vows from the realm of the academic to that of the practical and the immediate. He placed the emphasis on a consideration of simple human rights and duties, in the light of the will of God for the family. In a similar vein, ritual lustrations cannot displace the prime importance of a clean inner life (7:15, 20-23). A more calculated blow to the authority of scribal tradition could hardly be imagined, and by overturning the regime of the tradition of the elders, invested by the Pharisees with great dignity, Jesus declared the irreconcilable opposition of God's kingdom to their religious code.

C. An Extension of the Ministry in Scope and Depth. The journey beyond the northern bounds of the Galilean territory brought Him into quasi-gentile country for an indefinite period of time; but certainly the withdrawal cannot have been long after the springtime feeding of the multitude, dated by Mk. 6:39 (cf. Jn. 6:64). Encounter with the gentile people, with their varying needs, occupies the next and new section of the Gospel (7:24–8:26), although Jeremias (*Jesus' Promise,* p. 36) observes that the territory of Tyre and the region lying between Galilee and Caesarea Philippi were then still inhabited by descendants of the northern Israelite tribes. "It would have been," he comments, "to these outposts of Israelite population and Jewish religion that the mind of Jesus first turned when he extended his activity so far to the north," although the precise geographical data are uncertain (e.g., in 7:31 Sidon may be a misreading of Saidan, a variant form of Bethsaida). (*See* GALILEE VI.)

The incidents recorded in this section include: (1) blessing a Syrophoenician woman, explicitly named as a Gentile (7:26); (2) curing a deaf-mute (7:31-37), in which the technique of performing a miracle is unusual and has points of contact, at least in form, with Hellenistic magical cures (so M. Dibelius, *From Tradition to Gospel* [Eng. tr. 1934], pp. 83ff.; cf. J. H. Hull, *Hellenistic Magic and the Synoptic Tradition* [1974]); the rarity of this kind of narrative argues strongly for the essentially Jewish setting of the rest of the miracles in the historical career of Jesus; (3) feeding a crowd, numbered at "about four thousand" (8:9). This last story is sometimes taken as a "doublet" of the earlier pericope (6:30-44), but more probably it is to be regarded as an intentional insertion of a story, set in a non-Jewish milieu, designed to portray Jesus as the bread of life to the Gentiles (this suggestion goes back to Augustine; see Richardson, *Miracle-Stories of the Gospels* [1958], p. 98, who notes the striking vocabulary differences between the two accounts). And it cannot be accidental that in each chapter the miraculous provision of food sets in motion a cycle of events having a similar pattern (feeding; crossing the lake, 6:45-56 and 8:10; controversy with the Pharisees, 7:1-23 and 8:11-13; incidents in which there is "bread," 7:24-30 and 8:14-21; a healing miracle, 7:31-37 and 8:22-26). In the incidents of healing the parallels are especially precise. Vincent Taylor (*Gospel According to St. Mark* [1952], pp. 368f.) has set down the evidence in some detail. Both stories are also in a class apart in relation to the other healing miracles in the Gospels, e.g., no reference is made to human faith, a condition paralleled in certain Hellenistic healing accounts. R. H. Lightfoot offers an elaborate explanation for the peculiar nature of these stories. He goes on to account for the placing of the Bethsaida healing at this juncture on the ground that it forms a bridge connecting the blindness of the disciples in the earlier part of the Gospel with the illumination that came to them in the second part of the narrative, beginning with the turning point of the revelation at Caesarea Philippi (*History and Interpretation,* pp. 90ff.).

At all events, the subsequent pericope (8:27–9:1) marks a major crisis in the ministry, precipitated by Jesus Himself, who took the initiative in both the preliminary (8:27) and leading questions (v. 29). Peter, spokesman for the

Twelve, gave a direct answer to the momentous issue, "Who do you say that I am?" — "You are the Messiah." Jesus here, in contrast to the Matthaean parallel version of this incident (Mt. 16:12-28), accepted the title with little enthusiasm, for it is clear that Peter had no idea of the kind of Messiah Jesus was and would be. For that reason, the accompanying explanation in terms of a humiliated and suffering Son of man was warmly repudiated by the apostle, and Jesus, for good measure and with equal animation, rejected all that Peter's rebuke implied. Peter's thought was filled with notions of an all-conquering messianic prince, whose qualities are delineated in Ps. Sol. 17f.; and Jesus' disclosure of a pathway of suffering was totally unexpected. Moreover, "if it is the will of God that the Messiah should suffer, it might well be his will that the Messiah's disciples should suffer a similar fate; from that . . . the natural man shrinks" (Nineham, comm., *in loc.*).

The retort of Jesus takes up these two issues: His destiny required, as a divine necessity, accepting a cup of suffering and woe (8:31), and discipleship equally required a close identification with Him as corporate Son of man and Servant of God in a similar fate (vv. 34-38; v. 38 should probably read, "Whoever is ashamed of me and mine [i.e., the disciples]").

Mark 9:1 is a *crux interpretum*. C. H. Dodd (*Parables*, p. 35) gives full force to the perfect participle: "until they have seen that the kingdom of God has come with power." The disciples (he interprets) would soon be aware that the kingdom had already come, i.e., that it was a present reality in Jesus' ministry. But this view seems to strain the exegesis (cf. W. G. Kümmel, *Promise and Fulfilment* [Eng. tr., *SBT*, 23, 1957], pp. 25-28, on this verse; and on the whole question of "realized eschatology" note the significant footnote in J. M. Robinson, *Problem of History in Mark* [*SBT*, 21, 1957], p. 24); it is better to translate with the RSV. Later the disciples would be aware that the kingdom had come, but no indication is given of the duration of the interval that is envisaged elsewhere in His eschatological instruction (ch. 13).

The Transfiguration is dated with reference to the confession at Caesarea Philippi, and is the natural sequel to it. As the disciples have confessed Him to be the Messiah, they (or their representatives, the chosen three) are permitted to see His true stature and to share the secret of His filial relationship with the Father. The heavenly voice (9:7), "This is my Son, the beloved," combines two messianic titles and is coupled with an approbation that, even if men may reject and despise Him, He is to be followed by His own. "Hear Him" carries the thought "Obey Him" as in Dt. 6:4.

The ensuing snatch of conversation (9:9-13) as the disciples come down from the hill seems to have suffered some disorder in transmission, and C. H. Turner's emendation placing v. 12b after v. 10 has much to commend it (see C. Gore, *et al.*, eds., *A New Comm. on Holy Scripture* [1928], *in loc.*). The disciples are engaged in resolving a genuine perplexity. Current expectation of a Messiah associated Him with a triumphant reign, and awaited a returning Elijah (Mal. 4:5) to herald His arrival. Jesus had spoken about a rising of the Son of man, but why was this required? It seemed to imply a defeat and a death. Yet the OT (they would reason) knows nothing of such a defeat. Jesus points to what has already occurred: Elijah has come back in the person of John the Baptist, and has met a strange fate (unlike the prophet, who escaped the wrath of his enemies). The Son of man can expect no less.

The cure of the epileptic lad directs attention to the central place occupied by faith, defined by J. A. Findlay (*Jesus As They Saw Him* [1920], p. 107) as "a painstaking and concentrated effort to obtain blessing for oneself or for others, material or spiritual, inspired by a confident belief that God in Jesus can supply all human need." In this regard the present miracle story contrasts with the two earlier accounts from which the emphasis on faith is absent. Jesus' evaluation of the high place of faith in His miracles is classically recorded in 9:23: "Do you say 'ability'? Everything is within the ability of him who has faith" (cf. R. P. Martin, *Mark: Evangelist and Theologian* [1972], pp. 108f.).

A second announcement of the forthcoming rejection and death of the Son of man (9:30-32) is set within a stereotyped framework, observed by R. H. Lightfoot (*History and Interpretation*, pp. 117ff.), namely, in a scene in which the disciples have failed to perceive His ultimate destiny. This setting is clearest at the third prediction of the Passion (10:32-34), when "they were on the road going up to Jerusalem, with Jesus at the lead; and they were bewildered, and as they followed they were frightened." At no point in the Gospel story is there more vividly portrayed the gulf between Jesus' understanding of His messianic vocation and the disciples' hopes and fears of what they might expect — a vast distinction well described by H. E. W. Turner as the "Messianic cross-purpose" (*Jesus, Master and Lord*, p. 115). And in both the second and third predictions of the cross, the teaching of Jesus that follows each announcement was occasioned by the disciples' false ambitions and worldly aspirations (9:33-37; 10:35-45).

Chapter 10 removes the public ministry of Jesus from Galilee to Judea and Transjordan. At this point (10:1) the stage is being prepared for the final drama of Jesus' crucifixion, although it is likely that some considerable time elapsed between the events of chs. 10 and 15. The journey from Galilee may be dated in the late summer of A.D. 32, thereby allowing nine months or so before the events of the following year's Passover and permitting the five episodes recorded by John's Gospel (namely, a visit to the Feast of Tabernacles, an autumn and a winter in Jerusalem, an interval beyond the Jordan, a visit to Bethany, and a retreat to Ephraim).

Mark relates the breaking out of a fresh conflict as soon (apparently) as He set foot in Judea. The point at issue was the vexed question of marriage and divorce (10:2-12). Jewish law at that time gave the husband the sole right to divorce his wife in a most arbitrary way, by serving a written notice of the marriage's dissolution. No redress was possible for the wife, nor did she enjoy any corresponding right. Her sole method of obtaining a divorce was to persuade her husband to take the initiative and offer her release from the marriage vow. Jesus was concerned to issue a challenge to this obviously unfair situation, to uphold the ideal of the indissolubility of marriage, and to base His teaching on God's intention, declared in Gen. 2:24, that marriage is an equal partnership for all time (10:6f., 9). Divorce, therefore, followed by remarriage with another, runs counter to the divine purpose (vv. 10-12).

The following set of conversations and interviews is designed to show how clearly the demands of the kingdom of God are based upon its character. The kingdom is offered to (and understood by) the childlike spirit which takes it with simplicity, gratitude, and trustfulness (10:13-16); yet it also requires a priority and a fullhearted acceptance which brooks no rival. The riches of the man who was "very wealthy" (v. 22) proved to be a tragic stumbling block, not because they were evil per se but because they came to hold a place that God alone must have. In wealth Jesus found a terrible obstacle to human reliance on God Himself, and not surprisingly Paul characterizes "possessiveness" as idolatry (Col. 3:5). A trust in material possessions virtually excludes a trust in God and therefore entry into His realm (10:25).

An even greater tragedy, however, is that the professed followers of Jesus had still to learn the lesson of the kingdom's true nature. They were momentarily startled by the third reminder of what the journey to Jerusalem would entail (10:32); but the deep impression on their minds was clear from their actions and their words in these sections. They brushed aside the children as though their Master had more important business on hand (10:13); and they dealt just as summarily with blind Bartimaeus' request for healing (10:48), possibly on the same score that the Messiah was too busy at that time to attend to such trivia as the cure of a wayside beggar. Moreover, when two of their number, James and John, managed to get in a plea for special places at His heavenly court, the rest were incensed (10:41), because these two had sought preferential treatment and had jumped out of turn. Their minds, no less than the crude, vaulting ambition of James and John, were full of thoughts of earthly prestige to be enjoyed when Jesus entered upon "His glory" (v. 37), i.e., as messianic prince in Jerusalem in the soon-to-be-established kingdom.

They still needed to receive the solemn instruction of 10:42-45, with its climactic prophecy that the Son of man's title to lordship was to be gained along a road of self-denying service to mankind and the full and final offering of His life to God as a ransom for His people (v. 45), as the obedient and humiliated Servant of Yahweh (Isa. 53) and martyr figure (of 2 Macc. 7 and 4 Macc. 6:29; 17:22; these texts are discussed by C. K. Barrett in A. J. B. Higgins, ed., *NT Essays* [1959], pp. 12f.). And if verbal teaching failed to convince them, as it evidently did, they had a second chance to get the message from the acted symbolism of His entry into the holy city, according to the usual interpretation of 11:1-11.

D. Final Journey to Jerusalem. He came into the city as a king. So the narrative makes plain, with an undertone drawn from a passage in 2 K. 9:13 and more explicitly in the later Synoptics and in John, the arrival of the lowly king of Zec. 9:9. Yet, in Mark's account, to insist that He marched upon Jerusalem as a king goes beyond the evidence. The acclamation of the entourage (in 11:9f.) may be no more than an outburst from enthusiastic pilgrims bound for the festival, and a decisive point against the popular view that He stage-managed an entry to make a messianic claim apparent is that neither the Jews nor the Romans were compelled to act immediately against what had transpired. It could be argued, as E. Lohmeyer does in his *Lord of the Temple* (Eng. tr. 1961), pp. 34f., that He entered the city as Messiah incognito with a chief motive to claim the temple as His rightful possession as the sanctuary of God (so Lohmeyer understands v. 11); but this too remains doubtful.

The barren fig tree incident (11:12-14, 20-25) poses certain problems resulting from its obvious intent to make two points (so Nineham, comm., *in loc.*): to give an example of faith and prayer and to provide a didactic point, the fate of the fig tree symbolizing the fate that awaited Jerusalem and the Jewish people and religion. (For other reasons implicit in the story see L. A. Losie, *Studia Biblica et Theologica,* 7/2 [1977], 3-18.) This fate overtook them in A.D. 70 at the fall of Jerusalem. There are two chief problems. (1) This "miracle" involves a judgment on an inanimate object and is thus akin to the wonders related in the apocryphal gospels (cf. *ANT,* pp. 49ff. for examples). (2) If the event occurred after the traditional date of Palm Sunday, i.e., in March or April, no figs would be expected in any case — hence the editorial note added in v. 13: "for it was not the season of figs."

T. W. Manson (*BJRL,* 33 [1951], 271-282) offers some explanation of these two difficulties. The sentence "May no one eat . . ." (11:14) may be construed as a statement more than a curse, the tone of voice alone deciding which the speaker originally intended. A hypothetical Aramaic behind the Greek would allow of either, the imperfect and jussive in that language being consonantally identical. Thus what we have (apparently) as a curse may conceivably have been uttered as a statement of fact: "No one will ever again eat . . . ," couched in the form of a prophecy and implying various possibilities. For instance, it may be that the tree was dead already and could not yield fruit, or was in the process of dying, or that Jesus expected the end of the age or the fall of Jerusalem before the next harvest — or perchance the indefinite "no one" (in v. 14) veils an allusion to the speaker Himself, in which case it is a prophecy of His impending death, like Mk. 14:25 par.

The second difficulty — dating — involves the question of Gospel chronology. Manson (*BJRL*) suggests that this event (and what follows in the later parts of the Gospel) is to be dated at the time of an earlier festival, the Feast of Tabernacles, six months before Passover. Church calendar sequences are responsible for telescoping the events between the triumphal entry and the crucifixion into one week — a foreshortening explicitly denied in Mk. 14:49: "I was daily in the temple teaching." The advantage of this reconstruction is that it permits the story of the fig tree to be placed at a season when figs were possible, and so adds likelihood to Jesus' prophetic word and later appeal to the nation.

The sad condition of Judaism is illustrated by His visit to the temple (11:15-19). The outer court was a part of the temple precinct to which everyone, Jew and Gentile alike, was entitled to come for worship. Yet its facilities were being effectively denied to the Gentiles by the temple authorities, who were using the area as a marketplace and a money exchange. Consequently the area was a convenient thoroughfare for pedestrians (v. 16). Jesus' reform was designed to restore gentile privileges and to purify the temple of all that denied its importance as a house of prayer. (See further Jeremias, *Jesus' Promise,* pp. 65ff.)

Not surprisingly this action called forth a violent reaction (11:27-33), centering upon His authority to interfere in what was a priestly (i.e., Sadducean) preserve. Jesus' retort takes up the broad principle of the legitimacy of all decisions in religious affairs, citing the case of John as a test issue. The temple leaders, faced with an unenviable choice — to deny John's authority as an accredited prophet of God whose martyrdom was of recent memory in the minds of the people, or to admit that they had been wrong in refusing him — preferred to keep silence. To such men Jesus would not declare Himself.

But the question of his authority was not completely evaded. He did declare Himself by a parable, the point of which was taken by those who heard it (12:12). Based on Isa. 5:1-7, the story in 12:1-12 builds on a common feature of Palestinian economic life in the 1st cent., the existence of *latifundia,* which were rented out to the local peasants to be farmed in return for a share of the produce. This system was much resented, especially by those tenants who had strong nationalist feelings. Moreover, the story, as told by Jesus, has allegorical features intended to show the identity of the chief actors, and in particular the character of His enemies who would shortly encompass His death (cf. Dodd, *Parables,* pp. 93-98). In spite of His realistically assessing of the situation and His being under no illusion about how his fate would be decided (v. 7), Jesus looked beyond rejection to a vindication scene, borrowed from Ps. 118:22f. There is no valid reason why Jesus should not have quoted this Scripture, which was to figure prominently in the later Church's apologetic vis-à-vis Judaism (Acts 4:11; Eph. 2:20; 1 Pet. 2:7).

The following pericopes exemplify the various efforts made by His enemies to discredit Him in public debate, and may follow naturally from the embarrassment they suffered after the initial encounter of 12:12. The subtle and disingenuous questions challenged Him at different levels. On a political plane, the issue of tribute money was calculated to expose Him as either a pro-Roman sympathizer (and so turn the crowds against Him as a traitor to Israel's hopes, expressed in the Pharisaic Psalms of Solomon) or an anti-imperial nationalist, too dangerous to have His freedom. Either way He seemed to be caught in a trap. But Jesus refused to legislate as though Roman rule and Jewish freedom were mutually exclusive. Both political power and religious freedom are right in their respective spheres (cf. Rom. 13:1ff.; 1 Pet. 2:13-17) and must not be pitted against each other. "They marveled at Him" for this "simple" solution to a vexed question of state and church. When in later centuries the state turned persecutor and the church strove for territorial power, no such simple directive was possible.

Theologically, the question of post-resurrection marital status posed by the Sadducees (12:18-27) was in character, as the Evangelist notes (v. 18). See Acts 23:6-8 for a further indication that the Sadducees rejected the doctrine of the resurrection as novel. The question they formulated was an imaginary one, almost absurd, yet just possible (cf. a similar situation in Tob. 3). And it tried to show the ludicrous eventuality of what might happen in direct consequence of the levirate rubric of Dt. 25:5ff. Jesus replied that, if the only hope a person has is in vicariously surviving in his descendants, then his hope is illfounded. But, once grant a personal God who cares for His own in life and death — and the Hebrew patriarchs illustrate this par excellence; hence Moses is told that Yahweh is God of these men after their death — and life beyond the grave becomes transformed into personal existence in the love of God, and is not simply a prolonging of earthly conditions. The Scriptures thus speak of an eternal God who enters into a communion with His people that death cannot sever, and (for good measure) the synagogue prayers (one of the Eighteen Benedictions was called the "Power") confirm this hope of life and immortality.

A further query, ostensibly and almost certainly sincere, touched upon a matter debated at that time in Judaism. "Which commandment is first of all?" recalls the many attempts that had been made in Judaism to reduce religion to its essentials. Rabbi Simlai sought to reduce all the commandments to the one requirement of Hab. 2:4 (cited by Montefiore and Loewe, *A Rabbinic Anthology* [1938], p. 199). Jesus concentrated on the prior claims of love, in the order "love to God" issuing in "love to men" (Dt. 6:4f.; Lev. 19:18). Yet a theoretical acceptance of truth never suffices; it brings a person only in sight of the kingdom (12:34). Personal attachment to Jesus and the demands of discipleship are needed to bring a person, however well-meaning and sincere, into the kingdom (cf. Lk. 9:57-62). In other words, character comes before actions in both senses: it is more important and it explains why a person acts as he does.

After a series of interrogations, it was Jesus' turn to raise a question — "How can the scribes maintain that the Messiah is a descendant of David?" (12:35) — which apparently was of current interest in rabbinic circles (see T. W. Manson's pertinent comment [*Teaching of Jesus*, p. 266 n. 2]). The question is cast in the form of a so-called Haggadah question, i.e., one that indicates an apparent contradiction in Scripture, to which the answer is given that both passages are right, but they refer to different points (cf. D. Daube, *NT and Rabbinic Judaism* 1956], pp. 158-163). The point at issue is the precise relation of David, the traditional author of Ps. 110, and the Messiah. In Jewish expectation the messianic hope spoke of a coming nationalist leader who would revive the political fortunes and prestige of David's empire (cf. 2 S. 7:12; Jer. 30:9; Ezk. 34:23; and Ps. Sol. 17). Yet — and herein is the embarrassing difficulty to the Pharisaic notion — David not only looked forward to his illustrious successor, the Messiah, but looked up to Him as someone infinitely higher than any "second David" could be. David himself called Him Lord; how could He also be David's descendant (12:37)? A solution was eventually reached in Rom. 1:3f. (cf. 2 Tim. 2:8), where the qualification "in power" attached to "marked out as Son of God" in reference to David's Son implies that Christ in His post-Easter glory exercised the functions that belong to the OT Yahweh (for which the LXX uses the Gk. *kýrios*, "Lord"), as in Phil. 2:9-11.

The brief condemnation of the scribes (12:38-40) summarizes the philippic of Mt. 23, and is directed against the worst members of the Pharisee party. Not all Pharisees deserved this verdict, but it is ever a danger with a religious outlook such as Pharisaism that it is more deadly when it succeeds (conducing to pride) than when it fails (calling down on it the traditional judgment of "hypocrites"). In any case, with such a noble principle and high idealism, the maxim *corruptio optimi pessima* (the corruption of the best is the worst of all) is bound to apply.

The Pharisees' "love of money" (12:40; cf. Josephus *Ant.* xvii.2.4 [44]; I. Abrahams, *Studies in Pharisaism and the Gospels,* I [1917], ch. 10) serves as a background for the lovely story of 12:41-44, as Montefiore observes: "In contrast to the bad scribes, who 'eat' widows' property, we have now the tale of the good widow and her sacrifice" (*Synoptic Gospels,* I [1927], *in loc.*).

The apocalypse of ch. 13 is placed at this point to mark the closing stages of the Lord's activity and to give a hint of the final days. It thus forms a species of farewell discourse, patterned on the OT examples of farewell speeches delivered by Jacob (Gen. 48–49), Moses (Dt. 31–32), Joshua (Josh. 23–24), Samuel (1 S. 12), and David (1 Ch. 28–29). (On such literary genres, see J. Munck, in *Aux Sources de la tradition chrétienne. Mélanges offerts à M. M. Goguel* [1950], pp. 155-170.) But it has a more important function, namely, to invest the subsequent Passion narrative with an aura of glory and to suffuse it with the light of the ultimate triumph beyond the darkness of defeat, treachery, and death (see Nineham, comm., p. 341).

Whether the section existed before its incorporation into Mark's Gospel (the Little Apocalypse theory), and whether it represents the substance of Jesus' prophetic teaching or is the work of some Jewish-Christian apocalyptist, expanded by the insertion of dominical sayings by the Evangelist, are matters for debate. G. R. Beasley-Murray examines and is critical of the Little Apocalypse theory (in *Jesus and the Future* [1954], updated by his essay in *Southwestern Journal of Theology,* 21 [1978], 37-53) and champions the basic integrity of the chapter; D. E. Nineham supports the theory, arguing that a clear distinction should be made between what Jesus could have foreseen (e.g., 13:9-13; cf. 8:34ff.) and the use He is reported to have made of an apocalyptic, cosmically oriented genre of language and ideas (13:24-27), common in such treatises as Enoch, the Sibylline Oracles, and the Assumption of Moses, which are pseudonymous. Verses such as 14ff., which speak of "the desolating sacrilege set up where it [or he] ought not to be," clearly have the fall of Jerusalem in view (Lk. 21:10). It is possible, as many scholars hold, that Mark's recasting of this narrative —

assuming the Lukan priority of this apocalyptic section — has taken a prophetic utterance of Jesus, in the spirit of the Hebrew prophets who foretold the destruction of Zion (Mic. 3:12; Jer. 26), and turned it into an apocalyptic prediction-schema, based partly on a reminiscence of events in A.D. 40 when the mad emperor Caligula ordered his statue to be set up in the temple (Josephus *BJ* ii.10 [184-203]), as Antiochus Epiphanes had earlier done with the altar of Zeus in the Maccabean period (1 Macc. 1:54; cf. Dnl. 9:27; 11:31; 12:11). But this hypothesis of the origin of Mk. 13 has some doubtful features, and seems to credit Mark with overmuch ingenuity and creative skill at the expense of the historical truth of the discourse as delivered by the Lord Himself.

A time of fierce testing lay ahead of the disciples or their future representatives, according to 13:19. But beyond the cosmic upheaval and distress of vv. 24f. the ultimate vindication of the Son of man (as in Dnl. 7:13ff.) was assured — a note struck later when the conflict seemed to enter its darkest phase in Mk. 14:62 — and the final salvation of the elect is promised. The outbreak of the struggle was imminent (13:28f.), even though the time of the final denouement was a secret locked in the mind of the Father, to which even the Son has no access (vv. 30-32). Yet the disciples' duty was at least clear: faithfulness when bogus messiahs were on the rampage (vv. 5-8, 21-23) and the ruling authority was implacably hostile (vv. 9-13), added to watchfulness (vv. 33-37) lest His coming should find them ill prepared and irresponsible. So, "what I say to you, I say to all: be watchful" (v. 37 — a motif and a technical term, common in early Christianity: 1 Cor. 16:13; 1 Thess. 5:6; 1 Pet. 5:8; Rev. 3:2f.; 16:15).

The last three chapters of Mark cover a period between the plot to arrest Jesus (14:1f.) and the events of the crucifixion, the burial, and the visit of the women to the tomb in 16:1-8. As it stands, the record appears to compress all the happenings into a few days, set around the observance of the Jewish festival of Passover (cf. Jn. 12:1, where the anointing occurs six days earlier than Passover). Unfortunately it is not clear which day of the week coincided with the actual Passover observed in Judaism as Nisan 14 (sunset) or 15 (daylight hours). The preceding two days (14:1) were filled with the incidents of ch. 14, including the anointing at Bethany (14:3-9) by an unnamed woman (not Mary Magdalene nor the woman of Lk. 7), who wished, in her costly demonstration, to show her love and possibly to acknowledge His messianic status by supplying the consecrating oil (cf. 1 K. 19:16; 2 K. 9:3) for His kingly office. Perhaps, too, she glimpsed something of His destiny as one fated to die — at least this is how Jesus is reported to have received the action (v. 8). R. H. Lightfoot's comment is apposite here: "The Passion is the supreme act of the Messiah, and conversely the Messiahship of Jesus is the explanation of the Passion" (*History and Interpretation*, p. 141). The woman with the anointing oil perceived, as in a mystery, the interrelation between messiahship and Passion.

In stark contrast to such a "lovely deed" (14:6), the next incident reveals something of the hardness and callousness of the human heart. In exchange for money JUDAS ISCARIOT (probably "man of Kerioth" and therefore, unlike the other disciples, a southerner) agreed to betray the Lord by revealing something of His movements, so that the authorities could seize Him quietly (cf. Lk. 22:6).

The intention of the chief priests and scribes, reported in 14:2, was to apprehend Jesus before the festal season; but 14:12-16 seems to be at odds with the earlier chronological notice, and contains a difficult statement, apparently equating the first day of the unleavened bread with the time when the Passover lambs were slain in the temple. In fact, the lambs were killed during the hours from 2:30 p.m. to sunset on Nisan 14, and the "first day of unleavened bread" began at 6 p.m., the commencement of the next day, Nisan 15. Possibly, with W. C. Allen (comm. [1907], *in loc.*), we should accept that the text originally read (at 14:12) *pró tḗs hēméras*, "before the day of unleavened bread"; or perhaps Chwolson (*Das letzte Passamahl Christi* [1908], pp. 133ff.) is correct in arguing that the Aramaic underlying this verse has been misunderstood, and that the *Urschrift* read: "on the day before the feast of unleavened bread," i.e., Nisan 14 (cf. Jeremias, *Eucharistic Words*, pp. 2-4).

The following paragraphs represent the last meal of Jesus with His disciples as the Passover celebration (to be dated, from Mk. 14:17ff. onward, Nisan 15, according to the usual view of 14:12). This scheme contrasts with John, who dates the supper one day earlier and therefore regards it as an "anticipatory" Passover (or some other meal, such as sabbath kiddush or rabbinic *ḥ*ᵃ*ḇûrâ*), and makes the official Jewish Passover celebration on Nisan 14 coincide in time with the death of Jesus, God's paschal lamb (Jn. 1:29), on the cross (cf. Jn. 18:28, 39; 19:31, 42; etc.).

Whether the last meal was a regular (Jeremias, *Eucharistic Words*) or an anticipated (V. Taylor, *Gospel According to St. Mark* [1952], pp. 664ff.) Passover, it is clear that it must be understood against the background of the Passover ritual and Haggadah as a special example of Jewish table fellowship. From the latter come the notions of blessing God as the giver of food and drink (14:22) and the common life which binds the participants at the table. The paschal liturgy, drawn from Ex. 12 and interpreted in the Haggadah for Passover, explains the use of the bread and the cup as "interpretive symbols," recalling the events of the Exodus and enabling the Jewish families to relive the redemptive experience their fathers had known at first hand in Egypt (see A. J. B. Higgins, *Lord's Supper in the NT* [1952], and R. P. Martin, *Worship in the Early Church* [1974], pp. 110-19).

After singing the Hallel hymns (taken from Pss. 113–118) the band went out into the night, warned by the solemn announcement of impending desertion, betrayal, and death (14:26-31, 42). The failure of the disciples is typified (and aggravated) by the complete insensibility of the chosen three in Gethsemane (vv. 32-52); Peter's lack of vigilance received special rebuke (v. 37), and no exoneration (nor, it may be noted, explicit censure) was given to Judas' infamy. Jesus greeted his arrival with "He's got his money" (*apéchei*, a commercial term, used in the papyri for a receipt), and placed Himself in the hands of His foes. An attempt was made to defend Him, and an unnamed bystander lost his ear (possibly by accident). Jesus curtly rejected any such armed defense, which would have made Him appear a (Zealot?) brigand whose cause needed to be bolstered by violence and hatred. Up to the last, He was seen to be refusing all unworthy notions by which His destiny may be averted.

The tantalizing pericope (14:51f.) has been taken as an autobiographical insertion made by John Mark (so, e.g., Zahn); but had Mark been an eyewitness of these events, it is hard to explain why the dating of the last meal is so imprecise and uncertain. And the "awkward connexion" with the foregoing narrative "proves that he [the Evangelist] is dependent on a source for the story" (Nineham, comm., *in loc.*).

The trial scenes are divided into two parts (*see* JESUS CHRIST, ARREST AND TRIAL OF; and see *NBD*, pp. 1295f.).

Judas's betrayal of Jesus. Frieze (12th cent. A.D.) attributed to Michael Master, St.-Gilles-du-Gard Church, Provence, France (Rosenthal Art Slides)

First, the arraignment before the Sanhedrin appears to have had its object in fastening some accusation upon Jesus that would have made remission to Pilate a necessary next step. It is doubtful, then, if we should speak of the first hearing as a judicial "trial." More likely it was a preliminary investigation, of an informal character and somewhat careless about strict legal procedures. Hence the oft repeated discussions about the illegality and irregularity in this section: e.g., that witnesses were suborned (vv. 55-59); that Jesus' claims to be able to overthrow the temple (vv. 58ff.) and to be the Messiah (v. 61) were not per se tantamount to blasphemy; and that the session was at night and during the Passover season (see Jeremias, *Eucharistic Words*, pp. 52f.). All these points show that the nocturnal "trial" was more in the nature of a preparatory inquiry. Moreover, if the Jewish "trial" were self-contained, why did not the authorities, once the sentence had been passed (v. 64: "And they all gave their judgment against him as deserving of death"), carry out the prescribed penalty for blasphemy or heresy according to the law, stoning (Lev. 24)? (See Jn. 19:7.) The answer may be found in Jn. 18:31f., which records the Jews' inability to kill anyone (see C. K. Barrett's full note in his comm. on John, *in loc.*). G. D. Kilpatrick, in his pamphlet *The Trial of Jesus* (1953), has endeavored to show that the earlier investigation was an effort by the Sadducean aristocracy to prove to the Pharisees that Jesus was a public danger, while the Sadducees reserved the charge of treason, the crime of lese majesty, for Pilate's court, thereby intending to implicate the Romans with the major share of responsibility for His death. In keeping with this charge, the question presented to Pilate was one of politics. Jesus claimed to be a king and thus was guilty of anti-Roman activities (amplified in Lk. 23:2). Pilate was faced with an unenviable set of choices: either to release Jesus at the expense of incurring the increased enmity of the Jewish leaders, whose tender susceptibilities he had already aroused (Lk. 13:1ff.), or to bow to the claims of expediency and condemn Jesus in order to quiet the clamor of His enemies. He tried to escape the dilemma by offering the freedom of Jesus in exchange for another Jesus, surnamed Barabbas (given in some MSS in Mt. 27:16f.; see Deissmann, in Bell and Deissmann, eds., *Mysterium Christi* [1930], pp. 19-21). But the crowd, incited by the priests, opted for Barabbas, a Zealot leader.

In Mark's account the Roman authorities are presented in a neutral light, and Pilate in particular is viewed as a man caught in a very difficult position. The Jews, on the other hand, are the instigators (vv. 11, 13, 15) and are the pressure group, exerting a baneful influence on the procurator, who knows full well how they are motivated (vv. 10, 14). In the Matthaean version (27:24f.) this placing of the onus on the Jews is clearly emphasized, as P. Winter, *On the Trial of Jesus* (1961), remarks. But Winter's reconstruction is not free from difficulty, as A. N. Sherwin-White shows (*Roman Society and Roman Law in the NT* [1963]).

The tragedy moves now to its close, with the chief theme — that Jesus is the Messiah, incriminated by the Jewish leaders and so branded as a rebel against the empire by the Roman officials — picked up in the soldiers' mockery (15:16-20). Along the *Via Dolorosa* He stumbled and needed the help of a passerby, Simon, identified (perhaps because well known to the Christian community at Rome in Mark's day; cf. Rom. 16:13) as the father of Alexander and Rufus, to carry the *patibulum* or crosspiece of this "most cruel and hideous of punishments" (*crudelissimum taeterrimumque supplicium* in Cicero's onomatopoeic description, *In Verrem* v.64).

At the scene of the cross, the same charge as at the trial was leveled at Him as a mocking taunt: "Let the Messiah the king of Israel come down from the cross, that we may see and believe" (15:32). The Jews were hostile to the last as the Romans maintained a reserved impartiality, passively accepting an ugly situation. In fact, passivity turned to a more positive attitude when a Roman centurion announced the early Christian confession: "Truly this man was a (the) Son of God" (15:39; the absence of the definite article in the Greek is no proof that this statement should be understood in an indefinite sense; see E. C. Colwell, *JBL,* 52 [1933], pp. 12-21). Mark evidently intended that this confession should represent the firstfruits of gentile Christianity, as the earlier mention of a kindly deed (v. 36, where the "vinegar" means the soldiers' *posca,* a mixture of sour wine and egg with water, drunk by Roman soldiers on duty) seemed to follow the same tradition, namely, to present the Romans in a good light.

Early Christian understanding of Christ's death evidently included an overt reference to His burial (in 1 Cor. 15:4, which is usually taken to be a pre-Pauline credo, emanating from an Aramaic-speaking community [so A. M. Hunter, *Paul and His Predecessors* (2nd ed. 1961), pp. 117f.], and in Acts 2:29; 13:29). The pericope (15:42-47) that relates how Joseph of Arimathea made himself responsible for this office serves an evidential purpose. It certifies that He who was crucified really died, and tasted the bitterness of mortality. Included here may be the beginnings of Christian speculation about the *triduum mortis* (the three days of death), also tackled in 1 Pet. 3:18ff.; 4:6 to throw light on what the Lord did between Good Friday and Easter morn.

In primitive Christianity the validity of the assertion "Christ is alive" rested upon the personal appearances of the living Lord; the fulfillment of the prophetic Scriptures, notably (apparently) Hos. 6; and the conviction, of which Mk. 16:1-8 is a witness, that the tomb was open, with the great stone removed, when the women (who had been last at the cross, 15:40f.) were the first to visit it on Nisan 17 (16:4). It was open, but not exactly empty, for "a youth sitting on the right side, wearing a white robe," was inside and passed on the message: "He has risen, he is not here; here is the place where they laid him. But go and give this message to his disciples and Peter."

With the women's reaction in startled amazement to this news, the Gospel suddenly breaks off: "for they were afraid" (16:8a). This abrupt ending may be explained either as accidental (perhaps the last section was lost or destroyed) or intentional (perhaps the writer was caught in a pogrom and hurriedly concluded his work or intended in any case to end his Gospel at that exact point). No one knows. But whether by mishap or interruption or deliberate intention, the Evangelist expects his readers to be able to complete the story for themselves; in v. 7 he records the promise of an appearance in Galilee whither the risen Christ as shepherd will lead His scattered and bewildered sheep (cf. 14:28). In what is the final metaphor of the Gospel, Mark has pointed forward to the Parousia, for 14:27 ("I will strike the Shepherd, and the sheep shall be dispersed") uses the eschatological technical term (Gk.) *diaskorpízō* to indicate a time of tribulation before the end of the age (see Jeremias, *Jesus' Promise,* p. 64). Hence the promised gathering of the scattered flock is a symbol of the approaching redemption for all the Gentiles (Mt. 25:31f.; Jn. 11:51f.).

V. Theological Significance of Jesus' Life.–At this point we leave the area of historical inquiry and enter the field of Christian faith. The record of the Lord's earthly life and ministry inevitably raises the fundamental issue of what manner of man this is, and what is the Christian estimate of that life which, once lived out under a Palestinian sky long ago, was described by an early disciple as "the light of men" (Jn. 1:4). And the answer to this question lies at the very heart of what is called Christianity.

> From beginning to end, in all its various phases and aspects and elements, the Christian faith and life is determined by the person and work of Jesus Christ. It owes its life and character at every point to Him. Its convictions are convictions about Him. Its hopes are hopes which He has inspired, and which it is for Him to fulfil. Its ideals are born of His teaching and His life. Its strength is the strength of His spirit.
>
> (J. Denney, *Jesus and the Gospel* [1908], p. 1)

The simplest answer to the question posed above — and this is the classic statement of historic Christianity — is that He is true God and true Man. The discussion will follow this pattern, in the inverse order.

A. His Manhood. "The evangelists nowhere seek to prove Jesus' manhood; it is for them a tacit and self-evident assumption" (H. R. Mackintosh, *Person of Jesus Christ* [1913], p. 10). The evidence may be displayed in a number of complementary ways. The Jesus of the Gospels possessed a human body, which grew in the normal processes of development (Lk. 2:40, 46, 51f.). He was subjected to the ordinary human experiences of hunger and thirst, weariness and fatigue, pain and suffering; and at length He underwent a truly human death and burial (Mt. 21:8; Jn. 4:6; Mt. 8:24; Jn. 11:35; 19:28; and the Passion narratives).

He also shared our emotional life, entering into human joy and sympathy, and expressing affection and a desire for human companionship and support (Lk. 10:21; Mt. 9:36; Mk. 10:21; Mt. 26:37-40). At the other end of the emotional scale, He rose against the ravages of disease and sin with anger (Mk. 1:41 var.; 3:5; 11:15ff.). He. 4:15 sums up this twin aspect of the Lord's emotional life in a memorable sentence.

He possessed a true human mind, so that we find Him asking questions for information (Lk. 8:45; Jn. 11:34; Mk. 6:35; 9:21; but cf. Jn. 6:5f.). Mk. 13:32 poses something of a problem, with its apparent instance of Jesus' ignorance. Of this problem we may say: (1) it is not a confession of error but an admission of lack of knowledge; (2) as the church father Hilary of Poitiers realized (*De trinitate* ix.71, 75, cited by C. E. Raven, *Apollinarianism* [1923], p. 96), this admission is really an indirect witness to His greater-than-human power, for He knows that no one else knows except God, and that fits Jesus into a unique category.

He is described as sharing spiritual experiences, e.g., prayer. "No Christology is true which makes a Christ for whom prayer is either unnatural or impossible" (Mackintosh, p. 399). The record of His temptations (Mt. 4:1-11 par. Lk. 4:1-3; 22:44; cf. He. 4:15; 5:7) raises the question of how, if Jesus was sinless and divine, temptation could be a meaningful experience for Him. The minimal comment will include the following: (1) The temptations are convincing evidence of a real manhood, not a piece of play-acting. (2) The temptation in the wilderness came to Him from outside sources, not through inward depravity or a fallen nature. (3) The temptation was genuine, yet the victory was inevitable — a paradox on which the wise words of William Temple (*Christus Veritas* [1924], p. 217) throw some illumination. (4) Victory, therefore, required the personal exercise of His will to overcome the solicitation to evil. "He overcame . . . exactly as every man who does so overcomes a temptation — by the constancy of the Will" (Temple, p. 147). (5) Against the objection that if Jesus was sinless He could not have experienced real temptation, we may doubt the assumption that if a man does not commit certain sins, it must be because he has never felt the appeal of them. The man who yields to a specific temptation's pull has not felt its full power. He has given way to it while the temptation had yet (so to speak) something in reserve. Only the man who does not yield to a temptation knows the full force of the enticement. The entirely sinless one must therefore be the only one who really knows the full extent of temptation's power, because He has endured its utmost strength and never yielded (He. 2:18; cf. L. Morris, *Lord from Heaven* [1957], pp. 49-52).

The true humanity of Jesus Christ has important theological consequences, clearly exposed by H. R. Mackintosh, pp. 404f.; for the modern debate on the "impersonal manhood" of Christ and Barth's doctrine of His human nature, the books of D. M. Baillie, *God Was in Christ* (1948), and H. Johnson, *Humanity of the Saviour* (1962), may be mentioned.

B. His Deity. Confining our immediate attention to the Gospels, we may seek the data that portray the deity of Jesus; but first a caveat must be entered. The lines of evidence are more indirect and inferential than forthright and declarative. Jesus did not parade His divine relationship nor bludgeon His hearers into submission by a display of His deity, nor make (at least in the Synoptics) overt claims to divinity. The nearest there is to the last-mentioned feature is the Fourth Gospel's record of His use of the magisterial formula I AM (on which see E. Stauffer, *Jesus and His Story,* pp. 142ff.).

Jesus in His public and private teaching and in His recorded prayer life reveals something of His unique relationship to God. God is called by the tender name of *Abba* ("my dear Father," in itself a summary of Christology, as J. Jeremias, *Central Message of the NT* [Eng. tr. 1965], pp. 9-30, has shown), and Jesus knows Himself to be uniquely the Son of the Father (decisively in Mt. 11:25-30, on which the study of A. M. Hunter, reprinted in his *Teaching and Preaching the NT* [1963], pp. 41ff., should be consulted). Mackintosh sums up: "[Sonship] is the constitutive factor of His being. The life of the Father and the Son is one life; and either can be known only in the other" (p. 28).

The Lord's sense of authority shines through many of His deeds and words. As an interpreter of the OT (Mt. 5–7; 19:3-9), as the founder and head of the Church (Mt. 16:18f.; cf. O. Cullmann, *Peter* [Eng. tr. 1953], pp. 155ff.), as conveyer par excellence of the revelation of God (Jn. 8:12; 14:6-9), as the object of faith and the source of life (Mk. 8:34-38; Jn. 5:40; 6:29, 40; on which T. W. Manson comments, "in the last degree exacting, without being in the least degree arrogant," *Teaching of Jesus,* p. 211), in the exercise of divine prerogatives (such as declaring sins to be forgiven in His own name, Mk. 2:10; asserting His role as future judge of man, Mt. 7:21-23; 25:31-46; Jn. 5:22-30; and coupling His name with that of the Father and the Spirit, Mt. 28:18ff.; for the authenticity of this passage see R. P. Martin, *Worship in the Early Church* [1974], pp. 94-97), and in the names and titles He tacitly accepted (esp. the enigmatic "Son of man," which Stauffer declares to be "just about the most pretentious piece of self-description that any man in the ancient East could possibly have used" [*NT Theology* (1955), p. 108]) — in all these ways He shows Himself to be a unique figure in God's economy of salvation. The Scriptures point to Him, and are fulfilled in His ministry (Lk. 4:16-27). John the Baptist is His herald but is to be sharply distinguished from Him, for he prepared the way and bore witness to one greater than himself — Jesus, the inaugurator of a new age, the messianic era for which the OT prophets yearned.

Perfect manhood, seen at its highest and holiest; unique relationship to the Father, whose character is embodied in Jesus of Nazareth, in His life, death, and resurrection — these are the two facts that emerge from a reading of all the Gospels. They lay the foundation on which the Apostolic Fathers built their superstructure of Christology, and on which later the church fathers erected their doctrines and dogmas of the Incarnation and the trinity. But whether in embryo or in full growth, the truth to be discerned is nothing less than the ringing tones of the *Te Deum:* "Thou art the King of glory, O Christ; Thou art the everlasting Son of the Father."

See Plates 31-37.

Bibliography.–C. C. Anderson, *Critical Quests of Jesus* (1969); H. Anderson, *Jesus and Christian Origins* (1964); G. Bornkamm, *Jesus of Nazareth* (Eng. tr. 1960); F. F. Bruce, *Jesus and Christian Origins Outside the NT* (1974); H. Conzelmann, *Jesus* (Eng. tr. 1973); O. Cullmann, *Christology of the NT* (Eng. tr., 2nd ed. 1963); C. H. Dodd, *Founder of Christianity* (1970); *Parables of the Kingdom* (2nd ed. 1961); J. D. G. Dunn, *Jesus and the Spirit* (1975); W. R. Farmer, *The Synoptic Problem* (1964); R. H. Fuller, *Mission and Achievement of Jesus* (1954); *Foundations of NT Christology* (1965); J. Jeremias, *Eucharistic Words of Jesus* (Eng. tr. 1955); *Jesus' Promise to the Nations* (Eng. tr., *SBT,* 24, 1958); *NT Theology,* I (Eng. tr. 1971); R. H. Lightfoot, *History and Interpretation in the Gospels* (1935); T. W. Manson, *Sayings of Jesus* (repr. 1979); *The Servant-Messiah* (1953); *Teaching of Jesus* (2nd ed. 1935); D. E. Nineham, *Saint Mark* (Pelican Comm., 1963); G. Ogg, *Chronology of the Public Ministry of Jesus* (1940); N. Perrin, *Rediscovering the Teaching of Jesus* (1967); J. Reumann, *Jesus in the Church's Gospels* (1970); G. N. Stanton, *Jesus of Nazareth in NT Preaching* (1974); E. Stauffer, *Jesus and His Story* (Eng. tr. 1960); H. E. W. Turner, *Jesus, Master and Lord* (1953); G. Vermes, *Jesus the Jew* (1973); H. Zahrnt, *The Historical Jesus* (1963).

R. P. MARTIN

JESUS CHRIST, ARREST AND TRIAL OF.

I. Introduction.–The arrest, trial, and crucifixion of Jesus of Nazareth are facts of history. As events, their historicity is undoubted, and supported in both biblical and extrabiblical literature of the first Christian centuries. The theological significance of these events, on the other hand, admits the possibility of debate; and to this we shall return in due course. Moreover, the precise details of the *trial* of Jesus, as these appear in the four Gospels, need to be clarified as well as harmonized. In particular it will be necessary to decide what part is played in the whole episode by the SANHEDRIN on the one hand, and PONTIUS PILATE on the other.

That inquiries into the trial of Jesus have in the past been undertaken in the interests of anti-Semitic polemic is a matter for regret, and indicates the importance of elucidating the historical details of the incident so far as possible, and also of conducting this kind of investigation in a spirit of Christian devotion and humility.

II. Narratives.–The accounts of the arrest and trial of Jesus that we are given by the Synoptists and the fourth Evangelist apparently differ in some respects.

A. Synoptic Tradition. 1. Arrest. At the time of His arrest Jesus was in Gethsemane with the disciples. Mark and Matthew record that Jesus took Peter, James, and John, and withdrew with them from the main body of the disciples; Mark alone suggests that at the moment when Judas Iscariot arrived with the crowd, Jesus spoke the word about the Son of man being betrayed (14:41) to those three, and not to the disciples in general. All three Synoptic Gospels mention that the kiss of Judas was the signal for the actual arrest. It is likely that what Judas really betrayed was the whereabouts of Jesus, rather than His identity. In the darkness, however, the kiss would no doubt have assisted the recognition of Jesus by the authorities (Mk. 14:44); and probably Judas also hoped by this means to allay suspicion on the part of the Lord Himself.

Again, all the Synoptists record the defensive reaction of a disciple (Matthew and possibly Luke) or a bystander (Mark), who cut off the ear of the high priest's servant. Matthew alone adds the saying of Jesus at this point, "All who take the sword will perish by the sword" (26:52), followed by the claim that divine deliverance ("twelve legions of angels," v. 53) is available if needed, without recourse to arms. Luke alone preserves the tradition that Jesus healed the servant's ear (22:51). All three Gospels, finally, contain the dignified response of Jesus to His captors.

Both Mark and Matthew see this event as the fulfillment of Scripture (Mk. 14:49; Mt. 26:56), but Matthew alone says that Jesus Himself spoke of it in these terms (Mt. 26:54, 56); Luke has instead the dominical saying, "This is your hour, and the power of darkness" (22:53). Only in Mark appears the tradition of the young man, possibly the Evangelist himself, who then escaped capture by fleeing naked (14:51f.); and both Mark and Matthew record the desertion of Jesus by all the disciples.

That the arrest of Jesus took place during the Passover period does not necessarily contradict the decision of the authorities not to apprehend their prisoner "during the feast" in case of riot. The Greek (*mḗ en tḗ heortḗ,* Mk. 14:2; Mt. 26:5) is notoriously ambiguous in any case; but it is more than likely that the Jews regarded the subsequent offer of Judas as too good to miss, and allowing of no delay.

2. Jewish Trial. There follow in the Synoptic account two trials of Jesus in Jerusalem, the first before Caiaphas the high priest, named only by Matthew, and the second before Pilate. Luke's version differs from that of Mark and Matthew in placing the chief examination of Jesus by the Jewish authorities before the council (Sanhedrin), early on the day after the arrest and immediately before the Roman trial (22:66-71). According to him a plot had already been arranged to trick Jesus into treasonable speech, so that He could be delivered to the governor's jurisdiction (20:20). This duly happened the following morning; during

JESUS CHRIST, ARREST AND TRIAL OF

the intervening hours of the night the mocking of Christ took place. In Luke also, the leading questions were asked and judgment was given by the council at large.

In Mark and Matthew, however, the Jewish trial took place immediately. The first action of the chief priests and the whole council was to look unsuccessfully for evidence ("false testimony," Mt. 26:59) on which to prosecute Jesus. Having failed to agree among themselves, false witnesses (Mt. 26:60; Mk. 14:56) eventually accused Jesus of blasphemy under the Jewish law, for threatening to destroy the temple and rebuild it in three days. (No exact statement of this kind is attributed to Jesus in either Mark or Matthew; but cf. Mk. 13:2; Mt. 24:2.) Also, it was the high priest himself in Mark and Matthew who interrogated Jesus about His identity; although when the assembly as a whole was asked for a verdict, as in Luke's account, Jesus was declared by *them* to be "worthy of death" (Mk. 14:64; Mt. 26:66). Mark and Matthew report the reluctance of Jesus to answer His accusers, but in all three Gospels He claimed, explicitly (Mark) or implicitly (Matthew, Luke), the titles of Christ and Son (Mark "Son of the Blessed"; Matthew, Luke "Son of God"). The explicit claim of Jesus at Mk. 14:62, "I am [the Christ, the Son of the Blessed]," became in some unimportant witnesses, no doubt under the influence of the version in the other Evangelists, the more hesitant "You say that I am."

According to all three Evangelists this claim of Jesus, with its accompanying eschatological statement and (in Mark and Matthew) prediction of the Parousia, was regarded as the ultimate blasphemy, and sufficient reason by itself for condemning the prisoner to death.

The interlude of Peter's denial occurs at the same point in all the Synoptic accounts, i.e., on the night of the arrest. Mark and Matthew then report a second meeting of the chief priests and elders (and scribes, with the whole Sanhedrin, Mk. 15:1) the following morning, for the purpose of a joint consultation. (This is the point at which Luke places the actual trial of Jesus before Caiaphas.) The subject according to Matthew is how to secure the death of Jesus; but the debate is not reported by either Matthew or Mark in any detail, and Jesus was hurried off seemingly at once to Pilate.

Giotti di Bondone, Christ Before Caiaphas. Fresco (*ca.* A.D. 1305) in the Arena Chapel, Padua, Italy (Museo Civico, Padua)

3. Trial Before Pilate. Before the Roman governor, the charge against Jesus shifted from that of blasphemy in terms of the Jewish law to that of treason against the Roman state. Luke alone gives us the precise wording of the accusation (23:2); the general charge of "perverting our nation" is specified under the two subsidiary heads of "forbidding us to give tribute to Caesar" and "saying that he himself is Christ a king." A similar accusation is implied in Mark and Matthew by Pilate's opening question, "Are you the King of the Jews?" (Mk. 15:2; Mt. 27:11), which also appears in the Lukan narrative (23:3). In all three Synoptists the reply of Jesus is, "You have said so."

At this point Luke's tradition departs from the other Synoptists. According to Luke, Pilate protested the innocence of Jesus, at which the accusers became more insistent. They claimed that He had caused disturbance as far north as Galilee (23:4f.). Learning that Jesus was in fact a Galilean who belonged to the jurisdiction of Herod, Pilate (under the terms of the emerging legal practice of *forum domicilii*) sent the prisoner off to Herod, who happened to be in Jerusalem at the time. But the trial before Herod was an abortive affair, in spite of "vehement accusation" by the religious authorities (23:10). This is partly because Jesus maintained a dignified silence, and partly because Herod was interested only in gratifying his personal desire to see some "sign" performed. After a second mocking of Jesus, therefore, in which Herod himself participated, the prisoner was returned to Pilate for a second trial.

The Synoptic account thereafter follows a similar pattern in all three Gospels, except that Matthew alone includes the incident of the warning sent to Pilate by his wife (27:19). Pilate marveled at the silence of Jesus in the face of prosecution (Mark, Matthew), and finding Him not guilty, offered to scourge and release Him (Luke). At this point the *privilegium paschale* (the existence of which is questioned by some) was invoked, and Pilate asked whether the prisoner Barabbas (whose full name was probably Jesus Barabbas) or Jesus "who is called Christ" should be released under its terms (Mark, Matthew). In Luke the people themselves took the initiative in asking for the release of Barabbas. All three Synoptists represent Pilate as being in fact anxious to release Jesus; but under pressure from a crowd incited by the authorities (Mark, Matthew), he yielded to the demand for the crucifixion of Jesus in order to avoid further trouble, in spite of being unable to find any evil of which He could be justly accused. It is Matthew, not surprisingly, who records the incident of Pilate's washing his hands in public, and the willingness of the Jewish people to assume responsibility for the judgment (27:24f.). Pilate released Barabbas, and after scourging Jesus (Mark, Matthew), delivered Him to be crucified. It is at this point, after the trial before Pilate and before the crucifixion, that Mark and Matthew mention the mocking of Christ which Luke has already described.

Although the accounts in the Synoptic Gospels differ in a number of details, they agree on the general character of the trial of Jesus. In this tradition Jesus was arraigned before the Jewish tribunal, and judged worthy of death, on a charge of blasphemy. But the narratives appear to suggest that although the Sanhedrin could sentence a prisoner to death, the execution could not be carried out apart from reference to Roman authority, and indeed (although this is never stated in so many words) that only Pilate could actually cause Jesus to be put to death. Accordingly Pilate gave the final sentence, but on the grounds of what had by now been turned into a political charge.

B. Johannine Tradition. 1. Arrest. The account of the arrest and trial in the Passion narrative of the Fourth Gospel includes some notable but not necessarily conflict-

JESUS CHRIST, ARREST AND TRIAL OF

ing variations from the Synoptic record. According to John the arrest of Jesus took place in a garden, otherwise unnamed, "across the Kidron Valley" (18:1); it was apparently a familiar meeting place for Jesus and His disciples, and one therefore well known to Judas the betrayer. There is no mention of the kiss of Judas, since in this Gospel Jesus, portrayed as in complete command of the situation throughout, took the initiative in giving Himself up to the soldiers.

The effect of the self-identification of Jesus (using the theologically significant words *egṓ eimi,* Jn. 18:5f., 8) was to cause the virtual collapse of the opposition (v. 6); John specifies the character of the arresting crowd as partly military. Still in control, Jesus then ordered the release of His disciples (vv. 8f.). The fourth Evangelist identifies the supporter of Jesus who cut off the ear (Mk., Mt.; Lk., Jn., "right ear") of the high priest's servant as Simon Peter; and, no doubt following his own tradition, the writer further gives the name of the servant as Malchus. The rebuke of Jesus to Peter, "Put your sword into its sheath" (v. 11), also contains a typically Johannine reference to the Son's voluntary acceptance of the Father's will.

The Synoptic and Johannine narratives of the arrest, therefore, can be said to preserve a basically similar pattern. The chief divergences are most easily accounted for by the probable independence of the apostolic tradition lying behind the Fourth Gospel.

2. Jewish Trial. In John the trial of Jesus by the Jewish authorities is recounted briefly, and interwoven with the narrative of Peter's denial. According to the Textus Receptus the examination was apparently conducted before Annas (18:13), the father-in-law of Caiaphas; mention of Caiaphas himself does not occur until v. 24 (so, e.g., p^{66}, *ca.* A.D. 200). It is possible that the TR of Jn. 18:13-24 retains an early scribal error, and that following the Sinaitic Syriac version (4th-5th cents.), v. 24 should be read immediately after v. 13; or (so the twelfth-century minuscule 225) that its proper placing is between vv. 13a and 13b (see R. V. G. Tasker, comm. on John [*Tyndale,* 1960], p. 198). In this case the visit to Annas is extremely brief, and the Johannine tradition coincides with the Synoptic by making Caiaphas the president of the tribunal. But if Annas was indeed the president, there is no necessary error in the reference to him as "high priest," although he was deposed from that office in A.D. 15. The high-priesthood was regarded by the Jews as an office for life (cf. Mish. *Horayoth* iii.4); and in any case the influence of Annas on his successors seems to have been lasting (cf. also Lk. 3:2).

In the course of the Jewish "trial" Jesus was questioned about His disciples and His teaching (18:19), but not (except by implication) about His identity. There is no mention of either a charge or a sentence, and Jesus was sent off without delay to the residence of the procurator.

3. Trial Before Pilate. The second trial of Jesus in John is more extended in form than its Synoptic parallel. It is conducted almost dramatically on an "inner stage," the praetorium itself, and an "outer stage" before the crowds. The opening of the trial is *coram publico,* but when Pilate asked for the charge it was not specified; instead there was a vague reference to Jesus as an "evildoer" (18:30). Pilate's order, "Take him yourselves and judge him by your own law," was countered by a statement from the Jews, "It is not lawful for us to put any man to death" (v. 31), which seems to reflect the state of affairs implied in the Synoptic version.

The scene shifted to the inner stage, and a private discussion ensued between Pilate and Jesus on the subject of kingship. The sequence of remarks in 18:33-38 becomes even more intelligible if the words of Pilate, *Sý eí ho basileús tṓn Ioudaiōn* (v. 33), which are also found in the three Synoptic accounts, are taken not as a question but as a statement. Pilate then returned to the populace and protested the innocence of Jesus; but when he invoked the *privilegium paschale* in the hope of releasing his prisoner, the crowd cried instead for Barabbas.

The scourging and mocking follow at this point in the Fourth Gospel (19:1-3), after which Pilate brought Jesus out to the people, who demanded His death. Pilate tried again to transfer the responsibility for the execution to the Jews ("Take him yourselves and crucify him," 19:6), and only then did the gravamen of the charge against Jesus by the Jews emerge. It is the definitely theological accusation of blasphemy: "We have a law, and by that law he ought to die, because he has made himself the Son of God" (v. 7). The responsibility for the death of Jesus, as Matthew makes clear, rested from this point onward with the Jews, even if Pilate, afraid of being himself accused of treason against Rome, gave the final sentence of death (19:12-16).

We are now in a position to conclude that the Synoptic and Johannine versions of the trial of Jesus contain some interesting divergences. The chief variation is in the nature of the accusation preferred against the Lord. In the Synoptic Gospels He is charged with blasphemy before Caiaphas but with anti-Roman activity before Pontius Pilate, and sentence is given by the Roman governor on political grounds. In John the charge before the high priest is not explicitly stated, while before Pilate Jesus is accused of offenses against both the Roman and Jewish law (in that order). The title "King of the Jews" could be construed either politically or theologically, and no doubt provided the bridge between the double charge; but now Pilate's verdict, surprisingly enough, is apparently given on the basis of the charge of blasphemy. In neither tradition is the reason for the transfer of the trial of Jesus from the Jewish to the Roman authorities made really clear, although both contain the suggestion (especially strong in John) that Pilate was able to authorize an execution which the Jews could only recommend.

III. Proposed Solutions to the Problems.–Hans Lietzmann, followed by Paul Winter, resolved the apparent conflict between the Synoptic and Johannine traditions by simply denying the historicity of the trial before the Sanhedrin, and asserting that Pilate's sentence was given, and can only have been given, on political grounds. This runs counter to the appearance in all four Gospels of an examination by the Jewish authorities, and to the Johannine representation of Pilate's verdict against Jesus as one given on a theological charge.

Winter regarded the account of the trial of Jesus in the Gospels as "religious" rather than "historical" in its aim (p. 3). The idea that the Jews needed Pilate's authority to endorse their sentence of death is false, according to him, since the Sanhedrin was already in a position, at least before A.D. 70, to order execution (pp. 74, 87f.). As a result only certain features of the arrest and trial of Christ belong to what Winter called the stratum of "primary tradition." They are: the arrest itself, the transfer of Jesus to the high priest's residence, the brief Jewish council held the morning after the arrest and the dispatch to Pilate, the trial before Pilate, the Barabbas episode (already in Mark an editorial adaptation), the sentence of death passed on Jesus by Pilate on a charge of sedition, and the scourging and mockery (pp. 136f.). All the other incidents and details, in Winter's view, must be attributed either to "secondary tradition" or to "editorial accretion." The assumption made by both Lietzmann and Winter (who both follow Jean Juster) is that the Sanhedrin was able both to sentence prisoners to death *and* to carry out the execution. According to the truth of this premise their thesis stands or falls, since it is on the belief that the Sanhedrin possessed this power that the double trial, Jewish as well as Roman, is denied. The general critical position, to summarize, is that the Jewish law court had the authority to pass and carry out capital sentences, but that Jesus was in fact condemned to death by Pilate for political reasons, even though He Himself was without revolutionary ambitions (cf. Winter, pp. 10, 148).

Matthew Black (pp. 19-33) did not support the contention that the trial of Jesus by the Sanhedrin is unhistorical. Instead he restated the hypothesis (first put forward by John Hawkins) that the passion narrative in Luke is based on a non-Markan tradition into which material from the Second Gospel has been inserted. This would account for the notable addition in the Lukan version of a trial before Herod, and also for minor agreements in the trial narratives between Luke and Matthew against Mark. (Cf. also Catchpole, pp. 153-220.)

But Black also assumed that the Markan narrative telescopes the sequence of events between the arrest and crucifixion of Jesus, which resulted in an impression of undue if not impossible haste. It is noteworthy, however, that on the evidence of Dt. 17:12f. and Mish. *Sanhedrin* xi.4 the death penalty was prescribed for the man who disobeyed the Jerusalem high court; further, those accused of crimes specified under this head by the Torah (including false prophecy) were to be tried and sentence given before "all the people" during one of the feasts (Passover, Pentecost, or Tabernacles). The rushed assembly of the Sanhedrin at night, followed by the speedy trial and, after due reference to Rome, immediate execution of one who was accused of undermining Jewish authority and acting as a false prophet (Mk. 11:28; 14:58, 61), is perfectly consonant with this legal state of affairs. (See further J. Jeremias, *Eucharistic Words of Jesus* [Eng. tr. 1955], p. 53.)

Black suggested that the period occupied by the arrest and trial was "longer than our Gospels make it out to be" (p. 32), and that this accordingly affects the dating of the arrest and crucifixion, as well as of the Last Supper. Traces of a tradition that the arrest took place earlier in the Passion week than the eve of the crucifixion, which is the Synoptic date, are to be found in the Fourth Gospel, which almost certainly follows an independent and historically reliable tradition. There the arrest apparently occurred "before the feast of the Passover" (Jn. 13:1), immediately after the foot washing; and the crucifixion took place on the day of Preparation for the Passover (19:14), 14 Nisan, rather than as in the Synoptic version on 15 Nisan, the day of the Passover itself.

Black's conclusion was that the divergences between the Synoptic and Johannine chronologies reflect a dispute about the date of the Passover in the year of the crucifixion; and he noted that the patristic tradition that (as in John) the Last Supper and the arrest of Jesus took place early in the Passion week is possibly supported by a festival calendar of the Qumrân sectarians (pp. 30ff.). In spite of the degree of radical argumentation involved in Black's study, therefore, it provides a measure of support for the historicity of the Gospel records of the trial as a whole.

Winter (pp. 24f.), in denying the reliability of the Evangelists' report of the trial of Jesus before the Sanhedrin, was particularly skeptical about the claim in Mk. 14:53b, 55-64 that Jesus was tried by the Jewish authorities *at night*; although if the nocturnal hearing reported in Mark (Matthew and John) was purely informal, it would not necessarily have been illegal. Legal status was then formally conferred in the morning on the decisions of the night. But in light of the morning assembly, mentioned at Mk. 15:1, Winter regarded the night examination as a secondary importation into an earlier tradition (p. 25), although he was prepared to accept as factual the suggestion of all the Evangelists that Jesus spent the nocturnal interval between His arrest and the trial before Pilate in the residence of the Jewish high priest.

It is worth noting, however, that with the exception of Luke, who reports the single Jewish trial of Jesus as taking place in the morning, the Synoptists do not specify the purpose of the morning assembly of the Sanhedrin, except in general terms (they "held a consultation," Mk. 15:1; they "took counsel against Jesus to put him to death," Mt. 27:1). There is no reason to suppose that this refers to an actual trial in Mark and Matthew, which would then provide us with a curious doublet. In these accounts, as Sherwin-White pointed out (pp. 44-46), the Jewish authorities timed their proceedings so as to be in a position to arrive at the praetorium at precisely the right moment in the aristocratic working day. There were also legal reasons, as we have seen, for this particular timetable. The lighting of a fire similarly suggests that people were active rather than asleep (Mk. 14:54; Lk. 22:55f.; Jn. 18:18). The Lukan version makes the sequence of events smoother; but while there is every likelihood that the tradition underlying the Passion narrative of the Third Gospel is at least partly independent of the other Gospels, and not necessarily secondary, it is difficult to reconcile this point in Luke with the accounts in Mark and Matthew if they are correct.

G. D. Kilpatrick queried the overall position taken by Lietzmann and Winter, and argued convincingly that we are not compelled to dismiss the Sanhedrin trial as without historical basis. A case can be made out, he claimed, for the view that behind Mk. 14:55-65 "lies a tradition which need not be a fiction of the Early Church" (p. 20). One of his chief concerns in reaching this conclusion was to examine the actual role of the Sanhedrin in the incident of the trial of Jesus; and to this we now turn.

IV. Role of the Sanhedrin.–It has already been pointed out that the case of those who deny the historical nature of the initial trial of Jesus by the Jewish authorities rests on the assumption that the Sanhedrin was able to pronounce and carry out capital sentences. What is the evidence for their contention?

The details of Jewish and Roman legal procedure at this period are not as full or as certain as might be wished, but a number of conclusions are nonetheless possible. The Sanhedrin was the supreme Jewish judicial body in Roman Judea, and clearly possessed considerable authority. The execution of James in A.D. 62, according to Josephus (*Ant.* xx.9.1 [200]), followed trial by the Sanhedrin. The death of Stephen by the non-Roman method of stoning (Acts 7:54-60) was also preceded immediately by his trial before this council; and Peter and John were arrested and threatened with death by the same authority (Acts 5:21-33). Again, the Mishnah (*Sanhedrin* vii.1ff.) refers to the four kinds of death penalty (stoning, burning, beheading, and strangling) that the Sanhedrin was empowered to inflict, and records the execution by burning of a priest's daughter who was condemned by the Jewish court.

Even so, it is also certain that the power of capital jurisdiction was at this time reserved for leading provincial officials, and denied to local or even minor Roman authorities. In the 1st cent. A.D. the power of the Roman provincial ruler was considerable; only in the 2nd cent. was proconsular authority severely limited by the emperor himself. From Tacitus (*Ann.* xii.60) and Josephus

(*BJ* ii.8.1 [117f.]; *Ant.* xviii.1.1 [1f.]), we know that in the middle of the 1st cent. A.D. there were in Judea Roman equestrian "governors" called "prefects" ("procurators" from the time of Claudius onward), who exercised a power equivalent to the normal *imperium* held by any legate or proconsul; they wielded in fact the *ius gladii.*

Control of this kind may be confidently claimed for Pontius Pilate (described by the more military title of *hēgemōn* in Matthew and Luke, rather than by the Greek equivalent of *procurator,* which is *epítropos*; Mark and John use only the proper name), even if the evidence in Josephus refers to legislation for the abnormal circumstances of insurrection. It was this authority then that limited the powers of the Jewish Sanhedrin, and governed the relationship between the Roman and Jewish authorities of the 1st cent. A.D.

This situation is not necessarily called in doubt by the four examples cited above, since in none of them is it certainly established that the Sanhedrin was actually responsible for an execution. In the case of James, the evidence of Josephus, supported by that of the Palestinian Talmud as well as John, makes it clear that the Roman powers usually controlled the decisions and even the summoning of the Sanhedrin. The stoning of James was brought about by the Sadducean high priest Ananus, in the intervening period between the death of the procurator Festus and the arrival of his successor Albinus. This illegal exercise of authority displeased the people, who appealed first to Agrippa and then to Albinus, on the grounds that "it was not lawful for Ananus to assemble a Sanhedrin without [Albinus's] consent." When the new procurator arrived, therefore, he secured the dismissal of Ananus from the high priesthood for this action (*Ant.* xx.9.1 [199-203]).

The incident of the stoning of Stephen, secondly, admits the possibility that he died under the terms of lynch law, and not as the direct result of formal sentence by a Jewish tribunal. The third example is inconclusive, since the members of the Sanhedrin are described as anxious to bring about the deaths of Peter and John, but no indication is given of the intended method of achieving this aim. The bearing of the Mishnah episode is similarly doubtful, since there is no certainty that it relates to first-century Jewish legal practice.

The conclusion must be that normally the Sanhedrin could not and did not inflict the death penalty without consent of the Roman government. And yet isolated instances of capital sentences being passed and administered by the Sanhedrin do exist. One example is the manifestly irregular execution of James to which reference has just been made. We also know from Josephus (*BJ* vi.2.4) that the Romans allowed one exception to their rule about capital sentences; the Jewish authorities were able to arrest and put to death any non-Jewish and even Roman violator of the temple. (Cf. Acts 21:27-31. The wall inscription in question, however, is ambiguous regarding the actual manner of death that was permitted.) If this was the single exception, it becomes all the more likely that the norm was the one suggested, and that Jn. 18:31 is correct; it was not lawful for the Jews to put any man to death.

So far, then, the accuracy of the trial structure in all four Gospels need not be doubted. Jesus was sentenced by the Sanhedrin on the charge of blasphemy against the Jewish law, and then brought before Pilate for the sentence to be endorsed and carried out. But at the Roman trials the charge is altered, or at least made ambiguous (except possibly in Luke), in order to strengthen the case of the opposition and bring about the death of Jesus.

This conclusion cannot be regarded as certain, however, without a consideration of two further points. One concerns the precise grounds for the sentence of death passed on Jesus by the Sanhedrin, and the other the manner of His execution. The summary of the rabbinic law relating to capital sentences, which is contained in Mish. (*Sanhedrin* vii–ix), does not indicate that words spoken against the temple were regarded as either blasphemous or meriting death. Yet the Mishnah was finally codified long after the destruction of the temple, so that the omission of any reference to this kind of legislation is understandable. Moreover, at the trial of Stephen (Acts 6–7) the charge preferred is that of blasphemy "against Moses and God" (6:11), and when the accusation is specified in council, it concerns the alleged fact that Stephen spoke words "against this holy place" as well as against the law (v. 13), and had claimed that Jesus of Nazareth would "destroy this place" (v. 14). Evidently the enemies of Jesus were prosecuting Stephen before the Sanhedrin on grounds they regarded as likely to impress the Jewish authorities, hoping thereby to secure his removal. This supports the likelihood that speaking against the temple was regarded by the Jews of the 1st cent. as blasphemy and worthy of the death penalty, and that Jesus was condemned on these grounds.

In fact, it is only Mark and Matthew who mention this particular "blasphemy" as forming part of the Jewish charge; and as we have seen, only Mark represents the words of Jesus spoken against the temple as a *false* allegation. In view of the saying of Jesus prophesying the downfall of the temple (Mk. 13:2, 14; cf. Lk. 19:43f.), it is difficult to see what was "false" about this charge, unless the accusers' formulation of the saying is a deliberate attempt to misrepresent the teaching of Jesus by combining two different ideas (cf. the apparent confusion on this topic reflected at Jn. 2:19-21). It is also interesting to notice what may be regarded as almost an anticipation of this charge: the reference by Jesus at the time of the arrest to His having been until now daily exercising a ministry *in the temple* (Mk. 14:49 par.). But all the Synoptic Gospels, and indirectly the Fourth Gospel, suggest that blasphemy was the real reason for the Sanhedrin's verdict, even if the nature of that blasphemy was ultimately held to be the claims Jesus made for Himself rather than His words against the temple.

The second point of difficulty, and an important one in Lietzmann's discussion of this subject, is the manner of Jesus' execution. In Jewish law the penalty for blasphemy was death by stoning (cf. Lev. 24:16); but Jesus died by the Roman method of crucifixion. Must we therefore conclude with Lietzmann (and Winter) that the only sentence delivered and carried out against Jesus was Roman in character, and that the Jewish trial was therefore unnecessary and indeed fictional, invented to increase the responsibility of the Jews for the death of Christ? This is surely an unwarranted deduction, achieved only by the desperate device of first excluding the possibility that Jesus was examined by the Sanhedrin. If the records of the Gospels are at all accurate, and Jesus was tried and sentenced by the Roman authorities on the basis of an initial Jewish prosecution, the Roman form of death penalty is precisely what might be expected. There is therefore no reason to regard the trial of Jesus by the Sanhedrin and Pilate as out of accord with either Jewish or Roman legal procedure existing in the province of Judea during the 1st century. (For the legal position of the procurator, see further Sherwin-White, pp. 1ff.)

V. Roman Trial.–We have noticed that in the trial (Lk., trials) before Pilate, the charge shifts from blasphemy to sedition, and that except in the Fourth Gospel it is on political grounds that Jesus is sentenced. What justification is there, we may ask, for accepting this representation as historically reliable? What precisely was the nature of the Roman trial?

The Roman governor of the 1st cent. A.D. was in a position to try the cases of accused provincials without referring to any other authority (unless the prisoners were also Roman citizens). Advice could be sought from a *consilium* of friends and officials, but the trial itself followed the system of *cognitio* and was conducted without a jury. This accords with the extent of a Roman governor's powers at this period, already discussed (under IV above), which also typified, as again we have seen, the administration of a governor of the province of Judea.

Such a trial followed a regular pattern. The charge was specifically formulated and the accusation brought by the prosecutors concerned. The procurator heard the case in person, seated on the *bēma* (judgment seat). If the verdict of "guilty" was passed, as normally happened in the absence of defense, a particular penalty was inflicted. (See the evidence in Pliny *Ep.* ii.11, the case of Marius Priscus, the proconsul of Africa who was convicted in A.D. 100 of accepting bribes from prosecutors in order to sentence innocent persons to death; and *Ep.* x.96, the famous letter to Trajan, which indicates Pliny's readiness to punish Christians with death, although *extra ordinem*; see further Sherwin-White, pp. 13ff.)

These details agree very closely with the descriptions of the Roman trial of Jesus that appear in the Gospels. Pilate acted autonomously in decisions he made about his prisoner (Mk. 15:15 par.); there was no jury, although Pilate was considerably influenced by the Jewish leaders, and took their advice (Lk. 23:13-18). The charge against Jesus was formulated and brought by spokesmen from the Jews, although it is expressly stated only in the Lukan account (23:2). Pilate is described in Matthew and John as actually seated on the judgment seat (Mt. 27:19; Jn. 19:13, using *bēma*). There was no defense, so Pilate was forced to convict, and when sentence of death was given, crucifixion was specified (Mk. 15:15; Mt. 27:26; Jn. 19:16).

Three accounts also mention the scourging of Jesus that was administered by Pilate (Mk. 15:15; Mt. 27:26; Jn. 19:1); in Luke Pilate offered to beat his prisoner in lieu of further punishment. In both cases the details are correct, and correspond to actual Roman judicial procedure. Severe beating accompanied but never replaced other punishment (in this case, death); while lighter whipping could be used, and perhaps according to Luke was volunteered, as a means of admonishing the prisoner (although the verb in Lk. 23:16, *paideúsas*, is in fact ambiguous). Similarly, the repeated questioning of Jesus by Pilate or His accusers, in the face of both the silence of the prisoner and His evident innocence in the governor's eyes, agrees with a normative technique in Roman trials, whereby prisoners without defense were given the opportunity of recanting before sentence was passed. The younger Pliny's letter to the emperor Trajan, already cited, mentions this policy; his custom was to ask those accused of being Christians if they were such; "and if they admit it, I repeat the question a second and third time, with a warning of the punishment awaiting them" (x.96.3; cf. Acts 25:16).

We are left with a consideration of the apparent conflict between the Synoptists and the Fourth Evangelist over the grounds on which Jesus was sentenced to death in the Roman trial. We can account for the shift of the charge before Pilate from the theological to the political; almost certainly this was regarded as a surer way of securing the death of Christ. But how is it to be explained that in John Pilate sentences Jesus for blasphemy, while in the other Gospels the charge is evidently sedition?

It may well be asked whether in fact the differences between the charges brought against Jesus according to the Synoptic and Johannine reports are as clear-cut as they are often taken to be. We have already seen that a considerable degree of ambiguity surrounded the formulation of the charges in both trials, Jewish and Roman. Mark and Matthew reflect the confusion of the Sanhedrin prosecution, and the failure even to agree on a charge. Luke is equally unspecific, although the opening words of the Jewish company, "If you are the Christ, tell us" (22:67), point to a theological charge. In John no charge is formulated at all. The same is true in the reports of the trial before Pilate. No charge appears in Mark or Matthew. The Lukan account clarifies the allegation in language that is predominantly political; but the charge could also be said to contain a veiled accusation of blasphemy ("saying that he himself is Christ a king," 23:2). In John the prosecution is couched in notably vague terms, and Jesus is described merely as an "evildoer" (18:30).

All four Gospels agree, however, that Pilate asked Jesus whether He was the King of the Jews, and tried to release Him from a sentence on political grounds; but when in the end pressure from the opposition to Jesus forced his hand, the Roman governor agreed to the capital sentence. The conflict of interests between the Romans and the Jews at this period is well known and easily accounts for the tense and confused situation in which Pilate became involved. Whatever precise charge was formulated in the Roman trial, in all the Gospels the issue turns on the identity of Jesus as "King." The question of Caiaphas according to the Markan account, "Are you the Christ, the Son of the Blessed?" (Mk. 14:61; Mt., Lk., "Son of God"), is not the same as Pilate's question, "Are you the King of the Jews?" But with this form of the charge, the reason for which we have already noted, there is perhaps introduced a deliberate ambiguity.

The political and religious situation of first-century Judea was such that the phrase "King of the Jews" would carry a number of different overtones. It is therefore possible to conclude that when the Jews made the charge before Pilate they did so (at least by implication) on two counts. The predominant charge was political (as in Luke). Similarly, when Pilate condemned Jesus, there was possibly a doubt in his mind as to the precise significance of the charge brought, and even an intentional obscurity about the grounds on which he was sentencing the prisoner. If this duality exists and is in fact faithfully reflected in the Gospel accounts, to varying degrees, the apparent conflict among them in the matter of the actual grounds of sentence is resolved.

VI. Significance of the Trials.–Those who question the genuineness of the Sanhedrin trial of Jesus are forced to supply a motive for the inclusion of it in the records of the Evangelists. The usual explanation is that the Gospel writers are concerned to transfer the guilt for the death of Christ from the Romans to the Jews. Winter, for example (pp. 59-61), maintained that Pilate is represented as more and more sympathetic toward Jesus the later the Gospel accounts are written. These then become a powerful piece of apologetic in the face of an increasingly harsh imperial persecution of the Christian Church, and also reflect the normative first-century tension between Christianity and Judaism.

It is possible to see how the last point, the Jewish-Christian hostility of this period, *might* have influenced the Gospel writers in their accounts. But it remains difficult to understand any real reason for deliberately inventing the portrait of a friendly Pilate in order to gain favor with Rome. Even if they were flattered by this protestation of Roman innocence, would emperors who were intent upon the extermination or at best limitation of Christianity have been impressed by the action of a procurator who did his utmost to spare its founder? Further, how true is it that at this time the Gospels were written for the imperial court, let alone used in it, as apologetic documents? It is just possible to make out such a case for Luke-Acts; but even if it is established there, it does not seem arguable for the rest.

VII. Conclusion.–We may conclude that the Gospel records of the trial of Jesus preserve this piece of the tradition accurately. Certainly we have no reason to doubt that the main outline is correct. Jesus was tried by the Jewish authorities, and of necessity referred by them to the Roman procurator. Pilate, acting perfectly within his competence, endorsed the sentence against Christ, which by then, like the charge itself, had become intentionally balanced between political and theological motivation.

See Plates 34, 36.

Bibliography.–E. Bammel, ed., *Trial of Jesus* (1970); M. Black, "The Arrest and Trial of Jesus and the Date of the Last Supper," in A. J. B. Higgins, ed., *NT Essays* (1959), pp. 19-33; J. Blinzler, *Trial of Jesus* (Eng. tr. 1959); F. Bovon, *Les Derniers jours de Jésus* (1974); S. G. F. Brandon, *Trial of Jesus of Nazareth* (1968); T. A. Burkill, *VC,* 10 (1956), 80-96; 12 (1958), 1-18; O. Cullmann, *The State in the NT* (Eng. tr. 1957); C. H. Dodd, *Historical Tradition in the Fourth Gospel* (1963), pp. 82-120; J. Jeremias, *ZNW,* 43 (1952), 145-150; J. Juster, *Les Juifs dans l'empire romain* (1914); R. Kempthorpe, *Nov.Test.,* 19 (1977), 197-208; G. D. Kilpatrick, *Trial of Jesus* (1953); H. Lietzmann, *Der Prozess Jesu, Sitzungsberichte der Preussischen Akademie der Wissenschaften, Phil.-Hist. Klasse* (1931), pp. 313-322; E. Ruckstuhl, *Die Chronologie des Letzten Mahles und des Leidens Jesu* (1963); A. N. Sherwin-White, *Roman Society and Roman Law in the NT* (1963); P. Winter, *On the Trial of Jesus* (2nd ed. 1973).

S. S. SMALLEY

JESUS, GENEALOGY OF. *See* GENEALOGY OF JESUS.

JESUS JUSTUS jē'zəs jus'təs [Gk. *Iēsous ho legómenos Ioustos*–'Jesus who is called Justus'] (Col. 4:11). One of three friends of Paul — the others being Aristarchus and Mark — whom he associates with himself in sending salutations from Rome to the church at Colossae. Jesus Justus is not mentioned elsewhere in the NT, and there is nothing more known about him than is given in this passage in Colossians, viz., that he was by birth a Jew — "of the circumcision" — that he had been converted to Christ, and that he was one of the inner circle of intimate friends and associates of the apostle during his first Roman captivity.

J. RUTHERFURD

JETHER jē'thər [Heb. *yeṯer*–'abundance'].

1. Gideon's eldest son (Jgs. 8:20), who was called upon by his father to slay Zebah and Zalmunnah, but felt unable to execute them because of his youth. As a result Gideon himself put them to death.

2. Father of Amasa (1 K. 2:5,32); he was an Ishmaelite according to 1 Ch. 2:17, identical to "Ithra, the Israelite" of 2 S. 17:25.

3. A Jerahmeelite (1 Ch. 2:32).

4. A Judahite (1 Ch. 4:17).

5. A man of Asher (1 Ch. 7:38), the same as Ithran in v. 37.

D. F. ROBERTS

JETHETH jē'theth [Heb. *y^eṯēṯ*– meaning unknown]. A chief (or clan) of Edom (Gen. 36:40 par. 1 Ch. 1:51).

JETHLAH jeth'la [Heb. *yiṯlâ*]. *See* ITHLAH.

JETHRO jeth'rō, jē'thrō [Heb. *yiṯrô*–'pre-eminence'(?); Ex. 3:1; 4:18; 18:1f., 5f., 9f., 12; LXX Gk. *Iothor*]. Priest of Midian and father-in-law of Moses, also known as Reuel ("friend of God"[?]) in Ex. 2:18. Nu. 10:29 refers to a certain Hobab "the son of Reuel the Midianite, Moses' father-in-law," but by the period of the judges (cf. Jgs. 4:11) one generation represented by the phrase "the son of Reuel the Midianite" had dropped out of the genealogy, yielding a prima facie identification of Hobab with Reuel, which the earlier traditions did not support.

When Moses fled from Egypt he found refuge in Midian, where he received a hearty welcome into the household of Jethro on account of the courtesy and kindness he had shown to the priest's seven daughters in helping them to water their flock. This friendship resulted in Jethro's giving Moses his daughter Zipporah to wed (Ex. 2:15-21). After Moses had been for about forty years in the service of his father-in-law, the angel of the Lord appeared to him in the burning bush as he was keeping the flock at Horeb and commanded him to return to Egypt and deliver his enslaved brethren out of the hands of Pharaoh (ch. 3). With Jethro's consent Moses left Midian to carry out the divine commission (4:18).

When Jethro learned that Moses and the Israelites had been delivered from bondage to the Egyptians, he set out with his daughter Zipporah and her two sons to visit him in the wilderness (Ex. 18:1-6). A time of cordial fellowship ensued in which Jethro's own faith was strengthened by learning of Israel's deliverance through God's power (Ex. 18:7-12). It is noteworthy that in the religious service in which Jethro and Moses afterward engaged, when Jethro, as priest, offered a burnt offering, and Aaron with all the elders of Israel partook of the sacrificial feast, prominence was given to Jethro over Aaron, and thus a priesthood was recognized beyond the limits of Israel.

This visit of Jethro to Moses had important consequences for the future government of Israel (Ex. 18:13-27). The priest of Midian became concerned about his son-in-law when he saw him occupied from morning to night in deciding the disputes that had arisen among the people. The labor this entailed, Jethro said, was far too heavy a burden for one man to bear. Moses himself would soon be worn out, and the people, too, would become weary and dissatisfied, owing to the inability of one judge to decide all the cases that were brought before him. Jethro, therefore, urged Moses to make use of the talents of others and adopt a plan of gradation of judges who would dispose of all cases of minor importance, leaving only the most difficult for him to settle by a direct appeal to the will of God. Moses, recognizing the wisdom of his father-in-law's advice, readily acted upon his suggestion and appointed "able men from all the people" and placed them "over the people as rulers of thousands, of hundreds, of fifties, and of tens" (v. 21). Thereafter, Jethro returned to his own country.

The story of Jethro reveals him as a man of singular attractiveness and strength, in whom a kind, considerate disposition, a deeply religious spirit, and a wise judgment all met in happy combination. This ancient priest of Midian made Israel and all nations his debtors when he taught the distinction between the legislative and the judicial function, and the importance of securing that all law be the expression of the divine will, and that its application be entrusted only to men of ability, piety, integrity, and truth (Ex. 18:21).

J. CRICHTON

JETUR jē'tər [Heb. *y^eṭûr*–meaning uncertain]. A "son" of Ishmael (Gen. 25:15 par. 1 Ch. 1:31); against this clan the two and one-half tribes warred (1 Ch. 5:18f.). They are the Ituraeans of NT times. *See* ITURAEA.

JEUEL jə-ū'əl, jo͞o'əl [Heb. *y^eʿûʾēl*–'God has saved'(?)].

1. A man of Judah (1 Ch. 9:6); the name is not found in the parallel passage, Neh. 11:24.

2. A Levite, AV, NEB, Jeiel (2 Ch. 29:13).

3. A companion of Ezra (Ezr. 8:13, AV, NEB, Jeiel; 1 Esd. 8:39).

JEUSH jē'ush [Heb. *yeʿûš*–'may he protect'(?); *K yeʿîš,* in Gen. 36:5, 14; 1 Ch. 7:10].

1. A son of Esau (Gen. 36:5, 14, 18) who subsequently became an Edomite chieftain (cf. 1 Ch. 1:35).

2. A Benjaminite (1 Ch. 7:10), descended from Bilhan.

3. Another Benjaminite (1 Ch. 8:39), descended from King Saul; AV Jehush.

4. A Gershonite Levite (1 Ch. 23:10f.).

5. A son of King Rehoboam (2 Ch. 11:19).

D. F. ROBERTS

JEUZ jē'uz [Heb. *yeʿûṣ*]. A Benjaminite, son of Shaharaim by Hodesh and among the "heads of fathers' houses" (1 Ch. 8:10).

JEW [Heb. *yehûḏî*; Aram. *yehûḏāy*; Gk. *Ioudaios, ioudaízō* ("live like a Jew," Gal. 2:14), *Ioudaikōs* ("like a Jew," Gal. 2:14)]; **JEWESS** [Gk. *Ioudaia* (Acts 24:24)]; **JEWISH** [Heb. *yehûḏî*]; AV JEWS (1 Ch. 4:18; Neh. 5:1, 8; Est. 6:13), "Jehudijah" (a transliteration based on a misunderstanding of the text, 1 Ch. 4:18); NEB also JEWS (Neh. 5:1, 8); [Gk. *Ioudaikos* (Tit. 1:14), *Ioudaios*]; AV also JEWS (Jn. 19:42; Acts 13:6; 19:13f.), JEWESS (Acts 16:1), OF THE JEWS (Lk. 23:51; Jn. 2:6; Acts 10:22; 12:11; 14:1; 17:10; 25:24); NEB also JEW (Acts 13:6), OF THE JEWS (Acts 25:24), JUDAEAN (Lk. 23:51). "Jew" originally denoted one of the inhabitants of the southern kingdom of Judah (2 K. 16:6; 25:25; Neh. 1:2; 2:16; Jer. 32:12), or one of the postexilic Israelites in general as distinct from Gentiles (so in Jeremiah, Ezra, Nehemiah, Esther, Zechariah, Daniel, and the NT); strictly speaking, it is anachronistic to use the term with reference to Hebrews or Israelites of an earlier period. The word came into our language via French and Latin from the Greek transliteration of the Aramaic (Hebrew).

I. OT Usage.–Although Heb. *yehûḏî* means "person belonging to [the tribe of] Judah," it is never used this way in the OT. It comes into prominence only after the destruction of the northern kingdom and, more specifically, after the Babylonian Captivity. Thus it is used of an Israelite living in the province of Judea (Judah) during the Babylonian, Persian, Greek, and Roman periods. It is most frequent in Esther, where it denotes all Israelites (cf. the application of the term to Mordecai, who was of the tribe of Benjamin: 2:5; 3:5; 5:13; etc.); the same usage is found in Daniel (3:8, 12). Hence the term takes on a decidedly religious connotation, referring to adherents of the Hebrew religion (*see* JUDAISM), though there often remains a close connection with the land of Judah.

II. Intertestamental and Early Jewish Usage.–The term "Jew(s)" was only rarely used by Hebrew-speaking Jews in the land of Palestine, who tended to prefer the designation "Israel" (cf. the apocryphal books originally written in Hebrew, the Dead Sea Scrolls, the Mishnah, the Hebrew part of the Talmud, and the coins minted during the A.D. 70 and Bar Cochba rebellions). Thus among Hebrew-speaking Jews *yehûḏî* continued to have the connotation of an inhabitant of Judea rather than an Israelite in general. A striking illustration of this usage occurs in the reference of the Jewish leaders to Jesus as "King of Israel" (Mk. 15:32) in contrast to the Roman governor and the soldiers, who call him "King of the Jews" (Mk. 15:2, 9, 12, 18, 26; cf. also the question of the wise men, Mt. 2:2). It is interesting to compare this with Matthew's preference (*contra* John) for the term "Israel" rather than "Jews" for Palestinian Israelites.

III. NT Usage.–In the NT "Jew(s)" is used, with the exceptions mentioned above and a few other references (Mt. 28:15; Mk. 7:3; Lk. 7:3; Rev. 2:9; 3:9), primarily in the Fourth Gospel (68 times), Acts (79 times, but rarely in Luke) and the Epistles of Paul (35 times). A Jew is one who is not a Gentile (Gal. 2:14; 3:28; Acts 14:1, 5), a Samaritan (Jn. 4:9), or a proselyte (Acts 2:10). The term denotes not just one who is Jewish by religion, since proselytes are not "Jews" and Jewish Christians are (Acts 21:39; Gal. 2:13f.). In addition, from the NT point of view, it is possible to be a "Jew" by faith without having been born a Jew by race, nationality, or religion (Rom. 2:28f.; cf. Rev. 2:9; 3:9).

John's Gospel uses the term "Jews" not for all Israelites, or even all Israelites living in the province of Judea, but for those Israelite inhabitants of Judea, especially their religious and political leaders, who steadfastly opposed Jesus (though there are some positive references: 3:1; 11:33-36; 12:9-11; etc.). This should not be interpreted as Christian anti-Semitism (any more than similar references to "Israel" in the OT prophets), since it is clear that all the chief actors in the Gospel story, and probably also the author, are "Jews" in the broader sense (including Jesus!). Paul's reference to "the Jews, who killed both the Lord Jesus and the prophets" (1 Thess. 2:14-16; cf. 2 Cor. 11:24) should be interpreted along similar lines, since he himself was proud to be a Jew (Phil. 3:4f.; cf. Acts 21:39) and continued to believe that the Jewish people had a special place in God's plan (Rom. 11).

IV. Modern Usage.–There is no general agreement today concerning the use of the term. The question "Who is a Jew?" is being hotly debated in the context of the modern state of Israel. Orthodox Judaism accepts one as a Jew who has been born to a Jewish mother and who has not apostatized (e.g., converted to Christianity), while others would include also one who has a Jewish father or who has converted to Judaism (i.e., a proselyte). There is a clear preference among many Jewish leaders for the term "Israel" rather than "Jew" as a contemporary designation of the Hebrew people.

Bibliography.–*Encyclopedia Judaica* (1971), X, 22f.; M. Lowe, *Nov.Test.*, 18 (1976), 101-130.

W. W. GASQUE

JEWEL; JEWELRY. An ornament of gold, silver, or semiprecious stones in the form of an amulet, bracelet, headdress, anklet, or the like. Near Eastern archeological excavations have revealed many examples of such ornaments, demonstrating the widespread use of semiprecious stones in settings of precious metal. Accordingly, the MT frequently refers to jewels (Heb. *kelî*, "something manufactured") in connection with gold and silver (Gen. 24:53; Ex. 3:22; 11:2; etc.). In Cant. 7:1 (MT 2) Heb. *ḥalî* ("necklace, ornament"; cf. Prov. 25:12) describes any kind of ornamentation. Jewels were part of the high priest's regalia (Ex. 28:15-21; 39:8-14) and appeared similarly on the crowns (2 S. 12:20; 1 Ch. 20:2) and garments (Ezk. 28:13) of kings and queens. Wealthy people emulated these practices, and among articles of personal adornment the signet was popular in OT times (cf. Gen. 38:18; 41:42). Before coined money was introduced into the Near East in about the 6th cent. B.C., jewels were a highly negotiable form of wealth and during the monarchy constituted part of the royal treasury (1 K. 10:11; 1 Ch. 29:2, etc.).

See also ORNAMENT; GARMENTS; SIGNET; STONES, PRECIOUS.

R. K. H.

JEWELER [Heb. *ḥārāš 'eḇen*] (Ex. 28:11); AV ENGRAVER IN STONE; NEB CRAFTSMAN. The art of making jewelry was known in Palestine from prehistoric times. Artifacts reveal a considerable artistic sense and

Gold armlet (5th-4th cents. B.C.) showing Achaemenian influences from the Oxus Treasure of ancient Bactria. The hollows in the winged and horned griffins originally held inlays (Victoria and Albert Museum, London)

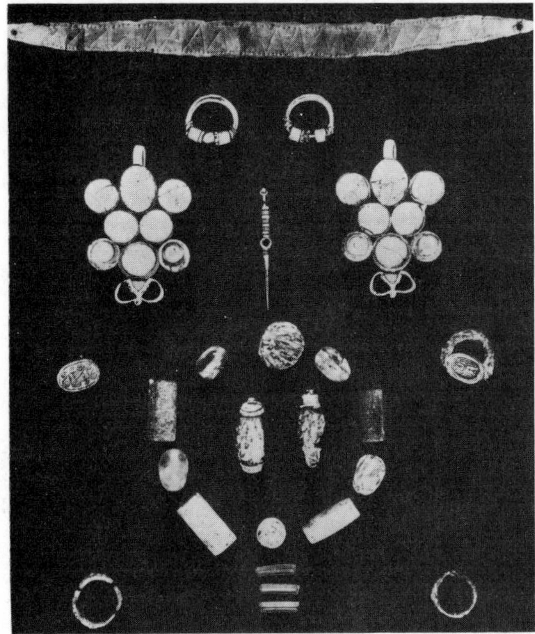

Jewelry found in a burial at Megiddo (from top to bottom): gold headband; gold rings; gold earrings; pins; scarabs and beads of gold, silver, amethyst, and crystal from a necklace; and two gold bands (*ca.* 1400 B.C.) (Oriental Institute, University of Chicago)

manual dexterity on the part of the craftsmen. The jewels of Ex. 28:11 were to be worn by the high priest.

JEWRY jo͞oʹrē. Used by the AV three times: once in the OT for Aram. *yᵉhûḏ* (Dnl. 5:13; RSV Judah); and twice in the NT for Gk. *Ioudaia* (Lk. 23:5; Jn. 7:1; RSV Judea).

JEWS. *See* JEW.

JEZANIAH jez-ə-nīʹə [Heb. *yᵉzanyāhû*–probably 'Yahweh hears'; cf. JAAZANIAH]. In Jer. 40:8 the name of a Judean leader who accompanied Johanan when he visited Gedaliah at Mizpah (cf. 2 K. 25:23). In Jer. 42:1 the RSV reads Azariah (cf. 43:2), following the LXX. The name seems to have been fairly common in sixth-century-B.C. Judah, occurring in one of the Lachish ostraca and on a contemporary seal inscription. Whether either is the biblical personage is unknown.

JEZEBEL jezʹə-bel [Heb. *'îzeḇel*; Gk. *Iezabel*]. The base of this Phoenician name is *zbl,* "prince," usually vocalized *zᵉḇûl.* Proposals for an original sentence name include *'y-zbl,* "where is the prince?" and *'ṯ-zbl,* "the prince exists." Both exclamations occur in passages concerning Baal's demise and return in the Ugaritic literature (*UT,* 49:III:20-21; IV:28-29, 39-40; *ANET,* pp. 140f.). The vowels of the MT, however, change the sense to *zeḇel,* "dung," thereby creating a wordplay in 2 K. 9:37, "the corpse of Jezebel shall be as dung" (*dōmen*). A seal from the 9th-8th cent. B.C. bears the Phoenician inscription *yzbl,* a form of the name which may have influenced the LXX spelling. Ahab's wife is the only person with this name in the OT.

The name of Jezebel usually evokes for us the image of a painted woman who is sexually alluring or trying to be, a manipulator of men, a political meddler, an idolatress. The Bible's condemnations of her, however, concern her role in public religious and political affairs, not her private (im)morality. Examination of the texts and related evidence shows that more was at stake for the biblical writers than the frivolous elements in her modern stereotype.

Jezebel is introduced in the listing of the evils of her husband Ahab's reign (869-850 B.C., 1 K. 16:31). Her father, Ethbaal king of the Sidonians, appears as Ithobalos in Josephus' account of Tyre (*Ant.* viii.13.1 [317]). A priest of Astarte, he killed his royal predecessor at Tyre to gain kingship over all the Phoenician cities, including the older Sidon, which were under the hegemony of Tyre (Josephus *CAp* i.18 [123]). Ahab's marriage probably sealed an alliance between Israel and Tyre just when the Aramean powers of Syria were threatening the small coastal states. Building a house and altar for Baal and an Asherah would have been required for alliance protocol as well as for Jezebel's devotions (cf. the shrines for Solomon's foreign wives, 1 K. 11:1-8), and they stood as Samaria's monuments to the religious heritage of its sister-city Tyre, whose landmark temples were dedicated to Baal Melqart (Lord of the City) and Astarte.

That the Phoenician temples in the capital of Israel were more than token shrines is evident from the events surrounding Elijah's confrontation with the prophets of Baal on Mt. Carmel (1 K. 18). Official royal support had shifted away from Yahwism, for Jezebel was able to cut off and kill the prophets of Yahweh (1 K. 18:4, 13) while maintaining the prophets of Baal (and of Asherah, according to a gloss) from the royal provisions, even in the drought and famine (1 K. 18:19). Josephus reported that Ithobalos was credited with having broken the same drought by his supplication to the gods, presumably Baal and Astarte whom he served (Josephus citing Menander, *Ant.* viii.13.2 [324]). Elijah used the occasion at Carmel to demonstrate Yahweh's power against such claims and to execute the prophets of Baal as a prelude to the end of the drought, but even he fled before Jezebel's wrath (1 K. 19:1-3).

The clash of religions is epitomized in the threatening message Jezebel sent to Elijah upon learning of the Carmel executions. The LXX and Latin versions preserve a variant wordplay that gives the passage a more forceful reading: "If you are Elijah, I am Jezebel! So may god(s) do to me, and more also, if I do not make your life as the life of one of them by this time tomorrow" (1 K. 19:2). Putting the names in opposition puts the respective deities in opposition as well, for Elijah's name means "Yahweh is my god," while Jezebel's invokes Baal "the prince." The RSV makes Jezebel speak here of "gods," translating all the plurals of the MT: *'ĕlōhîm,* "gods," and the verbs, "do" and "do more" (*see* GOD, NAMES OF II.A.2). In Codex Vaticanus of the LXX, however, *'ĕlōhîm* is matched to singular verbs, the common Israelite usage when referring to their singular God (cf. 2 K. 6:31: the king of Israel swears the same oath in the singular; and 1 K. 18:24: "the *'ĕlōhîm* who answers by fire, that one is the *'ĕlōhîm*"). The intensity of the cultic conflict and such verbal evidence suggest that Jezebel was promoting Baal as the *'ĕlōhîm* to replace Yahweh, not as an additional god in a polytheistic pantheon.

Further theological and legal tensions arose in the affair of Naboth's vineyard (1 K. 21). Ahab first appeared unhappy but bound by Naboth's refusal to sell or exchange his vineyard, a refusal "before Yahweh to give the inheritance of my fathers" to Ahab (1 K. 21:3). Similar concern for keeping property within the family is found in legal texts from Mari and Ugarit, and it brings to mind the theologically motivated statute in Lev. 25:23 regarding Hebrew property: "The land shall not be sold in perpetuity, for the land is mine" (cf. Lev. 25:29-31). Naboth's refusal to cede Hebrew land would be all the more understandable if the house of Omri was a family of Canaanite descent, as some have suggested on the basis of family names, the eagerness for Phoenician alliance and religion, the affinity for JEZREEL, and the purchase of the non-Israelite Samaria for its capital.

Jezebel circumvented all Naboth's possible objections by arranging a charge against him for cursing (piel of Heb. *bāraḵ,* lit. "bless"; cf. KoB, p. 154) God and king, with false witnesses and a sure guilty verdict and death sentence (1 K. 21:9f.). The legal details of the charge and consequences are unclear. Naboth may have been accused of blasphemy or of perjury regarding the sale; Ahab may have had royal rights to the property of a criminal or may have been judged the legal owner. Jezebel's manipulation of Hebrew law obtained what was the usual right of a Phoenician monarch over subjects' lives and property. In Israelite eyes, however, the crown had falsely condemned an innocent man to gain his property, and Elijah was sent to bear God's judgment (1 K. 21:19-24; cf. 2 S. 11–12: David had Uriah killed to gain Bathsheba and Nathan brought the judgment). Included in Elijah's message was the word of Jezebel's fate. Verse 19 is probably the original core of the judgment, the direct response to the royal outrage; this judgment is amplified with standard formulations about annihilating the male line (vv. 21f.; cf. 1 K. 14:10) and leaving the bodies unburied for dogs and birds to desecrate (v. 24; cf. 14:11; 16:4; Jer. 16:4). The opening and closing references to dogs in vv. 19 and 24 supply catchwords for interrupting Ahab's judgment with another introductory clause and the judgment against Jezebel (v. 23), a judgment echoed and expanded in 2 K. 9:10, 36f.

In the editorial remarks about the house of Ahab, Jezebel is blamed for the religious shortcomings of her royal spouse, sons, and extended family. This picture may be due partly to the Deuteronomic historian's tendency to use her as a model of Canaanite pollution, but it may also reflect the Phoenician practice of installing a royal woman as priestess of Astarte, thereby making her considerably more active in the close relations of temple and palace than was customary in the Hebrew monarchy. Amoʿashtart, who was daughter of Eshmunʿazar I, Tabnit's consort, and queen mother of Eshmunʿazar II, filled this role; she is inscribed with her son as builder of houses for the gods, especially for Astarte, Eshmun (the holy prince), and other deities of Sidon (*ANET,* p. 662). 1 K. 21:25 charges Jezebel with inciting Ahab to idolatry, and his son and successor Ahaziah is faulted for walking in the way of his father and the way of his mother (22:52). Although Jehoram/Joram avoids the associations with Jezebel and Ahab in some passages (2 K. 3:2, 13), he received the fatal thrust of Jehu's righteous attack on her account (9:22). The royal Judean in-laws were similarly judged. Jehoram of Judah, who married Athaliah of Israel (daughter of Ahab, 8:18; of Omri, 8:26), and their son Ahaziah were condemned for walking in the way of the house of Ahab (8:18, 27), and their kinsmen also fell under Jehu's sword (10:12-14).

By the time that Jezebel faced Jehu in Jezreel, she alone of the invested Israelite royalty remained a formal obstacle to his kingship (2 K. 9:30-37). Although Jehu appeared to the prophetic group and to his fellow officers as a properly anointed king, to her he was only a usurper like the seven-day king Zimri (1 K. 16:8-20). Jezebel's darkening her eyes and adorning her head (with formal wig and jewelry) should be seen less as a seductive attempt to distract Jehu from his zealous purpose than as the public appearance by the queen mother to confront the rebellious commander with the authority of the royal house and cult. The reversal of their positions is strikingly depicted in her being thrown from the window and in his entrance into the palace of his masters for a meal.

One can say, then, that the historical Jezebel was a princess and perhaps priestess of Tyre who used her role as wife and queen mother in the house of Ahab to promote Canaanite practices in the monarchy and cult of Israel. The biblical Jezebel, however, is a much more dramatic figure than her historical biography suggests because the literary presentation of her actions and speeches gives her unforgettable animation. One can almost feel the knife in her voice in the threat to Elijah, in her jab at Ahab's despondency over the vineyard, in her challenge to Jehu (1 K. 19:2; 21:5-7; 2 K. 9:31). Others speak of her in the strongest terms, in Obadiah's reports of her persecutions, in prophetic oracles of judgment, and in Jehu's scorching rebuke to Jehoram (1 K. 18:13; 2 K. 9:10, 22). Even the briefest assessments of her family's reigns cannot ignore her. She was probably impossible to ignore in life as well, but the text's portrait of her as the incarnation of the Canaanite cultic and political practices, detested by Israelite prophets and loyalists, has given her a literary life far beyond the existence of a ninth-century Tyrian princess. This is, ironically, the opposite effect of what was intended in the mutilation of her body and in Jehu's final observation "that they will not say, 'This is Jezebel' " (2 K. 9:37).

The NT was the first to say, "This is [a] Jezebel." The letter to the church of Thyatira warns against tolerating "the woman Jezebel, who calls herself a prophetess and is teaching and beguiling my servants to practice immorality and to eat food sacrificed to idols" (Rev. 2:20). As in the preceding letter's reference to Balaam and Balak (Rev. 2:14), the name typifies the errant Christian by an allusion to her OT counterpart. Here she is an influential woman within the congregation, whose teaching encourages members to depart from the preferred Christian practice of avoiding public festivities of city or trade guild that required feasting on dedicated food and sharing its accompanying entertainments.

The figure of Jezebel has remained a powerful literary referent. The combination of suspect political authority and religious antipathy that characterized the OT Jezebel also made several Roman Catholic queens her namesake in the attacks of their critics: Isabella I was called "the Catholic Jezebel" by Spanish Jews (F. W. Farrar, *Second Book of Kings* [1900], p. 124 n. 2), Mary Tudor and Mary Stuart received the name from John Knox ("He hath raised up these Jezebels [our mischievous Marys] to be the uttermost of his plagues," *First Blast of the Trumpet Against the Monstrous Regiment of Women* [1558]), and Titus Oates railed against *The Witch of Endor or the Witchcraft of the Roman Jezebel*. More recently, however, the heretical and political emphases of the allusion have faded in literary and slang references, leaving only the "harlotries and sorceries" of a manipulative and cosmetically carnal woman trying to control the men in her private life. If Jezebel had been only that, she would not have mattered in the biblical record of prophets and kings.

Bibliography.–F. I. Andersen, *JBL*, 85 (1966), 46-57; N. Avigad, *IEJ*, 14 (1964), 274-76; O. Eissfeldt, "Bist du Elia, so bin ich Isebel (I Kön xix 2)," in *Hebräische Wortforschung* (*SVT*, 16; 1967), pp. 65-70; J. Gray, *I & II Kings* (*OTL*, 2nd ed. 1970).

E. B. JOHNSTON

JEZELUS jə-zē'ləs [Gk. *Iezēlys*].

1. 1 Esd. 8:32, AV, NEB; RSV Jahaziel as in Ezr. 8:5 (*see* JAHAZIEL **5**).

2. 1 Esd. 8:35, AV, NEB; RSV Jehiel as in Ezr. 8:9 (*see* JEHIEL **7**).

JEZER jē'zər [Heb. *yeṣer*]; **JEZERITES** jē'zər-īts [Heb. *hayyiṣrî*]. Jezer was the third son of Naphtali (Gen. 46:24; Nu. 26:49; 1 Ch. 7:13), eponymous ancestor of the Jezerites (Nu. 26:49).

JEZIAH jə-zī'ə. *See* IZZIAH.

JEZIEL jē'zi-əl, jē-zī'əl [Heb. *K* *yᵉzûʾēl* or *yᵉzôʾēl*; *Q* *yᵉzîʾēl*–'God gathers'(?)]. One of David's Benjaminite recruits at Ziklag (1 Ch. 12:3).

JEZLIAH jez-lī'ə. *See* IZLIAH.

JEZOAR jə-zō'ar. *See* IZHAR.

JEZRAHIAH jez-rə-hī'ə. *See* IZRAHIAH.

JEZREEL jez'rē-əl, jez'rēl [Heb. *yizrᵉʿeʾl*–'God sows'; LXX usually *Iezrael*].

1. A city in northern Israel.

I. Identification.–Concerning *Iezrael*, Eusebius says, "Even now there is a very well known town, *Esdraēla* in the Great Plain between Scythopolis [=Beth-shean] and Legio [beside Megiddo]" (*Onom.* 108.12-14). The Bordeaux Pilgrim referred to it as *Stradela*, 16 km. (10 mi.) from Maximianupolis [=Legio] and 19 km. (12 mi.) from Scythopolis (*Itinerarium Burdigalense* 19.20). The Jewish scholar R. Eshtori Haparhi (between A.D. 1313-1322) recognized that the biblical name had been modified in Arabic to *Zerʿîn*. Edward Robinson, in 1838, was the first modern scholar to identify Jezreel with the Arab village of Zerʿîn, 11 km. (6⅝ mi.) N of Jenîn. The site is perched on the edge of a shelf that forms the southeast border of the great valley to which Jezreel has given its name. From this point the ground drops off steeply to the east to form the narrow valley of Beth-shean (Wâdī el-Jālûd).

II. History.–Jezreel is not mentioned in any of the Egyptian or cuneiform sources from the 2nd millennium B.C. Therefore, there are grounds for assuming that it was actually founded by the Israelites. Along with nearby Shunem (Sôlem), it is mentioned as a border town of the tribe of Issachar (Josh. 19:18) and must have shared the fortunes of that tribe, first submitting to servile status among the Canaanites (Gen. 49:15) and then rising in rebellion against them (Jgs. 5:15).

At the end of Saul's reign he and the Israelite troops marched out for a confrontation with the Philistines and encamped by "the fountain which is in Jezreel" (1 S. 29:1), evidently ʿAin el-Meiyiteh (now ʿEn Yizreʿel) rather than ʿAin Jālûd (now ʿEn Ḥarod). Meanwhile, the Philistines had mustered at Aphek on the Sharon Plain (1 S. 29:1) and then marched up to the Jezreel Valley (v. 11) and encamped at Shunem (1 S. 28:4). The battle must have taken place on the level ground around Jezreel (2 S. 4:4) until Saul and his forces retreated up the slope that runs along the Gilboa ridge SW of the town (1 S. 31:1).

Saul's son Esh-baal (Ishbosheth) was crowned king over the northern tribal areas formerly loyal to his father; these included (along with regions like Gilead, Ephraim, and Benjamin) Jezreel (2 S. 2:9), which must refer to more than just the town itself. Since Jezreel was evidently one of the earliest Israelite settlements in the "Great Plain" (contrast Jgs. 1:27, 30), its name came to be applied by them to the entire valley W of it. A comparison of Josh. 17:16, the earliest allusion to the Valley of Jezreel, with Jgs. 1:27 shows that the valley (or plain) refers to the territory of such towns as Taanach, Ibleam, and Megiddo in contrast to Beth-shean and its villages (cf. also Jgs. 6:33 and Ps. 83:9f. [MT 10f.]). The same situation prevailed in the Greco-Roman period; the "Great Plain" was Esdraelon (Jth. 1:8; cf. Eusebius *Onom.* 108.12-24 [see I above]).

During Solomon's reign, Jezreel (comprised of Taanach and Megiddo, i.e., most of the Great Plain) was governed by Baana son of Ahilud, the fifth district commissioner (1 K. 4:12). Under the Omride dynasty, Jezreel became a secondary capital of the Israelite kingdom (1 K. 18:44-46); Ahab's palace there (1 K. 21:1) was probably the "winter house" (Am. 3:15). The city was fortified, as evidenced by allusions to its gate (2 K. 9:31; 10:8) and tower (2 K. 9:17). Though the king and all his entourage — namely, high officials, familiar friends, and priests — might be in residence at Jezreel during certain periods of the year (2 K. 10:11), the affairs of the city were in the hands of the elders and free men (1 K. 21:8-14). One citizen, Naboth, was executed on a false charge of treason and his property confiscated by Ahab (ch. 21); otherwise, there was no legal means to force the landholder to relinquish his patrimony. The assassination of Joram, Jezebel, all the sons (members) of Ahab's family, and also of Ahaziah king of Judah took place during the coup d'etat of Jehu at Jezreel (2 K. 8:29; 9f.; 2 Ch. 22:5-9). The Jehu dynasty was to suffer defeat in the Valley of Jezreel as retribution for his excessive cruelty during his rise to power (Hos. 1:4f., 11 [MT 2:2]); but this scene of disaster would afterward become once again the center of agricultural productivity (Hos. 2:22 [MT 24]).

III. Archeology.–A brief sounding made on the site by Macalister early this century was ineffectual. More recent surveys have produced sherds of the Israelite, Roman, and Byzantine periods, as well as the remains of a medieval vaulted building and other structures.

Bibliography.–E. Robinson, *Biblical Researches*, II (1856), 318-325; *SWP*, II, 88, 130f.; R. A. S. Macalister, *PEQ*, 41 (1909), 175; A. Alt, *PJ*, 23 (1927), 48; A. Saarisalo, *Boundary Between Issachar and Naphtali* (1927), pp. 48ff.; W. Borée, *Die alten Ortsnamen Palästinas* (1930), p. 99; *HGHL*, cf. Index pp. 481f.; S. Yeivin, *Bulletin of the Israel Exploration Society*, 14 (1948), 89 (=*BIES Reader* B [1965], p. 113); I. Press, *Topographical-Historical Encyclopaedia of Palestine* (1948), II, 390; A. Alt, *Der Stadstaat*

Samaria, Berichte der Sächsischen Akademie der Wissenschaften, 101/5 (1954), 9-21 (=*KS*, III [1959], 260-270).

2. A settlement in the eighth district of Judah mentioned alongside Maon, Carmel, Ziph, and Juttah (Josh. 15:55f.). It is usually associated with Jezreel, a descendant of Hur in the genealogy of Judah (1 Ch. 4:3). David's wife Ahinoam, the mother of Amnon (2 S. 3:2; 1 Ch. 3:1), was undoubtedly from there (1 S. 25:43; 27:3; 2 S. 2:2). Abel's proposed identification with Khirbet Ṭarrâmā is impossible, since that site is not in the same topographical district as the other towns associated with Jezreel.

See *GP,* II, 365. A. F. RAINEY

JEZREEL, VALLEY OF jez-rēl' [Heb. *ʿemeq yizreʿʾel*]; NEB VALE OF JEZREEL. The vitally important lowland corridor extending southeastward from the Bay of Acco (modern Haifa Bay) area to the edge of the Jordan Valley at Beth-shean. It is known today as *Emek Yizreel,* or more simply the *Emek* (Arab. *Merj Ibn ʿAmir*). The whole valley is enclosed by steep scarps caused by geological faulting. On the southwest are the high limestone slopes of Mt. Carmel and Mt. Gilboa, and on the northeast the limestone Allonim hills near Nazareth, the isolated dome of Mt. Tabor (apparently the collapsed keystone of an arch) and Mt. Moreh (limestone with a thin covering of basalt). There are two subregions: the central plain of Megiddo and the eastern Beth-shean corridor, with the town of Jezreel at the junction of the two.

The plain of Megiddo is triangular, with its base of 32 km. (20 mi.) along the foot of the Carmel range and its apex just N of Mt. Tabor. It is drained by the tiny and sluggish river Kishon, whose course northwestward to the Bay of Acco is twice blocked, once by a narrow volcanic outcrop, extending northeastward from Megiddo, and again by a constricted defile between Mt. Carmel and the hills of lower Galilee, through which it enters the coastal region. The plain is floored with rich alluvium, about 100 m. (330 ft.) deep, brought down from the surrounding hills. It produced abundant wheat harvests in the early summer and well deserved the designation "rich valley" (Isa. 28:1). In winter, however, heavy rains could transform the whole valley into a sea of mud, and movement across it became almost impossible. Elijah advised King Ahab to make all haste to reach Jezreel before the rain began (1 K. 18:44), and Barak defeated Sisera in this plain because the Canaanite chariots could not move in the mud (Jgs. 4:15; 5:4). Both roads and villages clung to the lower slopes of the hills, the main road from Acco to Beth-shean following the base of the triangle.

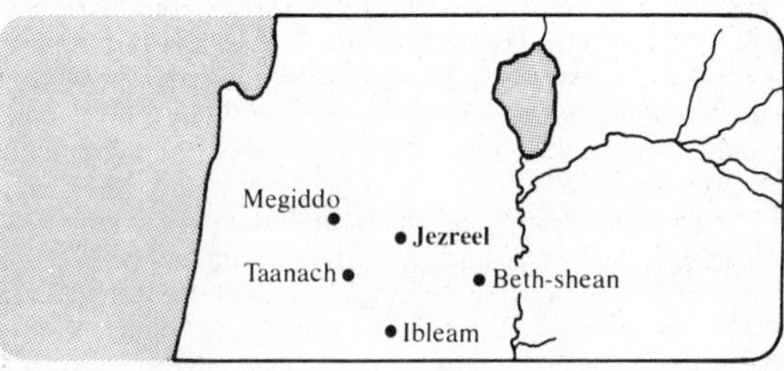

The plain of Jezreel as seen from Mt. Carmel (D. Baly)

The plain of Megiddo has five gates. One is the defile leading to the Bay of Acco, and another the threefold gate to the plain of Sharon, formed by narrow valleys across Carmel and guarded by the three fortresses of Jokneam, Megiddo, and Taanach. Of these Megiddo was by far the most important, because it controlled also the narrow volcanic causeway leading across the easily flooded plain. The third gate is the ascent of Gur (2 K. 9:27) leading southward through Dothan toward Samaria. Here Joseph came in search of his brothers (Gen. 37:17), and the king of Syria vainly tried to arrest Elisha (2 K. 6:13). Fourth is the passage on either side of Mt. Tabor, traditionally, though probably incorrectly, identified with the mount of transfiguration (Mt. 17:1; Mk. 9:2; Lk. 9:28). Here Barak mustered the warriors of Naphtali and Zebulun before the battle against Sisera (Jgs. 4:6). The great "Way of the Sea" from Damascus to Egypt ran N of Tabor and across the volcanic causeway to Megiddo. The other gate is the entrance to the Beth-shean corridor.

This corridor, guarded at its entrance by Jezreel (Zirʿîn), with its rich springs, and Shunem (Sôlem), slopes down toward the Jordan Valley between Mt. Gilboa on the south and Mt. Moreh on the north. Never more than 3 km. (2 mi.) wide, it is drained by the short river Harod (Arab. *Jālûd*) and is normally protected from the winter cold. It was the scene of the victory of Gideon over the Midianites (Jgs. 7) and later of the tragic defeat of Saul by the Philistines (1 S. 29:1; 31:1-7).

The plain of Megiddo was the territory of Zebulun and the Beth-shean corridor that of Issachar (Josh. 19:10-23), both of whom were said to "suck the affluence of the seas and the hidden treasures of the sand" (Dt. 33:19), because of their position on the great trade routes, but they were easily invaded and compelled to become "a slave at forced labor" (Gen. 49:15). Although the town of Jezreel was apparently a royal city in the kingdom of Israel and may have served as the king's winter residence, it could not withstand a siege, as could Samaria. With the collapse of the Syro-Israelite alliance against Assyria after the revolution against the dynasty of Omri in 842 B.C., Jehu was forced to submit to Shalmaneser III on Mt. Carmel in 841, and the southern edge of Jezreel became temporarily the northern frontier of Israel, marking, as it did, the northern edge of the better defended "heartland" of the country.

Bibliography.–*GB; HGHL;* Y. Karmon, *Israel: A Regional Geography* (1974); E. Orni and E. Efrat, *Geography of Israel* (1971).

D. BALY

JEZREELITE jez'ri-ə-līt [Heb. *hayizreʿēʾlî*]. A man of Jezreel, collectively the people of Jezreel. The term is always used of Naboth (1 K. 21:1ff.; 2 K. 9:21, 25), and refers to JEZREEL in the plain of Jezreel.

JEZREELITESS jez'ri-ə-līt'es [Heb. *yizreʿēʾlîṯ*]. A woman of Jezreel. The term is always used of Ahinoam the Jezreelitess (RSV also "of Jezreel"), one of David's wives (1 S. 27:3; 30:5; 2 S. 2:2; 3:2; 1 Ch. 3:1), and refers to Jezreel in Judah.

JEZRIELUS jez-ri-ē'lus [Gk. *Iezrielos*] (1 Esd. 9:27, NEB). *See* JEHIEL **8.**

JIBSAM jib'sam (1 Ch. 7:2, AV). *See* IBSAM.

JIDLAPH jid'laf [Heb. *yiḏlap*–'he weeps'(?)]. The seventh son of Nahor and Milcah (Gen. 22:22).

JIMNA, JIMNAH jim'na. *See* IMNAH **1.**

JIMNITES jim'nīts (Nu. 26:44, AV). *See* IMNITES.

JIPHTAH jif'tə [Heb. *yiptāḥ*] (Josh. 15:43, AV). *See* IPHTAH.

JIPHTHAHEL jif'tha-el (AV Josh. 19:14, 27). *See* IPHTAH-EL.

JOAB jō'ab [Heb. *yôʾāḇ*–'Yahweh is father'; Gk. *Iōab*].

1. Son of Zeruiah, David's sister. He was "commander of the army" (cf. 2 S. 19:13 [MT 14]) under David. He is first introduced in the narrative of the war with Abner, who supported the claims of Ishbosheth to the throne against those of David (2 S. 2:8–3:1). The two armies met, and on Abner's suggestion a contest took place between twelve men from each side; a general engagement followed, and in this Joab's army was victorious. Asahel, Joab's brother, was killed in his pursuit of Abner, but the latter's army was closely pursued, and he appealed to Joab for a cessation of hostilities. Joab called a halt, but declared that he would not have ceased if Abner had not made his plea.

In 2 S. 3:12-29 Abner visited David at Hebron, and made an alliance with him. He then left the town, apparently under royal protection. Joab was absent at the time, but returned immediately after Abner's departure, and protested to David for not avenging Asahel's death, and at the same time attributed a bad motive to Abner's visit. He sent a message, no doubt in the form of a royal command, for Abner to return; Abner did so and was taken aside "into the midst of the gate" (or as the LXX and some commentators read, "into the side of the gate" [3:27]), and slain there by Joab. David proclaimed his own innocence in the matter, commanded Joab as well as the people to mourn publicly for the dead hero (3:31), composed a lament for Abner, and pronounced a curse upon Joab and his descendants.

In 2 S. 10:1-14 (par. 1 Ch. 19:1-15) David sent ambassadors with his good wishes to Hanun on his ascending the throne of the Ammonites; the ambassadors were ill-treated, and war followed, David's troops being commanded by Joab. On finding himself placed between the Ammonites on the one hand, and their Syrian allies on the other, Joab divided his army, and himself led one division against the Syrians, leaving his brother Abishai to fight the Ammonites; the defeat of the Syrians was followed by the rout of the Ammonites.

2 S. 10:15-19 (par. 1 Ch. 19:16-19) describes a second war between Hadadezer and David. Joab is not mentioned here.

2 S. 11:1 narrates the resumption of the war against the Ammonites; Joab was in command, and the town of Rabbah was besieged. Here occurs the account of David's sin with Bathsheba, omitted by the Chronicler. David told Joab to send Uriah, her husband, to Jerusalem, and when Uriah refused to break the soldier's vow (11:6-13), Joab was used to procure his death in the siege, and the general then sent news of it to David (11:14-27). After capturing the "water-city" of Rabbah, Joab sent for David to complete the capture and lead the triumph himself (12:26-29).

The next scene depicts Joab succeeding in his attempt to have Absalom restored to royal favor. He had noticed that "the king's heart went out to Absalom" (14:1), and so arranged for "a wise woman" of Tekoa to bring a supposed complaint of her own before the king and then rebuke him for his treatment of Absalom. The plan succeeded. David saw Joab's hand in it and gave him permission to bring Absalom to Jerusalem. But the rebel had to remain in his own house, and was not allowed to see his father (14:1-24).

Absalom then attempted to secure Joab's intercession for a complete restoration to his father's confidence. Joab turned a deaf ear to the request until his field was set on fire at Absalom's command. He then saw Absalom and persuaded David to receive his prodigal son back into the royal home (14:28-33).

Afterward Absalom revolted, and made Amasa, another nephew of David, general instead of Joab (17:24f.). David fled to Mahanaim, followed by Absalom. Joab was given a third of the army, the other divisions being led by Abishai and Ittai. He was informed that Absalom had been caught in a tree (or thicket), and rebuked the informer for not having killed him. Although he was reminded of David's tender plea that Absalom be dealt with kindly, he killed the rebel himself, and afterward called for a general halt of the army. When David gave vent to his feelings of grief, he was sternly rebuked by Joab, and the rebuke had its effect (17:1–19:8a [MT 9a]).

On David's return to Jerusalem, Amasa was made commander of the army in place of Joab (19:13 [MT 14]). Sheba then revolted, Amasa lost time in making preparation for suppressing it, and Abishai was given command of the army (20:6; the Pesh. reads "Joab" for "Abishai" in this verse, and some commentators follow it, but the LXX supports the MT). Joab seems to have accompanied Abishai; and when Amasa met them at Gibeon, Joab, on pretense of kissing his rival, killed him. He then assumed command, was followed by Amasa's men, and arranged with a woman of Abel-beth-maacah to deliver to him Sheba's head. The revolt was then at an end.

Joab subsequently opposed David's suggestion of a census, but eventually carried it out (2 S. 24:1-9; 1 Ch. 21:1-6), yet 1 Ch. 21:6 and 27:24 relate that he did not carry it out fully. He was one of Adonijah's supporters in his claim to the throne (1 K. 1:7, 19, 41). For this he had to pay with his life, being slain at the altar in the "tent of the Lord" (1 K. 2:28-34) by Benaiah, who acted upon Solomon's orders. His murderer became his successor as head of the army. 1 K. 2:5 makes David advise Solomon not to forget that Joab slew Abner and Amasa, and 1 K. 11:14-22 contains a reference to the dread of his name in Edom. 1 Ch. 11:6 makes him gain the commander's position first at the capture of Jerusalem, but 2 S. 2–3 refers to a time before this event (cf. 2 S. 5:6-10; for a proposed solution of this difficulty, see KD, *in loc.*); 1 Ch. 11:8 makes him repair the city, and 1 Ch. 26:28 refers to a dedication of armor by him.

In summing up Joab's character, one should remember the stirring times in which he lived. That he was a most able general, there is no doubt. He was, however, very jealous of his position, and this accounts for Amasa's murder, if not partially for that of Abner too; if he was afraid that Abner would supplant him, that fear may be held to be justified, for Amasa, who had not been too loyal to David, did take Joab's place for a time. But blood revenge for Asahel's death was perhaps the main cause. Yet even when judged in the light of those rough times, and in the light of the blood-revenge custom (see R. de Vaux, *Ancient Israel* [Eng. tr. 1961], I, 11), the murder of Abner was a foul, treacherous deed.

Joab opposed the census probably because it was an innovation. His rebuke of David's great grief over Absalom's death can only be characterized as just; he is the stern warrior who, after being once merciful and forgiving, will not again spare a deceitful rebel; and yet David shows how a father's conduct toward a prodigal, rebellious son is not regulated by stern justice. Joab's unswerving loyalty to David leads one to believe that no disloyalty was meant by his support of Adonijah, who was really the rightful heir to the throne. But their plans were defeated by those of the harem.

Taken as a whole, his life, as depicted in the very reliable narrative of 2 Samuel and 1 Kings, may be said to be as characteristic of the times as that of David himself, with a truly Homeric ring about it. He was a great man, great in military ability and also in personal revenge, in his loyalty to the king as well as in his stern rebuke of his royal master. He was the greatest of David's generals, and the latter's success and glory owed much to this noblest of that noble trio whom Zeruiah bore.

2. A Judahite, father or founder of Ge-harashim (lit. "valley of craftsmen"; 1 Ch. 4:14), which is possibly to be identified with the Wâdī el-ʿArabah. *See* GE-HARASHIM.

3. A family of returned exiles (Ezr. 2:6 par. Neh. 7:11; Ezr. 8:9; 1 Esd. 8:35). D. F. ROBERTS

JOACHAZ jō'ə-kaz (1 Esd. 1:34, AV, NEB). *See* JEHOAHAZ **3.**

JOACHIM jō'ə-kim (Bar. 1:7, AV). *See* JEHOIAKIM **2.**

JOACIM jō'ə-kim.

1. (AV 1 Esd. 1:37-39; Bar. 1:3). *See* JEHOIAKIM **1.**

2. (1 Esd. 1:43, AV). *See* JEHOIACHIN.

3. (1 Esd. 5:5, AV). *See* JOAKIM **1.**

4. (AV Jth. 4:6, 8, 14; 15:8). *See* JOAKIM **2.**

5. (AV Sus. 1, 4, 6, 28f., 63). *See* JOAKIM **3.**

JOADANUS jō-ə-dā'nus (1 Esd. 9:19, AV, NEB). *See* JODAN.

JOAH jō'ə [Heb. *yôʾāḥ*–'Yahweh is brother'].

1. Son of Asaph and recorder under King Hezekiah (2 K. 18:18, 26; Isa. 36:3, 11, 22); he was one of the three officers sent by the king to speak to the Assyrian envoys at the siege of Jerusalem (*ca.* 701 B.C.).

2. In 1 Ch. 6:21 (MT 6); 2 Ch. 29:12, a Levite (son of Zimmah) = Ethan of 1 Ch. 6:42 (MT 27).

3. A son of Obed-edom (1 Ch. 26:4).

4. Son of Joahaz and recorder under King Josiah (2 Ch. 34:8).

JOAHAZ jō'ə-haz [Heb. *yôʾāḥāz*–'Yahweh has grasped']; (2 Ch. 34:8). Alternate form of JEHOAHAZ **1.**

JOAKIM jō'ə-kim [Gk. *Iōakeim*].

1. (1 Esd. 5:5); AV JOACIM. Son of Zerubbabel and leader of one of the groups of returning exiles.

2. (Jth. 4:6, 8, 14; 15:8); AV JOACIM. High priest in Jerusalem who, along with the "senate of the people of Israel," welcomed the heroine Judith back to the city after the death of Holofernes (Jth. 15:8).

3. (Sus. 1, 4, 6, 28f., 63); AV JOACIM. The husband of Susanna.

4. (1 Esd. 1:37-39, NEB). *See* JEHOIAKIM **1.**

5. (1 Esd. 1:43, NEB). *See* JEHOIACHIN.

JOANAN jō-ā'nan [Gk. *Iōanan*].

1. A grandson of Zerubbabel in the genealogy of Jesus according to Luke (3:27; AV JOANNA; NEB JOHANAN).

2. (1 Esd. 9:1, AV, NEB). *See* JEHOHANAN **3.**

JOANNA jō-an'ə [Gk. *Iōana* or *Iōanna*]. The wife of Chuza, Herod's steward. She was one of the "women who had been healed of evil spirits and infirmities" and who "provided for them [i.e., Jesus and His disciples] of their means" on the occasion of Jesus' tour through Galilee (Lk. 8:2f.). Along with other women she accompanied Jesus on His last journey from Galilee to Jerusalem, and was present when His body was laid in the sepulchre (Lk. 23:55). She was thus among those who prepared spices and ointments, who found the grave empty, and who "told this to the apostles" (Lk. 23:56–24:10). C. M. KERR

JOANNES jō-an'ēz [Gk. *Iōnnēs*]. An NEB variant of Johanan (1 Esd. 8:38; *see* JOHANAN **8**) and Jehohanan (1 Esd. 9:29; *see* JEHOHANAN **4**).

JOARIB jō'ə-rib [Gk. *Iōarib*]; AV JARIB. Ancestor of Mattathias (1 Macc. 14:29), given as Joarib in the AV of 1 Macc. 2:1; he was chief of the first of the twenty-four courses of priests in the reign of David. Varieties of the name are Jarib, Joarib, and Jehoiarib (1 Ch. 24:7).

JOASH jō'ash [Heb. *yehôʾāš, yôʾāš*–'Yahweh has bestowed' (cf. 2 K. 11:2, 21; 12:1-19; 2 Ch. 24:1; etc.)].

1. Also **JEHOASH** jə-hō'ash, the ninth king of Judah, and son of Ahaziah and Zibiah, a woman of Beer-sheba (2 K. 11–12; 2 Ch. 22:10–24:27). Joash was seven years old when be became king, and he is said to have reigned for forty years, though this figure may not be exact. The dates of his reign are given as 837-800 B.C. by W. F. Albright (*BASOR,* 100 [Dec. 1945], 16-22) and as 835-796 B.C. by Thiele (*MNHK*).

I. His Early Preservation.–When Athaliah usurped the throne and massacred the royal princes, Joash was saved from her fury by the action of his aunt Jehosheba, the wife of Jehoiada the high priest (2 K. 11:1f.; 2 Ch. 22:10f.). For six years he was concealed in the house of Jehoiada, which adjoined the temple; hence he is said to have been "hid in the house of Yahweh" — a perfectly legitimate use of the phrase according to the idiom of the time.

II. Counterrevolution.–During these formative years of Joash's early life, he was under the moral and spiritual influence of Jehoiada, a man of lofty character and devout spirit. At the end of the six years a counterrevolution was planned by Jehoiada, and was successfully carried out on a sabbath, at one of the great festivals. The accounts of this revolution in Kings and Chronicles supplement each other, and although the Levitical interest of the Chronicler is apparent in the details to which he gives prominence, the narratives do not necessarily collide, as has often been represented. The event was prepared for by the private exhibition of the young king to the five captains of the Carites and guards (2 K. 11:4; 2 Ch. 23:1); obviously the royal bodyguard had to be won over from its allegiance to Athaliah to support the legitimate heir to the throne. These entered into covenant with Jehoiada, and by his direction summoned the Levites from Judah (2 Ch. 23:2) and made the necessary arrangements for guarding the palace and the person of the king. In these dispositions both the royal bodyguard and the Levites seem to have had their parts. Joash next appeared standing on a platform in front of the temple, the law of the testimony in his hand and the crown on his head. Amid acclamations, he was anointed king. ATHALIAH, rushing on the scene with cries of "treason," was driven out and slain. A new covenant was made between Yahweh and the king and people; and at the conclusion of the ceremony a great procession was formed, and the king was conducted with honor to the royal house (2 K. 11:19; 1 Ch. 23:20). The boy king had full popular support, and his reign began auspiciously.

III. Repair of the Temple.–In early manhood Joash married two wives, and by them had sons and daughters (2 Ch. 24:3). His great concern at this time was the repair of the temple, which in the reign of Athaliah had been neglected, broken up, and plundered (2 K. 12:5, 12; 2 Ch. 24:7). To meet the expense of its restoration, the king ordered that all monies coming into the temple, whether dues or voluntary offerings, should be appropriated for this purpose (2 K. 12:4), and from the account in Chronicles he would seem to have contemplated a revival of the half-shekel tax appointed by Moses for the construction of the tabernacle (2 Ch. 24:5f.; cf. Ex. 30:11-16; 38:25). To enforce this impost would have involved a new census, and the memory of the judgments which attended David's former attempt of this kind may well have had a deterrent effect on Jehoiada and the priesthood. "The Levites did not hasten it," it is declared (2 Ch. 24:5).

Time passed, and in the twenty-third year of the king's reign (his thirtieth year) it was found that the breaches of the house had still not been repaired. A new plan was adopted. It was arranged that a chest with a hole bored in its lid should be set up on the right side of the altar in the temple court, under the care of two persons, one the king's scribe, the other an officer of the high priest, and that the people should be invited to bring voluntarily their half-shekel tax or other offerings, and put it in this box (2 K. 12:9; 2 Ch. 24:8f.). Gifts from worshipers who did not visit the altar were received by priests at the gate, and brought to the box. The expedient was a brilliant success. The people cheerfully responded, large sums were contributed, the money was honestly expended, and the temple was thoroughly renovated. There remained even a surplus, with which gold and silver vessels were made, or replaced, for the use of the temple. Jehoiada's long and useful life seems to have ended soon after.

IV. The King's Decline.–After Jehoiada died it soon became evident that the strongest pillar of the state was removed. It is recorded, "Jehoash [Joash] did what was right in the eyes of the Lord all his days, because Jehoiada the priest instructed him" (2 K. 12:2), but after Jehoiada had been honorably interred in the sepulchres of the kings (2 Ch. 24:16), a sad decline became manifest. The princes of Judah came to Joash and expressed their wish for greater freedom in worship than had been permitted them by the aged priest. With weak complaisance, the king "hearkened to them" (v. 17). Soon idols and Asherim were set up in Jerusalem and the other cities of Judah. Unnamed prophets raised their protests in vain. The high priest Zechariah, a worthy son of Jehoiada, testified in his place that as the nation had forsaken Yahweh, He also would forsake it, and that disaster would follow (v. 20). Wrathful at the rebuke, the king gave orders that Zechariah should be stoned at the temple court (v. 21). This was done, perpetrating the act of sacrilege, murder, and ingratitude to which Jesus referred in Mt. 23:35; Lk. 11:51.

V. Disaster and Assassination.–The high priest's dying words, "May the Lord see and avenge!" soon found an answer. Both Hebrew kingdoms were weak at this time, because they were disunited (for Jehu's wanton killing of King Ahaziah of Judah, the father of Joash, must have severed political relations), and more particularly because of the ascendancy of Damascus (due in turn to the temporary weakness of Assyria). So Hazael of Syria was able to overrun Israel, conquer the Philistine city of Gath, and advance on Jerusalem (2 K. 12:17; 2 Ch. 24:23f.). To save the capital from the indignity of foreign occupation, Joash, then in dire sickness, collected all the hallowed things of the temple and all the gold of the palace, and sent them to Hazael (2 K. 12:17f.). This failure of his policy excited such popular feeling against Joash that a conspiracy was formed to assassinate him. His physical sufferings won him no sympathy, and two of his own officers slew him while he slept in the fortress of Millo, where he was paying a visit (v. 20). He was buried in the city of David, but not in the royal sepulchres as Jehoiada had been (2 Ch. 24:25).

Joash is mentioned as the father of Amaziah (2 K. 14:1; 2 Ch. 25:25). His contemporaries in Israel were Jehu, Jehoahaz, and Joash. His own successor was his son Amaziah.

2. Also **JEHOASH.** The son of Jehoahaz, and twelfth king of Israel (2 K. 13:10-25; 14:8-16; 2 Ch. 25:17-24). Joash reigned for sixteen years, 801-786 B.C. (W. F. Albright, *BASOR,* 100 [Dec. 1945], 16-22; Thiele (*MNHK*) places him approximately three years later; cf. also A. Cody, *CBQ,* 32 [1970], 325-340). His reign marks the beginning of a resurgence of prosperity for Israel, which came to full fruition in the reign of his successor. This recovery was due to the total defeat of Syria by the Assyrian king Adadnirari III (811-783 B.C.); Damascus, under Ben-hadad II, was crushed in 802 B.C.

I. Elisha and Joash.–During the three previous reigns, for half a century, Elisha had been the prophet of Yahweh to Israel. He was now aged and on his deathbed. Hearing of his illness, the young king came and had a touching interview with him. His affectionate exclamation, "My father, my father, the chariots of Israel and the horsemen thereof" (2 K. 13:14; cf. 2:12), casts a pleasing light upon his character. Not only had Elisha repeatedly saved the armies of Israel from the ambushes prepared for them by the Syrians (2 K. 6:8-23), but he had given assurance of the relief of the capital when it was at its worst extremity (6:24ff.). To Joash, Elisha's presence was indeed in place of chariots and horses. The truth was demonstrated afresh by the promise the dying prophet now made to him. Directing Joash in the symbolical action of the shooting of certain arrows, he predicted three victories over the Syrians, and more would have been granted him had the faith of the king risen to the opportunity then afforded him.

II. Military Successes.–Now that Syria had been so weakened by Adadnirari III, Joash was able to recover the losses of the previous reign. He wrested from Ben-hadad the cities he had taken from Jehoahaz of Israel. The account of Joash's reign is very brief, but the favorable impression of him formed from the acts of Elisha is strengthened by another gained from the history of Amaziah of Judah (2 Ch. 25:17-24). For the purpose of a southern campaign, Amaziah had hired a large contingent of troops from Samaria. Being sent back unemployed, these mercenaries committed ravages on their way home, for which, apparently, no redress was given. On the first challenge of the king of Judah, Joash magnanimously refused the call to arms. Amaziah persisted, however, and the peace established nearly eighty years before by Jehoshaphat (1 K. 22:44) was broken at the battle of Beth-shemesh, in which Amaziah was defeated and captured. Jerusalem opened its gates to the victor, who looted its palace and temple. A portion of the city wall was broken down, and hostages to ensure Israel's obedience were taken to Samaria (2 K. 14:13f.).

III. Character.–Joash did not long survive his crowning victory, but left a resuscitated state, and laid the foundation for a subsequent rule which raised Israel to the zenith of its power. Josephus gives Joash a high character for godliness; but like each of his predecessors, he followed in the footsteps of Jeroboam in permitting, if not encouraging, the worship of the golden calves. Hence his conduct is pronounced "evil" by the historian (2 K. 13:11). He was succeeded by his son Jeroboam II.

3. A descendant of Judah and son of Shelah (1 Ch. 4:22).

4. The father of the "judge" Gideon (Jgs. 6:11, 25-32). He was of the tribe of Manasseh, of the clan of Abiezer, and had property at Ophrah. On his land stood an altar to Baal and an Asherah, until Gideon destroyed them. Gideon's action incensed the citizens of Ophrah, and they urged Joash to put his son to death; but he declined, remarking, "If [Baal] is a god, let him contend for himself" (v. 31).

5. One of the warriors who joined David at Ziklag (1 Ch. 12:3). He was a Benjaminite from Gibeah, and was related to Saul, David's bitter enemy.

6. A son of King Ahab. Evidently he was in charge of the prison at Samaria (1 K. 22:26f.; 2 Ch. 18:25f.).

W. S. CALDECOTT
D. F. PAYNE

JOASH [Heb. *yōʿāš*–'Yahweh has aided'].

1. A Benjaminite, one of the descendants of Becher (1 Ch. 7:8).

2. One of David's commissary officers supervising supplies of oil (1 Ch. 27:28).

JOATHAM jō'ə-thəm (Mt. 1:9, AV). *See* JOTHAM **3.**

JOB jōb. This book is named after its leading character, as are the books of Ruth, Ezra, and Nehemiah. It describes Job's trial and his struggle to be vindicated by God.

- I. Name
- II. Place in the Canon
- III. Text and Language
- IV. Date
- V. Background and Literary Parallels
- VI. Content
  - A. Prologue (1–2)
    1. The Setting (1:1-5)
    2. Job's Trial (1:6–2:10)
    3. Arrival of the Three Comforters (2:11-13)
  - B. Job's Curse-Lament (Ch. 3)
  - C. Dialogue Between the Three Friends and Job (4–27)
    1. First Cycle of Speeches (4–14)
    2. Second Cycle of Speeches (15–21)
    3. Third Cycle of Speeches (22–27)
  - D. Hymn to Wisdom (Ch. 28)
  - E. Job's Declaration of Innocence (29–31)
  - F. Elihu Speeches (32–37)
    1. Introduction and First Speech (32–33)
    2. Second Speech (Ch. 34)
    3. Third Speech (Ch. 35)
    4. Fourth Speech (36–37)
  - G. Yahweh Speeches (38:1–42:6)
    1. Yahweh's First Speech (38:1–40:2)
    2. Job's Response (40:3-5)
    3. Yahweh's Second Speech (40:6–41:34 [MT 41:26])
    4. Job's Response (42:1-6)
  - H. Epilogue (42:7-17)
- VII. Literary Form
- VIII. Unity and Integrity
- IX. Message

I. Name.–The central character's name is Job, Heb. *'îyôḇ* (Gk. *Iōb*). The precise meaning and origin of this name are debated. It is similar to the Hebrew word for "enemy," *'ôyēḇ*. If this root is the basis for the name, the etymology implies that Job is treated as God's enemy, or possibly that he is the object of enmity. In 13:24 (cf. 33:10) there is a play on this similarity; Job accuses God of treating him like His enemy. The form of this name, however, is that which designates a profession or habitual characteristic, and the root is not attested in this form. Another explanation turns to the Arabic root *'wb,* "return, repent," which suggests "the penitent one." If this were the meaning, only a small part of the whole drama would be reflected in the name.

Akkadian documents of the 2nd millennium B.C. from Mari, Alalakh, and Tell el-Amarna show a frequent use of this name. In the Execration Texts from Egypt (*ca.* 2000 B.C.) a Palestinian chief has the name *'ybm*. In a letter from Tell el-Amarna (no. 256) a prince of Ashtaroth in Bashar is named *Ay(y)âb*. W. F. Albright (*JAOS,* 74 [1954], 223-233) suggests that the name means "where is (my) Father?" This etymology fits in well with Job's longing for God, who is hiding His face from His servant. It also suggests that the name belonged to a patriarch prior to his testing.

II. Place in the Canon.–The canonicity of Job has never been seriously questioned. Its position, however, has fluctuated. In Protestant Bibles it falls after the historical works, which end with Esther, and thus heads the poetical books: Job, Psalms, Proverbs. This tradition is attested by Cyril of Jerusalem and Epiphanius, among others. Jerome preferred this order, and the Council of Trent established it for the Vulgate. In the Hebrew Bible it appears in the third division, the writings or Kethubhim; the order is Psalms, Job, Proverbs. The oldest tradition lists the books thus: Ruth, Psalms, Job, Proverbs, Ecclesiastes, Song of Solomon, etc. The Syriac Bible places Job after the Pentateuch in honor of the tradition that Moses was its author.

III. Text and Language.–The text of Job is frequently disturbed; many passages are obscure, either because of a rare word or because of a corrupt text. The versions testify to the difficulties of interpreting this poetical book even in ancient times. They offer variant readings, some of which help restore the correct Hebrew reading, but most of which are not very helpful.

The LXX is, for the most part, a literal, faithful translation of the Hebrew. Although it has many variant readings, the translators endeavored to be true to the Hebrew. Some variants bear witness to a different textual tradition, while many are paraphrases that attempt to handle an obscure text. The most unusual feature of the oldest Greek version is that it is shorter than the MT by some four hundred lines. One explanation of this brevity is that this book was translated into Greek before its growth process had ceased. A more likely position is that the LXX translators intentionally abridged the poem. This possibility is evident in the increasing number of omissions in the latter portions of the book and in the omission of many redundant passages. In a few places the translators made changes based on their theological perspectives, but such changes are infrequent. In his textual work Origen restored the missing lines to the LXX from Theodotion's Greek translation and marked them with an asterisk in his Hexapla. A Coptic version of the LXX attests the pre-Origen form.

The Targum follows the MT quite closely but with some

of its own idiosyncrasies; for example, it interprets some texts in light of Israel's history and sometimes adds theological explanations. Thus the Targum tends to expand the text.

A Targum of Job from Cave 11 of Qumrân (11QtgJob) is the oldest Targum known. The paleography of the MS led van der Ploeg and van der Woude to date it in the 1st cent. A.D., but Pope claims that the style of the language pushes its origin back to the 2nd cent. B.C. The text is extant from the middle of ch. 17 through 42:11, but unfortunately it is quite fragmentary; from ch. 32 on more of the text is preserved, including some extensive passages between 37:10 and 42:11. Interestingly this Targum ends at 42:11. On the whole the Qumrân Targum supports the MT, including the present status of chs. 24–27; however, there are numerous differences, and at times it sides with the LXX against the MT. Thus some evidence suggests that this book has had a diverse textual tradition.

The Peshitta is translated from the Hebrew and offers insight into some of the obscure passages. As the textual tradition of the MT is more fully understood, the Peshitta will most likely increase in value.

Soon after he translated Job into Latin from the LXX at the end of the 4th cent. A.D., Jerome decided to improve the translation by working directly from the Hebrew; he apparently continued to be influenced by the LXX Hexapla. A rabbi of Lydda was a resource who influenced him with the traditional rabbinic interpretation. The result of his labor was a fluid, smooth translation. Thus the Vulgate affords some assistance to understanding the text of Job.

Even with all these aids, plus the insights gained from recent discoveries of the Ugaritic texts and other inscriptions, numerous passages still require some emendation just to be translated. The more emendations increase, however, the further the interpretation moves from the original, so it is better to live with the difficulties and obscurities than to create a new work. Job remains the OT book with the most difficult text.

The language of the book, too, is most unusual. It is characterized by numerous rare words and unique examples of morphology and syntax; as a result numerous suggestions have been made to account for its singular nature. Since a most probable setting of the story is EDOM, it has been suggested that the poet was an Edomite. Although the Israelites detested Edomites, there was frequent interchange between the two countries. Also, Edom was famous for its wisdom; perhaps Job is an example from that wisdom tradition. Along with Ammonite and Moabite, the Edomite language is a dialect close to Hebrew. Since scant linguistic material from this region has come to light, the Edomite setting for this book remains hypothetical.

From the time of Ibn Ezra (12th cent. A.D.) some scholars have gone so far as to argue that Job was translated into Hebrew from another language. Arabic and Aramaic have been taken as the original languages. Guillaume places its origin in Teman from a poet whose language was permeated by Arabic. Tur-Sinai argues that the poem came from a partial Aramaic translation; many Aramaic words and phrases were left untranslated because of their similarity to the Hebrew while others were misunderstood and hence mistranslated. The Aramaic was the Babylonian Aramaic of the 6th cent. B.C. In addition, he thinks that many portions of the book became dislocated in the process. Tur-Sinai thus offers many new and different interpretations of Job, but his ingenious insights are buried amidst too many untenable speculations.

All interpreters dip into Arabic to explain numerous obscure words, since that language has a vast literature that offers many possible cognates. On the other hand, as our knowledge of Canaanite dialects increases, the importance of Arabic diminishes. The abundance, though, of Aramaic influence is beyond dispute.

The discoveries of the Ugaritic texts have greatly enhanced the linguistic knowledge of Northwest Semitic, and particularly the style of Semitic poetry. Articles by numerous scholars, especially the work of Gordon and Dahood, have applied the results of Ugaritic studies to improve the interpretation of many OT passages. Much insight into Job has resulted; Pope's commentary may be cited as the most noteworthy example.

The style of the book of Job suggests that the poet probably came from a region outside of Jerusalem; therefore his Hebrew was a dialect different from Jerusalem Hebrew and may have been very close to Aramaic. Further, the poet most likely had traveled much and was multilingual. As an artist he no doubt enriched the vocabulary of his poem to capture special nuances and to communicate subtle tones as he sought to grapple with the gravest human question, suffering. Since there were multiple dialects of these Northwest Semitic languages in a close geographical area, most people would know more than one dialect and thus would have little trouble understanding a presentation of this work.

IV. Date.–The date of composition is difficult to establish. The prose portions reflect the epic style of the patriarchal period. Numerous details bear witness to the patriarchal age and suggest the antiquity of the prose account. Job's wealth consists of flocks, slaves, and abundant offspring. The numbers three, seven, and ten dominate, in epic style, the accounting of his goods. His faith is simple and as head of the household he offers sacrifice for his household at a local shrine; he too may intercede for others. The Sabeans and the Chaldeans are still marauding tribes, rather than settled city dwellers. The unit of money (*qᵉśîṭâ*, 42:11) appears elsewhere only in Gen. 33:19 and Josh. 24:32. The description of Job's blessing contains ancient features: the naming of his three daughters without giving the names of his sons, his age of 140 years, his seeing his children's children to four generations, the report that he died an old man full of days. Conversely, the style of poetry has many characteristics of late Hebrew that lead many to date the work in the postexilic period.

The final form of the book was certainly reached by the 3rd cent. B.C., for it was known to Ben Sira and fragments of a manuscript from Qumrân are written in paleo-Hebrew script, suggesting further evidence that the work was viewed as coming from the patriarchal period. The lack of historical allusions suggests that the work was not written to address a particular national problem. Thus it is doubtful that this book was composed during the exilic period, for it has no specific allusions to the Exile. Also, the international flavor of the work and its primary concern with an individual's response to tragedy deny any connection with that issue. The greatest contrast between Job's suffering and Israel's is that his is undeserved whereas the entire OT tradition witnesses that the Babylonian Captivity is the result of Israel's disobedience of God's law.

Since the issue is the suffering of an individual, the work could have arisen in any period. Tragedy knows no time boundaries; it may strike during times of national prosperity or during times of adversity. Thus it is hard to reconstruct the social setting that would be the matrix which provided the impetus for such a masterpiece. The poet is searching for insight into the suffering of the righteous and at the same time is strongly resisting an easy application of the doctrine of retribution that condemns all who are in dire situation and blesses all the rich. Since the poet is taking up a polemic against various inadequate interpretations of suffering, one could suggest a date if more were known about the issues of concern in the wisdom school in the different periods. Another clue is the close affinity between the books of Job and Isaiah, most particularly their concepts of the righteous sufferer who bears his trial in faithful obedience to God. If the direction of literary influence could be unquestionably established, a reference point would be established, for the date of Isaiah's work is quite firm: an early seventh-century date for those who hold to the unity of Isaiah and a mid-fifth-century date for the scholars who accept the prophetic activity of Deutero-Isaiah. Job may be one of the prototypes for the figure of the Suffering Servant. Since Isaiah develops the vicarious virtue earned by the righteous sufferer, he may be influenced by the Jobian poet. Certainly the thesis of the atonement of mankind's sins by the suffering of an obedient, righteous servant would find a much greater acceptance among a people who had already wrestled with the concept that an innocent, righteous person might have to endure excruciating agony in a test of his faith as it is expressed in Job. Therefore if Job was prior to Isaiah, the work may come from the preexilic community. Thus a date in either the late 10th cent. during the energetic activity of the wisdom school or at the beginning of the 7th cent. under the revitalized activity of the wise under King Hezekiah may be seriously considered.

Although a seventh-century date should not be too readily dismissed, the majority of critical scholars date the work to the 4th cent. B.C. A definitive position, however, is not possible, and thus the question of date should not be a divisive issue.

*V. **Background and Literary Parallels.***–The book of Job stands alone in the OT, but it forms a part of the class of literature of the ancient Near East that struggles with the issues of suffering and turmoil in society. Various works challenge traditional ideas that have been reduced to simplistic laws: many of these works come out of the wisdom schools. In the OT the wisdom literature has close affinities with its Near Eastern counterparts, e.g., the same ideas and language are found in Prov. 22:17–24:22 and in the Egyptian *Wisdom of Amenemope*. The universal scope of the work, along with the wide knowledge of customs and nature from various parts of the Near East, indicates that the poet had traveled widely, or, if not, that he certainly belonged to a social class in which he had international contacts. Thus he most certainly was aware of the rich literature from surrounding countries.

In format the book of Job is comparable to *The Protests of the Eloquent Peasant* (*ANET*, pp. 407-410), which was written in Egypt in the 21st cent. B.C. It too consists of nine semipoetical speeches set between a prose prologue and epilogue; this A-B-A style appears in many ancient works. The greater point of contact is the use of long speeches to discuss matters of concern from a wisdom perspective. The peasant appeals to the pharaoh for redress of a violation of his justice. At first the peasant presents his case politely, but he becomes more irate and provoking as his case wears on. He would rather accept death than compromise his appeal for justice. In contrast, Job becomes more confident as his case drags out and his accusation of injustice focuses on God's governing the universe.

The book of Job may also be compared with *The Admonitions of Ipu-Wer* (*ANET*, pp. 441-44). In this work the sage protests the upheaval in Egyptian society and is distressed at the decline of morality. The emphasis, though, is more on a stable social order than on the issue of moral justice.

Other literature that addresses despondency over difficult circumstances may be compared with Job. *A Dispute over Suicide* (*ANET*, pp. 405-407), from the second half of the 3rd millennium B.C. and in A-B-A style, is cast in the form of a despondent man's debate with his soul. His contemplation of the values of death and suicide is similar to Job's longing for the rest of Sheol. Job, however, finds greater meaning in life, and his view of God and the worth of mankind causes him to reject any consideration of suicide. Although some of Job's speeches approach soliloquy form, particularly ch. 3, the bulk of the speeches are in disputation style, addressed to his companions or to God. Regarding a lyrical contemplation of death, there is similarity in *A Song of the Harper* (*ANET*, p. 467); its tone, however, is far more sentimental that that found in Job.

Numerous pieces of literature from Mesopotamia also treat the issue of suffering. The most famous one is entitled *I Will Praise the Lord of Wisdom* (*ANET*, pp. 434-37) and is known as *The Poem of the Righteous Sufferer* or *The Babylonian Job*. A man of high rank is reduced to inscrutable suffering. He laments his plight with a vivid description of the loathsome condition caused by his illness. He searches for an explanation, since he knows of no sin in his life. His disease stubbornly resists all efforts of the healing arts or exorcism. At last the god Marduk brings healing; thus the work concludes with a hymn of thanksgiving to Marduk. In contrast to Job, the Babylonian work contains no debate, and the victim recites his ritual acts but is willing to concede having sinned unknowingly.

Points of contact are also found with the Akkadian work known as *The Babylonian Ecclesiastes* or *A Dialogue about Human Misery* (*ANET*, pp. 438-440). A sufferer named Shagil-kinam-ubbib ("May Esagil [the name of Marduk's temple] declare the righteous pure") has a dialogue with a group of friends about divine justice and human suffering. The work contains twenty-seven speeches. The hero begins the discussion and answers each respondent in turn. Presenting his tale of woe to the friends, the sufferer complains, in contrast to Job, that he has endured trouble from his youth even though he has sought the help of the gods. The friends reply that his only hope is to pray for pardon and to avoid such windy talk. As the debate lengthens, the friends accuse him of despising the ordinances of the gods. At the end he pleads for mercy from Ninurta, Ishtar, and the king. The conclusion is missing, but most likely the gods responded to his petition. The speeches are shorter than those in Job and the nature of the hero's suffering and his approach to its solution differ extensively from those of Job. Yet it is possible that the poet of Job knew of this work.

The Akkadian poem *A Pessimistic Dialogue Between Master and Servant* (*ANET*, pp. 437f.) takes up the theme of the meaninglessness of human endeavors. A master discusses with his servant various possible activities to take up, e.g., dining, hunting, building a home, rebelling, loving a woman. The servant heartily agrees with his master; then when the master changes his mind the servant agrees and expresses the futility of the action. Since nothing has significance, death seems to be the only value. The master offers to send the servant on ahead, to which the servant responds that his master would live three days after him. Frustration with the sameness of life is evident. The book of Job, however, deals more with real losses than with mere pessimism, and for Job death is not the solution to his trial.

From the Hittite world comes the tale of Appu. Appu suffers much for lack of children. In his search for a solution, he bears reproach from a chiding wife. Except for this similarity, the accounts have little in common.

Tablet of the so-called Sumerian Job ("Man and His God") from Nippur (18th cent. B.C.). This poem, originating from the late 3rd millennium B.C., tells of an innocent man who, like Job, meets misfortune, prays for deliverance, is finally saved from his afflictions, and then praises his god (University Museum, University of Pennsylvania)

A Sumerian poem from the early 2nd millennium B.C. treats the theme of a wealthy, wise man who undergoes severe illness. The victim laments his plight without attacking his god. Nevertheless, he confesses his sin and receives divine deliverance.

Those who search for points of contact move to more distant lands. In India parallels are found in the story of Hariscandra, a wealthy ruler who was tested as the result of a wager between the gods Vasishta and Shiva. Hariscandra lost all but endured and was restored to his former estate.

The Greeks, too, treated the theme of suffering; particularly important are the tragedies. The one most often cited in comparison with Job is Aeschylus's *Prometheus Bound.* Prometheus aroused Zeus' anger by giving mankind the knowledge of fire. In punishment he was chained to a rock. His companions sought to have him confess his wrong, but he held on to his justice and pushed Zeus to relent. Prometheus, however, was sent to the netherworld. The broad framework is vastly different from Job. Prometheus is a Titan, consoled by his friends, while the fault of his plight resides squarely with a fickle deity. Indeed, the further away from the Semitic world parallels to the book of Job are sought, the fewer are the insights gained from the comparison.

The poet of Job has composed a singular masterpiece. The uniqueness of this work is vividly evident in comparison with all of these compositions. Job never yields to any pressure, be it pain or argumentation, that would have him abandon the certainty of his innocence. Job stands alone as the righteous sufferer; no other man ever showed such personal moral resolution. A comparison with these other texts shows that the poet was influenced by the rich literary tradition of the ancient Near East, but his poetic skill has produced a work which is marked by its originality.

In the context of the canon this book paved the way for the central message of the NT that a righteous person can suffer and be righteous, and that when he has triumphed his victory allows him to intercede for others. Numerous literary masterpieces through the centuries have been influenced by the book of Job in treating the vexing issue of unexplained suffering, e.g., Kafka's *The Trial,* Milton's *Samson,* Dostoevsky's *The Brothers Karamazov.* Even the psychologist Jung entered the debate with his *Answer to Job* (1963). The book of Job continues to speak profoundly. It is mentioned in nearly every serious discussion of suffering and theodicy. The power of this work is evident in its continuous impact on thinking minds and literary artists through the centuries.

VI. Content.–The book of Job consists of three basic parts: the prologue (1–2), the dialogue (3:1–42:6), the epilogue (42:7-17). The dialogue contains six sections: Job's opening lament-curse (ch. 3), a threefold cycle of dialogues between each of the three friends and Job (4–27), a hymn to wisdom (ch. 28), Job's declaration of innocence (29–31), the Elihu speeches (32–37), and the theophany and discourses of Yahweh (38:1–42:6). There are two Yahweh speeches (38:1–40:2; 40:6–41:34), each followed by a response from Job (40:3-5; 42:1-6).

The speeches, the bulk of the work, are composed in beautiful poetry that uses the richest variety of vocabulary and style found in the OT. The prologue (1–2) and the epilogue (42:7-17) are prose, as are the introductions to Job's first speech (3:1) and to the Elihu speeches (32:1-5) and the headings to the other speeches.

A. Prologue (1–2). The prologue presents an opening scene (1:1-5), an account of Job's trial set in duplicate stages (1:6–2:10), and the arrival of the three comforters (2:11-13).

1. Setting (1:1-5). The opening scene introduces Job, an upright, wealthy, wise nobleman. His wealth comprises a large family, abundance of flocks and servants, and a large estate. He has seven sons and three daughters who enjoy their family's wealth in a series of feasts. At the end of each feast Job scrupulously makes sacrifices to atone for any sins that might have been committed inadvertently by his children's frivolity. In all his ways Job has attained the stature of the most righteous and famous man of his day.

2. Job's Trial (1:6–2:10). The next scenes introduce the testing that Job must endure: each of two sessions of the heavenly council (1:6-12; 2:1-6) is followed by a stage in Job's testing (1:13-22; 2:7-10). In the first council scene Yahweh praises the genuine uprightness of His servant Job to the court's adversary, Satan. Satan acknowledges Job's pure character but argues that Job does not serve God out of genuine love, but rather for rewards that God bestows on him. Therefore he challenges Yahweh to let him afflict Job to determine the purity of Job's righteousness. Yahweh accepts the challenge and grants Satan permission to attack Job's possessions but not his body. In a series of four reports Job learns that all of his possessions and his children have been destroyed by marauding tribes and natural catastrophes. He dons mourning clothes and weeps before God without sinning.

At the next session of the heavenly council Satan acknowledges Job's faithful response, but argues that Job will not maintain his righteous character if his own body is abused. Again Yahweh, confident in His servant, makes a concession to Satan, granting him permission to afflict Job but not to kill him. Satan immediately curses Job with a disease that sorely distresses Job's body from the soles of his feet to the top of his head. In response Job's wife urges him to curse God so that he might die. Job resists the temptation, rebukes her, and mourns his plight in silence. In everything his attitude vindicates Yahweh's confidence; he does not sin at all.

3. Arrival of the Three Comforters (2:11-13). In the final scene of the prologue three comforters, Eliphaz, Bildad, and Zophar, friends of Job, come from distant lands to share in his suffering. So appalled are they at the sight of Job that they rend their garments and mourn in silence for seven days.

B. Job's Curse-Lament (Ch. 3). At the end of seven days Job breaks the silence with a long, bitter lament (3:2-26). This speech, which curses the day of his birth, is not a part of the dialogue since it is addressed not to the three friends but to God — here more an impersonal force than the personal God of his faith. In this curse-lament Job longs for peaceful rest; therefore, if he can remove the day of his origin from the calendar, he would be free from all trouble, for it would be as though he had never been. His words testify that his despair is total; only his righteous character forbids taking his own life. If rest is to be found in Sheol, death must come from the hand of God.

C. Dialogue Between the Three Friends and Job (4–27). Such scathing words provoke a response from Job's three friends, a dialogue in three cycles of speeches and responses. In each cycle Eliphaz, Zophar, and Bildad speak in order and each speech is followed by a response from Job.

The first two cycles are complete but the third cycle is broken, having suffered severely in its early stage of transmission (22–27). Only Eliphaz's homily is preserved intact (ch. 22). Job's reply is almost complete (23–24), but there are some severe difficulties in ch. 24. Bildad's address is far too short (26:1-6) and there is no word from Zophar. Numerous reconstructions have been offered. A moderate suggestion is to make Bildad's third speech out of 25:1-6; 27:13-22, and view Job's response as consisting of 26:1–27:12. Thus it is assumed that there never was a third speech for Zophar, the poet having intentionally truncated the third cycle. As the cycles progress, each comforter's speech becomes shorter, except for Bildad's, and throughout the dialogue Job's response is longer than the friend's presentation. Thus the emphasis falls on the words of Job, and a subtle negative connotation is cast on the friends' speeches.

1. First Cycle of Speeches (4–14). a. Eliphaz's Speech (4–5). Eliphaz, the highest ranking friend, is the first to speak. He commends Job for his past devout deeds (4:2-6) but is surprised by Job's words, for he thought that Job's reverence for God would be his confidence during misfortune (4:6). Afraid that Job has spoken too abrasively, Eliphaz instructs him in the doctrine of retribution (4:7-11). He supports his position by quoting from patterns he has observed in the course of nature. The kernel of his thinking — namely, that no one can be innocent before God — was a message received from a heavenly being in a nocturnal vision (4:12-21). Therefore it is impossible that Job's claim to innocence is correct, and there is no one who is qualified to serve as his defense attorney before God (5:1-8). In a more encouraging tone he alludes to a hymn that lauds God's majesty (5:9-16) and a wisdom saying that affirms God's protective care of His own (5:17-26). With this note of hope he concludes, confident that he personally knows the truth of his words (5:27).

b. Job's Response (6–7). Job responds with his first speech within the dialogue. In the first half he addresses the friends (ch. 6) and in the second half he laments before God. He defends his right to lament; anyone would groan under such a heavy burden (6:2-7). Thus he reiterates his wish that God would finish the suffering He has brought on Job by crushing him totally (6:8-13). Job turns to charge the friends with acting treacherously toward him in failing to help him overcome his suffering (6:14-23). If they would show some understanding of the uniqueness of his dilemma, he would gladly open himself to their teaching (6:24). Therefore he pleads with them to adopt a more congenial, accepting attitude toward him (6:24-30).

In the second portion Job takes up his lament again. He describes in vivid detail his present pain (7:1-6) and entreats God to act in a healing way toward him before it is too late (7:7-10). He defends his right to complain (7:11) and then charges God with unleashing His most powerful weapons against His servant as though he were His primordial enemy (7:12-18). In his final plea he asks God to leave him alone, even if it means passing over any sin, so that he might enjoy his few remaining days (7:19-21). Although Job is still despondent, his words are now calmer and more open to rational debate than in his opening curse-lament; he is beginning to cope with his affliction and he is forming the basis on which his trust in God will be built.

c. Bildad's Speech (Ch. 8). Bildad takes up Job's challenge. He fears that Job's words are a reproach against God. Thus he defends the justice of God's manner of acting (8:2-7). God does not pervert justice; whatever evil happens on earth is just retribution for some wrong. God's justice is defended by a referral to the testimony of past generations (8:8-10) and by vivid illustrations from nature — the growth of papyrus (8:11-13), a spider's web (8:14f.), the growth characteristics of a plant in a garden (8:16-19). Bildad concludes with a presentation of double retribution (8:20-22), with a word of hope to Job that his joy might return (8:21). Before Job's challenge Bildad strives to defend the "old-time" religion.

d. Job's Response (9–10). In his second speech Job pays little attention to the comforters, with the singular concession that no one is just before God (9:2). The point of this speech is Job's struggling with the possibility of arguing his case legally with God. A recitation of lines from hymns praising God's wisdom and power overwhelms Job with risks of taking on such a wise and powerful opponent (9:2-13). Even if God should appear to hear his concern, he does not know how to answer Him and fears that his own mouth would condemn him (9:14-20). Nevertheless, Job knows he is innocent (9:21). Thus he accuses God of failing to discriminate between the wicked and the righteous in His governance of the world (9:22-24). Abruptly Job turns to lament the meaninglessness of his plight (9:25-29). If his case could be decided by an ordeal, he feels that he would come out of it under greater condemnation (9:30f.). Next he longs for an arbiter to bring reconciliation between God and himself, but there is no one powerful enough to mediate the dispute (9:32f.). Therefore in desperation he pleads for God to remove His afflicting rod so that he might argue his case without fear.

In the next section Job accuses God of smiting him far beyond any wrong he could have committed, unmindful of the frail human constitution (10:1-17). Returning to his opening lament, he concludes with a wish that he had never been born and with a petition for God to give him some moments of peace before he descends to the darkness of Sheol (10:18-22).

e. Zophar's Speech (Ch. 11). Zophar takes up the issue and charges Job with idle, foolish talk (11:2-4). He wishes that God would reveal to Job true wisdom (11:5f.). He lauds the greatness of God (11:7-12) and concludes with an exhortation for Job to repent (11:13-20). The positive note in this speech is the vivid description of the blessing that attends the repentant person; otherwise Zophar has little to offer Job in encouragement.

f. Job's Response (12–14). Job brings the first cycle to an end with a long speech. He rejects the acclaimed wisdom of his friends and affirms his equality with them (12:2f.). He laments his having become a laughingstock and the prosperity of the wicked (12:4-6). These charges God must bear, for He is sovereign Lord over this world (12:7-25).

Since Job is not inferior to his friends and since their arguments are worthless and unable to stand the divine scrutiny, he resolves to make his plea to God alone (13:1-12). He will prepare his case to be heard in the heavenly court (13:13-19). He is beginning to realize fully that his only hope for vindication rests with God; therefore, he must defend his case before Him (13:15). So he asks for a reprieve in order that he may argue his case undisturbed and he laments the inhospitable treatment he is receiving from God (13:20-28).

Job turns to lament his plight (14:1-6). Since he can find no comfort in a doctrine of resurrection, he pleads for God to hide him until His wrath has passed (14:7-17). He concludes with a charge that God treats mankind far too harshly (14:18-22).

2. Second Cycle of Speeches (15–21). a. Eliphaz's Speech (Ch. 15). The second cycle opens with Eliphaz's second speech. He has become more disturbed at Job because of the nature of his arguments. He accuses Job of lacking wisdom and faith, regardless of his high claims to insight (15:15f.). In an effort to move Job to repentance, he teaches Job the doctrine of the certain, horrible fate of the wicked, including the most prosperous (15:17-35). His hope is that this description alone will move Job to adopt a new posture, for he adds no application.

b. Job's Response (16–17). Job responds with a defense of his right to speak and a charge that the friends are all miserable comforters (16:2-6). He then takes up his lament in vivid description of his pain with particular reference to God as his powerful attacker (16:7-14). Job's only response has been mourning and weeping as he holds to his innocence (16:15-17). Thus he petitions God to intervene and come to his defense (16:18–17:16). God could defeat his mockers by restoring his honor (17:1-10). He concludes with a struggle before the harsh realities of death that will destroy his last thread of hope (17:11-16).

c. Bildad's Speech (Ch. 18). Bildad rejects Job's accusations and counters by taunting Job for being so tormented (18:2-4). The bulk of his speech is a detailed description of the harsh punishment that the wicked must bear (18:5-21). They have no lasting benefits; not even a memory of them survives. Although he concludes without application, he is clearly warning Job that a worse fate awaits his blatant, angry words if he does not change.

d. Job's Response (Ch. 19). Job reproaches his friends for tormenting him and exalting themselves above him (19:2-6). In attacking Job they attack God, for He is the One who has made Job look guilty. Job again laments in detail his plight (19:7-22). God has attacked him mercilessly, stripping him of all his honor (19:7-12); thus he has been alienated from everybody, from his wife to his servants (19:13-19). His body has been reduced to skin and bones (19:20). He pleads for his friends to pity him and not to persecute him (19:21f.). In desperation his mind looks for a way of escape (19:23-27). He requests that his words be inscribed on a stone as a perpetual witness to his side of the case (19:23f.). In bold confidence he asserts that he knows his Redeemer (Kinsman, Helper) will vindicate him before all on earth even if it requires his rising from the dead (19:25-27). In conclusion he warns his friends against the dangers of pursuing a matter falsely (19:28f.).

e. Zophar's Speech (Ch. 20). Troubled by these words, Zophar feels compelled to defend his honor (20:2-4). Then he develops the thesis that the joy of the wicked is momentary, for hard punishment will begin on earth and continue in the darkness of Sheol (20:5-29). He cannot escape; his iniquity will certainly be revealed. This speech, like Bildad's last speech, stands as a pungent warning to Job to forsake his claim of innocence.

f. Job's Response (Ch. 21). Job directs his last speech of the second cycle solely to the friends. He pleads with them to attend more carefully to his words (21:2f.) and then asks them why such a troubled man should not give expression to his terror in lament (21:4-6). In direct opposition to Bildad's and Zophar's last speeches, he describes the success that attends the wicked (21:7-16). The curse against sinful deeds takes its effect too infrequently. If evil befalls a wicked man's children, what does he care since he has already enjoyed his own pleasure (21:17-21)? Since all people die and go to the same grave, what difference does morality make anyway (21:22-26)? He thus moves on to charge the friends with wronging him and having limited knowledge (21:27-33). Job comes to the conclusion that it is impossible for the friends to console him (21:34).

3. Third Cycle of Speeches (22–27). The third cycle begins in good form with a complete speech from Eliphaz (ch. 22), but the remaining speeches have suffered severely in their early transmission.

a. Eliphaz's Speech (Ch. 22). Eliphaz has lost patience with Job. The moderate, conciliatory manner evident in his first speech has turned to cold accusations of wickedness against Job. Holding to his thesis that no one can benefit God (22:2f.), he charges Job with having violated the standards of patriarchal generosity to the unfortunate (22:4-9). Therefore Job's peril is his just dessert (22:10f.). He defends his conclusions with a description of God's manner of governing the world (22:12-20). His more gentle side emerges with a powerful exhortation encouraging Job to repent (22:21-30). The motive to repent is based on the joy that attends the forgiven sinner.

b. Job's Response (23–24). Apparently ignoring Eliphaz, Job offers up a bitter complaint (23:2). He longs to present his case before God, for a judgment from God would be the only way to silence his critics (23:3-7). In despair Job returns to lament God's attitude toward him. God is distant and inattentive to His faithful servant (23:8-12), and God acts capriciously beyond control so that Job is filled with terror (23:13-17). Then in direct opposition to Eliphaz's counsel, Job ponders many situations that give evidence that God fails to determine the times of just judgment (ch. 24). In his position he remains unmoved by the rhetoric of the three friends.

c. Bildad's Speech (25:1-6; 27:13-23). Bildad's third speech is reconstructed from 25:1-6 and 27:13-23. Bildad opens with a hymn extolling God's dominion and sovereign, orderly rule (25:1-6). He develops in detail the aspect of God's governance that secures exact punishment for even the wicked who are the most powerful and wealthy (27:13-23). In his system none of the exceptions that Job has pointed out is allowed. Thus neither Job nor the friends are able to change each other's opinions.

d. Job's Response (26:1–27:12). Job concludes his retorts to the comforters by underscoring his conviction that their wisdom has failed to cope with his situation (26:1-4). He too can praise God; in using hymnic language he focuses on God's great power and shrewd wisdom that defeat every foe (26:5-14). Unmoved by the friends, he makes firm his commitment not to yield to their easy answers and to maintain the justice of his case without speaking wickedness (27:1-6). He finishes with a prayer requesting that his enemies be judged (27:7-12). In all his speaking Job holds tenaciously to his innocence.

D. Hymn to Wisdom (Ch. 28). Chapter 28 is a magnificent hymn praising the ultimate value of wisdom. Whether it belongs in the mouth of Job or is Zophar's third speech or is a hymn sung by a chorus is debated. It appears to be an interlude that forms a bridge between the dialogue with the friends and the series of speeches in the latter portion of the book, in which Job probes deeper for an answer to his trial. Therefore it seems best to assign the words to a neutral speaker, a chorus, or the poet himself.

The hymn has three major divisions. The first extols the great technological achievement by which mankind can extract the most precious minerals from the earth (28:1-11). Nevertheless, in all human searching one cannot find wisdom nor can one purchase her with the precious jewels he has gained (28:12-19). Where then is wisdom? She abides only with God, and she served as His architect in creating the world (28:20-27). Since wisdom is beyond human reach, one discovers her in personal experience only by shunning evil and fearing the Lord (28:28). This beautiful hymn ties together the two parts of the book and points beyond itself to the Yahweh speeches.

E. Job's Declaration of Innocence (29–31). After a pause Job takes up his case for the final time. He addresses God alone. In masterful style he argues the correctness of his stand throughout the debate and his trial. He formulates his declaration of innocence in order to compel God to respond. The declaration consists of three distinct parts: a description of his former state of mobility (ch. 29), a detailed account of his present suffering (ch. 30), and the declaration of innocence proper in which he enumerates the standards he has not violated (ch. 31).

The one who had championed the cause of the oppressed has become the object of rebuke even to the lowest levels of humanity. Nevertheless, Job remains so confident of his innocence that he places himself under a curse if he has ever committed any of a list of crimes. He has not lusted after a young lady, nor used deceit in business, nor committed adultery with a neighbor's wife, nor treated his servants harshly, nor withheld mercy from the poor and afflicted, nor trusted in wealth, nor worshiped the heavenly bodies, nor gloated over his enemies' misfortune, nor abused his land or its tenant. He signs his defense and demands a response from God (31:35-37). The lines are clearly drawn. Job has placed the resolution of his case squarely in God's hands; if God remains silent, Job must be righteous.

F. Elihu Speeches (32–37). The friends do not answer; they have conceded the argument to Job. Only God can answer Job's oath. The period of silence affords the opportunity for a young bystander to express his insight. Elihu, the son of Barachel the Buzite, apologetically but with great enthusiasm enters the debate.

1. Introduction and First Speech (32–33). Elihu is greatly disturbed that Job defends his own righteousness rather than God's and that the friends cannot refute Job but merely condemn him (32:1-5). His first speech is a long defense of his right to speak before such elders despite his youth (32:6-22). Since God gives wisdom to mankind, wisdom is not confined to the aged. Compelled to speak by agitation deep within him, he will answer Job directly with different arguments.

Elihu takes an open stance, inviting Job to debate with him as a fellow human (33:1-7). In debating style he quotes Job's position and then responds. He takes as the heart of his position Job's claim to innocence and his accusation that God has treated him like an enemy (33:8-11). His rebuttal is that God disciplines people through dreams and illness, hoping to preserve their lives from destruction (33:12-22). An angel may intervene to restore such a one to health and to lead him to repentance before he dies (35:23-28). God acts in this way many times to turn a person back to Himself (33:29f.). Elihu concludes his first speech with an exhortation for Job to listen carefully to his words (33:31-33).

2. Second Speech (Ch. 34). Since Job remains silent, Elihu takes up his second discourse. This time he addresses Job more harshly, rebuking Job for going too far in his questioning of God's justice (34:1-9). God is just and governs all in justice (34:10-20). God observes every action, nothing escapes His attention, and He speedily executes punishment on the wicked (34:21-30). In the light of this truth Job must humbly yield to being taught, for he presently adds rebellion to his sin (34:31-37).

3. Third Speech (Ch. 35). In this third speech Elihu answers Job's inquiry into the lack of benefits for righteous behavior. Elihu believes that God is too high to be injured by human sins or benefited by human righteousness. Since God does not answer the pleas of an empty cry, Job is guilty of uttering long, meaningless speeches.

4. Fourth Speech (36–37). In his last speech Elihu defends God's just governance of the world (36:1-4). He punishes the wicked and elevates the righteous (36:5-12). Although the godless relish God's anger, God still afflicts those who will amend their ways in order to activate their repentance (36:13-16). Job, however, must beware lest his trial harden his heart and cause him to scoff (36:17-23). Job needs to realize that God is wooing him back to Himself; therefore Job is exhorted to praise the God who manifests His greatness in the wonders of nature (36:24–37:13). Indeed mankind is far too ignorant and too weak to argue with such a Creator; therefore Job must submit to the divine superiority (37:14-20). Whenever the Almighty appears in a storm, His power and justice are manifest (37:21-24). The close of Elihu's speech thus prepares for the theophany.

G. Yahweh Speeches (38:1–42:6). Out of a whirlwind Yahweh answers Job. He addresses Job with a barrage of imponderable questions seeking to convince Job that his words have darkened counsel. Adopting this style, Yahweh chooses to enter into a wisdom debate with Job over His manner of judging the earth rather than into a legal dispute over the justness of Job's case. This last section comprises two speeches by Yahweh and two responses from Job.

1. Yahweh's First Speech (38:1–40:2). Yahweh accuses Job of speaking without knowledge (38:2f.) and turns to contemplate the wonders of the world He has created (38:4–39:30). First He asks Job about the origin of the world (38:4-15). He queries Job to discover if he knows how the world was constructed: how the foundations of the earth were laid, how the sea was confined behind doors, or how the morning was commanded to appear. Yahweh then shifts emphasis and questions Job about control of creation (38:16-38). Has Job traveled to the sources of the sea, or does he know the way to the dwelling place of light, or has he entered the storehouse of the rain? Can Job command the constellations or muster natural catastrophes? The obvious answer to all these questions is a loud "No!" God next concentrates on the specific qualities of selected animals that reveal God's wisdom, care, and sense of humorous wonder (38:39–39:30). God sets the time for the mountain goat to bear (39:1-4) and gives the wild ass the desert in which to roam freely (37:5-8). The wild ox cannot be tamed by man (39:9-12) nor can the horse outrun the strange-looking ostrich (39:13-18). The strength and splendor of the horse are also displayed in his lack of fear in battle (39:19-25). The eagle, which soars so high, at great distance detects food for its young and preys on corpses slain in battle (39:26-30). The entire order of creation is beyond the ability of mankind to manage, improve, or alter, and it bears witness to God's majestic wisdom and might.

After finishing His discourse on creation, God questions Job directly (40:1f.). He demands an answer from his litigant.

2. Job's Response (40:3-5). Job, however, strongly feels his own unworthiness in the divine presence and disclaims any ability to answer God (40:3-5). Therefore God resumes His discourse.

3. Yahweh's Second Speech (40:6–41:34 [MT 26]). God asks Job whether he will discredit God's justice to put himself in a favorable position (40:6-9). If he can, God will concede his ability to win his own victory. Then he will be able to adorn himself in majestic apparel and subjugate the proud wicked (40:10-14). God proceeds to defend His sovereign power by describing in detail two mighty creatures that He has made and that are subject to His word: Behemoth (40:15-24) and Leviathan (41:1-34 [MT 40:25–41:26]). Whether these are natural animals or mythical monsters is disputed. In the OT Leviathan usually symbolizes the primordial monster that embodies the essence of hostility against God (cf. Isa. 27:1). In these two poems, however, these creatures appear to be naturalized. Although their identity is also disputed, the most frequent identification equates them with the hippopotamus and the crocodile respectively. The vivid description of these creatures reveals God's masterful art in creation and His supreme lordship in controlling them. Mankind, conversely, cannot capture or master them, but is reduced to terror in their presence. Through this picture Yahweh demonstrates that no evil force is beyond His control. Yahweh stands supreme, unchallenged, sovereign.

4. Job's Response (42:1-6). This last Yahweh speech evokes from Job a confession of contrition and confidence in God (42:1-6). Job acknowledges God's authority over everything in the world; in contrast, his own speaking has been without understanding. The most amazing wonder of Yahweh's speaking is that Job has encountered God. Under the warmth and awe that attend the divine presence all of Job's complaints fade into insignificance, for his ear has heard God and his eye has seen Him. The personal vision of God has revitalized Job's faith, adding a new, rich, fuller dimension. In contrast to the Holy God, Job confesses his own depraved humanity; thus he despises himself and entreats God's compassion. He does not acknowledge any specific sin; rather he confesses his unworthy creatureliness before God. In his pride he had charged God with acting unjustly; now his contrite self bows willingly before God's superior wisdom and justice. His suffering is brought into perspective. Although his integrity would not permit him to repent of conjectured sins, his subordinate attitude in God's presence resonates with his deepest attitudes of trust and reverence before God. From this broad perspective his suffering no longer is a barrier between himself and his Creator. At last God and Job are reconciled. The distant, silent, unmoved God has reached out to His servant and spoken great insight into the wonders of the world. The stubborn, persistent Job has melted into eager submission before the dynamic love realized in God's appearing. God's love reaches out to, restores, and uplifts the resigned worshiper.

H. Epilogue (42:7-17). The epilogue details Job's restoration. God expresses His anger with the three comforters for misrepresenting Him (42:7-9). He instructs them to bring seven bulls and seven rams as a sacrifice for Job to offer on their behalf. They obey Yahweh's instructions; as a result, the faith of all four is affirmed; Job gladly intercedes for his friends and secures their acceptance by Yahweh.

God then vindicates Job by restoring him twofold for all his losses. His kinsmen and friends arrive to sympathize with him and assist in his recovery. Seven sons and three daughters are also born to him (42:10-17). The daughters, but not the sons, are named in epic style: Jemimah ("dove"), Keziah ("cinnamon"), and Kerenhappuch ("horn of eyepaint"); their beauty becomes legendary and they share with their brothers in the family inheritance. Since his deceased children still have existence even in the grave, Job is the father of twenty children. Job's life reaches the highest patriarchal standards of richness; he lives to the ripe old age of 140 years and sees his children to four generations. He dies "full of days." Job's vindication is complete.

The epilogue returns to the values of the patriarchal age to affirm Job's righteousness and his victory over the most gruesome trial. The restoration of Job testifies that God will vindicate His own faithful servants. Although He may allow them to endure austere trials, He will restore them and generously compensate them for the burdens they bear.

VII. Literary Form.–Scholars disagree on the precise literary classification of Job. The traditional opinion has been that the book contains a factual account of Job's experiences. A few, however, have considered the story to be a parable of the righteous sufferer — an idea that appears as early as the Talmud (T.B. *Baba Bathra* 15a). A less likely suggestion is that the story is an allegory of Israel's suffering during the Babylonian Captivity. This last interpretation may be discounted because of the complete lack of historical allusion and the absence of issues of national concern.

More likely the book is a wisdom discussion of the issue of suffering based on the epic account of an ancient hero. Many scholars argue that much of ancient epic literature was based on real people and events; thus there is little reason not to think of the book of Job along these lines. The impact of an idea is vastly multiplied in the human social consciousness when it becomes incarnate in human experience. Thus the truth that a righteous man actually endured so much excruciating pain provides the impetus for other righteous sufferers to hold to their integrity and endure their plight, confident of a just resolution.

Other classifications for this work include drama, epic, and tragedy. In many ways it resembles a drama, even having a chorus to sing the anonymous parts like ch. 28. The forms of the play and the tragedy, however, developed in Greece, and these forms seem not to have influenced Jewish writers before the 2nd cent. B.C. Although the story of Job as it stands could easily be adapted to the stage, the book has no stage directions for production and little dramatic movement in the speeches. Furthermore, the plot of Job differs radically from tragedy in the technical sense, development of the onerous consequences that flow from a flaw in character or an error in judgment.

Form-critical studies have uncovered the rich variety of forms from which the poet draws for development of the speeches. He employs proverbs, numerical sayings, hymns, laments, wisdom disputations, lawsuits, and lyrical nature poems. A few scholars have tried to define the form of the entire work. Richter has attempted to explain it as a lawsuit: the first section (4–14) constitutes the procedure to reach a settlement through a pretrial hearing, and a formal trial follows in 15–31; since Job appears to win by reason of the friends' silence, Elihu enters to appeal the decision (32–37); finally God appears as a litigant in a secular lawsuit, and under His questioning Job withdraws his complaint. In another direction C. Westermann has argued that Job is a dramatized lament: the dominant form throughout the work is the lament, and the legal language is used to develop the complaint and the accusation against God.

The last two efforts have offered fine insights into this work, but they fail in trying to level into one mold the rich variety of form and language in this artistic work. The poet has drawn heavily on four genres: the lament, the wisdom disputation, the lawsuit, and the hymn of praise. The lament form has influenced deeply the formation of the majority of Job's speeches as he gives expression to the real, persistent pain that he must constantly bear. Through this form he seeks to move God to act to relieve his suffering. The wisdom disputation provides the foundation for the dialogue between Job and friends who refuse to respond to his lament. Thus this genre provides the poet the opportunity to argue against superficial ideas current in the wisdom circles. Also woven through the speeches of Job is legal language. Since Job's illness is accepted by the friends and the community as incriminating evidence against his moral character, Job's deepest need is to be vindicated and to have his honor restored. He turns, therefore, to legal language in order to demand a hearing, which will result in an acquittal by the divine court. The lament form dominates Job's first speeches. As his confidence grows, he draws more heavily on legal language. Consequently his final speech, a declaration of innocence, serves mainly a legal function. Lines from hymns of praise appear as a part of numerous speeches. The focus in these beautiful lyrics is on God's majesty, His wisdom, and His power. They provide a touchstone between Job and his friends, and their recitation helps to encourage Job to pursue his case until God answers him. For the poet they disclose the vital relationship between God and the world He has created; they pave the way for the long Yahweh speeches. Consequently, the greatest insights into the issue of human suffering are to be found in the manner of God's creating and governing the world. As the poet employs these genres, he molds them to his overall purpose and thus they develop new nuances. Each pericope, then, must be interpreted more by its setting in the book than by its original life setting. Certainly the poet was influenced by numerous literary categories and genres from his environs, but his artistic skills have created a work that is *sui generis*.

VIII. Unity and Integrity.– The complexity of this book and its vastly different divisions have led many investigators to explain its growth and development in numerous ways. The most radical work was done by Baumgärtel. He found only the first cycle of speeches, though they too have received some embellishments, to be the core of the original work. On the other side a few, e.g., Budde and Gordis, have argued for the essential unity of the work. If the work is *sui generis*, the latter position appears to be the more likely. At least the bulk of the present work comes from a single author. Some obscure passages are most likely the result of difficulties in transmission. Probably the poet was dependent on an earlier epic work, which he reworked slightly to provide the framework for the dialogue. In composing the speeches he may have borrowed heavily from other sources, especially for the mouths of the different speakers, in his effort to articulate a position held with conviction during his day. In addition, this work may have been a lifetime project that went through many revisions. In the last analysis as interpreters we have only the final product. The analysis of stages of its growth gives insight into the whole, and work of this nature is most helpful. Nevertheless, the task of interpretation must move to treat the work in its final form as it has become a part of the sacred Scriptures. Two movements in interpretation have opened new avenues of discussion: the work of the structuralists, e.g., Polzin, and current efforts under the label of canon criticism, especially the work of Childs.

The first place of tension comes between the prose account and the poetic dialogue. The silent, enduring Job of the epic narrative is countered by the bitter, verbose, agonizing Job of the dialogue. The personal God Yahweh in the prose material becomes the distant God under the names El, Eloah, and Shaddai of the speeches. The epic nature of the prose account suggests that it is earlier than the dialogue. Most agree that the poet took over an old epic tradition that told of a righteous patriarchal hero who ranked with Noah and Daniel (Ezk. 14:14, 20). The exact nature of the epic tale and the amount the poet reworked it are debated. Although the epic portion is very old, some of the linguistic forms reflect a much later date and may be the work of the poet. The style of the epilogue strongly suggests that a response from Yahweh was an integral part of the earliest work; a portion of that work may stand at 38:1. The oldest narrative presents scenes in duplicate. Thus in its drama Job probably faced two temptations: one from his wife (2:9f.) and a second from his relatives (now mentioned in 42:11). At this juncture the poet reworked the epic and inserted the account of the friends (2:11-13) as the background for the dialogue.

The scenes regarding Satan are problematic. Satan never returns, and this name is usually considered to be a late form. The council scene, though, appears to be an integral part of the epic tradition; perhaps the name Satan is a later insertion, or quite possibly this name and the role of the antagonist in the divine court are older than present research has discovered.

Although the prose portions are considerably older, the poet accepted them as integral to his work and to the theology he wished to communicate. Thus the tensions between the two portions are intentional and must be treated in any attempt to discover the meaning of the book.

The core of the dialogue (chs. 3–31) is generally accepted as genuine with only a few additions and alterations. The biggest problem is chs. 24–28. The third cycle is incomplete, with far too short a speech from Bildad (ch. 25) and none from Zophar. This section has suffered great dislocation in the earliest period of its textual transmission, for the Qumrân Targum witnesses to the same order as the present MT. Another possible explanation suggests that the poet left the third cycle incomplete as an additional way of saying that the friends had nothing more to add and thus had failed both Job and God.

Many reconstructions of this cycle have been offered. A simple suggestion, as already noted, is to take 27:13-23, which is completely out of character in Job's mouth, with 25:1-6 as the remaining portions of Bildad's third speech and to form Job's reply out of 26:1–27:12. Obviously some lines have been lost from both of these speeches. It may be assumed also that there never was a third speech for Zophar.

The beautiful poem on wisdom (ch. 28) appears foreign in the mouth of any of the four speakers. It also seems to lack context, and some feel that it anticipates the Yahweh speeches so closely that it renders them redundant. The latter position, though, may be using the wrong principles of criticism for an ancient work. Some authors like to reverberate a theme throughout the entire piece, crescendoing to its final and full development. Thus the reader is prepared for its full presentation, for the concept has been imprinted indelibly on the audience's thinking. Recent critics recognize the stylistic similarities of this hymn to the rest of the poem. They attribute its origin, therefore, to the poet and its present location to a faithful student of the poet who wished to preserve this masterful poem. Nevertheless, this piece serves as a break between the dialogue and Job's final defense (29–31) and points the way to the Yahweh speeches. Its lack of context may be the result of the textual difficulties associated with the third cycle.

The Elihu speeches (32–37) are regarded by most critics as secondary. The lack of mention of Elihu elsewhere in the book is strange. The long, apparently redundant prose introduction is problematic. These speeches differ in style from those of the dialogue; the pompous, verbose nature, the quoting of Job followed by refutation, and the addressing of Job by his personal name are some of the differences. Although Elihu claims to take a different, more open stance toward Job, he seems offended by Job's words and feels a need to defend God's honor before Job's attack. As his speech progresses his position appears to be almost identical to that of the three friends he has condemned. Therefore some argue that these Elihu speeches were inserted to make this abrasive work more palatable to the established religious community. But to work from the position that these speeches make no significant contribution to the work fails to give any rationale for their inclusion, especially since they are not regarded as from the hand of the poet. In their present position they delay the divine response to Job's challenging oath. Thus they serve a good artistic function, especially for ancient Near Eastern literature, i.e., they create suspense. A space is needed between Job's final words and the appearing of Yahweh to set a tone and to convey the important theme of Yahweh's freedom; that is, Yahweh is not compelled by an oath to answer but rather chooses to respond because of His personal bond with His faithful servant.

Gordis's study has offered some new options regarding the origin and position of the Elihu speeches. Recognizing the differences in style, though he does not consider them as different as do other critics, he argues that these speeches came from the poet in later years as he continued to struggle with the issue of unjust suffering. In these speeches the poet wished to develop the concept that suffering is disciplinary. Since this is a partial truth, it would not belong in the Yahweh speeches, and since the poet wanted this idea to receive serious consideration, it must be developed outside the speeches of the three comforters. So Elihu was created. As these speeches were developed, the fourth one, describing God's power in the storm, was composed to prepare the way for the theophany from the storm. At best the Elihu speeches are problematic, but they stand in the final work and thus should never be lightly dismissed.

A response from Yahweh appears to belong to the oldest epic stratum. The poet took the opportunity to compose a most elegant speech addressing the issue of suffering against the backdrop of the wonders of creation. Although a few have rejected the first speech (38:1–40:5), the real problem rises with the long, detailed descriptions of the hippopotamus and the crocodile (40:7–41:34). Although their style is not as elegant as that of the first speech — perhaps partially due to textual problems and misunderstandings — they form a second speech from Yahweh that follows the integral twofold pattern evident in the prologue. Further, Yahweh appears to be pressing a point in order to move Job to a different disposition. Overall, the poet reaches his highest skill in these speeches, and his greatest insights into suffering are found here.

The epilogue (43:7-17) appears to many to be anticlimactic and inconsistent with the refutation of the doctrine of retribution in the dialogue. Although there are some rough seams where the poem joins the epic narrative again in 42:10-12, the epilogue belongs to the oldest form of the epic account. If Job has suffered innocently, his vindication must be evident at the conclusion. Since the author wished to resolve Job's case in this life, not in the next, Job's restoration must take place in a tangible form. On the other hand, it must be emphasized that the author did not reject the concept of retribution. Rather, he did not believe in immediate retribution for every matter. Events counter to a scheme of retribution could transpire for a long time before God settled accounts. Thus the wicked prospered, and conversely, many righteous had to bear suffering. One day, however, God will settle accounts justly, and those who have endured loss and maintained their integrity and faith in God will be justly and generously exalted by Him. The author sought to give insight into the ways of God and to correct misapplications of the doctrine of retribution rather than to create a new system of God's working with mankind. As a result, his insights strengthen the faith of those who endure suffering, giving a sense of freedom from a rigid application of theological principle, while at the same time the poet exalts one's confidence in the lordship of God, both in His justice and in His merciful concern for each of His followers.

In conclusion, the essential framework of this wisdom discussion has basically survived. Although the work is beset by textual difficulties, its essential integrity is established. As the knowledge of Near Eastern languages and literature increases, the interpretation of this great work will also become more exact.

IX. Message.–The book of Job seeks to demonstrate that a righteous person can suffer the most excruciating pain and maintain his integrity. Job was the most upright man that ever lived; no one was ever so rich, generous, and conscientious. Neither had anyone suffered so intensely. His suffering was experienced to the greatest extent on all levels — physical, emotional, social, and spiritual. The loss of his wealth was total, including houses, flocks, and children. His bodily pain was most severe, for he endured an illness with compounded complications from which he could not gain any repose. Emotionally he was torn between his love for God and God's apparent hostility toward him that aroused a deep sense of terror. Furthermore, his longing for an escape from his pain pulled against his absorbing desire to be vindicated. Socially, the most respected elder in the ancient Near East was plummeted from the respect he commanded to become a laughingstock, a taunt and object of reproach with no one willing to share his isolation from the community. Since no one else ever had so much or commanded such respect, Job stands alone as the one who has borne the greatest suffering. His agony was increased by God's silence. Job wished for some explanation, some word of perspective, but God failed to speak. He was willing to confess any wrong if it could be proved, but no insight came. Job was left completely alone to discover a way out of his dark abyss.

The poem especially attacks a simplistic application of the doctrine of retribution — only the righteous are blessed and the wicked suffer a just punishment. The corollary, that whoever experiences loss is surely guilty, falls under the poet's direct criticism. Although the OT certainly teaches that one's deeds are either rewarded or punished according to their nature (cf. Lev. 26; Dt. 28; Ps. 1; Isa. 58:6-14; Jer. 17:5-8; Hos. 10:11-14), it never succumbs to a deterministic application of this doctrine. The OT is aware that in this life some of the wicked enjoy a long life to the fullest and some of the righteous experience hardship and loss (Ps. 37:1-3; 49:5-12 [MT 6-13]; 73:1-9; Jer. 12:1-2; Hab. 1:5-11). Consequently the words of the friends that unequivocally accuse Job of heinous crimes become a grave violation of the intention that undergirds this doctrine. Their defensive attitude leads them to twist the redemptive nature of this divine truth into a damning force. Such a perversion of spiritual truth demands a most skillful repudiation, and one is found in this book. Thus the epilogue is not a leftover appendage to keep the older form of the epic intact; rather it makes an essential contribution to the message of the book. It reaffirms the doctrine that God rewards the righteous, with the implication that He just as certainly punishes the wicked. Although God does not execute immediate rewards for every action, a time will come when God will judge each person and render a just recompense. Therefore God can be both just and sovereign in allowing the righteous to suffer, for He will ultimately vindicate His own. On the human side, it is affirmed that one who endures great pain can challenge God to know why this is his lot and simultaneously hold on to his faith and be confident that the attack against him is not a proof that he has failed; one may endure the sharpest trials confident of his innocence before God. In this manner the poet presents a high view of mankind; mankind can transcend its present predicament for good.

The poem looks at the issue of suffering from many sides. Pain comes as a direct attack of a hostile force whose design is to coerce man into rebellion against God, according to the prologue. The friends argue that suffering is punishment for sins. Elihu develops in more detail the thesis that suffering is disciplinary, with the potential of leading to closer fellowship with God. The Yahweh speeches indicate that suffering is a mystery. It is not beyond God's sovereign rule nor does it indelibly mar the beauty and wonders in the world of God's handiwork. Out of the strangest and most obscure aspects of His creation God brings order and wonder. God faithfully maintains His creation and cares for all the animals He has made. Furthermore, no place nor creature is beyond His authority. In the final scene of the poem Job discovers that the agony of suffering dissolves in the affirming warmth of the divine presence. A vision of God absorbs his being and uplifts him to a complete sense of worth. The book fails to give a definitive answer to the question of suffering and rightly so, for it lies beyond the purview of any mortal. Great perspective, however, is extended by offering these different vantage points from which pain may be viewed. The greater purpose of the poem is to challenge mankind to endure its lot with an unadulterated confidence in God, for in so doing humanity attains to the noblest qualities inherent in its character. Each person's victory over suffering offers solace to others and gains for him the privilege of interceding for others, as is evident in the divine instruction to victorious Job to offer sacrifice for his wayward companions and thereby restore their relationship with God.

This work offers a model of the victorious value of endurance and unflinching confidence in God's justice during the most difficult trials. The greatest movement in the book is seen in the confidence that Job builds on the conviction of his own innocence and God's justice. Job moves from the deepest despair (ch. 3) to a bold challenge presented to God (ch. 31). In this development he is compelled to reject completely the simplistic positions articulated by his friends. Consequently, in his own thinking he must venture into new categories of possibility. His thinking is bound by three principal ideas: God is justice; he himself is innocent, undeserving of such affliction; and death will not vindicate him. Motivated by the burning desire to be vindicated with the restoration of his honor, he calls for a trial in which his case may be argued by God and himself.

After his curse-lament Job responds in chs. 6–7 to the first speech offered by one of his friends. Although he continues to lament his tormenting pain his words are more concrete; thus he is beginning to cope with the real situation that confronts him. It is not until his second speech in the dialogue, however, that he begins to formulate the possibility of entering into a lawsuit with God to gain a just verdict on his innocence. Since God appears to be treating him like an archenemy, Job longs for an umpire who might be able to arbitrate his case and bring reconciliation between the two of them (9:33f.). This wish is unrealistic, for the umpire by definition would be greater than God, an impossibility.

In his next speech Job pleads for two things: that God might remove his illness and that they together might dispute his case. Job expresses his firm confidence in God in a verse with some textual difficulties:

> Behold, he will slay me; I have no hope;
> yet I will defend my ways to his face. (13:15)

Another possible rendering is:

> If he slays me, I would have no hope;
> nevertheless, I will defend my ways to his face.

Job will not relinquish his right to a fair trial under any circumstances.

Afraid that death will take his life before he is acquitted, Job entertains the thought that he might be able to return to life and receive a just reward in his restored life. He observes that for a tree which has been cut down there is hope that it may send forth new shoots and grow again into a tree (14:7-9). This natural phenomenon, however, is without analogy in human experience; death is final (14:10-12). Thus Job fails to find any hope in a doctrine of resurrection (14:18-22). For justice to prevail, vindication must come for him in this life.

In the next speech Job prays that if he should die without vindication, the earth may not receive his blood until his case has been tried (16:18f.). The earth's refusal to cover his blood will mean that he has not been accepted by the grave and therefore can find no rest in Sheol. Thus God will have to overcome the injustice of an unavenged death before Job can take his place in the grave. In this context Job makes a strong affirmation of confidence in God:

> Even now, behold, my witness is in heaven,
> and he that vouches for me is on high. (16:19)

He believes that ultimately God will testify to his innocence.

Job continues to build his confidence in God's coming to his assistance. In a moment of insight he voices the most famous lines in the book:

> For I know that my Redeemer lives,
> and at last he will stand upon the earth;
> and after my skin has been thus destroyed,
> then from my flesh I shall see God,

whom I shall see on my side,
and my eyes shall behold, and not another. (19:25-27b)

These verses unfortunately are fraught with textual problems and with difficult syntax in crucial points. Thus translations of them differ markedly, e.g.:

But in my heart I know that my vindicator lives
and that he will rise last to speak in court;
and I shall discern my witness standing at my side
and see my defending counsel, even God himself,
whom I shall see with my own eyes,
I myself and no other. (NEB)

This I know: that my Avenger lives,
and he, the Last, will take his stand on earth.
After my awaking, he will set me close to him,
and from my flesh I shall look on God.
He whom I shall see will take my part:
these eyes will gaze on him and find
him not aloof. (JB)

In the broader context, Job expresses the wish that his words were engraved in a rock or a stele as an eternal witness to his righteousness. In order for him not to bear the eternal reproach of an ignominious reputation, there will have to be a counter-witness on earth to offset the incriminating evidence of his misfortune. An eternal record of his defense, however, is far inferior to a resolution of his case by a divine judgment. His deep-seated reverence for God, therefore, inspires the conviction that God will become his Advocate or Redeemer (*gôʾēl*) and that Job himself will witness his vindication with his own physical eyes even if he should die before the trial. That is to say, Job affirms his complete confidence in his ultimate vindication by God, who will act as his Redeemer. To be just, since Job has borne the shame of his suffering on earth, this acquittal must take place on earth before witnesses. Thus at his trial God must be visibly present and so, too, must Job. If, therefore, he should die before this trial takes place, it will be necessary to have his spirit reunited with his body for his vindication to be valid. These are powerful words evidencing Job's profound faith in God ultimately to rescue His own servants in a just way. God will act as his Redeemer even if the resurrection of Job would be required. Job is not defending a doctrine of resurrection that he had earlier rejected, but he is pushing the inner logic of his belief in God's vindicating justice. In the NT this inner logic will come to the foreground in a fully developed doctrine of resurrection as the seal of proof to the teaching that God's love for mankind is both just and redemptive. In a bold venture Job is pointing the way to that position, but he glimpses it only vaguely. Thus the emphasis of this great assertion must be kept on Job's faith in God as the final, sure Source of his redemption.

Job's confidence in God and the justice of his own ways continues to build even though God remains hidden. He affirms that he has held to God's ways firmly without any deviation (23:11-13). He is certain, therefore, that he will come through his trial an even better person:

But he knows the way that I take;
when he has tried me, I shall
come forth as gold. (23:10)

Job has prepared the way to make his final affirmation of innocence (29–31). He compares his former noble estate (ch. 29) with his present humbling affliction (ch. 30). Nevertheless, he knows he has not sinned and offers an oath of innocence (ch. 31). Thus he concludes with the challenge that God answer his pleas and his affirmation:

Oh, that I had one to hear me!
(Here is my signature! let the Almighty answer me!)
Oh, that I had the indictment
written by my adversary!
Surely I would carry it on my shoulder;
I would bind it on me as a crown;
I would give him an account of all my steps;
like a prince I would approach him. (31:35-37)

Job has conquered the confusion and distress created by his grievous losses and intense physical discomfort. By verbalizing details of his suffering, he has gained the means to cope with his affliction. As his body deteriorates, his mental resolve and moral conviction become stronger, for his thinking focuses on God in confidence that this God is his witness and and his Redeemer. Job has thus honored God's assurance, expressed in the prologue, that Job serves Him out of a genuine love and reverence, not for the gain he may receive. Consequently Job becomes the great example of a person's ability to suffer the gravest difficulties and severest shame yet preserve his faith in God. During such a trial a person may directly challenge God's ways of acting without tarnishing his moral integrity or destroying the basis of his faith. Indeed, by verbalizing his sorrow in deeply felt laments, he buttresses his mental attitude to avoid the pitfall of remorse and gains the moral strength to endure until God answers. The NT believer can be strengthened beyond Job's example by reason of the conquering love of Jesus Christ, for both His suffering and His righteousness surpassed Job's. Moreover, by rising from the dead, Jesus' righteousness has been proved and His death has been accepted as possessing vicarious virtue for anyone who will accept its merits. Inspired by the examples of Job and Jesus and drawing on their spiritual power, the believer can endure suffering in the confidence that "in all these things we are more than conquerors through him who loved us" (Rom. 8:37).

***Bibliography.*–*Comms.*:** F. I. Andersen (*Tyndale OT Comms.*, 1976); C. J. Ball (1922); K. Budde (1913); M. Buttenwieser (1922); F. Delitzsch (1866); E. Dhorme (Eng. tr. 1966); S. R. Driver and G. B. Gray (*ICC*, 1921); B. Duhm (1897); G. Fohrer (*KAT*, 1963); R. Gordis (1978); A. Guillaume (1968); N. C. Habel (*CBC*, 1975); G. Hölscher (*HAT*, 1937); F. Horst (*BKAT*, 1968); M. Jastrow (1920); E. J. Kissane (1939); M. H. Pope (*AB*, 3rd ed. 1973); H. H. Rowley (*New Century Bible*, rev. ed. 1976); S. Terrien (*IB*, III, 1954); N. H. Tur-Sinai (rev. ed. 1967); A. Weiser (*ATD*, 1974).

Other Works: A. C. M. Blommerde, *Northwest Semitic Grammar and Job* (1969); G. Fohrer, *Studien zum Buche Hiob* (1963); N. Glatzer, ed., *Dimensions of Job* (1969); R. Gordis, *The Book of God and Man: A Study of Job* (1966); L. L. Grabbe, *Comparative Philology and the Text of Job* (1977); A. R. King, *The Problem of Evil* (1952); J. Lévêque, *Job et son Dieu* (1970); J. Lindblom, *La Composition du livre de Job* (1945); R. Murphy, *Wisdom Literature* (*Forms of the OT Literature*, 1981), pp. 13-45; M. Noth and D. W. Thomas, eds., *Wisdom in Israel and in the Ancient Near East* (*SVT*, 3 [1960]); H. Richter, *Studien zu Hiob, Der Aufbau des Hiobbuches, dargestellt an den Gattungen des Rechtslebens* (1954); H. W. Robinson, *The Cross of Job* (1955); P. Sanders, ed., *Twentieth Century Interpretations of the Book of Job* (1968); N. H. Snaith, *Book of Job: Its Origin and Purpose* (*SBT*, 2/11, 1968); M. Sokoloff, *Targum to Job from Qumran Cave XI* (1974); E. F. Sutcliffe, *Providence and Suffering in the Old and New Testaments* (1955); J. van der Ploeg and A. S. van der Woude, *Le Targum de Job de la grotte XI de Qumran* (1971); G. von Rad, *Wisdom in Israel* (Eng. tr. 1972); C. Westermann, *Der Aufbau des Buches Hiob* (2nd ed. 1977).

Articles: A. Alt, *ZAW*, 55 (1937), 265-68; O. J. Baab, *Interp.*, 5 (1951), 329-343; M. Dahood, "Northwest Semitic Philology and Job," in J. L. McKenzie, ed., *The Bible in Current Catholic Thought* (1962), pp. 55-74; P. Dale, *ZAW*, 91 (1979), 268-282; H. A. Fine, *JBL*, 74 (1955), 28-32; D. N. Freedman, *HTR*, 61 (1968), 51-59; H. L. Ginsberg, *Conservative Judaism*, 21 (1967), 12-28; J. Gray, *ZAW*, 82 (1970), 251-269; A. Guillaume, "The Arabic Background of the Book of Job," in F. F. Bruce, ed., *Promise and Fulfilment* (1963), pp. 106-127; R. K. Harrison, *EQ*,

25 (1953), 18-27; J. A. Holland, *Australian Journal of Biblical Archaeology*, 2 (1972), 160-177; A. Hurvitz, *HTR*, 67 (1974), 17-34; W. A. Irwin, *JNES*, 5 (1948), 26-39; *JR*, 13 (1933), 150-164; 17 (1937), 37-47; H. Knight, *SJT*, 9 (1956), 63-76; K. Koch, *ZTK*, 52 (1955), 1-42; K. Kuhl, *TR*, 21 (1953), 163-205, 257-317; R. A. F. McKenzie, *Bibl.*, 40 (1959), 435-445; R. H. Pfeiffer, *ZAW*, 44 (1926), 13-25; R. Polzin, *Interp.*, 28 (1974), 182-200; H. Richter, *EvTh*, 18 (1958), 302-324; J. J. M. Roberts, *ZAW*, 89 (1977), 107-114; H. H. Rowley, *BJRL*, 41 (1958), 167-207; E. Ruprecht, *ZTK*, 73 (1976), 424-445; N. M. Sarna, *JBL*, 76 (1957), 13-25; D. S. Shapiro, *Judaism*, 5 (1956), 46-52; P. Skehan, *Bibl.*, 45 (1964), 51-62; *CBQ*, 23 (1961), 129-143; W. S. Taylor, *Theology Today*, 12 (1955/56), 451-463; K. T. Thompson, *Interp.*, 14 (1960), 51-63; M. Tsevat, *HUCA*, 37 (1966), 73-106; W. J. Urbrock, *Semeia*, 5 (1976), 111-137; J. W. Whedbee, *Semeia*, 7 (1977), 1-39; J. G. Williams, *ZAW*, 83 (1971), 231-255; J. K. Zink, *JBL*, 84 (1965), 147-152.

J. E. HARTLEY

JOB, TESTAMENT OF. *See* PSEUDEPIGRAPHA.

JOBAB jō'bab [Heb. *yôḇāḇ*; Gk. *Iōbab*].

1. Youngest son of Joktan (Gen. 10:29; 1 Ch. 1:23) and progenitor of an Arab tribe.

2. An Edomite king (Gen. 36:33f.; 1 Ch. 1:44f.).

3. King of Madon (Josh. 11:1).

4. 1 Ch. 8:9; and **5.** 1 Ch. 8:18, Benjaminites.

The name is confused with that of Job in the LXX of Job 42:17.

JOCHEBED jok'ə-bed [Heb. *yôḵeḇeḏ*–'Yahweh is glory'(?)]. Daughter of Levi, wife of Amram, and mother of Moses (Ex. 6:20; Nu. 26:59). According to Ex. 6:20, she was a sister of Kohath, Amram's father.

JODA jō'də [Gk. *Iōda, Iouda*].

1. A Levite, whose sons were to have charge "over the works of the Lord," corresponding to Sudias (1 Esd. 5:26), Hodaviah (Ezr. 2:40), Judah (Ezr. 3:9), Hodevah (Neh. 7:43).

2. An ancestor of Jesus in Luke's genealogy (Lk. 3:26; AV Juda).

JODAN jō'dən [Gk. *Iōdanos, Iōadanos*] (1 Esd. 9:19); AV, NEB, JOADANUS. A son of Jozadak and grandson of Jeshua; one of the priests who had a foreign wife. He is called Gedaliah in Ezr. 10:18 (*see* GEDALIAH **3**).

JOED jō'ed [Heb. *yô'ēḏ*–'Yahweh is witness']. A descendant of Benjamin (Neh. 11:7), missing in 1 Ch. 9:7.

JOEL jō'əl [*yô'ēl*–'Yahweh is God'; cf. *IP*, p. 140, but contrast BDB, p. 222]. A name of wide distribution in Israel, though attested mainly in postexilic texts.

1. The prophet (see the next article).

2. Samuel's elder son (1 S. 8:2; 1 Ch. 6:33 [MT 18]; 15:17). In 1 Ch. 6:28 (MT 13), the RV and RSV correctly restore the name. The AV follows the MT with "the firstborn Vashni"; here "Joel" must have fallen out by homoeoteleuton after "Samuel," the word following (*wᵉhaššēnî*, "and the second") being then misread as a proper name, "Vashni."

3. A Simeonite prince (1 Ch. 4:35).

4. A man of the tribe of Reuben (1 Ch. 5:4, 8).

5. A Gadite chief (5:12).

6. A Kohathite Levite (6:36 [MT 21]), apparently the same as Shaul in v. 24 (MT 9).

7. A man of the tribe of Issachar (7:3).

8. One of David's mighty men (11:38), brother of Nathan. 2 S. 23:36 has "Igal the son of Nathan." The difference between the two names in the Hebrew script is very slight, and the parallel lists in which the names occur show a large number of such variations. The Chronicler's account of the relationship with Nathan is defended by W. Rudolph, *Chronikbücher* (1955), p. 102, because of its more unusual nature.

9. A Levite (1 Ch. 15:7, 11). Many scholars further identify him with the Joel of 1 Ch. 23:8 and 26:22.

10. David's chief officer over the half-tribe of Manasseh (1 Ch. 27:20).

11. A Kohathite Levite of Hezekiah's time (2 Ch. 29:12).

12. A layman listed among those who married foreign wives in Ezra's time (Ezr. 10:43).

13. An overseer in postexilic Jerusalem (Neh. 11:9).

It is possible that some of these are identical (e.g., **4** and **5**, **8** and **10**, and cf. **9**), but the evidence is insufficient to advance beyond speculation.

H. G. M. WILLIAMSON

JOEL. The second of the twelve Minor Prophets. The MT consists of four chapters, but the English versions, following the LXX and Vulgate, have combined chs. 2 and 3 (=English 2:1-27 and 28-32) to give a total of three chapters.

- I. The Prophet
- II. The Book
  - A. Outline of Contents
  - B. Problems of Composition
    1. Date
    2. Quotations
    3. Unity
    4. Composition and Structure
  - C. Problems of Interpretation
    1. The Locusts and the Day of the Lord
    2. The Cult
    3. NT References

I. The Prophet.–Joel is introduced as "the son of Pethuel" (1:1; LXX Bethuel). Apart from this reference, no details concerning his life and person are supplied from either the book that bears his name or elsewhere. Even his date is still a subject of considerable controversy. His writing strongly suggests that he lived in the vicinity of Jerusalem; his interests seldom ranged further afield. He appears to have a detailed knowledge of temple procedures (e.g., 1:13f.; 2:12-17), and sympathetic concern for the cult is one of the features that distinguishes this book from some of the other prophetic books. Moreover, the formal structure of parts of chs. 1 and 2 may reflect contemporary liturgical practice. On the other hand, he does not seem to identify himself with the priests (1:9, 13; 2:17), even though on occasion he may pray representatively on behalf of the people (1:19f.). These facts have led many scholars to believe that Joel may have been a cultic prophet attached to the temple. This is a most attractive suggestion, although the understanding and the interpretation of his book are in no way dependent upon it.

II. The Book.–Since the only evidence we have for the setting and interpretation of Joel's ministry is the book itself, it will be helpful to start with a summary of its contents. The following paragraphs contain an outline of the prophet's message, without prejudice at this stage to the question of a more intricate literary structure (see B.4 below).

A. Outline of Contents. The book consists of two nearly equal parts. In the first (1:2–2:17) the prophet summons the people to lamentation and repentance because of drought and a devastating plague of locusts. In the second part (2:18–3:21), he promises salvation from the immedate effects of the disaster (2:18-27), eschatological blessing on Judah and Jerusalem, and judgment on the oppressing nations.

A general introductory statement claims that such complete and utter devastation had not struck within living memory, and was unlikely to recur within the foreseeable future (1:2-4). The stripping of vines and fig trees had left the drunkards without wine (vv. 5-7), while the laying waste of the fields at large had brought an end to the regular temple offerings (vv. 8-10) and had ruined the farmers (vv. 11f.). There was sufficient cause here for the priests to summon a penitential assembly (vv. 13-18), and the section concludes with a prayer by the prophet which indicates that a severe drought had also affected the country (vv. 19f.).

Already in 1:15 it has been indicated that the plague of locusts is a harbinger of the Day of the Lord, and this theme is developed in ch. 2 (cf. vv. 1, 11). The description shifts to the locusts themselves as the advancing army of the Lord (vv. 1-11) in a manner that occasionally resembles a theophany. The only appropriate response by Israel is repentance (vv. 12-17), which, though expressed through the cult, must give evidence of a genuine and individual change of heart.

We must assume that the people responded to Joel's preaching, for we next find him mediating God's promise that the locusts are to be driven off (v. 20), the drought ended (v. 23), and fertility restored to the land with abundant harvests that exceed the previous loss. This section is closely tied to the two that precede both in concept and phraseology (e.g., compare 2:17 with 27). Though it deals more directly with the problem of the locusts that has dominated the book up to this point than the sections which follow, 2:18 marks the decisive turning point in the book as the content moves from negative to positive (cf. Driver, p. 58; Wolff, pp. 6f., 67; Ahlström, p. 132; Allen, pp. 39-42).

Spiritual renewal will follow the physical restoration. Social and cultic barriers within Israel will be broken through by God. He will deal directly with all those in Jerusalem who have turned to Him for salvation (2:28-32).

The reversal in Israel's fortunes is highlighted by the summons to judgment of those nations who were former oppressors (3:1-3). Their own evil deeds will be turned against them in punishment (vv. 4-8), and the whole process is brought to a climax in a description of the Day of the Lord which resembles apocalyptic thought (vv. 9-16). (*See also* ESCHATOLOGY II.) The Lord Himself will then dwell in a secure and sanctified Jerusalem, which will become the center of fertility, blessing, and justice (vv. 17-21).

B. Problems of Composition. 1. Date. No issue raised by the book of Joel is more controversial than its date. Despite intense and protracted discussion, there is still no consensus of opinion, as the following survey will indicate.

a. Survey of Opinion. A more detailed survey may be found in Thompson ("The Date of Joel"). The main possibilities which various scholars have held in recent times are:

(1) Early Preexilic. Popular in the 19th cent. after the publication of Credner's comm. in 1831, this position has been upheld more recently by Bič as well as a number of conservative writers (e.g., the intros. to the OT of E. J. Young [rev. ed. 1964], pp. 254-57, and G. L. Archer [rev. ed. 1974], pp. 303-307). It is argued, for instance, that the position of Joel in the canon points to an early date, and that the conditions reflected in the book suit the rule of Joash while he was still underage (*ca.* 870-860 B.C.). Political allusions are explained by reference to 1 K. 14:25-28, 2 K. 8:20-22, and 2 Ch. 21:16f. In addition, Bič cites a number of Ugaritic parallels in order to interpret Joel as an early polemic against Baalism.

(2) Late Preexilic. Kapelrud, Keller, and Rudolph are notable proponents of a date for Joel immediately before the Exile. Rudolph, taking seriously the allusions of 3:2, gives a date between the first and second Babylonian sieges of Jerusalem (597 and 587 B.C.). Joel's origin within the cult is considered an adequate explanation for its allusions to other prophetic books, whereas its many close parallels with Jeremiah suggest that they were contemporaries. Many of the weaker arguments for a postexilic date are rightly rejected.

(3) Exilic. Reicke is among a few scholars who date Joel during the period before the building of the second temple. His main argument is that 2:17 ("between the vestibule and the altar") indicates that no full temple was standing at the time.

(4) Early Postexilic. A proposal which has gained a good deal of support (Myers, Ahlström, Allen) is to date Joel immediately after the rebuilding of the second temple (*ca.* 515-500 B.C.), thus making him a contemporary of Haggai and Zechariah. In addition to the general arguments in favor of a postexilic date (see 1.c below), precision is added by the reference in 3:8 to the Sabeans, who, it is claimed, lost control of the eastern trade routes after the 6th century.

(5) About 400 B.C. This is probably the position held by the majority of scholars, although, as we noted, another trend has been to favor a somewhat earlier date. Precision is given to the general indications of the postexilic period by the reference to the wall in 2:7, 9, said to be the one built by Nehemiah in 445 B.C., and by the citations from many other prophets (see B.2 below), which suggest that Joel is one of the latest books to have been written. On the other hand, the reference to Sidon's judgment as yet future (3:4 [MT 4:4]) suggests a date before 345 B.C. when that city was destroyed by Artaxerxes III and its inhabitants were sold into slavery.

(6) Late Postexilic. Those who find various layers of composition in Joel (see B.3 below) often date the secondary sections to the 4th or 3rd cent. B.C. This later date has further been upheld for the whole book by a few scholars. Earlier commentators pointed in particular to the mention of Greeks (3:6 [MT 4:6]) as a late element, while more recently Treves has suggested that 3:2f., 19 refer to Ptolemy I Soter's capture of Jerusalem in 312 B.C., and Stephenson, finding a reference to the firsthand experience of a total eclipse of the sun in 2:31 (MT 3:4), is obliged to date Joel later than 357 or 336 B.C., the dates of the only two total eclipses in the period under consideration.

b. Some Inconclusive Arguments. In view of such a wide diversity of opinion, few would dare to claim certainty for their position. Ibn Ezra and Calvin are only two of those who, even in the pre-critical period, expressed real uncertainty over the issue. Nevertheless, some of the arguments which have been adduced are far from convincing, and should therefore be dropped from the discussion. Those that have played a significant role in the debate may be mentioned here.

(1) Place in the Canon. Although it is true that generally the compilers of the "Book of the Twelve" appear to have been guided by chronological considerations, in the case of Joel uncertainty in this regard is shown because in the LXX Joel stands fourth, after Micah, not second. Moreover, Wolff has developed the argument that, since the book of Joel is in itself undated, its position in the canon may rest not on a tradition concerning its date, but on some close verbal parallels in its closing verses with Amos, which it immediately precedes (compare 3:16 with Am. 1:2, and 3:18 with Am. 9:13). As a result, its position in the canon cannot be determinative for us.

(2) The Greeks. The older argument that reference to the Greeks (Heb. *b^{e}nê hayy^{e}wānîm*) in 3:6 demands a date after the Hellenistic expansion (late 4th cent. B.C.) is un-

founded. Evidence for Greek contact with Palestine from much earlier times continues to accumulate (Myers, pp. 178-185; D. Auscher, *VT,* 17 [1967], 8-30), and it has been suggested that the reference in Joel is to the Greeks as a still somewhat remote people to whom the inhabitants of Judah and Jerusalem might be sold as slaves; this better suits a date before their conquests of 333 B.C.

(3) Lack of Reference to the King. This argument has been adduced in support of both a postexilic date and a date in which Joash was still a minor. This sufficiently demonstrates its ambiguity, but in any case the dangers of an argument from silence are such that little weight should be placed upon it.

(4) Reference to the Wall. A number of scholars have argued that the wall in 2:7, 9 is complete and that therefore, if the date of the book is postexilic, it cannot precede Nehemiah's time. It is unlikely, however, that no wall at all was in existence before Nehemiah, for Neh. 2:13 and 4:7 suggest that he needed only to repair certain sections, and the implication of Neh. 1:3 is that a wall surrounding postexilic Jerusalem had only recently been destroyed.

(5) Total eclipse of the sun. Stephenson's argument that 2:31 presupposes firsthand experience of a total eclipse of both moon and sun is striking, but ultimately not conclusive. In 2:10 and 3:15 (MT 4:15) similar phenomena are mentioned, and the statement is added that "the stars withdraw their shining," which cannot be explained on so natural a basis. It seems more probable, therefore, that the passage refers to elements drawn from the Day of the Lord traditions that were later associated with theophanic eschatological descriptions (cf. J. Jeremias, *Theophanie* [1965], pp. 97-100).

c. More Certain Indications. The following arguments, which all favor a postexilic date for Joel, seem to carry greater weight, particularly since they all point in the same direction. It should be stressed again, however, that a number of scholars propose alternative explanations, so that, though the following represents a majority opinion, it does not command full agreement.

(1) Reference to the Exile. The prophecy in 3:2f. seems most naturally to refer to the fall of Jerusalem, dispersion of the people, and foreign settlement of the land as past events. It is doubtful whether any situation prior to the final fall of Jerusalem in 587 B.C. can do justice to this description. In connection with this, 3:5 seems to refer to the destruction of the temple (contra Rudolph).

(2) Existence of the Temple. Despite Reicke's argument from 2:17, 1:2–2:17 clearly presupposes the existence of a temple in which the priests might expect in normal times to officiate over a full round of cultic ceremonies. Though we know little about conditions in Jerusalem during the Exile, it would be surprising if Joel could be fitted into that period. Taken with the first point, this would establish 515 B.C. (when the second temple was completed, cf. Ezr. 6:15) as a *terminus a quo.*

(3) Language. The argument from language and style has undoubtedly been overplayed in the past (cf. H. Holzinger, *ZAW,* 9 [1899], 89-131). Nevertheless, Ahlström (pp. 1-22) has surveyed the whole issue again with commendable caution in the light of the questions that have been raised about it and suggested that, although most of the evidence which has been advanced cannot be used to determine the date of Joel, a confluence of evidence from a limited number of items (e.g., "Judah and Jerusalem" in 3:1, 6, 20 and "sons of Zion" in 2:23) points to a period no earlier than Jeremiah. These findings would thus allow a late preexilic date, and would fit well with a postexilic one, but are an embarrassment to an early preexilic date.

(4) Names and Nature of the Community. Joel addresses his audience as "Judah and Jerusalem," and applies to them the title "Israel" (2:27; 3:16). The impression is of a small community, focused on the city of Jerusalem and its cult. These features are strikingly similar to those portrayed in the narratives of Ezra and Nehemiah (cf. H. C. M. Vogt, *Studie zur nachexilischen Gemeinde in Esra-Nehemia* [1966]), but appear quite out of place before the Exile.

(5) Quotations. These will be dealt with below (B.2) as a separate problem of composition. It is sufficient to say here that the evidence can be most naturally explained if Joel features among the later written prophets.

(6) References to Other Peoples. A *terminus ad quem* of 345 B.C. seems to be demanded by the manner in which Sidon is introduced in 3:4 (cf. B.1.a [5] above) and fits with the implication of 3:6 that the Greek expansion has not yet begun.

d. Conclusions. A date somewhere between 515 and 345 B.C. is the most likely on the basis of the evidence presented above, and this view presents fewer difficulties to the general outlook of the prophet as concerns both the cult and eschatology. It is difficult to specify further with any degree of certainty; Myers's argument from the decline of the Sabeans (3:8) at the end of the 6th cent. is questionable, since it is now known that the Sabean kingdom continued to flourish long after (cf. W. F. Albright, *BASOR,* 129 [Feb. 1953], 20-24; A. Jamme, *Sabaean Inscriptions from Maḥram Bilqîs [Mârib]* [1962]; A. K. Irvine, "The Arabs and Ethiopians," in D. J. Wiseman, ed., *Peoples of OT Times* [1973], p. 300). The evidence of the quotations perhaps brings us toward the latter part of the specified period, but the evidence on that basis alone is inconclusive in the final analysis.

2. Quotations. The book of Joel contains a striking number of verbal parallels with the writings of other prophets. The main examples are:

(1) 1:15=Ezk. 30:2f.; Isa. 13:6; Zeph. 1:7
(2) 2:2=Zeph. 1:14f.
(3) 2:3 reverses Isa. 51:3; Ezk. 36:35
(4) 2:6=Nah. 2:10
(5) 2:17=Ps. 79:10
(6) 2:27=Ezk. 36:11 (and frequently); Isa. 45:5f., 18
(7) 2:28=Ezk. 39:29
(8) 2:31=Mal. 4:5 (MT 3:23)
(9) 2:32=Ob. 17
(10) 3:4=Ob. 15
(11) 3:10 reverses Isa. 2:4; Mic. 4:3
(12) 3:16=Am. 1:2; Isa. 13:13
(13) 3:17=Ezk. 36:11
(14) 3:18=Am. 9:13

Many briefer parallels and allusions are also to be found.

Kapelrud in particular has argued that all this may be explained as a reflection of widely known cultic phraseology. Joel did not borrow directly from other prophets; all drew on a common stream of tradition. While this may well be so in some cases (e.g., 5), it does not, however, satisfy all the evidence. Kapelrud cannot account for the frequency of occurrence in Joel alone as opposed, for instance, to Nahum, Habakkuk, or Malachi, all of whom seem to have had equally close associations with the cult. Further, some of the arguments listed immediately below are also an embarrassment to his position.

Proponents of an early date for Joel are obliged to argue that it is from Joel that the other prophets quote. For the following reasons (cf. Gray), however, it seems more likely that it is Joel who is dependent: (a) at no. 9, Joel adds the words "as the Lord has said," indicating that it is a quotation; (b) some of the phrases (e.g., 6 and 13) are very characteristic of the prophets cited, but not of Joel; (c) several of the citations (e.g., 2, 4, 6) seem better suited to the wider context of the passages in the other prophets than in Joel; (d) sometimes Joel combines phrases from two or more other passages (e.g., 1, 3, 6, 12); to reverse the dependence in these cases would be much more unlikely; (e) twice (3, 11), Joel reverses sayings elsewhere. This is more probably the feature of a single writer than the result of coincidence in two other independent ones.

3. Unity. In a thesis of 1872, M. Vernes (*Le peuple d'Israël et ses espérances,* pp. 46-54) first challenged the unity of the book of Joel on the basis that the Day of the Lord in the first part was contemporary with the prophet, but future in the second part. A number of scholars, notably Duhm, Bewer, and Robinson, have adopted a comparable position. Duhm, e.g., argued that the apocalyptic sections were added to an original oracle about a locust plague in 1:1–2:17, though 1:15; 2:1b-2a, 11b also have to be attributed to the later writer. More recently, O. Plöger (pp. 96-105) has suggested later expansion as part of his influential theory on the early history of apocalyptic thought. He argues that 1:1–2:27 contains a record of Joel's oral preaching, ch. 3 a supplement to guarantee the eschatological interpretation of the Day of the Lord, and 2:28-32 a later, sectarian addition to apply the promises to a narrower group within Israel.

Nearly all modern commentators now accept the unity of the work, however, preferring to study in more detail the relationships between the two parts of the book. The Day of the Lord is a significant element in the first half (note especially its use as an *inclusio* in 2:1, 11), and this leads naturally to its development in the second part, for which the locust plague was a harbinger. Moreover, several characteristic features of Joel's style are evident in both parts: quotations from other prophetic books are distributed equally in both, and there are a number of verbal links between the two as well, e.g., 1:14 and 3:9; 1:15, 2:1f., and 3:14; 2:1b and 2:31b; 2:10a and 3:16a; 2:10b and 3:15; 2:11a and 3:16a; 2:11b and 2:31b, etc. (cf. Wolff, p. 7). Progress along this line shows itself to be exegetically more fruitful, and has led to a deeper appreciation of the structure of the book as a whole.

4. Composition and Structure. In recent years substantial attempts to explain the structure of the book on the presupposition of its unity include Bourke, Wolff, and Allen. The latter two argue for the main division at 2:18, and thus are able to balance the description of the plague and the lament of the first part with the change of fortune and promises of the second.

Wolff's analysis is simple, and restricts itself to a general outline. He finds the natural disaster of ch. 1 answered by the restoration described in 2:17-27; the eschatological disaster (as he interprets it) of 2:1-11 is answered in the final reversal of Israel's destiny promised in ch. 3, while the demand for repentance in 2:12-17 is matched by the oracle concerning the outpouring of the Spirit and salvation in 2:28-32.

Whereas this is of value in pointing to a general balance between the two sections of the book, it rests in part on an eschatological interpretation of 2:1-11 that not all scholars would accept. An alternative (and much more elaborate) series of correspondences is advanced by Allen (pp. 39-42). His theory incorporates detail of vocabulary parallels and other phenomena running throughout his commentary which cannot be dealt with here, but his overall analysis of parallel strophes within the various poetic units may be set out in tabular form as follows:

Part I. 1:2–2:17

A. 1:2-20	parallel with	B. 2:1-17
1. 1:2-12		1. 2:1-11
2-4		1f.
5-7		3-5
8-10		6-9
11f.		11f.
2. 1:13-20		2. 2:12-17
13f.		12-14
15-18		15f.
19f.		17

Part II. 2:18–3:21

A. 2:18-32	parallel with	B. 3:1-21
1. 2:18-27		1. 3:1-12
18-20		1-3
21-23		4-8
24-27		9-12
2. 2:28-32		2. 3:13-21
28f.		13f.
30f.		15-17
32		18-21

Like Wolff, Allen argues in addition that "the second half of the book takes up and reverses the destruction and deprivation characteristic of the laments of the first half," and he concludes: "the whole composition has been constructed as an intricate literary mosaic with remarkable skill and care" (p. 42).

Not all will agree with Allen's analysis in every detail, and some of the correspondences he finds are less striking than others. Nevertheless, it is hard to escape the impression that the various sections of the book are composed with conscious reference to the others in order to present a unified message. This factor, coupled with what has already been noted about citations from other prophets and phraseological repetition within the book, provides a strong indication that, though the prophet's ministry doubtless began in a concrete historical situation, the book as we now have it is the product of intensive literary activity. There is no reason to doubt that this was undertaken by the prophet himself.

C. Problems of Interpretation. In the light of what has been established about the nature and composition of the book, a few questions relating to its interpretation may finally be briefly treated.

1. The Locusts and the Day of the Lord. Since early times, there have been differences of opinion concerning the correct interpretation of the locusts in chs. 1–2. For instance, an allegorical-historical interpretation, in which the plague is seen as an allegory for historical human invaders, is found already in the Targum and early Christian writers. A. Merx (1877) went further, arguing that they represented the supernatural creatures of an apocalyptically described eschatological invasion. But in the present century, nearly all commentators have understood at least ch. 1 as a description of a literal plague of locusts. The accuracy of Joel's portrayal in this regard has been noted by some (cf. Thompson, 1955), and certainly the effects he lists, as well as the corresponding restoration in 2:18-27, suit this interpretation best.

The interpretation of 2:1-11 is less certain. Wolff, for instance, has drawn renewed attention to the differences between this section and ch. 1. It is certainly true that the description switches to the invaders themselves. The language becomes highly colorful, God's initiative in the affair is heightened, and the description is more closely related to the Day of the Lord (2:1, 11; but cf. 1:15). Nevertheless, these elements need not rule out a literal understanding — the invaders are compared to an attacking army, which would seem to suggest that they are not one in fact; 2:18 implies that the invasion is now past; and further elements of the description (especially 2:7-9) are still admirably suited to locusts, while none is incompatible with it. It is probably best, therefore, to understand our text in its final form as descriptive writing designed to draw warnings concerning the approach of the eschatological Day of the Lord from the impressions of this historical plague. Israel's repentance, presupposed by 2:18, means that judgment is averted, while in the future (2:28 — "afterward" may involve quite a long gap in view of 1:3) "all who call on the name of the Lord" (2:32) will similarly be kept safe. But the Day, prefigured in the plague, will come (note how the language of 1:15 and 2:1 is echoed in 3:14), bringing vindication to God's people, and judgment to those who have oppressed them.

2. The Cult. It is evident that Joel's outlook is very much dominated by a commitment to the postexilic cult of Jerusalem. He sees one of the major effects of the locusts to be the cessation of regular offerings; the response he demands is a solemn cultic assembly for penitential rites (1:13f.; 2:12-17); the message of assurance which comes to him (2:18-27) seems to have taken the form of an oracle of salvation familiar in the liturgy and imitated on occasions by the prophets (cf. C. Westermann, *Isaiah 40-66* [Eng. tr., *OTL,* 1966], pp. 11-13); and many of his hopes for the future are expressed in cultic terms familiar in particular from Ezekiel (e.g., 2:28f.; 3:16-18).

Yet Joel shows himself more than just a child of his time in this emphasis. At the heart of his exhortation lies a call to repentance (2:12-14), which, though taking cultic expression, is explicitly emphasized as requiring a moral change of will if it is to be effective ("rend your hearts and not your garments"), and at the same time is concerned to defend the ultimate freedom of God from cultic coercion ("Who knows whether he will not turn. . . ?"). Moreover, it is noteworthy that much of the concern for ritual holiness and detailed cultic prescription, familiar, e.g., in Ezekiel and Malachi, is here lacking. If the prophet was to communicate effectively, he had to speak through the forms that had meaning for his hearers, and in this he evidently succeeded; at the same time, he was unable to hide that he regarded these ultimately as forms only, the validity of which lay entirely in the essential message they were required to convey.

3. NT References. The book of Joel seems to have had a considerable impact on the preaching of Jesus and His first followers. The parable of the sheep and the goats (Mt. 25:31-46) probably bases its imagery in part on the trial of the nations in Joel 3; and C. H. Dodd, *According to the Scriptures* (1952), pp. 46-48 and 62-64, argued that Joel 2:28-32 and chs. 2–3 were parts of prophetic testimonies used more widely in the early Church.

Most interest centers on 2:28-32, which in its context in Joel makes promises of the Spirit and salvation to those in "Mount Zion and in Jerusalem." This passage is quoted in Acts 2:17-21, Peter claiming fulfillment of the prophecy in the events of Pentecost. Though the citation appears to be cut off in such a way as to open the promise to all without distinction, his continuation ("Men of Israel," 2:22), his allusion to Joel 2:32b in Acts 2:39, and the fact that his audience is presented as Jews from Jerusalem and the dispersion alone (2:5), suggest that at this stage the wider implications of the prophecy were not yet appreciated. A move toward a broader outlook, however, is evident in that the geographical limitation of Joel 2:32 gives way to the address to Jews from "every nation under heaven" (Acts 2:5). With Paul this progression is completed; in Rom. 10:12f. he applies Joel 2:32 to Jew and Greek with "no distinction." The Israel to whom Joel's words now apply is limited neither geographically nor ethnically, but rather, as he says, "the same Lord is Lord of all and bestows his riches upon all who call upon him."

***Bibliography.**–Comms.:* K. A. Credner (1831); J. Wellhausen (3rd ed. 1898); K. Marti (*Kurzer Hand-Commentar zum AT,* 1904); A. van Hoonacker (*EtB,* 1908); J. A. Bewer (*ICC,* 1912); S. R. Driver (*CBG,* 1915); W. Nowack (*Kurzer Hand-Commentar zum AT,* 3rd ed. 1922); E. Sellin (*KAT,* 3rd ed. 1930); J. A. Thompson (*IB,* 1956); A. Weiser (*ATD,* 7th ed. 1979); M. Bič (1960); H. W. Wolff (*BKAT,* 1963; Eng. tr., *Hermeneia,* 1977); T. H. Robinson (*HAT,* 3rd ed. 1964); C. A. Keller (*Comm. de l'AT,* 1965); W. Rudolph (*KAT,* 1971); L. C. Allen (*NICOT,* 1976).

Monographs: A. Merx, *Die Prophetie des Joel und ihre Ausleger von den ältesten Zeiten bis zu den Reformatoren* (1879); A. S. Kapelrud, *Joel Studies* (1948); T. Chary, *Les prophètes et le culte à partir de l'exil* (1955); O. Plöger, *Theocracy and Eschatology* (Eng. tr. 1968); G. W. Ahlström, *Joel and the Temple Cult of Jerusalem* (*SVT,* 21, 1971).

Articles: G. B. Gray, *Expos.,* 8 (1893), 208-225; B. Duhm, *ZAW,* 31 (1911), 184-88; O. R. Sellers, *AJSL,* 52 (1935), 81-85; J. A. Thompson, *JNES,* 14 (1955), 52-55; M. Treves, *VT,* 7 (1957), 149-156; J. Bourke, *RB,* 66 (1959), 5-31, 191-212; E. Kutsch, *Theologische Zeitschrift,* 18 (1962), 81-94; J. M. Myers, *ZAW,* 74 (1962), 177-195; H.-P. Müller, *Theologia Viatorum,* 10 (1965/66), 231-252; F. R. Stephenson, *VT,* 19 (1969), 224-29; B. Reicke, "Joel und seine Zeit," in H. J. Stoebe, ed., *Wort—Gebot—Glaube. Walther Eichrodt zum 80. Geburtstag* (1970), pp. 133-141; J. A. Thompson, "The Date of Joel," in H. N. Bream, *et al.,* eds., *A Light unto My Path: OT Studies in Honor of Jacob M. Myers* (1974), pp. 453-464; "The Use of Repetition in the Prophecy of Joel," in M. Black and W. A. Smalley, eds., *On Language, Culture, and Religion: In Honor of Eugene A. Nida* (1974), pp. 101-110.
H. G. M. WILLIAMSON

JOELAH jō-ē'lə [Heb. *yôʿē'lâ*]. A son of Jeroham of Gedor, one of David's recruits at Ziklag (1 Ch. 12:7 [MT 8]).

JOEZER jō-ē'zər [Heb. *yôʿezer*–'Yahweh is help']. One of David's Benjaminite recruits at Ziklag, though perhaps a Judean (1 Ch. 12:6 [MT 7]).

JOGBEHAH jog'bə-hə [Heb. *yogb^{e}hâ*]. A city in Gilead assigned to Gad and fortified by that tribe (Nu. 32:35). It lay on the line along which Gideon chased the Midianites (Jgs. 8:11), and the indication there leaves no doubt that it is represented today by Ajbeihât. The name attaches to three groups of ruins which date from Roman times. The position is about 11 km. (7 mi.) NW of ʿAmmân, and about midway between that city and the town of es-Salṭ. It stands 1057 m. (3468 ft.) above the level of the Mediterranean.

JOGLI jog'lī [Heb. *yoglî*]. Father of Bukki, a Danite chief (Nu. 34:22).

JOHA jō'ə [Heb. *yôḥā'*].

1. A Benjaminite (1 Ch. 8:16).

2. One of David's mighty men (1 Ch. 11:45).

JOHANAN jō-ha'nən [Heb. *yôḥānān*–'Yahweh has been gracious'; Gk. *Iōanan*]; AV Apoc. JOHANNES.

1. Son of Kareah, and one of "the captains of the forces in the open country" (i.e., probably guerilla bands), who allied with Gedaliah governor of Judah after the fall of Jerusalem in 586 B.C. (2 K. 25:23; Jer. 40:7–43:7). He warned Gedaliah of the plot of Ishmael ben Nethaniah, who was incited by the Ammonite king Baalis, to murder the governor; but the latter refused to believe him nor would he grant Johanan permission to slay Ishmael (40:8-16). After Ishmael had murdered Gedaliah and also seventy northern pilgrims Johanan went in pursuit. He was joined by the unwilling followers of Ishmael, but the murderer escaped. Thereupon Johanan settled at Geruth Chimham near Bethlehem (ch. 41). As Ishmael's plan was to take the remnant to the land of Ammon, so that of Johanan and his fellow-chiefs was to go to Egypt. They consulted the divine oracle through Jeremiah, and received the answer that they should remain in Judah (ch. 42). But the prophet was accused of giving false counsel and of being influenced by Baruch. The chiefs then resolved to go to Egypt, and forced Jeremiah and Baruch to accompany them (ch. 43).

2. The eldest son of King Josiah (1 Ch. 3:15), apparently = Jehoahaz (2 K. 23:30-33). *See* JEHOAHAZ **3.**

3. Son of Elioenai, and a Davidic postexilic prince (1 Ch. 3:24).

4. Father of the Azariah who was priest in Solomon's time (1 Ch. 6:9f. [MT 5:35f.]).

5. A Benjaminite recruit of David at Ziklag, but perhaps a Judean (1 Ch. 12:4 [MT 5]).

6. A Gadite recruit of David at Ziklag (1 Ch. 12:12 [MT 13]).

7. The MT has Jehohanan, an Ephraimite chief (2 Ch. 28:12).

8. A returned exile (Ezr. 8:12) = Joannes (1 Esd. 8:38; AV Johannes; NEB Joannes).

9. A postexilic high priest descended from the high priest Eliashib (Neh. 12:22f.) and probably the person with whom Ezra consorted (Ezr. 10:6). He was a younger contemporary of Nehemiah, and was called Jonathan in Neh. 12:11, this perhaps being a transcriptional error.

D. F. ROBERTS

JOHANNES jō-han'əz. An AV variant of Gk. *Iōanēs* (1 Esd. 8:38; *see* JOHANAN **8**) and Gk. *Iōnnēs* (1 Esd. 9:29; *see* JEHOHANAN **4**).

JOHANNINE THEOLOGY.

I. Introduction
II. Theme of Johannine Theology
III. Revelation of God in Jesus
 A. Glory
 B. Grace and Love
 C. Truth
 D. Signs and Works
 E. Witnesses
IV. Person of Jesus
 A. Messiah
 B. Son of Man
 C. Son of God
 D. Logos
 E. God
V. The World and Sin
VI. Savior of the World
VII. Entry to Eternal Life
VIII. Characteristics of Eternal Life
 A. Faith, Perseverance, and Assurance
 B. Knowledge
 C. Union with God
 D. Holy Spirit
 E. Obedience and Love
IX. Life in the Church
X. Eschatology

I. Introduction.–It is assumed from the outset that such an entity as Johannine theology exists and deserves study. For it could conceivably be the case that a Johannine theology is as illusory a concept as a "theology of the Catholic Epistles" is. There must be a certain unity within the Johannine writings that expresses itself in a common theology.

The five Johannine writings in the NT are generally agreed to have a common background and origin (E. Stauffer, *NT Theology* [1955], pp. 39-43; Barrett, pp. 49-52, 113f.). A common theological outlook also characterizes these five books, marking them off as a distinctive group within the NT, so that at first sight it is tempting to use them all as the source for Johannine theology. One book, however, Revelation, stands on its own, whether or not identity of authorship for it and the other writings in the Johannine corpus is assumed; it is of a distinct literary genre and pursues a sufficiently individualistic course to make it wiser for us not to use it as a theological source on a level with the other four writings. The remaining four writings, two of which are of comparatively minor theological importance due to their brevity, have a sufficiently close bond among them to make discussion of their theology a real and profitable possibility. Elsewhere reasons have been offered for assuming the common authorship of the Gospel and Epistles (*see* JOHN, EPISTLES OF), and the following exposition will attempt to demonstrate that they expound a unified theology, and that, with all their evidence of variety and development, they reflect a single theological outlook.

We assume that it is the Gospel and Epistles in their present form that are the objects of study. Theories of rearrangement and redaction, especially of the Gospel, have not commended themselves to many scholars (esp. British), and the theology of the Gospel can be satisfactorily interpreted without recourse to such theories (Barrett, *passim*; Dodd, *passim*). Theories that the author used and adapted sources reflecting a theology different from his own are too hypothetical to be made the basis of secure argument.

Our interest here and proper subject is the theology of the author of the literature and not that of Jesus Himself, whose words the author purports to record in the Gospel. The question as to how far the Gospel may be used as a source for the teaching of the earthly Jesus is not our present concern; it belongs to a study of the historical Jesus. But it may be taken for granted that what the author records as the teaching of Jesus can be used without scruple as a source for his own teaching. In our opinion the Fourth Gospel is based on reliable traditions of the words of Jesus, but John has made these words his own and wishes us to understand that he agrees with the teaching he attributes to his Master. His teaching is a true understanding of the words of Jesus and a legitimate development from them (cf. Hunter, p. 129).

A further preliminary concern is with the kind of background against which Johannine theology must be understood. Despite much detailed study (see esp. Dodd, pp. 3-130) there is as yet no unanimity concerning the results of this exploration, although certain facts are tolerably clear.

It is safe to say that a purely Greek approach is now ruled out (see Schnackenburg, *Gospel,* I, 119-152), and that the background of John is basically Hebraic and Christian. The sources of non-Christian influence upon John will be found to lie principally in the OT (F.-M. Braun, II) and in the Judaism of his day. On the Palestinian side the DSS provide the most recent addition to a rich range of background material which includes the rabbinic writings (see SB; A. Schlatter, *Der Evangelist Johannes* [1930]) and the apocalyptic literature (H. Odeberg, *The Fourth Gospel* [1929]); but opinions differ about the closeness of the parallels they present (F.-M. Braun, *RB,* 62 [1955], 5-44; Schnackenburg, *Gospel,* I, 120 n. 9, 128-135). On the Hellenistic side the writings of Philo show certain conceptual similarities, although the philosophical tone of Philo is far removed from the religious ethos of John (see Dodd, pp. 54-73; Feine, pp. 327-337). Increasing attention is being paid to the influence of the wisdom literature (Brown, I, cxxii-cxxv).

There is much dispute over the possibility of oriental influences, particularly of Gnosticism (W. G. Kümmel, *Intro. to the NT* [rev. ed., Eng. tr. 1975], pp. 217-228).

That a species of Gnosticism existed in the 1st cent. (in a rudimentary form) and that John was well aware of it are facts demonstrated by the polemic in his Epistles. But this very polemic speaks against the likelihood that John's thought was fundamentally based on Gnosticism (as advocated with varied emphasis by Bultmann, Käsemann, and L. Schottroff, *Der Glaubende und die feindliche Welt* [1971]), although he may have made some use of its concepts. It remains a problem, however, which documents may legitimately be used to reconstruct Gnostic thought in the 1st century. Attention has been drawn to the *Corpus Hermeticum* (Dodd, pp. 10-53; on the other side, G. D. Kilpatrick, "Religious Background of the Fourth Gospel," in F. L. Cross, ed., *Studies in the Fourth Gospel* [1957], pp. 36-44), to the Odes of Solomon (Bultmann, *Gospel*) and to the Mandean writings (Bultmann, *ZNW*, 24 [1925], 100-146; for a powerful criticism by E. Percy and Bultmann's reply, see *Orientalische Literaturzeitung*, 43 [1940], cols. 150-175). These documents (apart from one or two possible exceptions) are all later in date than the Johannine literature, and both the Odes and the Mandean writings are obviously dependent on Christian writings, so that they can be used only with the greatest caution. The same caveat must be issued with regard to recent attempts to find pre-Christian Gnosticism in the Nag Hammadi texts (L. Schottroff). In any case, the Gnostic concepts which John is supposed to have utilized are often so much altered and demythologized (as Bultmann himself admits) that it is worth asking whether John really used them at all, and whether other influences are not adequate to account for his language.

In the end, the most significant influence upon John remains that of the teaching of Jesus and of early Christianity. The theological statements made by John can be abundantly paralleled by other NT sources. What John expresses is the fundamental teaching of the early Church as molded by his own profound understanding and experience to meet the needs of his readers. There is room for difference of opinion as to his precise place in early Christian theology. His writings are not so much the coping stone of NT theology, erected on the foundation of the Pauline Epistles and the Synoptic Gospels (Scott, pp. 29-53), as an independent growth parallel to other developments in the same period (Bultmann, *Theology*, II, 2). John is probably independent of the written Synoptic Gospels, and his theology fits into the Palestinian milieu attested in the DSS.

The conclusions reached in the preceding paragraphs affect our understanding of what John was trying to do in his writings. It is impossible here to list in any detail the variety of modern interpretations of the general character of Johannine theology. Much recent thought is influenced positively or negatively by Bultmann, who holds that John made use of Gnostic language to present an existential message concerning the Revealer who reveals solely that He is the Revealer (*Theology*, II, 66). His deeds are empty symbols of a timeless message that calls people to "eschatological existence." Bultmann's pupil Käsemann argues somewhat differently; Jesus is viewed as a glorious divine being manifested in the earthly sphere, and the Johannine church that accepted this view was in fact heretical in outlook. A much more traditional interpretation from the fairly orthodox (but critical) Roman Catholic perspective is given by Brown and Schnackenburg. The influential British scholar C. H. Dodd has argued that John presents a message based on early tradition about Jesus but expressed in a manner intelligible to Hellenistic readers.

In the present article it is impossible to develop and justify at length a conservative view of John over against these various interpretations. (Such an attempt has been made by K. Haacker, who argues that John presents Jesus as the historical Founder of Christianity, who establishes the Church and appoints its way of life, and who is divinely authenticated for this task by His heavenly origin.) The most that can be done is to outline the key themes in Johannine theology and to show that they do not represent a deviation from primitive Christianity in the directions of Gnosticism, existentialism, or Hellenism.

II. Theme of Johannine Theology.–Both the Gospel and 1 John begin with a prologue, which sets the theme for Johannine theology. According to Jn. 1:1-18 the Gospel is about the Logos or Word of God, who from the beginning was with God and was Himself God. He created the universe, and through receiving Him, the only source of light and life, people receive the right to become children of God. This fact presupposes that people are actually in darkness, and John states that the light was not welcome to them, although there were some who believed and received the light.

It is difficult to be certain about the time and character of the manifestation of the light described in Jn. 1:1-13. From 1:14 onward it is clear that the Logos is a person who becomes incarnate in Jesus Christ, and that He is the theme of the book. The earlier verses of the chapter can then be regarded as an accurate summary of what took place in the life of Jesus, but it is also possible that they refer to the similar results of earlier manifestations of the light.

Although the subject of the Fourth Gospel is thus Jesus, the Word made flesh and the true light of humanity, this does not mean that the revelation of God came through Him alone. Two contrasts are drawn. The first is with John the Baptist, who appears in the role of a witness to the light. With him may be linked the disciples, who believe in Jesus and bear witness that they have seen His glory; they are witnesses to the Word in order that others too may believe. The second contrast is with the revelation of the law through Moses, and, although it will be shown later that Moses is also a witness to Jesus (Jn. 5:39, 46), the point emphasized here is that the law by itself is powerless to give life; grace and truth come only through Jesus, and in Him alone is the glory of His Father to be seen.

When we now glance back over this prologue, we see that most of the fundamental ideas of the Gospel are unfolded in it. It resembles the opening theme of a symphony. The rest of the Gospel is an elucidation and defense of what has been stated here. There will certainly be new ideas presented — e.g., the doctrine of the Spirit — but here we have Johannine theology in miniature. It is a theology that is centered on Jesus Christ and the eternal life He bestows on people. Confirmation of this is provided by comparison with 1 Jn. 1:1-4 and with the careful statements of purpose in Jn. 20:31 and 1 Jn. 5:13.

We can therefore say that the theology of John is a Christology, with which is clearly linked a soteriology. It is not primarily an anthropology (in effect the view of Bultmann), nor an ecclesiology (A. Corell, *Consummatum Est* [Eng. tr. 1958]), nor even an eschatology (Barrett) except insofar as this means that its subject is the eschatological person, Jesus. Our task, therefore, must be to "set forth the Meaning which the author of the Gospel has himself heard and seen in the concrete, historical life and death of Jesus of Nazareth, in His separate actions and in His audible words" (Hoskyns, p. 132).

III. Revelation of God in Jesus.–A basic contrast has often been drawn between the theology of Paul and that of John, in some such words as those of A. M. Hunter:

"Certainly Paul is more at home in the category of reconciliation, as John is in that of revelation" (p. 131). As Hunter himself goes on to affirm, such generalizations can be misleading if pressed too far (cf. J. Denney, *Death of Christ* [1951], pp. 139-148), but there is little doubt that the word "revelation" most adequately characterizes Johannine theology. Eternal life, which is for John the *summum bonum,* is defined as knowing God through Jesus Christ whom He has sent (Jn. 17:3). The Gospel is, therefore, a manifestation of the source of life (1 Jn. 1:2; 3:5, 8; 4:9) to mankind (Jn. 1:31; 2:11; 7:4; cf. 21:1, 14). It is thus a saving revelation, and it reveals God and His powerful name to those who are ignorant (Jn. 1:18; 9:3; 17:6).

The content of this revelation of God through Jesus Christ may be summed up in the words of John 1:14 as glory, grace, and truth.

A. Glory. Glory (*TDNT,* II, *s.v.* δόξα [Kittel, von Rad]; Bultmann, *Gospel,* p. 67 n. 2; Dodd, pp. 206-208) is the visible manifestation of the majesty and splendor of God. The purpose of Jesus was to reveal the glory of the Father (Jn. 11:4, 40), so that people would worship Him (i.e., give Him the glory which is His due, Jn. 9:24; 13:31f.; 15:8; 17:4; 21:19) instead of seeking glory from one another (5:41, 44; 8:50, 54; 12:43). At the same time Jesus Himself possessed glory; He shared the glory of His Father before His incarnation (17:5, 24; cf. 12:41), and was to resume it after His return to heaven (17:24). During His earthly life His glory was revealed (1:14; 2:11), and after His resurrection the Spirit continued to glorify Him (16:14). There is also a sense in which His disciples share in His glory (17:22).

It will be clear from these references that the word "glory" has a wide range of meaning in John, and that John's understanding of the manifestation of the majesty and splendor of God has two important characteristics. First, the splendor of divinity is to be seen — by those who have eyes to see it — in the love of God revealed in Jesus. Second, the divine glory is seen in Jesus when He seeks not His own but the Father's glory in His life of service, and supremely in His sacrificial death. For John the humiliation of Jesus is the supreme moment of His earthly glorification (7:39; 12:16, 23; 13:31f.; 17:1); He is lifted up in order to die (3:14; 8:28; 12:32, 34; W. Thüsing; Schnackenburg, *Gospel,* II, 398-410).

From this point of view we obtain the most satisfactory division of the Gospel into its various parts. In chs. 1–12 Jesus manifests His glory to the world; in chs. 13–17 He manifests His glory to the disciples; and in chs. 18–21 His glory is fully revealed at the cross.

B. Grace and Love. The revelation of Jesus to mankind is also one of grace (Jn. 1:14). Although the actual word is found only in this context (1:14-17; cf. 2 Jn. 3), the concept rules in the thought of John. Divine, unmerited favor is meant. The idea is developed in terms of love (*TDNT,* I, *s.v.* ἀγαπάω [Stauffer], esp. pp. 52f.; Schnackenburg, *Johannesbriefe,* pp. 231-39; C. Spicq, *Agapé dans le NT,* III [1959]).

The character of God is love (1 Jn. 4:8, 16). This fact is known to mankind from the revelation which has taken place in Jesus; His self-giving is the supreme testimony to both the fact and the character of divine love (1 Jn. 4:9). We may explore the meaning of this love in three directions.

First, love is the essential relationship between the Father and the Son; the Father loves the Son (Jn. 3:35; 5:20; 17:23-26) and the Son loves the Father (14:31).

Second, this love is shown by God to humanity. The greatest affirmation of John is that God so loved the world that He gave His Son (Jn. 3:16). This is a text of crucial importance because elsewhere in John it might appear that the love of God is solely for the disciples of Jesus; the truth is that God loves the world, but only those who respond to His love enjoy the fruits of it and enter into a loving relationship with Him (Schnackenburg, *Johannesbriefe,* p. 233). Both the Father and the Son love the disciples (13:1; 14:21, 23; 15:9-15; 1 Jn. 3:1; 4:9f., 16), and the disciples are to respond to that love by loving God (1 Jn. 2:5; 4:20f.) and Jesus (Jn. 14:15, 21; 21:15-17). Such love for God is expressed in the same way as it was by Jesus, namely, by keeping the commandments of God.

Third, the kind of love God has for His Son and for mankind is to be shown by people toward each other. This attitude is in fact the reverse of that which people naturally have for each other. Those who are still in the darkness hate not only God and His Son (Jn. 7:7; 8:42; 15:23-25) but also each other (1 Jn. 3:10-15). Believers who have known the love of God for themselves must love each other (e.g., Jn. 13:34f.; 1 Jn. 3:11; cf. Schnackenburg, *Johannesbriefe,* pp. 117-121). In this way the love of God continues to be revealed to the world.

C. Truth. The third characteristic of the revelation of God in Jesus is truth (*TDNT,* I, *s.v.* ἀλήθεια [Bultmann]; Dodd, pp. 170-78; I. de la Potterie, *La Vérité dans St. Jean* [1977]; S. Aalen, "'Truth,' a Key Word in St. John's Gospel," *SE,* II [1964], 3-24; Schnackenburg, *Gospel,* II, 225-237). The OT and Jewish background to this word links it to God's trustworthiness and righteousness and also to His wisdom. Thus the word refers to heavenly reality. For John the world to which Jesus came was a world that had lost contact with God and was characterized by error and lies (Jn. 8:44). Jesus brought to it a revelation of the true God (7:28). He bore witness to the truth and was Himself the truth (18:37; 14:6), and His activity was continued by the Spirit of truth (14:17). Thus the message of Jesus and of His followers can be called simply "the truth" (8:32, 40; 17:17; 2 Jn. 1f.). Through knowledge of it people are able to live and worship truly (Jn. 3:21; 4:23; 2 Jn. 4; 3 Jn. 3f.).

D. Signs and Works. John defines two ways in which this revelation is brought to mankind. The first of these is by means of the signs and works wrought by Jesus (*TDNT,* VII, *s.v.* σημεῖον [Rengstorf], esp. pp. 243-257; Dodd, pp. 141-43; Barrett, pp. 62-65; Schnackenburg, *Gospel,* I, 515-528; Wilkens; Brown, I, 525-532). The ministry of Jesus consisted of a series of signs (Jn. 2:11; 4:54; 20:30) and mighty works (6:30; 17:4). These were not meant merely to provide evidence of a miraculous, supernatural power (4:48); Jesus is not the wonder-working "divine man" of Hellenism (Bultmann, *Gospel,* p. 102 n. 1, makes too much of this, although he admits that the motif is not of decisive importance). Rather, the mighty works were meant to point beyond themselves to the character of Jesus as the Son of God and Savior of the world (Jn. 3:2; 6:14; 7:31; 9:16). They are not empty symbols, but themselves contain saving power and point to the saving significance of Jesus — as is often brought out in the accompanying discourses; their purpose was to lead people to faith (2:23; 12:37). Although faith ought to be possible apart from miraculous signs (20:29), Jesus did not refrain from signs, especially since through them the grace of God brought healing and salvation to men (9:3).

E. Witnesses. The second way in which the revelation comes to mankind is by means of witnesses (*TDNT,* IV, *s.v.* μάρτυς [Strathmann], esp. pp. 495-99). To witness is to give evidence of what one has seen and heard of a person in order to lead other people to belief in him. Jesus bore witness to the truth (Jn. 18:27), and could even say that He bore witness to Himself (8:13f., 18; there is no contradiction here with Jn. 5:31, since the kind of witness

Jesus refuses to give is that which would be for His own glory; cf. Bultmann, *Gospel*, p. 279). By their character His works bore witness to who He was (5:36; 10:25). Although He came to reveal the Father, it was also possible for the Father to bear witness to His Son (5:37; 8:18; 1 Jn. 5:9-11), so that those who claimed to know God must go on to recognize His Son. Even before Jesus appeared, testimony had been given to Him in the Scriptures (Jn. 5:39) and by John the Baptist (1:7-34; 3:26-30; 5:33), and during His ministry a variety of people substantiated His claims (4:39; 12:17; 19:35; 21:24). After His glorification the Spirit continued to testify to Him both in and through His disciples (15:26f.; 1 Jn. 1:2; 4:14; 5:7f.). Thus the revelation in Jesus was attested and continues to be affirmed to mankind.

IV. Person of Jesus.–From the manner of the revelation we now turn to a consideration of the person in whom the revelation was embodied. Various titles given to Jesus require examination.

A. Messiah. We are moving on thoroughly Jewish ground when we examine the presentation in John of Jesus as the Messiah (Dodd, pp. 87-93, 228-240; Schnackenburg, "Die Messiasfrage im Johannesevangelium," in J. Blinzler, *et al., NT Aufsätze für J. Schmid* [1963], pp. 240-264). First-century longings for the coming of a deliverer are reflected when John the Baptist answers the questions of the Jews by affirming that he is not the Christ (Jn. 1:20; 3:28), and when the Samaritan woman says that she looks forward to the coming of the Messiah (4:25). Throughout the first half of the Gospel there occur statements reflecting common Jewish traditions about the coming of the Messiah (7:27, 41f.; 12:34); the great question in controversy with the Jews is whether Jesus is the Messiah (4:29; 7:26, 31, 41; 9:22; 10:24ff.). The purpose of the Fourth Gospel is to lead people to see that this is the case (20:31) and thus to reecho the confession of the first disciples (1:41; 4:29; 11:27).

Various facets of Jewish messianic expectation are fulfilled in Jesus. He is the coming One (Jn. 11:27; 12:13), an idea that receives a characteristic Johannine nuance (1:9; 3:31; Barrett, p. 330). He is called the Holy One of God (6:69), the Savior (4:42; 1 Jn. 4:14), and the Lamb of God (Jn. 1:29, 36; Rev. 5:6; etc.). The people wonder whether He is the promised prophet (Jn. 6:14; 7:40). He is also spoken of as the King of Israel (1:49; 12:13; 18:33-38; 19:3, 14-22), an idea which receives new definition in John; the former of these ideas (and possibly also the latter) may be connected with the expectation of a prophet like Moses (W. A. Meeks).

Despite the rarity of its use in the Synoptic Gospels, in John the title of Messiah is given to Jesus during His lifetime. This does not mean, however, that the so-called messianic secrecy of the Synoptics is given up: although Jesus is willing to confess His identity to the true seeker, He refuses to do so to the unbelieving Jews (Jn. 4:26; 10:24-26).

B. Son of Man. The most common self-designation of Jesus in the Synoptic Gospels is the expression "Son of man." There the usage is derived principally from Dnl. 7 and other OT sources (the question of a background in Jewish apocalyptic is still not wholly clear), and the title appears in three main contexts: (1) the hidden messiahship of Jesus, (2) the necessity of His suffering (since the Son of man is also the Servant of Yahweh), and (3) His functions as judge and ruler at the Parousia. The problem is whether the title has the same significance in John (see *TDNT*, VIII, *s.v.* ὁ υἱὸς τοῦ ἀνθρώπου (Colpe), esp. pp. 464-470; Dodd, pp. 241-49; Schulz, *Untersuchungen*; Cullmann, pp. 182-87; A. J. B. Higgins, *Jesus and the Son of Man* [1964], pp. 153-184; Schnackenburg, *Gospel*, I, 529-542; F. J. Moloney, *The Johannine Son of Man* [1976]).

Although the title is overshadowed in importance by that of Son of God, it occupies a prominent place in John's Gospel with thirteen occurrences. Passages may readily be found in which the title bears a meaning corresponding to the Synoptic usage (e.g., Jn. 3:14; 5:27; 12:34). There is, however, an emphasis on the heavenly origin of the Son of man (3:13; 6:62) that has led many scholars to question whether the title can be adequately understood against the Synoptic background.

According to Bultmann two ideas are present (*Gospel, passim*, esp. pp. 107, 149 n. 4, 634; *Theology*, II, 37). The first is derived from Gnosticism, in which the totality of preexistent souls comprise the Son of man or *Urmensch*, who fell out of the world of light into the darkness and whose redemption and exaltation is fulfilled in the redemption of the individual souls. John, however, "degnosticizes" the title and makes it refer to Jesus, who came down from heaven and must ascend thither; whether the title still has a corporate reference is uncertain. This means that Jesus is the Son of man in His earthly life, and the Son of man is not merely a figure expected in the future (as in the Synoptic Gospels, on Bultmann's evaluation of their teaching). As Son of man, Jesus must ascend and be exalted, and in the end those who have not recognized Him during His earthly sojourn will be confronted by Him as their judge — which is the second idea present in the Johannine use of the title and stands closest to the apocalyptic teaching found in the Synoptics. Consequently, Jesus does not speak of His resurrection but of His ascent or departure to the Father. In brief, "Jesus is the Son of man, not, as understood by Jewish and early Christian apocalyptic, as he who one day will come on the clouds of heaven, but in his earthly presence; for in this earthly presence in which he enjoys continual communion with the Father, he shows to faith the miracle of his *doxa*" (Bultmann, *Gospel*, p. 107).

This view that the Johannine Son of man is related to the *Urmensch* of oriental and Gnostic speculation is found in several writers. Dodd (pp. 241-49, cf. 31f., 41-43, 69-71, 109-112) gives the theory a more philosophical presentation. According to this view the idea used by John is that of a Being who is the archetype of the human race, the real man (cf. the Platonic Idea of Man), and the inclusive representative of ideal or redeemed humanity. This philosophical understanding of the title seems most unlikely in the general context of Johannine thought, but Dodd is on surer ground when he proceeds to draw the idea of the exaltation of the Son of man from a use of the Servant passages in Second Isaiah.

Barrett (pp. 60f., 302f.) also finds that John's teaching is in line with speculations about the primal or archetypal Man; he stresses that the Son of man is essentially the heavenly Man, the ontological mediator between God and humanity and the sole means of union between heaven and earth (Jn. 1:51; cf. 6:27, 53). Cullmann stresses the element of majesty which characterizes the Johannine references and regards this as a pointer to the use of the idea of the preexistent divine Heavenly Man.

We should probably be very skeptical about the degree of influence of *Urmensch* speculation upon John. It is admitted by Bultmann that the idea has been to a certain extent modified by John himself, and that the characteristic apocalyptic usage is not absent from John. (Schulz, *Stunde* [pp. 96-124], thinks that the Son-of-man theme in John is derived ultimately from late Jewish apocalyptic, although the tradition has undergone considerable reinterpretation before being incorporated in John.) In the present state of study on the Son of man in the Synoptic Gospels, one dare not be dogmatic; but there would appear to be good grounds for criticizing Bultmann's failure to recognize the authenticity of the nonapocalyptic sayings in the Synoptics (cf. I. H. Marshall, *NTS,* 12 [1965-66], 327-351; *EQ,* 42 [1970], 67-87), and, more especially, his failure to reckon with their possible influence (whether or not as authentic sayings of Jesus) upon John. Further, John's equating of the Messiah and the Son of man (Jn. 12:34) indicates that the two terms are to be understood alongside each other. The following must be kept in mind: (1) "Son of man" is a title of majesty in Dnl. 7 and the Synoptics; (2) the idea of a descent by the Son of man (Jn. 3:13; cf. 6:62) is probably to be traced in Dnl. 7 and behind Daniel in Ezekiel; (3) the exaltation of the Son of man (Jn. 3:14; 8:28; 12:23, 34; 13:31) is presented in terms of the Servant traditions and in the light of His resurrection; and (4) John characteristically emphasizes the present anticipations of eschatological expectation. These characteristics indicate that an adequate background for the Johannine teaching about the Son of man is possible without going far beyond the bounds of Hebraic and early Christian thought (cf. S. S. Smalley, *NTS,* 15 [1968/69], 278-301).

C. Son of God. There can be little doubt that the title of Son or Son of God is fundamental in John's Christology; it occurs from twenty-seven to twenty-nine times in the Gospel (the text is uncertain at Jn. 1:18, 34) and twenty-four times in the Epistles. A number of ideas are linked together in the concept (*TDNT,* VIII, *s.v.* υἱός [Schweizer, *et al.*], esp. pp. 385-388; Dodd, pp. 250-262; Cullmann, pp. 297-303; Schnackenburg, *Gospel,* II, 172-186).

First, the metaphysical or essential relationship between Jesus and His Father is indicated. So close is the link between them that to deny the Son is to deny the Father (1 Jn. 2:22f.; 2 Jn. 9), and Father and Son are named together in such a way that the conclusion is irresistible that they belong inseparably to each other (Jn. 1:18; 5:23; 1 Jn. 1:3; 5:20). The Son is plainly described as preexistent (Jn. 3:17; 11:27; 1 Jn. 3:8; 4:9f., 14; Schnackenburg, *Gospel,* I, 494-506), and His relationship to God is designated by the adjective "only" (RSV, NEB), which indicates the special regard in which He is held by His Father (Jn. 1:14, 18; 3:16, 18; 1 Jn. 4:9; cf. Barrett, p. 180; Bultmann, *Gospel,* pp. 71 n. 2, 81f.).

This leads to the second idea contained in the title, that of the nature of the relationship between Father and Son. The NT is not as interested in the origin of the Son as Arius was, but prefers to draw out the meaning of Sonship in terms of the relationship to which it gives rise, namely, mutual love between Father and Son (Jn. 3:35; 5:20), expressed on the Son's side by obedience to His Father (5:19; cf. 4:34; 5:30; 6:38; 7:16-18; 8:28).

Third, the Son shares the functions of the Father, especially as the judge and the bringer of life (Jn. 5:17-30; see Dodd, pp. 255-57; Schulz, *Untersuchungen,* pp. 124-142).

Fourth, the Son is the mediator between God and mankind. This office stems from His incarnation. He was sent by the Father into the world (Jn. 3:17; etc.) and was given by Him that the world might be saved (3:16). But even while in the world He remains in constant communion with the Father (1:18; 3:13; 8:29; 16:32; cf. W. H. Cadman, *The Opened Heaven* [1969]). Consequently, He is able to reveal the Father to people (1:18), He lays down His life for them, and He is the source of life for those who believe in Him.

In this way the title of Son of God may be said to have been partly molded on a prophetic model (Dodd, pp. 254f.), but above all it expresses the fact that Jesus is the Savior; "Son of God" had messianic associations both in Judaism and Hellenism (Bultmann, *Gospel,* p. 93 n. 1), and the titles "Son of God" and "Christ" tend to have the same meaning in 1 John (Schnackenburg, *Johannesbriefe,* p. 157). But above all for John, Jesus is the Savior because of His metaphysical relationship with God, expressed in His filial consciousness (Jn. 11:41; 12:27f.; 17:1; etc.); this is why John is so concerned to stress that Jesus truly is the Son of God in a real and lasting incarnation (1 John; 2 Jn. 7-11).

D. Logos. Although the title of Logos or Word occurs only in Jn. 1:1-18 and 1 Jn. 1:1-4 (where it is a title, despite RSV and NEB), the character of Jesus as the Logos is determinative throughout John (see II above), and it is not surprising that much attention has been devoted to the background and meaning of the term (*TDNT,* IV, *s.v.* λέγω κτλ. [Kittel, *et al.*], esp. pp. 124-136; Bultmann, *Gospel,* pp. 20-31; Hoskyns, pp. 154-163; Dodd, pp 27-41, 65-73, 75-86, 263-285; Cullmann, pp. 249-269; Manson, pp. 136-159; Brown, I, 519-524).

(1) In the OT the creation of the world is explicitly attributed to the Word of God (Ps. 33:6; cf. Gen. 1; Jn. 1:3). What God says comes to pass, so that His word can be regarded in a sense as His deed (Ps. 145:13). Elsewhere in the OT the Word is God's means of self-revelation to people, the vehicle of His promises and commands. There is no personification or even hypostatization of the word of God here, although the Semitic tendency to regard sayings (such as blessings and curses) as having an independent existence once spoken may have prepared the way for the latter possibility.

(2) Hoskyns (pp. 159-163) drew attention to the way that early Christian thought tended to equate the word proclaimed with Christ Himself: cf. Col. 3:16, "Let the *word* of Christ dwell in you richly," with the parallel in Eph. 3:17, "That *Christ* may dwell in your hearts [cf. Col. 3:15] through faith." "Word" became a technical term for the Christian gospel, and the content of that word was Jesus Himself. John draws the identification elsewhere. He quotes the affirmations of Jesus that He is the way (Jn. 14:6; cf. the use of "the Way" in Acts 19:23; etc.) and that He is the Resurrection (Jn. 11:25; cf. Acts 17:18 — Paul "preached Jesus and the resurrection"). Alongside "If you continue in my *word*" (Jn. 8:31) can be placed "If you abide in *me* and my words abide in you" (15:7). It is a short step from here to the direct statement that Jesus is the Word.

(3) In the OT and Judaism God's wisdom is a concept closely parallel to His word. According to the vivid metaphor in Prov. 8, Wisdom was created by God before the world and stood by Him like a master workman at creation. In the later wisdom literature (esp. Wisd. 7) it occupies a prominent place and is described as sitting by the throne of God (Wisd. 9:4). A stoic element is present when it is spoken of as pervading the universe. There are very considerable parallels between the OT and Jewish description of wisdom and the Johannine description of the Word (tabulated in Dodd, pp. 274f.), and already in Judaism the identification of God's wisdom and word was beginning to be made (Wisd. 9:1f.), a fact that makes it easier to see how the description of wisdom has been transferred by John to the Word.

(4) The description of the Word in John is also parallel to that of the Torah or Law in Judaism. In several passages the Torah, especially in its concrete form in the Pentateuch, and wisdom are identified (Sir. 24; Bar. 3–4). Rabbinic Judaism assigned to the Torah a role of great importance; it was spoken of in personal terms, regarded as preexistent and an agent in creation, and described as the giver of light and life to men. The parallelism and contrast with the Torah is readily apparent in John (see esp. Jn. 1:17; cf. Dodd, pp. 75-86).

In the opinion of many scholars the material so far presented is an adequate background for the Johannine usage, but other suggestions have also been made.

(5) In Greek philosophy, particularly in Stoicism, the idea of the logos as the principle of rationality and order in the universe, and hence as the principle by which people ought to live, played an important part. But although this may have been important for other writers who formed a part of John's environment, this is not the obvious clue to the meaning of logos in John (cf. Bultmann, *Gospel,* p. 24). At the same time, however, by the use of the Logos terminology John secured a point of contact with those who were acquainted with its use in philosophy.

(6) The Jewish philosopher Philo attempted to express Jewish ideas in the terminology and thought forms of Platonism and Stoicism. His use of the term logos was extensive and varied. He identified the Platonic heavenly pattern of the visible world with the Stoic logos which gives structure and order to the visible world, and then equated both with the word which he described in the wisdom terminology as the preexistent, divine agent in creation and also as the intermediary between God and man. He also regarded it as the heavenly archetype of man and as the reason which indwells man; this gives a more personal nuance to what is in any case a highly fluid concept in his thought.

Several writers find in the Philonic logos the nearest parallel to the Johannine logos (Scott, pp. 145-175; Dodd; *NBD, s.v.* "Logos" [Birdsall]). But there is a vast difference in ethos between John and Philo, and the linguistic parallels between Philo and John are not as close as those between the wisdom literature and John.

(7) Bultmann (*Gospel,* pp. 24-31; cf. Schulz, *Untersuchungen,* p. 181 and n. 6) has raised the objections that in none of the Jewish sources mentioned above is logos used as a title — it is merely the name of a concept — and that the mythological personification in the wisdom and Torah speculation is not sufficiently living to have been the source of the Johannine personification of the Logos. The similarities between the wisdom literature and John are due to their common source in the Gnostic myth, according to which the figure of Logos or Nous (other names are also used) is conceived as descending into the world in human form as a disguise from the evil powers; in Christian thought this figure is identified with Jesus. Consequently Bultmann has ready-made answers to the questions posed by Hoskyns (p. 156): how did the description of wisdom come to be applied to the "word," and how has the "word" become a name for a clearly defined person?

This neat solution faces very considerable difficulties. It has already been mentioned that the sources from which the Gnostic myth is reconstructed are fragmentary and often of later date than John, and there is still no proof that the redeemer myth itself is of pre-Christian origin (R. M. Wilson, *The Gnostic Problem* [1958]; Schnackenburg, however, is more hospitable to the possibility, *Gospel,* I, 481-493, 543-557). Further, John preserves the more philosophical meaning of Logos which the name itself proves to have been original, whereas the Gnostic concept is much more mythological. Above all, the closeness of the parallels between John and the wisdom literature is such as to make any other *basic* source for John quite superfluous.

Thus, John teaches that Jesus is identified with the Logos of God, the creative and revealing Word who existed from the beginning with God and became a man. Despite the claims of E. Käsemann (p. 26 *et passim*), John does not fall into a naive docetism; the real manhood of Jesus is a cardinal point of Johannine Christology. Not only does the Gospel describe a real man who could be hungry and thirsty, but in 1 John the utmost importance is attached to the coming of Jesus by water and by blood, i.e., in a true and lasting incarnation (Jn. 4:6f.; 1 Jn. 5:6). Men were able to see, hear, and touch Him (1 Jn. 1:1f.). John thus emphasizes both the coming of the Savior from beyond space and time and the reality of His coming into this world as a man. History is of crucial importance for him (see esp. Hoskyns, pp. 107-135).

E. God. It is not a great step from saying that the Logos was God (this *must* be the translation of Jn. 1:1; see esp. Bultmann, *Gospel,* pp. 33f.; V. Perry, *EQ,* 35 [1963], 15-22) to saying that Jesus Himself was God. This step is taken in Jn. 20:28, which must be regarded as the christological climax of the Gospel. The textual evidence is strongly in favor of the reading "God" instead of "Son" in Jn. 1:18, but the contextual evidence here casts doubts upon the evidence of the MSS, and few scholars have accepted it. It is very likely that Jesus is designated as God in 1 Jn. 5:20 also.

Various writers (Dodd, pp. 93-96; E. Stauffer, *Jesus and His Story* [Eng. tr. 1960], pp. 142-160; cf. *TDNT,* II, *s.v.* ἐγώ; Schnackenburg, *Gospel,* II, 79-89; Brown, I, 533-38) have drawn attention to the significance of the formula "I am he" on the lips of Jesus (Jn. 4:26; 6:20; 8:24, 28, 58; 13:19; cf. Mk. 6:50; 13:6; 14:62); this formula is found in Second Isaiah as a self-affirmation of God (Isa. 43:10; 48:12), and the use of it by Jesus is consequently deeply significant.

Thus Johannine Christology culminates in the affirmation that the man Jesus is God come among men as their Lord and Savior. He receives from believing men and women this appellation of Lord, which is also the name given to God the Father (Jn. 1:23; 12:13, 38). This is clearly the case at Jn. 20:28 (cf. 20:2, 13, 18ff.; 21:7, 12), i.e., in the postresurrection narrative. Earlier in the Gospel the vocative form is used as the normal polite form of address, and is not restricted in application to Jesus alone (12:21; 20:15), but there are occasions when a deeper meaning may be intended (6:68; 9:38), and Jesus claimed to be the Lord of the disciples (13:13-16; 15:15, 20). There would, therefore, appear to be no reason (despite Bultmann, *Gospel,* p. 176 n. 2) for denying the possibility of the use of the title for Jesus by the Evangelist in 4:1; 6:23; 11:2 (see Cullmann, pp. 232f.).

V. The World and Sin.–The sphere of Jesus' activity in John is regarded as the lower realm in contrast to the upper realm, which is where God is (Jn. 8:23; cf. 3:3, 7, RSV mg.; 3:31; 19:11). More commonly it is spoken of as the world or "this world" in contrast to heaven as the divine sphere. The idea of God being above in heaven is one that is common to most religions, and there is no need to call it a Gnostic idea.

Although "world" is an ethically neutral concept in itself, it takes on a specifically moral and spiritual meaning in John (Schnackenburg, *Johannesbriefe,* pp. 133-37). It is the world of people who are separated from God. We may single out four main characteristics. First, the world is characterized by darkness or the absence of light (Jn. 1:5; 12:46; 1 Jn. 2:8-11; *TDNT,* VII, *s.v.* σκότος [Conzelmann]; IX, *s.v.* φῶς; Dodd, pp. 201-205; Schnackenburg, *Johannesbriefe,* pp. 76-79). When the true light did shine in it, it was not welcomed (Jn. 1:9), and people refused it because their deeds were evil (3:19); they were wilfully blind to the light (9:39-41), and consequently the judgment which came upon them was simply blindness from which they could not recover (12:37-40). It requires no proof that light and darkness are here moral and spiritual terms; light signifies both the revelation of God and the holy character of God.

Second, the state of the world is one of falsehood. It has cut itself off from the truth of God (see III above). The importance of this description is that it shows that what is primarily wrong with the world is not lack of true self-knowledge (so R. Bultmann, *Gospel*, pp. 40-48, etc.) but lack of knowledge of God.

Third, the world can also be spoken of as a place of bondage in which people lack freedom (Jn. 8:34). They are under a ruler whom they must obey, and that ruler is the prince of this world, the devil (Jn. 12:31; 14:30).

Fourth, the basic fact about the world is that it is characterized by sin; blindness or darkness, falsehood, and slavery are all ways of expressing this basic fact. Sin is incompatible with living in the light (1 Jn. 1:5-10), for in essence it is refusal to obey the law and commandments of God (3:4); it is expressed in lack of love for others, even to the point of murder (3:11-15). It is the mark of the children of the devil, and has no place in the life of the children of God (3:6, 8). Its most heinous expression is rejection of Jesus (Jn. 16:9).

Because of its sinful character the world stands under divine judgment. The coming of Jesus into the world is an act of divine judgment (Jn. 9:39), in which people have the opportunity of accepting salvation or passing judgment upon themselves. It can, therefore, be said that the purpose of Jesus was not to judge (i.e., condemn) the world but to save it, and that people judge themselves (3:17-19; 8:15; 12:47f.). But at the same time it can definitely be said that Jesus is the Judge who carries out the judgment of God upon the world; although His primary purpose was to save the world, judgment is the inevitable consequence of His coming (5:22, 27, 30; 8:16, 26, 50; cf. 16:8, 11 for the continuation of this work by the Spirit). Hence, although the final judgment is still future (Jn. 5:24, 29; 12:48), the world can be said to have been judged already (Jn. 3:18; 16:11) and is destined to pass away (1 Jn. 2:17). The verdict passed in the judgment is the sentence of death (Jn. 8:24; 1 Jn. 5:16), but the state of the world can be spoken of as already one of death, since it is separated from God who is the source of life; the wrath of God rests upon it (Jn. 3:36; 5:24f.; 1 Jn. 3:14).

Thus, John's description of the world is controlled by a basic dualism expressed in several pairs of opposites. That a similar dualism is to be found in Gnosticism is well known. But it remains questionable whether Gnosticism must be regarded as the source of Johannine dualism (as by L. Schottroff). The ethical dualism in John is thoroughly in line with the light and darkness terminology of the OT and Judaism, and need not be regarded as specifically Gnostic, although the presence of Gnostic heresy among his readers may have helped to influence John's formulations (Percy, pp. 63-76; Schnackenburg, *Johannesbriefe*, pp. 30-32; Böcher; Brown, I, lxii-lxiii).

That people are actually in the darkness does not prevent them from thinking they are in the light and possess the means of salvation. Since John is writing especially for people of Jewish background, he concentrates his attention on Jewish claims to possession of the light. The Jews thought that in the OT Scriptures they possessed eternal life (Jn. 5:39). But although the Scriptures possessed the highest religious authority for John (and for Jesus) — as is demonstrated both by his direct quotations and allusive use and by such statements as 5:45-47; 10:35 (Barrett, pp. 22-25) — the Jews' claim that they had found life in them was ill founded because they refused to come to the One to whom the Scriptures, rightly interpreted, bore witness (5:39f.). Those who have learned from the Father must come to the Son (6:44f.).

Nor is it sufficient to appeal to membership in the Jewish race. Descent from Abraham is all very well, but not if Abraham's children fall into sin and refuse to accept the One who is greater than Abraham (8:31ff.). If salvation is from the Jews (4:22), it is only because Jesus was a Jew.

The world, therefore, is bankrupt as far as eternal life is concerned; it is dead and cannot raise itself to life. It needs the Savior (Bultmann, *Theology*, II, 26-32).

VI. Savior of the World.–In the coming of Jesus the need of the world is fully met. To a world in darkness He appears as the light of the world (Jn. 8:12). In place of falsehood He brings the truth that He Himself embodies (14:6) and the knowledge of God the Father (17:3). Instead of slavery He offers freedom (8:32-36), and instead of sin and death He gives eternal life.

This last expression is John's favorite one for the blessing brought by Jesus (*TDNT*, II, *s.v.* ζάω κτλ. [von Rad, Bertram, Bultmann], esp. pp. 870-72; Dodd, pp. 144-150; Manson, pp. 110-19; Schnackenburg, *Gospel*, II, 352-361). Eternal life is originally life that does not end, i.e., life that continues beyond the grave and is thus a future possession. Such life is, however, of a divine quality, so that "eternal" has both a quantitative and a qualitative sense: life or eternal life (the terms are synonymous) means an everlasting life which is the life of God Himself. John emphasizes both these points. Those who possess eternal life shall never perish (Jn. 3:16; 6:27; 10:28), but will be raised from the dead (5:21-29; 6:40, 51, 54, 58). Further, that life is more abundant than the so-called life of this dead world (10:10). It is a life of fellowship with God (17:3), and it is received only from Jesus. He is the source of life (1:4; 11:25; 14:6; 1 Jn. 1:1f.). In metaphorical language He is the giver of living, i.e., life-bestowing, water (Jn. 4:10-14; cf. 7:38) and of living bread (6:27ff.; P. Borgen, *Bread from Heaven* [1965]). Jesus Himself can be called the bread of life, since it is by receiving Him that people receive His gifts (on this and similar "I am" statements, see E. Schweizer, *EGO EIMI* [2nd ed. 1965]; Bultmann, *Gospel*, p. 225 n. 3; Schnackenburg, *Gospel*, II, 79-89). He who has Jesus has life (1 Jn. 5:11f.).

What is new in John's teaching is implicit in the statements already made: eternal life is not merely a future possession for which believers hope, but also a present possession which they already enjoy (Jn. 3:36; 5:24; 6:47). The believer really has eternal life *now*, and not merely in the form of a promise (as Hartingsveld, p. 60; rightly Dodd, pp. 144-150).

We must now ask whether Jesus does anything in order that people may have eternal life. Is it sufficient that He appears among people to reveal God to them? Does Jesus save people primarily by coming to them and challenging them to decision? This, it would appear, is the view of Bultmann, who ascribes a monumental insignificance to what is at the center of the NT as a whole: the redemptive death of Jesus (*Theology*, II, 52-55; followed by E. Lohse, *Märtyrer und Gottesknecht* [1955], pp. 191f.). In order to achieve this conclusion a number of statements have to be emptied of their obvious meaning, and others have to be ascribed to a series of redactors. On this view, the death has significance only as the culmination of the whole life, which is said to be a sacrifice, but not an atoning sacrifice for sin.

In fact John's doctrine of the death of Jesus is not dissimilar from that of the NT as a whole (J. Denney, *Death of Christ* [1951], pp. 139-155; V. Taylor, *The Atonement in NT Teaching* [2nd ed. 1945]). The death of Jesus is the supreme demonstration of the love of God (Jn. 3:14-16; 13:1; 1 Jn. 4:9f.). He is presented as the Good Shepherd who lays down His life for the sheep (Jn. 10:11, 15, 17f.; cf. 1 Jn. 3:16), and His death is said to be a saving death on behalf of mankind (Jn. 11:50-52) by which they are drawn to God (12:32). As regards the manner of its efficacy, the death is a victory over Satan (Jn. 12:31; 1 Jn. 4:8), but the main category of understanding is undoubtedly that of sacrifice. Jesus is presented at the very outset of the Gospel as the Lamb of God who takes away the sin of the world (Jn. 1:29, 36) — an image that is definitely sacrificial, whatever be its precise force (cf. *TDNT,* I, *s.v.* ἀμνός κτλ. [J. Jeremias]). He was manifested to take away sin (1 Jn. 3:5), and His death is conceived as a propitiation for the sins of the whole world (2:2; 4:10; L. Morris, *Apostolic Preaching of the Cross* [3rd ed. 1965], pp. 205-208). It is through His blood that sin is cleansed (1:7), and He is said to be an advocate with the Father for sinners (2:1). Through His work the sins of believers are forgiven (2:12).

These citations show clearly not merely that the death of Christ is regarded by John as an objective act of atonement, but also that it lies at the center of his message (cf. R. V. G. Tasker, comm. on John [*Tyndale NT Comms.,* 1960], pp. 31f., *et passim*; F.-M. Braun, III, 137-182).

VII. Entry to Eternal Life.–The coming of Jesus into the world does not automatically result in the salvation of individual men and women. Rather, it creates a moment of crisis for everyone who comes into personal contact with Him; they are presented with the possibilities of receiving eternal life from the only One who can offer it, or of remaining in sin and darkness and thus confirming the judgment under which they already stand (Jn. 5:24; 12:46-48).

When this crisis leads to eternal life it is spoken of as a new birth or a birth from above (either translation is possible at Jn. 3:3, 7); without such a birth it is impossible to enter the kingdom of God. There has been considerable debate about the origin of this terminology (*TDNT,* I, *s.v.* γεννάω κτλ. [Büchsel, Rengstorf]; Barrett, pp. 172f.; Schnackenburg, *Johannesbriefe,* pp. 175-183). It was certainly common in the mystery religions and Gnosticism, and these are often regarded as the sources for John's usage; it is likely in any case that he knew of this language. But his teaching is more probably rooted in the teaching of Jesus (Mt. 18:3), and it may have a Jewish background: the Jewish saying about a proselyte, when newly baptized, being like a newly born child was originally not legal (Barrett, p. 172) but religious in its significance (J. Jeremias, *Jerusalem in the Time of Jesus* [Eng. tr. 1969], pp. 324f.; *Infant Baptism in the First Four Centuries* [Eng. tr. 1960], pp. 32-34).

Two sets of expressions are used to define how this crisis takes place. On the one hand, it is a birth from God (Jn. 1:13; 1 Jn. 2:29; 3:9; 4:7; 5:1, 4, 18) or from the Spirit of God (Jn. 3:6, 8). Its result is to make people children of God (1 Jn. 3:1; etc.); this is a relationship that is not simply moral (1 Jn. 2:29; 3:9; 4:7) but at the same time not physical (in 5:18b the slightly different Greek construction may indicate a reference to the unique begetting of Jesus by the Father; note also that whereas Jesus is called the Son, John never uses this word to describe believers). When we remember that the Spirit of God is His divine, superhuman power, working miraculously in human lives, it becomes clear that the new birth is an act of God Himself through which people are initiated into a life of divine quality.

On the other hand, the possibility of the new birth is dependent upon the fact that Jesus was lifted up to die (see J. Denney, *Jesus and the Gospel* [3rd ed. 1909], pp. 97-99); and the experience comes to those who believe in Jesus and receive Him (Jn. 1:12; 3:16).

The question now arises of the relationship between the act of God and the faith of people (Schnackenburg, *Gospel,* II, 259-274). John does not say that the work of the Spirit is dependent upon the faith of the individual. Nor does he say that the existence of faith is dependent upon the work of the Spirit; the doctrine of an inward regeneration of the individual prior to conscious faith is hardly to be deduced from Jn. 1:12f. (Barrett, pp. 136f.), although this does not mean that the activity of the Holy Spirit does not precede faith.

A number of passages teach plainly that nobody can come to Jesus and believe in Him without being drawn by the Father (Jn. 6:37, 44, 65; 10:29; 15:16, 19; 17:2, 6, etc.), and in one place at least (8:47) the impression is given that the world is divided, as in Gnostic thought, into two fixed groups — those destined to believe and those destined to perish. But the predestinarian inferences which may be drawn from these texts must be carefully qualified. There are other passages which teach a universal offer of salvation (Jn. 3:16f.; 6:45; 12:32; 1 Jn. 2:2), and besides that, the predestinarian language is not always applied rigorously (Jn. 12:37ff.; see Hoskyns, p. 429). When these facts are kept in mind, it appears that the predestinarian statements are intended to emphasize that the gift of eternal life is from start to finish the gift of God and is not something that man can grasp by his own endeavors; to go beyond this and find in John individual election (and reprobation) is distinctly precarious.

VIII. Characteristics of Eternal Life.–*A. Faith, Perseverance, and Assurance.* The new life to which entry is given by the new birth is preeminently a life of faith (*TDNT,* VI, *s.v.* πιστεύω κτλ. [Bultmann, Weiser], esp. pp. 222-28; Dodd, pp. 179-186; Schnackenburg, *Gospel,* I, 558-575). Although John uses the noun "faith" only once (1 Jn. 5:4), he uses the verb "to believe" 107 times; it has two distinct constructions: with the dative case or a noun clause to indicate credence in a person or acceptance of a statement as true, and with the preposition *eis* and the accusative case to indicate trust in and commitment to a person. (This is not an exhaustive analysis of the usage; there is, among other uses, a use of the verb absolutely with no object, where the meaning must be determined from the general context.) This usage is sufficiently consistent linguistically (despite Bultmann, *Gospel,* p. 252 n. 2) to be made the basis of a theological distinction between two levels of faith. The "lower" level is that of intellectual acceptance of the claims made by Jesus (Jn. 6:69; 8:24; 11:26f., 42, etc.); that this kind of faith is utterly indispensable is shown by the emphasis laid on right belief in the Epistles (1 Jn. 5:10; cf. 2 Jn. 7-9). But such faith is insufficient; it must culminate in the "higher" level of commitment of oneself to the person whose claims one has accepted intellectually (Jn. 1:12; 2:11, 23; 3:16, 18, 36, etc.; 1 Jn. 5:10, 13). No doubt intellectual faith is not truly intellectual faith unless it is accompanied by such commitment, but there can be an intellectual faith that falls short of the commitment that alone leads to eternal life.

The object of the believer's faith and trust is sometimes said to be God (Jn. 5:24; 14:1; 1 Jn. 5:10) or the revelation He has made (1 Jn. 5:10; cf. 4:16 and also Jn. 5:46f. of believing in the words of Moses), but usually it is Jesus Himself or the name of Jesus.

Faith is not merely a momentary act associated with the new birth. It is an attitude that is characteristic of the believer throughout his life, without which he would cease to be a partaker in eternal life. This aspect of faith is developed in John by the concept of abiding (J. Heise, *Bleiben. Menein in den Johanneischen Schriften* [1967]), which expresses both the close union between believers and their Lord (see below) and the continuing nature of the relationship between them. The disciples are commanded to abide in Jesus (Jn. 15:4-10; 1 Jn. 2:24, 28; 3:6), and are warned about the danger of failing to abide in Him (Jn. 15:6).

John thus emphasizes the need to abide in Jesus and warns against the danger of falling away (Jn. 16:1). Beside this teaching must be placed the statements that express the protection given by Jesus to His disciples (Jn. 6:39f., 44, 54; 10:28f.; 17:11ff.); it will then be apparent that we have in John the paradox of the possibility of falling away from faith and the promise of a divine protection that preserves the disciples from perishing. This paradox is no more to be explained away, whether from a Calvinist or an Arminian standpoint, than the paradox of faith and the Holy Spirit encountered previously. The believer needs to be warned against falling away, but at the same time he can be fully assured of his salvation (I. H. Marshall, *Kept by the Power of God* [1969]).

John stresses that the believer can know that he possesses eternal life (1 Jn. 5:13). The truth of the saving message is attested by witnesses (see above), including God Himself (Schnackenburg, *Johannesbriefe*, pp. 267-271). Further, the possession of the Spirit is a sign that a person is born of God (1 Jn. 3:24; 4:13). The believer is thus a person who is filled with joy (Jn. 15:11; 17:13; 1 Jn. 1:4).

B. Knowledge. A second main characteristic of the new life is knowledge (*TDNT,* I, *s.v.* γινώσκω κτλ. [Bultmann]; Dodd, pp. 151-169; Schnackenburg, *Johannesbriefe,* pp. 95-101). Eternal life can indeed be defined as knowing the Father and the Son (Jn. 17:3). What is distinctive in Johannine teaching is that the knowledge of believers is similar to the mutual knowledge of the Father and the Son (10:14f.). Believers know the Father (8:19; 14:7; 17:3; 1 Jn. 2:3, 13; 4:6; 5:20), they know the Son (Jn. 10:14; 1 Jn. 2:13f.; cf. 3:6) and are known by Him (Jn. 10:14), and they know the Spirit (14:17; cf. 1 Jn. 4:2, 6). Such knowledge is not a higher stage in Christian experience than faith (this is clear from the parallelism between the two concepts), but is the expression of the cognitive element in faith. The person who believes has personal fellowship with God (cf. 1 Jn. 1:3-7). This, and not knowledge of the mysteries of cosmogony or esoteric revelations, is the content of knowledge, according to John. Finally, it is worth noting that this knowledge is something present, and not merely future (Jn. 10:14; cf. the use of the perfect tense in 1 John).

C. Union with God. The third characteristic of the new life is union with God (Dodd, pp. 187-200). This is expressed in terms of fellowship with God (Schnackenburg, *Johannesbriefe,* pp. 66-72) and of abiding in Him. This last phrase has already been mentioned briefly; to what was said earlier must now be added that the abiding of the believer in Jesus (Jn. 15:4-10; 1 Jn. 2:24, 28; 3:6) is paralleled by the abiding of Jesus in the believer (Jn. 15:4f.), and that this mutual indwelling is patterned on the relationship of the Father and the Son with each other (14:10). The Father is also said to abide in believers and they in Him (1 Jn. 2:24; 3:24; 4:13f., 15f.), and the Spirit abides in believers (Jn. 14:17; see Bultmann, *Gospel,* p. 535 n. 1; Schnackenburg, *Johannesbriefe,* pp. 105-110).

These same relationships are also expressed by the use of the preposition "in" without the use of the verb "abide." The Father is in the Son (Jn. 14:11; 17:21, 23) and the Son in the Father (14:11, 20; 17:21). Following this archetypal relationship, the Son is in people (14:20, 23; 17:23, 26) and people are in the Son (14:20; 17:21; 1 Jn. 5:20). The Father is in people (Jn. 14:23; 1 Jn. 4:4) and people are in the Father (Jn. 17:21; 1 Jn. 5:20). There is no suggestion of any loss of identity in this relationship; it is one of loving communion (see esp. Dodd, pp. 187-200).

The concrete expression of communion with God is prayer. Just as Jesus was able to ask His Father for anything in prayer (Jn. 11:22), so the disciples may come to the Father and make known their requests (15:7; 16:23). Such prayer, however, must be made in the name of Jesus (14:13f.; 15:16; 16:24, 26) and must be in accordance with the will of the Father (1 Jn. 5:14) if it is to be sure of receiving an answer (3:22; 5:15).

D. Holy Spirit. The fourth characteristic of the new life is the presence of the Holy Spirit in the believer (*TDNT,* VI, *s.v.* πνεῦμα κτλ. [Schweizer, *et al.*], esp. 437-444). Jesus Himself possessed the Spirit (Jn. 1:32f.), and He passed on the gift to His disciples. He is the One who baptized with the Spirit (1:33; cf. 20:22), but, although the life-giving power of the Spirit was already present in the words of Jesus (6:63), the gift of the Spirit was fully given to people only after the glorification of Jesus (7:39). The Spirit is variously described as the Spirit of truth (14:17; 15:26; 16:13), the Holy Spirit (1:33, etc.), and the giver of life (6:63; cf. the verses associating the Spirit with the new birth). But the most characteristic description of Him in John is "another Paraclete" (14:16, 26; 15:26; 16:7; cf. 1 Jn. 2:1 of Jesus). The functions ascribed to the Spirit in this context are, first, that He will come and abide in the disciples after the departure of Jesus, to teach them, remind them of His words, and guide them into the truth; and, second, that He will bear witness to Jesus through the disciples before the world, and will convict the world of sin, righteousness, and judgment. These functions can be paralleled from the activities of Jesus Himself.

Recent studies suggest that the idea of the Paraclete has a complex background (*TDNT,* V, *s.v.* παράκλητος [Behm]; Bultmann, *Gospel,* pp. 566-572; O. Betz, *Der Paraklet* [1963]; Brown, II, 1135-1144; *NTS,* 13 [1966/67], 113-132; G. E. Johnston, *The Spirit-Paraclete in the Gospel of John* [1970]). The older view gave the term a forensic background (B. F. Westcott, comm. on John [1882], pp. 211-13); another traditional view assigns the meaning of "comforter" on the basis of the meaning of the cognate verb (cf. Hoskyns, pp. 465-470; Barrett, pp. 385f.). More recently attention has been directed to the ideas of intercession and heavenly intercessors in Jewish literature (cf. Job 16:19; 33:23, 26).

E. Obedience and Love. The fifth characteristic of the new life is that it is ethically conditioned. Not only is confession of sin a condition for walking in the light (1 Jn. 1:8-10); the new life is one of holiness, in which further sin is eschewed. The believer must follow the truth and do good (2 Jn. 4; 3 Jn. 3f., 11f.). Above all, he is to keep the commandments of God, since this is what love for God implies (Jn. 14:15, 21; 15:10; 1 Jn. 5:3; 2 Jn. 6) and is the proof that he knows God (1 Jn. 2:3f.). In particular, John draws attention to the new commandment given by Jesus that believers should love each other (Jn. 13:34; 15:12; 1 Jn. 2:9; 4:21; 2 Jn. 5f.). The whole matter is summed up by saying that the commandment is to love God (and, therefore, to keep His commandments) and one another (1 Jn. 3:23).

Such a life of obedience may also be described as one of sanctification in the truth. To be sanctified is to be set apart and dedicated for God's service (Jn. 10:36), and this thought is certainly present in Jn. 17:17, 19 also, but the full meaning of these verses is missed, if it is not remembered that this process of dedication includes the spiritual and ethical transformation of people to be suitable instruments for divine service. This means that believers are to eschew the sinfulness of the world (1 Jn. 2:15-17), even though they remain in the world (Jn. 17:15-18), and therefore Jesus prays that they may be kept from the evil one (17:15). The kind of life they are to live is thus a life that is free from sin (1 Jn. 3:4-10; on the problem of sinlessness, *see* JOHN, EPISTLES OF III; Schnackenburg, *Johannesbriefe*, pp. 281-88).

IX. Life in the Church.–The theology of John lays strong emphasis on the place of the individual and his faith in the divine purpose of salvation (C. F. D. Moule, *Nov.Test.*, 5 [1962], 171-190). This is not something for which the expositor need apologize; the modern stress on the corporate nature of Christianity can easily be carried too far. Nevertheless, this does not mean that John is deficient in teaching on the communal character of the Christian faith (E. Schweizer, "The Concept of the Church in the Gospel and Epistles of St. John," in A. J. B. Higgins, ed., *NT Essays* [1959], pp. 230-245; *Church Order in the NT* [1961], pp. 117-130; Brown, I, civ-cxi).

It is true that the word "church" is rare in John (3 Jn. 6, 9f., of the local church; cf. the "elect lady," 2 Jn. 1, 13), but the reality is there. A disciple is a member of the flock of Jesus; no doubt this metaphor is developed primarily in terms of the relation of the individual sheep to the shepherd, but there is also present the thought of the gathering together of other sheep to constitute one flock (Jn. 10:16). Similarly, while the imagery of the vine is primarily concerned with the relation of the individual branches to Jesus, there is teaching in the immediate context on the need for the disciples to love each other (15:12). This means that the disciples are constituted by their allegiance to Jesus into a group whose most noteworthy characteristic is mutual love. They form a fellowship (1 Jn. 1:3f.) in which the members show great love for each other; this concept is developed in 1 John to such an extent that love for those who are not in the fellowship tends to retreat into the background (see, however, Schnackenburg, *Johannesbriefe*, pp. 117-121). The outcome of such love is that the Church should manifest a oneness or unity, and the achievement of this unity is one of the chief objects for which Jesus prays (Jn. 17).

All this means that the Church forms a definite group over against the world, although it is possible for the visible Church to contain those who are not truly believers in Jesus and are eventually seen for what they are in reality (1 Jn. 2:19). It has a task of mission to the world, being sent by Jesus in the same way as He was sent by the Father (Jn. 20:21) in order to bear fruit, i.e., win converts (15:16); through seeing its love and unity the world may be led to believe (17:23). Jesus, therefore, prays not only for the world but also for the disciples through whose words and witness the world may be won (17:9, 20).

The world, for its part, indicates its separation from the Church by setting itself up in opposition to the Church and persecuting it. It hates believers, just as it hated Jesus, and persecutes them in order to force them to give up their faith; it can even do this under the false impression that it is thereby glorifying God (Jn. 15:18–16:4; 17:14; 1 Jn. 3:13).

Little is said in John about the inner life of the Church. Jesus speaks of the time which is already at hand when true worshipers will worship the Father in spirit and in truth without being tied to such places as Mt. Gerizim or Jerusalem (Jn. 4:19-24), but nothing is said about the manner of such worship. It is clear, however, that the task of witnessing to Jesus by means of words is an essential part of the activity of the Church, and the fact of pastoral care is hinted at in Jn. 21:15-19.

The place of the sacraments in Johannine teaching is disputed. The view of Cullmann (*Early Christian Worship* [1953]) that sacramental allusions are to be found in great abundance in John is far from convincing; even more unconvincing is the view of Bultmann (*Theology*, II, 9) and E. Lohse (*NTS*, 7 [1960/61], 101-125) that the sacramental references are all due to a redactor, although one can agree with Lohse that John puts the word above the sacraments in importance. In every case in the Gospel the references to the Lord's Supper are no more than allusive, and there is no narrative of its institution. The reason for this may lie in a *disciplina arcani* (J. Jeremias, *Eucharistic Words of Jesus* [Eng. tr. 1966], pp. 125-137; see, however, J. D. G. Dunn, *NTS*, 17 [1970/71], 328-338). It is, however, clear that John knows of baptism as a rite of initiation associated with the gift of the Spirit (Jn. 1:33; 3:5) and of the need for disciples to be nourished by the flesh and blood of the Son of man — language that almost certainly alludes to the Lord's Supper (6:53-58; the significance of 19:34 is obscure; on 1 Jn. 5:6-8 see W. Nauck, *Die Tradition und Charakter des ersten Johannesbriefes* [1957]).

John says little about the ministry. The Gospel teaches that Peter was entrusted with the task of a shepherd (21:15-19), and that the disciples collectively received authority to forgive and retain (i.e., not forgive) sins (20:23). There is no indication whether the group of disciples thus authorized was limited in number; this is in fact unlikely, since the group of twelve disciples or apostles is not significant in John. In the Epistles the Church situation is somewhat hazy, but there are indications that John himself exercised a general supervision over a number of churches and that a local leadership was beginning to develop. That a church discipline was operating is seen not only from Jn. 20:23 but also from the details recorded in the Epistles (1 Jn. 5:16; 2 Jn. 9-11; 3 Jn. 9-12).

X. Eschatology.–The temporal framework that conditions Johannine theology is a subject of lively debate among contemporary scholars (Schnackenburg, *Johannesevangelium*, II, 530-544; Brown, I, cxvi-cxxi). Elsewhere in the NT it is taught that the present evil era is destined to be succeeded by the new era of the kingdom of God, which will be inaugurated at the Parousia; but the saving intervention of God that will bring about this new era has already taken place decisively in the first coming of Jesus, so that the new era is already enjoyed proleptically by believers. In other words, there is an interim period between the first coming of Jesus and the Parousia during which the future era is partially realized; Christians already possess the earnest of future glory, and what is yet to come is merely the full manifestation of what has already been fully revealed in principle. The first coming of Jesus is the center of history, the decisive eschatological event, which nevertheless needs to be consummated at the Parousia.

According to Dodd (pp. 403-406, *et passim*) John teaches that the future era fully came at the first advent of Jesus, so that no decisive future event is still awaited. The place of the Parousia in early Christian expectation is taken by the coming of the Spirit. So far as believers are concerned, the return of Jesus is His spiritual return after His glorification; so far as the world is concerned, the visible Parousia of Jesus is replaced by the revelation of the loving unity of the Church. Thus John has decisively reinterpreted early Christian eschatology into a realized eschatology. A similar treatment of John is provided by J. A. T. Robinson (*Jesus and His Coming* [1957], pp. 160-185), but he differs from Dodd in believing that the Johannine nonapocalyptic and nonfuturistic eschatology was in fact the original Christian faith and was succeeded by the apocalyptic, futuristic hope of the Parousia. Bultmann (*Theology*, II, 57f.) reaches a somewhat similar conclusion by a different route: having removed all that savors of apocalyptic from John by the hypothesis of a redactor, he proceeds to regard Easter, Pentecost, and the Parousia as different expressions of the one existential event that is "the victory which Jesus wins when faith arises in man by the overcoming of the offense that Jesus is to him"; consequently, there is no impending cosmic drama to be awaited.

Something more akin to the traditional view is upheld by such scholars as Barrett, van Hartingsveld, and C. F. D. Moule (*op. cit.*). Barrett states that John has not abandoned the common NT eschatology, although he has emphasized its problems, and that according to John the promises (especially that of the resurrection of the dead) are already being fulfilled but in such a way as to leave over something for a future fulfillment also (p. 57).

The clue to the right answer lies in the formula, "The hour is coming and now is" (Jn. 4:23; 5:25; 16:32; cf. 16:25). This formula emphasizes both the presence and the futurity of certain events; the argument of Bultmann that the emphasis is placed entirely on the present time as the eschatological hour (*Gospel*, pp. 189f., esp. p. 190 n. 1) is not convincing and does not take into account the fact of statements with a purely future reference (e.g., Jn. 16:25). Moreover, what the formula shows is that certain future events are already taking place in the present time; what is taking place now is an anticipation of what will take place in the future. Thus already a number of people worship in spirit and in truth, and already a few dead are raised, but these are only partial anticipations of the worship and resurrection to take place in the future. Consequently, what takes place now is a foreshadowing of future events, and the emphasis is misplaced when it is suggested that John sees the future events as the finalizing of present realities and the visible unfolding of what now is (Hunter, p. 144).

This means that for all his immense stress on the present realization of eternal life, John looks forward to the fulness of life that is only partially realized by anticipation in the present time. To map out his expectations in detail is by no means easy, and according to van Hartingsveld (pp. 137-154) they cannot be fitted into a neat pattern; rather, John's expectations fall into three groups associated with the resurrection, the day of homecall for the disciples to their heavenly mansions, and the setting up of the messianic kingdom.

We may now briefly summarize the content of Johannine expectation regarding the future. We have already seen that John looked forward to the continuing life of the Church after the glorification of Jesus and to the presence of Jesus with His disciples through the Holy Spirit. During this time a period of woes and persecution is envisaged (Jn. 15:18–16:4; 16:32f.; 21:18f.); indeed it is already begun (16:32). It is the period of the revelation of antichrist, or rather of the antichrists, for John sees the spirit of antichrist as operative in all those who, though professing to be believers, deny that Jesus is the Christ. That they are already manifested indicates that the end time has begun (1 Jn. 2:18f.; 4:1-6).

After this comes the last day (Jn. 6:39f., 44, 54; 11:24; 12:48), which is associated with two events: the resurrection of the dead and the judgment. The resurrection is strictly of believers to eternal life, but John can also speak of a resurrection of judgment (5:25-29). There is also the possibility that a person may remain alive until the parousia of Jesus (21:22f.), when He comes again to take His people to be with Himself (14:3). But the relationship between living and dead believers at the time of the Parousia is not explicitly discussed; it would appear to be reasonable to assume that the voice that raises the dead is that of the Son of man at His coming. When Jesus comes again and His disciples see Him they will be transformed to become like Him (1 Jn. 3:2f.), and they will see His glory (Jn. 17:24). Their dwelling place will be the place Jesus has gone to prepare for them (14:3).

The center of Johannine eschatology is thus Jesus Himself. It is He who will gather together His people (Jn. 10:16; 11:52), and their expectations are directed toward Him. In the end, therefore, it is Jesus Himself who is the theme of Johannine theology.

Bibliography.–C. K. Barrett, *Gospel According to St. John* (1957); O. Böcher, *Der johanneische Dualismus im Zusammenhang des nachbiblischen Judentums* (1965); F.-M. Braun, *Jean le Théologien*, I-III (1959-66); H. Braun, *Qumran und das NT* (1966); R. E. Brown, *Gospel According to John*, I-II (*AB*, 1966, 1970); R. Bultmann, *Gospel of John* (Eng. tr. 1971); *Theology of the NT*, II (1955); O. Cullmann, *Christology of the NT* (Eng. tr. 1959); C. H. Dodd, *Interpretation of the Fourth Gospel* (1953); P. Feine, *Theologie des NT* (9th ed. 1953); T. F. Glasson, *Moses in the Fourth Gospel* (1963); K. Haacker, *Die Stiftung des Heils: Untersuchungen zur Struktur der johanneischen Theologie* (1972); E. C. Hoskyns and F. N. Davey, *The Fourth Gospel* (2nd ed. 1947); W. F. Howard, *Christianity According to St. John* (1943); *The Fourth Gospel in Recent Criticism and Interpretation* (4th ed. 1955); A. M. Hunter, *Introducing NT Theology* (1957); E. Käsemann, *Testament of Jesus* (Eng. tr. 1968); R. H. Lightfoot, *St. John's Gospel* (1956); T. W. Manson, *On Paul and John* (1963); J. L. Martyn, *History and Theology in the Fourth Gospel* (1968); W. A. Meeks, *Prophet-King* (1967); E. Percy, *Untersuchungen über den Ursprung der johanneischen Theologie* (1939); T. E. Pollard, *Johannine Christology and the Early Church* (1970); R. Schnackenburg, *Die Johannesbriefe* (*HTK*, 2nd ed. 1962); *Gospel According to St. John* (2 vols., Eng. tr. 1968, 1980); S. Schulz, *Untersuchungen zur Menschensohn-Christologie im Johannesevangelium* (1957), esp. bibliography; *Die Stunde der Botschaft: Einführung in die Theologie der vier Evangelisten* (1967); E. F. Scott, *The Fourth Gospel* (2nd ed. 1908); E. M. Sidebottom, *The Christ of the Fourth Gospel* (1961); W. Thüsing, *Die Erhöhung und Verherrlichung Jesu im Johannesevangelium* (2nd ed. 1970); L. van Hartingsveld, *Eschatologie des Johannesevangeliums* (1962); W. Wilkens, *Zeichen und Werke* (1969).

See also bibliographies to JOHN, EPISTLES OF and JOHN, GOSPEL ACCORDING TO. I. H. MARSHALL

JOHN (APOCRYPHA) [Gk. *Iōannēs*].

1. Father of Mattathias, grandfather of Judas Maccabeus and his brothers (1 Macc. 2:1).

2. Eldest son of Mattathias, surnamed Gaddi or Coddi in some MSS.

3. Father of Eupolemus, one of the envoys sent to Rome by Judas Maccabeus (1 Macc. 8:17; 2 Macc. 4:11).

4. John Hyrcanus, son of Simon and nephew of Judas Maccabeus (1 Macc. 13:53; 16:1). *See* HASMONEANS; MACCABEES.

5. One of the envoys sent to treat with Lysias (2 Macc. 11:17).

JOHN (NT) [Gk. *Iōannēs*].

1. JOHN THE BAPTIST.

2. The apostle, the son of Zebedee and brother of James (*see* JOHN THE APOSTLE).

3. A relative of Annas the high priest who sat in the Sanhedrin when Peter and John were tried (Acts 4:6). He may have been a son and the successor of Annas the high priest.

4. John Mark. *See* MARK, JOHN.

5. Father of Simon Peter (Jn. 1:42 [AV JONA]; 21:15-17 [AV JONAS]). The best MS witnesses have Gk. *Iōannēs*, instead of the *Iōna* of the MSS available to the AV translators. *Iōna* is probably scribal assimilation to Gk. *Bariōna* (from the Aramaic for "son of Jona") in Mt. 16:17.

JOHN, ACTS OF. *See* APOCRYPHAL ACTS: THE "LEUCIAN" ACTS III.

JOHN, EPISTLES OF.

The NT contains five books traditionally ascribed to John, and three of these are headed as epistles or letters. But only 2 and 3 John are strictly to be regarded as letters. Each is the length of an ordinary private letter, which could be written on a standard-size piece of papyrus (25 cm. by 20 cm. = 10 in. by 8 in.), and each has the typical form of a letter with a more or less stereotyped introduction and conclusion. The form of 3 John resembles that of the following letter on papyrus discovered in Egypt and dated in the 2nd or 3rd cent. A.D.:

> Irenaeus to Apollinarius his dearest brother many greetings. I pray continually for your health, and I myself am well. I wish you to know that I reached land on the sixth of the month Epeiph and we unloaded our cargo on the eighteenth of the same month. . . . Many salutations to your wife and to Serenus and to all who love you, each by name. Goodbye. Mesore 9. [Addressed] To Apollinarius from his brother Irenaeus (C. K. Barrett, *The NT Background: Selected Documents* [1956], no. 22, p. 29).

By contrast, 1 John lacks the typical stylistic features of a letter. It is not, however, to be regarded as a literary "epistle," for it bears all the marks of being addressed to a specific situation in some church or group of churches known to the author. It is probably best to regard it as a tract written to deal with a definite problem; we may perhaps think of it as a written sermon or pastoral address.

I. Situation of 1 John
II. Structure of 1 John
III. Contents of 1 John
IV. Contents of 2 John
V. Contents of 3 John
VI. External Attestation of the Epistles
VII. Provenance and Date
VIII. Relationship among the Five Johannine Writings
IX. Authorship of the Epistles

I. Situation of 1 John.–1 John was called forth by a crisis in the Church due to the rise of false teachers; the point had been reached at which they had seceded from the Church (2:19), but their influence was still upsetting the faithful (2:26). The author of the tract considered it necessary to write a careful statement of the apostolic faith for his friends, showing them where it was being distorted by the false teachers.

The false teachers appear to have been forerunners of the heretics who were responsible for the developed Gnostic systems of the 2nd century. The seeds of Gnosticism were already to be found in the NT period, although it is a confusing use of terminology if we apply the actual term "Gnosticism" to the incipient Gnosticism or pre-Gnosticism of this period (cf. R. M. Wilson, *The Gnostic Problem* [1958]). Three characteristics of the form of teaching combatted by John may be distinguished:

(1) The false teachers regarded themselves as an esoteric group, superior to ordinary Christians. They believed that they had a deeper knowledge than other Christians (cf 2:20, 27; 2 Jn. 9), and they showed little brotherly feeling toward them (cf. 4:20, which may have the false teachers particularly in mind).

(2) The precise content of this deep knowledge is uncertain. As far as doctrine was concerned, they denied that Jesus was the Christ (2:22), i.e., that He was the preexistent Son of God (1:1; 4:15; 5:5, 10) who had come in the flesh (4:2; 2 Jn. 7) to be the Savior of the world (4:9f., 14). Thus they rejected the basic Christian doctrine of the Incarnation and apparently also the doctrine of the Atonement. These views have generally been regarded as bearing some affinity to those of Cerinthus, a heretical teacher in Asia Minor at the close of the 1st century. According to Irenaeus, John was an opponent of Cerinthus and would not even bathe in the same bath-house at Ephesus with that "enemy of the truth" (*Adv. haer.* iii.3.4). Cerinthus taught that "the world was not made by the primary God, but by a certain power far separated from him, and at a distance from that Authority who is supreme over the universe, and ignorant of the God who is above all. He represented Jesus as having not been born of a virgin, but as being the son of Joseph and Mary according to the ordinary course of human generation, while he nevertheless was more righteous, prudent and wise than other men. Moreover, after his baptism, Christ descended upon him in the form of a dove from the Supreme Ruler, and that then he proclaimed the unknown Father, and performed miracles. But at last Christ departed from Jesus, and that then Jesus suffered and rose again, while Christ remained impassible, inasmuch as he was a spiritual being" (*Adv. haer.* i.26.1).

From this quotation it will be evident that the false teaching discussed in 1 John was by no means fully identical with that of Cerinthus, but it resembled it in distinguishing Jesus from the Christ who temporarily dwelt in Him; cf. especially 5:6, where John emphasizes that Jesus *Christ* came by the water (of baptism) and the blood (of the cross), and the repeated statement that Jesus *is* the Christ, the Son of God (2:22; 5:1, 5; cf. 4:2). It may be significant that the present tense is used; does it mean that Jesus remains the Christ? In 2 Jn. 7 the present participle "coming" may refer to the Incarnation as a continuous fact (C. H. Dodd). But the teaching of Cerinthus was more fully developed in a Gnostic direction, and R. Schnackenburg (pp. 17f.) denies any real connection between it and the false teaching in 1 John. (On the other side, see J. A. T. Robinson, "The Destination and Purpose of the Johannine Epistles," in *Twelve NT Studies* [1962], p. 134.)

In any case the teaching in 1 John appears to reflect the well-known distinction made by the Gnostics between spirit and matter. The spiritual was regarded as divine and good, and the material as created and evil; no lasting union was possible between them, and consequently a real incarnation of God in human flesh was impossible and could only be either apparent (the heresy known as Docetism) or temporary (Cerinthianism).

(3) These doctrinal views led to equally strange teaching about the life of the Christian. The false teachers claimed that they were "sinless" (1:8, 10), and it is probable that they felt they did not need cleansing by the blood of Jesus Christ. At the same time they were to some extent morally indifferent: they appear to have followed the ways of the world (cf. 2:15), they did not regard the commandments of Jesus as binding upon them (2:4), and they made little attempt to practice Christian love and generosity, although there is no indication that they fell into gross sin.

Perhaps this paradoxical behavior arose from their failure to regard sin as a moral category, namely, lawlessness (3:4, 7f.). They may have thought of sin as a spiritual matter, and hence saw no inconsistency in claiming sinlessness while at the same time indulging in selfishness and lovelessness. A Gnostic would have argued that, since the body (composed of matter) was evil and only the spiritual part of man was ultimately important, bodily behavior was irrelevant to Christian belief. Gnostic theology was more concerned with ignorance than with sin.

II. Structure of 1 John.–The argument of 1 John is best understood as an antidote to this false teaching, designed as a warning to those who had not yet succumbed to it (cf. K. Weiss, *ZNW,* 58 [1967], 247-255). Its structure is undeniably difficult.

Some commentators have adopted the view that the thought of the Epistle proceeds in spiral form, so that although the same ideas are repeated, the thought keeps ascending to higher levels. This view is especially associated with R. Law (*ISBE* [1939]). It yields the following analysis of the Epistle:

Prologue. 1:1-4.

(1) First Cycle. 1:5–2:28. The Christian life as fellowship with God (walking in the Light), tested by righteousness (1:8–2:6), love (2:7-17), and belief (2:18-28).

(2) Second Cycle. 2:29–4:6. Divine sonship tested by righteousness (2:29–3:10a), love (3:10b-24a), and belief (3:24b–4:6).

(3) Third Cycle. 4:7–5:21. Closer correlation of righteousness, love, and belief.

The weakness of this scheme is that the three themes common to the first and second cycles do not occur in the same manner in the third cycle.

A more elaborate scheme was adopted by A. E. Brooke (cf. W. G. Kümmel, *Intro. to the NT* [1966], pp. 306f.), which may be abbreviated as follows:

Introduction. 1:1-4.

(A) (1) Ethical Thesis. Walking in the light as the true sign of fellowship with God (1:5–2:17).

(2) Christological Thesis. Faith in Jesus as the Christ as the test of fellowship with God (2:18-27).

(B) (1) Ethical Thesis. Doing of righteousness as the sign that we are born of God (2:28–3:24).

(2) Christological Thesis. The Spirit which is of God confesses Jesus Christ come in the flesh.

(C) Combination of the two Theses:

(1) Love as the basis of faith (4:7-21).

(2) Faith as the basis of love (5:1-12).

Conclusion. 5:13-21.

This scheme also seems somewhat artificial.

If we must attempt to divide up the Epistle in a logical fashion, preference should be given to the divisions proposed by R. Schnackenburg:

Preface. 1:1-4.

(1) Fellowship with God as walking in the light, and its realization in the world (1:5–2:17).

(2) The present situation of the Christian Church: its defense against the antichrists, its expectation of salvation, and its religio-ethical task (2:18–3:24).

(3) The separation of those who belong to God from the "world" by true faith in Christ and love (4:1–5:12).

Conclusion. 5:13-21.

But even this scheme is not altogether free from difficulty. It seems best to regard the Epistle as composed of a series of connected paragraphs whose relation to each other is governed by "catch-words" as well as by logic. This does not mean that John is illogical, but simply that his Epistle is not adapted to division into large sections on a logical basis. The outline of contents below will show the flow of its thought.

It will not be surprising that various scholars have attempted to explain the difficulties in the structure of the Epistle by hypotheses of rearrangement, use of sources, and editorial revision.

(1) The simplest rearrangement is that proposed by K. Tomoi (*Expos.T.,* 52 [1940-41], 117-19), who wishes to place 4:1-6 between 4:21 and 5:1. In its present position 4:1-6 gives the impression of being a digression; but this is by no means impossible in John, and there is no objective evidence for the proposed reconstruction.

(2) The view that 1 John is an editorial revision of an earlier document was held by E. von Dobschütz (*ZNW,* 8 [1907], 1-8) and accepted by H. Windisch (p. 136). It was developed by R. Bultmann in two articles ("Analyse des ersten Johannesbriefes," in *Festgabe für A. Jülicher* [1927], pp. 138-158; "Die kirchliche Redaktion des ersten Johannesbriefes," in W. Schmauch, ed., *In Memoriam E. Lohmeyer* [1951], pp. 189-201). According to Bultmann, the original document consisted of 1:5-10; 2:4f., 9-11, 29; 3:4, 6-10, 14f., (24); 4:7, (8), 12, 16; 5:1, 4; 4:5, 6 (?); 2:23; 5:10, 12; (2 Jn. 9). Later the completed work was subjected to an "ecclesiastical" revision which added 5:14-21 and various small interpolations in order to bring the thought more into line with orthodox theology. These theories reappeared with minor modifications in Bultmann's commentary, where the author suggested that the original Epistle extended only to 2:27, the remainder being loosely attached discussions of the themes already treated.

(3) H. Preisker (in H. Windisch, *Die Katholischen Briefe* [*HZNT,* 3rd ed. 1951], ed. H. Preisker, pp. 168-171) holds that two source documents were combined: a "revelatory address" roughly identical with the original document isolated by Bultmann, and an "eschatological text" containing verses or parts of verses from 2:28; 3:2, 13f., 19-21; 4:17; 5:18f.

These views have not met with much acceptance, and have been effectively criticized by various scholars (W. Nauck, *Die Tradition und Charakter des ersten Johannesbriefes* [1957]; R. Schnackenburg, pp. 11-15).

(4) A more conservative line is taken by W. Nauck, who isolates a number of sets of antithetical statements in the Epistle. He thinks we can see traces of a previous work by John himself which he later wrote up in its present form. It may well be true that John used material which had already begun to assume a definite form through use in teaching and which was cast in a shape suitable for easy memorization (see F. F. Bruce in *EQ,* 30 [1958], 115f.), but the theory as a whole has not found favor.

(5) A novel analysis is offered by J. C. O'Neill (*The Puzzle of 1 John* [1966]), who argues that the author took up twelve poetic admonitions of Jewish provenance and adapted them in order to form a Christian document whose purpose is to show the fulfillment of Judaism in Christ. The theory is unconvincing, but at least the author has shown the Jewish affinities of the Epistle.

(6) On the basis of an analysis of numbers of syllables, J. S. Sibinga (in *Studies in John Presented to Professor Dr. J. N. Sevenster* [1970], pp. 194-208) has argued that the Epistle as we have it is a carefully balanced, rhetorical construction.

The variety of conclusions offered shows that the skepticism of such scholars as E. Haenchen (pp. 8-12, 15-20, *et passim*) and W. G. Kümmel (*op. cit.,* pp. 308f.) toward such theories is abundantly justified.

III. Contents of 1 John.–The Epistle begins with a statement of its purpose. John wishes to explain to his readers more about the word of life which was manifested in Jesus, so that there may be a true communion between them, himself, and God (1:1-4).

He then announces his starting point, that God is light; He is holy and He illuminates people who live in His presence. From this proposition, which would presumably be acceptable to his opponents, he now proceeds to quote and criticize various slogans which crystallized their teaching (1:6a, 8a, 10a; 2:41; cf. 4:20). Against them he asserts that it is impossible to claim fellowship with God while walking (i.e., living) in the darkness of sin; only those who walk in the light have fellowship with God through continual cleansing by the blood of Christ. Those who protest that they have no sin from which to be cleansed deceive themselves and deny the truth of God's verdict upon them. But those who confess their sin to God will find that He faithfully forgives them through the sacrifice provided by the righteous advocate, Jesus Christ. The practical test as to whether a person is a sinner in need of cleansing or truly knows God is whether or not he keeps God's commandments and lives as Jesus lived (1:5–2:6).

From the thought of God's commandments, John turns to the new commandment that Jesus gave. It is really an old commandment, but is now given afresh to Christians as the rule of life in the era of light that has already begun to shine in the darkness of the old, sinful world. We have here the typical NT idea of two eras or worlds, the old era of sin and the new era of salvation. But, whereas Jews looked forward to the coming of this new, messianic era in the future, Christians believed that it had already dawned in the midst of the old world and would one day (at the parousia of Jesus) entirely replace the old era; thus during the present time the two eras run side by side, and only the believer can see that the new age has already begun. In this new era people must live by the commandment of brotherly love. (The new commandment has two main aspects — faith and love (3:23) — and it finds expression in various commandments which John does not list in detail.) John is able to give his readers this new commandment because they belong to the new era and no longer walk in the darkness that blinds them and makes them a stumbling block; they enjoy the privileges of forgiveness, knowledge of the Son and of the Father, and victory over the devil. As citizens of the new world, they are not to cling to the sinful world with its temptations to lust and pride in material possessions, for it is doomed to pass away (2:7-17).

One of the signs that Christians live in the last hour before the old era passes away is the rise of false teachers. It was common knowledge that the Parousia would be preceded by the coming of antichrist; in the anti-Christian teaching of his opponents John saw part at least of the fulfillment of this prophecy. Through their secession from the Church the false teachers stood revealed as what they really were. They denied that Jesus was the Son of God, and since John thought of God as being the Father of believers only because He is the Father of Jesus Christ, this meant that they were denying the Fatherhood of God. (Jn. 20:17 is the only unambiguous reference in the Johannine corpus to God as the Father of believers.) To be sure, the false teachers based their claims on special knowledge, but John asserts that all Christians (RV mg., RSV, NEB), in virtue of their anointing by God (i.e., with the Spirit; perhaps, as Dodd suggests, with the Word of God), have true knowledge. Let them, therefore, keep to what they were originally taught (2:18-27).

John has spoken of the way in which their anointing abides in his readers. He now bids them for their part to abide in the Son, who is righteous, so that they will not shrink away from Him in shame at His parousia through being themselves unrighteous. Let them test themselves (and their teachers) by their likeness to Christ. For since Jesus is righteous, it follows that all who claim to be born of God, as He was, must be righteous also. This leads on to the thoughts of God's great love in making people His children and also of the prospect that when they see Him (probably Christ rather than God) they will be altogether like Him — all of which is a strong inducement to a holy life (2:28–3:3).

What, then, is the character of this holy life which God's children must lead? John begins by defining his terminology. Sin means failure to keep God's law. Since Jesus appeared on earth to remove sin, Christians do not sin by breaking God's law. Indeed they cannot sin, because they are born of God and His seed remains in them; on the other hand, the children of the devil, i.e., unbelievers, neither do what is right nor show love, and thus are clearly differentiated from believers. John's statement that believers cannot sin is strong and uncompromising. But it must be understood in the light of 1:8 and 2:1. The most probable explanation is that John is depicting the ideal character of the Christian; insofar as he really is a Christian and abides in Christ ("abide in him" is an imperative), he will not sin, and he will make it his purpose not to sin, in contrast with the false teachers who did not make it their aim to keep God's law despite all their professions of sinlessness (3:4-10). (On the theological problem, cf. the survey of various interpretations in Haenchen, pp. 30-35.)

While Christians have received the command to love each other, the false teachers, as has already been said, lack love. Consequently, Christians can expect to be hated by them, just as Abel was murdered by Cain. But the mark of the Christian must be love, demonstrated in the same spirit of sacrifice as was shown by Jesus and in practical charity (3:11-18).

Such acts help a person to be sure that he belongs to the truth and free him from the inward accusation that he is not really a child of God; for he can have perfect confidence in his judge, the God who knows his desire to love and serve Him (cf. Jn. 21:17). Freed from such accusations he can boldly approach the throne of grace in prayer, because he knows that he pleases God by keeping His commandments. Thus he really does abide in God, and God in him, as the Spirit of God inwardly assures him (3:19-24).

But how can a person be sure that it is the Spirit of God that abides in him? Do not the false teachers also claim to possess the Spirit? John answers that the sign of true inspiration is correct belief that Jesus Christ has come in the flesh. Anybody who does not confess this is inspired by antichrist (for "does not confess" some textual witnesses have "annuls" [Gk. *lýei*], i.e., repudiates the true doctrine about Jesus). Thus, there are two spirits, one of truth and the other of error, and it is not surprising that the world, inspired by antichrist, does not accept the witness of believers. Yet, although their opponents are many, believers may have confidence, because God is greater than their adversary and because believers have in reality already overcome the false prophets (4:1-6).

From this digression John returns to the theme of love, since love as well as faith is characteristic of those who possess the Spirit. Love is the sign that a person is born of God, for, as was supremely demonstrated in the sacrifice of Christ, God is love, and loved us before we began to love Him. (This is the second of John's great declarations about the nature of God. Cf. 1:5 and Jn. 4:24.) Even if people cannot see God, yet He abides in them if they show love (4:7-12).

A section now follows in which John gathers together much of what he has already said. He summarizes the grounds on which a person may be sure that he is a Christian: he possesses the Spirit of God; he confesses that Jesus is the Son of God; he abides in love. Consequently, God abides in him, and he may have complete confidence for the Day of Judgment because he shares in the character of God, and because there can be no cringing fear in a relationship of love. But to avoid any antinomian or spiritualistic misunderstanding, John reemphasizes that such love for God must be expressed by love for one's brethren. How, indeed, can those who love the Father fail to love His children also? It might be objected that it is not easy to love God and to keep His commandments, but John points out that through faith those who are born of God can overcome the world and all its temptations (4:13–5:4).

Thus John has returned to the theme of faith, and in a doctrinal section he now defines closely the content of true faith. It must be a faith that Jesus is the Son of God, and this is closely related to the fact that Jesus not only submitted to the water of baptism but also shed His blood on the cross, i.e., that the Son of God really became man and died for our sins, a fact which is corroborated by the witness of the Spirit to Jesus (cf. Jn. 15:26). It may be said, then, that there are three witnesses to Jesus — the Spirit, water, and blood — and they bring God's sure testimony about His Son to mankind. (For the text of 5:7f. see any modern translation or comm.; the AV contains a trinitarian interpolation, "in heaven . . . in earth," which is not part of the original text.) John possibly also means that the saving activity of the Spirit and the sacraments of baptism and the Lord's Supper continue this testimony in the Church (see the important discussion of this by W. Nauck, *op. cit.*). To disbelieve this testimony from God is to make Him a liar and to refuse His gift of eternal life in His Son (5:5-12).

The Epistle closes with a restatement of its purpose, which is to assure believers that, whatever false teachers may say and however strong the world may seem, they do possess eternal life and can be confident of a divine answer to their prayers. Thus they may pray for any erring brethren with confidence that they will be restored to fulness of life. In the case of mortal sin, however, prayer is apparently useless. (However, no one has ever established what John meant by "mortal sin." He probably meant apostasy, but we cannot be sure.) Next comes a reiteration of the great truths of the Epistle — that God's children have power not to sin and can overcome the devil, that the readers are in fact God's children, and that the Son of God has in very truth come in the person of Jesus to give them true understanding and eternal life. A final admonition warns against idolatry, and comes as something of a surprise (5:13-21).

IV. Contents of 2 John.–The situation and contents of 2 John are closely related to those of 1 John, but the tone is much more personal and practical. The letter is addressed from "the elder" (see IX below) to "the elect lady and her children." Although some scholars still think that an actual family is thus addressed, there can be little doubt that this is a cryptic manner of addressing a church (cf. 1 Pet. 5:13), and the whole manner of address is perhaps intended to baffle any hostile persons who might intercept the letter. W. Foerster (*TDNT,* III, 1095) thinks that the elder is respectfully addressing a church which he himself had not founded.

After expressing his joy that his readers are walking in the truth and exhorting them to love and to obey God's commandments, John comes to the main point of his letter. False teachers holding the doctrines attacked in 1 John have been going from church to church with their propaganda. John warns his readers lest they be led astray and lose their reward from God; those who "go on" (AV "transgresseth" is based on inferior MSS) to accept this "higher teaching" (as its proponents no doubt described it) are really abandoning true doctrine and with it their faith in God, the Father of Jesus Christ. False teachers should not be encouraged in any way, e.g., by offering them hospitality. John says that he would gladly write more, but he hopes to see his readers soon, and concludes his letter with greetings from his own church.

Since the false teachers are here apparently still within the church, it may be that 2 John was written earlier than 1 John, or else to a different church. In any case, it is clear that the two writings belong together.

V. Contents of 3 John.–The situation is somewhat different in 3 John, which is a private letter to an individual and deals more with ecclesiastical problems. It is addressed from the elder to his friend Gaius, who was a leading member in another church. Gaius is warmly commended for his loyalty to the truth, seen in the quality of his character. In particular, in an age when many Christian preachers traveled from church to church and were very much dependent on local hospitality, he is commended for looking after such preachers; by helping those who went out trusting in God, he has shown himself a fellow worker in (or with) the truth.

His attitude is contrasted with that of Diotrephes, whom John criticizes on two grounds. He refused to welcome traveling preachers and attempted to keep them out of the church. He also wished to have a place at the head of the church and refused to accept the authority of John; he was so successful in suppressing a letter of John that no trace of it has survived beyond the mention of it here. John, therefore, warns that he will come and deal personally with Diotrephes if necessary. Finally, he adds a word of commendation for Demetrius, who may have been one of the traveling preachers or the bearer of this letter, and concludes with cordial greetings.

The situation reflected here is not easy to reconstruct. Probably we are to see in it the troubles of a new system of church organization. At first the various churches were to a considerable extent under the guidance and leadership of apostles and similar people who traveled from place to place, and the authority of local leaders was correspondingly restricted. With the passage of time and the growth of the churches a new situation developed. The apostles died, leaving no defined system of succession, and local churches tended to develop more powerful leadership of their own. In various places there was a tendency for one person to become bishop and preside over the church and its other leaders. It looks as though Diotrephes was trying to hasten this process; he was seeking autonomy for his own church with freedom from the influence of the elder, and he himself wished to occupy the leading position in it. Possibly Gaius was a member of a neighboring church, for otherwise it would be strange for John to tell him what he must already have known.

It does not necessarily follow from this that Diotrephes had already become bishop in his own church (as is held by B. H. Streeter, *The Primitive Church* [1928], pp. 83-97; G. Bornkamm, *TDNT,*VI, 670-72; E. Schweizer, *Church Order in the NT* [1961], 12c, 14a), but simply that he was desirous of this position; thus the situation had not yet reached the stage of development reflected in the Epistles of Ignatius (cf. Dodd, pp. 161-65; Schnackenburg, p. 329).

It is also important to notice that no heretical views are attributed to him (despite W. Bauer, *Rechtgläubigkeit und Ketzerei im ältesten Christentum* [1934], pp. 96f.). Nor is there any reason whatever to assume that the elder was a heretic. This, however, is the assumption made by E. Käsemann (*ZTK,* 48 [1951], 292-311; similarly Bultmann, pp. 99f.); he holds that the elder was a teacher with sympathies toward Gnosticism. Although he opposed docetic views of Christ, he had the boldness to write a Gospel in which his own unorthodox opinions were expressed and was opposed by Diotrephes as the champion of orthodoxy. This hypothesis is entirely improbable; the Johannine writings are in fact a powerful defense against Gnosticism (for criticism of Käsemann, see G. Bornkamm, *TDNT,* VI, 671 n. 121; Schnackenburg, pp. 299f.; Haenchen, pp. 267-291).

VI. External Attestation of the Epistles.–The external attestation for 1 John is excellent, and certainly better than that for the Gospel of John. According to Eusebius (*HE* iii.39.17) it was used by Papias (*ca.* 130-140). It was quoted by Polycarp in *Phil.* 7 (*ca.* 110-140) and by Justin in *Dial.* 123.9 (*ca.* 150-160). Irenaeus (*Adv. haer.* iii.16.5, 8) accepted it as the work of John the disciple of the Lord, and this view was shared by Tertullian, Clement of Alexandria, Origen, and the Muratorian Canon. Eusebius states that its authenticity was never questioned (*HE* iii.24.17; 25.2).

The case of 2 and 3 John is less certain. It is uncertain whether the Muratorian Canon refers to all three Epistles or only to the first two (for the former view see J. Moffatt, *Intro. to the Literature of the NT* [3rd ed. 1918], pp. 478f.; P. Katz, *JTS,* N.S. 8 [1957], 273f.; for the latter see T. W. Manson, *JTS,* 48 [1947], 25-33). The Second Epistle was quoted by Irenaeus (2 Jn. 11 in *Adv. haer.* i.16.3; 2 Jn. 7f., wrongly ascribed to 1 John in iii.16.8) and by Aurelius a Chullabi (Council of Carthage, 256, Brooke, p. lix). According to Eusebius (*HE* vi.14.1), Clement of Alexandria commented on all the canonical Scriptures, but the fragments of his *Adumbrationes* that have survived do not include 3 John. Origen reflected current doubts about their status (comm. on John, v.3), and Eusebius reckoned them among the books that were disputed by some but generally recognized in the Church (*HE* iii.24.17; 25.2f.). On the basis of this and other evidence, T. W. Manson (*op. cit.*) concluded that 1 and 2 John were known in the Latin-speaking church in the West before 3 John, which was translated separately into Latin. In the East the Syrian church, which was slow in accepting the Catholic Epistles, took 1 John into the Peshitta, but 2 and 3 were only accepted much later in the Philoxenian Version. Undoubtedly the brevity and comparative unimportance of 2 and 3 John were responsible for their poor circulation and for the doubts expressed about them. There was some doubt about their apostolic authorship.

VII. Provenance and Date.–On the whole it is still most probable that the Epistles are to be connected with Asia Minor. If the teaching opposed in 1 John is linked with Cerinthus, this strengthens a case firmly based on the traditions that connect the author with Asia Minor. The claims of Syria have been urged by W. Nauck (*op. cit.,* p. 165); but this depends very much upon his interpretation of 1 Jn. 5:6f., which has not won general acceptance.

The date of composition cannot be determined with certainty. Resemblances to ideas found in the Qumrân literature indicate that the time required for the development of Johannine theology need not have been so long as formerly thought. On the other hand, the growth of heresy and the development of the ecclesiastical situation prevent an early date. Thus, a date between the 60's and 90's of the 1st cent. is probable.

VIII. Relationships among the Five Johannine Writings.– Before the question of authorship can be discussed it is necessary to consider the literary relations of the Epistles to each other and to the rest of the Johannine writings.

Some doubt was expressed in the early Church as to the common authorship of the three Epistles; Eusebius (*HE* iii.25.3) mentions the possibility that 2 and 3 John may not be the work of the Evangelist who was the author of 1 John, and similar doubts are mentioned in later writers, including Jerome (*De vir. ill.* 9, 18), Ambrose (*Ep.* 11.4), and the *Decretum Gelasianum.* This view was adopted by J. Moffatt (*op. cit.,* pp. 479-481), who cites a number of other scholars in support of his opinion. More recent scholarship affirms that all three Epistles are from the same hand (Brooke, pp. lxxiii-lxxix; R. H. Charles, *ICC* on Revelation [1920], I, xxxiv-xxxvii; Dodd, pp. lx-lxvi; Schnackenburg, pp. 297f.). Although 1 John is anonymous, we may now assume that its author was "the elder."

More serious doubts have been raised in recent years about the common authorship of the Gospel of John and 1 John. J. Moffatt, who himself was inclined to accept a difference in authorship, gave a lengthy list of supporters for his view (*op. cit.,* pp. 589-593); and the position has been popularized by C. H. Dodd (*BJRL,* 21 [1937], 129-156; summarized in his comm., pp. xlvii-lvi), who is followed by C. K. Barrett (comm. on John [1955], pp. 49-52; cf. also Windisch, pp. 109-111 and Haenchen, pp. 4-8). But convincing proof of common authorship is given by Brooke (pp. i-xix), W. G. Wilson (*JTS,* 49 [1948], 147-156), and W. F. Howard (*The Fourth Gospel in Recent Criticism and Interpretation* [4th ed. 1955], pp. 281-296; see also Law, pp. 339-363; Schnackenburg, pp. 34-39; Kümmel, *op. cit.,* pp. 310-12).

The relevant arguments may be summed up as follows:

(1) A number of linguistic differences between the Gospel of John and 1 John have been discovered. These include the absence of Gk. *oún* from 1 John (194 times in the Gospel), the much rarer use of *gár* and *dé,* and the substitution of *apó* (19 times in 1 John; 40 times in the Gospel) for *pará* (only 3 times in 1 John; 33 times in the Gospel); there is also a considerable diminution in the number of compound verbs used.

It is doubtful whether these stylistic differences can be regarded as very significant. R. Morgenthaler has pointed out that even if statistical investigations of this kind can produce fruitful results, they must always be carried out with very great caution; taken by themselves statistics can be deceptive (*Statistik des neutestamentlichen Wortschatzes* [1958], p. 65). That similar differences may be easily established between books whose common authorship is generally accepted should make us wary of attaching too much significance to these findings for the Johannine literature. (E.g., Gk. *mén* occurs only 10 times in Luke but 47 times in the slightly shorter book of Acts.) Inquiry must be made as to the possible causes of stylistic differences. In addition to difference of authorship the possibilities of use of sources and different amanuenses should be taken into account. Literary genre should also be noticed; *oún* is a historical rather than a consecutive particle in the Gospel. Finally, in this particular case it must be remembered that the Epistles stand closer in style and content to the Gospel than to any other writing. The very close stylistic similarities between the two groups may well be entirely adequate to outweigh the differences.

(2) Various words and word-groups found in the Gospel do not appear in 1 John, including: salvation and destruction, Scripture, glory, send and seek, above and below, judgment. These are carefully discussed by W. F. Howard, who finds reasonable explanations for their absence. In general it may be said that there are differences of emphasis between the Gospel and Epistles due to their having been written in different situations and with different purposes, and that it would be foolish to expect different books to have identical contents. Howard lists some similar omissions in and differences among the various writings of Paul: we may add to his examples the complete omission of the word "church" in Rom. 1–15.

(3) The crucial argument depends on a number of theological differences; the list that follows is based mainly on that given by J. Moffatt:

(a) In 1 John there is a transference to God of functions that in the Gospel are reserved for Christ; e.g., Christians are said to be "in God" directly, while in the Gospel this relationship is mediated through Christ.

(b) In 1 John eternal life depends on correct belief about the person of Christ rather than on faith in Him. Thus faith tends to be more intellectual.

(c) Christ is identified with Life rather than with the Logos.

(d) There is more emphasis upon sin and the need for propitiation.

(e) The signs that authenticate the messiahship of Jesus are not mentioned.

(f) There is more stress on the Parousia.

(g) The Holy Spirit is less personal, and is simply a witness to orthodox belief rather than an indwelling presence in believers.

(h) The Epistle stands nearer to Gnosticism than the Gospel does.

Of these arguments Moffatt himself regards (f) as weak. It is difficult not to believe that some of the others are equally weak. Point (e) does not seem important, and W. F. Howard deals adequately with (d) and (g). (See also Schnackenburg's criticism [pp. 37f.] of Dodd's interpretation of 2:20, 27; 3:9.) In view of the identification of Christ with Life in Jn. 1:4 it is doubtful whether much importance can be attached to (c); there is a difference of expression, but hardly a basic theological difference. As for (b), this point is adequately accounted for by the need to stress the importance of true belief against the false teachers; the same reason, the exigencies of polemic, will also account for (h). (That the Epistle stands nearer to primitive Christianity in certain points, as C. K. Barrett holds, may well be due to the use of traditional material.) Finally, it may be questioned whether Moffatt's references for (a) really prove his point.

When this evidence is fairly considered, it does not seem sufficient to overthrow belief in common authorship. Rather, we are seeing the same mind at work in two different situations in the production of two different kinds of literary work. The Gospel is, at least in part, an apologetic to the non-Christian, designed to lead him to faith in the incarnate Son of God; the Epistles are pastoral tracts called forth by particular situations in the Church.

To some extent the author's development of thought may also have contributed to these differences, if, as many scholars hold, the Gospel was written before the Epistles. But this argument can be used only with great hesitation, since it seems impossible to determine the order of composition. Although the Gospel is logically prior to 1 John, this does not necessarily mean that it was written first. It may be that 1 John was composed during the long period of meditation that went into the composition of the Gospel.

To complete the picture, some attention must be paid to the relation of the book of Revelation to the other Johannine literature. There is no doubt that Revelation is closely related to both the Gospel and the Epistles by a wealth of common theological concepts which mark the five Johannine books as a distinct group. The theory of common authorship of all five books has found some powerful support (E. Lohmeyer, *Die Offenbarung des Johannes* [2nd ed. 1953], pp. 198f., 202f.; P. Feine and J. Behm, *Einl. in das NT* [10th ed. 1954]; W. Michaelis, *Einl. in das NT* [2nd ed. 1954]), but the very considerable linguistic peculiarities of Revelation are such that the consensus of opinion is strongly against attributing it to the author of the other four books. J. Moffatt (*op. cit.*, p. 481) held that 2 and 3 John and Revelation had a common author. In any case, some connection between all five books must be posited, and it should be remembered that the external evidence for the apostolic authorship of Revelation is strong. (*See* REVELATION, BOOK OF.)

IX. Authorship of the Epistles.–The problems discussed in the last section show that the question of authorship is an intricate one, and a full treatment of it would require attention to the Gospel. The particular contribution of the Epistles to the general problem of the Johannine literature is found in their references to the elder who is named as the author of 2 and 3 John. It is generally agreed that this term does not mean here simply an elderly man or an elder in a local church (Haenchen, however, thinks that a leader of a local church is meant, pp. 288f.). The author claims an authority that is more than local, and this indefinite range of authority seems to be reflected in the title. There may have been a quasi-technical use of the term for the apostles and for those who formed the link between them and the next generation.

Was this elder the apostle John? Light on this problem is often sought from a well-known passage from Papias (cited in Eusebius *HE* iii.39.4): "And if anyone chanced to come who had actually been a follower of the elders, I would inquire as to the discourses of the elders, what Andrew or what Peter said, or what Philip, or what Thomas or James, or what John or Matthew or any other of the Lord's disciples; and the things which Aristion and John the elder, disciples of the Lord, say."

Here Papias refers to certain of the disciples of the Lord, including John, under the name of "elders" in the past tense, which presumably signifies that they were dead, and then speaks of two living disciples, Aristion and John the elder. Eusebius adds the comment that clearly two Johns are to be distinguished, and for his part he regards the former as the Evangelist and the latter as the probable author of Revelation.

These statements have given rise to considerable and inconclusive discussion (see G. Bornkamm, *TDNT,* VI, 676-680; J. Munck, *HTR*, 52 [1959], 223-243). Some scholars have held that this "John the elder" was a disciple of the apostle and was the author of the Gospel and the Epistles (B. H. Streeter, *The Four Gospels* [4th ed. 1930], pp. 430-461). But this cannot be more than a hypothesis, for it is still not finally settled whether Papias refers to two Johns or mentions the same person twice (because he alone of the apostles remained alive), although the former view commands greater support than the latter. If the former view is accepted, it is to be noted that Papias says nothing about any links between John the elder and John the apostle. Again, we cannot be sure that Papias used the term "elder" in the same sense as in 2 and 3 John, but it should be noted that he could use the term of apostles, and in this connection Peter's reference to himself as a "fellow-elder" may not be irrelevant (1 Pet. 5:1).

The evidence of Papias thus allows the possibility that John the apostle was the elder of the Epistles, although this is difficult if there was another "John the elder" alongside him. Haenchen holds that the opposition of Diotrephes to the elder is inconceivable if directed against an apostle (pp. 268f.), but the evidence of opposition to Paul in Corinth and elsewhere may be regarded as weakening the force of this argument. We are thrown back upon the evidence concerning the authorship of the Gospel, and our conclusions about the Epistles must rest upon our conclusions about the Gospel. Despite frequent assertions to the contrary, sufficient evidence connects the apostle John with the Gospel, and two possibilities thus arise. Either John the apostle was the author of the Epistles (doubtless with the aid of an amanuensis), or else the author was a close disciple of his, writing in his own name but incorporating his master's teaching. The tendency of modern scholars has been to think of a Johannine "school" in which various pupils transmitted the spiritual heritage of the apostle (C. K. Barrett, *op. cit.*, pp. 51f.); in this way E. Stauffer can say that all the Johannine writings are to be ascribed to the apostle or his influence (*NT Theology*

[1955], pp. 39-43). In the present state of scholarship it is thus still possible to associate the Epistles with John the apostle, although it would be rash to assert dogmatically the precise relationship which he bears toward them.

Bibliography.–Comms. by J. N. S. Alexander (*Torch*, 1962); A. E. Brooke (*ICC*, 1912); F. F. Bruce (1970); R. Bultmann (*KEK*, 1967; Eng. tr., *Hermeneia*, 1973); C. H. Dodd (*MNTC*, 1946); G. G. Findlay (*Fellowship in the Life Eternal* [1909]); J. H. Houldon (*HNTC*, 1973); M. de Jonge (*De Brieven van Johannes* [3rd ed. 1978]); R. Law (*The Tests of Life* [3rd ed. 1914]); G. P. Lewis (*Epworth Preacher's Comms.*, 1961); I. H. Marshall (*NICNT*, 1978); R. Schnackenburg (*HTK*, 5th ed. 1975); J. R. W. Stott (*Tyndale*, 1964); B. F. Westcott (5th ed. 1908); H. Windisch (*HNT*, 3rd ed. 1951).

See also the bibliographies in Brooke and Schnackenburg; and see the critical survey of recent studies provided by E. Haenchen, *TR*, N.F. 26 (1960), 1-43, 267-291.

I. H. MARSHALL

JOHN, GOSPEL ACCORDING TO.

I. Characteristics
II. Authorship
III. Background
IV. Method of Composition
  A. The *Aporiai*
  B. Theories of Dislocation
  C. Theories of Sources
  D. The "School" of John
  E. The Place of Preaching
V. Date
VI. Relation to the Synoptists
VII. Historicity
VIII. Purpose

I. Characteristics.–John's Gospel differs markedly from the other three. Though they have their differences and each has a character of its own, Matthew, Mark, and Luke all give us recognizably the same picture (as the name "Synoptic" indicates). But John does not fit into their scheme of things even though his book is sufficiently like theirs to be included in the class of writings known as "Gospels."

It has often been pointed out that there is not much movement in John. He does not give us a picture of the development either of the teaching of Jesus or of the growth of the opposition. The Synoptists do not do this as fully or as clearly as modern scholars would like, but at least there are some indications of development. Thus Peter's confession at Caesarea Philippi is a significant turning point, Jesus' later predictions of the Passion mark an advance on His earlier teaching, etc. In John there are fewer indications of the way the history developed (though it would not be true to say that there is none; John does have his hints at the way the events unfolded). He prefers to concentrate on the significance of what happened and of what Jesus taught. It matters more to him to convey meaning than to give precise indications of how Jesus' teaching progressed and how the Jewish opposition to Him grew.

John begins with a prologue that is unlike anything in the Synoptics. There is dispute about whether John wrote it, or found it and incorporated it, and even whether it should be understood as prose or as poetry. There is a good deal of subjective reasoning in all such discussions. As it stands the prologue introduces in impressive fashion some of the great thoughts that will be developed as the story unfolds.

John has a short section on Christian beginnings (1:19-51) in which he tells us something of the witness of John the Baptist and of the call of Jesus' first disciples. Then he has a long section in which he deals with some of the things Jesus said and did during His public ministry (2:1–12:50). This includes accounts of seven miracles, which John calls "signs" (Gk. *sēmeía*), and seven discourses, i.e., discussions with individuals (Nicodemus, the woman at the well) and groups (in the synagogue at Capernaum or the temple in Jerusalem). He proceeds to tell what happened in the upper room on the night before the crucifixion (13:1–17:26). The Synoptists, of course, give information about this evening, but John's account is for the most part unparalleled. Though his account is clearly the most detailed, he has puzzled all subsequent generations by omitting anything about the Last Supper. He proceeds to a narrative of the crucifixion and resurrection (18:1–20:31), where his account has its distinctives, notably in giving a good deal of information about the Roman trial of Jesus and some beautiful resurrection stories. Chapter 21 is an epilogue, which some think was appended by the original author, others by someone else. All this adds up to a Gospel that has had a wide appeal to Christians throughout the world and throughout the centuries. It is perhaps the most influential book that has ever been written.

It is written very simply. Not uncommonly the beginner in Greek starts with this Gospel and finds it no great problem. In translation the humble and unlearned have always known how to listen to these words and they have testified that in them they have found their deep needs met. But at the same time the simple language is profound. This Gospel presents the scholar with some of the most difficult problems in NT study. Perhaps it is the combination of simplicity and profundity that makes it so great.

The discourses present a particular problem because there is nothing like them in the other Gospels. There Jesus teaches mostly by parables and aphorisms. It would not be true to say that either is completely lacking in John, but it is certainly the case that the overall impression left is quite different. It is possible that here we have an aspect of Jesus' teaching which the Synoptists have not recorded. After all, any great teacher has different styles for different audiences, and it is not easy to think that the mind of Jesus was such that it could not encompass the Johannine discourses as well as the Synoptic teaching. It also must be remembered that, while in all probability Jesus spoke in Aramaic, what He said is reported in Greek. The Evangelist has translated what Jesus said, so that the final choice of words is his and not that of the Master. This does not mean that he has not faithfully reproduced the teaching, for it is possible for a translator to be accurate. But it does mean that we must allow for John's preference for various idioms and expressions.

Some find a problem with the ideas rather than the language. Here we should notice that John has a good deal to say about a variety of topics which receive little attention in the Synoptics. Thus he tells us a good deal more than they do about the Holy Spirit, particularly in the farewell discourse. He has much to say about light and life and love, about abiding in Christ, about believing in Him, about the world. But especially important under this heading is what he has to say about the Son and about the Father. The person of the Son looms large for John, and indeed he states that he writes that his readers may believe that Jesus is the Christ, God's Son, and thus enter into life (20:31). It is integral to this Gospel that in Jesus we see God incarnate ("the Word was made flesh"), that it is only through Him that we know God as He is, and that it is in Jesus that God has worked out the salvation of mankind. John sees eternal life as closely bound up with the mission of Jesus and specifically as something accomplished by His death (3:16).

II. Authorship.–Throughout most of its history the Church accepted without question the view that this Gospel was written by John the apostle. This view has been strongly criticized in modern times; indeed it has been abandoned and regarded as quite impossible by a great number of scholars. But there are still good grounds for accepting the traditional view.

The Gospel itself contains the claim that it was written by "the disciple whom Jesus loved" (21:20, 24). This attestation appears to be that of people who wished the facts of the case to be known. It seems impossible to hold that the author of the Gospel wrote this claim, but no known manuscripts omit it, so it appears to be contemporary with the original writing. An attestation as early as this by people who must have known the facts of the case must be regarded as weighty evidence. Some scholars hold that ch. 21 formed no part of the original Gospel and that the words refer only to this chapter. Whatever be the truth of the hypothesis that ch. 21 is an addition, it is preposterous to hold that there would be a solemn attestation of the authorship of this last chapter while the preceding chapters were left anonymous. There can be no doubt but that the words are intended to apply to the whole Gospel.

But the attestation does not reveal the identity of "the disciple whom Jesus loved." This expression appears in 13:23; 19:26; 20:2; 21:7, 20. He seems to be one of the unnamed disciples or one of the sons of Zebedee (21:2). He is close to Peter (13:24; 20:2; 21:7), which makes us think of the frequent linking of Peter, James, and John and of their being especially close to Jesus in the Synoptics. But James was martyred quite early (Acts 12:2), which leaves John. It is objected that it would be strange for a man to call himself "the disciple whom Jesus loved." But it would also be strange to use the title of someone else. It might conceivably be used by John in modesty. On this view, he does not even mention his own name but uses an oblique form of speech which emphasizes that he owes everything to the love of Jesus.

We should not pass over the curious fact that in this Gospel John and his brother James are never mentioned. The Synoptists make it clear that they were prominent in the apostolic band. We can understand John omitting reference to himself and his brother, but why should anyone else do this? With that we should notice the fact that the author habitually speaks of John the Baptist simply as John, though he takes care to differentiate people in other cases, e.g., Judas Iscariot in 12:4, Judas not Iscariot in 14:22. To refer to the Baptist in this way is natural if the writer himself was called John, but it would have been very confusing for anyone else.

This is not conclusive proof but it is the most natural way of taking the evidence, and it can be supported. As we shall see later, there is good reason for seeing in the author a Jew, more specifically a Jew of Palestine. He gives evidence of Jewish thinking and interests and he is at home in the customs and topography of Palestine. He is such a person as we would expect John to be.

Those who uphold the traditional authorship usually draw attention to indications that the writer was an eyewitness of the things of which he writes. Such touches are found throughout the Gospel; as an example notice the lively story of the giving of sight to the man born blind in Jn. 9 (cf. Morris, *Studies in the Fourth Gospel,* pp. 139-215). Unfortunately this kind of thing comes short of definitive proof. What seems to one set of critics nothing less than clear indication of an eyewitness seems to another nothing more than evidence of the author's power as a dramatist, little touches inserted to give the appearance of verisimilitude. They must be noted, for they are part of the evidence, but their force as proof must be qualified.

The controversies in this Gospel should be noted, for they are the kind of disputes that went on in Jesus' lifetime; they are not the sort of thing in which the later Church found itself involved. Thus there are disputes about the Messiah, when and where he would come, and what he would do. There are discussions about the manna, the right use of the sabbath, the importance of relationship to Abraham, true and false Judaism. There are no discussions of the Church as a body separate from Judaism, the place of bishops, the correct date for the observance of Easter, the existence of the aeons that meant so much to the Gnostics. The topics of the Gospel are those of Jesus' day and accord with authorship by someone who was there at the time and knew what happened. They do not accord with what we expect from someone from a later period and a different area who was simply concerned to produce a theological treatment of topics that would help the church of his day.

But there are some weighty arguments against Johannine authorship. It is pointed out that whereas John the son of Zebedee was a Galilean, this Gospel is concerned for the most part with happenings in and around Jerusalem. It may be countered that the author's theological interest dictated his choice of topics and that the question of messiahship had to be settled in Jerusalem. A further objection is that this Gospel omits some striking incidents at which we know from the Synoptists that John was present, e.g., the Transfiguration and the agony in Gethsemane. We might indeed have expected John to notice these, but we have to accept the fact that every author makes his own selection and these may not have appeared to John in quite the same light as they do to us. The story of the Transfiguration concentrates the glory into one story, but John sees it as pervasive. The whole incarnate life of Jesus shows God's glory, and the writer may well have felt it difficult to include a story which seems to concentrate it in one spot.

Similarly it has been pointed out that the whole Gospel shows Jesus' lowliness and dependence on God (the paradoxical combination of glory and lowliness is one of the features of John's portrait of Jesus). This is suggested as a reason for the omission of the story of Gethsemane. C. H. Dodd suggests that the omission is from motives of reverence, a veil being drawn over this intimate experience. In any case we must bear in mind that there are some extraordinary omissions from this Gospel. No one seems ever to have given a satisfactory reason for the absence of any account of the institution of the Lord's Supper. John has none of the great parables that are such a feature of Synoptic teaching, nor has he any equivalent of the Sermon on the Mount. In the light of these and other omissions we cannot say that he must include the Transfiguration or the agony of Gethsemane. He wrote what he wished to write and these omissions are no real indication that the son of Zebedee was not the author.

The biggest objections to apostolic authorship seem to be other than these. One is the difference from the Synoptists. If the Synoptic Gospels give us a reliable picture of Jesus, it is argued, then John's picture, which is so different, cannot be accurate and thus it cannot have been drawn by John the apostle. Here everything depends on what one thinks of the nature of the differences between the two portraits. If they are incompatible, then Johannine authorship is excluded. If Jesus was a large enough figure to inspire the two portraits, then the objection is not valid.

The other argument which convinces many scholars is that this Gospel gives every indication of being indebted to Gnosticism. This rules out the son of Zebedee on two counts: the Gospel is probably too late for him to have written it, and the ideas are not those of an early Palestinian but of a Hellenist of quite different outlook from that of the Galilean fisherman. If the premise be granted the objection is a strong one. But as we shall see in a later section, there are strong objections to seeing Gnosticism behind this Gospel. It seems that the objection is based on a too limited view of the range of thought available in first-century Palestine, to say nothing of the originality of Our Lord.

When we turn to external evidence, the Gospel is ascribed to John by Theophilus of Antioch (*ca.* A.D. 180), then by Irenaeus (*Adv. haer.* iii.11.1f.), and it seems by all others. There were objections by a few like the Alogi who appear to have disliked the doctrine of the Logos and accordingly ascribed the Gospel to the heretic Cerinthus. But there is no evidence that such views were ever held by other than a tiny group of dissenters (some think by only one dissenter, a certain Gaius). The tradition really knows of one name only, John son of Zebedee. It is worth adding that the Gospel was popular among the Gnostics when in due time they appeared. That the Church accepted it despite these heretical associations seems to show that it was known to come from the apostle. It could not be rejected, even though the heretics found it so congenial.

Probably there will never be full agreement about authorship. But where absolute certainty is unattainable we must choose on the basis of the probabilities. In this case the evidence is much more in favor of John the apostle than against him, and there is no other candidate with even a show of probability. We should accordingly accept John as the author.

III. Background.–For a long time the affinities of the Gospel with Greek thought were stressed and it could be described as "the Gospel of the Hellenists." More recently the Jewish affinities of the writing have received emphasis. But the Greek idea received a new impetus with the publication of R. Bultmann's comm. in 1941. Bultmann interpreted the Gospel in terms of the Gnostic redeemer myth. He discerned a signs source (the miracles), a discourse source (which he thought derived from non-Christian Gnosticism), and a Passion narrative. Some smaller units, such as the cleansing of the temple, were combined with these three by the Evangelist, who added his own contributions. Bultmann thought the manuscript somehow got into disorder and that a redactor rearranged it, putting in some comments of his own. This is a complicated analysis and it has not won very wide acceptance, but the thesis that at least part of the Gospel comes from Gnosticism has been looked on with favor by some scholars. Another way of seeing Gnosticism is to view the portrait of Jesus as an expression of "naive Docetism" as E. Käsemann holds (*Testament of Jesus* [Eng. tr. 1968], p. 70). Many scholars who reject the positions of Bultmann and Käsemann still find something Gnostic about John's language. They hold that many of John's ideas scarcely find a place within Palestinian Judaism and are convinced that we must see this Gospel against a Gnostic background. Whether or not John himself was a Gnostic, they think that he was using Gnostic tools.

The first objection to seeing Gnosticism behind this Gospel is that all the known Gnosticism is too late. Despite the confident assertions of some, there is as yet no evidence that Gnosticism was in existence early enough to be an influence on the NT (Yamauchi, pp. 184-86). Gnosticism was a system that gathered ideas from many sources as well as contributing its own, but it is the gathering of the sources into one system and not their existence separately that constitutes Gnosticism. Some of the ideas were early but that does not mean that Gnosticism was equally early. Characteristic Gnostic ideas are absent from John. He knows nothing of the idea that matter is evil. Nor does he have the concept of the *Demiourgos,* the being whom the Gnostics postulated as the creator of this evil material universe (which the Gnostics held the high good God would not have done). He makes no mention of the aeons or of many other important Gnostic concepts. Again, none of the known Gnosticism is early enough for John to have derived his portrait of the redeemer from it. Rather, Gnosticism seems to have taken the Christian picture of Jesus and combined it with features derived from other sources to make its redeemers. Bultmann puts emphasis on Mandaism, a specific form of Gnosticism, but Mandaism cannot be proved to have existed before Christianity, and some even doubt that its Gnosticism was there from its beginning. Some scholars hold that it was at first a baptist movement which somewhere along the way picked up some Gnostic ideas. This whole area is nothing but confusion and speculation. We cannot find a firm basis for the Gospel anywhere in Gnosticism as it is known to us. Indeed a quite fundamental divergence must be kept in mind. Where he is found the Gnostic redeemer is essentially a revealer: he brings mankind knowledge. But in John the Savior is more than a revealer. In John the Redeemer brings mankind salvation: He is the Lamb of God who takes away the sins of the world.

Gnosticism then can scarcely be held to be the milieu out of which this Gospel sprang. We have glanced at the idea that it might be from Hellenism, and such ideas have been put forward from time to time. But again, not too much can be made of this. Obviously a writing in Greek, probably published in a center of Greek culture, must have some Greek ideas in it. But it is not this that is characteristic of the Fourth Gospel. There can be found coincidences of language or thought with Philo or other Greek writers, but that is about as far as we can go. C. H. Dodd gave considerable attention to this aspect of the Fourth Gospel and noted affinities with the Hermetic literature, with Philo, and with other Greek writers. But not many have been persuaded that John should rightly be seen as a representative of this kind of writing, and even Dodd recognizes a Semitic basis.

There is considerable agreement that this Gospel must be seen as essentially Semitic. Some have held that it was written in Aramaic (C. F. Burney, *Aramaic Origin of the Fourth Gospel* [1922]; C. C. Torrey, *Our Translated Gospels* [n.d.]), but this has not convinced most scholars. More influential is the position of M. Black, who holds that there is Aramaic thinking behind a Gospel written in Greek (cf. *Aramaic Approach to the Gospels and Acts* [3rd ed. 1967]). W. G. Kümmel (*Intro. to the NT* [Eng. tr., rev. ed. 1975], p. 217) holds that either this must be the case or the author is from a bilingual environment. The Aramaic element is to be discerned especially in the sayings of Jesus.

This Gospel shows an accurate knowledge of Jewish customs. There are more references to the Jewish feasts than in any other Gospel, and clearly the writer is familiar with the Jewish liturgical year. He knows about Jewish purification rites (2:6), the inferior status of women (4:27), the sabbath regulations (5:10; 7:22f.), and much more of the same kind. He is aware of the time spent on building the temple (2:20). He knows the attitude of the Jews to the Samaritans (4:9).

The discoveries at Qumrân have given us a great deal of new information about Judaism in the time of Jesus (*see* DEAD SEA SCROLLS). One of the more unexpected results of the study of these documents is that they have more links with John than with any other writing in the NT. There are similarities in language and sometimes similarities in thought. Interestingly, quite often where the language is similar the ideas are different. Thus John speaks of "doing" the truth (Jn. 3:21), as does the Manual of Discipline (1QS 1:5; 8:2). But in John truth is connected with the person of Jesus who is the truth (14:6), whereas the covenanters connect it with keeping the law (for them Hab. 2:4 means "the men of truth, the doers of the law"). The fundamental difference is that for the people of Qumrân the wonderful days of the Messiah lie in the future, whereas for John the Messiah has come. But this does not prevent them from using a good deal of the same language and thought forms. The Scrolls help us to see that this Gospel is properly to be located in Palestine.

So does its accurate topography. John mentions a number of places, some of which, such as Cana, are not mentioned in any previous writing known to us. He has convinced experts like W. F. Albright ("Recent Discoveries in Palestine and the Gospel of St. John," in W. D. Davies and D. Daube, eds., *Background of the NT and Its Eschatology* [1964], pp. 153-171) and R. D. Potter (*SE,* I [1959], 329-337) of his accuracy. It cannot be shown that he has wrongly located any place he mentions. This would be almost impossible for a writer who did not know Palestine, particularly if, as many who object to the Johannine authorship hold, he was writing many years after the destruction of Jerusalem (when many landmarks were significantly affected).

A minor point is that John never refers to "the Gentiles," *tá éthnē*. When he uses the word *éthnos* he means the nation, i.e., the Jewish nation. He writes from the standpoint of someone within Judaism and does not reproduce the idea found elsewhere in the NT that the Jews' rejection of Jesus is followed by the Gentiles' acceptance of Him. There must have been effective Christian work among the Gentiles at the time John wrote. His interest, however, is not there but in the way Jesus came to Israel.

More important is the way the Gospel constantly reflects Judaism of the time of Jesus and not the environment of the Church at the time it was written. As we noted in the section on authorship, the controversies are not those of the second-century church but those of Palestine in the time of Jesus. How could a late, non-Palestinian writing so faithfully reflect conditions in the time and place of which it tells?

For these and other reasons most scholars are now convinced that the Fourth Gospel must be understood against an early Palestinian background. Whoever wrote it and whenever he wrote it, he had good and accurate knowledge of conditions in Palestine in Jesus' day.

IV. Method of Composition.–How was this Gospel written? Without actually saying so, most seem to have assumed that a writer sat down and wrote the book as it is, or dictated it to someone who did the scribal work for him. But some phenomena make such views difficult and to them we must turn our attention. In the process some of the important problems in Johannine studies will come under our notice.

A. The Aporiai. This Greek term refers to the "perplexities" which crop up in a close examination of this Gospel. Thus Jesus did "signs" in Jerusalem (2:23) but later we read of his having done his "second sign" (4:54). John the Baptist pointed Jesus out to his followers and told them who He was (1:29-34), but at a later time they do not know this (3:26-30). At the end of ch. 5 Jesus is in Jerusalem, but in 6:1 He went to the other side of the Sea of Galilee. Peter asks Jesus where He is going (13:36; cf. 14:5), but subsequently Jesus says that nobody has asked Him this (16:5). The Gospel appears to end at 20:31, but then comes another chapter. Quite a few such points can be adduced. Perhaps none of them is very serious, but they do raise questions. Why would anyone write a manuscript like this? A variety of answers has been given.

B. Theories of Dislocation. A view which has often been put forward is that the leaves of the manuscript were somehow disarranged and whoever put them together did so in the wrong order. It is felt by many that ch. 5 should follow ch. 6, this being a typical case of disruption of the natural order. As already noted, ch. 6 begins with Jesus going to the other side of the Sea of Galilee; this event follows strangely on ch. 5 where He is in Jerusalem. But it would follow ch. 4 quite naturally, for this ends with Jesus healing a boy in Galilee. There would be a better sequence

Text of Jn. 6:59-70 from the Bodmer Papyrus II (***p***[66]), the oldest (2nd cent. A.D.) considerable portion of John's Gospel now extant (Bodmer Library, Geneva)

also with ch. 7, which begins, "After these things Jesus was walking in Galilee; for he would not walk in Judea because the Jews were trying to kill him." This would follow more naturally on ch. 5 which has Him in Jerusalem than on ch. 6 where He is in Galilee. The Passover is said to be near in 6:4, and a feast, which might be the Passover, is present in 5:1. All this adds up to such a strong case that many are convinced by it.

But there are objections. There is no manuscript evidence for any order other than the one we have. To many it seems that the teaching on the divine Son in ch. 5 is the necessary basis for that on Jesus as the bread of life in ch. 6. The conflict in ch. 5 would quite naturally be followed by a move to Galilee. To some students the crisis point at 6:67 comes too early if it is before ch. 5.

Thus there are some considerable objections to this transposition, and we should bear in mind that this is probably the most plausible of all the transpositions that have been suggested. In the case of the others, as of this, good reasons may be urged against, as well as for, the suggested rearrangement.

Even if the rearrangements were accepted as on the whole giving better sequences, we would be faced with the problem of how the disruption came about. We would have to assume that the original of this Gospel was written in codex form rather than on a roll, and this is far from certain. And we have no reason for thinking that John would wish to use this form instead of the time-honored scroll. Granted that the leaves of a codex somehow became scattered, there are further problems. We must immediately ask whether we at this distance in time can arrive at the original order better than the first-century Christian who actually had the pieces in his hands. He must have seen the difficulties in the present order just as clearly as we do. The hypothesis moreover demands that all the pages out of order should conveniently begin and end with complete sentences. The chances are that at least some of the breaks would be in the middle of sentences and then there would be grammatical problems.

Some have tried to give a note of objectivity to the dislocation theory by calculating the lengths of the displaced sheets. Bernard thinks of each leaf (two pages) as having about 750 letters (thirty-four lines each of eleven letters). He tries to show that each of his major dislocations consists of multiples of this length. But the objectivity is only apparent. Scribes varied in their numbers of lines to a page and of letters to a line and allowance must be made for variation. When Bernard has one section consisting of 598 letters we must feel that he has strayed too far from his average. If variations of this magnitude must be allowed, then almost any length could be brought into the scheme and the objectivity vanishes. Again, if a codex were disarranged there would be units of two leaves (four pages), not single leaves.

All in all the objections are formidable and very few now accept this hypothesis. The theory has more ingenuity than probability.

C. Theories of Sources. There is a greater readiness to consider theories of sources than of dislocations. The thought is that the *aporiai* may be explained by the putting together of sections taken from a variety of sources (and with some editorial assistance) without the redactor having gone over the result carefully enough to smooth out the resulting rough places. We have already noticed Bultmann's view that there was a signs source, a discourse source, a Passion source, some smaller pieces, the contributions of the Evangelist, and, after the manuscript had in some unexplained fashion fallen into disorder, of the redactor who produced the final order. Few have completely agreed with Bultmann, but the signs source has appealed to many. The references to the first and second signs (2:11; 4:54) and to the many signs from which a selection has been made (20:30) seem to many to point irresistibly to a collection of miracle stories. They suggest that the Evangelist has made use of such a collection and has incorporated parts or all of it without bothering to correct the first two numerical references (though he has apparently tidied up the later ones). The reference to the many signs (20:30) is said to follow oddly on the Passion story (which is not called a "sign") while it would be the natural conclusion to a book consisting only of signs.

If there is a signs source the discourses are naturally taken together as evidence of another source. Most who work with the sources hypothesis think of the Passion narrative as a third main source, though some attach it to the signs source. There is always something left over, and this is ascribed to the redactor.

It must be agreed that such hypotheses would give an explanation of the unevennesses of the narrative as we have it. But before we can accept any such view we must reflect that a first-century author might not be as interested in producing a smooth-flowing writing as we are. He may have felt that his object would be attained without sifting carefully through what he had written to remove anything that would offend such susceptibilities as ours. In other words we must ask ourselves whether we are justified in looking for our modern standards of consistency in a first-century writer.

There are other objections. Probably the greatest difficulty in the way of all hypotheses of sources is the uniformity of style that marks this Gospel. From start to finish it is written in the same style, as a number of detailed examinations have shown. Some scholars have attempted to dispute this, drawing attention to grammatical minutiae and the localized presence of certain ideas, but they have not convinced very many. The unity of style remains an impressive fact. And, despite Bultmannn, most agree that the discourses show every sign of having been written by the Evangelist, not incorporated into his Gospel by someone who came across them. It is improbable that anyone who could write this kind of prose would simply take some other source, be it the "signs" or anything else, and add it to what he has composed. In any case the postulated signs source has many of the same characteristics as the discourses.

Moreover, source theories do not account satisfactorily for the fact that the signs and the discourses often fit in with each other so well. The feeding of the multitude and the discourse on the bread of life go together, as do the healing of the blind man and the discourse on the light of the world, while the raising of Lazarus fits the theme of Jesus as the resurrection and the life, a theme found often in the Gospel. We should probably also link the transforming of water into wine with the transformation that is the new birth, and the healing of the lame man on the sabbath with the discourse on the divine Son. It is not easy to see how such relatedness could result from the combination of disparate sources that were not originally intended to dovetail into one another.

It is further pointed out that those who see sources ask us to believe in the existence of documents of a kind for which we have no evidence and which are intrinsically unlikely. For example, consider the suggested signs source. Are we to believe that the early Christians had a source which in effect turned Jesus into a miracle worker? This source would have nothing of Jesus' teaching, no eschatology, no predictions of the Passion, no use of apocalyptic language. We know of no such document, and from what we do know of early Christian literature it seems most unlikely.

Some prefer to think of a series of editions. Thus it has been suggested that the author produced first a Gospel in which he outlined Jesus' ministry in Judea and later supplemented this with a Galilean edition. Others see him as writing first a narrative of Jesus' words and deeds and adding to that a Passion narrative. Or again it is possible that John took certain incidents and made a Gospel out of them, later adding other incidents without sufficiently smooth transitions.

R. E. Brown has enunciated a hypothesis with which many would be in substantial agreement. He sees five stages, beginning with a pool of traditional matter not dissimilar to what we see in the Synoptic tradition, but quite independent of it. Then came the preaching of the Evangelist and others (Brown thinks of some sections like Jn. 9 as being developed into "superb dramas" in this process). The third stage is the writing of a Gospel out of this matter, and the fourth a reediting of it (possibly a number of times). The final stage he sees as coming after the Evangelist's death when a redactor produced the Gospel we now have. Such views are not easy to refute, but it must be recognized that there is a good deal of speculative material here. And it is hard to see why the product of all this should be attributed to the apostle John. There have been many hands in it and the final shape is not in any way his, the hypothesis being that he was dead when it was produced. While this view takes account of some of the phenomena it overlooks others.

D. The "School" of John. Since the hypotheses of sources and editions are fraught with so much difficulty it seems better to look for some other solution to the problem of the *aporiai*. Many find it in the hypothesis of a Johannine "school," which would also account for the three epistles and the apocalypse associated with the name of John. Most agree that it is not easy to see how the same man could have written both the Gospel and the book of Revelation. There is more of a problem with the epistles. Here opinion is divided, with many holding that they must be ascribed to a writer (or writers) other than the author of the Gospel and others seeing enough evidence to support the traditional view that they come from the same pen. Those who see divergent authorship agree that there are links between all these writings, some linguistic and some conceptual. Add the persistent association of the name of John with these writings and the tradition that the apostle John lived to a great age and the scene is set for the hypothesis of a school. The idea now is that the apostle John had his own way of stating the Christian faith. He gathered disciples around him as he taught, and these in due time gave expression to much the same kind of thinking as that which characterizes the apostle. Their discussions enabled them to exchange ideas, and when in due course they began to write there turned out to be quite strong links among their writings. And in the Gospel are contributions from different members of the school that help account for the awkwardnesses.

Sometimes attention is drawn to the quotation by Eusebius of some words of Papias which have been taken to show that there was another John, who is usually referred to as "John the Presbyter" (*HE* iii.39.6). This is supported by a report Eusebius quotes from Dionysius that "it is said" there were two tombs in Ephesus, each bearing the name John. This is a very slender foundation on which to erect a hypothesis, but some hold that John the Presbyter existed and that he wrote the Gospel. They contend that confusion of the names caused the Church to ascribe it to the apostle. Despite the great names that have espoused this thesis it is difficult to see how it can stand. It is quite possible to take Papias's words as referring to only one John, John the apostle. The very existence of John the Presbyter is far from having been established. If he did exist there is no reason for linking him with the Gospel. There is no evidence that he wrote anything, let alone that he was of such a caliber as to be able to produce a writing like our Gospel. If the later Church could have been confused about apostles and elders it is equally possible for Papias, and if he was the one who was confused the theory has no basis.

The hypothesis of a school is difficult to refute, but it is also difficult to establish. The only evidence for it is the Johannine writings themselves, and for centuries the Church has managed to live with these documents without demanding a school to account for them. Other explanations are possible and throughout most of the history of the Church have been accepted without question. Further, there are great difficulties in the way of the school hypothesis. To take but one, what has happened to the apostle? It is a well-known fact, as noted in II above, that John the son of Zebedee is never mentioned in the Fourth Gospel. In this writing people of a similar name are usually distinguished, as when Judas is qualified by "Iscariot" (12:4) or "not Iscariot" (14:22), or when Thomas is described as "the Twin" (*dídymos,* 11:16), an epithet not found in the other Gospels. But in this Gospel the Baptist is habitually referred to only as "John" while John the son of Zebedee, whom we know from the other Gospels to have been a prominent figure in the apostolic circle, is never mentioned. But the school hypothesis asks us to believe that the revered founder of the school, the one to whose inspiration the school owed its very existence, the man who in the opinion of the school had the most significant insights into the Christian way, could be totally overlooked in the writing of a Gospel.

E. The Place of Preaching. Many students of this Gospel find indications of preaching behind it, as in the view of Brown noted earlier. There was obviously a good deal of preaching in the early Church. All the indications are that it was the most usual way of conveying the message of the Christian faith to the world outside (cf. Rom. 10:14). Unfortunately we know little about the mechanics of sermon preparation and the like in the early Church, though Acts does give accounts of some of the sermons preached by the first Christians. But there seems no reason why some sermons or at least sermon summaries might not have been written down.

Luke tells us that "many" had in fact written accounts of what had been fulfilled among the Christians (Lk. 1:1), and this should be taken seriously. Clearly much that the early Church wrote has perished. It is not unlikely that much of this material expressed "the gospel." It is worth bearing in mind that the canonical Gospels are not Mark's Gospel or Matthew's Gospel and so on. They are the gospel further described as according to Mark or Luke or one of the others. There was only one "gospel," though it might be given written form by more than one person.

What I am suggesting is that the apostle John, like other early Christians, preached the gospel. He may have written down some of the "gospel" he preached and made it available to other people. Like every preacher, he would have used some sermons more often than others (which may account for those phenomena that cause some students to discern much rehandling of the material in some sections of this Gospel). In due course he worked up some of the signs and discourses and other material which seemed to him important and thus produced a fuller account of the "gospel." In some such way he made the writing that has meant so much throughout the history of the Church. I do not mean that the Gospel is a record of his sermons and not of what Jesus said and did. That does not follow. Indeed, some scholars have held that the apostle may have made notes on Jesus' addresses not long after he heard them (e.g., D. Guthrie, *NT Intro.* [3rd ed. 1970], p. 286). I do not think the evidence for this is strong, though the theory is not improbable. If this was in fact the case, it would be quite in accordance with the above view for John to have included such notes in his Gospel. He must often have preached about what Jesus said and did, and the Gospel probably echoes some of his sermon material.

If there is enough evidence to justify this theory, we may allow for some intermediate composition, using only part of the material in the Gospel as some have held. But the main contention here is that most of the phenomena which puzzle us about the Fourth Gospel can be satisfactorily accounted for if we bear in mind that the apostle preached before he wrote. The *aporiai* are then evidence not that many sources or divergent writers were behind this Gospel, but rather that the records of the apostle's preaching were put together in such a way that all difficulties were not smoothed out. Even if we date the Gospel in the 60's we must allow for thirty or so years of preaching, and it seems that this is quite long enough to account for what we have. At any rate, the idea that the apostle preached a good deal and wrote his Gospel out of his experience as a preacher seems to have much more to be said for it than views of sources or editions and redactors.

*V. **Date.***–Traditionally this Gospel has been seen as the latest of the four. This has been accepted by liberal and conservative alike, and few have been found to date it earlier than the last decade of the 1st century. Some of course put it into the 2nd cent., but there has been a most unusual measure of agreement on the 90's or shortly thereafter. The conservatives thought John wrote to supplement the Synoptics, and the liberals thought that his concern was to correct them. But common to both has been the thought that he wrote last.

In recent years, however, it has been emphasized that the evidence for dependence on the Synoptists is thin. Since 1938 when P. Gardner-Smith's book *Saint John and the Synoptic Gospels* appeared, scholars have increasingly tended to see John as independent of the Synoptics. It is remarkable, if he knew them, that he has omitted so much that they contain and that he has worded what he has in just the way he has. On this last point, e.g., he records the Baptist as denying that he was Elijah (1:21), whereas in Mt. 11:14; 17:11-13; Mk. 9:11-13 Jesus said that he was that prophet. If John knew Matthew or Mark, it is difficult to think he would have left his statement quite as it is without showing how it relates to the other. It would have taken only a few words to show in what sense John was Elijah or in what sense he was not. But if this kind of thing shows that John is independent of the Synoptics the question of date is again raised. Perhaps the reason he does not refer to them is that he had not seen them, and perhaps the reason he had not seen them is that he wrote too early. At least the possibility must be considered.

It is worth noticing that there are several early locutions in John. Thus he does not speak of "apostles" but "disciples," and he often uses the expression "his disciples" rather than "the disciples." At a later time the Christians had no doubt as to whose disciples they were, but in the earlier period it was recognized that many rabbis had disciples. There had to be some way of differentiating Jesus' disciples from those of other teachers. Again the use of the present tense for the existence of the pool in Jn. 5:2 is most naturally taken as indicating that the pool was still in existence, i.e., it points to a date before A.D. 70. The affinities with Qumrân are also important, for the monastery was destroyed in the war of A.D. 66-70, so that contacts must be earlier. Such considerations fall short of proof but they indicate that a date in the 60's accounts for more of the phenomena than one in the 90's. Some would go further. F. Lamar Cribbs has assembled a mass of evidence to back up his contention that the date should be seen as in the late 50's or early 60's (*JBL*, 89 [1970], 38-55; see also J. A. T. Robinson, *Redating the NT* [1976], pp. 254-311). All in all it seems that we should accept a date in the 60's.

*VI. **Relation to the Synoptists.***–As already noticed, until recently it has been almost universally accepted that John wrote with the Synoptists either before him or in his mind. Some have held that he wished to fill out what they had to say with other matter in his possession; others saw him as trying to replace them or correct them. There have been doubts about the extent of his acquaintance with the Synoptists, but a common position is that of C. K. Barrett who thinks that John made use of Mark and possibly Luke, though his use of Matthew is much more problematic (Barrett does not think that any of these Gospels necessarily lay before John as he wrote; rather he had read Mark and been influenced by its contents and so probably with Luke).

Barrett's case rests heavily on the order in which certain key passages occur, for he feels that since John has the same order as Mark in ten incidents it is very likely that he knew Mark. But the order seems largely determined by the events themselves. The ministry of John the Baptist had to come first, and Jesus' departure for Galilee must follow that. The feeding of the multitude, which took place in Galilee, must come later than the departure for that region. Barrett next cites the walking on the lake, and this is the kind of sequence that would prove his point if there were enough examples. He goes on to Peter's confession, but it seems that Mk. 8:29 does not refer to the same incident as Jn. 6:68f. Jesus' departure for Jerusalem had to follow the Galilean ministry, and the entry to Jerusalem could scarcely come anywhere else in the sequence. Actually Barrett here links two events, the anointing and the entry, but has to note that they are in the reverse order in the two Gospels, so this is not very convincing. The Last Supper, arrest, Passion, and Resurrection follow, and there is nothing remarkable in their being in the same order in the two Gospels. Thus this argument is not a strong one. Nor is the argument from linguistic dependence, despite some interesting resemblances. Barrett lists twelve passages, which usually do not agree very closely; in any case Mark has about 12,000 words, so this is not a very convincing demonstration.

The case for dependence on Luke is, of course, less impressive and that for Matthew less still. It seems that there are no strong arguments for holding that John made use of any of the Synoptic Gospels, and there are some considerations on the other side. The bulk of the Fourth Gospel finds no parallel in the other three and even those incidents which are common to John and one or more of the others are treated so differently that it is difficult to postulate dependence. For example, both have a cleansing of the temple. But in John it comes at the beginning of Jesus' ministry and in the others at the end. When the accounts are compared closely it becomes evident that the two are as different as they could be and still speak of a temple cleansing. The common language is the barest minimum (there are really only five significant words in common, and without them it would be very difficult to tell a story of temple cleansing at all). John's references to the sheep and oxen and to the scourge of cords are not paralleled, nor his word for "money-changers" (Gk. *kermatistḗs*), nor his reference to the pouring out of money, nor the command "Take these things away." Contrariwise the Synoptists mention a command not to carry anything through the temple, a command John does not have. The Scripture passages cited are different in the two (Isa. 56:7; Jer. 7:11 in the Synoptists, and Ps. 69:9 [MT 10] in John). In the Synoptists objection is made to the dishonesty practiced (cf. "den of thieves"); in John it is to the practice in itself ("do not make my Father's house a shop"). This will be found typical. Most incidents in the Fourth Gospel differ from those in the Synoptics, and even where it is said there are links close examination usually reduces them to negligible proportions.

It seems that such resemblances are better explained in ways other than literary dependence. There can be no doubt that much of the story in the Gospels was carried on in oral tradition for quite some time, and there is no reason why John and the Synoptists should not have received stories in this way with similar wording. This point has its importance, for we should not think of any of the Gospels as descending on an astonished Church like lightning striking from the sky. The Church knew stories of Jesus, and told and retold them. The Gospels doubtless set out more than most early Christians would know, but it was essentially what the Church as a whole knew that found its place in these books.

This common knowledge has a further consequence. I have been arguing that the Fourth Gospel is independent of the Synoptists. But this does not mean that they are talking about something different. It is the same Jesus who is behind all four. The stories they tell are not the same stories but they are not in contradiction. In fact one can go further and assert that we need all four to get the complete picture. Again and again John can be shown to be necessary if we are properly to understand what the Synoptists wrote. For example, the Synoptists refer to a Galilean ministry that might be estimated to have lasted a year or less. Then Jesus went up to Jerusalem and was killed by the authorities in less than a week. This is all very astonishing. It is not so surprising when we learn from John that the ministry lasted three years or so, that during this period Jesus was in Jerusalem from time to time, and that on these visits He came into conflict with the religious leaders. This enables us also to make sense of Synoptic statements like "Day after day I was with you in the temple" (Mk. 14:49); "How often would I have gathered your children together" (Mt. 23:37).

All the Synoptists tell us that Peter was in the high priest's courtyard at the time of the denials. How did he get there? It is John who tells us that there was a disciple who was known to the high priest and who secured Peter's entrance. And at Jesus' trial people claimed that Jesus had said that He would destroy the temple and build it again in three days (Mt. 26:60f.; Mk. 14:58). Mockers said the same at Calvary (Mt. 27:39f.; Mk. 15:29) and the charge did not die, for Stephen's accusers said something of the sort (Acts 6:14). These people did not get the saying right (Mk. 14:59), but clearly Jesus said something that they were trying to reproduce. Once more we cannot find it in the Synoptists but John records it (Jn. 2:19). It is in an enigmatic form, and it is not surprising that the false witnesses did not agree when they tried to recall it.

Much more could be written along this line. The Johannine narrative interlocks with that of the Synoptists. The differences are such that it is more than difficult to think that the one was written in the light of a knowledge of the other. But there is no conflict. The two illuminate one another and help us get the complete picture.

VII. Historicity.–The great difference between the Synoptists on the one hand and John on the other, together with the evident concern of the fourth Evangelist with theology, has led many scholars to conclude that John is not very interested in historical accuracy. The thought is that he is trying to convey great theological truths rather than history. These scholars think that when John felt the Spirit of God was leading him to affirm some spiritual truth he expressed his certainty that this was what the teaching of Jesus meant by saying that Jesus said it. There is no conscious attempt to deceive but a way of stating things different from the way that we would naturally accept today. The Gospel of John is seen as something like the parables of Jesus rather than as a historical narrative. John's history is taken as very incidental: the Evangelist may have included some correct historical matter from time to time but this was not his aim. His aim was to teach theological truth; thus some scholars will refuse to accept any historical detail in John unless it is confirmed from some other source.

Now it is obvious that this Gospel has a profound interest in theology. That is an important part of its value to generations of Christians. But that does not mean that its history can be taken lightly. In fact, in this matter it does not differ significantly from the other Gospels. Redaction critics insist that the Synoptists were all theologians and that their writings cannot be properly understood unless their theological tendency is taken into account. Nobody today wants to affirm that any of the four is a straight historical narrative. All our Gospels were written by believers and all were written with a theological purpose. The problem may be more complex in John than in the others, but it is essentially the same problem.

That John has a theological interpretation of his history does not make what he writes void as history. It is widely recognized that we cannot have good history without interpretation. Interpretation is one of the important functions of the historian. The question is not whether John has an interpretation, but whether his interpretation is a good and helpful one. An interpretation may obscure the events or it may clarify them. It is contended here that John's interpretation is a clarifying and helpful one.

Such an interpretation is necessary when we are facing the Incarnation. For while the historical method is immensely valuable in dealing with the ordinary events of history it is lacking when it comes to what is more than history. It has no tools with which to evaluate the claim that in Jesus of Nazareth is One who is not less than God incarnate, God become man for mankind's salvation. As D. E. Nineham reminds us, "It is of the essence of the modern historian's method and criteria that they are applicable only to purely human phenomena, and to human phenomena of a normal, that is non-miraculous, non-unique, character" (*S.P.C.K. Theological Collections,* no. 6 [1965], 3). If then God has acted in history, the purely secular historian has no way of determining the fact. Such an interpretation as John's is essential if the real meaning of what happened is to be conveyed. Had Pilate or Caiaphas left an account they might well have conveyed something of the facts. But it is certain that their interpretation would have been erroneous. They did not understand the events in which they played such key roles. John did.

But that does not mean that John distorted the facts to bring out his interpretation. If all he wanted to do was convey theological teaching then why did he write a Gospel? An epistle is a very effective way of conveying teaching as 1 John, to name no other, clearly shows. That our author chose to write a Gospel shows that he was interested in the historical. He brings out his theological meaning by recounting what Jesus said and did, and he gives the impression that there is good history behind his theological teaching. We should notice that there are also some notable Johannine accuracies. We have already had occasion to notice John's topographical information and to see that this has convinced many that John knew Palestine well. To that we should add his habit of mentioning times of day at which things happened. Most students of the Gospel believe that this is because John had knowledge of those events and that his notices of time reflect accuracy of knowledge.

Perhaps the most important part of the Gospel from this point of view is the treatment of John the Baptist. It is interesting that in the Fourth Gospel this man of God is depicted in one capacity only, that of bearing witness to Jesus. Right at the beginning the Evangelist tells us that this is the case: the Baptist "came for witness, that he might bear witness of the light . . . he was not the light but came to bear witness of the light" (Jn. 1:7f.). There is not the slightest doubt about this. The Evangelist tells us little about the Baptist's teaching and not much about what he did. He does not even tell us that John baptized Jesus, though there can be no doubt that he refers to the occasion when this was done. Single-mindedly he brings out the point that the Baptist witnessed to Jesus. There can be not the slightest doubt that John's portrait of the Baptist is from a strong theological perspective.

Now one of the unexpected results of the study of the Qumrân scrolls is that they have many points of contact with what the Baptist says. In fact there is practically no element in the Baptist's teaching in this Gospel that does not have some point of contact in the Scrolls. This has convinced some critics that the fourth Evangelist's portrait of the Baptist corresponds to reality (e.g., J. H. Brownlee, *Interp.*, 9 [1955], 71-90; J. A. T. Robinson, "The New Look on the Fourth Gospel," *SE*, I, 345; A. Wikgren, "Biography and Christology in the Gospels," *SE*, I, 124). If John can be accurate when he is demonstrably concerned to make a theological point, this creates a presumption that he is accurate elsewhere. Specifically, if his portrait of John is a good one why should we think anything else about his portrait of Jesus?

John's stress on witness should also be considered here. He uses the noun *martyría* fourteen times (three times in Mark, once in Luke, not in Matthew) and the verb *martyréō* thirty-three times (Matthew and Luke once each, not in Mark). In both cases this is more often than in any other NT book. Clearly he puts unusual emphasis on witness. Now witness is a legal term. It refers to what goes on in a court of law to establish the truth. There is no point in talking about witness if one is concerned simply with theological romance. The use of the term shows that John's intention was to give facts and that he was confident that the facts would stand up. There was adequate testimony behind what he said.

Again, we should not overlook the fact that John has a good deal to say about truth. He uses the noun *alḗtheia*, "truth," twenty-five times, more than in any other book in the NT. The same can be said about his use of *alēthḗs*, "true" (fourteen times), and *alēthṓs*, "truly" (seven times), while his nine uses of *alēthinós*, "true," are just one below the highest (ten in Revelation). These statistics show that John is uncommonly interested in what is true. Perhaps it would not be impossible for a writer to put emphasis on the importance of the truth while himself conveying what is "true" by means of that which is not historically factual. But it would be unusual, so unusual that most of us would reject it. If a writer keeps talking about the truth and what is true, then it is incumbent on him to tell the truth. The counter to this is to affirm that John did not have an idea of truth like the modern scientific one and that he was quite able to promote the cause of truth by using what is not in full correspondence with historic fact. But this is conjecture. It must be proved; it is not enough to assert it. And it seems that the evidence is against it. John seems to be telling us the truth, in the sense of that for which there is adequate evidence.

It is usually held that one of John's aims was to combat heresy of a docetic type, the heresy that Jesus had no contact with matter but only seemed to have such contact. This ruled out a real incarnation and made nonsense of the Christian claim that in Jesus God had wrought salvation for mankind. Over against such ideas John insists that "the Word was made flesh" (Jn. 1:14). Now if John was in fact manufacturing stories with no historical basis (or using other people's stories of this kind), he was cutting the ground from under his own feet. The docetic heretics could easily allow an incarnation of this kind. It was the facts of the life of Jesus that bothered them. If John was to oppose them successfully it was very important that he did not make use of stories without factual basis.

Thus we have various reasons for holding that John is telling us what happened. He is not giving us a merely factual account. He has some theological points he wants to make, and he makes them. But he does not make them at the expense of historical accuracy. Thus a number of modern critics have come to respect at least some of John's history. To cite but one, C. H. Dodd argues that there is an early tradition behind this Gospel and that its historical judgments must be treated with respect (*Historical Tradition*). Dodd finds much that he cannot accept in John, but it is important that this great scholar is impressed with the amount of history he finds in this Gospel.

VIII. Purpose.–Various suggestions have been made concerning the purpose of this gospel. We have already noted one, namely, to combat Docetism. Put in this form it must be rejected, for Docetism as a developed heresy was known only from a much later time. But tendencies of a docetic type would later grow into Docetism, and it seems that John's emphasis on the reality of Jesus' humanity was in part aimed at such tendencies. But this can be no more than a side issue; it is not the main aim of the work.

A view with an honorable ancestry is that the author wrote to supplement the Synoptists. Clement of Alexandria thought that as far as the "bodily facts" were concerned John was content with what the Synoptists had written, but he wrote in addition "a spiritual Gospel" (Eusebius *HE* vi.14.7). The great objection to all such theories is that the evidence seems to show that John wrote independently of the Synoptists, as we have already noted. The same objection applies to other theories, e.g., that John wrote to correct or supersede the Synoptics.

There is more to be said for the view that John is concerned to oppose some continuing followers of John the Baptist. There is evidence that some who heard the Baptist did not heed his message that Jesus was the Christ, but preferred to carry on with the teachings and practices of John (cf. Acts 19:3). The Fourth Gospel makes it very plain that the place of the Baptist was a subordinate one, and it emphasizes the way John bore his witness to Jesus. But this occupies only a part of the Gospel, and it cannot be held to be John's main aim. As with the docetic tendencies, he was not averse to making some telling points in passing, but a polemic against the Baptist is not pervasive enough to be the purpose of the writing.

The same can be said about the two opposite views that John was written to oppose people who gave too much place to the sacraments or those who gave too little place to them. There is dispute as to whether chs. 3 and 6 refer to baptism and holy communion. But there can scarcely be dispute that any sacramental reference is too subdued to be thought the Evangelist's main thrust.

It seems that in determining the purpose of this Gospel we cannot do better than listen to the Evangelist's own words, "these are written that you may believe that Jesus is the Christ, the Son of God, and that believing you may have life in his name" (20:31). That is what the Gospel is all about. Throughout there is a determined attempt to show that Jesus was in fact the Christ of God, the One foretold through prophecy and the One through whom God would work His work of salvation. The whole Gospel bears on this theme in one way or another, and it makes it clear that life comes through believing in Him. Some feel that the Gospel has so much relevance to the building up of believers in their most holy faith that it ought not to be seen as primarily evangelistic. It is fair to retort that what has an evangelistic aim may well be of value also in building up the saints. We are not at liberty to ignore the Evangelist's own statement of purpose.

Bibliography.–*Comms.:* C. K. Barrett (rev. ed. 1978); J. H. Bernard (*ICC,* 1928); R. E. Brown (*AB,* 2 vols., 1966, 1970); R. Bultmann (Eng. tr. 1971); E. Hoskyns (1947); R. H. Lightfoot (1956); B. Lindars (*New Century Bible,* 1972); L. Morris (*NICNT,* 1971); R. Schnackenburg (Eng. tr., vol. I, 1968); R. V. G. Tasker (*Tyndale,* 1960); B. F. Westcott (1908).

Other works: C. H. Dodd, *Interpretation of the Fourth Gospel* (1953); *Historical Tradition in the Fourth Gospel* (1963); W. F. Howard, *The Fourth Gospel in Recent Criticism and Interpretation* (rev. ed. C. K. Barrett, 1955); R. Kysar, *The Fourth Evangelist & His Gospel* (1975); E. Malatesta, *St. John's Gospel 1920-1965* (1967); L. Morris, *Studies in the Fourth Gospel* (1969); H. Thyen, *TR,* N.F. 39 (1974/75), 1-69, 222-252, 289-330; 42 (1977), 211-270; E. Yamauchi, *Pre-Christian Gnosticism* (1973).

L. MORRIS

JOHN MARK. *See* MARK, JOHN.

JOHN, REVELATION OF. *See* REVELATION, BOOK OF.

JOHN THE APOSTLE. It is difficult to get a clear picture of John, for he is generally associated with other people. In the Synoptic Gospels he is usually mentioned along with his brother James and frequently with Peter also. In Acts he is linked with Peter on every occasion except in the expression "James the brother of John" (Acts 12:2). His father was Zebedee, apparently a successful fisherman (Mk. 1:20), and a comparison of Mt. 27:56 with Mk. 15:40 implies that his mother was Salome, who may be Jesus' "mother's sister" in Jn. 19:25. If so, John was a maternal cousin of Jesus. But this cannot be insisted upon, for it is not certain that the fourth Evangelist is making the same selection from the women by the cross (of whom there were many, Mt. 27:55) as the other Evangelists. The identification has much to be said for it, however.

John was one of the disciples called from their work by Jesus (Mt. 4:21 par.) and he appears, of course, in the lists of the Twelve (Mt. 10:2 par.). He was astonished at the miraculous catch of fish (Lk. 5:10), and at a later time, along with Peter, James, and Andrew, he asked Jesus when the end would be (Mk. 13:3f.).

More significant are some incidents in which he is singled out to be with Jesus on special occasions. Thus he was chosen, along with his brother James and with Peter, to be on the mountain when Jesus was transfigured (Mt. 17:1 par.). These three were the only ones whom Jesus allowed to go with Him into the house of Jairus when He raised Jairus's daughter from the dead (Mk. 5:37 par.), and at the close of Jesus' ministry it was these three again that Jesus asked to pray with Him in Gethsemane (Mt. 26:37 par.). On that occasion the weakness of the flesh was too much for them and they slept instead of praying. But it is noteworthy that in the hour of supreme crisis these were the men to whom Jesus looked for fellowship in prayer. We probably see something of the same attitude when Jesus entrusted to Peter and John the preparations for His last meal with His disciples (Lk. 22:8).

Thus it is plain that John was an important member of the Twelve. But there are indications that in those days he had much to learn about the spirit of Jesus and the cause to which he was so ready to commit himself. Thus James and John came to Jesus seeking the privilege of sitting on His right and His left in His glory (Mk. 10:35-45; in Mt. 20:20f. their mother made the actual request, but it is clear that the two sons were associated with her). In response to Jesus' question they affirmed their ability to "drink the cup" which He would drink and to be "baptized with the baptism" with which He would be baptized, evidently metaphors for suffering in the service of God. He assured them that they would indeed do this, but the places they sought were for those for whom the Father had prepared them. Not unnaturally the incident aroused the indignation of the other disciples.

A similar incident occurred when John spoke of encountering an exorcist who was casting out demons in Jesus' name. "We forbade him," John said, "because he does not follow with us" (Lk. 9:49 par.). Jesus, of course, told them not to forbid the man. An aggressive attitude toward their enemies surfaces when James and John wanted to call down fire from heaven on a Samaritan village which refused to receive the Twelve (Lk. 9:54). It is interesting that they thought this could be done. While they were clearly out of harmony with what Jesus stood for, equally clearly they were moved by a fiery zeal for His cause and the firm conviction that God in heaven would vindicate in the most striking manner those who called for vengeance on Jesus' opponents. Jesus gave the two brothers the name "Boanerges," which Mark translates as "sons of thunder" (Mk. 3:17). No explanation is given of the significance of this epithet, but the incidents just mentioned probably give us the clue. Thunder would point to noise and sudden disturbance and clearly anyone with such a nickname would not be expected to be gentle and considerate. The picture the Synoptists give us then is that the brothers were zealous and loyal but scarcely loving and helpful.

In Acts John appears in a list of the Twelve (Acts 1:13), and when James was killed it is noted that he was John's brother (Acts 12:2). Otherwise he appears only in company with Peter. These two went up to the temple at the ninth hour for prayer and were the means of bringing healing to the lame man (Acts 3:1-10). They were brought before the council on account of their teaching about Jesus and the resurrection (Acts 4:1f.). They were released but told to keep quiet, to which they retorted in the notable words: "Whether it is right in the sight of God to listen to you rather than to God, you must judge; for we cannot but speak of what we have seen and heard" (vv. 19f.). It was on this occasion that they were called "uneducated, common men" (v. 13), which probably means that they had not had the kind of formal education that the rabbis prized. John probably was included in the arrest of "the apostles" in Acts 5:18, which was followed by their release from prison by an angel. Finally John was sent with Peter to Samaria on the occasion when they laid hands on those whom Philip had evangelized and baptized (Acts 8:14).

In the Epistles John is mentioned only when Paul links him with Peter and James as "pillars" of the Church (Gal. 2:9). This indicates that he was an important ecclesiastical figure, but the interesting thing is that, here as elsewhere, there is nothing to show him taking a place of leadership. Except for his discussion with Jesus about the strange exorcist (Mk. 9:38 par.) he always appears in company with someone else, generally Peter, who is the one who speaks.

"The sons of Zebedee" are mentioned without the individual names in connection with the fishing expedition in Jn. 21:2. If we are correct in seeing John the son of Zebedee as the author of the Fourth Gospel we have some more important information about him. He was "the disciple whom Jesus loved." This should not be understood in an exclusive sense, for Jesus loved them all; nevertheless it does tell us something about the man. This beloved disciple was close to Jesus: he leaned on Jesus' breast at the Last Supper (Jn. 13:23), and he was the one who recognized Jesus on the occasion of the miraculous catch of fish (Jn. 21:7). It was to him that Jesus confided the care of His mother as He hung on the cross (Jn. 19:26f.). But the Gospel as a whole tells us more than do isolated expressions. It tells us that its author possessed an unparalleled insight into the message of Jesus and a powerful way of expressing it to others.

It is uncertain whether he was also responsible for the book of Revelation. This book claims John as its author, but does not specify which John. If it was the same John, we learn that he was "on the island called Patmos on account of the word of God and the testimony of Jesus" (Rev. 1:9), which presumably means that he was exiled for his faith. This book reveals its author to have been a fiery spirit and a man of vision. He apparently classes himself among the prophets (Rev. 22:9), and he repeatedly calls his book a prophecy (Rev. 1:3; 22:7, 10, 18f.).

It may seem curious that a man of whom we know so little, who habitually comes before us in company with someone else, and whose only recorded utterance is so much out of harmony with the spirit of Christ, should have such a high place in Christian regard and be seen as such a significant author. We should bear in mind that in fact we know little of the apostolic band, and further, that the positive achievements we can ascribe to any individual early Christian, apart from Paul, Peter, and Philip, are few.

Tradition has it that John lived at Ephesus to an old age (for refs. cf. Brown, pp. LXXVIII-XCII). We can neither prove nor disprove this. Sometimes it is said that John was martyred quite early (cf. Morris, pp. 280-83). If true this would rule him out as the author of any of our NT books. But the reasons are scarcely sufficient. A seventh-century summary of a fifth-century writer, Philip of Side, reports that Papias said that John and James were killed by the Jews. But Philip was a careless writer and nobody else seems to have found the reference in Papias. The ninth-century George the Sinner repeats the statement about Papias, or at least one manuscript says he does. But there is no evidence that he has any authority for this other than Philip of Side or his summarizer. To this is added the evidence of some church calendars (i.e., calendars which indicate the days on which the saints were commemorated) where James and John are commemorated together (cf. Morris, p. 281). But it is scarcely necessary to point out that commemoration together does not mean that both were martyrs, and even if they were it does not mean that they were martyred at roughly the same time. Those who favor the early martyrdom take Mk. 10:39 as a prophecy after the event, and say it indicates that John had already been martyred when Mark's Gospel was written. This is surely an argument without weight.

All in all the evidence brought forward for early martyrdom is very scanty and it is better to reject the whole idea. There is no solid argument against the tradition that John lived to a great age and was active in the service of his Lord. Tradition says that in his old age he was known as the apostle of love, so greatly had the love that is at the heart of the Christian faith possessed him. It was clearly of the utmost significance to the writer of 1 John.

Bibliography.–R. Brown, *Gospel According to John* (*AB*, 2 vols., 1966, 1970); F. Filson, *JBL*, 68 (1949), 83-88; L. Morris, *Studies in the Fourth Gospel* (1969), pp. 215-292; H. P. V. Nunn, *Authorship of the Fourth Gospel* (1952); P. Parker, *JBL*, 79 (1960), 97-110; 81 (1962), 35-43; J. N. Sanders, *NTS*, 9 (1962/63), 75-85.

L. MORRIS

JOHN THE BAPTIST [Gk. *Iōannēs ho baptistḗs*].

I. Sources
II. Parentage
III. Early Life
IV. Ministry
V. Baptism
  A. Origin
  B. Significance
  C. Baptism of Jesus
VI. Imprisonment and Death
VII. His Disciples
VIII. John and Jesus

I. Sources.–For trustworthy information concerning the life and work of John the Baptist we must go to the NT and Josephus. The Synoptic Gospels tell of his origin, ministry, message, and death. The Fourth Gospel focuses on his relation to Jesus. Josephus (*Ant.* xviii.5.2 [116-19]) reports his popularity, relation to Herod Antipas, and death.

II. Parentage.–Although in his ministry John was widely recognized as "a real prophet" (Mk. 11:32), he was of priestly descent (as were Jeremiah and Ezekiel). His mother Elizabeth was one "of the daughters of Aaron" and his father was a priest "of the division of Abijah" (Lk. 1:5), one of twenty-four divisions that took turns serving in the temple at Jerusalem (1 Ch. 24:10). "They were both righteous before God . . . had no child . . . and both were advanced in years" (Lk. 1:6f.). Their home was in "the hill country of Judea" (Lk. 1:65).

III. Early Life.–Lk. 1:36 indicates that John was born about six months before Jesus, whose birth cannot be dated later than early in 4 B.C. This suggests that John, like Jesus, began his ministry when he was about thirty years old (cf. Lk. 3:23). His father, an upright priest, lived in the hill country of Judea near the Qumrân sect, which was located in the wilderness of Judea near the northwest shore of the Dead Sea. This community had as its nucleus earnest priests who expected God to act soon to establish His rule. It has been suggested that Zechariah was in sympathy with the Qumrân group, and that when he and his wife died — both were already old when John was born — John was brought up at Qumrân and there was taught that the Scriptures promised God's early action to judge and redeem His people. This cannot be proved (cf. F. F. Bruce, *Second Thoughts on the Dead Sea Scrolls* [2nd ed. 1961], pp. 140-44; W. S. LaSor, *Dead Sea Scrolls and the NT* [1972], pp. 145f.). What is clear is that "the child grew and became strong in spirit, and he was in the wilderness [of Judea] till the day of his manifestation to Israel" (Lk. 1:80). It was a period of silence, study, thought, and preparation.

IV. Ministry.–John was still in the wilderness of Judea when "the word of God" called him to preach (Lk. 3:2), and there in the wilderness he began his ministry (Mt.

Traditional site of John's baptizing in the Jordan (W. S. LaSor)

3:1). This wilderness included not only the wild rocky region W of the Dead Sea but also the lower region of the Jordan Valley. At first John preached in the Jordan Valley just N of the Dead Sea; Jn. 1:28 places part of this ministry at Bethany beyond Jordan, which may be located E of Jericho on the east bank of the Jordan River, perhaps in the Wâdī el-Kharrâr. But John moved about; Jn. 3:23 speaks of a later ministry at Aenon near Salim, which may have been in Samaria, a few miles E of Jacob's Well, or further N, a few miles S of Scythopolis. At the end of his ministry he must have been either in Galilee or (probably) Perea, for Herod Antipas, who arrested him, ruled only these regions.

Luke 3:1f. gives an elaborate dating for the beginning of John's ministry. For Luke this event was important not only because John's prophetic ministry was influential but also because it heralded the new decisive action of God. The date cannot have been before A.D. 26, when Pilate became governor of Judea (cf. also Jn. 2:20), nor later than A.D. 28, for Jesus' ministry must have begun by then.

John dressed in rough garb, and ate the simple food available in the wilderness (Mk. 1:6); the leather girdle recalls the dress of Elijah (2 K. 1:8), and may suggest that John was conscious of a call to a ministry like that of Elijah. He did not go to Jerusalem or any city, but stayed in the wilderness and preached in the open. For his baptism he wanted running water, which was one factor in determining where he preached, and Jn. 1:28; 3:23 indicate that he preached where people passed by and he could easily be found. To fulfil his God-given mission he lived a life of stern hardship. That "John came neither eating nor drinking" (Mt. 11:18) is a dramatic way of describing his simple, self-denying way of life.

His preaching made no mention of ceremonial or priestly requirements. He addressed it to Jews (Mt. 3:9; Lk. 3:8), and announced the imminent coming of the messianic age, "the kingdom of heaven" (Mt. 3:2). He made no claim to be the Messiah, and even denied being Elijah (Mal. 4:5) or the prophet (Dt. 18:15); he was simply the warning "voice of one crying in the wilderness" (Mk. 1:3; Lk. 3:15f.; Jn. 1:20-23). The warning was urgent, for preliminary to the coming of God's final kingdom would be stern judgment, carried out by One mightier than John; it would bring blessing to those ready, but the fire of devastating judgment to the wicked (Mt. 3:11f.; Lk. 3:16f.). And instead of delivering the Jews from the foreign oppressor and honoring them, it would strike Israel first of all. Descent from Abraham would be no protection; Jews as well as Gentiles were sinners. The only escape was to repent, turn from sin, and change one's entire attitude and way of life. Those who did this and were baptized received forgiveness. But the repentance had to be real and thorough; the repentant person had to "bear fruits that befit repentance" (Lk. 3:8). All must share their goods and food, tax collectors must be honest, and soldiers must refrain from extortion and be content with their pay (Lk. 3:10-14).

John's method and message were urgent. He had no time for long discussions. Whether he addressed his warning of imminent judgment to "the multitudes" generally (Lk. 3:7), or particularly to "the Pharisees and Sadducees" (Mt. 3:7), it was a stern, fiery, fearless warning of imminent doom from which escape was possible only by prompt and genuine repentance matched by thorough obedience to God's will.

V. Baptism.–Though John was a prophet and gave no teaching requiring ceremonial priestly practices, he gave such prominence to baptism that his distinguishing title was "the Baptist" (*ho baptistḗs,* Mt. 3:1; etc.) or "the Baptizer" (*ho baptízōn,* only in Mk. 1:4; 6:14, 24), and his message was called "a baptism of repentance" (Mk. 1:4). This distinctive rite, evidently administered in the running water of the Jordan River (Mk. 1:5) or at springs (Jn. 3:23), was a symbolic expression of John's message.

A. Origin. The practice of ceremonial baths and washings was common throughout the ancient world, and persistent search has been made for the background that best explains why John gave baptism so prominent a place. Various washings were prescribed in the Mosaic law to remove defilement and infection and restore the normal clean state (Lev. 11–15). The messianic promises of the OT mention "a fountain opened for the house of Israel and the inhabitants of Jerusalem to cleanse them from sin and uncleanness" (Zec. 13:1); God was to "sprinkle clean water upon you, and you shall be clean from all your uncleannesses" and receive "a new heart" and "a new spirit" (Ezk. 36:25f.). Undoubtedly the cleansing promised included more than physical cleansing of the body.

By the time John began to preach, the Jews were requiring of proselytes from the gentile world not only circumcision but also baptism. This proselyte baptism was regarded as a cleansing from the ceremonial defilement that in Jewish eyes affected every Gentile. Frequent washings also were known among Jews. Josephus went into the wilderness and spent some time with Banus, an ascetic who "bathed himself in cold water frequently" (*Vita* 2). Josephus also reported that the Essenes "bathe their bodies in cold water" (*BJ* ii.8.5 [129]). The Qumrân Scrolls contain references to ritual lustrations, and some think that the reservoirs found at Qumrân attest frequent lustrations. The Jewish community at Qumrân probably was an Essene or Essene-type community, but it is doubtful that there was repeated ritual washing in such rather small reservoirs. In any case, a single initiatory baptism or bath is not attested at Qumrân, though no doubt some ritual washings were carried out there by this Jewish sect.

None of these ancient practices really explains the origins of John's baptism. They show that such a baptism would not have seemed strange in the ancient Near Eastern world, and they give clues to what John's baptism meant to the Jews; but his baptism was something new.

B. Significance. This baptism was administered but once to a person, and thus differed from the repeated washings so widely practiced. It was administered to Jews and so differed from proselyte baptism of Gentiles. It was not accompanied or immediately followed by the gift of the Holy Spirit, and so was not a full parallel to Christian baptism; John only promised the gift of the Spirit at some future time.

John's baptism had an eschatological focus. God's decisive action was imminent; judgment would strike all sinners, including unprepared Jews. Earnest repentance, divine forgiveness, and complete change of life were urgently necessary to escape judgment and enter the coming kingdom (Mt. 3:10; Lk. 3:9). Baptism was for penitent Jews, who thereby confessed their sins, renounced their old way of life, received forgiveness, dedicated themselves to a loyal and upright life, and looked expectantly for the coming of God's Mightier One to establish the divine kingdom. Contrary to Josephus (*Ant.* xviii.5.2 [117f.]), it was not merely for physical cleansing; it symbolized the spiritual cleansing and renewal of the repentant and reformed sinner.

C. Baptism of Jesus. It is historical fact that Jesus was baptized by John. Matthew, Mark, and Luke say so, and Jn. 1:31-33 implies it. But John baptized repentant sinners. Did Jesus confess personal sin? The NT rejects such an idea. Mt. 3:13-15 explains why He asked to be baptized: "to fulfil all righteousness." This means not that it was a hollow form to Him, but that He was so loyal a member of His people and so identified with them that He had to join with them in their confession and dedication (cf. 2 Cor. 5:21).

VI. Imprisonment and Death.–The exact date of John's imprisonment cannot be determined, but it occurred before Jesus returned to Galilee to open His ministry there (Mk. 1:14), and so *ca.* A.D. 28. The length of imprisonment is likewise uncertain. Since John died before Jesus' ministry ended (Mk. 6:14-29), it occurred not later than A.D. 29. Josephus reports a defeat of Herod Antipas in A.D. 36 which people thought was divine retribution on Herod for executing John (*Ant.* xviii.5.2 [116f.]). This might suggest a date later than A.D. 29. But John clearly died before Jesus did, and the story Josephus tells simply shows how deeply John impressed the people and how vividly they remembered him seven years after his death.

According to Josephus, Herod Antipas feared that John by his fiery preaching might stir up a revolt, so he seized him, imprisoned him at Machaerus E of the Dead Sea, and had him put to death. In the Gospels John's rebuke of Herod for marrying his brother's wife Herodias caused Herod to arrest him (Mk. 6:17f.; Mt. 14:3f.; Lk. 3:19f.). Quite possibly both explanations contain truth. Herod's fear of political results from John's preaching would explain the imprisonment; the scheming of Herodias explains best the extreme step of executing John by beheading him.

VII. His Disciples.–Most hearers of John, even those baptized, returned home after a time; but some became his disciples and lived as a group under his leadership. Even after his imprisonment they kept in touch with him; once a group of them came to Jesus with a question from him (Mt. 11:2; Lk. 7:19). Later, when John was executed, they buried his body and reported his death to Jesus. As during his ministry, they followed his teaching, fasted regularly (Mk. 2:18), and prayed as he had taught them (Lk. 11:1).

Little is known of their continuing work. Their loyalty to him during his imprisonment shows that they continued to live as his disciples. About twenty-five years later, when Apollos, a native of Alexandria, came to Ephesus, "he knew only the baptism of John," though he knew the OT prophecies of Jesus or some facts about Jesus' earthly life (Acts 18:25). Did he learn of John's message and baptism in Alexandria or in Jerusalem? At least the incident shows that John's movement continued and spread. The twelve men at Ephesus who had not heard of the Holy Spirit but had been baptized into John's baptism (Acts 19:1-7) are further evidence of this. The pointed insistence in Jn. 1:20; 3:28 that John was not the Messiah but had directed men to Jesus indicates that when the Fourth Gospel was written, probably late in the 1st cent. A.D., John's movement still continued, especially in Asia Minor, and some of his followers were claiming that John was the promised messianic leader. Some but by no means all of John's followers became followers of Jesus (Mt. 14:12?; Jn. 1:35-42).

VIII. John and Jesus.–Though many of John's followers gave John a rank superior to Jesus, John himself clearly claimed a preparatory and secondary role. He was sent by God but was subordinate to the Mightier One to come, and so could only hold the center of the stage for a limited time. His task was to proclaim the imminent coming of God's righteous kingdom and to call his hearers to repent and be baptized to escape the impending judgment and find a place in that kingdom. He announced the coming of the Mightier One, who would execute God's judgment, establish God's perfect order, and bestow the Holy Spirit on God's loyal people.

Matthew 3:14 suggests that John knew clearly that Jesus was the Greater One, and in Jn. 1:29, 33, 36 John explicitly identifies Jesus as the Greater One, the Lamb of God, and the Son of God. But in Mt. 11:2f. and Lk. 7:19 John sends from prison to ask Jesus if He is the Coming One, and Peter is said to have expressed a new, God-given revelation when at the end of the Galilean ministry he identifies Jesus as the Messiah (Mt. 16:17). These two groups of evidence are not contradictory. John sensed the greatness in Jesus without explicitly and immediately grasping and stating the full Christian gospel; the Fourth Gospel, in which men ascribe explicitly to Jesus in the first week of His ministry every great title the gospel story will contain, legitimately dramatizes the essential meaning of John's message and relation to Jesus without waiting for it to become clear, as it does in the other Gospels, in the ongoing development of His ministry. The Synoptic Gospels and the Fourth Gospel are in essential agreement. The latter's concern is always to bring out the full meaning of the story; John the Baptist had really pointed to Jesus without fully understanding what God was doing through him. Hence John's followers could think that they were true to him by continuing his independent movement, while the disciples of Jesus could rightly claim that they had grasped the final meaning of John's preaching and attitude.

Jesus' estimate of John was both positive and reserved. By coming to hear John preach and by being baptized Jesus recognized John's God-given mission. To Jesus, John was a true prophet of God, and more; he was Elijah who had come to prepare for God's final judgment and redemption (Mal. 4:5; Mt. 11:9-14). No greater man had lived. John's message and baptism, Jesus held, were as surely prompted by God as was His own ministry (Mk. 11:27-33). "Yet he who is least in the kingdom of heaven is greater than he" (Mt. 11:11), for John did not fully grasp the whole gospel and did not disband his followers when Jesus appeared, but continued to preach independently about the coming crisis, divine judgment, and the need of repentance and baptism. John prepared the way; the kingdom began to come in the ministry and work of Jesus. John had been divinely sent and was not repudiated, but once Jesus appeared John had to decrease while Jesus increased (Jn. 3:30).

Bibliography.–G. R. Beasley-Murray, *Baptism in the NT* (1962); A. Blakiston, *John the Baptist and His Relation to Jesus* (1912); W. H. Brownlee, "John the Baptist in the New Light of Ancient Scrolls," in K. Stendahl, ed., *The Scrolls and the NT* (1957); M. Dibelius, *Die urchristliche Überlieferung von Johannes dem Täufer* (1911); W. F. Flemington, *NT Doctrine of Baptism* (1948);

M. Goguel, *Au seuil de l'évangile: Jean-Baptiste* (1928); C. H. Kraeling, *John the Baptist* (1951); A. T. Robertson, *John the Loyal* (1911); J. A. T. Robinson, "The Baptism of John and the Qumran Community" and "Elijah, John, and Jesus" in *Twelve NT Studies* (1962); A. Schlatter, *Johannes der Täufer* (1956); J. Steinmann, *Saint John the Baptist and the Desert Tradition* (1958); J. Thomas, *Le Mouvement baptiste en Palestine et Syrie* (1935). F. V. FILSON

JOIADA joi'ə-də [Heb. *yôyāḏāʿ*–'Yahweh knows'].

1. A repairer of the Jerusalem walls (Neh. 3:6); AV "Jehoiada."

2. Son of Eliashib the high priest (Neh. 12:10f., 22; 13:28). *See* JEHOIADA.

JOIAKIM joi'ə-kim [Heb. *yôyāqîm*–'Yahweh raises up']. Son of Jeshua and father of Eliashib the high priest (Neh. 12:10, 12, 26). *See* JEHOIAKIM; JOKIM.

JOIARIB joi'ə-rib [Heb. *yôyārîḇ*–'Yahweh pleads, contends'].

1. A leading man of Ezra's time (Ezr. 8:16).

2. A Judahite (Neh. 11:5).

3. In Neh. 11:10; 12:6, 19 = JEHOIARIB.

JOIN; JOINED; JOINING [Heb. niphal of *lāwâ* (Gen. 29:34; Nu. 18:2, 4; Neh. 11:36; Est. 9:27; Ps. 83:8 [MT 9]; Isa. 14:1; 56:3; Jer. 50:5; Dnl. 11:34; Zec. 2:11 [MT 15]), *ḥāḇar*–'bind, unite' (Gen. 14:3; Ex. 28:7, 27; 39:4, 20; 2 Ch. 20:35-37; Job 16:4; Eccl. 9:4 *Q*; Hos. 4:17), *dāḇaq*–'cling to' (Josh. 23:12; 2 Ch. 3:12; Job 41:17 [MT 9]), also *'āḥaz*–'grasp' (1 K. 6:10), *bō' bᵉ-*–'enter into' (Gen. 49:6), *hāyâ ʿim*–'be with' (1 K. 5:6 [MT 20]), *hālaḵ . . . ʿal*–'go . . . with' (Jer. 3:18), *yāḥaḏ 'ēṯ*–'become united with' (Isa. 14:20), *'aḥᵃrê*–'after' (1 S. 13:4), hiphil part. of *nāgaʿ*–'cause to touch' (Isa. 5:8), hiphil part. of *ḥāzaq*–'hold on to' (Neh. 10:29 [MT 30]), *nāṯan . . . ʿal*–'place . . . upon' (Ezk. 37:19), niphal of *yāʿaḏ*–'meet by appointment' (Josh. 11:5), niphal of *yāsap* + *'el*–'add oneself to' (Ex. 1:10), *ʿāmaḏ*– 'stand, enter' (2 K. 23:3), *ʿāraḵ 'ēṯ*–'draw up in battle array with' (Gen. 14:8), *qāraḇ*–'come near' (1 K. 20:29; Ezk. 37:17), *qāšar*–'bind together' (Neh. 4:6 [MT 3:38]), *šîṯ . . . ʿim*– 'put . . . with' (Ex. 23:1), *tammîm*–'complete' (Ex. 26:24; 36:29); Gk. *kolláō*–'unite oneself with' (Mt. 19:5; Lk. 15:5; Acts 5:13; 8:29; 9:26; 17:34; 1 Cor. 6:16), also *prosklēróō*–'attach oneself to' (Acts 17:4), *prosklínō*–'attach oneself to' (Acts 5:36), *proskolláō*–'adhere to, join oneself to' (Mk. 10:7; Eph. 5:31), *syzeúgnymi*–'yoke together' (Mt. 19:6; Mk. 10:9), *synarmologéō*–'fit together' (Eph. 2:21; 4:16)]; AV CLEAVE UNTO, CONSORT WITH, COUPLE, UNITE, etc.; NEB AGREE TOGETHER, BE ATTACHED TO, BOND, MAKE COMMON CAUSE, etc.

The prohibition "you shall not join hands with a wicked man, to be a malicious witness" in Ex. 23:1 probably refers to collaborating with the unjust party in a suit by giving false testimony against his opponent. Job's claim in Job 16:4 that he could "join words together against" his friends is perhaps better translated "be noisy with words against" (relating Heb. *ḥāḇar* to Akk. *ḫabāru,* "be noisy" [O. Loretz, *CBQ,* 23 (1961), 293f.]; for alternative views see H. H. Rowley, *Book of Job* [*New Century Bible Commentary,* repr. 1980], pp. 116f.). The condemnation of those who "join house to house" in Isa. 5:8a refers to the buying up of the homes (and property, v. 8b) of the poor by wealthy landowners, thus leaving the poor homeless. Leah's hopeful statement in Gen. 29:34 that Jacob would "be joined" to her means that he would feel an emotional attachment to her because she had borne him three sons. "He who is joined [*Q*; read also by the LXX and Pesh.] with all the living" in Eccl. 9:4 simply refers to the living person, organically joined to all living persons. Hosea's lament that "Ephraim [i.e., Israel] is joined to idols" means that they are in confederation with false gods (cf. 4:12; 8:4f.; 13:2). In Mt. 19:5 (par. Mk. 10:7 according to some MSS), a quotation of Gen. 2:24 LXX, the phrase "be joined to his wife" probably refers generally to all aspects of the marital union, but Paul used the same verb (*kolláō*) in 1 Cor. 6:16 to refer specifically to sexual intercourse. In the familiar passage Mt. 19:6 (par. Mk. 10:9), "what God has joined together," the verb is *syzeúgnymi,* which originally meant "bring animals together in the yoke."

In the RSV the word "join" also renders the prefixed Greek preposition *syn-* in the words *symmimētḗs,* "fellow-imitator" (Phil. 3:17), and *synephístēmi,* "join in an attack" (Acts 16:22). J. E. H.

JOINTS (1 K. 22:34 par., AV). *See* SCALE ARMOR.

JOKDEAM jok'dē-əm [Heb. *yoqḏᵉʿām* (<*yāqaḏ*–'burn'?); LXX A *Iarikam*; LXX B *Iekdaam*; LXX L *Ieknaam*; Pesh. *nᵉqēmʿam*]. A city inherited by the tribe of Judah during the Conquest (Josh. 15:56), located by the biblical source near the cities of Maon, Carmel, Ziph, Juttah, Kain, etc. in "the hill country" (15:48) S of Hebron. It is perhaps to be identified with Khirbet Raqaʿ near Ziph. J. E. H.

JOKIM jō'kim [Heb. *yôqîm*–'Yahweh raises up']. A Judahite, descendant of Shelah (1 Ch. 4:22). *See* JEHOIAKIM; JOAKIM.

JOKMEAM jok'mē-əm [Heb. *yoqmᵉʿām*]. A town in Mt. Ephraim assigned to the Kohathite Levites (1 Ch. 6:68 [MT 53]), named along with Gezer and Beth-horon. The name Kibzaim in Josh. 21:22 may be another name for the same place (cf. *LBHG,* pp. 270f.). In 1 K. 4:12 the AV wrongly reads JOKNEAM, although this seems to be equated with Jokmeam in location. Identification is not yet possible. R. P. DUGAN

JOKNEAM jok'nē-əm [Heb. *yoqnᵉʿām*]. The LXX has many variants for this word; the closest to the MT is *Iek(o)nam,* while some (e.g., *Iekman* and *Iekommam*) show confusion in the labials, which has led some scholars to equate JOKMEAM with this place.

As a royal Canaanite city it was known as Jokneam in Carmel (Josh. 12:22). It also appears in the topographical list of Thutmose III as *ʿēn-q-n-ʿa-mu,* "the spring of Q." The boundary of Zebulon touched the stream in front of Jokneam (Josh. 19:11). According to Josh. 21:34, Jokneam was a Levitical city in the territory of Zebulon occupied by the members of the Merari clan. In the parallel passage, 1 Ch. 6:62, the MT (v. 47) does not have Jokneam, but LXX A and some other MSS add *Iekoman.* Later sources do not mention Jokneam.

Eusebius was unaware of the location of the site. The name had evidently been modified by the Hellenistic Age as demonstrated by Jth. 7:3, which refers to it as Gk. *Kyamōn.* Eusebius, therefore, gives no identification for Jokneam (*Onom.* 106.17f.; 108.27f.), though he is aware of the presence of Gk. *Kammōna,* "a village on the Great Plain, six miles from Legio to the north, on the way to Ptolemais (Acco)" (*Onom.* 116.21). During the Crusades a settlement existed there called Caïmont. This accounts for the name Tell Qeimûn (today Tel Yoqneam) beside the spring ʿAin Qeimûn, near the point where the Wâdī el-Milḥ (today Nahal Yoqneam) enters the plain of Jezreel.

The Wâdī el-Milḥ runs through the pass that separates the Carmel Range from the low-lying zone of hills that stands between the Valley of Jezreel and the Sharon Plain. (The name of this "low country" is Belâd er-Rûḥah [today Ramat Menashe]; it was called "shephelah" [Heb. *šᵉpēlâ*] in Josh. 11:2, 16b.) Thus ancient Jokneam occupied a strategic position guarding one of the passes leading to the Jezreel Plain.

Bibliography.–E. Robinson, *Later Biblical Researches* (1856), pp. 114f.; *SWP*, II, 69; W. F. Albright, *AASOR*, 2–3 (1921-1922), 24; *GP*, II, 365f.; A. Alt, *ZDPV*, 62 (1939), 3; W. F. Albright, *JBL*, 58 (1939), 184. A. F. RAINEY

JOKSHAN jok'shən [Heb. *yoqšān*, meaning unknown]. Son of Abraham and Keturah (Gen. 25:2f. par. 1 Ch. 1:32).

JOKTAN jok'tən [Heb. *yoqṭān*–'younger [son]?']. Son of Eber, and ancestor of thirteen tribes (Gen. 10:25f., 29; 1 Ch. 1:19f., 23) distributed throughout Arabia.

JOKTHEEL jok'thē-əl [Heb. *yoqtᵉʾēl*].

1. (Josh. 15:38). A town of Judah in the coastal lowlands. The site is unknown.

2. (2 K. 14:7). The city of SELA, capital of the Edomites, which Amaziah renamed Joktheel after he had captured it. It is possibly to be identified with Petra.

JONA jō'nə (Jn. 1:42, AV). *See* JOHN (NT) **5**; BAR-JONAH.

JONADAB jō'nə-dab. *See* JEHONADAB.

JONAH jō'nə [Heb. *yônâ*–'dove'; Gk. *Iōnas*].

1. According to 2 K. 14:25 Jonah the son of Amittai, of Gath-hepher, was the prophet of Yahweh who predicted the restoration of the land of Israel to its ancient boundaries through the efforts of Jeroboam II (793-753 B.C.). The life and ministry of the prophet may thus be placed in the early 8th century. His native village of Gath-hepher was in the territory of Zebulun (Josh. 19:13), and is commonly identified with Khirbet ez-Zurrâʿ, near Mashhad, about 5 km. (3 mi.) NE of Nazareth.

2. (1 Esd. 9:23). A Levite, the same as ELIEZER **9**. W. C. WILLIAMS

JONAH, BOOK OF. The fifth book of the Minor Prophets. Only four chapters long, it has so many serious problems that a brief article can treat them only by generalizing. Since the book is so well known and so short, a knowledge of it will be presupposed in the following article.

I. Structure and Unity
  A. Chapters 1–2
  B. The Psalm
  C. The Book as a Whole
II. Authorship and Date
  A. Language
  B. Parallels with Joel
  C. Nineveh as a Great City
III. Interpretation
  A. As Mythology
  B. As Midrash
  C. As Allegory
  D. As Symbol
  E. As History
IV. Message
  A. As a Postexilic Reaction
  B. As a Supplement to Nahum
  C. As a Prophetic Proclamation of Grace

I. Structure and Unity.–Early attempts to explain the book along traditional lines of source analysis (W. Böhme, *ZAW*, 7 [1887], 224-284, followed by H. Schmidt, *ZAW*, 25 [1905], 285-310) met with almost instantaneous rejection and were already discarded by König and Bewer as too artificial. Indeed, the resistance of the book to analysis by these means calls into question the method itself and cries for further investigation, using Jonah as the test case. Most modern scholars are inclined to regard the book as a unity, or as a compilation from two sources (chs. 1–3, and 4), or as a unity with the psalm added later.

A. Chapters 1–2. R. Pesch, following the pioneering work of N. Lohfink, argues for a concentric symmetry in the first section of the book, whereby the prophetic proclamation of faith is made the center of the pericope for reasons of stress. The analysis in Table 1 owes its stimulus to Pesch.

By this mode of analysis, whereby the proclamation of faith in Yahweh comes precisely in the center of the pericope (1:9, 10aα), three things may be shown: (1) the unity of the section; (2) the central position of Jonah's proclamation of faith in Yahweh; and (3) the climax of the section (2:10b [MT 11a]), in which Jonah's salvation from drowning follows Yahweh's word to the fish, that word itself paralleling God's word to Jonah (1:1). The motif of fear is developed in a similar pattern throughout the peri-

TABLE 1

Beginning of Pericope		Conclusion of Pericope	
1:1	Narrative: word of God to Jonah	2:10a	Narrative: word of God to the fish
1:2	Speech: Yahweh commissions Jonah to preach to Nineveh	2:2-9	Speech: Jonah's prayer from the belly of the fish
1:3	Narrative: Jonah's flight to Tarshish to avoid his prophetic mission	1:17	Narrative: for Jonah's deliverance God has appointed a great fish that swallows him
1:4,5aα	Narration and fear motif: the storm and the seamen's fear of it	1:15-16a	Narration and fear motif: the sea is stilled; the seamen fear Yahweh
1:5aβ	Prayers of the seamen: each man prays to his own god	1:14	Prayer of the seamen: to Yahweh
1:5cd,6aα	Narrative: Jonah goes to sleep in the ship's hold and the captain comes to him	1:13	Narrative: the seamen attempt to return the ship to land
1:6aβ,b	Speech: the sea captain to Jonah	1:12	Speech: Jonah to the seamen
1:7a	Speech of the seamen: to one another	1:11	Speech of the seamen: to Jonah
1:7b	Narrative: casting of lots	1:10c	Narrative: Jonah's past
1:8	Speech of the seamen: to Jonah	1:10aβ,b	Speech of the seamen: to Jonah
1:9, 10aα	Proclamation of faith in Yahweh		

TABLE 2

Focus on the Seamen		Focus on Jonah	
1:4	Crisis: destruction threatened by the storm	2:3	Crisis: drowning in the sea threatened
1:14	Seamen's response: prayer, finally to Yahweh	2:2	Jonah's response: prayer to Yahweh
1:15b	Reaction of Yahweh to prayer of the seamen: deliverance from the storm	1:17; 2:6b	Reaction of Yahweh to prayer of Jonah: deliverance from death in the sea
1:16	Concluding response of seamen to Yahweh's salvation: worship in cultic acts (sacrifice and vows)	2:9	Concluding response of Jonah to Yahweh's salvation: worship through praise, resolution to perform cultic acts (sacrifice and vows)

cope (1:5, 10, 16), documenting the progression of the faith of the seamen from a recognition of their own gods (5aβ) to the recognition of Yahweh as the God who has made heaven and earth (10a), where the central member is again primary.

B. The Psalm. The psalm (2:2-9 [MT 3-10]) has its own set of problems. (1) Is it earlier than, contemporary with, or later than the prose sections? (2) Is its location proper, or has it suffered a transposition? (3) What is its nature and how does this bear on the unity and meaning of the book?

First of all, it should be observed that the psalm is a song of thanksgiving for a deliverance already accomplished, as all commentators recognize. As such, it exhibits distinct parallels with other canonical psalms, although the details of these comparisons vary somewhat for each critic (cf. Feuillet, p. 181; Smart, *IB*, VI, 874; Scott, p. 22). Contrary to Feuillet, most hold these parallels to indicate the genre of the Jonah psalm, rather than sources on which the author drew.

While many moderns (e.g., T. H. Robinson, *Die zwölf kleinen Propheten: Hosea bis Micha* [*HAT*, 1954], p. 117) regard the psalm as a late composition and thus an even later insertion, Landes (*Interp.*, 21 [1967], 3-31) has argued (1) for its antiquity on the basis of its linguistic affinities with the poetry of the Bronze Age, and (2) for its traditional place in the book. Not only is this Letter witnessed by the earliest textual evidence (the LXX and the Qumrân scroll of the prophets), but there are real reasons for its present position: (1) it shows Jonah's anguish while drowning in the sea, and (2) it commemorates his deliverance. The parallels that Landes observes between chs. 1 and 2 are shown in Table 2.

See Table 3 for the parallels between the psalm and ch. 4.

The psalm, moreover, functions to slow the rapid pace of action in ch. 1, with the resulting suspense drawing the reader's attention to the act of deliverance in 2:10. The greater length of the psalm, when compared with its parallel in 4:2f., creates an admitted quantitative imbalance. But its omission would create an even more severe tilt in the other direction. In light of its important role in the structure of the book, it may be assumed that Landes is correct in regarding the psalm as older than the narrative portion of the book (as is the ancient cultic credo in 4:2cd), and that it was an integral part of the book's composition.

C. The Book as a Whole. Thanks to the labors of Lohfink, Pesch, Landes, and Ben Menahem (p. 3), the schema shown in Table 4 emerges for the entire book.

Thus although the book of Jonah appears at first glance to be a straightforward narrative, when examined in greater detail it reveals a remarkably formal structure that clearly indicates the compiler's intent to mark the contrast between the two major sections of the book, with the first section subordinated to the second section (Feuillet, p. 342). In 1:1–2:10, Jonah receives his command to preach to the Ninevites. But he attempts to escape his prophetic commission (cf. S. D. F. Goitein, *JPOS*, 17 [1937], 67) by fleeing to Tarshish aboard a Phoenician ship, only to wind up in the belly of a great fish. The second section (3:1–4:11) tells how Jonah receives Yahweh's command a second time and how he converts Nineveh by his forceful preaching, only to wind up in despair at the city's deliverance. The pattern A:B::A′:B′ emerges with such clarity and force that any argument for composite authorship or for a later insertion of the psalm seems merely to grope for the vestiges of legitimacy.

II. Authorship and Date.–A. Language. The language of the book of Jonah, once thought to point conclusively to a postexilic date (cf. S. R. Driver, *Intro. to the Literature of the OT* [9th ed. 1913], p. 322; Budde, p. 228, considers only Esther, Chronicles, and Daniel as later), can no longer be considered as pointing to some specific period in Israel's history. An Aramaic influence on the language of the book is not at all surprising in view of the Galilean origin of the prophet and, presumably, of the compiler. A

TABLE 3

Focus on the Ninevites		Focus on Jonah	
1:17	Focus shifts to Jonah	4:1-11	Focus shifts to Jonah
2:10	Jonah is spared	4:1	Jonah is angry that Nineveh is spared
2:1	Jonah prays	4:2a	Jonah prays
2:2-6a	Refers to his distress in the deep	4:2a	Refers to his distress in Palestine
2:6b-7	Asserts God's merciful deliverance	4:2bc	Draws the inference that God may save Nineveh; he must flee to Tarshish
2:8	Draws insight from his deliverance: idolaters forsake the One that loves them	4:2d	Asserts the mercy of God that leads to deliverance
2:9	Jonah's response to Yahweh: worship with sacrifices and vows	4:3	Jonah's response to Yahweh: a plea for death
2:10	Yahweh's response to Jonah: he acts so that the prophet may respond properly to the divine mission (yet to be accomplished)	4:4	Yahweh's response to Jonah: he acts so that the prophet may respond properly to the divine mission (already accomplished)

TABLE 4

Section I (Chapters 1–2)		Section II (Chapters 3–4)	
1:1f.	Word of Yahweh to Jonah	3:1f.	Word of Yahweh to Jonah
1:3	Jonah's flight to Tarshish	3:3-4a	Jonah's journey to Nineveh
1:4	Yahweh sends a storm on the sea	3:4b	Jonah's preaching in Nineveh
1:5	The fear of the seamen	3:5	The repentance and faith of the Ninevites
1:6	The captain comes to Jonah and speaks to him	3:6	The report reaches the king
1:7f.	Efforts of the seamen to learn why the storm had come upon them	3:7f.	Proclamation of the royal decree
1:9	Jonah's proclamation of faith	3:9	The king's hope in Yahweh
1:10a	The seamen recognize Yahweh	3:10	The Ninevites are delivered
1:11f.	Jonah willingly gives himself to spare the seamen	4:1	Jonah is angry because God has spared Nineveh
1:14	The seamen pray to Yahweh	4:2f.	Jonah's prayer of complaint to Yahweh
1:17	Yahweh appoints a fish to bring about Jonah's deliverance	4:6-8	Yahweh appoints a plant, a worm, and an east wind to bring about Jonah's repentance
2:10	Yahweh speaks and Jonah is delivered	4:9-11	Yahweh reasons with Jonah about Nineveh's deliverance

heavy Aramean presence could be felt in the territories of the northern kingdom throughout its brief history. Syria and Israel were rival powers, changing and exchanging the same tracts of land several times. Moreover, it is documented fact (2 K. 18:26 par. Isa. 36:11) that even educated Judeans and Assyrian army officers could converse in Aramaic during the reign of Hezekiah (late 8th-early 7th cent. B.C.).

Furthermore, many of the words formerly submitted as Aramaisms have themselves been called into question:

(1) The usage of the relative particle *še* in place of *'ᵃšer* (4:10) and in the compound forms *bᵉšellî* (1:12) and *ḇᵉšellᵉmî* (1:7) is not Aramaic (the Aramaic equivalent is *dî*), but Canaanite. It occurs as early as the Song of Deborah (Jgs. 5:7; cf. 6:17; 7:12; 8:26) and appears in Phoenician inscriptions (for the Phoenician influence in Jonah, see Loretz, *BZ*, N.F. 5 [1961], 19-24).

(2) Bewer (p. 12) cautions that *sᵉpînâ*, "ship" (1:5), often considered a word borrowed from Aramaic or Arabic, comes from the Hebrew root *spn,* meaning "to cover," and thus means either a decked vessel or the lower deck. Moreover, he warns that *mallāḥ,* "mariner" (1:5), often regarded as late because of its use by Ezekiel (27:9, 27, 29), is inconclusive because of the paucity of OT sea stories. The word *qᵉrî'â*, "preaching" (3:2), is a hapax legomenon in the OT and common only in later literature, but is derived from the common Hebrew verb *qārā'*, "to call or preach," using a common Hebrew noun pattern. The word *ṭa'am* (3:7) in the sense of "edict" may be derived from Aramaic (cf. Ezr. 6:14; Dnl. 3:10), or it may have been influenced directly by Akk. *ṭêmu*. Aside from the dubious Jer. 5:28, the verb *yiṯ'aššēṯ*, "will give a thought" (1:6), appears in the OT only in Dnl. 6:3 (MT 4), yet nouns from the same root appear in Job 12:5 and Ps. 146:4, leaving some room for doubting its Aramaic origin (Aalders, pp. 11f.).

B. Parallels with Joel. Oesterley and Robinson (pp. 372f.) observe the parallels with Joel (Jonah 3:9 par. Joel 2:14; Jonah 4:2d par. Joel 2:13c), but correctly warn that these are not to be overworked. Not only is it difficult to determine which writer influenced the other (the same may be said of the parallels found by Feuillet between Jeremiah and Ezekiel), but the date of the composition of Joel itself is hotly debated. Moreover, Jonah 4:2d par. Joel 2:13c reflects an old cultic credo, of a much earlier origin than either book.

C. Nineveh as a Great City. What appears at first glance to be the decisive indicator of a time for the book's composition is the clause *wᵉnînᵉwēh hāyᵉṯâ 'îr gᵉḏôlâ lē'lōhîm* (3:3b). Those who argue for the use of the verb as a narrative tense have not adequately considered its syntactical relationships. The meaning of the construction may be seen by means of contrasts with alternate forms that the writer rejected: *wattᵉhî nînᵉwēh 'îr gᵉḏôlâ,* "and Nineveh became a great city"; and *wᵉnînᵉwēh 'îr gᵉḏôlâ,* "and Nineveh was a great city." The former, with *wāw* consecutive and the imperfect, would most naturally make the growth of Nineveh subsequent to the last narrative tense (*wayyēlēḵ*, 3a), which makes no sense. The latter, with *wāw* disjunctive and the verbless clause, would mean that, at the time of Jonah's arrival, Nineveh was (already) a great city. But the extant text, utilizing *wāw* disjunctive and the perfect tense, would most naturally mean that at the time of Jonah's visit (viewed from a perspective some time in the future), Nineveh was a great city. If so, this clause would date the writing of the book as sometime subsequent to the fall of the Assyrian empire (*ca.* 612 B.C.). The clause is almost certainly a gloss, however (cf. J. H. Raven, *OT Intro.* [1910], p. 225); its intrusive nature may be recognized in the way it artificially disjoins v. 3 from v. 4a, whereas these elements are combined in one verse (1:3) in the first section.

Accordingly, there is no clear indication of when, or by whom, the book was written. Conservative scholarship has often identified the author as Jonah himself or one of his disciples (Young, *Intro. to the OT* [1960], p. 254). The argument (e.g., König, pp. 747f.) that the narration of the story in the third person suggests someone other than Jonah as the author seems vitiated when it is noted that Xenophon speaks of himself in *Anabasis* or Caesar of himself in *Gallic Wars* (Archer, p. 308) in a similar fashion. On the other hand, to indicate the possibility of a source near to Jonah for the story is not to demonstrate the probability, much less advocate such a conclusion. It should be kept in mind that nowhere does Jonah claim to have written the book, or any part of it.

In the light of the analysis given in the opening section of this article and the demonstrably formal character of the book, it seems better to regard the psalm as a cultic confession that was very early in its origins, yet had at some time acquired an association with Jonah and thus carried with it the substance of the narrative as it was transmitted (cf. the Psalms associated with David). The material would have been reworked subsequently by a single compiler, whose date is quite uncertain, into the formal structure that the book now manifests.

III. Interpretation.*–A. As Mythology.* Although it was once popular to dismiss the book of Jonah as a myth, such views have become increasingly difficult to defend. As the revelatory nature of biblical literature has become better understood, it has become evident that the materials are not mythical or legendary in the common sense of those words. Even though the Scriptures may, on occasion, borrow mythical motifs in a fashion reminiscent of Milton's *Paradise Lost* (cf. Weiser on Ps. 19:4 [MT 5]), the meaning extracted from these motifs is quite distinct from that ascribed to them by Israel's pagan contemporaries. Furthermore, if the fish be construed as representing the dragon of the deep (*tannîn* or *liwyāṯān*, a vital element for this interpretation), confusion results, for the fish is not the means of Jonah's destruction, but of his salvation (cf. Oesterley and Robinson, pp. 377-79).

B. As Midrash. One particularly difficult explanation of the book (advanced by Budde, p. 228 and followed by Schedl, p. 328) regards it as a midrash. This interpretation understands the ancient confession in 4:2d as the point of the book, developed as a story to illustrate Ex. 34:6 and its parallels (Nu. 14:18; Neh. 9:17c; Ps. 86:15; 103:8; 145:8; Joel 2:13c; Nah. 1:3). Although it is known that a literary genre called midrash existed in the early postexilic period (2 Ch. 13:22; 24:27), the form and content of these works seem so uncertain that the category may be somewhat meaningless (cf. Landes, *IDB, Supp.*, p. 489). Nor is J. Soggin's "prophetic novel" more useful, for he has invented a genre to contain a single piece of literature (*Intro. to the OT* [1974], p. 355).

C. As Allegory. The allegorical interpretation of Jonah was popularized by Cheyne. Most exegetes of this persuasion depend heavily on the meaning of Jonah's name ("dove") and conclude thereby that Hosea's use of the dove to symbolize mindless Israel (cf. Hos. 7:11; 11:11; Ps. 74:19), a people incapable of recognizing Yahweh's goodness to them, justifies the interpretation that Jonah represents Israel. The fish, then, represents the Babylonian captivity, which swallows Israel (cf. Jer. 51:34, 44) but preserves them from destruction and ejects them after three days (cf. Hos. 6:2) with a mission to the nations. While this theory appears tempting at first glance, at a closer inspection it not only suffers from a lack of consistency in terms (the word for "dove" in Ps. 74:19 is *tôr*, not *yônâ*), but there is no hint of any sort that the compiler intended the book to be so construed. This is not the case with other biblical allegories, particularly the longer ones (e.g., Jgs. 9:7-16; Isa. 5:1-7).

D. As Symbol. The symbolic or parabolic interpretation of Jonah avoids the problems posed by allegory in that meaning is sought for the story as a whole and not necessarily for each of its component parts. As such, a parable constitutes a compact, rapidly developing story that is not necessarily factual but is realistic enough for its hearers to form analogies with their own individual situations. Burrows's "satire" and Miles's "parody" are particular varieties of symbolic interpretation. Kleinert, recently echoed by Berlin, while refusing to forfeit the historicity of the book, argues for a "symbolic prophecy" wherein the sense, not the history, of Jonah's story constitutes the reason for its inclusion in the prophetic canon and therefore is the element of the book which must be considered prophetic. This is a powerful argument and is not to be set aside easily.

E. As History. The historical interpretation of the book has come under attack from many quarters, and, in order to consider it, the objections to it must first be weighed.

First, an assumption that the book of Jonah reflects a late date of writing cannot be adduced as evidence of nonhistoricity. Not only is the date of writing uncertain, but an understanding of the function of writing itself plays a role. It is widely accepted that the bulk of material from the ancient Near East was first transmitted orally, frequently as liturgy, and reduced to writing only when its existence was threatened (cf. E. Nielsen, *Oral Tradition* [*SBT*, 1/11, 1954], pp. 32f.). The tenacity of oral tradition, together with its demonstrably high degree of accuracy, robs this objection of much of its weight.

Second, appeal cannot be made to the fish story as evidence of nonhistoricity. While the throats of most whales are too narrow to swallow a man, the *cachalot* or sperm whale can (Harrison, p. 907). Moreover, G. Macloskie (*Bibliotheca Sacra*, 72 [1915], 334-38) has suggested that even other species of whales could preserve a man alive, were the man able to reach the great laryngeal pouch. This structure, with its thick, elastic walls, is large enough to contain a man and to supply him with air for breathing. A. J. Wilson (*Princeton Theological Review*, 25 [1941], 636) records the case of a man swept overboard by a harpooned sperm whale in the vicinity of the Falkland Islands. The whale was eventually killed and cut apart. After three days, the missing sailor was found in the animal's stomach, unconscious. He was successfully revived, although the skin of his face, neck, and hands was bleached white by the whale's gastric juices.

A third objection is frequently raised because Nineveh is called *ʿîr gᵉḏôlâ lēʾlōhîm mahᵃlaḵ šᵉlōšeṯ yāmîm* (3:3b; cf. 1:2; 3:2). Claus Schedl (p. 327) has argued that Nineveh could not be called a great city if the author wrote in the 8th cent. B.C. Moreover, the inner wall of historical Nineveh had a circumference of only about 13.5 km. (7¾ mi.), yielding a diameter that could in no way be construed as a three days' journey. While it is true that it was Sennacherib who extensively rebuilt the city, it had already become a royal residence by the time of Tiglath-pileser I (12th cent. B.C.) and both Ashurbanipal II (883-859 B.C.) and Sargon II (722-705 B.C.) had palaces there. Furthermore, D. J. Wiseman (*NBD*, *s.v.* "Nineveh") suggests that the Hebrew translation of *nînᵉwēh* does not distinguish between the *ninua(ki)*, or city district, and the *(al)-ninua*, or metropolis. Accordingly, Jonah 3:3b would refer to the entire administrative district of Nineveh, which was about 50 to 90 km. (30 to 60 mi.) across. Wiseman finds a remarkable agreement between Jonah 4:11 and the survey made by Felix Jones (1834), in which the population of Nineveh was estimated to have been about 175,000 persons.

The remaining objections are far less serious than those mentioned above. R. H. Pfeiffer's comment (*PIOT*, p. 588) that calling the Assyrian regent "the king of Nineveh" was tantamount to addressing the king of England as "king of London" can no longer be taken seriously, for subsequent investigation has revealed that this style of designation for a ruler was not uncommon among Israelite writers. Thus Ahab is occasionally designated the "king of Samaria" (1 K. 21:1; 2 K. 1:3). Moreover, it is always possible that the "king of Nineveh" was just that — a city governor — and not the Assyrian monarch.

Those who stress the improbability of a heathen city converting at the preaching of a foreign prophet have not adequately considered the tendency among polytheists in the ancient Near East to absorb whatever god seems most powerful into one's own pantheon and to nationalize him. It is possible to identify the revival at Nineveh with the religious reforms brought about by Adadnirari III *ca.* 800 B.C. that elevated Nabû to prominence. Archer (pp. 299f.), following Steinmueller, suggests that if Jonah had arrived in Nineveh during the reign of Aššur-dân III, he would have found the city psychologically prepared for a total catastrophe, since a plague had swept the city in 765, an eclipse of the sun had occurred in 763, and a second plague had followed in 759 B.C.

The mourning of the animals (3:8) may be explained as

a poetic description of their bawling for food and water. The miraculous growth of the *qîqāyôn* plant (4:10) may be taken as hyperbole, simply indicating extremely rapid growth.

With these objections answered, it should be concluded that there is no insurmountable obstacle to a historical approach to the book of Jonah. On the other hand, to demonstrate that it *could* be considered history is not the same thing as proving that it is, indeed, historical. The common appeal to the words of Jesus (Mt. 12:38-41 par. Lk. 11:29-32) must be tempered with considerable caution, for it may be argued that a typology is satisfied by the appearance of the type in the OT and does not demand real existence as well (C. Stuhlmueller, *Books of Aggai, Zacharia, Malachia, Jona, Joel, Abdia* [Pamphlet Bible, 1961], p. 48). No interpretation is without its problems, although it would seem that the symbolic and historical explanations are least objectionable.

IV. Message.–A. As a Postexilic Reaction. Because of its sweeping universalism, the popular trend has been to classify Jonah, like Ruth, as a polemic reacting against the excessive separatist zeal manifested by some of the followers of Ezra and Nehemiah (Oesterley and Robinson, Burrows). However, this constitutes a specimen of circular reasoning of classic proportions. Not only is there real reason to question a late date for the book of Ruth, but there is no hint of polemic in either composition (cf. R. E. Clements, "Purpose of the Book of Jonah," in *SVT,* 28 [1975], 18f.) or even the need for one in the books of Ezra and Nehemiah! Instead, the book of Jonah finds its nearest analogue in the traditions about Elijah and Elisha.

B. As a Supplement to Nahum. A more helpful suggestion has come from T. F. Glasson (*Expos.T.,* 81 [1969], 54f.). In comparing Jonah with Nahum — the other prophetic oracle to Nineveh — he observed that both books conclude with a question. Nahum's question implies judgment for Nineveh (3:19c, "For upon whom has not come your unceasing evil?"), whereas the conclusion of Jonah implies salvation and deliverance (4:11a, "and should not I pity Nineveh. . . ?"). The function of Jonah would then be to soften the harshness of Nahum and preclude the assumption that God had forever cast off the Assyrians. If it is incorrect to construe 3:3b as a gloss, this interpretation has much to commend it. Since the book of Jonah has proved so difficult to date conclusively, however, it would appear preferable to adopt an interpretation that does not automatically force the writing of the book later than 612 B.C.

C. As a Prophetic Proclamation of Grace. That the book of Jonah has a single didactic aim has been strongly suggested by the foregoing analysis of its literary structure. Moreover, the formal structure of the book would suggest that clues to its meaning are especially prominent in 2:10 (Jonah's deliverance), which prepares the way for the climax of the book, and in 4:9-11, the climax itself (God's justification of Nineveh's deliverance). Further insight is gained by the recognition of the central position enjoyed by 1:9, 10a (Jonah's confession of faith followed by the recognition of Yahweh by the seamen) and 3:9, 10 (the king's hope in Yahweh followed by God's deliverance of Nineveh) in their respective pericopes. Jonah's personal deliverance from the fish constitutes the grounds for God's justification of the collective salvation of Nineveh. The reader is led to this by Jonah's own confession of faith resulting in the deliverance of the seamen and by the king's confession of hope followed by the deliverance of Nineveh.

The message would seem to be, then, that faith in God leads to deliverance and salvation. The seamen confess their faith in Yahweh and are saved from the sea (ch. 1), Jonah confesses his faith in Yahweh and is saved from drowning (ch. 2), the Ninevites confess their faith in Yahweh and are saved from destruction (ch. 3), and at the conclusion of the book, God is reasoning with Jonah in an effort to bring him to a place of repentance and renewed faith that would bring about his final salvation.

In its abrupt end, the reader is suddenly addressed by the word of God: it is no longer a simple story about Jonah, but one about the reader himself (B. S. Childs, *SJT,* 11 [1958], 61). In the final analysis, "it is the prophet himself who is judged and, through him, those who read his story" (Scott, p. 19). The brutal Assyrians have been seen more ready to repent and to accept God's grace than one Israelite who has already been shown grace. The tale of Jonah, then, instead of a "fish story" that proves a perennial embarrassment, develops a theme (together with the other universalist passages of the prophets, e.g., Isa. 2:2-4 par. Mic. 4:1-3; Isa. 19:21; 60:1-9) that constitutes the grandest of the entire OT and prepares the way for the institution of the new covenant.

Bibliography.–Among the older commentaries, KD and Lange (Kleinert) are still useful. Among the more recent works listed below, Harrison's *Intro.* is invaluable for a survey of the critical problems.

G. Ch. Aalders, *Problem of the Book of Jonah* (1948); L. Allen, *Joel, Obadiah, Jonah, and Micah* (*NICOT,* 1976); G. Archer, *Survey of OT Intro.* (rev. ed. 1974); E. Ben Menahem, *Sēper Yônâ, Tᵉrê ʿᵃśār,* I (1973), 3-12; A. Berlin, *JQR,* 66 (1975/76), 227-235; J. Bewer, comm. on Jonah (*ICC,* 1913); M. Burrows, "Literary Category of the Book of Jonah," in H. T. Frank and W. L. Reed, eds., *Translating and Understanding the OT* (1970), pp. 80-107; *EB,* II, *s.v.* "Jonah" (T. K. Cheyne); A. Feuillet, *RB,* 54 (1947), 161-186, 340-361; R. K. Harrison, *Intro. to the OT* (1969); *HDB,* II, *s.v.* "Jonah" (E. König); *IDB, Supp., s.v.* "Jonah, Book of" (G. M. Landes); *Jew.Enc.,* VII, *s.v.* "Jonah" (K. Budde); N. Lohfink, *BZ,* N.F. 5 (1961), 185-203; W. O. E. Oesterley and T. H. Robinson, *Intro. to the Books of the OT* (1958); R. Pesch, *Bibl.,* 47 (1966), 577-581; C. Schedl, *History of the OT: The Age of the Prophets,* IV (1972), 325-29; R. B. Y. Scott, *Interp.,* 19 (1965), 16-25.

W. C. WILLIAMS

JONAM jō'nəm [Gk. *Iōnam*]; AV JONAN (TR *Iōnan*). An ancestor of Jesus in Luke's genealogy (3:30).

JONAN jō'nən. *See* JONAM.

JONAS jō'nəs [Gk. *Iōnas* < Heb. *yônâ*].

1. (1 Esd. 9:23, AV, NEB). *See* JONAH **2.**

2. The name given in the AV Apoc. and NT to the OT prophet Jonah (2 Esd. 1:39; Tob. 14:4, 8; Mt. 12:39-41; 16:4; Lk. 11:29-32).

3. The AV name for Simon Peter's father (Jn. 21:15f.). *See* JOHN (NT) **5.**

JONATH ELEM REHOKIM jō'nəth ē'lem rə-hō'kim [Heb. *yônaṯ 'ēlem rᵉḥōqîm*]. Title of Ps. 56 in the AV. Literally "the dove of the distant terebinths," perhaps the name of a popular melody to which the psalm was to be sung. *See* MUSIC; PSALMS.

JONATHAN jon'ə-thən [Heb. *yᵉhônāṯān, yônāṯan*–'Yahweh has given'; Gk. *Iōnathan*].

1. The young Levite of Jgs. 17–18, referred to by name in 18:30, where he is called "the son of Gershom, son of Moses," and where AV has Manasseh for Moses, following the MT in which the letter *nûn* of Manasseh is suspended. Rashi states the reason thus: "Because of the honor of Moses was the *nûn* written so as to alter the name." The original word was Moses, but it was thought undesirable that a descendant of his should have anything to do with images; and so Jonathan was made to have affinity (metaphorically) with Manasseh.

Jonathan was a Levitical Judahite of Bethlehem in Judah, who came to the house of Micah, in the hill country of Ephraim, and hired himself as a priest in Micah's sanctuary (17:1-13). The Danites sent five men north to spy for new territory, and on their way the spies came to the house of Micah, where they found Jonathan and consulted the oracle through him (18:1-5). Having received a favorable answer, they set out and came to Laish, and on their return south they advised that an expedition be sent there (18:6-10). Their clansmen accordingly sent out a band of warriors who on their way passed by Micah's house. The spies informed their comrades of the ephod and teraphim and images there, and they seized them, inducing Jonathan at the same time to accompany them as their priest (18:11-20). At Laish he founded a priesthood which was thus descended from Moses (18:30).

2. Son of King Saul. See the next article.

3. (2 S. 15:27, 36; 17:17, 20; 1 K. 1:42f.). Son of Abiathar the priest. He acted with Ahimaaz as courier to inform David of events at Jerusalem during Absalom's revolt. It was he who also brought to Adonijah the news of Solomon's accession.

4. (2 S. 21:21 par. 1 Ch. 20:7). Son of Shimei or Shimea, David's brother. He is said to have been the slayer of Goliath. *See* JEHONADAB **1.**

5. (2 S. 23:32; 1 Ch. 11:34). One of David's mighty men. *See* JASHEN.

6. (1 Ch. 2:32f.). A Jerahmeelite.

7. (1 Ch. 27:25, AV JEHONATHAN). Son of Uzziah, and one of David's treasurers.

8. (1 Ch. 27:32). A *dôḏ* or uncle (NEB "nephew") of King David. If the NEB rendering is correct, he would be identified with **4** above. He was a royal scribe and counselor to the king.

9. (Ezr. 8:6; 1 Esd. 8:32). Father of Ebed, a returned exile.

10. (Ezr. 10:15; 1 Esd. 9:14). One who either supported (RV) or opposed (RV mg., AV, RSV, NEB) Ezra in the matter of foreign marriages. *See* JAHZEIAH.

11. (Neh. 12:11). A priest, descendant of Jeshua (Joshua) = Johanan (12:22f.). *See* JEHOHANAN **3.**

12. (Neh. 12:14). A priest.

13. (Neh. 12:35). A priest, father of Zechariah.

14. (Jer. 37:15, 20; 38:26). A scribe in whose house Jeremiah was imprisoned.

15. (Jer. 40:8). Son of Kareah; a Judahite captain who joined Gedaliah after the fall of Jerusalem.

16. [Gk. *Iōnathēs,* 1 Macc. 2:5; 9:19; etc.; 2 Macc. 8:22]. The Maccabee surnamed Apphus in 1 Macc. 2:5, son of Mattathias.

17. Son of Absalom (1 Macc. 13:11). He was sent by Simon the Maccabee to capture Joppa (cf. 11:70, where a Mattathias son of Absalom is mentioned).

18. A priest who led in prayer at the first sacrifice after the return from exile (2 Macc. 1:23). D. F. ROBERTS

JONATHAN [Heb. *yᵉhônāṯān, yônāṯān*–'Yahweh has given'; Gk. *Iōnathan*]. The eldest son of Saul, the first king of Israel, of the tribe of Benjamin.

I. Three Periods.–The life of Jonathan, as far as we are told about him, falls naturally into three periods.

A. First Period. He came on the scene as the right hand and lieutenant of his father in his early struggles to beat off the hostile tribes, especially the Ammonites (1 S. 11), who beset the territory of Israel on all sides. As soon as Saul had gained his first decisive victory, the people rallied to him in great numbers, so that he was able to count upon three thousand men whenever they took the field. These were divided into two small armies, Saul retaining two thousand and making Michmash his headquarters, the rest being stationed at Gibeah under Jonathan, about 8 km. (5 mi.) distant. Jonathan thus commanded the base, while his father led the fighting force. Midway between the two camps was a Philistine outpost at Geba, facing Michmash across the pass of that name, a valley with steep sides, now the Wâdī Ṣuweinîṭ. Saul does not seem to have felt himself strong enough to commence hostilities against the Philistines, and took means to increase the forces at his disposal. The Philistines heard that the Israelites had cast off their yoke (1 S. 13:3b: for "Let the Hebrews hear," read "The Hebrews have revolted"; cf. the LXX), and came out in great numbers (13:5). They seem to have compelled Saul to evacuate Michmash, which they occupied. Saul fell back on Gibeah (13:16) and Gilgal with a greatly reduced following. In spite of this, Jonathan accompanied only by his armor-bearer surprised the Philistine outpost at Geba, who were killed to a man. This feat precipitated a general engagement, in which the Israelites, whose only weapons appear to have been their farming implements (Saul and Jonathan alone being armed with iron swords and spears), routed their enemies (13:20). The completeness of the victory was impaired by the superstitious action of Saul in refusing to allow the people to eat until the day was over (14:24). As this order was unwittingly broken by Jonathan, Saul wished to have him executed, but this the people refused to allow, as they clearly recognized that the credit for the victory was due to the energetic action of Jonathan in striking before the enemy had time to concentrate.

B. Second Period. The second period of the life of Jonathan was that of his friendship with David. The narrative is too well known to need recapitulating, and the simple tale would only be spoiled by telling it in other words. Jonathan's devotion to David was such that he not only supported him against Saul, his father (chs. 18–19), but was willing to surrender to him his undoubted claim to become Saul's successor (ch. 20). Their last meeting took place in the wilderness of Ziph, S of Hebron, some time after David had been driven into hiding (23:16-18).

C. Third Period. The third phase of Jonathan's life was that of the exile of David, when Saul was directing his energies to combat what he considered the rebellion of the son of Jesse. During this civil war, if that can be called war in which one of the two sides refuses to take the offensive against the other, Jonathan remained entirely passive. He could not take part in proceedings which were directed against his friend whom he believed to be destined to occupy the place which he himself should in the ordinary course of events have filled. We therefore hear no more of Jonathan until the encroachments of the Philistines once more compelled Saul to leave the pursuit of the lesser enemy in order to defend himself against the greater. Saul's last campaign against the Philistines was short and decisive: it ended in the defeat at Gilboa and the death of himself and his sons. The men of Jabesh-gilead, out of gratitude for Saul's rescue of their town at the beginning of his reign, crossed over to Beth-shan, on the walls of which town the Philistines had hung in chains the bodies of Saul and Jonathan, and took them down under cover of darkness and carried them to Jabesh. There they burned the bodies after the manner of the primitive inhabitants of the land, and buried the bones.

II. His Character.–Jonathan was a man of fine character, whose moral probity was matched by resolution and endurance. He was athletic and brave (1 S. 14:13; 2 S. 1:22f.). He could keep his plans secret when secrecy was necessary in order to carry them to a successful issue (14:1), and could decide on what course of action to follow and act upon it in an instant. His attack upon the Philistine garrison at Geba (or Gibeah, if we adopt the reading of the LXX and the Tg. of 13:3; cf. 10:5) was delivered at the right moment, and was as wise as it was daring. If he had a fault, from a military point of view, it may have been an inability to follow up an advantage. The pursuit of the Philistines on the occasion referred to ended with nightfall. In this respect, however, he perhaps cannot be justly censured, since he never had an entirely free hand.

III. Filial Piety.–Jonathan's independence and capacity for acting on his own responsibility were combined with devotion to his father. While holding his own opinion and taking his own course, he conformed as far as possible to his father's views and wishes. Filial duty could not have been more severely tested than was that of Jonathan, but his conduct toward both his father and his friend is above criticism. Only on one occasion did his anger get the better of him (1 S. 20:34) under gross provocation; Saul had impugned the honor of Jonathan's mother (20:30, LXX) Ahinoam (14:50), and made an attempt on Jonathan's life. The estrangement was momentary; Saul and Jonathan were undivided in life and in death (2 S. 1:23).

IV. Friendship with David.–But it is as the befriender of David that Jonathan will always be remembered. His devotion to David was altogether human; had it been dictated by a superstitious belief in David's destiny as the future ruler of his people (23:17), that belief would have been shared by Saul, which was not the case (20:31). In disinterestedness and willingness to efface his own claims and give up his own titles the conduct of Jonathan is unsurpassed, and presents a pleasing contrast to some of the characters we meet in the Bible. Jonathan and David stand for the highest ideal of Hebrew friendship, as do Damon and Pythias in Greek literature.

V. Inspired Affection.–We may be sure that Jonathan won the affection of the people. His armor-bearer was ready to follow him anywhere (14:7). David's devotion to him seems to have been sincere, although it also happened to coincide with his own self-interest. Jonathan appears to have inspired as great an affection as he himself felt (1 S. 20:41; 2 S. 1:26). His quarrel with his father was largely due to the solicitude of the latter for his son's interests (1 S. 18:29; 20:31).

VI. His Descendants.–Jonathan's sons were, in common with his brother's, killed in the wars. One alone — Merib-baal (Mephibosheth) — survived. Jonathan's posterity through him lasted several generations. A table of them is given in 1 Ch. 8:33-40 par. 9:40-44 (cf. 2 S. 9:12). They were famous soldiers and were, like their ancestors, distinguished in the use of the bow (1 Ch. 8:40).

T. H. WEIR

JOPPA jop'ə [Heb. *yāpô, yāpô'*–'beautify, beautiful'; Akk. *Ia-pu* (Am.Tab. 138:85; 294:20; 296:33), *Ia-a-pu* (Am. Tab. 138:6), etc.; Egyp. *Ya-pu* (e.g., list of Thutmose III, no. 62 [*ANET,* p. 242]); Phoen. *ypy*; Gk. *Ioppē*]; AV also JAPHO (Josh. 19:46). The ancient name is preserved in Arab. Yafa, modern Jaffa, just S of Tel Aviv. A small harbor town on the Palestinian coast, situated on a rocky promontory about midway between Mt. Carmel and Gaza (Strabo *Geog.* xvi.2.28; Pliny *Nat. hist.* v.14 [69]), 56 km. (35 mi.) NW of Jerusalem.

I. Description.–Though Joppa never became a major seaport, it was of some importance as a logistical base and an outlet to the Mediterranean. The entrance to the small cove is from the north and is not very safe. The cove is formed by a natural breakwater of rocks parallel to the shore and about 100 m. (330 ft.) from it. The Hellenes said that Andromeda was bound to a rock of this chain to be devoured by a sea monster to appease Poseidon, but Perseus rescued her in time (Josephus *BJ* iii.9.3. [419ff.]).

South of Joppa the coastal sands have penetrated inland, forming a barrier to access from the sea. To the north sandstone ridges also made the shore uninviting to seafarers; the next landing place was 6 km. (3 mi.) distant at the mouth of the Yarkon (Josh. 19:46; RSV ME-JARKON).

II. History.–*A. Late Bronze Age.* Though the site was fortified in the Middle Bronze Age, Joppa is first mentioned in historical sources in the topographical list of Thutmose III as one of the towns conquered during his first campaign (mid-15th cent. B.C.). There is also a legendary account of the conquest of Joppa by one of his generals (also called Thutmose) who used a ruse, smuggling troops into the city in baskets while he enjoyed a banquet with the local ruler (*ANET,* pp. 23f.).

From the Amarna Letters (14th cent. B.C.) it is clear that a royal granary (*shunuti*) was established there (294:22). A certain Yaʿtiru affirmed his responsibility for guarding both Gaza and Joppa (296:31-33). During the Ramesside period the "Satirical Scribe" depicted the beauty of the gardens at Joppa; more importantly, he detailed the work done there at the Egyptian ordnance center, where chariots were brought for repairs (*ANET,* p. 478). The gate of the city was ornamented with the cartouche of Ramses II.

Papyrus Anastasi I (cols. 24-25). This hieratic text describes the Syro-Palestinian geography of the 13th cent. B.C., including the area of Joppa (Trustees of the British Museum)

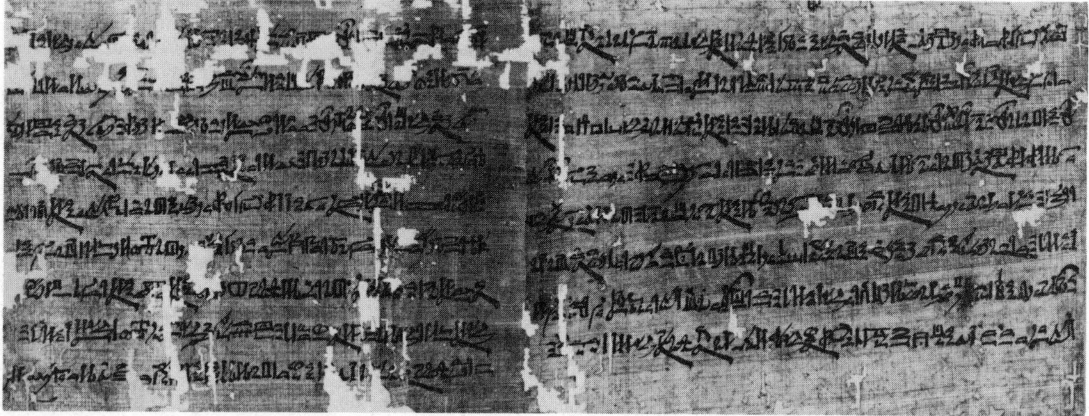

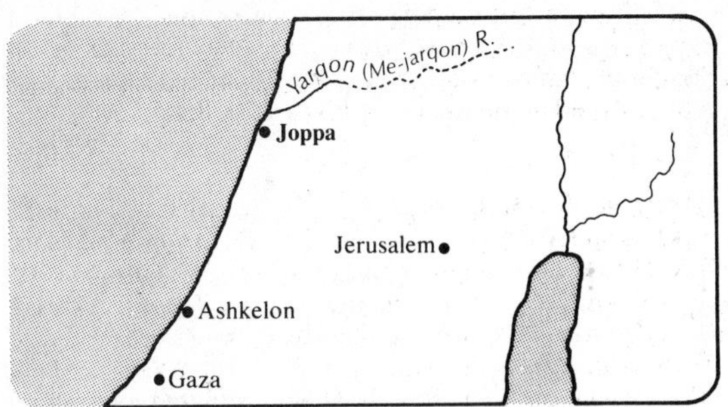

B. Israelite Period. Joppa does not appear often in the Bible, but it must have served as a seaport during the monarchal period (Jonah 1:3). It may have been included in the inheritance of Dan, though one can understand the passage differently (Josh. 19:46). Even if the Danites did not occupy their assigned place (19:47f.), the description of their inheritance seems to correspond to the second commissioner's district under Solomon (1 K. 4:9), and Joppa was the port to which timber was shipped for the Solomonic building projects in Jerusalem (2 Ch. 2:16 [MT 15]).

By the 8th cent. B.C. Joppa was not under Israelite control, but part of the dominion of Ṣidqia king of Ashkelon. Sennacherib occupied it, along with other towns in the immediate hinterland, during his march southward to quell the rebellion headed by Hezekiah and some Philistine city-states (*ANET,* p. 287b).

C. Persian Period. Those who returned to Jerusalem after the decree of Cyrus (*ca.* 538 B.C.) again hired Tyrians to ship lumber to Jerusalem via Joppa (Ezr. 3:7; 1 Esd. 5:55). It is not clear to whom the town belonged — perhaps the Phoenicians. During the 5th cent. B.C. the area called "Dor and Joppa, the mighty grain lands, which are in the territory of Sharon" was ceded to Eshmunʿazar king of Sidon by the Persian "Lord of Kings" (*ANET,* p. 505b), possibly Artaxerxes I.

D. Greco-Roman Period. Along with the rest of the Syrian coast, Joppa was taken by Alexander on his march from Tyre to Gaza (332 B.C.). He established a mint there. The hellenized name of the town was made to derive from that of Iope, a daughter of Aeolos the wind-god, and the wife of Kepheus, the alleged founder and first ruler of the town (Stephanus Byzantius 220.13ff.). After Alexander's death, Ptolemy I of Egypt occupied all of the Phoenician coast including Joppa (320 B.C.) and put garrisons there (Diodorus xviii.43; xix.59), but five years later Antigonus (of Phrygia) took the town for himself and stationed his own troops there. Ptolemy soon recaptured it, but razed the town, along with Acco, Samaria, and Gaza (312 B.C.), on his retreat to Egypt (Diodorus xix.93). The entire country returned to Egyptian hands after the battle of Ipsus (301 B.C.) and remained so until the battle of Paneion gave it to Antiochus III of Syria. (Ptolemaic control is reflected in the Zenon Papyri.)

During the Maccabean war against Antiochus IV the Jews of Joppa suffered at the hands of their neighbors (163 B.C.); two hundred were drowned in the harbor. For revenge Judas Maccabeus destroyed the harbor installations by fire, but could not take the city (2 Macc. 12:3-9). Jonathan later took it (147 B.C.), but was unable to hold it (1 Macc. 10:69-85; 11:1-6; Josephus *Ant.* xiii.4.4 [88-101]). Simon finally gained control over Joppa (1 Macc. 12:33f.; 13:11; 14:5, 34).

When the Romans took control, Pompey joined Joppa to the province of Syria (Josephus *Ant.* xiv.4.4 [74-76]; *BJ* i.7.7 [156-166, 169f.]). Caesar restored it to the Jews (*Ant.* xiv.10.6 [127-143]), Anthony gave it to Cleopatra (xv.4.1 [95]), and Caesar transferred it back to Herod (xv.7.3 [217]; *BJ* i.20.3 [396]).

The apostle Peter came to Joppa to raise Dorcas (Acts 9:36f.), and while he was there he had his vision of the ministry to the Gentiles (Acts. 10; 11:5-17).

During the war against Rome (A.D. 66-70) the Jews used Joppa as a sea base, but it was soon captured and destroyed by Vespasian (Josephus *BJ* iii.9.2 [414ff.]).

III. Excavations.–The site has most recently been investigated by J. Kaplan of the Tel Aviv Museum. Several seasons of excavations have illumined many facets of the city's history. Seven main strata, with some substrata, have been discerned, representing M.B., L.B., Iron Age, and the Persian and Hellenistic periods. Most noteworthy among the finds are the city gate from Ramesside times and a pre-Philistine temple.

Bibliography.–S. Tolkowsky, *Gateway of Palestine: A History of Jaffa* (1924); A. Alt, *KS,* I, 224 n. 2; *EAEHL,* II, *s.v.* "Jaffa" (H. and J. Kaplan); Y. Aharoni, *Tel Aviv,* 3 (1976), 5-15.

A. F. RAINEY

JORAH jō'rə [Heb. *yôrâ*–'early rain'(?)]; AV Apoc. AZEPHURITH; NEB Apoc. ARSIPHURITH. A family that returned with Zerubbabel (Ezr. 2:18; 1 Esd. 5:16), called HARIPH in Neh. 7:24.

JORAI jôr'ī [Heb. *yôray*–'Yahweh teaches'(?)]. A Gadite chief, but possibly the name of a clan (1 Ch. 5:13).

JORAM jôr'əm. *See* JEHORAM.

JORDAN jôr'dən [Heb. *yardēn*; Gk. *Iordanes*]. The most important river in Palestine and the valley or rift in which it flows.

I. Name
II. Prehistoric Times
III. Sources
  A. Nahr Bâniyâs
  B. Nahr Leddan
  C. Nahr Ḥasbânī
  D. Nahr Bereighith
IV. Huleh Valley
V. Sea of Galilee
VI. Jordan Valley
  A. Western Tributaries
  B. Eastern Tributaries

I. Name.–The name superficially means the "river that goes down." All rivers, however, flow downward, although some, like the Jordan, flow more precipitately than others. The root of the word "Jordan" may more correctly be related to the Arabic root *wrd,* "to come to," conveying the idea of people and animals seeking out a source of water. This idea is suggested in the term sometimes used by the Arabs for the Jordan, namely, esh-Sherîʿah, "the drinking place."

II. Prehistoric Times.–The Jordan River is situated in part of the Great Rift Valley, or geological fault, a series of depressions in the earth's crust, extending from Syria, in Western Asia, to the Gulf of Aqabah and continuing to southeast Africa.

During the Upper Pleistocene period a single body of water called the Lisan Lake stretched from the Beqaʿ Valley, between the Lebanon and Anti-Lebanon mountains, to the Wâdī el-ʿArabah. Evidences of early people and tools were found by D. A. E. Garrod and T. D. McCown in the Mt. Carmel caves, Mughâret el-Wâd, es-Sukul, and et-Tabun, from the Lower Paleolithic Age (before 70,000 B.C.), Middle or Mousterian (before 35,000 B.C.) and Upper (before 10,000 B.C.), as well as from the Natufian (before 7000 B.C.).

Since 1967 O. Bar-Yosef has directed excavations at another prehistoric site S of the Sea of Galilee called ʿUbeidiya. He has explained, in regard to the Lisan Lake, that "the advance and retreat of the water was repeated twice." Then the process was abruptly halted by "the very forces that had created the valley in the first place by tectonic movements." Sedimentary layers, "deposited both in the lake and on the land," and which generally "lay in horizontal strata, were suddenly folded and faulted until they became steep slopes." At the same time the "tilted formation was covered by a layer of lava" and other deposits. The final covering was the grayish-white marly sediment (Arab. *qattara*) of the salty water of the Lisan Lake, the top of which was about 392 m. (1286 ft.) below sea level, and the bottom about 783 m. (2570 ft.). The clay and gypsum sediments were similar to those found on the peninsula called el-Lisan ("tongue"), extending into the Dead Sea from its eastern shore. As the Lisan Lake finally retreated, the Huleh Valley, the Sea of Galilee, the Jordan River and Valley, and the Dead Sea (392 m. [1286 ft.] below sea level) were formed. Chunks of bitumen have been seen in the Dead Sea in modern times.

The Jordan River near prehistoric ʿUbeidiya is 70 m. (230 ft.) below sea level. Evidence of early hunters and food gatherers of four different cultural groups was found there. Lower Paleolithic stone tools, such as choppers, hand axes, and hammers were discovered, plus bones of amphibians and of numerous animals including bears, tigers, wild horses and oxen, deer, giraffes, rhinoceroses, hippopotami, and elephants.

Two main levels characterize the Jordan Valley. The upper one is called in Arabic *el-Ghôr,* "depression," in biblical Heb. *kikkār hayyardēn,* the "rift [or 'valley'] of the Jordan," a "garden of the Lord" (Gen. 13:10). The lower part is known as the *Zôr,* "thicket," equivalent to the biblical *geʾôn hayyardēn,* "jungle [NEB 'dense thickets'] of the Jordan" (Jer. 12:5; 49:19; 50:44; Zec. 11:3). Some sections are called *ʿēmeq,* "deep valley" (Ps. 60:6 [MT 8]; 108:7 [MT 6]), *biqʿâ,* "fissure" or "opening-out" (Dt. 34:3; Josh. 12:7), or *ʿarāḇâ,* "plain" (Nu. 22:1; Josh. 4:13). Between the Ghor and the Zor are the barren, strangely formed *Qattara* (Lisan) slopes of grayish-white marls and clays.

In Upper Galilee (Roman Tetracomia; M. Avi-Yonah, *Holy Land,* pp. 133f.) the Meiron Excavation Project conducted an archeological survey of many sites of importance in the Roman and Byzantine periods, and found synagogues and churches. At Khirbet Shemaʿ (Teqoʿah of Galilee) and Meiron they excavated synagogues (E. M. Meyers, *et al., AASOR,* 42 [1976], 73-98; 43 [1978], 45-118; *BASOR,* 230 [Apr. 1978], 1-24).

III. Sources.–The fairest part of the great geologic fault to which the Jordan belongs is the valley of the Lebanon, the Beqaʿ (Heb. *biqaṯ hallᵉḇānôn* (Josh. 11:17; modern Hollow- or Coelesyria). Its fertile fields and streams have helped to fill it with settlements and cities from earliest antiquity. A glittering crown was the fabulous city and sanctuary of Baalbek (Heliopolis). North of it the Orontes River (Nahr el-ʿAṣī) commenced its northward course to turn westward ultimately and flow through the ancient city of Antioch and into the Mediterranean. The evangelical efforts of early Christianity proved most fruitful at Antioch-on-the-Orontes, where Barnabas and Paul preached (Acts 11:19-26; 13:1-3), and the converts to the new faith "were for the first time called Christians."

South of the Lake of Homs, and several kilometers S of Baalbek, the Leontes River begins. It flows southeast around the base of the Lebanon Mountains through a deep canyon and empties into the Mediterranean N of Tyre. High in the hills commanding the sharp bend in the river

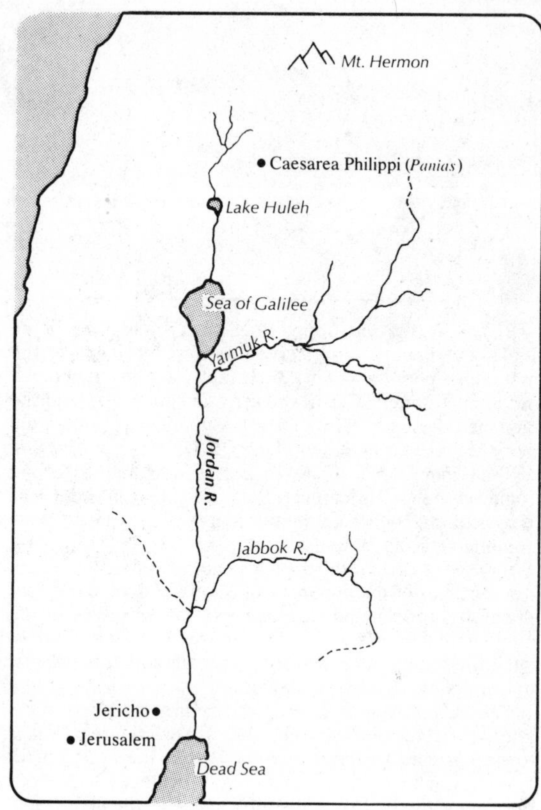

the Crusaders built the magnificent fortress of Beaufort (Belfort, Qalaʿat esh-Shaqif) in the late 12th century.

The union of four streams, born of springs originating from the snows of Mt. Hermon, forms the Jordan River. Also called the Jebel esh-Sheikh, the "mountain chieftain," Mt. Hermon seems to bestow grandeur and spirituality on the area (cf. Ps. 42:6 [MT 7]). The mountain range extends northeast and southwest for a distance of nearly 32 km. (20 mi.) and dominates the Jordan Valley. The principal peak is divided into three summits. The highest is 2814 m. (9232 ft.) above sea level, perpetually snow-capped, and is reflected in the waters of the Sea of Galilee; the other two are only a little lower. In later years a shrine was built there called Baal-hermon (Jgs. 3:3). Hermon was also known as "Sirion" by the Sidonians (Jer. 18:14), and "Senir" by the Amorites (Dt. 3:9).

A. Nahr Bâniyâs. The easternmost of the four sources of the Jordan is the Nahr (River) Bâniyâs, issuing forth with powerful flow from a cave (335 m. [1100 ft.] above sea level) at the base of a great limestone cliff of Mt. Hermon. It falls about 180 m. (600 ft.) in the 8 km. (5 mi.) of its course. Throughout the ages men have built shrines there. One of them was the seat of Baal-gad in the valley of Lebanon (Josh. 11:17; 12:7; 13:5). In Hellenistic times this cave was dedicated to the god Pan, and named Paneion; the town and district were known as Paneas (Arab. Bâniyâs).

Herod the Great received the whole district as a present from Augustus Caesar, for whom he built a white marble temple. When Herod Philip inherited Paneas he named the town Caesarea Philippi, to distinguish it from his father's Caesarea (Maritima) on the Mediterranean coast. Jesus and His disciples were in the district of Caesarea Philippi (Mt. 16:13-28; Mk. 8:27-33).

B. Nahr el-Leddan. The Nahr el-Leddan, "river of Dan," W of the Bâniyâs, is the shortest but strongest of

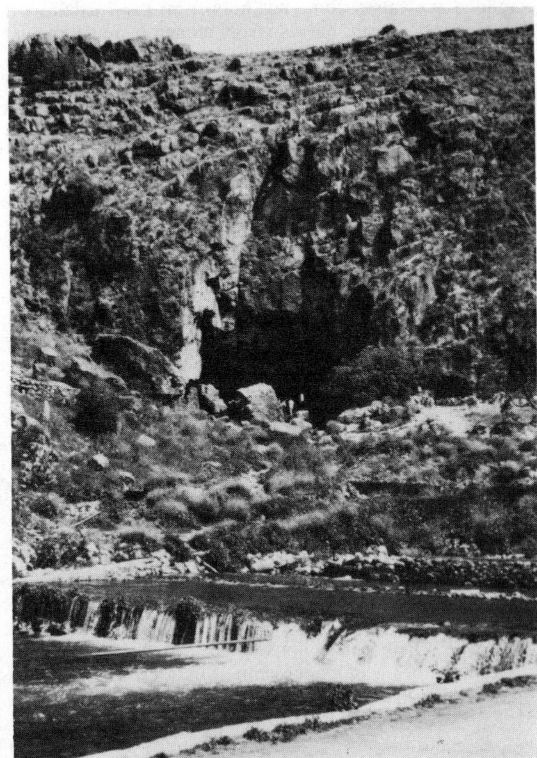

Two of the four sources of the Jordan: the Nahr Ḥasbânî (left) and the Nahr Bâniyâs (W. S. LaSor)

the sources of the Jordan. It originates in the powerful spring of ʿAin Leddan at the foot of the artificial mound of Tell el-Qâḍī ("the hill of the Judge"), known in Egyptian texts as Lus(i), and later as the Phoenician town of Laish or Leshem, before the tribe of Dan conquered it (Jgs. 18:27; Josh. 19:47) and made familiar the words "from Dan to Beer-sheba" (1 S. 3:20; 1 K. 4:25).

C. Nahr Ḥasbânī. The longest source of the Jordan, and most directly in line with it, is the Ḥasbânī, about 39 km. (24 mi.) long. It begins in an excellent spring (520 m. [1700 ft.] above sea level) at the foot of one of the western buttresses of Mt. Hermon, descends about 460 m. (1500 ft.), and parallels for a considerable distance the lower part of the southern course of the Leontes ("lion," Nahr Līṭânī). The two streams are separated less than 8 km. (5 mi.) from each other until the Leontes turns westward through a narrow deep gorge and empties into the Mediterranean Sea.

D. Nahr Bereighith. The westernmost source of the Jordan is the small mountain stream called the Nahr Bereighith, "the flea river." Through a small rocky gorge it rushes southward through the plain of Ijon (1 K. 15:20; modern Merj ʿAyûn) to enter into the Nahr Ḥasbânī about a kilometer above the junction of the Leddan and Bâniyâs streams.

All four streams lose their identities in the Jordan River, which plunges downward over 300 m. (1000 ft.) in less than 11 km. (7 mi.), as measured in a straight line from Bâniyâs, through rough basalt country to enter the Huleh Valley.

IV. Huleh Valley.–Formerly this area was called Lake Huleh, about 5 km. (3 mi.) long, over 3 km. (2 mi.) wide at its upper triangle, but narrowing to a point at the south, where the Jordan River emerged again, after meandering through malarial swamplands. Its maximum depth was almost 5 m. (15 ft.) and was known by Josephus as Lake Semechonitis.

In recent years the upper Jordan has been straightened and deepened by the state of Israel. The area has been transformed by an elaborate series of drainage canals into some 6000 hectares (15,000 acres) of lush farmland. Several hundred acres have been preserved as an indigenous habitat for papyrus, exotic plants, and wildlife.

In ancient times Huleh was guarded from the northwest by Abel of Beth-maacah (2 Sam. 20:14f., 18), the great mound of Tell Abil. It was once besieged by Joab, David's general. The fortified city of Hazor (Tell el-Qedaḥ; Josh. 11:10-12), about 8 km. (5 mi.) SW of Huleh, controlled the territory.

Emerging from the Huleh area with considerably increased volume, the Jordan flows quietly for about 3 km. (2 mi.), and then just beyond the Jisr Banât Yaʿaqub (the "Bridge of the Daughters of Jacob") it descends precipitously through a basalt gorge for about 11 km. (7 mi.) (falling from 70 m. [230 ft.] above sea level to 210 m. [690 ft.] below, almost 20 m. per km. [100 ft. per mi.]), before flowing for more than a kilometer through a plain and delta of its own deposits into the Sea of Galilee. *See* Plate 19.

V. Sea of Galilee.–Tiberias, Chinnereth, and Gennesaret are other names for the Sea of Galilee. It is 21 km. (13 mi.) long, 13 km. (8 mi.) across at its widest part, 5 km. (3 mi.) at the narrowest; at one point it is 46 m. (150 ft.) deep, and 210 m. (680 ft.) below sea level. Tell el-ʿOreimeh (Kinneret) is the site of the ancient fortified city of Chinneroth (probably from Heb. *kinnôr,* "harp"), situated just W of the Jordan River at its entrance to the Sea of Galilee. The Egyptians conquered it *ca.* 1468 B.C., and much later the Hebrews allotted it to the tribe of Naphtali (Nu. 34:11; Josh. 13:27; 19:35; 1 K. 15:20).

The clear waters come not only from the Jordan as it flows from the north, but also from numerous underground hot and cold springs. With the high, mainly volcanic hills of Galilee to the west and of Gaulanitis to the east, the Sea of Galilee has a comparatively narrow coast. This widens out for a distance of less than 6 km. (4 mi.) in el-Ghuweir (*ghôr,* "little valley") along the northwestern shore, to be identified with Gennesaret. The Jewish nobleman Josephus, who described himself as the military governor of Galilee (*BJ* ii.20.3-7 [562-582]) and who lived over a generation after the time of Jesus, wrote: "The lake of Gennesar takes its name from the adjacent territory. . . . Its water is sweet to the taste and excellent to drink . . . it is perfectly pure. . . . It has an agreeable temperature. . . . Skirting the lake of Gennesar, and also bearing that name, lies a region whose natural properties and beauty are very remarkable. There is not a plant which its fertile soil refuses to produce. . . . One might say that nature had taken pride in thus assembling . . . the most discordant species in a single spot. . . ." (*BJ* iii.10.7f. [506-521]).

Jesus chose Simon, Andrew, and the sons of Zebedee — James and John — as disciples when He "walked by the Sea of Galilee" (Mt. 4:18-22; Mk. 1:16-19). On the northwest side is the third-century synagogue of Capernaum (Tell Ḥûm), built over the original one in which Jesus preached on the Sabbath (Mk. 1:21). It was in Capernaum that He healed the centurion's servant (Mt. 8:5-13; Lk. 7:2-10). Peter had a house there (Mt. 8:14).

On the shore S of Capernaum at ʿAin et-Tabgha (Heptapegon) the fine Byzantine Church (*ca.* A.D. 400) of the Multiplication of the Loaves and Fishes has been excavated. Beautiful mosaic panels and floors were found in the basilica.

On the eastern side of the Jordan, as it enters the Sea of Galilee, is the "Fisherman's Village," Bethsaida (Julias). Outside of it Jesus healed a blind man (Mk. 8:22-26) and in a large open area miraculously fed the five thousand people who had gathered to hear Him (Lk. 9:10-17).

The Sea of Galilee was visible in wonderful perspective from the Horns of Hattin (Qarn Ḥaṭṭîn) that towered about 600 m. (2000 ft.) above it to the west and overlooked the large Roman toparchy of Tiberias. Around the western shore of the Sea of Galilee were such towns as Capernaum, Heptapegon, Gennesaret, Taricheae (Magadan, Dalmanutha, Mt. 15:39; Mk. 8:10), Arbel, Ammathus, Sennabris, and Philoteria in the south where the Jordan issues.

On the ruins of Rakkat Herod Antipas built the city of Tiberias *ca.* A.D. 20 and named it for the emperor Tiberius (A.D. 14-37). The city is mentioned in Jn. 6:23. After the destruction of Jerusalem by the Romans in A.D. 70, Tiberias was joined with Hammath (el-Hammam) about 2 km. (1 mi.) south, where there were popular hot springs. Hammath and Rakkat had been two of the fortified cities allotted to the tribe of Naphtali when the conquered land was divided (Josh. 19:35).

Over halfway down the eastern shore of the Sea of Galilee was the Roman district of Hippus. On a promontory about 2 km. (1 mi.) from the coast the Greeks built the city of Hippos (Sûsitâ, Qalʿat el-Ḥuṣn), probably to guard the road to Damascus. In 63 B.C. Pompey rebuilt some prominent Greek towns and organized them into a league of ten Roman cities, the Decapolis, to protect trade routes and military highways. Hippos (near Sussiyeh) was enlarged as a fortified city according to Roman town planning. During Christian times Hippos became the seat of the bishop, with at least three other churches besides the cathedral. In it is an inscription declaring "In the time of Procopius, Presbyter." Adjacent to the granite and marble cathedral was the baptistry with handsome mosaic floors that incorporated Greek inscriptions. There was an "intact dedicatory inscription to Saints Damian and Cosmas. . . , two Syrian brothers who, as physicians, gave free service to the poor and were martyred in the early fourth century." Another gave the date of its construction as A.D. 591. According to the latest excavator, there was a "massive basalt aqueduct that conveyed water into the city by gravitation from the 3.5 kilometer distant spring at Fiq [Aphek]" (C. Epstein, *EAEHL,* II, 521-23).

Gergesa (Chorsia, Kursī) was N of Hippos on the seashore near the northern boundary of the district of Hippos. M. Avi-Yonah (*Holy Land,* p. 174) favored it as a suitable location for the account of the demoniac in Mt. 8:28; Mk. 5:1; and Lk. 8:26, rather than Gadara, which is not close to the Sea of Galilee.

VI. Jordan Valley.–For some 21 km. (13 mi.) S of the Sea of Galilee the Jordan Valley is little more than 6 km. (4 mi.) wide in places. Where the Jālûd stream descends through the Beisan plain to the Jordan River the valley is from 9 to 10 km. (6 to 7 mi.) across. It narrows again because of the eastward extension of the hills of Samaria. For some distance S of the Wâdī Fârʿah the valley measures about 13 km. (8 mi.) across, and by the time it reaches the Jericho area it has achieved its maximum width of 22 km. (14 mi.). The straight distance between the Sea of Galilee and the Dead Sea is about 105 km. (65 mi.), but with all of its serpentine turns the Jordan River has a total length of about 320 km. (200 mi.). In that distance the Jordan falls about 180 m. (590 ft.), or an average of about 2 m. per km. (9 ft. per mi.). The width in its southward course is about 27-30 m. (90-100 ft.) and it is from 1 to 3 m. (3 to 10 ft.) deep, except in springtime when its waters rise to cover a much wider bed. Less than 8 m. (5 mi.) S of the Sea of Galilee, after the merger of the Yarmuk, the Jordan River becomes a muddy and turbulent stream, with a treacherous current that tears from one bank to the other as it rushes southward.

A. Western Tributaries. West of the Jordan River the tributaries are smaller and fewer in number; from N to S the chief ones are the wadis Fejjas, Bîreh, Jālûd, Mâliḥ, Fârʿah, ʿAujā, and Qelt.

In the peninsula formed by the southwestern shore of the Sea of Galilee and the emerging Jordan River, the ancient walled city of Beth-yerah (Khirbet Kerak, "temple of the moon") was discovered, which dates from 3000 B.C. and possessed an advanced agricultural community in 2700 B.C. It was famous for its unusual E.B. pottery (2600 B.C.), called by Albright Khirbet Kerak ware. Hellenistic remains were found in one section of the mound. In the area nearby existed the city of Philoteria built by Ptolemy II Philadelphus (285-246 B.C.). An extensive Roman town was uncovered there, including a fortress, thermal baths, and a synagogue. A large Christian church was constructed in A.D. 450 and modified several times as late as A.D. 529. M. Avi-Yonah (*Holy Land,* p. 138) explained that in this area near the Sea of Galilee the River Jordan "changed its course since antiquity." The remains of the "Crusader Bridge of Sinnabra" were found in the former river bed. Sennabris was probably near Philoteria. Just S of Beth-yerah the Neolithic site of Tell ʿEli (Khirbet esh-Sheikh ʿAli) was discovered where the Wâdī Fejjas (Naḥal Yavneel) joins a circular section of the Jordan River. On the other side of the Fejjas is prehistoric ʿUbeidiya.

Overlooking the Wâdī Bîreh (Naḥal Tabor) from the north as it approaches the Jordan, another Neolithic site, known as Munḥata (Ḥorvat Minḥa) was discovered. It was occupied *ca.* 7000 B.C. and produced decorated handmade pottery and elaborate clay figurines.

On the southern bank of the Wâdī Jālûd (Harod) is the strategic site of Beth-shan (Beth-shean, Tell el-Ḥuṣn, Beisan, Scythopolis, Nysa). The impressive tell has had a long history of occupation from the Chalcolithic period until the present day, and numerous levels have been explored. The territory of Beth-shan was conquered by the Egyptians, who called it Upper Retjenu. After three centuries of occupation they left a fortified city, rich temples and many other buildings, stelae, stone reliefs, anthropoid sarcophagi, statues, religious objects, and pottery. There was a square sanctuary from the Amarna period of Akhenaten (Amenhotep IV). Beth-shan was a cosmopolitan center with Syrian, Mesopotamian, and Hittite influences.

The Hebrews took over Beth-shan "and its villages" (Josh. 17:11; Jgs. 1:27). In the fighting with the Philistines Saul was slain and his body fastened to the wall of Beth-shan (1 S. 31:10-13). The administrative list of 1 K. 4:7-19 includes the territory of Beth-shan. During Hellenistic and Roman times the district was called Nysa-Scythopolis. Roman Scythopolis was a walled city of the Decapolis, with an acropolis, a large theater, a hippodrome, temples, bridges, and aqueducts.

During the Byzantine period Scythopolis, as the seat of the bishop, had a cathedral. Various churches and monasteries were constructed during the 5th cent. A.D. The curved walls and mosaic floors of a magnificent circular church from A.D. 435 were discovered there. Underneath it were the remains of a rectangular basilica of early Christian times. A large monastery was founded by "Christ-loving Lady Mary and her son Maximus" in A.D. 567, as recorded on the elaborate mosaic floor. Four synagogues were discovered.

The Wâdī Fâr'ah has its source in springs high in the rocky hills where the old Canaanite town of Tirzah was excavated. A little southwest is Mt. Ebal (940 m., 3084 ft. high), the ancient town of Shechem, and Mt. Gerizim (881 m., 2890 ft. high). Farther south, on top of a great hill commanding a view of much of the length of the Jordan Valley, is the towering Hasmonean fortress of Alexandrium (Qarn Sartabeh), constructed by Alexander Janneus (103-76 B.C.) and rebuilt by Pheroras at the order of his brother Herod. Farther south in the Jordan Valley, Herod erected the fortress of Phasaelis (Khirbet Faṣâ'il), in memory of his brother Phasaelus.

The hill country SW of Khirbet Faṣâ'il was found to have an amazing archeological history by P. W. Lapp. In tracing the source of the Samaria Papyri (*ca.* 375-365 B.C.) with Ta'âmireh tribesmen, he discovered labyrinthine caves in the desolate Wâdī ed-Dâliyeh gorge, and also the enormous necropolis of E.B.-M.B. shaft tombs of 'Ain es-Sâmiyeh, and Dhahr Mirzbâneh (P. W. Lapp, *The Dhahr Mirzbâneh Tombs* [1966]; P. W. and N. L. Lapp, eds., *Discoveries in the Wadi ed-Daliyeh* [*AASOR*, 41, 1974]; Z. Yeivin, *et al., IEJ*, 21 [1971], 73-85).

East of Jerusalem is one of the sources of the Wâdī el-Qelt, near 'Anâtâ (Anathoth, Jer. 1:1). The ancient Roman road trailed along the top of the southern cliff of the Wâdī el-Qelt, as it cut through the deep gorge, and descended to Jericho. The Greek Orthodox Monastery of St. George Choziba is an astonishing sight, perched on the northern side of the wadi, as though it is carved out of the vertical canyon wall. It is said to be over fifteen hundred years old and is approached by a precariously steep footpath cut into the rock. Farther along the Roman road are the excavated buildings of Hellenistic and Herodian Jericho (Tulûl Abū el-'Alâyiq), on both sides of the Wâdī el-Qelt, and the Roman aqueduct that furnished water for Herod's tropical winter capital, with its date palm, olive, and pomegranate trees, rich gardens, and balsam groves. There Jesus met Zacchaeus, the wealthy chief tax collector for the Romans, and transformed him (Lk. 19:1-10).

About 2 km. (1 mi.) N of the Herodian town is the mound of ancient Jericho (Tell es-Sulṭân), overshadowed by Jebel Qarantel, the traditional Mount of Temptation (Mt. 4:1-11). The modern city of Jericho (er-Riḥa) is SE of it. In the tell of ancient Jericho, near the spring of 'Ain es-Sulṭân (Elisha's fountain, 2 K. 2:19-22), K. M. Kenyon discovered seventeen distinct settlements, a Neolithic stone tower (*ca.* 7000 B.C.) 9 m. (30 ft.) high, and an astonishing collection of ten ancestral skulls with shell eyes, realistically sculptured with plaster.

John baptized Jesus in the Jordan River, probably at the traditional site of the Hijlah Ford, S of the place where the Wâdī el-Qelt flows into the Jordan. The Madeba Map shows at this ford what may be a guard-toll house with steps, perhaps to supervise the ferry boat "passing along ropes across the river" (M. Avi-Yonah, *Madaba Mosaic Map* [1954], p. 35, plate 1).

Near the northwestern shore of the Dead Sea the Wâdī Qumrân enters it, after cutting through the high cliffs that are pierced with many hidden caves. On a high marl terrace just N of the wadi, overlooking the Dead Sea about a kilometer (half a mile) away, G. L. Harding and R. de Vaux found the deserted ruins of Khirbet Qumrân, and excavated them in 1951-1956 (Harding, p. 195). In 1947 two local Ta'âmireh shepherds had found some pottery jars containing old parchment scrolls in a cave of the desolate wilderness. Albright in 1948 pronounced this "the greatest manuscript discovery of modern times." By 1949 Harding, de Vaux, and other scholars, with the help of the Arab Legion, had located and examined numerous caves, and had found many scrolls, fragments, and pottery.

The ruined buildings and caves in the surrounding cliffs had been occupied by covenanters of the Qumrân community, dedicated pious Jewish believers in God, who collected, copied, and preserved scrolls of the OT (except Esther) and probably buried old ones with appropriate ceremony in caves. In their library they also had commentaries and secular writings. They lived simply in the wilderness during dangerous times (*ca.* 130 B.C.-A.D. 68), reminiscent of the way of the Lord described in Isa. 40:3 and Mt. 3:1-3. They had strict rules for the order of the community, written in a long Manual of Discipline. Their buildings included a scriptorium, large meeting hall and refectory, pantry with over one thousand pottery dishes, kitchen with fireplaces and ovens, laundry, dyer's shop, kiln, a *mikveh* for ritual bathing, silos, many large cisterns, and an efficient system of conduits that brought water from a dam and waterfall. At certain periods during the years of occupation most of the members of the community probably slept in caves. About 2.4 km. (1.5 mi.) S of Khirbet Qumrân is the fine spring of 'Ain Feshkha, where the covenanters engaged in agriculture and possibly had a tanning operation. The building was excavated by de Vaux.

B. Eastern Tributaries. Where the Jordan River flows swiftly from the Sea of Galilee is a valley where ancient peoples lived. East of the Jordan, on a terrace, is the Neolithic site of Sha'ar ha-Golan, excavated by M. Stekelis (1949-1953). There he found early stone and bone tools and weapons with pottery from *ca.* 5000 B.C.

The streams E of the Jordan are more numerous and generally larger in volume and longer than those on the western side. Steep, westward-descending canyons, which level out when they reach the Jordan Valley, sever the high and broken Transjordanian plateau into distinctive segments. Between the Sea of Galilee and the Dead Sea eleven perennial streams enter the Jordan from the east.

View from the southwest of the Jordan near Adam. The Dome of Gilead is in the background, and at left the valley of the Jabbok (Wâdī Zerqā) comes down to meet the Jordan. The undercutting of these marl cliffs has occasionally dammed the river (D. Baly)

From N to S they are called the wadis Yarmûk, ʿArab, Tayibeh, Ziqlâb, Jurm, Yābis, Kufrinjeh, Râjeb, and Zerqā (biblical Jabbok), followed some 26 km. (16 mi.) farther south by the Nimrîn and Kefrein-Ḥesbân-Râmeh, the latter two joining together before flowing into the Jordan. Beyond them is the small Wâdī Azeimeh that flows into the northeastern corner of the Dead Sea, close to where the Jordan enters it at a point nearly 400 m. (1300 ft.) below sea level. On the eastern side of the Dead Sea (*Baḥr Lûṭ*, Sea of Salt, Lake Asphaltitis) are the Wâdī Zerqā-Māʿîn, the steep canyons of the Môjib (biblical Arnon) and of the Wâdī el-Ḥesā (biblical Zered).

The Yarmûk is about 9 m. (30 ft.) wide as it pours into the Jordan River about 6 km. (4 mi.) S of the Sea of Galilee. It forms a natural boundary between modern Syria and the Hashemite Kingdom of Jordan; in ancient times it separated Syria from northern Gilead. The territory of Og king of Bashan extended on both sides of it, with capitals at Ashtaroth (in Qarnaim) and Edrei (Derʿā). His sarcophagus or dolmen of black basalt was probably at Rabbath-ammon (modern Amman); Dt. 1:4; 3:11; Josh. 12:4).

In the gorge E of the confluence of the Jordan River with the Yarmuk (Hieromices) are the hot springs of Emmatha (Tell el-Ḥammeh) and the Roman baths. Elevated at the top of the cliff on the southern bank of the Yarmuk at Umm Qeis is the Hellenistic (Antiochia Seleucia) and Roman city of Gadara, once capital of the Roman territory with that name. The hot springs were then called the Springs of Gadara. The hill affords a marvelous view across the Sea of Galilee of the Jordan Valley to the south. Gadara was a city of the Decapolis on an important trade route and had a fortress, theaters, temples, a university (Harding, p. 56), and a synagogue.

Since Glueck's well-known surface explorations in Transjordan (1934-1951), other scientific, comprehensive surveys have been carried out in Jordan, with discoveries of many new sites and corrections of former dates (see bibliography). K. Prag and C.-M. Bennett have interpreted, evaluated, and placed in better perspective old and new discoveries.

North of the Wâdī Jurm and its springs, on the eastern slopes of the Jordan Valley, towers the great fortress of Tabaqat Faḥil, of importance from the Canaanite through the Byzantine periods. Early Egyptian records and Amarna Letters mentioned the site as Piḥilum. During Hellenistic and Roman times it was known as Pella, a walled city of the Decapolis. R. H. Smith found a large Christian church there from *ca.* A.D. 451.

East of the Jordan River, on the southern bank of the Wâdī Kufrinjeh, is the large Tell es-Saʿīdîyeh, excavated by J. B. Pritchard (1964-1967). Levels of occupation were established from the Late Bronze through the Roman periods but without direct evidence that it is Zarethan (1 K. 7:46; cf. N. Glueck, *River Jordan,* p. 119). East of it rises a tributary of the Wâdī Zerqā (Jabbok), where a Decapolis city of Gerasa (Jerash) was located. The Department of Antiquities of Jordan has continued to excavate and restore the beautiful Hellenistic-Roman buildings and theaters, plus the Byzantine churches of Jerash (Harding, pp. 79-105). South of it is another city of the Decapolis, Philadelphia, a site in ʿAmmân, capital of the Hashemite kingdom of Jordan, once known as Rabbath-ammon.

Below the junction of the Wâdī Zerqā (Jabbok) with the Jordan River is the small mound of Tell ed-Dâmiyeh, the biblical Adam(ah), which probably guarded the crossing there, one of the many old fords of the Jordan (Josh. 3:16f.). The AV of 2 S. 19:18 [MT 19] says: "there went over a ferry boat," perhaps a rope ferry. N. Glueck (*River Jordan,* p. 118) reported that "some years ago a decrepit rope-ferry plied its way across the swift current" of the Jordan. Earthquakes have occurred that blocked the river for hours. Near Dâmiyeh is a large dolmen field, containing various types of ancient megalithic tombs.

About 12.5 km. (7.5 mi.) NE of Tell ed-Dâmiyeh is Tell Deir ʿallā, where additional excavations have been made by H. J. Franken and M. M. Ibrahim.

The wadis Kefrein, Râmeh, and Ḥesbân join before flowing into the Jordan. A little S of the juncture, in the plains of Moab, is the huge Chalcolithic settlement of Teleilat el-Ghassul. In some of the buildings were found unique wall paintings, fine stone ware, decorated handmade pottery, bone and flaked tools (cf. Hennessy).

East of the Wâdī Ḥesbân in Moab is the site of Tell Ḥesbân, excavated from 1968 through 1976 under the direction of S. H. Horn and L. T. Geraty. They discovered levels of occupation from Iron I through the Islamic periods. This is the location of the biblical Heshbon (Nu. 21:26). A large Christian basilica was found at Tell Ḥesbân, destroyed in A.D. 612 by the Persians.

Heshbon, Medeba, Nebo, and other ancient towns of Moab along the King's Highway (Nu. 21:22) are mentioned in Isa. 15. Medeba was also prominent in Roman and Nabatean history (Harding, pp. 33, 73f.). During the Byzantine period Medeba was the seat of the bishopric and possessed many Christian churches; fourteen of them have been discovered already. One Greek Orthodox church contains priceless remnants of a mosaic floor from the 6th cent. A.D. depicting the earliest Palestinian map in existence. The artists created scenes with colored tesserae showing the Christian churches and towns extending around Jerusalem, probably from Byblos and Damascus to Thebes, from the Mediterranean Sea to Philadelphia (Rabbath-ammon) and Petra, and explained them with Greek inscriptions.

To commemorate the life of Moses in Moab (Dt. 34:1-5), early Christians erected churches on the two peaks of Mt. Nebo overlooking the Jordan Valley. Since 1973 M. Piccirillo has resumed the archeological work of Franciscan Fathers S. Saller and U. Corbo, with the assistance of architects and restorers. On the peak of Khirbet el-Mukhayyet (the town of Nebo) the Church of Saints Lot and Procopius was restored and mosaics were repaired and relaid. At the monastery on top of Siyagha, in the course of excavation, new discoveries were made of a funeral chapel, a baptistry with basin, unusual floors made of colored tesserae showing rural life, a dedicatory Greek inscription of five lines from A.D. 531 and another of two lines, giving the names of the artists who created the mosaic floors (M. Piccirillo).

Bibliography.–N. Glueck, *Explorations in Eastern Palestine*, *AASOR*, 14 (1934); 15 (1935); 18-19 (1939); 25-28 (1951); M. Avi-Yonah, *Quarterly of the Dept. of Antiquities in Palestine*, 5 (1936), 139-193; *The Holy Land* (1966); H. de Contenson, *ADAJ*, 4-5 (1960), 12-98; *ADAJ*, 8-9 (1964), 30-46; J. Mellaart, *ADAJ*, 6-7 (1962), 126-157; G. L. Harding, *Antiquities of Jordan* (1967); J. B. Hennessy, *Levant*, 1 (1969), 1-24; N. Glueck, *River Jordan* (rev. ed. 1968); *Other Side of the Jordan* (rev. ed. 1970); K. M. Kenyon, *Archaeology in the Holy Land* (1970); E. K. Vogel, *HUCA*, 42 (1971; offprint 1974); J. A. Sanders, *BA*, 36 (1973); R. H. Smith, *Pella of the Decapolis* (1973); K. Prag, *Levant*, 6 (1974), 69-116; O. Bar-Yosef, *Archaeology*, 26 (1975), 30-37; M. Ibrahim, J. A. Sauer, K. Yassine, *BASOR*, 222 (Apr. 1976), 41-66; L. T. Geraty, *ADAJ*, 21 (1976), 41-53; M. Piccirillo, *ADAJ*, 21 (1976), 55-59; T. M. Kerestes, J. M. Lundquist, B. G. Ward, K. Yassine, *ADAJ*, 22 (1977-78), 108-135; H. J. Franken, M. M. Ibrahim, *ADAJ*, 22 (1977-78), 57-80; C.-M. Bennett, "Some Reflections on Neo-Assyrian Influences in Transjordan," in P. R. S. Moorey and P. J. Parr, eds., *Archaeology in the Levant* (1978), pp. 164-171.

E. K. VOGEL

JORIBAS jō'rə-bəs (1 Esd. 8:44, AV). *See* JARIB **2.**

JORIBUS jō'rə-bəs. An AV and NEB variant of JARIB **3;** also an NEB variant of JARIB **2.**

JORIM jō'rim [Gk. *Iōreim* < Heb. *yᵉhôrām, yôrām*]. An ancestor of Jesus in Luke's genealogy (Lk. 3:29).

JORKEAM jôr'kē-əm [Heb. *yorqᵉʿām*]; AV, NEB, JORKOAM. A settlement in Judah established by Raham (1 Ch. 2:44). It is perhaps the same as the JOKDEAM of Josh. 15:56.

JOSABAD jō'zə-bad (1 Ch. 12:4, AV, NEB; 1 Esd. 8:63, AV), **JOSABDUS** jō-sab'dus (1 Esd. 8:63, NEB). *See* JOZABAS.

JOSAPHAT jos'ə-fat (Mt. 1:8, AV). *See* JEHOSHAPHAT.

JOSAPHIAS jos-ə-fī'əs (1 Esd. 8:36, AV, NEB). *See* JOSIPHIAH.

JOSE jō'sə. The AV form for Joshua in Luke's genealogy (3:29). *See* JOSHUA **4.**

JOSECH jō'sek [Gk. *Iōsech*] (AV JOSEPH). An ancestor of Jesus in Luke's genealogy (3:26).

JOSEDEC jō'sə-dek (AV Apoc.), **JOSEDECH** (AV Hag. 1:1, 12, 14; 2:2, 4; Zec. 6:11), **JOSEDEK** (NEB 1 Esd. 5:5, 48, 56; 6:2; 9:19). *See* JEHOZADAK, JOZADAK.

JOSEPH jō'səf, jō'zəf [Heb. *yôsēp*–'may he add' (i.e., may God add posterity), *yᵉhôsēp* (Ps. 81:5 [MT 6]); Gk. *Iōsēph, Iōsēs* (e.g., TR Mt. 13:55; Mk. 6:3)].

1. The eleventh son of Jacob and the first of Rachel. See separate article below.

2. The father of Igal, one of the twelve spies sent from the tribe of Issachar by Moses to spy out the land of Canaan (Nu. 13:7).

3. A son of Asaph (1 Ch. 25:2, 9).

4. A son of Binnui, who married a foreign wife after the Exile (Ezr. 10:42; cf. 1 Esd. 9:34, AV Josephus).

5. A priest of the family of Shebaniah in the days of Joiakim (Neh. 12:14).

6. A son of Zechariah. As a military commander under Judas Maccabeus, he, with Azariah, was commissioned to protect Judah while Judas went to do battle in Gilead. He was instructed by Judas not to engage in battle until the latter returned, but he ignored this directive and was defeated by Gorgias *ca.* 163 B.C. (1 Macc. 5:18, 56, 60).

7. A brother of Judas Maccabeus in 2 Macc. 8:22, although this is probably a mistake for John (as also in 10:19; cf. 1 Macc. 2:1-5).

8. Great-grandfather of Judith (Jth. 8:1).

9. The husband of Mary the mother of Jesus. *See* JOSEPH HUSBAND OF MARY.

10. An ancestor of Jesus Christ (Lk. 3:24).

11. An ancestor of Jesus Christ who lived sometime between King David and Zerubbabel the governor of postexilic Judah (Lk. 3:30; cf. vv. 27, 31).

12. A brother of James the Younger (AV Joses, Mt. 27:56; cf. Mk. 15:40).

13. A Jew of Arimathea in whose tomb Jesus was buried (Mt. 27:57; Mk. 15:43; Lk. 23:50; Jn. 19:38). *See* JOSEPH OF ARIMATHEA.

14. A brother of Jesus (Mt. 13:55; AV Joses), called Joses in Mk. 6:3 (*see* JOSES **1**).

15. A member of the early Church, called Barsabbas (but not the Barsabbas of Acts 15:22) and surnamed Justus, who was a candidate for the apostleship left vacant by Judas Iscariot (Acts 1:23; cf. vv. 15-26). *See* JOSEPH BARSABBAS.

16. The companion of Paul, surnamed BARNABAS (Acts 4:36; AV Joses).

S. F. HUNTER

JOSEPH jō′səf, jō′zəf [Heb. *yôsēp*–prob. 'may he (God) add' (i.e., other sons); LXX *Iōsēph*]. (Cf. Gen. 30:24; in vv. 23f. there may well be a pun on the verbs *'āsap,* "take away," and *yāsap,* "add," but not a rival etymology of Joseph. The place name *yšp-'ir* in an Egyptian topographical list of Thutmose III [*ca.* 1470 B.C.], often read as Joseph-El and compared with the name Joseph, is quite certainly not related to the name Joseph. The sibilants [*s, š*] are entirely distinct; *yšp-'ir* in the Egyptian list is of the same type as biblical Iphtah-el [Josh. 19:14, 27]. On *yšp-'ir,* cf. W. F. Albright, *JPOS,* 8 [1928], 249.) The eleventh (and favorite, Gen. 37:3; cf. 33:2) son of Jacob, his first by Rachel (Gen. 30:24; 35:24).

I. Literary Unity of the Joseph Story
II. Background of the Joseph Story
  A. Gen. 37: Sold into Egypt
  B. Gen. 39: Service in Egypt
  C. Gen. 40: Prison and Courtiers
  D. Gen. 41: Dreams, High Office, Egyptian Names
  E. Gen. 42–44: Border Control
  F. Gen. 45–47: Keepers of Cattle, Egyptian Economics
  G. Gen. 48–50: Shades of Death
  H. Date of Joseph

I. Literary Unity of the Joseph Story.–The story of Joseph is the story of a spoiled child and dreamer, sold into Egyptian slavery by jealous brothers, subjected to ups and downs culminating in his becoming real ruler of that ancient land, and divinely placed there, to save his people and countless others in dire need from famine. In Genesis, as it stands, the story is superbly told and is an obvious unity. However, Gen. 37; 39–50 have within the last few generations been subjected to precisely the same divisive literary analyses into fragments from supposed rival sources or "hands" as has the rest of the Pentateuch. In material assigned by some scholars to the so-called J document, the Joseph narratives are held to display considerable knowledge of Egyptian customs and institutions. The author, however, has been credited with "mistakes," the most obvious being the assumptions that the ancient Egyptians used camels (Ex. 9:3) and that straw was employed for making bricks (Ex. 5:5-19). The J source also seems to have been regarded by older liberals as depending to some extent upon the *Tale of the Two Brothers* (see below). The alleged E document, when dealing with Joseph, is held to exhibit a greater sense of divine purpose and power in the life of the hero (Gen. 45:5-8; 50:20; etc.), and to introduce more emotional elements into the narrative (cf. Gen. 37:29f.) than the J source. In the main, however, double narratives and appellatives are the usual criteria alleged. And even here the only doublet with any semblance of reality is the supposed double narrative of Joseph's being sold into Egypt, (1) by his brothers to merchants going to Egypt, and (2) by merchants who stole him from a pit. But as will be seen below, this doublet is imaginary. Double terms (Yahweh and 'Elohim for God; Israel and Jacob for Joseph's father; Ishmaelites and Midianites for the merchants; etc.) are worthless as criteria; such alternations in other ancient Near Eastern literatures employing closely similar turns of phrase show this clearly. See provisionally K. A. Kitchen, *JEA,* 47 (1961), 162f.; C. H. Gordon, *Christianity Today,* 4 (1959), 131-34; *HUCA,* 26 (1955), 67, 96f.

II. Background of the Joseph Story.–The story of Joseph itself needs no detailed rehearsal here; the Genesis narrative is a gem to be read in the pages of the OT itself. In what follows, therefore, knowledge of that narrative is presupposed, and special attention has been given to Egyptian and other background and to certain debated points.

A. Gen. 37: Sold into Egypt. The mark of Jacob's partiality or affection for Joseph was the "coat of many colors" (AV, RV), or "long-sleeved robe" (cf. RV mg., RSV) that he had given him. Either rendering of the Heb. *k^e^tōneṯ passîm* is possible archeologically, as Egyptian representations of Canaanite dress show it as often including both bright colors and long sleeves. Compare, e.g., the leader of the thirty-seven Semites shown visiting Egypt in the famous Beni-hasan tomb painting (*ca.* 1800 B.C.), D. J. Wiseman, *Illustrations from Biblical Archaeology* (1958), p. 29, fig. 25 (right); or *ANEP,* no. 3. Linguistically, *passîm* might possibly be compared with Assyr. *paspasu,* "brightly colored bird," and Arab. *fasafisa,* "mosaic" (Eisler, *Orientalische Literaturzeitung,* 11 [1908], cols. 368-371; cf. 14 [1911], col. 509), for the meaning "many-colored." "Long-sleeved" is arrived at by taking *k^e^tōneṯ passîm* as a "tunic of (i.e., reaching to) palms and soles," *pas* being the flat of the hand or foot (cf. BDB, p. 821a).

Shechem (37:13f.) and Dothan (v. 17) were both inhabited Canaanite cities in Joseph's day (Middle Bronze Age; on date, see below) as amply shown by excavations at both sites. For those at Shechem, see G. E. Wright,

Syrian tribute bearers with long-sleeved garments perhaps like Joseph's coat. Wall painting from the tomb of Thutmose IV (1421-1413 B.C.) (Trustees of the British Museum)

Campbell, Toombs, Kee, etc., in *BA*, 20 (1957), nos. 1, 4; 23 (1960); *BASOR*, 144 (1956); 148 (1957); 161 (1961). For Dothan, see J. P. Free, *BA*, 19 (1956), 43-48; *BASOR*, 131 (1953); 135 (1954); 139 (1955); 143 (1956); 147 (1957); 152 (1958); 156 (1959); 160 (1960).

The story of how Joseph was sold into Egypt is often considered to be one of the classic passages for demonstrating the alleged composite nature of the present pentateuchal narrative: according to the J account, Judah leads his brothers in selling Joseph to the Ishmaelites, while the E narrative portrays Reuben as suggesting that Joseph be left in a pit, but he is stolen by Midianites. In point of fact, this division of the existing narrative into two is unnecessary, and ignores certain points of Hebrew and allied Near Eastern stylistic usage.

The brothers would have killed Joseph, but Reuben (hoping to rescue him later) persuaded them to put him in a pit. Presently, while the brothers were having a meal, an Ishmaelite caravan appeared. Judah then suggested that they rid themselves of Joseph by selling him to the Ishmaelites instead of killing him. So, they took Joseph from the pit and sold him to "[some] Midianites, traders" — part of the Ishmaelite caravan — and this body of Ishmaelites (= Midianites = Medanites, so MT of v. 36) sold Joseph into Egypt (37:36; 39:1). The overlap of these terms is explicitly stated in Jgs. 8:24 (Gideon's Midianites had earrings "because they were Ishmaelites"), and for the close relationship of Medan and Midian, cf. Gen. 25:2. This overlap of terms is well known in the ancient Near East: thus, the Egyptian stela of Sebekkhu (*ca.* 1800 B.C.) uses three different terms — *Aamu, Mentyu-Setet,* and *Retenu khesyt* (=Asiatics, Asian bedouin, and vile Syrians) — for one and the same Palestinian foe, within a very short space of text.

When Reuben returned to the pit, he was evidently surprised to find Joseph gone; obviously, therefore, he was not with the other brothers when they sold Joseph. The simplest reason for his absence is that when the foreign caravan was sighted, he (the most dutiful) went off to guard their sheep until the foreigners were safely past; they (and Joseph) would be on their way south before Reuben returned to the pit and the meal. That the "they" who "drew Joseph up" in v. 28 are the brothers is no difficulty: as in other parallel literatures, a pronoun in Hebrew can often be separated from its antecedent by other agent nouns (e.g., Dt. 22:18f. — "he" in "he has brought an evil name" in v. 19 refers back not to the last noun preceding, the damsel's father, but to the man of v. 18). In Gen. 45:4, Joseph plainly reminds his brothers that they sold him into slavery; they might well be dismayed as well as surprised (45:3, 5) — the penalty for stealing and selling someone into slavery was death, both in Hammurabi's Code (§ 14) and among their own people still in Moses' time (Ex. 21:16; Dt. 24:7). But Joseph deliberately veiled the fact that it was his own brothers who stole him out of the land of the Hebrews when he was earlier pleading with the butler for his good offices (Gen. 40:14f.). To have admitted that he had been sold by his own brothers, on top of his imprisonment, would have made a bad impression on the butler and thus have wrecked his plea of innocence. When points like these are given their proper due, all need to cut up the narrative into insipid rival versions simply vanishes.

Joseph was sold for "twenty pieces [i.e., shekels] of silver" (Gen. 37:28), probably the current average price for a slave in the early 2nd millennium B.C., as attested also by Hammurabi's Code in the 18th cent. B.C. (one-third of a mina = 20 shekels: §§ 116, 214, 252, *ANET,* pp. 170, 175f.), in Old Babylonian tablets (I. Mendelsohn, *Slavery in the Ancient Near East* [1949], pp. 117, 155), and other contemporary documents from Mari (G. Boyer, *Textes Juridiques: Archives Royales de Mari* [1958], VIII, no. 10, lines 1-4). In earlier times (26th-20th cents. B.C.) the price was 10 to 15 shekels (e.g., Lipit-Ishtar code, §§ 12, 13, *ANET,* p. 160; Eshnunna code, §§ 55, 57, *ANET,* p. 163), while later it rose to 30 shekels (Nuzi, 15th cent. B.C.; Ugarit, 14th cent. B.C. [also 20 and 40 shekels]; Am.Tab., 30 shekels for ransom — E. F. Campbell, *BA,* 23 [1960], 19-20; the Mosaic laws, 13th cent. B.C.: Ex. 21:32), and then 50 shekels and upward in the Assyrian and later empires in the 1st millennium B.C. The figure of 20 shekels for Joseph thus fits well into the early 2nd millennium B.C., in the pattern of gradually rising prices in the ancient Near East.

B. Gen. 39: Service in Egypt. When Joseph was sold into Egypt (Gen. 37:36; 39:1), he was but one of many such Northwest Semitic-speaking slaves in the larger households and institutions of this land in the early 2nd millennium B.C. On the reverse of Papyrus Brooklyn 35.1446 is a list of some seventy-nine servants bequeathed by a man to his wife, *ca.* 1740 B.C. More than forty of these servants are explicitly labelled "Asiatics," and must at one time have been sold into Egypt as slaves like Joseph (but perhaps less dramatically), as the 13th Dynasty then reigning is not known to have fought in Asia, and so these would not be prisoners of war. Many of these slaves in Papyrus Brooklyn bear good Northwest Semitic names like Menahem or ʿAqabtu (related to "Jacob"). Study of this list and related material shows that these and other Semitic slaves in Egypt by their ability often received better positions than the less intelligent Egyptian fellahin, were employed about the house as domestics (*ḥery-per*) like Joseph (39:2), and — also like him — could rise to positions of trust under their masters (as shown by Posener), even performing the funerary functions that normally fell to an eldest son. See W. C. Hayes, *A Papyrus of the Late Middle Kingdom in the Brooklyn Museum* (1955); W. F. Albright, *JAOS,* 74 (1954), 222-233 (on the personal names); G. Posener, *Syria,* 34 (1957), 145-163 (on names and role of Semites in Middle Kingdom Egypt). Joseph as "overseer over his house" (39:4) would be *ʾimy-r pr,* "steward," a well-known title.

Hieratic papyrus listing slaves, including several with Northwest Semitic names, in Egypt about the time of Joseph (*ca.* 1700 B.C.) (Brooklyn Museum)

The incident of Potiphar's wife tempting Joseph and then trying to throw the blame on him has often been compared with the Egyptian *Tale of Two Brothers* in Papyrus D'Orbiney (late 13th cent. B.C.), and some have even asserted that the Egyptian tale inspired the production of the Hebrew narrative. But in point of fact, just this one incident of temptation to lust and transferred blame is the *only* point of contact between the two works, and (unhappily) a banal one at that; Egyptian sources indicate that both in literature and in daily life some other Egyptian women were no better than Potiphar's wife. In every other respect the two stories are entirely different; the Joseph narrative deals throughout, consistently and exclusively, with real people in real-life situations, while the D'Orbiney story's two brothers are apparently thinly disguised deities and the whole tale is permeated by fantasy (at one stage, the younger brother keeps his heart on top of a conifer tree that sports fine flowers; later he turns into a prize bull, two Persea trees, a chip of wood, etc.). This is best seen in reading a full-length translation of the story (e.g., in Erman and Blackman, *Literature of the Ancient Egyptians* [1927], pp. 150-161) and not just the "Potiphar" snippet usually reproduced in anthologies like *ANET.* In point of fact, there is quite certainly no direct link between the two works at all. That Joseph was not immediately put to death but simply imprisoned may be a hint that Potiphar doubted his wife's story, or at least perhaps intended to inquire more closely into the matter at leisure.

C. Gen. 40: Prison and Courtiers. Comparing Gen. 39:1, 20ff. with 40:1ff., it would appear that Joseph's master was directly employed in the personal palace service of the pharaoh as commander of the bodyguard. In Middle Egyptian terms, Potiphar would then be a *sḥḏ-šmsw* or instructor of retainers (for which function cf. R. O. Faulkner, *JEA,* 39 [1953], 39) attached to the court. Thus the household in which Joseph had first risen in service was probably in the capital and within reach of the palace and state administration. This would at once explain how it was that court officials like the butler and baker came to be put into ward with Joseph. Their imprisonment was real but not rigorous; Joseph was appointed to attend to their needs. Later Egyptian evidence indicates that this is realistic enough; during one treason trial of court notables in the time of Ramses III (*ca.* 1170 B.C.), three of the bench of judges were in turn punished for carousing with the prisoners on trial (cf. A. de Buck, *JEA,* 23 [1937], 156; and n. 2 to Judicial Papyrus of Turin, VI, 1-7)! The prison of Joseph and the two dignitaries was apparently a place of detention attached to the household of the captain of the guard (cf. 40:3f.), in proximity to the court. While the captain of the guard (probably still Potiphar) had senior oversight of the prison and so may have included *ỉmy-r ḫnrt,* "prison governor," among his titles, he had under him in actual charge of prisoners a keeper; the latter's Egyptian title would be *s3wty n ḫnrt,* "prison keeper" (see K. A. Kitchen, *Tyndale House Bulletin,* No. 2 [1956/57], 1f.). On Egyptian prisons and their functions, see W. C. Hayes, *op. cit.*

The title (chief) butler should be rendered (royal) cupbearer, Egyptian *wdpw-nsw,* later *wb3-nsw,* as is evident from his function in Gen. 40:11-13 and Egyptian data mentioned by Vergote, pp. 35-37. Potiphar, the cupbearer, and the baker are all described as *sārîs* in Hebrew, rendered "officer" in the English versions but often considered to mean "eunuch." Examination, however, of cognate *ša-rēš(-šarri)* in Akkadian and parallel terms in Hittite, etc., as well as of the occurrences of the Hebrew term *sārîs* in the OT, shows that in the 3rd and 2nd millennia B.C. these words were general ones for "dignitary," "official," "courtier," and only later (esp. in the 1st millennium B.C.) took on the narrower meaning "eunuch." In Egyptian also, for example, the word *sr,* "official," became in Coptic *siûr,* "eunuch." And as Potiphar was married, he obviously was no eunuch, though called *sārîs.* The fact is that the Joseph narrative is true to its origin in the early 2nd millennium B.C. and so uses *sārîs* in its early, general meaning, not the later more specialized meaning (see K. A. Kitchen, *JEA,* 47 [1961], 160, for references).

D. Gen. 41: Dreams, High Office, Egyptian Names. The prominence of dreams in the story of Joseph is characteristic of all Near Eastern antiquity. Joseph the boy has dreams foreshadowing his later exaltation, the cupbearer and baker each have a dream presaging their respective restoration and extinction, and it is by dreams that God warns the king of the prosperity and famine in store for Egypt. In Egypt and Assyria special textbooks existed for the interpretation of dreams; an Egyptian one (Papyrus Chester Beatty III, written in the 13th cent. B.C., but probably originally composed about five centuries earlier) follows the pattern, "If a man sees himself in a dream doing [such and such], it is good or bad and means that [so and so will befall him]." For a brief sample of this text, see *ANET,* p. 495; for the whole topic, see A. L. Oppenheim, *Interpretation of Dreams in the Ancient Near East* (1956); also *Les Sources Orientales, II: Les Songes et leur interprétation* (1959). The Hebrew word for "magician" used in Gen. 41:8, *ḥarṭummîm,* is from Egyp. (*ḫry-ḥbt*) *ḥry-tp* (Gardiner, *JEA,* 24 [1938], 164f., and Vergote, pp. 66-94, 206, for full study and bibliography).

Joseph's practical approach to the problem of impending years of plenty and then of famine (41:33-36) commended him to Pharaoh as the God-sent man for the situation (vv. 37ff.). Joseph was given the royal seal and supreme authority under Pharaoh, ceremonial investiture with linen raiment and gold necklace, and the second chariot. Opinions differ somewhat over the precise offices that Joseph held. Most scholars consider that the MT represents him as vizier, but some prefer to hold that in fact Joseph was more strictly a *ra-ḥery,* an official specially appointed to a given task (in this case, full charge of agriculture, economy, and antifamine measures) and directly responsible to Pharaoh. See J. M. A. Janssen, *Jaarbericht Ex Oriente Lux,* 14 (1955/56), 66f.; Vergote, pp. 102ff.; W. A. Ward, *JSS,* 5 (1960), 144-150 (who would make Joseph simply minister for agriculture directly responsible to the king). The investiture of high officials with linen and gold decorations is quite well attested from the monuments. The use of the chariot (41:43) and mention of horses (47:17) does not preclude a date for Joseph of *ca.* 1700 B.C.; the skeleton of a horse was found at the fortress of Buhen in Nubia in levels dating from well before the destruction of the fortress in the 17th cent. B.C. As horses at this period were never ridden but always used for chariots, this is a strong hint of the probable use of both horse and chariot to a limited extent in the Nile Valley as early as Joseph and for some time before his day (on the date of the skeleton, see W. B. Emery, *Kush,* 8 [1960], 8f. and plate IIIb).

Among the Egyptian names in Gen. 41, Potiphera is universally admitted to be Egyptian *P3-dỉ-P3Rʿ* or *Pedi-Prē,* "he whom Prē (=sun-god) has given"; and Potiphar is generally considered to be a variant of this. This type of name (i.e., *P3-dỉ-X,* where *X* is a deity) is known from the 19th Dynasty (13th cent. B.C.) onward, and replaced an older form with the same meaning; the writer of the Joseph story may have substituted a "modern" form *PediPrē* for older and obsolete *DidiRē.* Asenath is paralleled by Egyptian names like *ʾIw.s-n.t* or *-n-ỉt(.s)*: "she belongs to thee" (fem., the mother or a goddess) or ". . . to (her) father"; such names are well known in Egypt in the early 2nd millennium B.C. Zaphenath-paʿaneah may be for Zathenaph-paʿaneah, Egyptian (*Yōsēp*) *ḏd-n.f* (*ʾI*)*p-ʿnḫ*, i.e., "(Joseph) who is called Ip-ʿanekh" (the latter being a common name in the early 2nd millennium). For fuller details of these names, see K. A. Kitchen, *The Joseph Narrative and Its Egyptian Background* (forthcoming). These names are certainly not anachronistic as often alleged but are fully compatible with a date for Joseph in the first half of the 2nd millennium B.C. (on date, see below).

The wealth of Egypt's grainfields and granaries (Gen. 41:49) was proverbial throughout antiquity and was often illustrated on the walls of tombs of the great dignitaries of the Middle and New Kingdoms (cf. *Illustrations from Biblical Archaeology,* p. 33, fig. 27, and p. 37). But when the annual Nile flood failed, then the threat of famine stalked the land. Several famines are mentioned in Egyptian texts of all periods. Just before or after Joseph's time, in an oft-quoted inscription, a certain Bebi remarks, "When a famine came [lasting] many years, I gave grain to my town during each [year of] famine." On Egyptian famines, see J. Vandier, *La Famine dans l'Égypte ancienne* (1936). For a starving bedouin depicted on an Egyptian relief of *ca.* 2400 B.C., see *ANEP,* no. 102 (and cf. no. 101).

E. Gen. 42–44: Border Control. In chs. 42–43 the strict Egyptian border control that is presupposed by Gen. 42:9f. (when Joseph treats his brothers as "suspects") is again true to life for more than one period of Egyptian history: *ca.* 1960 B.C., Sinuhe had to evade the frontier guards on the forts called "Wall(s) of the Ruler" (cf. *ANET,* p. 19), while papyri of the 13th cent. B.C. reflect a similar close watch on frontier crossings then (*ibid.,* pp. 183f.; and *ANET,* pp. 258f.).

F. Gen. 45–47: Keepers of Cattle, Egyptian Economics. When Joseph's father and family finally arrived in Egypt, at Joseph's instigation and the pharaoh's express command, he told them to report their occupation to the pharaoh as keepers of cattle (Gen. 46:33f.), so that they might dwell in Goshen, for "every shepherd of flocks is an abomination to the Egyptians" (v. 34). As in the case of the Egyptians and Hebrews eating separately in Gen. 43:32, so the separation of foreign herdsmen from Egyptians rested largely or partly on ritualistic usage; in different Egyptian provinces, various animals were taboo (either honored or proscribed). See P. Montet, *L'Égypte et la Bible* (1959), pp. 99-101; Vergote, pp. 188f.

Joseph's aim in getting his people settled in Goshen by professing to be keepers of cattle and sheep was probably twofold. In the first place, the delta was still largely undeveloped in the 2nd millennium B.C.; much of it had not yet been reclaimed for cultivation, and the northeast delta was in some degree a semiforeign borderland in Egyptian eyes. Jacob and his clansfolk could live there peacefully, where Asiatics traditionally came and went, without close contact with the native Egyptian population (or their taboos). In the second place, the large, undeveloped tracts of the delta included marshes and rush- and scrub-covered plains excellent for keeping cattle, where the best Egyptian cattle were pastured; cattle from Upper Egypt were even sent to the delta seasonally each year, including during the latter part of the Hyksos period (*ca.* 1600 B.C.); see H. Kees, *Ancient Egypt: A Cultural Topography* (1961), pp. 29f., 88. This also explains the pharaoh's remark (Gen. 47:6) to Joseph concerning his brothers, "If you know any able men among them, put them in charge of my cattle": the royal cattle were kept in this favorable region, certainly "the best of the land" for this purpose. The settlement of the Hebrews in Goshen, the later "land of Rameses" (47:11, an editorial term), is one more example of the progressive colonization of the delta promoted by Egypt's rulers in successive periods of its history.

During the famine, Joseph bought up all private property in Egypt (except that of the temples) in exchange for grain for food and for cultivation (47:13-26), so that the pharaoh and the priests were the only landowners. This would fit well into the Hyksos period of Egyptian history, after the Middle Kingdom when the provincial governors at least were great landed families, and before the New Empire when Pharaoh and the state (sometimes barely distinguishable) and the great temples alone owned almost all land (the few known or probable cases of New Empire private land ownership are studied in contrast to the state and temple holdings by H. W. Helck, *Materialen zur Wirtschaftsgeschichte des Neuen Reiches* [1961], II, 237-39). In theory, the king owned all Egypt as successor to the gods on earth, but actual practice oscillated from period to period, in accordance with the successive economic and political changes during Egyptian history. The priests did not have to pay Joseph's one-fifth levy on the produce of all other land (Gen. 47:20), but this does not imply that they paid no taxes at all as some have inferred (on this, the evidence is ambiguous).

G. Gen. 48–50: Shades of Death. Eventually, Jacob reached the end of his long life, but first he blessed the sons of Joseph in particular (ch. 48) and his own twelve sons in general (ch. 49), in accordance with ancient Near Eastern and patriarchal custom (cf. Gen. 27; and C. H. Gordon, *BA,* 3 [1940], 8). For some linguistic background to Gen. 49, cf. J. Coppens, "La Bénédiction de Jacob," in *SVT,* 4 (1957), 97-115; the Middle Bronze Age tombs at Jericho with their many successive burials (K. M. Kenyon, *Digging Up Jericho* [1957], pp. 233ff.) illustrate Jacob's concern about and insistence on his being buried in the family grave with his forefathers (Gen. 49:29-33; cf. 50:5-14). Both Joseph in his turn (50:26) and his father (50:2f.) were embalmed, i.e., mummified in Egyptian fashion; and Joseph was put "in a coffin in Egypt." In the 17th cent. B.C., roughly mummiform wooden coffins with conventional portrait faces carved at the head end were the custom.

The seventy days' mourning (50:3) were traditional in Egypt (Vergote, p. 200 and references); also, Joseph's age of 110 years was that recognized as "ideal" by the Egyptians (Vergote, pp. 200f.) and this attainment would be regarded as a signal mark of divine favor by his contemporaries.

H. Date of Joseph. Those who regard the Joseph narratives as comprising historicized myth will have no great concern for establishing a firm chronological picture for the time of Joseph. Other scholars, however, who see in the patriarchal narratives a developing national saga, recorded much as similar material might be written today, will treat them as having a substantial basis of historical fact, and will make serious attempts to fit them into the chronology as carefully as possible. It must be stated at once that certain of the chronological problems associated with the patriarchal period are very complex, leading some scholars to assign a date of *ca.* 2000 B.C. to Abraham while others place him in the Egyptian Amarna Age (15th and 14th cent. B.C.). The preponderance of current archeological evidence, however, indicates that the topographical pattern of the patriarchal narratives is consistent with the situation in the Middle Bronze Age rather than with life in other periods, such as that of the Egyptian empire (*ca.* 1570-1200 B.C.), when Palestine was an Egyptian dependency.

One must distinguish carefully between the epoch in

which Joseph lived and the date of the present narrative in Gen. 37–50. The present narrative is most appropriately to be attributed to about the 13th cent. B.C. and to the hand of Moses. The use of the term "land of Rameses" in Gen. 47:11 (which will refer to Ramses II, *ca.* 1290-1224 B.C.) is one good indicator of this general date; certainly with the fall of the 20th Dynasty (*ca.* 1085 B.C.), this term was obsolete, and "field(s) of Zoan (Tanis)" replaced it. Particular emphasis on the age of 110 years occurs in the Ramesside period (1300-1100 B.C.); cf. Vergote. Nor are these the only reasons that favor a Ramesside (Mosaic) date for the present Joseph narrative.

Joseph himself, on all views, lived before the Ramesside period; most authorities put him in the Hyksos period (*ca.* 1700-1550 B.C.), and a few in the 18th Dynasty (in the 14th cent. B.C.). Chronologically, Joseph is inseparable from the patriarchs. Abraham, Isaac, and Jacob are a close series, on the unanimous testimony of Genesis and later tradition, while the life stories of Jacob and Joseph are inseparably interlocked. At present, the total available evidence favors dating the patriarchs in the early part of the 2nd millennium B.C.–*ca.* 1900-1700 B.C. in round figures; the destruction of Transjordanian settlements and of the Cities of the Plain in Gen. 14 and 19 would agree with a great reduction in population density in Transjordan after *ca.* 1800 B.C. (cf. N. Glueck, *The Other Side of the Jordan* [1940]), and archeologically attested seasonal occupation of the Negeb or Southland in Middle Bronze Age I and early II (21st-19th cents. B.C.) would agree with Abraham's journeys there in Gen. 12–13 (see N. Glueck, *Rivers in the Desert* [1959]). Four centuries or more from the 18th cent. B.C. (Gen. 15:13; Ex. 12:40f.) would agree with an Exodus in the 13th cent. B.C. As genealogies tend to be selective in the Near East and Scripture alike, their apparent shortness need not militate against the 430-year figure (*see* CHRONOLOGY OF THE OT III.A.; cf. also W. F. Albright, *BASOR*, 163 [1961], 49-54). Joseph at about 1700 B.C. would then fall into the Hyksos period of Egyptian history. With this would agree the use of "Egyptian" as a distinguishing epithet in Gen. 39:1; the strict observance of Egyptian habits (41:14) and taboos (43:32), combined with Joseph's ready acceptance in an Egyptian household (cf. Papyrus Brooklyn, etc., above), his rise at court, and the change in Egyptian land economics also noted above.

Bibliography.–Besides the references in the text, see the bibliography in J. Vergote, *Joseph en Égypte* (1959).

K. A. KITCHEN

JOSEPH AND ASENATH. *See* PSEUDEPIGRAPHA V.E.

JOSEPH BARNABAS. *See* BARNABAS.

JOSEPH BARSABBAS bär-sab'əs [Gk. *Barsabbas,* or *Barsabas*]; AV BARSABAS; for etymology, etc., of "Joseph," *see* JOSEPH. Joseph Barsabbas was surnamed Justus (Acts 1:23). Barsabbas was probably a patronymic, i.e., "son of Sabba or Seba." Other interpretations given are "son of an oath," "son of an old man," "son of conversion," "son of quiet." It is likely that the "Judas called Barsabbas" of Acts 15:22 was his brother.

Joseph Barsabbas was one of those who accompanied the apostles "during all the time that the Lord Jesus went in and out among us, beginning from the baptism of John until the day when he was taken up from us" (Acts 1:21f.). Therefore, when the brethren met in Jerusalem shortly after the Ascension and Peter proposed that they select someone to fill the place in the apostleship left vacant by Judas Iscariot, Joseph Barsabbas was nominated along with Matthias; Matthias, however, was the one on whom the lot fell, and he was therefore enrolled with the eleven apostles (Acts 1:15-26).

According to Eusebius (*HE* i.12), Joseph Barsabbas was one of the seventy (Lk. 10:1), and Papias records the oral tradition that he drank a cup of poison without harm (cf. Mk. 16:18). The Acts of Paul, a work belonging to the 2nd cent. and first mentioned by Origen, relates that Barsabbas, Justus the Flatfoot, and others were imprisoned by Nero for professing their faith in Christ; but when a vision of the newly martyred Paul appeared to the emperor, he ordered their immediate release.

C. M. KERR

JOSEPH HUSBAND OF MARY [Gk. *Iōsēph*] (Mt. 1:16ff.; 2:13, 19; Lk. 1:27; 2:4, 16; 3:23; 4:22; Jn. 1:45; 6:42). Joseph appears only in the narratives of the infancy and boyhood of Jesus in the Gospels of Matthew and Luke. The Gospel of Mark lacks any mention of him, and the Gospel of John mentions him only in a reference to Jesus as his son. This has led many to speculate that Joseph had died before Jesus entered His public ministry and that Mary was a widow during this period of Jesus' life. Such is quite probably the case, as in those times men were normally much older than the women they married.

The Gospel of Luke pictures both Joseph and Mary as residing in Nazareth before Jesus was born. Matthew makes no mention of their residence before Jesus' birth; he only makes it plain (as Luke does also) that Jesus was born in Bethlehem. It is quite possible that the families of Mary and Joseph were a part of the Jewish migration from Judea to Galilee which began during the time of the Maccabean ruler Aristobulus. Those who migrated were zealous Jews who desired to bring their religion to the pagan Galileans and were so successful that there was no question of the Jewish character of the region after that time. Yet these families kept their ties with their native cities, and for the purposes of the Roman census they were required to return. Joseph was a part of a poor carpenter's family. He not only followed this craft himself but also taught it to Jesus (Mk. 6:3). The Judean origin of Joseph's family is further emphasized by the repeated reference to his Davidic ancestry. Not only is this clear from the genealogies in both Matthew and Luke (*see* GENEALOGY OF JESUS) and the forced journey to Bethlehem for the census, but Mt. 1:20 also refers to Joseph's Davidic lineage; here the angel Gabriel addresses Joseph as David's son.

By the time of the Annunciation to Mary by the angel Gabriel, Joseph and Mary were already engaged. Engagement was a very formal occasion, usually sealed by a small gift or a written declaration, although the occasion could involve much more. The period of engagement for a virgin was normally one year, during which time she had the rights of a wife. Divorce was required to break the engagement, and the death of her intended husband before the marriage left her a widow. Infidelity during engagement was regarded as adultery (Dt. 22:13-21). Mt. 1:18-25 describes Joseph's situation. He found that Mary was obviously expecting a child and thus determined that he should divorce her quietly. The text notes that he was a just man, meaning that he lived as a pious Jew in accordance with the law. Although the law allowed him to make her a public example and thus have both Mary and her family disgraced, Joseph determined that a quiet divorce would be better.

At this point Joseph received the first of three direct revelations from God. During a dream the angel of the Lord appeared to him and disclosed that Mary had actually been faithful to him and that the child she had conceived was by the Holy Spirit and would be the Son of God. Thus instructed by the angel, Joseph did not fear to take Mary as his wife, although the text is explicit that he allowed her to remain a virgin until after the child Jesus was born.

Joseph's Davidic lineage required that he make the journey from Nazareth to Bethlehem for the purpose of the Roman census. It was necessary for each male to make the journey and pay a tax, but it was not necessary for women. Joseph's concern for Mary is shown in their journey. As the time of birth was close at hand, leaving her in Nazareth would have left her open to public ridicule during his absence. Luke seems to emphasize that God moved the entire Roman empire to fulfil Micah's prophecy that the Messiah would be born in Bethlehem (Mic. 5:1-4 [MT 4:14–5:3]). Upon their arrival in Bethlehem, Joseph was not able to obtain a place for them to stay in spite of Mary's condition. Thus, the child was born in a stable (probably a cave) and laid in a manger. There Joseph and Mary received the shepherds as recorded in Lk. 2:8-20.

An insight into the piety and poverty of Joseph is provided in the scenes involving the purification of Mary and the child. The law said that after a forty-day period the first-born male child and mother must be purified in the temple. Two offerings were to be given, a lamb and a turtle dove, except in the case of the poorest of people, who could offer two turtle doves. The latter was Joseph's offering. While in the temple Mary and Joseph met Simeon, who blessed them (Lk. 2:25-32); and as they marveled at Simeon's prophetic blessing they met Anna the aged prophetess, who also acknowledged their child as God's Messiah (Lk. 2:33-35).

God's second direct revelation to Joseph came immediately after the visit of the Magi. He was warned in a dream that he should not remain in Judea, as Herod was seeking to kill the young child. Joseph took Mary and the child and made his way into Egypt, where they lived until Herod's death. Joseph remained in Egypt until his third direct revelation from God, which occurred when the angel of the Lord told him to return to Israel, since those who had sought to kill Jesus were dead. Upon their return to Israel, Joseph and Mary found that Herod's son Archelaus reigned in Judea; so they returned to Nazareth and there raised their son (Mt. 2:19-23).

The final reference to Joseph shows again how he lived and raised Jesus as a pious Jew. The Scripture (Lk. 2:41) relates that Joseph and Mary made their pilgrimage to Jerusalem every year for the Passover feast. Jesus journeyed with them, apparently for the first time, when He was twelve years old. He undoubtedly was taken at this time so that He might prepare for His formal initiation into the Jewish nation the following year. After the seven days of the Passover, Jesus was inadvertently left in Jerusalem by His parents. Jesus' word concluding this passage shows His consciousness that Joseph was only His legal father and that His real father was God: "Don't you know that I must be about my father's business?" (Lk. 2:48).

The same emphasis is found in the references to Joseph in the Gospel of John. Since the formal narrative in the Gospel begins with the ministry of John the Baptist, no reference is made to Joseph's participation in the events of the story. Twice Joseph is recognized as Jesus' legal father. When Philip speaks of Jesus to Nathanael he calls Him Joseph's son (1:46). The same recognition is made by those who say that they know Jesus' father and mother and question Jesus' claim to have come down from above (6:42). Some scholars feel that the scornful question regarding Jesus' father is a reference to the presumed illegitimacy of His birth in the eyes of many Jews (Jn. 8:19). In the time of Justin Martyr (*ca.* A.D. 150) such a scandalous rumor was prevalent among the Jewish people. Throughout his Gospel, however, John is not as concerned to record the circumstances of Jesus' birth in Bethlehem as he is to indicate that the true origin of Jesus is with the Father and that He is the divine Word of God.

In the apocryphal NT literature the role of Joseph enlarges as the narratives about Jesus' childhood increase. In the Infancy Gospel of Thomas, Joseph plays a role in the story about Jesus giving life to clay sparrows He had created. He also is forced to admonish Jesus that He should not cause any more children to die by pronouncing curses on them. The Gospel of Peter and the Protevangelium of James both picture Jesus' brothers as children of Joseph by an earlier marriage. The glorification of Joseph in Egypt and the fostering of a cult around him seem to have been the source of an Arabic History of Joseph the Carpenter. This fourth- or fifth-century document is built around Joseph's life and death and includes material from the Infancy Gospel of Thomas and the Protevangelium of James, as well as a eulogy by Jesus over Joseph at his death.

Bibliography.–J. G. Machen, *Virgin Birth of Christ* (1930); B. Reicke, *NT Era* (Eng. tr. 1968); H. Daniel-Rops, *Jesus and His Times* (Eng. tr. 1955), pp. 108-151; B. Vawter, *The Four Gospels, An Intro.* (1969), I, 67-104.

D. W. WEAD

JOSEPH OF ARIMATHEA ar-i-mə-thē'ə [Gk. *Iōsēph apó Arimathaias*] (Mt. 27:57, 59; Mk. 15:43, 45; Lk. 23:50; Jn. 19:38). In all four Gospels the man who steps forth to bury Jesus' body is Joseph of Arimathea. As a member of the Sanhedrin, Joseph was undoubtedly a resident of Jerusalem at this time, but he was born and had lived previously in the Judean village of ARIMATHEA.

Joseph is described in both Mk. 15:43 and Lk. 23:50f. as being a member of the Sanhedrin, although he did not consent to their plot and action against Jesus. He was a rich man (Mt. 27:57) with good social standing (Mk. 15:43). His wealth is shown by the fact that he possessed a new tomb freshly cut out of stone. This undoubtedly indicates that he had made a permanent move from Arimathea to Jerusalem and expected to use this new tomb for his family burial plot in his new city. All four Gospels agree that Joseph became a disciple of Jesus, although John emphasizes that this was done secretly (Jn. 19:38). John seems to indicate that there were many such disciples (12:42). Mk. 15:43 and Lk. 23:51 disclose that he was "expecting the kingdom of God," thus indicating that he expected the Kingdom to come through Jesus. In addition, Luke stresses that he was a good and just man (Lk. 23:50). His desire to bury the dead despite personal risk shows that he was a pious Jew.

The four Gospels record that Joseph went to Pilate requesting that Jesus' corpse be given to him for proper burial. Although it was customary for the Romans to leave the crucified body on the cross for the birds to destroy, they seem to have respected the requirement of Dt. 21:23 that the bodies of executed criminals be taken down and buried. Normal Jewish practice allowed that such bodies be buried in a common tomb supplied by the court (Mish. *Sanhedrin* vi.5). Joseph broke this practice by stepping forth to bury Jesus in his own tomb. None of the Gospels reports that Jesus' followers had anything to do with the burial but only that they followed and observed the tomb in which he was laid (Lk. 23:55).

In the act of burial itself Joseph was accompanied by Nicodemus. Such an act brought with it the risk that neither man would be able to participate in the festivities of the Passover because of the ceremonial uncleanness caused by contact with a dead body (Nu. 19:11). It is probable that slaves performed the actual burial. According to Jewish custom the body was anointed with a spiced oil, in this case myrrh and aloes, wrapped with a linen sheet, and placed in the unused tomb. It was Jewish custom to lay a body on a shelf in the tomb until it had thoroughly decomposed. Then the skeleton was broken apart and placed in an ossuary, a small box for the bones, with an inscription to identify the deceased. The time for Jesus' burial was short, as only two or three hours remained between His death and the setting of the sun (the beginning of the sabbath). *See also* BURIAL II.

NT apocryphal literature portrays Joseph as a friend of Pilate. The Assumption of Mary shows him as caring for Mary, Jesus' mother, from Christ's ascension until her death.

Legends from a later period report that Joseph of Arimathea was sent by the Apostle Philip from Gaul to England, that he built the first church in Glastonbury and became its patron saint, that he brought the Holy Grail to England, and that he freed Ireland from snakes. Many legendary details of his life are found in the fifth-century Gospel of Nicodemus (*see* APOCRYPHAL GOSPELS III.B).

D. W. WEAD

JOSEPH, PRAYER OF. A pseudepigraphical writing. Of an original 1100 lines (according to Nicephorus) only two fragments can now be found in quotations by Origen (sixteen lines in *Comm. on John* ii.31; one line in *Philocalia* 23.15). The extant portion of the work portrays Jacob in exalted terms (e.g., "angel of God," "ruling spirit," "firstborn of every living thing"). The form of the work may have been a testament of Jacob. Scholars have differed about whether it is Jewish (perhaps anti-Christian), Jewish-Christian, Jewish-Gnostic, or even anti-Jewish. J. Z. Smith suggests that it is a product of mystical Hellenistic Judaism of the 1st or 2nd cent. A.D.

Bibliography.–J. Z. Smith, "Prayer of Joseph," in J. Neusner, ed., *Religions in Antiquity: Essays in Memory of Erwin Ramsdell Goodenough* (1968), pp. 253-294; J. H. Charlesworth, *Pseudepigrapha and Modern Research* (1976), pp. 140-42; M. R. James, *Lost Apocrypha of the OT* (1920), pp. 21-31.

E. W. S.

JOSEPH THE CARPENTER, HISTORY OF. *See* APOCRYPHAL GOSPELS II.G.

JOSEPHUS, FLAVIUS jō-sē'fəs, flā'vē-əs. Jewish historian and general in the war of the Jews against the Romans in A.D. 66-70. Josephus was born the son of a distinguished priestly family sometime between Sept. 13, A.D. 37, and March 16, 38, and died probably *ca.* A.D. 100 in Rome. His writings give some information about his life and family relationships. He was married four times and had five sons. His parents provided him an excellent rabbinic education, and at the early age of fourteen, so he boasted, he was so learned that the high priests and the leading men of the city of Jerusalem consulted him about matters of the law. Presumably he had also learned some Greek as a youth. When he was sixteen he undertook further training with the Pharisees, Sadducees, Essenes, and finally with a hermit. At nineteen he joined the Pharisees and remained for the rest of his life a faithful pharisaic Jew, perhaps of Shammaite tendency. He did not, however, take part in the new development of rabbinic Judaism after A.D. 70. In 64, when he was twenty-nine years old, he traveled to Rome to procure the release of several pious priests, his friends, who, as he said, had been arrested and sent there on insufficient grounds by the governor Felix. He was successful, thanks to a chance meeting with Nero's wife Poppaea.

When he returned to his homeland, probably impressed by the splendor and might of Rome, he tried first to extinguish the rising fires of insurrection against Rome but finally joined the rebels and became general of the Jewish forces in Galilee. His activities as regional commander, some of which were dubious, culminated in the heroic defense of the fortress Jotapata against Vespasian in 67. Taken prisoner and led before the Roman commander-in-chief, Josephus, who as a priest felt himself especially qualified to know and proclaim God's will, prophesied that Vespasian would become caesar. His prophecy was probably influenced by his insight that Rome was now called to rule the world and that the Jewish people probably could survive, independent and secure, in cooperation with Rome. Vespasian, evidently impressed with this man, spared his life and, when he actually was proclaimed caesar in 69, set Josephus free. Through this act of manumission Josephus became Josephus Flavius, i.e., Vespasian's family name (*gens Flavia*) was added to his own name. Vespasian's son Titus, whom Vespasian commissioned to end the war against the Jews, took Josephus to Judea, where Josephus was able to witness at firsthand the siege and capture of Jerusalem in the summer of 70. He returned with Titus to Rome, where he lived the life of an author as a favorite of Caesar's court. There he wrote, as a kind of court historian, his *Jewish War* (*De bello judaico* = *BJ*), a complete description of the war of 66-70, preceded by a thorough description of the events leading up to that war. After the death of Vespasian Josephus retained the favor of his successors Titus and Domitian (d. A.D. 96), but the end of his life is obscure.

Four of his works are extant: the *Jewish War* in seven books (A.D. 75-79); *Jewish Antiquities* (*Ant.*) in twenty books (completed 93/94); his autobiography (*Vita*) in one book, a kind of appendix to the *Antiquities* that contains mainly a comprehensive accounting of his activity in Galilee and relatively little about the remaining events of his life; and *Against Apion* (*Contra Apionem* = *CAp*), written certainly after 93/94 but probably before 96. This last is a thorough and convincing defense against the anti-Jewish polemic of non-Jewish authors and is at the same time a description of central Jewish religious convictions. It is uncertain whether Josephus wrote any other works. These alone make him a very important Jewish historian, perhaps the most important. His *Antiquities,* partly a free paraphrase and adaptation of the biblical books, comprise a history of the Jewish people from the creation of the world until his own time, as well as a kind of introduction to his earlier work. Not until H. Graetz, who in the 19th cent. wrote his *History of the Jews,* did anyone venture an undertaking of similarly great scope. Without the *Antiquities* and *Jewish War* little would be known about the historical events and the religious currents in Palestine in the two centuries before the destruction of Jerusalem in 70. The value of Josephus lies in his usefulness as a source for the history of Christianity as well as of Judaism; for his accounts are especially extensive precisely for those decades in which Christianity originated. Like Philo and the LXX, his writings were valued and used so much by the early Church that they were soon transmitted only by Christians and were almost forgotten in Judaism.

The way in which Josephus composed his writings is still subject to some scholarly debate. In writing *Jewish War* — which was originally in Aramaic — he did use helpers proficient in languages, because at the beginning of his writing career his command of Greek was insufficient to enable him to write with acceptable literary skill. His three other works, however, were probably written without any stylistic helpers. Any suggestion that Josephus continually rewrote his works and issued different editions is unfounded.

It is true that, very early in the transmission of Josephus's writings, Christians altered some sections and misrepresented Josephus as demonstrating some Christian beliefs. Thus the famous *testimonium Flavianum,* supposed to be the witness of the Jew Flavius Josephus to Jesus Christ, is certainly not genuine in its traditional form; at the most it contains a genuine nucleus. This *testimonium* was considered especially convincing because it had come from the enemy camp, so it was an important factor in the high honor given to Josephus by the early Church. (*See* JESUS CHRIST I.B.)

The value of Josephus for the reader and student of the OT and NT is so high that already in the Middle Ages he was often seen almost as a church father, and in more recent times his work has sometimes been regarded — half jestingly — as a "Fifth Gospel" or "Small Bible." The first half of the *Antiquities* is an especially invaluable witness to Jewish biblical exegesis, and Jewish traditions of all kinds, in the time of the origin of the NT. His works increase our knowledge of many historical and geographical details found in the Gospels. For example, Josephus's descriptions of the Jewish revolutionary parties and the Essenes are indispensable sources for the study of the Zealots and the Qumrân texts. His accounts of the fall of Jerusalem in 70 seemed to some early Christians to show the fulfillment of the NT threats of punishment for this city, which, for example, led to an old Syriac translation of his account of the destruction being taken into the Syriac canon as a "Fifth Maccabees." Parts of Josephus's works were even bound into some editions of the printed Bibles. As late as the 19th cent., especially in the English-speaking world, the reading of Josephus in many private homes was second only to the reading of the Bible.

Bibliography.–H. St.-J. Thackeray, *et al.*, eds., texts and translations in *LCL* (9 vols., 1926-1965); H. Schreckenberg, *Bibliographie zu Flavius Josephus* (1968), *Supplementband* (1979); D. M. Rhoads, *Israel in Revolution 6-74 C.E.: A Political History Based on the Writings of Josephus* (1976); S. J. D. Cohen, *Josephus in Galilee and Rome: His Vita and Development as a Historian* (1979); Eng. tr. by W. Whiston (1867, often reprinted).

H. SCHRECKENBERG

JOSES jō'sēz, jō'zez [Gk. *Iōsēs*].

1. One of the brothers of Jesus (Mk. 6:3), called Joseph in Mt. 13:55 (AV Joses). *See* BROTHERS OF THE LORD; JOSEPH **14.**

2. A brother of James the Younger and son of Mary, one of the women who stood by the cross of Jesus and went to His grave (Mk. 15:40, 47; cf. AV Mt. 27:56, where the RSV has Joseph). *See* MARY **3.**

3. A name of Barnabas (Acts 4:36, AV, where the RSV has Joseph). *See* BARNABAS.

JOSHAH jō'shə [Heb. *yôšâ*–'Yahweh's gift']. A descendant of Simeon, chief in his family (1 Ch. 4:34, 38).

JOSHAPHAT josh'ə-fat [Heb. *yôšāpāṭ*–'Yahweh has judged'; cf. JEHOSHAPHAT].

1. One of David's mighty men (1 Ch. 11:43), a Mithnite, but not included in the list of 2 S. 23.

2. A priest and trumpeter of David's time (1 Ch. 15:24), AV Jehoshaphat.

JOSHAVIAH josh-ə-vī'ə [Heb. *yôšawyâ*]. Son of Elnaam, one of David's mighty men (1 Ch. 11:46). He is omitted from the list of 2 S. 23, which is less complete and differs in detail.

JOSHBEKASHAH josh-bə-kä'shə, josh-bə-kash'ə [Heb. *yošbᵉqāšâ*] (1 Ch. 25:4, 24). A son of Heman appointed by David as a singer. Some commentators, by slightly modifying the MT, read the last eight or nine names as a prayer ("Be gracious to me, Yahweh, be gracious to me; You are my God; I have magnified and I will exalt [my] helper; sitting in adversity I said, 'Pour out visions in abundance'"), or as a series of incipits (cf. J. M. Myers, *I Chronicles* [*AB*, 1965], pp. 172f.). Whatever the words originally meant, clearly the Chronicler understood them as names.

JOSHEB-BASSHEBETH. *See* JASHOBEAM.

JOSHIBIAH josh-ə-bī'ə [Heb. *yôšiḇyâ*–'Yahweh sets' or 'causes to dwell']; AV, NEB, JOSIBIAH. A Simeonite (1 Ch. 4:35).

JOSHUA josh'o͞o-ə [Heb. *yᵉhôšu(a)*ʿ–'Yahweh saves'].

1. A man of Beth-shemesh. After the Philistines sent the ark away (1 S. 6:14) it stopped in Joshua's field by a stone.

2. A governor of Jerusalem during Josiah's reign (2 K. 23:8).

3. A high priest in postexilic Jerusalem. *See* JESHUA **3.**

4. [Gk. *Iēsous*]; AV JOSE (Lk. 3:29). An ancestor of Jesus in Luke's genealogy.

5. (AV also Jehoshua [Nu. 13:16; 1 Ch. 7:27]). Son of Nun, of the tribe of Ephraim. He was Moses' assistant and successor. The original form of the name was Heb. *hôšē(a)*ʿ, "salvation" (Nu. 13:8; LXX *Ausē*), but was changed by Moses to *yᵉhôšu(a)*ʿ, "Yahweh saves" (Nu. 13:16; LXX *Iēsoun*), perhaps reflecting the practice of assuming a regnal name; later pronounced *yēšû(a)*ʿ (Neh. 8:17; LXX *Iēsous* [cf. Mt. 1:21]). Joshua was a "servant" (or "second-in-command," *mšrt*; Ex. 24:13; cf. 32:17) of Moses. The Bible introduces him as the military field commander under Moses in Israel's battle against Amalek, their military engagement shortly after the Exodus (Ex. 17:9-13). He is presented next as a spiritual disciple of Moses: he accompanied him up the mountain for the reception of the Torah (Ex. 24:13), would not leave the sacred tent whenever Moses returned to the camp after talking to Yahweh face to face (Ex. 33:11), and zealously defended Moses' prerogatives when Eldad and Medad prophesied in the camp (Nu. 11:26-29).

He asserted his faith in Yahweh in the matter of spying out the land by vainly seeking together with Caleb to counteract the unbelieving, defeatist attitude of the other ten spies. Yahweh rewarded their courage and faith by promising them alone entrance into the land (Nu. 14:6, 22-24).

In spite of Joshua's apprenticeship and proven military and spiritual leadership, Moses would not choose him as successor apart from divine selection (Nu. 27:16-23).

Joshua is seen to be the successor of Moses both by legal appointment and by striking parallels between his and Moses' careers. N. Lohfink showed that the appointment of Joshua as Moses' successor follows a carefully worked-out schema (*Scholastik,* 37 [1962], 32-44).

As Israel's new leader he had two functions. He was a military commander to take the land, and an administrator to allot the land. This twofold responsibility was stated at his appointment while Moses was still alive (Dt. 1:37f.; 3:28; 31:7). After the death of Moses, Yahweh repeats his military responsibility (Josh. 1:2-5) and his administrative responsibility (1:6-9). His administrative functions commence in Josh. 13:7.

Moreover, the striking parallels of his career with that of Moses prove his selection. Yahweh was with him, as He was with Moses (1:5; 3:7); the people pledged to obey him, as they did Moses (1:17); he sanctified Israel before Yahweh's miracles as Moses did (3:5; cf. Ex. 19:14); the

Lord promised to exalt him as He had exalted Moses (Josh. 3:7; 4:14); both crossed the water miraculously and in both instances the waters stood in a heap and the tribes of Israel crossed on dry ground (3:17; cf. Ex. 14:21-23, 29; 15:8). At the outset of his mission against Yahweh's enemies he encountered the commander of Yahweh's army and was told, as was Moses, "Put off your shoes from your feet, for the place where you stand is holy" (5:15; cf. Ex. 3:5). Both interceded for the sinning people (7:7; Dt. 9:25-29); both wrote the law on stones (8:32). Yahweh hardened the hearts of their enemies (11:20; Ex. 9:12). At the end of their life-work, both Moses and Joshua delivered stirring addresses of appeal and warning to the assembled Israelites; both men died at symbolic ages (Moses, 120 or 3 full generations; Joshua, 110, the ideal life span for the Egyptians; cf. Gen. 50:22, 26, which give Joseph's age also as 110).

The true character of Joshua's leadership can be best appreciated by considering the decided military advantages belonging to his enemies. The Canaanites had experienced armies (cf. the accounts of the campaigns by the pharaohs of the New Egyptian empire into Palestine-Syria in *LBHG,* pp. 138-173), chariots (e.g., Thutmose III boasts of capturing 924 chariots in his decisive battle at Megiddo [*ANET,* p. 239]; Josh. 17:18; Jgs. 1:19; 4:3, 13 [900 chariots!]), and fortified cities (Nu. 13:28, 32f.; their military armament is depicted by Y. Yadin, *The Art of Warfare in Biblical Lands,* I [1963], 182ff.). Moreover, they were accustomed to forming alliances against a common foe from outside the land; e.g., in the war against Thutmose one hundred cities participated under the leadership of the kings of Kadesh on the Orontes and Megiddo, with the assistance of the king of Mitanni (cf. Josh. 9:1f.; 10:1-5; 11:1-5).

Against these odds Joshua could succeed only by strictly obeying the rules of holy war: complete dependence on Yahweh and strict obedience to His direction. Therefore, he stirred up the faith of his army by ceremony (e.g., 4:1-7), word (10:25), and life (24:15). Furthermore, he demanded of them exact obedience to Yahweh's word (cf. 8:25; 23:6).

Joshua serves as a model for all of Israel's future kings: here is a leader possessing Yahweh's spirit and having prophetic sanction (Nu. 27:18, 22), who is both a military genius and a spiritual giant (cf. Y. Kaufmann, *Biblical Account of the Conquest of Palestine* [1953], pp. 96f.). Later tradition spoke even more expansively of Joshua. Sir. 46:1-12 delineates him as Moses' successor "in prophesying" and as "a great savior" (v. 1), who "wholly followed" God (v. 6) and thus is an example for all (v. 10). Elsewhere he is called a judge (1 Macc. 2:55) and is included in lists of significant intercessors (2 Esd. 7:107) and of those who passed on the Torah (Mish. *Aboth* i.1).

B. K. WALTKE

JOSHUA, BOOK OF. The first book of the biblical section designated in the Jewish canon "the Former Prophets," which also includes Judges, Samuel, and Kings. In Hebrew the book bears the superscription *yᵉhôšu(a)ʿ*, after its central figure; in the LXX *Iēsous* (in some MSS with the addition of "son of Naue"); in the Peshitta it is called *"Ketaba di Yeshu bar Nun talmideh d'Mushe"* ("the book of Joshua, son of Nun, disciple of Moses"). In all but the last it immediately follows the Pentateuch, which is the natural order. The Peshitta, however, places the book of Job between the Pentateuch and Joshua, in accordance with the rabbinic view that Moses wrote Job (T.B. *Baba Bathra* 15a).

I. Outline
II. Purpose
III. Problems
  A. The Apparent Contradiction Between the Land Promised and the Land Possessed
  B. The Moral Problem of Annihilating the Canaanites
  C. The Conquest as Holy War
IV. Date of Composition
  A. The Traditional View
  B. The Generally Accepted View
  C. Kaufmann's Refutation of the Generally Accepted View
    1. The Problem of the D and P Imprint
    2. The Problem of the Contradiction with Jgs. 1
    3. The Problem of the Original Form of the War Stories
    4. The Problem of Inconsistencies Between the Boundary Lists and the City Lists
    5. The Archaic Character of the Book of Joshua
  D. Conclusion

I. Outline.

I. The Book of War: Taking the Land (Chs. 1–12)
  A. Preparation for War (Chs. 1–5)
    1. Charge to War (Ch. 1)
      a. Yahweh's Charge to Joshua (1:1-9)
      b. Joshua's Charge to the People (1:10-18)
    2. Reconnaissance of Jericho: Evidence of Canaan's Spiritual Weakness (Ch. 2)
    3. Miraculous Crossing of Jordan: Assurance of Yahweh's Presence and Joshua's Leadership (3:1–5:1)
    4. Final Spiritual Preparation (5:2-15)
      a. Ceremonies at Gilgal (5:2-11)
      b. Revelation of the Captain of Yahweh's Hosts (5:12-15)
  B. The Campaigns (Chs. 6–12)
    1. Central Campaign (Chs. 6–9)
      a. Conquest of Jericho (Ch. 6)
      b. Conquest of Ai (Chs. 7–8)
        1) Failure at Ai (7:1-5)
        2) Punishment of Achan (7:6-26)
        3) Success at Ai (8:1-29)
      c. Covenant Ceremony at Shechem (8:30-35)
      d. Alliance with Gibeon (Ch. 9)
    2. Southern Campaign (Ch. 10)
    3. Northern Campaign (Ch. 11)
    4. Summary (Ch. 12)
II. The Book of Distribution: Allotting the Land (Chs. 13–21)
  A. The Doctrine that Much Land Remains (13:1-7)
  B. The Territories of Transjordan Assigned by Moses (13:8-33)
  C. The Territories Assigned to Judah and Joseph at Gilgal (Chs. 14–17)
    1. Allotment to Judah (Chs. 14–15)
    2. Allotment to Joseph (Chs. 16–17)
  D. The Territories Assigned to the Remaining Seven Tribes at Shiloh (Chs. 18–19)
  E. The Assignment of Cities of Refuge (Ch. 20)
  F. The Assignment of Levitical Cities (Ch. 21)
III. Epilogue: Staying in the Land (Chs. 22–24)
  A. Consecration and Departure of the Tribes of Transjordan (Ch. 22)
  B. Consecration of the Rest of Israel: Joshua's Farewell Address (Ch. 23)
  C. Renewal of Covenant with All the Tribes of Israel (24:1-28)
  D. Death and Burial of Joshua (24:29-31)
  E. Burial of Joseph and Eleazar (24:32-33)

II. Purpose.–The book of Joshua intends to show the

historical fulfillment of Yahweh's promise made to the patriarchs and Moses to give Israel the land of Canaan by holy war. This intent is seen in the introductory charge (1:2-6), as well as in the summarizing refrains concluding the "Book of War" (11:23) and the "Book of Distribution" (21:43). Yahweh's opening charge reads: "Go over this Jordan, you and all this people, into the land which I am giving to them.... Every place that the sole of your foot will tread upon I have given to you, as I promised to Moses.... Be strong and of good courage; for you shall cause this people to inherit the land which I swore to their fathers to give them." The refrains at the end of the two "books" are similar: "So Joshua took the whole land according to all that the Lord had spoken to Moses; and Joshua gave it for an inheritance to Israel"; "Thus the Lord gave to Israel all the land which he swore to give to their fathers, and having taken possession of it, they settled there."

III. Problems.–*A. The Apparent Contradiction Between the Land Promised and the Land Possessed.* While the book asserts that the promises made to the fathers were fulfilled in Joshua's conquest (11:23; cf. 21:43), the historical reality is that the land promised was only partially given. Y. Kaufmann noted that the relationship between the promise pertaining to the dimensions of the land and its historical fulfillment can be divided into three categories: (1) a portion of this land was conquered and allotted; (2) another was allotted but not conquered — all the coastal strip (13:2-4), all the Emeq (17:11f.), almost all the portion of Dan (19:47), Jerusalem, Gezer, and other cities (15:63; 16:10); and (3) another was neither allotted nor conquered — from Baal-gad in the valley of the Lebanon to the Gateway to Hamath (Nu. 34:7f.; Josh. 1:4) (*Biblical Account*, p. 52).

The harmonization of these apparently contradictory statements lies in a correct understanding of "took [*lāqaḥ*] the whole land." The writer probably understood the taking of the land to mean the gaining of control without eliminating all opposition (cf. Wenham, p. 143; Kaufmann, pp. 84f.). Both the Book of War (chs. 10–11) and the Book of Distribution (chs. 13–21) recognize that the task of driving out the Canaanite was unfinished. Gibeon made a treaty with Israel (ch. 9); of the major northern cities only Hazor was burned (11:13); some Anakim remained in Gath, Gaza, and Ashdod (11:22). But the back of the Canaanite was broken, king after king was dead (ch. 12), and apart from an uprising by the Canaanites recorded in Jgs. 4–5 and the resistance of the Jebusites (2 S. 5:6-10), Israel's enemies from then on would not be the Canaanites but the Philistines, and others from outside the land (cf. the book of Judges).

To clarify the situation further it may be helpful to note that the concept of the land is both geographic and ethnographic (cf. Gen. 15:18-20; Ex. 23:28-31; Nu. 13:21; 34:2-12; Dt. 1:7; 11:24; 20:17; Josh. 1:4; 13:1-6). Now that the land in its ethnographic sense was defeated, it could also be said that the whole land in its geographic sense had been taken.

B. The Moral Problem of Annihilating the Canaanites. To many readers Moses' mandate to Israel "you shall save alive nothing that breathes, but you shall utterly destroy them [the inhabitants of the land of Canaan]" (Dt. 20:16f.) with its historical execution by Joshua in the ban at the end of each battle (Josh. 6:21; 8:24f.; 10:10, 28, 30, 35, 37, 39f.; 11:11, 14, 21) is a part of primitive religion. Now the book makes clear that involved in the concept of "possession" (*yrš*) by Israel is the notion of "dispossessing" (*yrš*) the inhabitants. The Gibeon episode shows that the Israelites intended to kill all within the Promised Land (9:18). In Josh. 13:6f. Joshua is told to allot the land even though much remains to be possessed according to Yahweh's promise: "I will myself drive them out from before the people of Israel" (13:6). Likewise Caleb offered to drive out the Anakim, if Joshua would give him the land (14:12), and Joshua told Ephraim and Manasseh to drive out the Canaanites from their area, "though they have chariots of iron" (17:18).

Although to many modern readers these wars seem immoral, from the biblical perspective they were fought precisely for moral reasons. The moral sanction behind these wars is not stated in Joshua, but two moral reasons for this type of warfare are indicated elsewhere.

First, Yahweh destroyed the Canaanites for their gross iniquity. To Abraham He implied that Joshua's sword would arrive when the iniquity of the Amorites was full (Gen. 15:16). Now the Bible normally refers to Canaan's pre-Israelite population as either Canaanites or Amorites, although these terms properly apply to two specific groups among Canaan's heterogeneous population. But these heterogeneous groups participated in a great cultural unit extending from the Egyptian frontier northward as far as Râs Shamrah (W. F. Albright, "The Role of the Canaanites in the History of Civilization" in P. W. Long, ed., *Studies in the History of Culture* [1942], pp. 11-50; K. M. Kenyon, *Amorites and Canaanites* [1966], p. 58). Moreover, the concept of holiness in this culture was diametrically opposed to Yahweh's standards of holiness. Albright pointed out that one of their principal goddesses, Anath, is called "the holy one" as a sacred prostitute. In addition to being a patroness of sexual life, both as a mother-goddess and a divine courtesan, she was also a goddess who delighted in butchery and sadism (*ARI*, pp. 73-76). Of their religion Bright wrote: "Canaanite religion, however, presents us with no pretty picture. It was, in fact, an extraordinarily debasing form of paganism, specifically of the fertility cult" (*BHI* [2nd ed. 1972], p. 116). The holiness and righteousness of God, then, demanded this judgment.

Second, the Bible regards the Canaanite religion as particularly contaminating. The intent of the mandate is to prevent God's righteousness from being turned against His own people (cf. Lev. 18:24-29; Dt. 20:18).

C. The Conquest as Holy War. Because these wars were moral in nature, the book presents them as holy war in which Yahweh is destroying Canaanite religion (for a description of "holy war," cf. G. von Rad, *Der heilige Krieg im alten Israel* [1951], p. 68; P. C. Craigie, *Problem of War in the OT* [1978], pp. 45-54). The central idea in the presentation of these stories is that this war begins with Yahweh's initiative and depends on Him for its success (Josh. 1:6, 9; 6:2; 10:8; 11:6). Because God is fighting, Israel need only trust and be confident. (On the concept of God as warrior, see P. D. Miller, *Divine Warrior in Ancient Israel* [1973]; Craigie, esp. pp. 33-44.) The events recounted in the section entitled "the preparation for the war" (chs. 1–5) are to boost Israel's morale by assuring them that Yahweh is directing the war. The function of the spies, according to 2:24, is not so much to bring back tactical information as to encourage Israel's faith (S. Wagner, *ZAW*, 76 [1964], 268).

The pattern of divine command (cf. ch. 1) followed by the obedience of the people is central in these stories. Repetition is used to emphasize the fidelity with which the command is obeyed (1:2, 11; 6:2-8; 8:1-27; 11:6f., 9).

Then, Yahweh fought for Israel: the walls of Jericho collapsed (ch. 6) and "the Lord threw down great stones from heaven" (10:11) and "fought for Israel" (10:14). Less apparent to the modern reader but perfectly obvious to the Canaanites was the theological significance involved in the standing still of the sun and moon (10:12-14). The sun

(Heb. *šemeš*) and the moon (Heb. *yārē(a)ḥ*) were principal deities among the Canaanites as indicated by such Canaanite place names as Beth-shemesh ("temple of the sun") and Jericho ("[temple of] the moon") (cf. *LBHG*, p. 97; W. F. Albright, *Yahweh and the Gods of Canaan* [1968], p. 83; J. Gray, *The Canaanites* [1964], p. 125). At the prayer of Israel's leader, Canaan's very gods were compelled to hide their faces (cf. R. D. Wilson, *Princeton Theological Review,* 16 [1918], 48; repr. in W. Kaiser, ed., *Classical Evangelical Essays in OT Interpretation* [1972], pp. 61-65). The enemy then panicked and Israel pursued.

In two incidents, however, Israel failed to obey the divine command. In the first assault on Ai (7:1-5), Israel was defeated because Achan had transgressed the ban at Jericho. But as Wenham pointed out, "even if the narrator had not said that Yahweh was angry with Israel, it might have been expected that the attack would fail, because there is no mention of a word from Yahweh to start the battle" (Wenham, p. 142). A similar thing occurred in the case of Gibeon (9:14, 18).

IV. Date of Composition.–A. *The Traditional View.* The author is nowhere mentioned in Scripture, although 24:26 refers to Joshua's writing down the words of the ordinances and the covenant made at Shechem "in the book of the law of God." Perhaps this verse was the basis for the talmudic attribution of the bulk of the book to Joshua, although the rabbis did recognize the work of others for at least some verses (T.B. *Baba Bathra* 14b, 15a). R. K. Harrison (*Intro. to the OT* [1969], p. 672) discusses some internal evidence for an early (premonarchic) date; e.g., 13:6 mentions the inhabitants of Sidon, but not the later, more important city of Tyre. Many scholars have pointed out the indications of a contemporary or eyewitness account (e.g., the first-person references in the MT of 5:1, 6 [cf. the AV], although the reference in v. 1 is textually uncertain). Even the most conservative scholars, however, admit evidence of later editorial work (obviously, e.g., 24:29-31).

B. The Generally Accepted View. A number of scholars discovered duplications, contradictions, derangements of sequence, etc. at many places in the book of Joshua. On this basis they concluded that the extant book comprises disparate material given shape in later times.

Until the work of A. Alt ("Das System der Stammesgrenzen im Buche Josua," in W. F. Albright, ed., *Sellin Festschrift: Beiträge zur Religionsgeschichte und Archäologie Palastinas* [1927], pp. 13ff.; repr. in *KS*, I [1953], 193-202; cf. also *KS,* I, 176-192), scholars posited a continuation of the pentateuchal sources (J, E, D, P) throughout Joshua, thus thinking in terms of a Hexateuch rather than a Pentateuch. But since the work of Alt, Noth, and Albright, scholars increasingly think of the book as an independent work derived from source material of various dates not connected with the pentateuchal sources (Wenham, p. 140). According to M. Noth, the book is the work of a collector (*Sammler*), a recensionist (*Bearbiter*), and an editor, plus various expanders. For all that, however, scholars do agree that in the final editing the book bears the impress of P and D. In particular, many contemporary scholars share the opinion that the Former Prophets (Joshua–2 Kings) are "a Deuteronomistic historical work," whether the product of editors belonging to the Deuteronomistic school, or of a single historian who set the Deuteronomistic stamp upon the whole. Moreover, most of these scholars believe that Joshua was edited in two stages and that chs. 13–21 and 24 represent secondary additions by the Deuteronomist to an earlier Deuteronomic book of Joshua (see the comms. by Noth, Hertzberg, and Gray; cf. Wenham, p. 140). According to this view the date of its composition cannot be placed earlier than the end of the 7th cent. B.C.

This inferred late date is buttressed by internal evidences as well. First, these scholars see a fundamental contradiction between the stories of the Conquest in Joshua and Jgs. 1. According to Joshua, they allege, Canaan was conquered in a full-scale national war and subsequently divided among the tribes in Joshua's lifetime. According to Jgs. 1, however, only part of the country was conquered, and that in separate tribal wars.

Second, Alt argued that the territory of Judah-Benjamin-Dan is identical with Josiah's kingdom, principally because the northern territory of Benjamin-Dan encroaches upon the land of Ephraim, which with Manasseh lacks mention in the city list. More specifically, in 18:21f. Jericho, Bethel, and Ophrah are assigned in the city list to Benjamin, though according to the boundary list these cities belonged to Ephraim and were included in the northern kingdom (cf. Josh. 16:1f.; 18:13; 1 K. 12:29; Am. 7:10-13, *et al.;* 1 K. 16:34; 2 K. 2:4f.). The cities of Dan reach to the outskirts of Jaffa (Josh. 19:45f.), thereby occupying an area N of Gezer, which is on the southern boundary line of Ephraim (16:3). Now in 2 K. 23:15 it is related that Josiah annexed part of Ephraim to his kingdom. Accordingly, Alt reasoned that the list of cities and the districts of the kingdom of Judah belong to a single official document at the time of Josiah, which a later editor cut up and from the pieces put together the territories of Judah, Benjamin, and Dan. F. M. Cross and G. E. Wright, however, rejected Alt's explanation for the inclusion of a portion of Ephraimite territory in a Judahite province (pp. 222f.). Instead they noted that according to 2 Ch. 13:19 Abijah (*ca.* 915-913 B.C.) annexed this portion, and according to 2 Ch. 15:8 Asa (*ca.* 913-873 B.C.) also controlled Ephraimite cities in the hill country, which were then garrisoned by Jehoshaphat (2 Ch. 17:2; cf. 19:4). Furthermore, they argued that Middin, Secacah, and Nibshan (Josh. 15:61f.) can be dated by archeology only during Iron II (9th cent. to early 6th cent. B.C.). Moreover, on other archeological grounds, especially on the basis of evidence from Beth-shemesh, they could not date the list later than the 9th cent. B.C. Accordingly they dated it to the reign of Jehoshaphat (*ca.* 873-849 B.C.). Finally, they concluded that the seventh- or sixth-century editor of Josh. 15–19 used it with other materials in order to give a full delineation of the territory claimed by Judah after the conclusion of the Conquest.

Third, it is believed that many stories in Josh. 1–11 are etiologies, especially from the tribe of Benjamin, and were originally local and tribal stories that were converted into national sagas by a later redactor.

C. Kaufmann's Refutation of the Generally Accepted View. Y. Kaufmann castigated those who examine the biblical text by the rules of Latin literary criticism, which assumes that an author must have a "schema," he must have a sequence from which he does not deviate, he must not repeat himself, etc. If such things occur in the biblical text they must be, according to these scholars, the result of multiple "redactors" or "expanders," who in most cases possessed little intelligence. Kaufmann observed, however, that in reality the biblical author allowed himself the freedom to compose in just this way (pp. 2f.).

Concerning alleged inconsistencies, one example will suffice to show the superficiality of such allegations. E. M. Good states: "According to Josh. 4:8, twelve stones were carried out of the Jordan and set up at Gilgal. According to verse 9, the stones were set up in the middle of the Jordan" (*IDB,* II [1962], 989). The contradiction, however, stands only in the English text. Verse 9 should be translated: "Now Joshua had set twelve stones in the midst of the Jordan. . . ." By inserting the noun "twelve stones" between the conjunction "and" and the verb "set," the

Hebrew writer compels the reader to interpret the perfect form of the verb as a pluperfect in sense (cf. S. R. Driver, *Treatise on the Use of the Tenses in Hebrew* [1892], p. 84). In other words, the setting up of the stones in the Jordan must be anterior to the action of taking them out of the Jordan and setting them up at Gilgal.

1. The Problem of the D and P Imprint. Some argue that the book contains literary elements related in style and subject matter to D and P and therefore was edited earlier than the late 7th cent. B.C., at the beginning of the second temple. This begs the issue, for it presumes the date of these pentateuchal sources. For Kaufmann, and now many others as well, P contains early, archaic material (*ZAW*, 48 [1930], 23-43), and the nucleus of D upon which Joshua is based is early (*Biblical Account*, pp. 4-7). Furthermore, the similarity in style and subject matter proves no more than that Joshua included material from the work of authors who wrote in the style of the Pentateuch. Affinity with the literature of the Pentateuch cannot decide the question of the book's date of composition. The date should be fixed by the internal evidence.

2. The Problem of the Contradiction with Jgs. 1. The whole conception that Jgs. 1 presents a parallel but contradictory account of the Conquest is based on the false assumption that the book of Joshua relates the conquest of all the cities of Canaan. The book contains no story about the conquest of Jerusalem and Gezer. Joshua defeated their kings but did not capture the cities. Similarly no story appears about the conquest of the five Philistine cities. In 11:22 it is explicitly stated that Anakim remained in Gaza, Gath, and Ashdod. In 12:7-24 no mention is made of Beth-shean, Jibleam, Harosheth-hagoyyim, Jezreel, Acre, Tyre, Sidon, Laish, the Philistine cities, Aijalon, Shaalbim, Jaffa, etc. That Joshua did not complete the conquest of Canaan within its borders is explicitly emphasized in chs. 13 and 23. Only 10:40-42, 11:16-23, and 21:41 speak of the conquest of all the land and the slaying of all its kings. Kaufmann (pp. 85f.), however, noted that the intent of these summaries is to show that the possession of Canaan had been decided in favor of the Israelites, rather than to present a picture of total conquest. Once this was stated, the author was able to incorporate in the Book of Distribution (chs. 12–21) passages taken from the same source as that from which Jgs. 1 is taken; these show that not all of the land was actually subjugated (cf. 14:6-15 in which Joshua gives his blessing to Caleb's plan to conquer Hebron, and 17:14-18 in which Joshua encourages the tribe of Joseph to conquer the Emeq; cf. also the necessity of a second battle by Joshua against Hebron [10:37; 11:21f.]).

Furthermore, Kaufmann noted, one must bear in mind the character of Joshua's wars as described in Josh. 1–11. They are wars of destruction and extermination, not of occupation by immediate settlement. Joshua always had the people return to camp after battle, for he knew that they were eager to possess land and could easily be diverted from the main objective of conquest if allowed to engage in "land-grabbing" (Kaufmann, p. 92). The natural consequence of conducting the war in this way was that the Canaanite survivors fortified themselves in various places as best they could. Hence the tribes had to continue their fight when they started settling in their positions. Jgs. 1, then, is the perfect continuation of Joshua. In this chapter there is no story about entering the land. On the contrary, Jgs. 1 mentions few Canaanite cities (see II.A above).

3. The Problem of the Original Form of the War Stories. The notion that the stories in Josh. 1–11 were local and tribal in their original form and were converted into national sagas by later redaction can only be maintained by question-begging techniques. On the basis of this dogma the text is erased, altered, etc., to fit the theory. Furthermore, it is held that both Joshua and Judges were subjected to a national, theocratic redaction. But concerning this Kaufmann asked: "Why has the tribal element completely disappeared from the stories in Josh and from them alone? It is clear that the 'national' redaction had no need to expunge the tribal element" (p. 70). The characteristic tradition-criticism treatment of these stories is subjective, lacks scientific controls, and introduces an unnecessarily novel theory in place of a stable, consistent, traditional text.

4. The Problem of Inconsistencies Between the Boundary Lists and the City Lists. Regarding the alleged inconsistencies between the two types of lists found in the Book of Distribution of the land, Kaufmann emphasized both that the apparent encroachment of Benjamin into the area of Ephraim is no more than a shifting of a border strip and that this fluctuation on a border is not unique. On almost every border fluctuations occur (cf. 15:10f. with 19:41-44; 15:60f. with 18:22, 28 [LXX]; 16:6 with 17:7; 16:63 with 18:28, etc.). This suggests that the boundaries mentioned in the book have no political or administrative significance at all, for such boundaries are required to be clear and unambiguous. In reality the purpose of the description of the distribution of land is historical; the author merely intends to describe the mixture of tribes that inhabited a given district or city, without intending to draw exact geographical boundaries. This description is chronologically earlier than any geographical or administrative division (cf. Kaufmann, pp. 14f.).

5. The Archaic Character of the Book of Joshua. Kaufmann also presented a forceful case for the archaic character of the book. At the time that Joshua fought his battles, the Philistines of the Pentapolis were not yet in Canaan. Joshua fought only against the Canaanites, even in the Shephelah (10:40-43; 11:16). In 11:22 it is stated explicitly that the Anakim occupy Gaza, Gath, and Ashdod, and no mention is made of the Philistines. Likewise, in Jgs. 1 there is still no mention of the Philistines (Kaufmann, pp. 50, 79). He further noted that the only mention of them is in Josh. 13, where the Israelites are promised the ability to expel them from the Shephelah. This suggests that "the real history of the Philistines is beyond the horizon of the Book of Joshua" (p. 80). Furthermore, the Gibeonites are enslaved, but continue to live in their cities; they are not yet dispersed "in all the territory of Israel" (2 S. 21:5). In addition, Dan is marked out in his unreal portion between Judah and Ephraim and W of Benjamin (Josh. 19:40-48) but not according to its real territory in the north. Dan's northward migration is mentioned (19:47), but none of its territory is marked out. Furthermore, Simeon resides in the midst of Judah (19:9) and its southward expansion to Mt. Seir (1 Ch. 4:34-43) is not mentioned (Kaufmann, pp. 22f.). Again, the Emeq is completely Canaanite (Josh. 17:16-18). What happened in the time of Deborah (*ca.* 1230 B.C.) is unknown to the book of Joshua. Jerusalem in the Book of War is an important Canaanite royal city, while in the Book of Distribution it is a city of no importance, called "Jebus," that still has no Israelite inhabitants (15:63) and is listed as a city of Benjamin. This is in accord with the fact that Hebron is called Kiriath-arbah (15:54), and Kiriath-jearim is called Kiriath-baal (15:60). Aijalon is in Dan's unreal portion, but is not yet Benjaminite. Lod, Hodid, and Ono are not mentioned (Kaufmann, pp. 79-82). The favor of the kingdom and its accouterments (temple, royal cities, priests, etc.) are unknown. The list of Levitical cities (Josh. 21:1-42) originated at a time when the heads of Levitical families rather than judges or kings were in a position to formulate or at least to influence the development of the social organizations.

D. Conclusion. Kaufmann (p. 7) concluded that the ancient book of Joshua was presumably composed by a recorder of events at the beginning of the period of the Judges, at the time of Dan's migration to the north, the latest event explicitly mentioned. The author also used "the Book of Jashar" (10:13), a pre-monarchic national epic that originated no later than the Conquest period.

Since ancient tradition holds that Sidon was the first Phoenician city to be founded, and since Tyre is absent from the list of cities conquered by Thutmosis III (*ca.* 1485), it is probable that Tyre had not yet been founded as a colony of Sidon at the time of the writing of this passage in Joshua. Its absence from the passage therefore suggests an early date for its composition.

See Vol. I, Map VI.

***Bibliography.**–Comms.*: F.-M. Abel (*La Sainte Bible,* 1950); F. Nötscher (*Echter-Bibel,* 1950); H. W. Hertzberg (*ATD,* 1953; 4th ed. 1969); M. Noth (*HAT,* 2nd ed. 1953); A. Cohen (*Soncino,* 1959); J. Gray (*New Century Bible,* 1967); J. Soggin (Eng. tr., *OTL,* 1972); M. Woudstra (*NICOT,* 1981).

Other Studies: A. Alt, *ZAW,* 45 (1927), 59-81; A. Saarisalo, *Boundary Between Issachar and Naphtali* (1927); J. Garstang, *Joshua, Judges* (1931; repr. 1978); B. Goff, *JBL,* 53 (1934), 241-49; M. Noth, *ZDPV,* 58 (1935), 185-255; K. Moehlenbrink, *ZAW,* 56 (1938), 238-268; W. F. Albright, *BASOR,* 74 (Apr. 1939), 11-23; "The List of Levitic Cities," in S. Lieberman, *et al.*, eds., *Louis Ginzberg Jubilee Volume* (1945), pp. 49-73; S. Mowinckel, *Zur Frage nach dokumentarischen Quellen in Joshua 13–19* (1946); G. E. Wright, *JNES,* 50 (1946), 105-114; M. Noth, "Überlieferungsgeschichtliches zur zweiten Hälfte des Josuabuches," in H. Junker, ed., *Alttestamentliche Studien* (Nötscher Festschrift; 1950); H. H. Rowley, *From Joseph to Joshua* (1950); A. Alt, "Joshua," *KS,* I (1953), 176-192; "Judas Gaue unter Josia," *KS,* II (1953), 276-288; Y. Kaufmann, *Biblical Account of the Conquest of Palestine* (1953); A. D. Tushingham, *BA,* 42 (1954), 98-140; E. Nielsen, *Shechem, a Traditio-Historical Investigation* (1955); J. Bright, *Early Israel in Recent History Writing* (*SBT,* 1/19, 1956); F. M. Cross, Jr., and G. E. Wright, *JBL,* 75 (1956), 202-226; Z. Kallai-Kleinmann, *VT,* 8 (1958), 134-160; G. E. Mendenhall, *BA,* 25 (1962), 66-86; G. J. Wenham, *JBL,* 90 (1971), 140-48; B. K. Waltke, *Bibliotheca Sacra,* 1929 (1972), 33-47.

B. K. WALTKE

JOSIAH jō-sī'ə [Heb. *yō'šîyāhû*–'Yahweh supports'; Gk. *Iōsias*]; AV Apoc., NT JOSIAS (1 Esd. 1; Bar. 1:8; Mt. 1:10f.). Son of Amon and king of Judah. The biblical account of Josiah is given in 2 K. 22:1–23:30 and 2 Ch. 34:1–35:27. He is mentioned in Jer. 1:1; 3:6. Sirach includes him in his Praise of Famous Men (Sir. 49:1-4).

Josiah was suddenly elevated to the kingship at the tender age of eight when Amon was slain. From 640 to 609 B.C. Josiah provided Judah with pious political leadership. During this period the extensive Assyrian empire not only declined in power but collapsed with the fall of Nineveh in 612. Simultaneously the Babylonian nation under King Nabopolassar (625-605) became a first-rate power in Mesopotamia and threatened further advance in the Fertile Crescent by challenging Egyptian might. In 609 Josiah's ambitious reign was suddenly terminated by his death at Megiddo in a battle with the Egyptians.

The decline of Assyrian control in Palestine provided favorable conditions in Judah for the rise of a nationalism that led to complete freedom from Assyrian vassalage. Likewise this era made it possible for Josiah to lead in a religious reformation without interference from Assyria, whence some of Judah's idolatrous practices had come in the days of Ahaz.

Apparently Josiah reacted personally against the apostate conditions that surrounded him during the first eight years of his reign. It is not improbable that he had godly tutors and pious political leaders who influenced him during these early years. At the age of sixteen (*ca.* 632 B.C.) he began to take God into account instead of conforming to the idolatrous practices that were so prevalent in Jerusalem. When he reached the age of twenty (*ca.* 628 B.C.) his convictions were so firmly established that he used his royal authority to initiate a religious reformation. By this time it was politically safe for Josiah to remove any religious practices that were associated with Judah's vassalage to Assyria. By 622 the reformation had progressed to the point of observing the Passover, which apparently had been neglected for a long time.

Drastic measures were necessary to rid the kingdom of its idolatry. Pagan practices were abolished throughout Judah as well as among the northern tribes. Altars of Baal were broken down, Asherim were destroyed, and vessels dedicated to idol worship were removed. In the temple, where women wove hangings for Asherah, chambers of cult prostitution were reclaimed. Horses that had been dedicated to the sun were removed from the entrance, and chariots were destroyed by fire. The horrible practice of child sacrifice was abruptly abolished. The altars erected by Manasseh in the court of the temple were crushed and scattered in the Kidron Valley. Even some of the high places erected by Solomon must have been in current use, for Josiah razed them and desecrated them with dead men's bones.

Religious personnel were also involved. Priests dedicated to idol worship were removed from office; they had been serving by royal appointment of former kings. Consequently, the burning of incense to Baal ceased. Josiah, however, made material provision for these deposed priests from temple revenue.

At Bethel the altar that had been erected by Jeroboam I was also destroyed. For over three hundred years this had been the public high place for idolatrous practice introduced by the first ruler of the northern kingdom. This altar was pulverized, and the Asherah, which probably had replaced the golden calf, was burned. When the bones from the adjoining cemetery were collected for public defilement of this high place, Josiah noticed the monument to the prophet of Judah who had so boldly denounced Jereboam (1 K. 13). Being informed that the man of God was buried there, Josiah ordered that the tomb should not be opened.

Throughout the cities of Samaria (the northern kingdom) reformation was the order of the day. High places were removed and priests were arrested for their idolatrous ministry.

The constructive aspect of this reformation came to fruition in the restoration of the temple in Jerusalem. When contributions came from Judah and the tribes in the north, the Levites were charged with the supervision of this fund. Since the time of Joash (two centuries earlier) the temple had been subject to long periods of neglect — especially under Manasseh. When Hilkiah the high priest began to gather funds to pay the workmen he found the book of the law. Hilkiah handed it to Shaphan, secretary to the king. He examined it and immediately read it to Josiah. The king was terribly disturbed when he realized that the people of Judah had not observed the law. Immediately, Hilkiah and the government officials were ordered to secure someone who could give them advice. Huldah, the prophetess residing in Jerusalem, had a timely message for them which was clear and simple: the curses and judgments for idolatry were inevitable. Jerusalem would not be spared the wrath of God. Josiah, however, would be spared the anguish of Jerusalem's destruction since he had penitently responded to the book of the law.

Under the king's leadership the elders of Judah, priests,

Levites, and the populace of Jerusalem assembled for the public reading of the newly found book. In a solemn covenant King Josiah, supported by the people, promised that he would devote himself wholly to obeying the law.

Plans were begun at once for the observance of the Passover. Priests were appointed and the temple services were reinstated. Careful attention was given to the pattern of organization for the Levites, as ordained by David and Solomon. In the Passover ritual great care was exercised to ensure conformity to that which was "written in the book of Moses" (2 Ch. 35:13). Because of this conformity to the law, and the extent of the people's participation, this Passover observance surpassed all similar festivities since the days of Samuel (2 Ch. 35:18).

The content of the book of the law found in the temple is not specifically indicated. Numerous references in the biblical account associate its origin with Moses. On the basis of that simple fact the book of the law may have included all the Pentateuch or contained only a copy of Deuteronomy. Those who regard the Pentateuch as a composite literary production which reached its final form in the 5th cent. B.C. limit the book of the law to the bulk of Deuteronomy or less. Since the reformation had already been in progress for six years when the book was recovered, Josiah had previous knowledge concerning the true religion. When the book was read before him he was terrified because of Judah's failure to obey the law. Nothing in the biblical record indicates that this book was published at this time or even ratified by the people. It was considered authoritative, and Josiah feared the consequences of disobedience. Having been given by Moses, the book of the law had been the rule of religious practice ever since then. Joshua, the judges, and the kings, together with the whole nation, had been under obligation to conform to its requirements. What alarmed Josiah when he asked for prophetic advice was that "our fathers have not kept the word of the Lord" (2 Ch. 34:21). Ignorance of the law was no excuse, even though the book of the law had been lost for some time.

Gross idolatry had prevailed for over half a century before Josiah began to rule. In fact, Manasseh and Amon had persecuted those who advocated conformity to true religion. Since Manasseh had even shed innocent blood, it is reasonable to charge him with the destruction of all copies of the law in circulation in Judah. In the absence of written copies, Josiah very likely associated himself with priests and elders who had sufficient knowledge of the law to give him oral instruction. From this came the firm conviction, during the first twelve years of his reign, that a national reform was necessary. When the book of the law was actually read before him he vividly realized that curses and judgment were due an idolatrous people. Knowing all too well the wicked practices common to his father, he still was shocked that destruction might come in his day.

Had the book of the law actually been lost? Probably there were those during Manasseh's reign who had enough interest to preserve some copies of the law. Since every copy was handwritten, relatively few were in circulation. After the voices of Isaiah and others had been silenced, the righteous people decreased rapidly under persecution. If Joash, the royal heir, could be hidden from wicked Athaliah for six years, it is reasonable to conclude that a book of the law could have been hidden from wicked Manasseh for half a century.

Another explanation concerning the preservation of this book of the law is suggested by an archeological observation (cf. J. P. Free, *Archaeology and Bible History* [1969], pp. 215f.). Since valuable records and documents were placed in cornerstones of important buildings in ancient as well as in modern times, this book of the law may have been preserved in the cornerstone of the temple. Here Josiah's workmen found it. David, before his death, charged Solomon as king of Israel to conform to all that is "written in the law of Moses" (1 K. 2:3). In building the temple it would have been appropriate to place the whole Pentateuch, or at least the laws of Moses, in the cornerstone. Perhaps this was a providential provision by which a copy of the Pentateuch was preserved for over three centuries and then rediscovered just when Judah, having been subjected to rulers who defied God's covenant with Israel, needed it most. Taken out of the temple in the reformation days of Josiah, it became the "living word" once more in a generation that was eventually to take the book of the law with it into Babylonian captivity.

Whether the reformation under Josiah represented a genuine revival among the common people is doubtful. Since it was initiated and executed under royal orders, the opposition was restrained as long as Josiah lived. Immediately after his death the people reverted to idolatry under Jehoiakim.

Jeremiah was called to the prophetic ministry in the thirteenth year of Josiah, 627 B.C. Since Josiah had already begun his reform it is reasonable to conclude that prophet and king worked hand in hand. Jeremiah's preaching (Jer. 2–4) reflects the strained relationship between God and Israel. Like a faithless wife who breaks her marriage vows Israel had forsaken God. Jeremiah realistically warned the people that Jerusalem could expect the same fate as had befallen Samaria a century earlier. How much of Jer. 1–20 is related to Josian times is difficult to ascertain. Although it may seem strange that when the book of the law was read the prophetic word came from Huldah instead of Jeremiah, the urgency for an immediate solution to the king's problem may have involved Huldah, who resided in Jerusalem. Jeremiah lived in Anathoth, 3 mi. NE of the city.

As the news of the fall of Ashur (614) and the destruction of Nineveh (612) circulated in Jerusalem, Josiah undoubtedly turned his attention to international affairs. In a state of military preparedness he made his fatal mistake. In 609 the Assyrians were fighting a losing battle; their government was in exile at Haran. Neco king of Egypt marched his armies through Palestine to aid the Assyrians. Since Josiah had little concern for the preservation of the Assyrians, he rushed his armies up to Megiddo in an effort to stop the Egyptians. Josiah was fatally wounded when his armies were routed. Suddenly the national and religious hopes of Judah vanished as the thirty-nine-year-old king was entombed in the city of David. After eighteen years of intimate association with Josiah, the great prophet Jeremiah is singled out by name in the concluding paragraph — "and Jeremiah lamented for Josiah."

S. J. SCHULTZ

JOSIAS jō-sī'əs.

1. (AV 1 Esd. 1; Bar. 1:8; Mt. 1:10f.). *See* JOSIAH.
2. (1 Esd. 8:33, AV; NEB JESSIAS). *See* JESHAIAH **4.**

JOSIBIAH jō-sib'ē-ə (1 Ch. 4:35, AV, NEB). *See* JOSHIBIAH.

JOSIPHIAH jos-i-fī'ə [Heb. *yôsipyâ*–'Yahweh adds']; AV Apoc. JOSAPHIAS. In Ezr. 8:10; 1 Esd. 8:36, the father of Shelomith, one of Ezra's companions.

JOT (Mt. 5:18, AV). *See* IOTA.

JOTBAH jot'bə [Heb. *yoṭbâ*–'pleasantness']. The home

of Meshullemeth, the mother of King Amon, daughter of Haruz (2 K. 21:19). The site cannot be identified with certainty, although some (e.g., J. Gray, comm. on Kings [*OTL*, 2nd ed. 1970], p. 711) identify it with ʿAin aṭ-Ṭaba, about 30 km. (20 mi.) N of Aqabah.

JOTBATHAH jot'bə-thə [Heb. *yoṭbāṯâ*]. A desert camp of the Israelites between Hor-haggidgad and Abronah (Nu. 33:33f.; Dt. 10:7, AV JOTBATH). It was "a land of brooks of water" (Dt. 10:7). *See* WANDERINGS OF ISRAEL.

JOTHAM jo'thəm [Heb. *yôṯām*–'Yahweh is perfect'; Gk. *Iōatham*].

1. The youngest son of Gideon-Jerubbaal, the sole survivor of the massacre of his seventy brothers by Abimelech. Although Jotham was the legitimate ruler after their death, he never gained national leadership. The people followed Abimelech, the son of Gideon's concubine at Shechem.

Jotham is best known for the fable he delivered at Mt. Gerizim to the men of Shechem (Jgs. 9:7-15). In this fable the trees request a number of useful trees to reign over them, but all decline the honor. Finally the bramble accepts. Although Jotham does not clearly delineate the application, in essence he pronounces a curse upon Abimelech, which was realized in subsequent developments (Jgs. 9:57).

After addressing the Shechemites on the summit of Mt. Gerizim, Jotham fled to Beer for safety while Abimelech continued to rule for three years.

2. A Judahite, son of Jahdai (1 Ch. 2:47).

3. King of Judah, son of Uzziah and Jerusha daughter of Zadok (2 K. 15:32-38; 2 Ch. 27:1-9). The chronological data are best interpreted by dating the beginning of Jotham's reign in 750 B.C. as co-regent with his father for ten years. After a ten-year co-regency with his father, he was sole ruler until 735 B.C. when he was replaced by Ahaz. Jotham died in 732 B.C.

Since Jotham was overshadowed by his father, who exerted such strong and forceful leadership, it is likely that he promoted the same economic and political policies. He erected citadels and towers throughout Judah. Cities were built in strategic places to strengthen the kingdom of Judah. Jotham's activity and influence at Ezion-geber are well attested. In the discovery of the eighth-century stratum a signet seal ring was found bearing Jotham's name. Although he did not remove high places maintained for idol worship, he promoted religious interest by building an upper gate at the temple in Jerusalem.

It is quite likely that the Ammonites rebelled when Uzziah died. Jotham subsequently regained supremacy and collected tribute during his second and third years (2 Ch. 27:15) but may not have been in a position to do so later because of Assyrian pressure.

With renewed Assyrian activity in the regions of Mt. Nal and Urartu in 736/735, Jotham faced difficulties maintaining an anti-Assyrian policy. Apparently the pro-Assyrian party in Jerusalem took advantage of this opportunity to elevate Ahaz, who favored friendship with the king of Assyria, to the Davidic throne as co-regent with his father, virtually placing the latter in retirement. In 732 Jotham died. He is listed in the royal genealogy in Mt. 1:9 (AV Joatham).

S. J. SCHULTZ

JOURNEY. *See* DAY'S JOURNEY; SABBATH DAY'S JOURNEY.

JOY.

I. Vocabulary
  A. Words for Joy or Rejoicing
  B. OT Expression of Joy
II. Joy in the OT
  A. Personal Joy
  B. National, Cultic Joy
  C. Messianic Joy
III. Joy in the NT
  A. Joy in Christ
  B. Joy Not of This World
  C. Joy in Affliction
  D. Joy in the Church
  E. Joy at the End of the Age

I. Vocabulary.–A. *Words for Joy or Rejoicing.* The NT vocabulary is simple, usually *chaírō, synchaírō,* or *chará*. Occasionally we find *agallíaō, agallíasis,* or *euphraínō*, especially in eschatological contexts or OT citations, for these last two words are the most frequently used in the LXX. Other words occurring less frequently are *kaucháomai* (Rom. 5:2f., 11; cf. NEB "exult" and AV "glory" in 5:3) and *skirtáō* (Lk. 6:23), translated by the RSV, AV, and NEB "leap for joy" (cf. Lk. 1:44). The OT vocabulary, on the other hand, is extremely varied and allows a great many possibilities in English translation (cf. esp. the NEB). The following words are translated "joy" (-ful, -fully, -fulness, -ous) and "rejoice" (-ing) in the RSV: *śimḥâ, śāmaḥ* or *śāmē(a)ḥ* (as an adj., cf. 1 K. 1:45; Est. 5:9), *rānan, rᵉnānâ* (Job 3:7; Ps. 63:5 [MT 6]), *rinnâ, śûś, śāśôn, māśôś, gîl, gîlâ* (Isa. 35:2; 65:8 [MT 9]), *ʿālaz, ʿallîz* (Isa. 32:13), *ḥāḏâ* (Job 3:6), *ḥeḏwâ* (1 Ch. 16:27; Neh. 8:10), *hêḏaḏ* (Jer. 48:33), *hēḏ* (Ezk. 7:7), *rûa(a)ʿ*, *tᵉrûʿâ* (Job 33:26; Ps. 27:6), *ṭôḇ* (Ps. 4:7 [MT 8]; Eccl. 7:14), *ṣāhal* (Est. 8:15), *śāḥaq* (Prov. 8:30f.). Even these, however, do not exhaust the list of synonyms for joy.

B. OT Expression of Joy. The basic and most common Hebrew root for joy is *śmḥ,* which reflects not only the inner emotion or state of well-being, i.e., "joy," but also its expression, i.e., "rejoicing." In fact, the OT more often refers to the expression than the emotion, as is evident in the Psalms and Prophets. The most frequently occurring words for "joy," besides *śimḥâ* (and *śāmaḥ*), are from the root words *gîl, śûś,* and *rānan*. These convey the sense of "expressing joy" or "exultation," and the last word group (*rānan, rᵉnānâ,* and *rinnâ*) is especially instructive, for it connotes a "ringing cry," whether in distress (Lam. 2:19), proclamation (1 K. 22:36), or, most frequently, exultation (cf. BDB, p. 943).

The sound of joy, and not just the state of joy, is also apparent from less common words. Heb. *hêḏaḏ* (cf. *hēḏ* in Ezk. 7:7) signifies "shouting" or "cheering" (Isa. 16:10; Jer. 48:33). The word *rû(a)ʿ* (cf. *tᵉrûʿâ,* e.g., Ezr. 3:13, "the sound of joyful shout") means "raise a shout," "give a blast," whether as a war cry, or as an alarm for battle, or in triumph and applause, in distress, or in joy. In Ezr. 3:13, e.g., the shout of joy is hardly distinguishable from the sound of weeping. The psalmist exhorts his fellows to "make a joyful noise" (*rû(a)ʿ*, cf. Ps. 66:1; 95:1f.; 98:4, 6; 100:1) and again, joy becomes a sound and not just a state of mind. The graphic and slightly uncomplimentary word *ṣāhal* means "neigh" or "cry shrilly." The word *pāṣaḥ* means "burst forth" (cf. the piel in Mic. 3:3) and is used seven times of bursting into joyful sound (five times of the earth or mountains bursting forth in joy: Isa. 14:7; 44:23; 49:13; 52:9; 55:12). In short, OT "joy" was not bottled up!

This exuberance is suggested, in fact, by the very wealth of Hebrew words for joy. One ancient scholar enumerates ten Hebrew words for joy (Midr. *Cant. Rabbah* i.4), but more realistically, D. W. Harvey lists thirteen Hebrew roots and twenty-seven separate words for joy or joyful participation in the cult (*IDB*, II, 1000). Frequently these synonyms are used in parallelism (the usual literary parallel is *śāmaḥ/gîl*). The most impressive example of this is Zeph. 3:14, 17, where in just two verses, eight different words are used for joy or joyful expression: *rānan, rû(a)ʿ, śāmaḥ, ʿālaz, śûś, śimḥâ, gîl,* and *rinnâ*.

> Sing aloud, O Daughter of Zion;
> shout, O Israel!
> Rejoice and exult with all your heart,
> O Daughter of Jerusalem!
>
> The Lord, your God, is in your midst,
> a warrior who gives victory;
> he will rejoice over you with gladness . . .
> he will exult over you with loud singing. . . .

The heaping of words for "joy" indicates the greatness of the cause of joy.

***II. Joy in the OT.**–A. Personal Joy.* On the one hand, the OT recognizes the personal joys of human existence. Birthdays should be the occasion for joy (Job 3:7), and a man, whether young or old, should take joy in his years (Eccl. 11:8f.). A man should rejoice in the wife of his youth (Prov. 5:18), and a wise son will make his parents glad (Prov. 23:24f.). One may even take joy in an apt answer or a word in season (Prov. 15:23). In the Psalms, especially those of David, personal joy reaches its highest expression, a joy in God. The grounds for this are His protection (Ps. 4:7 [MT 8]; 5:11 [MT 12]; etc.), His forgiveness and restoration (Ps. 30:5 [MT 6]; 51:8, 12 [MT 10, 14]; etc.) and His fellowship (Ps. 16:11: "in thy presence is fulness of joy," etc.). In fact, the Psalms anticipate the NT kind of joy (see III below).

B. National, Cultic Joy. On the other hand, the emphasis in the OT is upon national, communal rejoicing. In a sense, nothing seems unusual about Israel's joy in military victory (Jgs. 16:23; 1 S. 18:6; 19:5; 2 Ch. 20:27), feast days (Dt. 16:11-15; 2 Ch. 30:25f.; Ezr. 6:22), coronations (1 S. 11:15; 1 K. 1:40, 45; 1 Ch. 12:40 [MT 41]), or dedication of construction projects (1 K. 8:66; 2 Ch. 6:9; 7:10; Ezr. 3:12; 6:16); these are events that people in general celebrate. But in reality it is the Lord God in whom the Israelites rejoice. It is God who brings salvation, vindication (Pss. 68 and 149), and prosperity (Pss. 68; 85; 106:4f.; 126; and 132) to His people. God Himself is the king of all the earth (cf. Ps. 47:1-9 [MT 2-10]; 96:10-13; 97:1; 98:4-6), and it is He who dwells in Zion among His chosen people (e.g., Pss. 48; 84; 132). In fact, not only what God does for His people, but what He is, i.e., His character, evokes joy and gladness. They rejoice in His steadfast love (Ps. 21:6f. [MT 7f.]; 31:7 [MT 8]; 90:14), His salvation (Ps. 21:1 [MT 2]; Isa. 25:9; Hab. 3:18), His word and statutes (Ps. 119:74, 111, 162), His faithfulness (Ps. 33:1-4; 57:10f. [MT 11f.]; 100:1, 5), His justice (Ps. 48:11 [MT 12]; 67:4 [MT 5]; 96:11-13; 97:1f.; 98:4-9), His strength and greatness (Ps. 21:1 [MT 2]; 47:1f. [MT 2f.]; 66:1-3; 95:1-3), and His goodness (Ps. 100:1, 5).

C. Messianic Joy. On the whole, then, joy is a quality of the prosperous national life in the OT. As God blesses His people, there is joy. When the prophets proclaim God's judgment and withdrawal of Himself and of His blessing, there is a loss of joy (Isa. 22:1-13; 24:11; Ezk. 7:7, 12; Joel 1:15f.); what is true of Israel is also true of the other nations (Isa. 16:10; Jer. 48:33). But the prophets look past the Exile with its weeping and sad memories (Ps. 137) and see a vision of the restored blessing and prosperity of, especially, the messianic age, and joy is a dominant characteristic of that period. This is especially true in Isaiah (9:3 [MT 2]; 12:3, 6; 25:9; 26:19; 42:10-12; 51:3, 11; 52:7-10; 60:15; 61:7; 66:10), but it is true of other prophets as well (Jer. 31:13; Joel 2:21, 23; Zec. 2:10; 9:9; 10:7). In fact, in that day even the creation will rejoice (Isa. 35:1-10; 49:13) and God Himself will take joy in His people (Isa. 62:5; 65:18; Jer. 32:41; 33:9). It is this day of great rejoicing, which God and His people will share, that occasions the numerous words for joy in Zeph. 3:14, 17.

***III. Joy in the NT.**–A. Joy in Christ.* It is the NT insistence that these messianic expectations are fulfilled in Jesus Christ; Jn. 8:56 seems to indicate that Abraham anticipated such fulfillment (cf. L. Morris, comm. on John [*NICNT*, 1971], pp. 471f.; R. Brown, comm. on John, I [*AB*, 1966], 359f.). The joy of motherhood had special significance for Elizabeth (Lk. 1:14) and Mary (Lk. 1:47). Mary's joy is shared by the wise men (Mt. 2:10), the shepherds, the whole world (Lk. 2:10), and even by Elizabeth's unborn child, John (Lk. 1:44). As the bridegroom's friend, John rejoiced in the bridegroom's voice (Jn. 3:29).

The Gospels, especially Luke, note various occasions of joy in Jesus' ministry. The seventy return rejoicing that demons are subject to the name of Jesus, but Jesus suggests that they ought rather rejoice that their names are written in heaven (Lk. 10:17, 20). Zacchaeus rejoiced when Jesus called him down from the tree and went home with him (Lk. 19:6). When Jesus put His adversaries to shame, the crowd rejoiced at the things He did (Lk. 13:17). In fact, the crowd was generally exuberant as Jesus approached Jerusalem (Lk. 18:43) and rejoiced as He entered Jerusalem on a donkey (Lk. 19:37; cf. Zec. 9:9).

B. Joy Not of This World. In His farewell address Jesus seeks to comfort the disciples by assuring them of the Spirit's coming after He is gone (14:16-18). He acknowledges that for a little while they will not see Him (16:16) and that they will weep and lament (16:20). But He assures them that their sorrow will turn to joy, just as the woman in labor forgets her anguish for the joy of her newborn child (16:20f.). So notwithstanding their present sorrow, they will rejoice and no one will take their joy from them (16:22).

It is this joy that characterizes the kingdom of God — a kingdom, Jesus said, that is not of this world (Jn. 18:36). In this connection Paul says: "For the kingdom of God does not mean food and drink but righteousness and peace and joy in the Holy Spirit" (Rom. 14:17). It is the Holy Spirit who is the source of this joy (Gal. 5:22; 1 Thess. 1:6; cf. Acts 13:52; Rom. 15:13), and this joy is, on the one hand, joy in the hope of our inheritance (Rom. 5:2; 12:12; cf. Rom. 15:13) and, on the other hand, joy in suffering.

C. Joy in Affliction. In fact, it is this joy while suffering that most clearly distinguishes NT joy from that in the OT. First, there is joy in (or in spite of) suffering because of the great reward in heaven (Mt. 5:12; Lk. 6:23), the "inheritance" kept for us in heaven (1 Pet. 1:4, 6), the "better possession" (He. 10:34). We are to look to Jesus who, for the joy that was set before Him, endured the cross (He. 12:2). Furthermore, we should rejoice that we share the sufferings of Christ, so that we may be glad and rejoice when His glory is revealed (1 Pet. 4:13). Second, there is joy in suffering because suffering produces character (Rom. 5:3) and steadfastness (Jas. 1:2). But third, there is joy in suffering simply because it is for the sake of Christ and His body, the Church (Acts 5:41; Phil. 2:17f.; Col. 1:24; 1 Pet. 4:13). Thus Paul can write: "as sorrowful, yet always rejoicing" (2 Cor. 6:10). Here is the paradox of Christian faith, that our very human grief may be turned into and overcome by joy in the Holy Spirit (2 Cor. 7:4).

D. Joy in the Church. It follows then, that in spite of circumstances, joy should be a prominent characteristic of the Church, through which the kingdom of God is made manifest. Paul commands the Philippian church: "Rejoice in the Lord always; again I will say, Rejoice!" (Phil. 4:4; cf. 3:1; 1 Thess. 5:16). Christians should rejoice that they have received the word and believed in Christ (1 Thess. 1:6; 1 Pet. 1:8; cf. Acts 8:39; 16:34). Even the superficial believer does this much (cf. Mt. 13:20). They should rejoice that Christ is proclaimed (cf. Phil. 1:18) and that people are being won to Christ (Mt. 18:10-14; Lk. 15:3-10; Jn. 4:36; Acts 15:3; cf. Acts 8:8). Furthermore, those responsible for the "progress and joy in the faith" of the Church (Phil. 1:25; cf. 2 Cor. 1:24) may rejoice in the various evidences of maturity in other Christians: their following the truth (2 Jn. 4; 3 Jn. 4), their repentance from wrong (2 Cor. 7:9), their obedience (Rom. 16:19), their good order and firmness of faith (Col. 2:5), their unity and harmony with the brothers (Phil. 2:2), and their partnership in the gospel mission (Phil. 1:4f.). In fact, Paul rejoices in his Christian friends; they are his joy and his crown (Phil. 4:1; 1 Thess. 2:19f.). Among believers, one person's joy should be another's joy as well (Rom. 12:15; 1 Cor. 12:26; 2 Cor. 2:3; 7:13; Phil. 2:17f.).

E. Joy at the End of the Age. The joy that was seen by the prophets in their anticipation of the messianic age and that we experience proleptically through the Holy Spirit remains to be consummated at the end of the age, when we will all be presented "before the presence of his glory with rejoicing" (Jude 24). The saints will rejoice at the downfall of the great dragon, the ancient serpent called the devil and Satan (Rev. 12:7-12). Though the kings, merchants, and seafarers of the earth will mourn the fall of "Babylon the Great" (18:9-19), the angel calls out: "Rejoice over her, O heaven, O saints and apostles and prophets, for God has given judgment for you against her!" (18:20). Then the seer hears a great multitude praising God's judgment (19:1-8) and saying: "Hallelujah! For the Lord our God the Almighty reigns. Let us rejoice and exult and give him the glory. For the marriage of the Lamb has come, and his Bride has made herself ready" (vv. 6f.).

Bibliography.–*TDOT,* II, *s.v.* "gyl" (Bergman-Ringgren, Barth); *TDNT,* I, *s.v.* ἀγαλλίαομαι, ἀγαλλίασις (Bultmann); IX, *s.v.* χαίρω κτλ. (Conzelmann, Zimmerli).

H. VAN BROEKHOVEN, JR.

JOYE'S BIBLE. *See* ENGLISH VERSIONS III.C.

JOZABAD joz'ə-bad [Heb. *yôzāḇāḏ*–'Yahweh has bestowed'].

1. A Gederathite, and one of David's recruits at Ziklag (1 Ch. 12:4 [MT 5]). He is named with the Benjaminites, but possibly he was a native of the town Gedara in southern Judah.

2, 3. Two Manassite captains who joined David at Ziklag (1 Ch. 12:20 [MT 21]).

4. A Levite overseer in Hezekiah's time (2 Ch. 31:13); may be the ancestor of the chief of the priests in 2 Ch. 35:9 = Joram of 1 Esd. 1:9.

5. A Levite (Ezr. 8:33), mentioned again probably in Ezr. 10:23; Neh. 8:7; 11:16; AV Josabad (1 Esd. 8:63).

6. A priest who had married a foreign wife (Ezr. 10:22). He was named Gedaliah in 1 Esd. 9:22 (AV Ocidelus).

JOZACAR joz'ə-kär, jə-zā'kär [Heb. *yôzāḵār*–'Yahweh has remembered']; AV JOZACHAR. Servant and murderer (with Jehozabad) of Joash, king of Judah (2 K. 12:21 [MT 22]); called Zabad in 2 Ch. 24:26. Some MSS have "Jozabad" in 2 Kings.

JOZADAK joz'ə-dak. *See* JEHOZADAK.

JUBAL jo͞o'bal [Heb. *yûḇāl*; for meaning *see* JABAL]. Son of Lamech by Adah, and inventor of musical instruments (Gen. 4:21).

JUBILEE, YEAR OF [Heb. *šᵉnaṯ hayyôḇēl* (Lev. 25:13), or simply *hayyôḇēl* (25:28) < *qeren hayyôḇēl*–'the horn of the ram,' made into a trumpet (Josh. 6:5f.)]; AV JUBILE. According to Lev. 25:9 a loud trumpet should proclaim liberty throughout Israel on the tenth day of the seventh month (the Day of Atonement), after a lapse of seven sabbaths of years, or forty-nine years. In this manner the fiftieth year was to be announced as a Jubilee Year. It possessed the function of an ordinary sabbatic year, thus allowing the land to lie fallow for two successive years (Lev. 25:11, 22; *see* SABBATICAL YEAR). But in addition, real property was automatically to revert to its original owners (25:10, 13); and those who had been compelled by poverty to sell themselves for indentured service to their brothers were to gain release (v. 39).

I. Personal Liberty.–The fiftieth year was to be a time of proclaiming liberty to all the inhabitants of the land. God had redeemed His people from bondage in Egypt (Lev. 25:42); and none of them was again to be reduced to the status of an *'eḇeḏ,* or slave (v. 39). Poverty could, even at its worst, reduce an Israelite to a status no less than that of a hired servant, a wage earner, and then only until the Year of Jubilee (v. 40). God's chosen child was not to be oppressed (vv. 43, 46; *see* SLAVE). Indeed, as citizens of the theocratic kingdom, masters and servants had become brothers together (cf. Philem. 16). Thus, as seen in its widest application, only through its loyalty to God could Israel as a nation ever hope to be free and independent of other masters.

II. Restitution of Property.–A second feature of the Jubilee was that of the restitution of all real property. The purpose was to demonstrate that the earth is subject basically to God's law, and not to man's desires: "for the land is mine: for you are strangers and sojourners with me" (Lev. 25:23). God's specific legislation concerned the inalienability of Israel's land titles. It required the reversion of all hereditary property to the family that originally possessed it and the reestablishment of the initial arrangement regarding God's division of the land. It did not teach either the socialistic economic theory that a person is entitled to the ownership of goods on the basis of his need (in this case, the possession of the land that produced his living), or the free-enterprise system that allows an unlimited expansion of private property. On the contrary, it established a fixed title to the property assigned by God (cf. Dt. 21:16, on inheritance), so that the implied humanitarian factor is given a deeper theological foundation. It should also be noted that the restitution of Israel's property appears to have typical significance, for the possession of the land by its individual Hebrew owners served as an acted prophecy of the blessings of the messianic age (Isa. 61:1-3). The Year of Jubilee foreshadows the restoration of all that has been perverted by mankind's sin, the establishment of the true liberty of the children of God, and the deliverance of creation from the bondage of corruption to which it has been subjected on account of human depravity (Lk. 4:17-21; Rom. 8:19-23).

III. Resulting Property Values.–Since the institution of the Jubilee Year excluded the possibility of selling any piece of land permanently (Lev. 25:23), it necessarily became the means of fixing the prices of real property (vv. 15f.; cf. 25-28). The same rule applied to dwelling houses outside the walled cities (v. 31) and also to the houses owned by Levites, although they were built within walled cities (v. 32). In the same manner the value of Hebrew bondsmen was to vary according to the proximity of the Jubilee Year (vv. 47-54), and in 27:17-25 a similar arrangement related to such lands as were "sanctified unto Yahweh." In all these cases the original owner was at liberty to redeem his own property or to have it redeemed by some of his nearest relatives (25:25-27, 29, 48ff.; 27:19; Jer. 32:8; cf. ancient Babylonian parallels, B. Meissner, *Beiträge zum altbabylonischen Privatrecht* [1893], pp. 40ff.). He might take action at any time, at a price proportionate to the time lapse until the Jubilee.

IV. History.–After the initial revelation of the Jubilee law (Lev. 25:8-34), the Year of Jubilee is mentioned historically as a living feature within Israelite society (Nu. 36:4). Its first observance seems to have occurred after Joshua's entrance into Canaan (cf. Lev. 25:2), or midway in the judgeship of Othniel (Jgs. 3:11). No reference, however, to such a celebration appears in Scripture (apart from the idealistic anticipation of Ezk. 46:17), though this hardly justifies its usual relegation by liberal criticism to an assumed postexilic Priestly Code of arbitrary and utopian dreams (cf. R. H. Pfeiffer, *Religion in the OT* [1961], p. 187). The influence of the Jubilee law upon the culture of Israel, with the permanent property rights that it guaranteed, helps to explain the conduct of Naboth and Ahab, *ca.* 855 B.C. (1 K. 21:3f.; cf. 22:1), and such prophetic rebukes as Isa. 5:8; Mic. 2:2. These very passages, however, testify to a contemporary neglect (cf. W. Eichrodt's contention for its early date, *Theology of the OT,* I [Eng. tr. 1961], 96). Even as Israel's sabbatic years were not observed during the centuries before the Exile, so also the Jubilees were disregarded. But while the former were reinstated in the postexilic era (Neh. 10:31; 1 Macc. 6:49, 53; cf. frequent mention by Josephus), the latter are never mentioned again (cf. *Ant.* iii.12.3 [280-86]), living on only in principle and in the eschatological hope of the people of God.

Bibliography.–*Jew.Enc.* X, *s.v.* "Sabbatical Year and Jubilee" (J. D. Eisenstein); A. Jirku, *Reinhold-Seeberg-Festschrift* (1929), II, 169ff.; W. G. Moorehead, *Studies in the Mosaic Institutions* (*ca.* 1895); R. G. North, *Sociology of the Biblical Jubilee* (1954); G. Oehler, *Theology of the OT* (Eng. tr. 1883), pp. 342-45; J. B. Payne, *Theology of the Older Testament* (1962), pp. 400f.

J. B. PAYNE

JUBILEES, BOOK OF. *See* APOCALYPTIC LITERATURE III.B.

JUCAL jo͞o'kal. *See* JEHUCAL.

JUDA. AV variant of JODA (Lk. 3:26), JUDAH, JUDAS.

JUDAEA. *See* JUDEA.

JUDAH jo͞o'də [Heb. *y^ehûḏâ*–'praised'].

1. The 4th son of Jacob by Leah (see separate article).

2. An ancestor of Kadmiel, one of those who had the oversight of the rebuilding of the temple (Ezr. 3:9). He is the same as Hodaviah (Ezr. 2:40), Hodevah (Neh. 7:43), and Joda (1 Esd. 5:58).

3. A Levite who had taken a foreign wife (Ezr. 10:23).

4. A Levite who came up with Zerubbabel (Neh. 12:8).

5. A priest and musician who took part in the dedication of the wall of Jerusalem (Neh. 12:36).

6. A Benjaminite, the son of Hassenuah, who was second over the city of Jerusalem in the days of Nehemiah (Neh. 11:9).

7. One of the princes of Judah who took part in the dedication of the wall of Jerusalem (Neh. 12:34).

8. An ancestor of Jesus (Lk. 3:30; AV Juda).

S. F. HUNTER

JUDAH jo͞o'də [Heb. *y^ehûḏâ*; Gk. *Iouda, Ioudan, Ioudas*]; AV also JUDA, JUDAS. The meaning of the name is disputed. Some scholars explain it as "the child will thank God." Albright, arguing from the Arabic, suggests "the child will be led by God." J. Lewy proposes "belongs to God." All these explanations are doubtful.

Judah was the fourth son born to Jacob by Leah in Paddan-aram (Gen. 29:35, etc.). Of this patriarch's life only scanty details remain to us. He turned his brothers from their purpose to slay Joseph, persuading them to sell him to the Midianites at Dothan (37:26-28). A dark stain is left upon his memory by the story told in ch. 38. Reuben forfeited the rights of primogeniture by an act of infamy. Simeon and Levi, who came next in order, were passed over because of their cruel and treacherous conduct at Shechem. Judah, therefore, inherited the honors and responsibilities of the firstborn (ch. 34; 35:22; 49:5ff.). On the occasion of their first visit to Egypt, Reuben acted as spokesman for his brothers (42:22, 37). Then the leadership passed to Judah (43:3; 44:14-34). The sons of Joseph evidently looked askance upon Judah's promotion, and their own claims to hegemony were backed by considerable resources (49:22ff.). The rivalry between the two tribes, thus early visible, culminated in the disruption of the kingdom. To Judah, the "lion's whelp," a prolonged dominion was assured (49:9ff.). Many scholars think that the distinguished part played by Judah, the son of Jacob, reflects the important role of the tribe of Judah, which seemed to result from the prominence of certain families at the time of the patriarchs.

The tribe of Judah at the first census in the wilderness numbered 74,600 fighting men; at Sinai the number "from twenty years old and upward" was 76,500 (Nu. 1:27; 26:22; *see* NUMBERS, BOOK OF). The standard of the camp of Judah, with which were also the tribes of Zebulun and Issachar, was to the east of the tabernacle "toward the sunrising." The prince of Judah was Nahshon the son of Amminadab (Nu. 2:3). Caleb the son of Jephunneh represented Judah among the spies (13:6) and was also commanded to assist at the future allocation of the tribal portions (34:19). The Bible contains some genealogical lists of the sons of Judah; those in Genesis and Numbers are identical. But in Chronicles there are long and complicated lists, some of which do not derive directly from the eponym, and others seem to contradict each other. An additional list in the book of Ruth is the genealogy of the House of David, which repeats that of Judah. The lists of Judah are concentrated in Gen. 46:12; Nu. 26:19; 1 Ch. 2:3-52; 4:1-21.

The information given of the conquest of Judah's territory is meager and cannot be arranged in a self-consistent story. In Josh. 11:21ff. the conquest is ascribed to Joshua. Caleb is described as conquering at least a portion in Josh. 14:12; 15:13ff.; while in Jgs. 1 the tribes of Judah and Simeon play a conspicuous part; and Simeon founded a settlement in the south within the territory of Judah. The tribal organization seems to have been maintained after the occupation of the land, and Judah was so loosely related to the northern tribes that it was not expected to help them against Sisera. Deborah has no reproaches for absent Judah. It is remarkable that only one judge over Israel (Othniel, Jgs. 3:9-11) arose from the tribe of Judah. The first king of all Israel was chosen from the tribe of Benjamin. This made acquiescence by Judah easier than if Saul had sprung from the ancient rival Ephraim. But the dignity of Judah was fully vindicated by the splendid reigns of David and Solomon, from whom the Savior of the world should come in lineal descent (Lk. 3:33). The further history of the tribe is merged in that of Israel.

The boundaries of the territory of the tribe of Judah are fully described in Josh. 15:2-12; other quotations dealing with this subject are to be found in Nu. 34:1f., where the historical boundaries are described, and in Ezekiel, where the boundaries are utopian. *See* JUDAH, TERRITORY OF.

Bibliography.–W. F. Albright, *JBL*, 43 (1924), 363ff.; *BASOR*, 58 (1935), 10-18; *KS*, I, 49, 54f.; F. M. Cross and G. E. Wright, *JBL*, 75 (1956), 202ff.; S. Yeivin, *Encyclopaedia Miqraith* (1958).

A. A. SAARISALO

JUDAH, KINGDOM OF.

I. Origins of the Hebrew Monarchy
II. United Hebrew Kingdom
III. Kingdom of Judah
  A. Brief View of Judah's History
  B. Origins of the Kingdom of Judah
  C. Resources and Organization
  D. From the Division of the Kingdom to the Middle of the Eighth Century B.C.
    1. Beginnings of the Two Hebrew Kingdoms
    2. The Two Hebrew Kingdoms Stabilized
    3. Judah During the Jehu Dynasty of Israel
  E. Judah During the Period of the Assyrian Empire
    1. Assyrian Ascendancy: Israel's Decline and Fall
    2. Assyrian Decline: Judah Carries On Alone
  F. Decline and Fall of the Kingdom of Judah
    1. Assyria's End
    2. Babylon Revived

The present article is the exposition of the history of the southern Hebrew kingdom of Judah from the death of Solomon (922 B.C.) to the destruction of Jerusalem and the beginning of the Babylonian Exile (587 B.C.). For details on the earlier Hebrew kingdom *see* SAUL; DAVID; SOLOMON.

Judah is the name of one of the tribes of the Israelite nation. This tribe traced its ancestry to Judah, the fourth son of Jacob (Gen. 29:35; 49:8-12; Dt. 33:7). Upon the conquest of the land of Canaan, the Judah tribe possessed the southern hill country, the region from Jerusalem southward to the Negeb, and became one of the strongest elements in the nation (Josh. 15; Jgs. 1:1-20).

In time the Hebrews came to recognize two basic divisions among themselves, called Judah and Israel. It is not clear whether the special use of these terms was the result of the division of the kingdom or preceded it (the occurrence in 1 S. 18:16, e.g., could be a reflection of later usage). It is clear that long before the death of Solomon a polarization of tribal loyalties had begun, from which separate southern and central-northern identities were emerging.

I. Origins of the Hebrew Monarchy.–The Israelite tribes, upon entering Canaan, were formed into an AMPHICTYONY, a loose union of tribes around a central sanctuary, the tabernacle (Josh. 18:1, 8-10; 21:2; Jgs. 18:31). Leadership was furnished, in theory, by the tabernacle priest. As a matter of fact, the priesthood tended to degenerate quickly (1 S. 2:12-17, 27-36; 8:1-5), and so charismatic leaders — the judges — were raised up (Jgs. 2:16-19). These men were military deliverers who came to power at times of crisis and led the Hebrews against their enemies; they seem to have given little leadership in the more normal life of the nation. The amphictyonic union with its judges was much too loose to give the solidarity and leadership the nation needed to meet the threat of the strong hostile Canaanite peoples, and especially the Philistine menace.

Thus the Hebrews called for a king to "govern us and go out before us and fight our battles" (1 S. 8:20). While one account of the inauguration of the monarchy (1 S. 8) seems to indicate that the tribes were wrong in asking for a king, the monarchy was ultimately for the best. The nation, prone to individualism and strong tribal loyalties, needed a king to give it unity. Having a king did not mean the rejection of the theocracy; God always reigns through people and in the good kings, such as David, He continued to direct the nation (cf. Ps. 72).

II. United Hebrew Kingdom.–Saul, the first king (1 S. 9–31), a Benjaminite, was a transitional figure, often acting more the part of a charismatic judge than a king (1 S. 10:9-12; 11:5f.). The Israelite tribes (except for Benjamin) were reluctant to give him allegiance (1 S. 10:26f.; 11:12-15), and it appears that toward the end of his reign the tribes reverted to the unorganized life of the judges period.

David the son of Jesse, a Judean from Bethlehem, succeeded Saul upon his death (1 S. 16; 2 S. 2–1 K. 2). At first the non-Judean tribes were reluctant to surrender their dearly won freedom to him. Indeed, for a period of some seven and one-half years, David reigned in Hebron over the tribe of Judah only, while the other Hebrew tribes (at least for part of this time) gave their allegiance to a military government headed by Abner, Saul's cousin and chief-of-staff, who ruled in the name of Saul's son Ish-bosheth (2 S. 2:1-11). Here we have already a "divided kingdom" whose boundaries and tribal constituencies are quite similar to those of the later, better-known divided kingdom.

David, by his commanding personality and certain well-devised political moves, united the nation and bound the tribes to him. Among these moves the most important was his capture of Jerusalem, to which he gave a central place in Hebrew life. Jerusalem was in the territory of Benjamin, its southern boundary being the line separating Benjamin from Judah. Benjamin was a kind of buffer tribe between the strong Judah tribe to the south and the Joseph tribes N of it. David moved his residence to neutral Jerusalem (2 S. 5:6-10), which became the national capital and which gave a unity the city of Hebron could never have afforded. When David brought the ark to Jerusalem and placed it in a new tent, emphasizing the worship of Yahweh at this center, he was not only reviving the worship of God according to the divine command, but also strengthening his own regime (2 S. 6:1-19). This Judean control of Jerusalem was so strong that when the nation divided after Solomon's death, Jerusalem, although located in a tribe probably also hostile to Judah, remained in the possession of the Davidic line and thus became the capital of the southern kingdom, of which Judah was the prominent element.

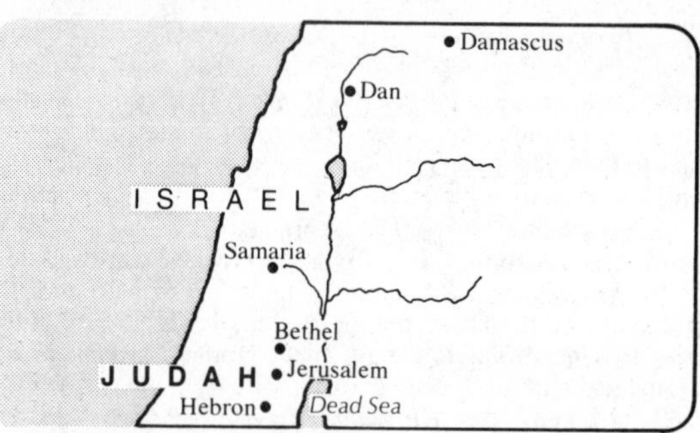

Under David, then, the Hebrews were a united nation and began to achieve national greatness. When David was old, however, the non-Judean tribes again became restive and listened to the appeals of revolutionaries. It is not clear that the Absalom revolt (2 S. 15–19) was an expression of discontent with the Judean rule over the nation, for Absalom was, of course, David's son. In the renewed submission of the tribes to David after Absalom's death, however, Judah took the lead (2 S. 19:9-15) and although the other tribes claimed an equal zeal in "bringing back the king," there was much bad feeling between Judah and the rest, as the old animosity between them reasserted itself (2 S. 19:41-43). The Sheba revolt (2 S. 20) was clearly an attempt by the non-Judeans to renounce Judean leadership, and it shows the fragility of the union of the tribes accomplished by David.

Solomon, David's son and successor, ruled the united nation with an iron hand. He strengthened its religious solidarity by building the temple in Jerusalem. The hold this "house" had on the religious affections of the whole nation is evident not only from such overt statements as those in the Psalms (e.g., Pss. 42, 122, 125, 132), but also from Jeroboam's first action after breaking away from Judah and establishing his own throne in Israel — the substitution of the Dan and Bethel religious centers, lest "the kingdom turn back to the house of David; if this people go up to offer sacrifices in the house of the Lord at Jerusalem" (1 K. 12:26f.). Studies of the tax-collecting system set up by Solomon (1 K. 4:7-19) indicate that his choice of centers for the collection and storage of the taxes was not along the old tribal lines. It probably represents a deliberate attempt to break down the old tribal loyalties, the better to control the often restive Israelites. It is not clear that Judah was included in this tax system. While the king's tribe may have been taxed according to an older scheme, the possibility that Judah was tax-exempt cannot be overlooked. When the provisions needed by Solomon's court for one day (1 K. 4:22-28) are considered, the complaint of the Israelites to Rehoboam about Solomon's "heavy yoke" (1 K. 12:4) seems entirely justified.

III. Kingdom of Judah.*–A. Brief View of Judah's History.* The history of the southern Judean kingdom from the death of Solomon to the Babylonian Exile can be divided into three parts. During the first two hundred years of its history, its sister kingdom Israel existed to the north of it. The two Hebrew kingdoms were very important to each other, and the relationships between them were constant. This period itself falls into two divisions.

(1) From the death of Solomon to the middle of the 8th cent. Judah carried on its political life in comparative isolation from the great powers of the Fertile Crescent. Shishak's invasion and Jehoshaphat's military alliance with Ahab brought Judah into contact with Egypt and the Arameans; nevertheless, except for the constant relations with its immediate neighbors, the Judean hill kingdom lived a life apart from the powerful world empires.

(2) From the middle of the 8th cent. to the fall of the northern kingdom (722 B.C.), and for a little while thereafter, the advance of the great Assyrian empire was the constant cloud under which both parts of the Hebrew nation had to live. This Assyrian juggernaut finally brought to an end the northern kingdom and nearly destroyed Judah.

After the fall of Samaria Judah carried on alone for more than a century. This, its third period, saw a change in the world empires. Assyria fell, and Babylon took its place as the dominant power in the Fertile Crescent. It was this new Babylonian empire that finally destroyed Jerusalem and the Judean state in 587 B.C.

B. Origins of the Kingdom of Judah. Although both David and Solomon had managed to unify and rule all the Hebrew tribes, during their reigns tensions continued to exist, and it was only because of their strong administration that they were able to maintain at least external peace and unity. During Solomon's old age, just as during David's, the non-Judean tribes had become restive. Jeroboam the son of Nebat had been in charge of the corvée of the Joseph tribes. After an encounter with the prophet Ahijah, who gave him "ten pieces" of Israel — ten tribes — Jeroboam rebelled and fled to Egypt for protection (1 K. 11:26-40). Shishak the king of Egypt was glad to keep an Israelite government in exile at his court, for anything that would weaken Solomon's strong empire would be to Egypt's advantage. Rehoboam's accession at the death of his father Solomon (922 B.C.) brought a weak new administration into power, and Jeroboam returned with his ultimatum of more freedom from the central authority at Jerusalem (1 K. 12:1-19). Rehoboam's foolish attempt to assert an absolute authority which he did not really possess gave Jeroboam and the Israelite tribes the excuse they wanted, and they revolted. So the ten tribes (i.e., Israel), which had constituted most of the Hebrews except Judah and part of Benjamin, again became independent of Judah and of David's line.

It must not be thought that the mere ineptitude of Rehoboam caused the split in the kingdom. The many tendencies toward tribal independence, and the dislike of Judean rule felt by the central and northern tribes, have already been noted. Probably it is best to consider the "divided kingdom" as the normal condition for the Hebrews, and the Davidic-Solomonic period of unity as an exception made possible only by the strong leadership manifested by this father-and-son administration.

C. Resources and Organization. Rehoboam continued to reign over a small southern region, roughly equal to the territory of Judah. Most of Benjaminite territory appears to have gone with the northern rebels (1 K. 12:20), but Jerusalem stayed with Judah, due to the presence of Rehoboam's army there, and it remained his capital. Thus the boundary between Judah and Israel must have run several kilometers N of Jerusalem. All southern Palestine (much of it desert) was held by Rehoboam. Even so, his territory was not more than half the size of the northern kingdom. His arable land was less than one-fourth that of Israel. Judah claimed suzerainty over Edom, and asserted it when possible. Judah's population (estimated at 300,000) was about half that of Israel. The northern kingdom had the best farm land and was favored with more rainfall than the south.

In spite of its small size Judah enjoyed certain advantages over Israel. Jerusalem, with its ancient heritage of the temple and its divinely ordained worship, together with the Davidic dynasty and the buildings and traditions of the strong Solomonic empire, were Judah's. Its location in the southern hill country removed it somewhat from the ever increasing Assyrian struggle for control of the road to Egypt — a struggle that was to result in Israel's destruction. Judah tended to be a city-state (no other Judean city could begin to compete with Jerusalem) with a homogeneous population and a strong centralization of authority, thus avoiding the weakness of decentralization that characterized the northern kingdom. The continuing Davidic dynasty (Israel had nine dynasties during the reigns of nineteen kings) and the Levitic priesthood attached to the Jerusalem temple were sources of continuing strength.

D. From the Division of the Kingdom to the Middle of the Eighth Century B.C. The detailed consideration of the history of the kingdom of Judah that follows is concerned only with the nation's continuity and its relations with other nations. For the internal history, see the articles on individual kings.

1. Beginnings of the Two Hebrew Kingdoms. Rehoboam's foolish attempt to assert power that he did not have was the immediate cause of the division of the kingdom. Solomon's empire was lost at once. In fact, Damascus soon became the head of a strong Aramean state, which was a constant threat to Israel and sometimes even to Judah. The other former subject states also asserted their independence, e.g., the Philistines (1 K. 15:27; 16:15) and Moabites (2 K. 3:4-27). Rehoboam (922-915 B.C.) was left so weak that he could not attempt to force the northern revolters to return to his rule (1 K. 12:18-24, although cf. 1 K. 14:30; 15:6), restricting himself to securing and fortifying certain border cities in Judah and Benjamin (2 Ch. 11:5-12).

Affairs in Judah were made much worse when the Libyan noble Shishak (Sheshonq I), founder of the 22nd Dynasty of Egypt, invaded Palestine (*ca.* 918) and sacked Jerusalem (1 K. 14:25-28; 2 Ch. 12:2-12). This brief attempt by Egypt to regain its Asiatic empire was futile, but the enormous tribute Shishak took from Rehoboam meant the immediate loss of most of the Solomonic treasure and grandeur. No doubt much of this loot was used to embellish the temples at Karnak; from the inscriptions on these buildings we learn that Shishak devastated all of Palestine, Israel as well as Judah.

Rehoboam's son Abijah (915-913) was succeeded by Asa (913-873), the first of a number of kings who sought to reform life and worship according to "the law and the commandment" (2 Ch. 14:4).

Sometime in Asa's reign occurred another Egyptian invasion, led by Zerah the Ethiopian (2 Ch. 14:9-15). It was repelled, the last direct Egyptian interference in Judean affairs for several centuries. Probably later, Baasha the king of Israel invaded Benjamin and placed Jerusalem in great jeopardy by fortifying Ramah, only 8 km. (5 mi.) N of the Judean capital. Asa sent gifts to Ben-hadad of Damascus, who attacked northern Galilee, compelling Baasha to pull back from Jerusalem. Asa hastily dismantled Ramah with conscripted labor, using the materials to strengthen the defenses of Geba and Mizpah, thus moving the frontier further to the north again and securing Jerusalem (1 K. 15:16-22). An inconclusive military struggle between Judah and Israel characterized this whole period.

2. The Two Hebrew Kingdoms Stabilized. Jehoshaphat's twenty-five-year reign (873-849) was important in several respects. It was a reign of peace and prosperity. Judah was strengthened in its defenses and military power (2 Ch. 17:1-5, 10-18), but especially by the religious revival sponsored by the king. Jehoshaphat inaugurated a policy of peaceful relations with surrounding nations that contributed to the internal tranquillity. Instead of the constant hostility and military pressure that had characterized the relations of Judah with Israel until this time, Jehoshaphat made peace with Israel, thus recognizing its right to separate existence (1 K. 22:44). He arranged for his son Jehoram to marry Athaliah, the daughter of Ahab king of Israel.

The Ahab dynasty, which was in power during the reign of Jehoshaphat, is infamous for its depravity and for its adoption of the Canaanite religion of Baal, which provoked the defiant protest of Elijah. No doubt this made Jehoshaphat's relations with Israel difficult; nevertheless the Judean king actively maintained his alliance, even going to battle several times with Ahab and his sons, for which he was reproved by the prophet Jehu son of Hanani (2 Ch. 19:1-3). At any rate, the alliance strengthened both sections of the Hebrew nation and enabled them to recapture some of the lands adjacent to Palestine proper which had been lost after the death of Solomon.

Jehoshaphat continued his father's policy of religious renewal. He worshiped Yahweh and "did not seek the Baals" (2 Ch. 17:3); thus the rampant Baalism of the Ahab regime in Israel did not penetrate Judah.

The full fruit of Jehoshaphat's treaty with Israel came to Judah during the reign of his son Jehoram (849-842), whose wife Athaliah was Ahab's daughter. Jehoram "walked in the way of the kings of Israel" (2 K. 8:18), introducing Baalism to Judah. Probably Athaliah was a strong power behind the throne, as was Jezebel in Israel. During his brief reign Judah lost control of Edom and Libnah (2 K. 8:20-22) and was invaded by Philistines and Arabians, who appear to have plundered Jerusalem (2 Ch. 21:16f.).

Ahaziah the son of Jehoram (842) met a violent death at the hand of the revolutionary Jehu son of Jehoshaphat, who slew him and his uncle Jehoram the king of Israel. Upon Ahaziah's death his mother Athaliah usurped the throne (842-837). She ruthlessly killed the royal family (2 K. 11:1-3) and fostered the worship of Baal. No doubt the conservatism of the hill-country Judeans made Athaliah's baalizing of Judah a slower process than Israel's had been, but Judah in time would probably have gone the paganizing way of Israel had not Athaliah's reign been cut short.

Fortunately for Judah, a strong reaction against the Baal influence quickly set in with the coup led by the high priest Jehoiada, who placed the child Joash on the throne (837-800). Jehoiada reformed the religious life of the nation (2 K. 12:1-16), but Joash, when he came to manhood and full power, favored paganism.

At this time Israel, having just come through Jehu's bloody revolution, was very weak, and the Arameans under Hazael of Damascus were in a period of ascendancy. Transjordan and the Philistine plain fell to Hazael, and he next attacked Jerusalem, but Joash bought him off by giving him the royal and temple treasuries (2 K. 12:17f.).

3. Judah During the Jehu Dynasty of Israel. The century of the reign of the dynasty of Jehu in Israel (842-746) saw many changes in the life of both divisions of the Hebrew nation. The power of Damascus was broken by King Adadnirari III of Assyria, who made a number of campaigns against the Aramean city-states, conquering Damascus in 802. The Hebrew kingdoms could thus enter a period of freedom from Aramean oppression. Jeroboam II revived Israel until it, together with Judah in the south, encompassed a large part of the old Solomonic empire (2 K. 14:25, 28). A time of prosperity ensued in which great wealth came to both kingdoms, probably as a result of trade. Israel's splendor is eloquently testified to by the excavations at Samaria, and Judah seems to have shared it (cf., e.g., Uzziah's expansion in the Negeb, 2 Ch. 26:10).

This time of prosperity was, however, a time of social and spiritual sickness, at least for Israel. The wealthy commercial class oppressed the peasants, whose condition was deplorable. The prophets Amos and Hosea testify to the social injustices of the time. Religion in Israel, while it seemed prosperous enough, was rotten to the core. It was a religion of outward ceremony and inward emptiness, devoid of true piety and social righteousness. Israel, although wealthy and optimistic, was on the brink of disaster. To what extent Judah shared these conditions our biblical sources do not tell us. Probably the southern kingdom, always more conservative, followed the same unhealthy trend, but to a lesser degree.

It was at this time that the first of the writing prophets appeared in Judah. The prophetic movement had been active for some time, but with the eighth-century prophets it reached a high peak. Amos and Hosea in Israel, and Isaiah and Micah in Judah (a little later), were among the greatest of the prophets and the first whose sermons have been recorded for all times. Isaiah began his ministry toward the end of this period and continued into the next, announcing God's judgment and calling for repentance.

Amaziah (800-783) succeeded his father Joash. During his reign the Israelites, led by Jehoash the grandson of Jehu, invaded Judah and sacked Jerusalem (792). Since Amaziah was taken captive at this time, his son Uzziah must have been co-regent until Amaziah died (783; *see* CHRONOLOGY OF THE OT V.B). Then Uzziah began his long reign of forty-two years (793-742). He and his famous contemporary Jeroboam II of Israel rode on the crest of the wave of the mid-eighth-century prosperity. Uzziah strengthened Judah, rebuilding Ezion-geber (2 K. 14:22) and controlling the Negeb and the Philistines (2 Ch. 26:6-8).

E. Judah During the Period of the Assyrian Empire. In the third quarter of the 8th cent. the political situation in the Fertile Crescent was alarmingly altered with the rise of the Assyrian empire. Under its vigorous king Tiglath-pileser III (745-727), the national policy became one of continuous powerful pressure westward, with Egypt as its ultimate objective. The nation of Israel, bestride the only road through Palestine to Egypt, first felt the Assyrian pressure, and finally fell before it. In time the Assyrians came even against the more isolated hill kingdom of Judah.

1. Assyrian Ascendancy: Israel's Decline and Fall. Jotham son of Uzziah (742-735) was attacked by Pekah king of Israel and Rezin king of Damascus in an attempt to force him to join them in a coalition against Assyria (2 K. 16:5-9; 2 Ch. 28:5-21; Isa. 7:1–8:15). Jotham died, leaving his son Ahaz (735-715) to face the invaders. Added to the crisis was an Edomite insurrection (2 K. 16:6) and a Philistine invasion (2 Ch. 28:17-19). Ahaz was one of Judah's most paganizing kings; he ignored Isaiah's offer of divine help and appealed to Tiglath-pileser for aid. The Assyrian king destroyed the coalition, overran Galilee and Transjordan, and reduced Israel to a small enclave in the hill country of Samaria. But Judah was now a vassal of Assyria and obliged to follow the Assyrian lead not only in politics but in religion as well. Assyria's gods must now have official recognition in Jerusalem. This is the background of Ahaz's changes in the temple, so condemned by the sacred historians. All kinds of heathen practices now flourished in Jerusalem (2 K. 16:10-18; 2 Ch. 28:22-25). Probably at this time also the nation suffered an economic decline; it had lost Ezion-geber and paid heavy tribute to Assyria. Later in the reign of Ahaz, Samaria was destroyed by the Assyrians and the Israelite kingdom ceased to be (722). Its territory became a part of the Assyrian empire. One can easily imagine the gloom Israel's fall produced in the sister nation to the south.

Hezekiah (715-686) inherited the policies of Assyrian vassalage from his father Ahaz, and his whole reign was devoted to the reversal of these and the reestablishment of Judean political and religious independence. There is every reason to believe that Hezekiah, a devout worshiper of Yahweh, was motivated by his religious convictions as much as by his desire to be free from the yoke of Assyria. The prophet Isaiah was his confidant and adviser. Early in his reign Hezekiah began to reform the religion of Judah (2 K. 18:3-6; 2 Ch. 29–31). Paganizing cults and local Yahweh shrines were prohibited, and the Passover was reinstituted. The king even tried to involve the remnant of the defunct Israelite kingdom in his reforms, but with little success.

In 705 Hezekiah rebelled against the Assyrian king Sennacherib by withholding tribute (2 K. 18:7). The succeeding events are described both in the Bible and upon the Assyrian monuments; scholars have not yet clarified all the details of the complex picture. It appears that all the Westlands were in revolt, abetted by Merodach-baladan of Babylon, who had thrown off the Assyrian yoke (2 K. 20:12-19; Isa. 39). Hezekiah appears to have been a leader, sending a delegation to Egypt for help (Isa. 30:1-7; 31:1-3). In 701 Sennacherib came to put down the revolt. One by one he conquered the rebellious allies until he came to Judah, which he overran, taking from Hezekiah a great tribute (2 K. 18:13-16). Events after this are not clear. Many scholars believe that the deliverance of Hezekiah from the Assyrians described in 2 K. 18:17–19:37 took place under a later attack by the Assyrians. At any rate, when Hezekiah died Judah was still maintaining a threatened independence, which his son soon lost.

2. Assyrian Decline: Judah Carries On Alone. The century between the death of Hezekiah and the destruction of the Judean state was a time of sudden political change; empires rose and fell almost overnight. Little could Manasseh realize how near to extinction was the fearful Assyrian power to which he paid tribute. And the Babylonian empire, which displaced the Assyrian, lasted only one human lifetime.

Manasseh, Hezekiah's son (686-642), completely reversed his father's policies, becoming a loyal vassal of Assyria. Both Esarhaddon and Ashurbanipal, his Assyrian lords, were vigorous conquerors, occupying Egypt and leaving Manasseh the choice between tribute and destruction. Once he seems to have dabbled in revolt, but a summons to appear before his Assyrian lord quickly cured him of it (2 Ch. 33:11-13). Manasseh's submission meant, of course, the reconstitution of Assyrian paganism in Jerusalem (2 K. 21:3-9). Many Judeans probably preferred the peace of wicked Manasseh's reign to the frequent crises and wars of pious Hezekiah's. Amon son of Manasseh (642-640) continued his father's policies.

Already in Manasseh's day the great Assyrian empire, overextended and full of dissensions, was slipping. Babylon, long a center of revolt, was with Median support constantly restive, and Egypt was never firmly held. Vigorous Indo-Aryan peoples infiltrated and weakened Assyria from the north. This situation was similar to that facing the Roman empire in the 4th and 5th cents. A.D. that led to its fall.

F. Decline and Fall of the Kingdom of Judah. 1. Assyria's End. After the death of Ashurbanipal (633) Assyria was fighting for its life. The Babylonians, led by Nabopolassar, were leaders in the coalition that finally destroyed the Assyrian capital Nineveh in 612. In 609 Assyria ceased to exist. It was in this period, with a brief power vacuum in the Levant, that Josiah reigned (640-609). Judah was now free for the first time in a century. Josiah is best known for his sweeping religious reforms, in which the finding of the book of the law played a prominent part (621 B.C.; 2 K. 22:1–23:25; 2 Ch. 34:1–35:19). All traces of Assyrian paganism, Canaanite rites, and magic were obliterated; and the king successfully centralized the worship of Yahweh by stamping out the local Yahweh shrines. These were days when all the world seemed to have turned upside down; a return to the old Hebrew faith would give the nation a sound foundation.

A new burst of prophetic activity characterized this period. Nahum sang for joy over Nineveh's fall. Zephaniah announced God's wrath against Judah. The young Jeremiah was unimpressed by the Josianic revival — it did not go deep enough. And Habakkuk (who probably flourished at this time) proclaimed a Chaldean invasion.

Josiah also extended Judean power by taking possession of the territory of the defunct Israel. There he died, foolishly (it seems to us) trying to stop Pharaoh Neco, as the Egyptian king was on his way to Carchemish to fight on the side of dying Assyria (2 K. 23:29f.).

2. Babylon Revived. For a brief time after Josiah's death, Judah fell under the power of Egypt. Neco, returning from Syria through Palestine, deposed and deported to Egypt Josiah's son Jehoahaz (609), setting in his place in Jerusalem his brother Eliakim (Jehoiakim, 609-598) as an Egyptian puppet (2 K. 23:31-37). Meanwhile, Nebuchadrezzar the son of Nabopolassar (605-562) had come to the throne in Babylon. During his long reign Babylon regained its ancient glory and dominion. Nebuchadrezzar was determined to crush Egypt and all that stood in the way of this objective; this led him to a series of campaigns against the Westlands, including Judah, and he soon took this area away from Egypt.

It appears that already in 605 Nebuchadrezzar had attacked Jerusalem, taking Daniel and other nobles hostage to Babylon (Dnl. 1:1f.; 2 Ch. 36:6f.). Certainly from this time on Nebuchadrezzar considered Judah part of his empire. Jerusalem's failure to see the finality of this, and its tendency to lean on Egypt for help — that "broken reed" — led to revolt several times, thus bringing about its destruction. Throughout these last years (from the death of Josiah to the destruction of Jerusalem) the nation was demoralized, led by irresolute and ungodly kings, disunited, and in a decline from which it could never recover. The book of Jeremiah is eloquent witness to those troubled days.

Jehoiakim rebelled against Nebuchadrezzar; as the Babylonian armies approached, the Judean king was killed in a palace coup and his son Jehoiachin (597) succeeded him. After a three-month siege the city surrendered, and the new king and many nobles and artisans (and the priest Ezekiel) were deported to Babylon (2 K. 24:5-16). Zedekiah, an uncle of Jehoiachin, was placed upon the throne, probably more as a regent than a king. After thirty-seven years in prison in Babylon, Jehoiachin was released and pensioned there (2 K. 25:27-30).

Zedekiah (597-587) should have understood the signs of the times and submitted to Babylon as Jeremiah urged him (Jer. 27–29). Instead, he was constantly planning rebellion. With deliberate finality the Babylonians came again, reducing all Judah and besieging Jerusalem (588). For a year and a half that desperate city held out. Zedekiah's final attempt to escape failed; he was led blinded to Babylon and Jerusalem was destroyed (2 K. 24:20–25:21). The Babylonians desolated the whole land of Judah and carried off to Babylon large numbers of its people. Many of the poor of the land who remained there finally went to Egypt (Jer. 43:1-7).

Thus Jeremiah's prediction of total destruction for the nation was tragically fulfilled (Jer. 25:1-11). Never again was there an independent Hebrew nation with its own king. That the Judeans even survived the destruction of their homeland and their exile to Babylon is without doubt one of the anomalies of history.

Bibliography.–W. F. Albright, *Biblical Period from Abraham to Ezra* (rev. ed. 1963); *BHI*; W. A. L. Elmslie, *IB* on Chronicles; J. H. Hayes and J. M. Miller, eds., *Israelite and Judaean History* (*OTL*, 1977); J. A. Montgomery and H. S. Gehman, comm. on Kings (*ICC*, 1951); *NHI*; *ORHI*, vol. I; N. H. Snaith, *IB* on Kings; *MNHK*.

J. B. GRAYBILL

JUDAH ON THE EAST. A place marking the eastern limit of the territory of Naphtali (Josh. 19:34). It is generally thought among scholars that the text is corrupt (cf. the LXX, which omits any reference to Judah, and many modern versions, e.g., NIV, JB, NAB); but no very probable emendation has been suggested. The full phrase, "Judah on the east at the Jordan" (Heb. *bîhûḏâ hayyardēn mizraḥ haššemeš*; AV "Judah upon Jordan toward the sunrising"; NEB "low-laying land by the Jordan on the east"), obviously cannot refer to the tribal territory of Judah, and it is difficult to imagine that any locale in this area would be named Judah. W. Thomson (*The Land and the Book* [1911], II, 466), however, proposed to identify it with Seiyid Jehûda, a small white-domed sanctuary about 5 km. (3 mi.) SE of Laish (Tell el-Qâḍī).

JUDAH, TERRITORY OF [Heb. *yᵉhûḏâ*; Josh. 15:1-62]. The land allotted to the tribe of Judah; later the territory

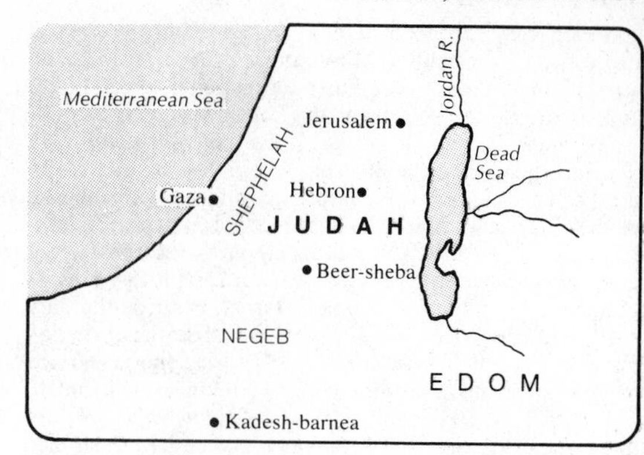

of the southern kingdom, and after the Exile the land occupied by Jews.

*I. **The Tribal Inheritance***.–The allocation of the tribe of Judah was the land from the boundary with Benjamin on the north to the boundary with Edom on the south, and from the Dead Sea on the east to the Mediterranean on the west. It is not to be understood that the tribe of Judah actually occupied all this territory from the time of the allotment, for both Joshua and Judges make clear that there was a lot of land to be possessed, there were many enclaves of non-Israelites (or perhaps better stated, there were many Israelite enclaves in the Canaanite territory), and there was almost constant warfare with other peoples over many parts of the land. Thus, e.g., the Philistine cities included in the allotment (Josh. 15:46f.) were only "taken" at a later time (Jgs. 1:18), and warfare with the Philistines over possession of the Shephelah continued into the days of David.

The inheritance is broken into parts in the description: "in the extreme South" (the Negeb, Josh. 15:21); "in the lowland" (the Shephelah, 15:33), which in turn is subdivided into five groups and includes the coastal plain; "in the hill country" (15:48), also subdivided into five groups; and "in the wilderness" (15:61). These divisions are according to the basic geographical divisions of southern Palestine, from west to east: (1) the coastal plain, (2) the Shephelah, (3) the central mountain range, and (4) the wilderness or Jeshimon. They also indicate the geographical separation of the Negeb from the region to the north. While a number of the cities cannot be identified, it seems clear that the subdivisions also are grouped geographically.

The northern boundary (Josh. 15:5-11) extended from the north end of the Dead Sea (v. 5) to the Mediterranean (v. 11), with landmarks including the ascent of Adummim, En-shemesh, En-rogel (v. 7), the valley of Hinnom, Mt. Ephron, Mt. Seir, Mt. Jearim, Beth-shemesh, and Jabneel; it came "to an end at the sea" (vv. 9-11). This boundary line approximately follows the modern road from the Jordan River to Jerusalem, and from there follows the old back road (Nahal Rephaim to Beth-shemesh) and Wâdī Sorek to the coast. The cities listed in 15:33-36 are along the western part of this border, and the cities in 15:37-42 are in the Shephelah further to the south, while those in 15:45-47 are located in the coastal plain extending to Gaza and Wâdī ʿArîsh.

The southern boundary (Josh. 15:2-4) extended from the south end of the Dead Sea to Wâdī ʿArîsh (the brook of Egypt) at the modern town of El-arish, including Scorpion Pass (ascent of Akrabbim), Kadesh-barnea, and Azmon. It is interesting to note that the cities listed along the southern boundary do not extend far S of Beer-sheba. Those in 15:21-32 are mostly E, N, and NW of Beer-sheba; those in 15:48-51 are between Beer-sheba and Hebron; those in 15:55f. are SE of Hebron; those in 15:58f. are N of Hebron; those in 15:52-54 are in the vicinity of Hebron; and those in the Greek addition to v. 59 (LXX 15:60) are in the vicinity of Bethlehem. The MT of 15:60 seems to be misplaced. The towns in 15:61 are in the wilderness from the area near Jericho to En-gedi.

II. Physical Features.–The physical features of Palestine in general apply to the territory of Judah. On the west is the coastal plain, often sandy or swampy, with no natural harbors, and the highway from Egypt to the north was located several kilometers inland. Between the coastal plain and the central mountain range in Judah is the rich piedmont (the foothills to those who live in the plain, but in the biblical view, as seen from above, the "lowlands" or Shephelah). This region is cut by numerous wadis, is reasonably well watered in the rainy season, and produces much of the food supply for all of Judah. The western part of the Shephelah is less rugged and more adaptable for farming; the eastern part is better used for orchards. The central mountain range in Judah is stony — increasingly so as we travel toward the south. According to an Arab legend, when Allah created the world, He sent two angels with large sacks of stones for the entire world, but while they were flying over this region one of the bags burst. From Jerusalem to Hebron, the legend becomes very real. As a result there are no main highways, and modern roads have been constructed only with considerable engineering. Agriculture was more difficult, except for olives and figs, and the domestication of small cattle was largely limited to goats; flocks of sheep had to be pastured often at a great distance (cf. Jacob's flock at Dothan, about 100 km. [60 mi.] from his home).

The etesian winds, mostly from the west, water the western slopes of the central range, but the eastern side is barren. This is the wilderness of Judah. Just at the end of the rainy season there is a green fuzzlike growth on the hills, but this quickly burns off and the land — called the Jeshimon — is completely barren. Only the oases watered by springs at Jericho, ʿAin Feshkha, and En-gedi provide water for the few settlements named.

The central range lies at an elevation of approximately 900 m. (3000 ft.), with an elevation of 895 m. (2936 ft.) just S of Jerusalem (Jebel Mukabbir), 1020 m. (3346 ft.) at the highest point near Hebron, and 302 m. (994 ft.) near Beer-sheba. The range rises again in the Negeb to an elevation of 1033 m. (3389 ft.) near Kadesh-barnea.

The mountainous wilderness of Judah between Bethlehem and the Dead Sea (D. Baly)

III. Judah in the Time of the Monarchy.–At an indeterminate time, the tribal allotment of Simeon (Josh. 19:1-9), which had been part of the territory of Judah, was absorbed, and there is no further record of the tribe of Simeon. The allotment of Dan also was in the territory of Judah, since some of the cities that are named appear in both lists (cf. Josh. 19:40-46), but Dan relocated in the northern end of the Jordan rift (19:47).

Saul, the first king of the monarchy, was of the tribe of Benjamin and had his capital at Gibeah of Saul, a short distance N of Jerusalem. David, the second king, was of the tribe of Judah, and he established his capital first at Hebron and later at Jerusalem. Jebus had not been conquered by the Israelites, and a portion of what is now Jerusalem (and probably was at that time) belonged to Benjamin. David's conquest, however, brought at least the Jebusite city into the territory of Judah, and brought Judah into a position of dominance over all the tribes.

David's kingdom extended far beyond the borders of what is known as Palestine. But this was known as "Israel" and not as "Judah." Strong tribal feelings still existed, and — while the theory that history can be rewritten on the basis of Rachel- and Leah-tribes seems improbable — tribal rivalry, particularly that of Benjamin and Ephraim ("Rachel-tribes"), provided the basis for the eventual division of the monarchy. Solomon, by realizing David's intention to build a house for Yahweh, succeeded in establishing a cult center for all the tribes at Jerusalem. But when Rehoboam, Solomon's son, proved to be insensitive to the feelings of the northern tribes, Jeroboam became king of the northern kingdom, and established a rival cult center in Benjamin and his capital in Ephraim.

Solomon had developed the southern part of Judah, both with coppermining and with his fleet located at Ezion-geber. David had subjugated the Edomites (2 S. 8:13f., reading *ʾdm* for *ʾrm* with the LXX), and there had been widespread slaughter of Edomites (cf. 1 K. 11:15f.). Solomon caught some of the backlash of this attempted purge of the Edomite royal line (1 K. 11:14-22), but was able to maintain control of the routes to the copper mines and the seaport.

IV. Judah in the Time of the Divided Kingdom.–Strong kings of Judah were able to maintain the operations in the deep south, but there must have been constant trouble and much bad blood between the Edomites and the Judeans. Amos reflects something of this in his prophecy (Am. 1:11f.). In the days of Jehoshaphat (873-848 B.C.), a coalition of Edomites, Moabites, and Ammonites attempted to invade Judah and reached Hazazon-tamar, above En-gedi (2 Ch. 20:1f.), but they were repulsed. Edom rebelled against Judah in the days of Jehoram (853-841 B.C.; 2 Ch. 21:8-10). Amaziah (796-767 B.C.) invaded Edom and slaughtered many Edomites. Uzziah (790-740 B.C.) restored the seaport at Ezion-geber, but when Ahaz (735-716 B.C.) was faced by the Syro-Ephraimite coalition, Edom revolted again, this time with permanent success (2 Ch. 28:17; cf. 2 K. 16:6, emending *ʾrm* to read *ʾdm,* and deleting the name Rezin). Against this background one can easily understand why Edom rejoiced when Jerusalem fell to the Babylonians (Ps. 137:7), and the prophecy of Obadiah may seem like a bit of chauvinism. In these movements and countermovements involving Judah and Edom, it is not clear how much of the Negeb was occupied by either party, since few geographical details are given. At the very least, the route to the copper mines and the seaport was involved. From later history it would seem that possibly even more of the Negeb was occupied at times by Edom.

V. Judah in the Postexilic Period.–The northern tribes had been taken into captivity by the Assyrians and have become known as "the lost tribes of Israel." The sole surviving identifiable tribe was Judah, and when this was conquered by Nebuchadrezzar, the captives became known as "Jews" — a word that developed from "Judeans." The returning exiles were henceforth known as Jews, and the name Judah was loosely used to refer to the region they occupied.

At first, this region was exceedingly small — not much more than Jerusalem and the surrounding region. The names of some of the towns or regions are recorded in the details of the rebuilders of Jerusalem in Neh. 3. It is obvious that some of these locations were formerly part of the northern kingdom (Y. Aharoni and M. Avi-Yonah, *Macmillan Bible Atlas* [rev. ed. 1977], p. 109). Samaritans occupied the region to the north, formerly the tribal portions of Ephraim and Cisjordanian Manasseh, and Idumeans (Edomites) occupied the region to the south, including Hebron. As the Nabateans moved into the Negeb from the east, the Idumeans were pushed northward, with the result that the border was not far S of Beth-zur, about 25 km. (15 mi.) from Jerusalem.

Under the Hasmoneans (Maccabees), Judah reached its greatest extent, incorporating Samaria and Galilee to the north, the coastal plain (except Ashkelon) to the west, Idumea to the south, and all of Transjordan on the east. For the several military campaigns that stretched over about a century, and for the regions that were involved, *see* MACCABEES.

Under the Romans, Judah — now more properly "JUDEA" — was a rather indefinite term. Herod the Great was named king of Judea, meaning approximately the region included in the Maccabean kingdom at its greatest extent. On the other hand, when Archelaus was named ethnarch of Judea, the region included only Samaria, the pre-Maccabean Judah, and Idumea. The Roman procurators of Judea controlled approximately this same territory, but their gubernatorial seat was at Caesarea (Maritima), not at Jerusalem.

***Bibliography*.**–*HGHL*, pp. 123-319; F. M. Cross and G. E. Wright, *JBL*, 75 (1956), 202-226; Y. Aharoni, *PEQ*, 90 (1958), 27-31; *LBHG, passim; GB* (rev. ed. 1974), pp. 177-190.

W. S. LASOR

JUDAISM jo͞o'di-iz-əm, jo͞o'dā-iz-əm [Gk. *Ioudaismos*]. The cultus and culture of the Jewish people, including political and social as well as strictly religious aspects. This term indicates that Judah rather than Israel figured in the reconstruction of the nation's life after the Babylonian captivity.

The word begins to appear in the intertestamental literature. 2 Macc. 2:21 relates that some in the days of Judas Maccabeus "vied with one another in manful deeds for the religion of the Jews," i.e., Judaism. In those days, when many Jews were succumbing to hellenization, the word Judaism connoted a mixture of godliness and patriotism, exemplified by one elder who "resolutely risked body and life for Judaism" (3 Macc. 14:38).

The word occurs only twice in the NT. In Gal. 1:13f. Paul cites his persecution of the Church before his conversion as the most obvious proof of his former devotion to Judaism. Incidentally, the apostle's testimony certifies that the Judaism of his time included the traditions of the fathers — the interpretations of the Mosaic law designed to help the covenant people cope with the changes in their life situation.

For a comprehensive treatment of Judaism, *see* RELIGIONS OF THE BIBLICAL WORLD: JUDAISM.

E. F. HARRISON

JUDAIZING jo͞o'di-īz-ing [Heb. hithpael of *yāhaḏ*–'become a Jew' (Est. 8:17); Gk. *Ioudaizō* (Gal. 2:14)]. The process of adopting Jewish religious and cultural practices, whether by choice or through coercion. The concept rarely occurs in Scripture. The single OT reference is Est. 8:17. A royal edict, inspired by Haman, called for the destruction of the Jews throughout the Persian empire. A second edict, issued after Queen Esther interceded for her people, permitted the Jews to destroy their assailants. This edict instilled fear in many who had planned to participate in the massacre, and they "declared themselves Jews." The LXX adds that they were circumcised. Their motivation was fear; hence their new alignment was insincere and their Judaizing doubtless temporary.

The only NT use of the term is in Gal. 2:14, where the RSV translates it as "to live like Jews." Peter had been eating with the gentile believers at Antioch, but when certain men arrived from the Jerusalem church, he discontinued this practice. Probably he recalled the rebuff he had received at Jerusalem for eating with gentile believers at Caesarea (Acts 11:2f.). Strict Jews would not do such a thing, since Gentiles who did not observe certain dietary prohibitions (Lev. 11) were "unclean." Christ, however, had instituted a change (Mk. 7:19).

Paul reproached Peter publicly because by his withdrawal Peter was compelling Gentiles in the Antioch church to adopt a strict Jewish mode of life if they wished to have table fellowship with him. If the gentile brethren were regarded as ceremonially unclean, it was questionable if they could sit down together with Peter at the Lord's Supper. In fact, the possibility of two church bodies, one Jewish and the other Gentile, would have to be faced. No wonder Paul was disturbed and asserted that Peter was not acting according to the truth of the gospel.

Early in the 2nd cent. A.D. Ignatius warned that believing in Jesus Christ and practicing Judaism were contradictory (Ign. Magn. x.3). The context does not provide any details except perhaps the remark that Christians do not live for the Sabbath but for the Lord's Day (ix.1).

For the few additional postapostolic references, see G. W. H. Lampe, ed., *Patristic Greek Lexicon* (4th ed., 1976), p. 674.

E. F. HARRISON

JUDAS jo͞o'dəs [Gk. *Ioudas* < Heb. *yᵉhûḏâ*–'Judah'].

1. Judas Maccabeus, third son of Mattathias (1 Macc. 2:4). *See* MACCABEES.

2. Judas, son of Chalphi, a Jewish officer who supported Jonathan bravely at the battle of Hazor (1 Macc. 11:70; Josephus *Ant.* xiii.5.7 [161]).

3. A person of good position in Jerusalem at the time of the mission to Aristobulus (2 Macc. 1:10); he has been identified with Judas Maccabeus and also with an Essene prophet (Josephus *Ant.* xiii.11.2 [311]; *BJ* i.3.5 [78]).

4. Son of Simon the Maccabee and brother of John Hyrcanus (1 Macc. 16:2). He was wounded in the battle that he fought with his brother against Cendebeus (1 Macc. 16:1ff.; Josephus *Ant.* xiii.7.3 [227]), and was murdered by Ptolemy the usurper, his brother-in-law, at Dok (1 Macc. 16:11ff.).

J. HUTCHISON

5. JUDAS ISCARIOT.

6. One of the brothers of Jesus (Mt. 13:55; Mk. 6:3). *See* BROTHERS OF THE LORD; JUDE, EPISTLE OF II.

7. An apostle, "not Iscariot" (Jn. 14:22). He is generally identified with Lebbaeus or Thaddaeus (Mt. 10:3; Mk. 3:18), and is also called "Judas the son of James" (Lk. 6:16; Acts 1:13; AV "Judas the brother of James"). If the RSV is accepted as the correct rendering of Lk. 6:16 and Acts 1:13, this Judas cannot be identified with the Judas of Mk. 6:3, or the Judas of Mt. 13:55, the brother of Jesus, or the author of the Epistle of Jude, who was the brother of James and possibly the same person as the Judas in Mt. 13:55. The only incident recorded of this Judas of James is in Jn. 14:22, where during Christ's address to the disciples after the Last Supper he put the question, "Lord, how is it that you will manifest yourself to us, and not to the world?" C. M. KERR

8. Judas of Galilee [Gk. *ho Galilaios*]. Mentioned in Acts 5:37 as the leader of an insurrection occasioned by the census of QUIRINIUS in A.D. 7. It is said that he and those who obeyed him perished in that revolt. Josephus also repeatedly mentions Judas by this same name, "the Galilean," and speaks of his revolt (*Ant.* xvii.1.6 [23]; xx.5.2 [102]; *BJ* ii.8.1 [118]; vii.8.1 [253]), but in *Ant.* xvii.1.1 (4) he names him a Gaulanite of the city of Gamala. As Gamala was in Gaulanitis, not far from the eastern shore of the Sea of Galilee, it may be regarded as belonging to that province. The party of Judas seems to have been identified with the Zealots. *See* ZEALOT.

9. One with whom Paul lodged in Damascus, whose house was in "the street called Straight" (Acts 9:11). Nothing further is known of him. *See* STRAIGHT STREET.

10. JUDAS BARSABBAS. J. ORR

JUDAS BARSABBAS bär-sab'əs [Gk. *Ioudas Barasabbas*]. Judas was, with Silas, a delegate from the church in Jerusalem to the gentile Christians of Antioch, Syria, and Cilicia. They were appointed to convey the letter containing the decision of "the apostles and the elders, with the whole church" regarding the attitude to be taken by gentile Christians toward the Mosaic law, and also to explain "the same things by word of mouth" (Acts 15:22-27). They accompanied Paul and Barnabas to Antioch, and since they "were themselves prophets," i.e., preachers, they not only handed over the epistle but stayed some time in the city preaching and teaching (v. 32). They seem to have gone no farther than Antioch, for "they were sent off in peace by the brethren to those who had sent them," and it was Paul and Silas who some time later strengthened the churches in Syria and Cilicia (vv. 40f.).

According to v. 34, AV, Judas returned to Jerusalem without Silas, who remained at Antioch and afterward became Paul's companion (v. 40). The oldest MSS, however, omit v. 34, and it is therefore omitted from the RSV (but cf. mg.). It was probably a marginal note to explain v. 40, and in time it crept into the text. Judas and Silas are called "leading men among the brethren" (v. 22), probably elders and "prophets" (v. 32).

Barsabbas being a patronymic, Judas was probably the brother of Joseph Barsabbas. He cannot be identified with any other Judas, e.g., "Judas not Iscariot" (Jn. 14:22). We hear no more of Judas after his return to Jerusalem (Acts 15:22ff.). S. F. HUNTER

JUDAS, GOSPEL OF. *See* APOCRYPHAL GOSPELS V.C.

JUDAS ISCARIOT jo͞o'dəs is-kâr'ē-ət [Gk. *Ioudas Iskariōtēs*]. One of Jesus' twelve disciples.

I. Name
 A. Man of Kerioth
 B. Man of the Lie
 C. Dagger Bearer
II. The Story
 A. Difficulties
 B. Interpretation

I. Name.–Iscariot is probably not the name of Judas's father, who is called Simon (Jn. 6:71; 13:2, 26). Many suggestions have been given to explain the name Iscariot. The most plausible are (1) "man of Kerioth," (2) "liar" or "man of the lie," (3) "dyer," and (4) "dagger bearer."

A. Man of Kerioth. One widely accepted explanation for the name is that it identifies Judas's origin, "Kerioth" (*qrywt*). This suggestion is strengthened by some texts that have *apó Karyōtou,* "from Karyoth," instead of Gk. *Iskariōtēs* or *Iskarioth.* The Kerioth mentioned is sometimes identified with Kerioth-hezron, a location later called Hazor (Josh. 15:15). It is very unlikely, however, that a man would be identified by a name no longer given to his home town. There is also a Kerioth in Judah and another in Moab (Jer. 48:14, 41). Some NT scribes, at least, understood the name to indicate the place of Judas's origin — "from Karyoth." But this is not the only possibility. Luke describes Judas as one who was "*called* Iscariot" (Lk. 22:3), as if this were a nickname of some kind. Other disciples who were given special names like this are: Simon, called Peter (the Rock), Simon the Cananaean (*qn'n,* "zealot"; see Lk. 6:15), James and John, sons of thunder (Mk. 3:17), and Matthew, the tax collector (Mt. 10:2). Named for their fathers are: James the son of Alphaeus (Mt. 10:3), James and John, sons of Zebedee (Mt. 10:2), and Judas himself, son of Simon (Jn. 6:71; 13:2, 26). None of the other apostles is identified by his place of origin, so it seems more likely that Iscariot, also, is a descriptive name. As a descriptive noun, Iscariot could be derived either from *šqr,* "lie," "liar," or *sicarius,* "dagger bearer."

B. Man of the Lie. It is philologically possible for the name Iscariot to be derived from Aram. *šqr'* ("liar") with the prosthetic *aleph* added for ease of pronunciation, or from *'yš šqr'* ("man of the lie"). The "man of the lie," then, is a traitor belonging to a typology similar to that of Ahitophel (2 S. 16:15–17:2; Midr. *Gen. Rabbah* xxxviii.1; *Cant. Rabbah* iii.7.5), one of David's inner circle who betrayed him at night when David was weak and weary. Like Judas, Ahitophel hanged himself after his plot (2 S. 17:23; Mt. 27:3-5). *Sanhedrin* 69b relates Ahitophel to Ps. 55:23 (MT 24), "Bloody and deceitful men shall not live out half their days." The Targum to Ps. 55:3 (MT 4) translates "enemy" by "the liar" (*šqr'*).

Another OT passage important as background for the Judas story is Ps. 41, which is perhaps referred to in Acts 1:16-20. Ps. 41:9 (MT 10), "For my close friend whom I trusted, while eating my bread, raised up his heel [Heb. *'qb*] against me," is quoted in Jn. 13:18 in reference to Judas, with the possible double meaning intended for the Heb. *'āqēḇ* (heel) and *'āqaḇ* (betray) in an original Semitic language. One of the villains in the Dead Sea Scrolls was the *'yš kzb* ("man of the lie") (1QpHab 2:2; 5:11; CD 20:15).

Evidence for classifying Judas in traitor categories also points out the close dependence of the Judas narrative on the OT. The relationship between prophecy and fulfillment is clear in Acts 1:16: "Men, brethren, it was necessary that the scripture be fulfilled which the Holy Spirit prophesied through the mouth of David concerning Judas who became a guide to those who seized Jesus." Furthermore, the tradition that the money that Judas returned was used to buy the potter's field to bury strangers (Acts 1:18 says Judas bought it himself) is another echo of the Scriptures (Zec. 11:12f.; Jer. 18:2f.; 32:6-14). In fact, the potter's field and the temple treasury of Mt. 27:5-7 seem to echo the Hebrew and Syriac respectively of Zec. 11:13. The relationship of the Judas story to traitor typology, fulfillment of Scripture, and satanology prompts some scholars (see Gärtner, p. 67; Lüthi, pp. 61, 64, 106) to conclude that the NT perspective toward Judas is not historically but theologically motivated.

C. Dyer. A proposal by Ehrman, further supported and clarified by Arbeitman, argues that Iscariot means "dyer" and refers to an occupation of dyeing cloth. The proposal makes sense etymologically but gives no clue about the character of the person so named.

D. Dagger Bearer. Iscariot may also be a Semitic form of *sicarius,* to which the prosthetic *aleph,* giving the initial

JUDAS ISCARIOT

vowel sound, was added for ease of pronunciation. This interpretation is supported by some texts which give *Skariōtes, Skariōth,* Syr. *Sᵉkariôtā', Sᵉkariûtā',* etc.

A *sicarius* is a "dagger [*sica*] bearer" or "assassin." In Palestine, during the lifetime of Jesus, the *sicarii* were extremely zealous Jewish nationalists, who carried daggers under their cloaks so that they could take advantage of every opportunity to kill Romans or Roman collaborators. A member of the *sicarii* would not be completely out of place among the disciples of Jesus. He would have as comrades Simon the Zealot, James and John, sons of thunder who wanted to bid fire come down from heaven and consume the Samaritans (Lk. 9:51-54), and Peter, who had a sword at Gethsemane (Jn. 18:10). Peter is also called Simon Bar-Jonah (Mt. 16:17; Jn. 1:42). Bar-Jonah is quite possibly a transliteration of Heb. *biryôn* or *baryônā',* which means "outlaw" or "zealot" (see T.B. *Gittin* 56a-b; Eisler, pp. 100, 252f., 356, 358; Hengel, pp. 55-57).

II. The Story.–A. Difficulties. The only sources dealing with Judas Iscariot are the four Gospels, Acts, and possibly 1 Cor. 11:23. The information they provide is very sketchy and unfavorable. Judas is described as the one who betrayed Jesus (Mt. 10:4; 26:25; 27:3; Mk. 8:19; Lk. 6:15f.; Jn. 6:71; 12:4; 13:2; 18:2, 5). He was under the direction of Satan (Lk. 22:3; Jn. 13:2), and his greed prompted him to steal (Jn. 12:4-6) and betray Jesus for the payment involved (Mt. 26:14; Mk. 14:10f.). Probably the amount of historical truth contained in these reports is colored by the feeling the Church had for him. But even from the reports of those who resented him, some good points are also evident. Furthermore, the Fourth Gospel indicates that Judas was the treasurer for the group (Jn. 12:4-6; 13:29), an office not usually given to one who is known to be greedy and irresponsible.

The many difficulties in the account of Judas caused Guignebert to conclude that "if the episode is founded on fact, which is doubtful, it remains unintelligible to us" (p. 457). In addition to the theological motivation, Guignebert (pp. 453-55) points out: (1) Paul does not mention Judas, although he describes some of the events that took place "on the night when he [Jesus] was betrayed" (1 Cor. 11:23); (2) Paul also described the resurrection when Jesus "appeared to Cephas, then to the twelve" (1 Cor. 15:5), as if Judas were still part of the group (see also Brandon, pp. 48f.); (3) the sum of thirty pieces of silver that Judas is reported to have been paid for betraying Jesus is a very small amount to expect for an assignment of this nature, and it is very closely related to Zec. 11:12 (see I.B above).

Although John anticipates the betrayal (6:71; 12:4) and Luke tells of previous plans (Lk. 22:3-6), the event apparently came at the Last Supper as a surprise to all except Jesus (Mt. 26:20ff.; Mk. 14:17ff.). In collaboration with the priests, Judas led the troops at night to Gethsemane to find Jesus. At that time Judas kissed Jesus in order to identify Him for those who had come to take Him captive (Mt. 26:47ff.; Mk. 14:43ff.; Lk. 22:47ff.; Jn. 18:2ff.). After the crucifixion, Judas repented and hanged himself (Mt. 27:3-6), or fell headlong and "burst open in the middle" so his "bowels gushed out" (Acts 1:18). He was replaced in the apostolic circle by a certain Matthias, not otherwise known (Acts 1:25).

It is true that the story is brief and has certain legendary features strikingly similar to OT Scripture, but it is unlikely that the whole story is a fabrication. It would have served no advantageous purpose for Christians to have invented a story that their Master had a betrayer in His innermost circle. Paul's reference to the betrayal (1 Cor. 11:23) may also indicate an early tradition about Judas (see Jeremias, pp. 66f., esp. n. 8). Hence its report in NT documents is evidently based on factual information.

B. Interpretation. The activity of Judas should be seen in comparison with other events that took place before, during, and after the crucifixion. The disciples had expected Jesus to restore the kingdom to Israel (Lk. 24:24; Acts 1:6). Peter rebuked Jesus when He suggested that He would go up to Jerusalem to be killed (Mt. 16:21-23). James and John had asked for official positions when Jesus became king (Mt. 20:20-24; Mk. 10:35-40). The disciples had quarreled about their respective ranks and positions before the Last Supper (Lk. 22:24-26). Jesus had promised that those who left all to follow Him would be repaid amply in terms of material goods in this life (Mt. 19:28f.; Mk. 10:28-30; see also Mt. 6:33). Evidently the disciples had expected Jesus to contest the authority of the Romans when He went up to the feast at Jerusalem, just as many aspiring messianic kings had done before Him. Had He

Judas is thought to have received Tyrian shekels among his "pieces of silver" (G. L. Archer; picture W. S. LaSor)

Akeldama, the traditional site of Judas's suicide (W. S. LaSor)

led a military revolution, there were those, like Peter, who would have been willing to die with Him in battle (Mt. 26:33; Mk. 14:29-31; Lk. 22:33f.). It was only after it became clear that Jesus was not going to lead an insurrection that Peter denied Jesus (Mt. 26:69-75; Mk. 14:66-72; Lk. 22:54-62) and Judas betrayed Jesus to the chief priests.

Judas's betrayal may have been done out of genuine patriotic devotion. According to this view, Judas, as a *sicarius,* was ready to employ military strength to overthrow Rome. When he learned that Jesus was not going to lead a military revolt, he considered Jesus to be a fifth columnist or saboteur of some sort who was weakening the military strength of Israel by recruiting some of the nation's leaders and then refusing to employ them in a military rebellion. Although he had responded favorably to Jesus' teaching, he could not follow a teacher who was not prepared to lead a war. So he parted company with Jesus, and as a disillusioned disciple, he retaliated against Jesus by turning Him over to the proper authorities — not so much because he loved money but because he loved his country and thought Jesus was delaying the movement that would free Palestine from the Romans. Another interpretation is that Judas was convinced that Jesus was the Messiah, but Judas was impatient. He acted as he did, therefore, in an attempt to force Jesus to take the stand Judas anticipated. Such attempts at historical understanding are, of course, tentative. It is not possible to trace with certainty the detailed course of events, nor to distinguish with confidence the background and motivation of Judas. The NT itself offers us an important theological interpretation, and it is in terms of this interpretation that our assessment of Judas is properly to be made.

Bibliography.–Y. Arbeitman, *JBL,* 99 (1980), 122-24; S. G. F. Brandon, *The Fall of Jerusalem and the Christian Church* (1951), 42f.; O. Cullmann, *The State in the NT* (Eng. tr. 1966); A. Ehrman, *JBL,* 97 (1978), 572f.; R. Eisler, *The Messiah Jesus and John the Baptist* (Eng. tr. 1931); *BC,* V, 22-30; B. Gärtner, *Svensk Exegetisk Årsbok,* 21-24 (1956-1959), 50-81; C. Guignebert, *Jesus* (Eng. tr. 1935), pp. 450-57; D. Haugg, *Judas Iskarioth in den NT Berichten* (1930); M. Hengel, *Die Zeloten* (1961); J. Jeremias, *The Eucharistic Words of Jesus* (Eng. tr. 1955); *Jew. Enc., s.v.*; K. Lüthi, *Judas Iskarioth* (1955); C. C. Torrey, *HTR,* 36 (1943), 51-62.

G. W. BUCHANAN

JUDE jo͞od [Gk. *Ioudas*]. A man usually said to be a brother of Jesus and author of the Epistle of Jude. *See* JUDE, EPISTLE OF.

JUDE, EPISTLE OF. The Epistle of Jude belongs in popular parlance to the classification of the General Epistles. Strictly speaking this is a misnomer, for the contents of the Epistle reflect a specific circle of readers. The author states that he switched themes in view of the perils confronting his readers. Instead of writing on "The Faith of our Fathers," he issues a broadside on "Avoiding Dangerous Heretics."

I. Contents
II. Author and Date
III. Jude and 2 Peter
IV. Heretics
V. Apocalyptic Sources
VI. Canonical History

I. Contents.–A demoralizing faction (vv. 4, 12) has slipped into the congregations that come under the writer's concern (v. 4). They are arrogant in their theological pretensions, boast of visions, and revile angelic beings (vv. 8-10); they impose on the credulity of the unsuspecting and create divisions by their stratification of the church membership (vv. 16, 19); they are self-centered, utilize religion as a spur to their own lusts (vv. 4, 8, 15f.), and leave in their wake desolate disappointment (v. 12).

To sharpen the picture of their deadly character, the writer draws heavily on two sets, three each, of OT examples. In the first group (vv. 5-7) he places (1) the murmuring Israelites, who were left to die in the wilderness (Nu. 14); (2) the angels who mingled with the daughters of men and produced a race of giants (Gen. 6:1-4; cf. 1 En. 10:4ff.); (3) Sodom and Gomorrah (Gen. 19). In the second group (v. 11) he refers to (1) Cain, according to late Jewish tradition a type of the sensualist and skeptic who has little regard for higher things; (2) Balaam, who misled the Israelites into idolatry and adultery (Nu. 25:1ff.; 31:16; cf. Rev. 2:14), and who in rabbinic tradition is the father of libertinists, traitors, and false teachers; the emphasis on Balaam's thirst for gain suggests the greed of the false teachers; (3) Korah, the rebel who challenged Moses' authority (Nu. 16), a type of the false teachers who refuse to recognize the authority of the duly constituted leaders in the congregations.

The presence of these false teachers, says Jude, should occasion no surprise. In line with the later Jewish view that everything that happens to Israel has been anticipated long before by God (cf. Ps. 56:8 [MT 9] and Isa. 37:26), the writer affirms that the judgment of these wicked deceivers has been duly prophesied (v. 4), with an apparent allusion to pseudepigraphical passages such as 1 En. 48 and 108. God's people are not to panic, but to cling to the faith as once delivered by the apostles to the saints (vv. 4, 17, 20). In contrast to the explicit statement of v. 4 regarding a written prophecy, v. 18 takes cognizance of a unanimous oral tradition stemming from the apostolic circle concerning the coming of false teachers (for similar statements see Acts 20:29f.; 1 Tim. 4:1-3; 2 Tim. 3:1-5; 2 Pet. 3:3). Against this opposition the Christians are to stress (1) praying in the Spirit (cf. Rom. 8:15f.; Eph. 6:18); (2) keeping themselves in the love of God, presumably a directive to ponder the prior love of God (cf. Rom. 5:8), but also an encouragement to avoid immorality, which separates Christians from this love; (3) awaiting the coming of the Lord Jesus Christ. The question of the Christian's personal attitude toward the victims of the false teachers is obscured by corruptions in the text of vv. 22f., which leave unclear whether two (AV and NEB) or three (RSV) groups are meant. If the triad is accepted, the writer is saying that the Christians are to (1) show mercy to those who are in doubt (not as AV renders, "making a difference"); (2) snatch others from the brink of disaster (cf. Am. 4:11; Zec. 3:2), and (3) avoid completely those who have fallen irrevocably under the spell of the false teachers (the second part of v. 23 makes little sense as it stands, and there is much to be said for the view that a word suggesting excommunication is called for; cf. 1 Cor. 5:5).

The doxology (vv. 24f.) underscores the theme notes of the Epistle. God alone can bring believers safely through their hazardous environment. He is their Savior through Jesus Christ. The libertinistic false teachers reject Christ's authority, but for the Christian He is Lord, now and forever.

II. Author and Date.–The writer of this tract lays such emphasis on the age of the apostles as a matter of history (vv. 3, 17) that it is difficult to associate him with the apostle Judas mentioned in Lk. 6:16; Acts 1:13 (cf. Jn. 14:22), even if we were to render in these passages "Judas brother of James," an unlikely translation. He calls himself simply "Jude, slave of Jesus Christ" and "brother of James." The latter designation appears to echo Mk. 6:3, where Jesus is called the "brother" of James and Jude. Of the life of this Jude we know little except for a hint in Eusebius (*HE* iii.19, 20.1-7; 32.5f.), who records an interesting tradition from Hegesippus regarding two grandsons of Jude. According to the account, Domitian feared an insurrection among the Jews and ordered all descendants of David to be put to death. Informers dragged Jude's grandsons before the emperor's tribunal, but they were released after the emperor noted their calloused hands and peaceful intentions. Thereafter they became leaders in the Church and died during Trajan's reign.

This story has complicated inquiry into the authorship of the tract, because it seems to suggest that Jude the grandfather must have died two to three decades before the trial took place, since the grandsons, now grown men, were the only surviving members of the family. But the argument is not conclusive, since we know next to nothing concerning the details of Jude's life and he may well have outlived his own son. If that is the case, the references to the apostolic era as a past phenomenon (v. 17) and to the "most holy faith" (v. 20) "once and for all delivered" (v. 3) would come naturally from Jude's pen, if he were writing in the closing years of his life, perhaps A.D. 70-80. On the other hand, if the words *adelphós dé Iakōbou* are a gloss, one cannot ignore the possibility that an otherwise unknown Jude held in esteem among a circumscribed group of Christians is to be held responsible for this little document. The recipients, as Streeter pointed out, would experience no difficulty in recognizing the writer of a letter sent by courier. The gloss, then, which must have been added very early, inasmuch as all MSS include it, represents either a scribe's honest mistake in identification or propaganda for canonical authority by associating the letter with a venerable link between the apostolic age and the later generations of Christians. A date anywhere in the last quarter of the 1st cent. or first decades of the 2nd cent. is feasible under this hypothesis.

Another suggestion is that a pseudonymous writer has put on the mask of Jude the Lord's brother. The words "brother of James," if they are his, would preclude any mistake regarding the writer's assumed role. If the words were added later, they suggest that the Epistle was known to be pseudonymous. The chief objection against pseudonymous authorship is the alleged obscurity of Jude. It should be noted, however, that our knowledge of Jude's activity in the Church, as was observed earlier, is extremely fragmentary, and that the little evidence we do possess in the accounts previously cited from Eusebius suggests that the family of Jude was significant in some Christian circles. Again, a pseudonymous writer who wished to call his generation back to their doctrinal senses might have utilized Jude's relative obscurity, if such it was, precisely because he required someone who was not himself an eminent apostolic voice but yet enjoyed sufficient prestige to mediate that authority to the writer's own generation. Dominical associations, together with the guarantee of "James," champion of orthodoxy, would have appeared to the author sufficient to achieve his purpose. Those who think the indications of a late date are a serious obstacle to any view that dates the letter earlier than the last decade of the 1st cent. find the hypothesis of pseudonymous authorship attractive. The *terminus ad quem* depends in some degree on the view one takes of the relation between Jude and 2 Peter.

III. Jude and 2 Peter.–Dependence of 2 Peter on Jude is suggested by the following considerations: (1) Jude is intelligible without 2 Peter, but the reader of 2 Peter requires Jude as a commentary. Thus, a knowledge of Jude 9 is presupposed by the writer of 2 Pet. 2:11, which apart from its parallel in Jude would be one of the most enigmatic sentences in the NT. Nor is the obscurity here in 2 Peter due to its alleged "prophetic character," for the story concerning Michael and the devil was current at the time of both writers. Note also how 2 Pet. 2:1 utilizes Jude 5 with its references to the "people of Israel," but eliminates the judgment pronounced on them in the wilderness; 2 Pet. 2:4 presupposed acquaintance with Jude 6; *hoútoi dé* comes rather abruptly in 2 Pet. 2:12, but fits comfortably in Jude 10; and *hymōn* (2 Pet. 3:2) is a clumsy underscoring of Jude 17.

(2) Jude's style is strikingly vigorous and clear compared with the more labored and cloudy rhetoric of 2 Peter (compare Jude 4 with 2 Pet. 2:3 and Jude 7 with 2 Pet. 2:4).

(3) It is more likely that the writer of 2 Peter would include Jude in his document than that Jude should merely reproduce in its essentials 2 Pet. 2. Moreover, if Jude had wished to accent the fulfillment of Petrine prophecy we would expect him to reproduce Peter's wording more precisely. It is often asserted in defense of the priority of 2 Peter that it would have been quite natural for Jude to copy from 2 Peter since his document indicates free use of other sources. Yet, while we do not have verbal correspondence with 2 Peter, Jude's use of apocalyptic literature is in the main much freer and more allusive than his alleged use of 2 Peter. It has also been stated that the picture painted in Jude is much darker and more sinister than in 2 Peter, but compare 2 Pet. 2:2f. with Jude 4 and the examples in 2 Pet. 2:6-8 with Jude 7, and note 2 Pet. 2:14. In fact, the picture in 2 Peter is vitriolically etched in comparison with the less bombastic prose of Jude.

Defenders of the priority of 2 Peter also stress the prophetic character of the letter, and since Jude makes allusion to "prescribed" heretics (v. 4) it is assumed that 2 Peter is the source. It is true that 2 Pet. 3:3, 17 look to the future, but 2:12-22 (esp. vv. 15, 17) assert that the heretics are already present. Moreover, it is not clear why Jude fails to make use of the reference to the scoffers mentioned in 2 Pet. 3, who must certainly have multiplied at the alleged later period. As will be seen below, Jude frequently refers to apocalyptic writings. These documents are filled with predictions of judgment for the wicked, and it is probably to these writings that Jude 4 refers.

If Jude is dependent on 2 Peter, and if 2 Peter, as most scholars hold, is to be assigned to the end of the 1st cent., a date somewhat later for Jude would take account of the survivors of the generations that had heard the apostles (v. 17).

IV. Heretics.–Identification of the heretics mentioned in the Epistle is a question of great importance for the historian of the early Christian era. The precise relationship of the heretics to the Christian community is not clearly spelled out, but they appear to have gained illegal admittance into the Christian community (v. 4) by ingratiating themselves with flattery and bombastic pretensions (v. 16). Ostensibly they identify themselves with the Christians in their most intimate gathering, the agape (v. 12), only to create divisions (v. 19) and confusion (v. 22). They refuse to accept direction, preferring to "shepherd themselves" (v. 12). They claim special visions, and speak disparagingly of angelic powers (vv. 8-10), apparently with a view to demonstrating their superior "spiritual" status. Their licentiousness (vv. 10, 16, 18), an evident outgrowth of this assumed superiority, only proves, however, that they are deficient in "spirit" (v. 19). Since Gnosticism was in the air also during the time when 1 Corinthians and Colossians were written, it would be an egregious blunder to locate the heretics mentioned by Irenaeus or other patristic writers in the generalized invectives hurled by Jude. The nature of the cosmological speculations and the christological viewpoints of Jude's heretics cannot be determined with any degree of certainty. The picture presented here rather reflects the common conflict between orthodoxy and heresy that we find depicted also in the Johannine letters, the Pastorals, and 2 Peter, and that ultimately led to solidification of the role of the bishop as theological arbiter.

V. Apocalyptic Sources.–The comparatively large percentage of references to noncanonical literature of an apocalyptic nature calls for special comment. The Ethiopic book of Enoch is one of the author's favorites. Reference has already been made to his use of 1 En. 48 and 108 (v. 4). The most obvious excerpt is found in vv. 14f., which parallels verbatim two-thirds of the Greek wording as found in the Egyptian MS discovered 1886/87 in Akhmim. The introductory phrase, "Enoch, the seventh from Adam" appears in 1 En. 60:8, "My grandfather was taken up, the seventh from Adam." 1 En. 10:4-20; 12:4f.; 54:1-5, etc., find a clear echo in the reference to the arrogant angels who mingled with the daughters of men (Jude 6). The story is reminiscent of Gen. 6:1-4, and the theme of judgment is sounded in Isa. 24:21f., "On that day the Lord will punish the host of heaven, in heaven. . . . They will be gathered together as prisoners in a pit; they will be shut up in a prison, and after many days they will be punished." From a similar reference to the fallen angels Jude derives his description of the "wandering stars, to whom is reserved the blackness of darkness forever" (Jude 13; cf. 1 En. 18:11–19:3). Augustine (*Civ. Dei* xv.23) and Chrysostom (*Hom. 22 in Gen.*) represent the few patristic voices who protest against this interpretation of Gen. 6:1-4 in Enoch, complaining that it makes of Moses' account a "baseless fable."

We have it on the authority of Clement of Alexandria, Origen, and Didymus that Jude employed for v. 9 a second apocryphal writing, the Assumption of Moses. The known fragments of this apocryphal writing do not include the account, but Jude 12-14 appear to echo Asm. Mos. 7, and Jude 16 has striking parallels to Asm. Mos. 5:5, "flatterers," and 7:9, "boastful."

VI. Canonical History.–Jude's heavy use of apocryphal writings retarded its canonical status in some quarters, but its relation to 2 Peter indicates the high prestige it enjoyed elsewhere. Did. 2:7 appears to echo Jude 22; and the distinctive greeting of Jude, as compared with Pauline letters, finds repetition in Polycarp's Epistle to the Philippians and the Martyrdom of Polycarp. The Muratorian Canon (A.D. 170-190) reflects a secure status in Rome: "Epistola sane Iudae et superscripti Iohannis duae in catholicis habentur" ("Further an epistle of Jude and two with the title [or: two of the above mentioned] John are accepted in the catholic Church" [H-S, I, 44f.]). In Alexandria, Clement refers to it in his *Paedagogus, Stromateis,* and *Hypotyposes.* Tertullian indicates that Carthage is familiar with the document, and the letter exists in the Old Latin version. After 200 the letter declined in importance, especially in Africa; and its absence in the Syriac canon marks its insecure status in some Eastern quarters. Eusebius, with some perplexity of terminology, observes that it is considered "spurious" (Gk. *notheúō*) by some and "disputed" (*antilégō*) by others (*HE* ii.23.25; 25.3; vi.13.6; 14.1). In the 4th cent. Jude overcame most of its opposition, and was listed without qualification in Athanasius's festal letter, A.D. 367.

See also PETER, SECOND EPISTLE OF.

Bibliography.–Comms. by C. Bigg (*ICC,* 2nd ed. 1902); M. R. James (*CGT,* 1912); J. N. D. Kelly (*HNTC,* 1969); R. Knopf (1912); A. R. C. Leaney (*CBC,* 1967); J. B. Mayor (1907; repr. 1979; *Expos. G.T.,* V); J. Moffatt (*MNTC,* 1947); K. H. Schelkle (*HTK,* 1964); J. Schneider (*NTD,* 1961); E. M. Sidebottom (*New Century Bible,* 1967); J. Wand (*WC,* 1934); J. Windisch and H. Preisker (*HNT,* 3rd ed. 1951); G. Wohlenberg (*KZNT,* 3rd ed. 1923).

G. H. Boobyer, *NTS,* 5 (1958/59), 45-47; E. Käsemann, *ZTK,* 49 (1952), 272-296; J. B. Mayor, *JTS,* 6 (1904/05), 569-577, and cf. 391-411; C. D. Osburn, *ZNW,* 63 (1972), 139-144; B. Reicke, *Diakonie Festfreude und Zelos in Verbindung mit der altchristlichen Agapenfeier* (1951), pp. 352-367; D. J. Rowston, *NTS,* 21 (1974/75), 554-563; B. H. Streeter, *The Primitive Church* (1929), pp. 183-86; H. Werdermann, *Die Irrlehrer des Judas- und 2 Petrusbriefes* (1913).

F. W. DANKER

JUDEA jōō-dē'ə [Gk. *Ioudaia,* for *ioudaía gē* or *ioudaía chōra,* "Judean land/region"]; AV, NEB, JUDAEA, JUDAH. The Greek and Roman equivalent of "Judah." Since the territory of Judah was approximately all that remained of the northern and southern kingdoms at the time of the Babylonian Exile, the exiles, particularly those who returned, were called "Judeans," shortened to "Jews," hence the name of the postexilic province (cf. Heb. *yehûḏâ,* Ezr. 9:9).

The Greek term is found first in Tob. 1:18, "any who came fleeing from the land of Judea" (*ek tḗs Ioudaias*), referring to the time of Sennacherib, but the story is from the Babylonian or the Persian period, and the Greek is probably a translation from Hebrew, in the light of Qumrân evidence. For the extent of Judea = Judah, *see* JUDAH, TERRITORY OF V. There is evidence, however, of a larger Judea.

Strabo (*Geog.* xvi.2.21), in discussing the term "Coelesyria," defines Judea as "the interior above [i.e., inland from] Phoenicia, as far as the Arabians, between Gaza and Antilibanus," which would include Samaria and Galilee as well as Judah. Luke seems to use the term with approximately the same meaning (Lk. 4:44, where some MSS have "Galilee"; 23:5 ["throughout all Judea, from Galilee even to this place," where "from" must be inclusive and not exclusive]; Acts 2:9; 10:37 [cf. Lk. 23:5]; etc.). In Acts 1:8, however, "Judea" is distinguished from "Samaria," possibly indicating that Luke was following a tradition of the *ipsissima verba* of Jesus. Matthew (4:25), Mark (1:5), and John (4:3) appear to use "Judea" in the more restrictive sense.

Josephus (*BJ* iii.3.5 [51-58]) places the northern border of Judea at Anuath Borcaeus, identified as Berkit, 14 km. (9 mi.) S of Shechem, therefore approximately the same as the northern border of the territory of Judah. The southern border he locates at "a village on the Arabian frontier, which the local Jews call Iardan." This has been identified as Arad, 26 km. (16 mi.) S of Hebron. The width is described as "from the river Jordan to Joppa." Jerusalem is located "at its very center" — which is geographically not accurate and therefore probably to be

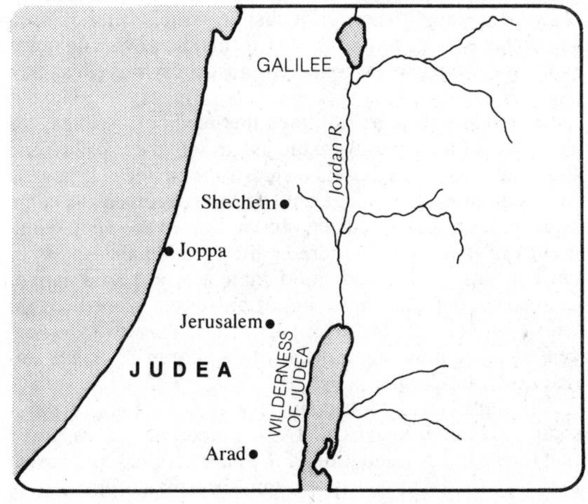

interpreted figuratively (cf. Jub. 8:19; T.B. *Sanhedrin* 37a). Josephus, however, continues, "[Judea] slopes down towards the coast on a ridge extending as far as Ptolemais" (§ 53), and he divides the land into "eleven districts." He names nine (including Pella) and as an afterthought says, "To these must be added Jamnia and Joppa . . . and lastly the territories of Gamala, Gaulanitis, Batanea, and Trachonitis, which form, moreover, part of Agrippa's kingdom" (§§ 55f.). Unless he has lost his train of thought, it would appear that Josephus, too, has a larger Judea, extending even beyond Galilee, equivalent to the Roman province of Judea after A.D. 44.

The wilderness of Judea (Mt. 3:1; cf. Mk. 1:4; Lk. 3:2), where John the Baptist began his preaching ministry, is probably the wilderness of Judah, i.e., the barren land between the central mountain range and the Dead Sea, approximately between the limits of Jerusalem and Hebron. For a discussion of the theory that John was raised at Qumrân, see W. S. LaSor, *The Dead Sea Scrolls and the NT* (1972), pp. 142-153. W. S. LASOR

JUDGE [Heb. *šōpēṭ* (Gen. 18:25; 19:9; Ex. 2:14; etc.), *pālîl* (Ex. 21:22; Dt. 32:31; Job 31:11), *p^e^lîlî* (Job 31:28), *dayyān* (1 S. 24:15 [MT 16]); Aram. *dînāyē'* (Ezr. 4:9), *dayyān* (Ezr. 7:25); Gk. *kritḗs, dikastḗs, krínō*]; AV also DINAITES (Ezr. 4:9); NEB also "assessment" (Ex. 21:22), "mere fools" (Dt. 32:31), "law" (Job 31:11, 28). On Ezr. 4:9, *see* DINAITES. The meaning of *pālîl* and *p^e^lîlî* is obscure (see *THAT,* II, *s.v. pll* [H.-P. Stähli]); in Dt. 32:31 the NEB apparently emends Heb. *p^e^lîlîm* to *'^e^lîlîm,* "fools," on the basis of LXX *anoētai,* "fools" (see the comms.). By far the most common Hebrew term for "judge" is *šōpēṭ,* a participle of the verb *šāpaṭ* meaning "decide, make a judgment." It is used for persons appointed to decide matters of law or justice, for God, and for the leaders of Israel in times of need during the premonarchial period. The meanings of the words built on the root *dyn,* as used in the OT, are generally the same as those of *šōpēṭ,* although only *dyn* seems to have had specifically forensic or juridical associations in its earliest known forms. See *TDOT,* III, *s.v.* "dîn" (Hamp, Botterweck).

The most common term in the NT is Gk. *kritḗs,* which, like Heb. *šōpēṭ,* can refer to the "judges" of premonarchial Israel (Acts 13:20) and to God (He. 12:23; Jas. 4:12; 5:9; cf. also 2 Tim. 4:8; Acts 10:42), as well as to officials who decide cases of law (e.g., Mt. 5:25 par. Lk. 12:58). John (8:50; 12:48) and Paul (Rom. 2:1) use forms of the related verb *krínō.* These words originally have to do with making a decision. The term used in Acts 7:27, 35 (OT quotation); Lk. 12:24 var., *dikastḗs,* is based on a root that is more definitely related to rendering justice. Precise understanding of these terms and of the OT terms, however, depends more on their use in context than on etymologies. *See also* JUDGING.

In the early patriarchal times the heads of families and the elders of the tribes were the judges (cf. Gen. 38:24), and their authority was based on custom. In the wilderness Moses alone was the judge until Jethro suggested a scheme of devolution. On his advice Moses divided the people into groups of thousands, hundreds, fifties, and tens, and over each group a wise and good man was set as a judge. Thereafter only the most important cases were brought before Moses (Ex. 18:13-26; Dt. 1:9-17). This arrangement ceased to be practicable when the children of Israel settled down in Canaan.

Although David took counsel with the heads of thousands and hundreds (1 Ch. 13:1), it need not be assumed that this was a continuation of the plan adopted by Moses. Probably the local courts were not organized till the time of David. In the days of the judges justice was administered by those who had risen by wisdom or valor to that rank (Jgs. 4:5; *see* JUDGES, BOOK OF). An organized circuit court was established by Samuel, who judged cases himself, and also made his sons judges (1 S. 7:16; 8:1). After the monarchy was instituted, the king tried all cases, when requested to do so by the wronged person, in the palace gate (1 K. 7:7; Prov. 20:8). There was no public prosecutor (2 S. 14:4; 15:2-6; 1 Ch. 18:14; 1 K. 3:16; 2 K. 15:5). Under David and Solomon there were probably local courts (1 Ch. 23:4; 26:29). Jehoshaphat organized a high court of justice (2 Ch. 19:8). The prophets often complained bitterly that the purity of justice was corrupted by bribery and false witness (Isa. 1:23; 5:23; 10:1; Am. 5:12; 6:12; Mic. 3:11; 7:3; Prov. 6:19; 12:17; 18:5). Even kings sometimes pronounced unjust sentences, especially in criminal cases (1 S. 22:6-19; 1 K. 22:26; 2 K. 21:16; Jer. 36:26). An evil king could also bend local courts to do his will, as may be gathered from the case of Naboth's vineyard (1 K. 21:1-13).

The first duty of a judge was to execute absolute justice, showing the same impartiality to rich and poor, to Jew and foreigner. He was forbidden to accept bribes or to wrest the judgment of the poor (Ex. 23:6-8; Dt. 16:19). He must not let himself be swayed by popular opinion, or unduly favor the poor (Ex. 23:2f.).

The court was open to the public (Ex. 18:13; Ruth 4:1f.). Each party presented his view of the case to the judge (Dt. 1:16; 25:1). Possibly the accused appeared in court clad in mourning (Zec. 3:3). The accuser stood on the right hand of the accused (Zec. 3:1; Ps. 109:6). Sentence was pronounced after the hearing of the case, and the judgment was carried out (Josh. 7:24f.). The only evidence considered by the court was that given by the witnesses. In criminal cases, not fewer than two witnesses were necessary (Nu. 35:30; Dt. 17:6; 19:15; cf. Mt. 18:16; 2 Cor. 13:1; 1 Tim. 5:19). In cases other than criminal the OATH was applied (Ex. 22:11; cf. He. 6:16). The lot was sometimes used (Josh. 7:14-18), especially in private disputes (Prov. 18:18), but this was exceptional. When the law was not quite definite, recourse was made to the divine oracle (Lev. 24:12; Nu. 15:34). P. LEVERTOFF

JUDGES, BOOK OF [Heb. *šōp^e^ṭîm*; Gk. *kritai*].

I. Title
II. Place in the Canon
III. Contents
IV. Chronological Problems
V. Sources and Authorship
VI. Relation to Other Biblical Books
VII. Text
VIII. Literary Importance
IX. Religious Message

I. Title.–The title is derived from the framework of the book, e.g., 2:17-19; 11:27. Even the verbal use of the root *špṭ* is, according to some scholars, mainly encountered in the framework (namely, 3:10; 4:4; 10:2f.; 11:27; 12:7-9, 11, 13f.; 15:20; 16:31). There is, however, doubt whether 4:4 should be placed in the framework. It is also uncertain whether the parts with chronological information should be regarded as framework. In spite of this, certain scholars regard the title as late and hold the opinion that the word *šōpēṭ* does not cover the activities of especially the so-called major judges. Oscar Grether proposed a better title for this group of judges, namely, *môšî(a)'*, "deliverer." This is unnecessary in light of the meaning of *šāpaṭ,* as is illustrated by tablets discovered at Ugarit and Mari. From this material it is clear that the root can mean "to govern" as well as "to judge." The title can thus be applied not only to the minor judges, but also to the major military leaders. It is also unnecessary to regard the minor judges as judicial sages only. The short notes in the book of Judges on the minor judges are too fragmentary to base far-reaching conclusions on them. Even so, the title *šōpēṭ* covers their activities as well as those of the major group. Since this stem was used in early Northwest Semitic as a title, we may assume that the title of this book is probably very old, and may even go back to the time of the judges.

II. Place in the Canon.–In the English Bible Judges is placed after Joshua as the seventh book of the OT. It takes the same place in the Hebrew Bible, where it is placed as the second book of the Former Prophets, which consist of Joshua, Judges, Samuel, and Kings; the Latter Prophets consist of Isaiah, Jeremiah, Ezekiel, and the Twelve Minor Prophets. The Greek Bible has a different division. Other historical books like Chronicles, Ezra, Nehemiah, etc., follow Kings, while one of the Megilloth, Ruth, is placed after Judges. This division is also followed by modern translations.

III. Contents.–*A. First Introduction (1:1–2:5).* These verses recapitulate the events of the Conquest of western Palestine. Here, however, it is emphasized that Israel did not succeed in expelling the enemy from the country (1:27-36), a failure regarded as a breach of promise and a cause of permanent weakness (2:1-3). The most common opinion among scholars is that this part of Judges stands in contrast to the narrative of the conquest of Palestine in Joshua. The difference is that the stories in Joshua refer to extermination and to the successive wars of an organized national army, while in Judges the impression is created that the country was taken by separate wars and individual tribes.

Various solutions are proposed to solve this problem. The best is that of Y. Kaufmann, who points out that in Josh. 1–11 the Hebrews fought in order to destroy and exterminate, not to occupy by immediate settlement. After certain cities were demolished and the central Canaanite forces were destroyed, the tribes went back to their allotted territories to clear the enemy from them. This is described in Jgs. 1.

B. Second Introduction (2:6–3:6). Reference is made to the apostasy of Israel and the misfortunes that befell them. They were chastised by foreign nations. If they repent and turn to Yahweh, He will save them from their oppressors. It is, in other words, a typical Deuteronomic trend.

C. General History of the Judges (3:7–16:31). A longer history is given of some of the judges, such as Deborah and Barak, Gideon, Jephthah, and Samson, and short notes on others such as Shamgar, Tola, Jair, Ibzan, Elon, and Abdon. There are also longer notes on Othniel and Ehud. In the history of Gideon is also incorporated a long chapter on the history of Abimelech and the failure of his kingship. The events are described as follows:

1. Othniel (3:7-11). He delivered Israel from the hand of the enigmatic Cushan-rishathaim.

2. Ehud (3:12-30). This Benjaminite delivered Israel from servitude to Moab by killing Eglon their king.

3. Shamgar (3:31). A very brief note on him does not even mention that he was a judge or of Israelite stock. According to some, the addition to his name "ben Anath" may suggest that he was a Canaanite, or that he was from the nomadic group of the Haneans, well known from the Mari Letters. He fought against the Philistines, which must have taken place at the beginning of the southern migration of the sea-peoples (cf. also 5:6, which suggests a very old date for the activity of Shamgar).

4. Deborah and Barak (4–5). Chapter 4 is written in prose and ch. 5 in verse. Scholars are unanimous that the so-called Song of Deborah is one of the oldest pieces of OT poetry, to be dated *ca.* 1125 B.C. A common opinion, based on certain discrepancies between ch. 4 and ch. 5, is that ch. 4 is much later. These differences exist because ch. 4 was written much later than ch. 5 and used a different strand of tradition. If the poetical form of ch. 5 is taken into consideration it must be conceded that the problem is not insoluble. Albright points out that songs of victory were used extensively in the Near East at the end of the 2nd millennium B.C. It is also very important to note that the victory of Ramses II is described both in prose and poetry. This is a clear parallel to the biblical account in Jgs. 4 and 5 (*see also* DEBORAH **2**).

Mt. Tabor as seen from the plain of Esdraelon. The armies of Deborah and Barak gathered at Mt. Tabor to fight Sisera's troops (Jgs. 4) (W. S. LaSor)

5. Gideon and Abimelech (6–9). There was a severe oppression by the bedouin of various tribes including the Midianites and Amalekites. Gideon was called as judge to deliver his people. Significantly, the religious position of the family of Gideon was strongly influenced by the service of Baal, which points to a decay of the Yahwistic religion; only a direct call by the Lord saved the situation.

Chapter 9 tells the story of Abimelech, who tried unsuccessfully to start the first Israelite kingdom. He shed the blood of seventy brothers and received the curse of the only one left. After some success in overthrowing a revolt by what may have been a Canaanite group in Shechem, he was to his shame killed by a woman in Thebez.

6. Tola and Jair (10:1-5). Short notes on these two judges are given. In the case of Jair his wealth is illustrated by the number of his sons. The expression Havvoth-jair means "camps of Jair." The word *hawwôṯ* is encountered in Ugaritic as well as in an Egyptian cognate from 2000 B.C., pointing to the antiquity of this expression.

7. Jephthah (10:6–12:7). An important part of the book of Judges is devoted to the history of Jephthah. This judge was despised by his own people because he was an illegitimate son of Gilead. Later he was called on to deliver Israel from the yoke of the Ammonites and other oppressing peoples. Some scholars distinguish two strands of tradition in this narrative. Noth, e.g., holds the opinion that the larger part of the story of Jephthah is an extension of, and a later insertion based upon, the short note in 12:7. Jephthah is then actually to be regarded as a minor judge, and a later redactor is said to have expanded the short note in 12:7 to a long story. There is in the narrative itself, however, no basis for this assertion.

8. Ibzan, Elon, and Abdon (12:8-15). Three short notes are included on these judges. Two of the names are attested in Ugaritic tablets, i.e., Abdon and, probably, Elon.

9. Samson (13–16). The history of Samson the Danite must be of great antiquity, because it describes the struggle between the Philistines and the Danites and Judahites. This was before the northern migration of Dan described in chs. 17–18. It was the beginning of a struggle with the

Philistines on a larger scale than before. The Philistines arrived in Palestine with the southern movement of the sea-peoples, probably at the beginning of Early Iron I (*ca.* 1200 B.C.).

10. Micah and the Levite (17–18). This story tells of the kidnapping of the hired Levite of Micah the Ephraimite by the Danites, who were on their way north to sack Laish (which they rebuilt on the same site and called Dan). The presence of the Levite in the Danite company explains the origin of the sanctuary at Dan.

11. The Outrage by the Benjaminites (19–21). The Benjaminites of Gibeah acted outrageously against the concubine of a Levite who sojourned in their city. In so doing they overthrew all principles of decency and the laws of hospitality. A war developed between the rest of Israel and Benjamin in which almost the whole of Benjamin was exterminated. By allowing the six hundred remaining Benjaminites to marry the women of Jabesh-gilead and abduct unmarried women during a festival at Shiloh, Israel enabled the guilty tribe to survive.

Chapters 17–21 stand in marked contrast to the rest of the book. In this part no judge is named, there is no common enemy to fight, and no danger threatens from outside. These chapters give an overview of the internal situation during the period of the judges, and the perversion and corruption of the time are contrasted with the peaceful times of the later monarchy. The author of this part was probably convinced that the monarchy of either David or Solomon was the only answer to such a corrupt situation.

IV. Chronological Problems.–The period of the judges extends from the death of Joshua to the death of Samson or the beginning of the activities of Samuel. The total of all the dates given in Judges is 410 years. But 1 K. 6:1 states that the temple of Solomon was constructed in his fourth year, 480 years after the Exodus. If we take 410 years and add the 40 years spent in the desert, then the years of Joshua, Eli, Samuel, Saul, and David, then add Solomon's years, a figure of approximately 599 years emerges, which is 119 years in excess of the 480 years given in Kings. Still another problem exists, for if we add 480 years to 957 (the fourth year of Solomon's reign) we get 1437, which is too early a date for the Exodus according to archeological evidence. The problem of the 480 years is solved if it is remembered that it is the result of reckoning forty years to a generation, for twelve generations. If we take twenty-five years for a generation we get the number 280, which, added to 957, gives 1237. This is fully in accordance with archeological results. But what of the 410 years according to the count in Judges? It is clear from certain parts of Judges that events happened simultaneously. If it is accepted that certain events were contemporaneous then it becomes difficult to draw any conclusions from the chronology of the book of Judges. Archeology has shown that *ca.* 1200 B.C. certain cities in Palestine were demolished. A flowering culture of Late Bronze was obliterated. The new developments of Early Iron I were of a lower culture than the preceding. The break is thus obvious and points to seminomadic groups in process of settling down. This evidence is clearly to be connected with the invading Israelite tribes. It is also the actual starting point of the book of Judges. The date of the activities of Samson is approximately 1100 B.C. The northern migration of the Danites happened after that. Thus, the book of Judges may cover a period from *ca.* 1200 to 1050. Another possible date in this book is given to the activities of Deborah and Barak, *ca.* 1125. This is the nearest we can come to any satisfactory chronology of Judges.

V. Sources and Authorship.–The greatest part of Judges is of considerable antiquity. The oldest part of the book is probably the poem of Deborah. The style of this poem is in accordance with the common style of poetry at the end of the 2nd millennium. Other parts were probably transmitted orally within certain Israelite families and tribes. It is quite possible that certain events were originally only of local importance, but later on, by oral transmission, they assumed national significance. The importance of these narratives cannot be overestimated, because this is the only historical material we have from a time in which documentary evidence is scarce. The value of the narratives is difficult to estimate, because in some instances they have been more carefully preserved than in others. Archeology gives no assistance in this problem.

These narratives are provided with a framework, but the date and background of this framework are problematic. Modern scholarship is apt to ascribe it to the activities of the Deuteronomic school. From certain parts it is clear that the style of the framework is analogous to that of the Deuteronomist. From other parts this is not clearly discernible. Y. Kaufmann holds the opinion that we must distinguish between an ancient Deuteronomist and a later one. The framework of Judges may be ascribed to the activities of the ancient Deuteronomist, who lived close to the events he described. There is, however, some difficulty with this view, for in 18:30 reference is made to the captivity of the land, which must be placed after the conquest of Tiglath-pileser III in 733/32 B.C. Furthermore, the whole idea of an ancient Deuteronomist is hypothetical and difficult to prove. We may safely assume that the ancient material of the book of Judges was arranged and annotated later than 732. It is unnecessary to ascribe all the religious policy or the political views in the book to the person(s) who produced the framework. Old material was arranged and molded into a unity with certain typical characteristics, e.g., interest in the role played by women in the critical moments of history (Jael, Deborah, the woman of Thebez, and Delilah). W. Beyerlin's view is that the framework was composed over a long period by various persons or groups, the latest of which is to be placed after the time of the Deuteronomist. Do we know the name of anyone who played a role in the formation of the book of Judges? The talmudic tradition says that Samuel wrote the book of Judges. This tradition is, however, without any historical basis. The book itself refers to the Song of Deborah as sung by her and Barak. Since Deborah was a judge of Israel and thus a sage, it is probable that she could have composed this song. This is the nearest we can come to naming the author of any part of the book. The final author is unknown, as is the case with many other OT books.

IV. Relation to Other Biblical Books.–As we have already seen, the material of the book is of two kinds, narrative and framework. In some places we can distinguish two threads of narrative. On this basis, some scholars endeavor to find the pentateuchal "sources" in the strands of tradition. The opinion is that J and E extend from the Pentateuch into Joshua and Judges. This standpoint is difficult to accept, because no clear-cut distinction can be made between the threads of narrative and there are no characteristics that enable us to identify them with the pentateuchal sources. As we have seen, the final composition of the book was probably undertaken by a member of the Deuteronomic school or someone even later.

The narratives of the book of Judges played an important role in later Israelite history and religion. This is shown, e.g., by Isa. 9:4, where reference is made to the day of Midian.

VII. Text.–It is of great importance that we have two different types of translation of Judges into Greek. Since 1705, when Grabe pointed out that there were two groups of text-types, this problem has been tackled by various scholars. The difference of these two types is the further problem of their relation to the MT. The following solutions have been proposed.

(1) G. F. Moore held the view that A (Alexandrinus) and B (Vaticanus) are two different translations.

(2) Soisalon-Soininen, and others in modern times, hold the opinion that both the large text-types sprang from a common original (*Grundtext*).

(3) Fritzsche, following Schulte, takes B as the original text and A as secondary.

(4) Others hold that the division into two text-types is only a broad classification. We have, according to Katz, four different text-types. This suggests a new approach to the problem, which must be left in the hands of scholars in this field.

The LXX might be a reliable translation of Judges. It may be that in this case the B text is not ancient, but of a later origin than A.

Only fragments of this book were discovered at Qumrân. Because they are not yet published, their value is difficult to assess.

VIII. Literary Importance.–From a literary standpoint this book must rank high among the books of the OT and other literatures. We have a masterly victory song in ch. 5. Its figurative language is beautiful. It is obviously composed by a literary genius and it is impossible to accept that there was no literary tradition before this song was composed. Some parts, and certain words, are difficult to interpret because our knowledge of poetry of Northwest Semitic in the latter part of the 2nd millennium is fragmentary. With the discovery and interpretation of the Ugaritic tablets a new approach to this poetry became possible that has clarified it to some degree.

The stories of Judges are of a very high standard and are fully equal to the best short stories of the world. Some of them are filled with brutal humor, e.g., the death of Sisera at the hand of a nomadic woman Jael, and the extermination of a group of Philistines by Samson, who at the same time caused his own death. In beautiful figurative speech one of the few fables of the OT is preserved, namely, Jotham's comparison of Abimelech with a thornbush (9:7ff.). These stories are beautiful in the compact expression of the original Hebrew, and even in translation they are of special quality.

IX. Religious Message.–In its final composition the book brings a message of the government of God in the history of His people. Israel abandoned the religion of the Lord and was punished by the oppression of its enemies. A judge was called by the Lord to deliver the people and as charismatic leader of the nation he brought deliverance, but with the deliverance came a new call to return to the worship of Yahweh. These judges were under the direct guidance of the Spirit of the Lord.

The book emphasizes the need for a close walk with the Lord. A person's life is to be judged by his love for, or disobedience to, the Lord. We can regard the final verse of ch. 5 as the message of the whole book: "So let all thine enemies perish, O Lord: But let them that love him be as the sun when he goeth forth in his might." Sometimes the impression is created that the enemies of the Lord are going to triumph, but in the end the enemies are punished, and righteousness and love for the Lord save the day. An example is the cunning of Delilah and her apparent triumph over the judge of the Lord, Samson; finally all her cunning is broken by the later renewal of strength granted to Samson by the Lord, to pull down the pillars of the Philistine temple (ch. 16).

This book emphasized for Israel the might of Yahweh. But to the Canaanites also who lived alongside Israel its message spoke of the almighty acts of the Lord. By reading this book, or by listening to the stories in oral transmission, they heard that Yahweh, not Baal, was king.

Bibliography.–Comms. by G. F. Moore (*ICC*, 1895); K. Budde (1897); G. A. Cooke (*CBSC*, 1913); C. F. Burney (1930); C. J. Goslinga (1938); K. Gutbrod (1951); J. M. Myers (*IB*); H. W. Hertzberg (*ATD*, 1953); F. C. Fensham (1958); A. Vincent (1958); R. Boling (*AB*, 1975); J. Gray (*New Century Bible*, 1977). Other works: W. Beyerlin, "Gattung und Herkunft des Rahmens im Richterbuch," in E. Würthwein and O. Kaiser, eds., *Tradition und Situation. Studien zur alttestamentlichen Prophetie* (Festschrift for A. Weiser, 1963), pp. 1-29; J. Bright, *Early Israel in Recent History Writing* (*SBT*, 1/19, 1956); O. Eissfeldt, *Die Quellen des Richterbuches* (1925); J. Garstang, *Joshua-Judges* (1931); N. Gottwald, *Tribes of Yahweh* (1979); O. Grether, *ZAW*, 57 (1939-40); Y. Kaufmann, *The Biblical Account of the Conquest of Palestine* (Eng. tr. 1953); H.-J. Kraus, *Die prophetische Verkündigung des Rechts in Israel* (1957); M. Noth, "Das Amt des Richters Israels," *Bertholet Festschrift* (1950); J. Schreiner, *Septuaginta-Massora des Buches der Richter* (1957); S. Sprank and M. Wiese, *Studien zu Ezekiel und den Buch der Richter* (1926).

F. C. FENSHAM

JUDGES, PERIOD OF.

I. Problems Concerning the Conquest
II. Political Situation
III. Religious Situation
IV. Civilization

Our main sources for the reconstruction of this period are the book of Judges, 1 S. 1–12, and certain archeological results. The oldest part of the book of Judges is the Song of Deborah. The prose narrative is based on ancient material, which gives us an adequate picture of the period. It is impossible, however, to write a history of this period. It is uncertain whether the events in the book of Judges are in a strict sequence. Furthermore, it is very difficult to get a clear picture of the relationship between the invading Israelites and the Canaanites.

I. Problems Concerning the Conquest.–Modern scholars often distinguish two strands of narrative concerning the Conquest; one is present in Joshua and the other in Judges. Joshua creates the impression that Canaan was conquered by the whole Israelite nation under the direction of Joshua. In Judges the impression is that the various tribes conquered their own allotted land. Y. Kaufmann (pp. 65f.) has argued convincingly that the difference between these two books is due to two different stages in the history of Israel. The part in Joshua refers to the beginning of the Conquest when united efforts were made to subject the Canaanites. Judges refers to a later period, after the death of Joshua, when every tribe had to conquer its allotted territory. It is, therefore, difficult to pin the Conquest down to a certain period. It is true that in certain parts of the Promised Land the Conquest was completed much later, even into the times of the monarchy.

The time of the judges was mainly a period of adjustment and adaptation to new circumstances. A seminomadic people arrived in a country with its own culture and institutions. In some cases the old culture of Canaan was regarded as taboo and was completely obliterated by using the ban (Heb. *ḥērem*). In other cases a kind of compromise was made wherein the new and the old were fused together. One of the great problems of OT study is to ascertain how far this fusion took place, and whether the product of the fusion was regarded as normative or as an unholy syncretism unacceptable to the pure religion of Yahweh.

Some scholars are ready to ascribe a considerable part of the Israelite culture reflected in the OT to Canaanite influence. On this view the Canaanite material was borrowed during the so-called peaceful conquest, or even in the period before the Conquest, when certain Israelite groups were in Palestine. Almost all such hypotheses are built on conjecture and cannot be proved. The evidence of the OT is that some fusion took place, but this was regarded as sinful and due to the backsliding of unfaithful Israelites. In almost every case this fusion or idolatry took place in the religious sphere. The possible borrowing of other things like literary forms, legal policies, etc., is left out of the picture. It is the task of the scholar to try to trace possible borrowing and fusion back to their very roots, but this is a very difficult task. One thing is certain, namely, that the religion of Yahweh was kept distinct from the Canaanitish religions. A comparison with material from Ugarit and the Amarna Tablets shows that nothing of the high ethical monotheism of the Yahwistic religion existed in Canaan and Syria. In other fields, e.g., literary forms, some fusion and even borrowing are probable.

*II. **Political Situation.***–The period of the judges coincided with a time of great political upheaval. The Hittites, whose highly civilized culture had exercised a stabilizing influence throughout the Near East, were overthrown by the southward surge of the sea-peoples. These peoples were possibly of Indo-European stock and included the Philistines, Cretans, and Lycians. In *ca.* 1186 they encountered the fleet of Ramses III king of Egypt, and were checked. Part of the remaining army settled down in Palestine, and was destined to dominate the history of that country for a very long period. The whole narrative of Samson shows the might and cunning of these peoples. In the period of the judges no one powerful country dominated the Near East. Egypt was becoming increasingly weak as a result of continual trouble with the new enemy. Just a few years before, Merneptah could boast that "Hatti [land of the Hittites] is pacified, Israel is laid waste" (the Egyptian scribe used the determinative for people and not for country with the word Israel, which may indicate that Israel had not settled); but after the arrival of the sea-peoples there was no domination by Egypt, only a few sporadic raids. The great Assyrian empire of Tiglath-pileser I was also contemporaneous with the time of the judges (1112-1074), but this king was absorbed with problems from another quarter and penetrated only into northern Syria. The great powers were thus busy with their own problems and Palestine was left to itself.

The foreign enemies of Israel mentioned in Judges are Cushan-rishathaim of Aram-naharaim, various nomadic groups of the desert, the Moabites and Ammonites, and the Philistines. Cushan-rishathaim is an enigmatic figure and might be the king of a certain nomadic or seminomadic group that was on its way to settle in Mesopotamia and made a raid into Palestine. We must not underestimate the mobility of certain groups in those days. The Mari Letters show that nomadic groups moved hundreds of kilometers over a wide area. The trouble the peoples of the desert or children of the East caused Israel was to be expected. It was the same kind of trouble they had caused the Canaanites a century before. The nomadic groups on the western fringes of the Arabian Desert looked at the cultivated land of Palestine with covetous eyes. The camel was now tamed, so they could travel faster and farther than before. Asses were in use in Palestine but they proved to be of little use in warfare against the taller and faster camel, which could move deeper into the desert.

Israel was also troubled by its eastern neighbors Moab and Ammon, who settled down just before the arrival of the Israelites. Some indication of the culture of these peoples has been discovered by Nelson Glueck. He points out that they had their own typical pottery and built cities and fortresses of large dimensions.

The western enemies of Israel, the Philistines, were under the influence of Cretan culture. Their contact with this culture is best illustrated by the parallelism between Late Helladic III, Late Minoan III, and Late Cypriote III pottery and Philistine pottery. They have the following common features: looped spirals, concentric arches, half circles, scale patterns, checkers, rhomboid patterns, net patterns, Maltese crosses, and the bird or swan pattern. These peoples were also advanced in the use of iron, and the Israelites had to go to them to sharpen their ironware. They were organized into a pentapolis of city-states that formed close ties against a common enemy.

From time to time the political situation became dark and confused and Israel was enslaved for long periods. In spite of this, the Israelite group did not always act as a unity. Intertribal differences arose, e.g., Deborah taunted the indifference of tribes like Reuben, Gilead, and Asher (5:15-17). The town of Meroz was cursed for its lack of cooperation (v. 23). After the success of Gideon in expelling the enemy, Ephraim protested their not being invited to fight against the enemy (8:1) — and their failure to get the greater part of the spoil (v. 2). The same tribe protested also against Jephthah for the same reason, but a rebellion ensued in which a great part of Ephraim was killed (12:1-6). In chs. 19–20 the story is told of the united effort of Israel to punish Benjamin for its outrage. Here again almost the whole tribe was obliterated. It is obvious from these facts, and also from the narratives on the various judges, that the tribes would not unite against their enemies. A few local tribes were moved to action, while other tribes went on with their daily business. This situation was highly unsatisfactory from a political point of view. On the western side the Philistines were rapidly developing into a formidable force. Only a king who could bind the goodwill of all the tribes to his person could succeed in saving Israel from political servitude.

*III. **Religious Situation.***–Here it is very important to distinguish the material of the narratives from that of the framework. We can deduce from the narratives that the transition from life in the desert to the agrarian way of life in Palestine was drastic. While wandering in the desert the Israelites worshiped Yahweh. They had entered into covenant with Him there, especially at Sinai. In Palestine they suddenly found themselves in an agrarian community where gods and goddesses of fertility were honored. A highly developed cult of Baal and Asherah existed that was based on the change of seasons and appealed to primitive human instincts. In the worship of Baal women were cultic prostitutes. The charm of this form of adultery and the enticements of this cult of nature and of fertility made Baal worship tempting to the ordinary man, especially to the ordinary Israelite who stood under the severe laws of Moses. The seductive joys of a higher culture and the death of religious leaders after the death of Joshua were causes of Israel's infidelity to the religion of Yahweh.

It is exactly this situation that is reflected in the book of Judges and in the first part of 1 Samuel. God came to Gideon almost as a stranger (6:13). All the acts of Abimelech, the son of Gideon, stood in contrast to the service of Yahweh (ch. 9). Even the Nazirite Samson acted in disobedience to the vow of his parents. His contact with Philistine women showed his weakness, which contrasted sharply with the Israelite ideal not to intermingle with paganism. The moral and religious decay is best illustrated, however, by the last five chapters of Judges. A Levite was abducted by the Danites and all the gods and images were also carried away. Another Levite's concubine was violated by the inhabitants of Gibea. All these cases point to spiritual demoralization within the Israelite community.

What about the pure Yahwistic religion during this period? The religion of the fathers was preserved in certain circles, possibly among the elite. There was a center of religious activity, namely, the tent of meeting, and the twelve tribes were annually compelled to gather around it. There were priests who maintained the worship of Yahweh. It is even possible that certain charismatic offices were established like those of judge and prophet. In these circles the Yahwistic religion was preserved and enabled to adjust itself to the new circumstances in Palestine. The tribal community and their covenant with Yahweh guaranteed their safety and the preservation of their religion. In the ferment of this period a religion was born which produced great men in the history of religion.

IV. Civilization.–The Israelites came into Palestine as seminomads. After the destruction of various towns and cities the reoccupation was slow. This reoccupation marks the change from Late Bronze to Iron I. The Israelites settled down in the hill country first, for they could not conquer the plains on account of the strong chariot force of the Canaanites. The difference between the civilization of Late Bronze and that of Iron I is made plain by archeology. In Iron I we have extraordinary simplicity and a lack of cultural sophistication, as Albright puts it. The structure of the Israelite community was different from that of the Canaanites. The result was that the Hebrews did not occupy the patrician houses of the Canaanites in the same way as the Canaanites had done. The ground floor was not used as a storehouse and a place for slaves. The houses built in these times were primitively constructed in comparison with those during Late Bronze. A new kind of pottery started, quite different from the beautiful forms of Late Bronze.

Although the Israelite tribes did not maintain such a high standard in architecture or in the construction of pottery forms, their literary and religious achievements were of immense importance. They had special talent for literature, especially poetry. This is obvious from the Song of Deborah, for example. On the other hand, the highly ethical and moral religion of Yahweh dominated the history of Israel right from its beginning. This religion stands in contrast to the sensual religion of the Canaanites. The period of the judges is to be regarded as the starting-point of new literary forms, the first steps of a nation in the direction of an organized state, and the beginning of the development of religious and judicial institutions.

See also JUDGES, BOOK OF.

Bibliography.–*AP*, pp. 110-128; *KS*, I, 89-175; *BHI*; N. Gottwald, *Tribes of Yahweh* (1979); Y. Kaufmann, *Biblical Account of the Conquest of Palestine* (1953); H.-J. Kraus, *Die prophetische Verkündigung des Rechts in Israel* (1957).

F. C. FENSHAM

JUDGING; JUDGE (verb) [Heb. *šāpaṭ* (Gen. 16:5; 31:53; Ex. 5:21; etc.), *dîn* (Gen. 49:16; 1 S. 2:10; etc.), *nāḵar* ("judge amiss," Dt. 32:27); Aram. *dîn* (Ezr. 7:25); Gk. *anakrínō* (1 Cor. 2:15; 4:3f.), *diakrínō* (1 Cor. 11:31), *dokéō* (He. 4:1), *kríma lambánō* (Jas. 3:1), *hēgéomai* (1 Tim. 1:12), *krínō* (Mt. 7:1f.; 19:28; etc.)]; AV also "seem" (He. 4:1), "counted" (1 Tim. 1:12), CONDEMN (Rom. 14:22; Jas. 5:9), etc.; NEB also "be found" (He. 4:1), "try" (Jn. 18:31), CONDEMN (Acts 13:46), etc.; **JUDGMENT** [Heb. *mišpāṭ* (Ex. 28:15, 29; Lev. 19:15; etc.), *šᵉpôṭ* (2 Ch. 20:9), *šepeṭ* (Ex. 6:6; 12:12), hiphil of *qāhal*–'assemble' ("call to judgment," Job 11:10), *ʿēṯ*–'time' ("time of judgment," Job 24:1), *pᵉlîlîyâ* ("giving judgment," Isa. 28:7), *pāqaḏ* ("execute judgment," Jer. 51:52); Gk. *dikaíōma* (Rev. 15:4), *dokéō* (Mt. 26:66), *gnṓmē* (1 Cor. 1:10; 7:40), *kríma* (Mt. 7:2; Jn. 9:39; Acts 24:25; etc.), *krísis* (Mt. 5:21f.; 10:15; etc.), *krínō* (Acts 15:19; 21:25; Rev. 16:5; "pronounce judgment," 1 Cor. 4:5; 5:3), *dikaiokrisía* ("righteous judgment," Rom. 2:5), *sōphronéō* ("sober judgment," Rom. 12:3)]; AV also "think" (Mt. 26:66), DAMNATION (Jn. 5:29; Rom. 13:2; 1 Cor. 11:29), CONDEMNATION (Jn. 3:19; 5:24), etc.; NEB also "just dealings" (Rev. 15:4), "opinion" (Mt. 26:66), "thought" (1 Cor. 1:10), etc.; **MAKE JUDICIOUS** [hiphil of Heb. *śāḵal* (Prov. 16:23)]; AV "teach"; NEB "guide." For *bēma*, "judgment seat," *see* JUDGMENT SEAT.

I. In the OT.–In ancient Israel and the ancient Near East judging and ruling were closely connected. The king was also a judge, so that it is not surprising that the most common terms for judging and judgment include the ideas of ruling or governing. Such is the case with *špṭ*, the root most frequently used for judging or judgment. The verb *šāpaṭ*, "decide, judge, govern," is occasionally translated "render judgment" (Zec. 7:9), and when the context indicates a negative connotation the NEB translates it "condemn" (Ezk. 23:45). In the niphal the verb means "enter into controversy, bring a charge" (Jer. 25:31). The RSV also translates the word as "rule," "punish," "defend." The related noun *mišpāṭ*, "judgment," is used in several ways. It refers to the act of deciding a case (Dt. 1:17), or the place of judgment (1 K. 7:7). When used with the verb *ʿāśâ* it refers to the execution of judgment (Ezk. 39:21). It also means "justice" (e.g., Mic. 6:8) and is usually so rendered by the newer translations. Another noun, *šᵉpāṭîm* (only in the pl.), occurs less frequently, mostly in Ezekiel, of acts of judgment (Ezk. 25:11). Identical in meaning is the noun *šᵉpôṭ*, which occurs only in 2 Ch. 20:9 and Ezk. 23:10.

Another root, *dîn*, is used much less frequently than *špṭ*, though with approximately the same meaning. The verb *dîn* means both "judge" and "govern." The noun means "judgment." In Est. 1:13 the noun refers to customary law and occurs alongside *daṯ*, meaning an edict of the king. The NEB translation "religion" is imprecise, although it should be understood that law and religion were interrelated in the ancient world.

Several Hebrew terms are translated "judgment" only once or twice by the RSV. In Ps. 119:66 *ṭaʿam*, "taste, judgment," refers to the discernment granted by God. In Jer. 51:52 *pāqaḏ ʿal* means "execute judgment" or "punish" (NEB) the idols. The RSV translates the verb *rîḇ*, "strive, contend," in Am. 7:4 as "judgment [by fire]." The passage is very difficult and has occasioned numerous emendations, none certain (see J. Morgenstern, *Amos Studies* [1941], pp. 59ff.). By redividing the text it could mean "a rain of fire" (D. Hillers, *CBQ*, 26 [1964], 221ff.). The verb *pillēl* in Ezk. 16:52 means "cause a reassessment" (E. Speiser, *JBL*, 82 [1963], 304). The sense is that Jerusalem was so evil that it made Sodom and Samaria look good. The cognate noun *pᵉlîlîyâ* in Isa. 28:7 refers to the "reasoning" that the priests could not give because of their drunken state. The NEB translation "hiccuping in drunken stupor" is too much of a paraphrase. In Isa. 32:4 no term for "judgment" occurs despite the RSV translation "good judgment." Here the NEB translation "understand and know" for *yāḇîn lāḏāʿaṯ* is preferable. The RSV understands *yaqhîl*, "call an assembly," in Job 11:10 to have a negative connotation, hence "calls to judgment." The AV preserves the ambiguity with "gathers together" but the NEB's "proclaims it" is unlikely. (See M. Pope, *Job* [*AB*, 2nd ed. 1973], p. 85.) In Prov. 18:1 *tûšîyâ* is a technical term used in wisdom literature to mean "sound, efficient wisdom." The RSV has "sound judgment," the NEB "competent [people]." Finally, in Job 24:1 the Hebrew has no term for "judgment," but the RSV understands *ʿēṯ*, "time," as "time of judgment."

There are several additional difficult passages. The NEB "flood" (*šṭp*) for "judgment" (*špṭ*) in 2 Ch. 20:9 assumes that there was a transposition of consonants.

This is possible, but unnecessary since "judgment" does fit the context. In Hos. 6:5 the NEB, without good reason, has omitted the last phrase "and thy (my?) judgment goes forth as the light." The difficult term *šaddîn* in Job 19:29 is often taken to be a relative particle, *šᵉ*, plus *dîn*, "judgment" (NEB "judge"). L. R. Fisher, however, suggested that it is a divine name, a variant spelling of Shaddai (see M. Pope, *Job*, pp. 147f.). Even more difficult is Job 36:17. The MT reading, "You are full of wicked judgment; judgment and justice take hold," remains unclear. (For discussion see Pope, *Job*, pp. 270f.) In Ps. 141:6, the RSV deletes Heb. *selaʿ* from the MT (cf. *BHS*), reading "those who shall condemn them." The AV retains the word ("judges . . . in stony places"), as does the NEB ("rock of justice").

II. In the NT. The word most frequently translated "judgment" in the NT is Gk. *krísis*, which is also the usual LXX translation of Heb. *mišpāṭ*. Often it refers to divine judgment (2 Pet. 2:4), sometimes on a special day of judgment (Mt. 10:15). Frequently the judgment implied is negative so that the translation "doom," "condemnation," or "punishment" best conveys the sense (Jn. 5:24, 29). It can also refer to human judgment, as in Jn. 7:24. Less frequent is *kríma*, referring to the decision of the judge. Usually it is used in an unfavorable sense, as in 1 Cor. 11:29 (AV "damnation") or Rom. 13:2 (NEB "punishment"). The very common verb *krínō*, "separate, distinguish, judge," is occasionally translated "pass judgment" (Rom. 14:3f., 10; etc.). Related terms are *diakrínō* (1 Cor. 11:31) and *anakrínō* (2:15; 4:3f. ["call to account" in 17:24]).

Several words in the NT are translated "judgment" only once or twice by the RSV. In Rev. 15:4 *dikaíōma* refers to the righteous acts (judgments) of God, and God's righteous judgments, *dikaiokrisía*, will be revealed on the day of wrath (Rom. 2:5). The verb *dokéō* means "think," and in Mt. 26:66 the question should be translated "What do you think?" or "What is your opinion?" (NEB). Similarly, *sōphronéō* refers to intellectual capacity, i.e., "be of a sound mind" (cf. "think your way to a sober estimate," Rom. 12:3, NEB). The noun *gnṓmē* is used of an opinion in 1 Cor. 7:40 and (unity of) thought or judgment in 1 Cor. 1:10.

The terms "damn," "damnation," etc., are found only in the AV, usually in contexts where the Gk. terms *apṓleia*, *kríma*, etc. imply an eternal judgment (e.g., 2 Pet. 2:3; Mt. 23:33; etc.).

See also ESCHATOLOGY VIII; LAW, JUDICIAL; ROMAN LAW.

Bibliography.–*TDNT*, II, *s.v.* δίκη κτλ.: δικαίωμα, δικαιοκρισία (Schrenk); III, *s.v.* κρίνω κτλ. (Büchsel, Herntrich); *TDOT*, II, *s.v.* "dîn" (Hamp, Botterweck); *Sacramentum Verbi*, II, *s.v.* "Judgement" (Pesch), 442-49.

J. C. MOYER

JUDGMENT, DAY OF. *See* JUDGMENT, LAST.

JUDGMENT HALL. The AV translation of Gk. *praitṓrion* in Jn. 18:28, 33; 19:9; Acts 23:35. Elsewhere the AV renders "Praetorium" (Mk. 15:16) and "the common hall" (Mt. 27:27). The RSV renders "praetorium" in every case except Phil. 1:13, where it reads "praetorian guard." *See* PRAETORIUM.

JUDGMENT, LAST. The biblical concept that at the end of history Jesus Christ will return in glory to earth, the dead will be raised, and they, together with all the living, will be finally judged by Christ and assigned their eternal destiny in heaven or hell. This great eschatological event will be a visible, public, and universal judgment; Christ's glory and His victory over sin, death, and Satan will be fully manifest; righteousness will be exalted; the perplexing discrepancies of history will be removed, and the mediatorial reign of Christ will reach its ultimate triumph as believers inherit the kingdom prepared for them.

The expectation of the final judgment permeates the entire Scripture. It is referred to as "the day of judgment" (Mt. 10:15; 11:22, 24; 2 Pet. 2:9; 3:7), "the day of the Lord" (Am. 5:18-20; Zeph. 1:14; 1 Thess. 5:2; 2 Pet. 2:9; 3:7), "the day of the Lord Jesus" or "the day of Christ" (1 Cor. 1:8; 2 Cor. 1:14; Phil. 1:6, 10), "the great day" (Jude 6), "the day" or "that day" (Rom. 2:16; 1 Cor. 3:13; 1 Thess. 5:4; He. 10:25), and "the day of wrath" (Zeph. 1:15, 18; 2:2f.; Rom. 2:5; Rev. 6:17; cf. 1 Thess. 1:10).

I. Earlier Judgments.–The last or final judgment implies that there were earlier judgments. Basic is the first judgment of God, which brought condemnation and death upon all people and a curse upon the creation as a result of Adam's fall in Paradise (Gen. 2:16f.; 3:14-19; Rom. 5:12-14; 1 Cor. 15:21f.). This first judgment continues in effect throughout all of history; the only way of escape from the condemnatory judgment is through faith in Jesus Christ.

Other specific judgments upon individuals and nations have been issued by God in history, e.g., the judgment of Cain, the flood in Noah's days, the confusion of tongues at Babel, the destruction of Sodom and Gomorrah, the Babylonian captivity of Israel. Justification by faith is a pardoning judgment of God declaring the believer righteous through Christ. At death the person as a disembodied soul is admitted to heaven or hell, a judgment that anticipates the final judgment. The perplexing discrepancies observable in life where the righteous often suffer while the unrighteous prosper (Ps. 73; Mal. 2:7; 3:14f.) will be finally resolved at the last judgment.

II. OT.–Abraham appealed to "the Judge of all the earth" as one who does right (Gen. 18:25). In the Psalms God is referred to as the king who will judge the earth with righteousness (Ps. 96:10, 13; 98:9). Ecclesiastes concludes with the warning that God will judge everything done in public as well as in secret (12:4). Dnl. 12:1-3 predicts the final judgment in words paralleled in Rev. 20:11-15.

The OT references to the final judgment are sometimes interwoven with the first coming of Christ. The prophets repeatedly referred to "the day of the Lord [*YHWH*]" as a special day of judgment upon Israel's enemies as well as upon unbelieving Israel. Amos warned that only the true believers in Israel would experience this day as victory, and he warned of its terror and horror for the unbelieving (5:18-20; cf. Isa. 24-26). Malachi predicted that the great event would be preceded by the coming of the Messiah and His forerunner (3:1ff.; 4:1, 5f.).

III. NT.–NT references to the final judgment are more numerous and clearer in the light of the Messiah's presence. John the Baptist's preaching emphasized the coming judgment and urgently called for genuine repentance as the only way of escape (Mt. 3:7-10). A similar emphasis upon the approaching judgment was central in Jesus' preaching and some extensive references are given (Mt. 13:24-50; 24; 25:31-46). Faith in Jesus as the Messiah is the only way to escape the judgment of wrath. The presupposition of God's sending His Son is that people are already under condemnation (Jn. 3:17f.) and whoever rejects Christ remains under God's wrath (Jn. 3:36). Paul taught that the Gentiles as well as the unbelieving Jews are under the wrath of God's judgment (Rom. 1:18ff.; 2:1–3:20). Other references to the last judgment are found in 1 Cor. 3:10-15; 2 Thess. 1:5-12; Rev. 20:11-15.

IV. Christ the Judge.–God triune, Creator and lawgiver, is also judge of all the earth. All of God's attributes, but especially His omniscience, power, righteousness, and holiness, are displayed in judgment. While God is judge

The Last Judgment. Tympanum (*ca.* A.D. 1130-1135) by Gislebertus, Cathedral of St. Lazarus, Autun, France (Rosenthal Art Slides)

(Ps. 50:6; Eccl. 12:14; Rom. 2:3, 5; 6:3; He. 12:23; Jas. 4:12; 1 Pet. 1:17), the Father has given authority to judge at the last day specifically to Jesus Christ, the Mediator (Jn. 5:22, 27; Mt. 25:31ff.; Acts 10:42; 17:31; Phil. 2:10; 2 Tim. 4:1, 8). Authority to judge the nations is part of Christ's exaltation and is one of the crowning features of His kingship. The Lamb is also the judge (Rev. 6:16f.), and this contributes to the confidence and comfort of the believer on that day (1 Jn. 4:17). When Christ completes His mediatorial work, He will deliver the kingdom to the Father (1 Cor. 15:24, 28).

While Jesus' first coming was preeminently for the purpose of salvation (Jn. 3:16ff.), His judging function accounts for His claim that "for judgment I came into this world" (Jn. 9:39). Because the Father judges through the Son, "the judgment seat of God" (Rom. 14:10) and "the judgment seat of Christ" (2 Cor. 5:10) are interchangeable. Angels and believers are associated with Christ in the final judgment (Mt. 19:28; 25:31; 1 Cor. 6:2f.; Rev. 20:4).

V. Universal Judgment.–The last judgment will be absolutely universal and worldwide. All men, women, and children will be judged; the angels, both good and fallen, and also Satan will be judged. The (resurrected) dead and the living, the just and the unjust — all will stand before the judgment seat of Christ to give account of what they have done in life. The books will be opened (Rev. 20:12) and everyone will be judged by what he has done, including every idle word and secret thought (Eccl. 12:14; Mt. 12:36; Rom. 2:16; 1 Cor. 3:13; Rev. 20:12f.). The issue of judgment is sealed at death, for everyone will be judged "according to what he has done in the body" (2 Cor. 5:10). Believers shall also be judged, although Scripture states that they do not come into judgment, in the sense of the condemnatory judgment, for they have already passed from death to life (Jn. 5:24; 1 Jn. 3:14). Christ refers to the judgment as a separation of the sheep from the goats (Mt. 25:32f.) and wheat from the tares (Mt. 13:36ff.). No partiality will be shown, for God is perfectly just. What a person sows, he will also reap; God cannot be mocked (Gal. 6:7f.). Believers will inherit the kingdom and enjoy the full bliss of heaven while unbelievers "shall suffer the punishment of eternal destruction and exclusion from the presence of the Lord and from the glory of his might" (2 Thess. 1:9).

VI. Criterion of Judgment.–Christ's judgment will be just. The ultimate criterion of judgment is the revealed will of God. Since God created man perfect, all are held responsible because of Adam's sin (Rom. 5:13ff.; 1 Cor. 15:21ff.). Gentiles who have received only the revelation of God from Creation are guilty for their sinful suppression (Rom. 1:18ff.). But unbelieving Jews are doubly guilty, for they have had the additional revelation of redemption (Rom. 2–3:20). The whole world is held accountable, and all have sinned and fall short of the glory of God (Rom. 3:19-23). Although the final judgment will take account of the degree of revelation received (Rom. 2:12), acquittal comes only to those who believe in Jesus Christ. The announcement of the coming judgment is part of the gospel (Rom. 2:16) and constitutes the background for the urgency of preaching and the call to faith in Jesus Christ. The eternal destiny of the individual and the sentence in the last judgment is fixed at death and will not change during the intermediate state between death and the final judgment. Faith in Jesus Christ brings justification now and eternal life at the last judgment. For the unbeliever the appointed day of judgment is a day of wrath (Rom. 2:5), but for believers it is the day of redemption (Eph. 4:30; 1 Jn. 4:17) when they shall inherit the kingdom prepared for them by Christ their king (Mt. 25:34; 1 Cor. 6:9f.).

VII. Historical Views.–In Roman Catholicism the last judgment has often been depicted in terms of terror connected to its penitential system. Medieval art and sculpture on cathedral entrances frequently reflect this perspective. The Reformers regained the biblical perspectives and Reformed creeds reflect the comfort of the last judgment for believers (Heidelberg Catechism, qq. 1, 52; Belgic Confession, art. XXXVII; Westminster Confession, ch. 35; Westminster Larger Catechism, qq. 88-90; Westminster Shorter Catechism, q. 38). With the Enlightenment, judgment was reduced either to progressive education or to a present immanent process only, and Schiller's dictum that "the history of the world is the judgment of the world," while open to various interpretations, became axiomatic for many in this sense. Dialectical theology restricts eschatology to the present, eliminating future eschatology, and thus regards the "last judgment" as the crisis involved in the revelational encounter here and now. Evangelical Bible interpreters differ about the time of the judgment and the number of judgments.

See also ESCHATOLOGY; ETERNAL.

Bibliography.–*TDNT*, III, *s.v.* κρίνω κτλ. (Büchsel, Herntrich); J. P. Martin, *The Last Judgment* (1963); L. Morris, *The Biblical Doctrine of Judgment* (1960).

F. H. KLOOSTER

JUDGMENT SEAT [Gk. *bēma*–'step' < *bainō*]; (Mt. 27:19; Jn. 19:13; Rom. 14:10; 2 Cor. 5:10); **THRONE** (Acts 12:21); **TRIBUNAL** (Acts 18:12, 16f.; 25:6, 10, 17); NEB also COURT, BENCH (Acts 18:17), ROSTRUM (12:21). The Greek word is used in its literal sense only once in the NT: Acts 7:5, "not even a step of a foot," RSV "not even a foot's length" (similar expression in Dt. 2:5, LXX). The extended meaning, "raised platform," "tribunal," "judicial bench," occurs nine times literally, twice figuratively. This meaning is well attested in classical Greek and Hellenistic Greek and is found in the LXX.

In their accounts of the trial of Jesus before Pilate, Mt. 27:19 and Jn. 19:13 refer to the *bēma* of Pilate, located outside the Praetorium proper in the courtyard called the PAVEMENT (Gk. *lithóstrōton*), in Aramaic "Gabbatha." Obviously, this was a raised platform, perhaps ornately decorated (as at Corinth, see below), with possibly a chair or bench from which Pilate delivered his judicial decisions.

When Herod Agrippa I met his sudden death in Caesarea, he was seated on a *bēma* making a speech to a deputation from Tyre and Sidon after negotiating a treaty with them (Acts 12:21, 23 D).

When the Corinthian Jews accused Paul before Gallio, they brought him before the *bēma* (Acts 18:12, 16f.). Excavations at CORINTH, begun in 1896 by the American School of Classical Studies at Athens and continuing intermittently to the present, have revealed extensive features of the ancient city. Among the ruins are the remains of a richly decorated platform overlooking the agora, which is considered to be the *bēma* at Corinth (cf. O. Broneer, *BA*, 14 [1951], 91f.). Hence, the riot scene in which Sosthenes was beaten (Acts 18:17) took place in the agora or marketplace before the *bēma*. These impressive ruins, with the inscription using the term *rostra* (the Latin equivalent of the Gk. *bēma*), make the above identification very plausible.

When Paul appeared before Festus at Caesarea, Festus was seated upon the *bēma* (Acts 25:6, 17). Paul refers to this as the *bēma* of Caesar (Acts 25:10), suggesting that this was the official judicial bench in the praetorium at Caesarea where the Roman governor resided and functioned.

The term has a spiritual significance in Rom. 14:10 ("judgment seat of God") and 2 Cor. 5:10 ("judgment seat of Christ"); both passages refer to the appearing of all people (including Christians) before God (or Christ) to be judged. This term is an apt figure to describe this significant eschatological event. B. VANELDEREN

JUDICIAL BLINDNESS. *See* JURISPRUDENCE, ABUSE OF.

JUDICIAL COURTS. *See* COURTS, JUDICIAL.

JUDICIAL HARDENING. *See* HARDEN.

JUDITH jōō'dith [Heb. *yᵉhûḏîṯ*–'a Jewess'] (for etymology, see next article).

1. A wife of Esau, daughter of Beeri the Hittite (Gen. 26:34).

2. The heroine of the book of Judith in the Apocrypha — a pious, wealthy, courageous, and patriotic widow who delivered Jerusalem and her countrymen from the assault of Holofernes, the general of Nebuchadnezzar who had arranged the expedition which aimed at making Nebuchadnezzar the object of universal human worship. *See* JUDITH, BOOK OF.

JUDITH, BOOK OF. A book of the OT Apocrypha.

I. Textual Evidence.–Judith probably rests on a lost Hebrew original, which the Greek translates faithfully but in Hebraic manner. Swete (*OTG*, II, 781-814) prints the B text in full, noting the variants of א and A in his *apparatus criticus*. See also A. E. Brooke, N. McLean, and H. St. J. Thackeray, *The OT in Greek*, III (1906), pt. 1. The further textual evidence in Greek, Syriac, and Latin need not be detailed here, as the critical problems are not acute in this realm. See A. E. Cowley in *APOT*, I, 245f.; *HNTT*, pp. 298f. The interesting but late Hebrew midrashic versions, which are not of great critical value, are translated by C. J. Ball in Wace, I, 252-57.

II. The Story.–The story may be conveniently perused in full in Wace, I, 262-360; or *APOT*, I, 248-267; and it is minutely analyzed in *HNTT*, pp. 285-290. In historical and geographical blunders it outshines TOBIT.

Nebuchadnezzar achieves outstanding westward conquests, largely through his commander Holofernes. The book of Judith makes him king of Assyria, resident in Nineveh, whereas he was really king of Babylonia; and Nineveh had fallen in 612 B.C., several years before his reign commenced, *ca.* 605 B.C. (chs. 1–3). The churlish Jews, alone of the nations threatened, refuse immediate submission — though they are really quite afraid. They have just returned from Babylonian Captivity, and are rebuilding their temple — another glaring anachronism. Achior, leader of the Ammonites, in a fascinating lightning sketch of Jewish history, assures Holofernes that he can easily conquer this people if he catches them in sin against God; free from such sin, they are invincible. This is interpreted as a slight on the imputed deity of Nebuchadnezzar; and Achior, narrowly escaping with his life, is left to the Jewish mercies in bonds at the unidentified and probably fictitious city of Bethulia — a disastrous policy error for Holofernes! The dramatic irony of his contempt for information so vital is magnificent. Losing his golden opportunity, he decides to subjugate the Jews by the more realistic means of troop concentrations and cutting off water supplies (chs. 4–7).

The rich and pious widow Judith, armed by prayer and fasting, plans to save the city in her own way. Casting off her mourning garments, she dons her most magnificent adornments, and, simulating treachery to her own people, seeks the face of Holofernes, who is easily beguiled by her charms. She declares, giving the unheeded words of Achior a new twist, that the desperate Jews are about to sin in the matter of tithes and sacred offerings, and this has caused her to leave for conscience' sake. This sin will mark the psychological moment for the attack of Holofernes, and she will lead him to absolute victory (chs. 8–11).

Holofernes, blinded and reckless in his love or lust, grants Judith all the liberties she requests, only requiring her presence at a private banquet, which eventually reduces itself to the pair of them. (This situation would scarcely be thinkable for an Eastern lady, least of all for one of deep religious convictions.) The commander is too drunk to violate the person of his guest; but she violates his person drastically, grabbing his hair and hewing right through his neck with his own sword. Then she and her maid calmly walk out of the camp, carrying the bloody trophy of the severed head in a bag. After that, battle fortunes favor the Jews. Among other events, Achior becomes a proselyte (chs. 12–15), Judith utters a psalm of triumph, and her later years are succinctly recorded (ch. 16).

III. Selected Exegetical Notes.–*3:8.* The iconoclastic zeal of a reforming Josiah and the martyr-breeding pagan cult of an emperor, both familiar enough in separate contexts, make strange bedfellows in one verse. Cf. 6:2.

4:9-15. Penitential fasting and earnest prayer, little known outside periods of national crisis.

5:8. Interesting picture by a proselyte-to-be of the birth of monotheism. See note on 14:10.

5:17-19. Apostasy in religion engenders defeat in battle — an OT leitmotiv powerfully stated. The advice of Achior in vv. 20f., to base battle strategy on hamartiological observation, would, if genuine, indicate acute insight in an enemy. There is delicious irony both in the contemptuous rejection by Holofernes of something he cannot begin to understand and in the true picture of affairs on the Israelite side in 7:19-28.

8:1. Judith (Heb. *yᵉhûḏîṯ*) is both a proper name and the normal term for Jewess. The subjoined genealogy, genuine or spurious, is designed for verisimilitude, and militates against any purely allegorical interpretation of the book.

8:6. Here and elsewhere, Judith is a remarkable Pharisee, a female counterpart of the unconverted Saul of Tarsus.

8:11-20. Judith rightly denounces as irreligious the attempt by the elders to circumscribe God's power by a conditional oath. The reference to idolatry as outmoded is revealing.

8:31. The conviction of the elders that Judith's godliness will bring rain in answer to their prayers recalls the talmudic Onias the Circle-drawer, who vowed to stand inside his ring till God answered his prayers with rain and then further instructed the Almighty on intensities and volumes. For a priceless example of talmudic humor, see Mish. *Taanith* iii.8 (T.B. *Taanith* 23a).

9:10. With fullest allowances for circumstances, it cannot be maintained that Judith's prayer for the success of her deceit is a pleasing one.

10:8. The prayer of the elders is somewhat secular and mundane in spirit.

10:19. A fascinating remark, probably meaning that it is not safe to spare the Israelite men, because, possessing such beautiful women, they may well employ them as deceivers and decoys. The irony of the sentiment is underlined by the complete subsequent success of Judith in all her wiles.

11:5f. Judith's deceit raises very pointedly the question as to whether the end does or does not justify the means. See below.

11:10. A skillful echo of the declaration of Achior; see 5:17f. Holofernes is singularly more open to persuasion when he hears the same thing from female lips.

11:17. For the many usages of *theosebḗs,* "religious," see *TDNT,* III, *s.v.* Θεοσεβής (Bertram). There is a secondary suggestion of the mantic, reiterated in the claim to *prógnōsis* or foresight (see *TDNT,* I, *s.v.* γινώσκω κτλ.: πρόγνωσις [Bultmann]); but the primary meaning is that as a good Jewess, fervent in prayer, she expects to be heard of God.

11:19. Cf. Ezk. 34:5; Mt. 9:36; etc.

12:2. Gk. *skándalon,* offense or moral stumbling block, is another word significant in both Testaments.

13:6-10. Cf. Jael and Sisera, Jgs. 4:17-22; 5:24-27. Cf. Jgs. 9:53f.

13:16. The Eastern mind would be little inclined to receive Judith's statement at its face value.

14:10. Achior is an Ammonite; Dt. 23:3 makes his acceptance as a proselyte another glaring improbability.

16:17. An interesting statement of retributive eschatology.

IV. Historicity and Date.–Few contemporary Protestant scholars would care to fight the losing battle for the historicity of Judith; the contradictions of known facts and psychological probabilities are too numerous and too serious. Fewer still would defend its inspiration and canonicity, whatever the verdict of the Roman Church. This does not exclude a possible substratum of truth, magnified and distorted in folklore. The allegorical refuge has also been tried. Jerome equated Judith with the Christian Church, the decapitated Holofernes with the devil. The dispassionate reader is not convinced that this is altogether polite to the Church. The book is much more comprehensible as an ultranationalistic Jewish manifesto in the guise of fiction, a didactic novel, like Tobit, but patriotic rather than ethical in slant. On this interpretation there is no need to take the history or geography too seriously. Bethulia may be Shechem, the modern Nablus, as some have maintained, or it may be a mere figment of the writer's imagination.

It is generally agreed that Judith was not written in the age it professes to portray and so ludicrously distorts. A dating in Christian time is improbable; that of the Bar Cochba revolt, A.D. 132, taking Nebuchadnezzar as a cryptogram for Hadrian, is discountenanced by Christian quotation of the book at an earlier date. An approximation of 150 B.C. enjoys wide scholastic acclaim. Pfeiffer (*HNTT,* p. 295 n. 13) conveniently lists its supporters, but suggests that the psalm in ch. 16 may be earlier than the rest of the book. Wace (pp. 244-48) would advance the date to the reign of Alexandra Salome (79-70 B.C.). This could make the book, like Susanna, a pro-Pharisaic tract, applauding aspects of theology and upholding certain property rights of married women and widows. Judith has been interpreted as an indirect compliment to Alexandra, and Simeon ben Shetah has been given a place in the picture. This is hypothetical but interesting. An earlier date might not even exclude later Pharisaic adaptation.

V. Theology and Evaluation.–Reactions to Judith must inevitably be personal and subjective. On the assumption that patriotism overrides all other virtues, that duty to the state outweighs duty to God or mankind, and on the further assumption that a worthy end justifies the use of dubious or shabby means, Judith is a heroine altogether shining and admirable. She possesses incredible courage and pertinacity; her devotion to ritual Judaism under the most impossible circumstances is extraordinary. Many have objected to her lying and imposture, to the cool and calculating way she sexually entices a man she detests in her heart, to the bloodiness of the deed she commits without scruple or tremor. Her later denial of misconduct with Holofernes is almost anticlimactic. She was faithful to Jewish ritual, but what of her morals? Many modern Westerners find her duplicity detestable, and her Pharisaic righteousness unattractive. The assessment of the ancient Easterner would be entirely opposite: to him Judith was a female savior, a patriot without equal, a Jewess without reproach. Judaism, fighting against overwhelming odds for its very existence, was not the aggressor; and any weapons would seem justified against the monster Holofernes.

The main theological interest centers in the cardinal OT teaching of national sin and divine retribution, cleverly introduced, first through the Ammonite, an enemy, later through Judith, the female patriot.

Bibliography.–M. S. Enslin and S. Zeitlin, *Book of Judith* (1972); J. C. Daucy, *et al.,Shorter Books of the Apocrypha* (1972), pp. 67-131; A. M. Dubarle, *Judith* (*Analecta Biblica,* 24, 1966); E. Haag, *Studien zum Buche Judith* (1963); H. Lamparter, *Die Apokryphen,* II (1972), 135-182.

R. A. STEWART

JUICE [Heb. *mišrâ* (Nu. 6:3), *ʿāsîs* (Cant. 8:2)]. In Nu. 6:3 the term describes the pulp or liquid pressed from grapes, while in Cant. 8:2 the reference is to the juice of pomegranates.

JULIA jo͞o'lē-ə [Gk. *Ioulia*]. The name of a Roman Christian to whom Paul sent greetings; the wife or sister of Philologus with whose name hers is coupled (Rom. 16:15). The name points to a member of the imperial household.

JULIUS jo͞o'lē-əs [Gk. *Ioulios*]. The centurion of the Augustan cohort under whose charge Paul was sent a prisoner to Rome (Acts 27:1, 3). *See* ARMY, ROMAN II.A.

JUNIAS jo͞o'nē-əs [Gk. *Iounias, Iounia*]; AV JUNIA. One to whom, with Andronicus, Paul sent greetings at the close of his letter to the Romans (Rom. 16:7). The name may be masculine, "Junias," a contraction of Junianus, or feminine, "Junia"; it is *Iounian,* the accusative form, that is given. In all probability this is the masculine, "Junias." Paul defines the two as (1) "my kinsmen, (2) "my fellow prisoners," (3) who are "of note among the apostles," and (4) have been "in Christ before me."

(1) They were Jews. Paul calls the Jews "my brethren," "my kinsmen according to the flesh" (Rom. 9:3). Because Prisca and Aquila, a Jewess and Jew, are not designated as kinsfolk, W. J. Conybeare and J. S. Howson (*Life and Epistles of St. Paul* [rev. ed. 1856], p. 535) suppose "the epithet to denote that the persons mentioned were of the tribe of Benjamin."

(2) They had been companions of Paul in some unrecorded imprisonment. The phrase denotes more than the fact that they, like Paul, had suffered imprisonment for the sake of Christ.

(3) This may mean that they were well known to the apostolic circle or distinguished as apostles. The latter is probably correct, "apostle" being used in a wide sense (cf. 1 Cor. 15:7). The prophetic ministry of the early Church consisted of apostles, prophets, and teachers (1 Cor. 12:28; Eph. 4:11), the apostles being missionaries in the modern sense (see T. M. Lindsay, *The Church and the Ministry in the Early Centuries* [1903], ch. 3). Some apostles were missionaries sent out by particular churches (Acts 13:2f.; 2 Cor. 8:23; Phil. 2:25).

(4) They were among the first converts, "early disciples" like Mnason of Cyprus (Acts 21:16).

S. F. HUNTER

JUNIPER jōō'nə-pər. *See* BROOM TREE.

JUPITER jōō'pə-tər (AV 2 Macc. 6:2; Acts 14:12f.). The AV uses the Latin name Jupiter for the Greek god Zeus because of the influence of the Vulgate. *See* ZEUS.

JURISDICTION [Heb. *kissē'*] (Neh. 3:7); AV THRONE; NEB SEAT; [Gk. *exousía*] (Lk. 20:20; 23:7); AV also AUTHORITY. The power and authority to govern or legislate. Heb. *kissē'* literally means "seat" or "throne"; *see* THRONE. Gk. *exousía* has a broad range of meaning; in the NT it means "right, authority, capability" (Rom. 9:21); "power, strength" (Mt. 9:8); "right and might" (Jn. 5:27). Thus it gets the meaning of the powers of the magistrate, which it bears in later Greek (Tit. 3:1; Rom. 13:1-3). And in this sense it is used in Lk. 20:20; 23:7, where it is translated "jurisdiction."

JURISPRUDENCE, ABUSE OF. Among the Hebrews before the conquest of Canaan, disputes in the family or clan would be settled by the natural head (Heb. *'āḇ*) of the family or clan. This custom was prevalent in nomadic or seminomadic societies. According to Ex. 18, Moses as leader of the tribes settled all disputes. But he was compelled to appoint a body of elders to act in conjunction with himself. In the more complex society after the Conquest it was necessary to alter the position. This was done by David (1 Ch. 26:29-32) and again by Jehoshaphat (2 Ch. 19:5-11). In every case the structure was adapted to new circumstances and certain abuses among the officials and judges were eliminated.

The abuse of jurisprudence and the miscarriage of justice was of such frequent occurrence that it is especially mentioned in the ancient code of Hebrew law, the Book of the Covenant (Ex. 23:1-3, 6-8). This law is taken up again in Dt. 16:19. In fact the OT abounds with allusions to the corruption and venality of the judicial bench (Lev. 19:15; Ps. 15:5; Prov. 17:23; Isa. 1:23; 5:23; Am. 5:12; Mic. 3:11; 7:3; Zeph. 3:3).

A common image used to depict such practices is that of judicial blindness. In Ex. 23:8 the blindness (Heb. *'wr*) is connected with the open-eyed (*piqᵉḥîm*), and in Dt. 16:19 with the wise (*ḥᵃkāmîm*). The meaning, however, is the same, namely, the bribe blinds the eyes of the judge (cf. also 1 S. 12:3). The related word "make blind" in Ugaritic (*'wr*) means "blind the one eye" or, as an adjective, "one-eyed" (*UT,* pp. 454f.). But this cannot be the meaning in Hebrew, where we can infer from the word "open-eyed" in Ex. 23:8 that both eyes are affected by the bribe.

The abuse of jurisprudence was very ancient. It is said in the Code of Hammurabi § 5 that if a judge should alter his decision, he must be expelled from the assembly of judges (*ina puḫrim*) and must never be allowed to act as judge again. But it is not only the bribe that may influence the judgment of a judge. All over the ancient Near East the idea existed that the judge should act impartially toward the widow, orphan, and poor. The god is regarded as protector of the poor in the ancient law code of Ur-Nammu (*ca.* 2050 B.C.), in the Code of Hammurabi, and in various other documents of the Near East. The same attitude is also to be encountered in the tablets of Ugarit. The protection of the poor thus became an obsession with certain judges, and the rights of the rich were overlooked. Against this attitude the law of Ex. 23:3 was made. A judge should be impartial in every decision and should not be influenced by any person or any gift.

In OT times bribery and the abuse of jurisprudence were well known. Job 9:24 says that God "covers the faces of its [the earth's] judges" to be blind to justice in the world. Judicial corruption was the burden of prophetic preaching (cf., e.g., Isa. 1:23; 5:23; Mic. 3:11). Prov. 17:23 defines the wicked person as one who is always prepared to take a "bribe out of the bosom, to pervert the ways of justice."

Bibliography.–H. Cazelles, *Études sur le code de l'alliance* (1946); W. F. Albright, "The Judicial Reform of Jehoshaphat," *A. Marx Jubilee Volume* (1950); G. Driver and J. Miles, *Babylonian Laws* (2 vols., 1952-55).

F. C. FENSHAM

JUSHAB-HESED jōō'shəb-hē'səd [Heb. *yûšaḇ ḥeseḏ*–'may steadfast love be returned']. Son of Zerubbabel. The name is probably symbolic (1 Ch. 3:20).

JUST [Heb. *mišpāṭ* (Job 35:2; Ps. 9:4 [MT 5]; 117:7; Prov. 16:11; Jer. 10:24; etc.), *šālēm* (Prov. 11:1), *ṣaddîq* (Ezr. 9:15; Job 12:4; 27:17; Ps. 145:17), *ṣeḏeq* (Lev. 19:36; Dt. 25:15; Job 31:6; Ps. 17:1; etc.); Gk. *díkaios* (Mt. 1:19; Lk. 1:17; 14:14; Jn. 5:30; Acts 22:14; 24:15; Rom. 7:12; etc.), *éndikos* (Rom. 3:8; He. 2:2)]; **JUSTICE** [Heb. *mišpāṭ* (Ex. 23:6; Dt. 10:18; 16:19; 24:17; 1 S. 8:3; etc.), *ṣeḏeq* (Dt. 16:20; etc.), *ṣᵉḏāqâ* (Gen. 18:19; etc.); Gk. *dikaiosýnē* (Acts 24:25; Rom. 3:5; He. 11:33), *díkē* (Acts 28:4), *krísis* (Mt. 12:18; Lk. 11:42; etc.)]; **JUSTLY** [Heb. *ṣaddîq* (2 S. 23:3), *ṣeḏeq* (Isa. 59:4); Gk. *dikaíōs* (Lk. 23:41; 1 Pet. 2:23), *díkaios* (Col. 4:1)]; AV also RIGHTEOUS (Ezr. 9:15; Ps. 145:17; etc.), "even" (Job 31:6), "right" (Job 35:2; Ps. 9:4 [MT 5]; 17:1), "judgment" (Ps. 111:17; 119:121; 145:17), etc.; NEB also TRUE (Lev. 19:36), "correct" (Dt. 25:15; Ps. 11:1), RIGHTEOUS (Job 27:17; Ps. 145:17; Acts 22:14), "punish you as you deserve" (Jer. 30:11; 46:28), "act without principle" (Ezk. 18:25f.; 33:17), etc. The AV translates *mišpāṭ* as "judgment" 294 times, but the RSV most frequently translates *mišpāṭ* as "justice" in distinction from *ṣeḏeq* or *ṣᵉḏāqâ* as "righteousness." In any case, the Hebrew terms are often interchangeable, as the famous parallelism of Am. 5:24 demonstrates. Moreover, the terms righteousness and justice (in either order), whether referring to God or to man, are frequently combined for emphasis (Gen. 18:19; 1 K. 10:9; 2 Ch. 9:8; Ps. 89:14 [MT 15]; 119:121; Prov. 2:9; Isa. 9:7 [MT 6]; 56:1; 59:9, 14; Jer. 22:15; 23:5; Ezk. 45:9).

I. General Usage.–In Judaism (especially Proverbs) as elsewhere, wisdom literature abounds in common definitions and descriptions of the "just" or "righteous" person. Further, what makes weights and measures "just" (Lev. 19:35f.; Dt. 25:13-16; Prov. 11:1; 16:11; Ezk. 45:9f.; Am. 8:5) is common knowledge among Israel's neighbors.

The famous list of virtues in Phil. 4:8, though used in a specifically Christian context, comes from Hellenistic popular philosophy, and presupposes common agreement about what is "just." Christians may well "have respect . . . for everything that is humanly true and good" (K. Barth, comm. on Philippians [Eng. tr. 1962], p. 124). The distinction between the just and the unjust on whom God sends rain may also be a matter of common understanding (Mt. 5:45). Pilate's wife, with no theological intention, allegedly described Jesus as "that just man" (Mt. 27:19; RSV "righteous").

II. God's Character.–The people of God not only appropriate common views of justice and righteousness, but contribute distinctive understandings based on the character of God, who is uniquely "just" (RSV "righteous"; Neh. 9:33; Ps. 7:9 [MT 10]; Isa. 45:21; Zeph. 3:5). It is unthinkable that God would pervert either justice or what is right (Job 8:3).

The major point is that God's justice is no abstraction at odds with an equally abstract mercy. To the contrary, as the description "a righteous God and a Savior" implies (Isa. 45:21), God's justice seeks concretely to express His mercy and to accomplish His salvation (Jgs. 5:11; Ps. 7:17 [MT 18]; 35:23f.; 51:14 [MT 16]; 71:15; 103:17; Isa. 46:13; 51:5f.). The expected Messiah, accordingly, will judge not by the usual criteria (empirical data perceived by his eyes and ears) but by righteousness (*ṣeḏeq,* Isa. 11:4). "Righteousness and justice [*ṣeḏeq ûmišpāṭ*] are the foundation of thy throne" (Ps. 89:14 [MT 15]). Steadfast love, faithfulness, and righteousness characterize God (Ps. 85:10-13 [MT 11-14]).

In the NT God's justice remains bound to His mercy. Paul insists, for instance, that God's justice is not shaken when the sinner, whose wickedness demonstrates "the justice of God" (AV "righteousness"), is forgiven (Rom. 3:5). This position is essential to Paul's thesis that God, who is not unjust (Rom. 9:14), has not rejected His people Israel for being disobedient and contrary (10:21–11:1; Munck, p. 57). Later writers described God as One who "judges justly" (1 Pet. 2:23), who is "faithful and just" when He forgives us (1 Jn. 1:9), and whose ways are "just and true" (Rev. 15:3).

Jesus is described as righteous, just, "the Just One" (Acts 3:14; 7:52; 22:14; 1 Jn. 2:1; 3:7; cf. Jn. 5:30). The Lukan texts may well reflect the suffering servant song of Isa. 52:13–53:12 (so I. H. Marshall, *Luke: Historian and Theologian* [1970], p. 171).

III. Consequent Expectations for Social and Economic Justice.–These characteristics of God do not appear in isolation from His people, who mature and build on the basis of God's actions on their behalf. He commands: "You shall have just balances, just weights . . ." because "I am the Lord your God, who brought you out of the land of Egypt" (Lev. 19:36). Because God gave them the land, His people "shall not pervert justice" (Dt. 16:18-20; 24:17f.). The reason, the basis, for keeping God's justice and doing His righteousness is that God's salvation and deliverance are on the way (Isa. 56:1).

Thus the kind of justice that accords with God's character is, accordingly, dynamic rather than static, creative rather than codified, realistic rather than idealistic. It is neither merely forensic, nor merely religious, for it is covenantal justice. It rightly orders the relation of people to God, and thereby to one another. What is the good? That is the same as to ask: "What does the Lord require of you?" The answer is: "To do justice, and to love kindness [*ḥeseḏ*], and to walk humbly with your God" (Mic. 6:8). By these requirements God's goodness is structured into the social order. (Who God is, for instance, affects our daily uses of balances and weights [Prov. 11:1].) The justice that God inaugurates remains restless so long as the poor are oppressed, the needy crushed, and justice turned to wormwood (Am. 4:1; 5:7). "But let justice roll down like waters, and righteousness like an ever-flowing stream" (Am. 5:24).

It is equally true that when a people distance themselves from God, a true prophet must write of them: "Therefore justice is far from us, and righteousness does not overtake us" (Isa. 59:9; cf. 59:2). That is, God's justice already exists, and it cannot be ignored and denied with impunity (Isa. 1:17-20; Hos. 2:19; 4:1; Am. 5:15).

It is remarkable, in view of greatly changed political circumstances, that this theme of God's social and economic justice was not lost within the early Church. It is not that social justice became less important to God in NT times, but rather that the Church was in a very different situation from that of tribal amphictyony or theocratic monarchy. "Masters, treat your slaves justly" (Col. 4:1) is not merely an appeal to common sensibilities about slaves, but also a reminder "that you also have a Master in heaven" (4:1b). "Justice [*krísis*] and mercy and faith" remain more essential to the law than tithing (Mt. 23:23). Luke's commitment to "the people of the land" is in the same tradition. NT apocalyptic writings abound in this understanding of justice, even if not in the same terminology (Mt. 24–25; Mk. 13; Lk. 21:8-36).

IV. Norm for Persons in Authority.–From the Yahwist (early 10th cent. B.C.) comes a persistent norm for kings and, implicitly, others in authority (P. Ellis, *The Yahwist* [1968], pp. 203f.): the way of the Lord can be kept, and His promises received, only by actually doing "righteousness and justice" (Gen. 18:19). God made Solomon king "that you may execute justice and righteousness" (1 K. 10:9 par. 2 Ch. 9:8). Only "with justice and with righteousness" will the Davidic kingdom be upheld, according to Isaiah's ideal (9:7). Ps. 72:1 refers to the same model: "Give the king thy justice, O God, and thy righteousness to the royal son."

It is by this norm that a monarch's misconduct was measured. What makes a king, wrote Jeremiah, is not successful competition with other rulers for more luxury (a reference to Jehoiakin's use of slave labor to build a new palace), but only doing "justice and righteousness" (Jer. 22:15; cf. J. Bright, *Jeremiah* [*AB,* 1965], pp. 142, 144f.; cf. also 23:5). Micah puts to "the heads of Jacob" and "rulers of the house of Israel" the rhetorical question: "Is it not for you to know justice?" Judged by that standard they have, on the contrary, cannibalized their own subjects (Mic. 3:1-3).

Similarly, Luke emphasizes a triple woe (11:42-44) descending on Pharisees who neglected "justice and the love of God." Roman officials appear, through Luke's eyes, to have been more committed to justice than were those particular Jewish authorities who condemned "the Holy and Righteous One" (Acts 3:14; cf. Lk. 23:47; F. W. Danker, *NT Witnesses for Preaching: Luke* [*Proclamation Comms.,* 1976], pp. 64-67).

V. Just Persons.–Several persons are "just" in that they have upheld God's justice within the covenant community. Mary's husband Joseph is "a just man" in this sense (Mt. 1:19). Both the piety and actions of Joseph from Arimathea mark him off as "a good and righteous [AV "just"] man" (Lk. 23:50). Another such person is "Cornelius, a centurion, an upright and God-fearing man, who is well spoken of by the whole Jewish nation" (Acts 10:22). There is also "righteous Lot" (2 Pet. 2:7).

VI. Acts 28:4.–After Paul was shipwrecked on his journey to Rome and he and his company landed on Malta, he was bitten by a viper. The natives inferred that he must have been a murderer and that, though he escaped from the sea, "justice" (Gk. *díkē,* AV "vengeance") would not allow him to live. "Justice" here is not an abstract principle, but a goddess (cf. NEB "divine justice") who personified justice, according to Schrenk (*TDNT,* II, 181).

F. F. Bruce (comm. on Acts [2nd ed. 1952; repr. 1970], p. 471) suggests that Luke has replaced a Maltese deity by *díkē*, just as he substituted Zeus and Hermes for the Lycaonian deities in 14:12 (cf. E. Haenchen, comm. on Acts [Eng. tr. 1971], p. 713 n. 5).

Bibliography.–J. Bright, *Kingdom of God* (1953), pp. 59-70; R. E. Brown, *The Birth of the Messiah* (1979), pp. 275-79; V. P. Furnish, *Theology and Ethics in Paul* (1968), pp. 81-92; J. Munck, *Christ and Israel* (Eng. tr. 1967), pp. 55-60; E. F. Scott, *Epistles of Paul to the Colossians, to Philemon, and to the Ephesians* (*Moffatt's NT Comms.*, 1930), pp. 81f.; R. B. Y. Scott, *Relevance of the Prophets* (1954), pp. 158-179; *TDNT*, II, *s.v.* δίκη κτλ. (Quell, Schrenk).

J. G. GIBBS

JUSTICES [Aram. *d^eṯāḇār* < Old Pers. *dātabara*–'law-bearers'] (Dnl. 3:2f.); AV COUNSELLORS; NEB JUDGES. Officials whose function is uncertain, although the Persian word that lies behind the Aramaic word suggests a judicial function. They are probably inferior in status to the first three officials mentioned in both uses of the list, since the conjunction *w^e*, "and," attached to the third term seems to distinguish the first three as a separate and superior group (L. F. Hartman and A. A. di Lella, *Book of Daniel* [*AB*, 1978], p. 156).

J. E. H.

JUSTIFICATION [Heb. *ṣeḏeq*, vb. *ṣāḏēq*; Gk. *dikaíōma*, *dikaíōsis*, vb. *dikaióō*]. In a legal sense, the declaring just or righteous. In biblical literature *dikaioún*, without denying the *real* righteousness of a person, is used invariably or almost invariably in a declarative or forensic sense. (See *DNTT*, III, 352-377; *TDNT*, II, *s.v.* δίκη κτλ. [Quell, Schrenk]; Bauer, rev., pp. 195-98.)

- I. Pauline Epistles
  - A. Universality of Sin
  - B. Perfection of the Law of God
  - C. Life, Work, and Death of Christ
    - 1. Paul's Own Experience
    - 2. The Resurrection Connected with the Death
    - 3. Faith, Not Works, the Means of Justification
    - 4. Baptism Also Eliminated
    - 5. Elements of Justification
    - 6. Justification Has to Do with the Individual
- II. Other NT Writings
  - A. Synoptic Gospels
  - B. Johannine Tradition
  - C. 1 Peter and Hebrews
  - D. Epistle of James
- III. OT
- IV. Later Development
  - A. Apostolic and Early Church Fathers
  - B. Council of Trent
  - C. Luther
  - D. Schleiermacher
  - E. Twentieth Century

I. Pauline Epistles.–In this article reference will first be made to the writings of Paul, where justification receives its classic expression, and from there as a center, the other NT writers, and finally the OT, will be treated.

A. Universality of Sin. According to Paul, justification rests on the presupposition of the universality of sin. All men are not only born in sin (Eph. 2:3), but they also have committed many actual transgressions, which render them liable to condemnation. Paul proves this by an appeal to the OT witnesses (Rom. 3:9-18), as well as by universal experience, both of the heathen (1:18-32) and of the Jews (2:17-28; 3:9).

B. Perfection of the Law of God. The perfection of the law of God and perfect observance of it are necessary if justification is to come by it (3:10). The modern notion of God as a good-natured and more or less nonchalant ruler to whom perfect holiness is not inexorable is not Paul's notion. If one had indeed kept the law, God could not hold him guilty (2:13), but such an obedience never existed. Paul has no trouble with the law as such. Those who have tried to find a difference here between Galatians and Romans have failed. The reminder that the law was ordained by angels (Gal. 3:19) does not mean that it was not also given by God. It might be reckoned in a sense among the elements of the world (Gk. *kósmos*, 4:3), as it is an essential part of an ordered universe, but that does not at all mean that it is not also holy, right, and good (Rom. 7:12). It was added on account of transgressions (Gal. 3:19), for it is only a world of intelligent, free spirits capable of sin that needs it, and its sanctions make sin seem all the more sinful (Rom. 7:13).

C. The Life, Work, and Death of Christ. It is fundamental in Paul's thinking that Christ died for our sins, according to the Scriptures (1 Cor. 15:3). In due season He died for the ungodly (Rom. 5:6); while we were yet sinners He died for us (v. 8); we are justified in His blood (v. 9), and it is through Him that we are saved from the wrath (v. 9). While we were enemies we were reconciled to God through the death of His Son (v. 10), being justified freely by His grace through the redemption that is in Christ Jesus whom God set forth as a propitiation (3:24f.). There is no reconciliation, no justification, except through and by Christ (cf. Gal. 5:4).

1. Paul's Own Experience. Paul's own experience cannot be left out of the account. He lived through the doctrine, as well as finding it through illumination of the Spirit in the OT. It was not that he had only outwardly kept the law. He had been zealous for it, and had been blameless in every requirement of its righteousness (Phil. 3:6). What was borne in upon him was how little such blamelessness could stand before the absolute standard of God. Just how far he was shaken with doubts of this kind we cannot say with certainty; but it seems impossible to conceive the Damascus conversion scene in the case of such an upright man and strenuous zealot without supposing that Paul had undergone a psychological preparation and had questioned whether his fulfilling of the law enabled him to stand before God. For a Pharisaically educated man like himself, there was no way to overcome these doubts except in a renewed struggle for his own righteousness shown in the fiery zeal of his Damascus journey, pressing on even in the blazing light of noonday. This conversion broke down his philosophy of life, his assurance of salvation through works of the law done ever so conscientiously and perfectly. The revelation of the glorified Christ, with the assurance that He, the God-sent Messiah, was the very one whom he was persecuting, destroyed his dependence on his own righteousness, a righteousness that had led him to such shocking consequences. Although this was for him an individual experience, it had universal applications (Gal. 3:8). It showed him that there was an inherent weakness in the law through flesh, i.e., through the whole physical, psychical, and spiritual nature of man, which is considered sinful. Paul learned that the law needed bracing and illuminating by the Son, who, though sent in the likeness of the flesh of sin, yet as an offering for sin condemned sin and cast it out (Rom. 8:3), to the end that the law might be fulfilled in those who through Him walk not after the flesh but after the Spirit (v. 4). That was the glory of the new righteousness thus revealed. If the law had been able to do that, to give life, Christ need not have come, and righteousness would have been by the law (Gal. 3:21). But the facts show that the law was not thus able — neither the law written on the heart given to all, nor the law given to Moses (Rom. 1:18–3:19; cf. Gal. 2:16f.). Therefore every mouth is stopped, and all flesh is silent before God. On the ground of lawkeeping, what the modern man would call morality, our hope of salvation has been shattered. The law has spoken its judgment against us (Gal. 3:10). It cannot therefore lead us to righteousness and life, nor was that its supreme intention: it was a pedagogue or tutor (Gk. *paidagōgós*) to lead us to Christ that we might be justified by faith (v. 24; cf. Rom. 10:4). What made Paul differ from his companions in the faith was that his own bitter experience under the revelation of Christ had led him to these facts.

2. The Resurrection Connected with the Death. It was remarked above that the ground of justification according to Paul is the work of Christ. This means especially His death as a sacrifice, in which, as Ritschl well says (*Rechtfertigung und Versöhnung,* II [3rd ed. 1899], 157), the apostles saw exercised the whole power of His redemption. But that death cannot be separated from His resurrection, which first awakened them to a knowledge of its decisive worth for salvation and finally confirmed their faith in Jesus as the Son of God. "The objective salvation," says Ritschl (p. 158), "which was connected with the sacrificial death of Christ and which continued on for the church, was made secure by this, that it was asserted also as an attribute of the resurrected one," who was delivered up for our trespasses, and was raised for our justification (Rom. 4:25). But this last expression is not to be interpreted with literal preciseness, as though Paul intends to distinguish between the forgiveness of sins as brought about by the death and justification by the Resurrection, for both forgiveness and justification are identified in 4:6-8 (cf. 1 Cor. 6:11). It was the Resurrection that gave Christians their assurance concerning Christ (Acts 17:31); by that resurrection He has been exalted to the right hand of God, where He makes intercession for His people (Rom. 8:34). Christ's mediatorship is founded upon His death — the Lamb slain from the foundation of the world (Rev. 13:8).

B. Weiss well says: "It was from the certainty of the exaltation of Christ to Messianic sovereignty, an exaltation which was brought about by the resurrection, . . . that Paul has attained to faith in the saving significance of His death, and not conversely. Accordingly, the assurance that God cannot condemn us is owing, primarily, to the death of Christ, but still more to His resurrection and exaltation to God's right hand (Rom. viii.34), inasmuch as these first prove that His death was the death of the mediator of salvation, who has redeemed us from condemnation. . . . The objective atonement was accomplished by the death of Christ; but the appropriation of it in justification is only possible, if we believe in this saving significance of His death, and we can attain to faith in that, only if it is sealed by means of the resurrection" (*Biblical Theology of the NT,* I [Eng. tr. (of German 3rd ed.) 1882], 436f.).

3. Faith, Not Works, the Means of Justification. The means or condition of justification is faith (Rom. 3:22-28; cf. Gal. 3:11; etc.), which rests upon the pure grace of God and is itself, therefore, His gift (Eph. 2:8). The making of faith to be the only instrument of justification is not arbitrary, but rests on its receptive nature. Faith is the hand outstretched to the divine Giver, who, though He sends rain without our consent, does not give salvation except through an appropriate spiritual response. This faith is not simply belief in historical facts, though this is presupposed as to the atoning death (Rom. 3:25) and the resurrection (10:9) of Jesus, but is a real reception of the gift with the heart (v. 10), and is therefore able to bring peace in our relation to God (5:1). The object of this faith is Jesus Christ (3:22, etc.), through whom alone comes the gift of righteousness and the reigning in life (5:17) — not Mary, not angels, not doctrine, not the Church, but Jesus only. To be sure, God the Father is not thereby excluded as an object of faith, as the redeeming act of Christ is itself the work of God (2 Cor. 5:19), whose love expressed itself toward us in this way (Rom. 5:8). Faith in the one God is always presupposed (1 Cor. 8:6), but it was the apostolic custom to refer repentance to God and faith to Christ (Acts 20:21). The oneness of God the Father and Christ the Son in a work of salvation is the best guarantee of the divinity of the latter, both as an objective fact and as an inner experience of the Christian.

Since justification is by faith, it is not by works or by love, or by both in one. Justification cannot be by works, because they are lacking in time or amount or quality; nor can they be accepted in any case until they spring from a renewed heart, for which faith is the necessary presupposition. Justification cannot be by love, for love exists only where the Spirit has put it into the heart (Rom. 5:5), and the indispensable prerequisite for receiving love is faith. This statement does not deny that the crown of Christianity is love (1 Cor. 13:13); it means only that the root of love is faith. Nor can love be regarded as a partial condition of justification on the strength of the phrase often quoted for that purpose, "faith working through love" (Gal. 5:6). The apostle is speaking here only of those who are already "in Christ," and he says that over against the Galatian believers bringing in a lot of legal observances, the only availing thing is not circumcision or its lack, but faith energizing through love. Here the interest is, as Ritschl says (II, 343), in the kingdom of God, but justification proper has reference to the sinner in relation to God and Christ. At the same time this text reveals the tremendous religio-ethical force abiding in faith, according to Paul.

4. Baptism Also Eliminated. Not only are good works and love removed as conditions or means of justification of the sinner, but baptism is also eliminated. According to Paul, it is the office of baptism not to justify, but to cleanse, i.e., symbolically to set forth and seal the washing away of sin and the entrance into the new life by a dramatic act of burial, which for the subject and all witnesses would mark a never-to-be-forgotten era in the history of the believer. "Baptism," says Weiss (I, 454), "therefore presupposes faith in Him as the one whom the Christian Church designates with the name of their Lord, and also binds to an adherence to Him, which excludes every dependence upon any other, inasmuch as He has acquired a claim upon their devotion by the saving deed of His self-surrender on the cross." Baptism points to a complete parting with the old life by previous renewal through faith in Christ, which renewal baptism in its turn sealed and announced in a climax of self-dedication to Him. This act, while symbolically and in contemporary parlance of both Jew and Gentile called a new birth, was probably often actually so in the psychological experience of the baptized. But while justification is often attributed to faith, it is never to baptism.

5. Elements of Justification. What are the elements of this justification? The first is the forgiveness of sins (Rom. 4:5-8; cf. Acts 13:38f.). With this are connected peace and reconciliation (Rom. 5:1, 9f.; cf. 10:11). The second is the declaring or approving as righteous or just (3:21-30; 4:2-9, 22; 5:1, 9-11, 16-21, etc.). C. F. Schmid is perfectly right when he says that Paul (like James) always uses *dikaioún* in the sense of esteeming, pronouncing, and treating as righteous, both according to the measure of the law (Rom. 2:13; 3:20) and also according to grace (*Biblical Theology of the NT* [Eng. tr., 2nd ed. 1877], p. 497). The word is a forensic one, and Godet goes so far as to say that the word is never used in any Greek literature for making righteous (comm. on Romans [Eng. tr. 1883], I, 157). It is the ungodly who are justified (Rom. 4:5), and the justification is a reckoning or imputation (Gk. *logízesthai*) of righteousness (vv. 6, 22), not an infusing or making righteous. The opposite of "justify" is not "be a sinner," but is "accuse" or "condemn" (8:33f.), and the opposite of "justification" is "condemnation" (5:18). Besides, it is not the infusing of a new life, of a new holiness, that is counted for righteousness, but it is faith that is so counted (4:5; Phil. 3:9). What God looks upon when He justifies is not the righteousness that He has imparted or is to impart, but the atonement that He has made in Christ. It is one of the truest paradoxes of Christianity that unless a righteous life follows, there has been no justification, while the justification itself is for the sake of Christ alone through faith alone. It is a "*status,* rather than a character," says Stevens (*Pauline Theology* [1892], p. 265); "it bears the stamp of a legal rather than of an ethical conception." Stevens refers to the elaborate and convincing proof of the forensic character of Paul's doctrine of justification (in Morison, *Exposition of Romans,* pp. 163-200). An interesting illustration of how further study may correct a wrong impression is given by Lipsius, who, in *Die Paulinische Rechtfertigungslehre* (1853), maintains that righteousness or justification mean not "exclusively an objectively given external relation to God, but always at the same time a real inner condition of righteousness" (p. 10). In his *Lehrbuch der evangelisch-protestantischen Dogmatik* (3rd ed. 1893), however, Lipsius calls the righteousness of God properly an "objective gift of grace, not simply in the sense in which the OT just one judged his position of salvation as a gift of grace, but as a righteousness specially reckoned and adjudicated by way of grace and acknowledged before the judgment [or court; German *Gericht*] of God (Rom. 4:6; cf. vv. 1-8, 11; 3:23; Gal. 3:6). This is always the meaning of *dikaioún, dikaioústhai,* or *dikaíōsis* in Paul. It consists in the not-reckoning of sins" (p. 658). Of course justification is only a part of the process of salvation, which includes regeneration and sanctification, but these are one thing and justification is another.

6. Justification Has to Do with the Individual. Finally it is asked whether justification in Paul's mind has to do with the individual believer or with the society or Christian congregation. Ritschl (II, 217f.) and Sanday-Headlam (comm. on Romans [*ICC,* 3rd ed. 1897], pp. 122f.) say the latter; Weiss (I, 442) says the former. It is indeed true that Paul refers to the church as purchased with Christ's blood (Acts 20:28; or God's blood, according to the two oldest MSS and ancient authorities; cf. Eph. 5:25; Rom. 8:30; Gal. 3:8), and he uses the pronoun "we" to designate the recipients of redemption (Col. 1:14; Eph. 2:18). But it is evident on the other hand that faith is an individual matter, a thing first between man and his God, and only after a person has been united to Christ by faith can he enter into a spiritual fellowship with fellow believers. The subject of justification, therefore, must be in the first place the individual and only in the second place and by consequence the society. Besides, those justified are not the cleansed and sanctified members of churches, but the ungodly (Rom. 4:5).

As to the argument from baptism urged by Sanday-Headlam, it must be said that Paul always conceives of baptism as taking place in the Christian community with believers and for believers and that for and to which they are baptized is not justification, but the death and resurrection of Christ (6:3f.). The righteousness of God has been manifested not through baptism but through faith in Jesus Christ unto all that believe (3:22), being justified freely, not through baptism, but through the redemption that is in Christ Jesus (v. 24). With Paul baptism symbolizes and externally actualizes union with the death of the Lord, and would be both impossible and inappropriate in the case of those not already believers in Christ and thus inwardly united to His society.

II. Other NT Writings.–It is a commonplace of the theology that is called "modern" or "critical," that Paul and not Jesus is the founder of Christianity as we know it, that the doctrines of the divinity of Christ, atonement, justification, etc., are Paul's work, and not his Master's. There is some truth in this. Though we may never separate Christ's teaching ministry from His redemptive commitments and accomplishments, and though it is a false contrast to say that Christ did not come to preach the gospel but to do something so that there would be a gospel to preach, yet it is the work of obedience and suffering unto death as the demand and price of redemption that is central in Christ's humiliation. It was not only Jesus' method but also the requirements of His mission to do His own work and not that of the disciples. It was His to die, to rise from the dead, to ascend to the Father, and to give the Holy Spirit to lead His disciples into all truth.

A. Synoptic Gospels. Harnack's statement (*What is Christianity?* [2nd rev. ed. 1901], p. 68) that the "whole of Jesus' message may be reduced to these two heads: God as Father, and the human soul so ennobled that it can and does unite with Him" is simply not true, for it omits an essential part of His message, namely, that salvation is bound up in His (Christ's) own person (cf. Mt. 10:37-39; 16:24-27). Confession of Him (not simply of the Father) determines acknowledgment above (10:32), where judgment is rendered according to our attitude to Him in His unfortunate ones (25:35-46). No sooner was His person rightly estimated than He began to unfold the necessity of His death and resurrection (16:21). The evening before that death occurred, He brought out its significance, perpetuated the lesson in the institution of the Supper (Mk. 14:24), and reinforced it after His resurrection (Lk. 24:26). Paul himself could hardly have expressed the fact of the atonement through Christ's death more decisively than Mt. 20:28; 26:28. With this foundation, could the Christian doctrine of salvation take any other course than that it actually did take? Instead of referring men to the Father, Christ forgives sins Himself (9:2-6), and He reckons all men as needing this forgiveness (6:12). While the time had not arrived for the Pauline doctrine of righteousness, Jesus prepared the way for it, negatively, in demanding a humble sense of sin (5:3), inner fitness and perfection (vv. 6, 8, 20, 48), and positively in requiring recourse to Him by those who felt the burden of their sins (11:28) — to Him who was the rest-giver, and not simply to God the Father, a passage of which Rom. 5:1 is an echo. For it was especially to those to whom, as to the awakened Paul, the law brought condemnation that He came to heal and to save (Mk. 2:17; Mt. 9:13; Lk. 15:7). It was for sinners that He came (Lk. 15:2; 7:39; 19:7; Mt. 11:19), just as Paul understood; and the way for their salvation was not better law-keeping, but trusting prayer in the confession of sin (Lk. 18:13), the humble heart and a hunger for righteousness (= faith). See Mt. 5:3, 6. He who brings most of himself, of his own pride and works, must undergo radical transformation if he is to obtain the kingdom of heaven (18:3f.; Mk. 10:14). Not only entrance, but the final reward itself is of grace (Mt. 19:30; 20:1-16), and in anticipation of Paul's message was the promise of Paradise to the penitent robber (Lk. 23:43). At the very beginning the message sounded out, "Repent ye, and believe in the gospel" (Mk. 1:15), the gospel which was summed up in Christ, who would gather the people, not directly to God the Father,

JUSTIFICATION

but to Himself (Mt. 23:37). All this means justification through faith in Himself, in His divine-human manifestation (Mt. 16:13-16). This is the faith of which He expressed Himself with anxiety in Lk. 18:8, and the presence of which He greeted with joy in Mt. 8:10. Paul's proclamation was continuous with the self-witness of Jesus, which conversely pointed as a consequence to the witness of Paul.

B. Johannine Tradition. Justification by faith is not more implicit in John's Gospel than in the first three; it is only more explicit (Jn. 3:14-16). Eternal life is the blessing secured, but this of course is only possible to one not under condemnation (3:36). The new Sonship of God came also in the wake of the same faith (1:12). The Epistles of John vary from Paul in word rather than in substance. The atoning work of Jesus is still in the background; walking in the light is not conceivable in those under condemnation and without faith; and the confession of sins that leads to forgiveness seems only another name for the justification that brings peace (1 Jn. 1:9f.; cf. 2:1f.). Everything, as with Paul (Eph. 2:7; Tit. 3:4), leads back to the love of God (1 Jn. 3:1), who sent His Son to be the propitiation for our sins (4:10).

C. 1 Peter and Hebrews. Paul gave justification a full treatment which other NT writers presuppose but do not unfold. Peter's "Repent ye, and be baptized . . . in the name of Jesus Christ" (Acts 2:38) is meaningless unless faith be exercised in Christ. It is He in whom, though we see Him not, yet believing, we rejoice greatly with joy unspeakable (1 Pet. 1:8), receiving the end of our faith, the salvation of our souls (v. 9). It is only, however, through the precious blood as of a lamb without blemish, even that of Christ (v. 19); only through Him are we believers in God (v. 21). The familiar expression, "Come to Jesus," which simply means "Have faith in Jesus for justification and salvation," goes back to Peter (2:4). The Epistle to the Hebrews has other interests to look after, but it does not deny faith; rather, it exhorts us to draw near with a true heart in fulness of faith (He. 10:22), which it lays at the foundation of all true religion, thinking, and achievement (ch. 11). The writer can give no better exhortation than to look unto Jesus the author and perfecter of our faith (12:2), an exhortation in the true spirit of Paul, whose gospel of faith for justification is also summed up in 4:16.

D. Epistle of James. We come lastly to the core of the matter in regard to NT representations of justification — the famous passage in Jas. 2:14-26, which at first sight seems to be a direct blow at Paul. We cannot enter here into the interesting question of the date of James (*see* JAMES, EPISTLE OF), but a careful look at this vigorous and valuable letter will show us that contradiction on the part of James to Paul is apparent and not real.

(1) In this section James uses the word "faith" simply for intellectual belief in God, and especially in the unity of God (2:19; see also context), whereas Paul uses it for a saving trust in Christ. As Feine says (*Theologie des NT* [2nd ed. 1911], pp. 660-63), for Paul faith is the appropriation of the life-power of the heavenly Christ. Therefore he knows no faith which does not bring forth good works corresponding to it. What does not come from faith is sin. For James faith is subordination of man to the heavenly Christ (2:1), or it is the theoretic acknowledgment of one God (2:19). Justification is for James a speaking just of him who is righteous, an analytical judgment. (2) James uses the word "works" as meaning practical morality, going back behind legalism, behind Pharisaism, to the position of the OT prophets, whereas Paul uses the word as meritorious action deserving reward. (3) When James is thinking of a deeper view, faith stands central in Christianity (1:3, 6; 2:1; 5:15). (4) Paul also on his part is as anxious as James vitally to connect Christianity and good works through faith (1 Thess. 1:3; Gal. 5:6; 1 Cor. 13:2; Rom. 2:6f.). (5) The whole argument of James is bent on preserving a real practical Christianity that is not content with words merely (2:15-16), but shows itself in deeds. He is not trying to show, as Paul, how men get rid of their guilt and become Christians, but how they prove the reality of their profession *after* they receive the faith. He is not only writing to Christians, as of course Paul was, but writing to them *as* Christians ("my brethren," v. 14), as already justified and standing on the "faith of our Lord Jesus Christ" (v. 1), whereas Paul was thinking of men, Gentile and Jew, shivering in their guilt before the Eternal Justice, and asking, How can we get peace with God? "There is not," says Beyschlag (*NT Theology*, I [1895], p. 367f.), "an objective conflict between the Pauline and Jacobean doctrines; both forms of teaching exist peacefully beside each other. James thought of justification in the simple and most natural sense of *justificatio justi*, as the Divine recognition of an actually righteous man, and he thought of it as the final judgment of God upon a man who is to stand in the last judgment and become a partaker of the final *sōtēría* ["salvation"]. Paul also demands as a requisite for this last judgment and the final *sōtēría* right works, the love that fulfils the law and the perfected sanctification, but he (except in Rom. 2:13) does not apply the expression *dikaioústhai* ["to be justified"] to the final judgment of God, which recognizes this righteousness of life as actual. He applies it rather to that first sentence of God with which He graciously receives the believing sinner returning to Him, and takes him into fellowship with Himself." Beyschlag rightly insists that James undoubtedly taught with the first apostles that whoever believes in Christ and is baptized receives the forgiveness of sins (Acts 2:38; 3:19; 10:43), and that he would not have contested the Pauline idea of justification by grace through faith, insisting only that works must follow. Theologically, the chief if not the only difference is that James did not make the cross of Christ the center of his teaching, while the atonement was fundamental for Paul (*see* JAMES, EPISTLE OF).

III. OT.–All the NT writers built on the OT. That there should be a cleft or contradiction between the OT and what we call the NT would have been to them inconceivable. Abraham believed in Yahweh; and He reckoned it to him for righteousness (Gen. 15:6; Rom. 4:3). Whoever does not keep all parts of the law all the time is condemned (Dt. 27:26, LXX; Gal. 3:10; cf. Ps. 14; 143:2; Rom. 3:20; see vv. 9-20, and the references to the OT in the ASV). The prophets insisted upon the practical works of righteousness — "What does the Lord require of you but to do justice and to love kindness and to walk humbly with your God?" (Mic. 6:8). No religious attitude or services could take the place of uprightness of life. This does not mean that the OT writers understood that men were justified by their good deeds, for it was always believed that underneath all was the mercy and loving-kindness of God, whose forgiving grace was toward the broken and contrite spirit, the iniquities of whom were to be carried by the Servant of the Lord, who shall satisfy many (Ps. 103:8-13; 85:10; Isa. 57:15; 53:11, and many other passages).

IV. Later Developments.–*A. Apostolic and Early Church Fathers.* It is humiliating to confess that the witness immediately after the apostles (the Apostolic Fathers) did not reach the serene heights of Paul. There are passages which remind one of him, but the atmosphere is different. Christianity is conceived of as a new law rather than as a gospel of the grace of God. We cannot go into the reasons for this: suffice it to say that in gentile Christendom the presuppositions for that gospel failed, and the NT writings were not yet in the consciousness of the church to the extent that they dominated her thinking. The fine passage in Clement of Rome (A.D. 97; 32:3f.: "All of them therefore were all renowned and magnified, not through themselves or their own works or the righteous actions which they had wrought, but through his will; and therefore, we who by his will have been called in Christ Jesus are not made righteous by ourselves, or by our wisdom or understanding or piety or the deeds which we have wrought in holiness of heart, but through faith, by which Almighty God has justified all men from the beginning of the world; to him be glory for ever and ever. Amen") is not at all on a par with his whole epistle, as he coordinates faith with other virtues in ch. 35, makes hospitality and godliness the saving virtues for Lot in ch. 11, couples hospitality and faith together as equal for Rahab in ch. 12, and represents forgiveness of sins through keeping commandments and love in ch. 1. Ignatius (about 110-15 A.D.) speaks in one place about Jesus Christ dying for us, that believing on His death we might escape death (Trall. 2:1), but with him the saving things seem to be love, concord, obedience to bishops, and the indwelling God = Christ, though he has also the excellent passage: "None of these things is hidden from you if ye be perfect in your faith and love toward Jesus Christ, for these things are the beginning and end of life — faith is the beginning and love the end, and the two being found in unity are God, while all things else follow in their train unto true nobility" (Eph. 14). The so-called Barnabas (date uncertain) puts the death of Christ Jesus at the foundation of salvation, which is expressed by the remission of sins through His blood (ch. 5), the kingdom of Jesus being on the cross, so that they who set their hope on Him shall live forever (ch. 8). At the time even believers are not yet justified (ch. 4), for which finally a whole series of works of light must be done and works of darkness avoided (ch. 19). The Shepherd of Hermas and 2 Clement are even more moralistic; whatever their praise of faith, they have the beginning of the idea of merit. The same legalistic tone is found in the Didache. This trend went forward till it was almost full-fledged as early as Tertullian (after A.D. 200) and Cyprian (A.D. 250). And thus it continued until it struck Augustine, bishop of Hippo, who united, so far as they could be united, the Pauline thoughts of sin, grace, and justification with a regular legalism. His book *De Spiritu et Littera* (A.D. 412) was largely after Paul's own heart, and the Reformers hailed it with joy. But he kept the legalistic elements, for instance, that in justification a good desire and a good will are infused, that justification grows, that our merits must be taken into the account even though they are God's merits, that the faith which justifies is a faith which works by love, that faith is the holding true of what God (and the church) says (though occasionally a deeper view of faith is seen), and that works play an important part, as in *De fide et operibus*. Augustine made a bridge by which we could go either back to Paul or forward to Aquinas. As Harnack well says, Augustine experienced, on the one hand, the last revival in the ancient church of the principle that "faith alone saves," and, on the other, he silenced that principle for a thousand years. The very Catholic theologian who stood nearest to that principle overcame it (*ZTK*, 1 [1891], 177). His misunderstanding of Paul's "faith that worketh through love" had momentous consequences.

B. Council of Trent. Those consequences are best seen in the decrees of the Council of Trent (Session 6, 1547), which are the definite and final crystallization of the medieval development. (1) Justification is a translation from a natural state to a state of grace. With this works prevenient grace, awakening and assisting, and with this in his turn man cooperates and prepares himself for justification. This cooperation has the merit of congruity, though the first call comes before any merit. (2) Faith is an element in justification. "Receiving faith by hearing, they of free will draw near to God, believing those things to be true which have been divinely revealed and promised." Faith as a living trust in a personal Savior for salvation is lacking. Among the truths believed is the mercy of God and that He wishes to justify the sinner in Christ. (3) This faith begets love to Christ and hatred to sin, which are elements also of the justifying process. (4) Now follows justification itself, "which is not a bare remission of sins, but also sanctification and renewal of the inner man through the voluntary reception of grace and of gifts." (5) But this renewal must take place through baptism, which, to the prepared adult, both gives and seals all the graces of salvation, forgiveness, cleansing, faith, hope and love. (6) Justification is preserved by obeying the commandments and by good works, which also increase it. (7) In case it is lost — and it can be lost, not by venial, but by mortal sin and by unbelief — it can be regained by the sacrament of penance. (8) To get it, to keep or regain it, it is also necessary to believe the doctrines as thus laid down and to be laid down by this Council (see Mirbt, *Quellen zur Geschichte des Papsttums* [4th ed. 1924], pp. 291-337).

C. Luther. Luther's early writings show that almost from the beginning of his earnest study of religious questions, he mounted up to Paul's view of justification by faith alone (Loofs, *Lehrbuch der Dogmageschichte* [4th ed. 1906], pp. 696-98). Faith is the trust in the mercy of God through Christ, and justification is the declaring righteous for His sake, which is followed by a real making righteous. From the beginning to the end of his life as a religious teacher these are the elements of his doctrine. Speaking of 1513-15, Loofs says (p. 697): "Upon these equations [to justify = to forgive, grace = mercy of the non-imputing God, faith = trust in His mercy] as the regulators of his religious self-judgment, Luther's piety rests, and corresponding to them his view of Christianity, and even later" (than 1513-15); and he adds that "to reckon as righteous" (*reputari justum*) must not be understood with Luther as an *opposition* "to make righteous," for his "to be justified without merits" in the sense of "to forgive" (*absolvi*) is at the same time the beginning of a new life: *remissio peccati . . . ipsa resurrectio*. "His constantly and firmly held view, even more deeply understood later than in 1513-15, that 'to be justified without merit' = 'to be resurrected [to be born again]' = 'to be sanctified' is a pregnant formulation of his Christianity." So much being said, it is not necessary to draw out Luther's doctrine further, but it will suffice to refer to the Histories of Doctrine, to Köstlin, *Luthers Theologie* (2nd ed. 1901; see Index, *s.v.* "Rechtfertigung," and I, 349), and especially to Thieme, *Die sittliche Triebkraft des Glaubens: eine Untersuchung zu Luthers Theologie* (1895), pp. 103-314.

From Luther and the other Reformers the NT doctrine went over to the Protestant churches without essential modification, and has remained their nominal testimony until the present. A classic expression of it, which may be taken as representing evangelical Christendom, is the 11th of the 39 Articles of Religion of the Church of England: "We are accounted righteous before God only for the merit of Our Lord and Saviour Jesus Christ by faith, and not for our own works or deservings: wherefore that we are justified by faith only is a most wholesome doctrine and very full of comfort, as more largely is expressed in the Homily of Justification." It is true that at one time

Wesley's opponents accused him of departing from this doctrine, especially on account of his famous Minute of 1770, but this was due to a radical misunderstanding of that Minute, for to the last he held staunchly Paul's doctrine (see *Lutheran Quarterly* [Apr. 1906], pp. 171-75).

D. Schleiermacher. A new point of view was brought into modern theology by Schleiermacher, who started from the fundamental fact of Christian experience that we have redemption and reconciliation with Christ, which fact becomes ours by union with Christ through faith. This union brings justification with other blessings, but justification is not considered as even in thought a separate act based on Christ's death, but as part of a great whole of salvation, historically realized step by step in Christ. The trend of his teaching is to break down the distinction between justification and regeneration, as they are simply different aspects of union with Christ.

Ritschl carried forward this thought by emphasizing the grace of the heavenly Father mediated in the first instance through the Son to the Christian community, "to which God imputes the position toward him of Christ its founder," and in the second instance to individuals "as by faith in the Gospel they attach themselves to this community. Faith is simply obedience to God and trust in the revelation of his grace in Christ." This brings sinners into fellowship with God which means eternal life, which is here and now realized, as the Fourth Gospel points out, in lordship over the world (cf. Franks in *DCG,* I, 922f.). The judicial or forensic aspect of justification so thoroughly in-wrought in Paul's thought is denied by Ritschl. "In whatsoever way we view the matter," he says, "the attitude of God in the act of justification cannot be conceived as that of a judge" (*Christian Doctrine of Justification and Reconciliation* [Eng. tr. 1900], p. 90). W. N. Clarke agreed with Schleiermacher in eliminating justification as a separate element in the work of salvation, and harked back to the legalistic view in making it dependent on the new life and subsequent to it (*Christian Theology* [1898], pp. 407f.). No book had as much influence in destroying the NT conception of justification among English-speaking readers as that of J. H. Newman (*Lectures on Justification* [3rd ed. 1874]), which contains some of the finest passages in religious literature (pp. 270-73, 302, 338f.), but which was so sympathetic to the Tridentine view that the author had nothing essential to retract when he joined Rome in 1845. "Whether we say we are justified by faith, or by works, or by sacraments, all these but mean this one doctrine that we are justified by grace which is given through sacraments, impetrated by faith, manifested in works" (p. 303).

E. Twentieth Century. If many nineteenth-century theologians tended to regard the biblical and evangelical doctrine of justification as artificial, several forces came together in the 20th cent. to reverse the situation. Of these the most important are as follows.

New lexical and exegetical study showed that, while the righteousness of God is certainly not an imparted righteousness, nevertheless in a verse like Rom. 10:4 it implies an element of power (cf. E. Käsemann, *Romans* [Eng. tr. 1980]) that prevents it from being a purely verbal matter. The many passages which suggest a *fait accompli* when speaking of justification (e.g., Rom. 8:30; 1 Cor. 6:11) support the view that this dimension has also to be taken into account even though it may not be the dominating aspect.

Schweitzer's eschatological reassessment of the teaching of Jesus (*Quest of the Historical Jesus* [1906]), while it found few supporters in its original form, opened up a parallel train of research in which emphasis has come to be placed on the element of eschatological realization in the work of Jesus. Hence it is no longer possible to think of a *purely* forensic justification. Certainly believers do not yet enjoy the sanctity that will be theirs at the last day. To that extent one may truly speak of a declared or imputed righteousness. The forensic aspect is not in dispute. On the other hand, there is an element of the "already" as well as the "not yet" in the justifying work of God in Christ. The righteousness which is declared to be ours is a real and not a fictional righteousness. The crucial victory has been won, the critical decision made, the turning point passed. Believers belong even now to the new age in which the true reality is that which is reckoned to be theirs because they have put their faith in Christ. The last things, being future, are also present. Justification carries a reference to the future which is present because, as God's future, it impinges already on the present.

Renewed study of the Reformation reinforced this understanding by focusing on the creative power of the Word of God. Luther, Zwingli, Calvin, and indeed all the leading Reformers found in God's Word a vital force which made it totally impossible to think of any statement of God's as merely a matter of words. As Zwingli pointed out in *The Clarity and Certainty of the Word of God* (*LCC* [XXIV], pp. 59ff.), when God says a thing it infallibly comes to pass according to His will. This finds illustration at creation. God says: "Let there be light," and at once light exists and begins to shine. The healing ministry of Jesus provides further examples of this certainty of God's Word to accomplish what it declares or commands. The leper finds instantaneous restoration when Jesus issues the creative imperative: "Be clean." Similarly God's justifying of the ungodly has the force of more than a mere declaration. On the basis of Christ's atoning work, God pronounces righteous those who believe in Him even though they are unquestionably sinful and guilty in themselves. When He does this, they do not at once become intrinsically sinless and innocent, but they do enter into the new life in Christ in which the innocence and sinlessness which will finally be theirs is already the true reality of their life and being in virtue of the divine acquittal. The words of justification are judicial but they are not on that account empty of all the force of the God who creates as well as justifies by the Word.

A fresh appreciation of the vicarious nature of the ministry of Christ cooperated with the other factors to shed a new and powerful light on justification. Emil Brunner in *The Mediator* and even more so Karl Barth in *CD,* IV/1, 211-283 ("The Just Judge Judged in our Place") and 514-642 ("The Justification of Man") (cf. also II/2, 552-781) gave prominence to this aspect. God spoke His Word of justifying power in Jesus Christ, who by His representative death and resurrection brought the old life of sinners to its end and initiated the new life of righteousness. The righteousness which is God's gift in justification has power because it is the righteousness of Jesus Christ for us. The last things have come in virtue of the work of God done in our place and on our behalf in His Son. The justifying Word accomplishes what it declares because this Word is Christ, in whom the sin of the world has in fact been carried away and the righteousness of God's believing people has in fact come. When the vicarious nature of Christ's work is ignored, forgotten, or resisted, justification unavoidably loses its reality. Conversely an understanding of this factor leads naturally and necessarily to the new facts of God which provide the rationale and the reality of the divine sentence.

These facts enable us to say, as Barth emphasized, that God justified Himself in His justification of the wicked. He did this in three ways. First, He justified His creation of beings that could bring upon themselves the misery and ruin of the fall and temporal and eternal death. He did this by His gracious intervention on their behalf. Second, He justified His omnipotence by not allowing the rebellious will of the creature to prevail over His own righteous will as the Creator. Third, He justified His intervention by protecting it against any possible accusation of caprice, injustice, or unreality. No one can come before God and say that He is unjust in His creating, overruling, or justifying work. He spoke and acted in Jesus Christ in such a way that He is both just and justified in all His ways, not least in His justifying work.

Finally, biblical and historical investigation brought out afresh the strength of the bond between justification and sanctification. Barth again took the lead here in *CD*, IV/1, 514-642 and IV/2, 533-553 ("Justification and Sanctification"). He pointed out that Calvin himself incorporated justification in his more general teaching on the Christian life. This emphasis in turn opened the door for Roman Catholic reappraisal, as in Hans Küng's *Justification* (Eng. tr. 1964), which advanced the audacious thesis that Calvin held the Catholic doctrine that Luther had distorted on the one side and Trent (in necessary correction) had also distorted on the other. Roman Catholicism in general seems not to have been persuaded by Küng, and many scholars view with reservations the attempt to relate justification and sanctification more closely in Calvin, who undoubtedly understood justification itself very much as Luther did. Nevertheless, there is incontestable truth and value in the insight that justification in no sense stands alone but forms part of a divine sequence which begins with God's foreknowledge and predestination, includes sanctification, and concludes only with glorification (Rom. 8:30; cf. 1 Cor. 6:11). Precisely for this reason the righteousness of God that comes to expression in His justifying of the ungodly carries with it all the power of God in His eschatological work (Tit. 3:7), the work accomplished in the incarnate Word, which begins here and now with Christ's vicarious death and resurrection and concludes with His *parousia* and the death and resurrection of believers with Him.

With this twentieth-century restatement of the truth, and with the new facets that have been discovered, the older objections to the doctrine of justification have lost their cogency. The place of justification at the heart of the gospel can again be affirmed with confidence. It can be preached as well as taught with renewed vitality, urgency, and conviction as a realistic message of redemption for this and every age.

Bibliography.–In addition to the standard commentaries, dictionaries, and NT theologies, and the older books mentioned in the text, the following books may be particularly noted: *CD*, II/2; IV/1; IV/2; K. Barth, *Comm. on Romans* (Eng. tr. 1933); *Ethics of 1928-1929*, II (1978); J. Bennett, *Justification as Revealed in Scripture* (1840); H. Berkhof, *Christian Faith* (Eng. tr. 1979); G. C. Berkouwer, *Faith and Justification* (1954); E. Boehl, *Reformed Doctrine of Justification* (1946); G. Bornkamm, *Paul* (Eng. tr. 1971); J. Buchanan, *The Doctrine of Justification* (1867; repr. 1954); J. Calvin, *Inst.* iii.11-18; G. Downame, *A Treatise of Justification* (1633); H. Küng, *Justification* (Eng. tr. 1964); M. Luther, *Lectures on Romans* (*LCC*), XV; J. Owen, *The Doctrine of Justification by Faith* (*Works*, V, 1862); H. Ridderbos, *Paul* (Eng. tr. 1975); P. Schaff, *Creeds of Christendom*, III: *Evangelical Creeds* (1919); H. Thielicke, *The Evangelical Faith*, III (Eng. tr. 1982).

J. A. FAULKNER
J. MURRAY
G. W. BROMILEY

JUSTIFY; JUSTIFIED. These terms translate (1) various forms of Heb. *ṣāḏaq*; (2) various forms of Gk. *dikaióō*; (3) the Greek phrase *apodoúnai lógon*. (1) In Job 32:2, Elihu was angry at Job because he "justified himself rather than God" (NEB "made himself out more righteous than God"), i.e., he considered himself morally "in the right" and God "in the wrong" concerning his physical trial. Later, in 33:32, Elihu challenges Job to "speak, for I desire to justify you" (NEB "I would gladly find you proved right"). By this he means that he would gladly acknowledge Job to be "in the right" if the latter could produce sufficient evidence to convince him. In 40:8, God asks Job, "Will you condemn me that you may be justified?" (NEB "Dare you . . . put me in the wrong that you may be right?"), i.e., will you assert that I am "in the wrong" in this trial, thus leaving yourself as the one who is "in the right"? In Ps. 51:4 (MT 6), the guilt-ridden psalmist acknowledges that God is "justified in [His] sentence and blameless in [His] judgment" (NEB "proved right in [His] charge and just in passing sentence"), i.e., He is completely within the bounds of moral propriety in judging him. In Prov. 17:15 occurs the maxim "He who justifies the wicked . . . [is] an abomination to the Lord." The forensic nature of *ṣdq* is well illustrated here, since the proverb refers to those perverse judges who acquit the guilty and convict the innocent (often for a bribe; cf. Isa. 5:23). In Isa. 43:8-15, a trial speech with many interpretative difficulties, God challenges the gods of the other nations to "bring their witnesses to justify them" (v. 9c; NEB "produce witnesses to prove their case"), i.e., bring forward their people who will attest their past record of seeing into the future and thus wisely guiding their people (v. 9b; the forensic nature of *ṣdq* is also clearly demonstrated here). (2) In Mt. 11:19, which is also difficult, the Evangelist applies to Jesus the proverb "wisdom is justified by her deeds" (var. "her children"; cf. Lk. 7:35; NEB "God's wisdom is proved right by its results"), by which he probably means that Jesus, the divine Wisdom (or the One through whom the divine wisdom works), is shown to be "in the right" by the results He obtains, i.e., His miraculous healings. In Lk. 7:29, another difficult passage, Luke is probably making a parenthetical comment in his narrative with the statement that "all the people and the tax collectors justified God, having been baptized with the baptism of John" (NEB "all the people, including the tax-gatherers, praised God, for they had accepted John's baptism"), i.e., they acknowledged, by being baptized by John, that God's judgment on them as announced by John was just. In 10:29, after Jesus implies that the young lawyer is deficient in duty (v. 28), he seeks "to justify himself," i.e., to vindicate himself for not doing that duty. In 16:15, Jesus characterizes the Pharisees as those who "justify [themselves] before men" (NEB "impress [their] fellowmen with [their] righteousness"), i.e., make it a point to demonstrate publicly their righteousness by various acts of piety. In the familiar story of the Pharisee and the tax-collector in 18:14, Jesus declares that the latter "went down to his house justified rather than the other" (NEB "went home acquitted of his sins"), by which He means that he was morally "in the right" and the Pharisee was not. (3) The phrase *apodoúnai lógon* (lit. "give a reason") occurs in Acts 19:40, another difficult passage, where the town clerk of Ephesus warns an agitated crowd, "We are in danger of being charged with rioting today, there being no cause that we can give to justify this commotion," i.e., to warrant the existence of the meeting. For the theological doctrine *see* JUSTIFICATION.

J. E. H.

JUSTLE jus'əl [hithpalpel of Heb. *šāqaq*]. An archaic AV term for "rush to and fro" (cf. NEB "jostle") in Nah. 2:4 (MT 5).

JUSTUS jus′təs [Gk. *Ioustos*]. Three men of this name are mentioned in the NT.

1. Joseph Barsabbas, whose Roman surname was Justus (Acts 1:23).

2. A Corinthian proselyte (Gk. *sebómenos tón theón*), whose house adjoined the synagogue and who received Paul when the Jews opposed him (Acts 18:7). He was probably a Roman citizen, one of the *coloni,* and so he would have been of assistance to the apostle in his work among the better class of Corinth. There is some disagreement among MSS regarding the name. The TR gives Justus alone. The RSV, following WH, Tisch., B, D, gives Titius Justus; but other MSS give Titus Justus. E. J. Goodspeed identifies him with the Gaius of Rom. 16:23 (*JBL,* 69 [1950], 382f.). Paul continued to lodge with Aquila and Priscilla but made the house of Justus his own synagogue.

3. A Jew, Jesus Justus.

S. F. HUNTER

JUTTAH jut′ə [Heb. *yuṭṭâ* (Josh. 21:16), *yûttâ* (15:55); LXX *Tany, Itan* (15:55), *Ietta* (15:55 A)]. A town in the hill country of Judah, mentioned with Maon, Carmel, and Ziph; a Levitical city (Josh. 21:16). In some versions of the LXX it occurs (Gk. *Iota*) in 1 Ch. 6:57. In Eusebius's *Onom.* (266.49; 133.10) a large village called Juttah is described as eighteen Roman miles from Eleutheropolis. This agrees with the position of Yuṭṭā, a large and prosperous Moslem village, 1140 m. (3740 ft.) above sea level, 8.5 km. (5.3 mi.) S of Hebron and 25 km. (15.5 mi.) from Beit Jibrîn (Eleutheropolis). There are many rock-cut tombs and ancient winepresses all around the village.

E. W. G. MASTERMAN